W9-COZ-704

The Encyclopedia of New York City

The Encyclopedia

of New York City
Second Edition

Edited by KENNETH T. JACKSON

Executive Editor LISA KELLER

Managing Editor NANCY V. FLOOD

Yale UNIVERSITY PRESS *New Haven & London*

THE NEW-YORK HISTORICAL SOCIETY *New York*

Published with assistance from the Annie Burr Lewis Fund.

Yale University Press books may be purchased in quantity for educational, business, or promotional use. For information, please e-mail sales.press@yale.edu (U.S. office) or sales@yaleup.co.uk (U.K. office).

Set in Garamond type by Westchester Book Group.

Printed in the United States of America by RR Donnelley.

Library of Congress Cataloging-in-Publication Data

The encyclopedia of New York City / edited by Kenneth T. Jackson.—2nd ed.
p. cm.
ISBN 978-0-300-11465-2 (alk. paper)
1. New York (N.Y.)—Encyclopedias. I. Jackson, Kenneth T. II. New-York Historical Society.
F128.3.E75 2010
974.7'1003—dc22

2010031294

A catalogue record for this book is available from the British Library.

This paper meets the requirements of ANSI/NISO Z39.48-1992 (Permanence of Paper).

10 9 8 7 6 5 4 3 2 1

SPONSORS

Major support for the second edition of
The Encyclopedia of New York City
was provided by

FOUNDING SPONSOR
The Peter Jay Sharp Foundation

SPONSORS
William A. Ackman
Peter Aron
Kenneth and Kathryn Conboy
Elizabeth B. Dater
Joan K. Davidson
Furthermore: a program of
the J.M. Kaplan Fund
Richard Gilder
Robert Goelet
Tom and Leatrice Gochberg
Susan and Roger Hertog
Barbara and Kenneth T. Jackson
Ira and Barbara K. Lipman
Henry Luce Foundation
Dan Lufkin
M. Myers Mermel
Cheryl and Philip Milstein
John Moore
The McGraw-Hill Companies
The New York Times Company Foundation
Pershing Square Foundation
Rockefeller Brothers Fund
Susan and Elihu Rose Foundation
Jack Rosenthal
Surdna Foundation
Bernard and Irene Schwartz Foundation
Sue Ann Weinberg

ASSOCIATE SPONSORS
University Seminars, Columbia University
Michael Weisberg

The editor expresses appreciation to the Warner Fund at the University Seminars at Columbia University for their help with publication. Material in this work was presented to the University Seminar "The City."

COUNCILORS
William A. Ackman
Kenneth Conboy
Elizabeth B. Dater
Joan Davidson
Richard Gilder
Robert Goelet
Tom Gochberg
Roger Hertog
Kenneth T. Jackson
Ira Lipman
Dan Lufkin
M. Myers Mermel
Cheryl Milstein
John Moore
Elihu Rose
Jack Rosenthal
Donald Rubin
Bernard S. Schwartz
Ed Skloot
Sue Ann Weinberg

Major support for the first edition of
The Encyclopedia of New York City was provided by

The National Endowment for the Humanities
McGraw–Hill, Inc.
Frederick P., Daniel, and Elihu Rose
The Susan and Elihu Rose Foundation

Additional support was received from

The Lucius N. Littauer Foundation
The Frederick W. Richmond Foundation
The Frances and Benjamin Benenson Foundation
The Charles H. Revson Foundation
The Weiler–Arnow Investment Company
The Josiah Macy, Jr. Foundation
The J. M. Kaplan Fund
The Horace W. Goldsmith Foundation
Citicorp
The Consolidated Edison Company of New York
The Durst Foundation
The J. Aron Charitable Foundation
The New York Times Company Foundation
The Pattee Charitable Lead Trust
The Philip Morris Companies
The Jill and Marshall Rose Foundation
The Robert Schalkenbach Foundation
The Seth Sprague Charitable and Educational Foundation
The Lawrence A. Wien Foundation
Chase Manhattan Bank
The Vincent Astor Foundation
The Young & Rubicam Foundation
Lester Wunderman
The Bernhill Fund
Sidney J. Bernstein
Brooklyn Union Gas
Ann L. and Lawrence B. Buttenwieser
Brown, Harris, Stevens
The Edison Parking Corporation
The Edward S. Gordon Company
Home Life Insurance Company
HRO International
Kenneth T. and Barbara B. Jackson
Lintas: New York
Maidenform Inc.
Marine Midland Bank
The Port Authority of New York and New Jersey
Proskauer Rose Goetz & Mendelsohn
Sheldon H. Solow
Silverstein Properties
J. Walter Thompson USA
The Zeckendorf Company
Abrams Benisch Riker
Tishman Speyer Properties
The Bronx County Historical Society
History of New York City Project, Inc.
Joel and Bonnie Fox Schwartz

ADVISORY BOARD FOR THE FIRST EDITION

An asterisk denotes "deceased."

ASSOCIATE EDITORS FOR THE FIRST AND SECOND EDITIONS

Note: A superscript "1" following an author's name signifies first edition; "2" signifies second edition. An asterisk denotes "deceased."

Gerard Koeppel[2]
Independent Historian

Jeffrey A. Kroessler[2]
John Jay College

Margaret Latimer[1]
Jackson Homestead, Newton, Massachusetts

Bara Levin[1]
Michael Shipley Communication

Richard K. Lieberman[1]
LaGuardia Community College

Paul Magocsi[1]
University of Toronto

John Manbeck[2]
Former Brooklyn Borough Historian

Roland Marchand*[1]
University of California, Davis

Arnold Markoe[1,2]
Brooklyn College

Brooks McNamara[1]
New York University

August Meier*[1]
Kent State University

David Ment[1]
New York City Municipal Archives

James E. Mooney[1]
Independent Historian

Robert C. Morris*[1]
National Archives—Northeast Region

Mark Naison[1]
Fordham University

Philip Pauly*[1]
Rutgers, the State University of New Jersey

Elisabeth Israels Perry[1]
Saint Louis University

Jon A. Peterson[1]
Queens College

Jan Seidler Ramirez[1]
National September 11 Memorial and Museum

Naomi Rosenblum[1]
Photographic Historian and Author

David Rosner[1]
Columbia University

John Rousmaniere[2]
Historian and Author

Charles L. Sachs[1]
New York Transit Museum

Virginia Sánchez Korrol[1,2]
Brooklyn College

Joel Schwartz*[1]
Montclair State University

Vincent Seyfried[1]
Independent Researcher, New York

Martin Shefter[1]
Cornell University

Barnett Shepherd[1,2]
Staten Island Historical Society

Robert W. Snyder[1]
Rutgers, the State University of New Jersey

Andrew Sparberg[2]
TCI College of Technology

Bayrd Still*[1]
New York University

John Tauranac[2]
Cartographer

John Tebbel*[1]
New York University

Emmanuel Tobier*[1]
New York University

Frank Vos*[1]
Independent Scholar

Mike Wallace[1]
Graduate Center, City University of New York

Alan Wallach[1]
College of William and Mary

Harold Wechsler[1]
New York University

Howard Weiner[1,2]
College of Staten Island

Sean Wilentz[1]
Princeton University

Elliot Willensky*[1]
New York City Landmarks Preservation Commission

Carol Willis[1,2]
Columbia University

Don B. Wilmeth[1]
Brown University

Sherrill Wilson[2]
African Burial Ground Project

Mary Ellen Zuckerman[1]
Geneseo College

PROJECT STAFF

SECOND EDITION

Encyclopedia of New York City Staff

Editor-in-Chief	Kenneth T. Jackson	
Executive Editor	Lisa Keller	
Managing Editor	Nancy V. Flood	
Deputy Managing Editors	Holly Cronin David White	
Senior Project Editors	Meghan Lalonde Kate Lauber	
Project Editors	Anne Epstein Cecilia Magnusson Jessica Montesanto Frank Nestor	
Assistant Editors	Patrick Barrett Ben Berger Joseph Breen Meryl Cates Briana Dema Garrett Felber Leila Forrence Ella Foshay Irina Ikonsky Emily Johnson	Andrew Kryzak Aleeza Lubin Stephanie Miller Rowan Moore Gerety Nathan Morgante Dianna Ng Max Seppo Ben Silk Caleb Smith Sarah Wansley
Interns	Henry Cooper Alison Flood Gussie Foshay-Rothfeld Penelope Gelwicks Michelle Hutt Kendra Johanson Nicholas Kelly	Phillip Nontel Joe Piscina Alex Poole Samantha Rothberg Jessica Schott Marlena Slowik Liza Weingarten
Senior Illustrations Editor	Lisa Keller	
Associate Illustrations Editor	Alexander Heilner	

Yale University Press Staff

Sponsoring Editor Vadim Staklo

Project Manager Joyce Ippolito

Production Editor Susan Laity

Chief Copy Editor Jessie Dolch

Copy Editors Robin DuBlanc
Karen Gangel
Laura Hensley
Noreen O'Connor

Proofreaders Robin Charney
Jessie Hunnicutt
Jennie Kaufman
Noreen O'Connor
Millie Piekos
Marnie Wiss

Indexers Marcia Carlson
Suzanne Mackzum
Marian Rhys

Designers Nancy Ovedovitz
Lindsey Voskowsky

Production Controller Maureen Noonan

FIRST EDITION
Executive Editor Fred Kameny

Sponsoring Editor Edward Tripp

Managing Editors Peter Eisenstadt (1990–92)
Deborah S. Gardner (1988–90)

Deputy Managing Editors Alana J. Erickson
Walter Friedman

Senior Project Editor	James Bradley	
Project Editors	Eric Wm. Allison Kerry Candaele Eileen K. Cheng Marc Ferris Nancy Flood Janet Frankston Shan Jayakumar Erica Judge Kevin Kenny Laura Lewison Joseph S. Lieber Chad Ludington Melissa M. Merritt	Ruth Morris Becky Nicolaides Edward T. O'Donnell Sandra Opdycke Grai St. Clair Rice Cara Sadownick Allen J. Share Joanna Usher Silver Jeff Sklansky Robert W. Snyder Robert Sanger Steel Naomi Wax
Senior Illustrations Editor	Grai St. Clair Rice	
Illustrations Editors	Deborah S. Gardner Melissa M. Merritt	
Associate Illustrations Editor	Dale L. Neighbors	
Senior Copy Editor	Pamela H. Sturner	
Copy Editors	Amy Balser William J. Moses Shawn Simmons	
Chief Proofreader	Lawrence Kenney	
Production Controller	Cele Syrotiak	

PREFACE

This is the second edition of a book that first appeared in 1995. At that time, it was both a critical and commercial success, and it inspired similar efforts in many other cities. At last count, it had received four awards for reference excellence, had been through seven printings, and had sold more than 70,000 copies.

But that was before the Internet revolution and before third graders could Google anything or turn to Wikipedia for a reference on millions of topics. What, then, is the justification for hundreds of expensive pages of paper bound between two hard covers? Is this volume the literary equivalent of a livery stable in the 1920s?

The Encyclopedia of New York City may be an old model, but it is an enduring and necessary one. When Denis Diderot invented the genre of the encyclopedia in the middle of the eighteenth century, he offered what was then a novel and radical idea: bring all the knowledge of the world to anyone who wanted to discover it. Such easy access then was considered an affront to the establishment of the time, which tried to ban the book. Opposition crumpled in the face of support by progressive Enlightenment thinkers, who were delighted by the prospect of sharing knowledge. Diderot's genius also lay in his idea of assembling experts in different areas who would prepare authoritative entries that were both thorough and accessible to the reading public.

Like Diderot's project, *The Encyclopedia of New York City* provides the distilled knowledge of hundreds of experts and presents their entries in that same accessible way. In the twenty-first century, when books compete with electronic sources, there is still an important niche for reference materials such as this. Although third graders may know how to use an Internet browser, browsing a book is a very different experience. There is a joy in leafing through the pages to make unexpected discoveries about topics in which you did not think you had an interest. You look up MALCOLM X, and your eyes fall also to the MALBONE STREET WRECK, a train disaster in Brooklyn that claimed at least 93 lives in 1918. Or you look up TENEMENTS and also happen to read about the TENDERLOIN, a Manhattan neighborhood that once contained the city's greatest concentration of saloons, brothels, gambling parlors, and dance halls. On the Internet you cannot look up something that you do not know exists. Serendipitous discoveries are often the best kind. In New York City, there are mysteries on every block, and this encyclopedia is similar, with new mysteries on every page. Furthermore, this book has been created by experts who have spent decades specializing in specific areas, and the reader is able to identify these authors, whose entries cannot be changed by other people who may not have the same knowledge and expertise.

But why bother with a second edition? To put it simply, New York City is always evolving, and especially so in the past two decades. When the first edition was written, B. Altman was a department store, the World Trade Center dominated the city's skyline, J. P. Morgan and Chase Manhattan Bank were separate companies, crime was going up, and the worst day ever for the New York City Fire Department was 17 October 1966, when 12 firefighters were killed at 23rd Street and Broadway. We have eliminated several hundred entries and added almost a thousand new ones, from KAREEM ABDUL-JABBAR to the ZIEGFIELD FOLLIES. The new entries greatly expand the story of New York City: ARSON, BRICKS, the CENTRAL PARK JOGGER, COMPSTAT, JOE DIMAGGIO, E-ZPASS, HIGH LINE, HOUSE NUMBERING AND STREET NAMING, HUDSON SQUARE, ARCHBISHOP IAKOVOS, KLEINFELD BRIDAL, MICKEY MANTLE, EVELYN NESBIT (the Girl in the Red Velvet Swing), PUBLIC ORDER, SIDEWALKS, the SUBWAY HERO (Wesley Autrey), and SYNAGOGUES. We have also updated virtually every retained entry. In a city that has grown by a million people since 1990, the 450 neighborhoods have also grown and changed, with new ethnic groups continuing to make New York City the most diverse spot on the planet. And we have added hundreds of new illustrations, both historical and contemporary, to help bolster the reader's understanding of people and places. But even with all of the revisions, it remains impossible to capture all of New York City in one book, or to be flawless in every entry.

How does one take the measure of New York City? Even casual visitors can see and feel and sense that it is different from other places. Its buildings are bigger, its pace quicker, its streets noisier, and its sidewalks more crowded than those of other communities. It often overwhelms tourists from around the world, who are typically told that New York City is the least "American" of cities and that they must travel far from it if they are to understand and know the "real" United States.

In this case the stereotype is correct: New York City *is* different. For one thing, it is older than virtually every other American city. Boston, Philadelphia, Charleston, Savannah, Newport, and Williamsburg come to mind when one thinks of historic places, yet New York City is older than all of them. As for the settlements that were already established when Dutch traders first landed at the southern tip of Manhattan—St. Augustine, Jamestown, Fort St. George, Hampton, Plymouth, and Santa Fe—Jamestown, Plymouth, and Fort St. George disappeared, and the other three failed to prosper for the first three centuries of their existence.

New York City is also unusual because of its high population density. In 1900 the Lower East Side was the most densely inhabited place in the world. As late as 1960 Manhattan contained half of all the world's skyscrapers of 50 stories or higher. The city's midtown office district in 1960 had more office space per acre than any other central business district on earth; in fact, only lower Manhattan and the Chicago Loop were even half as dense. In recent years Hong Kong and Shanghai have matched New York City's skyscraper total; and Tokyo, Mexico City, and São Paulo have populations and densities that match or exceed those of New York City. Suburbanization has greatly reduced the worst overcrowding in the United States. But the city remains far more crowded than any other in the country, with twice the population density of Chicago and many times the density of Houston and Los Angeles.

New York City has long been unusual because of its sheer size. Even before 1775, when its population was never more than 25,000, it ranked with Boston, Philadelphia, Charleston, and Newport as one of the five leading cities in the colonies. It had surpassed Philadelphia by 1810 to become the largest city in the United States, and Mexico City by 1830 to become the largest in the western hemisphere. By 1900 it was the second-largest city in the world (after London) and by 1930 the largest. It remains the only U.S. municipality ever to exceed four million residents. And in 2010 each of its five boroughs is large enough to be an important city in its own right, with Queens having more inhabitants than Philadelphia or Phoenix, Brooklyn several times as many as Boston and San Francisco, the Bronx far more than Detroit, and Staten Island more than St. Louis.

Figures for the metropolitan area are even more impressive. When the Regional Plan Association in 1930 defined the metropolitan region as comprising the city and 31 adjacent counties in New York, New Jersey, and Connecticut, the region was already the first in the history of the world to exceed 10 million residents, and in 1970 it became the first to exceed 15 million. Although eventually surpassed by Tokyo and a few other places, the New York City metropolitan region still counted 22 million people in 2010, or as many as lived in all the cities of the earth combined in 1700.

Unlike other urban encyclopedias, which typically include suburbs in their coverage, this one is about the city of New York and its five constituent boroughs. No disrespect to the suburbs is intended, but to include all 1500 such places would have made the book so huge as to be unwieldy. However, New York City is inextricably linked to its suburbs, and the reader will note that we occasionally refer to *Greater New York* or to the *metropolitan region*. In such cases, the definition used is that of the 31-county area defined by the Regional Plan Association.

Capturing the essence of this vibrant and still-growing metropolis has not been easy. More than 10,000 books have been written about the city, with new ones appearing yearly. In the nineteenth century, guidebooks proliferated to service the booming tourist industry, and they provided a de facto history of the city. I. N. Phelps Stokes's six-volume *The Iconography of Manhattan Island, 1498–1909* remains unsurpassed. Edwin Burrows and Mike Wallace's *Gotham* is a beautifully written interpretive narrative of life up to 1898. Specialized studies address everything from prison ships to police to prostitution to public order. *The Encyclopedia of New York City* is the rare publication that addresses all aspects of life in the Big Apple (and this book explains where that term came from).

The format of this second edition is similar to that of the first. Its alphabetical entries range from prehistory to the present and cover all five boroughs, although most of the boroughs did not become part of New York City until 1898. Entries reference people, places, neighborhoods, ethnicities, events, generic and thematic topics, and time periods. This edition includes more than 5000 entries by more than 800 authors. The length of the entries ranges from 50 to nearly 7000 words, with most entries running about 200 to 800 words.

Like the first edition, this one adheres to principles of reference publishing, which is to provide basic information and a place to begin research, not to end it. As a synthetical work, it aims to gather existing information rather than present research on new material. Many entries have brief bibliographical citations to help the reader who is interested in more information. While the editor in chief has aimed to keep the entries as factual and impartial as possible, some interpretation has crept in, and this reflects the view of the individual author, not the editorial staff. The encyclopedia also has some useful cross-referencing. In addition to 750 illustrations, half of which are new, there are also more than 100 charts and tables, which show, for instance, which television shows were filmed and set in New York City, how many ticker-tape parades the city has organized, how tall the tallest buildings are, and a host of other fascinating aspects of the city. Certain entries have not been included for pragmatic reasons; city agencies, for instance, are covered in thematic entries, and advertising and law firms are shown in tables. Some of the entries are not only new, but they exist in no other encyclopedia: RAILROADS, SONGS, ARMORIES, TELEVISION SHOWS, PUBLIC EXECUTIONS, NEWSPAPERS, and SQUARES are examples of these.

New York City has never been a static entity, and neither is *The Encyclopedia of New York City.* An electronic edition of this print one is planned, with updates that will mirror the vibrancy of the city it reflects. And although every word in this book has been read by the editor in chief and many other editors, the encyclopedia no doubt includes errors. The editor accepts responsibility for them and asks that suggestions, criticisms, and comments be e-mailed to ktj1@columbia.edu.

These thousands of entries are meant not only to convey the history of this great metropolis, but also its spirit. A final word comes from E. B. White, connoisseur of New York City: "New York blends the gift of privacy with the excitement of participation; and better than most dense communities it succeeds in insulating the individual . . . against all enormous and violent and wonderful events that are taking place every minute."

ACKNOWLEDGMENTS

In 2001, even before the terrorist attacks on the World Trade Center transformed all of our lives, many friends and colleagues began urging me to put out a revised second edition of the encyclopedia. Even the idea of such an effort was daunting, but I and they knew that the community of people who care about the city and its history would assist and support me at every step. The first individual to offer material assistance was Dan Lufkin. Over lunch in Manhattan Valley, he reviewed my justification for such a volume and thought about my time and monetary estimates. Two weeks later he telephoned to say that the Peter Jay Sharp Foundation would become the major sponsor. Without Dan's enthusiasm and help, this project would not have moved forward. And he has remained committed to the encyclopedia in all the years since we began our work. Following Dan's lead, other funders soon joined him in support. Jack Rosenthal of the New York Times Company Foundation became a particularly engaged councilor. Kenneth Conboy, Joan K. Davidson, Tom Gochberg, and Sue Ann Weinberg offered both financial advice and personal friendship. Roger Hertog and Richard Gilder contributed even though their primary interests lay elsewhere. Special thanks go also to the Henry Luce Foundation for its generous matching program, and to the Warner Fund at the University Seminars at Columbia University.

Writing about New York City is often a labor of love. Fortunately, people who feel this way revised pieces they had written 20 years before, or better yet, submitted completely new pieces. John Tauranac, who drew a half dozen maps for the first edition, started all over again to update all of his original work. When I missed deadlines and when promised submissions never arrived, Jeffrey Kroessler, John Rousmaniere, and Barnett Shepherd generously gave their time to quickly plug the hole in the dike. Eric Goldstein of the Natural Resources Defense Council and Helene Amato of the Department of Environmental Protection ensured that our knowledge of New York City's remarkable water supply system was correct. Danniel Maio of Identity Maps quickly revised the complicated Manhattan street maps.

Librarians and archivists were essential at critical points. At the New-York Historical Society, Jean Ashton of the library made available work space; Marilyn Kushner, Sue Kriete, Miranda Schwartz, and Eleanor Gillers helped access a treasure trove of photographs. Thanks also go to Donna Jeffrey, Kieran Garvey, and Valerie Crane at the New-York Historical Society for their support. And Louise Mirrer, president of the New-York Historical Society, whose plate was always full with other concerns and responsibilities, was always willing to pause, consult, and encourage.

Ken Cobb, assistant commissioner of the New York City Department of Records and Information Services and former director of the Municipal Archives, offered his matchless knowledge and city records; he never hesitated to help answer the most difficult questions and supply photographs, too. Steve Saks and Tom Lisanti of the New York Public Library, and Susan Henshaw Jones and Robbi Siegel of the Museum of the City of New York made possible many of the hundreds of new illustrations.

Our digital files could not have made their way to the printed page without the guidance of Yale University Press. Joyce Ippolito, an extraordinary editor, spearheaded the effort to get this book out and oversaw every aspect of its editing and publication. She and her talented team of copy editors—Jessie Dolch, Robin DuBlanc, Karen Gangel, Laura Hensley, and Noreen O'Connor—demonstrated wisdom as they expeditiously went through masses of material. Susan Laity, production editor, gave valuable production advice, and Nancy Ovedovitz and Lindsey Voskowsky, designers, made the book as beautiful as it is. Thanks go to Maureen Noonan, production controller; Marcia Carlson, indexer, and her team, Suzanne Mackzum and Marian Rhys; and proofreaders Robin Charney, Jessie Hunnicutt, Jennie Kaufman, Noreen O'Connor, Millie Piekos, and Marnie Wiss. John Donatich, director of Yale University Press, was a source of support and encouragement, as was reference editor Vadim Staklo.

So many people spent so many hours with entries. Particular thanks go to David White and Holly Cronin for their hard work and boundless enthusiasm. Others who put special efforts into this project include Aleeza Lubin, Meghan

Lalonde, Kate Lauber, Cecilia Magnusson, Frank Nestor, Anne Epstein, and Meryl Cates. Alexander Heilner did a heroic job with his stunning new pictures and encouraged other talented photographers to contribute their work. Nancy Flood took over as managing editor at the start and spent countless hours organizing files, contacting authors, and providing a supportive environment for our many interns. Even as the first edition was pouring into bookstores, she was examining every page, warning me about textual biases and shortcomings, and suggesting new entries. Her love for New York City helped make this book come to fruition.

The last 18 months of a major reference effort are inevitably the most difficult. Fortunately, Professor Lisa Keller of Purchase College stepped into the breach and invested her enormous energy and talent into the project. As an author, she knew about prose style; as a New York historian, she knew about sources; and as a former journalist, she knew about deadlines. Each of these skills was critical as she edited entries, cajoled authors, pulled together hundreds of new illustrations, checked thousands of entries, and watched over production schedules. Her unbounded passion for New York City propelled her in the completion of this project.

Finally, Barbara Bruce Jackson supported my decision to contribute my time and our money to a project that in the end delivers neither academic glory nor financial reward. We made this choice because we left Memphis together 48 years ago and together found happiness in the place that we both continue to regard as the greatest city in the world.

KENNETH T. JACKSON

ABBREVIATIONS

AB	Artium Baccalaureus
AM	amplitude modulation; Artium Magister
app.	appendix
b	born
BA	Baccalaureus Artium / Bachelor of Arts
BArch	Bachelor of Architecture
B.C.	British Columbia
BD	Bachelor of Divinity
BS	Bachelor of Science
C	centigrade
ca	circa
chap(s).	chapter(s)
comp(s).	compiler(s), compiled by
d	died
DDS	Doctor of Dental Surgery
diss.	dissertation
DPhil	Doctor Philosophiae / Doctor of Philosophy
Dr.	Doctor
ed(s).	editor(s), edited by
EdD	Doctor of Education
edn	edition
F	Fahrenheit; Federal Reporter [in legal contexts]
fl	flourit [he/she flourished]
FM	frequency modulation
HMS	His/Her Majesty's Ship
introd.	introduction
JD	Juris Doctor [Doctor of Laws]
kHz	kilohertz
LLB	Legum Baccalaureus [Bachelor of Laws]
LLD	Legum Doctor [Doctor of Laws]
LLM	Legum Magister [Master of Laws]
Ltd.	Limited
MA	Magister Artium / Master of Arts
MArch	Master of Architecture
MBA	Master of Business Administration
MD	Medicinae Doctor / Doctor of Medicine
MFA	Master of Fine Arts
MHz	megahertz
MPhil	Magister Philosophiae / Master of Philosophy
MS	Master of Science
n.	note
n.d.	no date
no(s).	number(s)
n.p.	no place
n.pub.	no publisher
Ont.	Ontario
O.P.	Ordo Praedicatorum [Order of Preachers (Dominicans)]
orig.	originally
PhD	Philosophiae Doctor / Doctor of Philosophy
pop.	population
pubd	published
repr.	reprinted
rev.	revised
Rev.	Reverend
Sask.	Saskatchewan
SS	Steamship
St(s).	Saint(s)
Ste.	Sainte
STL	Sacrae Theologiae Licentiatus [Licentiate in Sacred Theology]
STM	Sacrae Theologiae Magister [Master of Sacred Theology]
suppl(s).	supplement(s)
unpubd	unpublished
USS	United States Ship
v.	versus
WPAG	*New York City Guide: A Comprehensive Guide to the Five Boroughs of the Metropolis: Manhattan, Brooklyn, the Bronx, Queens, and Richmond* (New York: Random House, 1939; repr. New York, Pantheon, 1982, as *The WPA Guide to New York City: The Federal Writers' Project Guide to 1930s New York*)
YIVO	Yidisher visnshaftlekher institut
YMCA	Young Men's Christian Association
YM–YWHA	Young Men's and Young Women's Hebrew Association
YWCA	Young Women's Christian Association

ABBREVIATIONS USED ON MAPS

Amer	American
Assoc.	Association
Av(s)	Avenue(s)
Bldg.	Building
Blvd	Boulevard
Bway	Broadway
Ctr	Center
E	East
Ex	Exchange
Expwy	Expressway
Ft	Fort
Hgts	Heights
HQ	Headquarters
LIRR	Long Island Rail Road
Mt	Mount
N	North
Pct.	Precinct
Pkwy	Parkway
Pl	Place
PO	Post Office
PS	Public School
R.C.	Roman Catholic
Rd	Road
RR	Railroad
Sq	Square
St	Street
Vill	Village
W	West

NOTES ON THE USE OF THE ENCYCLOPEDIA

COVERAGE

There is no more difficult and contentious issue facing the editors of a reference work than what to put in and what to leave out. In this encyclopedia the criteria vary according to whether the subject is a person, a neighborhood, an institution, an ethnic or religious group, or a broad, thematic topic, as well as varying from one historical period to another. Such criteria will ease the task of selection, but only to a degree. In the end subjectivity plays a part, as it must in any reference work other than a directory.

The people included in the encyclopedia are those whom the editors judged to have left a permanent mark on the city's history or culture. Most of them lived in the city for much of their lives; some are influential visitors (such as Lafayette, Lincoln, and Dickens) and one—the Duke of York, for whom the city is named—never set foot in the city. After the mid-twentieth century residence is a more elusive criterion. On the one hand there are figures who had important careers in New York City but lived outside it. On the other hand are prominent figures in the worlds of film, music, and sports with national and international careers, who may have had a residence in New York City, but also lived and worked in other places. Some people are mentioned only in tables and the index, as they are not significant enough to merit entries but are too important to be neglected altogether. Examples include most of the city's early mayors, who were appointed to what was a largely ceremonial office; in many cases little is known about them.

The more than 400 entries on neighborhoods include all those generally recognized as extant, as well as the best known of those that are defunct. In other categories—businesses, restaurants, magazines, radio stations—the choice of subjects is highly selective. National organizations and firms are generally included only if based in New York City. And to keep the encyclopedia to a manageable size, certain categories have been excluded entirely, notably line agencies of the municipal government and individual creative works such as novels and films.

In every entry the focus is on the connection of the subject to New York City, with careers outside the city compressed or omitted entirely. For example, the entry on Thomas Jefferson does not discuss his presidency or his writing of the Declaration of Independence: it deals solely with the six months that he spent in New York City in 1790.

USAGE

Given the great interest in New York City, this encyclopedia is written for both an American and international audience. Measurements are given in imperial and metric systems. Place names and institutional names are given in the form that prevailed at the time being discussed. This practice extends to spelling changes (Williamsburgh is used in references before 1855, Williamsburg thereafter), but not to changes in spacing or hyphenation (the Long Island Rail Road is referred to consistently as such, even though it was known as the Long Island Railroad until 1944). The city is referred to either as New York City or (in exceptional cases) as the City of New York. The form New York is used only in bibliographies, for the colony of New York, and in references to New York State where it is unmistakable that the state is being referred to (otherwise the form New York State is used).

The ampersand in corporate names is generally expanded, although it is used where necessary to avoid confusion (notably with the Ringling Brothers and Barnum & Bailey Circus) and in acronyms (such as AT&T). The en dash (–) is used rather than the hyphen (-) in institutional names like Helmsley–Spear, which are derived from two surnames rather than a single hyphenated surname. Transliteration follows the Pinyin system for Chinese and the YIVO system for Yiddish.

ALPHABETIZATION

The encyclopedia follows a letter-by-letter system, in which a heading of more than one word is treated as if it were spelled solid: spaces, hyphens, diacritical marks, and periods are disregarded, as are elements in brackets and parentheses. In accordance with established dialoguing practice, names beginning with "St." are alphabetized as if beginning with "Saint." Corporate and institutional names that begin with a person's forename (such as R. H. Macy and the Solomon R. Guggenheim Museum) are alphabetized under the first letter of the forename, not the surname. The reader who looks for such entries under their latter part (Macy and Guggenheim) will be referred to the appropriate place by a cross-reference.

HEADINGS

The heading of an entry about a person takes this form:

Washington, George (*b* Bridges Creek, near Fredericksburg, Va., 22 Feb 1732; *d* Mount Vernon, Va., 14 Dec 1799).

Parentheses are used to show parts of a name not ordinarily used by a person (or institution or other entitity). These parts are in boldface:

Ives, Charles (Edward)
Koch, Edward (Irving)
Catholic Medical Center (of Brooklyn and Queens)

Brackets are used for alternative names. These are in lightface:

Ellington, Duke [Edward Kennedy]
Clermont [North River Steamboat]

A person who has more than one name is entered under the best-known one, with alternative names given in brackets:

Twain, Mark [Clemens, Samuel (Langhorne)]

The formula "née" is used for maiden names:

Astor [née Schermerhorn]**, Caroline Webster**

Where there is more than one bracketed name these are separated by semicolons and the order is that of reverse chronology:

Malcolm X [Shabazz, el-Hajj Malik e-; Little, Malcolm]

Titles of nobility are given in lightface:

Bing, Sir **Rudolph**
Hyde, Edward, Viscount Cornbury
Moody [née Dunch]**, Deborah,** Lady Moody

For a firm or institution, the name appearing in the heading will be the current form if the entity is extant and based in New York City, and the best-known form if the entity is defunct or based elsewhere.

Where two or more entries have an identical heading they are distinguished by lowercase roman numerals:

West Brighton (i). Name by which West New Brighton is sometimes known.
West Brighton (ii). Neighborhood in southwestern Brooklyn.

When a person, place, institution, or other entity that is the subject of an entry is referred to in running text elsewhere, the form used is that of the boldface heading of the entry (including the lowercase roman numeral if there is one, unless the reference is unmistakable without it); anything in lightface, parentheses, or brackets is disregarded.

DATES

The dates appearing in the heading of an entry about a person provide the fullest information available on that person's birth and death. Question marks indicate uncertainty over that part of the date they are next to. If the specific date or part of it is unknown, circa or baptismal date is given, or just a year.

STRUCTURE OF ENTRIES

Each entry starts with a tagline—a short, verbless definition that describes the subject's principal activity or activities. Definitions of neighborhoods include the latest available population figures (if known) and approximate boundaries. In cases where such boundaries cannot be fixed with any certainty, the definition identifies the center of the neighborhood, the names of surrounding neighborhoods, or the location within the borough.

Most entries are ordered chronologically. The longest are divided into sections, each beginning with a subheading.

CROSS-REFERENCES

A cross-reference directs the reader to another entry or to another part of the same entry. If referring to another entry it is printed in small capitals. Cross-references are of three types:

1. The cross-reference from an acronym or alternative name to the main entry:

ACLU. See American Civil Liberties Union.
North River Steamboat. See Clermont.
Clemens, Samuel (Langhorne). See Twain, Mark.

2. The cross-reference from one entry to a second entry, used where the second entry contains a substantial amount of additional information about the subject of the first. It may appear in text, or at the end of the entry, after any bibliography and before the signature.

These measures contributed to widespread homelessness.
For further illustration see Riis, Jacob A.
See also Theater, §5.

3. The cross-reference from one part of an entry to another:

(see also §6, above).

Cross-references are used to direct the reader to substantive discussions, not passing mentions. Entries from thematic entries may cross-refer to other thematic entries, but not to entries on individual persons or institutions: thus the entry on science refers the reader to those on anthropology, biology, geology, physics, and psychology, but not to entries on individual scientists and scientific institutions.

BIBLIOGRAPHIES

The bibliographies are intended to provide suggestions for further research. They are selective and will not necessarily include all of the sources consulted by the authors or editors.

The first edition of a book is usually cited. For books with more than one edition the most recent is cited as well if it appeared at least ten years after the first edition (a subsequent edition that appeared sooner may be cited if it is bibliographically significant). Only one place of publication is given for each publisher. Places of publication and names of publishers for revisions and subsequent editions are given only if they differ from those of the first edition. The abbreviation "p(p)." is used only where necessary to avoid confusion. We have included Web sites that are not likely to change, usually for specific organizations rather than specific documents.

Articles in periodicals are cited thus:

Ellen G. Landau, "Lee Krasner's Early Career," *Arts Magazine* 56 (1981), no. 2, pp. 110–22; no. 3, pp. 80–89

Fascicle numbers (2 and 3 in the example above) are given only if each fascicle is separately paginated. If the periodical is through-paginated only the volume number is given.

Bibliographic items are ordered chronologically, earliest items first. Two or more items published in the same year are ordered alphabetically by authors' surnames.

CLOSING DATE

Information in the encyclopedia is believed to have been accurate as of 31 March 2010.

A&P. See Great Atlantic and Pacific Tea Company.

Abbott, Berenice (*b* Springfield, Ohio, 17 July 1898; *d* Monson, Maine, 10 Dec 1991). Photographer. She moved to Greenwich Village in 1918 to pursue journalism. During her first few years in the city she developed an interest in the arts, prompting her to move to Paris in 1921 to study sculpture and drawing. She fell into photography when Man Ray recruited her to work as his darkroom assistant, and she soon developed a talent and passion for the medium, becoming a well-known portraitist and photographing such luminary figures as James Joyce and Sylvia Beach. In Paris she met French photographer Eugène Atget, and when she returned to New York City in 1929, she brought the bulk of his images with her, publicizing his documentary work and arranging for the Museum of Modern Art to purchase the collection in 1968.

Fascinated by the contrasts between old buildings awaiting demolition and tall buildings under construction, Abbott—inspired by Lewis Mumford's writings on technological eras—embarked on an ambitious project to systematically chronicle the entire city. Initially, she worked on the project independently while supporting herself with commercial work and teaching at the New School for Social Research, where she established the photography program and continued to teach until 1958. In 1935 she moved into a Greenwich Village loft with the art critic Elizabeth McCausland, who was supportive of Abbott's documentary work and later wrote much of the text to accompany her New York photographs. That same year the Federal Arts Project took interest in Abbott's study of the city and gave her financial support to hire assistants and devote her time to completing the project. In 1939 the set of 305 photographs was given to the Museum of the City of New York, and the images became the subject of her book *Changing New York,* which is still considered the best record of the city made before World War II. Although most of her photographs were taken in Manhattan, all boroughs are represented in this collection of images that emphasize physical structure and capture the energy of New York City's rapid transformation during the interwar period.

A pioneer in the straight photography movement, which advocated the importance of unmanipulated images, Abbott published the acclaimed *Guide to Better Photography* in 1941. She also designed several photographic devices, including the telescopic lighting pole or "autopole," and held U.S. patents for four of her inventions. A number of her portraits of local artists, along with photographs of downtown streets and interiors, were collected in the book *Greenwich Village Today and Yesterday* (1948). Later projects included the documentation of scientific phenomena for high school textbooks and automobile culture in small-town America. Abbott moved to Maine in 1966. Many of her New York City photographs are archived at the New York Public Library, where a major retrospective of her work was exhibited in 1989.

Hank O'Neal, *Berenice Abbott: American Photographer* (New York: McGraw–Hill, 1982); Douglas Levere, *New York Changing: Revisiting Berenice Abbott's New York* (New York: Princeton Architectural Press, 2004); George Sullivan, *Berenice Abbott, Photographer: An Independent Vision* (New York: Houghton Mifflin, 2006)

Holly Cronin

Abbott, George (Francis) (*b* Forestville, N.Y., 25 June 1887; *d* Miami Beach, 31 Jan 1995). Director, producer, and playwright. He began his career as an actor in 1913–34 and later produced, directed, and wrote more than 75 plays and musicals, including *Twentieth Century* (1932), *Boy Meets Girl* (1935), *Where's Charley?* (1948), *The Pajama Game* (1954), and *A Funny Thing Happened on the Way to the Forum* (1962). With Richard Rodgers and Lorenz Hart he wrote the book for *On Your Toes* (1936), directed and wrote *The Boys from Syracuse* (1938), and produced and directed *Pal Joey* (1940). He also worked on the adaptation for the stage of Betty Smith's *A Tree Grows in Brooklyn* (1951), which he produced and directed, and was an author and the director of *Damn Yankees* (1955) and *Fiorello!* (1959). He worked on a revival of *Damn Yankees* in 1994.

George Abbott

Sara J. Steen

Abbott, Lyman (*b* Roxbury [now in Boston], 18 Dec 1835; *d* New York City, 22 Oct 1922). Minister. After a brief period in the Midwest he wrote for *Harper's Magazine* and moved to New York City, where he worked with Henry Ward Beecher on the publication *Christian Union* (later renamed *Outlook*). He became the editor in 1881, and the journal was soon known as the leading exponent of progressive Christian social thought, especially the Social Gospel. Abbott took part in Henry George's mayoral campaigns, was active in the Progressive Party, and wrote four books on Christianity and contemporary issues. In 1890 he succeeded Beecher as pastor of the Plymouth Congregational Church in Brooklyn Heights.

Ira V. Brown, *Lyman Abbott, Christian Evolutionist: A Study in Religious Liberalism* (Cambridge, Mass.: Harvard University Press, 1953)

Eileen W. Lindner

ABC. See American Broadcasting Company.

Abdul-Jabbar, Kareem [Alcindor, Lew] (*b* New York City, 16 Apr 1947). Basketball player. Born in Harlem, he led the elite Catholic high school Power Memorial to a 95–6 record during his four years on the basketball court, including a 71-game winning streak. He earned all-American honors three times and graduated as the leading scorer and rebounder in New York City high school basketball history. He later became one of the most successful college and professional basketball players of all time, winning three National Collegiate Athletic Association (NCAA) championships at the University of California, Los Angeles, and playing most of his professional career with the Los Angeles Lakers and Milwaukee Bucks. In 1971 he changed his name to reflect his Muslim faith, which he began practicing in college. He has made two brief returns to the New York City basketball scene since his retirement as a player: he applied for the position of head basketball coach at Columbia University in 2003 and was hired for a brief time as a scout by the New York Knicks in 2004. Abdul-Jabbar has also authored several books, including *On the Shoulders of Giants: My Journey through the Harlem Renaissance* (2007).

David White

Abel, Rudolf (Ivanovich) [Golfus, Emil R.; Fisher, William August] (*b* England, 11 July 1903; *d* Moscow, 15 Nov 1971). Cold war spy. A colonel in the Soviet security agency (KGB), he began his career in espionage in 1927. In 1948 he is said to have entered the

United States through Canada with a forged passport. He then lived in Brooklyn under the alias Emil R. Golfus and worked at an art and photographic studio at 252 Fulton Street. In 1957 fellow Soviet Reino Hayhanen defected, became a counter spy, and helped the Federal Bureau of Investigation (FBI) locate Abel, thereby dismantling a Soviet spy ring. After he was arrested on 21 July 1957, a search of his home revealed spy equipment. He was convicted by a federal district court in Brooklyn and sentenced to 30 years in prison. On 10 February 1962, he was exchanged for American U-2 pilot Francis Gary Powers.

Louise Bernikow, *Abel* (New York: Trident, 1970)

Martin Ebon, Stephanie Miller

Abercrombie and Fitch. Firm of retailers formed during the late nineteenth century as an outdoor-supply store by David T. Abercrombie, a railroad engineer and prospector. It opened on South Street in Manhattan, where one of the first customers was Ezra H. Fitch, a wealthy lawyer and sportsman who became Abercrombie's partner. In 1908 the store provided President Theodore Roosevelt with equipment for an African safari, including snake-proof sleeping bags. Abercrombie left in 1912, and in 1917 Fitch moved the store to Madison Avenue at 45th Street, where a fly-casting pond was installed on the roof and a shooting range in the basement (which closed after a friend of Ernest Hemingway injured his shoulder while firing an elephant gun). Well-known customers in the following years included Admiral Richard Byrd, Charles Lindbergh, and Amelia Earhart, as well as Presidents William Howard Taft and Warren G. Harding (who both bought golf clubs), Woodrow Wilson (riding equipment), Herbert Hoover (fishing tackle), and Dwight D. Eisenhower (boots for weekends at Camp David); King Hussein of Jordan outfitted his yacht there, and Katharine Hepburn occasionally rode a bicycle across the main floor. In 1977 the firm, which operated a chain of nine stores, declared bankruptcy. The name was bought in 1978 by Oshman's Sporting Goods, which opened its first Abercrombie and Fitch store in 1979 in California and another at South Street Seaport in 1984. Abercrombie and Fitch was sold to the Limited in 1988. In the early twenty-first century the company operated over 300 stores nationwide, selling clothing geared toward young adults.

Eric Wm. Allison

Abigail Adams Smith Museum. Former name of the Mount Vernon Hotel Museum and Garden.

Abingdon Square. Name given to the intersection of West 12th Street, Eighth Avenue, and Hudson Street in Manhattan, and by extension to the surrounding neighborhood.

Abingdon Square, 1904

Its eponym is Charlotte Warren, by marriage the countess of Abingdon; she was the daughter of Susannah de Lancey and the English privateer Admiral Peter Warren, whose estate of 300 acres (121 hectares) encompassed most of what is now the West Village. The neighborhood has a varied architecture that includes nineteenth-century row houses, apartment buildings, tenements, and commercial buildings, as well as factory buildings and warehouses at Westbeth and the Gansevoort Meat Market that have been converted into residences for artists and expensive condos. Its principal commercial thoroughfares are Hudson Street and Bleecker Street, which are lined with specialty shops and restaurants. A restoration in 2004 transformed the 0.22-acre (0.09-hectare) Abingdon Square Park from an asphalt triangle into a green park, emphasizing its historic character.

Joyce Mendelsohn

abolitionism. The course of abolitionism in New York City followed that within the state in general in many matters. Gouverneur Morris introduced a resolution to eliminate slavery in New York State at the state constitutional convention in 1777; a large majority of the delegates approved it. However, no further action was taken until 1785 when the state legislature debated several abolitionist measures. Among them was a plan introduced by Aaron Burr to free all slaves immediately, which won the support of Federalists (who sought to extend civil rights to blacks) but was soundly defeated; another plan calling for gradual emancipation, which a majority of the legislature supported, failed because it would also have extended suffrage to blacks. Federalists concentrated on ending the slave trade and in 1785 passed a bill banning the sale of slaves in New York State but allowing slaves to be brought into the state and remain there for no longer than nine months. During the same year such well-known figures as John Jay, Alexander Hamilton, Chancellor Livingston, Philip Schuyler, and Hector St. John de Crèvecoeur established the New York Manumission Society to encourage public support for abolition. The society mediated indentureship negotiations and provided legal assistance to African Americans who were denied their freedom; its efforts to ensure compliance with the law of 1785 were largely unsuccessful because slave owners often found loopholes that allowed sales of slaves out of state. The legislature in 1799 passed the Act for the Gradual Emancipation of Negroes and Other Slaves, which declared free the children of slaves born on or after 4 July, granted freedom to slaves born before that date at the age of 24 for women and 28 for men, and required the registration of children indentured to their masters until the age of manumission. To end abuses of the law the legislature in 1817 declared all slaves free as of 4 July 1827. In 1841 the state rescinded the provisions allowing nonresidents to hold slaves for as long as nine months.

Abolition did not end discrimination against blacks in New York, who were denied full rights of citizenship. The Democrats controlling the state constitutional convention of 1821 redefined the property requirement for voting along racial lines: blacks could vote only if they owned property worth at least $250, whereas the property qualification was eliminated for white male voters. Meanwhile, many free blacks joined the abolitionist movement, which was also taken up by the first black newspapers in New York City, *Freedom's Journal* (1827–29) and the *Rights of All* (1829). The city became an abolitionist center during the 1830s and in 1833 home to the American Anti-Slavery Society, the first national organization of its kind. Some of its most influential members were leaders of the city's black community, including Samuel E. Cornish and Theodore S. Wright. Under the society's auspices Wright and Henry Highland Garnet made speaking tours of the northern and western states and with other black abolitionists from the city became leading spokesmen for the antislavery movement: they argued that blacks would not enjoy the full rights of citizenship until slavery was eradicated throughout the country. By demonstrating political acumen and oratorical skills, they also sought to destroy myths of inferiority that provided a basis for discriminatory legislation.

Interracial tensions mounted during the 1830s. Many white abolitionists advocated repatriating blacks to Africa, leading blacks to build a separate movement against racism while continuing to work with whites. Such prominent African Americans from Manhattan as Philip Bell Cornish and J. W. C. Pennington attended the first National Negro Convention in Philadelphia from 15 to 24 September 1830, the first of several such conventions held during the 1830s. At the New York State Negro Convention, held in New York City on 25 January 1831, a number of delegates denounced efforts by the New York Colonization Society to resettle blacks in Africa as a scheme to perpetuate slavery and proclaimed their dedication to abolition and the uplift of free blacks. Abolitionism failed to win much support among whites and even intensified antiblack sentiment among white workers who viewed blacks as competitors in the labor market. During a several-day rampage in 1834 known as the Journeymen's Riot, white day laborers disrupted a meeting of abolitionists at Chatham Street Chapel and attacked the homes of Lewis Tappan and scores of African Americans.

The *Colored American,* launched in 1837, provided coverage of the movement until ceasing publication in 1841. Black churches became the most important venues for abolitionism. Through astute biblical exegesis, hard-nosed political analysis, and fiery oratory, black clergymen inspired their congregations to embrace "moral suasion," a policy of eschewing political action and converting slaveholders to abolitionism through moral argument. In 1840 a number of blacks left the American Anti-Slavery Society after disagreeing with members who favored moral suasion and helped to form the American and Foreign Anti-Slavery Society. African Americans during the 1840s continued to hold state and local conventions where speakers protested racism, criticized business for maintaining ties to the southern economy, and encouraged blacks to vote for candidates of the Liberty and Free Soil parties, hoping that in return for the support of black voters the parties would oppose limitations on black suffrage in New York State. Such leaders as Garnet, who at a convention in Buffalo in 1843 urged slaves to fight for their freedom, adopted a more militant stance. The *Ram's Horn* (1847) also took up the abolitionist cause.

Protecting the freedom of African Americans also became an abolitionist cause in the city, where slave hunters sought to kidnap the many fugitive slaves who settled there. Concern mounted after the passing of the Fugitive Slave Act (1850), which outlawed efforts to help runaway slaves and required officials to cooperate in recapturing them. The case of James Hamlet, a resident of Williamsburgh captured by local authorities and transported to Baltimore, became a cause célèbre: the New York Vigilance Committee (1835), an organization dedicated to helping fugitives, raised $800 to buy his freedom, and on 5 October 1850 his return to the city was celebrated with a rally at City Hall Park.

Resentment against blacks reached a peak during the DRAFT RIOTS of July 1863 when a mob of Irish workers protested the federal draft act by attacking the local draft office and killing several state militiamen who had been called in. During the course of the day they destroyed the homes of blacks and the shops of whites who traded with them and dragged their occupants into the street. They set fire to the Colored Orphan Asylum on Fifth Avenue between 43rd and 44th streets, where they murdered an infant. New York State began accepting blacks for military service in 1864 to meet a quota imposed by the federal government. African Americans from the city were incorporated into the 20th Regiment by 5 May 1864 and the 31st Regiment by 27 March 1865 and accounted for 877 casualties by the end of the war.

Benjamin Quarles, *Black Abolitionists* (New York: Oxford University Press, 1969)

See also AFRICAN AMERICANS.

Thelma Foote

Abraham and Straus. Firm of retailers, originated in 1865 in Brooklyn as a small dry-goods shop called Wechsler and Abraham by Abraham Abraham, who was 22 at the time, and Joseph Wechsler. When the Brooklyn Bridge was completed in 1883 Abraham and Wechsler foresaw that a new shopping district would emerge at its eastern terminus, and they moved the business to a five-story building at 422 Fulton Street (on the block bounded by Fulton, Hoyt, and Livingston streets and Gallatin Place) that by 1889 was the largest dry-goods store in New York State. In 1893 Abraham joined with Isidor and Nathan Straus to buy out Wechsler's share of the business and gave the store its current name; the new partnership dissolved in 1920. The store was incorporated, joined the American Merchandising Corporation, and in 1925 became publicly owned. It expanded outside of Brooklyn in 1934 when a store opened in Jamaica, and became a division of Federated Department Stores in 1949. With 15 stores, Abraham and Straus was the second-largest department store chain in the metropolitan area until 1995, when Federated dropped the name completely in favor of Macy's, which it had acquired in 1994.

Leon A. Harris, *Merchant Princes: An Intimate History of Jewish Families Who Built Great Department Stores* (New York: Harper and Row, 1979)

Laura Gwinn

Abrams, Charles (*b* Vilnius [now in Lithuania], 16 Feb 1902; *d* New York City, 22 Feb 1970). Lawyer, public official. Abrams left a highly successful law practice to participate in the drafting of the Municipal Housing Authorities Law of New York State in 1934 and became the first counsel of the New York City Housing Authority (NYCHA) (1934–37). His victory in *New York City Housing Authority v. Muller* (1936) established the authority's right to employ the power of eminent domain for slum clearance. As the chairman of the New York State Commission against Discrimination (1955–59) he challenged broad patterns of discrimination by launching wide-ranging investigations. He also taught at Columbia University, worked as a housing consultant, and traveled on behalf of the United Nations. His published writings include *Revolution in Land* (1939), *The Future of Housing* (1946), *Forbidden Neighbors* (1955), and *The City Is the Frontier* (1965).

A. Scott Henderson, *Housing and the Democratic Ideal: The Life and Thought of Charles Adams* (New York: Columbia University Press, 2000)

Rosalie Genevro

Abrams v. United States. Pivotal case decided by the U.S. Supreme Court in 1919 (250 U.S. 616). It upheld the ruling of a lower court that had convicted five non-naturalized Russian citizens on Manhattan's Lower East Side of violating the Espionage Act. The defendants, some of who were self-described revolutionaries, anarchists, and socialists, had distributed pamphlets intended to foster solidarity between immigrant Russian workers and the freedom fighters in their homeland. The pamphlets criticized President Woodrow Wilson for American involvement against the Russian Revolution. Assistant Attorney General Robert Stewart argued the case for the government, while Harry Weinberger led the defense effort. Justice John Hessin Clarke wrote the Court's majority opinion, which argued that the pamphlets' appeal to workers threatened the government and American foreign policy. The ruling expressed prevalent fears of communism, anarchism, and revolution, as well as the government's intense efforts to contain political dissent. The creation of the Committee for Public Information and the passage of the Espionage and Sedition Acts during World War I reflected efforts to quell opposition toward the government. Many newspapers ceased publication or avoided coverage of the war. Individual dissenters faced 20-year jail sentences and $10,000 fines. The Russian Revolution in 1917, a growing American socialist movement, and a wave of union strikes perpetuated fears after the war during the "first Red Scare." Only Justices Oliver Wendell Holmes and Louis Brandeis dissented from the majority opinion, claiming that the pamphlets posed no direct threat to the government and citing an infringement upon the Russians' First Amendment rights. The minority opinion conveyed concern over government suppression of free speech. The decision set the legal precedent for future rulings on government regulation of free speech and press, but also stirred a movement of First Amendment activists.

David White

Abyssinian Baptist Church, 2009

Abyssinian Baptist Church. One of the oldest, largest, and most influential Protestant congregations in the United States. It traces its origins to 1808, when a few free black parishioners left the First Baptist Church of New York City because they were unwilling to accept racially segregated seating in a house of worship. Together with a group of Ethiopian merchants, they established themselves in a building on Anthony Street (later Worth Street). After meeting in a series of buildings on Anthony, Thompson, and Spring streets, the congregation moved to Waverly Place and then to 40th Street. In 1908 Adam Clayton Powell, Sr., a young preacher from New Haven, Connecticut, became the pastor. Under his leadership the congregation in 1920 purchased lots on 138th Street between Lenox and Seventh avenues in Harlem. After a successful tithing campaign to which 2000 members responded, a cavernous Gothic and Tudor structure, replete with imported stained-glass windows and an Italian marble pulpit, was dedicated on 17 June 1923. In 1937, by which time the congregation had grown to 7000 members, Powell gave up the pastorate in favor of his only son, Adam Clayton Powell, Jr. An intrepid preacher and civil rights leader who also served 14 terms in the U.S. House of Representatives, the younger Powell made Abyssinian what he called the "church of the masses," combining the Christian message of justice and equality with the militant oratory of liberation. Powell's successors, Samuel DeWitt Proctor and Calvin O. Butts III, continued his tradition of political activism. In the early twenty-first century the church continued to serve thousands of communicants each week, many of them attracted by the superb choir and the 67-rank organ. The New York Philharmonic has performed at the church, as have such internationally acclaimed musicians as Leontyne Price and André Watts.

Kenneth T. Jackson

Abzug [née Savitzky], **Bella** (*b* Bronx, N.Y., 24 July 1924; *d* Manhattan, 31 March 1998). Politician. Born to Russian-Jewish immigrants who ran the Live and Let Live Meat Market on Ninth Avenue, Abzug gave her first speech at age 11 in a subway station. A graduate of Hunter College and Columbia Law School, Abzug represented accused communists and tried civil rights cases in New York and the South in the 1950s. In 1961 Abzug co-founded Women's Strike for Peace, a group that lobbied against the House Un-American Activities Committee and the Vietnam War and for a nuclear test ban. A self-proclaimed radical known for her trademark wide-brimmed hats, Abzug gained notoriety for brash rhetoric; Norman Mailer said her voice "could boil the fat off a taxicab driver's neck." In 1970 she won the congressional election in New York's nineteenth district (parts of lower Manhattan and the Upper West Side). In this campaign she actively campaigned to gay voters and ran on the slogan "This Woman's place is in the house—the House of Representatives." In Washington Abzug co-wrote the Freedom of Information Act; the "sunshine law," which provides guaranteed access to information held by the state; and the Right to Privacy Act. She favored cutting the Pentagon's budget to pay for national health care. Abzug was one of the first members of Congress to call for Richard Nixon's impeachment, and she responded to an invitation to the White House from him by writing on the acceptance line that her constituents demanded a withdrawal from Vietnam. The state legislature split the nineteenth district following Abzug's election; she was elected from the twentieth district (the Upper West Side and Riverdale) in 1972 and 1974. In 1974 Abzug and Ed Koch proposed the first-ever federal gay rights bill. Abzug gave up her congressional seat to run an unsuccessful campaign for Senate in 1976. After leaving Congress, Abzug briefly worked for Jimmy Carter, ran for Congress in 1978 and 1986, practiced law, and worked for women's groups.

Ben Silk

Academy of American Poets. Organization founded in 1934 that supports American poets and fosters the appreciation of contemporary poetry, located at 584 Broadway. It administers awards (including the Wallace Stevens Prize), sponsors readings, publishes a literary journal, and maintains a poetry Web site, an audio archive, and an array of online poetry resources for teachers. The organization also hosts workshops for New York City high school students. In April 1996 the academy inaugurated National Poetry Month. In 2008 the organization's 14 chancellors included such prominent poets as Sharon Olds and C. K. Williams. There have been more than 70 past chancellors, among them W. H. Auden, John Berryman, Robinson Jeffers, Robert Lowell, and Marianne Moore.

Helen Graves

Academy of Arts and Letters. See American Academy of Arts and Letters.

Academy of Medicine. See New York Academy of Medicine.

Academy of Mount St. Vincent. Original name of the College of Mount St. Vincent.

Academy of Music. Opera house opened in 1854 at the northeast corner of 14th Street and Irving Place. It was built at a time when the area near Union Square was an affluent neighborhood. The building was lavish and had a stage sufficiently large for grand opera, many private and stage boxes, and about 4000 seats upholstered in crimson velvet; the interior of the hall was painted white and gold and illuminated by thousands of gaslights. Irving Hall, an annex at Irving Place and 15th Street, was the home of the New York Philharmonic in 1861–63. In several seasons during 1856–86 the Philharmonic performed in the main theater, which for 30 years was the principal venue for foreign opera singers visiting the city. The building was destroyed by fire in 1866 but rebuilt by 1868; a more serious blow was the opening in 1883 of the Metropolitan Opera House, which drastically reduced its audience. The Academy of Music was unable to compete and closed in 1886; its manager, Colonel James Mapelson, lamented his inability to "fight Wall Street." The space continued to be used for several years for labor meetings, plays, vaudeville acts, and motion picture screenings; the site is now occupied by a building of Consolidated Edison.

John Frederick Cone, *First Rival of the Metropolitan Opera* (New York: Columbia University Press, 1983)

Nancy Shear

Academy of Sciences. See New York Academy of Sciences.

Academy of the Fine Arts. See American Academy of the Fine Arts.

accounting. Until the late nineteenth century most accounting in New York City was handled by clerks with only basic bookkeeping skills: the pace of business was slow and transactions uncomplicated. Certified financial statements were considered unnecessary because many businessmen based their dealings on informal assessments of character. A demand for new services arose during the 1880s with the development of large corporations. Investors required audits to verify financial statements by corporate managers, and the managers sought advice in developing and improving their accounting systems. The number of accountants in the city increased, and in 1882 the Institute of Bookkeepers and Accountants was formed; it later became the New York Institute of Accounts (NYIA). Among the directors of the organization was Charles Waldo Haskins, who operated one of the city's largest accounting firms, Haskins and Sells (later Deloitte Touche Tohmatsu). Training in accounting was offered through an apprenticeship system based on the British model and in proprietary bookkeeping academies such as that of Silas S. Packard in Manhattan, which was highly successful. Several accounting associations were soon formed in the city. One of the first was the American Association of Public Accountants (AAPA; from 1957 the American Institute of Certified Public Accountants [AICPA]), which began operations in 1887 after an English chartered accountant, Edwin Guthrie, traveled to the city seeking reputable American accountants to engage as correspondents. It attracted an elite membership based in the East that was often called on to devise new accounting methods for transactions of unprecedented complexity. Seeking recognition as specialists, the members promoted auditing as an element of corporate governance that had proved its effectiveness in investment banking; they also set standards for internal regulation based on those adopted by British chartered accountants earlier in the century.

Efforts to set standards for education and licensing were undertaken in the following years. In 1895 the AAPA opened the College of Accounts, which offered a one-year certification course consisting of a thousand hours of instruction; it closed soon after the New York State Board of Regents refused it the right to grant degrees. During the 1890s separate efforts to establish state licensing were pursued by accountants in the NYIA and by the AAPA. The accountants of the NYIA prevailed because they were concentrated in New York City and because they were led by Haskins, who through his connection by marriage to the Havemeyer family was able to win the support of Melvil Dewey, secretary of the Board of Regents (which controlled professional licensing). Haskins's colleagues in the NYIA formed the New York Society of Certified Public Accountants in 1897. Dissatisfied with existing training and apprenticeship programs, Haskins made plans for a university curriculum: he believed that the quantitative nature of accounting made it akin to the physical sciences and shared the hope of many Progressives that its precision might allow a high degree of control over the affairs of business and government. His enthusiasm and financial guarantees led to the formation of the College of Commerce, Accounts and Finance at New York University in 1899, of which he was the first dean. His ideas were reinforced by his close associate Charles Ezra Sprague, a faculty member whose book *The Philosophy of Accounts* (1908) and other writings were among the first to define a theory of accounting. The college became a model for institutions nationwide, and by 1927 its graduates accounted for 57 of the 179 college-educated members of the AAPA.

Accounting developed rapidly between 1900 and 1904, owing to a sudden increase in corporate mergers. The demand for audits rose sharply as bankers in the city floated securities in London, where statement certification was common practice. The importance of accounting became firmly established in 1901 when the House of Morgan engaged the firm of Price Waterhouse to certify statements of U.S. Steel, the country's first manufacturing corporation with more than $1 billion in assets. The AAPA set ethical standards prohibiting such practices as using knowledge of accounting contrary to the public interest; these standards proved durable as the profession developed in later years. After the federal income tax was introduced in 1913, accountants were increasingly engaged in preparing tax returns. A uniform certifying examination was introduced by the AAPA in 1917 and later adopted by all state licensing boards nationwide. By the 1920s most firms listed on the New York Stock Exchange presented annual certified statements; they were required to do

The Academy of Music, 14th Street and Irving Place, ca *1910*

so after the formation of the Securities and Exchange Commission, which considered such statements vital to restoring public confidence in the country's financial markets. From the 1930s the AAPA set standards for such practices as accounting and auditing, and later tax preparation, consulting, attestations, and reviews. Educational standards rose, largely because of Haskins's efforts, leading New York State in 1940 to require candidates for certification to have a baccalaureate degree, the first such mandate in the country. Doctoral programs were established by New York University (1944), Columbia University (1954), and Baruch College (1974). During the 1970s the AICPA assumed new responsibilities for review and oversight, through which it sought to protect the public; it also published books and periodicals to promote competence and achieve consensus about matters of practice. New York City remained a leading center for education in accounting in the early twenty-first century.

Paul J. Miranti, Jr.

Ackerman, Frederick L(ee) (*b* Edmeston, N.Y., 9 July 1878; *d* New York City, 17 March 1950). Architect and urban planner. He was the chief designer of low-rent housing and the town planner for the Fleet Corporation, an organization formed during World War I to provide emergency housing for shipyard workers. In collaboration with Clarence S. Stein and Henry Wright he developed Sunnyside Gardens in Queens (1924) and led the movement toward building housing units in clusters and constructing apartment buildings with common social space. As the director of the New York City Housing Authority from 1934 to 1938 he advocated low-rise, walk-up apartment buildings within the cost limits of public housing. Later he conducted site studies used by housing authorities during the late 1940s, and with Lafayette Goldstone he designed the Lillian Wald Houses (1949) on the Lower East Side. Ackerman wrote *The Housing Famine: How to End It* (1920).

Joel Schwartz

ACLU. See AMERICAN CIVIL LIBERTIES UNION.

ACNielsen. Marketing firm. Established in 1923 by Arthur C. Nielson, Sr., the firm is headquartered in New York with offices in more than 100 countries worldwide. In the early twenty-first century, their headquarters were located at 700 Broadway. The firm is best known for its Nielsen ratings that measure radio, television, and newspaper audiences and the receptivity of programming. It also created Homescan, a program that measures grocery and retail purchases for a group of subjects to track purchasing patterns as related to household demographics.

Acosta Vice, Celia M. (*b* Guayanilla, Puerto Rico, 20 June 1919; *d* Puerto Rico, 30 Jan 1993). Civic leader. Acosta Vice arrived in New York City in 1926 and lived in Brooklyn until 1979. In the late 1930s, she opened a small business in Williamsburg that became a hub for information about jobs, housing, income taxes, and other concerns in the Spanish-speaking neighborhood. She worked with local Democratic clubs and helped found the Fernando Sierra Vardeci Independent Democratic Club in Brooklyn in 1954. She also organized the 50-member Council of Brooklyn Organizations. The first Puerto Rican woman real estate agent in New York City, in 1960 she was the first female grand marshal of the city's Puerto Rican Day Parade. Acosta Vice established the Puerto Rican Heritage Bookstore in the 1970s. This collection of artifacts and books is considered the foundation for El Museo del Barrio.

Virginia Sánchez Korrol

acquired immune deficiency syndrome. See AIDS.

Actors' Equity Association. Labor union of professional actors and stage managers working in the legitimate theater. It was formed in New York City in May 1913 by 112 actors committed to fighting the arbitrary work rules and low wages then prevalent in the American theater. In August 1919 it mounted a strike for recognition, which increased its membership to more than 8000 and led to a five-year contract between the union and the Producing Managers' Association. The union is affiliated with the AFL–CIO through its parent organization, the Associated Actors and Artistes of America, and has its headquarters in Manhattan. As of the early twenty-first century, Actors' Equity had more than 45,000 members nationwide.

Alfred Harding, *The Revolt of the Actors* (New York: William Morrow, 1929)

Martha S. LoMonaco

Actors Studio. School opened in 1947 by Elia Kazan, Robert Lewis, and Cheryl Crawford of the Group Theatre to encourage actors to develop their craft without the demands of public performance. Its artistic director from 1951 was Lee Strasberg, who introduced the Method, a controversial psychological approach to acting that stressed the actor's life experiences and was greatly influenced by the work of Russian actor and director Konstantin Stanislavsky. Among the members of the studio was Marlon Brando, whose visceral acting style came to exemplify the Method. After Strasberg's death in 1982, joint leadership was assumed by Ellen Burstyn and Al Pacino, who continue to head the program today along with Harvey Keitel. In the fall of 1994, the Actors Studio Drama School (ASDS) began a Master of Fine Arts (MFA) program at the New School in New York City. In 2005 ASDS broke with the New School, and beginning in 2006 the studio offered a joint MFA program with Pace University. In 1994 the Actors Studio started broadcasting the Emmy-nominated television program *Inside the Actors Studio* on the Bravo television network; it features seminars with influential actors and directors discussing how they developed their talents and careers. The Actors Studio remains one of the most influential theater schools in the world, training such well-known actors, directors, and playwrights as Robert De Niro, Marilyn Monroe, Tennessee Williams, Paul Newman, Norman Mailer, Jane Fonda, Julia Roberts, and Dustin Hoffman.

Foster Hirsch, *A Method to Their Madness: The History of the Actors Studio* (New York: W. W. Norton, 1984)

D. S. Moynihan

ACT UP [AIDS Coalition to Unleash Power]. Organization formed in 1987 by activists in New York City to advocate stronger measures against acquired immune deficiency syndrome (AIDS) and to defend those suffering from it. Offering information on the medical and social consequences of AIDS, pharmaceuticals, and treatments, the group gave rise to dozens of similar groups throughout the United States and the world. ACT UP became especially known for its confrontational tactics toward government at all levels, the medical profession, and the pharmaceutical industry. In the early twenty-first century it held weekly meetings at 200 West 13th Street and maintained headquarters at 332 Bleecker Street.

Robert A. Padgug

Adams, Franklin P(ierce) (*b* Chicago, 15 Nov 1881; *d* New York City, 23 March 1960). Columnist. After working for the *Chicago Tribune* he moved to New York City in 1904 and in 1913 joined the *New York Tribune* to write a column called "The Conning Tower," which appeared in various newspapers in the city until 1941; he usually wrote under the pseudonym "F.P.A." He was also a regular guest on the radio quiz program *Information Please* (from 1938) and a member of the Algonquin Round Table. He lived at 124 West 13th Street (1925–28) and 26 West 10th Street (1929 to the mid-1930s). A humorist with a taste for the epigrammatic and the sardonic, Adams was among the most widely read journalists in New York City. His newspaper column was a forum for literary opinion, gossip, commentary, and light verse by him and others (including Ring Lardner, Sinclair Lewis, and Dorothy Parker); to be published in it was considered an honor.

Robert E. Drennan, ed., *The Algonquin Wits* (New York: Citadel, 1968)

Brenda Wineapple

Adams, Thomas (*b* Scotland, 10 Sept 1871; *d* England, 24 March 1940). Urban planner. He managed England's first "garden city," founded the British Town Planning Institute, and served as adviser to the Commission of Conservation of Canada, before being named director of the Regional Plan of New York in 1923. Sponsored by the Russell Sage Foundation, this grand scheme was a 40-year outline for the city's development into a vast supermetropolis of 20 million people. Adams served as the plan's director until 1929; his colleagues included Frederick Law Olmsted, Jr., and George B. Ford. In addition to supervising extensive survey and planning work, Adams oversaw publication of the plan in a book titled *The Building of the City.* Although generally applauded, the Regional Plan of New York was condemned by the critic Lewis Mumford as "nothing more than the orderly dilution of New York over a 50-mile circle."

Susan Kriete

Addams, Charles (Samuel) (*b* Westfield, N.J., 7 Jan 1912; *d* New York City, 29 Sept 1988). Cartoonist. He attended Colgate University, the University of Pennsylvania, and the Grand Central School of Art and first published cartoons in 1935 in the *New Yorker,* which carried his work for more than half a century. Known for their macabre humor, his cartoons were shown at the Metropolitan Museum of Art, the Museum of the City of New York, and Harvard University. They inspired the television series *The Addams Family* (1964–66), which was also made into several motion pictures (1991, 1993, 1998), cartoon series, video games, and a Broadway show (2010). Addams published a dozen books, including *Addams and Evil* (1947), *Monster Rally* (1950), and *Favorite Haunts* (1976).

James E. Mooney

Addisleigh Park. Housing development in central Queens, just north of the former site of a golf course in St. Albans later occupied by the Veterans Administration Extended Care Center. It was begun in 1927 when the Addisleigh Homes Company and the Rodman and English Building Company built several blocks of houses in the English style on large plots on 179th and 180th streets between Murdock Avenue (114th Street) and Linden Boulevard. The houses cost $12,000 to $30,000 at a time when prices in Queens typically ranged from $8000 to $12,000. Buyers were drawn by the proximity of the golf course and the train station at St. Albans. Among the residents were such prominent African Americans as Lena Horne, Count Basie, Percy Sutton, Ella Fitzgerald, and Jackie Robinson. The Depression and the building up of available land put an end to development in 1939. In 2010 the neighborhood was still predominately middle-class African Americans, with about 650 homes, and efforts were under way to have the neighborhood designated a historic district by the Landmarks Preservation Committee.

Vincent Seyfried

Adler, Felix (*b* Alzey, Germany, 13 Aug 1851; *d* New York City, 24 April 1933). Religious leader and educator. His family emigrated from Germany and settled in New York City in 1857, when his father was invited to assume the rabbinate of Temple Emanu-El. Educated at Columbia College (BA 1870) and in Semitic studies at the University of Heidelberg (PhD 1874), he was influenced by Kantian religious idealism, studied European approaches to the problems of labor and industrial society, and taught Hebrew and Oriental studies at Cornell University for two years. With the support of German businessmen and professionals who were adherents of Reform Judaism he formed the New York Society for Ethical Culture in 1876, which drew on traditional creeds, ritual, and prayer, and at the same time emphasized activism, secularism, and universalism. He also helped to train leaders for societies in St. Louis, Philadelphia, Chicago, and London and remained the leader of the society to the end of his life. Active in causes of civic and social improvement in the city between 1876 and 1925, he strongly supported industrial education, kindergartens, settlement houses, good-government clubs, tenement reform, child labor legislation, and the construction of small parks, public baths, and laundries. His interest in labor and his belief in providing young people with training in ethics led to the opening by the society of a kindergarten in 1878 (the first in the eastern United States) and a workingman's school in 1880, the first of several Ethical Culture schools in the city. In his writings and lectures Adler discoursed on the philosophical, ethical, and practical applications of Ethical Culture and his belief that religion should be based on intellectual truth, that the moral development of the individual and of society was paramount, and that morality need not rely on theology.

Howard B. Radest, *Toward Common Ground: The Story of the Ethical Societies in the United States* (New York: Ungar, 1969); Robert S. Guttchen, *Felix Adler* (New York: Twayne, 1974); Benny Kraut, *From Reform Judaism to Ethical Culture: The Religious Evolution of Felix Adler* (Cincinnati: Hebrew Union College Press, 1979); Horace Leland Friess, *Felix Adler and Ethical Culture: Memories and Studies* (New York: Columbia University Press, 1981)

Jane Allen

Adler, Jacob (*b* Odessa, Ukraine, 1855; *d* New York City, 1 April 1926). Actor, father of Stella Adler. In 1879 he made his debut in the Ukraine in the Yiddish theater, then a developing genre. After performing in eastern Europe he settled in 1882 in London, where he became well known for his performance in the title role of Karl Gutzkow's *Uriel Acosta.* By the time he moved to New York City in 1887, Adler enjoyed an international reputation. He was most popular in grand emotional roles and was associated with such literary repertory as Jacob Gordon's *Der yidishe kenig Lear.* A glamorous figure, Adler married several prominent actresses, including Sara Heine-Haimovitch and Dina Stettin Feinman. Stella Adler and several of his other children, including Celia Adler, Luther Adler, and Frances Adler, worked in the Yiddish and English-language theater.

Lulla Rosenfeld, *Bright Star of Exile: Jacob Adler and the Yiddish Theater* (New York: Thomas Y. Crowell, 1977); Jacob Adler, *A Life on Stage: A Memoir* (New York: Knopf, 1999)

Nahma Sandrow

Adler, Samuel (*b* Worms, Germany, 3 Dec 1809; *d* New York City, 9 June 1891). Rabbi. After earning a doctorate in Germany in 1836 he became a leader of the Reform movement in Judaism. In 1857 he moved to New York City to lead the congregation of Temple Emanu-El, where he continued his reform work and sought to raise the level of religious consciousness. His revised version of the Hebrew prayer book became widely used. Adler formed the Hebrew Orphan Asylum of New York, which stressed religious training for children, and worked toward equality for women in religious matters. His published writings include *Leitfaden für den israelitischen Religionsunterricht* (1864).

James E. Mooney

Adler, Stella (*b* New York City, 10 Feb 1901; *d* Los Angeles, 21 Dec 1992). Actress and acting teacher who pioneered the teaching of Method acting in American theater and founded one of the nation's most prominent acting schools. Born into a theatrical family, she was the daughter of Jacob and Sara Adler, both Russian immigrants and leaders of the Yiddish stage movement in New York; her five siblings were also actors. She first appeared on stage at the Grand Street Theater on the Lower East Side when she was four. After enrolling in the American Laboratory Theater School in 1925, she began studying the Method, the revolutionary technique created by Konstantin Stanislavsky. While Classical acting focused on the development of external skills, Method acting emphasized the development of an actor's internal sensory, psychological, and emotional abilities. During the Depression she joined the Group Theatre, an experimental union of writers, directors, and actors who promoted socially relevant theater in the United States. With one of the company's founders, Lee Strasberg, she became a leading authority on the application of the Method, though she and Strasberg often differed on the role that imagination should play in the acting craft. While Strasberg encouraged students to utilize their own personal memories in order to convey emotion, Adler emphasized the development of imagination as the key component of the acting craft. Throughout her long career she appeared in nearly 200 stage productions and won high praise for both her acting and directing talents. She also appeared in three Hollywood films: *Love on Toast* (1938), *Shadow of a Thin Man* (1941), and *My Girl Tisa* (1948). In 1949 she founded the Stella Adler Conservatory of Acting in Manhattan on West 27th Street, which soon became one of the premier acting institutions in the United States. A demanding and impassioned teacher, she shaped the careers of hundreds of notable performers, including Marlon Brando, Warren Beatty, and Robert De Niro. In 2003 the Stella Adler Outreach Program was established by the school to offer free actor training, internships, and scholarships to disadvantaged inner-city children.

Robert Sanger Steel

Adler v. Board of Education of the City of New York. U.S. Supreme Court case (342 U.S. 485) of 1952 that challenged the constitutionality of New York's Feinberg Law, which prohibited anyone who belonged to a list of "subversive" organizations from teaching in the public schools. Passed in 1949, this law was a product of the government's far-reaching efforts to subvert communist activity in the United States by removing dissenters from positions of influence. It was directed at communist activity but seemingly threatened much broader applications. The New York Teachers' Union organized a small group to challenge the law's constitutionality before it could be implemented. The case bore the name of Irving Adler, a math teacher at the Textile High School in Manhattan who was listed first alphabetically of the appellants. The teachers won their case in the state supreme court, but the decision was overturned by the state appellate court and made its way to the U.S. Supreme Court, where the Feinberg Law was upheld by a 6–3 decision in March 1952. The court's ruling set an important precedent for the restriction of political dissent and the role of the government in the education system during the McCarthy era. A number of city teachers, including Adler, lost their jobs in the ensuing years when they refused to answer questions about their political beliefs. In 1967 the Supreme Court essentially reversed its *Adler* decision in *Keyishian v. Board of Regents* (385 U.S. 589). Many of the city's teachers who had been fired during the previous decade, including Adler, applied successfully for reinstatement.

David White

Adriance Farmhouse. Historic house in Queens. It was built in 1772 by Jacob Adriance and is now at 75–50 Little Neck Parkway in Floral Park; it is part of the Queens County Farm Museum. The first farm on the site, built in 1697, was one of many farms established by colonial settlers who were drawn to the region by the rich soil deposited by glaciers. The farmhouse that now stands in its place was built in the Dutch style with a steeply pitched roof and a shingled exterior; it was doubled in size in the 1830s. From 1890 to 1926 the property was a truck farm; it was acquired in 1927 by the Creedmoor State Hospital, and until the 1960s patients tilled the soil. Two years after the last members of the hospital staff left the premises, the house and farm were opened as a museum in 1975.

Jonathan Kuhn

adult education. During the colonial period adult education consisted of instruction in English and the Bible. In 1857 the philanthropist and inventor Peter Cooper opened the Union for the Advancement of Science in New York City to provide free evening technical training for people who worked during the day and to sponsor lectures and discussions through the Cooper Union Forum. In the early nineteenth century night schools offered classes in English and civics to immigrants. In 1919 James Robinson and Charles Beard opened the New School for Social Research at 66 West 12th Street as a center for adult education, with emphasis on the social sciences and psychology. Adult education was greatly increased by the passage of the Servicemen's Readjustment Act of 1944 (popularly known as the GI Bill) and the Universal Military Training and Services Act of 1951, which provided veterans with the opportunity to complete high school and college. In the 1970s and 1980s a large number of women entered adult education programs. In the twenty-first century the public school system in New York City provides a wide range of free courses for adults. Most colleges have special programs for older students: at the City University of New York people 65 years old may enroll in any course for a minimal charge. The New York City Adult Literacy Initiative prepares adult students for tests in English as a second language and high school equivalency tests; it offers classes free of charge at community organizations, public schools, branches of the City University of New York, and public libraries.

Huey B. Long, *Adult and Continuing Education: Responding to Change* (New York: Teachers College Press, 1983); Nell Eurich, *The Learning Industry: Education for Adult Workers* (Princeton, N.J.: Carnegie Foundation for the Advancement of Teaching, 1990)

Rachel Shor

advertising. During the eighteenth century advertising in New York City appeared mainly in newspapers. Classified advertisements took up half or more of the printed page in the *New-York Gazette* (1725), the *New-York Weekly Journal* (1733), and the *New York Daily Advertiser.* By 1800 the city was beginning to surpass Philadelphia in its number of newspapers, and advertisements became more common and more vivid, often carrying display type and crude illustrations. By the first quarter of the nineteenth century, more than 500 magazines also provided important advertising space. The first advertising agent in the United States, Volney B. Palmer, opened an office in New York City a few years after he began operations in the early 1840s in Philadelphia: his commission of 25 percent was charged not to the merchants who placed advertisements, but to the newspapers that printed them. An early competitor of Palmer, S. M. Pettingill, in 1852 became the first agent to prepare advertisements himself, a practice that gave rise to the modern advertising agency.

After the Civil War advertising became more important. Magazines were more numerous, and George P. Rowell made several innovations in newspaper advertising: his practice of buying up advertising space in bulk from newspapers and then selling it to advertisers, which he developed in Boston, prompted him to move to New York City. There he issued *Rowell's American Newspaper Directory* (1869), which listed all the newspapers in the country and for the first time gave an accurate estimate of their circulations, a service of great value to advertisers. In 1888 he launched *Printer's Ink,* the first advertising trade magazine. In 1875 N. W. Ayer and Son introduced the "open contract," which made it clear that the agent represented the advertiser rather than the newspaper and which specified the amount to be spent on the advertising, as well as the commission to be paid by the advertiser to the agent (12 percent, later raised to 15 percent). In 1879 Ayer conducted the first marketing survey. J. Walter Thompson began his career in New York City in the 1860s by placing advertisements in magazines, and in 1880 Cyrus H. K. Curtis conceived magazines that were not primarily literary publications but rather vehicles for the growing advertising industry. P. T. Barnum is often regarded as a primary innovator in advertising, as he astutely promoted a woman who he alleged was the 161-year-old nurse of George Washington, the midget Charles Stratton (advertised as General Tom Thumb), the Swedish soprano Jenny Lind, and a circus advertised as the "Greatest Show on Earth."

The electrification of New York City led to the introduction in the 1890s of enormous illuminated advertising signs, and by 1893 Broadway was known as the "Great White Way." The city had 25 small advertising agencies by the turn of the twentieth century. Criticisms of advertising being fraudulent reached a peak, and in 1911 the vigilance committee of the Advertising Club of New York supported a "truth in advertising" bill in the state legislature. The bill was enacted and soon inspired similar measures in 36 other states. The image of advertising improved further as a result of World War I, during which representatives of advertising agencies aided the war effort through the Council of National Defense. From 1918 to 1929 advertising agencies in the city grew along with a rapidly industrializing economy that produced and marketed everything from cigarettes and toothpaste to piano lessons and soft drinks. Radio broadcasts began in 1920, and within two years more than two million sets were in use, providing agencies with another advertising medium. Radio advertisements were resisted at first but eventually became an important means of selling inexpensive and often-purchased items as well as durable goods such as refrigerators.

During the 1920s J. Walter Thompson emerged as the leading advertising agency in the United States, in part through its emphasis on market research, which it began in 1923 when it conducted a quantitative study of magazine circulation that proved widely influential. Another important agency, Young and Rubicam, began in 1923 in Philadelphia and moved to New York City in 1926. Raymond Rubicam was a brilliant copywriter who helped to focus greater attention on the creative side of the business. The agency also engaged George Gallup in 1932 to conduct research into copy testing and marketing. Advertising continued virtually unabated during World War II, when advertisements showing how a firm's products were helping to win the war were common. Advertisers also prepared to satisfy the pent-up demand for products that would be released when the war ended.

The late 1940s and 1950s, which saw an enormous expansion of the advertising business in New York City, included the advent of television. By 1952 there were 18 million television sets and 110 commercial transmitters in the United States, and by 1954 the Columbia Broadcasting System was the largest advertising medium in the world. Radio as an advertising medium was hit hard by the introduction of television and struggled for many years to recover. By 1957 television advertising accounted for $1.5 billion in spending by advertisers.

By the 1960s a new emphasis was placed on the creative side of the advertising business, in what came to be called the "creative revolution." William Bernbach, a native of Brooklyn, was influential in this change; his work sought drama in the natural, everyday language and expression of ordinary people, for example in his advertisements for Levy's Jewish Rye and his campaign for Volkswagen based on the slogan "Think small." Two other leading figures were Leo Burnett (who conceived the Marlboro man and the Jolly Green Giant) and David Ogilvy (who conceived the man in the Hathaway shirt and Commander Whitehead for Schweppes). During the 1960s many advertising agencies in the city were formed with creativity as their guiding principle. At the same time the advertising business was becoming ethnically more heterogeneous: the agency Doyle Dane Bernbach employed Jews, thus breaking with a long discriminatory practice of most agencies (with the notable exception of Grey Advertising). Gradually other ethnic exclusions were removed, and by the 1980s the advertising business in New York City was essentially open to whoever had sufficient talent to work in it.

The creative revolution faltered during the 1970s, and a renewed emphasis was given to the "hard sell," which stressed the product rather than the style of presentation. During the same period a number of the major advertising agencies in the city changed from partnerships to publicly owned corporations, including Doyle Dane Bernbach; Foote, Cone and Belding; Grey Advertising; Ogilvy and Mather; and J. Walter Thompson. Some agencies consolidated through merger and acquisition, including Ted Bates; Interpublic; Ogilvy and Mather; Wells, Rich, Greene; and Young and Rubicam. The trend toward consolidation continued into the 1980s: under the leadership of Martin Sorrell, the WPP Group acquired J. Walter Thompson and the Ogilvy Group, and the Omnicom Group was formed through the merger of BBDO International, Doyle Dane Bernbach, and Needham Harper Worldwide. The number of multinational advertising agencies decreased from 12 in 1978 to eight in 1988, and at the end of the 1980s only four of the 15 largest agencies in the country had the same ownership and structure as they had had at the beginning of the decade. With the recession of the late 1980s and early 1990s consolidations became less frequent and the advertising business entered a period of retrenchment. Nonetheless, New York City remained the advertising capital of the country, with half the people in the United States working in advertising being based in the city. With the rise of the Internet and e-mail into the twenty-first century, advertisers found new ways to revitalize marketing strategies as well as to work with older media such as cable television and film. New York City is home to the Association of National Advertisers (708 Third Avenue) and the American Association of Advertising Agencies (405 Lexington Avenue), both founded in 1917.

To the PUBLIC.

THE FLYING MACHINE, kept by John Mercereau, at the New-Blazing-Star-Ferry, near New-York, ſets off from Powles Hook every Monday, Wedneſday, and Friday Mornings, for Philadelphia, and performs the Journey in a Day and a Half, for the Summer Seaſon, till the 1ſt of November; from that Time to go twice a Week till the firſt of May, when they again perform it three Times a Week. When the Stages go only twice a Week, they ſet off Mondays and Thurſdays. The Waggons in Philadelphia ſet out from the Sign of the George, in Second-ſtreet, the ſame Morning. The Paſſengers are deſired to croſs the Ferry the Evening before, as the Stages muſt ſet off early the next Morning. The Price for each Paſſenger is *Twenty Shillings*, Proc. and Goods as uſual. Paſſengers going Part of the Way to pay in Proportion.

As the Proprietor has made ſuch Improvements upon the Machines, one of which is in Imitation of a Coach, he hopes to merit the Favour of the Publick.

JOHN MERCEREAU.

Auguſt 23, 1771.

An advertisement in the New York Gazette and Weekly Post-Boy, *1771*

Stephen R. Fox, *The Mirror Makers: A History of American Advertising and Its Creators* (New York: William Morrow, 1984)

See also OUTDOOR ADVERTISING.

Chauncey G. Olinger, Jr., Meghan Lalonde

Afghans. The extent of Afghan immigration to the United States was difficult to measure before 1953; only after passage of the 1952 McCarran–Walter Immigration and Nationality Act were members of the former Asiatic Barred Zone (non-Europeans and non-Africans) allowed to enter the country. The number of Afghan immigrants to New York City increased markedly after Marxists, with help from the army, seized control of the government in 1978 by assassinating the prime minister, Mohammad Daoud Kahn, who had overthrown King Zahir Shah in 1973. This later group represented all classes of Afghan society, though most of its better-educated members found themselves underemployed in their new home. According to immigration statistics, 1868 Afghans entered New York City between 1982 and 1987, a number that excludes those who entered the country illegally. After the Taliban took control of Afghanistan in 1996, many Afghans fled to New York, and following the attacks of 11 September 2001, the U. S. War on Terror drove even more inhabitants from Afghanistan. In response the United States initiated a special immigration program that opened up 500 special immigration visas annually for Afghans and Iraqis who had helped U.S. military forces. In 2008 there were just over 9000 Afghans living in New York City. A section of Flushing is sometimes referred to as Little Afghanistan; small Afghan communities have also taken root in several

Queens neighborhoods including Elmhurst, Jackson Heights, and Corona, and in Midwood, Brooklyn. The majority of Afghans in New York City are Muslims. The most visible Afghan organization in the country, the Afghan Community in America, based in Queens, has expended considerable effort to dislodge the Soviet Union from Afghanistan and influence American political leaders and public opinion.

Marc Ferris

AFL. See American Federation of Labor.

African Americans. New York City has played a pivotal role in the history of African Americans. During the nineteenth century it was a center of abolitionism; the site of influential black churches, benevolent organizations, and schools; and a focus of sometimes violent conflict between blacks and European immigrants. After the turn of the twentieth century Harlem became internationally known as a center of black nationalism and other forms of political activism, and of the literary and artistic movement known as the Harlem Renaissance. In later years the city's black community increased its political power and eventually accounted for more than a quarter of the total population.

1. From the Colonial Period to 1900

The African presence in what is now New York City dates to the Dutch settlement of New Amsterdam in 1626 when the West India Company imported enslaved Africans to build public works and to labor in the prosperous fur trade. The Dutch recorded the names of nine of the first male slaves as Paulo Angola, Simon Congo, Big Manuel, Little Manuel, Manuel de Gerrit de Reus, Anthony Portuguis Garcia, Peter Santomee, Jan Francisco, and Little Anthony. The first female slaves arrived on the island in 1628. Those enslaved by the company were given the right to be baptized, to marry, and to own property and were allowed to work for themselves when their services were not required by the company or other slave owners. They could also obtain legal recourse and could testify against and sue whites. Because of these privileges slavery in New Netherland was less severe than in other colonies of the western hemisphere. On 25 February 1644 the 11 male slaves who had been the first to arrive in the colony and their wives were declared "half free" on petition; in exchange for this conditional freedom they were required to make an annual payment to the Dutch West India Company of 22.5 bushels (800 liters) of beans, corn, peas, or wheat and a fat hog valued at 30 guilders. They received deeds to land that some had farmed before their emancipation, near that deeded to Africans who had always been free, in the area between what are now Astor Place and Prince Street in Greenwich Village. The children (born and unborn) of the half-freed slaves remained the property of the company.

The English conquest of New Netherland in 1664 resulted in harsher and more restrictive bondage. Most free Africans were disfranchised, any public assembly of more than three Africans or Indians was deemed illegal, curfews were set for blacks and Indians, and free Africans were penalized for harboring fugitive slaves. In 1703 there were 630 blacks in what is now New York City. An uprising of slaves on 6 April 1712 culminated in the death of several whites, for which 19 African participants were executed, and led to the passage of a law that barred Africans from owning property. The enslaved population continued to rise: Africans accounted for about 20 percent of the city's 11,000 residents by 1741. In the same year Africans were accused of conspiring to burn down the colony, for which more than 30 people were executed and 71 deported.

Lured by the promise of freedom, enslaved Africans fought on both sides of the conflict in the American Revolution. In 1781 the state assembly passed a law freeing all Africans who had served in the state's military forces. But the political and civil rights of all black New Yorkers were severely limited: they could not vote or hold public office, interracial marriage was prohibited, and a statute passed in 1785 precluded them from testifying against whites in court. In the same year the New York Manumission Society was formed. Its members argued that slavery was incompatible with the democratic rhetoric that fueled the American Revolution. Abolitionists persuaded the state legislature in 1799 to enact the Act for the Gradual Emancipation of Negroes and Other Slaves, which stipulated that every male slave born after 4 July 1799 was to be freed at the age of 28 and every female at 24.

In 1796 a group of free Africans in New York City began to hold meetings that eventually led to the formation of the African Methodist Episcopal Zion Church, the first black congregation in the city (eventually known as "Mother Zion," it later occupied a church built at Church and Leonard streets in 1801). The first black Baptist church in the city, the Abyssinian Baptist Church, was formed in 1808 on Worth Street and directed by Thomas Paul. In the same year the African Association for Mutual Relief, the first insurance company that catered to blacks, was opened on Baxter Street by several black civic and political leaders. African American members of the White Sands Street Methodist Church in Brooklyn left in 1812 to form the High Street African Wesleyan Methodist Episcopal Church, and the first congregation of black Episcopalians, led by Peter Williams, Jr., built St. Philip's Protestant Episcopal Church on Centre Street in 1818. Out of the early African American churches grew literary and musical societies, church schools, and benevolent organizations such as the New York African Society for Mutual Relief (formed in 1808).

In 1821 the state legislature ruled that African Americans could vote only if they owned property worth at least $250, while at the same time it eliminated the property qualification for white male voters. Not surprisingly there were only 16 qualified African American voters in 1825 and 68 in 1835. Most employed African Americans in the nineteenth century were unskilled; men often were laborers and women domestic servants. In 1825 more than one-fifth of the African American residents of Manhattan lived in the sixth ward, which spread from Five Points north and west to the Hudson River.

A group of free blacks set up separate schools for black children, which were open only sporadically and were always underfinanced. The New York Manumission Society founded African Free Schools during the late eighteenth century. The nation's first black newspaper, *Freedom's Journal*, was launched in 1827 by the abolitionist minister Samuel Cornish and John Russwurm, one of the first blacks in the United States to receive a college degree. Its goal was to improve the political and economic standing of free blacks and agitate for the end of slavery. The newspaper later changed its name to *Rights for All* before ceasing publication in 1830. Other black newspapers in New York City in the nineteenth century were the *Colored American* (1837), the *Ram's Horn*, the *Anglo-African* (1859), and Frederick Douglass's *North Star* (1847). Williams helped to form the African Dorcas Society (1828), a women's sewing group that made clothing for young black students so that they could attend the African Free Schools. Many middle-class blacks opened restaurants, the most successful of which were Thomas Van Renesselaer's Eating House on Wall Street, Katy Ferguson's Pastry Shop on Thompson Street, Downing's Oyster House on Broad Street, and Cato's in lower Manhattan. The all-male African Clarkson Association, formed in 1829, was both a literary society and a benevolent organization. Its members paid monthly dues of 25 cents and could receive financial help when they or their families fell ill.

There were more than one dozen black literary and book-lending societies in Manhattan and Brooklyn by the mid-nineteenth century. The Philomethean Society (1830) owned more than 600 volumes by 1837, and the Phoenix Society (1833) sponsored lectures on history and science that regularly attracted more than 300 listeners; its members included Williams, Cornish, the abolitionist and book merchant David Ruggles, and the poet Charles B. Ray. Literary groups for women included the Female Literary Society (1834) and the Ladies Literary Society (1836). The Garrison Literary

Association (1834), a group for children and young adults, was open to any person of good moral character between the ages of four and 20 willing to pay annual dues of 12.5 cents. In 1845 a group of white abolitionists and politicians in New York City formed the African Education and Civilization Society (more commonly known as the African Civilization Society), which prepared black students to teach in Africa. The Society for Promoting Education among Colored Children was formed in 1847 by the poet and educator Charles Reasoner at 49 Frankfort Street.

In the 1840s many white European immigrants moved to New York City, leading to a great deterioration in the employment opportunities available to free blacks. Their political status remained weak as well: in 1846 a proposed amendment to the state constitution that would have granted blacks the same voting rights as whites was rejected by the local electorate. The fight for suffrage and against American colonization led to the formation of the Negro Convention movement in the 1830s. In 1834 a black minister delivering an abolitionist sermon to a predominantly black audience at the Chatham Street Chapel was assaulted, triggering five days of antiabolitionist agitation in which white mobs attacked blacks and abolitionist white churches as well as the Bowery Theatre. Two black churches were extensively damaged before the militia ended the violence on the night of 11 July by arresting about 150 ringleaders of the mob. By 1850 most of the city's blacks were living in or near Greenwich Village, and by 1860 others had settled on the West Side between 10th and 30th streets, the infamous Tenderloin. After accounting for 5 percent of the city's population in 1840, blacks in 1860 accounted for less than 2 percent.

A rash of antiblack incidents beset New York City during the Civil War. In the summer of 1862 a mob of Irishmen attempted to burn down a tobacco factory in Brooklyn where two dozen black women and children were working. The DRAFT RIOTS of 13–17 July 1863 began as a protest against a clause in the draft law exempting from service those who paid a $300 fee but soon assumed racial dimensions as an Irish mob assaulted blacks, hanging many and mutilating others, and destroyed black institutions and homes. This was the bloodiest riot in the history of the United States, and at least 105 people died. In 1869 a proposal to eliminate the property qualification for black voters was rejected by the electorate in New York State. Blacks in the city did not obtain the vote on an equal basis with whites until three-fourths of the states ratified the 15th Amendment to the U.S. Constitution in March 1870.

The Afro-American League (1889) and the Afro-American Council (1898), both formed by the militant black editor of the *New York Age,* T. Thomas Fortune, were short-lived. Black Democrats had no power in Tammany Hall, which tried to appease them in 1898 by creating an all-black group called the United Colored Democracy. Although there were 60,666 blacks in New York City by 1900, they still accounted for less than 2 percent of the total population, as immigrants from southern and eastern Europe flooded the city. Competition among blacks and immigrants for jobs and housing resulted in mutual distrust and hostility. A riot erupted in the Tenderloin on the night of 15 August 1900 after a white policeman was killed by a black man. Blacks were pulled from streetcars and beaten by the mob, and many fought back by hurling bricks and bottles. The police made little effort to intervene, and some joined the rioters in their racial attacks. In response to what they saw as a police cover-up of the incident, 3500 blacks met at Carnegie Hall on 12 September 1900 to form the Citizens' Protective League.

2. After 1900

In 1904–5 the real estate market in Harlem collapsed, leaving unfilled many new apartment houses along Seventh and Lenox avenues in the West 130s and 140s. To find tenants landlords reduced rents, allowing many blacks to move into the area. Several real estate firms purchased a number of these properties, among them the Afro-American Realty Company, formed in 1904 by Philip A. Payton, Jr. Blacks also established a community in San Juan Hill that stretched from 60th to 64th streets between 10th and 11th avenues; the area was the site of another race riot in 1905. By 1914 Harlem had 50,000 black residents, and several black churches moved there from midtown, including St. Philip's Episcopal Church (to 133rd Street) and the Abyssinian Baptist Church (to 138th Street), which had become the largest black church in the city. White residents and landlords opposed to the rapid increase in the area's black population were active in the Harlem Property Owners' Improvement Corporation from 1910 to 1915. The Gates Avenue Association protested the more modest influx of blacks into Brooklyn.

The expansion of the black community in New York City was fueled by migration from the South, a desire to escape southern racism and deprival of voting rights, and a search for economic opportunity and political freedom. The northward migration created the large black residential ghettos of northern cities and simultaneously a growing and eventually significant black electorate. Between 1910 and 1930 the white population of Manhattan decreased by 633,249 while its black population increased by 154,135. In 1917 Edward Johnson, a Republican from the 19th assembly district in Harlem, became the first black elected to the state legislature. Many blacks from the city fought in World War I: the all-black 369th Regiment (known as the Harlem Hellfighters) received the Croix de Guerre from the French government and returned to Manhattan for a triumphant victory parade on 17 February 1919. At the same time landlords were overcharging blacks in a racially restricted market, companies and unions were practicing blatant racial discrimination, and Harlem had the worst health record in the city. These racial inequities, coupled with antiblack race riots in 26 cities in the summer of 1919, converted many blacks to the nationalistic philosophy of the Universal Negro Improvement Association (UNIA), based in New York City and led by MARCUS GARVEY, who argued that blacks in the New World should be repatriated to Africa and that Africa should be liberated from European colonial rule. The core of Garvey's support was the large West Indian population of Harlem, but the group recruited members from all over the city through parades and conventions in Madison Square Garden. The UNIA disintegrated in the mid-1920s after Garvey was convicted of mail fraud, sentenced to federal prison, and later deported. Although other militant black organizations such as the Marxist nationalist African Blood Brotherhood had large followings, as did radicals like Cyril Briggs, Hubert Henry Harrison, and William Bridges, who were all active in New York City, they failed to capture the imagination of blacks in the city as Garvey had.

In the 1920s writers and artists traveled to Harlem from all over the United States to be part of the literary and artistic movement known as the Harlem Renaissance. Charles S. Johnson, editor of the magazine *Opportunity* (published by the National Urban League), held a meeting of leading black writers and white publishers at the Civic Club in March 1924 that helped to launch the careers of such talented black writers as Langston Hughes, Claude McKay, Zora Neale Hurston, Countee Cullen, Jean Toomer, and Rudolph Fisher. The painters Aaron Douglas, William H. Johnson, Palmer Hayden, and Malvin Gray Johnson and the sculptor Augusta Savage strove to invent a black American art by studying African art and emulating its styles and themes. Plays with black themes and actors enjoyed great success, notably *The Emperor Jones* (1920) and *All God's Chillun Got Wings* (1924) by Eugene O'Neill and *The Green Pastures* (1930) by Marc Connelly.

During the Depression 50 percent of blacks in New York City were unemployed, double the unemployment rate of whites. In 1929 the Republican Charles W. Fillmore was elected the city's first black district leader, but many blacks soon shifted their support from the Republicans to the Democrats, who for the first time received a majority of the black vote in elections for the presidency (1932), mayoralty (1933), and governorship (1934). By the mid-1930s the first effective black political organization in Brooklyn had developed among the Democrats of Bedford–Stuyvesant. At the same time white merchants on 125th Street in Harlem refused to employ black sales clerks, and a boycott against them was organized in 1934 by Sufi Abdul Hamid. The Citizens League for Fair Play, a middle-class black organization led by John H. Johnson, became a powerful force in the boycott. The boycott ultimately failed when a court order prohibited the picketing of white merchants and the groups became riven by disagreements. A rumor that the police had killed an adolescent boy, Lino Rivera, for stealing a penknife sparked a riot in Harlem in 1935. In 1938 a second boycott of the white merchants on 125th Street, led by ADAM CLAYTON POWELL, JR., and the Greater New York Coordinating Committee, was more successful in ending employment discrimination. Additional boycotts were launched against the bus and telephone companies, which also refused to employ blacks. The Communist Party received much publicity by protesting police brutality against blacks, racial bias in the city's public schools, and inadequate services and discrimination at Harlem Hospital.

Blacks as a Percentage of Total Population in Selected Counties of New York State, 1790–1890

	New York	Kings	Queens	Richmond	Westchester
1790	10.47	32.88	19.46	23.10	7.42
1800	10.53	31.55	17.52	16.61	6.35
1810	10.19	22.32	16.36	13.30	6.38
1820	8.80	15.74	14.90	9.94	5.65
1830	6.90	9.77	13.77	7.79	5.80
1840	5.23	5.98	11.57	4.40	4.73
1850	2.68	2.93	9.37	3.92	3.56
1860	1.55	1.79	5.90	2.59	2.28
1870	1.39	1.35	5.14	2.38	1.91
1880	1.63	1.53	4.20	2.39	2.37
1890	1.56	1.35	2.76	1.86	2.33

Note: During the period 1790–1890 New York, Kings, and Richmond counties are assumed to be substantially equivalent to the present Manhattan, Brooklyn, and Staten Island. Queens included what is now Nassau County, and Westchester included what is now the Bronx.

Sources: U.S. Bureau of the Census, Reports for 1790, 1800, 1810, 1820, 1830, 1840, 1850, 1860, 1870, 1880, 1890; Ira Rosenwaike, *Population History of New York City* (Syracuse: Syracuse University Press, 1972)

The outbreak of World War II and the U.S. military buildup did not benefit blacks in the city to the same extent that it did whites: 40 percent of the city's black population in 1940 remained on relief or dependent on federal funds for temporary work relief. A survey of 72 defense plants in Brooklyn taken by the Urban League in 1941 revealed that they employed only 234 blacks in a total workforce of 13,840, and almost half the plants excluded blacks entirely. In the same year A. Philip Randolph formed the March on Washington Committee in New York City to prevail on the federal government to end the political disfranchisement of blacks in the South, desegregate the army, and prohibit discriminatory employment practices by defense contractors. Fearful of a potential threat to national unity, President Franklin D. Roosevelt asked Eleanor Roosevelt and Mayor Fiorello H. La Guardia to persuade Randolph to call off the protest march. Randolph agreed, provided that the government ban discrimination in companies with defense contracts; in response, Roosevelt on 25 June 1941 issued an executive order banning discrimination in defense industries. Even then blacks were relegated to less lucrative forms of work: they tended not to work in defense industries but rather to take the place of whites who did, as well as whites who had gone to war.

World War II saw the emergence of Powell as an important political figure. After serving as the pastor of Abyssinian Baptist Church he won a seat on the City Council in 1941. Although La Guardia had supported his candidacy, the two men were soon at odds over Powell's charges of racial discrimination and police brutality in New York City. In 1942 Powell protested the refusal of City College to reappoint a black leftist professor, Max Yergan, at a time when the school did not have any full-time tenured black professors. He also criticized La Guardia for allowing the U.S. Navy to use Hunter College and Walton High School as training facilities for the Women's Reserve, which practiced racial segregation, and for contracting with the Metropolitan Life Insurance Company to build Stuyvesant Town, a tax-exempt, quasi-public housing project on the Lower East Side that excluded blacks from its properties. The city eventually agreed to prohibit the discriminatory selection of tenants in all its future projects.

The shooting of a black military policeman by a white policeman in mysterious circumstances at a hotel in Harlem on 1 August 1943 led to a riot in which five people were killed and 307 were injured. Plate-glass windows of stores along 125th Street were smashed, and the total damage exceeded $5 million. The anger of the community was evident that autumn when the communist Benjamin Davis was elected to the City Council because of his strong sponsorship of civil rights. Davis replaced Powell, who had resigned from the council and won a seat in Congress as a Democrat in 1944. In 1953 Assemblyman Walter Gladwin became the first black elected official in the Bronx, and Hulan E. Jack, a seasoned Democratic politician, became the first black borough president of Manhattan. Brooklyn elected its first black city councilman, J. Daniel Diggs, in 1957.

The unemployment rate of blacks in New York City during the 1950s remained double that of whites. Of the students who entered academic high schools in Harlem in 1959, about 53 percent failed to graduate, as did 61 percent of those entering vocational schools. By the mid-1960s only about half the children in Harlem lived with their parents, compared with 83 percent in New York City as a whole. As the population of Harlem declined and the black population of the other boroughs increased, poverty and unemployment remained. In 1961 the Congress of Racial Equality (CORE) demanded that a milk plant operated by Sealtest–Sheffield Farms in Bedford–Stuyvesant increase its black labor force, which then consisted of seven out of 367 employees, and in 1963 it demanded that more blacks work on the construction of the Downstate Medical Center. Constance Baker Motley served as the borough president of Manhattan (1965–66), as did Percy Sutton. In 1964 J. Raymond Jones, known as the "Harlem Fox," became the first black leader of Tammany Hall, and Kenneth Brown became the first black elected to the state assembly from Queens. In the same year Milton Galamison and the City-Wide Committee for Integrated Schools led two student boycotts of classes to demand the removal of the president of the Board of Education, and Jesse Gray organized rent strikes in Harlem by black tenants to obtain affordable housing. The killing of a black youth by a white police lieutenant in the summer of 1964 led to a riot in Harlem that lasted three nights; one person was killed, 141 were seriously injured (including 48 police officers), and 519 were arrested. Amid this unrest militant black leaders like Malcolm X and organizations like the Nation of Islam gained increasing popularity. After the riot Mayor Robert F. Wagner invited

Martin Luther King, Jr., to New York City to obtain his advice on racial matters, and charges of police brutality led to the formation of a civilian police review board. Mayor John V. Lindsay's efforts to promote better race relations in the city contributed to its escape from the massive rioting that besieged other U.S. cities during the 1960s.

In 1968 Shirley Chisholm of Brooklyn became the first black woman to be elected to the U.S. Congress by defeating James Farmer, a nationally known civil rights leader and former head of CORE. Despite his troubles with CORE stemming from charges of conflict of interest, Powell was repeatedly reelected until he lost his seat to Charles B. Rangel in 1970. During the administration of President Lyndon B. Johnson the Bedford Stuyvesant Restoration Corporation, an antipoverty agency in Brooklyn, obtained about $50 million from government and foundation sources, an impressive sum that nevertheless amounted to only $125 for each resident of the area over a seven-year period. With the de-escalation of the war on poverty and the shift from manufacturing to a service economy that relied on a more highly educated and technically skilled labor force, employment prospects for many lower-income blacks diminished: in New York City between 1970 and 1984 industrial employment requiring only a minimum of education fell from 492,000 to 239,000. The city's black population increased from 458,000 in 1940 to 1,668,000 in 1970, while suburbanization reduced the white population from 6,977,000 to 6,048,000. Many blacks left Manhattan to live in less crowded areas, and consequently the number of blacks living in the outer boroughs increased sharply.

In November 1989 David N. Dinkins was elected the first black mayor of New York City after asking residents to vote their hopes, not their fears. He made strenuous efforts to manage the city, which he frequently referred to as a "gorgeous mosaic" of racial, ethnic, and religious groups, but he was unable to stem the tide of economic decay and ethnic factionalism abetted by years of official neglect. This lack of success led to his narrow defeat in 1993 by Rudolph W. Giuliani, although his record was consistent with that of other mayors of large American cities in the early 1990s.

According to the federal census the non-Hispanic black population of New York City in 1990 stood at 1,847,049 (including 417,506 foreign-born), accounting for 25.2 percent of the total population and representing an increase of 9 percent over the preceding decade.

Blacks as a Percentage of Total Population in Selected Counties of the Colony of New York, 1698–1786

	New York	Kings	Queens	Richmond	Westchester
1698	14.2	14.7	5.6	10.0	13.7
1703	14.4	17.9	9.7	19.2	10.2
1712	16.7	N/A	N/A	N/A	11.8
1723	18.8	20.0	15.6	16.9	10.2
1731	18.3	22.9	15.8	16.7	11.5
1737	16.1	24.0	14.5	18.5	12.6
1746	20.9	27.7	16.4	18.4	7.3
1749	17.8	34.3	16.7	19.0	10.8
1756	17.5	31.2	20.1	21.8	10.1
1771	14.3	32.1	20.4	20.9	15.8
1786	8.9	33.0	16.7	22.0	6.1

N/A = Not Available
Note: Counties are not necessarily coextensive with present counties.
Source: U.S. Bureau of the Census, *A Century of Population Growth* (1909)

3. Post-1990 Gentrification

The economic boom of the 1980s barely reached Harlem. By 1990 high unemployment rates, high crime rates, poor schools, and deteriorating social services contributed to the continuing suburbanization of the black middle class. Between 1960 and 1990 Harlem lost approximately one-third of its population and half of its housing stock, but because of its illustrious history as the epicenter of the African American renaissance of the 1920s, the neighborhood continued to hold the attention of urban planners and community activists.

At the turn of the twenty-first century, Harlem had a dearth of bank branches, grocery stores, chain stores, and upscale coffee shops, but that changed during the following years with the establishment of major department store outlets, movie complexes, and "higher end" stores. Questions of housing affordability became important in the community. In May 2008 the City Council approved the rezoning of 125th Street to pave the way for high-rise office towers and some 2100 new market-rate condominiums. Such changes could cause the loss of small businesses and the displacement of some long-term residents. With renovated brownstones in Harlem selling for $1 million and new condominium apartments selling for almost that much, working-class Harlem residents cannot afford the newer upscale housing.

The arrival of the black and white "gentrifiers" is changing the class and racial composition of Harlem. Black urban professionals profess a desire to redeem Harlem and other historic black communities from decay and despair. White urban professionals seeking quality housing at affordable prices claim a color blindness and a willingness to live in an integrated neighborhood. Nevertheless, both black and white gentrifiers have similar effects upon the working class. Lawsuits, calls for economic boycotts, community-wide meetings, and denunciations to block gentrification have become commonplace. The return of middle-class people to Harlem may improve city services, but integrating lower income urban residents into the economic mainstream transcends gentrification.

Gilbert Osofsky, *Harlem: The Making of a Ghetto; Negro New York, 1890–1930* (New York: Harper, 1963); Shane White, *Somewhat More Independent: The End of Slavery in New York City, 1770–1810* (Athens: University of Georgia Press, 1991); Sherrill D. Wilson, *New York City's African Slave Owners: A Social and Material Culture History* (New York: Garland, 1994); Craig Steven Wilder, *A Covenant with Color: Race and Social Power in Brooklyn* (New York: Columbia University Press, 2001); Ira Berlin and Leslie M. Harris, eds., *Slavery in New York* (New York: New Press, 2005)

Sherrill D. Wilson (§1), Larry A. Greene (§2, §3)

African Burial Ground. Seven-acre (2.83-hectare) burying place for enslaved and free Africans from the late 1600s to 1794. The Negroes Burial Ground, situated north of present-day Wall Street, may be related to Trinity Church, at Broadway and Wall Street, which received its charter and land title in 1697. That same year the church declared that Africans who were not members of the church would no longer be buried in the churchyard. Prior to the establishment of Trinity Church as the Church of England in New York, the land had been designated as the city's burial ground for paupers, who were interred there without regard to race. The establishment of the African Burial Ground created a segregated location for the burial of Africans and people of African descent outside the official city limits.

The northern portion of the cemetery at Duane and Elk streets was excavated in 1991–92, when the federal government began the construction of an office building at Broadway and Duane Street. The remains of 419 men, women, and children were unearthed and analyzed at Howard University, in Washington, D.C. The number of human remains buried in the cemetery is estimated at more than 15,000, nearly 50 percent of which are children under the age of 12. The skeletal remains of these children indicate malnutrition and early disease; those of adult men and women show evidence of hard labor. Artifacts associated with the burials included African trade beads, shroud pins, fragments of shroud cloth, coins, buttons, bits of smoking pipes, coffin hardware, and a few items of silver and copper jewelry. Approximately 200 to 300 human remains are estimated to lie below the excavated portion of the site; these were not unearthed owing to community and public protest over the defilement of a previously unknown sacred site.

The Negroes Burial Ground became the African Burial Ground in 1993 because use of the term *Negro* was considered derogatory. The word *African* was used throughout the late eighteenth and early nineteenth centuries in the names of organizations created for and by people of African descent and was thereby viewed as historically in keeping with what Africans called themselves during the time the cemetery was in use. The African Burial Ground is a National Historic Landmark, and New York City designated the surrounding area the African Burial Ground and Commons Historic District in 1993. In 2003 the excavated ancestral remains and artifacts were reinterred on a portion of the historic site. More than 8000 "ancestor cards," which contemporary people had used to express love, honor, and gratitude for their African ancestors, were also buried at the site. In 2004 Elk Street, which borders the reburial site to the east, was renamed the African Burial Ground Way.

The African Burial Ground National Monument was established by proclamation of President George W. Bush on 26 February 2006 and is now administered and managed by the National Park Service. In fall 2007 a 25-foot (7.62-meter) granite memorial by the architect Rodney Leon, entitled *Door of No Return,* was dedicated at the site.

Sherrill D. Wilson, *New York City's African Slave Owners: A Social and Material Culture History* (New York: Garland, 1994); Ira Berlin and Leslie Harris, eds., *Slavery in New York* (New York: W. W. Norton, 2005); Warren R. Perry, Jean Howson, and Barbara A. Bianco, eds., *New York African Burial Ground Archaeology Final Report,* vol. 1 (Washington, D.C.: Howard University, 2006)

Sherrill D. Wilson

African Dorcas Society. New York City's earliest African American women's association. Founded by members of St. Philip's Church in 1827 at the urging of church leaders, the society was created the same year that African slavery ended in New York. Its primary purposes were to collect monies and to gather and sew clothing for impoverished African American children to enable them to attend classes at the African Free Schools.

Sherrill D. Wilson

African Free Schools. Schools opened by the New York Manumission Society during the late eighteenth century to provide children of African ancestry with moral and practical instruction. The first African Free School, under the instruction of Cornelius Davis, admitted both boys and girls and offered training in reading, penmanship, arithmetic, grammar, geography, and (after 1791) needlework. In 1797 trustees added an evening school for adults taught by William Pirsson and his assistant John Teasman, one of the few early teachers who were black. On Pirsson's retirement Teasman took charge and in 1809 introduced a highly efficient monitorial method of teaching developed in London by Joseph Lancaster. By training a group of student monitors who eventually became teachers themselves, Teasman increased the average attendance at the free school from 60 to more than 350. The first schoolhouse was destroyed by fire in 1814, and the society soon built another one at 245 William Street. A second school was established closer to the city's black population at 135 Mulberry Street in 1820; between 1827 and 1829 the society employed the editor and minister Samuel Cornish to increase enrollment. Five schools opened in 1831–33 under Benjamin H. Hughes, and the curriculum of the schools expanded as Charles C. Andrews, the principal instructor, added classes in navigation, business, and skilled trades.

In the early 1830s William Hamilton, Henry Sipkins, and Thomas Downing mounted a successful campaign to remove Andrews because of his support for the African colonization movement. Under increasing local demands for more black teachers the schools appointed John Peterson, Sarah M. Douglass, Ransom F. Wake, and Charles Reason; by 1834 blacks taught in five of the seven schools and held all but one of the assistants' positions. In the same year the Manumission Society transferred control of all seven of its schools to the New York Public School Society, a charity group not belonging to the abolitionist movement. Two of the schools were designated as public schools and the rest at a lower level as public primaries; all became part of the public school system in 1847. During their 60-year history the African Free Schools prepared many of their students for more advanced education and trained future leaders like the physician James McCune Smith, the abolitionist ministers Samuel Ringgold Ward and Henry Highland Garnet, the Episcopal clergyman and scholar Alexander Crummell, the antislavery leader and Liberian government official John B. Russwurm, the businessman Peter Williams, the abolitionist Theodore S. Wright, the engraver Patrick Reason, and the Shakespearean actor Ira Aldridge. Largely denied entry into the skilled trades, other products of the practical curriculum had to settle for work as waiters, coachmen, barbers, servants, shipwrights, and seamen.

Charles C. Andrews, *The History of the New York African Free-Schools from Their Establishment in 1787* (New York: Mahlon Day, 1830)

Robert C. Morris

African Methodist Episcopal Church. A denomination formed by black members of the St. George Methodist Episcopal Church in Philadelphia, who withdrew in 1787 because of racial discrimination. Most who withdrew became Episcopalians, but a small group led by Richard Allen formed a congregation named Bethel African Methodist Episcopal Church. Repeated efforts by white Methodists to assert control led Allen to gain autonomy for the congregation in 1807 and to form an independent denomination in 1816, the African Methodist Episcopal Church, of which he became the first bishop. In 1819 Allen sent William Lambert to New York City to hold the first New York Annual Conference; independent congregations in Brooklyn (1766) and Flushing (1810) were among the first to join the church. During the years before the Civil War the church grew rapidly. In 1918 Reverdy C. Ransom, the pastor of Bethel Church in Manhattan and later a bishop, became the first black to seek election to the U.S. House of Representatives, from the 21st congressional district. Floyd H. Flake, the pastor of Allen Church in Jamaica, was elected to the U.S. House of Representatives in 1986 (from the sixth district, in Queens). In the beginning of the twenty-first century, the church had 2.5 million members in the United States, 20 bishops, and 19 episcopal districts in North America, South America, the Caribbean, Africa, and Europe. It operates missions and financial agencies, issues publications, and sponsors housing, institutions of higher education, and social service centers.

Daniel A. Payne, *History of the African Methodist Episcopal Church* (Nashville: Publishing House of the A.M.E. Sunday School Union, 1891)

Dennis C. Dickerson

African Methodist Episcopal Zion Church. Church formed by black members of the John Street Church in New York City. Increasing tension with white members led some black members of the John Street Church to ask Bishop Francis Asbury for permission to conduct separate services in 1796. Although officially autonomous, the African Chapel remained within the jurisdiction of the Methodist Episcopal Church until 1820, when a group led by William Stillwell, a supporter of the independent black church movement, broke away. After failing to win independence within the white church, blacks formed the African Methodist Episcopal Zion Church in 1821; congregations were organized in Manhattan, Philadelphia, and New Haven, Connecticut, and on Long Island. James Varick was elected the first superintendent in 1822 and reelected in 1826; Christopher Rush succeeded him in 1828. At the urging of the African Methodist Episcopal Church during preparations for a merger in 1864, the church replaced its superintendency with a lifetime episcopacy. Although the merger failed, the superintendents of the church became bishops in 1868. From 1880 they served without term restrictions. Congregations formed in New England and the Middle Atlantic states, and the church became associated with abolition through the work of such noted members as Sojourner Truth, Harriet Tubman, Jermain Loguen, and Frederick Douglass. After Emancipation missionaries opened churches in the South. Expansion was most rapid in North Carolina and Alabama; many congregations were also formed in other parts of the South, the Midwest, and the West. Membership increased from 13,702 in 1864 to 349,788 in 1890. Well-known members of the church in New York City during these years included T. Thomas Fortune, who between 1881 and 1907 launched the newspapers the *Freeman*, the *Globe*, and the *Age*, and Bishop Alexander Walters, an important black spokesman in the Democratic Party, especially during the presidential election of 1912. At the beginning of the twenty-first century the church had more than 1.2 million members in 13 episcopal districts in the United States, South America, the Caribbean, West Africa, and England and 13 bishops, who oversaw missions, publications, pension funds, and evangelical efforts. Its principal educational institutions were Livingstone College and Hood Theological Seminary in Salisbury, North Carolina.

Dennis C. Dickerson

Agee, James (Rufus) (*b* Knoxville, Tenn., 27 Nov 1909; *d* New York City, 16 May 1955). Essayist, poet, and novelist. After graduating from Harvard University in 1932 he moved to New York City to work as a reporter for *Fortune*. He took a basement apartment at 38 Perry Street in Greenwich Village and had an office on the 52nd floor of the Chrysler Building, where he became known for working all night while smoking cigarettes, drinking whiskey, and listening to classical music. He published a volume of poetry, *Permit Me Voyage*, in 1934. In 1936 he received a commission from the magazine to write a series of articles about tenant farming in the South; the result was an impressionistic mixture of prose and poetry that was 10 times longer than required. After the magazine relinquished the rights to the story, Agee worked alone to complete it, living at times in Brooklyn, as well as in Frenchtown and Stockton, New Jersey; Harper and Brothers provided a small advance but dropped the project after receiving the revised manuscript. Financially ruined and drinking heavily, Agee lived at 322 West 15th Street from 1939 until 1941 when he began working for *Time*. His book was published by Houghton Mifflin as *Let Us Now Praise Famous Men*. He lived at 172 Bleecker Street from the autumn of 1941 until 1951, and in the mid-1940s he worked in a studio at 33 Cornelia Street. His film reviews for *Time* and the *Nation* were among the most influential in the country; he also wrote scripts for three films, including *The African Queen* (1951) and *The Night of the Hunter* (1955), and the novel *The Morning Watch* (1950). He spent the end of his life at 17 King Street in a house built by Aaron Burr. Agee's novel *A Death in the Family* was published in 1957 and won a Pulitzer Prize in 1960; a collection of his essays, *Agee on Film*, was published in 1958–60. He died of a heart attack at age 45 and was buried on his family farm in Hillsdale, New York.

David Madden, ed., *Remembering James Agee* (Baton Rouge: Louisiana State University Press, 1974); Lawrence Bergreen, *James Agee: A Life* (New York: E. P. Dutton, 1984)

See also DOCUMENTARY FILMMAKING.

Walter Friedman

agriculture. The first farmers on Manhattan Island were Lenape women, who adopted agriculture sometime after the year 1300. Like other Indians in eastern North America, the Lenape grew Northern Flint corn, with its small 3- to 4-inch ears and multicolored kernels; pole and runner beans; and summer and winter squash, including pumpkins. These new crops supplemented the wild plants, nuts, fish, and game that made up the Late Woodland diet of the American Indian. Perhaps as early as the late sixteenth century, and certainly by the early 1600s, the Lenape dehydrated and stored vegetables in granaries and pits, which were drawn upon as exchange for trade goods from European fishermen. Although Manhattan's first permanent European settlers sowed wheat, oats, and rye in the spring of 1626, over the next two decades they intermittently relied on Indian stores for a portion of their subsistence.

In 1630 the Dutch West India Company encouraged agriculture by providing settlers with shelter, livestock, seed, and tools. The company also recognized slavery, which was to remain legal for the next two centuries. As elsewhere along the eastern coast of North America, seventeenth-century agriculture in New Amsterdam borrowed from the crops and methods of both the New and Old Worlds. The Europeans adopted the practice of burning brush and planting in hills, while the Indians diversified their diets with the addition of cherries and peaches and adopted the use of iron hand tools. This transformation was not without friction, however. With so much open land, the Europeans allowed their cattle and swine to graze freely, a practice that led, inevitably, to incursions onto Indian fields. Gardens and cultivated fields also served as targets of vengeful armies on both the Dutch and Lenape sides during the periodic violence that plagued the colony between 1637 and 1674.

As the Lenape retreated west under pressure of Europe's advance, the new settlers cleared land for grain, corn, and garden crops. Owing to the small size of their farms and their limited labor resources, most families functioned as semisubsistence producers. They raised livestock and foodstuffs sufficient for home use, in addition to producing small surpluses of wheat, butter, and pork. In the pre-Revolutionary era, western Long Island, the Hudson Valley, and southeastern Pennsylvania became well known for exporting wheat. Farm tenancy was common throughout the seventeenth and eighteenth centuries, and a somewhat limited use of slave labor on farms continued through the period into the nineteenth century.

The rise of New York as a port city after 1815 came at a time when farmers in the Northeast sought to replace wheat as a cash crop. Declining soil fertility, endemic losses to disease and insects, and higher operating costs forced New York's farmers to yield to western competitors. Despite such problems, the huge local market, the abundance of experienced labor, and the unlimited availability of fertilizer influenced the choices made by those living within a day's travel of the city. These conditions invited agricultural specialization, and from the 1820s through the 1870s agriculturalists switched from mixed farming to milk and vegetable production. As the growing city's demand for fresh milk outstripped local supplies, entrepreneurs in the 1840s established confinement dairies. Built in conjunction with whiskey distilleries in industrial sections of Manhattan and Brooklyn, these low stables housed thousands of cattle that consumed a diet consisting almost entirely of distillery mash; detractors labeled the resulting product swill milk. The unsanitary conditions of these businesses drew the attention of the reform press and, eventually, of legislators, who outlawed this means of milk production—though it held on past 1900 regardless. However, in the twentieth century, and due to the unhealthy production of milk, the Department of Health closely regulated dairies in New York City (this is when pasteurization began). In 1916 the nearly 100 dairies housed a total of 10,000 to 15,000 cows. The last dairy in Manhattan closed in the late 1920s, and by 1960 only five dairies remained citywide. These included Oscar Prasse's certified goat dairy in Staten Island and Balsam Farms, a 200-head dairy established in 1900 by Isaac Balsam. Located at 88-25 Pitkin Avenue in Ozone Park, Balsam Farms was the last dairy in the city when it closed in the mid-1960s. The site became the Balsam Village housing development.

In the mid-1800s New York's farmers faced constant pressure from developers to sell their land. Even though the process of converting farmland to housing led to the ultimate destruction of agriculture within the city, it initially encouraged vegetable farming. As property changed hands over generations, heirs who might once have viewed land in terms of its agricultural potential began to consider its value as real estate. In this way land slowly trickled away from farm families into the hands of speculators and developers. In other instances retired farmers oversaw the development of their properties. Both processes resulted in the creation of numerous small, unconnected plots of vacant land that were often held off the real estate market for one or more seasons. The new landowners generated income by leasing these plots to recently arrived immigrants from Germany and the United Kingdom, many of whom had prior experience as market gardeners.

Between 1850 and 1880, owing to the availability of horse manure from Manhattan and Brooklyn and the adoption of intensive production methods, New York, Queens, and Kings counties consistently ranked among the top vegetable producers in the United States. In the latter year, Kings and Queens counties ranked first and second nationally, and Queens County continued as a top vegetable producer into the twentieth century.

At the turn of the twentieth century there were more than 2000 farms in New York City, averaging 25 acres (10.12 hectares) each. Thirty years later, nearly 90 percent had disappeared. In 1937 Vincenzo and Mary Bendetto, who worked as vegetable growers in Manhattan, converted their square-block lot of leased land at 10th Avenue and 214th Street to an automobile parking lot; in this manner the last commercial farm in Manhattan quietly passed from existence. Commercial agriculture continued elsewhere in the city, however, particularly in Queens and Staten Island, although only a handful of tiny, isolated farms were left by 1960. Commercial farming persisted in New York City until 2003, when the family of John Klein, Jr., sold the remaining 2 acres (0.81 hectares) of the family farm, located at 194-15 73rd Avenue in Fresh Meadows.

Although commercial farming disappeared from New York City, three agricultural museums keep farming traditions alive: the Queens County Farm Museum, Wyckoff House, and the Sylvanus Decker Farm. The agriculture program at John Bowne High School continues to prepare students for agriculture-related employment, as it has since 1917. In the first decade of the twenty-first century more than 1300 community gardens stretched across the city, a handful of publicly funded "farmer" training programs were in place, and backyard poultry hobbyists, beekeepers, and hydroponics enthusiasts continued to be in evidence. Hydroponic farming has a long history in New York, dating back at least to the 1930s, yet it remains current; in 2007 a hydroponic demonstration garden floated on a barge in the Hudson River as a means to promote urban agriculture.

Ulysses P. Hedrick, *A History of Agriculture in the State of New York* (New York: Hill and Wang, 1933; repr. 1966); Edward K. Spann, *The New Metropolis: New York City, 1840–1857* (New York: Columbia University Press, 1986); David S. Cohen, *The Dutch-American Farm* (New York: New York University Press, 1992); Marc Linder and Lawrence Zacharias, *Of Cabbages and Kings County* (Iowa City: University of Iowa Press, 1999)

Louis P. Tremante

AIA. See American Institute of Architects.

AIDS [acquired immune deficiency syndrome]. During the decade following the identification of AIDS by public health officials in the early 1980s, New York City was more severely affected by the disease than any other American city. In 1986 epidemiologists estimated that more than half the homosexual men in the city and three-fifths of intravenous drug users were infected with the human immunodeficiency virus (HIV), the precursor of AIDS. By the end of 1987 one in 61 women giving birth in the city was infected. Toward the end of the 1980s AIDS became the leading cause of death in the city among men 25 to 44 years of age and black women 15 to 44 years of age. By 1988 the city's health care and social welfare systems were becoming increasingly overwhelmed: 13 percent of the inpatient beds in facilities maintained by the Health and Hospitals Corporation were occupied by AIDS patients that year. In response the city and private organizations worked to increase inpatient and outpatient services as well as home health care.

AIDS raised a number of controversial issues of public policy. A debate over mandatory testing for HIV and whether the names of those who tested positive should be kept confidential was settled when the state legislature passed the Testing Confidentiality Act of 1988, which required informed consent before testing and assured those tested of confidentiality. In addition, health care workers were empowered to help individuals who tested positive in disclosing their status to intimate partners. In the twenty-first century city officials continued their policy against mandatory testing and treatment while stressing the importance of both. While patient confidentiality remained crucial, a 1998 law, which became effective in 2000, reaffirmed mandatory reporting procedures for both health care providers and laboratories. In 2004 New York City correctional facilities expanded the availability of voluntary rapid testing, a move that resulted in a fourfold increase in testing among the incarcerated population of New York City.

In the twenty-first century the development of more effective pharmaceutical therapies and the increased spread of information about HIV and AIDS prevention led to a dramatic drop in the number of both AIDS-related deaths and new infections. In 2008, 3305 new AIDS cases were reported in New York City; this was 2020 fewer than in 2004. The number of AIDS-related deaths that same year was 1108, an 8 percent drop from 2007. While the overall number of diagnoses began to decline in 2001, diagnoses in young women and men between the ages of 13 and 29 increased. As of 2007 infection rates in New York City were three times the national average, and AIDS was the third leading cause of death among individuals younger than 65. The disease disproportionally affects minority communities; in the early part of the twenty-first century 80 percent of new AIDS diagnoses occurred in African American and Hispanic individuals. According to 2008 data from the New York Department of Health and Mental Hygiene, one in 70 New Yorkers is infected with HIV, and one in 40 African Americans. New York City remained the epicenter of the pandemic in the United States in 2008, with more AIDS cases than Los Angeles, San Francisco, Miami, and Washington, D.C., combined, with more than 100,000 people in the city living with HIV/AIDS.

The pandemic inspired early activism by such groups as the Gay Men's Health Crisis and the more militant organization AIDS Coalition to Unleash Power (ACT UP). Between 1986 and 2006 the New York City AIDS Walk raised more than $100 million, with more than 40,000 walkers annually. In 1991 Thomas Duane became the first openly gay and openly HIV-positive member of the New York City Council. He was elected to the New York State Senate in 1998 and continued to speak out against discrimination and the stigma associated with the disease. The Broadway community, always deeply affected by the disease, formed the largest industry-based HIV/AIDS fund-raising and grant-making organization, Broadway Cares/Equity Fights AIDS. Artists in New York City take part in fund-raising and educational efforts, including an annual event known as the Day with(out) Art sponsored by the city-based nonprofit organization Visual AIDS. Begun in 1989 as the Day without Art, the event initially shut down museums and other art organizations so staff could volunteer their time to AIDS charities. In 1997, however, the national day of remembrance was reframed to emphasize works of art focusing on the disease or created by artists with HIV/AIDS. Many artists, choreographers, and writers have produced art related to the AIDS pandemic, including paintings by Keith Haring, Larry Kramer's play *The Normal Heart,* and the Pulitzer Prize–winning play *Angels in America* by Tony Kushner. Several municipal landmarks are dedicated to acknowledging the effect of AIDS on New York City. Park Row between Beekman and Spruce Streets was renamed People with AIDS Plaza. On 30 November 2008, the day before the annual World AIDS Day, the AIDS Memorial was dedicated in Hudson River Park.

Peggy McGarrahan, *Transcending AIDS: Nurses and HIV Patients in New York City* (Philadelphia: University of Pennsylvania Press, 1994); Susan M. Chambre, *Fighting for Our Lives: New York's AIDS Community and the Politics of Disease* (New Brunswick, N.J.: Rutgers University Press, 2006)

David F. Musto, Anne Epstein

air rights. Zoning regulation. *Air rights* refers to the difference between the actual floor area of an entire building and the maximum amount of floor area allowed on a lot. Developers commonly use air rights to build taller skyscrapers than city zoning regulations allow. These rights can be bought and sold in order to raise revenue or create larger buildings. This transfer can be done in two ways. The first is to combine two adjacent lots into one, which is called a zoning lot merger. Once this has been done, any unused air rights of one lot may be transferred to the other. The other method of obtaining air rights is a transfer of development rights to shift the air rights from one building to another within the vicinity. This is only applicable in special circumstances, usually protecting a historic building, an open space, or cultural resources. This method is only used when a zoning lot merger is impossible, such as when a street separates a historic building from another lot. In 2005 Christ Church at Park Avenue and 60th Street set the record for air-right sales, selling for $430 per square foot, which totaled over $30 million.

Nathan Morgante

AirTrain (JFK). An 8.1-mile (13-kilometer) light rail mass transit service. Opened in 2003 by the Port Authority of New York and New Jersey, the AirTrain provides passenger service within John F. Kennedy International Airport (JFK); connecting service between JFK and the New York City subway system's A-train at Howard Beach Station, in Queens; and connecting service between JFK and the E, J, and Z trains as well as the Long Island Railroad at Jamaica Station, also in Queens. Replacing shuttle buses, the AirTrain decreases local road traffic and shortens commute times. The trip takes between 8 and 16 minutes to get from the airport to Howard Beach and Jamaica; trains run around the clock, leaving every 2 to 8 minutes during peak hours and every 6 to 12 minutes late at night.

Ben Silk

AirTrain, 2009

Alan Guttmacher Institute. Nonprofit organization in New York City and Washington, D.C., formed in 1968 as the Center for Family Planning Program Development, a division of the Planned Parenthood Federation of America. Its founders, Frederick S. Jaffe and the obstetrician and gynecologist Alan F. Guttmacher, then president of the federation, intended that the new organization should protect reproductive rights throughout the world (especially among the young and the poor) and communicate to policy makers and the public the findings of research in the fields of reproductive rights, reproductive health, and population. The institute became independent and separately incorporated in 1977. As of 2010 its New York City office was located at 125 Maiden Lane.

Albanians. Albanian peasants and unskilled workers settled in New York City early in the twentieth century; most found work in shoe, glass, and textile factories. They formed neighborhoods according to religious affiliations: Catholics on South Fordham Road opened the Albanian Catholic Center, Muslims in central Brooklyn created the Albanian American Islamic Center, and Eastern Orthodox in Jamaica founded the St. Nicholas Albanian Church. Another influx of immigrants began after World War I and again after World War II when refugees, political exiles, and professionals settled in the city and launched a number of periodicals and organizations. The Free Albania Committee, an alliance of various political groups, promoted freedom and democracy in Albania and in 1957 began publishing *Shqiptari i Lire* (The Free Albanian). The farmers' organization the Agrarian Democratic Party (also known as Balli Kombetar) issued the publication *Shgrbistari* (The Serviceman, 1950–61) for its youth branch and also introduced the newspaper *Zeri i Ballit* (The Voice, 1950–). *Jeta Katholike Shkiptare* (Catholic Albanian Life, 1966–) and the Muslim publication *Perpejka e Jone* (Our Effort, 1974–) were intended to provide religious, social, and political news. The Albanian Kosovar Youth reported on violations of the political rights of Albanians living in Yugoslavia. Small business owners belonged to the Albanian Owners Association.

In the mid-1990s between 20,000 and 25,000 Albanians lived in New York City. Many were professionals, office workers, small business owners, and food-service and maintenance workers; they promoted education and also sought to preserve their customs and ethnic heritage. Well-known Albanians in the city have included the writer and social activist Nemnie Zaimi and the writer and literary scholar Arshi Pipa. In 2007 more than 31,000 people in the city were reported to be of Albanian ancestry.

Vladimir Wertsman

Albee, Edward (Franklin) (*b* Washington, D.C., 12 March 1928). Playwright. He achieved some notoriety with his early works *The Zoo Story* (1959), which is set in Central

Park, and *The American Dream* (1961), and won a Tony Award and a New York Drama Critics Circle award for *Who's Afraid of Virginia Woolf?* in 1962. During his early career he lived in a duplex in Greenwich Village; in 1978 he began dividing his time between a loft in Tribeca and homes in Long Island and Florida. He later wrote three Pulitzer Prize–winning plays, *A Delicate Balance* (1966), *Seascape* (1975), and *Three Tall Women* (1994). A number of his plays were performed Off-Broadway in honor of his 80th birthday in 2008, including two of which he directed himself at the Cherry Lane Theater.

Kenneth T. Jackson

Aldridge, Ira Frederick (*b* New York City, 1807; *d* Łódź, Poland, 1867). Internationally acclaimed African American actor. He attended the African Free School in New York City and received awards for his oratory skills. His fondness for theater developed while living in the city. He worked with the African Company, also known as the African Grove Theatre, formed in 1821, where he performed his first role as Rolla from *Pizarro.* Feeling stifled by his race in the United States, Aldridge left the country in 1825 for England in hopes of receiving better roles. Abroad he achieved recognition and praise from audiences; he is regarded as the first black American to become established as an actor in another country, performing Shakespeare and debuting at London's Covent Garden in 1833. He lived and toured in Europe for the remainder of his life. The Ira Aldridge Memorial Chair at the Shakespeare Memorial Theatre in Stratford-upon-Avon, England, and a theater at Howard University in Washington, D.C., were named in his honor.

Meryl Cates

Alexander, William, Lord Stirling (*b* New York City, 1726; *d* Albany, N.Y., 15 Jan 1783). General. After receiving his education in New York City he went to England to claim his title, which was refused by the House of Lords; he then returned to the city, where he became a governor of King's College and held several offices after his marriage to Governor William Livingston's sister. He opposed the Stamp Act, and as a colonel during the American Revolution in January 1776 he captured the *Blue Mountain Valley,* a British transport ship. He was then promoted to brigadier general of the Continental Army and oversaw the construction of fortifications including Forts Lee and Washington. Captured during the Battle of Long Island, he was freed during an exchange of prisoners and fought in the battles of Westchester, Trenton, Brandywine, and Germantown; his attack on British forces on Staten Island was repulsed. By the end of the war Alexander was promoted to the rank of major-general.

Paul David Nelson, *William Alexander, Lord Stirling* (Tuscaloosa: University of Alabama Press, 1987)

James E. Mooney

Alexander Hamilton. Side-wheel steamboat designed by J. W. Millard and built by the Bethlehem Shipbuilding Corporation of Maryland in 1924. It measured 349 feet (106 meters) by 77 feet (23 meters). From 1924 until 6 September 1971 the ship was operated by the Hudson River Day Line between New York City and other points along the Hudson. Its retirement marked the end of the scheduled steam service along the Hudson that had begun in 1807. Efforts to preserve the vessel failed: the hulk lies in Sandy Hook Bay, New Jersey.

Arthur G. Adams

Alexander Hamilton U.S. Custom House. See U.S. Custom House.

Alexander Robertson School. Private elementary school, opened in 1789 in Manhattan by the Second Presbyterian Church and originally situated at Broadway and King's Street (now Pine Street). It is the oldest fully coeducational institution in New York City. The school is named for the principal benefactor of the church, a Scotsman who lived in New York City and raised money to repair the church after Hessian mercenaries used it as a barracks during the American Revolution. The school moved in 1813 to West 14th Street and in 1900 to 95th Street and Central Park West. A Scottish flavor persists despite the diverse populations of both school and church: the emblem of the school is a thistle, bagpipes are played at special events, and each graduation ceremony ends with the singing of "Auld Lang Syne."

Richard Schwartz

Alexander's. Firm of retailers. Its first department store was opened in 1928 at Third Avenue and 152nd Street in the Bronx by George Farkas (1902–80) and named after his father. The firm built its reputation by selling fashionable clothes at discount prices and concentrating on lower- to middle-income customers. In 1963 Farkas moved the main store to 59th Street and Lexington Avenue, just across from Bloomingdale's. Alexander's filed for bankruptcy in May 1992 and closed its eleven retail outlets in the city. The building at 59th Street remained unoccupied until it was torn down in 1999. The Bloomberg Tower opened on the 59th Street site in 2004.

Leslie Gourse, Kenneth T. Jackson

Alger, Horatio(, Jr.) (*b* Chelsea, Mass., 13 Jan 1832; *d* Natick, Mass., 18 July 1899). Writer. In 1866 he was asked to leave the Unitarian ministry and moved to New York City, where he worked for the benefit of the Newsboys Lodging House. Before long he was writing dime novels for the juvenile market about street boys who go from rags to riches by virtue of hard work and good luck. From 1872 to 1876 he lived at 26 West 34th Street. Alger wrote 103 juvenile novels, among them the best seller *Ragged Dick* (1868); though modestly received during his lifetime these works were popularized after World War I, when they were marketed to adolescents as models for achieving success.

Michael Joseph

Algerians. The first Algerians to settle in New York City were 200 college students who arrived in the early 1970s on government scholarships to attend New York University, Columbia University, Brooklyn's Polytechnic University, and Stevens Institute of Technology (in New Jersey). This group stayed on in the country as professionals in scientific and technical fields. In the 1980s a second wave of mostly middle-class families came seeking relief from economic hardship. In the 1990s young, single Algerians from France began immigrating to escape French racism toward North Africans. Even so, the population remained small: in the early 1990s Algerian New Yorkers probably did not exceed 600. Owing mainly to the diversity lottery, which creates visas for countries with low rates of immigration, however, there has been a steady influx of Algerians since then; by the early twenty-first century between 10,000 and 12,000 Algerians were residing in New York City. Algerians maintain cultural solidarity through the Algerian American National Association (AANA, established 1987). AANA helps Algerians achieve American citizenship and sponsors educational and cultural programs that promote good relations between Algeria and the United States. Algerian *rai,* a mix of Arab, African, and rock music with themes of social commentary and protest, has become popular in the city through the performances of such musicians as Cheb Khaled.

Paula Hajar

Algonquin Hotel. Hotel opened in 1902 on West 44th Street between Fifth and Sixth avenues. Frank Case operated the hotel from 1907 until his death in 1946. The building, designed by Goldwyn Starrett, has a facade of red brick and limestone and is decorated with eighteenth-century English and American furnishings. In the 1920s and 1930s the hotel was a center of literary and theatrical life: it was closely associated with the *New Yorker* and hosted the Algonquin Round Table, a meeting of famous writers and literary personalities. Alan Jay Lerner wrote the musical *My Fair Lady* in room 908. Control of the hotel passed to Ben Bodne in 1946; upon his retirement in 1987 Caesar Park Hotels acquired the Algonquin.

Algonquin Hotel, ca *1910*

Frank Case, *Tales of a Wayward Inn* (New York: Frederick A. Stokes, 1938)

B. Kimberly Taylor

Algonquin Round Table. Name given to a group of lively theatrical and literary figures who met daily for lunch at the Algonquin Hotel on West 44th Street for about a decade beginning in 1919. The group met first in the Pergola Room (now the Oak Room), until Frank Case, manager of the Algonquin, moved it in 1920 to the round table in the larger Rose Room so that the members would be more visible to the public. The central figure in the group was Alexander Woollcott, drama critic of the *New York Times.* Its other members included the writer Franklin P. Adams, author of the highly popular newspaper column "The Conning Tower" and generally considered the dean of the table; the press agents Murdock Pemberton and John Peter Toohey; the writers Heywood Broun and his wife, Ruth Hale; Jane Grant of the *New York Times* and her husband, Harold Ross, who founded the *New Yorker;* Dorothy Parker, Robert E. Sherwood, and the humorist Robert Benchley, all writers for *Vanity Fair;* Art Samuels of *Harper's Bazaar;* the writers Marc Connelly, George S. Kaufman, and Donald Ogden Stewart; and the illustrator Neysa McMein. From time to time others were invited to the table, including the actors Douglas Fairbanks, Harpo Marx, Alfred Lunt and Lynn Fontanne, Tallulah Bankhead, Ina Claire, and Margalo Gilmore; the novelists Edna Ferber, Margaret Leech, and Alice Duer Miller; the playwrights Noël Coward and Charles MacArthur; the screenwriter Herman Mankiewicz; and the young violinist Jascha Heifetz. The group was celebrated for being at once glamorous, irreverent, acerbic, worldly, and clannish. Its influence stemmed largely from the power that newspaper columnists wielded during the prosperous 1920s. By the end of the 1920s the Algonquin Round Table had virtually ceased to exist. They remain the symbols of a literate humor that is inextricably associated with New York City and reminders of a time when urban living and urbanity were often combined.

Margaret Case Harriman, *The Vicious Circle: The Story of the Algonquin Round Table* (New York: Rinehart, 1951); James R. Gaines, *Wit's End: Days and Nights of the Algonquin Round Table* (New York: Harcourt Brace Jovanovich, 1977)

Brenda Wineapple

Alice Austen House. Historic structure in Staten Island. The first house on the site was built by the Dutch in the 1690s as part of a farm near the Narrows. The property was acquired in 1844 by the grandfather of the photographer Alice Austen, who expanded the house and added peaked windows and a gingerbread trim, giving it the appearance of a Victorian cottage. The family moved into the house shortly after Austen was born in 1866, and she remained there until 1945; the more than 7000 photographs that she took while living at the house are now at the Staten Island Historical Society. The house and grounds were restored in the 1980s and reopened as a museum, with temporary exhibitions.

Ann Novotny, *Alice's World: The Life and Photography of an American Original, Alice Austen, 1866–1952* (Old Greenwich, Conn.: Chatham, 1976)

Jonathan Kuhn

All Angels' Church. Founded in the 1830s by St. Michael's Church (99th Street and Amsterdam Avenue) as the "colored Sunday School" for residents of Seneca Village, a racially mixed community in what is now Central Park. All Angels' relocated from park ground and incorporated in 1859. It then purchased the old building and moved it to donated land at West End Avenue and 81st Street. A stone church designed by Samuel B. Snook replaced it by 1890 but was razed in 1979. In the early twenty-first century the congregation continued to meet in the old parish house on 80th Street, maintaining traditional and innovative worship and a vigorous social program.

John B. Snook

Allen [Israel], **Mel(vin)** (*b* Birmingham, Ala., 14 Feb 1913; *d* Stamford, Conn., 16 June 1996). Sports broadcaster. Raised in Alabama, he came to New York City in 1937 to work in radio; he broadcast New York Yankees and Giants home baseball games from 1939 until 1943. After military service he returned to New York City in 1946, broadcasting Yankee games through 1964 on radio and television, after which time the Yankees did not renew his contract. Allen broadcast baseball in Milwaukee (1965) and Cleveland (1968), then returned to New York City in 1978 to call Yankee games on cable television through 1985. He also served as host of the long-running

Alice Austen House, 2009

weekly syndicated television series *This Week in Baseball,* nearly until his death.

Andrew Sparberg

Allen, Stephen (*b* New York City, 2 July 1767; *d* Hudson River at Riverdale, 28 July 1852). Mayor. Apprenticed to a sail maker during the American Revolution, he later formed a partnership with his former employer. Soon after starting his own business he amassed a fortune by bypassing ship chandlers to deal directly with wholesalers. A staunch Jeffersonian, he became president of the Mechanics City, a director of the Mechanics Bank, and a city alderman. Allen was appointed mayor and served for three terms (1821–24) and in his later years became a Jacksonian Democrat. He died aboard the steamboat *Henry Clay* when it caught fire on the Hudson River in 1852.

Howard Rock

Allen, Woody [Konigsberg, Allan (Stewart)] (*b* Brooklyn, 1 Dec 1935). Musician and award-winning film director, writer, and actor. He grew up in Flatbush and during his first year at Midwood High School wrote material for the columnist Earl Wilson; in 1952 he took his current name partially based on his musical idol, clarinetist Woody Herman. After briefly attending New York University and City College of New York, he was hired as part of NBC's internship program for writers and contributed material to major programs during television's "Golden Age." During the 1960s Allen appeared as a stand-up comedian at venues such as the Bitter End and the Blue Angel, on the *Ed Sullivan Show,* and on the *Tonight Show,* of which he was also a guest host. His play *Don't Drink the Water* (1966) ran for 18 months on Broadway. In 1965 he wrote and acted in *What's New, Pussycat?,* and in 1969 he directed his first complete feature film, *Take the Money and Run.* Many of the films he directed, which numbered 45 by 2009, were set in New York City and largely autobiographical. Notable examples include *Manhattan* (1979), *Radio Days* (1987), and *Manhattan Murder Mystery* (1993). *Hannah and Her Sisters* (1986), much of which was filmed at the Langham, an apartment building at 135 Central Park West, includes an architectural tour of Manhattan; other films were made at locations ranging from Sutton Place to Coney Island. In the early twenty-first century, Allen's filming location preferences tended toward Europe, primarily London, where his creative freedom was challenged less by financiers and audiences were more receptive. Allen has played traditional jazz clarinet since the age of 15 and performs with his band on a regular basis in New York City.

Eric Lax, *Woody Allen* (New York: Alfred A. Knopf, 1991); Maurice Yacowar, *Loser Take All: The Comic Art of Woody Allen* (New York: Continuum, 1991); Peter J. Bailey, *The Reluctant Film Art of Woody Allen* (Lexington: University Press of Kentucky, 2003)

Val Ginter

Alley Pond. Name formerly applied to a neighborhood in northwestern Queens, at the head of Little Neck Bay along a valley 125 feet (38 meters) deep made by Alley Pond. A royal grant for the land was given in 1673 to Thomas and Christopher Foster, who soon built the first house. By 1691 a grist mill was operated by John and Stephen Hicks just south of what is now Northern Boulevard; Alley Pond was dammed just upstream to provide power for a second mill (1752), to the east of which Thomas Foster built a house in 1758 that survived until the 1930s. In the 1820s a wool mill operated at or alongside the site of this second mill, and from 1821 to 1826 the hamlet of Alley Pond provided a post office for Flushing (the second in Queens County). The mill was bought in 1828 by Benjamin Lowerre of Flushing, who operated it and a country store until 1859. His son-in-law William C. Buhrmann took over the business and repaired and improved the mill machinery as late as 1878; Buhrmann's sons continued to operate the store from his death in 1898 until 1920. The film *Zaza* was made in the neighborhood in 1908. By 1926, when the mill was destroyed by fire, the hamlet of Alley Pond had grown to include about a dozen houses. The store was demolished to make way for the Cross Island Parkway in October 1939; Alley Pond was filled in and the mill was demolished in 1955 during the construction of an embankment for the Long Island Expressway. In the 1970s row houses were built on new streets to the south, and a shopping mall opened on the east side of the valley.

Vincent Seyfried

Alley Pond Park. Second-largest public park in Queens, measuring 624.78 acres (253 hectares) and bordered to the north by Little Neck Bay, to the east by Douglaston, to the south by the Union Turnpike, and to the west by Bayside. The park is transected by the Belt Parkway from north to south, by the Long Island Expressway south of Oakland Lake, and by the Grand Central Parkway at its southernmost corner. Most of the park was acquired and cleared by the city in 1927, but the area was moderately augmented in 1936 by small sections south of Grand Central Parkway (on either side of the old Motor Parkway) and around Oakland Lake; meadowlands north of Northern Boulevard were added in 1961–62. In the northern end of the park Lake Oakland flows into Alley Creek and on to Little Neck Bay. North of the Long Island Expressway there are meadowlands and to the south woodlands. The Alley Pond Environmental Center has a library, museum, animal exhibits, guided nature walks, and trails for horseback riding.

Vincent Seyfried

Allied Chemical. Firm of chemical manufacturers, formed on 17 December 1920 as the Allied Chemical and Dye Corporation, one of two major American holding companies that sought to counter German control of the chemical industry during World War I. On its formation the firm commanded assets of $282.7 million from five large makers of related products: the Solvay Process Company, maker of alkalis and nitrogen products; the Semet–Solvay Corporation, a pioneer in the production of soda ash, caustic soda, and coke by-products; the Barrett Company, a maker of coal tar products; the General Chemical Company, the first maker of synthetic ammonia and contact acid in the United States; and the National Aniline and Chemical Company, which erected the first integrated dyestuffs plant in the United States. In 1922 Allied Chemical and Dye acquired Heyl Laboratories and began to produce medical products; during the 1940s the original five corporations were liquidated and a large research laboratory was constructed. The firm took the name Allied Chemical Corporation in 1958. In 1971 it moved its corporate headquarters from New York City to a large complex at Morris Township, New Jersey. Later it was renamed the Allied Corporation before merging with the Signal Companies in 1985 to become Allied–Signal, which merged with and took on the name of Honeywell in 1999.

Williams Hayes, ed., *American Chemical Industry,* vol. 6, *The Chemical Companies* (New York: D. Van Nostrand, 1949)

David B. Sicilia

almshouses. The first almshouse in what is now New York City was built in 1653 on Beaver Street in New Amsterdam; it was replaced under Dutch and English rule by structures on Broad and Wall streets called deacons' houses, which were privately supported by charitable contributions to churches. A publicly financed almshouse opened in 1736 on the site of the present City Hall and included a range of facilities for the poor: a workhouse for those fit to work, a poorhouse for the unfit, and a house of correction for "unworthy" paupers who were considered criminals. In 1784 the city appointed commissioners of the Alms-House and Bridewell (the prison), and in 1832 it formed the Alms House Department. The commissioners shared the prevailing attitude of the day that the problems of health, housing, and unemployment resulted from moral deficiencies and could be solved by hard work, thrift, and temperance. In the almshouse

The Female Almshouse on Blackwell's Island, ca *1885–90*

Protestant clergymen preached to predominantly Irish Catholic inmates. Strict rules were prescribed and harsh measures imposed to enforce proper behavior, including physical punishment, solitary confinement on bread and water, and leg irons. Overcrowding was acute, particularly during the years of cholera and yellow fever; as a result larger almshouses were built, such as the one opened in April 1816 at 26th Street near the East River in Bellevue. Over the years separate facilities opened for paupers with contagious diseases, for prostitutes, for criminals, and for mental patients. Children living at the almshouse were moved in 1832 to the Long Island Farms in Queens County and then in 1848 to "nurseries" on Randalls Island. A workhouse was set up on Blackwell's (now Roosevelt) Island in the following year. During the same period almshouses also opened in Brooklyn, Queens, and Staten Island. The commissioners of the almshouses complained that immigrants overburdened their facilities; by 1854–60 the almshouse population was on average 86 percent foreign born. Reports of the period abound with descriptions of destitution, disease, and death. In the 1870s and 1880s, New York State passed laws requiring that children over two years of age be removed from almshouses and placed with families or in hospitals, orphan asylums, or other institutions.

The agency charged with overseeing the almshouses was restructured and renamed several times. After consolidation (1898) the city began to subsidize the care of poor children in private institutions, and in 1902 the board of trustees of the Bellevue and Allied hospitals assumed responsibility for the public charity hospitals. In 1936 the last of the almshouse facilities was abolished when the penitentiary at Blackwell's Island was moved to Rikers Island. The Almshouse Department became the Department of Welfare in 1936, which in turn became the Department of Social Services in 1967.

David M. Schneider, *The History of Public Welfare in New York State,* vol. 1, *1609–1866* (Chicago: University of Chicago Press, 1938); Raymond A. Mohl, *Poverty in New York, 1783–1825* (New York: Oxford University Press, 1971)

Juliana F. Gilheany

Alphabet City. Neighborhood in Manhattan in the East Village, bounded to the north by 23rd Street and Avenue C, the west by FDR Drive, the south by Houston Street, and the east by Avenue A. Its name derived from avenues A, B, C, and D, which run only in this part of Manhattan. In the 1840s and 1850s, the area had a large German population and was referred to as Little Germany, or Kleindeutschland. In the mid-nineteenth century, the population shifted to eastern European immigrants, mostly Irish, Italian, and Jewish. The area underwent another major population change in the twentieth century, with a large influx of Puerto Ricans. It has long been known as a low-rent neighborhood for immigrants. Since about 1980, however, higher rents have brought increased commercial activity with the opening of new restaurants, bars, and shops, as well as a more affluent population. Notable places include Tompkins Square Park, Stuyvesant Town, and the Christodora House. The area also contains several community gardens.

Jessica Montesano

alternate-side-of-the-street parking. System of regulations imposed in 1950 that limits curbside parking to one side of the street on certain days of the week. The regulations began as an experiment on the Lower East Side to facilitate street cleaning, which had recently become mechanized, and were soon extended to all of Manhattan, the Bronx, Brooklyn, and Queens. In many areas parking was allowed only on the south side of the street during three-hour periods on Mondays, Wednesdays, and Fridays, and only on the north side during three-hour periods on Tuesdays, Thursdays, and Saturdays. Fines levied against violators were at first nominal but increased as the city began to rely more heavily on parking tickets as a source of revenue: by 2008 the fine for alternate-side-of-the-street violations reached $65 and receipts from parking citations of all kinds exceeded $550 million. More than 10,000 miles (16,000 kilometers) of street fell under alternate-side-of-the-street rules. Motorists, in what some sarcastically refer to as the "New York Grand Prix," ritualistically moved their vehicles each morning from one side of the street to the other, often just ahead of the street cleaners. In 2001 Calvin Trillin published *Tepper Isn't Going Out,* a humorous novel about a man who found the perfect parking spot and decided to stay in his car forever. Initially the regulations were suspended only on Sundays and civic holidays such as Veterans Day, but in 1952 the City Council added the Jewish high holy days, with Catholic holy days following soon after. Greek Orthodox holy days were added in 1990. In more recent years the number of suspended days has grown to 34 with the addition of Muslim (Idul-Fitr and Eid al-Adha) and Hindu (Divali) holy days and the Asian Lunar New Year. The regulations are also routinely suspended after heavy snowfalls. The high fines and seemingly greater competition for a fixed number of parking spaces have given rise to several thriving businesses that offer car-moving and ticket-fixing services.

Edward T. O'Donnell

alternative press. Term used for periodicals with a nontraditional content and readership, often combining characteristics of newspapers and magazines and sometimes published irregularly. *Freedom's Journal,* launched in 1827 by and for blacks, was the first newspaper of its kind in the country and remained in operation until 1829. The *Free Enquirer,* published from 1829 to 1830 by the communitarian theorist Robert Dale Owen and the feminist Fanny Wright, supported women's rights and birth control and encouraged frank debates about religion. It influenced George Henry Evans, who published the *Working Man's Advocate* (weekly, 1829–45), the most widely read labor newspaper during the 1830s and 1840s, as well as the *Man* (1834–35), the *Radical* (1841–42), and *Young America* (1844–49); he eventually aligned himself with advocates of land reform who adopted the slogan "vote yourself a farm." During the labor movement of the 1830s advocates of prison reform, broad-based education, and democratic changes in suffrage presented their ideas in alternative publications. Craft unions in the city formed the General Trades Union during the mid-1830s and published the *Union* (1834–36) under the editorship of the labor leader John Commerford. Although efforts to organize workers diminished during a severe depression in 1837, capitalist speculators and their sympathizers in Tammany Hall remained the target of several newspapers, among them the *Subterranean,* published by the politician Mike Walsh from 1845 to 1847. The newspaper *Sybyl* promoted women's rights in the 1840s, and Victoria Woodhull and her sister Tennessee Claflin published *Woodhull and Claflin's Weekly* from 1870 to 1876, which advocated women's rights and also included articles on marriage (attacked as a form of slavery), extramarital sex, prostitution, abortion, and venereal disease.

After organizing the Socialist Labor Party in 1877 a number of German intellectuals published the first English-language socialist newspaper that became widely read, as well as the *People* (1891–99) and the *Daily People* (1900–14), the most important publications of the party. Such alternative newspapers were crucial to politics in the city; almost every socialist, radical, and anarchist group produced a newspaper to recruit and educate members. New York City became the national center of the alternative press. In 1883 John Swinton, a former managing editor of the *Sun,* launched a newspaper to encourage workers to engage in politics. Known as *John Swinton's Paper,* it was read by trade unionists throughout the country but ceased operations in 1887 after consuming $40,000 of Swinton's savings. When the Socialist Party was at its peak, *The Masses* (1911–17), a literary and political journal based in Greenwich Village, challenged the cultural status quo. Edited by Max Eastman, it attracted such writers as John Reed and Walter Lippmann but was eventually undermined by tension among radical intellectuals, artists, and labor leaders whom it sought to bring together. The Bolshevik Revolution divided the socialist movement: the communist ideology of the Soviet Union was embraced by *Class Struggle* (1917–19), *Revolutionary Age* (1918–19), and *Worker's Council* (1921) and rejected by the *Socialist Review* (1919–21), *Labor Age* (1921–33), and the *American Socialist Monthly* (1935–37).

The relationship of the American left and the Soviet Union remained the most divisive issue in the alternative press during the following decades and led to the formation of several new publications. The editors of the *New Masses* (monthly, 1926–33), Mike Gold and Joseph Freeman, supported strict revolutionary communism, argued for a "proletarian literature," and excluded writers such as Ernest Hemingway, Theodore Dreiser, Langston Hughes, and Richard Wright; strident factionalism gradually abated as the left coalesced in support of the Popular Front in the mid-1930s. At the same time the *Daily Worker* (1924–58), sponsored by the Communist Party, sought a wider audience by adding a sports page and book and film reviews; it was one of the first newspapers in the country to

The Revolution.

PRINCIPLE, NOT POLICY: JUSTICE, NOT FAVORS.

VOL. I.—NO. 1. NEW YORK, WEDNESDAY, JANUARY 8, 1868. $2.00 A YEAR.

The Revolution;

THE ORGAN OF THE

NATIONAL PARTY OF NEW AMERICA.

PRINCIPLE, NOT POLICY—INDIVIDUAL RIGHTS AND RESPONSIBILITIES.

THE REVOLUTION WILL ADVOCATE:

1. IN POLITICS—Educated Suffrage, Irrespective of Sex or Color; Equal Pay to Women for Equal Work; Eight Hours Labor; Abolition of Standing Armies and Party Despotisms. Down with Politicians—Up with the People!

2. IN RELIGION—Deeper Thought; Broader Idea; Science not Superstition; Personal Purity; Love to Man as well as God.

3. IN SOCIAL LIFE.—Morality and Reform; Practical Education, not Theoretical; Facts not Fiction; Virtue not Vice; Cold Water not Alcoholic Drinks or Medicines. It will indulge in no Gross Personalities and insert no Quack or Immoral Advertisements, so common even in Religious Newspapers.

4. THE REVOLUTION proposes a new Commercial and Financial Policy. America no longer led by Europe. Gold like our Cotton and Corn for sale. Greenbacks for money. An American System of Finance. American Products and Labor Free. Foreign Manufactures Prohibited. Open doors to Artisans and Immigrants. Atlantic and Pacific Oceans for American Steamships and Shipping; or American goods in American bottoms. New York the Financial Centre of the World. Wall Street emancipated from Bank of England, or American Cash for American Bills. The Credit Foncier and Credit Mobilier System, or Capital Mobilized to Resuscitate the South and our Mining Interests, and to People the Country from Ocean to Ocean, from Omaha to San Francisco. More organized Labor, more Cotton, more Gold and Silver Bullion to sell foreigners at the highest prices. Ten millions of Naturalized Citizens DEMAND A PENNY OCEAN POSTAGE, to Strengthen the Brotherhood of Labor; and if Congress Vote One Hundred and Twenty-five Millions for a Standing Army and Freedman's Bureau, cannot they spare One Million to Educate Europe and to keep bright the chain of acquaintance and friendship between those millions and their fatherland?

Send in your Subscription. THE REVOLUTION, published weekly, will be the Great Organ of the Age.

TERMS.—Two dollars a year, in advance. Ten names ($20) entitle the sender to one copy free.

ELIZABETH CADY STANTON, } EDS.
PARKER PILLSBURY, }

SUSAN B. ANTHONY,
Proprietor and Manager.
37 Park Row (Room 17), New York City,
To whom address all business letters.

KANSAS.

THE question of the enfranchisement of woman has already passed the court of moral discussion, and is now fairly ushered into the arena of politics, where it must remain a fixed element of debate, until party necessity shall compel its success.

With 9,000 votes in Kansas, one-third the entire vote, every politician must see that the friends of "woman's suffrage" hold the balance of power in that State to-day. And those 9,000 votes represent a principle deep in the hearts of the people, for this triumph was secured without money, without a press, without a party. With these instrumentalities now fast coming to us on all sides, the victory in Kansas is but the herald of greater victories in every State of the Union. Kansas already leads the world in her legislation for woman on questions of property, education, wages, marriage and divorce. Her best universities are open alike to boys and girls. In fact woman has a voice in the legislation of that State. She votes on all school questions and is eligible to the office of trustee. She has a voice in temperance too; no license is granted without the consent of a majority of the adult citizens, male and female, black and white. The consequence is, stone school houses are voted up in every part of the State, and rum voted down. Many of the ablest men in that State are champions of woman's cause. Governors, judges, lawyers and clergymen. Two-thirds of the press and pulpits advocate the idea, in spite of the opposition of politicians. The first Governor of Kansas, twice chosen to that office, Charles Robinson, went all through the State, speaking every day for two months in favor of woman's suffrage. In the organization of the State government, he proposed that the words "white male" should not be inserted in the Kansas constitution. All this shows that giving political rights to women is no new idea in that State. Who that has listened with tearful eyes to the deep experiences of those Kansas women, through the darkest hours of their history, does not feel that such bravery and self denial as they have shown alike in war and peace, have richly earned for them the crown of citizenship.

Opposed to this moral sentiment of the liberal minds of the State, many adverse influences were brought to bear through the entire campaign.

The action of the New York Constitutional Convention; the silence of eastern journals on the question; the opposition of abolitionists lest a demand for woman's suffrage should defeat negro suffrage: the hostility everywhere of black men themselves; some even stumping the State against woman's suffrage; the official action of both the leading parties in their conventions in Leavensworth against the proposition, with every organized Republican influence outside as well as inside the State, all combined might have made our vote comparatively a small one, had not George Francis Train gone into the State two weeks before the election and galvanized the Democrats into their duty, thus securing 9,000 votes for woman's suffrage. Some claim that we are indebted to the Republicans for this vote; but the fact that the most radical republican district, Douglass County, gave the largest vote against woman's suffrage, while Leavenworth, the Democratic district, gave the largest vote for it, fully settles that question.

In saying that Mr. Train helped to swell our vote takes nothing from the credit due all those who labored faithfully for months in that State. All praise to Olympia Brown, Lucy Stone, Susan B. Anthony, Henry B. Blackwell, and Judge Wood, who welcomed, for an idea, the hardships of travelling in a new State, fording streams, scaling rocky brinks, sleeping on the ground and eating hard tack, with the fatigue of constant speaking, in school-houses, barns, mills, depots and the open air; and especially, all praise to the glorious Hutchinson family—John, his son Henry and daughter, Viola—who, with their own horses and carriage, made the entire circuit of the state, singing Woman's Suffrage into souls that logic could never penetrate. Having shared with them the hardships, with them I rejoice in our success.

E. C. S.

THE BALLOT—BREAD, VIRTUE, POWER.

THE REVOLUTION will contain a series of articles, beginning next week, to prove the power of the ballot in elevating the character and condition of woman. We shall show that the ballot will secure for woman equal place and equal wages in the world of work; that it will open to her the schools, colleges, professions and all the opportunities and advantages of life; that in her hand it will be a moral power to stay the tide of vice and crime and misery on every side. In the words of Bishop Simpson—

"We believe that the great vices in our large cities will never be conquered until the ballot is put in the hands of women. If the question of the danger of their sons being drawn away into drinking saloons was brought up, if the mothers had the power, they would close them; if the sisters had the power, and they saw their brothers going away to haunts of infamy, they would close those places. You may get men to trifle with purity, with virtue, with righteousness; but, thank God, the hearts of the women of our land—the mothers, wives and daughters—are too pure to make a compromise either with intemperance or licentiousness."

Thus, too, shall we purge our constitutions and statute laws from all invidious distinctions among the citizens of the States, and secure the same civil and moral code for man and woman. We will show the hundred thousand female teachers, and the millions of laboring women, that their complaints, petitions, strikes and protective unions are of no avail until they hold the ballot in their own hands; for it is the first step toward social, religious and political equality.

First issue of the Revolution, *8 January 1868, launched by Susan B. Anthony* report on racial conflict and also published articles by Wright on politics and culture in Harlem. As a newspaper of the Communist Party it remained closely tied to the interests of the Soviet Union: it did not protest the internment of Japanese Americans and condemned wartime strikes. Always in debt, it never had more than 38,000 subscriptions and ceased operations after its circulation fell below 10,000 during the 1950s.

A number of young writers who became activists in the 1960s worked in the 1930s and 1940s for newspapers that were not aligned with the Communist Party. The *Catholic Worker,* formed in 1933 by Dorothy Day and the French philosopher Peter Maurin, stressed the virtues of voluntary poverty and nonviolent action and urged readers to take responsibility for achieving social justice. Former Trotskyists including Irving Howe, C. L. R. James, Dwight Macdonald, and James Burnham wrote for the *Militant* (weekly, 1928–) and the *New International* (1934–58); among the political and cultural journals published in the city by former Trotskyists were *Dissent* (1954–) and *Politics* (1944–49). The independent newspaper the *National Guardian,* which began publication in 1948 and was renamed the *Guardian* in 1967, covered national liberation movements in Africa and Southeast Asia long before there was widespread interest in them. The *Daily Worker* resumed publication as the *Daily World* in 1968 and was successively renamed the *People's Daily World* in 1986 and the *People's Weekly World* in 1990.

During the 1960s and early 1970s an "underground" press developed in the city. Several newspapers sought to introduce the politics of the New Left to the counterculture, including the *Village Voice* (1955– , edited by Ed Fancher and Daniel Wolf), the *Realist* (1958–74, Paul Krassner), the *East Village Other* (1965–72, Walter Bowart), and the *New York Rat* (1968–70, Jeff Shero). Oriented toward youth and irreverent toward both right and left, these newspapers were known for their psychedelic graphics and sexual frankness. The *East Village Other* called for rent control, safer streets, and investigations of unscrupulous landlords; the *New York Rat* had close links to the antiwar movement. As new, more radical groups were formed, the alternative press became increasingly angry and militant: stories appeared under such headlines as "The Year of the Heroic Guerilla," and radical feminists took over the *Rat,* which they renamed *Women's Liberation.* After homosexual patrons of the Stonewall Inn resisted a police raid in June 1969, the periodical *Come Out!* was launched by the Gay Liberation Front. Most publications introduced during these years soon ran out of funds or were abandoned. A few, such as the *Village Voice,* survived by revamping themselves to reach a wider readership and attract more advertisers. In the twenty-first century many alternative newspapers are published online where they can be updated quickly and regularly. They also feature columnists and bloggers to present varying viewpoints and encourage discussion between writer and readers.

Alternative Press: A Guide to the Microform Collection (Ann Arbor, Mich.: University Microfilms International, 1990)

Kerry Candaele

Altria Group. See Philip Morris.

Alvin Ailey American Dance Theater. Dance company. Alvin Ailey (*b* Rogers, Tex., 5 Jan 1931; *d* New York City, 1 Dec 1989) studied dance with Lester Horton and Martha Graham before moving to New York City in 1954 after an invitation to perform in Truman Capote's Broadway show *House of Flowers.* In 1958 he formed the Alvin Ailey American Dance Theater with the aim of bringing black dancers into the mainstream of dance. The company's first performance took place at the 92nd Street Y, and in 1960 the Alvin Ailey American Dance Theater became the resident company of the Clark Center for the Performing Arts at the 51st Street Young Women's Christian Association. From the early days of the company, Ailey and his dancers were tapped to be international ambassadors of dance performing tours in Africa, Europe, Asia, and Australia as part of President John F. Kennedy's President's International Program for Cultural Presentations. In 1969 the company temporarily moved to the Brooklyn Academy of Music, where Ailey established the Ailey School. For the most part, the Ailey organization has tended to make the West Side of Manhattan its home, with studios in such varied locations as a renovated church at 229 East 59th Street, 1515 Broadway, 211 West 61st Street, and City Center at 151 West 55th Street. Ailey dancers were repeatedly invited to perform for White House functions. In 1976 the company performed at the opening night at Studio 54. After Ailey's death in 1989, dancer and choreographer Judith Jamison was named artistic director. In 2008 the entire Ailey organization, including the Alvin Ailey American Dance Theater, the Ailey School, Ailey II, and the Alvin Ailey Foundation, was located in the Joan Weill Center for Dance at 405 West 55th Street in Manhattan. In 2008 the block between Ninth and 10th avenues was officially renamed Alvin Ailey Place as part of a 50th anniversary celebration of the company.

The troupe performs Ailey's dances as well as the work of such established choreographers as Horton, Katherine Dunham, Pearl Primus, Ted Shawn, Talley Beatty, John Butler, and Donald McKayle and such younger ones as Ulysses Dove, Elisa Monte, and Bill T. Jones. A versatile choreographer himself, Ailey skillfully blended ballet, modern dance, and jazz dance in works set to music by diverse composers such as Ralph Vaughan Williams, John Coltrane, and Duke Ellington, who in 1970 composed *Les trois rois noirs* and *The River* for the company. Some of Ailey's dances are thematic, often drawing on black culture (including his best-known work, *Revelations,* and *Blues Suite*); others focus on abstract movement and have often been performed by ballet companies (*Streams, The River,* and *The Lark Ascending*).

Susan Cook and Joseph H. Mazo, *The Alvin Ailey American Dance Theater* (New York: William Morrow, 1978)

Brenda Dixon Gottschild, Anne Epstein

Alwyn Court. Elegant apartment building in Manhattan, erected in 1909 at 180 West 58th Street by the architectural firm of Harde and Short. The building is notable for its exuberantly decorated French Renaissance facade of terra-cotta, depicting salamanders (symbol of François I of France), flowers, leaves, dragons, and crowns. It has a central courtyard containing an architectural mural by Richard Haas. Designed at the time that large apartment buildings were just beginning to win acceptance as upper-class residences, Alwyn Court originally contained only 22 apartments, ranging in size from 14 rooms to 34. The Depression forced a change, and in 1938 the building was modified to contain 75 apartments, each with three to five rooms.

Sandra Opdycke

Amalgamated Bank of New York. Commercial bank opened in 1923 in Union Square by the Amalgamated Clothing Workers of America. It became instrumental in supporting unions by providing low-interest loans and a loan support program for strikers, and was the first bank in New York City to offer unsecured personal loans and free checking with no minimum balance. In the early twenty-first century, Amalgamated was the only bank in the United States owned entirely by a union. It had assets of more than $4 billion and nine New York branches, which provided pension trust and custodial services, consumer and commercial loans, mortgages, and health care financial services.

The Evolution of Banking: A Story of the Transition from the Medieval Moneylender to the Labor Bank (New York: Amalgamated Bank of New York, 1926)

Laura Gwinn

Amalgamated Clothing Workers of America. Labor union formed in 1914 by men's clothing workers, most of them Jewish and Italian immigrants. It had its roots in a bitter strike at the end of 1912 by employees seeking higher wages and relief from conditions in disease-ridden tenements and dark, poorly ventilated sweatshops. The first enduring institution to defend against abuses in the garment trade, it took an approach that became known as the "new unionism": unlike its affiliate in the American Federation of Labor, the United Garment Workers, which promoted nativism and craft elitism, it sought the membership of immigrants and introduced a method of collective bargaining, sometimes called "industrial democracy," that encouraged workers to help resolve grievances on the shop floor. In the 1930s and 1940s these innovations became the model for labor relations throughout much of American industry. In 1936 the union was one of the founding members of the Congress of Industrial Organizations (CIO). The union also achieved success in a number of social innovations, including unemployment insurance, group health care, affordable credit (through the Amalgamated Bank), and cheap cooperative housing (in Manhattan and the Bronx); these measures prefigured the core reforms of the New Deal and represented a remarkable degree of social conscience at a time when such concepts were uncommon.

These gains were threatened by the Depression, and the union survived partly because it organized aggressively and in 1932 rid itself of members with ties to organized crime, an effort carried out with the reluctant help of Mayor James J. Walker. Unable to escape calamity on its own, it strengthened its relations with government and shifted its support from socialism to the Democratic Party and the welfare state. In the city it helped to form the American Labor Party, which delivered the votes of former radicals to Franklin D. Roosevelt, Herbert H. Lehman, and Mayor Fiorello H. La Guardia. After World War II the union changed as blacks, Asians, Latin Americans, and Puerto Ricans became the majority. Membership reached 96,000 in 1952 but declined to 57,000 by 1970, reflecting the decline of garment manufacturing in the city. In 1976, as imports flooded the American market, the union merged with the Textile Workers Union of America, a measure first considered during the early 1920s. In 1995, the Amalgamated Clothing and Textile Workers Union merged with the International Ladies' Garment Workers' Union to form UNITE, which merged again in 2004 with the Hotel and Restaurant Employees Union and formed UNITE HERE. In 2009 the combined organization had more than 265,000 members, who worked primarily in the hotel, food service, casino gaming, laundry, and warehousing industries.

Steve Fraser

Amalgamated Housing Corporation. Organization formed in 1926 by the Amalgamated Clothing Workers of America (ACW). Its incorporation followed an attempt in the preceding year by Abraham Kazan, manager of the credit union of the ACW, to build reasonably priced cooperative housing for the union's workers by forming the ACW Corporation. With his colleagues he chose a site in the Bronx accessible to the subway, near Van Cortlandt Park and the Jerome Park Reservoir, but was unable to raise sufficient funds to begin construction. The Amalgamated Housing Corporation was formed by the union as a means of furthering Kazan's project after the state legislature in 1926 passed the Limited Dividend Housing Companies Law to encourage low-cost housing through tax incentives. Kazan was named president of the new corporation by Sidney Hillman, president of the ACW, and he also remained as president of the ACW Corporation, which became the construction company for the project. In addition to capital raised from cooperative members, the Metropolitan Life Insurance Company and the publishers of the *Jewish Daily Forward* provided a credit fund and a mortgage, enabling groundbreaking to take place in November 1926. The following year the Amalgamated Cooperative Apartments, designed by the architects George W. Springsteen and Albert Goldhammer, were built north of Sedgwick Street between Saxon and Dickinson avenues in the Bronx. The apartments accommodated 303 families who paid $11 a room a month and $500 a month to buy into the cooperative: because of Kazan's insistence on open membership not all the families were associated with the ACW. Among the first tenants was the family of David Dubinsky, president of the International Ladies' Garment Workers' Union. The building was luxurious by the standards of the time, with large rooms and interior garden courtyards. Ice, dental, medical, and children's services were provided cooperatively, along with a newspaper (*Community News*) and various cultural activities; house committees oversaw day-to-day functions. In January 1929 construction of an additional 192 apartments began on land adjacent to the original building. That same year Kazan and the Amalgamated Housing Corporation purchased a block of land on Grand Street, in the Lower East Side, and built the Amalgamated Dwellings (six stories, 236 apartments), also designed by Springsteen and Goldhammer. The complex won an award in 1931 from the American Institute of Architects, and a local street was renamed Kazan Street. Another 115 units were added to the original housing in the Bronx in 1931, and a large complex of five- and six-story buildings in a Gothic style was built in 1937. Norman Avenue, which adjoins these extensions, was renamed Hillman Avenue after the union's president.

Tenants in the early decades of the Amalgamated projects were primarily Jewish and Italian. In 1950 the three Amalgamated groups, along with several cooperatives in the city, labor unions, and neighborhood and fraternal organizations, formed the United Housing Foundation to promote cooperative housing, with Kazan as president. The following year the Hillman Housing Project, comprising three 12-story buildings, their gardens, and their playgrounds, was constructed at Grand Street between Abraham Kazan Place and Lewis Street, requiring clearance of 65 slum tenements in a four-block area; by 1990 the complex contained more than 4000 units. Like the rest of the city the Amalgamated projects became more ethnically diverse in the 1970s and housed an increasing number of black, Latin American, Korean, and other Asian residents. In 2008 the Amalgamated Housing Corporation maintained housing for more than 1500 families. Both the Amalgamated Houses and the Amalgamated Dwellings were managed by independent cooperative boards composed of local residents, and state law required that residency be open only to those of middle or limited income.

Asher Aschinstein, *Report of the State Board of Housing on the Standard of Living of 400 Families in a Model Housing Project, the Amalgamated Housing Corporation* (Albany, N.Y.: Burland, 1931); *Thirty Years of Amalgamated Cooperative Housing, 1927–1957* (New York: Warbasse Memorial Library, 1958)

Marjorie Harrison

Amato Opera Theater. Opera company formed in 1947 by Anthony Amato and Sally Bellantoni Amato. It initially sponsored performances at unused auditoriums around the city before moving to a site on Bleecker Street now occupied by the Circle in the Square Theatre, and then to a white brick building in the East Village at 319 Bowery at Second Street. Although the theater seats only 107 persons and the stage is only 20 feet (6 meters) wide, the productions were ambitious, and as many as 70 performers have been onstage at one time. Aspiring singers who had hoped to be discovered by major companies performed for no pay. In May 2009 the Amato ceased operations, and Anthony Amato sold the theater building. Their last performance was of Mozart's *Marriage of Figaro* on 31 May 2009.

Kenneth T. Jackson

AMAX. Firm of ferrous-metal miners. It was formed in 1887 at 80 Wall Street by a prominent German family as the American Metal Company (Amco), a trader of metals, and moved to 61 Broadway in 1913. Its financial interest in the discovery of molybdenum ore in the Rocky Mountains in 1916 made it internationally known, and it soon developed molybdenum for commercial use and focused increasingly on mining rather than trading. The Climax Molybdenum Company was formed in 1934 with headquarters at 500 Fifth Avenue and worked closely with Amco until the two companies merged in 1957 to form American Metal Climax, with offices in Rockefeller Center. Renamed AMAX in 1974, it became one of the most successful firms in the city. In 1993 AMAX merged with the Cyprus Minerals Company to form Cyprus Amax Minerals Company.

James Bradley

Ambassador Hotel. Hotel at 51st Street and Park Avenue, designed by the firm of Warren and Wetmore and erected in 1921. An aristocratic structure, it differed from some of its contemporaries in having individually designed rooms and suites. The furnishings and interior ornamentation, loosely inspired by eighteenth- and nineteenth-century English and French styles, were supplied by John Wanamaker.

Shan Jayakumar

Ambrose, John W(olfe) (*b* Newcastle West, Ireland, 10 Jan 1838; *d* New York City, 15 May 1899). Engineer who developed docks and channels in New York Harbor and constructed elevated railroads. In the 1880s Ambrose founded the 39th Street South Brooklyn Ferry and became president of the Brooklyn Wharf and Dry Dock Company. He devoted his last years to seeking funds for enlarging New York Harbor from Congress, which shortly before his death voted an appropriation for a channel 45 feet (13.7 meters) deep, 2000 feet (610 meters) wide, and 10 miles (16 kilometers) long. The Ambrose Channel and Light are named for him.

Elliott B. Nixon

A.M.E. Church. See African Methodist Episcopal Church.

Amerada Hess Corporation. Firm of petroleum distillers formed as the Amerada Corporation in 1920 by Everett de Golyer (1885–1954), with headquarters at 65 Broadway. Initially a small firm that sought new methods for finding petroleum, it became one of the largest independent oil companies in the country after discovering an important oil field in North Dakota in 1952. Through the efforts of Leon Hess (1914–1999) it merged with the Hess Oil and Chemical Corporation and became the Amerada Hess Corporation; the offices were moved in 1973 to Rockefeller Center. In 2006 the company changed its name to the Hess Corporation.

James Bradley

American Academy of Arts and Letters. Society of composers, artists, architects, and writers founded in 1904 by elite members of the National Institute of Arts and Letters, who took the Académie Française as their model. The initial seven members were William Dean Howells, Augustus Saint-Gaudens, Edmund Clarence Stedman, John La Farge, Mark Twain, John Hay, and Edward MacDowell. Now numbering 250, the academy's members are elected for life. Since 1923 the academy has been housed in the Audubon Terrace complex in upper Manhattan on Broadway between 155th and 156th Streets. In 1976 the academy and its parent organization voted to merge into one institution with a two-tiered membership structure, called the American Academy and Institute of Arts and Letters. In 1993 all members were enrolled in a single organization, again known as the American Academy of Arts and Letters. The organization exhibits art and manuscripts, funds readings and performances of new works, purchases works of art to be donated to museums, and administers awards. Each year more than 50 individuals are recognized with awards and honors ranging from $5000 to $75,000.

Helen Graves

American Academy of Dramatic Arts. A school for film, television, and stage acting. Founded in 1884, the academy celebrated its 125th anniversary in 2009. It offers classes in acting, voice and speech, theater history, and makeup. The academy also provides an education in the business aspect of an acting career. The school is designed around a two-year program with conservatory classes and programs, including performances. Academy alumni, many of whom have won Emmy, Tony, and academy awards, include Grace Kelly, Adrien Brody, Kim Cattrall, and Danny DeVito.

Meryl Cates

American Academy of the Fine Arts. Formed in 1802 as the New York Academy of Arts, the first art school and museum in the city. Its founders were Edward Livingston, then the mayor of New York City, and his brother Robert R. Livingston, the American minister to France. The Livingstons attracted nearly 80 merchants, physicians, lawyers, and other prominent citizens to a subscription for the purchase of casts after antique sculptures in the Louvre. Later the academy was led by De Witt Clinton (1813–16), who deployed it for political purposes, and by John Trumbull (1817–35), who sought to professionalize the arts. The name was changed to the American Academy of the Fine Arts in 1817, and annual exhibitions were held at the New York Institution for the Arts in City Hall Park (1816–30) and at 81/2 Barclay Street (1831–42). In 1826 members of the academy reacted to the contemporary American art exhibits of the newly formed National Academy of Design by increasing their display of paintings by old masters, a gambit that eventually failed but nonetheless jump-started the market for European painting in the city. In 1842 the remaining officers disbanded the academy and sold its sculpture to the National Academy and paintings to Daniel Wadsworth.

Mary Bartlett Cowdrey, *The American Academy of Fine Arts and American Art Union, 1816–1852* (New York: New-York Historical Society, 1953); Carrie Rebora, "The American Academy of the Fine Arts, New York, 1802–1842" (PhD diss., City University of New York, 1990)

Carrie Rebora Barratt

American Anti-Slavery Society. Abolitionist organization. It was formed in Philadelphia in 1833 by the merger of a group of evangelical

American Academy of Dramatic Arts, 2009

—VOL. I. NO. 5.—

THE
AMERICAN
ANTI-SLAVERY
ALMANAC,
FOR
1840,

BEING BISSEXTILE OR LEAP-YEAR, AND THE 64TH OF AMERICAN INDEPENDENCE. CALCULATED FOR NEW YORK; ADAPTED TO THE NORTHERN AND MIDDLE STATES.

Slave State — Free State

NORTHERN HOSPITALITY—NEW YORK NINE MONTHS' LAW.
The slave steps out of the slave-state, and his chains fall. A free state, with another chain, stands ready to re-enslave him.

Thus saith the Lord, Deliver him that is spoiled out of the hands of the oppressor.

NEW YORK:
PUBLISHED BY THE AMERICAN ANTI-SLAVERY SOCIETY,
NO. 143 NASSAU STREET.

The Anti-Slavery Almanac, *1840*

reformers in New York City led by Lewis Tappan and a group from Boston favoring immediate abolition led by William Lloyd Garrison. The society was based in New York City and was dominated by New Yorkers until 1840. Tappan served on the executive committee with such prominent merchants and reformers as John Rankin and William Green; his brother Arthur Tappan was president of the society. In the 1830s the society flooded the mails with abolitionist literature and organized a massive petition campaign. It was crippled in 1840 when the faction from New York City led by the Tappans withdrew and formed the American and Foreign Anti-Slavery Society. Control of the American Anti-Slavery Society was assumed by Garrison, who advocated moral suasion, northern secession, and black civil rights. The society disbanded in 1870 after Congress ratified the 15th Amendment.

Peter J. Wosh

American Art-Union. Nonprofit organization formed in 1839 by a group of merchants, bankers, lawyers, and railroad directors in New York City as the Apollo Association for the Promotion of the Fine Arts in the United States; it changed its name in 1844. The stated goals were "cultivating the talent of artists" and "promoting the popular taste." The group bought paintings from American artists such as William Sidney Mount and Thomas Cole and distributed them by lottery to subscribers, who paid an annual membership fee of $5. At the height of its influence in 1849 it distributed 1010 works of art among 18,960 subscribers across the nation. It also published an illustrated periodical (April 1848 to December 1851) and issued one or more engravings to members each year. At a time of growing sectional strife between North and South, the American Art-Union promoted themes of patriotic cohesion. It ceased operations in 1853 as the result of legal actions brought against it because of its lotteries.

Mary Bartlett Cowdrey, *The American Academy of Fine Arts and American Art-Union, 1816–1852* (New York: New-York Historical Society, 1953)

Patricia Hills

American Ballet Theatre [ABT]. Dance company. Formed in 1939 under the name Ballet Theatre, it gave its first performance in January 1940. The founders, Richard Pleasant and Lucia Chase, previously gave financial support to ABT's forerunner, Mordkin Ballet, led by the Russian dance teacher Mikhail Mordkin. Pleasant encouraged Chase to build a larger company on the European model, and the two recruited many performers, including Europeans fleeing the hostilities of World War II, and signed on Antony Tudor as their resident choreographer. Since its founding, ABT emphasized classical technique, such as the Vaganova method, and adaptability in its dancers. Its repertoire consisted of classical full-length ballets from the nineteenth and early twentieth centuries and contemporary works, including *Giselle, Apollo,* and *Duets.* ABT also encouraged the development of new works and has performed pieces by twentieth-century choreographers such as Agnes de Mille and Twyla Tharpe.

The impresario Sol Hurok expanded the audience for the company by booking performances at the Metropolitan Opera House but damaged its reputation by disregarding Tudor's seriousness of purpose and seeking to impose his view that ballet should be frothy, high-spirited entertainment. The company nevertheless gave successful performances of *Fancy Free* (1944) by Jerome Robbins, ABT's first collaboration with scenic designer Oliver Smith, and *Theme and Variations* (1947) by George Balanchine. Oliver Smith, who emphasized the interaction between moving scenery and the human form, later became codirector of ABT in 1945 and held the position until 1980.

From the late 1940s to the early 1960s the company suffered from its lack of a permanent performance venue in New York City. After breaking with Hurok, it was unable to depend on the Metropolitan Opera House, and when Balanchine's company, the New York City Ballet, became an affiliate of the City Center of Music and Drama in 1950, this venue became unavailable as well. The company was reduced to performing in various theaters on Broadway, an arrangement that proved unsatisfactory. Tours took on an increasingly important role: the company visited small U.S. cities throughout the 1950s and 1960s, Europe in 1956–57 (at which time the company took its current name), and the Soviet Union with the sponsorship of the U.S. Department of State in 1960. These years were marked by such a lack of artistic focus that the tour of the Soviet Union took place only after one early supporter, John Martin of the *New York Times,* failed to dissuade the government from funding it.

The fortunes of the company revived in 1964 when the New York State Theater opened as part of the Lincoln Center for the Performing Arts. By providing a home for the New York City Ballet, the theater again freed up the City Center for ABT; the New York State Theater was itself available when the New York City Ballet and the City Opera were not in residence there. In 1967 the company gave a well-received performance of the complete *Swan Lake,* staged by David Blair of the Royal Ballet. In the same year Cynthia Gregory emerged as a promising dancer and Eliot Feld made his debut as a choreographer. The company continued to emphasize international talent: among those who performed with the company after taking up residence in the United States were the prominent Russian dancers Natalia Makarova (1970) and Mikhail Baryshnikov (1974) and Balanchine's leading ballerina, Gelsey Kirkland. In 1977 public television showed ABT's production of *The Nutcracker* featuring Baryshnikov and Kirkland, regarded by many as a classic. The late 1970s were the company's most successful years since its first few seasons.

In 1980 the board of directors, in a controversial move, forced the retirement of Chase and placed Baryshnikov as the new artistic director. He received continual popular and internal criticism during this time. With Baryshnikov as the head, the company refined its classical tradition and staged and restaged many classical ballets. Baryshnikov resigned from the directorship in 1989 and a year later was replaced by Oliver Smith and Jane Hermann, a former director in the presentations department in the Metropolitan Opera Association. This change was characterized by bitterness, threats of strikes and financial collapse, and fears for the company's financial and artistic survival.

In 1992 Kevin McKenzie, a former ABT principal dancer, became the artistic director. He wished to maintain the company's traditional repertoire and recognized the importance of touring as a source of revenue, publicity, and spreading dance to people all over the world. In the fall of 2000 ABT visited

Members of the American Ballet Theatre in Fancy Free *(1940; Jerome Robbins, third from left)*

China, Singapore, and Taiwan, the latter two for the first time. The company supports the development of dance and choreography by holding various programs, such as ABT II, and summer intensive sessions for young artists from across the United States. In 2004 ABT opened the Jacqueline Onassis School, a facility that teaches dancers from 12 to 18 years old. Its curriculum uses principles from the classic French, Italian, and Russian schools of training in order to provide its students with classical technique and the ability to adapt to all styles of dance; thus they are instructed in the ideals of the company that they may later join. ABT annually tours the United States, reaching more than 600,000 people. Its repertoire continues to consist of classical ballets and contemporary works, many with American themes. While ABT remains at City Center in the fall, during its main season the company performs at the Metropolitan Opera House for eight weeks in the spring.

Anita Finkel, Frank Nestor

American Bank Note Company. Firm of engravers formed in 1858 by the merger of seven banknote engraving firms. It was originally housed in the Merchants' Exchange Building on Wall Street and soon after its formation became the most renowned financial engraver in the country. In addition to paper money the firm printed stamps and stock certificates. It built headquarters on Broad Street in 1908. The firm was acquired by the United States Bank Note Corporation in 1990 and left New York for suburban Pennsylvania.

William H. Griffiths, *The Story of American Bank Note Company* (New York: American Bank Note Company, 1960)

James Bradley

American Bible Society. Interdenominational religious society formed in New York City in 1816 by delegates representing local Bible societies from across the country and having as its aim the circulation of the Bible without doctrinal note or commentary. Despite some early contact with Roman Catholics it remained essentially Protestant until the 1960s. The society first occupied quarters on Nassau Street. During its early years it used new forms of printing technology to produce unprecedented quantities of inexpensive Bibles and testaments, and subsidized missionary translators overseas. From 1836 it set up agencies overseas to coordinate the translation, production, and distribution of Bibles; this trend increased dramatically after the Civil War. The society directed special efforts at urban youths, immigrants, mariners, and American Indians. In 1853 it moved to Bible House on Astor Place, a six-story building that housed its extensive pressroom, bindery, and sales operations while also providing a headquarters for a wide range of Protestant benevolent organizations. Later the offices moved successively to Park Avenue at 57th Street (1936) and Broadway at 61st Street (1966). The society maintained a visible presence in the Near East, the Far East, and Latin America well into the twentieth century. By the middle of the century it began to focus its efforts on distributing not only the Bible in its entirety but also biblical excerpts. At the same time the work of the society was marked by a growing cooperation with Roman Catholics after the Second Vatican Council and by support for the world Bible fellowship known as the United Bible Societies, a consortium of national organizations that the society had helped to form in 1946. In the early twenty-first century the society's headquarters were at 1865 Broadway.

Henry Otis Dwight, *The Centennial History of the American Bible Society* (New York: Macmillan, 1916); Creighton B. Lacy, *The Word-Carrying Giant: The Growth of the American Bible Society* (South Pasadena, Calif.: William Carey Library, 1977); Peter J. Wosh, *Spreading the Word: The Bible Business in Nineteenth Century America* (Ithaca, N.Y.: Cornell University Press, 1994)

Peter J. Wosh

American Booksellers Association. Trade association for American retail bookstores. Formed in 1900 in New York City, it was originally intended to stabilize book prices and eliminate price cutting. The association offers programs to facilitate book distribution, issues manuals and handbooks, and is a sponsor of the National Book Awards. In 1992 the association moved from New York City to suburban Tarrytown in Westchester County, New York.

Eileen K. Cheng

American Brands. Firm of consumer-product manufacturers, formed as the American Tobacco Company in 1890 by James B. Duke with headquarters at West 22nd Street, off the Hudson River. In 1904 Duke formed the American Tobacco trust by consolidating most of the nation's major tobacco companies, and he moved the headquarters to the Constable Building (Fifth Avenue and 18th Street). The trust was broken up after the U.S. Supreme Court ruled in 1911 that it violated antitrust laws, but the firm nonetheless remained tremendously successful. At Duke's death it was taken over by George Washington Hill and soon became the leading tobacco company in the United States. The firm moved its offices in 1955 to Lexington Avenue and 42nd Street; it was renamed American Brands in 1968. American Brands expanded during the 1980s, when it bought life insurers and manufacturers of office products, hardware, rubber products, and optical goods. The firm moved its headquarters from New York City in 1986.

John K. Winkler, *Tobacco Tycoon: The Story of James Buchanan Duke* (New York: Random House, 1942)

James Bradley

American Broadcasting Company [ABC]. Television and radio network based in New York City. It began as the second radio network of the National Broadcasting

Company (NBC), called the Blue Network; put up for sale by a ruling of the Federal Communications Commission in 1943, it was acquired by Edward J. Noble for $8 million and given its current name. Although Noble bought five television stations in major markets in 1946, NBC and the Columbia Broadcasting System (CBS) still had more affiliates and more talent. At first ABC specialized in animated cartoons from Hollywood and in action and Western series such as *Cheyenne* and *Maverick*. The news division was run by John (Charles) Daly, also the host of the quiz program *What's My Line?* on CBS. Financial difficulties in 1953 forced a merger with United Paramount Theatres, the president of which, Leonard Goldenson, ran the new company for the next 32 years. ABC was the only network to broadcast the Army–McCarthy hearings live in 1954, but the network was known for the low quality of its news programs, which relied on films supplied by newsreel companies until 1963. During the 1960s it broadcast such popular programs as *77 Sunset Strip* and *Hawaiian Eye,* but it did not pose a threat to CBS and NBC until 1975–76, when Elton T. Rule became president and the network overtook both its competitors in the ratings (a position it held for three consecutive years). In 1976 it offered Barbara Walters the unprecedented salary of $1 million a year to become the first female anchor of a network news program, and it broadcast the series *Roots* (based on the book by Alex Haley), which attracted more viewers than any television program had done before. The network also became known for the sports programs *Wide World of Sports* and *Monday Night Football* and for its coverage of the Olympics; its sports producer Roone Arledge introduced such techniques as slow motion and instant replay. Arledge became president of the news division in 1977. He made an aggressive attempt to improve it by persuading journalists from CBS to join ABC-TV and by developing such highly regarded programs as *Nightline* (with Ted Koppel) and *Sunday Morning with David Brinkley.* In the 1980s the evening news program (with Peter Jennings) surpassed those of the other networks in the ratings. Emboldened by its success, the company expanded its facilities on West 66th Street and built more studios in the West 60s. In 1986 ABC was acquired for $3.5 billion in a friendly takeover by Capital Cities Communications. The joint company was acquired by the Walt Disney Company in 1996. After several years of lackluster ratings ABC experienced an increase in viewership in 1999 with its popular game show *Who Wants to Be a Millionaire?* hosted by Regis Philbin and aired from the company's New York City studios. In the early twenty-first century ABC continued to broadcast many programs nationally from studios in New York City.

Les Brown, *Television: The Business behind the Box* (New York: Harcourt Brace Jovanovich, 1971); Sterling Quinlan, *Inside ABC: American Broadcasting Company's Rise to Power* (New York: Hastings House, 1979); Barbara Matusow, *The Evening Stars* (Boston: Houghton Mifflin, 1983)

Judith Adler Hennessee

American Chicle Company. Firm of chewing gum manufacturers, formed as Adams Sons and Company in 1876 by the glass merchant Thomas Adams (1818–1905) and his two sons. As a result of experiments in a warehouse on Front Street, Adams made chewing gum that had chicle as an ingredient, large quantities of which had been made available to him by General Antonio de Santa Anna of Mexico, who was in exile in Staten Island and at whose instigation Adams had tried to use the chicle to make rubber. Adams sold the gum with the slogan "Adams' New York Gum No. 1—Snapping and Stretching." The offices and factory were on Vesey Street and were later moved to Murray Street. The firm was the nation's most prosperous chewing gum company by the end of the century: it built a monopoly in 1899 by merging with the six largest and best-known chewing gum manufacturers in the United States and Canada, and achieved great success as the maker of Chiclets. It was renamed the American Chicle Company, with headquarters on 44th Street in Manhattan, but it moved in 1923 to Thomson Avenue in Long Island City, where the firm had two factories. During World War II many of the facilities were used for packing and shipping war rations. The firm merged with the Warner–Lambert Pharmaceutical Company in 1962 and soon left the city; its factories in Long Island City closed in 1981.

Robert Hendrickson, *The Great American Chewing Gum Book* (Radnor, Pa.: Chilton, 1976)

James Bradley

American Civil Liberties Union [ACLU]. Organization devoted to the defense of individual liberties guaranteed by the Bill of Rights of the Constitution of the United States. Its national office is in New York City, as is the office of its affiliate, the New York Civil Liberties Union (NYCLU). On its formation in 1920 the ACLU was seen as the successor to the Civil Liberties Bureau (CLB), which had been formed in 1917 to protect freedom of speech, freedom of the press, and the rights of conscientious objectors during World War I. The leaders of the CLB and of its parent organization, the American Union against Militarism (AUAM), included many social workers and reformers associated with the Henry Street Settlement.

The ACLU is active in the areas of First Amendment rights (freedom of speech, of the press, and of assembly), due process (search and seizure, the right to counsel), equal protection (civil rights for racial minorities and women), and privacy (abortion rights). It is perhaps best known for defending adherents of controversial groups, including communists, American Nazis, and members of the Ku Klux Klan. It has also aroused controversy by advocating a strict separation of church and state that precludes prayer in public schools and religious displays on government property.

During its first decades the national office of the ACLU in New York City handled virtually all the work of the organization, and members of the board of directors and staff lived in the city. Roger Baldwin, the director from 1920 to 1950, was active in many other political and social causes, including pacifism, the labor movement, and civil rights. In the 1950s the ACLU began to develop a network of state affiliates, which took on most of the local and regional work of the organization. The national office coordinates the affiliates, works on special projects in such areas as reproductive freedom, women's rights, and children's rights, and maintains a legislative office in Washington. The NYCLU grew out of the New York Civil Liberties Committee (NCLC) and became a semiautonomous affiliate with its own professional staff in 1951.

The activities of the ACLU include litigation, lobbying, and public education. At any one time the organization works on about 1000 cases, most of which are handled by volunteer lawyers. Its most notable successes have come about in Supreme Court litigation: by one estimate the organization played a part in four-fifths of the important civil liberties and civil rights cases decided by the Supreme Court between the mid-1920s and the mid-1990s. As of 2008 the ACLU had about 500,000 members.

Samuel Walker, *In Defense of American Liberties: A History of the ACLU* (New York: Oxford University Press, 1990)

Samuel Walker

American Council of Learned Societies. Organization of scholarly societies formed in 1919 for the study of the humanities. The council promotes research, offers fellowships, and sponsors the International Research and Exchanges Board, the Council for International Exchange of Scholars, a program to encourage American studies in Europe and Asia, committees on Chinese civilization, and exchanges with scholars from Russia and eastern Europe. Books published under its auspices include grammars of Azerbaijani, Armenian, Finnish, Mongol, and Bashkir, the papers of Charles Darwin, the census of medieval manuscripts, and such reference works as the *Dictionary of Scientific Biography* (1970–80), the *Dictionary of the*

Middle Ages (1982–89), and the *Dictionary of American Biography* (1928–). The council also produces an annual report, a quarterly newsletter, and an occasional papers series. The offices are at 633 Third Avenue in Manhattan. In the early twenty-first century it had 69 organizations as members, among them the American Philosophical Society (formed in 1743 by Benjamin Franklin), the American Dialect Society, the History of Science Society, and the Metaphysical Society of America.

James E. Mooney

American Craft Museum. See Museum of Arts and Design.

American Cyanamid. Firm of chemical and pharmaceutical manufacturers. It had headquarters in New York City at Rockefeller Center from 1928 to 1962 and a plant on Willoughby Street in Brooklyn where surgical sutures and ligatures were manufactured from 1945 to 1952. It left the city for suburban Connecticut in 1963.

James Bradley

American Ethnological Society. Oldest professional anthropological organization in the United States. It was formed in New York City in 1842 by a group including Albert Gallatin, who was also its first president. Weakened by factionalism and financial difficulties during the 1850s and 1860s, it nevertheless continued to meet sporadically through the end of the nineteenth century. After 1900 the society was revitalized under the direction of Franz Boas, who drew on the anthropological resources of Columbia University and the American Museum of Natural History. It published an important monograph series beginning in 1940. In the mid-1950s the American Ethnological Society moved beyond its focus primarily on New York City to become a national organization, with publications issued from the University of Washington in Seattle. In the early 1980s it became a subsection of the American Anthropological Association.

John V. Murra, ed., *American Anthropology: The Early Years* (St. Paul: West Publishing, 1976)

Ira Jacknis

American Express. Firm that began in 1850 as a joint stock corporation formed by the merger of three former rivals: Wells and Company; Butterfield, Wasson and Company; and Livingston, Fargo and Company. The new firm constructed a building on Jay and Hudson streets in Manhattan and enjoyed a virtual monopoly on the transport of goods, currency, and securities throughout New York State. In 1874 it moved to 65 Broadway. Soon the firm offered services nationwide by reaching agreements with other express companies (including Wells Fargo), railroads, and steamship companies. It expanded to include financial services by offering money orders from 1882 and introducing the world's first traveler's check in 1891. By the early twentieth century the express companies came under scrutiny from the Interstate Commerce Commission. The firm discontinued its express business altogether when the government took over the railroads during World War I. It opened a travel division in 1915, constructed a new building at 65 Broadway (1917), opened branches in several countries, and set up a banking subsidiary with offices throughout the world. During the 1920s the firm offered around-the-world cruises and one of the first air travel arrangements, from London to Zurich. In 1929 Chase Securities Corporation, an affiliate of the Chase National Bank, purchased 97 percent of the firm in an attempt to gain access to its extensive international network, but the Depression prevented Chase from acquiring full ownership, and when the government ruled in 1933 that banks could not conduct nonbanking operations, Chase divested itself of American Express entirely. After World War II the firm increased the number of its foreign offices from 50 to 139 in response to a markedly increased demand for tours and excursions, and in 1958 it introduced its charge card. An attempt by a fraudulent subcontractor to sell large quantities of water as soybean oil in November 1963 left the firm with enormous liabilities (the incident became known as the salad-oil scandal), but creditors' claims were quickly settled. The charge card operation was at first unprofitable, but by 1967 cardholders numbered more than two million, and the volume of charges reached $1.1 billion.

In 1968 American Express acquired the Fireman's Fund Insurance Company, which became one of its largest subsidiaries, and in 1971 it launched the magazine *Travel and Leisure*. It acquired the data processing firm First Data Resources as well as the brokerage house Shearson, Loeb, Rhoades in 1981 and Investors Diversified Services in 1984; in the following year it began selling off the Fireman's Fund Insurance Company, which had proved to be a financial drain because of cyclical losses. It moved its headquarters to the World Financial Center at Battery Park City in 1986, constructing the 51-story American Express Tower. On 11 September 2001, when two hijacked airliners crashed into the twin towers of the World Trade Center, the American Express headquarters across the street were heavily damaged and 11 American Express employees were killed. It took more than half a year for the company to move back into its former location.

Peter Z. Grossman, *American Express: The Unofficial History* (New York: Crown, 1987)

Mary Hedge

American Federation of Labor [AFL]. Trade union organization formed in 1886. Among its forerunners was the Cigar Makers International Union (CMIU), based in New York City, which was organized along craft lines and offered generous benefits to members in exchange for high dues. Under Adolph Strasser, the international president, and Samuel Gompers, the president of Local 144, the organization responded to a recent depression and the political activism of socialists, greenbackers, and others by joining with Peter McGuire, who had organized carpenters in St. Louis, to form the Federation of Organized Trades and Labor Unions in 1881; this remained smaller than its rival, the Knights of Labor, but played an important role in agitating for the eight-hour day. After a bitter dispute in the city between the CMIU and District 49 of the Knights, labor leaders including Strasser and Gompers called for the formation of a stronger federation, and in December 1886 the American Federation of Labor held its first convention in Columbus, Ohio, electing Gompers its president. The most influential trade unionist in New York City, he held the position until his death in 1924 (except for a year in 1894), his tenure marked by the growth of skilled craft unionism in many industries, including the building trades. Under his direction the federation became the most powerful organization of its kind in the United States; during a time when it had little money he made his apartment its headquarters.

Gompers came to believe that political activities and trade unionism should remain separate, and in 1889 he came into bitter conflict with Daniel DeLeon, the socialist leader of the Central Labor Federation (CLF), an organization chartered in the AFL. DeLeon refused to dissociate his Socialist Labor Party from the federation, which from 1894 responded by discouraging the participation of socialists and opposing socialist alternatives to capitalism. The national organization made no effort to organize unskilled workers and became increasingly conservative: Gompers eventually joined the National Civic Association, which was dominated by business and dedicated to rationalizing relations between labor and management. In 1922 Rose Schneiderman of the Women's Trade Union League resigned from the New York City Central Trades and Labor Council, the governing body of the federation in the city, because she was convinced that it would never seriously support women's labor issues.

During the 1920s and early 1930s the AFL suffered nationwide from a fierce campaign against unions waged by corporations, and at the onset of the Depression membership declined from about five million to about three million. During 1933 and 1934 New York City experienced a resurgence of organizing in the garment trade. Both Sidney Hillman's

Amalgamated Clothing Workers of America (ACWA) and David Dubinsky's International Ladies' Garment Workers' Union (ILGWU) won strikes in the city. Eventually Hillman took the ACWA into the newly formed Committee of Industrial Organizations (CIO; later renamed the Congress of Industrial Organizations), formed by Hillman and John L. Lewis to organize workers in mass-production industries who had been ignored by the AFL. The ILGWU at first also joined the CIO, but it returned to the AFL in 1940. The AFL denounced the CIO for its links to communism even as some of its affiliates, including the teamsters, adopted the organizing methods of the CIO. One of the most important trade unionists at the time was George Meany, president of the AFL in New York State, who built alliances with city and state political leaders that ensured the passage of laws requiring unemployment insurance and workers' compensation.

The AFL gained strength by adapting to the anticommunist movement after World War II: its unions readily accepted the anticommunist provisions of the Taft–Hartley Act (1947), while the CIO suffered from internal struggles that led to the expulsion of unions with links to communists. A merger of the two organizations took place in 1955 to form the AFL–CIO but was not completed in New York City until 1959, when the Greater New York Central Trades and Labor Council of the CIO was replaced by the New York City Central Labor Council (CLC) as the central body of the AFL–CIO in the city. The first president of the CLC was Harry Van Arsdale of the International Brotherhood of Electrical Workers (IBEW); he was largely responsible for persuading Mayor Robert F. Wagner to recognize the right of public workers to organize and for winning strong encouragement from the CLC for the organizers of Local 1199 of the Hospital Workers' Union, most of whom were black women.

The CLC was politically involved in elections, such as the election of Mario M. Cuomo as governor of New York in 1982. After Harry Van Arsdale's death in 1986, a rift developed between building-trade unions and municipal unions during the disputed election of Van Arsdale's son, Thomas Van Arsdale, as the council's president. The younger Van Arsdale charged Victor Gotbaum, his rival, with supporting communist governments abroad. Van Arsdale won the election after a ruling by Lane Kirkland, then president of the AFL–CIO. In 1995, Kirkland resigned; Thomas Donahue took his place as acting president until John Sweeney was elected president of the AFL–CIO. In the beginning of the twenty-first century, the AFL–CIO suffered from severe cutbacks in industrial employment and the withdrawal of three large unions from the federation in 2005.

Stuart Bruce Kaufman, *Samuel Gompers and the Origins of the American Federation of Labor, 1848–1896* (Westport, Conn.: Greenwood, 1973); Leon Fink and Brian Greenberg: *Upheaval in the Quiet Zone: A History of the Hospital Workers' Union, Local 1199* (Urbana: University of Illinois Press, 1989)

Richard Yeselson

American Federation of State, County and Municipal Employees [AFSCME]. Labor union formed in Wisconsin in 1932. Its first local in New York City dates to 1937. In 1944 District Council 37 was chartered to coordinate its locals in the city. Several thousand municipal employees joined AFSCME by 1949, but in 1952 its two largest units defected to the International Brotherhood of Teamsters: one became the Uniformed Sanitationmen's Association, the other Local 237. Under the leadership of Jerry Wurf, the union slowly recovered, capitalizing on Mayor Robert F. Wagner's commitment to collective bargaining. By 1961 District Council 37 had 20,000 members. When Wurf was elected international president of AFSCME in 1964, he was succeeded as executive director of District Council 37 by Victor Gotbaum. In 1965 District Council 37 won a recognition election involving 20,000 hospital workers and became the largest municipal union; its certification as the representative of most employees of mayoral agencies gave it the right to bargain for pensions and benefits for most city workers, including those represented in wage negotiations by other unions. Its strength, organizing campaigns, favorable contracts, and occasional job actions helped increase its membership to nearly 100,000 by the early 1970s. The union offered its members, many of whom held low-paying jobs, a wide range of benefits, including legal, medical, and social services, educational programs, and cultural activities. In 1974 AFSCME set up District Council 1707 to represent its growing membership among employees of nonprofit social service agencies.

AFSCME's financial contributions, telephone banks, and volunteers made it a powerful force in local and state politics, usually providing support for liberal Democrats. During the fiscal crisis of the mid-1970s Gotbaum helped negotiate agreements among leaders in government, business, and labor that saved the city from bankruptcy. With other unions District Council 37 agreed to wage deferrals, reductions in benefits, and a massive purchase of municipal bonds with pension funds, even as thousands of its members were put out of work. Gotbaum emerged from the crisis as the city's most prominent labor leader, known for his blustering style and close ties to business leaders. He retired in 1987; his successor was Stanley Hill, who started working for the city as a caseworker in 1959. The leading African American unionist in the city, Hill played important roles in the presidential campaign of Jesse Jackson in 1988 and the election of Mayor David N. Dinkins in 1989.

During the 1980s and 1990s the leaders of individual District Council 37 locals became increasingly powerful and in some cases corrupt. A series of investigations that began in 1997 ultimately led to the conviction of 32 AFSCME officials on charges of embezzlement and rigging a membership vote to ratify a controversial 1996 contract with the city. National AFSCME forced Hill to retire and placed District Council 37 under their supervision and administration. It regained its autonomy in 2002 with the election of Lillian Roberts as its executive director (she had served as a top AFSCME leader under Gotbaum). AFSCME remained the city's largest union of public employees but without the widespread influence it once had.

Jewel Bellush and Bernard Bellush, *Union Power and New York: Victor Gotbaum and District Council 37* (New York: Praeger, 1984)

Joshua B. Freeman

American Federation of Television and Radio Artists [AFTRA]. Labor union formed as the American Federation of Radio Artists (AFRA) in New York City in 1937; its first president was the entertainer Eddie Cantor. In 1952 the union broadened its scope to include television performers and took its current name. During the 1950s the union fined, censured, and expelled members who failed to cooperate with the House Committee on Un-American Activities. The local union in New York City had about 25,000 members in the early twenty-first century, roughly one-third of the national membership. The union's national headquarters moved to Los Angeles in 2006. AFTRA represents actors, broadcasters, musicians, dancers, disc jockeys, puppeteers, and other performers who work in radio, television, Internet and digital programming, and a few other areas unrelated to broadcasting. It has successfully organized performers in public broadcasting, but met with some challenges in cable television, video recording, and digital media. The union establishes minimum salaries and fees through collective bargaining with networks, local stations, advertisers, and other producers. Initiation fees and dues are used primarily to support contract negotiations and enforcement. The union is affiliated with the American Federation of Labor–Congress of Industrial Organizations (AFL–CIO).

Gerard Koeppel

American Folk Art Museum. Museum originally chartered as the Museum of Early American Folk Arts in 1961. Its founders believed that folk art should be studied not only as historical and ethnographical artifacts, but as serious art. It first showed works to the public in a gallery located on the parlor floor of a townhouse at 49 West 53rd Street. Robert Bishop was appointed director of the museum in 1977. During his tenure he greatly expanded its collection and promoted it to a wide audience. The museum partnered with New York University in 1981 to create the first graduate program in folk art studies in the nation. In 1989 it opened a branch location in Columbus Circle, opposite Lincoln Center. Over the following years the museum increasingly focused on contemporary folk artists and gained recognition for its acquisition of the archives of and 24 paintings by Henry Darger. In 2001 the museum changed its name to the American Folk Art Museum and opened its new building at 47 West 53rd Street, which was critically and publicly acclaimed for its innovative architectural design.

Breanne Scanlon

American Geographical Society. Organization formed at 179 Broadway in Manhattan on 9 October 1851 as the American Geographical and Statistical Society. The original membership numbered about 100 and included some of the most prominent figures in New York City, among them Alexander Isaac Cotheal, Henry Evelyn Pierrepont, Charles A. Dana, Henry J. Raymond, Freeman Hunt, and Judge Alexander Warfield Bradford. Early activities of the society included publication of its *Bulletin* (from 1852) and the reading of papers on such topics as the exploration of South America and the polar regions, construction of a railroad to the Pacific, and the extension of the telegraph. Despite concerns about insufficient funds and membership, the society was granted a charter by the state legislature in 1854. It moved its headquarters to Cooper Union in 1866 and took its current name in 1871; it later moved successively to 11 West 29th Street (1876), West 81st Street, 3755 Broadway, at Audubon Terrace (1911), and 156 Fifth Avenue. In the 1880s the society focused on such concerns as development of the Congo basin and the siting of a ship canal between the Atlantic and the Pacific oceans. Its president between 1903 and 1906 was Commander Robert E. Peary, explorer of the North Pole. In 1912 the society gained international recognition when it sponsored the Transcontinental Excursion, which introduced distinguished European geographers to the American landscape. The *Bulletin* became the *Geographical Review* in 1916.

The society was an important source of strategic information to the American military during both world wars. In 1950 it launched a quarterly magazine for the general reader called *Focus* and the following year published the *Millionth Map of Latin America*. It played an important role in preparing the *Columbia Lippincott Gazetteer of the World* (1952) and assembled an important map collection (now at the University of Wisconsin at Milwaukee). In later years the society reaffirmed its commitment to strengthening geographical education in American schools. A travel program was begun in 1985 to sponsor educational voyages throughout the world. At the turn of the twenty-first century the American Geographical Society was located at 120 Wall Street.

Elizabeth J. Kramer

American Heart Association. Organization for the prevention and cure of heart disease. Among its forerunners was the Society for the Prevention and Relief of Heart Disease, formed by physicians in New York City concerned with the management of heart disease. Organizational meetings were held at the New York Academy of Medicine in 1915, the first annual meeting on 26 January 1916. During the next eight years the society provided information and assistance to physicians in other cities who were organizing similar groups. At the initiative of the society the American Heart Association was formed in 1924 and held its first meeting in February 1925. The national headquarters moved to Dallas, Texas, in 1975. In the early twenty-first century the American Heart Association Heritage Affiliate was located at 122 East 42nd Street.

William Lee Frost

American Indians. Indian people have been living in and around what is now New York City for at least 11,500 years.

1. Early Hunters and Gatherers

Remains associated with early Paleo-Indians represent the oldest known verifiable physical record of human occupation in the area. The most direct evidence comes from Clovis points, which are lance-shaped chipped-stone projectile points with a long, narrow channel flake removed from the center; they have been found at North American sites occupied between 11,500 and 10,000 B.P. and have been recovered on Staten Island, notably at Port Mobil. Paleo-Indians and people who lived during the Archaic period (circa 10,000 to 3000 B.P) and the Early and Middle phases of the Woodland period (circa 3000 to 1000 B.P) were hunters and gatherers.

Artifacts made and used by these hunting and gathering people have been found at sites throughout the metropolitan area and were crafted almost entirely between 3300 and 3000 B.P from the Late Archaic period to the Early Woodland period. Thousands of stylistically distinct objects have also been found in the city, including pottery, which was first introduced into the Northeast during Early Woodland times. Most of these objects have been found in large sites repeatedly reoccupied by different peoples at different times, among them the Ryder's Pond site near Sheepshead Bay in Canarsie, the Bay Terrace site on Little Neck Bay in Queens, and the Ward's Point National Historic Landmark on Staten Island. Others have been discovered in small sites briefly occupied and used for special purposes, such as the rock shelters in Inwood Park at the northern tip of Manhattan Island and the many garbage heaps of shells, called shell middens, that formerly lined the local waterways.

Studies suggest that Paleo-Indians and succeeding hunting and gathering peoples in the metropolitan area belonged to small, mobile bands that divided into flexibly organized groups consisting of family and friends; these

Jacob A. Riis, Mountain Eagle and His Family of Iroquois Indians *(1895)*

groups traveled on foot or in watercraft and used tools, weapons, and ornaments crafted from stone, bone, shell, horn, and wood. Hunters and warriors used spears and darts tipped with antler projectile points or chipped stone that often came from local cobbles and rock outcrops; discoveries of projectile points made from cherts, flints, and other stones quarried in Pennsylvania, New Jersey, Connecticut, and upstate New York suggest contact with people from those areas. At specific times of the year members of these groups traveled to particular places to quarry stones; gather wild plants, shellfish, and eggs; and catch fish using spears, nets, or weirs. Gathering together in villages or camping separately, they lived in dome-shaped, sapling-framed houses covered with bark or grass mats and stored their goods in bark or skin containers, in pits, in wooden-splint or woven-grass baskets, and (during Woodland times) in fired clay pots and jars.

Living in Ice Age times, Paleo-Indians hunted such animals as caribou and elk roaming dense spruce and pine forests similar to those now found in northern Canada and Siberia. Remains of plants and animals adapted to more temperate environments have been found in deposits postdating Paleo-Indian times. The presence of deer bones, oyster and clam shells, and pollen from deciduous trees indicates that present-day climatic conditions arose in the region about 8000 B.P. and continued to change over the following years, with changes in air temperature and humidity as well as water temperature, salinity, and sea level.

Variations in the types and styles of artifacts and the frequency with which they are found may reflect social responses to environmental changes. Archaeological evidence indicates that direct and indirect contact with people from more interior portions of the continent influenced the life of Indians in the metropolitan area during Woodland times. Sites have yielded Meadowood and Adena projectile points from the Early Woodland period of a kind most commonly found farther north and west and dated to between 3000 and 2000 B.P. Several of these sites contain the oldest pottery yet found in the Northeast. Middle Woodland sites dating from 2000 to 1000 B.P. have provided evidence of increasing contact with groups in other regions. One group was people from upstate New York of the Kipps Island phase, whose presence within the present city limits became traceable through discoveries at Ward's Point of tools made from jasper stones quarried in Pennsylvania, olivella shells from the southern Atlantic coast, mica from the Carolina highlands, copper from the Great Lakes, and a platform pipe similar to others usually found in the Ohio Valley. Many archaeologists believe that the arrival of Indians later known as Delawares is confirmed by discoveries at several sites (including Ward's Point) of pottery belonging to the Abbott Farm series, as well as stone projectile points in the Fox Creek style made of argillite quarried from the Delaware Valley.

2. Late Woodland Period

Evidence of sweeping changes in social organization has been found in deposits dating to the earliest phases of the Late Woodland period, between 1200 and 800 B.P., at Ward's Point and Bowman's Brook on Staten Island, Ryder's Pond in Brooklyn, and Clason's Point in the Bronx. Thick midden layers of occupational debris and dense clusters of hearths and storage or refuse pits at these sites indicate that Late Woodland people spent much of their time in towns of unprecedented size and density. New styles of pottery and small, triangular, chipped-stone projectile points used with newly introduced bows and arrows have been found in these towns and smaller campsites like those discovered at the Cold Spring Harbor site in northern Manhattan, the Van Cortlandt site in the Bronx, and the Aqueduct site in Queens.

Other evidence suggests that during these times Indians in the area also began to live in bark- or grass-covered longhouses and to grow or consume cultivated plants, including corn, beans, squash, and tobacco. This was the culture encountered by the Florentine navigator Giovanni da Verrazano when he made the first recorded landfall by a European in New York Harbor in 1524. Neither he nor Henry Hudson, who conducted the next documented voyage to the area in 1609, noted the names or identities of the people they met. They were eventually called Delawares, a name given to all linguistically and culturally related Indians living along the Atlantic seaboard between the Delaware and Hudson valleys at the time of initial contact with Europeans; the name was originally applied to those living along the Delaware River.

3. Munsees

According to Delaware traditionalists currently living in such places as Oklahoma, Wisconsin, and Ontario, the Indians of the metropolitan area called themselves *Lenape* (people) and their homeland *Lenapehoking* (land of the people). It is widely believed that those living in the northernmost reaches of Lenapehoking spoke variants of a Delaware dialect known as Munsee (stony country). Colonial records documenting relations with Indians indicate that kinship, political ties, and economic ties linked Munsee speakers into a widespread social network that extended across the lower Hudson and upper Delaware valleys from southeastern New York to northeastern Pennsylvania.

Early European records are unclear about the structure of Munsee society; ethnographic evidence provided later by Delawares indicates that all Munsees belonged to one of several maternally linked clans consisting of related women, their children, and husbands from other families living together in sapling-framed longhouses. They lived near reliable sources of water, well-drained soils, and places favorable for hunting, fishing, and foraging. In the spring they felled trees, burned undergrowth, and planted crops between tree stumps. They also fished for shad, eel, and herring; gathered greens, nuts, roots, and berries; and collected bird eggs. During communal hunts they burned sections of forest to drive game off cliffs or into pens or rivers. In the summer they dispersed to small camps, traded, traveled, made war, undertook vision quests, and held thanksgiving celebrations. They gathered together again during the fall to harvest crops, gather nuts, catch fish, collect shellfish, and hunt deer and migrating waterfowl. During the winter they made and repaired tools and weapons, told stories, and held religious festivals.

Munsee society lacked institutionalized inequalities. The people followed both men and women of proven ability who governed by the power of persuasion. Unfettered by coercive governments or authoritarian leaders, Munsees could move to any community willing to accept them. Women usually owned their homes and fields and moved infrequently; men moved more often because of customs that required a husband to move into his wife's household. Men retained membership in their original clans throughout their lives, but many shifted their political loyalties when they moved. Such shifts were essential for those who took on leadership responsibilities in new communities. One figure who did was Waumetompack, known in the 1650s as a Rockaway chief in Queens County but later prominent among Matinecocks living farther east along the northern shore of Long Island.

4. Colonial Times

There were a number of Munsee communities in the area during the seventeenth century. In addition to Rockaway (sandy place) and Matinecock (at the lookout point), there was Maspeth (bad water place) and Jamaica (beaver place) in Queens, as well as five communities in Brooklyn: Marechkawick (sandy place) near Borough Hall, Nayack (point of land), Wichquawanck (sandy bank) at Fort Hamilton, Techkonis (translation unknown) in Gravesend, and Canarsie (grassy place), a village in the marshy Flatlands. Settlers often referred to Indians from what are now the Bronx and Westchester County as Wiechquaesgecks (birch bark or swampy country), the Indian name for what became Dobbs Ferry, New York. Indian communities formed in the Bronx along Long Island Sound at Hunt's Point, Soundview, Throgs Neck, and Pelham Bay; along the Harlem River in Hell Gate,

Mosholu, and Marble Hill; and at various places in Manhattan, including Cold Spring Harbor. According to two accounts from the early seventeenth century, there was a group in the eastern Bronx called Siwanoys (southerners). Other documents indicate that the Rechgawawancks (sandy hillside), who were believed to have lived in the western Bronx, were more probably the Haverstraws, another Munsee group on the western bank of the Hudson River living in a town bearing their name in Rockland County. Another Munsee village, Aquehonga (sandy hillside), sat on bluffs overlooking Raritan Bay near what is now the Ward's Point National Historic Landmark. Colonists on Staten Island noted other Munsee communities on the banks of the Great Kills, the Narrows, the Kill van Kull, and the Arthur Kill.

Manhattan (possibly derived from the Munsee word *menatay,* or island) stood at the center of this world. In 1626 the island was reportedly sold by Indians for 60 guilders' worth of goods to Peter Minuit, the first governor of New Netherland, who established the capital of New Amsterdam at its southern tip. Munsees sold Staten Island to the Dutch in 1630. Both islands soon became important trading centers where visiting Munsees exchanged pelts, food, and cylindrical blue and white shell beads known as wampum for European textiles, glass beads, and implements made of iron, brass, and copper. Many also managed to obtain guns, ammunition, and liquor from colonists who ignored laws prohibiting the sale of such items to Indians. Firearms allowed game to be killed with unprecedented ease and efficiency and also made raids and warfare more dangerous.

5. Conflict with Europeans and Other Indians

Alcohol presented a serious threat to Munsee communities, which were disrupted and demoralized by the violence of drunkards. But the threats posed by guns and alcohol paled in comparison to the devastation caused by deadly epidemics of smallpox, measles, and malaria, which struck Indian communities every five to 10 years throughout the colonial era and may have killed nine out of every 10 Munsees. Weakened by losses from disease, alcohol abuse, and warfare, Munsees found themselves caught between powerful rivals desiring control over their lands. Armed with Dutch guns, such powerful interior nations as the Mohawks and Mahicans denied Munsee hunters access to trapping grounds; they also extorted wampum and other commodities. Desiring their land, Dutch settlers quickly came to regard the impoverished Munsees as unwanted neighbors, and an increasingly violent struggle ensued in which insults, thefts, and assaults gave way to a series of unpunished murders.

War finally broke out in 1640 when Governor Willem Kieft sent a military detachment to Staten Island to investigate the theft of a pig. Instead, the soldiers attacked a Raritan Indian community. This set off what became known among Europeans as Governor Kieft's War, part of a wider struggle sparked by the European invasion of the Northeast and often pitting Indians against each other during the seventeenth century. The first phase of the war ended when Munsee warriors from Long Island and the lower Hudson Valley attacked and defeated the Raritans. A Mahican attack on Wiechquaesgecks and Hackensacks during the winter of 1643–44 set the stage for the war's second and more violent phase. Seizing the opportunity to avenge several settlers' murders, Kieft ordered an attack on the more than 120 Wiechquaesgeck and Hackensack refugees sheltering among the Dutch in camps at Pavonia (in what is now Jersey City) and Corlear's Hook (in lower Manhattan); most of the refugees were killed during a surprise attack on the night of 23 February 1643. Munsee warriors united by hatred of the Dutch soon attacked outlying settlements throughout New Netherland, where they killed or captured scores of colonists, among them the well-known Puritan dissenter Anne Hutchinson and most of her family; they also drove colonists from Staten Island and much of the adjacent mainland. The Dutch retaliated quickly, killing hundreds of Munsees in Westchester County and Long Island in 1644. Despite devastation on both sides, the struggle remained indecisive, and a peace treaty was signed on 30 August 1645.

But the peace proved uneasy, and Munsees resentful of Dutch encroachments on their lands attacked settlements in and around Manhattan in 1655. The renewed hostilities became known as the Peach War, after a Dutch settler who was alleged to have murdered an Indian woman for picking peaches in his orchard, and dragged on for several years. The outbreak of war with Esopus Indians living farther upriver in 1658 further weakened the Dutch colony, which was denied adequate support by the Netherlands and fell easily to an English squadron in 1664 after years of almost continual Indian warfare. Eager to avoid these mistakes, the English quickly signed treaties of friendship with Indian leaders.

6. Dissolution of the Munsees

Although rumors of Indian conspiracies circulated throughout the region for the next 100 years, Munsees never again took up arms against settlers in the metropolitan area. English leaders compelled the Munsees to sell all their remaining lands within what are now the city limits; by 1701 they had put their marks to 39 deeds to lands there. Staten Island was resold in 1657 by Indians who had driven settlers away during Governor Kieft's War and again in 1670 by English colonists eager to secure clear and uncontested title to the land. All lands in Brooklyn were alienated from Indians through 22 deeds signed between 1636 and 1684; among the last areas of the county to be handed over was Canarsie.

Indians unwilling to leave their lands then lived as tenants on colonial farmsteads or moved to remote or unwanted swamplands. The Munsees grew poorer and subsisted as best they could. Most dressed in English clothes and spoke a trade jargon of mixed English, Dutch, and Delaware words when speaking to colonists; many also sought to master English. Men found work as laborers, farmhands, and sailors; women worked as servants and sold homemade straw brooms, splint baskets, and grass mats. Elderly Munsee herbalists and healers found many patients among both Indians and Europeans.

Most Munsees gradually moved away, often settling in mountainous enclaves in the Hudson Highlands of northern New Jersey and southern New York State. Others moved to small tracts of land set aside as reservations in Nassau County at Cow Neck, Matinecock Neck, and Fort Neck. Many of these people ultimately joined other Munsees at the large Minisink towns along the upper Delaware Valley; all were finally forced westward into exile at the end of the Seven Years' War in 1762. Some Munsees refused to abandon their old homes, among them a number of Matinecock families who continued to live in small communities scattered along the northern shore of Queens and Nassau counties. Other Indians lived quietly in unwanted backlots in Washington Heights and Canarsie and on Staten Island. Increasingly unable to find spouses among the few remaining Indians in the region, most married non-Indians. Children born into these households rarely learned Indian language or customs. The Munsee language finally died out in the city as the last elders fluent in it died during the early nineteenth century.

7. Nineteenth to Twenty-first Centuries

Indians from elsewhere began moving to New York City in search of work during the nineteenth century. Men found work as longshoremen, factory workers, and laborers; women as artisans, seamstresses, washerwomen, and servants. A number took an active interest in their Indian heritage. A Chibcha artist from Colombia named Emilio Cabral Diaz worked with such local non-Indian historic preservationists as Reginald Pelham Bolton and William L. Calver to establish an "Indian life reservation" in Inwood Park during the 1920s; it was the site of powwows and encampments until the 1950s. Many of those in attendance were Mohawks from reservations in upstate New York and Canada uniquely skilled in high steel work and readily able to find work in bridge and skyscraper construction. They formed a small community at Gowanus in Brooklyn during the 1920s; most left by the 1960s.

The federal census of 2000 counted 41,289 Indian people in New York City (about 0.3 percent of the total population). Most Indians descended from communities in the metropolitan area call themselves Delawares or Lenapes, and those from Queens are usually known as Matinecocks. An important center of Indian life is the American Indian Community House, founded in 1969, at 11 Broadway, which administers cultural programs and service projects.

Alanson B. Skinner, *The Indians of Manhattan Island and Vicinity* (New York: American Museum of Natural History, 1932); Reginald Pelham Bolton, *Indian Life of Long Ago in the City of New York* (New York: Joseph Graham, 1934); Allen W. Trelease, *Indian Affairs in Colonial New York: The Seventeenth Century* (Ithaca, N.Y.: Cornell University Press, 1960); Robert S. Grumet, *Native American Place Names in New York City* (New York: Museum of the City of New York, 1981); Herbert C. Kraft, *The Lenape: Archaeology, History, and Ethnography* (Newark: New Jersey Historical Society, 1986)

Robert S. Grumet

American Institute of Architects [AIA]. Organization formed on 23 February 1857 in New York City by 13 architects, including Richard Upjohn, Richard M. Upjohn, Jacob Wrey Mould, Richard M. Hunt, and Leopold Eidlitz. These founders invited 12 other architects to become members, of whom at least two, Thomas U. Walter and Alexander Jackson Davis, had belonged to a similar organization in 1836 that quickly disbanded because its membership was small and widely dispersed. The institute stated in its constitution (signed 18 May 1857) that its purpose was "to promote the scientific and practical perfection of its members and to elevate the standing of the profession." It soon focused its attention on the concerns of an emerging profession, including fee schedules, training for students and young practitioners, professional ethics, and fair standards for architecture competitions. The institute inaugurated a system of local chapters when it formed one in New York City in 1867. It admitted its first female member, Louise Bethune, in 1888, merged with the Western Association of Architects in 1889, and in 1898 moved its headquarters from New York City to the historic Octagon House in Washington. In the early twenty-first century the local chapter in the city worked through an extensive structure of volunteer committees; it offered continuing education and formulated positions on public building and planning issues. The *AIA Guide to New York City* (1967; 4th edn 2000) by Eliot Willensky and Norval White is the standard architectural guide to the city.

Rosalie Genevro

American Institute of Physics [AIP]. Organization formed with a grant from the Chemical Foundation in 1931 to foster communication among physicists dispersed through different fields and facing rising costs of publication. It was proposed at a joint committee of physicists at Columbia University and set up quarters in offices owned by the Chemical Foundation; it soon moved into its own office on East 57th Street and then to larger quarters at 335 East 45th Street after World War II. In the following years the institute became one of the largest and most important physical science organizations in the country, gaining tens of thousands of members in dozens of chapters nationwide. It opened a publishing facility in suburban Woodbury, Long Island, and in the early twenty-first century produced the publications of more than 25 physics and engineering societies. Its office in Manhattan houses the Niels Bohr Library.

Chad Ludington

American International Group [AIG]. Firm of insurers. It was founded in 1919 by Cornelius Vander Starr as C. V. Starr and Company of Shanghai, which arranged insurance for the China trade of American businesses and was the first American company to sell insurance products to Chinese buyers in Shanghai. Following World War II the company greatly expanded its operations, growing its business in Asia and branching out into the Caribbean, the Middle East, and Africa. In 1962, Starr turned over the company's American operations to Maurice R. "Hank" Greenberg, who built up the company's highly profitable corporate insurance coverage. Throughout the 1960s the firm acquired numerous insurance companies in the United States, including National Union Fire (1968), New Hampshire Insurance Company (1969), and American Home (1969), and established its headquarters on Pine Street in Manhattan. In 1968 Greenberg succeeded Starr as chief executive, and the company quickly became the largest underwriter of commercial and industrial insurance in the United States. The company went public in 1969 and continued to expand both its domestic and overseas operations under Greenberg, eventually becoming the 18th largest company in the world with revenues in excess of $100 billion. In 2008, due to AIG's large exposure to rapidly deteriorating mortgage-backed securities on which it had sold insurance protection, Standard & Poor's downgraded the company's credit rating to below AA levels, which restricted AIG's access to the credit it required to do business. The company was saved from bankruptcy on 17 September 2008, by the provision of $85 billion (later expanded to nearly $183 billion) in emergency credit from the Federal Reserve Bank of New York, as well as the Federal Reserve's assumption of a 79.9 percent equity stake in the company. On 22 September, AIG's stock was removed from the Dow Jones Industrial Average. As of 2010, the company's headquarters remained at 70 Pine Street in Manhattan.

Ronald Kent Shelp, *Fallen Giant: The Amazing Story of Hank Greenberg and the History of AIG* (Hoboken, N.J.: Wiley, 2006)

Andrew A. Kryzak, Robert J. Gibbons

American Irish Historical Society. Organization formed in Boston in 1897 and later based in New York City. In 1940 it moved its offices to 991 Fifth Avenue. The society focuses on Irish contributions to the history of the United States, and it holds lectures, concerts, and art exhibits. It also has a literary journal and public library.

The American Irish Historical Society, 1897–1972: Seventy-fifth Anniversary (New York: American Irish Historical Society, 1972)

William D. Griffin

American Jewish Committee. Jewish defense agency formed in New York City in 1906 in response to pogroms in Russia. It initially drew much of its membership from among wealthy Jews of German descent and had an executive committee of 15. Because the organization remained exclusive it was threatened with marginalization as Jews from eastern Europe moved to the city in large numbers. It responded by forming the New York Kehillah in 1908, which became its local chapter. Under its second president, Louis Marshall, the committee fought the Ku Klux Klan and the restrictive Immigration Act of 1924. Its journal, *Commentary,* began as a publication of a group of Jewish thinkers and writers on political and cultural subjects. Not originally a Zionist organization, the committee became a strong defender of Israel after 1948. It has headquarters in New York City.

Naomi Cohen, *Not Free to Desist: The American Jewish Committee, 1906–1966* (Philadelphia: Jewish Publication Society of America, 1972); Henry L. Feingold, *A Jewish Survival Enigma: The Strange Case of the American Jewish Committee* (New York: American Jewish Committee, 1981); Marrianne R. Sanua, *Let Us Prove Strong: The American Jewish Committee, 1945–2006* (Waltham, Mass.: Brandeis University Press, 2007)

Henry Feingold

American Jewish Congress. Organization inspired by the Congress movement in New York City and Philadelphia, which sought to make Jewish organizations democratic, and formed to give American Jews a voice at the peace conference in Versailles. It was formally established as a national organization after communal elections were held in June 1917.

After the peace conference it made its headquarters in New York City until 1922, when it adjourned. In the following years the Congress was reorganized to become the most politically activist Jewish secular organization in the United States. Under Stephen S. Wise it enjoyed success through its Commission on Law and Social Action and offered staunch support to the Zionist movement. Unlike other Jewish defense agencies it took part directly in local and national politics, relying on coalitions with other organizations representing minority groups to accomplish its goals. It focused its efforts on political reform and often used the courts to implement its program of social justice, which pursued improvements in public housing, education, and civil rights. With the advent of Nazism it sought to focus public attention on the issue of rescue by sponsoring protest rallies and boycotts; a rally at Madison Square Garden inspired dozens of others in cities nationwide. After 1945 the American Jewish Congress shifted its efforts to civil rights, public housing, women's rights, and the Labour Party in Israel. During the 1960s, many of the organization's civil rights efforts paralleled the American civil rights movement while membership during the 1980s and 1990s slowly declined. The establishment of the Commission of Women's Equality in 1984 was heavily influenced by the Congress's practice as one of the first Jewish organizations to devote considerable time and resources specifically to women's issues by both male and female members of the organization. Resurgence during the late 1990s and early 2000s was largely due to growing support for Israel and the challenging of contemporary anti-Semitism abroad.

Morris Frommer, "The American Jewish Congress: A History, 1914–1950" (PhD diss., Ohio State University, 1978)

Henry Feingold

American Jewish Joint Distribution Committee. Organization formed as the Joint Distribution Committee on 27 November 1914 in New York City to help displaced eastern European Jews. It soon merged with the American Jewish Relief Committee, an organization of German Jews, and the Central Relief Committee, an organization of Orthodox Jews. It took its current name in 1915 after merging with the People's Relief Committee, which represented workers. After the war the committee took part in reconstruction and formed loan cooperatives. During the 1930s it aided European Jews; its office in Paris offered vocational training and provided relief for Jews fleeing the Nazis, and the organization played a vital role in rescuing 80,000 Jews from occupied Europe, guiding them mainly through Spain and Vichy France. Between 1945 and 1952 the committee spent more than $350 million to assist 250,000 displaced persons, and from 1949 it cooperated with the Israeli government to form Malben, an organization that helps ill, handicapped, and elderly immigrants. It also maintained medical, educational, and vocational programs in North Africa, Iran, France, eastern Europe, and the former Soviet Union. One of the most effective organizations of its kind, the American Jewish Joint Distribution Committee had helped millions of Jews worldwide by the early twenty-first century. In 2004 the committee spent nearly $200 million on its services.

Oscar Handlin, *A Continuing Task: The American Jewish Joint Distribution Committee, 1914–1964* (New York: Random House, 1964); Yehuda Bauer, *My Brother's Keeper: A History of the American Jewish Joint Distribution Committee, 1929–1939* (Philadelphia: Jewish Publication Society of America, 1974)

Michael N. Dobkowski

American Labor Party. Political party formed in New York City in 1936 by leaders of various garment trade unions. It endorsed Democratic and Republican candidates in local, state, and national elections and occasionally sponsored independent candidates; many of its votes came from adherents of the Socialist Party who wished to support Franklin D. Roosevelt and other candidates committed to the New Deal but were reluctant to vote for a "bourgeois" party like the Democrats. Despite the anticommunist leanings of its founders, David Dubinsky and Alex Rose, the American Labor Party quickly came under the influence of communists; its most prominent spokesman was the congressman from East Harlem, Vito Marcantonio, a sympathizer with the communists on many issues. In the late 1930s the Labor Party played an important role in the politics of New York City by helping to provide more than one-fifth of the votes for the reelection of Mayor Fiorello H. La Guardia in 1937; it also supported Mike Quill, president of the Transport Workers Union, who maintained close ties to the Communist Party and was elected to the City Council as a candidate of the American Labor Party in 1937, 1943, and 1945. When communists gained control of the party early in World War II, Rose and others left it to form the Liberal Party. The Labor Party received an average of 13 percent of the vote in elections in the city between 1938 and 1949 and was strongest in Jewish, black, and Puerto Rican neighborhoods. As the surrogate in New York State for the Progressive Party in 1948 it helped Leo Isacson to win a special election for a seat in Congress as a representative from the southern Bronx, and in November it gave the presidential candidate Henry Wallace more than half the votes that he received nationwide (Isacson failed to win reelection to a regular term in the same election). Marcantonio lost his seat in 1950. Attacked as a communist front, the American Labor Party lost support during the cold war and was dissolved in 1956.

Kenneth Waltzer, "The Party and the Polling Place: American Communism and the American Labor Party in the 1930s," *Radical History Review* 23 (autumn 1980): 104–29; Max Gordon, "A Response," *Radical History Review* 23 (Autumn 1980): 130–35; Gerald Meyer, *Vito Marcantonio, Radical Politician, 1902–1954* (Albany: State University of New York Press, 1989); Gerald Meyer, *The American Labor Party, 1936–1954* (New York: Garland, forthcoming)

Maurice Isserman

American Lung Association. Organization formed in New York City in 1907 as the National Tuberculosis Association to coordinate the activities of various state affiliates, including the New York Lung Association.

American Museum of Natural History. One of the largest and most important museums in the world, conceived by the scientist Albert Bickmore in the early 1860s and established in 1868. It opened in 1869 at the New York Arsenal, where several specimen collections were put on display the following year. The many business leaders and politicians on the museum's board of trustees helped secure funds from the city and private donations. In 1874 President Ulysses S. Grant took part in the groundbreaking for a new building on Central Park West between 77th and 81st streets. The trustees soon purchased many collections, but the museum lacked a systematic process for acquiring specimens and adequate means for displaying them. Situated well north of the center of the city and closed on Sundays during the 1870s, the museum attracted few visitors and eventually fell into debt.

Important changes were made by Morris K. Jesup, a wealthy railroad securities broker who became the third president of the museum in 1881. He employed a taxidermist to create displays that were attractive and comprehensible and supported Bickmore's plan to inaugurate lectures on nature for schoolteachers. This program and a new policy that kept the museum open on Sundays increased the popularity and visibility of the museum. Jesup had a strong interest in evolution and scientific research. He appointed the zoologist Joel A. Allen as the curator of mammalogy and ornithology, asked Henry Fairfield Osborn to develop a new program in vertebrate paleontology (1891), and invited Franz Boas to join the department of anthropology (1896). The primary objective of the museum, as defined by Jesup, was to provide an uplifting

American Museum of Natural History, 1937

place where the public could both learn about nature and find respite from the bustling city.

As the curator of vertebrate paleontology Osborn furthered Jesup's interests by promoting expeditions and publications that illuminated evolutionary biology. A wealthy aristocrat, he formed close ties to the trustees and rose quickly through the ranks of the museum's administration, becoming president in 1908. During a tenure that lasted 25 years he sponsored the search for human ancestors in Mongolia, led by Roy Chapman Andrews, and expeditions to Africa, led by Carl Akeley. These dramatic undertakings captured public attention and led to the establishment of new scientific departments and large exhibit halls. Osborn drew considerable philanthropic support for these and other expeditions and tripled contributions from the city, efforts that allowed the museum to build a new wing in the 1930s. Like Jesup he channeled contributions into disciplines that documented evolution, such as vertebrate paleontology, anthropology, mammalogy, and ornithology. New exhibits such as the Hall of the Age of Man and the Akeley African Hall revealed his interest in protecting nature from encroaching urbanization and his attachment to maintaining the power and prestige of peoples of northwestern European ancestry. A program in astronomy, promoted by Osborn in the 1920s, was given greater attention by the museum in the 1930s with the construction of the Hayden Planetarium (1935).

In the 1940s and 1950s traditional taxonomic studies continued, while at the same time scientists such as Ernst Mayr and George Gaylord Simpson offered important new interpretations of evolution and Margaret Mead, head of anthropology at the museum, emphasized social and cultural anthropology. G. K. Noble and other scientists conducted research on animal behavior at the department of experimental biology, and Albert E. Parr, appointed director of the museum in 1942, replaced many of the displays on evolution with ones that reflected new findings in ecology and physical geography. The importance given to expeditions continued and in the 1950s led to the opening of several new field stations for biological research. In the 1960s civil rights groups attacked the few remaining displays that reflected Osborn's racist beliefs; the Hall of the Age of Man was replaced in 1961 by a Hall of the Biology of Man. Efforts were begun in the 1980s to revamp mammal and dinosaur displays in the light of new knowledge and interpretations. The Rose Center for Earth and Space was opened in 2000, containing the new Hayden Planetarium. In 2007 the Bernard and Anne Spitzer Hall of Human Origins replaced the Hall of the Biology of Man and depicted the process of human evolution. In 1999 the *New York Times* helped choose the items and design for a time capsule that was on display briefly and is now permanently stored in the building. In 2008 the museum had about four million visitors annually, a staff of about 1300, and an operating budget of over $120 million.

Geoffrey T. Hellman, *Bankers, Bones, and Beetles: The First Century of the American Museum of Natural History* (Garden City, N.Y.: Natural History Press, 1969); Ronald Rainger, *An Agenda for Antiquity: Henry Fairfield Osborn and Vertebrate Paleontology at the American Museum of Natural History, 1890–1935* (Tuscaloosa: University of Alabama Press, 1991)

Ronald Rainger

American Numismatic Society. Association formed in 1858 by collectors of coins, medals, and similar items. In 1907 the society settled at its first permanent home at Audubon Terrace, a beaux-arts complex in Washington Heights in Manhattan. The society moved to 96 Fulton Street in 2004, and again to One Hudson Square at Varick and Canal streets in 2008. In the early twenty-first century it maintains one of the world's largest and most valuable collections, composed of 800,000 coins, bills, medals, and other artifacts; its library contains 100,000 items. With 2000 members, it offers training programs and fellowships and publishes monographs and journals. The society's collection includes one of the oldest coins in the world, issued in 650 B.C. by a Lydian king, as well as a rare 1861 $1000 bill of Confederate money.

Howard L. Adelson, *The American Numismatic Society, 1858–1958* (New York: American Numismatic Society, 1958)

Kate Lauber

American Peace Society. Its forerunner was the New York Peace Society, formed in 1815 by the devout Presbyterian layperson David Low Dodge (1777–1852) and dedicated to the condemnation of all warfare, defensive as well as offensive, based on biblical principles. This group joined with others of similar beliefs in May 1828 to form the American Peace Society. The society favored negotiation, arbitration,

Medal commemorating the tercenary of the purchase of Manhattan Island, struck for the American Numismatic Society (designed by Hermon A. MacNeil)

and a "Congress of Christian Nations" to resolve international conflicts. After a period of stagnation in the years following the Civil War the society reemerged during the Progressive movement. In the early twenty-first century its national offices were in Washington, D.C.

Edson Leone Whitney, *The American Peace Society: A Centennial History* (Washington, D.C.: American Peace Society, 1928)

Peter J. Wosh

American Research Bureau. Original name of Arbitron Inc.

American Revolution. New York City in the eighteenth century embodied many of the complexities of the Revolution and experienced all of its turmoil. Politically, it was an important base for the Sons of Liberty, but it was also the capital of Loyalist America, a position solidified by the British conquest of the city in 1776. Militarily, the city was considered the greatest strategic prize on the continent by both sides. By controlling the Hudson River, and the city at its mouth, the British hoped to split New England from the rest of the colonies and crush the rebellion. George Washington spent the next seven years trying to retake the city, and failing that, to turn the occupation into a liability for the British. With the end of the war in 1783 the city had been heavily damaged.

1. Early Developments, 1764–74

New York City in the late colonial period was second in importance in British America only to Philadelphia. By the mid-eighteenth century it was wealthier and more populous than Boston, and at independence it had about 25,000 inhabitants, who were crowded into the area below what is now City Hall. Well to the north lay the village of Harlem; most of Staten Island and the counties of Queens, Kings, and Westchester (which began at the Harlem River) were farmland. The racial, ethnic, religious, and economic divisions in the city helped to build a tradition of turbulent politics. Some New Yorkers gained wealth in transatlantic trade and wartime supply contracts: the Loyalist Oliver De Lancey (1718–85) asserted after the Revolution that his confiscated estate had been worth £115,000. These traders had luxuries and maintained connections with people of high social rank in England; they adapted elements of English culture to their colonial environment. Their culture was denounced in New York's first literary magazine, the *Independent Reflector,* which folded under political pressure in 1753 only a year after it started. Written by William Livingston, William Smith, Jr., and John Morrin Scott and modeled after the *Independent Whig* of London, the magazine took aim at petty royal functionaries and showy affluence; it was an influential early expression of the ideals and rhetoric that culminated in the Revolution. Artisans and independent craftspeople, another important group, made products that competed with merchants' imports, and to protect their interests they banded together, sometimes instigating riots.

The city prospered when the British made it their headquarters during the Seven Years' War (1756–63) but experienced a depression when the war ended. Spending on relief for the poor tripled, and merchants' profits were halved. The growing poverty was denounced in the press, especially in the *New-York Journal,* a militant newspaper operated by John Holt. Merchants were incensed by the Sugar Act of 1764, which imposed British control on the American sugar market, and the provincial assembly, in which many had seats, inveighed against it. The Stamp Act of 1765, which mandated the use of stamps on all legal and commercial documents, led the colonies to create the Stamp Act Congress, which met in the city. About this time a group of popular leaders emerged who came to be known as the Sons of Liberty. They included both artisans like Holt and Marinus Willett and small merchants like Isaac Sears and Alexander McDougall. They had a network throughout the colonies. The Sons of Liberty were committed to direct action and in late October 1765 led their first uprising, in which they destroyed carriages and sleighs belonging to Lieutenant Governor Cadwallader Colden, the enforcer of the Stamp Act, and an elegant house rented by Major Thomas James, who had trained the guns of Fort George on the city. One of their last public riots was the sacking the following May of a new theater that was considered an irresponsible luxury in a time of public distress.

Tensions continued to rise over issues of commerce and military supply. The Quartering Act required the colonial assemblies to appropriate supplies for British troops garrisoned in America. When the assembly in New York refused to grant supplies for redcoats stationed in the city, Parliament passed the New York Restraining Act of 1767. This forbade the city to act at all until it appropriated the supplies. By the time news of the act arrived, the assembly had in fact complied, but John Dickinson's influential *Letter from a Pennsylvania Farmer* cited the Restraining Act as a major colonial grievance. During the same year that the act was passed, many merchants joined in the nonimportation movement against the Townshend taxes, but their alliances shifted as they quarreled among themselves and with other revolutionaries. The elections of 1768 and 1769 led to a division in the assembly between the Livingstons, who were landholders, and the De Lanceys, who were merchants who gained the support of the Sons of Liberty by berating the Livingstons for supplying British troops. The presence of such troops in Manhattan led to increased tension. They competed with New Yorkers for work, which they were permitted to seek while off duty; and they made relations worse by tearing down successive liberty poles erected by colonists in the Fields (later City Hall Park). The Sons of Liberty were alarmed by the large garrison at the upper barracks (near the Fields) and lower barracks (near the Battery), and they ended their alliance with the De Lanceys when the assembly controlled by the De Lanceys voted that surrounding British troops should receive supplies. The De Lanceys became Loyalists, and under their control from 1769 to 1775 the assembly ceased to be militant. In his broadside "To the Betrayed Inhabitants of the City and Colony of New-York," McDougall in 1769 lambasted the assembly for voting to supply the British and was imprisoned. In the same year the merchants of New York City joined those of Philadelphia and Boston in a boycott of British commerce to protest the Townshend taxes. In January 1770 tensions between colonists and British troops led to the Battle of Golden Hill and the Nassau Street Riot; although no lives were lost, the issues being fought over were the same as those that led to the killing of five civilians in the Boston Massacre two months later. Merchants in the city repealed their boycott of British commerce later that year after Parliament rescinded all the Townshend taxes except the one on tea. Artisans protested the

By His EXCELLENCY

GEORGE WASHINTON, Eſquire,

General, and Commander in Chief of the Army of the United States of North-America.

WHEREAS a Bombardment and Attack upon the City of New-York, by our cruel, and inveterate Enemy, may be hourly expected: And as there are great Numbers of Women, Children, and infirm Perſons, yet remaining in the City, whoſe Continuance will rather be prejudicial than advantageous to the Army, and their Perſons expoſed to great Danger and Hazard: I Do therefore recommend it to all ſuch Perſons, as they value their own Safety and Preſervation, to remove with all Expedition, out of the ſaid Town, at this critical Period,—truſting, that with the Bleſſing of Heaven, upon the American Arms, they may ſoon return to it in perfect Security. And I do enjoin and require, all the Officers and Soldiers in the Army, under my Command, to forward and aſſiſt ſuch Perſons in their Compliance with this Recommendation.

Given under my Hand, at Head-Quarters, New-York, Auguſt 17, 1776.

GEORGE WASHINGTON.

NEW-YORK:—Printed by John Holt, in Water-Street.

George Washington's notice to the citizens of New York City, August 1776

rescission because they had benefited from the boycott and been excluded from the decision to end it, and when rumor arose about a new crisis over the tax on tea, they formed their own Committee of Mechanics and purchased a place to hold meetings. The first tea ship headed for the city during this time was turned back at Sandy Hook, New Jersey. When tea was found aboard the *London* in April 1774, revolutionaries began costuming themselves as "Mohawks," as the participants in the Boston Tea Party had done; during their preparations a crowd boarded the ship, dumped the tea, and burned the empty chests at the Fields.

2. Tensions Leading to War, 1774–76

A month after the *London* was stormed, the city elected 51 men to its first Revolutionary committee, in which moderates outnumbered radicals. At the meeting that chose the committee, the young aristocrat Gouverneur Morris likened members of the city's "mob" to "poor reptiles" who were casting off "their winter's slough" and would bite "ere noon."

Eleven radical members resigned from the committee in July 1774 to protest its timid policies. The second Revolutionary committee comprised 60 members elected in November to enforce the Continental Association; this was the trade boycott ratified by the Continental Congress in response to measures taken by the British in retaliation for the Boston Tea Party. It was replaced by a Committee of One Hundred, elected in April 1775 after the battles at Lexington and Concord. The province of New York had already chosen the first of its Revolutionary congresses, which elected delegates to the Second Continental Congress. At the outset of the war full power was gradually assumed by the congress, which met in the city, and by local committees such as the Committee of One Hundred. Governor William Tryon called an assembly election at the end of 1775 to undercut these Revolutionary bodies, but the new assembly never met; he escaped to a British ship in the harbor, and the mayor and aldermen found themselves powerless. Loyalists nevertheless remained strong in the city, and the Sons of Liberty met fierce resistance from merchants engaged in transatlantic trade: 57 members of the Chamber of Commerce became Loyalists, 21 remained neutral, and only 26 were revolutionaries. The De Lanceys strongly opposed the Revolution, as did the printer James Rivington and the Anglican ministers Samuel Seabury and Myles Cooper.

In the rural counties around the city the Revolution found virtually no support: the sparsely populated counties of Queens, Kings, and Richmond (Staten Island) were prosperous and shunned the political turmoil of the city, even after resistance had turned to revolution. In January 1776 Queens was captured, its firearms seized, and its leaders arrested by General Charles Lee, one of Washington's most zealous officers. He inspired no support there, and when British troops invaded during the following August, 1300 people signed a congratulatory address, and 800 joined the first militia under the renewed royal government.

After the American siege of Boston forced British commander in chief General William Howe to evacuate in March, Washington prepared for a British invasion of New York by moving his troops to the city and its environs, occupying lower Manhattan, Brooklyn Heights, and Bay Ridge. By this time, 80 percent of the prewar population had fled, leaving 5000 inhabitants, a sign that the British had overestimated the depth of loyalism, which prevailed among a once-powerful minority. *Common Sense* by Thomas Paine had become popular in the city for its condemnation of monarchy and its call for simple republican institutions. In May the Committee of Mechanics, the largest radical faction that remained, called for the popular acceptance of whichever new constitution the province might adopt to become an independent state. Although some in the city urged the abolition of the old order, many others, especially the mercantile elite, had to be forced to accept independence and wanted no political experiments. On 2 July 1776, the day Congress approved the Declaration of Independence, General Howe landed his expeditionary force—then the largest in British history—on Staten Island. Meeting no resistance, he established a staging area for an invasion of Long Island, Manhattan, and Westchester County. A week later, New Yorkers toppled the statue of George III that had stood at Bowling Green.

General Howe's brother, Admiral Richard Howe, arrived from England on 12 July. He had convinced the Crown to empower the two brothers not only as commanders in chief, but as peace commissioners authorized to grant pardons to the American rebels if they renounced independence. The Howe brothers' feelings of friendship for the Americans—stemming from the Massachusetts government's funding of a marble monument to their slain brother George—apparently made them ambivalent in battle and had important repercussions during the impending military campaign. On 22 August they invaded western Long Island, crossing below the Narrows and establishing camps of British and Hessian soldiers in an arc from Gravesend Bay to Jamaica Bay. Most of Washington's troops on Long Island were dug in on Brooklyn Heights to protect that vital ground dominating lower Manhattan. Others were stationed along Gowanus Heights, an east–west ridge that provided an outer line of defense where they planned to ambush the British at four passes, including two still visible today in Green-Wood Cemetery and Prospect Park. The Jamaica Pass, the farthest to the east, was defended only lightly, and the British used it to turn the American flank during the Battle of Long Island on 27 August, the largest battle of the war and the first for the United States as an independent nation. Washington's forces were routed, with some 200 Americans killed and 800 captured. With the Americans nearly trapped on Brooklyn Heights, General Howe declined to storm their lines, and Washington organized a nighttime withdrawal across the East River (29–30 August). Instead of pursuing the Americans, the British convened a fruitless peace conference on Staten Island (11 September) and did not invade Manhattan until 15 September. Again they failed to cut off an American retreat, this time to the northern end of the island. Mary Murray served cakes and Madeira to the British generals during the invasion (at today's 37th Street and Park Avenue), giving rise to the legend that she deliberately detained them for two hours and saved thousands of fleeing American troops. On 16 September the Americans won a small, morale-building victory, the Battle of Harlem Heights. A mysterious fire on 20–21 September destroyed a quarter of the city, some 1000 buildings, angering the British, who hanged Nathan Hale as a spy the following day.

In October the British again tried to encircle Washington's forces, by landing troops in lower Westchester County. Again Washington escaped, by marching his troops to White Plains, fighting a battle there, and retreating into the hills to the north. Howe gave up the chase and on 16 November captured Fort Washington, which, in conjunction with Fort Lee, the Americans had hoped would keep British ships out of the Hudson River. Instead, some 2800 American soldiers were captured, the second-worst loss of the war (after Charleston, South Carolina, where 5500 Americans were captured). Until the loss of Fort Washington, American commanders were satisfied that the campaign in New York—and the Americans' many escapes—had done more damage to General Howe's reputation than it had to the American cause. With the American victories at Trenton and Princeton, the importance of Howe's missed opportunities to end the war at a stroke in New York became clear. The city remained under British control, but enough of Washington's forces had survived to prolong the war indefinitely.

3. From the Center of Loyalism to the National Capital, 1776–89

Loyalists fled to the city in large numbers, and the poorest lived in "canvas town," a foul-smelling encampment patched together amid the ruins of the fire. The failure to rebuild quickly, food shortages, hyperinflation, and the persistence of martial law all contributed to the gradual alienation of Loyalists from the British war effort. Nonetheless, promises of freedom and skilled employment attracted many escaped slaves to the city and into the king's service. The population far exceeded what it had been before independence, and merchants reopened their businesses to serve the British army. Rivington, whose press had been smashed in November 1775 by a group under the leadership of Sears, began publishing the *Royal Gazette*, a Loyalist paper. Tryon returned, and Smith, once an advocate of rebellion and later a member of the royal council, was appointed the chief justice. Wealthy Loyalists and officers in the British army and navy entertained one another in style. Real power remained in the hands of the military, and although some talked of restoring civil government, no attempt was made to reconvene the provincial assembly. The British commanders Sir William Howe, Sir Henry Clinton, and Sir Guy Carleton maintained martial rule, and for much of the war the city was governed by the aged major-general James Robertson, who had a reputation for promiscuity and corruption. When commerce with the mainland was almost closed off, privation set in and worsened when American privateers were successful against British merchant vessels.

The colonial government had convened in the city, but the state's Revolutionary government-in-exile met in Kingston, New York. In April 1777 the state's "Convention of the People" adopted a relatively conservative state constitution, with a strong governor and state senate. The occupied counties were represented in both the assembly and the senate by appointed members until the British evacuation. The British preoccupation with holding the city continued to influence events, even as major combat moved elsewhere. General Howe unhinged the British grand strategy by sailing for Philadelphia in July 1777, leaving General Henry Clinton to protect the city and assist General John Burgoyne's invasion of the Hudson River corridor from Canada. Without that support, Burgoyne surrendered at Saratoga, precipitating a French alliance with the Americans the following year. Howe was soon replaced by Clinton. Hoping to retake the city with help from the French navy, Washington settled his forces in an arc stretching from New Jersey through the Hudson Highlands to Connecticut. He also developed an extensive spy network in the city that relayed intelligence to Long Island and across the Sound. James Rivington was later revealed as one of Washington's best sources. From 1778 to 1781 the war in the north became a stalemate between the field armies, focused on New York City. When the British captured Charleston in 1780, they opened a new front in the war, but Clinton left his second-in-command, General Charles Cornwallis, in the south and returned to New York, fearful of a Franco-American assault on the city. Washington preyed on this fear, keeping pressure on New York City to weaken British efforts in the south.

In the city itself some 3800 Loyalists organized themselves into a militia to aid the British; this was not much more than a home guard and was never deployed against the American army. Early in 1781 the Associated Loyalists were organized under their own board of directors. The group was led by Loyalist gentlemen, including Oliver De Lancey and Benjamin Franklin's son William, who had been governor of New Jersey, and included in its ranks many refugees from areas under Revolutionary control. Until April 1782 they conducted raids across the Hudson and into Westchester and southern New England but were disbanded after one of their captains, Richard Lippincott, incurred the anger of both Americans and British by hanging a prisoner, Joshua Luddy, whom he had agreed to exchange. New York City became the main site for holding American prisoners of war, who were kept initially in public buildings and warehouses; ships moored in Wallabout Bay later became the most infamous prisons. As many as 1100 men at a time were held on the *Jersey*, where misery was extreme and death rates high. Some prisoners were soldiers, but many were privateers captured at sea. Their conditions did not improve until Carleton became the British commander of the city in 1782.

By the summer of 1781 the French and Americans had shifted their plans for a joint attack from New York City to Chesapeake Bay. Pinning the British to the city with a feigned attack, the allies marched to Virginia. Like Burgoyne at Saratoga, Cornwallis surrendered at Yorktown in October after pleading in vain for assistance from British forces concentrated in New York. The city's large harbor provided a naval base but proved to be a trap: the sandbars between Coney Island and Sandy Hook delayed the movement of the British fleet, which left to rescue Cornwallis the day he surrendered. The war continued for two more years, and Washington kept up his vigil outside New York City.

The Treaty of Paris in 1783 created two difficult tasks for Carleton: to evacuate British troops and Loyalists, and to transfer power. Many Loyalists realized that they could not regain their confiscated property or escape punishment under the laws that the independent state had passed to punish them, and they sought refuge in Britain. The large number of black Loyalists knew that returning to their American owners meant reenslavement; some who tried to evacuate were taken off their ships by their owners. The reincorporation of the city and the rest of the southern district by the government of New York State caused other hardships for Loyalists who stayed. Those whose property had not been confiscated had to pay double tax and were denied the protection of the courts, and the entire southern district was made to pay a special tax to share the cost of the war. The Citation Act allowed patriots to bring damage suits against people who had used their property during the occupation.

After the peaceful transfer of the city to the Americans on Evacuation Day, 25 November 1783, the city faced tremendous obstacles to prosperity. Its physical structure was seriously damaged, its currency devalued, its commerce in chaos owing to the dumping of British goods, and its political and economic prospects in doubt. In 1784 the formation of a new city government paved the way for restructuring, and from 1789 to 1790 New York City was the nation's capital. Most of those who had fled the city returned, businesses emerged, and a stable municipal and federal government laid the foundation for a strong city that became the largest and most successful in the nation during the following decades.

Edward Countryman, *A People in Revolution: The American Revolution and Political Society in New York, 1760–1790* (New York: W. W. Norton, 1989); Judith Van Buskirk, *Generous Enemies: Patriots and Loyalists in Revolutionary New York* (Philadelphia: University of Pennsylvania Press, 2002); Richard Ketchum, *Divided Loyalties: How the American Revolution Came to New York* (New York: Holt, 2003); Barnet Schecter, *The Battle for New York: The City at the Heart of the American Revolution* (New York: Penguin, 2003); Edwin Burrows, *Forgotten Patriots: The Untold Story of American Prisoners during the Revolutionary War* (New York: Basic Books, 2008)

See also Evacuation Day; Hale, Nathan; Hudson River; Prison ships.

Edward Countryman, Barnet Schecter

American Society for the Prevention of Cruelty to Animals [ASPCA]. Humane society, formed in 1866 by Henry Bergh as the first humane society chartered in the United States. In addition to performing rescue work its agents were empowered by state legislation to issue summonses for violations of animal cruelty and animal control laws. The national headquarters on East 92nd Street in Manhattan house the Bergh Memorial Animal Hospital, an animal shelter open 24 hours a day, and an adoption center. The society also maintains a shelter and hospital in Brooklyn, and pet receiving centers in the Bronx, Queens, and Staten Island. The concerns of the organization now include education; the treatment of animals used for food, for clothing, and in laboratory research; and the protection of endangered species.

John J. Gallagher

American Society of Composers, Authors, and Publishers [ASCAP]. Performance rights organization. It was founded in 1914 at the Claridge Hotel in Manhattan largely by artists associated with Tin Pan Alley, including Victor Herbert. Its purpose was to protect the copyrighted materials of its members and to provide compensation when their works were performed publicly. The advent of radio provided a new source of income for ASCAP, which was responsible for implementing the first radio-licensing fees. As new media such as television and the Internet became part of the culture, ASCAP continued to expand its oversight of artists and artistic material. As of 2008 ASCAP had 330,000 members, among them Lauryn Hill, Dr. Dre, and Marc Anthony. Former members include Jimi Hendrix, the Ramones, the Beatles, the Rolling Stones, John Denver, Carly Simon, and Janis Joplin.

Max Seppo

American Standard. Firm of plumbing and building-fixture manufacturers. It was formed in 1929 as the American Radiator and Standard Sanitary Corporation after a merger of the American Radiator Company (formed in the city in 1905) and the Standard Sanitary Corporation, and took its current name in 1967. Between 1968 and 1971 the firm sponsored vocational training, improvements in public transit, and affordable housing. Among its programs was Construction for Progress, which sponsored several low-income housing projects in Harlem and the southern Bronx. During the 1980s the firm sold mostly plumbing and air conditioning supplies. It was taken private in 1988 and moved its executive offices to 1114 Sixth Avenue the following year. The company again became public in 1999 and moved its corporate headquarters to suburban Piscataway, New Jersey. The American Standard Building on 40 West 40th Street, Raymond M. Hood's first commission in the city, is a municipal landmark.

James Bradley

American Stock Exchange. Stock exchange in the financial district of New York City. It was originally composed of dealers with insufficient funds to become members of the New York Stock and Exchange Board (1817; later the New York Stock Exchange, NYSE) and was known as the Curb because members met their clients in the streets and became known as "curbstone brokers" who traded mostly the stocks of firms smaller, younger, and riskier than those represented on the older exchange. In the 1860s shares were sold in mining companies formed after the discovery of gold in California in 1848. The volume of activity was heavy: on a busy day, when 6000 shares of stocks might be sold at the New York Stock and Exchange Board, 70,000 shares might be sold at the Curb, where after the Civil War new securities and stocks in small manufacturing companies were first sold. By tacit agreement the New York Stock and Exchange Board concentrated on established issues and on maintaining high standards for listing and trading. Determined to cleanse the Curb of marginal brokers and securities, a curbstone broker named Emmanuel S. Mendels, Jr., in 1904 published an official Curb directory of 209 reliable brokers and in 1908 organized the New York Curb Market Agency. In 1911 the exchange became known simply as the New York Curb Market and drew up a constitution; it moved indoors to 113–23 Greenwich Street in 1921 and in 1929 was renamed the New York Curb Exchange.

The volume of stocks and bonds traded during the 1920s, especially that of foreign securities, grew rapidly. By 1930 the exchange had more foreign issues on its list than all other American securities markets combined. The price of a seat rose from $6800 in 1921 to $254,000 in 1929. As firms became well known, they often moved to the NYSE, but the Curb continued to attract new and foreign firms. It took its current name in 1953 and soon became known as Amex. During the 1960s and 1970s it introduced a number of innovations, including the listing of stock options, automation, and surveillance of trades. In 1998 the American Stock Exchange merged with NASDAQ, which had overtaken it as the main competitor to the NYSE. The American Stock Exchange, located near the World Trade Center, was significantly affected by the terrorist attacks of 11 September 2001 but recovered in the ensuing years. In 2008 the exchange was acquired by NYSE Euronext and was later renamed the NYSE Amex Equities.

Stuart Bruchey, *The Modernization of the American Stock Exchange, 1971–1989* (New York: Garland, 1991)

Stuart Bruchey

American Sunday School Union. Interdenominational Protestant philanthropic organization formed in 1824 as an offshoot of the Sunday and Adult School Union and based in Philadelphia. It organized a national network of Sunday school supporters, developed standardized curricula and pedagogical techniques, and published moral and religious literature for American youths. Chapters in New York City were active throughout the nineteenth century. The union altered its focus toward rural areas after the Civil War and ultimately evolved into the American Missionary Fellowship in 1974.

Peter J. Wosh

American Symphony Orchestra. Orchestra formed in 1962 in New York City by Leopold Stokowski, who announced that his aims were "to afford opportunity to gifted musicians, regardless of age, sex, or racial origin, and to offer concerts of great music within the means of everyone." Carnegie Hall was chosen as the site of its concerts, which initially numbered six each season. Perhaps its most notable performance was the world premiere of Burl Ives's Symphony no. 4 in 1965. The orchestra was reorganized as a cooperative in 1973. In the 1980s it suffered a decline in subscribers, but it regained visibility under the direction of Leon Botstein, who became its conductor in 1992 and reoriented the programming to emphasize lesser-known works of the nineteenth century. In the early twenty-first century the orchestra's main subscription series was at Avery Fisher Hall in Lincoln Center. It also performed at Columbia University and Bard College, toured regularly, and recorded various classical pieces.

American Telephone and Telegraph [AT&T]. Telecommunications firm, formed in 1885 in Boston as a subsidiary of the American Bell Telephone Company to develop long-distance communications channels and maintain the parent company's control of telephony in the United States. In 1899 the offices were moved to 195 Broadway in New York City, where AT&T became the parent firm of several regional telephone companies and of the manufacturing subsidiary Western Electric. It briefly acquired control of Western Union in 1909 before the two firms were separated by antitrust action. AT&T kept competitors out of the long-distance market by providing "universal service" at low cost and making constant technological improvements. Its control of telephony was strengthened by passage of the Mann–Elkins Act (1910), the "Kingsbury Commitment" (1913), and subsequent federal regulation, which established the Bell system as the manager of the national telephone network. In 1925 Bell Telephone Laboratories was incorporated as a subsidiary. The firm launched a number of radio stations in the 1920s, and on 7 April 1927 it made the first television broadcast from its laboratory on West Street. In the late 1930s the Federal Communications Commission reaffirmed the firm's position as the dominant carrier of telecommunications, but in 1949 AT&T and Western Electric were sued for antitrust violations, and a consent decree prevented AT&T from engaging in business other than telephony. During the following years the firm's monopolies in telephone equipment and long-distance service were gradually weakened by regulators, and in 1982 an antitrust action led to a settlement under which the firm (then the largest in the world) agreed to divest itself of its regional operating companies, though it remained free to enter such new, unregulated fields of business as computer hardware and data transmission. In 1983 AT&T moved its offices to 550 Madison Avenue. From the mid-1990s through the first decade of the twenty-first century AT&T became increasingly involved in new technologies related to computer, broadband, and wireless services. Over that time AT&T formed several entities from divisions of the original company that specialized in various aspects of the new technologies. In 2010 AT&T was based in New Jersey, and its former location on Madison Avenue had been taken over by the Sony Corporation.

N. R. Danielian, *AT&T: The Story of Industrial Conquest* (New York: Vanguard, 1939); John Brooks, *Telephone: The First Hundred Years* (New York: Harper and Row, 1976); Peter Temin, *The Fall of the Bell System: A Study in Prices and Politics* (New York: Cambridge University Press, 1987)

See also Western Union Company, Telephony.

George David Smith

American Temperance Union. Union formed in 1836 in Saratoga, New York, and based in New York City for its three decades of existence. It sought to unify, coordinate, and structure the work of hundreds of societies throughout North America favoring abstinence from alcohol. Its first president was Stephen Van Rensselaer. The union relied on moral suasion, religious publications, and legislative action to further its goals and was influential in reformist circles from its founding to the late 1840s. It represented the wealthier, more evangelical, avowedly prohibitionist wing of the temperance movement. In 1865 the union was absorbed by the newly formed National Temperance Society and Publication House, also based in Manhattan.

Permanent Temperance Documents of the American Temperance Union (New York: American Temperance Union, 1846)

Peter J. Wosh

American Tract Society. Protestant organization formed in 1825 by the merger of societies based in New York City and Boston. It became one of the largest publishers in the antebellum United States, producing each year thousands of religious books, pamphlets, tracts, and hymnals that enterprising peddlers circulated throughout the country as they preached salvation. After the Civil War the society increasingly concentrated its efforts on freed slaves, and the focus of its publishing operations shifted away from tracts and toward books and foreign-language publications. In the late 1940s it reaffirmed its traditional emphasis on small, English-language gospel tracts. The society left its landmark building at 150 Nassau Street in 1963 and eventually moved to Garland, Texas.

Stephen Elmer Slocum, "The American Tract Society, 1825–1975: An Evangelical Effort to Influence the Religious and Moral Life of the United States" (diss., New York University, 1975)

Peter J. Wosh

America's Cup. International yacht racing trophy and competition. Created and long dominated by New Yorkers, America's Cup racing took place off the city for 50 years. In 1850 the founding commodore of the New York Yacht Club, the steamboat tycoon John Cox Stevens, formed a syndicate to build a 100-foot yacht called *America* and take her to England to represent New York shipbuilding at the Great Exhibition, and also to race English yachts. (Other members of the syndicate were Alexander Hamilton's son James and his son-in-law George L. Schuyler.) *America* was designed by a Brooklyn naval architect, George Steers, along the lines of his breakthrough New York pilot schooners.

On 22 August 1851, *America* beat 14 English yachts in a 53-mile race around the Isle of Wight. The prize was a silver ewer presented by the Royal Yacht Squadron that the New York Yacht Club donated for international competition in accordance with a few simple rules: racing is held after a foreign yacht club challenges the club that last won the cup, the defender chooses the waters for the race course, and other details are negotiated between challenger and defender. The America's Cup trophy came to be called for the yacht that first won it.

The first match, in 1870, consisted of one race between the lone English challenger, *Cambria,* and the New York Yacht Club's fleet. They raced on the club's "inside course," starting off Staten Island, sailing out into New York Bay, and returning. *Magic* won the race, with *America* in fourth place and *Cambria* finishing tenth. The race was a public sensation. According to one reporter, "New York emptied itself out through the Narrows until the offing was like a crowded port with pillars of steam and glimmer of sails, and the shores of Staten Island were like swarming cities." From 1871 onward, it was a true match, with one yacht in each side. Most competitors were big schooners or, beginning in 1881, huge single-masted racing sloops sailed by professional crews. The race course was eventually moved to the New York Yacht Club's "outer course" in the Atlantic Ocean off Sandy Hook. Public interest remained immense; U.S. Navy patrol boats were required to prevent spectators from interfering with the racing yachts.

Thanks to better organization and to sailing in familiar waters, the New York Yacht Club's defenders won all 13 New York matches against English, Canadian, and Irish yachts, although Sir Thomas Lipton's *Shamrocks* came close to winning in 1901 and 1920. After cup racing was moved to Newport, Rhode Island, in 1930, the New York Yacht Club continued to win through 11 matches, until Australia's victory in 1983. Several defenders were built or equipped at shipyards on City Island and in the Bronx, or were owned by the New York Maritime College, at Fort Schuyler. When Dennis Conner (representing the San Diego Yacht Club) won the cup in 1987, he and his crew were accorded a parade down Fifth Avenue.

In seven matches between 1987 and 2007 in Australia, California, New Zealand, and Spain, the New York Yacht Club mounted three challenges, none successful. Many of its members were active in the cup as sailors or administrators.

John Rousmaniere, *The Low Black Schooner: Yacht America, 1851–1945* (Mystic, Conn.: Mystic Seaport Marine Stores, 1986); John Rousmaniere, *America's Cup Book, 1851–1983* (New York: W. W. Norton, 1983)

John Rousmaniere

Americas Society. Organization dedicated to education, debate, and dialogue in the Americas. In 1965 a group of business leaders led by David Rockefeller founded the Center for Inter-American Relations to educate leading government officials, artists, and businesspeople about Latin America, the Caribbean, Canada, and North America in order to better establish their impact on U.S. national interests. The center was absorbed by the Americas Society in 1985. Its programs promote its agenda of free trade, democracy, and general cultural awareness. The society also works closely with the Council of the Americas, a business organization dedicated to free trade and open markets between countries in the western hemisphere. The Americas Society is located at 680 Park Avenue.

Stephanie Miller

Ammann, Othmar H(erman) (*b* Schaffhausen, Switzerland, 26 March 1879; *d* Rye, N.Y., 22 Sept 1965). Engineer. He graduated from the Swiss Polytechnic Institute and left for America in 1904. For several years he worked in engineering firms in Pennsylvania and New York City, where in 1912 he joined the firm of Gustav Lindenthal, serving as the chief assistant on the Hell Gate Bridge (1917). He left the firm in the early 1920s to design a bridge over the Hudson River. In 1925 the Port of New York Authority adopted his plan and appointed him the chief engineer of what would later be named the George Washington Bridge (1931). Ammann also built the Bayonne Bridge (1931) for the Port Authority. For the Triborough Bridge and Tunnel Authority he designed the Triborough Bridge (1936), the Bronx–Whitestone Bridge (1939), the Throgs Neck Bridge (1961), and the Verrazano–Narrows Bridge (1964).

Rebecca Read Shanor

AM New York. Free daily newspaper owned by the Tribune Company. Launched in 2003, *AM New York* is distributed primarily by employees who hand out the paper at major commuting hubs during the morning rush hour and at newspaper boxes located on street corners throughout the city. *AM New York* competes primarily with the New York edition of *Metro.*

Michael C. Repka

Office of the Amsterdam News

amphibians and reptiles. At the time of European settlement, amphibians and reptiles thrived in the varied estuarine, aquatic, and terrestrial habitats of what is now New York City. In 1927 G. K. Noble, curator of herpetology at the American Museum of Natural History, listed 70 species for the New York City area, including 3 lizards, 5 marine turtles, 11 aquatic turtles, 15 salamanders, 15 frogs and toads, and 21 snakes, among them the Copperhead and the Rattlesnake, which were rapidly disappearing. As the city grew, streams, marshes, and swamps were filled in or drained, uplands cleared, and critical habitats lost, severely reducing the number and diversity of amphibians and reptiles.

Species that survived in the area tend to be aquatic species found in large lakes, and small, secretive species with simple requirements and the ability to live in parks, cemeteries, and other green areas. In addition, beginning in the 1980s, efforts to restore species to natural areas of parks were undertaken by the National Park Service and the New York City Department of Parks and Recreation. These efforts helped to reverse some of the declines. Among the native species still common in New York City are the Spring Peeper, Fowler's Toad (in Staten Island and Long Island), Green Frog, Bullfrog, Red-Backed Salamander, Eastern Garter Snake, Northern Brown Snake, Snapping Turtle, Painted Turtle, and Diamond-Backed Terrapin (in Jamaica Bay). Several rarer species are still found in the Greenbelt in Staten Island, in Pelham Bay and Van Cortlandt parks in the Bronx, in Floyd Bennett Field in Brooklyn, and in Jamaica Bay Wildlife Refuge, Forest Park, and Alley Pond Park in Queens. Aquatic turtles are among the only species in the ponds of such landscaped and heavily trafficked parks as Central Park, Prospect Park, and Flushing Meadows–Corona Park; many exotic pet turtles are also released into these ponds, but few survive.

Robert P. Cook

Amsterdam News. James Henry Anderson published the first edition of this Harlem newspaper from his home at 135 West 65th Street in 1909. It sold at two cents per copy and covered local African American achievements and social events. The paper soon moved to 17 West 135th Street and in 1916 moved again, to 2293 Seventh Avenue. C. B. Powell and P. M. H. Savory purchased the weekly in 1935. Under their ownership the paper became a nationally recognized voice for black Americans and supported Republican politics until the 1930s. In the early 1970s the tabloid changed hands again; its new owners included Percy E. Sutton, H. Carl McCall, and Clarence E. Jones, who became its publisher and editor. In the 1980s Wilbert A. Tatum became editor and was succeeded by his daughter Elinor Tatum in 1997. In 2007 a new magazine section called "The Focus" was introduced, the purpose of which was to highlight topical information and offer in-depth reporting.

Mario A. Charles

Amtrak [National Railroad Passenger Corporation]. Government-owned corporation that provides intercity and interstate passenger rail service in the United States. Amtrak trains in New York run on tracks formerly operated by the New York Central Railroad and the Pennsylvania Railroad. The first Amtrak train left from Pennsylvania Station en route to Philadelphia in 1971. Pennsylvania Station, owned by Amtrak, is the busiest train station in the United States, serving 600,000 passengers daily, and Amtrak's only station in New York City. Amtrak trains from Pennsylvania Station operate in the Northeast and Empire corridors, providing service to Boston, Washington, D.C., Albany, and as far north as Montreal.

Max Seppo

anarchism. New York City became a center of anarchism during the mid-nineteenth century, when European anarchists moved there and joined with libertarians in challenging perceived injustices of capitalism and the state. Many radicals were inspired by the writings and rousing speeches of Johann Most, who published the newspaper *Freiheit* (1882–1910) and organized German anarchists. The leading advocate of terrorism, he sought to redress class grievances with dynamite. The execution of anarchist leaders in 1886–87 after a riot in Haymarket Square in Chicago incited anarchists in New York City to action. Jews on the Lower East Side formed the Pioneers of Liberty (1886), protested the Haymarket affair, organized workers' educational clubs, and between 1880 and 1930 launched more than a dozen anarchist publications, including the Yiddish-language newspaper *Fraye arbeter shtime* (1890–1977), which became the most prominent and enduring periodical of its kind in the country. Italian anarchists settled in Brooklyn and Paterson, New Jersey. *L'Anarchico,* the first Italian anarchist newspaper in the United States, was launched in 1888.

The assassination of President William McKinley by the anarchist Leon Czolgosz in 1901 led to widespread violence against anarchists in the city: anarchist headquarters were vandalized, immigrants were attacked, and many public figures called for the "lynch law" and the "extermination" of anarchists. Johann Most was arrested and imprisoned for inciting violence, and in 1903 foreigners known to be anarchists were barred by federal legislation from entering the country. Among anarchists, McKinley's assassination widened the division between advocates of violence and those who sought change peacefully. Education and aid were emphasized in modern schools, among them one named for the Spanish anarchist and educational reformer Francisco Ferrer: they stressed the history of revolution and of the working class and avoided that of religion and capitalism. In 1907 an anarchist Red Cross was formed in the city to assist political prisoners of the Russian Revolution. After Most's death in 1906 Emma Goldman and Alexander Berkman became leading figures of anarchism in the United States; they published the journal *Mother Earth* (1906–17), addressed May Day rallies in Union Square, protested against World War I, organized strikes, gave lectures on contraception and "free love," and helped to renew the intellectual vigor of anarchism. Carlo Tresca published the newspaper *L'Avvenire* in New York City from 1913 and also helped to organize a strike by hotel workers that was led by the Industrial Workers of the World.

In 1918 Mollie Steimer, Jacob Abrams, and other anarchists in Harlem affiliated with the journal *Der Shturm* were convicted of criticizing American intervention in the Russian Revolution. Their cause was taken up by Louis Brandeis and Oliver Wendell Holmes, who together dissented from a decision by the Supreme Court to uphold the conviction. The anarchist movement was weakened after 1919, when Steimer, Goldman, Berkman, and others were exiled during a "red scare" inspired by fear of the Russian Revolution, and between 1920 and 1960 most anarchist newspapers ceased publication. Although the decline of anarchism was partly due to repression, a more important cause was the rise of communism, which attracted many of those on the fringes of the anarchist movement. Libertarian ideals were preserved by anarchists, liberals, and socialists opposed to fascism; anarchist philosophy was the basis of Dwight Macdonald's periodical *Politics* and of Dorothy Day's newspaper the *Catholic Worker* (1933), and the Libertarian Book Club was formed in the 1940s. The assassination of Tresca in July 1943 marked the end of a period when anarchism was inextricably associated with immigrants.

The civil rights movement and the Vietnam War revitalized interest in anarchist ideals during the 1960s and 1970s. At the New School for Social Research Herbert Marcuse inveighed against consumerism and political conformity. Ayn Rand praised capitalism in discussions of objectivism broadcast by the radio stations WKCR and WBAI; her books were available at the Objectivist Book Service on 34th Street. Paul Goodman denounced statist policies and "compulsory miseducation" and argued that student protests of the time were anarchic in origin. Many anarchists scorned the radical group Students for a Democratic Society for being too conciliatory toward established society. Abbie Hoffman and other "yippies" organized relief for the poor and in 1967 aided blacks during riots in Newark, New Jersey. In March 1968, 6000 radicals including Hoffman disrupted service at Grand Central Terminal until dispersed by police officers in full riot gear. During the early 1980s self-described anarchists took over abandoned buildings on the Lower East Side. In the early twenty-first century anarchism continued to be supported in the city by the Libertarian Book Club, which organized lectures and provided information about anarchist history as well as contemporary social and political issues.

David E. Apter and James Joll, eds., *Anarchism Today* (New York: Doubleday, 1971); William O. Reichert, *Partisans of Freedom: A Study in American Anarchism* (Bowling Green, Ohio: Bowling Green University Press, 1976); Paul Avrich, *Anarchist Portraits* (Princeton, N.J.: Princeton University Press, 1988)

David A. Balcom

Anastasi, Anne (*b* New York City, 19 Dec 1908; *d* New York City, 4 May 2001). Psychologist. She was a key architect of psychological testing in the twentieth century and author of *Psychological Testing* (1954), which is still considered a classic in the field. She attended Rhodes Preparatory School in Manhattan for two years and then went to Barnard College when she was only 15 years old, majoring in psychology and receiving her bachelor's degree in 1928. She completed her doctoral degree at Columbia University in 1930 at age 21 and then taught at Barnard (1930–39); Queens College of the City University of New York (1939–47), where she was chair of the psychology department; and Fordham University (1947–79). In 1972 she became the third woman to be elected president of the American Psychological Association. Her many awards included the National Medal of Science in 1987, the nation's highest award for scientific achievement. She died in her home at 138 East 39th Street.

Harold Takooshian

Anastasia, Albert (*b* Calabria, Italy, 1902; *d* New York City, 25 Oct 1957). Organized-crime figure. After growing up in Sicily he moved to New York City, where with his brother "Tough Tony" he took control of the waterfront in Brooklyn in the 1920s and gained power in its union. After killing a fellow longshoreman he spent 18 months on death row at Sing Sing, the state penitentiary at Ossining, New York; he was released after key witnesses disappeared. With Louis "Lepke" Buchalter he became an enforcer for Murder Incorporated, a criminal organization responsible for 500 deaths and disappearances. Nicknamed the "Mad Hatter," he was protected and controlled by Lucky Luciano (until he was deported) and Frank Costello (until he became preoccupied with his own legal problems). Shortly after threatening Meyer Lansky, Anastasia was murdered by two gunmen in a barber shop at the Park Sheraton Hotel.

Salvatore Anastasia, *Anastasia mio fratello,* ed. Benedetto Mosca (Rome: Novissima, 1967)

James E. Mooney

Anchor Savings Bank. Established as the Bay Ridge Savings Bank in 1909 to serve a neighborhood of sailors. In 1968, looking to expand, it took on the name Anchor Savings Bank in honor of its original customers. The following year it merged with Bushwick Savings Bank. By 1994, when it merged into Dime Savings Bank, Anchor had taken over 15 banks, had $9.9 billion in assets, and operated 65 branches in New York State, New Jersey, and Florida.

Leslie Gourse

Ancient Order of Hibernians. Roman Catholic society formed in Ireland in 1565. Its first branch in the United States was founded as a social and benevolent society in 1836 at St. James Roman Catholic Church in Manhattan. The society is made up of separate men's and women's groups that work in close cooperation. There are about 80 local divisions in New York City, based mainly in neighborhoods that have a large Irish population. The Ancient Order of Hibernians is nonpartisan in American politics but has a strong tradition of support for nationalist movements in Ireland. It organizes dances, concerts, educational programs, and religious celebrations.

Thomas F. McGrath, *History of the Ancient Order of Hibernians* (Cleveland: Thomas F. McGrath, 1898); John T. Ridge, *Erin's Sons in America: The Ancient Order of Hibernians* (New York: Ancient Order of Hibernians, 1986)

John T. Ridge

Anderson, Alexander (*b* New York City, 21 April 1775; *d* Jersey City, N.J., 17 Jan 1870). Engraver and physician. Apprenticed to a physician after his 14th birthday, Anderson graduated with an MD from Columbia College in 1796, at the same time providing engraved illustrations for the New York City book trade in his spare time. His parents discouraged him from pursuing a career in art. He worked at Bellevue Hospital during the yellow fever epidemic of 1795, and again in 1798, when he lost his mother, father, wife, infant son, brother, and close relatives. After the tragedy, he abandoned medicine in favor of his preferred calling, engraving. Inspired by the illustrations on end-grain boxwood that he had seen in Thomas Bewick's *General History of Quadrupeds* (1790), Anderson taught himself the requisite skills; his edition of the *Quadrupeds* (1804) brought him wide recognition. He was the first to introduce this artistic and commercially successful medium to American bookmaking and has been called the father of American wood engraving. In the next three or four decades, he was this country's most popular illustrator, with his work appearing in fiction, poetry, history, religion, Bibles, medical texts, and, particularly, children's books. His skill and his amused and affectionate portrayals of children in storybooks and in Webster's spellers have claimed a permanent place for him in the history of American illustration. He continued to work until he died in his 95th year.

His proof books, with over 9000 engravings, are in the New York Public Library. A selection of his tools is at the New-York Historical Society and the Connecticut Historical Society. The majority of his surviving woodblocks are at the New-York Historical Society, the University of Florida, Gainesville, and Columbia University. His manuscript diary, from 1793 to June 1799, is at Columbia University.

Benson John Lossing, *A Memorial of Alexander Anderson, M.D., the First Engraver on Wood in America* (New York: privately printed, 1872); Frederic M. Burr, *Life and Works of Alexander Anderson, M.D., the First American Wood Engraver* (New York: Burr Brothers, 1893); Jane R. Pomeroy, *Alexander Anderson (1775–1870), Wood Engraver and Illustrator: An Annotated Bibliography* (New Castle, Del.: Oak Knoll Press for the American Antiquarian Society and the New York Public Library, 2005)

Jane R. Pomeroy

Anderson, Charles W(illiam) (*b* Oxford, Ohio, 28 April 1866; *d* New York City, 28 June 1938). Public official. After moving to New York City in 1886 he became active in Republican politics, and in 1890 he was elected president of the Young Men's Colored Republican Club of New York County. He was a gauger in the district office of the Internal Revenue Service, the private secretary to the treasurer of New York State (1895–98), and the supervisor of accounts for the state racing commission (1898–1905). In 1905 President Theodore Roosevelt appointed Anderson as the collector of internal revenue for the second district of New York City (encompassing Wall Street and the major piers), considered one of the most important federal positions in the city. He reportedly received the appointment through the influence of his friend and close political associate Booker T. Washington. Dismissed from office by President Woodrow Wilson in a purge of black Republicans, he later held senior positions in state government and again served as collector of internal revenue from 1923 to 1934.

James S. Kaplan

Andrew W. Mellon Foundation. Charitable organization. It began operations in June 1969 with the merger of two foundations set up by the children of Andrew W. Mellon: the Avalon Foundation, formed in 1940 by Ailsa Mellon Bruce (*d* 25 Aug 1969) and based in New York City, and the Old Dominion Foundation, formed in Virginia in 1941 by Paul Mellon (*d* 1 Feb 1999). The foundation makes grants in the areas of higher education, cultural affairs and the performing arts, population, conservation and the environment, and public affairs. In 2008 the foundation had an endowment of more than $5 billion, with annual grants making appropriations of about $210 million. Its offices are at 140 East 62nd Street.

Kenneth W. Rose

Androvetteville. Name applied in the eighteenth century to CHARLESTON.

Annadale. Neighborhood in southwestern Staten Island, overlooking the Raritan Bay. It was once inhabited by Raritan Indians and was given its current name about 1860 in honor of Anna Seguine, a member of a prominent local family. The first houses in the area were fishing bungalows. There was relatively little development until the opening of the Verrazano–Narrows Bridge in 1964; the construction of private houses on a large scale began only about 1975. The neighborhood is the site of Blue Heron Pond Park, to the north of which is a station of Staten Island Rapid Transit. The housing stock in Annadale varies from the modest to the opulent; there is a large Italian population, and the neighborhood is ethnically diverse.

Gertrude M. Egish, *Next Stop, Annadale!* (New York: Staten Island Historical Society, 1997)

Martha S. Bendix

Annexed District. Name applied to the lands annexed by New York City in 1874 (the present neighborhoods of Kingsbridge, Morrisania, and West Farms in the Bronx) and 1895 (the rest of what is now the Bronx).

Gary Hermalyn, "The Bronx at the Turn of the Century," *Bronx County Historical Society Journal* 36 (1989): 92–112

Gary D. Hermalyn

Ansonia. Seventeen-story apartment building on Broadway between 73rd and 74th streets. Designed in a beaux-arts style by the architectural firm of Graves and Duboy, it was built in 1904 by the developer W. E. D. Stokes and soon became well known for attracting such residents as Babe Ruth, Enrico Caruso, Theodore Dreiser, Igor Stravinsky, Arturo Toscanini, Florenz Ziegfeld, Mischa Elman, Sol Hurok, Lauritz Melchior, Ezio Pinza, and Lily Pons. During renovations in the 1980s some portions were converted into studios for voice coaching and space for theater rehearsals. Ornamented facades, balconies, and corner towers make the Ansonia Hotel an outstanding structure on the West Side. It was declared a New York City landmark in 1972.

Thomas E. Bird

Anthology Film Archives. Museum dedicated to avant-garde cinema. Formed in 1969 by the filmmakers Jonas Mekas and Jerome Hill, it was the first of its kind in the United States. From 1970 it mounted exhibitions at Joseph Papp's Public Theater in an "invisible cinema" designed by Peter Kubelka, in which viewers were separated from each other by black partitions and a seat hood that minimized perceptual interference while allowing for a communal sense of viewing. Its collection, the Essential Cinema Repertory, was selected by a committee of theoreticians, filmmakers, and poets to celebrate the aesthetics of cinema and provoke discussion about alternative cinema. The archive introduced the Independent Film Preservation program and began its library collection in 1972, introduced video exhibitions in 1974, and maintained a theater at 80 Wooster Street from 1973 to 1980. In 1979 the Anthology Film Archives acquired a former courthouse building at Second Avenue and Second Street, which came to house two theaters, a film preservation department, a library, and a gallery. As of the early twenty-first century, the archives held 11,000 films and 3,000 videotapes. In 2007 it was among several institutions that received funding from a $20 million grant provided by the Carnegie Corporation. The building itself has also been used in film, most recently in *Spider-Man 2* (2004).

Grai St. Clair Rice

anthropology. New York City became noted for its contributions to the field of anthropology even before the Civil War through the work of Albert Gallatin, who conducted research on American Indian languages and helped to organize the American Ethnological Society in 1842. The American Museum of Natural History opened an anthropology department in 1874, but it was not directed by trained curators until 1894, when it was reorganized by Frederic Putnam of Harvard University. Prominent anthropologists in the department included Franz Boas, who was curator from 1895 to 1905, Clark Wissler, Robert Lowie, Herbert Spinden, Harry Shapiro, Margaret Mead, and Colin Turnbull. The New York Academy of Sciences opened an anthropology division in 1896. After 1900 the center of anthropology in New York City gradually shifted toward Columbia University, where Boas began teaching in 1896. Among his first students were Alfred Kroeber (to whom Columbia awarded its first PhD in anthropology in 1901), Lowie, Edward Sapir, Paul Radin, and Alexander Goldenweiser, who all centered their work on salvaging the vanishing culture of the American Indian. In the 1920s Boas's students included Mead, Ruth Benedict, Gladys Reichard, Ruth Bunzel, and Melville Herskovits. Ralph Linton, who like Benedict studied culture and personality, became a professor at Columbia in 1937 after Boas's retirement.

Between the two world wars many schools in the city introduced anthropology into their curricula, including all four public colleges in New York City (City College, Hunter College, Brooklyn College, and Queens College) and the New School for Social Research, where Elsie Clews Parsons and Goldenweiser taught when the school opened in 1919. The French anthropologist Claude Lévi-Strauss taught at the New School from 1942 to 1945 and was the cultural attaché to the French embassy from 1946 to 1947. In 1941 the Viking Fund (later known as the Wenner–Gren Foundation for Anthropological Research), an important source of grants for anthropological study abroad, established its headquarters in the city. Although the city's preeminence as a center of anthropology declined as the field gained popularity throughout the country after World War II, in 1966 doctoral programs in anthropology were launched at New York University, the New School, and City University of New York. In the early twenty-first century the New York Academy of Sciences also remained an important center for anthropologists throughout the city.

Ira Jacknis

Anti-Defamation League. Nonprofit organization formed as an affiliate of B'nai B'rith in 1913 to combat negative portrayals of Jews in books, periodicals, and advertising. Initially the league supported the censorship of texts that it believed would encourage anti-Semitism, including works of Shakespeare and Dickens. In 1946 the organization moved to New York City from Chicago and broadened its mission to include defending the rights of all Americans: it filed a brief in the school desegregation case *Brown v. Board of Education* (1954) and drafted the first anti-discrimination bill, the Ives–Quinn Act. In later years the league supported the Civil Rights Act of 1964 and defended the rights of Jews in the Soviet Union. In the late twentieth and early twenty-first centuries, the league's activities included monitoring terrorist groups, working on Israeli–Palestinian relations, and promoting Holocaust awareness. The league's headquarters in the twenty-first century remain in Manhattan, although it has offices all over the United States and in Israel, Russia, and Italy.

Deborah Dash Moore, *B'nai B'rith and the Challenge of Ethnic Leadership* (Albany: State University of New York Press, 1981)

Jean Ulitz Mensch

Anti-Slavery Society. See American Anti-Slavery Society.

Antonetty, Evelina Lopez (*b* Salinas, Puerto Rico, 19 Sept 1922; *d* New York City, 19 Nov 1984). Activist. She moved in 1933 with her family to New York City, where in the 1940s she organized unions and worked to improve educational opportunities for Puerto Ricans. In 1965 she founded and became the first executive director of United Bronx Parents, an organization that encouraged parents to take part in the school system and that offered various social services in the South Bronx. After her death, the Puerto Rican Studies Library and Archives at Hunter College were named for her.

Nélida Pérez

Antonini, Luigi (*b* Vallata Irpina, Italy, 11 Sept 1883; *d* New York City, 29 Dec 1968). Labor leader. He joined the International Ladies' Garment Workers' Union as a dress presser in 1913 and became a leader of Italian workers in New York City. In 1919 he organized Italian Dressmakers Local 89, of which he served as general secretary. Elected vice president of the union in 1934, he joined with its president, David Dubinsky, to form the American Labor Party in New York City in 1936 and the Liberal Party in 1944. Antonini later led the Italian-American Labor Council in opposition to Mussolini and assisted in rebuilding democratic trade unions in Italy after World War II.

Philip V. Cannistraro, "Luigi Antonini and the Italian Anti-Fascist Movement in the United States, 1940–1943," *Journal of American Ethnic History,* vol. 5, no. 1 (Fall 1985): 21–40; John Stuart Crawford, *Luigi Antonini: His Influence on Italian-American Relations* (New York: Education Department, Italian Dressmakers' Union, Local 89, International Ladies' Garment Workers' Union, 1950)

Robert D. Parmet

A.P. See Associated Press.

apartments. The first apartment building in New York City was the Stuyvesant, designed in 1869 by the architect Richard Morris Hunt, the first American to attend the École des Beaux-Arts. The building was also called the French Flats, a term later used more broadly for any dwellings of the same kind (which were not known as apartments until the 1880s). Early apartment buildings in Manhattan were constructed at a time when most middle-class families in the city lived in row houses. In contrast to row houses and their descendants, the brownstones, which had dark interiors and were costly to maintain, apartment buildings symbolized modern technology and new ways of family living. Apartments signaled a shift in the cultural ideals of the upper middle class from its colonial Anglo-Saxon origins to the culture of the Continent, especially that of Second Empire Paris. In 1871 Hunt completed the Stevens House, an eight-story building with a passenger elevator and other technological innovations. Dozens of similar apartment buildings were erected in Manhattan in the 1880s, some having as many as 20 rooms: one of the best known was the Dakota (1884, Henry J. Hardenbergh). To counter the prejudice against apartments that was still common among wealthy residents, many of the new buildings were developed as cooperatives; this arrangement gave residents a financial interest in their apartment that was tantamount to ownership and offered services such as catered meals and domestic help.

Not all apartment buildings were luxurious, however. Tenements provided compact rental housing for poor and working-class immigrants at a monthly rent of two to three dollars a room. Before the late nineteenth century most tenements in New York City were railroad apartments, or railroad flats, which contained several rooms in a line, usually without windows, that entered into one another and lacked a hallway. The Tenement House Law of 1879 set standards for space, ventilation, and hygiene and implemented the dumbbell design: between the front and back rooms the exterior walls were indented, creating large air shafts between adjacent buildings. In 1901 the law was amended to mandate a toilet for each dwelling, separate living and sleeping rooms, and adequate light, which brought the tenement closer to the level of other apartment buildings in the city. At the same time the number of luxury apartments increased in Manhattan, especially on the Upper East Side and Upper West Side, where three large apartment buildings along Broadway were each briefly promoted as the world's largest: the Ansonia (1904, 17 stories, Graves and Duboy), the Apthorp (1908, 12 stories, Clinton and Russell), and the Belnord (1908, 12 stories, Hiss and Weeks). The great number of apartments built in the 1920s had become less luxurious than their forerunners, for the new large-scale apartment building was now the modest domain of the middle class. The gap between tenement and apartment building was further narrowed by the Multiple Dwellings Law (1929), which eliminated the legal distinction between the two types of dwelling and united all categories of housing under a uniform set of design controls. With the onset of the Depression, luxury apartments became smaller: in the Century on Central Park West (1931, Jacques Delamarre), each apartment had only one or two bedrooms.

Most innovations in the building of apartments from the late 1920s on were made in the outer boroughs, where low-rise garden apartments for the expanding middle class were built on cheap land newly accessible by subway. Large developments were constructed in Jackson Heights and later along the Bronx River Parkway, the Pelham Parkway in the Bronx, and the Eastern Parkway in Brooklyn. Some apartment buildings in Manhattan had small gardens enclosed in courtyards, among them the Hudson View Gardens (1924, George F. Pelham), Tudor City (1928, H.

Douglas Ives), and London Terrace (1930, Farrar and Watmaugh). Many of the housing projects built with government sponsorship in the 1930s were garden apartments, including Hillside Homes in the Bronx (1935, Clarence Stein) and Harlem River Houses in Manhattan (1937, Archibald Manning Brown); public funds also subsidized the construction of such large complexes as Parkchester in the Bronx (1940, Richmond H. Shreve) and Stuyvesant Town in Manhattan (1949, Gilmore D. Clarke). After World War II, pressures to reduce construction costs and the movement of the middle class to the suburbs encouraged the development of a design known as "tower in the park," characterized by a large apartment building surrounded by open space. The design was further encouraged by changes in zoning in 1961 and was seen in such developments as the Kips Bay Plaza (1965, I. M. Pei and Partners) and Co-op City (1968–70, Herman J. Jessor), the largest postwar apartment complex in New York City. Among the most innovative apartment complexes of the 1960s and 1970s were Riverbend (1967, Davis, Brody), made up of duplex apartments facing terraces, several projects sponsored by the Urban Development Corporation at Twin Parks in the Bronx, and Battery Park City in lower Manhattan (1979, Alexander Cooper and Associates).

Tax policy and rent regulation encouraged landlords in the 1980s to convert several hundred thousand rental apartments in New York City to cooperatives and condominium units. There was considerable new construction in Hell's Kitchen (which became known as Clinton) and along upper Broadway. Trump Tower on Fifth Avenue (1983, Swanke, Hayden, Connell) became a symbol of the lavish lifestyle of the 1980s. In the outer boroughs many of the spacious apartment buildings of the 1920s were abandoned or destroyed by arson. The city made plans to replace them not with apartment buildings but with owner-occupied houses, entailing subsidized home-ownership programs. By the turn of the twenty-first century, this strategy was eclipsed by several factors. As land became less available, low-density housing could no longer be expected to satisfy housing-production requirements related to increased population growth.

The demand for increased production has been effectively met only on the luxury level, with little innovation in terms of the basics of New York apartment design. There have been some spatial influences related to "loft-style living," and the first "green" apartment buildings have appeared, such as the Solaire in Battery Park City (2003, Cesar Pelli and Associates), but perhaps the most pervasive new tendency in luxury housing has been project branding by high-style practitioners. The marketing success of the Perry Street Towers in the West Village (1999–2002, Richard Meier and Partners) set an important precedent. Numerous international architects including Frank Gehry, Zaha Hadid, Santiago Calatrava, and Jean Novel have followed suit.

Richard Plunz, *A History of Housing in New York City: Dwelling Type and Social Change in the American Metropolis* (New York: Columbia University Press, 1990)

See also Dumbbell tenements.

Richard Plunz

Apgar, Virginia (*b* Westfield, N.J., 7 June 1909; *d* New York City, 7 Aug 1974). Anesthesiologist who invented the Apgar Score. She worked for most of her professional life at the Columbia–Presbyterian Medical Center, where in 1938 she became the first woman to lead a department; she was also the first female physician to hold a full professorship at the College of Physicians and Surgeons and in 1949 became the first professor of anesthesiology there, remaining until 1959. She is best known for developing the Apgar Score (1952), a quick method for determining whether newborn infants require special medical attention. Apgar ended her career at the National Foundation–March of Dimes, where she held several prominent positions. With Joan Beck she wrote *Is My Baby All Right?: A Guide to Birth Defects* (1972).

Joseph S. Lieber

Apollo Association for the Promotion of the Fine Arts in the United States. Original name of the American Art-Union.

Apollo Theater. Constructed by New York architect George Keister in 1913 as an all-white theater named Hurtig and Seamon's Burlesque at 253 West 125th Street, it opened as a black theater in 1934, borrowing its name from owner Sidney Cohen's other nearby venture. Harlem had just undergone the cultural resurgence of the Harlem Renaissance, and along with popular nightspots like the Cotton Club, Connie's Inn, Minton's Playhouse, Monroe's Uptown House, and Smalls' Paradise, several theaters had opened to black audiences by the 1920s—namely, the Lafayette Theatre and neighboring Crescent. The Lafayette, which preceded the Apollo as a performer's rite of passage, featured acts such as Louis Armstrong, Bill "Bojangles" Robinson, and Bessie Smith. However, the emergence of Cohen's Apollo Theater, managed by Morris Sussman, eventually created healthy competition for cutthroat businessman Frank Schiffman, who managed the Lafayette and worked for Leo Brecher at the nearby Harlem Opera House on 125th Street. Though Cohen reportedly contacted notorious talent scout John Hammond to book shows, he died just before the arrangement could be finalized, and consequently the Apollo and Harlem Opera House merged, with the latter turned into a movie house and the Apollo as the sole interest of Brecher and Schiffman, billed as "The Only Stage Show in Harlem."

The Apollo quickly became central to Harlem's social life and gained national notoriety for its "Amateur Night in Harlem," broadcast live on WMCA and 21 of its affiliates across the country. Initially, the Apollo presented what was essentially a vaudevillian act, equipped with a line of chorus girls that rivaled the Cotton Club's. Despite being a black theater, the early years also featured top white performers such as Harry James, Woody Herman, and Charlie Barnet; furthermore, the audience was roughly 40 percent white during the week and as high as 75 percent on Amateur Night. During the swing era the theater acted as the stringent trial ground for bandleaders Duke Ellington, Count Basie, and Andy Kirk, as well as a nascent star of Basie's orchestra, Billie Holiday. Much to the consternation of the Harlem elite and the National Association for the Advancement of Colored People (NAACP), the theater featured comedy acts in blackface, many—such as Butterbeans and Susie's "I Want a Hot Dog for My Roll"—embedded with sexual innuendo. The Apollo also offered dance performers such as the Berry Brothers, Nicholas Brothers, Bill "Bojangles" Robinson, and the act of Buck and Bubbles.

What distinguished the Apollo Theater was its Amateur Night, which launched the careers of countless artists, including King Curtis, Wilson Picket, Pearl Bailey, Sarah Vaughan, Rush Brown, James Brown, and Dionne Warwick. The amateur night idea was a remnant of Schiffman's Harlem Amateur Hour with Ralph Cooper at the Lafayette Theatre. Apollo crowds were notorious for their willingness to show displeasure with a poor performance, and stagehand Norman Miller, known as Porto Rico, began a tradition that lasted until the 1970s of chasing a floundering singer offstage by firing a cap gun. From then on, the audience's displeasure would be buttressed by a wailing siren from backstage and a wild Porto Rico (later played by Bob Collins) chasing the chastised performer offstage with his cap pistol.

The 1950s saw the decline of the Apollo variety show, largely because of the great success of a rhythm-and-blues group, the Orioles, which Schiffman billed alongside a range of older acts throughout the decade. The theater continued to have occasional variety shows and comedy acts. Gospel acts also became popular, including the Staple Singers, Sister Rosetta Tharpe, Clara Ward, and the Soul Stirrers with Sam Cooke. The 1960s was the Apollo's most successful decade, in no small part because of the charismatic James Brown. The Schiffmans (Frank and his son Bobby) also became more active in community politics and the civil rights movement. Along

Apollo Theater, 2009

with soul performers like Ray Charles, Aretha Franklin, and Sam Cooke, the Apollo responded to the surge in jazz with hard boppers Art Blakey and Horace Silver, as well as white acts Dave Brubeck, Stan Getz, and Apollo favorite Buddy Rich, who once charmed the audience by playing drums with one arm broken and in a cast. Comedians like Richard Pryor and Redd Foxx also continued to make their mark at the theater.

In early 1976, after the community's drug and theft problems overflowed to the theater and a shooting killed an 18-year-old boy, the Apollo Theater closed. Two years later it reopened with old performers such as James Brown and newer groups like George Clinton and Parliament-Funkadelic. The theater gained landmark status in 1983 and was purchased by Inner City Broadcasting Company, led by former borough president Percy E. Sutton. New York State bought the Apollo in 1991 and ran it as the nonprofit Apollo Theater Foundation, Inc. It became home to a syndicated television show, *Showtime at the Apollo,* in 1987. In the early twenty-first century the Apollo attracted about 1.3 million visitors annually and began a significant renovation and expansion. To celebrate its 75th anniversary season during 2009–10, the theater created an archive of documents, photographs, and other historic materials and collaborated on an oral history project with Columbia University.

Garrett Felber

Apple Bank for Savings. Savings bank formed in 1863 as the Harlem Savings Bank. It took its current name in May 1983. In the early twenty-first century the bank was the fourth largest savings bank in New York State and had 33 branches in New York City.

David White

apprenticeship. During the colonial period apprentices in New York City trained in crafts through legal attachments to master tradesmen. In return for labor they received food, clothing, shelter, rudimentary education, and religious training. Although the standard period of apprenticeship in America was seven years or until age 21, terms were often shorter in colonial New York City because of a labor shortage. Indeed, apprenticeship was most common in the wealthier crafts and among orphans, with short-term labor contracts often used in other trades, contracts that allowed apprentices to become in part wage-earning journeymen. This trend was reinforced by the growth of the marketplace after independence and led semi-skilled youths to enter the workshop as journeymen at progressively earlier ages. The authority of the master was further undermined by the individualistic emphasis of republican ideology and evangelical religion, and by technological advances that obviated full understanding of a trade. In the early nineteenth century an apprentice would often live apart from his master's household and demand a cash wage. Between 6000 and 8000 apprentices labored in the city in 1820. With the introduction of heavy machinery in many trades at the time of the Civil War apprentices virtually disappeared from New York City.

W. J. Rorabaugh, *The Craft Apprentice: From Franklin to the Machine Age in America* (New York: Oxford University Press, 1986)

Howard Rock

Apthorp Apartments. Residential building between Broadway and West End Avenue south of 79th Street. Designed for the Astor estate as luxury rental housing by the firm of Clinton and Russell and built in 1908 in the style of an Italian Renaissance palazzo, it covers 86 percent of the block, is 12 stories high, and has two vaulted carriageways leading from the street to an interior courtyard with an impressive fountain. At the time the Apthorp was completed its size and full range of concierge services surpassed those of the Ansonia, its rival in luxury hotel housing. In 2008 conversion of the 100 rental apartments to condominiums was completed.

Joel Schwartz

Aquarium. See New York Aquarium.

Aqueduct. Neighborhood in southwestern Queens, adjoining the western edge of Aqueduct Racetrack between Rockaway Boulevard and the Southern Parkway. One of the first developments was a cemetery (now nearly obliterated), begun in 1680 at what is now 149th Avenue and Redding Street. In the eighteenth and early nineteenth centuries the area was sparsely populated and tilled by families of Dutch descent, including the Ryders, Duryeas, and Rapalyes. The neighborhood was first known as South Woodhaven; the current name became used locally after a conduit for the Brooklyn Water Works was

Apthorp Apartments, 2009

built in 1854–58 south of what is now the parkway, and more widely after the Long Island Rail Road opened a station there in 1880. The railroad station, paid for by the track's owners, later became the Aqueduct subway station. The Centerville (Eclipse) Race Course stood south of Rockaway Boulevard and east of Cross Bay Boulevard and was popular in the 1850s and 1860s. The Queens County Jockey Club bought land in 1892 and opened a racetrack on 15 September 1894, which was rebuilt in 1959. A new winter track was installed in 1978. A flea market operates there three days a week. In 2005 the grandstands were renovated, and 4500 lottery machines were installed. The racetrack and nearby John F. Kennedy International Airport provide many jobs to residents.

Vincent Seyfried

Aqueduct Racetrack. Thoroughbred racetrack in Ozone Park, opened on 27 September 1894 and operated by the Queens County Jockey Club. A minor facility at its inception, it eventually became the site of such famous races as the Carter Handicap on 10 July 1944, which ended in a triple dead heat. In 1959 the New York Racing Association spent $33 million to renovate the track, which opened on 14 September with a capacity of 80,000. Thirty minutes by express subway from Times Square, it became the leading betting track in the United States in 1960, when it achieved a daily handle of $2,698,419. By the early 1990s attendance had declined. The track underwent renovations in 2001 and 2006. Beginning in 2007 the racing season ran from October through late April.

Steven A. Riess

Arabs. The first Arabic-speaking residents of New York City were Syrians and Lebanese who began immigrating to New York from the Ottoman province of Greater Syria in the late 1870s. By the 1890s the area around Rector and Washington streets in lower Manhattan had become known as Little Syria; eventually other Syrian neighborhoods would form in Cobble Hill, Park Slope, and Bay Ridge in Brooklyn. Much later, Steinway Street in Astoria, Queens, would become another recognizably Arab neighborhood, the inhabitants being largely North African.

Many early immigrants started out as peddlers and went on to become business people and merchants. Some became wealthy in the import-export trade. In the early 1900s New York City had a vibrant Arabic literary establishment: such émigré writers as Kahlil Gibran and Elia Abu Madi greatly influenced Arabic letters, both in the Americas and in the Arab world. Because of its size, vibrant press, and commercial strength, New York's Arab community was considered the mother colony of all other Arabic-speaking communities in the United States, and until the 1960s it was the most influential. In 1965, when the immigration restrictions imposed in 1924 were lifted, immigration from Arab countries resumed, spurred this time by military and political upheavals, the unfulfilled economic expectations of a newly educated Arab elite, and economic pressures in the poorer Arab countries. Between 1965 and 2008 the number of New Yorkers of Arab origin more than tripled, to over 200,000. In addition to descendants of the early immigrants, there were newcomers from Syria, Lebanon, Palestine, Yemen, Egypt, Morocco, Sudan, Jordan, Iraq, Algeria, Tunisia, Libya, Saudi Arabia, and Kuwait. Christians accounted for 95 percent of the early immigrants, but Muslims account for the overwhelming majority of arrivals in the twenty-first century.

Among most Arabs, religious affiliation defines public identity, an attitude fostered by the Ottoman practice of governing subjects according to their membership in a religious community. The Arab world is the birthplace of Islam, Christianity, and Judaism, and in a reflection of this varied heritage Arabs in New York City practice all three in about a dozen variations, almost all indigenous to the Arab East. These include Sunni and Shiite Islam, whose followers worship with their coreligionists from other nations and language groups at more than 100 mosques in all five boroughs, the most prominent of which is the Islamic Cultural Center at 96th Street and Third Avenue in Manhattan (opened 1989). Also represented is the Druze religion, whose adherents are served by the head of the Druze Council of North America in New Jersey. Arabs, both here and in the Middle East, also practice Roman Catholicism and various forms of Protestantism.

Arab-owned store, Atlantic Avenue, 2009

Arab Christianity is 2000 years old; its diversity stems from the development of local liturgies and theological differences among Christian communities in the early centuries of the church, localisms that were further complicated by the split between the Roman Catholic and Eastern Orthodox churches in 1054 and by the succession, over the centuries, of alliances and realignments among smaller Christian groups. The Lebanese Maronites, whose liturgy is partly in Aramaic, the language of Jesus, are Catholic; they worship at Our Lady of Lebanon Cathedral on Remsen Street in Brooklyn Heights. Melchites, also under papal jurisdiction, were actually aligned with the Antiochian Arab Orthodox until the two split in 1724, but they still share the same Byzantine rites and liturgy. Melchites worship at the Church of the Virgin Mary in Park Slope, in Brooklyn; Antiochian Orthodox worship at St. Nicholas Orthodox Cathedral on State Street and St. Mary's Orthodox Church in Bay Ridge, also in Brooklyn. New York's Egyptian Copts, also Orthodox, worship at St. George's Coptic Orthodox Church in Brooklyn, St. Mary's and St. Anthony's Coptic Orthodox Church in Queens, and the Coptic Orthodox Church of Archangel Michael and St. Mena in Staten Island.

In addition to its Arab Christians and Muslims, New York has roughly 100,000 Arab Jews. Seventy-five percent descend from Syrians who immigrated at the beginning of the twentieth century; the rest immigrated later from Syria, Iraq, Yemen, and North African countries. Arab Jews have much in common linguistically and culturally with other Arabs, and many, particularly Syrian Jews from Aleppo, a city in northern Syria, have retained their Arabic language and cultural values at least as successfully as other Arabs have.

Although second-, third-, fourth-, and fifth-generation Arabs are for the most part assimilated and middle class, more recent immigrants have a wider range of experiences and ways of life. Those on the bottom of the economic ladder are drawn to the city's fluid service economy and work at whatever jobs they can find, living in enclaves scattered around the city, particularly in Brooklyn, and maintaining a traditional way of life as best they can. For wealthier, educated Arabs, immigration often reflects a decision to start a new life, despite the personal social costs that some aspects of Americanization may entail. Many Arabs are self-employed. Arab entrepreneurs work in wholesale and retail trades (food, clothing, furniture, jewelry) and services (automotive repair, food catering, real estate, accounting, insurance). In the professions of medicine, law, architecture, academia, banking, and finance, Arabs are prominent. Professional societies include the Arab Bankers Association of North America (ABANA) and the New York chapter of the National Arab American Medical Association. Interest in Arabic culture has been growing since the 1990s. It was during that decade that Simon Shaheen, perhaps the most well known of the city's Arab (Palestinian) musicians (as an oudist, violinist, composer, and teacher), produced a series of annual Arabic arts extravaganzas called *Mahrajan al-Fan* (Festival of the Arts) at the Brooklyn Museum of Art, bringing poets and dancers from all over the country and the Arab world for days of performance and celebration.

When the World Trade Center was attacked on 11 September 2001, Arab Americans suffered twice, for they were the group that was subsequently blamed for the event—or at least associated with those who were to blame. In the months following the attacks, hundreds of hate crimes and incidents of discrimination were perpetrated on members of the community, and, along with other Middle Easterners and South Asians, almost 3000 Arab Americans were detained, and many were deported. The tragedy had an unanticipated impact: it intensified the cultural ferment that had been building in the previous decade. In early 2002, the Museum of the City of New York mounted a huge installation entitled "A Community of Many Worlds: Arab Americans in New York City." The exhibit had actually been in the planning stages since 1997, but after the events of 11 September, the opening was delayed and its size was tripled, because it had suddenly become, in the words of its president, "the most important exhibit the museum had ever put on."

After the 2001 attacks, new Arab American cultural outlets were born. One was the New York Arab American Comedy Festival, which, since 2004, has been an annual multi-evening event featuring dozens of Arab American standup comics from all over the country. Each July New York celebrates Arab Heritage Week, when over a dozen Arab American organizations from many countries and interest groups hold performance events and street festivals around the city, attracting thousands. Inaugurated in 2004 by Mayor Michael Bloomberg, the festivities begin with the Arab American Street Festival, at Bond Street and Broadway in Greenwich Village, under the aegis of the Network of Arab-American Professionals (NAAP). In March 2008 the Brooklyn Arts Council sponsored the Brooklyn Maqam Arab Music Festival, which presented a full month of free Arabic music making in 15 venues in Brooklyn and Manhattan, showcasing more than 100 Arab, Arab American, and other artists.

Kathleen Benson and Philip Kayal, eds., *A Community of Many Worlds: Arab Americans in New York City* (New York: Museum of the City of New York and Syracuse University Press, 2002)

Paula Hajar

Arbeiter Ring. See Workmen's Circle.

Arbeiter Union. Central labor council formed to consolidate 26 German unions in 1864. Led by Conrad Kuhn, it published the *Arbeiter Union* (edited by Adolf Douai), the first daily German labor newspaper in New York City, which was published weekly between 13 June 1868 and 15 May 1869, and daily between 20 May 1869 and 17 September 1870. The union became the leading labor organization in the city, and with affiliated unions it led a strike for the eight-hour workday in 1872. Although more than 100,000 persons took part, the strike was crushed and the Arbeiter Union disbanded.

Stanley Nadel

Arbitron Inc. Largest U.S. provider of audience measurement for the radio industry and a major research firm. Formed in 1949 as the American Research Bureau by Jim Seiler, it launched television viewing surveys in New York City in 1950 and opened an office in the city in 1953. By 1955 the bureau issued television ratings for more than 140 markets; in 1964 it began issuing ratings of radio broadcasts, which became its primary business. The bureau was acquired in 1961 by the Council for Economic and Industry Research, which was then bought in 1967 by the Control Data Corporation. The name was changed to Arbitron in 1973, and in 1995 the firm stopped producing local television ratings. Early in the twenty-first century the company had about 1900 employees and was headquartered in Columbia, Maryland.

George Winslow

Arbus [née Nemerov], **Diane** (*b* New York City, 14 March 1923; *d* New York City, ?27 July 1971). Famous photographer. She began her career as a fashion photographer in New York City, studied with Lisette Model from 1958 to 1960, and became known during the 1960s as a photographer of the absurd who often captured her subjects in unflattering poses: her subjects ranged from beauty contestants to nudists. She taught at the Parsons School of Design (1965–66) and Cooper Union (1968–69) and had an exhibition of her work at the Museum of Modern Art in 1967.

A posthumous traveling exhibition sponsored by the Museum of Modern Art in 1972 established Arbus as an important figure in photography. She lived at 319 East 72nd Street (1954–58), 71 Washington Place (1958–59), where she also opened a studio, 121l/2 Charles Street (1959–68), 120 East 10th Street (1968–70), and 463 West Street (from 1970 until her death).

Patricia Bosworth, *Diane Arbus: A Biography* (New York: Alfred A. Knopf, 1987)

Laura Gwinn

archaeology. The first formal, professional archaeological investigations in New York City were undertaken after deposits of seventeenth-century artifacts were discovered during construction at Old Slip and excavations for the World Trade Center. Other excavations began in 1979 at the former site of the Stadt Huys, built as a tavern at Pearl Street and Coenties Alley and used as the town hall of New Netherland and then New York City from 1653 to 1699. Sites at Broad Street (1983) and 60 Wall Street (1984) were also dug in the original part of Manhattan. Excavations were conducted at Hanover Square (1981), the Telco (telephone company) Block (1981), 175 Water Street (1981–82), the site of Barclays Bank (1984), and the site of the Assay Office (1984), blocks built on landfill amassed from the seventeenth century onward. The excavations uncovered such architectural remains as the foundations of houses, warehouses, taverns, and shops as well as hundreds of thousands of artifacts, both whole and fragmentary, including ceramics, bottles, smoking pipes, buttons, coins, gun parts, toys, large deposits of food, and materials used as ballast in merchant ships, such as English flint, coral from the Caribbean, and yellow bricks from the Netherlands. Smaller deposits from later periods were found before construction of the American Express Building at the World Financial Center and of a block at 53rd Street near Third Avenue, as well as a site at Sullivan and Third streets, which contained important material from a late eighteenth-century "suburb."

Excavations for a new federal building in 1991 led to the discovery of the African Burial Ground, used for slaves and free New Yorkers of African descent throughout the eighteenth century. That site provided from human remains information on health, disease, and some kinds of physical trauma. A Five Points site, examined about at the same time, revealed material from the city's most notorious nineteenth-century slum. Excavations have also occurred at a number of prehistoric sites, including Ryder's Pond in Brooklyn, Clason's Point and several sites in Pelham Bay Park in the Bronx, and Ward's Point in Staten Island; at the site of such historic houses as those of Pieter Claessen Wyckoff (circa 1641) in Brooklyn, Adrian Onderdonck (1731) in Queens, and John Bowne (1661) in Flushing; and in the nineteenth-century free black communities of Weeksville in Brooklyn and Sandy Ground in Staten Island.

Artifacts from these studies have provided important insight into the history of New York City, especially during the colonial period. Aspects of community planning were revealed in a number of sites, especially methods of landfill in swampy areas, a procedure controlled by the local legislature throughout colonial times. At Hanover Square archaeologists discovered a wall built shortly after 1687 by six Dutch families to hold fill in place. A similar joint effort was made almost 60 years later at 175 Water Street where a vessel used in the Caribbean trade until the 1740s (now known as the Ronson Ship, after the developer of the office building on the site) was sunk across several lots, also to hold fill. By the next stage of filling, which occurred after the American Revolution as revealed at the Assay site, the techniques for making land had become more sophisticated.

Most of the excavations were done in what was at the time an affluent neighborhood, and some of the deposits have been linked to important colonial figures, including the merchants Robert Livingston (Hanover Square), Cornelius Van Tienhoven (Broad Street), and Lewis Carre (Stadt Huys); the well-known silversmith and goldsmith Simeon Soumaine (Hanover Square); and the physician Hans Kierstede (Broad Street). Information about colonial social life has been inferred from objects found at such tavern sites as that of the Lovelace Tavern, which stood next to the Stadt Huys and served briefly as the city hall. Taverns were important social centers of the early city, and analysis of ceramics and pipes from the Lovelace Tavern reveals not only that its patrons did more drinking and smoking than eating but also that smuggling from the Netherlands occurred during the English trade embargo and that fashions in the city were different from those in surrounding areas. Deposits from later periods have yielded evidence about changing family organization and sex roles and health practices.

Excavations continued in the early twenty-first century. In 2003 archaeologists were granted permission to dig at the former Tomb of the Martyrs, an 1808 crypt containing the remains of Americans who died in British prison ships during the American Revolution. The coffins were moved to Fort Greene Park in 1873, but archaeologists believed some remains had been left behind in Vinegar Hill; a portion of the tomb's wall was uncovered, but no remains were found. Construction of Coenties Slip Park in 2004 revealed pre-1808 water mains made of bored logs, part of the Manhattan Water Company system. As the city built a new South Ferry subway station in 2005–6, workers encountered four pre-Revolutionary stone walls that were likely part of a military battery, plus dishes, glass, bones, and a 1744 British coin. Another dig continued at Lott House, an eighteenth-century Dutch house in Flatlands, Brooklyn. In the early twenty-first century artifacts from local sites were held by several institutions, including the South Street Seaport Museum, Columbia University, and New York University. A permanent outdoor exhibition about the Stadt Huys was maintained at the headquarters of Goldman Sachs at 85 Broad Street.

Edward Staski, "Living in Cities: Current Research in Urban Archaeology," *Historical Archaeology*, special publication 5 (1987); Nan A. Rothschild, *New York City Neighborhoods: The 18th Century* (New York: Academic Press, 1990)

Nan A. Rothschild

Archbishop Molloy High School. Catholic high school for boys at 85-53 Manton Street in Briarwood, Queens, opened in 1892 as an elementary and secondary school by the Marist Brothers at 151 East 76th Street in Manhattan. Later named St. Ann's Academy, it drew most of its students from Brooklyn and Queens by the 1950s, when the Marist Brothers decided to replace the aging plant at 76th Street. In 1957 it moved to its new building in Queens and was renamed for Thomas Molloy, the bishop of Brooklyn from 1921 to 1956. In the early twenty-first century enrollment was around 1500.

Gilbert Tauber

Architectural League of New York. Organization formed on 18 January 1881 at a meeting of 50 young architects convened by Cass Gilbert, who sought to promote their artistic development. Most of the members recognized that their training was inferior to that offered by the École des Beaux-Arts in Paris but doubted whether they could look to the American Institute of Architects for help. At frequent meetings that continued for several years members took turns assigning sketch problems and having their solutions evaluated by prominent architects. After a brief dormant period the league was reconstituted in 1886 by Russell Sturgis, who inaugurated a program of exhibitions, lectures, dinners, and tours. The same year marked the inception of annual exhibitions of the best new work in architecture and the related arts (continued to 1938), and the league soon became influential in defining architectural taste in New York City and nationally. By the early 1930s the league had become staid, and it was overtaken as an aesthetic arbiter by the Museum of Modern Art, newly established and vehemently modernist. The league reemerged in the 1960s as an important forum for architectural debate through exhibitions of the work of a new generation of architects, a series of avant-garde installations called

"Environments." It also sponsored design studies and held an annual competition for young architects. Its presidents have included George B. Post, Henry Hardenbergh, Grosvenor Atterbury, Raymond M. Hood, Wallace K. Harrison, Ulrich Franzen, and Robert A. M. Stern.

Rosalie Genevro

architecture. Architecture has reflected New York City's rise as the country's economic and cultural capital. The city's architects have led the nation in innovative design and engineering techniques, making the city famous for its vertical skyline, among the first in the world. This produced an extraordinary population density in Manhattan.

Early New York City architecture was influenced by Dutch settlers. Seventeenth-century New Amsterdam adopted the style of its mother city, with narrow multistory buildings marked by stepped gables and low swooping roofs. In the late seventeenth and eighteenth centuries, British style dominated, featuring mostly Georgian and Federal row houses that were characterized by design symmetry; the use of brick, timber, and masonry; and ornate sashes and linteled doorways. The few examples that survive include residences in Historic Richmond Town in Staten Island, the Friends Meeting House (1694, 1719) in Flushing, St. Paul's Chapel (1768, 1794) in Manhattan, and the Old New Dorp Moravian Church (1764) in Staten Island.

1. Federal and Antebellum New York City, 1784–1860

Local builders, rather than architects, were responsible for most of the design and construction in the growing metropolis. They copied the work of others or relied on pattern books that supplied everything from the detail of a stair banister to a complete plan. Most early nineteenth-century buildings were small, stood one to three stories tall, and were used for both work and residence. Three- and four-story brick buildings near the piers of South Street had merchants' countinghouses on the first story and manufacturing and storage facilities in lofts in the upper stories. Until the mid-1820s the few buildings with architectural details copied those of the late Georgian and early Federal styles. A notable exception was the French-inspired City Hall, one of the first important public buildings in the city, designed by the émigré architect Joseph-François Mangin with his American-born colleague John McComb, Jr.

During the 1840s and 1850s, as land became more costly in the business districts of Manhattan and Brooklyn, houses were demolished or converted to commercial use. Residential neighborhoods moved away from the original downtown area. Brooklyn Heights and Greenwich Village became popular residential areas, with new row houses modeled after the terraces of English cities. Built by speculators for craftspeople and the middle class, these row houses were suited to the city's grid plan, which created narrow lots, and to its market, shaped by high land costs. The wealthy often supplemented their small town houses with large country houses on the outskirts of the city, among them Gracie Mansion (1804, now the mayor's residence), Hamilton Grange and Wave Hill (1802, 1844, now museums), and Litchfield Villa (1857, now borough offices of the city's parks department).

The few formally trained architects in New York City during this time were usually educated in England, France, or Germany. They took on American pupils, as there were no architectural schools in the United States; a few Americans were self-taught. Their residential designs included mansions on Fifth Avenue and the grander row houses of the 1840s and 1850s surviving around Washington Square, at Colonnade Row on Lafayette Street in Manhattan, and in Brooklyn Heights. The leading architects of the time, Alexander Jackson Davis and his partner Ithiel Town, Minard Lafever, Richard Upjohn, and Detlef Lienau, received commissions for religious, institutional, commercial, and government buildings. These public buildings were large, costly structures with complex plans or "programs" that required knowledge of sophisticated construction technology and appropriate style. In 1857 two dozen architects in the city founded the American Institute of Architects (AIA), which continues in the twenty-first century as the main professional organization. Their goals were to distinguish architects from carpenters, to improve architectural training, and to educate the public through newspaper and journal articles.

Architects and builders favored Greek Revival style in the first half of the nineteenth century. It was used by Lafever as early as 1833 for Sailors' Snug Harbor, a home for retired mariners in Staten Island, and in 1848 by Gamaliel King for Brooklyn City Hall (now Brooklyn Borough Hall). After the Great Fire of 1835, new architecture included the U.S. Custom House (now Federal Hall) by Town and Davis and the Merchants' Exchange (now Citibank) by Isaiah Rogers, both completed in 1842. Greek Revival details also adorned two innovative commercial buildings. The Astor House (1836) was the city's first modern hotel: it had ornate public rooms, comfortable bedrooms, and running water, unusual for the time. The most important antebellum store, which revolutionized retail practices and paved the way for the department store, was A. T. Stewart's "Marble Palace," opened in 1846 on Broadway. Sizable religious buildings also appeared during this period. In the third Trinity Church (1846) Richard Upjohn introduced the Gothic Revival style to American religious architecture, followed by St. Patrick's Cathedral, begun in 1853 and designed by James Renwick, Jr., in a style inspired by German Gothic.

In the 1850s two technological advances originated in the city. The use of cast iron for mass-produced structural columns and ornamental facade elements, first promoted in the 1840s by James Bogardus as a means of fireproofing, made it possible to build larger and better-lit commercial buildings (see CAST-IRON ARCHITECTURE); and after the introduction of the passenger elevator, first installed in 1857 in the Haughwout Building at Broadway and Broome streets, space in the upper stories of buildings became more accessible and profitable. These innovations later led to the development of steel cage construction and the skyscraper. Cast-iron architecture flourished from the mid-1850s to the 1880s and created the streetscape of loft buildings and stores in the neighborhoods of lower Manhattan now called Tribeca and SoHo, and in Williamsburg and the Fulton Ferry district in Brooklyn.

2. From the Civil War to the Depression, 1860–1930

From the 1870s through the 1930s, the skyline of Manhattan took shape and became world famous as the city's population soared to seven million from one million. The development of steel cage construction, along with fast elevators, electric lighting, and sophisticated heating and plumbing systems, made possible the construction of SKYSCRAPERS, which became icons of the city's global importance. The skyscraper and the apartment building became the two definitive architectural norms.

In 1913 Cass Gilbert's Woolworth Building was one of the first skyscrapers in lower Manhattan. Most skyscrapers were office towers housing national and international corporations and their thousands of workers. Along with the Woolworth Building, the Singer Building (1908) and Metropolitan Life Insurance headquarters (1909) became world famous, as did the Empire State Building (1931), reaching the equivalent of 102 stories and setting a record for height that remained unbroken for more than 40 years. The completion of the 40-story Equitable Building at 120 Broadway in 1915 helped to ensure the passage in 1916 of the city's first comprehensive zoning code, which regulated land use and limited the height of buildings according to a formula involving their street frontage. As a result, the straight tower was replaced by the setback form, some striking examples of which are the Williamsburgh Savings Tower (1929, Halsey, McCormack and Helmer), the only skyscraper built outside Manhattan; the Chrysler Building (1930, William van Alen); the Bank of Manhattan Building (1930, H. Craig Severance with Yasuo Masui); and the

Cities Service Building (1932, Clinton and Russell).

Entertainment architecture boomed and produced opulent buildings such as Carnegie Hall (1891), the Brooklyn Academy of Music (1907), the Metropolitan Opera (1883), and the Palladium (1949); these had fantastic ornamentation ranging in style from Baroque to Egyptian. During the 1920s and 1930s majestic movie houses were built for the national chains of Loews and Paramount. A few firms specialized in such projects, such as Rapp and Rapp, and Herts and Tallant; their commissions in the city set the standard for the country. Motion-picture production facilities were built in both Astoria and Manhattan before the industry moved west. Hotel construction rose dramatically and resulted in opulent, dramatic buildings, such as the Plaza Hotel and Waldorf=Astoria. At the same time, New York City became an important manufacturing center, filled with slaughterhouses, markets, warehouses, breweries, and sugar-refining plants.

The need to house the surging immigrant population resulted in the construction of thousands of TENEMENTS. These basic multiunit buildings, built at low cost, lacked sufficient windows, running water, and indoor toilets and were so badly constructed that they posed health and safety hazards, leading eventually to municipal regulation. The infamous DUMBBELL TENEMENTS, so-called for their shape, were finally outlawed by the Tenement House Law of 1901. American architects such as Ernest Flagg and I. N. Phelps Stokes pursued schemes for model housing for the poor that originated in Europe. Examples included the Home and Tower Buildings (1877, 1879, Hicks and Baltic streets, Brooklyn) and the York Avenue Estate (1901–13, 79th Street and York Avenue, Manhattan); investors like Alfred T. White and the limited-dividend housing company City and Suburban Homes sought to create housing that was affordable for the working class yet had basic amenities and returned a small profit. Increasingly, a market emerged for apartments for the working and middle classes, built in upper Manhattan, Queens, Brooklyn, and the Bronx from 1910 to the 1930s.

The Daily News Building, designed by Raymond M. Hood and John M. Howells, 1950

The small but growing number of architectural firms focused on designing residences for the wealthy; these included Edward and George Blum, Schwartz and Gross, George Pelham, Emory Roth, and J. E. R. Carpenter. Richard Morris Hunt popularized the "French flat" in 1869 with the Stuyvesant on East 18th Street. In the 1880s Henry J. Hardenbergh created even more elegantly finished and larger apartments such as the Dakota (1884) on 72nd Street and Central Park West, which pioneered the design of the large internal courtyard. The architectural firm of Clinton and Russell made the courtyard a prime feature at the Apthorp (1908) at Broadway and 79th Street. By the 1920s Park and Fifth avenues were lined with luxury apartment buildings that had rooms for servants, and large complexes such as Tudor City and London Terrace occupied full city blocks surrounding courtyard gardens. Delano and Aldrich designed 925 Park Avenue (1907) and 1040 Park Avenue (1923); the work of Charles A. Platt ranged from the palazzo-like Studio Building (1906) on East 66th Street to the austere tower at 120 East End Avenue (1929) commissioned by Vincent Astor, which contained apartments ranging from five to 23 rooms. As early as the 1880s a number of apartment buildings for the wealthy were set up as cooperatives, a financial arrangement later adopted more broadly. Decorative styles of apartment houses of the 1920s and 1930s were varied: Georgian was fashionable in Manhattan, Tudor in Jackson Heights, and art deco on the Grand Concourse. Some architects specialized in free-standing one-family houses, ranging from modest brownstones to luxurious MANSIONS. A. T. Stewart's mansion (1869), designed by John Kellum, was the first of the luxury mansions to move to Fifth Avenue, which at 34th Street was considered uptown at the time. Babb, Cook and Willard designed the Upper East Side mansion of Andrew Carnegie (1901) and J. A. Stenhouse and C. P. H. Gilbert that of Otto H. Kahn (1918). The Astors and Vanderbilts built their mansions on Fifth Avenue in the 1880s and 1890s. "Country estates" were built from the 1870s to the 1920s in Staten Island (New Brighton), the Bronx (Riverdale), and Queens (Jamaica Estates), and successful business leaders built mansions in Brooklyn Heights, Park Slope, and Fort Greene.

Row houses, often called BROWNSTONES because of the local stone used in construction, became popular among the middle classes and proliferated in Manhattan and Brooklyn from the 1870s until the eve of World War I, when the need for more housing drove up the price of land and resulted in taller units. Brownstones were popular in the Upper East Side, Harlem, Park Slope, Carroll Gardens, and Mott Haven. Town houses, individually designed large row houses, were built in Manhattan for the wealthy, especially on the Upper East Side where such families as the Roosevelts, the Pratts, and the Morgans lived. The simplest row houses, intended for workers in the trades and factories, were usually erected by local builders and consisted of two stories with brick facades. The most elaborate stood four, five, or six stories tall; had libraries, multiple parlors, bedrooms, and servants' quarters; and featured ornate facades of limestone, brownstone, or combinations of masonry and brick.

New York City also attracted architects interested in innovative urban housing design. Grosvenor Atterbury and Frederick Law Olmsted, Jr., designed the planned community of Forest Hills Gardens (begun 1910), a gardenlike suburb of one-family houses and terraces; Clarence S. Stein, Henry Wright, and Frederick Ackerman designed Sunnyside Gardens (1924–28), a neighborhood of densely developed row houses. These experiments were sponsored by groups that favored more rational land use to lower housing costs and create better communities. Springsteen and Goldhammer designed apartments in the Bronx for the Amalgamated Clothing Workers Union (Amalgamated Cooperatives, 1927–37) that allowed working-class residents to be owners instead of tenants and to enjoy a large number of communal social activities.

In the twentieth century New York City became a magnet for talented designers who practiced in firms, contracting their services one job at a time; a few were employed by government agencies supervising public construction projects and sometimes designing buildings. Patrician firms such as Carrère and Hastings and McKim, Mead and White obtained the majority of large public commissions. Ethnicity played a role too: firms run by Jews and Catholics were usually small and often specialized in particular building types such as churches or apartment houses. Firms varied in size, from one principal employing a single draftsman to large establishments with several prominent partners supported by a large staff. Platt had a medium-sized firm with 17 employees in 1920. McKim, Mead and White employed 110 people in 1909; they designed the Municipal Building (1914) and Pennsylvania Station (1911). Architect training often took place in these firms through a studio system brought to the city in 1857 by Richard Morris Hunt, the first American to graduate from the École des Beaux-Arts in Paris. Dozens of others followed him to France, studying at the École after obtaining a college degree or an architectural degree in the United States. (Although drafting courses had been offered in New York City since the founding of Cooper Union in 1859, the city had no degree program in architecture until one was established in 1881 at Columbia University by William R. Ware.) On their return they apprenticed young students who studied the classical architecture of Greece and Italy, as well as the interpretations of the classics in the Renaissance and seventeenth- and eighteenth-century Europe that were at the heart of the beaux-arts curriculum.

Until the 1920s few female or minority architects practiced in New York City. Marcia Mead (1879–1967) became the first woman to graduate from the Columbia School of Architecture in 1913. She established her own firm in the city but built most of her important commissions elsewhere. The best-known building by a woman before 1930 was the reconstructed Theodore Roosevelt Birthplace (1923), designed by Theodate Pope Riddle (1868–1946), a wealthy and successful designer of country houses and private schools in Connecticut. There were even fewer black architects. Vertner Tandy (1885–1949) was a graduate of Tuskegee Institute and the designer of a number of buildings in Harlem, including St. Philip's Church and Rectory (1911, with George W. Foster), Madame C. J. Walker's town house (1917), and Smalls' Paradise (1925), a jazz club. Among those who trained with him was John L. Wilson (1898–1989), who became the first black graduate of Columbia in 1928. He worked on the plans for the Harlem River Houses (1936–37, Archibald Manning Brown) and then was employed by the parks department and had his own practice. Julian Abele (1882–1950), the first black graduate of the École des Beaux-Arts and the chief designer for the firm of Horace Trumbauer and Associates in Washington, D.C., designed the James B. Duke Mansion (1912, now the Institute of Fine Arts) at Fifth Avenue and 78th Street.

IAC Building (designed by Frank Gehry), 2009

Between 1890 and 1920 the beaux-arts style dominated, with its ornamental language, a preference for monumental scale, and use of symmetry, axial composition, and grand spatial progressions. Buildings in this style include the New York Public Library (1911), the Brooklyn Museum (1897), Audubon Terrace (1904), the Metropolitan Museum of Art (1902), the American Museum of Natural History (founded in 1869), Grand Central Terminal (1913, by Reed and Stem, and Warren and Wetmore), the New York Stock Exchange (1903), and the campuses of Columbia University (planned 1894) in Morningside Heights and New York University (planned 1892–94) in the Bronx (both designed by McKim, Mead and White). Among the largest public commissions of these years were the Municipal Building (1913), the U.S. Custom House (1907, Cass Gilbert) at Bowling Green, the Hall of Records (1899–1907, John R. Thomas and Horgan and Slattery, also known as the Surrogate's Court) on Chambers Street, and Grand Army Plaza in Brooklyn. Architects also designed bathhouses, precinct stations, firehouses, public toilets, and public schools; a leader in this last area was Charles B. J. Snyder, who worked for the Board of Education from 1891 to 1923. New York City supported innovative designs of public hospitals, including Bellevue Hospital (1908, McKim, Mead and White) on First Avenue at 25th Street, and Seaview Hospital (1914, Raymond F. Almiral) in Staten Island, the largest municipal tuberculosis hospital. The firm of Heins and LaFarge designed the New York Zoological Park, or Bronx Zoo (1899), and all the stations of Interborough Rapid Transit (1904), the first subway line in Manhattan. The New York Public Library engaged several firms, among them Carrère and Hastings and McKim, Mead and White, to design its branch buildings.

Other designs were also used in this prosperous period from the 1870s through the 1920s. Religious buildings favored the medieval style: the Episcopal Cathedral of St. John the Divine (1892–1911, Heins and LaFarge; 1911–42, Cram and Ferguson) combined Byzantine, Romanesque, and French Gothic elements, and many smaller neighborhood Episcopal churches were influenced by English parish buildings. Large synagogues often drew on sources that were "Moorish":

Washington Mews, nineteenth- and twentieth-century low-rise buildings, 2009

examples include the Central Synagogue (1871–72, Henry Fernbach) on Lexington Avenue and the Eldridge Street Synagogue (1886–87, Herter Brothers). Settlement houses, such as the University Settlement (1901, Howells and Stokes, 184 Eldridge Street), favored the Colonial Revival style. Building in the city was marked by an eclecticism of styles, including Second Empire, Romanesque, Italianate, Renaissance, Victorian Gothic, neo-Greco, and art deco. George B. Post, for example, designed the Long Island (now Brooklyn) Historical Society (1881) in the Queen Anne style, the campus of City College (1897–1908) in Collegiate Gothic, and the New York Stock Exchange (1903) in beaux-arts Roman Revival. Buildings designed in one style were often enlarged or completed in another, such as the former New York County Courthouse (1861–71, John Kellum; also called the Tweed Courthouse), a building in Renaissance style with a medieval wing (1874–77) added by Leopold Eidlitz.

Professional architectural associations flourished. In 1881 the Architectural League of New York was formed; this was followed by the Society of Beaux-Arts Architects in 1893 and the Beaux-Arts Institute of Design in 1916. Architects secured a position on the Art Commission created by the new municipal charter of 1898, worked to raise state standards for education and licensing, and were influential members of the Improvement Commission and the Committee of the Regional Plan of New York and Its Environs (1922–31). Architectural criticism was published in specialized journals as well as in newspapers and magazines such as *Harper's.* Mariana Griswold Van Rensselaer's essays were published in the *Century* in the 1880s, and in the 1890s Russell Sturgis and Montgomery Schuyler wrote a column for that publication. Herbert Croly edited and wrote for the *Architectural Record,* and Royal Cortissoz was the art critic of the *New York Tribune* for more than 50 years and the author of monographs and articles on local architects. Lewis Mumford made the *New Yorker* a forum for architectural comment beginning in the 1920s.

3. From the New Deal to the Twenty-first Century

The Great Depression hit the architecture profession deeply. A few large projects already under way were completed, such as the Daily News Building (1930, Howells and Hood) and the McGraw–Hill Building (1931, Raymond M. Hood, Godley and Foulhoux). In the 1930s, under the auspices of the Public Works Administration and later the New York City Housing Authority, the city became the site of the country's first public housing projects: the Harlem River Houses (1937) and the Williamsburg Houses (1937). Among the federally funded projects of the time were the charming buildings of the Central Park and Prospect Park zoos, designed by Aymar Embury. Local architects also designed post offices, hospitals, schools, playgrounds, municipal swimming pools, and beach facilities, as well as the new roads and bridges that reshaped the city. One of the few major private commissions to proceed was Rockefeller Center (designed 1929, built 1932–40), sponsored by John D. Rockefeller, Jr., who was also responsible for Riverside Church (1930) and the Cloisters (1934–38), the medieval branch of the Metropolitan Museum of Art.

By the late 1940s the International style became popular. Based on the sleek lines and modern materials favored in Europe by the 1920s and formally introduced in a major exhibition at the Museum of Modern Art in 1932, the style sought to convey an image of modernity and industrial progress. The World's Fair of 1939–40 was an example of its use, and it increasingly became popular for office buildings from the 1950s to the early 1980s. One element associated with the International style was the glass curtain wall, which became common after it was introduced at the United Nations Building (1947–53), designed by an international group of architects led by Wallace K. Harrison, and at Lever House (1952), designed by Gordon Bunshaft of Skidmore, Owings and Merrill. The metal-and-glass Seagram Building (1958, Ludwig Mies van der Rohe with Philip Johnson) and the Chase Manhattan Bank Tower (1955–61, Gordon Bunshaft, Skidmore, Owings and Merrill) were the first office towers set in plazas, a model adopted in the zoning code in 1961 that replaced the setback and prevailed for 30 years.

During the 1950s and 1960s the federal government encouraged new construction with slum clearance and urban renewal programs. Sites of several acres called "superblocks" were initially used for public housing projects as well as for housing projects sponsored by labor unions, insurance companies, and private developers. These projects contained hundreds to thousands of units of working- and middle-class housing, stores, schools, and other amenities. The largest projects included Stuyvesant Town, Peter Cooper Village, Park West Village, and Washington Square Village and Washington Square South in Manhattan; Parkchester and Co-op City in the Bronx; Lefrak City, Rochdale Village, and Electchester in Queens; and Cadman Plaza and Starrett City in Brooklyn. Although many of these complexes became successful communities, urban renewal also changed neighborhoods and displaced people and small businesses. Jane Jacobs's seminal book *The Death and Life of American Cities* (1961) provoked discussions of the impersonal nature of urban renewal projects and the importance to the city's vitality of small-scale buildings and neighborhoods. Her ideas eventually led to scaled-down housing projects: "scatter-site" building and smaller scale construction prevailed in the 1970s and 1980s. Promoted by variously sponsored local development corporations such as the church-sponsored Nehemiah Houses and the Housing Partnership, middle-income families were provided with row houses, small apartment buildings, and garden apartments, and in one instance with one-family houses of suburban character (1986, Charlotte Street in the Bronx). Urban renewal also resulted in the construction of Lincoln Center, a cultural hub that inspired similar projects elsewhere. Lincoln Center

Largest Architecture Firms in New York City

Name and Address	Founded	No. New York Architects, 2008/2007	Total Construction Volume (in millions)	No. New York Area Projects	2008 Area Projects Total Square Footage (in millions)	Notable New York Area Projects and Clients
Perkins Eastman, 115 Fifth Ave.	1981	161/182	$4,500.0	200	5.8	TKTS booth; Sky View Parc
Gensler Architecture, Design and Planning, 1230 Sixth Ave.	1965	158/139	$16,600.0	1037	20.9	St. John's University; Ogilvy
Kohn Pedersen Fox Associates, 111 West 57th St.	1976	146/139	N/D	N/D	N/D	Related Companies; Port Authority of New York and New Jersey
HOK, 620 Sixth Ave.	1955	130/142	$13,000.0	92	N/A	Canon USA headquarters; SUNY Downstate Medical Center
Skidmore, Owings and Merrill, 14 Wall St.	1936	90/92	N/A	181	N/A	Multipurpose building at the New School; Katz Women's Hospital at LIJ Medical Center
RMJM, 275 Seventh Ave.	1956	87/88	N/A	65	N/A	East River Science Park; Gouverneur Healthcare Services
Polshek Partnership Architects, 320 West 13th St.	1963	77/67	$500.0	45	0.2	Weill Cornell Medical College's Biomedical Research Building; Staten Island Courthouse
Perkins + Will, 215 Park Ave. South	1935	71/52	$5,097.4	24	0.1	NYU's Leonard Stern School of Business; United Nations Capital Master Plan
HLW, 115 Fifth Ave.	1885	65/65	$700.0	135	3.0	Google; Nassau County Courthouse
Ismael Leyva Architects, 48 West 37th St.	1996	60/99	N/D	11	1.4	785 Eighth Ave; Yves at 166 W. 18th St.
Spector Group, 19 West 44th St.	1965	58/57	$595.0	109	3.6	NASDAQ Stock Market; New Jersey School Construction Authority
NBBJ, 2 Rector St.	1943	56/54	$9,400.0	N/D	N/D	N/D
Cetra/Ruddy Inc., 583 Broadway	1991	56/73	$752.0	3	2.8	1 Madison Park; Audubon Sanctuary
FXFOWLE Architects, 22 West 19th St.	1978	56/74	$650.0	60	4.0	11 Times Square; Lincoln Center redevelopment—Alice Tully Hall
GreenbergFarrow, 44 West 28th St.	1974	55/85	N/D	85	N/D	East River Plaza; Fordham Place
Cooper, Robertson and Partners, 311 West 43rd St.	1979	51/58	$305.0	25	0.004	Hunter College School of Social Work; Whitney Museum expansion
Swanke Hayden Connell Architects, 295 Lafayette St.	1906	50/52	N/A	75	2.5	Moody's; Federated Department Stores
Robert A. M. Stern Architects, 460 West 34th St.	1977	50/53	$1,464.1	44	0.9	15 Central Park West; Kaufman Center
Beyer Blinder Belle Architects and Planners, 41 East 11th St.	1968	48/51	$407.0	159	0.6	New York City Hall; Cooper–Hewitt National Design Museum
Mancini•Duffy, 39 West 13th St.	1955	42/68	$725.0	208	N/A	Cushman and Wakefield; Fitzpatrick Cella Harper and Scinto
Gruzen Samton, 320 West 13th St.	1936	42/39	$16.0	210	1.2	Academic and laboratory building at Cooper Union; El Museo del Barrio

(*continued*)

Largest Architecture Firms in New York City (*Continued*)

Name and Address	Founded	No. New York Architects, 2008/2007	Total Construction Volume (in millions)	No. New York Area Projects	2008 Area Projects Total Square Footage (in millions)	Notable New York Area Projects and Clients
Davis Brody Bond Aedas, 315 Hudson St.	1969	41/42	$431.1	32	0.5	September 11 Memorial and Museum; Columbia University's Manhattanville expansion
STV Inc., 225 Park Ave. South	1912	40/39	$950.0	101	4.5	Bronx Adult Psychiatric Center; Spring Creek Intermediate School/High School
SLCE Architects, 841 Broadway	1941	37/48	$2,625.0	50	9.2	10 West End Ave.; Avery Condominium
Pei Cobb Freed and Partners, 88 Pine St.	1955	37/48	$155.0	9	0.2	Fordham University; St. Vincent's Hospital

Firms are ranked by number of area architects. N/A=Not available, N/D=not disclosed.
Source: *Crain's New York Business,* 2009. New York Area's Largest Architecture Firms, 6–12 April.
Compiled by Andrew A. Kryzak

Largest New York City–Based Construction Companies by 2007 Revenue

Name and Address	New York Area Revenue (millions)	Companywide Revenue (millions)	Recent Projects
Tishman Construction Corp., 666 Fifth Ave.	$2,297.7	$3,555.4	Freedom Tower; Bank of America Tower; Four Seasons Hotel and Condos
Structure Tone Inc., 770 Broadway	$2,100.7	$3,333.0	St. Patrick's Cathedral; New York University
Turner Construction Co., 375 Hudson St.	$1,900.0	$9,315.0	Yankee Stadium; Lincoln Center
Bovis Lend Lease LMB Inc., 200 Park Ave.	$1,706.5	$4,983.8	Archstone Clinton; Rego Park Center
Plaza Construction Corp., 260 Madison Ave.	$1,253.0	$1,253.0	Battery Park City; 11 Times Square
Hunter Roberts Construction Group, 2 World Financial Center	$509.6	$606.2	188 Ludlow Tower; P.S./I.S. 260
Gilbane Building Co., 2 Rector St.	$332.2	$4,166.6	Brooklyn Museum expansion and renovation
VJB Construction Corp., 555 Eighth Ave.	$325.0	$325.0	The Adagio; the O'Neill Building
Gotham Construction Co., 1010 Sixth Ave.	$306.0	$306.0	600 W. 42nd St., La Guardia Airport
Henegan Construction Co., 250 West 30th St.	$230.0	$230.0	Lehman Brothers; Merrill Lynch
Barr and Barr Inc., 460 West 34th St.	$188.0	$401.0	New York Hospital Queens modernization
Shawmut Design and Construction, 3 East 54th St.	$168.3	$850.6	Apple Inc.; Tom Ford
Americon Construction Inc., 44 West 18th St.	$140.0	$166.0	Marc Ecko; TV Guide
Citadel Construction Corp., 250 Fifth Ave.	$113.6	$173.0	MLB Advanced Media; Flack+Kurtz

Source: *Crain's New York Business,* 6–12 October 2008
Compiled by Frank Nestor

also proved influential in having been designed by a team of architects, an approach taken in designing Roosevelt Island and Battery Park City in the 1970s, Metrotech Center in the 1980s, and Queens West in the 1990s, all sponsored by local development authorities.

The number of women and African American architects increased. Natalie de Blois was a senior designer at Skidmore, Owings and Merrill from 1944 to 1965; Lynda Simmons worked on Riverbend Houses (1967) while at Davis, Brody and then became president of Phipps Houses, the largest nonprofit manager of middle-income housing in New York City; Kathryn Wilde became president of the innovative Housing Partnership; Frances Halsband became dean of the Pratt School of Architecture; Susana Torre became head of the architecture department at Parsons School of Design. Architectural critics included Catherine Bauer, who condemned public housing design in the 1950s; in 1963 Ada Louise Huxtable was appointed architectural critic of the *New York Times.* The foremost black architect of the postwar years was J. Max Bond, Jr., dean at the City College School of Architecture; from 1969 to 1990 his firm (Bond, Ryder Associates) designed the Schomburg Center for Research in Black Culture in Harlem and apartment towers in Battery Park City and elsewhere. The firm eventually merged with Davis, Brody, for which Bond worked on several buildings at the Audubon Biomedical Science and Technology Park (Broadway and 165th Street) of Columbia University, site of the assassination of Malcolm X. Harry J. Simmons, Jr., of Simmons Architects, founded the Coalition of Black Architects; Robert Washington designed the Harlem International Trade Center; and William E. Davis, Jr., became a member of the New York City Landmarks Preservation Commission and the head of the African Burial Ground Competition Coalition in 1994.

Tallest Building in Each Borough, 2009

Borough	Name	Height, feet / (meters)*	Floors
Manhattan	Empire State Building (1931), 350 Fifth Ave.	1250 / (381)	102
Queens	Citicorp Building (1990), One Court Square	658 / (200.5)	50
Brooklyn	Brooklyner (2009), 111 Lawrence St.	515 / (156.7)	51
Bronx	Tracey Towers Apartment I (1972), 20 West Mosholu Pkwy. South	400 / (121.9)	41
Staten Island	Church at Mount Loretto (1894), 6581 Hylan Blvd.	225 / (69)	N/A

*Antenna masts are not included in height; spires and architectural details are included in height.
Sources: Emporis.com, "The World's Building Website," http://www.emporis.com; SkyscraperPage .com, http://skyscraperpage.com
Compiled by Frank Nestor

By the 1950s architecture in New York City was characterized by innovative design. The Guggenheim Museum (1959), a concrete spiral by Frank Lloyd Wright (his only major building in New York City); the Whitney Museum of American Art (1966, Marcel Breuer), a cantilevered, masonry-covered concrete box; the Trans World Airlines Terminal at John F. Kennedy International Airport (1960, Eero Saarinen), singular for its expressionistic curves; and the undulating, aluminum-sheathed buildings of the Bronx Developmental Center (1976, Richard Meier) all attracted widespread comment. The twin towers of the World Trade Center (1970, Minoru Yamasaki) became the city's tallest buildings. The Jacob K. Javits Convention Center (1986, James Ingo Freed of I. M. Pei and Partners) is a faceted glass box supported by an innovative space frame. The granite facing of the IBM Building (1983, Edward Larrabee Barnes) marked the first departure from the ubiquitous glass and metal. The North River Sewage Treatment Plant was designed with a 20-acre (8-hectare) state park (1991, Richard Dattner) on its roof overlooking the Hudson to provide recreational space to a densely populated neighborhood. Citicorp broke with the flat-roofed profile that had become the norm in the 1950s and 1960s when it adopted a steeply slanted roofline for its headquarters building (1978, Hugh Stubbins) in Manhattan. The company also built a 48-story tower (1989, Skidmore, Owings and Merrill) in Long Island City, the first postwar skyscraper outside Manhattan. In the last decades of the twentieth century, postmodern architecture became popular, with its softening of hard modernist lines and use of eclectic and unusual forms and ornamentation. Robert Venturi became a pioneer of this form, along with Robert Stern (15 Central Park West, 2008); Michael Graves; Skidmore, Owings and Merrill (Time Warner Center, 2003); and Johnson/Burgee (AT&T Building, 1984, later the Sony Building).

In 1965 the Landmarks Preservation Law was passed to prevent the destruction of older buildings, spurred on after the tearing down of Pennsylvania Station failed in 1963. Private groups took on the care of preserving historic buildings such as the Bowne House (1661) in Flushing, the Old Merchant's House (1832) on East Fourth Street, and the Weeksville Houses (circa 1830–70) in Brooklyn, while the city's parks department administered more than a dozen historic houses, including the Alice Austen House (circa 1695) in Staten Island and King Manor (1733–55) in Queens. The South Street Seaport area was developed as a multiuse area for commercial and museum purposes. Preservationists promoted "adaptive reuse" projects, such as Giorgio Cavaglieri's conversion into a public library of the Jefferson Market Courthouse, a Victorian Gothic structure in Greenwich Village. Warehouses became artists' housing at Westbeth and market-rate housing at the Eagle Warehouse and the Ansonia Piano Factory in Brooklyn; churches became apartments and discothèques; mansions became libraries, organizational headquarters, and museums. The Carnegie Mansion on Fifth Avenue was converted into the Cooper–Hewitt Museum (under the direction of Hardy Holzman Pfeiffer Associates). The International Design Center in Long Island City was developed from commercial buildings that had been chewing gum, cracker, and electric battery factories. Artists gained loft space, studios, and galleries from the transformation of Public School 1, a century-old building in Long Island City, while an old city asphalt plant became a neighborhood recreation center, Asphalt Green. Unused motion-picture studios in Astoria were converted into the Museum of the Moving Image. In the 1980s Ellis Island, New York's immigration center, was restored and turned into a museum (Beyer Blinder Belle, restoration specialists, oversaw the project). The gradual renovation of Grand Central Terminal and the New York Public Library started in the 1980s and 1990s. B. Altman's beaux-arts department store (1906, 1914, Trowbridge and Livingston) was transformed into an office center and New York Public Library branch in the early 1990s (Hardy Holzman Pfeiffer). The refurbished U.S. Custom House at Bowling Green, a project directed by Ehrenkranz Eckstut and Whitelaw, created space in the 1990s for the Museum of the American Indian as well as federal offices and courts.

From the 1950s to the 1980s large architectural firms came to dominate the market: Eggers and Higgins; Davis, Brody; Emery Roth and Sons; Fox and Fowle; Gruzen Sampton Steinglass (originally Kelly and Gruzen); Gwathmey Siegel; Harrison and Abramovitz; Pei Cobb Freed (originally I. M. Pei); Kohn Pedersen Fox; and Skidmore, Owings and Merrill. At the same time, much of the city's commercial and residential architecture was designed by small firms, such as Schuman Lichtenstein Claman and Efron (SLCE Architects), which developed thousands of typical middle-class apartment buildings. By the 1980s architectural plans had to pass through an increasingly complex approval process before construction could begin. Community planning boards involved neighborhoods in decisions regarding construction; civic organizations such as the Municipal Art Society and architectural critics weighed in on historic preservation and design; city and state environmental agencies enacted measures to protect resources; and special needs organizations, such as the Mayor's Office for the Handicapped, ensured that new buildings would accommodate all. Architects took advantage of new laws that gave developers more building space in return for constructing open, semipublic spaces; allowed for the sale of air rights in return for more building flexibility; and gave concessions to developers in return for reducing the number of market-rate apartments in any building to allow for rent-reduced apartments, called "80–20."

New York City Guide: A Comprehensive Guide to the Five Boroughs of the Metropolis: Manhattan, Brooklyn, the Bronx, Queens, and Richmond (New York: Random House, 1939; repr. New York: Pantheon, 1982, as *The WPA Guide to New York City: The Federal Writers' Project Guide to 1930s New York*); Andrew Dolkart, *Guide to New York City*

Landmarks (Washington, D.C.: Preservation Press, 1992); Matthew A. Postal, *Guide to New York City Landmarks* (New York: John Wiley and Sons, 2008); Norval White and Elliot Willensky, eds., *AIA Guide to New York City* (New York: American Institute of Architects, New York Chapter, 1967; 4th edn New York: Three Rivers Press, 2000)

Lisa Keller, Deborah S. Gardner

archives. The history of archives in New York City mirrors the broader development of archival management in the United States, where a strong archival tradition did not exist before the first half of the twentieth century. It was not until 1934 that the National Archives and Records Service (now the National Archives and Records Administration) was created. New York State was the last state in the country to have a formal archives program, which was established by legislation in 1971 but not in full operation until the late 1970s.

The most efficiently managed collections were within libraries. The Astor Library, formed in 1848, included among its holdings the extensive records of the U.S. Sanitary Commission, a private relief organization of the Civil War era. The Astor Library's holdings were supplemented by those of the Lenox Library when the two institutions merged to form the New York Public Library (NYPL) in 1895. The New-York Historical Society, founded in 1804, collected the records of the John Jacob Astor's American Fur Company, the New York Board of Trade and Transportation, and the records of the American Art Union, as well as numerous eighteenth- and nineteenth-century account books of merchants from New York City and New York State. By the middle of the twentieth century, organizations such as the Carnegie Endowment for International Peace and Citizens Union had transferred their records to the Columbia University Libraries. The papers of individuals and families were also collected by these libraries and others, including the Brooklyn Historical Society (formerly the Long Island Historical Society) and the Staten Island Institute of Arts and Sciences. Archives were kept less formally by some cultural and nonprofit organizations (such as the New York Philharmonic) and by some businesses. In 1946 Time Inc. became the first corporation in the city to establish a formal archival program; others followed after nearly a decade.

In the middle and late twentieth century, the city's archival repositories increased in number and in importance, and they were found in a wide range of government agencies, nonprofit organizations, and corporations. *A Guide to Archives and Manuscripts in the United States* (1961), edited by Philip M. Hamer, counted 56 repositories in New York City; its successor, the *Directory of Archives and Manuscript Repositories in the United States* (1988), counted 168, and according to the New York State Historical Documents Inventory, the number of publicly accessible archives in the city in the late 1980s was 285. Inspired by the growing influence of social history, new and often identity-centered archives were established, such as the Lesbian Herstory Archives (1974) and the archives of the Center for Puerto Rican Studies at Hunter College (1981). Archival management emerged as a professional field, owing in part to the growing historical awareness fostered by the bicentennial of the United States in 1976. That year, New York University's graduate history department established a two-year master's degree program in archives and documentary editing. Later, Columbia University, St. John's University, Pratt Institute, and Long Island University (with campuses in Manhattan and Brooklyn) added courses in archival management to their graduate library schools. The Archivists Round Table of Metropolitan New York was formed in 1979; in the early twenty-first century it had almost 300 individual members representing 155 institutions, making it one of the largest regional archival organizations in the nation. In 1989 the Archivists Round Table initiated the first annual "Archives Week," which featured publicity campaigns, family history fairs, awards, tours, and exhibitions to increase public awareness of archives. The idea spread to many states and cities; since 2007 American Archives Month has been observed annually across the country in October.

In difficult economic times, archives in many corporations and nonprofit institutions were seen as expendable. Chemical Bank, the Bowery Savings Bank, and the Young Men's Christian Association of Greater New York all ended their archival programs; after a corporate merger the archives of J. Walter Thompson were closed and the records given to Duke University. As the cost of real estate in New York City increased in the 1980s, some corporations (such as J. C. Penney) and nonprofit organizations (such as the American Institute of Physics and the Salvation Army) left the city, taking their archives with them. Columbia University closed its School of Library Service in 1992. In 2002 the Teachers College Library closed its Special Collections Department, which had held almost 3000 linear feet (915 linear meters) of records of the history of education and nursing.

The largest repositories in the city are those of governmental and quasi-governmental agencies, in particular the Municipal Archives, which holds most of the records of city government. This collection is complemented by the holdings of the Office of the New York County Clerk and autonomously held city agency records, such as those of the Department of Environmental Protection. The records of federal agencies with offices in the Greater New York area are in the custody of the National Archives–Northeast Region in lower Manhattan. The archives of the United Nations (UN) contain historical records relating to the UN and its agencies.

Libraries, historical societies, and research institutes account for the next largest segment of repositories, holding personal papers and organizational records from a wide range of sources. The collections of archival materials in the NYPL are divided among several divisions within the Research Libraries. The largest of these is the Manuscripts and Archives Division in the Center for the Humanities, housing general historical and literary collections as well as the records of the library itself. Also at the NYPL are the Berg Collection of English and American Literature; important special collections in the Theater, Dance, and Music Divisions of the Performing Arts Research Center at Lincoln Center; and original records that chronicle the African diaspora at the Schomburg Center for Research in Black Culture. The New-York Historical Society holds more than two million items that illuminate the history of New York City and New York State from colonial times to the twenty-first century. Its collections include the papers of Rufus King, the Livingston family, Aaron Burr, and James and William Alexander, as well as extensive military records. Smaller but nonetheless important collections of original records are maintained at the Pierpont Morgan Library, the Brooklyn Historical Society, the Bronx County Historical Society, and the Staten Island Historical Society. In 2000 five major Jewish archival and cultural organizations joined as partners in the Center for Jewish History, bringing under one roof the archival holdings of the American Jewish Historical Society, the Leo Baeck Institute, the YIVO Institute for Jewish Research, and the American Sephardi Federation along with the art and artifact collections of the Yeshiva University Museum.

Among colleges and universities in the city, the largest repositories are at Columbia University and New York University. The Rare Book and Manuscript Library at Columbia includes not only extensive general holdings with particular strengths in publishing and political history, but also the distinctive collections of the Herbert H. Lehman Papers, the Bakhmeteff Archive of Russian and East European History and Culture, the Carnegie Collections, the Center for Human Rights Documentation and Research, and the Oral History Research Office. Columbia's Avery Architectural Library houses one of the most important collections of architectural archives in the world. Notable repositories at New York University include the Wagner Labor

Archives, the Tamiment Library, the University Archives, and the Fales Collection of literary manuscripts. University archives and historical collections are also maintained by Fordham University, Pace University, Yeshiva University, the Jewish Theological Seminary, and the City University of New York, as well as by many of the latter's individual colleges, particularly City College, the College of Staten Island, and the LaGuardia and Wagner Archives at LaGuardia Community College.

Other important archives in New York City are maintained by businesses (for example, the JPMorgan Chase Bank, the New York Stock Exchange, MetLife, Teachers Insurance and Annuity Association–College Retirement Equities Fund, the Shubert Organization); religious institutions (Trinity Church, Central Synagogue, the Roman Catholic Archdiocese of Brooklyn); museums (the Museum of Modern Art, the Brooklyn Museum, the Frick Collection); cultural organizations (Carnegie Hall, the New York Philharmonic); medical and scientific institutions (New York Hospital–Cornell Medical Center, the Mount Sinai Medical Center, the New York Zoological Society); and a variety of not-for-profit organizations (the 92nd Street Young Men's and Young Women's Hebrew Associations; the Ford Foundation). The role of New York City as a center of the arts and the communications industry is reflected by the presence of such diverse repositories as the Anthology Film Archives, the Archive of Contemporary Music, and archives of film and video at the major television networks.

The terrorist attacks of 11 September 2001 prompted a response among the city's archivists and historians seeking to document the catastrophe. Within a few weeks of the attacks, the Columbia University Oral History Research Office began interviewing individuals who were in some way affected by the attacks and their aftermath, eventually sponsoring five different projects that recorded more than 300 interviews. Similarly, city archivists began meeting in late September 2001 to discuss documentation strategies, and the Archivists Round Table subsequently undertook a two-year study funded by the New York State Documentary Heritage Program, identifying more than 260 major repositories holding 9/11 documents and objects. Some institutions, notably the New-York Historical Society, found themselves inundated with memorabilia such as banners and posters, which were costly to preserve and often of negligible informational value, but so laden with symbolic significance that any discussion of sampling or deaccessioning could engender accusations of sacrilege.

As they moved into the twenty-first century, the city's archival repositories faced the unprecedented challenges of the information age—challenges ranging from the ways information about holdings was delivered, to the content of the records themselves, to the preservation of "born-digital" records. Most major academic and research libraries made collection-level information for their archival collections available online via their Web sites. Some, such as the NYPL, Columbia University, and the New-York Historical Society, began to provide Web access to selected digitized documents from their collections. In 2005 Columbia University's School of Continuing Education inaugurated a new Master of Science program in Information and Archive Management. The curriculum reflected society's shifting understanding of the meaning of archives, de-emphasizing the historical significance of documents in favor of the management of current or recent electronic records.

Phyllis A. Klein, *Our Past Before Us: A Five-Year Regional Plan for METRO's Archives and Historical Records Program, July 1, 1989–June 30, 1994* (New York: New York Metropolitan Reference and Research Library Agency, 1989), METRO Miscellaneous Publications, no. 40

Mary B. Bowling

Arden, Elizabeth [née Graham, Florence Nightingale] (*b* Woodbridge, Ont., 31 Dec 1878; *d* New York City, 18 Oct 1966). Pioneering cosmetics businesswoman. After moving to New York City in 1908 to work for the chemical firm Squibb she worked as a cashier in Eleanor Adair's beauty salon and in 1910 changed her name and opened the Salon D'Oro at 509 Fifth Avenue, which offered elaborate and expensive beauty treatments. With $6000 borrowed from her brother she opened other salons and in 1915 developed her first important product, Venetian Cream Amoretta. She later made such preparations as Ardena Skin Tonic and Venetian Cleansing Cream, and was the first person to introduce mascara into the United States and to employ traveling demonstrators as saleswomen. She produced her cosmetics in small quantities, sold them at high prices through exclusive department stores, and attracted customers with innovative packaging and strategically placed advertisements. By 1929 she had moved her salon to 691 Fifth Avenue, bought a factory at 212 East 52nd Street and a penthouse at 834 Fifth Avenue, and become a prominent member of fashionable society in Manhattan. By the mid-1930s she sold 108 products in 595 shapes and sizes. She weathered the Depression partly by developing a line of multicolored lipsticks designed to match clothing. Her salons numbered 29 in the United States and 19 abroad and continued to thrive; in 1939 she bought a factory in Long Island City. During the 1940s Arden opened two resort spas. By the time of her death in 1966 she oversaw an immensely profitable cosmetics conglomerate, which was purchased in 1970 by the pharmaceuticals firm Eli Lilly.

Nancy Shuker, *Elizabeth Arden: Cosmetics Entrepreneur* (Englewood Cliffs, N.J.: Silver Burdett, 1989)

Marc Ferris

Arden Heights. Neighborhood in west central Staten Island. Some houses were built before the Civil War, but the area remained mostly rural into the twentieth century. The neighborhood was once the site of a resort called the Woods of Arden. Townhouses, schools, and shopping centers were built from the 1960s; a few of the older houses remain. The Village Greens (1972–74) is the largest housing complex in the area and one of the more thoughtfully planned developments in Staten Island. The principal thoroughfare in the neighborhood is Arden Avenue.

Martha S. Bendix

Arendt, Hannah (*b* Hannover, Germany, 14 Oct 1906; *d* New York City, 4 Dec 1975). Philosopher. After studying at the universities of Königsberg (BA 1924), Marburg (where she was a student of Martin Heidegger), and Heidelberg (PhD 1928), she lived as an exile in Paris (1933–40) and in 1941 fled to New York City. She lived first on West 95th Street (1941–51) and then at 130 Morningside Drive (from 1951 to the late 1960s). At this time Arendt worked as research director of the Conference on Jewish Relations, editor of Schocken Books, and executive secretary of Jewish Cultural Reconstruction. She was a guest professor at Columbia University in the 1950s. Arendt devoted her intellectual life to exploring the philosophy of Immanuel Kant and the conflicts facing a Jew living in a Christian culture. In *The Origins of Totalitarianism* (1951) she examined the relationship between anti-Semitism, imperialism, and the "phenomenology" of totalitarianism. In *The Human Condition* (1958) she explored the nature of freedom within the realm of politics. Her report on the trial of Adolf Eichmann, *Eichmann in Jerusalem* (1963), contrasted Kantian rationalism with the "banality of evil" inherent in Nazism. In 1967 Arendt joined the graduate faculty of the New School for Social Research in Manhattan, where she taught until her death. She and her husband are buried at Bard College in Annandale-on-Hudson, New York.

Elisabeth Young-Bruehl, *Hannah Arendt, for Love of the World* (New Haven: Yale University Press, 1982); Elisabeth Young-Bruehl, *Why Arendt Matters* (New Haven: Yale University Press, 2006)

Peter M. Rutkoff, William B. Scott

Argosy Book Store and Gallery. Retail bookshop opened in 1925 by Louis Cohen, specializing in secondhand books and initially situated on Fourth Avenue, then known as Book Row. It moved in 1931 to 114 East 59th Street and in 1964 to its present location, a curious nineteenth-century structure with an indented facade at 116 East 59th Street. Cohen used the lower stories of the building before acquiring it in the 1950s and expanding to all six stories. In addition to secondhand books Argosy deals in antique prints, first editions, and other rare printed items, many of which are displayed in the store's gallery. In the twenty-first century the store is in its third generation of family ownership and maintains its overflow in a warehouse in Brooklyn.

Thomas M. Hilbink

Arion Gesangverein. German singing society formed by a group that split from the Deutscher Liederkranz in 1854. The comic performances were popular, especially after 1863, when they adopted the carnival format of the Mainzer Karneval-Verein. It met in Pythagoras Hall in 1863–71, and after absorbing the Teutonia Männerchor bought its own clubhouse in the German neighborhood of Kleindeutschland and brought Leopold Damrosch from Germany to direct its chorus. The club built a lavish new clubhouse in upper Manhattan in 1885, and by 1892 it was the leading German social organization in the United States. After World War I the Arion merged with the Liederkranz.

Arion, New York, von 1854 bis 1904 (New York: Arion Gesangverein, 1904)

Stanley Nadel

Arledge, Roone (*b* Forest Hills, Queens, 8 July 1931; *d* New York City, 5 Dec 2002). Television broadcaster and producer. After receiving his undergraduate degree from Columbia in 1952, he worked briefly at WRCA (later WNBC) and at the DuMont Television Network. In 1960 Arledge started working for the struggling American Broadcasting Company (ABC). Taking control of ABC Sports, he transformed sports broadcasting by using such techniques as slow-motion instant replays and freeze-frames and by moving sports to prime time. In 1961 he created *Wide World of Sports,* which would become the longest-running sports show in history. He also popularized *Monday Night Football* and produced 10 Olympic Games. In 1977 Arledge was made president of ABC News. There he produced the shows *World News Tonight* and *Nightline,* among others.

Max Seppo

Arlen, Harold [Arluck, Hyman] (*b* Buffalo, N.Y., 15 Feb 1905; *d* New York City, 23 April 1986). Composer, singer, and songwriter. The son of a cantor, he moved to an apartment on West 57th Street in 1925 and played at venues such as the Palace Theater and Monte Carlo. In the early 1930s he wrote music for and performed at the Cotton Club in Harlem, and he composed scores for Broadway musicals and films into the early 1950s. Some of his songs are in a jazz and blues idiom, others in the ballad style of Tin Pan Alley. Among his outstanding works are his first hit, "Get Happy" (1930, lyrics by Ted Koehler), "Over the Rainbow" (1939, lyrics by E. Y. Harburg), and "Blues in the Night" (1941, lyrics by Johnny Mercer). Some of his pieces were inspired by New York City: "Harlem Holiday" (1932), "Let's Take a Walk around the Block" (1934), "It's a Long Way to Broadway" (1937), and "I Love a New Yorker" (1949). At age 81, Arlen died in his apartment on Central Park West in Manhattan. He is buried in suburban Hartsdale, New York.

Edward Jablonski, *Harold Arlen: Happy with the Blues* (Garden City, N.Y.: Doubleday, 1961)

Nicholas E. Tawa

Arlington. Neighborhood in northwestern Staten Island bounded to the north by Richmond Terrace, to the east by the neighborhood of Mariners Harbor, to the south by the Staten Island Expressway, and to the west by South Avenue. The area was originally the western part of the township of Northfield and at one time was the site of a station of Staten Island Rapid Transit on the North Shore line (now defunct). To the west of the neighborhood is a rail yard that once belonged to the Chesapeake and Ohio Rail Road. The area consists principally of Victorian houses, high-rise apartment buildings, and small businesses. Many of the oldest houses belonged to oystermen in the nineteenth century. Arlington has grown considerably since the 1980s; major developments have included Arlington Terrace and Heron Place Apartments.

Martha S. Bendix

Armenian Apostolic Orthodox Church. The first Armenian liturgy was offered at Grace Episcopal Church on 22 September 1889 by Hosvep Sarajian. After resigning from his missionary assignment in 1894 he left the United States, was consecrated a bishop in Armenia, and returned to America in October 1898; he established his headquarters in Worcester, Massachusetts, and in 1927 moved to New York City, where the church rented space until May 1949 and then occupied a complex at St. Vartan Cathedral, at 630 Second Avenue. Before 1920 an administrative split within the church formed two parishes, each named St. Gregory the Illuminator: the older, at 221 East 27th Street, became known as St. Illuminator's Cathedral; the other began in a rented space at 337 East 17th Street, made several moves within midtown, and from 1950 was located on East 35th Street. St. Vartan Cathedral was rebuilt as a diocesan cathedral; it absorbed St. Gregory's parish and was consecrated as St. Vartan on 28 April 1968.

The Holy Cross Church of Armenia (580 West 187th Street), purchased in 1928 and rebuilt in 1952–53, houses the tomb of the diocesan primate Archbishop Ghevont Tourian, who was assassinated on 24 December 1933. In Queens the Armenian Church of the Holy Martyrs (209–15 Horace Harding Expressway) was completed in 1955. The St. Sarkis Church of Bayside was destroyed by lightning on 21 May 1985; the new St. Sarkis Church was built in Douglaston in 1990. Early in the twenty-first century the Armenian church had about 50,000 adherents in New York City.

Arten Ashjian

Armenian Evangelical Church. Dating from 1921, the Armenian Evangelical Church at 152 East 34th Street is the oldest of the 13 Armenian church buildings (Protestant, Roman Catholic, or Orthodox) in New York's five boroughs. In 1881 a series of Manhattan prayer meetings was begun by the Reverend Garabed Nergararian upon his arrival from Constantinople. These meetings grew over the years, and on 14 November 1896 the congregation held its first Sunday service as the Armenian Evangelical Church, in rented space on East 13th Street. With the influx of Armenian refugees following the 1915 Turkish massacre of Christian Armenians, the church in 1921 purchased the imposing building it currently occupies (a former bank). This is the flagship church among the 32 congregations in the Armenian Evangelical Union of North America. This church had had 15 pastors by the time it celebrated its 100th anniversary in 1996, which also marked the 150th anniversary of the origin of Armenian Protestantism on 1 July 1846 in Constantinople.

Harold Takooshian

Armenians. Armenians descend from an ancient ethnic group that inhabited eastern Anatolia (now in Turkey) from 800 B.C. The first Armenian in the United States, a sericulturist known as Martin the Armenian, arrived at the Virginia colony in 1619, and Armenians settled in New York City from the 1830s. The 70 Armenians in the United States before 1870 included Khachadur Osganian, who became president of the New York Press Club and wrote *The Sultan and His People* (1857), a popular book introducing Americans to the Ottoman Empire; and pharmacist Kristapor Seropian, who invented the durable green dye still used in U.S. currency. During the nineteenth century many Armenians developed successful import-export firms (some dealing in Oriental rugs); others became craftspeople or managers in the photoengraving trade.

After the Ottoman Empire began its decline in 1890, Armenians were systematically persecuted by Turkish authorities. About 64,000 Armenian refugees reached the United States by 1914, and another 30,771 arrived between 1919 and 1924. Perhaps 20,000 remained in New York City, where they concentrated in the East 20s or Washington Heights in Manhattan. A vibrant first-person account of this Armenian community later appeared in the best-selling novel *A House Full of Love* (1954) by Marjorie Housepian Dobkin.

In 1915 a group of business leaders led by Cleveland H. Dodge met at 1 Madison Avenue to form the Near East Relief Foundation, which aided Christian victims of the Ottoman Empire, most of whom were Armenians; by 1930 it had sent $110 million overseas, more than any other humanitarian organization in history up to that time. In the 1920s Armenian political parties reestablished themselves in the city, and the continuation of old rivalries resulted in bloodshed. On Christmas Eve 1933 members of the Armenian Revolutionary Federation (known as Dashnags) assassinated the Armenian archbishop of New York, Leon Elisee Tourian, during Mass at the altar of the Holy Cross Church of Armenia, causing a deep schism within the Armenian Apostolic Church of North America (as a result of which the parishes of the original diocese and the new prelacy are now under separate archbishops). The next phase of immigration (1948–91) brought an additional 70,300 Armenians to the United States from the Soviet Union and a somewhat larger number from Eastern Europe and the Muslim countries of the Middle East. Perhaps 10 percent of these immigrants settled in New York City.

The Armenian community remains factional, especially in religious affairs. In the United States more than 85 percent of Armenians identify with the Armenian Apostolic Church of North America; about 10 percent are Protestant and 3 percent Roman Catholic. As of 2008, 10 of the 19 Armenian churches in Greater New York are in the city's five boroughs, including the Armenian cathedral at 34th Street and Second Avenue (headquarters of the Eastern Diocese of the Armenian Apostolic Church of North America), seven Orthodox Apostolic churches (four under the diocese, two under the prelacy), one Armenian Catholic cathedral, and one Protestant church.

The *Armenian Reporter International,* by far the largest of a dozen U.S. Armenian weeklies, was launched in Queens in 1967 by Edward K. Boghosian (1927–2006); a large Armenian collection is housed in Queens College.

Many Armenians have gained notice in the life of the city, such as political reformer Edward N. Costikyan, educator Vartan Gregorian, and television personality Arlene Francis. As of 2000 about 100,000 Armenians lived in Greater New York, the third-largest community in the United States after Los Angeles and Boston.

Silva Barsumyan and Harold Takooshian, *Armenian Organizations in Metropolitan New York* (New York: Privately printed, 1973)

Harold Takooshian

armories. Headquarters for the civilian volunteer militia in the United States. In New York City they housed the National Guard of the State of New York and were built in the nineteenth and early twentieth centuries. Prior to 1872, only a few armories existed in New York City, including the Centre Market Armory, the Downtown Arsenal, the Central Park Arsenal, the Tompkins Market Armory, and the Twenty-second Regiment Armory; most militia units were housed in rented quarters. A burst of construction occurred from 1872 to 1936, when 24 armories were built in the city under state mandate. From 1872 to 1895, six publicly funded armories went up in Manhattan and five in Brooklyn; one privately funded armory was constructed in Manhattan. In the twentieth century, four were built in Manhattan, three in Brooklyn, two in the Bronx, two in Queens, and one in Staten Island. The demand for armories reflected the fact that the National Guard was the nation's main military body until the early twentieth century, when new laws established professional military forces (prior to that the 1792 Militia Act had required states to establish forces of white males aged 18 to 45). The name National Guard came into use in New York State in 1862; previously, it had been used only by the Seventh Regiment. Often referred to as citizen-soldiers, these volunteers were supported by private funds, whereas the armories were paid for by public money. The National Guard and the armories served a variety of nonmilitary purposes (though in the twenty-first century they were once again pressed into active military service in Iraq and Afghanistan). As membership and activity declined in the nineteenth and twentieth centuries, so did the place of the armory, which had originally provided space for drill rooms, weapons storage, and sleeping quarters. After the Civil War armories increasingly became the setting for major social and cultural events, and the Guard became known for its popular dress parades on city streets. By the twentieth century armories gradually became community centers, emergency resource facilities, and homeless shelters; many were torn down or sold. With membership in the Guard on the decline, the armory itself became an inducement for joining, in that the structures built after 1872 were famous for their clublike facilities and well-appointed interiors.

The history of the armory in New York differs from that of the state and the nation, where armories were built because of fears of popular uprisings and labor agitation in the latter half of the nineteenth century. Although the

Seventh Regiment Armory, ca *1910*

Eighth Regiment Armory, ca *1900*

Ninth Regiment Armory, ca *1900*

National Guard was often used elsewhere to quell strikes and labor unrest, in post–Civil War New York it was deployed for peacekeeping purposes only during the 1871 Orange Riots (which resulted in dozens of deaths) and the 1895 Brooklyn Transit strike. Afterward, most deployments were for noncivil disturbances, such as natural disasters and assistance during the terrorist attack of 11 September 2001 on the World Trade Center. New York built armories reluctantly, a reflection of the conviction that the city could control its own security, that police were in charge, that diversity would benefit the city, and that money would be better spent on other things. City authorities resisted legal mandates to build, claiming that no sites were available, costs were too high, and alternative drill spaces were available. The public complained that armories would produce higher taxes, infringe on private property, displace businesses, and result in eminent domain or eviction.

Until the 1870s, most National Guard units in New York had only temporary, rented quarters, which were notorious for poor quality and high rent. A major change took place in 1873, when the state legislature established a board of commissioners of armories and drill rooms, with the power to purchase or take public land through taxes and floating bonds (Central Park, Reservoir Square, Union Square, and Madison Square were specifically excluded from available sites). City politicians did not want to relinquish valuable real estate for armories or use public money to build them, but they were left with little choice after 1884, when the state established the Armory Board, charged with building local armories. This board consisted of the mayor, the commissioner of Public Works, the commander of the First Division, three guardsmen, and other public officials. Although New York State paid for most armories, the city had to pay for its own. In response, city officials pursued a policy of delaying or deterring such construction, particularly under the influence of Andrew Haswell Green, a civic leader and comptroller, who was an outspoken critic of the costs involved in supplying armories to the militias. In 1884, the Armory Board succeeded in getting the Sinking Fund to authorize $2 million in bonds in order to purchase sites for new armories for the Eighth, Ninth, Twelfth, and Twenty-second regiments; funding was later obtained for armories for the Seventy-first and Sixty-ninth regiments. A major scandal rocked the Armory Board in 1885, when the Gibbs Commission learned of huge profits from real estate deals involving land for armories; this event resulted in the indictment of Alexander Shaler, head of the New York State National Guard First Division. Shaler resigned in disgrace following two hung juries.

In the early twenty-first century, the 20 structures that still existed in the city were used mainly for nonmilitary purposes, such as cultural centers or homeless shelters. Only seven of the old armories continue to be used for their original purposes. The six publicly funded headquarters for the National Guard are at 68 Lexington Avenue and 2366 Fifth Avenue in Manhattan; 355 Marcy Avenue and 1579 Bedford Avenue in Brooklyn; 168th Street in Jamaica, Queens; and 321 Manor Road in Staten Island. Two other buildings currently in use as armories are at 150-74 Sixth Avenue in Queens and 10 West 195th Street in the Bronx. Of the nine armories or arsenals built prior to the 1870s only one exists, the arsenal in Central Park, which serves as headquarters for the Department of Parks and Recreation. The only privately built armory was that of the prosperous Seventh

Temporary/Rented Headquarters (Armories/Arsenals) of National Guard Regiments, through the 1870s

First Militia

- 69th (Irish or Highlanders) Regiment, at the Essex Market (Delancey) until 1857, and then at 23rd Street and Sixth and Seventh avenues
- 11th (German) Regiment, moved into the Essex Market at Chrystie and Delancy until it disbanded
- Fifth (German or Jefferson Grenadiers) Regiment, moved from a saloon on Hester Street to stables at Ninth Avenue and 27th Street
- 79th Regiment, on the fifth floor at Greene and Houston streets
- 96th Regiment, moved from Germania Hall in the Bowery to Centre Street
- Sixth Regiment, at the top of Tammany Hall at 14th Street
- First Regiment, over a stable at 32nd Street
- 12th Regiment, at Broadway and 45th and 46th streets
- 22nd Regiment, at 14th Street and Sixth Avenue
- 71st Regiment (consolidated with the 37th), at Broadway and Sixth Avenue
- 84th Regiment, at Broadway and Fourth Street

Third Brigade

- Eighth Regiment, at the Excelsior Building at 23rd Street and Seventh and Eighth avenues
- Ninth Regiment, over a stable at West 26th Street
- Seventh Regiment, at Tompkins Market
- Washington Grays, at Broadway and 45th Street
- First Cavalry, at 46th Street and Broadway
- Third Cavalry, at the Bowery
- B, C, G, and K Batteries, shared the City Arsenal on Elm Street

Compiled by Lisa Keller

Regiment (known as the "Silk Stocking" regiment) at 643 Park Avenue. The Seventh fought for two decades for a new building, failing to get Reservoir Square (now Bryant Park) and Washington Square as sites; it raised half a million dollars to construct its castlelike and well-appointed Upper East Side headquarters, now used for art exhibitions and social soirees. In 2008 it was in the process of conversion into a major cultural center,

Fourteenth Regiment Armory (designed by William A. Mundell), ca *1900*

Armories Built in New York City, 1872–1936

Regiment	Armory Location	Date Built
Seventh Regiment	643 Park Ave., Manhattan	1877–81
23rd Regiment	Clermont Ave., Brooklyn	1872–73
47th Regiment	Marcy Ave., Brooklyn	1883–84
12th Regiment	Columbus/61st–62nd Sts., Manhattan	1887
Eighth Regiment	Madison Ave. and 94th St., Manhattan	1889–90
22nd Regiment	Broadway/Columbus and 67th–68th Sts., Manhattan	1889–92
23rd Regiment	Bedford Ave., Brooklyn	1891–95
14th Regiment	Eighth Ave., Brooklyn	1891–95
71st Regiment	Park Ave. and 33rd–34th Sts., Manhattan	1892–94
13th Regiment	Sumner Ave., Brooklyn	1892–94
Squadron A	E. 94th–95th Sts., Manhattan	1894–96
Ninth Regiment	West 14th St., Manhattan	1894–97
First Battery	West 66th St., Manhattan	1901
Troop C	Bedford Ave., Brooklyn	1903–7
69th Regiment	Lexington Ave. and 25th–26th Sts., Manhattan	1904–6
17th Separate Company	Northern Ave., Queens	1904–5
Second Battery	Franklin Ave., Bronx	1908–11
22nd Regiment	168th and Ft. Washington, Manhattan	1909–11
Second Signal Corps	Dean St., Brooklyn	1909–11
Eighth Coastal Artillery Regiment	Kingsbridge Rd., Bronx	1912–17
101st Cavalry Squadron	Manor Rd., Staten Island	1922
Brooklyn Arsenal	Second Ave., Brooklyn	1924–26
369th Regiment	142nd–143rd Sts. and Fifth Ave., Manhattan	1932
Fourth Regiment	168th St., Queens	1936

Note: Until 1898 Brooklyn was a separate city.
Compiled by Lisa Keller

though it still serves as headquarters for the Seventh Regiment.

Architecturally, the armories are distinctive for the medieval or castellated style that dominated in the nineteenth century. In the twentieth century, architectural styles included Collegiate Gothic, beaux arts, art deco, and art moderne. Among the prominent architects and architectural firms that designed the armories were Clinton and Russell, Hunt and Hunt, William Mundell, John Rochester Thomas, Horgan and Slattery, Walker and Morris, Pilcher and Tachau, and Van Wart and Wein.

Ann Beha Associates, *The Armory: Armories of New York City* (New York: New York Landmarks Conservancy, 1978); Robert Fogelson, *America's Armories* (Cambridge, Mass.: Harvard University Press, 1989); Nancy Todd, *New York's Historic Armories: An Illustrated History* (New York: State University of New York Press, 2006); Lisa Keller, *Triumph of Order: Public Space and Democracy in New York and London* (New York: Columbia University Press, 2008)

Lisa Keller

Armory Show [International Exhibition of Modern Art]. Art exhibition held from 17 February to 15 March 1913 at the 69th Regiment Armory, at Lexington Avenue and 25th Street in Manhattan. It presented modernist trends in European and American art and had an immeasurable influence on the American public. The show was conceived in December 1911 at a meeting of the artists Walt Kuhn, Jerome Myers, Elmer MacRae, and Henry Fitch Taylor, who soon gained the sponsorship of the Association of American Painters and Sculptors; Mabel Dodge, Gertrude Vanderbilt Whitney, and other arts patrons also agreed to contribute funds. Kuhn, the secretary of the association, went to Paris with the painter Arthur B. Davies and met with the critic Walter Pach to secure the loans of European art. The controversial show was both praised and denounced in the press. It consisted of about 1600 works of art, including van Gogh's *Mountains at Saint-Rémy,* Marcel Duchamp's *Nude Descending a Staircase,* Constantin Brancusi's *Mademoiselle Pogany,* and Francis Picabia's *Dances at the Spring.* Works from abroad accounted for about a third of the total and for 123 of 174 works sold. A smaller version of the show traveled to Boston and Chicago.

Milton W. Brown, *The Story of the Armory Show* (Greenwich, Conn.: New York Graphic Society, 1963; rev. New York: Abbeville, 1988)

Patricia Hills

Armory Track and Field Center. Indoor track and field facility and site of the National Track and Field Hall of Fame located at 168th Street and Broadway in the Washington Heights section of Manhattan. Built initially in 1909 as a training center for the National Guard, the 168th Street armory hosted a number of track meets beginning in the 1920s. By the 1960s it had become one of the city's leading indoor track and field facilities. The economic downturn of the 1970s and 1980s led the city to turn the building into a homeless shelter, and track competitions ceased by 1987.

In 1993 the Armory Foundation was established to convert the building back into a track facility that would serve the community and the city's youth. The foundation refurbished the building and installed a new Mondo-surface track (a fast and durable synthetic surface ideal for top-level track competitions) that made the armory a world-class facility and one of the best venues for indoor track in the country. Adjacent to the 200-meter track is a throwing cage for the shot put, a sand pit for the long and triple jumps, a pole-vault runway, and a high-jump bar and mat. By the early twenty-first century the facility was the center of high-school track in the city, if not the nation. Nicknamed "the fastest indoor track in the world," the armory garnered national attention in 2001 when Alan Webb, a boy from Virginia and a future Olympian, became the first American high-school student to run a mile in less than four minutes indoors. In addition to holding more than 100 high-school meets and a number of collegiate and professional competitions each winter during the indoor season, the track is heavily used and sought after by local high-school teams and athletes for practice throughout the year. It also hosts children from the Police Athletic League and many free clinics in which former track and field stars come to teach and coach aspiring young athletes. The facility sold corporate naming rights in 2003 and was renamed the New Balance Track and Field Center.

David White

Armstrong, Edwin H(oward) (*b* New York City, 18 Dec 1890; *d* New York City, 31 Jan 1954). Electrical engineer and inventor. While a student at Columbia University (graduated 1913) and a faculty assistant to Michael Pupin, he experimented in the basement of Philosophy Hall with Lee De Forest's Audion tube, enabling him to amplify, as well as transmit, radio signals through regenerative circuits (1912). This earned him the Institute of Radio Engineers' Medal of Honor. Stationed in France during World War I, he invented the superheterodyne circuit (1918)—the basic circuit in analog radio and television receivers—for tuning in frequencies of the ignition systems of enemy aircraft. In 1931 he improved the frequency modulation (FM) method of radio broadcasting, which eliminated the static of amplitude modulation (AM) radio while increasing fidelity. He ran tests from atop the Empire State Building and broadcast the opening of the World's Fair of 1939–40. In 1942 he won the Edison Medal of the American Institute of Electrical Engineers. Legal battles ruined Armstrong financially and contributed to his suicide; by 1967, however, his widow had won millions in damages on his behalf. Armstrong was inducted into the National Inventors Hall of Fame in 1980.

Lawrence P. Lessing, *Edwin Howard Armstrong: Man of High Fidelity* (New York: Bantam, 1969); Tom Lewis, *Empire of the Air: The Men Who Made Radio* (New York: Harper Perennial, 1993)

Val Ginter

Armstrong, Louis [Pops; Satchmo] (*b* New Orleans, 4 Aug 1901; *d* New York City, 6 July 1971). Trumpeter, singer, and important jazz performer. After an apprenticeship in New Orleans he became the second cornetist in King Oliver's Creole Jazz Band in Chicago (1922–24). As a member in New York City of Fletcher Henderson's big band (1924–25) Armstrong introduced a conception of tone, technique, improvisation, and swing previously unknown in the city. In Chicago he made recordings with his Hot Five and Hot Seven (1925–28) that document his position as one of the most important figures in jazz. During this period he changed from the cornet to the more brilliant and penetrating trumpet, and developed a technique of improvising delightful nonsense syllables called scat singing. He began working with big bands, often mediocre ones. While appearing in the Broadway revue *Hot Chocolates* (music by Fats Waller) he popularized "Ain't Misbehavin' " and the racial protest song "(What Did I Do to Be So) Black and Blue(?)" (1929). He also appeared in films, including *Pennies from Heaven* (1936). A concert at Town Hall on West 43rd Street in 1947 marked his return to playing with small groups, which he continued to do in performances for the remainder of his career. On record he played with other ensembles as well, and he had several popular hits: "Blueberry Hill" (1949), "Mack the Knife" (1955), "Hello, Dolly!" (1963), and "What a Wonderful World" (1967). His home from 1942 to the end of his life was at 34-56 107th Street in Corona in Queens; it is now the Armstrong House National Historic Landmark. Armstrong is buried in Flushing Cemetery in Queens.

Max Jones and John Chilton, *Louis: The Louis Armstrong Story, 1900–1971* (London: Studio Vista, 1971); James Lincoln Collier, *Louis Armstrong: An American Genius* (New York: Oxford University Press, 1983); Gary Giddins, *Satchmo* (New York: Doubleday, 1988)

Barry Kernfeld

Arno, Peter [Peters, Curtis Arnoux] (*b* New York City, 8 Jan 1904; *d* Port Chester, N.Y., 22 Feb 1968). Cartoonist and writer. He graduated from Yale in 1924 and in the following year joined the staff of the *New Yorker,* where his urbane, satirical cartoons of café society helped to set a breezy tone. He also wrote and produced musical reviews and motion pictures, designed automobiles, painted, and played the piano. A member of the Society of Illustrators, he published several collections of cartoons, including *Whoops Dearie* (1927), *Peter Arno's Parade* (1929), and *Sizzling Platter* (1949). Arno lived for many years at the Dorset Hotel at 30 West 54th Street.

James E. Mooney

Arnold Constable. Firm of retailers, one of the oldest in New York City. It was formed in 1825 by Aaron Arnold (1794–1876) and his nephew George Arnold Hearn (1835–1913), who opened a small dry-goods shop at the corner of Mercer and Canal streets; Hearn left the firm in 1837 and was replaced by James Mansell Constable. The firm in 1868 opened a lavish store of five stories on Broadway and 19th Street, in the fashionable shopping district later known as Ladies' Mile. The store became known especially for its mourning clothes and also sold household goods. In addition to retailing the building was used for wholesaling and manufacture. In 1914 the firm followed many other large retailers by moving its store uptown, to Fifth Avenue and 39th Street. The store closed in 1975.

Leslie Gourse

Arrochar. Neighborhood in northeastern Staten Island bounded to the north by the Staten Island Expressway, to the east by Fort Wadsworth, and to the west by Hylan Boulevard. The area was originally inhabited by Lenni Lenape Indians. Its name is derived from that of a sizable estate built in 1840 by the first European settler, W. W. MacFarland, which was named in turn after the village in Scotland from which he originated; his house is now the oldest building on the grounds of St. Joseph Hill Academy. At the turn of the century the area was the gateway to the popular resort areas of South and Midland beaches, and in 1914 the local chamber of commerce described it as the "Riviera of the harbor." In the following decades the neighborhood became settled by Italians and later by members of other ethnic groups. Arrochar is a quiet enclave of large homes and small businesses.

Martha S. Bendix

arson. Arson has been a problem in New York City since its earliest days. The fear of conflagrations in extremely fire-prone structures made arson a real concern throughout the seventeenth, eighteenth, and nineteenth centuries; a fire set in one building could spread to others.

Following the seizure of New Amsterdam by the British in 1664, laws prohibiting arson (based on English common law) were passed in an attempt to control the problem. While most arson crimes were the acts of individuals, the first organized arson scheme was the alleged "Great Negro Plot" during the winter of 1741. Soon after the arrest of several black slaves for burglary, a series of fires erupted throughout lower Manhattan. Believed to be arson, one of these fires was started in Fort George, the key to the city's military defense. Although the supposed plan to burn down the city never reached significant proportions, more than 200 people were arrested and more than 30 executed. The city's first large conflagration was the Great Fire of 21 September 1776. As George Washington's Continental army was withdrawing from Manhattan, a fire began in the Fighting Cocks tavern in Whitehall Street. It was alleged that the retreating soldiers set fire to the city to leave little of value to the advancing British soldiers. Some believe that Nathan Hale, who was executed as a spy, was part of a Revolutionary plot in which fire destroyed nearly 500 buildings in the southwestern portion of the city, including Trinity Church. As the city grew after the Revolutionary War, the number of fires increased.

The Great Fire of 1835, which destroyed much of the southeast districts of the city, was not thought to have been arson related. A number of minor fires in the city at that time, however, were thought to have been related to economic discontent. In 1838 insurance companies called for the passage of a city ordinance to appoint commissioners specifically for investigating fires. It was not until 1854, however, that the idea became a reality when *New York Herald* reporter Alfred Baker called on Chief Engineer Alfred Carson to create the post of fire marshal. Baker noted that a number of fires of "doubtful origin" needed to be investigated and prosecuted. Insurance companies paid the marshal's salary and allowed for the hiring of an assistant in subsequent years. The marshal was also given a police sergeant's shield. Arson was at the center of the Civil War draft riots of 1863. Numerous buildings were burned throughout Manhattan between 13 and 16 July, including the Colored Orphan Asylum on Fifth Avenue. The following year, at the behest of President Jefferson Davis of the Confederate States of America, a mission to torch the city was hatched. Presumably, a conflagration would demoralize New Yorkers and cause them to seek an end to hostilities. Although six Confederate soldiers started fires in 12 of the city's hotels, the flames were quickly extinguished.

Thomas Brophy, a news reporter, became the city's most famous fire marshal. Hired in 1907, he ascended to the rank of chief fire marshal in 1915 and held the title until his retirement in 1949, having investigated more than 100,000 fires (more than any other person in the world). Brophy was called in to investigate the 1916 BLACK TOM EXPLOSION in Jersey City, the 1942 Cocoanut Grove nightclub fire in Boston (492 killed), and the Barnum & Bailey Circus fire in Hartford, Connecticut, in 1944 (167 killed). Early in World War II he led the investigation of the burning and capsizing of the French luxury liner NORMANDIE, which was being converted into a troop carrier. Brophy's investigation concluded that the fire was an accident, not sabotage. More than 1000 people attended his 1949 retirement dinner at the Waldorf-Astoria hotel.

The largest arson wave in the city occurred from the late 1960s through the early 1980s in Bushwick in Brooklyn, East Harlem in Manhattan, and the South Bronx. At the heart of the arson epidemic were a variety of motivating factors: tenants who burned their own apartments to be put at the head of the list for public housing, apartment building owners seeking insurance payouts (which led to "redlining" by insurance companies, making it impossible for legitimate apartment building owners to get insurance), and vandals who set fires in order to make structures uninhabitable so that they could steal copper tubing. The best-selling book *Report from Engine Company 82* by Dennis Smith chronicled this period. The fire department stemmed the tide of arson by the 1980s. The "red cap" program placed highly visible fire marshals wearing red baseball hats in a specific community as a deterrent to arson. In addition, the Fair Access to Insurance Requirement (FAIR) program was instituted to combat redlining and make insurance accessible to building owners in areas with high levels of arson.

The deadliest arson fire in New York City's history (excluding the terrorist attacks of 11 September 2001) was the HAPPY LAND FIRE, which occurred in the Bronx at the Happy Land Social Club on 25 March 1990. Eighty-seven people died when their only means of escape was blocked by fire.

Glenn P. Corbett

art. See ARCHITECTURE, ART CRITICISM, MURALS, PAINTING, PHOTOGRAPHY, and SCULPTURE, as well as entries on individual figures and institutions.

Art Commission. Appointed group authorized to approve public art projects and to regulate the permanent installation on city property of works of art and architecture (including parks and bridges). Modeled after similar commissions in Europe, Boston (1890), and Baltimore (1895), it was established by the charter of 1898 through the efforts of the architect John M. Carrère and art organizations such as the Municipal Art Society, the Society of Beaux-Arts Architects, and the Fine Arts Federation. By 1907 the commission had to approve the plans and designs of all structures proposed for city-owned lands, a mandate that eventually came to encompass fire stations, schools, libraries, hospitals, parks and recreational facilities, bridges, sewage disposal plants, streetlights, and newsstands. The members of the commission, who serve without pay, include the mayor and representatives of the Metropolitan Museum of Art, the New York Public Library, and the Brooklyn Museum; the commission must also include one painter, one sculptor, one architect, one landscape architect, and three laypersons. All are appointed by the mayor and serve staggered three-year terms. The commission meets at City Hall and holds a monthly hearing and confidential ballot on the fine art and urban design proposals of various city agencies. Its many influential members have included the painters John La Farge and Robert Ryman, the sculptors Daniel Chester French and Alexander Calder, and the architects Charles F. McKim and Wallace K. Harrison. Under the administration of Mayor Edward I. Koch (1978–89) the commission assumed a larger and more active role than previously: it took inventory of the art owned by the city, began several conservation programs, and became responsible for the administration of the Tweed Gallery at 52 Chambers Street, which mounts exhibitions in conjunction with other municipal agencies.

Michelle H. Bogart, *The Politics of Urban Beauty: New York and Its Art Commission* (Chicago: University of Chicago Press, 2006)

Harriet F. Senie

art criticism. Critical writings on art range widely in their aims and methods: from personal appreciation of subject matter and artistic skills, to didactic essays aimed at a popular audience, to highly theoretical treatises. In early nineteenth-century New York City painters were measured against the perfection of the Old Masters and the advanced techniques of contemporary European artists. Such standards informed William Dunlap's *History of the Rise and Progress of the Arts of Design in the United States* (1834) and the criticism found in the periodicals *Port Folio, New York Review,* and *Atheneum Magazine.* James Jackson Jarves, in *The Art-Idea* (1864), valued art that strove toward an ideal perfection.

In the 1830s and 1840s excellence in landscape painting meant fidelity to the scenic details of the American countryside. Truth to nature, a principle advanced by John Ruskin, was supported by William James Stillman and John Durand, editors of the art journal *Crayon* (1855–61), and by the Society for the Advancement of Truth in Art (1863) in its publication *New Path.* Simultaneously, the American Art-Union (1839–52), in its *Bulletin,* called on artists to paint patriotic subjects for a democratic patronage. Similarly, Henry T. Tuckerman, in his *Book of the Artists* (1867), praised genre artists such as Eastman Johnson, who met the needs of cultural nationalism while painting pictures with a moral sentiment.

Postbellum art criticism became increasingly professionalized within newspaper journalism. By the 1880s American artists turned from a moralizing and didactic art to one concerned with beauty and art for art's sake. Critics open to the new aesthetics included Russell Sturgis, Jr., Clarence Cook, Mariana Griswold Van Rensselaer, S. G. W. Benjamin, and Charles de Kay.

In the first decade of the twentieth century Mary Fanton Roberts (writing under the name of Giles Edgerton) praised Robert Henri and the Ashcan School for painting "the spirit of the people." Influenced by European cubism and fauvism, New York artists strove to be modern, which meant antitraditional, antiacademic, and experimental. Critics sympathetic to the modernizing tendencies were Charles Caffin, James Gibbons Huneker, Sadakichi Hartmann, Benjamin de Casseres, Paul Haviland, Waldo Frank, and Marius De Zayas, all of whom contributed to Alfred Stieglitz's journal *Camera Work.* Willard Huntington Wright and Arthur Jerome Eddy wrote influential books explaining the new art to the American public.

More traditional views were taken by Royal Cortissoz and Peyton Boswell, founders of *Art Digest.* Art critics during the 1920s and 1930s, more moderate about semi-abstract art and urban realism, included Frank Jewett Mather, Jr., Joseph Edgar Chamberlain, Elizabeth Luther Cary, Edwin Alden Jewell, Henry McBride, Lloyd Goodrich, and Forbes Watson. Cultural critics such as Edmund Wilson, Lewis Mumford, and Alain Locke also made forays into art criticism. During the 1930s many art critics returned to a populist standard, measuring art by its capacity to communicate with working people; among them were Meyer Schapiro (writing as John Kwait for *New Masses*), Elizabeth McCausland (writing as Elizabeth Noble for *Art Front* and *New Masses*), and Harold Rosenberg.

In the late 1940s abstract expressionism was championed by Rosenberg, Schapiro, Tom Hess, and especially Clement Greenberg, who became the city's most theoretically oriented and influential mid-century art critic. Unlike Hess, Dore Ashton, Brian O'Doherty, and Robert Coates, Greenberg was unreceptive to experimental art forms. The artist Fairfield Porter and the poet Frank O'Hara wrote with a heightened sensitivity toward postwar art, without Greenberg's theoretical apparatus. The art historian Leo Steinberg, who had written art criticism in the 1950s, was one of the first to challenge Greenberg's theories in his book *Other Criteria* (1972). The early writings of Rosalind Krauss, Michael Fried, and Barbara Rose followed Greenberg's lead but eventually moved away from what Fried saw as his reductionist views.

By 1970 art criticism had become more diverse. Lawrence Alloway and Lucy R. Lippard wrote favorably on pop art, photorealism, feminist art, and political art. Cindy Nemser launched the *Feminist Art Journal,* and in 1977 a collective of New York women published the first issue of *Heresies,* a feminist journal on art and politics. Max Kozloff, of *Artforum,* wrote on photography, which along with video art had become a vanguard art form. In 1976 Annette Michelson and Krauss began the journal *October,* which included features on conceptual art. Gregory Battcock, Carter Ratcliff, John Perreault, Kim Levin, Kay Larsen, Robert Pincus-Witten, Grace Glueck, Thomas McEvilley, Peter Schjeldahl, and Arthur Danto displayed openness toward different artistic styles. Among the most influential magazines were *Art in America, Arts, Artnews,* and *Artforum.*

More traditional critics included Robert Hughes of *Time,* Douglas Davis of *Newsweek,* and John Canaday and John Russell of the *New York Times.* The art critic Hilton Kramer left the *New York Times* in the 1980s to launch the *New Criterion,* which took a purist approach to evaluating art. His successors at the *Times,* Michael Brenson, Roberta Smith, Michael Kimmelman, and Holland Cotter, were more willing to write about political and feminist artists, while criticism by feminists, gays and lesbians, and racial minorities became more prominent. The New Museum of Contemporary Art published the writings of Marcia Tucker, Brian Wallis, Craig Owens, Kate Linker, Lowery Stokes Sims, and William Olander. This diversity continues into the early twenty-first century; among the newer critics are Douglas Crimp, Robert Storr, and John Perrault.

Patricia Hills

art galleries. The earliest commercial art galleries in New York City opened around 57th Street, largely because of the proximity of the Museum of Modern Art (1929) on West 53rd Street. Among the most important early galleries were the Julien Levy Gallery and Peggy Guggenheim's Art of This Century on 56th Street, which launched the career of Jackson Pollock. During the 1950s the Betty Parsons Gallery, the Sidney Janis Gallery, the Hirschl and Adler Galleries, the Leo Castelli Gallery, and the Ronald Feldman Gallery became some of the leading outlets of the pop art movement. At the same time, several new galleries along East 10th Street, largely artists' collectives, showed works by the second generation of abstract expressionists. In 1969 Paula Cooper opened the first art gallery in SoHo on Wooster Street, launching the evolution of the neighborhood into an artistic center. Artists could take advantage of large, open loft and warehouse spaces both for living and for exhibitions. The hub of the SoHo scene was 420 West Broadway, which housed the Leo Castelli Gallery (which moved downtown in 1971), the Sonnabend Gallery, and the Charles Cowles Gallery. In the same area two important alternative spaces, White Columns (1969) and Artists Space (1972), provided exhibition space for socially engaged art that was regarded as unsalable.

A new gallery district took shape in the East Village after the Fun Gallery opened in 1980. Within a few years the area was the site of about 50 galleries, including the Gracie Mansion Gallery, the Civilian Warfare Gallery, and the International with Monument Gallery. These establishments were run for little money (often out of private residences) and helped bring about the gentrification of the neighborhood. But when the aesthetic represented by virtually all the galleries fell out of favor around the time the stock market crashed in 1987, the district disappeared.

By this time SoHo was enjoying a revival. Several gallery owners from the East Village attempted to move their operations to the thriving neighborhood, but because of higher costs in the area, most failed. The continuing search for cheaper rents eventually led to the development of a gallery district on 22nd Street between 10th and 11th Avenues, aided by a sense that the former edginess of SoHo had been superseded by an ostentatious consumerism.

In the early twenty-first century there were about 600 galleries in New York City focused in four major neighborhoods. About 300 of those galleries were located in Chelsea, mostly exhibiting contemporary, oftentimes avant-garde artists. Galleries on Madison Avenue on the Upper East Side of Manhattan were known for exhibitions featuring museum-quality works by well-established and historically renowned artists. Modern masters were often exhibited in 57th Street galleries, while other neighborhoods like Williamsburg in Brooklyn offered space to experimental artists with little name recognition.

Arthur, Chester A(lan) (*b* Fairfield, Vt., 5 Oct 1829; *d* New York City, 18 Nov 1886). Twenty-first president of the United States. The son of a Baptist minister, he moved to New York City in 1852, four years after graduating from Union College. An ambitious lawyer, Arthur focused on civil rights cases. His success in *Jennings v. Third Avenue Railroad Co.* (1855) helped make possible the racial integration of passenger railroads in the city. He was also an active member of the newly formed Republican Party and as the quartermaster general for New York State was responsible for providing care to troops passing through the state. In 1871 President Ulysses S. Grant, influenced by Republican city boss Roscoe Conkling, appointed Arthur customs collector for the Port of New York, but Arthur was soon accused of corruption and was forced from office in 1878. Arthur was then elected vice president in 1880 on a ticket with Republican James Garfield. Upon Garfield's assassination in September 1881, Arthur became the first president since George Washington to take the oath of office in New York City. He was sworn in at his townhouse at 123 Lexington Avenue, near 28th Street. Arthur returned to the city after failing to be renominated for the presidency. In 1899 a 17-foot (5-meter) bronze statue of Arthur designed by George Edwin Bissell was erected on the northeast corner of Madison Square Park.

Thomas C. Reeves, *Gentleman Boss: The Life of Chester Alan Arthur* (New York: Alfred A. Knopf, 1975)

Mollie Keller

Arthur Ashe Stadium. Open-air tennis stadium located on the grounds of the National Tennis Center in Flushing Meadows–Corona Park in Queens. It is named in honor of Arthur Ashe, a champion tennis player and civil rights pioneer who became the first African American man to win a major tennis tournament when he won the 1968 US Open tennis tournament. In the early 1990s Mayor David Dinkins negotiated with the United States Tennis Association to keep the US Open in Queens for the next 25 years in return for 21 acres (8.5 hectares) of parkland; it was paid for through tax-exempt bonds. Opened in 1997, the stadium seats more than 22,000 and is the largest tennis stadium in the world. In the twenty-first century the US Open drew more than 700,000 fans annually during the two-week event in late summer. Unlike Wimbledon and the French Open, the two major tennis tournaments held each summer in Europe, the US Open plays matches under stadium lighting at night, and Arthur Ashe Stadium is well known for capacity crowds filled with celebrities who remain past midnight.

David White

Arthur Kill. Tidal strait about 10 miles (16 kilometers) long between Staten Island and New Jersey. It opens at its northern end into Newark Bay and at its southern end into Raritan Bay, and is lined with industrial sites (mostly in New Jersey) and salt marshes (in Staten Island). Two islands in the waterway belong to Staten Island: Pralls Island (a bird sanctuary of about 30 acres, or 12 hectares) and the Island of Meadows (about 40 acres, or 16 hectares), which is situated at the entrance to a deepwater creek known as the Fresh Kills. Arthur Kill sees considerable marine traffic, which led the New York Port Authority to deepen it from 35 feet (10.7 meters) to 41 feet (12.5 meters) in 2007 to accommodate larger ships. It is spanned by the Goethals Bridge, by a lift bridge of Conrail (formerly used by the Baltimore and Ohio Railroad), and by the Outerbridge Crossing.

Gerard R. Wolfe

artisans. Skilled craftsmen played a critical role in early America. They were most heavily concentrated in towns and cities, especially the major seaports, where they constituted the largest sector of the population. They worked in a panoply of trades ranging from goldsmithing, silversmithing, and cabinetmaking at the top to baking, butchering, and carpentry in the middle, to tailoring and shoemaking at the bottom. The most populous trades were the building crafts, particularly carpentry and masonry, that might

Arthur Ashe Stadium, 2009

employ 40 percent of craftsmen during construction season. Tailoring and shoemaking followed in size.

Mid-eighteenth-century artisans could be classified as either wage earners (the beginning of a working class) or master craftsmen, (incipient bourgeois entrepreneurs), and in the course of a colonial career they were often both. Normally a lad of 13 or 14 would contract with a master craftsman to learn a trade. He boarded with his master, who was responsible for his rudimentary education and clothing as well as teaching the secrets of the trade. Learning cabinetmaking or watchmaking took many hours at the hands of the ablest craftsmen. Shoemaking, with awl and hammer skills, took less time to master.

Following release from indentures at age 21, an artisan would be a wage earner or journeyman, often working for master craftsmen. If competent and savvy he would subsequently open his own business. A master's dwelling commonly included a lower-story shop with his family living above. Mobility to master craftsman standing was common except in the poorest trades. Artisans in those trades, even those owning small shoemaker or tailoring shops, often earned only a subsistence living. Shoemaker George Robert Twelves Hewes, the last survivor of the Boston Tea Party, was imprisoned early in his career for small debts, such were the perils of his trade. Still, artisans were above unskilled laborers, indentured servants, and slaves.

Skilled craftsmen were products in part of English guild traditions that supervised their trades, limiting admission, controlling prices, and setting rules of their trade. Colonial America had no guild tradition, nor did it develop one. On the one hand this meant that it was a more open society. Also, artisans were generally literate and politically aware and proud of their craft skills, even if they lacked the legal imprimatur of a guild. On the other hand, they were unable to gain guild privileges with regard to price control, limitation of craft membership, or status. Moreover, while men who possessed demanding skills and well-fashioned tools were clearly above the level of laborers who worked on the docks, they were subject to a tradition that classified anyone who performed manual labor, however refined, as beneath the rank of gentlemen. Lacking breeding, wealth, and education, they were expected to defer to their mercantile and professional betters who regarded mechanics (as they were commonly known) with a measure of condescension. There was no guild membership to mediate that standing.

Skilled craftsmen had a strong social identity. They dressed in a common manner, kept common hours, and shared social traditions that separated them from the elite as well as unskilled laborers. As independent entrepreneurs who owned their shops, they were freemen entitled to vote, part of the political mix in eighteenth-century urban politics. Although they seldom attained significant political positions, their voices were considered by elite factions seeking office. They could easily make the difference in factional struggles such as the one between the De Lanceys and Livingstons in New York.

During the Revolutionary era skilled craftsmen became central players in the movement toward independence. In Boston, New York, and especially in Philadelphia artisans formed their own committees and took on part of the ad hoc governing committees that emerged in New York and Philadelphia.

The period from 1790 to 1830 was the golden age of the American craftsman. The era left a great legacy in craftsmanship; federal furniture remains the greatest craft work produced in the American experience, and artisan crafts gave birth to the American labor movement and to manufacturing and entrepreneurship innovation.

The work of such cabinetmakers as Duncan Phyfe and Charles-Honoré Lannuier, to name but two, are almost priceless in the antique market of the twenty-first century. Replacing the Chippendale style that dominated the eighteenth century, a style that combined Chinese, rococo, and pseudo-Gothic styles in ornately carved furniture, was a new style emphasizing grace, linearity, proportion, and artful display of color, including inlays and painted designs. Based on neoclassical design, this new design became popular in England beginning in the 1770s. American furniture and craftsmanship drew on the English, Greek, and Roman models but with subtle differences in proportions. Given the spirit of republicanism that pervaded the era, it is not surprising that much of the furniture and silver and grandfather clocks and other fine works displayed American eagles and other symbols of the new American nation, blending them with classical republican symbols.

The business of a craft in the early national period was more extensive than in the colonial era. First, independence meant the opportunity to enter the marketplace. Craftsmen were deft users of advertisement, credit, and banking. Indeed, New York in 1810 incorporated the Mechanics Bank, the highest capitalized bank ($1.5 million), which specified that $600,000 be devoted to mechanics. Duncan Phyfe employed more than 100 journeymen, with sections of turners, upholsterers, carvers, and gilders. His quarters included a workshop, a warehouse, and display rooms. Furniture was built and stocked in Manhattan, ranging in quality, for sale to the mercantile elite in the city and to brokers in the West Indies and other American cities.

Many crafts prospered with the economic growth of the Napoleonic Wars. Shipbuilding contractors employed large numbers of craftsmen in production of clipper and naval vessels. In construction master builders would contract to construct a home and then hire carpenters, masons, and stonecutters. The city's most common crafts, notably printing, cabinetmaking, construction, shoemaking, and tailoring, became large-scale enterprises requiring considerable capital investment; type and printing presses, for example, cost well beyond the means of an aspiring journeyman. In these trades masters tended to become cost-conscious employers rather than the paternal master craftsman who nurtured journeymen and apprentices on their way to master standing. Journeymen, as well, had to accept that fact that they were unlikely to become master craftsmen. In so doing, journeymen formed their own benevolent associations to provide benefits in case of illness or death, and negotiate with employers. More and more journeymen lived in boardinghouses rather than with masters, and more apprentices left their indentures early for wages in crafts that demanded less skill.

In the age of Andrew Jackson the labor supply was increased by the influx of Irish and German immigrants. In addition, work now turned to ready made or "slop" production rather than custom orders. Masters became foremen who were pressured by competition to lower wages. A few highly skilled cutters might do well, as would a number of industrialists, but the average wage for an artisan slipped below the subsistence level, and all family members had to work to stay afloat. Not surprisingly, artisans resented the loss of their income and standing and in 1829 organized a Workingman's Party that was influenced by radical thinkers such as Thomas Skidmore, who called for the equalization of property, and George Henry Evans, who demanded free land distribution. This party lasted only a couple of years and was beset by divisions, but the new economy pushed artisans to form stronger unions such as, in New York City, the General Trades Union that called 40 strikes and included 50 separate unions in the early 1830s. The union movement was hurt by the Panic of 1837 but reemerged in the 1850s.

Artisans became the core of the emerging working class of America, forming organizations that would lead to the modern labor unions and third parties that would offer ideas that would influence major party politics in years to come.

Howard B. Rock, *The New York City Artisan, 1789–1825: A Documentary History* (Albany: SUNY Press, 1989); Howard B. Rock, *Artisans of the New Republic: The Tradesmen of New York City in the Early Republic* (New York: New York University Press, 1979); Sean Wilentz, *Chants Democratic: New York City and the Rise of the American Working Class, 1788–1850* (New York: Oxford University Press, 1984)

Howard Rock

Artkraft Strauss Sign Corporation. Firm of billboard and sign makers formed in 1935 by Jacob Starr, a Russian electrician. In the 1930s Starr was among the first advertisers to use electric signs to promote motion pictures. Douglas Leigh, a designer for the firm in the 1950s, created such well-known signs as one for Camel cigarettes on the Hotel Claridge that depicted a man blowing smoke rings (with steam provided by Consolidated Edison) and one for Pepsi-Cola atop the Bond Building in which the company's logotype glimmered behind a waterfall that circulated 10,000 gallons (38,000 liters) of water. Artkraft Strauss later controlled most of the sign display space in Times Square, where it was also responsible for lowering the "time ball" at midnight on New Year's Eve. In 2000 the firm employed more than 170 artists, designers, engineers, carpenters, welders, electricians, plumbers, and sign painters to build its signs, which are as large as 1000 square feet (93 square meters).

Kathleen Hulser

Art Students League. Art school founded in 1875 as an offshoot of the National Academy of Design. Founded by a group of male students from the academy, along with several female artists, it sought to be a more liberally minded school for aspiring artists. The first classes were held in rented rooms on the top floor of a building on the corner of Fifth Avenue and 16th Street. In 1878 the league received a charter from New York State establishing a 12-member Board of Control, a governing council including no fewer than three students from the school. In 1892, after assisting in the founding of the American Fine Arts Society, the league, along with several other arts associations, commissioned a headquarters on 57th Street between Broadway and Seventh Avenue. This landmarked building designed by Henry J. Hardenbergh has been the location of the school's main campus ever since. Many of the country's most popular and influential artists have either taught or studied at the Art Students League. Early instructors included Augustus Saint-Gaudens, Daniel Chester French, Thomas Eakins, Thomas Hart Benton, and Childe Hassam. The league's influence stretched into the twentieth century with George Bellows, Helen Frankenthaler, Georgia O'Keeffe, Norman Rockwell, Man Ray, Jackson Pollock, Robert Rauschenberg, Roy Lichtenstein, and Mark Rothko all maintaining some connection to the school. The school opened a second campus in Sparkill, New York, in the Hudson River Valley in 1995.

Anne Epstein

Art Students League (building designed by Henry J. Hardenbergh), ca 1900

Arverne. Neighborhood on Rockaway Peninsula in southeastern Queens. It began as a number of streets and villas laid out in April 1882 between Beach 47th and Beach 74th streets by the developer Remington Vernam, whose signature on checks, "R. Vernam," inspired the community's name. A fashionable resort between 1888 and 1908, the neighborhood declined in the 1950s owing to an increase in low-income housing. The area became an urban-renewal site in 1964 and in 1990 was sold by the city to private companies for the expansion of condominiums. Two new and upscale projects, Waters Edge and Waters Edge II, were completed in 1999 and 2001. Arverne by the Sea is an ongoing and larger high-end development of one- and two-family homes. Plans for the Arverne by the Sea community include a new school, parks, a transportation center, retail space, and a Young Men's Christian Association.

Vincent Seyfried

Ashbery, John (Lawrence) (*b* Rochester, N.Y., 28 July 1927). Poet and art critic. He published poems in a number of well-known literary magazines and anthologies by the late 1940s. After studying at Harvard College (BA in English 1949) and Columbia University (MA 1951), he worked as a copywriter for Oxford University Press (1951–54) and McGraw–Hill (1954–55). During these years he became the most prominent member of the New York School of poets. In 1958 he moved to Paris, and after returning to New York City in the autumn of 1965 he became the executive editor of *Art News*, a position he held until 1972. In 1983 Ashbery received the New York City Mayor's Award of Honor for Arts and Culture. In 2006 April 7th was declared "'John Ashbery Day' in the City of New York" by the New York City Council in conjunction with a three-day tribute to the artist's work at the New School's John Ashbery Festival. Ashbery has published about 30 volumes of learned, witty, elliptical poetry informed by a strong visual sense, including *Self-Portrait in a Convex Mirror* (1975, Pulitzer Prize), and half a dozen plays; translated (sometimes under the name Jonas Berry) and edited a dozen other volumes; and taught at Brooklyn College, New York University, and Bard College.

Allen J. Share

Ashcan School. Popular name for a group of realist artists, including John Sloan, Stuart Davis, Maurice Becker, George Luks, William Glackens, Everett Shinn, Glenn O. Coleman, and Henry Glintenkamp, who drew naturalist depictions of street life for the radical socialist publication *The Masses* in the early twentieth century. They were also influenced by the growth of visual advertisements and commercial art in the entertainment and fashion industries. The term (also Ash Can School) was coined in March 1916 by the cartoonist Art Young and was intended to be derogatory, but it soon lost its negative connotations and came to be applied to all the early realists, including Robert Henri and George Bellows.

Rebecca Zurier, *Picturing the City: Urban Vision and the Ashcan School* (Berkeley: University of California Press, 2006)

Patricia Hills, Meghan Lalonde

Asia Society. International nonprofit organization created to initiate awareness of Asian culture and to strengthen relationships and cultural understanding between Asians and Americans. Founded in 1965 by John D. Rockefeller III, the Asia Society has headquarters at 725 Park Avenue and 70th Street. The society offers art exhibitions, including a collection of nearly 300 pieces of Asian art, dating from 2000 B.C.E. Additionally, the society holds dance and music performances, films, and lectures, and produces publications to educate Americans about the 30 countries and their respective cultures that compose the Asia–Pacific region, including Japan, China, Korea, Iran, New Zealand, and others.

Stephanie Miller

Asimov, Isaac (*b* Petrovichi, Russia, 2 Jan 1920; *d* New York City, 6 April 1992). Science fiction writer. His family emigrated from Russia to the East New York neighborhood of Brooklyn when he was three years old. He spoke both Yiddish and English at home, graduated from Boys' High School at the age of 15, and attended Columbia University (BS 1939, MA 1941, PhD 1948 in chemistry); he taught biochemistry at Boston University from 1949 to 1958. He sold his first science fiction story at age 18. A prolific writer, Asimov consistently released between 10 and 12 books a year, including the *Foundation* and *Robot* series. Although his best-known works were science fiction novels and stories, he also wrote nonfiction, history, mysteries, and literary guides to the Bible and the works of Shakespeare. In 1975 Asimov moved into the Park Ten Apartments overlooking Central Park with his second wife, Janet. He lived there until his death from complications associated with the human immunodeficiency virus, which he contracted from a blood transfusion during heart surgery in 1983.

James E. Mooney, Anne Epstein

ASPCA. See American Society for the Prevention of Cruelty to Animals.

Aspinwall, William Henry (*b* New York City, 16 Dec 1807; *d* New York City, 18 Jan 1875). Merchant. After attending public schools he worked as an apprentice in the mercantile firm of his mother's brothers, G. G. and S. Howland, and by the age of 30 was a partner in Howland and Aspinwall, the city's largest mercantile firm. He set up railroads and steamship lines in Latin America in time to profit from the traffic of miners across the Isthmus of Panama during the California gold rush and by the time of the Civil War was among the city's wealthiest men. Aspinwall supported Abraham Lincoln, formed the Union League Club, and amassed an art collection that he opened to the public; he was also a director of the Lenox Library and the Chamber of Commerce.

James E. Mooney

William Henry Aspinwall

ASPIRA. Nonprofit organization formed in 1961 in New York City by Antonia Pantoja and other Puerto Rican leaders. ASPIRA engenders Puerto Rican leadership development through educational attainment. School-based ASPIRA chapters, youth conferences, and career, college, and financial aid counseling encourage young Puerto Ricans to complete high school and attend college. Thousands of ASPIRA graduates have become leaders in the public and private sectors, including politician Fernando Ferrer, actor Jimmy Smits, journalist Aída Alvarez, and educator Isaura Santiago. In 1972 the Puerto Rican Legal Defense and Education Fund represented the group in a suit against the New York City Board of Education. The resulting consent decree mandated the provision of transitional bilingual education programs in New York City. Serving Puerto Rican and Latino youth beyond New York City, ASPIRA of America was formed in 1968, with offices in six states, Puerto Rico, and Washington, D.C.

Antonia Pantoja, *Memoir of a Visionary* (Houston: Arte Público Press, 2002)

Virginia Sánchez Korrol

Associated Press [AP]. News service formed in 1848 by six newspapers in New York City: the *Sun*, the *New York Herald*, the *Courier and Enquirer*, the *Journal of Commerce*, the *New York Tribune*, and the *New York Express*. The original members were joined in 1851 by the *New York Times*. The organization faced competition from the Western Associated Press (1865), which criticized it for monopolistic practices in gathering news and setting prices. An investigation in 1891 revealed that several principals of the AP had entered into a secret agreement with a rival organization, a disclosure that led to the complete reformation of the service in 1892 as a nonprofit cooperative called the Associated Press of Illinois. In 1900 the service reincorporated in New York State and took its present name, while retaining its nonprofit cooperative status.

The AP grew rapidly under the direction of Kent Cooper from 1925 to 1948, adding a photographic service in 1927 and a wirephoto network in 1935, and greatly enlarging its overseas distribution. In later years it expanded into radio, television, automated picture reception, and satellite transmission. In 2006 the AP had 242 bureaus worldwide, providing material for over 10,000 subscribers in 121 different countries, and its headquarters were at 450 West 33rd Street in Manhattan.

Shan Jayakumar

Association for a Better New York. Civic foundation. Founded in the 1970s by real estate developer Lew Rudin and several others, it serves as a forum where elected officials and private sector leaders come together to explore potential solutions to New York City's economic and social problems. In the twenty-first century the foundation was under the leadership of Lew's son, William Rudin.

Jessica Montesano

Association for Improving the Condition of the Poor. Charity organized in 1843 to morally uplift and help the deserving poor. An offshoot of the New York City Mission Society, it was led by such prominent New Yorkers as the merchant Robert Minturn. Its first general secretary, Robert M. Hartley, supervised more than 300 upper-class men who volunteered to visit persons in need; his careful records demonstrated a relationship between mortality and filthy, crowded living conditions and became an example for scientific philanthropists in the late nineteenth century. The association constructed public bathhouses in 1852, 1892 (the People's Baths), and 1904 (the Milbank Memorial Bath, donated by Elizabeth Milbank Anderson). In 1855 it sponsored the Working Men's Home for black men at 151 Elizabeth Street, considered by many the country's first model tenement, and it was an important advocate of the Metropolitan Health Act of 1866 and other sanitary reforms. After Hartley's retirement in 1876 the association no longer relied solely on men as volunteers, and in 1879 it became one of the first organizations of its kind to employ women as visitors. With the Charity Organization Society, the New York City Mission and Tract Society, and the Children's Aid Society the association in 1891 became an owner of the United Charities Building at 105 East 22nd Street, donated by John M. Kennedy. Among the other facilities that it established and supported were medical dispensaries and dental clinics, the Neponsit Beach Hospital at Rockaway Beach for nonpulmonary tuberculosis patients, summer camps for children, families, and the elderly, and Sea Breeze, a vacation home for mothers and children at Coney Island. In 1939 the Association for Improving the Condition of the Poor merged with the Charity Organization Society to form the Community Service Society.

Alana Erickson Coble

Association of American Publishers. Trade association for book publishers, formed in 1970 by the merger of the American Book Publishers Council and the American Educational Publishers Institute. In addition to informing its members on such issues as copyright and marketing, it represents the publishing business to both government and the public. The association has offices at 51 Fifth Avenue in New York City, as well as in Washington, D.C.

Eileen K. Cheng

Association of Catholic Trade Unionists [ACTU]. Labor organization formed in New York City in 1937 by John Cort, Martin Wersing, and John P. Monaghan, who hoped to "make Catholic social principles an effective force for sound unionism and industrial relations." It established "labor schools" where Catholic workers studied religious and social principles, and published the *Labor Leader*, a national newspaper dedicated to Catholic social teaching and workers' rights; it also mediated labor disputes, supported more than 300 strikes nationwide, and provided legal defense for striking workers. The association was closely allied with the Congress of Industrial Organizations (CIO). At its peak in 1940 there were 10,000 members drawn from many occupations; non-Catholics were welcomed as associate members and numbered 90,000. By the early 1940s the association had its national headquarters in New York City and 24 chapters nationwide. It lost support in the following years as it worked with growing intensity to eliminate the influence of communists in the CIO and other labor organizations, and by 1950 its membership declined and many chapters closed. The chapter in New York City lasted until 1973.

Douglas P. Seaton, *Catholics and Radicals: The Association of Catholic Trade Unionists and the American Labor Movement, from Depression to Cold War* (Lewisburg, Pa.: Bucknell University Press, 1981)

Edward T. O'Donnell

Association of Neighborhood Workers. Nonprofit organization formed in December 1900 by Mary Simkhovitch and John Elliott to "effect cooperation among those who are working for neighborhood and civic improvement, and to promote movements for social progress." It met regularly at neighborhood centers, which provided some financial support. The association accomplished much of its work through committees; it investigated conditions in housing, the workplace, and schools; published pamphlets; organized neighborhood groups; produced exhibitions; and promoted legislative reforms. In 1919 it incorporated as the United Neighborhood Houses at 70 Fifth Avenue.

Betty Boyd Caroli

Association of the Bar of the City of New York [ABCNY]. Association organized on 1 February 1870 after Manhattan lawyers were disturbed by the corruption and judicial malfeasance rampant in William M. "Boss" Tweed's government; a petition to organize the bar for "mutual protection and benefit" circulated in December 1869 was endorsed by more than 200 lawyers by late January 1870. William Evarts was chosen as the first president on 15 February and remained in office for a decade. Most original members were Protestant graduates of elite universities who worked for large firms. The association formed law, grievance, and judicial committees in November 1870 and became a model for subsequent bar associations in Brooklyn (1872), New York State (1876), and the nation (1878). It quickly gained influence through its battles with Tweed and assumed the authority to discipline members of the profession and establish ethical standards. In 1884 the ABCNY's responsibility for policing professional conduct was recognized by the appellate division of the state supreme court, which lacked the resources to carry out the task itself. It opened elegant headquarters, first at 20 West 27th Street and then at 7 West 29th Street, while elaborate screening procedures and high fees ensured that membership remained exclusive. Until the 1920s every president of the ABCNY was listed in the *Social Register*, and the organization resisted incorporation into the state bar association. Its conservative leadership opposed David Dudley Field's civil codification of legal precedents, preferring to rely on the traditional but arcane system of common-law precedents. In the 1890s Joseph Choate and Elihu Root led a successful ABCNY campaign that changed the state constitution and established the appellate division that consolidated the process of legal review. In 1896, when the association moved to 42 West 44th Street, a New York City Landmark building designed by Cyrus Eidlitz, it had fewer than 1400 members but enjoyed unparalleled influence. Its plan for international arbitration was presented to the Hague Conference of 1899.

From the 1920s the association consolidated its influence, as its leadership included national figures such as Charles Evans Hughes, Henry L. Stimson, and John W. Davis. A progressive–conservative split among its membership became apparent during a bitter fight that condemned the state legislature for expelling five duly elected socialists (1920). As the society's president from 1924 to 1925, Henry Taft sought to expand membership, only to have his efforts nullified by his successor. In 1929 President Charles C. Burlingham orchestrated investigations of municipal corruption that led to the resignation of Mayor James J. Walker. Not until 1937 did the ABCNY amend its charter to admit women; the first female attorney was installed three years later. Under Harrison Tweed (1945–48) it established the position of executive secretary and began publishing the *Record*. From 1953 to 1956 it led the fight against the Bricker Amendment (which would have empowered Congress "to regulate all Executive and other agreements with any foreign power or international organization"), opposed the American Bar Association by denouncing federal loyalty oaths, and published reports that led to the New York State Court Reorganization Act of 1962.

Long reluctant to recognize the importance of Jewish lawyers in Manhattan, the ABCNY began to appoint them to important committees, and in 1956 elected its first Jewish president, Louis Loeb. Archaic membership requirements were eased during the 1960s, and a more liberal association actively joined social protest movements: it defended the Civil Rights Acts (1964–65), supported the civil rights efforts of Martin Luther King, Jr., and sent 1200 lawyers to Washington, D.C., to protest intervention in Cambodia (1969). By the 1970s some positions on the board were reserved for women and members of ethnic and racial minorities. In 1980, after a century of policing the profession, the association ceded authority for disciplining lawyers but continued to advocate high professional standards, efficiency in the courts, and increasing the number of elective judgeships. In the 1980s and 1990s, the ABCNY worked to reform New York's mental health and divorce laws, encouraged lawyers to work pro bono for charities, and established committees on the environment, sex and law, and consumer affairs. It opposed the nomination of Robert H. Bork to the U.S. Supreme Court, elected Conrad K. Harper as its first black president, and led opposition to American detainee policy during the second Gulf War. In the early twenty-first century it had over 23,000 members and maintained a reference library of almost half a million volumes.

George Martin, *Causes and Conflicts: The Centennial History of the Association of the Bar of the City of New York* (Boston: Houghton Mifflin, 1970); Michael S. Powell, *From Patrician to Professional Elite* (New York: Russell Sage, 1980)

George J. Lankevich

Astor [née Russell]**, (Roberta) Brooke** (*b* Portsmouth, N.H., 30 March 1902; *d* Briarcliff Manor, N.Y., 13 Aug 2007). Philanthropist and socialite. As a child she lived in Beijing and Shanghai. Married at 16 to J. Dryden Kuser, she divorced him and moved to New York with her son, where she studied creative writing at Columbia University. She remarried stockbroker Charles Marshall, who died in 1952, and then worked as a feature editor for *House and Garden*. She married Vincent Astor in 1953 and assisted him in philanthropic pursuits; upon his death in 1959 she devoted herself to the Vincent Astor Foundation. When the foundation closed in 1997, she had overseen the donation of nearly $200 million in grants benefiting cultural and educational organizations, notably the New York Public Library and the Metropolitan Museum of Art, as well as projects for the poor and the disadvantaged. She believed that Astor money, which was made in New York real estate, should be spent in New York. Astor socialized and danced well into her 90s, and the New York Landmarks Conservancy named her a living landmark in 1996. Astor, who suffered from Alzheimer's disease in her waning years, died at her country home at age 105. Her published memoirs include *Patchwork Child* (1962) and *Footprints* (1980); she also wrote two novels, *The Bluebird Is at Home* (1965) and *The Last Blossom on the Plum Tree* (1986).

Kate Lauber

Astor [née Schermerhorn]**, Caroline (Webster)** (*b* New York City, 22 Sept 1830; *d* New York City, 3 Oct 1908). Society figure. She was born into an established family and was educated in New York City and in France. Determined to lead the city's elite, she married William Astor and with Ward McAllister chose a group known as the "400," named for the number of guests who could be accommodated in her ballroom; her dinner parties, balls, and musicales became well known. After McAllister's death she chose Harry Lehr, a much more flamboyant figure, as his successor. In 1894 she had a mansion built at Fifth Avenue and 65th Street, where she remained until the end of her life.

James E. Mooney

Astor, John Jacob (*b* Waldorf, Germany, 17 July 1763; *d* New York City, 29 March 1848). America's richest man before the Civil War. He began his career as a fur trader in the Pacific Northwest and in March 1784 arrived in New York City, where he lived at what are now 362 Pearl Street (1785–90) and 149 Broadway (1794–1803). In the following years he amassed a real estate empire that included buildings and parcels of land in Manhattan acquired from 1810. Unlike most real estate investors he did not engage in short-term speculation or develop property for sale: instead he bought land at low prices and waited for the market to change and for urban growth to drive up the value of his properties. While waiting for these long-term increases he collected a large income in rents from his extensive commercial and residential holdings, seldom investing in improvements; he generally sold only if he needed money to buy more property and occasionally when values were increasing quickly. After selling his fur business in 1834 he focused solely on real estate in Manhattan, particularly in what is now midtown.

For a time Astor lived at 223 Broadway in a building that became the Astor House hotel in 1836 (demolished 1913) and later at 585 Broadway; he also had a summer home known as "Astoria" or "Hell Gate Farm" at what is now East 87th Street between York and East End avenues. During the panic of 1837 he bought many distressed properties and foreclosed on hundreds of others for which he held or obtained mortgages. By 1840 he was the country's wealthiest man and one of the city's best-known businessmen, owning an estate worth more than $20 million; his urban properties were estimated to have increased ten times in value from the time he purchased them. In twenty-first century terms, his fortune would have been worth more than $100 billion. Shortly before his death he declared: "Could I begin life again, knowing what I now know, and had money to invest, I would buy every foot of land on the island of Manhattan."

When Astor died in 1848, his wealth was already legendary. The *New York Daily Tribune's* obituary stated, "The question is often asked, how rich is Mr. Astor? But who can answer." The New York press pointed out that Astor's fortune reflected the economic success of the city, but that Astor had not left much to the city to show his gratitude; his estate was left to his family. His only major gift to New York was $400,000, which was used to create the Astor Library in 1849. The Astor Library, located at Sixth Avenue and Lafayette Street, opened to the public in 1854 and offered a large collection of free-of-charge noncirculating books. The holdings were later incorporated into the New York Public Library. The Astor Library building became home to the Joseph Papp Public Theater in 1967.

Astor's vast empire was managed by his heirs and descendants into the twentieth century. A great-grandson, William Waldorf Astor, built luxury hotels and apartment buildings in Manhattan during the 1890s, including the Waldorf Hotel, erected on the site of the family's mansions at Fifth Avenue and 34th Street and later merged with the Astoria Hotel (owned by John Jacob Astor IV) to form the Waldorf=Astoria. Astor's great-great-grandson Vincent Astor worked from 1942 with the developer William Zeckendorf to increase the value and returns of the family's holdings, which declined after World War II in a changing market.

Marc A. Weiss

Astor House. A five-story hotel on the west side of Broadway between Barclay and Vesey streets. Designed by Isaiah Rogers in the Greek Revival style for John Jacob Astor and erected in 1834–36, it was the first luxury hotel in New York City. There were many fine public rooms and more than 300 guest rooms, and running water was pumped by steam even to the upper stories before the Croton water system opened in 1842. For several decades the hotel was an internationally renowned meeting place for prominent statesmen and literary figures; it was the site of an impromptu speech by President-elect Abraham Lincoln on 19 February 1861. In its later years newer uptown hotels surpassed its services, and in 1913 construction of the subway system forced demolition of part of the building. The rest was destroyed in 1926.

May N. Stone

Astoria. Neighborhood in northwestern Queens, constituting the part of Long Island City north of Broadway. The area was originally called Hallett's Cove after William Hallett in the mid-seventeenth century. Renamed for John Jacob Astor, who invested $500 in local real estate, it was developed in 1839 by Stephen A. Halsey, a fur merchant. During the 1840s and 1850s it grew slowly inland from the ferry landing at the foot of Astoria Boulevard. Wealthy New Yorkers built mansions on 12th and 14th streets and on 27th Avenue. The German United Cabinet Workers bought four farms in 1869 between 35th and 50th streets and developed a German town. In the following year Schuetzen

Astor House, 1899

Park was laid out at Broadway and Steinway Street. William Steinway, an immigrant piano maker who founded the famous piano company in 1853, bought a large tract on both sides of what became Steinway Street from Astoria Boulevard to the East River. He built Steinway village, home to factories, housing, and community services. In 1870 Astoria, Hunter's Point, Steinway, and Ravenswood consolidated to form Long Island City. Treacherous reefs in Hell Gate were dynamited in 1876 and 1885 at the behest of the federal government.

In the late nineteenth and early twentieth centuries Astoria became a popular residential neighborhood with booming commercial construction spurred on by new bridges and public transport. A signature building style for the area was the six-family apartment building, which created a low-skyline profile for the neighborhood. In 1909 the Queensboro Bridge was finished, connecting the area to Manhattan. The shore of the East River became a park in 1913, and the first rapid transit line, the Astoria elevated, opened on 31st Street on 1 February 1917. The Independent subway connected Astoria to Manhattan in 1933, extending service along Steinway Street and Broadway. On 11 January 1936 the Triborough Bridge (now the Robert F. Kennedy Memorial Bridge) connected it to Manhattan and the Bronx. In the twenty-first century it is connected to Manhattan by four subway lines, two of them elevated lines.

Astoria is home to the Museum of the Moving Image; the Isamu Noguchi Museum; the Socrates Sculpture Park; Astoria Park, site of the city's largest public swimming pool; and Bohemian Hall, the city's oldest beer garden, founded in 1910. The area has been particularly popular for movie and television projects. The Kaufman Astoria Studios, part of which was converted to the Museum of the Moving Image, filmed movies with Rudolph Valentino, the Marx Brothers, and Paul Robeson. In the 1970s the defunct studio was revitalized for television filming, including *All in the Family* and *The Cosby Show*. Astoria has become a popular location for movie shoots, including *Goodfellas* and *A Bronx Tale*.

Always a popular ethnic enclave, Astoria has changed significantly in the past century. Originally populated by Dutch and Germans, it attracted Czechs (Bohemians) and Slovaks in the early twentieth century. After World War II Italians settled there, and by the 1960s it became the center for Greeks. One-third of all Greeks who moved to New York City in the 1980s settled in the neighborhood, and by the mid-1990s they accounted for almost half its population. St. Demetrios Cathedral, one of 11 Greek Orthodox churches in the area, is probably the largest outside of Greece. Greek immigrants who settled in the neighborhood received aid from the Hellenic Americans Neighborhood Action Committee, a locally based social services agency.

At the start of the twenty-first century Astoria was one of the most diverse neighborhoods of New York City, attracting a broad array of ethnic groups. While the Greek population remained large, the area included Brazilians, Colombians, Bangladeshis, Chinese, Guyanese, Koreans, Ecuadorians, Romanians, Indians, Filipinos, Albanians, and Bosnians. Astoria's Arab population included immigrants from Lebanon, Egypt, Tunisia, Yemen, and Morocco, all of whom settled in the Steinway Street area in the 1990s.

Lisa Keller, Vincent Seyfried

Astoria Federal Savings and Loan Association. Thrift institution, formed in 1888 as the Central Permanent Building and Loan Association by residents of Long Island City. Soon one of the chief lenders of home mortgages in Queens, in 1937 it adopted its current name and built headquarters at 37-16 30th Avenue in Long Island City. It opened branches in Ditmars, Forest Hills, and Flushing from the late 1950s, merged with the Metropolitan Federal Savings and Loan of Middle Village (1973), and bought Citizens Savings and Loan of Woodside (1979) and the Whitestone Savings and Loan (1990). The firm moved its headquarters in 1989 to Bulova Corporate Center in Jackson Heights. In 1997 it acquired the Greater New York Savings Bank. By the early twenty-first century, Astoria Federal was the largest thrift depository headquartered in New York, with deposits of $13.1 billion.

James Bradley

Astoria Silk Works. Factory in Astoria, Queens, established in 1820. Part of the West Point foundry owned by Gouverneur Kemble, it was one of two factory sites; the other was in Cold Springs, Long Island. Astoria Silk Works was owned by investors that included Jacob Ruppert and William Steinway. The mill was located on Steinway Avenue (now Street) near Potter Avenue (now 23rd Avenue). It was composed of brick buildings, marked by "ASW," that still stand today. A fire in 1914 closed the factory permanently.

Jessica Montesano

Astoria Studio. See KAUFMAN ASTORIA STUDIOS.

Astor Library. See NEW YORK PUBLIC LIBRARY.

Astor Place. Neighborhood on the East Side of Manhattan, bounded to the north by Eighth Street, to the east by Third Avenue, to the south by Fourth Street, and to the west by Broadway. On 10 May 1849 the Astor Place Riot broke out at the Astor Place Opera House on a site now occupied by the District 65 Building (1890, George E. Harney), which houses the district offices of the United Auto Workers. For a brief period before the Civil War some of the city's wealthiest families lived at Astor Place, including the Astors, the Vanderbilts, and the Delanos. By the 1860s manufacturing and warehousing concerns moved into the neighborhood, which fell into disrepair after the turn of the twentieth century. It was revitalized in the 1960s and 1970s as a shopping district catering largely to students, and Broadway and Fourth Street became lined with shops selling clothes, records, books, and novelties. Notable buildings in the neighborhood include the Astor Place Building at 444 Lafayette Street (1876, Griffith Thomas), an attractive structure of brick and painted cast iron; and 428–34 Lafayette Street, which is all that remains of a once-elegant row of buildings known as Colonnade Row (1833). The Public Theater, in a building that once housed the Astor Library and from 1921 to 1965 was the headquarters of the Hebrew Immigrant Aid Society, is where the producer Joseph Papp first staged the musicals *Hair* and *A Chorus Line;* it is now a complex of seven performance spaces for plays, concerts, films, and readings and also houses the headquarters of the New York Shakespeare Festival. A subway station at the corner of Eighth and Lafayette streets, restored in 1986, has a cast-iron replica of the original kiosk and bas-relief ceramic plaques depicting beavers, an allusion to the fur trade, in which John Jacob Astor made his first fortune. Balanced en point between Lafayette Street and Fourth Avenue is Bernard Rosenthal's steel cube *Alamo* (1967). The magnificent Cooper Union Foundation Building (1859) dominates Astor Place between Third and Fourth avenues. In the early twenty-first century the area has experienced a gentrifying influence, especially from New York University students.

Linda Elsroad

Astor Place Riot. Violence that occurred from 10 to 11 May 1849 at the Astor Place Opera House, triggered by a feud between the English actor William C. Macready and the American actor Edwin Forrest. See RIOTS.

Astral Apartments. Housing project at 184 Franklin Street between Java and India streets in Greenpoint, Brooklyn, built in 1886 for kerosene refinery workers and Charles Pratt's Astral Oil Company nearby. A Queen Anne structure a block long with many entrances, it became known for its light and airy rooms. There was a settlement house, library, and kindergarten on the premises. At the beginning of the twenty-first century, the Astral Apartments remained a monument to the hopes of nineteenth-century housing reformers.

Kenneth T. Jackson

AT&T. See American Telephone and Telegraph.

Atlantic Basin. Basin constructed in the mid-1800s in a swampy area of south Brooklyn known as Red Hook to accommodate shipping. Along with Erie Basin in the same area, it was a relatively rare feature in U.S. seaports. Construction was begun in 1841 on the shore of Buttermilk Channel directly opposite Governors Island. It was eventually completed in the form of a large H parallel to the channel, adding many berths for cargo transfer to the Brooklyn waterfront. Most berths were lined with cargo sheds, but large multistory warehouses were built on the inland side of the basin with grain elevator towers, making Atlantic Basin an important facility for the shipment of grain. The original brick warehouses were replaced with fireproof reinforced concrete warehouses early in the twentieth century. Atlantic Basin and the second-generation warehouses survive into the twenty-first century. The warehouses underwent preliminary renovation for conversion into apartments, but the stevedoring company operating the Red Hook Container Port immediately to the north would like to see them returned to warehouse use. The outer berth south of the entrance to Atlantic Basin is now a passenger terminal built specifically for the Cunard ocean liner *Queen Mary 2*.

Norman J. Brouwer

Atlantic Mutual Insurance Company. Chartered by the state legislature on 11 April 1842, it opened offices at the corner of Wall and William streets and took over the business of a former marine insurer, Atlantic Insurance, a stock company established in 1824. The appeal of the reorganized firm to shipowners and merchants seeking a share of the profits from marine insurance lay in its structure as a mutual firm (owned by policyholders rather than stockholders). A reinsurance agreement with the Insurance Company of North America enabled it to provide larger amounts of insurance for single ships. Under the leadership of Walter Restored Jones, Atlantic Mutual prospered while American clipper ships were in demand: it was the only major American mutual marine insurer to survive the intense competition from British companies at the end of the nineteenth century. Even as the market for marine insurance was declining, the firm expanded by organizing subsidiaries in 1931 to provide fire and casualty insurance. Except for the disastrous year of 1854 it paid a dividend every year for a century and a half. Located at 100 Wall Street, it employed 1200 people and had sales of $93 million in 2007.

Robert J. Gibbons

Atlantic Yards. Large rail yard complex located in central Brooklyn adjacent to the intersection of Flatbush and Atlantic avenues and operated by the Long Island Rail Road and the Metropolitan Transit Authority. A predecessor to the Long Island Rail Road built a line in 1836 to the end of Atlantic Avenue at the East River to connect with a ferry to Manhattan, although efforts to restrict or outlaw steam locomotives by the City of Brooklyn led to construction of a tunnel and the use of horses; the line west of Flatbush Avenue was abandoned in 1877. The freight-handling facilities at Flatbush Avenue were expanded over the next century, but in 2008 they were the focus of a large-scale redevelopment project that would be built over them and include a basketball arena, hotel, retail and office space, and middle-income and market-rate housing, along with landscaped public spaces. The project encountered opposition from neighborhood residents concerned about potential crowds and traffic, lack of low-income housing, and the condemnation of adjacent buildings. As of 2010, however, the project had received court approval and was slated to proceed.

Norman J. Brouwer

Atlantic Basin, 2009

Atlantic Yards, 2009

Atterbury, Grosvenor (*b* Detroit, 7 July 1869; *d* Southampton, N.Y., 18 Oct 1956). Architect and planner. He grew up in New York City and after graduating from Yale University studied architecture at Columbia University; he later joined the firm of McKim, Mead and White and received a patent for prefabricated construction materials. Some of his first commissions were for country houses and townhouses of family and friends, followed by model tenements on East 31st Street and Forest Hills Gardens in Queens, a development of prefabricated houses that became a model for garden suburbs. He also helped to design City Hall, another building for the Russell Sage Foundation at Lexington and 22nd Street, the American Wing of the Metropolitan Museum of Art, and the Amsterdam Houses. Atterbury formed the National Housing Association and the National City Planning Institute and was president of the Architectural League of New York.

James E. Mooney

Auburndale. Neighborhood in north central Queens. It was laid out in 1901 by the New England Development and Improvement Company on 90 acres (36 hectares) of farmland previously owned by Thomas Willet, the first mayor of New York City, and bounded to the north by Crocheron Avenue, to the east by Auburndale Lane, to the south by Northern Boulevard, and to the west by the Clearview Expressway. A railroad station was opened by the Long Island Rail Road in May 1901. The name is derived from that of Auburn, Massachusetts, hometown of the president of the company. It is home to the Flushing Cemetery, established in 1853, and borders on the Kissena Park Golf Course and Kissena Park. At Martins Field on 46th Avenue between 164th and 165th streets lies an old African American and Native American cemetery that was paved over to build a playground opened in 1935. In the early twenty-first century Auburndale was a residential suburb of one-family brick houses and tree-lined streets known for its fine homes and well-kept neighborhood.

Vincent Seyfried

Auchincloss, Louis (Stanton) (*b* Lawrence, N.Y., 27 Sept 1917; *d* New York City, 26 Jan 2010). Writer and lawyer. He grew up in New York City, joined the law firm of Sullivan and Cromwell, and from 1954 until his retirement in 1987 practiced law at the firm of Hawkins, Delafield and Wood on Wall Street. He also served as president of the Museum of the City of New York from 1966 to 1990. He authored 31 novels, 17 nonfiction works, and 17 short-story collections. Auchincloss is often regarded as a novelist of manners in the tradition of Henry James and Edith Wharton. *Tales of Manhattan* (1967), *Skinny Island* (1987), and *Manhattan Monologues* (2002) center around life in New York City. He received the National Medal of Arts in 2005.

B. Kimberly Taylor

auction system. The auction system of sales dates to the early years of colonial rule, with the first regulatory laws enacted in 1676. The state in 1784 passed a tax of 2½ percent on goods sold at auction. In 1801 the law allowed for 24 auctions licenses, a number increased to 36 in 1813. Yet auction sales amounted to little until the Jeffersonian Embargo of 1807 and the British blockade during the War of 1812 created the conditions for the vast expansion of auction sales. Denied access to their largest foreign market for almost a decade, British manufacturers were eager to rid themselves of excess inventories, and at the same time Americans were eager for British imports. Auctions allowed British manufacturers to reduce inventories and quickly reestablish their market dominance. Manufacturers' agents based in New York City sold directly to auction houses and offered long credit periods of 12 to 18 months. In 1817 the city consolidated its dominance of the auction trade by passing laws lowering the tax on auction sales and requiring that all goods put up for auction be sold regardless of the price offered. Opportunities for bargains drew rural retailers and (more importantly) local jobbers who assembled various goods into packages for rural retailers while offering one-year credits. In turn the auction houses made the most of their money by offering six and eight months' credit, called *del credere,* to the large jobbers and shorter credits to rural retailers. The dominance of auction sales was felt in the 1820s when $160 million passed through such important auction houses as John Hone and Sons; Hicks, Lawrence, and Company; and Haggerty and Austin. This figure accounted for 44 percent of the city's imports and a fifth of the nation's.

At first auctions outraged traditional merchants. Having bought quantities of goods in the months immediately following the peace of 1815, merchants were caught with inventories at high and inflexible prices in a quickly glutted market. The dominance of auctioneers produced a futile political backlash among regular merchants, who mounted an unsuccessful slate of candidates in the elections of 1828. The merchants' economic response proved more successful. After 1830 American merchants began sending representatives to Europe, and by offering immediate cash sales to manufacturers they regained control over the import trade. Specializing in one line of business and buying in quantity allowed for more competitive pricing.

After peaking in the late 1820s auction sales stagnated during the 1830s at about $160 million for the decade. This figure, the same as that for the preceding decade, now represented less than 20 percent of the city's vastly expanded trade. Ultimately, auction sales were destroyed by the credit crunch of 1836–37 and the subsequent depression: because of their low selling prices, auctioneers' profits accrued from the credit they offered their customers, and they suffered when credit dried up after 1836. Despite its brief history the auction system radically transformed the ways goods were sold throughout the United States.

Robert G. Albion, *The Rise of New York Port, 1815–1860* (New York, n. pub.: 1939)

James Ciment

Auden, W(ystan) H(ugh) (*b* York, England, 21 Feb 1907; *d* Vienna, 28 Sept 1973). Poet and writer. He grew up and was educated in England, where he became well known as a writer before moving to New York City in 1939. During World War II he abandoned Marxism and became an Anglican. He lived at 7 Cornelia Street from about 1945 until 1953, when he moved to quarters at 77 St. Mark's Place, remaining there until April 1972. His long poem *The Age of Anxiety* (1947), set in a bar and an apartment in the city, won the Pulitzer Prize. Auden also wrote librettos for operas including Igor Stravinsky's *The Rake's Progress* (1951), edited collections of poetry, and taught at Oxford University and a number of colleges in the city.

James E. Mooney

Audubon, John J(ames) (*b* Les Cayes [now in Haiti], 26 April 1785; *d* New York City, 27 Jan 1851). Artist and ornithologist. He worked as an apprentice clerk in New York City in the winter of 1806–7 and practiced taxidermy for Samuel Latham Mitchill. During 1808–26 he engaged in the study of birds, working in various capacities around the United States, and in 1824 he became a member of the Lyceum of Natural History. In 1826 he traveled to England, where he found a publisher for *Birds of America*, a series of his watercolors engraved by Robert Havell, Jr.; the series was published in installments between 1827 and 1838 in London, where he sought subscribers and exhibited the original watercolors for the prints in 1839. He settled with his family at 86 White Street in New York City in 1836. The mayor granted him permission in 1841 to shoot rats on the Battery at dawn in order to obtain specimens for the illustration of his *Viviparous Quadrupeds of North America* (1845–48). In the early 1840s he bought a parcel of 24 acres (10 hectares) overlooking the Hudson River near what is now 155th Street and Audubon Terrace; he built a mansion there and named the estate Minnie's Land after his wife. He died at Minnie's Land and was buried in Trinity Cemetery. In 1863 the New-York Historical Society purchased

John J. Audubon, American Avocet *(1821)*

from his widow 430 of the 433 original watercolors in *Birds of America* for $4000.

Alice Ford, *John James Audubon* (Norman: University of Oklahoma Press, 1964; rev. New York: Abbeville, 1988); Richard Rhodes, *John James Audubon: The Making of an American* (New York: Alfred A. Knopf, 2004)

Susan M. Sivard

Audubon Park. An obsolete name for a hilly plot of land in northern Manhattan, bounded to the north by 156th Street, to the east by Amsterdam Avenue, to the south by 153rd Street, and to the west by the Hudson River. It was part of the site in 1776 of the Battle of Washington Heights. In 1841 the land was acquired by John J. Audubon, who named it Minnie's Land and built his estate there. In the following year he sold a parcel of 23 acres (9 hectares) to Richard F. Carmen; in 1843 this became Trinity Cemetery, where Audubon is buried under a runic cross 16 feet (5 meters) tall. Much of the rest of the land is occupied by the museums and institutions of AUDUBON TERRACE.

George Bird Grinnell, *Audubon Park: The History of the Site* (New York: Trustees of Audubon Park, 1927)

Rachel Shor

Audubon Terrace. Beaux-arts complex on Broadway between 155th and 156th streets in Manhattan, built as an educational and cultural center by Archer Milton Huntington (1870–1955), a railroad magnate, philanthropist, and devotee of Hispanic culture. In 1904 Huntington bought sections of Audubon Park, the former estate and game preserve of the naturalist John J. Audubon and formed the Hispanic Society of America, dedicated primarily to establishing a free public museum and library for the study of Hispanic culture. The nucleus of its holdings consisted of books, paintings, sculptures, architectural fragments, and examples of the decorative arts that Huntington had collected from the Iberian peninsula. The Italianate headquarters of the society were designed by his cousin Charles Pratt Huntington and opened in 1908. Anna Hyatt Huntington, Archer's wife, produced the equestrian statue of El Cid in the courtyard, the lions flanking the doorway of the society, and the bas-reliefs of Don Quixote and Boabdil in its library. During the next few decades Charles Pratt Huntington designed much of the rest of the complex, including the buildings for the American Numismatic Society (built 1906–7), the Church of Our Lady of Esperanza (1909–11, the second Spanish Roman Catholic Church in New York City), the American Geographical Society (1909–11), and the Museum of the American Indian (1916–22). Those for the American Academy of Arts and Letters and the National Institute of Arts and Letters (1921–30) were designed in an Italian Renaissance Revival style by William Mitchell Kendall of McKim, Mead and White and Cass Gilbert. As the surrounding neighborhood of Washington Heights changed, the institutions of Audubon Terrace, which was designated a city historic district in 1979, attracted fewer patrons. The Geographical Society moved in the early 1970s and was replaced by Boricua College, which serves the Latino community. The Smithsonian Institution took over the Museum of the American Indian in the 1980s and moved most of the collections to Washington, D.C.; the remainder became the George Gustav Heye Center of the National Museum of the American Indian at the U.S. Custom House in lower Manhattan. The American Numismatic Society left in 2004 and sold its building to the Academy of Arts and Letters.

Ella M. Foshay

Audubon Theatre and Ballroom. Building at Broadway and West 165th Street that covered a full block and contained a 2368-seat theater, street-level retail space, offices, and a ballroom on the second story. It was designed by THOMAS W. LAMB and built in 1912 by Hungarian immigrant William Fox; the Audubon was known for its polychrome terracotta facade on Broadway, adorned with a line of three-dimensional fox heads. One of the first theaters in Fox's chain, it showed films and presented vaudeville shows; by the 1920s Fox had built a film production empire worth $300 million. After the Depression he lost his fortune and was jailed for fraud; the Fox Film Corporation merged with Twentieth Century Pictures in 1935 and became Twentieth Century–Fox Film Corporation. The theater was successively called the Beverly Hills and the San Juan. During the 1930s the ballroom was the site of efforts to organize transit workers. The IRT Brotherhood and Transport Workers Union of America both met there, with labor leader Michael Quill in attendance. In 1964 MALCOLM X formed the Organization of Afro-American Unity and held weekly meetings in the ballroom; in February 1965 it was the site of a rally during which he was assassinated. The Audubon was closed and the city took ownership when back taxes accumulated. Columbia–Presbyterian Medical Center announced plans to demolish the deteriorating Audubon and to build a new research center during the late 1980s; the announcement met with opposition from preservation groups that stressed the building's importance to the history of the civil rights movement. Columbia compromised and restored portions of the facade and ballroom; the Malcolm X and Dr. Betty Shabazz Memorial and Educational Center, designed by Davis Brody Bond, opened there in 2005. Most of the building was incorporated into the Audubon Biomedical Science and Technology Park, managed by Columbia and jointly developed by the university and the state and city of New York.

Eric Wm. Allison, Kate Lauber

Austen, (Elizabeth) Alice (*b* Staten Island, N.Y., 17 March 1866; *d* Staten Island, 9 June 1952). Renowned photographer. Born to a middle-class family, she learned techniques of photographic processing at an early age. She depicted the life of the middle class in the 1890s by photographing objects and buildings, as well as everyday events and unusual pastimes in her circle of friends; Austen also photographed scenes in lower Manhattan, including many that captured the animation and vitality of immigrant street life. Photographs, such as *Hester Street: Egg Stand* (18

April 1895), were taken solely for her own interest and pleasure. Emotionally more distant than the work of her contemporaries Jacob A. Riis and Lewis Hine, her photographs are elegantly composed and display fine technique. In her later years Austen supported herself with income from an inheritance, the value of which was drastically reduced by the stock market crash of 1929, so she was forced to vacate her home, Clear Comfort, on bluffs overlooking New York Bay. Just before her death, her work was acquired by the Staten Island Historical Society. Later her home was preserved as a landmark and is now open to the public as a museum.

Ann Novotny, *Alice's World: The Life and Photography of an American Original, Alice Austen, 1866–1952* (Old Greenwich, Conn.: Chatham, 1976)

See also PHOTOGRAPHY.

Naomi Rosenblum

Auster, Paul (Benjamin) (*b* Newark, N.J., 3 Feb 1947). Writer. A graduate of Columbia University (1970), Auster spent several years as a translator in France in the mid-1970s before returning to the United States in 1979. He has received international recognition for his fiction and nonfiction pieces, often set in New York, such as *The Invention of Solitude* (1982), *The New York Trilogy* (1987), *Timbuktu* (1999), and *The Brooklyn Follies* (2005). Auster, one of the more prominent postmodern American writers, is noted for his absurdist crime-fiction works, for his conflation of French metaphysical and American transcendental thought, and for his use of the New York landscape (especially Brooklyn). He has lived for many years in Park Slope and has been vice president of the PEN American Center.

Cecilia Magnusson

automats. Self-service restaurants operated by the Horn and Hardart Company of Philadelphia; the first in New York City opened at 1557 Broadway in Times Square on 2 July 1912. Initially automats offered only buns, beans, fish cakes, and coffee (widely considered the best in the city). Each item cost five cents, was displayed in a compartment behind a glass door, and was bought by dropping a nickel into a slot. By the early 1930s the automats introduced a full range of lunch and dinner entrees. Soon a symbol of life in the city, automats reached the height of their popularity during the 1940s and 1950s, when more than 50 automats in the city served more than 350,000 customers a day. In 1952 Horn and Hardart raised the price of coffee to ten cents, news met with grief by New Yorkers who regarded the nickel coffee of the automats as one of life's great certainties. After fast-food restaurants opened in the early 1970s automats declined in popularity; during the 1970s and 1980s Horn and Hardart replaced many automats with Burger King restaurants. The last automat in the city stood at 42nd Street and Third Avenue and closed on 8 April 1991.

Jack Alexander, "The Restaurants That Nickels Built," *Saturday Evening Post,* Dec. 1954

James Bradley

automobile manufacture. During the first decade of the twentieth century New York City was a center for the manufacture of steam and electrically powered vehicles for both passenger and freight transport. In 1900 six factories that together employed nearly 500 people manufactured automobiles in the city. The largest producer of electric cars, the Electric Vehicle Company, made cars in factories just outside the city limits but was owned by financiers on Wall Street. In 1899 the firm launched a fleet of taxicabs in several major cities, and several hundred ran on the streets of New York City. By 1916 the internal combustion engine had proved itself more powerful, reliable, and cost-effective than its competitors, and the automobile industry shifted to the Midwest, the center for the development of gasoline-powered automobiles that ran on internal combustion engines.

See also TRAFFIC.

Joanne Abel Goldman

Autrey, Wesley (*b* New York City, 1956). Construction worker known variously as the Subway Hero or Subway Samaritan for a random act of bravery in New York City. On 3 January 2007 he and his two daughters were waiting for a downtown no. 1 train at 137th Street and Broadway. As the train approached Cameron Hollopeter, a 19-year-old student at the New York Film Academy, suffered a seizure and fell off of the platform onto the tracks. Autrey jumped to the track bed, covered the ailing passenger with his body, and pressed him into the roughly 1-foot-deep (30.5-centimeter deep) trench between the rails as the train passed overhead. The pair remained under the train until workers were able to shut down the electrified third rail and free them. Both he and Hollopeter suffered only minor injuries. As a result Autrey garnered national and even international acclaim for his courage. In the aftermath of the event Autrey received New York City's Bronze Medallion from Mayor Michael Bloomberg, $10,000 from Donald Trump, and $5000 in cash plus $5000 in scholarship money for each of his daughters from the New York Film Academy. The Metropolitan Transit Authority (MTA) rewarded him with a year's worth of free subway rides. On 23 January 2007 Autrey attended the State of the Union address in Washington, D.C., and was honored by President George W. Bush. In late 2008 Autrey announced his intentions to start a foundation aimed at keeping children off of the street.

Michael C. Repka

Avedon, Richard (*b* New York City, 15 May 1923; *d* San Antonio, Tex., 1 Oct 2004). Photographer. Son of Russian-Jewish immigrants

Berenice Abbott, Automat (ca *1935*)

in New York City, he briefly attended DeWitt Clinton High School and was appointed poet laureate of the New York City high schools. After studying at Columbia University (1941–42), serving in the U.S. Marine Corps (1942–44), and studying photography at the New School for Social Research, he joined *Jr. Bazaar* in 1945, later moving to *Harper's Bazaar*. During these years he worked principally as a fashion photographer. From 1966 his photographs appeared in such varied publications as *Vogue* and *Rolling Stone*. Over the years his work covered a wide range, from portraits to journalistic photographs of the civil rights and antiwar movements. Published collections of Avedon's photographs include *Observations* (1959), *Nothing Personal* (1964), *Portraits* (1976), *Avedon Photographs, 1947–1977* (1978), *In the American West* (1985), and *Evidence, 1944–1994* (1994). His work is also held in the permanent collections of the Metropolitan Museum of Art, the Smithsonian Institution, and the Victoria and Albert Museum. He was the visual consultant for the film version of George Gershwin's musical *Funny Face* (1956).

Shan Jayakumar

aviation. The first "aeronaut" born in the United States, Charles Durant of Jersey City, New Jersey, made a 30-mile (48-kilometer) balloon flight on 9 September 1830, commencing at Castle Garden in lower Manhattan and witnessed by more than 30,000 spectators. Similar exploits remained popular with New Yorkers throughout the nineteenth century: the first major attempt to fly across the Atlantic took place in Brooklyn in 1873.

In 1906 James Gordon Bennett, Jr., publisher of the *New York Herald,* sponsored the first international aviation races, which were staged in New York City the following year. In 1910, by which time the city had more than a dozen firms catering to flyers, the world's largest air meet to date was held at Belmont Park, just outside the city limits. European and American aviators raced inside the park, then ended the meet with a dash across New York City, around the Statue of Liberty, and back to Belmont. Among several bankers who played an important role in promoting aviation in its early days were August Belmont and Cornelius Vanderbilt, who financed the manufacture of the Wright brothers' airplanes after 1909. The first transatlantic flight was launched in 1919 from Rockaway Naval Air Station (later Jacob Riis Park). In New York City, as elsewhere, one of the first practical uses of the airplane was the delivery of mail. From 1918 the U.S. Army Air Corps delivered mail destined for the city to Belmont Park, but this arrangement proved unsatisfactory. Newark Airport in New Jersey was designated the airmail terminus for the city by the United States Postal Service after the Kelly Act (1925), which allowed the letting of contracts with private carriers.

Colonial Airways established the first regular flights from the metropolitan region on 18 June 1926, with service to Boston. The manufacture of airplanes and related equipment became an important local industry. In 1929, 34 firms in the city and in nearby communities on Long Island were involved in aviation, including Curtiss–Wright Aviation Company, Curtiss Airports Corporation, Fairchild Aviation Corporation, and Sikorsky Aircraft; Wright engines were manufactured in suburban Paterson, New Jersey. The New York, Rio, and Buenos Aires line, based in Manhattan and led by Ralph O'Neill, began international seaplane service in 1930. With the connivance of the post office this line was taken over in 1930 by Pan American Airlines, based in suburban Port Washington, Long Island, and led by Juan Trippe. Pan American also used seaplanes, which at the time were both larger and easier to fly into the city than land planes. Daniel Guggenheim's Fund for the Promotion of Aviation sponsored important innovations in the late 1920s and 1930s and in 1929 helped form the first modern airline in the nation (Western).

By this time it was apparent that the city needed to build a new airport or expand an existing one. Roosevelt Field, the starting point for Charles Lindbergh's transatlantic flight in 1927, was considered too remote from the city's post office, and Mayor James J. Walker believed that there was insufficient space for expansion at Holmes Field (in Jackson Heights) or at Glenn H. Curtiss Airport (later North Beach Airport, now La Guardia Airport). Walker instead favored building an airport on Governors Island, but cost and military considerations foreclosed this plan, as well as a plan widely backed in 1930 for an artificial island of 783 acres (317 hectares) between Governors Island and Staten Island, complete with subway connections. In 1930 the city decided on Barren Island in Brooklyn. The following year the Ludington Line introduced hourly flights between Newark and Washington, D.C., and a flying school based in North Beach began scheduled sightseeing flights between Newark and North Beach Airport. By 1934 the airport at Barren Island was completed. Named for Floyd Bennett, a member of Admiral Richard Byrd's expedition to the North Pole, this field covered 367 acres (149 hectares) and accommodated the first scheduled land-plane service in the city (by American Airlines), but poor accessibility to Manhattan precluded airmail service. Some airlines continued to use Newark Airport, which after a major expansion in 1928–29 became the busiest airfield in the world. Several triumphant flights during what is considered the heyday of aviation (1929–39) ended in the city, including Howard Hughes's circling of the globe in three and a half days in 1937.

The dominant commercial position of the city, its topography, and its large population combined to make it a leader in domestic and international aviation and in related industries in the late 1930s. When La Guardia Airfield opened in 1939, it handled more than 250 flights a day in its first year of operation, giving New York City the heaviest air traffic in the United States. By 1938 the number of manufacturers of airplanes and related equipment in the region had fallen to 12 (reflecting consolidation during the Depression), but among these were such large firms as Fairchild, Grumman Industries, North American Aviation, and Chance–Vought Industries. World War II brought prosperity to these manufacturers and others in the area, notably Charles L. Norden and Company (1929–49), which produced the Norden bombsight in both Manhattan and suburban White Plains, New York.

The opening in 1948 of Idlewild International Airport (now John F. Kennedy International Airport) and the Port of New York Authority's takeover in 1947–48 of Idlewild, La Guardia, Newark, and Teterboro airports strengthened the position of the city as an innovator in regional airport planning and as the dominant force in intercontinental air travel. American Overseas Airlines (a subsidiary of American Airlines) began transatlantic land-plane service from La Guardia Airport on 25 October 1945; it was followed by Trans World Airlines on 5 February 1946 and by Pan American soon after. Commercial jet service began in New York City on 4 October 1958, with flights to London on the Comet IV by British Overseas Airways.

Plans for a fourth large airport in the region foundered in the 1960s, but New York City retained a central role in several new developments in aviation, including the establishment of the first modern air shuttle (by Eastern Airlines in 1961 to Boston and Washington, D.C.) and the introduction of the Boeing 747 (by Pan American). Military aviation manufacturing continued to prosper on Long Island: North American Aviation produced the F-105 (to 1986) and the A-10, Grumman the F-14 "Tomcat," the A-6A, and the space shuttle. In 2007 the three major airports in greater New York served more than 109 million passengers and employed about 65,000 people.

Roger Pineau, *Ballooning, 1782–1972* (Washington, D.C.: Smithsonian Institution Press, 1973); Roger E. Bilstein, *Flight in America, 1900–1983: From the Wrights to the Astronauts* (Baltimore, Md.: Johns Hopkins University Press, 1984); Joshua Stoff, *Aerospace Heritage of Long Island* (Interlaken, N.Y.: Heart of the Lakes, 1989)

Paul Barrett

Avon Products. Global firm of cosmetics manufacturers formed in 1886 by David McConnell as the California Perfume Company. Originally a door-to-door Bible salesman based in Manhattan, McConnell began including a free vial of perfume with each book purchase as an incentive. He joined the cosmetics industry when he realized that his perfume was more popular than his Bibles. His company operated from a warehouse at 126 Chambers Street, and the products were manufactured in Suffern, a town in nearby Rockland County, New York. In 1939 the firm took the name Avon Products, Inc., in honor of Shakespeare's Stratford-on-Avon. After World War II it maintained McConnell's original door-to-door approach and grew into the world's largest direct seller of beauty-related products, with 5.1 million independent representatives and sales of $8.1 billion in 2005. Although the firm dispersed most of its manufacturing plants and administrative staff across the country in 1986, it still maintained corporate headquarters at 1251 Avenue of the Americas in Manhattan in the early twenty-first century.

Ayres, Anne (*b* London, 3 Jan 1816; *d* New York City, 9 Feb 1896). Nun. An admirer and associate of William Augustus Muhlenberg, the Episcopal rector of the Church of the Holy Communion, she dedicated herself to celibate religious service. Although no Episcopal sisterhoods existed at the time, she was unilaterally consecrated a sister of the Holy Communion by Muhlenberg in 1845. In 1859 she undertook the organization of his most ambitious enterprise, St. Luke's Hospital, on Fifth Avenue between 54th and 55th streets.

Allen C. Guelzo

B

Bacall, Lauren [Perske, Betty Jean] (*b* New York City, 16 Sept 1924). Actress. After working briefly in the theater she made her film debut opposite Humphrey Bogart in *To Have and Have Not* (1944), loosely based on the novel by Ernest Hemingway, in which she spoke the memorable phrase "If you want something, just whistle." She became known for her portrayal of assertive, elegant women and her languid delivery of scathing lines. One of her most celebrated roles was that of the older sister in a motion picture adapted in 1944 from Raymond Chandler's novel *The Big Sleep,* in which she engages in witty exchanges with Bogart. She married Bogart in 1945 and after settling in New York City continued to appear in plays (*Cactus Flower,* 1966–68), musicals (*Applause!,* 1969–71, winning a Tony Award for her portrayal of a fading actress modeled after Tallulah Bankhead), and films (*Harper,* 1967; *Murder on the Orient Express,* 1974; *Health,* 1980). Bacall wrote several books, including the autobiography *By Myself and Then Some* (2006), and lived for decades at the Dakota at 72nd and Central Park West.

S. D. R. Cashman

Bache and Company. Investment bank. Founded in 1879 in Manhattan, it was originally called Leopold Cahn and Company. Jules Bache, the nephew of the founder, renamed the company J. S. Bache and Company in 1892. By the turn of the twentieth century, the company was a leader on Wall Street, with seats on several stock exchanges. When Jules Bache died in 1944, his nephew, Harold Bache, became the head of the company and shortened its name to Bache and Company. It became a publicly traded company in 1971. In 1981 Bache and Company was acquired by Private Finance Initiative for $385 million. In 2007 the company was rebranded Bache Commodities, and as of 2010, in the United States, it operated as Prudential Bache Commodities.

Jessica Montesano

Badillo, Herman (*b* Caguas, Puerto Rico, 21 Aug 1929). Congressman, borough president, and deputy mayor. Orphaned at an early age, Badillo moved in 1941 to East Harlem, where he was raised by his aunt, Aurelia Rivera. He lived briefly near Chicago and Los Angeles, and then returned to New York City, where he graduated from Haaran High School (1947), City College of New York (1951), and Brooklyn Law School (1954). A progressive liberal as a young man, Badillo immersed himself in the organizational activities of the community, becoming involved in confrontational issues such as bilingual education, the establishment of Hostos Community College, and numerous other initiatives dedicated to advancing the Puerto Rican community. He became one of the first Puerto Rican political leaders in the city to achieve prominence in the Democratic Party. He served as commissioner of the city's Department of Relocation (1962–65); the first Puerto Rican borough president of the Bronx (1966–69); and the first Puerto Rican voting member of the U.S. House of Representatives, representing the city's 21st district (1970–77). Badillo ran unsuccessfully for the mayoralty in 1969, 1973, 1977, 1981, and 1985. He was a deputy mayor under Edward I. Koch. In 1993 Badillo was part of the fusion ticket formed by the mayoral candidate Rudolph W. Giuliani, remaining a registered Democrat but nominated for the office of comptroller by the Republican and Liberal parties; he lost the election to Alan G. Hevesi, but served as Mayor Giuliani's special counsel on educational policy. In 1999 Governor George Pataki appointed Badillo chairperson of the City University's board of trustees. Badillo formally joined the Republican Party and ran for mayor in 2001, losing the primary to Michael Bloomberg. More conservative in his later years, in the early twenty-first century he continued to practice law in New York City and became a senior fellow of the Manhattan Institute of Policy Research.

Herman Badillo, *One Nation, One Standard: An Ex-Liberal on How Hispanics Can Succeed Just Like Other Immigrant Groups* (New York: Sentinal HC, 2007)

Virginia Sánchez Korrol

bagels. Ring-shaped rolls first produced in Poland in the seventeenth century, made with malt (rather than sugar) and high-gluten processed flour, then boiled and baked, for a crisp outer crust and a chewy inside. The New York City bagel is typically fluffier and softer than the bagels from Montreal and other eastern European varieties. Eastern European Jews brought the bagel to New York City during the 1880s, and it soon became closely associated with the city. They were sold by street vendors who carried them around on dowels through the hole in the middle. In 1907 the International Bagel Bakers Union was founded in New York City, joining 300 local bakers together. Only sons of union members could know the secrets of the trade, making bagel apprenticeship more competitive than medical school admission during the years following the union's conception. Bagel Bakers Local 338, based in New York City, had nearly 300 members by 1915. By the 1950s the popularity of bagels extended beyond Jewish neighborhoods and continued to spread during the 1960s with the development of the bagel-making machine (before which they were produced by four-person teams: two rolled the dough, one boiled the dough, and one baked the bagels) and the frozen bagel.

Thomas M. Hilbink, Cecilia Magnusson

Baha'is. Members of a religion founded in 1897 in Persia by followers of Baha'u'llah (1817–92), a Persian nobleman whom adherents of the faith accept as the last messenger of God after Muhammad. The Baha'i religious community in New York City numbers about 900 ethnically diverse followers in the metropolitan area. Followers are committed to the elimination of prejudice, the equality of women, the achievement of universal education, and tolerance of all religions; the religion is governed through local, self-governing communities. The Baha'i Center on East 11th Street and First Avenue in lower Manhattan provides public meetings, including weekly jazz and children's theater programs, worship services, and offices for the local assembly. New York City was home to the Second Baha'i World Congress (1992) held at the Jacob K. Javits Convention Center and attended by nearly 30,000 individuals, according to organizers.

Leyli Shayegan

Baker, Ella Josephine (*b* Norfolk, Va., 13 Dec 1903; *d* New York City, 13 Dec 1986). Civil rights leader. She lived in Littleton, North Carolina, from the age of eight. After graduating from Shaw University she moved to New York City in 1927. During the Depression she taught consumer education in Harlem for the Works Progress Administration and also helped to organize the Young Negroes' Cooperative League and chapters of the National Association for the Advancement of Colored People (NAACP) throughout the South. She directed the branch of the association in the city during World War II and in 1953 ran unsuccessfully as a Liberal for a seat in the state assembly. At the request of Martin Luther King, Jr., she led the Southern Christian Leadership Conference in 1958. After a meeting of sit-in protesters at Shaw University in 1960, she helped to form the Student Nonviolent Coordinating Committee and became its adviser. In 1964 she attended the Democratic National Convention and helped to organize the Mississippi Freedom Summer and the Mississippi Freedom Democratic Party office in Washington, D.C. Baker returned to Harlem after the 1960s.

Sule Greg C. Wilson

Baker, Russell Wayne (*b* Morrisonville, Va., 14 Aug 1925). Journalist, humorist, and author. He was raised in an itinerant family that, he would write, "treasured words," which could "take you all the way to New York City."

H & H Bagels, 2009

Baker was a correspondent for the *Baltimore Sun* and, beginning in 1954, was the chief White House correspondent for the *New York Times*. In 1962 the *Times* gave him a twice-weekly column called "Observer," which won Baker the Pulitzer Prize for Distinguished Commentary in 1979. He also won the Pulitzer for Biography with a memoir of his youth, *Growing Up* (1982). In 1974 Baker and his wife moved to Manhattan, where they lived in a town house on the East Side. He regarded his adopted city with a New Yorker's mixed skepticism and affection. For instance, he explained the large plant in his living room this way: "All the vital people in New York go in heavily for parlor greenery, which is natural, considering that when they step outside the landscape is mostly cement and high blood pressure." He also wrote: "Life in New York is a matter of constantly testing laws, most of which prove much less inflexible than the law of gravity, at least if you can afford a lawyer." Baker later moved to Virginia and wrote his final "Observer" in 1998. He has served as host of PBS Television's *Masterpiece Theater* and written essays and book reviews for the *New York Review of Books*.

Russell Baker, *The Good Times* (New York: William Morrow, 1989)

John Rousmaniere

Baker Field. Columbia University's athletic complex. Located in upper Manhattan along 218th Street, it includes a football stadium; tennis courts; soccer, softball, and baseball fields; boathouses; and a field hockey venue. Financier George F. Baker purchased the 26-acre (10.5-hectare) area for the university on 30 December 1921 for $700,000. It was dedicated in April 1922 and hosted spring football practice that same year. In the fall of 1923 the first stadium at the site, then known as Baker Field, opened with 15,000 seats in temporary stands. Five years later the university built the 32,000-wooden-seat stadium that served Columbia until the spring of 1983. A new stadium was constructed the following year and used for football, lacrosse, and track and field. In the twenty-first century the field remained Columbia's primary athletic complex.

Jessica Montesano

bakeries. Although most baking was done at home in the eighteenth century, there were seven retail bakeries in New York City in 1700, which sold mostly bread. Some of the bakers in lower Manhattan were V. J. Cortlandt (Broadway), Coevrad and House (Broad Street), and George Dieterich (Pearl Street). Bakery workers conducted their first strike in the city in 1741. The number of retail bakeries rose to 12 in 1800 and 38 in 1840, but by 1850, after an influx of immigrants, there were 476 in the city. At the time the leading bakers were Robert Spier, Erastus Titus, and C. T. Goodwin; Treadwell and Harris, formed by E. Treadwell in 1825, was one of the most popular establishments until the end of the nineteenth century. By the 1850s bakeries offered not only bread, but cakes and other sweets, biscuits, and bagels. Wholesale bakeries, formed during the second half of the nineteenth century, established routes and sales territories, delivering their products by horse and wagon to grocery stores. Among the first successful firms were Holmes and Coutts, the Purssell's Manufacturing Company, and the S. B. Thomas Company, which introduced English muffins. The first large bakers' union in the city, the Journeymen Bakers Union of New York and Brooklyn, was formed in 1880 and had its headquarters alternately in Manhattan and Brooklyn until the turn of the twentieth century, when the headquarters were moved to Chicago and the union was renamed the Bakery and Confectionery Workers International Union. There were more than 100 locals in New York City, most divided along ethnic lines; some of the best-known were those operated by Germans, Italians, Jews, and Bohemians.

By the 1890s mergers and trusts characterized the business. The most important trust was the New York Biscuit Company, an amalgamation of firms from the Northeast. Its plant at 10th Avenue and 14th Street housed its headquarters and the country's largest baking factory. The National Biscuit Company (formed in 1898; later Nabisco), which dominated baking in the Northeast, had headquarters in Chicago and many factories in New York City (including one on 10th Avenue), where it developed Animal Crackers, Lorna Doones, and other well-known

Cheesecakes at Junior's, 2009

products. By 1900 there were nearly 2500 bakeries in New York City.

Antitrust battles exacerbated tension between management and labor. The Ward Baking Company, which made Tip-Top Bread and operated in Brooklyn and the Bronx, was the dominant baker in the city during the 1920s. Innovations were made in baking technology, and many firms became manufacturers of baking ovens and machines; the most prominent was Fowler and Rockwell. The Continental Baking Company, which was formed by Ward and which made Wonder Bread and Hostess cakes, had its headquarters in New York City from 1923 to 1984. Other manufacturers included Dugan Brothers of Queens Village, Silver Cup Bread of Long Island City, Fink Baking, and the General Baking Company.

By the early twenty-first century more than 1000 bakeries remained in the city. Wonder Bread had a factory in Jamaica, the Taystee Baking Company had headquarters in Flushing, and Drake Bakeries was in the Bronx; two other major Bronx bakeries closed: Stella D'Oro Biscuit Company (2009) and Old London Foods (2010). Brick-oven bread remained popular, and bakeries of a traditional sort were scattered throughout the city, among them Orwasher's on East 78th Street in Manhattan (1916), Parisi Bakery on Mott Street in Little Italy, and Mosha's Bakery on Wythe Avenue in Williamsburg (1890). Notable bakery chains included Au Bon Pain and Hot and Crusty; notable independent bakeries included Magnolia Bakery, City Bakery, and Blue Ribbon Bakery. Among the leading ethnic bakeries were Patisserie J. Lanciani in Greenwich Village (French), the White Eagle in Greenpoint (Polish), the Franczoz Bakery Shop in Borough Park (kosher), the Damascus Bakery on Atlantic Avenue in Brooklyn (Middle Eastern), and the International Bake Shop in Ridgewood (eastern European). There were also many shops specializing in Caribbean, Latin American, and Asian baked goods.

William G. Panschar, *Baking in America* (Evanston, Ill.: Northwestern University Press, 1956); Stuart Kaufman, *A Vision of Unity: A History of the Bakery and Confectionery Workers International Union* (Urbana: University of Illinois Press, 1986)

James Bradley

Berenice Abbott, Bread Store *(1937)*

Balanchine, George (*b* St. Petersburg, 22 Jan 1904; *d* New York City, 30 April 1983). Choreographer. He trained in Russia and became a successful choreographer in western Europe with Serge Diaghilev's Ballets Russes. At the invitation of the arts patron Lincoln Kirstein he immigrated to the United States and settled in New York City in 1933, with a vision of creating a permanent ballet company. In 1934 the two opened the School of American Ballet at 637 Madison Avenue. His first ballet in the United States, the group composition *Serenade* (to Tchaikovsky's music), was performed by students in June 1934; the ballet's emphasis on choreography rather than plot, costumes, or star dancers reflected principles that Balanchine followed for the rest of his career. During these years he lived at 11 East 77th Street and 120 East End Avenue in Manhattan. He continued his collaboration with Kirstein in his work for such companies as the American Ballet, which was the resident dance troupe of the Metropolitan Opera (1935–38), and the Ballet Society (1946–48), a chamber company that produced original ballets with newly commissioned music and decor. He also provided choreography for several Broadway shows, notably *On Your Toes* (1936) by Richard Rodgers and Lorenz Hart, which includes the famous ballet "Slaughter on Tenth Avenue." Between 1944 and 1946 he was a choreographer for the touring company Ballet Russe de Monte Carlo.

From the 1940s Balanchine forged a new style of classical dance. In the ballets *Concerto Barocco* (1941), *Ballet Imperial* (1941), and *Symphony in C* (1947) he heightened, quickened, and inverted traditional movements, but unlike other revolutionaries such as Martha Graham and Merce Cunningham he never abandoned classical technique. He further developed this idiom in *The Four Temperaments* (1946). At the invitation of Morton Baum, chairman of the executive committee of the City Center of Music and Drama, he joined with Kirstein in 1948 to form a resident company that became known as the New York City Ballet. With the company he created such reductive masterpieces as *Agon* (1957), *Episodes* (1959), *Movements for Piano and Orchestra* (1963), *Violin Concerto* (1972), and *Symphony in Three Movements* (1972). He also provided choreography for such narrative ballets as *The Nutcracker* (1954) and *Coppélia* (1974), spectacles such as *Vienna Waltzes* (1977) and *Jewels* (1967), and many classical display pieces.

In 1964 the New York Ballet moved to the New York State Theater at Lincoln Center. Balanchine trained many dancers there in a style characterized by sharp, precise, and often large movements. Among the most celebrated dancers with whom he worked were Maria Tallchief, Tanaquil LeClercq, Melissa Hayden, Suzanne Farrell, Patricia McBride, Merrill Ashley, Jacques d'Amboise, Edward Villella, and Peter Martins, who with Jerome Robbins became a ballet master of the company on Balanchine's death. In 1990 a segment of West 63rd Street near the New York State Theater was renamed George Balanchine Way.

Bernard Taper, *Balanchine: A Biography* (New York: Harper and Row, 1963; rev. Times Books, 1984); Nancy Reynolds, *Repertory in Review: Forty Years of the New York City Ballet* (New York: Dial, 1977); *George Balanchine: A Catalogue of Works* (New York: Viking, 1984)

Nancy Reynolds

Baldwin, James (Arthur) (*b* New York City, 2 Aug 1924; *d* St. Paul de Vence, France, 1 Dec 1987). Writer and civil rights activist. Born in Harlem to Emma Berdis Jones, he was raised by his mother and David Baldwin, the man she married when James was three years old. At Frederick Douglass Junior High School, he began contributing short stories and editorials to the school magazine at the encouragement of a French instructor, Countee Cullen, a notable poet of the Harlem Renaissance. In 1938, at age 14, he underwent what he later described as a "prolonged religious crisis" and became a preacher at the Fireside Pentecostal Assembly at 71 Thayer Street. He preached for three years while attending the prestigious DeWitt Clinton High School in the Bronx, where he stood apart both for his color and for his intellectual gifts, working as an editor of the *Magpie,* a school magazine. At age 16 he was introduced to the artist Beauford Delaney at his Greenwich Village studio. Baldwin credits Delaney with introducing him to the music (not allowed in his home) of Ma Rainey, Bessie Smith, Louis Armstrong, and Marian Anderson. In 1942, Baldwin graduated, left the church, and took a job laying railroad track in New Jersey. During the following year of odd jobs, he wrote short stories and essays (many of which would be published in his 1955 collection *Notes on a Native Son*) before returning to Harlem in June 1943. Encouraged by Delaney, Baldwin moved from his family's apartment to a Greenwich Village room. In 1944, struggling to write an autobiography of his childhood titled *Crying Holy,* Baldwin became friends with the influential author Richard Wright.

In 1948 Baldwin moved to Paris. His first novel, *Go Tell It on the Mountain,* was published in 1953. After a frustrated attempt at theater, he published *Notes on a Native Son* in 1955 and his second novel, *Giovanni's Room,* which drew controversy surrounding its homoeroticism, the following year. In 1957, he returned to the States, feeling the need to participate in the burgeoning civil rights movement. Commissioned for an article by *Harper's* magazine, Baldwin traveled to the South for the first time, where he was deeply impressed upon meeting Dr. Martin Luther King, Jr.; Baldwin would later remember his time during the civil rights years in essays published in *No Name in the Street* (1972). In 1961, his second collection of essays, *Nobody Knows My Name,* received critical attention and was also a surprising financial success.

Baldwin had become a national figure by this time and was also engaged politically through his writing. His long essay "Down at the Cross" (later published in *The Fire Next Time* [1963]) explored themes of race and religion, in particular the relationship between Christianity and the Black Muslim movement. While immersed in the civil rights struggle, he wrote *Blues for Mr. Charlie* (1964), a play based on the murder of Emmett Till that explored themes of racism and oppression. By the late 1960s, however, he seemed to fall out of favor politically as the Black Power movement took hold, and he was criticized by the Black Panthers' Eldridge Cleaver in his autobiography *Soul on Ice.* Baldwin lent support through his writing to various causes and continued to publish through the mid-1980s; he divided time between living abroad and in the United States until his death in 1987. A memorial service was held at the Cathedral of St. John the Divine at 112th Street and Amsterdam Avenue in Manhattan.

Garrett A. Felber

Baldwin, Roger (Nash) (*b* Wellesley, Mass., 21 Jan 1884; *d* New York City, 26 Aug 1981). Civil libertarian. After graduating from Harvard he became a nationally known social worker in St. Louis. In April 1917 he moved to New York City to assist Crystal Eastman and the Civil Liberties Bureau (CLB) in defending conscientious objectors, freedom of speech, and freedom of the press during World War I. He spent nearly a year in prison (1918–19) for refusing to be inducted into the armed forces. In 1920 he helped reorganize the CLB as the American Civil Liberties Union (ACLU), of which he became the director. After retiring from the ACLU in 1950 Baldwin devoted himself to international human rights issues. He was awarded the presidential Medal of Freedom in early 1981.

Samuel Walker, *In Defense of American Liberties: A History of the ACLU* (Carbondale: Southern Illinois University Press, 1999); Robert Cottrell, *Roger Nash Baldwin and the American Civil Liberties Union* (New York: Columbia University Press, 2001)

Samuel Walker

Ball, Thompkins and Black [Ball, Black and Company]. Firm of jewelers that later became Black, Starr and Frost.

Ballantine Books. Firm of book publishers, formed in 1952 by Ian Ballantine, formerly of the firm Bantam, and his wife, Betty. The firm distinguished itself by publishing paperbound books simultaneously with clothbound editions issued by established houses, and by offering royalties to authors of 7.5 percent, then thrice the going rate. The book trade was aghast but the firm was a success. It published science fiction by Ray Bradbury and others, as well as anthologies based on the magazine *Mad.* After the firm was acquired in 1973 by Random House, Ballantine resigned to form a book packager, Rufus Publications, that had a short life.

James E. Mooney

Ballet Hispanico of New York. Dance company founded in 1970 by Tina Ramirez to represent Hispanic culture through performance dance. It is known for its innovative fusion of Latin, classical, and contemporary dance. The company has commissioned more than 70 pieces from internationally acclaimed choreographers and performs nationally and internationally. In addition to its performance group, the Ballet Hispanico also operates a school, which trains 600 students in dance and performance techniques and has such notable alumni as Nancy Ticotin, Jennifer Lopez, and Michael DeLorenzo. It also administers programs such as "Primeros Pasos" or "First Steps," which provides after-school programs, classroom programs in public schools, and residency programs to students throughout New York City. It is located on

West 89th Street between Columbus and Amsterdam avenues.

Stephanie Miller

Ballet Tech. See Feld Ballet.

Ballet Theatre. See American Ballet Theatre.

B. Altman. Firm of high-end clothing retailers, founded in April 1865 by Benjamin Altman as a small dry-goods shop at 39 Third Avenue between Ninth and 10th streets. It moved in the early 1870s to larger quarters on Sixth Avenue between 21st and 22nd streets and in 1876 to an elegant six-story building at 627 Sixth Avenue (at 19th Street). Altman began buying land in the block diagonally across from the Empire State Building bounded by 35th Street, Madison Avenue, 34th Street, and Fifth Avenue, and in 1905 work began on a twelve-story building in the Italian Renaissance style. Completed in 1914, it was built largely of French limestone and took up the entire block; its elegant interior had broad aisles, high ceilings, parquet floors, and crystal chandeliers. Known as one of the most fashionable department stores and for its extravagant Christmas decorations, Altman attracted many visitors with its window displays of mechanized tableaux during the winter holidays. The building received landmark status in 1985. In 1987 Altman's was bought by L. J. Hooker, a firm owned by the Australian corporate raider George Herscu, and at the end of 1989 it ceased operations. At the end of the twenty-first century the building was occupied by the New York Public Library's Science, Industry, and Business Library as well as the CUNY Graduate Center.

Allen J. Share

BAM. See Brooklyn Academy of Music.

Bancroft [Italiano], **Anne (Maria Louisa)** (*b* Bronx, 17 Sept 1931; *d* New York City, 6 June 2005). Actress. Born to an Italian immigrant family, her mother a telephone operator and her father a patternmaker, Bancroft was intrigued by performance art at a young age. After graduating from the Christopher Columbus High School in the Bronx in 1948, she attended a series of acting schools in New York City and Los Angeles. She made her film debut in *Don't Bother to Knock* in 1952 and then continued her career in Hollywood and on Broadway with hits like *New York Confidential* (1955), *Two for the Seesaw* (1958), *The Miracle Worker* (1962), and, most prominently, *The Graduate* (1967). A Catholic, she converted to Judaism to marry director and writer Mel Brooks in 1964 at New York City Hall after meeting him on the set of a talk show. Bancroft was known for her Method acting, her sultry voice, and the versatility of her roles. The Emmy-, Tony-, and Academy Award–winning actress split her time between Los Angeles and New York City homes until her death in 2005. Her memorial service in New York City featured Paul Simon singing Simon and Garfunkel's song "Mrs. Robinson," which was written about her role in *The Graduate*. Bancroft is buried at the Kensico Cemetery in suburban Valhalla, New York.

Cecilia Magnusson

bands. The first military band in New York City was the 11th Regiment Militia Band, led by Thomas Brown and stationed on Bedloe's Island (now Liberty Island). The military tradition inspired a civilian brass band movement in the early to mid-nineteenth century. Thomas Dilks's Independent Band, formed in 1825 as the city's first professional wind band, played for several seasons at Castle Garden before dividing into two factions in 1835, one of which was directed from the following year by Allen Dodworth and became the most successful and influential band in the city. Dodworth invented and patented specially designed marching instruments in 1838 and published the highly regarded manual *Brass Band School* in 1853. He managed the group until 1860, when his brother Harvey took charge. In the same year John F. Stratton, a manufacturer based in New York City, began mass production of brass instruments. After the Civil War a number of leading bandmasters were based in the city: Harvey Dodworth led the Dodworth Band and the 13th Regiment Band of the New York National Guard, Claudius Grafulla led the 7th Regiment Band until he was succeeded in 1881 by the trombonist Carlo Cappa, and David L. Downing led the 9th Regiment Band. All three derived prestige and steady financial support from their association with the armed forces, and all were given free artistic rein. In 1873 Patrick S. Gilmore assumed leadership of the 22nd Regiment Band, widely known from then on as Gilmore's Band. Under his direction the 22nd regularly toured the nation with the best-known soloists of the time and set new standards for performance. After Gilmore's death in 1892 19 of his musicians joined a band based in the city and formed by John Philip Sousa that became nationally renowned.

One of the most popular bands in New York City was that formed in 1887 by Frederick Innes, a trombonist and former leader of the 13th Regiment Band in Brooklyn. It often gave summer concerts at Prospect Park and performed regularly throughout the city until Innes moved to Denver in 1913. After 10 years as a renowned trombone soloist with Sousa's band, which he also helped to lead, Arthur Pryor in 1903 formed his own ensemble, which in the same year made its debut at the Majestic Theatre (3 November) and recorded the first commercial discs issued by the Victor Company; for several seasons it also played at Luna Park in Coney Island. By this time several bands based in New York City maintained regular touring schedules and appeared at such venues as Manhattan Beach, Hamilton Fish Park, and Madison Square Garden. In 1915 Sousa's band gave daily concerts between May and September at the Hippodrome, and Pryor performed during the summers of 1921–25 at Lido Beach in Coney Island. The New York Military Band was formed in 1911 by Edwin Franko Goldman, formerly a cornetist with the Metropolitan Opera Orchestra and an instructor at Columbia University; known from 1918 as the Goldman Band, it performed annual summer concerts at Columbia and the Central Park Mall, commemorated in Goldman's popular march "On the Mall" (1923). Other Goldman compositions inspired by New York City include "Central Park," "New Yorker," "Hail, Brooklyn," and "On the Hudson." The Goldman Band also played on the first radio broadcast of the National Broadcasting Company on 15 November 1926.

From the 1920s professional concert bands diminished in number, and bands became associated primarily with school, civic, and fraternal organizations. Bands were formed by the fire department (1922), the police department, the Knights of Columbus, City College (1925), Columbia University (1928), and Fordham University (1928). The Goldman Band performed until 1979 under the direction of Goldman's son Edward, who died the following year; under the direction of Ainslee Cox the group continued as the Goldman Memorial Band and performed throughout the five boroughs into the 1990s, by which time it was the city's longest-lived band and the third-oldest professional musical association of any kind. The city's most visible bands are those of local high schools, which regularly perform at parades throughout the city.

Marc Ferris

Bangladeshis. Immigration to the United States from Bangladesh began in the early 1970s and grew slowly into the 1990s. In 1990 about 5000 Bangladeshis lived in the five boroughs, the majority in Queens (2567) and Brooklyn (1313). In Manhattan, Bangladeshis formed a small enclave on East Sixth Street. By 2000 the Bangladeshi population had grown to about 28,000, 18,310 of which lived in Queens and 6243 in Brooklyn. According to the Department of City Planning, about 4000 Bangladeshi immigrants were arriving legally in New York City each year early in the twenty-first century, making them one of the fastest-growing immigrant groups. Unofficial estimates that account for undocumented immigrants put the Bangladeshi population as high as 100,000 in 2009, when the Consulate General of Bangladesh in New York was located at 211 East 43rd Street.

Jessica Montesano

Bangs, Nathan (*b* Stratford, Conn., 2 May 1778; *d* New York City, 3 May 1862). Minister and editor. A leading exponent of American Methodism in New York City, he served the Methodist Book Concern as its director from 1820 to 1828. He also edited the important Methodist periodicals *Christian Advocate and Journal and Zion's Herald* and the *Methodist Quarterly Review,* and led the American Methodist missionary organization. Bangs was later the pastor of three congregations in the city.

Charles Yrigoyen, Jr.

Bankers Trust Company. Firm of commercial bankers formed in 1903 by Henry Davison with J. P. Morgan and his associates in response to stricter regulations of trusts. It was designed to perform fiduciary work for commercial banks. The first head office was in the Jersey Central Building at 143 Liberty Street, but it soon moved to 7 Wall Street. In 1909 the firm leased a building at 16 Wall Street and added a pyramid to the top, which became a symbol of the financial district. The firm pursued commercial banking in the 1920s and 1930s. It moved its headquarters to Fifth Avenue and 44th Street in 1936 and introduced retail banking operations after World War II. Between 1955 and 1965, 22 branches were added. In 1962 executive headquarters were erected at 280 Park Avenue. In 1974 a new headquarters was opened adjacent to the World Trade Center. In 1999 it was acquired by Deutsche Bank.

Susan Aaronson

Headquarters of the Bankers Trust Company (designed by Trowbridge and Livingston), 1912

Bankhead, Tallulah (Brockman) (*b* Huntsville, Ala., 31 Jan 1902; *d* New York City, 12 Dec 1968). Actress. The daughter of a Speaker of the U.S. House of Representatives, she made her debut on Broadway in 1918 and after a number of mixed performances became well known in *Dark Victory* (1934), by George Brewer, Jr., and Bertram Bloch, and a revival of W. Somerset Maugham's *Rain.* From 1931 to 1938 she lived at the Hotel Elysée at 56–60 East 54th Street. One of her most memorable roles was that of Regina Giddens in Lillian Hellman's *The Little Foxes* (1939). Her performance in Thornton Wilder's *The Skin of Our Teeth* (1942) was well received, and she toured in a successful revival of Noël Coward's *Private Lives* (1945–50). During the 1940s she had permanent quarters at the Hotel Gotham at 2 West 55th Street. Known for her deep voice, she was the host of the city's last important radio variety program, *The Big Show* (1945–50). Bankhead made a few motion pictures; of these only Hitchcock's *Lifeboat* (1943) conveys her distinctiveness. She bought the building at 230 East 62nd Street in 1956 and lived there until 1962, when she moved to 447 East 57th Street, her home for the last six years of her life.

Lee Israel, *Miss Tallulah Bankhead* (New York: G. P. Putnam's Sons, 1972)

David J. Weiner

banking. See Commercial banks, Credit unions, Investment banking, Savings and loan associations, and Savings banks, as well as entries on individual figures and institutions.

Bank of New York. The first chartered bank in New York City. Its formation followed the placing of a small advertisement in the *New York Packet* on 23 February 1784, only three months after British troops left New York City, calling on the "Gentlemen of this City to establish a Bank on liberal principles." The bank was organized during a meeting at the Merchants' Coffee House, with Alexander Hamilton authoring its constitution. It opened for business at the Walton House on 9 June 1784. The charter called for a capital stock of $500,000; shares of $1000, payable in gold or silver, were all bought up immediately. In 1797 the bank erected its headquarters at 48 Wall Street. The center of the city's financial life, it provided financing for importers and

Bank of New York, 2009

helped the federal government to establish a firm financial basis. After four years on the board of directors Hamilton became the secretary of the Treasury under President George Washington in 1789 and soon negotiated the government's first loan from the bank, which put up $200,000 against warrants drawn by the U.S. Treasury. The bank became a major lender to New York City, New York State, and foreign governments. The bank eventually merged with such prominent institutions as the New York Life Insurance and Trust Company (1922), the Fifth Avenue Bank (1948), the Empire Trust Company (1966), Empire National Bank (1980), and the Long Island Trust Company (1987). After acquiring the Irving Bank in 1988 the Bank of New York became the tenth-largest bank holding company in the United States, with assets of about $50 billion. As of 1 October 2007 the bank changed its name to the Bank of New York Mellon following its merger with the Mellon Financial Corporation. Before this, it had been the oldest bank in the United States operating under its original name. In 2008 its headquarters remained at 48 Wall Street.

Herbert S. Parmet, *200 Years of Looking Ahead: Commemorating the Bicentennial of the Founding of the Bank of New York, 1784–1984* (Rockville, Md.: History Associates for the Bank of New York, 1984)

Allis Wolfe

Bank of United States. Commercial bank formed in 1913 by Joseph Marcus, formerly a garment manufacturer. It was situated at first on the corner of Orchard and Delancey streets; from 1918 the head office was at Fifth Avenue and 32nd Street. The bank catered specifically to a clientele of Jews and recent immigrants. Control of the bank was assumed in 1927 by Bernard Marcus (son of the founder) and his partner Saul Singer, who acquired five other banks at inflated prices and used depositors' money to pursue speculative personal ventures. By the time of its failure on 11 December 1930, the bank had 440,000 depositors and 59 branches, making it then the largest bank in American history. In the ensuing crisis in the banking system some members of the New York Clearing House were accused of anti-Semitism for having allowed the bank to fail, although even those who made the accusation acknowledged that the bank had engaged in questionable practices. Bernard Marcus and Singer were sent to Sing Sing Prison in March 1931.

M. R. Werner, *Little Napoleons and Dummy Directors: Being the Narrative of the Bank of United States* (New York: Harper and Brothers, 1933)

Joan L. Silverman

Bank Street College of Education. Private institution formed in 1916 as the Bureau of Educational Experiments by Lucy Sprague Mitchell (1878–1967), a former pupil of John Dewey at Columbia Teachers College who sought to study the physical, social, and emotional growth of children and to develop environments conducive to learning. With her colleague Harriet Johnson she organized the first all-day nursery schools (1918) and adopted a scientific and creative approach to pedagogy. Under her leadership the bureau funded health and nutrition studies, vocational projects, sex education programs, and schools where educational theories could be tested and students' behavior observed. In 1930 the bureau moved from six brownstones on West 12th and 13th streets to 69 Bank Street and organized the Cooperating School for Student Teachers; it was granted a charter by the Regents of the State of New York in 1941 and certified under its current name in 1950. Bank Street College has been active in public and private schools in the city and has gained national recognition for its participation in such programs as Head Start, Follow Through, and Right to Read and for its role in publishing the Little Golden Books and Bank Street Readers for children. In 2010 it was located at 610 West 112th Street in Manhattan and enrolled about 1000 students, all at the graduate level, and conferred master of science in education and master of education degrees. It also operated the Bank Street School for children which, in 2010, enrolled about 450 students.

Bank Street College of Education, 2009

Lucy Sprague Mitchell, *Two Lives: The Story of Wesley Clair Mitchell and Myself* (New York: Simon and Schuster, 1953); Joyce Antler, *Lucy Sprague Mitchell: The Making of a Modern Woman* (New Haven: Yale University Press, 1987)

Linda Elsroad, Alfonso J. Orsini

Bank Street School. Nursery school opened in 1918 by Lucy Sprague Mitchell under the auspices of the Bureau of Educational Experiments (later known as the Bank Street College of Education). Initially situated in her brownstone in Greenwich Village, the school moved with the bureau in 1930 to a disused factory of the Fleischmann Yeast Company on 69 Bank Street, where it expanded into a full elementary school. The educational methods at the school reflected the influence of Mitchell's study with John Dewey at Teachers College and her collaborations with Caroline Pratt at the Play School and Elisabeth Irwin at the Little Red School House. The school is a demonstration school with a curriculum that focuses on the emotional, social, physical, and intellectual well-being of its students. Eventually the school moved to West 112th Street, where it served both as a community school and as an experimental facility for education students and experts. In 2006 it enrolled 450 children from 3 to 13 years old.

Joyce Antler, *Lucy Sprague Mitchell: The Making of a Modern Woman* (New Haven: Yale University Press, 1987)

Alfonso J. Orsini

Bantam Books. Firm of paperback book publishers, formed in 1945 by Ian Ballantine. He opened his headquarters at 1107 Broadway and moved to 25 West 45th Street in 1950. With its parent firm, Grosset and Dunlap, Bantam was sold in 1968 to National General Corporation. Headquarters were moved to 666 Fifth Avenue in 1970, and the firm was sold in 1974 to IFI International, an Italian conglomerate. In 1977 a controlling interest was bought by the Bertelsmann Publishing Group, which became the sole owner in 1981. Bantam produced the popular children's "Choose Your Own Adventure" series from 1979 to 1998. It was also known for its science fiction and mystery novels, and the Bantam Classics series included such books as Jane Austen's *Pride and Prejudice* and Fyodor Dostoevsky's *Crime and Punishment.* In 1999 Bantam merged with Dell Publishing.

Clarence Petersen, *The Bantam Story: Twenty-Five Years of Paperback Publishing* (New York: Bantam, 1970)

Allen J. Share

Bantam Dell Publishing Group. Book publisher. In 1999 Bantam Books and Dell Publishing were merged to form the Bantam Dell Publishing Group. This became the largest division of Random House, which had been acquired the year before by Bertelsmann Publishing Group International, one of the largest media companies and mass-market book publishers in the world. Bantam Dell Publishing Group superseded Bantam Doubleday Dell, which had been created in 1988 after Bertelsmann acquired Doubleday and Company late in 1986. The Bantam Dell Publishing Group includes books published under the following imprints: Bantam Hardcover, Bantam Mass Market, Bantam Trade Paperback, Spectra, Delacorte Press Hardcover, Dell Mass Market Paperback, Delta Trade Paperback, the Dial Press Hardcover, and Dial Press Trade Paperback. In the early twenty-first century the firm's offices were at 1745 Broadway.

Allen J. Share

Baptists. The first notice of Baptist activity in New Netherland is a report from the pastors of the Reformed Church in 1657 that "a fomenter of error," a cobbler from Rhode Island named William Wickenden, "began to preach at Flushing, and then went with the people into the river and dipped them," for which he was banished from the province. A congregation was organized in 1724 by Nicholas Ayres, who had been converted to the Baptist position in meetings held in his house. A meetinghouse was built, and Ayres remained its pastor until he resigned in 1731. In the following year the property was claimed by one of the trustees, and the congregation dissolved. First Baptist Church (1762) was organized by a group that had first met informally and had then become members of the Scotch Plains Baptist Church in New Jersey. John Gano was called as pastor, and a meetinghouse was built on Gold Street. The church was closed during the Revolution and used for a stable by British troops. Gano served as a chaplain to the Continental army and returned in 1784, finding only 37 of the 200 members still in the city. Abyssinian Baptist Church (1808) was organized by "free colored" members of First Baptist. The first Baptist churches in what later became the other boroughs were Baptist Temple (organized as First Baptist Church, 1823) in Brooklyn, Park Baptist Church (1841) in Staten Island, Ridgewood Baptist Church (organized as First German Baptist Church, 1855) in Queens, and Fulton Avenue Baptist Church (organized as German Bethel Baptist Church of Morrisania, 1857) in the Bronx. The first African American congregations in Brooklyn, Queens, and the Bronx were, respectively, the Concord Baptist Church of Christ (1847), Ebenezer Baptist Church of Flushing (1870), and Day Star Baptist Church (organized 1888 in Manhattan). In 1830 Baptists were among the four leading denominations in New York City, with 2931 members. By 1870 this number increased to 11,203 in Manhattan and 6812 in Brooklyn. Successive phases of immigration brought new groups of people to the city from Europe, the Caribbean, Latin America, Asia, and Africa, prompting the formation of many foreign-language Baptist congregations: First German Baptist Church (1846), Trinity Baptist Church (First Swedish Baptist Church, 1853), First Italian Baptist Church (1897), First Norwegian–Danish Baptist Church (1903), First Czechoslovak Baptist Church (Bohemian Baptist Church, 1905), First Latvian Baptist Church (1905), First Hungarian Baptist Church (1906), First Estonian Baptist Church (1919), First Spanish Baptist Church (1919), First Russian Baptist Church (1923), First Chinese Baptist Church (1926), First Polish Baptist Church (1926), Haitian Baptist Church (1965), Korean Baptist Church (1976), First Rumanian Baptist Church (1979), First Portuguese-Speaking Baptist Church (1982), Bronx Bible Church (Filipino, 1986), and First Indonesian Baptist Church (1993).

The first organization of Baptists in Greater New York was the New-York Association, formed in 1791 by three churches in the city, three from New Jersey, and one from Long Island. In time this body became the Southern New York and the Long Island Baptist associations, in fellowship with American Baptist Churches USA. The Baptist Female Missionary Society (1806), Baptist Sunday School Society (1816), and Baptist Widows and Orphans Fund (1839) were also sponsored by churches in New York City. In 1841 they organized the Representative Mission Society of the Baptist Association, incorporated in 1893 as the New York City Baptist Mission Society, which together with the Baptist Church Extension Society of Brooklyn and Queens (1918) conducted mission work throughout the city. Edward S. Judson developed Judson Memorial Baptist Church (1890) as an institutional church serving the Italian community in Greenwich Village. In 1901 the Mission Society conducted five daily vacation Bible schools, the first in the city. Charles Hatch Sears, executive secretary from 1904 to 1943, was an outstanding mission planner and administrator who greatly increased the scope of the society's work in the city to encompass the organization of many new churches, educational work with African American churches, and Christian Friendliness programs to serve immigrant families. In 1972 the two Baptist associations (Southern New York; Long Island) and the two city mission societies (New York; Brooklyn and Queens) merged to form American Baptist Churches of Metropolitan New York (ABC Metro), which by the mid-1990s had 148 member churches in the five boroughs; because of congregational autonomy, many of these also belong to other Baptist bodies.

A strong sense of ethnic identity, as well as theological and political conflicts, led to the formation of other bodies of Baptist churches that also included congregations in the city. Among these were the North American Baptist Conference (1865, with two churches in the city in the mid-1990s), founded by German Baptists, and the Baptist General Conference (1879, with six churches), founded by Swedish Baptists. African American churches have three national conventions: National Baptist Convention USA (1895, with 285 member churches in New York City), the parent convention of black Baptists; the National Baptist Convention of America (with 23 churches), which divided from the other body in 1915; and the Progressive National Baptist Convention (1961, with 63 churches), which had as its first president Gardner C. Taylor, then pastor of Concord Baptist Church of Christ in Brooklyn. Theological controversies with American Baptists caused the formation of the General Association of Regular Baptists (1932, three churches in New York City) and the Conservative Baptist Association of America (1947, 27 churches). The Southern Baptist Convention, organized in 1845, began missionary activity in the city in 1957; in the mid-1990s the Metropolitan New York Baptist Association included 75 churches in the five boroughs.

New York City has also been a center for national Baptist organizations. The American Baptist Home Mission Society was organized on 27 April 1832 in the Mulberry Street Baptist Church. Some sessions were also held at the Oliver Street Baptist meetinghouse: its pastor, Spencer H. Cone, was elected the first president. The Northern Baptist Convention, founded in 1907 in Washington, D.C., with Governor Charles Evans Hughes of New York as its president, was incorporated in the state and established headquarters in the city. In 1911 American Baptists organized the Ministers and Missionaries Benefit Board, which was incorporated with offices in New York City. From 1920 to 1963, when national American Baptist headquarters were moved to Valley Forge, Pennsylvania, the city was the site of the national offices of the American Baptist Foreign Mission Society, the Woman's American Baptist Foreign Mission Society, the American Baptist Home Mission Society, the Woman's American Baptist Home Mission Society, and the Northern Baptist Convention, as well as the Benefit Board, which all remain in the city. Many important Baptist national meetings and conferences have been held in the city, but only the National Baptist Convention USA has conducted its national convention there (in 1935 and 1993).

Several leading Baptist leaders and thinkers have lived and worked in New York City. William Colgate, founder of the soap manufacturing company bearing his name, was a Baptist deacon. Walter Rauschenbusch, a leading exponent of the Social Gospel, developed his theological perspective as the pastor of a German congregation near Hell's Kitchen from 1886 to 1902; he joined with his fellow Baptist pastors Samuel Zane Batten, Nathaniel Schmidt, and Leighton Williams to form the Brotherhood of the Kingdom, devoted to social thought and action. The first woman to be ordained by a Baptist congregation was Mabel Lee in 1925: she succeeded her father as minister of the Morningstar Chinese Mission, which became First Chinese Baptist Church. John D. Rockefeller, Jr., was a Baptist layman and philanthropist who financed the move of Park Avenue Baptist Church to Morningside Heights, where it became the Riverside Church. Its first pastor was Harry Emerson Fosdick, an advocate in the pulpit of liberal theology and biblical criticism, whose sermon "Shall the Fundamentalists Win?" was bitterly attacked by John Roach Straton, pastor of Calvary Baptist Church. Adam Clayton Powell, Jr., who succeeded his father as pastor at Abyssinian Baptist Church, led civil rights demonstrations in Harlem before being elected to Congress in 1944. Bertha Grimmell Judd was president of the Woman's American Baptist Home Mission Society from 1937 to 1942 and wrote the society's 50-year history. Marguerite Hazzard was its president from 1951 until 1955 when it merged with the American Baptist Home Mission Society. In the early twenty-first century, there were about 600 Baptist churches in New York City and almost 400,000 members of Baptist congregations in the five boroughs.

George D. Younger

Barbadians. Immigrants from Barbados began settling in New York City around 1900. The Sons and Daughters of Barbados Benevolent Society, formed in 1913, was an early center for the community. Several thousand Barbadians, most of them black, arrived during the following decades. Throughout the 1950s racial prejudice confined them almost exclusively to the black neighborhoods of Harlem and Bedford–Stuyvesant and to menial and unskilled work even though most were literate and skilled. Tens of thousands of Barbadians arrived in the city after the passage of the Hart–Celler Act in 1965. They settled primarily in Brooklyn and in a few racially integrated neighborhoods.

Barbadians in New York City work in management, technical occupations, and the professions; the unskilled continue to account for a large part of the workforce. Barbadians are active in the Combermere School Alumni Association of New York, the Barbados Nurses' Association of New York, and the Barbados Ex-police Association of New York, as well as in a number of cricket clubs. In 2000 more than 27,000 New Yorkers claimed Barbadian ancestry, and two-thirds of them live in Brooklyn.

Veronica Udeogalanya, *A Comparative Analysis of Caribbean Immigrants Admitted into the United States, 1985–1987* (New York: Medgar Evers College, Caribbean Research Center, 1991)

Calvin B. Holder

Barber, Red [Walter] (*b* Columbus, Miss., 17 Feb 1908; *d* Tallahassee, Fla., 22 Oct 1992). Sports broadcaster. Raised in Florida, he began broadcasting baseball in Cincinnati, covering the Reds from 1934–38. In 1939 the Brooklyn Dodgers hired Barber to broadcast games, breaking a 1934 radio ban the Dodgers, Yankees, and Giants had signed. That same year he broadcast the first-ever televised baseball game when the Dodgers hosted the Cincinnati Reds, his former employer. His accurate, unbiased descriptions and homespun southern wit earned Barber a reputation as baseball's best broadcaster. He also announced football and was the first sports director for Columbia Broadcasting System Radio. After 1953 Barber left the Dodgers for the New York Yankees, broadcasting on radio and television for the Yankees through 1966, when he was fired after reporting that only 413 spectators were at a rainy Yankee Stadium for a meaningless September game. He retired to Florida, writing and broadcasting until his death.

Andrew Sparberg

Barbetta. Restaurant. Located at 321 West 46th, it is the oldest restaurant in New York City that is still owned by the family that started it. Founded in 1906 by Sebastiano Maioglio, it serves Italian Piemonte cuisine in the midst of eighteenth-century Italian furnishings. In 1963 the owner Laura Maioglio added a garden for open-air dining behind four nineteenth-century row houses that she bought from the Astor family on West 46th Street. Several rooms in the row houses serve as private party spaces.

Jessica Montesano

Barbicide. Brand of disinfectant products. Invented by Maurice King in 1947 in Brooklyn, the trademark blue liquid that disinfects combs and brushes has become a standard at barber shops and salons nationwide. King also invented a solution that dissolves the hair off synthetic brushes. King, a chemist and chemistry teacher, began King Research in a one-story factory on 12th Street and Second Avenue in Brooklyn. In 1988 King died and his son Ben took over the business, expanding the product line to include hospital-grade salon disinfectants and hair and skin care. In 1997 Ben King gave a gift of Barbicide to the Smithsonian Institution; it is now on display at the National Museum of American History. In the twenty-first century the company's production is located in Wisconsin.

Jessica Montesano

Bard, Samuel (*b* Philadelphia, 1 April 1742; *d* Hyde Park, N.Y., 24 May 1821). Educator and physician. The son of the prominent physician John Bard, he moved to New York City as a young man. He studied medicine from 1760 to 1765 in London and Edinburgh and in 1767 helped found at King's College the first medical school in New York City; this was later absorbed by the College of Physicians and Surgeons, of which he became the second president (1811–21). Throughout his career in New York City he maintained an extensive private practice; he was also at one time George Washington's physician. Bard wrote several major works, including *A Compendium of the Theory and Practice of Midwifery* (1808).

John Brett Langstaff, *Doctor Bard of Hyde Park* (New York: E. P. Dutton, 1942)

Joseph S. Lieber

Barent Eylandt. Former name of Randalls Island.

Bargemusic. Floating concert hall moored in the East River at Fulton Ferry Landing, Brooklyn Heights, since its founding by Olga

Bloom in 1978. A former violinist and violist, Bloom purchased a 100-foot-long (30.48 meters) decommissioned coffee barge built in 1899, which she renovated as a "safe harbor" for chamber music. The only enduring nautical establishment of its sort in the world, Bargemusic boasts a spectacular setting, the windows backing its stage offering a view of lower Manhattan. Its scale and limited seating for an audience of about 100 make it well suited to chamber music. Directed since 2000 by the violinist Mark Peskanov (in association with Bloom), Bargemusic produces four concerts each week, featuring a changing lineup of small ensembles.

James M. Keller

Barnard College. Undergraduate college for women within Columbia University, formed on 1 April 1889 with its own buildings, faculty, curriculum, administration, budget, and trustees. It was named for Frederick A. P. Barnard, the president of Columbia from 1864 to 1888, who was unable to persuade the trustees of Columbia to admit women as undergraduates. Annie Nathan Meyer, the young wife of a doctor, was largely responsible for raising the initial funds and assembling the first board of trustees, of which Barnard was a member. The first secular institution in New York City to grant the AB degree to women, it opened with a student body of 14 and a faculty of six and occupied a brownstone building at 343 Madison Avenue, near the site then occupied by Columbia at Madison Avenue and 49th Street. After Columbia moved to Morningside Heights in 1897, Barnard followed in 1900 to a site of 1 acre (0.4 hectares) at Broadway and 119th Street where a single building was erected. The college was led by a dean until 1952 and from that time by a president; among those to occupy these positions were Virginia C. Gildersleeve (1911–47), Millicent Cary McIntosh (1947–62), Ellen Futter (1980–93), Judith Shapiro (1994–2008), and Deborah L. Spar (2008–present). Most students lived off campus until 1980, but many dormitories were built in the following years and by the mid-1990s about 90 percent of the students lived on campus. Despite several proposals to merge with Columbia College, Barnard remained independent, even after Columbia decided to admit women for the first time in 1983. In 2007 construction began of a new multifunction student center called the Nexus. As of 2009 the campus occupied 4 acres (1.6 hectares) and had 11 buildings, 319 faculty members, 2400 students, and more than 25,000 alumnae. Famous alumnae include Martha Stewart, Joan Rivers, Zora Neale Hurston, and Twyla Tharp.

Barnard College, 2009

A History of Barnard College: Published in Honor of the Seventy-fifth Anniversary of the College (New York: Barnard College, 1964); Robert A. McCaughey, *Stand Columbia: A History of Columbia University* (New York: Columbia University Press, 2003)

Jane Allen

Barnes, Djuna (*b* Cornwall-on-Hudson, N.Y., 12 June 1892; *d* New York City, 18 June 1982). Novelist and playwright. As a reporter for the *Brooklyn Daily Eagle* shortly before World War I she wrote about Greenwich Village, where she settled about 1915. Associated with a circle of radical poets and artists who frequented Bruno's Garret on Washington Square South, she wrote innovative plays for the Provincetown Players, experimental verse, and droll vignettes of manners, and at the end of the war moved to Paris, where she wrote her best-known work, the novel *Nightwood* (1936). After returning from Europe in 1940 she lived in Patchin Place. Some of her later novels draw on the eccentric types of Greenwich Village. Toward the end of her life she became regarded as one of the earliest exponents of an avowedly lesbian sensibility in American letters.

Andrew Field, *The Life and Times of Djuna* (New York: G. P. Putnam's Sons, 1983); Andrew Field, *The Formidable Miss Barnes* (Austin: University of Texas Press, 1985)

Jan Seidler Ramirez

Barnes and Noble. Firm of book publishers and booksellers. It began in 1873 as a firm of wholesale book jobbers operated by William R. Barnes and G. Clifford Noble, who supplied schools, colleges, libraries, and book dealers with new and used books; they opened their first bookstore at 105 Fifth Avenue in

1917. The first publishing venture, launched in 1931, was the College Outline Series, which provided summaries of college courses. The firm was bought by Ampel in 1969 and the publishing division was sold to Harper and Row in 1971. During the 1970s Barnes and Noble became one of the country's first discount retail booksellers; it bought the firm of B. Dalton in 1986 and Doubleday Book Shops, a chain of 40 stores, in 1990. The firm went public in 1993 and throughout the 1990s opened a number of megastores. In 2010 a typical Barnes and Noble store averaged 25,000 square feet (7620 square meters) and held as many as 200,000 books; the company sells 300 million books per year. Its headquarters are at 122 Fifth Avenue. Just down the block the original 105 Fifth Avenue location remains the flagship store.

Allen J. Share

Barnet and Doolittle. Firm of lithographers formed in 1821 by William Armand Barnet and Isaac Doolittle (*b* New Haven, Conn., 13 Oct 1784; *d* Rochester, N.Y., 17 April 1852), both trained in France. Situated at 23 Lumber Street (later Trinity Place), it was the first commercial lithography firm in the United States. The firm was responsible for creating the incunabula of the lithographic art, and it produced the first American book with lithographs (*A Grammar of Botany,* comp. Henry Muhlenberg, 1822, drawings by Arthur J. Stansbury), an untitled view of the Black River falls, bridge, and mill near Brownville, New York, illustrations for the *American Journal of Science* (1822), and other works, some of which are held by the New-York Historical Society.

Harry T. Peters, *America on Stone: The Other Printmakers to the American People* (New York: Doubleday, Doran, 1931)

Wendy Shadwell

Barneys New York. Firm of men's clothing retailers, formed in 1923 at Seventh Avenue and 17th Street by Barney Pressman (1895–1991). In the early years Pressman angered competitors and manufacturers by purchasing brand-name suits from independent retailers in the South and reselling them at low prices. The firm owed its early success in part to his skill at developing clever promotions and radio and print advertising. By the 1960s Pressman's son Fred shifted the focus from discount toward high-priced retailing, and the store became the first in New York City to sell the work of famous European designers. It added women's apparel and elegant housewares in 1976, and in 1986 opened a separate women's branch in six brownstone buildings adjacent to the main store. An outlet at the World Financial Center opened in 1988, and in the following year three joint venture agreements were reached with the Japanese retailing concern Isetan, which called for the opening of stores across the United States and in Japan and Southeast Asia. In 1993 Barneys opened a large uptown branch at Madison Avenue and 61st Street. It remained privately held in the beginning of the twenty-first century.

Marc Ferris

Barnum, P(hineas) T(aylor) (*b* Bethel, Conn., 5 July 1810; *d* Bridgeport, Conn., 7 April 1891). Impresario. In 1841 he took over the site and contents of Scudder's Museum, a defunct institution at the intersection of Broadway and Ann Street, and opened the American Museum. His astute promotion of appearances there by such performers as the midget Charles Stratton (General Tom Thumb) and the Swedish soprano Jenny Lind made this the most successful of the many dime museums in the city. The museum was destroyed by fire on 13 July 1865, reopened on Broadway at Spring Street, then burned again in 1868. Barnum retired briefly to work on a revised edition of his autobiography (first published 1855, revised 1927), and on 10 April 1871 he opened with William Coup in Brooklyn what is generally acknowledged to have been the first three-ring circus. The various circuses with which he was associated were the first large-scale entertainments to travel by railway; they performed annually in New York City at the Hippodrome on 27th Street and later at the original Madison Square Garden. In 1882 he had the giant elephant Jumbo sent from England and paraded him through the streets of New York City. Often accused of perpetrating hoaxes (he once exhibited a "Fejee mermaid"), Barnum cheerfully capitalized on the gullibility of an amused public. Along with baby contests, melodramas, and poultry shows he exhibited live animals, scientific specimens, and curiosities of the natural world, providing inexpensive entertainment to a wide and varied audience. Although a permanent resident of Bridgeport (where he served as mayor), he maintained homes in Manhattan throughout his career, including one at 52 Frankfort Street from 1835 to 1840 and another at 438 Fifth Avenue from 1868.

P. T. Barnum

Neil Harris, *Humbug: The Art of P. T. Barnum* (Boston: Little, Brown, 1973); A. H. Saxon, *P. T. Barnum: The Legend and the Man* (New York: Columbia University Press, 1989)

See also Circuses.

Jean Ashton

Baron, Salo Wittmayer (*b* Tarnow, Galicia, 26 May 1895; *d* New York City, 25 Nov 1989). The most prominent scholar of Jewish history in the twentieth century. He taught from 1930 at Columbia University, where he directed the Center of Israel and Jewish Studies from 1950 to 1968. His apartment on Claremont Avenue was known nationally as a gathering place for scholars. Baron was president of the American Academy for Jewish Research, the Conference on Jewish Social Studies, and the American Jewish Historical Society. He wrote hundreds of articles and 13 books, including *A Social and Religious History of the Jews* (1937–89), published in 18 volumes.

Robert Liberles, *Salo Wittmayer Baron: Architect of Jewish History* (New York: New York University Press, 1995)

Michael N. Dobkowski

Baron de Hirsch Fund. Charitable organization. It was incorporated in February 1891 with $2.4 million from Baron Maurice de Hirsch (1831–96), a German immigrant who also established the Jewish Colonization Association in London. The fund is dedicated to assisting Jewish immigrants from Russia and Romania and offers various forms of aid, including English instruction. It operated solely within the United States until a change in its constitution in 1970 enabled it to begin assisting immigrants in Israel, providing financial assistance for education in the United States.

Samuel Joseph, *History of the Baron de Hirsch Fund: The Americanization of the Jewish Immigrant* (New York: Baron de Hirsch Fund, 1935)

Kenneth W. Rose

Barondess, Joseph (*b* Kamenets-Podolsk [now Kamanets-Podolski], Ukraine, 3 July 1867; *d* New York City, 19 June 1928). Labor leader. He emigrated from England to the United States, where he helped organize a union for cloakmakers in New York City. In 1891 he was unjustly convicted of extortion in a labor dispute, but he was pardoned in the following year. He later helped to organize the International Ladies' Garment Workers' Union, the Hebrew Actors' Union, and the Hebrew–American Typographical Union. A Zionist from 1900, he represented American Jewry at the Paris Peace Conference in 1919; he also served two terms on the New York City Board of Education. Barondess spent the last years of his life as an insurance broker.

Robert D. Parmet

"barrel murder." A murder committed in 1903, discovered on 14 April when a man was found stabbed and nearly decapitated in an ash barrel on a corner of East 11th Street. The crime led to widespread panic that an international criminal syndicate based in Sicily was preparing to launch attacks on non–Italian Americans. Public fears diminished after police identified the man as Benedetto Madonia and determined that the crime had been motivated by a matter within the syndicate. Tomasso Petto was suspected of complicity in the crime but never convicted.

Mary Elizabeth Brown

Barren Island. A former island in Jamaica Bay near the shoreline of Flatlands, lying within the borough of Brooklyn and far from residential areas. In the mid-nineteenth century it was the site of the largest dump in New York City, fed by barges carrying garbage and animal remains. Local factories used the remains, boiling bones and making fertilizer, glue, and fish oil. The last factory closed in 1935. In 1930 the island became the site of Floyd Bennett Field after the municipal government filled in marshland to connect it to the mainland. The island's population of 400 was evicted in 1936 to make way for the Belt Parkway. The U.S. Navy bought the airfield in 1942 and owned it until 1971, when control reverted to the city. Since 1972 Barren Island has been part of the Jamaica Bay Unit of the Gateway National Recreation Area.

Stephen Weinstein

Barrymore, John (Sidney Blythe) (*b* Philadelphia, 15 Feb 1882; *d* Los Angeles, 29 May 1942). Actor. Born into "America's First Family of Theater," Barrymore's good looks earned him the nickname "The Great Profile." In 1920, at the Plymouth Theater in New York City, Barrymore made his Shakespearean debut in *Richard the Third.* His performance was hailed by critics as the beginning of a new era for Shakespeare on the American stage. He went on for 101 performances—one more than Edwin Booth—before withdrawing from the production. Barrymore's starring role in *Hamlet* (1922) also won critical praise in both New York and London. An early star of silent films, he was acclaimed as one of the screen's greatest performers; during his 25-year career, he played the leading man in more than 60 films. By the mid-1930s, Barrymore's reckless lifestyle and hard drinking had taken its toll. To pay off debts to his ex-wives and the Internal Revenue Service, Barrymore accepted whatever roles were offered, but his memory became erratic and he had to resort to cue cards to remember his lines. He married four times and had three children; he is the grandfather of the popular actress Drew Barrymore. His sister, Ethel, and brother, Lionel, both had long and illustrious careers on the stage and in Hollywood. The Ethel Barrymore Theater, on West 47th Street, is named for his sister.

Frank Dyer

bars, taverns, and saloons. In 1641 the Stadt Herbergh, or City Tavern, sold wine and beer imported by the Dutch East India Company to the citizens of New Amsterdam, and the tavern became so central to the community that it was later made the town hall. Peter Stuyvesant complained in 1648 that 25 percent of the houses in the city were taverns and proceeded to impose strict regulations on their hours of business. The King's Arms at Cedar Street and Broadway became the rendezvous for opponents of Jacob Leisler in the 1680s. After the British captured New Amsterdam, the design of the English tavern came to predominate. Elaborately painted signs were mounted in front of such taverns as the Black Horse, the St. George, and the White Lion. At the center of the typical tavern stood a large fireplace that provided heat and was used for cooking; around the fireplace were tables and chairs for customers. The bar had a small, secure liquor cabinet to protect against thievery and destructive brawls. Ales and porters were the most widely consumed beverages, though rum, brandy, and Madeira also were popular. Most taverns offered two meals: a hot dinner at noon and a cold supper in the evening. Visitors from other cities and those in need of accommodations were quartered in small rooms on the second story or given pallets near the fireplace. Taverns were frequented only by men—merchants, lawyers, artisans, and sailors—and ranged in grade from the luxurious Fraunces Tavern (now rebuilt on its original site at 54 Pearl Street) to cheap taverns near the East River. Many were stopping places for stagecoaches, as well as centers for such entertainments as lectures, animal shows, bear baitings, cockfights, and rat killings. They served many other functions as well: in the early eighteenth century sailors seeking employment went to the Sign of the Pine Apple near the docks on the East River; politicians and businessmen often negotiated at the Merchants' Coffee House on Broad Street (from 1754) and the Black Horse Tavern at William Street and Exchange Place; drovers and butchers haggled over the price of cattle at the famous Bulls Head Tavern on the east side of the Bowery north of Canal Street; and early in the nineteenth century the Blue Boar on William Street was a national employment center for carpet weavers.

In the mid-nineteenth century the functions of the tavern were assumed by various other establishments: the hotel emerged as a place specifically for lodging, and the barroom or saloon (a term derived from the drinking salon of the 1850s) became a place where a working-class clientele consumed beer and other

Steve Brodie's Bowery Saloon, ca *1895*

liquors. As tens of thousands of Irish and German immigrants settled in the city, the saloon evolved into a central institution. Usually situated on a street corner, it was a single room dominated by a long, straight bar, usually without any chairs or seats. The change from tavern to saloon was accompanied by a growth in the popularity of lager beer, first brewed in the city in the late 1840s by Frederick and Maximilian Schaefer. By the 1860s and 1870s "stand-up" barrooms, owned mostly by breweries, were found throughout New York City. Some taverns suffered from the effects of the temperance movement and in particular from a decline in patronage among the middle class, but in tenement neighborhoods barrooms became integrated into the local way of life.

The saloon came to be regarded as the "poor man's club," providing young men with an appealing alternative to the lodging house and the tenement. Because saloons had no seats they could accommodate the rush of factory workers at midday and after work, and as early as the 1850s they served a free lunch to those purchasing beer. Workers could spend the evening playing shuffleboard, billiards, and cards or reading newspapers that the saloons provided; some men even received their mail there. Tammany Hall recognized the importance of saloons in working-class life and used them to muster votes from immigrants. Its last great leader, Charles Francis Murphy, began his career in politics in the 1880s as the owner of a saloon on 19th Street and Avenue C that sold customers a glass of beer and a bowl of soup for 5 cents. Toward the end of the century Jacob A. Riis took photographs of customers at "black-and-tans" (underground bars that were dimly lit and often dangerous). By 1885 there were 10,000 drinking places in the city, or one for every 140 residents. The great majority were local stand-up bars, but some were specialized establishments: beer gardens in Little Germany with tables, chairs, and brass bands (see Beer halls); elegant saloons in hotels; "sporting saloons" such as Harry Hill's at Crosby and Houston streets, where boxing matches attracted both the wealthy and the working class; concert saloons that provided musical and theatrical entertainment before the rise of vaudeville; and sailors' barrooms such as Jimmy the Priest's on Fulton Street (the model for the saloon in Eugene O'Neill's *The Iceman Cometh*).

Between the 1860s and 1919 there were only modest changes in the function and design of saloons. Although they remained overwhelmingly male, by 1910 women were sometimes admitted with a male escort. During Prohibition drinking moved from legal establishments to illegal speakeasies, which were ubiquitous and well attended despite a common view that they lacked ambience. Saloons reopened after the repeal of Prohibition but failed to regain the central position in the life of the city that they had occupied earlier, in part because improvements in housing conditions made evenings at home more bearable, and in part because restrictions on immigration in the 1920s decreased the city's population of single men. Female customers increased in number after World War II and were admitted to most drinking places by about 1960. The few bars that continued to admit men only were gradually forced by the women's movement to relent: the last was McSorley's Old Ale House in 1970, which had long been known by the slogan "good ale, raw onions, and no ladies." In the 1960s and 1970s bars were the backdrop for the city's changing sexual mores: singles bars began to open, especially on the Upper East Side (the best-known was Maxwell's Plum), as did gay bars, such as the Stonewall Inn on Christopher Street (site of the well-known rebellion in June 1969). Both types of bar declined in the 1980s and 1990s, however, owing to the spread of AIDS and other sexually transmitted diseases, as well as a worsening economy. At the same time brew pubs (which brewed their own beer) and sports bars increased in popularity.

The New York City Indoor Smoke-Free Air Act of 2002 banned smoking from nearly every business in New York, including bars. It was met with widespread opposition from bar and restaurant owners, who predicted a loss of income. Among the bars that have become well known in the history of New York City are the White Horse Tavern in Greenwich Village, Pete's Tavern at Irving Place, the Landmark Tavern at 46th Street and 11th Avenue, and the Ear Inn on Spring Street.

W. Harrison Bayles, *Old Taverns of New York* (New York: Frank Allaben Genealogical Company, 1915); Joseph Mitchell, *McSorley's Wonderful Saloon* (New York: Pantheon, 1992)

Richard Stott

Bartholdi Inn. Theatrical boardinghouse founded in 1899. Theresa Bartholdi, often called "Mother" Bartholdi, was the founder of the boardinghouse, which began as two floors at 1536 Broadway. Five years later, it moved to a 110-room location on the corner of 45th Street and Broadway. The inn catered mainly to vaudeville performers, including Eva Tanguay, Fanny Brice, Pearl White, D. W. Griffith, John Gilbert, Mack Sennett, and Charlie Chaplin. The Bartholdi Inn was replaced by a movie theater and office building in 1920.

Max Seppo

Bartók, Béla (*b* Nagyszentmiklós, Hungary [now Sînnicolau Mare, Romania], 25 March 1881; *d* New York City, 26 Sept 1945). Composer and pianist. After spending most of his career in Budapest, he fled from the Nazis and in October 1940 arrived in New York City, living first at 110-31 73rd Road in Forest Hills in Queens. During the same year he was appointed a research assistant in music at Columbia University, where he transcribed and edited a collection of Serbo-Croatian women's songs. For three years he lived at 3242 Cambridge Avenue in Riverdale in the Bronx. He composed the Concerto for Orchestra (1943), a commission by Serge Koussevitzky that won him the attention of a wider public, and the Sonata for Solo Violin (1943), commissioned by Yehudi Menuhin. From 1944 until his death he lived at 309 West 57th Street in Manhattan.

S. D. R. Cashman

Bartow–Pell Mansion. Historic house in the Bronx. It stands on a tract now in Pelham Bay Park bought in 1654 by the English physician Thomas Pell. Built between 1836 and 1842 by Robert Bartow, a publisher and a

Bartow–Pell Mansion, 2009

descendant of Pell, it remained in the family until 1888, when it was acquired by the city. The mansion is an elegant stone building with lavishly decorated Greek Revival interiors and a grand spiral staircase. In 1914 an orangerie was added and the International Garden Club took over the maintenance of the mansion, carriage house, and grounds. The mansion served Mayor Fiorello H. La Guardia as a summer office in 1936 and was opened as a public museum in 1947. The carriage house was restored and opened to the public in 1993.

Lockwood Barr, *Genealogical Charts and Biographical Notes on the Pell Family, with Special Reference to the Lords of the Manor of Pelham, Westchester County, New York, also the Allied Bartow Family of the Bartow Mansion* (Pelham Manor, N.Y.: n.pub., 1946); *Historic Houses in New York City Parks* (New York: Department of Parks and Recreation/Historic House Trust of New York City, 1989)

Jonathan Kuhn

Baruch, Bernard (Mannes) (*b* Camden, S.C., 19 Aug 1870; *d* New York City, 20 June 1965). Legendary financier. After moving to New York City with his parents and three brothers in 1880 he lived with his family at 144 West 57th Street, later at 345 West End Avenue, and until 1899 at 51 West 70th Street. He graduated from City College in 1889 and joined the brokerage firm of A. A. Housman as a clerk; by the time he was 30 he had amassed a fortune of more than $1 million. At age 33 he was elected to the governing committee of the New York Stock Exchange. A supporter of Mayor William J. Gaynor, he became a trustee of City College in 1910. His most successful investment was in the Gulf Sulphur Company (later Texas Gulf Sulphur) in 1912. He was appointed by President Woodrow Wilson as chairman of the War Industries Board in 1918, and after the war to a senior advisory position with the American peace delegation in Paris. In the 1920s he bought a mansion at 1055 Fifth Avenue, where he lived until 1946 (the site is now occupied by 1050 Fifth Avenue). Although he lost money during the stock market crash of 1929 he recovered quickly; his fortune was estimated at $20 million to $25 million during the Depression. In the early 1930s he had the foresight to buy gold. A conservative Democrat, he was a sometimes reluctant ally of President Franklin D. Roosevelt and an adversary of President Harry S. Truman, who named him the American representative to the United Nations Atomic Energy Commission in 1946. As a longtime member of the Committee on Unlisted Securities he worked to advance the acceptance of mining issues by the other governors. His greatest disappointment in business was his inability to gain control of a railroad. In his later years Baruch warned repeatedly against inflation. Bernard Baruch College of the City University of New York is named in his memory. From the mid-1940s until his death he lived at 4 East 66th Street. He wrote *Baruch: My Own Story* (1957) and *Baruch: The Public Years* (1960).

Bernard Baruch

Jordan A. Schwartz, *The Speculator: Bernard M. Baruch in Washington, 1917–1965* (Chapel Hill: University of North Carolina Press, 1981); James Grant, *Bernard M. Baruch: The Adventures of a Wall Street Legend* (New York: Simon and Schuster, 1983)

James Grant

Baruch College. College of the City University of New York (CUNY), formed in 1919 at 17 Lexington Avenue in Manhattan as a branch of City College dedicated to business and civic administration. Its landmark building is located on the site of the Free Academy, the first free institution of public education in the United States. In 1953 it was named after the financier Bernard Baruch, one of the most successful graduates of City College, who gave the college $9 million in 1965; it became an independent college of the city university system in 1968.

In the early twenty-first century it has three schools: the Zicklin School of Business, which enrolled 80 percent of its students; the School of Public Affairs; and the Weissman School of Arts and Sciences. The college also offers nondegree and certificate programs through its Division of Continuing and Professional Studies. Zicklin School of Business is the largest collegiate school of business in the nation and the only CUNY school that offers business programs accredited by the Association to Advance Collegiate Schools of Business. Formerly a predominantly male student body, by 2009 more than half the students were women; 65 percent of the almost 17,000 students were full time.

Selma C. Berrol, *Getting Down to Business: Baruch College in the City of New York* (Westport, Conn.: Greenwood, 1989)

Lisa Keller

Baryshnikov, Mikhail (*b* Riga, Latvia, 28 Jan 1948). Dancer, choreographer, and dance promoter. He joined the Kirov Ballet in Leningrad (now Saint Petersburg, Russia) in 1967, and soon rose to prominence for his technical virtuosity and emotional fire before defecting to the West in 1974. He joined American Ballet Theatre, quickly becoming a star and helping to launch the "ballet boom" of the 1970s. In 1979 he moved briefly to New York City Ballet, returning to ABT in 1980 as principal dancer and artistic director, a position he held for 10 years. While at ABT he choreographed a number of works, including *The Nutcracker*. Active in both modern dance and ballet, he has performed with major companies worldwide, in films, on television (including *Sex and the City*), and in the theater. A dance promoter as well as a performer, he

The first home of Baruch College, Lexington Avenue and 23rd Street

founded the Baryshnikov Dance Foundation (1979) and the White Oak Dance Project (2002, with MARK MORRIS) and is currently artistic director of the Baryshnikov Arts Center (established 2005). Located at 450 W. 37th Street, the center offers performance space (including the Jerome Robbins Theater) and dance studios, as well as residencies and other support for artists.

Barzun, Jacques (Martin) (*b* Créteil, France, 30 Nov 1907). Historian. His association with Columbia University began when he enrolled there at age 15 in the fall of 1923 (AB 1927, MA 1928, PhD 1932). He went on to positions as a professor (1928–55), dean of the graduate faculties (1955–67), dean of the faculties and provost (1958–67), and university professor (1968–75). One of the most prominent intellectuals in the United States, he was featured on the cover of *Time* magazine in 1956. After retiring from Columbia, he was literary adviser to Charles Scribner's Sons (1975–93). He moved to San Antonio, Texas, but continued writing about his academic specialty, cultural history, and about higher education. His most recent works in these fields are *From Dawn to Decadence: 500 Years of Western Cultural Life, 1500 to the Present* (2001), *Begin Here: The Forgotten Conditions of Teaching and Learning* (1991), and *A Stroll with William James* (1991). A sampling of his work can be found in *A Jacques Barzun Reader* (2002).

Mary Elizabeth Brown

Postcard showing the Polo Grounds, home of the New York Giants, ca *1918 (Inset Johnny McGraw)*

baseball. Manhattan and Brooklyn played an important role in the early development of baseball. In 1846 a set of rules defining the "New York game" was issued by a committee led by Alexander J. Cartwright and comprising members of the New York Knickerbocker Club, an organization of white-collar workers from Madison Square and Murray Hill. The rules provided for a diamond-shaped infield with bases separated by a distance of 90 feet (27 meters); the pitcher stood in the center of the diamond at a distance from home plate of 45 feet, or 14 meters (changed in 1893 to 60 feet and 6 inches, or 18 meters). The first game played under these rules reportedly took place on 19 June 1846 in Hoboken, New Jersey. When Cartwright later joined the gold rush of 1849 he introduced the New York game in San Francisco. With continuing modifications it eclipsed such rival versions of baseball as "town ball" and the "Massachusetts game" and became standard. During the next 15 years some 60 organized baseball clubs played matches in and around New York City. In the 1850s the popularity of baseball in eastern cities surpassed that of cricket, and baseball was soon being called the national game. Its acceptance was promoted by the journalist Henry Chadwick, who reported on games for local newspapers and devised a box score for recording each player's achievements. In 1860 organized baseball was most popular in cities in the Northeast. Among the best-known teams in the area were the Knickerbockers, Eagles, Empires, and Gothams of Manhattan; the Eckfords, Atlantics, Putnams, and Excelsiors of Brooklyn; and the Unions of Morrisania. Some clubs like the Knickerbockers and the Excelsiors limited membership to white-collar workers; a few like the Uniques of Brooklyn were composed of black players. During the Civil War soldiers of both armies learned the game and helped to spread it to other areas of the country. At the same time strong amateur teams attracted large crowds.

The National Association of Base Ball Players was formed in 1857 by amateurs seeking to promote the game, and although it never organized a league or a championship schedule, more than 300 clubs belonged to it by 1867. Leading teams erected fenced parks, charged admission, and paid good players for their services. Gamblers openly accepted wagers and sometimes offered bribes to players. The association was unable to curb either these practices or the growth of professionalism. By 1869 the New York Mutuals paid their starting players; the first team to pay all its players, the Cincinnati Red Stockings, was managed by Harry Wright, a former professional cricket player with the St. George Club of Staten Island. The Red Stockings toured the nation and remained unbeaten until losing a game in extra innings to the Atlantics in the summer of 1870 before a large crowd at the Capitoline Grounds in Brooklyn. A meeting at Collier's Cafe on Broadway and 13th Street on 17 March 1871 led to the formation of the National Association of Professional Base Ball Players, which hastened the demise of the National Association of Base Ball Players. The new association lasted five seasons and is considered the first major league. Its teams in the metropolitan region included the Mutuals (1871–75), the Atlantics (1872–75), and the Eckfords (1872). Between 1872 and 1875 the Boston Red Stockings won the championship of the league in each year; the best effort during this period by a team from New York City was the second-place finish in 1874 by the Mutuals.

The National League of Professional Base-Ball Clubs was formed in 1876 by a group of club owners meeting at the Grand Central Hotel in New York City. The Mutuals were one of the first eight members of the league but were expelled after refusing to play their final games in the first season. From 1877 to 1882 no team from New York City played in the league, although several strong teams played from 1877 to 1879 in a rival one, the International Association. In 1882 the National League admitted a team from the city called the Giants, which won the championship of the league and the World Series in 1888 and 1889 and inspired several other teams in later years to take its name. In the following decade the fortunes of the New York Giants plummeted: they were able only to place second in 1894, and in the following year they came under the ownership of Andrew Freedman, a politician from Tammany Hall whose quixotic and abortive effort to dominate the league stirred dissension among other owners. New York City was also represented in the American Association, which was recognized by the National League as a major league under the National Agreement of 1883. The association lasted to the end of 1891 and fielded two teams in the area. The New York Metropolitans joined in 1883 and in the following season won the championship of the association before losing the first World Series to the champions of the National League (from Providence, Rhode Island). The owner of the Metropolitans, John Day, also owned the Giants of the National League, the team to which he shunted his best players; the Metropolitans were severely weakened as a result and left the American Association in 1887. In the same year the Brooklyn Bridegrooms joined the association. Owned by Charles Byrne, they won the championship of the association in 1889, which had been won for four consecutive seasons by the St. Louis Browns. After losing the World Series to the Giants the Bridegrooms moved in the following year to the National League and won its championship, becoming the only team ever to win consecutive pennants in different major leagues. In the World Series of 1890 the Bridegrooms played to a draw against the champions of the American Association (from Louisville, Kentucky). In 1890 a third major league, the Players National League, was organized by John Ward, the captain of the New York Giants and the head of the Brotherhood of Professional Base Ball Players. The league opposed several practices of the owners in the other leagues, including those of selling players, extending their contracts unilaterally, and limiting their salaries. It had teams in Manhattan and Brooklyn and attracted many players from the other leagues but was declared bankrupt after one season. The American Association disbanded in 1891 under pressure from the National League, which absorbed four of its eight teams: the result was a single major league with 12 teams, the National League and American Association of Professional Base Ball Clubs. This operated to the end of 1899, when its championship was won by the team from Brooklyn, then known as the Superbas. The same team won the championship in 1900, when the league reduced the number of its teams to eight.

New York City in the early twentieth century was the home of several important baseball teams as well as the birthplace of some of the best-known baseball traditions: local fans were among the first to eat hot dogs at the ballpark (introduced at the Polo Grounds by Harry M. Stevens after 1900) and the first to hear the song "Take Me Out to the Ball Game" (1908), by Al Von Tilzer and Jack Norworth (who were both from New York City). The American League was formed in the city in 1901 and recognized as a major league under the National Agreement of 1903. Under the new system of two major leagues the World Series was revived and major league baseball began a half-century of unprecedented stability: after a team moved from Baltimore to New York City in 1903 and became the Highlanders, no other teams changed their location until 1952. The Highlanders played at a wooden stadium at 165th Street and Broadway called Hilltop Park until 1913, when they became tenants of the New York Giants at the Polo Grounds and were renamed the Yankees; in 1923 they moved to Yankee Stadium at East 161st Street and Jerome Avenue

World Series Appearances of New York City Baseball Teams

Season	Winner	Opponent	Series	Most Valuable Player
1905	New York Giants	Philadelphia Athletics	4–1	—
1911	Philadelphia Athletics	New York Giants	4–2	—
1912	Boston Red Sox	New York Giants	4–3	—
1913	Philadelphia Athletics	New York Giants	4–1	—
1917	Chicago White Sox	New York Giants	4–2	—
1921	New York Giants	New York Yankees	5–3	—
1922	New York Giants	New York Yankees	4–0	—
1923	New York Yankees	New York Giants	4–2	—
1924	Washington Senators	New York Giants	4–3	—
1926	St. Louis Cardinals	New York Yankees	4–3	—
1927	New York Yankees	Pittsburgh Pirates	4–0	—
1928	New York Yankees	St. Louis Cardinals	4–0	—
1932	New York Yankees	Chicago Cubs	4–0	—
1933	New York Giants	Washington Senators	4–1	—
1936	New York Yankees	New York Giants	4–2	—
1937	New York Yankees	New York Giants	4–1	—
1938	New York Yankees	Chicago Cubs	4–0	—
1939	New York Yankees	Cincinnati Reds	4–0	—
1941	New York Yankees	Brooklyn Dodgers	4–1	—
1942	St. Louis Cardinals	New York Yankees	4–1	—
1943	New York Yankees	St. Louis Cardinals	4–1	—
1947	New York Yankees	Brooklyn Dodgers	4–3	—
1949	New York Yankees	Brooklyn Dodgers	4–1	—
1950	New York Yankees	Philadelphia Phillies	4–0	—
1951	New York Yankees	New York Giants	4–2	—
1952	New York Yankees	Brooklyn Dodgers	4–3	—
1953	New York Yankees	Brooklyn Dodgers	4–2	—
1954	New York Giants	Cleveland Indians	4–0	—
1955	Brooklyn Dodgers	New York Yankees	4–3	Johnny Podres
1956	New York Yankees	Brooklyn Dodgers	4–3	Don Larsen
1957	Milwaukee Braves	New York Yankees	4–3	—
1958	New York Yankees	Milwaukee Braves	4–3	Bob Turley
1960	Pittsburgh Pirates	New York Yankees	4–3	—
1961	New York Yankees	Cincinnati Reds	4–1	Whitey Ford
1962	New York Yankees	San Francisco Giants	4–3	Ralph Terry
1963	Los Angeles Dodgers	New York Yankees	4–0	—
1964	St. Louis Cardinals	New York Yankees	4–3	—
1969	New York Mets	Baltimore Orioles	4–1	Donn Clendenon
1973	Oakland Athletics	New York Mets	4–3	—
1976	Cincinnati Reds	New York Yankees	4–0	—
1977	New York Yankees	Los Angeles Dodgers	4–2	Reggie Jackson
1978	New York Yankees	Los Angeles Dodgers	4–2	Bucky Dent
1981	Los Angeles Dodgers	New York Yankees	4–2	—
1986	New York Mets	Boston Red Sox	4–3	Ray Knight
1996	New York Yankees	Atlanta Braves	4–2	John Wetteland
1998	New York Yankees	San Diego Padres	4–0	Scott Brosius
1999	New York Yankees	Atlanta Braves	4–0	Mariano Rivera
2000	New York Yankees	New York Mets	4–1	Derek Jeter
2001	Arizona Diamondbacks	New York Yankees	4–3	—
2003	Florida Marlins	New York Yankees	4–2	—
2009	New York Yankees	Philadelphia Phillies	4–2	Hideki Matsui

Note: In 1904 the owners of the New York Giants refused to compete against the Boston Red Sox (then the Boston Americans); however, it is still considered a World Series appearance.

As of 2009 the New York Mets went to four World Series and won two, the Brooklyn Dodgers went to seven and won one, the New York Giants went to 15 and won five, and the New York Yankees went to 40 and won 27.

There have been 14 all–New York match-ups in the World Series. New York teams have played in 65 of the 104 World Series and won 34.

Compiled by Frank Nestor

Major League Ballparks of New York City

Year(s)	Name	Location	Team (League)
1853, 1886–89	St. George Grounds	St. George, Staten Island	Washington Club (later Gotham Club), Metropolitans (AA), Giants (NL)
1858	Fashion Race Course [National Course]	Willets Point, Queens	New York–Brooklyn Series
1865–76	Capitoline Grounds	Halsey St. and Marcy, Putnam, and Nostrand Aves., Brooklyn	Excelsiors, Atlantics (NA), Mutuals (NL)
1867	Satellite Grounds	Brooklyn	Uniques
1871–77	Union Grounds	Lee Ave. and Rutledge St., Brooklyn	Mutuals (NA), Eckfords (NA), Atlantics (NA)
1880–88	Polo Grounds (i)	100th to 112th Sts. between Fifth and Sixth Aves., Manhattan	Gothams (NL), Giants (NL), Metropolitans (AA)
1883–91	Washington Park (i)	Third to Fifth Sts. between Fourth and Fifth Aves., Manhattan	Dodgers (AA, NL)
1884	Metropolitan Park	107th to 109th Sts. between First Ave. and East River, Manhattan	Metropolitans (AA)
1886	[Name unknown]	Near Melrose Station of the Harlem Railroad, Manhattan	Unions
1887	Wild West Grounds	Tompkinsville, Staten Island	Metropolitans (AA)
1889–90	Ridgewood Park [Wallace's Ridgewood Grounds, Horse Market, Meyerrose's Union League]	Onderdonk and Elm Aves., Queens	Trolley Dodgers (AA)
1889–90	Manhattan Field [Polo Grounds (ii)]	155th St. and Eighth Ave., Manhattan	Giants (NL), Gladiators (AA)
1890	Maspeth Ball Grounds [Long Island Recreation Grounds]	Maspeth, Queens	Trolley Dodgers (AA)
1890–97	Eastern Park	Eastern Pkwy., Belmont Ave., Sackman St., and Van Sinderen Ave., Brooklyn	Wonders (PL) Bridegrooms (NL)
1890–1963	Polo Grounds (iii and iv) [Brotherhood Park, Brush Stadium]	115th to 157th Sts. between Eighth Ave. and Harlem River Speedway, Manhattan	Giants (NL), Yankees (AL), Mets (NL)
1898–1915	Washington Park (ii)	First to Third Sts. between Third and Fourth Aves., Brooklyn	Dodgers (NL), Tip Tops (FL)
1903–12	Hilltop Park	165th to 168th Sts. between Broadway and Washington Ave., Manhattan	Highlanders/Yankees (AL), Giants (NL)
1913–57	Ebbers Field	Bedford Ave., Montgomery St., McKeever Pl., and Sullivan Pl., Brooklyn	Dodgers (NL), Eagles (NNL), Brown Dodgers (USL)
1920s	Jasper Oval [Hebrew Orphan Asylum Oval]	136th to 138th Sts. between Convent Ave. and St. Nicholas Terrace, Manhattan	Bacharach Giants (ECL)
1922–32	Dyckman Oval [Inwood Hill Park Oval]	Inwood Hill Park, 214th and Seaman Sts.	Cuban Stars (NNL, NE-WL), Cuban Stars West, Cuban Stars East (ECL, ANL), Bacharach Giants (ECL)
1923–36	Catholic Protectory Oval	East Tremont Ave. and Unionport Rd., Bronx	Lincoln Giants (ECL), Cuban Stars West (NNL)
1923–1940s	Dexter Park [Bushwick Park, Sterling Oval]	Jamaica Ave., Woodhaven, Queens	Royal Giants (ECL)
1923–2008	Yankee Stadium	157th to 161st Sts. between Fifth and Madison Aves., Bronx	Yankees (AL), Black Yankees (NNL)
1928–29	Olympic Field	135th to 138th Sts. between Convent Ave. and St. Nicholas Terrace, Manhattan	Lincoln Games (ECL, ANL)
1938	John J. Downing Stadium [Randalls Island Stadium, Triborough Stadium]	Randalls Island, Manhattan	Black Yankees (NNL)
1939	19th St. Sandlot	19th to 60th Sts. between First Ave. and Sutton Place, Manhattan	Cubans (NNL)
1964–2008	Shea Stadium [William A. Shea Municipal Stadium]	Flushing Meadows–Corona Park, Queens	Mets (NL), Yankees (AL)

(continued)

Major League Ballparks of New York City (*Continued*)

Year(s)	Name	Location	Team (League)
2009–	New Yankee Stadium	East 161st St. and River Ave., Bronx	Yankees (AL)
2009–	Citi Field	126th St. and Roosevelt Ave., Flushing, Queens	Mets (NL)

AA=American Association, AL=American League, ANL=American Negro League, ECL=Eastern Colored League, FL=Federal League, NA=National Association, NE-WL=Negro East-West League, NL=National League, NNL=Negro National League, PL=Players League, USL=United States League

Source: Michael Benson, *Ballparks of North America* (Jefferson, N.C.: McFarland, 1989)

Compiled by Laura Lewison; updated and edited by Frank Nestor

in the Bronx. Between 1903 and 1923 the Giants of the National League emerged as the most powerful and profitable team in the major leagues. During the tenure of their manager John McGraw (1902–32) they won the championship of the league 10 times and the World Series three times (their loss of the league championship in 1908 was brought on by the failure of "Bonehead" Fred Merkle to touch second base). During these years the league championship was won twice by the team from Brooklyn, now renamed the Dodgers. In 1914–15 the Federal League sought unsuccessfully to be recognized as a major league. One of its members was the Brooklyn Federals, a mediocre team owned by Robert Ward, an important financial backer of the league whose death in 1915 soon led to its dissolution.

A far more enduring challenge to the major leagues was mounted by the Negro leagues, the first of which was formed in 1920 by Rube Foster as the Negro National League and included teams from the Midwest. New York City was represented by the Lincoln Giants and the Brooklyn Giants in the Eastern Colored League, formed in 1923 by Nat Strong. Among the best-known players on these teams were the pitchers Smokey Joe Williams and Cannonball Dick Redding, the shortstop John Henry Lloyd (known as the "black Honus Wagner"), and the catcher Louis Santop. Both the Eastern Colored League and the Negro National League disbanded at the onset of the Depression. By this time the New York Yankees of the American League had begun to overshadow the New York Giants of the National League and during the next four decades were undeniably the best team in baseball. Between 1921 and 1964 they won 29 league pennants and 20 World Series, led by such prominent players as Babe Ruth, Lou Gehrig, Joe DiMaggio, and Mickey Mantle. The Yankees played against the Giants in six World Series (known as "subway series"), of which they lost two (1921, the first series to be broadcast on radio, and 1922) and won four (1923, 1936, 1937, and 1951). Among the best-known players on the Giants in these years were Mel Ott (1926–47) and Carl Hubbell (1928–43). A second Negro National League was formed in 1933, followed by a Negro

Major League Professional Baseball Teams in New York City

Years	Team	League
1871–76	New York Mutuals	National Association, 1871–75 National League, 1876
1872	Brooklyn Eckfords	National Association
1872–75	Brooklyn Atlantics	National Association
1883–87	New York Metropolitans	American Association
1883–1957	New York Giants	National League
1884–1957	Brooklyn Dodgers[1]	American Association, 1884–89 National League, 1890–1957
1890	Brooklyn Wonders[2]	Players League
1890	New York Phillies	Players League
1903–	New York Yankees[3]	American League
1914–15	Brooklyn Tip Tops[4]	Federal League
1922	Cuban Stars	Negro National League
1923–29	Lincoln Giants	Eastern Colored League, 1923–26, 1928 American Negro League, 1929
1923–29	Cuban Stars East	Eastern Colored League, 1923–28 American Negro League, 1929
1923–29	Bacharach Giants	Eastern Colored League, 1923–28 American Negro League, 1929
1923–30	Cuban Stars West	Negro National League
1923–27	Brooklyn Royal Giants	Eastern Colored League
1935	Brooklyn Eagles	Negro National League
1935–50	New York Cubans	Negro National League, 1935–48 Negro American League, 1949–50
1936–48	New York Black Yankees	Negro National League
1962–	New York Mets	National League

1. Although primarily known as the Trolley Dodgers from the 1890s and as the Dodgers from 1910, the team had several other names. Official names: Bridegrooms (1884–98), Superbas (1899–1926), Robins (1927–31, for the manager Wilbert Robinson), Dodgers (1932–33), Brooklyns (1934–37), Dodgers (1938–57). Unofficial names: Ward's Wonders (for John M. Ward, who joined the team after the Brooklyn Wonders of the Players League disbanded in 1890), Foutz's Phillies (for Dave Foutz, manager 1893–96), Barney's Boys (for Billy Barney, manager 1897–98), Byrne's Boys (for Charles Byrne, president 1890–98), Infants (about 1910).

2. Also called Ward's Wonders, for the star player John M. Ward.

3. Originally called the Highlanders; the name Yankees first used in 1905, both names used for the next eight years. In 1912 the team moved to its new stadium, the Polo Grounds on East 155th Street, and in 1913 the name was officially changed to the Yankees.

4. The name Brookfeds was introduced but never widely adopted.

Sources: Frank G. Menke, *The Encyclopedia of Sports* (New York: A. S. Barnes, 1953); Harold Seymour, *Baseball* (New York: Oxford University Press, 1960); Donn Rogosin, *Invisible Men* (New York: Atheneum, 1983); Michael Benson, *Ballparks of North America* (Jefferson, N.C.: McFarland, 1989)

Compiled by Laura Lewison

American League in 1937. The Negro National League in 1935 included the Brooklyn Eagles and the New York Cubans, who won the second of two championships contested during each half of the season. From 1936 both the Cubans and the New York Black Yankees belonged to the league, but after Major League Baseball at last became racially integrated in 1947 when Jackie Robinson joined the Brooklyn Dodgers, the Negro

National League disbanded in the following year. The Cubans and the Black Yankees in 1949 joined the Negro American League, which played its final game in 1950 (by which time the Cubans were its only remaining team from the city).

The audience for baseball expanded rapidly with the introduction of broadcasts on television, the first of which was made from New York City in 1939 by Red Barber. In the 1940s the Dodgers became a formidable team in the National League, owing largely to the accomplishments of Duke Snider, Gil Hodges, and Robinson. The team played seven World Series against the Yankees but won only one (1955) and lost six (1941, 1947, 1949, 1952, 1953, 1956). Competition for the league championships and in the World Series during these years was marked by intense rivalry and several dramatic successes and failures: a missed third strike by the Dodgers' catcher Mickey Owen that helped the Yankees to win the World Series in 1941, a streak by DiMaggio in the same year during which he hit safely in 56 consecutive games, a home run by the Giants' outfielder Bobby Thomson that won a playoff against the Dodgers for the championship of the National League in 1951, and a perfect game pitched by Don Larsen of the Yankees against the Dodgers in the World Series of 1956. The popularity of baseball nationwide was encouraged by the status of New York City as the center of print and broadcast journalism: some 25 newspapers were published there in 1950.

Baseball in the city was dealt a severe blow in the winter of 1957, when both its teams in the National League announced plans to move to California in the following season: the Giants and their popular outfielder Willie Mays to San Francisco, and the Dodgers to Los Angeles. In 1962 the city was awarded one of two new teams in the league, the New York Mets, who performed at a rarely matched level of ineptness in their early seasons before astonishing observers by winning the World Series in 1969, earning the nickname "Miracle Mets." Led by Dwight Gooden and Darryl Strawberry, the Mets again won the series in 1986 against the Boston Red Sox after a critical error by Boston first baseman Bill Buckner allowed the Mets to win the sixth game of the series and force a decisive seventh game, which they won. The Yankees played poorly in the late 1960s and early 1970s but revived under owner George Steinbrenner (from 1973), winning the World Series in 1977 and 1978 with the play of such stars as Thurman Munson, Rich "Goose" Gossage, Bucky Dent, and Reggie Jackson, who famously hit three home runs in game six of the 1977 series at Yankee Stadium. The Yankees failed to make the playoffs from 1982 through 1994, but with stars such as Derek Jeter and Mariano Rivera and the leadership of manager Joe Torre, the team won four World Series in five years from 1996 to 2000 (losing only in 1997) and made the playoffs every year from 1995 through 2007. Under new manager Joe Girardi, the Yankees won the 2009 World Series. The Mets experienced more moderate success, with their best season ending at the hands of the Yankees in the 2000 World Series. Two minor league teams also played in the city in the early twenty-first century, with the Brooklyn Cyclones, a Mets affiliate, playing at Keyspan Park and the Staten Island Yankees playing at Richmond County Bank Ballpark since 2001. In the early twenty-first century many New Yorkers remained ardent fans of baseball, and the city continued to exert a strong influence on the game.

Melvin L. Adelman, *A Sporting Time: New York City and the Rise of Modern Athletics, 1820–1870* (Urbana: University of Illinois Press, 1986)

See also SPORTS.

David Q. Voigt

Basie, Count [William] (*b* Red Bank, N.J., 21 Aug 1904; *d* New York City, 26 April 1984). Pianist and bandleader. He moved to New York City about 1924; there he learned to play the pipe organ from Fats Waller. In 1927 he left New York City and became a leading performer of the hard-driving swing that developed in Kansas City. He returned to New York City in 1936 as the leader of the Count Basie Orchestra, which attracted such well-known soloists as the tenor saxophonists Lester Young and Herschel Evans, the trombonist Dicky Wells, the trumpeters Buck Clayton and Harry "Sweets" Edison, and the singers Billie Holiday, Jimmy Rushing, and Helen Humes; he played in the rhythm section with Walter Page, Jo Jones, and Freddie Green. For a while the members of the band lived at the Woodside Hotel in Harlem, inspiring the composition "Jumpin' at the Woodside" (1938). Basie dismantled the big band in 1950 and organized another one in 1951 that had tighter and more polished arrangements and performed around the world. With his wife, Catherine, he moved to St. Albans in the borough of Queens in 1946. His book *Good Morning Blues: The Autobiography of Count Basie* was published in 1985.

Stanley Dance, *The World of Count Basie* (New York: Da Capo Press, 1985)

Douglas Henry Daniels

basketball. New York City is widely acknowledged to have become the spiritual home of basketball soon after the sport was invented in Springfield, Massachusetts, in 1891, and to have remained so for the next century. By 1900 basketball was played throughout the metropolitan area at chapters of the Young Men's Christian Association and in settlement houses, school gymnasiums, lofts, armories, and dance halls, and amateur and semiprofessional teams soon flourished. The year 1914 marked the formation of the New York Celtics, who played for three seasons before disbanding when the United States entered World War I. After the war the promoter Jim Furey and his brothers sought to reorganize the team, which became known as the Original Celtics when the owner of the New York Celtics refused to relinquish his rights to their name. Along with the New York Whirlwinds, which had been organized by the well-known promoter Tex Rickard, the Original Celtics were one of the outstanding teams of the period. Their success and popularity stimulated the interest of the public in professional basketball, and in 1925 the American Basketball League (ABL) was formed with teams in Brooklyn, Washington (D.C.), Cleveland, Rochester (New York), Fort Wayne (Indiana), Boston, Chicago, Detroit, and Buffalo. The Original Celtics did not at first join the league (the owners believed that they could make more money by barnstorming), but teams that did belong to the league hoped to capitalize on the popularity of the

NBA Finals Appearances by New York City Basketball Teams

Year	League	Winner	Opponent	Series	Most Valuable Player
1951	NBA	Minneapolis Lakers	New York Knicks	4–3	—
1952	NBA	Minneapolis Lakers	New York Knicks	4–3	—
1953	NBA	Minneapolis Lakers	New York Knicks	4–1	—
1970	NBA	New York Knicks	Los Angeles Lakers	4–3	Willis Reed
1972	ABA	Indiana Pacers	New York Nets	4–2	—
1973	NBA	New York Knicks	Los Angeles Lakers	4–1	Willis Reed
1974	ABA	New York Nets	Utah Stars	4–1	—
1976	ABA	New York Nets	Denver Nuggets	4–2	—
1994	NBA	Houston Rockets	New York Knicks	4–3	—
1999	NBA	San Antonio Spurs	New York Knicks	4–1	—

Abbreviations: NBA=National Basketball Association, ABA=American Basketball Association, league founded in 1967 that later merged with the NBA in 1976.
Compiled by Nathan Morgante

Original Celtics by challenging them to exhibition games, only to be embarrassed by losing decisively and regularly. The Original Celtics finally joined the ABL as a replacement for Brooklyn, which had the worst record in the league, and in two seasons won 72 games and lost only 14; in the playoffs the team won eight games and lost one. Professional basketball had a precarious existence in New York City in the next two decades, and by 1929 the ABL was defunct.

A number of notable black teams were formed in the 1920s. The best of these was the New York Renaissance (popularly known as the New York Rens), formed in 1922 by Bob Douglas and named after the Renaissance Casino in Harlem where the team played its home games. By the mid-1930s the Rens were acknowledged to have succeeded the Original Celtics as the leading team in New York City; they continued to play until after World War II. The well-known team the Harlem Globetrotters, notwithstanding its name, was based in Chicago.

New York University, St. John's College, and Fordham University all had powerful teams during the 1920s. Between 1928 and 1936 St. John's won 179 games and lost only 32 under the coaching of Buck Freeman, probably the greatest exponent of the deliberate style of play associated with the Original Celtics and the Rens. College basketball reached a new level of popularity in 1934, when both City College of New York and New York University finished their seasons undefeated and played against each other in March for the unofficial championship of the city. The game was staged at the 168th Street Armory by Ned Irish (1905–82), a sportswriter who had arranged games to benefit the city relief fund at the behest of Mayor James J. Walker, and drew a crowd of 16,000.

The city and the metropolitan area were the site during these years of some of the best collegiate basketball in the country. City College and New York University were always competitive, St. John's remained a consistent winner after Joe Lapchick replaced Freeman as the head coach in 1937, and other schools such as Long Island University, St. Francis College, and St. Peter's College and Seton Hall College in New Jersey were emerging as basketball powers. This success in collegiate basketball culminated in 1938 in the first staging of the National Invitation Tournament (NIT), sponsored by the Metropolitan Basketball Writers Association; the success of the NIT inspired the National Collegiate Athletic Association (NCAA) to organize its own tournament in 1939. In its first 13 years the NIT was won five times by teams from New York City, and in 1950 City College became the first school to win both the NIT and the championship of the NCAA. In the following year college basketball in the city was devastated by the results of an investigation led by the district attorney of Manhattan, Frank Hogan, into allegations of "point shaving" (deliberately reducing the margin of victory in a game to accommodate bettors). Thirty-two players were indicted from seven local schools, including City College, Manhattan College, New York University, and Long Island University. Madison Square Garden soon ceased to be a major venue for college games, the NIT lost some of its glamour, and most local colleges severely reduced their basketball programs or eliminated them entirely. Not until the late 1970s did another local school, St. John's University, field a team that achieved a high national ranking.

Professional basketball began to arouse the interest of fans after World War II. The Basketball Association of America, formed in 1946, included as one of its original members the New York Knickerbockers; after two years the association merged with the National Basketball League to form the National Basketball Association (NBA), which had 17 teams. The Knicks were among the first racially integrated teams in basketball: Nat "Sweetwater" Clifton, one of the first black players in the NBA, joined the team in the autumn of 1950. On the court the Knickerbockers achieved little distinction in their first 23 years and won only two divisional titles, but after several astute trades and drafts they won the championship of the NBA in 1969–70 and again in 1972–73. After a period of poor play the team's fortunes improved in the 1990s, but the Knicks failed to win the NBA championship, losing twice in the finals.

New York City is noted for having outstanding basketball players in its high schools and playgrounds. Hundreds of players each year are recruited in the city by colleges throughout the country, and brokers of high school basketball players, called "street agents," are often seen at high school and playground games. Among local players who have become prominent in college and as professionals are Kareem Abdul-Jabbar, who played in the city as Lew Alcindor, Connie Hawkins, Roger Brown, Julius Erving, Albert King, Nate "Tiny" Archibald, and Nancy Lieberman. The best-known playground players include Hermann "Helicopter" Knowings, Joe "the Destroyer" Hammond, Pablo Robertson, Jumpin' Jackie Jackson, Bobby Hunter, Ron Jackson, and Earl "the Goat" Manigault, considered by his peers to have been as talented as Abdul-Jabbar.

Basketball is a popular and visible game in the city's playgrounds in the early twenty-first century, reflected by the presence of weekend tournaments such as the Rucker Pro Tournament (first staged in 1950), played at the Holcombe Rucker Memorial Playground opposite the site of the old Polo Grounds on 155th Street and Frederick Douglass Boulevard (Eighth Avenue). Professional and college basketball played at Madison Square Garden also remains popular, with the Knicks playing their home games there and the NIT and Big East Conference tournaments held annually each spring.

Michael Benson, *Everything You Wanted to Know about the New York Knicks: A Who's Who of Everyone Who Ever Played on or Coached the NBA's Most Celebrated Team* (Lanham, Md.: Taylor Trade Publishing, 2007).

See also Abdul-Jabbar, Kareem; Harlem Renaissance; New York Knicks; Rucker Tournament; Sports.

Albert Figone

Basquiat, Jean-Michel (*b* Brooklyn, 22 Dec 1960; *d* New York City, 12 Aug 1988). Artist. When he was a child his family encouraged him to be artistic, and at the age of 17 he began spraying graffiti on blighted buildings in lower Manhattan with the tag "SAMO"; the *Village Voice* wrote a piece on his graphics the following year. In 1978 he moved to Manhattan and was involved in the thriving East Village art scene. His first recognition as a neoexpressionist artist was in 1980 when he participated in the exhibition *The Times Square Show*; in the early 1980s he continued to have his works shown around the city. In 1985 he was featured on the cover of the *New York Times Magazine* for the piece "New Art, New Money: The Marketing of an American Artist." He died of a drug overdose in his loft at 67 Great Jones Street. In 1996 a film biography *Basquiat* was made about his life. His work has soared in value since his death; in 2008 *Untitled (Boxer)* fetched $12 million.

Jessica Montesano

Bates USA. Advertising agency, formed in 1987 as Backer Spielvogel Bates Worldwide after Saatchi and Saatchi merged two of its subsidiaries: Ted Bates (founded in 1940 by Theodore L. Bates) and Backer and Spielvogel. In 1994 the firm was renamed Bates Worldwide; in 1997 its parent company was split into two companies, with Bates becoming part of Cordiant Communications Group. In 2003 the WPP Group acquired Cordiant and closed Bates.

George Winslow

Bath Beach. Neighborhood in southeastern Brooklyn, bounded to the north by 86th Street, to the east by Bay Parkway, to the south by Gravesend Bay, and to the west by 14th Avenue; a section of Bensonhurst. Named for the English spa of Bath, it was a resort known for its yacht clubs, fashionable villas, and a restaurant called the Captain's Pier at the foot of 19th Avenue until the creation of the Belt Parkway paved over the beachfront in 1939. The housing consists mostly of two- and three-family redbrick houses and six-story apartment buildings. The population is mostly Italian, and many residents work in Manhattan. In the early twenty-first century many

Bath Beach, 1992

Asian, Russian, and Jewish immigrants have moved into the neighborhood.

Stephen Weinstein

Bathgate. Neighborhood in the central Bronx, immediately west of Crotona Park. It is often said to include the neighborhood of Claremont. The name derives from a family that worked the lands of Morris Manor before establishing its own farm in Morrisania in 1841 on a tract of more than 140 acres (57 hectares), with a farmhouse situated near what is now Third Avenue and East 172nd Street. The land was sold to the city about 1883 as part of the Parks Act and became Crotona Park (plans to name it after the Bathgates were forestalled by a dispute between the family and the surveyors). Many Jews from the Lower East Side moved to new five-story apartment buildings in the area after the Third Avenue elevated line was extended north in the 1890s. By the mid-1950s there were increasing numbers of blacks and Puerto Ricans, and Bathgate Avenue became a thriving commercial strip known into the 1960s for its ethnic restaurants. The Bathgate Industrial Park occupies eight blocks along Bathgate Avenue between the Cross Bronx Expressway and Claremont Parkway. Built on the site of apartment buildings that were burned and abandoned in the 1970s, it is one of the most successful business zones in the Bronx. In the first decade of the twenty-first century the population is largely black and Hispanic, with a large Puerto Rican community.

John McNamara, *History in Asphalt: The Origin of Bronx Street and Place Names* (New York: Bronx County Historical Society, 1984)

Gary D. Hermalyn

bathhouses. A quick sponging off was considered adequate for personal cleanliness during colonial times in New York City. Gradually the elite began to enjoy bathing, and in 1792 Nicholas Denise opened a "very convenient Bathing House, having eight rooms, in every one of which Baths may be had with either fresh, salt or warm water . . . prices fixed at 4s per person." The opening of the Croton Aqueduct in 1842 made bathing easier for those who could afford to install running water in their homes; most of the city's population continued to rely on public hydrants. Interest in building public baths in New York City mounted about the mid-nineteenth century, when a national movement was organized to promote personal cleanliness in crowded tenements lacking adequate bathing facilities. The movement in New York City achieved its first success in 1849, when the Association for Improving the Condition of the Poor built the People's Bathing and Washing Establishment at 141 Mott Street, the first public bath. Open only during the summer, it provided laundry facilities, a swimming pool, and baths for men and women. The rates were prohibitive for the poor: 3 cents an hour to use the laundry, and from 5 to 10 cents to take a bath. Initially the bath attracted 60,000 persons a year and was hailed by the association as a great success, but it closed in 1861 for lack of patronage.

Concern over the cleanliness of the poor intensified after the Civil War, as immigrants from southern and eastern Europe crowded into the city's slums. In 1870 the Department of Public Works built its first floating baths, large wooden structures installed in the Hudson and East rivers that formed pools for bathing free of charge from June to October. By 1888 15 such baths attracted about 2.5 million men and 1.5 million women a year. Insisting that the pools were designed for cleanliness and not for recreation, the authorities imposed a 20-minute limit on their use. On hot days young boys evaded this regulation by moving from pool to pool, dirtying themselves en route. Soon after construction was completed, pollution became a serious problem, and from 1914 the floating baths were required to be watertight and filled with purified water. Spurred by the germ theory of disease, which lent new importance to the battle against dirt, reformers and the press urged the city government to open free baths during the 1880s. The city refused, on the grounds that the proposals lacked public support, and the physician Simon Baruch launched a campaign to seek

The Asser Levy Recreation Center, designed by Arnold W. Brunner and William Martin Aiken, opened as a public bath in 1908 (photo 1991)

Public bathhouse

other sponsors. He eventually persuaded the Association for Improving the Condition of the Poor to build a new bathhouse on the Lower East Side. Contributions to the venture included $27,000 from various sources and 80 pounds (36 kilograms) of soap from the firm of Colgate. The People's Baths opened in the early 1890s, its grand arch inscribed with the maxim "Cleanliness Next to Godliness"; this was the first successful indoor bathhouse in the country and was widely imitated. Built of concrete and iron and fitted with showers instead of tubs, it was easy to keep clean and inexpensive to operate. A 5-cent fee provided for a towel and soap. In 1898 alone the bathhouse attracted 115,685 patrons. Its success inspired other private charities to build similar facilities, and some businesses introduced baths for their employees.

The city did not begin to build a public bath until 1895, when the state legislature passed a law requiring municipalities with populations of 50,000 or more to build free bathhouses. During the same year the reform Republican William L. Strong won the mayoral election and endorsed the public bath movement. The first free bath began operation in March 1901 on Rivington Street. By 1914 the city had built 16 more public baths in Manhattan, seven in Brooklyn, and one each in Queens and the Bronx, most of them in neighborhoods populated by immigrants; the result was the most elaborate and expensive bath system in the country. Men and women entered separate waiting rooms and took a number. Once called, they were given 20 minutes to shower in a small cubicle divided into a changing area and a shower stall. Attendants controlled the timing and the temperature of the water. Most of the baths built after 1904 included gymnasiums and swimming pools to attract more patrons. People generally preferred to bathe at home if they could, and bathing facilities were increasingly provided by landlords under the Tenement House Law of 1901, which required tenements to have running water on all stories. Use of public baths declined, even before the last one was completed in 1914, whereas commercial bathhouses thrived. In 1897 there were 62 such facilities, including Russian (steam) baths, Turkish (hot-air) baths, vapor baths, and medicated baths, as well as swimming pools. More than half were owned and used by Jews from eastern Europe seeking to uphold religious and social traditions of bathing. The best known included the Russian and Turkish Baths on 10th Street between Avenue A and First Avenue.

Many municipal baths were renovated during the 1930s by the Works Progress Administration; after World War II most were demolished or converted to other uses (the last one, the Allen Street Baths, was shut down during the 1970s). Commercial bathhouses catering to gays played a central role in the gay liberation movement of the 1970s. A bitter controversy erupted during the 1980s over whether these bathhouses contributed to the spread of Acquired Immune Deficiency Syndrome by allowing casual sex on their premises; local health officials were ultimately given the power to close them by the state legislature in 1985. During the same years the growth of homelessness prompted the city to reintroduce free showers, this time in municipal shelters.

Few of the original municipal baths remain in the first decade of the twenty-first century. One, the Asser Levy Bath on East 23rd Street, was designated a landmark and reopened in 1990 as a swimming pool (without a bath) after $8 million in restorations. Private bathhouses, however, can still be found, and many gay bathhouses continue to operate, despite the closure of some by the Health Department. Russian bathhouses also remain, notably the Russian and Turkish Baths in the East Village.

Richard L. Bushman and Claudia L. Bushman, "The Early History of Cleanliness in America," *Journal of American History* 74 (1988), 1213–38; Marilyn Thornton Williams, *Washing "The Great Unwashed": Public Baths in Urban America, 1840–1920* (Columbus: Ohio State University Press, 1991)

Corinne T. Field, Marilyn Thornton Williams

Batten, Barton, Durstine and Osborn [BBDO]. Advertising agency formed in 1928 when the George Batten Company merged with Barton, Durstine and Osborn. Its accounts included General Electric and General Motors. In 1940 Alex Osborn, one of the company's founders, coined the term "brainstorming" to describe his technique for devising ideas for advertising campaigns. The agency was the first to set up a radio department and made plans for television advertising as early as 1931. Under the management of Ben Duffy in 1946–57 its work in television increased billings to more than $200 million, and the agency shifted its emphasis from advertising for banks, insurers, electric utilities, and other institutions to advertising for packaged goods. During the 1960s and 1970s it remained among the four largest advertising agencies in the United States, and in 1986 it merged with Doyle Dane Bernbach and Needham Harper to form a new public holding company, the Omnicom group, with total billings of $5 billion. In 1994, BBDO was selected advertising agency of the year by *Adweek* and *Advertising Age,* and in 2007 BBDO Worldwide was named Network of the Year at the Cannes Lions Advertising Festival. In 2008, BBDO New York was named Agency of the Year.

Chauncey G. Olinger, Jr.

Battery Maritime Building [BMB]. New York City's last intact, early-nineteenth-century ferry structure. Designed by the architects Walker and Morris, who also designed its neighboring twin, the original Whitehall Ferry Terminal, it opened in 1909 at the foot of Whitehall Street on the southern tip of Manhattan. At a time when 17 ferry lines plied the East River, the BMB served commuters who took the ferry from Manhattan to 39th Street in South Brooklyn. The BMB is an example of Beaux-Arts Structural Expressionism, mirroring the architecture of the Paris Exposition of the late nineteenth century. It is composed of several materials, including cast-iron columns, rolled-steel plates and angles, stucco-paneled walls and arches, lead-patterned glass windows, and a copper-paneled mansard roof. The ceiling vaults of the second-floor loggia deck are decorated with Gustavino tiles.

The BMB has had several lives. For 29 years ferry passengers lined up in the Great Hall, a 34-foot-high (7.3-meter-high), 8500-square-foot (790-square-meter) waiting area, one of the city's grand spaces. From there they boarded vessels at slips 5, 6, and 7 on the south side of the building. In 1938 the Brooklyn ferry service was discontinued, leaving the slips unused and the BMB structure to deteriorate. The U.S. Army, followed by the Coast Guard, ran ferry service to Governors Island from the BMB; the Governors Island Preservation and Education Corporation and the National Park Service continue that operation at slip 7. An occasional commuter ferry to New Jersey ran from slip 5 in the 1980s.

Various city agencies have found homes in the BMB, including the Department of Ports and Terminals (originally the Docks Department, housed in Pier A). In the 1980s the ferry level housed mothballed records of the Docks Department dating from 1870, a basketball court, and an out-of-tune piano. The latest tenant, the Department of Transportation, used the Great Hall for storage and the third and fourth floors for offices. The building was designated a city landmark in 1967; nine years later it earned a place on the National Register of Historic Places.

From 2001 to 2006, under the aegis of the city's Economic Development Corporation (EDC), the BMB underwent a $60 million structural restoration and exterior face-lift. With that work complete, EDC has selected developers from the Dermot Company and the downtown restaurateur Harry Poulakakis to bring the BMB back to life. Its latest reincarnation includes a specialty-foods market in the Great Hall and a new addition housing a boutique hotel and rooftop restaurant.

Ann L. Buttenwieser

Battery Park, with office district in background, ca *1935–40*

Battery Park. Public park at the southernmost edge of Manhattan. Dutch settlers in 1623 called the site Capske Hook, from the Native American word *kapsee,* which means "rocky ledge." Fort Amsterdam was constructed at the site in 1626, and Governor Thomas Dongan began building batteries along the shore in 1683, thus lending the area its name. Fort Amsterdam (which was successively renamed Fort James, Fort Willem Hendrick, Fort William, and Fort Anne) was occupied by the British and renamed Fort George during the Revolutionary War. In 1788 the fort was demolished, the rubble from which was used as landfill to expand the Battery, which became a public waterfront promenade. Between 1808 and 1811, a new, circular fort was built 200 feet offshore on an artificial island to prepare for the War of 1812.

Originally called the West Battery, it was named Castle Clinton in 1815 and was reborn in 1824 as Castle Garden, an entertainment venue. As Castle Garden, it was the leading entertainment hall in the city for more than 30 years, perhaps best known for a performance there in 1850 by the singer Jenny Lind, presented by P. T. Barnum. The building was later used as the federal immigration center for the East Coast (1855–90, before the opening of the facility at Ellis Island), and after being reconfigured by Stanford White as the New York Aquarium (1896–1941) was operated by the parks department. From 1940 to 1952 the park was closed while the Brooklyn-Battery Tunnel was built beneath it; on reopening it had new landscaping and an additional two acres of land. In 1963 President John F. Kennedy dedicated the East Coast Memorial to the 4596 servicemen who lost their lives in the Atlantic during the Second World War, one of the many monuments in the park honoring soldiers, explorers, inventors, and immigrants. In 1982 New York State designated Battery Park as part of Harbor Park, a group of historic waterfront sites.

By the late twentieth century the park had deteriorated; in response, the Battery Conservancy, a private nonprofit organization, was created in 1994. The conservancy has followed other public-private partnerships at city parks

Battery Park, 2010

and implemented improved landscaping, programming, and amenities; it has brought musical entertainment back to Castle Clinton, which is also slated for restoration. In the early twenty-first century a sea-themed carousel with a ferry link to the aquarium at Coney Island was planned, and a Frank Gehry–designed playground was in the works. The park today spans 25 acres (10.12 hectares) and receives 5 million visitors annually. Its more than 20 monuments include *The Sphere,* a sculpture by Fritz Koenig that originally stood in the World Trade Center plaza as a monument to peace. After the sculpture was damaged during the attacks of 11 September 2001, it was moved to Battery Park, where it now stands as a memorial to those killed.

Jonathan Kuhn, Kate Lauber

Battery Park City, 2009

Battery Park City. Commercial and residential complex in lower Manhattan, bounded to the north by Chambers Street, to the east by West Street, to the south by Pier A, and to the west by the Hudson River. It is built on 92 acres (37 hectares) of landfill, a quarter of which were dredgings from the construction of the World Trade Center. The complex was developed by the Battery Park City Authority, a public-benefit corporation formed in 1968 by the New York state legislature. The authority sold state bonds to fund the work, including landfill, infrastructure, and public parks. A portion of the profits was used to finance public amenities as well as to build and rehabilitate low- and middle-income housing elsewhere in New York City.

Wallace K. Harrison, one of Governor Nelson Rockefeller's main architects, oversaw the initial plans for the mixed-use community in the 1960s. M. Paul Friedberg and Partners were the original landscape architects. Construction began in 1974 on Gateway Plaza, a residential complex. A master plan drawn up in 1979 by Alexander Cooper and Stanton Eckstut allocated 42 percent of the land for housing, 30 percent for open space (including an esplanade along the river), 19 percent for streets and avenues, and 9 percent for commercial and office space. In the first phase, Olympia and York was the sole developer of the commercial area, the World Financial Center, which was adjacent to the financial district around Wall Street and connected to it by two walkways.

Battery Park City experienced serious problems during and after the terrorist attacks of 11 September 2001, which brought down the twin towers of the World Trade Center. Virtually all residents were required to leave their homes for an extended time. Environmental hazards that resulted from the destruction and the resultant fires, including airborne toxins, smoke, ash, and other pollutants, were major problems. But by 2009 Battery Park City had fully recovered. It consists of residential areas, including Gateway Plaza, a high-rise building complex; the Rector Place Residential Neighborhood and the Battery Place Residential Neighborhood; a hotel; Stuyvesant High School, which opened in 1992 (designed by Alexander Cooper and Partners); shopping and commercial outlets; the World Financial Center, designed by Cesar Pelli; and North Cove, a yacht basin. A ferry service was established in 1989 to Hoboken, New Jersey. Additional building in the 1990s and early 2000s resulted in the creation of an extensive waterfront park of 8 acres (3.2 hectares), designed by Carr Lynch Associates in conjunction with Oehme, van Sweden and Associates, and a park of 3 acres (1.2 hectares) at the southern end of the complex, designed by Alexander Cooper, Nicholas Quennell, and the artist Jennifer Bartlett. Also added was the Museum of Jewish Heritage, a Holocaust memorial, an Irish famine memorial, a luxury hotel, and more housing.

Among the architects who are represented at the complex are Charles Moore; Cesar Pelli; Davis, Brody and Associates; Skidmore, Owings and Merrill; Menz and Cook; Mitchell/Giurgola; the Gruzen Partnership; Bond Ryder James; Ulrich Franzen; the Vilkas Group; James Stewart Polshek and Partners; Ehrenkrantz, Eckstut and Whitelaw; Costas Kondylis; and Gruzen Samton Steinglass. Artists whose work may be seen at Battery Park City include R. M. Fischer (*Rector Gate,* 1989, a whimsical entryway between park and esplanade), Richard Artschwager (*Sitting/Stance,* 1989, a collection of fanciful street furniture), Ned Smyth (*Upper Room,* 1987, a small park with a variety of decorative architectural motifs), Siah Armajani, Scott Burton, and Mary Miss.

In 2006 city and state officials announced the creation of the New York City Housing Trust Fund, which would use revenue from Battery Park City for 4300 affordable units of housing; this was to be followed by another 30,000 units of affordable housing in the following decade. In 2009 approximately 10,000 people lived in Battery Park City's mostly middle-class and upper-middle-class apartments.

Lisa Keller, Nan Ellin

Battista, Vito P(iranesi) (*b* Bari, Italy, 7 Sept 1908; *d* Brooklyn, 24 May 1990). Architect and political leader. With his family he moved to New York City at the age of three and settled in the Brooklyn neighborhood of Bushwick. After attending night school he studied architecture at the Carnegie Institute, the Massachusetts Institute of Technology, the École des Beaux-Arts in Paris, and Columbia University. He helped to design structures for the World's Fair of 1939–40 and Cadman Plaza, became president of the Society of Architects in Brooklyn, and organized the Institute of Design and Construction (1947). A Republican in a predominantly Democratic city, he was known as a gadfly with a showman's flair and a perennial candidate for municipal office who spoke for ordinary people while inveighing against taxes, rent control, welfare abuse, and municipal waste. Battista was a state assemblyman from 1965 to 1975.

George J. Lankevich

Bauer, Catherine. See Wurster, Catherine Bauer.

Bayard, Nicholas (*b* Alphen, Netherlands, 1644; *d* New York City, ?1709). Mayor. A nephew of Peter Stuyvesant, he began his career as a clerk for the provincial secretary of New Amsterdam and held a similar position after the English conquest; he was appointed receiver general when the Dutch returned to power in 1673 but was removed from his offices when the English returned and was subsequently imprisoned by Governor Edmond Andros. He was a favorite of Governor Thomas Dongan, who appointed him mayor of New York City in 1685 and a member of the governor's council in 1687. A leading opponent of Jacob Leisler, Bayard was imprisoned by the Leislerians in early 1690 (see Leisler's Rebellion). On his release in 1691 he was reappointed to the governor's council and helped to ensure that Leisler was executed on charges of treason later the same year. Bayard was dismissed from office in 1697 and was himself convicted of treason and sentenced to death in 1702 when Leisler's former allies controlled the provincial government, but he was pardoned before the sentence was carried out.

David William Voorhees

Bayard, William (*b* New York City, 1761; *d* New York City, 18 Sept 1826). Merchant. The son of Loyalist parents, he remained in New York City after his family moved to England in 1783. With Herman LeRoy, Bayard formed an international shipping company that was one of the strongest of its kind for four decades. He also speculated in land upstate, was a privateer in the War of 1812, tried to obtain loans for the Erie Canal, was president of the Morris Canal Company and the Bank of America, and belonged to the Chamber of Commerce. Toward the end of his life Bayard was troubled by accusations that his firm, then managed by his sons, engaged in questionable practices. Bayard wrote *An Exposition of the Conduct of the Two Houses* (1826).

James E. Mooney

Bayard–Condict Building. Office building at 65 Bleecker Street between Broadway and Lafayette Street, erected in 1898. It is the only building in New York City designed by Frank Lloyd Wright's teacher Louis H. Sullivan. The building is ornamented with terracotta. Between the columns and an intricately filigreed cornice are six angels said to have been added over Sullivan's objections. The original capitals from the first-floor columns are now in the sculpture garden of the Brooklyn Museum.

John Voelcker

Baychester. Neighborhood in the northeastern Bronx and the site of Co-op City, bounded to the east by the Hutchinson River and Pelham Bay Park and to the southwest and west by the New England Thruway. The area was a marsh until it became the site of a cucumber farm and pickle factory from the 1870s to 1895; it was then used to farm strawberries and in the 1890s was given its current name by real estate developers. A few years later the land was sold to the Curtiss-Wright Aviation Company for a municipal airport that was never built; it was also considered a possible site for a racetrack. An amusement park called Freedomland occupied the area from 1960 until the construction in 1968–70 of Co-op City, one of the largest housing developments in the United States. Sixty thousand persons live in 15,372 apartments in the development, which has 35 buildings (mostly high-rise), movie theaters, eight multistory garages, five shopping centers, a firehouse, a heating plant, and an educational park. Apart from Co-op City the neighborhood consists principally of one- and two-family houses and a large shopping mall. Some residents of the area west of the New England Thruway also consider their neighborhood part of Baychester. At the beginning of the twenty-first century the population was largely black and Latin American.

John McNamara, *McNamara's Old Bronx* (New York: Bronx County Historical Society, 1989)

Gary D. Hermalyn

Bayonne Bridge. The longest steel arch bridge in the world when it opened in 1931, in the early twenty-first century it was the third largest in the world. The bridge serves vehicular traffic crossing the Kill van Kull waterway between Port Richmond in Staten Island and Bayonne, New Jersey. Designed by Othmar H. Ammann, a bridge engineer at the Port of New York Authority, it was completed in 1931 at a cost of $13 million. It has a dramatic, high arch of 266 feet (81.1 meters) that carries the roadbed for 1675 feet (511 meters) without intermediary piers. The total length of the bridge, including approaches, is 8460 feet (2580 meters), and the clearance above water at mid-span is 150 feet (46 meters). The original plan called for granite sheathing to be laid over the steelwork of the arch abutment, but this was eliminated to lower costs. In 1932 the Bayonne Bridge was awarded a prize as the most beautiful structure of steel completed in 1931, winning against Ammann's other 1931 project, the George Washington Bridge. The initial hope was that the Bayonne and Goethals bridges would serve as major routes across New Jersey to the Holland Tunnel. Alternative highways proved faster, however, and the Bayonne has typically carried only modest traffic.

Darl Rastorfer, *Bayonne Bridge* (New York: Port Authority of New York and New Jersey, 2007)

Rebecca Read Shanor, Jameson W. Doig

Bay Ridge. Neighborhood in southwestern Brooklyn, bounded to the north by 61st Street, to the east by the Gowanus Expressway, to the south by 86th Street, and to the west by Upper New York Bay. The land was part of a tract bought by the Dutch West India Company from the Nyack Indians in 1652. The neighborhood was called Yellow Hook for the color of the clay found in the area; so as not to evoke unpleasant associations with the yellow fever epidemic of 1848–49 this name was abandoned in 1853 in favor of the current one, which recalls the position of the neighborhood by the bay and the glacial ridge that runs along what is now Ridge Boulevard. After the Civil War the area became a retreat of the wealthy, whose mansions lined the bluffs above the Narrows. The Crescent Athletic Club (now Fort Hamilton High School) was the center of fashionable society. After the opening of the Fourth Avenue subway in 1915, high-rise apartment buildings replaced most of the earlier houses. At the turn of the twentieth century, the population

View of Bayonne Bridge from Staten Island to New Jersey, 1932

consisted largely of Italians and Scandinavians; after World War II Irish, Greeks, and Arabs joined the community. In the 1960s the building of the Verrazano–Narrows Bridge required that more than 8000 residents be displaced. The neighborhood was the setting in 1978 for the film *Saturday Night Fever,* several scenes of which were filmed at a local nightclub. During the 1980s the Chinese community centered at Sunset Park expanded into the neighborhood, and a number of abandoned factories and warehouses were converted into garment factories run by Chinese entrepreneurs. The Chinese are by far the largest single group in the first decade of the twenty-first century, accounting for more than one-quarter of all immigrants; there are also large numbers from Italy, Russia, Ukraine, Lithuania, Greece, Korea, Lebanon, Egypt, Syria, and Jordan. The neighborhood has an active army installation at Fort Hamilton and is the terminus in Brooklyn of the Verrazano–Narrows Bridge. Two mansions remain: the Fontbonne Hall Academy, at 9901 Shore Road (now a private school), and the Gingerbread House, at 82nd Street and Narrows Avenue (designated a landmark). Bay Ridge is a community of one- and two-family row houses and frame houses with bay fronts, garages, basements, and lawns. The main shopping streets are 86th Street and Third and Fifth avenues.

Elizabeth Reich Rawson

Bay Ridge Savings Bank. Original name of ANCHOR SAVINGS BANK.

Bayside. Neighborhood in northeastern Queens, on Little Neck Bay, for which it is named. First inhabited by Matinecock Indians, it was part of the area for which William Lawrence received patents from King Charles I in 1644. During the American Revolution it was settled first by John Rodman, a Quaker, and later by Thomas Hicks, a resident of Flushing whose land was included in a parcel of 246 acres (100 hectares) bought in 1824 by Abraham Bell. About this time the Lawrence family also settled in Bayside, which grew after the North Shore Railroad was extended in 1866. During the next 30 years many mansions were built on the high ground around the bay by wealthy New Yorkers, including F. N. Lawrence, G. Howland Leavitt, and G. W. Harway; many of their estates were dissolved in the 1920s and 1930s, when film stars and sportsmen built houses there, among them Pearl White, Norma Talmadge, John Golden, and James J. Corbett. Between 1908 and 1928 J. Wilson Dayton and the McKnight Realty Company put up many houses on side streets of Bell Boulevard and on new streets built inland from Little Neck Bay. After World War II the character of Bayside was altered by highways and bridges built to the east and west, including the Cross Island Parkway, which cut off access to Little Neck Bay, the Throgs Neck Bridge (1961), and the Clearview Expressway (1961–63). Large apartment complexes such as Bay Terrace and Clearview Gardens were built in the late 1950s. Queensboro Community College opened in 1967 on the former site of the Oakland Golf Course. Bayside is a comfortable middle-class, suburban neighborhood, with a growing Chinese, Korean, and Indian population.

Vincent Seyfried

Bayswater. Neighborhood in southwestern Queens, constituting the part of Far Rockaway north of Bayswater Avenue and Mott Avenue. It was developed by William Trist Bailey, who built cottages and a brick hotel called the Bayswater House on land bought in 1878 from J. B. and W. W. Cornell, descendants of Richard Cornell, the first settler in Rockaway. Summer mansions were later built on large lots by many prominent residents of Brooklyn. In June 1905 Trist was declared bankrupt and his tract was sold piecemeal at auction. Bayswater Point, a site of 12 acres (5 hectares) on Jamaica Bay, was acquired in 1986 by New York State, which in 1991 designated the area a state park to be administered by the Audubon Society. By this time many older houses in the neighborhood had been demolished and replaced by housing for the middle class. In the twenty-first century Bayswater has a diverse population with significant numbers of African Americans and Orthodox Jews and remains an upscale neighbor to Far Rockaway.

Vincent Seyfried

Bay Terrace. Neighborhood in east central Staten Island, centered at a station of the same name of Staten Island Rapid Transit and lying within the neighborhood of Oakwood. It consists mainly of modern estates.

Martha S. Bendix

BBDO. See BATTEN, BARTON, DURSTINE AND OSBORN.

Beach, Alfred Ely (*b* Springfield, Mass., 1 Sept 1826; *d* New York City, 1 Jan 1896). Newspaper and magazine publisher and inventor. With his brother Moses Sperry Beach he acquired control of the *New York Sun* in 1848 from their father, the newspaper publisher Moses Yale Beach; in 1852 he relinquished his share of the paper. An owner and editor of *Scientific American,* he helped to transform the magazine into a publication of national stature. He also contributed to the invention of the typewriter and took out a patent for a model in 1847; he invented a typewriter for the blind in 1857. Among his other inventions were pneumatic tubes for mail and passengers (1865) and a shield used for tunneling under streets and rivers (1868). In 1870 he built a section of pneumatic subway under lower Manhattan that many consider to have been the prototype for the subway system that was eventually built.

Steven H. Jaffe

Beach, Moses Yale (*b* Wallingford, Conn., 15 Jan 1800; *d* Wallingford, 19 July 1868). Newspaper publisher and inventor, father of Alfred Ely Beach. After inventing a rag-cutting machine for the manufacture of paper and a combustion engine, in 1834 he became the manager of the mechanical department at the *New York Sun,* which was owned by his brother-in-law Benjamin Day. He bought the *Sun* from Day in 1838 and transformed it into one of the country's most prosperous and widely read "penny papers." A prominent Democrat, he was sent by President James K. Polk on a secret mission to Mexico (1846), where he tried unsuccessfully to negotiate an end to the Mexican–American War. Between 1842 and 1855 he published a pamphlet, *The Wealth of New York,* in which he included himself on a list of the city's thousand richest citizens. He retired from the *Sun* in 1848 and turned it over to his sons, Alfred Ely Beach and Moses Sperry Beach (*b* Springfield, Mass., 5 Oct 1822; *d* Peekskill, N.Y., 25 July 1892). With five other newspaper publishers in 1848–49 he formed the cooperative news-gathering organization that later became the Associated Press.

Frank M. O'Brien, *The Story of the Sun, New York: 1833–1928* (New York: D. Appleton, 1928)

Steven H. Jaffe

beaches. The New York City Department of Parks and Recreation maintains beaches in four of the five boroughs, constituting 14 miles (22.5 kilometers) of shoreline. Orchard Beach and Promenade is located in the Bronx; Brighton Beach, Coney Island, and Manhattan Beach in Brooklyn; and Rockaway Beach in Queens. Midland Beach, South Beach, and Wolfe's Pond Beach comprise most of the beach land in Staten Island. The beaches are open annually from Memorial Day through Labor Day.

New York City Parks and Recreation Public Beaches

Bronx: Orchard Beach
Brooklyn: Brighton Beach, Coney Island Beach, Manhattan Beach
Queens: Rockaway Beach
Staten Island: South Beach, Midland Beach, Wolfe's Pond Beach

Source: New York City Department of Parks and Recreation Web site, http://www.nycgovparks.org.
Compiled by Frank Nestor

Orchard Beach, 2009

Beals, Jessie Tarbox (*b* Hamilton, Ont., 23 Dec 1870; *d* New York City, 31 May 1942). Photographer. She pursued photography as a hobby, married her darkroom assistant Alfred Tennyson Beals in 1897, and became a full-time photojournalist in 1900. After traveling widely she settled in New York City in 1905. There she recorded subjects ranging from society figures to the slums of the Lower East Side, and gained regular assignments for leading newspapers and magazines. After separating from her husband in 1917 she opened a tea shop in Sheridan Square that doubled as a photography studio, and in the following years she documented the bohemian milieu of Greenwich Village in a series of memorable print and postcard views. Other favorite photographic subjects were city gardens and cigar-store Indians.

Jessie Tarbox Beals, Great Lurid Blobs of Color on a Wooden Box and Bobby Edwards in his Garret 'neath the Stars Creating Eukalalies *(Postcard of a painter in his studio in Greenwich Village)*

Alexander Alland, *Jessie Tarbox Beals: First Woman Photographer* (New York: Camera / Graphic Press, 1978)

See also Photography.

Jan Seidler Ramirez

Beame, Abraham D(avid) (*b* London, 20 March 1906; *d* New York City, 10 Feb 2001). Mayor. His family emigrated from Warsaw via London to the United States in 1906 and settled in New York City. He earned an accounting degree from City College of New York, taught public school, and at the age of 24 joined the Madison Democratic Club in Brooklyn. During his early years in public service, he was appointed budget director (1952) and elected comptroller (1961). In 1965 he became the first Jewish candidate since the consolidation of New York City (1898) to win the Democratic nomination for mayor, but he lost the general election to John V. Lindsay. After winning reelection as comptroller in 1969, he was elected mayor in 1973. During his term, a serious fiscal crisis forced him to spend his time conducting financial negotiations with state and federal officials, banks, and municipal unions. To avert bankruptcy, he laid off large numbers of city employees and delayed maintenance and important capital expenditures. He was accused by the Securities and Exchange Commission of using unsound budgeting practices, but defended by others for having made politically difficult decisions in a time of economic difficulty. The formation of the Municipal Assistance Corporation and the Emergency Financial Control Board in 1975 severely restricted Beame's ability to exercise the traditional powers of the mayor. Discredited by the fiscal crisis, he sought reelection in 1977 but lost the Democratic primary election and retired from politics.

Ken Auletta, *The Streets Were Paved with Gold* (New York: Random House, 1979)

Chris McNickle

Beamon, Robert [Bob] (*b* New York City, 29 Aug 1946). Olympic champion long jumper. He was raised by his grandmother in Jamaica, Queens, where he became involved with gangs and ran afoul of the law several times. At age 14 he struck a teacher after a gang dispute spilled into his Queens Public School 40 classroom, and he was sent to the 600 School, a Manhattan facility for juvenile delinquents. Beamon then worked to resurrect his life so he could attend Jamaica High School and participate on the track team under legendary coach Larry Ellis. Beamon set numerous city high school track records, culminating with a New York State record in the long jump at age 16. Five years later he made the United States Olympic team and at the 1968 Mexico City Olympics won the gold medal and set a world record in the long jump.

Abraham D. Beame, 1974

Aided by the altitude of Mexico City and favorable weather conditions, Beamon's leap of 29 ft. 2.5 in. (8.9 meters) eclipsed the previous mark by more than 2 ft. in an event in which records typically fell by no more than a few inches. His record stood for 23 years and the term "Beamonesque" became a common phrase in sports for describing an unexpected and incredible record-breaking accomplishment. Beamon never again jumped within 2 ft. of his record. In the early twenty-first century Beamon lived in Florida and remained active in promoting sports for inner-city children and the Olympic movement.

David White

Beard, Charles A(ustin) (*b* near Knightstown, Ind., 27 Nov 1874; *d* New Haven, Conn., 1 Sept 1948). Historian. In 1902 he enrolled at Columbia University (MA 1903, PhD in political science 1904), where he became a lecturer in history (to 1907) and then taught public law as an adjunct professor, associate professor (from 1910), and professor (from 1915). He became an expert in municipal government, helped to establish public administration as a field of study, and wrote *American City Government: A Survey of Newer Tendencies* (1912). His highly influential work *An Economic Interpretation of the Constitution* (1913) reflected his belief in the primacy of economic forces in history. Several of his later works were written in collaboration with his wife, Mary Ritter Beard. In 1915 he became the director of the Training School for Public Service (the first graduate school of public administration in the United States), a branch of the New York Bureau of Municipal Research (the first research institute in the United States designed to promote efficiency in municipal government), and in 1918 he became the director of the entire bureau. He resigned from Columbia in 1917 (to protest the dismissal of his colleague James McKeen Cattell), and in 1919 he was one of the founders of the New School for Social Research. After leaving the Bureau of Municipal Research (1921) and the New School he moved to New Milford, Connecticut, and spent the rest of his life writing and lecturing. In his later years he appeared to disavow the progressivism of his early career when he became an outspoken critic of President Franklin D. Roosevelt.

Jane S. Dahlberg, *The New York Bureau of Municipal Research: Pioneer in Government Administration* (New York: New York University Press, 1966); Richard Hofstadter, *The Progressive Historians: Turner, Beard, Parrington* (New York: Alfred A. Knopf, 1968)

Allen J. Share

Beard, James (Andrews) (*b* Portland, Ore., 5 May 1903; *d* New York City, 23 Jan 1985). Chef. After moving to New York City in 1938 he wrote his first book in 1940. He served in the army during World War II. In 1955 he launched Beard's Cooking Classes, which were later held in his townhouse in Greenwich Village. A food editor for the *New York Times* for many years, he also wrote a syndicated column for United Press and gave demonstrations on the television program *Elsie Presents*. Beard wrote more than two dozen books, including *Fowl and Game Cookery* (1944), *Cook It Outdoors* (1941), and his autobiography, *Delights and Prejudices* (1981).

Evan Jones, *Epicurean Delight: The Life and Times of James Beard* (New York: Alfred A. Knopf, 1990); Robert Clark, *James Beard: A Biography* (New York: Harper Collins, 1993)

James E. Mooney

Beard, Mary Ritter (*b* Indianapolis, 5 Aug 1876; *d* Scottsdale, Ariz., 14 Aug 1958). Historian and feminist. She moved to New York City in 1902, pursued graduate study in sociology at Columbia University until 1904, and worked with the National Women's Trade Union League in organizing the shirtwaist makers' strike of 1909. In the following year she became active in the Woman Suffrage Party of New York State, serving briefly as the vice chairman of its branch in Manhattan (1910–11) and as the editor of its official organ, the *Woman Voter* (1911–12). Her interest in municipal reform led to the publication of her book *Women's Work in Municipalities* (1915). She collaborated on several other works with her husband, Charles A. Beard. From 1935 she attempted to establish the World Center for Women's Archives, which incorporated and set up an office in New York City but disbanded in 1940 for lack of support and funds. At the age of 70 she published her most important and influential book, *Woman as a Force in History* (1946).

Nancy F. Cott, ed., *A Woman Making History: Mary Ritter Beard through Her Letters* (New Haven: Yale University Press, 1991)

Allen J. Share

Beard, William Holbrook (*b* Painesville, Ohio, 13 April 1824; *d* New York City, 20 Feb 1900). Painter. At about age 20 he moved to New York City and became a portrait painter; he later worked in Buffalo and studied in Europe before returning to the city in 1860, where he became known for such paintings as *Bulls and Bears, Teddy Bear's Picnic,* and *Deer in a Wood* depicting animals behaving like people. Beard was a member of the National Academy of Design, the Century Association, and the Artists' Fund Society.

William H. Gerdts, *William Holbrook Beard: Animals in Fantasy* (New York: Alexander Gallery, 1981)

James E. Mooney

Bearden, (Fred) Romare (Howard) (*b* Charlotte, N.C., 2 Sept 1911; *d* New York City, 11 March 1988). Painter. The son of a well-known political activist and newspaper editor in Harlem, he became acquainted as a youth with such jazz musicians and writers as Fats Waller and Langston Hughes. He studied in 1936–37 at the Art Students League with George Grosz and then joined the 306 Group of black artists in Harlem; a friendship with Stuart Davis developed in part because of a shared interest in jazz. In the mid-1940s shows devoted exclusively to his work were mounted at the Samuel Kootz Gallery, where Robert Motherwell and Adolph Gottlieb also exhibited. After living in Paris in 1950 he returned to New York City, where he continued to paint, organize exhibitions, and write. From 1963 he created collages for the Spiral Group, initially as part of a collaboration with other black artists on themes drawn from black life, and in the following year he was appointed the art director of the Harlem Cultural Council. He was also an organizer of the Cinque Gallery, which showed the work of young black artists. A retrospective of his work at the Museum of Modern Art entitled *Romare Bearden: The Prevalence of Ritual* (1971) brought him wider recognition. Bearden worked in an improvisatory manner that he likened to that of a jazz musician. His work is characterized by a vivid and often jarring juxtaposition of disparate images from urban life. With the artist Carl Holty he wrote *The Painter's Mind: A Study of Structure and Space in Painting* (1969).

Albert Murray and Dore Ashton, *Romare Bearden, 1970–1980* (Charlotte, N.C.: Mint Museum, 1980); Ruth E. Fine, *The Art of Romare Bearden* (New York: Harry N. Abrams, 2003)

Mona Hadler

Beatrice International Holdings. See TLC Beatrice International Holdings.

Bear Stearns. Firm of investment bankers formed as a brokerage firm in New York City in 1923 by Harold C. Mayer, Joseph Ainslie Bear, and Robert B. Stearns. It initially had offices at 100 Broadway and by 1940 had departments for institutional bonds, risk arbitrage, and municipal bond trading. The firm opened its investment banking division in 1943 and an international department in 1948; several domestic and European offices were opened in the 1950s and 1960s. Under the leadership of Alan C. Greenberg in the 1980s the firm became a leading worldwide investment banking and securities trading firm, with major American and international corporations among its clients. In March 2008 the firm collapsed, preceding a wider downfall of the investment bank industry on Wall Street in September 2008, and was sold to JPMorgan Chase.

Mary E. Curry

beats. Members of a literary movement centered from about 1950 to the mid-1960s in lower Manhattan (as well as San Francisco), characterized by bohemianism, a hostility toward commercialism and conformity, and an enthusiasm for visionary states induced by hallucinogenic drugs. The movement had its roots in informal discussions held in 1944 by Allen Ginsberg and Lucien Carr, both undergraduates at Columbia University, and William Burroughs and Jack Kerouac, all seeking what they called a new vision in literature; they often met at the West End Cafe, on Broadway and 113th Street near Columbia.

The most important texts of the beat movement date from the early 1950s: Kerouac's first novel, *The Town and the City* (1950); his most popular work, *On the Road* (1951, published 1957), written in an apartment at 454 West 20th Street in Manhattan; *Go* (1952), by John Clellon Holmes, a vivid description of the beat movement, which by the time the book was published had grown to include many friends and acquaintances of the original members; Burroughs's first novel, *Junkie: Confessions of an Unredeemed Drug Addict* (1953, under the pseudonym William Lee), which depicts the author's early years of drug addiction; and Ginsberg's *Howl and Other Poems* (1956), an influential collection of free verse. The members of what became known as the beat generation gained visibility after *On the Road* was reviewed in the *New York Times* and became a best seller. In 1957 Norman Mailer analyzed the aesthetics of the movement in his essay "The White Negro" (published in *Dissent*), Norman Podhoretz attacked the beats for "expressing contempt for coherent, rational discourse" in the spring issue of *Partisan Review* (his criticism was rebutted by LeRoi Jones and others), and an unruly symposium on the beats was held at Hunter College. In the same year Ginsberg returned from a visit to Europe to settle on the Lower East Side, where he joined other beat writers including Jones, Gregory Corso, Peter Orlovsky, and Diane Di Prima, poets like Frank O'Hara who did not belong to the movement but were sympathetic toward it, and poets associated with Black Mountain College (such as Robert Creeley) and San Francisco (such as Michael McClure). The work of the beats was circulated by small publishers like Grove Press, Totem Press, and Corinth Books, and by bookshop owners such as Ted Wilentz of the Eighth Street Bookshop, Robert A. Wilson of the Phoenix Bookshop, Andreas Brown of the Gotham Book Mart, and Ed Sanders of the Peace Eye Bookshop. Poetry readings and experimental plays flourished downtown at the Living Theater, the Artist's Studio, and the Gas Light Cafe. In 1959 Ginsberg, Corso, and Orlovsky read their poetry to a receptive audience at Columbia and made a film entitled *Pull My Daisy* with Kerouac, the artist Larry Rivers, the musician David Amram, and the photographer Robert Frank in the studio of the painter Alfred Leslie in Manhattan.

Kerouac described his favorite scenes of New York City in *Lonesome Traveler,* a collection of travel sketches published in 1960. That same year three popular anthologies of beat writing were published in New York City: *The Beats,* edited by Seymour Krim; *The Beat Scene,* edited by Elias Wilentz, with photographs by Fred McDarrah of the *Village Voice;* and *Beat Coast East: An Anthology of Rebellion,* edited by Stanley Fisher, who tried to define the word *beat* by walking the streets of Greenwich Village and asking "an assortment of squalid squares and plastered saints what they thought the word meant" (he was given 20 definitions). In 1961 Ted Joans, a young painter and poet, satirized the "beatniks" of Washington Square and the tendency of the press toward sensational coverage of the beat movement in his witty collage book *The Hipsters.*

In the early 1960s little magazines dedicated to experimental writing proliferated in Greenwich Village and on the Lower East Side, among them *Yugen, Floating Bear,* and *Fuck You: A Magazine of the Arts.* This period has been described by Di Prima in *Memoirs of a Beatnik* (1969), Sanders in *Tales of Beatnik Glory* (1975), Joyce Johnson in *Minor Characters* (1983), and Hettie Jones (at one time married to LeRoi Jones) in *How I Became Hettie Jones* (1990).

The beat movement was largely spent by the mid-1960s, but it strongly influenced the hippie movement of the late 1960s and early 1970s, in which some beat figures were active: Sanders and Tuli Kupferberg took part in protests on Fifth Avenue against the Vietnam War by performing with their rock group the Fugs, and Kupferberg's book *1001 Ways to Beat the Draft* (1966) enjoyed wide circulation. A new generation of experimental writers carried on the beat traditions of small-press publishing and poetry reading in New York City, perhaps best exemplified by the Poetry Project at St. Mark's Church in the Bowery. Ginsberg became a Distinguished Professor of English at Brooklyn College, continued to live on the Lower East Side, and remained a prominent figure in the literary, musical, and artistic avant-garde until his death on 5 April 1997.

Ann Charters, "The Beats: Literary Bohemians in Post-war America," *Dictionary of Literary Biography,* vol. 16 (Detroit: Gale Research, 1983); Barry Miles, *Ginsberg: A Biography* (New York: Simon and Schuster, 1989); Bill Morgan, *The Beat Generation in New York: A Walking Tour of Jack Kerouac's City.* (San Francisco: City Lights, 1997)

Ann Charters

Beaux-Arts Institute of Design. Institute opened by the Society of Beaux Arts Architects (1894) to promote the classical values of the French school among architects in the United States. It offered free classes to draftsmen and had unparalleled influence in architectural instruction from 1900 until the 1930s. The principal function of the institute was to sponsor juried competitions. Its programs were used by nearly three-quarters of the country's architecture students. Headquarters in an art deco style were designed in 1927 by Frederick C. Hirons and built at 304 East 44th Street (now a city landmark). With the rise of modernism the institute lost much of its influence and was reorganized as the National Institute for Architectural Education.

John Frederick Harbeson, *The Study of Architectural Design, with Special Reference to the Program of the Beaux-Arts Institute of Design* (New York: Pencil Points Press, 1927)

Carol Willis

Becker–Rosenthal case. Case involving the shooting of Herman Rosenthal on 16 July 1912 in New York City. It generated much interest because it involved public figures and had political and anti-Semitic overtones. Rosenthal operated a gambling house on the Lower East Side and was reputedly a minor figure in organized crime. Police lieutenant Charles Becker (1869–1915), who led a "strong arm squad" to eradicate gambling, was charged with his murder; Rosenthal had accused Becker of graft in a long article in the *New York World* published two days before Rosenthal's death. Leading citizens dedicated to rooting out police corruption supported the investigation of the murder. Mayor William J. Gaynor briefly defended Becker in public before Jewish leaders criticized the mayor for his attack on "lawless foreigners" (a group in which he included Rosenthal). The district attorney who successfully prosecuted the case,

Charles Whitman, embarked on a career in politics: as governor of New York he approved Becker's execution, which took place at Sing Sing Prison on 7 July 1915. Herbert Bayard Swope, an enterprising reporter for the *World*, became the best-known journalist of his day for his coverage of the case.

Andy Logan, *Against the Evidence: The Becker-Rosenthal Affair* (New York: McCall Publishing, 1970)

Norris Randolph

Beckman, John (*b* New York City, 22 Oct 1895; *d* Miami, 22 June 1968). Professional basketball player. Known as the "Babe Ruth of basketball," he was only 5 ft. 10 in. (1.8 meters) tall and never played ball in college, but in his 28 years in the game he was a top attraction. Beckman played with the New York City–based Original Celtics, was their top scorer, and led the team to the 1922 Eastern League title. He played for teams in eight different leagues between 1911 and 1930, winning championships on four of those teams. He was inducted into the Basketball Hall of Fame in 1973.

Frank Dyer

Bedford Corners. Early name for a part of Brooklyn now lying within Bedford–Stuyvesant.

Bedford Park. Neighborhood in the northwestern Bronx, bounded to the northeast by Mosholu Parkway, to the east by the New York Botanical Garden, to the south by 198th Street, and to the west by the Jerome Park Reservoir. Lehman College abuts the reservoir in the neighborhood's southwestern corner. It was planned in the 1880s and named after the town of Bedford, England, which also inspired its design as a suburban park and the Queen Anne architecture of its original houses. With the opening of the Jerome Avenue subway line in 1917 and the Third Avenue elevated line in 1920, the area became more accessible and more heavily built up. In spite of the Depression a large number of buildings were erected in the 1930s, including many apartment buildings in the art deco style. Among those who resided in the neighborhood was William Fox, a founder of the film company that later became 20th Century Fox. After World War II the neighborhood remained middle class, with a large population of Irish and Jews and later of Latin Americans, blacks, and Koreans. In the first decade of the twenty-first century the area contained many ethnic groups, including Dominicans, Jamaicans, Guyanese, Cambodians, Koreans, Mexicans, Bangladeshis, and Vietnamese.

Bedford Park's Art Deco Treasures (New York: Bronx County Historical Society, 1981)

Gary D. Hermalyn

Bedford–Stuyvesant. Neighborhood in north central Brooklyn (2000 pop. about 150,000), bounded to the north by Flushing Avenue, to the east by Broadway and Saratoga Avenue, to the south by Atlantic Avenue, and to the west by Classon Avenue. Before 1977 it extended as far south as Eastern Parkway. Its name is derived from those of two middle-class communities in nineteenth-century Brooklyn—Bedford (to the west) and Stuyvesant Heights (to the east)—and is often abbreviated as Bed–Stuy. Bedford–Stuyvesant has one of the largest African American communities in the United States.

In the 1630s and 1640s the Dutch West India Company purchased from the Canarsee Indians the woodlands that became Bedford, a community recognized by the English governor Richard Nicolls in 1667. Its central location between the towns of Bushwick, Jamaica, and Flatbush influenced the farmer Thomas Lambertse to build a public inn in 1668. Seventeenth-century Bedford was a farming hamlet inhabited by Dutch families and African slaves. Farmers carted surplus goods, to be sold in neighboring communities, to the Breuklen Ferry down the main road, which was close to Fulton Street, and to Hunterfly Road. After the Battle of Long Island (1776), the area was invaded by English troops. Later, the farmland was divided into housing lots and sold to new arrivals. As early as 1790, more than one-quarter of the residents were blacks (mostly slaves). Eventually, the Lefferts family bought land from the Lambertses, who were prominent developers in the area. Leffert Lefferts became a judge and town clerk in Bedford after he graduated from King's College, and his family was among the first to sell land to blacks. In 1835 John Lefferts sold the land that became known as Weeksville to Henry C. Thompson, a free black; Carrsville was built on the land bought in 1832 by another free black, William Thomas. These transactions and others affected the ethnic composition of Bedford, which by 1834 was also referred to as Bedford Corners.

The neighborhood was the site of a station of the Brooklyn and Jamaica Railroad (forerunner of the Long Island Rail Road), which was constructed in 1836 and traversed Atlantic Street (now Atlantic Avenue). Its population reached 14,000 in 1873 and included Irish, Germans, Jews, Scots, Dutch, and blacks. The ethnic diversity of the neighborhood was reflected in the names of its institutions: the Jewish Hospital, the Colored Orphan Asylum, St. John's Episcopal Church, and St. Mary's Hospital. The opening of the elevated railway (about 1885) and the Brooklyn Bridge (1883) linked the area more closely with Manhattan and spurred the construction of brownstones and the growth of new neighborhoods called East Brooklyn, New Brooklyn, and St. Marks (all in what is now Bedford–Stuyvesant). At the turn of the century, Bedford Corners and particularly Stuyvesant Avenue attracted residents from the middle and upper classes, including the retailing entrepreneurs F. W. Woolworth and Abraham Abraham. More than 45,000 persons lived in the neighborhood in 1920.

As the population continued to grow, brownstones that had formerly housed one family were subdivided into several units. The opening of a subway in 1936 gave the community a new link to Manhattan. The neighborhood attracted large numbers of eastern European Jews, Italians, and later blacks from the South and the Caribbean, many of whom settled in the western section. As the population rose, the communities of Bedford and Stuyvesant Heights became one large area of black settlement, and the neighborhood

Bedford–Stuyvesant, 2009

acquired its current name. By 1940 it had more than 65,000 black residents, and members of other ethnic groups began to leave.

Organizations were established to give financial and social assistance to blacks, among them the Paragon Progressive Federal Credit Union, formed by F. Levi and other West Indians in 1937. Black churches moved to Stuyvesant Avenue and other parts of the neighborhood and worked with the National Urban League, the National Association for the Advancement of Colored People, and other institutions to fight racial discrimination, segregation, and poverty, but inadequate housing and unemployment persisted and impoverished the neighborhood. At the same time residents began to exert a stronger political influence, and in 1968 they elected Shirley Chisholm to the U.S. Congress, where she was the first black woman to serve.

Senator Robert F. Kennedy's visit to the neighborhood in the late 1960s inspired his support for the Bedford Stuyvesant Restoration Corporation. The Society for the Preservation of Weeksville and Bedford–Stuyvesant History was formed in 1971 to commemorate the role that blacks played in developing the neighborhood, and the Bedford–Stuyvesant Restoration Plaza, which includes the Billie Holiday Theatre, was completed in 1976. The 1980s saw large-scale settlement of black immigrants from the Caribbean, primarily Guyana, Jamaica, and Barbados, and to a lesser extent Trinidad and Tobago, Haiti, and St. Vincent and the Grenadines.

By the late twentieth century Bedford–Stuyvesant was the largest black neighborhood in New York City. Immigrants came from the Caribbean, but also from the French Antilles, Latin America, and Africa. At the same time, in the 1990s second- and third-generation black southerners and Caribbeans with higher levels of education and middle- and upper-class incomes began to relocate or return to the community. The district became economically sounder.

Early in the twenty-first century, most of the neighborhood consists of well-maintained brownstone and brick-front housing that was built before World War I. Among the historic features of Bedford–Stuyvesant are the Weeksville Historic District, the Stuyvesant Heights Historic District, and the Brooklyn Children's Museum (built in 1899). Boys High School (1891) is an enormous, striking terra-cotta building in a Romanesque Revival style; among those who attended the school were Isaac Asimov and Norman Mailer.

Mary H. Manoni, *Bedford–Stuyvesant: The Anatomy of a Central City Community* (New York: Quadrangle/New York Times Books, 1973); David Ment and Mary S. Donovan, *The People of Brooklyn: A History of Two Neighborhoods* (New York: Brooklyn Educational and Cultural Alliance, 1980)

Mario A. Charles

Bedford Stuyvesant Restoration Corporation. The first nonprofit community development corporation in the United States, formed in 1967. It was founded through the bipartisan efforts of Senators Robert F. Kennedy and Jacob K. Javits, who worked with residents of Bedford–Stuyvesant to improve the quality of life and economy of the neighborhood. Among the buildings that it helped to construct with private and public capital were a commercial center of 300,000 square feet (28,000 square meters) known as Restoration Plaza, a major health care facility (55,000 patients' visits annually), and 2225 residential housing units. The corporation also created a joint venture with Pathmark Stores to develop a supermarket of 30,000 square feet (2800 square meters), found employment for 25,000 persons, and provided loans to 134 local businesses. Cultural facilities sponsored by the corporation included the Billie Holiday Theatre (seating 214), the Skylight Gallery at the Center for Art and Culture, and the Restoration Dance Theatre. The corporation is governed by a board of 26 community members, assisted by a business advisory board of nine members from the greater metropolitan area. The success of the Bedford Stuyvesant Restoration Corporation prompts a large number of national and international visitors, academic institutions, and foundations to study its methods of community development.

Charles Palms

Bee, Clair (*b* Grafton, W.Va., 2 March 1900; *d* Cleveland, 20 May 1983). Basketball coach. As the coach of the men's basketball team at Long Island University he won 410 games and lost only 86 between 1931 and 1952. The team was undefeated in two seasons (1935–36 and 1938–39) and won the National Invitation Tournament in 1939 and 1941; it also won 43 consecutive games from February 1935 to December 1936 as well as 139 consecutive home games at the gymnasium of the Brooklyn College of Pharmacy and at Madison Square Garden, where some of its more important games were played. After Long Island University eliminated its basketball program in 1952 in response to the gambling scandal of the preceding year, Bee coached professional basketball for a few years, taught at the New York Military Academy, operated basketball camps, wrote fiction, and maintained a farm in upstate New York.

Neil D. Isaacs, *All the Moves: A History of College Basketball* (Philadelphia: J. B. Lippincott, 1975)

Albert Figone

Beecher, Henry Ward (*b* Litchfield, Conn., 24 June 1813; *d* Brooklyn, 8 March 1887). Prominent Protestant minister of nineteenth-century America and brother of Catharine Beecher and Harriet Beecher Stowe. He studied in Massachusetts and Ohio and for eight

Henry Ward Beecher

years was a pastor in Indianapolis. On 10 October 1847 he took charge of the prosperous Plymouth Congregational Church at 75 Hicks Street in Brooklyn Heights, where he gave sermons that attracted large crowds every Sunday. By the time of the Civil War he was the most famous minister in the United States, and even Abraham Lincoln visited Beecher's church just before he became president of the United States. He lived at 124 Hicks Street from the 1860s. Beecher exerted tremendous influence over public morality in New York City as a lecturer and as the editor of the weekly publications the *Independent* (1861–64) and the *Christian Union* (1870–81). Some of his most enthusiastic supporters were middle-class women who inspired him to endorse the woman suffrage movement. His career suffered after Theodore Tilton, editor of the *Independent* (1864–70), accused him of committing adultery with his wife and filed suit for damages in 1874. The trial lasted six months; it ended with Beecher's acquittal, and although he continued to lead the Plymouth until the end of his life his public influence was reduced.

Theodore Tilton vs. Henry Ward Beecher: Action for Crim. Con. (New York: McDivitt, Campbell, 1875); Clifford E. Clark, *Henry Ward Beecher: Spokesman for a Middle-Class America* (Urbana: University of Illinois Press, 1978)

Jeff Finlay

Beechhurst. Neighborhood in northeastern Queens, lying within Whitestone. It began as a tract of 135 acres (55 hectares) bounded to the north by the East River, to the east by 162nd Street, to the south by Cryder's Lane, and to the west by 154th Street and laid out as a residential park in 1906 by the Shore

Acres Realty Company. Some lots measured only 20 by 100 feet (6 by 30 meters), but more than half were a quarter acre, designed to encourage the construction of larger houses, especially along the shore and to the east. In the 1920s Beechhurst attracted many people active in the theater, including the producer Arthur Hammerstein, whose house was later made a landmark. The Whitestone branch of the Long Island Rail Road offered convenient commuter service until the Depression. In the 1960s large apartment buildings were erected east of 162nd Street and on the shore of the East River, on land by then considered part of the neighborhood. Early in the twenty-first century, Beechhurst became a seaside community for the upper middle class.

Vincent Seyfried

Beekman, Gerard G. (*b* New York City, 29 July 1719; *d* Flushing, Queens, 1797). Political and mercantile leader, grandson of Gerardus Beekman. He was active in international trade and engaged in marine insurance underwriting and other legitimate ventures as well as in smuggling. A Loyalist, he chose to remain in New York during its occupation by the British. He moved to Flushing (now in the borough of Queens) in about 1780 and remained there until his death.

Philip L. White, ed., *The Beekman Mercantile Papers, 1746–1799* (New York: New-York Historical Society, 1956); Philip L. White, *The Beekmans of New York in Politics and Commerce, 1647–1877* (New York: New-York Historical Society, 1956)

Jacob Judd

Beekman, Gerardus (baptized New Amsterdam, 17 Aug 1653; *d* New York City, 10 Oct 1723). Political and mercantile leader. He was the son of William (Wilhelmus) Beekman (1623–1707), a merchant who after emigrating to New Amsterdam in 1647 with Peter Stuyvesant was active in municipal and provincial politics and acquired extensive properties on Manhattan Island and in the Hudson River valley. After studying medicine he began a practice in Midwout (Flatbush) about 1677. An adherent of Jacob Leisler (see LEISLER'S REBELLION), he was arrested by Governor Henry Sloughter, convicted of treason, and sentenced to death in 1691, but his life was spared and he continued to take part in politics. He later acquired additional property in Kings County and lower Manhattan and opened the Beekman Slip on the East River in 1722. The holdings of his family came to encompass three large farms: one between what are now Beekman and William streets; a second bounded by what are now Pearl, Gold, Ann, and Fulton streets; and a third along the East River bounded by what are now 49th Street, Second Avenue, and 61st Street; some of this land remains in the family's possession. His brother Henry Beekman (1652–1716) was a provincial legislator who fought for a general assembly strong enough to withstand the powers of the Crown and its appointed governor. His later descendants included Gerard Beekman (1842–1918), a great-great-great-grandson, who donated to the New-York Historical Society the family's coach, acquired in 1771; the blue room from its mansion, where the British had their headquarters during the American Revolution; and the bedroom of the mansion, used by Major John André; and the physician Fenwick Beekman (1882–1962), a great-great-great-great-grandson, who was a major donor to the New-York Historical Society and its president from 1947 to 1956. Beekman, Ann, and William streets are all named for family members, as are the New York Infirmary Beekman Downtown Hospital at 170 William Street and the R. Livingston Beekman House at 854 Fifth Avenue (1903–5), now the Serbian Mission to the United Nations.

For bibliography, see BEEKMAN, GERARD G.

Jacob Judd

Beekman Place. Neighborhood on the Upper East Side of Manhattan, bounded to the north by 51st Street, to the east by the East River, to the south by 49th Street, and to the west by First Avenue. It is a small residential enclave named after the Beekman family, whose mansion stood there from 1765 to 1874. The building was used briefly during the American Revolution as a British headquarters and was the site of the trial and execution of Nathan Hale. The mansion was demolished as the city grew northward, and the property was subdivided and developed. The neighborhood was at first favored by the working class, but soon after the successful redevelopment of Sutton Place (1920) its character changed: writers and actors moved into the neighborhood and formed the Beekman Hill Association to oversee its transformation into a quiet and secluded domain of the elite. The first of several luxury apartment buildings along Beekman Place was developed by Joseph G. Thomas and his wife, the muralist Clara Fargo Thomas. The couple was responsible for the construction of Beekman Terrace (1924), the Beekman Mansion (1926), and the Campanile Apartments (1926–30). In addition to a number of lavishly appointed town houses there are other luxury apartment buildings in the area, including 1 Beekman Place (1930), 2 Beekman Place (1931), and the Beekman Tower (1928), originally a residential hotel for sorority women known as the Panhellenic Tower. It is famous for its rooftop ballroom and cocktail lounge. In the first decade of the twenty-first century many of the houses were owned by foreign governments as missions or consulates.

Owen D. Gutfreund

Beene, Geoffrey (*b* Haynesville, La., 30 Aug 1927, *d* New York City, 28 Sept 2004). Fashion designer. He moved to New York in 1947 to study at the Traphagen School of Fashion. After designing clothing for several firms on Seventh Avenue, including Harmay and Teal Traina, he formed his own business in 1963. His distinctive juxtaposition of modern fabrics and old-fashioned craftsmanship and techniques made him one of the most highly acclaimed designers in the United States. Beene, who resided on Manhattan's Upper East Side, often used embroidery, top-stitching, and appliqué in his work.

Caroline Rennolds Milbank

beer halls. Beer halls were a prominent feature of Kleindeutschland and other German

Interior of the German Winter Garden and Theatre, a popular beer hall, at 45 Bowery

neighborhoods in New York City, which from 1855 to 1880 had the largest German-speaking community in the Americas. A variety of *lokale,* the general term for German neighborhood eating and drinking establishments, lined Avenue A and the Bowery and provided relief from crowded tenements. Basement bars catered to the rough and loose, while other bars, meeting rooms, ballrooms, and even bowling alleys served as social niches for neighbors, colleagues, congregations, political groups, and newly arrived immigrants. Among the well-known halls were Hillenbrands on Hester Street, the Concordia on Avenue A, and Germania on the Bowery. There were also opulent halls where families gathered to drink, eat, sing, dance, and—especially on Sundays—to be entertained by music and drama; the best known were the Deutsches Volksgarten, the Atlantic Gardens, Niblo's Saloon, and Magar's Concert Hall. During the summer, beer halls of all kinds moved outdoors into the lots behind their buildings to form beer gardens. After 1880 the city's German population began moving to Yorkville on the Upper East Side, where beer halls survived until the mid-twentieth century.

Zelda Stern, *The Complete Guide to Ethnic New York* (New York: St. Martin's, 1980); Stanley Nadel, *Little Germany* (Urbana: University of Illinois Press, 1990)

Chad Ludington

Beiderbecke, Bix [Leon Bismarck] (*b* Davenport, Iowa, 10 March 1903; *d* New York City, 6 Aug 1931). Jazz musician. Born into a middle-class German family, he dropped out of school at age 18 and moved to New York City in 1924. He began touring with his band, the Wolverine Orchestra, and continued performing with a number of other jazz groups, most notably saxophonist Frankie Trumbauer's ensemble (1925–26) and Paul Whiteman's Orchestra (1927–29). Most famous for his cornet and piano abilities, he joined Whiteman's as one of the most popular and highly paid acts as a soloist in the 1920s. Beiderbecke died at the age of 28 from alcoholism.

Richard M. Sudhalter and Phillip R. Evans, *Bix: Man and Legend* (New Rochelle, N.Y.: Arlington House, 1974)

Jessica Montesano

Belafonte, Harry [Harold George Belafonete, Jr.] (*b* New York City, 1 March 1927). Singer, actor, and human rights activist. British West Indian Belafonte attended George Washington High School. He joined the navy during World War II and in 1945 returned to New York, where he studied drama at Erwin Piscator's Dramatic Workshop while performing with the American Negro Theater. In the early 1950s, Belafonte made his debut at the Village Vanguard. He recorded music from 1949 to 2003 and was best known for his album *Calypso* (1956), the first album to sell over one million copies, earning him the title the "King of Calypso." He appeared on television and in films such as *Carmen Jones* (1954), *Uptown Saturday Night* (1974), and *Swing Vote* (1999). He was a supporter and confidant of Martin Luther King, Jr., and helped raise money to release civil rights protesters from jail, finance Freedom Rides, support voter-registration drives, and organize the March on Washington in 1963. In the early 1960s Belafonte was appointed a cultural adviser to the Peace Corps. In 1985 Belafonte produced the song "We Are the World," which raised funds for Africa. In 1987 he was appointed as a goodwill ambassador for the United Nations Children's Fund. After being diagnosed with cancer in 1996, he became an activist for prostate cancer survivorship. Belafonte retired from performances in 2003 but remains involved in social and political activism.

Stephanie Miller

Belarusians. The first Belarusian settlers moved to New York City in the 1890s and quickly became incorporated into the city's life. When the Slavic and Baltic division of the New York Public Library opened its doors on 24 May 1911, the first reader was from Belarus. The number of Belarusian immigrants peaked between 1910 and 1913; many were from Minsk, Vilna, Hrodna, Vicebsk, Homiel, Mahiloŭ, Smalensk, Brest, and Pinsk. The U.S. Immigration Service counted them as Russians if they were Eastern Orthodox and as Poles if they were Roman Catholic. The first Belarusian organization in New York City was the White Russian National Committee (1921). One of the members of this organization was Alex Wojciechowicz, an American of Belarusian descent who was the center on Fordham University's famous "seven blocks of granite" offensive line in the 1930s and a member of both the college and professional football halls of fame. More Belarusians moved to the city from 1948 to the early 1950s. During this period several Belarusian churches were formed (most under the jurisdiction of the Belarusian Autocephalous Orthodox Church), as were such organizations as the United Belarusian–American Relief Committee (1948), the Belarusian–American Association (1949), the Belarusian Institute of Arts and Sciences (1951), the Belarusian–American Relief (1957), the philanthropic organization the Krečeŭski Foundation (1958), and the Belarusian–American Union (1965). The Belarusian Institute of Arts and Sciences (1951) became one of the most productive publishers of Belarusian scholarship. The institute was also the founder and publisher of the scholarly annual *Zapisy* (Transactions) (since 1952). The monthly newspaper *Bielarus* (1950) and the annual collection of poetry and fiction by Belarusian émigré writers under the same title (2007) are published by the Belarusian–American Association, which in the early twenty-first century sponsored youth programs and a supplementary school. It is the largest Belarusian organization in the United States.

Of the half-million Belarusians who settled in the United States between 1909 and the early 1990s, between 50,000 and 75,000 remained in the New York City metropolitan area. After Alaksandr Łukašenka became president of Belarus (1994), the number of refugees increased to 5369 (1999–2005). Of these, political asylum recipients were common (913 from 1999–2005). The new generation formed the Belarusian–American Youth Association (2006). The center of Belarusian life in New York City is at St. Cyril of Turaŭ Cathedral (401 Atlantic Avenue in Brooklyn), a former Episcopalian church built in 1850. The parish holds an annual Belarusian Festival, which is part of the annual Atlantic Antic street festival.

Vitaŭt Kipel, *Belarusans in the United States* (Lanham, Md.: University Press of America), 1999

Liavon Yurevich

Belasco, David (*b* San Francisco, Calif., 24 July 1853; *d* New York City, 14 May 1931). Producer and playwright. He began working as a stage manager in New York City in 1882 and achieved some renown for the way he adeptly devised and managed stage effects. As a producer he was responsible for 121 productions in New York City (including revivals). He also wrote some 70 plays, many in collaboration with others. In 1902 he broke with the Theatrical Syndicate, after which he became known for the extreme realism of his stage productions. Many of these were mounted at the innovative structure he built in 1907, named the Belasco Theatre and still standing at 111 West 44th Street. He lived from about 1926 at the Hotel Gladstone, 114 East 52nd Street, and retired in 1930. Belasco's most important plays include *The Heart of Maryland* (1895), *Madame Butterfly* (with John Luther Long, 1900), and *The Girl of the Golden West* (1905).

Lise-Lone Marker, *David Belasco: Naturalism in the American Theater* (Princeton, N.J.: Princeton University Press, 1974)

See also Stage design.

Don B. Wilmeth

Bel Canto Opera Company. Opera company formed in 1969 by Theodore Sieh to present bel canto works and infrequently performed operas of many periods and styles. It produced more than 120 works during its first 20 seasons in New York City, including Daniel Auber's *Manon Lescaut,* Johann Christian Bach's *Temistocle,* Gaetano Donizetti's *Ca-*

terina Cornaro, Ferencz Erkel's *Bank Ban,* William Henry Fry's *Leonora,* Stanisław Moniuszko's *The Haunted Manor,* and Nikolai Rimsky Korsakov's *The Snow Maiden.* Several singers who performed with the company became well known, including Claudia Catania, Elizabeth Hynes, and Samuel Ramey. The unusual repertory of the company has attracted such renowned conductors and directors as Cynthia Auerbach, Victoria Bond, Janet Bookspan, Igor Chichagov, Frank Corsaro, Thomas Martin, Frederick Roffman, and Johannes Somary.

Thomas E. Bird

Bellaire. Neighborhood in east central Queens, centered on Jamaica Avenue and 211th Street between Hollis and Queens Village. Originally a tract of farmland of 42 acres (17 hectares) owned by the Haubitzer family, it was bought in June 1899 by J. A. H. Drissel, the secretary and treasurer of the National Pigeon Shooters Association, who built a grandstand and casino on the site and named it Interstate Park. Many shooting events were held there from 1900, including the Grand American Handicap in 1901 and 1902. The park was declared bankrupt after the shooting of birds was prohibited in November 1902. In 1907 a realty company demolished the grandstand and developed the land as a suburb named Bellaire Park; Bellaire Gardens was promoted as a development in 1921. Later the area was usually considered part of Queens Village.

Vincent Seyfried

Belle Harbor. Neighborhood in southwestern Queens, lying within Rockaway Beach and bounded to the north by Jamaica Bay, to the east by 129th Street, to the south by the Atlantic Ocean, and to the west by Beach 141st Street. The first sections were developed in 1907 by Frederick J. Lancaster, president of the West Rockaway Land Company; the waterfront between Beach 125th and Beach 128th streets was later added for the Belle Harbor Yacht Club. The company installed sewers, wide streets, sidewalks, and utilities and sold lots measuring 20 by 100 feet (6 by 30 meters) for year-round homes. In 1915 the area was remapped to provide for 234 beachfront and bay-front lots; trolley service was begun in 1917. In the early twenty-first century Belle Harbor was a well-kept, upper-middle-class suburban neighborhood and overwhelmingly Caucasian. On 17 November 2001 a large airliner taking off from John F. Kennedy Airport crashed into the neighborhood, killing five people on the ground. There is a memorial to this event in Rockaway Park.

Vincent Seyfried

Bellerose. Neighborhood straddling the border between Nassau County and Queens. Its original expanse (now entirely in Nassau), bounded to the north by Jericho Turnpike, to the east by Remsen Lane, to the south by the Long Island Rail Road, and to the west by Colonial Road, was laid out by Helen M. Marsh, a real estate agent from Lynn, Massachusetts, who around 1897 bought five parcels of land and in 1906 formed the United Holding Company, which supervised development until 1927. Streets were configured in a semicircular pattern with the railroad station at its center; some were given the names of states and of the Great Lakes. A large adjoining area across the city line in Queens was opened to residential development in 1910 and was also named Bellerose. Bounded to the north by Grand Central Parkway, to the east by Little Neck Parkway, to the south by Jericho Turnpike, and to the west by the Cross Island Parkway, this section became a densely built-up neighborhood of one-family houses shaded by trees. In 2008 the portion of Bellerose lying in Queens was a comfortable neighborhood, largely white and middle class to upper middle class. Many residents consider it more like Nassau County than Queens. The neighborhood is the site of the Queens County Farm Museum, which has a working chicken coop and an array of other barnyard animals. Around the turn of the twenty-first century Bellerose developed a strong Indian community.

Vincent Seyfried

Bellevue Hospital. Municipal hospital opened in 1736 as a six-bed infirmary by the Public Work House and Home of Correction at lower Broadway (now City Hall). In 1794 the city purchased a building on 5 acres (2 hectares) at 26th Street and First Avenue to house victims of epidemics, and in 1811 it purchased a site for an almshouse occupying 150 acres (60 hectares) bounded by 28th Street, the East River, 23rd Street, and Second Avenue. The almshouse, completed in 1816, became known as the Bellevue Establishment. The hospital at 26th and First took its current name in 1825 and was used mainly for the victims of epidemics. Filth, neglect, and high mortality rates were rampant until mid-century, when the hospital was separated from the almshouse and reorganized by a medical board. The hospital averaged between 550 and 850 beds by the 1850s. It was the first hospital in the United States to use hypodermic syringes (1856) and to develop a hospital-based ambulance service (1869). Its services were expanded to include an outpatient dispensary (1867), a reception hospital on Canal Street (1869), and an auxiliary hospital on 95th Street and 10th Avenue for accident cases (1871). Wards for alcoholics and a pavilion for the insane were added in the late 1870s, as well as new pavilions for emergencies (1876) and women and children (1882). At the pavilion for gynecology and obstetrics (1887), in 1887 doctors performed the first cesarean section in an American hospital. As the hospital gave greater attention to services for outpatients, it opened a tuberculosis clinic (1904), a social services department (1906), a psychopathic clinic (1908), a dental clinic (1908), and the nation's first ambulatory cardiac clinic (1911). Several schools were founded at the hospital: the Bellevue Hospital Medical College (1861), nursing schools for women (the first Nightingale School of Nursing in the United States, 1873) and men (1888), and a school of midwifery (1911). Bellevue treated American soldiers during the Civil and Spanish–American wars and organized base hospital units to serve overseas in the world wars. Bellevue was overseen by various charities and correction boards until it came under the jurisdiction of municipal hospital boards in the twentieth century. In 1970 control of Bellevue was transferred to the New York

Bellevue Hospital, ca 1905. The balconies provided fresh air, which was thought to speed patients' recovery.

City Health and Hospitals Corporation, with Bellevue serving as the flagship facility. Until the late twentieth century, Bellevue dwarfed all other hospitals in New York City: it had about 1150 beds by 1920 and about 2700 by the 1950s. Expansion continued, with a new outpatient facility (1973), an inpatient facility (1975), and a psychiatric hospital (1985). By 2006 Bellevue had decreased its bed capacity to 768 and had six intensive care units, 1200 house staff, and 500 residents and interns. Bellevue, known as a center for trauma, limb reimplantation, head and spinal cord injury, and cardiac care, has also been rated number one in the United States for psychiatry and emergency medicine. The New York University–Bellevue Medical Center was formed in 1947. Bellevue has been affiliated with the New York University School of Medicine since 1968 and serves as a teaching hospital.

Sandra Opdycke, *No One Was Turned Away: The Role of Public Hospitals in New York City since 1900* (New York: Oxford University Press, 1999)

Jane E. Mottus

Bellows, George (Wesley) (*b* Columbus, Ohio, 12 Aug 1882; *d* New York City, 8 Jan 1925). Painter and printmaker. The son of an architect, he studied under Robert Henri at the New York School of Art and developed a bold, naturalistic style. In 1909 he became the youngest artist elected to the National Academy of Design. His scenes of everyday city life allied him with the Ashcan School; he also depicted boxing matches, seascapes, and portraits. After rooming with friends at 352 West 58th Street he moved in 1906 to the Lincoln Arcade Building on Broadway. In 1910 he moved to a house at 146 East 19th Street and renovated the third floor for a studio. Many of Bellows's paintings are at the Brooklyn Museum.

Marianne Doezema, *George Bellows and Urban America* (New Haven: Yale University Press, 1992); Michael Quick et al., *The Paintings of George Bellows* (New York: Harry N. Abrams, 1992)

Judith Zilczer

Bellows, Henry Whitney (*b* Boston, 11 June 1814; *d* New York City, 30 Jan 1882). Clergyman. After receiving his education at Harvard College and the Harvard Divinity School he became the pastor of the First Congregational Church in New York City (later renamed the Church of All Souls). Known as an orator, he led the U.S. Sanitary Commission during the Civil War and oversaw its efforts to improve sanitation in army camps and to provide ambulances, doctors, and nurses on the battlefield. In an address to the alumni of the Harvard Divinity School in 1859 he deplored the lack of faith in the institution of the church and called for a universal church based on freedom in religious matters and a statement of purpose. In April 1865 he played an important role in forming the National Conference of Unitarian Churches. Bellows presided over All Souls until the end of his life.

Walter Donald Kring, *Henry Whitney Bellows* (Boston: Unitarian Universalist Association, 1979)

Walter Donald Kring

Bell Telephone Laboratories. Research and engineering firm. It was an outgrowth of the engineering department of Western Electric, a manufacturing division of American Telephone and Telegraph (AT&T) that began operations at 463 West Street, just south of the meatpacking district, in 1907. The main purpose of Bell Laboratories was to develop practical improvements in telephony, but its activities expanded to such an extent that by the time AT&T underwent reorganization in 1913 the laboratories were among the most advanced in the world for research in the electrical sciences. In 1925 the firm was incorporated as a subsidiary owned equally by AT&T and Western Electric. It remained independent of the daily operations of its parent firms, which provided it with a sustained competitive advantage in telephony through such innovations as coaxial cable, microwave radio, and direct long-distance dialing. It also made innovations in fields less directly related to telephony: the first synchronous-sound motion picture system, the negative-feedback amplifier, the electrical-relay digital computer, advances in information theory, and the transistor (1947, for which John Bardeen, William Shockley, and Walter H. Brattain were awarded the Nobel Prize in physics in 1956). In 1947 Bell Laboratories moved to suburban New Jersey.

M. D. Fagan, ed., *A History of Engineering and Science in the Bell System* (n.p.: Bell Telephone Laboratories, 1975); Leonard S. Reich, *The Making of American Industrial Research: Science and Business at GE and Bell, 1876–1926* (New York: Cambridge University Press, 1985); George David Smith, *The Anatomy of a Business Strategy: Bell, Western Electric, and the Origins of the American Telephone Industry* (Baltimore: Johns Hopkins University Press, 1985)

George David Smith

Belmont. Neighborhood in the west central Bronx, bounded to the north by Fordham University, to the east by the Bronx Zoo, to the south by Tremont, and to the west by the Grand Concourse. It was originally the easternmost part of the manor of Fordham, which was eventually donated to the Dutch Reformed Church in New York City as a source of income to pay its ministers. The church leased the land to farmers before selling it in 1755. The area remained farmland into the early nineteenth century, when a privately owned Episcopal boys' boarding school operated by William Powell opened on part of the property. Later most of the farms were included in Jacob Lorillard's estate, called Belmont. After the Civil War the Lorillards bequeathed their mansion to the Home for Incurables (now St. Barnabas Hospital). From the 1880s the City of New York cut streets through the farms and real estate developers built housing on the land. The great spur to development in the 1890s was the extension to Fordham Road of the elevated line along Third Avenue at the western edge of the neighborhood. During that same time the New York Zoological Society was developing the Bronx Zoo in Bronx Park to the east, a project that required many workers to landscape the grounds and construct the buildings that would house the animals. This type of work had already drawn millions of Italian immigrants to the United States; further, real estate interests openly appealed to Italians to settle in Belmont. By the beginning of the twentieth century the neighborhood had become densely populated. It eventually became known as the Little Italy of the Bronx, and its ethnic character is still reflected in the presence of the Enrico Fermi Cultural Center and by a large market and many Italian food shops along Arthur Avenue. Until 1940 there were also pushcarts, but Mayor Fiorello H. La Guardia had these removed to the New York Retail Market Building on the avenue. In the 1980s a large number of Catholic Albanian immigrants also settled in the neighborhood. Puerto Ricans, Mexicans, and other Latinos, as well as American blacks, have moved in at the edges of the area, but its heart remains Italian. The housing stock includes one-family frame and brick houses, two-family houses, four-story brick walkup apartment buildings dating from the early twentieth century, five-story apartment buildings from the 1920s, and a few tall apartment towers from the mid-1970s. In 1986 Fordham Plaza was built at the northwest corner of the neighborhood, the first new office building in the Bronx in decades. Most of the northern section of Belmont along Fordham Road consists of automobile showrooms. At the turn of the twenty-first century Belmont remains among New York's most culturally distinctive areas, and Arthur Avenue continues to attract thousands of shoppers every day.

Lloyd Ultan

Belmont [Vanderbilt; née Smith], **Alva (Ertskin)** (*b* Mobile, Ala., 17 Jan 1853; *d* Paris, 26 Jan 1933). Suffragist and society figure. Educated in France, she moved to New York City in the early 1870s, married William K. Vanderbilt in 1875, and persuaded her husband to commission the architect Richard Morris

Hunt to build a château at Fifth Avenue and 52nd Street costing $3 million; this was the site in 1883 of a famous and extravagant costume ball. After her scandalous divorce from Vanderbilt in 1895 and her remarriage to Oliver Belmont she devoted her time and considerable resources to woman suffrage: she formed and presided over the New York Political Equality League, in 1909 rented an entire floor of a building on Fifth Avenue for the National American Woman Suffrage Association, and in 1921 was elected president of the National Woman's Party. Belmont later moved to France, where she spent the rest of her life.

Thea Arnold, James E. Mooney

Belmont, August (*b* Alzey, Germany, 8 Dec 1816; *d* New York City, 24 Nov 1890). Banker, diplomat, and horse-racing enthusiast. Of German Jewish background, he was the American agent for the Rothschilds of Frankfurt am Main. He settled in New York City in 1837 and formed his own firm on Wall Street, which engaged in arbitrage, commodity speculation, private lending, foreign exchange, and corporate, real estate, and railroad investment. The rapid success of the firm made him a prominent figure in society, well known for his lavish parties. In 1849 he married Caroline Perry, a daughter of Commodore Matthew C. Perry, at the Church of the Ascension; their children were brought up as Episcopalians. An active Democrat, he was rewarded in 1853 for supporting Franklin Pierce's presidential campaign with a diplomatic post in the Netherlands, to which he was later appointed minister (1855–57); he was also chairman of the Democratic National Committee (1860–72) and a founder of the Manhattan Club (1865). Belmont owned one of the finest stables of thoroughbred horses in the country: he was a founder in 1866 of the American Jockey Club, and in 1867 he inaugurated the now-famous Belmont Stakes, first held at Jerome Park in the Bronx.

August Belmont

Irving Katz, *August Belmont: A Political Biography* (New York: Columbia University Press, 1968); Vincent P. Carosso, *Investment Banking in America: A History* (Cambridge, Mass.: Harvard University Press, 1970); David Black, *The King of New York: The Fortunes of August Belmont* (New York: Dial, 1981)

Theresa Collins

Belmont Island [U Thant Island]. Artificial island in the East River off East 42nd Street in Manhattan, less than half an acre (0.2 hectare) in size. Originally built over a small, dangerous granite outcropping known as Man-o'-War Reef, it was enlarged during the 1890s with rocks and soil excavated by workers digging a trolley tunnel under the river between Queens and Manhattan. This ill-fated tunnel project was planned by piano manufacturer William Steinway, who died before it could be completed. The tunnel excavation was finished in 1907 by financier August Belmont, Jr., and the island then became known as Belmont Island. The tunnels themselves, known as the "Steinway Tunnels," went on to serve the No. 7 Flushing line subway from Manhattan, which has tracks running directly beneath the island. In 1977 the island was adopted by a group of United Nations (UN) employees, followers of Buddhist chaplain Sri Chimnoy. They leased the island from New York State, landscaped it, and began referring to it as U Thant Island for the UN's third secretary general, who was from Burma. A 30-foot (9-meter) "Oneness Arch" containing personal memorabilia of U Thant was then erected and dominates the islet that popularly, but unofficially, still bears his name.

Gerard R. Wolfe

Belmont Stakes. Thoroughbred horse race for three-year-olds, first run in 1867 and now one of the oldest races in the United States. Held each June, it is the third event in the Triple Crown, after the Kentucky Derby and the Preakness. The race was first run at Jerome Park in the Bronx before being moved east of the Bronx River in 1890 to the Morris Park Racecourse, where it remained until 1905, when it was moved to Belmont Park in Elmont, Long Island, just outside New York City. The length of the race, one and a half miles (2.4 kilometers), is the same as that of the Epsom Derby in Britain and the longest of any major horse race in the United States. Perhaps the most memorable running of the Belmont Stakes was in 1973, when Secretariat won the race by 31 lengths and set a track record for the distance, becoming the first horse in 25 years to win the Triple Crown. As of 2008 only 11 horses had won the Triple Crown, the last being Affirmed, in 1978.

Ashbel Green

Belnord Apartments. Residential building occupying the entire block between Broadway and Amsterdam avenues and between 86th and 87th streets. Designed in an eclectic Renaissance style by the architectural firm of Hiss and Weeks and opened in 1908, it is a 12-story palazzo with an interior court entered by carriage vaults on 86th Street; a delivery entry on 87th Street leads underground, thus insulating the building's residents from tradesmen. Reportedly the largest apartment building in the world for several years, the Belnord has 175 apartments arranged in suites of eight to 14 rooms; at one time it had full concierge services and pneumatic mail delivery. It maintains a standard of luxury beyond that of the smaller Ansonia and Apthorp apartment buildings.

Joel Schwartz

Belter, John Henry [Heinrich, Johann] (*b* Ulm, Württemberg, 1804; *d* New York City, 23 Sept 1863). Cabinetmaker and furniture manufacturer. He was first listed as a cabinetmaker at 40½ Chatham Street in directories in New York City in 1844. Within two years he moved to more fashionable quarters on Broadway. In 1853 he exhibited an ebony and ivory center-table at the New York Crystal Palace (now part of the Manney Collection). John H. Belter and Company opened a factory on Third Avenue at 76th Street in 1854 and showrooms at 552 Broadway in 1856, moving them to 772 Broadway in 1861. In mid-1847 Belter secured his first patent, which covered machinery for sawing "Arabesque" chairs; he later received others for an improved bedstead (1856), a technique for laminating and molding gilded layers of veneer into a cylinder from which multiple chair backs were cut (1858), and improvements to a bureau drawer and its locking device (1860). In his work he used from five to 16 layers of veneer and carved decorations ranging from scrolls to complex patterns of flowers, fruit, and animals. His partners continued the business until they were forced to declare bankruptcy in 1867. In later years Belter's name became a generic term for ornate Rococo Revival furniture of laminated construction.

Marvin D. Schwartz, Edward J. Stanek, and Douglas K. True, *The Furniture of John Henry Belter and the Rococo Revival* (New York: E. P. Dutton, 1981)

Deborah Dependahl Waters

Benchley, Robert (Charles) (*b* Worcester, Mass., 15 Sept 1889; *d* New York City, 21 Nov 1945). Essayist, humorist, and actor. After graduating from Harvard University in 1912 he moved to New York City to write. Initially he had little success, publishing his work only occasionally. His first humorous piece appeared in *Vanity Fair* in October 1914, and in 1916 he was engaged by Franklin P. Adams as an associate editor of the Sunday magazine of the *New York Tribune.* As the managing editor of *Vanity Fair* he met Dorothy Parker and Robert E. Sherwood. A member of the Algonquin Round Table, he was well known for such quips as "I'd like to get out of this wet suit and into a dry martini." He lived at the Algonquin Hotel in 1919 and later moved to the Royalton Hotel at 44 West 44th Street, where he kept a suite for 24 years. In 1920 he resigned in protest when Parker was fired for criticizing actress Billie Burke. After leaving *Vanity Fair* he took an office with Parker and turned to freelance writing, producing the column "Books and Other Things" for the *New York World* and working as a drama critic for *Life* and the *New Yorker.* At the same time he became a popular comedian, best known for the monologue "The Treasurer's Report," which he performed in many stage revues and in a film made at the Fox studios in Astoria in 1928; he later made more than 40 other films. Often self-deprecating in his humor, Benchley wrote of his own career: "It took me fifteen years to discover I had no talent, but I couldn't give it all up because by that time I was too famous."

Babette Rosmond, *Robert Benchley: His Life and Good Times* (Garden City, N.Y.: Doubleday, 1970)

Walter Friedman

Benedict [née Fulton], **Ruth** (*b* New York City, 5 June 1887; *d* New York City, 17 Sept 1948). Anthropologist, feminist, and poet. After graduating from Vassar College in 1909 she married and settled near New York City in 1914, and in 1919 she became a student of the anthropologists Alexander Goldenweiser and Elsie Clews Parsons at the New School for Social Research. She transferred to Columbia University in 1921 to study with Franz Boas and earned her PhD there in 1923. She was also influenced by the linguist Edward Sapir and by Margaret Mead, a former pupil who became her friend and lover. During the 1920s she wrote poetry under the name Anne Singleton. At Columbia she worked closely with Boas and rose from the rank of lecturer (1923) to full professor (1948). Instrumental in popularizing the field of anthropology, she was credited with making New York City a center for its study in the 1930s and 1940s. Benedict carried out fieldwork among several American Indian peoples, notably the Zuni of the southwestern United States, focusing on the relationship between individual personality and culture. She wrote two popular and influential works: *Patterns of Culture* (1934) and *The Chrysanthemum and the Sword: Patterns of Japanese Culture* (1946). After World War II she directed the project known as Research in Contemporary Cultures at Columbia.

Judith Schachter Modell, *Ruth Benedict: Patterns of a Life* (Philadelphia: University of Pennsylvania Press, 1983); Lois W. Banner, *Intertwined Lives: Margaret Mead, Ruth Benedict, and Their Circle* (New York: Knopf, 2003)

Ira Jacknis

Benét, Stephen Vincent (*b* Bethlehem, Pa., 22 July 1898; *d* New York City, 13 March 1943). Writer, brother of William Rose Benét. He was educated at Yale University (BA 1919, MA 1920), where he was a writer and editor for the *Yale Literary Magazine* and the *Yale Record.* New York City figured prominently in his work. *Heavens and Earth* (1920) included a section of poems entitled "The Tall Town" that depicted everyday experiences there. Of two minds about the city's literary life, he spent much of his time in Paris. In 1929 he won a Pulitzer Prize for *John Brown's Body* (1928), an epic poem depicting the Civil War through sketches of historical and fictional characters set in rhymed verse. In the same year he was elected to the National Institute of Arts and Letters, later becoming its vice president. He lived at 326 East 57th Street during the late 1920s and at 220 East 69th Street during the 1930s before moving in 1939 to 215 East 68th Street, where he remained for the rest of his life. Inspired by the collapse of the American economy, the rise of fascism in Europe, and his own financial and physical difficulties, he turned to apocalyptic themes in such works as "Metropolitan Nightmare," a poem published in *Burning City* (1936) about tropical heat and a fictional steel-eating termite in New York City. Benét lectured widely, wrote book reviews for the *New York Herald Tribune* and the *Saturday Review of Literature,* and was elected to the American Academy of Arts and Letters (1938). His written works include operettas, short stories such as "The Devil and Daniel Webster" (1936), and *Western Star* (1943, Pulitzer Prize 1944), the first volume in what was to have been a series about a pioneer's experiences.

Charles Andrews Fenton, *Stephen Vincent Benét: The Life and Times of an American Man of Letters, 1898–1943* (New Haven: Yale University Press, 1958)

Naomi Wax

Benét, William Rose (*b* Brooklyn, 2 Feb 1886; *d* New York City, 4 May 1950). Writer, brother of Stephen Vincent Benét. He attended the U.S. Military Academy before graduating from Yale University in 1907. In a collection of colorful, romantic poems entitled *The Falconer of God and Other Poems* (1914) he juxtaposed images of the streets of New York City with others of visionary dreamlands. After working as an assistant editor at *Century Magazine* he joined with Henry Seidel Canby, Amy Loveman, and Christopher Morley to launch the *Literary Review* of the *New York Evening Post* in 1920, where he was chief contributor, and the *Saturday Review of Literature* in 1924, where he was the poetry critic, author of the column "The Phoenix Nest" (1924–50), and an editor until the end of his life. For a time he lived in a studio at 37 West 10th Street before moving with his wife, the poet Elinor Wylie, to 142 East 18th Street (1923–26). Benét also worked as a translator and children's storyteller. His published writings include verse and prose for children, short stories, textbooks, the verse novel *Rip Tide* (1932), and *The Dust Which Is God,* a fictionalized autobiographical narrative in verse that won a Pulitzer Prize in 1942.

Laura Benét, *When William Rose, Stephen Benét, and I Were Young* (New York: Dodd, Mead, 1976)

Naomi Wax

Benjamin, Park (*b* British Guiana [now Guyana], 14 Aug 1809; *d* New York City, 12 Sept 1864). Writer and editor. Born to slaveowners, he settled in New England as a young man and joined a literary circle that included Oliver Wendell Holmes and Henry Wadsworth Longfellow. After moving to New York City he became the literary editor of the *New Yorker* under Horace Greeley. In 1839 he began publishing the *New World,* a weekly literary journal that soon had a national circulation and was dedicated to promoting distinguished American and European literature. As the editor of the daily newspaper the *Evening Signal* he engaged in frenzied controversies of public life. Benjamin spent his last years as one of the most popular lecturers on the American Lyceum circuit, where he presented satirical and humorous verse and often appeared with Greeley and Henry Ward Beecher.

Merle M. Hoover, *Park Benjamin, Poet and Editor* (New York: Columbia University Press, 1948)

Andrew Wiese

Bennett, D(eRobigne) M(ortimer) (*b* Springfield, N.Y., 23 Dec 1818; *d* New York City, 6 Dec 1882). Freethinker, publisher of *The Truth Seeker* journal, and opponent of New York City's leading censor, Anthony Comstock. Raised in rural New York, Bennett left home as a teenager and joined a Shaker community in New Lebanon, New York. After defying the celibate community by marrying a fellow Shaker, Mary Wicks, Bennett moved around the Midwest, working at farming, pharmacy, and patent medicine sales; he also took up journalism because the local papers in Paris, Illinois, would not print his letters. By this time, he had become a freethinker, or "infidel" from Christianity. In 1873 he and Mary moved *The Truth Seeker* to Manhattan, where it was published from offices at 335 Broadway. Reflecting the intellectual and spiritual tumult of the times, *The Truth Seeker* had 50,000 readers, among them

Mark Twain, Clarence Darrow, and Robert Ingersoll, "the Great Agnostic." Its pages challenged the arrests of individuals and seizures of literature undertaken by Comstock and his New York Society for the Suppression of Vice; in return, Comstock had Bennett arrested twice for distributing the free-love advocate Ezra Heywood's pamphlet, *Cupid's Yokes.* (There was nothing sexually explicit in the pamphlet, but it did attack Comstock.) The second arrest, in 1879, was followed by conviction and 11 months in Albany Penitentiary. The 1879 U.S. Court of Appeals decision *United States v. Bennett,* which affirmed Bennett's conviction, set the precedent for American censorship law for the next three-quarters of a century. After his release from prison, Bennett was honored by a standing-room-only crowd at Chickering Hall, at 437 Fifth Avenue in Manhattan. He traveled around the world for the next year and died a few months after returning home to New York City. He is buried in Brooklyn's Green-Wood Cemetery.

Roderick Bradford, *D. M. Bennett: The Truth Seeker* (Amherst, N.Y.: Prometheus Books, 2006)

Marjorie Heins

Bennett, James Gordon, Jr. (*b* New York City, 10 May 1841; *d* Beaulieu, France, 14 May 1918). Newspaper publisher. He took control of the *New York Herald* when his father, the publisher, retired in 1867, and he continued the newspaper's tradition of sparing no expense to collect news. In 1869 he sent the reporter Henry Morton Stanley to Africa to find the missionary David Livingstone. An eccentric society figure and commodore of the New York Yacht Club, Bennett lived off the newspaper's profits while supervising operations from his home in Paris. In 1887 he launched the Paris edition of the *Herald,* which later became the *International Herald Tribune.* Perhaps better known as a sportsman than as a journalist, Bennett sponsored many regattas and horse, automobile, and airplane races.

Don C. Seitz, *The James Gordon Bennetts: Father and Son* (Indianapolis: Bobbs–Merrill, 1928)

Steven H. Jaffe

Bennett, James Gordon, Sr. (*b* Keith, Scotland, 1 Sept 1795; *d* New York City, 1 June 1872). Newspaper publisher and editor. In 1829 he became the associate editor of the *Courier and Enquirer,* and in May 1835 he launched the *New York Herald* from a basement on Wall Street with $500; its financial reportage, coverage of crime and scandal, and enterprise in collecting national and international news soon made it one of the most successful "penny papers" in the United States. Bennett's editorial attacks on his competitors and iconoclastic contempt for religious norms made him arguably the most controversial American newspaperman of his day. Outraged subjects of his articles physically assaulted him at least six times, and he was excluded from polite society in New York City. The *Herald* had the highest circulation of any American daily newspaper. Although it initially disavowed party politics, Bennett editorialized regularly against abolition and for U.S. territorial expansion, and after 1840 he tended to support Democratic presidents. Although initially critical of Abraham Lincoln, the *Herald* became supportive of him after 1864, presumably because Lincoln offered Bennett the mission to France (which he declined). Bennett is considered one of the inventors of American popular journalism.

Don C. Seitz, *The James Gordon Bennetts: Father and Son* (Indianapolis: Bobbs–Merrill, 1928); Frank Luther Mott, *American Journalism: A History of Newspapers in the United States through 260 Years, 1690–1950* (New York: Macmillan, 1941; 3rd edn 1962); James L. Crouthamel, *Bennett's New York Herald and the Rise of the Popular Press* (Syracuse, N.Y.: Syracuse University Press, 1989)

See also Advertising.

Steven H. Jaffe

Bennett [DiFighlia], **Michael** (*b* Buffalo, N.Y., 8 April 1943; *d* Tucson, Ariz., 2 July 1987). Choreographer and director. He made his debut on Broadway as a dancer in *Subways Are for Sleeping* (1961) and as a choreographer in *A Joyful Noise* (1966). He provided choreography for television variety programs taped in New York City, including *Hullabaloo* and *The Ed Sullivan Show* in the late 1960s. His first major success was the musical *Promises, Promises* (1968), and he won his first Tony Award for the musical *Follies* (1971). His most widely known musical, *A Chorus Line* (1975), was born of a series of taped sessions with veteran dancers and Bennett's desire to honor a dancer's life. Under Bennett's direction and with choreography of Bob Avian, the show opened on 15 April 1975 at the Joseph Papp Public Theater. After 101 performances the show moved to the Shubert Theatre for a 15-year, 6137-show run, during which it broke box office records and won nine Tony Awards. In 1977 Bennett bought an eight-story building located at 890 Broadway between 19th and 20th Streets. He turned it into his personal office as well as some of the most sought-after rehearsal space in New York City. In October 1986 he sold the building to several of the companies that made their home there. After Bennett's death in 1987 a memorial service was held in the Shubert Theatre and the lights on Broadway were dimmed.

Ken Mandelbaum, *A Chorus Line and the Musicals of Michael Bennett* (New York: St. Martin's, 1990)

Barbara Cohen–Stratyner

Benny, Jack [Kubelsky, Benjamin] (*b* Chicago, 14 Feb 1894; *d* Beverly Hills, Calif., 27 Dec 1974). Comedian. He played the violin in vaudeville theater and in 1927 lived for a few years at the Hotel Edison (228 West 47th Street). Benny made his radio debut on Ed Sullivan's program in 1931 and within a year had his own show in New York City. In 1935 he relocated the program to California and led the national ratings, eventually expanding to television.

James E. Mooney

Benson, Egbert (*b* New York City, 21 June 1746; *d* Jamaica [now in Queens], 24 Aug 1833). Statesman. He graduated from King's College in 1765 and during the American Revolution became a patriot; he was later active in state government and in the provincial congress, was a delegate to the Congress of the Confederation and the Annapolis Convention of 1786, and served two consecutive terms in the U.S. Congress. Benson was appointed to the state supreme court in 1794 and to the chief judgeship of the U.S. Circuit Court, a position he left to return to Congress. He was also a trustee of Columbia College and helped to form the New-York Historical Society.

James E. Mooney

Bensonhurst. Neighborhood in southwestern Brooklyn, adjoining Bay Ridge, Borough Park, and Coney Island and bounded to the north by 61st Street, to the east by McDonald Avenue, to the south by Gravesend Bay, and to the west by 14th Avenue. Once a small section of New Utrecht, it was covered by farms and had fewer than 4000 inhabitants before the construction of steam railroads in the 1870s. In the late 1880s the developer James Lynch bought large parcels of land from several members of the Benson family and built the suburb of Bensonhurst-by-the-Sea on a plot of 350 acres (142 hectares) bounded to the north by 78th Street, to the east by 23rd Avenue, to the south by Gravesend Bay, and to the west by 20th Avenue. He planted 5000 shade trees and designed villas for 1000 families. The area was 6 miles (10 kilometers) from City Hall in Brooklyn, and middle-class families were attracted by its rural character and proximity to Manhattan; 22nd Avenue became Bay Parkway, built by the City of Brooklyn as part of a tree-lined route from Prospect Park to the sea. Along Gravesend Bay the Bensonhurst Yacht Club, the Atlantic Yacht Club, and the Crescent Athletic Club catered to an affluent sporting population. When the town was annexed to Brooklyn in 1894, the population was less than 10,000.

The area became heavily populated soon after being linked to Manhattan in 1915 by the Fourth Avenue subway along a route formerly used by the Sea Beach and West End steam railways. Brick houses for two to three

Loading hay in Bensonhurst, 1900

Backyards in Bensonhurst, 1977

families and apartment buildings of four to six stories built in the 1920s were occupied mostly by Italians and Jews from the Lower East Side. The population increased dramatically during the first quarter of the twentieth century, to nearly 150,000 by 1930. An increasing number of Jews turned to local institutions for education and recreation, including the Jewish Community House, which opened in 1927 at Bay Parkway and 78th Street.

Residential growth continued after World War II. In 1949 the Shore Haven Apartments complex was built by Fred Trump at 21st Avenue off the Belt Parkway; with 5000 apartments this was then the largest private housing development in Brooklyn. The 1950s saw an influx of immigrants from southern Italy (primarily Sicily and Naples). Several local residents became well known, among them the opera singer Robert Merrill, the actor Elliott Gould, the comedian Buddy Hackett, and the baseball pitcher Sandy Koufax. The neighborhood also became famous through the popular television series *The Honeymooners* as the home of Ralph Kramden, a boisterous bus driver portrayed by Jackie Gleason. For many years the neighborhood was one of the most homogeneous in the city. In 1980 the population was 93 percent white and about 80 percent Italian; more than 70 percent of the residents occupied one- and two-family houses. In the 1980s immigrants from Asia and the Soviet Union moved into the neighborhood; Chinese immigrants settled mostly in one- to three-family houses between Bay 25th and Bay 50th streets, Russians in the many apartment buildings lining Bay Parkway. Other ethnic groups that moved into the neighborhood late in the twentieth century included Greeks, Koreans, Israelis, Poles, and Arabs, especially from Egypt, Lebanon, Syria, and Jordan. Tensions between whites and blacks in the neighborhood erupted in August 1989 when a black teenager was murdered by a gang of whites.

In the early twenty-first century the population of Bensonhurst remains largely Italian, Chinese, and Russian and mostly lower middle class. Family and church are central in many residents' lives, and several generations of a family are likely to live on the same block. The Regina Pacis Roman Catholic Church stands on 65th Street. Blacks live mostly in the Marlboro public housing project, which lies at the eastern edge of the neighborhood. The Jewish Community House offers social service programs for senior citizens and Russian immigrants. Most Italians live along 18th Avenue between 63rd and 86th Streets and along 86th Street between 14th Avenue and Bay Parkway. In September a feast is held for Santa Rosalia, the patron saint of Sicily.

Stephen Weinstein

Benton, Thomas Hart (*b* Neosho, Mo., 15 April 1889; *d* Kansas City, 19 Jan 1975). Painter and muralist. A grand-nephew of the senator of the same name from Missouri, he studied in Paris (1908–11), where he befriended Morgan Russell and Stanton Macdonald-Wright, and worked in New York City from 1912. There he experimented with synchromist color abstraction and took part in exhibitions of the Peoples Art Guild and the Forum Exhibition (1916). After 1918 he developed a monumental figurative style that celebrated the folk culture of the United States. His first mural commission was a nine-part cycle for the New School for Social Research called *America Today* (1931, now at the Equitable Life Assurance Society of the United States), which depicts industry and city life before the Depression. Later murals, such as those for the Whitney Museum of American Art (1932), focused on native, rural, and folk themes central to the Regionalist movement. Benton left New York City in 1935. He wrote *An American in Art: A Professional and Technical Autobiography* (1969).

Henry Adams, *Thomas Hart Benton: An American Original* (New York: Alfred A. Knopf, 1989)

Judith Zilczer

Benton and Bowles. Advertising agency and market research firm formed several months before the stock market crash of 1929 by William Benton and Chester Bowles, who met while working at the George Batten Company, an advertising firm in New York City. Benton was president of the new firm and Bowles took charge of the creative side. The firm began with capital of $1800 and occupied an office in the Chanin Building at 122 East 42nd Street before moving in 1930 to 5 East 45th Street. To research the public's opinion of a gelatin product made by the General Foods Corporation, their first important account, Benton and Bowles surveyed housewives door to door. The success of the ensuing advertising campaign led General Foods to place more business with the firm, enabling it to survive the Depression and to emerge as a leading advertising agency. Other major accounts included Procter and Gamble, and Bristol–Myers. In 1932 the agency moved to 444 Madison Avenue. It was one of the first agencies to use radio for advertising purposes and also produced the radio programs *Beauty Box* (for Palmolive), *Showboat* (for Maxwell House), Fred Allen's *Town Hall Tonight,* and *Gang Busters.* Benton became chairman of the board in 1935 but resigned the following year, and Bowles left the firm in 1941; each later served in several high-ranking government positions. The firm moved to 666 Fifth Avenue in 1957 and to 909 Third Avenue in 1969. In 1986 Benton and Bowles merged with the midwestern advertising firm D'Arcy MacManus Masius to form D'Arcy Masius Benton and Bowles, with headquarters in New York City.

Sidney Hyman, *The Lives of William Benton* (Chicago: University of Chicago Press, 1969); Chester Bowles, *Promises to Keep: My Years in Public Life* (New York: Harper and Row, 1971)

See also Advertising.

Marjorie Harrison

Bergdorf Goodman. Firm of clothing retailers. Formed in 1894 as Bergdorf and Voight by Herman Bergdorf and Herman Voight, it first operated a small tailoring and fur shop at 125 Fifth Avenue, later moving to Ladies' Mile. A tailor in the shop, Edwin Goodman (1878–1953), bought a share of the business, and a few years later Bergdorf retired to France. The firm specialized in high fashion and catered to an elite clientele. Its success made necessary a move to new quarters on the site of the former Vanderbilt Mansion at 58th Street and Fifth Avenue. A small store was built there in 1928 and was eventually expanded to 57th Street. In 1987 the store was acquired by the Neiman-Marcus Group, and in 1990 the men's department was moved across the street to 745 Fifth Avenue. In 1997 the ninth floor, formerly the Goodman family's private penthouse apartment, was converted into an upscale salon and day spa.

Booton Herndon, *Bergdorf's on the Plaza: The Story of Bergdorf Goodman and a Half-Century of American Fashion* (New York: Alfred A. Knopf, 1956)

Leslie Gourse

Bergen Beach. Neighborhood in southeastern Brooklyn, bounded to the north by Paerdegat Basin and Canarsie, to the east by Jamaica Bay, to the south by Mill Basin, and to the west by Flatlands. A family descended from Hans Hansen Bergen, a Dutch settler of the seventeenth century, owned the land and eventually sold it to Percy Williams, an entrepreneur who developed it as a summer resort. His enterprise thrived in the 1890s and the early twentieth century but became unable to compete with Coney Island and Rockaway Beach; by 1926 the last section had been sold for a development of one-family houses. Several houses were built and onetime picnic groves were run through with streets, but most of the area remained undeveloped into the 1980s. In the early twenty-first century this largely Italian neighborhood contained single-family homes with small lawns and almost no commercial activity.

Ellen Marie Snyder-Grenier

Berger, [Mike] **Meyer** (*b* Brooklyn, 1 Sept 1898; *d* New York City, 8 Feb 1959). Reporter for the *New York Times.* Berger focused on ordinary New Yorkers and received a Pulitzer Prize in 1950. His column "About New York" appeared in the *Times* from 1939 to 1940 and from 1953 until his death in 1959. He wrote *The Story of the New York Times,* and a collection of his columns was titled *The Eight Million.* Berger is considered a reporter's reporter. The Meyer Berger Award is presented each year by Columbia University's School of Journalism for outstanding reporting on the lives of ordinary people.

Frank Dyer

Bergman, Bernard (*b* Hungary, 1911; *d* Manhattan, 16 June 1984) Rabbi. He immigrated to the United States in the 1920s and lived in Brooklyn. In the 1940s he was a rabbi at a Jewish nursing home on the Lower East Side, served as editor and publisher of the Yiddish-language daily the *Jewish Morning Journal,* and was the head of the Zionist organization Hapoel Hamizrachi. In 1955 he established the Towers Nursing Home on Central Park West and 106th Street in the building that formerly was the New York Cancer Hospital as well as the Park Crescent home on Riverside Drive and 87th Street. At the height of his career he was a leader of New York's Orthodox Jewish community and had a $24 million real estate and nursing-home empire. In the 1970s the Towers home was charged with Medicare fraud, and residents testified that they had endured physical abuse, pest infestations, and inadequate heat. The site was closed in 1974. In 1976 Bergman was sentenced to four months in federal prison after he was convicted on Medicare and tax fraud charges; he also served eight months for convictions on state offenses.

Jessica Montesano

Berkman, Alexander (*b* Vilnius [now in Lithuania], 21 Nov 1870; *d* Nice, France, 28 June 1936). Anarchist. He moved in 1888 to the Lower East Side where he joined the Pioneers of Liberty. During a steelworkers' strike in 1892 in Homestead, Pennsylvania, he tried to assassinate Henry Clay Frick and was subsequently imprisoned for 14 years; he remained one of the best-known anarchists in the United States from 1906 to 1919. In New York City he edited *Mother Earth* (a publication launched by Emma Goldman), organized opposition to World War I, and helped to form the Ferrer School, which was devoted to libertarian causes and the working class. Exiled in 1919, Berkman moved to Paris where he wrote for the Jewish Anarchist Federation of New York.

David A. Balcom

Berle, A(dolf) A(ugustus), Jr. (*b* Boston, 29 Jan 1895; *d* New York City, 17 Feb 1971). Scholar and public official. He earned a degree from Harvard Law School at age 21 and worked for the firm of Louis D. Brandeis before volunteering for the army in 1917; he later moved to New York City, where he taught law at Columbia University, provided financial advice to Mayor Fiorello H. La Guardia, and directed the Planning Commission and the Housing Authority while also serving as chamberlain of New York City between 1934 and 1938. As an adviser to President Franklin D. Roosevelt he promoted central planning, and he worked as a Latin American expert and diplomat for him and for presidents Harry S. Truman and John F. Kennedy. He also helped to organize the Liberal Party and wrote a number of books on law and politics, including *The Modern Corporation and Private Property* (1932).

Jordan A. Schwarz, *Liberal: Adolf A. Berle and the Vision of an American Era* (New York: Free Press, 1987)

James E. Mooney

Berle [Berlinger], **Milton** (*b* New York City, 12 July 1908; *d* Los Angeles, 27 March 2002). Actor. After years in vaudeville he made his debut on Broadway in Earl Carroll's *Vanities* (1932) and the *Ziegfeld Follies* (1936, 1943). Never wholly successful in film or on radio, he became well known in *Texaco Star Theater* (1948–56), a television program produced in New York City by the Columbia Broadcasting System. His broad humor and antics came across well on television and were important in spurring sales of television sets. Known often as "Uncle Miltie" or "Mr. Television," Berle was one of the best-known television actors of his time.

David J. Weiner

Berlin. Former name of a section of northwestern Queens at the eastern edge of Laurel Hill, bounded to the north by the Long Island Expressway, to the east by 50th Street, to the south by Newtown Creek, and to the west by 48th Street. It was promoted as Berlinville in 1871 and developed to draw German immigrants; all the streets were named after German cities. By the early twenty-first century the area had been given over almost entirely to industry.

Vincent Seyfried

Berlin, Irving [Baline, Israel] (*b* Tyumen, Russia, 11 May 1888; *d* New York City, 22 Sept 1989). Composer, songwriter, and producer. The son of a cantor, he moved to New York City from Russia in 1893 and without formal musical instruction began his career on the Lower East Side as a street singer and singing waiter, and in Tin Pan Alley as a song plugger. He performed in vaudeville and Broadway revues and achieved his first great success with the song "Alexander's Ragtime Band" (1911). In 1919 he formed Irving Berlin Music and with Sam Harris in 1921 he opened the Music Box Theatre, at 239 West 45th Street, where he introduced his newest songs. He lived for most of his life on the Upper East Side of Manhattan and spent his last years as a recluse in a mansion on Beekman Place.

Berlin usually wrote the lyrics to his own songs. Because he was a self-taught pianist able to play in only one key, he was able to write songs in other keys only by having his piano equipped with a unique keyboard-shifting device. His songs are remarkable for their unforced melodies and rhythms and their forthright sentiments; they captured the public fancy and were eagerly sought after by musicians in Tin Pan Alley and elsewhere. The best-known include "God Bless America" (1918), "White Christmas" (1942), and many songs inspired by New York City, among them "Where Is My Little Old New York" (1924), "Puttin' on the Ritz" (1929), "Manhattan Madness" (1932), "Harlem on My Mind" (1933), "Easter Parade" (1933), "Slumming on

Irving Berlin

Park Avenue" (1937), and "Washington Square Dance" (1950). Berlin's successful Broadway shows *Annie Get Your Gun* (1946) and *Call Me Madam* (1950) both featured Ethel Merman; his last Broadway production was *Mr. President* (1962).

Laurence Bergreen, *As Thousands Cheer: The Life of Irving Berlin* (New York: Viking, 1990)

Nicholas E. Tawa

Bernstein [née Frankau], **Aline** (*b* New York City, 22 Dec 1882; *d* New York City, 7 Sept 1955). Theatrical designer. The daughter of Rebecca and Joseph Frankau, an actor, she was born on West 34th Street and grew up in a theatrical boarding house on West 44th Street. She attended the New York School for Applied Design and Hunter College before studying painting at the New York School of Art under Robert Henri. In 1902 she married Theodore Bernstein, a Wall Street stockbroker, but in 1925–30 had a tumultuous affair with writer Thomas Wolfe. Bernstein began her career by working with Irene and Alice Lewisohn in the Henry Street Settlement as a costume designer and became the primary stage and costume designer when they established the Neighborhood Playhouse in 1915 and remained until it closed in 1927. Her productions at the Playhouse for *The Little Clay Cart* (1924) and *The Dybbuk* (1925) and several of the *Grand Street Follies* helped build her early reputation. Later she designed for the Civic Repertory Company and for the Theatre Guild, including *Ned McCobb's Daughter* (1926) and *Reunion in Vienna* (1931). Among her late works was *Regina* (1949), which won the Tony Award for best costume design. After a two-year battle, Bernstein in 1926 became the first woman admitted to Local 827 of the United Scenic Artists Union. In 1937 she cofounded the Museum of Costume Art, which was later incorporated into the Metropolitan Museum of Art. Bernstein also wrote three novels, an autobiography titled *An Actor's Daughter* (1941), and the posthumously published *Masterpieces of Women's Costume of the 18th and 19th Centuries* (1959). Bernstein died in her apartment at 875 Park Avenue.

Dianna Ng

Bernstein, Leonard [Louis] (*b* Lawrence, Mass., 25 Aug 1918; *d* New York City, 13 Oct 1990). Conductor, composer, and educator. In 1943 he was named assistant conductor of the New York Philharmonic and soon after gave a dramatic performance leading the orchestra as a substitute for Bruno Walter, who had become ill. He conducted the New York City Symphony from 1945 to 1948 and in 1957 returned to the New York Philharmonic as its co-conductor (with Dimitri Mitropoulos). In the following year he became the first music director of the orchestra both born and trained in the United States, and he remained in this position until he was named its laureate conductor in 1969. A committed and enthusiastic advocate of modern works, he projected an image strikingly different from that of the stern, foreign-born conductor to which American audiences were accustomed. He performed more concerts with the orchestra than any other conductor in its history, giving 36 world premieres and 14 American premieres. He was the first

Leonard Bernstein

conductor to understand and master television as a medium for music education: after making several programs in 1954 for the television series *Omnibus,* he began two series with the New York Philharmonic in 1958: Young People's Concerts, which continued for 15 years, and a series geared toward adults that continued until 1962.

In addition to being the focus of much of Bernstein's career as a conductor, New York City provided the inspiration for many of his compositions. His first ballet, *Fancy Free* (1944, choreography by Jerome Robbins), was so well received at its premiere by the Ballet Theatre at the Metropolitan Opera House that it was soon transformed into the full-length Broadway musical *On the Town* (1944). His other works for the stage include *Wonderful Town* (1953), *Candide* (1956), *West Side Story* (1957), and *Mass* (1971), and two operas, *Trouble in Tahiti* (1952) and *A Quiet Place* (1984). He also wrote three symphonies (*Jeremiah,* 1942; *The Age of Anxiety,* 1949; and *Kaddish,* 1963), the orchestral works *Facsimile* (1946) and *Serenade* (1954), and chamber and vocal music. Bernstein wrote *West Side Story* while living at the Osborne on West 57th Street; for many years until the end of his life he lived in the Dakota on West 72nd Street.

John Briggs, *Leonard Bernstein: The Man, His Work and His World* (New York: World, 1961); Humphrey Burton, *Leonard Bernstein* (New York: Doubleday, 1994)

See also Musical theater.

Barbara Haws

Berra, Yogi [Lawrence Peter] (*b* St. Louis, 12 May 1925). Baseball player. Born to parents from Italy, he spent his entire playing career as a catcher and outfielder for teams in New York City. From 1946 to 1963 he was a central figure with the Yankees as the team won 10 World Series. Berra set many World Series records, including those for most series played (14), most series games played (75), most hits (71), and most times at bat (259). In 1956 he caught pitcher Don Larsen's perfect game, the only one in World Series history. Berra was named Most Valuable Player in the American League in 1951, 1954, and 1955. He also played briefly for the Mets in 1965. After his playing days, he was a manager of the Yankees in 1964 (they won the American League pennant that year), 1984, and the first 16 games of the season in 1985. He also managed the New York Mets from 1972 to 1975, winning the National League pennant in 1973. After Yankees owner George Steinbrenner fired Berra as manager in 1985, Yogi vowed never to return to Yankee Stadium while Steinbrenner owned the team. Berra remained estranged from the Yankees franchise until 1999, when he reconciled his differences with Steinbrenner. On 18 July 1999 he finally returned to Yankee Stadium on "Yogi Berra Day." Berra is perhaps the most-often-quoted figure in baseball. His aphoristic, colorful malapropisms, known as "Yogi-isms," have entered the American vernacular; an extensive selection is included in the first chapter of his autobiography, *Yogi: It Ain't Over* (1989). He was inducted into the Baseball Hall of Fame in 1972.

Joseph S. Lieber

Best & Co. Firm of women's and girls' clothing retailers. Formed in 1879 by Albert Best and James A. Smith, its first establishment was a children's store at 315 Sixth Avenue. The firm moved its retail operations to a 12-story building at Fifth Avenue and 51st Street in 1947 and later opened several branches. At its peak it operated 14 stores, of which three alone reportedly had $10 million worth of inventory. The firm ceased operations in 1970; its main store was replaced by Olympic Tower, an office and residential building.

Leslie Gourse

Bethany Baptist Church. Church at 460 Sumner Avenue in Brooklyn, founded in 1883. It is notable for having been the first black congregation to move into the heart of Bedford–Stuyvesant. It moved to its present site in 1924 during the height of white resistance to black migration.

Kenneth T. Jackson

Bethel Tabernacle African Methodist Episcopal Church, Brooklyn. Church in Weeksville, Brooklyn. Founded in 1847, it continued to thrive past the 1870s, when the predominantly black community of Weeksville was slowly overwhelmed by the larger white community around it. In 1978 the church moved to 1630 Dean Street, directly across the street from its original home. The new building had earlier been Public School 83, an all-white school that had been integrated in 1864 by students from Colored School no. 2, which had itself been founded a few years earlier by some of the leading citizens of Weeksville.

Kenneth T. Jackson

Bethesda Fountain. Fountain in Central Park; it was the only sculpture commissioned as part of Frederick Law Olmsted and Calvert Vaux's original park design. Emma Stebbins, the first woman to receive a major art commission in New York City, sculpted the angel that is the fountain's centerpiece. Vaux designed the base, which features detailing by Jacob Wrey Mould. Inspired by a passage in the Gospel of John about the healing waters of Jerusalem's Bethesda Pool, Stebbins designed the sculpture in tribute to the 1842 Croton Aqueduct system, which provided clean water to the city. The angel holds a lily symbolizing purity in one hand and with the other blesses the fountain's water, which flows over four cherubs that represent temperance, purity, health, and peace. The fountain, which cost $63,000 and was designed in Rome and cast in Munich, was unveiled in 1873 to mixed reviews. In the 1960s it became a gathering place for hippies, young African Americans and Puerto Ricans, and political radicals. The fountain subsequently deteriorated until the

Bethesda terrace

Bethesda Fountain

Central Park Conservancy was founded in 1980. It was restored in 1980–81 as one of the conservancy's first projects to rehabilitate the park. Also known as the "Angel of the Waters," the fountain has been featured in many films and plays, including Tony Kushner's *Angels in America* (2003).

Kate Lauber

Beth Israel Medical Center. General-care hospital in Stuyvesant Square, opened in May 1891 as a facility for Orthodox Jews by the Beth Israel Hospital Association, which in 1889 had opened a dispensary at 97 Henry Street. It began with 20 beds at 196 East Broadway and later occupied quarters at 206 East Broadway and 195 Division Street. The hospital served kosher food and had a Yiddish-speaking staff. It relied heavily on donations from wealthy Jews and from 1894 also received support from the Saturday and Sunday Association; as late as 1915 about 93 percent of the patients received medical treatment free of charge. In 1917 the hospital became a member of the Federation of Jewish Philanthropic Societies. In 1929 the hospital moved to a facility at Jefferson and Cherry streets and opened the Beth Israel Training School for Nurses (now the Phillips Beth Israel School of Nursing); by this time it had acquired a prestigious reputation and no longer served only the poor. In 1945 it became a teaching hospital of the New York University School of Medicine. Beth Israel purchased Manhattan General Hospital in 1964. During the next two years it opened the Linsky Pavilion, the Bernstein Institute, Fierman Hall, and Gilman Hall, and formed an affiliation with the New York Eye and Ear Infirmary. It set up the nation's largest methadone program in 1977, was named a center for AIDS care by New York State in 1987, and in 1988 acquired a nursing home with 230 beds in suburban White Plains, New York, and an inpatient unit with 12 beds for AIDS patients. In the beginning of the twenty-first century the medical center had 1368 beds.

Tina Levitan, *Islands of Compassion: A History of the Jewish Hospitals of New York* (New York: Twayne, 1964)

Bernadette McCauley

Bettmann Archive. Photographic archive. It was formed in 1935 in New York City by Otto L. Bettmann, a refugee from the Nazis who began the business with a few prints and negatives that he had taken with him from Germany. The archive began at just the time when large picture magazines such as *Life* and *Look* were beginning publication, and these magazines became its first important customers. The archive moved in 1961 from two crowded basement rooms at 215 East 57th Street to a suite at 136 East 57th Street. In 1984 the archive took over the photographic library of United Press International, thus increasing the number of its images from about 3 million to more than 16 million, and in the following year it became the photographic library for Reuters. These two transactions changed the business from an almost exclusively historical archive into a news archive as well, known as the Bettmann Archive/Bettmann Newsphotos. By 1990 it contained 17 million images and was the world's largest commercial repository of prints and photographs. Bettmann sold the business to the Kraus–Thompson organization in 1981. In 1989 the family of H. P. Kraus became the sole owners. In 1995 the Bettmann Archive/Bettmann Newsphotos was bought by the Corbis Corporation, a company founded in 1989 and wholly owned by William H. Gates, chairman of the Microsoft Corporation, who planned to digitize the entire collection and amass a vast archive of digital images. In 2002 the prints and negatives from the Bettmann Archive were transferred from Manhattan to the Iron Mountain/National Underground Storage Facility, a former limestone mine in western Pennsylvania where, 220 feet (67 meters) underground, their preservation would be easier to secure.

Otto Bettmann, *Bettmann: The Picture Man* (Gainesville: University Press of Florida, 1992)

Allen J. Share

Betts, Samuel Rossiter (*b* Richmond, Mass., 8 June 1786; *d* New Haven, Conn., 3 Nov 1868). Judge. He attended Lenox Academy and Williams College (graduated 1806), studied law in Hudson, New York, and began a practice in Monticello, New York. A major in the army during the War of 1812 defending New York Harbor, he then represented Orange and Sullivan counties in Congress (1816–18), moved to Newburgh, New York, and became district attorney of Orange County. Appointed circuit judge of the New York State Supreme Court in 1823, he was appointed to the U.S. District Court for the Southern District of New York in 1827 by President John Quincy Adams. He heard mostly maritime cases; during the Civil War his cases concerned the blockade, the rights of neutral ships, and prize law. He lived at 16 St. Mark's Place. He retired in 1867 and moved to New Haven; he is buried in Woodlawn Cemetery. Betts wrote *Admiralty Practice* (1838) and is credited with having established an American practice distinct from English precedents.

Jeffrey A. Kroessler

Biaggi, Mario (*b* New York City, 26 Oct 1917). Congressman. After becoming the most decorated police officer in New York history he won election to the House of Representatives in 1968 as a Democrat from the tenth district (Astoria and parts of the Bronx). He remained in office for 10 years, eventually representing the nineteenth district (part of the Bronx and Yonkers). An important member of the Democratic machine in the Bronx and a champion of Irish and Jewish causes, he sought the mayoralty in 1973, ultimately withdrawing when it was revealed that he had invoked the Fifth Amendment before a federal grand jury. In 1987 he was convicted of having accepted bribes from Coastal Dry Dock, a firm that received nearly $500 million in U.S. Navy ship rebuilding contracts during the 1980s and gave nearly $2 million a year in insurance business to a company owned by Meade Esposito, leader of the Democratic machine in Brooklyn; the bribes came in the form of free vacations that Biaggi took with his mistress while his wife was fatally ill. In 1988 he was defeated for reelection by Eliot Engel in a primary and later was convicted of illegally helping Wedtech, a defense contractor based in the Bronx, to obtain city-owned property. After spending 21 months in federal prison in Fort Worth, Texas, he was released in early 1991 for reasons of health. In 1992 Biaggi ran for his old seat in Congress, losing again to Engel.

Jesse Drucker

Bialystoker Synagogue. Synagogue in lower Manhattan. A group of Jews from Bialystok, Poland, founded Congregation Beth Haknesseth Anshe Bialystok in 1878, meeting in a rented space on the Lower East Side. In 1905 the congregation purchased the Willett Street Methodist Episcopal Church, now 7–13 Bialystoker Place, and converted it into an Orthodox synagogue. Erected in 1826, the fieldstone building is one of four houses of worship surviving from the late Federal period in lower Manhattan and is the oldest building used as a synagogue in New York City. The sanctuary, decorated with Depression-era wall and ceiling paintings, was restored in 1988, and work on the stained-glass windows was completed in 1999. By the early twenty-first century the synagogue's membership exceeded 300 families; three prayer services were conducted daily, 365 days a year.

Joyce Mendelsohn

Bialystoker Synagogue, 2009

Bible Teachers Training School [Biblical Seminary in New York]. Institution that later became the New York Theological Seminary (ii).

bicycle messengers. New York bicyclists paid to rapidly deliver packages and letters. A large number of bicycle-messenger services were formed in the 1970s and 1980s as entrepreneurs recognized that heavy vehicular traffic was making it difficult for businesses in Manhattan to deliver and receive packages and documents. Because the messengers were generally paid in proportion to the number of packages they delivered, they had an incentive to ride quickly and sometimes recklessly, and near misses and even collisions with automobiles and pedestrians were common. Some companies dispatching the messengers disclaimed responsibility for any injuries and damages resulting from these accidents on the grounds that the messengers were not their employees but rather were independent contractors. By 1990 the number of messenger services had been reduced by the growth of facsimile transmission and overnight package services. That number would decline again over the next decade as broadband Internet service altered the nature of business transactions. Nonetheless, in the early twenty-first century many messengers are still employed for same-day package delivery in Manhattan.

Though most messengers did not participate in officially sanctioned bicycle races, Nelson Vails gained prominence in competitive cycling and won a silver medal in the match sprints at the 1984 Olympic Games. Messenger culture was imitated and adopted by portions of New York City's burgeoning cycling community around the turn of the twenty-first century as many commuters and recreational riders opted to ride the single-speed, fixed-gear bicycles favored by messengers. This trend exploded with the custom paint jobs and rebuilding of vintage bicycles in many of the city's more hip neighborhoods.

See also Bicycling.

Trudy E. Bell, Michael C. Repka

bicycle racing. The first of many venues that carried the name Madison Square Garden was designed for bicycle racing. These races took place on an oval wooden track and were well attended in the late nineteenth century. The garden even gave its name to a popular type of team race still run in venues around the world: the madison. In recent decades bicycle racing in New York City has focused on public roads rather than on a track. The racing scene is dominated by several clubs, most of which field amateur squads of varying abilities. Among them is the Century Road Club Association, founded in 1898, which is the largest club dedicated to racing in the United States. Several professional riders began racing in New York City before reaching international prominence, among them George Hincapie, a native of Queens who won the U.S. National Road Race Championships in 1998 and 2006. Though bicycle racing has traditionally been a European interest, the increasingly global nature of the sport has caused its popularity in the city to skyrocket. Races occur weekly in-season on the park drives of Central Park and Prospect Park and on the inactive airstrips of Floyd Bennett Field. Annual events hosted at other venues include the Grant's Tomb Criterium in Morningside Heights and the Harlem Skyscraper Criterium around Marcus Garvey Park. The BMC Software New York City Cycling Championship was held in the financial district in 2002, 2003, and 2004. The Kissena Velodrome in Queens, one of only 22 bicycle tracks remaining in the United States, stages multiple races each week. In 2007 the Department of Parks and Recreation opened an expansive network of mountain biking trails in Highbridge Park in Washington Heights, which was used as a race venue on its opening day, bringing mountain bike racing to Manhattan for the first time.

See also Bicycling.

Michael C. Repka

bicycling. Mode of transportation and recreation heavily used in New York City. An early bicycle with a large front wheel called the velocipede was introduced at the New York Athletic Games in November 1868. Like much of the United States, the city experienced a bicycle craze during the 1890s. Riding schools proliferated, and some recruited fashionably dressed women known as "bicyclettes" to ride around the city promoting bicycling and bicycling instruction. By 1894 bicycle exhibitions were being held annually at Madison Square Garden. An especially notable one in 1896 attracted some 120,000 people, including a number of the city's most socially prominent residents. By 1899 there were 53 bicycle clubs in New York City.

The Depression in the 1930s brought about a renewed interest in bicycling, and bicycles

Mercury Wheel Club, Flushing race track, June 1894

Bike memorial for cyclists and pedestrians killed, 2009

appeared on Fifth Avenue for the first time since the 1890s. Organizations such as the Century Road Club Association, founded in 1898, and the New York Cycle Club, founded in 1937, became major proponents of racing and riding bicycles in the city. One of the first American bicycle touring companies, Country Cycling Tours, was formed in New York City in the 1970s to offer bicycle tours ranging from one day in the metropolitan region to two weeks overseas. About this time recreational cycling became more popular, especially in Central Park and Prospect Park, where the city provided paved bicycle paths. Despite tension and occasional skirmishes among cyclists and runners, joggers, and pedestrians, these groups coexist relatively peacefully in the city's parks. The Five-Boro Bicycle Tour, held each May and covering about 40 miles (64 kilometers), was inaugurated by American Youth Hostels in the late 1970s; later renamed Bike New York, it annually draws 30,000 registrants and has inspired similar tours in San Francisco and other cities.

Bicycle commuting became popular for a number of reasons: a growing concern for fitness and the environment, a sharp increase in gasoline prices in the 1970s, heavy traffic, shortcomings in public transit and public transit strikes, and the development in the 1980s of heavier mountain bikes and city bikes better suited to the uneven surfaces of city streets than lightweight, narrow-tire racing bikes. In response to the demands of the growing number of bicycle commuters, the city designated bicycle lanes on Broadway and across the Brooklyn Bridge and laid down concrete dividers along Sixth Avenue in 1980—though these were quickly removed after they were deemed ineffective. In 2007, however, a fully separated bike lane was installed on a several-block stretch of Ninth Avenue below 23rd Street as a trial for further expansion. Among problems plaguing commuting cyclists is theft; one well-known manufacturer of bicycle locks specifically exempted New York City from the guarantee offered with its products. Nonetheless, in 1999 a spokesperson for Transportation Alternatives estimated that the number of bicycling commuters had surpassed 100,000, and studies by the Department of Transportation indicated a 77 percent increase in the number of riders between 2001 and 2008.

In a 1993 announcement the Department of City Planning embarked on an ambitious project to create a 350-mile-long comprehensive network of bicycle trails fully separated from roadways. These "Greenways" run through the city's expansive park system and complement the proposed 550 miles of on-street bicycle paths, part of the master plan announced by the Department of City Planning, Department of Transportation, and the City of New York in 1997. In 2007 the Department of Parks and Recreation opened a large network of mountain biking trails and a BMX (bicycle motocross) park in Highbridge Park, a densely forested area adjacent to Washington Heights in upper Manhattan. In 2009 the administration of Mayor Michael Bloomberg continued to increase the number of bicycle lanes in the city.

See also Bicycle messengers, Bicycle racing.

Trudy E. Bell, Michael C. Repka

Big Allis. Nickname for the largest of three generating units (also known as Ravenswood 3) at Ravenswood Generating Station in Long Island City. Consolidated Edison announced the decision to build a 1000-megawatt fossil fuel–burning plant in 1961, thus more than doubling the size of its largest existing generating plant; it would be the largest generating unit in the world. Ravenswood eventually was chosen as the site, which also was to be home to a proposed nuclear power plant. Allis–

Chalmers Manufacturing Company was given the contract to build the giant turbine, hence the nickname. Because other utilities were concerned over its effect on the electric grid, the unit was put on line at just over a third of its capacity in June 1965. Five months later the great Northeastern blackout of November 1965 caused the generator to grind to a halt, resulting in serious damage. From the 1965 blackout to the end of 1972 Big Allis experienced frequent reliability problems, with outages occurring for 630 days during that period. The loss of capacity led to annoying "brownouts." Once, after six months of work, Big Allis ran for 87 minutes before conking out for another four months. Since that time outages have been routine or normal for a generator of its type. In 1999 Consolidated Edison sold the Ravenswood station to KeySpan Energy, which was acquired by the British electric utility National Grid in 2007. As part of the regulatory approval process, the state Public Service Commission required National Grid to sell its Ravenswood generating unit. In March 2008 an agreement to sell the unit to the Canadian firm TransCanada Corporation for $2.8 billion was announced. The Ravenswood station provided about 25 percent of New York City's power requirements in 2008.

Joseph A. Pratt, *A Managerial History of Consolidated Edison, 1936–1981* (New York: Consolidated Edison, 1988)

William J. Hausman

Big Apple. Nickname for New York City. John J. Fitz Gerald, a reporter for the *Morning Telegraph,* originally used the term in the 1920s to refer to the city's racetracks; he had heard it used by black stablehands in New Orleans in 1921. Black jazz musicians in the 1930s used the name to refer to the city (and especially Harlem) as the jazz capital of the world. The nickname was largely unknown by the 1950s. In 1971 Charles Gillett, president of the New York Convention and Visitors Bureau, revived the nickname as part of a publicity campaign to attract tourists to the city.

Gerald Leonard Cohen, *Origin of New York City's Nickname "The Big Apple"* (Frankfurt am Main: Peter Lang, 1991)

Gerald Leonard Cohen

Bigelow, John (*b* Bristol [now Malden-on-Hudson], N.Y., 25 Nov 1817; *d* New York City, 19 Dec 1911). Editor and diplomat. He attended Union College in Schenectady, New York, moved to New York City at 17, and at 20 was admitted to the bar. In 1848 with William Cullen Bryant he became an owner and editor of the *New York Post.* As American consul general in Paris during the Civil War he helped to persuade Napoleon III not to grant diplomatic recognition to the Confederacy. While in Paris he unearthed Benjamin Franklin's manuscript autobiography, which he edited and published. After the death of his close friend Samuel J. Tilden he helped to unite Tilden's trust with the Astor and Lenox libraries to form the New York Public Library. Bigelow was a longtime resident at 21 Gramercy Park in Manhattan.

Margaret A. Clapp, *Forgotten First Citizen: John Bigelow* (Boston: Little, Brown, 1947)

Ormonde de Kay

Big Manuel (*b* Africa; *d* New Amsterdam, *ca* 1680). Seventeenth-century African American landowner. He was one of the first Africans in New Amsterdam and may have been one of the 11 Angolan men brought to the colony by the Dutch West India Company in 1626. Soon after this group became part of the colony one of the Africans was murdered; when questioned the rest confessed in solidarity, and Big Manuel was chosen by the company to be hanged. He was spared when the noose snapped and the hangman, Black Peter, complied with the spectators' demand that he not be hanged again. In 1644, after nearly 20 years of service, he and 10 other Africans petitioned successfully for their freedom. They were given title to land north of the city, where many already tilled plots. Big Manuel received swampy land just north of Minetta Brook that later became Washington Square.

Sule Greg C. Wilson

bilingual education. The most multilingual city in the nation has taught its school population wholly or partly in languages other than English since 1968, when Spanish was introduced into the public school curriculum. At Public School 25 in the southeastern Bronx, 900 pupils took part in a voluntary, experimental bilingual program funded by the school district; half of the students spoke mostly English, and the other half spoke mostly Spanish (of these, 86 percent were Puerto Rican and most of the rest were black). At Public School 155, a bilingual program prepared students for full English instruction by the third grade. Both programs received the support of local, state, and national community organizations, policy groups, and legislators. In 1970, 32 schools serving 2332 students from Spanish-speaking backgrounds received federal funding. The city's Office of Bilingual Education was formed in 1972. A lawsuit filed by various Puerto Rican community organizations led by ASPIRA resulted in a consent decree in 1974 that established standards for entitlement programs; these standards dealt with instructional, organizational, personnel, and other matters. The number of students in the city who are English Language Learners (ELLs) leveled to approximately 140,000 annually in the early twenty-first century, and the languages of instruction expanded to include Spanish, Chinese, Haitian Creole, Korean, Polish, Arabic, Russian, and Yiddish. In 2006–7, approximately 31 percent of the ELLs were served by Transitional Bilingual Education (TBE) or Dual Language Education (DLE) programs. Ninety percent of the ELLs using the native language for instruction were in TBE programs that aim to transfer the ELLs as quickly as possible to English-only classrooms. The DLE programs expand services to native English speakers and aim to develop full bilingualism and biliteracy, high academic achievement, and cross-cultural communication among both ELLs and native English speakers.

Maria Torres-Guzmán

Billboard. Weekly trade magazine. It was originally a journal for the billposting and advertising business when it began publication in 1894; eventually it became best known for its "charts," which measure the sales of recorded music and are highly influential in the popular-music business. *Billboard* is headquartered in New York City with offices in London, Los Angeles, and Miami. From its inception the magazine was owned by founder William H. Donaldson; it later was taken over by the Littleford family, Donaldson's grandsons, who sold it to private investors in 1985 for an estimated $40 million. The magazine was sold again in 1987 for about $100 million to Affiliated Publications. In 1994 the Dutch media company VNU acquired it. In 2005 *Billboard* began to cover other forms of digital and mobile entertainment as well as music. It continues to be published weekly, and Billboard.com, launched in 1995 as *Billboard* online, attracts four million visitors a month as one of the top music Web sites.

Galen Gart, *First Pressings: Rock History as Chronicled in Billboard* (Milford, N.H.: Big Nickel, 1986–)

Owen D. Gutfreund

billboards. See Outdoor advertising.

billiards. Various forms of billiards and pocket billiards became popular pastimes for New Yorkers in the 1730s. Billiard tables were found chiefly in hotels and coffeehouses until billiards gained favor with the general public about 1840. By the time Tobias O'Connor and Hugh W. Collender manufactured the first billiard tables in the city in 1850, about 60 billiard saloons thrived in lower Manhattan, and the game was strongly associated with gambling, drinking, and Irish immigrants. The person who did the most to popularize billiards in New York City was Michael Phelan (*b ca* 1814; *d* 1871), a player, manufacturer, and owner of billiard parlors who wrote *Billiards without a Master* (1850) and *The Game of Billiards* (1857) and published *The Billiard Cue,* the nation's first periodical devoted exclusively to the game. He was an aggressive promoter who helped make New York City the billiards capital of the United States. With Collender he operated a table factory and showroom at the corner of Crosby and Spring streets from 1854. Phelan's most lasting contribution to billiards was his invention of a sharp-edged cushion made of India rubber, perfected in 1854 and still in use. Phelan's chief competitors, Dudley Kavanagh and Levi Decker, introduced a catgut cushion in the following year that did not prove popular with the city's billiards enthusiasts. By 1858 four firms in the city turned out billiard tables in a business characterized by bitter rivalries. Manufacturers published magazines in which they disparaged their competition, and after Phelan formed the American Billiard Players Association in September 1865 he was accused of engaging in monopolistic practices by Kavanagh, who in 1866 formed the National American Billiards Association and began manufacturing his own tables with Decker at a five-story factory on the corner of Centre and Canal streets.

Billiards benefited from an explosion of popularity in the city during the last three decades of the nineteenth century, and by 1900 New Yorkers supported at least 130 "public rooms" and 13 manufacturers of billiard tables. Billiard parlors, or pool halls, increased in number during the following decades, although they continued to be associated in the public mind with drinking, prostitution, and gambling (they were the first places where off-track wagering on horse races was conducted systematically). By the 1920s the 4000 pool halls in the city attracted a steady business. Billiards declined in popularity after World War II. Only 257 pool halls were left in the city in 1961. In the early twenty-first century billiard tables were still found in many bars, and a few fashionable pool halls catered to young professionals.

Willie Hoppe, *Thirty Years of Billiards* (New York: G. P. Putnam's Sons, 1925; repr. Dover, 1975)

Marc Ferris

Billopp's Point. Southeastern portion of the former Billopp estate at the southern tip of Staten Island, facing Perth Amboy, New Jersey, bounded to the north and east by Tottenville, to the south by Raritan Bay, and to the west by the Arthur Kill. The area is named for the Billopp family, who lived on the land for four generations. Christopher Billopp (*d* 1724) was an English naval officer and a favorite of the Crown. In 1675 he laid claim to 932 acres (377 hectares) here and erected near the shore an imposing two-story stone house, now known as the Conference House. In 1687 he was given a royal charter for 1600 acres (647 hectares) (including the original 932 acres) and was made Lord of the Manor of Bentley. Christopher Billopp (1737–1827), great-grandson of the first Christopher Billopp, was a leading citizen of Staten Island and a Loyalist. In 1783 he sold the manor and left for St. John, New Brunswick, Canada. During the nineteenth century the area was called Ward's Point after the Ward family, who had purchased the area from Billopp. In 2010 it was part of Conference House Park.

Barnett Shepherd

Biltmore Hotel. A 26-story hotel between 43rd and 44th streets and Madison and Vanderbilt avenues. Designed by the firm of Warren and Wetmore as part of a grand plan for Terminal City (a proposed complex of seven hotels), it was built in 1913 by the New York Central Railroad and opened with a gala dinner on New Year's Eve. The cornice of the building was uniform with that of Grand Central Terminal, and its lower floors were in the neo-palazzo style. Above the cornice the facade was of brick and terra-cotta in a modernized Italian Renaissance style. A floor plan in the shape of the letter "H" allowed for 1000 outside rooms, of which 900 had private baths; the stairs and elevators of the building were linked to the pedestrian passageways of the terminal. The hotel was the national campaign headquarters for the Democratic Party from 1936 to 1952, and in the 1940s it became famous for offering reduced rates to college students to attract weekend business; the hotel is referred to in J. D. Salinger's *Catcher in the Rye.* The hotel closed in 1981, and there were plans to strip the building down to its steel frame and rebuild it as the Bank of America. Preservationists sought to protect at least the Palm Court, but developers moved in a wrecking crew on a Friday night. A large clock from the Biltmore was installed in the atrium of the building occupying the site of the hotel.

John Tauranac

Biltmore Program. Declaration issued by members of the Zionist movement during a conference at the Biltmore Hotel in New York City between 6 and 11 May 1942, urging the transformation of Palestine into a Jewish commonwealth and the replacement of the British mandate there by the Jewish Agency.

Michael N. Dobkowski

Bing, Alexander Max (*b* New York City, 1879; *d* New York City, 29 Nov 1959). Community planner. With his brother Leo Bing he built a number of successful luxury apartment buildings in Manhattan in the early twentieth century. While working for the U.S. Housing Corporation he became interested in affordable housing for low-income communities. In the early 1920s he formed the City Housing Corporation of New York (CHC) to build a development in Queens called Sunnyside Gardens, based on the English garden city concept of Ebenezer Howard. For this he engaged the architects Clarence Stein and Henry Wright and sought help from such reformers as Eleanor Roosevelt, Richard Ely, Lewis Mumford, and Catherine Bauer. The success of the project enabled him to buy a large parcel of land in Fair Lawn, New Jersey, through the CHC; there he built Radburn in 1928, a "town for the motor age" within commuting distance of New York City. Construction ceased during the Depression, and the CHC encountered serious problems with its cash flow, eventually declaring bankruptcy. In the early twenty-first century Radburn remained one of the country's best-known experiments in community planning by a private developer.

Daniel Schaffer, *Garden Cities for America: The Radburn Experience* (Philadelphia: Temple University Press, 1982)

Marc A. Weiss

Bing, Sir **Rudolf** (*b* Vienna, 9 Jan 1902, *d* Yonkers, N.Y., 2 Sept 1997). Opera manager. He worked in Germany before emigrating to England due to the rise of the Nazi party. During the war he managed the Glyndebourne Opera in London and was later a founder and manager of the Edinburgh Festival (1947–49). He moved to New York City in 1949 to become general manager of the Metropolitan Opera, a position he would hold until 1972. Bing undertook important revivals of Verdi and Mozart, for which he engaged stage directors from the legitimate theater (among them Margaret Webster, Alfred Lunt, and Tyrone Guthrie), and oversaw the company's move into its new theater at Lincoln Center in 1966. Brusque and intransigent, Bing sometimes clashed with singers, notably Maria Callas, but he maintained high production standards. In 1972 he unwillingly left the Metropolitan after a tenure second in length only to that of Giulio Gatti-Casazza. He became a consultant in the following year to Columbia Artists Management and lectured at Brooklyn College. Bing wrote a memoir, *A Knight at the Opera* (1981).

John W. Freeman

Binkerd, Robert S(tudebaker) (*b* Dayton, Ohio, 7 Nov 1882; *d* New York City, 28 Oct 1969). Reformer. Concerned about municipal corruption, he became the secretary of Citizens Union (1908–9), which owing to his efforts was transformed into a civic organization immune from political control. He was the secretary of the Fusion Committee of 1909 during its unsuccessful campaign to defeat Tammany Hall in the mayoral election, and as secretary of the City Club of New York (1909–13) he was the city's unofficial representative in Albany, New York. In 1911 he helped to defeat a proposal backed by Tammany Hall to revise the city charter. He wrote *Home Rule for Cities* (1912).

Bernard Hirschhorn

Biograph Company. Film studio formed early in 1896 as the American Mutoscope Company, with offices at 841 Broadway in Manhattan. It soon produced short comedies with somewhat risqué scenes on the roof of the building, which by early March 1897 was covered with an elaborate open-air stage that could be turned to catch the rays of the sun. After its name was changed to the American Mutoscope and Biograph Company in 1899, the firm opened a new, indoor studio at 11 East 14th Street in May 1903: this was the first motion picture studio in the world to rely exclusively on electric lights for illumination of the stage. Many films were directed there by Wallace McCutcheon (*A Search for Evidence*, 1903) and D. W. Griffith (*The Lonely Villa*, 1909). The company was renamed the Biograph Company in 1908, and in early 1913 it completed construction on a third and much larger studio at 175th Street and Prospect Avenue in the Bronx, which Griffith did not have a chance to use before he joined a rival organization. Biograph made films at the facility to the end of 1916, when it ceased production. The space became a rental studio in 1917 and was used by most of the major production companies during the silent period, including Metro Film Corporation, Fox Film Corporation, Warner Brothers, Selznick Pictures, and First National. It was leased by the U.S. Signal Corps during World War I, closed in 1927, and in 1933 was converted to sound and rented by various independent producers. After being used by the Army Signal Corps during World War II the building fell into disrepair. It was revamped in the 1950s, when as Gold Medal Studios it was employed for such films as Elia Kazan's *A Face in the Crowd* (1957), Sidney Lumet's *The Fugitive Kind* (1959), Daniel Mann's *Butterfield 8* (1960), and Peter Yates's *John and Mary* (1969), as well as for television series such as *Car 54 Where Are You?* and *Naked City*. By the mid-1970s it had been abandoned to vandals.

Charles Musser, *The Emergence of Cinema: The American Screen to 1907* (New York: Charles Scribner's Sons, 1990)

Charles Musser

biology. The first graduate program in biology in New York City was set up at Columbia University in the early 1890s by Henry Fairfield Osborn. In its early years the program emphasized evolutionary biology and became affiliated with the American Museum of Natural History, where Osborn laid the foundation for a research program in vertebrate paleontology. He and his students used the large collection of specimens at the museum to help answer a wide range of questions about morphology and evolution. Edmund Beecher Wilson helped to make the university a center of research in cellular biology and embryology, and made careful microscopical studies that he summed up in his classic text *The Cell in Development and Heredity* (1896). Important research in genetics was conducted at Columbia during the first two decades of the twentieth century by Wilson and Nettie M. Stevens, who in 1905 discovered the chromosomal pairings that determine sex. Beginning in 1910 Thomas Hunt Morgan conducted important experiments with fruit flies, which provided additional evidence that genes on chromosomes influence the inheritance of particular traits and formed the basis for classical transmission genetics. Theodosius Dobzhansky and L. C. Dunn, who joined Columbia respectively in 1927 and 1928, made additional contributions to the field. Dobzhansky documented the role of genetic mutations in evolution, and his work, along with studies done by Ernst Mayr and George Gaylord Simpson of the American Museum of Natural History, helped lead the way to the evolutionary synthesis of the 1940s.

The Rockefeller Institute for Medical Research also made important advances in the field of biology. In 1910 Jacques Loeb, a biochemist at the institute who was well known for his work on artificial parthenogenesis, began a research project with his assistant John Howard Northrop on nucleoproteins. Another biologist at the institute, Alexis Carrel, improved techniques for cultivating tissues outside the body. In 1935 Wendell M. Stanley confirmed the crystalline structure of the tobacco mosaic virus, a discovery that won him the Nobel Prize in chemistry in 1946. Experiments by Oswald T. Avery, Colin MacLeod, and Maclyn McCarty in 1944 suggesting the role played by DNA (deoxyribonucleic acid) in transforming benign bacteria into virulent strains promoted the development of molecular biology, particularly molecular genetics.

In the twenty-first century New York City has continued to be home to centers and research institutions focusing on the biological sciences. In December 2002 the New York Structural Biology Center was opened by a group of 10 research centers, located next to the campus of the City University of New York at Convent Avenue and 133rd Street. It is governed by a board representing institutional members in the city, including Albert Einstein College of Medicine of Yeshiva University, City University of New York, Columbia University, Memorial Sloan–Kettering Cancer Center, Mount Sinai School of Medicine, and New York University. That same year, the Joan and Joel Smilow Research Center of New York University opened, including investigators in the fields of cancer, cardiovascular biology, neuroscience, and other areas.

George W. Corner, *History of the Rockefeller Institute, 1901–1953: Origins and Growth* (New York: Rockefeller Institute Press, 1964); Garland E. Allen, *Thomas Hunt Morgan: The Man and His Science* (Princeton, N.J.: Princeton University Press, 1978); Philip J. Pauly, *Controlling Life: Jacques Loeb and the Engineering Ideal in Biology* (New York: Oxford University Press, 1987)

Ronald Rainger, Danielle Molinski

Birdland. Jazz club. It opened on 15 December 1949 in a basement at 1678 Broadway, just north of 52nd Street. Named by its owners Morris and Irving Levy for the alto saxophonist Charlie Parker (known as "Bird"), who performed there, it seated 400 and was the site of performances by such leading musicians as Dizzy Gillespie, Bud Powell, and Count Basie. The impresario Symphony Sid broadcast some of his radio programs from the club. In 1965 the club closed because of increased rents; it reopened for one night in 1979. Birdland inspired George Shearing's song "Lullaby of Birdland" (1952). An unrelated club with the same name was opened in 1986, at 2745 Broadway, near 106th Street; in 1996 this club moved to 315 West 44th Street, between Eighth and Ninth avenues.

Peter Eisenstadt, Marc Ferris

birds. Proximity to the Hudson–Raritan estuary makes New York City along the Atlantic flyway a potentially ideal habitat for birds: 10 percent of the species identified in the continental United States have been observed in and around Jamaica Bay. Birds remain an important means of monitoring the city's environmental quality. However, pollution from pesticides and the loss of habitat to development during the twentieth and twenty-first centuries have driven several species of birds to extinction in New York City. Others have been threatened, especially harriers such as the Osprey and the Peregrine Falcon, which absorbed large quantities of pesticide in the fish they ate and produced thin-shelled eggs that usually broke before reaching maturity. Their numbers and those of Grasshopper Sparrows, Piping Plovers, and Roseate Terns increased after endangered species laws were passed, pesticides were banned, and nesting poles were erected in the early twenty-first century. To compensate for the loss of farmlands in the metropolitan area, more than 18 nesting boxes for Barn Owls were installed in the Jamaica Bay Wildlife Refuge during the summer of 1992 where the first recorded nest of a Peregrine Falcon was discovered in

1993. At Floyd Bennett Field in Brooklyn one Barn Owl box began producing four to six young a year during the early 1980s.

One of the best locations for observing land birds in New York City is Central Park, where 15 species are common. Mourning Doves, Downy Woodpeckers, Blue Jays, American Crows, Black-capped Chickadees, Northern Mockingbirds, Cardinals, and House Finches are seen year round. American Robins, Common Yellowthroats, Red-winged Blackbirds, Common Grackles, American Goldfinches, and Rufous-sided Towhees are often seen during warmer months; Dark-eyed Juncos are seen in winter. More than 100 species may be observed during the spring migration in April and May, and more than 320 species have been observed breeding, migrating, or roosting in the Jamaica Bay Wildlife Refuge. This major bird migratory area provides a year-round opportunity to see a diversity of species. Five species of water birds can be seen in the bay, ponds, and marshes at the refuge: the Double-crested Cormorant, the Glossy Ibis, the Canada Goose, the Mallard, and the Herring Gull. During spring, summer, and autumn Egrets are easily identified by their white plumage, Glossy Ibises by their long, decurved bills. Each September and October the autumn migration of Marsh Hawks, Sharp-shinned Hawks, Kestrels, and Red-tailed Hawks is a spectacular event over Jamaica Bay and Breezy Point. More than 1500 hawks were once counted in a single season at Fort Tilden, an abandoned Nike missile defense base that is now part of the Gateway National Recreation Area.

John Bull, *Birds of the New York Area* (New York: Harper and Row, 1964); John Bull, *Birds of New York State, including the 1976 Supplement* (Ithaca, N.Y.: Cornell University Press, 1985); *Macmillan Field Guide to the Birds of North America: Eastern Region* (New York: Macmillan, 1985)

See also Fauna; Pale Male; Parrots, wild; and Rock Pigeon.

John Bull, John T. Tanacredi

Bishop McDonnell Memorial High School. Catholic high school for girls, opened in 1926 at 260 Eastern Parkway in Brooklyn. At its height it had more than 2000 students drawn from the entire diocese of Brooklyn, which until 1957 included all of Long Island. In later years enrollment was limited to girls from Brooklyn and Queens. The school closed in 1973; its building was taken over by the St. Francis de Sales School for the Deaf.

Gilbert Tauber

Bitter, Karl (Theodore Francis) (*b* near Vienna, 6 Dec 1867; *d* New York City, 9 April 1915). Sculptor. After studying architectural sculpture in Vienna he emigrated to the United States in 1889 and settled in New York City, later establishing a home and studio in suburban Weehawken, New Jersey. Through the patronage of the prominent architect Richard Morris Hunt he quickly gained recognition in the fields of public and architectural sculpture, and he executed several fine works of sculpture at the appellate court, the customs house, and the Metropolitan Museum of Art. A founding member of the National Sculpture Society in 1893, he was its president in 1906–7 and again in 1914. He was also the director of sculpture for the world's fairs of 1901 (Buffalo), 1904 (St. Louis), and 1915 (San Francisco). The collaborative planning of the fairs instilled in him a vision of urban improvement and provided the early inspiration of the "city beautiful" movement. At a time of increasing hostility toward Germans and Austrians before World War I he executed a large monument of the German-American statesman and reformer Carl Schurz at Morningside Drive and 116th Street (1909–13). Appointed to the New York City Art Commission in 1912, he oversaw the development of Grand Army Plaza on Fifth Avenue, to which he contributed the Pulitzer Fountain. Bitter died after being struck by an automobile while crossing the plaza.

James M. Dennis, *Karl Bitter, Architectural Sculptor, 1867–1915* (Madison: University of Wisconsin Press, 1967)

Susan Rather

B. Kreischer and Sons. Firm of firebrick makers. Formed in 1845 as Kreischer and Mumpeton by Balthazar Kreischer (*b* 13 March 1813; *d* 25 Aug 1886), an immigrant from Bavaria, it became one of the leading manufacturers in the metropolitan area of firebricks, gas retorts, and molded decorative clay building materials (briefly including terra-cotta). It operated the New York Fire-Brick Manufactory at Delancey and Goerck streets in Manhattan from 1845 to 1876 and from 1854 to 1927 managed clay mines and an extensive factory complex in Staten Island called Kreischerville (now known as Charleston) that resembled a company village. Its administrative headquarters were at Goerck and Mangin streets in Manhattan. The company bought additional clay mines in New Jersey and Pennsylvania, and during the 1860s and 1870s also had a factory in Philadelphia. During the 1890s the plant in Staten Island employed more than 300 persons. The factory closed just before the Great Depression and was destroyed by fire in 1936. Several prominent architects based in New York City used the firm's products: terra-cotta by Kreischer decorates Barnard College, St. Luke's Hospital, and other buildings. Remains of the enterprise at Charleston include the Charles Kreischer Mansion and a row of workers' housing (both designated landmarks by the city), and the Clay Pit Ponds State Park Preserve. Product samples and documents are preserved at the Staten Island Historical Society, the Staten Island Institute of Arts and Sciences, and the New-York Historical Society.

Asher and Adams' Pictorial Album of American Industry (New York: Asher and Adams, 1876; repr. New York: Routledge, 1976), 82; Shirley Zavin and Elsa Gilbertson, *Staten Island Walking Tours* (New York: Preservation League of Staten Island, 1986); Charles L. Sachs, *Made on Staten Island: Agriculture, Industry, and Suburban Living in the City* (New York: Staten Island Historical Society, 1988)

Charles L. Sachs

Black, Starr and Frost. The oldest firm of jewelers in the United States. Formed in 1801 in Savannah, Georgia, as Marquand and Paulding, it was moved in 1810 to New York City by Isaac Marquand, who in 1813 bought out the jewelry shop of James H. Hyde at 166 Broadway. In 1819 he merged his business with that of Erastus Barton, whom he bought out in 1823; his son Frederick then took over the business and changed the name first to F. Marquand and in 1833 to Marquand and Company. Henry Ball and William Black entered the firm and opened a new shop at 181 Broadway. When the Marquands withdrew from the business in 1839, Erastus O. Thompkins became a partner and the firm was renamed Ball, Thompkins and Black, in new quarters at 247 Broadway; on the death of Thompkins in 1852 it became Ball, Black and Company. The firm offered household and gift items such as porcelain, silver, paintings, and bronze statuary as well as gemstone jewelry and precious objects. It was one of few American retailers to display its wares in London at the Crystal Palace in 1851. Shops were opened at Broadway and Prince Street in 1860 and at several locations along Fifth Avenue: at 28th Street in 1876, when Cortlandt Starr and Aaron V. Frost became partners and the name became Black, Starr and Frost; at 39th Street in 1898; and at 48th Street in 1912. The company was immortalized in the original lyrics to the song "Diamonds Are a Girl's Best Friend" sung by Marilyn Monroe in the film *Gentlemen Prefer Blondes.* After the company changed hands several times in the late twentieth century, Black, Starr and Frost moved its headquarters to California.

Janet Zapata

Black Ball Line. First regularly scheduled cargo ship service in the world. It was founded in 1817 by a group of New York City merchants led by Jeremiah Thompson who believed that greater profits could be made by offering scheduled sailing ship departures on the service between New York City and Liverpool, England. Previously, ships had sailed when fully loaded with cargo, a process that took weeks during which shippers had little idea when their goods would be leaving port and passengers had to seek nearby accommodations to be ready to leave on short notice. To offer scheduled departures the company had to have a large enough fleet so that one vessel would be available on the designated day each week at both ends of the service. Thompson and his associates believed people would be willing to pay higher rates for this service, more than compensating for any unused cargo space. Their gamble paid off and was soon copied by other shipowners in the city and other major East Coast ports. The vessels became known as packet ships, a name taken from earlier fast sailing vessels used to carry mail and consular dispatches. The new packet ships were also built for speed, reducing the average crossing time by weeks. To compete for high-paying passengers, they also provided fine dining and accommodations. For these reasons many people continued to cross the Atlantic in packet ships long after the first regular steamship services were established in 1838. The Black Ball Line survived until 1878. The last packet ship line, Grinnell, Minturn and Company of New York, lasted until 1881, carrying only cargo in its final years. Throughout the Black Ball Line's history its vessels were immediately identifiable at sea by a large black ball in the center of the fore topsail.

Norman J. Brouwer

blacklisting. In October 1947, during hearings before the House Un-American Activities Committee, a group of screenwriters and directors refused to reveal whether they had ever belonged to the Communist Party. When it became clear that the "Hollywood 10" would be held in contempt of Congress, the heads of the major movie studios met in New York City at the Waldorf-Astoria and decided to fire them. In the Waldorf Statement, issued on 3 December 1947, the Association of Motion Picture Producers declared that its members would not knowingly employ "a Communist or a member of any party or group which advocates the overthrow of the Government of the United States by force or by illegal or unconstitutional methods." On 22 June 1950 the blacklist expanded when three former agents of the Federal Bureau of Investigation published *Red Channels,* a listing of the "subversive" associations of 151 writers, directors, and performers, including Leonard Bernstein, Lee J. Cobb, Aaron Copland, Lena Horne, Langston Hughes, Gypsy Rose Lee, Arthur Miller, Zero Mostel, Edward G. Robinson, Pete Seeger, Artie Shaw, William L. Shirer, and Orson Welles. Advertising agencies on Madison Avenue enforced the blacklist by requiring radio and television producers to submit the names of the people they wanted to use as writers, directors, and actors. The lists were then vetted to ensure that no one with communist connections was hired. The producer David Susskind would later testify that in seeking to fill positions for one show over a one-year period he submitted 5000 names to the advertising agency Young and Rubicam. The blacklist began to weaken in 1956, when the radio entertainer John Henry Faulk filed a libel suit against AWARE, Inc., an anticommunist group that had accused him of having communist ties. Faulk charged that AWARE had attacked him in an effort to silence his criticism of the blacklist. The case came to trial in New York City in 1962 and resulted in a record judgment of $3.5 million against AWARE and two other defendants. Although many blacklisted entertainers began to work again in the late 1950s and early 1960s, Faulk's career never recovered.

John Henry Faulk, *Fear on Trial* (New York: Simon and Schuster, 1964); David Everitt, *A Shadow of Red: Communism and the Blacklist in Radio and Television* (Chicago: Ivan R. Dee, 2007); Christopher M. Finan, *From the Palmer Raids to the Patriot Act: A History of the Fight for Free Speech in America* (Boston: Beacon Press, 2007)

Christopher M. Finan

Black Muslims. See Nation of Islam.

blackouts. Complete loss of utility-supplied electricity. Electric power blackouts have been common in New York City since the Brush arc lighting system failed on 10 June 1881. The blizzard of 1888 toppled overhead power lines and shut off lights for three hours. These early blackouts produced no reports of people trapped because elevators and subways were not yet heavily used.

A 1936 explosion and fire at the Hell Gate generating station on 133rd Street knocked out power in the Bronx and in Manhattan north of 59th Street; Hell Gate again shut down when it was flooded by a hurricane on 21 September 1938. Burned cables caused a blackout in 1948 that lasted two hours between Walker and 74th streets on the East Side of Manhattan, and one in 1959 that lasted eight to 14 hours in 5 square miles (13 square kilometers) of upper Manhattan. Hundreds of thousands were affected by a rush hour blackout 13 June 1961 between 42nd and 80th streets.

Widespread extended blackouts occurred on 9 November 1965, 13 July 1977, and 14 August 2003. Both the 1965 and 2003 blackouts involved massive cascading transmission system failures that affected multiple states and parts of Canada. Both blackouts induced little civil disorder in New York. The urban legend that good cheer New Yorkers experienced during the 1965 blackout led to a spike in births nine months later has now been refuted. By contrast, the 1977 blackout, which affected only the New York City region, resulted in widespread civil disorder. More than 3000 people were arrested for looting, rioting, and arson. Damage in downtown Brooklyn, East Harlem, and the Upper West Side exceeded $300 million. In 2003 there was virtually no looting or disorder, and the city remained calm.

Localized blackouts mostly have been caused by fires (often underground electrical fires) or weather problems, including snow, rainstorms, and high temperatures. Notable examples occurred on 9 September 1981 in lower Manhattan; 13 August 1983 in the garment district, affecting both Macy's and Gimbels on 34th Street; 15 August 1985 in lower Manhattan; 5 August 1988 in Harlem and Morningside; 13 August 1990 in lower Manhattan, shutting down Wall Street for six hours; 9 July 1993 in south central Brooklyn; 21 May 1996 in Queens; 6 July 1999 in northern Manhattan; 7 July 1999 on the Lower East Side; 20 July 2002 in lower Manhattan, shutting down several subway lines across the city during morning rush hour; 8 June 2005 in Staten Island; and 17 July 2006 in Queens, leaving some residents in the sweltering heat for five days.

Stanley Altman, *Electric Utilities, What Can Be Expected?: A Study of the 1977 New York City Blackout* (Case Studies in Technology and Public Policy) (New York: New York University Press, 1982)

John L. Neufeld

Black Panther Party. African American radical organization. It was founded in 1966 by Huey Newton and Bobby Seale for the purpose of black empowerment. In 1968 party members established branches in Harlem and Brooklyn. In April of the following year, after repeated confrontations with the police, 21 members of the New York City chapter were arrested on numerous conspiracy charges. Civil rights attorney William Kunstler provided legal defense for the group, and in May 1971 the members were acquitted of all charges.

Emilyn L. Brown

Black Star Line. Shipping line established by Marcus Garvey as an economic outlet for his organization, the United Negro Improvement Association (UNIA). Founded in 1919, the shipping line derived its name from the British shipping company the White Star Line. In response to reports of discrimination by passengers, seamen, and African traders who suffered from the privilege given to European merchants, Garvey created the line with the central aim of stimulating trade between Africa, the United States, the West Indies, and Central America; this business worked toward his belief in the need for an independent black economy. Another goal was to transport people traveling on business or for pleasure without inferior accommodation. The line also provided work for underemployed, skilled black laborers. Initially meant to be the property of a small group of UNIA members, ownership was opened to the masses in an effort to gain necessary capital. Stock was sold at $5 a share, and nearly $800,000 was reportedly raised. The first ship purchased was the SS *Yarmouth,* renamed the *Frederick Douglass,* which made trips to the West Indies and Central America. A riverboat was also acquired for excursion trips on the Hudson River. An investigation soon began, however, and Garvey was accused of mail fraud surrounding the purchase of a ship, the SS *Phyllis Wheatley.* Garvey was sentenced to five years in prison in 1923, but President Calvin Coolidge commuted the sentence. Though it closed in 1922 after losses of over a half-million dollars, the Black Star Line helped internationalize Garveyism and widen the UNIA base by appealing outside the usual black elites for financial support.

Garrett A. Felber

black theater. African American actors, playwrights, and producers have taken part in the rich theatrical history of New York City, and themes drawn from African American life have been the subject of numerous productions. Black theater in the city probably began in 1821 when William A. Brown opened the African Theatre off lower Broadway. The company produced Shakespeare, musical comedies, pantomimes, and Brown's own play *The Drama of King Shotoway* (1823), the first play by a black American. Although city authorities closed the African Theatre in 1823, from its ranks emerged the celebrated actor Ira Aldridge (1807–67), a native of the city who left the United States in 1825 and earned international recognition as a tragedian.

The most popular black performers of the antebellum period were not "black" at all but were white minstrels in blackface. The first performance occurred in 1843 at the Bowery Amphitheatre by four white entertainers calling themselves the Virginia Minstrels, whose comic song-and-dance routines were intended to depict life on southern plantations. Minstrel shows dominated the musical stage for decades and fixed Negro stereotypes that inhibited the acceptance of African American actors on the legitimate stage. After the Civil War minstrel shows more often included African American performers; some who excelled in the genre included Ernest Hogan, Sam Lucas, and James Bland, composer of the song "Carry Me Back to Ol' Virginny."

A break in the minstrel tradition occurred in 1898 when the vaudeville performers Bob Cole and Billy Johnson produced the first African American musical comedy, *A Trip to Coontown,* in which Cole performed out of blackface. Cole then joined J. Rosamond Johnson to write and produce two other shows. Another pair of vaudevillians, Bert Williams and George Walker, joined with the writer Jesse Shipp and the composer Will Marion Cook to produce elaborate musicals. They achieved great success with *In Dahomey* (1903): the show was staged in London, where a royal command performance was given. On the dramatic stage openings for African American actors came first with black companies in plays written by whites. In 1884 J. A. Arneaux organized the Astor Place Company of Colored Tragedians in New York City, which produced *Othello, Richard III,* and John Banim's *Damon and Pythias* (1821). From 1915 black companies appeared regularly at the Lafayette Theatre in Harlem (for illustration see LAFAYETTE THEATRE). Although still absent from Broadway, African Americans also worked downtown, in productions of Ridgely Torrence's *Three Plays for a Negro Theatre* (1917) and of Eugene O'Neill's *The Emperor Jones* (1920), in which Charles Gilpin played the leading role. Paul Robeson began his career on Broadway in 1925 in a revival of *The Emperor Jones;* he later appeared in *Stevedore* (1935), by Paul Peters and George Sklar. After a somewhat fallow period, the 1920s saw several new black musicals, including *Shuffle Along* (1921), by Eubie Blake and Noble Sissle, which had a run of 504 performances. Other important musicals of the decade included *Runnin' Wild* (1926), by James P. Johnson and Cecil Mack after a book by Flourney Miller and Aubrey Lyles, and *Hot Chocolates* (1929), by Fats Waller and Andy Razaf. For several decades after 1930, African Americans wrote relatively few Broadway musicals. After the call for a new Negro theater "about, by, for, and near" blacks by W. E. B. Du Bois, editor of the *Crisis,* repeated attempts were made to establish a viable African American theater that would present plays in Harlem by blacks. The Krigwa Players (1926), the New Negro Art Theatre (1927), and the Harlem Experimental Theatre (1928) were organized, none lasting more than a few years. The late 1920s and 1930s saw the production of a number of plays on aspects of African American life, many of them by white authors. Perhaps the trend can be dated to *Show Boat* (1927), by Jerome Kern and Oscar Hammerstein II, and its memorable songs on black themes such as "Ol' Man River"; Robeson appeared in a revival of the work in 1932. Marc Connelly's *The Green Pastures* (1930), an evocation of black conceptions of Heaven, led to a vogue for Broadway shows with white authors and all-black casts. Two memorable American operas of the 1930s were staged with African American casts: *Four Saints in Three Acts* (1933), by Virgil Thomson and Gertrude Stein, and *Porgy and Bess* (1936), by George Gershwin. In 1935 Langston Hughes's melodrama *Mulatto,* dealing with racial tensions in a household in Georgia, opened at the Vanderbilt Theater and won praise for the actress Rose McClendon. Hughes also wrote *Don't You Want to Be Free?* (1937), a music drama about working-class solidarity that played in his Harlem Suitcase Theatre (1937) and ran for 135 weekend performances. His collaboration with Zora Neale Hurston, *Mulebone,* had its belated premiere in New York City in 1991.

As the Federal Theatre of the Works Progress Administration closed in Harlem, new groups surfaced to take its place. The Rose McClendon Players (1938), organized by Dick Campbell, mounted six productions including Abram Hill's *On Striver's Row* (1939), a satiric comedy of social climbing in Harlem. The Negro Playwrights Company managed only one production before closing, Theodore Ward's *Big White Fog* (1940). The American Negro Theatre, formed in 1940 by a group including Frederick O'Neal (later the president of the Actors' Equity Association), successfully produced Philip Yordan's *Anna Lucasta* in 1944 and transferred it to Broadway in the same year, thus losing valued members to the commercial theater and helping to bring about its own demise. About this time two African American actors gained recognition for their work on Broadway: Canada Lee for his performance as Bigger Thomas in the stage adaptation of Richard Wright's novel *Native Son* (1941), and Robeson for his portrayal of Othello for 296 performances in a production sponsored by the Theatre Guild in 1943. African Americans continued to appear in works of musical theater written and produced by whites, such as *Carmen Jones* (1944), produced by Billy Rose with a libretto by Hammerstein, and Harold Arlen's *St. Louis Woman* (1946).

The 1950s introduced two black female playwrights. Alice Childress, in *Trouble in Mind* (1955), warned against stereotyping in racially mixed plays, while Lorraine Hansberry in *A Raisin in the Sun* (1959) showed a family in turmoil as it sought to escape the slums of Chicago. Other plays of the decade with a strong social content included *In Splendid Error* (1954), by William Branch, about the role of Frederick Douglass in John Brown's raid, and Loften Mitchell's *A Land beyond the River* (1957), on the fight for equal rights in the education of black children.

The production in 1961 of Jean Genet's revolutionary play *The Blacks,* with a cast of prominent actors, signaled a new direction for African American theater. As the civil rights movement gained force, black playwrights were called to arms by LeRoi Jones (Amiri Baraka) in such plays as *Dutchman* and *The Slave* (both 1964). Less militant playwrights who sought their own response to the stresses of the period included Ed Bullins, whose lyrical prose plays depicted characters yearning hopelessly for a better life. Charles Gordone won a Pulitzer Prize for *No Place to Be Somebody* (1969), a play dealing with irredeemable barroom types. With *Cities in Bezique* (1965) and *For Colored Girls Who Have Considered Suicide When the Rainbow Is Enuf* (1976), Adrienne Kennedy and Ntozake Shange respectively found new symbolic and narrative forms for their plays, seeking liberation for black women. The most critically acclaimed production on Broadway of the time was Howard Sackler's *The Great White Hope* (1968), with James Earl Jones in an impressive performance as the heavyweight boxing champion Jack Johnson.

The demands of the Negro Ensemble Company (1967) and the New Federal Theatre (1970) for plays brought the work of Caribbean and African writers to the stage. Chief among these were the Caribbean authors Lennox Brown and Derek Walcott, Wole Soyinka of Nigeria (the last two being winners of the Nobel Prize for literature), and Athol Fugard, a white South African. During this period of theatrical ferment Broadway contributed several black musicals. From Vinnette Carroll's Urban Black Corps came the hit production *Don't Bother Me, I Can't Cope* (1972), with book and music by Micki Grant, which ran for more than 1000 performances. Carroll achieved further success in 1976 with *Your Arms Too Short to Box with God,* a gospel version of the Book of Matthew. There were also black versions of earlier musical successes, such as *The Wiz* (1975), adapted from *The Wizard of Oz,* and tributes to black musicians, such as *Ain't Misbehavin'* (1978), which celebrated the work of Fats Waller. This trend continued into the 1980s with *Sophisticated Ladies* (1981), featuring the music of Duke Ellington, and *Dreamgirls* (1981), based on the career of the singing group the Supremes. The most encouraging sign for serious playwrights was the emergence of the playwright August Wilson, who worked closely with the director Lloyd Richards on a series of plays about African American life in different decades, including *Ma Rainey's Black Bottom* (1984) and *The Piano Lesson* (1990); his work was well received by audiences and critics and earned him a Pulitzer Prize for *Fences* (1987).

The 2008 revival of Tennessee Williams's *Cat on a Hot Tin Roof,* which premiered on Broadway in 1955, marked the first time the play was performed by an all-black cast. Terrence Howard, in his Broadway debut; James Earl Jones; and Phylicia Rashad were part of the original cast. The show ran for 125 performances. Many African American theater companies and groups that formed across the city have continued to thrive. The Negro Ensemble Company has provided more than 200 new plays and produced many well-known actors, including Denzel Washington, Samuel L. Jackson, and Angela Bassett. The Billie Holiday Theatre has also become a recognized playhouse and source of reputable productions and acting for more than 30 years. The Apollo Theater, which celebrated its 75th anniversary in 2009, has been a beacon for African American performers and known for discovering new talent and launching careers for black actors, singers, comedians, and dancers.

James Weldon Johnson, *Black Manhattan* (New York: Alfred A. Knopf, 1930); Loften Mitchell, *Black Drama: The Story of the American Negro in the Theatre* (New York: Hawthorn, 1967); Errol Hill, ed., *The Theatre of Black Americans* (Englewood Cliffs, N.J.: Prentice Hall, 1980)

See also THEATER, §§5, 6.

E. G. Hill, Meryl Cates

Black Tom explosion. A New Jersey explosion that killed seven people on 30 July 1916 at the Lehigh Valley Railroad terminal on Black Tom Island, just west of Ellis Island. Barges and railroad cars loaded with dynamite and munitions destined for World War I battlefields in France exploded, breaking windows along the waterfront of Brooklyn and as far north as Times Square. In 1939 a claims commission ruled that the explosion was an act of sabotage by agents of the imperial German government.

Jules Witcover, *Sabotage at Black Tom: Imperial Germany's Secret War in America, 1914–1917* (Chapel Hill, N.C.: Algonquin, 1989)

Elliott B. Nixon

Blackwell, Elizabeth (*b* Bristol, England, 3 Feb 1821; *d* Hastings, England, 31 May 1910). Physician, sister of Emily Blackwell. She moved to New York City with her family in 1832 and remained there for about six years before moving to Ohio. In 1849 she became the first woman to earn a doctorate of medicine in the United States. She practiced medicine in Manhattan, where she opened a dispensary that later became the New York Infirmary and College for Women, a hospital run entirely by women; during the Civil War she organized a nursing unit. Blackwell lived at 126 Second Avenue from 1860 until 1869, when she returned to England.

Jordan Brown, *Elizabeth Blackwell* (New York: Chelsea House, 1989)

James E. Mooney

Blackwell, Emily (*b* Bristol, England, 8 Oct 1826; *d* York Cliffs, Maine, 7 Sept 1910). Physician, sister of Elizabeth Blackwell. With her sister in 1856 she formed the New York Infirmary for Women and Children, a health care center operated by women that trained female physicians and provided gynecological care. In 1858 she secured state funding, and in 1860 the infirmary moved to larger quarters at Second Avenue and Eighth Street. The infirmary offered "tenement house service" (instruction in hygiene for the poor) and in 1868 expanded into a full-fledged medical school for women. After twice moving to larger facilities, the infirmary merged with the New York University Medical Center in 1996. The infirmary treated more than one million patients.

Thea Arnold

Blackwell Hospital. Name commonly used to refer to two hospitals on Blackwell's Island (now Roosevelt Island). The Lunatic Asylum opened in 1839 at the northern end of the island. It accepted patients transferred from Bellevue Hospital and later added buildings for acute care (1881) and chronic care (1892). When the state took charge of caring for the insane in 1894, patients from Blackwell were transferred to other state facilities. Meanwhile, the Island Hospital opened at midcentury on the island's southern end for patients suffering from alcoholism and venereal diseases, or both. The hospital was reorganized in 1866 as Charity Hospital and renamed City Hospital in 1892.

Jane E. Mottus

Blackwell's Island. Name applied until 1921 to ROOSEVELT ISLAND.

Blake, Eubie [James Hubert] (*b* Baltimore, 7 Feb 1887; *d* New York City, 12 Feb 1983). Pianist and songwriter. He first worked in cabarets in New York City as a ragtime pianist about 1905. He traveled along vaudeville

Eubie Blake and his orchestra, 1921

circuits with various singers, notably Noble Sissle, and shortly before 1920 settled in New York City, where he lived in Harlem (eventually on Strivers' Row); about 1946 he moved to Bedford–Stuyvesant. In 1921 he composed music for the successful black Broadway musical *Shuffle Along.* He retired in 1946 and studied music at New York University, but a renewed interest in ragtime in the 1950s led him to resume his career as a performer and to accept speaking engagements. He gained a large following during the revival of the music of Scott Joplin in the 1970s and performed almost to the end of his life. Sissle and Andy Razaf were the two principal writers of lyrics to Blake's songs, the best known of which include *I'm Just Wild about Harry* (1921) and *Memories of You* (1930).

Robert Kimball and William Bolcom, *Reminiscing with Sissle and Blake* (New York: Viking, 1973); Al Rose, *Eubie Blake* (New York: Schirmer, 1979)

Edward A. Berlin

Blake, Lillie Devereux [née Devereux, Elizabeth Johnson] (*b* Raleigh, N.C., 12 Aug 1833; *d* Englewood, N.J., 30 Dec 1913). Writer and suffragist. Born into a wealthy family, she moved to New York City in 1857 and published her first short story; from 1859 she supported herself by writing short stories and novels. She became active in the women's movement in 1869. Blake played a leading role in suffragist efforts to attract support from socially prominent women, and became president of the New York State Woman Suffrage Association in 1879 and of the New York City Woman Suffrage League in 1886. Unlike Susan B. Anthony and others she refused to focus on suffrage exclusively, and as a result she left the suffrage movement to found the National Legislative League in 1900, which promoted a variety of women's causes.

Eileen K. Cheng

Blakelock, Ralph A(lbert) (*b* New York City, 15 Oct 1847; *d* Elizabethtown, N.Y., 9 Aug 1919). Artist. The son of a physician, he studied painting briefly at the Free Academy of New York City, the predecessor of City College, intending to follow in his father's profession. After three terms, however, Blakelock dropped out and began taking classes at Cooper Union and became known for his large landscapes in the style of the Hudson River School. He married in 1877 and raised nine children in New York City. In 1899 he was awarded the Hallgarten Prize by the Manhattan-based National Academy of Design, which inducted him as an associate member in 1913 and a full member in 1916. Blakelock's painting career was largely ended after he suffered a mental breakdown, and he spent many years in an institution. Among his works are *Pipe Dance* and *Indian Encampment,* which are held by the Metropolitan Museum of Art.

James E. Mooney

Blass, Bill [William Ralph] (*b* Fort Wayne, Ind., 22 June 1922; *d* New Preston, Conn., 12 June 2002). Fashion designer. He worked for several firms on Seventh Avenue before designing clothes from 1959 for Maurice Rentner, a firm that he purchased in 1970 and renamed Bill Blass Limited. Using fabrics and workmanship of high quality, he distinguished himself as a designer of crisp, sporty clothing. His signature items include a tennis sweater made with red, white, and blue sequins, and a cashmere sweater set that can be converted into a ballroom gown with full satin skirts. In 1994 the public catalog room at the New York Public Library was renamed in his honor for his substantial contributions to the institution.

Caroline Rennolds Milbank

Blatch [née Stanton], **Harriot (Eaton)** (*b* Seneca Falls, N.Y., 20 Jan 1856; *d* Greenwich, Conn., 20 Nov 1940). Suffragist. The daughter of Elizabeth Cady Stanton, she formed the Equality League of Self-Supporting Women and with Carrie Chapman Catt led the woman suffrage movement in New York City. She helped to modernize suffragism by recruiting wage-earning women, introducing militant tactics, and pursuing a political strategy. Between 1910 and 1913 she organized mass demonstrations in New York City and pressed the state legislature to authorize a referendum on giving women the right to vote. After women were enfranchised she was the socialist candidate for city comptroller and worked for economic equality for women. Her book *Challenging Years: The Memoirs* was published in 1940.

Ellen Carol DuBois

Blatchford, Samuel (*b* New York City, 9 March 1820; *d* Newport, R.I., 7 July 1893). Supreme Court justice. He graduated from Columbia College and studied law before becoming private secretary to Governor William Seward. Admitted to the bar in 1842, he practiced in his father's office for three years, and then worked as a partner in Seward's law practice in Auburn, New York, for nine years. He established the firm of Blatchford, Seward, and Griswold in New York City with Seward's nephew. A specialist in admiralty and maritime law, he collected and published 24 volumes of federal court decisions in that field that had been decided in New York's Second Circuit. He was appointed as district judge for the Southern District of New York in 1867 and as judge for the Second Circuit in 1878. In 1882 President Chester A. Arthur appointed Blatchford to the U.S. Supreme Court. He wrote 430 majority opinions and only two dissents during his 11 years on the Court.

Frank Scaturro

Blazing Star. Village on the western shore of the Arthur Kill on Staten Island, named after a local tavern of the late seventeenth century, renamed Rossville in 1836. In 1778 British forces held a ball in Blazing Star where Captain Christopher Billopp was captured by the Americans. The town became noted for the Winant House (1690; demolished 1932) and a luxury hotel (1829).

James Bradley

Bleibtrey, Ethelda (*b* Waterford, N.Y., 27 Feb 1902; *d* West Palm Beach, Fla., 6 May 1978). Olympic swimmer. She began swimming to recover from the polio she had suffered as a child. In 1918 she joined the Women's Swimming Association (WSA) in New York at 145 West 55th Street. By 1919 she was the top American swimmer. In 1920 she won all three women's Olympic swimming gold medals available at the 1920 Antwerp Olympics (the first American to win a gold medal in swimming). She set numerous world records throughout her career in freestyle and backstroke and was the national champion in distances ranging from 50 yards (45.7 meters) to the mile (1.6 kilometers). She was arrested for public nudity in 1919 for swimming without stockings at Manhattan Beach; her arrest helped to repeal the law requiring women to wear stockings while swimming. In 1928 she was arrested a second time for swimming in the Central Park Reservoir, after the *New York Daily News* had paid her to do so. Mayor James Walker released her, and Central Park soon opened its first large swimming pool. She resigned from the WSA in 1921. Bleibtrey turned professional in 1922 and later became a well-known coach in New York and Atlantic City.

Henry Cooper

blindness. The earliest recorded instance of municipal assistance to the blind in New York City dates to 1718, when the city allocated funds to help a blind artisan buy tools to support his family. In the 1850s the New York Eye and Ear Infirmary (founded in 1820 as the New York Eye Infirmary) served several thousand patients a year across the state, receiving grants from the state and the city to cover its free services to the poor. Further medical services became available when the New York Ophthalmic Hospital opened at 6 Stuyvesant Street in 1852, serving the poor and offering training to physicians in exchange for their free services. The New York Institute for the Blind (1832) was the first school in the country to offer formal education to blind children. In 1866 its director, William Wait, developed a method of reading called the

New York point system; this gained currency nationwide but was ultimately supplanted by the Braille system, which proved better adapted to machine embossing. The financial needs of the blind became clear in the 1860s and city funds were allocated from 1866, when a grant of $35 a year was made to each needy person. The private Society for the Relief of the Destitute Blind (1869) opened a residence at 219 West 14th Street for impoverished blind men and women. Soon after, the city government designated four wards of the municipal almshouse on Blackwell's Island as the Asylum for the Indigent Blind.

As orphanages and other institutions became crowded during the 1880s, contagious eye diseases spread, infecting one-quarter of children in city institutions. A subsequent state law requiring more rigorous medical examinations of institutionalized children and isolation of those infected helped reduce the rate of blindness among children. The depression of 1893 and the arrival of thousands of immigrants to the city made it increasingly difficult for the blind to obtain employment. In response, the Industrial Home for the Blind began a small workshop in Brooklyn in 1893 and added a home for blind mechanics. St. Joseph's Asylum for Blind Girls in Pleasant Plains opened in 1897. When a survey showed that nearly one-fifth of the city's schoolchildren had eye diseases, the health department in 1902 opened an eye hospital and clinic at Gouverneur Hospital.

Private agencies for blind children were formed in the early twentieth century, including the Sunshine Home, Nursery, Hospital, and Kindergarten for Blind Babies (1904) in Dyker Heights. Organizations that served adults as well as children began operations during these years, notably the libraries for the blind of the New York Public Library (1905) and the New York Association for the Blind (1905; now Lighthouse International). Initially children with communicable eye diseases were denied entrance to public schools, but in 1912 the Board of Education opened its first "vision" school for these children. The state began to provide services and advocacy for blind city residents through the New York State Commission for the Blind (1913). During the Depression the federal government began to play a larger role, taking full responsibility for the needy blind in 1974 with the establishment of Supplementary Security Income; further legislation increased federal support to public and private programs in the city. The Andrew Heiskell Braille and Talking Book Library, part of the New York Public Library, opened at 40 West 20th Street in 2001; in the early twenty-first century the city's public university system provided undergraduate and graduate degree programs for the blind. In March 2008 David Paterson, a legally blind former state senator from Harlem, became governor of New York, bringing to the city a new awareness of the blind community. In the early twenty-first century more than 110,000 people with severe visual impairment lived in New York City, including more than 20,000 who were legally blind.

David M. Schneider, *The History of Public Welfare in New York State, 1867–1940* (Chicago: University of Chicago Press, 1938–41); John Duffy, *A History of Public Health in New York City* (New York: Russell Sage Foundation, 1968, 1974)

Sandra Opdycke

Bliss, Henry H. (*b* New York City, 13 June 1830; *d* New York City, 14 Sept 1899). First person killed in the United States in a motor vehicle accident. In 1899 he was hit by a taxi as he got off a trolley at Central Park West and West 74th Street, a place on the Eighth Avenue rail line referred to as "Dangerous Stretch." Bliss, a real estate man, died the next day. A plaque was erected there in 1999 to mark the centennial of the first American traffic fatality.

Bliss, Lillie P(lummer) (*b* Boston, 11 April 1864; *d* New York City, 12 March 1931). Music and arts patron. She was one of the three founders of the Museum of Modern Art and as a vice president of the museum helped to establish its international reputation. In 1934 she gave to the museum 122 works by European and American artists, including Arthur B. Davies, Walt Kuhn, Jean Renoir, Edgar Degas, Paul Gauguin, Georges Seurat, Henri Toulouse-Lautrec, Henri Matisse, Paul Cézanne, Amedeo Modigliani, and Pablo Picasso. Bliss also founded the Kneisel Quartet.

Linda Elsroad

Bliss, Neziah (Hezekian) (*b* Hebron, Conn., 1790; *fl* 1810–1850) Entrepreneur and developer. In 1810 he moved to New York City, where he learned about steam engines from Robert Fulton. The following year he built a steamboat with Daniel French. He then moved to Cincinnati, where he continued his research on steam engines with backing from William Henry Harrison. In 1827 he returned to the city and founded Novelty Iron Works on East 12th Street in Manhattan. In 1832 he bought 30 acres (12.1 hectares) in Greenpoint, Brooklyn, which became home to his company. He eventually purchased most of Greenpoint and then bought land across the Newtown Creek, designating the site Blissville, which is now part of Long Island City. He had the land surveyed, laid out streets, and in 1838 built bridges across the Bushwick Creek and the Newtown Creek (this bridge is now known as the Greenpoint Avenue Bridge). In 1850 he started a ferry service between Greenpoint and lower Manhattan. He also supported construction of a highway and railroad in and out of Greenpoint. In 1861 Bliss's Novelty Iron Works built the rotating turret for the USS *Monitor,* the United States' first ironclad warship.

Henry Cooper

Blissville. Neighborhood in northwestern Queens, lying within Long Island City just north of Newtown Creek between Dutch Kills Creek and Greenpoint Avenue. It was named after Neziah Bliss, who with Eliphalet Nott in 1837 bought the Hunter farm, which included all of Hunter's Point. Monument works, hotels, and saloons opened after Calvary Cemetery was laid out in 1848 on the eastern edge. Borden Avenue was extended through Blissville in 1870 and a horsecar line began operations in 1874. Distilleries and oil refineries were built along Newtown Creek; many who worked in industry and in the cemetery lived in plain frame houses along Bradley, Starr, and Review avenues. In the early twenty-first century the neighborhood remained heavily industrial.

Vincent Seyfried

Blitzstein, Marc (*b* Philadelphia, 2 March 1905; *d* Fort-de-France, Martinique, 22 Jan 1964). American composer. An early piano prodigy, he studied music at the Curtis Institute of Music in Philadelphia. He became an advocate of the socially conscious popular theater created by Bertolt Brecht and Hanns Eisler and moved between Philadelphia and New York City for much of his professional life, producing most of his works on Broadway. His most famous creation is *The Cradle Will Rock*, a pro-union opera whose premiere was directed by Orson Welles in 1937. He developed a close friendship with Leonard Bernstein, who produced the play at Harvard University in 1939. Blitzstein's other major works include the opera *Regina*, an adaptation of Lillian Hellman's *The Little Foxes;* the Broadway musical *Juno,* based on Season O'Caset's *Juno and the Paycock;* and his Off-Broadway translation and adaptation of Bertolt Brecht and Kurt Weill's *Threepenny Opera*. At the time of his death Blitzstein was working on a series of one-act operas based on various stories by Bernard Malamud.

Benjamin Yakas

blizzard of 1888. Major snowstorm that began just after midnight on Monday, 12 March 1888, and lasted until just before midnight on Tuesday, 13 March. It was caused by the collision of a cold-weather front from Canada and an unusually warm front from the South, by way of New Jersey. When the fronts collided over New York City, the dry and intensely cold air chilled the moisture of the warm front and caused a blinding snowfall; by 7:00 a.m. on Monday all the roads

Woodbine between Broadway and Bushwick Avenue in Bushwick two days after the blizzard of 1888

and highways of the city were blocked. The snowfall was made worse by powerful northern gales of up to 60 miles (69 kilometers) per hour, which in some places blew the streets clear and in others piled up drifts to the second story of buildings. Hopes of clearing the streets quickly were ruined when the temperature sank to 5°F (−15°C). The blizzard was the worst in New York City since 1857: the total accumulation of snow was 21 inches (53 centimeters), property damage was estimated at $20 million to $25 million, and the city did not fully recover for 10 to 14 days. One consequence of the blizzard was a directive by Mayor Hugh J. Grant in January 1889 that all overhead wires be placed underground.

Mary Cable, *The Blizzard of '88* (New York: Atheneum, 1988)

Vincent Seyfried

Block, Adriaen (*b* Amsterdam, *ca* 1567; *d* Amsterdam, 27 April 1627). Dutch trader, explorer, and cartographer and one of the first white residents of what is now New York City. On his three or four voyages to the New York City region between 1611 and 1614, he established a fur trade with Native Americans and charted much of the coast between New Jersey and Massachusetts as well as sections of the Hudson and Connecticut rivers. He is credited with determining Long Island and Manhattan to be islands, coining the term *New Netherland* on his 1614 map, and being the first European to sail into the Long Island Sound. During his last voyage, Block's ship, *Tyger*, was destroyed by fire off Manhattan, forcing the crew to set up a winter camp—reputedly the first European settlement on Manhattan. With the help of Native Americans they built the first Dutch sailing vessel made of North American timber, *Onrust* (Restless), in which Block sailed up the East River. He was the first known European to navigate the straits off Wards Island and is responsible for naming the passage *Hellegat* (Hell Gate). The information he presented to the Dutch Republic upon returning from his exploratory voyages secured three years of exclusive fur-trading rights for the New Netherland Company, the predecessor of the Dutch West India Company, which Block established with a group of merchants, including fellow explorer Hendrick Christiaensen. Block Island at the mouth of the Long Island Sound and the Independent School 25 Adrien Block School in Flushing, Queens, are named in his honor.

See also Dutch.

Holly Cronin, Matthew Kachur

bloodsports. In colonial New York City bloodsports included such traditional English recreations as cockfighting, dogfighting, bear and bull baiting, and ratting (contests pitting men or dogs against rats), as well as gander pulling, in which a greased gander was hung by the neck between horizontal sticks and men rode by and tried to pull the gander from its head. Bloodsports were popular among all classes before the nineteenth century, but with increased social stratification they became restricted largely to working-class males in antebellum New York City in the rough camaraderie of saloons, pool halls, volunteer firehouses, and gambling parlors. The height of popularity for bloodsports was reached during the 1860s and 1870s when contests took place in saloons like Kit Burns's Sportsman's Hall (273 Water Street) and Harry Hill's (22–34 East Houston Street). Although bloodsports were illegal, they remained popular to the end of the century. Cockfighting enjoyed widespread support, especially among immigrants from the Mediterranean and the Caribbean. Breeders in the rural South supplied many of the birds used in the city. The rise of such spectator sports as baseball and football after the turn of the twentieth century caused the popularity of bloodsports to decline, and cockfighting was made a felony. Some Latin American immigrants continued to engage in the sport in the late twentieth century: in 1988 77 spectators at a cockfighting festival in Bushwick in Brooklyn were arrested, and in 1989 an illegal Cuban social club in Morrisania in the Bronx where cockfights were staged was raided. Though not extensive, illegal dogfighting still existed in New York City in the early twenty-first century as gamblers, breeders, and fight organizers tried to keep their profitable activities hidden from public view. One local newspaper alleged that the city was the "capital of illegal dogfighting." In July 2008 the New York state legislature combated the problem by making it illegal to attend a dogfight even if there was no evidence of gambling or paid admission.

Elliott J. Gorn, *The Manly Art: Bare-Knuckle Prize Fighting in America* (Ithaca, N.Y.: Cornell University Press, 1986)

Elliott J. Gorn

Bloomberg, Michael Rubens (*b* Boston, 14 Feb 1942). The 108th mayor of New York City; he assumed office 1 January 2002. Born to a family of Russian and Polish immigrants, he attended Johns Hopkins University (BS 1964) and Harvard Business School (MBA 1966). He founded Bloomberg L.P. in 1981, a financial services software company of which he owns 88 percent. In 2009 Bloomberg was probably the richest person in New York City. In 2001 the lifelong Democrat ran for mayor as a member of the Republican Party, campaigning that in the wake of the terrorist attacks of 11 September 2001, the city's economy needed a mayor with business experience. His election to office was the first time in city history that two different Republicans held office consecutively. Bloomberg was reelected as a member of the Republican Party in 2005, but he switched party allegiances in

2007 when he declared himself an independent. After the two-term limit of the City Charter was extended in 2008, Bloomberg ran in 2009 for a third term on the Republican and Independence Party lines, citing that the city required a leader with experience in finance and business because of the financial crisis and recession of 2008–9; he won the election on 3 November 2009. He is considered by colleagues to be socially liberal, supporting abortion rights, gay marriage, and immigration reform. On foreign and fiscal policy, however, he is widely considered to be conservative. During his first two mayoral terms, his accomplishments included placing the Board of Education under the control of City Hall, further reducing crime; creating 3-1-1, an all-purpose city helpline; expanding small business loans; and extending smoking bans in workplaces and other venues.

Kenneth T. Jackson, Meghan LaLonde

Bloomberg L.P. Information, news, media, and financial services company. It was founded in 1981 by Michael Bloomberg; in 1990 it launched Bloomberg News and two years later purchased the radio station WBBR, which airs daily financial news. In 1994 Bloomberg Television was launched. In 2008 the firm was valued at $22.5 billion and had its headquarters in the Bloomberg Tower at 731 Lexington Avenue.

Jessica Montesano

Bloomfield. Neighborhood in northwestern Staten Island. It lies southwest of Old Place and is bisected by the West Shore Expressway. Known during the seventeenth century as Daniell's Neck, it was later called Merrell Town (after a local farmer) and Watchogue. Merrill Avenue, which ran straight for 1 mile (1.6 kilometers), was once called "the long, long lane that has no turning." The western section was sometimes called "Beulah Land." For many years the area was sandy and rural. In 1973 a tank of liquefied natural gas owned by the firm of Texas Eastern exploded as it was being repaired, killing 40 workers. Many houses were built during a flurry of development in the 1970s and 1980s. To the north lies Gulfport, the shipping complex of the Gulf Oil Corporation. The neighborhood is largely residential.

Martha S. Bendix

Bloomingdale. Name used until the mid-nineteenth century for the Upper West Side of Manhattan; it is a corruption of the Dutch name Bloemendael, or Bloomendal (vale of flowers). The area was named for a town near Haarlem in the Netherlands and was largely rural, with a few farmhouses and villages. The Bloomingdale Road, opened in 1703, ran between what are now 23rd and 147th streets and followed roughly the same route of the present Broadway. The name Bloomingdale became obsolete as farms and country estates gave way to urban development, but in the early twenty-first century it was still used by the Bloomingdale House of Music and as a name for a local branch of the New York Public Library.

Michele Herman

Bloomingdale Insane Asylum. The first mental hospital in New York State, it opened in 1821 in Morningside Heights at the behest of Thomas Eddy as a branch of New York Hospital (1791). It combined traditional medical interventions with a form of reeducation known as "moral treatment." During its first two decades the asylum received a subsidy from the state and cared for a heterogeneous population that included members of the lower classes. The number of poor patients declined after the opening of a municipal institution in 1839 and a state hospital in 1843, and the subsequent elimination of state support. The asylum grew more slowly than public mental hospitals: between 1830 and 1875 the average number of patients increased only from 136 to 182. The resident physicians who directed the institution included James Macdonald (1825–37), Pliny Earle (1844–49), Charles F. Nichols (1849–52, 1877–89), and D. Tilden Brown (1852–77). By the 1880s real estate promoters seeking to develop the Upper West Side put increasing pressure on the governors of New York Hospital to move the asylum, and in 1891 the governors approved plans to move it to a site in White Plains, New York, acquired in 1868. The move was completed by the end of 1894, and the site of the asylum became part of the Morningside Heights campus of Columbia University.

William Logie Russell, *The New York Hospital: A History of the Psychiatric Service, 1771–1936* (New York: Columbia University Press, 1945)

Gerald N. Grob

Bloomingdale Road. Early road, the precursor of Broadway. Opened in 1703, it ran from what is now 23rd Street to the northern end of Bloomingdale Village, today's 114th Street. In 1795 the road was extended north to 147th Street and linked to the old Kingsbridge Road. In 1869 the Western Boulevard was built over Bloomingdale Road north of 59th Street. Known popularly as The Boulevard, in 1899 "Broadway" was formally applied to the entire route from South Ferry through Manhattan's northern tip and to the boundary between The Bronx and Yonkers. Broadway between 59th and 168th streets retains its 150-foot (46-meter) width and wide median as legacies from The Boulevard. In the vicinity of 125th Street east of Broadway, a short street (Old Broadway) today follows the original Bloomingdale Road.

Andrew Sparberg

Bloomingdale's. Department store. It opened as a dry-goods store in 1872 founded by Lyman Bloomingdale and his brother Joseph Bloomingdale and was known as the "great East Side bazaar." Located at 938 Third Avenue near 56th Street (well north of the fashionable shopping district), it had a large

Bloomingdale Insane Asylum, ca *1890*

Bloomingdale's

beehive decoration on the roof. The store attracted customers from miles away after the Third Avenue elevated line was built in 1879, leading the store to adopt the slogan "all cars transfer to Bloomingdale's." In 1886 it moved to larger quarters at Third Avenue and 49th Street. By 1927 it occupied the entire block bounded by 60th Street, Third Avenue, 59th Street, and Lexington Avenue, where a building was completed in 1931 at a cost of $3 million. The store catered to the middle class, offering "the best possible value for the least possible price." In 1930 it became part of Federated Department Stores and had annual sales of $25 million. In the late 1940s the store began selling higher quality merchandise and adopted new advertising strategies to appeal to chic customers worldwide. After the Third Avenue line was razed in 1954, the surrounding neighborhood was revitalized. As part of a reorganization the firm opened a series of boutiques within its stores during the 1970s and 1980s. In 2003 Federated changed the names of all its properties to Macy's, with the exception of Bloomingdale's, which kept its brand. In the early twenty-first century Bloomingdale's maintained 36 stores nationwide; its two locations in New York City were at 504 Broadway in SoHo and 59th Street and Lexington Avenue, its flagship store.

Maxine Brady, *Bloomingdale's* (New York: Harcourt Brace Jovanovich, 1980); Marvin Traub and Tom Teicholz, *Like No Other Store . . . : The Bloomingdale's Legend and the Revolution in American Marketing* (New York: Times Books/Random House, 1993)

Allen J. Share

Bloomingdale Square. One of the five open spaces provided for on the 1811 Commissioners' Plan, New York City's master plan. The privately owned 20-acre (8-hectare) site extended from 53rd to 57th streets between Eighth and Ninth avenues. It was eliminated in 1857 after the establishment of Central Park in order to extend 54th, 55th, and 56th streets.

Lisa Keller

Bloomingview. Former name of HUGUENOT.

Blue Cross Blue Shield. See EMPIRE BLUE CROSS AND BLUE SHIELD.

Blue Note Records. Jazz recording label. Blue Note Records was founded in New York City in 1939 by Alfred Lion, a young German immigrant who was joined at the label two years later by his childhood friend Francis Wolff. Together, the two of them built Blue Note into a successful record label that was to become synonymous with innovation in jazz. Although Blue Note's first hit was clarinetist Sidney Bechet's version of *Summertime*, the label became renowned for its association with more modern jazz artists like Thelonious Monk, John Coltrane, Horace Silver, Miles Davis, Art Blakey, Jimmy Smith, and Ornette Coleman. Saxophonist Ike Quebec's work for Blue Note in the Artists and Repertoire division throughout the 1950s and early 1960s helped to build the label's roster into a who's who of jazz. Blue Note was unique in that it paid musicians for rehearsal time prior to recording sessions. Along with Lion's reputation as a producer who was willing to listen to musicians, the practice of paid rehearsal made the label popular among recording artists and earned their loyalty. Blue Note gave artists the freedom to experiment and the time to pull it off. This company policy and reputation epitomizes Lion's hands-off but perfectionist production style and, along with the work of engineer Rudy Van Gelder, gives Blue Note releases their distinctive sound. They are also well known for their cover art, designed by Reid Miles and often featuring Wolff's photographs of recording sessions. After more than 25 years in the business, Lion and Wolff sold the Blue Note name and catalogue to the record company EMI in 1965. EMI has contributed to a resurgence of the Blue Note name in recent years through an extensive reissue campaign, releases from new artists like Norah Jones, Madlib, and Ravi Coltrane, and a partnership with Starbucks Coffee.

Rowan Moore Gerety

Blunt, Edmund March (*b* Portsmouth, N.H., 20 June 1770; *d* New York City, 1860). Mariner, author, publisher, and ship chandler. He published *The American Coast Pilot*, along with many charts of harbors, thereby easing the danger of coastal navigation, which was unreliable before the federal government began providing charts in the 1830s. The first collection of sailing directions in the United State, the *Coast Pilot*, was published by Blunt in Newburyport, Massachusetts, in 1796, and he soon was the country's premier publisher of maritime books. The *Coast Pilot* contained detailed directions for avoiding shoals, as well as articles by the pioneering meteorologist William Redfield, who developed the method of tracking storms by tracking wind direction and barometer readings. In 1811 Blunt moved to New York City and established a ship's chandlery and publishing house at 202 Water Street. Blunt and his sons, George W. and Edmund, published the *Coast Pilot* in 21 editions until the government's Coast Survey acquired the rights in 1867. Blunt also published one of the first general guides to the city, its laws, and its institutions, *Blunt's Stranger's Guide to the City of New-York* (1817).

Robert Greenhalgh Albion, *The Rise of New York Port, 1815–1860* (New York: Scribner's, 1939); John Rousmaniere, *After the Storm: True Stories of Disaster and Recovery at Sea* (New York: McGraw-Hill/International Marine, 2002)

John Rousmaniere

Bly, Nellie [Seaman (née Cochran), Elizabeth] (*b* Cochran's Mills, near Ford City, Pa., 5 May 1867; *d* New York City, 27 Jan 1922). Journalist. She began her career at the *Dispatch* in Pittsburgh. As a "stunt" journalist for the *New York World* in New York City in the late 1880s she became well known for making an undersea descent in a diving bell and an ascent in a hot-air balloon, for exposing the horrors of an asylum by feigning insanity, and for circling the globe in 72 days. After marrying the industrialist Robert Seaman in 1895, she interrupted her career. On his death in 1915 Bly joined the *New York Journal*, where she worked for the rest of her life. She wrote *Nellie Bly's Book: Around the World in Seventy-two Days* (1890).

Nellie Bly. Halftone printed in a supplement of the New York World, *2 February 1890.*

Kathy Lynn Emerson, *Making Headlines: A Biography of Nellie Bly* (New York: Dillan, 1989)

Julian S. Rammelkamp

BMT. See Brooklyn–Manhattan Transit Corporation.

B'nai B'rith International. Secular Jewish fraternal order formed in 1843 by a group of German-speaking immigrants who met at Sinsheimer's saloon on Essex Street in Manhattan. Initially a mutual aid society, the order devoted itself to philanthropy as its members achieved a measure of financial security. The order sponsored orphanages, hospitals, and old-age homes during its early years and by 1882 had chapters in 30 countries. The influx of eastern European Jews to the United States during the late nineteenth century prompted the organization to establish employment bureaus; one of these, the Industrial Removal Office, sought to secure employment for recent immigrants outside New York City. B'nai B'rith also sponsored "Americanization" programs. A women's auxiliary became the independent B'nai B'rith Women's Organization in the early twentieth century, and the Anti-Defamation League was formed as an affiliate in 1913 to combat negative portrayals of Jews in books, periodicals, and advertising. The 1920s saw the emergence of youth groups and of Hillel, a service agency for Jewish college students. During World War II B'nai B'rith helped European Jews to obtain visas and provided religious and recreational programs for a government refugee encampment in Oswego, New York. Like many other American Jewish agencies it did not fight immigration quotas during the Holocaust. The organization moved its headquarters to Washington in 1957. Each year, the organization gives out several awards including a Presidential Gold Medal awarded to honor the recipient's commitment to the Jewish people and for the support of Israel.

Deborah Dash Moore, *B'nai B'rith and the Challenge of Ethnic Leadership* (Albany: State University of New York Press, 1981)

Jean Ulitz Mensch

B'nai Jeshurun. Conservative synagogue formed in 1825 by a faction that seceded from Shearith Israel after a dispute regarding the distribution of communal honors; it was the second synagogue in New York City. Initially it occupied a former church on Elm Street and had a largely English congregation. During the 1870s it sought to replace segregated seating with family pews, a plan that met with opposition and led to a heated civil trial. The congregation moved northward and during the 1920s built a lavish temple in a Moorish style on West 88th Street. B'nai Jeshurun is the city's oldest Ashkenazic congregation and the oldest Conservative synagogue in continuous operation.

Jenna Weissman Joselit

Board of Education. The chief governing body of the public school system in New York City from 1842 to 2002. The Board of Education was formed in 1842 to resolve religious and political controversies over the role of the Public School Society, which had managed the city's schools until then. At the time it was recognized that the schools in the city could not be effectively governed like those in most school districts in New York State, where the popular election of school boards and the financing and management of schools all occurred at the district level. In New York City a single board chosen at large would have been unrepresentative, and dividing the city into districts would have been inequitable. The system of governance that was chosen as a compromise provided for the election of school commissioners, trustees, and inspectors in each ward and for the representation of each ward committee on a central board of education. After 1871 these ward trustees were appointed, but they continued to provide an important element of local influence to the system. Having the responsibility to appoint teachers and contract for school repairs, trustees helped to bridge the gap between city leadership and neighborhood interests.

Ward trustees continued to function until 1896 when reformers effectively pointed out the failure of the localized system to satisfy the educational needs generated by immigration and economic development. A movement to entrust the management of the schools to educational experts resulted in the elimination of ward trustees in Manhattan and the Bronx; a somewhat parallel "local committee" system in Brooklyn was continued under a borough school board initially created upon city consolidation. The reformers' model was

Former Board of Education offices, 110 Livingston Street, Brooklyn, 2009

Superintendents of the New York City Board of Education

William H. Maxwell, 1898–1918
William L. Ettinger, 1918–24
William J. O'Shea, 1924–34
Harold G. Campbell, 1934–42
John E. Wade, 1942–47
William Jansen, 1947–58
John J. Theobald, 1958–62
Bernard E. Donovan, 1962–63
Calvin E. Gross, 1963–65
Bernard E. Donovan, 1965–69
Nathan Brown, 1969–70
Irving Anker, 1970
Harvey B. Scribner, 1970–73
Irving Anker, 1973–78
Frank J. Macchiarola, 1978–83
Richard F. Halverson, 1983
Anthony J. Alvarado, 1983–84
Nathan Quinones, 1984–87
Charles I. Schonhaut, 1988
Richard R. Green, 1988–89
Bernard Mecklowitz, 1989
Joseph A. Fernandez, 1990–93
Ramon C. Cortines, 1993–95
Rudolph Crew, 1995–99
Harold O. Levy, 2000–2002
Joel I. Klein, 2002–

Source: New York City Department of Education, http://schools.nyc.gov/default.htm

fully implemented in 1902, with the city's schools centralized under a single board and management of the schools delegated to the superintendent of schools and associate superintendents.

The centralized board retained primary authority over the school system until the 1960s when it was challenged by advocates of more effective education for black and Spanish-speaking children and other children in poor neighborhoods. Experiments with various forms of shared power included "community control" in three demonstration districts and the decentralization of authority under the community school board system adopted in 1970. Under this system the central board (consisting of seven members, two appointed by the mayor and one appointed by each of the five borough presidents) appointed the chancellor and administered the high schools centrally. Elected community school boards (the first democratically elected school officials since 1871) could select their own community superintendents to manage elementary and junior high schools and could, in theory, select principals and teachers on the basis of local needs. However, districts relied for funding on centrally generated city and state appropriations and centrally defined allocation formulas. Since the overall financ-

Changes in the Board of Education

1842: First Board of Education for New York City: 34 commissioners popularly elected, two from each of 17 wards (later increased to two from each of 22 wards). Board of five trustees popularly elected in each ward; it appoints teachers and manages most affairs of the schools; two inspectors elected in each ward to inspect schools and to certify teachers' qualifications.

1853: Board of Education acquires schools of the Public School Society. Board has 59 members: 44 commissioners popularly elected (two from each of 22 wards) and 15 members transferred from the former board of the Public School Society for a transition period until 1855.

1855: Board has 44 members: two commissioners from each ward. Ward trustees and inspectors as in 1842.

1864: Board has 21 members: three commissioners elected from each of seven school districts. Districts contain between two and seven wards, thus producing a roughly equal number of pupils in each district. Board of five trustees elected in each ward. Trustees retain major role in appointing teachers and in managing schools. Each school district has three inspectors appointed by the mayor with responsibilities for inspecting schools and for certifying teachers' qualifications.

1869: Board has 12 members, appointed by the mayor to serve until the end of 1871. Local elections continue to determine ward trustees and inspectors.

1871: Board of Education replaced by a municipal Department of Public Instruction under direct authority of the mayor, who appoints its 12 members. Mayor also appoints ward trustees and inspectors.

1873: Board of Education reestablished with 21 members appointed by the mayor, three from each of seven school districts; five ward trustees in each ward, appointed by the Board of Education; three inspectors in each school district, appointed by the mayor.

1896: Ward trustees abolished. Most direct powers of appointment and management of schools transferred to a board of superintendents composed of professional educational managers. Board of Education has 21 members appointed by the mayor; five inspectors in each of 15 inspection districts also appointed by the mayor.

1898: Consolidation of Greater New York and confederation of school boards. Borough school boards retain powers of appointment and of school management. New York City Board of Education (21 members) is retained and becomes School Board for the Boroughs of Manhattan and the Bronx; future appointments to be made by the mayor. Brooklyn Board of Education (45 members) is retained and becomes School Board for the Borough of Brooklyn; future appointments to be made by the mayor. School Board of the Borough of Queens (nine members) and School Board of the Borough of Richmond (nine members) also appointed by the mayor. Board of Education of the City of New York ("Central Board") composed of 19 representatives chosen by the borough boards (11 from Manhattan and the Bronx, six from Brooklyn, one each from Queens and Richmond).

1901: Full powers transferred to citywide Board of Education and superintendent of schools. Borough boards abolished. Board has 46 members appointed by the mayor (22 from Manhattan, 14 from Brooklyn, four from the Bronx, four from Queens, two from Richmond); executive committee has 15 members; each of 46 local school boards (largely advisory) has seven members (five appointed by the borough president, one each by the Board of Education and by the district superintendent).

1917: Smaller Board of Education reflects a larger trend toward streamlining urban school systems. Board has seven members appointed by the mayor (two from Manhattan and from Brooklyn, one from each of the other boroughs).

1948: Board enlarged to reflect shifts in population: nine members appointed by the mayor (two each from Manhattan, the Bronx, Brooklyn, and Queens; one from Richmond).

1961: Former board removed during scandal; nine members now appointed by the mayor from names submitted by a screening panel.

1968: Decentralization: board expands to 13 members appointed by the mayor and acquires authority to delegate powers to local boards; board appoints 25 local school boards composed of nine members each.

1969: Further decentralization: community school boards acquire powers of appointment and of management in elementary and junior high schools. Interim Board of Education has five members, one appointed by each borough president; 32 school districts each have one community school board with nine members, to be popularly elected in special school elections from 1970.

(*continued*)

Changes in the Board of Education (*Continued*)

1973: Expansion of central board to seven members (two appointed by the mayor, one by each borough president) and formation of 32 community school boards whose members are popularly elected.

2002: Mayor Michael Bloomberg receives authorization from New York state legislature to reform and reorganize school system. He eliminates community school boards and changes Board of Education's name to the Department of Education. Headquarters moved from Livingston Street in Brooklyn to Tweed Courthouse in Manhattan.

2009: In June New York State Senate declines to renew Mayor Bloomberg's authority over school system; authority reverts to Department of Education. In August mayoral control restored and set to expire in 2015.

CITY OF BROOKLYN

1835: Separate school districts with citywide control: three trustees in each district appointed by the Brooklyn Common Council, three citywide inspectors, and three citywide commissioners also appointed by the Common Council.

1843: First Brooklyn Board of Education: two members from each school district (initially numbering 14), appointed by the Common Council.

1850: Central Board of Education with substantial powers of appointment and school management delegated to local committees. Board has 33 members, at least one from each school district appointed by the Common Council. Committees of the board with extensive powers of oversight formed for each school.

1854: Expansion reflects incorporation of Williamsburgh and Bushwick. Board has 45 members, 13 from the new Eastern District, appointed by the Common Council.

1862: Mayor given power to appoint members, though Common Council must approve choices.

1882: Mayoral appointments no longer subject to approval by Common Council.

1898: Consolidation of Greater New York. Brooklyn Board of Education becomes School Board of the Borough of Brooklyn.

ing levels were generally insufficient, the districts found they had very little flexibility in practice.

Tension over the selection, operation, and relative powers of the central board, the community boards, and other officials continued during the 1970s and 1980s. Problems in school governance increased during the 1990s. Members of the central board increasingly divided into factions that faced off on several major controversies over curriculum reform. Mayor Rudolph Giuliani, ending the tradition of partial autonomy for the Board of Education, intervened directly to force the resignations of two chancellors in succession.

In 2002, arguing that the governance structure had contributed to a general failure to meet the educational needs of the city's youth, Mayor Michael Bloomberg succeeded in persuading the state legislature and governor to abolish the Board of Education, to abolish the elected community school boards, and to give full control of the school system to the mayor. Henceforth, the mayor would appoint the chancellor, who would administer the entire system, and, in Bloomberg's words, the citizens of New York could "hold their Mayor accountable for the success or failure of their schools."

David Ment

Board of Elections. Political body that administers elections in New York City. Its creation in 1901 was a major political reform intended to eliminate corruption of the city's elections. It replaced the Bureau of Elections, which worked under the police department but had more sweeping powers, including the preparation of ballots for primary, special, and general elections; the enforcement of election laws; and the counting of votes. The board's first commissioner was John Voorhis, a Tammany Democrat who served until 1931. The mayor decided appointments to the board until 1911, when Tammany Hall, facing an unfriendly mayor, gave this power to the Board of Aldermen. In the mayoral election of 1925 the board introduced mechanical voting machines to replace the paper ballots previously used. Originally the board consisted of four commissioners of elections, two Democrats and two Republicans from Brooklyn and Manhattan, selected by the party leaders and confirmed by the City Council. By the early 1970s this arrangement was under attack from reformers, who believed that it was unrepresentative and encouraged political cronyism. These criticisms intensified after a court in 1972 reversed the victory in a primary election of Representative John J. Rooney over Allard K. Lowenstein because of vote fraud. In the following year the board was reconfigured to consist of one Democrat and one Republican from each borough, with terms fixed at four years. At the time the president of the Board of Elections was David N. Dinkins, the future mayor, who resigned in 1973 because of the board's failure to enact voter registration reforms. Throughout the 1980s the board struggled with modernizing its voting and registration systems. Early in the twenty-first century the commissioners are appointed from each borough upon the recommendation of both the Republican and Democratic parties and then sent to the City Council for a confirmation vote. The commissioners hire a bipartisan staff to handle the day-to-day operations of the board.

James Bradley, Nathan Morgante

Board of Estimate. A major institution of New York City government between 1902 and 1990. It commonly rivaled the mayoralty in power from the time of Mayor William J. Gaynor (1910–13) through the first two administrations of Mayor Robert F. Wagner (1953–61). The board exercised authority over the city's budget, land-use zoning, the use of city-owned property, and the issuance of franchises to private companies performing public services. It considered proposals prepared by subordinate agencies such as the Bureau of Engineering and the Bureau of Franchises, which recommended the companies that should receive permits for building and operating subways, street railways, buses, and utility lines. For example, the Board of Estimate authorized the Interborough Rapid Transit Company and the Brooklyn–Manhattan Transit Corporation to build and operate the city's first subway lines. An important source of the Board of Estimate's preeminence was its exercise of the municipal government's "residual powers."

The board was composed of the mayor, the president of the City Council, the comptroller, and the presidents of the five boroughs. It often was dominated by a coalition of the comptroller and the borough presidents. Each citywide official had four votes and each borough president two, and for many years voting was conducted privately with the understanding that there would be public unanimity on resolutions. The five borough presidents and comptroller commonly were allied with the city's regular Democratic Party organizations. Mayors elected with the support of these same organizations generally had little of an independent political base that might press the mayor to oppose the board's majority coalition and provide them with the political support they would need to prevail in such a conflict. "Fusion" or "reform" mayors (for example, Fiorello H. La Guardia, John Lindsay, and Edward Koch) were more likely to resist that coalition, thereby pitting the mayoralty against the Board of Estimate.

The Board of Estimate was abolished by a charter reform commission established in 1986 after the U.S. Court of Appeals ruled unconstitutional its system of giving equal representation to boroughs as disparate in size and racial composition as Staten Island (small and predominantly white) and Brooklyn (large and heavily nonwhite). The city charter provisions abolishing the Board of Estimate took effect in 1990 and transferred to the City Council the board's powers over the municipal budget and zoning. Most of the other powers of the old Board of Estimate were reassigned to the mayor.

Wallace S. Sayre and Herbert Kaufman, *Governing New York City: Politics in the Metropolis* (New York: Russell Sage Foundation, 1960); Charles Brecher and Raymond D. Horton, with Robert A. Croft and Dean Michael Mead, *Power Failure: New York City Politics and Policy since 1960* (New York: Oxford University Press, 1993)

Martin Shefter

Board of Estimate v. Morris. Case decided in 1989 (489 U.S. 688) by the U.S. Supreme Court that invalidated the voting structure of the Board of Estimate. The board at the time consisted of the three citywide elected officials (the mayor, the president of the City Council, and the comptroller), who each cast two votes, and the five borough presidents, who each cast one vote. Because of the wide disparity of population among the five boroughs, the Supreme Court unanimously held that giving equal voting power to each borough violated the constitutional requirement of "one person, one vote." The decision led to a revision of the city charter that abolished the Board of Estimate and redistributed its powers.

Richard Briffault

Board of Examiners. An agency responsible for creating and administering licensing examinations for employees of the Board of Education. Created in 1898, under the charter that took effect upon consolidation, it initially comprised the superintendent of schools together with four examiners appointed by the Board of Education. Its formation was one of several steps taken by the public schools to phase in the "merit," or civil service, system, under which the school authorities were required to hire from among the top three people on an eligible list. Although the board's licensing system largely eliminated patronage, its examinations were often criticized for favoring members of ethnic groups already working in the schools. In 1969 much of the board's power was undermined by a decentralization law permitting the 45 percent of schools scoring lowest in reading to appoint teachers on the basis of the National Teachers Examination. The board was further weakened in 1971 when a federal district court ruled that the examination for the position of principal was unconstitutional because it lacked proven validity and produced eligible lists containing disproportionately few black candidates; the ruling authorized community school boards to appoint acting principals without regard to the eligible lists. The Board of Examiners remained a target of reformers until it was eliminated in 1990 by legislation proposed by Chancellor Joseph A. Fernandez; thereafter, the school system could select applicants from among the pool of educators holding state certification.

David Ment

Board of Standards and Appeals. Municipal agency formed in 1916 in conjunction with the zoning regulations of the same year. It is empowered to modify zoning and construction laws for builders and developers. The board is composed of five commissioners, appointed by the mayor to six-year terms. One must be a registered architect, one a professional planner, and one a professional engineer, and each of these three must have at least 10 years of experience. No more than two members of the board may be residents of any one borough. Because of its broad powers to exempt developers from the city's zoning laws, the board has frequently been an object of controversy. Mayor James J. Walker was charged with receiving payoffs in return for zoning variances. During the administration of Mayor Edward I. Koch the board came under repeated criticism, sometimes from the mayor himself, for permitting the conversion of lofts in manufacturing areas to residential use and for contributing to overdevelopment and a glut of office space by being too eager to award variances to developers. It is empowered by the City Charter to interpret the Zoning Resolution, Building and Fire Codes, Multiple Dwelling Law, and Labor Law. As of 2010 its offices were at 40 Rector Street.

James Bradley

Boas, Franz (*b* Minden [now in Germany], 9 July 1858; *d* New York City, 21 Dec 1942). Anthropologist. After obtaining a doctorate in physics from the University of Kiel in 1881, he turned first to geography, then to anthropology, undertaking fieldwork among the Baffinland Inuit from 1883 to 1884. He spent three months with the Indians of the Northwest Coast before settling in January 1887 in New York City, where he became the geography editor for the magazine *Science* (1887–88) and married his Austrian American fiancée, Marie Krackowizer. In 1896 he was appointed assistant curator of ethnology at the American Museum of Natural History; in the same year he became a lecturer in anthropology at Columbia University, and from 1897 to 1902 he led Morris K. Jesup's expedition to the northern Pacific coast. A full professor at Columbia from 1899, he resigned his position at the museum in June 1905 to devote himself to teaching full-time. After his retirement from Columbia in 1936, he continued to teach and often spoke out against racism. Boas is credited with making New York City the center of American ANTHROPOLOGY during the first half of the twentieth century. His research challenged the existing emphasis in anthropological theory on biological heredity, replacing it with a culturally based environmentalism that had a profound influence on the field.

George W. Stocking, Jr., *The Shaping of American Anthropology, 1883–1911: A Franz Boas Reader* (New York: Basic Books, 1974); Douglas Cole, *Franz Boas: The Early Years, 1859–1906* (Vancouver: Douglas and McIntyre; Seattle: University of Washington Press, 1999)

Ira Jacknis

boat basins. Although New York City has 578 miles (930 kilometers) of shoreline, it has few boat basins for pleasure craft. Staten Is-

79th Street Boat Basin, 2009

land has several such dockages, and the World's Fair Marina in Flushing, Queens, in operation since 1964, offers about 300 slips along a 1.4-mile (2.2-kilometer) promenade that encircles Flushing Bay. Sheepshead Bay in Brooklyn provides 10 fixed piers for commercial charter vessels. The best known of New York City's boat basins is located at the intersection of West 79th Street and the Hudson River. Created in 1937, and supposedly the home of as many as 100 boat owners who live year-round alongside the 110 slips, 60 moorings, and five main docks, the area is popular because of its bucolic setting and gorgeous views.

Kenneth T. Jackson

bocce. Game of Italian origin in which players take turns trying to throw a larger *bocce* ball closest to a smaller *pallino* ball. Closely related to the Dutch pastime of LAWN BOWLING, which was introduced to New York City in the seventeenth century, bocce is played on a narrow and rectangular dirt court that is enclosed by wooden backboards. Italian immigrants popularized the game during the late nineteenth century in San Francisco and New York City. In 1935 the New York City Parks Department maintained six bocce courts, four in Brooklyn and two in Staten Island. By 2008 there were more than 40 public courts in the city, with the majority in Queens, Brooklyn, and the Bronx, and an annual citywide tournament begun in 1995 drew roughly 80 teams, which were made up predominantly of players in their fifties or older. There is also a well-known indoor court on East 62nd Street in Manhattan in the dining room of Il Vagabondo, a once popular local bar and playing spot during the 1960s that was expanded and converted into a restaurant.

David White

bodegas. Small neighborhood convenience stores that sell a wide variety of food and nonfood items. The word reflects their ethnic connection to Latino areas in New York City, where they are often the only food supply source because of the lack of local supermarkets. They sell goods that reflect a direct connection to the specific homelands of Latino immigrants.

Bodega, 2009

Smith Street in Boerum Hill, 2009

Boerum Hill. Neighborhood in northwestern Brooklyn, covering 36 blocks and bounded to the north by State Street, to the east by Fourth Avenue, to the south by Warren Street, and to the west by Court Street. It is named for the colonial farm of the Boerum family that once stood in the area. Most of the housing consists of three-story row houses built between 1840 and 1870. In 1973 an area of six blocks around Dean Street was designated a historic district by the Landmarks Preservation Commission. As of the early twenty-first century the population was mostly upper middle class. There is a commercial district with shops and restaurants on Atlantic Avenue and Fulton, Smith, and Court streets.

John J. Gallagher

Bogardus, James (*b* Catskill, N.Y., 14 March 1800; *d* New York City, 13 April 1874). Inventor. After fulfilling an apprenticeship to a watchmaker he moved to New York City, where in 1820 he was awarded the Gold Medal of the American Institute for a clock design; he later patented a complex clock mechanism and invented machinery for cotton spinning, sugar grinding, and metal engraving. He is best known for developing construction methods that allowed entire buildings to be made of cast iron (see CAST-IRON ARCHITECTURE); he first used these methods in constructing a facade at 183 Broadway (1848) and a row of five stores at the corner of Murray and Washington streets (1849). A few of his buildings remain at an intersection named for him in SoHo.

James E. Mooney

Bogart, Humphrey (DeForest) (*b* New York City, 25 Dec 1899; *d* Beverly Hills, Calif., 14 Jan 1957). Actor. He was born in a four-story row house at 245 West 103rd Street in Manhattan and attended Trinity School from 1913 to 1917. Bogart became a road manager and assistant stage manager for the theatrical producer William S. Brady and also worked at Brady's film studio in the city. In 1920 he took a two-line walk-on part in a play he was managing, and other roles followed. He moved to 43 East 25th Street and in 1930 secured a role in a 10-minute short film titled *Broadway's Like That.* His stage role as the gangster Duke Mantee in *The Petrified Forest* (1935) helped him to become well known, and the 1936 film version made him a star. He moved to Hollywood, where he frequently played big-city hoodlums in such films as *The Racket Busters* (1938), in which he played a gang leader trying to muscle his way into the trucking business in Manhattan. He is best known for his role as Rick Blaine, the witty, jaded café owner in *Casablanca* (1942). In that film, when he mentions that he was born in New York City and is asked by Major Heinrich Strasser whether he can imagine the Germans in his home town, he replies, "Well, there are certain sections of New York, Major, that I wouldn't advise you to try to invade." In 1945 he married the actress Lauren Bacall. Bogart appeared in more than 75 films, including John Huston's *The African Queen* (1951).

Alan G. Barbour, *Humphrey Bogart* (New York: Galahad, 1973); Robert Sklar, *City Boys: Cagney, Bogart, Garfield* (Princeton, N.J.: Princeton University Press, 1992)

Allen J. Share

Bohemian Hall and Beer Garden. Beer garden, auditorium, and recreation center in Astoria, Queens. The Bohemian Citizens' Benevolent Society constructed the main building in 1910 and added the beer garden in the 1930s. The hall was built to function as a neighborhood gathering place for Czechs. It has a Czech bar and restaurant and a Czech language school, and often features performances of Sokol, or Czech gymnastics. The outside beer garden is a large area of picnic tables with a performance space that accommodates up to 1000 people for food and drinks. It is the last of the large beer gardens left in New York City. Czechs and people of other nationalities from all over the city come to the hall and garden for festivals, performances, and socializing.

Maurita Baldock

Boissevain, Inez Milholland (*b* Brooklyn, 6 Aug 1886; *d* Los Angeles, 25 Nov 1916). Suffragist. As an undergraduate at Vassar College (graduated 1909) she was active in advocating socialism and female suffrage. She earned a law degree at New York University, married the merchant Eugen Boissevain, and became prominent in the women's rights and radical labor movements by writing for *McClure's Magazine* and taking part in the "shirtwaist strike" of 1909, the Women's Trade Union League, the Women's Political Union, and the National Woman's Party. Her death from pernicious anemia followed an exhausting national tour in which she campaigned for woman suffrage.

Jan Seidler Ramirez

Bonanno, [Giuseppe] **Joe** (*b* Castellammare del Golfo, Sicily, 18 Jan 1905; *d* Tucson, Ariz., 12 May 2002). Mafia chieftain. Bonanno is said to be one of the models for the character Vito Corleone in Mario Puzo's novel *The Godfather.* He was the boss of one of New York City's five original Mafia families; and despite gangland wars, being kidnapped during a power struggle, and decades of prosecution by local and federal officials, he survived to die of natural causes at the age of 97 in 2002. Because he was the reputed leader of a powerful criminal enterprise, investigators in earlier years trailed him 24 hours a day, searched his home, and went through his trash, but he was never convicted of anything more serious that obstructing justice. He disappeared from public view for more than a year during the mid-1960s, an apparent kidnapping, during a power struggle within the Bonanno family, which the media called the Bananas War. He was often referred to as Joe Bananas, a nickname he despised. He wrote an autobiography, *A Man of Honor,* and was the subject of a cable television movie, *Bonanno: A Godfather's Story.*

Frank Dyer

Boni and Liveright. Firm of book publishers founded by Horace Liveright and Albert Boni in 1917. The two met in an advertising agency, where Liveright pooled his father-in-law's fortune (amassed as vice president of International Paper Company) with Boni's joint publishing experience with his brother, Charles. The new venture attracted many eager young and radical writers (e.g., Rudyard Kipling, Robert Louis Stevenson, H. G. Wells, and Friedrich Nietzsche) who could not persuade larger and more conservative firms to publish their works. Their objective was to publish modern classics under the banner of the Modern Library. The partners split up in 1918, when they could not agree on the direction of the firm, and Liveright took control after betting the firm on a coin toss. Boni left for the USSR, where he was imprisoned as a spy, and returned in 1920 to resume publishing with his brother. Liveright started to sell increasingly edgier material and came under fire from conservatives like the Society for the Suppression of Vice. In 1924 Liveright began using profits from the firm to fund theatrical productions, many of which failed, forcing him to sell the Modern Library to the vice president, Bennett Cerf, who changed the name of the firm to Random House. Meanwhile, Horace Liveright became perhaps the only book publisher whose life became the subject of a Hollywood film, *The Scoundrel,* starring Noel Coward.

Gilmer Walker, *Horace Liveright: Publisher of the Twenties* (New York: D. Lewis, 1970)

See also BOOK PUBLISHING.

James E. Mooney

Bonwit Teller. High-end women's apparel store founded in 1897 by Paul J. Bonwit and Edmund B. Teller. Initially located at Sixth Avenue and 23rd Street, the flagship store moved first to Fifth Avenue and 38th Street in 1911 and finally to Fifth Avenue and 56th Street in 1930. The store became an internationally renowned chain with locations in Paris, Philadelphia, and London, selling everything from custom-made clothing to high-end American designs including those by New York designer Nettie Rosenstein. In 1934 the company was sold to the Atlas Corporation in what was to be the first of several transitions in ownership. In 1946 the Hoving Corporation bought the store, followed by Genesco in 1956, Allied Stores Corporation in 1979, and L. J. Hooker in 1979. Bonwit Teller closed permanently in May 1990 to make way for Trump Tower.

Sarah Brafman

book publishing. New York City has the largest concentration of publishers and book-related enterprises in the United States. Books were first produced in the city by WILLIAM BRADFORD, a printer trained in London. After 1752 HUGH GAINE printed almanacs, books for children, and classics in addition to a newspaper. James Rivington published poetry and sermons from 1773, imported music and law books, and was one of the earliest publishers to "pirate" British editions of popular works (international copyright law did not exist until 1891). Thomas Swords and James Swords (1785) produced literary works, college and religious texts, and children's books. During the early nineteenth century New York City surpassed Boston and Philadelphia as the country's most important publishing center. John Wiley (1807, later JOHN WILEY AND SONS) initially issued literary works and later became a major publisher of technical, scientific, college, professional, and medical books. Harper and Brothers (1817) bought stereotype plate-making machinery, roller presses for high-speed mass production, and a steam press; it was among the first to use electrotyping in producing illustrations. The AMERICAN BIBLE SOCIETY (1816) aimed to circulate the Bible without doctrinal note or commentary: it eventually published or sold most English-language editions of the Bible and distributed editions in many languages worldwide.

Initially most publishers offered broad lists. The firm of D. APPLETON, formed in 1831 by Daniel Appleton, published religious books, children's books, travel books, science books such as Darwin's *The Origin of Species*, and Spanish-language materials. DODD, MEAD (1839) was known for serious religious and general books but also the *Elsie Dinsmore* series for girls and the Red Badge detective mystery series. George Palmer Putnam, a former partner of Wiley, in 1848 launched the firm that later became G. P. PUTNAM'S SONS; he opposed piracy and sought to extend international copyright laws. Charles Scribner opened a firm in 1846 that published religious books, secondary school textbooks, and imported books; it was renamed CHARLES SCRIBNER'S SONS in 1871. The city's first important specialized publisher was David Van Nostrand, who from 1848 published and imported works of military history, science, and technology. Picture books and storybooks for children were offered at low prices from the late 1840s, notably by the firm of John McLoughlin, Jr., from 1858 MCLOUGHLIN BROTHERS. In 1866 Frederick W. Leypoldt and HENRY HOLT opened a firm specializing in foreign-language books and translations, including German pocket-sized paperbacks known as Tauchnitz Editions. After the partnership dissolved in 1872, Leypoldt and Richard Rogers Bowker launched *PUBLISHERS WEEKLY;* their firm took the name R. R. Bowker and became known for directories, bibliographies, and reference works. E. P. DUTTON (1858) moved to New York City in 1869 and specialized in religious books. The British firm of MACMILLAN, eager to exploit new markets and combat piracy, opened a branch in the city under George Edward Brett that became an important general publisher in its own right. Leypoldt's and Holt's firm evolved into Henry Holt and Company in 1873.

The first two university presses in the city were established at the turn of the century:

Columbia University Press (1893) and the American branch of Oxford University Press (1896). Grosset and Dunlap was formed in 1898 by Alexander Grosset and George Dunlap and became the leading publisher of inexpensive hardcover reprints and popular children's books. During the same year the *New York Times Book Review* was launched as the first publication of its kind in the city. In 1897 Doubleday was formed, originally as a partnership between Frank Nelson Doubleday and the magazine publisher J. S. McClure, as the Doubleday and McClure Company; in 1900 Walter Hines Page replaced McClure, and the firm became Doubleday, Page and Company. George H. Doran began his distinguished literary imprint in 1908, and in the same year Yale University Press (now of New Haven, Connecticut) opened at an office in Manhattan; New York University Press followed in 1916. The demand for technical books increased: McGraw–Hill (1917) became one of the largest publishers of college textbooks, business magazines, and economics, engineering, and professional books; and Prentice Hall, formed in 1913 by R. P. Ettinger and Charles Gerstenfeld, published business books, financial information services, and some trade titles. By 1915 Alfred A. Knopf left Doubleday to form a company with his wife, Blanche, which in the following decades stressed quality in its offerings. The firm introduced foreign writers to the United States and set new standards in typography and book design. Among the scores of writers whom it attracted were Dashiell Hammett, H. L. Mencken, John Hersey, Thomas Mann, and John Updike.

After World War I Horace Liveright and Albert Boni in 1917 founded Boni and Liveright and began publishing the Modern Library of reprinted classics, providing funds for more controversial new literature. In 1918 Liveright bought out Boni's share of the company. The firm remained known as Boni and Liveright until 1928, afterward continuing as Horace Liveright and Company, and it became a groundbreaking publisher in the literary renaissance of the 1920s. Alfred Harcourt and Donald Brace, both previously with Holt, established Harcourt, Brace in 1919. In 1921 George Delacorte founded the Delacorte Press. At this firm, and at its descendant Dell Books, Helen Meyer exerted a strong influence on the trade from the 1920s to the 1950s. In the nonfiction and college fields the firm of W. W. Norton (1923) announced as its motto "Books That Live." It maintained an unusually large, selective backlist, later including many trade paperbacks. Book reviewing was increasingly important: in 1924, competing with the *New York Times Book Review, New York Herald Tribune Books* began publication, as did the *Saturday Review of Literature,* an outgrowth of a weekly review section in the *New York Post.* During the same year Simon and Schuster was formed by Richard L. Simon and M. Lincoln Schuster, who enlivened book publishing and advertising. The firm was scorned by its more traditional competitors but consistently had best sellers; some of its most successful ideas were provided by Leon Shimkin, the financial adviser and later owner. In 1925 Bennett A. Cerf, an editor for Liveright, and Donald S. Klopfer took over the Modern Library. They adopted the corporate name Random House in 1927 and earned early fame for issuing James Joyce's *Ulysses.* Another former editor at Liveright, Saxe Commins, brought luster to the firm as the editor of Eugene O'Neill and William Faulkner.

A number of publishing ventures begun in the mid-1920s became successful. William Morrow began operations in 1926, following Viking Press, which had formed the previous year under Harold K. Guinzburg and George S. Oppenheim. Viking soon acquired the firm of Ben W. Huebsch, an editor with a distinguished list of American and foreign writers, and became known for literary excellence, distinctive design, and children's books. The firm of John Day was formed by Richard Walsh and later specialized in books about Asia under the direction of Pearl S. Buck. Vanguard Press, led by James Henle, issued politically progressive, well-designed books at low cost (it ceased operations in the 1960s). The year 1926 also saw the acquisition of the Literary Guild from Guinzburg by Doubleday, Page and the launching of the Book-of-the-Month Club by Harry Scherman.

Doubleday merged with Doran in 1927 to form Doubleday, Doran, known after 1946 as Doubleday and Company. About this time a number of publishers began producing fine books for collectors. The longest-lived effort was that of George Macy, whose Limited Editions Club (1929) attracted some of the leading designers and illustrators. Many publishers flourished during the 1930s despite the Depression. Farrar and Rinehart, founded in 1929 by the editors John Farrar, Stanley Rinehart, and Frederick Rinehart, became highly successful. Under Cass Canfield from 1931 Harper and Brothers published such well-known writers as J. B. Priestley, J. B. S. Haldane, Robert E. Sherwood, and Jacques Cousteau. The city's first specialized publisher of art books was Studio Books, which moved from London in 1932 and set high standards in art printing (it later became known as Viking Studio). Crown Publishers (1936) grew out of Outlet Books, a remainder bookselling company bought by Nat Wartels and Robert Simon in 1934. New Directions Press, formed in 1936 by James Loughlin to publish avant-garde works, became known for its list of modern prose and poetry, including William Carlos Williams, Ezra Pound, and E. E. Cummings. In 1932 paperback production in pocket-sized (later "rack-size") format began with the release of the first 10 Pocket Book titles by Robert De Graff. The nonprofit Armed Services Editions, given to thousands of enlisted personnel during World War II, helped to create a prospective audience for cheap paperbacks. Mass circulation of inexpensive books became possible by linking the popular paperbacks with the nation's wholesale magazine distributors. Early competitors included Avon Books (1941), of the Hearst Corporation; George Delacorte's Dell Books (1942); and Popular Library (1942). Dover Publications, formed by Hayward Cirker in 1941, issued facsimiles and reprints of out-of-print titles in a variety of sizes and sold them cheaply in stores and through the mail. Ian Ballantine left Penguin to help form Bantam Books in 1945. Competition intensified among paperback publishers, who vied for display space, aided by eye-catching cover designs.

Publishers explored new avenues during the 1940s and 1950s. In 1942 Simon and Schuster introduced a line of children's storybooks called Golden Books, produced by leading writers and artists under the direction of Albert Rice Leventhal and sold for 25 cents each. German wartime and postwar émigré publishers appeared in New York City: Helen and Kurt Wolff founded Pantheon Books in 1942; Salman Schocken established Schocken Books in 1946, issuing books of Jewish and general interest. Farrar left Farrar and Rinehart in 1944 and in 1946 joined Roger Straus to form Farrar, Straus (later Farrar, Straus and Giroux), which became well regarded for the works of T. S. Eliot and Edmund Wilson; Rinehart later was absorbed by Holt. In 1947 Victor Weybright and Kurt Enoch, editors at Penguin, launched the New American Library, applying mass-market manufacturing techniques to serious nonfiction, sold largely through college and major general bookstores. Cambridge University Press opened an office in the city in 1949. Advances in color lithography and offset printing in the 1950s changed the appearance of books. New technology in color separation and multicolored printing, which allowed for spectacular fine arts reproductions, were exploited by Harry N. Abrams, who established a firm under his own name in 1950 (and later the Abbeville Press, 1977). Art publishers and such specialized photography publishers as Aperture (1952) applied refined techniques of reproducing black-and-white photographs. A bold direction in literature was taken by Barnet Rosset, who in 1951 acquired Grove Press and published work by unknown writers (much of it in translation) and writers associated with the beat movement; he also successfully defended himself against censorship in publishing D. H. Lawrence's *Lady Chatterley's Lover* and Henry Miller's *Tropic of Cancer.* In 1952 Macmillan of London set up a branch known as St. Martin's Press, and Ian Ballantine formed Ballantine Books, publishing original and reprint paperbacks and some titles in simultaneous hardcover and paperback editions.

In the early 1950s Jason Epstein developed the idea of high-quality paperback editions of literary and scholarly works to be sold in general and college bookstores. At Doubleday he successfully initiated the first titles in the Anchor Books line in 1953. "Quality paperbacks" (later known as trade paperbacks) were soon produced by other publishers such as Knopf, which added the paperback division Vintage Books in 1954 and later engaged Epstein to expand it. In 1955 William Jovanovich gained control of Harcourt, Brace. In 1957 Alfred A. (Pat) Knopf, Jr., left his father's firm, joining Simon Michael Bessie, who left Harper, and Hiram Haydn, who left Random House, to form Atheneum Publishers. It built a respected list and in 1961 added a children's book department. Knopf assumed control after Bessie and Haydn left in 1963. Harper and Brothers introduced Harper Torchbooks and took the name Harper and Row after buying the textbook publisher Row, Peterson. The publishers of *Time* set up Time–Life Books in 1959: its heavily illustrated series on world cultural history and the sciences sold in large quantities, primarily through the mail. Doubleday developed a line of religious books, and Yeshiva University Press was begun in 1960 to publish books of religious scholarship.

The 1960s saw a rash of mergers, takeovers, and reorganizations among many of the city's publishers. In 1960 Harcourt, Brace bought the World Book Company and became Harcourt, Brace and World (in 1970 the name changed to Harcourt Brace Jovanovich). The Columbia Broadcasting System (CBS) bought Holt, Rinehart and Winston, and Knopf became an autonomous division of Random House, retaining its identity during later acquisitions. The encyclopedia publisher Crowell–Collier took control of the Macmillan Company from George P. Brett and other stockholders in 1961. Time–Life Books bought the Book-of-the-Month Club in 1966 and the firm of Little, Brown (Boston) in 1968. In the same year R. R. Bowker sold itself to the Xerox Corporation. Holt sold its educational line to Harcourt Brace Jovanovich and its trade list to the German firm Verlagsgruppe Georg van Holtzbrinck, which retained the name Henry Holt. D. Van Nostrand, bought by Litton Industries during the same year, became Van Nostrand Reinhold after another acquisition and was later bought by International Thomson Publishing. McGraw–Hill was strengthened during the 1960s and 1970s by Curtis Benjamin, who found markets for exports, and by Harold W. McGraw, Jr., who worked to improve relations with the retail book trade.

Mergers continued to reshape publishing in the 1970s and 1980s. Warner Publishing (1972), which merged the film and communications divisions of Warner, became a force in the mass-market book trade. Led by Thomas J. MacCormick from 1972, St. Martin's Press expanded its programs in publishing original and imported titles. After buying Jove Publications (from Harcourt Brace Jovanovich), the Berkley Publishing Corporation, and Coward McCann, G. P. Putnam's Sons was itself bought in 1975 by MCA, an entertainment and media conglomerate, to form the Putnam Berkley Group, later led by Phyllis Grann. It acquired Grosset and Dunlap in 1982. The highly regarded Simon and Schuster, led by Richard Snyder, was bought in 1975 by Gulf and Western Industries (later Paramount Communications). In the same year Viking Press merged with the American subsidiary of Penguin to form Viking Penguin. Doubleday acquired the Dell Publishing Company in 1976. In 1977 the German publishing conglomerate Bertelsmann bought Bantam. Harper and Row acquired Thomas Y. Crowell (1977) and J. B. Lippincott of Philadelphia (1978), and Atheneum became a subsidiary of Scribner's (1979). After William Morrow's death his firm continued under Thayer Hobson, sustaining its reputation as a publisher of children's books and good commercial fiction. It was bought in 1981 by the Hearst Corporation (which already owned Avon Books) but continued to operate independently. The merger by Werner Mark Linz in 1980 of several firms including Crossroads, Herder and Herder, and Frederick Ungar resulted in the Crossroad/Continuum Publishing Group, publishers of scholarly and general religious works.

By the 1990s scores of publishers were owned by about 12 conglomerates. In 1980 Advance Publications, owned by S. I. Newhouse and Donald Newhouse, took over Random House, including Knopf, Pantheon, and the trade paperback line Vintage. The Newhouses also acquired Times Books (1984), Schocken Books (1988), and Crown Publishers (1988) with its affiliates, notably Clarkson N. Potter. Prentice Hall in 1984 became a division of Simon and Schuster (under Paramount) and was reorganized into departments devoted to trade, educational, professional, and electronic publishing. The British firm of Reed Holdings bought R. R. Bowker from Xerox in 1985, later placing the Bowker magazines under its subsidiary Cahners, in New York City; Bowker became a division of Reed Reference (New Providence, New Jersey). In 1986 Bertelsmann bought Doubleday (which had previously acquired Dell) and formed the Bantam Doubleday Dell Publishing Group in 1988. In the same year Viking Penguin bought E. P. Dutton and New American Library, which became operations of the parent company, Penguin USA. Warner Communications and Time Inc. merged in 1990 to form Time Warner, and the newspaper magnate Rupert Murdoch bought Harper and Row and merged it with William Collins to form HarperCollins. Harcourt Brace Jovanovich, after several acquisitions, was known in 2010 as Houghton Mifflin Harcourt. The firm of Crowell Collier Macmillan was taken over in 1988 by the British entrepreneur Robert Maxwell and became part of a conglomerate that in 1992 owned the Macmillan Publishing Company, Charles Scribner's Sons, Atheneum Publishers, Audel Technical Books, and Schirmer music books. In the breakup of Maxwell's properties that followed his death, Macmillan school books went to McGraw–Hill in 1993, and in 1994 Paramount Communications bought the rest of Macmillan. Also in 1994 Paramount was bought by Viacom, a multimedia conglomerate. As publishing mergers continued into the twenty-first century, the largest English language publishers, Simon and Schuster, Random House, Penguin Group, and HarperCollins, maintained headquarters in New York.

See also Children's book publishing, Literature.

Chandler B. Grannis, Martha W. Grannis

Book Row. Area of secondhand bookstores concentrated from the late nineteenth century in seven blocks along Fourth Avenue between Union Square and Astor Place. It contained about a dozen stores during the 1920s and 1930s and about 25 in the years after World War II, among them the Arcadia Bookshop, Biblo and Tannen, the Fourth Avenue Bookstore, the Green Bookshop, the Pageant Bookshop, the Raven Bookshop, Stammer's Bookstore, the Strand Book Store, and the Samuel Weiser Bookstore. As rents increased and buildings were demolished during the mid-1950s, a number of the shops moved nearby to Broadway. The secondhand book business declined, and early in the twenty-first century only a few bookshops remained in the area.

Marvin Mondlin and Roy Meador, *Book Row America: An Anecdotal and Pictorial History of the Fourth Avenue Antiquarian Book Trade* (New York: Carroll and Graf, 2004)

Allen J. Share

booksellers. The city's colonial bookstores functioned as post offices and listening posts; many booksellers engaged in printing as well. The first bookshop in New York City was opened in 1693 by William Bradford, the colony's official printer. Catherine Zenger opened the second bookshop in 1742, specializing in pamphlets and stationery. Her husband, John Peter Zenger, had been one of Bradford's apprentices in 1694; apprenticeships continued to lead to new establishments throughout the colonial period. The growth of the fiction market after the American Revolution led to a growth in the number of bookshops. By 1802 booksellers and publishers held their first literary fair; half a million books were sold in five days. The first secondhand bookshop in the city was that of Samuel Wood on Pearl Street in 1804. Charles Wiley opened a shop in 1807 at 6 Reade Street and moved in the 1820s to 3 Wall Street, a newly developing booksellers' neighborhood; his back room became known as the Den, a meeting place for such intellectuals as William Cullen Bryant, James Fenimore Cooper, Fitz-Greene Halleck, and Samuel F. B. Morse (see John Wiley and Sons). George Palmer Putnam worked for Wiley and later founded his own bookshop and publishing house. Daniel Appleton began selling books in his shop on Exchange Place in 1825 and became a publisher in 1831: his shop was the most popular in New York City until it closed in 1881. Isaac Baker and Charles Scribner opened a bookshop in 1846 on Nassau Street and a publishing firm during the 1850s. After the Astor Library opened on Lafayette Street, fashionable bookstores moved during the 1850s to Astor Place and secondhand dealers moved from Nassau Street to Fourth Avenue, which between Astor Place and 14th Street became known as "booksellers' row."

August Brentano, an Austrian immigrant, had a newsstand on lower Broadway specializing in foreign and hard-to-find materials in 1853. During the 1870s Brentano's Literary Emporium on Union Square was a meeting place for Henry Ward Beecher, Edwin Booth, and Artemus Ward. Booksellers became more specialized during the 1880s as department stores began to sell discounted books as "loss leaders." By the turn of the twentieth century several fashionable booksellers had moved near Madison Square, including those of Brentano, Putnam, Scribner, and E. P. Dutton.

Shops established in the early twentieth century included Womrath's (1902), the first in a network of bookshops that operated rental libraries; Doubleday and Page (Pennsylvania Station, 1910); and Barnes and Noble (105 Fifth Avenue, 1917). Smaller shops specialized in books on women (Woman's Book-Shop, Lexington Avenue and 52nd Street, 1916), modern literature (Gotham Book Mart, 128 West 45th Street, 1920), the theater (Drama Bookstore, 723 Seventh Avenue, 1923), used and rare books (Argosy Book Store, 116 East 59th Street, 1924; the Strand, 828 Broadway, 1928), the occult (Samuel Weiser, 132 East 24th Street, 1926), black and African subjects (Lewis H. Michaux's National Memorial African Bookstore, 125th Street, 1930–74; University Place Bookshop, 821 Broadway, 1932), and beat poetry (Elias Wilentz's Eighth Street Bookstore, 1947–79).

Chains like Barnes and Noble, Doubleday, B. Dalton, and Waldenbooks proliferated during the late twentieth century. By the 1990s few booksellers remained on Fourth Avenue; Barnes and Noble acquired Doubleday and B. Dalton and opened megastores across the city. Small bookshops were rare by the early twenty-first century, with venerable stores like Gotham Book Mart and Coliseum Books closing in 2007. Some independent booksellers managed to survive, including the Strand, 192 Books (192 10th Avenue, 2003), and Shakespeare and Company, with locations in Manhattan and Brooklyn. Used and new books were also increasingly sold by sidewalk vendors in Harlem, Morningside Heights, and Greenwich Village.

See also John Wiley and Sons.

Henry Walcott Boynton, *Annals of American Bookselling, 1638–1850* (New York: John Wiley and Sons, 1932)

Marc H. Aronson, Kate Lauber

Booth, Edwin (Thomas) (*b* Bel Air, Md., 13 Nov 1833; *d* New York City, 7 June 1893). Actor. The son of the actor Junius Brutus Booth (1796–1852), he spent much of his career in New York City. His first major appearance in the city was at Burton's Theatre in May 1857. During 1864–65 he set a record by giving 100 performances as Hamlet, arguably his greatest role. On 25 November 1864 he appeared in *Julius Caesar* at the Winter Garden in his only performance with his brothers John Wilkes Booth (1839–65), better known as the assassin of Abraham Lincoln, and Junius Brutus Booth, Jr. (1821–83). He also excelled as Sir Giles Overreach in Philip Massinger's *A New Way to Pay Old Debts* (1625), and as Betruccio in Tom Taylor's *The Fool's Revenge* (1859). He managed, successively, the Winter Garden (1864–67) and Booth's Theatre (1869–74), at the southeast corner of Sixth Avenue and 23rd Street. In 1888 he donated his home at 16 Gramercy Park South to the Players Club, then newly established, while retaining an apartment where he remained until the end of his life. He gave his last performance, as Hamlet, at the Brooklyn Academy of Music in 1891. A statue of Booth erected in 1918 in Gramercy Park stands opposite the Players.

Eleanor Ruggles, *Prince of Players: Edwin Booth* (New York: W. W. Norton, 1953); Charles H. Shattuck, *The Hamlet of Edwin Booth* (Urbana: University of Illinois Press, 1969)

Don B. Wilmeth

Booth Memorial Hospital and Medical Center. Nonprofit general-care hospital in Flushing, Queens, opened in 1957 by the Salvation Army. It began as a rescue home for women, opened in 1892 by the Salvation Army, which offered shelter and medical care to all comers, especially mothers and women addicted to alcohol and drugs. After moving to several sites on the East Side it was given more permanent quarters on East 15th Street, and in 1914 the name was changed to Booth Memorial Hospital. In 1918 the facility was licensed as a general hospital. In 1957 the hospital moved to Flushing, where it had 210 beds and provided general and maternity care. It eventually expanded to 487 beds, treated more than 150,000 patients annually, and became an important teaching hospital affiliated with the New York University School of Medicine. In 1992 it changed its name to New York Hospital Queens.

Jane Allen

boots. See Shoes, boots, and leather.

Borden. Firm of food processors, the descendant of a dairy business formed in 1856 by Gail Borden, who operated a milk depot on Canal Street and a factory in Wollcottsville, Connecticut. The business sold sanitary, condensed milk produced with a patented vacuum evaporation method. It failed twice, owing to a wariness on the part of New Yorkers toward milk that was not fresh from the dairy, bad economic times, and a lack of financial backing. In 1858 Borden met Jeremiah Milbank, a wholesale grocer on Front Street who provided adequate capital. Renamed the New York Condensed Milk Company, the business was helped by *Frank Leslie's Illustrated Newspaper*, which exposed the filthy conditions at other dairies in New York City and suggested that they were responsible for the city's high infant mortality rate. Demand soared after Borden took out an advertisement in Leslie's newspaper in May 1858 vaunting his product's "purity, durability, and economy." Delivery routes were established between lower Manhattan and 51st Street, with additional offices at 53 South Street and in Brooklyn at Fulton and Front streets. With the onset of the Civil War, Borden supplied canned milk to soldiers, who were often too far from a dairy to get fresh milk. Soldiers who returned home told of the miraculous product from New York City, pushing production yet higher. In 1861 the factory moved from Connecticut to Wassaic, New York, 55 miles (90 kilometers) north of Manhattan, to which the milk was transported by train. Borden bought from local farmers virtually all the milk they could provide, freeing them from the task of finding retail customers and from the risk of losing excess supplies to spoilage. In return the firm required that farmers follow strict sanitary guidelines.

The firm continued to expand after the Civil War, and its success helped to create the modern dairy industry. Incorporated in 1899 as the Borden Condensed Milk Company, it remained in the dairy business almost exclusively during the first quarter of the twentieth century, buying other dairies and ice cream companies. In 1928 massive diversification began, with entities purchased in Europe and Canada, and in 1932 the firm introduced Elmer's Glue-All, which eventually became the largest-selling household glue in the United States. During World War II the firm supplied dairy products to America's armed forces and also manufactured synthetic adhesives for military purposes. It expanded into plastics and chemicals in the 1950s and into rubber in the 1960s, when sales reached $1 billion. In the 1980s Borden further expanded its food business. By 1994, when the firm was bought out by Kohlberg, Kravis, Roberts and Company (a food conglomerate with holdings that included RJR Nabisco), it had moved its corporate headquarters to Columbus, Ohio, and shut down its factories in New York City.

Joe B. Frantz, *Gail Borden, Dairyman to a Nation* (Norman: University of Oklahoma Press, 1951)

Thomas M. Hilbink

Boricua College. A private, nonprofit college opened in 1974. The main campus is at 3755 Broadway at Audubon Terrace in Manhattan (the former site of the American Geographical Society), and there are also campuses at 186 North Sixth Street and 9 Graham Avenue in Brooklyn. The students live off campus and the curriculum is oriented toward the interests of Puerto Ricans and other Latin Americans. The college was the first in the United States to offer bilingual education in Spanish and English. Although all courses are taught in English, the faculty are required to be bilingual in English and Spanish to help the students. Fully accredited in 1980, Boricua offers associate and bachelor's degrees in liberal arts, elementary education, business administration, human services, and inter-American studies. In the early twenty-first century enrollment was about 1200 students.

Marc Ferris, Rachel Shor

Borough of Manhattan Community College. College of the City University of New York, opened in 1964. It began as a small business-oriented community college with an additional liberal arts focus, allowing students to transfer to four-year colleges. Since 1983 it has been located at 199 Chambers Street and occupies four blocks between Chambers and North Moore streets. Students can also take classes uptown at Inwood/Washington Heights and in Harlem. The school offers associate degrees in more than 20 fields and in the early twenty-first century had an enrollment of 17,000 students, making it the largest of the City University of New York colleges and the only community college in Manhattan.

Stephanie Miller

Borough Park. Neighborhood in southwestern Brooklyn (2009 est. pop. 110,000), lying within New Utrecht southeast of Green-Wood Cemetery and covering 200 blocks bounded to the north by 37th Street, to the east by McDonald Avenue, to the south by 64th Street, and to the west by Eighth Avenue. Often called Boro Park, the area was the site of commercial nurseries in the early nineteenth century and was developed in the 1880s as Blythebourne by Electus B. Litchfield. Initially the residents were comfortably middle class. Jews from Williamsburg arrived by the 1920s and Italians from the Lower East Side of Manhattan in the 1930s. During the 1960s many Reformed Jewish residents moved to the suburbs; they were replaced by Orthodox Jews from Williamsburg and Crown Heights. The population continued to grow as Hasidic Jews moved to the neighborhood from other parts of Brooklyn, Israel, central Europe, and Russia and as the birth rate rose (bringing the average number of children in a family to seven). Among the organizations that were formed were the Council of Jewish Organizations, a consortium of 170 educational, religious, and service institutions; and the Jewish Youth Library, offering education in the Orthodox tradition. By 2009 Orthodox or Hasidic Jews accounted for about 80 percent of the population; there were about 200 temples, 50 yeshivas (including those in the Bais Yakov school system, which enrolled more than 20,000 students), and more than 20 Hasidic sects, including the Belz(er), the Bobov, the Ger, the Satmar, and the Spinka. Many residents work in Manhattan or in northern Brooklyn, often riding to work on the buses of locally organized lines. An important local event is the celebration of Purim every spring, which draws crowds from throughout the metropolitan area. Borough Park has many immigrants from Israel and the Soviet Union, and to a lesser extent from India, Romania, Poland, Guyana, and Italy. The neighborhood is densely populated and mostly residential; the housing consists mostly of one- and two-family houses. There are few parks. In the early twenty-first century it was considered the "baby boom capital" of New York City because of its high birth rate.

John J. Gallagher

borough presidents. The offices of borough president were established by charter in 1898 to preserve "local pride and affection for the old municipalities" after consolidation. When the charter was revised in 1901 the five borough presidents became members of the Board of Estimate and gained administrative power over the physical development of the city. Their influence on the board was enhanced by an agreement to vote as a bloc on certain local issues, and they often helped to resolve conflicts between neighborhoods and City Hall. Charters written after 1901 tended to centralize financial functions (such as assessment) and services (such as building inspection), thus reducing the borough presidents' authority. This movement culminated in the outright elimination of the Board of Estimate in 1990. Although the borough presidents lost many powers they gained new ones, including the authority to appoint the members of community boards, the Board of Education, and the City Planning Commission. The borough presidents serve four-year terms that are coterminous with those of the mayor. Although the borough presidency does not usually lead to higher office, Robert F. Wagner (ii) and David N. Dinkins did proceed from the office of borough president of Manhattan to that of mayor.

Nora L. Mandel

Borough Presidents in New York City since Consolidation

BRONX

Louis F. Haffen (D), 1898–1909
John F. Murray (D), 1909
Cyrus C. Miller (D), 1910–13
Douglas Mathewson (D), 1914–17
Henry Bruckner (D), 1918–33
James J. Lyons (D), 1934–61
Joseph Periconi (R/L), 1962–65
Herman Badillo (D), 1966–69
Robert Abrams (D), 1970–77
Stanley Simon (D), 1978–87
Fernando Ferrer (D), 1987–2001
Adolfo Carrión, Jr. (D), 2002–9
Ruben Diaz, Jr. (D), 2010–

BROOKLYN

Edward M. Grout (D), 1898–1901
J. Edward Swanstrom (F), 1902–3
Martin W. Littleton (D/I), 1904–6
Bird S. Coler (D/I), 1906–9
Alfred Steers (D/I), 1910–13
Lewis H. Pounds (R/F), 1913–17
Edward J. Riegelman (D), 1918–24
Joseph A. Guider (D), 1925–26
James J. Byrne (D), 1926–30
Henry Hesterberg (D), 1930–33
Raymond V. Ingersoll (D), 1934–40
John Cashmore (D), 1940–61
John F. Hayes (D), 1961
Abe Stark (D), 1961–70
Sebastian Leone (D), 1970–76
Howard Golden (D), 1976–2001
Marty Markowitz (D), 2002–

MANHATTAN

Augustus W. Peters (D), 1898–99
James J. Coogan (D), 1899–1901
Jacob A. Cantor (D), 1902–3
John F. Ahearn (D), 1904–9
J. Cloughen (D), 1909 (four days)
George McAneny (F), 1910–13
Marcus A. Marks (F), 1914–17
Frank L. Dowling (D), 1918–19
Henry H. Curran (R), 1920–21
Julius Miller (D), 1922–30
Samuel Levy (D), 1931–37
Stanley M. Isaacs (R), 1938–41
Edgar J. Nathan (R), 1942–45
Hugot Rogers (D), 1946–50
Robert F. Wagner, Jr. (D), 1950–53
Hulan E. Jack (D), 1954–61
Louis Cioffi (D), 1961 (acting)
Edward R. Dudley (D), 1961–64
Constance Baker Motley (I/D), 1965–66
Percy Sutton (D), 1966–77
Andrew J. Stein (D), 1978–85
David Dinkins (D), 1986–89
Ruth Messinger (D), 1990–97
C. Virginia Fields (D), 1998–2005
Scott Stringer (D), 2006–

QUEENS

Frederick Bowley (D), 1898–1901
Joseph Cassidy (D), 1902–5
Joseph Bermel (D), 1906–8

(continued)

Borough Presidents in New York City since Consolidation (*Continued*)

Lawrence Gresser (D), 1909–11
Maurice E. Connolly (D), 1911–28
Bernard M. Patten (D), 1928
George U. Harvey (R), 1929–41
James A. Burke (D), 1942–49
Maurice A. Fitzgerald (D), 1950–51
James J. Lundy (R), 1952–57
James J. Crisona (D), 1958–59
John T. Clancy (D), 1959–62
Mario J. Cariello (R), 1963–68
Sidney Leviss (D), 1969–71
Donald Manes (D), 1971–86
Claire Shulman (D), 1986–2001
Helen M. Marshall (D), 2002–

STATEN ISLAND

George Cromwell (R), 1898–1913
Charles J. McCormack (D), 1914–15
Calvin VanName (D), 1915–21
Matthew J. Cahill (D), 1922
John A. Lynch (D), 1922–33
Joseph A. Palma (R/CF/AL), 1934–45
Cornelius A. Hall (D/I), 1946–53
Edward G. Baker (D), 1953–55
Albert V. Maniscalco (D), 1955–65
Robert T. Connor (R/C), 1966–77
Anthony R. Gaeta (D), 1977–84
Ralph J. Lamerti (D), 1984–89
Guy Molinari (R), 1990–2001
James Molinaro (R/C), 2002–

Note: Party affiliations are given in parentheses.
Abbreviations: AL, American Labor; C, Conservative; D, Democratic; CF, City Fusion; F, Fusion; I, Independent; L, Liberal; R, Republican.

boroughs. The five administrative divisions of New York City, created by consolidation in 1898. Each borough elects a borough president and is coextensive with one county: Manhattan with New York County, the Bronx with Bronx County, Brooklyn with Kings County, Queens with Queens County, and Staten Island with Richmond County.

Boston Post Road. One of the earliest major thoroughfares in New York City, also known as the King's Highway and the Great Road. The road followed the course of an American Indian trail that existed before the time of European settlement. During the colonial period it was the main overland link between Boston and New York City, and at the behest of King Charles II in 1673 it became the first official post road in North America. The road originated near the Battery at the southern tip of Manhattan, headed north along what is now the Bowery to Union Square, then roughly followed the present Park Avenue. It continued north through Harlem, crossed over to the mainland at Kingsbridge (near the present Broadway and 228th Street), and cut diagonally from southwest to northeast through the Bronx. Regularly improved to facilitate efficient travel and postal service, it promoted the growth of several roadside towns in New York, Connecticut, and Massachusetts. As postmaster general of the colonies, Benjamin Franklin installed milestones along the road, some of which still exist in the twenty-first century. During the American Revolution the road was used by retreating American soldiers after their defeat in the various battles around New York City. In 1789 the road was chosen for President George Washington's inaugural tour of New England. It continued to carry post riders until the advent of the railroad in the 1840s. Although the Boston Post Road eventually became engulfed by the growing metropolis, vestiges remain in the form of the Bowery in Manhattan, Boston Road in the Bronx, and U.S. Highway 1 in New England.

Robert Sanger Steel

botanical gardens. The Elgin Botanic Garden in New York City was established in 1801 by David Hosack, a professor of botany and materia medica at Columbia College, to provide plant materials for study by medical students. The first public botanical garden in the United States, it covered 20 acres (8 hectares) of land then considered remote from the center of the city and later occupied by Rockefeller Center. Hosack's own finances were insufficient to continue maintaining the garden, and in 1810 he sold it at a loss to the state; the land was granted in 1814 to Columbia College and was held by Columbia University until 1985. John Torrey (1796–1873), a pupil of Hosack, in 1817 published a catalogue of plants growing within 30 miles (48 kilometers) of the city; his work established the approach to fieldwork that distinguished botanists in New York City during the nineteenth century. In 1856 Torrey became a trustee of Columbia, where he was given a house in exchange for opening his library and herbarium to the university. By 1867 he had formed the Torrey Botanical Club, which in 1870 began publishing the first American periodical on botany, the *Bulletin of the Torrey Botanical Club.*

Members of the club, notably Nathaniel Lord Britton (1859–1934), a professor of botany at Columbia, and his wife, Elizabeth Knight Britton (1858–1934), an expert on lichens, campaigned for the establishment of a major American botanical garden, and on 28 April 1891 the New York Botanical Garden was created by an act of the state legislature. The site chosen was at the northern end of Bronx Park along East Fordham Road, and it was designed by a committee that included Calvert Vaux and Calvert Parsons, Jr. Some earlier structures from the Lorillard estate were retained, including a stone snuff mill, built on the present site in 1840. The city would not aid the establishment of the garden before sufficient funds were raised from private sources: this was accomplished through the philanthropy of such businessmen as Cornelius Vanderbilt, Andrew Carnegie, and J. P. Morgan, all of whom later served on the board of managers. In 1896 Nathaniel Britton became the first director of the garden; he began a program of scientific publication and initiated a research program in plant exploration and field collection that emphasized systematic botany and taxonomy. He consolidated the libraries and herbaria of Hosack and Torrey to form the research collections of the New York Botanical Garden, and in 1900 he organized public lectures, the beginning of an education program that came to include botanical and horticultural education at all levels, from children's gardening classes to advanced degree programs. Tropical and economic plants were first housed indoors at the garden in 1902 in a conservatory modeled after the Palm House at the Royal Botanic Gardens in Kew, England, and built of glass and iron by Lord and Burnham. A rose garden designed by the noted landscape gardener Beatrix Farrand was begun in 1916 and became an important specialty garden. T. H. Everett by 1932 established a formal program for the training of gardeners, which was continued by the School of Horticulture. The rock garden was initially designed in 1934 by Everett. The Institute for Economic Botany was set up in 1981 to apply botanical science to ecological problems, as was the Institute for Ecosystems Studies (now a separate institution based in Millbrook, New York). In May 2006 the Pfizer Plant Research Laboratory opened: a $23 million, 28,000-square-foot (2601-square-meter) facility designed by Polshek Partnership Architects. The garden's one million curated plants grow on 250 acres (101 hectares).

The Brooklyn Botanic Garden, originally part of the Brooklyn Institute of Arts and Sciences, was built in 1910 next to the Brooklyn Museum along Washington and Flatbush avenues, on rough meadowland previously used by the parks department as an ash dump. Under its first director, C. Stuart Gager (1872–1943), the garden became known for its emphasis on plant physiology and genetics and for its efforts in public education: the world's first children's gardening program was established there in 1914. Gager oversaw the making of a Japanese hill-and-pond garden that incorporated four styles (designed by Takeo Shiota in 1915), the Cranford Memorial Rose Garden (opened in June 1927), and the grove collection of flowering Japanese cherry trees. A popular series of handbooks began publication in 1945. The Steinhardt Conservatory (completed in 1988) was designed by Davis, Brooks and Associates to house the Trail of Evolution and several habitat groups, as well as the bonsai collections begun in 1925. The garden spans 52 acres (21 hectares) and receives 700,000 visitors annually. In 2003 the garden partnered with the Prospect Park

Alliance and the city to open the Brooklyn Academy of Science and the Environment, a public high school adjacent to the garden and park.

The Queens Botanical Garden was initially a horticultural display called Gardens on Parade, built on 5 acres (2 hectares) on a reclaimed ash dump for the World's Fair of 1939–40. It was enlarged in 1941 to 26 acres (11 hectares) and managed by the Queens Botanical Garden Society as a public garden. When this land was needed for the World's Fair of 1964–65, the garden was moved to a site adjoining Flushing Meadow Park. Its specialty gardens include a rose garden, a bird garden, and a Victorian wedding garden. In 2001 the garden launched the Sustainable Landscapes and Buildings Project, a $24 million capital plan, and in 2007 it opened the visitor and administration center, an award-winning green building designed by Joan Krevlin of BKSK Architects.

The Staten Island Arboretum (now the Staten Island Botanical Garden) was founded in 1960 and moved to Snug Harbor Cultural Center in 1977. Designed to match its setting, a community established in 1831 along Richmond Terrace for retired sailors, it lies on 80 acres (32 hectares) and includes Victorian plantings, a perennial border, a butterfly garden, and special collections of Siberian iris, orchids, and rhododendrons. It boasts the first Chinese Scholar's Garden in the country, which opened in 1999 and was designed and built by the Landscape Architecture Corporation of China in Suzhou.

See also Horticulture.

Bernadette G. Callery

Boucicault, Dion (*b* Dublin, 26 Dec 1820; *d* New York City, 18 Sept 1890). Actor and playwright. After achieving success in London he arrived in New York City in 1853 and found work writing and acting for Lester Wallack and Laura Keene, each of whom owned theaters bearing their name. He made his local acting debut on 10 November 1854, and on 8 December 1857, at the Wallack Theatre, he produced his first play, *The Poor of New York,* which was immediately successful. Known for melodrama, comedy, and sensational special effects, his later works were also popular, among them *The Octoroon* (1857) and *The Colleen Bawn* (1860), which was enthusiastically received by Irish audiences in the city. *The Shaughraun* (1874) ran four months at Wallack's theater. Boucicault produced 33 plays in New York City. He is buried in Mount Hope Cemetery in the Bronx.

Marion R. Casey

Boudin, Leonard (B.) (*b* Brooklyn, 20 July 1912; *d* New York City, 24 Nov 1989). Lawyer. He graduated from St. John's Law School in 1936 and practiced labor law before forming a partnership in the late 1940s with Victor Rabinowitz. In 1958 he won the case of *Kent v. Dulles,* in which the U.S. Supreme Court ruled that the U.S. Department of State could not refuse to issue passports for political reasons. During the 1960s he represented several clients in cases related to the Vietnam War, among them Julian Bond, a young state legislator from Georgia denied his seat for opposing the war, Benjamin Spock, who with others was charged with conspiracy to violate the Selective Service Act, and Daniel Ellsberg, charged with disclosing the Pentagon Papers, a classified account of the war.

Jonathan D. Bloom

Bourne, Randolph (Silliman) (*b* Bloomfield, N.J., 30 May 1886; *d* New York City, 23 Dec 1918). Critic. At Columbia University (graduated 1913) he came under the influence of John Dewey, Franz Boas, and Charles Beard. Deformed by spinal tuberculosis, he wrote anonymously of his disability in the *Atlantic* and was a regular contributor to the *New Republic.* In his writings Bourne drew a distinction between a "beloved community" arrived at through democratic association and the coercive cohesion of the nation-state. Bourne died in the influenza epidemic of 1918 in his apartment at 18 West Eighth Street.

Alexander Bloom

Bowery. A street in lower Manhattan that stretches for about 1 mile (1.6 kilometers) from Chatham Square to Cooper Square. Following the route of an American Indian path from the southern tip of the island to Harlem, it derives its name from *bowerij,* the Dutch word for farm, because in the seventeenth century it was a farming area north of the city. Governor Peter Stuyvesant bought much of the land there in 1651. The Bowery remained on the outer fringe of the city until about 1800, and it was most important as part of the main route to Boston. As the city's exploding population moved northward, the Bowery became broad and elegant, the home of such diverse personages as the philanthropist Peter Cooper and the songwriter Stephen Foster. It was especially important for entertainment, and its sidewalks were lined with taverns, oyster bars, and minstrel theaters. The largest auditorium on the continent, the Great Bowery Theater, was dedicated on 23 October 1826. Damaged and rebuilt on several occasions as a result of disastrous fires, it was one of several theaters in the area that dominated the theatrical life of the city between 1850 and 1875. After the Civil War the Bowery ceased to compete with Broadway as a commercial thoroughfare and with Fifth Avenue as an elegant residential address. Its specialty became nickel museums featuring mermaids, snakes, sword swallowers, lions, dwarfs, and women in various states of undress. At the same time that the Bowery became more closely associated with cheap entertainment, it was dealt a blow by the transportation system, from which it never recovered, when the Third Avenue elevated line was placed over it. After 26 August 1878 little steam engines showered pedestrians below with oil drippings and hot coals. Middle-class men and women could easily avoid such nuisances by walking along other streets, such as Broadway, that were not degraded by the ugly elevated lines. Meanwhile, the Bowery became synonymous with homeless derelicts and tramps. It was the site of cheap lodging houses, missions, and late-night saloons, and its brothels were so numerous that it became a veritable magnet for visiting sailors. In 1892 the Bowery was the butt of a popular song by Charles M. Hoyt:

> The Bowery, the Bowery!
> They say such things and they do such things
> On the Bowery, the Bowery!
> I'll never go there any more!

Early in the twentieth century the Bowery was even more infamous as a place of squalor, alcoholism, and wretchedness. Even prostitutes gravitated to other neighborhoods. In 1907 the street had 115 clothing stores for men and none for women. In the same year the nightly population of the "flop houses," missions, and hotels on the Bowery was estimated at 25,000. No other skid row in the United States attracted so many vagrants or so much notoriety. At the same time many stores along the street developed successful specialties in lighting fixtures and secondhand restaurant equipment.

After 1970 the homeless population of the Bowery sharply declined, as New York City dispersed its indigent to other neighborhoods. Efforts at gentrification also had powerful effects, and in the twenty-first century there was scarcely a vagrant in sight. Luxury apartment buildings and new restaurants began to appear, and with a few exceptions the Bowery no longer remained a sanctuary for the forgotten in American society.

Kenneth T. Jackson

Bowery Bay Beach. Original name of North Beach.

Bowery Mission. Christian mission founded in 1879 by Rev. A. G. Ruliffson. It is the third-oldest mission in the United States. In 1895 the Bowery Mission was purchased by the *Christian Herald,* a magazine and organization that today comprises the Bowery Mission and Kids with a Promise. The mission provides shelter, meals, medical services, and clothing for the homeless. It also runs a summer camp for impoverished children, after-school programs, and substance rehabilitation programs. It was founded at 14 Bowery and has moved several times since, always remaining in the same area. In the early twenty-first century it was located at 227 Bowery.

Max Seppo

Bowery Savings Bank. Savings bank formed on 2 June 1834 by a group of local business leaders who included Hamilton Fish, Peter C. Stuyvesant, and Anson G. Phelps. It initially occupied rent-free quarters in the Butchers' and Drovers' Bank (later a rival) on Bowery Street. Within two years the bank bought a building on 130 Bowery Street; this was redesigned in 1894 by the firm of McKim, Mead and White and declared a city landmark in 1966. The bank expanded and became one of the city's leading banks by 1860, when it had almost 42,000 depositors. The bank granted home loans and loans for large-scale construction projects. It built executive offices on 42nd Street near Park Avenue (a branch was moved into the building at 130 Bowery Street) in 1921. The bank funded such projects as Fordham Plaza, the Albee Square Shopping Mall, and the renovation of Times Square. The bank was acquired by the Greenpoint Savings Bank in 1995, which was sold to North Fork Bank in 2004 and to Capital One Bank in 2007.

Oscar Schisgall, *The Bowery Savings Bank of New York: A Social and Financial History of the Bowery Savings Bank* (New York: American Management Association, 1984)

James Bradley

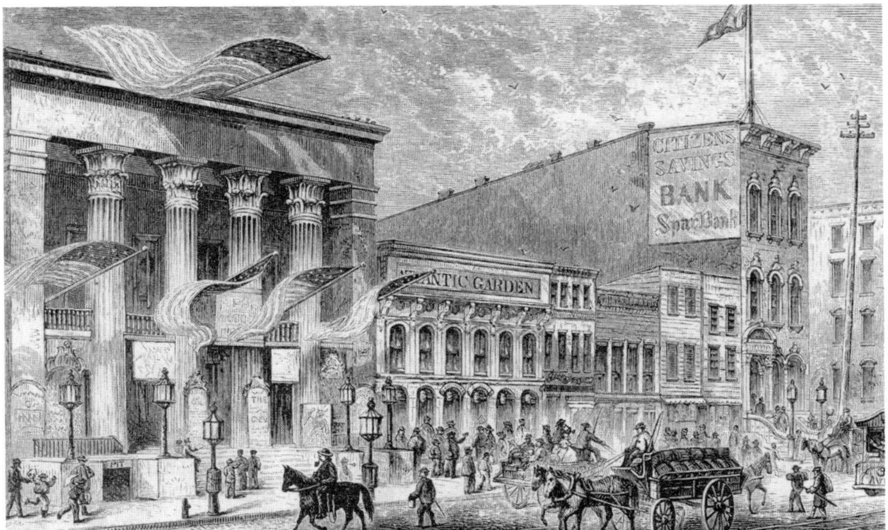

The Old Bowery Theatre

Bowery Theatre. Opened in 1826 at the corner of Canal Street and the Bowery, the Bowery Theatre was in competition with the Park Theatre on Park Row and offered a similar repertory. By the 1830s, however, it specialized in the melodrama and spectacle that appealed to residents of its immigrant neighborhood; foreign-language productions were mounted beginning in 1879. The theater burned in 1828, 1830, 1836, 1838, and 1845 and was rebuilt each time. It burned for the last time in 1929.

Don B. Wilmeth

Bowes, Edward (*b* San Francisco, 14 June 1874; *d* Rumson, N.J., 13 June 1946). Radio entertainer and real estate entrepreneur. Brought up in San Francisco, he did well in real estate, and the earthquake of 1906 proved only a temporary setback. After moving to New York City in 1918, he bought and built several theaters, including the Capitol, which he promoted on the radio. By 1935 he was the host of *Major Bowes' Amateur Hour,* broadcast first by the National Broadcasting Company (NBC) and then by the Columbia Broadcasting System (CBS) (his military title was from a reserve commission given to him as an entertainment specialist during World War I). The program's popularity led to road shows, a magazine, a staff of 65, and great wealth.

James E. Mooney

Bowling Green at Broadway, ca *1925–30, flanked by the Standard Office Building (right) and the Cunard Building (left)*

Bowling Green. Oldest existing park in New York City. Situated in lower Manhattan opposite the original fort at the foot of an

American Indian path (later Broadway), it was a parade ground and cattle market during the seventeenth and early eighteenth centuries. It became public property with the Dongan Charter of 1686. The Common Council leased it to three residents in 1733 at one peppercorn a year to use as a bowling green, "for the Beauty & Ornament of the Said Street" and "the Recreation & Delight of the Inhabitants of this City." In 1770 the British erected a gilded, equestrian statue of George III, which was toppled by irate citizens in 1776 and supposedly melted into ammunition. After the Revolution, elegant townhouses were built around the park, and during the early nineteenth century the small, ellipsoidal green was largely the private domain of their occupants. The public did not gain full access until about 1850 when the northward movement of residential Manhattan had led to the conversion of the townhouses to shipping offices. Eventually such nonresidential structures as the Produce Exchange and the U.S. Custom House replaced the townhouses. The city has modernized and restored the park numerous times: after the construction of the Interborough Rapid Transit Company subway station in 1905, just before the 1939 World's Fair, during the U.S. Bicentennial, and again in 1990 and 2004. Arturo Di Modica's bronze *Charging Bull* (1989) sits at the park's north end.

Margaret Latimer

Bowne, John (*b* Matlock, England, 1628; *d* ?Flushing, 1695). Religious dissenter. Dissatisfied with the Congregational town church in Boston, he moved from New England to Flushing, where in 1657 he converted to Quakerism. In 1662 he was arrested, imprisoned, and fined for holding Quaker meetings in his home. He sought an appeal from the directors of the Dutch West India Company, who instructed Governor Peter Stuyvesant not to persecute dissenters as long as they were not socially disruptive. His house at Bowne Street and 37th Avenue in Flushing still stands (see Bowne House).

Arthur J. Worrall

Bowne and Company. Firm of stationers and printers. Formed in 1775 at what is now 149 Pearl Street in Manhattan by Robert Bowne, it is one of the oldest continuously operating businesses in the United States. Initially it sold various goods that included stationery, cloth, cutlery, and furs. John Jacob Astor was an employee before he began his own fur-trading business. By the late 1820s the firm had narrowed its focus to stationery and commercial printing; later it became a leading financial printer. Bowne and Company became publicly owned in 1968 and is traded on the New York Stock Exchange. In the early twenty-first century its principal location was 55 Water Street, and there was also a retail branch at the South Street Seaport.

Bowne and Co., 1775–1952 (New York: Bowne and Company, 1952); *Nineteenth-Century Job Printing Display: The Poster* (New York: Bowne and Company, 1991)

Owen D. Gutfreund

Bowne House. Historic house. Built in Queens in 1661 by John Bowne and standing at Bowne Street and 37th Avenue in Flushing, it is a wood-frame English colonial saltbox, notable for its steeply pitched roof with three dormers. It was altered and expanded several times during the late seventeenth and early eighteenth centuries. Nine generations of Bowne's descendants lived in the structure until 1945, when the Bowne Historical Society assumed control of it. The house has original architectural details as well as seventeenth- and eighteenth-century documents, furniture, and artifacts that belonged to the family.

Jonathan Kuhn

boxing. One of the first noted American fighters was a former slave from Staten Island, Bill Richmond (1763–1829), who had a distinguished career in England. The first recognized boxing match in the United States was between Jacob Hyer and Tom Bealey in New York City in 1816. The city was the national center of boxing when the sport became popular in the 1840s, when it was illegal. Fighters were mainly Irish and English professionals or tough Americans associated with rival ethnic and political gangs. The first national championship was won by Tom Hyer of New York City (son of Jacob Hyer) over Yankee Sullivan in 1849. Sullivan claimed the title after Hyer's retirement but lost it to John Morrissey of New York City in 1853. The sport declined during the 1860s and had little following. Matches were either impromptu or arranged in sporting taverns like Harry Hill's Dance Hall. World heavyweight champion John L. Sullivan defended his title in the city in 1883, but because of interference by the police there were no important matches from 1885 until the early 1890s, when boxing was revived at Coney Island under the protection of political bosses. In 1896 the state legislature liberalized the restrictions on boxing by passing the Horton Act, and New York City again became the national boxing capital. Notable bouts included Jim Jeffries' defeat of James J. Corbett for the world heavyweight championship on 11 May 1900. The Horton Act was repealed in the same year, and from that time bouts were held in secret on barges, in the backrooms of saloons, or at ostensibly private clubs where restrictions on boxing went unenforced. In 1911 the state legislature, controlled by the Democrats, passed the Frawley Act, which permitted 10-round "no decision" bouts under the supervision of an athletic commission. Venues ranged from small neighborhood firetraps like the Sharkey Athletic Club to Madison Square Garden and Ebbets Field. In 1913 alone there were 49 licensed clubs in the city. The Frawley Act was repealed in 1917 by Republican reformers.

A supervisory athletic commission reestablished boxing in 1920 with the Walker Act. Madison Square Garden became the leading venue for boxing in the nation. Control of the ring passed from politicians to members of organized crime, like Waxey Gordon, Dutch Schultz, and Owney Madden. Poor neighborhoods continued to produce the majority of fighters, including the Irish heavyweight champions Gene Tunney (1926–29) and Jimmy Braddock (1935–37). Among the many famous bouts of the interwar years were several for the heavyweight championship, including victories by Jack Dempsey over Luis Firpo on 14 September 1923 (drawing 82,000 spectators at the Polo Grounds), by Joe Louis over Max Schmeling on 19 June 1936, in 2:04 of the first round (drawing 75,000 at Yankee Stadium), and by Louis over Billy Conn on 18 June 1941 (drawing 54,487 at the Polo Grounds). Louis was associated with the nation's dominant promoter, Mike Jacobs, who staged three-eighths of all championships in the United States between 1937 and 1949. After Jacobs retired, the main promoter was the International Boxing Club; run by James Norris and closely tied to the organized-crime figure Frankie Carbo, it arranged 80 percent of all championship fights from 1949 to 1953. Prominent local fighters during these years included the middleweight champions Rocky Graziano (1947–48) and Jake La Motta (1949–51). Boxing's popularity declined in the late 1950s from overexposure on television (audience shares fell from 31 percent to 10.6 percent); investigations of its corruption; the level of its violence, which could lead to the death of fighters (such as that of Benny Paret, who died on 24 March 1962, several days after a televised fight with Emile Griffith for the welterweight championship); and competition from other sports. In 1956 Floyd Patterson, a native of New York City, won the world heavyweight championship at the age of 21; he held it for three years until being knocked out in an upset by Ingemar Johansson at Yankee Stadium. Only 18,215 attended the fight, and net receipts were only $407,000, but media income, which included closed-circuit television, exceeded $900,000. In 1960 Patterson became the first heavyweight to regain the title, which he lost again in 1962 to Sonny Liston. On 8 March 1971 the city was the site of a historic fight between Joe Frazier and Muhammad Ali at Madison Square Garden before 29,445 spectators and a closed-circuit audience of 1.3 million. The fight was nicknamed the Fight of the Century and advertised as the only one ever held between two undefeated heavyweights, each of whom had a legitimate claim to the world championship.

Frazier won by a unanimous decision. In 1987 Mike Tyson, originally from Brooklyn, became the first world heavyweight champion from the city in a quarter-century; in 1990 he lost the title, which in the following years was held by two more fighters from Brooklyn, Riddick Bowe (1992–93) and Michael Moorer (1994).

While the emergence of cable and pay-per-view television lessened the importance of gate receipts for promoters and many of the most glamorous fights were held by gambling casinos in Las Vegas and Atlantic City, New Jersey, Madison Square Garden continued to host memorable fights in the 1990s and early twenty-first century. The 11 July 1996 heavyweight bout between Riddick Bowe and Andrew Golota ended in chaos that spread from the ring into the audience after Golota was disqualified for punching below the belt; more than a dozen spectators and a number of police officers had to be taken to the hospital, and 16 people were arrested. Evander Holyfield and Lennox Lewis fought for the heavyweight title on 13 March 1999; Holyfield was awarded the victory, but the crowd and most experts believed that Lewis had clearly been the superior fighter and that the bout may have been fixed. Several important fights were held at the Garden in the early twenty-first century, including the middleweight championship won by Bernard Hopkins over Felix Trinidad on 29 September 2001. In 2007 the 82-year-old boxing ring that had been transported from the two previous Madison Square Gardens was replaced and sent to the International Boxing Hall of Fame after a final welterweight fight in which Miguel Cotto defeated Zab Judah of Brooklyn. The new Garden ring soon began to develop a legacy of its own as it hosted a January 2008 fight in which Roy Jones, Jr., defeated Trinidad in a contest that was publicized as a clash between the two best fighters of their generation.

Steven A. Riess, *City Games: The Evolution of American Urban Society and the Rise of Sports* (Urbana: University of Illinois Press, 1989)

Steven A. Riess, David White

Boys and Girls Clubs of America. National nonprofit organization formed to provide youths with a positive alternative to roaming the streets. Established in 1906 as the Boys' Club Federation of America by the incorporation of 53 local clubs, in 1930 it moved to New York City where it occupied offices near Grand Central Terminal. Herbert Hoover was its chairman from 1936 until his death in 1964. In 1960 the organization dedicated a national headquarters at 771 First Avenue, across the street from the United Nations building, where it was based until moving to Atlanta in 1994. In the early twenty-first century more than a dozen local clubs throughout New York City were active in fulfilling the organization's mission to build character and leadership skills in young people through educational programs, the arts, athletics, and community outreach.

James Bradley

Boys and Girls High School. Secondary school opened in 1878 as the Central Grammar School at Court and Livingston streets in Brooklyn. It is the oldest public high school in New York City. The girls' division moved in 1886 to a new building designed by James W. Naughton at Nostrand Avenue, and in 1891 the names of the schools were changed to reflect their status as two separate institutions: Boys High School and Girls High School. Boys High School moved to a building designed by Naughton in the Romanesque Revival style on Madison Street. Girls High School closed in 1964. In 1976 Boys High School moved to 1700 Fulton Street, began admitting girls, and was again named Boys and Girls High School; its former building was designated a city landmark in 1975 and now houses the Street Academy, an alternative high school. In 2010 Boys and Girls High School enrolled about 4300 students. Well-known alumni include Aaron Copland, Isaac Asimov, Norman Mailer, Lena Horne, and Shirley Chisholm.

Erica Judge

Boys' Club of New York. Organization founded in 1876 by Edward H. Harriman, a Wall Street tycoon and railroad magnate who gave the organization about $500,000 over the next 33 years. It began operations in the basement of the Wilson Mission School at Avenue A and Eighth Street near Tompkins Square in lower Manhattan. From the beginning the club welcomed any boy between the ages of six and 17 and sought especially to serve the needs of the immigrant poor. In 1901 it moved to a new six-story brick and sandstone building at Avenue A and 10th Street. A seven-story addition, replete with an indoor pool, a gymnasium, and a library, opened in 1917. In 1927 the club added a branch at 321 East 111th Street in Jefferson Park, a heavily Italian section of East Harlem. E. Roland Harriman, son of the founder, became president in 1934 at the age of 38. He served the club for 57 years, successively as a trustee, president, and chairman. The building at Tompkins Square was renamed the Harriman clubhouse in 1988. In the early twenty-first century the organization had tens of thousands of alumni throughout the United States.

Sharon Zane, *The Boys' Club of New York: A History* (New York: Boys' Club, 1990)

Kenneth T. Jackson

Boys' High School. Original name of DeWitt Clinton High School.

BQE. See Brooklyn–Queens Expressway.

Brace, Charles Loring (*b* Litchfield, Conn., 19 June 1826; *d* Switzerland, 11 Aug 1890). Minister and social worker. He graduated from Yale University in 1846 and later studied at the Union Theological Seminary in Manhattan. In the early 1850s he began working with homeless, unschooled, immigrant boys in New York City. With the assistance of several prominent New Yorkers he formed the Children's Aid Society in 1853, of which he was the executive officer for the next 37 years. A staunch believer in self-help, he opposed charitable aid that might encourage dependence. He acquired an international reputation as a practitioner of the "new philanthropy" by explaining the basic principles of assistance to the poor in books and articles such as *The Dangerous Classes of New York and Twenty Years' Work among Them* (1872). At his death his son Charles Loring Brace, Jr. (1855–1938) succeeded him as executive secretary of the society. His memoir *The Life of Charles Loring Brace, Chiefly Told in His Own Letters, Edited by His Daughter* was published in 1894.

Jane Allen

Bradford, William (*b* Leicestershire, England, 1663; *d* New York City, 1752). Printer. Generally considered to be the first printer in colonial New York City, he was apprenticed to the English Quaker printer Andrew Sowle, whose daughter he married in 1685, shortly before immigrating to Pennsylvania. He ran into a series of problems with Quaker authorities in that city and in 1692 was jailed for printing pamphlets by the contentious heretic George Keith. Governor Benjamin Fletcher brought him to New York City some months later, where he became the official—and only—printer in the colony until 1726, when his onetime apprentice John Peter Zenger set up a rival press.

Bradford printed official documents, including the first edition of the *Laws of New York* in 1710, as well as private publications. The first book printed in the colony, appearing in May 1693, shortly after Bradford's move to the city, was Keith's *New-England's Spirit of Persecution Transmitted to Pennsilvania.* Among the other "firsts" that came from Bradford's establishment on Hanover Square were the first play published in the colony, the first printed map of New York (the Bradford–Lyne map of 1731), and the first newspaper (the *New-York Gazette* in 1725).

Jean Ashton

Brady, Diamond Jim [James Buchanan] (*b* New York City, 12 Aug 1856; *d* Atlantic City, N.J., 13 April 1917). Businessman. The son of a saloon keeper on the West Side, he was born at 90 West Street and lived there until the age of 11. After working as a bellboy and messenger and for the New York Central Railroad he began selling portable rail-cutting saws in 1879, beginning a successful career as a salesman of railroad equipment, during which he earned as much as $1 million a year. He frequented well-known restaurants, nightclubs, and theaters and became known for his voracious appetite, lavish attire (he owned 30 complete sets of jewelry with a total value of more than $1 million), sweet and sympathetic nature, willingness to spend money on himself and others, and partiality toward attractive women. His friendship with Lillian Russell was the subject of much speculation. From about 1900 Brady's home was at 7 West 86th Street.

George A. Thompson, Jr.

Brady, Mathew B. (*b* Warren County, N.Y., *ca* 1823; *d* New York City, 15 Jan 1896). Early photographer. He mastered the daguerreotype process from the photographic pioneer Samuel F. B. Morse and foresaw a role for photography in preserving the historical record. In 1844 he opened the Daguerrian Miniature Gallery, a studio and portrait gallery on Broadway at Fulton Street. This proved successful both artistically and commercially, and from 1845 to 1850 he photographed the most important figures of his time. *A Gallery of Illustrious Americans* (1850), published with the lithographer Francis D'Avignon, includes portraits from Brady's daguerreotypes of Andrew Jackson, Daniel Webster, and John J. Audubon. In 1853 Brady built a larger and more lavish studio at 359 Broadway, near Franklin Street. A third studio stood at 643 Broadway, and his last and most lavish studio opened in the summer of 1860 at 785 Broadway, at 10th Street. His profits rose as thousands of customers returned to be photographed with the new collodian wet-plate process, which allowed multiple prints from a single negative. Brady seldom operated the camera himself and instead employed "operators," many of whom later established their own careers as photographers, including Timothy O'Sullivan (*b ca* 1840; *d* 1882) and Alexander Gardner (1821–82). One of Brady's most well-known pictures was of Abraham Lincoln taken the day Lincoln spoke at Cooper Union on 27 February 1860. He was forced to declare bankruptcy in 1871 after incurring debts from his best-known and most ambitious project, the documentation of the Civil War. He never regained the popularity he had enjoyed earlier but remained one of the most influential American photographers of the nineteenth century. His last residence was at 127 East 10th Street.

James D. Horan, *Mathew Brady: Historian with a Camera* (New York: Crown, 1955); Roy Meredith, *Mathew Brady's Portrait of an Era* (New York: W. W. Norton, 1982)

Dale L. Neighbors

Brady, William V(ermilye) (*b* New York City, 1811; *d* New York City, 31 March 1870). Mayor. A fiscally conservative Whig, he served as mayor of New York City from 1847 to 1848. During his tenure his proposal to eliminate the newly created police department was rejected by the Common Council. He later served as the city's postmaster.

Howard Kaplan

Brando, Marlon (*b* Omaha, Neb., 3 April 1924; *d* Los Angeles 1 July 2004). Actor. He moved to New York City as a 19-year-old ditch digger who had been expelled from his military high school. He enrolled in the Dramatic Workshop of the New School for Social Research, under Stella Adler, where he quickly impressed his peers with his mastery of the Method style of acting. In 1947, after acting in a number of smaller productions, Brando landed the role of Stanley Kowalski in the Broadway opening of Tennessee Williams's *A Streetcar Named Desire.* The show went up at the Ethel Barrymore Theater on 3 December 1947 under the direction of Elia Kazan. Brando's performance electrified audiences and critics alike, and many say it revolutionized acting technique in the United States. He went on to play the same role in the play's film adaptation. Brando is perhaps most famous for his film portrayals of two fictional but quintessentially New York characters: Terry Malloy, a longshoreman on the Red Hook piers in Elia Kazan's *On the Waterfront* (1954); and Don Vito Corleone, an Italian immigrant and Mafia patriarch, in Francis Ford Coppola's *The Godfather* (1972). He spent most of his life in Hollywood and Tahiti.

Rowan Moore Gerety

Bratton, William J. (*b* Boston, 6 Oct 1947). Former New York City police commissioner. After serving for several years in Boston's police department, in 1990 he was appointed chief to New York City's transit police. In 1994 he was appointed the 38th commissioner of the New York Police Department by Mayor Rudolph Giuliani. Bratton introduced the CompStat system of tracking crimes, a real-time police intelligence computer system, which the police department continued to use into the twenty-first century. Bratton left his position in 1996 after alleged personal conflicts with Giuliani and afterward directed police operations in Los Angeles (where he resigned in 2009).

William Bratton and Peter Knobler, *Turnaround: How America's Top Cop Reversed the Crime Epidemic* (New York: Random House, 1998)

Jessica Montesano

Brearley School. Private girls' secondary school opened in 1884 in Manhattan by Samuel Brearley, Jr., who had intended to teach at a boys' school but was persuaded by Mrs. Joseph H. Choate to remedy the shortage of good schools for young women. To fund its operations he borrowed several thousand dollars from a classmate at Harvard, Charles Bonaparte (a great-nephew of Napoleon). The school was so successful that by the second year it had to turn away students. After occupying many locations Brearley moved to 610 East 83rd Street in 1930. In the early twenty-first century it had an enrollment of about 670 students.

Richard Schwartz

Breezy Point. Neighborhood in southwestern Queens at the western tip of the Rockaway Peninsula; it includes the communities of Breezy Point, Rockaway Point, and Roxbury. The area remained undeveloped until the early twentieth century, when the Rockaway Point Company rented tent sites for about $20 a summer to visitors, most of whom were Irish. By the 1920s a colony of residents owned bungalows on rented land. In 1961 the firm of Northern Properties paid $17.5 million for all the land west of Jacob Riis Park (except Fort Tilden) to erect a high-rise development to house 220,000. To protect their cottages, residents formed the Breezy Point Cooperative and paid $11.5 million for the land. Construction began on two 14-story apartment buildings but ceased when the city announced plans to acquire the peninsula for parkland in 1963; the unfinished apartments were demolished in 1978. The city intended to condemn the three communities, but residents forced a compromise that permitted all to remain; city-owned land became part of the Gateway National Recreation Area, while property of the Breezy Point Cooperative was excluded. After this, more residents winterized their property. In the early twenty-first century the private, gated communities had 2836 houses, about three-quarters inhabited year-round, the rest seasonal cottages; no buildable lots remain. Full-time residents number about 5000, but the population swells by thousands more in summer. In 2009 Breezy Point was nearly 99 percent white, the majority Irish American. The communities have three of the last volunteer fire companies in the city: Rockaway Point, Point Breeze, and Roxbury.

Jeffrey A. Kroessler

Breslin, Jimmy [James] (*b* Jamaica, Queens, 17 Oct 1930). Journalist and novelist. With his Irish Catholic working-class roots, he brought an outer borough perspective to the New York City media. Along with writers like Tom Wolfe, Breslin embodied the style of New Journalism, often becoming a participant in his own stories. After attending Long Island University (1948–50), Breslin worked as a sportswriter for a number of city newspapers and magazines, including the *New York Journal-American*. He was later a columnist for the *New York Herald-Tribune* and the *New York Post;* in the early 1960s he and Wolfe became staff writers for the *Herald-Tribune*'s Sunday supplement, which in 1968 became *New York* magazine. In 1969 Breslin blurred the line between journalism and politics and ran for president of the City Council under mayoral candidate Norman Mailer, with a platform that sought to make New York City the 51st state of the United States. Breslin maintained an extensive network of contacts with city officials, police officers, politicians, and mobsters. He endured a violent beating by the Lucchese mob family in 1970 after writing an article about a family member; the same year, he published his first novel, *The Gang That Couldn't Shoot Straight,* a Brooklyn Mafia comedy. Since 1982 Breslin has been married to former New York City Council member Ronnie Eldridge; his first wife died in 1981. Through the twentieth century Breslin continued to write novels about working-class cops, mobsters, immigrants, and race and religion in New York City; he won the Pulitzer Prize in 1986 for his newspaper columns. In 2008 Breslin, who lived on Central Park West, published *The Good Rat,* a collection of stories about the Mafia.

Kate Lauber

Bretons. Bretons began immigrating to the United States from Brittany in the early twentieth century. They were distinguished from other French citizens by their Celtic origin, and about 40 percent of those who immigrated spoke a Celtic language closely related to Welsh. Although at first most entered the United States through the Port of New York and settled in central New Jersey, during the late 1940s New York City became the center of Breton American life. Soon after their arrival, Bretons were widely distributed in the workforce and were well known for the crepe restaurants they owned and managed. Additionally, Bretons formed the Stade Breton, a sporting association in New York City, and the Breton Association of the United States, a sponsor of cultural and social events. At the end of the twentieth century, an estimated 90,000 Breton immigrants and their descendants lived in New York City.

Paul Robert Magocsi

Brevoort, James Renwick (*b* Yonkers, N.Y., 20 July 1832; *d* Yonkers, 15 Dec 1918). Landscape painter. He grew up in Williamsbridge and Fordham, in what is now the Bronx, and in 1850 began to study architecture, working as an assistant to his cousin James Renwick, Jr., whom he helped to prepare designs for St. Patrick's Cathedral. In 1854 he earned a certificate in architecture from the School of Design at New York University, and he soon enrolled at the National Academy of Design, where he mounted exhibitions from 1856 to 1901. His work was also shown at the Brooklyn Art Association between 1861 and 1881. He lived on 10th Street from 1858 to 1861 and at 212 Fifth Avenue from 1863 to 1872. During the 1870s and 1880s he often traveled and worked in Europe, primarily in England, Italy, and the Netherlands; he returned to Yonkers in 1890, built a house at 390 North Broadway, and between 1898 and 1906 also maintained a residence at 52 East 23rd Street. Brevoort's paintings are leading examples of a phase in American landscape painting known as Native Impressionism and American Luminism.

Allen J. Share

brewing and distilling. Brewing was a small-scale industry in New York City during the seventeenth century. English techniques and a top-floating yeast were used to produce beer, ale, and porter, which did not require cooling. Sold in local markets, they were consumed warm. The first brewery was established by the Dutch governor Peter Minuit in 1633 in a log cabin in Marckvelt (Market Field), which would today lie in the financial district. Distilling was a separate undertaking confined mostly to the production of rum, using sugar cane transported from the West Indies by colonial merchants. By 1770 there were four distilleries in Manhattan and 12 others nearby that produced rum for sale locally and abroad. When whiskey displaced rum as the most popular liquor during the early nineteenth century, the distilling industry gradually moved west. Both industries were transformed by new technology. Spirits were bought by wholesale firms in the city that colored, flavored, and bottled them and sent them to retailers, often saloons. German brewers who settled in the city during the 1840s introduced yeasts that required cool temperatures and produced "lager," or stored beer, which became especially popular in the summer heat. Brewing flourished for a time after water of good quality became widely available. The Hell Gate Brewery, opened by the German immigrant George Ehret in 1866, was the country's largest in 1877, and that of Jacob Ruppert was the eighth largest. In 1879 the number of breweries reached 78 in Manhattan and 43 in Brooklyn; those numbers declined after 1880, when cheap rail transportation and mechanical refrigeration allowed entrepreneurs in Milwaukee, St. Louis, and Cincinnati to make inroads into local markets. As successful breweries made larger investments in production and distribution facilities, small firms disappeared. In 1895 the Hell Gate Brewery was the country's fourth largest, Ruppert the 12th largest. By 1910 there were only 39 breweries in the city; they usually sold their beverages in kegs through saloons under their control. Formed by western suppliers in 1899, the Distilling Company of America made its headquarters in New York City and sought unsuccessfully to dominate the spirits trade. It was reorganized as National Distillers Products in 1932.

Advertisement of Bernheimer and Schwartz, Pilsner Brewing Company, 1911

Under the 18th Amendment the manufacture, transportation, and sale of alcoholic beverages became forbidden in 1920. Some breweries declared bankruptcy, while others reorganized to make such products as soft drinks and ice cream. Many New Yorkers defied Prohibition, and illegal factories opened locally to supply their needs. Such efforts became known nationally through news media based in the city and led much of the country to conclude that Prohibition had failed to reduce liquor consumption effectively. After the repeal of the 18th Amendment in 1933, 23 of the city's brewers resumed business, most aiming their products only at the large local market. Stores displaced saloons as the most important retail outlets, and brewers expanded their sales of bottled beer. Canned beer was introduced that same decade. Only the firm of F and M Schaefer Brewing sought to compete in national markets. After 1937 the firm of Seagram's had its headquarters in the city and was the world's largest distiller. National Distillers Products became National Distillers and Chemical after 1948 and was one of four large companies that dominated the American distilling industry to the end of the 1960s. Between the late 1940s and the mid-1970s brewing in the city declined, as small firms were forced out of business by large companies with national distribution. The country's four largest firms (none in the city) increased their share of the national market from 21 percent to 59 percent. By 1950 only five local firms brewed beer, and brewers blamed the city's high electricity and water rates for their inability to compete. The country's second-largest brewer, Joseph Schlitz, bought the Hell Gate Brewery in 1949 and maintained operations there until 1973, when it withdrew to escape the city's high labor costs and invest in newer facilities. The city's last brewery closed in 1976. During the 1980s expensive beers were produced in small quantities for exclusive markets by newly opened microbreweries. In 1987 National Distillers and Chemical sold its liquor division to American Brands. The Brooklyn Brewery opened in 1987 and produces most of its beer upstate in Utica. In 1996 the Harlem Brewing company started its Sugar Hill brand, which is brewed in Saratoga Springs (the name was inspired by the Sugar Hill neighborhood in Harlem). Two well-known microbreweries are the Times Square Brewery, at 210 West 42nd Street, and the Chelsea Brewing Company, on Pier 59.

Stanley Wade Baron, *Brewed in America: A History of Beer and Ale in the United States* (Boston: Little, Brown, 1962)

K. Austin Kerr

Briarwood. Neighborhood in east central Queens, bounded to the north by Union Turnpike, to the east by Parsons Boulevard, to the south by Hillside Avenue, and to the west by the Van Wyck Expressway. The area was first developed about 1905 by Herbert A. O'Brien; the name was suggested by his wife, Adeline, for the thick woods and briars covering the land. The Briarwood Land Company later declared bankruptcy and the area remained largely undeveloped until the mid-1920s, when it was divided into lots that were sold at auction. Together with the New York Life Insurance Company the United Nations built Parkway Village in 1947 to provide housing for its staff members. The development became a cooperative in 1983 and housed residents of many nationalities, although by that time few worked for the United Nations. Several apartment buildings rise above the surrounding one- and two-family houses. Briarwood has been traditionally, and remained in the twenty-first century, a diverse community with a population nearly equally divided among many ethnic groups. Well-known residents have included the diplomat Ralph Bunche, the feminist and social activist Betty Friedan, and the civil rights leader Roy Wilkins.

Plan for New York City, 1969: A Proposal, vol. 5 (Cambridge, Mass.: MIT Press, 1969)

Patricia A. Doyal

Brice, Fanny [Borach, Fannie] (*b* New York City, 29 Oct 1891; *d* Los Angeles, 29 May 1951). Comedian. She became known for performing songs and parodies of the arts and society in such revues on Broadway as Florenz Ziegfeld's *Follies* between 1910 and 1920. She lived from 1914 to 1918 at 8 West 58th Street and from 1918 to 1921 at 230 Central Park West. In the early 1920s she bought a house at 306 West 76th Street, where she lived with Nicky Arnstein until their divorce in 1927. She then had an apartment at 15 East 69th Street (now the Westbury Hotel) and lived there with Billy Rose after they were married in February 1929. She became well known in Rose's musical revues *Sweet and Low* (1930) and *Crazy Quilt* (1931). During the 1930s and 1940s she performed as "Baby Snooks" on the radio. Brice was portrayed by Brooklyn-born Barbra Streisand in the musical *Funny Girl* (1964, film version 1968) and the motion picture *Funny Lady* (1975). Brice was the first female Jewish comedian to work successfully in musical comedy and radio in the commercial mainstream.

Barbara Wallace Grossman, *Funny Woman: The Life and Times of Fanny Brice* (Bloomington: Indiana University Press, 1991)

Barbara Cohen–Stratyner

Brick Presbyterian Church. Church founded in 1767 by the Reverend John Rodgers. The church was first located on Beekman Street, but moved to Fifth Avenue and 37th Street in 1858 as many of its members moved uptown to that area. It moved again in 1940 to Park Avenue and 91st Street, where it remains today. The church has been in continuous operation since its founding, save for a brief closure during the Revolutionary War, and currently has more than 1200 members. Noted members of the congregation have included New York governor Edmund Morgan, U.S. Secretary of State John Foster Dulles, and IBM founder Thomas J. Watson. Charles Dickinson, the church organist and choirmaster from 1909 to 1965, founded the School of Sacred Music at Union Theological Seminary and the American Guild of Organists.

Sarah Brafman

bricks. From Dutch times, brick has been the most popular construction material used in New York City buildings. It is fireproof and, since the soft clay of the nearby lower Hudson Valley was ideal for making bricks, both readily available and inexpensive. The demand for bricks went through four stages before 1900. In colonial times it was the common material for almost all buildings, residential and commercial, and there were kilns throughout the city (one in the 1740s was located on the site of City Hall Park). From 1800 to 1840 brick was identified with fashionable construction in Federal-style houses, often with a brownstone facade produced by applying a layer of soft New Jersey sandstone. At mid-century there appeared a new, ornamental style of brick residential construction in the Greek Revival style, which had originated in Philadelphia and used fine-grained, smooth-faced "pressed brick" of a uniform red. After the Civil War the upper classes favored stone houses, and brick houses tended to be occupied by workers. ("Brick is getting too common for first-class fashionable houses," sniffed a newspaper in the 1860s.)

Bricks were made in many sizes, shapes, and colors. "No regulation appears to exist in the United States beyond the custom of the place and the caprice of the maker," one observer of American construction observed in 1839. Brick size was finally standardized in 1899 at 8¼ by 2½ by 4 inches. During a boom in building brick apartment houses in the 1940s and 1950s, a new "jumbo" size brick was developed, and later bricks the size of tiles were used in city buildings.

Brickworkers and bricklayers were united in craft unions from the early 1800s, maintaining prices by collectively shutting down works and pressing employers for shorter working days. The 10-hour work day, which arrived in New York in the 1830s, was largely brought about by brickworkers. Their efforts in favor of the eight-hour day failed in a wave of unsuccessful strikes in 1868. Long independent of the other building trades, bricklayers finally united with plasterers and masons to form a union with 130,000 workers in 1928 and 149,000 in 1973.

Charles Lockwood, *Bricks and Brownstones: The New York Row House* (New York: Abbeville Press, 1972); Irwin Yellowitz, "Eight Hours and the Bricklayers' Strike of 1868," in *Essays in the History of New York City: A Memorial to Sidney Pomerantz,* ed. Irwin Yellowitz (Port Washington, N.Y.: Kennikat Press, 1978); John D. Stewart, ed., *The Schermerhorn Row Block: A Study in Nineteenth-Century Building Technology in New York City* (Waterford, N.Y.: New York State Parks, Recreation, and Historic Preservation, Bureau of Historic Sites, 1981)

John Rousmaniere

Bridewell. A name once used to refer to certain prisons in Manhattan. The first Bridewell in the city was built in 1734, the second in 1775 at City Hall, near where the Sons of Liberty fought to maintain the liberty pole. The site became a rallying point for protests against the British, and the jail was first used to imprison and punish patriots and revolutionary soldiers. After the Revolutionary War it was used as a city jail.

William Jackson Davis, *Reminiscences of the City of New York and Its Vicinity* (New York: Privately printed, 1855)

Joseph P. Viteritti

bridge. Card game. It was introduced to New York City in 1893 by Henry I. Barbey, a banker and yachtsman who lived in Europe for many years and wrote the first book of rules for the game. Initially called auction bridge, it became popular in clubs, schools, and hotels but was supplanted in the mid-1920s by a new version known as contract bridge, for which rules were set and published by the Whist Club of New York. The Cavendish Club was formed in 1925 by Wilbur F. Whitehead and for the next eight years met at the Mayfair Hotel, which became the most important gathering place for bridge players and sponsored the Cavendish Trophy from 1928. The club itself met in a succession of hotels that included the Ritz Tower and Carlton House, and in 1941 it became a nonprofit membership corporation. The city was made the site of the Eastern States Regionals, first held in 1929. Local newspapers published bridge columns edited by such experts as Albert H. Morehead, who worked for the *New York Times* from 1935 until 1963, when he was succeeded by Alan F. Truscott. New York City lies in the 24th district of the American Contract Bridge League and is the site of the Fun City Regionals, launched in 1970.

James E. Mooney

Bridge Apartments. Four high-rise buildings above the Manhattan approach to the George Washington Bridge between Audubon and Wadsworth avenues and West 178th and 179th streets. In 1960 Kratter Corporation made the innovative purchase of the air rights above the public highway; Brown and Guenther designed the 32-story towers, which were New York City's first housing with aluminum curtain walls. The 960 Mitchell–Lama subsidized apartments filled quickly in 1964, but tenants complained of traffic noise and fumes. Later the U.S. Environmental Protection Agency demonstrated that the buildings acted like chimneys, drawing fumes up from the roadway, which should have been covered over and mechanically ventilated. Rents increased and services declined; a rent strike in 1972 changed little. In the early twenty-first century, the buildings, though still occupied, were in deteriorated condition.

See also Mitchell–Lama.

Cathy Alexander

Bridge Café. Historic restaurant located at 279 Water Street in Manhattan. In 1794 Newell Narme opened a "grocery and wine and porter bottler" in the then-two-and-a-half-story wooden building with a peaked roof. Since that time the building has been the site of a series of food and drinking enterprises, eventually becoming the oldest continuous business establishment in New York City. In 1888 the exterior of the building was altered to its present form. During much of the nineteenth century, the building was described in city directories variously as a grocery, a porterhouse, or simply a liquor establishment. (The New York City Board of Excise issued tavern licenses to groceries throughout much of the nineteenth century, allowing alcoholic beverages to be consumed on the premises.) One notable tenant was Henry Williams, who operated a porterhouse and brothel there from 1847 to 1860. The prostitutes were actually listed in the 1855 New York census. Then in 1859 Thomas Norton became a lessee and porterhouse keeper and remained until 1881. The current owners bought the building in 1979 and named it the Bridge Café. They upgraded the restaurant and bar but kept the charming 1920s interior. While in office, Mayor Edward I. Koch regularly had dinner there and declared it to be his favorite restaurant.

Richard McDermott

Bridgemarket. High-end commercial complex. The $24 million, 98,000-square-foot (9104-square-meter) space opened in 1999 under the Queensboro Bridge. In the early twenty-first century the complex includes a flagship Food Emporium, Guastavino's restaurant, the Terence Conran shop, and a public plaza designed by Lynden Miller. Before its conception the Bridgemarket space was run down and inhabited by vagrants. The design process of the space began as early as 1977. The building combines a modern glass and steel pavilion with historic preservation of tile vaults and terra-cotta details under the bridge's vaults.

Jessica Montesano

bridges. There are 2027 bridges serving New York City, of which 76 are over water, 329 are used by railroads, 1011 are over land, and the rest are in parks, serve subways, or are private pedestrian bridges. Because the city is virtually an archipelago (only the Bronx is connected to the mainland), bridges are necessary for motor vehicles, trains, subways, and to a lesser extent pedestrians. The first bridge in the city was the King's Bridge (1693; demolished and buried in 1917), a small structure of stone and timber that spanned Spuyten Duyvil Creek between Manhattan and what is now the Bronx. It was built by the Philipse family and a toll was required to cross it until 1759, when the Farmer's Free Bridge (demolished 1911) opened over the Harlem River and forced the King's Bridge to become free as well. Other bridges over the Harlem River included Dyckman's Bridge (1756); Coles Bridge (1795, also known as the Harlem Bridge), a toll timber drawbridge at East 129th Street with a span of 300 feet (91.5 meters) and a width of 24 feet (7.3 meters); and Macombs Dam Bridge (1813), a low stationary toll bridge at 155th Street, built to furnish power for milling, that allowed the tide to flow in but not out. The dam was destroyed in 1838 in a raid by more than 100 angry citizens who believed that it illegally blocked a navigable stream. An unsuccessful suit by the owners of the bridge against those who had destroyed the dam established the precedent that the right to free passage to "an arm of the sea" can be limited only by the U.S. Congress. The High Bridge was built in 1837–48 to carry the large water pipes of the Croton Aqueduct system over the Harlem River. The early vehicular bridges provided access to the post roads leading to Albany (New York) and Boston but were of lesser use to most New Yorkers, who were concentrated in lower Manhattan and surrounded on two sides by water that could be crossed only by sloop, raft, canoe, or dinghy, and later by steam-powered ferry. In 1869 the parks department of New

Throgs Neck Bridge, 2009

Marine Parkway Bridge, 2009

took several attempts. Two train tunnels and two vehicular tunnels were built beneath before the construction of the GEORGE WASHINGTON BRIDGE (1931), a graceful structure designed by Othmar H. Ammann. Unlike the Brooklyn Bridge and other suspension bridges before it, the George Washington Bridge was built of bare steel, without granite cladding or architectural ornament. Ammann adhered to the same principle in his later bridges: the Triborough Bridge (1936), the BRONX–WHITESTONE BRIDGE (1939), the THROGS NECK BRIDGE (1961), and the VERRAZANO–NARROWS BRIDGE (1964). Severe cutbacks in bridge maintenance and repair in the 1970s and 1980s led to structural problems and occasional closings. In the late 1990s and in the twenty-first century the city began spending more than $3 billion on major rehabilitations of many of the city's aging bridges, including the Manhattan, Queensboro, Williamsburg, and Brooklyn bridges. Over the Harlem

York City was given authority over the bridges spanning the Harlem River and their approach streets, thus extending the city's direct jurisdiction beyond its northern border before it annexed what later became the Bronx.

The city's economy depended on a system of waterborne transport that was frequently interrupted by ice and fog, prompting demands for more reliable links, especially between Manhattan and Brooklyn. In the 1850s builders of suspension bridges became confident of their ability to span the East River, and in 1883 John Augustus Roebling and his son Washington completed the BROOKLYN BRIDGE, the first modern vehicular crossing over water in the region. A period of extensive bridge building followed: the WILLIAMSBURG BRIDGE (1903), MANHATTAN BRIDGE (1909), and QUEENSBORO BRIDGE (1909) were constructed over the East River, as were eight over the Harlem River, including the Spuyten Duyvil railroad bridge (in the 1880s), the WASHINGTON BRIDGE (1889), the Third Avenue Bridge (1899, the third structure on the site originally occupied by Coles Bridge), and the WILLIS AVENUE BRIDGE (1901). A respected bridge engineer of the time was Alfred Pancoast Boller, who designed the Park Avenue Railroad Bridge (1891), the second MACOMBS DAM BRIDGE (1895), the 145th Street Bridge (1905), the Broadway Bridge (1908, replacing a bridge dating from 1895 that was floated downstream to become the University Heights Bridge at West Fordham Road), and the second Madison Avenue Bridge (1910). By 1910 bridges also spanned Dutch Kills, Newtown Creek, and the Gowanus Canal. The HELL GATE BRIDGE (1917), at one time the world's longest steel arch bridge, carried trains of the Pennsylvania Railroad over the Hell Gate Channel into Manhattan. Traversing the formidably wide Hudson River

Selected Bridges of New York City

NAME (YEAR OPENED)	UNDERLYING BODY OF WATER OR LAND	CONNECTING BOROUGHS
High (1848)	Harlem River	Manhattan–Bronx
Brooklyn (1883)	East River	Manhattan–Brooklyn
Washington (1888)	Harlem River	Manhattan–Bronx
Carroll Street (1889)	Gowanus Canal	Brooklyn
Third Avenue (1889)	Gowanus Canal	Brooklyn
City Island (1901)	Pelham Bay Narrows	Bronx
Willis Avenue (1901)	Harlem River	Manhattan–Bronx
Grand Street (1903)	Newton Creek	Queens–Brooklyn
Williamsburg (1903)	East River	Manhattan–Brooklyn
Ninth Street (1905)	Gowanus Canal	Brooklyn
145th Street (1905)	Harlem River	Manhattan–Bronx
Third Street (1905)	Gowanus Canal	Brooklyn
Union Street (1905)	Gowanus Canal	Brooklyn
Borden Avenue (1908)	Dutch Kills	Queens
Pelham (1908)	Eastchester Bay	Bronx
University Heights (1908)	Harlem River	Manhattan–Bronx
Manhattan (1909)	East River	Manhattan–Brooklyn
Queensboro (1909)	East River	Manhattan–Queens
Hunters Point Avenue (1910)	Dutch Kills	Queens
Madison Avenue (1910)	Harlem River	Manhattan–Bronx
Hell Gate (1917)	East River	Queens–Wards Island
Ocean Avenue (pedestrian) (1917)	Sheepshead Bay	Brooklyn
Eastchester (1922)	Eastchester Creek	Bronx
North Channel (1925)	North Channel	Queens
Roosevelt Avenue (1925)	Flushing River	Queens
B&O Railroad (1928)	Arthur Kill	Staten Island–New Jersey
East 174th Street (1928)	Bronx River	Bronx
Goethals (1928)	Arthur Kill	Staten Island–New Jersey
Outerbridge Crossing (1928)	Arthur Kill	Staten Island–New Jersey
Greenpoint Avenue (1929)	Newtown Creek	Queens–Brooklyn
Stillwell Avenue (1929)	Coney Island Creek	Brooklyn
George Washington (1931)	Hudson River	Manhattan–New Jersey
Bayonne (1931)	Kill van Kull	Staten Island–New Jersey
Cropsey Avenue (1931)	Coney Island Creek	Brooklyn
Fresh Kills (1931)	Richmond Creek	Staten Island

(*continued*)

Selected Bridges of New York City (*Continued*)

NAME (YEAR OPENED)	UNDERLYING BODY OF WATER OR LAND	CONNECTING BOROUGHS
Hook Creek (1931)	Hook Creek	Queens–Nassau
Little Neck (1931)	Alley Creek	Queens
Metropolitan Avenue (1933)	English Kills	Brooklyn
Henry Hudson (1936)	Harlem River	Manhattan–Bronx
Robert F. Kennedy (formerly Triborough) (1936)	East River, Harlem River, Bronx Kills	Queens–Wards Island, Manhattan–Randalls Island
Marine Parkway–Gil Hodges (1937)	Rockaway Inlet	Brooklyn–Queens
Westchester Avenue (1938)	Bronx River	Bronx
Bronx–Whitestone (1939)	East River	Bronx–Queens
Cross Bay–Veterans' Memorial (1939; reopened 1970)	Jamaica Bay	Queens
Flushing (Northern Boulevard) (1939)	Flushing River	Queens
Kosciuszko (1939)	Newtown Creek	Queens–Brooklyn
Whitestone Expressway (1939)	Flushing River	Queens
Midtown Highway (1940)	Dutch Kills	Queens
Mill Basin (1940)	Mill Basin	Brooklyn
Hutchinson River Park Extension (1941)	Eastchester Creek	Bronx
Hamilton Avenue (1942)	Gowanus Canal	Brooklyn
Wards Island (pedestrian) (1951)	East River	Manhattan–Wards Island
Bruckner Boulevard (1953)	Bronx River	Bronx
Unionport (1953)	Westchester Creek	Bronx
Pulaski (1954)	Newtown Creek	Queens–Brooklyn
Roosevelt Island (1955)	East River	Queens–Roosevelt Island
Lemon Creek (1958)	Lemon Creek	Staten Island
Throgs Neck (1961)	East River	Bronx–Queens
Broadway (1962)	Harlem River	Manhattan–Bronx
Alexander Hamilton (1963)	Harlem River	Manhattan–Bronx
Hawtree Basin (pedestrian) (1963)	Hawtree Basin	Queens
Verrazano–Narrows (1964)	Narrows	Brooklyn–Staten Island
Rikers Island (1966)	Bowery Bay	Queens–Rikers Island

Source: Norval White and Elliot Willensky, eds., *AIA Guide to New York City* (New York: American Institute of Architects, New York Chapter, 1967; 3rd edn San Diego: Harcourt Brace Jovanovich, 1988)

River, the High Bridge, a national landmark and the city's oldest surviving bridge, is involved in the first major reconstruction of the entry paths to the bridge from the Bronx and Manhattan sides since their original construction.

I. N. Phelps Stokes, *The Iconography of Manhattan Island, 1498–1909* (New York: Robert H. Dodd, 1915–28; repr. Arno, 1967); Carl W. Condit, *American Building: Materials and Techniques from the First Colonial Settlements to the Present* (Chicago: University of Chicago Press, 1968); Sharon Reier, *The Bridges of New York* (New York: Quadrant, 1977)

Gary D. Hermalyn, Rebecca Read Shanor

Bridge Street African Wesleyan Methodist Episcopal Church. Church formed in Brooklyn in 1766. The first congregation included whites and blacks and was led by a British army officer. After racial discord erupted, black members withdrew and formed the African Wesleyan Methodist Episcopal Church (1818), which became part of the African Methodist Episcopal Church in 1820. Richard H. Cain, the pastor between 1861 and 1863 and later a bishop, was elected to the U.S. House of Representatives from South Carolina in 1873. Susan Smith McKinney-Steward, the first black woman physician in New York State, was the organist during the 1890s. In the early twenty-first century the church still held regular services.

Dennis C. Dickerson

Briggs, Cyril (*b* Nevis, 28 May 1887; *d* ?Los Angeles, 18 Oct 1966). Political activist. He became one of the earliest and most articulate advocates of black nationalism in Harlem as a writer for the *Colored American Review* (1915) and the *Amsterdam News* (1914–19). In 1919 he launched his own journal, the *Crusader*, and founded the African Blood Brotherhood, a paramilitary group intended to further black nationalism in the United States and Africa. He wrote favorably about the Bolshevik Revolution by 1920 and called for alliances between blacks and progressive whites; he probably joined the Communist Party at this time. Over the next two years he sought to join the black nationalist group the Universal Improvement Association but was rebuffed by its leader, Marcus Garvey, because of his socialist connections. Under his leadership the African Blood Brotherhood formed an affiliation with the Communist Party (1925) and thus became the first black communist group in New York City. In the late 1920s and 1930s he edited the communist newspaper the *Harlem Liberator* but clashed frequently with the party's leadership over black nationalism. Briggs was expelled from the party in 1942; he moved to California in 1944.

Harold Cruse, *The Crisis of the Negro Intellectual* (New York: William Morrow, 1967); Mark Naison, *Communists in Harlem During the Depression* (Urbana: University of Illinois Press, 1983)

Calvin B. Holder

Brighton Beach. Neighborhood in southwestern Brooklyn (2000 pop. 75,574), lying between Manhattan Beach and Coney Island and bounded to the north by Neptune Avenue, to the east by Corbin Place, to the south by the Atlantic Ocean, and to the west by Ocean Parkway. Initially developed by William A. Engeman in 1868, the area was named for the resort in England in 1878 by Henry C. Murphy and a group of business leaders who bought a large parcel on which to build the elegant Hotel Brighton. North of Brighton Beach Avenue Engeman built the Brighton Beach Racetrack, which made the area an important center of thoroughbred horse racing. In 1907 the Brighton Beach Baths opened on the site of a former amusement park to provide swimming, tennis, and entertainment. (By the twenty-first century the Brighton Beach Baths had been replaced by a huge housing development.) To meet the increased demand for housing in the 1920s developers built more than 30 six-story apartment buildings with elevators south of Brighton Beach Avenue between Coney Island Avenue and Ocean Parkway. The population consisted mostly of Jews from Brownsville, East New York, and the Lower East Side. Convenient transportation to Manhattan was provided by an express subway route with four tracks. On the former site of the racetrack, the wood-frame houses and bungalows had deteriorated severely by 1970. After the Soviet Union relaxed emigration policies during the 1970s, about 30,000 Jews settled in the neighborhood and its environs; many were from Odessa in the Ukraine and were attracted by the proximity of the neighborhood to the ocean. Of the

Boardwalk at Brighton Beach, Coney Island, ca *1905*

immigrants who settled in Brighton Beach during the 1980s, the great majority were from the Soviet Union; many of the rest were from China, India, Pakistan, and Vietnam. In the mid-1990s much of the population was elderly and the housing consisted mostly of dense rows of apartment buildings. In 2009, while condominiums began to replace the older bungalows and apartment buildings, the neighborhood remained home to one of the largest Russian-speaking populations outside Russia. Along Brighton Beach Avenue Russian restaurants, nightclubs, fruit stands, and bookstores owned by immigrants stand in the shadow of the elevated train.

Annelise Orleck, "The Soviet Jews: Life in Brighton Beach, Brooklyn," in *New Immigrants in New York,* ed. Nancy Foner (New York: Columbia University Press, 1987), 273–304

Stephen Weinstein

Brighton Beach Bath and Racquet Club. Private athletic club established as the Brighton Beach Baths in 1907 and occupying 15 acres (6 hectares) on the Atlantic Ocean at 3205 Coney Island Avenue in Brooklyn. Once advertised as the world's largest beach resort, it had more than 13,000 members by the 1960s. The club featured knish-eating contests, ferocious mah-jongg and one-wall handball games, three swimming pools, a miniature-golf course, steam rooms, a solarium, and an area reserved for card playing. On weekends the band shell was the site of performances by entertainers such as Milton Berle, Lionel Hampton, Herman's Hermits, and Tallulah Bankhead. By the early 1990s the neighborhood had been transformed and the club had declined. In 1994 a court gave the owners the right to close the complex, and in 1997 it was sold and its memorabilia put up for auction. In 1999 Muss Development broke ground on the Oceana Condominium and Club, a complex of 850 luxury condominiums with indoor and outdoor pools, a 1-acre (0.4-hectare) park, and a complete health club in the spirit of the original Bath and Racquet Club. In 2003 the $250 million Oceana project was honored by the National Association of Home Builders as one of the "Best For Sale Housing Communities in America."

Kenneth T. Jackson

Brighton Heights. Neighborhood in northeastern Staten Island, lying between Silver Lake Park and Randall Manor and bounded to the north by Castleton Avenue, to the south by Forest Avenue, and to the west by Brighton Avenue. Once part of the Village of New Brighton, it consists primarily of small houses and businesses. The most prominent building is Morris Intermediate School, which stands at the corner of Castleton and Brighton avenues and is named for William Morris, a prominent black businessman who lived in the area in the early twentieth century; some of his descendants still live in Staten Island.

Martha S. Bendix

Brill, A(braham) A(rden) (*b* Kanczuga [now in Poland], 12 Oct 1874; *d* New York City, 2 March 1948). Pioneering psychoanalyst. A native of Galicia, he moved alone to New York City at age 15. After several years of training in Europe, where he became a disciple of Freud, he returned to the city in 1908 and became the first practicing psychoanalyst in the United States. He taught at New York University (1913–20), New York Post-Graduate Medical School (1914–18), and the College of Physicians and Surgeons (1927) and was also affiliated at various times with many other institutions, including Bellevue Hospital, Bronx Hospital and Dispensary, and the Vanderbilt Clinic. Best known as the translator into English of Freud's works, Brill was also the leading spokesman in the United States for the new science of psychoanalysis. His published writings include *Basic Principles of Psychoanalysis* (1949). In 1947 the New York Psychoanalytic Institute and Society dedicated the Abraham A. Brill Library.

Joseph S. Lieber

Brisbane, Arthur (*b* Buffalo, 12 Dec 1864; *d* New York City, 25 Dec 1936). Newspaper executive. The son of the utopian socialist Albert Brisbane, he began his career as the editor of Charles A. Dana's newspaper the *Sun.* In 1896 Joseph Pulitzer named him the editor of the Sunday edition of the *New York World.* He became the circulation director of the *World* during a period of intense competition with William Randolph Hearst's *New York Journal.* As an assistant to Hearst he became well known for his unrestrained editorials and for encouraging the frenzied newspaper war.

Oliver Carlson, *Brisbane: A Candid Biography* (New York: Stackpole and Sons, 1937)

Julian S. Rammelkamp

Bristol–Myers Squibb. Firm of pharmaceutical manufacturers, incorporated in New York City as Bristol–Myers in 1900. Its forerunner was the Clinton Pharmaceutical Company, formed in 1887 in Clinton, New York, by William McLaren Bristol and John R. Myers. By 1928 the firm manufactured proprietary drugs at plants in New Jersey and had markets in 26 countries. It was taken over and operated by Drug Inc. from 1928 to 1933 but later grew by acquiring other firms, including Harris Laboratories in 1942 and Cheplin Biological Laboratories in 1943. It merged in 1989 with the Squibb Corporation and took its present name. The new firm was large enough to finance modern pharmaceutical research and development. By 2005, when it had $19.2 billion in global sales, Bristol-Myers Squibb was active in research on AIDS and cancer drugs and had headquarters at 345 Park Avenue.

David J. S. King

Bristow, George F(rederick) (*b* Brooklyn, 19 Dec 1825; *d* 13 Dec 1898). Composer. Born to a respected conductor, pianist, and clarinetist, he was surrounded by music from a young age. He joined the violin section of the New York Philharmonic at the age of 17, rising to the position of concertmaster seven years later. His opera *Rip van Winkle* is one of the first operas about an American subject as well as the second opera by an American composer to be performed by a professional company. Bristow spent 44 years teaching music in the New York City public school system. Public School 134 in the Bronx is named for him.

Anne Epstein

Broad Channel. Neighborhood in southeastern Queens (2008 pop. 3000) on the only inhabited island in Jamaica Bay, which occupies 150 acres (60 hectares) west of a waterway also called Broad Channel. It consisted at first of a few anglers' shacks and could be reached only by boat. In 1880 it was made the site of one of four fishing platforms built alongside a railroad trestle 5 miles (8 kilometers) long across the bay from southern Queens to the Rockaway Peninsula. A hotel and saloon were opened the following year; visitors rented rowboats and baymen continued to fish and to dig for clams. The Board of Health in 1916 declared Jamaica Bay polluted and prohibited fishing. Cross Bay Boulevard was opened through the center of Broad Channel in 1924, and a large residential community took shape within five years; nine inlets were dredged along the western shore and about 15 short streets were laid out. The city retained title to the land, giving the householders renewable 10-year leases. Because of the marshy ground, many of the houses were built on stilts. Between 1950 and 1955 the city realigned the railroad route and radically changed the shape of the islands in the bay. A subway station opened on 28 June 1956. In 1982 the city permitted local residents to buy their houses, the average value of which rose rapidly from $10,000 to $100,000. For many years most houses used septic tanks and there was no sewage system. Broad Channel is a largely Irish community with many firefighters and police officers and their families and a reputation for being insular and suspicious of city government.

Vincent Seyfried

Broadway, 2010

Broadway. New York City's most famous street begins at the Battery and extends for 21 miles (34 kilometers) through Manhattan and the Bronx, reaching Yonkers at 262nd Street and continuing north to Albany and beyond. It was originally the Weckquasgeek trail, built by Native Americans along a natural ridge in lower Manhattan. Named Heere Straat (High Street) by the Dutch, it led to a fort at the southern tip of the island and became an important trade route linking the harbor with the colony of New Netherlands. Most of the street was exempted from the grid of the 1811 commissioner's street plan and was allowed to maintain a diagonal route across the city. The street was consolidated with the Bloomingdale and Kingsbridge roads in upper Manhattan in 1899, and the entire route was renamed Broadway. Until the early nineteenth century Broadway was largely residential, but it soon became crowded with fashionable department stores, dry-goods merchants, hotels, and, later, skyscrapers. Parks and town squares were created at the intervals where Broadway crossed a north-south avenue, and the intersecting east-west streets were made wider. These intervals, including Columbus Circle and Union, Madison, Herald, and Times squares, became commercial focal points and locations for subway stations after 1904. The city's first theaters opened on lower Broadway in the eighteenth century, and the theater district migrated north along its route throughout the nineteenth century; by the time it reached Times Square in the early twentieth century, Broadway's name had become synonymous with theater and entertainment. In 1918 a study by the deputy commissioner of traffic reported that it was the busiest street in the world. Descriptive names have been applied to various sections of the street, including the Canyon of Heroes, between Battery Park and City Hall, named for the route of ticker-tape parades; Ladies' Mile, between Ninth and 23rd streets, named for a fashionable nineteenth-century shopping district; the Great White Way near 42nd Street, for the proliferation of electric lights in the area; and Silicon Alley between SoHo and 23rd Street, for the numerous Internet and new media companies located there. Broadway remains one of New York City's principal commercial and cultural thoroughfares in the twenty-first century.

Lloyd Morris, *Incredible New York* (New York: Random House, 1951); Mary C. Henderson, *The City and the Theatre: New York Playhouses from Bowling Green to Times Square* (Clifton, N.J.: James T. White, 1973); Carin Drechsler-Marx and Richard F. Shepard, *Broadway* (New York: Harry N. Abrams, 1988); David Dunlap, *On Broadway* (New York: Rizzoli, 1990)

Linda Elsroad, Caleb Smith

Broadway Junction. Neighborhood in northeastern Brooklyn (2000 pop. *ca* 2500), bounded to the north by Broadway, to the east by Van Sinderen Avenue, to the south by Atlantic Avenue, and to the west by Rockaway Avenue. Known as Jamaica Pass during colonial times, it was used during the Battle of Long Island in August 1776 by British troops as a passage to Gowanus, where they trapped and defeated colonial troops. It is residential, has light industry, and is the transfer point for the Fulton Street "A," the Canarsie "L," and the Broadway "J" elevated rapid transit lines. The neighborhoods of East New York and Stuyvesant Heights meet at the intersection of Jamaica Avenue, Broadway, and Fulton Street. Highland Park and the Cemetery of the Evergreens are nearby.

Stephen Weinstein

Broadway Presbyterian Church. Currently located at 601 West 114th Street at Broadway, it was founded in 1825 at 65 Bleecker Street. The present site was purchased in 1910, the cornerstone laid on 16 March 1912, and the first service held on 10 November 1912. The architect who built the English Gothic sanctuary, Louis E. Jallade, modeled it after the Brown Memorial Tower on which he worked at nearby Union Theological Seminary. As of 2008 the church operated a nursery school and a soup kitchen for the poor.

Jessica Montesano

Broadway theaters. The major commercial theaters in New York City are mostly located in the midtown theater district, which takes up the blocks between Sixth and Eighth avenues from West 41st Street to West 54th Street. One of the city's first theaters was the Playhouse on Broadway in the early eighteenth century. Gradually the city's theaters moved northward, primarily along Broadway, until a theater district was established around Times Square. In 2008 there were 39 Broadway theaters. The term refers not to location but to theater size. A playhouse with more than 499 seats is officially a Broadway theater wherever it is located. Only three Broadway theaters are actually located on Broadway: the Marquis, the Palace, and the Broadway. One, the Vivian Beaumont at Lincoln Center, is located outside the theater district. While approximately one-third of the theaters bear traditional, mostly British names (the Lyceum, the Longacre, the St. James), the majority of names recall the history of Broadway itself: its leading artists (Belasco, Barrymore, Booth) and playwrights (Eugene O'Neill, Richard Rodgers, August Wilson, Neil Simon), plus critic Walter Kerr and legendary theater cartoonist Al Hirschfeld. The Shubert Organization, America's oldest professional theater company and the largest owner of Broadway houses, is memorialized not only in the Shubert Theatre, but in the Gerald Schoenfeld and Barry Jacobs theaters, named for the current chairman and a former president of the organization.

Mary C. Henderson, *The City and the Theatre: New York Playhouses from Bowling Green to Times Square* (Clifton, N.J.: James T. White, 1973)

Marvin Carlson

Broadway United Church of Christ. Congregational church organized in 1836 as the Broadway Tabernacle Church with funds from the reformers Lewis and Arthur Tappan, partly in an attempt to attract to New York City the evangelist Charles Grandison, who served as pastor for the first year. The abolitionist preacher Joseph P. Thompson was pastor from 1845 to 1871. Over the years the church underwent several changes of location and name. The congregation worshipped until 1857 in the Broadway Tabernacle (1836) on Broadway between Leonard and Worth streets, from 1859 in a new building at Sixth Avenue and 34th Street, and from 1905 in a new building on Broadway and 56th Street (demolished 1970). The name was changed in the early 1950s to Broadway Congregational Church, and after the merger in 1957 of the Congregational church with the Evangelical and Reformed church to Broadway United Church of Christ. Later the church shared space: from 1970 with the Church of St. Paul the Apostle (Roman Catholic) at 59th Street and Ninth Avenue, from 1980 with Rutgers Presbyterian Church on 73rd Street and Broadway, and from 1985 with St. Michael's Church (Episcopal) on 99th Street between Broadway and Amsterdam Avenue.

History of Broadway Tabernacle Church (New York: S. W. Benedict, 1846)

Kevin Kenny

Brodie, Steve (*b* New York City, 1863; *d* San Antonio, Tex., 1 Jan 1901). Famously jumped off of the Brooklyn Bridge on 23 July 1886. The stunt was probably faked, but he capitalized on his celebrity to star in vaudeville shows and open a popular bar at 347 Bowery. The phrase "taking a Brodie" or to "pull a Brodie" describes a daring or foolish feat.

Caleb Smith

Brodsky, Joseph (*b* Leningrad, 24 May 1940; *d* New York City, 28 Jan 1996). Poet. Forcibly exiled from the Soviet Union in 1972, he moved to the United States and ultimately made his home in New York City. Brodsky authored nine volumes of poetry, as well as translations and several collections of essays. He taught at numerous colleges and universities, including Queens College, City University of New York, New York University, and Columbia University. In 1987 he received the Nobel Prize for literature. In 1991 he was appointed poet laureate of the United States. The literary community valued Brodsky for both the quality of his work and his passionate advocacy for poetry, characterized by Seamus Heaney as a "total conviction about the trustworthiness of poetry as a force for good." Although he was a professor for many years at Mount Holyoke College in Massachusetts, Brodsky always returned to New York City. He died at his home in Brooklyn Heights.

Helen Graves

broken windows policy. Theory of criminality that many credit with the historic drop in crime rates in New York City, then nationally, starting in 1992. The theory was introduced by the criminologists James Q. Wilson and George Kelling in the *Atlantic Monthly* (March 1982) following a 1969 essay on "deindividuation" by Philip Zimbardo, a psychologist at New York University. This two-part theory posits that (1) crime naturally increases in unkempt neighborhoods that fail to quickly repair broken windows and other eyesores; and that (2) government policy can reduce crime by quickly repairing rather than ignoring such blight. Put another way, police who enforce minor violations such as littering and graffiti painting will see a drop in major crimes like robbery and murder. When mayors such as New York City's Rudolph Giuliani first implemented this "quality of life enforcement," or "zero-tolerance policy," crime rates plummeted. Although the verity of the broken windows theory is a topic of academic debate, popular support for this policy remains high in the city and nationally.

Harold Takooshian

Bronck, Jonas (*b* Komstad, Småland, Sweden, 1600; *d* Broncksland, north of the Harlem River, Westchester County, 1643). Colonist. He lived on his father's farm in Sweden before moving to Amsterdam, where he taught himself navigation and became a sea captain. With his wife and indentured servants he settled in New Netherland in 1639. His stone house contained the largest library in the colony and was the site of a peace conference with the Weckquasgeek Indians in 1642. The Bronx River and, by extension, the borough of the Bronx are named for him.

Lloyd Ultan, *The Bronx in the Frontier Era: From the Beginning to 1696* (New York: Bronx County Historical Society, 1993)

Lloyd Ultan

Bronx. Northernmost borough of New York City. It encompasses 42 square miles (109 square kilometers) and is the only section of New York City that belongs to the North American mainland. Undulating hills and valleys mark the western half; east of the Bronx River the land slopes gently toward Long Island Sound. The borough has a population of about 1.3 million (federal census of 2000), and by the late 1980s its bridges, highways, and railroads were more heavily traveled than those of any other part of the United States. There are 11 colleges and universities in the borough: Fordham University, the Maritime College of the State University of New York, three branches of the City University of New York (Lehman College, Bronx Community College, and Hostos Community College), the Albert Einstein College of Medicine of Yeshiva University, the College of Mount St. Vincent, Manhattan College, Mercy College, the College of New Rochelle, and Monroe College. About 25 percent of the area is parkland (more than in any other borough); this includes the Bronx Zoo and the New York Botanical Garden, which is the site of the last remnant of a hemlock forest that once covered the city and contains such artifacts as the earliest known petrograph in the area, a turtle drawn by Weckquasgeek Indians, Algonquin speakers who inhabited the land thousands of years before European exploration.

1. From 1609 to the 1890s

Henry Hudson, probably the first European to see the shoreline, in 1609 sought cover from a storm for his vessel the *Halve Maen* in Spuyten Duyvil Creek. The eastern shore was described by Adriaen Block, the first European to navigate the East River (1614). The mainland was settled in 1639 by Jonas Bronck, a Swedish sea captain from the Netherlands who eventually built a farmstead at what became 132nd Street and Lincoln Avenue; a small group of Dutch, German, and Danish servants settled with him. In 1642 a peace treaty ending a war between the Dutch and the Weckquasgeeks was negotiated in Bronck's home. During the same year two settlements were established by colonists from Rhode Island: one by Anne Hutchinson near the river that was later named for her, another by John

Arthur Avenue Indoor Market, 2009

Throckmorton in what is now Throgs Neck; both settlements were destroyed in a war between the Dutch and the Weckquasgeeks. Bronck's servants scattered after his death in 1643. In 1646 a patroonship was formed by Adriaen van der Donck in an area that now includes Riverdale and a part of Westchester County (he was given an enormous land grant in return for attracting 50 families to it), and Thomas Cornell, a colonist from Rhode Island, built a farm in what became Clason Point. In 1655 both settlements were destroyed during another conflict between the Dutch and the Weckquasgeeks. Most of the eastern half of the area was bought in 1654 by Thomas Pell of Connecticut, who invited 16 families to form the village of Westchester near what is now Westchester Square. Between 1683 and 1714 Westchester was the seat of Westchester County (which included the Bronx until the second half of the nineteenth century) and as a chartered borough was the only town in the colony with an elected mayor. It was the first town without a property qualification for suffrage: settlers chose a representative to the provincial assembly and had their own municipal court. Horses, cattle, sheep, and wheat were the main agricultural products, and a cottage industry in cloth making thrived. A semiannual fair was held to promote manufacturing and commerce. St. Peter's Church on Westchester Avenue organized the first parish in 1693. That same year Frederick Philipse, a wealthy merchant of New York City, obtained from Governor Benjamin Fletcher the hereditary right to build and operate a toll bridge (the King's Bridge) across Spuyten Duyvil Creek to Manhattan.

During English rule most inhabitants were English, of English descent, or Dutch. Anglicanism was the religion sanctioned by colonial law, but Presbyterians, Quakers, and members of the Dutch Reformed Church were in the majority. The first blacks, slaves from the West Indies, soon made up 10 to 15 percent of the population; in most households there were one or two who worked as farmhands or housemaids. In 1698 the first free black was recorded. Indians left the area soon after 1700. At this time the Bronx was composed of two towns and all or part of four huge manors (feudal grants allowing the proprietor exclusive rights to build grain mills and establish courts to try tenants): lying entirely within the present Bronx was the town of Westchester; to the north and including part of the present Westchester County was the town of Eastchester; to the northeast and including another part of the present Westchester County was the manor of Pelham, owned by the Pell family; to the southwest was the manor of the Morris family, Morrisania; in most of the western section was the manor of Fordham, settled in 1671 by John Archer (later owned by the Dutch Reformed Church of New York City, then absorbed by Westchester in 1755); and to the northwest and including much of the present Westchester County was the manor of Philipsburgh, owned by the Philipse family. The first Catholics moved to the area in 1744, the first Jewish settlers about ten years later. The King's Bridge fell into disuse, and the toll was eliminated in 1759 after a parallel bridge (the Farmers' Free Bridge) was built by farmers under the leadership of Benjamin Palmer. He planned subsequently to build a city to rival New York City. Hoping to lure the commercial traffic of Long Island Sound he formed a consortium to buy an island in Pelham Manor that he named City Island, but the project failed.

The area experienced constant conflict during the American Revolution. Fortifications erected by General George Washington to protect the Harlem River valley proved ineffective on 12 October 1776, when British troops outflanked the Continental army by landing at Throgs Neck. During the battle of Pell's Point in today's Pelham Bay Park, on 18 October about 750 men led by Colonel John Glover of Marblehead, Massachusetts, stayed the march of 4000 British and Hessians, enabling Washington to evacuate his army to White Plains. For much of the rest of the war the Bronx remained in British hands and was subjected to raids by rebels that caused widespread destruction. In November 1783 Washington and Governor George Clinton began a march from the Van Cortlandt mansion (now in Van Cortlandt Park) to take possession of New York City from the departing British. A recommendation in 1783 by Lewis Morris that Morrisania be the capital of the United States was rejected, but during an epidemic of yellow fever in Philadelphia in October 1797 President John Adams governed from the farmhouse of his daughter and son-in-law in what was then the southern part of Eastchester.

In the early nineteenth century the chief means of livelihood in lower Westchester County were growing wheat and raising livestock; between 1800 and 1830 the population rose from 1755 to 3023. Severe famine in Ireland and the growth of industry and commerce in the city drew thousands of Irish to the Bronx as laborers. There was a brief period of industrial growth during the War of 1812, when paint, glass, pottery, and bleaching factories opened in West Farms. Many Irish immigrants were employed in the construction of the High Bridge over the Harlem River (1837–48), the New York and Harlem Railroad (1841, the first railroad in the area), and the Croton Aqueduct (1842); the Irish also worked in the first iron foundry and industrial village at Mott Haven (1841), developed by Jordan L. Mott. After the building of the Erie Canal, New York City was inundated with wheat from the Midwest, whose fertile lands yielded fruits, vegetables, and dairy products for sale in the city. The first railroad tracks were laid over these lands, and rural stations eventually became the centers of new villages such as Melrose, Morrisania, Tremont, Fordham, Williamsbridge, Wakefield, Highbridge, Morris Heights, Kingsbridge, and Riverdale; the campus of St. John's College (later Fordham University) was built near a station in 1841. Increasing numbers of New Yorkers chose to live in the country and work in the city. Summer homes were built along waterways in the Bronx by industrialists and financiers, among them Richard M. Hoe, William E. Dodge, and Collis P. Huntington. As the railroad was extended, the center of population shifted west from the area east of the Bronx River, and the towns of West Farms (1846) and Morrisania (1855) were established.

Economic opportunity in the United States and a failed revolution in Germany in 1848 led thousands of Germans to move to the Bronx. Many settled in Melrose and Morrisania and became shopkeepers, brewers, and saloon owners. They also organized choral societies, *Turnvereine* (athletic clubs), and social clubs such as the Tallapoosa Club and the Schnorer Club, which became social centers for business leaders. In 1863 the Janes and Beebe ironworks at 149th Street and Brook Avenue produced the dome for the Capitol in Washington, D.C. The Johnson Iron Foundry on Spuyten Duyvil Creek made munitions during the Civil War and the Spanish–American War. Many Irish immigrants settled near new factories and in areas where construction work could be found. Developments intended largely for wealthy residents of Manhattan and other sections included Woodlawn Cemetery (1863), where they were buried, and the Jerome Park Racetrack (1866), where the Belmont Stakes was first run. By this time it was generally assumed that towns on the mainland would be annexed by New York City as it expanded northward. In 1868 Mott Haven, in Morrisania, numbered its streets to have them conform to those of the city, and the following year the municipal parks department was given control of the bridges over the Harlem River and the streets leading to them. In 1874 the towns of Morrisania, West Farms, and Kingsbridge (all of which lay west of the Bronx River) were annexed to the city; known as the Annexed District, they were placed under the jurisdiction of the parks department and became the city's 23rd and 24th wards. The journalist John Mullaly organized a movement urging the city to buy huge tracts and set them aside for parks while land in the Bronx was still cheap; in 1888 a commission purchased what later became Van Cortlandt, Crotona, Claremont, St. Mary's, Bronx, and Pelham Bay parks and the Mosholu, Pelham, and Crotona parkways. In 1888 the Third Avenue elevated line was extended to 132nd Street, precipitating the most rapid growth that the Bronx had ever seen.

Beginning in 1890 a commissioner of street improvements was elected in response to complaints by inhabitants of the Annexed District that the parks department did not repair or build roads. Under the direction of the commissioner (and later of the borough president) the Grand Concourse was designed and built. Modeled after the Champs-Élysées, this wide avenue was lined with trees and had an innovative design based on the use of underpasses at major street crossings. The Belmont Stakes was moved east of the Bronx River in 1890 to the Morris Park Racecourse, where it remained until moving again to Belmont Park in Nassau County in 1905. In the northern section of Bronx Park, the New York Botanical Garden opened in 1891 and soon became known worldwide; the Bronx Zoo, in the southern section in 1899, displayed and bred many species (the American Bison Society used a herd at the zoo to restock western ranges). During the late nineteenth century New York University opened a campus in University Heights; the principal buildings were designed by Stanford White and included a colonnade that became the Hall of Fame for Great Americans, the first hall of fame in the world.

2. From the 1890s to the 1990s

By the 1890s there was strong support in parts of Eastchester, Pelham, and the village of Wakefield for consolidating with New York City the area east of the Bronx River, along with Brooklyn, Queens, and Staten Island. Most people assumed that high real estate values in Manhattan would cover the public debt already incurred by the towns and pay for further public improvements being planned, such as a sewer system in Wakefield. In a nonbinding referendum in 1894 consolidation was favored by voters in New York City and its outlying areas but was defeated overwhelmingly in the city of Mount Vernon and by one vote in the town of Westchester. The state legislature defeated a bill inspired by the referendum but in 1895 passed another bill annexing to the city the area east of the Bronx River, parts of the towns of Pelham and Eastchester, the village of Wakefield, and the town of Westchester, which because of its central location was included despite its negative vote in 1894. The newly annexed area became part of the 24th ward and was placed under the jurisdiction of the commissioner of street improvements (the office eventually became the model for that of borough president).

After consolidation in 1898 the 23rd and 24th wards became the borough of the Bronx, which with Manhattan remained part of New York County (the other boroughs were already separate counties). But the journey from the Bronx to the courts in southern Manhattan was so long that inhabitants of the Bronx soon petitioned for county designation. Morris High School, the first public high school in the Bronx, opened in 1897. Many of the Italian immigrants who moved to the city at the turn of the twentieth century settled in the Bronx, often near the factories of Melrose, or in Belmont, where they found work in the building trades or in landscaping the nearby New York Botanical Garden and the Bronx Zoo. Others helped build the Jerome Park Reservoir, and some bought farms in the rural northeastern Bronx. In 1904 the first subway connecting the Bronx to Manhattan was built under 149th Street, providing cheap rapid transit that, along with the Third Avenue elevated line, enabled hundreds of thousands of residents during the first third of the twentieth century to leave tenements in Manhattan for spacious new apartments in the Bronx. Yugoslavians, Armenians, and Italians were among those who made the move, but the largest group was Jews from central and eastern Europe. In 1912 the state legislature established the County of Bronx as the 62nd county in the state, effective 1 January 1914.

With the influx of population in the first third of the century the economy of the Bronx grew rapidly. The Third Avenue elevated line was gradually extended northward, and in the process trolley lines were connected to it, forming a rapid transit line that provided access from lower Manhattan to expanses of undeveloped land. Many apartment buildings and commercial buildings were soon erected along the corridor of the elevated line, which reached its northern terminus at Gun Hill Road in 1920. In 1923 Yankee Stadium was opened at 161st Street and River Avenue as the home of the New York Yankees, who became known as the "Bronx Bombers" because of the large number of home runs hit in the following decades by such players as Babe Ruth, Lou Gehrig, Joe DiMaggio, Mickey Mantle, Roger Maris, and Reggie Jackson. Eventually the stadium was also used for football games, championship boxing matches, and religious gatherings. Grocery stores, restaurants, vegetable and fruit markets, tailors, and hardware stores became common in neighborhood shopping districts. Inhabitants throughout the borough shopped in department stores and boutiques at 149th Street and Third Avenue, an area known as the Hub that also had movie palaces and vaudeville theaters. Alexander's opened a department store there in 1928, and a branch on Fordham Road in 1938, which soon had more sales per square foot than any department store in the nation. Eventually a section of Fordham Road eclipsed the Hub as the main shopping district. In 1929 Loew's theater syndicate built the Paradise Theatre for $4 million on the Grand Concourse immediately south of Fordham Road; it had 4000 seats and a Baroque decor that included a ceiling painted dark blue to suggest a nighttime sky, small lightbulbs that resembled stars, and simulated clouds that were projected across the ceiling by machine.

The onset of the Depression ended the period of tremendous growth that had begun in 1888, but privately financed apartment buildings continued to be constructed (most in the predominant style of the time, art deco). This was especially true of the Grand Concourse area, which became a symbol of social and economic success; many apartment buildings there had five or six stories with

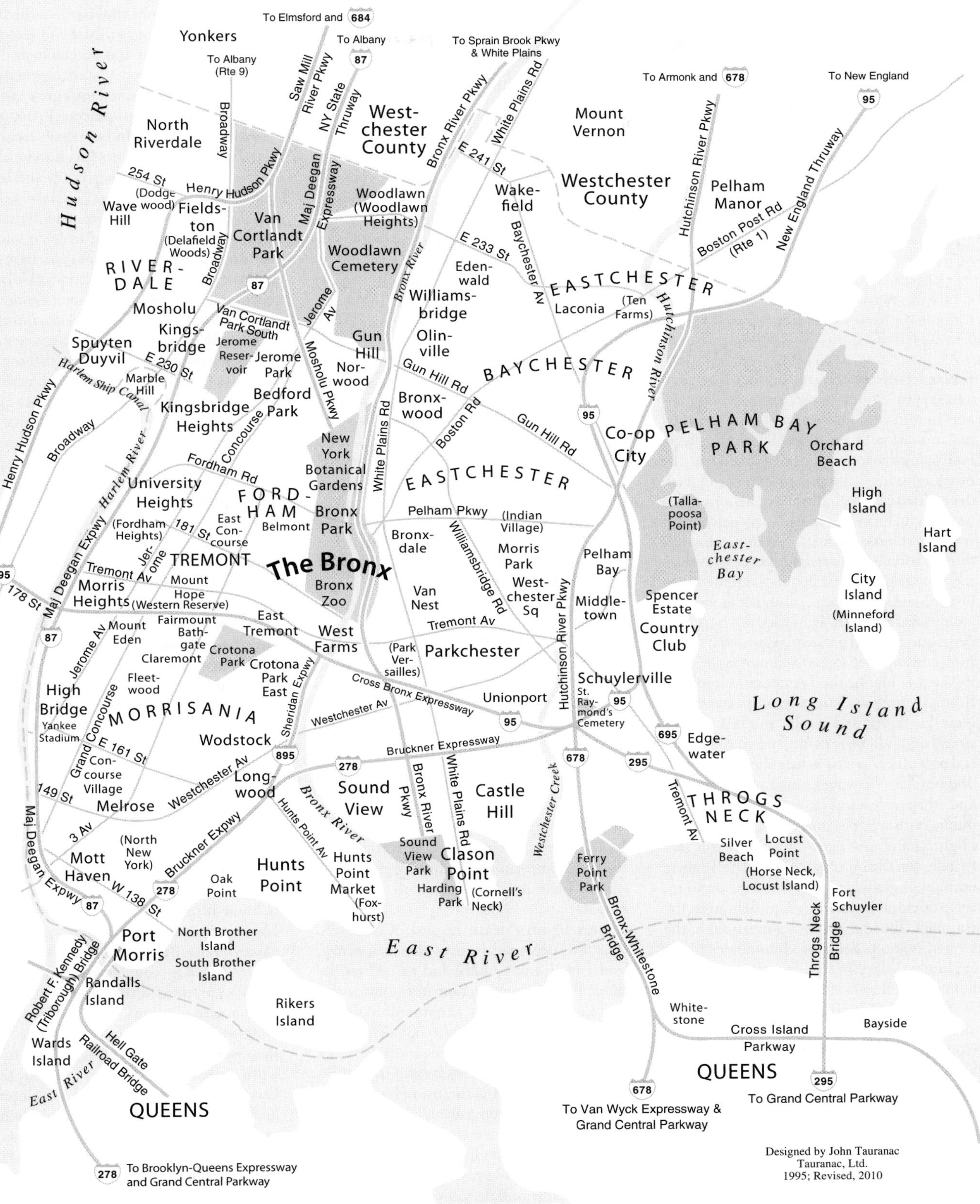

To Elmsford and 684
Yonkers
To Albany
87
To Sprain Brook Pkwy & White Plains
To Albany (Rte 9)
Saw Mill River Pkwy
NY State Thruway
Bronx River Pkwy
White Plains Rd
To Armonk and 678
To New England
95
Hudson River
North Riverdale
Broadway
West-chester County
Mount Vernon
Hutchinson River Pkwy
New England Thruway
254 St
Henry Hudson Pkwy
Maj Deegan Expressway
E 241 St
Wake-field
Westchester County
Pelham Manor
Boston Post Rd (Rte 1)
(Dodge Wave wood) Hill
Fields-ton
(Delafield Woods)
Van Cortlandt Park
Woodlawn (Woodlawn Heights)
Woodlawn Cemetery
E 233 St
Baychester Av
Eden-wald
RIVER-DALE
EASTCHESTER
Jerome Av
Bronx River
Williams-bridge
Laconia
(Ten Farms)
Hutchinson River
Mosholu
Van Cortlandt Park South
Kings-bridge
Spuyten Duyvil
E 230 St
Jerome Reser-voir
Jerome Park
Gun Hill
Olin-ville
Harlem Ship Canal
Marble Hill
Nor-wood
Mosholu Pkwy
Gun Hill Rd
BAYCHESTER
Henry Hudson Pkwy
Kingsbridge Heights
Bedford Park
Bronx-wood
Boston Rd
Gun Hill Rd
95
Co-op City
PELHAM BAY PARK
Orchard Beach
Broadway
Harlem River
Concourse
New York Botanical Gardens
White Plains Rd
Fordham Rd
EASTCHESTER
University Heights
FORD-HAM
High Island
(Talla-poosa Point)
Hart Island
Maj Deegan Expwy
(Fordham Heights)
181 St
East Con-course
Belmont
Bronx Park
Pelham Pkwy
(Indian Village)
Bronx-dale
Williamsbridge Rd
Morris Park
East-chester Bay
Jer-ome
TREMONT
The Bronx
Pelham Bay
95
Tremont Av
Morris Heights
Mount Hope (Western Reserve)
Bronx Zoo
Van Nest
West-chester Sq
Middle-town
Spencer Estate Country Club
City Island (Minneford Island)
178 St
Hutchinson River Pkwy
Mount Eden
Fairmount
East Tremont
West Farms
Tremont Av
87
Jerome Av
Bath-gate
Claremont
Crotona Park
Crotona Park East
(Park Ver-sailles)
Parkchester
Fleet-wood
Cross Bronx Expressway
Schuylerville
High Bridge
MORRISANIA
Sheridan Expwy
Westchester Av
Unionport
St. Ray-mond's Cemetery
95
Long Island Sound
Yankee Stadium
Grand Concourse
E 161 St
Wodstock
Bruckner Expressway
895
278
678
295
695
Edge-water
Con-course Village
Westchester Av
Long-wood
149 St
Melrose
Sound View
Bronx River Pkwy
White Plains Rd
Castle Hill
Westchester Creek
Tremont Av
THROGS NECK
Maj Deegan Expwy
3 Av
Bronx River
Hunts Point Av
(North New York)
Mott Haven
Bruckner Expwy
Hunts Point
Hunts Point Market (Fox-hurst)
Sound View Park
Clason Point
Harding Park
(Cornell's Neck)
Ferry Point Park
Silver Beach
Locust Point (Horse Neck, Locust Island)
W 138 St
278
87
Oak Point
Fort Schuyler
Port Morris
North Brother Island
South Brother Island
East River
Bronx-Whitestone Bridge
Throgs Neck Bridge
Robert F. Kennedy (Triborough) Bridge
Randalls Island
Rikers Island
White-stone
Cross Island Parkway
Bayside
Wards Island
Hell Gate Railroad Bridge
East River
QUEENS
QUEENS
678
295
To Van Wyck Expressway & Grand Central Parkway
To Grand Central Parkway
278
To Brooklyn-Queens Expressway and Grand Central Parkway
Designed by John Tauranac
Tauranac, Ltd.
1995; Revised, 2010

Population of Selected Towns within the Present Boundaries of the Bronx, 1790–1890

	Eastchester	Morrisania	Pelham	Westchester
1790	N/A	133	199	1,141
1800	1,581	258	N/A	992
1820	1,021	N/A	283	2,162
1830	1,030	N/A	334	2,362
1840	1,502	N/A	789	4,154
1850	1,679	N/A	577	2,492
1860	5,582	9,245	1,025	4,250
1870	7,491	19,609[1]	1,790	6,015
1880	8,737		2,540	6,789
1890	15,442		3,941	10,029

1. Incorporated into New York City in 1874.
N/A = Not Available
Note: Population figures for towns were not included in the census of population of 1810.
Compiled by James Bradley

wide entrance courtyards bordered by grass and shrubs. About 49 percent of the inhabitants in 1930 were Jews, most of whom worked in Manhattan. By 1934 housing in the Bronx had many more amenities than that of the other boroughs: almost 99 percent of residences had private bathrooms, about 95 percent central heating, more than 97 percent hot water, and more than 48 percent mechanical refrigeration. The largest housing development of the time, Parkchester, was undertaken by the Metropolitan Life Insurance Company. Completed in 1942, it housed 40,000 residents and boasted parks, playgrounds, sculpture, convenience stores, and movie theaters. Edward J. Flynn, the Democratic leader of Bronx County and an early supporter of the New Deal, secured public funds to repair streets and build the county jail and the central post office, as well as neighborhood parks. The borough became known for its colleges and universities and its growing number of public high schools, among them the Bronx High School of Science for gifted students (which by the mid-1990s had the highest number of graduates who had gone on to receive doctorates than any high school in the country). The first important meetings of the United Nations Security Council were held at Hunter College in the Bronx (later renamed Lehman College).

After World War II new housing was built, and the makeup of the population changed. Construction ranged from luxury apartment buildings in Riverdale to public housing in the southern Bronx. Longtime residents and former members of the armed services left older housing in the southern neighborhoods of Hunts Point, Morrisania, and Mott Haven to move to privately built housing in the northern Bronx, to other boroughs, or to the suburbs. About 170,000 persons displaced by slum clearing in Manhattan, mostly black and Puerto Rican, moved to Hunts Point and Morrisania, as well as to Melrose, Tremont, and Highbridge. In 1950 social workers reported enduring poverty in a section of the southern Bronx. Systematic rent control was introduced during World War II to prevent rents from skyrocketing as empty apartments became scarce; it soon prevented conscientious landlords from paying for repairs to their aging buildings. Buildings were often set afire, sometimes by unscrupulous landlords hoping to collect insurance or by unscrupulous tenants taking advantage of the city's policy that burned-out tenants should be given priority for public housing and receive money for new furnishings. A period of rampant arson in the late 1960s and early 1970s ended only after this policy was changed and a limit was imposed on insurance payments for reconstructing burned-out apartment buildings. From that time one-family houses and row houses were built, hundreds of apartment buildings restored, and several apartments converted to cooperatives and condominium units, permitting more residents of the southern Bronx to own their homes.

After Flynn's death in 1953, Charles A. Buckley succeeded him as the Democratic leader of Bronx County and gained federal funds for the construction in the 1950s and 1960s of housing and a network of highways linking the Bronx with the rest of the city, among them the Major Deegan Expressway, the Cross Bronx Expressway, and the Bruckner Expressway. As commuting by automobile became more convenient, high-rise apartment buildings were erected in southern and eastern neighborhoods along the new roads, including Soundview, Castle Hill, Spuyten Duyvil, and Riverdale. Co-op City, a complex of 15,372 units built in the northeastern Bronx between 1968 and 1970, housed 60,000 persons and was one of the largest housing developments in the world. The distribution of products to the metropolitan area and the rest of the East Coast became easier for industries occupying new industrial parks in the Bronx, such as those along Bathgate and Zerega avenues, and for fruit and vegetable dealers in the Hunts Point Food Market (opened 1965). Puerto Ricans accounted for a growing share of the population (20 percent in 1970) and became more active in politics: Herman Badillo was the first Puerto Rican to be elected to the borough presidency (1965) and later to the U.S. Congress; Robert Garcia was elected to Congress in 1978; Fernando Ferrer was elected borough president in 1987; and José Serrano succeeded Garcia in 1990. In 1974 the campus of New York University at University Heights was taken over by Bronx Community College. In the late 1970s condominiums were being built on City Island and elsewhere along Long Island Sound, whereas the southern Bronx had by then become known nationally as a symbol of urban blight. In 1977 the Bronx became a national symbol of urban crisis when President Jimmy Carter walked on the rubble of destroyed apartment houses and the sportscaster Howard Cosell announced that "the Bronx is burning" during a nationally televised World Series game at Yankee Stadium.

During the 1980s and 1990s cooperation between grassroots organizations, neighborhood groups, and local government spurred a massive rebuilding of formerly devastated neighborhoods. Much of the new housing consisted of privately owned one-, two-, and three-family homes. The Fulton Fish Market moved to Hunts Point in 2007. In 2009 the Metro–Hutchinson office complex was completed, making it one of the largest in the city, and a new Yankee Stadium, erected across the street from the original arena, on the north side of 161st Street, opened in 2009.

By the early twenty-first century the population of the Bronx was increasing, the ethnic breakdown being about a third black, a third Latin American, and a third Asian and white. Musicologists maintain that this ongoing cultural diffusion led to the popularity of hip-hop music and break dancing, which originated in the Bronx in the 1970s. By 2000 Puerto Ricans accounted for a quarter of the population, though the number of Koreans, Vietnamese, Indians, Pakistanis, Cubans, Dominicans, Jamaicans, Greeks, and Russians was also growing. Albanians settled in Belmont, Cambodians in Fordham. Co-op City remained a successful development, luxury apartments built in Riverdale in the 1950s became cooperatives, and the housing stock continued to include the world's largest concentration of art deco–style buildings. Entrepreneurs formed new businesses, and the borough's public schools became overcrowded with new immigrant students.

Stephen Jenkins, *The Story of the Bronx* (New York: G. P. Putnam's Sons, 1912)

Gary D. Hermalyn, Lloyd Ultan

Bronx Community College. Junior college of the City University of New York, opened in 1957 at the former site of the Bronx High School of Science on 184th Street and Creston Avenue. In 1973 it moved to a disused campus of New York University at University Avenue and 181st Street. In 2007 it enrolled 4994 full-time and 3723 part-time students. The campus is the site of the Hall of Fame for Great Americans.

Marc Ferris

Bronx County Historical Society. Private, nonprofit cultural and educational institution opened in 1955 to document and interpret the social and economic history of the Bronx from the seventeenth century to the present. It has a research library and more than 18,000 photographs and slides; it also runs Poe Cottage (circa 1812), Edgar Allen Poe's last home and now a historic museum, and the Valentine–Varian House (circa 1758), now the Museum of Bronx History. The society also offers tours of the Bronx. Its offices and collections are at 3309 Bainbridge Avenue.

Gary D. Hermalyn

Bronxdale. Neighborhood in the central Bronx, bounded to the north by Allerton Avenue, to the west by the Bronx River Parkway, to the south by Pelham Parkway, and to the east by Esplanade Avenue. It was settled in the nineteenth century as a village on the eastern bank of the Bronx River. When Bronx Park was laid out in 1888, a cloth-tape and cloth-printing mill and bleachery built in the mid-nineteenth century was forced to move, along with its resident workers. Jews moved to the neighborhood in large numbers after the opening in 1917 of the White Plains Road branch of the Interborough Rapid Transit. A predominantly residential area, Bronxdale has attracted varied ethnic groups over the past century. White Plains Road and Lydig Avenue remain the main commercial streets and the Bronx headquarters of the city parks department is in Bronk Park.

Lloyd Ultan

Bronx Empowerment Zone. Under the administration of Bill Clinton, nine economically underdeveloped areas of the country were designated to receive special incentives and programs to encourage new business growth. In 1996 the Bronx became one of these Empowerment Zones. Under the Empowerment Zone program, small businesses receive tax breaks for moving into the Bronx and hiring neighborhood residents. There are also measures that minimize the financial burden of taking out business loans. The goal is to mobilize entrepreneurs and increase employment in this largely depressed area of the city. The Bronx has seen substantial investment through the Empowerment Zone programs. The *New York Post* and the Fulton Fish Market moved to the Bronx. Borough President Adolfo Carrión drafted the Yankee Stadium Neighborhood Development Plan to build a new high school for sports medicine near the stadium, a new park and hotel, and a Yankee Hall of Fame. The Bronx Empowerment Zone was able to partially finance the Venture Center, a state-of-the-art office complex, to accommodate startup businesses.

Penelope Gelwicks

Bronx High School of Science. One of the most distinguished secondary schools in the United States. It opened in 1938 at 184th Street and Creston Avenue for gifted students interested in science and mathematics. In its first year it admitted 300 boys on the basis of a written examination, and in 1946 it began to admit girls. The school moved in 1958 to a building at 205th Street and Jerome Avenue, north of Lehman College. The curriculum includes advanced college placement courses in science and mathematics, as well as independent research programs. Students at the Bronx High School of Science have won many city, state, and national academic honors, and nearly all go on to attend engineering, technical, or liberal arts colleges. In 2007 the school had an enrollment of nearly 3000 and was one of several selective specialized high schools in the city's public education system. Distinguished alumni of the Bronx High School of Science include seven Nobel laureates in physics: Leon Cooper (1972), Sheldon Glashow (1979), Steven Weinberg (1979), Melvin Schwartz (1988), Russell A. Hulse (1993), H. David Politzer (2004), and Roy J. Glauber (2005). Other notable graduates of the school include the former secretary of defense Harold Brown, the journalists William Safire and Joseph Lelyveld, the writer E. L. Doctorow, the electrical sound engineer Robert Moog, the singer Bobby Darin (Walden Robert Cassotto), the activist Stokely Carmichael, and the astrophysicist Neil deGrasse Tyson.

Gerard Koeppel

Bronx Home News. Newspaper launched by James O'Flaherty (1874–1939), published weekly from 1907 and daily from 1922 from offices at East 148th Street and Third Avenue. It focused on local news and always named as many residents of the Bronx as possible. Perhaps its most famous headline was "Bronx Man Leads Russian Revolution," a reference to Leon Trotsky, who had lived in the Bronx in 1917. In 1939 the newspaper had a circulation of 110,000 (with a heavy reliance on home delivery) and published neighborhood editions in upper Manhattan, but it soon went into decline and was sold to the owners of the *New York Post* on 30 May 1945. The *Bronx Home News* ceased publication on 18 February 1948.

Stephen A. Stertz

Bronx Hospital. Private hospital in the Bronx. It opened in 1911 and served Jewish immigrants. In 1918 the hospital moved to the Eichler estate at 169th and Fulton avenues. A new building was completed in 1932, and the old hospital became a nursing home. The hospital merged in 1962 with Lebanon Hospital to form Bronx–Lebanon Hospital Center.

Andrea Balis

Bronx–Lebanon Hospital Center. Non profit, voluntary hospital in the Bronx, the largest serving the southern part of the borough. Its two major divisions are 1 mile (1.6 kilometers) apart on the Grand Concourse and on Fulton Avenue. Together, they house 858 beds. The hospital was formed in 1962 by the merger of Lebanon Hospital and Bronx Hospital. In 1971 it became a teaching hospital of the Albert Einstein College of Medicine. Bronx–Lebanon has two inpatient facilities, extensive outpatient facilities, and a center for the treatment of AIDS; it also maintains housing, nutrition, and food distribution programs.

Andrea Balis

Bronx Municipal Hospital Center. See Jacobi Medical Center.

Bronx Museum of the Arts. Founded in 1971 to bring visual arts to the Bronx, until 1982 it was housed in the rotunda of the Bronx County Courthouse, located on the Grand Concourse and 161st Street; it then moved to a former synagogue on the Grand Concourse and 165th Street. The museum displays primarily local artists of African American, Asian, and Latin American descent. It also has an educational department, which offers art classes and workshops. In 2007 the architectural firm Arquitectonica completed a new facility that nearly doubled the museum's space.

Max Seppo

Bronx Opera Company. Community opera company. Founded in 1967 by artistic director and principal conductor Michael Spierman, the Bronx Opera Company (BOC) performs in English, with costumes and a full orchestra. BOC presents two operas per year, holding four performances each at the Bronx High School of Science and various high schools and colleges. The company moved in 1980 to the Lovinger Theatre of Lehman College. Performances in Manhattan were held at the Hunter College Playhouse (later the Sylvia and Danny Kaye Playhouse), John Jay College, City University of New York. In 1995 BOC started an arts education program for Bronx public school students that includes a Job Shadow Program and showing students an abridged performance.

Mark Laiosa

Bronx Park. Public park in north central Bronx, covering 662 acres (268 hectares) and bounded to the north by Gun Hill Road; to the east by Bronx Park East and Unionport Road; to the south by East 180th Street, Boston Road, and Bronx Park South; to the west by Southern Boulevard and Dr. Theodore Kazimiroff Boulevard; and to the northwest by Webster Avenue. It is bisected by Fordham Road, and within its borders the Bronx River Parkway runs roughly parallel to the Bronx River. The park was laid out during the 1880s as part of a plan to reserve parkland in undeveloped areas annexed or soon to be annexed to New York City. During the 1890s it was chosen as the site for the city's zoological and botanical gardens. The area south of Fordham Road was to be used by the New York Zoological Society (now the Wildlife Conservation Society), and what later became known as the Bronx Zoo opened to the public in 1899. Most of the area north of Fordham Road (about 250 acres [100 hectares]) became the site of the New York Botanical Garden (1891), which became one of the finest gardens of its kind in the world and contains virgin hemlock forest, covering 40 acres (16 hectares).

Evelyn Gonzalez and Timothy Rub, *Building a Borough: Architecture and Planning in the Bronx, 1890–1940* (New York: Bronx Museum of the Arts, 1986); John Mullaly, *The New Parks beyond the Harlem* (New York: 1887; repr. New York: Bronx County Historical Society, 2008)

Peter Derrick

Image of the Bronx River, 1905

Bronx River. A meandering, scenic waterway whose source is in the hills of Westchester County near the Kensico Dam. The river was known as Aquahung to the Native Americans until the surrounding lands were purchased by Jonas Bronck in 1639. The river drains a valley 24 miles (38 kilometers) long and flows south past White Plains, dividing Yonkers from Mount Vernon, passing through the middle of the Bronx into the East River between Hunts Point and Clason Point. It is especially picturesque at the Bronx River Gorge in the New York Botanical Garden, where the historic Lorillard Tobacco Mill is preserved. The river also bisects the Bronx Zoo. The rocky shores and outcroppings show clearly the glacial action of the retreating Wisconsin Ice Sheet. The Bronx River is navigable for only 2.6 miles (4.2 kilometers), to East 172nd Street. In 1913 a dredging project by the U.S. Army Corps of Engineers was begun; it was about 90 percent complete by the early twenty-first century with the depth averaging 10 to 12 feet (3 to 4 meters). At the outbreak of the American Revolution, it was said that the British War Office was so ignorant of the topography of the Bronx that it ordered Admiral Richard Howe to sail his fleet up the river and attack "whatever American ships he found there." The Bronx River has had a long history of severe pollution caused primarily by the dumping of effluents from surrounding towns. By the early twenty-first century most communities had agreed to stop dumping raw sewage, as efforts to stock the river with such fish as the alewife were undertaken to combat eutrophication. In February 2007 biologists reported the sighting of a beaver—the first seen in New York City in more than two centuries.

Gerard R. Wolfe

Bronx Symphony Orchestra. Community orchestra formed in 1940. It disbanded after one concert season but was re-formed in 1947 by Irwin Hoffman, conductor, and Edward I. Cohen, orchestra manager, as part of the Walton Community Center. Rehearsals and performances took place at Walton High School in the Bronx. Later conductors included Leon Hyman (1952–59), Paul Wolfe (*ca* 1959–62), Saul Schectman and Moshe Budmore (*ca* 1962–63), Louis F. Simon (*ca* 1964–68), Michael Spierman (1968–81, 1989–91), Joseph Delli Carri (1981–84), Robert Black (1986–89), George Rothman (1991–93), and Gheorghe Costinescu (1993–94). In early 1968 the orchestra moved to the Bronx High School of Science, before moving in 1980 to the Performing Arts Center at Lehman College, City University of New York, giving four to six concerts a year. In 1995 the Bronx Symphony Orchestra became independent of Lehman College, used various conductors, and began touring the Bronx. José Alejandro Guzman became music director and conductor in 1998.

Mark Laiosa

Bronx Terminal Market. Indoor market complex covering 32 acres (13 hectares) along the Harlem River between 149th and 152nd streets in Mott Haven. Construction on a cold-storage warehouse began under Mayor John F. Hylan in 1917 and was completed in the 1920s, when other buildings were added to form an indoor market. The market was not successful until the 1930s, when Mayor Fiorello H. La Guardia expanded it as part of his program to eliminate pushcarts. Ten buildings were added to the south of the original warehouse, and the market became the city's main wholesale distribution center for ethnic foods. In December 1935 Mayor La Guardia prohibited the sale and possession of artichokes there to end the inflation of their price by organized crime; in the following year the price declined and the ban was lifted. The complex was leased to the firm of Arol Development under Mayor John V. Lindsay in 1972. This arrangement came into conflict with the rebuilding of Yankee Stadium during the 1970s, which called for the construction of a parking area on land already leased to Arol. In 1993 about 75 percent of the market lay empty, and Mayor David N. Dinkins condemned the lease with Arol after George Steinbrenner, owner of the New York Yankees, threatened to move the team out of the Bronx. In the late 1990s the city lost a legal battle with the developer, who has the lease until 2052. As of 2010 the site had not been redeveloped.

Melissa M. Merritt

Bronx–Whitestone Bridge. Suspension bridge that spans the East River, connecting the Hutchinson River Parkway and Ferry Point Park in the Bronx to Whitestone in Queens. Designed by the engineer Othmar H. Ammann and the architectural firm Cass Gilbert and Company, it was constructed in 23 months at a cost of $17,785,000 and opened on 30 April 1939; at the time it was the fourth-longest suspension bridge in the world. The bridge reaches a maximum clearance above mean high water of 150 feet (46 meters), and the total length of its main span (excluding approach drives) is 2300 feet (701 meters). It has six traffic lanes, each 30 feet (9 meters) wide. Connected a few years after its completion to the parkways of the Bronx and Queens, it greatly improved access between Long Island and Westchester County and points north and east, and it spurred a housing boom in the adjacent areas of Queens that was interrupted only by World War II. The Bronx–Whitestone Bridge is operated by the Triborough Bridge and Tunnel Authority.

Stephen A. Stertz

Bronx Zoo entrance, 2009

Bronxwood Park. Name formerly applied to a development built in 1880 in the north central Bronx and bounded to the north by North Oak Drive, to the east by Bronxwood Avenue, to the south by South Oak Drive, and to the west by White Plains Road. All the streets were named for trees. The area later became a residential section of Williamsbridge. At the turn of the twenty-first century most of the housing consisted of small one-family houses and apartment buildings.

John McNamara, *History in Asphalt: The Origin of Bronx Street and Place Names* (New York: Bronx County Historical Society, 1984)

Gary D. Hermalyn

Bronx Zoo. The largest metropolitan zoo in the United States. After a campaign led by the Boone and Crockett Club, the state of New York in 1895 awarded a charter to the New York Zoological Society that empowered it to build a zoological garden. William Hornaday (1844–1937), a well-known zoologist and one of the founders of the National Zoological Park in Washington, D.C., became the director of the project in 1896 and selected a site for the new zoo in southern Bronx Park. Plans were drawn up by the architects George Lewis Heins and C. Grant Lafarge in 1897, and construction on the zoo's beaux-arts pavilions began the following year. The New York Zoological Park, which became known as the Bronx Zoo, opened in November 1899, housing 843 animals. Its naturalistic, parklike settings were in marked contrast to the small exhibits in the Central Park Zoo. In 1902 the zoo appointed Reid Blair as the first full-time veterinarian at a zoo in the United States. In 1906 Hornaday incited controversy when he exhibited Ota Benga, a Congolese pygmy brought to the United States for the St. Louis World's Fair, in the monkey house. African American clergy immediately protested, and the exhibit was closed.

Hornaday, an authority on the nearly extinct American bison, set aside breeding sanctuaries for the species in the American West. In 1907 the zoo sent 15 bison to the new Wichita National Bison Reserve in Oklahoma, a project that influenced cooperative wildlife conservation efforts among zoos and nature reserves worldwide. In 1916 it opened an animal hospital, the first of its kind in the United States. Early in the tenure of Fairfield Osborn (1887–1969) as president of the New York Zoological Society (1940–68), hidden moats were added to the African Plains exhibit (1941), and a children's zoo (1941) and "farm in the zoo" (1942) were opened. William Conway, who joined the Bronx Zoo in 1956 as an assistant curator of birds, was appointed general director in 1966. Believing that zoos should serve as nature refuges and breeding centers for endangered species of wildlife, he developed exhibits that allowed the animals to live in naturalistic replicas of their habitats rather than cages. To lend emphasis to its role in international conservation, the New York Zoological Society in 1993 changed its name to the Wildlife Conservation Society; the formal name of the zoo became the Bronx Zoo / Wildlife Conservation Park. In the twenty-first century the zoo has used its influence to focus on environmental sustainability not only in New York City but throughout the world. In 2004 eco-friendly composting restrooms were installed in the zoo out of concern for the nearby Bronx River, and in 2008 the 1903 lion house was restored to environmentally green standards. The zoo, one of the largest in the world, is home to over 4000 animals of more than 500 species—many rare and endangered—and draws some two million visitors annually.

William Bridges, *Gathering of Animals: An Unconventional History of the New York Zoological Society* (New York: Harper and Row, 1974)

Steven Johnson, Kate Lauber

Brook. Exclusive social club formed in 1903. It was intended to offer uninterrupted service day and night and was named for Tennyson's poem (the last two lines of which read: "For men may come and men may go, / But I go on forever"). Among the founding members was Stanford White, who designed the first clubhouse (at 6 East 35th Street) and the second (at 7 East 40th Street), a brownstone with an added classical facade to which the club moved after one year. These buildings were furnished with libraries, antique furniture, fine china, and paintings by Benjamin West and Gilbert Stuart. Later the club moved to a building at 111 East 54th Street designed by another member, William Adams Delano.

James E. Mooney

Brookdale Hospital Medical Center. Private nonprofit hospital. It started in 1921 as a single building with 75 beds and gradually added more buildings and departments over the years. By 2008 it had grown to 539 beds and 30 buildings situated on a 14-acre (6-hectare) plot at 1 Brooksville Plaza. The hospital has specialized long-term care at the Schulman and Schachne Institute for Nursing and Rehabilitation, which relocated to Brookdale in 1973.

Max Seppo

Brookfield Properties. Real estate development firm based in Toronto, Canada, founded as Olympia and York. Under the ownership of Albert, Paul, and Ralph Reichmann it attracted widespread attention for buying eight distressed skyscrapers on prime sites in Manhattan during a real estate slump in 1977. This risky purchase helped to launch a wave of foreign investment in the city's real estate during the 1980s after a boom in financial services led the eight buildings to triple in value. Olympia and York became an important force in the local real estate market; it later built the World Financial Center in Battery Park City, a complex of four towers completed from 1981 to 1988 containing 8 million square feet (743,000 square meters) of office space. The firm went bankrupt in the early 1990s and reorganized as Brookfield Properties, maintaining many of its New York City properties, including the World Financial Center; despite the terrorist attacks of 11 September 2001, the firm has grown to be one of the largest publicly traded property managers and developers in the world.

Marc A. Weiss

Tollgate at Jamaica Avenue and Van Wyck Boulevard in Brooklyn, 1897 (demolished 1897)

Brooklyn. The most populous borough in New York City (2000 pop. 2,465,326), occupying 71 square miles (184 square kilometers) on the southwestern tip of Long Island and situated on New York Harbor across the East River from Manhattan. Once an independent municipality, it was the nation's third-largest city for nearly half a century. Although it became a borough of New York City in 1898, it still retains the qualities of a large urban complex, with an independent central business district and government center; remains of a sizable industrial base; distinguished educational and cultural institutions; many varied and lively neighborhoods; about 65 miles (105 kilometers) of natural shoreline, including some 7 miles (11 kilometers) of sandy beaches; 5959 acres (2413 hectares) of parkland; and about a quarter of the Gateway National Recreation Area.

1. From Settlement to Consolidation

At the time of European settlement, the territory was the home of Munsee-speaking native people known as the Lenapes or Delawares. Some 2000 Lenape Indians inhabited several villages in the southwestern section of Long Island, among them Keschaechquereren, Marechkawieck, and Canarsie. Until the arrival of Europeans the Indians lived harmoniously and subsisted on fish, shellfish, wild animals, and harvested produce. The first European ship to sight what became Brooklyn was probably that of Giovanni da Verrazano in 1524, but the first contact was most likely made by the crew of Henry Hudson's *Halve Maen* in 1609.

Basing its claim on Hudson's voyage, the Dutch West India Company settled what is now Brooklyn as part of the Dutch colony of New Netherland in about 1635, or around a decade after New Amsterdam (Manhattan). The company found the natural harbor, fertile lands, forests, and wetlands an ideal locale. The earliest recorded European land purchases were made in 1636 in what became Flatlands and Flatbush by a director of New Netherland, Wouter van Twiller, and his associates. Over the next several years other purchases were made in the areas of Gowanus and Wallabout bays for which the next director, Willem Kieft, issued patents. Regular ferry service to Manhattan began in the early 1640s, primarily to serve the needs of local farmers.

Antagonism between the Indians and Europeans emerged almost immediately in Brooklyn as well as other parts of New Netherland, owing partly to differing concepts of land ownership and efforts by the director to collect taxes from the Indians. A conflict in the mid-1640s, referred to as Governor Kieft's War, resulted not only in a marked decrease of the Indian population but also in a weakening of the Dutch colony's economy.

For both political and economic reasons the Dutch West India Company encouraged the formation of towns. Within about a decade the company formally and informally chartered the original six towns of what is now Brooklyn. Five of these were Dutch settlements: Breuckelen (Brooklyn) in 1646, directly across the East River from New Amsterdam and apparently named for the community in the Netherlands south of Amsterdam; New Amersfoort (Flatlands) in 1647; Midwout (Flatbush) in 1652; New Utrecht in 1657; and Boswick (Bushwick) in 1661. The sixth was the English town of Gravesend, founded by a group of followers of the Anabaptist Lady Deborah Moody and chartered in 1645.

The original towns tended to be situated on existing Indian paths: Breuckelen was settled along a path leading from Marechkawieck, which became known as the "road from the ferry" and later formally named Fulton Street. Only Gravesend adapted a formal layout. Its four-square plan of 1646, constituting one of the country's first planned communities, survives at an angle to the surrounding grid.

The director of New Netherland appointed magistrates for most of the towns, but they held minimal authority. Except in Gravesend the major town institution was the Dutch Reformed Church. Town settlers maintained their affiliations with the Dutch church in New Amsterdam until 1655, when a church was constructed in Flatbush. Soon the other towns erected their own churches. With the church came schools, and modest town centers began to take shape. The colony exhibited a degree of religious tolerance, and, in addition to the English settlers, early residents included Walloons (generally Huguenots from what are now southeastern Belgium and nearby France), French, and immigrants from elsewhere in Europe.

The six farming towns grew slowly, and the English takeover of the colony in 1664 had little effect. In 1683 Kings County was established as an administrative entity of the province of New York. Over the next several decades, county administration evolved from simple colonial courts and a county clerk to a board of supervisors, with representatives from each town. Elected town officials, usually chosen from among prosperous farmers, were concerned primarily with regulations governing the collection of taxes, the use and subdivision of land, and the laying out of roads. Intertown highways were the responsibility of the Board of Supervisors. Farming remained the chief occupation, with surplus produce brought to market in the town of Brooklyn across the river from Manhattan, or directly to Manhattan by the ferry, which was adjacent to the market.

By the 1680s the remaining Indian population of Brooklyn was virtually annihilated, its ability to subsist eroded by the relinquishing of virtually all Indian land, and its health ravaged by diseases imported from Europe. The European settlers increasingly relied on African slaves to provide an assured labor force, supplemented by indentured servants. At the end of the seventeenth century the county's population was about 2000.

The quiet life of the towns continued for much of the eighteenth century, and the population grew slowly over the next hundred years. Although most residents remained passive in the drive for independence that pervaded the colonies in mid-century, Kings County was the site of the Battle of Long Island (August 1776), the largest contest of the American Revolution and a disaster for the Continental Army, after which the British controlled both Kings County and Manhattan. After seven years of British occupation, marked by the notorious mistreatment of thousands of prisoners in British ships moored in Wallabout Bay, the county resumed its docile, rural existence.

Only one area of Kings County exhibited strong growth. As New York City evolved into the nation's urban center, the town of Brooklyn close to the ferry experienced gradual commercial development. Ropewalks, breweries, distilleries, slaughterhouses, and shops began to appear, and, in a clear sign that the area around the ferry was losing its rural character, the town officials in the late 1780s demarcated it as a separate fire district. In 1799 the county's first newspaper, the *Long Island Courier,* began publication there. The growth of business encouraged a spurt in population; within the next two decades the population of the town of Brooklyn tripled while the other five towns grew by less than a third.

With the introduction of Robert Fulton's steam ferry in 1814, farsighted entrepreneurs began to transform Brooklyn into one of the world's first commuter suburbs. Brooklyn Heights, on the hill above the ferry, was promoted as the ideal residence for affluent businessmen from Manhattan. In 1816 the town's built-up area was incorporated as the Village of Brooklyn, with its own elected trustees. The first urban street improvement project began in the village in 1819 with a survey and mapping of streets, followed by the grading and graveling of major roads and the installation of sidewalks along Fulton Street. In 1834, overcoming the opposition of New York City, the entire town of Brooklyn was chartered as the City of Brooklyn. At the time Brooklyn had fewer than 16,000 residents, and all of Kings County fewer than 25,000, compared with New York City's more than 200,000. Also in response to the city's progress, a second area of growth was emerging farther up the East River. In 1801 the U.S. Navy purchased a small shipyard on Wallabout Bay between the ferry district and the Town of Bushwick, a second ferry to Manhattan began operation just north of the yard, and in 1827 this part of Bushwick was incorporated as the Village of WILLIAMSBURGH.

After the establishment of the City of Brooklyn, local officials asked the state legislature to appoint a commission to map streets and public squares. The resulting plan of 1839 consisted of a rectangular grid of streets, overlaid by wider diagonal avenues and interspersed with several small parks. The subsequent development of Brooklyn generally followed this plan. In 1869 the state established the Town Survey Commission to map the towns of Flatbush, Flatlands, New Utrecht, and Gravesend; its plan of 1874 extended the street grid as far as Jamaica Bay. The grid changed angles slightly at town boundaries and shifts in topography. As the steam railway and the elevated railway reached the outlying towns, each town was annexed by Brooklyn.

The remainder of Kings County continued its measured growth, enjoying agricultural prosperity as a result of the development of both Brooklyn and New York City. Even with the adoption of state laws requiring gradual emancipation, slaveholders in Kings County seemed more reluctant than those of the state's other counties to abandon slavery. In 1800 more than a quarter of the county's residents were slaves, and not until mandatory emancipation in New York State in 1827 were they all freed. Many formerly enslaved residents remained in Kings County, securing employment as farmworkers or fishermen. In the 1830s and 1840s they founded several communities in central Brooklyn such as Weeksville and Carrville.

Brooklyn continued to grow as New York City became the country's dominant metropolis. After the opening of the Erie Canal in 1825 new waterfront warehouses, tanneries, and factories manufacturing such commodities as paint, glass, and glue began operations along the East River. These new enterprises generated the need for artisans such as wheelwrights and coopers as well as retail businesses, banks, and insurance companies, along with schools, churches, newspapers, libraries, and benevolent organizations. New ferry routes were initiated in the 1830s, and a steam railroad from the harbor to Jamaica began running in 1836.

City Hall (now BROOKLYN BOROUGH HALL), a Greek Revival structure completed in 1849 on Fulton Street uphill from the ferry landing, became the center of the downtown civic, business, shopping, and entertainment district. Municipal services—water supply, fire and police protection, and street lighting—and school systems expanded. Gaslights were introduced in Brooklyn in 1848, and the first horse-drawn street railways began operating in 1854. In the mid-1850s a board of water commissioners was established, and soon water was being pumped through Brooklyn from a new supply system.

Until the mid-nineteenth century, residents of Brooklyn depended largely on Manhattan's theaters and concert halls for cultural enlightenment. The origins of most major cultural institutions in Brooklyn may be traced to the Apprentices Library (1823), which was intended to provide youth with training in industry and intellectual subjects. After two unsettled decades its founders formed a new corporation, the Brooklyn Institute, which included an art gallery, a public hall for lectures and readings, and space for classes and natural history exhibits. By the 1850s the institute had become the center of Brooklyn's cultural life. To encourage an interest in music and literature and lessen reliance on institutions in Manhattan, wealthy citizens organized the BROOKLYN ACADEMY OF MUSIC in 1859. Its original building was completed in 1861 one block from City Hall, and from time to time it housed programs of the Brooklyn Institute. Other cultural institutions included the Mercantile Library, erected across the street several years later, and the Long Island Historical Society (1863; now the Brooklyn Historical Society).

Brooklyn at mid-century experienced tremendous growth. The Village of Williamsburgh became a city in 1851, and in 1854 Brooklyn annexed both Williamsburgh and the Town of Bushwick. By 1855 nearly half of Brooklyn's 205,000 residents were foreign born; of these more than half were Irish, and slightly less than a quarter each were German and English. The immigrant growth led to a proliferation of churches and ethnic social service organizations, and Brooklyn became known as both the city of homes and the city of churches.

By 1860 Brooklyn had 266,661 inhabitants, a figure exceeded only by New York City and Philadelphia. The remaining towns of Kings County were still largely rural, with a

Population of Selected Towns in Brooklyn, 1790–1890

	Brooklyn	Bushwick	Flatbush	Flatlands	Gravesend	New Utrecht	Williamsburgh
1790	1,603	540	941	423	426	562	N/A
1800	2,378	656	946	493	489	778	N/A
1820	7,175	930	1,027	512	534	1,009	N/A
1830	15,396	1,620[1]	1,143	596	565	1,217	N/A
1840	36,233	1,295	2,099	810	799	1,283	5,094
1850	96,838	3,739	3,177	1,155	1,064	2,129	30,780
1860	266,661	N/A	3,471	1,652	1,286	2,781	N/A
1870	396,099	N/A	6,309	2,286	2,131	3,296	N/A
1880	566,663	N/A	7,634	3,127	3,674	4,742	N/A
1890	806,343	N/A	12,338	4,075	6,937	8,854	N/A

1. Includes Williamsburgh.
N/A = Not Available
Note: Williamsburgh and Bushwick were annexed by Brooklyn in 1855. Population figures for towns were not included in the census of population of 1810.
Compiled by James Bradley

combined population of less than 12,500. Gradually those nearest Brooklyn began to be influenced by its phenomenal growth: a part of Flatbush was chartered as the Town of New Lots; farms gave way to row houses; and ferry lines, street grids, and transportation systems emerged. Meanwhile, the working-class and immigrant residents began settling in neighborhoods different from those inhabited by the middle class. The annexed area of Bushwick (by now called the Eastern District), for example, was heavily German; its many breweries helped give the community a distinctive character.

As the port in Manhattan became overcrowded, more firms moved to Brooklyn. And as the original waterfront district in Brooklyn filled up, shipbuilding and other heavy industries became concentrated along the waterfront of the Eastern District. By 1865 manufacturing employment in Brooklyn reached almost 14,000, with many more thousands working in transportation, warehousing, and related industries. Manufacturers found the waterfront of Brooklyn ideal for the region's heavy and bulky industries, including grain storage, sugar refining, and glass manufacturing. Some 7 miles (11 kilometers) of docks, warehouses, basins, grain elevators, drydocks, and freight terminals lined the shore from Red Hook in South Brooklyn to Newtown Creek in Greenpoint at the city's northern boundary.

As the center of population moved east away from the harbor, cultural institutions followed. The Brooklyn Institute reorganized in 1890 as the Brooklyn Institute of Arts and Sciences. Its directors planned a grand museum on land adjacent to PROSPECT PARK, the great landscaped green space designed by Frederick Law Olmsted and Calvert Vaux and completed in the early 1870s. Although the museum's imposing plans by McKim, Mead and White were never fully realized, the BROOKLYN MUSEUM, renowned for an outstanding permanent collection of Egyptian, American, and African materials, became one of the country's major art institutions.

Growth continued unabated during the last years of the nineteenth century, with Brooklyn's population reaching nearly 567,000 by 1880. Steady migration from Europe and rural America transformed the social and political life of the community. A number of major Republican figures came out of the Eastern District, and the Irish of South Brooklyn produced leading Democrats. New industries moved into Williamsburgh (by then spelled Williamsburg) and Greenpoint, including printing firms (D. Appleton and A. S. Barnes both moved their operations from Manhattan), oil refineries (Pratt Astral Oil Works being the largest), and iron foundries (such as the Hecla Architectural Iron Works and the firm of Cheney and Hewlett). By the 1880s Brooklyn was handling more waterborne tonnage than New York City, and it was the nation's fourth-largest industrial city.

Transportation advances also influenced growth. Horsecar lines were supplanted by steam railroads, which were built out to the beach resorts of Coney Island in Gravesend and Canarsie in Flatlands during the 1860s and 1870s. In 1885 the first elevated railroad in Brooklyn was completed, and within a few years more elevated lines began to extend into the county's outlying areas. These lines, along with the simultaneous conversion of the street railways from horse power to electricity, hastened the growth of suburbs and signaled the imminent development of the rural outer regions. Working conditions on the electrified railways, or trolleys, deteriorated as the companies recoiled from the costs of electrification and frequent reorganization, and in 1895 Brooklyn experienced an explosive trolley strike. The completion of the Brooklyn Bridge in 1883, the first physical link between the country's largest and third-largest cities, symbolized both their economic interdependence and their impending political union. Brooklyn was growing not only in population and commerce but also in physical size. In 1886 it annexed the Town of New Lots, and between 1894 and 1896 it annexed the remaining four original towns of Kings County. By the turn of the century the amusement parks and grand hotels of CONEY ISLAND, BRIGHTON BEACH, and MANHATTAN BEACH provided new entertainment forms for thousands of visitors from Brooklyn and Manhattan.

Having nearly reached its allowable state debt limit and nearly exhausted its ability to issue bonds, the governmental apparatus in Brooklyn could no longer support its impressive development. For some decades the Democratic machine, led by Hugh McLaughlin, controlled the government, with an occasional interruption by Republican reformers such as Seth Low. After years of contention the Democrats, supported by working-class and immigrant residents, lost out to the reformers, who joined their counterparts in New York City and New York State to move toward consolidation. On 1 January 1898 the City of Brooklyn became the Borough of Brooklyn.

2. From Consolidation through the Late Twentieth Century

The loss of political independence did nothing to hinder growth. By 1900 the population of Brooklyn exceeded one million. The expansion of existing transit lines, the arrival of subways, and the extension of public utilities made possible widespread residential and commercial development. During the first decades of the twentieth century, the outlying towns of Flatbush, Gravesend, New Utrecht, and Flatlands began to urbanize. The first subway into Brooklyn, which opened in 1908, and two additional bridges crossing the East River from Manhattan, completed by 1909, contributed to rapid residential and industrial development. Electrification of the elevated railways and steam railways by 1900 and the takeover of many of the existing lines by the Brooklyn Rapid Transit Company enabled the connection of various routes.

Industry in Brooklyn was still expanding, with more than 100,000 factory workers by 1905 and more than 165,000 by the 1920s. Industrial complexes such as Bush Terminal (1902) that fused docking, factory, warehousing, and transportation functions continued to draw large manufacturers, and industrial and business expansion brought more population. Until the passage of new immigration laws, culminating in 1924, Brooklyn attracted hundreds of thousands of immigrants, many of them from eastern and southern Europe. Rural Americans, including many African Americans from the South, were also arriving. Following the movement of population, the cultural institutions moved from the older downtown area farther into central Brooklyn. Schools and libraries multiplied. And with the arrival of the automobile, suburban developments, attached houses, and apartment buildings began filling in the street grids in outlying areas.

By the 1920s the Brooklyn Dodgers were becoming a symbol of fortitude for masses of local residents. Brooklyn had more than 2.5 million residents by 1930, making it New York City's most populous borough. The new modes of transportation were rendering the old obsolete. In 1924 the Fulton Ferry was discontinued, and the first airport in New York City, Floyd Bennett Field, was dedicated in 1931. The Independent Subway System opened in Brooklyn in 1936, followed by the cessation of elevated service on Fulton Street in 1940.

As outlying residential areas developed, neighborhoods closer to downtown were transformed. Older one-family houses and row houses were converted into rental apartments and rooming houses, and already congested working-class communities became more so. Decline and deterioration, the arrival of the "slum," seemed inevitable. The New Deal brought several public housing projects and other public improvements, such as community swimming pools. And World War II brought new jobs: the Brooklyn Navy Yard alone employed some 70,000 men and women in continuous shifts. The postwar years brought general prosperity to Brooklyn, and its population peaked in 1950 at 2.7 million. In the 1950s a renewal project of the borough's civic center eliminated a substantial amount of older housing and businesses; the resulting housing, parks, and wide thoroughfares left the district devoid of its former cosmopolitan vitality.

Postwar prosperity did not last as the borough fell into a decline, symbolized by the demise in 1955 of its one nationally known daily newspaper, the *Brooklyn Eagle,* and the departure in 1957 of its fabled baseball team, the Dodgers. The same automobile that had stimulated development of the borough's suburban areas now took residents beyond its borders to yet newer suburbs. Spurred by new federal housing mortgage and highway construction programs and the completion of the Verrazano–Narrows Bridge in 1964, hundreds of thousands of white, middle-class residents abandoned Brooklyn for Long Island, Staten Island, and New Jersey, to be replaced largely by working-class and immigrant populations.

Brooklyn experienced a severe loss in jobs at the same time. Total manufacturing employment fell from more than 235,000 in 1954 to less than 200,000 by 1970, as companies looked beyond the borough for vacant land on which to build more efficient facilities, as well as for cheaper labor and utilities and lower taxes. Taking advantage of federal tax credits for new capital investment, whole industries such as shipping and brewing abandoned the borough outright. In 1956 the Port of New York Authority purchased and renovated 2 miles (3 kilometers) of deteriorating waterfront, but in less than two decades, after failing to provide the requisite facilities for containerization, the piers were all but abandoned. In 1966 the federal government shut down the Brooklyn Navy Yard, leaving the waterfront almost inactive. By 1970 entire industrial and residential districts had taken on the appearance of bombed-out communities of wartime.

After 1970 Brooklyn experienced considerable renewal, but even where the city intervened with new subsidized housing, as in Coney Island, the new projects often failed to stimulate community rebirth. In other neighborhoods, efforts by longtime residents and new arrivals were more successful. With a combination of public and private funds, organizations such as the Bedford Stuyvesant Restoration Corporation and the Pratt Center for Community and Environmental Development and businesses such as the Brooklyn Union Gas Company and Consolidated Edison helped to improve housing conditions and create new amenities. Brooklyn was the birthplace of the brownstone revival movement, and the landmarks preservation movement inspired the renaissance of many of the borough's historic neighborhoods. In 1965 Brooklyn Heights became New York City's first Historic District.

Through government and private intervention, Brooklyn strove to revitalize its economic core, although there were some dramatic declines. In the early 1970s the City of New York, in cooperation with local nonprofit groups, began to transform the decommissioned Brooklyn Navy Yard into an industrial park. A number of national companies such as International Business Machines (IBM) collaborated on economic redevelopment with the Bedford Stuyvesant Restoration Corporation.

The downtown business district, which during the 1970s declined from third- to sixth-largest in the United States, still employed some 40,000 workers, although manufacturing employment in Brooklyn fell below 100,000 by the early 1980s. In the mid-1990s MetroTech, a multiblock academic and high-technology office and research complex, began adding thousands of workers and a new vitality to downtown.

3. The Twenty-First Century

The twenty-first century has seen an enormous burst of residential and commercial activity in Brooklyn. Adding a fresh vibrancy to many neighborhoods are new boutiques, eateries, artists' and designers' lofts, "big-box" chain stores, performance spaces, and hotels. In 2001, the minor-league Brooklyn Cyclones began playing out of Coney Island. And in 2006 a cruise-ship terminal opened in Red Hook.

The borough remains widely known for its cultural institutions. The Brooklyn Public Library (formed in 1896, merged in 1903 with the Mercantile Library) occupies a headquarters erected in the 1930s near Prospect Park and also oversees some 58 branches and a business library. The Brooklyn Botanic Garden, opened in 1911 next to Prospect Park, is one of the world's great public horticultural institutions and was the first botanical garden to establish a garden specifically for children. Other notable institutions include the Brooklyn Academy of Music, one of the nation's premier avant-garde performing arts centers; the Brooklyn Museum, a major American art institution; the Brooklyn Children's Museum (1899), the first museum of its kind in the world; the Brooklyn Historical Society, which features an excellent research library; the New York Aquarium, which moved to Brooklyn in 1957; and many educational institutions, including Brooklyn College, Pratt Institute, Long Island University, and Polytechnic University.

Major residential, commercial, cultural, and recreational projects are in planning throughout the borough. A number of them, however, face opposition concerning their possible environmental impact and potential residential displacement.

Both the periods of phenomenal growth and devastating declines have contributed to the richness of Brooklyn. While the growth has allowed the borough to prosper, the declines have resulted inadvertently in the survival of

Roosevelt Island
New Jersey
Hudson River
Manhattan
East River
Newtown Creek
Greenpoint
Queens
278
Bedford Av
Brooklyn–Queens Expressway
Metropolitan Av
Williamsburg Bridge
DUMBO
Manhattan Bridge
Brooklyn Bridge
(Dutchtown)
WILLIAMSBURG
Broadway
DeKalb Av
Brooklyn Navy Yard (Wallabout)
Vinegar Hill
Fulton Ferry
Brooklyn Heights
(Cripplebush)
Bushwick
Cypress Hills Cemetery
Ellis Island
Liberty Island (Bedloe's Island)
Governors Island
Buttermilk Channel
Flatbush Av
Fort Greene
Clinton Hill
DeKalb Av
BEDFORD-STUYVESANT
Ridgewood
Downtown Brooklyn
Cobble Hill
(Punkiesberg)
(South Brooklyn)
Boerum Hill
Fulton St
Atlantic Av
(Bedford Corners)
Stuyvesant Heights
Ocean Hill
Cemetery of the Evergreens
Cypress Hills
(Union Place)
Jamaica Av
Highland Park
Fulton St
Atlantic Av
Queens
Upper New York Bay
Red Hook
Carroll Gardens
Prospect Heights
Broadway Junction
(Carrville)
(Weeksville)
Eastern Pkwy
Pitkin Av
City Line
Erie Basin
Gowanus
Park Slope
Crown Heights
(Crow Hill)
(Jamaica Pass)
EAST NEW YORK
(Plunders Neck)
Gowanus Bay
Brooklyn Botanic Garden
(Pigtown)
East New York Av
Prospect Expressway
7 Av
Prospect Park
Prospect-Lefferts Gardens
(Lefferts Manor)
Brownsville
New Lots
Spring Creek
Windsor Terrace
Wingate
(Oostwoud)
Penn Av
Belt Parkway
Bush Terminal
Gowanus Expressway
Green-Wood Cemetery
Parkside
Parade Grounds
Utica Av
Kings Highway
Flatlands Av
Starrett City
Rugby
Remsen Village
Rockaway Pkwy
Sunset Park
Ft Hamilton Pkwy
Prospect Park South
Holy Cross Cemetery
East Flatbush
4 Av
Farragut
Ditmas Av
Kensington
FLATBUSH
Brooklyn
Canarsie
Borough Park
Ditmas Av
BAY RIDGE
Parkville
Ditmas Park
Flatlands Av
Paedergat Basin
(Blythebourne)
Mapleton
New Utrecht Av
Ditmas Av
(Greenfield)
Flatbush Av
86 St
Georgetown
Dyker Heights
Midwood
(Yellow Hook)
18 Av
Bay Parkway
Ocean Pkwy
Coney Island Av
Flatlands
Mill Basin
Bergen Beach
New Utrecht
86 St
Avenue P
BENSONHURST
Marine Park
Narrows
Verrazano Narrows Bridge
Fort Hamilton
Av P
Kings Highway
Mill Island
Jamaica Bay
Bath Beach
Kings Highway
Homecrest
Marine Park
Flatbush Av
Mill Basin
Staten Island
Avenue U
Avenue U
Gravesend
86 St
Floyd Bennett Field
(Barren Island)
Lower New York Bay
Gravesend Bay
Stillwell Av
Ocean Pkwy
Sheepshead Bay
Gerritsen Beach
Belt Parkway
Sheepshead Bay
Plum Beach
Sea Gate
Neptune Av
(West Brighton)
Brighton Beach
Manhattan Beach
CONEY ISLAND
Marine Parkway Bridge
Queens
Rockaway Inlet
Atlantic Ocean
The Rockaways
Designed by John Tauranac
Tauranac, Ltd.
1995; Revised, 2010

aspects of local history that might have disappeared had the prosperity been constant—Dutch street names, architecturally distinguished houses, handsome factories, prominent cultural institutions, ethnically diverse neighborhoods, and even remnants of the original town centers. The combination of these vestiges of the past with the energy of the present gives Brooklyn its continued promise for the future.

Henry R. Stiles, ed., *History of the City of Brooklyn* (Brooklyn: Published by subscription, 1867–70) and Stiles, *The Civil, Political, Professional and Ecclesiastical History and Commercial and Industrial Record of the County of Kings and the City of Brooklyn, New York, from 1683–1884* (New York: W. W. Munsell, 1884); David Ment, *The Shaping of a City: A Brief History of Brooklyn* (New York: Brooklyn Educational and Cultural Alliance, 1979); Margaret Latimer, *Brooklyn Almanac: Illustrations, Facts, Figures, People, Buildings, Books* (New York: Brooklyn Educational and Cultural Alliance, 1984); Ellen Snyder–Grenier, *Brooklyn: An Illustrated History (Critical Perspectives on the Past)* (Philadelphia: Temple University Press, 2004)

Margaret Latimer

Brooklyn, Bath and West End Railroad. The successor to the Brooklyn, Bath and Coney Island horsecar line, founded in 1862, which connected 25th Street and Fifth Avenue in Brooklyn and the ferry slip at 39th Street in Brooklyn with the Tivoli Hotel and Amusement Park in Coney Island. The line was completed in 1867, and in 1870 steam power replaced the horses. In 1885 the Atlantic Avenue Railroad acquired the line and renamed it the Brooklyn, Bath and West End. It merged in 1898 with the Nassau Electric Railroad and in the following year became part of the Brooklyn Rapid Transit Company. Electric trolley service began in 1901, and an elevated line was completed in 1917 (it is now part of the "B" line). The trolley service continued on the original grade until 1947.

James C. Greller and Edward C. Watson, *Brooklyn Elevated* (Hicksville, N.Y.: N.J. International, 1987)

John Fink

Brooklyn, Canarsie and Rockaway Beach Rail Road. Railroad opened on 21 October 1865 as a subsidiary of the Long Island Rail Road (LIRR). It connected eastern New York City to Canarsie Landing by rail, from where a ferry took passengers to Rockaway Beach. The LIRR added train connections from Valley Stream and Woodhaven Junction to Rockaway Beach in 1870. The line became electric-powered in 1906, when it was leased to the Brooklyn Union Elevated Railroad (a subsidiary of Brooklyn Rapid Transit). During the early years of the twentieth century the line offered the most popular route for New Yorkers seeking to visit the amusement park at Canarsie Beach. Service between Canarsie Landing and Rockaway Avenue was provided from October 1917 by a trolley shuttle and from 1951 by buses. In 1928 the elevated tracks of the railroad were connected to the subway line of Brooklyn Manhattan Transit running to 14th Street in Manhattan.

James C. Greller and Edward C. Watson, *Brooklyn Elevated* (Hicksville, N.Y.: N.J. International, 1987)

John Fink

Brooklyn, Flatbush and Coney Island Railway. Railroad opened on 2 July 1878. It began as a steam railroad connecting the Brighton Hotel near Coney Island with the Long Island Rail Road at Atlantic and Franklin avenues. In 1887 the line merged with the Brooklyn Union Elevated Railroad (a subsidiary of Brooklyn Rapid Transit) and was renamed the Brooklyn and Brighton Beach Railway. An extension was then built between Prospect Park and Fulton Street (now known as the "S" line, or Franklin Avenue Shuttle) to provide direct access between Brighton and downtown Brooklyn. In 1905 electric power replaced steam and the line was rebuilt, with an "open cut" between Prospect Park and Avenue H and an elevated structure south of Avenue H. The company extended the elevated line in 1917 to Stillwell Avenue on Coney Island, thus forming a double-level structure that became commonly associated with Coney Island. Direct service between Brighton Beach and midtown Manhattan was established in 1920 when the subway between Prospect Park and DeKalb Avenue was completed. The railroad was the forerunner of the "D" and "Q" subway lines in Brooklyn.

John Fink

Brooklyn Academy of Music [BAM]. Performing arts center at 30 Lafayette Avenue in the Fort Greene neighborhood of Brooklyn. The present building was erected by the firm of Herts and Tallant in 1908, replacing one at Montague and Clinton streets opened on 15 January 1861 and destroyed by fire on 30 November 1903. Actor Edwin Booth first performed at the academy in 1862, and on 4 April 1891 he gave the last performance of his career at the Montague Street building, drawing thousands to see him in his signature role as Hamlet. The academy is a stately, cream-colored brick building in the neo-Italianate style that includes three major performance spaces: the Howard Gilman Opera House (seating 2109), the Harvey Lichtenstein Theater (seating 874), and BAMcafé, formerly Leperq Space, an old ballroom remodeled in 1997 as a restaurant and live music venue. From 1935 to 1970 BAM was one of several organizations in the borough affiliated with the Brooklyn Institute of Arts and Sciences. At the initiative of Harvey Lichtenstein, president and executive producer, the academy expanded its offerings in 1967 to encompass ethnic music, dance, and theater. The Next Wave Festival, an avant-garde series, was launched in 1981. In the same year the academy formed a local development corporation that purchased and refurbished several performing sites nearby. In 1998 a four-screen movie theater, BAM Rose Cinemas, was added to the performance space. The academy emphasizes new and unusual repertory and

Brooklyn Academy of Music, 2009

draws audiences from throughout the metropolitan area. The Brooklyn Philharmonic is the resident orchestra.

Martha McGowan, *Growing Up in Brooklyn: The Brooklyn Academy of Music: Mirror of a Changing Borough* (New York: Brooklyn Union Gas, 1983)

Bruce C. MacIntyre

Brooklyn Apprentices Library. Forerunner of the Brooklyn Museum.

Brooklyn Army Terminal. Military ocean supply facility situated in Sunset Park along Second Avenue from 58th to 65th streets. It was designed by Cass Gilbert and completed in 1919. The terminal covers 97 acres (39 hectares) and at its peak consisted of 19 structures, including two eight-story warehouses of reinforced concrete, one of which was at the time the largest warehouse in the world. A unique interior well permitted direct loading and unloading to any level of the building, and three enclosed two-story piers permitted the simultaneous loading of 20 oceangoing vessels. During World War II three million troops and 37 million tons of supplies sent overseas by the New York Port of Embarkation passed through the terminal. In 1984 the New York Public Development Corporation bought the facility, which was converted to manufacturing space for many small businesses.

Joseph F. Meany, Jr.

Brooklyn Atlantics. Baseball team. Formed in August 1856 in the village of Bedford in what is now Brooklyn, it was one of the dominant teams of the early years of baseball. The social club that sponsored the team had as members many butchers and others from the food trades and enjoyed close ties with local political factions. The team had a large working-class following and won several unofficial championships during the 1860s. Originally an amateur organization, it fielded a few paid players after the Civil War. Perhaps its greatest achievement was its defeat in 1870 of the first entirely professional baseball team, the Cincinnati Red Stockings, which until then had won 84 consecutive games. Reorganized as an all-professional team, the Atlantics competed in the National Association of Professional Base Ball Players from 1872 to 1875.

George B. Kirsch

Brooklyn–Battery Tunnel. Longest continuous underwater tunnel for motor vehicles in North America, spanning Upper New York Bay between the southern tip of Manhattan (called the battery for an artillery battery that used to stand there) and the Brooklyn–Queens Expressway in Brooklyn. It was designed by Ole Singstad. In order to finance it Mayor Fiorello H. La Guardia ceded control of the New York City Tunnel Authority (which was short on funds and could not get assistance from the Public Works Administration) to Robert Moses's Triborough Bridge Authority, which had enough money to complete the project. Moses tried to change the plan from a tunnel to a bridge but was denied permission by President Franklin D. Roosevelt, who was concerned that a bridge would be vulnerable to attack and would block the Brooklyn Navy Yard's access to the sea. Construction began in 1940 and was suspended during World War II owing to iron and steel shortages; construction resumed in 1945, and the tunnel opened to traffic on 25 May 1950. Two tubes lined in cast iron and measuring 31 feet (9.5 meters) in diameter span 9117 feet (2781 meters). Air is circulated through the tunnel by four ventilating towers, including one situated near Governors Island. Some 60,000 vehicles use the Brooklyn–Battery Tunnel each day.

Rebecca Read Shanor

Brooklyn Borough Hall. Building at 209 Joralemon Street, opened in 1848 as the city hall of Brooklyn. Plans were laid in 1835, a year after Brooklyn was granted its city charter. The winning entry in a design competition was submitted by the architect Calvin Pollard, who proposed a majestic building in a Greek Revival style. Construction began in 1836 but was halted after the foundation was completed owing to the city's precarious financial condition and the panic of 1837. Interest in resuming construction revived in the early 1840s. In 1845 a bond issue of $50,000 was authorized by the state legislature, and Gamaliel King, an architect from Brooklyn, was commissioned to design a building for the existing foundation. His design, a simplified version of Pollard's, called for a structure of Tuckahoe marble with an Ionic portico and a wooden cupola. In 1895 the cupola and sections of the interior were destroyed by fire; in 1898 Vincent Griffith and the firm of Stoughton and Stoughton designed and installed a cupola of cast iron. On the consolidation of Brooklyn and New York City in 1898 the building became the borough hall. The room formerly used by the Common Council was converted into a courtroom in a beaux-arts style by the architect Axel Hedman in 1902. Brooklyn Borough Hall deteriorated steadily until its restoration was completed in 1989 under the direction of the firm of Conklin Rossant.

William J. Conklin and Jeffrey Simpson, *Brooklyn's City Hall* (New York: Department of General Services, 1983); Andrew S. Dolkart, *Borough Hall, 1848–1949* (New York: Fund for the Borough of Brooklyn, 1989)

Andrew S. Dolkart

Brooklyn Brewery. Brooklyn-based brewing company. Started in 1987, it is one of the few breweries in New York City in the early twentieth century. Owned by Steve Hindy, a former reporter, and Tom Potter, a former banker, it produces Brooklyn Lager, a draft

Brooklyn Borough Hall, 2009

beer. It is located at #1 Brewer's Row, 79 North 11th Street, Williamsburg.

Holly Cronin

Brooklyn Bridge. Steel suspension bridge across the East River between Brooklyn and Manhattan, opened on 24 May 1883. Its span of 1595.5 feet (486.3 meters) between towers was for a time the longest in the world. The bridge was the inspiration of the engineer John Augustus Roebling, the inventor of wire cable and an accomplished bridge builder who in 1867 put forth a plan to William C. Kingsley, publisher of the *Brooklyn Eagle*. He envisioned two massive stone towers, a network of steel cables suspended from the towers and embedded in anchorages at either end, vertical wires connecting the roadbed to the cables and reinforced by diagonal stays running down from the towers, and iron trusses underpinning the suspended floor from tower to tower to stiffen the roadbed. The unprecedented use of steel in a suspension bridge was intended to provide unmatched strength and stability. A bill to incorporate the New York Bridge Company, introduced in the state legislature at the behest of Kingsley by Henry Murphy, a state senator and former mayor of Brooklyn, was passed in April 1867 after an unusually cold winter that emphasized the vulnerability of ferry service to the elements. The project suffered a severe setback in June 1869, when just as the necessary approvals had been secured Roebling was fatally injured by a ferry that toppled him from a waterfront piling. His place was taken by his son Washington Roebling, who solved many structural problems in what remained a difficult and dangerous project. So that the towers of the bridge would sit firmly on bedrock, the riverbed was excavated by men working in huge, bottomless wooden boxes called caissons. The risk of fire was ever present, and the men were susceptible to the bends (then called caisson disease and poorly understood). Roebling himself fell victim to the bends while working alongside the men sinking the western caisson in the summer of 1872 and was an invalid to the end of his life. He continued nevertheless to supervise operations through a telescope from his room on Columbia Heights while his wife, Emily Warren Roebling, relayed his instructions to workers and managers. The project continued to be plagued with difficulties: in 1878 Washington Roebling found that defective wire rope had been woven into the bridge cables, the result of graft on the part of the suppliers (he used sound wire to reinforce the cables), and soon afterward the project ran short of money (new appropriations were made in 1879). On its completion the bridge was widely acclaimed as the "new eighth wonder of the world." Its lavish dedication was attended by the mayors of Brooklyn and New York City, Governor Grover Cleveland, and President Chester A. Arthur, but not by Roebling, whose relations with the bridge company for the last four years of the project had been deeply strained. The opening of the bridge to the public a week later was marred by the deaths of 12 pedestrians who were trampled during a panic set off by a shouted warning, anonymous and groundless, that the bridge was in danger of imminent collapse.

The Brooklyn Bridge became a highly recognizable landmark and an important cultural icon, and many artists and writers saw it as a symbol of American urbanization and industrialization. To Walt Whitman it was the work of engineering that completed Columbus's mission and helped to create a more closely linked world; to Hart Crane in the 1920s it was an affirmation of love, beauty, and the divine wholeness and unity of all history. The early twentieth-century painters John Marin and Joseph Stella saw the

Brooklyn Bridge, 2009

bridge and the skyscrapers nearby as the embodiment of the evolving new world. Henry James detested the bridge, which he characterized as a mechanical monster and a soulless loom across which the "electric bobbins" of trains wove together two cities and by extension the world. But the critic Lewis Mumford believed that the Brooklyn Bridge had become "a source of joy and inspiration to the artist, perhaps the most completely satisfying structure of any kind that [has] appeared in America." No other bridge has ever been so richly woven into American culture.

Alan Trachtenberg, *Brooklyn Bridge: Fact and Symbol* (New York: Oxford University Press, 1965); David G. McCullough, *The Great Bridge* (New York: Simon and Schuster, 1972)

Ellen Fletcher

Brooklyn Bridge Park. Park stretching from Atlantic Avenue to Jay Street along the East River in Brooklyn. The park's conception began in 1998 when the Port Authority of New York and New Jersey put the 1.3-acre (0.5-hectare) site, which included six defunct cargo shipping piers, up for sale to a private developer. In 2002 Governor George Pataki and Mayor Michael Bloomberg created the Brooklyn Bridge Park Development Corporation to develop a park instead. The nonprofit Brooklyn Bridge Park Conservancy manages its funding and operations to comply with the requirement that the park be financially self-sufficient. A plan was announced in 2004 to build luxury condominiums within the park's borders; residents of these apartments will pay fees to fund the park's maintenance in lieu of taxes. The unprecedented placement of private homes inside a public park has drawn ire from the plan's opponents. An organization called the Brooklyn Bridge Park Defense Fund filed a lawsuit to stop the plan; the suit was defeated and was being appealed as of 2008. The first phases of the park opened in 2010, and the park will eventually comprise 85 waterfront acres (34.4 hectares).

Kate Lauber

Brooklyn Children's Museum. Museum opened in 1899 in two Victorian mansions at 5 Brooklyn Avenue and St. Mark's Avenue as the first children's museum in the United States. In 1976 a spacious new building was erected on the same site. The museum was the first to use interactive, "hands-on" exhibits to help children understand the physical and cultural world. Most of the museum is underground and not visible from the street.

Laura J. Lewison

Brooklyn College. College of the City University of New York, opened in 1910 as an extension division of City College for Teachers. In 1917 it began offering first-year evening classes to male high school graduates. In 1926 the Board of Higher Education opened the Brooklyn Collegiate Center of City College for men and the Brooklyn Collegiate Center of Hunter College for women in an office building at Willoughby and Bridge streets. The board authorized a new coeducational, four-year college in Brooklyn in 1930. The newly constructed neo-Georgian campus between Flatbush and Ocean avenues opened in 1937. Harry D. Gideonse, the president from 1939 to 1966, presided over the college's growth in the turbulent years surrounding World War II. After an investigation by the New York state legislature's Rapp–Coudert Committee in the early 1940s, the college was reputed to hold leftist sympathies and was sometimes referred to as the "little red schoolhouse" (see Communism). After the war it expanded its programs, increased enrollment, and began to enhance its academic reputation. During the Vietnam War the campus was plagued by student unrest. One demand of the protesters was an open admissions policy. When it was implemented in 1970, enrollment soared from nearly 20,000 to more than 35,000 students, putting an enormous strain on the institution's resources and causing the college to install temporary buildings on campus. Many of the new students were ill prepared, resulting in the need for remedial programs. Critics' assertions that open admissions had lowered academic standards helped scuttle the policy when the fiscal crisis struck in 1975 and free tuition was eliminated. In the 1980s the college adopted a core curriculum that garnered national attention. Newly hired distinguished professors included the poet Allen Ginsberg and the violinist Itzhak Perlman. A new state-of-the-art library opened in 2002.

Murray M. Horowitz, *Brooklyn College: The First Half Century* (New York: Brooklyn College Press, 1981)

Selma Berrol, William M. Gargan

Brooklyn Collegiate and Polytechnic Institute. Original name of Polytechnic University.

Brooklyn Cyclones. Baseball team formed in 2001 as a minor league farm team of the New York Mets. Playing in MCU Park in Coney Island, the Cyclones, named after the Coney Island roller coaster, are in the New York Penn League, the lowest level in the minor leagues. The team has drawn large crowds. They were co-champions of the New York Penn League in 2001 and won division titles in 2003, 2004, and 2007. The Cyclones became the first professional team in Brooklyn since the Dodgers left in 1957.

Steven Levine

Brooklyn Daily Times. Name from 1855 to 1932 of the Brooklyn Times–Union.

Brooklyn Dodgers. Baseball team, formed in 1883 when the Interstate Minor League granted a franchise in Brooklyn to Charles Byrne and Joseph Doyle, both businessmen from Manhattan, and Ferdinand Abell, a casino owner from Rhode Island. The team joined the major leagues in 1884 when it moved to the American Association; in 1890 it moved to the National League. The name derived from the reputed skill of residents of Brooklyn at evading the streetcars of the burgeoning trolley system; other names applied to the team in its early years included the Bridegrooms (inspired by a series of marriages by team members in 1889), the Superbas (because the manager at the turn of the century was Ned Hanlon, and a popular theatrical group at the time was called Hanlon's Superbas), and the Robins (after the manager from 1914 to 1931, Wilbert Robinson). The team played at two stadiums in South Brooklyn, each called Washington Park, and at Eastern Park in Brownsville near Broadway

Keyspan Park (now MCU Park), home of the Brooklyn Cyclones, 2009

Junction before moving to Ebbets Field in 1913. The strong pitching of Jeff Pfeffer and Burleigh Grimes and the consistent batting and fielding of the left fielder Zach Wheat helped the team to win the National League pennant in 1916 and 1920, but it lost the World Series to the Boston Red Sox and the Cleveland Indians. In 1920 it played a 26-inning game at Boston that ended with the score tied at one, and it also suffered the embarrassment of hitting into an unassisted triple play at Cleveland in the World Series. From 1909 to 1925 Wheat established team records for games played, hits, doubles, triples, and total bases. The first member of the Dodgers other than a pitcher to be elected to the Baseball Hall of Fame, Wheat was highly popular with fans throughout his career.

From 1925 to 1938 the Dodgers played an inept and unintentionally comic brand of baseball that earned them the nickname the Daffiness Boys. Their fortunes changed after Larry MacPhail became the general manager in 1938: he named Leo Durocher the manager, acquired young players like Pee Wee Reese and Pete Reiser, and engaged as the team's radio broadcaster Red Barber, whose relaxed southern manner and knowledge of the game along with the Dodgers' improved play greatly increased the team's following. The fans in Brooklyn became widely known for their eccentricity. During the 1930s and 1940s Hilda Chester sat in the bleachers in center field bellowing at players and ringing a cowbell, and the Sym-Phony Band paraded through the stands serenading opposing players and umpires. The unofficial symbol of the team was a depiction by the cartoonist Willard Mullin of a Dodger player as an amiable bum. During the war years Branch Rickey assumed control of the team, and in 1945 he signed Jackie Robinson to a contract with the Dodgers' minor league affiliate in Montreal. Robinson joined the team in 1947 as the first black player in the modern major leagues. His strength of character in withstanding severe racial bigotry united the team, and his outstanding play brought it wide acclaim. Between 1947 and 1957 the Dodgers benefited from a powerful offense led by Reese, Robinson, Duke Snider, Gil Hodges, Roy Campanella, and Carl Furillo that enabled them to win six National League pennants. Opposed each time in the World Series by the New York Yankees, they were able to win only in 1955, largely because apart from Don Newcombe and Carl Erskine they were lacking in strong pitchers. After the 1957 season the Dodgers' president Walter O'Malley moved the team to Los Angeles, an act that provoked enduring anger and resentment among residents of Brooklyn.

Roger Kahn, *The Boys of Summer* (New York: Harper and Row, 1971); Jules Tygiel, *Baseball's Great Experiment: Jackie Robinson and His Legacy* (New York: Random House, 1983)

See also SPORTS, §§3, 4.

Stephen Weinstein

Brooklyn Eagle. Daily newspaper. It began in 1841 as an organ of the Democratic Party called the *Brooklyn Eagle and King's County Democrat* and published daily. For two years its chief editor was Walt Whitman, who in 1846 articulated the principle that partisanship should not prevent the newspaper from speaking to all the people of Brooklyn. By the time of the Civil War it was the most widely read afternoon newspaper in the United States, and during the war it was one of several publications that the federal government threatened to suspend. It remained the largest daily and Sunday newspaper in Brooklyn and in 1937 absorbed its last major competitor, the *Brooklyn Times–Union*. Over the years the newspaper won the Pulitzer Prize four times, once for exposing corruption in the police department during the administration of Mayor William O'Dwyer. After a decline in daily circulation to 125,000, a long-running dispute with the New York Newspaper Guild, and a lengthy strike it ceased publication in 1955. For a few months in 1960 it resumed publication as a weekly newspaper, and it was published daily for a year ending in mid-1963. Among those who wrote for the *Brooklyn Eagle* were St. Clair McKelway, Hans von Kaltenborn, Edward Bok, Nunnally Johnson, and Winston Burdett. Until 1955 the offices were on what is now Cadman Park East.

Raymond A. Schroth, *The Eagle and Brooklyn* (Westport, Conn.: Greenwood, 1974)

John J. Gallagher

Brooklyn Female Academy. Original name of PACKER COLLEGIATE INSTITUTE.

Brooklyn Ferry. Former name of BROOKLYN HEIGHTS.

Brooklyn Friends School. Coeducational elementary and secondary school founded by the Brooklyn Meeting of the Religious Society of Friends and opened in 1867 in the basement of the Quaker Meeting House on Schermerhorn Street. In 1972 it moved to 375 Pearl Street in Brooklyn Heights (the former site of the Brooklyn Law School). The school adheres to Quaker educational principles and emphasizes academic excellence, tolerance, community service, and pacifism. It was among the earliest schools in New York City to promote ethnic and racial diversity in its student body, which enrolls children ages 20 months through the 12th grade. The school sponsors a chorus consisting of students and the elderly that was the subject of the documentary film *Close Harmony* (1981), which won an Academy Award.

Richard Schwartz

Brooklyn Gas Light Company. Utility chartered in 1825. It failed but was revived in 1847 after receiving a contract to light streets. From 1849 it delivered gas manufactured from coal in a plant beside the Brooklyn Navy Yard. In 1895 it was one of seven firms that merged to form the Brooklyn Union Gas Company.

William J. Hausman

Brooklyn Heights. Neighborhood in northwestern Brooklyn (2009 est. pop. 20,000), bounded to the west and north by Columbia Heights and the Brooklyn–Queens Expressway, to the east by Court Street and Cadman Plaza West, and to the south by Atlantic Avenue. Canarsee Indians lived on the bluffs above the East River and called the place Ihpetonga. By 1642 farms in the area were served by ferries, the most important of which was run by Cornelis Dircksen from the foot of what is now Fulton Street to Peck Slip in Manhattan. The village of Brooklyn thrived around the ferry landing and along Fulton Street, but until the second decade of the nineteenth century the high ground overlooking the river was sparsely settled with a few good-sized farms; there were some factories along the wharves at water level. General Israel Putnam withdrew his troops to the area after the American defeat in the Battle of Long Island, during which George Washington

Brooklyn Heights, ca *1904; foreground shows docks along the shore of Manhattan*

maintained his headquarters in a house at the foot of what is now Montague Street. Washington evacuated the troops across the river under cover of fog on 29–30 August 1776.

Speculative development in the area began soon after Robert Fulton's steam ferry began its dependable schedule of crossings of the East River in 1814. Streets were laid out and graded after Brooklyn was incorporated as a village in 1816, and from 1823 the merchant Hezekiah Pierpont advertised his property as "the nearest country retreat" convenient for people working in lower Manhattan. Soon other landowners including John Hicks, Jacob Middagh Hicks, John Middagh, Henry Remsen, and Teunis Joralemon divided their farms into lots measuring 25 by 100 feet (8 by 30 meters), still the common unit of property in the neighborhood. The building boom of the 1820s began at the northern end of the district, on Hicks Street and the adjacent cross streets. Frame and brick buildings two and a half stories high in a late Federal style with pitched and gambrel roofs were standard; many belonged to tradespeople, sailors, and waterfront workers, and a number still stand. Essentially, Brooklyn Heights became the world's first commuter suburb. By the 1830s and 1840s more substantial houses of brick and brownstone with Greek Revival details were being built farther south. During the following decades the houses grew larger, exhibiting the entire range of revival styles that swept American architecture: Italianate, Second Empire, Victorian Gothic, Romanesque, neo-Greco, and Classical Revival. Some of the houses belonged to merchants whose ships docked at the wharves below. Throughout the nineteenth century the neighborhood had an unmatched elegance. Warehouses along Furman Street below the bluff had trees and grass planted on their roofs: these were the back gardens of the houses of Columbia Heights.

In 1908 Interborough Rapid Transit opened its subway, breaking the seclusion of Brooklyn Heights and making it easier to live there and work in Manhattan. Many of the patricians fled, and their mansions were partitioned into apartments and boarding houses. Artists and writers were attracted by the character of the neighborhood. Several large hotels were built, including the St. George on Clark Street, once the largest in New York City. By the time of the Depression much of the middle class was gone. The boarding houses had deteriorated into low-grade rooming houses, and social planners were describing parts of the neighborhood as slums. A section of the neighborhood was later designated for clearance and redeveloped under the Cadman Plaza project. During the 1940s and 1950s Brooklyn Heights suffered some stunning blows, notably the loss of its entire northwest corner for the construction of the Brooklyn–Queens Expressway in 1953. Brownstone row houses gave way to large apartment buildings and institutional dormitories. An important step in redeveloping the neighborhood was taken when local civic groups such as the Brooklyn Heights Association cooperated with Robert Moses in planning the Esplanade, a park along the East River completed in 1950. In 1958 a group of residents formed the Community Conservation and Improvement Council (later absorbed by the Brooklyn Heights Association), which in 1965 succeeded in having the neighborhood listed on the National Register of Historic Places and designated the first historic district in New York City. In the 1970s and 1980s gentrification transformed boarding houses into middle-class residences and multifamily condominiums. One of the more prominent structures in the neighborhood is the world headquarters of the Jehovah's Witnesses at 124 Columbia Heights. By the early twenty-first century Brooklyn Heights had recovered its reputation as one of New York City's most pleasant and attractive neighborhoods.

Clay Lancaster, *Old Brooklyn Heights: New York's First Suburb* (New York: C. E. Tuttle, 1961; repr. Dover, 1979); David Ment, *The Shaping of a City: A Brief History of Brooklyn* (New York: Brooklyn Educational and Cultural Alliance, 1979)

Ellen Fletcher

Brooklyn Historical Society. Organization formed in 1863 as the Long Island Historical Society. It is one of the oldest historical societies in the country. The association first occupied quarters in the Hamilton Building at Court and Joralemon streets near Borough Hall and later moved to 128 Pierrepont Street in Brooklyn (where it remained into the twenty-first century). Designed by George B. Post and completed in 1880, the new building originally housed an auditorium, offices, a museum on the fourth story, and a research library on the second story with black ash woodwork and stained glass windows. It was the first major structure in greater New York to use extensive terra-cotta ornament and in 1991 was declared a National Historic Landmark; the library is one of few interior landmarks in Brooklyn. In the early twentieth century the society suffered a decline in membership and income, the auditorium was converted into commercial space, and the museum closed. Renewed growth in the early 1980s enabled the society to expand its public programs and mount changing exhibitions; in 1985 it took its current name. A permanent exhibition on the history of Brooklyn opened in the renovated former auditorium in 1989. The society's collection of materials related to Brooklyn, the largest in existence, includes paintings, sculptures, and other works of fine art and decorative art, archaeological artifacts, books, photographs, manuscripts, and ephemera. After complete renovation of the building between 1999 and 2004, the Brooklyn Historical Society attracted an increasingly diverse group of visitors.

Ellen Marie Snyder–Grenier

Brooklyn Historical Society headquarters, 2009

Brooklyn Howard Orphan Asylum. The first orphanage and philanthropic institution controlled and operated by blacks in greater New York. It was opened in 1866 at the corner of Dean Street and Troy Avenue by Sarah A. Tillman, a black minister's widow who took in 20 children of emancipated slaves when they could not be accommodated at the Colored Orphan Asylum. She was assisted in her efforts by Oliver Otis Howard, later a founder of Howard University. Black control of the asylum was maintained for more than 50 years, much of that time under the leadership of the preacher William F. Johnson. Under increasing financial pressure, the all-female, all-black board of managers was replaced in 1913 by an all-male board with a white majority and a white president. Wartime shortages and the deterioration of its physical plant forced the orphanage to close in 1918. It was then transformed into the Howard Memorial Fund, which provided scholarships for needy children into the 1990s.

Seth M. Scheiner, *Negro Mecca: A History of the Negro in New York City, 1865–1920* (New York: New York University Press, 1965); Carleton Mabee, "Charity in Travail: Two Orphan Asylums for Blacks," *New York History* 55 (1974), 55–77

Mike Sappol

Brooklyn Jewish Center. Conservative synagogue on Eastern Parkway, designed in a neoclassical style in 1919 by Louis Abramson. The building had an enormous sanctuary, a gymnasium, a swimming pool, and a kosher restaurant. For over half a century, Israel H. Levinthal presided over the congregation, which by the 1940s included more than 2000 families. The Brooklyn Jewish Center offers a wide range of classes, lectures, and publications and helps to enlarge the role of the American synagogue.

Jenna Weissman Joselit

Brooklyn Law School. Private law school in Brooklyn Heights founded in 1901 by William Payne Richardson, who served as the dean until his death in 1945, and Norman Heffley, who became president of the Board of Trustees. It merged with St. Lawrence University in 1903 but returned to its independent status in 1943. It was accredited by the American Bar Association in 1937 and in the early twentieth century was known for its admission policy, which disregarded race, gender, ethnicity, or socioeconomic status. The law school has occupied a number of buildings, including the Brooklyn Eagle Building (from 1904), a building at 375 Pearl Street (from 1928), and finally a 10-story building at its current location at 250 Joralemon Street (from 1968). In 1973, under Dean Raymond Lisle, the school became a member of the Association of American Law Schools. A year later, the *Brooklyn Journal of International Law* was first published and has since become one of the nation's leading legal journals. In the early twenty-first century Brooklyn Law School offered 180 diverse law courses and had an enrollment of over 1500 full- and part-time students.

Stephanie Miller

Brooklyn–Manhattan Transit Corporation [BMT]. One of two privately operated subway companies in New York City in the early twentieth century. Formed in 1896 as the Brooklyn Rapid Transit Company (BRT), a securities holding firm, it was greatly enlarged over the next five years through a series of mergers and leases that combined the Brooklyn Union, Kings County, and Seaside and Brooklyn Bridge elevated lines; the Sea Beach, Brighton, and West End steam surface railroads; and a number of electric and horse railways, all previously independent entities. In 1899 the company made an important traffic-sharing deal with the Long Island Rail Road: the railroad was allowed to develop transit lines in Queens, and the BRT took over some of its routes in Brooklyn, such as the Culver and South Brooklyn lines.

The Brooklyn Rapid Transit Company controlled nearly all the street and elevated lines in Brooklyn by 1901, yet its multiple, overlapping routes were not combined into a coherent network. Although the company served many passengers who commuted to the financial district in downtown Manhattan, its elevated lines ended at ferry terminals at the edge of the East River in Brooklyn (except for one short shuttle line across the Brooklyn Bridge). These shortcomings and the extension of service to Brooklyn by Interborough Rapid Transit (IRT) in January 1908 prompted the company to build its own subways. In March 1913 the BRT signed a contract with the New York Public Service Commission known as Contract no. 4, which provided for the construction of 111 miles (179 kilometers) of new rapid transit routes in Brooklyn, Manhattan, and the Bronx. These new lines unified the company's sprawling system and allowed its riders to travel directly from Manhattan to Brooklyn. Contract no. 4 affected the single largest expansion of the subway system in the city's history.

Inflation after World War I affected the Brooklyn Rapid Transit Company severely. The price of materials like coal and iron escalated, but Contract no. 4 limited the fare that the company could charge to five cents. On 1 November 1918 a train derailed at Malbone Street in Brooklyn, killing 102 passengers. This accident and continuing financial problems forced the company to declare bankruptcy on 31 December 1918. When it emerged from bankruptcy on 15 March 1923 the company changed its name, largely in an attempt to erase the stigma of the crash. The Depression ruined the BMT: its ridership declined 12 percent from 1928 to 1937. On 1 June 1940 the City of New York under Mayor Fiorello H. La Guardia acquired the assets of the Brooklyn–Manhattan Transit Corporation, and its rapid transit lines became a division of the city's transit system.

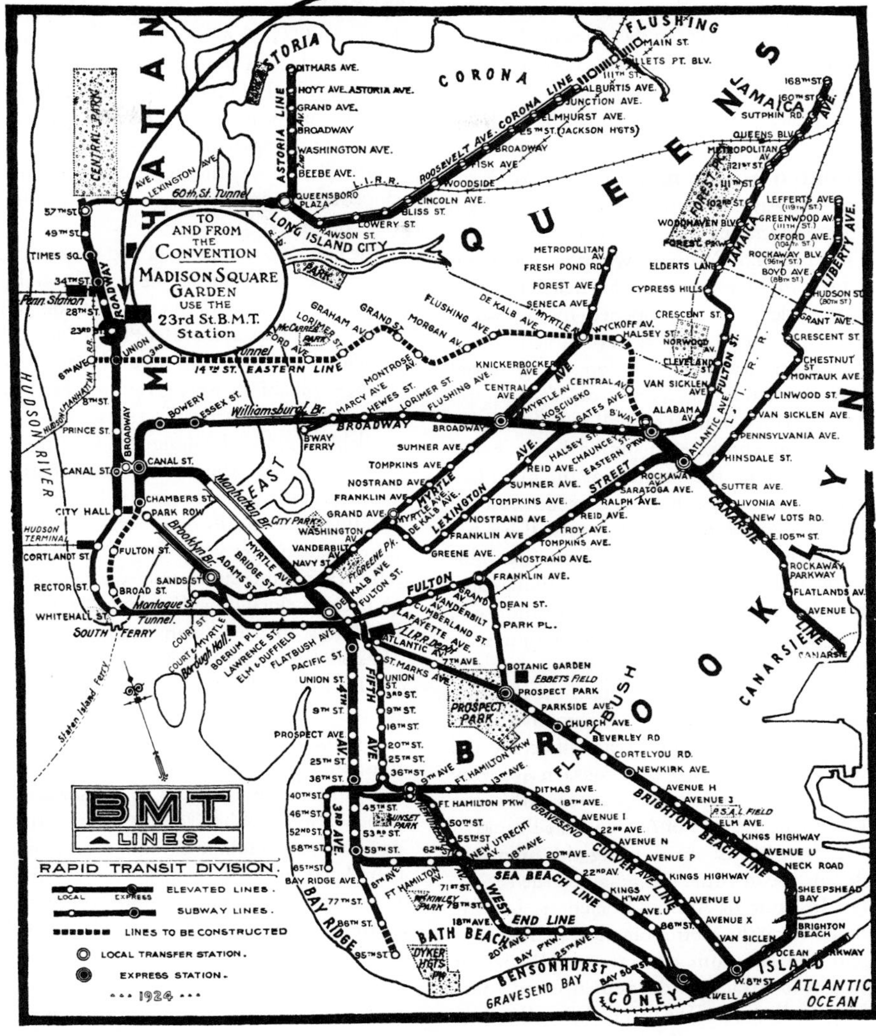

Map of the Brooklyn–Manhattan Transit system issued for the Democratic National Convention at Madison Square Garden, June 1924

Clifton Hood, *722 Miles: The Building of the Subways and How They Transformed New York* (Baltimore: Johns Hopkins University Press, 1995)

Clifton Hood

Brooklyn Manor. Section of Woodhaven in southwestern Queens, lying on both sides of the abandoned Rockaway branch of the Long Island Rail Road. It was once the Vanderveer farm between Woodhaven Boulevard and 96th

Street, from which 603 building lots were made in 1892 north of Jamaica Avenue. Brooklyn Hills was developed in 1905 from the former estate of the Napier family and extended from Forest Park to Atlantic Avenue between 100th and 104th streets.

Vincent Seyfried

Brooklyn Museum. Museum at 200 Eastern Parkway. Its forerunner was the Brooklyn Apprentices Library, formed in 1823 by the local merchant William Wood for the moral education of apprentices. Modeled after the Apprentice's Library opened by Benjamin Franklin in Philadelphia, it occupied a number of sites successively before being moved into the Brooklyn Lyceum on Washington Street, which housed a small natural history collection and offered public lectures and classes. Under the auspices of the manufacturer Augustus Graham, the lyceum and the library merged in 1843 to form the Brooklyn Institute, which soon offered small exhibitions and more extensive educational programs; Graham endowed a library and a fine arts gallery. In 1890 the Citizens' Committee on Museums of Art and Science publicly advocated continued support of the institute to accommodate the growing population of Brooklyn. In the same year it became the parent organization of the Brooklyn Academy of Music, the Brooklyn Botanic Garden, the Brooklyn Museum of Art, and the Brooklyn Children's Museum. During the following decade the institute was renamed the Brooklyn Institute of Arts and Sciences. Loosely modeled on the Metropolitan Museum of Art and the Museum of Natural History, it sought to attract a wider audience and house larger collections. The first director, Franklin W. Hooper, reorganized the existing collections and amassed new ones. He also oversaw the construction of a new building designed in 1893 by the architecture firm of McKim, Mead and White to be the largest of its kind in the world. Based on a design by the French theorist J. N. L. Durand, the plans called for a series of beaux-arts quadrant pavilions (square buildings with a glass-enclosed central court), linked together to represent an encyclopedia of human culture; only one quadrant was completed (1927).

The collections expanded and the museum reorganized again during the second and third decades of the twentieth century under William Henry Fox, and under Philip Youtz, the director from 1933. The natural history and science collections were given to other institutions, and the art collections were made available for study by designers. Controversy erupted in 1934 when Youtz had the grand staircase at the entrance removed to make the building symbolically more accessible and less imposing. In later years the collections were refined as the museum attracted a larger group of patrons, including the Havemeyers, the Friedsams, the Kevorkians, and the Cantors. The collections of Egyptian and African art at the Brooklyn Museum are among the finest in the United States. Following a well-publicized competition for a "master plan," the museum unveiled its newly organized Egyptian galleries, designed by Arata Isozaki and James Stewart Polshek, in 1993; a new entrance pavilion with dramatic Baroque fountains was completed in 2004. Under director Arnold Lehman, a controversial administrative reorganization in 2006 diminished curatorial authority. The Elizabeth A. Sackler Center for Feminist Art opened in 2007.

Joan Darragh, Leland Roth, et al., *A New Brooklyn Museum: The Master Plan Competition* (New York: Brooklyn Museum, 1988); Linda Ferber, "History of the Collections," *Masterpieces in the Brooklyn Museum* (New York: Harry N. Abrams, 1988)

Peter L. Donhauser

Brooklyn Museum, 2009

Brooklyn Navy Yard. Popular name of a shipyard on the East River at Wallabout Bay, officially known as the New York Naval Shipyard. The purchase of land was authorized in 1800 by Secretary of the Navy Benjamin Stoddart; the commandant's house, designed by Charles Bulfinch and completed in 1806, is on the National Register of Historic Places. In its early years the shipyard fitted out ships for ventures against Caribbean and Barbary pirates and during the War of 1812 readied more than 100 vessels for raids on British merchant shipping. In the first half of the nineteenth century it benefited from the growth of the Port of New York and from developments in steam propulsion at private shipyards on the East River. Among the ships launched were the *Fulton,* the first oceangoing steamship in the U.S. Navy, and the steam frigate *Niagara,* which helped lay the first transatlantic cable. The United States Naval Lyceum was formed at the shipyard in 1833; a professional and cultural organization, it included among its members James Fenimore Cooper and Matthew C. Perry. During the Civil War more than 6000 workers built 16 vessels, converted more than 400 merchant and private ships to naval service, and fitted out the ironclad *Monitor.* The shipyard was the central base for ship repair and for distributing supplies to the Union fleet. During a worldwide race toward larger warships, the battleship *Maine* (6682 tons) was launched in 1895, and the shipyard became the navy's principal supply depot during the Spanish–American War. The USS *Arizona* and six other battleships were built between 1906 and 1926, and in 1918 employment at the shipyard reached 18,000.

During World War II the Brooklyn Navy Yard was the largest naval construction facility in the United States. Among the vessels completed there were the *Missouri* (45,000 tons), on the decks of which World War II officially ended on 2 September 1945. More than 71,000 men and women worked in shifts around the clock by 1944; in addition to battleships they built aircraft carriers and auxiliary vessels, repaired more than 5000 ships, and converted another 250. The shipyard by then included six huge drydocks, two building ways, eight piers, 270 buildings, 19 miles (30 kilometers) of streets, and 30 miles (48 kilometers) of railroad track. It was the largest industrial center in the navy, as well as the largest employer in New York State. Naval construction declined in the late 1940s but revived during the cold war. In December 1960, 50 people were killed when the aircraft

Launching of the USS Bon Homme Richard *at the Brooklyn Navy Yard, 29 April 1944*

Brooklyn Navy Yard, 2009

carrier *Constellation* was ravaged by fire. From that time only six ships were built, as shipbuilding operations shifted to such southern ports as Newport News (Virginia) and Pascagoula (Mississippi).

By 1965 fewer then 7000 men and women worked at the shipyard. In 1966 Secretary of Defense Robert McNamara closed the facility as part of a nationwide base closing initiative. In the following year, at a cost of $24 million, New York City purchased 260 acres (105 hectares) at the site, which was reopened as an industrial park in 1971. Managed by the not-for-profit Brooklyn Navy Yard Development Corporation since 1981, the yard expanded to house more than 240 businesses by the early twenty-first century, employing more than 5000 workers in a variety of firms, including film and television studios, trucking companies, ship repair facilities, design companies, and wholesale fish distributors. Plans for a history center to retain the yard's connection to its past as well as to refurbish landmarks within the yard are under way.

Arnold Markoe

Brooklyn Philharmonic. Orchestra in Brooklyn founded in 1954 by conductor Siegfried Landau. His successors include Lukas Foss, Dennis Russell Davies, and Robert Spano. The orchestra is known for its premieres of new works, including those of John Adams, Steve Reich, Philip Glass, and Bright Sheng. Since 1991 it has been the resident orchestra of the Brooklyn Academy of Music. In the early twenty-first century it was under the direction of Michael Christie.

Steven Levine

Brooklyn Public Library. Library system founded in Brooklyn in 1892 and opened in 1897. Director Mary E. Craigee oversaw the library's development from its inception until 1898. The first branch, opened at Brooklyn Public School 3 in Bedford, had separate reading rooms for men and women and was one of the first libraries that allowed readers to browse. Between 1901 and 1923 the library received $1.6 million from philanthropist Andrew Carnegie and built 21 branch libraries. A children's branch opened in Brownsville in 1914; the first public library solely for children, it was equipped with child-sized furniture and fancifully decorated with scenes and figures from well-known stories (it is now the Stone Avenue Branch). By 1905 a triangular site fronting Grand Army Plaza and flanked by Flatbush Avenue and Eastern Parkway was chosen for the main library. Architect Raymond Almirall designed a grand beaux-arts building and construction began in 1912, but by 1930 little more than one wing was completed. Library director Milton J. Ferguson began anew with architects Githens and Keally, who during the 1930s demolished most of Almirall's wing and constructed an art moderne building shaped like an open book, with the spine facing Grand Army Plaza and the covers stretching along Flatbush Avenue and Eastern Parkway. The building's front entrance featured limestone pylons and huge bronze doors 40 feet (12.2 meters) tall covered in gilt renditions of literary figures and quotations. Completed in 1941, it was named Ingersoll Memorial Library after the borough president. The Business Library grew out of the Brooklyn Athenaeum (1852) and Brooklyn Mercantile Library (1857), both housed at Atlantic Avenue and Clinton Street; they consolidated and moved to 197 Montague Street in 1869. The new library included a business reference department and was renamed the Brooklyn Library in 1878, becoming part of the Brooklyn public library system in 1943. The Business Library's current building opened in 1962 at 280 Cadman Plaza West, where it shared space with the Brooklyn Heights branch. In 2007 the Central Library completed renovations that included the 200-seat Dr. S. Stevan Dweck Auditorium and an improved front plaza; planning also began for a Visual and Performing Arts Library (designed by Enrique Norten of TEN Arquitectos) to be built on Flatbush Avenue adjacent to the Brooklyn Academy of Music. In the early twenty-first century the Brooklyn Public Library is the fifth largest library system in the country, with 60 libraries. It serves the 2.5 million residents of Brooklyn with more than five million circulating and reference items in 50 languages; more than one million people hold Brooklyn Public Library cards, and there is a library within a half mile (0.8 kilometer) of every resident in the borough.

GraceAnne A. DeCandido, Kate Lauber

Brooklyn–Queens Expressway [Interstate 278, BQE]. Expressway that stretches from the Brooklyn–Battery Tunnel to the Grand Central Parkway in Queens. Originally called the Brooklyn–Queens Connecting Highway, it spans 11.7 miles (18.8 kilometers). Construction began in 1937, and under the guidance of Robert Moses the six-lane expressway was completed in sections through 1964 at a total cost of $137 million of city, state, and federal funds. Moses ran into opposition when he tried to build the expressway through historic Brooklyn Heights and agreed to an alternate plan drawn up by neighborhood residents that resulted in a cantilevered section topped by the Brooklyn Esplanade. Planned before the interstate highway system was developed, the expressway's design was obsolete almost immediately, with narrow lanes and no shoulders; it has seen many reconstruction projects since its completion. In 2007 the Brooklyn Academy of Music commissioned musician Sufjan Stevens to write a symphony and accompanying film about the expressway titled *The BQE*.

Kate Lauber

Brooklyn Rapid Transit Company [BRT]. A precursor of the BROOKLYN–MANHATTAN TRANSIT CORPORATION, formed in 1896. See also SUBWAYS.

Brooklyn Surface Railroad Riots. Violence that erupted throughout Brooklyn between 14 January and 2 February 1895 among striking surface railroad workers. See RIOTS.

Brooklyn Technical High School. Specialized high school at 29 Fort Greene Place. Plans for a science high school were promoted at the end of World War I by Albert L. Colston, chairman of the mathematics department at Manual Training High School, who recognized the need for an advanced science, mathematics, and engineering curriculum in the city. Under his direction the technical program at Manual Training High School was overhauled, and an innovative engineering program was introduced that won approval from the Board of Superintendents in November 1918 and attracted more than 1200 students the following year. The need for a modern facility was soon apparent, and in May 1922 the Board of Education announced plans for a technical high school. A renovated factory loft building at 49 Flatbush Avenue Extension (near the Manhattan Bridge) was the first site of Brooklyn Technical High School, which opened on 11 September 1922 with nearly 2500 students; Colston was named its principal. Mayor James J. Walker broke ground in 1930 for the present nine-story building on the block between South Elliott Place and Fort Greene Place, built at a cost of $5 million (unprecedented in the United States) and opened in September 1933. Students were admitted only after passing a demanding entrance examination. From November 1938 the school had a radio station, WNYE, that was used by the Board of Education. There were 6000 students from throughout the city by 1960; in 1970 the school became coeducational. Facilities for high-technology programs were added as part of $13 million in renovations begun in 1984. Enrollment stood at nearly 5000 in the early twenty-first century. Among the graduates of Brooklyn Tech are the Nobel laureates George Wald (class of 1923; prize in physiology or medicine, 1967) and Arno Penzias (class of 1951; prize in physics, 1978).

Elliot Willensky, *When Brooklyn Was the World, 1920–1957* (New York: Harmony, 1986)

Allen J. Share

Brooklyn theater fire. Fire on 5 December 1876 in an elegant theater at 313 Washington Street, where 1000 spectators saw Miss Kate Claxton perform in *The Two Orphans*. The fire broke out backstage shortly before the end of the play. Although there was enough time for all to evacuate the building, the stairs became blocked when 500 patrons in the balcony rushed for the exits, and 295 people were killed. The fire consumed the entire theater: more than 100 victims were so badly burned that they were buried in a common grave in Green-Wood Cemetery. The disaster became internationally known and compelled Brooklyn and New York City to impose stricter standards for fire inspections in theaters. In its number of casualties the fire was exceeded only by that at the Iroquois Theater in Chicago in 1903.

Report of the Executive Committee (Brooklyn: Brooklyn Theatre Fire Relief Association, 1879)

Edward T. O'Donnell

Brooklyn Times–Union. Daily newspaper. Launched in 1848 as the *Williamsburgh Daily Times*, it became the *Brooklyn Daily Times* on the unification of Brooklyn and Williamsburgh in 1855. The newspaper supported the antislavery movement and the presidential candidacy of Abraham Lincoln. Walt Whitman was a reporter and later the managing editor after he left the *Brooklyn Eagle*. Published seven days a week, the newspaper at one point had a circulation area that included all of Brooklyn and parts of Long Island. It became known as the *Brooklyn Times–Union* after buying the *Standard Union* in 1932. In 1937 it was bought by the *Brooklyn Eagle*.

Raymond A. Schroth, *The Eagle and Brooklyn* (Westport, Conn.: Greenwood, 1974)

John J. Gallagher

Brooklyn Union Gas Company. Utility formed in 1895 that consolidated all the gas companies in Brooklyn through the merger of the Brooklyn Gas Light Company (1825), Fulton Municipal Gas, Citizens' Gas Light, Metropolitan Gas Light, Williamsburg Gas Light, People's Gas Light, and Nassau Gas Light. It later purchased several smaller companies and expanded into Queens. The company originally manufactured gas but began to convert to natural gas after New York City was connected by the transcontinental pipeline in 1950 to the gas fields of the southwestern United States. By August 1952 the conversion was complete. Later it acquired the New York and Richmond Gas Company (1957), which served Staten Island, the Kings County Lighting Company, and the Brooklyn Borough Gas Company (1959). Supply problems in the early 1970s led the company to produce synthetic gas, to import liquefied natural gas, and to purchase subsidiaries engaged in exploration and production. In 1997 the company reorganized as a holding company, changed the parent name to KeySpan Energy, and the following year purchased the generating assets of Long Island Lighting Co. In 2007 the U.K.-based company National Grid acquired KeySpan for $11.8 billion.

Elwin S. Larson, *Brooklyn Union Gas: Fueling Growth and Change in New York City* (New York: Newcomen Society, 1987)

William J. Hausman

Brooks Brothers. One of America's oldest continually operated retailers of men's clothing; opened in 1818 by Henry Sands Brooks at Catherine and Cherry streets, the center of the wholesale clothing trade. It became known for fine quality and was among the first stores to offer both custom- and ready-made clothing. After Brooks's death in 1833 the business was taken over by his sons Henry, Daniel, John, Elisha, and Edward. They gave the firm its current name in 1850 and opened a store at Broadway and Grand Street in 1858. The firm supplied uniforms for Union soldiers during the Civil War, efforts that made its original store a target of mob violence during the draft riots in 1863; it remained a military outfitter for many years. The years after the war were marked by several important developments. The store on Cherry Street closed in 1874, and the remaining one moved with the retail district to successive sites uptown until finally settling at Madison Avenue and 44th Street in 1915. In 1900 the firm became the first in the country to offer shirts with button-down collars. Partners were increasingly drawn from outside the Brooks family, and in 1903 the firm was transformed from a partnership into a corporation. In the following years stores were opened in Boston, San Francisco, Los Angeles, and Newport, Rhode Island. From the mid-1920s Brooks Brothers faced increasing financial difficulties. Its earnings dropped steadily during the 1930s, and by the end of 1935 it had an operating deficit of more than $1 million. In 1946 it was taken over by Julius Garfinckel, a retail firm in Washington, ending control by the Brooks family. Under the new management unprecedented sales and profits were achieved during the mid-1950s. Between 1955 and 1988, when the business was bought by the retail chain of Marks and Spencer, Brooks Brothers expanded its operations from six to 47 stores in the United States and 21 in Japan. It nonetheless suffered during an economic recession in the late 1980s as it was forced to compete with more stylish designers and stores. To attract younger customers it brought its conservative "Ivy League" styling up to date and adjusted its standards to produce more affordable clothing. In 2001 the company was sold to Retail Brand Alliance, a privately held firm. By the early twenty-first century most of Brooks Brothers' sales came from its outlet and online stores. In 2010 there were four stores in New York City: the flagship building at 345 Madison Avenue, 1270 Sixth Avenue, 1234 Broadway, and One Liberty Plaza.

The World Trade Center's twin towers were directly across the street from the One Liberty branch, and during the terrorist attack of 11 September 2001, the store was used as a triage center and makeshift morgue. The building was one of the first in the immediate vicinity to reopen after the attacks.

Eileen K. Cheng

Brown, Claude (*b* New York City, 23 February 1937; *d* New York City, 2 February 2002). Author. He published *Manchild in the Promised Land* (1965), a memoir of his brutal childhood in Harlem during the 1940s and his escape from street life as an adolescent. Brown had a troubled youth. He was shot in the abdomen at age 13 during an attempted robbery, and he spent three stints at a reform school, Warwick. Each time he returned to Harlem. Brown eventually moved to Greenwich Village, began playing piano, and took high school classes at night. He went on to Howard University, where he turned an article he had written for *Dissent* into his book *Manchild*. It sold four million copies worldwide and earned Brown social respect from critics such as Ralph Ellison, James Baldwin, and Richard Wright. Brown published another account of life in Harlem—this time, about other people's lives—*The Children of Ham*, in 1976. He died of respiratory failure.

Rowan Moore Gerety

Brown, Elmer E(llsworth) (*b* Kiantone, near Jamestown, N.Y., 28 Aug 1861; *d* New York City, 3 Nov 1934). Educator. He graduated from the State Normal College in Illinois in 1881, became a superintendent in Belvidere County (Illinois) later that year, and earned an AB at the University of Michigan (1889) and a PhD at the University of Halle-Wittenberg in Germany (1890). After working as a high school principal and teaching at the University of Michigan and the University of California at Berkeley he was appointed commissioner of education by President Theodore Roosevelt in 1906. In 1911 he resigned to become the seventh chancellor of New York University. There he continued the expansion begun by his predecessor, Henry Mitchell MacCracken, by developing a coeducational facility called Washington Square College (1914), improving the professional schools, establishing New York University Press (1916), enlarging the library system, and renovating buildings and property (including the School of Education in 1929). On his retirement in 1933 the university had more than 40,000 students and was the largest private university in the United States.

Theodore F. Jones, *New York University, 1832–1932* (New York: New York University Press, 1933)

Paul H. Mattingly

Brown Brothers Harriman. Firm of commercial bankers. It was formed by Alexander Brown in Philadelphia in 1818 as the firm of John A. Brown, an offshoot of a firm of Irish linen importers. In 1825 a branch called Brown Brothers was opened in New York City by James Brown, a son of Alexander Brown; with the firm of William and James Brown of Liverpool, it became an important commission house and merchant bank. The branch moved its offices to 59 Wall Street in 1843. Brown Brothers was known as a conservative house that helped to reorganize railroads during the late nineteenth century, and it was a leading provider of letters of credit throughout the world. In 1907 seven of the 14 partners were members of the Brown family. After becoming independent of the firm in England in 1918 the American operation expanded during the 1920s and opened a large bond department. On 1 January 1931 it received its current name after merging with the private banks of W. Averell Harriman (formed in 1919) and the Harriman brothers (formed in 1927 by Harriman and his brother E. Roland Harriman). With the passage of the Banking Act of 1933 the firm ceased underwriting corporate securities and became a commercial bank. By 1994 Brown Brothers Harriman was the oldest and largest private commercial bank in the United States. In 2001 it moved its headquarters to 140 Broadway after 168 years at its Wall Street location; in the early twenty-first century it had 15 offices worldwide and 2700 employees.

John A. Kouwenhoven, *Partners in Banking: An Historical Portrait of a Great Private Bank* (Garden City, N.Y.: Doubleday, 1968; repr. 1983)

Mary E. Curry

Brownson, Orestes A(ugustus) (*b* Stockbridge, Vt., 16 Sept 1803; *d* Detroit, 17 April 1876). Philosopher and writer who lived in New York City from 1826 to 1831. In 1838 he launched the *Boston Quarterly Review* as a radical publication. His indictment of capitalism in his essay "The Laboring Classes" was seized on by the Whigs in 1840 as a means of tarring President Martin Van Buren, whom Brownson supported. The demagoguery of the election led Brownson to doubt the possibilities of democratic reform. He discontinued the *Review* in 1842 to write for the *U.S. Democratic Review*, published in New York City by John L. O'Sullivan. After exploring several faiths and organizing his own church in 1836, he caused a sensation by converting to Catholicism in 1844. As the editor and principal writer of *Brownson's Quarterly Review* (1844–64, 1873–75) he became an important critic of developments in literature, philosophy, science, religion, and government. Among the topics he explored were the relationship between church and state and the nature of civil and religious liberties. He moved the *Review* to New York City in 1855 and to Elizabeth, New Jersey, after a quarrel with Archbishop John Hughes. Brownson wrote an autobiography, *The Convert* (1857), and *The American Republic* (1866), a philosophical essay on the solubility of the Union.

Arthur M. Schlesinger, Jr., *Orestes A. Brownson: A Pilgrim's Progress* (Boston: Little, Brown, 1939)

Robert Emmett Curran

brownstones. Residential, sandstone row houses of two to four stories built throughout New York City during the nineteenth century. They evolved when the rising price of property in Manhattan during the 1840s and 1850s caused developers to modify the design of the traditional Federal or Greek Revival row house: a front setback was carved out to provide a feeling of spaciousness; the basement was raised to admit light, so that it could be used as a scullery and servants' work area; a large staircase with rails of wrought iron was installed, leading to a high stoop with a balustrade; and the entire building was extended into the rear yard to enlarge the space for family and servants. Brownstones were built in blocks of several at a time, and their flat cornices, continuous string-coursing, and regular stoops gave them an imposing regularity. Italianate windows and door hoods above the entrances accentuated the facades with striking shadows. "Jersey freestone," a reddish-brown sandstone of varying hues, was quarried in Passaic County, New Jersey, sawed by modern steam machinery into sheets 4 or 6 inches (10 or 15 centimeters) thick, and mounted over a brick structural frame. Weathering eventually changed the stone to a chocolate brown and darkened the mortar to give the buildings a somber veneer. Although wealthy families at first resisted the new structures they came to appreciate their stolid private space, and during the social turbulence of the 1850s many families moved to the areas of major brownstone development, such as Gramercy Park and Brooklyn Heights. In the 1880s and 1890s creative and eclectic stylistic innovations appeared: heavy arched windows in the Richardsonian Romanesque style, asymmetrical features in the Queen Anne style, and the triangular roof lines, gabled niches, and three-paneled window bays of Charles Eastlake. The trim of some buildings was decorated with red, yellow, and tan brick and terra-cotta, and several blocks of brownstones on the Upper West Side displayed a stunning variety of color.

The interior of a brownstone was cramped. One entered the front door into a vestibule about five feet (1.5 meters) square. Straight ahead were an ascending staircase and a hallway leading to the rear of the building; to the side of the vestibule lay a front parlor, at the rear of which overlooking the backyard lay a nearly identical dining room, where most entertaining took place. The parlor and the dining room could be united by opening a set of double doors surrounded by a decorative molding. Brownstones were often sufficiently deep that between the front and back rooms a third room could be interposed, usually a formal dining hall with a marbleized fireplace and gilt mirror. In a typical brownstone the family quarters were on the second story and the servants' quarters on the third, which sometimes contained interior rooms ventilated by air shafts.

The confining and expensive brownstones could not compete with the sprawling luxury apartments of the Dakota and the Ansonia or the suburban homes that became popular at the turn of the century, and in the early 1930s blocks of brownstones were leveled to allow for the construction of offices, notably around Rockefeller Center. Of those brownstones that remained many in midtown were subdivided before World War II into cheap rental apartments and rooming houses. Further demolition of brownstones funded by Title I of the Housing Act of 1949 and overseen by Robert Moses angered many residents and inspired them to political action. A renewal of interest in historic preservation led to the renovation of brownstones in Greenwich Village, on the Upper West Side, in Chelsea, and later in Park Slope. The Landmarks Preservation Commission, formed in 1965, protected the brownstone heritage of areas such as the Metropolitan Museum Historic District, Riverside Drive, and West 80th and 81st streets.

Charles Lockwood, *Bricks and Brownstones: The New York Row House, 1783–1929: An Architectural and Social History* (New York: McGraw-Hill, 1972)

Joel Schwartz

A row of brownstone houses

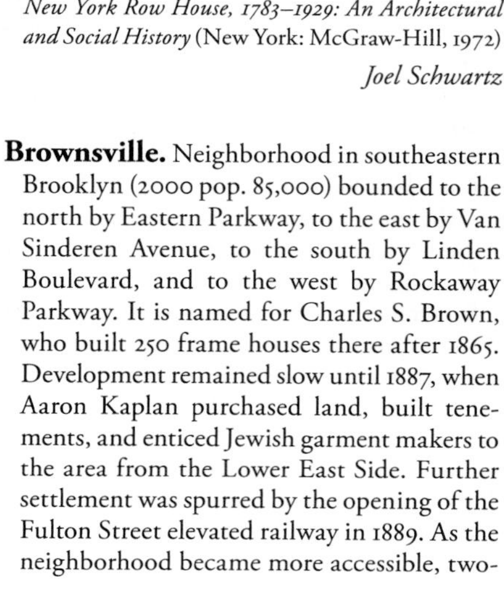

Brownsville. Neighborhood in southeastern Brooklyn (2000 pop. 85,000) bounded to the north by Eastern Parkway, to the east by Van Sinderen Avenue, to the south by Linden Boulevard, and to the west by Rockaway Parkway. It is named for Charles S. Brown, who built 250 frame houses there after 1865. Development remained slow until 1887, when Aaron Kaplan purchased land, built tenements, and enticed Jewish garment makers to the area from the Lower East Side. Further settlement was spurred by the opening of the Fulton Street elevated railway in 1889. As the neighborhood became more accessible, two-family homes and small tenements with storefronts at street level replaced earlier houses, and by 1910 large multifamily buildings dominated. The area was largely Jewish, with sweatshops and pushcarts and few sewers or paved streets. Living conditions improved after 1920, as did rapid transit connections to Manhattan with the completion in 1922 of the New Lots branch of Interborough Rapid Transit. The neighborhood prospered from the 1920s to the 1940s and was a center of labor radicalism: it elected socialists to the state assembly between 1915 and 1921 and a candidate of the American Labor Party in 1936. Margaret Sanger opened the first birth control clinic in the United States at 46 Amboy Street on 16 October 1916 (it was closed nine days later by the vice squad). During these years the neighborhood inspired some of the most evocative accounts of the Jewish experience in New York City, including Henry Roth's novel *Call It Sleep* (1934) and Alfred Kazin's memoir *A Walker in the City* (1951). Some local residents who later became prominent include the composer Aaron Copland, the actor Danny Kaye, and the impresario Sol Hurok.

Many of its residents moved to the suburbs after World War II. There followed a cycle of decay, abandonment, vandalism, and arson, which high-rise public housing projects built during the 1950s and 1960s did little to alleviate. Later housing renewal efforts were more successful, notably those sponsored by the Council of East Brooklyn Churches to provide affordable one-family houses at Marcus Garvey Village and Nehemiah Housing. At the beginning of the twenty-first century, Pitkin Avenue, the main commercial thoroughfare, was lined with small businesses, shoe and clothing outlets, and restaurants. Loew's Pitkin Theater, a lavish movie theater built in 1930 by Thomas W. Lamb, remained at the corner of East New York Avenue and Pitkin Avenue as a retail store. The heavyweight boxing champions Mike Tyson and Riddick Bowe both grew up in the neighborhood. Brownsville attracted many immigrants from the Caribbean during the 1980s, especially from Jamaica (accounting for 30 percent of all immigrants), Guyana and Haiti (each about 15 percent), Grenada, Barbados, and Trinidad and Tobago. In the early twenty-first century the population of Brownsville was largely African American, with smaller groups of Latinos and West Indians. The neighborhood remained mostly low-income, with one of the highest densities of public housing projects in the city.

David W. McCullough, *Brooklyn and How It Got That Way* (New York: Dial, 1983); John Manbeck and Kenneth T. Jackson, *The Neighborhoods of Brooklyn* (New Haven: Yale University Press, 2001)

Elizabeth Reich Rawson

Bruce, Lenny [Schneider, Leonard Alfred] (*b* Mineola, N.Y., 13 Oct 1925; *d* Los Angeles, 3 Aug 1966). Comedian. Raised in Mineola on Long Island, he ran away from home at age 16 to work on a farm before serving in the navy from 1942 to 1945. Bruce performed on a small scale in New York City area nightclubs and burlesque houses after the end of the war; in 1948 he first performed for a wider audience on *Arthur Godfrey's Talent Scouts*. In the 1950s Bruce moved from nightclubs to Hollywood and a television audience. During this time he became among the first comedians to attract large followings for performing routines that involved profane language and discussion of topics such as religion, race, sex, and drug use. In his bit "Christ and Moses," Bruce described a confused Jesus wondering why 40 Puerto Ricans should live in one room in Spanish Harlem while Francis Cardinal Spellman wore an $8000 ring. This style earned Bruce enemies in law enforcement; he was arrested on a series of obscenity and drug charges in California, Chicago, Philadelphia, and New York City over the following years and was denied entry into Australia and the United Kingdom. The arrests made nightclub owners hesitant to hire him. His 1964 conviction on obscenity charges after a show at Cafe au Go Go in Greenwich Village effectively excluded him from working in New York City. Bruce left New York for California, where he died in 1966 of a drug overdose. In 2003 Governor George Pataki posthumously pardoned Bruce for his obscenity conviction.

Ben Silk

Bruckner, Henry (*b* Bronx, 17 June 1871; *d* Bronx, 14 April 1942). Public official. After representing the Bronx as a state legislator (1900) he was a commissioner of public works (1901–12), a member of the U.S. Congress (1912–17), and a borough president (1918–33). His loyal adherence to Tammany Hall enabled him to win elections consistently. During the same time he developed Bruckner Beverages, the city's largest bottler of soda water. Bruckner's political career ended when Judge Samuel Seabury recommended his removal from the borough presidency after an investigation of Tammany Hall. Although Bruckner declined to resign, Edward J. Flynn, Democratic leader of Bronx County, did not designate him for reelection. Bruckner Boulevard is named for him.

Ada Louise Huxtable, *Will They Ever Finish Bruckner Boulevard?* (New York: Macmillan, 1970)

Neal C. Garelik

Bruckner Boulevard. Highway that runs from the Lower Bronx to the Bronx River, formerly known as Eastern Boulevard. Designed to connect the Bronx–Whitestone and Triborough bridges with Pelham Bay Park, it was formed in 1895 from three roads that were originally separated by swamps: Ludlow Avenue, which connected the Bronx River and Unionport; Sixth Street, which lay in Unionport; and Willow Lane, which ran from Unionport to Pelham Bay Park and covered portions of an ancient Native American path. On 29 July 1942 Eastern Boulevard was renamed for Henry Bruckner, a former Bronx borough president. In the late 1940s the road was widened, in anticipation of the Bruckner Expressway that was to be built over it, and a drawbridge was added over the Bronx River. In 1956 Robert Moses's plan to build the Bruckner Expressway was approved by the city; the project was completed in 1972 at more than six times the original projected cost. In December 1996 the boulevard underwent a makeover, which included new curbs, plantings, sidewalks, and lighting.

Henry Cooper

Bruère, Henry (Jaromir) (*b* Saint Charles, Mo., 15 Jan 1882; *d* Winter Park, Fla., 17 Feb 1958). Reformer. After moving in 1905 to New York City, in 1907 he formed the New York Bureau of Municipal Research, which studied the structure of the city government and its administration of social services. He became city chamberlain during the administration of Mayor John Purroy Mitchel in 1914 and chairman of the Committee for Better Housing under Mayor Robert F. Wagner. Bruère wrote *The New City Government: A Discussion of Municipal Administration, Based on a Survey of Ten Commission-governed Cities* (1912). He lived at 340 West 86th Street.

Bernard Hirschhorn

Bruno, Guido [Kisch, Curt Joseph] (*b* Mladá Boleslav, Bohemia, 15 Oct 1884; *d* Bala Cynwyd, Pa., 31 Dec 1942). Book dealer and printer. He grew up near Prague, emigrated to the United States in 1907, and from 1914 to 1916 was the proprietor of Bruno's Garret on Washington Square South, which functioned as an art gallery, lecture hall, talent agency, and print shop specializing in the offbeat. He published local news gazettes, literary chapbooks, and whimsically illustrated pamphlets, as well as *Fragments from Greenwich Village* (1921). He was also a partner in the short-lived Thimble Theater at 10 Fifth Avenue. In his later years Bruno sold rare American manuscripts and autographs.

Arnold I. Kisch, *The Romantic Ghost of Greenwich Village: Guido Bruno in His Garret* (Frankfurt am Main: Peter Lang, 1976)

Jan Seidler Ramirez

Brushville. Former name of Queens Village. Named Little Plains in the 1640s, it was renamed after Thomas Brush, who established a wheelwright and blacksmith shop there in 1824. Later he built a tavern, a general store, and a tobacco-curing warehouse. In 1865 residents voted to adopt the name Queens despite the risk of confusing the village with the county; the word Village was added in 1924 by the Long Island Rail Road when it erected an elevated station.

Vincent Seyfried

Bryant, Louise (Anna Louisa) (*b* San Francisco, 5 Dec 1885; *d* Sèvres, France, 6 Jan 1936). Journalist. She graduated from the University of Oregon in 1909, became editor of the Portland-based *Society* magazine, and married her first husband. In 1914 she met John Reed, a journalist and activist, whom she later married, and moved to Greenwich Village. While in New York City, she wrote for several socialist and radical magazines. She traveled to Russia with Reed during the Bolshevik Revolution and wrote *Six Red Months in Russia* (1918). After Reed's death in 1920 she went to central Asia for reporting and published *Mirrors of Moscow* (1923). She became a foreign correspondent and notably conducted the first interview by a non-Italian with Mussolini. A retrospective film *Reds* (1981) about her life with Reed starred Diane Keaton as Bryant.

Mary V. Dearborn, *The Queen of Bohemia: The Life of Louise Bryant* (Boston: Houghton Mifflin, 1996)

Jessica Montesano

Bryant, William Cullen (*b* Cummington, Mass., 3 Nov 1794; *d* New York City, 12 June 1878). Poet, editor, and civic leader. He was initially a staunch Federalist. After moving to New York City in 1825 he succeeded E. L. Godkin as the editor of the *New York Review* and the *Evening Post*. In 1829 he bought the *Post*, where he continued to work until nearly the end of his life. Initially revered as a poet, he became the city's most influential resident through his public work, and he abandoned Federalism for liberal positions on a number of issues, including abolition and free soil; he also supported Abraham Lincoln. In 1867 he bought his last home, a house at 24 West 16th Street. An influential advocate of public parks, public health, and other civic causes, Bryant was among those who created the Century Association in 1846, Central Park in the 1850s, and the Metropolitan Museum of Art in 1870, and he was the first president of the board of trustees of New York Medical College. Bryant Park on 42nd Street honors his memory.

Charles Henry Brown, *William Cullen Bryant* (New York: Charles Scribner's Sons, 1971)

Jeff Finlay

Bryant High School. Former name of William Cullen Bryant High School.

William C. Bryant

Bryant Park. Nine-acre (3.6-hectare) public park in Manhattan, located between Fifth and Sixth avenues and 40th and 42nd streets. Designated a public space in the Dongan Charter of 1686, the site was a potter's field from 1823 to 1840. The city subsequently constructed the Croton Distributing Reservoir on the eastern portion of the site, while the western side became a public park named Reservoir Square. The Crystal Palace, an iron and glass exhibition building constructed for New York's first world's fair, stood in Reservoir Square from 1853 until it burned down in 1858. In 1884 the park was renamed for poet, newspaper editor, and parks advocate William Cullen Bryant. In 1899 the city demolished the reservoir and replaced it with the New York Public Library, completed in 1911. During the early twentieth century the park became a haven for the homeless, especially after the Rapid Transit Board used it as a dumping ground during construction of the Queensboro Subway. In 1932 the George Washington Bi-Centennial Celebration Committee constructed a temporary replica of Federal Hall in Bryant Park, fencing the park off and charging an admission fee. The city paid to demolish the structure after mismanagement and corruption emptied the committee's coffers, and the park remained a vacant lot. Robert Moses made redesigning Bryant Park top priority when he became parks commissioner in 1934, choosing a beaux-arts plan by Queens architect Lusby Simpson. By the following year the park had been raised 4 feet (1.2 meters) above street grade, surrounded by an iron fence and graced with a large central lawn, bluestone walkways, and London plane trees. Moses and Simpson sought to create an oasis in midtown, but by the mid-twentieth century the park had instead become a refuge for alcoholics, panhandlers, and prostitutes. In 1966 Parks Commissioner Thomas P. F. Hoving and the Avenue of the Americas Association implemented a plan to enliven Bryant Park with weekly fashion shows, concerts, and performances. During the city's fiscal crisis of the 1970s, however, the park—known as Needle Park because of its resident drug dealers—further deteriorated. In 1979, the independent Parks Council constructed bookstalls and cafes in the park to attract passersby. Simultaneously, the Bryant Park Restoration

Bryant Park looking toward the New York Public Library, 1937

Corporation (now Bryant Park Corporation, BRC), a private nonprofit organization formed by trustees of the New York Public Library and the Rockefeller Brothers Fund, began an ambitious program to privately manage the park by creating a business improvement district to fund its restoration and future operations. Led by BRC executive director Daniel Biederman and founded on the ideals of urbanist William H. Whyte, the decade-long restoration process resulted in a meticulously maintained and financially self-sustainable park that today features a restaurant, Wi-Fi Internet access, ice skating, and outdoor movies. Crime almost disappeared. The park maintained a close relationship with the New York Public Library and in the twenty-first century housed more than 80 miles (129 kilometers) of book stacks underneath its great lawn. The privatization of the park, which is wholly managed and funded by BRC, remains a controversial issue. Critics contend that BRC focuses on commercial events such as the biannual Fashion Week rather than on public access, while BRC argues that commercial events bring in fees that help maintain and improve the park for its users.

Kate Lauber

Buchalter, Louis "Lepke" (*b* New York City, 1897; *d* Ossining, N.Y., 4 March 1944). Organized-crime figure. He grew up on the Lower East Side and worked in extortion, protection rackets, loan sharking, and various illegal enterprises for both labor and management. Known for his violent tactics and his quiet but luxurious style of life, he was soon a target of the district attorney of Manhattan, Thomas E. Dewey. After violating narcotics and antitrust laws he went into hiding in 1937, spending most of his time on Third Street in Brooklyn. He surrendered in 1939. While in prison he was convicted of masterminding the murder of a store owner in Brooklyn, and he was executed at Sing Sing State Prison.

Margaret Latimer

bucket shops. Fraudulent businesses that ostensibly buy and sell stocks, bonds, and commodities on behalf of customers but in fact use their money to engage in deceptive and speculative practices. During the nineteenth century bucket shops had little effect on stock prices because they failed to execute most orders that their customers placed. In other cases they would bilk their customers by freezing orders to buy when a downward trend was expected in the market and then pocketing the difference. Bucket shops were forced to discontinue their practices after an investigation by Charles Evans Hughes in 1909. The long bear market of 1919–21 saw new firms open that executed orders and then reversed them through dummy accounts; rising stock prices after 1922 forced these operations out of business. In March 1923 an investigation by the district attorney Joab Banton was joined by the attorney general of New York State. By this time it was estimated that scores of customers had been cheated out of $800 million since November 1918. The New York Stock Exchange barred its members from dealing with bucket shops, and in 1924 a "padlock" injunction closed the National Stock, Cotton and Grain Exchange. Despite this success Banton estimated in June that fraud still exceeded $1 billion a year. It was not until October 1934 that a federal law outlawed bucket-shop techniques and the Securities and Exchange Commission declared all such operations illegal.

George J. Lankevich

Buckley, Charles A(nthony) (*b* New York City, 23 June 1890; *d* New York City, 22 Jan 1967). Congressman and Bronx political leader. As a young man he worked as a construction laborer and was an active member of the North End Democratic Club. Elected to Congress in 1934, he became the chairman of the public works committee, which oversaw federal construction contracts. In 1953 he became the Democratic leader of Bronx County. Buckley's political influence in the city weakened after he opposed Mayor Robert F. Wagner's successful reelection campaign in 1961, and he lost his congressional seat to the reformer Jonathan Bingham in a Democratic primary in 1964. He nonetheless remained in charge of the Democratic Party in the Bronx to the end of his life. He lived at 21 West 192nd Street.

Chris McNickle

Buckley, William F(rank), Jr. (*b* New York City, 24 Nov 1925; *d* Stamford, Conn., 27 Feb 2008). Writer, publisher, and commentator. Born into a wealthy family, he served in the U.S. Army during World War II and graduated from Yale in 1950. In 1955 he founded *National Review* in New York City, which became the leading journal of conservative opinion in the United States. As the candidate of the Conservative Party for mayor of New York City in 1965 he attacked the city's liberal social policies and advocated fiscal responsibility and law and order. He finished third behind the Republican candidate John V. Lindsay and the Democratic candidate Abraham D. Beame but exceeded expectations by winning 13.4 percent of the votes. In 1966 he became the host of *Firing Line,* an interview program taped weekly in New York City and broadcast nationwide on public television until 1999. Buckley retired as editor in chief of *National Review* in 1990 but continued to write a syndicated newspaper column and publish spy novels and works on politics and history. Buckley maintained residences on Park Avenue in Manhattan and in Stamford, Connecticut.

John B. Judis, *William F. Buckley, Jr.: Patron Saint of the Conservatives* (New York: Simon and Schuster, 1988); Linda Bridges and John R. Coyne, Jr., *Strictly Right: William F. Buckley Jr. and the American Conservative Movement* (New York: John Wiley and Sons, 2007)

Edward T. O'Donnell

Buddhists. New York City is an important center of American Buddhism, in part because its residents include immigrants from most countries that have a strong Buddhist tradition, among them China, Japan, Thailand, Korea, Tibet, Burma, Vietnam, Cambodia, Laos, and Sri Lanka. The first Buddhists in the city were Chinese who settled there in the mid- to late nineteenth century. It is not known where they established their first temple because they often worshipped in nondescript rooms at the headquarters of secular Chinese associations. Buddhism became a subject of wide interest after the Theosophical Society was formed in the city in September 1875 by Helena Blavatsky. Japanese Buddhism established a presence in the city in 1930 when the artist and writer Sokei-an Sasaki, an adherent of Rinzai Zen Buddhism, formed the Buddhist Society of America (renamed the first Zen Institute of America in 1945). Later led by Mary Farkas and situated at 113 East 30th Street, this organization began publishing *Zen Notes* in 1954. Another important Japanese sect, Jodo Shinshu, was represented by the New York Buddhist Church, formed in 1938 at 331 Riverside Drive as an affiliate of Buddhist Churches of America. The church held separate Sunday services in Japanese and English and in 1948 began supporting the American Buddhist Academy, which ordains priests and offers a master's degree in Buddhist studies. During the 1960s Buddhism was popularized by such beat poets as Allen Ginsberg and Jack Kerouac and other figures in the counterculture. The Zen Studies Society was formed in 1968 at 223 East 67th Street, and the Chinese (Ch'an) Institute of Chung-Hwa, Buddhist Culture Meditation Center, opened in 1979 in Elmhurst.

Tibetan Vajrayana Buddhism also gained a large following, with institutions ranging from such formal ones as the Tibet Center (Gelugpa school) and the Dharmadhatu of New York (Kagyu school) to less formal ones like the Buddhist Center (Sakya school), led by the guru Lama Pema Wangdak. The New York Buddhist Vihara, an enclave of monks formed in 1980 in Kew Gardens, Queens, and directed by a Sri Lankan spiritual leader, represented Heravada Buddhism, an ascetic tradition most closely associated with Thailand and Southeast Asia. American-born Buddhists in the city took an early interest in efforts to modernize the religion, to make its hierarchy more democratic and open to women, and to encourage dialogue between its sects. The American Buddhist Movement, formed at 301 West 45th Street in 1980 by

Kevin O'Neil, published the *American Buddhist* between 1980 and 1988 and by 2000 had more than 500 members, mostly middle class and American born. By this time there were 11 Buddhist temples in Chinatown and several more in Flushing, and the Buddhist Association of the United States, which was primarily Chinese, supported the Temple of Enlightenment at 3070 Albany Crescent in the Bronx. Most Buddhist organizations in the city maintain rural retreats in upstate New York.

Charles S. Prebish, *American Buddhism* (North Scituate, Mass.: Duxbury, 1979)

Marc Ferris

budget. Municipal spending was relatively low in seventeenth- and eighteenth-century New York City, when efforts at social betterment were conducted largely by private charities and religious organizations, and the city's taxing power was strictly circumscribed. The city's total budget in 1850 was $3,368,163, or $6.53 per inhabitant. Spending increased after the city established a system for the comprehensive collection and assessment of property taxes in 1859.

After consolidation in 1898 the government of the newly enlarged New York City spent $78 million in its first year. Nearly continuous growth between 1898 and 1933 raised the municipal budget to $578 million. Its expansion during this period reflected the substantial infrastructure investments required to tie the new city together, as well as the demand for improved services in the 1920s. During this 35-year period, municipal expenditures rose at an average annual rate of 6 percent.

Municipal spending did not decline until 1933, four years after the collapse of the New York Stock Exchange, because of a fiscal crisis in 1932 that stopped the city's ability to borrow. Although the rate of growth in the 1930s was slower than in the 1920s, World War II affected the municipal budget more profoundly than the Depression. The war forced advocates of the New Deal to redirect federal resources toward defending the nation and away from economic "pump-priming" (an activity that included federal aid to cities like New York City). From 1933 to 1945 municipal spending rose to $737 million, an average of 2 percent a year.

After the war the budget followed a pattern of steady growth that lasted until the mid-

Growth of New York City's Budget, 1830–2009

	1830	1840	1850	1860	1869	1880	1890
Fire	$23,462	$76,788	$44,969	$167,573	$907,940	$1,387,991	$2,123,367
Police	$99,521	$271,709	$487,541	$1,395,122	$2,901,133	$3,227,069	$4,587,599
Health	$1,252	$4,677	$7,229	$161,070	$194,936	$256,425	$390,434
Streets, sewers, and public health	$50,378	$160,840	$287,188	$914,784	$1,333,210	$1,005,129	$1,656,458
Education	$25,995	$94,411	$374,553	$1,278,781	$3,150,000	$3,422,307	$4,149,563
Charities and correction	$131,021	$254,000	$400,000	$746,199	$953,000	$1,318,793	$2,124,750
Asylums and related institutions	$4,000	$6,921	$9,863	$109,661	$939,219	$930,399	$1,154,644
Other	$340,989	$736,396	$1,756,820	$5,012,866	$16,153,323	$18,206,420	$18,798,865
Total	$676,618	$1,605,742	$3,368,163	$9,786,056	$26,532,761	$29,754,533	$34,985,680

	1900	1910	1920	1930	1940	1950
Debt service	$18,033,269	$46,443,695	$76,486,538	$175,405,957	$153,620,293	$189,076,993
Police	$11,992,503	$15,110,797	$24,595,186	$50,137,369	$58,873,297	$101,964,808
Fire	$4,840,767	$8,153,542	$13,186,753	$20,676,528	$33,119,278	$58,087,070
Education	$17,160,097	$28,578,432	$50,831,347	$100,637,912	$103,180,322	$288,646,779
Charities	$2,857,084	$4,734,252	$8,149,387	$9,855,150	$15,275,502	$197,036,034
Street cleaning	$5,031,282	$7,531,362	$13,163,523	$28,252,188	$28,466,356	$52,069,339
Health	$1,055,515	$2,747,723	$7,565,455	$23,478,454	$34,141,500	$91,715,932
Corrections	$762,775	$1,271,351	$2,445,551	$3,222,207	$3,976,475	$7,040,504
Other	$29,045,680	$48,559,116	$77,265,745	$153,104,063	$156,856,816	$201,230,072
Total	$90,778,972	$163,130,270	$273,689,485	$564,769,828	$587,509,839	$1,186,867,531

	1960	1970	1980	1990	2000	2009
Debt service	$294,389,265	$724,598,084	$1,720,434,679	$2,098,847,435	$3,327,000,000	$1,837,000,000
Police	$208,258,278	$616,358,752	$674,037,283	$1,627,487,683	$3,084,000,000	$7,651,000,000
Fire	$109,476,530	$273,230,862	$321,290,820	$690,242,803	$1,078,000,000	$2,864,000,000
Education	$578,124,929	$1,750,635,119	$2,808,791,726	$6,669,264,270	$10,674,000,000	$11,017,000,000
Social services	$327,596,170	$1,562,911,121	$3,099,814,418	$5,530,878,823	$5,409,000,000	$6,319,000,000
Sanitation	$88,931,612	$280,001,882	$629,371,133	$629,371,133	$829,000,000	$1,952,000,000
Health	$162,324,383	$671,392,699	$508,344,450	$1,529,579,049	$1,526,000,000	$1,050,000,000
Corrections	$15,840,800	$61,224,999	$139,067,231	$708,882,488	$833,000,000	$1,738,000,000
Other	$390,004,990	$939,532,696	$2,938,015,937	$7,142,662,776	$11,416,000,000	$6,885,000,000
Total	$2,174,946,957	$6,879,886,214	$12,839,167,677	$26,627,216,460	$38,126,000,000	$41,313,000,000

Note: Numbers are rounded for 2000 and 2009.
Compiled by Kenneth T. Jackson and Alex Poole

1960s. Pent-up demand for the expansion of the municipal government was financed primarily by the growth of revenues from municipal taxes on real property and sales, though by this time transfers from the State of New York and the federal government were beginning to make substantial contributions as well. Between the end of World War II and 1965 the budget grew an average of 8 percent a year, reaching $3.34 billion.

From the mid-1960s municipal spending grew at unprecedented rates. It surpassed $4 billion in 1967, $5 billion in 1968, $6 billion in 1969, $7 billion in 1971, $8 billion in 1972, $9 billion in 1973, and $10 billion in 1974, reaching $11.654 billion in 1975. From 1965 to 1975 the budget grew by an average of 13 percent a year, driven largely by three forces. First, in 1965 the federal government and New York State required the city to help finance public assistance and Medicaid for poor New Yorkers. Under the federal mandate the state paid half of the program's costs, and the state in turn compelled the city to pay half of that. This requirement that the city pay for 25 percent of welfare and Medicaid costs from municipal revenues, coupled with socioeconomic changes that were increasing the number of dependent poor, drove municipal spending up by $3.3 billion between 1965 and 1975. Second, the municipal government expanded the municipal bureaucracy by 60,000 positions, partly to provide the mandated welfare and health services. In addition the expansion of a collective bargaining program introduced in the 1950s provided the leaders of municipal unions with a new forum for winning higher wages and benefits for their members. The expansion in the number and compensation of municipal employees added $3.6 billion to the municipal budget between 1965 and 1975. Third, debt service, or payments of principal and interest to the holders of municipal bonds and notes, rose by nearly $1.5 billion as the city enlarged its program of capital projects financed by borrowing.

The rapid growth of expenditures required that municipal officials find new revenue sources, notwithstanding the boom in revenues that accompanied the expansionary economy of the 1960s. During the second half of the 1960s the city raised rates on existing sales and property taxes and also introduced new taxes on business and personal income. After 1969, when the local economy began to experience a long recession, municipal officials stopped raising taxes and began using proceeds from note and bond sales to pay day-to-day operating expenses. These practices contributed to a steep rise in debt service costs during the first half of the 1970s. By 1975 the city had accumulated a budget deficit of more than $3 billion and needed to borrow $7 billion simply to pay off notes that were coming due.

The second of the city's twentieth-century fiscal crises began in May 1975, when the financial institutions that had been underwriting municipal bond and note sales ceased doing so. In the face of municipal default the state created the MUNICIPAL ASSISTANCE CORPORATION in June. The corporation was to issue long-term bonds, backed by municipal revenues, in order to pay off municipal creditors. In September, after it became clear that a refinancing strategy would not be sufficient, the state also created the Emergency Financial Control Board to control municipal spending. During the control period expenditure growth was limited by freezing welfare benefits to the poor and wages of municipal employees as well as eliminating 60,000 municipal positions. Furthermore, capital spending was stopped, except for projects supported by intergovernmental funds. The state also helped limit the growth of expenditures by assuming the cost of certain services previously funded by the city, including higher education. Because of these measures and more favorable economic conditions, the city's budget was brought into balance by 1981, enabling the city to begin to regain access to public credit markets. Between 1975 and 1982 municipal spending rose an average of only 4 percent annually.

During the 1980s economic growth and the desire to make up for the effects of the fiscal crisis led to an expansionary period in municipal budgeting. Between 1982 and 1990 the budget grew an average of 7 percent a year, to $26.6 billion. The greater part of the increase, $7.8 billion, reflected an attempt to restore the size and wages of the municipal workforce to the levels that had prevailed before the fiscal crisis. Some 50,000 workers were added to the payroll.

Between 1990 and 1994 the budget grew to $31.8 billion, despite worsening national and local economic conditions. Increasing fiscal stress resulted from the expansion of municipal employment and higher debt service, reflecting the refinancings during the fiscal crisis and the resumption of capital spending during the 1980s.

In 1995 the city's adopted budget called for a reduction in spending for the first time since 1980. Continued local economic stress and conservative fiscal policies pursued by newly elected Mayor Rudolph Giuliani led to a relatively slow pace of budget growth, just 2 percent annually from 1994 to 1998. During Giuliani's second term a better economy and changed policies led to more rapid growth of 6.3 percent annually, bringing the budget to $41.7 billion in fiscal year 2002.

The terrorist attacks of 11 September 2001 created fiscal problems that newly elected Mayor Michael Bloomberg was forced to address. In response to large projected budget gaps, the city borrowed about $2 billion to help cover operating expenses and raised property taxes 18 percent. The local economy recovered quickly, and municipal spending continued to rise relatively rapidly, with the adopted budget for fiscal year 2008 reaching $59.4 billion.

Raymond D. Horton and Charles Brecher, eds., *Setting Municipal Priorities, 1981* (Montclair, N.J.: Allenheld, Osman, 1980); Martin Shefter, *Political Crisis, Fiscal Crisis: The Collapse and Revival of New York City* (New York: Basic Books, 1985); Gerald Benjamin and Charles Brecher, eds., *The Two New Yorks: State-City Relations in the Changing Federal System* (New York: Russell Sage Foundation, 1988); Charles Brecher and Raymond D. Horton, *Power Failure: New York City Politics and Policy since 1960* (New York: Oxford University Press, 1993)

Charles Brecher, Raymond D. Horton

building trades. Most builders in colonial New York City were known as "mechanics"; some were politically active as Sons of Liberty and members of the General Committee of Mechanics, which opposed the importation of British manufactured goods. As the market economy grew after the American Revolution, such groups evolved into trade societies and unions, among them the New York Society of Journeymen House Carpenters. A group of journeymen stonecutters in 1823 engaged in the first known strike by masons. At issue was the 10-hour day, which was later won by masons, bricklayers, and other workers. In 1867 New York City and Brooklyn bricklayers joined the first national union in that trade, but the union met with competition and fractured in a dispute over secret oaths; its membership shrank from 7000 to fewer than 300, only to be revived in a joint union with masons. Those in the building trades later organized citywide in the General Trades' Union of New York City under the leadership of John Commerford. Union action in favor of the eight-hour day was aggressive but failed. During a severe depression in the 1870s, the Committee of Safety was formed to demand more public works projects. Skirmishes between workers and the police culminated in a riot at Tompkins Square on 13 January 1874. Building trades unions adopted restrictive entry requirements, including steep initiation fees and stringent rules of apprenticeship, and organized joint actions and sympathy strikes against builders who did not recognize unions. By the turn of the twentieth century contractors came to regard the union hiring hall as a convenient source of highly skilled workers, whose wages were the highest in the country. Corruption and an effort by contractors to regain control led to a total halt to construction in the city in 1903. Later, unions shut out immigrants, and Jewish and Italian workers formed their own unions and locals. Unions expanded through all the building trades during the skyscraper boom of the 1920s. As some union officials extorted bribes, organized crime appeared, at first to protect picket lines and then to become embedded in locals for many years. The political conservatism of the New York City building trades was highlighted during the "hard hat" demonstration of May 1970 when 200 construction workers attacked a rally against the Vietnam War. The reputation of the building trades was solidified in the weeks after the terrorist attacks on the World Trade Center in 2001 when workers flooded to Ground Zero to clear it and prepare it for new construction.

Walter Hugins, *Jacksonian Democracy and the Working Class: A Study of the New York Workingman's Movement, 1829–1837* (Stanford, Calif.: Stanford University Press, 1960); Howard B. Rock, *Artisans of the New Republic: The Tradesmen of New York City in the Age of Jefferson* (New York: New York University Press, 1979); Grace Palladino, *Skilled Hands, Strong Spirits: A Century of Building Trades History* (Ithaca, N.Y.: Cornell University Press, 2005)

Colin J. Davis, John Rousmaniere

Bulgarians. Bulgarians settled in New York City about 1900 along avenues B and C at Third and Fourth streets on the Lower East Side. The Bulgarian American Mutual Aid Society, formed in 1906, was the first organization of its kind in the United States. It was soon followed by the Bulgarian Subsidiary Committee (1915–17), which helped immigrants and orphans of World War I. Promoting Bulgarian culture was the goal of the Bulgarian Students Association (1924–27), the Bulgarian Society (1929), and the Bulgarian Institute (1935). Political organizations were formed by refugees and political exiles who settled in New York City after World War II. The Bulgarian National Committee, formed in 1946, was a coordinating organization that eventually moved its headquarters to suburban New Jersey. Through its publication *American-Bulgarian Review,* the American Bulgarian League (1947–68) sought to unite anticommunist groups in fighting for democracy in Bulgaria; a similar goal was later pursued by the Bulgarian National Front (1958–67) through its publication *Borba* (Fight). The Bulgarian Social Democrats (1955–57) published *Svoboden Narod* (Free People) before moving their organization to Austria. During the 1950s and 1960s most of New York City's Bulgarian population moved to neighborhoods throughout Manhattan and to the Bronx (especially Tremont Avenue and Fordham Road) and suburbs in New York, New Jersey, and Connecticut. There was also a Bulgarian National Council (1960–65) that served as an umbrella organization for all political entities. In the early twenty-first century more than 3800 Bulgarians lived in the city, including teachers, writers, artists, small business owners, food-service and maintenance workers, and painters. Many were Eastern Orthodox and belonged to the church of Sts. Cyril and Methodius in Manhattan or St. Apostol Andrew in the Bronx, a popular site for social gatherings and cultural events and a center for the study of the Bulgarian language.

Francis J. Brown and Joseph S. Roucek, eds., *Our Racial and National Minorities* (New York: Prentice Hall, 1937; rev. Englewood Cliffs, N.J.: Prentice Hall, 1960, as *One America: The History, Contributions and Present Problems of Our Racial and National Minorities*), 179–83; Nikolay G. Altankov, *The Bulgarian-Americans* (Palo Alto, Calif.: Ragusan, 1979)

Vladimir Wertsman

Bulls Head. Neighborhood in central Staten Island, at the intersection of Victory Boulevard and Richmond Avenue. The area was named for a ferocious bull with large eyes and short horns that adorned the sign of a tavern said to be a gathering place for Tories during the American Revolution. After the tavern was destroyed by fire, the town was known as Phoenixville and later as London Bridge. Residents in 1849 formed the Asbury Methodist Episcopal Church (now the Son-Rise Charismatic Interfaith Church), named after the American Methodist preacher Francis Asbury, who visited Staten Island as early as 1771. In the graveyard lies Ichabod Crane, whose name was borrowed by his friend Washington Irving for the short story "The Legend of Sleepy Hollow." A number of farmers who settled in the neighborhood in the 1920s were the first members of a sizable Greek community that built Holy Trinity–St. Nicholas Greek Orthodox Church on Richmond Avenue in 1930. A new church building was constructed facing Victory Boulevard in 1965, and the Hellenic Cultural Center was added in 2002, retaining part of the 1930 church. Until the mid-1960s Richmond Avenue was lined with truck farms. In later years the area became more ethnically diverse, with a large influx during the 1980s of immigrants from India, Korea, and the Philippines. Bulls Head is commercial and residential.

Christine Victoria Charitis, *Staten Island's Greek Community* (Arcadia, 2005)

Martha S. Bendix, Barnett Shepherd

Bulova. Firm of watchmakers. Formed as the J. Bulova Company in 1875, it was incorporated in 1911 and reincorporated under its current name in 1923. It achieved immense commercial success in the mid-twentieth century, especially under the leadership of Arde Bulova (1889–1958). At its operations in Queens neighborhoods of Woodside and Flushing it made innovations in watchmaking and developed a number of watchmaking tools. Foreign competition and outmoded technology brought on its decline during the late 1960s and 1970s. In 1979 the firm was bought by the Loews Corporation, which reversed its decline by improving quality control, introducing many new styles of watches, and advertising extensively. The firm returned to profitability in 1986. In 2007 the Loews Corporation sold Bulova to the Japanese-held Citizens Holdings Company, which closed its Queens headquarters on Grand Central Parkway.

Peter A. Coclanis

Bunshaft, Gordon (*b* Buffalo, 8 May 1909; *d* New York City, 6 Aug 1990). Architect. He attended the Massachusetts Institute of Technology (BArch 1933, MArch 1935), worked briefly in Buffalo, and was introduced to modern architecture while visiting Europe on a traveling fellowship. On his return he worked at intervals in New York City in the offices of Edward Durell Stone and Raymond Loewy before joining the firm of Skidmore, Owings and Merrill, where he became a full partner in 1949 and remained until 1979. Bunshaft's precise, refined architecture was influenced by Le Corbusier and Ludwig Mies van der Rohe, while displaying a sensitivity to local, technological, and financial constraints. His best-known works are commercial buildings for which he was a design partner: Lever House (1952), the first glass-walled private office building, which introduced the idea of a plaza beside a high structure and helped to inspire the zoning revisions of 1961; the Veterans Administration Hospital in Brooklyn (1951); Chase Manhattan Plaza (1961), a catalyst for the renewal of Wall Street; and the controversial but powerful 9 West 57th Street (1974), which slopes to fit into the zoning "envelope." An art collector, Bunshaft placed works by important artists in most of his buildings.

Carol H. Krinsky, *Gordon Bunshaft of Skidmore, Owings and Merrill* (New York: Architectural History Foundation/Cambridge, Mass.: MIT Press, 1988)

Carol Krinsky

Bureau of City Betterment. Civic organization, a forerunner of the Institute of Public Administration.

Bureau of Educational Experiments. Original name of the Bank Street College of Education.

Bureau of Municipal Research. Civic organization, a forerunner of the Institute of Public Administration.

burlesque. The evolution of theatrical burlesque in New York City at first paralleled its evolution elsewhere: traditional parodies of standard theatrical works, exemplified by John Gay's *Beggar's Opera* (performed in New York City in 1750 by the English company of

Walter Murray and Thomas Kean), gradually gave way to more unsophisticated forms of entertainment less concerned with lampooning works of literature than with displaying female bodies. The beginnings of this trend may be traced to the early nineteenth century, when female stage performers began to appear in tights. The first of these was Francisque Hutin at the Thalia Theater in New York City in 1827. Adah Isaacs Menken wore beige tights for her role in *Mazeppa* at the Broadway Theatre in April 1866, thus giving an illusion of nudity and causing a sensation. Tights were worn by an entire female chorus when *The Black Crook* opened in September of the same year at Niblo's Garden (an event that also marked the first performance in New York City of the cancan), and by the English troupe the "British Blondes," which in September 1868 performed a burlesque of Greek mythology, *Ixion,* under the direction of Lydia Thompson at Wood's Theatre. By May 1869, 14 of the 16 theaters in New York City were offering "naked drama." The person perhaps most responsible for Americanizing the burlesque show was Michael B. Leavitt, the producer of the Rentz–Santley shows. He combined ideas borrowed from the productions of Thompson with elements of minstrelsy, variety shows, and theatrical extravaganzas, all performed in an unvarying sequence: musical numbers and comedy, a series of specialty acts (the olio), and an after-piece and finale. Dancing figured prominently in Leavitt's productions, which drew large audiences in New York City and elsewhere in the 1870s and 1880s. One of the first women from his troupe to gain recognition as a performer in her own right was May Howard, who by 1888 appeared at variety houses in Manhattan as the leader of a company that bore her name and that later achieved great prominence. Another important troupe in this period was the Rose Sydell Burlesque Company, better known as the "London Belles." One of the first theater owners in New York City to offer burlesque entertainment was Henry Clay Miner, first at the Bowery and then at the Eighth Avenue Theatre (built 1881). Joseph Weber and Lew Fields did so as well at their Broadway Music Hall (opened September 1896).

By the turn of the century the characteristics of the modern burlesque show had become fixed: chorus girls in tights, bare-bellied solo cooch dancers (female dancers whose routines were derived from belly dancing and featured erotic movements), and comedians. The years 1900 to 1914 were the heyday of burlesque in New York City. The best-known performers included Billy Watson, who appeared with a "beef trust" of chorines each weighing as much as 200 pounds (90 kilograms), "Sliding Billy" Watson, Bozo Snyder, Leon Errol, and Alexander Carr, and in later years Al Jolson, Jack Pearl, Fanny Brice, Eddie Cantor, Joe Cook, Bud Abbott and Lou Costello, Phil Silvers, and Joey Faye. The importance of New York City as a center of burlesque grew with the establishment of national burlesque chains, called wheels. The first of these, the Columbia wheel, was formed in 1905 by Samuel Scribner and Lawrence Weber and devoted to "clean" burlesque, or burlesque suitable for families. Its flagship theater, the Columbia, opened in New York City in January 1910 at Seventh Avenue and 47th Street; in Brooklyn, Columbia controlled the Star Theater on Jay Street. Many other theaters were controlled by the Minsky family. Among those that were not were the Olympic and Irving Place, both near 14th Street, and the Eltinge on 42nd Street. As the burlesque of the wheels became increasingly hard to distinguish from vaudeville, the burlesque of resident stock companies, which was most closely identified with the Minskys, became increasingly risqué. The character of burlesque changed markedly with the introduction about 1927 of the striptease, which began as an encore and in the following years grew in explicitness and prominence; by 1930 the Irving Place Theater was known specifically for this brand of entertainment. Among the best-known strippers were Ann Corio, Margie Hart, Gypsy Rose Lee, and Georgia Sothern. When Fiorello H. La Guardia became mayor in 1934, he began a crusade against burlesque, which by then had acquired an unsavory reputation. Although burlesque was allowed in 1937 to continue in modified form, it was banned in May 1942. Theatrical burlesque had a resurgence in New York City in the early twenty-first century, although its audience does not match that patronizing strip clubs throughout the city.

Bernard Sobel, *Burleycue: An Underground History of Burlesque* (New York: Farrar and Rinehart, 1931); Irving Zeidman, *The American Burlesque Show* (New York: Hawthorn, 1967); Morton Minsky and Milt Machlin, *Minsky's Burlesque* (New York: Arbor House, 1986)

William Green

Burlingham, Charles C(ulp) (*b* Plainfield, N.J., 31 Aug 1858; *d* New York City, 6 June 1959). Admiralty lawyer and civic reformer. Known as "New York's first citizen," he served two terms as president of the Association of the Bar of the City of New York and was later a confidential adviser to Mayor Fiorello H. La Guardia. For half a century Burlingham remained highly influential in judicial appointments and politics.

Frank Vos

Burr, Aaron (*b* Newark, N.J., 6 Feb 1756; *d* Port Richmond [now in Staten Island], 14 Sept 1836). Vice president of the United States. After a distinguished military career, he arrived in New York City in 1783 as a colonel after British forces evacuated, settling at 3 Wall Street (1783–84). He established a thriving legal practice, became active in politics, and served in the state assembly (1784–85, 1797–99), as the attorney general of New York State (1789–91), and in the U.S. Senate (1791–99). During these years he lived at 10 Maiden Lane (1784–90), 4 Broadway (1790–94), and Mortier House in Greenwich Village (most of the time from 1794 to 1804). In 1799 he was instrumental in chartering the Manhattan Company, which was the second bank in New York City, and in the following year he mounted a successful candidacy for the vice presidency. From the 1780s he was a political rival of Alexander Hamilton, whom he blamed for his own loss of the presidency in 1800 and of the governorship of New York in 1804. He eventually challenged Hamilton to a duel that took place on 11 July 1804, at Weehawken, New Jersey, in which Hamilton was killed. The duel ended Burr's political career. Enmeshed in political intrigues in the West, he stood trial for treason (of which he was acquitted), spent several years in Europe, and returned to New York City in 1812 to resume the practice of law. Houses at 127 and 131 MacDougal Street were built for him in 1829. In 1833 he married Eliza Jumel, with whom he lived for several months in a house at Edgecombe Avenue near West 160th Street (now known as the Morris–Jumel Mansion). He spent the end of his life in genteel poverty and his last weeks at Winant's Inn at 2040 Richmond Terrace in Port Richmond (later named the St. James Hotel and the Port Richmond Hotel).

Portrait of Aaron Burr by John Vanderlyn, 1802

Milton Lomask, *Aaron Burr* (New York: Farrar, Straus and Giroux, 1979–82); Nancy Isenberg, *Fallen Founder: The Life of Aaron Burr* (New York: Viking, 2007)

See also Abolitionism.

Barbara A. Chernow

Burroughs, William Seward (*b* St. Louis, Mo., 5 Feb 1914; *d* Lawrence, Kans., 2 Aug 1997). Writer. A central figure of the beat generation, he was born into a family of moderate wealth with a legacy of American corporate life: his grandfather on his father's side was an inventor credited with perfecting the adding machine, and his uncle on his mother's side worked as a publicist for John D. Rockefeller. While attending Harvard University, Burroughs frequently visited New York City and the homosexual subculture of Greenwich Village. After graduating in 1936 he traveled throughout Germany and Austria, where he studied medicine and married a German Jew to help her escape the Nazis (the two separated once back in New York yet remained friends for many years).

Moving between Chicago and New York City, he avoided the draft in the early 1940s owing to his psychiatric record. While in the city in 1943, he was introduced to Allen Ginsberg, a student at Columbia University, and Jack Kerouac, a recent graduate. During this same period Burroughs married a Barnard student by common law, Joan Vollmer Adams, who had converted her apartment on 115th Street into a bohemian gathering spot. He also quickly became a mentor to the younger Ginsberg and Kerouac and would later coauthor a novel with Kerouac titled *And the Hippos Were Boiled in Their Tanks.* In 1946 Burroughs began experimenting with several drugs, including morphine, marijuana, and heroin, and left New York City to move to Texas (to be joined later by Joan and her daughter from a previous marriage); the following year the couple had a son. After a brief stint in New Orleans he found himself an expatriate in Mexico City, where he began his first book, *Junk* (later published as *Junkie* and, finally, *Junky*). Although the novel deals predominantly with the subaltern communities of 1940s America, it ends with the autobiographical event that took place on 6 September 1951 in which Burroughs shot and killed his wife in a drunken game of "William Tell" at a party. After a few weeks in jail, he was released on bail and eventually acquitted of manslaughter; it was during the laborious trial that he wrote his short novel *Queer.* Burroughs returned to New York City in 1953 to live with Allen Ginsberg. The two writers had a brief affair, and Burroughs again left the city for Mexico.

He eventually returned to the city in 1974, having secured a teaching position at City College with the help of Ginsberg. Despite struggling to pay the rent on his Lower East Side apartment, he was frustrated with teaching and rejected a position at the University of Buffalo. Instead he supported himself by doing reading tours; in 1978 the Nova Convention (held throughout the state of New York) was organized in his honor, with guests such as Frank Zappa, Timothy Leary, and John Cage. In 1974 he left New York City for the final time, moving to Kansas to once again escape his heroin addiction.

Garrett A. Felber

buses. The first person to operate horse-drawn omnibuses in New York City was Abraham Brower in 1831. The Fifth Avenue Coach Company operated horse-drawn buses from 1885 and motorbuses from 1905, and established single- and double-decker buses as durable mass transit vehicles. By 1908 all horse-drawn buses had been retired. Mayor John F. Hylan provided bus franchises to private operators from 1920. Bus service began in Staten Island in 1921 after the local streetcar company discontinued its operations. By 1925 Fifth Avenue Coach had developed a large network in Manhattan, including a route connecting with Jackson Heights, Queens, that it served primarily with double-deckers. In 1926 Fifth Avenue Coach acquired Manhattan's leading streetcar operator, New York Railways. Fifth Avenue Coach operated two bus routes along the Grand Concourse from 1924 to 1928. It then yielded the franchise to the Third Avenue Railway, which operated a far-reaching streetcar network in the Bronx and received an exclusive bus franchise; many of its routes entered upper Manhattan by means of the bridges across the Harlem River. In Queens fledgling bus operators emerged in the 1920s and developed a large network, and from 1931 the Brooklyn–Manhattan Transit Corporation (BMT) ran buses in Brooklyn that provided access to its streetcars and subways. Trolley buses, which were hybrid vehicles combining features of motor buses and streetcars, were first introduced in the 1920s in Staten Island and quickly abandoned. In 1932 and again in 1948, trolley buses were installed on some Brooklyn routes before being eliminated in 1960.

Mayor Fiorello H. La Guardia set out in 1934 to establish a coherent, citywide policy on surface transit: he eliminated some streetcar lines and granted franchises to strong private bus operators in each borough. In Queens the eastern part of the borough was served by North Shore Bus, the southwestern part by Green Bus, and the northwestern part by Triboro Coach; there were also three smaller operators that evolved from former trolley operators, specifically Jamaica Bus, Queens Transit, and Steinway Omnibus. Between February 1935 and June 1936, Fifth Avenue Coach formed the subsidiary New York City Omnibus and converted all the routes formerly operated by New York Railways to bus routes. The only streetcar routes left in Manhattan by 1936 were those of Third Avenue Railway, which operated along Broadway, Third Avenue, and Amsterdam Avenue, and across 42nd, 59th, and 125th streets. In 1936 Fifth Avenue Coach introduced the first of 160 double-decker buses in its network; between 1938 and 1950 Fifth Avenue Coach and Third Avenue Railway introduced large, single-deck diesel-powered buses on heavily traveled routes. In Staten Island, La Guardia granted franchises to two companies, the more powerful of which, Staten Island Coach, took over all the routes in the borough in 1937.

Berenice Abbott, Greyhound Bus Terminal, *244–48 West 34th Street, 14 July 1936*

Queens Transit and Steinway Omnibus came under common ownership in 1939. In 1940 the city bought the BMT and inherited the huge streetcar network in Brooklyn. Between 1941 and 1956 this entire network was converted to bus service, using large (typically 400–500) orders for large diesel-powered buses. Third Avenue Railway and the city signed a new franchise agreement in 1940 that provided for complete conversion of its streetcar lines in Manhattan and the Bronx to bus service by 1960. The conversion took place between March 1941 and August 1948, after which Third Avenue Railway became the Surface Transportation Corporation.

In Staten Island the bus franchise of Staten Island Coach was sold in March 1946 to Isle Transportation, which abandoned the operation in February 1947 and sold it to the city's Board of Transportation, preserving important services to the Staten Island Ferry at St. George. In March 1947 the core of the Queens Bus Division of the New York City Transit Authority (NYCTA) was formed when North Shore Bus returned its franchise to the city, forcing the Board of Transportation again to rescue a local bus operation. Green Bus continued to operate independently and obtained ownership of Triboro Coach (1947), Jamaica Bus (1949), and Command Bus (1979). In 1948 the city acquired two small bus companies in Manhattan with five routes, including ones along First and Second avenues and across 49th and 50th streets. Fifth Avenue Coach and New York City Omnibus merged in 1954, and in 1956 they acquired Surface Transportation. In April 1957 surface transit routes became converted entirely to buses with the replacement of the last streetcar route, which crossed the Queensboro Bridge.

Between 1948 and 1962 the bus routes of New York City were controlled entirely by the city in Brooklyn and Staten Island, by the city and five private companies in Queens, and largely by the combined operation of Fifth Avenue Coach and Surface Transportation in Manhattan and the Bronx. Transfers were eliminated in Manhattan and the Bronx in 1962, after which the NYCTA and private companies in every borough except the Bronx allowed selective transfers between their own routes only. Early in the same year an investment group led by Harry Weinberg purchased Fifth Avenue Coach, prompting a strike by drivers on 1 March when the new management sought to discharge some unionized employees as a cost-cutting measure. The city quickly intervened and took over the entire system, creating a subsidiary of the NYCTA, the Manhattan and Bronx Surface Transit Operating Authority (MABSTOA); from 1962 until 2006 MABSTOA and the NYCTA operated virtually all local routes except for those of private companies in Queens and Brooklyn (Green, Triboro, Jamaica, Command, and Queens–Steinway). Bus drivers stopped making change on 31 August 1969, requiring customers to use exact coins, subway tokens, or more recently, Metrocards (see below). Fare boxes do not accept bills.

Express buses that transported passengers from the outer boroughs to Manhattan for a premium fare began in 1968. These routes are now operated by the NYCTA and until 2005 by a number of private companies, including Command Bus (which served Brooklyn), New York Bus Service and Liberty Lines (which served Riverdale, Co-op City, Williamsbridge, and other outlying sections of the Bronx), and the aforementioned Queens private concerns.

In 1980 the NYCTA discovered structural problems with its new fleet of Flxible buses, manufactured by Grumman. Used buses were borrowed from Washington, D.C., while the buses were being repaired, but the repairs were unsuccessful and the Flxible buses were permanently taken out of service in 1984. Small, private bus lines continued to be acquired by larger lines and by the city, which in 1980 took over Avenue B and East Broadway Transit of Manhattan. Queens Transit and affiliate Steinway (Omnibus) Transit were sold in 1986 and then merged as the Queens Surface Corporation. In 2005–6, the remaining private companies in Queens, Brooklyn, and the Bronx (Command, Green, Triboro, Jamaica, Queens Surface, Liberty Lines, and New York Bus Service) were purchased outright by the Metropolitan Transportation Authority (MTA) and combined into a new public corporation called MTA Bus Company, ending 100 years of privately operated bus service in New York City.

Since 2008 NYCTA and MABSTOA have operated virtually all local bus routes in Manhattan, the Bronx, Brooklyn, and Staten Island, as well as express routes between Manhattan and Staten Island, Brooklyn, and Queens. Local routes in Queens are divided between the NYCTA and MTA Bus Company, which also operates important express routes between Manhattan and Queens, the Bronx, and Brooklyn. The combined NYCTA, MABSTOA, and MTA bus systems in 2007 taken together comprised 320 routes (250 local and 70 express) and carried 850 million passengers a year on 5800 buses. Brooklyn alone had 60 routes and 1400 buses. In Manhattan buses carried fewer passengers than subways: they were perhaps most useful to passengers traveling crosstown (who cannot easily do so by subway) and to the elderly and handicapped (half fares for passengers older than 65 were introduced in 1969, "kneeling buses" in 1976, and wheelchair lifts in 1980). Beginning in 1997, 60-foot- (18-meter-) long, three-axle, articulated buses, which carry 50 percent more people than conventional 40-foot (12-meter) models, were introduced in the Bronx and Manhattan. In 2004 hybrid-electric buses, which combine a small diesel engine with an electric motor, were introduced as a means to reduce diesel fuel consumption and resulting exhaust emissions.

Since 1997 the bus system has had increased ridership. The Metrocard system integrated the subways with all bus operations (both NYCTA/MABSTOA, the former private companies, and MTA's Nassau County buses) and permitted free transfers between and within both modes. Subway tokens were eliminated as a bus fare medium in 2003. For most of transit history in New York City, bus and subway fares have been the same, differing only from 1 July 1948 to 1 July 1950, when subways cost 10 cents and buses 7 cents. While there were some small differences in bus fares in the 1948–56 period, depending on whether the Board of Transportation/NYCTA or a private operator controlled a particular route, by 1956 all local bus fares were standardized at 15 cents and have since then remained tied to the subway fare.

Intercity buses first served New York City in 1924. With the construction of the Holland and Lincoln tunnels, intercity services expanded, and many small, independent terminals were built in the western part of midtown. Plans by the city to develop a single, off-street bus terminal with ramps leading directly to the Lincoln Tunnel took shape in 1945 and led to the construction in 1947–50 of the Port Authority Bus Terminal, where all intercity buses now depart and arrive.

Andrew Sparberg

Bush Terminal. Industrial park in northwestern Brooklyn, bounded to the north by Upper New York Bay, Gowanus Bay, and 32nd Street; to the east by Third Avenue; to the south by 41st Street; and to the west by Upper New York Bay. The first facility of its kind in New York City to have many tenants, it was planned as a center of manufacturing and distribution by Irving T. Bush, who hoped to make of it "an industrial city within a city." It consisted of one warehouse in 1890 but later had its own rail system, fire and police forces, steam and power plants, deep-water piers, and access to the highway. New buildings were erected from 1902. At its greatest extent the facility occupied about 200 acres (81 hectares) between 27th and 50th streets, handled 50,000 railroad freight cars, and had 18 piers that were the port of call for 25 steamship lines. By the 1960s it was called Industry City and had 150 tenants employing 25,000 workers, most of whom lived nearby in Sunset Park. It was bought by a group led by Harry B. Helmsley in 1965. The active port was deemed unusable in the 1970s because of industrial contamination. In the early 1990s Bush Terminal had 6.5 million square feet (600,000 square meters) of floor space in 16 buildings of six to 12 stories each and was managed by the firm of Helmsley–Spear. Most of the occupants are manufacturers and distributors of garments, printed products, women's fashion accessories, processed food, plastics, electronics, and toys. In the twenty-first century the city and state gave $36 million to develop a new park on the 23 acres (9.3 hectares) between 43rd and 51st streets and new waterfront access points to link upland communities.

John J. Gallagher

Bushwick. Neighborhood in northeastern Brooklyn (est. 2000 pop. 100,000), bounded to the north by Flushing Avenue, to the east by Queens County, to the south by the Evergreens Cemetery and Conway Street, and to the west by Broadway. One of the original six towns of Brooklyn during Dutch rule, it was established as Boswijck (heavy woods) in 1660 between Bushwick Creek and Newtown Creek and remained a farming community well into the nineteenth century. Many German immigrants lived there after 1840, and between 1850 and 1880 at least 11 breweries were located within a 14-block area known as brewer's row. Peter Cooper's first factory made glue in Bushwick in the 1840s. With Williamsburgh the town became part of the City of Brooklyn in 1854. In 1869 Adrian Martenses Suydam broke up the family farm to build housing, and the land was the site of 125 residences by 1884. Development increased after the opening in 1888 of an elevated line to Manhattan. After the Depression of the 1930s, the German population gave way to Italians, and after World War II blacks and Puerto Ricans moved to Bushwick. Many factories closed between the 1950s and the 1970s. Of the seven local breweries remaining after World War II, the last two, Rheingold and F and M Schaefer, ceased operations in 1976. Arson and looting during the blackout of 1977 further damaged the neighborhood. In the 1980s some sections were revitalized by new and refurbished housing. About one-third of the new immigrants who settled in Bushwick in the 1980s were from the Dominican Republic, with smaller numbers from Guyana, Ecuador, Jamaica, India, and China. Notable buildings in the neighborhood include the Reformed Church of South Bushwick at 15 Himrod Street (1853) and St. Mark's Lutheran Church and School at 626 Bushwick Avenue (1892). Knickerbocker Avenue and Broadway are the main commercial streets. The population is primarily composed of African Americans and Latinos, with smaller groups of Italians and Asians. In the early twenty-first century Bushwick remained economically disadvantaged and plagued by violence and drug use. However, young artists and students catalyzed the development of a burgeoning cultural and commercial presence in the neighborhood.

Tony Sanchez, *Bushwick Neighborhood Profile* (New York: Brooklyn in Touch Information Center, 1988)

Elizabeth Reich Rawson

Bushwick Savings Bank. Bank that merged with the Bay Ridge Savings Bank to form ANCHOR SAVINGS BANK.

BusinessWeek. Weekly magazine launched in 1929 by the McGraw–Hill Publishing Company, originally titled *The Business Week.* It grew into the nation's largest business publication: from 1975 it traditionally carried more advertising pages annually than any magazine in the United States. Starting in 1988 the magazine began publishing annual rankings of business programs (master's of business administration, MBA), later adding undergraduate school rankings. Its worldwide circulation at the beginning of the twenty-first century was nearly one million worldwide, and in 2008 it won the National Magazine Award for the second year in a row. The company's headquarters are at 1221 Avenue of the Americas.

The Business Week Almanac (New York: McGraw–Hill, 1982)

Donald S. Rubin

Butler, Nicholas Murray (*b* Elizabeth, N.J., 2 April 1862; *d* New York City, 7 Dec 1947). Influential university president. At Columbia College he was a student (AB 1882, PhD in philosophy 1884) and a teacher of philosophy (1885–90). In 1889 he founded the New York College for the Training of Teachers (now Teachers College), of which he was president until 1891. As the dean of the faculty of philosophy at Columbia (from 1890) he opposed a curriculum narrowly based on the classics and worked to ease admission and graduation requirements for undergraduates. He also launched the *Educational Review* (which he edited from 1891 to 1919), was active in efforts to reform the public schools in New Jersey and centralize those in New York City, as well as in the movement for municipal consolidation, and was president of the National Education Association (1893–94) and an initiator of its Committee of Ten (1892–94), which advocated a liberalization of the high school curriculum. He also helped to form the College Entrance Examination Board in 1900 and was its first chairman (to 1914). In 1902 he became the president of Columbia University after the incumbent, Seth Low, was elected mayor of New York City. During his long tenure (to 1945) he greatly increased the size and standing of the university as well as the power of his office, enabling Columbia to add five divisions (including a summer school, an extension division, and a school of journalism), 30 buildings, 2800 faculty members, and more than 23,000 students. He also continued to be active in other fields and was instrumental in forming the Carnegie Foundation for the Advancement of Teaching (1905), which sponsored an influential report on reforming medical education by Abraham Flexner, and the Carnegie Corporation (1911), of which he was later chairman (1937–45). In 1912 he was nominated by the Republicans as their vice-presidential candidate after the death of Vice President James S. Sherman, and he unsuccessfully sought the Republican presidential nomination in 1920. A staunch advocate of international peace through conciliation, he was chairman of the Lake Mohonk Conferences on International Arbitration, president of the Carnegie Endowment for International Peace (1925–45), and a sponsor of the Kellogg–Briand treaty (1929). For these efforts he shared the Nobel Peace Prize with Jane Addams in 1931. Butler's published writings include *Across the Busy Years: Recollections and Reflections* (1939–40).

Richard Whittemore, *Nicholas Murray Butler and Public Education, 1862–1911* (New York: Teachers College Press, 1970); Michael Rosenthal, *Nicholas Miraculous: The Amazing Career of the Redoubtable Dr. Nicholas Murray Butler* (New York: Farrar, Straus, and Giroux, 2006)

Harold S. Wechsler

Butter and Cheese Exchange. Original name of the NEW YORK MERCANTILE EXCHANGE.

butterflies. Butterflies thrive in New York City, where they are supported by a variety of habitats including fields, shrub thickets, developing woodlands, shaded trails and glades, wet meadows, and salt marshes. Community gardens throughout the city also host a wide variety of butterflies. The most abundant species are Swallowtails, Whites, Sulphurs, Gossamer Wings (*Lycaenidae*), Brushfoots (*Nymphalidae*), Skippers, and Milkweeds. Monarchs can be seen at Ocean Breeze Park in Staten Island; this species may travel up to 2100 miles (3379.6 kilometers) during its migration from New York City to Mexico. In autumn the Viceroy, a common orange-and-black butterfly that mimics the Monarch, can be seen throughout the city before its migration south; it is especially common in Staten Island, where large stands of seaside goldenrod provide food for its larval caterpillar. Alkaloids from the plant make both the caterpillar and its metamorphosed adult distasteful to predators.

Don Reipe, Jim Ingraham, and Guy Tudor, *Butterflies of the Jamaica Bay Wildlife Refuge* (Washington, D.C.: National Park Service, U.S. Department of the Interior, 1993)

John T. Tanacredi

Butterick, Ebenezer (*b* Sterling, Mass., 29 May 1826; *d* Brooklyn, 31 March 1903). Businessman. He worked as a tailor and in 1863 was one of the first people to produce clothing patterns in a variety of sizes. In 1864 he moved to New York City, where with two partners he formed E. Butterick and Company at 589 Broadway. By 1871 his firm made patterns in more than 12,500 styles and had sales of $4 million a year. Through Butterick's patterns, fashionable, closely fitting apparel was made available to women who could not afford the services of dressmakers.

E. Butterick's report of New York fashions, summer 1873

E. Butterick's report of New York fashions, autumn and winter 1872–73

Claudia B. Kidwell, *Cutting a Fashionable Fit: Dressmakers' Drafting Systems in the United States* (Washington, D.C.: Smithsonian Institution Press, 1979)

Wendy Gamber

Buttermilk Channel. A body of water separating Governors Island from the southeastern tip of Red Hook in Brooklyn. Its name may have been inspired by the white water of its shallow rapids. Over the years the channel was dredged to at least 40 feet (12 meters). In Brooklyn it adjoins the entrance to the Atlantic Basin and Docks (built in the 1840s), now the site of the Red Hook container port.

Elizabeth Reich Rawson

Butts, Calvin O(tis), III (*b* New York City, 19 July 1949). Pastor, activist, and president of the State University of New York College at Old Westbury. A graduate of Morehouse College, Union Theological Seminary, and Drew University, in 1989 he became the pastor at Abyssinian Baptist Church in Harlem, which in the twenty-first century has a membership of almost 10,000. Butts has led campaigns against police brutality, negative billboard advertisements for alcohol and tobacco products in the inner city, and rap lyrics that advocate violence and demean women.

Sherrill D. Wilson

Byrnes, Thomas F. (*b* Dublin, Ireland, 15 June 1842; *d* New York City, 7 May 1910). Detective and superintendent of police. He became widely known in the 1880s when he solved the robbery of $3 million from the Manhattan Bank. In 1883 the state legislature placed under his command all precinct detectives, whose primary activity until then had been to collect payoffs for the precinct captain. He advanced to the rank of chief inspector in 1888 and became superintendent of the force in 1892. Byrnes was a brutal man who purportedly invented the "third degree" and modernized the police force. He enjoyed cooperative relations with the underworld, which eventually led to his firing in 1895 by the Board of Police Commissioners. Upon his retirement, he was said to have amassed a fortune.

Joseph P. Viteritti

cable cars. The first commercial passenger cable railway in the United States ran on the world's first elevated line, on Greenwich Street and Ninth Avenue in Manhattan, from 1868 until the introduction of steam locomotives in 1871. The country's only bridge cable railway opened on the Brooklyn Bridge in 1883; in 1885 the cars that ran along it installed cable grips similar to the grip patented by A. S. Hallidie. A cable street railway was built along 10th Avenue (now Amsterdam Avenue) north of 125th Street. Cable street railways were also constructed along 125th Street in 1886 (the nation's only crosstown line), Seventh Avenue south of Central Park to Broadway to Bowling Green in May 1893 (later extended to South Ferry), Third Avenue in December 1893 (extended to City Hall in February 1894), Columbus Avenue in 1894, and Lexington Avenue in 1895.

The first cable car lines were long and had few curves. Cars were pulled by "ropes"—long, braided cables of iron and hemp that rested on pulleys and moved at a steady speed of 9 miles (14.5 kilometers) an hour. Each car was run by a "gripman" who operated a clamp (or "plough") that protruded below the car, passed through a slot between the rails, and gripped the cable. Although cables accelerated service, they were expensive to operate: loose cable strands could snag on the car grip and cause the car to be dragged forward and smash into cars ahead of it, and a cable lasted only a few months.

Cable railways in Manhattan were distinctively designed: their cables and their drive machinery were installed in pairs so that a car could be easily switched from a line requiring work or inspection to its duplicate, a system that was effective except when tangles developed. For such emergencies the railways used electrical signaling systems to have the cable stopped by the appropriate powerhouse. One of the powerhouses occupied a basement 40 feet (12 meters) deep under the eight-story Cable Building at Broadway and Houston Street (designed by McKim, Mead and White) that was constructed to minimize noise and vibration. Around the turn of the century electric streetcars replaced cable cars; one cable powerhouse became an electrical substation. The cable railway on the Brooklyn Bridge converted to electric traction after the completion of a subway tunnel under the East River in 1908. The Brooklyn Heights line was the last cable line in the city, going electric in 1909. In 1976 an aerial cableway was built between Manhattan Island and Roosevelt Island, the first such facility for commuters in an American city.

Sheldon C. Silberstein

cable television. The city's Board of Estimate awarded the first cable television franchises in 1965, at a time when civic groups and consumer advocates saw cable technology as a means of increasing public access to the airwaves. Their hopes were borne out initially by such experiments as the Washington Heights Neighborhood Action Program.

Manhattan was the first borough to be wired for cable television, which was seen as a means of circumventing the problems that tall buildings created for broadcast reception. Cable service in Riverdale in the Bronx was provided by Community Antenna TV (CATV). In 1970 the city granted 20-year monopoly franchises to two cable companies, each for roughly half of Manhattan: Teleprompter (later renamed Manhattan Cable TV), controlled by Howard Hughes, and Sterling Manhattan (later renamed Paragon Cable), owned by Time Inc. This scheme was criticized by consumer advocates, who wanted the cable business regulated as a public utility. By the mid-1970s all of Manhattan was wired for cable television, as was Staten Island (by Staten Island Cable). For the rest of the city, progress was slow. Companies competed for the franchises, but the process was marred by corruption, politics, changes in laws and technology, and financial problems. In 1988 only 39 percent of the city had access to cable television, which was still largely unavailable outside Manhattan and Staten Island. The deadlock was broken in the following years, and a number of cable franchises offered services to the other boroughs, such as Brooklyn Queens Cable, owned by Warner Communications, and Queens Inner Unity Cable System, part of Inner City Broadcasting (a firm controlled by Percy Sutton, a former borough president of Manhattan).

By the mid-1990s cable television was available in all of New York City. When Time and Warner Communications merged in 1990 they created a new entity that inherited the customers of Brooklyn Queens Cable, thereby becoming the largest cable provider in the city, with more than 700,000 subscribers. Richard Aurelio of Time Warner, a former deputy mayor under Mayor John V. Lindsay, became a major figure in cable television. In 1992 he founded New York 1 News, the city's first 24-hour television news station. Public-access cable also emerged in the 1990s. Fledgling stations like Manhattan Neighborhood Network, Bronxnet, Brooklyn Community Access Television (BCAT), and Queens Public Television (QPTV) began offering a variety of news, education, and entertainment programs. On 17 November 1998 the City Council authorized nine franchises to sell cable television to New York City residents for a period of 10 years: Time Warner Cable of New York City (five), Time Warner Cable Partners (two), Cablevision Systems, and Queens Inner Unity Cable System.

After 2006 the cable provider companies of Time Warner Cable and Cablevision split off from their parent companies, leading to speculation that one would acquire the other. Both companies increased telecommunication capacity so that they could provide both telephony and broadband services. Meanwhile, programming costs rose so dramatically after 1995 that even traditional broadcasters like NBC, CBS, and Fox were asking for payment for programming services. By 2010 Time Warner Cable had a near monopoly on cable service in Manhattan, while Cablevision had a significant presence in the outer boroughs. New York City remained the headquarters of the dominant players in the industry: News Corp, Viacom, and Time Warner.

James Bradley, Kevan Jackson

Cabrini, Frances Xavier [Maria Francesca] (*b* Sant'Angelo Lodigiano, Italy, 15 July 1850; *d* Chicago, 22 Dec 1917). Catholic saint and missionary. In 1880 she formed the Missionary Sisters of the Sacred Heart, and in 1889 she moved to New York City to open a mission. With the order she taught at St. Joachim's Chapel (defunct), the Church of Our Lady of Pompeii, and Transfiguration Catholic Church in Manhattan; St. Rita of Cascia in the Bronx; and the Church of St. Stephen (in 1941 renamed Sacred Heart–St. Stephen) in Brooklyn. In 1892 she opened Columbus Hospital (later known as Cabrini Medical Center). The order opened a school in 1899 that is now Cabrini High School. Mother Cabrini was the first American citizen to be canonized. The Shrine Chapel at Cabrini High School contains her remains. A statue of her stands in St. Patrick's Cathedral, and a parish on Roosevelt Island was named for her.

Theodore Maynard, *Too Small a World: The Life of Francesca Cabrini* (Milwaukee: Bruce, 1945); Pietro Di Donato, *Immigrant Saint: The Life of Mother Cabrini* (New York: McGraw-Hill, 1960); Mary Louise Sullivan, *Mother Cabrini: Italian Immigrant of the Century* (New York: Center for Migration Studies, 1992)

Mary Elizabeth Brown

Cabrini Medical Center. Hospital opened in 1892 by Mother Frances Xavier Cabrini and the Missionary Sisters of the Sacred Heart at 41 East 12th Street. Originally called Columbus Hospital, it moved in 1906 to its current site on East 19th and 20th streets. In 1920 the Missionary Sisters purchased St. Lawrence Hospital at 163rd Street and Edgecombe Avenue in the Bronx; this site served as an extension of Columbus Hospital until 1937. In the early 1970s it was renamed Cabrini Medical Center after a merger with the Italian Hospital. In the early twenty-first century, the hospital had 519 beds and included an ambulatory surgery program, a psychiatric day hospital, the Cabrini Home Health Agency, and the Cabrini Hospice. Other related facilities include the Stuyvesant Polyclinic (outpatient services) and St. Cabrini Nursing Home in suburban Dobbs Ferry. Cabrini is a teaching affiliate of the Mount Sinai School of Medicine and is still sponsored by the Missionary Sisters of the Sacred Heart.

Bernadette McCauley

cabs. See TAXICABS.

Cadman, Samuel Parkes (*b* Wellington, Shropshire, England, 18 Dec 1864; *d* Plattsburgh, N.Y., 12 July 1936). Minister. He led the influential Methodist Metropolitan Temple from 1895 to 1901 and the Central Congregational Church in Brooklyn from 1901 until the end of his life. A leader in the ecumenical movement, he was president from 1924 to 1928 of the Federal Council of Churches and from 1928 to 1936 was the host of its radio program, broadcast on Sunday afternoons by the National Broadcasting Company. Cadman was sympathetic to Darwinian thought and critical biblical scholarship.

Fred Hamlin, *S. Parkes Cadman: Pioneer Radio Minister* (New York: Harper and Brothers, 1930)

Charles Yrigoyen, Jr.

Cadman Plaza. Area in northwestern Brooklyn bounded to the north by approaches to the Brooklyn Bridge, to the east by Adams Street, to the south by Court and Joralemon streets, and to the west by Cadman Plaza West. When the name came into use in 1939, it referred only to the approach to the Brooklyn Bridge. To build the plaza several blocks were demolished during the 1940s, which in the following decade became the site of a complex of grassy, tree-lined malls. Standing on or near the plaza are the New York State Supreme Court (1957), the Brooklyn General Post Office (1885–91), the Federal Building and Courthouse (1961), and the Brooklyn War Memorial (1951); there is sculpture throughout. On some days a farmers' market is held in front of Borough Hall, which was renovated between 1982 and 1988. In the early twenty-first century Cadman Plaza functions as a recreation area for the residents of Brooklyn Heights.

Ellen Marie Snyder-Grenier

Cadman Plaza, 2009

Cadmus, Paul (*b* New York City, 17 Dec 1904; *d* Weston, Conn., 12 Dec 1999). Painter. He studied at the National Academy of Design (1919–26) and the Art Students League (1929–31) and became known for his satirical views of modern society. Local sites inspired much of his work, including his well-known painting *The Fleet's In!* (1934), which won him national attention for its explicit sexual depiction of sailors and prostitutes in Riverside Park. Egg tempera became his primary medium in 1940, and in the following decade he perfected magic realism, the style for which he was best known, using a precise and delicate technique to portray scenes of sex and horror in everyday settings. Cadmus produced comparatively few works after the 1940s and moved to Connecticut in 1975.

Philip Eliasoph, *Paul Cadmus: Yesterday and Today* (Oxford, Ohio: Miami University Art Museum, 1981)

Eileen K. Cheng

Caesar, Sid (*b* Yonkers, N.Y., 8 Sept 1922). Comedian. Having studied saxophone and clarinet at the Julliard School in Manhattan, he worked at resorts in the Catskills and played in several prominent big bands led by Charlie Spivak, Claude Thornhill, Shep Fields, and Art Mooney, among others. While serving in the U.S. Coast Guard during World War II he was stationed in Brooklyn, where he met the composer Vernon Duke. Together they worked on the military revue *Tars and Spars* (1944) and also its motion-picture version. After appearing in the revue *Make Mine Manhattan* (1948), he won a role in the television program *Admiral Broadway Revue* (1949). For much of his career he worked as part of a team with Imogene Coca, Carl Reiner, and Howard Morris. His skill as a sketch comic and dialectician were well served in the popular television series *Your Show of Shows,* which was filmed at NBC's New York studios from 1950 to 1954. He maintained his popularity in *The Sid Caesar Show* on television and returned to Broadway in *Little Me* (1962), for which he received a Tony Award nomination the following year. He continued to act in film and television through the early twenty-first century, collecting two Emmy Awards and another eight nominations between 1951 and 1997. In 1982 he wrote his first autobiography, *Where Have I Been,* and in 2004 he wrote a second, *Caesar's Hours.*

David J. Weiner

Café des Artistes. Restaurant in Manhattan. It is located on the ground floor of the HOTEL DES ARTISTES.

Café Society. One of the only integrated downtown jazz clubs in New York City, Café Society opened in Greenwich Village in 1938. The club was modeled after European political cafes and named in jest after the phrase coined for the lifestyle of chic, upscale society types. Its owner, Barney Josephson, was a New Jersey shoe salesman. Journalist Helen Lawrenson described it as "The Wrong Place for the Right People" and "our first political nightclub. Jazz and politics were what it was all about." Some early founders, such as Lawrenson and John Hammond, were members of the Communist Party's Popular Front; Hammond was in charge of the booking and Lawrenson acted as hostess and publicity writer. Café Society featured impressive artists such as pianists Mary Lou Williams, Art Tatum, Earl Hines, Bud Powell, Albert Ammons, and Hazel Scott; singers Billie Holiday and Lena Horne; and blues musicians Big Joe Turner, Josh White, and Big Bill Broonzy. It was here that Holiday first performed the controversial song about lynching, "Strange Fruit." The club also attracted notable personages such as Frank Sinatra, Paul Robeson, Joe Louis, and Adam Clayton Powell, Jr. (who met his second wife, Hazel Scott, at the club). Jazz critic Leonard Feather lived above the club. In 1940 Josephson opened the Café Society Uptown on East 58th Street between Lexington and Park avenues. With the club and its owner under continued surveillance by J. Edgar Hoover and the Federal Bureau of Investigation, Josephson's brother Leon, who had invested money in the club's formation, was subpoenaed in 1947 and sent to prison the following year after refusing to testify before the House Un-American Activities Committee (HUAC). The Society Uptown, which was considered more chic than the more informal downtown club, was sold in 1947 to Max Gordon, owner of the rival club the Village Vanguard. The revamped bistro, Le Directoire, featured French music and failed shortly after opening. The Society Downtown suffered as well because of negative publicity after the HUAC hearings and closed in 1948.

Garrett A. Felber

Caffin, Charles H(enry) (*b* Sittingbourne, England, 4 June 1854; *d* New York City, 15 Jan 1918). Art critic and writer. The son of an Anglican minister, he graduated from Pembroke College, Oxford University, in 1873 and moved in 1892 to the United States. He moved in 1897 to Long Island and in about 1908 to Manhattan. His perceptive criticism on new trends in painting, sculpture, and photography was published in the *Evening Post* (1897–1900), the *Sun* (1901–4), and the *New York American* (1913–18).

Sandra Lee Underwood, *Charles H. Caffin: A Voice for Modernism, 1897–1918* (Ann Arbor, Mich.: UMI Research Press, 1983)

Patricia Hills

Cage, John (Milton, Jr.) (*b* Los Angeles, 5 Sept 1912; *d* New York City, 12 Aug 1992). Composer and writer. A supporter of the composers' organization New Music, he moved to New York City in 1943 and became an important figure in the musical avant-garde. In the 1950s much of his work came to be influenced by eastern philosophy and Zen Buddhism, and indeterminacy (chance methods) began to play a large role in the composition and performance of his music. His works are scored for instruments ranging from toy piano and prepared piano (a piano that is altered by the addition to its strings of nuts, bolts, and other objects) to plants, juice blenders, and transistor radios; one of his best-known works, *4'33"* (1952), calls for the performer or performers to remain silent and consists only of random sounds heard in the auditorium. Among his compositions are several scores for the choreographer Merce Cunningham. Cage was known for his facility with styles and moods from the stark to the numbingly complex. His published writings include *Silence* (1961) and *A Year from Monday* (1967).

Paul Griffiths, *Cage* (New York: Oxford University Press, 1981); Richard Fleming and William Duckworth, eds., *John Cage at Seventy-five* (Lewisburg, Pa.: Bucknell University Press, 1989)

Barbara L. Tischler

Cagney, James (*b* New York City, 17 July 1899; *d* Stanfordville, N.Y., 30 March 1986). Actor. The son of an Irish bartender and a Norwegian mother, he grew up on the Upper East Side working as a waiter and poolroom racker to help support his family. After graduating from Stuyvesant High School he attended Columbia College. He sang in a production of *Pitter-patter* on Broadway in 1920 and joined the vaudeville circuit; he later returned to Broadway, where his performance in *Penny Arcade* (1929) won him roles with Joan Blondell in motion pictures, often as characters from the city. He played a gangster in *Public Enemy* (1931) and won an Academy Award for his portrayal of George M. Cohan in *Yankee Doodle Dandy* (1942). Cagney left retirement to portray a police commissioner in the film *Ragtime* in 1981. His autobiography, *Cagney by Cagney*, was published in 1975.

James E. Mooney

Cago, Joe. See Valachi, Joseph.

Cahan, Abraham (*b* Podberezye [now Pabrade, Lithuania], 7 July 1860; *d* New York City, 31 Aug 1951). Editor, writer, and political leader. He was educated at the state teachers' seminary in Vilnius, where he was introduced to the radical ideas of the Narodnaya Volya (People's Will Party), which was responsible for assassinating Tsar Alexander II in March 1881. After evading the Russian police he moved to New York City in June 1882, where he soon became active in politics: he gave his first socialist lecture in Yiddish on 18 August 1882. A leader of Yiddish-speaking radical unionists, he helped to launch the *Jewish Daily Forward* in 1897; as its editor from 1901 until his death he made it a forum for immigrants seeking to organize industrial unions. He also edited *Tsukunft*, wrote for the *Naye Zeit* and the *Arbeiter Tsaytung*, and published articles, stories, and literary criticism in the *Sun*, the *New York World*, the *Evening Post*, the *Workman's Advocate*, and the *Atlantic Monthly*. Cahan also worked on Lincoln Steffens's *Commercial Advertiser* for four years. His published writings include *Yekl: A Tale of the New York Ghetto* (1896), which William Dean Howells called the "vanguard of New York," *Imported Bridegroom* (1898), *The White Terror and the Red* (1905), and *The Rise of David Levinsky* (1917), his well-known novel about an immigrant's experience in New York City. Cahan lived for many years at 224 East 11th Street.

Moses Rischin, *The Promised City: New York's Jews, 1870–1914* (Cambridge, Mass.: Harvard University Press, 1962)

Seth Kamil

Calatrava, Santiago (*b* Valencia, Spain, 28 July 1951). Architect, engineer, and sculptor. A graduate of the Institute of Architecture in Valencia and the Federal Institute of Technology in Zurich, Calatrava integrates his architecture and civil engineering background into his innovative designs. In 1999 the *New York Times* chose his design for its time capsule chronicling life in the late twentieth century. In the early twenty-first century Calatrava was working on the World Trade Center Transportation Hub for the Port Authority of New York and New Jersey. He has had two major exhibitions in New York City: "Sculpture Into Architecture" (Metropolitan Museum of Art, 2005) and "Structure and Expression" (Museum of Modern Art, 1993).

Dianna Ng

Calisher, Hortense (*b* New York City, 20 Dec 1911; *d* New York City, 13 Jan 2009). Author of novels and short stories. She attended Hunter College High School and graduated from Barnard College in 1932. Her short stories, first appearing in the *New Yorker* in 1948, earned her recognition for her well-defined style and identifiable themes. Inspired by elements of her own life and childhood, she produced around 24 novels and short stories. Calisher was a finalist for the National Book Award for her first novel, *False Entry* (1961), and was nominated twice afterwards. She was awarded the Kafka Prize in 1987 for the novel *The Bobby-Soxer* (1986), and a Lifetime Achievement Award in 1989 from the National Endowment for the Arts. President of PEN American Center (1986–87) and the American Academy of Arts and Letters (1987–90), Calisher also taught at many prestigious universities, including Barnard College from 1956 to 1957 and Columbia University from 1968 to 1970 and 1972 to 1973.

Meryl Cates

Callas, Maria [Kalos, Sophia] (*b* New York City, 2 Dec 1923; *d* Paris, 16 Sept 1977). Soprano. Born to Greek immigrants, she grew up in Astoria. In 1937 her family returned to Athens, where she began her formal musical education. She returned in 1945 to the United States, and in the fall of 1956 debuted at the Metropolitan Opera with the leading role in *Norma*. She later performed the leading roles in *Tosca* and *Lucia di Lammermoor*. From 1971 to 1972 she gave a series of master classes at Julliard. Callas is considered one of the greatest sopranos and operatic actresses of all time.

Jessica Montesano

Calloway, Cab(ell) (*b* Rochester, N.Y., 25 Dec 1907; *d* Hockessin, Del., 18 Nov 1994). Singer and bandleader. After growing up in Baltimore and Chicago he briefly played the drums and worked as a master of ceremonies. For a time he led the band the Alabamians before taking over another one known as the Missourians, which he renamed Cab Calloway and His Orchestra. Within a few years of his debut at the Cotton Club in 1931 he became a sensation known for his dancing and his white suits as well as his singing. Calloway's band attracted such musicians as Milt Hinton and Dizzy Gillespie and remained one of the most successful bands of the swing era until it was dismantled in 1948. Many of his songs, such as "Minnie the Moocher" (1931), celebrate the drug culture and disreputable aspects of nightlife in New York City. He performed and recorded music for various entertainments, including animated films, the motion pictures *Stormy Weather* (1943) and *The Blues Brothers* (1980), the opera *Porgy and Bess* (1952), and the musical *Hello, Dolly!* (1968). Calloway wrote an autobiography, *Of Minnie the Moocher and Me* (1976).

Douglas Henry Daniels

Calvary Cemetery. Roman Catholic cemetery in Woodside, Queens. Owned by the Archdiocese of New York and managed by the trustees of St. Patrick's Cathedral, it is the largest cemetery in the United States in terms of interments or bodies buried there, which numbered almost three million in the early twenty-first century. Located near the Long Island Expressway and Queens Boulevard, it comprises Old Calvary Cemetery and New Calvary Cemetery. The original tract of land occupied 80 acres (32 hectares) of the Alsop farm on the northern bank of Newtown Creek on Laurel Hill; it was purchased by the trustees of St. Patrick's Cathedral in 1846 for $18,000. The first burial was on 31 July 1848. Initially most burials were of children and poor Irish immigrants from the tenements of lower Manhattan. Early burial parties arrived by ferry across Newtown Creek, but in 1870 there was overland access. By 1867 the original tract was full and church authorities began to annex neighboring farms. The northern edge of the cemetery reached Queens Boulevard in 1888. Tracts were later added south and then north of what is now the Brooklyn–Queens Expressway (1879), and south of what is now the Long Island Expressway between 50th and 58th streets (1900). For many years there were more burials at this cemetery than at any other in the city, but by the twenty-first century almost all the space had been filled. Those buried in Calvary include three generations of Robert F. Wagners, the comedian Lou Costello, presidential candidate Alfred E. Smith, actor Lionel Barrymore, and mobster Thomas Lucchese.

The Visitor's Guide to Calvary Cemetery, with Map and Illustrations (New York: J. J. Foster, 1876)

Vincent Seyfried, John Rousmaniere

Calvary Church. Episcopal congregation formed in 1835. The church, designed in the Gothic Revival style by James Renwick, Jr., was built at the northeast corner of Park Avenue and 21st Street in 1846. Renwick, who later designed St. Patrick's Cathedral on Fifth Avenue between 50th and 51st streets, originally intended for the Calvary's facade to be built of white marble but eventually decided to use brown sandstone instead. Part of the Gramercy Park neighborhood, Calvary was the family church of such prominent New Yorkers as the Roosevelts (including Theodore and Eleanor) and Edith Wharton. Samuel Shoemaker, rector in the 1930s, initiated extensive outreach activities, including evangelistic efforts aimed at local office workers and programs for alcoholics upon which the popular Alcoholics Anonymous "12 Steps" program was based. The church was also a center of the Oxford Group Movement, which emphasized personal transformation. In the mid-1970s it formed a united parish with Sixth Avenue's Church of the Holy Communion and St. George's Episcopal Church of Stuyvesant Square; the building continues to be used for worship services.

Robert Bruce Mullin

Calyo, Nicolino (*b* Naples, 1799; *d* New York City, 9 Dec 1884). Painter. In 1834 he emigrated to the United States, where he worked in Philadelphia and Baltimore and then settled in New York City in 1835. He is best known for a series that he painted in gouache of the Great Fire (16–17 December 1835), which was engraved by William James Bennett (1787–1844) and enjoyed wide circulation. Between 1839 and 1846 he depicted street vendors in two series called "The Cries of New York." He made dioramas, panoramas, and theatrical set designs with his sons John Calyo (1829–93) and Hannibal Calyo (1835–83) and also painted portraits, miniatures, and landscapes.

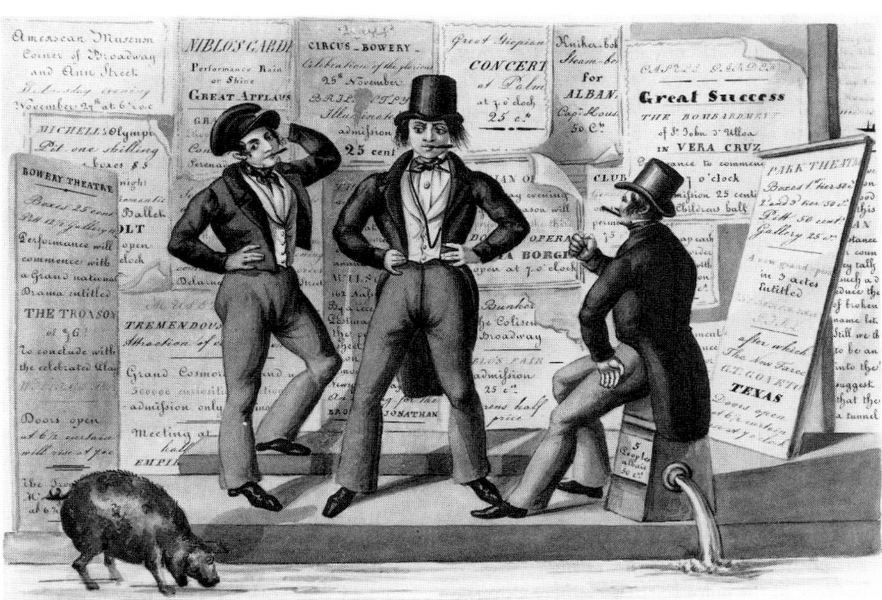

Nicolino Calyo, The Soap-Locks, *1847*

Annette Blaugrund

Cambreleng, Churchill C(aldom) (*b* Washington, N.C., 24 Oct 1786; *d* Huntington, N.Y., 30 April 1862). Prominent congressman. He grew up in North Carolina and in 1802 moved to New York City, where he later became a close associate of John Jacob Astor. Elected to the U.S. House of Representatives in 1820, he was the first congressman from the city to earn national recognition as a Jacksonian, and he led the powerful Committee on Ways and Means during the Bank War of 1836, during which controversy sparked over the Second Bank of the United States. He remained in office for 18 years, a record that went unbroken in the city for almost a century. After leaving Congress he remained active in Democratic politics. Cambreleng is buried in Green-Wood Cemetery.

James Bradley

Cambria Heights. Neighborhood in southeastern Queens. It lies within St. Albans and is bounded to the north by 115th Avenue, to the east by Nassau County, to the south by 120th Avenue, and to the west by Springfield Boulevard. It acquired the name "Cambria" in the 1920s from the Cambria Title Savings and Trust Company, a coal company in Pennsylvania. "Heights" was added because of the area's relatively high elevation of 49 feet (15 meters). The area was developed in 1923 on 163 acres (66 hectares) of farmland formerly owned by the Buck, Fausner, and Hartmann families and acquired by Oliver B. LaFreniere, a real estate agent from East New York. It was first populated by Jewish, German, Irish, and Italian residents. After World War II the neighborhood developed into a largely African American, middle-class suburb. In the 1980s there was an increase in immigration from the Caribbean. About half of this population immigrated from Jamaica, while many others did so from Haiti, Guyana, Trinidad and Tobago, and Barbados. In the early twenty-first century the population consisted largely of Jews, Latinos, and African Americans.

Vincent Seyfried

campaign finance. The New York City Campaign Finance Act, enacted in 1988 pursuant to a charter amendment, provides for partial public funding in primary, runoff, and general elections for qualifying candidates for mayor, other citywide offices, borough president, and City Council. The campaign finance program is one of a very few operated by an American city, and in its coverage of offices and elections it is one of the most extensive in the United States at any level of government. Participation in the program is voluntary. Candidates who wish to qualify for public funds must limit contributions and expenditures and abide by reporting and disclosure rules. Those who raise a minimum amount of private contributions (the amount varying according to the office sought) are eligible for a dollar-for-dollar match of public funds, to a maximum of $500 per private contribution. The program is administered by a five-member campaign finance board, which is a nonpartisan, independent city agency. It publishes an annual voter's guide that it distributes to every household having at least one registered voter. Unlike his opponents, Michael Bloomberg did not use public financing in his campaigns for mayor in 2001, 2005, and 2009.

Richard Briffault

Campanella, Roy (*b* Philadelphia, 19 Nov 1921; *d* Woodland Hills, Calif., 26 June 1993). Baseball player. His father was Italian and his mother African American, so he was at first barred from playing Major League Baseball because of the color barrier. He played in the Negro Leagues until he joined Jackie Robinson on the then–Brooklyn Dodgers and was their regular catcher from 1948 to 1957. Campanella was one of Major League Baseball's first African American players. He played in the All-Star Game eight times and was Most Valuable Player in the National League three times. He played in six World Series, winning against the Yankees in 1955. In 1958 he was driving to his suburban Long Island home when his car skidded on a slick road, hit a telephone pole, and flipped over. As a result of the accident, Campanella was paralyzed from the shoulders down. He spent the rest of his life in a wheelchair. In 1969 Campanella became the second player of African American descent to be inducted into the Major League Baseball Hall of Fame, following Jackie Robinson.

Frank Dyer

Campbell, Tunis (*b* Middlebrook, N.J., 1 April 1812; *d* Boston, 4 Dec 1891). Abolitionist, minister, author, and politician. As an abolitionist and minister in New York City, he lectured frequently in the Five Points neighborhood, often under dangerous conditions. As a headwaiter at Manhattan's Howard House, Campbell developed a formal style of table service, modeled loosely on military maneuvers, that challenged the obsequious servility that most nineteenth-century whites expected of black service workers. In 1865 Campbell became the governor of five Sea Islands off the coast of Georgia, and during Reconstruction he built a strong political machine and militia in McIntosh County, Georgia. He won several elective offices, including state senator, but at the end of Reconstruction he was jailed on trumped-up charges by his Democratic political enemies. After serving a year in a convict labor camp, he returned to the North and died in Boston in 1891.

Russell Duncan, *Freedom's Shore: Tunis Campbell and the Georgia Freedmen* (Athens: University of Georgia Press, 1986)

Daniel Levinson Wilk

Canadians. Canada's relationship with New York City dates to the seventeenth century, when traders from New France competed with the Dutch for peltry and access to American Indian trade networks. By the early eighteenth century, mission Indians from Montreal and Canadian fur traders known as *coureurs des bois* had opened up a lucrative smuggling route to Albany, from whence furs were sent on to New York City and exported to England. Among the earliest Canadian settlers in New York City were a handful of coureurs des bois, defecting French soldiers, and colonists welcomed by Governor Thomas Dongan, a Catholic, in the 1680s.

The largest single exchange of people between New York City and Canada occurred during and immediately after the American Revolution, when some 30,000 evacuated Loyalists settled in the future Canadian provinces of New Brunswick, Nova Scotia, Ontario, and Quebec. Among them were David Mathews, a former mayor of New York City; the Reverend Charles Inglis, the departing rector of Trinity Church; and the lawyer William Smith, Jr., an early historian of New York State and later a chief justice of Quebec. Landseekers from New York State, known as "late Loyalists," streamed into Canada until the outbreak of war in 1812, when perhaps eight in ten residents of Upper Canada (later Ontario) had roots in the former American colonies.

The flow of migrants reversed in the mid-nineteenth century, as Canadians began flooding across the border amid land pressures and dwindling economic opportunities at home. The number of Canadians born in the United States rose from 147,711 in 1850 to 980,938 in 1890 (a figure equivalent to 20.3 percent of Canada's population at that time) and 1,286,389 in 1930. The Canadian-born population of New York City remained relatively low, reaching 15,546 in 1890 and 45,423 (including 6863 French Canadians and 5305 Newfoundlanders) in 1930. Yet Canada also served as a way station for an untold number of European immigrants later destined for New York City.

Many Canadian-born New Yorkers eventually retraced their footsteps across the 49th parallel, and most who stayed assimilated quickly and tended not to form a distinct group. French Canadians, however, clung to their ethnic and linguistic identity, founding a New York chapter of the Société de Saint-Jean Baptiste des Etats-Unis, a nationalist fraternal organization, in 1850, and briefly supporting a newspaper, *Le Public Canadien* (1867–68). In 1882 the Roman Catholic Saint Jean-Baptiste Church was built on Lexington Avenue at 76th Street to serve the French Canadians of Yorkville, some of whom had previously worshipped in a nearby stable. By this time, the city had begun to attract English-speaking Canadian professionals and businesspeople, some of whom gravitated to such elite social clubs as the Canadian Club of New York (initially launched in 1885), the Canadian Society of New York (1897), and the Canadian Women's Club of New York (1920). On Prospect Park West in the 1930s there lived a small colony of Newfoundlanders who worked on fishing smacks that sailed from Sheepshead Bay.

Canadian emigration slowed in the latter half of the twentieth century. The 1960 U.S. census listed 40,345 Canadian-born New Yorkers, including 6270 French speakers and 4838 Newfoundlanders, and another 25,641 American-born children of Canadian parents. The number of Canadian-born New Yorkers dipped to 15,874 in 1980 before creeping back up to 21,039 in 2006, when some 45,000 Canadians lived in the metropolitan area. According to the 2000 census, some 10,645 New Yorkers claimed French Canadian ancestry, compared to 9744 who claimed Canadian ancestry—this despite the vastly higher numbers of non-French Canadians arriving in the city throughout the nineteenth and twentieth centuries. Regardless, tourists formed the most prominent group of Canadians in New York City in the new millennium: buoyed by a strong Canadian dollar, some 880,000 visited the great metropolis in 2007.

The list of notable Canadian New Yorkers includes the financier Morris Robinson (1784–1849), a son of Nova Scotia Loyalists and the founding president of the Mutual Life Insurance Company of New York; Edward P. Doherty (1840–97), who as a first lieutenant with the 16th New York Cavalry during the Civil War commanded the troops that pursued and killed John Wilkes Booth, and who later served as the New York City inspector of street pavings; the political scientist, philanthropist, and urban reformer Elgin R. L. Gould (1860–1915); the entrepreneur Elizabeth Arden (1878–1966), who moved to New York City in 1908 and founded one of the largest cosmetics firms in the world. Canadian journalists include Peter Jennings (1938–2005), American Broadcasting Company (ABC) and *World News Tonight* anchor from 1983 to 2005; Robert MacNeil (*b* 1931), cohost of *The MacNeil–Lehrer Report* from 1975 to 1995; the real estate developer Mortimer B. Zuckerman (*b* 1937), also editor-in-chief of *U.S. News and World Report* and owner of the *Daily News*; and Malcolm Gladwell (*b* 1963), an essayist for the *New Yorker* and author of *The Tipping Point* (2000). Canadian comedians include Dan Aykroyd (*b* 1952), Martin

Short (*b* 1950), and Mike Myers (*b* 1963), who starred on the television show *Saturday Night Live,* produced by the Canadian-born Lorne Michaels (*b* 1944).

Mike Woodsworth

Canal Street. Major thoroughfare running east–west in southern Manhattan. It connects Brooklyn in the east (via the Manhattan Bridge) across Manhattan to New Jersey (via the Holland Tunnel). Canal Street forms the main spine of Chinatown and borders the Little Italy, Tribeca, and SoHo neighborhoods. It takes its name from an actual canal dug in the area in the early nineteenth century to drain contaminated water from the Collect Pond to the Hudson River. The pond was eliminated in 1811, and Canal Street was completed in 1820, built to follow the path of the canal. During the early twentieth century it was the center of the bustling jewelry trade. In the 1920s the Citizens Savings Bank built its domed headquarters at the Bowery, which remained a landmark on the street in the early twenty-first century. In recent years Canal Street has become a successful commercial district and tourist area filled with open storefronts, street vendors, banks, and jewelry stores.

Benjamin Yakas

Canal Street, 2009

Canarsie. Neighborhood in southeastern Brooklyn, lying on a low section of shore along Jamaica Bay and bounded to the north by East 108th Street and Fresh Creek Basin, to the east by Jamaica Bay, and to the south and west by Jamaica Bay, Paerdegat Basin, Ralph Avenue, and Ditmas Avenue. Originally part of Flatlands, the land was named for the Indians who occupied it at the time of European settlement. It remained a quiet area of fishing and farming for much of the eighteenth century. Germans arrived during the 1870s, soon followed by Dutch, Scotch, and Irish settlers. By the 1920s there were also Jews and Italians, many of whom made their living fishing in oyster beds in Jamaica Bay. In 1907 a seaside resort called the Golden City Amusement Park opened at Seaview Avenue and Canarsie Road, which was destroyed by fire in 1934 and leveled for the construction of the Belt Parkway in 1939. In the 1920s pollution in Jamaica Bay devastated the fishing industry, and the local economy suffered severely during the Depression. As marshes were filled in during the 1950s and 1960s several apartment complexes and one- and two-family houses were built. Soon row houses covered the area. The rapidly growing population consisted mostly of middle-class whites, including many Italians and Jews from Crown Heights, East New York, Brownsville, Bedford–Stuyvesant, Bushwick, and Williamsburg. The ethnic composition underwent marked change in the 1980s, as the neighborhood and especially its northeastern section attracted a large number of blacks from the Caribbean nations of Jamaica (accounting for a quarter of the total), Haiti, Guyana, Barbados, Trinidad and Tobago, and Grenada, as well as immigrants from China, the Soviet Union, and Israel. The main commercial streets in Canarsie are Flatlands Avenue, Avenue L, and Rockaway Parkway, and there are two large recreation areas (the Canarsie Pier and Canarsie Park); the neighborhood has a suburban ambiance.

Jonathan Rieder, *Canarsie: The Jews and Italians of Brooklyn against Liberalism* (Cambridge, Mass.: Harvard University Press, 1985)

Ellen Marie Snyder-Grenier

canning. In New York City the processing of foods in glass bottles was begun in 1818 by the English immigrant Thomas W. Kensett. He employed a process developed by Nicholas Appert that consisted of packing food in wide-mouth glass bottles, which were then sealed with corks and submerged in vats of boiling water. With his father-in-law, Ezra Daggett, he opened a business in the city in 1819 for bottling salmon, lobster, oysters, meats, and vegetables. In 1825 the two obtained a patent for a process of preserving foods in tin-plated canisters, which soon replaced glass. Canning was seen as a means of preventing scurvy during the long voyages of sailing ships: in 1828 the *Journal of the Franklin Institute* suggested that canned vegetables would be both more nutritious and more palatable than other ships' provisions, and the first canneries opened in the port cities of New York City, Boston, and Baltimore (to which Kensett moved his operations in 1828 to be closer to the supplies of oysters and fruits in which his firm specialized). Canning was also used to preserve luxury foods for the wealthy. There was only one canning establishment in New York City in 1846, the firm of Wells, Miller and Provost, on Front Street near Peck Slip. From 1856 Gail Borden sold canned condensed milk in the city and maintained his headquarters there, although the milk was processed at Wolcottville (now Torrington), Connecticut, and from 1861 at Wassaic, New York, the site of a large factory built with financial backing from Jeremiah Milbank. In 1887 the French immigrant Alphonse Biardot and his sons Octave and Ernest opened a canning operation at the corner of Warren and Greenwich streets in Manhattan, where they canned meat soups and vegetable soups as the Franco-American Company.

By the mid-nineteenth century canneries were common in areas such as upstate New York where fruits and vegetables were grown, and the city became a place where canned foods were not so much processed as distributed and consumed.

Edward F. Keuchel

Cannon, Harriet Starr (*b* Charleston, S.C., 7 May 1823; *d* Peekskill, N.Y., 5 April 1896). Religious leader. After the death of her sister in 1856 she joined the Sisterhood of the Holy Communion (formed 1852), an Episcopal order run by Ann Ayres and William Augustus Muhlenberg that assisted the poor in New York City. In 1858 she was placed in charge of a ward at St. Luke's Hospital. Her tendencies toward traditional monasticism were resisted by Muhlenberg and Ayres for being too "popish," and she was dismissed from the sisterhood in 1858. At the invitation of Bishop Horatio Potter later that year she and her associates took over the management of the House of

Mercy, a refuge for prostitutes at 86th Street and Broadway, and so impressed Potter with their success that he helped them to form a community along traditional, Catholic lines. The Community of St. Mary, formally organized on 2 February 1865, was the first monastic community officially constituted by an Anglican bishop since the sixteenth century, and Cannon was elected its first mother superior. Although resisted at first by some Protestants the community soon prospered. Among its many enterprises in New York City were St. Mary's Free Hospital for Poor Children and St. Mary's School on West 46th Street. In 1872 the order purchased as a headquarters an extensive property at Peekskill-on-Hudson where Cannon spent the rest of her life.

G. F. Seymour, *Mother Harriet of the Sisterhood of St. Mary: A Sketch* (Milwaukee: n.pub., 1896)

Kevin Kenny

Cantor, Eddie [Itzkowitz, Isidore] (*b* New York City, 31 Jan 1892; *d* Los Angeles, 10 Oct 1964). Comedian and singer. Born on Eldridge Street on the Lower East Side, he became successful performing songs and skits in vaudeville, in the *Follies* of 1917–19, 1923, and 1927 and other musicals produced by Florenz Ziegfeld, and in some of the first sound motion pictures produced by Samuel Goldwyn (including *Whoopee*, 1930, and *Roman Scandals*, 1933). He was popular on radio and television for more than 30 years. His best-known songs, "Whoopee" and "You'd Be Surprised," combined cynicism with naïveté. Cantor wrote a number of books, including *My Life Is in Your Hands* (1928), *Caught Short!: A Saga of Wailing Wall Street* (1929), and *Take My Life* (1957). He was the first president of the American Federation of Radio Artists, forerunner of the American Federation of Radio and Television Artists.

Barbara Cohen-Stratyner

Eddie Cantor

Cantor Fitzgerald. Global financial services firm. It was founded in 1945 by Bernard Gerald Cantor and John Fitzgerald as a limited partnership. The firm specializes in bond trading, as well as investment banking, asset management, and market data and brokerage services. It is one of 17 primary dealers that trade U.S. government securities directly with the Federal Reserve Bank of New York. During the 11 September 2001 terrorist attacks on the World Trade Center, the firm lost 658 employees, more than any other company and two-thirds of its workforce, in its offices on high floors of the North Tower. The firm distributed 25 percent of its profits over the following five years to families of the victims and paid for 10 years of health insurance for them.

Benjamin Yakas

Canyon of Heroes. Term for an area in lower Manhattan that is the route of TICKER-TAPE PARADES.

capital, federal. For a discussion of New York City as an early capital of the United States, see CONGRESS.

Capital Cities Communications. Corporation formed in 1954 that acquired FAIRCHILD PUBLICATIONS in 1968 and the AMERICAN BROADCASTING COMPANY in 1986.

Capote, Truman (Garcia) [Persons, Truman (Streckfus)] (*b* New Orleans, 30 Sept 1924; *d* Los Angeles, 25 Aug 1984). Novelist. He moved to New York City in 1935 at age 10, then to Connecticut, and returned to the city in 1942, where he graduated from Dwight School and began working for the *New Yorker.* He also wrote short stories for numerous publications including the *Atlantic Monthly* and *Harper's Magazine.* He first achieved recognition in 1948 with his novel *Other Voices, Other Rooms,* which stayed on the *New York Times* best-seller list for nine weeks and catapulted him into celebrity. His newfound acclaim brought him into contact with an elite social circle in New York City, where he made acquaintances that shaped the character Holly Golightly, heroine of *Breakfast at Tiffany's* (1958). On the publication of *In Cold Blood* in 1966 Capote hosted the celebrated Black and White Ball at the Plaza Hotel in Manhattan, called the party of the century. From the late 1960s his literary output declined with his increasing fame and deteriorating health.

Gerald Clarke, *Capote, a Biography* (New York: Simon and Schuster, 1988)

Robert Morrow, Max Seppo

Cardinal Hayes High School. School for boys at 650 Grand Concourse in the Bronx, opened in 1941 by Francis Cardinal Spellman as a memorial to his predecessor, Patrick Cardinal Hayes. To accommodate a surge in the high-school-age population during the late 1950s and early 1960s the school opened three annexes and reached an enrollment of 3400; with the opening of additional high schools by the archdiocese the last of the annexes was closed in 1970. Enrollment stood around 1100 in the early twenty-first century. The school's building, designed in an art deco style by the firm of Eggers and Higgins, has a distinctive curved facade built to parallel the curve of the Grand Concourse. Among the notable alumnae are filmmaker Martin Scorsese and entertainer Regis Philbin.

Gilbert Tauber

Cardozo, Benjamin (Nathan) (*b* New York City, 24 May 1870; *d* Port Chester, N.Y., 9 July 1938). Justice of the Supreme Court. The son of the judge Albert Cardozo, he was considered a brilliant jurisprudent, and by 1900 was recognized as one of the most adept lawyers in New York City. Shortly after winning a seat on the New York Supreme Court he was appointed in 1914 to fill a vacancy on the state court of appeals. Elected its chief judge in 1926, he won widespread admiration for his well-crafted opinions, which balanced respect for legal precedent with a belief that the law should adapt to social change. In 1932 he left the court of appeals when he was appointed to the U.S. Supreme Court to fill the seat vacated by Oliver Wendell Holmes, to whom he was widely regarded as the most fitting successor. His view that innovative legislation may ease social problems often placed him in the minority of the court as it struck down some of the reforms of the New

Benjamin Cardozo, 1914

Deal. His ideas eventually prevailed: among his last opinions was one written for the majority upholding the Social Security Act. The Cardozo School of Law, opened in 1976 at 55 Fifth Avenue, is part of Yeshiva University.

Beryl H. Levy, *Cardozo and the Frontiers of Legal Thinking* (New York: Oxford University Press, 1938); Richard A. Posner, *Cardozo: A Study in Reputation* (Chicago: University of Chicago Press, 1990)

Frederick S. Voss

Carey, Hugh L(eo) (*b* Brooklyn, 11 April 1919). Governor and congressman. Born to Irish parents in Park Slope, where he attended parochial schools, he fought during World War II as part of the army's 104th Timberwolf Division, crossing the Rhine at the Bridge at Remagen and helping to liberate the Nordhausen (Dora–Mittelbau) concentration camp. He was released from five years of active duty as a decorated lieutenant colonel. Carey earned a bachelor's degree in 1949 and a law degree in 1951 from St. John's University. In 1960 he was elected to the U.S. House of Representatives; in 1974 he was elected governor of New York State in a landslide against Republican governor Malcolm Wilson. Facing state budget deficits and New York City's financial crisis, Carey kept the city out of bankruptcy through state aid, through the creation of the Municipal Assistance Corporation and the Emergency Financial Control Board, and by successfully lobbying for federal aid and loan guarantees to the city. In 1975 he signed the Willowbrook Consent Decree, which began the process of releasing people from large mental health institutions. He centralized administration of the unified court system and created a nonpartisan merit system for the appointment of judges to the court of appeals. He vetoed death penalty legislation. Reelected in 1978, he cut income taxes and streamlined the government. Carey declined to run for a third term and became a partner at the law firm Harris Beach PLLC.

Gerald Benjamin and T. Norman Hurd, eds., *Making Experience Count: Managing Modern New York in the Carey Era* (Albany, N.Y.: Nelson A. Rockefeller Institute of Government, 1985); Daniel C. Kramer, *The Days of Wine and Roses Are Over: Governor Hugh Carey and New York State* (Lanham, Md.: University Press of America, 1997)

Steven A. Levine

Carlin, George (*b* New York City, 12 May 1937; *d* Santa Monica, Calif., 22 June 2008). Comedian. Raised on West 121st Street in Morningside Heights in Manhattan, Carlin drew much of the inspiration for his early material from his working-class, Irish American upbringing in New York City. Carlin joked that his childhood friends referred to the neighborhood as "White Harlem" in order to sound tough. He attended parochial schools before dropping out of Bishop Dubois High School in 1953. He then joined the U.S. Air Force and began in show business as a radio disc jockey at an off-base station in Shreveport, Louisiana. Carlin performed mainstream material in the 1960s, working mostly in nightclubs, and in television and movies to a lesser extent. He shed his conventional image in 1970, appearing in long hair and jeans and discussing drugs and the Vietnam War. In 1972 Carlin released the albums *FM & AM,* his first Grammy winner, and *Class Clown,* which featured his famous routine "Seven Words You Cannot Say on Television." A lawsuit followed the airing of the routine on WBAI, a New York City radio station operated by the Pacifica Foundation. In 1978 the U.S. Supreme Court's ruling in the case of *Federal Communications Commission [FCC] v. Pacifica Foundation* affirmed the FCC's right to regulate "indecent" material on radio and television. Carlin hosted the first-ever episode of *Saturday Night Live* in New York City in 1975. He recorded many of his 14 Home Box Office (HBO) specials at New York City venues, including Carnegie Hall and the Beacon Theater. From the 1980s on Carlin dealt with a vast array of topics, including deceptive language ("language that takes all the life out of life"), religion, consumerism, and civic ideals ("Rights aren't rights if someone can take them away. They're privileges. All we've ever had in this country is a Bill of Temporary Privileges."). His 1998 book *Brain Droppings* became a best seller; in 2004 Comedy Central named Carlin the second-greatest stand-up comedian of all time, behind only Richard Pryor.

Ben Silk

Carlisle DeCoppet. Firm of securities brokers. Formed in 1891 in New York City as DeCoppet and Doremus by Edward J. DeCoppet and Robert P. Doremus, it became the leading trader on the New York Stock Exchange of odd lots (transactions of fewer than 100 shares of stock). It was one of half a dozen such traders in the 1920s, when odd lots accounted for 25 percent of all trading on the exchange. It was renamed Carlisle DeCoppet after merging with the firm of Carlisle and Jacquelin in 1969. Working solely with other brokers and conducting no business with the public, the firm by 1975 was the last one dealing in odd lots, which by this time accounted for only 3 percent of all stock-market trading in the United States. After losing its most important customer, the firm of Merrill Lynch, Pierce, Fenner and Smith, in 1975, Carlisle DeCoppet offered its securities processing system to the New York Stock Exchange, which assumed responsibility for odd lots in December 1976.

Mary E. Curry

Carlson, Chester F(loyd) (*b* Seattle, 8 Feb 1906; *d* New York City, 19 Sept 1968). Inventor of photocopying. After graduating from the California Institute of Technology in 1930 he worked in the patents section of Bell Laboratories in New York City, where he became concerned with the need to copy documents quickly and accurately. He perfected a dry copying process in his laboratory in a rented room in Astoria in Queens, where the first successfully photocopied image was made in October 1938. He received his first patent for the process in November 1940, but he had great difficulty convincing investors that xerography had commercial potential. While working for the Mallory Company in 1944 he visited the Battelle Memorial Institute in Columbus, Ohio, and granted the patent for xerography to the development corporation of the institute in return for being allowed to use its facilities to improve the xerographic process. His work at Battelle was sponsored from 1947 by the Haloid Company, a paper manufacturing firm in Rochester, New York, after its president, Joseph Wilson, read about the research in *Radio News.* In the following year Haloid announced that a breakthrough in xerography had been achieved; it copyrighted the trade name XeroX and in 1949 introduced the XeroX Copier Machine, model A.

Carnegie, Andrew (*b* Dunfermline, Scotland, 25 Nov 1835; *d* Shadowbrook, Mass., 11 Aug 1919). Industrialist, author, philanthropist, and peace activist. He moved to the United States with his parents in 1848 and settled in Allegheny City, which is today part of Pittsburgh. After working briefly in a cotton mill, he took a job as a telegraph messenger, then secured a position as secretary to Thomas Scott, then a divisional superintendent of the Pennsylvania Railroad. Carnegie eventually rose in the ranks to become the Pittsburgh division superintendent of the railroad. He retired from the railroad in 1865 to go into business for himself, primarily bridge-building and iron mills. Within only a few years, he had earned his first millions. In 1872 he became one of the nation's first—and soon its most successful—steelmakers. He married Louise Whitfield in 1887; their daughter, Margaret, was born in 1897. Carnegie devoted his later years to writing, philanthropy, and peace activism. He was a fierce opponent of the Spanish–American War and an outspoken advocate for treaties and world organizations devoted to international peace. In 1901 he sold his majority share in Carnegie Steel, worth $226 million, to J. P. Morgan, who was organizing the U.S. Steel Corporation. Considered by many to be the founder of modern philanthropy, he gave away most of his fortune during his lifetime. The remainder was bequeathed to the Carnegie Corporation of New York. Among his many gifts was Carnegie Hall at 57th Street and Seventh Avenue, considered by many professionals to

Andrew Carnegie's mansion (designed by Babb, Cook, and Willard), ca *1910. The house with its gardens and conservatory occupied half a block between 90th and 91st streets on Fifth Avenue; it became the Cooper–Hewitt Museum in 1977*

be the most prestigious concert venue in the world.

Joseph Frazier Wall, *Andrew Carnegie* (New York: Oxford University Press, 1970); David Nasaw, *Andrew Carnegie* (New York: Penguin Press, 2006)

David Nasaw

Carnegie [Carnagey]**, Dale** (*b* Harmony Church, near Maryville, Mo., 24 Nov 1888; *d* Queens, 1 Nov 1955). Pioneer in teaching public speaking, personality development, and corporate solutions. After moving to New York City he became business manager for the legendary journalist Lowell Thomas, who was on a lecture tour. After the tour was completed, Carnagey opened an office in the Carnegie Hall Building (which led him to change his surname), where he taught public speaking. Employing a staff to research habits of successful people, he devised a method of instruction that combined acting, writing, and sales techniques, which he outlined in *How to Win Friends and Influence People* (1936). The book ultimately sold 30 million copies and has been translated into more than 35 languages. His motivational principles were adopted by figures ranging from Norman Vincent Peale and Pope John Paul I to Frank Perdue and Lee Iacocca. More than seven million people took the Dale Carnegie courses in 75 countries and 29 languages. Carnegie's residences in New York City included 244 West 56th Street in Manhattan and, during the last 25 years of his life, 27 Wendover Road in Forest Hills Gardens, Queens.

Giles Kemp and Edward Claflin, *Dale Carnegie: The Man Who Influenced Millions* (New York: St. Martin's, 1989)

Val Ginter

Carnegie, Hattie [Kanengeiser, Henrietta] (*b* Vienna, 14 March 1886; *d* New York City, 22 Feb 1956). Fashion designer. Her adopted surname was apparently inspired by that of the industrialist Andrew Carnegie. Between the 1930s and 1940s she was one of the foremost designers in the United States. She employed more than 1000 persons at her couture house on East 49th Street and in businesses that made ready-to-wear clothing as well as perfume and accessories. Among the designers who worked for her were Jean Louis, Norman Norell, Claire McCardell, and Pauline Potter (later known as Pauline de Rothschild).

Caroline Rennolds Milbank

Carnegie Corporation of New York. Philanthropic organization formed in 1911 by Andrew Carnegie and endowed with $135 million to "promote the advancement and diffusion of knowledge and understanding among the people of the United States and the British dominions and colonies." It was the largest single foundation established by Carnegie, who was its first president and served until his death in 1919. Under Carnegie's stewardship the corporation reflected his interests in libraries and pipe organs. Its first major effort was to fund the construction of the Carnegie Free Public Libraries throughout the English-speaking world; by the time the program ended in 1917, it had constructed 2509 library buildings at a cost of $56 million. After Carnegie's death the corporation broadened its scope, and between 1919 and 1923 it created the National Research Council, the American Law Institute, and the National Bureau of Economic Research. Frederick P. Keppel, the corporation's president from 1923 to 1942, emphasized cultural philanthropy and in particular programs in adult education and the arts. During his tenure the corporation provided funds for promoting arts societies and the study of art in public schools to the American Federation of Arts (founded by Carnegie's associate Elihu Root in 1909 in opposition to the Ashcan School). It also helped the People's Institute to sponsor lectures by philosophers and social scientists like Morris Raphael Cohen and Lewis Mumford, and funded classes at the Workers' Education Bureau of America (formed in 1921 by Charles A. Beard and others).

After the 1940s the influence on public policy of the Carnegie Corporation lessened as that of newer and larger foundations like the Ford Foundation increased, and as the federal government formed new agencies and markedly increased its role in education with the passage of the Elementary and Secondary Education Act of 1965. The corporation continued nonetheless to finance research and writing projects, including Gunnar Myrdal's study of race problems, *An American Dilemma* (1944), and David Riesman's study of alienation, *The Lonely Crowd* (1950), as well as such educational projects as the Children's Television Workshop and *Sesame Street,* first broadcast in 1969. By the early 1990s the Carnegie Corporation had donated more than $500 million to universities, libraries, and research institutes to further the goals of individualism, liberty, equal opportunity, internationalism, and peace. By 2005 its capital fund had a market value of $2.2 billion.

Ellen C. Lagemann, *The Politics of Knowledge: The Carnegie Corporation, Philanthropy and Public Policy* (Middletown, Conn.: Wesleyan University Press, 1989)

Stephen Weinstein

Carnegie Hall. Concert hall situated at the southeast corner of 57th Street and Seventh Avenue. It was built between 1889 and 1891 and was known until 1894 as the Music Hall. The hall cost $1 million and was paid for by Andrew Carnegie, after a suggestion from conductor Walter Damrosch that a home was needed for the Oratorio Society and the New York Symphony Society. The building was designed in a neo-Renaissance style by the architect William B. Tuthill and built by the firm of Isaac A. Hopper and Company entirely of terra-cotta and brick, with an iron framework on a natural foundation of solid granite. Originally the building comprised four public spaces: the Main Hall, now seating 2804; the Chamber Music Hall (renamed Carnegie Recital Hall in 1898 and Weill Recital Hall in 1986), seating 268; Chapter Hall, used for lectures, meetings, and religious services until its renovation in 1985, when it was renamed

Carnegie Hall, 2009

the Kaplan Space and became used primarily for rehearsals and recordings; and the Recital Hall, which became the home of the Carnegie Lyceum in 1898, the Carnegie Playhouse in 1960, and the Carnegie Hall Cinema in 1970. In 1894 and 1896 two towers housing 150 studios were constructed around and atop the original building as a means of providing supplemental income. These residential and working spaces, designed by the architect Henry J. Hardenbergh, later housed such tenants as Charles Dana Gibson, the Authors' Club, Isadora Duncan, the American Academy of Dramatic Arts, Agnes de Mille, and the studios of the Victor Talking Machine Company, where Enrico Caruso made his first American recordings in 1904.

Carnegie Hall officially opened on 5 May 1891 and was widely praised for its acoustical excellence, favorable sightlines, and intimate ambience. The inaugural music festival lasted five days and was highlighted by an appearance by Tchaikovsky, who conducted several of his own works. The American debut of the Polish pianist Jan Ignace Paderewski at the hall on 17 November 1891 was followed by the debut of virtually every important classical musician of the next hundred years.

In its first century more than 50,000 events took place at Carnegie Hall. From 1892 the principal tenant was the Philharmonic Society of New York (from 1928 the Philharmonic–Symphony Society of New York, later known generally as the New York Philharmonic), which remained there until 1961. During these first 100 years more than 1300 compositions received their world premiere or American premiere at the hall, among them Antonín Dvořák's symphony *From the New World* (world premiere, 16 December 1893), George Gershwin's *Concerto in F* (1928), and Duke Ellington's *Black, Brown and Beige* (1943). Many well-known composers took part in performances of their own works, including Camille Saint-Saëns, Gustav Mahler, Sergei Prokofiev, Maurice Ravel, Ottorino Respighi, Aaron Copland, Igor Stravinsky, Virgil Thomson, William Schuman, John Cage, and Philip Glass. The hall was the site of performances by leading orchestras, chamber ensembles, and soloists from throughout the world, and by performers of jazz, folk music, popular music, and rock, among them James Reese Europe and his Clef Club (1912), Fats Waller (1928), Benny Goodman (1938), Dizzy Gillespie (1947), Woody Guthrie (1946), Pete Seeger (1946), Miles Davis (1957), Edith Piaf (1957), Judy Garland (1961), Frank Sinatra (1964), the Beatles (1964), and the Rolling Stones (1964). The acoustics of the hall also made it a forum for public speakers, including explorers, authors, politicians, and religious leaders.

Carnegie retained ownership of the hall until his death in 1919. His wife, Louise Whitfield Carnegie, sold the building in 1924 to the real estate developer Robert E. Simon; on his death in 1935 ownership passed to his son Robert E. Simon, Jr., who maintained the building until 1960. Scheduled for demolition as the New York Philharmonic prepared to move to a new home in Lincoln Center, Carnegie Hall was saved by a coalition of musicians, politicians, and civic figures led by the violinist Isaac Stern. It was bought by the City of New York in 1960 and registered as a National Historic Landmark in 1964.

On 18 May 1986 Carnegie Hall closed for the most comprehensive renovation and restoration in its history. In seven months at a cost of $60 million the firm of James Stewart Polshek and Partners restored much of the building to the way it had appeared in 1891, while improving its technical features. At the same time steps were taken to help ensure the financial stability of the hall: an adjacent lot on 57th Street (which had been acquired by Andrew Carnegie in 1903) was subleased by the Rockrose Development Corporation from the Carnegie Hall Corporation to allow for the construction of a 60-story building, Carnegie Hall Tower. During the late 1990s it added many educational programs, including a Family Concerts series, as well as its acclaimed Professional Training Workshops. In 2003 the new Judy and Arthur Zankel Hall opened to accommodate the hall's expanded educational programming, in addition to hosting a wide variety of performances.

Ethel Peyser, *The House That Music Built: Carnegie Hall* (New York: Robert M. McBride, 1936); Richard Schickel, *The World of Carnegie Hall* (New York: Julian Messner, 1960); Theodore O. Cron and Burt Goldblatt, *Portrait of Carnegie Hall: A Nostalgic Portrait in Pictures and Words* (New York: Macmillan, 1966); Richard Schickel and Michael Walsh, *Carnegie Hall: The First One Hundred Years* (New York: Harry N. Abrams, 1987)

Gino Francesconi

Carnegie Hill. Neighborhood on the Upper East Side of Manhattan, bounded to the north by 98th Street, to the east by Lexington Avenue, to the south by 86th Street, and to the west by Fifth Avenue. The area was the rural site of a few charitable institutions, modest houses, and squatters' shacks when the steel magnate Andrew Carnegie built an imposing neo-Georgian mansion at 91st Street and Fifth Avenue in 1902. An affluent residential neighborhood took shape after he sold nearby lots to such wealthy businessmen as Otto H. Kahn, James A. Burden, and John Henry Hammond. Along with such mansions, gracious townhouses and luxury apartment buildings were erected until the Depression. The neighborhood boasts many private schools and cultural institutions, among them the Cooper–Hewitt Museum, the Guggenheim Museum, and the Jewish Museum. Elegant shops and restaurants now line Madison Avenue, the main commercial street. Much of the area is protected by landmark designation.

Kate Simon, *Fifth Avenue: A Very Social History* (New York: Harcourt Brace Jovanovich, 1978); *Carnegie Hill: An Architectural Guide* (New York: Carnegie Hill Neighbors, 1989)

Joyce Mendelsohn

carousel manufacturing. Brooklyn was a center of carousel manufacturing between

1875 and 1918, when animal carvers such as Charles I. D. Looff, M. C. Illions, Charles Carmel, Solomon Stein, and Harry Goldstein developed a wildly exuberant "Coney Island style." The style is exemplified in horses by Carmel at Prospect Park, Coney Island, and Playland Park (Rye, New York), by Illions at Flushing Meadows, and by Stein and Goldstein at Central Park.

Stephen Weinstein

Carpatho-Rusyns. The Carpatho-Rusyns are a Slavic people. They are also known as Rusyns, Ruthenians, Carpatho-Russians, Carpatho-Ukrainians, and Lemkos. During the 1880s they began immigrating to the United States from the north-central ranges of the Carpathian Mountains, until 1918 part of the Austro-Hungarian Empire. Most of the Carpatho-Rusyns in New York City are descendants of immigrants who arrived between 1880 and 1914. They settled primarily on the Lower East Side and in Brooklyn, working as laborers in the garment industry, in small factories, and in the service trades. When most of their homeland became part of Poland and Czechoslovakia after World War I, a few thousand more Carpatho-Rusyns immigrated; many were Lemkos from the Polish province of Galicia. In New York City Lemkos formed the League for the Liberation of Carpatho-Russia (1917), which published a newspaper and strove to unify the Carpathian homeland with a democratic Russia. During the 1930s Carpatho-Rusyns settled in Yorkville alongside Czechs and Hungarians, and their numbers increased by several hundred after World War II, when Carpatho-Rusyns fled the communist regimes of Eastern Europe, the Ukraine, Czechoslovakia, and Poland.

Carpatho-Rusyns have sometimes aligned themselves with Russians, Slovaks, Ukrainians, and Czechs, but have also maintained their own religious and secular organizations. Their political organizations in New York City have supported a range of solutions for the Carpatho-Rusyn homeland: unity with the Soviet Union (Carpatho-Russian National Committee, 1939), unity with an independent Ukraine (Organization for the Defense of the Lemko Land, 1940), and unity with Czechoslovakia (Council of Free Carpatho-Ruthenia in Exile, 1951). These groups have issued their own publications in Russian, Ukrainian, and the Carpatho-Rusyn vernacular. The predominant faith of Carpatho-Rusyns is Eastern Christianity, and New York City has several parishes belonging to the Byzantine Ruthenian Catholic Church and the American Carpatho-Russian Orthodox Greek Catholic Church. The most architecturally striking sanctuary is the Byzantine Ruthenian Church of St. Mary, built in 1963 on the corner of East 15th Street and Second Avenue in Manhattan. Many Carpatho-Rusyns also belong to parishes of the Orthodox Church in the United States, which is oriented toward Russian Orthodoxy. Carpatho-Rusyn Jews include a community of Hasidim in Borough Park led by the grandson of the renowned rabbi of Mukachevo (Ukraine). Several Carpatho-Rusyn cultural organizations have their headquarters in New York City: the Carpathian Research Center (1958), the Lemko Research Foundation (1978), and the Carpatho-Rusyn Research Center (1978). Perhaps the best-known Carpatho-Rusyn in the cultural history of the city was the artist and filmmaker Andy Warhol.

Paul Robert Magocsi, *The Carpatho-Rusyn Americans* (New York: Chelsea House, 1989)

Paul Robert Magocsi

Carpenter and Vermilye. Original name of the investment banking firm Dillon, Read.

Carrère and Hastings. Firm of architects formed in 1884 by John M(erven) Carrère (1858–1911) and Thomas Hastings (1860–1929), former students at the École des Beaux-Arts in Paris who had worked as draftsmen in the offices of McKim, Mead and White. The partners were successful from the outset, receiving commissions for large country estates, churches, and hotels. In 1897 the firm achieved national prominence after winning the design competition for the New York Public Library with a plan that combined a majestic facade with rich interior spaces. Later the firm completed the First Christian Science Church (1903) at Central Park West and 96th Street, the triumphal arch and colonnade at the approach to the Manhattan Bridge (1905), Richmond Borough Hall (1906), Grand Army Plaza (1912) in Manhattan, the Frick mansion (1914), and the Richmond County Courthouse (1919). After Carrère's death Hastings continued to practice under the firm's name. In association with other architects he designed several notable office buildings, including the Cunard Building (1921) and the Standard Oil Building (1922). Marble busts of Carrère and Hastings were placed on the first landing of the main staircase at the New York Public Library.

Rebecca Read Shanor

Carroll, Earl (*b* Pittsburgh, 16 Sept 1893; *d* Mount Carmel, Pa., 17 June 1948). Theater producer. In 1923–32 he produced the revue *Vanities,* which along with Florenz Ziegfeld's *Follies* and George White's *Scandals* was one of the best-known Broadway shows of the jazz age. Critical reaction was mixed; the *Brooklyn Eagle* once remarked that "Carroll's showmanship consisted in selling gutter humor and naked female flesh to morons," but reviews in the *New York Times* were more positive. In 1927 Carroll was found guilty of perjury for denying that the champagne in which a nude showgirl bathed at one of his late-night parties contained alcohol, and he was sent to prison. After his release he had an inconsequential career in Hollywood.

Ken Murray, *The Body Merchant: The Story of Earl Carroll* (New York: W. Ritchie, 1976)

George A. Thompson, Jr.

Lounge of the Earl Carroll Theatre, 755 Seventh Avenue

Carroll Gardens. Neighborhood in northwestern Brooklyn, occupying 40 blocks and bounded to the north by Degraw Street, to the east by Hoyt Street, to the south by Ninth Street, and to the west by the Gowanus and Brooklyn–Queens expressways. It was originally considered part of Red Hook. The current name was adopted in the 1960s by real estate agents; the eponym of the neighborhood is Charles Carroll, an immigrant from Ireland and a signer of the Declaration of Independence. The area was settled by Irish immigrants in the early nineteenth century. From the late nineteenth century to the 1950s it attracted many Italians, and between 1920 and 1950 most of the Irish population left for more affluent communities. The Carroll Gardens Association, formed in 1964, gradually succeeded in improving the image of the neighborhood and in breaking a political machine that had dominated since the 1930s. In the 1960s many young, middle-class professionals moved to the area, drawn by its safety, tranquility, and proximity to Manhattan. Carroll Gardens is distinguished by its brownstones and its exceptionally large front yards, a feature resulting from a plan drawn up in 1846 by the land surveyor Richard Butts. These yards may be seen on First to Fourth places between Henry and Smith streets and on President, Carroll, and Second streets between Smith and Hoyt streets. Part of this area was designated a historic district in 1973 (President and Carroll streets between Smith and Hoyt streets and Hoyt Street between President and First streets). In the early twenty-first century Carroll Gardens remained a mostly middle-class, Italian enclave where several dialects of Italian are spoken. There are a number of fraternal and benevolent societies representing towns in Italy, frequent bocce games, a procession on Good Friday, extravagant fireworks displays on Independence Day, and a large number of Italian restaurants, delicatessens, bakeries, and pastry shops.

Nan Ellin

Carroll Gardens, 2009

Carrville. Former neighborhood in west central Brooklyn, lying in Bedford next to Weeksville. Along with Weeksville it was settled in the 1830s by free black farmers, laborers, and craftspeople. The name is of unknown origin but may be a corruption of Crow Hill, a name applied to the surrounding area. A church opened in 1839 but soon closed. An African free school was established about the same time, but in 1841 white trustees of school district no. 3 took over its management and renamed it Colored School no. 2; it later moved to Weeksville. A racially integrated organization laid out Citizens Union Cemetery in the area in 1851 (black burials were often prohibited in white cemeteries). In the 1850s Carrville and Weeksville became demographically one large black community, large sections of which were destroyed along with the cemetery when a road that became Eastern Parkway was cut through the area in 1869–70. Carrville was all but obliterated when streets were laid out from 1870 to 1875.

Ellen Marie Snyder-Grenier

Carson, Johnny (John William) (*b* Corning, Iowa, 23 Oct 1925; *d* Los Angeles, 23 Jan 2005). Television host and comedian. He began his career in the Midwest and California, working as a comic and television host. In October 1962 he became the host of *The Tonight Show Starring Johnny Carson* on the National Broadcasting Company (NBC), which was filmed in New York City. On the show, the city was often the butt of his monologues; he famously joked, "Anytime four New Yorkers get into a cab together without arguing, a bank robbery has just taken place." In May 1972 the show moved to Burbank, California; he went on to host *The Tonight Show* until 1992. Carson was inducted into the Television Academy Hall of Fame in 1987.

Jessica Montesano

Carter, Elliott (Cook), Jr. (*b* New York City, 11 Dec 1908). Composer. Born into a prosperous family, he was educated in France, at the Horace Mann School in New York City, and at Harvard University before studying composition with Nadia Boulanger in Paris. After finding his distinctive voice during the late 1940s, he produced a large corpus of music marked by intricate rhythmic relationships and complex melodic counterpoint. Long a resident of West 12th Street, he served on several college faculties, including a two-decade involvement (1964–84) at the Juilliard School. He was widely honored by the city's musical community during his centennial year when he participated in many concerts and symposia.

David Schiff, *The Music of Elliott Carter* (Ithaca, N.Y.: Cornell University Press, 2nd edn. 1998)

James M. Keller

Carter, Henry. Given name of Frank Leslie.

Cartier. Firm of jewelers formed in Paris in 1847. It opened its first American branch on 1 November 1909 at 712 Fifth Avenue under the direction of Pierre Cartier (1878–1965). In exchange for a pearl necklace the firm in 1917 acquired the Renaissance palace of the banker Morton F. Plant at 653 Fifth Avenue, which became its new location. The branch in New York City offered jewels from the main shop in Paris before setting up its own workshop, where art deco jewelry was produced based on Egyptian and Oriental models as well as on modern designs. Cartier's nephew Claude Cartier (1925–75) took over the branch in 1948 and remained president until 1962, when the company was taken over by outside interests. Robert Hocq, Joseph Kanoui, and Alain-Dominique Perrin assumed control of the firm in 1972 and of the branch in New York City in February 1976. The result was the formation of Cartier International, again bringing the management of all the houses under one hand. In 1984 Alain Dominique Perrin founded the Cartier Foundation for Contemporary Art.

Gilberte Gautier, *Cartier, the Legend* (London: Arlington, 1983); Hans Nadelhoffer, *Cartier: Jewelers Extraordinary* (New York: Harry N. Abrams, 1984)

Janet Zapata

carting. During the first two centuries of the history of New York City, cartmen dominated intracity transport. They pledged to obey municipal ordinances derived from English and Dutch law, in consideration of which they were given a monopoly on licenses. The cartmen refused employment to blacks, juveniles, and nonresidents and held strikes in 1677 and 1684 to protect their monopoly and resist further municipal regulation. In 1691 the city set fees for cartage and rules for the ownership of carts, standardized the measurement of loads, and required that cartmen serve any orderly person seeking their assistance; these laws remained in effect with little change until 1844. By the colonial period there were about 400 cartmen in the city, some of whom specialized in the transport of furniture, mercantile goods, firewood, hay, or food. The typical cartman was recognizable by his white frock, farmer's hat, and clay pipe. After the American Revolution cartmen helped to rebuild the city's economy. A political controversy arose when Mayor Richard Varick in 1789 ended the custom of awarding freemanships to licensed carters, a loss that denied suffrage to many impoverished carters. In an effort to have the custom reinstated, the cartmen aligned themselves with the emerging Democratic Republican Party and in 1795 helped to elect the cartman Alexander Lamb to the state assembly.

In the first decades of the nineteenth century cartmen defended their monopoly against Irish immigrants looking for work. After a bitter dispute in 1818, Mayor Marinus Willett divided the business between general carting, to be performed by citizens, and dirt carting, to be performed by the Irish. In 1825 a new law restricted general carting licenses to citizens. Despite the protests of black residents of New York City the business remained rigidly segregated. Throughout the nineteenth century cartmen evoked the anger of the middle class because of their reckless driving, surly behavior, cruelty to horses, and rate gouging during plagues and fires. They raised their rates each year on 1 May, when the city's residents traditionally moved into new dwellings. Their monopoly was again attacked during the Workingman's Movement of 1829 and remained a political controversy throughout the 1830s, when 3500 cartmen sided with the Whig Party against the Democrats, who favored the elimination of restrictive licensing. In 1844 the Board of Aldermen abolished licensing restrictions and the requirement that each driver own his cart, partly because more cartmen were needed in the expanding city. The business began to collapse in the 1850s as the carters' monopoly became unenforceable in the growing metropolis and larger express wagons replaced small carts.

Howard B. Rock, *Artisans of the New Republic: The Tradesmen of New York in the Age of Thomas Jefferson* (New York: New York University Press, 1979); Graham Hodges, *New York City Cartmen, 1676–1850* (New York: New York University Press, 1986)

Graham Hodges

cartooning. During the last quarter of the nineteenth century cartoons emerged as a medium that captured the dynamism and adventure of New York City. As a cartoonist for *Harper's Weekly* Thomas Nast lambasted William M. "Boss" Tweed and popularized such characters as the Democratic donkey and the Tammany Hall tiger. *Puck,* launched in 1876, provided a forum for such cartoonists as Joseph Keppler and Bernard Gillam; the *Judge* followed in the same vein from 1881. Charles Dana Gibson contributed caricatures of social and political figures to *Harper's* and other magazines, and in 1895 R. F. Outcault introduced "Hogan's Alley" in Joseph Pulitzer's newspaper the *New York World.* In a single, crowded panel, each installment depicted the pathos, tumult, and squalor of life in the Irish slums through the experiences of a baby-faced urchin in a yellow nightshirt. The harsh, mischievous humor of the strip became so popular that Outcault was persuaded by William Randolph Hearst to move to the *New York Journal,* where the series was renamed "The Yellow Kid." Outcault portrayed a childhood robbed of its innocence by ugliness, menace, and delinquency. In a typical panel from 1897 a chaotic dog show takes place in an alley while a parrot sagely advises in the customary slang of the strip: "Children if you want to live tro dis stay on yer perch." The yellow ink used to print the cartoon gave rise to the term "yellow journalism."

Outcault's success inspired the first comic strips, so named because they included several panels: the "Katzenjammer Kids" (1897) by Rudolph Dirks, based on the German strip "Max und Moritz" by Wilhelm Busch; "Happy Hooligan" (1899) by Frederick Burr Opper; "Buster Brown" (1902) by Outcault; and "Mutt and Jeff" (1907) by Bud Fisher, the first strip to appear daily. From 1913 the *New York American* printed the first strip in which each installment was an episode in a continuing story: "Bringing Up Father," by the Irish immigrant George McManus (1884–1954), satirized wealthy New Yorkers and romanticized the Irish working class through the adventures of Jiggs and Maggie, an Irish working-class couple who struck it rich and were suddenly thrust into a life of leisure. Jiggs constantly sought to slip away from his elegant surroundings and return to the corner saloon and the corned beef and cabbage of his old neighborhood, but whenever his ambitious and showy wife, Maggie, discovered his escapades she pummeled him with "fisticuffs" and kitchenware. McManus contrasted the haughty silliness of the rich and vacuous with the earthy charm, wisdom, and good humor of the slums. Although he showed respect for a society that allowed a hod carrier and a washerwoman to acquire great wealth, he suggested that no one could ever fully leave poverty behind and questioned whether anyone should want to. The strip became hugely popular, appeared in about 500 newspapers, and at its height reached 80 million readers in 46 countries, running for 41 years. Rube Goldberg's comic strip recounting the adventures of Boob McNutt was popular for 20 years. Other cartoons served political ends or were aimed at a more sophisticated readership: from 1911 to 1917 the leftist magazine *Masses* published cartoons by such artists as French Sloan, George Bellows,

"Sixty Seconds Make One Minute," Bud Fisher cartoon

Boardman Robinson, and Art Young; cartoons by James Thurber, Peter Arno, and Charles Addams also appeared in the *New Yorker.*

From the 1920s newspapers and pulp magazines printed comic strips based on detectives and adventure characters. *Famous Funnies* (1934) began by reprinting comic strips from newspapers and then introduced strips of its own, many with humorous animal characters. Other early comic books included *Tip Top Comics* and *King Comics.* The first "superhero," Superman, was created by Jerry Siegel and Joe Shuster and first appeared in *Action Comics* (1938), published by Detective Comics (later known as DC Comics), which soon after introduced Batman (by Bob Kane and Bill Finger, first featured in *Detective Comics* in 1939). In 1941 Marvel Comics introduced Captain America (by Joe Simon and Jack Kirby). From 1940 to 1952 Will Eisner (*b* New York City, 1917) produced his influential weekly strip "The Spirit," chronicling the adventures of a masked crime fighter in a seamy version of New York City called Central City. Judith O'Sullivan has described the city as at once the Spirit's "adversary and amour," which "is blighted but possesses a cunning life of its own. . . . Unlike the Spirit itself, the city is vigorously aggressive, asserting itself immediately in the strip's first frame." The Spirit was the product in part of the Yiddish theater, an insecure, confused, lower-middle-class New Yorker given to self-deprecating monologues. One of the many cartoonists influenced by Eisner was Jules Feiffer, whose weekly comic strip popularized a distinctive brand of humor infused with neurosis, angst, and the absurdities of urban life. A rather more sophomoric approach was taken by William M. Gaines: in April 1955 he launched the satirical magazine *Mad,* in which cartoons and comic strips parodied advertisements and popular culture. Gaines began the magazine after spending part of his earlier career publishing comic books devoted to crime and horror, a type of publication that provoked a strong reaction from the political right. In the face of growing pressure and hearings by subcommittees of the U.S. Senate, comic book publishers in the 1950s adopted a form of self-censorship called the Comics Code of America. Among the less controversial comics of the period was "Apartment 3-G" (1961), a conventional soap opera in the form of a comic strip by Nick Dallis and Alex Kotzky, in which three young women share an apartment in Manhattan next door to a bearded sage who offers them paternal guidance. After assuming control of Marvel Comics, Kirby and Stan Lee in 1962 introduced Spider-Man, an anguished teenager turned crime fighter. The company later published a large number of comic strips set in New York City and helped revitalize the comic book business. Although in the 1970s and 1980s both Superman and Batman gained new life in big-budget motion pictures, by the 1990s New York City was no longer the undisputed center of comic book publishing.

Comic strips continue to be published in newspapers ranging from the *Daily News* (which also prints cartoons in its sports section) to the *Village Voice* (which publishes Feiffer, the politically oriented comic strips of Mark Alan Stamaty, and the "Real Life Funnies" of Stan Mack). Caricatures of literary and political figures by David Levine appear regularly in the *New York Review of Books.* The *New Yorker* runs numerous single panel cartoons. The School of Visual Arts offers a Bachelor of Fine Arts in cartooning and was known as the School of Cartoonists and Illustrators when it opened in 1947.

Ron Goulart, ed., *The Encyclopedia of American Comics* (New York: Facts on File, 1990); Judith O'Sullivan, *The Great American Comic Strip: One Hundred Years of Cartoon Art* (Boston: Little, Brown, 1990)

Jeff Sklansky

Cartwright, Alexander Joy, Jr. (*b* New York City, 17 April 1820; *d* Honolulu, 12 July 1892). Inventor of baseball. In 1842 he joined the Knickerbocker Fire Fighting Brigade, where he started playing town ball. From 1843 to 1845 he worked as a bank teller; after the bank was lost to a fire, he opened a stationery shop and bookstore. In 1845 he formed the Knickerbocker Base Ball Club, which set down 20 rules for the game. On 19 June 1846 his club played the New York Nine club in the first baseball game ever (Cartwright was the umpire). In 1849 he moved to California in search of gold, teaching the game to those he met along the way. In 1852 he moved to Honolulu, where he founded a fire department, hospital, and library; managed the finances of the Hawaiian royal family; and founded baseball leagues that are considered the predecessors of the modern American League and National League.

Henry Cooper

Caruso, Enrico [Errico] (*b* Naples, 27 Feb 1873; *d* Naples, 2 Aug 1921). Singer. Caruso sang opera in Italy before traveling to the United States, where he gave his first performance at the Metropolitan Opera in November 1903, in Verdi's *Rigoletto.* He soon became the best-known operatic tenor of his generation. With the Metropolitan Opera he sang 37 roles in 626 performances in New York City and 235 on tour. He also made more recordings than any other singer of his time (for Victor) and many concert appearances, some to promote Liberty Bonds during World War I. On 11 December 1920 he suffered a throat hemorrhage while performing at the Brooklyn Academy of Music; he gave his last performance on 24 December 1920 in New York City. Caruso was known for a robust yet warm, mellow voice, and reissues of his recordings remain popular. He lived from 1908 to 1920 at the Hotel Knickerbocker (42nd Street and Broadway) and from 1920 to the end of his life at the Vanderbilt Hotel (34th Street and Park Avenue).

Enrico Caruso

Howard Greenfield, *Caruso* (New York: G. P. Putnam's Sons, 1983)

See also Carnegie Hall.

John W. Freeman

Cascade Linen and Uniform Service. Firm of laundry and linen suppliers in Brooklyn, formed in 1898 as General Linen Supply and Laundry by Charles Bonoff, a Russian immigrant. It eventually became the largest firm of its kind in the world. The main plant at Myrtle and Marcy avenues in Brooklyn incorporates the original building and uses the oldest operating electric generator in New York City. In 2005 the company was indicted on charges of violating federal antitrust laws by allegedly agreeing not to compete for customers with other linen suppliers.

Kenneth T. Jackson

Casey, William (Joseph) (*b* Elmhurst, Queens, 13 March 1913; *d* Glen Cove, N.Y., 6 May 1987). Businessman and political leader. After earning a BA at Fordham University (1934) and a law degree at St. John's University (1937) he worked during World War II in the Office of Strategic Services, where he developed a passion for espionage and politics. In the late 1940s he returned to the city to give lectures on tax law at New York University. Soon considered an expert, he gained wealth and power through his extensive knowledge of financial markets and in 1957 joined the law firm of Hall, Casey, Dickler and Howley, where he remained until 1971. He was a powerful insider in both New York City and Washington, D.C., and gained several government posts while maintaining strong ties to businesses and law firms in the city. In 1978 he formed the Manhattan Institute, a nonprofit education and research institute. He was appointed director of the Central Intelligence Agency in 1981 by President Ronald Reagan. Casey's tenure was marked by controversy and suggestions that he had taken part in an illegal scheme to sell arms to Iran and finance an insurgent movement in Nicaragua with the proceeds; subpoenaed by a congressional committee, he died shortly before he was scheduled to testify.

Joseph E. Persico, *Casey: From the OSS to the CIA* (New York: Viking, 1990)

James Bradley

Casita María. Oldest settlement house serving New York City's Latino population. It opened its doors in El Barrio in 1934 on the first floor of a building at 32 West 113th Street. Founded by educators Elizabeth and Claire Sullivan and an organizing committee of local leaders, it was created to combat rising juvenile delinquency and to provide a center for organized sports and recreation. Although initially intended for children's after-school programs, the addition of adult activities, including English-language workshops, resulted in the need for larger quarters. Satellites appeared on East 110th Street, East 102nd Street, and East 107th Street. The growth of the settlement house paralleled the rapid increase of the Puerto Rican community following World War II. In 1958 Casita María moved its headquarters to 928 Simpson Street in the South Bronx. Among the largest multiservice organizations in the city, Casita María offers social services and educational programs such as preschool Head Start, summer and day camps, youth clubs, and occupational training. It runs the Corsi and Carver Centers in East Harlem and the Mount Pleasant Senior Housing Complex in Mount Pleasant, New York.

Virginia Sánchez Korrol

casitas. Wood-framed buildings of one story and one or two rooms built on vacant, city-owned lots by Puerto Rican residents of the southern Bronx, East Harlem, and the Lower East Side. Once a common form of housing among the poor of the Puerto Rican rural highlands, coastal regions, and urban shantytowns, the casita first appeared in New York City in the late 1970s, where it became used variously as a shelter and meeting place for social clubs, block associations, cultural centers, and horticultural groups. Constructed from recycled scrap lumber and store-bought materials, it is characterized by a pitched roof, an entrance at the gabled end, and a porch (or "balcón"), the railings of which are commonly fashioned with decorative X's, and is often painted in the vibrant colors of the Caribbean. A casita may have a working kitchen with a refrigerator, stove, and running water and is frequently surrounded by a landscaped, dooryard garden and a nonvegetated, clean-swept yard (or "batey"), which simulates the rural, preindustrial Caribbean topography. The casita and its surrounding property are protected from vandals by a chain-link fence. A number of casita builders lease property from the city as participants in the Green Thumb community garden program. Members of neighborhoods often construct a casita in an attempt to keep neglected city property from being used for dumping, drug abuse, "chop shops," and prostitution, yet the city considers casitas "illegal structures" and routinely demolishes them.

Joseph Sciorra, "'I Feel Like I'm in My Country': Puerto Rican Casitas in New York City," *Drama Review* 34 (1990), 156–68

Joseph Sciorra

Castelli, Leo (*b* Trieste, Italy, 4 Sept 1907; *d* New York City, 21 Aug 1999). Art dealer. He moved to the United States in 1941, studied at Columbia University, and in 1957 opened the Leo Castelli Gallery at 4 East 77th Street. In the following decades the gallery displayed the work of some of the leading figures in contemporary American art, including Jasper Johns and Robert Rauschenberg (mounting their first exhibitions in 1958), Frank Stella (1959), Roy Lichtenstein (1961), John Chamberlain, Dan Flavin, Donald Judd, Ellsworth Kelly, Claes Oldenburg, James Rosenquist, Richard Serra, Cy Twombly, and Andy Warhol. In 1971 the gallery moved to 420 West Broadway, where it helped to fuel the development of SoHo as an art district. In the early twenty-first century the Leo Castelli Gallery was located at 18 East 77th Street in Manhattan.

Avis Berman

cast-iron architecture. Architectural use of cast-iron components for major structural purposes, particularly entire iron fronts for commercial buildings in mid-nineteenth-century American cities. By the late eighteenth century, technological advances made the high-carbon ferrous alloy known as cast iron available in quantity and at affordable prices, leading to its use in Britain and France for pipes, bridges, and aqueducts, and later for interior columns of market halls and libraries. American engineers and architects adapted the medium to the needs of rapidly growing American cities, creating storefronts and eventually entire building facades of cast iron.

Cast iron had major advantages for builders. Inexpensive, versatile, and lighter than stone, it was strong in compression, meaning that slender cast-iron columns could bear great weight and allow large window openings. While not completely fireproof, it was fire-resistant. Although behind most iron fronts were conventional interior structures of timber with brick walls, the fronts themselves, often highly ornate, were weight-bearing walls of repeating arches and panels supported by cast-iron columns. Cast iron required far less hand labor than brickwork and no hand carving, as ornamental detailing was achieved in the casting process. The Italianate designs then fashionable were well suited to mass production in iron. Construction was rapid because the many iron parts were prefabricated, then

Cast-iron architecture at 620 Avenue of the Americas, 2009

Poster for D. D. Badger's Architectural Iron Works

bolted together at the building site to form a frame that was raised into place.

New York City became the center of cast-iron architecture in the United States. At first cast iron was employed for small exterior decoration of the sort still seen on Greek Revival and Federal houses in Greenwich Village and Brooklyn Heights. Later, slender columns provided structural support in building interiors (for example, holding up balconies in the Park Theatre, rebuilt in 1822). In 1823 New York City specified iron for gas mains. By the end of the 1820s, shop fronts with cast-iron columns and glass show windows were introduced; they occupied the ground floors of otherwise conventional brick or stone commercial buildings, offering more light and floor space to display merchandise. Such a storefront was advertised for rent in 1825 on John Street near the East River. In 1837 inventor Jordan L. Mott offered for sale complete prefabricated iron storefronts.

In the 1840s New Yorker James Bogardus began an impassioned campaign for buildings made entirely of cast iron, inside and out. During a stay in England and on the Continent (1836–40), he had learned about pioneering British uses of cast iron and about Italian Renaissance architecture. Eager to demonstrate the advantages of cast iron and to silence scoffers, he built for himself on Centre Street a four-story iron factory for producing a grinding mill he invented. Casting of the iron components was contracted out to several small foundries in the city. As the factory was being erected, Bogardus found two customers: pharmacist John Milhau ordered a full iron facade to modernize his existing small brick building at 183 Broadway (1848), and the merchant Edgar Laing had a row of five stores with four-story iron fronts erected at the corner of Murray and Washington streets (1849). Bogardus filled both orders from the supply of parts cast for his own factory, so that all three buildings were created from the same few basic iron elements. With these three buildings Bogardus demonstrated the feasibility of constructing complete iron fronts, and other architects and engineers quickly adopted the new construction method.

In 1850–51 Bogardus constructed in Baltimore a large five-story building with two iron facades for A. S. Abell, publisher of the *Baltimore Sun.* In 1854, after a huge fire in December 1853 destroyed the publishing plant of Harper and Brothers, Bogardus rapidly constructed a new headquarters at 333 Pearl Street, reusing patterns from his *Sun* iron building. To achieve fire-resistant construction he employed an interior frame of cast-iron columns and exposed bowstring trusses with wrought-iron beams and brick jack arches.

The strength and relative lightness of cast iron allow construction of tall structures. Bogardus built four high, freestanding cast-iron towers in Manhattan. Two were open-frame watchtowers for the fire department, one 100 feet (30 meters) tall on Ninth Avenue (1851) and another 125 feet (38 meters) tall on Spring Street (1853). The Bogardus watchtowers were later destroyed, but a similar one still stands in Marcus Garvey Park in Harlem and is now on the National Register of Historic Places; built in 1856 by engineer Julian Kroehl, it is 47 feet (14 meters) tall. In 1855 Bogardus built a tower 175 feet (53 meters) tall on Centre Street for a manufacturer of gunshot, and in 1856 he erected a 217-feet- (66-meter-) tall shot tower on Beekman Street. Gunshot was produced by dropping molten metal through a sieve from a great height into a vat of cold water below. To prevent hot pellets from being blown into the street, Bogardus's iron-frame shot towers had infill brick walls that were not load bearing. This use of a brick wall in a self-supporting iron frame is often cited as a precursor of skyscraper curtain-wall construction.

Also innovative were constructions with glass walls supported by iron frameworks, creating vast spaces flooded with light. This technique was employed for the Crystal Palace (1853), a huge pavilion of iron and glass designed by the firm of Carstensen and Gildemeister, built in Bryant Park to house the first American World's Fair. Among later examples of glass-and-iron buildings, none was grander or caught the public fancy more than the train shed at Cornelius Vanderbilt's Grand Central Depot (1869). Its soaring, filigreed iron arches and glass roofs made it a tourist attraction second only to the U.S. Capitol, whose low dome had been replaced with a soaring cast-iron dome (completed in 1865).

Architectural iron was supplied by established foundries, which made stock parts sold through catalogues and also did custom work. The modest foundries that produced cast iron were scattered throughout Manhattan, Brooklyn, and the Bronx, mostly along waterways, so that pig iron, coal, and special sand

Hugh O'Neil Building, 2009

for molding could be brought in by water, and finished products readily shipped out. The first foundry in the city to offer architectural iron was that of James L. Jackson; founded in 1840, from 1857 the firm occupied a large site on East 28th Street, near the present site of Bellevue Hospital. In 1846 the ironsmith Daniel D. Badger moved his operations from Boston to Manhattan, establishing a small foundry at 42 Duane Street. He was known for a patented iron storefront that combined cast-iron columns with rolling shutters made of iron, giving strong protection against burglars and above all against fire. He later set up a foundry on East 14th Street, one of the largest in the city, which shipped iron building elements all over the country. Other important ironworks in the city included Aetna, Excelsior, Atlantic, Jordan Mott's foundry (from 1828 on the shore of the Harlem River in the southern Bronx, where Mott also built a village for his workers called Mott Haven), the foundry of the brothers J. B. and W. W. Cornell (on the Hudson River near 26th Street), and Jones, Beebe and Company, which provided iron for the U.S. Capitol and bridges in Central Park. Later, the Hecla ironworks, established by Neil Poulsen in 1876 in Greenpoint, excelled at large-scale ornamental ironwork for what were then called elevator buildings.

The heyday of cast-iron architecture in New York City began in the mid-1850s and lasted for about three decades. Scores of large, handsome structures were built with cast-iron fronts, and many still stand in the early twenty-first century, notably the Haughwout Building (1856) on Broadway at Broome Street, the Cary Building (1856) on Chambers Street, and a restrained classical building by Bogardus at 254 Canal Street (1857). In 1869 Peter Gilsey used a lavish Second Empire style for his eight-story hotel on Broadway, with large iron fronts on both Broadway and 29th Street, which became a favorite of theatergoers. Cast iron also was used for large public buildings since demolished, such as the Tompkins Market on Third Avenue at Sixth Street (1860) and the Manhattan Market at 34th Street and the Hudson River (1877), for large ferry terminals such as the Brooklyn Ferry at Fulton Street (1863), as well as for modest iron-front buildings of no more than five stories built on lots 25 feet (8 meters) wide throughout the commercial districts of lower Manhattan and downtown Brooklyn.

Retailers who catered to the carriage trade built some of the most stylish cast-iron fronts along the Ladies' Mile, a historic district from the Flatiron Building to Madison Avenue and Broadway at Fifth Avenue; few of these buildings still stand. Among the best known were A. T. Stewart (1862; later known as Wanamaker's), which gradually expanded to fill an entire city block, becoming one of the largest iron structures in the world; the James McCreery Store (1868); Lord and Taylor on Broadway (1869), perhaps the exemplar of the retail emporium; Arnold Constable on Fifth Avenue (1876); B. Altman on Sixth Avenue at 18th Street (1876); and Stern Brothers on West 23rd Street (1878). Fabric merchants and other wholesale firms that drew buyers from around the country occupied imposing iron-front headquarters, particularly in the areas now known as SoHo and Tribeca, where many survive with historic district protection. Most surviving buildings are in the Italianate or Second Empire styles and are intended to resemble stone—for example, the Gunther Building (1871) at the corner of Broome Street; 72 Greene Street (1872), a many-columned building with a pedimented entrance, known as "the king of Greene Street"; and 30 Greene Street (1872). Richard Morris Hunt received critical acclaim for the Roosevelt Building at 478 Broadway (1874), a highly original Greek revival structure, and for a now-demolished building next door done in a brightly painted Moorish style (1876). The expanse of glass windows in cast-iron buildings could be remarkable—for example, in 1 Bond Street (1880) or 361 Broadway (1881).

In the last two decades of the nineteenth century, use of cast iron for entire building facades tapered off; the safety elevator allowed brick and stone commercial buildings to become progressively taller, and steel was increasingly employed as a structural medium from the mid-1880s. Cast iron continued to be used for interior structural columns, often in combination with timber and rolled-iron beams, and was still used for smaller structures or in decorative ways, giving business to small foundries in the city into the twentieth century. In 1904 the Hecla ironworks provided 133 ornamented kiosks of cast iron and glass for the new subway entrances of Interborough Rapid Transit. Cast iron was also used in decorative window enframements, such as the elegant glass and iron front of Charles Scribner's bookstore on Fifth Avenue at 48th Street (1913), and the front of 181 Madison Avenue, a 19-story art deco building at the corner of 34th Street (1928). The ubiquitous, simple, one-story storefront continued to be made of cast-iron elements into the 1920s, but thereafter the use of cast iron for architecture was practically at an end.

From the time of the Depression, cast-iron buildings were endangered by neglect, changing patterns of commerce, and demolition. Whole cast-iron districts were threatened by urban renewal after World War II. These dangers stimulated a new interest in iron architecture and efforts at preservation. Several iron-front buildings received landmark designation, and an area of SoHo encompassing 139 iron-front buildings on 26 city blocks was designated a historic district by the city in August 1973 and a National Historic Landmark in June 1978.

Daniel D. Badger, *Badger's Illustrated Catalogue of Cast-Iron Architecture* (New York: Baker and Godwin, 1865; repr. New York: Dover, 1981); John G. Waite, ed., *Iron Architecture in New York City* (Albany: New York State Historic Trust, 1972); *SoHo: Cast Iron District Designation Report* (New York: New York City Landmarks Preservation Commission, 1973); Margot Gayle and Edmund V. Gillon, *Cast-Iron Architecture in New York: A Photographic Survey* (New York: Dover, 1974); Donald Friedman, *Historical Building Construction* (New York: W. W. Norton, 1995); Margot Gayle and Carol Gayle, *Cast-Iron Architecture in America:*

The Significance of James Bogardus (New York: W. W. Norton, 1998)

Margot Gayle, Carol Gayle

Castle [née Foote], **Irene** (*b* New Rochelle, N.Y., 7 April 1893; *d* Eureka Springs, Ark., 25 Jan 1969). Dancer. In 1911 she married the English dancer Vernon (Castle) Blythe (1877–1918), a member of Lew Fields's comedy troupe. The two performed with Fields in his popular musical comedy *The Summer Widowers* (1911) before beginning their career in Paris as the dance team Vernon and Irene Castle. For the next five years they were the most popular team of ballroom dancers in the world, appearing mostly in cabarets and at their salon at the Castle House, 26 East 46th Street; they also made a number of films, performed in musicals on Broadway (including Irving Berlin's *Watch Your Step* [1914]), commissioned dance music from such composers as Berlin and James Reese Europe, and wrote the book *Modern Dancing* (1914). After her husband's death in an airplane crash in 1918 Irene Castle continued to act in films before retiring in 1924. She wrote *My Husband* (1919) and *Castles in the Air* (1958). The Castles were portrayed in a 1939 film *The Story of Vernon and Irene Castle*, starring Fred Astaire and Ginger Rogers. They are buried together in Woodlawn Cemetery in the Bronx.

Barbara Cohen-Stratyner

Castle Clinton (left), ca *1900; on the right is a fireboat station at the edge of Battery Park*

Castle Clinton. Fort built between 1808 and 1811 on an artificial stone island 100 yards (90 meters) off the Battery. Originally known as the West Battery, it was one of seven forts proposed in 1807 by Lieutenant Colonel Jonathan Williams to protect New York Harbor from invasion by the British. The current name dates to 1815. Although the design is traditionally attributed to John McComb, Jr., it was probably the work of Williams; McComb probably designed only the entranceway to the fort and served as the building contractor. The original plan called for many tiers of massive brownstone blocks, but because of financial constraints, only one tier with 28 gun mountings was built. The fort was never used in combat, and after the War of 1812 it ceased to be an important military facility; it was given to the city in 1823 and converted into Castle Garden, a center for popular entertainment. It was the starting point on 9 September 1830 of a balloon flight of 30 miles (48 kilometers) made by the "aeronaut" Charles Durant, and the site in 1850 of a performance by the singer Jenny Lind presented by P. T. Barnum. The fort was reclaimed by the city in 1855 and used as an immigration station until 1890; it was converted in 1896 into the New York Aquarium by the firm of McKim, Mead and White. Robert Moses forced the aquarium to move in 1941 and sought to demolish the fort to accommodate a bridge between Brooklyn and the Battery and later a ventilation unit for the Brooklyn–Battery Tunnel. After the aquarium was demolished, a conflict ensued over preserving the remaining walls of the fort. In 1950 the fort was ceded to the U.S. Department of Interior and designated a national monument. Restored during the 1970s, Castle Clinton then housed ticket booths for the ferries to the Statue of Liberty and Ellis Island. In the early twenty-first century the castle was used as a venue for performing arts, as a transportation hub for heritage tourism and the recreational use of New York Harbor, and as an interpretive center focusing on the history of the castle.

Thomas M. Pitkin, *Historic Structures Report: Castle Clinton National Monument* (Washington, D.C.: U.S. Department of the Interior, 1960)

Andrew S. Dolkart

Castle Hill. Neighborhood in the southeastern Bronx lying on a peninsula bounded to the north and east by Westchester Creek, to the south by the East River, and to the west by Pugsley's Creek. Its most striking topographical feature is a small hill that led Captain Adriaen Block, the first European observer, to characterize the land as a castle; later it was owned by the Wilkins family and named after their estate. By the 1920s there were a few one-family houses scattered among truck farms that gradually diminished in number before disappearing in the 1940s. Low-income housing projects were built on empty lots in the 1960s. In the mid-1990s the Young Men's Christian Association and the Elias Karmon Gymnasium occupied Castle Hill Point. In the early years of the twenty-first century the neighborhood experienced a slight revival, owing to the renewed interest in the neighboring "SoBro," a nickname for the South Bronx, and Parkchester neighborhoods.

Gary D. Hermalyn

Castleton. Former township in northern Staten Island, covering about 3880 acres (1570 hectares) and bounded to the north by the Kill van Kull and to the east by Upper New York Bay. Its area encompasses the neighborhoods of New Brighton, Brighton Heights, Randall

Jenny Lind at Castle Garden, 1850

Manor, Silver Lake, Castleton Corners, St. George, Tompkinsville, Four Corners, and West New Brighton. One of the original four subdivisions of the County of Richmond, it was the governor's manor and was named for Governor Thomas Dongan's manor of Cassiltowne in County Kildare, Ireland. The manor house, which stood on a lot bounded to the north by Richmond Terrace, to the east by Dongan Street, to the south by Castleton Avenue, and to the west by Bodin Street, was reportedly a place for assembly and celebration by local Indians before being destroyed by fire on 25 December 1878.

Martha S. Bendix

Castleton Corners. Neighborhood in northern Staten Island bounded to the east by Manor Road and to the south by Victory Boulevard. Once called Centreville, the neighborhood lay at a corner of Governor Thomas Dongan's land grant and was the site of a brewery during the nineteenth century. After the Verrazano–Narrows Bridge was completed in 1964, the Staten Island Expressway was extended to the area, spurring the construction of houses. During the 1980s there were modest levels of immigration to the area from India, Korea, the Philippines, China, Israel, and Egypt. Castleton Corners early in the twenty-first century is largely a white, middle-class residential area, with a growing number of Asians and some commercial sections.

Martha S. Bendix

Castle Williams. Fort on Governors Island, begun in 1807 and completed in 1811 according to the designs of Jonathan Williams. It was popularly known as the "cheese box" because of its circular shape. Two hundred feet (60 meters) in diameter, with ivied red sandstone walls 40 feet (12 meters) high and 8 feet (2.5 meters) thick, it housed three tiers of guns and was intended to blast away at any enemy ships that managed to force their way past Forts Wadsworth and Hamilton at the southern entrance to the harbor. During the Civil War, Castle Williams housed Confederate prisoners of war; in the first half of the twentieth century it was a disciplinary barracks for the U.S. Army, and later it was operated by the U.S. Coast Guard.

Kenneth T. Jackson

Castro, Bernard (*b* Palermo, Sicily, 11 Aug 1904; *d* Ocala, Fla., 24 Aug 1991). Businessman. He moved to New York City in 1919, worked as an apprentice upholsterer, and learned English at night school. In 1931 he invented the fold-out sofa bed, or convertible, and in the same year opened a retail store at Fifth Avenue between 14th and 15th streets. Sales were sluggish until he began running advertisements on local television in 1948 that featured his daughter Bernadette. He eventually opened 48 stores in 12 states and maintained a conspicuous billboard in Times Square for about 30 years, until September 1983. Under his daughter's management the firm operated five stores in the city in 1991. The Castro Convertibles Corporation was bought by Krause's Sofa Factory in 1993 after declining sales.

Marc Ferris

Caswell–Massey. Pharmacy. It was established in 1752 by William Hunter in Newport, Rhode Island, and later moved to New York City, where it was acquired by John Caswell and William Massey. Situated successively at Fifth Avenue and 25th Street and then at 48th Street and Lexington Avenue, it is reportedly the oldest pharmacy in the city. The business was taken over in 1906 by the brothers Ralph and Milton Taylor, and it remained in their family until it was sold in 1989 to a holding company based in Hong Kong. Under the name Caswell–Massey the company operates more than two dozen outlets and distributes nationwide an array of specialty soaps, colognes, and beauty care products. In 1999 Anne Robinson, a descendant of President John Quincy Adams, bought the company and restored it to profitability. Early in the twenty-first century it was a small national chain.

Owen D. Gutfreund

Cathedral College. Private college, opened in Brooklyn in 1914 as the Cathedral College of the Immaculate Conception. In 1967 it moved to Douglaston, Queens, where it provided undergraduate education to candidates for the Catholic priesthood. After the school closed in 1989 the building became a pastoral center and a house for seminarians attending local colleges and for retired priests.

Christina Plattner

Cathedral of St. John the Divine. The largest church in the United States, situated at Amsterdam Avenue and West 112th Street in Morningside Heights and incorporated in 1873; the principal church of the Episcopal Diocese of New York. The firm of Heins and LaFarge drew up plans in 1891 and the first stone was laid in 1892. In 1911 the commission for the design was transferred to the firm of Cram and Ferguson, and the east end and the crossing were completed. The sanctuary and choir were built in a Romanesque style; the nave was designed in a French Gothic style by Ralph Adams Cram, its main vault built to a height of 124 feet (38 meters). After the entire length of 601 feet (183 meters) was finished in 1941, construction halted until 1979. Stained-glass windows depicting biblical characters and modern personages were installed, and the traditional decor was embellished with modern themes. During the 1980s and early 1990s the Cathedral of St. John the Divine became known for its attention to the arts, the community, youth, the elderly, ecumenism, the environmental movement, and international issues. It is reportedly the world's largest cathedral and the third-largest church, after the Basilica of Our Lady of Peace of Yamoussoukro in the Ivory Coast and St. Peter's in Rome. Construction resumed on the southwest tower from 1982 to 1992, employing young city dwellers apprenticed to a master mason from England, and in 2007 the scaffolding surrounding it was removed. After the gift shop in the north transept was destroyed by fire in December 2001, scaffolding was erected throughout the cathedral and the

Castle Williams, 2009

Cathedral of St. John the Divine, 2009

entire interior was cleaned of soot. This work was completed, and the full length of the cathedral was reopened in 2008. Construction of a new residential building on the southeast site of the cathedral close also began in March 2007.

Howard E. Quirk, *The Living Cathedral of St. John the Divine: A History and Guide* (New York: Crossroad, 1993)

J. Robert Wright

Cathedral School. Episcopal elementary and secondary school, occupying 13 acres (5 hectares) on the grounds of the Cathedral of St. John the Divine at Amsterdam Avenue and West 112th Street in Manhattan. Founded by Bishop Henry Potter in 1901, it was a boarding school for 40 boys, originally to provide the boys choir for a large Gothic cathedral. The choir earned a long-standing reputation as one of the finest in the United States. In 1964 the school began admitting non-singing boys, and in 1974 it became coeducational under Bishop Paul Moore. In the early twenty-first century it enrolled around 250 students from nursery school and pre-kindergarten through eighth grade.

Richard Schwartz

Cather, Willa (Sibert) (*b* Winchester, Va., 7 Dec 1873; *d* New York City, 24 April 1947). Novelist. At nine she moved with her family to Nebraska, where she grew up among European pioneers who inspired much of her writing. She graduated from the University of Nebraska at Lincoln in 1895 and moved to Pittsburgh, where she worked as a journalist. After publishing her first collection of poems and short stories she was invited to join the editorial staff of *McClure's* in New York City in 1906. From 1908 to 1913 she lived at 82 Washington Place. On the success of her novel *O Pioneers!* (1913) she left her editorial position and moved to 5 Bank Street, where she remained until 1927. Her portrayals of simple, courageous men and women living on the prairie in such novels as *My Ántonia* (1917) reflected her nostalgia for the American West, a feeling intensified by her increasing awareness of materialism in the city during the early twentieth century. She won a Pulitzer Prize for the novel *One of Ours* (1922). Cather lived at the Grosvenor Hotel at 35 Fifth Avenue from 1927 until 1932, when she moved to 570 Park Avenue.

James Leslie Woodress, *Willa Cather: A Literary Life* (Lincoln: University of Nebraska Press, 1987)

James E. Mooney

Catholic Charities of the Archdiocese of New York. Charitable organization formed in 1920 by Archbishop Patrick Hayes to centralize Catholic charities after a 1919 diocesan survey revealed waste and duplication in staffing and services. At the outset it was responsible for 32 charitable institutions, including hospitals, orphanages, nurseries, and homes for the aged, as well as various other groups. It set up divisions responsible for families, health, children, protective care, social action, and finance. Via the 9/11 Neediest Fund and the 9/11 United Services Group, it was instrumental in providing assistance to residents after the 2001 terrorist attacks. In 2008 it delivered approximately $577 million in services.

Matthew J. Brennan

Catholic Club of the City of New York. Organization formed in March 1871 to promote Catholic service and the study of Catholic history, literature, science, and art. Initially known as the Xavier Union, it was an offshoot of the Xavier Alumni Sodality (1863), an organization of graduates of St. Francis Xavier College. The club was incorporated in 1873 and renamed the Catholic Club on 22 November 1888. The club was a lay organization with its own administration but had the approval of the Roman Catholic Archdiocese of New York. It operated a building at 120 Central Park South from March 1892 and published a bulletin from 1891 to 1930. In 1925 it had a reference library of 30,000 volumes, the largest of its kind in the country open to the public. The club declined after 1930 and ceased operations in 1958.

Marion R. Casey

Catholic Medical Center (of Brooklyn and Queens). Hospital system formed in 1967 by the Diocese of Brooklyn to reduce costs through centralized management; it was the first network hospital system approved by New York State. The center comprised Holy Family Nursing Home (1879) and St. Mary's Hospital (1882) in Brooklyn, and St. John's Hospital (1891), Mary Immaculate Hospital (1902), St. Joseph's Hospital (1962), and the Monsignor Fitzpatrick Skilled Nursing Pavilion (1987) in Queens, as well as the country's largest hospital-based home care program. The center merged with Manhattan's St. Vincent's Hospital in 2000 to form the Saint Vincent Catholic Medical Center (SVCMC); this organization closed in 2010. In order to regain solvency, in 2006 SVCMC sold Mary Immaculate Hospital and St. John's Hospital and closed St. Mary's Hospital. SVCMC retained Holy Family Nursing Home and the Monsignor Fitzpatrick Skilled Nursing Pavilion.

Matthew J. Brennan

Catholics. At the end of the Revolutionary era Catholics in New York City numbered no more than 200, but they became the city's largest religious denomination by the mid-nineteenth century and have remained so to the present day.

1. Colonial and Early Federal Periods, 1640–1815

For much of the colonial period Roman Catholic worship in New York City was clandestine because the Dutch and English prohibited the public practice of Catholicism. In 1643 the French Jesuit missionary Isaac Jogues visited New Amsterdam and found only two

Roman Catholic Bishops of the Diocese of Brooklyn

John Loughlin (1853–91)
Charles Edward McDonnell (1891–1921)
Thomas Edmund Molloy (1922–56)
Brian J. McEntegart (1957–68)
Francis J. Mugavero (1968–90)
Thomas V. Daily (1990–2003)
Nicholas Anthony DiMarzio, Jr. (2003–)

Compiled by Edward T. O'Donnell

Roman Catholic Bishops, Archbishops, and Cardinals of the Archdiocese of New York

Richard Luke Concanen, O.P.,[1] bishop (1808–10)
John Connolly, O.P., bishop (1815–25)
John DuBois, bishop (1826–42)
John Hughes, bishop (1842–50), archbishop (1850–64)
John Cardinal McCloskey, archbishop (1864–85), cardinal (1864–75)
Michael Corrigan, archbishop (1885–1902)
John Cardinal Farley, archbishop (1902–11), cardinal (1911–18)
Patrick Cardinal Hayes, archbishop (1919–24), cardinal (1924–38)
Francis Cardinal Spellman, archbishop (1939–46), cardinal (1946–67)
Terence Cardinal Cooke, archbishop (1968–69), cardinal (1969–83)
John Cardinal O'Connor, archbishop (1984–85), cardinal (1985–2000)
Edward Cardinal Egan, archbishop (2000–01), cardinal (2001–2009)
Timothy Dolan, archbishop (2009–)

1. Concanen never arrived in New York City from Europe because of embargoes during the Napoleonic Wars; he fulfilled his duties through priests based in the city.
Compiled by Edward T. O'Donnell

Catholic inhabitants. With the restoration of the Stuarts in 1660 Catholics enjoyed a brief period of toleration in England and the colonies. In New York Catholics were able to practice their religion from 1674 to 1688. Under Governor Thomas Dongan (1682–88), an Irish Catholic, the colonial assembly passed the "Charter of Liberties and Privileges" on 30 October 1683, granting religious freedom to all Christians. Dongan also brought to the colony three English Jesuits, who opened a school and celebrated Mass. The Glorious Revolution in England in 1688–89 and Leisler's Rebellion in New York City in 1689–91 brought a temporary end to religious toleration of Catholics. By 1696 there were only 10 known Catholics, and in 1700 a law barred Catholic priests from entering the colony under penalty of life imprisonment. A combination of anti-Catholic and antiblack hysteria swept the city during the "Negro plot" of 1741, when rumors circulated that Catholics had encouraged a slave revolt. Among the victims executed for treason was John Ury, an Anglican clergyman who was mistaken for a Catholic priest.

The repeal of the antipriest law in 1784 and the arrival of the Irish Capuchin friar Charles Whelan led to the organization of the first Catholic parish in the city. Whelan found a poor community of about 200. A group of 22 Catholic laymen organized the first parish, and on 10 June 1785 "The Roman Catholic Church in the City of New York" was incorporated. In little more than a year a small brick church was erected at the corner of Barclay and Church streets on three lots leased from Trinity Church. The building was formally dedicated as St. Peter's Church on 4 November 1786.

In 1808 Pope Pius VII established the Diocese of New York, which contained all of New York State and northern New Jersey. The first bishop, Richard Luke Concanen, O.P., died in Italy in 1810, unable to reach his diocese because of the Napoleonic Wars. The initial development of the see in 1808–15 was due to an Alsatian Jesuit, Anthony Kohlmann. He built the original St. Patrick's Cathedral (1815) on Mott Street and opened the New York Literary Institute, a short-lived Jesuit college that closed in 1813.

2. The Immigrant Church

New York's first resident bishop (1815–25) was John Connolly, O.P., another Irish Dominican. On his arrival in 1815 he found only three churches and six or seven priests in the whole diocese. But between 1815 and 1842 the number of Catholics increased from about 15,000 to 200,000, most then Irish, but also many Germans and a few French. The massive influx of immigrants intensified ethnic rivalry within the Catholic community. Despite these problems the Catholic Church in New York City became larger and stronger (and poorer) during the decades before the Civil War. The Sisters of Charity founded in 1809 by Elizabeth Ann Bayley Seton, a native New Yorker, opened a Catholic orphanage in 1817. Father John Power, the pastor of St. Peter's Church in 1819–49, launched the *Truth Teller,* the first Catholic newspaper in the city, in 1825, and in the following year helped to establish St. Mary's Church on Grand Street, the third Catholic church in the city. The popular Cuban-born priest, Felix Varela, founded Christ Church (1827), which was divided into the parishes of St. James and Transfiguration in 1833. Chronic debt plagued many of the parishes.

During the 1840s John Hughes became the most influential Catholic prelate in the United States. Born in Ireland in 1797, he became the coadjutor (assistant) bishop to Bishop John DuBois in 1838 and successfully eliminated "trusteeism" by shifting the control of parish property from lay parish trustees to the pastors and the bishop. In 1840, at the invitation of Governor William Seward, Hughes challenged the monopoly of public education in New York City by the Public School Society, a government-subsidized Protestant organization, and demanded comparable funding for Catholic schools. After an acrimonious political struggle the state legislature replaced the Public School Society in 1842 with elected school boards and prohibited religious instruction in public schools. As a consequence Hughes decided to build his own system of parochial schools. Ironically, his success in Albany led to the secularization of the public schools, a result that he neither intended nor desired.

Hughes became the fourth bishop of New York on 20 December 1842 and continued to attract national attention by his vigorous response to anti-Catholic bigotry. In 1844 a nativist mob killed 13 Irish Catholics and destroyed three churches in Philadelphia. When nativists threatened similar attacks in New York City, Hughes posted armed guards around his churches. He warned the nativist mayor-elect James Harper that if harm should come to his churches, he would transform the city into "a second Moscow" (a reference to tactics against Napoleon in 1812). His leadership maintained the peace and prevented the sort of bloodshed that occurred elsewhere. To alleviate the chronic shortages of priests and sisters, Hughes invited 10 religious communities to the diocese.

The enormous growth of the Catholic community led the Holy See to restructure the church in New York State by establishing new dioceses in Buffalo and Albany (1847) and in Brooklyn and Newark, New Jersey (1853). Within six years the original Diocese of New York was reduced to one-tenth its former size and made an archdiocese on 19 July 1850 with Hughes as the first archbishop. The first two bishops of Brooklyn, John Loughlin (1853–91) and Charles E. McDonnell (1892–1921) were both priests of the Archdiocese of New York.

During the massive Irish and German immigration of 1840–65 the number of Catholics in the diocese reached almost 400,000, making them the single largest denomination in the city. "National parishes," which were ethnic rather than territorial, were formed to meet the pastoral needs of German- and French-speaking Catholics. The same practice was followed later for Italian and Slavic immigrants. At the close of the Civil War there were 32 parishes in Manhattan, of which 23 were territorial (and mainly Irish), eight were German, and one was French. In all, Hughes was responsible for the establishment of 61 new parishes within the present confines of the Archdiocese of New York and for the construction of the new St. Patrick's Cathedral on Fifth Avenue (begun 1858, consecrated 1879). On his death in 1864 perhaps as many as one of every two New Yorkers was a Catholic, and the parochial schools educated 16 percent of the 100,000 children in the city.

Hughes's successor, John McCloskey, was the first native-born archbishop of New York (1864–85) and the first American cardinal (1875–85). In 1872 John Kelly replaced William M. "Boss" Tweed as the head of Tammany Hall and inaugurated a period of Catholic political domination (his wife was a niece of McCloskey). William R. Grace, a successful businessman, became the city's first Catholic mayor in 1880. Catholic charitable institutions continued to provide health and social services, notably St. Vincent's Hospital (1849), the Catholic Protectory (1863), the New York Foundling Hospital (1870), and the Mission of the Immaculate Virgin for the Protection of Homeless and Destitute Children (1871). The first black Catholic church north of the Mason–Dixon line, St. Benedict the Moor, opened in 1883 in a former Protestant church on Bleecker Street in Greenwich Village and later moved to the new black neighborhood around West 53rd Street.

Michael Augustine Corrigan, archbishop 1885–1902, was a leading figure in the conservative wing of the American Catholic hierarchy and a conscientious administrator who added 99 parishes to the archdiocese. However, his administration was marred at the outset by his public clash over local politics with Edward McGlynn, the charismatic pastor of St. Stephen's Church. McGlynn defied Corrigan to support Henry George, the reform candidate in the mayoral campaign of 1886, leading to McGlynn's suspension and excommunication. The McGlynn Affair had a polarizing effect in the archdiocese and was an embarrassment to the American hierarchy. Significantly, Corrigan was the only archbishop of New York in 150 years who was not made a cardinal.

3. Two Dioceses in One City

The creation of Greater New York City in 1898 left the city's Catholics divided between two dioceses, the Archdiocese of New York and the Diocese of Brooklyn. The former was composed of Manhattan, the Bronx, and Staten Island (as well as seven upstate counties) and the latter of Brooklyn, Queens, and the rest of Long Island. Both dioceses grew rapidly during the early twentieth century. In the Diocese of Brooklyn the Catholic population increased from 500,000 in 1900 to 800,000 in 1920; in the Archdiocese of New York the Catholic population increased from 825,000 in 1900 to 1.3 million in 1920, with much of the growth occurring in the Bronx, Westchester, and Staten Island.

Many of the new Catholics were Italian immigrants whose numbers grew from 12,223 in 1880 to 554,449 in 1910. In the Archdiocese of New York both Corrigan and his successor, John Cardinal Farley (1902–18) responded to this pastoral challenge by recruiting priests from Italy. The most famous of the Italian missionaries was not a priest, however, but Mother Frances Xavier Cabrini, who arrived in New York City in 1889 and was canonized in 1946, the first U.S. citizen to receive this honor.

The heyday of Irish domination of the Catholic Church in New York City occurred in the early twentieth century under Cardinal Farley and his successor, Patrick Cardinal Hayes (1919–38), a first-generation Irish American from the Lower East Side. Their counterpart in Brooklyn was Thomas E. Molloy (1922–56). At the celebration of the centennial of the Diocese of New York in 1908, 40,000 men marched up Fifth Avenue to the cathedral while hundreds of thousands watched from the sidelines. Hayes's most notable contribution was the organization of several hundred charitable institutions and agencies of the archdiocese into the Catholic Charities of the Archdiocese of New York.

Francis Cardinal Spellman (1939–67) was the last of the brick-and-mortar archbishops of New York. He added 45 new parishes, spent almost $600 million building and renovating Catholic educational and charitable facilities, and centralized the financial and administrative operations of the archdiocese. In the late 1940s the Catholic population of the Archdiocese of New York increased markedly because of a huge influx of Latin American Catholics, first from Puerto Rico and then from Cuba, the Dominican Republic, and other countries. Spellman established an archdiocesan office for Hispanic Catholics, sent large numbers of diocesan priests to learn Spanish, and welcomed the newcomers into his diocese.

In 1957 the Diocese of Brooklyn was reduced in size when Nassau and Suffolk counties were made a separate diocese with its seat in Rockville Centre. Brooklyn became the only totally urban diocese in the United States under Bryan J. McEntegart (1957–68) and the smallest in area, though it remained one of the largest in population, with more than one million Catholics. On 4 October 1965 Pope Paul VI became the first pope to visit New York City; he addressed the United Nations and celebrated an outdoor Mass at Yankee Stadium.

Both Terence J. Cooke (1968–83) in New York and Francis J. Mugavero (1968–90) in Brooklyn assumed their posts amid major changes in the church in the wake of the Second Vatican Council and widespread turmoil in American society. In both dioceses the total Catholic population remained relatively stable, but only because Latin American immigrants replaced older middle-class Catholics. In New York Cooke used his financial acumen to establish a cooperative system whereby wealthier parishes were taxed to support poorer ones. In October 1979 Pope John Paul II visited the city, celebrating Mass at both Shea Stadium and Yankee Stadium, and returned again for a another visit in 1995.

4. The Contemporary Scene

John Cardinal O'Connor (1984–2000) assumed a high media profile as archbishop of New York, clashing with local and state officials over the issue of abortion and establishing warm relations with both the New York Jewish community and labor leaders. His successor, Edward Cardinal Egan (2000–2009), revamped the finances of the archdiocese and initiated the first comprehensive consolidation of parishes. Egan was succeeded in 2009 by Archbishop Timothy Dolan. In Brooklyn, Thomas V. Daily (1990–2003) succeeded Bishop Mugavero and was succeeded by Nicholas A. DiMarzio (2003–).

In 2007 the Catholic Church in New York City consisted of 410 parishes, 193 in the Archdiocese of New York and 217 in the Diocese of Brooklyn. The Catholic population of the archdiocese (including the seven upstate counties) was 2.5 million, with 1505 priests; the Catholic population of the Diocese of Brooklyn was 1.5 million, with 722 priests. Both New York and Brooklyn maintained extensive school systems, with 93,548 and 57,318 students, respectively. Both dioceses also remained home to large numbers of immigrants, mainly Hispanic, but also growing numbers of Haitians, Asians, and Africans. Each Sunday Mass was celebrated in more than 30 languages in New York City.

John K. Sharp, *History of the Diocese of Brooklyn, 1853–1953* (New York: Fordham University Press, 1954); Robert I. Gannon, *The Cardinal Spellman Story* (Garden City, N.Y.: Doubleday, 1962); Jay P. Dolan, *The Immigrant Church: New York's Irish and German Catholics, 1815–1865* (Baltimore: Johns Hopkins University Press, 1975); Richard Shaw, *Dagger John: The Unquiet Life and Times of Archbishop John Hughes of New York* (New York: Paulist Press, 1977); Robert Emmett Curran, *Michael Augustine Corrigan and the Shaping of Conservative Catholicism in America, 1878–1902* (New York: Arno, 1978); Florence D. Cohalan, *A Popular History of the Archdiocese of New York* (Yonkers, N.Y.: United States Catholic Historical Society, 1983); Joseph Coen, Patrick J. McNamara, and Peter I. Vaccari, *Diocese of Immigrants: The Brooklyn Catholic Experience, 1853–2003* (Strasbourg: Editions du Signe, 2003); Thomas

J. Shelley, *The Bicentennial History of the Archdiocese of New York* (Strasbourg: Editions du Signe, 2008)

Thomas J. Shelley

Catholic schools. The first Roman Catholic school in New York City opened in 1800 at St. Peter's Church in lower Manhattan. It remained the only Catholic school until 1817, when a "free school" was set up in the basement of St. Patrick's Old Cathedral under the leadership of Bishop John Connolly. Both schools were characterized by poor conditions because their parishes could not afford to maintain them. During the tenure of John DuBois, appointed Connolly's successor in 1826, the first school building in the Diocese of New York was erected at St. Patrick's Cathedral in 1837, and a second school was built in the following year at St. Peter's. DuBois also helped to establish Catholic secondary education in New York City, opening St. Joseph's Select School for girls in 1833 (which became Mount St. Vincent's Academy in 1847) and St. Mary's Academy in 1835. While DuBois was indisposed, his duties as the diocesan administrator were assumed by John J. Hughes, who in 1840 oversaw the opening of St. Joseph's Seminary in the Bronx, staffed successively by Italian Vincentians and French Jesuits before the Diocese of New York took charge. Hughes was appointed bishop in 1842, at a time when anti-Catholic sentiment in the public schools was strong. Children were not allowed to read from the Catholic version of the Bible, and with the passing of the Maclay Bill in 1842, religious instruction was prohibited in public schools. In response Hughes announced that the archdiocese would give priority to building Catholic schools, a task that until then had been handled primarily by individual parishes. Hughes in effect committed himself and other leaders of the church to establishing a Catholic parochial school system in New York City. By 1858 the assets of the Catholic educational system of New York City were valued at about $2 million. At the time of Hughes's death in 1864, there were about 15,000 children attending the 12 select schools and 31 free schools in the Archdiocese of New York.

Parochial schools served the city's growing immigrant population. German parochial elementary schools and high schools began opening in the city in the 1860s. Not all Catholics supported parochial education: some feared that it would further separate Catholics from the mainstream of society, and others believed that Catholic leaders should focus on churches, not schools. Most Catholics were concerned about the financial burden that schools placed on their parishes. By a decree of the Third Plenary Council of American bishops, held in 1884 in Baltimore, each pastor was required to build a parochial school in his parish within two years; anyone who failed to do so was subject to removal from his pastorate. A strong advocate of the council's decrees concerning Catholic education was Michael A. Corrigan, under whose leadership the Archdiocese of New York opened 75 schools and 3 academies by the time of his death in 1902 (although it fell short of the goal of a school in every parish). Under Corrigan's successor, John Cardinal Farley, the Cathedral Girls' High School, a free parochial school, opened in 1905. By 1908 there were 3736 girls attending Catholic secondary schools in the Archdiocese of New York. St. Peter's, a Catholic high school opened in 1915 in Staten Island, attracted many Catholic students who could not afford the tuition of a private high school. The Jesuits established Regis High School in 1914 exclusively for scholarship students; other religious orders ran Catholic secondary schools and met their operating expenses by charging tuition. The Sisters of Charity, who maintained 10 academies, were the main order providing secondary education for girls; the Jesuits and the De La Salle Brothers directed most of the secondary schools for boys. Farley invited a number of other communities into the archdiocese to help support secondary education, including the Christian Brothers of Ireland and the Religious of the Sacred Heart of Mary. By the time of his death in 1918, he had opened 50 schools with about 28,000 students. Most parish churches in New York City that did not have a school had plans to build one by the time Francis Spellman was appointed archbishop in 1939. He expanded parochial education for boys, opening Cardinal Hayes High School (1941) in the Bronx, the first secondary school to be administered by diocesan clergy. During his tenure a controversial bill was introduced in Congress by Representative Graham Barden that would have required the federal government to pay the states $50 for each child enrolled in public primary and secondary schools. The Catholic church fought passage of the bill because parochial schools would not receive any of the money. This led Spellman to disagree publicly with Eleanor Roosevelt and others who did not support state aid for parochial education.

The number of parochial schools grew between 1940 and 1965 (the peak year for Catholic parochial school attendance in the United States). In Manhattan, the Bronx, and Staten Island the number of schools increased from 146 to 183. Despite this growth most Catholic schoolchildren were not enrolled in parochial schools, which in 1966 enrolled about 40 percent of all Catholic students and 27 percent of Catholic high school students. The 1970s saw the opening of parochial schools at each of the seven African American parishes; many of the students attending these schools were non-Catholics. The staffs of Catholic schools, historically composed of members of male and female religious orders, gradually changed after about 1965. By the early twenty-first century the majority of Catholic schoolteachers were laypersons.

Jay P. Dolan, *The Immigrant Church: New York's Irish and German Catholics, 1815–1865* (Baltimore: John Hopkins University Press, 1975); Florence D. Cohalan, *A Popular History of the Archdiocese of New York* (New York: United States Catholic Historical Society, 1983)

Margaret M. McGuinness

Catholic Worker. Weekly newspaper launched in 1933 by Dorothy Day.

cat shows. Madison Square Garden was the site of the first cat show in North America, sponsored by the Englishman James T. Hyde on 8 May 1895. The Atlantic Cat Club held its first show at Madison Square Garden in 1903 and about 10 more in later years; in 1906 the club became affiliated with the Cat Fanciers Association. Another affiliate of the association, the Empire Cat Club, was formed in 1913 and in 1917 began staging annual shows in New York City, until 1984 usually at Madison Square Garden and occasionally at hotels in Manhattan. Later venues included the New York Passenger Ship Terminal at Pier 90 in Manhattan (1985), the Jacob K. Javits Convention Center (1986), the Borough of Manhattan Community College (1988), and the Seaview Home on Staten Island (from 1989). Madison Square Garden was also the site of shows held by the Knickerbocker Cat Club (in the 1970s) and the International Cat Association (annually from 1985). In 1971 the Brooklyn Cat Fanciers, a club affiliated with the Cat Fanciers Federation, began holding an annual show at the Hall of St. Finbar's, at Bay 20th Street and Bath Avenue. In 2008 the annual Cat Championship, sponsored by the Cat Fanciers' Association, was held at Madison Square Garden.

Joseph S. Lieber, Kayla Soyer Stein

Catt [Chapman; née Lane], **Carrie (Clinton)** (*b* Ripon, Wis., 9 Jan 1859; *d* New Rochelle, N.Y., 9 March 1947). Suffragist. After serving briefly as the president of the National American Woman Suffrage Association she shifted her attention to New York City, where in 1909 she organized the New York City Woman Suffrage Party to unify local suffragists. She organized efforts to hold a referendum in 1915 on giving women the vote by amending the state constitution; after this failed she regained the presidency of the national suffrage association, a post she held until the 19th Amendment to the U.S. Constitution was passed. She reorganized the association after 1920 as the League of Women Voters but concentrated her energies on pacifism and international feminism. With Nettie Rogers Shuler she wrote *Woman Suffrage and Politics: The Inner Story* (1923). Her office was at 171 Madison Avenue; she lived at 404 Riverside Drive.

Carrie Chapman Catt and Al Smith

Jacqueline Van Voris, *Carrie Chapman Catt: A Public Life* (New York: Feminist Press at the City University of New York, 1996)

Ellen Carol DuBois

Cattell, James McKeen (*b* Easton, Pa., 25 May 1860; *d* Lancaster, Pa., 20 Jan 1944). Psychologist. He graduated from Lafayette College, studied at Johns Hopkins University and the University of Göttingen, and earned a doctorate in 1886 at the University of Leipzig. He became the first professor of psychology in the world in 1889 at the University of Pennsylvania and in 1891 was appointed the first professor of psychology at Columbia University, where he was the head of the psychology department. During the next two decades he helped to establish psychology as a discipline and an independent experimental science. He shared the functionalists' interest in measuring intelligence and developed the first tests based on pain thresholds and reaction times. His contributions to studies of intelligence testing and individual differences continued to be widely acknowledged, and many of his students became well known. He helped to form the American Psychological Association in 1892 and was its president in 1895. With J. M. Baldwin he launched *Psychological Review,* of which he remained the editor until 1903, and *Psychological Monographs* (now *Psychological Abstracts*). He also oversaw the weekly journal *Science,* which he converted into the journal of the American Association for the Advancement of Science; *Popular Science Monthly* (1900), which he renamed *Scientific Monthly;* and the magazine *American Naturalist* (1908). He also published the biographical directories *American Men of Science* (1906) and *Leaders in Education* (1932). In 1915 he began publishing *School and Society* and helped to form the American Association of University Professors. He was known for his outspokenness on controversial issues and his contentious relationship with the president of Columbia, Nicholas Murray Butler; he was nearly dismissed in 1910 for criticizing the university's pension plan and again in 1913 when he published *University Control,* which attacked Wall Street for its influence on American colleges. He was finally dismissed in October 1917 after the trustees charged him with treason and sedition for defending conscientious objectors during World War I (the historian Charles A. Beard resigned to protest their decision). Cattell never returned to teaching but continued conducting research, writing, and working as a science editor. He also helped to form the Psychological Corporation, a firm that provided psychological services to businesses (1921), and Science Press and was president of the American Association for the Advancement of Science (1924), the International Congress on Psychology (1929), and the Science Service in Washington (1930–34). He was the first psychologist elected to the National Academy of Sciences (1890) and the American Academy of Science (1901).

A. T. Poffenberger, ed., *James McKeen Cattell, 1860–1944: Man of Science* (Lancaster, Pa.: Science Press, 1947)

See also Science.

Kevin Kenny, Sandra Opdycke

CBGB (& OMFUG) [Country, Bluegrass, Blues and Other Music for Uplifting Gourmandizers]. A rock club at 315 Bowery near Bleecker Street in lower Manhattan, opened in 1973 by Hilly Kristal. After a brief, undistinguished period as a venue for its namesake musical styles it began featuring rock groups in 1974. It soon became the center of an emerging music scene that came to be known as punk rock. Among those who appeared there were such pioneering punk and new wave groups as the Ramones, Television, the Patti Smith Group, Blondie, the Dead Boys, Richard Hell and the Voidoids, and the Talking Heads. Over the next three decades it became the best-known rock club in the United States, and possibly the world. CBGB closed in October 2006 after a protracted rent dispute, with a final concert performed by Patti Smith.

Caleb Smith

CBS. See Columbia Broadcasting System.

Cedar Grove. Neighborhood in east central Staten Island. Once known as Cedar Grove Beach, it was first shown on maps in 1850 as a small colony of summer houses for sport fishermen. The Cedar Grove Beach Club was formed in 1938. The 67 bungalows in the area were condemned by the City of New York in 1962 for a highway that was never built; the occupants of the bungalows still rent them from the city.

Martha S. Bendix

Cedar Tavern. Drinking establishment. It first opened its doors on Cedar Street in 1866. It moved to its Greenwich Village location, at 24 University Place, in 1945. In the 1950s it gained a reputation as a gathering place for avant-garde artists, writers, filmmakers, and musicians, including Jackson Pollock, Larry Rivers, Frank O'Hara, John Ashbery, Jack Kerouac, Alfred Leslie, and David Amram. The leading figures of the New York School and Beat Generation found the bar a congenial place to meet, drink, socialize, and exchange ideas on life and art. The Cedar, in turn, accepted the artists' eccentricities and forgave their excesses. In 1964 the bar moved to 82 University Place, where it continued to attract celebrities like F. Murray Abraham as well as neighborhood drinkers and New York University students. It closed in November 2006.

William M. Gargan

Celler, Emmanuel (*b* New York City, 6 May 1888; *d* New York City, 15 Jan 1981). Democratic congressman. After graduating from Columbia College and Columbia Law School, he was admitted to the bar in 1912. In 1922, running for Congress in a Brooklyn district that had never gone Democratic, Celler squeaked to victory, denouncing prohibition and nativism to its Jewish, Italian, Greek, and

Irish voters. As his district became increasingly multiethnic, multiracial, and Democratic, Celler, ever sensitive to his minority constituents, was reelected to 24 consecutive terms. From the first, he opposed the discriminatory national origins quota system in U.S. immigration law. During World War II, he lambasted the Roosevelt administration and the State Department for their strict application of the quotas, which made the rescue of Europe's Jews from the Holocaust nearly impossible. After the war, Celler authored measures permitting Indians and Filipinos to immigrate and become naturalized U.S. citizens and 300,000 displaced persons to enter the country. With the 1965 passage of the Hart-Celler immigration reform act, which he cosponsored, he finally achieved his goal of ending immigration quotas based on national origins. Celler was a staunch supporter of the New Deal, Fair Deal, and Great Society programs. As chairman of the House Judiciary Committee (1949–53, 1955–73), he introduced and steered through Congress each of the civil rights bills from 1957 to 1968 and four constitutional amendments (23rd through the 26th). After Elizabeth Holtzman defeated Celler in the 1972 Democratic primary, he continued practicing law in New York City. His autobiography is titled *You Never Leave Brooklyn* (1953).

Lawrence Rubin, "Oral History Memoir of Congressman Emanuel Celler." 24 June 1970 and 1 August 1972, William E. Wiener Oral History Library of the American Jewish Committee, New York

Barbara Blumberg, James E. Mooney

Lutheran Cemetery, Middle Village, Queens

cemeteries. During the city's first two centuries, most burials were in churchyards or synagogue plots in or near residential areas in Manhattan and Brooklyn, or in family plots on farms or estates. In 1820 there were 100 cemeteries in Manhattan alone, 23 of them between City Hall and the Battery. Thirty years later, however, there were only 23 cemeteries on the entire island, and New Yorkers were being buried in remote parts of Kings and Queens counties. There were two reasons for this development, and they added up to a burial crisis in New York City. One was the rapidly increasing demand for downtown land for real estate development as the metropolitan area's population tripled between 1830 and 1850. The other was the city's long, bleak history of recurring yellow fever and cholera epidemics for which the blame was almost universally assigned to "miasmic vapors" rising from graves.

One solution to the burial crisis was to contain miasmic vapors in costly underground, marble-clad burial plots, two of which (the New York Marble Cemetery and the New York City Marble Cemetery) were built near Third Street and Second Avenue in the early 1830s. They are still maintained and very occasionally accept new burials. Another solution was to build or pave over old burial grounds, making little or no effort to honor the remains. An untold number of cemeteries in all the boroughs, most of them used by the working class or African Americans, disappeared in this fashion in the nineteenth and twentieth centuries. Among the few that have been restored is the African American Burial Ground at Duane Street in Manhattan. The city's potter's field for indigent people was moved in 1823, with its remains, from its original site (now Washington Square) to the site of Bryant Park, and then in 1869 to Hart Island, off the Bronx. The most lasting solution to the burial crisis of the early nineteenth century was to close burial grounds and churchyards in heavily populated parts of Manhattan and Brooklyn and transfer the remains to, and make new burials in, large new cemeteries in outlying rural areas. After burials were banned south of South Street in 1830 (the line was moved northward with the population), many churches and cemetery associations sold their land and founded new cemeteries in Kings and Queens counties or acquired sections in existing cemeteries. Many families were outraged to have their ancestors taken away from nearby crypts and graves. *The New York Times* reported that when remains were exhumed from a Baptist churchyard in 1863 it caused a great fervor.

The few colonial-era burial grounds that survive include those of the Staten Island Reformed Church and the Spanish–Portuguese synagogue, Shearith Israel, in Manhattan; the Revolutionary Cemetery in Bay Ridge, Brooklyn; the Moore-Jackson Cemetery in Woodside, Queens; and Trinity Churchyard in Manhattan. All are inactive. Trinity Church's other cemetery, at 155th Street and Broadway, is the only Manhattan cemetery that conducts burials on a regular basis. The first of the new cemeteries that received transfers and new burials was Green-Wood Cemetery, in Brooklyn, founded in 1839. At 474 acres (192 hectares), it was so large that when the state legislature passed the 1847 Rural Cemeteries Act permitting the construction of other nonsectarian burial grounds outside the city, no new cemetery was permitted to have more than 200 acres (81 hectares) in any one county. The first cemeteries created under the authority of the act, Cypress Hills (1847) and the Evergreens (1849), were built on the Queens–Kings border. Many of their initial burials included mass transfers from old downtown churchyards or members of numerous fraternal societies and military, ethnic, and other associations that acquired plots in cemeteries. In 2008 there were 17 cemeteries on or near the Jackie Robinson Parkway running along the county line. The first major nonsectarian cemetery in the Bronx was Woodlawn, founded in 1865. At the same time as these very large public cemeteries appeared in what became the outer boroughs, wealthy families founded private cemeteries in suburban New York City, reacting to the theft of the body of department-store tycoon A. T. Stewart in 1878.

To make the new rural cemeteries attractive, Andrew Jackson Downing, Alexander Jackson Davis, Frederick Law Olmsted, Richard Morris Hunt, and other leading architects and landscape architects were retained to design and build them. A rural cemetery served multiple uses—as a burial ground, as a patriotic emblem where the bodies of war heroes and other veterans were interred, and also as a public park where families picnicked on summer afternoons. The new cemeteries grew very rapidly, and in 1893 the Brooklyn *Daily Eagle* estimated that more than two million remains lay in Brooklyn and Queens. Rural cemeteries were nonsectarian, but

Moravian Cemetery, 2009

many burial grounds were built for the whole range of religious communities, including Jews, Friends, Protestants, Muslims, and Roman Catholics. The oldest Roman Catholic cemetery is St. Patrick's Old Cathedral, in Manhattan, dedicated in 1815.

At the end of the twentieth century many of New York City's old rural cemeteries were nearly filled and new, large burial grounds appeared in New Jersey and upstate New York. Amid continuing concern about maintenance, the New York State legislature mandated that one-fourth of burial fees be set aside in a fund for perpetual care (later called permanent maintenance) of graves. Still, many old, underfunded cemeteries suffered from neglect and were adopted by historical and genealogical societies that engaged in energetic conservation and preservation projects. In the early twenty-first century the largest cemetery in the city was Calvary, in Queens, the cemetery of the Roman Catholic Archdiocese of New York, with more than three million remains.

Judi Culbertson and Tom Randall, *Permanent New Yorkers: A Biographical Guide to the Cemeteries of New York* (Chelsea, Vt.: Chelsea Green, 1987); David Charles Sloane, *The Last Great Necessity: Cemeteries in American History* (Baltimore: Johns Hopkins University Press, 1991); Jeffrey I. Richman, *Brooklyn's Green-Wood Cemetery* (New York: Green-Wood Cemetery, 1998); John Rousmaniere, *Green Oasis in Brooklyn: The Evergreens Cemetery, 1849–2008* (Brooklyn: The Evergreens/Smith-Kerr, 2008)

John Rousmaniere

censorship. Many struggles over the censorship of speech and the press have been waged in New York City, long considered the national center of publishing and broadcasting. One of the earliest cases in the United States occurred in the city in 1735, when John Peter Zenger, a German immigrant, was charged with seditious libel for printing in his *Weekly Journal* that William Cosby, the royal governor of New York, was among other things a "rogue"; Zenger's lawyer persuaded the jury to acquit him by arguing that the truth was sufficient to defend against a charge of libel, an argument contrary to the prevailing doctrine of English law. No major cases arose during the eighteenth and nineteenth centuries, although conflicts over freedom of the press were common. In 1873 Anthony Comstock, perhaps the best-known censor in the history of the city, formed the New York Society for the Suppression of Vice and became its secretary. The organization was later renamed the New York Society for the Improvement of Morals by John S. Sumner, who became its director. Comstock was largely responsible for the passage of the federal statute on obscenity of 1873, which was popularly known as the Comstock Act and barred from the mails any "obscene, lewd, and lascivious" publications. He and others were influential in censoring many works, including those of Ovid, Boccaccio, Rabelais, Rousseau, Fielding, Flaubert, and André Gide; they also condemned *The Genius* by Theodore Dreiser (1916) and *God's Little Acre* by Erskine Caldwell (1933). In response to the Comstock Act many publishers practiced informal censorship by urging authors to change the words and tone of their books before publication. The publishing house of D. Appleton pressured Stephen Crane to make such changes when it agreed to issue his novel *Maggie: A Girl of the Streets* in 1896. Even films were subject to censorship. In 1913 producers attempted to show *The Inside of the White Slave Traffic,* a film depicting the sexual coercion of innocents into a life of brothels, at the Park Theater. When a half-dozen police officers arrived with orders to confiscate the film, the 500 women waiting to see the next screening nearly broke into a riot, rushing toward the door. When several thousand sympathetic protesters joined their cause, the police had to send for reinforcements to disperse the crowd. Section 211 of the Comstock Act also barred from the mails devices used for birth control and was invoked to suppress Margaret Sanger's newspaper the *Woman Rebel* in 1914 and to close her birth control clinic in Brownsville in 1916.

Sections of the police department regulations known as the "New York cabaret laws" set the precedent for the censorship of artistic expression by the city. Section 20 of the regulations reads as follows: "No person shall be permitted to appear in any scene, sketch or act with breasts or lower part of torso uncovered or so thinly covered or draped as to appear uncovered." In 1947 the police commissioner denied dancer Helen Gould Beck (Sally Rand) the identification card that she needed to perform legally because he believed that her performance would violate section 20. Beck received her permit when the judge who heard her case ruled that this denial was a prior restraint on free expression and symbolic speech (*Beck v. Wallender,* 71 N.Y.S. 2d 237 [1947]). The regulations also banned obscene language in public performances, which led to the prosecution of many performers, including the comedian Lenny Bruce in 1964, and prevented performers with police records from working in the city, among them the musicians Billie Holiday and Thelonious Monk.

Many precedents for federal standards of censorship have been set in New York City, especially those defining obscenity and pornography. In 1934 the national statute defining obscenity was overruled in federal court in New York City in a case concerning *Ulysses* (1922) by James Joyce (*United States v. One Book Entitled Ulysses,* 72 F. 2d 705 [1934]); it was held that obscenity should be determined by the effect that a book read in its entirety would have on a person of average sexual instincts. This definition became known as the "Ulysses standard" and was refined and made more specific by subsequent decisions. The rule that prevailed before the Ulysses standard was nonetheless applied in New York City as late as 1952, when a city magistrate determined that magazines containing pictures of nude and seminude women were obscene. The case of *New York Times Company v. Sullivan* (1964), heard in a county court in Alabama, helped to set guidelines for freedom of the press: it concerned an advertisement placed in the *New York Times* containing some false statements about the civil rights record of the city of Montgomery. The *Times* was fined $500,000 by the court in Alabama, but the U.S. Supreme Court reversed the verdict by ruling that a public official suing for libel must prove that the material in question was published with knowledge of its falsity or with reckless disregard for its truth or falsity. The standard set by the court, which became known as the "Sullivan rule," continued to be tested in courts in the city; two of the most prominent cases were *General William Westmoreland v. CBS* (1985) and *General Ariel Sharon v. Time Magazine* (1985).

A furor was created in 1989 when homoerotic photographs by Robert Mapplethorpe were included in federally funded exhibitions. The National Endowment for the Arts responded to the controversy by requiring the recipients of its grants to eschew obscenity. Opposition to the new rules was led by a number of performers and arts administrators in the city, including Karen Finley and Joseph Papp. The Giuliani administration's aggressive tactics in reducing crime and improving the quality of life in New York City often brought it into conflict with free speech advocates such as the New York Civil Liberties Union, which participated in 34 lawsuits against the city during Giuliani's mayoralty. Efforts by the Giuliani administration to block the use of amplified sound for rallies in Times Square and charge $100,000 fees for First Amendment events in public parks were defeated in court, as was an attempt to revoke sound permits from the "Black Israelites" preaching in Times Square. The administration also denied a rally permit to the Ku Klux Klan, which ultimately was permitted to hold the rally as long as its members did not wear masks.

The most famous censorship case of the Giuliani administration involved an art piece at the Brooklyn Museum by British artist

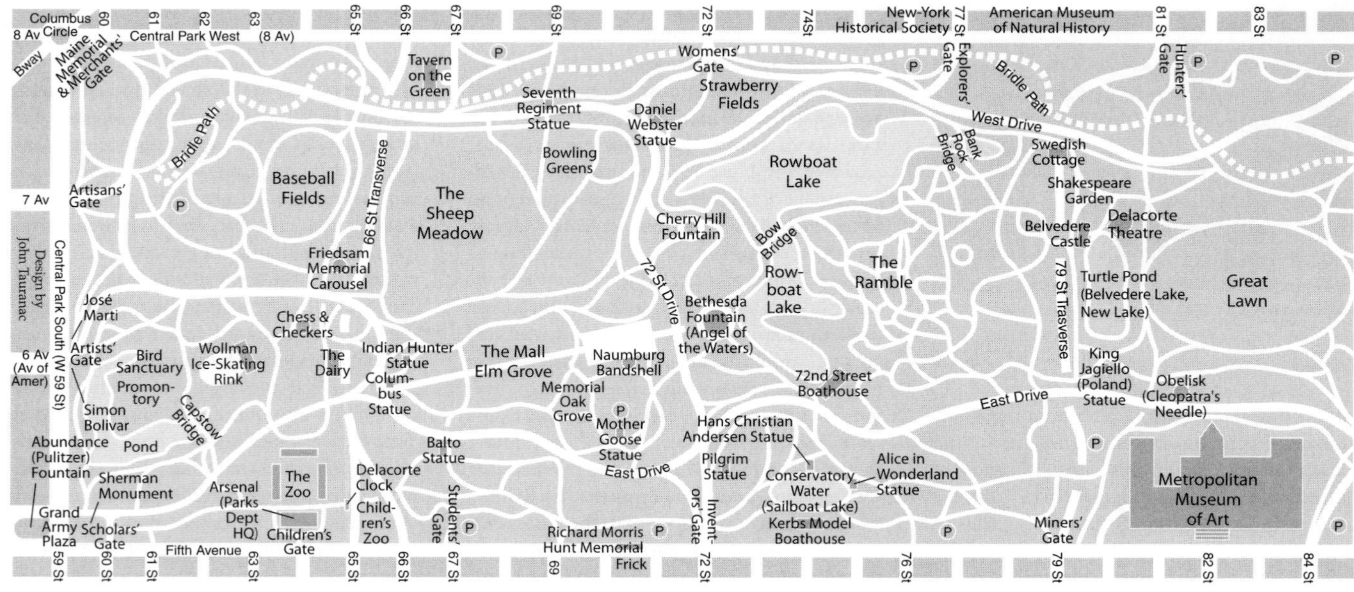

Chris Ofili. His painting *The Holy Virgin Mary,* part of the *Sensation* exhibit, featured a black African depiction of the Virgin Mary surrounded by images from blaxploitation movies, close-ups of female genitalia cut from pornographic magazines, and, most notoriously, elephant dung. Exclaiming, "There's nothing in the First Amendment that supports horrible and disgusting projects," Giuliani attempted to penalize the museum for conveying offensive ideas, including an attempt to evict the museum from its city-owned building. The Eastern District Court found that the city's actions violated the First Amendment, and the city chose to settle the case in 2000, paying the museum and withdrawing its eviction efforts.

In the early twenty-first century there were a few high profile incidents relating to censorship. Attempts to limit public demonstrations in order to preserve order were viewed as censorship by some. Mayor Michael Bloomberg was criticized by free speech advocates for restricting large demonstrations such as that of 15 February 2003, an anti–Iraq War protest, and that of the August 2004 Republican Convention. While pornography in its various forms has traditionally been considered legal, in 2009 Governor David Paterson proposed taxing Internet downloads of pornography as part of an attempt to close a massive budget deficit.

Censorship: 500 Years of Conflict (New York: Oxford University Press, 1984); Leon Hurwitz, *Historical Dictionary of Censorship in the United States* (Westport, Conn.: Greenwood, 1985)

Leon Hurwitz, Janos Marton

Center for Migration Studies [CMS]. Nonprofit organization founded at 209 Flagg Place, Staten Island, in 1964 by the Society of Saint Charles–Scalabrinians under Silvano M. Tomasi to collect and disseminate information on contemporary human international migration. The CMS holds conferences, including one annually on American immigration laws and policies; publishes the quarterly *International Migration Review,* books, and papers; and maintains a library and archive rich in Italian Americana. Lydio F. Tomasi, CS, served as executive director from 1967 to 2001; Joseph Fugolo, CS, succeeded him. In 2003 CMS's editorial office moved to 27 Carmine Street in Manhattan.

Mary Elizabeth Brown

Central Baptist Church. Church at 166 West 92nd Street designed by Walter Cook and built in 1915 to serve Baptists descended from the congregation of the Laight Street Baptist Church, founded in 1842.

Sharon Wilkins

Central Grammar School. Original name of Boys and Girls High School.

Central Park. Public park in Manhattan, covering 843 acres (340 hectares) bounded to the north by 110th Street, to the east by Fifth Avenue, to the south by 59th Street (Central Park South), and to the west by Central Park West. It was the first landscaped public park in the United States. Advocates of its construction were mostly wealthy merchants and landowners who admired the public grounds of London and Paris and argued that comparable facilities would give New York City an international reputation; they also believed that a public park would offer their families an attractive setting for carriage rides and provide workers with a healthful alternative to the saloon. After three years of debating the size and cost of the park, the state legislature in 1853 authorized the city to use the power of eminent domain to acquire a parcel of more than 700 acres (285 hectares) in the middle of Manhattan. A site bounded by 106th Street, Fifth Avenue, 59th Street, and Eighth Avenue was chosen, where an irregular terrain of swamps, bluffs, and rocky outcroppings made the land undesirable for private development.

Control over the park was initially set by the state legislature, which was predominantly Republican. It appointed the Central Park Commission in 1857 to prevent local New York City Democrats from gaining control. The commission was the city's first planning agency and, under the leadership of Andrew Haswell Green, oversaw the planning of upper Manhattan as well as management of the park itself. In 1857 it held a contest to design the park, the first such contest in the country: the winning entry was the "Greensward plan," which called for a pastoral landscape in the English romantic tradition and was submitted by Frederick Law Olmsted, the superintendent of the park, and Calvert Vaux, a former partner of Andrew Jackson Downing. Their plan called for a combination of the pastoral (open, rolling meadows), the picturesque (the Ramble), and the formal (the dress grounds of the Mall, or Promenade, and Bethesda Terrace). An impression of uninterrupted expanse was maintained by building four transverse roads 8 feet (2.5 meters) below the park's surface to carry crosstown traffic. Pressure from local critics soon led Olmsted and Vaux to separate carriage drives, pedestrian walks, and equestrian paths from each other. Assisted by Jacob Wrey Mould, Vaux designed more than 40 bridges to eliminate grade crossings between the various routes.

The construction of the park was one of the most extensive public works projects undertaken in the city during the nineteenth century. About 1600 residents of shantytowns in the area were displaced, including Irish pig

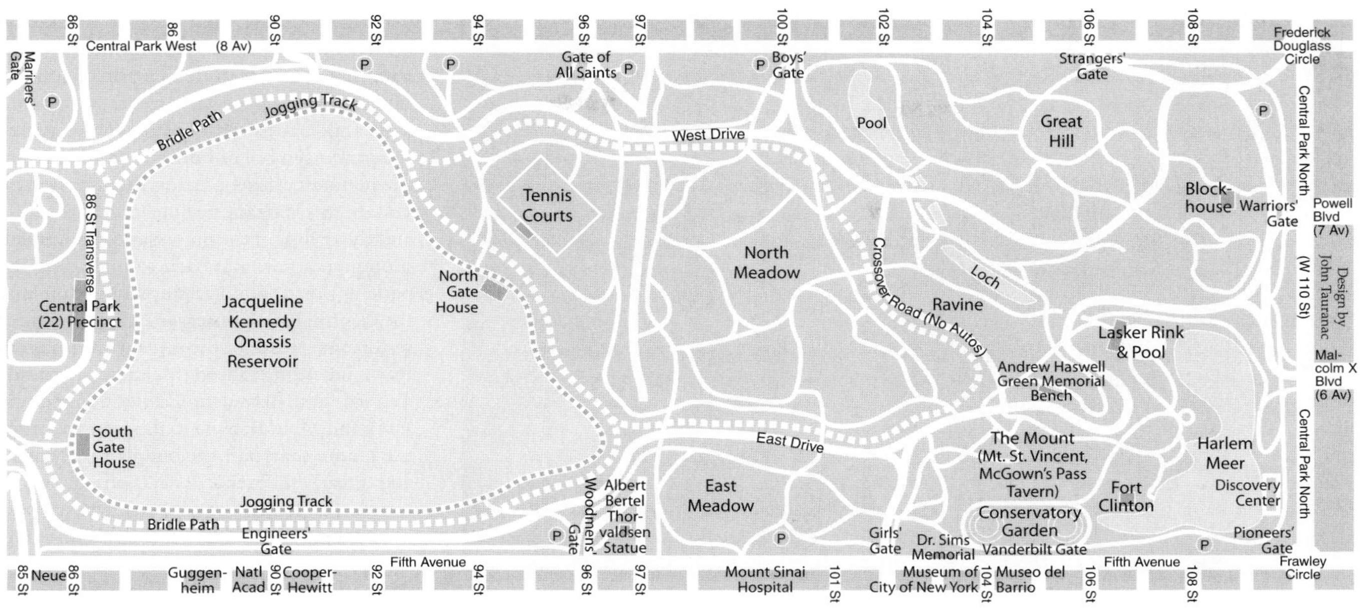

farmers and German gardeners. Seneca Village, a black settlement at Eighth Avenue and 82nd Street that had three churches and a school, was also demolished. About 20,000 workers were engaged, including native-born stonecutters, engineers from New England, Irish laborers, and German gardeners. They blasted out ridges with gunpowder (more than was used in the Battle of Gettysburg), removed nearly 3 million cubic yards (2.3 million cubic meters) of soil, planted more than 270,000 trees and shrubs, and built a curvilinear reservoir just north of an existing rectangular one. The park opened to the public in the winter of 1859, when thousands skated on lakes built over former swamps. In 1863 the northern boundary was extended to 110th Street.

In the decade after the opening, more than half of those visiting the park arrived in carriages (which less than 5 percent of the city's population could afford to own), and each day there were elaborate carriage parades in the late afternoon. Middle-class residents

Central Park, 2009

Central Park entrance, 2009

went skating in winter and attended concerts on Saturday afternoons in summer. Many Irish and Germans were discouraged from going to the park by stringent rules, especially a ban on group picnics. Small tradesmen were not allowed to use commercial wagons for family drives, and only schoolboys with a note from their principal could play ball on the meadows. These rules were repeatedly contested. By 1865 there were more than seven million visitors to the park a year, and during the late nineteenth century the park was opened to a wider range of uses. Under a new city charter (1870) the park came under local control and the mayor appointed park commissioners, who gradually authorized new facilities, including a carousel, goat rides, tennis on the lawns, and bicycling on the drives. The zoo moved into permanent quarters in 1871 and soon became the most popular feature. In the 1880s workers successfully campaigned for concerts on Sunday, their only day of rest.

In the early twentieth century, neighborhoods populated mostly by immigrants developed at the park's borders, and the number of visitors to the park reached a peak. Progressive reformers joined with workers in advocating facilities for active recreation. In 1927 August Heckscher donated the first equipped playground, which was built on the southeastern meadow. When plans were announced to drain the rectangular reservoir, Progressives pushed to have a sports arena, a swimming pool, and playing fields built over it. Others, inspired by the "city beautiful" movement, proposed a formal civic plaza and promenade to connect the museums at the eastern and western borders. Landscape architects and preservationists campaigned against these suggestions, and the site was made into the Great Lawn. Mayor Fiorello H. La Guardia gave control of a new centralized park system in 1934 to Robert Moses, who during his 26 years in office provided many of the facilities requested by Progressive reformers. During the Depression he used federal money to build 20 playgrounds on the periphery of the park, renovate the zoo, realign the drives to accommodate automobiles, build athletic fields in the North Meadow, and expand recreational programs. He later added permanent ball fields to the Great Lawn for corporate softball teams and neighborhood little league teams. In the early 1950s and early 1960s private benefactors contributed the Wollman Skating Rink, the Lasker Rink and Pool, new boathouses, and a chess and checkers house. The park became the site of summer performances by the New York Shakespeare Festival in 1957 and by the New York Philharmonic in 1965.

Thomas Hoving and August Heckscher (grandson of the philanthropist), the parks commissioners appointed by Mayor John V. Lindsay, encouraged such events as rock concerts and "be-ins" during the 1960s, making the park a symbol of both urban revival and the counterculture. During the 1970s severe budget cuts, a steady decline in maintenance, and the revival of the preservation movement prompted a new approach to managing the park. A private fund-raising body known as the Central Park Conservancy took charge of restoring features of the Greensward plan in 1980, including Sheep Meadow, Bethesda Terrace, and Belvedere Castle (designed by Vaux and Mould); by 1990 the group contributed more than half the budget for the park and greatly influenced decisions about its future. In the early twenty-first century, the conservancy established a long-term agreement with the city to oversee maintenance of the park, combining its private funds with public monies. Public events, always limited in number, became severely restricted in 2005 when they were capped at six cultural events a year on the Great Lawn.

Henry Hope Reed and Sophia Duckworth, *Central Park: A History and a Guide* (New York: Clarkson N. Potter, 1967); Frederick Law Olmsted, Jr., and Theodora Kimball, eds., *Forty Years of Landscape Architecture: Central Park* (Cambridge, Mass.: MIT Press, 1973); Galen Cranz, *The Politics of Park Design: A History of Urban Parks in America* (Cambridge, Mass.: MIT Press, 1982); Roy Rosenzweig and Elizabeth Blackmar, *The Park and the People: A History of Central Park* (Ithaca, N.Y.: Cornell University Press, 1992)

Elizabeth Blackmar, Roy Rosenzweig

Central Park Casino. Nightclub in Central Park near Fifth Avenue and 66th Street, designed in 1864 by Calvert Vaux. Under the name Ladies' Refreshment Salon, it was used

Central Park Casino

as a small nightclub in the early 1920s. After JAMES J. WALKER was elected mayor in 1925, it was leased to his friend the restaurateur Sidney Solomon and lavishly redesigned by Joseph Urban. From 1926 to 1934 the club was a high-priced establishment that became widely known as the center of the mayor's active social life. After he resigned in 1932 there were plans to have the structure serve a wider public, but the parks commissioner, Robert Moses, a political rival of Walker, demolished it and replaced it with a playground.

Sandra Opdycke

Central Park Conservancy. The Central Park Conservancy, a not-for-profit organization composed of a board of private citizens authorized by contract with New York City to restore, manage, and preserve Central Park, was founded in 1980 by Mayor Edward I. Koch, Parks Commissioner Gordon J. Davis, and Central Park Administrator Elizabeth Barlow Rogers. In 2007 it provided more than 84 percent of Central Park's annual $25 million operating budget and was responsible for all basic care of the park. It has a 60-member board consisting of two city officials ex officio (the parks commissioner and the Manhattan borough president), five trustees appointed by the mayor, and many who represent the business, banking, and legal community of New York City.

Elizabeth Barlow Rogers

Central Park jogger. Name popularly applied to a 28-year-old investment banker who was raped and assaulted by a gang of youths near the northern part of Central Park on the evening of 19 April 1989. The crime gained notoriety because of its randomness and brutality, as well as its racial overtones (the victim was white and her attackers black). In 1990 five of the assailants were convicted of various charges in two trials; the victim returned to work after eight months, but suffered permanent injuries. In the late 1990s Trisha Meili released her identity and story to the public and authored a book about her experience. She also became a prominent motivational speaker and advocate, through the Achilles Foundation, of individuals with disabilities participating in running.

Central Park West. Avenue in Manhattan running from 59th Street at Columbus Circle to 110th Street at Fredrick Douglass Circle along the western edge of Central Park. Buses and cars run both north and south along the avenue, which is also served by the local B and C trains and the express A and D trains. The avenue is home to the American Museum of Natural History, the New-York Historical Society, and a large number of residential buildings, some of which command the highest real estate prices in the city.

Ben Silk

Central Park West, 2009

Central Park Zoo. Zoo located at 830 Fifth Avenue (and 64th Street) in Central Park. The zoo began as a de facto menagerie in 1860, when New York City residents and local circuses began "donating" or dropping off unwanted animals—72 black swans and a bear cub, for instance—at the Arsenal, a munitions depot for the New York National Guard. Converted into the Central Park Menagerie in 1864 (and not included in the original design for Central Park), the Arsenal housed a variety of animals in metal cages, including Mike Crowley, the first chimpanzee ever shown in the United States. As part of a Works Progress Administration project in 1934, Parks Commissioner Robert Moses renovated the site behind the Arsenal as a zoo, moving his own Parks Department offices to the building itself (where they remain today).

Moses's renovations and new zoo design were state-of-the-art for the 1930s. Prior study of sea lion behavior and habitat had even informed the architect's design of the sea lion pool, which was almost unheard of for the day. Admission was free of charge. But the facilities eventually proved inadequate, and in 1980 the Wildlife Conservation Society signed an agreement with the New York City Department of Parks and Recreation to oversee the renovation and management of the zoo. After five years of demolition and construction, the zoo reopened in 1988 with a design by Kevin Roche and John Dinkeloo following the safari zoo model, which seeks to replicate animals' natural habitats.

In the early twenty-first century the zoo was home to more than 130 species of animals in habitats ranging from the Antarctic (penguins) to the equatorial tropics (toucans), including several endangered species (red pandas, thick-billed parrots, and Wyoming toads) and two species that have been at the zoo since its original incarnation in the 1860s: polar bears and sea lions. The zoo attracts one million visitors annually.

Rowan Moore Gerety

Central Synagogue. Reform temple at the corner of 55th Street and Lexington Avenue in Manhattan. The building is a twin-towered structure erected in 1870–72 as the fifth house of worship of Ahawath Chesed (formed in 1846 by Bohemian Jews on the Lower East Side); the congregation merged in 1898 with the members of Shaar Hasomayim and took its current name in 1920. Designed by Henry Fernbach, one of the first Jewish architects in the United States, the building was erected of sandstone with limestone trim in a Moorish Revival style and modeled after the Dohany Street Synagogue in Budapest. The synagogue is the oldest in continuous use in New York City; it was designated a city landmark in 1966 and is the only synagogue in the state to have been designated a National Historic Landmark (1975). Across 55th Street is the Phyllis and Lee Coffey Community House (1965–68, designed by Kahn and Jacobs), built as a memorial to Jonah B. Wise, one of the congregation's distinguished rabbis.

Herbert Maier Schwarz, *Your Temple: A Unique Story of Devotion* (New York: Central Synagogue, 1958); Stella F. Fuld, ed., with Janet Stone and Mildred Ross, *Central Synagogue, 140 Years* (New York: Harry N. Abrams, 1979)

Joy M. Kestenbaum

Centreville. Name formerly applied to Castleton Corners.

Century Association. Private club of about 2000 men and women who are authors, artists, and amateurs of letters and the fine arts. For the club's purposes, amateurs are defined as "men and women of any occupation provided their breadth of interest and qualities of mind and imagination make them sympathetic, stimulating, and congenial companions in a society of authors and artists." The club was formed in the early nineteenth century, when a group formed the Bread and Cheese Club; after its demise, some of its members, together with members of the National Academy of Design, created the Sketch Club in 1829. It met fortnightly at the homes of its members. At a meeting in 1847, when it became clear that the number of artistically minded New Yorkers who wanted to join was too large for anyone's living room, the Century was formed; it took its name from the number of men who were invited to join. The Century made its home in a variety of odd places around the city until it finally settled down, on 10 January 1891, in its present Renaissance-style building at 7 West 43rd Street, designed by McKim, Mead and White (all three of whom were members). Much of the furniture still in the building was designed by the firm. Many of the artist members, several from the Hudson River School, contributed paintings in lieu of entry fees. In the early twenty-first century the Century added musicians as members.

Henry S.F. Cooper, Jr., *Inside the Century* (New York: The Century Association, 1997)

Henry S. F. Cooper, Jr.

Century Illustrated Monthly Magazine. Periodical launched in 1870 as *Scribner's Monthly,* edited by the poet and essayist Josiah Gilbert Holland. In 1881 it became independent of Charles Scribner's Sons and was renamed. An engraving process developed by Alexander W. Drake and the printing of Theodore Low De Vinne made the magazine the most visually appealing publication of its day. Edited by Richard Watson Gilder, it sought to inspire, uplift, and unite the nation. "The War Series," which consisted of memoirs of Union and Confederate veterans and ran for three years, raised circulation to 250,000 in the 1880s. *Century* declined in the face of competition from mass-market magazines like *McClure's* and ceased publication in 1930.

Arthur John, *The Best Years of the Century: Richard Watson Gilder, Scribner's Monthly and Century Magazine, 1870–1909* (Urbana: University of Illinois Press, 1981)

Marc H. Aronson

Century 21. Department store. Located at 22 Cortland Street across from the World Trade Center Plaza, it sells brand-name and high-end clothing, accessories, shoes, and home wares at discounted rates. Century 21 has several locations throughout New York and New Jersey. The Manhattan flagship store, which is the firm's headquarters, was renovated and reopened in the summer of 2002 after the terrorist attacks of 11 September 2001.

Jessica Montesano

ceramics. The production of pottery in New Amsterdam began after the necessary raw materials were discovered there in abundance. The first documented potter in the settlement was Dirck Claesen, who worked in Manhattan during the 1650s. During the seventeenth century most potters in the city produced simple household containers and roof tile of an unrefined red earthenware. In later years suitable clay was found for making stoneware, which unlike redware could be made hard and watertight. Stoneware was produced by Dutch, German, and English potters in New York City as early as the 1730s, long before it was made elsewhere in the colonies in comparable quantities. In 1718 a stoneware pottery was opened on Pottbaker's Hill between Reade and Duane streets by William Crolius, a potter from Neuwied. It became one of the most enduring potteries of its kind in the city, carried on by his sons William Crolius and John Crolius; by John's four sons, including Clarkson Crolius, who was also city collector, an assemblyman, and a member of the Common Council; and later by Clarkson Crolius, Jr., a civic leader and the last member of the family to run the pottery, from which he retired in 1850. A small porcelain factory staffed by skilled French workers was opened about 1813 by Henry Mead. After it failed in 1824, another factory was opened in the following year on the same site by two Frenchmen, Louis François Decasse and Nicolas Louis Édouard Chanou. It was known for producing products of high quality before being destroyed by fire in 1828.

Toward the mid-nineteenth century the demand for stoneware declined, in part because of the invention of glass canning jars. The city's prosperity as a marketing center pushed ceramics manufacturers to the outskirts, especially Brooklyn, Staten Island, and New Jersey. At the same time the demand for porcelain and white earthenware manufacture increased. During the 1840s and 1850s handwork and small shops in the porcelain industry were gradually replaced by mechanized production in larger factories that could produce goods at lower cost, making porcelain available to the middle class for the first time. Between 1840 and 1860 many porcelain workers were skilled German and English immigrants, and Brooklyn became one of the country's leading ceramic centers, along with Trenton, New Jersey, and East Liverpool, Ohio. Hotels, boardinghouses, and saloons proliferated and required dinnerware, bar vessels, and toilet accessories. At the Crystal Palace Exhibition of the Industry of All Nations in 1853, the country's first international exposition, the firms of Charles Cartlidge and William Boch and Brothers exhibited their wares. Both had factories in Greenpoint, in Brooklyn, and produced heavy porcelain tableware and a wide range of house trimmings, including name plates, keyhole covers, and knobs for doors, drawers, and shutters. Cartlidge's firm closed in 1854. In 1867 Thomas C. Smith joined Boch and Brothers, which was renamed the Union Porcelain Company and later the Union Porcelain Works. Soon the largest and most successful ceramics manufacturer in the area, it had a sizable factory complex that in 1884 employed 200 workers and made an average of $250,000 in annual sales. It designed art wares that were exhibited nationally and remained in operation until about 1922. From the time of World War I traditional ceramic forms were often rejected for more sculptural ones. In the following decades New York City became an international center for ceramic art, where many artists, especially European and Asian immigrants, settled near the universities where they worked and taught.

William C. Ketchum, Jr., *Potters and Potteries of New York State, 1650–1900* (Syracuse, N.Y.: Syracuse University Press, 1987)

Alice Cooney Frelinghuysen

Cerf, Bennett (Alfred) (*b* New York City, 25 May 1898; *d* Mount Kisco, N.Y., 27 Aug 1971). Publisher and writer. After attending

Columbia College (BA 1919) and the Columbia School of Journalism (1920), he briefly worked at the *New York Herald Tribune* and a brokerage firm on Wall Street. In 1923 he joined the publishing firm Boni and Liveright, where he became a vice president. Cerf left in 1925 to found the Modern Library with his business partner Donald Klopfer, which led to the creation of Random House in 1927 (named so because he thought they would be publishing "a few books on the side at random"). In his 40-year tenure at Random House he published such writers as Franz Kafka, Eugene O'Neill, William Faulkner, and Theodor Geisel (Dr. Seuss). After a drawn-out court case in 1933 he published James Joyce's *Ulysses.* Cerf compiled numerous volumes of jokes and riddles and was a panelist on the television quiz show *What's My Line?* from 1951 to the show's end in 1967. In 1969 he bequeathed to Columbia University the Random House archives, which contain records of such writers as Gertrude Stein, William Faulkner, and Sinclair Lewis. Among Cerf's more than two dozen books are *Try and Stop Me* (1945), *The Book of Riddles* (1960), and his memoir *At Random: The Reminiscences* (1977).

James E. Mooney, Irina Ikonsky

Chabad. See Lubavitchers.

Chadwick, Henry (*b* Exeter, England, 5 Oct 1824; *d* Brooklyn, 20 April 1908). Sportswriter and father of baseball. He moved to New York City with his family in 1837, settling in Brooklyn. In 1856 he filed cricket reports for the *New York Times* and later that year became a cricket and baseball editor for the *Brooklyn Daily Eagle,* a position he held until 1894. He was the best-known promoter of "New York," or "Brooklyn," baseball and helped to make it more popular than both "Massachusetts" baseball and cricket. While writing about baseball for the *New York World* and the *Sun* he developed the box score, a method of compiling game statistics. From 1881 to 1908 he edited the *Spalding Baseball Guide,* the leading publication of its kind. Throughout his career he promoted baseball as an outlet for competitive energies and an alternative to drinking and fighting; he devoted much of his time to combating gambling, which threatened the wholesome reputation of what he called "America's game." In 1896 the National League voted to give him a lifetime pension. Known to many as the "father of baseball," Chadwick worked in baseball journalism to the end of his life. He is buried in Green-Wood Cemetery.

Edward T. O'Donnell

chamberlain. The office of chamberlain was established in 1868 to maintain financial records, deposit public moneys, and compile quarterly financial reports. Appointed by the mayor, the chamberlain received a commission on the accounts that he supervised. The establishment of the comptroller's office in 1802 diminished the chamberlain's powers. The office of the chamberlain became a part of the department of finance in 1916 and was abolished in 1938.

Neal C. Garelik

Chambers, Whittaker [Jay Vivian] (*b* Philadelphia, 1 April 1901; *d* Westminster, Md., 9 July 1961). Journalist and spy. He graduated from Columbia University and worked as a freelance journalist. After joining the Communist Party in 1931 he was a spy courier for the Soviet Union until the Nazi–Soviet pact of 1939 led him to abjure communism. From 1939 to 1948 he enjoyed a prominent career as a senior editor at *Time,* specializing in cultural and world affairs. He achieved notoriety in 1948 when in testimony before the House Un-American Activities Committee he accused Alger Hiss, then president of the Carnegie Endowment for International Peace in New York City, of having removed and copied classified documents while working at the State Department. Hiss claimed innocence but in 1950 was convicted of perjury and served four years in prison. Chambers spent his later years issuing apocalyptic warnings of the Soviet threat and became something of a hero for American conservatives. He wrote a memoir, *Witness* (1952).

Allen Weinstein, *Perjury: The Hiss–Chambers Case* (New York: Alfred A. Knopf, 1978)

Martin Ebon

Champion, Gower (*b* Geneva, Ill., 22 June 1919; *d* New York City, 25 Aug 1980). Choreographer, director, and dancer. He grew up in Los Angeles, and at the age of 15 began a career as a dancer when he won a contest at the Coconut Grove with Jeanne Tyler. While serving in the U.S. Coast Guard (from 1942) he met Sid Caesar, and after leaving the service he became reacquainted with high school friend Marjorie Belcher (later known professionally as Marjorie Bell). The two formed a dance team, married on 5 October 1947, and appeared on Milton Berle's television program and at the Persian Room of the Plaza Hotel. With Caesar and Imogene Coca they worked on the *Admiral Broadway Review* (1947–48), an important early television program that was a forerunner of *Your Show of Shows.* In the following years Champion worked as a choreographer, winning the first of his seven Tony Awards for the Broadway show *Lend an Ear* (1948). He conceived of and directed the musical revue *Three for Tonight* (1955) at the Plymouth Theatre in New York City and also directed *Bye Bye Birdie* (1960), *Carnival* (1961), *Hello, Dolly!* (1964), *I Do! I Do!* (1966), and *Sugar* (1972). In 1980 he directed David Merrick's production of *42nd Street*; he died hours before the curtain rose on opening night.

Alana Erickson Coble

Chanin, Irwin (*b* New York City, 29 Oct 1891; *d* New York City, 24 Feb 1988). Real estate developer. With his brother Henry Chanin (1894–1973) he opened a firm to build houses in Brooklyn, the Bronx, Queens, and Staten Island; the two eventually expanded their operations to Manhattan, where they erected apartment buildings and many theaters and hotels on Broadway and became leading developers in the 1920s. Irwin worked with the firm of Sloan and Robertson to design the Chanin Building, a dramatic structure of 56 stories with a terra-cotta facade on 42nd Street and Lexington Avenue near Grand Central Terminal. Completed in 1929, it was the Chanins' most ambitious project, containing more commercial space than the Woolworth Building and known as the tallest building north of Wall Street until the Chrysler Building was completed in 1930. With the onset of the Depression, the Chanins experienced financial difficulties and eventually lost most of their properties.

Marc A. Weiss

Chapin, Alfred C(lark) (*b* South Hadley, Mass., 8 March 1848; *d* 2 Oct 1936). Mayor of Brooklyn. He practiced law and belonged to the Democratic Party. As mayor from 1888 to 1891 he brought improved police protection, an increased water supply, a growth in park acreage, and the construction of the monumental arch at the entrance to Prospect Park.

Ellen Fletcher

Chapin School. Independent elementary and secondary school for girls and young women founded by teacher Maria Bowen Chapin. It opened in 1901 at 12 West 47th Street as Miss Chapin's School for Girls and Kindergarten for Boys and Girls, with 78 students and 7 teachers. After occupying two larger buildings, the school moved in 1928 to a neoclassical-style building at 100 East End Avenue. Designed and built for the school by the New York firm of Delano and Aldrich, the building stood in enlarged form at the same location in the early twenty-first century. The Chapin School, Ltd. became the school's official name in 1934. In 2007 it had 665 female students (K–12) and more than 100 full-time faculty members.

Charlotte Johnson Noerdlinger, *And Cheer for the Green and Gold: An Anecdotal History of the Chapin School* (New York: The Chapin School, 2000)

Ella M. Foshay

Charging Bull. Sculpture. *Charging Bull* is a 7000-pound (3175-kilogram) bronze sculpture in Bowling Green Park, near Wall Street in Manhattan. Created by the Sicilian artist Arturo Di Modica at his own expense (some $360,000), the bull was illegally installed in front of the New York Stock Exchange just before Christmas 1989, only to be impounded by the police several days later. It was reinstalled in its present location in 1990 as a response to public outcry, where it remains on long-term loan to the city's Department of Parks and Recreation.

Rowan Moore Gerety

Charity Hospital. Hospital on Blackwell's Island; a forerunner of Elmhurst Hospital Center.

Charity Organization Society [COS]. Society organized in 1882 in New York City by the reformer Josephine Shaw Lowell to evaluate and refer applicants for charity. It kept extensive records about living conditions in the city and concentrated on poverty, an approach that led other groups to shift their focus from charity and moral correction to social welfare. Known for taking an active interest in those with whom they worked, the society's "friendly visitors" later became a model for social caseworkers. Among the directors was the reformer Edward T. Devine. With the Association for Improving the Condition of the Poor and the Children's Aid Society, the society in 1891 became an owner of the United Charities Building at 105 East 22nd Street, which was donated by John M. Kennedy. During the same year the society formed a national publication committee that launched the journal *Charities Review,* which after several changes of name eventually became the *Survey,* the most influential publication of its kind in the country. The society also sponsored Laurence Veiller's tenement exhibition in 1900 and his work in drafting the city's Tenement House Law of 1901. In 1939 the Charity Organization Society merged with the Association for Improving the Condition of the Poor to form the Community Service Society.

Grace Florence Marcus, *Some Aspects of Relief in Family Casework* (New York: Charity Organization Society, 1929)

Alana Erickson Coble

Charles H. Revson Foundation. Charitable organization formed in 1956 by Charles H. Revson (*b* 11 Oct 1906; *d* 24 Aug 1975), a founder of the cosmetics firm Revlon. During his lifetime the foundation donated $10 million to medical, educational, and Jewish organizations in New York City: these gifts funded a diagnostic center at the Albert Einstein College of Medicine, an institute of ophthalmology at New York Medical Center, Revson Plaza at Columbia University, and the fountain at Lincoln Center for the Performing Arts. Enlarged by an endowment after Revson's death, the foundation in 1978 took on a full-time staff, began a formal grant-making process, and defined four areas of activity: urban affairs, education, biomedical research policy, and Jewish philanthropy. Contributions are aimed in particular at projects relating to the future of New York City, the changing role of women in society, government accountability, and the impact of modern communications on education. By the early twenty-first century, the foundation's endowment had grown to $200 million and it dispersed over $9 million annually. Its offices are at 55 East 59th Street in Manhattan.

Kenneth W. Rose

Charles Scribner's Sons. Firm of book publishers formed in 1846 by the booksellers Charles Scribner and Isaac Baker, who specialized in didactic material. The firm was led from 1871 to 1930 by Charles Scribner and employed William Crary Brownell as its literary advisor from 1888 to 1928; it also published *Scribner's Magazine* (1886–1914), edited by Edward I. Burlingame, and operated a bookstore at 597 Fifth Avenue (now a landmark) designed by Ernest Flagg, whose sister Louise married Charles Scribner, Jr. From 1910 to 1947 Maxwell Perkins redefined the image of the editor and championed such authors as F. Scott Fitzgerald, Ernest Hemingway, and Thomas Wolfe. Owned and managed for many years by the same family, Scribner's was long highly regarded as a publishing house. In 1984 it was acquired by Macmillan and the bookstore was sold.

Roger Burlingame, *Of Making Many Books: A Hundred Years of Reading, Writing, and Publishing* (New York: Charles Scribner's Sons, 1946); Charles Scribner, Jr., *In the Company of Writers: A Life in Publishing* (New York: Charles Scribner's Sons, 1990)

Marc H. Aronson

Charleston. Neighborhood in southwestern Staten Island (2000 pop. 17,000) bounded to the north by Clay Pit Ponds, to the east by Sandy Ground, to the south by Tottenville, and to the west by Arthur Kill. It was known as Androvetteville in the eighteenth century. The area is rich in the type of clay needed for making bricks, and in 1854 a Bavarian immigrant named Balthazar Kreischer opened a factory where heat-resistant bricks were made by German and Irish workers. By the 1890s these workers numbered more than 300. A company town called Kreischerville took shape that consisted of Kreischer's Italianate mansion, the residences of two of his sons, an inn, a hotel, a grocery store, and housing for workers. The family also built St. Peter's Evangelical Reformed Church (1883), now known as the Free Hungarian Reformed Church. After the factory closed in 1927, the neighborhood took its current name. Some of the old clay pits may be seen at Clay Pit Ponds State Park. In the 1970s there were discussions about using municipally owned land for an amusement park and including Charleston in various development schemes, one of which for a new town was advanced by James Rouse. A much-reported anti-gay crime in 1990 brought negative notoriety, as did the closing of a restaurant at the Kreischer Mansion. In 2005 over 130 acres (53 hectares) of city-owned land, first called the Charleston Retail Site, became the Bricktown Centre, a shopping center with nearby ball fields, recreational land, and a school planned.

Howard R. Weiner

Charlotte Gardens. Famous urban renewal project in South Bronx, bounded to the north by East 174th Street, to the east by Southern Boulevard, to the south by Jennings Street, and to the west by Crotona Park. By 1975 the abandoned and devastated area was being compared to bombed-out Germany after World War II. In October 1977 President Jimmy Carter visited the area and pledged federal aid for its redevelopment. Ronald Reagan also expressed concern about the neighborhood during his presidential campaign in 1980. The South Bronx Development Organization

Charlotte Gardens

received $3 million in federal aid, and in the summer of 1983 a complex of 94 ranch houses was completed, each house selling for a subsidized price between $49,500 and $60,000, depending on amenities. The project was the most successful attempt to redevelop South Bronx during the 1980s, and in the twenty-first century, Charlotte Gardens was a suburban presence amid many similar small-scale neighborhoods throughout the surging borough.

Joel Schwartz

Charlotteville. Neighborhood in northwestern Queens, lying within Woodside and bounded to the north by 31st Avenue, to the east by 68th Street, to the south by Northern Boulevard, and to the west by Hobart Street. Development was begun by John A. Mecke but was interrupted by his death in May 1867. In June and August 1868 his heir auctioned off lots, and in 1880 the area was annexed to Woodside. A large unsold portion was redeveloped in the 1890s as North Woodside. The name gradually fell into disuse as Woodside expanded after consolidation.

Vincent Seyfried

charter. New Amsterdam was incorporated by a charter of the Dutch West India Company in 1653. Under English rule "the Mayor Aldermen and Commonality of the City of New York" was incorporated in response to local petition. According to the charters of Governors Richard Nicolls (1665), Thomas Dongan (1686), Lord Cornbury (1708), and John Montgomerie (1731), the mayor and other officials were appointed by the provincial governor and council.

Until the late eighteenth century, the charter change process assured New York City a measure of independence. When the city requested powers from the state beyond those given in Montgomerie's charter, its autonomy began to diminish. Popular election of the mayor (1834) and some department heads (1849) followed. By the mid-1850s the city's affairs were virtually controlled by the state; changes to the municipal charter were made only by the (usually) Republican state legislature. The charter of 1870 re-empowered the city. It was said to have been "bought" by William M. "Boss" Tweed for $600,000. The reform charter of 1873 strengthened the powers of the comptroller. In 1881 the state legislature granted a charter to Brooklyn that became a model for other American cities. The Charter of Greater New York (1898) set the present boundaries of the city and provided for central governing institutions.

A new charter in 1901 decentralized city government by strengthening the borough presidents and establishing a powerful board of estimate. The legislature in 1914 gave all cities in the state except New York City a role in defining their charters; that right was extended to New York City in 1924. A referendum in 1935 on the proposals of the (Thomas Day) Thatcher Commission brought about proportional representation for City Council elections.

From the 1960s changes to the charter were usually introduced not in the City Council but by commissions formed by the mayor under powers granted by state law in 1961. The (John T.) Cahill Commission (1961) established an electoral system for the City Council that assured representation for minority parties, strengthened the mayor's budgetary powers, and weakened the borough presidents and the comptroller. The (Roy) Goodman Commission (1973–75), formed by the state legislature, proposed decentralizing city government.

In response to a federal lawsuit over equal representation, the (Michael I.) Sovern Commission (1983) eliminated council seats filled by at-large (borough-wide) elections and introduced a reapportionment scheme for the council. A second suit challenging the system of representation used by the Board of Estimate, *Morris v. Board of Estimate* (1989), inspired the formation of (Richard) Ravich (1986–88) and (F.A.O.) Schwartz, Jr. (1988–89), commissions, appointed by Mayor Edward I. Koch. They recommended (and achieved) abolishing the Board of Estimate and redistributing its powers; changing procedures for budgeting, land use, elections, and administration; devising safeguards of governmental integrity; and transforming the City Council into a more effective legislature.

Over the following two decades Mayors Rudolph W. Giuliani and Michael Bloomberg appointed six charter commissions (1998, 1999, 2001, 2002, 2003, 2004–2005), more than for any similar period in the city's history. Critics alleged that the mayors used the revision process inappropriately to advance their political agendas or to seek policy changes in a manner that bypassed the City Council. Commissions appointed by Mayor Bloomberg failed to achieve nonpartisan elections in the city, but the 2004–2005 commission, headed by Ester R. Fuchs, did gain voter approval of significant charter changes, creating an ethical code for administrative law judges and entrenching good financial management practices first adopted during the 1970s fiscal crisis. See table of changes beginning on p. 230.

James Kent, *Charter of the City of New York, with Notes thereon; Also a Treatise on the Powers and Duties of the Mayor, Aldermen, and Assistant Aldermen, and the Journal of the City Convention* (New York: Childs and Devoe, 1836); Mark Ash, *The Greater New York Charter* (New York: Baker, Voorhis, 1898; 5th edn 1925); Frank J. Mauro and Gerald Benjamin, eds., *Restructuring the New York City Government: The Reemergence of Municipal Reform* (New York: Academy of Political Science, 1989)

Gerald Benjamin

Chase, Edna Woolman (*b* Asbury Park, N.J., 14 March 1877; *d* Sarasota, Fla., 20 March 1957). Magazine editor. She began working for the fashion magazine *Vogue* in 1895 and was appointed editor in chief in 1914 by its owner, Condé Nast. In the same year she staged a fashion show in New York City, the first in the United States. Throughout her career she made innovations in graphic design and photography, adhered to high standards in fashion, and encouraged American fashion designers. She was put in charge of all editions of the magazine in 1948 and retired in 1952. With Ilka Chase she wrote *Always in Vogue* (1954).

Mary Ellen Zuckerman

Chase, William Merritt (*b* Williamsburg, Ind., 1 Nov 1849; *d* New York City, 25 Oct 1916). Painter. After studying art in Indiana he moved to New York City in 1869, where he attended the National Academy of Design. He studied in Munich, Germany (1872–78), and returned to New York in 1878 to teach at the Art Students League. Setting up a number of studios, including one at 51 West 10th Street and another in the Tiffany Building, Chase painted still lifes and impressionistic landscapes of the parks and harbors of Brooklyn and Manhattan. He also opened the Chase School of Art (now Parsons The New School for Design) in 1896. Among his pupils were Georgia O'Keeffe, Edward Hopper, and Rockwell Kent. President of the Society of American Artists and part of the Ten American Painters, Chase was known for his Tenth Street studio, which represented the novelty and status of the nineteenth-century artist. An exhibition of his landscape paintings was held at the Brooklyn Museum of Art in 2000.

Keith L. Bryant, *William Merritt Chase: A Genteel Bohemian* (Columbia: University of Missouri Press, 1991)

Irina Ikonsky

Chase Manhattan. Commercial bank formed in 1955 through the merger of the Manhattan Company and Chase National Bank. Its total resources of $7.6 billion made it the then-largest bank in New York City and the second-largest bank in the United States. Although the new bank was nominally governed by the charter of the Manhattan Company (written in 1799), in practice Chase National managed its operations. A 60-story building designed by the firm of Skidmore, Owings and Merrill was the headquarters for the new bank; built in 1955–61 at a cost of $121 million at 1 Chase Manhattan Plaza, near Pine Street and Liberty Street, it spurred a revival of office building construction in the city's financial district. David Rockefeller, son of John D. Rockefeller, Jr., was president of the bank from 1961 to 1969 and

Changes to the City Charter, 1653–2008

1653

Legislative: New Amsterdam receives its first charter from the Dutch West India Company, establishing the offices of schout, two burgomasters, and five schepens, all of whom are appointed by the director general. Together these officeholders form a court of inferior jurisdiction as well as a legislative body.

Executive: The burgomasters are responsible for nominating church wardens, fire inspectors, and surveyors, subject to the approval of the colony's director general.

1665

Legislative: Under English rule the Dutch form of government continues briefly, but is replaced by a mayor, five aldermen, and one sheriff. Serving together as the city's governing body, these officials are appointed by the governor.

Executive: The mayor is empowered to grant tavern licenses.

1686

Legislative: The charter of Governor Thomas Dongan calls for the freemen in each of the city's six wards to elect one alderman and one assistant, who together with the mayor and the recorder form the Common Council. This body possesses most of the power for governing the city, including the power to regulate markets, transportation of goods, and access to docks; it may also levy fines on offenders. All legislation passed expires after three months unless confirmed by the governor and the council.

Executive: The mayor is appointed annually by the governor. He is a justice of the peace and judge of the court of common pleas; he also has the power to award tavern licenses, to appoint the city's high constable, and (with the Common Council) to grant citizenship.

Courts and Boards: The mayor, recorder, and alderman are justices of the peace. The mayor, recorder, and any two aldermen constitute a court of sessions of peace. The mayor or recorder and any two others qualify as a court of common pleas.

1689

Legislative: Liesler's Rebellion results in the overthrow of the colonial government established by Dongan's charter. A province-wide convention calls for elections in the autumn of 1689.

Executive: Peter Delanoy becomes the city's first elected mayor, but is overthrown in 1691.

1730

Legislative: The charter of Governor Thomas Montgomerie leaves the function of the city's government virtually unchanged. It does create a seventh ward (the Montgomerie Ward), thereby increasing the number of aldermen and assistant aldermen to seven each. Laws passed by the Common Council expire after one year unless confirmed by the governor and by the council.

Executive: Receiving advice from the council of state, the governor continues annually to appoint the mayor to a one-year term.

Courts and Boards: The mayor, recorder, and aldermen are *ex officiis* justices of the peace. The mayor or recorder and any three others may hold general courts of session of peace. The mayor or recorder and three or more aldermen constitute a court of record to hear civil cases.

1777

Executive: On advice from the council of state, the governor of the state appoints the mayor.

1791

Legislative: The city eliminates the names of wards in favor of using numbers.

1813

Legislative: The state legislature declares that the Common Council will perform the same duties required of supervisors of other state counties.

Executive: The Common Council takes over the powers of clerk of the market from the mayor.

1821

Executive: An amendment to the state constitution authorizes the Common Council to select the mayor, a power formerly exercised by the state legislature and the governor.

1830

Legislative: A new charter separates the Board of Aldermen and the Board of Assistant Aldermen into distinct bodies, which together form the Common Council. Each ward elects one alderman and one assistant alderman for one-year terms. Legislation may originate in either chamber, but must be approved by both before being sent to the mayor. Restraints are placed on the fiscal powers of the Common Council: it may not draw money from the treasury except for purposes previously specified by legislation and it may not borrow against the credit of the corporation except in anticipation of future revenues. The council does retain the power to appoint the heads of the executive departments.

Executive: Removed from the Common Council, the mayor nonetheless gains power of veto over the ordinances and resolutions it passes. This veto may be overridden if a majority of both boards re-passes the legislation. The office of deputy mayor (since 1675 a position held by an alderman chosen by the mayor to act in his absence) is transferred to the president of the Board of Aldermen. No city departments fall under the direct control of the executive.

1834

Executive: An amendment to the state constitution calls for annual public mayoral elections.

1849

Legislative: The term for aldermen, but not assistants, is increased to two years. Assistants receive the sole power to impeach city officials. The Common Council surrenders the power to appoint the heads of executive departments and to perform executive business; still, it retains the powers to tax and spend and to administer municipally owned lands. Though now elected, the heads of executive departments remain beholden to the Common Council, as their appointments must be approved.

Executive: The mayor's term of office is increased to two years and he becomes head of the police department (but not chief). He lacks full executive powers, as the 10 executive department heads are elected rather than named by the mayor, and most appoint their own subordinates.

(*continued*)

Changes to the City Charter, 1653–2008 (*Continued*)

1853
Legislative: A Board of Councilmen replaces the Board of Assistant Aldermen and together with the Board of Aldermen comprises the Common Council. The Board of Councilmen is made up of 60 men elected annually from as many newly drawn districts of roughly equal population. The councilmen take charge of all legislation concerning expenditures; the Board of Aldermen may only suggest amendments. Denied the right to sit as judges in municipal courts and to appoint policemen, members of the Common Council also lose control of the police department, which is placed under a Board of Commissioners. All contracts, leases, and sales in excess of $250 must be open to public bidding.
Executive: The mayor accrues further power, as the Common Council now needs a two-thirds majority in each chamber to override his veto. The elected heads of executive departments remain largely independent of the mayor. A Board of Commissioners composed of the mayor, recorder, and city judge presides over the police department.
Courts and Boards: The removal of councilmen as judges in municipal courts yields a more independent judiciary.

1857
Legislative: The city's aldermen are no longer elected by ward, but rather one each from 17 larger districts. The Board of Councilmen is made up of six members elected from each senate district in the city for one-year terms. The Common Council loses powers to the comptroller, who becomes administrator of the city's real estate and auditor of its accounts, its overseer of disbursement, and its collector of taxes. No longer members of the Board of Supervisors of New York County, aldermen gain power to remove department heads by a two-thirds vote (without the mayor's approval).
Executive: Empowered to appoint and to remove most heads of executive departments, albeit with the aldermen's consent, the mayor shores up control over the executive branch. At the same time the state supplants the Municipal Police with its own Metropolitan Police, combining New York, Kings, Richmond, and Westchester counties; a commission of five state-appointed overseers along with the mayors of New York City and Brooklyn (as *ex officiis* members) supervises the Metropolitan Police.
Courts and Boards: A separate New York County Board of Supervisors is created as a check on city government. A board of six elected and six appointed (by the mayor) supervisors replaces the mayor, recorder, and alderman as the members of the board.

1864
Board of Estimate: The Board of Estimate and Apportionment is established; it includes the commissioners of the Metropolitan Police and the comptrollers of New York City and Brooklyn and is responsible for estimating the annual cost of operating the Metropolitan Police.

1868
Council: An amendment to the city charter abolishes the Board of Councilmen, replacing it with the Board of Assistant Aldermen. Each assembly district elects an assistant and an alderman to two-year terms.

1870
Council: The charter of William M. "Boss" Tweed and its amendments of 1871 modify the Board of Aldermen to consist of 15 men elected from the city at large. The Board of Assistant Aldermen consists of one man elected from each assembly district. Members of each board serve one-year terms. All legislation involving expenditures requires a three-fourths vote of approval from each board. The comptroller, corporation counsel, commissioner of public works, and heads of various municipal departments receive non-voting seats on the Board of Aldermen.
Mayor: The mayor augments his power as he receives the right to appoint officials in executive departments (except those of finance and law) without the Common Council's approval. Groups of commissioners with terms of between four and eight years lead most departments; thus the mayor further expands his influence in city government beyond his two-year term. His veto is enhanced as a three-fourths majority vote of each board of the Common Council is required to override his veto. After 13 years of state control, the police department is placed under the mayor's authority.
Board of Estimate: The Board of Supervisors of New York County is terminated as a distinct body and its powers are returned to the former supervisors (see 1813), the aldermen, the mayor, and the recorder. A newly created Board of Apportionment includes the mayor, the comptroller, the commissioner of public works, and the president of the department of public parks. The board's duties include estimating and apportioning money sufficient to run each department of city government for each given year. It sends this budget for certification to the county supervisors (the mayor, recorder, and alderman). By taxing real and personal estate, the supervisors raise funds sufficient to meet expenditures and interest due on the city's bonds.

1873
Council: The "Reform Charter" eliminates the Board of Assistant Aldermen, making the Board of Aldermen alone the Common Council. Three aldermen are elected from each senate district along with six others as at-large candidates, totaling 21 members. To forestall one-party domination of the council, voters may vote for no more than two aldermen from their senate district and four at-large candidates. The term of office for aldermen is reduced from two years to one. These changes do not take effect until 1875.
Mayor: Pending approval by the Board of Aldermen, the mayor appoints all department heads and commissioners except the commissioners of public instruction, the comptroller, the corporation counsel, the president of the police department, and the commissioner and president of public works.
Board of Estimate: The Board of Apportionment becomes the Board of Estimate and Apportionment; its reorganized membership includes the mayor, the comptroller, the president of the Board of Aldermen, and the president of the Department of Taxes and Assessment. Based on requests from individual departments, it estimates the cost of government operations, apportions a sum to each department, and establishes a tax rate. The aldermen make non-binding recommendations on the budget; the comptroller certifies it. The board is given the power to issue stocks and bonds.

1874
Council: The number of aldermen making up the Common Council is set at 22. Six aldermen are elected at large and 16 others are elected as representatives of as many aldermanic districts.

(*continued*)

Changes to the City Charter, 1653–2008 (*Continued*)

Board of Estimate: The mayor and the recorder are removed as supervisors of the County of New York, thereby making the Board of Supervisors and the Board of Aldermen equivalent.

1884

Council: The president of the Board of Aldermen is no longer elected by his fellow aldermen, but rather by the general electorate as an at-large candidate.

1888

Council: One representative from each of the city's 25 assembly districts and a president elected at large now comprise the Board of Aldermen. All serve one-year terms (increased to two years in 1892).

1898

Council: A Municipal Assembly consisting of a Council and a Board of Aldermen replaces the Common Council. The Council includes 28 members elected to four-year terms from 10 council districts (four in Manhattan, three in Brooklyn, and one each in the Bronx, Queens, and Staten Island). Each district elects three members, though Staten Island elects only one. Elected at large, the president serves as the 29th member. The Board of Aldermen includes one member from each of the 60 assembly districts who serves a two-year term. Board members elect a president from among their number. Allowed to attend meetings, the heads of various municipal departments may not vote. This marks the demise of the Common Council.

Mayor: The term of the mayor is increased to four years, though he may not seek reelection. His appointments must transpire within the first six months of his tenure, but they do not require confirmation by the Municipal Assembly. The mayor's hand in financial and franchise issues benefits from a clause mandating a five-sixths majority in the Municipal Assembly to override his veto. The office of comptroller remains elective.

Board of Estimate: The office of borough president is created. Elected to four-year terms, the borough presidents take responsibility for local administration and public works (streets and sewers). Members of the Board of Estimate include the mayor, the comptroller, the corporation counsel, the council president, and the president of the Department of Taxes and Assessments. The board submits an annual city budget to the Municipal Assembly, which may vote only to decrease individual apportionments. However, the mayor may veto such decreases.

1901

Council: The city charter is amended to eliminate the Municipal Assembly in favor of a single Board of Aldermen. Seventy-three aldermen are elected from as many districts to two-year terms. The president of the board is once more elected at large. A majority vote of the board determines the filling of vacancies; the person filling the vacancy must hail from the same party as his predecessor.

Mayor: The term of the mayor is reduced to two years, though he is again eligible for reelection.

Board of Estimate: The Board of Estimate and Apportionment is now made up of the mayor, the comptroller, the president of the Board of Aldermen (each of whom has three votes), and the five borough presidents (each of whom has one vote). The borough presidents' terms of office are reduced to two years but they gain new powers, including those formerly assigned to the Board of Public Improvements, as well as the power to regulate buildings, sewers, and highways. In 1902 the Board of Estimate and Apportionment takes over the duties and the powers of the Board of Public Improvements.

1905

Mayor: The term of the mayor is increased to four years.

Board of Estimate: The Board of Estimate and Apportionment takes the power to grant franchises over from the Board of Aldermen.

1911

Board of Estimate: Empowered to authorize public improvements, the Board of Estimate and Apportionment also may determine the tax revenue needed to pay for them.

1917

Board of Estimate: The Board of Estimate and Apportionment is empowered to regulate buildings and zoning.

1924

Council: An amendment to the state constitution grants the city home rule: its legislature is free from virtually all state interference in the city's governance; pending approval by public referendum, the legislature is empowered to amend the city charter. A new Municipal Assembly is established; the Board of Aldermen constitutes the lower chamber, the Board of Estimate and Apportionment the upper. The Board of Aldermen is comprised of a president elected at large, five borough presidents, and 65 men elected from as many districts for two-year terms.

Board of Estimate: The Board of Estimate and Apportionment is composed of the mayor, the comptroller, the president of the Board of Aldermen, and the five borough presidents.

1938

Council: A smaller City Council replaces the 65-member Municipal Assembly. Council members are elected by a system of proportional representation: each borough elects one councilman for each 75,000 voters. Councilmen serve two-year terms.

Mayor: The office of deputy mayor is created; it is eliminated in 1939.

Board of Estimate: Renamed the Board of Estimate, the Board of Estimate and Apportionment is empowered to veto any legislation of the City Council. The Commissioners of the Sinking Fund surrender their powers to the board, which now represents the most powerful governing body in the city.

1945

Council: The term for councilmen is increased to four years, matching the length of the mayor's term.

1946

Mayor: The office of deputy mayor is restored as a full-time position.

1949

Council: Proportional representation is abolished; subsequently one councilor is elected from each state senate district within the city.

(*continued*)

Changes to the City Charter, 1653–2008 (*Continued*)

1958

Board of Estimate: The voting powers within the Board of Estimate are changed. The mayor, comptroller, and president of the City Council each have four votes; the five borough presidents have two.

1963

Council: A new charter provides for the election of one councilman from each state senate district within the city and two councilmen-at-large from each borough.

Mayor: Empowered to appoint additional deputy mayors, the mayor also may estimate general fund revenues for budget purposes, a responsibility previously within the comptroller's purview. The mayor may also estimate the maximum debt that the city may incur for capital projects.

1975

Board of Estimate: Six amendments to the city charter pass via referendum. Overall they represent an attempt to improve governmental efficiency and to increase oversight of individual agencies, particularly in fiscal matters. The powers of the City Council, the Board of Estimate, and the office of the mayor remain unchanged.

1978

Board of Estimate: The number of votes on the Board of Estimate changes, giving two each to the mayor, the comptroller, and the president of the City Council, and one to each borough president. But the proportions remain the same, so the change is not substantive.

1989

Council: The City Council is expanded from 35 to 51 seats to improve the prospects of racial and ethnic minority candidates. The council receives full power over the municipal budget as well as authority over zoning, land use, and franchises.

Mayor: The mayor controls municipal agencies and approves contracts through them, proposes an annual budget and an estimate of revenues, and appoints seven members to the newly created City Planning Commission.

Board of Estimate: A new City Planning Commission replaces the Board of Estimate, which is eliminated. Empowered to recommend zoning changes, to grant special land-use permits, and to vote on sites chosen for city projects, the City Planning Commission consists of 13 members: seven appointed by the mayor, one by the president of the City Council, and one by each of the borough presidents.

1993

Council: The City Council votes to rename the president of the City Council the public advocate. The public advocate presides over all stated meetings of the City Council. He or she also serves as an *ex officio* member of council committees and thus retains the right to introduce and co-sponsor legislation. Additionally, the outcome of a referendum imposes a two-term limit on City Council members and on citywide elected officials.

1996

Council: Voters reject a City Council proposal to extend term limits.

2008

Mayor: At the urging of Mayor Michael Bloomberg (who would have exhausted his term limit in 2009), the council votes 29 to 22 to extend the term limit to three terms; this occurs after the defeat (22 to 28 with one abstention) of an amendment to submit the issue to public referendum. Legal challenges to the extension fail in federal court; similarly, a proposed law in the New York State legislature fails to pass.

Source: New York City Charter Revision Committee, http://www.nyc.gov/html/charter/html/home/home.shtml

Compiled by Edward T. O'Donnell, Alex Poole

chairman from 1969 to 1981. One of the most influential corporate leaders of his time, he introduced electronic automation and expanded the bank's international activities. Chase helped to bring about several major projects in Manhattan during the late 1960s and early 1970s, including Madison Square Garden, New York Plaza, South Street Seaport, the World Trade Center, and Lincoln Center. In the mid-1970s inflation, the oil embargo, poor real estate investments, and loans to developing countries caused the most severe crisis for the bank since the Depression. Although Chase Manhattan recovered in the 1980s, the city's investment banks then dominated the financial stage. The bank greatly expanded its global operations in these years, opening 30 international branches, 11 representative offices, and 65 subsidiaries in more than 50 countries. A recession in the city's banking sector led to Chemical Bank's acquisition of Chase Manhattan in 1996; the merger, valued at $10.4 billion, created the then-largest bank in the United States. The new entity continued to operate under the name Chase Manhattan Bank until its acquisition of the J. P. Morgan and Company in 2000, when it became JPMorgan Chase and Company.

John Donald Wilson, *The Chase: The Chase Manhattan Bank, N.A., 1945–1985* (Boston: Harvard Business School Press, 1986)

Ann C. Gibson, Tao Tan

Chase National Bank. Commercial bank founded in 1877 at 104 Broadway by John Thompson and named after Salmon P. Chase, secretary of the treasury under President Abraham Lincoln. After Henry W. Cannon became chairman in 1887 it moved its offices to Nassau Street and became an established correspondent bank, providing capital through short-term loans to other banks. Its growth continued under the leadership of A. Barton Hepburn, president from 1904 to 1911 and chairman from 1911 to 1917. The Chase Securities Corporation, formed in 1918, underwrote and managed large securities, which it sold to individuals and institutions from 1927; it was liquidated after the passage of the Glass–Steagall Act (1933), which prohibited commercial banks from underwriting securities. During the 1920s Chase also merged with several important banks in the city, such as the Metropolitan Bank (1851) in 1921, the Mechanics National Bank (1810) in 1926, and Equitable Trust (1902) in 1930. The merger with Equitable Trust made Chase the largest bank in the world and established its connection with the Rockefeller family: John D. Rockefeller, Jr., the largest shareholder in Equitable, eventually owned nearly 4 percent of the stock in Chase. These mergers were largely the work of Albert H. Wiggin, chairman of the bank from 1911 to 1933. His reputation was sullied when investigations by the Senate Banking and Currency Committee in 1933 revealed that he and his colleagues at Chase had made a profit of $10 million during the stock market crash of 1929 by short-selling shares in their own bank. Wiggin was succeeded in 1933 by Rockefeller's brother-in-law Winthrop W. Aldrich. By 1946 Chase had more than $6 billion in assets. John J. McCloy, a businessman and government official who became chairman in 1953, introduced retail banking and engineered the formation in 1955 of Chase Manhattan Bank through a merger with the Manhattan Company, a bank with more than 50 branches in New York City.

Ann C. Gibson

Chase School of Art. Original name of Parsons The New School for Design.

Chatham Square. Two-block square in Chinatown at the intersection of the Bowery, East Broadway, Oliver Street, St. James Place, Park Row, Worth Street, Mott Street, Doyers Street, Division Street, and Catherine Street. Once home to large numbers of saloons and brothels in the Five Points district of nineteenth-century New York City, Chatham Square now features the Kim Lau Memorial Arch, erected in 1962 in memory of the Chinese Americans who died in World War II, and a statue of Lin Ze Xu, a nineteenth-century Chinese anti-drug hero.

Ben Silk

Chayefsky, Paddy [Sidney] (*b* New York City, 29 Jan 1923; *d* New York City, 1 Aug 1981). Playwright. Brought up in the Bronx, he graduated from City College and wrote realistic, intimate dramas for television. The best known of these early works was *Marty* (1953), the story of a lonely butcher in the Bronx who typified the urban working class in the 1950s. His screen adaptation of *Marty* (1955) and his scathing social satires *The Hospital* (1971) and *Network* (1975) won Academy Awards for best screenplay. His stage plays *The Tenth Man* (1959), *Gideon* (1961), and *The Passion of Josef D* (1964) were all produced on Broadway.

Shaun Considine, *Mad as Hell: The Life and Work of Paddy Chayefsky* (New York: Random House, 1994)

Sara J. Steen

Chebra Ansche Chesed. Original name of Temple Ansche Chesed.

Chelsea (i). Neighborhood on the West Side of Manhattan (2000 est. pop. 42,000), bounded to the south by West 14th Street and to the west by the Hudson River. The northern and eastern boundaries correspond roughly to 30th Street and Sixth Avenue. A farm owned by Jacob Somerindyck and his wife covered a parcel bounded by what became 24th Street, Eighth Avenue, and 21st Street, and by the Hudson River, the eastern bank of which lay along what is now 10th Avenue. The farm was bought on 16 August 1750 and named Chelsea by Thomas Clarke, a retired British army captain. It was extended to what is now 19th Street by his daughter Charity and her husband, Benjamin Moore. They opposed a plan of 1807–11 to add streets north of 14th Street and in 1813 deeded the property to their son, Clement Clarke Moore. He eventually became a developer and a faculty member of General Theological Seminary, which in 1825 accepted a site that he donated on Ninth Avenue; he also donated land on 20th Street for St. Peter's Episcopal Church (1836–38). For the next 30 years one-family houses were built by speculators and residents, among them faculty of the seminary, building tradespeople, and merchants. A mansion was built on Ninth Avenue facing the seminary by the merchant and banker Don Alonzo Cushman, who developed other properties including a row on 20th Street that was named for him. The neighborhood expanded to include adjacent properties that had been owned by Robert Ray and Henry Eckford, and an industrial area took form along the Hudson. Ray donated land at Ninth Avenue and 28th Street for the Church of the Holy Apostles (consecrated 1848).

In the 1820s Scottish weavers formed Paisley Place east of Seventh Avenue and south of what is now 17th Street; there were also German, Italian, and British enclaves. Several Baptist, Methodist, and Presbyterian churches were formed, as were the Church of St. Vincent de Paul (by French Catholics in 1840), St. Columba Roman Catholic Church (by Irish Catholics in 1845), and Congregation Emunath Israel (1851). By 1869 a theater district extended along 23rd Street from Sixth Avenue to Eighth Avenue, and Samuel Pike opened an opera house west of Eighth Avenue. This was soon acquired by Jay Gould and Jim Fisk and renamed the Grand Opera House. About 50 people were killed during a riot between Irish Catholics and Irish Protestants on 12 July 1871 at Eighth Avenue and 24th Street. Freight handling and warehousing became important industries in the area, and the area west of 10th Avenue became the site of lumberyards, breweries, factories, rail yards, and piers.

About 1900 the population peaked at 85,000. The opera house flourished into the early twentieth century, and many performers stayed at the Chelsea Hotel. Several motion picture studios opened in the neighborhood after 1907, the most productive of which was Adolph Zukor's Famous Players (1912). The Hellenic Orthodox Community of St. Elefthe-

Chatham Square

rios Church (1918) was the site in 1931 of Athenagoras's enthronement as the archbishop of North and South America; later destroyed by fire, the church was rebuilt in 1976. In 1930 a block dating from the time of Clement Clarke Moore was replaced by London Terrace, a high-rise apartment complex bounded by 24th Street, Ninth Avenue, 23rd Street, and 10th Avenue. A few other high-rise structures were also built, but additional plans for development were abandoned during the Depression. The announcement of the Elliott Housing Project in 1939 marked the beginning of urban renewal, although construction was delayed during World War II when the site was used to house 1000 members of the U.S. Coast Guard. The West 400 (21st–23rd) Block Association—the oldest continuously operating block association in the country—was formed in 1952. About 1960 the Chelsea Houses were built on a parcel bounded by 27th Street, Ninth Avenue, 25th Street, and 10th Avenue, and the Robert Fulton Houses were built on Ninth Avenue between 16th and 19th streets. Penn South (1962), a housing cooperative circumscribed by 29th Street, Eighth Avenue, 23rd Street, and Ninth Avenue, was sponsored by the International Ladies' Garment Workers' Union. The Chelsea Residence was established to allow mentally disabled adults to live independently.

Several piers dating from the 1960s were obsolete at completion because they could not handle containerized cargo. At the same time townhouses were refurbished and the neighborhood became fashionable. In 1973 22 rooming houses (on 22nd and 23rd streets west of Ninth Avenue) were sold by Louise Gard, a major holder of such accommodations, and eventually became the Fitzroy Place cooperative apartments. The neighborhood also became a center for television production. Warehouses were converted into nightclubs and restaurants replaced bodegas. Humanities High School was renamed in 1990 for the civil rights activist and local resident Bayard Rustin. Like much of Manhattan, Chelsea experienced a renaissance during the 1990s and into the early twenty-first century, becoming one of New York City's most sought after addresses.

Samuel White Patterson, *Old Chelsea and Saint Peter's Church: The Centennial History of a New York Parish* (New York: Friebele, 1935); Rhetta M. Arter, *Living in Chelsea: A Study of Human Relations* (New York: New York University Center for Human Relations Studies, 1954); Robert Baral, *Turn West on 23rd: A Toast to New York's Old Chelsea* (New York: Fleet, 1965)

Hilda Regier

Chelsea (ii). Small neighborhood in northwestern Staten Island, bounded to the north by South Avenue, to the east by the William T. Davis Wildlife Refuge, to the south by Meredith Avenue and Victory Boulevard, and to the west by the Arthur Kill. The area was sometimes called Prallstown, after the Prall family that was granted the land in 1675, and during the American Revolution it was facetiously known as Peanutville because the villagers stored nuts for those who rode the ferries between New York and New Brunswick, New Jersey. It consists mostly of open marshland and is little developed apart from a few businesses, among them the large communications complex known as the Teleport. There are also several small pockets of older, one-family houses.

John-Paul Richiuso

Chelsea Hotel. Hotel located at 222 West 23rd Street in Manhattan and opened in 1884 as an apartment building with 40 units. One of the first residential cooperatives in New York City, the building is a 12-story brick structure with iron balconies in an eclectic Victorian style that has French and British influences. Early residents included several artists, among them Charles Melville Dewey (from 1885). The building became a hotel in 1905 and was visited by the actresses Sarah Bernhardt and Lillian Russell and the writers Mark Twain and O. Henry. In the 1930s Thomas Wolfe wrote *You Can't Go Home Again* at the hotel, and the artist John Sloan lived there. It later attracted the writers James T. Farrell, Dylan Thomas, Brendan Behan, and Arthur Miller and the composer Virgil Thomson (from 1940 until his death in 1989). Andy Warhol's film *The Chelsea Girls* (1966) was made there. In the lobby are displayed works by artists associated with the hotel, including Larry Rivers, André François, and Patrick Hughes.

Robert Baral, *Turn West on 23rd: A Toast to New York's Old Chelsea* (New York: Fleet, 1965); Florence Turner, *At the Chelsea* (New York: Harcourt Brace Jovanovich, 1987)

Hilda Regier

Chelsea Market. Mixed-use public space and indoor mall located between Ninth and 11th avenues between 15th and 16th streets. Located in the original National Biscuit Company (Nabisco) headquarters, the complex that was built in the 1890s was renovated in 1997. It is comprised of 22 buildings that total over 2 million square feet (185,800 square meters). The birthplace of the Oreo cookie now houses bakeries, restaurants, and upscale stores on its ground floor and broadcasting companies, including Oxygen Network, Food Network, and NY1, on its higher levels. The opening of Chelsea Market helped speed gentrification in Chelsea and the Meatpacking District at the end of the twentieth century. With the opening of the High Line in 2009, the market became one of the focal points of the elevated park, which runs through the upper floors of the main building.

Anne Epstein

Chelsea Market, 2009

Chelsea Piers. Manhattan piers on the Hudson River between Little West 12th and West 23rd streets completed in 1910 by the firm Warren and Wetmore. They were the primary piers for the White Star and Cunard lines and served as a major embarkation point for troops and materiel during World War I and World War II. The piers were involved in critical events surrounding the RMS *Titanic* and RMS *Lusitania* disasters: the *Titanic* was

Chelsea Piers, 1909

Chelsea Piers, 2009

en route to pier 59 when it sank, and survivors were dropped off at White Star pier 54 by the RMS *Carpathia* on 18 April 1912. The *Lusitania* left Cunard pier 54 on 1 May 1915 before being torpedoed. By the 1950s the piers were primarily used for cargo and gradually fell into disuse. By the 1990s five of the original piers had been demolished or destroyed by fire, and in 1994 the remaining four were converted into the Chelsea Piers Sports and Entertainment Complex, which houses new sports facilities, restaurants, a marina, and film studios.

Caleb Smith

Chemical Bank. Commercial bank formed in 1824 as a subsidiary of the New York Chemical Manufacturing Company, a maker of drugs and chemicals in Greenwich Village. It was situated first at 216 Broadway, opposite St. Paul's Church, well north of most of the 12 banks then operating in the city, which were clustered around Wall Street. Chemical owed much of its early success to its second president, John Mason, a leading merchant and founder of the New York and Harlem Railroad. Mason served the bank from 1831 until his death in 1839 and reduced its reliance on chemical manufacturing. After Mason's death the bank was run successively until 1878 by his cousins by marriage, Isaac Jones and John Jones, who disbanded the chemical works and renewed the bank's charter in 1844. In the following year the bank moved to large headquarters at 270 Broadway at Chambers Street. The bank was instrumental in 1853 in forming the New York Clearing House, the first such organization in the United States. During the panic of 1857 it acquired the nickname "old bullion" for its policy of paying specie on demand. As the bank's reputation grew during the nineteenth century, the value of its stock reached $425 a share in 1860 and $1500 a share in 1875, the highest of any bank based in New York City.

During the early twentieth century Chemical Bank continued to expand. It bought the Citizens National Bank in 1920 and opened its first branch office in 1923, at Fifth Avenue and 29th Street. The first international office opened in London in 1929, and in the same year the bank converted to a state charter that enabled it to merge with the United States Mortgage Trust Company. Later, Chemical acquired more than a dozen banks in New York City, including the Corn Exchange Bank Trust Company in 1954, from which it gained many additional branches; the New York Trust in 1959, operator of an extensive wholesale banking network; and Security National Bank in 1975, a leading bank on Long Island. It was one of the founding members in 1985 of the New York Cash Exchange (NYCE), an automated teller network that radically transformed consumer banking, and in 1991 it merged with Manufacturers Hanover Trust to create the second-largest bank in the United States. In 1996 Chemical Bank acquired Chase Manhattan Bank, but retained Chase's name for the combined entity until the acquisition of J. P. Morgan and Company in 2000, when it became JP Morgan Chase and Company.

History of the Chemical Bank, 1823–1913 (New York: privately printed, 1913)

Stephen Weinstein

chemicals. As early as 1626 the chief commercial agent of the Dutch West India Company remarked on the potential in New Amsterdam for processing lime, used in the manufacture of mortar and glass. Although before 1700 most chemicals were produced and used within private households, entrepreneurs continued to explore opportunities for commercial mineral refinement. Large naval stores used tar oil and pitch, and a number of small firms tanned hides; produced paints, dyes, and varnishes; refined sugar; made soap and candles; and operated breweries and distilleries. The noxious odors and chemical dangers that accompanied the development of the industry drove out many residents, and others demanded regulation within the city limits: tar pits were banned in 1676, as were lime-burning pits and rum distilleries in 1703. By the early eighteenth century factories produced glass, dyes, paper, potash, and linseed oil, and the city became a leading center of sugar refining, with large factories owned by John van Cortlandt, William Rhinelander, Peter Livingston, and Nicholas Bayard (who in 1730 opened a multistory refinery on Wall Street between William and Nassau streets). Tanning was centered on Beekman's Swamp; tanneries and starch factories, breweries, tar houses, furnaces, and potteries were on the shores of the Collect. In 1744 tanning and water pits for the dressing of leather were banned from the city. The Society for the Promotion of Arts, Agriculture, and Economy was formed in 1766, and professorships in chemistry were established at King's College (now Columbia University) in 1767 and 1792.

The manufacture of fine chemicals dates to 1793 when the Schieffelin family began to mix drugs at a shop on Pearl Street; the firm remained an important manufacturer of pharmaceuticals into the twentieth century. In 1797 restrictions were placed on the manufacture of glue, soap, and tallow. With the development of coal and petroleum destructive distillation (slow cooking in homemade ground kilns or in kettles), the production of heavy chemicals increased markedly. From 1823 alums and acids were manufactured by the New York Chemical Manufacturing Company (a forerunner of Chemical Bank); Martin Kalbfleisch opened a color works in Harlem in 1835 and later diversified into sulfuric acid, sulfates, mineral acids, and salt production at factories in Harlem and Brooklyn. New York City had 3387 chemical factories in 1850, and at the end of the century it was a leading producer of heavy industrial chemicals such as acids, bleaches, soda, potashes, alums, coal-tar products, fertilizers, wood products, and cyanide; one of few areas in which it could not compete was dyemaking, which was dominated by German concerns. Chemical and paint factories were clustered along the East River in Brooklyn and its tributary Newtown Creek and near abattoirs, metal refineries, and other nuisance industries. But the industry was soon compelled to move away from heavily populated neighborhoods, first to upper Manhattan and then to outlying areas such as Hunts Point and Hudson County, New Jersey, where costs were low, restrictions on industry few, waterways deeper than Newtown Creek, riverbanks less crowded than those of the East River, and settlements sparser than those of lower Manhattan.

By the early twentieth century Manhattan had 1350 chemical plants that produced a quarter of the nation's heavy chemicals; the average plant employed 52 workers, and 11 plants employed more than 1000. Rapid growth occurred in the production of such heavy chemicals as soda acids, ammonia, potash bleaching compounds, and compressed and liquefied gases. Procter and Gamble erected a large facility at Port Ivory on Staten Island in 1907. Most of the fertilizer manufacturers moved out of Manhattan and into New Jersey. In 1922 only one in 10 chemical workers in the city worked below 59th Street in 29 small plants; Brooklyn and Queens had 43 large plants. After World War II many chemical manufacturers set up facilities around Newark and Raritan bays and along their linking waterways. At the same time petrochemical plastics became a major product for giant firms like Union Carbide and the Allied Chemical and Dye Corporation. Thirty-seven factories produced plastics in 1947, and it was partly because of plastics manufacturing that even as the number of chemical firms based in the city continued to decline, their total output increased: in 1947 there were 1696 manufacturers in the metropolitan area, in 1963 there were 986, with a value added of $794.3 million, and in 1977 there were 685, with a value added of $1.6 billion.

Several leading chemical firms retained corporate headquarters in Manhattan during the 1970s, including makers of industrial products (Air Reduction, Allied Chemical, Celanese, National Distillers and Chemical, NL Industries, Texas Gulf Sulphur, and W. R. Grace) and of consumer products (American Home Products, Bristol–Myers, Colgate–Palmolive, and Pfizer). But only four chemical firms remained in the city in the early twenty-first century: W. R. Grace (food and agricultural products, industrial chemicals, videotapes, sealing compounds, plastic adhesives, paper, oil and gas field machinery, business research, and software), Quantum Chemical (propane, butane, and other gases; soaps and detergents; plastics and resins; polypropylene sheet and film; polyethylene and polypropylene resins; and industrial inorganic materials), Witco Chemical (cleaning and polishing preparations, organic plasticizers, plastics and resins, petroleum products, rubberized fabrics, filtering clays, and oils and greases), and Inspiration Resources (fertilizers and agricultural chemicals, herbicides and insecticides, and anhydrous ammonia).

C. A. Browne, *The Story of Chemistry in Old New York* (New York: American Chemical Society, 1935)

See also Shoes, boots, and leather and Soap and toiletries.

David B. Sicilia

Chemists' Club. Organization formed on 29 November 1898 to promote the interests of chemists. The first offices were at 108 West 55th Street. Under the leadership of its first president, C. F. Chandler, the club began assembling a library. By 1901 there were 140 resident and 119 nonresident members. With financial assistance from its president, Morris Loeb, the club purchased new quarters at 50–54 East 41st Street in 1909 and moved there in 1911. As chemical firms after World War I moved to midtown the club's membership greatly expanded and came to include business leaders as well as scientists. In the early twenty-first century the Chemists' Club had 2500 members and a staff of 90 was located at 3 West 51st Street.

Elizabeth J. Kramer

Cherry Lane Theatre. Off-Broadway theater. Located at 38 Commerce Street in Greenwich Village, it is New York City's oldest continuously running Off-Broadway theater. The building had served as a brewery, tobacco warehouse, and box factory prior to its conversion to a 250-seat theater in 1924 by Edna St. Vincent Millay and the Provincetown Players. In the 1960s the theater presented works by Samuel Beckett, Edward Albee, Eugene Ionesco, and Harold Pinter. Cherry Lane premiered Beckett's *Happy Days* in 1961 and Amiri Baraka's (then known as LeRoi Jones) *Dutchman* in 1964. Play-development programs begun by the theater in the late 1990s sought to develop the work of black and female playwrights in particular. In 1998 the theater opened a 60-seat black-box theater space dedicated to staging new works by Americans.

Sarah Wansley

Chesebrough–Pond's. Firm of cosmetics manufacturers. It was formed on Sullivan Street in Brooklyn in 1870 as the Chesebrough Manufacturing Company by Robert A. Chesebrough (1837–1933), who developed Vaseline petroleum jelly in the early 1850s in his oil refinery on Delevan Street. The firm was immediately successful and in the early 1880s became part of the Standard Oil trust, opened several branches in Europe, and built headquarters on State Street in Manhattan, where it remained for the next 75 years. After the breakup of Standard Oil in 1911, the firm became independent again. In 1955 it merged with Pond's Extract Company to become Chesebrough–Pond's and opened headquarters on Lexington Avenue. During the following decades the firm bought many cosmetics, perfume, and toiletry companies. Although its main offices were moved out of the city in 1972, many of its subsidiaries remained there. Unilever United States bought Chesebrough–Pond's in 1987.

James Bradley

chess. The first national chess tournament in the United States, the First American Chess Congress, was held in New York City in 1857. The tournament was won by Paul Morphy, a 20-year-old prodigy from New Orleans who the following year proved himself the best player in the world by defeating European masters during a Continental tour (in Paris he played blindfolded against eight players, winning against six and drawing with two). His stunning victories popularized the game in the United States, and he was acclaimed on his return to New York City in 1859. He later showed antipathy toward the game, and after returning to New Orleans in 1860 he never again played in public. Morphy's passage through New York City invigorated a chess community that became the center of American chess for a century, attracting the nation's strongest players and many prominent émigrés, among them the next three world champions: Wilhelm Steinitz (*b* Prague, 1836), Emmanuel Lasker (*b* Berlinchen, Germany [now Barlinek, Poland], 1868), and José (Raúl)

A street game of chess, 2009

Capablanca (*b* Havana, 1888). All took up residence in New York City, although Lasker did so late in life (1937), and Capablanca did so unofficially, first as a student at Columbia University and later as a nominal member of the Cuban diplomatic service. Steinitz, recognized as the world's best player when he moved to New York City in 1883, became the first official world champion in 1886 by defeating Johannes Zukertort of Germany in a match played in New York City, St. Louis, and New Orleans.

Tournaments held in New York City in 1924 (won by Lasker) and 1927 (won by Capablanca) were probably the most important international competitions ever held in the United States. The high point of American chess was the 1930s, during which the United States won the world team championships known as the Chess Olympiads four consecutive times (1931, 1933, 1935, and 1937). Competition in the United States at the time was organized primarily through chess clubs, the most influential of which were in New York City and belonged to the Metropolitan Chess League. An annual match between the Manhattan Chess Club (uptown) and the Marshall Chess Club (downtown) in which the strongest players in the country took part was the last and most important event of the season. All members of the four teams that won the Chess Olympiads were drawn from these two clubs: Reuben Fine, Samuel Reshevsky, Frank J. Marshall, Arthur Dake, Isaac Kashdan, Israel Horowitz, and Herman Steiner. After World War II the United States no longer dominated international chess, but the clubs in New York City continued to produce such prominent players as Larry Evans, William Lombardy, Robert Byrne, Donald Byrne, and most notably Bobby Fischer. After winning the World Championship in 1972 Fischer withdrew from public competition for two decades, eerily recalling the example of Morphy a century earlier. The 1960s and 1970s saw the development of a strong national chess federation sanctioning open tournaments throughout the country. The chess clubs lost their role as the leading organizers of the game, although the Manhattan and Marshall clubs remained exceptionally active and the city continued to attract leading players, both Americans and émigrés (especially from Russia and eastern Europe). The World Chess Federation chose New York City as the site for the first half of the World Championship Match of 1990, making it the fifth such event held there (more than in any other city except Moscow). In the twenty-first century chess in New York City flourishes not only at the grandmaster level but also in informal settings outdoors, particularly in Washington Square Park. Matches there are often accompanied by wagering, and a few enterprising players are able to make a living at their game. In Bryant Park the New York Chess and Backgammon Club rents out chess sets by the hour.

David Lawson, *Paul Morphy, the Pride and Sorrow of Chess* (New York: McKay, 1976); Edward G. Winter, ed., *World Chess Champions* (Elmsford, N.Y.: Pergamon, 1981); David Hooper and Kenneth Whyld, *The Oxford Companion to Chess* (New York: Oxford University Press, 1984)

James Glass

Chickering Hall. Concert hall opened by the piano makers of the same name in November 1875 at the northwest corner of Fifth Avenue and 18th Street. It was intended to compete with Steinway Hall on East 14th Street, and became well known in 1875 when Hans von Bülow played a series of piano recitals there. As fashionable society moved uptown the hall suffered from its location, and in 1893 the building was remodeled into retail stores.

Marc Ferris

child labor. Child labor reformers organized on a large scale during the late nineteenth century. In 1902–3 the New York Child Labor Committee was formed by settlement-house workers and reformers such as George Alger. Backed by wealthy business leaders and soon also by organized labor, scholars, and the clergy, the organization had on its staff such reformers as George Hall and Jeanie Minor. To gain the support of the public, reformers needed to destroy the prevailing notions that children required only a simple education and could build a lifetime career on work done in childhood. Another large obstacle was the esteem held for children who supported poor or ailing parents. The committee employed innovative techniques in attacking these attitudes. It conducted investigations establishing the detriment of work to children and then presented its findings to the public in flyers, leaflets, and photographs showing that child workers were defenseless, exploited, robbed of their childhood and often their lives, and limited in adulthood. Eventually persuaded of the moral and economic evil of child labor, the public supported legislative campaigns that focused on changing the law, and the child labor movement became one of the most sustained and widely supported in the city. Although far from complete, reform efforts had considerable success between 1903 and the 1930s. The age at which children could leave school was raised from 14 to 16 in 1935, the number of hours they could work daily and weekly was steadily reduced, and children were barred from working at night and under dangerous conditions. The laws also broadened in scope to include work not only in factories but also in stores, canneries, the home, and the street.

Adequate enforcement was difficult to achieve, and with regard to homework it was nearly impossible. There were not enough inspectors, the laws were often vague and contained loopholes, and enforcement was resisted by parents, employers, and even some public-school officials seeking to reduce class size and remove disruptive students. The situation gradually improved. Machines designed for semiskilled adults took over the work previously assigned to children, and during the Depression many children lost their jobs to adults. Enforcement of existing laws became more stringent. In the late 1930s homework was reduced after it was barred in many industries by the federal government, which also banned child labor under the age of 16 and established a minimum wage. Violations

Jacob A. Riis, In a Sweatshop *(ca 1890), showing a 12-year-old boy pulling basting threads*

of child labor laws in New York City increased after federal restrictions on homework were eased (while continued in the garment industry).

Jeremy Felt, *Hostages of Fortune: Child Labor Reform in New York State* (Syracuse, N.Y.: Syracuse University Press, 1965); Hugh Hindman, *Child Labor: An American History* (Armonk, N.Y.: M. E. Sharpe, 2002)

Irwin Yellowitz

Children's Aid Society. Philanthropic organization formed in 1853 by Charles Loring Brace. It was one of the first agencies of its kind in the United States and became well known for opening lodging houses (five for boys and one for girls) in the poorest districts of New York City. A night's lodging cost 10 cents and a meal cost 7 cents. The society also operated 21 industrial schools (six of them associated with lodging houses) where carpentry, woodworking, printing, dressmaking, laundry work, and typewriting were taught at no charge. Eventually it opened kindergartens, free reading rooms, night schools, baths, gymnasiums, and seaside vacation houses, as well as a convalescent home for sick children. It also found foster homes for about 90,000 children in Michigan, Iowa, Illinois, and Wisconsin. Although a few of the children were bound to trades, most were placed with farm families, on the assumption that farmers' homes were the best place to bring up homeless orphans or outcast children. (Most children were eventually adopted by their foster families.) In the 1890s the society organized a farm school in suburban Westchester County to give older boys training in agriculture before they were sent to the farms. At his death in 1890 Brace was succeeded by his son Charles Loring Brace, Jr.; together their tenures amounted to 75 years, during which they raised $25 million for the society.

Charles Loring Brace, *The Dangerous Classes of New York and Twenty Years' Work among Them* (New York: Wynkoop and Hallenbeck, 1872); *Children's Aid Society of New York: Its History, Plan and Results* (New York: Children's Aid Society, 1893); *The Crusade for Children: A Review of Child Life in New York during 75 Years, 1853–1928* (New York: Children's Aid Society, 1928)

Jane Allen

Jacob A. Riis, Children's Aid Society: Going West *(ca 1890). The last group of boys sponsored by Mrs. John Jacob Astor, posing in front the offices of the Children's Aid Society at 24 St. Mark's Place*

children's book publishing. Until the early nineteenth century the only children's books produced in New York City were reprints of English works drawn from the popular publications of John Newbery. Amusing but moralistic fare devised from the educational precepts of John Locke was issued for a liberal Anglican audience by Hugh Gaine of Hanover Square and William Durell of Queen Street, his chief successor. The first publisher in the city to specialize in children's books was Samuel Wood, who began operations on Pearl Street in 1806 and published *Cries of New York* (1808), which gave children a glimpse of city life. About this time engraving techniques were introduced by Alexander Anderson: these replaced clumsy woodcut and copper-plate engraving as the primary means of producing illustrations and transformed the design of children's books. Other technological advances also fostered the growth of children's literature. The country's first stereotyping plant was opened in the city by David Bruce, allowing publishers to reissue popular works without maintaining extensive supplies of type. In 1839 Joseph A. Adams, a pupil of Alexander Anderson, invented a process to render multiple copies from a copper plate using engraved woodblocks. This process proved invaluable in augmenting a publisher's stock of illustrations.

During the 1840s New York City became the center of the book trade. A distinctly American style emerged in the work of F. O. C. Darley, who abandoned the custom of copying English conventions and based his style on observations of American life. Some of his best-known illustrations were those for "The Night before Christmas" (1862) by Clement Clarke Moore depicting Santa Claus in a rural landscape like those described by Washington Irving; his work became a model for other American illustrators. About the time of the Civil War the firm of R. Hoe and Company in the city introduced the power-driven press, which increased the profitability of longer prose works. The firms of James Harper, Charles Scribner's Sons, G. P. Putnam's Sons, and D. Appleton soon took advantage of this form of technology to publish children's stories by distinguished writers of mature fiction, often after the stories had been serialized in such popular children's periodicals as *St. Nicholas Magazine.* Unable to compete, many small specialty publishers suffered.

"A Misunderstanding," by Margaret Johnson, in St Nicholas's Baby World, *1884*

One such publisher, McLoughlin Brothers on Beekman Street, made important advances in illustration by adapting several color printing processes. Between 1860 and 1900 the firm introduced chromoxylography, chromolithography, and photo-engraving and helped to make popular a kind of picture book that led to other innovations during the early twentieth century. Another important publisher of children's books about the turn of the century was Grosset and Dunlap, formed in 1898.

Between 1916 and 1955 publishers in the city produced about 74 percent of the country's children's books, and their offerings often reflected a local bias. By 1926 children's departments had been set up by Harper and Brothers, Macmillan, Doubleday, Longman, E. P. Dutton, and Harcourt Brace. Output expanded, and illustrations became more sophisticated as the photo-offset process simplified color printing and refined its palette. Advanced technology and the artistic guidance of such astute editors as Louise Seaman (Bechtel) at Macmillan and May Massee at Doubleday led to the publication of stunning picture books. Other publishers followed suit, creating new openings for talented female editors and artists, including Ursula Nordstrom, director of the children's department at Harper from 1940 to 1973. In 1942 Simon and Schuster introduced a line of storybooks called Golden Books. They were produced by leading writers and artists under the direction of Albert Rice Leventhal and sold for 25 cents each; the books attained great popularity.

Children's book publishing in the city continued to flourish after World War II. A number of classic postwar children's books were deeply associated with the city, including *Stuart Little* by E. B. White, published by Harper in 1945, and Eloise, by Kay Thompson, published by Simon and Schuster in 1955, although by the early twenty-first century the partiality toward New York City had given way to a broader outlook.

Jane Bingham and Grayce Scholt, *Fifteen Centuries of Children's Literature: An Annotated Chronology of British and American Works* (Westport, Conn.: Greenwood, 1980)

See also Book publishing.

Michael Joseph

Children's Museum. See Brooklyn Children's Museum.

Children's Television Workshop. Former name of Sesame Workshop.

Childs. Restaurant chain founded in 1889 by William and Samuel Childs. Their original self-service restaurant, on Cortlandt Street, catered mainly to office workers. The early expansion of the chain was aided by the pressure of the temperance movement against taverns. By 1916 there were more than 40 outlets, typically with white-tile walls to emphasize cleanliness and discourage loitering, a decor that was imitated by competitors. Childs later operated more expensive restaurants with waitress service. The flagship of the chain, opened in 1925, was at 604 Fifth Avenue. In 1961 the chain was acquired by the Riese Organization, which converted the remaining Childs restaurants into fast-food outlets. In 2003 the building on Coney Island that once housed one of the most prized Childs restaurants received landmark status from the city.

Gilbert Tauber

Childs, Richard S(pencer) (*b* Manchester, Conn., 24 May 1882; *d* Ottawa, Ont., 26 Sept 1978). Businessman and reformer. He was the son of the founder of the Bon Ami Company, a soap manufacturer that produces hypoallergenic soap from feldspar and tallow. His father founded the company in 1886 with the J. T. Robertson Soap Company. In 1904 Richard joined the Erickson Company, an advertising firm owned by one of his father's friends. In 1911 he began to work for his father's company, Bon Ami. In 1910 he formed the Short Ballot Organization with Woodrow Wilson (offices at 383 Fourth Avenue), which sought to reduce the number of elective offices at the state, county, and municipal levels. Childs believed that by reducing the number of elected offices, reformers could weed out corruption and increase the efficiency of the government; this would allow the few officials important enough to be elected to have cooperative and streamlined administrations, much in the manner that the president chooses his cabinet. These beliefs were likely inspired by his managerial experience in business, trying to streamline government like a company and use highly technically trained administrative experts. Childs promoted the Short Ballot through magazines like *McClure's, Collier's,* and *Everybody's.* In response to Childs's efforts toward simplifying local government, the city appointed a citywide medical examiner in 1918 and a citywide sheriff and register in 1942. Childs was the president of the City Club of New York (1926–38) and chairman of Citizens Union (1941–50). He wrote *Short Ballot Principles* (1911) and *Civic Victories: The Story of an Unfinished Revolution* (1952).

Childs

Bernard Hirschhorn, *Democracy Reformer: Richard Spencer Childs and His Fight for Better Government* (Westport, Conn.: Greenwood Press, 1997)

Bernard Hirschhorn

child welfare. During the eighteenth and nineteenth centuries New York City made innovative efforts to help neglected and delinquent children. The New York Poorhouse, opened in 1736, was the first public institution in the city to provide care for children, who at the time constituted a large number of those living in almshouses. In 1797 concern for the quality of care in poorhouses led to the formation of the New York City Ladies' Society for the Relief of Poor Widows with Small Children, a volunteer child-care agency. Reorganized as the Orphan Asylum Society, it established the New York Orphan Asylum (1807–19), where children received shelter until they were old enough to be apprenticed. In 1825 efforts to separate juvenile offenders from adult criminals in Bellevue Prison led to the opening of the nation's first and best-known juvenile reformatory, the House of Refuge. Although its founders, John Griscom and Thomas Eddy, envisioned a progressive, rehabilitative institution, a harsh penal attitude was soon assumed toward the juvenile inmates. Other institutions for needy children that were supported by private citizens in New York City included the Catholic Orphan Asylum, the Leake and Watts Orphan Asylum (opened in 1830–31), and the Colored Orphan Asylum (1836–63). Children and adults were housed together until nurseries opened on Randalls Island in 1848.

Having led the movement toward placing children in institutions, New York City was also a leader in removing them from congregate care and placing them in foster homes. The New York Juvenile Asylum (1851–60) sheltered children for as long as five years before placing them with families. The most important large-scale attempt to remove children from congregate institutions was that of the Children's Aid Society (1853), under the direction of Charles Loring Brace, which removed impoverished children from the streets and placed them in foster homes in the western United States. Although the society and other groups like it were nonsectarian, their work was perceived by some as a Protestant attempt to convert young Catholic and Jewish children. It was partly in response to this perception that the Hebrew Benevolent Society (1860) and the New York Catholic Protectory (1863) were incorporated. The New York Society for the Prevention of Cruelty to Children (1874) also protected children from homes that it deemed improper. Although private, it enjoyed the status of a law-enforcement agency and came to exercise a powerful influence in New York City. Efforts to remove children from the almshouse altogether culminated in the Children's Law (1875), which prohibited the retention of children between three and 16 years of age in almshouses throughout the state. The first law of its kind in the country, it led to the abolition of the nurseries on Randalls Island and contributed to the proliferation of private child-care agencies in the late nineteenth century. A direct outgrowth of the child protection movement was the establishment in New York City of the first children's court in the state (1900); reorganized as an independent tribunal by the New York City Children's Court Act (1924), it had the power to place neglected and delinquent children on probation and to refer them to diagnostic and treatment facilities.

In the early twentieth century New York City established a system under which child-care services were performed by private agencies under contract to the city. The city also experimented with its own foster home and adoption service, the Children's Home Bureau (1916), under the auspices of the Department of Public Charities. This service failed to take hold and was discontinued in 1917 because of a prevailing belief that children were better served by private organizations. The government again took on a role in institutional and foster care when private efforts diminished during the Depression and World War II: the Works Progress Administration opened 27 nursery schools in New York City from 1933 to 1943, which later came under the control of local child-welfare agencies. The Racial Discrimination Amendment (1942) and the more stringent Brown–Isaacs Law (1952) forbade racial discrimination in agencies receiving municipal funds.

New York City continued to strengthen its child-care system during the mid-twentieth century. The Citizen's Committee for Children of New York was organized in 1944 to investigate inadequate care for children whose mothers worked in war industries, and day care in the city continued to be characterized by effectiveness and activism. Although state aid to day care in the city ceased in 1947, 97 centers were opened by the Day Care Council of New York City (1948), a nationally recognized body that helped focus attention on day care and in 1961 gained the support of President John F. Kennedy. In the twenty-first century New York City was a nationally acknowledged leader in such early childhood education programs as Project Giant Step.

David M. Schneider and Albert Deutsch, *The History of Public Welfare in New York State*, vol. 2, *1867–1940* (Chicago: University of Chicago Press, 1941); Merril Sobie, *The Creation of Juvenile Justice: A History of New York's Children's Laws* (Albany, N.Y.: New York Bar Foundation, 1987)

Mary McDonald

China Institute in America. Nonprofit educational institution focused on the understanding and appreciation of traditional and contemporary Chinese civilization, language, and culture. Founded in 1926 by American and Chinese educators John Dewey, Hu Shih, Paul Monroe, and Kuo Ping Wen, it was located at 2 West 45th Street until it moved to its current location at 125 East 65th Street in 1944. Since 1933 the institute has offered courses on Chinese civilization, language, and culture, in addition to sponsoring American and Chinese scholarship programs. In 2005 it established the Confucius Institute, which prepares and accredits Mandarin teachers to teach in New York City schools.

Stephanie Miller

Chinatown. Neighborhood on the Lower East Side of Manhattan, covering about 35 blocks and bounded to the north by Kenmare and Delancey streets, to the east by Allen

Food market in Chinatown, 1992

Chinatown, 2009

Street, to the south by East and Worth streets, and to the west by Broadway. The first Chinese in New York City were mostly sailors and merchants working in trade between China and the United States from 1784 to 1850; usually they remained only briefly in the city, but some took English names and married local women, and by 1850 there was a Chinese American enclave. According to the state census of 1855, the first documented Chinese immigrant in New York City was a man who had taken the name William Brown and married an Irish woman after moving to the city in 1825. By 1859 the *New York Times* estimated that there were 150 Chinese men living in lower Manhattan, many of whom found work as sailors, cooks, candy and cigar vendors, and operators of boardinghouses catering to Asian sailors. In the 1870s the population of the neighborhood grew to more than 2000, spurred by a violent anti-Chinese movement in the West and the completion of the transcontinental railroad (1862–69).

Prospective Chinese immigrants were prevented from settling in the United States and becoming American citizens by the Chinese Exclusion Act (1882). Immigration laws also prevented most men from having their wives and families join them; as a result, the neighborhood became known as the "bachelor society," and the population remained under 4000 until World War II. Chinatown began as a tiny enclave bounded by Pell and Doyer streets and including the lower portion of Mott Street. Chinese immigrants could engage in only a few kinds of business, including hand laundries, which required a small initial investment and minimal knowledge of English and in which there was no competition from other ethnic groups. About the 1890s entrepreneurs opened restaurants in the neighborhood to attract tourists; soon there were also gift shops and Buddhist temples. For aid and the resolution of disputes, residents turned to traditional Chinese organizations, many of which were respectable; some fraternal ones known as tongs became embroiled in disputes over membership and gambling that sometimes became violent. In the early years of the twentieth century a series of battles between tongs became known by outsiders as the "tong wars."

After China and the United States became allies in World War II, President Franklin D. Roosevelt signed a measure in 1943 repealing the Chinese exclusion acts, and Chinese immigrants were granted the right to become citizens. At the same time a quota for Chinese immigration was set at 105 persons a year, and Chinatown continued to grow slowly. The neighborhood was seen as a community of hardworking people who respected law and family, and outsiders called it the "gilded ghetto" and its population the "model minority." By 1965 the neighborhood occupied seven blocks and had a population of 20,000 that was still disproportionately male. During the same year legislation was introduced to abolish the system of immigration quotas based on national origin, and after 1 July 1968, 20,000 Chinese immigrants a year were allowed to enter the United States. With the rapid growth of the Chinese community after 1965 and the easing of prejudices that had kept its housing patterns limited, Chinatown expanded beyond its traditional boundaries, absorbing much of Little Italy and parts of the Lower East Side, and becoming the most populous Chinese community in the western hemisphere. But over time the neighborhood lost its status as the only center of the Chinese population in New York City, as Chinese settlements took root in Elmhurst, Flushing, Sunset Park, and Bay Ridge. By the 1980s only about 30 percent of all Chinese in the city lived in Chinatown. At the same time the neighborhood became ethnically more diverse: although more than three-quarters of all immigrants who settled in Chinatown in the 1980s were Chinese, there were also enclaves of immigrants from Bangladesh, Burma, Vietnam, the Philippines, and Malaysia, as well as a Latin American population that was largely Dominican and Puerto Rican.

In the early twenty-first century Manhattan's Chinatown was the most populous and densely settled Chinese community in the nation, and the third largest in area. As of 2000, at least 150,000 ethnic Chinese inhabited the neighborhood. After the 9/11 attacks, given Chinatown's proximity to the afflicted area, business and tourism were temporarily stunted in the neighborhood. Much of the economy was underground, or was otherwise found in the grocery, jewelry, and technology industries; there was also a burgeoning bus line industry, aptly named the "Chinatown bus" lines, that was made up of buses from several companies that all departed from Canal Street. As high-end real estate in Manhattan continued to move downtown, Chinatown became the site of the construction of several luxury condominiums, although the vast majority of the population lived in either traditional tenement houses or in the subsidized housing projects in the area.

Peter Kwong, *The New Chinatown* (New York: Hill and Wang, 1987)

Charlie Chin, Cecilia Magnusson

Chinese. Chinese sailors and peddlers lived in New York City as early as the 1820s and 1830s, and in the 1850s about 150 sailors lived in lower Manhattan. Most planned to return to China after making a fortune, but some wanted to remain in the United States. In 1868 at least 10 Chinese in Manhattan had American citizenship. By the 1860s and 1870s, Chinese became targets of racism promoted by some politicians and union organizers. Mutual aid and protection societies known as *fang,* or *fong* ("house"), were organized according to kinship and geographical origin; they provided temporary lodging and financial assistance and sponsored social events, cultural festivals, and funerals. One of the first was Gongsi Fang, which remained an important institution well into the 1940s. During the 1870s many miners and railroad workers moved east to escape anti-Chinese agitation in the West, and their neighborhood in New York City grew as they settled along Pell, Mott, Bayard, Doyer, and Canal streets and later on Chatham Square; the area was soon known as Chinatown. The first grocery in the neighborhood was probably the Wo Kee store, opened in 1872 at 34 Mott Street and soon

Stafford M. Northcote, Hi Hee Chinese Theater *(1900)*

followed by other groceries and by vegetable stands and fish markets. About 300 Chinese were sent from San Francisco by James B. Harvey to replace militant Irish women employed in his Passaic Steam Laundry in Belleville, New Jersey. By the early 1880s all the Chinese workers were discharged, and many of them moved to Manhattan to open hand laundries. Relatives joined them from the Far West, Hong Kong, and China. Chinese scattered throughout the city, often in quarters attached to hand laundries, and Chinatown became the headquarters for a wide range of organizations.

According to the census of 1890 there were 2048 Chinese in the city in the 1880s; the true figure was probably between 8000 and 10,000, as immigrants often remained in New York City only temporarily. Before the 1940s most Chinese immigrants in the city were from Guangdong (Canton) and largely preserved their cultural traditions and ethnic identity. They adhered to traditional ethical principles, among them Confucian ideals of filial piety, loyalty, righteousness, and reciprocity, and celebrated important festivals, including the lunar New Year, Qing Ming (Tomb-Sweeping Day), and Mid-Autumn. Dragon and lion dancing took place on every proper occasion. Deities in Chinese popular religion were worshipped in temples, or "joss houses" (two were built in the 1880s), and ancestor shrines were erected. A Cantonese theater opened and newsstands sold Chinese-language newspapers that provided news from the homeland. Anti-Chinese sentiment intensified during the late nineteenth century, forcing Chinese to move to Chinatown to escape discrimination. Tourism nonetheless was an important source of income for the community by the 1880s. Excluded from most occupations except those requiring cheap labor, many Chinese ran "chop suey" restaurants, which like laundries required little capital or knowledge of English. They also exploited American curiosity about Chinese culture aroused by the visit to New York City in 1896 of a high-ranking Chinese official, Li Hongzhang (Hung-Chang), to promote the chop suey business. Stores in Chinatown imported food, clothing, and other goods from China, and souvenir shops offered items made with Chinese silk and porcelain.

Under the Chinese exclusion acts passed by the U.S. Congress during the late nineteenth and the early twentieth centuries, Chinese immigrants were barred from naturalization, becoming the first ethnic group to be excluded from the United States. Subsequently, they had ambiguous status and were subject to intimidation and political, social, and economic exploitation, especially if they had entered the country illegally. Clan associations of persons bearing the same surnames sponsored welfare programs and were usually dominated by wealthy merchants. Several dating from 1887 became some of the largest: Ng's Association, Loong Kung Kong Saw (formed by Liu, Guan, and Zhang), and Lee's Family Association. Organizations known as *hui guan,* or *gong suo* ("meeting halls"), were larger than clan associations and fang and were organized by persons from the same district in China. They provided medical services, cared for the elderly and the poor, built cemeteries, shipped the remains of deceased members to China, and built temples in which members performed sacrificial rites. The New York Ning Yang Hui Guan (Ning Yung Association), formed in 1890 by immigrants from Taishan (Toishan) in Guangdong, became the most powerful. Fang, clan associations, and hui guan belonged to an umbrella organization called Zhonghua Gong Suo (1883), or New York Chinese Consolidated Benevolent Association (CCBA). For many years the association was an informal local government: it acted as a liaison to other segments of American society, settled disputes among Chinese organizations, collected funds for legal expenses incurred defending the community's interests, and sponsored various social welfare programs. Its leaders were chosen by the merchant elite from the largest hui guan. Until the 1950s all Chinese in the metropolitan area were automatically members of the CCBA. Other influential organizations included the Chinese-American Citizens Alliance (organized by American-born Chinese), the Chinese Chamber of Commerce, and the Chinese Restaurants Association.

Chinese women were barred from joining their husbands in the United States, leading to a severe imbalance: for every Chinese 15-year-old girl in New York City there were 40 boys in 1910, 16 in 1920, 14 in 1930, and 9 in 1940. Many men turned to fang, which served as substitute families, and others to gambling, prostitutes, and opium, which were controlled by secret societies known as *tang,* or *tong.* During the early twentieth century the most powerful of these organizations in the city were Hip Sing and On Leong, which often fought bloody battles to defend their spheres of business. The "tong wars" did not end until the mid-1930s, after American authorities threatened to deport the tong leaders. Meanwhile, many immigrants became active in Chinese politics and supported Sun Yat-sen in overthrowing the Manchu Qing dynasty, donating money and even returning to China to take part in the revolution, which dominated Chinese-language newspapers in the city and often split the community. The number of social organizations increased. In response to the Ning Yang Hui Guan, non-Taishan Cantonese organized the Liancheng (Lun Sing) Gong Suo in 1900, which did not admit non-Cantonese organizations until after the 1970s and even then remained predominantly Cantonese. Prominent clan associations of the early twentieth century included the Wing Chun Tong of Chan's Family Association, known as Sam Yip Gung Saw (1900), Shao Lum Gung Saw (1911), and Wong Kong Har Tong (1911). The New York Chinese Public School (Niuyue Huaqiao Gongli Xuexiao) opened in 1908 to teach children the rudiments of Chinese language and culture. Supported by tuition and donations from associations and individuals, it operated after school and on weekends and survived frequent financial crises, continuing to operate into the early twenty-first century. The quality of its offerings was criticized, and before the 1940s wealthy merchants often sent their children to China for middle school.

During the exclusion era, Chinese in the city did not remain silent. Wong Ching Foo founded *Chinese American* (*Huan Mei Xin Bao,* 1883–84), a bilingual weekly to fight for legal rights. In 1892 Wong and other community leaders formed the Chinese Equal Rights League to fight against the exclusion. In the 1920s Chinatown became a base for Chinese seamen, who formed organizations there and sought support in their struggle for equal treatment. Fang were especially vital during the Depression and saved many Chinese from starvation. In response to the Japanese invasion of China during the 1930s, Chinese in the city banded together to form the New York Overseas Chinese Anti-Japanese Salvation General Committee for Military Funds (1937), an organization that cut across all clan, district, and political lines to collect money for relief in China, expose Japanese atrocities against the Chinese, and arouse American sympathy for the Chinese cause. A leading organization, the Chinese Hand Laundry Alliance, adopted the slogan "To Save China, to Save Ourselves" and linked the struggle against exploitation and discrimination in the United States to patriotic support for China. During World War II many Chinese joined the American armed forces, and others worked for the merchant marine. They formed a number of organizations in the city, among them the Chinese Seamen's Patriotic Association, the Chinese Seamen's Union, and the Chinese section of the National Maritime Union. A labor shortage and an improvement in their public image also allowed many Chinese to find work in war-related industries, and in 1943 the Chinese Exclusion acts were repealed.

After the war Chinese veterans were granted legal residency, and many took advantage of the G.I. Bill of Rights to advance their education and careers. With the passage of the War Bride Act (1945) and the G.I. Fiancées Act (1946), women were allowed to join their husbands, and the ratio of men to women in the Chinese community gradually stabilized. Most of the women did not speak English and provided cheap labor for garment factories, where they worked in sweatshop conditions. Many sailors settled in the city, and the population grew to include northern and eastern Chinese, among them speakers of Mandarin and Fujian (Fukienese). Hand laundries declined as washers and dryers became widely available, but restaurants remained an economic mainstay, many of them specializing in the cuisines of Beijing, Hunan, Sichuan (Szechuan), and Shanghai. The establishment of the People's Republic of China in 1949 left thousands of Chinese students stranded in the United States. Many later settled in the metropolitan area, and some later became known internationally for their professional achievements, among them T. D. Lee of Columbia University and C. N. Yang of the State University of New York at Stony Brook, who together won the Nobel Prize for physics in 1957. The American-born children of immigrants often became professionals and moved out of Chinatown.

From the mid-1960s the population grew rapidly. Immigration accelerated after the Immigration Act of 1965 abolished restrictions on immigration according to race. New York City became the most popular destination for Chinese immigrants because of its employment opportunities, especially in garment factories, which from the 1960s accounted for an increasing portion of the economy in Chinatown. The largest social welfare agency, the Chinatown Planning Council, provided English classes, vocational training and placement, legal assistance, and mental health services and sponsored day-care centers, youth facilities, low-income housing projects, and a senior citizens' center. Other important social agencies formed during the 1960s and 1970s included the Chinatown Manpower Project, Asian Americans for Equality, and the Asian American Legal Defense and Education Fund. As its influence declined the CCBA was criticized, especially for its policy of appointing rather than electing officials, and during the 1980s demands were made for structural reforms. From this time on, all groups in the Chinese community, including the traditional CCBA and new immigrant organizations (such as the United Chinese Associations of New York, which mainly consisted of Fujian and other mainland Chinese immigrant organizations) as well as those organized by American-born Chinese, worked together to promote Chinese participation in local and national politics. John Liu became the first Chinese American (and the first Asian American) to be elected to the New York City Council in 2002. He was reelected in 2005. More Chinese American candidates have joined the race for seats in the New York City Council and the state assembly in recent years.

By 1980 the Chinese community in New York City was the largest in the country, surpassing that of San Francisco. Immigrants who settled in the city during the 1960s and 1970s were often professionals who had to take unskilled jobs because they did not speak English. Chinatown in lower Manhattan expanded and other Chinese communities grew in Brooklyn and Flushing; while Cantonese remained in the majority, immigrants from other regions such as Fujian and northeast China increased dramatically in the late twentieth century. Fashion, food, and ideas from throughout Asia were introduced, and from the late 1970s wealthy immigrants from Taiwan, Hong Kong, and Southeast Asia invested large amounts of capital in real estate and various businesses. Tens of thousands of well-educated Chinese professionals took jobs in city government, finance, law, medicine, technology, and academia. English replaced Chinese as the primary language in many families, and the number of interracial marriages increased.

At the beginning of the twenty-first century, several daily, weekly, and monthly Chinese newspapers and magazines were circulated in the metropolitan area, encouraging integration while also strengthening ties to China. The recognition by mainstream society and international audiences of the artistic accomplishments of New York City–based Chinese artists, such as those of film director Ang Lee (*Crouching Tiger, Hidden Dragon,* 2000, and other films) and playwright David Henry Hwang (*M. Butterfly,* 1988, and other plays), was celebrated in the Chinese community. Many cultural organizations became influential, such as Chen and Dancers, the Four Seas Players, the Asian American Dance Theater, and the Museum of Chinese in the Americas. Major landmarks in Chinatown include the statue of Confucius in Confucius Plaza and the statue of Commissioner Lin Zexu in Chatham Square.

Renqiu Yu, *To Save China, to Save Ourselves: The Chinese Hand Laundry Alliance* (Philadelphia: Temple University Press, 1992); Min Zhou, *Chinatown: The Socioeconomic Potential of an Urban Enclave* (Philadelphia: Temple University Press, 1992); Xiaolan Bao, *Holding Up More than Half the Sky: Chinese Women Garment Workers in New York City, 1948–92* (Champaign: University of Illinois Press, 2001)

Renqiu Yu

Chinese Hand Laundry Alliance of New York [CHLA]. Organization formed on 23 April 1933 to protest an ordinance forcing Chinese hand laundries in New York City to cease operations. It defeated the ordinance and became the foremost agency in the struggle for the economic, political, and civil rights of Chinese laundry workers; it also helped launch the Chinese-language newspaper *China Daily News* (1940–89). At its peak in the 1940s the organization had about 5000 members. During the 1950s it was harassed by the Federal Bureau of Investigation for alleged ties to communism, and several members were deported. The alliance took part in the civil rights movement of the 1960s and remained in operation into the 2000s. In the 1990s the organization had about 300 members. In the early twenty-first century its offices were located at 149 Canal Street.

Renqiu Yu

Chisholm [née St. Hill], **Shirley (Anita)** (*b* New York City, 30 Nov 1924; *d* Daytona Beach, Fla., 1 Jan 2005). Congresswoman. The daughter of Quakers, she moved with her family at the age of two from Brooklyn to Barbados, her mother's native country, and remained there until the age of 10. She received her BA from Brooklyn College and an MA from Columbia University, and in 1964 she was elected to the state assembly as a Democrat from Bushwick and Bedford–Stuyvesant. In 1968 she became the first African American woman elected to the U.S. House of Representatives, from New York City's twelfth district. During her seven terms in office she supported legislation promoting education, employment, and the rights of Haitian refugees, served on the House Rules Committee, and was the secretary of the House Democratic Caucus. She sought the Democratic presidential nomination in 1972. Chisholm retired from Congress in 1982, owing partly to discouragement over the policies of President Ronald Reagan; in that same year she was appointed to the Purington Chair at Mount Holyoke College. She later led the National Political Congress of Black Women. She wrote *Unbought and Unbossed* (1970) and *The Good Fight* (1973).

Sule Greg C. Wilson

Choate, Joseph (Hodges) (*b* Salem, Mass., 24 Jan 1832; *d* New York City, 14 May 1917). Lawyer. He moved to New York City in 1855 and was a clerk for the law firm of William Evarts, where he soon became a partner. At the height of his career in the last decades of the nineteenth century he was the counsel for Standard Oil and the American Tobacco Company, and he also played a central role in the struggle by the Bell System to protect its telephone patent rights. In *Pollock v. Farmer's Trust* (1895) his emotional argument against the federal income tax persuaded the U.S. Supreme Court to void it. He was one of the most popular "club men" in the city and a favorite after-dinner speaker. He was also a founding trustee of the American Museum of Natural History and the Metropolitan Museum of Art. Known for his charm and keen intellect, Choate was for many years one of the best corporate lawyers in the nation.

Theron G. Strong, *Joseph H. Choate* (New York: Dodd, Mead, 1917)

Frederick S. Voss

Chock full o'Nuts. Firm of coffee importers formed in 1922 by William Black and incorporated in 1932. It began as a retailer of coffee beans and opened a restaurant in 1933 that soon expanded into one of the first fast-food chains in the city, well known for its simple menu, low prices, and takeout counters; its headquarters were at 425 Lexington Avenue. In 1953 the firm owned 25 restaurants in Manhattan and two in Brooklyn and introduced a commercial brand of coffee, which became a great success in part because of a catchy advertising jingle. At the height of its growth in the 1960s and 1970s, the firm owned more than 150 restaurants in the city. It concentrated increasingly on coffee in the late 1970s and in 1983 sold its remaining restaurants. In May 1994 the firm capitalized on the growing popularity of cafés by opening one on Madison Avenue and returning to New York City for the first time in 20 years. In 1999 the company was purchased by the Sara Lee Corporation, the second-largest coffee roaster in the world. In the mid-1990s Chock full o'Nuts had its headquarters at 370 Lexington Avenue, but it has since moved them to suburban Harrison, New York.

James Bradley

choirs. The Episcopal tradition of choirs of men and boys is maintained in New York City in St. Thomas Church on Fifth Avenue, with a unique boarding school for its boys. The Abyssinian Baptist Church in Harlem has a noted gospel choir. The Boys Choir of Harlem, a concert choir, was founded in 1968 by Walter Turnbull and later opened a large school. Early in the twenty-first century financial and other difficulties reduced its activities. Turnbull died early in 2007.

See also Choruses.

John B. Snook

cholera. A relative stranger to American shores until the 1830s, cholera was the most feared epidemic disease of the nineteenth century. As transatlantic steamship travel and immigration from impoverished regions of the world to the United States increased, serious cholera epidemics in New York City occurred in 1832 (3513 deaths), 1849 (5071 deaths), 1854 (2509 deaths), and 1866 (1137 deaths). The blame for the epidemics during the 1830s rested on its victims: "intemperate" and impoverished New Yorkers, especially the Irish. In 1866 a new Metropolitan Board of Health was effective in drastically reducing the death rate from cholera in New York City. After Robert Koch's discovery in 1883 of the etiologic agent *Vibrio cholerae,* the means by which the cholera bacterium is transmitted became better understood. The first use of cholera culture methods to prevent entry of the disease at a seaport was performed by Hermann M. Biggs and T. Mitchell Prudden on behalf of the New York City Department of Health and the New York Quarantine Station in 1887. The last cholera epidemic in New York City, in 1892, was contained to fewer than 120 deaths, despite a number of political skirmishes.

Charles Rosenberg, *The Cholera Years: The United States in 1832, 1849, and 1866* (Chicago: University of Chicago Press, 1962); John Duffy, *A History of Public Health in New York City* (New York: Russell Sage Foundation, 1968, 1974); Howard Markel, *Quarantine! East European Jewish Immigrants and the New York City Epidemics of 1892* (Baltimore: Johns Hopkins University Press, 1997)

Howard Markel

choruses. The first choruses in New York City sang in Anglican and Episcopal churches in the late eighteenth century. The nineteenth century saw the rise of men's chamber choruses like the Mendelssohn Glee Club (1866, professional) and the University Glee Club (1894, amateur) and of such large, independent choral societies as the Oratorio Society. Formed in 1873 by Leopold Damrosch, the Oratorio Society gave the first of many annual performances of Handel's *Messiah* at Christmas of the following year, and in 1891 performed Berlioz's *Te Deum* for the opening of Carnegie Hall. Important choruses begun

Concert by the Choral Society at Madison Square Garden, 1883

in the first half of the twentieth century include the St. Cecilia Chorus (1906); the Schola Cantorum (1909–71), conducted from 1926 to 1971 by Hugh Ross; the Dessoff Choirs (1930), which originally specialized in music of the fourteenth to seventeenth centuries; the Cantata Singers, formed in 1934 by Paul Boepple and active into the late 1960s; and the Collegiate Chorale, formed in 1941 by Robert Shaw at the Marble Collegiate Church. The All-City High School Chorus was organized in 1936 by P. J. Wilhousky.

The New York Choral Society was formed as an amateur chorus in 1959 by Robert DeCormier, and several chamber choruses were established from the 1960s, including amateur ensembles like the Canby Singers (led by Edward T. Canby, 1960), the Sine Nomine Singers (Harry Saltzman, 1968), the Canticum Novum Singers (Harold Rosenbaum, 1973), and the New York City Gay Men's Chorus (Gary Miller, 1980), and such professional ones as the Amor Artis Chorale (Johannes Somary, 1961), the Gregg Smith Singers (1961), Musica Sacra (Richard Westenburg, 1964), the National Chorale (Martin Josman, 1969), Melodious Accord (Alice Parker, 1984), and the New York Concert Singers (Judith Clurman, 1988). The National Choral Council was formed in 1968 by Martin Josman and others to encourage and strengthen choral singing in the city and elsewhere through performance, community service, and education; it became the sponsor of a "Messiah Sing-In" each December at Lincoln Center. Several unique choruses were founded in the late twentieth century, including the New York City Labor Chorus (1991), the City Bar Chorus, composed of legal professionals (1993), and the New York City Housing Authority Youth Chorus (1997).

Among the notable church choirs in the city are those of St. Bartholomew's Church, the Church of the Ascension, Riverside Church, St. Patrick's Cathedral, St. Peter's Episcopal Church, St. Ignatius Loyola Church, St. Thomas Church (Fifth Avenue and 53rd Street), the Church of Our Saviour, First Presbyterian Church, Fifth Avenue Presbyterian Church, Church of the Incarnation (Episcopal), Marble Collegiate Church, Trinity Church Wall Street, and the Church of St. Mary the Virgin. Several churches in Manhattan have boys' choirs, including St. Thomas Church, the Church of the Transfiguration, Grace Church, and the Church of St. Luke-in-the-Fields. The Boys Choir of Harlem, formed in 1968 by Walter Turnbull, has toured throughout the world. In addition to the permanent choruses of the Metropolitan Opera and the New York City Opera, choruses are often engaged by opera and musical theater companies through the American Guild of Musical Artists, an organization of professional choristers. In the outer boroughs most choruses are affiliated with educational institutions (for example, the Brooklyn College Chorus, the Queens College Glee Club, and the Richmond Choral Society). Special events and festivals sponsored by local choruses include "Summer Sings" of the New York Choral Society and the "Messiah Sing-In" of the National Choral Council. Of the many performances by visiting choruses, perhaps the most popular are those of the Vienna Boys Choir at Carnegie Hall.

Bruce C. MacIntyre

Christ Church. Episcopal church in the Bronx, built in 1866 along what is now the Henry Hudson Parkway. Its members have included the baseball player Lou Gehrig, whose funeral was held there, and Fiorello H. La Guardia, in whose honor stained-glass windows were installed. It is a designated city landmark.

Thomas M. Hilbink

Christ the King Regional High School. Catholic high school at 68-02 Metropolitan Avenue in Queens, occupying a four-story building completed in 1964 as the last of six high schools built by the Diocese of Brooklyn to accommodate children born after World War II. Planned for 3000 students, the school originally consisted of a boys' school run by the Marist Brothers and a girls' school run by the Daughters of Wisdom. These were separated by a central block housing the library and other shared facilities. The school became coeducational in 1973 and eventually had a predominantly lay faculty. In 2006 enrollment was 1300.

Gilbert Tauber

Christian Scientists. Members of a religious organization based on the beliefs of founder Mary Baker Eddy. The Christian Science Society held its first meeting in New York City on 27 November 1887. It was incorporated as the Church of Christ, Scientist, in 1888 and renamed the First Church of Christ, Scientist, in 1896. In 1891 a splinter group founded the Second Church of Christ, Scientist, which in 1900 built its headquarters, designed by Frederick R. Comstock, at 68th Street and Central Park West. The First Church commissioned the architectural firm of Carrère and Hastings to design its beaux-arts building, completed in 1903. In 2004 the First Church sold its 2400-seat building to Crenshaw Christian Center East and joined the Second Church; the 68th Street congregation was renamed the First Church. In the early twenty-first century Christian Scientists maintained churches and reading rooms throughout the five boroughs.

Kevin Kenny, Kate Lauber

Christie's. Auction house formed in London in 1766 by James Christie. The success of its first salesroom in New York City, opened at 520 Park Avenue in 1977, led to the addition of a second, Christie's East, at 219 East 67th Street in 1979. Several records have been set at its operations in the city: the Tremaine Collection of Contemporary Art sold for $25,824,700 in 1988, the largest sum paid for the modern collection of a single owner, and in 1990 Vincent van Gogh's *Portrait of Dr. Gachet* sold for $82.5 million, the largest sum paid for any lot at auction. In 2000 a price-fixing scandal between executives at Christie's and Sotheby's, a rival auction house, became an issue of major concern. In the early twenty-first century Christie's New York City salesrooms served as anchors for operations in 13 other American cities and over 30 countries.

Janet Frankston

Christo [Javacheff, Christo Vladimirov] **and Jeanne-Claude** [Denat de Guillebon, Jeanne-Claude] (*b* Gabrovo, Bulgaria, 13 June 1935; *b* Casablanca, Morocco, 13 June 1935; *d* 18 Nov 2009, New York). Artists. The married couple are known for environmental installation art. They permanently moved to New York City in 1964. Their work, which has appeared on four continents, includes the wrapping of the Reichstag in Berlin and the Pont Neuf bridge in Paris. Their work *The Gates* was installed in New York City's Central Park in 2005.

Sarah Brafman

Christodora House. Young women's settlement house. Founded in the East Village in 1897 by the philanthropists Sara Libby

Christodora House, 2009

Carson and Christina MacColl, it originally occupied two floors in a tenement house at 1637 Avenue B. New Russian, Polish, and Ukrainian immigrants settled in New York City in increasing numbers after the turn of the century, and the settlement house provided them with essential social services. In 1928 funds donated by the railroad magnate Arthur Curtis James facilitated the construction of the present building, a 17-story edifice at 147 Avenue B on the corner of East Ninth Street. Because this was the world's tallest structure dedicated to social service, it became known as the "skyscraper settlement house." It had a music school, a poets' guild, a playhouse, a gymnasium, a swimming pool, and a dining hall with a river view. George Gershwin, whose brother led the poets' guild, gave his first public performance at a recital on the third floor in 1914. Christodora House continued to serve as a social settlement until shortly after World War II, when it fell into disrepair and was taken over by the city. Occupied by community groups in the 1960s, it was sealed after a fire destroyed its electrical system. It was sold at public auction in 1975, then renovated 10 years later and converted into luxury condominiums. The organization, however, continued to provide educational opportunities and leadership training for New York City youth into the early twenty-first century.

Robert Sanger Steel

Christy, Howard Chandler (*b* Morgan County, Ohio, 10 Jan 1873; *d* New York City, 3 March 1952). Illustrator. Trained as a painter, he became known for his drawings, which appeared in periodicals such as *Harper's* and *Scribner's* and in books by James W. Riley and others. He was also the creator of an ideal female type known as the "Christy Girl" that was featured in several books of drawings, including *The American Girl as Seen and Portrayed by Howard Chandler Christy* (1906) and *The Christy Girl: Drawings by Howard Chandler Christy* (1906). About 1920 he resumed painting, executing portraits, figure subjects, and *plein air* landscapes, as well as murals for the Park Lane Hotel and the Café des Artistes. His last studio was in the Hotel des Artistes at 1 West 67th Street. Christy is recognized as one of the foremost illustrators of the early twentieth century in New York City.

Carol Lowrey

Chrysler Building. Art deco skyscraper at 405 Lexington Avenue, standing 1046 feet (319 meters) tall and designed by William Van Alen. It began as a speculative venture by William H. Reynolds, the developer of Dreamland at Coney Island. In 1927 the entire project, including leases and architectural plans, was bought by the automobile magnate Walter P. Chrysler, for whom were added such details as the decorative stainless-steel eagle heads and Chrysler radiator caps and the helmet-like top, known as the vertex. Inside the pinnacle was a private executive dining hall known as the Cloud Club; the 71st story, which also afforded stunning views, was set aside for a visitors' center that displayed Chrysler's first tool kit. Upon completion in 1930, the building was the tallest in the world (surpassed a few months later by the Empire State Building). Tube lighting that illuminated the vertex at night was included in the original plans but not installed until 1981. The facade was designated a landmark in 1978, as was the lobby, known for its splendid ceiling mural and marble veneers and the marquetry on its elevator doors. In July 2008 the building was purchased by the Abu Dhabi Investment Council.

Carol Willis

Chumley's. Speakeasy, bar, and restaurant. Started by Leland Stanford Chumley in 1928 in a former blacksmithery at 86 Bedford Street, at the corner of Barrow Street, in the West Village. With its plain, unmarked door on Bedford Street and another with a small peephole on Barrow Street, it became famous for not displaying a sign or indication that the structure was anything other than a private residence. The square room inside, with tables set against walls decorated with old book jackets, was perfect for surreptitious meetings of the Industrial Workers of the World or for illicit drinking during the Prohibition era. It is widely thought that the address of Chumley's is at the root of the term "to 86" something, meaning to kill or end it. Legend has it that police would call the owner in advance of raids during Prohibition, prompting him to "86" everyone by sending them out the bar's Bedford Street exit or through windows and balconies onto the building next door.

Chumley's has long been known as a favorite hangout of American literary figures who found their way to its unmarked doors, including James Agee, Heywood Broun, Willa Cather, E. E. Cummings, John Dos Passos, Theodore Dreiser, William Faulkner, Edna Ferber, Allen Ginsberg, Lillian Hellman, Norman Mailer, Edna St. Vincent Millay, and John Steinbeck. On 5 April 2007 a wall collapse forced Chumley's to shut down indefinitely.

Kenneth T. Jackson, Rowan Moore Gerety

Church, Frederic(k) E(dwin) (*b* Hartford, Conn., 4 May 1826; *d* New York City, 7 April 1900). Painter. He studied painting in Catskill, New York, from 1844 to 1846 with Thomas Cole, who taught him to consider landscape painting as a means of expressing noble ideas. In 1847 he moved to New York City, where he worked in studios in the American Art Union building (1847–58) and in the Tenth Street Studio (1858–89); he was elected to the National Academy of Design in 1849 and to the Century Association in 1850. His aesthetic was shaped in part by the writings of John Ruskin, which encouraged artists to depict nature as a reflection of divine creation, and by the works of J. M. W. Turner, whose spectacular lighting effects he emulated. Soon he was known internationally as the foremost painter of the Hudson River School. Inspired by the German scientist Alexander von Humboldt, who urged artists to evoke cosmic truths by synthesizing art and science in depictions of nature, he traveled to South America (1853, 1857), Labrador and Newfoundland (1859), Jamaica (1865), and Europe and the Middle East (1867–68). His greatest rival was Albert Bierstadt (1830–1902), known for his detailed panoramic paintings of Western scenes, especially the Rocky Mountains. Church's reputation declined after the Civil War. Between 1867 and 1872 he designed a farmhouse in a Persian style with Calvert Vaux for Olana, a farm overlooking the Hudson River near Hudson, New York, to which he retired in 1889. His studio at Olana has been preserved, along with 2000 books, several thousand manuscripts, and more than 700 artworks.

David C. Huntington, *The Landscapes of Frederic Edwin Church: Vision of an American Era* (New York: George Braziller, 1966); Franklin Kelly et al., *Frederick Edwin Church* (Washington, D.C.: National Gallery of Art, 1990)

Timothy Anglin Burgard

Church Club of New York. Club formed in 1887 in Manhattan by laymen of the Episcopal Diocese of New York. Among its aims were to promote interest in the history and theology of the church and to engage in good works for the benefit of the poor. Early members included such prominent figures as Nicholas Murray Butler, J. P. Morgan, and Cornelius Vanderbilt. Membership was at first limited to white males; racial restrictions were removed in 1954, and women were admitted after 1975. Over time the club became an important meeting place, independent of clerical influence, for active Episcopal laypeople from many of the churches in the city and the surrounding dioceses. It also made contributions to Episcopal theological seminaries. Although the Church Club has occasionally organized to pursue a particular aspect of church policy, more often its influence has been exerted by individual members acting in their local parishes and on diocesan committees.

James Elliott Lindsley, *The Church Club of New York: The First Hundred Years* (New York: Church Club of New York, 1994)

Chauncey G. Olinger, Jr.

churches. The first congregation in New York City was the Collegiate Dutch Reformed Church in Manhattan, formed in 1628. It eventually included Middle, Marble, West End, and Fort Washington Collegiate churches. The first house of worship, the Friends Meeting House in Flushing, was built in 1694. In 1697 Trinity Church built its first sanctuary at Broadway and Wall Street. In 1768 the John Street United Methodist Church in Manhattan was established as the first Methodist church in the United States. One of its sextons, Peter Williams, later left to form the African Methodist Episcopal Church. St. Peter's, the first Roman Catholic parish, was organized in Manhattan in 1785. By 1786 the city had 17 Protestant churches serving Presbyterians, members of the Dutch Reformed Church, Episcopalians, German Lutherans, Quakers, Baptists, Methodists, and Moravians. The Abyssinian Baptist Church (1808) was the first black church in the city and became one of the most influential, later providing a political base for Adam Clayton Powell, Sr., and Adam Clayton Powell, Jr. After the formation of the Roman Catholic Diocese of New York in 1808, St. Patrick's Old Cathedral was completed in 1815 and was the bishop's see until 1879 when a new St. Patrick's Cathedral came into use (1858–77, designed by James Renwick, Jr.). St. Philip's Episcopal Church (1818) bought scores of apartments in Harlem, playing a critical role in the development of the area and becoming the country's wealthiest black congregation.

During the mid-nineteenth century Gothic Revival styles dominated church architecture, owing largely to the influence of Richard Upjohn. He designed the Church of the Ascension in Manhattan (1841, Episcopal); Christ Church in Cobble Hill (1841–42, Episcopal); the Congregational Church of the Pilgrims (1844, now Our Lady of Lebanon Maronite Cathedral), which has a piece of Plymouth Rock jutting from one wall and was the first Romanesque-style church in the country; the Church of the Holy Communion in Manhattan (1844–46, Episcopal; now a nightclub); Trinity Church in Manhattan (1846, Episcopal); Grace Church in Brooklyn (1847, Episcopal); Trinity Chapel in Manhattan (1850–55, Episcopal; now the Serbian Orthodox Cathedral of St. Sava); St. George's Church in Flushing (1853, Episcopal); and Christ Church in the Bronx (1866, Episcopal). His most important rival was Renwick, who worked principally in the Gothic Revival style and designed Grace Church in Manhattan (1843–45, Episcopal); Calvary Church, also in Manhattan (1847, Episcopal); the Riverdale Presbyterian Church (1863); and St. Ann's Church (1869, Episcopal). Using Gothic Revival, Greek Revival, and Italianate styles, Minard Lafever designed St. James Church in Chinatown (1835–37, Roman Catholic), the Mariner's Temple on the Lower East Side (1842, Baptist), the Church of the Savior in Brooklyn Heights (1844, now First Unitarian Church), Holy Trinity Church, also in Brooklyn Heights (1847, Episcopal), the Church of the Holy Apostles in Manhattan (1848, Episcopal), and the Strong Place Baptist Church in Cobble Hill (early 1850s, now St. Francis Cabrini Chapel).

St. Patrick's, Richmond, 2009

Several churches were centers of movements for temperance, Sabbatarianism, and abolitionism. One of the best-known was the Plymouth Church of the Pilgrims in Brooklyn Heights, which under Henry Ward Beecher led campaigns against slavery from 1847. Several Eastern Orthodox congregations of

Greeks, Russians, and eastern Europeans built churches from the late nineteenth century. By 1890 the city directory listed 450 churches, including Congregationalists, Evangelicals, African Methodist Episcopalians, Reformed Presbyterians, United Presbyterians, Unitarians, Universalists, Disciples of Christ, Swedenborgians, and members of the Salvation Army. There were also churches formed by such ethnic groups as Germans, Swedes, French, French Canadians, Chinese, Italians, Latin Americans, Poles, and Irish. Storefront churches became common in some neighborhoods, often opened by charismatic preachers without a larger denomination. During the first decades of the twentieth century Bertram Grosvenor Goodhue introduced a new level of sophistication to the Gothic Revival style in his designs for St. Thomas Church in midtown Manhattan (1909–14, Episcopal), the Church of the Intercession in Harlem (1911–14, Episcopal), the Church of St. Vincent Ferrer in Manhattan (1916–18, Roman Catholic), and St. Bartholomew's Church in midtown Manhattan (1917–19, Episcopal), which incorporated Byzantine elements.

In the twenty-first century there were more than 2200 Protestant and Orthodox churches and 350 Roman Catholic churches in the city. With more than 40,000 members, the Church of the Incarnation in Inwood (Washington Heights) was the largest Roman Catholic parish in the city; St. Patrick's Cathedral had the largest Sunday attendance, with 6900 communicants. The Concord Baptist Church of Christ in Bedford–Stuyvesant, with 12,000 members, was the largest black congregation in the country. In some neighborhoods Anglican immigrants from the West Indies enlarged Episcopal congregations that had long declined; St. Mark's Church in Crown Heights had 3000 members and was the city's largest Episcopal congregation. From 1995 to 2008 the congregation of the Fifth Avenue Presbyterian Church grew by 50 percent to more than 3550 members. Among the few churches that remained devoted to a single ethnic or national group were congregations of Swedes, Norwegians, Finns, Czechs, and Hungarians. The number of Roman Catholic churches offering services in Spanish increased, and Chinese and Korean Protestant congregations were formed as well: one of the largest was the Korean Presbyterian Church of Queens in Flushing, which had 1800 members. The Cathedral of St. John the Divine, the seat of the Episcopal Bishop of New York, remained the largest church in the United States and one of the largest cathedrals in the world. Among the city's newest churches were Grace Methodist Church on West 86th Street in Manhattan and the Norwegian Seaman's Church on East 52nd Street. By the early twenty-first century New York City was central to Christianity's growth among non-Western populations. Reflecting contemporary immigration patterns, many fast-growing churches, such as the Seventh Day Adventists, had congregations around the city focusing on diverse ethnic groups, especially Latinos, West Africans, West Indians, Asians, and Eastern Europeans.

Susanna A. Jones

Church of Jesus Christ of the Latter Day Saints. See Ellis Island, Mormons.

Church of Our Lady of Mount Carmel (Manhattan). Roman Catholic church on East 115th Street in East Harlem. Migrants from Polla, Salerno, first celebrated the church's namesake feast day in East Harlem on 16 July 1881. The Archdiocese of New York secured Pallottine missionaries to organize the church and a school in 1884. Pope Leo XIII named the church a shrine on 12 May 1903. The Madonna's statue was installed over the altar on 23 June 1923. The school merged with nearby Holy Rosary, and the school building closed in 2004; in the early twenty-first century the building housed the National Catholic Museum of Art and History.

Robert Anthony Orsi, *The Madonna of 115th Street: Faith and Community in Italian Harlem, 1880–1930* (New Haven: Yale University Press, 1985)

Mary Elizabeth Brown

Church of Our Lady of Pompeii. Roman Catholic church at 25 Carmine Street in Manhattan. A chapel was opened for a new parish on 8 May 1892 by Pietro Bandini, chaplain of the Society of St. Raphael for the Protection of Italian Immigrants. From 1897 to 1926 the congregation met at the Church of St. Benedict the Moor, which was demolished during the widening of Sixth Avenue. The current building, modeled after southern Italian churches, contains a church (dedicated 27 October 1928), a school (opened 1930), and a convent. The plaza in front honors Antonio Demo, pastor from 1899 to 1933.

Constantino Sassi, *Parrochia della Madonna di Pompei in New York: Notizie storiche dei primi cinquant' anni dalla sua fondazione, 1892–1942* (Rome: Santa Lucia, 1946); Michael Consenza, *Church of Our Lady of Pompeii in Greenwich Village: History of the Parish, 1892–1967* (New York: Parish of Our Lady of Pompeii, 1967); Mary Elizabeth Brown, *From Italian Villages to Greenwich Village: Our Lady of Pompei, 1892–1992* (New York: Center for Migration Studies, 1992)

Mary Elizabeth Brown

Church of St. Ann and the Holy Trinity. Episcopal church in Brooklyn, incorporated in 1787. In the nineteenth century it became a national center of the Low Church movement in American Episcopalianism, and it supported missionary work, Sunday schools, Bible classes, an orphanage, and societies to help educate poor children. In 1869 it moved to a Gothic Revival church (Clinton and Livingston streets) designed by the firm of Renwick and Sands, which was sold by the congregation in 1969 to the Packer Collegiate Institute after St. Ann's merged with the Church of the Holy Trinity. From that time the congregation met in the neo-Gothic Church of the Holy Trinity (1847) at Montague and Clinton streets. They established a school and a performing arts center that became known nationally. In the twenty-first century they continued to support both institutions and had organized the restoration of the Church of the Holy Trinity.

Peter J. Wosh

Church of St. Benedict the Moor. Roman Catholic church formed by African American parishioners in 1883 at the former Third Universalist Church, a building in a Greek Revival style on Bleecker and Downing streets that closed on 1 May 1898. The building was demolished in 1927 to widen Sixth Avenue. The parish reconvened on 20 November 1898 at the former Second Evangelical Church, a Corinthian building at 320 West 53rd Street. On 28 February 1954 members of the clergy from the Franciscan Third Order Regular opened a ministry for Latin Americans at St. Benedict's. A number of African American nuns from the community of the Handmaids of the Most Pure Heart of Mary formed a convent and day nursery of St. Benedict uptown, which eventually moved to 34 West 134th Street. As of 2010 the parish was located at 457 West 51st Street in Manhattan.

Jorge Coll, *Una iglesia pionera: Ensayo histórico sobre la parroquia de San Benito de Palermo, en la ciudad de Nueva York, EE.UU. de America* (New York: Privately printed, 1989)

Mary Elizabeth Brown

Church of St. Brigid. Roman Catholic Church at 119 Avenue B and East Eighth Street. Built in 1848 and 1849 to the design of Irish-born architect Patrick Keely, it served the East Village's growing Irish community in the wake of the Irish Potato Famine. As the neighborhood changed, the church welcomed the area's other immigrant communities, including Germans, eastern Europeans, and Puerto Ricans. In 2001 the church was closed because of structural problems. Years of fighting ensued between the Archdiocese of New York, which wanted to permanently close it, and parishioners, who wanted to reopen it. On the eve of demolition in 2008 an anonymous gift of $20 million saved the

Church of St. Brigid (designed by Patrick Keely), 2009

church and provided for its restoration as well as establishing an endowment and support for the religious school.

Melissa Baldock

Church of St. Luke-in-the-Fields. Episcopal parish church on Hudson Street in the West Village, between Christopher and Barrow streets. It occupies the third-oldest church building still in use in Manhattan. The congregation was formed in 1820 by a group including Clement Clarke Moore, who served as the first warden and helped design the building, a simple, rectangular, late Federal brick version of an English village church with a tower at the eastern end. The building opened in 1822; extensions in the Gothic style were added on the south side in 1859 and the north side in 1875. Throughout its history the church has emphasized service to a changing community and the liturgical piety of the Anglican High Church tradition. During the 1840s its rector John Murray Forbes helped to introduce the principles of the Oxford Movement in New York City, and in 1847 it was the site of one of the first professions of monastic vows in the Episcopal Church. A fire in 1981 gutted the building; rebuilt after a fund-raising campaign, the church reopened in 1985. The interior design by Hardy, Holtzman, Pfeiffer Associates restored much of the lost simplicity of the original Federal style while evoking other features of the old church with graceful restraint.

Mrs. H. Croswell Tuttle, *History of Saint Luke's Church in the City of New York, 1820–1920* (New York: Appeal Printing Company, 1926)

Donald F. M. Gerardi

Church of St. Mary the Virgin. Episcopal parish church at 145 West 46th Street, near Times Square. The congregation was formed in 1868 by Thomas McKee Brown under a state law allowing religious organizations to incorporate and remain self-governing. Affiliated from the outset with the Episcopal Diocese of New York, it emphasized the Catholic tradition of ritual and music in Anglicanism. Its church building became known as the Mother Church of Anglo-Catholicism and informally as Smoky Mary's because incense was (and is) often used during services. The congregation moved into its present building in 1895, the architect being Napoleon LeBrun and the style French Gothic. It is said to be the first church in North America constructed on a steel frame. During the 1970s the church took part in the liturgical renewal that inspired a revision of the Book of Common Prayer in 1979. St. Mary's also became known for its neighborhood ministries during the 1980s and early 1990s. Extensive restoration and redecoration of the nave interior was undertaken in 1997.

Newbury Frost Read, *The Story of St. Mary's* (New York: Privately printed, 1931)

J. Robert Wright

Church of St. Peter. Roman Catholic church organized in 1785. Its first parishioners included Elizabeth Ann Bayley Seton, Pierre Toussaint, and representatives of the Spanish Crown. The current church, dedicated in February 1838, stands at 18 Barclay Street. From 1800 to 1940 it operated the nation's first free parochial school. The congregation was largely Irish in the 1880s and Polish and Ruthenian in the 1920s; eventually many parishioners worked in the area but did not live there. The congregation was almost nonexistent in the 1960s, but grew as it attracted new members among residents of Battery Park City.

Leo Raymond Ryan, *Old Saint Peter's: The Mother Church of Catholic New York (1785–1935)* (New York: United States Catholic Historical Society, 1935); *St. Peter's Church: The Oldest Catholic Parish in New York State* (New York: Parish of St. Peter, n.d. [?1985])

Mary Elizabeth Brown

Church of St. Vincent Ferrer. Roman Catholic church. Located at 869 Lexington Avenue, the French Gothic Revival church was originally conceived by Dominican priests during the 1860s. The present building, designed by Bertram Grosvenor Goodhue, was completed in 1918. It was dedicated on 5 May, with more than 50,000 people in attendance. In 1967 it was declared a landmark by the New York City Landmarks Preservation Commission. The St. Vincent Ferrer High School is affiliated with the place of worship. As of 2008 the Dominican order continued to run the church.

Church of the Annunciation. Catholic house of worship. Located at 88 Convent Avenue, the it was established to serve the Irish Catholic population of upper Manhattan, specifically residents of Manhattanville. When established in 1854, it was the first Catholic church to be built on the West Side above Second Street.

Sharon Wilkins

Church of the Good Shepherd. Episcopal house of worship located at 240 East 31st Street. Famous for its protracted history of ministry and service and originally known as the Church of the Incarnation, it was at various times designated a mission, a chapel, and an independent church. In the mid-1800s the Church of the Incarnation separated from Grace Church, forming the Association for the Home Mission of the Church of the Incarnation. The first services were held on East 28th Street, but a new building was soon erected on East 31st Street. Renamed the Church of the Reconciliation, it was admitted into the Episcopal Diocese of New York in 1863. Within a few years, owing to financial difficulties, the church again became a mission of Incarnation.

Shortly after the turn of the twentieth century Edward Severin Clark offered to build a new church. The cornerstone was laid in 1902, and additional buildings were added to the complex over the next few years. For several decades the chapel was a model for how to blend spiritual and social services. By the 1960s Incarnation was no longer able to support the chapel and became a mission. In 1963 the name was changed to the Church of the Good Shepherd, which became independent through an endowment created by the sale of former Incarnation property.

Sharon Wilkins

Church of the Heavenly Rest. Episcopal house of worship founded in 1865 by a group of Civil War veterans. The original location was on the corner of Fifth Avenue and 45th Street. In 1925 the church moved to its current location, a building at Fifth Avenue and 90th Street designed by Bertram Goodhue.

Max Seppo

Church of the Holy Apostles. Episcopal parish church formed in 1844 at Ninth Avenue and 28th Street in Manhattan. In 1848 it moved into its current building, designed in an Italian Tuscanate style by William Maynard LeFevre and soon known for its stained-glass windows by William Jay Bolton and John Bolton, brothers widely considered the first stained-glass makers in the United States. Extensions designed by Richard Upjohn in the 1850s were added to the transepts and sanctuary. It opened a soup kitchen in 1982 that by the end of 1990 had served more than 1.5 million meals and was the largest facility of its kind in the city. The day after a devastating fire destroyed much of the church on 9 April 1990, the kitchen served 943 cold meals by candlelight. In 2008 Holy Apostles boasted the largest soup kitchen in the city on a single site, having served more than six million meals to the hungry and homeless from its opening in 1982 through its 25th anniversary in 2007.

Lucius A. Edelblute, *The History of the Church of the Holy Apostles (Protestant Episcopal), 1844–1944* (New York: Privately printed, 1944)

J. Robert Wright

Church of the Holy Communion. Episcopal church at Sixth Avenue and 20th Street in Manhattan, formed by W. A. Muhlenberg in 1844 as a "free" church, or one in which pew rents were abolished. It was noted both for its service to the community and for practices in worship that were unusual for the Episcopal church in the nineteenth century: daily prayer, weekly Eucharist, lighted candles, antiphonal chanting, and altar flowers. In the mid-1970s it formed a united parish with Calvary Church and St. George's Episcopal Church; in the twenty-first century the building is used for nonreligious purposes.

Robert Bruce Mullin

Church of the Holy Trinity. Episcopal house of worship located at 316 East 88th Street in Manhattan. The first Church of the Holy Trinity, at 42nd Street and Madison Avenue, was consecrated in 1865; a second was erected in 1873. Jacob Wrey Mould crafted the original design. Leopold Eidlitz used his vision in art and architecture to build a church in High Victorian Gothic style, featuring a steeple and tower. At the end of the nineteenth century, with the growth of Grand Central Terminal, the area changed and Holy Trinity merged with St. James Church at Madison Avenue and 71st Street in 1895. An endowment was created through the sale and demolition of Holy Trinity's 42nd Street property. The congregation became the Church of the Holy Trinity in the Parish of St. James. Meanwhile Serena Rhinelander donated construction funds and property on East 88th Street to erect a church complex to be supervised by St. James. The new Church of the Holy Trinity was consecrated in 1899. Its mission was to serve the spiritual, intellectual, and social needs of Yorkville and East Harlem residents. The Church of the Holy Trinity once again became an independent parish in 1950.

Sharon Wilkins

Church of the Most Holy Redeemer. Roman Catholic church at 173 East Third Street in Manhattan. It was founded in 1844 on Third Avenue as a German national parish by the Redemptorists. A school staffed by the School Sisters of Notre Dame opened in the same year, and Gabriel Rumpler was appointed the first pastor by Archbishop John Hughes. A new church was dedicated in 1851. As a result of the changing ethnic composition of the area, by the early twenty-first century the church ministered principally to Latin American Catholics.

Margaret M. McGuinness

Church of the Most Holy Trinity. German Catholic church founded in 1841 on Montrose Avenue in Williamsburgh, which is now in Brooklyn. The parish was formed by John Stephen Raffeiner to serve the area's growing German population, and the first church building was erected in 1841. In 1853 a larger church was built on an adjacent lot to house the growing congregation and to provide a parish for the sisters of St. Dominic (from Regensburg, Germany). Parishioners and clergymen formed the Orphan Home Society (1861) and St. Catherine's Hospital (1868) on Bushwick Avenue. A third church, a large Gothic cathedral, was built in 1885. Membership declined along with the German population of the neighborhood after the turn of the twentieth century. Many Latin Americans joined the church in the 1960s, and in 1981 Franciscan friars took over the administration of the parish.

Bernadette McCauley

Church of the Transfiguration (i). Roman Catholic church at 29 Mott Street in Manhattan, known as the English Lutheran First Church of Zion when it was built in 1801. It was purchased in 1853 for $30,000 by John McClellan and his congregation, who at the time occupied a church at 45 Chambers Street formerly known as the Dutch Reformed Presbyterian Church. Profits from the sale of their old church helped to retire the debts incurred by the parish, which consisted mainly of poor Irish immigrants from the Five Points. More than 1000 students attended a girls' school run by St. Elizabeth Seton's Sisters of Charity that opened at the church in 1856 (where one of the teachers was Mother Cabrini), and a boys' school run by the Christian Brothers that opened in 1857 (where one of the students was Patrick Hayes, later a cardinal). In the 1890s the Irish leaders in the parish relegated the more than 8000 Italian immigrants to a basement congregation. Tensions between the Irish and the Italians in the parish remained strong until 1902, when Ernest Coppo arrived from Italy with a group of Salesian priests, took over as pastor, and moved the Italians upstairs.

Coppo also established a Chinese mission at the church to minister to the more than 2000 Chinese who lived nearby. From the 1920s to the 1950s, the parish thrived as a central institution in Little Italy and Chinatown; Jimmy Durante belonged to the church as a youth, and the opera singer Enrico Caruso was known to attend services. In the 1940s Francis Cardinal Spellman assigned the church to the Maryknoll Fathers, an order that had served in China, and in the 1950s the parish added masses with sermons in Cantonese. The archdiocese took over the administration of the church in 1975, and in 1976 it named Mark Cheung as its first Chinese pastor. In the early twenty-first century the Church of the Transfiguration remained an important institution in Chinatown.

Edward T. O'Donnell

Church of the Transfiguration (ii). Located on 29th Street near Fifth Avenue, and one of the first Anglo-Catholic parishes of the Episcopal Church, it formed in 1848 and became known as the Little Church around the Corner. The church was a station of the Underground Railroad and a refuge for blacks during the Civil War. Well-known members who took part in the abolitionist movement were the mother of Theodore Roosevelt and G. H. Houghton, a rector who in 1863 repelled white lynch mobs by brandishing a cross. The outline of the present neo-Gothic building was completed by 1864; notable features include the Lich Gate (1896) and the Mortuary Chapel (1908). In 1988 the interior

Lich Gate (designed by Frederick Clarke Withers), Church of the Transfiguration (ii)

was refurbished and a new organ was built by the firm of C. B. Fisk. The Church of the Transfiguration is the headquarters of the Episcopal Actors' Guild and has the oldest boys' choir in the city, formed in 1881. In 2005 a new 55-story residential building was begun on the site of the old parish house, the first four floors designated for parish use; it was completed in 2008.

J. H. Randolph Ray, *My Little Church around the Corner* (New York: Simon and Schuster, 1957)

J. Robert Wright

Cigar Makers' International Union. Labor union organized in 1864 by Czech, German, and Hungarian immigrants in New York City who sought to protect their cigar shops from sweeping industrial changes. The United Cigarmakers joined the union as Local 144 in 1875, at a time when innovations such as molds, bunching machines, and suction tables threatened the hand-rolled cigar industry. Weakened by a series of costly strikes in 1869, 1873, and 1877, the union was reorganized by Samuel Gompers and Adolph Strasser (both from Local 144), who introduced financial and administrative reforms associated with the "new model" unions of Great Britain. Its longtime rivalry with the Progressive Cigarmakers culminated in the formation of the American Federation of Labor; it absorbed the Progressive Cigarmakers in 1886, the year its membership in New York City reached 8000 (almost one-third of the union's total). Continued technological innovation caused fears of job displacement and triggered many strikes. In 1915 lowered initiation fees were used to encourage women in the industry to join the union. Cigar makers during the interwar years began to move from union enclaves such as New York City to other parts of the United States, and national membership in the union fell from 40,000 in 1919 to 7000 in 1940. The union left New York City after World War II.

Norman Ware, *The Labor Movement in the United States, 1860–1895: A Study in Democracy* (New York: D. Appleton, 1929); Willis Nissley Baer, *Economic Development of the Cigar Industry in the United States* (Lancaster, Pa.: Art Printing, 1933); Patricia Cooper, *Once a Cigar Maker: Men, Women and Work Culture in American Cigar Factories, 1900–1919* (Urbana: University of Illinois Press, 1987)

See also Knights of Labor, District Assembly 49.

Ronald Mendel

CIO. See Congress of Industrial Organizations.

Circle in the Square. Theater company formed by the producer and director Theodore Mann and the director José Quintero in 1951. It was the first nonprofit theater on Broadway. Early on it became known for its acclaimed productions of such commercially unsuccessful plays as Tennessee Williams's *Summer and Smoke* (1952) and Eugene O'Neill's *The Iceman Cometh* (1956). Among the many prominent actors who launched their careers at the theater are Geraldine Page, Jason Robards, George C. Scott, and Colleen Dewhurst. In 1972 Circle in the Square moved from Bleecker Street to a theater in the Paramount Plaza on 235 West 50th Street; the Circle in the Square Theatre School is housed in the same location. The theater was designed by Alan Sayles and seats 682. Since it opened in 1951, it has produced more than 150 shows, including *Death of a Salesman* (1975), *Tartuffe* (1977), *A Streetcar Named Desire* (1988) and *Sweeney Todd* (1989). Circle in the Square stopped staging its own productions in 1998, but the theater is still in use by other companies.

Robert Hatch, *Circle in the Square* (New York: Horizon, 1960)

See also Theater.

D. S. Moynihan

Circle Line. Two sightseeing boat lines. The original Circle Line company was formed in 1945 by Francis J. Barry (1906–86) through the merger of several earlier lines. From a pier at West 43rd Street its boats initially circled Manhattan Island clockwise; the direction was later changed to counterclockwise. Tour guides pointed out historic and architectural landmarks and the residences of well-known figures. In 1962 Circle Line acquired the Hudson River Day Line. In 1982 Circle Line split into two separate companies: Circle Line Downtown and Circle Line at 42nd Street. Both offered speed-boat rides, private reservations, and various tours around the city, including a three-hour tour around Manhattan. During the terrorist attacks of 11 September 2001 the companies ceased normal activities and transported people from Manhattan to New Jersey. Circle Line was the exclusive provider of transportation to Liberty and Ellis islands, transporting about 70 million people there from 1953 to 2007, when the service was taken over by Hornblower Cruises and Events. Circle Line remained a popular tourist attraction during the first decade of the twenty-first century.

Max Seppo, George A. Thompson, Jr.

Circumnavigators Club. International organization founded in 1902 by three travelers en route to New York City. The club's mission is to encourage and inspire global fellowship and to provide a forum for intellectual exchange among those who have traveled around the world. In the early twenty-first century the club maintained 14 chapters worldwide and international headquarters at the Williams Club, at 24 East 39th Street in Manhattan.

Holly Cronin

circuses. New York City became a favored destination of circus acts during colonial times because of its large population. A live lion was exhibited there as early as May 1728. In the decades after the American Revolution New York City was one of few in the United States where leisure pursuits were not prohibited for moral reasons. The first circus was probably that of the Englishman John Bill Ricketts, which ran between 1793 and 1799. An elephant, the first in the country, was shown in 1796. Exhibitions were mounted several times by the team of Victor Pépin and John Breschard between 1808 and 1813 and by the Englishman James West between 1817 and

1822. Seeking to eliminate competition, two theater producers bought out West and engaged the first bareback rider, James Hunter, who made his debut in New York City in 1823. These circuses and a few others, most of them managed by Europeans, performed for weeks or months in temporary buildings and at such pleasure gardens as Vauxhall, Niblo's Garden, and one at Richmond Hill (as early as 1823). By the late 1820s there were a dozen or more circuses and many traveling shows, most operated by Americans. The introduction of tents made circuses less dependent on long engagements in cities. Several menageries toured the country, and in the 1830s they became able to move wagonloads of caged animals and tenting equipment daily. In 1834 nine such menageries merged to form the Zoological Institute, headquartered at 37 Bowery, where an exhibition hall was also built. In 1835 the institute controlled all 13 American touring menageries and merged several with circuses, leaving only five touring circuses still independent. In a rigged stock sale the institute raised $329,325 from 123 investors but was forced to declare bankruptcy during the panic of 1837.

Various theaters, exhibition halls, and vacant lots in the city were sites of one-ring circuses that competed with one another annually until after the Civil War. From the winter of 1838–39 the hall at 37 Bowery was known as the Bowery Amphitheatre, a major venue for circuses until it was refitted as the Stadt Theatre in 1854. Franconi's Hippodrome, an impressive canvas-covered building, occupied two acres (one hectare) at Broadway and 23rd Street. On 8 February 1864 an iron structure known as the Hippotheatron opened on 14th Street between Third and Fourth avenues. In 1865 the facility was taken over and renovated by Lewis B. Lent. From 1866 to 1876 he ran Lent's New York Circus, one of the first to travel cross country by rail. The building was bought in 1872 by P. T. Barnum, who moved his circus there in November, and was destroyed by fire the same year.

The following years saw the mergers of several large circuses. In the autumn of 1873 Barnum leased land formerly used by the New York and Harlem Railroad between Madison and Fourth avenues at 26th and 27th streets. There he erected the New York Hippodrome and presented his circus from 1874 to 1875. Known as Gilmore's Garden during the late 1870s, the building was also used by other circuses, including that of James Cooper and James A. Bailey; it was renamed Madison Square Garden in May 1879 by the new owner, Cornelius Vanderbilt. In 1881 Barnum's circus merged with Bailey's to form a three-ring circus that was introduced at Madison Square Garden and dominated the city's circus business in the years that followed. The building was replaced in 1890 with another of the same name that was the venue of the Adam Forepaugh–Sells Brothers Circus (owned by Bailey) while Barnum and Bailey toured Europe from 1898 to 1902; the new building was demolished in 1925. In 1905 another structure called the New York Hippodrome was erected at Sixth Avenue between 43rd and 44th streets. After Bailey's death from an insect bite at Madison Square Garden in 1906, Barnum and Bailey was sold to the Ringling brothers in 1907; in 1909 it opened in Chicago and the Ringling circus was moved to Madison Square Garden. The shows combined in 1919 to form the Ringling Bros. and Barnum & Bailey Circus, whose performances in New York City became associated with the arrival of spring.

Ringling Bros. enjoyed a virtual monopoly in the city. Cole Brothers, which featured the animal trainer Clyde Beatty, opened for only one season in New York City, appearing for three weeks at the New York Hippodrome in 1937. As the Clyde Beatty–Cole Brothers Circus it opened unsuccessfully at the New York Coliseum. After that time it usually held its spring opening at the Commack Arena on Long Island. After abandoning the canvas big top in 1956 in favor of arenas, Ringling Brothers no longer opened its season at Madison Square Garden, but its springtime engagement in the city still remained the longest of the season, averaging six weeks or more. As part of a Soviet-American exchange program the Moscow Circus performed at the Felt Forum in September 1963 and in later years. An important innovation in the style of American circuses was the Big Apple Circus. Conceived by Paul Binder as the nonprofit New York School for Circus Arts, it was modeled on European one-ring circuses and supported mostly by local philanthropists. It opened under canvas at Battery Park on 20 July 1977 and in the following years toured the city and other sites in the Northeast; it appeared under canvas on 4 December 1981 at Damrosch Park near Lincoln Center, which became the site of an annual engagement that gradually lengthened to more than two months during the holiday season. By 2008 both the Ringling Bros. and Big Apple circuses had lessened their focus on New York City, instead touring major cities across the United States.

George Speaight, *The History of the Circus* (San Diego, Calif.: A. S. Barnes, 1980)

Richard W. Flint

Citibank. Commercial bank. It was formed by a group of merchants in New York City on 14 September 1812 as a state-chartered institution called the City Bank of New York. Its name was changed successively to National City Bank of New York (1865, after the bank joined the national banking system), First National City Bank of New York (1955, after a merger with the First National Bank of the City of New York), First National City Bank (1962), and Citibank (1976). A holding company, First National City Corporation, was formed in 1968 with the bank as its principal subsidiary; it became known as Citicorp in 1974. The headquarters of the bank remained for almost a century at 52 Wall Street, before moving in 1908 to 55 Wall Street (previously the Merchants' Exchange and the U.S. Custom House), then in 1961 to 399 Park Avenue. Citicorp Center, containing additional offices, opened in 1977 at Lexington Avenue and 53rd Street.

The first president of the bank, Colonel Samuel Osgood (1812–13), had been the first postmaster general of the United States, a naval officer of the Port of New York, and a director of the Bank of the Manhattan Company. Isaac Wright, the fifth president (1827–32), was the founder of the Black Ball Shipping Line, which provided the first regularly scheduled sailing routes between New York City and Liverpool. After the panic of 1837, control of the bank passed to Moses Taylor, who as a director and then as the president of the bank (1856–82) took a comprehensive approach to finance, offering a full range of commercial and investment banking services, and stressed liquidity, or "ready money," for commodity merchants. Under the leadership of James Stillman (1891–1918) the bank grew from a small commercial institution into the largest bank in the United States. During the panic of 1893 its reputation for safety attracted the deposits of leading corporations, and the bank also became a major underwriter of securities for American business. Frank A. Vanderlip (1909–19), whom Stillman had chosen as his successor, formed the National City Company, which sold foreign and domestic bonds to retail customers. As president of the bank Charles E. Mitchell (1921–33) expanded on Vanderlip's strategy of diversification. He increased the number of local branches, offered compound interest, and extended personal loans to small depositors. From 1927 the National City Company sold common stocks to its customers, using the world's largest private telegraph line, and in 1929 the Farmers Loan and Trust Company became part of the bank, which now offered trust services nationwide.

The Depression led to a drastic reversal of the bank's fortunes. A planned merger with the Corn Exchange Bank collapsed. The bank also had political problems: the chief counsel of the Senate Banking Committee, Ferdinand Pecora, blamed the bank and Mitchell in particular for the stock market crash, and Mitchell resigned on 26 February 1933. The Glass–Steagall Act separated commercial and investment banking and forced the liquidation of the National City Company. A need for funds in the late 1950s led to the development in 1961 by Walter B. Wriston of the negotiable certificate of deposit, a financial instrument that allowed the bank to enter a highly competitive market for funds and expand its assets. As its president (1967–70) and then chairman (1970–84), Wriston transformed the bank into a global financial services institution. The bank expanded its businesses across state lines and emphasized consumer products as regulatory barriers fell. It was the first bank to introduce automatic teller machines on a large scale (1978) and became a national leader in credit cards, student loans, and home mortgages. In response to the oil shocks of the 1970s, it led other banks to "recycle" petrodollars (using excess funds deposited by Arab oil-producing nations by extending loans to the third world, primarily Latin America), and after the government of Mexico defaulted on its loans in August 1982 it organized an effort to restructure these loans. Wriston was succeeded as the chairman of Citibank by John S. Reed (1984–2000), who streamlined the back offices of the bank and led its consumer bank to profitability. After Reed's retirement in 2000 he was replaced by Victor Menezes, who was replaced three years later by William Rhodes. Citibank announced in 2006 that it would be the corporate sponsor of the new New York Mets stadium, which would be called CITI FIELD. In 2008 the bank became a subsidiary of Citigroup Incorporated and suffered during the global financial crisis, requiring a government bailout to survive that same year. In 2009 the company split into two companies: Citicorp and Citi Holdings, Inc.

Harold van B. Cleveland and Thomas F. Huertas, *Citibank, 1812–1970* (Cambridge, Mass.: Harvard University Press, 1985)

Joan L. Silverman

Citicorp Building. A 48-story skyscraper, 663 feet (202 meters) tall, at 44th Drive and 45th Avenue in Hunter's Point, Queens. Designed by the firm of Skidmore, Owings and Merrill and built in 1989, it provides backup office space for the Citicorp Center across the East River in Manhattan, which is one subway stop away. The Citicorp Building is taller than any other building in Queens, Brooklyn, or Long Island.

Citicorp Center. Skyscraper between 53rd and 54th streets on the east side of Lexington Avenue; at the northern end the base of the building extends as far east as Third Avenue. Designed by Hugh Stubbins with Emery Roth and Sons and completed in 1977, it has a height of 915 feet (279 meters) and is one of the tallest buildings in midtown Manhattan. The building is a sleekly modern aluminum and glass tower in the shape of a square column, entirely supported at its base by four 127-feet- (38.7-meters-) tall stilt-like pillars that are centered on each side. The asymmetrical roof is stepped and steeply sloped on its southern face and is a recognizable feature in the New York City skyline. A sunken plaza functions as an entrance to the lower level and to the subway. Originally the building was intended to have apartments on the upper stories, each with a southern terrace, but the plan was abandoned when a request for a zoning variance was denied. The Citicorp Center is arguably the most dramatic skyscraper built in the United States in the half-century after World War II.

John Tauranac

Citi Field. Baseball stadium in Flushing Meadows–Corona Park in Queens, home of the New York Mets. In July 2006 construction for the stadium began in a lot adjacent to Shea Stadium, the Mets' home field at the time. The cost of construction, which was completed in time for the 2009 season, was $900 million. New York City leases the stadium to the Mets; the current lease expires in 2049. In 2006 the New York City–based financial services company Citigroup agreed to purchase naming rights for $20 million per year, for a duration of 20 years.

Citi Field seats 41,800 fans. The design by the architecture firm Populous includes several features from Ebbets Field, the original home of the Brooklyn Dodgers, among them a rotunda dedicated to Jackie Robinson and a red brick and granite facade. The field has a natural grass surface and open-air design, as well as one of the deepest center fields in the major leagues and varied wall height. The iconic apple that was raised every time the Mets got a home run in Shea Stadium was made larger in Citi Field; the original apple from Shea Stadium is located inside Citi Field's bullpen entrance gate. Amenities at Citi Field include the Pepsi Porch, a section of right field that extends 8 feet (2.4 meters) into fair territory. The Taste of the City food court includes several of the city's trendiest eateries, and there are luxury restaurants and clubs on each level. Located behind the center field scoreboard is the 2KSports area, which caters to younger fans and features a variety of games.

Citi Field, 2009

See also SHEA STADIUM and NEW YORK METS.

Meghan Lalonde

Citizens Budget Commission. Civic association formed during the fiscal crisis of 1932 to advocate low taxes, efficiency, and tight controls over the finances of New York City. It was sponsored by real estate owners, banks, and large retail and wholesale businesses but sought to appeal to all citizens. The commission's staff publishes information about the city's revenues, borrowing, expenditures, and operations; testifies at city hearings; and advises municipal officials. Among the best-known leaders of the Citizens Budget Commission have been the real estate attorney Peter Grimm, the Republican leader Harold Riegelman, the budget analyst Herbert J. Ranschberg, and Columbia Professor Raymond Horton, who led key studies during the response to the fiscal crisis of the mid-1970s. Consistent with its long history, in 2008 the commission listed as its functions those of a "watchdog," researcher, monitor of municipal performance, and information provider.

Wallace S. Sayre and Herbert Kaufman, *Governing New York City* (New York: Russell Sage Foundation, 1960)

David C. Hammack

Citizens' Housing and Planning Council. An organization formed as the Citizens' Housing Council in 1937 by Harold S. Buttenheim, editor of the *American City,* to unite the many constituencies for housing reform and development in New York City, formulate and analyze housing policy, and support housing legislation. Its members included bankers; representatives of construction, real estate, and other businesses;

architects; engineers; labor and tenant leaders; and social workers. The council's early studies of how tax policy and rent control affected housing filled gaps in existing research and were published as a report called *Housing the Metropolis* in 1938. From 1941 it published *Legislative Information Bulletin,* which tracked and evaluated bills related to housing and community development. *A Housing Program for New York City* (1945) forecast the supply of housing that the city would need after the war and proposed financing and administrative means to achieve it. The council assumed its current name in 1948. In the following decades it analyzed public housing management (1958), offered an approach to neighborhood conservation (1962), gave an overview of the property market in the city (1975), and predicted financial difficulties in Mitchell–Lama housing (1977). In the report *On Its Own: New York City Approaches Affordable Housing* (1985), the council evaluated the effects of the federal government's virtual withdrawal from the production of subsidized housing and outlined actions that the city might undertake to address its still-urgent need for affordable dwellings. Its later reports included *The Challenge and the Change* (1989) and *Preserving New York's Low-Income Housing Stock* (1992). The council relies heavily on the technical and political expertise of its board of directors, which in the early twenty-first century consisted largely of development executives (from both profit-making and nonprofit ventures), lawyers, and bankers.

Rosalie Genevro

Citizens Union. Civic association. It began as a political party formed on 22 February 1897 by Elihu Root and 164 other prominent citizens to oppose Tammany Hall in the first municipal election after consolidation; R. Fulton Cutting was its first chairman (to 1908). The organization was committed to separating municipal elections from those at the state and national levels. Forming clubs in various districts in the city, it declined to join with local Republicans to nominate fusion candidates in the mayoral election of 1897, naming instead an independent ticket led by Seth Low, then the president of Columbia University. Low lost the election but won in 1901 after the union agreed to a slate of fusion candidates. By 1908 patronage seekers were infiltrating the party, and it became a nonpartisan civic organization. Located at 198 Broadway early in the twenty-first century, Citizens Union evaluates candidates for local office, publishes an annual voters' directory, and monitors city legislation, as well as state legislation affecting New York City. It advocates the selection of judges on the basis of merit, reforms in campaign finance and election law, and other legislative reforms to improve governmental efficiency and integrity. Among those who have served as its chairman are William Jay Schieffelin (1909–41), Richard S. Childs (1941–50), Milton M. Bergerman (1950–70), Robert B. McKay (1971–77), Terence H. Benbow (1977–83), Malcolm MacKay (1983–86), Robert F. Wagner (1986–93), and Richard J. Davis as of 2007.

Bernard Hirschhorn

City and Suburban Homes. Firm of real estate developers formed in 1896, specializing in limited-profit housing projects for low-income workers. It built model apartments on West 68th and 69th streets (now demolished), using a design by Ernest Flagg that had won a competition in 1896. In 1898 it engaged James E. Ware to adapt his own design, which had won second prize in the same competition, as the plan for a housing project in Manhattan, the First Avenue Estate, that eventually occupied sites at 1168–90 First Avenue, 1194–1200 First Avenue, 401–29 East 64th Street, and 402–30 East 65th Street. Refinements were later made by Phillip H. Ohm, who with Percy Griffin and the firm of Harde and Short was engaged to design the Avenue A Estate at 1470–92 Avenue A, 501–31 East 78th Street, and 502–28 East 79th Street; this was the largest housing project of its kind from its completion in 1913 until the 1930s. City and Suburban Homes continued to build model apartments in the city until shortly after World War II. Its most successful ventures became the basis for many other housing developments, including those built by the federal government from the 1930s. The First Avenue Estate and the Avenue A Estate were designated city landmarks in 1990. A portion of the estates was later stripped of its landmark designation by the Board of Estimate at the request of Peter Kalikow, who owned the site and wished to build luxury apartment buildings there. In 1993 the courts overturned the action of the Board of Estimate, restoring landmark designation to the entire complex.

Eric Wm. Allison

City Bank of New York. Bank formed in 1812 that eventually became known as Citibank.

City Center of Music and Drama. Concert hall at 131 West 55th Street in Manhattan, dedicated in 1924 as the Mecca Temple by the Ancient and Accepted Order of Nobles of the Mystic Shrine, or Shriners. After a foreclosure on the hall, Mayor Fiorello H. La Guardia and the producer Jean Dalrymple saved it from demolition in 1943 and purchased it for the city; it reopened on 11 December with a concert by the New York Philharmonic. City Center was the first performing arts center in the United States that could legitimately claim to be a people's arts center. It offered dramatic, musical, and dance performances at ticket prices of no more than $2. In its early years the hall was the home of the City Center Opera Company (later the New York City Opera) and the New York City Ballet, both of which encouraged American performers, composers, and choreographers. The City Center Orchestra was conducted by such figures as Leopold Stokowski and Leonard Bernstein during its relatively brief existence, and actors such as Gertrude Lawrence and Orson Welles appeared at the hall in theatrical productions. After the opening of the New York State Theater at Lincoln Center in 1966, the New York City Opera and the New York City Ballet left the City Center, which continued to stage various cultural events; starting in 2004 it hosted an annual Fall for Dance Festival.

Martin Sokol, *The New York City Opera: An American Adventure* (New York: Macmillan, 1981)

Barbara L. Tischler

City Club. Organization formed in 1892 to promote social interaction among men interested in efficient city government and the election of "fit persons" to municipal office. The management of the affairs of the club and the political campaigns that it sponsored were traditionally in different hands. The club publishes an annual report as well as books and pamphlets on such diverse subjects as rapid transit, bridges, public charities, the water supply, the school calendar, the police department, and the city charter.

James E. Mooney

City College of New York. Original college of the City University of New York, formed in 1847 by citywide referendum as the Free Academy. First housed in a building at 17 Lexington Avenue, the school offered a pre-freshman year and four years of liberal arts instruction by five faculty members, and was administered by a president. It conferred its first baccalaureate degrees in 1853 and took its current name in 1866.The college also administered Townsend Harris High School. The student body consisted in the early years largely of German Jews and by the turn of the century of Russian Jews, and attendance at the college soon came to be regarded as a means of escaping the poverty of the Lower East Side. Jews accounted for three-fourths of the students by 1903 and for at least four-fifths during the 1920s and 1930s. In 1907 construction was completed on a new campus of 35 acres (14 hectares) at 138th Street and Convent Avenue, designed in a neo-Gothic style and built of Manhattan schist excavated during the digging of subway tunnels, with a trim of white terra-cotta. An amphitheater carved into the slopes of upper Manhattan was given to the college in 1915 by the mining

City College (designed by George B. Post), ca *1910; right assembly hall*

magnate Adolph Lewisohn and named Lewisohn Stadium (demolished 1973).

City College became known for academic excellence after World War I, and enrollment increased sharply, reaching the unprecedented level of 32,030 in October 1929. To ease the strain on facilities, campuses were set up in Brooklyn and Queens that later became Brooklyn College and Queens College. In the early 1930s the college emerged as a leader in collegiate basketball, and in 1950 it became the first school to win both the National Invitational Tournament and the championship of the National Collegiate Athletic Association; these achievements were tarnished in the following year when several players were found to have been guilty of "point shaving" (deliberately reducing the margin of victory in a game to accommodate bettors). Between the 1930s and the 1950s the student body also became known for its leftist sympathies, and many socialist, communist, and Trotskyist groups were formed on the campus. As the school improved its reputation, it increased the minimum high school average required for admission, from 60 in 1928 to 88 in 1941. In 1961 the school became a part of the City University of New York, which in 1970 instituted a controversial policy of open admissions that guaranteed a place in the university system to every graduate of a high school in New York City. In 1976 the city imposed tuition fees for the first time.

After decades of expansion the school added five professional schools in the last decades of the twentieth century: the School of Architecture, the School of Nursing, the School of Engineering, the School of Education, and the Sophie Davis School of Biomedical Education. It completed a performing arts center called Aaron Davis Hall in 1979 and the North Academic Center in 1984, and housing laboratories, classrooms, and the largest library in the university system. In part because of open admissions, the college's student body by the 1980s began to the reflect the city's ethnic diversity. City College continued to make a number of renovations to its campus in the early twenty-first century, including a large investment to replace the original terracotta on many of its buildings, which had begun to erode. The annual undergraduate population in the first decade of the new millennium was around 8500. Well-known alumni of City College include the financier Bernard Baruch (1889), the novelist Upton Sinclair (1897), Senator Robert F. Wagner (1898), Justice Felix Frankfurter (1902), the actor Edward G. Robinson (1914), the lyricist Ira Gershwin (1918), the historian Lewis Mumford (1918), the labor leader A. Philip Randolph (1919), the physician Jonas E. Salk (1934), the politicians Edward I. Koch (1945) and Herman Badillo (1951), Secretary of State and General Colin L. Powell (1958), and eight Nobel laureates, the most from any public college.

Solomon Willis Rudy, *The College of the City of New York: A History, 1847–1947* (New York: City College Press, 1949; repr. Arno, 1977); Louis G. Heller, *Death of the American University, with Special Reference to the Collapse of City College* (New Rochelle, N.Y.: Arlington House, 1973)

Marc Ferris

City Council. The legislative branch of municipal government. The first charter after consolidation provided for a bicameral legislature called the Municipal Assembly, but this was abandoned in 1901 in favor of a Board of Aldermen that initially had one member from each of 73 districts who served two-year terms. The number of districts was reduced to 67 in 1916 and 65 in 1921. Several charter reforms were undertaken to strengthen the council, which in 1936 was reshaped into a single house based on proportional representation. Between the elections of 1937 and 1945 the size of the membership varied from 26 in 1937 and 1941 to 17 in 1943. Proportional representation was abandoned in 1949 when the council became a body of 25 members, elected one to a district by majority vote. Charter revisions effective in 1963 called for 10 more members, two elected at large from each borough: to promote pluralism in a body that was overwhelmingly Democratic, it was stipulated that in each borough the at-large members must not be drawn from the same party. For many years City Council districts were coextensive with state assembly districts and later with state senate districts; when the boundaries of assembly districts were redrawn in the early 1960s in compliance with a decision by the U.S. Supreme Court to apply the doctrine of "one person, one vote" to state legislatures, the city increased the number of council districts to 27 in time for the municipal elections of 1965.

After a state law established the New York City Health and Hospitals Corporation, the council was required to appoint five of the 16 members of the board. Council seats were reapportioned after the federal census of 1970, and in 1973 elections were held for 33 districts. The amended boundaries were successfully challenged in court, leading to federally mandated elections using a new set of boundaries in 1974. In the following year the council was required to approve several appointments that previously had been made at the mayor's discretion. The elections scheduled for 1981 required redistricting on the basis of figures from the census of 1980. The boundaries drawn by the council were found to violate the Voting Rights Act (1966) because they reduced the representation of racial minorities, and the elections were postponed until 1982 while new boundaries were drawn; the number of districts was increased to 35, benefiting racial minorities and incumbents. The 10 at-large seats were ruled unconstitutional because they violated the principle of "one person, one vote," and no new at-large members were elected in 1981 or 1982; the seats were abolished by referendum in 1983. Elections were held for all 35 district seats in 1985 and 1989. Charter reforms passed in 1989 increased the size of the council to 51 in 1992 and abolished the Board of Estimate, leaving the council with sole legislative authority over the operating and capital budgets; authority over zoning and land use also was transferred to the council from the Board of Estimate.

Elections for the 51 district seats were held in November 1991 on the basis of district boundaries drawn using data from the census of 1990. In 1993 council members were elected to four-year terms. The president of the City Council was elected citywide and stood next in the line of succession to the mayor's office until 1993–94 when, as a result of the charter revisions of 1989, the office was replaced by that of the public advocate. The public advocate also was given the responsibility of presiding over the council and serving as a member ex officio of all its committees, but with greatly reduced powers because of the newly enlarged role of the council's speaker. The speaker is a member of the council elected by the other members.

In 1993 voters approved an amendment to the City Charter limiting council members and other elected officials to two terms. The referendum was supported primarily by a wealthy businessman, Ronald Lauder, who financed the campaign in favor of the change. In 1996 the council speaker led an effort to amend the term limit provision to allow three terms. This was defeated at the polls with Lauder lending support to the effort to retain stricter limits. The effect of the term limit provision was evident in elections during the early twenty-first century, when several council members were prevented from seeking an additional term.

The 1989 charter reforms, the "new blood" attracted by the effects of term limits, transformed a previously weak legislature into a more active one. Council committees began playing an increased role in oversight and zoning, and the council leadership exercised initiative in bargaining with the mayor over the size and distribution of the municipal budget.

Wallace Sayre and Herbert Kaufman, *Governing New York City: Politics in the Metropolis* (New York: Russell Sage Foundation, 1960); Frank J. Mauro and Gerald Benjamin, eds., *Restructuring the New York City Government: The Reemergence of Municipal Reform* (New York: Academy of Political Science, 1989); Charles Brecher and Raymond D. Horton, with Robert Cropf and Dean Michael Mead, *Power Failure: New York City Politics and Policy since 1960* (New York: Oxford University Press, 1993)

Charles Brecher

city directories. City and business directories were an important resource for consumers and commercial establishments before the advent of the telephone and remain valuable tools for research in the twenty-first century. In 1786 David C. Franks published the first directory of New York City, a slim volume containing 856 entries. Other directories were issued by the printing firm of Hodge, Allen, and Campbell (1789–92) and by William Duncan (1792–95). David Longworth and his son Thomas published 45 editions of the *American Almanac, New-York Register, and City Directory.* Although not a formal census, the almanac provided a listing of the names, occupations, and addresses of the city's "heads of households" (mostly men), "homemakers" (mostly widows and women who owned their own businesses), and business partnerships, as well as lists of judges, politicians, ministers, and fraternal organizations. Some residents refused to give their names accurately to avoid tax collectors, military service, or jury duty. To increase revenues in 1813 David Longworth inserted a small advertising section in the front of his directory. From 1841 until 1849 directories were published by John Doggett, Jr., the first printer to interleave pages of advertising and listings. In 1860 John F. Trow emerged as the dominant printer. When advertising revenues fell during the Civil War, Trow responded by selling advertisements on the borders of pages. He also published a street guide, a directory of partnerships, and *Wilson's Business Directory,* which was organized according to occupation or service and was an important outlet for advertising.

The *Brooklyn City Directory* was first issued by Alden Spooner (from 1822); between 1832 and 1860 seven firms published the directory, along with a separate street guide and business directory. Later directories of Brooklyn were published by J. Lain and Company (from 1861), the Lain and Healy Company (from 1892), and George Uppington (from 1900).

The spread of telephones around 1900 rendered city and business directories redundant. In 1898 the publishers of the nation's directories organized into the American Association of Directory Publishers in an effort to stem the decline. Ralph L. Polk, a directory magnate from Detroit, bought out Trow's publishing interests in 1915 and continued to issue directories under Trow's name after consolidating the city directory, the street guide, and the directories of businesses and partnerships into one volume. The city directory of Manhattan appeared sporadically during the 1920s. The last was published in 1932 by the Emergency Unemployment Relief Committee.

Marc Ferris

city halls. A tavern facing Coenties Slip on Pearl Street was the center of colonial administration for New Amsterdam and became the first city hall on 6 February 1653. Administrative offices were moved on 14 October 1703

Entrance to City Hall facing City Hall Park, ca *1905*

to a building on Wall Street, which saw the trial of John Peter Zenger for libel (1735) and meetings of the Stamp Act Congress (1765) and the Continental Congress (1785); it was remodeled in 1788 by Pierre L'Enfant. On 4 October 1802 the city announced plans for a new building near what is now the intersection of Broadway and Park Row designed by John McComb, Jr., and Joseph François Mangin. One of the most prominent structures of its time, it was set in a park and had a marble exterior, a dome, a rotunda, and a cupola affording spectacular views of the surrounding countryside. At its completion in 1812 offices and legislative and judicial chambers were moved there and the former city hall on Wall Street was demolished. During festivities in 1858 celebrating a demonstration of a transatlantic cable, the cupola, dome, and rotunda were set on fire by fireworks launched from the roof; reconstruction was supervised by Leopold Eidlitz. The body of President Abraham Lincoln lay in state there for a few days during the funeral procession from Washington, D.C., to Illinois. All judicial offices were moved elsewhere by the time of the consolidation of the five boroughs in 1898, and from that time the building has been used by the mayor and the city legislature solely for offices and legislative chambers. The interior was restored between 1907 and 1918 by Grosvenor Atterbury: the Governor's Room, among his most representative works, has furniture from the Federal period and a portrait collection that includes many works by John Trumbull. In the early twenty-first century it was still used as a museum that housed important American artwork and artifacts.

Mary Beth Betts

City Hospital (Center at Elmhurst). Hospital that later became Elmhurst Hospital Center.

City Housing Corporation. Limited-profit corporation formed in 1924 by members of the Regional Planning Association of America to put into practice their theories of planning and housing design. It sponsored the construction between 1924 and 1928 of Sunnyside Gardens in Queens, which spanned about 16 contiguous city blocks and provided affordable housing for 1202 families. The innovative features of Sunnyside Gardens included common ownership of shared courtyards and the mixing in the same development of different types of buildings and apartments and different forms of ownership. The corporation also sponsored the building of Radburn Garden City in New Jersey.

Clarence S. Stein, *Toward New Towns for America* (Cambridge, Mass.: MIT Press, 1951); Carl Sussman, ed., *Planning the Fourth Migration: The Neglected Vision of the Regional Planning Association of America* (Cambridge, Mass.: MIT Press, 1976)

Michael Kwartler

City Island. Island in the northeastern Bronx and the site of a neighborhood of the same name. Nearly 1¾ miles (3 kilometers) long at its longest point, it is connected at its northern end by a bridge to the mainland but is separated from the nearest residential area there by the expanse of Pelham Bay Park. Because of its isolation the neighborhood has retained the feel of a village in New England. At the northeastern tip is a causeway connecting the island to High Island, an uninhabited island of 3 acres (1.2 hectares). Initially called Minnewits by the local Indians and Minneford Island by the British, the island received its current name when it was purchased on behalf of a syndicate in 1761 by Benjamin Palmer, who envisioned it as a potential commercial rival to New York City. Although his plans were thwarted by the onset of the American Revolution, local residents earned an income from fishing and clamming, and from 1830 the Solar Salt Works retrieved salt from evaporated seawater. In the late nineteenth and the early twentieth centuries many marine pilots lived on the island, boarding steamships from New England to guide them through the treacherous waters of Hell Gate to Manhattan. The island also became a center for building yachts, and several financiers and industrialists anchored their boats there. In the twentieth century City Island became a center for boat building and sailmaking. Landing craft were manufactured there during World War II; after the war five yachts designed at the island won the America's Cup. The island also became a summer resort of rented cottages and summer homes. Minneford Shipyard, the last boatyard on the island, closed in 1982, but sailmakers and other maritime businesses continued to flourish. City Island Avenue, the main street, has seafood restaurants and marinas along with antique shops, boutiques, and the North Wind Undersea Institute, a marine museum. Most residents live in one-family houses, although there are also some condominiums.

John McNamara, *McNamara's Old Bronx* (New York: Bronx County Historical Society, 1989)

Lloyd Ultan

City Line. Neighborhood in east central Brooklyn, bounded to the north by Atlantic Avenue, to the east by the border with Queens County, and to the south and west by North Conduit Boulevard. It was named before Brooklyn was incorporated into New York City. In 1943 residents erected a war memorial by private subscription at Liberty Avenue and Eldert Lane. Once Italian and Irish, the population became predominantly Latin American during the latter half of the twentieth century and into the twenty-first century, with some residents from the Caribbean and Guyana. Just north of the area at Grant and McKinley avenues stands St. Sylvester's Roman Catholic Church, where services are given in both Spanish and English; it is an important community center. Liberty Avenue is the main commercial district (the City Line Cinema once stood there). One- and two-family houses predominate, but there are also several small apartment buildings.

Ellen Marie Snyder-Grenier

Citymeals-on-Wheels. Charitable program launched in 1981 in New York City by the writers Gael Greene, James Beard, and Barbara Kafka to supplement Meals-on-Wheels, a federal program offering five hot meals a week to the homebound elderly. It provides hot meals on Saturdays, Sundays, and holidays for thousands of homebound elderly residents. The program is funded privately and overseen by the city's Department for the Aging.

Alana Erickson Coble

City of New York v. State of New York. Court case decided in 1990 (76 N.Y. 2d 479) by the New York State Court of Appeals. It sustained a state law authorizing a referendum of voters in Staten Island to determine whether they wished to create a commission to draft a charter that would make Staten Island an independent city. Noting that the referendum would not actually authorize secession or commit the state to support secession, the court held that the referendum would not violate the city's home rule. In the referendum, conducted in November 1990, the charter commission proposal was supported by 82 percent of the borough's voters.

Richard Briffault

city planning. City planning in colonial New York City consisted of little more than providing for defense, regulating port activities, and isolating noxious industry. A more comprehensive approach was taken during the nineteenth century to accommodate rapid growth (from 60,000 to half a million during the first half of the century). The government devised a visionary plan based on efficient transport and on uniform, easily marketable parcels of property: it laid out a comprehensive street grid, installed a citywide water system, built Central Park, and passed legislation regulating tenements and allowing the city to build a rapid transit system. Calls to increase the role of government followed during the late nineteenth century, and on consolidation in 1898 responsibility for city planning was divided among the borough presidents, the municipal legislature (consisting of the Board of Aldermen and the Board of Estimate and Apportionment), and the mayor. Among the most important jurisdictions was street mapping and park planning (only about 40 percent of the city was mapped at the time); this was overseen by the borough presidents and subject to approval by the Board of Estimate. The legislature had authority over infrastructure, purchases of land for public use, and building and housing codes; the mayor supervised the agencies responsible for delivering services and enforcing codes.

By the turn of the century progressives led by George McAneny identified planning as a vital element of municipal reform.and pressed for a nonpartisan, expert municipal commission responsible for developing a master plan and a capital budget. A citizens' advisory group was appointed to draft a plan to beautify streets and parks, and secure the passage of state legislation that gave the city jurisdiction over local planning and zoning.

At the same time, the Board of Estimate formed two committees to deal with the question of regulating land use more strictly. Each was directed by McAneny and composed of the borough presidents, and each had a paid staff and established citizens' advisory commissions. The first report recommended expanding the police power for zoning, an idea inspired by legislation limiting the height of buildings in other American cities and by the German practice of restricting land use. The second report called for a permanent planning commission patterned on those in 20 other cities. A Commission on Building Districts and Restrictions drafted a zoning code for the city. Based on a broad legal framework conceived by Edward M. Bassett, the code divided the city into residential, commercial, and unrestricted districts and regulated building density to provide more light and air; the code was adopted as law by the Board of Estimate in 1916. The requirement that skyscrapers be built with setbacks soon altered the skyline of Manhattan, as needle-like towers such as the Chrysler and Empire State buildings defined the prevailing style in commercial architecture. The Committee on the City Plan reviewed almost 50 subjects for the Board of Estimate, functioning essentially as a planning commission.

At the same time the Russell Sage Foundation sponsored a model housing community in Queens known as Forest Hills Gardens in 1911; this was followed by Sunnyside Gardens, a similar but smaller community built by the City Housing Corporation, a limited-dividend company. In 1921 the Port of New York Authority was formed to plan and operate regional transportation. During the 1920s the Russell Sage Foundation funded an ambitious initiative for the city and the 22 counties around it. Published as *The Regional Plan for New York and Its Environs,* the plan focused on transportation, open space, and the relations between the city and its suburbs. Many of its recommendations, especially for highways and regional parks, were implemented in the following decades.

In the wake of the *Regional Plan* the campaign to establish a permanent planning commission resumed, and at the insistence of such advocates as McAneny and Bassett, Mayor James J. Walker formed the City Committee on Plan and Survey. The committee made recommendations that led in 1930 to the appointment of a planning commissioner supported by a planning department and a nine-member citizens' advisory board. One of the commissioner's first tasks was to draw up a master plan for reviewing capital programs (his own power in this regard was weak). In 1932 both the commissioner's position and the department were eliminated as the city descended into fiscal crisis.

At the urging of planning advocates, Mayor Fiorello H. La Guardia in 1934 formed the Mayor's Committee on City Planning. With funds from the Works Progress Administration the group conducted real estate surveys, amended the zoning ordinance, drafted a new street plan, and mounted a large exhibition on city planning at the Russell Sage Foundation. More important, it made certain that city planning was a central issue in the charter revision of 1935. Under the new charter, approved in 1936, a permanent planning commission was formed to draw up a master plan and the capital budget, maintain the official map, and oversee the zoning ordinance. The commission had seven members (six appointed by the mayor in addition to the chief engineer of the Board of Estimate, who served ex officio) and several mandates, and its chairman oversaw a city planning department of 27 members. Each borough president was given the power to appoint a citizens' advisory board on land use. Mayor La Guardia appointed as the first chairman Rexford Tugwell, an advisor to President Franklin D. Roosevelt. Among the other commissioners were Vernon Moon, chief engineer of the Board of Estimate; Cleveland Rogers, editor of the *Brooklyn Daily Eagle;* the architect Edwin A. Salmon; Arthur V. Sheridan, chief engineer of the Bronx; and Lawrence Orton, secretary of the Regional Plan Association, who served for four terms until 1969. Initially the commission focused on the zoning ordinance of 1916, which it brought up to date by strengthening protection for districts with one-family housing and reclassifying unrestricted areas for retail, business, or manufacturing. In response to pressure for development and affordable housing, the commission revamped sections of the street system. One result was that the grid was eliminated in the area in the Bronx that became Parkchester, a housing development built by the Metropolitan Life Insurance Company.

During these years the commission began to draw up a master plan, and by 1941 it announced plans for slum clearance, low-cost housing, parks, transportation, and education. The most controversial element was the land-use scheme, which addressed the flight of the middle class to the suburbs. It assumed that the population would stay virtually unchanged at 7.3 million and focused on placing residents near their places of work and recommended reclaiming blighted areas for residential use, building high-density housing developments near parks and riverfronts and low-density ones beyond transit lines, and establishing business districts at transport hubs; it also sought to increase the amount of open space from 29,000 acres (11,745 hectares) to 76,000 acres (30,780 hectares), allowing for "greenbelts" separating incompatible districts and for a reserve surrounding Jamaica Bay. But the commission never adopted the plan. Parks Commissioner Robert Moses promptly arranged for his own appointment to the commission, where he remained a dominant figure for 18 years. During his tenure he blocked the notion of comprehensive planning and led the commission to focus instead on specific projects and the zoning ordinance. As the city's construction coordinator and the head of the Mayor's Committee on Slum Clearance he also directed the city's efforts in public building, slum clearance, and urban renewal, thus performing a highly personal and unorthodox brand of planning that was totally unimaginable to its original promoters.

The years after World War II saw the scope of city planning expand rapidly. By the late 1940s the zoning ordinance had become unworkable: it had three maps for each district, allowing hundreds of combinations, carried 1400 amendments, and made provision for a population of 70 million. The *Plan for Rezoning the City of New York* recommended a zoning ordinance based on a single map, 18 categories of land use, and 38 districts. It also sought to regulate building density according to the floor–area ratio (a measure expressing the "total permitted floor area as a multiple of the area of the lot, for all lots regardless of use"), defined an acceptable angle of light obstruction known as the sky exposure plane, and introduced requirements for open space, yards, and parking.

Little effort was made to implement these measures until the real estate magnate James Felt was appointed chairman in 1956 by Robert F. Wagner, who had become mayor in 1954. Felt soon engaged the firm of Voorhees, Walker, Smith and Smith to prepare the text and maps for a new ordinance. These were completed in less than two years and published as *Zoning New York City: A Proposal for a Zoning Resolution for the City of New York.* By 1961 the new ordinance was in place: providing for a population of 11 million (while assuming a population of eight million for 1975), it designated half the city's area for infrastructure (streets, open space, and airports), reserved almost one-third for residential development, and divided one-fifth evenly between commercial development and manufacturing.

Another central element of planning after the war was a massive rebuilding program stimulated by such federal legislation as the Housing Act of 1937, the Housing and Slum Clearance Act of 1949, and successive amendments encouraging urban renewal. Seeking to preserve the city's stature in commerce, culture, education, and health care, the commission planned to replace factories and tenements with modern apartment buildings and middle-income housing; it approved such projects as Lincoln Center, the Brooklyn Civic Center, the expansion of Pratt Institute and New York University, and the development of enormous residential districts like the West Side Urban Renewal Area, Washington Market, and Kips Bay. With federal money the city eventually built more than 100,000 units of public housing, mostly in large developments on slum-cleared land.

These efforts met with anger from community activists, who protested the destruction of their neighborhoods and the massive displacement of population. Some of the best-known leaders of the movement were Charles Abrams and Jane Jacobs, residents of Greenwich Village who fought a plan to greatly enlarge a roadway going through Washington Square Park, and who became increasingly outspoken in their criticism. *The Death and Life of Great American Cities* (1961), Jacobs's first of three major works on cities, was an attack on both the methods and goals of orthodox city planning, and Abrams later led the planning program at Columbia University, which along with Hunter College and Pratt Institute developed advocacy planning, an approach that strengthened the role of local communities. Such measures helped to increase popular activism, and after a charter revision in 1963 mandated the establishment of community districts, 59 planning areas with community boards were formed. In 1961 Elinor Guggenheimer became the first woman appointed to the city planning commission.

Both public and private concerns undertook ambitious projects. Under David Rockefeller's leadership during the 1950s, the Downtown Lower Manhattan Association sponsored a plan for the redevelopment of 564 acres (228 hectares) in lower Manhattan. This called for improved transportation and redevelopment of Washington Market and South Street Seaport as well as rezoning, all of which was accomplished in succeeding years, triggered by the decision of Chase Manhattan Bank to build new headquarters in the area. In the 1960s the planning commission oversaw new initiatives, and the staff of the planning department expanded to more than 400. After his appointment by Mayor John V. Lindsay, Donald H. Elliott formed the Urban Design Group to sponsor innovative approaches to urban problems, opened borough branches, and oversaw the creation of 59 community planning districts, an idea promoted by a predecessor, Robert F. Wagner. Concern about the waterfront became a persistent issue, although a general waterfront plan was achieved only in the early 1990s under Richard Schaffer. New York State also took a larger role in city planning at this time.

In 1969 the planning commission published its long-awaited master plan as the six-volume *Plan for New York City,* which was controversial and never adopted. At various times the commission amended the zoning ordinance of 1961 to promote specific types of development and preservation: it protected unique features by providing for special districts, offered incentives to achieve such aims as adding open public spaces to densely built-up areas, and introduced contextual zoning to make new construction visually compatible with its surroundings. Several of the most important changes resulted from charter revisions made in 1975 and 1989. The first of these revisions guaranteed the public a larger voice in project reviews. Both revisions perfected the uniform land use review process to assess zoning and planning matters; under this process community boards and borough presidents hold public hearings and review planning issues before their consideration by the planning commission and City Council. The charter of 1989 enlarged the planning commission to 13 members appointed by the mayor, the borough presidents, and the public advocate, and assigned it a new set of functions.

Although the planning commission continued to oversee the zoning ordinance and the uniform land use review process, the charter no longer mandated that it develop a single master plan. Instead the charter called for the commission to adopt local plans (known as 197a plans) submitted by community boards or other parties, the waterfront revitalization plan in compliance with the Federal Coastal Zone Management Act, and its own or other agency-generated plans. In the early twenty-first century the department of city planning continued to perform staff functions for the commission. It also worked with other municipal agencies to maintain a citywide geographic information system and prepare a series of planning reports mandated by the charter.

In 2007 Mayor Michael Bloomberg issued PlaNYC, a strategic plan prepared by the Office of Long Term Planning and Sustainability, a part of the Mayor's Office of Operations. This plan aimed to reduce the city's greenhouse gas emissions by 30 percent by 2030 while accommodating a million new residents. Its 127 initiatives dealt with improving the city's infrastructure (especially water and transportation) and environment. Among its goals was the planting of a million trees by 2017.

Eugenie Ladner Birch

City University of New York [CUNY]. The roots of the municipal college system of New York City began in 1847 with the Free Academy, which in 1866 became City College of New York. In 1926 the state legislature of New York created the Board of Higher Education to administer City College, Hunter College, and two extensions in Brooklyn and Queens (later Brooklyn College and Queens College). Because Jews

CUNY Institutions, by Date of Founding

- The City College, 1847 (4-year, Manhattan)
- Hunter College, 1870 (4-year, Manhattan)
- Bernard M. Baruch College, 1919 (4-year, Manhattan)
- Brooklyn College, 1930 (4-year, Brooklyn)
- Queens College, 1937 (4-year, Queens)
- New York City College of Technology, 1946 (4-year, Brooklyn)
- Bronx Community College, 1957 (2-year, Bronx)
- Queensborough Community College, 1958 (2-year, Queens)
- Graduate Center, 1961 (Graduate/professional, Manhattan)
- Kingsborough Community College, 1963 (2-year, Brooklyn)
- Borough of Manhattan Community College, 1963 (2-year, Manhattan)
- John Jay College of Criminal Justice, 1964 (4-year, Manhattan)
- York College, 1966 (4-year, Queens)
- Hostos Community College, 1968 (2-year, Bronx)
- Lehman College, 1968 (2-year, Bronx)
- Medgar Evers College, 1970 (4-year, Bronx)
- LaGuardia Community College, 1968 (4-year, Queens)
- Sophie Davis School of Biomedical Education, 1973 (Graduate/professional, Manhattan)
- College of Staten Island, 1976 (4-year, Staten Island)
- School of Law, 1983 (Graduate, Queens)
- Macaulay Honors College and The Teacher Academy, 2001 (4-year, multiple locations)
- School of Professional Studies, 2003 (Graduate/professional, Manhattan)
- Graduate School of Journalism, 2006 (Graduate/professional, Manhattan)

were limited by quotas at several private colleges in the city, Jewish students predominated at these colleges from the 1890s to the mid-1950s, when Italians and Irish became numerous. After World War II a rising birthrate and the ensuing demand for higher education led to a period of modest expansion, culminating in the formation in 1961 of the tuition-free City University of New York. CUNY consisted of four senior colleges (City College, Hunter College, Brooklyn College, and Queens College) and four community colleges (Bronx Community College, Queensborough Community College, Staten Island Community College, and New York City Community College, renamed New York City College of Technology in 2002). In subsequent decades CUNY gained a reputation as a top-notch public university and opened graduate and professional schools as well as additional community and senior colleges.

The system grew rapidly after chancellor Albert Bowker instituted a policy of open admissions in 1970 that guaranteed a place in the university to every high school graduate in the city. The policy was widely criticized for lowering educational standards at a university that had produced scores of well-known graduates, including Bernard Baruch, Bella Abzug, Ira Gershwin, and Colin Powell. The number of first-year students initially increased from 24,000 to more than 35,000, and the cost of the expansion contributed to a fiscal crisis at CUNY during 1975–76. Beset by its own financial problems, the city for the first time imposed tuition on CUNY students. In 1979 the state assumed financial responsibility for the senior colleges and agreed to share in the costs of the community colleges. The university's reputation had dropped dramatically by the 1990s, when more than half the students enrolled in senior colleges required remedial courses to keep up.

In 1999 the university ended open admissions at the senior colleges; that same year CUNY alumnus Matthew Goldstein became chancellor, and under his leadership the university made significant improvements. Goldstein led efforts to hire more faculty and increase private fund raising to offset decreased public funding (tuition and fees, however, continued to account for an increased percentage of the university's $2 billion operating budget). Macaulay Honors College, an elite tuition-free program, opened in 2001. By 2007 every student at the top five senior colleges passed reading, writing, and math proficiency tests, up from 58 percent in 1978. In 2008 Goldstein raised admission standards at the senior colleges; university-wide enrollment had increased after 1999 although some voiced concerns about maintaining diversity when the percentage of black students fell. CUNY remains the largest urban public college system in the country, with 23 institutions educating more than 231,000 degree-credit students and 230,000 adult, continuing, and professional education students with 6100 full-time faculty. Black, white, and Latino students each compose about one-quarter of the student body, with Asian students accounting for 15 percent; 68 percent of CUNY students attend public high schools in the city.

A Long-Range Plan for the City University (New York: Board of Education, 1962); *A New College Student: The Challenge to City University Libraries* (Rockaway Park, N.Y.: Scientific Book Service, n.d. [?1969])

Selma Berrol, Kate Lauber

civic associations. Organizations that work outside the political party system to further their views of the public interest and nonpartisan government. The Chamber of Commerce of the State of New York, arguably the city's first civic association, formed in 1768 to protest the Townshend Acts. Other early civic associations such as the Free School Society (1805), the Society for Prevention of Pauperism (1818), and the Association for Improving the Condition of the Poor (1843) advocated services. Most early associations won municipal subsidies from city officials who shared their social and family connections. Universal suffrage for white men increased the diversity of the City Council after 1850; wealthy merchants responded by creating the Citizens' Association (1863), a self-styled nonpolitical advocate of good government that sought to reform sanitary and housing conditions and evaluated the city government. Like the Chamber of Commerce of the State of New York, the Citizens' Association provided a sort of unofficial or private government until it ventured directly into politics at the behest of Peter Cooper and others. It remained active in municipal affairs well into the 1870s when some of its most prominent members formed the New York County Democracy, an overtly partisan group opposed to Tammany Hall.

Chamber of Commerce of the State of New York, ca *1905*

Civic associations allied with the Republican Party of the period included the Union League Club (1863), the New York Civil Service Reform Association (1877), and the City Reform Club (1882), in which Theodore Roosevelt was briefly prominent. Efforts by the People's Municipal League (1890), the City Club (1892) and its Committee of Seventy (1894), and Citizens Union (1897) to encourage the participation of "independent" Democrats and Republicans in mayoral campaigns brought civic associations to their high point. The vast, diverse electorate created by consolidation in 1898 made it more difficult for civic associations to compete against Democratic and Republican organizations with sophisticated leaders (such as Democrat Charles F. Murphy) and statewide networks.

With the expansion of municipal government at the end of the nineteenth century, most civic associations narrowed their focus. Women led many of the new groups, including the Charity Organization Society, the New York State Charities Aid Association, the Women's Health Protective Association, the Kindergarten Association, and the Public Education Association. Organizations concerned specifically with women's issues included the Women's City Club, the New York City Federation of Women's Clubs, several woman suffrage organizations, and the League of Women Voters (1920). Citizens Union alone continued to enjoy considerable electoral success with fusion mayoral candidates such as Seth Low and John Purroy Mitchel and ultimately Fiorello H. La Guardia. After World War II the Regional Plan Association of New York and the Citizens Budget Commission sought to play a broad role in policy planning comparable to that of the "private governments" of the nineteenth century. Notable associations with sharply defined purposes include the United Parents Association, the Citizens Committee on Children, the Citizens' Housing and Planning Council, the Friends of Central Park, and the Gay Men's Health Crisis. Citywide and neighborhood chambers of commerce and block associations are also civic associations, as are ethnic associations such as B'nai B'rith, the National Association for the Advancement of Colored People (NAACP), and the Italian-American Defense Fund. So many groups are now well organized in New York City that this is in truth a vast and complex field.

David C. Hammack

civil defense. There was little fear of foreign military attack in New York City during World War I, despite rumors of sabotage, but World War II brought a different perception and a different reality. Early in the war German U-boats sank thousands of tons of shipping near the entrance of New York Harbor. New Yorkers were reminded that "loose lips sink ships." After the Allies bombed Berlin in 1942, German radio vowed retribution against New York City, and blackout drills took on an understandable urgency. Mayor Fiorello H. La Guardia warned that the city was the "world's number-one target."

Rejected for a commission in the military, Mayor La Guardia in May 1941 was named the unpaid head of the U.S. Office of Civilian Defense, a position that he vigorously discharged but held only until early 1942. In the following year he appointed Grover A. Whalen, the guiding spirit behind the World's Fair of 1939–40, to lead the city's Civilian Defense Volunteers Office. During the war more than 400,000 New Yorkers enrolled. Organized at the local level by block leaders, about half the volunteers were assigned to "civilian protective groups," which included aircraft spotters, air raid wardens, and auxiliary firemen and policemen. Blackout drills were held at three-month intervals, and sirens were tested each Saturday at noon. The other volunteer programs, designated "community war services," involved activities such as child care, nutrition education, housing information, carpooling, and rationing. The rationing of gasoline, rubber, sugar, coffee, meat, and processed food by the U.S. Office of Price Administration (OPA) was supervised in New York City by 15 local offices. Regulations were so specific that they differentiated between hard and soft salami. Barrels to collect rubber, rags, and metal were placed in the lobbies of apartment buildings and public buildings. Schoolchildren collected tinfoil. Colleges provided training for military units, Columbia University offered courses to improve the efficiency of defense plants, and students at Brooklyn College went upstate to help bring in the crops. The city's branch of the American Association of University Women sponsored lectures on the psychological effects of war.

Near the war's end plans were made to sell the air raid sirens and close the city's civil defense offices. But the cold war strategy of nuclear deterrence assumed an atomic survival plan, and the U.S. Civil Defense Act of 1950 "assigned the main responsibility for action to state and local authorities with appointed local volunteer staffs." The New York City Office of Civil Defense, at 135 East 55th Street in Manhattan, coordinated all matters affecting civil defense and natural disasters, and had the power to mobilize civil defense forces and direct other municipal agencies. Schools held "duck and cover" drills; newspapers printed air raid instructions; shelter sites were designated in basements and subways; sirens were placed in firehouses; dehydrated foods, medicines, and supplies, including postcards to be mailed to relatives, were stockpiled throughout the city; buses were designed for conversion into ambulances; and documentary films as well as a 34-page pamphlet entitled "You and the Atomic Bomb" were widely distributed. There was, however, little support from the legislature, implementation was haphazard, with few dollars and fewer volunteers, and the public was essentially apathetic. The military editor of the *New York Times,* Hansen Baldwin, described the city's civil defense effort as "non-existent."

In 1955 Mayor Robert F. Wagner and Governor W. Averell Harriman argued that civil defense was a federal responsibility. Although the city was seen as a prime target of Soviet missiles, many New Yorkers questioned the value of shelters to protect against the immense destruction of a hydrogen bomb. Ulster and Sullivan counties were examined as evacuation sites, despite widespread doubt that evacuation from a missile attack was possible. One county executive in Westchester said that in the event of an attack he would close the boundaries with New York City. In the early 1960s Governor Nelson A. Rockefeller promoted shelters, notwithstanding continued debate about their worth, and sought to stock them with federal agricultural surpluses. During the 1960s and 1970s public concern with civil defense declined in New York even as the ability of the Soviet Union to destroy the city increased. With the collapse of the Union of Soviet Socialist Republics in the early 1990s, the military threat against North America virtually disappeared.

By the early twenty-first century, terrorism by fanatics became more of an issue than hostile actions by a powerful nation-state.

See also Counter-terrorism.

Arnold Markoe

Civilian Review Board. A panel dating back to 1953 to hear complaints of misconduct by the police. Mayor John V. Lindsay's proposal in 1966 that the panel consist entirely of private citizens provoked bitter opposition from the Patrolmen's Benevolent Association, which failed to defeat the plan in court but then succeeded in doing so by an overwhelming margin in a referendum. The board was then put in place with a membership consisting solely of employees of the police department (under the name Civilian Complaint Review Board). There was little public discussion or controversy in 1986 when Mayor Edward I. Koch signed a bill changing the composition of the board so that half its members would be private citizens. During the late 1980s the board heard allegations of police brutality in connection with several incidents, including a riot involving the police and advocates for the homeless in Tompkins Square Park in 1988. At the urging of Mayor David N. Dinkins, the City Council in 1993 passed a bill requiring all members of the board to be civilians (five selected by the mayor, five by the City Council, three by the police commissioner). The new board was also granted subpoena power. In 2001 Mayor Rudolph Giuliani adopted a practice that allowed the board to prosecute cases, although all substantiated disciplinary cases must still be given administrative hearings within the department regardless of whether a criminal prosecution takes place.

Joseph P. Viteritti

civil service. Nonelected government workers. Political loyalties were openly considered when public offices were filled in New York City during colonial times and after independence. In the late eighteenth century there were three appointed offices in the city for every eight persons in the electorate. Not all appointments were desirable; the charter of Governor John Montgomerie stipulated a penalty for appointees who refused to serve.

Among the positions filled by the state council of appointment was the mayoralty, which commanded such patronage that to accept it DeWitt Clinton resigned in 1803 from the U.S. Senate. During the 1830s the electorate expanded, the mayoralty and other municipal offices became elected positions, and municipal appointments were used to build and sustain broadly based "political machines." In some cases appointees engaged only in political work collected city salaries. During the mid-nineteenth century, Democrats in the city and Republicans in state government battled for control of municipal appointments. Tammany Hall played an important role in dispensing patronage, especially by its leaders, William M. "Boss" Tweed and John Kelly.

In reaction, the first civil service reform association in the United States, the Civil Service Reform Association, was formed in the city in 1877, and in 1883 New York City and Brooklyn became the first cities in the nation to adopt civil service regulations. (These inspired a national civil service movement.) Also in 1883 the first state civil service commission in the nation was established in New York. The application of civil service regulations in cities with populations of 50,000 or more, at first optional, was mandated by state law for certain groups of employees in 1884. In 1894 the new state constitution stipulated that state and local employees should be appointed and promoted according to "merit and fitness" determined in competitive examinations.

In the decades after consolidation, civil service reformers and party leaders struggled for control of municipal appointments. Initially the conflict was marked by issues of ethnicity and class: most reformers were Protestant and middle or upper middle class, while most members of party organizations were immigrants and Irish Catholics. Realizing its popularity, the parties embraced the notion of merit and fitness but simultaneously worked to constrain its reach by excluding certain positions from civil service requirements, establishing temporary appointments, and manipulating civil service rules and procedures.

Ironically, civil service rules sometimes proved to be an obstacle to reform—for example, by preventing employment of outside experts in city government. Mayors John Purroy Mitchel, Fiorello H. La Guardia, and John V. Lindsay were accused by their partisan adversaries of bypassing the civil service system to build political bases in the city's neighborhoods. The efforts of Mayor Robert F. Wagner (ii) led to a state law establishing a personnel department for city government (1954), collective bargaining with municipal employees' labor unions (1958), and a reduced role for the municipal civil service commission in policy making.

After it was disclosed in 1989 that Mayor Edward I. Koch maintained a "talent bank" of supporters seeking municipal appointments, the State Commission on Government Integrity (led by John Feerick) argued that to make municipal employment more widely accessible the number of posts requiring special qualifications should be limited. Allegations of bypassing civil service requirements continued to arise periodically, for example with regard to personnel administration in the Parks Department during the mayoralty of Rudolph W. Guiliani. A 1996 charter change under Mayor Guiliani created a Division of Citywide Personnel Services within a newly established Department of Citywide Administrative Services. At the end of 2005 there were 223,824 city employees under civil service administration. The Civil Service Commission remained as a quasi-judicial oversight and appeals body, seeking to ensure the continued application of the "merit and fitness" principle in city government.

William L. Riordon, *Plunkitt of Tammany Hall* (New York: McClure, Phillips, 1905); Wallace S. Sayre and Herbert Kaufman, *Personnel Administration in the Government of New York City* (New York: Mayor's Committee on Management Survey of the City of New York, 1952); Theodore J. Lowi, *At the Pleasure of the Mayor: Patronage and Power in New York City, 1898–1958* (New York: Free Press, 1964)

See also Government and politics.

Gerald Benjamin

civil service unions. Some of the first municipal workers who organized in New York City were street cleaners; they joined the Knights of Labor and the International Brotherhood of Teamsters but ceased their efforts after an unsuccessful strike in 1911. The New York Teachers' Union (1916) was succeeded by the United Federation of Teachers, which did not sign its first contract until mid-century. A number of organizations were formed that provided mutual aid and fought for better working conditions, but they did not engage in collective bargaining. Among these were the Patrolmen's Benevolent Association (PBA), the Firemen's Mutual Benefit Association, and the Civil Service Forum. Interest in unions among city employees increased during the 1930s as the Civil Service Forum declined, the national labor movement revived, and the political left grew in importance (many municipal unions were led by socialists and communists). By the time of World War II, unions had a foothold in the public welfare, hospital, and sanitation departments and the boards of transportation and education. Mayor Fiorello H. La Guardia (1934–45) allowed employees to join unions but barred them from striking and the city from engaging in collective bargaining. His stand was tested in 1940 during the city takeover of private transit lines that employed unionized workers. After a series of clashes with the Transport Workers Union, La Guardia entered into negotiations about wages and other issues but refused to allow formal bargaining. In 1947 the state's Condon–Wadlin Act outlawed strikes by public employees and made the dismissal of strikers automatic.

Municipal unions made some of their most important gains under Mayor Robert F. Wagner (1954–65). Seeking the support of labor during the 1953 mayoral election, Wagner pledged to institute collective bargaining for city workers. In 1954 he established employee grievance procedures and guaranteed the right of city workers to organize without reprisal. In 1956 the city allowed unions to collect dues from employees by means of voluntary withholding from paychecks and held its first union recognition election. Executive Order 49, issued by Wagner in 1958, granted many workers the right to bargain with the city through exclusively recognized unions of their choice. Blue-collar employees were among the first to take advantage of these gains. Some were represented by unions within single agencies, such as the Uniformed Sanitationmen's Association. Employees scattered throughout city government were sought out by Teamsters Local 237 and District Council 37 of the American Federation of State, County, and Municipal Employees, which soon became the largest municipal union. During the mid-1960s professional and clerical workers, many of whom were women, joined unions in large numbers, and several police officers' and firefighters' benevolent associations became collective bargaining agents. There were few strikes during Wagner's term, and those that occurred had little effect on the public, except for one by welfare workers in 1965 that lasted for 28 days. Under Mayor John V. Lindsay (1966–73) strikes were frequent and disruptive. In January 1966 transit workers held a 12-day strike that virtually paralyzed the city. During the next three years physicians, nurses, teachers, social workers, and sanitation workers went on strike, and the PBA held a five-day "sick-out."

The unions' militancy brought about dramatic improvements in wages, benefits, and pensions and led to the replacement of the Condon–Wadlin Act in 1967 by the Taylor Law, which continued the ban on strikes but placed greater emphasis on resolving disputes.

The growth of municipal unions, at a time when unionized employment in private industry was declining, bolstered the labor movement in the city. By 1970 civil service unions had more than 250,000 members and represented more than 90 percent of the city workforce in collective bargaining. Most civil service unions supported the civil rights movement and the liberal wing of the Democratic Party, but police unions generally followed a more conservative path. During the fiscal crisis of the mid-1970s civil service unions helped the city to avoid bankruptcy by agreeing to wage deferrals, benefit reductions, large-scale dismissals, and the use of pension funds to buy $2.5 billion in municipal bonds. Union backing was crucial in the election of Governor Mario M. Cuomo in 1982 and Mayor David N. Dinkins in 1989.

By the end of the twentieth century civil service unions had well over 300,000 members and remained influential in the routine operations and long-term development of municipal government. However, the city practice of signing contracts with one or two of its unions and then forcing the rest to accept the established pattern, along with reluctance of civil service unions after the fiscal crisis to engage in illegal strikes, restrained wage gains even during periods of prosperity.

Raymond D. Horton, *Municipal Labor Relations in New York City: Lessons of the Lindsay-Wagner Years* (New York: Praeger, 1973); Bernard Bellush and Jewel Bellush, *Union Power and New York: Victor Gotbaum and District Council 37* (New York: Praeger, 1984); Mark H. Maier, *City Unions: Managing Discontent in New York City* (New Brunswick, N.J.: Rutgers University Press, 1987); Joshua B. Freeman, *Working Class New York: Life and Labor since World War II* (New York: New Press, 2001)

Joshua B. Freeman

Civil War. New York City's role in the Civil War has often been underappreciated. In part, this derives from two prominent events in the city that hardly advanced the Union cause. The first of course was the secession, or "free city" movement, associated with Mayor Fernando Wood, who called in early 1861 for New York City to remain neutral in a future North–South conflict. Manhattan was already the commercial entrepot of the entire United States, and its merchants and factories had already "lent" tens of millions of dollars, all of it at risk in case of war, to enterprises in the southern states. In the event of armed insurrection, such trade would be disrupted, and the worst-case scenario, feared by the New York City elite, was that the new Confederate government would unilaterally declare all debts to persons and businesses in the North null and void. New York City businessmen would lose $100 million or more in an instant. Not surprisingly, they proposed that Manhattan simply secede from Washington, remain neutral, and continue to do business with all comers in any forthcoming conflict. There would be no disruption of commerce, no deaths, and no inconvenience. This scenario never played out, the secession movement disintegrated, and New York City businessmen became enthusiastic supporters of the Union cause.

The second disruptive event in New York City during the Civil War was a riot in July 1863 that continues to rank as the worst civil disturbance in all of American history. The week-long violence resulted in at least 100 deaths, dozens of burned out buildings, and thousands of injuries. There was ample justification for anger among the rioters, in the form of a draft policy that allowed affluent men, such as Theodore Roosevelt's father, to buy their way out of uniformed service, but the riots gave the city a bad reputation on both sides of the Mason–Dixon line.

Yet New York City was the backbone of the Union cause. For example, in April 1861, after Confederate batteries in Charleston harbor had fired upon the American flag at Fort Sumter and after Abraham Lincoln had called for 75,000 volunteers to defend the union, more than 150,000 New Yorkers, the largest assemblage of people ever seen in the western hemisphere, gathered in and around Union Square in a public expression of support for the president. By the end of 1861, 66 regiments from New York State were already in uniform. By the end of the war, 448,000 residents of New York State had been drawn to the colors, comprising 248 infantry regiments, 27 cavalry regiments, and 23 regiments of engineers or artillery. New York City alone put about 100,000 men into the field, or more than any other city and almost as many as any state. Some New Yorkers served with particular distinction. The 69th infantry, better known as the Irish Brigade, for example, was blessed by Archbishop John Hughes at St. Patrick's Cathedral just before departing for war on 23 April 1861. It soon developed a reputation as one of the toughest units in the Union Army, and its soldiers made a decisive contribution to the federal victory at Antietam. Similarly, at Gettysburg in early July 1863, five of the six Union generals in action on the first day were from New York. On the second day, when Little Round Top was in extreme peril, five Union regiments, two of them from New York, saved the left flank of the army of the Potomac and thus the entire Union position. And the two officers whose quick thinking and decisive action made possible that epic defense were both from New York—Brigadier General Gouverneur Kimble Warren and Colonel Strong Vincent.

The New York 20th, 26th, and 31st regiments were major formations in what was known then as the United States Colored Troops (USCT). African Americans in those units trained on Hart Island and Rikers Islands in 1864, and the 31st was one of the Union regiments that cornered Robert E. Lee at Appomattox on 9 April 9 1865 and effectively ended the war.

But it was New York's industries and financiers as much as its soldiers who eliminated all hope for the Confederacy. New York State alone produced more manufactured goods than all 11 southern states combined, and it had more railroad track mileage than the entire Confederacy. At the great Continental Iron Works in the Greenpoint section of Brooklyn, skilled craftspeople produced gun carriages and mortar beds for the Navy, and they did most of the work on the Union's first ironclad warship, the *Monitor,* which engaged the Confederate ironclad *Merrimac* in 1862 in Virginia, thus ending the 2000-year history of wooden navies.

New York City, already the nation's largest city in 1860 and about twice the size of Philadelphia, outproduced every other city, let alone then-backward Richmond, where a few enterprises like the Tredegar Iron Works tried unsuccessfully to keep up with northern workshops. The city's carriagemakers made hundreds of supply wagons and ambulances for the Union Army, while Phelps Dodge made iron forgings and casings. The city's fledgling garment industry standardized men's suit sizes and made enough uniforms to literally outfit an army. Pharmaceuticals poured out from the shops of Pfizer and Squibb, while the Hendricks Brothers Copper Rolling Mills operated at full capacity around the clock to meet war needs. By the end of the Civil War in 1865, New York City was thriving as never before and poised to join London and Paris as one of the three greatest urban agglomerations in the world. The result would probably have been the same even if President Lincoln had somehow avoided war, but there can be little doubt that the foundation for New York City's industrial, financial, cultural, and commercial supremacy had been strengthened by the conflict between 1861 and 1865. And over those four years New York City and New York State made it possible for the United States to remain one nation.

Kenneth T. Jackson

Claiborne, Liz [Ortenberg, Elisabeth Claiborne] (*b* Brussels, 31 March 1929; *d* 26 June 2007). Fashion designer. She emigrated to the United States in 1939, at the age of 20 won the Jacques Heim National Design Contest (sponsored by *Harper's Bazaar*), and in

1949 moved to New York City to work as a sketch artist at the sportswear house Tina Leser. She worked as a designer for Dan Keller and Youth Group Inc. before forming a business under her own name in 1976. She broadened her line by 1984 to include accessories, men's and children's clothes, and fragrances. In 1989 she retired to pursue environmental and philanthropic interests, establishing the Liz Claiborne and Art Ortenberg Foundation that year. As of 2008 her company was valued at $5 billion.

Anne E. Kornblut

Clare, Ada (McElhenney) (*b* Charleston, S.C., July 1834; *d* New York City, 4 March 1874). Actress, feminist, and writer. Born to an aristocratic southern family, she moved to New York City in 1854 and took up acting. During the height of her acting career she frequented Pfaff's Cellar, where she became known as the "queen of Bohemia"; she also wrote a column for the *Saturday Press,* an iconoclastic weekly magazine of the arts. Her sole novel, *Only a Woman's Heart* (1866), was so poorly received by reviewers that she abandoned writing and spent the rest of her career acting in a provincial stock company. She died of rabies, which she contracted from a dog bite suffered in her theatrical agent's office.

Jan Seidler Ramirez

Claremont. Neighborhood in the southwestern Bronx (2000 pop. 15,064), lying in the northernmost section of Morrisania and bounded to the north by the Cross Bronx Expressway, to the east by Crotona Park, to the south by East 169th Street, and to the west by Claremont Park. The name Claremont was first applied to the estate of the Zborowski family, which occupied 38 acres (15.4 hectares) west of Webster Avenue; it was separated from the neighboring estate of the Bathgate family (later Crotona Park) by a carriage road that became Claremont Parkway. The Zborowski and Bathgate estates were bought for parkland by New York City in 1888 and later became Claremont Park and Crotona Park. The neighborhood developed in between the parks on lower ground. It became populous in the 1920s and 1930s and was predominantly Jewish until the 1950s, when the community became increasingly black and Spanish-speaking. By the 1990s, crime, drugs, abandoned housing, demolished blocks, and a large concentration of high-rise low-income public housing left Claremont one of the poorest sections of the southern Bronx. Since then, a decrease in crime and new construction of affordable housing have improved the neighborhood.

Jill Jonnes, *South Bronx Rising: The Rise, Fall, and Resurrection of an American City* (New York: Fordham University Press, 2002)

Evelyn Gonzalez

Claremont Riding Academy. A riding school housed in an equestrian stable at 175 West 89th Street in Manhattan. It was the oldest continuously operated equestrian stable in New York City and perhaps the oldest in the United States. The building (now a landmark), designed by Frank A. Rooke in Romanesque Revival style and completed in 1892, was a common structure for its time and housed a succession of livery businesses. The academy was formed in 1927, at a time when many stables in the city had been razed or converted into parking garages. In the 1960s the city condemned the academy to make way for public housing, but the housing was never built, and Paul Novograd, son of the academy's previous owner, bought it back in 1998. In April 2007 Novograd closed the academy because of rising costs and a decline in business.

Clarissa L. Bushman

Clarenceville. An obsolete name for a small section of Richmond Hill in central Queens. It began as a development in January 1853, when a group led by the prominent lawyer W. T. B. Milliken bought a farm on the south side of Jamaica Avenue, extending from 100 feet (30 meters) west of 110th Street to 100 feet east of 112th Street. A post office and a railroad station opened in July 1869. By August 1872 the community had essentially become absorbed by the surrounding development of Richmond Hill and abandoned its original name. The Long Island Rail Road nevertheless continued to use the name Clarenceville for a station at 111th Street until service there ceased in 1940.

Vincent Seyfried

Clark, Aaron (*b* Northampton, Mass., 16 Oct 1787; *d* New York City, 2 Aug 1861). Mayor. A lawyer and wealthy landowner, he became a Whig alderman and won a three-way election during the panic of 1837 to become the second popularly elected mayor of New York City. In 1838 he was reelected by a margin of 500 votes; he narrowly lost the election in the following year.

James E. Mooney

Clark, Kenneth (Bancroft) (*b* Panama Canal Zone, 24 July 1914; *d* Hastings-on-Hudson, N.Y., 1 May 2005). Psychologist. When he was five years old he moved to Harlem with his mother, a seamstress and union organizer for the International Ladies' Garment Workers' Union. His father remained in the Canal Zone, working with the United Fruit Company as an agent. Clark attended local public schools and George Washington High School in upper Manhattan. He earned a bachelor's degree in 1935 and a master's in 1937 from Howard University. He completed his doctorate at Columbia University in 1940, the first African American to earn a doctorate from its Psychology Department. While at Columbia he studied with Otto Klineberg, the eminent social psychologist. Clark became the first black faculty member at City College of New York. During World War II he worked on Gunnar Myrdal's *An American Dilemma,* the massive study of American racism. Clark's work with his wife, Mamie Phipps Clark, on racial awareness in children played a critical role in the U.S. Supreme Court's decision in *Brown v. Board of Education* (1954) that ruled racial segregation in public schools unconstitutional. Clark formed the organization Harlem Youth Opportunity Unlimited and began several experimental programs in education. His published writings include *Dark Ghetto* (1965), his classic discussion of the effect of racism and social and political powerlessness among urban blacks during the 1960s; *The Pathos of Power* (1974); and *A Relevant War on Poverty* (1969), with Jeannette Hopkins, his longtime editor. Clark became president of the American Psychological Association in 1970. He retired from teaching in 1975 but continued to be active at City College for the remainder of his life. He was dedicated to the Northside Center for Child Development, the social service and psychological service for children that he established with Mamie Clark in 1946. Initially, Clark hoped to establish an integrated center that would exemplify the principles of integration, but resistance from referral agencies and the school system combined with the reality of de facto segregation led to a largely minority client population. Clark's later life was marked by a certain cynicism about the future of American society's willingness to change, but he remained true to his belief that a truly integrated society remained the last, best hope.

Kenneth B. Clark, *Dark Ghetto, Dilemmas of Social Power* (New York: Harper and Row, 1965); Gerald Markowitz and David Rosner, *Children, Race, and Power: Kenneth and Mamie Clark's Northside Center* (New York: Routledge, 2000)

David Rosner

Clark [née Phipps], **Mamie (Katherine)** (*b* Hot Springs, Ark., 1917; *d* Hastings-on-Hudson, N.Y., 11 Aug 1983). Psychologist. She spent her youth in Hot Springs, attended Howard University, and earned a doctorate in psychology from Columbia University. Her research on racial awareness in young children was furthered by her husband, Kenneth Clark, and played a critical role in the decision *Brown v. Board of Education* (1954), in which the U.S. Supreme Court ruled racial segregation in public schools to be unconstitutional. Clark was the director of the Northside Center for Child Development from 1946 to 1979.

David Rosner

Clason Point. Neighborhood in the south central Bronx, bounded to the north by White Plains Road and the Bruckner Expressway, to the east by Pugsley's Creek, to the south by the East River, and to the west by the Bronx River. The neighborhood is mainly residential and contains a few small shops and a strip mall on Soundview Avenue. The first inhabitants were Siwanoys, whose village, Snakapin, was one of the largest Indian settlements along the shoreline of the Bronx. Known as Cornell's Neck by European settlers (for Thomas Cornell, a farmer who settled there in 1654), it was later named for Isaac Clason, a wealthy merchant of the nineteenth century, and became the site of the Clason Military Academy. The view and proximity to the East River and the mouth of the Bronx River led to the development of resorts that included dance halls, bathing piers, and restaurants. During World War II the last pedestrian ferry from Clason Point to College Point in Queens ended service; after the war Kane's Casino became the Shorehaven Beach Club, which was later the site of a housing development. The singer Jennifer Lopez began her career performing at the local Boys and Girls Club. Since the 1980s more than a quarter of new immigrants settling in Clason Point and its environs have been Dominican. The neighborhood is also populated by large numbers of immigrants from Ecuador, Honduras, Colombia, Jamaica, Guyana, and China.

John McNamara, *History in Asphalt: The Origin of Bronx Street and Place Names* (New York: Bronx County Historical Society, 1984); John McNamara, *McNamara's Old Bronx* (New York: Bronx County Historical Society, 1989)

Gary D. Hermalyn

classical music. New York City has been the national musical capital since the mid-nineteenth century. Its continued dominance into the twentieth and twenty-first centuries was ensured by its orchestras, opera companies, concert halls, and conservatories and by its role in music publishing and recording.

1. Beginnings to 1890

The Dutch sang psalms in their own language long after the English captured the colony (1664) and formed Trinity Church (1697). Musical life in eighteenth-century New York City was undistinguished. The earliest documented public performance, advertised in the *New–York Gazette* as a "consort of musick, vocal and instrumental," was held in 1736 at the home of the vintner Robert Todd. The first concert hall in the city was the Nassau Street Theatre at 64–66 Nassau Street where operas were staged from about 1750. A singing school opened in 1753 by William Tuckey, a clerk at Trinity Church, offered biweekly classes and helped the church to develop an accomplished choir. Music dealers and instrument makers often supplemented their incomes by giving music lessons; two of the best known were W. C. Hulett (a violin teacher and dancing master from 1759 to 1799) and Alexander Reinagle (who gave keyboard lessons to George Washington's adopted daughter, Nellie Custis). About 1760 Francis Hopkinson, later a signer of the Declaration of Independence, provided translations in English for the Psalter. The New Theatre opened in 1798 on Park Row facing City Hall Park and later became known as the Park Theatre. During these years musical life remained dominated by England: the theater in New York City was in effect a provincial branch of the theater in London, and many English immigrants were musicians and singing actors, some of whom also worked as teachers, publishers, composers, and entrepreneurs. Among the most important were James Hewitt (1770–1827), who moved to the city in 1792 and wrote the music for the play *Tammany; or, the Indian Chief* (1794); Benjamin Carr (1769–1831), composer of the opera *The Archers; or, The Mountaineers of Switzerland* (1796); and Victor Pelissier (*b ca* 1740; *d ca* 1820), composer of the opera *Edwin and Angelina* (1796). John Jacob Astor, who later made a fortune in the fur trade and in real estate in Manhattan, opened a music shop in the city in 1786 and within a decade found himself competing with Hewitt and Carr in importing and distributing music and instruments, principally from England.

Music in New York City developed rapidly during the nineteenth century as the number of inhabitants and especially of immigrants steadily increased. Traveling theatrical companies presented a variety of English, French, and Italian works in newly constructed theaters, and after the War of 1812 several notable European musicians arrived in the city. At the Park Theatre in 1825 Manuel García's troupe mounted a production of Rossini's *Il barbiere di Siviglia* (the first Italian opera performed in the city in its entirety) and another of Mozart's *Don Giovanni* that was attended by the author of the libretto, Lorenzo Da Ponte, a resident of New York City since 1805. Da Ponte was a leading backer of the Italian Opera House at Church and Leonard streets (opened in 1833, closed in 1835, reopened in 1836 as the National Theatre), a successful opera and entertainment hall that was destroyed by fire in 1841. Washington Irving, the city's leading literary figure, an amateur flutist, and the author of another English version of *Der Freischütz,* took part in the negotiations surrounding the production of *Il barbiere* (an effort also supported by Astor). He also joined with other literary figures to help bring about the first complete American production in 1839 of Beethoven's *Fidelio,* which attracted full houses to the Park Theatre for 14 consecutive nights.

One of the most important concert venues in the nineteenth century was Niblo's Garden at Broadway and Prince Street (built by William Niblo in 1829, destroyed by fire in 1846, rebuilt in 1849, again destroyed by fire in 1895). There, Gaetano Donizetti's *Lucia di Lammermoor* received its first staging in New York City in 1843. Italian opera also established a strong following at the Richmond Hill Theatre at Charlton and Varick streets, where Vincenzo Bellini's *Il Pirata* was given its American premiere; the theater was also known as Tivoli Garden and changed its name successively to the New Greenwich Theatre and the New York Opera House before closing in 1849. The American premiere of Bellini's *I Puritani* in 1844 was the opening production of Palmo's New York Opera House, the most distinguished opera house in early nineteenth-century New York City, which also staged the first opera by Giuseppe Verdi in the United States (*I Lombardi* in 1847); after a change in ownership in 1848 the repertory changed from music to theater. In 1847 a group of wealthy patrons opened the Astor Place Opera House. The riot that took place nearby in 1849 tarnished its reputation irretrievably, and in 1854 the owners sold the opera house to the Mercantile Library Association, which converted the building to Clinton Hall. The same year marked the opening of the Academy of Music, the first permanent opera house in New York City. Concerts were given from 1859 at the Great Hall at Cooper Union (still in operation in the 1990s) and from 1861 at the Brooklyn Academy of Music on Montague Street (destroyed by fire in 1903).

Although New York City in the middle of the nineteenth century did not have a school of composers equal to the Knickerbocker poets or the painters of the Hudson River School, a number of resident composers wrote music of lasting merit. One was Anthony Philip Heinrich (1781–1861), composer of fanciful orchestral pieces such as *The Ornithological Combat of Kings; or, The Condor of the Andes and the Eagle of the Cordilleras* (1836), who lived in New York City from 1837 until his death. Another important composer who flourished in the city was William Henry Fry (1813–64), an ebullient lecturer and a writer for Horace Greeley's *New York Tribune* whose works include *Leonora* (1845), the first American bel canto opera in English, and the symphony *Santa Claus* (1853). The popular composer Stephen Foster spent some of the most important years of his songwriting career in the city and died at Bellevue Hospital. The first internationally recognized American keyboard virtuoso, Louis Moreau Gottschalk (1829–69), made New York City his home during much of his peripatetic later career. His piano compositions, based on Caribbean music, influenced later developments in popular music that led to ragtime and jazz, and his two-movement symphony *A Night in the Tropics* (1858) foreshadows by almost a century the style of much twentieth-century American music. George F. Bristow (1825–98), a native of Brooklyn, became the best-known American composer in England when the Andante from his Symphony no. 2 was performed there in 1854 by the Jullien Orchestra, and his *Rip Van Winkle* (1855), the first American opera on an American subject, ran for four weeks at Niblo's Garden. Lesser-known composers included Caryl Florio (the pseudonym of William Robjohn, 1843–1920) and Horace Nicholl (1848–1922). Musical life in New York City at mid–nineteenth century was so active that the prominent diarist George Templeton Strong could attend a concert almost every night of the week. The city was also the most important center for organ builders, piano makers, and music publishers, especially on lower Broadway. Leading music publishers included the firms of William Hall; Firth, Pond and Company; and Charles H. Ditson. The first foreign music publisher to establish a branch in the city was the German firm of André and Company, which offered among other items a complete inventory of music by Mozart; it was followed shortly by the British firm of Novello, which sold sacred music from its shop at 389 Broadway. Many of the hymnbooks distributed throughout the United States were published in Manhattan, and the *Jubilee Songs,* the first published sheet music of blacks that eschewed caricature, were issued from East Ninth Street. The piano-making firm Steinway and Sons was formed in 1853 and opened a large factory at 53rd Street and Fourth Avenue in 1860.

Music education at mid–nineteenth century was increasingly the domain of such small academies as the New York Conservatorio at 417 Houston Street (opened in 1836 by Elam Ives, Jr.) where classes were held during the day for women and in the evening for men; John Watson's Musical Academy at 385 Broadway (from 1839), which offered lessons in singing, organ, piano, harmony, and composition; and the American Musical Institute at 466 Broadway (1846–48), which during its final year had on its faculty the acclaimed pianist Henri Herz (he taught at the neighboring offices of André and Company, 477 Broadway). Amateur singing societies proliferated as German-speaking immigrants increased in number and formed social organizations; the more notable included the Deutsche Liederkranz (which performed its first concert in 1847 with Thomas L. Damas conducting) and its offshoot the Männergesangverein Arion (1854).

Religious music also flourished. A widespread interest in congregational singing spurred mass education in vocal music. Lowell Mason (1792–1872), originally from Boston, formed the New York Musical Normal Institute for training music teachers in 1853 along with other such influential musicians as Thomas Hastings (1784–1872), George James Webb (1803–87), William S. Bradbury (1816–68), and George F. Root (1820–95). The institute's novel teaching methods and instructional hymnbooks influenced generations of amateur American singers, as did its large repertory of new tunes, many of which became classics; the school moved to Massachusetts in 1856. From 1846 to 1859 the organist at Trinity Church was Edward Hodges (1798–1867), born and trained in England, who helped to revitalize church music through his performances of organ masterworks, founding of a male choir, and composition of services and anthems. His efforts culminated in the founding of such secular and nondenominational organizations as the Church Choral Society (1869) and the Oratorio Society (1873). A breach widened about this time between the populist tradition of vocal hymnody and a movement for higher aesthetic standards that saw music as a morally efficacious force. The extent of the division was made clear when the award by New York University of honorary doctorates in music to Mason (1853) and Hastings (1855), the first granted by a major institution of higher learning in the United States, was criticized by such leading professional composers as Fry and Bristow. By 1880 there were about 370 houses of worship in the city, most of which required the services of organists, choir directors, and professional singers.

Such advocates of the Episcopal liturgical revival as Hodges and W. A. King, aided by enlightened vestry members such as P. A. Schermerhorn and H. C. De Rham of Grace Church, were active in 1842 in forming the Philharmonic Society of New York (later known as the New York Philharmonic), the first permanent symphonic ensemble in the United States. The orchestra gave its first concert on 7 December at the Apollo Rooms, which stood on the site formerly occupied by the Broadway Theatre at Canal and Walker streets; it later was based at Niblo's Garden (1854–56, 1858–59); the Academy of Music, built in 1854 at 14th Street and Irving Place (at intervals, 1856–86); Irving Hall, an annex of the academy at Irving Place and 15th Street (1861–63); and Steinway Hall at 73–77 East 14th Street (1866), an important concert hall until it closed in 1890. Strong was president of the society from 1870 to 1874. Opera and especially Italian opera continued to flourish in the city during the second half of the nineteenth century. Built in 1868 as (Samuel) Pike's Opera House, the Grand Opera House at Eighth Avenue and 23rd Street presented the American premiere of Ruggiero Leoncavallo's *Pagliacci.* The New York Stadt Theatre at 45 Broadway opened in 1868 and presented the first American performance of Richard Wagner's *Lohengrin* in 1871.

By the mid–nineteenth century New York City had become the focal point of international concert tours, and many artists made extended stays. Among the operatic singers to appear in the city were García's daughter Maria Malibran (1808–36), who married a French merchant while living in the city; Jenny Lind (1820–87), whose concert appearances at Castle Garden in 1850 (promoted by P. T. Barnum) were enthusiastically received; and Adelina Patti (1843–1919), who at the age of seven made her operatic debut in the city at a charity concert in 1850 at Tripler's Hall, 667–77 Broadway, an important venue that was damaged by a series of fires during the following years, reopened in 1854, and took several other names before closing in 1867. Other popular visitors included Jullien (at the Crystal Palace, 1853), the eccentric Norwegian violinist Ole Bull (1810–80), the pianist Hans von Bülow (1830–94), and the composer Arthur Sullivan (1842–1900).

Professional schools of music began in earnest after the Civil War. Among the best known were the Grand Conservatory (1874), the New York College of Music (1878, absorbed in 1920 by New York University), and the National Conservatory of Music (opened in 1885 at 128 East 17th Street, closed in the 1920s). Under the directorship of Jeannette Thurber the National Conservatory had on its faculty the pianist Rafael Joseffy and the composer and cellist Victor Herbert; its director from 1892 to 1895 was Antonín Dvořák, who during his tenure wrote his symphony *From the New World* (also known as the *New World Symphony*). The Metropolitan Conservatory opened in 1886. During these years the city's primacy in music was reinforced by its growing number of music publishers, including G. Schirmer (1861) and Carl Fischer (1872), and by the formation in 1883 of the Metropolitan Opera, which staged its first performances on Broadway between 39th and 40th streets.

Music in New York City in the late nineteenth century was heavily central European. Germans both Jewish and Christian dominated the city's musical life, and German music was ubiquitous. Wagner was performed not only at the Metropolitan Opera but by brass bands. At the centenary in 1889 of Washington's inauguration as president, massed German singing societies supplied most of the music. Some émigré musicians distinguished themselves as impresarios, notably Max Maretzek (1821–97), Bernard Ullman (1817–85), and the brothers Maurice Strakosch (1825–87) and Max Strakosch (1834–92).

Prominent German-born conductors included Leopold Damrosch, who formed the New York Symphony Society in 1878 and excelled as a conductor of German opera, and Theodore Thomas, leader of the Thomas Orchestra (1867–91), the Philharmonic Society (1871–91), and later the Chicago Symphony, who set a high standard of orchestral performance, encouraged a generation of American composers by programming their works, and conducted young people's concerts as early as 1883. Among the leading musicians who were not of German origin the most famous was the composer Edward MacDowell, an accomplished pianist and inventive harmonist who early achieved wide recognition for his two concertos for piano and orchestra, four epic keyboard sonatas, and many elegant character pieces. In his last works he adapted the tuneful manner of Anglo-Celtic melody to his sophisticated harmonic style and made a point of exclusively using English rather than Italian terms as tempo indications and marks of expression. Among MacDowell's friends was George Templeton Strong, Jr. (1856–1948), who on deciding to pursue a career in music was nearly disowned by his father. Schooled abroad and an expatriate for most of his life, he composed several large-scale symphonic works, of which the most accomplished was the symphony *Sintram* (1888).

2. From the Opening of the Music Hall to World War II

The opening concerts on 5 May 1891 of the Music Hall (now Carnegie Hall) at 57th Street and Seventh Avenue were conducted by Peter Ilich Tchaikovsky and reinforced the emergence of New York City as one of the world's major musical centers. The city was soon visited by the pianists Jan Ignace Paderewski (1860–1941) and Teresa Carreño (1853–1917). The Church Choral Society and the Oratorio Society gave the first performances of such important American works as *Phoenix Expirans* (1892) by George W. Chadwick (1854–1931), *Hora Novissima* (1893) by Horatio Parker (1861–1919), and *Vexilla Regis* (1894) by Harry Rowe Shelley (1858–1947). Toward the end of the nineteenth century the first settlement schools provided music instruction to poor children, among them the Henry Street Settlement (1892), which later opened a music wing (1927). Emilie Wagner and David Mannes in 1894 opened the Music School Settlement, which later moved successively to Third Street (where it took the name Third Street Musical School Settlement) and East 11th Street and eventually became the nation's oldest community arts school. Columbia University formed a department of music in 1896 under MacDowell. New York City was one of the last major American cities to include music in the standard public school curriculum. In 1898 the Symphony Society began a regular series of children's concerts under Leopold Damrosch's son Frank Damrosch, later succeeded by his brother Walter Damrosch.

After the turn of the twentieth century the city was changed markedly by the immigration of thousands of Italians, Germans, Russian Jews, and Irish. Anton Seidl's 13 years in the city with the Metropolitan Opera Orchestra and the New York Philharmonic bolstered the performance of the German repertory, as did Gustav Mahler's years as the conductor of the Metropolitan Opera and the Philharmonic (1908–11). Walter Damrosch conducted the Metropolitan Opera, the New York Symphony, and the Philharmonic; composed operas (*The Scarlet Letter,* 1896; *The Man without a Country,* 1937); and at the end of his career was a popular radio personality. Frank Damrosch became a leading choral director with the Metropolitan Opera and the Oratorio Society (founded by his father) and in 1905 formed the Institute for Musical Art (later renamed the Juilliard School). In 1903 the Metropolitan Opera gave the first staged performance outside Bayreuth of Wagner's last opera, *Parsifal.* Italian music was also well represented. In his almost 20 years in New York City, Enrico Caruso became the most famous operatic singer who had ever lived, and through the city's fledgling recording industry the first international recording artist.

Efforts to strengthen a largely ineffectual system of copyright protection led to the formation in the city in 1914 of the American Society of Composers, Authors, and Publishers (ASCAP), which included among its founding members Herbert, Irving Berlin, and John Philip Sousa (whose works were the focus of several early lawsuits won by the association). At first, licensing fees were payable to ASCAP only for live performances of music by its members; eventually the association also monitored broadcasts and recordings.

In time, the operatic and symphonic repertory broadened, as the Philharmonic and the New York Symphony performed less music by German, Austrian, and Hungarian composers and French, Russian, and American works began to enter the repertory. At the same time classical music continued to reach a wider audience. The mining magnate Adolph Lewisohn endowed Lewisohn Stadium (1915) at City College, between 136th and 138th streets and Amsterdam and Convent avenues, with the stipulation that inexpensive concerts be given there during the summer (an annual feature that lasted until 1966). Two important music schools opened about the same time: the David Mannes School (1916, later the Mannes College of Music) and the Neighborhood Music School (1917, later the Manhattan School of Music). In 1923 New York University introduced a baccalaureate music degree, and the School of Sacred Music opened at Union Theological Seminary (this lasted until 1973 when it moved to Yale University). Major concert halls opened during these years included Town Hall at 123 West 43rd Street, built by suffragists in 1921 as a site for public meetings; and the Mecca Temple (now known as City Center of Music and Drama), constructed at 131 West 55th Street in 1923 by the Ancient and Accepted Order of Nobles of the Mystic Shrine, or Shriners. The Philharmonic Symphony Society of New York and the New York Symphony merged in 1928, by which time the city was regularly visited by orchestras from throughout the country and the world. Smaller orchestras were also based in New York City, such as the American National Orchestra (to 1923), the State Symphony Orchestra (to 1926), and the City Symphony (1940–47). In 1924 the Philharmonic began a series of children's concerts under the direction of Ernest Schelling.

As concert life became more active, American composers broke with European models and forged distinctive styles. Charles Ives, a prosperous partner in a life insurance business whose independent means freed him from the constraints imposed by a conservative public, wrote works that were often dissonant and modern for their time. He moved to New York City soon after his graduation from Yale University in 1898 and remained there until 1911, during which time he wrote his piano trio, first piano sonata, first two violin sonatas, second and third symphonies, and various smaller pieces. Prominent modernist composers based in New York City during the early twentieth century included Edgar Varèse, who moved to the city in 1915; Carl Ruggles, who moved there in 1917; and Henry Cowell. Among composers in a more conservative vein were Daniel Gregory Mason (professor at Columbia) and the opera composer Deems Taylor. A number of organizations promoted the performance of modern music, such as the International Composers' Guild, formed in 1921 partly through the efforts of Varèse; the League of Composers and the American section of the International Society for Contemporary Music (both formed in 1923, merged in 1954); the Pan-American Association of Composers, in which Cowell played a leading role; and later the Composers' Forum (active 1935–40, revived 1947).

During the years surrounding World War I the concert tradition and the vernacular influenced each other considerably. Ragtime composers often worked in classical forms, and many classical composers looked to ragtime for inspiration. The bandmaster James Reese Europe led a concert by the Clef Club at Carnegie Hall in 1912 that displayed a number of hybrid ragtime and classical pieces; George Gershwin wrote his *Rhapsody in Blue,* given its premiere in 1924 by Paul Whiteman and his orchestra, and his *Concerto in F* (1925) for piano and orchestra; the Harlem stride pianist James P. Johnson composed several works of "symphonic jazz," notably *Yamekraw* (1928, orchestrated by William Grant Still); Scott Joplin during the last years of his life made a desperate and largely unsuccessful attempt to interest backers in producing his opera *Treemonisha* (which was widely acclaimed when it was finally staged long after his death, in 1976); and the early output of Aaron Copland included several works strongly informed by jazz, among them *Music for the Theater* (1925) and *Four Piano Blues* (1926). Copland was also an influential member of the League of Composers and a contributor to its journal *Modern Music*. Another composer well known for his critical writings was Virgil Thomson, who with Gertrude Stein wrote the operas *Four Saints in Three Acts* (1928) and *The Mother of Us All* (1947, about Susan B. Anthony) and from 1940 to 1954 was the principal music critic at the *New York Herald Tribune*. A number of modernist composers were active in leftist politics, particularly those associated with the Composers Collective, and contributed to two workers' songbooks published by the Workers Music League. Workers' rounds were written by Elie Siegmeister (1909–91), who used the pseudonym L. E. Swift, and Charles Seeger (1886–1979), who wrote as Carl Sands. Copland in 1934 won a song competition sponsored by the *New Masses* with his composition "Into the Streets of May," and Marc Blitzstein's opera *The Cradle Will Rock* (1937) was imbued with the ideology of the Popular Front. At the same time the phonograph achieved greater commercial viability. In New York City the recording firms Victor and Columbia Talking Machine were among early leaders of the field, which they continued to dominate after electric recording was introduced in 1925. During the 1920s both firms evolved into conglomerates active in such areas as broadcasting and theater management. They also expanded beyond New York City, especially after the 1930s when the advent of radio and the Depression prompted the industry to move most of its popular-music divisions to the West Coast. Long an important center for music management, the city about 1920 became the base of operations for the impresario Sol Hurok, who remained in the forefront of the business for five decades.

The rise of Nazism brought a number of distinguished émigré musicians to the city, including the conductors Bruno Walter and Erich Leinsdorf; the pianists Rudolf Serkin and Claudio Arrau; the singers Lauritz Melchior (1890–1973), Lotte Lehmann, Elisabeth Schumann, Friedrich Schorr, and Alexander Kipnis; and the composers Stefan Wolpe, Béla Bartók (who worked at Columbia), and Paul Hindemith (who taught at Yale). New symphony orchestras were formed, notably the NBC Symphony Orchestra, conducted by Arturo Toscanini from 1937 to 1954, principally on the radio. The New York Philharmonic broadcast over the Columbia Broadcasting System (CBS) from 1930, and from 1931 Texaco sponsored nationwide radio broadcasts by the Metropolitan Opera, which staged French, German, Italian, American, English, and Russian works performed by such singers as Rosa Ponselle (1897–1981), often in spectacular productions. Walter Damrosch gave radio broadcasts for schoolchildren during the 1930s, and the pianist Olga Samaroff-Stokowski offered "audience development" courses from the mid-1930s to 1948, first at the David Mannes School and later at Town Hall. The New Friends of Music presented concerts of chamber music between 1936 and 1953. The dominance of ASCAP in licensing was challenged when it failed to reach a contract agreement with radio broadcasters in 1939, and a consortium of 600 broadcasters then formed a competing organization, Broadcast Music Inc. (BMI), which specialized in popular genres such as folk music and blues. The radio station WQXR began broadcasting in 1936 as the first full-time classical music station in the United States; the municipal station WNYC also broadcast a large amount of classical music, especially during the administration of Mayor Fiorello H. La Guardia. From 1935 to 1943 the Music Project of the Works Progress Administration provided free concerts, educational programs, and music instruction to New Yorkers, and in 1935 the Composers' Forum began a series of lecture-performances at which a featured composer took questions from the audience.

From the 1920s to the 1940s many composers wrote works celebrating American history, the city, and the American West. These works were usually programmatic and often patriotic: well-known examples include Copland's *A Lincoln Portrait* (1942); Earl Robinson's *Ballad for Americans* (1938); Blitzstein's *Airborne Symphony* (1943–46), composed during World War II for the Eighth Air Force; John Alden Carpenter's *Skyscrapers* (1926); Adolph Weiss's *American Life: Scherzo Jazzoso* (1928); and Duke Ellington's symphonic jazz piece *Harlem Air Shaft* (1940). For the centenary of the New York Philharmonic in 1942–43 nine conductors programmed 22 compositions by Americans, and between October 1943 and January 1945 the Philharmonic played nine pieces commissioned by the League of Composers and CBS, some of which had been inspired by the war; these reached a large audience when broadcast by CBS over the radio. After a foreclosure on the Mecca Temple Mayor La Guardia saved it from demolition in 1943 and bought it for the city. Renamed City Center of Music and Drama, the building became the home in the following year of the City Center Opera Company (later the New York City Opera), which featured young American singers in high-quality productions at low prices. During its early years the company presented a short season devoted to the music of Gilbert and Sullivan, and later its offerings were often more adventurous than those of the Metropolitan Opera.

3. After World War II

New chamber ensembles were formed in New York City after the war, among them the Juilliard String Quartet (1946), and in 1948 the Metropolitan Opera began broadcasting performances on television. Composers living in the city worked in diverse styles. The art songs of Ned Rorem (*b* 1923), on texts by American poets as disparate as Walt Whitman and Sylvia Plath, were indebted to Maurice Ravel and Claude Debussy. Copland exerted an influence on a large group of composers, including David Diamond (1915–2005); William Schuman, composer of the opera *The Mighty Casey* (1951–53); Peter Mennin (1923–1983); and Siegmeister, who based his cantata *I Have a Dream* (1967) on the life of Martin Luther King, Jr., and also wrote such works as *A Sunday in Brooklyn* (1946). In addition to composing, Siegmeister was a tireless advocate of modern music, and both Schuman and Mennin were presidents of the Juilliard School. Ellington continued to write quasi-symphonic works, notably *Harlem (A Tone Parallel to Harlem)* (1950). The most influential and most difficult to categorize among composers in the city was Leonard Bernstein, who wrote compositions ranging from successful Broadway musicals to operas, ballets, and symphonic pieces composed in an eclectic, accessible style, and who was also the music director of the New York Philharmonic from 1958 to 1969. Composers of electronic music worked at the Columbia–Princeton Electronic Music Center, formed in the city in 1959 by Milton Babbitt (*b* 1916), Otto Luening (1900–1996), Vladimir Ussachevsky (1911–90), and Roger Sessions (1896–1985). John Cage, a resident of the city from 1943, wrote several compositions based on chance methods, a notorious, completely silent work called *4'33'* (1952), and music for "prepared piano" (the sound of which was altered by having nuts, bolts, and other objects inserted between its strings). He collaborated frequently with Merce Cunningham's dance company. The dense, rhythmically intricate, and often daunting music of Elliott Carter, perhaps more successful among critics than with audiences, constituted one of the most impressive bodies of work written by an American. Not all composers were tolerant of the stylistic diversity that characterized classical music in the city. Some of them, especially those affiliated with universities and with such organizations and ensembles as the League of Composers/International Society for Contemporary Music (ISCM), the Group for Contemporary Music, Speculum Musicae, and the New York New Music Ensemble, espoused an orthodox view of composition that accepted as legitimate only the 12-tone techniques of Arnold Schoenberg and Anton Webern and their disciples.

Concert life in the city continued to be centered at Carnegie Hall, the home of the New York Philharmonic until the opening of Philharmonic Hall (eventually renamed Avery Fisher Hall) at the LINCOLN CENTER FOR THE PERFORMING ARTS on 24 September 1962. Carnegie Hall later survived efforts by real estate developers to have it razed. Lincoln Center was also the site of the New York State Theater, which became the home of the New York City Opera in 1966. In the same year the New York Philharmonic and the Metropolitan Opera began presenting regular seasons of outdoor concerts on the Great Lawn in Central Park and at other parks throughout the five boroughs. The Chamber Music Society of Lincoln Center, formed in 1969, presented concerts in Alice Tully Hall at Lincoln Center by a resident ensemble supplemented by guest soloists.

Far from the mainstream of classical music there developed schools of composition that flourished in the lofts, art galleries, and nightclubs of lower Manhattan. Inspired by the work of Cage, "minimalists" such as La Monte Young (*b* 1935), Meredith Monk (*b* 1943), Steve Reich (*b* 1936), and Philip Glass (*b* 1937) repudiated the complexity of modern composition and built extended works by frequently repeating simple rhythmic and melodic fragments. Groups such as Experiments in Art and Technology (EAT), which was associated with Bell Laboratories in New Jersey, explored novel combinations of technology and art. Composers such as Laurie Anderson and John Zorn attempted a fusion of classical music and avant-garde rock. The festival New Music/New York of 1979 led to the formation of the New Music Alliance, a group dedicated to promoting performances of new music throughout the United States.

By the early twenty-first century a large number of performing ensembles were based in New York City, ranging from symphony orchestras (which numbered more than 40 in the metropolitan area), to groups specializing in early music (for instance the Waverly Consort and the New York Cornet and Sackbut Ensemble) founded by graduate students and inspired by the study of pre-Baroque music at universities, to groups specializing in modern music (the Contemporary Chamber Ensemble, the Group for Contemporary Music, and Speculum Musicae). Operas were staged by the Metropolitan Opera and the New York City Opera, as well as by such smaller companies as the New York Grand Opera (which in 1994 launched a seven-year festival of all of Verdi's operas, the first such project ever), the Amato Opera Company, the Opera Orchestra of New York, the Brooklyn Academy of Music, and the opera companies of the Juilliard School, the Manhattan School of Music, and the Mannes College of Music. Although music programs in the public schools had suffered from budgetary reductions (fewer than 1000 licensed music teachers were in the system in the mid-1990s, compared with 3000 in the 1960s), in 2006 Carnegie Hall Academy and the Juilliard School partnered with the public schools in a program to train music teachers. High-quality musical training was also offered at the FIORELLO H. LA GUARDIA HIGH SCHOOL OF MUSIC AND ART AND PERFORMING ARTS (opened in 1936). In addition to its well-known conservatories the city had several notable community music schools, including the Greenwich House Music School, the Turtle Bay Music School, the Bloomingdale House of Music, and the Harlem School of the Arts.

The city's many concert venues cover a wide range. Carnegie Hall remains the favored auditorium for visiting orchestras, chamber ensembles, and recitalists; others perform at Avery Fisher Hall, Alice Tully Hall, and the Walter Reade Theater (all at Lincoln Center). Kaufman Concert Hall at the 92nd Street Y(M-YWHA) (1930, seating 916) supports resident orchestras and presents renowned guest orchestras and soloists. In 1978 the Hebrew Arts School added a concert hall seating 457 to its building at 129 West 67th Street, renamed Merkin Concert Hall in 1981. Classical music is also performed at several schools and universities, including Columbia (at the Kathryn Bache Miller Theatre), Hunter College (at the Sylvia and Danny Kaye Playhouse), City College (Aaron Davis Hall), Lehman College (the Lehman Center for the Performing Arts), and Queens College (the Colden Center), and at such museums as the Metropolitan Museum of Art, the Guggenheim Museum, the Asia Society, the Museum of Modern Art, and the Whitney Museum of American Art. Many churches offer performances of classical music at Christmas and Easter. Performance spaces specializing in the avant-garde include Public School 122 (First Avenue and Ninth Street), the Clocktower Gallery (108 Leonard Street), Franklin Furnace (112 Franklin Street), and the Kitchen (512 West 19th Street), which became a leading venue for performance art and experimental music soon after its opening in SoHo in 1971. Bargemusic, a floating concert hall moored in Brooklyn beneath the Brooklyn Bridge, began presenting a notable chamber music series in 1978. Symphony Space, at 95th Street and Broadway, is a disused movie theater that was converted into a concert hall in 1978.

Although some music businesses left New York City for California after the 1930s, the large record companies Polygram, Bertelsmann Music Group (BMG) (bought by Sony in 2008), and Sony kept their headquarters in the city, as did such specialized labels as Composers Recordings, Inc. (CRI), New World, and Nonesuch (now part of Elektra/Warner). The Recording Industries Association of America (RIAA), a trade organization formed in 1952, is also based in the city. Along 57th Street, near Carnegie Hall, are most of the country's large music management agencies, many of which were established by former associates of Hurok: Columbia Artists Management, ICM Artists, and Thea Dispeker. ASCAP has offices on Broadway across from Lincoln Center, and BMI is on 57th Street.

The study of music history in general and American music in particular owes much to the work of scholars based in New York City, such as Frédéric Louis Ritter in the late nineteenth century and especially John Tasker Howard (author of *Our American Music,* 1931). The American Musicological Society was organized in 1939 in a townhouse on Washington Square. Otto Kinkeldey, Gustave Reese, Curt Sachs, Paul Henry Lang, Eric Werner, and Oscar Sonneck established the city as a center for musicology through their activities as university professors, writers on music history, and librarians. Two institutions of great importance are the *Musical Quarterly* (1915–) and the music division of the New York Public Library for the Performing Arts, which has a unique collection of Americana and remains unsurpassed in the metropolitan region for the breadth of its holdings.

George Whitney Martin, *The Damrosch Dynasty: America's First Family of Music* (Boston: Houghton Mifflin, 1983); John Rockwell, *All American Music: Composition in the Late Twentieth Century* (New York: Alfred A. Knopf, 1983); Barbara L. Tischler, *An American Music: The Search for an American Musical Identity* (New York: Oxford University Press, 1986); Gilbert Chase, *America's Music: From the Pilgrims to the Present* (New York: McGraw–Hill, 1966; 3rd edn Urbana: University of Illinois Press, 1987); Vera Brodsky Lawrence, *Strong on Music: The New York Music Scene in the Days of George Templeton Strong, 1836–1875,* vol. 1, *Resonances* (New York: Oxford University Press, 1988)

James M. Keller, Nancy Shear,
Barbara L. Tischler, Victor Fell Yellin

Clearing House Association. See NEW YORK CLEARING HOUSE ASSOCIATION.

Clearwater. Sloop used for teaching about the ecology of the Hudson River. Designed like the sloops used for trade on the Hudson River during the nineteenth century, the ship was built during a campaign led by the folk singer Pete Seeger to clean up the Hudson. It first sailed in New York Harbor in the summer of 1970, serving as a mobile classroom and laboratory. In 2004 the *Clearwater* was listed on the National Register of Historic Places for its role in environmental advocacy and education about the Hudson River.

Clemens, Samuel (Langhorne). See Twain, Mark.

Cleopatra's Needle [Obelisk]. Red granite shaft 69 feet (21 meters) tall and weighing 200 tons (181 metric tons) that stands in Central Park near the Metropolitan Museum of Art. It was erected in Heliopolis about 1475 B.C. by Pharaoh Thutmose III. Roman soldiers moved it in 12 B.C. to Alexandria, where it remained until it was shipped to New York City in 1880 as a gift to the United States from the khedive of Egypt. Unloaded at Staten Island, it was sent on pontoons up the Hudson River, then rolled on cannonballs to its present site. Another obelisk known as Cleopatra's Needle, also a gift of the khedive, stands in London. Despite their name neither is known to have any connection with Cleopatra.

Ernest Alfred Wallis Budge, *Cleopatra's Needles and Other Egyptian Obelisks* (London: Religious Tract Society, 1926)

Sandra Opdycke

Clermont [North River Steamboat]. The first commercially successful steamboat in America. Designed by Robert Fulton and built by Charles Brown(e) in New York City, it measured about 140 feet (42.6 meters) by 16 feet (4.9 meters), although the size was modified several times; the side paddle wheels were powered by an engine made by the English firm Boulton and Watt. Commercial service between New York and Albany quickly followed the first demonstration trip of the steamboat in 1807. The *Clermont* was retired in 1814, replaced by larger and more technically advanced steamboats. During Fulton's life it was known as the *North River Steamboat* and came to be called the *Clermont* only after his death in 1815.

Cynthia Owen Philip, *Robert Fulton: A Biography* (New York: F. Watts, 1985)

Arthur G. Adams

Cleveland, (Stephen) Grover (*b* Caldwell, N.J., 18 March 1837; *d* Princeton, N.J., 24 June 1908). Twenty-second and 24th president of the United States. He was a mayor of Buffalo and a governor of New York before being elected president as a Democrat in 1884. After failing to win reelection in 1888 he moved with his wife, Frances, to New York City, where they lived in an elegant, four-story town house of red brick and brownstone at 816 Madison Avenue (near 68th Street). He was of counsel to the law firm of Bangs, Stetson, Tracy and MacVeagh (15 Broad Street), where he formed close alliances with many financiers on Wall Street, including J. P. Morgan. After he regained the presidency in 1892 the family sold the house on Madison Avenue and lived briefly at 12 West 51st Street before returning to the White House. Cleveland returned to the city in 1893 for an operation for throat cancer: this was performed aboard a yacht at Pier A in the East River and kept secret for fear that news of it would exacerbate a severe financial crisis, which ended in 1895 when Cleveland enlisted Morgan's help.

Cleopatra's Needle, ca 1900

Allan Nevins, *Grover Cleveland: A Study in Courage* (New York: Dodd, Mead, 1932); Henry F. Graff, *Grover Cleveland* (New York: Henry Holt, 2002)

James Bradley

Clews, Henry (*b* Staffordshire, England, 14 Aug 1834; *d* New York City, 31 Jan 1923). Financier. After immigrating to the United States in 1850 he opened the securities firm of Stout, Clews and Mason in 1859, which became the second-largest underwriter of American government bonds during the Civil War. He was active in Republican politics and helped to form the Committee of Seventy, a reform group that forced William M. "Boss" Tweed from office. Renamed Henry Clews and Company in 1877, the firm by the 1890s was the largest negotiator of railroad loans in America or Europe. Clews wrote *Wall Street Point of View* (1900) and *Fifty Years in Wall Street* (1908).

George Winslow

Clifton. Neighborhood in northeastern Staten Island bounded to the north by Stapleton, to the east by Upper New York Bay, to the south by Rosebank, and to the west by Van Duzer Street. A neighborhood of the same name laid out in 1837 occupied a somewhat larger area; its early history was closely tied to that of the Vanderbilt family. As a young man Cornelius Vanderbilt carried passengers and cargo by boat to Manhattan from the foot of the avenue that now bears his name. In the neighborhood was the former U.S. Public Health Service Hospital, a sprawling complex that housed the original headquarters and laboratories of the National Institutes of Health (now in Bethesda, Maryland). In 2009 a large portion of the former hospital property was acquired by the Salvation Army for development as a recreation and community center. By the early twenty-first century, Liberians and other West Africans were living in the area. Most residents of Clifton live in one-family homes, with a few in apartment complexes. The principal thoroughfares are Tompkins Avenue and Bay Street. Clifton has a Staten Island Rapid Transit station.

Henry G. Steinmeyer, *Staten Island, 1524–1898* (New York: Staten Island Historical Society, 1950; repr. 1987)

John-Paul Richiuso

Clinton. Name given in 1959 to a neighborhood on the West Side of Manhattan bounded to the north by 59th Street, to the east by Eighth Avenue, to the south by 42nd Street, and to the west by the Hudson River. It occupies most of the area formerly known as Hell's Kitchen. The name comes from DeWitt Clinton Park, located between 52nd and 54th streets west of 11th Avenue.

Clinton, DeWitt (*b* Little Britain, N.Y., 2 March 1769; *d* Albany, N.Y., 11 Feb 1828). Mayor and governor. The son of the Revolutionary general James Clinton, he entered elite circles of government and society in New York State after being employed as a private secretary by Governor George Clinton, his uncle, about 1790. Within a decade he became

DeWitt Clinton

one of the most powerful politicians in the state and was appointed to the U.S. Senate in 1802. He returned to the city in 1803 after being appointed mayor, a position to which he was reappointed every year until 1815 (with the exceptions of 1807 and 1810, when political opponents controlled the state's Council of Appointment). While in office he helped found the Free School Society, the New-York Historical Society, the Literary and Philosophical Society, and the Orphan Asylum; as mayor he also improved sanitation, administered public markets, guided plans to expand the city northward, and strengthened the defenses of New York Harbor to prepare for war with Britain. In the presidential election of 1812 he ran against James Madison, seeking the support of both Federalists, who opposed the war, and Republicans, who wished to wage it more successfully; he won 89 electoral votes to Madison's 128.

After his defeat Clinton was overshadowed in popularity by Governor Daniel D. Tompkins (whose election he had engineered in 1807) and by 1815 no longer held public office. He soon returned to politics to promote the plan for the Erie Canal, for which he managed to secure the legislature's approval despite opposition from the Bucktails of Tammany Hall. When Tompkins resigned in 1817 to become vice president of the United States, Clinton was elected to replace him as governor, winning 43,310 votes to his opponent's 1479. As mayor and governor Clinton had a vision of the city's future as a great commercial center, and by means of commercial success he hoped to raise the city to cultural eminence as well. To this end he sponsored many measures to aid education and cultural institutions, although a good number were weakened or blocked by political opponents. His plans for the city, like the plan for the Erie Canal, called for the active participation of government. He won reelection in 1820 against Tompkins but did not seek another term in 1822 because of strong opposition from the Bucktails, led by Martin Van Buren. In 1824 he was again elected governor, with the support of voters outraged that the Bucktails had dismissed him from his position as an unsalaried canal commissioner. Clinton presided over the opening ceremonies of the canal in 1825 and remained in office until his death. Two neighborhoods, a high school, and several parks in the city are named for him.

Jabez D. Hammond, *Political Parties in the State of New York, from the Ratification of the Federal Constitution to December 1840* (Albany, N.Y.: C. Van Benthuysen, 1842); Evan Cornog, *The Birth of Empire: DeWitt Clinton and the American Experience, 1769–1828* (New York: Oxford University Press, 1998)

Evan Cornog

Clinton, William Jefferson (Bill). (*b* Hope, Ark., 19 Aug 1946) Forty-second president of the United States. After serving two terms as president from 1992 to 2000, he started the William J. Clinton Foundation in 1997, a nongovernmental organization that works for international community building. In 2001 a New York branch of the Clinton Foundation opened in Harlem at 55 West 125th Street. In addition the former president set up his office in Harlem and with his wife, Senator Hillary Rodham Clinton, purchased a home in suburban Chappaqua.

Jessica Montesano

Clinton Cove Park. Two-acre park in Manhattan between 54th and 57th streets and the northernmost part of Hudson River Park. Funded by the city, the Hudson River Park Trust, and private donations, Clinton Cove Park opened in spring 2005 and features a boathouse for nonmotorized vessels, a sculpture of a 30-foot-long wine bottle, a lawn, a public walkway extending to the western end of Pier 94, and a "get-down," which allows visitors to sit at the level of the river.

Ben Silk

Clinton Hill. Neighborhood in northwestern Brooklyn. Overlooking Wallabout Bay and centered at Pratt Institute, it is bounded to the north by the Brooklyn–Queens Expressway, to the east by Classon Avenue, to the south by Atlantic Avenue, and to the west by Vanderbilt Avenue. The neighborhood is named for DeWitt Clinton and occupies the highest ground in the area. In 1832 Clinton Avenue was laid out as a tree-lined boulevard along the crest of the hill, and some grand villas had been built by the 1840s. The area was considered a rural retreat until the speculative development in the 1860s of row houses, which by 1880 lined most of the streets and attracted affluent professionals. Between 1880 and 1915 the wealthiest industrialists of Brooklyn built mansions on Clinton and Washington avenues. Development was spurred by the decision of the oil executive Charles Pratt to build a house at 232 Clinton Avenue in 1874; this magnificent residence, now part of St. Joseph's College, was surrounded by three of the four other houses that Pratt gave to his sons as wedding gifts. In 1887 Pratt founded Pratt Institute at 200 Willoughby Street, an art and industrial school that became the focus of the neighborhood and remained so for more than a century. Apartment buildings were constructed from about 1900, and during the 1920s and 1940s they largely replaced the mansions along Clinton and Washington avenues. During the 1950s and 1960s one-family houses became rooming houses. Robert Moses in 1954 cleared a five-block area south of Pratt Institute for renewal, and in the 1970s many of the fine brownstones of the neighborhood were restored.

Clinton Hill is a neighborhood of shingled, clapboard, brick, limestone, and brownstone houses, interspersed with frame houses and mansions predating the Civil War as well as apartment buildings. It is inhabited by a large number of artists, architects, photographers, and craftspeople and is racially diverse (45 percent black, 55 percent white and Asian), with many Italians and a number of black immigrants from the Caribbean. There is a wide range in the quality and price of housing, from elegant brownstones and mansions to inexpensive apartments for students.

Designated a Historic District in 1981, the neighborhood includes such city landmarks as the Emmanuel Baptist Church (1887) and the Steele-Skinner House (1812), both on Lafayette Avenue, and the Church of St. Luke and St. Matthew (1889) and the Royal Castle Apartments (1910), both on Clinton Avenue. The main buildings of the Pratt campus on Hall Street are all landmarks, as are the Mechanics Temple (1889, formerly the Lincoln Club) at 67 Putnam Avenue and St. Mary's Episcopal Church (1859) at 230 Classon Avenue. DeKalb Avenue is the main thoroughfare. As of the early twenty-first century, the neighborhood was experiencing an upswing in popularity, spurring gentrification and the growth of a burgeoning upper-middle-class population.

Clinton Hill Brooklyn (New York: Society for Clinton Hill, n.d.); Nanette Rainone, ed., *The Brooklyn Neighborhood Book* (New York: Fund for the Borough of Brooklyn, 1985)

Elizabeth Reich Rawson

Cloisters. Museum. Located in Manhattan at Fort Tryon Park, it houses a collection of European medieval art and architecture chiefly assembled by the sculptor George Grey Barnard. It was known as the Barnard Cloisters until its purchase in 1925 by the Metropolitan Museum of Art, with a donation from John D. Rockefeller, Jr. The Metropolitan Museum then expanded and remodeled the building and opened it as a branch in 1938. Rockefeller also purchased 700 acres (290 hectares) across the Hudson River in New Jersey to maintain the natural views from the museum. The museum incorporates architectural monuments from the cloisters of five French monasteries: Saint-Michel-de-Cuxa, Saint-Guilhem-le-Désert, Bonnefont-en-Comminges, Trie-en-Bigorre, and Froville. Its chapels and exhibition halls contain approximately 5000 works of Romanesque and Gothic art, the most notable of which are the Unicorn Tapestries, and its meticulous gardens feature plantings representative of the medieval period.

Elliot S. Meadows

Cloisters, ca *1938*

Clove Lakes Park. Public park in Staten Island, occupying 200 acres (80 hectares) in West New Brighton. It contains several freshwater lakes, adjoined by a brook that extends through the park from Victory Boulevard to the Kill van Kull. From the seventeenth to the nineteenth centuries, several dams were built to create water pressure for local mills. Many ponds were used for ice harvesting. Brooks Pond provided the island's water supply in the late nineteenth century and the early twentieth. In 1926 the area was acquired by the Parks Department and given its current name. In the early twenty-first century Clove Lakes Park offered facilities for boating, fishing, hiking, and horseback riding.

James Bradley

clubs. See Political clubs, Social clubs, University clubs, and Women's clubs.

Clurman, Harold (*b* New York City, 18 Sept 1901; *d* New York City, 9 Sept 1980). Drama critic, director, teacher, and actor. He became interested in the theater after seeing the Yiddish actor Jacob Adler in *Uriel Acosta* at the Grand Street Theatre in 1907. After studying at Columbia University and the Sorbonne, where he lived with Aaron Copland, he settled in New York City. There he made his acting debut as a walk-on in Stark Young's play *The Saint* at the Greenwich Village Theatre in 1924. With Cheryl Crawford and Lee Strasberg he formed the Group Theatre (1931–41) to produce plays with aesthetic and social relevance. He directed premieres for Carson McCullers's *A Member of the Wedding* (1950, Empire Theatre) and William Inge's *Bus Stop* (1955, Music Box Theatre), wrote reviews for the *New Republic* (1949–52), the *Nation* (1953–80), and the *Observer* (1955–63), and taught directing at Hunter College (1964–80). Clurman's published writings include *The Fervent Years* (1945), a history of the Group Theatre; three volumes of criticism, *Lies like Truths* (1958), *The Naked Image* (1966), and *The Divine Pastime* (1974); and *On Directing* (1972), a widely read text among theater students.

Cobble Hill. A 40-block neighborhood in northwestern Brooklyn, sandwiched between Brooklyn Heights, Boerum Hill, and Carroll Gardens, bounded to the north by Atlantic Avenue, to the east by Court Street, to the south by Degraw Street, and to the west by the Brooklyn–Queens Expressway. It is one of several small neighborhoods that once made up South Brooklyn. The area was settled in the mid-seventeenth century by Dutch farmers, who called it Punkiesberg. A hill at what is now the corner of Atlantic Avenue and Court Street was known as Cobbleshill at the time of the American Revolution, but the name became disused during the nineteenth century. The area remained rural until 1836, when ferry service to Atlantic Avenue spurred suburban development. Between 1840 and 1880 many brownstones and brick row houses were built in the Greek Revival and Romanesque styles; the population was upper middle class. In the 1870s the philanthropist Alfred T. White built two experimental housing projects in the area: the Towers (439–45 Hicks Street), a Romanesque Revival apartment building intended for working-class tenants, and Warren Place, a mews of tiny one-family experimental housing developments built around a private courtyard for middle-class tenants; both remained standing into the 1990s. In the early twentieth century there was an influx of immigrants from Ireland, Italy, and the Middle East. The neighborhood contains many churches predating the Civil War and one of the city's finest collections of nineteenth-century houses, including the birthplace of Winston Churchill's mother, Jennie Jerome, at 154 Amity Street. Long Island College Hospital (1848) occupies several buildings on Henry Street and Amity Place. The Israel Ashei Emes Synagogue, in an early Romanesque former church building on Kane Street, is the home of the oldest Jewish congregation in Brooklyn. Brownstone enthusiasts moved in during the late 1950s and revived the name Cobble Hill; they organized a successful effort to resist public housing and were instrumental in having the neighborhood designated a historic district in 1969. Housing prices rose steadily from the 1970s through the 1990s, and by the beginning of the twenty-first century Cobble Hill was arguably Brooklyn's most sought-after neighborhood. By that time, almost all of its east-west streets had become a continuous line of elegant and renovated brownstones.

Kenneth T. Jackson, Philip Kasinitz

Cobble Hill Cinemas, 2009

Cocclestown. Original name of RICHMONDTOWN.

cockroaches. In New York City the cockroach has a notorious reputation and ubiquitous presence. The city's roach population was inadvertently introduced by trade and includes the American (also known as the "water bug"), German (common during the 1970s), Oriental, Australian, and brownbanded species, measuring 0.1 to 0.2 inches (0.3 to 0.5 centimeters) in length, although some reach 1.75 inches (4.4 centimeters). Scavengers that feed on garbage, dead insects, and human food, they are common household pests and are found everywhere, from subways to fine restaurants. Cockroaches are especially visible in poorly maintained buildings because wall voids and debris provide good shelter, although they enter new apartments as well, often by riding in on the clothing or shopping bags (they prefer paper over plastic) of residents. They seek the water around pipes and sinks, and are known to be attracted to toothpaste. Evidence that cockroaches spread disease is conclusive; this has encouraged the development of insecticides, although chemical control often forces roaches into neighboring apartments or buildings, and some roaches have become resistant to widely used substances. Research into effective roach control focuses on growth regulators, pheromones, and molting hormones to disrupt life processes and cause populations to fall.

Louis N. Sorkin

coffee. Coffee was available in New York City when it was a Dutch trading post. The Dutch dominated the coffee trade during the seventeenth century just as the British came to dominate the tea trade, and Dutch residents of New Amsterdam consumed coffee as a luxury item, sucking the drink through cubes of sugar held between their teeth at home or in coffeehouses, or having it prepared at the apothecary as a headache remedy. Over the course of the eighteenth century, the city's proliferating COFFEEHOUSES became hubs of business and politics and gathering places for high society. They served as offices for meetings that led to the founding of both the Bank of New York and the New York Stock and Exchange Board; the Sons of Liberty and the earliest manumission society in the United States both held meetings in coffeehouses as well. After Alexander Hamilton's duel with Aaron Burr, bulletins on the state of Hamilton's health were posted outside the Tontine Coffee House. When President George Washington arrived in New York City in 1789, the city's mayor chose to greet him at the Merchants Coffee House in Manhattan.

In 1790 the coffee-roasting industry was born in New York City when a factory opened on Great Dock Street (now Pearl Street). At the time coffee was still prepared largely in commercial establishments. Roasting coffee beans at home was time-consuming and impractical, and wholesale roasting made coffee more suitable for home consumption. Roasted coffee beans began to show up in New York City dry-goods stores in the first half of the nineteenth century.

Two Civil War–era New York City inventions helped usher in the modern coffee industry. In his factory on Warren Street, Jabez Burns invented and manufactured an industrial coffee roaster that could be emptied without removing the roasting drum from the fire. In Brooklyn the invention of the paper bag meant that packaging no longer needed to be made by hand in the style of "sugar loafs" (a cone of paper filled with sugar with the ends twisted shut) and that roasted coffee beans could be packed for retail in advance. John Arbuckle, who moved his business from Philadelphia to be closer to coffee's port of entry, was the first to successfully capitalize on these inventions in building a national brand. Some of the warehouses for his factory in Brooklyn's DUMBO neighborhood still stand. The majority of coffee businesses—from importers and brokers to roasters and "jobbers" (wholesale distributors)—were concentrated on Washington Street in Manhattan along the Hudson River. In 1882 local coffee merchants founded the Coffee Exchange in the City of New York. After more than a century of mergers and consolidations, the Coffee Exchange became the New York Board of Trade, where more coffee was traded than anywhere else in the world (more than $1 billion daily) early in the twenty-first century and where the global price standards for Arabica coffee were set each day.

At the end of the nineteenth century, the coffee port and corresponding businesses consolidated on Manhattan's East Side, on Water and Front streets. By the early twentieth century coffee warehouses moved across the East River to the Brooklyn waterfront, the point of entry for nearly 60 percent of coffee consumed in the United States in 1920. Coffee roasters remained in Manhattan. Eminent domain in the mid-1960s reduced the area in which they did business, and many closed; of those who could afford to move, only Gillies Coffee Company, founded in 1840, continued to do business in New York City in 2007. Several newer companies contributed to the approximately 100 million pounds of coffee roasted in New York City in 2007, but that number decreased each year. New Yorkers, however, continue to enjoy the brew in large quantities, from the 50-cent cups available from carts or bodegas on most corners in Manhattan to the $4 concoctions at any one of the city's 158 Starbucks Coffee locations (as of 2007—the first opened only 10 years before). On the retail side, New York City's coffee industry has grown considerably since cappuccino made its 1956 U.S. debut at MacDougal Street's Caffe Reggio, to more than half a billion dollars annually.

Rowan Moore Gerety

Coffee, Sugar and Cocoa Exchange. A commodities market incorporated as the Coffee Exchange of the City of New York in 1885. It was relatively small, sustained by connections to producers in Latin America and banks, as well as by daily reports from local business newspapers and other commodity exchanges and by monthly estimates of crop conditions and other harvest news from government agencies in provinces and shipping centers. The name was changed to the New

York Coffee and Sugar Exchange in 1916 when the sugar markets in Europe were closed by World War I and trade shifted to New York City. Coffee futures trading was plagued with difficulties caused by grading standards that could allow substitution of one variety for another, so that the need for arbitration of disputes between buyers and sellers increased. Importers complained during the 1950s to the Federal Trade Commission that the narrow definitions of grades excluded them from hedging opportunities. After an investigation the exchange entered into a consent decree that broadened its standard contract to cover about 70 percent of the world's coffee. The exchange in the 1960s had 350 members and controlled much of the world spot and futures business in sugar. In 1979 it absorbed the New York Cocoa Exchange (opened 1925), which was an important center of trading in Latin American cocoa, an increasingly important commodity as supplies from Africa diminished. Trading volume during the 1980s quintupled for cocoa (largely because lower output worldwide led to a sextupling of prices) and more than doubled for coffee. The Federal Trade Commission responded with more rigorous scrutiny of traders and efforts to bring about better self-governance. In 1998 the Coffee, Sugar and Cocoa Exchange partnered with the New York Cotton Exchange to form the New York Board of Trade. Its headquarters moved to the World Financial Center after its previous trading site was destroyed during the terrorist attacks on the World Trade Center of 11 September 2001.

New York Coffee and Sugar Exchange, Inc.: Its Role in the Marketing of Sugar (New York: Hobbs, Dorman, 1965)

Morton Rothstein

coffeehouses. During the colonial period coffeehouses were important meeting places for politicians, merchants, and military officers in New York City. Like their English counterparts these coffeehouses sold alcohol and were centrally situated. In 1696 John Hutchins opened the King's Arms, also known as the Coffee House, on the west side of Broadway just north of the cemetery of Trinity Church. A focal point for opponents of Jacob Leisler, it was frequented by a genteel clientele. By 1747 new owners referred to the King's Arms as the Exchange Coffee House to reflect its function as a marketplace for many commodities, including slaves, ships, horses, and real estate. Another important center of commerce and conviviality was the Merchants' Coffee House, opened about 1737 at the southeast corner of Wall and Water streets. Along with George Burns' Coffee House, which supplanted the old King's Arms, the Merchants' was an important meeting place for the Sons of Liberty; there, Isaac Low, Alexander MacDougall, James Duane, and John Jay on 23 May 1774 drafted the famous letter of the New York Committee of Correspondence protesting the Intolerable Acts and supporting the formation of the Continental Congress. In later years the Merchants' Coffee House was the site of meetings that led to the formation of the Chamber of Commerce (1768), the Bank of New York (1784), the New York Hospital Society (1785), the Society of the Cincinnati (1786), and the Manhattan Company (1799). The Merchants' also oversaw the first public auction of stock in 1790 and remained in operation until the building was destroyed by fire on 18 December 1804. The Tontine Coffee House, opened in 1794 on the northwest corner of Wall and Water streets, was perhaps the best known establishment of its kind in New York City and an important institution until 1826. Coffeehouses diminished in number by the 1830s as the city's boundaries expanded and various populist movements created a hostile climate that persuaded the rich and powerful to take their business to exclusive private clubs and other institutions.

Frederic De Peyster, *History of the Tontine Building* (New York: Nesbitt, 1855); Elizabeth Brown Cutting, *Old Taverns and Posting Inns* (New York: G. P. Putnam's Sons, 1898)

Marc Ferris

Coffin, Henry Sloane (*b* New York City, 5 Jan 1877; *d* Lakeville, Conn., 25 Nov 1954). Minister. He was brought up in Manhattan at 13 West 57th Street and attended Yale University and the Union Theological Seminary. While serving at the Bedford Park Presbyterian Church in the Bronx and the Madison Avenue Presbyterian Church (1905–26), he became known for his impassioned preaching style and his writings on the Social Gospel movement. He rallied immigrants in support of educational programs, Bible classes, and missionary work in China, and increased the size of the congregation at Madison Avenue Presbyterian Church from 600 to 2500. During his tenure as the president of Union Theological Seminary (1926–45), the seminary occupied new buildings, appointed the first women to its faculty (1927), added a School of Sacred Music (1928), and absorbed Auburn Seminary from upstate New York (1939). Among the notable faculty that he drew to the school were the eminent theologians Reinhold Niebuhr and Paul Tillich and the biblical translator James Moffatt. In addition he expanded seminary opportunities for African Americans and helped students to reconcile religious pacifism with American involvement in World War II. As a leader of the local presbytery's Board of Church Extension, he helped to support new congregations. He was also a member of the Board of Home Missions (1903) of the American Presbyterian church and a charter member of the Board of National Missions (1923). Elected moderator of the General Assembly (1943), the highest post in the Presbyterian church, he advocated ecumenism after World War II and committed himself to unifying the northern and southern branches of the Presbyterian church, an objective that was achieved 40 years later. Coffin's published writings include *Social Aspects of the Cross* (1908), *A More Christian Industrial Order* (1920), and *A Half-Century of Union Theological Seminary, 1896–1945: An Informal History* (1954).

Morgan Phelps Noyes, *Henry Sloane Coffin: The Man and His Ministry* (New York: Charles Scribner's Sons, 1964); Robert T. Handy, *A History of Union Theological Seminary in New York* (New York: Columbia University Press, 1987)

David Meerse

Cohan, George M(ichael) (*b* Providence, R.I., ?4 July 1878; *d* New York City, 5 Nov 1942). Singer, actor, playwright, composer, and producer. As a child he toured with his family in vaudeville. During the first decades of the twentieth century he wrote and often performed in fast-paced musical melodramas and revues notable for their unabashed flag-waving, settings in New York City, slang, and widely popular songs. For some years he lived in the Hotel Knickerbocker at 142 West 42nd Street. Cohan wrote and produced Broadway plays and musicals throughout the 1920s, often appearing in them. From the 1930s he lived in an apartment at 993 Fifth Avenue. Toward the end of his career he received critical acclaim for his performances in *Ah, Wilderness!* (1933), by Eugene O'Neill, and *I'd Rather Be Right* (1937), by Richard Rodgers and Lorenz Hart. Cohan wrote "Give My Regards to Broadway" and "I'm a Yankee Doodle Dandy." A statue of him stands in Duffy Square in midtown Manhattan.

Patrick McGilligan, *Yankee Doodle Dandy* (Madison: University of Wisconsin Press, 1981)

Cohen, Morris Raphael (*b* Minsk, Ukraine, 25 July 1880; *d* Washington, D.C., 28 Jan 1947). Philosopher. He moved with his parents to New York City in 1892, where he attended public schools and City College of New York (BS 1900). While an undergraduate he became active in the Educational Alliance, and with Thomas Davidson he opened a night school for workers where he taught philosophy and history; he later taught at Townsend Harris Hall (1902–4, 1906–12) and City College (1912–38). After beginning graduate work at Columbia he transferred to Harvard University (PhD 1906). A philosophic naturalist, he favored the use of rational methods in pursuing knowledge. He made critical reflections on social morals and laws in much of his work and adhered to a social philosophy calling for government intervention to eliminate social inequities. Cohen was president of the American Philosophical Association (1928).

Among his published writings are *Reason and Nature: An Essay on the Meaning of Scientific Method* (1931), *Law and the Social Order* (1933), *Preface to Logic* (1944), *The Faith of a Liberal* (1945), *The Meaning of Human History* (1947), *A Dreamer's Journey: The Autobiography* (1949), and *American Thought: A Critical Sketch* (1954). The Cohen Library at City College is named for him.

Leonora Cohen Rosenfield, *Portrait of a Philosopher* (New York: Harcourt, Brace and World, 1962)

Walter Friedman

Cohn, Roy (Marcus) (*b* New York City, 20 Feb 1927; *d* Bethesda, Md., 2 Aug 1986). Lawyer. He graduated from Columbia Law School at age 20; worked in Manhattan for the U.S. attorney, whom he assisted in the celebrated espionage trial of Julius and Ethel Rosenberg; and became known for his combative style in the courtroom. In Washington, D.C., during 1953–54 he was the chief counsel to the committee led by Senator Joseph R. McCarthy that held hearings on purported communist influence in the army; he then returned to New York City and joined the law firm that became Saxe, Bacon and Bolan. During the following decades he acquired a reputation as one of the most powerful, flamboyant, and controversial lawyers in the city. He defended a number of organized-crime figures and was associated with conservative causes. Acquitted on federal charges of conspiracy, bribery, and fraud, Cohn was disbarred in New York State for misuse of his clients' funds only weeks before his death of AIDS. He is buried at Union Field Cemetery in Ridgewood, Queens.

Nicholas Von Hoffman, *Citizen Cohn* (New York: Doubleday, 1988)

Lisa Gitelman

Cohnheim, Max (*fl* 1848–61). Humorist, playwright, and political activist. In Germany he was associated with the humor magazine *Kladderadatsch* in Berlin. After the revolution of 1848 he immigrated to the United States and settled in New York City. He wrote comic songs for the Arion Gesangverein, edited the *New Yorker Humorist* in 1858–60, and became one of the leading German playwrights in the city. One of his plays, about a triumphant German revolution, was partly set in the Shakespeare Hotel in New York City. He worked briefly for the Republican Party in 1856 before joining other German American radicals in 1857 to form the Kommunisten Klub. He later served as a captain of artillery in the Civil War.

Stanley Nadel

Cole, Thomas (*b* Bolton-le-Moors, England, 1 Feb 1801; *d* Catskill, N.Y., 11 Feb 1848). Painter. He moved to the United States in 1818 and worked as an engraver and portrait painter in Philadelphia, Pittsburgh, and Steubenville, Ohio. In 1825 he moved to New York City and made his first sketching tour up the Hudson River to the Catskill Mountains. That same year he became well known after three of his landscapes were bought by John Trumbull, William Dunlap, and Asher B. Durand, an event considered to have marked the beginning of the HUDSON RIVER SCHOOL. Cole traveled to Europe (1829–32, 1841–42) and throughout New York State and New England, often using the sites he visited as inspiration when he returned to his New York studio to paint. The first artist to treat landscape as a metaphor for the new nation, he argued in his "Essay on American Scenery" (1835) that the United States was a new Eden in which the landscape revealed the presence of God and a future of promise. The allegorical series "The Course of Empire" (1833–36, painted for Luman Reed) and "The Voyage of Life" (1839–40, painted for Samuel Ward) were based on his conception that landscape painters should combine morality and imagination with observations of nature. Among his pupils was Frederic E. Church; he also encouraged Durand to become a landscape painter. In 1836 he left the city and settled in Catskill. Considered the most influential member of the Hudson River School, Cole helped form the National Academy of Design (1826) and the Sketch Club (1827).

Thomas Cole, The Course of Empire: The Consummation of Empire *(1835–36)*

Ellwood C. Parry III, *The Art of Thomas Cole: Ambition and Imagination* (Newark: University of Delaware Press, 1988); William H. Truettner and Alan Wallach, eds., *Thomas Cole: Landscape into History* (New Haven: Yale University Press, 1994)

Timothy Anglin Burgard

Coleman, Ornette (*b* Fort Worth, Tex., 9 March 1930). Saxophonist and composer. He made his debut in New York City in November 1959 at the Five Spot Café, where his group was so well received by those ranging from the Modern Jazz Quartet to Leonard Bernstein that the engagement was extended for six months. In the following year he recorded the album *Free Jazz,* the title of which came to refer to a genre that he played a large role in developing. Coleman returned to Greenwich Village in 1965 at the Village Vanguard. His performances and recordings during the 1960s and early 1970s were characterized by jagged rhythms, harmonies that were at least outwardly atonal, and the sequential repetition of short melodic motifs and helped to earn him a reputation as one of the most radical innovators in the history of jazz. He often performed with the trumpeter Don Cherry, the double bass player Charlie Haden, and the drummer Ed Blackwell. In 1971 he opened a performance space called Artist's House at 131 Prince Street in SoHo, and in 1976 he formed the band Prime Time, which blends free jazz, funk, and soul. His 2006 album *Sound Grammar* won the Pulitzer Prize for music in 2007. That same year, he was awarded a Grammy Award for lifetime achievement.

Barry McRae, *Ornette Coleman* (London: Apollo, 1991)

Ira Berger

Coler, Bird S(im) (*b* Champaign, Ill., 9 Oct 1867; *d* Brooklyn, 12 June 1941). Public official. He worked in his father's private bank and as a young man amassed a fortune trading securities. He then turned to politics and with the backing of Tammany Hall was elected in 1898 as the first comptroller of the consolidated city. Defeated in the gubernatorial election of 1902, he won public office in 1906 as the borough president of Brooklyn. He was the commissioner of charities under Mayors John F. Hylan and James J. Walker. In 1929 he broke with the Democrats to seek the presidency of the Board of Aldermen on Fiorello H. La Guardia's unsuccessful mayoral ticket. Coler wrote widely on municipal government and finance. A hospital on Roosevelt Island is named in his honor.

See also WATER, §2.

Frank Vos

Coler–Goldwater Specialty Hospital and Nursing Facility. Municipal hospital specializing in rehabilitation and chronic care, administered by the New York Health and Hospitals Corporation. It was built on Welfare Island on the site of a city prison that had been demolished during the 1930s and opened in July 1939 as the Welfare Hospital for Chronic Disease; it was renamed in 1942 for S. S. Goldwater. An initial focus on the research and treatment of chronic illness was broadened during the 1950s to include comprehensive rehabilitation for the disabled. A skilled nursing facility was established in the 1970s. In 1996 Goldwater Memorial Hospital merged with Coler Memorial Hospital to become Coler–Goldwater Specialty Hospital and Nursing Facility, creating one of the largest subacute care facilities in the world.

Sandra Opdycke

Coles, Honi [Charles] (*b* Philadelphia, 1911; *d* Queens, 12 Nov 1992). Dancer. He began tap dancing in Philadelphia and later became famous for sustained involvement in the dance world of Harlem and New York City. During the 1930s he performed at the Harlem Opera House and the Apollo Theater, and by 1940 he was a soloist with Cab Calloway. With Charles "Cholly" Atkins he formed the team of Coles and Atkins: their specialty was synchronized, identical-step dance routines, and in 1949 they began a two-year engagement on Broadway in the show *Gentlemen Prefer Blondes*. Although public interest in tap dancing subsided during the 1950s, their team was one of the longest-lived. Coles became the production manager of the Apollo in 1960, continued to perform occasionally, and worked with younger dancers. In 1988 he received the Capezio Award for providing an "inspiration to a new generation of tap dancers." He lived in East Elmhurst in Queens.

Robert Seder

Colgate, William (*b* Hollingbourne, England, 25 Jan 1783; *d* New York City, 25 March 1857). Soap maker and toothpaste pioneer. In 1795 Colgate moved to the United States with his family to escape public hostility toward his father, who had supported the French Revolution. After settling in New York City in 1804 he became a manager of Slidell and Company, the city's largest tallow chandler. In 1806 he opened his own firm, Colgate and Company, which introduced and began marketing the first commercial brand of toothpaste in 1873 and later evolved into COLGATE–PALMOLIVE, a global consumer products company. A leading philanthropist, Colgate was active in the American Bible Society and helped to found what later became Colgate University, in Hamilton, New York.

James Bradley

Colgate–Palmolive. Firm of soap and toiletry manufacturers formed in 1806 at 6 Dutch Street in Manhattan by William Colgate as a starch, soap, and candle enterprise called Colgate and Company. Its first advertisement for "Soap Mold and Dipt Candles" appeared in 1817. During the early years its main products were toilet essence, soap, and pearl starch. In 1847 the company moved its factory to New Jersey but kept its business office in New York City. In 1873, it began marketing the first commercial brand of toothpaste, which was sold in jars until 1896, when Colgate introduced the collapsible tube system to the industry. The firm merged with Palmolive–Peet Company of Chicago in 1922, adopted the Colgate–Palmolive name in 1953, and established domestic and international headquarters at 300 Park Avenue in Manhattan in 1956. Colgate–Palmolive manufactures a wide range of consumer products relating to oral care, personal care, home care, and pet nutrition. Prominent brands include Mennen, Ajax, Irish Spring, Hill's Pet Nutrition, Protex, Softsoap, and Murphy Oil Soap.

Richard Kobliner

Coliseum. See NEW YORK COLISEUM.

Collect. A large pond 60 feet (18 meters) deep, formerly in lower Manhattan just north of the present City Hall Park; it was also called Fresh Water Pond. It was fed by an underground spring, and its overflow ran through the marshes of Lispenard Meadows to the Hudson River. The name is a corruption of the Dutch word *kolch* (a small body of water), erroneously written as *kalch* (lime) by some nineteenth-century writers, probably in reference to the lime from the heaps of oyster shells left around the pond by American Indians. During the eighteenth century the pond was a favored spot for picnics in the summer and ice skating in the winter. It also provided drinking water at the Tea Water Pump in Chatham Street and water for the tanneries, breweries, ropewalks, and slaughterhouses that were built on its southern and eastern banks; by the late eighteenth century the pond was already considered "a very sink and common sewer." Several proposals for new uses of the pond were submitted to the Common Council, including one for a park designed by Pierre L'Enfant and another for a canal between the Hudson and the East rivers, but the pond was instead filled in between 1803 and 1811 by earth from the surrounding hill. By 1813 the pond was virtually covered as Centre Street was extended northward.

Carol Groneman

College Board. Nonprofit membership educational association formed to develop standardized college admission tests for secondary-school students. Its first meeting was held on 17 November 1900 in the library of Columbia University. The board was conceived by Charles William Eliot, president of Harvard University, as a means of simplifying the college admission process by eliminating the separate entrance examinations administered by each college. The idea was energetically taken up by Nicholas Murray Butler, soon the president of Columbia, who was the first secretary of the board and later its president. Initially the board offered essay examinations in history, mathematics, physics, chemistry, and ancient and modern languages. In 1926 it introduced the Scholastic Aptitude Test (SAT), a multiple-choice examination divided into verbal and mathematical sections that displaced the essay examinations by 1940. In 1947 the board joined with the Carnegie Foundation and the American Council on Education to form the Educational Testing Service, which took over many of the board's testing and other services. The board reintroduced examinations in 1955 not unlike the early essay examinations as part of the Advanced Placement (AP) Program, which allowed high school students to enroll in college-level courses. The College Scholarship Service also was introduced in the 1950s; it provided a common application form for financial aid and promoted scholarships based on financial need. The board was chartered in 1957 by the University of the State of New York as a nonprofit educational association governed by a board of trustees. For many years the College Board was housed in offices provided by Columbia University. It moved into the Interchurch Center on Riverside Drive in 1960 and then to 888 Seventh Avenue before purchasing the nine lowest floors of the Sofia Building at 45 Columbus Avenue in 1985; in the early twenty-first century it maintained its headquarters there. The association is composed of more than 5400 schools, colleges, universities, and other educational organizations. Well-known tests it administers include the SAT, AP subject tests, and the

Preliminary SAT/National Merit Scholarship Qualifying Test (PSAT/NMSQT).

Claude M. Fuess, *The College Board: Its First Fifty Years* (New York: College Entrance Examination Board, 1967); John A. Valentine, *The College Board and the School Curriculum: A History of the College Board's Influence on the Substance and Standards of American Education, 1900–1980* (New York: College Entrance Examination Board, 1987)

John C. Aubry

College of Mount St. Vincent. Independent liberal arts college formed in 1847 by the Sisters of Charity of Mount St. Vincent as a secondary school for women. Originally called the Academy of Mount St. Vincent, the school was first located at Mount St. Vincent at McGowan's Pass in what is now Central Park; it moved to its current site in Riverdale in the Bronx in 1857, when the Sisters of Charity purchased Fonthill, the estate of the actor Edwin Forrest. The curriculum was expanded to include postsecondary education in 1910, and the following year the school took its current name and opened with 28 first- and second-year students; degrees were awarded from 1913. The first president was the archbishop of New York, John Cardinal Farley, and the first dean was Mary Ambrose Dunphy of the Sisters of Charity. In 1964 the college initiated a cooperative program with Manhattan College. Male students were first admitted in 1974. The college received authorization from the New York State Board of Regents in 1988 to confer a master of science in nursing. It also added a master's program in business. By the early twenty-first century Mount St. Vincent had an enrollment of more than 1600 undergraduate and graduate students.

Marie De Lourdes Walsh, *The Sisters of Charity of New York, 1809–1959* (New York: Fordham University Press, 1960); Mary Oates, ed., *Higher Education for Catholic Women: An Historical Anthology* (New York: Garland, 1987)

Bernadette McCauley

College of Physicians and Surgeons (P&S). Medical school of Columbia University located at the Columbia–Presbyterian Medical Center. See also Medical schools.

College of Staten Island. Part of the City University of New York, it was formed in 1976 by the merger of Staten Island Community College (1955) in Sunnyside and Richmond College (1965) in St. George. Senator John Marchi played a key role in creating the institution, and he and Governor Mario Cuomo worked to move the college to a new 204-acre (83-hectare) campus at Willowbrook in 1993. This campus, the largest of any college in New York City, incorporates 19 neo-Georgian buildings from the former Willowbrook State School with new library, performing arts science, and athletic and student activities facilities. The college offers two- and four-year undergraduate degrees, as well as graduate degrees and doctorates in nursing and physical therapy. In 2007 it had more than 12,000 students and 335 full-time faculty members.

The College of Staten Island at Willowbrook (New York: City University of New York, 1985)

Howard R. Weiner

College Point. Neighborhood in north central Queens, northwest of Flushing along the East River and Flushing Bay. It was built in 1854 by Conrad Poppenhusen to accommodate the workers at his hard-rubber factory, and Poppenhusen personally guided the development of its streets, houses, businesses, and schools. In 1870 it became a village incorporating the neighborhoods of Flammersburg and Strattonport. In the 1880s and 1890s, breweries, silk mills, and paint works proliferated, and the area grew rapidly and attracted mostly a German population. Its beer halls and amusement parks, especially Point View Island, made it popular for outings, steamboat excursions, and political clubs. During Prohibition the resorts declined in popularity and were eventually replaced by aircraft and aviation-parts factories built by Sikorsky Aircraft, the LWF Company, and the Edo Corporation. In the early twenty-first century, College Point remained predominantly residential, with a minor industrial presence throughout the neighborhood. Commercial and residential development increased, resulting in the demolition of many older buildings.

Vincent Seyfried

colleges and universities. The first institution of higher learning in New York City was King's College, opened at Trinity Church on Wall Street in 1754 by Anglicans allied with members of the Dutch Reformed Church and offering a traditional curriculum of Greek, Latin, and mathematics. Closed during the American Revolution, it reopened in 1784 as Columbia College. General Theological Seminary was formed in 1822, followed by Union Theological Seminary (Presbyterian) in 1836. The University of the City of New York (1831), later renamed New York University (NYU), was established in response to the conservative curriculum and dominance of Episcopalians at Columbia but nonetheless offered a curriculum of Greek, Latin, and mathematics for much of the nineteenth century; a law school was added in 1835. The first college for women was Rutgers Female Institute (1838); renamed Rutgers Female College in 1867, it ceased operations in 1895. St. John's College (1841), in what is now the Bronx, was the first Catholic college in the metropolitan area. It was turned over to the Jesuits in 1846 by Bishop John Hughes and later became Fordham University. Institutions for women included Packer Collegiate Institute (1845) and the Academy of the Sacred Heart (1846), which was renamed Manhattanville College in 1917 and eventually moved to suburban Purchase, New York. The Academy of Holy Infancy, established by Brothers of the Christian Schools in 1853, later became known as Manhattan College and moved from Manhattanville to the Bronx in 1923. Public higher education was first offered at the Free Academy (1848), which in 1866 changed its name to City College of New York and introduced college-level courses. The Polytechnic Institute of Brooklyn, founded

Rutgers Female College, 489 Fifth Avenue

in 1854 as an academy called the Brooklyn Collegiate and Polytechnic Institute, was chartered as a college in 1890 and later became Polytechnic University.

During the second half of the nineteenth century NYU Law School and the Columbia School of Law (1858) dominated legal education in the city. Cooper Union for the Advancement of Science and Art (1859), endowed by Peter Cooper, distinguished itself by offering training in architecture, engineering, and the fine arts without cost to students. St. Francis Academy (1859), organized by the Franciscan Brothers in Brooklyn, was taken over by Jesuits in 1884. The Homeopathic Medical College of New York opened in 1860, as did the Long Island College Hospital Medical School in Brooklyn (renamed the State University of New York [SUNY] Downstate Medical Center in 1950). At the invitation of John D. Loughlin, archbishop of Brooklyn, St. John's College, founded by the Vincentian Fathers in Brooklyn in 1870, later moved its main campus to Jamaica. In 1971 it assumed control of Notre Dame College in Staten Island.

Most nineteenth-century colleges continued to exclude women; among the exceptions was the Normal College for Women (1870, later renamed Hunter College for its founder, Thomas Hunter), which trained many of the teachers in the city's public schools. The Jewish Theological Seminary of America opened in 1886 to train Conservative rabbis and eventually had five divisions at its Morningside Heights campus. The same year saw the opening of the Isaac Elchanan Seminary, an Orthodox institution that eventually became Yeshiva University (first based on the Lower East Side and then moved to Washington Heights in 1929). Pratt Institute (1887) expanded from a technical secondary school in Brooklyn into a university with six divisions. Barnard College (1889), an undergraduate college for women, developed a close affiliation with Columbia but retained its own faculty and administration. The Webb Institute of Naval Architecture moved from Fordham Heights to suburban Glen Cove, Long Island, in 1949.

At the end of the nineteenth century the metropolitan region became a center for professional education. Three of the best-known institutions were medical schools: New York University School of Medicine (founded 1841 as University Medical College), the College of Physicians and Surgeons (founded in 1807; part of Columbia from 1860; coeducational since 1917), and Cornell University Medical College (1898, now Weill Cornell Medical College). Others were schools of law, including New York Law School (1891), formed by Theodore Dwight, who had resigned his position as dean of Columbia Law School after a dispute with President Seth Low; Brooklyn Law School (1901); and law schools at St. John's and Fordham. Other schools that opened during these years include Teachers College (1886, a part of Columbia from 1898); a school of pedagogy at New York University (1890); Adelphi College (1896, now Adelphi University), which moved from Brooklyn to Garden City, on Long Island; the Juilliard School (founded 1905 as the Institute of Musical Art), a conservatory that later became known as well for dance and drama; Pace University (1906), which began as a school of accounting on a site near City Hall; and the New York College for Podiatric Medicine (1911), now the site of the largest foot clinic in the United States. Cathedral College of the Immaculate Conception opened in Brooklyn in 1914 to train Catholic priests, moved to Douglaston in 1967, and closed in 1988. St. Joseph's College, formed in 1916 as a college for Catholic women in Brooklyn, admitted men in 1969, and added a branch campus in Patchogue in 1979. The Bureau of Educational Experiments (1916) became known for such innovative projects as the country's first nursery school (1918): as the Bank Street College of Education (1950) it was responsible in the 1960s for the Bank Street readers, among the first primers to depict characters of different races. The Mannes College of Music (1916) provided instruction at the undergraduate and graduate levels and also introduced high school and extension programs. The college merged with the New School in 1989. The New York School of Interior Design (1916) first granted degrees in 1976. The Manhattan School of Music (1917–18), awarded bachelor's degrees from 1943 and doctorates from 1973; it moved to Morningside Heights in 1969. Wagner College (1883, affiliated with the Evangelical Lutheran Church in America), originally Rochester (New York) Lutheran Proseminary, moved to Staten Island in 1918, where it became coeducational (1933) and introduced a comprehensive undergraduate program.

The number of institutions in the city increased after World War I. Charles A. Beard, John Dewey, Alvin Johnson, James Harvey Robinson, and Thorstein Veblen organized the New School for Social Research (1919). The country's first university for adults, its University in Exile and its École Libre des Hautes Études became a haven for European intellectuals in exile during World War II. Other colleges introduced adult divisions and weekend programs that attracted workers and parents. City College opened a school of business and civic administration (1919), a school of technology (1919), and a school of education (1921). The Jewish Institute of Religion, a rabbinical college founded by Stephen S. Wise in 1922, merged in 1950 with Hebrew Union College of Cincinnati. The resulting Hebrew Union College–Jewish Institute of Religion moved from the West Side to Greenwich Village in 1979. Long Island University, opened in Brooklyn in 1926, expanded to Southampton (1963, purchased 2005 by SUNY) and Brookville, Long Island (1954), and added a college of pharmacy and health sciences. Berkeley College, now with seven locations in New York and New Jersey, opened in 1931 as a business college. To meet an increasing demand for public higher education the state legislature in 1926 replaced the City College Board of Trustees with the Board of Higher Education, which soon opened a branch of City College in downtown Brooklyn (1926) that was absorbed by Brooklyn College (1930); Queens College (1937); and a division of Hunter College in the Bronx (1931) that became Herbert H. Lehman College (1968).

The first two-year independent colleges offered programs that permitted students to transfer to four-year colleges as well as vocational programs. From 1928 to 1936 Seth Low Junior College operated as an affiliate of Columbia, accepting Jewish and Catholic students who transferred to professional schools requiring fewer than four years of college for admission. Hofstra University opened on Long Island in 1935 as a branch of New York University. A two-year women's college formed in 1936 by the Religious of the Sacred Heart of Mary was renamed Marymount Manhattan College and became a four-year college after being chartered as a branch of Marymount College in Tarrytown, New York (1946, merged with Fordham University, 2002). Marymount Manhattan College became independent in 1961. The Kings College (1938), originally an interdenominational Protestant seminary in Belmar, New Jersey, moved from suburban Briarcliff Manor to the Empire State Building in 1999 and is now a Christian liberal arts college. Bramson ORT, a technical college under Jewish auspices, opened in 1942 to serve refugees and immigrants; it gained college status and moved from Manhattan to Forest Hills, in Queens, in 1977.

The demand for higher education rose sharply after World War II. The New York Institute of Technology (1955) moved from Brooklyn to Manhattan in 1958. Jurisdiction over New York City Community College (founded in 1946 as the New York State Institute of Applied Arts; now New York City College of Technology) was transferred from the State Education Department to the Board of Higher Education in 1964. The School for Cartoonists and Illustrators (1947, renamed the School of Visual Arts in 1956) offered degrees in fine arts, film, media arts, and photography. To make college education more generally accessible, the state legislature established the State University of New York (1948), which eventually took over the Fashion Institute of Technology (1944); Long Island College Medical Center (1950, now SUNY Health Science Center at Brooklyn); the Maritime

College at Fort Schuyler (1874), a regional center of Empire State College (1971); and the State College of Optometry (1971). In 1954 the Rockefeller Institute for Medical Research became a degree-granting institution called Rockefeller University. Yeshiva University opened Stern College for Women in 1954 in midtown Manhattan and the Albert Einstein College of Medicine in 1955 in the Bronx. Polytechnic University in Brooklyn (1854) opened a graduate center in Farmingdale, Long Island, in 1954, absorbed the NYU School of Engineering and Science in 1973, and announced a merger with NYU in 2008.

The first public community college of the City University of New York (CUNY) was Staten Island Community College (1955); other community colleges opened by the Board of Higher Education specialized in programs for adults and immigrants, including Bronx Community College (1957), which moved to the former campus of New York University in University Heights in 1973; Queensborough Community College (1958); Borough of Manhattan Community College (BMCC, 1964); and Kingsborough Community College (Brooklyn, 1963). The board also oversaw the founding of the Graduate Center (1961) and the John Jay College of Criminal Justice (1967) and took over Baruch College (1919). The New York City government ratified creation of the City University of New York as a coordinating administrative entity in 1957.

Rising enrollments in the 1960s led to a rapid expansion of higher education, both public and private. Marymount Manhattan College (1946), a branch of Marymount College in Tarrytown that became independent in 1961, established the Malcolm–King Harlem College Extension Center in 1968; the center closed in 1989. The College for Human Services (1964, renamed Audrey Cohen College in 1992 and Metropolitan College in 2002) offers "purpose-centered" liberal arts and professional curricula. Touro College (1970), a private, multicampus liberal arts college, emphasized Jewish history and culture in its curriculum. The Mount Sinai School of Medicine (1963, the first medical school opened by a hospital since the 1910 Flexner Report) moved affiliations from CUNY (1967) to NYU (1999). Several additional units of CUNY opened to accommodate the baby boomers and the city's racial and ethnic minorities, including York College in Jamaica (1966, four-year program); Eugenio Maria de Hostos College in the Bronx (1968, two-year); Medgar Evers College in Brooklyn (1969, four-year); and Fiorello H. La Guardia College in Long Island City (1971, two-year). Efforts by CUNY to build new facilities accelerated after 1970, when it adopted a policy of open admissions (guaranteeing a place at the uni-

Private Colleges and Universities in New York City

American Academy of Dramatic Arts, 1884 (2-year, Manhattan)
American Academy McAllister Institute of Funeral Service, 1926 (2-year, Manhattan)
Art Institute of New York City, 1980 (2-year, Manhattan)
ASA Institute of Business and Computer Technology, 1985 (2-year, Manhattan)
Bank Street College of Education, 1916 (Graduate, Manhattan)
Bard Graduate Center for Studies in the Decorative Arts, Design and Culture, 1993 (Graduate, Manhattan)
Barnard College, 1889 (4-year/graduate, Manhattan)
Berkeley College, 1931 (2-year/4-year, Manhattan)
Bethel Seminary of the East, 1985 (Graduate, Queens)
Boricua College, 1973 (4-year/graduate, Manhattan)
Boston Graduate School of Psychoanalysis, New York, 1973 (Graduate, Manhattan)
Bramson ORT College, 1942 or 1977 (2-year, Queens)
Brooklyn Law School, 1901 (Graduate, Manhattan)
Christie's Education, 1978 (Graduate, Manhattan)
College of Mount Saint Vincent, 1847 (4-year/graduate, Bronx)
College of New Rochelle, 1940 (4-year/graduate, Brooklyn)
Columbia University, 1754 (4-year/graduate, Manhattan)
Cooper Union for the Advancement of Science and Art, 1859 (4-year/graduate, Manhattan)
DeVry College of New York, 1931 (4-year, Queens, Manhattan)
Fordham University, 1841 (4-year/graduate, Bronx, Manhattan)
Gamla College, 1996 (2-year, Brooklyn)
The General Theological Seminary of the Episcopal Church, 1817 (Graduate, Manhattan)
Gerstner Sloan–Kettering Graduate School of Biomedical Sciences, 2004 (Graduate, Manhattan)
Globe Institute of Technology, 1985 (4-year, Manhattan)
Hebrew Union College–Jewish Institute of Religion, 1875 (4-year/graduate, Manhattan)
Helene Fuld College of Nursing, 1945 (2-year, Manhattan)
Institute of Design and Construction, 1947 (2-year, Brooklyn)
Jewish Theological Seminary of America (JTS), 1886 (4-year/graduate, Manhattan)
Juilliard School, 1905 (4-year/graduate, Manhattan)
Katharine Gibbs School, 1911, closed (2-year, Manhattan)
The King's College, 1938 (4-year/graduate, Manhattan)
Laboratory Institute of Merchandising, 1939 (4-year, Manhattan)
Long Island Business Institute (Flushing campus), 1968 (2001) (2-year, Queens)
Long Island College Hospital of Brooklyn School of Nursing, 1833 (2-year, Brooklyn)
Long Island University, 1926 (4-year/graduate, Brooklyn)
Mandl School, 1924 (2-year, Manhattan)
Manhattan College, 1853 (4-year/graduate, Bronx)
Manhattan School of Music, 1917 (4-year/graduate, Manhattan)
Marymount Manhattan College, 1936 (4-year/graduate, Manhattan)
Mercy College, 1950 (4-year/graduate, Bronx, Manhattan)
Metropolitan College of New York, 1964 (4-year/graduate, Manhattan)
Monroe College, 1933 (4-year, Bronx)
Mount Sinai School of Medicine of New York University, 1963 (Graduate, Manhattan)
The New School of Interior Design, 1919 (4-year/graduate, Manhattan)
New York Studio School, 1964 (4-year/graduate, Manhattan)
New York Theological Seminary, 1900 (Graduate, Manhattan)
New York University, 1831 (4-year/graduate, Manhattan)
Pace University, 1906 (4-year/graduate, Manhattan)
Pacific College of Oriental Medicine (4-year, Manhattan)
Phillips Beth Israel School of Nursing, 1904 (2-year, Manhattan)
Plaza College, 1916 (2-year, Queens)
Polytechnic Institute of New York University (independent until spring 2009, when it merged with New York University), 1854 (4-year/graduate, Brooklyn)
Pratt Institute, 1887 (4-year/graduate, Brooklyn, Manhattan)
Professional Business College, 1990 (2-year, Manhattan)
Rabbi Isaac Elchanan Theological Seminary, 1896 (4-year/graduate, Manhattan)
Richard Gilder Graduate School at the American Museum of Natural History, 2006 (Graduate, Manhattan)
Rockefeller University, 1901 (Graduate, Manhattan)

(continued)

Private Colleges and Universities in New York City (*Continued*)

St. Francis College, 1859 (4-year/graduate, Brooklyn)
St. John's University, 1870 (4-year/graduate, Queens)
St. Joseph's College, 1916 (4-year/graduate, Brooklyn)
St. Vincent Catholic Medical Center/St. Vincent's Hospital Manhattan, 1849 (2-year/graduate, Staten Island, Brooklyn, Queens/Manhattan)
School of the International Center of Photography, 2001 (Undergraduate/graduate, Manhattan)
School of Visual Arts, 1947 (4-year/graduate, Manhattan)
Swedish Institute, 1916 (Proprietary 2–3-year, Manhattan)
Teachers College, 1887 (Graduate, Manhattan)
Technical Career Institutes, 1909 (2-year, Manhattan)
Touro College, 1970 (4-year/graduate, Brooklyn, Manhattan, Queens)
Tri-State College of Acupuncture, 1949 (4-year, Manhattan)
Union Theological Seminary, 1836 (Graduate, Manhattan)
Vaughn College of Aeronautics and Technology, 1932 (4-year/graduate, Queens)
Wagner College, 1883 (4-year/graduate, Staten Island)
Weill Cornell Medical College of Cornell University, 1898 (Graduate, Manhattan)
Wood Tobé–Coburn School, 1879 (2-year, Manhattan)
Yeshiva University, 1886 (4-year/graduate, Manhattan)

For lists of public colleges and universities in New York City, see the tables in City University of New York and State University of New York

versity to every graduate of the city's public high schools). CUNY opened a School of Law in 1983 and a Graduate School of Journalism in 2006.

The city's fiscal crisis of the mid-1970s caused a severe retrenchment. CUNY discontinued its policy of open admissions and began charging tuition for the first time. Richmond College (1965) and Staten Island Community College were forced to merge in 1976, to form the College of Staten Island. St. Vladimir's Orthodox Theological Seminary moved from Manhattan to suburban Crestwood, New York, in 1962, and New York Medical College moved to suburban Valhalla, New York, in 1978, after becoming affiliated with Pace University in 1973.

The attacks of 11 September 2001 on the World Trade Center affected several colleges and universities in lower Manhattan. Damage to Fiterman Hall, part of BMCC located near the destroyed 7 World Trade Center, forced a move to temporary classrooms. But several existing colleges expanded into the area later in the decade by leasing relatively inexpensive space. Meanwhile, Columbia embarked on a major expansion into Manhattanville.

Frank C. Abbott, *Government Policy and Higher Education: A Study of the Regents of the University of the State of New York, 1784–1949* (Ithaca, N.Y.: Cornell University Press, 1958); Harold S. Wechsler, *The Qualified Student: Selective College Admission in America, 1870–1970* (New York: Wiley-Interscience, 1977); Robert McCaughey, *Stand Columbia* (New York: Columbia University Press, 2003)

Harold S. Wechsler

College Settlement. First college settlement in the United States, opened in 1889 at 95 Rivington Street as an educational exchange for educated and underprivileged women. Initially there were seven full-time residents who were recent graduates of Smith, Vassar, and Wellesley colleges; they organized clubs for the neighborhood's children and adults, most of whom were German (eventually there were also Russian and Polish Jews). The organization soon expanded: by 1895 it had a kindergarten, a circulating library, a Penny Provident Fund, and a vacation home and provided instruction in sewing, cooking, woodcarving, basketwork, singing, literature, politics, history, and debating. The first head residents included Jean Fine Spahr (1889–92), Jane E. Robbins (1893–97), Mary Kingsbury Simkhovitch (1898), and Elizabeth Sprague Williams (1899–1915). Encouraged by the success of the organization, a group of alumnae from several eastern women's colleges formed the College Settlements Association in 1890, which, through membership subscriptions and the recruitment of resident staff, opened additional college settlements in Philadelphia, Boston, and Baltimore. As the neighborhood changed, the settlement decided to focus on teaching arts and dramatics and organizing leisure activities. In 1903 a 19-year-old Eleanor Roosevelt returned from a trip to Europe and became actively involved with the organization. For her contribution she taught immigrant children on the Lower East Side how to dance and stretch. Her experiences with poverty were later passed on to Franklin D. Roosevelt, whom she was dating at the time and who accompanied her on several visits. The organization closed in 1930.

Jane Allen

Collegiate School. Independent day school for boys from kindergarten through 12th grade and the oldest institution in New York City. Efforts to provide education in the Dutch Reformed Church were first made in 1628 by Jonas Michaëlius, the first Dutch Reformed minister in New Netherland. The school opened in 1687 at the first of its 17 successive sites, on Beaver Street between Broadway and Broad Street; it closed from 1776 to 1783 during the British occupation of New York City. Eventually the school settled on West End Avenue in 1892 between 77th and 78th streets. Collegiate became an independent corporation in 1940 but maintained close ties with the Reformed Protestant Dutch Church. In 2010 the school had 640 students.

Henry W. Dunshee, *History of the School of the Reformed Protestant Dutch Church in the City of New York from 1633 to the Present Time* (New York: Collegiate Reformed Protestant Dutch Church, 1853); Jean Parker Waterbury, *A History of Collegiate School, 1638–1963* (New York: C. N. Potter, 1965)

William Lee Frost

Colles, Christopher (*b* Dublin, 9 May 1739; *d* New York City, 4 Oct 1816). Civil engineer and inventor. After moving to New York City he built the city's first public waterworks (1774–76), which employed a steam engine of his own design. Destroyed before its completion during the British occupation, the system was later adapted by the Manhattan Company. His plan to link the Hudson River with the Great Lakes by way of the Mohawk River (1785) is regarded as having inspired the Erie Canal. He drew the routes leading north and south from New York City in *A Survey of the Roads of the United States of America* (1789), the first comprehensive mapping of the nation's highways. He was also the first superintendent of the New York Institution (1816), also known as the Old Almhouse. Although Colles died impoverished, his friend John Pintard arranged for him to be buried at St. Paul's Chapel.

Gerard Koeppel

Collier's. Weekly magazine. Launched in 1888 by Peter Collier in New York City, it soon became a leading popular magazine, specializing in muckraking and the work of such writers as Henry James and Richard Harding Davis and of such artists as Frederic Remington and Charles Dana Gibson. The magazine was commended for its reportage of World War II, notably that of Ernest Hemingway and Quentin Reynolds. Members of the editorial staff included Theodore H. White and George J. W. Goodman (who later wrote under the pseudonym Adam Smith). After the war the magazine declined under ineffective management. In the early 1950s it lost 40 percent of its advertising, and although circulation reached a peak of four million, *Collier's* ceased publication in December 1956. It was perhaps the first major casualty of the growing influence of advertising on magazines.

Ashbel Green

Collins, Ellen (*b* ?31 Dec 1828; *d* New York City, 8 July 1912). Housing reformer. She came from a Protestant background and was a member of the New York Mission Society and the Association for Improving the Condition of the Poor. During the 1880s she bought and repaired four dilapidated dwellings, known as rookeries, on Water Street on the Lower East Side and organized model tenements; these were rented to working-class tenants who were held to a strict code of moral behavior. She limited her profit to 6 percent in this venture and along with Olivia Dow and Edith Miles introduced tenement reforms that were adopted by the more systematic limited-dividend housing programs of corporate philanthropists in the 1890s.

Joel Schwartz

Collins Line. Passenger ship line. It was formed in 1850 by Edward Knight Collins (1802–78), an operator of sailing ships, and had five luxury liners. One of these, the *Baltic*, won a prize in 1852 for its speed in crossing the Atlantic. Two other ships were lost: the *Arctic* sank in a collision off Newfoundland that cost many lives, including those of Collins's wife and two children, and the *Pacific* vanished en route from Liverpool to New York City. The Collins Line ceased operations soon after the federal subsidy for transporting mail was withdrawn in 1857, owing to Southern opposition.

Warren Armstrong, *The Collins Story* (London: R. Hale, 1957)

Frank O. Braynard

Collyer brothers. Collectors and recluses. Langley Collyer (1886–1947), a concert pianist, and his brother Homer (1883–1947), a former admiralty lawyer who had been blinded and paralyzed by a stroke in the early 1930s, spent their retirement barricaded in a dilapidated brownstone at Fifth Avenue and 128th Street in Harlem. They had no gas, water, electricity, or sewer connection; admitted no one to the house; had only an old crystal set radio for contact with the outside world; and never disposed of anything. Langley explained to an acquaintance that he kept thousands of old newspapers in the house because Homer would want to read them when he regained his sight, and that he had 14 grand pianos because Homer liked to hear him play. On 21 March 1947 the police received a mysterious telephone call reporting that Homer had died in the house. Officers were dispatched to the scene only to find that all the doors and windows were blocked. After many attempts they were able to break through an upper-story window; they found the house filled with rats and honeycombed with passages between piles of junk. Homer's body was found in an upstairs room, but there was no sign of Langley, and rumors circulated that he was still inside the house hiding. The investigation received extensive coverage in the local press, and crowds gathered to catch a glimpse of Langley Collyer or at least his fantastic collections. After clearing out the house for several weeks the police discovered the body of Langley, who had apparently triggered one of many booby traps he had set for thieves who he believed were plotting to break in; he had died of heart failure after a suitcase, three breadboxes, and several bundles of newspapers fell on him, and Homer had died of starvation several days later. In addition to the 14 pianos the police found tons of newspapers, several old chandeliers, many cats, and the chassis of an old automobile in the basement.

Jonathan Aspell

Colón, Jesús (*b* Cayey, Puerto Rico, 1901; *d* New York City, 1974). Community activist and writer. Colón spent his early years in Cayey, the birthplace of the Socialist Party in Puerto Rico. In 1917 he moved to New York City, where he became a columnist for several newspapers, including *The Daily Worker, La Vida Obrera,* and *Gráficio.* He was active in much of the grass roots political activity of the 1920s and 1930s that involved the Puerto Rican community in the city. He was a founding member of Ateneo Obrero and La Liga Puertorriqueña e Hispana in 1928. During the 1930s, as violence against Puerto Ricans increased, Colón regarded himself as a guardian of the community and reported acts of violence in his columns. He spearheaded a series of exposés, including one reporting police harassment and brutality against community leaders. In the 1940s Colón worked along with the American Labor Party and the Communist Party to organize workers. In 1953 he made an unsuccessful run for public office in New York City under the banner of the Socialist Party. The House Un-American Activities Committee investigated him later in the decade.

Linda Delgado

Colonnade Row. A row of nine attached Greek Revival mansions constructed in 1833 by Seth Geer in Manhattan on the west side of Lafayette Place (now Lafayette Street), just below Astor Place. Originally named La Grange Terrace after the Marquis de Lafayette's country home in France, the row was distinguished by its marble facade, which consisted of 27 Corinthian columns rising from a rustic base. All the stonework was done by inmates of the state penitentiary at Sing Sing. The houses were occupied by several prominent figures, including John Jacob Astor, before it became fashionable to move uptown. In 1902 the five southernmost houses were demolished to make way for an annex to Wanamaker's department store. Four houses remained in the twenty-first century.

Elliott B. Nixon

Colonnade Row, ca *1910*

Colony Club. Social club for women, the first of its kind in New York City. It was formed in 1903 by Florence "Daisy" Jaffray (Mrs. J. Borden) Harriman (1870–1967), who modeled it on clubs for prominent men. With other wealthy women, including Anne Tracy Morgan (1873–1952), a daughter of J. P. Morgan, she raised half a million dollars and commissioned Stanford White to build a luxurious facility at 120 Madison Avenue near 30th Street. Decorated by the well-known designer ELSIE DE WOLFE, the club had a swimming pool, rooftop garden, gymnasium, squash court, library, card room, cocktail bar, smoking room, dining facilities, reception areas with a musician's gallery, and 10 bedrooms. The 1000 or so members attended lectures, entertained, secured support for charitable causes, and held their daughters' debutante balls at the club. By 1913 more space was needed, and the firm of Delano and Aldrich was engaged to build a new facility at 564 Park Avenue at 62nd Street. This one was more elaborate: its 12 levels contained more bedrooms than the first, as well as a floor of servants' quarters and a room for pets.

Anne O'Hagan, "A Beautiful Club for Women: The Colony Club of New York," *Century*, December 1910, pp. 216–24

Karen J. Blair

Colored American. Weekly newspaper launched in New York City in March 1837 by Samuel Cornish and Philip Bell, a prominent black journalist. It was financially supported by abolitionists and dedicated to the advancement of black Americans. Cornish resigned as the editor in 1839 and was replaced by Charles Bennett Ray, pastor of the Bethesda Congregational Church and an active supporter of the Underground Railroad in New York City. Bell continued his association with the newspaper until it ceased publication in 1842.

Martin E. Dann, *The Black Press, 1827–1890: The Quest for National Identity* (New York: G. P. Putnam's Sons, 1971); Roland E. Wolseley, *The Black Press, U.S.A.* (Ames: Iowa State University Press, 1971)

Sandra Roff

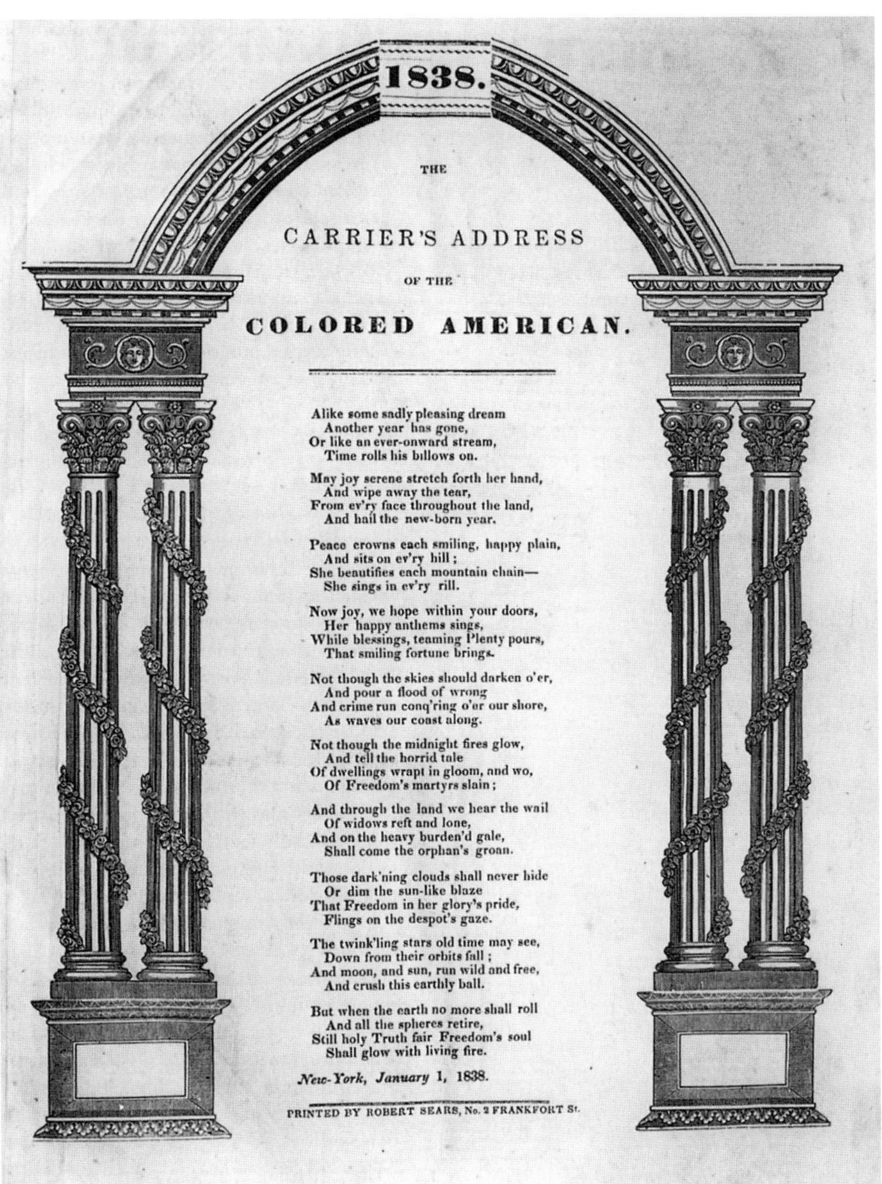

1838.

THE

CARRIER'S ADDRESS

OF THE

COLORED AMERICAN.

Alike some sadly pleasing dream
  Another year has gone,
Or like an ever-onward stream,
  Time rolls his billows on.

May joy serene stretch forth her hand,
  And wipe away the tear,
From ev'ry face throughout the land,
  And hail the new-born year.

Peace crowns each smiling, happy plain,
  And sits on ev'ry hill;
She beautifies each mountain chain—
  She sings in ev'ry rill.

Now joy, we hope within your doors,
  Her happy anthems sings,
While blessings, teaming Plenty pours,
  That smiling fortune brings.

Not though the skies should darken o'er,
  And pour a flood of wrong
And crime run conq'ring o'er our shore,
  As waves our coast along.

Not though the midnight fires glow,
  And tell the horrid tale
Of dwellings wrapt in gloom, and wo,
  Of Freedom's martyrs slain;

And through the land we hear the wail
  Of widows reft and lone,
And on the heavy burden'd gale,
  Shall come the orphan's groan.

Those dark'ning clouds shall never hide
  Or dim the sun-like blaze
That Freedom in her glory's pride,
  Flings on the despot's gaze.

The twink'ling stars old time may see,
  Down from their orbits fall;
And moon, and sun, run wild and free,
  And crush this earthly ball.

But when the earth no more shall roll
  And all the spheres retire,
Still holy Truth fair Freedom's soul
  Shall glow with living fire.

New-York, January 1, 1838.

PRINTED BY ROBERT SEARS, No. 2 FRANKFORT St.

"The Carrier's Address of the Colored American," poem for the New Year, 1838

Colored Home and Hospital for the Sick, Aged and Indigent. A charitable institution for blacks founded in 1839 by the Society for the Relief of Worthy Aged Colored Persons (a Quaker women's organization). Initially called the Colored Home, it housed, according to its own literature, "respectable, worn out colored servants." In the mid-1840s the commissioner of almshouses authorized it to shelter all sick and destitute blacks in the city, and a facility was constructed on First Avenue between 64th and 65th streets with a grant of $10,000 from the state legislature. This included not only a home for the aged and infirm but a men's hospital, women's hospital, lying-in hospital, nursery, "house of industry," chapel, and school. Children, the sick, and the destitute of all ages were received, excluding only the insane and those afflicted with smallpox. Among the first occupants were a number of retired black sailors who had been denied admission to the city almshouse and Sailors' Snug Harbor despite having contributed to the mariners' fund. During the 1850s there were 200 beds, enough to house virtually all the city's sick black population. By paying the weekly fee of 60 cents charged to each resident, the city contributed 80 percent of all revenues. In 1872 the name was changed to the Colored Home and Hospital for the Sick, Aged and Indigent. The institution expanded its capacity in the 1890s to 300 beds and began charging its patients fees and accepting voluntary contributions; eventually public funds accounted for only about 30 percent of annual income. In 1898 the home and hospital moved to 141st Street and Southern Boulevard in the Bronx; outpatient dispensary services were added, and the Training School for Colored Nurses opened as the first formal nursing school for black women in the country. Because the Bronx was then predominantly white (most residents were recent immigrants), the move meant that the institution became distanced from the blacks whom it was originally intended to serve. In 1902 it began to admit white patients and was renamed the Lincoln Hospital and Home. The old-age home continued to operate as an institution for blacks (until 1927), as did the nursing school (until the early 1970s).

Mary W. Thompson, *Broken Gloom: Sketches of the History, Character, and Dying Testimony of Beneficiaries of the Colored Home, in the City of New-York* (New York: J. F. Trow, 1851); Seth M. Scheiner, *Negro Mecca: A History of the Negro in New York City, 1865–1920* (New York: New York University Press, 1965); Rhoda G. Freeman, "The Free Negro in New York City in the Era before the Civil War" (Ph.D. diss., Columbia University, 1966); Leonard P. Curry, *The Free Black in Urban America, 1800–1850* (Chicago: University of Chicago Press, 1981)

Mike Sappol

Colored Orphan Asylum. School and shelter for black children opened in 1836 by Mary Murray and Anna Shotwell. It was managed solely by women for more than a century and attained celebrity before the Civil War as a model institution. Fewer than one-third of the asylum's inmates were orphans, and by about the age of 12 most were returned to their parents or placed in positions as farm laborers or domestic servants. After its building at Fifth Avenue between 43rd Street and 45th Street was destroyed by a mob during the draft riots (1863), the asylum was rebuilt in 1867 at 143rd Street and Amsterdam Avenue. In 1907 facilities were constructed in Riverdale according to the "cottage plan," a reform of the Progressive era that reorganized large, dehumanizing philanthropic institutions into campuses of smaller, homelike "cottages." The first black member of the board of directors was appointed in 1939. In 1944 the asylum was renamed the Riverdale Children's Association. After a controversy over conditions in the orphanage was aired in the press, it was decided in 1946 to discontinue institutional care and concentrate on foster care and dispersed small-group settings. The campus in Riverdale was sold to the Jewish Home for the Aged. It moved to Riverside Drive and 168th Street, changing its name to the Westside Center for Family Services. In March 1988 the Westside Center merged with Harlem–Dowling Children's Services.

From Cherry Street to Green Pastures: A History of the Colored Orphan Asylum at Riverdale-on-Hudson, 1836–1936 (New York: Riverdale Children's Association, 1936); *Riverdale Children's Association: 120th Anniversary, 1836–1956* (New York: Riverdale Children's Association, 1956)

Mike Sappol

Colored Orphan Asylum, 1861

Coltrane, John (William) (*b* Hamlet, N.C., 23 Sept 1926; *d* New York City, 17 July 1967). Saxophonist and composer. He grew up in Philadelphia and played in various groups before moving to New York City in 1955. During the next four years he became prominent as the tenor saxophonist in the small groups of Miles Davis and Thelonious Monk. He lived from 1957 to 1959 in an apartment on the second floor of 203 West 103rd Street in Manhattan and from 1959 to 1963 at 116–60 Mexico Street in Queens. He recorded the album *Giant Steps* (1959), his first major album as a musician at the forefront of jazz, and then formed a quartet with the pianist McCoy Tyner, the double bass player Jimmy Garrison, and the drummer Elvin Jones. In the following years his music grew increasingly dissonant. Coltrane became the leading figure of the jazz avant-garde, a circle of musicians based principally in the city who were seeking to overcome what they considered the limitations of bop and its offshoots. He was also the key figure in the resurgence of the soprano saxophone, which had been an obscure instrument in jazz for several years until he took it up in 1960. In his later career he obliterated the boundaries of jazz harmony and often performed solos of unprecedented length. Coltrane's important recordings include *My Favorite Things* (1960), *A Love Supreme* (1964), *Ascension* (1965), and three albums recorded at clubs in New York City—*Live at the Village Vanguard* (1961), *Live at Birdland* (1963), and *Live at the Village Vanguard Again* (1966). More than any other jazz musician of his time he enjoyed a reputation well beyond the usual audience of aficionados.

Cuthbert Ormond Simpkins, *Coltrane: A Biography* (New York: Herndon House, 1975)

Peter Keepnews

Columbia Broadcasting System [CBS]. Television and radio network. It was formed in January 1927 as United Independent Broadcasters, comprising 16 radio stations and operating from the Paramount Building. It was financially unsuccessful until it was bought in September 1927 for $503,000 by William S. Paley, the heir to a cigar fortune, who renamed the network the Columbia Broadcasting System (CBS). He engaged Lowell Thomas in 1930 as the newscaster of the first daily network news broadcast on radio, and Frank Stanton in 1935 to develop methods of surveying audiences. In 1938 he acquired the American Record Company and renamed it CBS Records. Stanton took charge of corporate matters and became president of the network in 1946, a position he held until 1972; Paley continued to make the decisions about programming. Initially CBS had fewer affiliates than the National Broadcasting Company (NBC) because it lacked radio personalities. Paley persuaded Jack Benny, Edgar Bergen, and others to leave NBC and join his network. He also had success with Ed Sullivan, Jackie Gleason, and Lucille Ball. Having less capital than his competitors, he decided to focus on news programs that were relatively cheap to produce. The network is considered to have originated broadcast journalism. Its leading newscaster was Edward R. Murrow, who during World War II broadcast *This Is London* with a team of reporters that included Charles Collingwood, Eric Sevareid, Howard K. Smith, and Richard C. Hottelet. In New York City Murrow and his producer, Fred W. Friendly, broadcast the first news documentary series on television, *See It Now* (1951–58). The best-known episode of this program, which discussed the activities of Senator Joseph R. McCarthy, aired in 1954. During the 1950s, which were regarded as the "Golden Age" of television, CBS produced *Studio One* and *Playhouse 90* (live broadcasts of dramas and comedies in which well-known actors from the Broadway theater appeared) out of New York City, and it soon had the highest ratings of the three networks. In the 1950s CBS developed its famous "eye" logo. The anchor of the network's evening news program, Douglas Edwards, was replaced in 1962 by Walter Cronkite, who held the position for almost 20 years. In 1965 the company moved its corporate headquarters from 485 Madison Avenue to a new building designed by Eero Saarinen at 51 West 52nd Street; its news division worked out of a renovated dairy at 524 West 57th Street. In 1968 the network first broadcast the news-magazine program *60 Minutes,* which became the longest-running program of its kind.

Between 1962 and 1979 the net annual income of CBS rose from $41.8 million to $200 million, and by 1977 the network was a conglomerate with holdings of $2.5 billion. Its diverse holdings included the baseball team the New York Yankees, the piano maker Steinway and Sons, the toymaker Creative Playthings, and the book publisher Holt, Rinehart and Winston. In 1981 CBS launched a cable television service focused on the performing arts. These businesses proved hugely unprofitable, and the company divested itself of most of them. With the rise of the American Broadcasting Company (ABC) and the Cable News Network (CNN) in the 1980s, profits fell and CBS was no longer the most successful network in television. It was taken over in 1985 by Laurence Tisch, president of Loews Corporation, who closed or sold most of its remaining subsidiary businesses.

In December 2005 Westinghouse Electric Corporation acquired CBS for $5.4 billion. Viacom bought out this company in 2000 at a cost estimated at $37 billion. In 2005 Viacom split off CBS, which once again became a publicly traded company. Beginning in 2008 both Viacom and CBS were controlled by Sumner Redstone.

A. M. Sperber, *Murrow: His Life and Times* (New York: Freundlich, 1986); Peter J. Boyer, *Who Killed CBS?: The Undoing of America's Number One News Network* (New York: Random House, 1988); Sally Bedell Smith, *In All His Glory: The Life of William S. Paley* (New York: Simon and Schuster, 1990)

Judith Adler Hennessee

Columbia Grammar and Preparatory School. Coeducational high school opened in 1764 in Manhattan as the preparatory school for King's College (now Columbia University). Samuel Johnson, the first president of the college, advocated for the school because of his conviction that before entering college a student should be well trained in grammar. The school was affiliated with the university until 1864. It moved several times throughout the city and now occupies four buildings on West 93rd and 94th streets, including a new high school building completed in 2001. As of 2007 enrollment in both schools was 1100.

Ross Dixon and McDonald Sullivan, eds., *Columbia Grammar School, 1764–1964: A Historical Log* (New York: Columbia Grammar School, 1965)

Richard Schwartz

Columbia Journalism Review. Bimonthly magazine published under the auspices of the Graduate School of Journalism at Columbia University. It was launched in 1961 by Edward W. Barrett as a quarterly publication that monitored print and broadcast news in the United States; beginning in 1971 it was published bimonthly. The largest, oldest, and most widely respected magazine of its kind, it is written for professional journalists and is known for the popular features "The Lower Case" and "Darts and Laurels."

Laura Gwinn

Columbia–Presbyterian Medical Center. See New York Presbyterian Hospital.

Columbia University. The oldest, richest, and most famous educational institution in New York City, situated principally on a 36-acre (14.5-hectare) campus in Morningside Heights in Manhattan. Chartered by George II on 31 October 1754 as King's College, it opened with eight students in the vestry room of Trinity Church and moved to its own building in 1760. The first president was Samuel Johnson (to 1763), a convert from the Congregational to the Anglican Church and the first in a line of Anglican and Episcopalian presidents lasting for nearly 200 years. His successor was Myles Cooper (to 1775), a Loyalist under whom the college nevertheless attracted as students such revolutionaries as Alexander Hamilton (1773–75), John Jay (AB 1764), Robert Livingston (AB 1764), and Gouverneur Morris (AB 1768). The college added a medical department in 1767. The college building was a military hospital during the American Revolution, when classes were suspended.

The state legislature, which envisioned the college as part of a projected state university, rechartered the school in 1784 as Columbia College. It returned control of the college to locally based trustees in 1787. Columbia divested itself of its medical department in 1813 by allowing it to merge with the New York College of Physicians and Surgeons. This college itself became a division of Columbia in 1860 during the presidency of Charles King (1849–64). King also supervised a move in 1857 to a campus at Madison Avenue and 49th Street and oversaw the opening of the School of Law (1858) and the School of Mines (1864, now the Henry Krumb School of Mines, part of the Fu Foundation School of Engineering and Applied Science). Other professional schools were added during the administration of Frederick A. P. Barnard (1864–89): the School of Architecture (1881, now the Graduate School of Architecture, Planning, and Preservation) and the School of Library Service (1887), led by Melvil Dewey. The university opened the School of Nursing (1892) during Seth Low's presidency (1890–1901) and affiliated in 1898 with Teachers College

Presidents of Columbia University

Samuel Johnson (1754–63)
Myles Cooper (1763–75)
Benjamin Moore (in president's absence,* 1775–76)
William Samuel Johnson (1787–1800)
Charles H. Wharton (1801)
Benjamin Moore (1801–11)
William Harris (1811–29)
William A. Duer (1829–42)
Nathaniel Fish Moore (1842–49)
Charles King (1849–64)
Frederick A. P. Barnard (1864–89)
Seth Low (1890–1901)
Nicholas Murray Butler (1902–45)
Frank D. Fackenthal, acting (1945–48)
Dwight D. Eisenhower (1948–53)
Grayson Kirk (1953–68)
Andrew W. Cordier (1969–70)
William J. McGill (1970–80)
Michael I. Sovern (1980–93)
George Rupp (1993–2002)
Lee C. Bollinger (2002–)

* Classes were suspended in 1776 because of the American Revolution and resumed in 1784. A Board of Regents governed the college until 1787.
Source: Columbia University Libraries, "President Profiles," http://www.columbia.edu/cu/lweb/indiv/uarchives/presidents.html.
Compiled by Frank Nestor

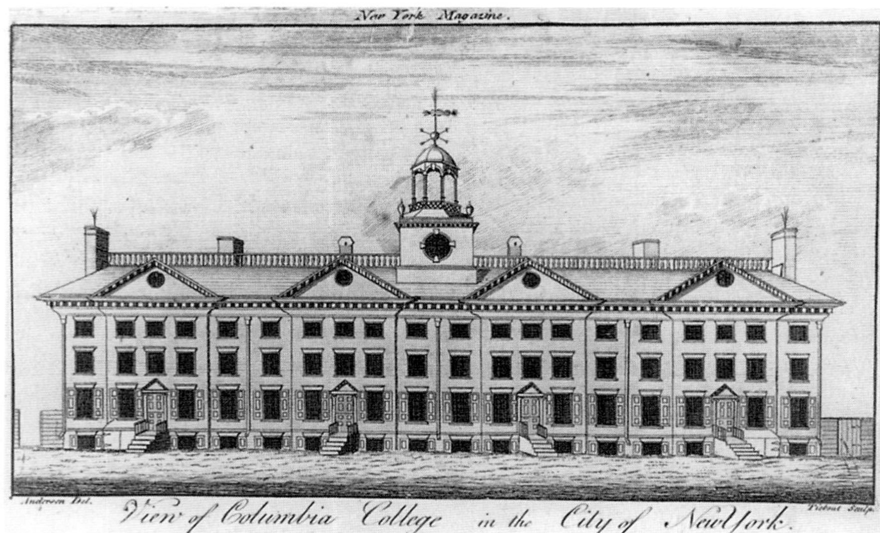

Original building of Columbia College, 1790

(opened in 1889). Columbia favored a broad and "scientific" rather than a narrow and practical brand of professional education. This emphasis caused some controversy: Theodore Dwight, who dominated the law school for 30 years, resigned as its dean in 1891 after a dispute with Low and founded New York Law School. Graduate faculties were established in political science (1880), philosophy (1890), and pure science (1892), and the name of the institution was changed to Columbia University in 1896 (changed again to Columbia University in the City of New York in 1912).

In 1897 the university moved to its current location, a rectangular campus with buildings designed in an Italian Renaissance style by the firm of McKim, Mead and White. Low Memorial Library, a classical Roman building with Grecian detail, became the centerpiece of the new campus. The harmonious design of its undergraduate, graduate, and professional buildings marked the rest of the campus, a symbol of the continuity of liberal and professional education.

Nicholas Murray Butler, president of the university from 1902 to 1945, and professors such as political scientist John W. Burgess spearheaded the move to emphasize graduate and professional schools in the early twentieth century. A prominent figure in local and national politics, Butler oversaw the absorption in 1904 of the New York College of Pharmacy (1831–1976) and in 1905 of the School of Philanthropy (founded 1898, renamed the School of Social Work in 1963), as well as the opening of the Graduate School of Journalism (1912), the Business School (1916, renamed the Graduate School of Business in 1949), the School of Dental and Oral Surgery (1917, merged in 1923 with the New York College of Dental and Oral Surgery, renamed the College of Dental Medicine in 2006), the School of Optometry (1910–56), University Extension (1920, renamed the School of General Studies in 1947), and the School of Public Health (1921, renamed the Mailman School of Public Health in 1999). Butler also liberalized admission and graduation requirements for undergraduates (increasing the number of permissible electives) and made it easier for them to pursue liberal arts and professional degrees simultaneously (an option exercised by more than 60 percent of all students at Columbia College in 1939).

During these same years Columbia became known for a distinctive approach to the social sciences. A belief that events were determined by social forces rather than by a priori laws and that conclusions about human behavior emerged from induction rather than deduction informed the work of John Dewey in education, psychology, and philosophy; James McKeen Cattell in psychology; James Harvey Robinson in history; E. R. A. Seligman in economics; Franz Boas in anthropology; and Charles A. Beard in political science and history. Tensions beset the university during World War I: the Student Army Training Corps was active on campus, and many faculty members worked on military research and propaganda; at the same time Dewey helped to form the American Association of University Professors to protect the academic freedom of faculty members, and Cattell defended the rights of conscientious objectors, for which he was dismissed in 1917 by Butler (prompting the resignation of Beard, who then joined with Dewey and Robinson to form the New School for Social Research in 1919). One indirect result of the war and its propaganda efforts was the introduction in 1919 of a compulsory survey course for undergraduates called Contemporary Civilization, which traced the development of Western thought from Plato to the present. Columbia introduced a complementary course in the humanities in 1937. In 1921 the College of Physicians and Surgeons moved from midtown to Washington Heights and formed an affiliation with Presbyterian Hospital.

During the interwar years Columbia College remained in the university's shadow, although its course in contemporary civilization became widely known and imitated. Several faculty members were active in local, national, and international affairs: philologist John D. Prince served in the New Jersey state legislature and was an ambassador to Denmark (1921–26) and Yugoslavia (1926–33); law professor A. A. Berle was a member of President Franklin D. Roosevelt's "brain trust," as was the economist Rexford Guy Tugwell (who later led the New York City Planning Commission from 1938 to 1940). Economists Seligman and Robert Haig worked for the League of Nations, and the historian Carlton Hayes was ambassador to Spain (1942–45). Nobel Prize–winning physicist Michael Pupin advocated electrification with direct current rather than alternating current, which led to clashes with local utility companies.

Butler worked toward adoption of the Kellogg–Briand treaty and for international reconciliation and was awarded the Nobel Peace Prize in 1931. Many World War II refugees found their way to the university during the 1930s, including sociologist Paul Lazarsfeld. Lazarsfeld founded the Bureau of Applied Social Research at Columbia and undertook important work with Robert K. Merton and members of the Institute of Social Research, which moved from Frankfurt am Main in Germany to a brownstone owned by the university. A number of physicists connected with the Manhattan Project studied nuclear fission at Columbia until the project moved to the University of Chicago in 1942, among them I. I. Rabi, Enrico Fermi, John R. Dunning, Harold Urey, and George B. Pegram (later head of the university's Division of War Research). Literary and cultural critics who became prominent during these years included art historian Meyer Schapiro; literary scholars Lionel Trilling, Gilbert Highet, Mark Van Doren, and Rufus Mathewson; sociologists Daniel Bell and C. Wright Mills; and historians Jacques Barzun, Allan Nevins, and Richard Hofstadter. An upset by the Columbia football team of Stanford University in the 1934 Rose Bowl and frequent demonstrations by left-wing students highlighted a multifaceted campus student life during the 1930s.

After World War II the university introduced area studies programs and in 1946 opened the School of International Affairs

Low Library (center) at Columbia University, 1898

(renamed the School of International and Public Affairs in 1981). By the early 1950s the university was the center of a group of cultural iconoclasts and bohemians known as the beats, whose most important members were Allen Ginsberg and Jack Kerouac. Completion of five buildings with designs strikingly at odds with those of McKim, Mead and White signaled the continued dominance of the professional schools. Dwight D. Eisenhower, president of the university from 1948 until he left for the White House in 1953, was the first head of the university who was not an Anglican or Episcopalian. Columbia opened the School of the Arts (1965) during the administration of his successor, Grayson Kirk (1953–68).

The growing national and international reputation of Columbia stood in contrast to the university's strained relations with its neighbors. Increasingly selective admissions policies worked against applicants from New York City, and the university, the largest owner of real estate in Morningside Heights, was accused of excluding working-class and minority tenants from its residential housing. Many students leveled the same criticisms; they also objected to the role of some professors in secret defense research during the Vietnam War and to a mode of governance at the university that they considered autocratic. These tensions culminated in April 1968 in demonstrations by students against the construction of a new gymnasium in Morningside Park. Demonstrators occupied five buildings, the university called in the police, and many students were arrested. One consequence of the demonstrations was the formation of the University Senate, a deliberative body in which the administration, students, faculty, staff, and alumni are represented.

Columbia College in 1983 became the last division of the university—and the last Ivy League school—to admit women. Affiliated Barnard College (1889), for women only, has its own administration, governing board, and faculty. Columbia faculty members who played prominent roles in the federal government since the 1960s include law professor William Cary (head of the Securities and Exchange Commission, 1961–64), economist Arthur Burns (head of the Federal Reserve, 1970–78, and ambassador to Germany, 1981–85), and political scientist Zbigniew Brzezinski (national security adviser to President Jimmy Carter, 1977–81). Politically prominent university alumni include Barack Obama (president of the United States, 2009–); senators Judd Gregg (R-N.H., 1993–) and Frank Lautenberg (D-N.J., 1982–2001, 2003–); U.S. attorneys general Michael B. Mukasey (2007–9) and Eric Holder (2009–); and New York State governor David A. Paterson (2008–).

Recent university presidents include Andrew W. Cordier (1969–70), William J. McGill (1970–80), Michael I. Sovern (1980–93), George E. Rupp (1993–2002), and Lee C. Bollinger (2002–). In 2003 Bollinger proposed a campus expansion onto a 17-acre (6.9-hectare) parcel in Manhattanville; the university offered housing, open space, and commitments to sustainable development in exchange for community support. Bollinger presided over the university's 250th anniversary in 2004 and announced a $4 billion capital drive in 2006, focused on endowment, physical plant, and scholarships.

In the twenty-first century the university reported the deaths of 107 alumni, family members, and friends of Columbia University during the terrorist attacks of 11 September 2001. Controversies related to Middle Eastern politics preoccupied the campus during mid-decade, culminating with a September 2007 speech delivered by Iranian prime minister Mahmoud Ahmadinejad, preceded by Bollinger's frosty remarks.

In addition to 65 buildings on its Morningside campus, Columbia sites include the Columbia University Medical Center and the Audubon Biomedical Science and Technology Park in Washington Heights; the Lamont–Doherty Earth Observatory in Palisades, New York; Nevis Laboratories in Irvington, New York; and Reid Hall in Paris, France. The university is also the site of more than 100 centers and institutes for specialized research. Its endowment was $7.2 billion on 30 June 2007—the seventh-largest endowment among U.S. universities. In autumn 2006 Columbia enrolled 24,644 students and had 263,137 living alumni. Columbia College had 4212 students in 2006 (51.7 percent women). The university's 25 libraries held 9.3 million volumes, 6.2 microform units, 28 million manuscript items, and 600,000 rare books, making the system the seventh largest in the United States. As of 2010, 79 Nobel laureates studied or taught at Columbia. Recent faculty recipients include Barack Obama (Peace, 2009), Martin Chalfie (Chemistry, 2008), William Vickery (Economics, 1996), Horst Stormer (Physics, 1998), Robert Mundell (Economics, 1999), Eric Kandel (Medicine, 2000), Joseph Stiglitz (Economics, 2001), Richard Axel (Medicine, 2004), Edmund Phelps (Economics, 2006), and Orhan Pamuk (Literature, 2006).

David C. Humphrey, *From King's College to Columbia, 1746–1800* (New York: Columbia University Press, 1976); Robert McCaughey, *Stand Columbia: A History of Columbia University* (New York: Columbia University Press, 2003); Rosalind N. Rosenberg, *Changing the Subject: How the Women of Columbia Shaped the Way We Think about Sex and Politics* (New York: Columbia University Press, 2004); Michael Rosenthal, *Nicholas Miraculous: The Amazing Career of the Redoubtable Dr. Nicholas Murray Butler* (New York: Farrar, Straus and Giroux, 2006)

Harold S. Wechsler

Columbia University Press. University press formed in 1893 by 10 trustees of Columbia University. It was the first university press in New York City and one of the first in the United States. The press publishes both scholarly works in a wide range of fields and books of general interest. Its best-known publications are *Granger's Index to Poetry* (1904–, first published by Columbia in 1945) and the *Columbia Encyclopedia* (first published 1935; 6th edn 2000). Columbia University Press is located at 562 West 113th Street in Manhattan.

Eileen K. Cheng

Columbus Circle. Site in Manhattan from which distances to and from New York City are measured, lying at the intersection of Broadway, Central Park West, Eighth Avenue, and 59th Street. On 12 October 1892 the area was named to honor Christopher Columbus after local Italian Americans donated a rostral column of Carrara marble 70 feet (21 meters) high; Gaetano Russo's statue of the explorer was placed atop the column

Columbus Circle, ca *1910*

in 1894. Early in the twentieth century subway service was installed below the monument, but incessant traffic prevented development of the new theater district predicted by leaders such as William Randolph Hearst. In 1913 a monument to those lost on the battleship USS *Maine* (Harold Van Buren Magonigle, sculptures by Attilio Piccirilli) was constructed at the Merchants' Gate into Central Park. Both the column and the monument were refurbished before centennial celebrations in 1992. Area attractions included Reisenweber's Café, where the original Dixieland Jazz Band debuted in 1917, the Colonnade Building, and the Park Theatre, but visitors rarely entered the area west of the circle known as San Juan Hill. Urban redevelopment razed much of that ghetto in the 1960s, and the circle was for a time dominated by the New York Coliseum (Leon Levy and Lionel Levy, 1956), the unique Huntington Hartford Gallery of Modern Art (Edward Durell Stone, 1965; renovation Brad Cloepfil, 2008), and the Gulf and Western Building (Thomas Stanley, 1970; renovation Costas Kondylis and Philip Johnson, 1997). Another cycle of redevelopment began in the 1990s, when the Gulf and Western Building became the Trump International Hotel and Tower, and in the early twenty-first century the Time Warner Center (David Childs, 2003) was built on the former site of the New York Coliseum. Cultural institutions include the Rose Theater and Jazz at Lincoln Center (both inside the Time Warner Center), while the former Huntington Hartford Gallery in 2007 became the Museum of Arts and Design. A 2005 redesign of the circle created a fountain and quiet pedestrian sanctuary around the statue of Columbus.

George J. Lankevich

Columbus Hospital. Original name of Cabrini Medical Center.

Columbusville. Name formerly applied to a section of Maspeth in northwestern Queens. It was developed by Edward Dunn during 1854–55 on 69th Place (old Fifth Avenue) between Grand and Caldwell avenues and was soon absorbed by Maspeth, which lay a few blocks away. The name fell into disuse in the 1890s.

Vincent Seyfried

Comden and Green. Team of lyricists. Its members, Betty Comden (*b* Brooklyn, 3 May 1918; *d* Manhattan, 23 Nov 2006) and Adolph Green (*b* New York City, 2 Dec 1915; *d* New York City, 24 Oct 2002), met in the 1930s and formed a nightclub act called the Revuers that also included Judy Tuvim (later known as Judy Holliday) and Alvin Hammer and that wrote its own material because it could not afford to pay copyright fees. The two wrote the lyrics for Leonard Bernstein's musicals *On the Town* (1944) and *Wonderful Town* (1952), which won a Tony Award. They also won the award for *Hallelujah, Baby* (1969), *Applause* (1970), and *On the Twentieth Century* (1978). Their work was noted for its elegance, enthusiasm, and wit.

Robert Seder

Commandment Keepers Ethiopian Hebrew Congregation. Synagogue located at 31 Mount Morris Park West at 123rd Street in Manhattan. It was established in 1930 under the leadership of a Nigerian-born rabbi Wentworth Arthur Matthew, who immigrated to the United States from the British West Indies. The followers of this sect, many of West Indian heritage, believe that people of Ethiopian descent compose one of the lost tribes of Israel. The congregation has been housed at the Marcus Garvey Park location since 1962.

Sharon Wilkins

Commentary. Monthly journal launched by the American Jewish Committee in November 1945. Elliot E. Cohen served as editor from 1945 to 1959, and the art critic Clement Greenberg as associate editor from 1945 to 1957. Early contributors included such prominent intellectuals as Harold Rosenberg, George Orwell, Reinhold Niebuhr, Hannah Arendt, Arthur M. Schlesinger, Jr., Martin Buber, John Dewey, Daniel J. Boorstin, Philip Roth, Lionel Trilling, and Albert Camus. Initially considered liberal, the journal gradually became more conservative under Norman Podhoretz, who served as editor-in-chief from 1960 until his retirement in 1995, when he became editor-at-large. By the early twenty-first century, it was considered one of the key bastions of neoconservatism. The magazine is no longer associated with the American Jewish Committee. *Commentary* has editorial offices at 165 East 56th Street.

Melissa M. Merritt

commercial banks. Commercial banking in New York City had its beginnings less than seven months after the British evacuation. Favored by location, leadership, and legislation, the city developed into the world's largest commercial banking center by the mid-twentieth century.

1. To 1900

The Bank of New York, the first in the state and today the oldest surviving bank in the nation, opened on 9 July 1784. It has occupied the corner of Wall and William streets since 1798. It received a charter on 21 March 1791. By then its deposits aggregated 50 percent more than its bank-note liabilities. In 1792 the First Bank of the United States (1791–1811) located a branch on Wall Street. Nathaniel Ward organized what may have been the first private (unincorporated) bank in 1796. The Manhattan Company bank was sponsored by Republicans as a counterweight to the Federalist-dominated existing banks. Merchants Bank opened on 2 July 1803 but had to wait until March 1805 for a charter because of a strong opposition from other city banks. A benevolent society for poor members of more than 30 trades, the General Society of Mechanics and Tradesmen, received a charter for the Mechanics' Bank in 1810. Directors of Jersey Bank in Jersey City formed the Union Bank in 1811. Congress refused to renew the charter of the First Bank of the United States. Its closing in 1811 led to the formation of the Bank of America, City Bank (today Citibank), and the bank of the New York Manufacturing Company. The city had eight chartered banks by 1812, all located on Wall Street. Franklin Bank, located on Franklin Square, opened in 1818. These banks could receive deposits, deal in coin and bullion,

Interior of the National Park Bank at 214 Broadway, ca *1910*

make loans by discounting merchants' notes and accepting bills of exchange, facilitate payments, and issue banknotes, which served as currency. Private banks were forbidden to issue banknotes but otherwise performed the same functions as incorporated banks. They dominated foreign-exchange transactions in the early nineteenth century.

As the local economy expanded, new banks formed. Almost one-third of the loans to the U.S. Treasury during the War of 1812 came from New York City banks. These banks resented the branch of the Second Bank of the United States at 65 Broadway (1817), which they regarded as an egregious incursion against their business by the federal government. The branch eventually relocated to Wall Street, where it functioned until 1836, when the Philadelphia bank's federal charter expired. Thereafter, the largest bank in the United States was New York City–based until the mid-twentieth century. In the 1820s eight banks were formed, beginning with the North River Bank (1821). In 1824 Fulton Bank and the Chemical Bank on Broadway opposite City Hall Park were authorized. The latter started out as an affiliate of the Chemical Manufacturing Company, a producer of medicines and dyes. The Delaware and Hudson Canal Company began operations in 1824; the Bank of the New York Dry Dock Company received a perpetual charter in 1825. The firm of James G. Brown opened a private bank in October 1825; in 1931 the name was changed to Brown Brothers Harriman, the sole remaining private bank in the city. By the 1830s New York had become the nation's largest banking center. Banks in upstate New York as well as the Midwest kept balances on Wall Street, which they used to clear banknotes and checks. During the spring and summer deposits flowed to the city; in the autumn money was withdrawn to move crops to market. Call loans, introduced in the 1830s, became a fixture of the New York money market by the 1850s. In 1837, 78 percent of all bankers' deposits were in nine of the city's 23 banks; by 1846 eight of the 24 held 82 percent. Until 1838 bank charters were issued on the basis of political bargaining in Albany. As a result only 40 of 3170 shares of the Seventh Ward Bank (1833) were sold to the general public; one-third went to friends of the commissioners distributing the shares, and the rest to state officials. The landmark General Banking Law of April 1838 opened the field, providing free banking. A bank charter no longer required a special act of the legislature. Many other states and even the federal government copied the act. North American Banking and Trust Company was the first to be organized under the new law (16 July 1838), followed by 15 other free banks in the next two years.

By the 1840s the major city banks were attracting deposits from about 600 of the 700 banks in the nation. In exchange, various services were rendered. Financial panics prevented bank customers from converting their claims into specie on several occasions. This lasted from May 1837 to April 1838 and for two months beginning on 13 October 1857. New York had 5.1 percent of the nation's banks and 11.2 percent of its total assets in 1850. To ensure the smooth functioning of check and note collection among the numerous local banks, the New York Clearing House Association opened on 11 October 1853. Fifty-one city banks and the recently organized National Bank of Brooklyn joined at the start. The clearinghouse's usefulness was demonstrated during the panic of 1857, when loan certificates were issued to the member banks to quell the crisis.

In August 1861 New York bankers joined with colleagues in Boston and Philadelphia to lend $150 million to the Union cause. Restrictions on cash payments went into effect in December 1861 and were not lifted until April 1862. Specie payments were suspended on 30 December 1862 and were not resumed until 1 January 1879. Gold was now traded as a commodity. In the autumn of 1864 the Bank of New York took charge of examining, bagging, and sealing gold coins on behalf of the Board of Gold Dealers. The private bank of J. P. Morgan opened in 1862 and developed into a major force in American business history.

The National Currency Act of February 1863 made it possible to obtain a bank charter from Washington. Eleven national banks soon organized in the city: the First, Second, Third, Fourth, Fifth, Sixth, Eighth, Ninth, and Tenth National Banks as well as the Central National Bank and the National Currency Bank. At the outset the Clearing House would not admit the First National

Bank and refused to exchange its banknotes. Only one state bank converted to a national institution: the New York Exchange Bank (1864). Seeking to attract all state-chartered banks to the national system, Congress amended the National Currency Act in 1864, making New York the sole central reserve city where national banks throughout the country could redeposit a fraction of their required reserves. New York retained its leading position even after Chicago and St. Louis also became reserve cities in 1887. The Bank of Commerce, the largest in the United States, became a national bank in January 1865, followed by Seventh Ward Bank in April (renamed the Seventh National Bank) and eventually 43 other Albany-chartered banks. Of the state banks opened before the war, only four never converted to national bank status: Peoples, Oriental, Bank of Manhattan, and Corn Exchange. By 1866 there were 11 state banks; except for the Bank of America, Bank of Manhattan Company, Nassau Bank, and Corn Exchange, they were small, with capital under $1 million.

In 1864 two newly organized banks ran counter to the national bank trend: New York Exchange Guaranty and Indemnity Company and the New York Gold Exchange Bank. In 1867 the state chartered Stuyvesant Bank and the Eleventh Ward Bank (which absorbed Dry Dock). A state law made it easy for national banks to convert to a New York charter, and three did so in 1869. That same year no fewer than five new state banks opened in the city.

The first trust company, Farmers' Fire Insurance and Loan Company, opened in 1822. Renamed Farmers' Loan and Trust Company in 1836, it was bought by National City Bank in 1929. New York Life Insurance and Trust Company appeared in 1830; it was acquired by Bank of New York in 1922. These institutions focused on executing and administrating trusts but over time encroached on the traditional activities of commercial banks. United States Trust (1853) became a leading firm. By the early 1870s, the dozen trust companies that had been established began to offer serious competition to the city's commercial banks. Trust companies were not then subject to legal reserve requirements and (unlike banks) offered interest on deposits.

By 1876 there were 70 banks, 15 of which lined Wall Street; one was as far north as 123rd Street and Third Avenue. It was natural that the nationwide organization of the industry, the American Bankers Association, would select Manhattan for its headquarters. Comptroller of the Currency John Jay Knox hailed New York as the "clearinghouse of the western world" in 1882. In 1883 there were 506 private banks in the city. In 1885 Bank of America's capital reached $8 million, the largest in New York. The first bank merger in the city produced Market and Fulton National Bank (1887), which merged with Southern National Bank (1896). The Twenty-third Ward Bank (1888) was the first commercial bank in what became the borough of the Bronx a decade later. Also in 1888 the Bank of Harlem and Hamilton Bank opened in northern Manhattan; they merged in 1892. By 1890 New York City had more state banks and trust companies than national banks. Some were associated with particular trades and industries. Central National Bank (1863) catered to dry-goods firms. Market National Bank (1852) was involved with shipping and the metal and stone trades. Shoe and Leather Bank (1852) focused on hardware and other "conservative trades." Hide and Leather National Bank opened in 1891 and changed its name to the National Bank of the United States in New York (1902), merging to become the Western National Bank of the City of New York in February 1903.

The Bank of New York opened the first foreign-exchange department in 1897; in 1902 National City Bank advertised that it could pay out any sum in any city worldwide within 24 hours. In 1887 the Jarvis–Conklin Mortgage Trust Company opened a London branch—the first foreign office of a New York institution. In 1914 only four city banks had branches overseas. Meanwhile a few Canadian banks opened branches in New York toward the end of the nineteenth century.

Financial crises interrupted growth. After Marine National Bank closed in 1884 a stock market panic nearly resulted in a suspension of cash payment. In 1893 most of the city's banks suspended such payments, which brought the premium for currency to 4 percent. By 1900, as more prosperous times returned, the city's banks held 25.4 percent of the country's banking resources, though accounting for only 1.2 percent of the nation's banks.

2. After 1900

Trust companies offered increasingly stiff competition to commercial banks: trust deposits increased 150 percent between 1897 and 1902, while bank deposits grew only 40 percent. National banks, barred by law from offering trust services until 1914, organized Bankers Trust Company (1903). Banks began to establish affiliates that enabled them to underwrite securities. First National Bank formed First Security Corporation (1907). National City Bank's National City Company (1911) became the leading investment bank by the end of the 1920s. By 1910 the city's national banks had 15 percent of the loans made by all U.S. national banks.

As early as 1891 the Knickerbocker Trust Company (234 Fifth Avenue) opened a branch on 18 Wall Street, possibly the first bank branch in the city. Under a law enacted in 1898 chartered banks could establish branches throughout the five boroughs, which by then composed Greater New York. By 1905 there were 15 banks and nine trust companies in the four outer boroughs; the oldest included Brooklyn Bank of Long Island (1824), Brooklyn Bank (1832), Mechanics Bank (1852), Staten Island Bank (1838–42), Flushing and Queens County Bank (1873), the Bank of Staten Island (1886), First National Bank of Staten Island (1888), the Bank of Jamaica (1889), and Citizens Trust Company of Brooklyn (1905). Citizens acquired Manufacturers National Bank of Brooklyn (opened 1853) in 1914 and renamed it Manufacturers Trust Company in 1915. The latter relocated its headquarters to the Wall Street area. The spread of branch banking was accompanied by 148 mergers within the city between 1899 and 1925.

The Federal Reserve Act of 1913 aimed to diminish the power and influence of New York's great banks nationally. The country was divided into 12 Federal Reserve districts. The Federal Reserve Bank of New York opened 16 November 1914 with only 33 national banks as members. The first state-chartered bank to join, Broadway Trust Company, waited until the summer of 1915, followed by Corn Exchange Bank (1916) and Guaranty Trust (1917). Wartime patriotism led others to become member banks. The district bank in New York dominated monetary policy making nationwide under Benjamin Strong, governor of the institution from 1914 until his death in 1928.

Restrictions on foreign exchange and gold exports by World War I combatants helped turn New York into the main source of financing for American foreign trade and most European trade with Latin America and Asia. Deposits from foreign governments and investors accumulated in New York, and by 1917 the city surpassed London as a financial center. National City Bank had 35 branches overseas, which grew to 83 by 1930. Many foreign banks opened subsidiaries in New York: the French–American Banking Corporation (1919), Anglo–South American Trust Company (1923), and J. Henry Schroder Banking Corporation (1923).

In 1923, 33 of the 100 largest American banks were in New York. Of the 93 banks headquartered in Manhattan in 1916, 40 were south of Fulton Street. Ninety-seven banks merged between 1926 and 1930, including 29 in 1929 alone. Most were small neighborhood banks; among the larger were Guaranty Trust Company's acquisition of National Bank of Commerce (1929) and Chase National Bank's merger with Equitable Trust to form what was for a time the largest bank in the world. At 927 feet (282 meters), the Bank of Manhattan skyscraper (40 Wall Street) was briefly the tallest building in the world (1929). That year the city's banks held just under 23 percent of the nation's banking assets and had a combined total of 630 branches in the five boroughs. Corn Exchange Bank led with 67,

Ladies' department at the New Amsterdam National Bank, 1906. To encourage gentile women to do business in what was essentially a male institution, banks provided separate areas to make them feel more comfortable

followed by Bank of Manhattan, 64; Bank of United States, 58; Manufacturers Trust, 45; National City, 37; Bank of America, 34; and Public National, 33.

The Great Depression brought significant changes. By 1930, 79 of the 100 largest U.S. banks were outside New York. National City Bank took over Bank of America in November 1931; Manufacturers Trust's acquisition of Chatham and Phenix National Bank early in 1932 was the last significant merger for the next 20 years. To cut costs, branches were closed; by 1932 the number had declined to 552. Cash payments were suspended from 4 March to 13 March 1933, this time under an order from the White House.

During the stock market booms of the 1920s securities affiliates such as Chase Securities (1917), the Guaranty Company (1920), and the Bankers Company of New York (1928) enjoyed tremendous success. Congressional hearings after the stock market crash of 1929 uncovered questionable actions by security affiliates, especially by National City and Chase. Some banks dissolved their affiliates even before all member banks were required to do so by the Banking Act of 1933 (the Glass–Steagall Act).

During World War II, the city's banks were major purchasers and promoters of Treasury securities. In 1940 they had more than 30 percent of U.S. deposits. The financial district remained south of Chambers Street, where 37 of 51 Manhattan banks had their headquarters. Interbank balances declined relative to other cities. Chase National Bank was the largest in the city until 1948, when it was surpassed by National City. The amount of American bank assets held in the city dropped below 19 percent in 1949. In 1954–55 major Wall Street banks combined with other commercial banks known for their large neighborhood networks. Manufacturers Trust led with 112 offices; Chemical merged with Corn Exchange to form Chemical Corn Exchange, which had 98; Chase and the Bank of Manhattan Company formed Chase Manhattan Bank, which had 96 offices and became the city's largest bank once again; First National City, combining First National Bank and National City (1955), had 73 offices; and after merging with Public National, Bankers Trust had 42. At this time half of the commercial loans made by the city's banks went to borrowers outside the metropolitan area. Chase Manhattan introduced a consumer charge plan in the city in 1958 but abandoned it after a few years. In 1928 National City had been the first major bank to offer consumer loans. Its success encouraged banks all over the United States to finance household spending on autos and major appliances after 1945.

At the end of 1958, 26 foreign banks had agencies, and 41 had representative offices in the city. National City, Chase Manhattan, Morgan Guaranty, Bankers Trust, and Hanover had, among them, 64 foreign branches in 1959. Meanwhile, in 1961 foreign banks were authorized to open branches that accepted deposits in the United States. About one-fourth of the city's bank employees worked in its 366 foreign banks. In 1960, at long last, city banks were permitted branches in adjacent Nassau and Westchester counties. Nevertheless, city banks had only 15 percent of the nation's bank deposits in mid-1965, a decline from about 17 percent in 1959.

In 1961 the city's financial center moved from lower Manhattan to midtown, as Citibank relocated its headquarters to 399 Park Avenue (at 53rd Street) and other important banks such as Chemical, Manufacturers Hanover, and Bankers Trust opened offices nearby. In February 1961 First National City became the first major bank to pay interest to large business depositors, offering negotiable certificates of deposit (CDs) at a rate competitive with those of Treasury bills. The innovation spread throughout the United States as banks sought to attract funds for lending purposes. Chase Manhattan formed the first small-business investment company in 1962. Major banks were now cultivating small businesses, as sizable firms turned increasingly to securities for financing.

Eurodollar deposits in overseas banks, with London as the center, denominated U.S. dollars. Eurodollar loans had begun to appear in the late 1950s; they increased greatly over the next decade as a result of a federal tax on long-term bank loans to foreigners and regulatory restrictions on foreign-credit extensions, which were introduced in 1965 as part of an attempt to correct American balance-of-payment difficulties.

During the late 1960s major institutions introduced bank credit cards: the Everything Card (First National City, 1967); Master Charge, later renamed Master Card (Manufacturers Hanover, Chemical, and Marine Midland, 1968; First National City, 1969); Unicard (Chase Manhattan, 1969); and Bank Americard, later renamed Visa (Chase Manhattan, 1972). Chemical Bank installed the first automated teller machine (ATM) in 1969. Citibank launched a program of covering its New York market with cash-dispensing machines in the fall of 1975. With the exception of Citibank, all the major banks in New York City formed an ATM consortium called the New York Cash Exchange into the 1970s. By the late 1980s almost every bank in the city offered ATM facilities.

Bank holding companies could operate nonbank financial subsidiaries devoted to such services as mortgages and consumer lending anywhere in the country. In October 1968 the owners of First National City Bank exchanged their stock for shares in a bank holding company, First National City Corporation (now Citicorp), with the aim of becoming the leader in global finance. By 2006 Citicorp had more than 2000 subsidiaries in more than 100 countries. Chase shareholders became owners of Chase Corporation in June 1969. A merger with Morgan Guaranty in

2000 created JPMorgan Chase and Company, which described itself as "a leading global finance services firm with operations in more than 50 countries." Within a few years all the nation's major banks had become subsidiaries of bank holding companies.

In 1975 New York banks held about 10 percent of the city's $12 billion municipal debt. Deficit spending in the 1950s and 1960s had brought indebtedness to such a level that lenders were no longer willing to finance the city. (See BUDGET.) At the height of the city's fiscal crisis during the summer of 1975, leading banks exchanged short-term notes for bonds issued by the Municipal Assistance Corporation. When the city again faced default that autumn, Ellmore Patterson of Morgan, Walter Wriston of Citibank, and David Rockefeller of Chase sought a federal loan or loan guarantee; Congress extended to the city an unprecedented $2.3 billion line of credit. The municipal debt was refinanced and timely payments made.

Manhattan's banks focused increasingly on foreign markets, where they were permitted to engage in all aspects of investment banking. In 1977 Chase extended more credit abroad than in the United States. To enable American financial institutions to compete in overseas Eurocurrency markets, the New York Clearing House proposed international banking facilities (IBFs); approved in December 1981, by 1989 they numbered 527. Half of these were in New York City and belonged to 150 American banks, 49 Edge Act corporations (subsidiaries of American banks engaged exclusively in international banking), and 37 foreign banks and agencies. Although IBFs had little direct effect on employment, they helped to stem the growth of offshore shell branches in the Caribbean.

As Europe and Japan prospered during the 1980s the city's banks ceased to lead in international lending. Meanwhile, between 1975 and 1989 the number of foreign banking facilities increased from 68 to 255; these held 74 percent of total assets in the United States. Commercial bank employment in the city increased from 5.2 percent in the private sector in 1983 to 5.7 percent in 1987 but declined soon after. By 1984 Chase Manhattan had 331 branches in every major market in New York State and by 1985 operated in 71 countries, which were the source of half its deposits and loans. Citicorp became the country's largest bank, and its holding company the ninth largest in the world; in 1987 Citicorp, Chase, Morgan, and Bankers Trust had more than half their assets overseas. Bank of New York merged with Irving Trust in 1989, the largest local merger to that time. In July 1991 Chemical Bank and Manufacturers formed the third largest banking organization in the United States, then merged into Chase in March 1996. A consortium of European banks acquired the failed Franklin National Bank in October 1974; Citibank bought European American Bank (EAB) in 2001, attracted by EAB's significant presence on Long Island. Deutsche Bank, one of the world's largest, bought Bankers Trust in 1999, as part of the German bank's plan to become a global investment bank. The most significant consolidation in recent years was the 1998 merger of Citicorp and the Travelers Group to form Citigroup. Citi led the move to modify the Gramm–Leach–Bliley Act of 1999, making it possible for Citi to keep its Travelers insurance and investment-bank holdings. The banking industry could now engage in universal banking on the European model. Repeal of the 1933 Glass–Steagall Act permitted commercial banks to be combined with investment banks, a long sought-after goal. By the early 2000s JPMorgan Chase and Citigroup were the leaders in investment-banking revenues, ahead of Morgan Stanley, Merrill Lynch, and especially Goldman Sachs, which had earlier dominated the industry.

In the early 2000s, leading banks moved credit and consumer-lending subsidiaries to states offering less restrictive regulations and lower taxes, especially Delaware and South Dakota. As part of the global financial crisis that began in 2007 and continued for several years, some financial institutions, such as Merrill Lynch and Lehman Brothers, either merged or went out of business entirely. Other giant institutions such as Citgroup and AIG needed massive assistance from the federal government in the form of loans; in some cases such as Citigroup, the government took part ownership.

Benjamin J. Klebaner, *Commercial Banking in the United States: A History* (Hinsdale, Ill.: Dryden, 1974; rev. Boston, Mass.: Twayne, 1990, as *American Commercial Banking: A History*)

Benjamin J. Klebaner

commercial fishing. Cod, mackerel, bluefish, and striped bass were once plentiful in the waters surrounding New York City, as were shad, sturgeon, and eels in nearby bays and the Hudson River; there were also abundant lobsters and oysters. For decades a fish known as menhaden that was valued for its oil rather than its meat was also caught in the metropolitan area. Although most East Coast whaling was done off Nantucket and New Bedford, Massachusetts, whaling vessels sailed from the Port of New York as early as 1768, and between 1792 and 1877 at least 49 whaling ships were based there, making extended voyages to grounds in the Pacific and Indian oceans. During the colonial period shallow water off Communipaw (now in Jersey City, New Jersey) was the local center for oystering and Upper New York Bay was the center for fishing, but both areas ceased to be used in the early nineteenth century because of depleted stocks and increasing pollution. About this time the Fulton Fish Market on the East River in lower Manhattan became the regional distribution center for seafood. From March to June mackerel was

HSBC Bank, Williamsburg, Brooklyn, 2009

brought there by a large fleet of schooners from New England that operated between North Carolina and eastern Long Island. Farmers living near the shore supplemented their income by fishing and delivered their catch to the market themselves or loaded it onto steamboats that operated between local landings and Manhattan. A number of styles of net were used: seine nets hauled ashore by teams of men or horses; moored, cylindrical "fyke" nets; pound nets hundreds of feet long erected on poles offshore, which trapped fish in a pocket at one end; and gill nets, which were attached to poles or allowed to drift and entangle the gills of fish (these were outlawed in much of the area during the 1940s because they depleted the stock too rapidly).

Raritan Bay became a vital area for fishing, clamming, and oystering during the nineteenth century. Along with oysters harvested in Long Island Sound those harvested in Raritan Bay were sold late in the century in the oyster markets of Manhattan, which consisted of distinctive barges moored in groups along the waterfront; these barges were the headquarters of various wholesalers. On each barge stood a two-story structure with doors and windows facing the shore: the first story was used for packing and distribution, the second for offices.

For over a century the piers at the Fulton Fish Market were home to a large fleet of fishing vessels. These were mainly schooner- or sloop-rigged sailing vessels during the nineteenth century; in the twentieth century the development of gasoline and diesel engines led to their replacement with motored fishing boats. After World War II the expansion of the country's network of paved highways and expanded use of refrigerated trucks led most of the boats to leave lower Manhattan for smaller harbors closer to fishing grounds off the upper coast of New Jersey and off the south shore and east end of Long Island. By the early 1970s few fishing boats still delivered their catch directly to the Fulton Market. The last to do so was the scalloper *Felicia,* which called for the final time around 1978, shortly before the historic fishing slip between piers 17 and 18 was eliminated as part of the construction of a large dining and shopping pavilion.

During the 1980s the city attempted to attract fishing boats back to the harbor with the construction of a modern "Fishport" on the Brooklyn shore of the Upper Bay at the foot of Columbia Street. After seven years of planning and construction and the expenditure of over $25 million, the city had to abandon the project. Most fish wholesalers preferred to remain in Manhattan and continue one-on-one trading rather than switch to the auction system instituted at the new facility. Wholesalers also believed that fish would remain fresher if brought to the city in refrigerated trucks from points near where they were caught, as opposed to spending increased time in the holds of boats. By the first decade of the twenty-first century, the survival of commercial fishing in the region—including the last enclave within the city at Sheepshead Bay, Brooklyn, also home to a fleet of party fishing boats—was being threatened. This was due to depletion of the fish supply and the federal catch quotas intended to maintain fish stocks; steadily rising costs of fuel and crew wages; gentrification, the rising values of waterfront real estate, and the construction of upscale developments along the water; and the new residents' complaints about the noise and smells associated with commercial fishing.

Norman J. Brouwer

Commercial High School for Girls. Original name of Washington Irving High School.

Commerford, John (*fl* 1830–1874). Labor leader. In 1830 he supported the New York Working Men's Party, and shortly thereafter, he was elected president of the New York Chairmakers' and Gilders' Union Society. He represented the 15th ward of the city when he joined the committee of New York Workingmen Opposed to Paper Money and Banking and to All Licensed Monopolies. In 1834 the Chairmakers' Society elected him its representative to the National Trades' Union, where he served as secretary and treasurer. In the mid-1830s he agitated for prison labor reform in New York City, involved himself in Democratic politics, and joined the Locofoco movement, a radical branch of the party opposed to state banks, monopolies, tariffs, special interests, and Tammany Hall. In 1835 he succeeded Ely Moore as the president of the General Trades' Union of New York City. He helped to found the General Trades' Union journal, *The Union,* and served as its editor. In 1842 he was elected president of the Free Trade Association, became the owner of a chair-making shop, helped to found the National Reform Association, and was nominated by this group for U.S. Congress. In 1850 he was a delegate to the New York City Industrial Congress. He moved to the Republican Party in 1859 on account of its land-reform platform and became a candidate for the state assembly. In 1860 he stood as a Republican candidate for Congress, but was defeated.

Sean Wilentz, *Chants Democratic: New York City & the Rise of the American Working Class, 1788–1850* (Oxford: Oxford University Press, 1984)

Henry Cooper

Committee of Fourteen. Antiprostitution committee. In 1905 it was constituted by wealthy business leaders, university professors, and other progressive reform members of the New York Anti-Saloon League to combat the phenomenon of "Raines Law" hotels (saloons that got hotel licenses to sell liquor on Sundays). These hotels were venues for Prostitution, the main target of the committee. It promoted legislation to require investigation of such venues, and by 1911 the hotels had largely been shut down. Thereafter the committee investigated prostitution in massage parlors, restaurants, tenements, or other institutions deemed likely to produce "immoral" conditions. It worked closely with the police and gathered information on prostitution, venereal disease, rehabilitation of the females involved in the sex trades, and related public health topics. The committee began to deal with crime prevention as well before its dissolution in 1932 because of financial difficulties.

Michelle Hutt

commodity exchanges. Merchants handling commodities in New York City first gathered in the 1750s in small quarters on Broad Street and in 1768 moved to an area outside the New York Chamber of Commerce. The completion of the Erie Canal in 1825 and increased business activity led to the construction of the Merchants' Exchange (1827) on William Street, destroyed by fire in 1835 and rebuilt on Wall Street. New York City led the nation in handling goods such as sugar, coffee, and cocoa from Latin America and in conducting export business in cotton, breadstuffs, tobacco, and other farm produce. The New York Mercantile Exchange extended futures trading to perishable commodities in 1872, with limited effect. The informal, unregulated methods in commodity trading gave way in the 1860s and 1870s to organized exchanges in major American and European ports, where most trading was in a limited number of nonperishable commodities and in futures contracts. It was rare for contracts to be settled by delivery of the commodity in question; instead the difference between a contracted price and a market price was usually paid in cash. This practice led to the development of "hedging" facilities, where prices were more stable and the risk of price changes was shifted from merchants and processors to speculators. Gradually this system spread to a range of commodities during the late nineteenth and early twentieth centuries, surviving a period of stagnation during the Depression.

The federal government first imposed regulations on commodities exchanges in the 1920s. The Commodity Exchange Act and laws governing grains and cotton required exchanges to make accurate reports of their transactions and to improve their self-governance. Greater pressure was later placed on exchanges when investigations exposed instances of insider trading and manipulation of reported transactions (mostly in Chicago). A major target of these regulations was the Commodity

Exchange (COMEX), formed in 1933 by the merger of the New York Rubber, National Silk, National Metal, and New York Hide exchanges. During World War II the New York Mercantile Exchange opened a successful futures market in potatoes, eggs, butter, and rice. During the 1950s and 1960s most trading on COMEX was in gold, silver, and copper. It grew steadily by offering trading in government securities futures, foreign exchange, and stock index futures; aluminum futures met with less success. In the 1960s and 1970s the formal trading system that developed in the late nineteenth century was extended to precious metals, raw materials, and a range of financial instruments. This system required exchanges to adhere to complex rules, to use clearinghouse functions to settle differences in gains and losses, and to accept limits on the number of their members, who alone were entitled to serve as brokers.

The New York Mercantile Exchange, the chief rival of COMEX, became an important market during the energy crisis of 1973 because of its contracts for crude oil, heating oil, and unleaded gasoline. The Commodity Futures Trading Commission, formed in 1974, provided much broader, stricter regulation of futures trading in commodities than its predecessor, established under the relatively weak Commodities Exchange Act of the 1930s. In 1981 the New York Mercantile Exchange revived its potato trading, in addition to expanding into platinum and palladium. By 1990 it was the fastest-growing and most prosperous commodity exchange in New York City. Four major commodity exchanges shared trading facilities in the World Trade Center in the mid-1990s: the New York Mercantile Exchange, the New York Cotton Exchange, the Commodity Exchange, and the New York Coffee, Sugar, and Cocoa Exchange. After the terrorist attacks of 11 September 2001 on the World Trade Center, the New York Mercantile Exchange relocated its headquarters to the World Financial Center.

Sonny Kleinfield, *The Traders* (New York: Holt, Rinehart and Winston, 1983); Michael Atkin, *Agricultural Commodity Markets: A Guide to Futures Trading* (London: Routledge, 1989); Martin Mayer, *Markets* (New York: W. W. Norton, 1989)

Morton Rothstein

Commodore Hotel. Hotel in Manhattan that later became the Grand Hyatt.

Common Council. Legislative branch of the government of New York City, established by the charter of Governor Thomas Dongan of 1686. In addition to the mayor and the recorder the council included one alderman and one assistant alderman elected to one-year terms from each of the city's six wards. Although it had the power to regulate commerce and public safety, from monitoring strangers to setting the price of bread, drawing up the rules of the city market, and controlling ever-present hogs, its actions could be vetoed by the governor and his council or simply allowed to become null if they were not approved within three months. The city's government lacked a clear separation of powers: the mayor presided over the council, and both the mayor and aldermen served as justices of the peace and as justices in the court of common pleas. In 1813 the state legislature empowered the council to act as a Board of County Supervisors for New York County, and in 1821 the council gained the power to appoint the mayor.

The charter of 1830 divided the council into a board of aldermen and a board of assistant aldermen and removed the mayor from the council. Legislation could originate in either board but required the approval of both before being forwarded to the mayor. The council could override a mayoral veto by majority vote of both boards and retained the power to appoint the heads of executive departments. The nature of the council was again

Presidents of the Board of Aldermen, Board of Assistant Aldermen, and Board of Councilmen, 1831–1897

BOARD OF ALDERMEN

1831–32	Samuel Stevens
1832–33	Henry Meigs
1833–34	John Y. Cebra
1834–35	James Monroe
1835–36	Isaac L. Varian (1 July 1835 to 28 Dec 1836)
1836–39	Egbert Benson (from 28 Dec 1836)
1839–40	A. V. Williams
1840–42	Elijah F. Purdy
1842–43	Caleb S. Woodhull
1844–45	Richard L. Schieffelin
1845–46	Oliver Charlick
1846–47	David S. Jackson
1847–49	Morris Franklin
1849–50	James Kelly (8 May 1849 to 7 Jan 1850)
1850–51	Morgan Morgans
1852–53	Richard T. Compton
1854	Nathan C. Ely
1855–56	Isaac O. Barker
1857–58	John Clancy
1859	Thomas McSpedon
1860	William J. Peck
1861	Henry W. Genet
1862	John T. Henry
1863	William Walsh
1864	John T. Henry
1865	Morgan Jones
1866	John Brice
1867	Joseph Shannon
1868–71	Thomas Coman
1872	John Cochrane
1873–74	Samuel B. H. Vance
1875–76	Samuel Lewis
1877	Henry D. Purroy
1878	William R. Roberts
1879	Jordan L. Mott
1880	John J. Morris
1881	Patrick Kiernan
1882	William Sauer
1883	John Reilly
1884	William P. Kirk
1885	Adolph A. Sanger
1886	Robert B. Nooney
1887	Henry R. Beekman
1888	George H. Forster (*d* 8 Nov)
1889–92	John H. V. Arnold
1893–94	George B. McClellan
1895–97	John Jeroloman

BOARD OF ASSISTANT ALDERMEN

1831–32	James B. Murray
1832–34	William Van Wyck
1834–35	George W. Bruen
1835–36	James R. Whiting
1837–39	Caleb S. Woodhull
1839–40	Nathaniel Jarvis, Jr.
1840–41	Frederick R. Lee
1841–42	Thomas R. Lee
1842–43	William Adams
1843–44	Charles P. Brown
1844–45	William Everdell
1845–46	Nathaniel Pierce
1846–47	Neil Gray
1847–48	Linus W. Stevens
1848–49	Wilson Small
1849–50	Edwin D. Morgan (8 May to 7 Jan)
1850	Oscar W. Sturtevant
1851	Alonzo A. Alvord
1852–53	Jonathan Trotter

BOARD OF COUNCILMEN

1854	Edwin J. Brown
1855	Daniel D. Conover
1856	Benjamin F. Pinckney
1857	Jonas N. Phillips
1858	Charles H. Haswell
1859	Charles G. Cornell
1860–61	Morgan Jones
1862	Charles T. Pinckney
1863	Morgan Jones
1864–65	James Hayes
1866	J. Wilson Green
1867	James G. Brinkman
1868	John Stacom
1869	James A. Monaghan
1870	John Riley (Jan–June)

BOARD OF ASSISTANT ALDERMEN

1870–71	John Galvin (June–Jan)
1872	Otis T. Hall
1873	William Wade
1874	Joseph P. Strack

Compiled by Edward T. O'Donnell

altered when the charter of 1849 increased the terms for aldermen (but not assistant aldermen) to two years, took away the council's power to appoint executive department heads, and required the council to muster a two-thirds majority in each board to override the mayor's veto.

In 1853 further changes in the charter eliminated the board of assistants in favor of a 60-member board of councilmen in charge of all legislation concerning expenditures. Members of the Common Council lost the right to sit in city courts and to control the police department. The comptroller assumed power over city finances in 1857, and the council no longer acted as the board of supervisors for the county. The board of assistant aldermen was reinstated in 1868 and eliminated for the last time by the "reform charter" of 1873, which vested all legislative power in a board of aldermen whose 21 members were elected annually. The board was empowered to approve or reject the mayor's appointments to executive offices; the powers of finance and taxation were increasingly the province of the Board of Estimate and Apportionment. With consolidation in 1898 the Common Council ceased to exist, and the city gained a bicameral legislature, which lasted until 1901. From that time the legislative branch of city government was a unicameral body called, successively, the Municipal Assembly, the Board of Aldermen, and the City Council.

Edward T. O'Donnell

common starling. A chunky bird about 8 inches (20 centimeters) long with a short tail that is mostly black but has some iridescent green and purple feathers; it has white spots and a dark bill in autumn and winter and a yellow bill in spring and summer. Introduced to Central Park in 1890 from Europe, it was well established by the early 1920s. It begins breeding in early spring and builds nests in nearly all available bird boxes and dead trees, thereby excluding such species as woodpeckers, tree swallows, purple martins, and eastern bluebirds.

John Bull, *Birds of the New York Area* (New York: Harper and Row, 1964)

John Bull

Commonwealth Fund. Charitable organization formed in 1918 with an endowment of $10 million from Anna M. Harkness for "benevolent, religious, educational and like purposes." In its early years the fund supported projects related to medical education and the welfare of women and children; it also contributed to war relief. Later the fund made contributions in the fields of public health (including mental hygiene), community health, and medical research. In New York City the fund has contributed to Columbia University, the Union Theological Seminary, the New York Red Cross, public television, and many settlement houses. Additional gifts to the endowment were made by Harkness, her son Edward S. Harkness (1874–1940), and his wife, Mary S. Harkness (1874–1950). In 2008 the Commonwealth Fund had assets of $750.8 million.

A. McGehee and Susan L. Abrams, *For the Welfare of Mankind: The Commonwealth Fund and American Medicine* (Baltimore: Johns Hopkins University Press, 1986)

Erwin Levold

communism. The role played by communism in New York City was at one time so large that the drama critic Lionel Abel, a former Trotskyist sympathizer, remarked in his memoirs that in the 1930s the city "went to Russia and spent most of the decade there." In the city many former socialists joined the communist movement after the founding of the Communist International in 1919. New York City was the place of publication of two daily newspapers issued by the Communist Party USA, *Morgen Freiheit* (in Yiddish, 1922) and the *Daily Worker* (1924), as well as its influential literary magazine the *New Masses* (1926). The party also established its publishing house International Publishers in New York City and a number of schools, cultural groups, immigrant fraternal organizations, and political auxiliaries. Throughout the 1920s factional disputes among American communists mirrored those occurring in the Soviet Union. In the middle of the decade the party found strong support among workers in the garment trades, including many members of Local 25 of the International Ladies' Garment Workers' Union, with which the party lost influence after leading an unsuccessful six-month strike in 1926. During the early years of the movement most communists in the city were of foreign origin; as late as 1931 the foreign-born made up more than four-fifths of the membership in the metropolitan district.

In 1927 the party moved its national headquarters to New York City from Chicago. For the next two decades its activities were directed from the ninth floor of a building that it owned at 35 East 12th Street, one block south of Union Square. The party came close to developing a mass following in the city: at the height of its strength it drew tens of thousands to march in its annual parade on May Day and filled Madison Square Garden with 20,000 cheering spectators. On 6 March 1930, four months after the crash of the stock market, the Communist Party in the city called for a demonstration of the unemployed in Union Square; the number of participants was estimated as more than 100,000 by the *Daily Worker* and as 35,000 by the *New York Times*. Like many other communist gatherings in the early 1930s this one ended violently when mounted police swinging clubs rode into the crowd to prevent it from marching on City Hall. Later that year and in the years that followed, communists throughout the city organized councils of the unemployed, led protest marches on city relief offices, and gathered crowds to resist evictions. Some neighborhoods were likened to the "red belt" surrounding Paris; cooperative apartments organized by the Communist Party on Allerton Avenue in the Bronx were a stronghold of party support, as were parts of Harlem, East Harlem, Brooklyn, the Lower East Side, and the waterfront.

The party grew during the mid-1930s as it became more adept at attracting American-born adherents. In accord with the policies of the Popular Front approved in Moscow, American communists eschewed the revolutionary rhetoric of earlier years in favor of uniting people in a coalition against fascism. The party leader Earl Browder described communism as "twentieth-century Americanism." Communists now agreed to endorse liberal politicians they had once despised, including Fiorello H. La Guardia. Increasingly the party was made up of the native-born children of immigrant parents; it also developed a large following among blacks. Many young members had taken part in radical student politics at City College of New York and Brooklyn College.

After the formation in the 1930s of the Committee for Industrial Organization (CIO; later renamed the Congress of Industrial Organizations) communists gained unprecedented influence within the union movement. In the city they were instrumental in organizing the Transport Workers Union of America, led by their close ally Mike Quill. They were also influential in the National Maritime Union, the United Electrical Workers, District 65 of the United Retail and Wholesale Employees, and the American Newspaper Guild. Ben Gold, president of the Fur Workers Union, was one of few labor leaders in the United States who openly avowed his affiliation with the party. Although their greatest strength was in the new unions of the CIO, the communists also retained a following in locals of the American Federation of Labor (AFL), such as the Painters Union, the Hotel and Restaurant Workers Union, and the American Federation of Teachers. Communism was popular among writers, intellectuals, and artists in the city. The John Reed Clubs were formed in the 1930s, as was the League of American Writers, which sponsored congresses in the city in 1935, 1937, and 1939 that were well attended. Many who were not communists but were concerned by the spread of fascism in Europe were drawn to support antifascist groups controlled by the Communist Party, including the American League against War and Fascism, which had as its chairman in the late 1930s Harry F. Ward, a professor at Union Theological Seminary.

By 1938 the Communist Party had 38,000 members in New York State, about half its national membership, and most of these lived in New York City. A communist candidate for the presidency of the city's Board of Aldermen received nearly 100,000 votes in 1938, and during World War II two avowed communists, Peter V. Cacchione of Brooklyn and Benjamin Davis of Harlem, held seats on the City Council. The loyalty of the party to the Soviet Union did not hinder its growth as long as Moscow advocated international collective security against the Nazis. Despite such events as the Moscow trials of the late 1930s, the faith of most communists in the virtues of the "workers' fatherland" remained unshaken. The nonaggression pact between Germany and the Soviet Union in August 1939 ended the respectability of the Popular Front in the United States; former allies dropped away and right-wing opponents of communism went on the attack. The Rapp–Coudert investigations (1940–41) by the state legislature into communist influence in the municipal colleges led to the dismissal or resignation of about 60 faculty members from City College and Brooklyn College. The party briefly regained strength during the "grand alliance" that followed the Nazi invasion of the Soviet Union in June 1941, but after the Nazis were defeated, communists came under sustained attack. The trial of 11 communist leaders in 1949 for conspiring to overthrow the government and the trial of Julius and Ethel Rosenberg in 1951 for espionage were both held in New York City, and both ended in convictions. In 1956, by which time membership had fallen to about 20,000, the party was further weakened by Nikita Khrushchev's denunciation of Josef Stalin and the suppression of the Hungarian revolution by the Soviet Union; by the end of the 1950s the party was a small sectarian group. Leadership of the party was assumed in 1959 by Gus Hall (1910–2000), a four-time candidate for the presidency of the United States. When communism collapsed in the Soviet Union in the early 1990s, the party lost many longtime members, but it remained loyal to its Leninist ideology. In the early twenty-first century its national headquarters remain at 235 West 23rd Street in Manhattan.

Irving Howe and Lewis Coser, *The American Communist Party: A Critical History* (Boston: Beacon, 1957); Maurice Isserman, *Which Side Were You On?: The American Communist Party during the Second World War* (Middletown, Conn.: Wesleyan University Press, 1982); Mark Naison, *Communists in Harlem during the Depression* (Urbana: University of Illinois Press, 1983); Harvey Klehr, *The Heyday of American Communism: The Depression Decade* (New York: Basic Books, 1984)

Maurice Isserman

community gardens. New York City's community gardens have served a variety of purposes—including basic subsistence, education, social uplift, and political expression—since the first garden was founded at the municipal almshouse in 1736. Community members worked the almshouse gardens both for their own maintenance and to offset the costs associated with institutionalization. Almshouses, asylums, and other public and private social service institutions of the nineteenth and twentieth centuries, such as the New York City Farm Colony on Staten Island and the Creedmoor Psychiatric Center in Queens, had community gardens, which were worked by their residents. Public and private emergency relief programs of the late nineteenth and early twentieth centuries offered temporary subsistence relief to unemployed New Yorkers during times of economic strife. During the Depression of the 1890s families received tools, seeds, and 1-acre (0.4-hectare) allotments in Long Island City to grow vegetables, thus reducing dependence on public assistance. This idea was revived during the Great Depression of the 1930s; between 1934 and 1938 some 700 acres (283 hectares)—amounting to some 5000 allotments—were provided to unemployed men and their families so that they could raise their own food.

Other New Yorkers formed subsistence gardens on their own. Mid-nineteenth-century squatter communities such as Manhattan's Dutch Hill were surrounded by garden plots dug out among the swamps and bedrock that constituted the island's soil. It was a difficult living; during the summer of 1854, for instance, one official commented on the distress expected for these families in the coming winter due to crop failure brought on by drought. Squatter gardeners also risked eviction at a moment's notice, as happened to hundreds during the construction of Central Park in the late 1850s.

Twentieth-century urban reformers viewed community gardening as a means to teach city children about nature and the environment. In 1902 they established the DeWitt Clinton Farm School in DeWitt Clinton Park, which for 30 years provided children in impoverished neighborhoods with an alternative to the streets, and linked classroom science instruction to practical examples in the garden. The movement to integrate gardening and public school curricula declined after World War I, but two programs, the Brooklyn Botanic Garden Children's Garden (1914, the oldest community garden in the city) and the agricultural program at John Bowne High School (1917), continue. After World War I the New York City Department of Parks and Recreation assumed responsibility for the children's garden program, operating more than 1800 garden plots by 1927. The department's Farm Garden Program peaked around 1950, although many children's gardens remain in the city.

Real estate developers established community gardens in the early twentieth century as a means to encourage healthful living in modern apartment projects. The oldest of these, the "garden apartments" of Jackson Heights, dates to 1917. Later, during the 1960s, designers of public housing also adopted the private community garden concept. As of 2007, the Department of Housing Preservation and Development managed 572 community gardens, the largest single set of managed community gardens in the city.

Community gardening experienced a surge in popularity during both world wars as city residents grew vegetables in "victory gardens" created in parks, schools, and vacant lots to show their patriotism and offset increased food costs. During the 1960s, as the last few commercial farms disappeared from the city, community groups began to advocate for permission to convert vacant building lots into public gardens. These initial efforts on the part of local residents to combat crime and improve neighborhoods magnified in the 1970s through the assistance of activists, most notably the Green Guerillas (1973). In 1978 the city began offering short-term leases to community groups through the Green Thumb Program. By the twenty-first century there were more than 1300 community gardens across New York City.

Since the beginning of the twenty-first century some community garden proponents have joined a national locally grown food movement to address a range of urban social and economic problems through gardening. Private, nonprofit organizations have taught gardening techniques and business skills and promoted agriculture as means to combat poor nutrition and other effects of poverty. In eastern New York members of the United Community Centers garden sold more than $4000 worth of vegetables at a local farmers market in 2006, and the New Farmer Development Project, sponsored by Cornell University Cooperative Extension, trains immigrants with agricultural experience to become successful market gardeners and small business owners.

Laura J. Lawson, *City Bountiful: A Century of Community Gardening in America* (Berkeley: University of California Press, 2005)

Louis P. Tremante

Community Service Society. Organization formed in 1939 by the merger of the Association for Improving the Condition of the Poor and the Charity Organization Society, two of the most influential private charities in New York City. Initially it concentrated on family casework, fresh-air programs, and community health (one of its legacies is establishing the prototype for the federal school lunch program) but gradually closed its clinics and summer camps. Influenced by the poverty programs of the 1960s, it shifted its focus to legislative work and pilot antipoverty programs. During the early 1970s it gradually eliminated its social casework and sought instead to empower the poor in their own communities by helping eligible persons obtain welfare, encouraging the formation of tenants' councils in public housing, and sponsoring local programs for the elderly. In the mid-1990s it provided short-term rent grants to those facing eviction and emergency funds for public-benefits applicants, coordinated the 10,000 members of its Retired and Senior Volunteer Program, sought to develop permanent housing for the homeless, and conducted studies on poverty. It also launched a voter registration program for the poor and remained one of their most important advocates in health care, education, and housing. In the early twenty-first century it provided aid for World Trade Center employees affected by the attacks on 11 September 2001. Its advocacy efforts extended to the housing crisis and health care debates in 2009–2010.

Marilyn Thornton Williams

commuter tax. Earnings tax levied by New York City from 1966 to 2000 on nonresidents working within the city. It was first imposed 1 July 1966 as part of the city's new income tax; the rate was initially 0.25 percent of salary earned in New York City and was raised to 0.45 percent in 1971. The New York State Legislature repealed the commuter tax in May 1999 for New York suburban residents only; the tax was still levied on out-of-state commuters. New Jersey and Connecticut state governments successfully challenged that proviso; in April 2000 New York's court of appeals ruled that the repeal must include out-of-state commuters as well.

Andrew Sparberg

Composers Collective. Musical association. Founded in 1931, the collective brought together New York City–based composers and musicologists in an effort to create a new music for the American proletariat. Meeting in lofts rented by the Communist Party and in the homes of its members, the group followed in the tradition of the Pierre Degeyter clubs (named for the composer of the "Internationale") that had met in various cities for the same purpose. The group also drew inspiration from the work of Austrian-born composer Hanns Eisler, a close friend of the playwright Bertolt Brecht and himself a committed socialist. Counting among its members Henry Cowell, Jacob Schaefer, Charles Seeger, Elie Siegmeister, and Aaron Copland, the collective was in large part a response to the worsening economic conditions of the 1930s, and it viewed music as a way to unite the American working classes. Viewing classical, "bourgeois" music as inadequate for this task, the collective sought to develop an original style of music suited to the common people—one that blended modern harmonies and rhythms with tunes that were simple enough to be sung by those without musical training.

Though the collective was never officially associated with the Communist Party and most of the composers associated with the group were not communists, many of its members (especially Seeger) published frequently in such journals as the *Daily Worker* and the *New Masses.* In conjunction with the latter, the collective held a nationwide competition in 1934 for the best musical setting of Alfred Hayes' poem "Into the Streets May First." The group produced two *Workers' Songbooks* before disbanding in 1936.

Patrick Barrett

Compstat. Crime tracking system. Short for "computer comparison statistics," it was developed in 1994 by the New York Police Department (NYPD) under Deputy Commissioner Jack Maple. It uses statistical analysis and advanced technology to track and anticipate crime. Compstat involves the collection of information on crimes area by area into one citywide centralized database, enabling officers to see patterns in crime and identify and police high-risk areas. Information is overlaid onto a city map, which then allows the NYPD to use its forces more effectively. Compstat represented a new stage in the professional culture of the NYPD, as officers were required to attend weekly meetings involving patrol officers, detectives, and narcotics officers in order to coordinate their efforts. The NYPD also invited community organizations to these meetings for community feedback. Since the creation of Compstat the city has seen a drop in almost all categories of crime. The program has been copied in cities from New Orleans to Los Angeles. In 2000 New York City started a program called Healthstat to use the same idea to combat health problems.

Nathan Morgante

comptroller. The chief financial officer of New York City. The position was established in 1801 to countersign all warrants drawn on the chamberlain and was initially filled by appointment. The comptroller became the head of the department of finance in 1831, an elected official in 1884, and the head of a separate office in 1938. Elected citywide to a four-year term and second in the line of succession should the mayor's office fall vacant, the comptroller issues an annual report advising the mayor and City Council and audits all financial transactions. The abolition in 1989 of the Board of Estimate, of which the comptroller had been a member ex officio since 1874, significantly reduced the comptroller's power.

Comptrollers of New York City since Consolidation

Bird S. Coler, 1898–1901
Edward M. Grout, 1902–5
Herman Metz, 1906–8
W. A. Pendergast, 1910–17
Charles L. Craig, 1918–25
Charles W. Berry, 1926–32
George McAneny, 1933
Arthur Cunningham, 1934
Joseph D. McGoldrick, 1935
Frank J. Taylor, 1936–37
Joseph D. McGoldrick, 1938–41
Lazarus Joseph, 1946–53
Lawrence E. Gerosa, 1954–61
Abraham D. Beame, 1962–65
Mario Procaccino, 1966–69
Abraham D. Beame, 1970–73
Harrison J. Goldin, 1974–89
Elizabeth Holtzman, 1990–93
Alan G. Hevesi, 1994–2004
William Thompson, 2002–

Rebecca B. Rankin, *The Treasurer, Chamberlain and the Comptroller of the City of New York* (New York: New York Municipal Reference Library, 1949); Thelma E. Smith, *Guide to the Municipal Government of the City of New York* (New York: Mellen, 1973)

Neal C. Garelik

computers. New York City has an important history as a center of innovations in computing technology. The Computing-Recording-Tabulating Company, formed in the city by Thomas J. Watson, was an early leader in data processing and later became well known as International Business Machines (IBM). The Columbia Statistical Bureau, a laboratory for educational test scores, was opened at Columbia University in 1928 by Ben D. Wood with equipment borrowed from Watson; in 1930 IBM developed for the bureau the "Columbia machine," an electromechanical calculator that could interpolate tables, calculate correlation coefficients, and automatically shift numbers between its 10 registers (allowing it to handle both 10-digit numbers and 10 numbers at one time). The bureau did important work in scientific computing for the astronomy department at Columbia, and its experiments also proved useful in demographic studies and led to machines such as the IBM 600-series calculating punches. Further advances in computer technology were made during the 1930s at Columbia when the astronomer Wallace J. Eckert opened a laboratory in Pupin Hall with IBM accounting machines and other equipment: this made possible a rudimentary program for complex calculations, an important step toward the first computer. In 1939 IBM experimented with the vacuum tube, a relatively new device, with the aim of using it in computing. Research at the firm's headquarters in New York City and at its engineering laboratory in Endicott, New York, led to the development of multipliers that were 1000 times faster than electromechanical calculators.

After the outbreak of World War II, some work in computing in New York City continued. Work on the transistor, the first generation of a silicon-based semiconductor that had a profound effect on computing technology, was conducted in the city in 1947. Fortran (formula translation), the first widely used programming language, was developed in the mid-1950s at the IBM Watson Scientific Computing Laboratory near Columbia University and at the corporate headquarters of IBM (590 Madison Avenue) by a team of scientists led by the mathematician John Backus. They also designed a compiler, a set of 28,000 programming instructions for translating Fortran into machine code. Based on algebra and containing grammar and syntax rules, Fortran was an efficient language that enabled programmers to communicate with the computer by means of straightforward mathematical instructions rather than in long strings of binary code. Because Fortran was easier to learn than earlier languages, programming was no longer the exclusive domain of the computer specialist. During the 1960s Fortran was standardized, and it long remained the most widely used scientific programming language.

After the 1960s the West Coast eclipsed New York City as a center of computer innovation and development. IBM moved its corporate headquarters to suburban Westchester County in 1964 and was soon followed by other firms, many of which nonetheless retained important offices in Manhattan. In the 1990s a number of Internet and new media firms developed in Manhattan in a corridor extending down Broadway from the Flatiron district into SoHo and Tribeca, an area that subsequently gained the nickname Silicon Alley. In the early twenty-first century the local new media industry continued to grow, and the city was home to companies such as advertising technology firm DoubleClick, new media conglomerate IAC/InterActiveCorp, and search giant Google's second-largest corporate office, located in the former Port Authority Commerce Building at 111 Eighth Avenue in Chelsea.

Stan Augarten, *Bit by Bit: An Illustrated History of Computers* (New York: Ticknor and Fields, 1984); John Case, *Digital Future: The Personal Computer Explosion: Why It's Happening and What It Means* (New York: William Morrow, 1985)

Elliot S. Meadows

Comstock, Anthony (*b* New Canaan, Conn., 7 March 1844; *d* Summit, N.J., 21 Sept 1915). Sex reformer. Brought up in a devout Congregationalist household, he moved to New York City after the Civil War, married, and worked in a dry-goods establishment. In 1872 he helped to form the New York Society for the Suppression of Vice, a private agency given limited powers by the police to regulate and monitor sexual behavior, and in the following year he successfully sought a federal anti-obscenity statute known as the "Comstock Law." He enforced the law as a special agent of the Post Office Department, arresting more than 3600 persons from 1872 to 1915 for selling obscene pictures, contraception articles, abortifacients, and gambling materials. He achieved his best-known exploit in 1878, when after posing as an impoverished father unable to support another child he arrested the prominent abortionist Ann Lohman, known as Madame Restell; she took her own life in prison. In 1906 he raided the Art Students League and confiscated paintings of nudes. By this time George Bernard Shaw had introduced the word *comstockery* to describe the American obsession with regulating morality and suppressing sexuality. Although Comstock's activities in New York City inspired groups around the nation, his indiscriminate raids on art galleries, newspapers, and businesses eventually called into question his campaign against obscenity. He also wrote several books about urban dangers: *Frauds Exposed* (1880), *Traps for the Young* (1883), and *Morals versus Art* (1887). From 1871 he lived at 354 Grand Avenue in the Williamsburg neighborhood of Brooklyn.

Heywood Broun and Margaret Leech, *Anthony Comstock: Roundsman of the Lord* (New York: A. and C. Boni, 1927); Nicola Beisel, *Imperiled Innocents: Anthony Comstock and Family Reproduction in Victorian America* (Princeton: Princeton University Press, 1997)

Timothy J. Gilfoyle

Anthony Comstock

concert saloons. Bars offering alcohol and entertainment in New York City from the 1840s until the end of the nineteenth century. They ranged from the palatial to the seedy and were initially clustered in lower Manhattan along Broadway and the Bowery, where they drew a male clientele from the working class and a few from the slumming middle class. Women who appeared in the saloons were usually waitresses or prostitutes, and sometimes both. One of the best-known establishments was Harry Hill's on Houston Street. At the beginning of the Civil War concert saloons became popular among soldiers and war contractors stationed in the city, and in 1861, 40 of the saloons advertised in local newspapers. Increased patronage caught the attention of moral reformers, who attacked the saloons for promoting drunkenness and prostitution. In April 1862 the state legislature banned the sale of alcohol and the employment of waitresses in saloons and required all places of amusement to obtain a license, the fees from which were used to support the Society for the Reformation of Juvenile Delinquents; saloon owners soon became adept at obtaining political protection and circumventing the law. The saloons became central to the culture of sporting men and eventually moved north to midtown and the Tenderloin. With the decline of prostitution in the early twentieth century, these establishments were replaced by cabarets, nightclubs, and vaudeville theaters, which offered forms of entertainment developed by such saloon performers as Tony Pastor.

Lewis A. Erenberg, *Steppin' Out: New York Nightlife and the Transformation of American Culture* (Westport, Conn.: Greenwood, 1981); Robert W. Snyder, *The Voice of the City: Vaudeville and Popular Culture in New York* (New York: Oxford University Press, 1989); Timothy J. Gilfoyle, *City of Eros: New York City, Prostitution, and the Commercialization of Sex, 1790–1920* (New York: W. W. Norton, 1992)

Robert W. Snyder

Concord. Neighborhood in northeastern Staten Island, bounded to the north by Cypress Hill, to the east by Grasmere, to the south by Dongan Hills, and to the west by Emerson Hill. The area was called Dutch Farms until about 1845, when, having been visited by Ralph Waldo Emerson and Henry David Thoreau, it was renamed after their hometown in Massachusetts. In the early nineteenth century it was inhabited chiefly by German immigrants. The neighborhood now consists of one-family houses, small

Concert saloon on the Bowery presenting a "re-fined singing and dancing act," ca *1890*

apartment buildings, and new condominiums. The center of the neighborhood is traversed by some of the most heavily traveled roads in Staten Island, among them Clove Road, Richmond Road, Targee Street, and the Staten Island Expressway. In the early twenty-first century, the neighborhood's population was ethnically diverse.

John-Paul Richiuso

Concord Baptist Church. Church at 833 Marcy Avenue in Bedford–Stuyvesant, formed in 1848 by members of the Abyssinian Baptist Church of Manhattan. One of the first black churches in Brooklyn, it was initially led by the noted abolitionist Sampson White and took an active role in the antislavery movement. Over the years the church became noted for its commitment to education, adding a director of religious education in 1919, a preschool nursery in 1948, and the Concord Elementary School in 1960. It also sponsored a nursing home, a clothing exchange, a credit union, and various other enterprises. From 1942 to 1990 the church was led by Gardner Taylor, known as the dean of black pastors in the United States.

Aileen Laura Love

Condé Nast Publications. Firm of magazine publishers formed in 1909 by Condé Montrose Nast through his purchase of *Vogue* (1892), a high fashion magazine that quickly gained success. The company created publications geared toward a specific class or interest. Its reputation grew with the launching of *Dress and Vanity Fair* (September 1913, renamed *Vanity Fair* in 1914), which was edited by Frank Crowninshield and featured the art of Pablo Picasso, the photographs of Edward Steichen, and the writing of Dorothy Parker, Robert Benchley, and Colette. Nast took over *House and Garden* (1901) in 1915 and *American Golfer* in 1928. His operations were severely affected by the Depression, as a result of which *Vanity Fair* and *American Golfer* ceased publication in 1935. In 1939 he introduced *Glamour.* After his death in 1942 the firm was owned and operated by a British publisher, experiencing international growth with British and French *Vogue.* It was purchased in 1959 by newspaper magnate S. I. Newhouse, Sr., whose son S. I. Newhouse, Jr., remained chairman into the early twenty-first century. In 1993 the firm acquired Knapp Communications, the publishers of *Architectural Digest* and *Bon Appétit.* Condé Nast in 2010 published 27 titles, including *Vogue, Vanity Fair* (reintroduced in 1983), the *New Yorker* (1925), *Gentleman's Quarterly* (1957), and *Bride's* (1959). The headquarters are at 4 Times Square.

Laura Gwinn, Emily Johnson

Coney Island. Neighborhood in southwest Brooklyn (2000 pop. 106,120), bounded to the north by Coney Island Creek and the Belt Parkway, to the east by Ocean Parkway, to the south by the Atlantic Ocean, and to the west by Norton's Point. It is also home to one of the most famous amusement parks in the world. The area was named by the Dutch for the wild rabbits (*konijn*) that abounded there during the seventeenth century. The area's first resort hotel, the Coney Island House, opened in 1824 and played host to P. T. Barnum and Daniel Webster, among others. After the Civil War, development of the beachfront area accelerated, and five railroads were built connecting the area to the rest of Brooklyn. With the encouragement of the well-connected Brooklyn politician John Y. McKane, entrepreneurs began to set up innovative seasonal concessions at the shoreline, including the first American hot dog cart, carousels, and roller coasters. Other early attractions included heavyweight championship boxing matches, gambling dens, dance halls, and brothels, earning Coney Island the nickname of "Sodom by the Sea."

Between 1897 and 1904 three amusement parks opened along Surf Avenue, the avenue closest to the ocean: Steeplechase Park at West 17th Street (George C. Tilyou, 1897), Luna Park at West 10th Street (Frederick Thompson and Elmer Dundy, 1903), and Dreamland at West Fifth Street (William H. Reynolds, 1904). The new parks had several features that transformed the amusement industry: they charged admission, banned alcohol, promoted "polite vaudeville," and offered elaborate mechanical rides.

Steeplechase Park was presided over by "The Funny Face," a cartoon figure whose expression of slightly unhinged hilarity set the tone for the park's amusements, including the namesake Steeplechase Race, in which visitors rode mechanical horses attached to high iron rails; the Blowhole Theater, where jets of air sent women's skirts skyward; and the revolving Barrel of Love. In contrast, Luna Park offered an environment more fantastical than funny: buildings adorned with Moorish spires and minarets, lit at night by tens of thousands of incandescent bulbs. In keeping with the "lunar" theme, the park's attractions included a "Trip to the Moon" in the winged airship *Luna.* In 1904 the average daily attendance at Luna Park was 90,000. Dreamland was designed as a cosmopolitan, genteel antidote to rival parks and to the crowds and noise of New York City in general. The spacious grounds were decorated with replicas of international landmarks (such as the Alps and the Tower of Seville). The amusements were less sedate: two popular attractions were the Leap-Frog Railway, in which two electric railroad cars hurtled toward each other on a single track; and the Fighting Flames show, an elaborately staged tableau vivant of a burning tenement building. Dreamland was itself destroyed by fire in 1911.

On an average weekend in 1907 visitors mailed about 250,000 picture postcards from Coney Island, spreading the reputation of the three parks nationwide. After the subway was extended to the area in 1920, there were a million visitors a day in high season. A boardwalk, built by the city in 1924, helped to ease crowding on the busy stretch between Brighton Beach and Sea Gate.

Despite the neighborhood's summertime attractions, there was almost no year-round population in Coney Island until the early twentieth century, when Italian and Jewish immigrants settled around Surf, Neptune, and Mermaid avenues. This population remained virtually unchanged until the 1940s, when then–Parks Commissioner Robert

Coney Island Beach, ca *1898. Ropes strung above the water helped bathers to keep their footing*

Coney Island, 2009

Luna Park, 1911

Moses widened the beach, demolishing many commercial amusements in favor of a new municipal aquarium and skating rink. Although Moses did not succeed in having the entire area rezoned for residential use, these developments, combined with the destruction by fire of Luna Park in 1944 and the rise in neighborhood street gangs, led to a steep decline in tourism, investment, and year-round population. By the 1960s, the development of high-rise, public housing projects near the amusement district brought a new residential population that was largely African American and Hispanic.

Steeplechase Park and the Parachute Jump closed in 1964, and the land was purchased by developer Fred Trump, who lobbied unsuccessfully for its rezoning for more than a decade before selling the property to the city. In 2001 the city used a portion of the Steeplechase Park property to build Keyspan Park, a stadium for the Brooklyn Cyclones, a minor league baseball team. A small amusement district remains in Coney Island, adjacent to the boardwalk between West Eighth and West 15th streets. Many of the surviving attractions are National Historic Landmarks, including the Wonder Wheel (a Ferris wheel with sliding and stationary cars), the Cyclone roller coaster, and the Parachute Jump (not currently in operation). A merry-go-round known as the B&B Carousel was also purchased by the city and restored prior to its reinstallation. Several historic restaurants are still in operation, including Gargiulo's (West 15th Street, 1907), Nathan's Famous Frankfurters and Seafood (Mermaid Avenue, 1916), and Totonno's Pizzeria Napolitano (Neptune Avenue, 1924).

In the early twenty-first century the future of Coney Island's beachfront real estate was the subject of ongoing negotiation and intense community concern. Private developers such as Thor Equities purchased the majority of the available properties during the first decade of the century and evicted many amusement operators, with the stated intent of transforming the area into a year-round luxury resort with hotels, high-rise condominiums, and a new theme park. A development of this scale would require the city to rezone the historical amusement area.

Coney Island's brash charms have been the subject of artists (Reginald Marsh), songwriters (Woody Guthrie, Lou Reed), filmmakers (Woody Allen, Spike Lee) and writers (including O. Henry, Neil Simon, and Lawrence Ferlinghetti, author of *A Coney Island of the Mind*). Among the area's more recent champions is the arts organization Coney Island USA, founded by Dick Zigun, which has revitalized some of the area's traditional, affordable entertainments, such as the freak show, burlesque, the popular annual Mermaid Parade, and a Coney Island Museum. The Coney Island History Project and the Lola Staar boardwalk roller rink (in the stucco and terra-cotta Child's Restaurant building) are additional examples of recent local engagement and preservation work in and around the amusement park area.

John F. Kasson, *Amusing the Million: Coney Island at the Turn of the Century* (New York: Hill and Wang, 1978); Charles Denson, *Coney Island: Lost and Found* (Berkeley: Ten Speed Press, 2002)

Elizabeth Bradley

Coney Island Hospital. Hospital that started as a first aid center for Coney Island beachgoers. In 1909 it moved to its current location at 2601 Ocean Parkway in southern Brooklyn. It was expanded in 1954 and again in 2006 when an extensive inpatient tower was built. The hospital offers general and specialty ambulatory care services, emergency services, and inpatient services. In the early twenty-first century it has 371 beds.

Max Seppo

confectioners. Some of the first confectioners in the colonies were Dutch bakers in New Amsterdam in the mid-seventeenth century. Confections of the sort that they made (including sugar wafers, sugar plums, and macaroons) were bought mostly by the elite until the early nineteenth century. Some of the largest firms were those of Ridley and Company (1806) on Hudson Street, R. L. Stuart, which had a factory on Greenwich Street (Stuart himself later became a prominent sugar refiner), John Stryker, James Thompson and Sons, and the Delmonico brothers. By the 1850s production increased owing to new technology such as the revolving steam pan, and the manufacture of confections became important in Manhattan, where the sugar industry was concentrated and there was a large market. A candy shop was opened on Canal Street in 1860 by William Loft and his wife; the firm, which remained in the city for almost 130 years, eventually produced more than 350 kinds of candy and operated one of the largest chains of candy stores in the

United States. Henry Heide, an immigrant, formed a business under his own name in 1869, which sold a variety of chocolates and hard candies, including Jujyfruits, Jujubes, and Red Hot Dollars. Milton S. Hershey had a candy firm in the city in the late nineteenth century before building a chocolate empire in Pennsylvania. Tootsie Rolls were introduced by Leo Hirschfield in 1896 and for a time were made in the city by the Sweets Company of America.

The number of confection factories in the city increased from 108 in 1900 to more than 1100 in 1922, but they did not gain a larger share in the national industry: many were small and sold their products directly to druggists and cigar shops. Most candy workers were immigrant women who worked in squalor for long hours and little pay. An investigation of their working conditions led to the passage of the New York State Fair Wage Bill in 1928. The chocolate bar known as Chunky was introduced in the mid-1930s by the confectioner Philip Silverstein and named after his granddaughter (who had been plump as an infant). Many popular candies were made in the city: Bonomo's Turkish Taffy by the Gold Medal Candy Corporation of Brooklyn, Mike and Ikes and Hot Tamales in Brooklyn in the 1920s by the firm of Just Born, Hopalongs by the Ryan Candy Company, and Now and Laters during the 1950s and 1960s by the Phoenix Company. Eventually the industry became automated, the demand for workers diminished, and the confection industry consolidated. As the cost of factory maintenance rose and the sugar industry declined, most confection firms left the city, went out of business, or were acquired by larger companies. In the early twenty-first century some established confectioners were holding steady, such as the 100-year-old Joyva Corporation (makers of halvah) in Brooklyn and Mondel Chocolates in Morningside Heights, founded in 1943 and a favorite of actress Katharine Hepburn. Retail sales of candy have continued to remain high, particularly those of "premium" chocolates, exquisite candies sold by department stores and mail-order firms. Confectioners such as Jacque Torres Chocolate in the DUMBO area of Brooklyn, specializing in unique, high-end chocolates, have been expanding their retail operations throughout the city.

James Bradley

Conference Board. Organization formed in 1916 in suburban Bronxville, New York, as the National Industrial Conference Board. It represented employers' associations and was intended to combat a perceived antipathy toward business among the public. During World War I it made recommendations that led to the formation of the National War Labor Board as an adjudicator of labor disputes. In its early years it also helped businesses improve relations with their employees and took stands on legislative and regulatory issues. Eventually it withdrew from its role as a partisan advocate of business interests, and in 1924 it was reconstituted in New York City as a nonprofit organization with open membership and the support of labor, which earlier had been an opponent. During the following decades the focus gradually shifted away from industrial relations and government regulation and toward broader economic concerns. Among other activities the board was responsible for beginning the scientific measurement of the cost of living. The board took its current name in 1970. Its offices are at 845 Third Avenue. Although it maintains offices in New York City, it has expanded into aiding international countries.

David Schorr

Conference House. Historic house in Staten Island at 7455 Hylan Boulevard, beside the Raritan Bay near the southernmost point of New York City and New York State. It was built as a stone farmhouse about 1680 by Christopher Billopp, a captain of the British navy. A rear lean-to added in 1720 created the present saltbox structure. The house is named after a peace conference held on 11 September 1776 between Admiral Richard Howe of the British forces and a group of American patriots, including Benjamin Franklin and John Adams, the failure of which led to the continuation of hostilities for seven more years. Later the dwelling served variously as a hotel and a small-scale factory. The Conference House Association was established in 1925 and deeded the property to the city the following year; the structure was restored and dedicated as a museum in 1937. The house is situated among large shade trees and has a spacious colonial kitchen and several period rooms.

William Thompson Davis, *The Conference or Billopp House* (Lancaster, Pa.: Science Press, 1926); *Historic Houses in New York City Parks* (New York: Department of Parks and Recreation/Historic House Trust of New York City, 1989)

Jonathan Kuhn

Confucius Plaza. Limited-equity housing cooperative located in Manhattan's Chinatown. It was constructed in 1975 for about $38 million. At 44 stories, it was the tallest building in Chinatown. In the early twenty-first century Confucius Plaza contains 762 apartments, which are largely occupied by Chinese Americans, as well as shops, community spaces, a day-care center, and Public School 124. A statue of the Chinese philosopher Confucius stands at the entrance to the plaza.

Max Seppo

Congregationalists. The origins of Congregationalism in New York City date to 1643, when English settlers from New England and Virginia formed a church in New Amsterdam. Congregationalists were given considerable freedom by the Dutch, who found no theological objections to their beliefs. A few more churches were established during the second stage of the Great Awakening (1740–60), but Congregationalists remained few in number and often sought the fellowship of Presbyterians until the early nineteenth century. Congregationalism remained largely concentrated in New England, and the General Association of New York was not formed until 1824. The oldest churches moved north as the city expanded, among them the Worth Street congregation, which was formed in 1840 and moved to 34th Street in 1857. The New Congregational Church was organized in Brooklyn Heights by 20 congregants who engaged as their first pastor Henry Ward Beecher, a nationally known proponent of progressive liberal Christianity. Soon renamed Plymouth Church, the congregation became the city's most influential Congregational church largely through Beecher's efforts. He was succeeded in 1890 by Lyman Abbott, whose writings also circulated nationally. The congregation left the General Association in 1882. Important contributions were also made by the revivalist Charles G. Finney, who as pastor of the Chatham Street Chapel stressed warm personal piety and moral conduct with attention to social improvement. Others also linked spiritual and social renewal, among them Samuel Cochran, pastor of the Sullivan Street Congregational Church. Liberal evangelical ideas about the relation of religious faith to society were explored in the *Independent,* a noted Congregational journal published in the city.

From about 1900 Congregationalists in the city focused on mission work and drew attention to the needs of immigrants and the poor. In 1902 the Worth Street congregation ceased to exist, but its ministry was continued by the Broadway Tabernacle Church at 56th Street and Broadway, which formed a mission congregation known as Bethany Church at 10th Avenue and 35th Street that extended ministries to the poor. During the first decades of the twentieth century some of the most influential work was done by college students from New England. Settlement houses were opened on the Lower East Side and in Hell's Kitchen by a number of institutions, including Yale University, Wellesley College, and Smith College, often with the help of pastors active in the Social Gospel movement. Through such measures Congregationalists gained influence disproportionate to their small number.

In 1957 the Congregational Christian churches merged with the Evangelical and Reformed church to form the United Church of Christ. In the following decades social responsibility and enlivened spirituality remained the fundamental concerns of several

Congregationalist church on Forest Avenue, 1903

parishes of the new organization. In an enduring expression of congregationalism, RIVERSIDE CHURCH retains its affiliations to both the United Church of Christ and the American Baptist Church.

Eileen W. Lindner

Congregation Ansche Chesed. Former name of TEMPLE ANSCHE CHESED.

Congregation Baith Israel Anshei Emeth. Former name of the KANE STREET SYNAGOGUE.

Congregation Kehilath Jeshurun. Orthodox synagogue, formed by immigrants as Anshe Jeshurun in Yorkville in 1872. The congregation built a large Romanesque temple on East 85th Street between Park and Lexington avenues in 1902. Before World War I many of the members were Russian Jews; under the direction of Joseph H. Lookstein (1936–79) the congregation set standards for American Orthodox Judaism.

Jenna Weissman Joselit

Congregation Rodeph Sholom. Reform synagogue. Founded on the Lower East Side in 1842 by members of a Bikkur Cholim society, the congregation moved to Lexington Avenue and 63rd Street in 1891 and joined the Reform movement in 1901. In 1930 the congregation moved to its current location at 7 West 83rd Street, a Romanesque structure designed by architect Charles B. Meyers. In 1970 Rodeph Sholom established the first Jewish day school in the United States.

Kate Lauber

Congress. New York City was the seat of the national legislature, and was the nation's capital from January 1785 to 1790. For most of this time the national government operated under the Articles of Confederation (in effect from 2 March 1781). This document vested authority in a unicameral legislature, the Continental Congress, in which each state had one vote and appointed from two to seven delegates. A vote of the Continental Congress on 23 December 1784 designated New York City as its 10th meeting place, pending the construction of a federal district on the banks of the Delaware River near Philadelphia. Because no existing structure was suitable for housing the congress, a state lottery was conducted to raise funds and Pierre Charles L'Enfant (1755–1825) redesigned the Old City Hall (later Federal Hall) at the intersection of Broad and Wall streets.

The congress was overseen by a president who was given the impressive title of "President of the United States in Congress Assembled" but nevertheless wielded little power. While the congress met in New York City the presidency was held by Richard Henry Lee (11 January 1785 to 12 November 1785), John Hancock (23 November 1785 to 6 June 1786), Nathaniel Gorham (6 June 1786 to 2 February 1787), Arthur St. Clair (2 February 1787 to 22 January 1788), and Cyrus Griffin (22 January 1788 to 21 October 1788). Increasingly, power was exercised by the heads of executive departments appointed by the congress, including the postmaster general (Ebenezer Hazard, 1782–89), the secretary of foreign affairs (Robert Livingston, 1781 to 1784; John Jay, 1784 to 1789), the superintendent of finance (Robert Morris, who resigned under pressure on 1 November 1784), the members of the Board of Treasury, which replaced the superintendent of finance (Arthur Lee, Samuel Osgood, and Walter Livingston), and the secretary of war (Henry Knox, elected 8 March 1785). Jay conducted much of his business from FRAUNCES TAVERN and from his home at 11 Broadway, at the corner of what later became Exchange Place. In April 1785 the tavern was leased to the Department of Foreign Affairs, which made the structure its virtual headquarters. Until 1788 the war and treasury departments also occupied space in the building.

The first session of the congress in New York City began on 11 January 1785, by which time the limits on its power and effectiveness had fueled growing demands for a new government; absenteeism was rampant, long adjournments were common, and so many congressional delegates attended the Constitutional Convention in Philadelphia in 1787 that the congress was virtually shut down. Nonetheless, several important pieces of legislation were ratified by the Continental Congress, notably the Northwest Ordinance of 13 July 1787, which provided the framework for the expansion of the United States.

New York State approved the Constitution of the United States on 26 July 1788, amid much rejoicing in the city. At the first session of the new congress under the U.S. Constitution (4 March 1789), the organization of the national government was the first order of business. George Washington was inaugurated president of the United States at Federal Hall on 30 April. The executive departments were organized within a year, with the Department of Foreign Affairs renamed the Department of State on 15 September 1789. The Federal Judiciary Act (24 September 1789) organized the structure of the federal judiciary and the Supreme Court, and the Department of Justice was formed on 26 September. Other important legislation included the first Tariff Act (4 July 1789), the Census Act (1 March 1790), and the Naturalization Act (26 March 1790); measures establishing a coast guard (4 April 1790) and putting into effect Alexander Hamilton's refunding plan (26 July 1790), under which the federal government assumed debts incurred by the states during the American Revolution; and the Treaty of New York (signed in Federal Hall on 7 August 1790), whereby the Creek Indians recognized the sovereignty of the United States. The crowning legislative achievement of the federal congress in New York City was the formal submission to the states on 25 September 1789 of 12 proposed amendments to the Constitution, the first 10 of which were ratified in 1791 as the Bill of Rights. On 10 July 1790 the House of Representatives voted to begin construction of a national capital on the Potomac River and to move the capital in the interim to Philadelphia. The final session of Congress in New York City concluded on 12 August 1790.

Charlene Bickford Bangs and Kenneth R. Bowling, *Birth of the Nation: The First Federal Congress, 1789–1791* (New York: Second Circuit Committee, 1989)

Robert I. Goler

Congress of Industrial Organizations [CIO]. Council of industrial unions formed in New York City. Its forerunner was the Committee for Industrial Organization, an association formed in Washington in November 1935 by union presidents, including John L. Lewis of the United Mine Workers, who were frustrated by the refusal of the American Federation of Labor (AFL) to organize unskilled workers in mass production. Directed by Lewis, it did not formally break with the AFL and received crucial support from labor leaders in New York City, especially David Dubinsky of the International Ladies' Garment Workers' Union (ILGWU) and Sidney Hillman of the Amalgamated Clothing Workers of America (ACWA). From the 1930s the Communist Party provided many organizers who were welcomed by Lewis, largely out of expediency, but not by Hillman, who led a faction opposed to communism. After victories at U.S. Steel and General Motors in 1936 and 1937, which set American unionism in a new direction, the committee held its first convention in 1938, where it took the name Congress of Industrial Organizations and became independent, leading Dubinsky to transfer his allegiance back to the AFL in 1940. Hillman's influence steadily increased. A supporter of state intervention to rationalize relations between labor and management, he sought to align the CIO with the Democratic Party. After a number of setbacks Hillman formed the CIO Political Action Committee in 1943 to accept money and provide support for political candidates (usually Democrats) who were sympathetic toward unions. It won a large following in heavily unionized areas and played an important role in the reelection of President Franklin D. Roosevelt in 1944, cementing the relationship between organized labor and the Democratic Party and dashing the hopes of activists who sought to form an independent labor party.

Tensions within the CIO between communists and anticommunists mounted during the 1940s. The Greater New York Industrial Council, formed in 1940 as the central body of the CIO in the city, was controlled by a powerful leftist faction that Hillman opposed. The conflict grew increasingly bitter after he withdrew the ACWA from the council, but a number of leaders with ties to the Communist Party nonetheless became highly influential, among them Mike Quill, president of the Transport Workers' Union (TWU), and Lee Pressman, Lewis's chief aide and the counsel to the CIO. In 1948 disagreements erupted over whether to support Harry S. Truman, the presidential nominee of the Democratic Party, or Henry Wallace, the nominee of the Progressive Party, which was dominated by communists. Pressman resigned to work for Wallace, Quill renounced the Communist Party at a convention of the TWU, and in 1949–50 the CIO expelled 11 unions with communist ties, ending its internal struggles. The decline of its influence was nonetheless signaled by the election of Dwight D. Eisenhower as president in 1952. Except for a few powerful unions, such as the United Auto Workers and the United Steelworkers of America, CIO affiliates were small and financially weak compared to their counterparts in the AFL. As the country moved increasingly toward the right, the leadership decided that organized labor might best close ranks, and in 1955 the CIO merged with the AFL to form the AFL–CIO. The election as its first president of George Meany, president of the AFL, indicated that the social concerns of the CIO would be subordinated to the administrative ones of the AFL.

Irving Bernstein, *The Turbulent Years: A History of the American Worker, 1933–1941* (Boston, Mass.: Houghton Mifflin, 1969); Joshua B. Freeman, *In Transit: The Transport Workers Union in New York City, 1933–1966* (New York: Oxford University Press, 1989); Steven Fraser, *Labor Will Rule: Sidney Hillman and the Rise of American Labor* (New York: Free Press, 1991)

Richard Yeselson

Congress of Racial Equality [CORE]. Civil rights organization. After its establishment in 1942, the Congress of Racial Equality began as an interracial civil rights organization advocating nonviolent resistance. It organized the first "freedom ride" (1947); helped to integrate interstate bus transportation in the South; and, by utilizing sit-ins and protests, worked to change the 1940s civil rights landscape by influencing integration practices in northern cities. Over time, CORE became an unflinching and often controversial advocate of black power, emphasizing economic development, community-controlled education, and community self-determination. Early in its history, CORE's organizational structure transitioned from a decentralized network of regionally based affiliates to a more centralized program based on national direction and leadership. Roy Innis became national director in 1968; in the early twenty-first century he remained national president and CEO. In addition to his long involvement in civil rights activism, Innis was a cofounder of the Harlem Commonwealth Council. Other noted activist CORE leaders included James Farmer, cofounder, first national director, and leader of a protest aimed at ending discrimination and racism during the 1964 World's Fair in New York City; Floyd B. McKissick, the second national director; and, Bayard Rustin, a cofounder of the New York City office. In the early twenty-first century CORE's national headquarters were at 817 Broadway.

Sharon Wilkins

Connelly, Marc[us Cook] (*b* McKeesport, Pa., 13 Dec 1890; *d* New York City, 21 Dec 1980). Playwright. Son of two actors, he worked as a journalist in McKeesport until moving to New York City in 1917 to cover theatrical news for the *Morning Telegraph.* He soon struck up a friendship with fellow theatrical journalist George C. Kaufman, and the two collaborated on a series of successful comedies, beginning with *Dulcy,* which opened in 1921 at the Frazee Theatre. A member of the illustrious Algonquin Round Table, Connelly is best known for his Pulitzer Prize–winning play *The Green Pastures.* Opening at the Mansfield Theatre in 1930, *The Green Pastures* playfully retells the story of the Old Testament through the lens of a small African American town in the South. At the time, critics hailed the production for being the first show on Broadway to have an entirely black cast, but a planned revival in 1954 failed to open because of the belief that the play perpetuated negative stereotypes of African Americans. In 1968 Connelly published his autobiography *Voices Offstage: A Book of Memoirs.*

Sarah Wansley

Connolly, James (*b* Edinburgh, 5 June 1868; *d* Dublin, 12 May 1916). Political activist. He visited New York City in 1902 and moved to the United States in the following year. Disillusioned with the Socialist Labor Party under Daniel DeLeon, he turned to the Industrial Workers of the World (IWW), which offered him a position as a union organizer in the city. He lived in Newark, New Jersey, before moving to Elton Avenue in the Bronx at the end of 1907. From his office at 60 Cooper Square in Greenwich Village he launched the Propaganda League of the IWW and organized workers, focusing his efforts in the building trades. With a number of Irish labor leaders, including Elizabeth Gurley Flynn, he formed the Irish Socialist Federation in March 1907 at 79 MacDougal Street; to report and promote its work he launched a monthly newspaper in January 1908, the *Harp,* which had a circulation of 3000 by 1909 and ceased publication in 1910. His work with the federation led him away from the IWW and toward the brand of socialism advocated by Eugene V. Debs. In 1909 Connolly was appointed organizer of the Socialist Party of America and on its behalf embarked on an 11-month national tour in May. He was given a farewell dinner by the Irish Socialist Federation in New York City on 14 July 1910 and left for Dublin on 16 July. Later the same year he published *Labor in Irish History,* much of which he had written while in New York City. After signing the Irish declaration of independence in 1916, Connolly commanded Republican forces during the Easter insurrection of the same year and was executed by the British.

Austen Morgan, *James Connolly: A Political Biography* (Manchester, England: Manchester University Press, 1988)

Kevin Kenny

Connolly, John (*b* Slane, Ireland, 1750; *d* New York City, 6 Feb 1825). Roman Catholic bishop. He joined the Dominican order, was ordained about 1774, and from 1775 to 1814 lived at San Clemente in Rome, where he was the librarian of the Casanate Library, an agent for several Irish bishops, and a prior (1782–96). After his appointment as bishop of the Diocese of New York on 4 October 1814, he moved to New York City on 25 November 1815. He approved new parishes, welcomed the Sisters of Charity, opened an orphanage, and dealt with conflict over the ownership by lay trustees of church property. Connolly is buried beneath St. Patrick's Old Cathedral.

Mary Elizabeth Brown

Connolly, Maurice E. (*b* Queens, 22 June 1881; *d* Queens, 24 Nov 1935). Disgraced Queens borough president. He earned a bachelor's degree from St. John's College and a law degree from Columbia University; after working as an attorney he was appointed a city magistrate. He became well known in 1911 for criticizing the administration of the borough president of Queens, Lawrence Gresser, who was soon removed from office by Governor John A. Dix for corruption. Amid calls for reform the Board of Aldermen selected Connolly as his successor. From 1911 Connolly oversaw the construction of streets, sewers, and subways. Eventually homeowners protested high assessments for sewer construction, and in December 1927 charges of fraud were filed with Governor Alfred E. Smith against Connolly, who resigned only days before public hearings were to begin. In June 1928 he was indicted by a grand jury along with the sewer contractor, John M. Phillips, and two engineers; testimony revealed that Phillips had illegally received millions of dollars from sewer contracts issued by Connolly's administration, and a jury of the state supreme court found both men guilty of conspiracy to defraud the city. Connolly was sentenced to a year in prison, which he served on Welfare Island (known today as Roosevelt Island) from 9 May 1930 to 4 March 1931.

Edward T. O'Donnell

Conservative Party. Statewide political party formed in 1962 in New York City by the lawyers J. Daniel Mahoney and Kieran O'Doherty to free the Republican Party in New York State from the influence of liberals such as Jacob K. Javits and Nelson A. Rockefeller. It opposed civil rights legislation and favored a strongly anticommunist foreign policy; its manifesto, the Declaration of Principles, expressed concern about inflation, education, taxation, labor unions, and laxness in prosecuting crime. First sponsoring candidates for office in 1962, the party sometimes nominated its own candidates and at other times endorsed Republicans or (less often) Democrats for local, state, and national offices. It became widely known in 1965 during the mayoral campaign of William F. Buckley, Jr., which was intended as a protest against John V. Lindsay's liberal Republicanism. Buckley won 13 percent of the vote, an unexpectedly high total drawn mostly from middle-class homeowners in the outer boroughs. The party outpolled the Liberal Party in the city in the gubernatorial election in 1966 and during the same year was instrumental in defeating a referendum proposing a civilian review board to oversee the police department. It reached the peak of its influence in 1970 when Buckley's brother James Buckley was elected to the U.S. Senate as its nominee, defeating the liberal Republican incumbent Charles E. Goodell and the Democratic nominee Richard Ottinger; Buckley failed to win reelection in 1976. In the 1980s and early 1990s the party lost some of its adherents to the Right-to-Life Party. James P. Molinaro, a member of the Conservative Party, was elected to be borough president of Staten Island in 2001 and reelected in 2005. The party had about 155,000 members in 2010.

J. Daniel Mahoney, *Actions Speak Louder* (New Rochelle, N.Y.: Arlington House, 1968); Charles Lam Markmann, *The Buckleys: A Family Examined* (New York: William Morrow, 1973)

Lawson Bowling

Consolidated Edison. Power company. Consolidated Edison (Con Edison) was initially formed in 1823 as the New York Gas Light Company. Publicly traded since 1824, the company is the longest continuously listed stock on the New York Stock Exchange. The Edison Electric Illuminating Company was formed in 1880 as Thomas Edison applied to New York City for a permit to build the country's first commercial electric power station, located at Pearl Street, which initially supplied 59 customers in lower Manhattan. By 1884 the six major gas companies in New York City, pressured by the increased popularity of electricity, combined to form the Consolidated Gas Company of New York. Between 1898 and 1899, much of New York City's electric power supply was collected under the title of the New York Gas & Electric Light, Heat & Power Company. In 1901 Consolidated Gas became the main electric supplier to New York City, forming a new company, New York Edison, from the companies it controlled, including Edison Electric Illuminating and the New York Gas & Electric Light, Heat & Power Companies. By 1932 Consolidated Gas and New York Edison were providing more electricity to consumers than any other power company in the world. In 1936 the two merged to form the Consolidated Edison Company of New York, the city's only power supplier. In 1998, following the deregulation of New York State utilities, the newly created Consolidated Edison, Inc., became one of the largest investor-owned energy companies in the United States. In 2009 Con Edison's revenues topped $14 billion, providing electricity and natural gas to more than three million customers in Greater New York City.

Anne Epstein

Consolidated (Stock and Petroleum) Exchange [CSE]. Stock exchange formed in 1885 by the merger of four smaller exchanges to handle odd lots, which brokers belonging to the New York Stock Exchange (NYSE) discouraged because of the low commissions they generated. Four hundred brokers who began to sell odd lots contrary to the rules of the NYSE attended the formation of the Consolidated Exchange, which soon became known as the "Little Board." The new exchange printed the transactions of the New York Stock Exchange with Western Union tickers and drew away some of its business. Although its issues and brokers were marginal, the Consolidated Exchange was one of the city's first workable clearinghouses and made innovations in recruiting small investors. It eventually became the second-largest stock exchange in the city and for a time was the only major rival of the NYSE, which sought to destroy it. The exchange suffered from poor leadership, and in 1903 a series of government investigations began. The Consolidated Exchange had only a marginal role in securities trading by the early 1920s and ceased operations in 1928.

Jonathan Aspell

consolidation. The incorporation on 1 January 1898 of New York City within its present boundaries. It grew out of efforts by the merchant elite, led by Andrew Haswell Green, to improve the harbor and promote the development of shipping, railroads, and utilities by substituting centralized municipal government for the existing system, which was highly fragmented with control shared among 40 separate local governments. During its first two centuries New York City was coextensive with Manhattan; Kingsbridge, Morrisania, and West Farms, then in Westchester County, were annexed in 1874. As early as 1868 Green had advanced a plan to annex to New York City all the territory now making up the Bronx, Brooklyn, Queens, and Staten Island. The Chamber of Commerce of the State of New York and Mayor Abram S. Hewitt endorsed Green's plan in 1888, and through Thomas C. Platt, the "easy boss" of the state Republican Party, who considered consolidation to be politically advantageous, saw it through the state legislature in 1894. Many residents of Brooklyn and outlying districts objected; they feared consolidation would deprive them of local control over taxes, expenditures, development policies, and even the racial and ethnic composition of their neighborhoods. The Loyal League of Brooklyn and the *Brooklyn Eagle* argued outspokenly that consolidation would destroy what they described (not entirely correctly) as the homogeneously Protestant character of their community. But the City of Brooklyn was so deeply in debt that it could not build needed water mains, sewer lines, or schools. Property owners there and in northern Manhattan and the Bronx favored consolidation so that their communities could draw on revenues from real estate taxes in central Manhattan. A nonbinding 1894 referendum in all areas to be affected approved consolidation everywhere except in two villages in eastern Queens, with a total vote of 176,170 in favor and 131,706 opposed; the governor approved the plan in 1896. In 1895 the city annexed the rest of the territory now making up the Bronx. A charter of the greater city was issued by a state commission under the direction of Seth Low and approved in 1897, and the new city's first elections were held in the same year. The consolidated city was known as Greater New York, a term later more often applied to a larger area including parts of Westchester, Long Island, New Jersey, and Connecticut.

Consolidation made New York City the most extensive and populous city in the United States (its population increased instantaneously from two million to 3.4 million), brought property tax rates and assessments under a consolidated system, and gave the city jurisdiction over nearly all areas to be developed as suburbs during the next 50 years (with the significant exception of northern New Jersey). For 50 years the bulk of the suburban development of the New York metropolitan region actually took place within the enlarged City of New York. But the new city's bicameral legislature was unwieldy, and procedures for planning and making public improvements were complicated. As a result a commission appointed by the state legislature drafted a new charter, which provided for an elected mayor and comptroller, a powerful Board of Estimate that included the five borough presidents, and a single Board of Aldermen composed of members from 73 districts; the new charter took effect in 1901. Consolidation made it possible for the Greater City to use Manhattan's large tax base to borrow money needed to build streets, water and sewer lines, schools, firehouses, rapid transit, and parks throughout its vast territory; inevitably, electoral politics led to standardization in those facilities. "Local control" was often lost, but for decades, at least, New Yorkers often expressed pride in the high standard of the facilities their city provided.

David C. Hammack, *Power and Society: Greater New York at the Turn of the Century* (New York: Russell Sage Foundation, 1982)

David C. Hammack

consulates. The first consulates in New York City were set up by France, Spain, and the Netherlands shortly after the American Revolution. The city now has more than 100 consulates, most of which are on the Upper East Side and in east midtown. Established by foreign governments to promote their interests abroad, consulates and their employees enhance the city's status as an international center and, along with the United Nations, annually contribute tens of millions of dollars to the local economy. The city strives to maintain good relations with diplomats: the Commission for the United Nations, Consular Corps and Protocol meets newly appointed consuls general; provides information about diplomatic immunities and privileges; advises on housing, schools, and cultural events in New York City; sponsors outings and seminars; and mediates disputes between diplomats and the city's government, businesses, and private citizens. The security of the Consular Corps is the responsibility of the New York Police Department. Local precincts assign regular patrols to consulates, and the department assigns extraordinary security concerns to the dignitary protection unit of its intelligence division. The city absorbs much of the cost for these services, but the federal government partially reimburses expenses associated with the protection of consulates and periodic visits from foreign dignitaries. Consular employees are typically posted to the United States for two to four years. New members must be accredited by their embassy in Washington, D.C., and by the U.S. State Department. Some members of the consular community live in the suburbs, but most prefer to spend their few years in the United States within the five boroughs.

Lauren Markoe

Consumers' League. See National Consumers' League.

Continental Corporation. Holding company based in New York City for a group of insurers active principally in commercial, personal-property, and casualty insurance. Its origins can be traced to 1853, when a group of 12 prominent businessmen from New York City set up the Continental Insurance Company, a fire-insurance firm with capital of $500,000. The first president was William V. Brady, a former mayor of the city, and the first office was in the basement of 6 Wall Street. In 1860 the offices were moved to Broadway, where many other insurers soon followed. During the Civil War the sympathies of the firm lay squarely on the Union side, and leaves of absence with full pay were granted to employees who volunteered for the Union army. The firm also donated funds to establish a local guard for the city's financial institutions while the militia was at war; this guard served during the draft riots of July 1863. In 1864 the firm contributed to the establishment of a full-time, professional fire department in New York City. The company opened an office in Brooklyn in 1868, but during the next 40 years most of its capital was spent outside the metropolitan area on claims that followed devastating fires in Chicago, Boston, Baltimore, and San Francisco. Rapid growth occurred after 1911, when the firm began issuing automobile and, later, aviation insurance. By 1918 it owned other smaller insurers that formed a corporation called the America Fore Group. The Continental Insurance Company weathered the Depression and World War II, prospered during the 1950s, and later evolved into the Continental Insurance Companies (1962) and the Continental Corporation (1968). As of 2007 Continental was a publicly owned, multinational firm with more than $60 billion in assets.

Chad Ludington

Continental Grain. Firm of commodity traders, formed and incorporated in New York City in 1944 by the Fribourg family of Belgium. Its headquarters were originally at 2 Broadway and were moved in 1974 to Park Avenue and 43rd Street. During the 1980s the firm entered the international agribusiness market while continuing to trade commodities. Continental Grain was the most profitable privately held company in the city by the mid-1980s, with sales in 1990 of more than $15 billion. In 1996 the company went public and in 1999 Continental Grain sold its commodity marketing business and became known as ContiGroup Companies.

James Bradley

Continental Iron Works. Foundry and shipyard. In 1859 Thomas F. Rowland and Samuel Sneeden opened a large factory at Calyer and West streets on the Greenpoint, Brooklyn, waterfront. This firm made wrought- and cast-iron pipes for the Croton Aqueduct. The next year, Rowland took control of the business, renamed it Continental Iron Works, and with the outbreak of the Civil War, began making mortar beds and gun carriages for the U.S. Navy. Soon Rowland contracted to build the hull of the groundbreaking Union ironclad, the *Monitor.* The *Monitor* was launched from the shipyard's docks on 30 January 1862. Hundreds of men had labored on the vessel, often working in shifts around the clock; the firm received seven and a half cents for each pound of iron used. With peace, Continental Iron Works fabricated steamboats, ferryboats, steam boilers, and engines; after 1887 an internal furnace designed for boilers was a core product. The family continued to operate the firm after Rowland's death in 1907 until its closing in 1928.

Joshua Brown and David Ment, *Factories, Foundries, and Refineries: A History of Five Brooklyn Industries* (Brooklyn: The Brooklyn Educational & Cultural Alliance, 1980); James L. Nelson, *Reign of Iron: The Story of the First Battling Ironclads, the Monitor and the Merrimack* (New York: HarperCollins, 2004)

Cathy Alexander

Convent of the Sacred Heart. Catholic school for girls spanning all grades from kindergarten through high school. It was opened in 1881 at 533 Madison Avenue and run by the Society of the Sacred Heart, an order formed in France in 1801. The school moved in 1934 to the former mansion of Otto H. Kahn at 1 East 91st Street (1918, designed by J. Armstrong Stenhouse with C. P. H. Gilbert) and expanded in 1966 to the adjacent Burden House (1905, designed by Warren and Wetmore); both buildings are designated city landmarks. From 1976 the board of trustees was composed predominantly of laity. In 2008 the student enrollment was 670.

Convent of the Sacred Heart: A History, 1881–1981 (New York: Alumnae Association of the Convent of the Sacred Heart, 1981)

Gilbert Tauber

Convent of the Sacred Heart, ca *1900*

Coody, Abimelech. Pseudonym of Verplanck, Gulian C.

Coogan's Bluff. Neighborhood in northern Manhattan, bounded to the north by 160th Street, to the east by the Harlem River, to the south by 155th Street, and to the west by the Harlem River Drive. The area is known for a steep escarpment that descends 175 feet (53 meters) to sea level. It is named for James Jay Coogan, a real estate merchant who served as borough president of Manhattan (1899–1901), was twice an unsuccessful mayoral candidate, and owned much property in the area, including the Polo Grounds (built in 1890 as Brotherhood Park), a stadium that was the home of the (baseball) New York Giants and the New York Mets, among other teams. After the Giants moved to California the city took over the stadium, which it demolished in 1964 to make way for a public housing project. From that time the name Coogan's Bluff fell into disuse.

John Kieran, *A Natural History of New York City* (Boston: Houghton Mifflin, 1959)

James Bradley

Cook, Will Marion (*b* Washington, D.C., 27 Jan 1869; *d* New York City, 20 July 1944). Musician and composer. In 1889 he made his musical debut at Carnegie Hall. In his twenties, he moved to New York City and studied at the National Conservatory of Music under Antonín Dvořák. Working toward creating a "Negro" statement in music, he utilized the genre of musical theater. In 1898 he wrote the first black musical, *Clorindy,* and five years later he wrote *In Dahomey,* the first full-length Broadway musical written and performed by African Americans. He was a regular diner at the Marshall Hotel on 53rd Street, where he discussed black musical theater with prominent black Broadway stars. Cook notably composed ragtime-style syncopated numbers, and his musicals had distinctively "Negro" lyrics. In 1910 he formed the New York Syncopated Orchestra. From 1918 to 1944 he lived at 221 West 138th Street. The house became a National Historic Landmark in 1976. He was also a mentor to jazz greats Duke Ellington and Eubie Blake.

Jessica Montesano

Cooke, Terence Cardinal (*b* New York City, 1 March 1921; *d* New York City, 6 Oct 1983). Archbishop. The son of Irish immigrants, he was born on the Upper West Side, grew up in Throgs Neck in the Bronx, and attended Catholic schools. He received his bachelor's degree from Cathedral College, entered St. Joseph's seminary (1940), and was ordained a priest in 1945; his first posting was Bronx parish St. Athanasius (1946–47). After receiving his master's in social work from Catholic University (1949) he worked for the Catholic Youth Organization, taught at Fordham University (1949–56), and was procurator at St. Joseph's Seminary in suburban Yonkers (1954–57). In 1957 he became secretary to Francis Cardinal Spellman, archbishop of New York, and later became a vice chancellor (1958–61), chancellor (1961–65), and vicar general and titular bishop (1965–67). After Spellman's death in 1967 Cooke rose to archbishop (1968) and then cardinal (1969). He also succeeded Spellman as military vicar for the United States Armed Forces (1968).

Matthew J. Brennan

Co-op City. Housing development. One of the largest housing developments in the United States, it is located in Baychester, in the Bronx, next to the Hutchinson River, and consists of 15,372 apartments on 338 acres (137 hectares). In colonial times Sir Thomas Pell, for whom nearby Pelham Manor and Pelham Parkway are named, owned the land. The main road to Co-op City, Bartow Avenue, is named for John Bartow, owner of a Revolutionary War–era grist mill on the site. Before construction for Co-op City began in 1966, it was the site from 1960 to 1964 of Freedomland U.S.A., the world's largest outdoor family entertainment center at the time. When it opened in 1968, Co-op City was the largest cooperative housing project in the United States. Under the state's 1955 Limited Profit Housing Law, also known as the Mitchell–Lama program, it was a racially diverse, moderate-income housing development. The basic room price started in the late 1960s at $450; by 2008 room prices were $3,500. Minimum and maximum income requirements have always been in place for each apartment size. Co-op City has been plagued with several problems throughout its history, including major structural issues in some of the buildings; a payment strike in the mid-1970s in response to increases in monthly maintenance costs; the management corporation's mounting debt from repairs; as well as various controversies, such as one in 2002 over a parking shortage. In 2004, heavily in debt, it reached a $475 million agreement with the state to refinance and fix many of its facilities. In the early twenty-first century, Co-op City had three shopping centers, which included supermarkets, dry cleaners, restaurants, shops, and community rooms; a 25-acre (10-hectare) educational park of three elementary schools, two middle schools, a high school, and a planetarium; and 15 houses of worship. The complex had approximately 55,000 residents, with more than 8300 over the age of 60; about 55 percent were African American, 25 percent Hispanic, and 20 percent white. Well-known former residents include Representative Eliot L. Engel (D-N.Y.), actress Queen Latifah, and novelist Richard Price.

Jessica Montesano

Cooper, Edward (*b* New York City, 26 Oct 1824; *d* New York City, 25 Feb 1905). Mayor and industrialist, son of Peter Cooper. He graduated from Columbia College and with Abram S. Hewitt opened a firm of iron manufacturers. During the 1870s he investigated William M. "Boss" Tweed's bank accounts and promoted sanitation reform; he won the mayoral election of 1879 as a fusion candidate supported by Republicans and by fellow Democrats opposed to Tammany Hall. An earnest reformer, Cooper helped to enact the Tenement House Law of 1879. He lived at 8 Lexington Avenue.

James E. Mooney

Cooper, James Fenimore (*b* Burlington, N.J., 15 Sept 1789; *d* Cooperstown, N.Y., 14 Sept 1851). Novelist, social critic, and historian. He first lived in New York City in 1808 as a naval recruiter and frequently visited it for social reasons while residing in Westchester County (1811–13; 1817–22). After he started writing in 1820, he traveled often to the big city—he finished *The Spy* (1821) and began *The Pioneers* (1823) in a series of stays at the City Hotel in the fall of 1821—and in 1822 he and his family relocated to Manhattan and remained until leaving for Europe in 1826. During his city years he became the first American novelist to make a living by his pen, writing *The Pilot* (1824), *Lionel Lincoln* (1825), and *The Last of the Mohicans* (1826) and starting *The Prairie* (1827). Collectively, these six early books included the first fictional treatment of the sea, of ordinary Americans at war, and of interracial friendship based on equality. In addition, *The Pioneers* and *The Last of the Mohicans* gave inspiration to the Hudson River School of artists and helped shape American attitudes toward nature, conservation, and the environment. After returning home from his seven-year European stay in 1833, Cooper divided much of his time between New York City and Cooperstown. His many friends in Manhattan, most associated with his 1820s Bread and Cheese Club (forerunner of the Century Association), included lawyers, artists, businessmen, politicians, and other writers. Among his better fictional portrayals of city life are those in *The Water Witch* (1830), *Afloat and Ashore* (1843–44), *Satanstoe* (1845), and *The Ways of the Hour* (1850). Of Cooper's *Towns of Manhattan,* intended as the first history of Greater New York, only fragments survive, the rest having been lost in a fire at his printer's shop.

Wayne Franklin, *James Fenimore Cooper: The Early Years* (New Haven: Yale University Press, 2007)

Wayne Franklin

Cooper, Peter (*b* New York City, 12 Feb 1791; *d* New York City, 4 April 1883). Inventor, manufacturer, and philanthropist. He had almost no formal education but was trained in business by his father and demonstrated unusual talents as an inventor and entrepreneur. During the War of 1812 he prospered by making equipment for cutting cloth. He then

Peter Cooper, 1882

became a grocer and by his early twenties was a wealthy glue manufacturer. In 1828 he opened the Canton Iron Works in Baltimore, where he built the country's first functional steam engine, the "Tom Thumb," and greatly enlarged his fortune. Among his later ventures were rolling mills and wire factories; eventually he controlled more than half the telegraph lines in the United States. He also manufactured the first structural beams for fire-retardant buildings, introduced the Bessemer process to the United States, invented a number of mining devices, and helped finance the first transatlantic telegraph cable. An adherent of Jacksonian principles, Cooper was elected to the Common Council of New York City (1828–31), with the backing of Tammany Hall, and the Civic Reform Party (1840–41). As a member of the council and the Citizens' Association, a nonpartisan group of politically engaged citizens in the city, he sought to free the police and fire departments from political interference, ensure an adequate water supply and better sanitation, provide public education for the poor, and improve prison conditions. In 1857–59 he formed the Cooper Union for the Advancement of Science and Art to provide a free education to gifted students from the working class. Cooper unsuccessfully sought the United States presidency as a Greenback in 1876. The campaign of his Democratic opponent, Samuel J. Tilden, was led by Cooper's son-in-law Abram S. Hewitt, who served in Congress and was later elected mayor, as was Cooper's son Edward. Cooper is buried in Green-Wood Cemetery in Brooklyn.

Allan Nevins, *Abram S. Hewitt, with Some Account of Peter Cooper* (New York: Harper and Brothers, 1935); Edward C. Mack, *Peter Cooper, Citizen of New York* (New York: Duell, Sloan and Pearce, 1949)

Evan Cornog, Jerome Mushkat

cooperage. Manufacture of barrels and casks. The barrel was once a unit of measurement, and cooperage played such a large role in the development of commerce in New York City that two casks are prominently depicted on the city's official seal. In the late seventeenth century the flour trade depended on barrels; so, too, did the city's sugar refineries (after 1730), local distilleries, breweries, taverns, and coffee merchants. Until the Civil War most barrel wood was floated down the Hudson River from upstate and stored at docks in Brooklyn and Manhattan. Coopers worked in small artisanal shops near the wharves, and traditional methods of production were employed longer than in most other trades. In 1855 there were 1018 coopers in the city, almost three-fourths of whom were immigrants. In 1860 Anson T. Briggs of Brooklyn became one of the first coopers in the United States to employ mechanical production. When the Brooklyn Cooperage Company of Lowell M. Palmer began manufacturing staves by machine in 1865, employees staged a four-month strike in protest; by 1895 the firm was sufficiently prosperous to expand nationwide. In 1900 there were 90 coopering firms in Manhattan and 36 in Brooklyn. In the following decades coopering plants left the city for locations closer to large forests, and by 1922 they employed only 1258 unskilled employees citywide, most of them near the sugar refineries in Brooklyn. There were only 21 coopering shops in the city by 1930. Prepackaging of goods formerly sold in barrels and the use of plastic, fiberboard, and steel containers virtually eliminated commercial coopering from New York City, except for a few firms that built the wooden water tanks seen on the roofs of apartment buildings.

Franklin E. Coyne, *Development of the Cooperage Industry in the United States, 1620–1940* (Chicago, Ill.: Lumberers, 1940)

Marc Ferris

Cooper and Hewitt. Firm of iron manufacturers. It was opened about 1850 by Edward Cooper and Abram S. Hewitt, the son of an engineer, after they were given the Trenton Iron Works by Peter Cooper. It had the country's first open-hearth furnace and produced some of the first iron beams and girders, at one time employing 3000 men. During the Civil War it provided steel for gun barrels.

James E. Mooney

cooperatives. Apartment buildings with ownership arranged on a corporate basis. They first became popular in the late nineteenth century. Cooperatives differ from condominiums in that they provide for ownership of shares in a corporation rather than outright ownership of an individual residential unit. Residents of a cooperative may usually sell their shares at any price, provided that the board of directors approves of the prospective buyer. The first cooperative in New York City was probably the Rembrandt on West 57th Street, designed by Philip Hubert in 1881 (demolished). Buildings with a similar form of ownership were soon erected, including the Gramercy at 34 Gramercy Park East (1883, George da Cunha) and the Chelsea at 222 West 23rd Street (1884, Hubert, Pirsson and Company; later converted into the Chelsea Hotel). All these buildings had spacious apartments planned for prosperous upper-middle-class families. The Central Park Apartments at Central Park South and Seventh Avenue (1883, Hubert, Pirsson and Company; often called the Navarro) failed in 1888. This ended the construction of cooperatives until 1901, when a group of artists began the 67th Street Studios at 23 West 67th Street (1903, Sturgis and Simonson), which had large units containing studios two stories tall and adjacent duplex living spaces. Their success led to a wave of cooperative construction during the first two decades of the twentieth century. Duplexes planned for artists or those who wished to live in an artistic milieu were especially popular, among them the Hotel des Artistes on West 67th Street (1918, George Mort Pollard). The Bryant Park Studios on West 40th Street (1901, Charles A. Rich) and the Gainsborough Studios on Central Park

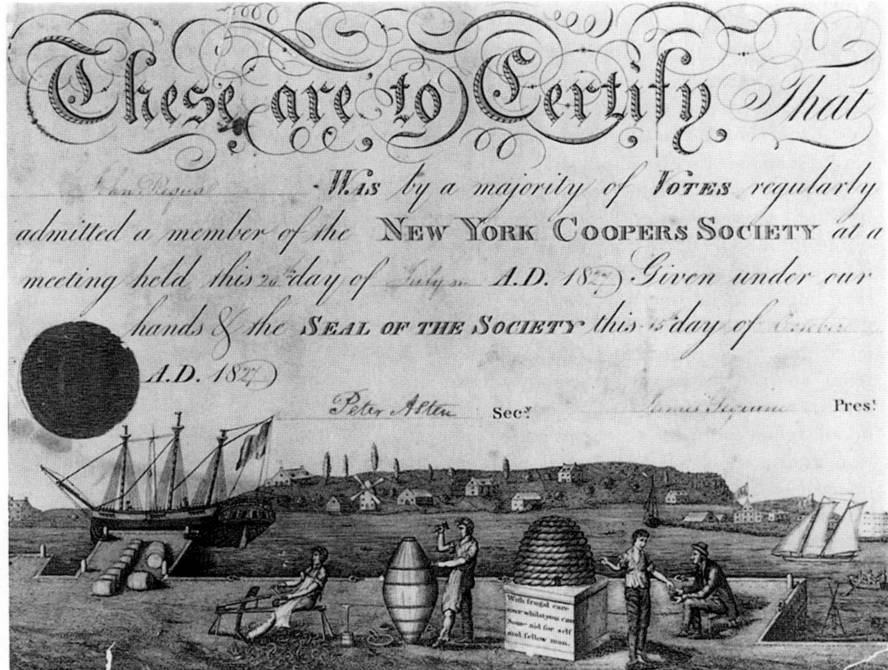

These are to Certify That

Was by a majority of Votes regularly admitted a member of the New York Coopers Society at a meeting held this 20th day of July A.D. 1827 Given under our hands & the Seal of the Society this 15 day of

A.D. 1827

Peter Allen Secy Pres!

Certificate of membership in the New York Cooper Society, 1827

South (1908, Charles Buckham) were erected on sites with unobstructed northern exposure. Cooperatives were also built on Gramercy Park and the Upper East Side, most of them by syndicates or clubs of prospective tenants rather than by firms of developers. Generally, not all the units were individually owned; some were rented for income.

By the 1920s cooperatives were so popular in New York City, especially on the Upper East Side, that speculators became active in their construction. At the same time middle-class cooperatives became common: the first was Linden Court (1919, Andrew J. Thomas) in Jackson Heights, built by the Queensborough Corporation as a complex of 10 buildings and interior gardens on one city block. Many similar developments were built in Jackson Heights. Elsewhere in the city the most important middle-class cooperative was Hudson View Gardens in Washington Heights (1924, George Pelham), a picturesque complex in a Tudor style built around a semicircular drive and a large garden.

The first nonprofit, or limited-dividend, cooperative was the Alku at 816 43rd Street in Sunset Park (1916, Maxwell Cantor), one of several cooperatives built by Finnish immigrants. In these cooperatives residents usually owned a single share, and shareholders could not sell at a profit; the idea was to create high-quality rather than profit-making housing. The number of nonprofit cooperatives increased during the 1920s, many built by labor unions and other groups seeking to provide comfortable housing for workers. The largest such complexes were in the Bronx and were known for their high quality, among them the Amalgamated Houses on Van Cortlandt Park South and the United Workers Houses (known as the coops) on Bronx Park East.

Many cooperatives failed during the Depression and were converted into rental housing. After World War II government programs such as Mitchell–Lama and Section 13 (overseen by the Federal Housing Administration) provided incentives for building nonprofit cooperatives for working- and middle-class families. Cooperatives regained their popularity during the 1970s, leading to new construction (generally at the luxury level) and the conversion of thousands of rental apartments. By the early twenty-first century condominiums had become more popular than cooperatives for new construction, and many of the limited-dividend cooperatives, including many Mitchell–Lama projects, had been converted into market-rate housing.

Christopher Gray, "The 'Revolution' of 1881 Is Now in Its 2d Century," *New York Times,* 28 Oct 1984, §12, pp. 57–64; Andrew S. Dolkart, "Hudson View Gardens: A Home in the City," *SITES* 20 (1988), 34–44; Dolkart, "Homes for People: Non-profit Cooperatives in New York City, 1916–1929," *SITES* 21–22 (1989), 30–42; Richard Plunz, *A History of Housing in New York* (New York: Columbia University Press, 1990)

Andrew S. Dolkart

Cooper–Hewitt Museum. Art museum opened at Cooper Union in 1897 as the Cooper Union Museum of Art and Decoration. A small museum for instruction in the applied arts at Cooper Union was planned by Peter Cooper but did not open until his granddaughters Eleanor Hewitt and Sarah Hewitt raised sufficient funds to form and maintain a collection. Modeled after the Musée des Arts Décoratifs in Paris, it contained scrapbooks, patterns, drawings, prints, and decorative art objects and was intended to instruct professional designers and workers. With the help of such well-known patrons as the merchant George A. Hearn, the Hewitts amassed holdings during the first decades of the twentieth century that included several important collections of textiles given by J. P. Morgan, more than 300 drawings and small paintings from the estate of Winslow Homer, and 2000 sketches by Frederic E. Church given by Church's son. The museum became part of the Smithsonian Institution in 1969 and moved in 1976 to the former Andrew Carnegie mansion at Fifth Avenue and 91st Street. The museum expanded its exhibitions and programs for the public and introduced a graduate curriculum in decorative arts in conjunction with Parsons School of Design.

Russell Lynes, *More Than Meets the Eye: The History and Collections of the Cooper–Hewitt Museum* (New York: Smithsonian Institution, 1981)

Peter L. Donhauser

Coopers and Lybrand. Accounting firm formed as Lybrand, Ross Brothers and Montgomery on 1 January 1898 in Philadelphia by William Lybrand, T. Edward Ross, Adam A. Ross, and Robert H. Montgomery. On 1 June 1902 it opened an office at 25 Broad Street that became influential in local and national affairs. From 1916 it often handled funding reports and party records during presidential campaigns. The office donated its services to the city through the Emergency Unemployment Relief Committee in 1930, and several partners acted as comptrollers from 14 September 1931 to 8 February 1932. In 1947 one of the partners, Prior Sinclair, led opposition to a bill that would have allowed accountants to become licensed without passing the state examination for certification. In 1998 the firm merged with Price Waterhouse to form PricewaterhouseCoopers.

Janet Frankston

Cooper Union (for the Advancement of Science and Art). Private, tuition-free college at 41 Cooper Square offering degrees in engineering, architecture, and art. Formed by Peter Cooper to provide higher education for workers, it opened at Astor Place in 1859 and initially had a free reading room, classrooms, and exhibitions of art and technology. It also absorbed the Female School of Design, formed in 1846 to provide women with an alternative to menial employment. Public debates, lectures, and speeches were often held in the Great Hall (Abraham Lincoln spoke there in 1860). Under the direction of Cooper's son-in-law Abram S. Hewitt, the school became more like a traditional college

Cooper Union, 1876

after the Civil War, offering degrees in engineering from 1886. Its practical curriculum and nonsectarian, coeducational approach were emulated by other institutions such as Rice University and the Tuskegee Institute. Hewitt and the department store owner George A. Hearn encouraged a plan by Cooper's granddaughters to form the Museum for the Arts of Decoration, which opened in 1897 and was later renamed the Cooper–Hewitt Museum. An autonomous school of architecture opened in the same year. At the turn of the twentieth century the School of Art became less of a philanthropic venture and more of a professional school. Between 1898 and 1933 the People's Institute directed public programs in the Great Hall, where Felix Frankfurter, Samuel Gompers, and Jacob A. Riis were among those introduced to political activism and higher learning. Programs in the Great Hall led to the formation of the National Woman Suffrage Association, the International Ladies' Garment Workers' Union, and the National Association for the Advancement of Colored People (NAACP). As of 2010 Cooper Union had about 900 students in its three schools: the Irwin S. Chanin School of Architecture, the School of Art, and the Albert Nerken School of Engineering.

Peter G. Buckley

Copacabana. Nightclub at 10 East 60th Street in Manhattan, opened in 1940. Until the late 1950s it was a glamorous venue for performances by such entertainers as Frank Sinatra, Ella Fitzgerald, Nat King Cole, and Jimmy Durante. It then declined in popularity and closed in 1973. During the 1980s the space was used as a discothèque and as a facility for various functions. In 1992 a new club by that name opened at 617 West 57th Street. In 2001 it moved to West 34th Street and 11th Avenue and played mostly hip-hop and salsa music. In 2007 the building was condemned and the club was forced to close.

James E. Mooney

Copland, Aaron (*b* New York City, 14 Nov 1900; *d* North Tarrytown, N.Y., 2 Dec 1990). Composer. The son of Russian immigrants, he studied composition with Rubin Goldmark at 140 West 87th Street from 1917 to 1921. From 1921 to 1924 he was one of the first of the many young American composers who studied with Nadia Boulanger in Paris. After his return to the United States he provoked controversy with dissonant, angular compositions influenced by jazz, such as *Music for the Theater* (1925). He also wrote for the journal *Modern Music,* spoke on musical topics at the New School for Social Research, and with Roger Sessions organized concerts in 1928 to introduce new compositions; during the Depression he was allied with the Composers Collective and took an interest in writing music with an overtly political content. Copland's compositional style became less astringent in the 1930s and 1940s: he frequently evoked American legend and folklore, especially in his well-known ballet scores for Agnes de Mille (*Billy the Kid,* 1938; *Rodeo,* 1942) and Martha Graham (*Appalachian Spring,* 1944). In the 1950s and 1960s his compositions again became less accessible. His *Connotations* (1962), commissioned for the opening of Philharmonic Hall in 1962, was written in a densely serial style. He lived at the Empire Hotel, just across from Lincoln Center, until 1961, when he moved to Peekskill, in Westchester County. After a rich and varied compositional life his output ebbed after 1970. Copland was the most influential American composer of the twentieth century. Although best remembered for his celebrations of rural America, he proved equally adept at portraying the urban pastoral in such works as *Quiet City* (1940) and *Music for a Great City* (1963). In 1982 Queens College of the City University of New York named its music school in his honor. With Vivian Perlis he wrote two volumes of memoirs (1984, 1989).

Barbara L. Tischler

Copperheads. Name applied to Confederate sympathizers in the North during the Civil War, of whom New York City had many. Denounced by Republicans as traitors, poisonous snakes-in-the-grass within the "loyal" states, Copperheads responded by wearing badges made from copper Liberty-head pennies to condemn northern oppression. New York's extensive commercial ties to the South led much of the city's merchant and white working classes—mostly Democrats—to call for a negotiated settlement, allowing the South to return to the Union with slavery intact or to secede peacefully. In January 1861 the Copperhead mayor, Fernando Wood, even proposed that the city should also secede, becoming a duty-free port trading equally with the North and South. President Abraham Lincoln countered the forces of secession by concentrating unprecedented power in the federal government. His Emancipation Proclamation, on 1 January 1863, angered white workers in the North, who had been told by Copperhead politicians and newspapers, including the *Daily News,* the *Express,* the *Caucasian,* and the *Copperhead,* that freed slaves would take their jobs at lower wages. In May, Wood and other so-called Peace Democrats held mass meetings in the city to denounce the arrest by federal troops of the prominent Ohio Copperhead Clement Vallandigham on charges of sedition. In July, the first federal draft—with a $300 exemption fee—triggered four days of rioting and attacks on the city's African American population. Charges of a Copperhead and Confederate conspiracy behind the draft riots were never proved, but the riots did inspire Confederate attempts to sabotage cities across the North with support from local Copperheads. On 25 November 1864 a failed attempt to burn New York City damaged 19 hotels and Barnum's Museum. The Copperheads' ultimate triumph came after the Civil War, with the defeat of Reconstruction in 1877 by a resurgent Democratic Party, led by New York politicians including Congressman Fernando Wood.

Sidney David Brumer, *Political History of New York State during the Period of the Civil War* (New York: Columbia University Press, 1911); Jerome Mushkat, *Tammany: The Evolution of a Political Machine, 1789–1865* (Syracuse, N.Y.: Syracuse University Press, 1971); Iver Bernstein, *The New York City Draft Riots: Their Significance for American Society and Politics in the Age of the Civil War* (New York: Oxford University Press, 1990); Barnet Schecter, *The Devil's Own Work: The Civil War Draft Riots and the Fight to Reconstruct America* (New York: Walker and Company, 2007)

See also Civil War; Draft riots; and Wood, Fernando.

Barnet Schecter

Corbett, Harvey Wiley (*b* San Francisco, 8 Jan 1873; *d* New York City, 24 April 1954). Architect. After studying at the University of California, Berkeley, and the École des Beaux-Arts he moved to New York City in 1901, where he worked for several firms before forming a partnership with F. Livingston Pell in 1903. The two were known for their designs in revival styles, among them the neoclassical New York School of Applied Design for Women at 160 Lexington Avenue (1909). In 1912 Corbett became a partner of Frank J. Helmle, who had a practice in Brooklyn. In the 1920s he became a leading defender of skyscrapers and increased urban density, wrote extensively on the effect of the zoning law of 1916, and offered futuristic proposals for multilevel traffic separation and pedestrian bridges. Among the many skyscrapers he designed was the Bush Tower at 132 West 42nd Street (1918), which was widely acclaimed and housed his offices in its two top stories. The firm was renamed Corbett, Harrison, and MacMurray after Helmle's retirement in 1928 and later became Harvey Wiley Corbett Associates. Other commissions included the Master Apartments at 310 Riverside Drive (1929), the National Title Guaranty Building of Metropolitan Life Insurance on Madison Square (1932, with D. Everett Wald), and the Criminal Courts Building at 100 Centre Street (1939).

Carol Willis

Corbett, James J(ohn) (*b* San Francisco, 1 Sept 1866; *d* Queens, 18 Feb 1933). Boxer. The son of Irish immigrants, in May 1891 he fought 61 rounds over four hours with Peter Jackson, and in September 1892 he won the world heavyweight championship from John L. Sullivan. Known as "Gentleman Jim," he was popular among fans for his speed and finesse in the ring. Corbett was the world heavyweight champion from 1892 to 1897, losing the world title to Bob Fitzsimmons in March 1897 (in 14 rounds). After retiring from the ring in 1903 he moved to New York City, where he engaged in fight promotion, as well as broadcasting and stage and screen acting. He also wrote a book, *The Roar of the Crowd: The True Tale of the Rise and Fall of a Champion* (1925). In 1954 he was posthumously inducted into the Ring Boxing Hall of Fame and in 1990 into the International Boxing Hall of Fame.

John J. Cancannon

Corbin, Austin (*b* Newport, N.H, 11 July 1827; *d* Newport, R.I., 4 June 1896). Railroad tycoon. He formed the Corbin Banking Company in New York City in 1865, and while on vacation in Coney Island in 1873 made plans to develop a lavish summer resort at its eastern tip called Manhattan Beach, which eventually included the Manhattan Beach Hotel and the Oriental Hotel. Corbin was the owner (1880–96) and president (1881–96) of the LONG ISLAND RAIL ROAD.

Stephen Weinstein

Corigliano, John (*b* New York City, 16 Feb 1938). Composer. Born in Brooklyn into an Italian American family of professional musicians, he studied at the Manhattan School of Music and Columbia University where he received his bachelor's degree in 1959. He has composed symphonies, concertos, works for solo instruments and chamber groups, operas, and film scores, including Sonata for Violin and Piano (1963). The New York Philharmonic commissioned Corigliano to write several works, as did the Chamber Music Society of Lincoln Center and the New York State Council on the Arts. He was awarded the Grawemeyer Award for Symphony no. 1 (1991), which was inspired by his feelings of loss and anger over the AIDS crisis. Corigliano also won an Academy Award in 1999 for his work on the film *The Red Violin.* In 2001 he was awarded the Pulitzer Prize for Symphony no. 2. He has taught at the Manhattan School of Music, Lehman College, and the Juilliard School.

Max Seppo

Corlear's Hook. Former neighborhood in lower Manhattan, covering 50 acres (20 hectares) and bounded to the north by Delancey Street, to the east by the East River, to the south by Montgomery Street, and to the west by east Broadway. Before Dutch settlement it was known as Rechtauck but was renamed for a Dutch family that settled there in the seventeenth century. In 1776 the American army built a fortification there. It became home to shipbuilding in the late eighteenth century. Into the nineteenth century it struggled with crime and vice, and large tenements sprang up during the 1830s and 1840s. In the early twentieth century activists from the Henry Street, University, and Grand Street settlements advocated the removal of the area's "old law" tenements (tenements built before passage of the 1901 Tenement House Act) and decaying piers so that low-income housing could be constructed. The Amalgamated Dwellings (1930) and the Vladeck Houses (1940) were developed through municipal and federal financing and built by the city housing authority; the Hillman Houses (1949) and Corlear's Hook project (1955), conducted under Title I of the Housing Act of 1949, were sponsored by the United Housing Foundation, with the intention of transforming slums into middle-income developments. The New York City Housing Authority started $50 million of improvements on the Vladeck Houses in 1998.

Joel Schwartz

Cornbury, Lord. See HYDE, EDWARD.

Cornell, Joseph (*b* Nyack, N.Y., 24 Dec 1903; *d* Queens, 29 Dec 1972). Sculptor. In 1929 Cornell moved into an ordinary house at 37-08 Utopia Parkway in Flushing where he lived and worked to the end of his life. He frequented the city's museums and galleries as well as Woolworth's. An avid collector, Cornell often visited the secondhand book dealers on Fourth Avenue in search of old books, engravings, and souvenirs. He is best known for his typically small assemblages—sectioned wooden boxes filled with photographs, maps, and an array of found objects. He characterized his work as "a natural outcome of love for the city."

Diane Waldman, *Joseph Cornell: Master of Dreams* (New York: Harry N. Abrams, 2002)

Harriet F. Senie

Cornell, Katharine (*b* Berlin, 16 Feb 1893; *d* Vineyard Haven, Mass., 9 June 1974). Actress. Made independently wealthy by a legacy, she moved to New York City in 1916 to become an actress. She joined the Washington Square Players, performed her first important roles with Jessie Boustelle's stock company, and in 1924 appeared on Broadway as the star of George Bernard Shaw's *Candida.* She later acted in such classics as *Romeo and Juliet, St. Joan,* and *Three Sisters* and a number of inferior plays that she sustained by her talent. Her greatest roles were Candida and Elizabeth Barrett in Rudolf Besier's *The Barretts of Wimpole Street.* In 1921 she married Guthrie McClintic, with whom she formed Cornell and McClintic Productions in 1930; with Cornell in starring roles and McClintic as the director the two mounted shows on Broadway and toured the country. She lived from 1921 to 1952 at 23 Beekman Place and from 1961 on East 51st Street.

Katharine Cornell

George A. Thompson, Jr.

Cornell University Medical College. Former name of WEILL MEDICAL COLLEGE OF CORNELL UNIVERSITY.

corners and panics. Financial crises brought on by speculation in securities markets have played an important role in the economic and political history of New York City. During the early Federal period an increase in trading in government bonds helped to bring about the formation in 1790 of the New York Stock Exchange, and eventually rampant speculation that one writer characterized as "scriptomania" caused a panic in 1792. Alexander Hamilton, the secretary of the treasury, was criticized for his handling of the crisis, which ultimately had little effect on the economy. As finance and industry took on a larger role in the city, however, panics assumed larger proportions. In the 1830s Jacob Little and other speculators made huge profits by organizing pools of investors and manipulating stock prices. A period of speculation in railroads, canals, cotton, and real estate ended in 1837 when a financial panic ruined many banks and speculators. The depression that followed constrained Wall Street until the 1850s, when economic growth and easy credit ignited another round of speculation, primarily in railroads. The market collapsed in August 1857, and by December the streets of New York City were filled with rioters and unemployed workers, who blamed the banks and speculators for their troubles. The panic of 1857 brought about a generational change on Wall Street, and a new breed of speculator dominated the market after the Civil War, at a time when the markets had gained such a powerful influence on the U.S. economy that financial panics frequently led to severe economic dislocation. One of the most profitable schemes of the speculators during these years was known as executing a corner, that is, buying all available supplies of a stock or commodity to drive up the price. This speculative maneuver created a financial panic in 1869 when Jay Gould made $40 million by trying to corner the market for gold. Speculators like Daniel Drew and Cornelius Vanderbilt also manipulated share prices during their takeover battles for the Erie Railroad and other firms. A major national financial scandal resulted from the bankruptcy in 1873 of Crédit Mobilier, which had bribed scores of politicians to obtain government subsidies for the building of the Union Pacific Railroad. The scandal caused stock prices to plunge, producing the worst depression of the nineteenth century, and ruined Jay Cooke, then the most powerful man on Wall Street. The failure of a brokerage house owned by Ulysses S. Grant after his presidency produced a minor panic in 1884, and the federal government nearly became bankrupt between 1893 and 1895; it recovered only when J. P. Morgan bought several bond issues on the condition that the federal government return to the gold standard. Panics were caused by attempted corners in 1901 (by James Hill and Edward H. Harriman for control of the Northern Pacific Railroad) and 1907 (by Frederick Heinze and Charles Morse for control of United Copper), when Morgan again played an important, stabilizing role; after several banks closed and the stock market fell sharply, he joined with the U.S. Department of the Treasury to shore up the banking system with fresh capital.

After the turn of the twentieth century it became more difficult to manipulate prices because of the creation of the Federal Reserve in 1913 and because more shares were traded.

"The Great Financial Panic—Closing the Doors of the Stock Exchange on Its Members, Saturday, Sept. 20th," Frank Leslie's Newspaper, *4 October 1873*

Even so, Allan Ryan in 1920 was able to increase the price of shares in the Stutz Motor Company by buying all the stock, and Jesse Livermore, working at the behest of Clarence Saunders, was able to corner the stock in the grocery firm Piggly Wiggly. The New York Stock Exchange forced Ryan and Saunders to give up their shares, but throughout the 1920s easy credit fueled widespread speculation by allowing corporations to go heavily into debt and encouraging speculators to buy stocks on credit. In 1928 a pool of speculators organized by William Durant cornered the stock in the Radio Corporation of America (RCA), which increased in price by 60 points a share in just four days. The market finally stalled in September 1929 and crashed in October, the economy slipped into the worst depression of the twentieth century, and the stock market lost 80 percent of its value by 1933. By this time it was clear that the nation's financial markets suffered from enormous structural weaknesses, which the reforms of the New Deal were intended to remedy: the federal government formed the Securities and Exchange Commission in 1934, outlawed manipulation of the stock market, and strengthened regulations. These reforms made panics and corners considerably more rare but did not eliminate them. Prices dropped 27 percent in a panic between December 1961 and June 1962 known as the Kennedy slide, and the Dow Jones Industrial Average lost 37 percent of its value between 1968 and 1970. As late as 1979 the brothers Nelson Bunker Hunt and W(illiam) H(erbert) Hunt unsuccessfully tried to corner the market in silver, but federal regulators intervened to prevent a financial crisis, and the Hunts lost more than $4 billion (they eventually declared bankruptcy). On 19 October 1987 the Dow Jones Industrial Average underwent a decline of 508 points, or 23 percent, the largest single day percentage decline in its history. In the late 1990s speculation in Internet and technology stocks pushed the markets into a new bubble. When it burst, the tech-heavy NASDAQ index fell from a peak of 5048 on 10 March 2001 to less than half that by October 2002. Investigations by then New York State Attorney General Eliot Spitzer and federal regulators led to multibillion dollar settlements with brokerage firms and banks that had touted a number of Internet companies and telephone companies that eventually went broke; ultimately, investors in Internet and tech stocks lost some $7 trillion in equity from the market's peaks.

In the twentieth century, steep stock market declines were often followed by slumps in the New York City housing and commercial real estate markets; in the years following the 1907, 1929, 1968–70, and 1987 stock market crashes, a number of prominent New York City developers declared bankruptcy. After the 1907 crash, discounted sales of homes in the 1910s helped transform Harlem, and the 1987 crash caused commercial property values to fall by nearly half in some parts of Manhattan. The collapse of the Internet bubble of 2001 hurt commercial real estate in some areas, particularly the so-called Silicon Alley areas of lower Manhattan, but the slump was temporary and a booming global property market soon pushed the price of New York City real estate to record levels. During the summer of 2007, worries that U.S. borrowers might default on $200 billion to $300 billion worth of home mortgages roiled global stock markets and produced a global credit crunch that made it difficult for companies and investors to borrow money or sell mortgage-backed securities. That forced New York–based banks and brokerages to write off large losses in mortgage-backed securities and prompted widespread litigation and government investigations into fraud in the mortgage markets.

Robert Sobel, *Panic on Wall Street: A History of America's Financial Disasters* (New York: Collier, 1972)

George Winslow

Cornish, Samuel Eli (*b* Sussex Co., Del., *ca* 1795; *d* Brooklyn, 6 Nov 1858). Civil rights leader. He formed the First Colored Presbyterian Church (later renamed Shiloh Presbyterian Church) in 1821 and was its pastor until 1827, when with John B. Russwurm, a proponent of the "Back to Africa" movement, he launched *Freedom's Journal*, the first black newspaper in the United States, from an office at 150 Church Street. After the journal ceased publication in 1829 he edited several others devoted to abolition and civil rights, including *Rights for All* (1829) and the *Colored American* (1837–41). Cornish attended the first National Negro Convention, held in Philadelphia in 1830, as a delegate from New York City and became a prominent figure in the black convention movement. An advocate of practical education, he promoted literacy among blacks in the North and with philanthropists raised money to build schools dedicated to preparing black youths for industrial work. In 1833 he was appointed to the executive committee of the American Anti-Slavery Society.

Lawrence D. Reddick, "Samuel E. Cornish," *Negro History Bulletin* 5 (Nov. 1941), 38

Thelma Foote

Corona. Neighborhood in north central Queens (2009 pop. *ca* 70,000), adjoining Flushing Bay and Flushing Meadow Park. It was developed in 1854 by a group of speculators from New York City and named West Flushing. The same year marked the beginning of service by the Long Island Rail Road and the opening of the National Race Course (later Fashion Race Course), which continued to operate until the Civil War. Developers planned the streets according to the route of the railroad. In 1872 the village changed its name to Corona (the "crown" of villages on Long Island). Early factories made china, portable houses, and from 1893 into the 1930s, Tiffany glass. The population reached 2500 by 1898 and 6200 by 1910, and it continued to grow after the introduction of rapid transit in 1917. The commercial center shifted in the 1920s from near the railroad station to Northern Boulevard. From 1943 to 1971 the great jazz trumpeter Louis Armstrong lived in the neighborhood, which was then largely Italian and Jewish. The area attracted a large Latino community after World War II, at first Puerto Rican and after 1965 increasingly Dominican. Immigration to the neighborhood in the 1980s was heavy: the Dominican Republic accounted for almost half of all immigrants who settled there, while China and Colombia accounted for about one-tenth each. Other countries that were well represented included Korea, India, the Philippines, Ecuador, Pakistan, Peru, and Guyana. In the early 1970s the neighborhood was the site of heated conflicts between middle-class homeowners and advocates of low-income housing. Corona was the fictional home of Archie Bunker in the popular television series *All in the Family* (1971–83). In the early twenty-first century, Corona remained ethnically diverse, inhabited mostly by Latinos, with smaller populations of Italian Americans, Asian Americans, and African Americans.

Vincent Seyfried

coroner and medical examiner. Under English law, which from the 10th century mandated that the government investigate deaths, colonial governors appointed coroners for Manhattan and other counties. While some coroners were medical doctors, many were not, and reports were unreliable. The job was often a lucrative political sinecure that paid a fee for each body that was examined. Coroners were known to recycle corpses and take bribes from families or the police to come up with desirable rulings. Among the 20 inquest reports that City Coroner Thomas Shreve filed with his invoice for £66 to the Common Council on 19 April 1771 was a verdict that a certain Samuel Belknap, described as "a prisoner confined in jail," had died by "the hand of God." Attempts to reform the coroner's office were generally ineffectual. Richard Croker, a young blacksmith and Tammany Hall functionary, was named one of the city's four coroners in 1873 with the promise of earning $15,000 a year in fees. He was no more qualified for the job than two of the other coroners, a lawyer turned editor and another Tammany ward heeler (the fourth coroner was the only physician). Mayor William F. Havemeyer's attempts to unseat him failed, and Croker held the position for three years. A state senate committee investigating the city government reported that Croker had no conception of his duties and was skilled only in getting the same corrupt individual, who had been convicted of necrophilia, appointed to coroner's juries a total of 118 times. Croker was nevertheless elected to his second three-year term (he later became the boss of Tammany Hall). Of the 65 coroners elected between the consolidation of New York City in 1898 and 1915, none was chosen for ability. Nineteen were physicians with political pull; eight were undertakers; seven were politicians; six were real estate agents; two were saloon keepers; two were plumbers; and the remainder included a musician, a dentist, and a butcher.

Critics of the system were concerned that even honest coroners were unaware of advances in medical science and developments in pathology. They pressed Albany to follow the lead of Massachusetts and replace coroners with certified medical doctors. In 1914 Mayor John Purroy Mitchel and the City Club, a reform group, commissioned a report that concluded that the position was political and many coroners unqualified. An additional accusation, that the physician appointed by the coroner "is a law unto himself," reflected a widespread conviction that coroners tolerated abortions and, to please families, reported that persons committing suicide had died of natural causes. In 1915 a new law replaced the coroner as of 1918 with a medical examiner. This official was required to be both a medical doctor and a pathologist, pass a written test, and demonstrate an ability to perform a successful autopsy. The first chief medical examiner was the former head of Bellevue Hospital, Charles Norris.

At the end of the twentieth century, the medical examiner became a lightning rod for controversies concerning poor administration and apparent cover-ups of causes of the deaths, not only of well-known individuals (such as former Governor Nelson Rockefeller) but also of several African American men while in police custody. Three medical examiners in succession were fired by mayors. As one of them, Elliott Biden, observed, "These days, it's a rare M.E. who manages to stay out of trouble for any length of time and still maintain his independence."

"Archives of Coroner and Office of Chief Medical Examiner, 1823–1946," http://www.nyc.gov/html/records/html/collections/collections_coroner.shtml; Michael Baden, *Unnatural Death: Confessions of a Medical Examiner* (New York: Ivy Books, 1989)

John Rousmaniere

corporate headquarters. Corporate headquarters concentrated in New York City at the end of the nineteenth century, when proximity to centers of transportation and communication was increasingly important to businesses with operations extending across the country. Because of its role in finance the city attracted a disproportionate number of the country's corporate headquarters, which were initially clustered in lower Manhattan around Wall Street. The city's position was solidified when Standard Oil moved its headquarters from Cleveland in 1882. After the rapid transit system opened and tracks north of Grand Central Terminal were covered (1910), publishers, chemical and drug companies, and eventually airlines formed a second business district between 42nd and 60th streets, and for the next 50 years construction east of Sixth Avenue slowed only during the Great Depression and World War II. By the mid-1960s New York City was home to headquarters of 136 of the nation's 500 largest firms, vastly more than any other U.S. city.

When an economic decline during the late 1960s and 1970s severely hurt the city, a number of firms moved to suburban New York State, New Jersey, and Connecticut where they found larger and cheaper facilities, lower taxes, and less crime. Between 1969 and 1976 only four corporations opened headquarters in the city and 55 among the largest 500 moved out. By the mid-1970s some companies followed shifting markets and moved to such cities as Dallas, Houston, and Los Angeles. Despite economic growth during the 1980s and 1990s New York City continued to have a net loss of corporate headquarters as more companies left then came, but it also achieved some gains, as industries such as banking, insurance, and transportation became stronger.

Zoning changes eventually encouraged the construction of offices west of Sixth Avenue. Largely because of corporate headquarters and the ancillary businesses they attracted, midtown emerged as the largest central business district in the world. As many firms became part of conglomerates and multinational corporations or were decentralized, the continuing role of the city as a hub of corporate headquarters remained unclear, especially as developments in communications and information technology threatened to diminish the importance of headquarters by permitting central operations to be carried out in offices across the country and overseas. There was apprehension after the terrorist attacks of 11 September 2001 that fear of future attacks would speed up corporate departures, especially from the downtown business district. New York City, however, rebounded quickly. A turning point was the decision of Goldman Sachs to remain in downtown rather than relocate across the Hudson. This decision was in response to the city's giving Goldman Sachs $1 billion in tax-free bonds to build a new office tower in lower Manhattan as well as the reluctance of many top employees to leave the city. In 2010 the city housed 44 of the Fortune 500 companies as compared with 41 in 1990.

Stanley Buder

Fortune 500 Firms Based in the New York City Metropolitan Area

1955 (131)[1]
1. Standard Oil of New Jersey (2)[2]
2. U.S. Steel (3)
3. General Electric (4)
4. Socony–Vacuum Oil (9)
5. Western Electric (12)
6. Texas Co. (Texaco) (14)
7. Shell Oil (16)
8. National Dairy Products (17)
9. Sinclair Oil (21)
10. Union Carbide and Carbon (24)

1960 (160)
1. Standard Oil of New Jersey (2)
2. General Electric (4)
3. U.S. Steel (5)
4. Socony Mobil Oil (6)
5. Texaco (8)
6. Western Electric (10)
7. General Dynamics (15)
8. Shell Oil (17)
9. National Dairy Products (20)
10. Union Carbide (24)

1965 (163)
1. Standard Oil of New Jersey (2)
2. General Electric (4)
3. Socony Mobil Oil (5)
4. U.S. Steel (7)
5. Texaco (8)
6. International Business Machines [Armonk, N.Y.] (9)
7. Western Electric (11)
8. Shell Oil (14)
9. National Dairy Products (23)
10. Union Carbide (26)

1970 (156)
1. Standard Oil of New Jersey (2)
2. General Electric (4)
3. International Business Machines [Armonk, N.Y.] (5)
4. Mobil Oil (7)
5. Texaco (8)
6. International Telephone and Telegraph (9)
7. Western Electric (11)
8. U.S. Steel (12)
9. Shell Oil (16)
10. General Telephone and Electronics (19)

1975 (134)
1. Exxon (formerly Standard Oil of New Jersey) (1)
2. Texaco (4)
3. Mobil Oil (5)
4. General Electric [Fairfield, Conn.] (8)
5. International Business Machines [Armonk, N.Y.] (9)
6. International Telephone and Telegraph (11)
7. U.S. Steel (12)
8. Western Electric (18)
9. Continental Oil [Stamford, Conn.] (16)
10. Union Carbide (21)

1980 (135)
1. Exxon (1)
2. Mobil (3)
3. Texaco [Harrison, N.Y.] (5)
4. International Business Machines [Armonk, N.Y.] (8)
5. General Electric [Fairfield, Conn.] (9)
6. International Telephone and Telegraph (13)
7. Conoco [Stamford, Conn.] (15)
8. Western Electric (19)
9. Union Carbide (25)
10. RCA (36)

1985 (120)
1. Exxon (1)
2. Mobil (3)
3. Texaco [Harrison, N.Y.] (5)
4. International Business Machines [Armonk, N.Y.] (6)
5. American Telephone and Telegraph (8)
6. General Electric [Fairfield, Conn.] (9)
7. International Telephone and Telegraph (21)
8. Allied Chemical [Morris Township, N.J.] (25)
9. Philip Morris (32)
10. Union Carbide [Danbury, Conn.] (35

1990 (86)
1. Exxon (3)
2. International Business Machines [Armonk, N.Y.] (4)
3. General Electric [Fairfield, Conn.] (5)
4. Mobil (6)
5. Philip Morris (7)
6. Texaco [White Plains, N.Y.] (10)
7. Xerox [Stamford, Conn.] (21)
8. Pepsico [Purchase, N.Y.] (23)
9. RJR Nabisco Holdings (24)
10. Allied–Signal [Morristown, N.J.] (31)

1995 (98)
1. AT&T (5)
2. General Electric [Fairfield, Conn.] (6)
3. International Business Machines [Armonk, N.Y.] (7)
4. Philip Morris (10)
5. Prudential Insurance Co. of America [Newark, N.J.] (13)
6. Texaco [White Plains, N.Y.] (16)
7. Citicorp (17)
8. Pepsico [Purchase, N.Y.] (20)
9. ITT (23)
10. American International Group (26)

2000 (84)
1. General Electric [Fairfield, Conn.] (5)
2. International Business Machines [Armonk, N.Y.] (6)
3. Citigroup (7)
4. AT&T (8)
5. Philip Morris (9)
6. American International Group (17)
7. TIAA–CREF (19)
8. Lucent Technologies [Murray Hill, N.J.] (22)
9. Texaco [White Plains, N.Y.] (28)
10. Merrill Lynch (29)

2005 (82)
1. General Electric [Fairfield, Conn.] (1)
2. Citigroup (8)
3. American International Group (9)
4. International Business Machines [Armonk, N.Y.] (10)
5. Verizon (14)
6. Altria Group (17)
7. J. P. Morgan Chase and Co. (20)
8. Pfizer (24)
9. Johnson and Johnson [New Brunswick, N.J.] (30)
10. Time Warner (32)

1. Numbers in parentheses following the year indicate the total number of Fortune 500 firms based in the metro area.

2. Numbers in parentheses following the name of each firm indicate the rank of that firm within the Fortune 500.

Note: From 1955 to 1994 firms included in the Fortune 500 derived more than 50 percent of their sales from manufacturing and mining, or both. From 1995 the list includes the top 500 closely held and public corporations across industries, ranked by gross revenue.

Source: *Fortune* magazine

Compiled by Andrew A. Kryzak

corporation counsel. Lawyer appointed to defend the legal interests of New York City. A similar office was held first by James Graham, the city's recorder from 1683 to 1701, and in the following century by such distinguished men as Robert R. Livingston and Richard Varick. It was merged into a new position known as attorney of the corporation in 1801. After the offices became separate again on 14 May 1839, Peter A. Cowdrey became counsel and Samuel J. Tilden attorney. In April 1849 the counsel became an elected official in charge of the new Municipal Law Department; the election held soon after was won by Henry Davies. The position became appointive again under William M. "Boss" Tweed's charter of 1870, and the corporation counsel then exercised nearly complete control over litigation involving the city. While in office, William C. Whitney (1875–82) introduced divisional specialization. The city's counsel was used by Mayor John F. Hylan to block proposals for increasing transit fares and utility fees, and by Mayor Fiorello H. La Guardia to prepare a new administrative code. By the mid-1970s the office performed so poorly that it was denounced by Judge Bentley

Kassal, leading Allen Schwartz to carry out reforms and secure agreements from major law firms to provide lawyers to the city free of charge. The corporation counsel continued to serve the city in the early twenty-first century.

George J. Lankevich

Corporation of the City of New York. In addition to wielding government powers, the city is a corporation, a status giving it the legal capacity to own property, sue and be sued, and exercise other functions. New Amsterdam was granted a limited municipal government in 1653. The charter promulgated by Governor Richard Nicolls (1665) changed the "Forme and Ceremony" of government to conform with British practice but recognized the city as a "body Politick and Corporate." Under the laws of that time the corporation, although having governmental powers, was treated as a private institution. Successive colonial charters, especially that of Governor John Montgomerie (1731), defined its rights and privileges and gave it an endowment of "private" land that included most of Manhattan Island north of the present Canal Street as well as the underwater land adjacent to the shoreline in lower Manhattan. Voting and the holding of municipal office were limited to freemen (Dutch burghers), who were required to meet certain property and residence qualifications and were the only people allowed to engage in trade or skilled occupations in the city. The freemanship was gradually expanded, but it persisted as a distinct class even after American independence. The early Corporation of the City of New York did not have the authority to levy direct taxes. Its revenue derived mainly from regulatory and licensing fees, franchises, and income from its property. Throughout the eighteenth century the corporation made numerous grants of underwater land to be filled in. The grantee typically paid a modest quit rent in cash but was also required to build specific public improvements such as streets, piers, and bulkheads. In this way the city was able to manage its expansion and provide improved facilities for its growing maritime trade. The growth of population in the late eighteenth century and the early nineteenth created a need for additional public services and facilities. The corporation became increasingly dependent on the state legislature for the authority to levy taxes and do other things not contemplated in the colonial charters. Through a series of court decisions and charter revisions, the Corporation of the City of New York by the 1860s had lost nearly all of its former autonomy and like other municipal corporations was an instrumentality of the State of New York. By this time the corporation had also divested itself of most of its former landholdings or turned them over to public purposes such as parks.

Murray Hoffman, *A Treatise upon the Estate and Rights of the Corporation of the City of New York, as Proprietors* (New York: McSpedon and Baker, 1853); George W. Edwards and Arthur E. Peterson, *New York as an Eighteenth-Century Municipality* (Port Washington, N.Y.: I. J. Friedman, 1917); Hendrik Hartog, *Public Property and Private Power: The Corporation of the City of New York in American Law, 1730–1870* (Ithaca, N.Y.: Cornell University Press, 1989)

Gilbert Tauber

Corridan, John M. See Waterfront priest.

Corrigan, Michael A(ugustine) (*b* Newark, N.J., 13 Aug 1839; *d* New York City, 2 May 1902). Archbishop. He was a coadjutor bishop to Cardinal John McCloskey from 1880 until being appointed archbishop of New York City in 1885. Responding to the needs of Catholic immigrants, he opened 75 parochial schools, centralized the parochial system, and built St. Joseph's Seminary (Dunwoodie) in Yonkers, New York. He also formed a number of charitable institutions (consolidated in 1902 as the Association of Catholic Charities), which he staffed by attracting 24 religious orders to the archdiocese, including the Scalabrinians and the Missionary Sisters of the Sacred Heart. He emerged as a conservative leader and drew sharp criticism from many Catholics after excommunicating the priest Edward McGlynn for supporting Henry George in the mayoral campaign of 1886 (over Corrigan's protests, McGlynn was reinstated by the Vatican in 1892). Corrigan's antiprogressive position was nonetheless supported by papal encyclicals, culminating in *Testem Benevolentiae* (1899).

Michael A. Corrigan, 1888

Robert Emmett Curran, *Michael Augustine Corrigan and the Shaping of Conservative Catholicism in America, 1878–1902* (New York: Arno, 1978)

Robert Emmett Curran

Corso, Gregory (*b* 26 March 1930, New York City; *d* 17 Jan 2001, Robbinsdale, Minn.). Poet and member of the Beat literary movement. He grew up in orphanages and foster homes and was sentenced to three years in Clinton State Prison for robbery when he was 16. He spent his time in jail reading classic works of literature and writing poetry. After he was released from prison in 1950, he met the poet Allen Ginsberg at the Pony Stable, a bar in Greenwich Village. Ginsberg introduced Corso to Jack Kerouac and William Burroughs, who were also living in New York City at the time. These writers influenced Corso, and his poetry developed from conventional verse to a more free-form style. Corso, Ginsberg, Burroughs, and Kerouac formed the nucleus of the Beat literary movement during the 1950s and 1960s, and they alternated living in New York City and San Francisco. Corso briefly taught at the State University of New York at Buffalo in the early 1960s but was dismissed in 1965 when he refused to certify that he was not a member of the Communist Party. Corso published 13 books of poetry, one novel (*American Express*), and two plays and taught and lectured extensively. He died of prostate cancer.

Breanne Scanlon

Cortelyou, Jacques (*b* Utrecht, Netherlands, *ca* 1625; *d* ?New Utrecht, New Netherland, between 28 Feb and 27 July 1693). Landowner and surveyor. Of French parentage, he attended the University of Utrecht and worked as a tutor and land surveyor in America. In 1652 he settled in New Netherland, where he tutored the children of Cornelis Van Werckhoven, a member of the Dutch West India Company. After Van Werckhoven's death he secured a patent in 1657 for land that is now the site of Fort Hamilton in Brooklyn; Cortelyou then divided this land into 20 lots and established the town of New Utrecht. As the surveyor general of New Netherland he drew the first map of New Amsterdam in 1661. He lived at Fort Hamilton and traveled daily to his office on Whitehall Street. Cortelyou's descendants include Isaac Cortelyou, a fence viewer (an official who administered fence laws) and an overseer of the poor in the 1770s who lived in a stone house in Gowanus (eventually known as the Vechte–Cortelyou House) that was the scene of fierce fighting during the Battle of Long Island (August 1776), and George B. Cortelyou, a prominent Republican politician who was chairman of the Republican National Committee (1904), postmaster general (1905), and secretary of the treasury (1907).

Stephen Weinstein

cosmetics. Wigs, rouge, and face powder were used by both men and women in colonial New York City. After the American Revolution most face and hair powder, toilet waters, and lotions were made at home; chemists prepared more complex products such as oils, creams, pomades, perfumes, and dyes; and such prominent merchants in New York City as Nicholas Low and James Rivington imported cosmetics from England and France. The nineteenth century saw a decline in the use of cosmetics, but the city remained the site of many cosmetics firms and of several innovations in the industry, as well as the central receiving point for English and French cosmetics bound for the United States. The English chemist Robert Bach, who set up shop at 128 Pearl Street in 1798, imported most of his preparations. His business evolved by 1872 into the prosperous firm of Dodge and Olcott, which distilled raw materials for export and operated from 88 William Street until it moved to New Jersey in 1904. Two cosmetics firms in the city during the early nineteenth century later evolved into multinational conglomerates: those of Robert Chesebrough and the chemist Theron Pond (whose enterprises merged to form Chesebrough–Pond's in 1955), and of the candle and fancy soap maker William Colgate at 6 Dutch Street (1806), which eventually became the Colgate–Palmolive Company. Both businesses also had operations in Brooklyn: Pond bottled his immensely popular witch hazel there from 1846, and Chesebrough manufactured petroleum jelly at 24 State Street from 1870. Pond later manufactured cold cream, for which he became widely known.

In New York City there were 90 hairdressers operating in 1890, most of whom visited customers in their homes. Commercial beauty salons and makers of hair-care products gradually increased in number. Manuel Besosa manufactured a brand of hair dye called Orija at 66 West 125th Street, and 44 perfumers and seven importers did a thriving business. In a brochure in 1882, Simonson's Human Hair Emporium at 34 East 14th Street advertised not only its usual supply of wigs, toupees, and human hair but also cosmetics imported from France, including the cream Fountaine de la Beauté, the hair color Fluide Magique, and Velontine Face Powder. Mary E. Cobb offered complete beauty treatments in 1886 at her salon at 66 West 23rd Street and remained in business until 1906. The nation's largest cosmetics firm, Avon, began in the city in 1886 and within a decade employed 100 salesmen and operated from a warehouse at 126 Chambers Street.

New York City is the hub of the cosmetics industry

Several developments in the first decades of the century solidified the city's position as the center of the world's cosmetics industry: manufacturers, importers, and marketers believed that an address on Fifth Avenue would lend their products an aura of elegance and gentility, and as they relied increasingly on advertising, transportation, and distribution through department stores, the need to locate in New York City became more pressing. Beauty products, salons, and exclusive sales outlets multiplied rapidly in the early twentieth century, spurred primarily by such locally based pioneers as Elizabeth Arden and her business rival, Helena Rubenstein. Among their successful competitors was Dorothy Gray, who began her career as a custom cosmetician for Elizabeth Arden in 1915 and in the following year opened her own salon at 57th Street and Madison Avenue (moved in 1926 to 753 Fifth Avenue); her business was eventually acquired by the firm of Lehn and Fink.

The Manufacturers' Perfumers Association of the United States was formed in New York City in 1894. In 1920 the group, which later became known as the Toilet Goods Association, published a comprehensive register of wholesalers, manufacturers, and importers of cosmetics and raw materials that listed 480 cosmetics firms operating in Manhattan, 48 in Brooklyn, three in Long Island City, and one in Flushing. Among these were a number of large chemical firms that supplied raw materials for cosmetics, including Pfizer, Squibb, Burroughs–Wellcome, Merck, Schmid, and Schiefflin, as well as the firm of Maurice Levy, who invented the lipstick case. In 1937 the catalogue listed 506 cosmetics businesses in Manhattan, of which many were branches of foreign firms like Chanel, Fabergé, and Jean Naté; others were chemical factories like the Adams Chemical Laboratories at 561 West 147th Street. One of the smaller firms in the catalogue was Revlon, a five-year-old business led by Charles Revson and based at 125 West 45th Street. One of the city's most important cosmetics manufacturers from the 1950s was Estée Lauder. By 1965 Lauder's firm was encroaching on Revlon's market, and a strong rivalry ensued.

Very little cosmetics manufacturing remained in the city after World War II. Although the largest firms maintained their headquarters there, high land costs, wages, and taxes made it more economical for them to operate their factories elsewhere. The industry also experienced a trend toward consolidation, exemplified by the acquisition of Almay, a small firm based in Brooklyn, by the conglomerate TLC Beatrice. In the early twenty-first century, virtually every major cosmetics firm in the world maintained at least an office in the city, including such French firms as Lancôme, L'Oréal, and Chanel, and the giant Japanese firm Shiseido. The cosmetics industry remained an integral part of the magazine, television, department store, chemical firm, and fashion industries.

Maggie Angeloglou, *A History of Make-Up* (New York: Macmillan, 1970); Margaret Allen, *Selling Dreams: Inside the Beauty Business* (New York: Simon and Schuster, 1981)

See also Soap and toiletries.

Marc Ferris

Cosmopolitan. Monthly magazine. It was launched in Rochester, New York, in 1887 and moved to New York City, where in 1888 it was purchased and developed into a magazine of domestic and foreign policy by John Brisben Walker, a former newspaperman who had made a fortune in iron and real estate. During the Spanish–American War two reporters covered the front, while Theodore Dreiser wrote a story on a munitions factory and Stephen Crane reported on the Boer War. Walker was not averse to influencing public policy: in 1895 he used the magazine to offer Spain $100 million in exchange for Cuban independence; in 1902 he proposed a world congress of nations; and he also advocated nationalizing the railway system. He was an early proponent of aviation, and in 1892 he used the magazine to provide one of the first forums for articles on "aerial navigation." In 1905 Walker sold the magazine for $400,000 to William Randolph Hearst, who was more assertive than Walker in using the magazine as a vehicle for venting his opinions. A *Cosmopolitan* story published in 1905 called "The Treason of the Senate," about the alliance between big business and several senators, led President Theodore Roosevelt to coin the term *muckraking* to describe what he saw as sensationalistic but incisive reporting. From 1912 the magazine emphasized fiction: a serial by Robert W. Chambers entitled "The Common Law" and illustrated by Charles Dana Gibson increased circulation by 70 percent. Fiction continued to be published for the next 30 years. By 1965, with circulation foundering, the Hearst Corporation appointed as its editor Helen Gurley Brown, the author of *Sex and the Single Girl,* who sought out a readership of single working women by celebrating a decadent, materialistic way of life. She briefly published centerfold photographs of male nudes and introduced various changes in format that eventually increased circulation from 700,000 to two million. Clearly, the sexual explicitness of the magazine became one of its main selling points. In the early twenty-first century *Cosmopolitan* had 58 international editions, was printed in 34 languages, and was distributed in more than

100 countries. It also expanded to include three American television networks and Cosmo Radio.

Benjamin Yakas, Rachel Sawyer

Cosmopolitan Club. Private women's club located at 122 East 66th Street in Manhattan. Its 10-story clubhouse was designed by Thomas Harlan Elett and opened in 1932, but the club organization itself dates to 1909. "The Cos," as it has since been dubbed, counts Eleanor Roosevelt, Helen Hayes, Pearl Buck, Marian Anderson, Margaret Mead, Willa Cather, and Abby Aldrich Rockefeller among its distinguished past members.

Elizabeth L. Bradley

Costello, Frank [Castiglia, Francesco] (*b* Laurapoli, Calabria, Italy, 1891; *d* New York City, 18 Feb 1973). Gangster. When he was nine years old, his family moved to East Harlem. After being jailed several times as a youth for petty crimes and concealed weapons, he refined his trade, buying favors from political leaders, judges, and the police. For many years he had a penthouse in the Majestic Apartments at 115 Central Park West. After his release from prison, he formally changed his name to Frank Costello. He was nicknamed the "Prime Minister of the Underworld" for his infamous negotiating skills and in 1916 forged an alliance with Ciro Terranova, head of the Morello crime family and the 107th Street gang. Through Morello, Costello was introduced to Charles Luciano, the Sicilian leader of the Lower East Side gang. In 1931, after the killing of several rival bosses, Luciano became the new leader of the crime family and appointed Costello the *consigliare*, or the second in command. Luciano was later convicted for his role in a prostitution ring, leaving Costello in charge of the family. Members of the Luciano crime family, notably Vito Genovese, made an unsuccessful assassination attempt in 1956 to gain control. After serving a short term at the federal penitentiary in Atlanta in 1959, Costello retired to his estate on Long Island. He died of a heart attack.

See also Organized crime.

James E. Mooney

Frank Costello, May 1935

Cotton Club. Dance hall and supper club. Established in 1920 by the former heavyweight boxing champion Jack Johnson, "Club Deluxe" was located in a dance hall of the Douglas Casino at 142nd Street and Lenox Avenue in Harlem. The notorious gangster "Owney" Madden soon purchased the club and struck a deal that allowed Johnson to remain as manager. The renamed Cotton Club was a whites-only cabaret famous for its fake jungle decor, exotic draperies, and lavishly costumed dancers. The club premiered in 1923 as a replication of popular Broadway "Negro Revues," featuring chorus girls and male dancers. In 1927 Duke Ellington's Washingtonians began a five-year booking and, owing to the primitive backdrop and exotic dancing of Earl "Snakehips" Tucker, were quickly dubbed Duke Ellington's Jungle Band. The club garnered national attention after the Columbia Broadcasting System (CBS) began broadcasting the performances, which had previously been aired by local station WHW. Because Ellington was a valuable commodity, the club acknowledged his request for racial inclusion and relaxed the "whites only" policy for relatives of the band. It was not until 1932, however, that Lucille Wilson, the future wife of Louis Armstrong, successfully challenged the "nothing darker than a light olive tint" policy for Cotton Club dancers. By this time, Cab Calloway headlined and gained fame with his hit "Minnie the Moocher." The club also became a fashionable spot for celebrities; it was there that Adam Clayton Powell, Jr., who was light-skinned enough to gain admission, met his first wife, Isabel Washington, a Cotton Club girl.

In 1936 the Cotton Club closed in Harlem and reopened at Broadway and 48th Street. With the arrival of the swing era, the newly designed interior featured a mural of the white bandleaders Benny Goodman, Gene Krupa, and Tommy Dorsey all in blackface. In 1939 Louis Armstrong and Stepin Fetchit headlined, but the club had been handed indictments for income tax evasion and closed in 1940. Ultimately, America's changing appetite for swing bands led to the demise of lavish venues like the Cotton Club.

Garrett A. Felber

Cotton Exchange. See New York Cotton Exchange.

Council of Jewish Women. Volunteer organization formed in 1893. A local chapter formed in New York City the following year was led by Rebekah Kohut and Sadie American, who developed programs to aid Jewish immigrants, especially women and children. It sent volunteers to the docks to help women traveling alone, founded the Lakeview Home for Girls, and maintained recreation rooms on the Lower East Side. It also served refugees from both world wars, set up programs to aid the blind, handicapped, and hospitalized, and worked with other civic groups to pass social legislation.

Elisabeth Israels Perry

Council of Learned Societies. See American Council of Learned Societies.

Council on Foreign Relations. Nonprofit organization formed in 1921 to bring together leading figures in academia, business, law, and journalism to study issues of foreign policy; it occupied offices at 45 East 65th Street, next door to Franklin D. Roosevelt's townhouse, before moving in 1945 to the Harold Pratt House, a five-story mansion on the southeast corner of 68th Street and Park Avenue, across from Hunter College. The building was given to the council by the widow of Harold Pratt, one of the original directors of the Standard Oil Company; John D. Rockefeller donated a fund for its maintenance. The leadership of the council reflected its strong ties to the Morgan family of bankers until the early 1950s, when David Rockefeller and other members of his family became prominent among its senior officers and directors. The council played an important role in both Democratic and Republican presidential administrations after World War II and was an early supporter of the presidential candidacy of Dwight D. Eisenhower, who, while serving as president of Columbia University, led a group at the council during 1949–50 that studied aid to Europe. The council publishes the influential quarterly journal *Foreign Affairs,* sponsors meetings and conferences at Pratt House and occasionally on Wall Street, and produces a program for the city's radio station (WNYC). The members of the council join by invitation; the by-laws require that a third of them live or work near the city. In 2010 membership stood at about 4300; more than 160 people work at its offices in New York City.

Robert D. Schulzinger, *The Wise Men of Foreign Affairs: The History of the Council on Foreign Relations* (New York: Columbia University Press, 1984)

Marjorie Harrison

Couney, Martin A. (*b* Alsace, 30 Dec 1870; *d* Brooklyn, 1 March 1950). Pediatrician. He studied in Paris under the pediatrician P. C. Budin, and in 1896 at an international exposition in Berlin he demonstrated an incubator for infants modeled after a device used in poultry breeding. The invention proved a medical and financial success and was demonstrated in London, Paris, Omaha (Nebraska), and Buffalo between 1897 and 1901. In 1903 he opened a nursery on Coney Island where he was able to offer free treatment for premature infants by charging an admission fee of 25 cents to sightseers. His work was exhibited in New York City at the World's Fair of 1939–40 and at Luna Park and Dreamland until 1943, about which time the Cornell Medical Center opened a central hospital ward for premature infants. Couney lived at 3728 Surf Avenue in Sea Gate.

A. J. Liebling, "Patron of the Preemies," *New Yorker,* 3 June 1939, 20–24; William A. Silverman, "Incubator-Baby Side Shows," *Pediatrics* 64, no. 2 (1979), 127–41

George A. Thompson, Jr.

counterfeiting. Counterfeiting was rampant in colonial New York City, even though it was a capital offense. Few counterfeiters were executed, however, as juries usually acquitted defendants regardless of the evidence against them. When a bag of halfpence was examined in 1753, a third were found to be counterfeit, many having been cast in sand. During the American Revolution the British counterfeited Continental currency on a warship in New York Harbor. Foreign coins that predominated in the circulation of New York City, such as the Spanish colonial 2-reale coin, were widely counterfeited. Counterfeiters forged the notes of good state-chartered banks, printed up others for nonexistent banks, and raised the denominations of small notes. Fruit-stand owners who sold produce near the ferries in lower Manhattan passed off counterfeit coins regularly. Counterfeiting became riskier during the Civil War, when uniform banknotes were introduced and the Secret Service was formed, but it revived in the 1930s during the Depression. New York City subway tokens were extensively counterfeited from 1970 until 1995; in the twenty-first century attempts have been made to counterfeit the subway MetroCard, but none is known to have succeeded.

Kenneth Scott, *Counterfeiting in Colonial New York* (New York: American Numismatic Society, 1953); John M. Kleeberg, ed., *Circulating Counterfeits of the Americas* (New York: American Numismatic Society, 2000)

John M. Kleeberg

counter-terrorism. Counter-terrorism, the actions the government takes both to thwart potential terrorist acts and to react to any acts that occur, is of paramount concern in New York City.

Public attention focused on terrorism following the 26 February 1993 attack on the North Tower of the World Trade Center that killed six and injured more than 1000 people. Counter-terrorism steps in response to this included monitoring vehicle access to the basement parking garage and requiring personal identification for admission to the World Trade Center buildings. In 1999 the city's emergency command center was moved to the 23rd floor of 7 World Trade Center.

After the attacks of 11 September 2001, when al Qaeda terrorists destroyed both towers of the World Trade Center, killing more than 2600 people, new security measures were put into place to protect the city. The USA Patriot Act, which expanded federal jurisdiction, became law 26 October 2001. Federal counter-terrorism forces under the umbrella of the Department of Homeland Security gained major responsibilities in New York City. U.S. Customs and Border Protection stepped up terrorist and weapons interdiction at John F. Kennedy International Airport. Inspection was augmented on merchant and cruise ships entering the New York–New Jersey seaport, the East Coast's largest. Agreements with foreign nations allowed U.S. customs agents stationed overseas to check shipping containers dockside before they are transferred to vessels headed for U.S. ports. The regional Joint Terrorism Task Force based in Manhattan accelerated operations. Staffed primarily by Federal Bureau of Investigation agents and New York City police officers, the Task Force integrates additional federal law enforcement and intelligence resources. The Federal Emergency Management Agency revised its Urban Search and Response System mandate, originally to respond to natural disasters, to include terrorist attacks.

The most visible aspect of counter-terrorism is the protection of structures and public spaces. Police contingents are positioned at bridges, tunnels, landmarks, and transportation centers. Truck traffic is limited to the upper level of the George Washington Bridge. Visitors can no longer climb the stairs above the Statue of Liberty's pedestal, and public tours of the New York Stock Exchange have been discontinued. Police conduct random sweeps and bag searches in the subway system. NYPD harbor and aviation units and U.S. Coast Guard crews from Staten Island and Kings Point patrol New York City's vast port, 578 miles (930 kilometers) of waterfront, including the United Nations frontage on the East River and the Statue of Liberty in the Lower Harbor. "Operation Hercules" units, the NYPD's version of "showing the flag," make unannounced lightning displays of force. Massed police vehicles, sirens, flashing lights, and helmeted officers with assault weapons flood target areas to create a "curtain of mystery," a Rand Corporation concept that attempts to complicate terrorists' plans by adding additional layers of uncertainty. Security has been hardened in the downtown financial district, home to the New York and American Stock Exchanges, the Federal Reserve Bank, and an intricate road, tunnel, bridge, and subway network. The NYPD's Lower Manhattan Security Initiative has an around-the-clock uniformed presence, comprising combat-equipped officers, canine teams, emergency service units, and a video surveillance system. Unauthorized vehicular traffic is barred from core streets in the Wall Street area, and plans have been advanced to scan all traffic below Canal Street.

Counter-terrorism is also a function of the Port Authority of New York and New Jersey police who patrol the Port Authority Trans-Hudson train system, the Holland and Lincoln tunnels, the George Washington Bridge, Kennedy and LaGuardia airports, and the World Trade Center site. The Metropolitan Transportation Authority has its own police force, supervising security on the seven bridges and two tunnels entirely within the city and an enormous regional transportation system of buses, subways, and Metro–North and Long Island Rail Road trains. It has also developed a widespread counter-terrorism ad campaign: "If You See Something, Say Something; call the terrorism hotline at 1-800-NYC-Safe."

The NYPD assigns more than 1000 of its officers to counter-terrorism duty every day. Ever-expanding intelligence operations include financial investigations and cyberintelligence. Law enforcement officials are concerned about threats from domestic as well as international terrorists. New York City's diverse population provides a reservoir of foreign-language skills, enhancing police operations. Arabic-speaking New York City police officers monitor jihadist Internet sites. To gather intelligence about international terrorist activities, New York City detectives have been deployed abroad at sites including Madrid, London, Tel Aviv, Toronto, Amman,

Abu Dhabi, Singapore, and Interpol headquarters in Lyon, France.

Nexus, the NYPD program that educates and enlists the support of the private sector, aims to deny sensitive resources to terrorists. To share and collect information, each year detectives visit thousands of businesses, including tourist attractions, hotels, retail stores, garages, theaters, self-storage warehouses, and salvage yards. Among the items they monitor are fertilizer and other bomb components, as well as other chemical, biological, radiological, and nuclear materials, which are available—by purchase or theft—from commercial sources. Oil tanker trucks as well as aircraft are subject to hijacking and subsequent use as weapons. Police specialists also coordinate private barrier construction and conduct seminars for private security personnel. Most funding for counterterrorism operations in New York City, which annually runs over $200 million, comes from the municipal budget.

Arnold Markoe

counties. New York City is made up of five separate and complete counties (New York County, Bronx County, Kings County, Queens County, and Richmond County), unlike other American cities, which are either parts of counties (Los Angeles is part of Los Angeles County, Chicago is part of Cook County, Miami is part of Dade County, Detroit is part of Wayne County), coterminus with a single county (Philadelphia, for example), or stand outside of any county (Baltimore and St. Louis). Among other things, the counties administer the court system.

See also Courts.

Kenneth T. Jackson

Country Club. Neighborhood in the northeastern Bronx, bounded to the north by Pelham Bay Park, to the east by Long Island Sound, to the south by Throgs Neck, and to the west by Bruckner Boulevard. The land was owned by the Ferris family during the eighteenth century and most of the nineteenth. Country Club Road once led to the Westchester Country Club, which was patronized by yachtsmen and polo players during the nineteenth century. A development called the Country Club Land Association was mapped in 1892, and in the 1920s more lots were added after the adjoining estate of the Spencer family was dissolved. In the twenty-first century the area is known for its stately homes and quiet streets.

John McNamara, *McNamara's Old Bronx* (New York: Bronx County Historical Society, 1989)

Gary D. Hermalyn

courthouses. In the 1650s courts of law in New Amsterdam were usually housed in buildings also used for other government offices. In 1802 the city sponsored a competition to design a new city hall, specifying that the building must include chambers for both the local legislature and the judiciary. The winning entry, designed by John McComb, Jr., and Joseph François Mangin, was completed in 1812 and had a broad flight of exterior stairs, an entrance portico, classical details, and a cupola adorned with John Dixey's statue *Justice.* During the early nineteenth century courts that became too large for their quarters were moved to other buildings in City Hall Park. The Richmondtown Courthouse (1837–39) on Staten Island was built in a Greek Revival style that incorporated severe classical details, an exterior flight of stairs, an entrance portico, and a cupola. It housed all judicial offices of the county until consolidation in 1898; it became part of the Richmondtown Restoration during the 1990s and is now the oldest courthouse in the city.

Several police courts, such as the Jefferson Market Courthouse, were constructed during the late 1840s and 1850s. In 1861 construction began on a county court building in City Hall Park. Designed by John Kellum and often called the Tweed Courthouse, it was one of the first eclectic style courthouses (called Anglo-Italianate by some). Kellum used such traditional features as a broad flight of exterior stairs, a portico, and classical details; the southern wing, designed by Leopold Eidlitz, has Romanesque details. The city paid for labor that was never performed and overpaid for materials, and this extra money lined the pockets of William M. "Boss" Tweed and his cronies. The courthouse was not completed until 1880, and the scandals eventually led to Tweed's imprisonment. The building was restored during 1999–2001 and became the Department of Education's offices. Eclecticism also marked the beaux-arts courthouse of the state supreme court in Long Island City (1876, George Hathorne; rebuilt in 1908 by Peter Coco) and a Romanesque courthouse in Harlem (1893, Thom and Wilson).

In the early twentieth century several majestic courthouses were built as elements in well-designed clusters of buildings, according to the principles of the "city beautiful" movement. A courthouse at 26th Street and Madison Square for the appellate division of the state supreme court (1900, James Lord Brown) was praised for its stylistic coherence. Its park setting and marble colonnades gave it an urban grandeur; judicial themes were depicted in exterior allegorical sculptures by Daniel Chester French and interior murals completed under the supervision of John La Farge. Similar principles guided the design of the borough courthouse at East 161st Street and Brook Avenue in the Bronx (1906, Michael Garvin) and the county courthouse on Richmond Terrace in Staten Island (1913–19, Carrère and Hastings).

In 1912 Guy Lowell won a competition to design a county courthouse to replace Tweed. His entry called for a monumental scale, austere details, and a circular plan with traditional exterior stairs, classical porticoes, and allegorical sculptures. Many feared the building site in City Hall Park would detract from

Foley Square, ca *1940. Diagonally from lower left: New York County Courthouse; left, New York City Department of Health; right, Department of Motor Vehicles; New York City Criminal Courts Building and Men's House of Detention*

Brooklyn Courthouse, 2009

City Hall, and in 1915 Lowell and the city chose the area now known as Foley Square. Concerns about expense forced Lowell to make his design smaller and hexagonal, though he retained the stairs, portico, sculpture, and austerity of the first design. The rotunda and interior balcony were decorated with a cycle of frescoes, *Law through the Ages* (1936–38, Attilo Pusterla). After the courthouse was completed in 1926 a cluster of others were built in Foley Square; Lowell's innovations inspired the plans for several. Cass Gilbert integrated a skyscraper with a base similar to that of the county courthouse in his design for the federal courthouse (1936). In planning the state criminal courts building (1939; also known as "the Tombs") Harvey Wiley Corbett rejected traditional styles for a setback shape and a simplicity typical of American skyscrapers of the 1920s. He also included a huge granite base that made an abstract portico at the entrance. For the appellate court building on Monroe Place and Pierrepont Street in Brooklyn (1937) the firm of Slee and Bryson adopted pared-down versions of traditional elements, including a short stairway leading to a door flanked by two Doric columns and sculptural medallions across the attic depicting judicial figures. Foley Square was extended by the civil courthouse (1960, William Lescaze), in which a modern metal-and-glass, non–load-bearing curtain wall made up the exterior.

Conrad Duberstein Bankruptcy Courthouse, 2009

A shortage of courtroom space in the 1990s resulted in several new courthouses. Kohn Pedersen Fox designed the United States Courthouse annex (1991–94) located behind Lowell and Gilbert's buildings on Foley Square. Its massive, abstracted piers and simplified moldings echo the older buildings without overtly quoting classical forms. Maya Lin's *Sounding Stones* sculpture (1996) is located in the plaza. Many of the new buildings reject the traditional forms associated with courthouse architecture. Rafael Viñoly's high-style modernist Bronx Housing Court (1997) on the Grand Concourse juxtaposes large windows with expanses of brick and sandstone, an overscaled entry canopy, and the eye-catching extruded glass volume of the ninth-floor library. Pei Cobb Freed and Partners and Gruzen Samton's Queens Family Courthouse (2003) on Jamaica Avenue places different functions in separate volumes of varying heights and clads the rationalist exterior with curtain walls and window grids. The grand public entry has Ursula von Rydingsvard's *Katul Katul* sculpture.

Mary B. Dierickx, *The Architecture of Public Justice: Historic Courthouses of New York City* (New York: Department of General Services, 1993)

Mary Beth Betts

courts. The Dutch established the first judicial system, and after the English took New York the city had the first provincial courts. When Albany became the state capital in 1797, the principal state courts moved there. New York City was the site of the first federal court, and the U.S. Supreme Court held its first sessions there. Many important federal cases have been heard in U.S. district courts for the Southern District of New York and the Eastern District of New York.

1. Municipal

In the early years of New Amsterdam, the director and his appointed council heard all cases, civil and criminal, brought by the schout-sifcall (the sheriff-prosecutor). In 1653 a new charter gave the city autonomy from the province of New Netherland and the West India Company. The judicial system consisted of a schout, who prosecuted cases and executed the court's orders and judgments, two burgomasters, and five schepens (aldermen), all appointed by the director. Similar courts were soon set up in Harlem and the five Dutch towns in what is now Brooklyn. In 1665, a year after taking the colony from the Dutch, Governor Richard Nicolls installed an English system, with a mayor, five aldermen, and a sheriff, who together formed the mayor's court. From 1684 the mayor and aldermen and a recorder held a court of sessions to try felonies, misdemeanors, and ordinance violations. The charter promulgated by Governor Thomas Dongan (1686) designated the mayor's court a court of common pleas with common-law jurisdiction over contract, tort, and property disputes; it consisted of the mayor and recorder (one presided) and at least two of the aldermen. The charter of Governor Richard Montgomerie (1730) retained the court. Provincial acts in 1732 and 1744 authorized magistrates to hold a special court of sessions to try minor offenders who were unable to post bail within two days of arrest (those convicted were publicly flogged).

With New York under British occupation during the American Revolution, city courts were suspended between 1776 and 1783, and the civilian population of the city and Long Island was subject to courts-martial. Soon after resuming in early 1784 the mayor's court tried the case of *Rutgers v. Waddington,* with Alexander Hamilton defending the wartime tenant of a brewery against a suit by its previous owner for back rent. Mayor James Duane's ruling awarded only partial damages, weakening the state's Trespass Act (aimed at Loyalists) and helping to establish the principle of judicial review of legislation. The city's rapid growth led to the formation of lower civil courts. Under a statute of 1782 magistrates were permitted to try lawsuits involving claims of less than £10. Beginning in 1787 assistant justices presided over such cases, and in 1800 they gained jurisdiction over lawsuits between seamen and ship captains or owners. Reorganized as a justice's court in 1807, in 1819 the assistant justice's court was renamed the marine court, where seamen could have a jury trial and plead their cases orally instead of filing written pleadings. Its civil jurisdiction increased incrementally, reaching $2000 by 1875. Assistant justices' courts established in 1807 were the lowest civil courts, organized initially by wards and later by districts; from 1822 the assistant justices were appointed by the Common Council, and in 1852 the courts were renamed the district courts. The lowest criminal tribunal, the police court, was formally named the police office in 1798 and was overseen by "police justices" who issued warrants, arraigned suspects, granted bail, and in lieu of bail committed arrested individuals to jail pending trial; they were appointed by the Common Council from 1797. Corporal punishment for misdemeanors was limited by statute in 1785 and 1789 and abolished in 1801 (hard labor or fines were substituted).

The city's court system continued to grow during the nineteenth century. In 1821 the mayor's court became the court of common pleas (the mayor had long since ceased presiding), with a chief judge and associate judges (Charles P. Daly served variously in both capacities for 41 years); the aldermen were removed in 1847. The Village of Brooklyn had justices of the peace and in 1827 received a municipal court to handle civil cases. In 1828 a superior court began operation in New York City to handle a backlog of civil cases from the court of common pleas and the supreme court. After 1847 its jurisdiction and that of the court of common pleas were the same, giving the city three higher civil courts (common pleas, superior, and supreme), each with its own judges, clerks, trial and appellate terms, and case reports, sometimes handing down conflicting decisions. Under the state constitution of 1894 the superior and common pleas courts were merged into the supreme court, effective in 1896. There were three levels of criminal courts. The court of general sessions tried felony cases: the recorder presided and any two of the common pleas judges, the mayor, and the aldermen completed the bench. The court of special sessions tried misdemeanors and ordinance violations, but with a panel of three judges instead of juries as in the rest of the state. This consisted of the recorder and two common pleas judges from 1830 until 1858, when they were replaced by the police justices. In 1849 the courts in Brooklyn were reorganized so that justices of the peace tried small civil cases, and police justices held preliminary hearings and courts of special sessions. A city court with higher civil and criminal local jurisdiction equivalent to that of the supreme court was also formed and in 1896 was merged into the supreme court.

Police court at the Tombs, ca *1870*

The selection of judges became a highly contentious issue in the mid-nineteenth century. Originally, city magistrates were not locally elected or appointed; rather, the governor, with the consent of the state senate, appointed the recorder and the judges of the common pleas, superior, and marine courts. Statutes enacted between 1847 and 1850 made these and the police justices elective. Beginning in 1848 police justices were assigned to districts, and in 1860 a board of police justices was formed to supervise the system. By the 1860s Tammany Hall controlled the judicial nominations for the police and district courts and filled court jobs at all levels with party hacks and no-shows. Many cases were dismissed by recorder John Hackett and superior court judge John McCunn, both chosen by the Tweed Ring, in exchange for political favors and bribes. The police courts were especially lax and corrupt, and after the fall of the Tweed Ring in 1873 the police justices ceased to be elected and were instead appointed by the mayor, who remained the city's chief magistrate; aldermen were barred from becoming police justices. In 1883 the marine court was renamed the city court.

Efforts at reorganization and reform began in the last decades of the nineteenth century. Problems in the police courts persisted, leading to an investigation into the courts and the police force by State Senator Clarence Lexow in 1894 that began a municipal reform movement. In 1895 the police courts were replaced by magistrates' courts and a separate court of special sessions was also established, the justices appointed by the mayor. After 1892 state law required that children under 16 charged with crimes be detained and tried separately from adults, and between 1902 and 1910 children's courts opened in each borough as divisions of the court of special sessions. After consolidation in 1898 the city court replaced the district and justice's courts in Brooklyn and Long Island City, and the magistrates' and special sessions courts of New York City were extended to Brooklyn, Queens, and Staten Island, which continued to have their own county courts; in 1914 the Bronx became a separate county and gained its own county court. Specialized magistrates' courts were set up after 1900, among them a women's court (1910) in Manhattan and the Bronx to handle prostitution cases; night, felony, and homicide courts for arraignments; and traffic, probation, gambler's, and commercial-frauds courts to relieve the caseloads of the district

Court System in New York State, 1777–1847

Court	Jurisdiction	Appeals to
Court for the Correction of Errors	Final Appeals and Impeachment	
Supreme Court, General Term	Intermediate Appeals	Court for the Correction of Errors
Supreme Court		
Circuit Courts	Civil	Supreme Court, General Term
Courts of Oyer and Terminer	Criminal	Supreme Court, General Term
Court of Exchequer (to 1823)	Fines and Penalties	Supreme Court, General Term
Court of Chancery	Civil (Equity)	Court for the Correction of Errors
Court of Probates (to 1823)	Probate	Court of Chancery
Surrogate Courts (after 1787)	Probate	Court of Probates (to 1823); Court of Chancery (1823–47)
Courts of Common Pleas	Civil	Supreme Court, General Term
Courts of Sessions	Criminal	Supreme Court, General Term
Justices of the Peace Courts (to 1824) Courts of Common Pleas (after 1824)	Limited Civil	Supreme Court, General Term
Courts of Special Sessions (to 1824) Courts of Common Pleas (after 1824)	Limited Criminal	Supreme Court, General Term
City and Village Courts	Limited Civil and Criminal	Various
Surrogate Courts	Probate	Supreme Court, General Term or Appellate Division or Appellate Term
City Courts	Limited Civil and Criminal	County Courts; Supreme Court, Appellate Term, Long Island
Town and Village Justice Courts	Limited Civil and Criminal	County Courts; Supreme Court, Appellate Term, Long Island
District Courts (Long Island only, after 1973)	Limited Civil and Criminal	Supreme Court, Appellate Term

Compiled by James D. Folts with the assistance of Kevin Kenny

magistrates' courts. Despite these structural changes, ethical problems remained. A legislative commission under Alfred R. Page in 1910 criticized the treatment of women and children in magistrates' courts and recommended improvements in decorum and facilities; legislative acts during the same year and in 1915 provided for better administration. The children's court became a separate division with its own probation department in 1915, and a family court opened in 1918 as a division of the magistrates' court to handle spousal and child-support cases.

During state constitutional conventions in 1915 and 1921, proposals were made to combine the city's lower civil courts and abolish the four county courts; these were voted down by the public, but a constitutional amendment in 1925 transferred the civil jurisdiction of the county courts to the city court, effective in 1927. The children's court became independent in 1924 and was given jurisdiction over juvenile criminals and delinquents, as well as cases of child neglect. From this time the courts of general and special sessions tried criminal defendants between the ages of 16 and 19 as "youthful offenders," with probation the usual outcome. Public policy increasingly directed the court to rehabilitate young offenders rather than punish them. In 1932 Judge Samuel Seabury issued a report on the magistrates' courts and found that bribery, extortion, and the use of political influence were widespread. A domestic relations court was set up to administer the family and children's courts in 1933. Branches of the magistrates' courts known as adolescent courts opened in Brooklyn and Queens in the 1930s and later in the other boroughs to try youths between the ages of 16 and 18 as "wayward minors"; these were intended to separate minors from older and more hardened offenders, but failed to stem the rise in juvenile crime after World War II. In 1934 a small-claims division of the municipal court was formed to clear a backlog of small suits. During the same year the women's court was extended citywide.

After the war the city's caseload increased rapidly, first in automobile accident claims and later in criminal and family cases. From 1951 jurisdiction over delinquent girls between the ages of 16 and 20 was given to a girls' term. Overlapping jurisdictions and uncoordinated administration hampered city courts, and in 1955 a state commission under Harrison Tweed recommended the consolidation of all the city's lower civil and criminal courts into one court. The plan failed, largely because of opposition from politicians who relied on the courts to distribute patronage, but reorganization was finally mandated under a constitutional amendment in 1961. In September 1962 the Court of Special Sessions and the magistrates' courts merged into a criminal court responsible for trying misdemeanors and ordinance violations and for preliminary felony hearings; the mayor was empowered to appoint the judges to 10-year terms. The court of general sessions in each of the five counties was abolished, their criminal business transferred to the state supreme court, and the domestic relations court was replaced by a statewide family court. The city court and the municipal court were merged in 1962 into a civil court responsible for lawsuits up to $25,000 under judges elected to 10-year terms. The women's court was abolished in 1967. Cases involving minor traffic and housing codes were removed from the criminal courts; in 1970 moving violations were handled by the state department of motor vehicles, and in 1972 a new housing section of the civil court handled housing code and rent cases. The development of a statewide judicial administration during the 1970s helped to unify the city's court system. A deputy administrative judge supervised all state and local courts in the city after 1974 and assigned judges wherever needed. The state assumed all operating costs for the city courts in 1977 in the wake of the fiscal crisis.

2. State

New York City was the seat of the major colonial and state courts until 1797, when the capital was moved to Albany. The "Duke's Laws" of 1665, issued under authority of the duke of York, established a court of assizes composed of the governor, his council, and other officials meeting yearly in the city to try important cases. With the division of the province into counties in 1683 came new county courts of oyer and terminer empowered by the first colonial assembly to "hear and determine" major criminal and civil cases, with two provincial judges and designated local magistrates. A court of chancery handled matters of equity including injunction, the foreclosure of mortgages, the discovery of evidence, and the appointment and supervision of trustees. It met in New York City beginning in 1683 and the royal governor was chancellor. Probate jurisdiction was vested in the colonial governor and (after 1691) his delegate or "surrogate."

An act of the assembly in 1691 replaced the courts of oyer and terminer with a supreme court of judicature possessing all the civil, criminal, and appellate jurisdictions of English common-law courts; court terms were held in the city by an appointed chief justice and two associates. The act also established courts of common pleas (civil) and sessions (criminal) in each county. In 1692 the assembly empowered a supreme court justice to preside over circuit courts in each county and try major civil and criminal cases. The governor objected to the assembly's attempts to reenact the judiciary act of 1691, and after 1698 ordinances of the governor were the legal basis for the supreme and chancery courts. English court procedure was introduced rapidly, allowing the city's merchants to use the courts to collect debts more easily.

The most notable, and divisive, political trial began in 1733, when incoming Governor William Cosby sued Acting Governor Rip Van Dam for back salary. He ordered the state supreme court to sit as a court of exchequer so that the case could be tried without a jury. When Chief Justice Lewis Morris challenged the legality of this arrangement, he was dismissed and replaced by James de Lancey. Morris and his supporters then launched the *New-York Weekly Journal,* a publication dedicated to attacking Cosby. Cosby bypassed the grand jury in having the editor, John Peter Zenger, charged with seditious libel. Andrew Hamilton, a lawyer from Philadelphia, won that historic case for Zenger by arguing brilliantly for freedom of the press and for the jury's right to decide not only the fact of publication but also the truth of the libel. The supreme court was at the center of controversy again during the 1760s, when a political faction led by the Livingston family opposed Acting Governor Cadwallader Colden's plan to appoint supreme court justices to serve at pleasure rather than for life. Colden stubbornly sought to review on appeal the facts as well as the law in *Forsey v. Cunningham,* a case argued before the state supreme court, but failed and was denounced by the provincial elite for undermining the right of juries to determine facts.

Court System in New York City

Court	Jurisdiction	Appeals to
CIVIL COURTS (ARRANGED CHRONOLOGICALLY)		
Mayor's Court, 1665–73, 1674–1821[1] (also known as Court of Common Pleas after 1686)	Civil and criminal	Court of Assizes, 1665–73, 1674–84; Court of Oyer and Terminer, 1683–91; Supreme Court after 1691
Court of Common Pleas, 1821–95 (merged into Supreme Court)	Civil	Court of Common Pleas (General Term), 1848–95; Supreme Court (General Term), 1828–48, 1877–95; Court of Appeals, 1848–77
Superior Court, 1828–95 (merged into Supreme Court)	Civil (commercial)	Superior Court (General Term), 1848–95; Supreme Court (General Term), 1828–48, 1877–95; Court of Appeals, 1848–77
Assistant Justices' Courts, 1787–97 (succeeded by Justices' Courts)	Limited civil	Supreme Court
Justices' Courts, 1797–1819	Limited civil; marine after 1800	Supreme Court
Marine Court, 1819–83 (succeeded by City Court)	Intermediate[2] civil; marine	Supreme Court, 1819–28; Superior Court, 1828–53; Marine Court (General Term),[3] 1853–83; Court of Common Pleas (General Term), 1853–83
City Court, 1883–1962 (succeeded by Civil Court)	Intermediate civil; marine	City Court (General Term), 1883–1902; Court of Common Pleas (General Term), 1883–95; Supreme Court (Appellate Division), 1896–1902; Supreme Court (Appellate Term), 1902–62 (New York, Bronx[4] counties), 1914–62 (Kings, Queens, Richmond counties)
Assistant Justices' Courts, 1807–52 (succeeded by District Courts)	Limited civil	Supreme Court, 1807–18; Court of Common Pleas, 1818–28; Superior Court, 1828–52
District Courts, 1852–98 (succeeded by Municipal Court)	Limited civil	Superior Court (General Term), 1852–77; Court of Common Pleas (General Term), 1877–95; Supreme Court (Appellate Division), 1896–98
Municipal Court, 1898–1962 (succeeded by Civil Court)	Limited civil; small claims after 1934	Supreme Court (Appellate Division), 1898–1902; Supreme Court (Appellate Term), 1902–62 (New York, Bronx counties), 1911–62 (Kings, Queens, Richmond counties)
Civil Court, 1962–	Limited civil; small claims	Supreme Court (Appellate Term)
CRIMINAL COURTS (ARRANGED CHRONOLOGICALLY)		
Court of Special Sessions, 1732–1962 (succeeded by Criminal Court)	Limited criminal	Court of General Sessions to 1895; Supreme Court (General Term), 1895; Supreme Court (Appellate Division)
"Police Court," 1798–1895 (succeeded by Magistrates' Court)	Limited criminal	Court of General Sessions
Magistrates' Court, 1895–1962 (succeeded by Criminal Court)	Limited criminal	Court of General Sessions, or (outside New York County) County Court, 1895–1922; Court of Special Sessions (Appellate Part), 1922–62

(continued)

Court System in New York City (*Continued*)

Court	Jurisdiction	Appeals to
Criminal Court, 1962–	Limited criminal	Supreme Court (Appellate Term)
Family Court (branch of Magistrates' Court), 1918–33 (merged into Domestic Relations Court)	Family	Same as Magistrates' Court
Children's Court, 1923–33 (formerly branch of Court of Special Sessions; merged into Domestic Relations Court)	Juvenile	Supreme Court (Appellate Division)
Domestic Relations Court, 1933–62 (succeeded by Family Court: see table of New York State courts)	Family and juvenile	Supreme Court (Appellate Division)

1. The Mayor's Court was also known as the Court of Common Pleas from 1868. In 1821 the name was legally changed to Court of Common Pleas, as the mayor no longer presided.

2. Intermediate and limited civil jurisdiction were defined in terms of the value of cases heard by each court.

3. General Term courts were appellate panels, in this case selected from the Marine Court and in others selected from the Marine Court and in others selected from other courts. For clarity the General Terms of the Marine Court, Superior Court, and Court of Common Pleas have been omitted from this table.

4. Bronx County existed legally from 1898, although it was not organized until 1914.

Compiled by James D. Folts with the assistance of Kevin Kenny

Under the first state constitution of 1777, the trial court system was retained unchanged and a court was added for the correction of errors, replacing the governor and council as the highest appellate court. During the colonial period the governor had served as chancellor and set up the court of chancery without legislative consent. After 1778 there was an appointive chancellor. In 1787 the court of chancery received jurisdiction over divorce cases and a surrogate's court was established in each county. Until 1823 a court of probates heard appeals from the county surrogates' courts and supervised the settlement of estates of persons who had died out of state. The office of public administrator opened in 1799 to settle estates of city residents without heirs. The 1822 state constitution created circuit judges in eight circuits who would travel to each county to try civil cases originating in the supreme court and to hold courts of oyer and terminer for felonies, including all capital crimes. (New York City was in the first circuit.) The supreme court heard appeals from the lower courts and ruled on points of law raised in the circuit courts. From 1823 equity powers were divided between the court of chancery and a supreme court circuit judge or a vice chancellor assigned to New York.

During the 1820s William Sampson and Henry D. Sedgwick, prominent lawyers in the city, called for a reform of the state's antiquated common-law court procedure; a code of civil procedure became law in 1848. Under the constitution of 1846 the state courts were reorganized, and in 1847 an elective court of appeals replaced the court of errors as the highest appellate court. An elective supreme court was established in 1847 to combine law and equity jurisdictions. A second division of the court of appeals was established in the city to handle a large backlog of cases between 1889 and 1892. Supreme court justices appointed to hear appeals in a general term took appeals from higher trial courts, while appeals from the superior and common pleas courts in New York County and from the city court in Brooklyn went directly to the court of appeals. Circuit courts and courts of oyer and terminer remained the county-level trial terms of the supreme court until 1896, when the supreme court justices continued to preside over trial terms of the supreme court in each county. The state constitution of 1894 established a supreme court appellate division, which began in 1896 and had in its first department New York County (and later Bronx County as well) and in its second Kings, Queens, and Richmond counties. A court of claims was formed in 1897 to handle claims against the state, holding sessions in New York City.

The early twentieth century saw the construction of several court buildings, among them the ornate courthouse of the supreme court appellate division (first department) at 27 Madison Avenue in 1900, the Queens County Courthouse in Long Island City (1908), and the Hall of Records on Chambers Street (1911), erected to house the many books and files of the surrogate's court of New York County, the busiest in the state. Special terms were added in the first and second departments to hear appeals from the city and municipal courts in 1914 and later from the court of special sessions as well. A number of courts moved to new quarters during the following decades: the Richmond County Courthouse (1919) replaced a courthouse erected in Richmondtown in 1839; the New York County supreme court building on Foley Square (1927) took over the functions of the courthouse built under William M. "Boss" Tweed from 1861 to 1872; and new quarters were assumed by the Bronx County civil courts (in the county building, opened in 1934), the Bronx County appellate division, second department (in a building at 45 Monroe Place in Brooklyn, 1938), the supreme court of Queens County (in a building completed in Jamaica in 1939), and the supreme court of Kings County (in the civic center, 1957). In response to a report prepared by James A. Foley, the New York County surrogate, practice of the surrogate's court and the law of estates was reformed during the 1930s.

Justices are elected to the state supreme court by district to 14-year terms. In New York City, New York County is the first district; the second district was Kings and Richmond counties until 2008, when the state legislature established a long-sought thirteenth district, separating Staten Island from Brooklyn; the eleventh district was Queens County, established 1963; and the twelfth district was the Bronx, established 1983.

3. Federal

The most important federal court in New York City is the District Court for the Southern District of New York State. Its precursor, the U.S. District Court of New York, was established under the Judiciary Act of 1789 and was the first federal court to meet under the Constitution, convening on 3 November 1789 in the Exchange Building on Broad Street, across from Fraunces Tavern (the supreme court did not meet until February 1790). Like the Admiralty Court in Britain, the court had jurisdiction over cases arising under the Constitution and federal statutes, admiralty and maritime cases, disputes between citizens of different states and between states and the federal government, and all "Controversies to which the United States shall be a Party." President Washington appointed distinguished lawyer James Duane as the court's first justice; attorneys admitted to practice in the court on its first day included Alexander Hamilton and Aaron Burr. The number of cases was at first small but grew so rapidly that on 9 April 1814 Congress divided the court into the Northern and Southern districts of New York State.

The earliest cases dealt with admiralty and maritime law, and in both precedent and practice the court followed the tradition of the British Admiralty Court in the Province of New York. The court inherited the records of the British court as well, cases involving piracy and privateers (such as letters of marque from the French and Indian War), the treatment of seamen (who often had to sue ships' owners and captains for their wages), and smuggling or other violations of the Navigation, Townshend, Sugar, and Tea acts. Many cases involved American ships trading with French and Dutch ports in the Caribbean. When the British confiscated a ship and its cargo on charges of smuggling, officials responsible for enforcing the law often acquired the goods at auction, a blatant conflict of interest that fed the growing discontent of colonial merchants in the years before the American Revolution. Precedents established in the admiralty court remained in force after independence. During the undeclared naval war with France, the USS *Constitution* brought a captured merchantman into New York Harbor and asked the court to declare it a legitimate prize of war, the proceeds from its sale to be distributed among the officers and crew. This traditional law of the sea remained in practice as late as the Civil War, when ships of the U.S. Navy brought in captured Confederate blockade runners as prizes. Other maritime cases involved accidents at sea; the court was the venue for lawsuits against owners of the *General Slocum, Titanic, Lusitania,* and *Andrea Doria.*

Important obscenity cases were also heard in the Southern District of New York, because under federal law the court was responsible for determining whether materials imported into the United States were obscene or indecent. In the nineteenth century the articles in question included books, photographs, playing cards, and drugs, articles, and medicines "used for the prevention of conception or for causing unlawful abortion." The court ruled in 1932 that D. H. Lawrence's *Lady Chatterley's Lover* was obscene and in 1939 that James Joyce's *Ulysses* was not. During World War I John Reed was among many who were indicted on charges of sedition. In 1919 Emma Goldman was deported to Russia as an "alien anarchist" after her writ of habeas corpus was denied in the court. Her lawyer had unsuccessfully argued that an individual could not be deported for an "attitude of mind or the holding of political, social or economic views, or the expression thereof." During the "Red Scare" after World War II the court was the venue for three major trials: the conviction of 11 communists under the Smith Act (1949), the perjury trial of Alger Hiss (1950), and the espionage trial of Julius and Ethel Rosenberg, with Justice Irving Kaufman presiding (1953). It also heard a large number of cases in corporate law, antitrust law (including the landmark prosecution of the American Tobacco Company), and bankruptcy (including those of Mathew Brady and the City Housing Corporation). During Prohibition there were prosecutions under the Volstead Act, ranging from the sale of a single glass of beer to the tax evasion trial of Dutch Schultz. In the area of patent law and copyright infringement, Thomas Edison, Rudyard Kipling, Irving Berlin, and the creators of the Lone Ranger, Mickey Mouse, and Batman have all at one time or another asked the court to protect their copyrights. The terrorists who bombed the World Trade Center in 1993 were convicted in the Southern District of New York (1994, 1995).

Congress created the U.S. District Court for the Eastern District of New York in 1865, splitting Long Island and Staten Island from the Southern District of New York, but both courts held jurisdiction over the harbor. The first judge appointed to the bench of the new court was Charles Linnaeus Benedict; the number of judgeships was later increased to two in 1910, six in 1940 (after Prohibition and the Depression had swelled the caseload), and eight in 1960. The courthouse is in downtown Brooklyn. A second courthouse opened in Westbury (Nassau County) in 1971, moving to Uniondale in 1981; the third opened in Hauppauge (Suffolk County) in 1987. Major cases tried in the Eastern District of New York include *Schechter Poultry Corp. v. United States* (1935), which resulted in a ruling that the National Industrial Recovery Act was unconstitutional; a case concerning the deplorable conditions for the severely mentally challenged at the Willowbrook State Development Center on Staten Island (1975); the successful challenge to the constitutionality of the Board of Estimate (1984); the bribery trials of Brooklyn Democratic leader Meade Esposito (1987) and Representative Mario Biaggi (1988); the mail fraud and extortion trial of Nassau County Republican leader Joseph Margiotta (1981); the bribery trial of Judge William Brennan of the New York State supreme court (1985); the prosecution of Staten Island Congressman John Murphy and others in the "Abscam" case, an FBI "sting" operation (1980); *Beekman v. City of New York* (1979), which challenged the physical examination administered by the Fire Department of the City of New York on the grounds that it discriminated against women; *Arthur v. Starrett City* (1985), over the use of quotas to maintain racial balance in a housing complex; the prosecution of individuals involved with the Puerto Rican terrorist organization Fuerzas Armadas de Liberación Nacional (FALN) for as many as 30 bombings in New York City (1983); and the conviction of mob boss John Gotti (1992). Ronell Wilson, the killer of two undercover police officers on Staten Island in 2003, was convicted in the Eastern District Court and sentenced to death (2007), the first such sentence since the Rosenbergs; Staten Island District Attorney Daniel Donovan handed the prosecution to federal prosecutors in the Eastern District after New York's death penalty was ruled unconstitutional.

David McAdam, ed., *History of the Bench and Bar of New York* (New York: New York History Company, 1897); Alden Chester, *Courts and Lawyers of New York: A History, 1609–1925* (New York: American Historical Society, 1925); Richard B. Morris, ed., *Select Cases of the Mayor's Court of New York City, 1674–1784* (Washington, D.C.: American Historical Association, 1935); Alfred J. Kahn, *A Court for Children: A Study of the New York City Children's Court* (New York: Columbia University Press, 1953); *Bad Housekeeping: The Administration of the New York Courts* (New York: Association of the Bar of the City of New York, n.d. [?1955])

James D. Folts, Jeffrey A. Kroessler

Cousy, Robert Joseph [Bob] (*b* New York City, 8 Aug 1928). Basketball player. The son of French immigrants, Cousy grew up playing stickball and boxball on Manhattan's East Side. At age 12 Cousy moved with his family to St. Albans, Queens, where he began playing basketball. Despite being twice cut from the Andrew Jackson High School team, he won the city scoring championship as a senior and earned a scholarship to Holy Cross College in Worcester, Massachusetts. An innovative guard with unprecedented ball handling and passing skills, Cousy became known as "the Houdini of the Hardwood." He won a collegiate title at Holy Cross and six professional titles with the Boston Celtics; in 1996 a National Basketball Association (NBA) panel named him one of the 50 greatest players in NBA history.

Ben Silk

Covello, Leonard (*b* Avigliano, Italy, 26 Nov 1887; *d* Messina, Sicily, Italy, 19 Aug 1982). Teacher and principal. When he was nine, his family moved to East Harlem, where he found schools indifferent or hostile to Italians. He became a high school language teacher in 1913 and in 1922 persuaded officials to make Italian an elective language; he also advocated academic rather than vocational education for Italians. In 1934 he was appointed the first principal of Benjamin Franklin High School, which he made an integrated school despite racial tensions in East Harlem. On his retirement in 1956 he became the educational consultant to the Puerto Rican Migration Division and continued to write about education. He returned to Italy in 1972. Covello wrote a memoir, *The Heart Is the Teacher* (1958).

Mary Elizabeth Brown

Covenant House. Nonprofit charitable organization that operates shelters for homeless and runaway youths. The first Covenant House was opened in 1968 by Bruce Ritter, a Franciscan friar, in two abandoned tenements in the East Village. The organization went on to open several shelters throughout New York

City, including one on 41st Street near Times Square kept open 24 hours a day, and an outreach center on West 44th Street. In 1990 Ritter was forced to resign amid allegations of sexual and financial misconduct. In the early twenty-first century Covenant House was the largest privately funded organization in the world devoted to helping teenage runaways, serving over 70,000 a year through its 20 shelters in the United States, Canada, and Latin America.

Mary Rose McGeady, *God's Lost Children: Letters from Covenant House* (New York: Covenant House, 1991)

Frank Morrow

Cowley, (David) Malcolm (*b* Belsano, Pa., 24 Aug 1898; *d* New Milford, Conn., 27 March 1989). Writer, editor, and literary historian. He volunteered as an ambulance and munitions truck driver in France during World War I and reported from the Western Front for the *Pittsburgh Gazette*. In 1920 he graduated from Harvard University and wrote for the *New York Daily Post* and *The Dial* until he moved to Paris, where he was exposed to the emerging styles of Dadaism and Surrealism and edited *Gargoyle*, the first continental European English-language publication between the world wars. While living abroad, he was associated and worked with members of the "Lost Generation," including F. Scott Fitzgerald, Ernest Hemingway, John Dos Passos, and Ezra Pound, among others. In 1929 he published his first book of poetry, built around his poem "Blue Juniata." He then started a 15-year career at the *New Republic* magazine, where he wrote book reviews. In 1934 he published *Exile's Return: A Literary Odyssey of the 1920s*, which came to be regarded as the definitive chronicle of the 1920s. He helped to organize the first American Writer's Congress in 1935. From the early 1930s to November 1935 he lived at 360 West 22nd Street. In 1941 he was hired as a deputy for the Office of Facts and Figures, a government agency responsible for disseminating information about the government's defense efforts during World War II. He resigned in 1942 under pressure from the Federal Bureau of Investigation because of his past ties to communists and left-wing organizations.

B. Kimberly Taylor

Craft Museum. See Museum of Arts and Design.

Crain's New York Business. Business magazine. Launched in 1985 by Crain Communications, Inc., the magazine provides local New York City business news and coverage. It also has an online version, complete with industry coverage, New York City industry lists, and research guides.

Jessica Montesano

Crane, (Harold) Hart (*b* Garretsville, Ohio, 21 July 1899; *d* Gulf of Mexico, 27 Apr 1932). Poet. Born to Clarence Crane, inventor of the Life Saver candy, he moved to New York in 1917 but rarely settled down, spending much of his time in Cleveland, Mexico, Cuba, and Europe. It was in New York City, however, that he developed his career as a poet, socializing with such writers as E. E. Cummings and Allen Tate. Influenced by Walt Whitman and T. S. Eliot, Crane focused on urban scenes and developed a unique poetic style that readers sometimes found challenging. Many of his poems were set in New York City, such as "The Bridge" (1930), in which the Brooklyn Bridge served as the poetic centerpiece. He at one time lived near the bridge at 110 Columbia Heights in Brooklyn but wrote the collection of poems while living on the Isle of Pines in the Caribbean. Crane lived a mostly troubled life, struggling with bouts of depression and alcoholism, which worsened during 1931–32 while in Mexico on a Guggenheim Fellowship. He committed suicide by jumping from the deck of the SS *Orizaba* off the coast of Florida en route to New York City from Mexico.

David White

Crane, Stephen (*b* Newark, N.J., 1 Nov 1871; *d* Badenweiler, Germany, 5 June 1900). Novelist. He briefly attended Lafayette College and Syracuse University but left to pursue a writing career. In 1891 he moved in with his brother in suburban New Jersey, where he wrote stories and articles for various newspapers, including the *New York Tribune* and the *New York Herald*. During this period, he began taking trips to the Bowery, exploring its tenements and nightlife. His experiences there would serve as the foundation for *Maggie: A Girl of the Streets* (1893), *George's Mother* (1896), and an article for *New York Press* entitled "An Experiment in Misery." In 1892 he moved to Manhattan, living at 165 West 23rd Street between Sixth and Seventh avenues. *The Red Badge of Courage*, an unromanticized account of the Civil War written despite Crane's never having been a solider, was first published in 1894 in various newspapers. After its publication Crane went on a long journalistic tour of North America, one of many in his lifetime. He would later cover the Spanish–American War in a brief stint for the *New York World*. When he returned to New York City after five months traveling, Crane joined the Lantern Club, a group of writers who gathered at 126 William Street. After 1894 Crane published mostly short stories (*Wounds in the Rain*, 1900) and poems (*The Black Riders and Other Lines*, 1895). He died of tuberculosis.

Max Seppo

Crater, Joseph F(orce) (*b* Easton, Pa., 1889; *d* ?1930). Judge who disappeared. He earned a law degree at Columbia Law School, opened a private practice that became successful, and took up quarters at 40 Fifth Avenue; he also became politically active and was made president of the Cayuga Democratic Club, an organization closely associated with Tammany Hall. In April 1930 he was appointed to the state supreme court by Governor Franklin D. Roosevelt. After dinner at a restaurant in Manhattan on 6 August he stepped into a taxicab with about $5000 in his wallet, waved goodbye to a friend, and disappeared. An investigation by a grand jury hinted at corruption in the Cayuga Club; Crater was never found.

James E. Mooney

Crazy Eddie. Chain of retail electronics stores opened by Eddie Antar, an entrepreneur from Brooklyn and the grandson of Syrian immigrants. It began as a store which Antar opened in Brooklyn in 1969 that sold electronic equipment (mainly televisions and stereos) nearly at cost. The firm prospered during the early 1980s with the rising popularity of videocassette recorders; more stores opened throughout the metropolitan area, and television commercials were made featuring Jerry Carroll, who waved his arms and frantically screamed, "Crazy Eddie's prices are insane!" At its peak the chain consisted of 43 stores. Sales declined from late 1986, and the firm filed for bankruptcy protection in 1989. Antar was arrested in Israel in June 1992 on suspicion of having passports under three names and of carrying millions of dollars stolen from the stockholders of Crazy Eddie; he was later sentenced to 12 and a half years in prison for fraud and ordered to repay $121 million in restitution.

Melissa M. Merritt

Credit Suisse. Firm of investment bankers. It was formed in New York City as the First Boston Corporation in June 1934 by a merger of the investment banking divisions of First National Bank of Boston and Chase National Bank after the Glass–Steagall Act required the separation of commercial and investment banks. In the 1930s and 1940s First Boston was the only large publicly owned firm of its kind and underwrote securities for many corporations and public utilities, including electric and oil companies, as well as for commercial banks and securities firms. After the stock market crash of October 1987 the firm sought to refinance temporary loans that it had made during the 1980s; it received capital from Credit Suisse and was restructured in December 1988, becoming a privately held subsidiary of an international investment bank controlled by CS Holding, the parent company of Credit Suisse. The firm took the name CS First Boston in September 1993. In 1990 CS Holding gained a majority share in CS First Boston by increasing its holdings from 44.5 percent to 64 percent. In 1996 CS First Boston became Credit Suisse First Boston when the CS Holding Group reorganized itself into the

Credit Suisse Group. In 2006 the name First Boston was dropped entirely and the company became known as Credit Suisse. It retains investment banking headquarters at 11 Madison Avenue.

Mary E. Curry

credit unions. The first credit union in New York City was organized in 1914 by the employees of Bing and Bing after the Russell Sage Foundation had prevailed on New York State to make credit unions legal. By the following year there were 19 credit unions in the state, 11 of which were in New York City. Mayor John Purroy Mitchel organized a credit union in 1916 for municipal workers, in order to end the practice of garnishing their salaries. During the 1920s credit unions increased in number and size, though many failed during the Great Depression of the 1930s. Those that survived benefited from a loss of faith in commercial banks and other financial institutions that were perceived as impersonal. Credit unions grew slowly in the 1940s, but picked up again in the 1960s and, with assistance from the provision of the federal "share-draft" insurance in 1971, rapid expansion resumed thereafter.

In the early 1970s, the Municipal Credit Union of New York City became one of the largest credit unions in the country. In 1977, however, rumors that it was in difficulty generated a run by shareholders that threatened its existence, despite the protection of federal insurance. It recovered after a temporary takeover by the New York State superintendent of banking. In 1980 there were about 440 credit unions in New York City; congressional legislation to "deregulate" banking in 1980 and 1982 freed credit unions from restrictions on the interest rates they could pay and expanded the kinds of loans and investments they could make. Among other things, it allowed them to provide checking accounts and to make commercial loans. The legislation also imposed Federal Reserve System reserve requirements.

In the last decades of the twentieth century, credit unions emerged as full-service banks for consumers. But the common bond—their distinguishing quality—weakened. In a quest for growth, credit unions with different common bonds have merged. The number of credit unions has also declined due to conversions into savings institutions and banks. By the early twenty-first century, the number of credit unions in New York City had fallen to less than 140.

Carrol J. Moody and Gilbert C. Fite, *The Credit Union Movement: Origins and Development, 1850–1980* (Dubuque, Iowa: Kendall/Hunt, 1984); Dean F. Amel, "Trends in Banking Structure since the Mid 1970s," *Federal Reserve Bulletin,* March 1989, pp. 120–3; *Annual Report of the New York State Banking Department* (Albany: New York State Banking Department, 2005)

Bernard Shull

Creedmoor. A tract of land in east central Queens, one mile (1.6 kilometers) north of Queens Village and centered on Braddock Avenue and old Rocky Hill Road (now Braddock Avenue), named for the family that farmed there. The name is used only locally and does not refer to any village or settlement, past or present. Conrad Poppenhusen of College Point ran a railroad through the area parallel to Braddock Avenue in 1871 and donated some of the surplus land to the National Rifle Association for use by the state National Guard, which opened firing ranges in 1873. The growth of Queens Village from the 1890s and the hazards connected with the firing ranges led to the eviction of the National Guard in 1908. In 1910 the tract became the site of a large state mental hospital.

Vincent Seyfried

Creedmoor Psychiatric Center. State mental hospital on Winchester Boulevard near Queens Village, built on land originally owned by the Creed family. It opened in 1912 as a "farm colony" for the Brooklyn Psychiatric Center in facilities formerly used as barracks for the National Guard. With the construction of new buildings in 1926, 1929, and 1933 Creedmoor became a separate state hospital. Although its nominal capacity was 3300 patients, there were 6000 patients by the 1940s, and overcrowding was exacerbated by staff shortages and limited funds. During these years various new treatments for mental illness were introduced at Creedmoor, including hydrotherapy, insulin therapy, electroshock therapy, and in a few cases lobotomy. A more important innovation was the introduction of antidepressant and tranquilizing drugs, which became widely used in the state mental health system in 1955. At Creedmoor the new drugs meant quieter wards, fewer injuries to staff members and patients, and a dramatic increase in the number of patients who could manage daily life in the community. As a result the number of inpatients at the hospital declined to 1100 by 1991, while outpatient services and residential placements were expanded in keeping with the new policy of deinstitutionalization. When it became clear during the late 1980s that many of the homeless in New York City had urgent psychiatric needs, Creedmoor established a special inpatient program of psychiatric rehabilitation intended specifically for the homeless. The Living Museum, presenting art by patients, was founded by Bolek Greczynski in 1984 in the hospital. In 2001 the city sold part of the mental hospital to residential developers and used another portion to develop three schools and athletic fields.

Sandra Opdycke

Creelman, James (*b* Montreal, 12 Nov 1859; *d* Berlin, 12 Feb 1915). News correspondent. He moved from Montreal to New York City in 1872 and worked for several newspapers, including the *Brooklyn Eagle* and the *New York Herald.* Creelman was considered a "yellow journalist," actively inputting his own opinion during interviews and articles and traveling to find and report on stories. He covered the tensions between Japan and China in 1894 for the *New York World.* William Randolph Hearst hired Creelman to cover the war between Cuba and Spain in 1898 for the *New York Journal.* He favored Cuba so strongly that he convinced the U.S. general in command to let him help American soldiers invade a Spanish blockhouse. Creelman was injured from gunfire during the invasion. He wrote editorials for the *World* until 1906 when he became a civil servant. He returned to the *Journal* to cover World War I and did so until his death. He wrote *On the Great Highway: The Wanderings and Adventures of a Special Correspondent* (1901).

Max Seppo

Cremin, Lawrence A(rthur) (*b* New York City, 31 Oct 1925; *d* New York City, 4 Sept 1990). Educator and historian. After graduating from Townsend Harris High School and City College he took his master's and doctoral degrees at Columbia University. He served as president of Teachers College at Columbia (1974–84), the Spencer Foundation (1985–90), the National Academy of Education (1969–73), the History of Education Society (1959–60), and the National Society of College Teachers of Education (1961–62). Among his many honors were a Guggenheim Fellowship (1957), the Bancroft Prize (1962), the award of the American Education Research Association (1969), and the Pulitzer Prize for history (1981). He wrote more than a dozen major books and was writing a biography of the educator John Dewey at the time of his sudden death of a heart attack. A lifelong resident of Manhattan, Cremin was the foremost historian of education in the United States.

Kenneth T. Jackson

cricket. Organized cricket in New York City began in 1838, with the founding of the St. George Cricket Club; in 1844 John Richards and William T. Porter formed the New York Cricket Club. English-born merchants, professionals, diplomats, and military officers dominated these clubs, but some native-born Americans also joined. From the mid-nineteenth century until the early twentieth, teams representing these and other organizations from Manhattan, Brooklyn, and Staten Island competed against teams from Boston, Philadelphia, and Newark, New Jersey. Several of the clubs from Manhattan established playing grounds in Staten Island and in or near Hoboken, New Jersey. The St. George Cricket Club arranged international contests that matched select teams from the United States against teams from Canada and England.

Cricket was eclipsed in popularity first as a team sport by baseball in the 1860s, then as a pastime for the elite by tennis and golf in the early twentieth century. After World War I, immigrants from Great Britain and its colonies kept cricket alive. In the early twenty-first century several thousand West Indians and other immigrants continued to pitch their wickets in public parks throughout the city.

Melvin Adelman, *A Sporting Time: New York City and the Rise of Modern Athletics, 1820–1870* (Urbana: University of Illinois Press, 1986); George B. Kirsch, *The Creation of American Team Sports: Baseball and Cricket, 1838–1872* (Urbana: University of Illinois Press, 1989)

George B. Kirsch

crime. A growth in crime during the eighteenth century paralleled the growth of New York City as a cosmopolitan center. Crime surged with the population and economic fluctuations of the 1730s and 1760s. The number of thefts and assaults rose as the city became more crowded: maritime trade brought more sailors to the city and more prostitution (often prosecuted as "keeping a disorderly house"). In general the legal system could not control crime, especially theft. RIOTS were tolerated as expressions of political discontent.

The crime rate remained low during the first two decades of the nineteenth century but rose rapidly from the 1820s when immigration and the growth of manufacturing and trade gave rise to ethnic and class tensions. Recent immigrants often fell prey to swindlers and were also blamed for disorderliness, public drunkenness, and more serious crimes; Irish immigrants who moved to the city in the 1840s were especially singled out. Temperance advocates tried to close saloons frequented by immigrants, especially the Irish, whose gangs often fought against nativist gangs. The number of murders per 100,000 inhabitants increased from 2.5 in the late 1840s and early 1850s to 4.4 in the 1850s and 1860s. In the middle of the century ethnic and racial hostility and economic inequities led to racist assaults on blacks and made riots more common and more dangerous. The worst riots in the history of the city were the DRAFT RIOTS of 1863, which began as a protest against the first federal conscription policies and degenerated into a race riot. During the second half of the century violent crime decreased owing to the ministrations of political machines, improved policing, and residents' adaptations to the strains and discipline of urban life; but vices such as prostitution and gambling flourished, often with the cooperation of the political machines. Most criminal operations were run by successive members of immigrant groups—at mid-century the Irish, and at the turn of the twentieth century Jews and Italians. Eventually moral reformers pressured government to control saloons, brothels, and gambling dens, which turned for protection to Tammany Hall and other political organizations. The red-light district in the city, the TENDERLOIN, became a national symbol of urban depravity that was widely depicted in novels and tabloid newspapers.

The number of murders declined by the turn of the twentieth century. Widely differing murder rates among whites and blacks continued to reflect economic disparities: the rates per 100,000 inhabitants for whites and blacks, respectively, were 3.7 and 9.8 in 1900, 5.1 and 21.7 in 1910, 5.0 and 23.0 in 1920, and 5.8 and 28.7 in 1930. Murders reached a peak during Prohibition, when violence worsened as crime GANGS were reorganized. As the gangs imported liquor and distributed it throughout the nation, they adopted conventional business techniques and redefined their relations with government; they continued to do so after the repeal of Prohibition in 1933. At the same time, organized crime in the city focused increasingly on narcotics, gambling, and waterfront racketeering. In 1935 acute economic trouble in black neighborhoods caused the murder rate among blacks to reach 35.1 citywide (compared with 4.3 per 100,000 for whites citywide).

During the 1960s New York City, like most American cities, witnessed a dramatic increase in violent crime. Riots in minority neighborhoods and the overrepresentation of blacks among criminals and victims inevitably linked discussions of crime and race, much as nineteenth-century New Yorkers had linked their crime problem to the Irish. The number of murders reached 1116 in 1969, after which the number remained above 1000 into the 1990s. People felt unsafe and routines of life changed. Many businesses retained private security guards, and features intended to thwart criminals became incorporated into the design of buildings. Signs reading "no radio" were routinely placed in the windows of automobiles to discourage thieves. Despite some fluctuations, crime continued to increase during the 1970s and 1980s, virtually overwhelming the municipal justice system. The number of reported incidents of rape nearly doubled, from 2141 in 1970 to 3875 in 1979 (perhaps in part because it became a crime that women were more willing to report). Other American cities had proportionately more crime, but New York City became a symbol of urban lawlessness because of its size and prominence. On average more than 1500 murders a year were committed during the 1970s and 1980s. The increase in the number of assaults, automobile thefts, and other thefts was linked to the abuse of drugs, especially heroin, cocaine, and crack cocaine, which became enduring features of urban life. Aided by the Racketeer Influenced and Corrupt Organizations (RICO) laws, federal law enforcement agencies continued to fight organized crime but could not extinguish it. Frustration with crime undermined the city's reputation for liberalism. In 1977 Edward I. Koch, a congressman from the East Side with a liberal voting record, was elected on a platform emphasizing law enforcement and the death penalty.

During the 1980s the boom on Wall Street created opportunities for corrupt practices like insider trading that led to prosecutions of prominent financial figures such as Ivan Boesky. Felonies remained a major concern of voters and politicians, but racial and ethnic divisions among New Yorkers prevented the formation of a united front against crime. Investigations of racial bias among police officers, and the racially motivated killings of black men in Howard Beach and Bensonhurst and of a Hasidic Jew in Crown Heights, elicited much controversy. In 1989 David N. Dinkins, a liberal black Democrat, was elected mayor after promising to be firm with criminals. His victory suggested that a stern attitude toward crime was widely shared by New Yorkers of all races. Dinkins expanded the police force and saw crime decline during his term in office, but he failed to increase his political base, suffered from the charge that he was indecisive, and battled with the police over departmental reforms. In 1993 he was

Homicides per 100,000 Residents in New York City, 1866–2009

Year	Homicide Rate
1866–70	4.0
1871–75	6.5
1876–80	4.8
1881–85	4.9
1886–90	4.5
1891–95	3.5
1896–1900	2.5
1901–5	3.8
1906–10	5.5
1911–15	5.8
1916–20	4.9
1921–25	5.4
1926–30	6.0
1931–35	7.4
1936–40	4.5
1941–45	3.5
1946–48	4.7
1949–51	4.0
1952–55	4.3
1956–60	4.7
1961–65	7.6
1966–70	12.6
1971–75	21.7
1976–80	23.5
1981–85	24.9
1986–90	25.4
1991–95	24.1
1996–2000	10.0
2001–5	7.4
2006–9	6.3

Number of Offenses Reported to Police in New York City, 1945–2008

Year	Murder	Rape	Robbery	Burglary	Theft	Automobile Theft
1945	292	N/A	1,417	4,348	11,981	12,226
1955	306	N/A	7,133	38,963	69,790	12,383
1960	435	841	6,597	36,049	88,176	21,069
1965	681	1,154	8,904	51,072	115,782	34,726
1966	734	1,761	25,539	120,903	163,683	44,914
1967	809	1,905	35,934	150,245	182,151	58,169
1968	976	1,840	54,405	173,559	216,245	77,448
1969	1,116	2,120	59,152	171,393	190,540	85,796
1970	1,201	2,141	74,102	181,694	193,005	94,835
1971	1,513	2,415	88,994	181,331	187,232	96,624
1972	1,757	3,271	78,202	148,046	134,664	75,865
1973	1,740	3,735	72,750	149,311	127,500	82,731
1974	1,607	4,054	77,940	158,321	163,157	73,731
1975	1,690	3,866	83,190	177,032	188,832	83,201
1976	1,647	3,400	86,183	195,243	232,069	96,682
1977	1,553	3,899	74,404	178,907	214,838	94,420
1978	1,503	3,882	74,028	164,447	200,110	83,112
1979	1,733	3,875	82,572	178,162	220,813	89,748
1980	1,812	3,711	100,550	210,703	249,421	100,478
1981	1,826	3,862	107,475	205,825	258,369	104,706
1982	1,668	3,547	95,944	172,794	264,400	107,430
1983	1,622	3,662	84,243	143,698	253,801	92,725
1984	1,450	3,829	79,540	128,687	250,759	88,478
1985	1,384	3,880	79,532	124,838	262,051	79,426
1986	1,582	3,536	80,827	124,382	281,713	85,853
1987	1,672	3,507	78,890	123,412	289,126	95,654
1988	1,896	3,412	86,578	127,148	308,479	119,940
1989	1,905	3,254	93,377	121,322	287,749	133,861
1990	2,245	3,126	100,280	119,937	268,620	147,123
1991	2,154	2,892	98,512	112,015	256,473	139,977
1992	1,995	2,815	91,239	103,476	236,169	126,959
1993	1,946	2,818	86,001	99,207	235,132	112,464
1994	1,561	2,666	72,540	88,370	209,808	95,420
1995	1,177	2,317	59,278	73,879	180,949	72,679
1996	983	2,332	49,672	61,270	162,246	60,379
1997	770	2,157	44,708	54,099	157,039	51,893
1998	633	2,046	39,359	46,185	147,018	44,056
1999	664	1,702	36,091	40,469	140,370	39,693
2000	673	1,630	32,558	37,112	139,661	35,846
2001	714*	1,664	30,520	34,432	146,112	32,628
2002	587	1,689	27,229	30,102	129,655	27,034
2003	597	1,609	25,989	28,293	124,846	23,628
2004	570	1,428	24,373	26,100	124,016	21,072
2005	539	1,412	24,722	23,210	120,918	18,381
2006	596	1,071	23,511	22,137	115,363	15,936
2007	496	875	21,787	20,914	115,318	13,256
2008	523	890	22,186	19,867	117,682	12,440

N/A = Not Available.

* This figure does not include the 2,823 homicides reported as a result of the terrorist attacks of 11 September 2001.

Source: U.S. Department of Justice, Bureau of Justice Statistics; Federal Bureau of Investigation, Uniform Crime Reports, http://www.fbi.gov/ucr/ucr.htm

Number of Homicides in New York City, 1960–2009

Year	Homicides
1960	390
1970	1,117
1980	1,812
1985	1,384
1986	1,582
1987	1,672
1988	1,896
1989	1,905
1990	2,262
1991	2,154
1992	1,995
1993	1,946
1994	1,561
1995	1,181
1996	1,030
1997	803
1998	629
1999	671
2000	673
2001	649
2002	587
2003	597
2004	570
2005	539
2006	596
2007	496
2008	523
2009	471

Sources: Federal Bureau of Investigation, "Crime in the United States: Uniform Crime Reports" (1999–2008) and "Uniform Crime Reports for the United States" (before 1999); New York Police Department weekly CompStat sheet, http://www.nyc.gov/html/nypd/downloads/pdf/crime_statistics/cscity.pdf (2009)

Compiled by Andrew A. Kryzak

defeated for reelection by Rudolph W. Giuliani, a former prosecutor who made fighting crime a major theme of his campaign.

The Giuliani administration combined strong support for the police with aggressive crime-fighting strategies that mixed active street-level enforcement with computerized statistical analysis of crime. Crime declined throughout Giuliani's two terms in office, but his mayoralty saw clashes over police shootings and charges of police brutality; his lack of close ties to the city's minority communities sharpened disputes when victims of police action were black or Hispanic.

When Giuliani left office in 2001, New York City led the nation in levels of crime reduction. The drop in crime confounded beliefs that policing had little effect on crime and that crime could not be reduced without addressing the "root causes" of crime in inequality. Crime continued to fall during the first and second terms of Giuliani's successor, Michael Bloomberg, who maintained the strategic approach to crime fighting that marked the Giuliani years but was more solicitous of black and Hispanic concerns in confrontations with police. In the twenty-first century New York City streets once known for fearsome levels of danger became dramatically safer.

Robert W. Snyder

Crimmins, John D(aniel) (*b* New York City, 18 May 1844; *d* New York City, 9 Nov 1917). Businessman and art collector. He was a partner in his family's firm, the Crimmins Company, which made a fortune in the construction of the Croton Aqueduct, the extended waterfront, sewers, gas mains, electric duct lines, streets, and elevated railways. From 1883 to 1887 Crimmins was the president of the Board of Commissioners of Public Parks of New York City, and he belonged to the Greater New York Charter Revision Commission of 1901; he was also on the boards of many financial institutions, including the New York Title and Mortgage Company, of which he was president from 1901 to 1914. A trustee of several cultural and charitable organizations, he also funded the building of St. Patrick's Cathedral's Chapel of St. Anne and in 1888 dedicated it to his late wife, Lily Lalor Crimmins. Crimmins had the most complete collection of maps and pictures of old New York City (about 5000 items), as well as a large collection of Gaelic manuscripts and books on Irish subjects. He wrote two books, *St. Patrick's Day: Its Celebration in New York and Other American Places, 1737–1845* (1902) and *Irish American Historical Miscellany* (1905).

Marion R. Casey

Cripplebush. Name applied to Williamsburg until the 1820s, centered around the intersection of Nostrand and Flushing avenues. The Dutch West India Company bought the land from the Canarsie tribe in 1638. The area was named for the thickets of scrub oak that proliferated until the American Revolution and which British troops harvested for fuel. The first school was established there in 1775. Farms were built after the war; the area remained sparsely populated.

James Bradley

Crisis. Monthly periodical. Launched in 1910 in New York City with W. E. B. Du Bois as editor, it became the official publication of the National Association for the Advancement of Colored People (NAACP). Du Bois covered activities of the association as well as incidents of antiblack discrimination; he also published articles by young black authors. Although Du Bois built a sizable circulation, his independent way of operating and certain viewpoints prompted criticism, which led to his resignation in 1934. The magazine has always kept its subscription prices extremely low. The NAACP continued to publish the *Crisis* into the early twenty-first century, focusing predominantly on issues of political and legal discrimination.

Elliott Rudwick, *W. E. B. Du Bois: Propagandist of the Negro Protest* (New York: Atheneum, 1968)

Seth M. Scheiner

Croatians. A Croatian community formed in New York City about 1888 and consisted mostly of young Dalmatian men who lived on the West Side in the area bounded by 48th Street, 10th Avenue, 34th Street, and 11th Avenue. Poor economic conditions, compulsory military service, and political unrest due to an increased Magyarization policy in Croatia also led men to move to New York City, where they found work as stevedores, longshoremen, tugboat crewmen, freight handlers, and railroad employees, often with the New York Central Railroad. They frequently lived as boarders with relatives or fellow villagers, or in cooperative households known as *društvo*. The weekly newspaper *Narodni List* (National Gazette) was launched by 1898 and published daily from 1902. A number of other newspapers were published at the time, including *Hrvatski Svijet* (Croatian World) and *Domovina* (The Homeland); they provided news of developments in Croatia and the United States, and their nationalistic editorial policies divided the community. Men often gathered at Croatian groceries, barber shops, and steamship agencies; Croatian saloons were the center of their social life, and saloon keepers acted as bankers, steamship agents, and subscription agents for Croatian newspapers.

Before World War I, Croatian immigrants were listed in immigration records as Austrians, Hungarians, Slovenians, or members of southern Slavic groups. In 1912 the Croatian population in Manhattan was estimated at between 2500 and 3000 and included few women and children and only 150 to 200 families; most were men between the ages of 17 and 45, 60 percent were from Dalmatia, few became American citizens, and nearly 50 percent returned to Croatia after saving money for their families. The war and the southern Slav unification movement in Croatia intensified nationalistic sentiments and led many Croatians to understand the importance of American citizenship and the vote. A Croatian Roman Catholic Church, Saints Cyril and Methodius, was formed in 1913 by the Franciscan Fathers to offer religious services in Croatian. The chuch was located at 552 West 50th Street from 1913 to 1974, when the congregation began to share space with the Irish Catholic parish of St. Raphael at 502 West 42nd Street. At the end of World War I rates of immigration and repatriation increased as news of American prosperity spread. The incorporation of Croatia into a kingdom dominated by Serbs led many Croatian immigrants to remain in the United States. In the following years immigration decreased after quotas were imposed and the economy declined. A few Croatians were drawn to the city for the World's Fair of 1939–40 and remained after the outbreak of World War II. The community in New York City became divided over the issue of support for the fascist Ustaša government of Ante Pavelic but reunited against the communist dictatorship of Josip Broz Tito after receiving reports of atrocities in Yugoslavia.

The political refugees who settled in the city after World War II were usually educated and led opposition to the Yugoslavian government. An educational organization known as the Croatian Academy of America was formed in 1953 to focus on Croatian history and culture and by 1960 published the *Journal of Croatian Studies*. The *Croatian Press* moved to the city in 1956 and became a leading proponent of Croatian independence. Croatians held liberation parades along Fifth Avenue, raised funds to repair churches and establish ambulatory services in Croatia, and also sent food, clothing, and medical supplies. At the same time a number of Croatian doctors settled in the city. Other immigrants found employment as kitchen workers, waiters, longshoremen, construction workers, and painters and often held two jobs; women worked in factories, cleaned offices, and took clerical positions. In many families both husband and wife worked, one during the day and the other at night if there were children, allowing them to buy homes in Brooklyn and Queens. After a failed attempt to separate from Yugoslavia in 1971, Croatian nationalists sought refuge in the United States, especially New York City: according to the 1980 census, 22,000 Yugoslavs lived there at the time. During the following decade the number who settled in the city declined to a few hundred a year.

In 2000 there were 12,000 Croatians living in New York City, most of them American citizens; the largest concentration was in Queens. Well-known Croatians in the city have included the artist Ivan Mestrovic, the opera singers Zinka Kunc-Milanov and Milka Trnina, and the conductor Ivan Cerovac.

Gerald Gilbert Govorchin, *Americans from Yugoslavia* (Gainesville: University of Florida Press, 1961); Frances Kraljic, *Croatian Migration to and from the United States, 1900–1914* (Palo Alto, Calif.: Ragusan, 1978); George J. Prpic, *South Slavic Immigration in America* (Boston: Twayne, 1978)

Frances Kraljic

Croker, Richard (*b* Blackrock, near Dublin, 24 Nov 1841; *d* Dublin, 29 April 1922). Powerful Tammany Hall political leader. He immigrated with his parents to New York City at age two. In his youth he was a machine-tool worker, earned a reputation as a fighter, and became the leader of the Fourth Avenue Tunnel Gang, which he used as a political base. He was elected an alderman in 1869 and held a series of appointed and elected city government offices until 1886, when he became the leader of the Democratic organization in New York County, known as Tammany Hall. His tenure was marked by widespread disclosures of political corruption that hurt his candidates. Revelations in 1894 by a state investigating committee that Tammany Hall had

Richard Croker

abused the Police Department cost it the mayoralty in 1895. An investigation in 1900 led to the election of the fusion candidate Seth Low as mayor in 1901 and weakened Croker's credibility. He ceased to lead Tammany Hall in 1902. By then a wealthy man, Croker retired to Ireland to breed horses and engage in philanthropy.

Alfred Henry Lewis, *Richard Croker* (New York: Life Publishing, 1901); M. R. Werner, *Tammany Hall* (New York: Doubleday, Doran, 1928); Theodore Lothrop Stoddard, *Master of Manhattan: The Life of Richard Croker* (New York: Longmans, Green, 1931)

Chris McNickle

Croly, Herbert (David) (*b* New York City, 23 Jan 1869; *d* Santa Barbara, Calif., 17 May 1930). Writer and magazine editor. Born to a middle-class family of New York City journalists (his parents were David Goodman Croly of the *New York World* and Jane Cunningham Croly of the *New York Herald* and the *New York World*), he learned the value of education and expertise as the foundation of social improvement. He promoted big government and labor unions, considering them an inevitable result of industrialization, and supported an interventionist foreign policy despite his disillusionment with the outcome of World War I. After attending City College and Harvard University, he returned to New York City in 1899 and became the editor of *Architectural Record.* In 1909 he wrote *The Promise of American Life,* in which he took issue with what he perceived as a Jeffersonian bias toward small-scale organization among American reformers. In 1914 he launched the *New Republic* with the help of a young Walter Lippmann. Croly remained editor of the magazine until his death.

David W. Levy, *Herbert Croly of the New Republic: The Life and Thought of an American Progressive* (Princeton, N.J.: Princeton University Press, 1985)

Lawson Bowling

Croly, Jane Cunningham [June, Jenny] (*b* Market Harborough, Leicestershire, England, 19 Dec 1829; *d* New York City, 23 Dec 1901). Journalist. She moved to New York State as a child and to New York City in 1855, where she remained for most of her life. Through her work for several newspapers she became well known as one of the first female syndicated columnists in the country; she also contributed regularly to the *New York World* and several popular periodicals. She formed Sorosis in 1868, one of the first women's clubs in the nation, and the General Federation of Women's Clubs in 1890, a national network of volunteer organizations. Her pen name, "Jenny June," recalls Fanny Fern, the pseudonym of antebellum female columnist Sarah Willis. *Memories of Jane Cunningham Croly, "Jenny June"* (1904) was compiled by friends after her death.

Karen J. Blair

Cromwell Recreation Center. Public park and recreation facility named for the first borough president of Staten Island, George Cromwell. Built by the Works Progress Administration on the northwestern coast of Staten Island from 1934 to 1936, the recreation center offers athletic, social, and educational activities, in addition to swimming off Cromwell Pier. Recent additions include gymnastics equipment, facilities for computer and photography classes, exercise rooms, and Staten Island's first sports gallery, in the center's lobby. An estimated 100,000 people use the center annually.

Ben Silk

Cross Land Savings Bank. Formed as the East Brooklyn Savings Bank by Samuel C. Barnes, it opened at Myrtle Avenue in Bedford (now Bedford–Stuyvesant) in 1860 and primarily served customers in the neighborhood. Its headquarters were moved to Bedford Avenue in 1922 and to Montague Street in Brooklyn Heights in 1962. The firm was renamed the Metropolitan Savings Bank in 1969 and acquired the Fulton Savings Bank in 1978, before merging with Brooklyn Savings Bank and Greenwich Savings Bank in 1981. It became a federal mutual savings bank in 1985, at which time it took its current name. By 1988 the bank had assets of more than $15 billion and was New York's largest savings bank, as well as a major lender in the city's commercial and residential real estate market. It was severely weakened by its large-scale investments in "junk bonds," leveraged buyouts, and real estate during the 1980s. The federal government seized control of the bank in January 1992 and renamed it the Crossland Federal Savings Bank. Many of the bank's housing projects were subsequently sold.

James Bradley

Crotona Park East. Neighborhood lying north of Hunts Point and east of Morrisania in the west central Bronx, bounded to the north by the Cross Bronx Expressway, to the east by the Bronx River, to the south by Westchester and Prospect avenues, and to the west by Crotona Park; it is sometimes considered part of Hunts Point and Morrisania (2000 combined pop. 68,574). The area was the site of large estates in the town of West Farms in Westchester County until it was annexed to New York City in 1874. Some sections were developed in the 1890s after trolley connections were built to the Third Avenue elevated line; the rest became densely covered by apartment buildings after the subway was extended in 1904. The population became predominantly Jewish, but there were also German, Irish, and Italian immigrants. During the 1950s an increasing number of blacks and Puerto Ricans settled there. By the 1970s the many burnt-out apartment buildings of the neighborhood became a national symbol of inner-city decay. Charlotte Street was visited by presidential candidates: Jimmy Carter in 1976 and Ronald Reagan in 1980. (Later, Bill Clinton visited in 1997.) With funds from public programs, one-family houses were built on Charlotte Street in the early 1980s, put up for sale in 1983, and first occupied in the summer of 1984. Other new housing was also built during the 1980s using funds from community groups and public programs. By the early twenty-first century most of the neighborhood had been rebuilt and had a suburban character.

Evelyn Gonzalez

Croton Aqueduct. The first public water supply for New York City. Opened in 1842, the Croton Aqueduct bought pure and ample water from a mainland watershed, ending the city's long reliance on inadequate and increasingly polluted well water. The aqueduct was conceived in 1832 after a cholera epidemic killed more than 3500 residents (one in 60). It was authorized by the state legislature (1834) and overwhelmingly approved in a referendum of city voters (1835). A state-appointed commission, led by former mayor Stephen Allen, supervised the project. David Bates Douglass conducted the original surveys of the Croton River and its tributaries in Westchester and Putnam counties and laid out the route of the aqueduct (1833–36); John Bloomfield Jervis perfected the engineering plans and oversaw construction (1836–42). A dam on the lower Croton River created a 500-million-gallon reservoir, from which an unpressurized conduit of brick and masonry, averaging 7.5 feet (2.3 meters) wide and 8.5 feet

Croton Aqueduct, 1893

(2.6 meters) high and laid mostly at or just below ground level, led the water by gravity south to the Harlem River. The High Bridge (completed 1848) carried the water in iron pipes onto rural upper Manhattan at what became 174th Street. The water continued in conduit or pipe to a 150-million-gallon receiving reservoir on open ground in what became Central Park between 79th and 86th streets; pipes carried the water down to a landmark 20-million-gallon distributing reservoir on high ground at the future intersection of Fifth Avenue and 42nd Street, then 1 mile (1.6 kilometers) north of the city limits. The total distance from dam to distributing reservoir was 40.5 miles (65.2 kilometers); a network of cast iron pipes distributed Croton water in the city. The completion of the aqueduct was commemorated with a citywide celebration in October 1842, one of the largest in the city's history. "Croton" became a byword for good water, and the aqueduct a model for American urban water supplies.

New Yorkers, formerly limited to a few daily pails of well water, became prodigious water users. As use rose beyond the aqueduct's daily capacity of 90 million gallons in the mid-1880s, work began on the New Croton Aqueduct, a pressurized tunnel three times the size of the old aqueduct and the world's longest and largest tunnel when completed (1893). The 240-foot (73-meter)–high New Croton Dam, the largest masonry dam in the world when opened (1905), submerged the original dam. New Croton water entered Manhattan in a pressure tunnel under the Harlem River. The addition of nine mainland reservoirs by 1911 increased the total daily supply of the Croton system to 400 million gallons and obviated the need for the original receiving reservoir (filled during the 1930s to become Central Park's Great Lawn) and the distributing reservoir (demolished during the 1890s to allow construction of the New York Public Library).

As the vast Catskill and Delaware aqueduct systems came into service during the twentieth century, the Old Croton was gradually cut back and stopped supplying water to the city (1955). It was designated a National Historic Landmark in 1992. In 2007 High Bridge, the city's oldest bridge, was in the early stages of rehabilitation as a park. The New Croton Aqueduct continues to supply 10 percent of the city's water.

Gerard T. Koeppel, *Water for Gotham: A History* (Princeton, N.J.: Princeton University Press, 2000); *Water-Works: The Architecture and Engineering of the New York City Water Supply*, ed. Kevin Bone (New York: Monacelli Press, 2006)

Gerard Koeppel

Crouch and Fitzgerald. Firm of luggage and leather-ware retailers, formed in 1839 by George Crouch as a harness and luggage maker. The firm achieved early success by supplying wood-framed leather trunks to traveling salesmen. By 1892 it had a factory on West 41st Street, three retail outlets in Manhattan, and 200 employees. In 1988 the firm was bought by Lenox, Inc., a division of the Brown–Forman Corporation.

Kenneth T. Jackson

Crow Hill. Former neighborhood in northeastern Brooklyn, stretching from the hills east of Prospect Park to East New York. According to folklore it was named for the largest hill in the area, which was infested with crows; the *Brooklyn Eagle* in 1873 suggested that the area was named for a settlement begun in the 1830s by blacks, who were called "crows" by whites. Many residents worked in the fish and meat markets in Manhattan and lived in shanties on the hill. As the city limits were extended and whites bought property in the area, blacks were forced out. The Kings County Penitentiary was built on the crest of Crow Hill after a land purchase in 1846; eventually considered a blight, the penitentiary was demolished in 1907 and the land became the site of Brooklyn Preparatory School and the Church of St. Ignatius Loyola. By a slight change of orthography, the area was renamed Crown Heights in the early twentieth century.

Ellen Marie Snyder-Grenier

Crown Heights. Neighborhood in west central Brooklyn, bounded to the north by Atlantic Avenue, to the east by Ralph Avenue, to the south by Empire Boulevard, and to the west by Washington Avenue. The first settlements in the area, Weeksville and Carrville, were formed by free blacks in the 1850s. Mansions were built after mid-century on former farmland in the northern section and were eventually followed by limestone row houses. The street grid was laid out in 1855 and Eastern Parkway was completed in 1874, facilitating the development of mansions, row houses, detached houses, and apartment buildings. Originally called Crow Hill, the name *Crown Heights* came into use in the early twentieth century. The construction of the Interborough Rapid Transit Company Eastern Parkway subway increased land values and expanded suburban development south of Eastern Parkway. But by the 1960s there was significant decay, and efforts to improve the neighborhood were made in the 1970s and 1980s; preservationists recognized the distinctive brownstones that marked the neighborhood.

Caribbean immigrants arrived in the area in the early twentieth century. In the 1920s German, Scandinavian, Irish, Italian, and Jewish immigrants also settled in the area in large numbers. The neighborhood attracted the Hasidic sect of Lubavitchers; by 1950 the neighborhood's population was half Jewish. After World War II many white residents moved to the suburbs, while Caribbeans and African Americans moved in. Tensions increased following an incident in 1991 in which an African American child was accidentally killed by an automobile driven by a Lubavitcher. A riot followed during which a visiting Lubavitcher was killed.

The principal thoroughfare of the neighborhood is Eastern Parkway; the main commercial districts center on Franklin, Nostrand, Kingston, and Utica avenues. The neighborhood is home to many cultural institutions and landmarks: Prospect Park (which borders it), the Brooklyn Museum, the Brooklyn Children's Museum, the Botanic Gardens, the central branch of the Brooklyn Public Library, the Society for the Preservation of Weeksville and Bedford–Stuyvesant History, and Medgar Evers College. The West Indian Day Parade held on Eastern Parkway every Labor Day is the largest parade in New York City, attracting millions of spectators. The

Lubavitch world headquarters are at 770 Eastern Parkway.

Ellen Marie Snyder-Grenier, Kate Lauber

Cruger, John (*b* Germany, *ca* 1680; *d* New York City, 13 Aug 1744). Mayor, father of John Cruger, Jr. He moved to New York City from Bristol, England, in 1698. After becoming successful as a shipper and slave trader, he won election as an alderman from the dock ward in 1712, a position he retained until 1735. Appointed mayor in 1739, he remained in office for five consecutive one-year terms. Cruger is remembered for having ruthlessly suppressed the "Negro plot" of 1741.

Thomas J. Davis, *A Rumor of Revolt: The "Great Negro Plot" in Colonial New York* (New York: Macmillan, 1985)

David William Voorhees

Cruger, John, Jr. (*b* New York City, 18 July 1710; *d* New York City, 27 Dec 1791). Mayor. A son of Mayor John Cruger, he was a New York City alderman from 1754 until being appointed mayor in 1756. In 1765, the last year of his tenure, he saw the city through the Stamp Act protests. Cruger was the last speaker of the provincial assembly, where he held a seat from 1759 to 1775. In 1768 he helped to organize the New York Chamber of Commerce and Industry, of which he was the first president.

David William Voorhees

Crystal Palace, ca *1853*

Crystal Palace. Cast-iron and glass building completed in 1853 on a site bounded to the north by 42nd Street, to the east by the Croton distributing reservoir, to the south by 40th Street, and to the west by Sixth Avenue. Designed by the architects Georg J. B. Carstensen and Charles Gildemeister, it was built in the shape of a Greek cross with a dome at its center and reputed to be fireproof. The building opened on 14 July 1853 as the site of the first World's Fair in the United States, an event entitled "Exhibition of the Industry of All Nations" that was inspired by the Great Exhibition at the Crystal Palace in London of 1851. The fair had more than 4000 exhibitors from around the world, of which those from the United States were the most numerous. Like its predecessors in London and Dublin (1852), the fair in New York City exhibited the products of agriculture and industry and housed a collection of sculpture; it was also the first World's Fair to exhibit paintings in a picture gallery. Although paid attendance at the exhibition exceeded one million, the sponsors were left with $300,000 in debt when the exhibition closed on 1 November 1854. In the following years space was leased out to various organizations for events such as one celebrating the laying of the transatlantic telegraph cable. The Crystal Palace caught fire on 5 October 1858 and was completely destroyed, purportedly within 15 minutes. Bryant Park was later developed on the site.

Charles Hirschfield, "America on Exhibition: The New York Crystal Palace," *American Quarterly* 9 (1957), 101–16; Ivan D. Steen, "America's First World's Fair: The Exhibition of the Industry of All Nations at New York's Crystal Palace, 1853–54," *New-York Historical Society Quarterly* 47 (1963), 257–87

I. Steen

Cuban Giants. Baseball team. Formed in the summer of 1885, it was the first black ball club to play professionally. Its amateur forerunners included the Brooklyn Uniques (in the late 1860s) and other teams that often played against white teams with support from wealthy sponsors, until a growing prohibition against interracial games took hold after Reconstruction. The founder of the Cuban Giants was Frank Thompson, the head waiter at the Argyle Hotel in Babylon, Long Island, and the players included a number of his fellow waiters. The name of the team was taken in the belief that the players would encounter less racial discrimination if they were thought to be foreigners, and for this reason they also spoke gibberish on the field. Bought by John L. Lang, who was white, soon after it was formed, the team achieved a record in 1885 of six wins, two losses, and one tie. George Williams, Abe Harrison, and Shep Trusty were signed by Lang from the Philadelphia Orions and helped the Cuban Giants to become the best black team before 1890. Lang then sold the team to another white man, Walter Cook, who engaged a black manager, S. K. Govern. Salaries typically ranged from $10 a week for pitchers and catchers to $12 a week for outfielders; white major leaguers earned about $50 a week at the time. In the first Colored Championships of America in New York City in 1888, the Cuban Giants finished first and the New York Gorhams third. After the Cuban Giants moved to Pennsylvania and became the York Monarchs, there emerged a new team called the Cuban Giants (later the Genuine Cuban Giants); another team with a similar name, the Cuban X Giants, was formed by E. B. Lamar and won the Colored Championships in 1895 against the Page Fence Giants.

Solomon White, *Sol. White's Official [Negro] Base Ball Guide* (Philadelphia: n.pub. [Camden House], 1907); Robert Peterson, *Only the Ball Was White* (Englewood Cliffs, N.J.: Prentice Hall, 1970); Arthur Ashe, *A Hard Road to Glory* (New York: Amistad/Warner, 1988)

Arthur Ashe

Cubans. A few Cuban immigrants settled in New York City during the 1870s and 1880s. Most had fled the Cuban struggle for independence from Spain, were Catholic, and worked in cigar factories opened by fellow immigrants. The most important member of this community was José Martí, a writer, politician, and leader of the Cuban independence movement who escaped prison in Spain and moved to the city in 1880. Living among tobacco workers, he continued to lead the independence movement, formed the Partido Revolucionario Cubano in 1892, gave the order to resume hostilities against Spain in 1895, and left the city to join the battle. During the 1940s and 1950s musicians such as Machito, his wife, Graciella, and her brother Mario Bauzá introduced Afro-Cuban jazz to the city, which profoundly influenced such jazz musicians as Dizzy Gillespie. Immigration from Cuba reached a peak between 1959 and 1962, when 155,000 members of the Cuban elite fled Fidel Castro's communist government. The New York City area was the second-most popular destination (after southern Florida), a pattern that held during an influx of white-collar and unskilled workers between 1962 and 1973. During the early 1970s between 12 and 13 percent of the Cuban immigrants who moved to the United States settled in the city. After declining in the mid-1970s, Cuban immigration increased during the 1980s and early 1990s, when more than 5000 Cubans settled in New York City, about 4 percent of all those who moved to the United States. The cigar factories eventually closed and unemployment among Cubans rose above the national average, but many family businesses were successful, among them restaurants popular for their fish, pork, and chicken dishes accompanied by rice and black beans. Although known to be sometimes divided by racial antagonism, the Cuban community in New York City is conspicuously tight-knit and politically conservative. The largest Cuban neighborhoods in the early twenty-first century were Washington Heights, Morris Heights, Crown Heights, East Flatbush, Astoria, Elmhurst, and Jackson Heights. In 2000 Cubans were the 26th-largest foreign-born population in New York City.

Chad Ludington

Cullen, Countee (Porter) (*b* New York City, 30 May 1903; *d* New York City, 9 Jan 1946). Poet and novelist. After graduating from DeWitt Clinton High School in the Bronx, he earned his bachelor's degree from New York University and a master's degree from Harvard University in 1926. He worked briefly as an assistant editor of *Opportunity: A Journal of Negro Life* before winning a Guggenheim fellowship to travel in France, where he wrote *Black Christ and Other Poems* (1929) and the novel *One Way to Heaven* (1932). In 1934 he returned to New York City, where he taught at Frederick Douglass Junior High School and wrote until the end of his life. A branch library and a school in Harlem are named for him.

Margaret Perry, *A Bio-Bibliography of Countee P. Cullen* (Westport, Conn.: Greenwood, 1971)

See also Harlem Renaissance.

James E. Mooney

Cullen, Michael J(oseph) (*b* Newark, N.J., 10 April 1884; *d* Queens, 24 April 1936). Businessman. He worked as a clerk in an A&P store in Newark from 1902 until 1919, when he moved to the Midwest to work for other grocery chains. He developed a plan for selling food on a large scale, but his attempts to have it put into effect were rebuffed in 1929 by Kroger (a grocery chain for which he worked as a manager in Illinois) and then by A&P. In August 1930 he opened King Kullen, the country's first supermarket, in a garage at 171-06 Jamaica Avenue in Queens. The store attracted customers by offering ample parking and merchandise in convenient displays. The business controlled expenses by keeping furnishings to a minimum and emphasizing self-service. Cullen called himself the "world's greatest price wrecker," advertised in newspapers, and distributed circulars that read "Save, Save, Save . . . Low, Low, Low Prices." By 1932 he had eight supermarkets that earned $6 million a year in sales.

John J. Concannon

Culver Line. Railway incorporated in 1869 as the Prospect Park and Coney Island Railroad by the lawyer Andrew R. Culver, to whom the state legislature granted permission to build a line along McDonald Avenue from Ninth Avenue and 20th Street in Park Slope to Gravesend. Culver proceeded to consolidate a route to the beachfront at Coney Island by successively leasing Gravesend Road, buying out the Coney Island Bridge Company, and then buying out a horse-car line on Vanderbilt Avenue (1871) to gain access to downtown Brooklyn. In June 1875 he opened a steam line that popularized the day excursion to Coney Island and transported as many as 20,000 passengers each Sunday. The line was extended to Norton's Point in 1879, and during the 1880s patrons were attracted by the addition of parlor cars and a newly constructed pier and observatory at Coney Island. In 1885 the Long Island Rail Road (LIRR) permitted Culver to run trains from Parkville to the 65th Street ferry terminal over its tracks in Bay Ridge, and in 1889 the Brooklyn Union Elevated Railroad permitted the connection of the line to the elevated terminus at Fifth Avenue and 36th Street; to make this connection the Culver Extension was built over the West End line from McDonald Avenue to Fifth Avenue and 37th Street. Service began in June 1890, and the extension was soon the most heavily used section of the line. In January 1893 Culver sold the line to the LIRR, and in August 1895 its president, Austin Corbin, arranged with Brooklyn Union Elevated to run elevated trains on both the Culver Line and the Culver Extension, making the entire system a continuous rapid transit line. Despite these developments the line lost money in the 1890s. In 1899 it was electrified: elevated trains on Fifth Avenue ran to 36th Street on power from a third rail, and then to Coney Island on trolley wire. In 1902 the line was leased and then sold to the Brooklyn Rapid Transit Company. It was completely integrated into the rapid transit system in 1919, when the entire line from Ninth Avenue to Coney Island was elevated and converted to operate with Fourth Avenue subway trains. In 1954 a connection was built between Church and Ditmas avenues, integrating the Culver Line into the Independent Subway System.

Vincent Seyfried

Cummings, E(dward) E(stlin) (*b* Cambridge, Mass., 14 Oct 1894; *d* North Conway, N.H., 3 Sept 1962). Poet. Educated at Cambridge University, he drove an ambulance in France during World War I and later moved to New York City, settling in Greenwich Village; he made extended trips to Paris and to New Hampshire, where he wrote and painted. After returning from travels in Europe in 1923 he moved to quarters at 4 Patchin Place in Greenwich Village that he retained for the rest of his life. Cummings's poetry was highly personal; he saw conventional capitalization and punctuation as impediments to expression and generally eschewed them in his poems (he also omitted capital letters from his name). Because publishers often rejected his work, he used family money to produce his first collections *W* (1931), *no thanks* (1935), and *Is 5* (1926) and the play *Him* (1927). He received the Dial Award in 1925 and became well known during the 1950s when he was elected to the National Institute of Arts and Letters and published *95 Poems* (1958).

Norman Friedman, *E. E. Cummings: The Growth of a Writer* (Carbondale: Southern Illinois University Press, 1964)

James E. Mooney

Cunard Line. First transatlantic passenger line. An English company formed in 1840 by Samuel Cunard (1787–1865), of Nova Scotia, its first scheduled trips connected England with Halifax, Nova Scotia, and with Boston. The company chose New York City in 1847 as its western terminal port and later occupied offices at the Cunard Building, 25 Broadway (built 1921). The steamers of the Cunard Line were at first recognizable by their assonant names: the *Britannia* (its first steamer), the *Mauritania* (built in 1907 and long known as the "speed queen" of the Atlantic), and the *Lusitania* (sunk by a German U-boat in 1915 off the coast of Ireland). Perhaps its best-known ships were the *Queen Mary,* the *Queen Elizabeth,* the *Queen Elizabeth II,* and the *Queen Mary II.* The first *Queen Mary* arrived in New York City in 1936 and gained an enduring popularity for its speed, service, and beautiful interiors. It carried soldiers between New York City and the United Kingdom during World War II and later resumed commercial service from New York City. The flagship of Cunard after 2004 was the superliner *Queen Mary II,* which sailed between New York City and the Caribbean during the winter and across the Atlantic during the summer. In 2005 Carnival Cruise Lines took over the Cunard Line but continued to operate the cruise ships *Queen Mary II, Queen Elizabeth II,* and *Queen Victoria* under the Cunard name.

Francis Edwin Hyde, *Cunard and the North Atlantic, 1840–1973: A History of Shipping and Financial Management* (London: Macmillan, 1975)

Frank O. Braynard

Cunningham, Merce (*b* Centralia, Wash., 16 April 1919; *d* New York City, 26 July 2009). Dancer and choreographer. After moving to New York City he was a principal dancer in Martha Graham's company from 1939 to 1945. In 1942 he began collaboration with the composer John Cage that lasted until Cage's death in 1992. The two performed together in the city in 1944 and were commissioned by Lincoln Kirstein in 1947 to create *The Seasons* (sets and costumes by Isamu Noguchi), performed by the Ballet Society (forerunner of the New York City Ballet). In the early 1950s Cage began radical, influential experiments in which random methods such as tossing coins were used to determine musical pitch, duration, and dynamics. Cunningham also began to use such processes for choreographic elements like sequence, the number of dancers involved, and their location in space. Another cardinal principle of their aesthetic was that the music and the dance should be independent of one another. Merce Cunningham Dance Company was formed in the summer of 1953 at Black Mountain College in North Carolina and has since been based in New York City. The original members included Carolyn Brown, Viola Farber, Remy Charlip, and Paul Taylor (dancers), Cage (music director), and David Tudor (composer and pianist); later members included the painters Robert Rauschenberg (resident designer, 1954–64), Jasper Johns (artistic adviser, 1967–84), and Mark Lancaster (artistic adviser, 1980–85). Cunningham also collaborated with many other visual artists, including Frank Stella, Andy Warhol, Robert Morris, and Bruce Nauman, as well as with the composers Morton Feldman, Earle Brown, Christian Wolff, David Behrman, John King, and Takehisa Kosugi, who was appointed music director in 1995. In the early 1970s Cunningham began making choreography specifically for the camera in conjunction with filmmakers Charles Atlas and later Elliot Caplan. These works were later adapted for the stage, notably *Channels/Inserts* (1981) and *Points in Space* (1986). Both have produced documentaries: *Cage/Cunningham* (Caplan, 1991) and *Merce Cunningham: A Lifetime of Dance* (Atlas, 2001). In 2003 the company celebrated its 50th anniversary; in those 50 years Cunningham created upward of 150 works.

Merce Cunningham

James Klosty, ed., *Merce Cunningham* (New York: Saturday Review Press, 1975; rev. Limelight, 1986); David Vaughan, *Merce Cunningham/Fifty Years* (New York: Aperture, 1997)

David Vaughan

CUNY. See City University of New York.

Cuomo, Mario M(atthew) (*b* Queens, 15 June 1932). Governor. The son of Italian immigrants, he attended St. John's University Law School and was admitted to the bar in 1956. He worked for liberal causes, defended community groups, and proved an adept mediator during a dispute over low-income housing in Forest Hills in the 1960s. Appointed secretary of state of New York by Governor Hugh L. Carey in 1975, Cuomo investigated abuses in nursing homes and negotiated solutions to various disputes on the governor's behalf. In 1977 he was persuaded by Carey to seek the mayoralty of New York City, but lost the Democratic primary to Edward I. Koch, whom Carey supported in the general election—even though Cuomo remained on the ballot as the candidate of the Liberal Party. During Carey's second term (1979–83), Cuomo served as lieutenant governor. Cuomo sought the governorship when Carey declined to seek reelection in 1982, defeating Koch in the Democratic primary and the Republican businessman Lewis Lehrman in the general election. As governor, Cuomo was an independent thinker and eloquent speaker who differed with his own (Catholic) church by favoring abortion rights and with a large segment of the electorate by opposing the death penalty. He was reelected to the governorship by overwhelming margins in 1986 and 1990. Widely regarded as a prospective candidate for the presidency, he spent a good deal of time in 1991 considering whether to mount a campaign before deciding to remain in Albany. In 1994 he was defeated in his attempt to win a fourth consecutive term. After 1995 Cuomo became of counsel to the corporate and financial services department and litigation department of Willkie Farr and Gallagher LLP in New York City.

Robert S. McElvaine, *Mario Cuomo: A Biography* (New York: Charles Scribner's Sons, 1988)

Leslie Gourse

Curb. Original name of the American Stock Exchange.

curling. Game of Scottish origin in which a disc of stone or iron is slid toward a target by two teams of four players each. It became popular in New York City during the late nineteenth century. Among the many clubs formed, the best known was the New York Caledonian Curling Club, which had headquarters on Sullivan Street; others included the St. Andrew's Curling Club, the New York Thistle Curling Club, and the Brooklyn Caledonian Curling Club. Matches were often held on Central Park Lake, and the Grand National Curling Club championships attracted crowds from throughout the Northeast. In Brooklyn matches were held at Prospect Park Lake. Curling was soon eclipsed in popularity by baseball and other sports.

Curling match, 1870

James Bradley

Currier and Ives. Firm of lithographers, formed in New York City in 1857. Its elder partner was Nathaniel Currier (*b* Roxbury [now in Boston], 27 March 1813; *d* New York City, 20 Nov 1888), who served an apprenticeship in Boston with the lithography firm of William and John Pendleton before settling in New York City, where he was in business as N. Currier by 1835. Originally he was a job printer who produced tickets, billheads, flyers, and certificates commissioned by others; one highly successful image was *Awful Conflagration of the Steam Boat Lexington,* a dramatic scene of the disaster of January 1840 that appeared in editions of the *Sun.* About 1840 Currier put into effect a plan to produce and market works by his own firm. Among the decorative and timely lithographs that he offered were *City Hotel: Broadway, New York, Jenny Lind: Als Tochter des Regiments,* and a temperance caricature, *The Drunkard's Progress.* In 1852 Currier engaged as his bookkeeper James Merritt Ives (*b* New York City, 5 March 1824; *d* Rye, N.Y., 3 Jan 1895), who proved an indispensable businessman and became a partner. The firm of Currier and Ives had two main locations in lower Manhattan, at Nassau Street and 33 Spruce Street, near Gold Street.

During the following decades the firm of Currier and Ives virtually abandoned job printing and focused on providing reasonably priced decorative images to the general public. The firm's work displayed little artistic or technical superiority, but its skill at marketing enabled it to become the most successful lithography firm in the United States. Currier and Ives's huge inventory of about 7000 titles included sporting prints (such as *The Yacht Dauntless of N.Y.* and *Mr. William H. Vanderbilt's Celebrated Team Small Hopes and Lady Mac: Driven by their Owner*), views (*Great East River Suspension Bridge, Central Park, the Drive, The Narrows from Staten Island,* and *New York and Brooklyn*), comic series (*Life in New York*), fashion prints (*The Grecian Bend: Fifth Avenue Style*), romantic images (*The Belle of New York*), and political portraits (*Hon. Wm. A. Wheeler: of New York*). Among the artists whose works the firm reproduced were Louis Maurer, James Buttersworth (who specialized in depicting ships), George Henry Durrie (who made country scenes, especially seasonal ones), and Fanny Palmer (who made still lifes and rural views). The best-known lithographers employed by the firm were James Cameron and Napoleon Sarony.

Currier retired in 1880, and under Ives's direction the firm worked in chromolithography until 1888. Both men are buried in Green-Wood Cemetery in Brooklyn. The business closed in 1907. After World War I businessman Harry Peters formed a major collection of the work of Currier and Ives: his collection is now held by the Museum of the City of New York. Other important holdings are at the Library of Congress and the New-York Historical Society.

Harry T. Peters, *Currier and Ives: Printmakers to the American People* (Garden City, N.Y.: Doubleday, Doran, 1929); Bernard F. Reilly, Jr., introd., *Currier and Ives: A Catalogue Raisonné* (Detroit: Gale Research, 1984)

Wendy Shadwell

Curry, John F(rancis) (*b* Ireland, 2 Nov 1873; *d* Coral Gables, Fla., 25 April 1957). Tammany Hall political leader. After election to the state assembly in 1902, he became the leader of his district on the West Side in 1905 and commissioner of records (1911–29). Long at odds with the "new Tammany," he was elected by his colleagues to lead Tammany Hall in 1929, with the backing of Mayor James J. Walker and powerful Tammany politician James J. Hines. In 1931 he refused to waive immunity during the investigation of municipal government led by Samuel Seabury. His fatal mistake was to try to block the nominations of Franklin D. Roosevelt for president and Herbert H. Lehman for governor in 1932. In the following year the mayoral candidate whom he backed, John P. O'Brien, was defeated; Curry was himself ousted from the leadership of Tammany Hall in 1934.

Frank Vos

Curtis, George William (*b* New York City, 24 Feb 1824; *d* New York City, 31 Aug 1892). Writer, editor, and reformer. After a youth spent in New England and abroad he returned in 1850 to New York City and began a career in book publishing and journalism at a time when the city was increasingly dominating the fields. He first gained recognition for a series of popular travel narratives and social satires, including *Nile Notes of a Howadji* (1851), *The Potiphar Papers* (1853), and *Prue and I* (1856). During the mid-1850s he edited the short-lived but influential *Putnam's Monthly* with his friend Frederick Law Olmsted and began an association with the leading publishing house Harper and Brothers that lasted for 35 years. From his office in the Harper Building on Franklin Square and more often from his suburban villa on Staten Island, he composed monthly essays for *Harper's New Monthly Magazine* under the rubric "Editor's Easy Chair" (1854–92), a series of moral and social sketches entitled "Manners upon the Road" for *Harper's Bazar* (1867–73), and the editorial columns for *Harper's Weekly* (from 1863 until his death). In his writings he advocated woman suffrage and attacked high tariffs and patronage politics; he also led the campaign for a professional civil service and was the president of the National Civil Ser-

Currier and Ives, The Age of Brass *(1869; also known as* The Triumph of Woman's Rights)

Currier and Ives, The Age of Iron *(1869)*

vice Reform League during 1881–92. With E. L. Godkin at the *Nation,* Curtis was a powerful shaper of elite public opinion during the Gilded Age. His career exemplified the close links between professional journalism, literary culture, commerce, and public activism among upper-class intellectuals in the late nineteenth century. Curtis High School in Staten Island is named after him.

Edward Cary, *George William Curtis* (Boston: Houghton Mifflin, 1894); Gordon Milne, *George William Curtis and the Genteel Tradition* (Bloomington: Indiana University Press, 1956)

See also INTELLECTUALS.

David Scobey

Curtis High School. First secondary school opened in St. George, Staten Island, in 1904 at Hamilton Avenue and St. Mark's Place. Named after the editor, writer, and reformer George William Curtis, it was the first public high school in Staten Island. In 1982 the school was designated a New York City landmark. As of 2007 it had 2600 students and offered programs in fashion design, theater arts, computer science, and international service as well as an international baccalaureate degree.

Erica Judge

Cushman, Charlotte (Saunders) (*b* Boston, 23 July 1816; *d* Boston, 18 Feb 1876). Actress. She made her debut in New York City as Lady Macbeth (1836) and in several appearances abroad became the first American-born actress to earn an international reputation. She gave successful performances in many roles in 1871 at Booth's Theatre on the corner of West 23rd and Sixth Avenue (1869–83, demolished in 1965). She also gave her farewell performance as Lady Macbeth on 7 November 1874 at Booth's.

Don B. Wilmeth

Cushman, Don Alonzo (*b* Coventry, Conn., 1 Oct 1792; *d* New York City, 1 May 1875). Businessman. He made his fortune in wholesale dry-goods trade during the 1820s. In 1830 he purchased a sizable piece of land at what is now 172 Ninth Avenue in Chelsea and built a house that still stands. He later became a principal developer of the area and built several buildings, a handful of which survive in the twenty-first century. Cushman was a leading member of both Trinity Church and St. Peter's Church, founder of the Greenwich Savings Bank, and director of the Erie Railway Company. Cushman Row (406–18 West 20th Street), a series of four-story Greek Revival buildings, built in 1840, and the residential Donac apartment building (402 West 20th Street), built in 1898, are named for him. He was the great-grandfather of J. Clydesdale Cushman, who cofounded the global real estate service company Cushman and Wakefield.

Val Ginter

Custom House. See U.S. CUSTOM HOUSE.

Cutter, Bloodgood H(aviland) (*b* Little Neck [now in Queens], 5 Aug 1817; *d* Queens, 26 Sept 1906). Poet. Born to a long-established Flushing family, he was the master of a coastal schooner before inheriting his grandfather's estate, settling into the life of a gentleman farmer; in 1840 he married Emmaline Allen, daughter of a prosperous Little Neck farmer. Known as the Long Island Farmer Poet, he penned verse for any and all occasions; several refer to incidents of the Civil War. His best-known include "On Laying the Corner Stone of the Town Hall at Flushing, Long Island," "To the Health Authorities of Naples," "On Tobacco Smoking in Queens County Court House," and "Spare That Cottage." Cutter's 500-page collection, *The Long Island Farmer's Poems,* appeared in 1886. He was the "poet lariat" in *Innocents Abroad* (1869) by Mark Twain, who described his verse as "barbarous rhyme." Cutter is buried in Zion Episcopal Church in Douglaston, Queens, and left the bulk of his $1.5 million estate to the American Bible Society.

Jeffrey A. Kroessler

cycling. See BICYCLE MESSENGERS; BICYCLE RACING; and BICYCLING.

Cyclone. Roller coaster at Astroland Amusement Park at Coney Island. The site had previously been occupied by the first modern roller coaster, the Switchback Railway, as well as the world's first successful looping roller coaster, Loop the Loop. The Cyclone opened on 26 June 1927; it was designed by Vernan Keenan and built by Harry Baker. The wooden structure had steel tracks over a distance of 1.6 miles (2.6 kilometers) with a ride time of one minute and 50 seconds and a 24-person seating capacity. Its first owners, Jack and Irving Rosenthal, passed operation to Chris Feuchts, and he to the city. It was operated for some time by the city's Parks Department until the new owners of Astroland Park, Dewey and Jerome Alberts, were authorized to operate the coaster in 1975; major renovations were done that year. The Cyclone was designated a New York City landmark in 1988 and was added to the National Register of Historic Places in 1991. In 2002 the ride celebrated its 75th anniversary. Astroland closed in 2008 and so too did the famed Cyclone.

Jessica Montesano

Cypress Hills. Neighborhood in northeastern Brooklyn, lying on a terminal moraine and bounded to the north by the Queens county line, to the east by Eldert Lane, to the south by Atlantic Avenue, and to the west by Pennsylvania Avenue. It was called Union Place after a local racecourse during the 1820s before being renamed for the trees growing on hills in the area. To the north lie Highland Park and 18 cemeteries that contain the graves of 20,000 veterans from the Civil War and later wars, as well as those of Harry Houdini, Mae West, Edward G. Robinson, and Sholem Aleichem. Cypress Hills residents are predominantly working class, and the housing consists of one-, two-, and three-family structures; Fulton Street is the main commercial thoroughfare.

Alter Landesman, *A History of New Lots, Brooklyn to 1887* (Port Washington, N.Y.: Kennikat, 1977)

John J. Gallagher

Cypriots. Cypriots first immigrated to the United States during the early twentieth century; they entered through Ellis Island, and the great majority settled in New York City. Large numbers followed in the 1950s, and many Greek Cypriots arrived after the Turkish invasion of Cyprus in 1974. Greek Cypriots initially settled in Manhattan and later moved to Queens, New Jersey, and Long Island. They formed many cultural organizations under the auspices of the Cyprus Federation of America (1951), as well as three Greek Cypriot community centers in Astoria. Their high level of education enabled Greek Cypriots to rise socially and economically along with other Greek Americans. Turkish Cypriots settled at first in the Bronx and formed the Turkish-Cypriot Aid Society (1931) and the Inonou School (1979) to teach Turkish language and culture to children. In later years a number of Turkish Cypriots moved to Queens, upstate New York, and New Jersey.

Antonia S. Mattheou

Czechs. Czech immigrants, originally known as Bohemians after the medieval kingdom that became part of the Austrian Empire, began arriving in New York City in large numbers during the middle of the nineteenth century. Although not a Czech major center like Chicago, New York was the only coastal city with a significant Czech population, numbering almost 41,000 at its peak in 1910. The first wave of immigrants settled on Manhattan's Lower East Side, where Avenue B was known as the Czech Boulevard. An estimated 75 percent of these immigrants worked as cigar makers living in the city's slums, whose wretched living conditions were depicted in Jacob Riis's landmark photojournalistic study *How the Other Half Lives* (1890). In the 1880s the factories and their workers began to relocate to the Upper East Side of Manhattan, transforming the area between 65th and 78th streets from Second Avenue to the East River into a Czech enclave. Czech immigrants also dominated the pearl button industry, which used a manufacturing process invented in Bohemia. By 1920 there were 19 pearl button manufacturers in Manhattan, 12 in Winfield (now part of Woodside) in Queens, and seven in Astoria. In addition, Czech tradespeople worked as furriers, piano makers, brewers, stonecutters, and metalworkers. During World War I the Czech community supported the drive for an independent Czechoslovakia led by the émigré politician and future president Tomáš Masaryk, whose wife, Charlotte Garrigue, was a Brooklyn native. After the creation of this new country in 1918, the term *Czech* to designate the immigrant community replaced the older usage *Bohemian*. Although the golden age of Czech immigration ended in 1930, the turbulent history of Czechoslovakia, especially the Nazi occupation in 1939, the communist coup in 1948, and the Soviet invasion in 1968, brought fresh waves of immigrants. In the 2000 census 18,813 inhabitants of New York City listed their ancestry as Czech or Czechoslovakian.

Although most Czech immigrants were Roman Catholic, Free Thought flourished among them before World War I, and others became Protestant. The Jan Hus Presbyterian Church at 351 East 74th Street, named after the fifteenth-century Czech martyr, had a Neighborhood House that served the Czech community for more than 50 years. In addition to religious institutions, club life flourished. The gymnastic club Sokol (Falcon), founded in 1867 as part of a Prague-based movement, erected a training hall in 1896 at 420 East 71st Street that remains its headquarters in the twenty-first century. In 1892 a socialist gymnastic club originated in New York City called the Workers–American Sokol, and in 1909 a Catholic gymnastic club called Orel (Eagle) was founded as an affiliate of an organization in the Czech lands. In 1894 the Bohemian Benevolent and Library Association, an umbrella organization of various Czech clubs, built the Bohemian National Hall at 321 East 73rd Street, a grand structure featuring a ballroom, library, and numerous meeting rooms. Owned by the Czech Republic in the twenty-first century, it is being refurbished to house the country's Consulate-General, a government-run cultural organization called the Czech Center, and other facilities. The Bohemian Hall and Park, completed in 1919 at 29-19 24th Avenue in Astoria, Queens, is still run by the Bohemian Citizens Benevolent Society of Astoria and boasts the only original outdoor beer hall in the city.

Czechs were especially prominent in the musical life of the city, among them Antonín Dvořák, who lived at 327 East 17th Street from 1892 to 1895 when he was director of the National Conservatory of Music; the soprano Emma Destinn (Ema Destinnová), who starred at the Metropolitan Opera for eight seasons until 1916; Jarmila Novotná, another soprano who headlined in the same house from 1940 until her retirement in 1956; and the pianist Rudolf Firkušný, who settled in the city in 1940 and taught at the Juilliard School.

Thomas Capek, *The Czech (Bohemian) Community of New York* (New York: Czechoslovak Section of America's Making, 1921); Vratislav Bušek and Ján Shintay, "The Czechs and Slovaks of New York," *Panorama: A Historical Review of Czechs and Slovaks in the United States of America* (Cicero, Ill.: Czechoslovak National Council of America, 1970), 18–29

Claire E. Nolte

D

Daché, Lilly (*b* Beigles, France, ?1892; *d* Louvecienne, France, 31 Dec 1989). Milliner. At the age of 14 she left school to assist her aunt, a milliner, and after an apprenticeship in Paris she moved to the United States in 1924. She began by selling hats at R. H. Macy and soon was able to open her own shop, where she introduced one of her signature designs, a hat molded snugly to the head. In 1937 she moved into a building on East 57th Street that served as her work studio, sales floor, and home. She created custom hats for fashionable customers, including many film stars, and also began selling ready-to-wear hats through department stores. Her turban, snood, and war worker's hats were among her most famous designs. As her store became more successful, she expanded her design repertory to include gloves, lingerie, dresses, perfumes, and men's shirts and ties. When she retired in 1968 her daughter Suzanne pursued millinery in her stead. Daché wrote *Talking through My Hats* (1946) and *Glamour Book* (1956).

Anne E. Kornblut

D'Agostino. Firm of food retailers. It was formed by brothers Nicola and Pasquale D'Agostino, who moved to New York City from Abruzzi, Italy, in 1921. The brothers became pushcart peddlers and later worked in a butcher shop. In 1932 they combined several specialized food shops into one emporium at Lexington Avenue and 83rd Street that was a forerunner of the modern supermarket. After Pasquale died in 1960, Nicola retired four years later and passed the business on to his sons. In 1986 Nicholas D'Agostino, Jr., became chairman of the board; Nicholas D'Agostino III, the son of Nicholas, Jr., was named president and chief operating officer during the same year. The supermarket had 26 locations in New York City and Westchester County in the early twenty-first century.

Mary Elizabeth Brown

Dahesh Museum of Art. Art museum. The Dahesh Museum of Art has its origins in the collection of Salim Moussa Achi, a Lebanese writer and philosopher who was known by his pen name as Dr. Dahesh, which means "wonder" in Arabic. For 50 years Dahesh, the leader of a universalist religious movement called Daheshism, collected paintings, sculptures, drawings, and other artworks by nineteenth- and twentieth-century European artists with academic training, with the intention of eventually creating a museum to show his collection. When the Lebanese Civil War began in 1975, Dahesh moved his home and vast art collection to suburban Greenwich, Connecticut. He died there in 1984 and willed the collection to the Zahid family, who incorporated the Dahesh Museum of Art in 1987. In 1995 the Dahesh Museum officially opened in a small gallery space at 601 Fifth Avenue. Although it was named after Dahesh, museum administrators took strides to distance the museum from the spiritual life of its founder and to focus attention instead on the European academic art collection, which is characterized by highly detailed, realistic depictions of historic and mythological subjects. These artworks were largely in vogue before the rise of the impressionist art movement. After a failed attempt to purchase gallery space at 2 Columbus Circle, the museum reopened at 580 Madison Avenue in September 2003.

Breanne Scanlon

Daily Mirror. Newspaper launched in 1924 in New York City by William Randolph Hearst. It began as a tabloid indistinguishable from its competitor, the heavily illustrated *Daily News,* but later developed a more sensational style characterized by manufactured stories and heavy use of doctored photographs and "picture snatching" (the taking of unauthorized photographs). Its writers included the gossip columnist Walter Winchell and the political commentator Drew Pearson. Although the newspaper drew many advertisers, it was second in both advertising and circulation to the *Daily News* for many years and in the 1950s experienced declining profits. A newspaper strike that lasted 114 days in 1962 further weakened the *Daily Mirror,* which on 16 October 1963 printed its final edition.

Lindsay Chaney and Michael Cieply, *The Hearsts: Family and Empire: The Later Years* (New York: Simon and Schuster, 1981)

Madeline Rogers

Daily News. Newspaper. First published on 26 June 1919 as the *Illustrated Daily News* by Joseph Medill Patterson; the name changed to its current form during the first year. Inspired by Lord Northcliffe's *Daily Mirror* of London, Patterson intended to publish the first successful American tabloid by reaching a mass audience. The newspaper became noted for halftone photographs and its focus on popular feature stories, local news, and personality profiles. The offices were situated first in the Evening Mail Building at 25 City Hall Place and moved after two years to 25 Park Place. During the early years Patterson oversaw operations from Chicago where his family's Tribune Company, the parent company to the *Daily News,* was located. The earliest editions were cheaply printed on rented presses and circulation was disappointing, but by late 1920 the newspaper began to show a profit as New Yorkers responded to its convenient size and gritty sensationalism. In 1922 circulation reached 400,000 and a Sunday edition was introduced, and in 1924 circulation reached 750,000, making the *Daily News* the most widely read newspaper in the United States.

The popularity of the *Daily News* during the 1920s was due to its numerous photographs, illustrations, comic strips, contests, and coupons as well as its sensationalist coverage of scandals, fires, and crime. A famous front-page photograph in January 1928 of the execution of the murderess Ruth Snyder, taken surreptitiously by a photographer who had strapped a camera to his leg, sold thousands of extra copies of the newspaper. Techniques were developed to include sex and violence in otherwise mundane articles, and great effort was taken to make reading the newspaper a participatory experience, for example by including the full names and addresses of those interviewed. The most popular items were the "Inquiring Photographer" (a feature widely imitated) and a section of letters called "Voice of the People." In the spring of 1926 circulation exceeded one million on weekdays and 1.25 million on Sundays. In 1930 the newspaper moved to a 37-story art deco skyscraper at 220 East 42nd Street, designed by John Mead Howells and Raymond M. Hood and erected at a cost of more than $10 million.

Patterson tempered the newspaper's sensationalism during the 1930s and began to address the issues brought on by the Depression and by the New Deal, which the newspaper supported for most of the decade. But it continued to exemplify tabloid journalism as it inaugurated a "beautiful baby" contest, sponsored dance marathons, and defended itself against libel suits by Lou Gehrig and others. By 1939 the Sunday edition was the most widely read newspaper in the world, selling more than three million copies. Notwithstanding its support for Franklin D. Roosevelt, the *Daily News* took a staunchly isolationist stand toward Nazi aggression in Europe, opposing the Lend–Lease bill in 1940 and gasoline rationing in 1941 and eventually likening Roosevelt to Napoleon and Mussolini. On Patterson's death in 1946 control of the newspaper passed to Roy Hollis, who died in an automobile accident three months later. Richard Clarke was then named executive editor, reporting to the new head of the News Syndicate Company, Eleanor "Cissy" Patterson (sister of the founder).

After World War II the newspaper became more conservative in its politics. It continued to be identified with a lively writing style characterized by breeziness, puns, and aphorisms: a front-page headline that appeared when the federal government refused to extend help to the city during its fiscal crisis in 1975, "Ford to City: Drop Dead," became a classic of tabloid journalism. In the meantime readership steadily declined as the newspaper lost much of its traditional base of blue-collar workers, immigrants, and members of racial minorities to the suburbs and television and to a lesser extent to the foreign-language press. The *Daily News* lost $11 million in 1981 and the owners made an unsuccessful attempt to sell the newspaper in the following year. By that time circulation stood at 1.5 million on weekdays and 2.1 million on Sundays.

A crippling strike by deliverers begun in October 1990 threatened the newspaper's survival and led to profound changes. The owners continued to publish by urging employees to cross picket lines and securing replacement workers, and the union urged boycotts by advertisers and news dealers. In March 1991 negotiations collapsed, and it was announced that the newspaper would cease publication unless a buyer was found. Robert Maxwell, a successful newspaper publisher from Britain, then purchased the *Daily News* when the union agreed to drastic staff reductions. Maxwell drowned under mysterious circumstances in November; in the following year control was assumed by Mortimer B. Zuckerman, a successful real estate developer. By the mid-1990s the *Daily News* had recovered much of the circulation that it had lost during the strike, and at the opening of the twenty-first century it broke with the national trend and saw a gain in circulation to more than 700,000.

Frank Luther Mott, *American Journalism: A History of Newspapers in the United States through 250 Years, 1690 to 1940* (New York: Macmillan, 1941); John Tebbel, *An American Dynasty* (New York: Greenwood, 1968); Leo E. McGivena et al., *The News: The First Fifty Years of New York's Picture Newspaper* (New York: News Syndicate, 1969)

Steve Rivo, Thorin Tritter

Daily Worker. Newspaper of the American Communist Party, later known as the People's Weekly World.

dairying. Cattle were introduced to New Amsterdam in 1625, including a few milk cows. According to a report by Jonas Michaëlius in 1628, dairy products were sought after but scarce in Manhattan. Local herds proliferated, and in 1644 colonists built a wall near what is now Wall Street to prevent cattle from leaving pastures in Battery Park. Larger grounds near City Hall were used for summer pastures from 1653, and meadows in northern Manhattan were used into the nineteenth century. Each morning summer herdsmen employed by the city blew horns to move the cattle to fresh pasture; in the evening they returned each animal to its owner, ready to be milked and bedded down. Winter fodder was mostly corn or wild marsh-hay from Long Island. Throughout the seventeenth and eighteenth centuries dairying remained a practice of general farming, and milk, butter, and cheese (which was especially scarce) were sometimes bartered to neighbors or traded to local retailers. Ice cream made by skilled confectioners became popular in the city during the American Revolution, and by 1779 it was made for home delivery by Joseph Corree in his shop at 17 Hanover Square; it soon became known as "everyman's dessert." In 1806 the cheese maker Ephraim Perkins urged wheat farmers of Herkimer County, New York, to shift to dairying and produce cheese for the city market. He himself opened a dairy farm in Herkimer County that by 1828 had 78 cows and shipped as much as 16 tons (14.5 metric tons) of cheddar cheese a year to the city; farms in the surrounding counties soon also became suppliers. The merchant and geographer John Melish wrote in 1807 that the first milkmen walked around the city carrying two buckets of tepid milk suspended from a yoke.

As the city grew during the nineteenth century, farmland and cattle became scarce in Manhattan and dairy farmers moved to Williamsburgh, other parts of Brooklyn, and Queens County. Haphazard breeding practices and poor management left dairying primarily in the hands of farmers who sought large profits and followed advice given in newspapers and agricultural tracts by Zadock Pratt, Silas L. Loomis, and Xerxes A. Willard. Local dairies were unable to satisfy demand, and in the 1820s swill milk was first offered; it was produced by cows fed a mixture of mash, warm slop from stills, and brewer's grain and kept in sheds attached to breweries and distilleries. Swill milk producers rented stalls to cattle owners in Manhattan for $5 a year and sold their milk (labeled "pure country milk") for four or five cents a quart (or liter); the largest firm was that of William M. Johnson and Son on 16th Street. The cows were often unhealthy, tied in stalls 3 feet (1 meter) wide and fed 32 gallons (120 liters) of slop and 3 pounds (1.4 kilograms) of hay daily. As early as 1826 some farmers who sold milk and butter in the city used as middlemen such captains on the Hudson River as Joel D. Hunter, who opened the firm of Hunter Walton. One enterprising farmer, Thomas W. Decker, used flatboats to transport milk from his farm in Fordham to markets on the East Side, where he had a thriving business; he later joined with other milkmen to form Sheffield Farms, which became one of the largest milk producers in the Northeast. By 1830 large-scale producers used horse-drawn carts for home delivery, and in the 1840s "hokey-pokey men" first sold homemade, hand-dipped ice cream from small wagons pulled by goats; after 1848 they used small freezers.

Milk was first shipped to the city regularly in special ice-cooled cars in 1842 by the New York and Erie Railroad, which by 1850 shipped 13,428,311 gallons (56,758,785 liters) a year. As demand rose, farms in Queens, Orange, and Westchester counties supplied milk to the city. Such improved cattle breeds as the Ayrshire, Holstein–Frisian, and Simmental were imported about this time. The New York and Harlem Railroad shipped four million gallons (17.1 million liters) in 1847 and double that quantity by 1852, when there were 25 milk companies in the city, with 1200 employees and nearly 800 horses. Even after they were connected to the city by rail, farms in outlying areas faced stiff competition from factories in the city; in the 1850s two-thirds of the city's milk was supplied by cows fed distillery grains. From 1842 the reformer Robert M. Hartley contended that New Yorkers' health was deteriorating because of swill milk, which had a bluish tint and uneven consistency that prompted retailers to add borax, chalk, starch, flour, sugar, calves' brains, or water, an especially dangerous additive because the city's supply was often impure. Other reformers joined Hartley in fighting horrendous conditions in swill milk factories in northern Manhattan and Brooklyn. In the 1850s Hartley's findings were published in *Frank Leslie's Illustrated Newspaper,* which with John Mullaly's pamphlet *The Milk Trade of New York and Vicinity* (1853) argued that swill milk caused the deaths of thousands of children in the city. Swill milk maintained its hold on the fluid market until legislation in 1862 reduced its market share; legislation in 1864 prohibited retailers from diluting milk with water.

Jacob Fussell, the first ice cream wholesaler, sold his product for 25 cents a quart in 1864 (confectioners charged $1.25). Butter from Goshen and other towns in Orange County, New York, dominated the city's market until 1873, when the Oleo–Margarine Manufacturing Company opened in Manhattan and produced oleomargarine that tasted like butter and cost less. Children continued to suffer from the effects of adulterated and spoiled milk. Harvey D. Thatcher developed the "Common Sense Milk Bottle" (patented in 1884), a glass bottle fitted with a rubber O-ring, as well as a complex system of packing, shipping, and reusing bottles that allowed milk to be delivered under more sanitary conditions. In 1889 Henry Koplik opened the first milk depot that pasteurized milk for poor infants. "Certified" milk, which was approved by physicians and supposedly sold only to children, was introduced by Henry L. Coit in the 1890s. Milk depots became popular after Nathan Straus's laboratory on the East Third Street Pier offered "sterilized milk" at four cents a quart. In 1912 Ernest J. Lederle, the health commissioner, made pasteurization mandatory for all milk for children despite opposition from dealers seeking to avoid the expense; nonetheless, 10 percent of the milk consumed in the city was still unpasteurized in 1920. Cottage cheese, cream cheese, and sour cream were made by the firm of Breakstone Foods on the Lower East Side from 1882, and in 1900 the Constantinople-on-the-Pike, or Cornucopia (ice cream in a cone), was served in stores that flourished on Chatham Street. After the turn of the twentieth century parmesan and mozzarella cheese also became popular as restaurants increasingly catered to a diverse population.

After 1913 bowls of ice cream were offered for five cents at Horn and Hardart automats; Cho-Cho novelty bars, Cherio-bars, and Sidewalk Sundaes were introduced in the 1920s but were overshadowed by the Mel-O-Rol, a specialty at the World's Fair of 1939–40. Such local producers as the J. M. Horton Ice Cream Company in Manhattan and the Reid and Union Dairy and the Blue Ribbon Ice Cream Company in Brooklyn became unable to compete. By 1930 they were bought by the Pioneer Ice Cream Division of Borden Food Corporation, which in 1932 became the first ice cream plant in the metropolitan area to abandon metal cans for paper cartons. As the city grew, dairy producers could no longer offer personal service, and cooperative marketing associations were formed to run processing plants and sell dairy products in retail stores and along home delivery routes in the city. New Deal policies during the 1930s set strict government guidelines for quality control, and in 1933 New York State enacted milk control laws to stabilize prices and protect small, independent dealers, a practice that inspired similar efforts by other states and soon had the effect of restricting entry into the market. In 1942 Daniel Carasso and Joe Metzger began making Dannon yogurt in the Bronx, a product that became highly successful after the firm changed from whole milk to skim milk in the 1970s.

Dairying in New York City and its environs declined sharply during the following decades in the face of increasing urbanization, rising taxes and land costs, and improved technology for storing milk and transporting it over long distances. As late as 1940 the federal census of agriculture counted six farms with 328 cows in Brooklyn, nine farms with 563 cows in Queens, and nine farms with 127 cows in Staten Island. By 1978 only one farm in Queens and one in Staten Island remained. Local ice cream brands including Borden and Sealtest lost a large portion of the market during the 1970s and 1980s to "premium" and "super premium" brands. In an effort to balance the needs of producers, middlemen, and consumers, New York State continued to regulate the production and sale of milk; the Milk Control and Milk Producers Security Reform Act of 1987 effectively eliminated both intrastate and interstate competition.

Robert M. Hartley, *An Historical, Scientific and Practical Essay on Milk* (New York: Jonathan Leavitt, 1842); John Mullaly, *The Milk Trade of New York and Vicinity* (New York: n.pub., 1853); Ralph Selitzer, *The Dairy Industry in America* (New York: Dairy and Ice Cream Field, 1976)

Thomas D. Beal

Daitch–Shopwell. Chain of supermarkets formed in New York City in December 1955 from the merger of Daitch Crystal Dairies and Shopwell Foods. By 1962 it had grown to include 103 stores. It declined during the 1960s and 1970s. Most of the stores had been renamed Shopwell or Food Emporium by 1986, when the chain was acquired by the Great Atlantic and Pacific Tea Company.

Howard Kaplan

Dakota. Apartment building at 1 West 72nd Street at Central Park West in Manhattan. It was built between 1882 and 27 October 1884 by Henry J. Hardenbergh, later the designer of the Plaza Hotel, at the initiative of Edward Clark, president of the Singer Manufacturing Company. Despite its inconvenient location and a feeling on the part of many wealthy New Yorkers that apartments were no better than tenement housing, the building was fully rented by the time of its completion, without benefit of paid advertising. It had 85 apartments of 4 to 20 rooms each, with drawing rooms as large as 25 by 40 feet (8 by 12 meters), ceilings ranging in height from 15 feet (4.5 meters) on the second floor to 12 feet (3.6 meters) on the seventh floor, and interior walls paneled in fine woods. The roof was steeply gabled, and decorative patterns were etched on an exterior of yellow brick, rose marble, and dark brownstone (over time these darkened to various shades of brown). The tenants were served by a staff of 150. A 10-room apartment in the building cost $250 a month, an extravagant sum by the standards of the day. Over the years the Dakota became perhaps the most recognizable apartment building in the city. It was the setting for Roman Polanski's film *Rosemary's Baby* (1968) and the home of many figures in the arts and entertainment, including Leonard Bernstein, Boris Karloff, Judy Garland, Lauren Bacall, Mia Farrow, and Judy Holliday. One of the best-known residents, John Lennon, was fatally shot in front of the building in December 1980.

Stephen Birmingham, *Life at the Dakota: New York's Most Unusual Address* (New York: Random House, 1979)

Clarissa L. Bushman

Dalton School. Private elementary and secondary school at 108 East 89th Street in Manhattan, opened in 1919 by Helen Parkhurst, who was active in the progressive education movement. Originally called the Children's University School and situated at West 74th Street, it moved in 1922 to another building on the same street and in 1929 to its current elementary school location on East 91st Street and its secondary school location on East 89th Street. As the school's headmistress, Parkhurst implemented the Laboratory Plan, which stressed cooperation between students and teachers to set individualized goals. The school used no tests or grades and virtually no discipline. It remained true to Parkhurst's principles after she retired in 1942 and continued operating into the twenty-first century. Its enrollment in 2010 was 1300, including students from kindergarten through the 12th grade.

Diane Lager, "Helen Parkhurst and the Dalton Plan" (diss., University of Connecticut, 1983)

Alfonso J. Orsini

Ice skating in Central Park in front of the Dakota, ca *1890*

The Dakota, 2009

Daly, (John) Augustin (*b* Plymouth, N.C., 20 July 1838; *d* Paris, 7 June 1899). Producer and playwright. As a young man he moved to New York City and worked as a theater critic for several newspapers, including the *Sunday Courier,* the *Sun,* and the *New York Times.* His plays *Under the Gaslight* (1867), *Horizon* (1871), and *Divorce* (1871) were well received, and in 1869 he formed his own company at the Fifth Avenue Theatre. After the theater was destroyed by fire in 1873 he leased another one and named it Daly's Fifth Avenue Theatre. He also ran the Grand Opera House, where his *Roughing It* was a tremendous success and where he presented adaptations of English and European works. By the end of his life Daly had written and adapted more than 90 plays and had been a producer for more than 30 years.

Joseph Francis Daly, *The Life of Augustin Daly* (New York: Macmillan, 1917); Marvin Felheim, *The Theater of Augustin Daly: An Account of the Late Nineteenth-Century American Stage* (Cambridge, Mass.: Harvard University Press, 1956)

James E. Mooney

D'Amato, Cus [Constantine] (*b* Bronx, 17 Jan 1908; *d* Catskill, N.Y., 4 Nov 1985). Boxing trainer and manager. He grew up fighting on the streets of a tough Bronx Italian neighborhood before opening the Empire Sporting Club at Gramercy Gym on 14th Street in Manhattan. D'Amato trained many fighters before helping New Yorker Floyd Patterson win the heavyweight championship in 1956. Known for his psychological toughness and integrity, D'Amato refused to allow his fighters to take part in bouts promoted by the corrupt International Boxing Club. D'Amato later moved to upstate New York, where in 1980 he met and began training Brooklyn fighter Mike Tyson, then a 14-year-old reform school student. D'Amato adopted Tyson in 1984 and died in 1985, one year before Tyson won his first heavyweight title.

Ben Silk

Damrosch, Leopold (*b* Posen, Germany [now Poznań, Poland], 22 Oct 1832; *d* New York City, 15 Feb 1885). Violinist, conductor, and composer, father of Frank and Walter Damrosch. After taking a degree in medicine he became the first violinist in the ducal orchestra at Weimar and a friend of Franz Liszt's and Richard Wagner's. In 1871 he took his family to New York City, and until 1883 he led the Männergesangverein Arion. He founded the Oratorio Society of New York (1873) and the Symphony Society (1878), and he conducted the Metropolitan Opera; he remained associated with each institution until his death. Committed to the German repertory, he gave the American premiere of Brahms's Symphony no. 1, conducted at the first large-scale music festival in the city in 1881 (with an orchestra of 250 and a chorus of 1200), and in 1884–85 gave the American premieres of Wagner's *Der Ring des Nibelungen* and *Tristan und Isolde.* Damrosch and his sons determined the shape of opera in New York City. The outdoor musical amphitheater just south of the Metropolitan Opera House at Lincoln Center is named for his family.

Nancy Shear

Damrosch, Walter (Johannes) (*b* Breslau, Germany [now Wrocław, Poland], 30 Jan 1862; *d* New York City, 22 Dec 1950). Conductor and educator, son of Leopold Damrosch. He became a director of the Metropolitan Opera with Anton Seidl on the death of his father in 1885, and remained with the company until 1891. From 1885–98 he conducted the Oratorio Society of New York, and in 1894 he formed the Damrosch Opera Company, which introduced opera in many cities across the United States. Between 1885 and 1928 he periodically conducted the New York Philharmonic, and in 1899 he returned to the Metropolitan for two seasons of German opera. He produced a European tour by the New York Symphony Society in 1920, the first by an American orchestra, and in 1925 he conducted the first orchestral concert broadcast nationally on radio. Damrosch was the host of a weekly music appreciation program with the National Broadcasting Company (NBC) Symphony in 1928–42.

Nancy Shear

Dana, Charles A(nderson) (*b* Hinsdale, N.H., 8 Aug 1819; *d* Glen Cove, N.Y., 17 Oct 1897). Newspaper editor and publisher. After a sojourn at the utopian colony Brook Farm, he joined the *New York Tribune* in 1847, becoming Horace Greeley's assistant and arguably the first American journalist to hold the position of managing editor. During 1867–68 he bought and became the chief editor of the *Sun,* which under his direction became noted for its independence from both political parties and its opposition to civil service reform and the labor movement. Dana was among the most influential journalists of the century, and his emphasis on colorful human interest stories and eye-catching headlines prefigured the practices of yellow journalism.

Candace Stone, *Dana and the Sun* (New York: Dodd, Mead, 1938)

Steven H. Jaffe

dance. The first documented dance performance in New York City was "The Adventures of Harlequin and Scaramouch, or the Spaniard Trick'd," a pantomime performed by the English dancer Henry Holt in February 1739. From the eighteenth century to the early nineteenth century, acrobats (or "posture-makers"), harlequins, jugglers, hornpipe dancers, and rope dancers were common entertainers; some dances performed on stage were based on social dances such as the minuet. Dance until the early nineteenth century was usually part of variety programs that often included plays, operas, burlesques, pantomimes (harlequinades), short recitations, singing, and acrobatics, but there were also a few one-act ballets. By 1750 the Nassau Street Theatre offered regular seasons of variety programs in which dance was included. John Gay's *The Beggar's Opera* was presented for the benefit of the actor Thomas Kean on 15 January 1751, and the dance at the end of each act was performed by "a Gentleman lately from London," possibly Robert Upton. From the early 1750s performances were given by William Hulett, a dancing master and expert in hornpipes and harlequin dances. Lewis Hallam's American Company presented the pantomime "Harlequin Collector" at the John Street Theatre in April 1768; afterward a group of Cherokee chiefs and warriors in the audience performed a war dance on stage. One of the first known African American impersonations was a "Negro dance" performed at the John Street Theatre in 1767 by Mr. Tea. Performances of this sort eventually became a genre that formed the basis of minstrelsy in the nineteenth century.

At this time, audiences did not have a difficult time decoding the storybook ballets, usually based on fairy tales and fables. A resolution against public amusements was passed by the Continental Congress in 1774, and theaters closed during the American Revolution before reopening somewhat cautiously in the 1780s. New York City became part of a tour circuit that included Philadelphia and Charleston, South Carolina. Because of the prevailing sentiment that theater was too frivolous an amusement for a new nation emerging from war, some theater companies disguised their entertainments as edifying recitations. John Durang, the first well-known American dancer, performed the hornpipe and patriotic dances in the city from 1784 to 1796 with the Old American Company. In 1794 he performed in "Tammany; or, the Indian Chief," the first American production incorporating opera and ballet. During the early 1790s dance flourished in the city as many French dancers settled there after escaping the French Revolution. Among them was Alexandre Placide, an acrobat, mime, and dancer who sometimes performed on a tightrope; he moved to the city in 1792, and with his common-law wife, Suzanne Vaillande, produced 15 European ballets and pantomimes, many of which became popular. His ballets were also staged in the city by Durang, who presented his own dancers and worked with the Dutch dancer William Francis, the English ballet master James Byrne, and M. Francisquy, a dancer in the Paris opera who introduced pantomimes based on American themes. Durang was a partner of Mme Gardie, a talented Dominican-born dancer who performed in *Sophia of Brabant* (1794), the first classical ballet given in the city.

The 1820s saw an influx of European dancers who introduced classical French ballet technique, among them Claude Labasse, Francisque Hutin, M. and Mme Achille, and Charles and Marietta Ronzi Vestris. The more precise execution of ballet technique recaptured audiences. By the 1830s and 1840s romantic ballets were regularly presented by Europeans. In 1832 Philippe Taglioni first choreographed *La Sylphide,* which epitomizes the romantic era of ballet, with a revolutionary change in dance technicality and story premise. His daughter, legendary dancer Marie Taglioni, was known for her role in *La Sylphide.* The year 1839 marked the debut of Jean Petipa and his son Marius Petipa (later the choreographer of the Russian Imperial Ballet). With James Sylvain as her partner, the well-known Fanny Elssler of the Paris Opéra performed *La Tarentule, La Sylphide,* and several character dances in 1840 before embarking on a two-year national tour during which she trained local dancers to augment her casts; her performances inspired an American "balletomania." Several American-born ballet dancers became successful, among them Augusta Maywood, who in 1838 at age 13 made her debut in the city in *Le Dieu et la bayadère* (she moved to Europe in 1839), and Mary Ann Lee, who also made her debut in the city (at 16), studied with Jean Coralli in Paris, and returned to the United States to introduce such classics from the French repertory as *Giselle.* One of her regular partners was George Washington Smith, who also toured in Elssler's American company in 1840, studied with Sylvain, and was later the partner of Julia Turnbull, Giovanna Ciocca, Giuseppina Morlacchi, and Pepita Soto. He became the ballet master of the Bowery Theatre in 1847 and of the Lyceum Theatre in 1850; he also arranged dances for Lola Montez during her tour in 1851 and at times was her partner. Ballets and pantomimes were often performed at the Park Theatre and Vauxhall Gardens. Audiences were generally white and of mixed social class.

Competitive tap dancing, a blend of Irish clogging and African syncopated rhythms, was first performed in saloons and dance halls in the Five Points neighborhood. By the end of the nineteenth century black minstrel shows were performed in theaters, and there was also an African American vaudeville circuit. Some black entertainers, such as Bert Williams, performed in white vaudeville shows. The extravagant ballet *The Black Crook* opened in 1866 at Niblo's Garden on Broadway and soon became one of the most popular productions of its kind in the city. The production lasted nearly six hours and incorporated dazzling fairyland transformations, a troupe of child precision dancers, and female dancers with their legs bared below mid-thigh. It became a model for musical theater, vaudeville, music hall productions, and variety spectacles such as *America,* a lavish celebration of technological invention produced by Imre Kiralfy for the World's Columbian Exposition in Chicago in 1893 and performed in the same year at the Metropolitan Opera.

About this time modern dance was developed in the city by Loie Fuller, Isadora Duncan, Ruth St. Denis, and others, some of whom had studied with Italian ballet dancers. They were also influenced by vaudeville skirt dancing, the expressive techniques of François Delsarte, acting, and Hindu and Japanese dances presented by international expositions and amusement parks. In their work they explored the theme of rugged American individualism, recasting elements of popular entertainment and genteel parlor dances. Fuller and Duncan began their careers in New York City in the 1890s and then, after becoming well known in Europe, returned to the United States. Duncan became a sensation, commonly known as the "mother of modern dance." She is recognized for her unorthodox (for the time) dress code, which featured flowing dresses that discarded the traditions of tight, corseted costumes. St. Denis made New York City her headquarters after her debut there in 1906 and a subsequent successful European tour; she performed her mystical Orientalist dances on the national vaudeville circuit. She married Ted Shawn, and in 1915 the couple organized the Ruth St. Denis and Ted Shawn School of Dancing and Related Arts, known as Denishawn, in Los Angeles; it had branches in several cities, including New York City.

There was no American school of ballet until 1909, when the Metropolitan Opera engaged Malvina Cavallazzi as a teacher for its company. Interest in ballet was revived in the city by Anna Pavlova and Mikhail Mordkin, former dancers in Sergei Diaghilev's Ballets Russes. In 1910 they danced in *Coppélia, Aziade,* and such divertissements as *The Dying Swan,* which was performed at the Metropolitan Opera for two years. In 1911 Theodore Kosloff danced with Gertrude Hoffman at the Winter Garden Theatre in works from the repertory of the Ballets Russes, of which he had been a member. The Ballets Russes made two tours of the country in 1916–17, reproducing ballets that had enjoyed tremendous success in Paris, including *Petrouchka, Schéhérazade, Les Sylphides,* and *Afternoon of a Faun.* During the second tour Vaslav Nijinsky presented his last ballet, *Till Eulenspiegel,* based on the story of the medieval Flemish trickster and set to music by Richard Strauss.

From the end of the nineteenth century until the 1940s, many of the ballets in New York City were offered by the Metropolitan Opera, which presented its own company and touring companies. Versions of Diaghilev's works were performed by the Ballets Russes and others. The engagement of Rosina Galli, a graduate of the La Scala school in Milan, as the lead dancer in 1914 and as the ballet master in 1919 gave luster to the opera's company, which until the Depression presented full-scale ballets as part of operas or on their own. Several small ballet companies performed elsewhere. Michel Fokine worked at the Hippodrome and performed in Florenz Ziegfeld's *Follies* during the 1920s, and in 1924 he organized a small company to perform his works. In 1926 Mordkin formed the Mordkin Ballet Company, which performed in the Greenwich *Follies* and toured briefly. Martha Graham, Doris Humphrey, Charles Weidman, and Louis Horst, the music director of St. Denis's company, left the Denishawn school during the 1920s for New York City. Dissatisfied with the fin de siècle decorativeness of her training, Graham worked to extrapolate a specifically American form of dance from the rhythms of city life, and deep, emotionally driven choreography. Horst became her mentor and an influential composition teacher to successive groups of modern dancers. Humphrey and Weidman formed their own school and company in 1928, basing their technique on Humphrey's principles of fall and recovery. Weidman's gift was for comedy; Humphrey combined principles of musical visualization that she had explored with St. Denis and embodiments of social utopias and social conflicts.

In the 1920s many African American entertainers found work in the Cotton Club and other nightclubs where the owners and the audiences were white. New York City became a hotspot for tap dancing, a truly American form of dance. The Hoofer's Club was where many of the great tappers and steps were born, providing a place where black tap dancers could get together and share technique and styles. African Americans first became concert dancers during the Harlem Renaissance, when they gained access to theaters, financing, and work as dancers, composers, musicians, and writers for the stage. A number of musicals intended for mixed audiences and produced entirely by African Americans were introduced, often based on racial stereotypes traditional in minstrel shows. Among these were *Shuffle Along* (1921, Flourney Miller and Aubrey Lyles; Noble Sissle and Eubie Blake), *Plantation Revue, From Dixie to Broadway, Runnin' Wild,* and *Chocolate Dandies.* Many performers found employment in these productions, and a number became internationally known, including Josephine Baker and Bill "Bojangles" Robinson. Initially presented in Harlem, the musicals eventually moved to Broadway and were performed for white audiences, after which the Charleston became a social dance and tap dancing was incorporated into many mainstream musical comedies. At the same time a number of black dancers sought to develop forms of concert dancing shaped by African American history. In 1931 Hemsley Winfield formed the Negro Art Theater Dance Group, which in its first concert presented dances based on African themes and set to black spirituals by Edna Guy, who had studied at the Denishawn school. As the witch doctor in *The Emperor Jones* in 1933, Winfield became the first black dancer to perform at the Metropolitan Opera. Asadata Dafora, a musician born in Sierra Leone and trained in Europe, moved to the city in 1929 and in 1934 produced *Kykunkor,* a program of African music and dance elegantly arranged for the theater and performed by a cast of Africans and black Americans; it met with success and became a model for others.

By the 1930s New York City had become the world's foremost center for dance, especially modern dance. Mary Wigman sent one of her pupils, Hanya Holm, to open a branch of her school of German modern dance there in 1931, and by the late 1930s it was the Hanya Holm Studio. Holm worked with Graham, Humphrey, and Weidman to help shape the modern dance movement. Her critique of capitalism through dance influenced many younger dancers, some of whom belonged to Graham's and Humphrey's companies, took part in the unionization movement, and were allied with cultural organizations of the Communist Party. With the support of the Workers' Dance League they formed political dance troupes like the Red Dancers, the New Duncan Dancers, the Modern Negro Dance Group, the New Dance Group, and the Theater Union Dance Group. They treated such themes as the Spanish Civil War, German fascism, and American racism. While the Popular Front was active, the league softened its treatment of class conflict and renamed itself the New Dance League, which celebrated American folk themes and invited less politically radical dancers to take part in its performances. Several modern dance groups included black dancers and choreographers by 1937, when an evening of the works of Guy, Dafora, Katherine Dunham, and Talley Beatty was presented at the 92nd Street Young Men's Hebrew Association, a central venue for modern dance. During the same year Eugene von Grona organized the American Negro Ballet, which after its debut at the Lafayette Theatre in Harlem received criticism that reflected long-standing prejudices about dance and race. Dunham moved to New York City in 1939 to direct the Labor Stage, for which she provided choreography for a production of *Pins and Needles* before embarking on a long career of synthesizing Caribbean, African, and European styles. Several of her pupils became well known, including Beatty, Janet Collins, Lavinia Williams, Jean-Léon Destine, and Charles Moore, and she remained an important influence in African American concert dances.

Regular ballet seasons were introduced in the city in the 1930s. Managed by Wassily de Basil, the Ballet Russe de Monte Carlo had several successful seasons from 1933 during which Léonide Massine was its ballet master; it presented Diaghilev's repertory as well as comedies and new symphonic ballets by Massine, including *Les Présages* and *Symphonie fantastique.* In 1938 Sergei Denham became its impresario and it presented *Gaîté parisienne,* a new character ballet by Massine that became one of the company's staples. The Original Ballet Russe was formed by de Basil in 1938, and the two companies became rivals. From 1935 Sol Hurok and other impresarios regularly sponsored visiting dance companies at the Metropolitan Opera before and after the resident company's season. On Galli's retirement the resident company became the American Ballet, led by George Balanchine (1935–38). Although the new director of the Metropolitan Opera, Edward Johnson, had promised artistic reforms, Balanchine's dances were considered too nontraditional and overpowering, and in 1938 Boris Romanov, a member of the Ballets Russes, became the resident choreographer, a position he held until 1941. The Mordkin Ballet was revived in 1937; several of its members formed the Ballet Theatre in 1939.

New York City became the international center of ballet during the 1940s. The Ballet Theatre committed itself to preserving traditional ballet and encouraging new work, and was soon one of the most important companies in the city. Its first choreographer was Jerome Robbins, who produced *Fancy Free* in 1944 and, with the English choreographer Antony Tudor, trained such dancers as Nora Kaye, Harold Lang, Michael Kidd, Alicia Alonso, and Hugh Laing. The Ballet Russe de Monte Carlo became the most popular touring company in the country during and after World War II. From 1938 it engaged such renowned dancers as Alexandra Danilova, Alicia Markova, Mia Slavenska, Igor Youskevitch, Mary Ellen Moylan, Leon Danielian, and Maria Tallchief, and many of its dancers became influential teachers. In 1942 Massine left the company, which produced several ballets by Balanchine as well as Agnes de Mille's *Rodeo,* and in 1944 Frederick Franklin became the ballet master. At times the company competed for audiences with the Original Ballet Russe, and in 1950 it ceased to offer regular seasons in New York City; it was dissolved in 1962. For a few seasons a number of companies organized by Balanchine and Lincoln Kirstein joined forces as the Ballet Society, a subscription organization that performed at the New York City Center for Music and Dance. The group changed its name to the New York City Ballet when it became the resident company there in 1948 and was quickly embraced by the city's intelligentsia for incorporating classical values in abstract works set to music by modern composers like Stravinsky and Paul Hindemith. They have continually been an authority on Balanchine/Stravinsky ballets, from the oldest surviving work *Apollo,* choreographed in 1928 for Diaghilev's Ballet Russes, all the way through their final collaborative ballet, *Agon* (1957). In 1964 the New York City Ballet became the resident company of the New York State Theater in Lincoln Center, renamed the David H. Koch Theater in 2008. Still performing Balanchine's works in the early twenty-first century, the company is often regarded as a benchmark in neoclassical ballet, which Balanchine created.

After World War II, a new group of modern dancers emerged. Humphrey's humanist themes and balanced orchestration of weighted movements were adopted by one of her pupils, José Limón, in such works as *The Moor's Pavane* (1949). The political and mythical themes of the 1920s and 1930s were abandoned for an abstract approach by Alwin Nikolais, who had studied at the Hanya Holm Studio, and by Merce Cunningham, who danced with Graham and worked from the premise that music and dance are independent partners in time and space. Paul Taylor, who danced with both Graham and Cunningham, initially embraced minimalism in his choreography, but during the early 1960s he became more accessible and eclectic, often using symphonic music. Pearl Primus, born in Trinidad and trained as an anthropologist, studied at the New Dance Group and in 1943 made her debut in *African Ceremonial,* an "anthropological" modern dance. After a research trip to the South in 1944 she provided choreography for dances like *Strange Fruit* (about a lynching) and *Hard Times Blues* (about sharecropping). She specialized in African dances and in 1948 made the first of many trips to Africa, where she found material that inspired her later work. With such choreographers as Anna Sokolow, Jane Dudley, Sophie Maslow, William Bales, and Daniel Nagrin she took part in group concerts throughout the 1940s and early 1950s at the studio of the New Dance Group, which also sponsored a performing group and offered dance classes at rates affordable to working people (a policy that it continued to provide until it closed in 2009). Donald McKayle, a pupil of Primus who had also been trained in ballet, formed a company in 1951. Among his dances are *Games* (1951), about city children, *Rainbow 'round My Shoulder* (1959), about a chain gang, and *District Storyville* (1962), set to New Orleans jazz. In the 1960s he began providing choreography for Broadway productions, television, and films.

Choreographers for the Metropolitan Opera in these years included Tudor (1950–51, 1956–61) and Markova (1963–69). Several small troupes assembled by Robert Joffrey in the 1950s together formed the Joffrey Ballet in 1960, which became one of the major companies in the city. It was disbanded in 1964, but reorganized the following year when Gerald Arpino became its principal choreographer and was soon renowned for its youthfulness. Alvin Ailey formed a company in 1958 that presented dances set to black music and based on themes of the civil rights movement (including *Revelations,* 1960, set to spirituals). The company, under the direction of Judith Jameson, a former Ailey dancer, celebrated its 50th anniversary from 2008 to 2009.

In the early 1960s a number of choreographers called themselves postmodernists to distinguish themselves from others who became prominent in the years between the world wars. Influenced by visual art and "happenings," a genre of live art produced in the late 1950s and 1960s, many postmodernists were pupils of Cunningham. Robert Dunn, a composer and a pupil of John Cage, taught a choreography workshop from 1960 to 1962 that led to the formation of a cooperative group known as the Judson Dance Theater, which flourished from 1962 to 1964 and continued into the late 1960s. Among its choreographers were Yvonne Rainer, Steve Paxton, Trisha Brown, David Gordon, Judith Dunn, Deborah Hay, and Lucinda Childs; there were also composers, filmmakers, and visual artists such as Robert Rauschenberg and Robert Morris. Although the group was never aesthetically united, its members shared an interest in nontraditional physical techniques, chance juxtapositions, cooperative production, and the incorporation of untrained dancers into their works. Intimate performances were given at the Judson Memorial Church in Greenwich Village and in unconventional venues like lofts and the outdoors.

In the 1960s and 1970s some members of the Judson group formed companies and in their own work explored reductive structures such as repetition and mathematics; they often performed in silence and used uninflected phrasing. Some of their best-known works include *Trio A* by Rainer (1966), *Structured Pieces* by Brown (1973), and *Calico Mingling* by Childs (1973). Several choreographers formed the Grand Union, an improvisation group. Meredith Monk and Kenneth King experimented with theater that incorporated several media. Hay and Simone Forti explored natural movement and the meanings of non-Western physical disciplines like Tai Chi Chuan. Prejudices about dance and race lingered into the late 1960s, when the Dance Theatre of Harlem began operations (1969). In the 1970s a number of young black choreographers became prominent, among them Rod Rogers, Eleo Pomare, Garth Fagan, and Dianne McIntyre. In the 1970s the experimental dancer Twyla Tharp formed the Twyla Tharp Dance Company and joined the artistic mainstream. Her intellectually rigorous works, often set to popular music, blended elements of African American social dancing, jazz dancing, and ballet. Later, Tharp choreographed the hit musical *Movin' Out* on Broadway to the music of Billy Joel, which opened in 2002 and ran for a total of 1303 performances. Many touring ballet companies visited the city, and the Harkness and Feld ballets were formed.

Choreographers well known during the 1960s and 1970s collaborated on large-scale productions with visual artists and composers during the 1980s, often making use of refined movements and performing before large audiences. They and some younger dancers like Jim Self and Susan Marshall also received commissions to write ballets. Under the leadership of Mikhail Baryshnikov, the American Ballet Theatre encouraged adventurous new works, including some by Gordon, Karole Armitage, and Mark Morris, a major choreographer of the 1980s who directed the Mark Morris Dance Group and became known for his musicality and his experiments with gender roles. Venues for postmodern dance included the Dance Theater Workshop, the Kitchen, P.S. 122, and the Next Wave Festival at the Brooklyn Academy of Music. Many dancers prominent in the 1980s and early 1990s linked postmodern dance with contemporary movements in art and architecture. Works concerned with questions of identity were produced by Self, Bill T. Jones, Arnie Zane, Tim Miller, Ishmael Houston-Jones, Fred Holland, Viveca Vazquez, Dancenoise, and the Urban Bush Women, a group led by Jawole Willa Jo Zollar that drew on black culture in Africa and the United States to explore themes of black women's identity.

Relying on the movement and shapes that can be created by the body alone, companies like Pilobolus, first founded in 1971, and MOMIX, created in 1980, gained significant momentum in the early twenty-first century. Many companies have surfaced under the genre of contemporary ballet, including

Alonzo King's LINES Ballet, founded in 1982, and Complexions, created in 1994 by Ailey dancers Dwight Rhoden and Desmond Richardson. Creating a new ripple in ballet with his innovative works, Christopher Wheeldon, a dancer turned choreographer, became resident choreographer at New York City Ballet. In 2007 Wheeldon started Morphoses/The Wheeldon Company, using members of other renowned companies as a platform to present his critically acclaimed choreography.

An early attempt to establish a dance archive in the Museum of Modern Art ended in 1948, and most of the materials were eventually transferred to the New York Public Library. The museum nevertheless retained a collection of stage and costume designs to which it has continued to add, as well as materials on dance in its motion-picture archive. The New York Public Library for the Performing Arts at Lincoln Center contains the world's largest dance archive, which traces the early days of classical ballet in the United States and the development of modern dance. Documents in the archive include the papers of the American Ballet Theatre and of the Ballet Russe de Monte Carlo, photographic scrapbooks of St. Denis and Shawn, Duncan's correspondence with Gordon Craig, and the manuscripts of the choreography of Balanchine, donated by Kirstein. Also available are videotaped performances by such choreographers as Cunningham and Tharp, and videotapes from the Brooklyn Academy of Music, the Dance Theater Workshop, and the Dance Theatre of Harlem. There are also dance collections at the Asia Society, the Kitchen, the Paley Center for Media (formerly the Museum of Television and Radio), the Shubert Archives, and the Anthology Film Archives, as well as archives maintained by dance companies.

Paul Magriel, ed., *Chronicles of the American Dance from the Shakers to Martha Graham* (New York: Dance Index, 1948; repr. New York: Da Capo, 1978); Lynn Fauley Emery, *Black Dance in the United States from 1619 to 1970* (Palo Alto, Calif.: National, 1972); Deborah Jowitt, *Time and the Dancing Image* (New York: William Morrow, 1988); Francis Mason, *101 Stories of the Great Ballets* (New York: Random House, 1989); Nancy Goldner, *Balanchine Variations* (Gainesville: University Press of Florida, 2008)

See also Folk and ethnic dancing.

Sally Banes, Meryl Cates

dance criticism. Dance writing in New York City began during the mid-nineteenth century, when it consisted mainly of short, descriptive pieces discussing dance as a social event or as a costume spectacle. Dance reviews were frequently placed on the society page of local newspapers, mixed in with other arts stories. With an increase in technique-based dance, as early as the 1800s and certainly in the 1900s, there was a need for journalists with a technical vocabulary, leading to the rise of the modern dance journalist. When Carl Van Vechten (1880–1964) began writing about dance for the *New York Times* (1906–13), dance reviews became a respected form of criticism. By explaining technical terms and defending innovative performances, he expanded public awareness of dance. While working for the *Times* and the *New York Press* (1913–14) he wrote about crucial events in the history of dance in New York City, including the debuts of Anna Pavlova, Mikhail Mordkin, Maud Allan, and Loie Fuller. In *Interpreters and Interpretations* (1917) and other books, he introduced the work of Isadora Duncan and Vaslav Nijinsky to a wider audience. Although he retired by 1920, his vivid accounts helped to establish dance as a recognized art form. In earlier dance writings, the dancer was often the primary focus, but as the role of the critic evolved, the spotlight was placed on the choreography.

The first full-time dance critic in the city was John Martin (1893–1985), hired in June 1927 by the *New York Times.* He was known for his controversial treatment of ballet, especially some of the neoclassical ballets choreographed by George Balanchine. His close association with Martha Graham, Doris Humphrey, and other pioneers of modern dance made him an influential dance writer in the United States until his retirement from the *Times* in 1962.

Walter Terry (1913–82), dance critic for the *New York Herald Tribune* from 1936 until 1966, was a trained dancer who reviewed performances more as a friend of dance than as an aesthetic judge. Edwin Denby (1903–83) wrote for the bimonthly magazine *Modern Music* (1936–43), for the *Herald Tribune* while Terry was fulfilling military service (1942–45), and for the periodicals *Dance* and *Center.* Arlene Croce (*b* 1934) founded the quarterly journal *Ballet Review* in 1965 and was its editor for 14 years. She became the dance critic for the *New Yorker* in 1973. Her detailed articles, many of which were collected in *Sight Lines* (1987), were sympathetic toward the works of Balanchine, Mark Morris, and David Gordon. Martin's successor at the *Times,* Allen Hughes (1921–2009), was in turn succeeded in 1965 by Clive Barnes (1927–2009), who from 1967 was also the newspaper's drama critic; shortly after he left the *Times* in 1977 he became a critic for the *New York Post.* He also wrote a monthly column for *Dance* magazine called "Attitudes," provided his perspectives on the WQXR radio station, and published many books. Anna Kisselgoff (*b* 1938) took over the post of chief dance critic at the *Times* in 1977 and, using her vast historical knowledge of dance and straightforward approach, became an influential force of the time. Other prominent dance critics include Deborah Jowitt (*b* 1943) of the *Village Voice,* who was recognized for her unaffected reviews and veneration for the art form and artist; Tobi Tobias (*b* 1938) of *New York;* Marcia Siegel (*b* 1932) of the *Hudson Review;* and Joan Acocella (*b* 1945), the dance critic for the *New Yorker* since 1998, whose works include *Mark Morris* (1993) and an edition of the diary of Nijinsky (1999). Jennifer Dunning (*b* 1942) of the *Times* has written books on dance topics, including *But First a School* (1985) and *Alvin Ailey: A Life in Dance* (1998). In April 2007 Alastair Macaulay became chief dance critic at the *Times,* following the retirement of John Rockwell (*b* 1940), critic since 2005. Macaulay was previously the chief theater critic for the *Financial Times* and chief dance critic for the *Times Literary Supplement,* both in London.

Meryl Cates, William C. MacKay

dance halls and discothèques. Dance halls for members of the working class were present in New York City by the middle of the nineteenth century and soon acquired an unsavory reputation. John Allen, known as the "wickedest man in New York," ran a dance hall during the 1860s at 304 Water Street that was also a bordello. Local residents commonly referred to Harry Hill's famous dance hall at 26 East Houston Street (1868–90) as the city's "most respectable disreputable house" and to the Black and Tan Concert Hall at 153 Bleecker Street as the "Chemise and Drawers." At the same time members of fashionable society danced waltzes, polkas, and the lancers in stylish dress and sumptuous surroundings. Allen Dodworth, a bandmaster and a violinist with the New York Philharmonic, opened a dancing school at 402 Broadway in 1842 and became so closely associated with the city's social elite that one of the studios he opened later, at 681 Fifth Avenue, was a temporary site for the Metropolitan Museum of Art. One of the nation's preeminent dancing masters, Dodworth published *Dancing, and Its Relation to Education and Social Life* in 1885 and retired in the following year, leaving control of the school to his nephew George, who bought a building at 12 East 49th Street where he taught the daughters of such prominent families as the Astors, the Gallatins, the Hones, the Belmonts, the Vanderbilts, and the Dwights. The Dodworths were more than simply dance teachers: they hoped to bring good manners to the dance floor and believed that proper dance technique and etiquette could help to refine society.

The growing influence of ragtime music and dance between 1890 and World War I complicated the Dodworths' mission. Rental halls that were the primary venues for dancing between 1890 and 1910 gained in popularity in neighborhoods inhabited by immigrants and the working class. By one estimate there were 130 dance halls in the city in 1895 (most on the Lower East Side) and 195 by 1910. Social dancing peaked between 1911 and 1915, and venues ranging from cabarets in Times Square and elegant hotels to large, nondescript dance halls struggled to keep pace with a rapidly increasing demand. Two types of dance hall played the largest role. The first were dance palaces that accommodated from 500 to 3000 patrons and included Grand Central Palace, the city's first (opened in 1911 at 488 Lexington Avenue); the Manhattan Casino (2926 Eighth Avenue); and the Harlem Casino (100 West 116th Street). Such halls catered mostly to teenagers and featured professional musicians and promotional events. Other dance halls such as Tangoland on East 86th Street, known as "closed" or "taxi" dance halls, were situated above street level, had amateurish bands, and were sparsely decorated; patronized solely by single males (and therefore popularly associated with prostitution), they offered female dancing partners for hire at a fixed price for each dance, which the dancer split equally with the owner of the hall. This practice was commemorated in the song "Ten Cents a Dance" (1930) by Richard Rodgers and Lorenz Hart.

The proliferation of dance halls raised the ire of reformers. They joined such groups as the Committee of Fourteen (1905–32) and the Committee on Amusement Resources of Working Girls (1909–15), which prevailed on the state legislature to amend the city charter in 1910 to provide for the licensing of dance halls, and then helped to refine the state law by securing passage at the municipal level of the Dance Hall Law of 1911. To ensure propriety on the city's dance floors George Dodworth and other concerned dance teachers organized the New York Society of Teachers of Dancing in 1914. This group was less influential than Vernon and Irene Castle, whose refined versions of the latest dance steps met with huge success on the floors of cabarets and hotels. To counter the reformers many owners of dance halls renamed their establishments academies and schools, and some opened large dance spaces that offered refined surroundings, among them Roseland, opened by Louis J. Brecker on New Year's Eve 1919, and the Savoy Ballroom in Harlem, which opened in 1925. During the 1920s and 1930s Arthur Murray ran a chain of studios in the city to teach social dancing. In 1925 there were 786 licensed dance spaces in the five boroughs, of which 238 were in Manhattan. The Advisory Dance Hall Committee calculated that about 14 percent of the city's males and 10 percent of its females aged 17 to 40 frequented at least one dance hall a week.

Dance halls remained popular during the 1930s. At the Savoy Ballroom in Harlem a racially mixed crowd numbering as many as 5000 danced the Lindy hop to the accompaniment of the country's leading jazz bands. Fashionable hotels such as the Pennsylvania, the Lincoln, and the New Yorker opened ballrooms that featured swing and "sweet society" bands such as that of Eddy Duchin. Many dance palaces closed during the Depression, but taxi dance halls continued to draw customers and criticism. In 1936 the police raided 20 such establishments around Sands Street near the Brooklyn Navy Yard, and as late as 1964 Bernard J. O'Connell, the city's license commissioner, revoked the permits of six dance halls in Times Square for offending public decency. Developers razed the Savoy Ballroom to make way for a housing project in 1958, and eventually taxi dancing disappeared from New York City.

The decline of the dance hall coincided with the rise of the discothèque. The Peppermint Lounge, opened on West 45th Street in 1959, was associated from the following year with the dance called the twist and remained a popular venue for celebrities until it closed in December 1965. Other early discothèques that attracted a fashionable clientele included Ondine (308 East 59th Street), the private discothèques Le Club (416 East 55th Street) and L'Interdit (in the Gotham Hotel), and Arthur (154 East 54th Street, 1965–69), which was owned by several stage and film performers and was known for the bold dress of its patrons. Cheetah, opened at Broadway and 53rd Street in April 1966 and owned by Borden Stevenson (a son of the politician Adlai Stevenson), featured rock dancing and was frequented by teenagers. By the mid-1960s several large dance clubs were situated in the theater district and in Greenwich Village. The Electric Circus, at 23 St. Mark's Place, presented an opening gala on 27 June 1967 that attracted celebrities, hippies, and the curious, who were entertained by trapeze acts and performance artists as well as dizzying lights and a deafening sound system that required the laying of a special cable in St. Mark's Place by Consolidated Edison. Dom, directly downstairs from the Electric Circus, was the primary dance club for blacks in Greenwich Village during the late 1960s.

Those who patronized discothèques during the 1970s danced not to rock but to the four-square rhythms of disco. The most exclusive clubs admitted only the prominent and fashionably dressed and were written about relentlessly by gossip columnists. Lighting and sound systems were increasingly elaborate, and illegal drugs widely used. The best-known club of the period was Studio 54, owned by Stephen Rubell and Ian Schrager, which opened on 26 April 1977 at 254 West 54th Street in the shell of the abandoned Gallo Theater. Its chief competitor was Xenon, also in a former theater, at 124 West 43rd Street. Other discothèques catered to the working class, especially in the outer boroughs; a club of this sort is vividly depicted in the film *Saturday Night Fever* (1977). The decadent excesses of the more lavish clubs ended about 1980, when the owners of Studio 54 were sentenced to three and a half years in prison for tax evasion. At the same time other venues opened in disused warehouses in Chelsea, lower Manhattan, and the meatpacking district; at these clubs racially mixed crowds danced to rap, "house," and other forms of music on enormous dance floors. Among the few clubs of this kind to last more than a year or two were the Palladium at 126 East 14th Street (1984), an ultramodern club opened by Rubell and Schrager; the Limelight (1985), in a disused church at 47 West 20th Street; and Area at 157 Hudson Street (1983–87), which redesigned its interior every season and drew huge crowds. Other notable establishments included the Tunnel (a former railroad station at 12th Avenue and 28th Street) and Mars (a warehouse at 28 10th Avenue), both frequented by fashionable young people and residents of the suburbs; 12 West at 491 West Street, opened in 1975 by Michael Fesco as the city's first discothèque with an overtly homosexual clientele; the Mudd Club at 77 White Street (during the late 1970s and early 1980s); and Nell's, an intimate club at 246 West 14th Street (opened in 1986).

Ballroom dancing retained its appeal. By the time Murray retired from dance instruction in 1964 he oversaw an empire that included a thriving mail-order business and more than 300 franchised dance studios. In the same year there were at least 25 other ballroom dance schools and studios in Manhattan. Refined social dancing continued to be practiced at Roseland and at the Red Parrot (617 West 57th Street). Latin American dances and rhythms, which first gained popularity during the 1940s and 1950s, became more prevalent as the number of Spanish-speaking immigrants increased. At the Palladium (Broadway and 53rd Street) Frank "Killer Joe" Piro taught such Latin dances as the samba, the mambo, and the conga. The city's Spanish-speaking population also frequented unlicensed social clubs, a practice that was usually ignored by other residents of the city until it was brought to their attention by such tragic incidents as the Happy Land fire of 1990, in which 87 people died at 1959 Southern Boulevard in the Bronx. During the 1980s influential Latin dance clubs included the Corso (205 East 86th Street) and the Copacabana (10 East 60th Street). In the first decade of the twenty-first century the trendiest clubs tended to be on the West Side of Manhattan, especially the meatpacking district in Chelsea.

Marc Ferris

Dance Theater Workshop. Organization for contemporary choreographers and dancers. In 1965 it was founded to sponsor and support choreographers, especially those early in their careers. Hundreds of artists have worked with the organization, including Whoopi Goldberg, Mark Morris, David Gordon, Bill T. Jones, and Molissa Fenley. Under the directorship of David White (1975–2003), the

Dance Theater Workshop expanded greatly and introduced the New York Dance and Performance Awards, or Bessie Awards; the Suitcase Fund; the New York State Dance-Force; and the National Performance Network, a program to support experimental dance outside the city. The organization also helps its members with publicity and other practical aspects of presentation. In 2002 the Dance Theater Workshop opened its Doris Duke Performance Center, which houses administrative offices, two large rehearsal studios, and the Bessie Schönberg Theater. Each year the Dance Theater Workshop presents more than 110 performances from about 45 different companies and artists.

Joan Acocella

Dance Theatre of Harlem. Dance company formed in New York City in 1969. Its artistic director, Arthur Mitchell (*b* New York City, 27 March 1934), had been the first full-time black member of the New York City Ballet (1955–68) and one of its most popular soloists, creating many roles in ballets by George Balanchine. Its ballet master was Karel Shook. The company made its debut at the Guggenheim Museum in 1971, gave successful performances in the United States and abroad, and became known for flouting racial stereotypes and what Mitchell called "the myth that ballet has something to do with race, creed, and class." It assembled a large, varied repertory that included nineteenth-century Russian classics, many ballets by Balanchine, and works by such contemporary choreographers as Glen Tetley and Garth Fagan. In the 1980s it revisited *Giselle* in a Creole setting. Among those who have been associated with the company are Ronald Perry, Mel Tomlinson, and Paul Russell. Its school at West 152nd Street in Manhattan continues to train hundreds of students.

Brenda Dixon Gottschild

Danes. Danish sailors were among the crew of Henry Hudson's ship the *Halve Maen,* which sailed into New York Harbor in 1609. Among the many Danish settlers who lived in New Amsterdam was Jonas Bronck, who moved there in 1629 and bought large tracts of land just north of Manhattan that became known as the Bronx (probably after him). At least 100 Danes lived in New York City by 1675, and in 1704 they joined with Norwegians to build a small Lutheran chapel near the intersection of Broadway and Rector Street. Immigration from Denmark reached a peak during a period of political unrest there between 1850 and 1900, and most Danes passed through the city on their way west; those who remained usually lived in the Scandinavian section of Bay Ridge in Brooklyn. Danish men were often mechanics, sailors, carpenters, and bricklayers. Many of them belonged to unions, and some were prominent musicians and professionals. Most Danish immigrants were Lutheran, but many married members of other ethnic and religious groups. Dania, a health insurance organization for Scandinavian immigrants, opened a branch in Brooklyn in 1886. A Danish-language paper, *Nordlyset* (The Northern Light), was published in the city from 1891 to 1953, and in 1903, 17 Danish organizations were listed within the paper, none with more than 100 members. By 1930 the Danish-born accounted for less than 1 percent of the population of New York City, but about 200,000 persons were of Danish descent. One of the best-known Danes in the city was Jacob A. Riis, a photographer, reformer, and writer whose book *How the Other Half Lives* (1890) exposed the destitution of the city's slums; he was called "New York's most useful citizen" by President Theodore Roosevelt, and his work led to many reforms in tenement regulations.

Chad Ludington

Danilova, Alexandra (*b* Peterhof, Russia, 20 Nov 1903; *d* Manhattan, 13 July 1997). Dancer. She trained in St. Petersburg and in 1924 left Russia with schoolmate and choreographer George Balanchine. The two traveled and worked together, sharing a lifelong professional and personal relationship. In the 1920s she danced with Sergei Diaghilev's Ballets Russes and during the peak of her career (1938–51) with the Ballet Russe de Monte Carlo, which became an American company at the beginning of World War II. An immensely versatile ballerina, she danced heroic, glamorous, and mischievous principal roles. Danilova was known for her commanding stage presence and beautiful legs and became one of the most popular ballerinas of her time. In 1958 she made her Broadway debut in *Oh, Captain!,* in which her only scene was a well-received dance sequence with Tony Randall. However, the show was a failure and closed. Balanchine then hired Danilova to work at his School of American Ballet, where she taught from 1964 to 1989. She and Balanchine staged the ballet "Coppélia" for the New York City Ballet in 1974. Through her dancing and teaching Danilova helped to incorporate the charm and glamour of late nineteenth-century Russian classical ballet into the sleek classical styles developed in the United States during the late twentieth century, especially by the New York City Ballet under Balanchine's direction. In 1986 she wrote *Choura: The Memoirs of Alexandra Danilova,* and after her retirement from teaching, she became a dance lecturer.

Frank Nestor

Dannon Yogurt. Firm of yogurt makers formed in 1942 in the Bronx by Daniel Carasso, the son of a Spanish yogurt maker, and Joe Metzger. It moved in the following year to Long Island City in Queens, and was acquired in 1959 by Beatrice Foods and in 1981 by the French firm BSN Groupe. It moved its main office to suburban White Plains, New York, in 1986. In the early twenty-first century it sold and produced over six million cups of yogurt a day, encompassing more than 100 flavors and styles, making Dannon the top-selling yogurt brand in the world.

Leslie Gourse

Danticat, Edwidge (*b* Port-au-Prince, Haiti, 19 Jan 1969). Novelist, memoirist, and short-story writer. After her parents immigrated to New York City to escape dictator Jean-Claude Duvalier's regime, Danticat remained in Haiti under the care of her aunt and uncle. In 1981 she and her younger brother reunited with their parents in Brooklyn. She received a BA from Barnard College and an MFA from Brown University. Channeling her personal experiences as an immigrant into her writing, Danticat became the predominant English-speaking voice of Haiti, and her books worked to diversify the American canon. She moved to Miami in 2002.

Clare Richfield

Da Ponte, Lorenzo [Conegliano, Emanuele] (*b* Ceneda [now Vittorio Veneto], Italy, 10 March 1749; *d* New York City, 17 Aug 1838). Librettist, bookseller, impresario, and teacher. After writing the librettos of many celebrated operas, notably Mozart's *Don Giovanni* and *Le Nozze di Figaro,* he moved to New York City in 1805 with the intention of spreading Italian culture. Soon after arriving he was befriended by Clement Clarke Moore, who helped him to establish a school where he taught students the language and literature of Italy, France, and Spain. After seven years in an unsuccessful foray into commerce in Sunbury, Pennsylvania, he returned to New York City and with his brother Carlo began importing Italian books to the United States. First operating out of his home on Broadway and later from a store, he wrote a widely read annotated catalogue for his customers that contained a history of Italian literature. From 1825 he taught Italian at Columbia College, to which he sold his library of Italian books. In November 1825 he helped to bring about productions by a visiting opera company of Rossini's *Il Barbiere di Siviglia* and of *Don Giovanni.* Convinced of the need for a full-fledged professional opera company in New York City, he pursued patrons and in 1833 proposed, commenced, and completed construction of the Italian Opera House. The neoclassical building was considered the most sumptuous theater in the United States and displaced the Park Theatre as the leading theater in the city. Da Ponte had succeeded in establishing opera as an art form in New York City by the time the theater was destroyed by fire in 1841.

Sheila Hodges, *Lorenzo Da Ponte* (London: Granada, 1985); *Lorenzo Da Ponte: A Vision of Italy from Columbia College* (New York: Columbia University, 1991)

Thomas M. Hilbink

D. Appleton. Firm of publishers formed by Daniel Appleton, the owner of a general store at 16 Exchange Place. Appleton published his first book, an inspirational volume of biblical texts, in 1831, and during the next few years became known for publishing devotional and theological books as well as reprints of British fiction. He made his son William Henry Appleton a partner in 1838, and together they produced Spanish-language and children's books, ventures that proved shrewd and profitable. After his father's death in 1849, William Henry Appleton took over the firm and engaged his brothers as partners; his association with editor and author Edward L. Youmans led to the publication of many important scientific works by such writers as Charles Darwin and Herbert Spencer. Known for its varied list, the firm also produced sentimental fiction, medical books, the novels of Edith Wharton, *Alice's Adventures in Wonderland*, General William T. Sherman's memoirs, and such reference works as the *New American Cyclopaedia*, a work in 16 volumes. D. Appleton remained in the Appleton family until a business failure in 1900. In 1933 it merged with the firm of Century to become Appleton–Century.

Charles A. Madison, *Book Publishing in America* (New York: McGraw–Hill, 1966); John Tebbel, *Between Covers: The Rise and Transformation of Book Publishing in America* (New York: Oxford University Press, 1987)

Alice Fahs

Darin, Bobby [Cassotto, Walden Robert] (*b* Bronx, 14 May 1936; *d* Los Angeles, Calif., 20 Dec 1973). Performer. After graduating from the Bronx High School of Science, he signed with Decca Records in 1956. After he recorded "Splish Splash" in 1958 with Atlantic Records, his career took off. In 1959 he recorded the ballad "Dream Lover," and a year later his album *Mack the Knife* won the Grammy Award for Record of the Year. In the 1960s he became involved in politics and worked on Robert F. Kennedy's campaign. Noted for his big-band sound, he continued recording and also acted in several films until his death. In 1990 he was posthumously inducted into the Rock and Roll Hall of Fame. The 2004 movie *Under the Sea* was a biopic of Darin's life.

Jessica Montesano

Darley, F(elix) O(ctavius) C(arr) (*b* Philadelphia, 23 June 1822; *d* Claymont, Del., 27 March 1888). Illustrator. He moved to New York City in 1848 and became one of the most popular and influential illustrators of his time. During the late 1840s and 1850s he illustrated works by Washington Irving and James Fenimore Cooper and a collection of comic essays by William Evans Burton, *The Yankee among the Mermaids* (1854–58). His style was one of the first with a distinctively American point of view and brand of humor; he had a talent for satire and subtle overstatement, and his work encouraged other illustrators to develop their own styles rather than imitate English ones. He was best known for his engravings for *Rip Van Winkle* (1848) and *The Legend of Sleepy Hollow* (1849). Darley helped to form the American Society of Painters in Water Colors and also belonged to the Artists' Fund Society of New York and the National Academy of Design.

Ethel M. King, *Darley, the Most Popular Illustrator of His Time* (New York: T. Gaus' Sons, 1964)

Michael Joseph

David Mannes Music School. Original name of the Mannes College of Music.

Davies, J. Clarence (*b* 1868; *d* 13 April 1934). Real estate developer. Educated at City College, he opened a real estate office in the Bronx in 1889 with funds borrowed from his family. He was one of the organizers of the Bronx Board of Trade, had important local political connections, and became known for his collection of historical memorabilia connected with New York City, including more than 15,000 items that he willed to the Museum of the City of New York. He was also a longtime trustee of the Association for the Improvement of the Education of the Deaf. Davies called himself the "king of the Bronx" because of his prominent role in the development of real estate in the area.

Stephen A. Stertz

Davis, Alexander Jackson (*b* New York City, 24 July 1803; *d* West Orange, N.J., 14 Jan 1892). Architect. With Ithiel Town he designed the U.S. Custom House on Wall Street (1833–42, now Federal Hall) in the Greek Revival style. In buildings such as the chapel of New York University (1835–37, formerly at Washington Square), designed in the Gothic Revival style, he introduced an irregular picturesque style that reached its height in the villas of Grace Hill in Prospect Park (1854–56,

Advertisement for D. Appleton's "stereoscopic views," ca *1870*

commissioned by Edwin Litchfield) and Lyndhurst in Tarrytown, New York (1838–42, enlarged 1864–67). With the landscape architect Andrew Jackson Downing he promoted these as an ideal form of domestic architecture. A member of the short-lived American Institution of Architects (1836–37) and later of the American Institute of Architects, he actively took part in attempts to professionalize American architecture by forming organizations to promote standards of education and practice. Considered a leading architect of his time, Davis introduced many of the revival styles that became popular during the mid- to late nineteenth century. He is also known for his design of the nation's first planned suburb, Llewellyn Park in New Jersey, a model of picturesque design that he laid out in 1853.

Amelia Peck, ed., *Alexander Jackson Davis, American Architect, 1803–1892* (New York: Rizzoli, 1992)

Mary Beth Betts

Davis, Benjamin Jefferson (*b* Dawson, Ga., 8 Sept 1903; *d* New York City, 22 Aug 1964). Civil rights leader and editor of the *Negro Liberator,* as well as the *Daily Worker.* He was elected as a communist to the City Council from Harlem, replacing Adam Clayton Powell, Jr., after his election to the U.S. Congress in 1944. Davis was expelled from his office for alleged subversive activities before his second term ended. In 1959 he was elected to the National Committee of the Communist Party and served as its secretary.

Gerald Horne, *Black Liberation/Red Scare: Ben Davis of the Communist Party* (Newark: University of Delaware Press, 1994)

Janet Frankston

Davis, John W(illiam) (*b* Clarksburg, W.Va., 13 April 1873; *d* Charleston, S.C., 24 March 1955). Lawyer, diplomat, and presidential candidate. He attended Washington and Lee University (BA 1892, LLB 1895) and was elected to the U.S. Congress as a Democrat in 1910 and 1912, later serving as solicitor general of the United States (from 1913) and ambassador to Great Britain (1918–21). After settling in New York City he formed the law firm that later became Davis Polk and Wardwell. At the Democratic National Convention in New York City in 1924, where the atmosphere was tense because of the high summer temperature and a controversial proposal to denounce the Ku Klux Klan by name, Davis received the presidential nomination on the 103rd ballot. But he campaigned ineffectively against Calvin Coolidge and lost the general election by a wide margin. He then resumed his legal career, during which he argued 141 cases before the U.S. Supreme Court.

William H. Harbaugh, *Lawyer's Lawyer: The Life of John W. Davis* (New York: Oxford University Press, 1973; repr. Charlottesville: University Press of Virginia, 1990)

Davis, Miles (Dewey, III) (*b* Alton, Ill., 26 May 1926; *d* Santa Monica, Calif., 28 Sept 1991). Jazz trumpeter and bandleader. The son of a dentist and a musician, he grew up in East St. Louis (Illinois) and at age 13 learned to play the trumpet from one of his father's patients, Elwood Buchanan, who taught him to play cleanly and without vibrato. He was taken to bars around St. Louis by his next teacher, Clark Terry. He soon joined a local rhythm-and-blues band, the Blue Devils, and became its music director. After graduating from high school, he moved to New York City to enroll at the Juilliard School in 1945, dropping out shortly thereafter, as he developed a reputation in jazz clubs as a first-rate bebopper. He made his recording debut the same year and was a sideman on many of Charlie Parker's seminal Savoy and Dial sides. After leaving Parker at the end of 1948, he made his first real recordings as a leader in 1949, with a nonet that included Johnny Carisi, the saxophonists Gerry Mulligan and Lee Konitz, and the pianist John Lewis, as well as arranger Gil Evans, in a lighter though bebop-derived sound that became known as the *Birth of the Cool* sessions. After several years of somewhat intermittent work because of a heroin addiction, he signed with Prestige in 1954 and organized his so-called first quintet, with John Coltrane, Red Garland, Philly Joe Jones, and Paul Chambers. The group stayed together through 1958, with Cannonball Adderly making it a sextet in 1957. Davis became known for rendering ballads with a unique emotional intensity; for his improvisations on such standards as "Bye, Bye Blackbird," "Surrey with the Fringe on Top," and "My Funny Valentine"; for his own compositions, such as "Four"; and for an aggressive, unembellished blues style on "Walkin'" and "Bags' Groove." In 1955 he signed a recording contract with Columbia Records, with whom he would record for the next three decades. His best-known albums of the period were *'Round about Midnight* (1956), *Milestones* (1958), and *Straight, No Chaser* (1958). With Gil Evans he also made a series of remarkable big band recordings, *Miles Ahead* (1957), *Porgy and Bess* (1958), and *Sketches of Spain* (1960). *Kind of Blue* (1959), probably his best-known album, with pianist Bill Evans on most tracks, was an exemplar of modal improvising. After several years of changing personnel and moving to a more forceful and impressionistic style, he formed his "second quartet" in 1964 with Ron Carter, Herbie Hancock, and Tony Williams, joined the following year by Wayne Shorter. The group played mostly original material and lasted until 1968, when Davis began to experiment with rhythm and blues, rock, and electronic instrumentation, which remained the basis of his improvisations for most of the remainder of his career. He produced *In a Silent Way* (1969), *Bitches Brew* (1969), and *Jack Johnson* (1970), playing with noted instrumentalists such as pianists Chick Corea and Joe Zawinul, the electric guitarist John McLaughlin, and others. By the early 1970s Davis was plagued by ill health, and he retired in 1974. He resumed playing in 1981, but his playing during his last decade generally was not as well-regarded as his earlier work. In all, he recorded about 35 albums. Throughout his career Davis made New York City his base, and he lived in a series of hotel rooms and apartments before purchasing a brownstone at 312 West 77th Street in 1961. Later, he moved to Fifth Avenue and 79th Street, where he lived until his death. He was buried in the Woodlawn Cemetery in the Bronx.

Miles Davis

Miles Davis, with Quincy Troupe, *Miles: The Autobiography* (Simon and Schuster: New York, 1989); Ian Carr, *Miles Davis: The Definitive Biography* (New York: Harper Collins, 1999)

S. D. R. Cashman, Peter Eisenstadt, Marc Ferris

Davis, Ossie [Raiford Chatman] (*b* Cogdell, Ga., 18 Dec 1917; *d* Miami Beach, Fla., 4 Feb 2005). Actor. In 1939 he dropped out of Howard University to pursue his acting career with the Rose McClendon Players in Harlem. He later graduated from Columbia University. Although his acting career was interrupted by World War II, Davis returned to New York City and Broadway after his army service. In 1950 he made his film debut in *No Way Out,* and in 1970 he made his directorial debut with the film *Cotton Comes to Harlem.* Davis was also known for his involvement in the civil rights movement, and along with his wife, Ruby Dee, he helped organize the 1963 March on Washington. He was nominated for two Tony Awards, first in 1958 for Best Supporting Actor in a Musical for *Jamaica,* and in 1970 (as coauthor) for Best Book of a Musical for *Purlie.* Throughout his career he acted in movies, on Broadway, and directed several movies; he continued acting until his death.

Jessica Montesano

Davis, Reverend Gary (*b* Laurens, S.C., 30 April 1896; *d* Hammonton, N.J., 5 May 1972). Guitarist. Born partially blind, by his youth he had completely lost his vision. He began learning guitar at the age of six and went on to play both secular and religious songs. In 1940 he moved to New York City, playing "gospel blues" and preaching on the streets of Harlem. Later in his life he became more religious and was ordained at the Missionary Baptist Connection Church in Brooklyn. A master of the finger-picking style of guitar playing, his style influenced many famous musicians, such as Jerry Garcia and Ry Cooder. He recorded a few albums in the 1950s and 1960s, songs from which were rerecorded by the likes of Bob Dylan and Peter, Paul and Mary.

Jessica Montesano

Davis, Richard Harding (*b* Philadelphia, 18 April 1864; *d* Mount Kisco, N.Y., 11 April 1916). Journalist. He entered journalism in Philadelphia as a young man. After reporting on the Johnstown Flood in 1889 he joined the *New York Sun* and later became the editor of *Harper's Weekly.* As a war correspondent for several journals he covered the Greco–Turkish, Boer, Spanish–American, Russo–Japanese, and Balkan wars, and World War I, often using sensational prose. Davis also wrote and published fiction, plays, and a popular musical comedy.

Gerald Langford, *Richard Harding Davis Years: A Biography of a Mother and Son* (New York: Henry Holt, 1961)

Julian S. Rammelkamp

Davis, Stuart (*b* Philadelphia, 7 Dec 1892; *d* New York City, 24 June 1964). Painter. The son of two artists, he moved to New York City in 1909 to study with Robert Henri. His work was exhibited at the Armory Show in 1913, and in the same year he joined the staff of the independent socialist magazine the *Masses* as a protégé of the realist artist John Sloan; he left the magazine in 1916 over a dispute with the editors. Exhibitions of his work at the Newark Museum in New Jersey and at the Whitney Studio Club sponsored by Gertrude Vanderbilt Whitney encouraged his new interest in experimenting with formal problems. Seeking to create an unsentimental, uniquely American art and influenced by jazz, he developed a cubist style that used flat, overlapping, brightly colored shapes and motifs from everyday life, such as gasoline pumps, commercial logotypes, and billboard advertisements. Many consider his images, such as *Lucky Strike* (1921), prototypes for pop art. During the 1930s he sought to develop an art with social content through his abstract style. He also belonged to the Artists' Union and edited its publication, *Art Front,* and was the executive secretary of the American Artists' Congress (1936–40). Under the auspices of the Federal Art Project he painted murals for the Williamsburg Housing Project and for the radio station WNYC. In 1991 the Metropolitan Museum of Art held a major retrospective of his work.

Patricia Hills, *Stuart Davis* (New York: Harry N. Abrams, 1996)

Patricia Hills

Day, Benjamin (Henry) (*b* West Springfield, Mass., 10 April 1810; *d* New York City, 21 Dec 1889). Newspaper publisher and editor. After beginning his career as a printer he launched the *Sun* in September 1833, which under his direction attained the highest circulation of any daily newspaper in the United States. His innovations included using newsboys to sell newspapers in the streets, eschewing party journalism, and emphasizing crime reportage and sensational hoaxes. In 1838 Day sold the *Sun* to Moses Yale Beach, and in 1842 he assumed management of the illustrated literary periodical *Brother Jonathan.*

Francis Beacham Whitlock, *Two New Yorkers, Editor and Sea Captain, 1833* (New York: Newcomen Society, 1945)

Steven H. Jaffe

Day, Dorothy (May) (*b* Brooklyn, 8 Nov 1897; *d* New York City, 29 Nov 1980). Social activist. She became interested in the socialist movement while attending the University of Illinois and on her return to New York City worked as a reporter for the *New York Call,* a socialist daily newspaper. During the 1920s she married and divorced, published a novel, and bore a daughter out of wedlock. After converting to Catholicism she founded the weekly newspaper the Catholic Worker in 1933 with the French religious mystic and social critic Peter Maurin. The paper sold for one cent and had a circulation that reached 185,000 in 1940; it explored pacifism, anarchist utopianism, and Catholic social thought through spiritual essays and radical reporting. In 1933 the newspaper inspired a social movement when Day and her followers opened a soup kitchen on the Lower East Side. By 1938 1200 people were fed there every day, and other "houses of hospitality" opened in dozens of other cities by the end of the decade. The *Catholic Worker* lost many supporters when its opposition to violence provoked hostility during World War II, but it influenced later generations of Catholic social activists. After Day's death St. Joseph House on East First Street and Maryhouse on East Third Street continued to operate. Among other books, she wrote *The Long Loneliness: The Autobiography of Dorothy Day* (1952). In 2000 Pope John Paul II granted the Archdiocese of New York permission to open a cause for Day's sainthood, thereby granting her the title of a "Servant of God" according to the Catholic Church.

Mel Piehl, *Breaking Bread: The Catholic Worker and the Origin of Catholic Radicalism in America* (Philadelphia: Temple University Press, 1982)

Maurice Isserman

DC Comics. Firm of comic book publishers formed in 1935 in New York City as National Allied Publications. In the year of its founding it introduced *New Fun Comics,* a comic book containing adventure stories. In 1936 the firm became Detective Comics, a name that it also used as the title for a comic book of crime and suspense published in the following year. It introduced Superman, its first "superhero," in *Action Comics* in 1938. Batman, who first appeared in *Detective Comics* in 1940, fought crime in Gotham City, a fictitious version of New York City. The company soon developed the Flash (1940), the Green Lantern (1941), and Wonder Woman (1942), who were early members of the Justice Society of America, the first superhero team. Although interest in superheroes declined after 1945, the firm revived its fortunes by revamping its characters in 1956. In 1977 it officially took the name DC Comics, after using it unofficially for years. DC Comics published a 12-issue series called *Crisis on Infinite Earth* in 1985 and an acclaimed "graphic novel" featuring Batman called *The Dark Knight Returns* in 1986. A division of Time Warner, DC moved to 1700 Broadway in the mid-1990s. In the twenty-first century DC published more than 80 titles each month and close to 1000 issues per year. It catered to a diverse readership through several imprints, including DC Universe, Vertigo, CMX, and Zuda.

Will Jacobs and Gerard Jones, *The Comic Book Heroes: From the Silver Age to the Present* (New York: Crown, 1985); Mike Benton, *The Comic Book in America: An Illustrated History* (Dallas: Taylor, 1989)

Patricia A. Perito

DDB Needham Worldwide. Advertising agency formed in 1986 through a merger of Needham Harper Worldwide and the Doyle Dane Bernbach Group. Needham Harper was founded in 1925 in Chicago by Maurice H. Needham and opened its first office in New York City in 1939. Doyle Dane Bernbach was formed in 1949 in New York City by Ned Doyle, Maxwell Dane, and the well-known copywriter William Bernbach, who in the 1960s was the most influential figure in the "creative revolution" in advertising. In the twenty-first century the agency was known as DDB Worldwide and had its headquarters at 437 Madison Avenue.

Chauncey G. Olinger, Jr.

Dead End. Name sometimes applied in the early twentieth century to a small neighborhood in the East 50s along the East River, so named because of the extreme poverty of the area and because the streets "dead-ended" there at the edge of the river. A play about the neighborhood, Sidney Kingsley's *Dead End,* was produced in 1935; it inspired several films in which the street gang the Dead End Kids appeared.

Irving Lewis Allen

Dead Man's Curve. Nickname for a sharp curve on Manhattan's Broadway cable car line at Union Square just north of 14th Street. The name came into use after 1891, when cable cars replaced the horse-drawn cars between South Ferry and Central Park. Gripmen knew that if they applied the brakes in the middle of the curve, the cars would become stranded, and as a result the cars were driven quickly around the curve with no concession for other vehicles or pedestrians, causing many accidents. The danger persisted until electric streetcars were introduced after the turn of the century.

Andrew Sparberg

Dead Man's Curve, ca *1900*

Dead Rabbits. Irish gang in the sixth ward; the term *dead rabbit* was a slang term for a rowdy. The gang supported Mayor Fernando Wood and was apparently known as the Mulberry Street Boys until a riot with the rival nativist gang the Bowery Boys in the Five Points neighborhood on 4 July 1857, which was prompted by the formation of a new state police force and the enactment of liquor laws intended partly to undermine Wood's power. The Metropolitan Police were driven from the neighborhood by the Mulberry Street Boys and were then replaced by the Bowery Boys. The violence of the riot (12 people were killed) prompted the renaming of the Mulberry Street Boys by the press and the police. Although little is known about the gang apart from hearsay, later chroniclers considered the Dead Rabbits the most violent gang of the mid-nineteenth century. The gang was popularized in director Martin Scorsese's 2002 motion picture *Gangs of New York.*

Joshua Brown

deafness. One of the first of several important institutions for deaf New Yorkers was the New York School for the Deaf, opened in 1818 in the city almshouse as the second institution of its kind in the United States. In 1829 a building was dedicated on 50th Street between Fourth and Fifth avenues. The school floundered until 1831, when Harvey Pringle Peet became the principal; he developed a vocational program that became standard in residential schools for deaf children (1831), replaced a weak staff with several of the school's finest graduates and college-educated hearing teachers (including F. A. P. Barnard, later president of Columbia University), and introduced home instruction of deaf children, who by law were not permitted to attend the school until the age of 12. Recognized as one of the finest schools of its kind in the country, it used the French method of instruction, which relied on sign language as the primary mode of communication. The school was the site of the first Convention of American Instructors of the Deaf in 1850 and in 1852 introduced a "high class" for its most promising students, who received three years of college preparatory work after completing the regular course. Their success led to the formation in 1864 of the world's first collegiate institution for deaf students in Washington, D.C., now known as Gallaudet University. In 1852 Thomas Gallaudet, the hearing son of a deaf woman, formed in New York City St. Ann's Church for Deaf-Mutes, the first church in the country designed for a deaf congregation. Afternoon services were signed, and morning services were spoken for the family and friends of deaf parishioners. The popularity of the church led to the introduction of deaf services nationwide and to the ordination of deaf ministers in the Episcopal Church and other denominations. In 1856 the New York School for the Deaf moved to a property in Washington Heights known as Fanwood, which became its popular name.

In 1867 the New York Institution for the Improved Instruction of Deaf-Mutes opened on Lexington Avenue between 67th and 68th streets as a private school for the deaf children of German-speaking immigrants; it later became known as the Lexington School. The director was Bernhard Engelsman, who had taught deaf children in Vienna according to the German tradition of teaching deaf students without sign language, relying instead on speech and speechreading. He was the first in the United States to make successful use of this method, which was also adopted by his successors. In 1870 Fanwood became the world's largest school of its kind with 616 pupils, and Lexington secured state support on the same basis as Fanwood, guaranteeing its survival. The Manhattan Literary Society for the Deaf was formed by the deaf artist and intellectual John Carlin. It was followed by the Deaf-Mutes' Union League, which was organized in 1887 by graduates of Lexington and united deaf professionals around common goals, especially philanthropic activities; the league was unusual in its acceptance of oral education. The country's most important publication during this period was the *Deaf-Mutes' Journal,* launched in Mexico, New York, by Henry Rider, a graduate of Fanwood. It eventually became affiliated with the school and under the direction of Edwin Hodgson during the 1890s and early twentieth century became a fierce advocate of educational, professional, and personal rights for deaf people. The success of the Lexington School lent strength to the growing popular support of the oral method. German-speakers established similar institutions in Milwaukee, Detroit, and Baltimore, and by 1920 the oral method was in virtually universal use in the United States. Fanwood moved to suburban White Plains, New York, in 1938; enrollment declined to about 300 by 1970.

The deaf community in New York City has had a number of prominent members, especially in the arts. Helen Keller lived in Forest Hills from 1917 to 1938. The poet James Nack lived in the city, as did the photographer Alexander Pach. In 1934 Emerson Romero, a graduate of the Wright Oral School, set up a theater guild in the city for deaf actors unwelcome in Hollywood after the advent of "talkies." From 1937 to 1963 Ernest Marshall, a graduate of Fanwood, made motion pictures in sign language. Bernard Bragg, also a graduate of Fanwood, helped to form the National Theatre of the Deaf, which presented productions with deaf actors for hearing audiences. Such efforts were instrumental in the success that deaf actors began to achieve by the early 1990s.

St. Ann's ceased operations as a separate church in 1949 but as of 2007 remained a mission affiliated with the Episcopal Diocese of New York. Some of the most important political activists for the deaf were Hodgson and Thomas Fox, teachers at the New York School for the Deaf who later led the National Association of the Deaf, and Fred Schreiber, a graduate of Lexington and Fanwood who during the 1960s transformed the association into a powerful advocacy organization.

John Vickrey Van Cleve and Barry A. Crouch, *A Place of Their Own: Creating the Deaf Community in America* (Washington, D.C.: Gallaudet University Press, 1989)

John Vickrey Van Cleve

Dean, James (*b* Marion, Ind., 8 Feb 1931; *d* Cholame, Calif., 30 Sept 1955). Actor. After growing up in California, he moved in 1951 to New York City, appearing on several television shows and enrolling in the famed Actor's Studio under the instruction of Lee Strasberg. His first Broadway role was a small part in a production entitled *See the Jaguar,* which closed after only five performances. While in New York City, Dean lived at 19 West 68th Street from 1953 until his death. He also spent time at the Iroquois Hotel at 49 West 44th Street, and at the Young Men's Christian Association (YMCA) on West 63rd Street. Dean went on to star in three motion pictures: *East of Eden* (1955), *Rebel without a Cause* (1955), and *Giant* (1956). He died in a car wreck at age 24. He is the only actor to have received two posthumous Academy Award nominations.

Anne Epstein

Dean Witter Reynolds. Firm of securities brokers formed in 1978 by the merger of Dean Witter and Company (1924) and Reynolds Securities (1931). At the time the merger was the largest in the history of the securities business. In 1981 the firm was acquired by Sears, Roebuck and Company and became the nucleus of its financial services network. It launched the Discover credit card in 1986. In 1993 Sears spun the company off and it became an independent, publicly traded company called Dean Witter, Discover and Company. In 1997 it merged with Morgan Stanley Group, headquartered in Manhattan, and became Morgan Stanley Dean Witter for a brief period before the Dean Witter name was dropped entirely.

Chad Ludington

Dearie, Blossom (Margrete) (*b* East Durham, N.Y., 29 April 1926; *d* New York City, 7 Feb 2009). Jazz cabaret singer. Famous in the jazz and cabaret circuit for her clear, girlish voice, perfect diction, light piano style, and witty and sophisticated lyrics, she moved to New York City in the 1940s, where she absorbed the city's rich jazz scene and joined the Blue Flames, a vocal group connected with the Woody Herman Band. She spent a few years in Paris in the 1950s performing with the Blue Stars, but returned in the late 1950s to New York City, where she lived in Greenwich Village until her death. She recorded six Verve albums from 1956 to 1960, which are today regarded as classics; these include *Blossom Dearie, Once upon a Summertime,* and *My Gentleman Friend.* In the 1970s she founded her own label, Daffodil Records, which produced an album with all original lyrics and music, *Blossom Dearie Sings.* Until 2006 she regularly performed in Manhattan at Danny's Skylight Room and often traveled to London to perform at Ronnie Scott's Jazz Club. Known as a perfectionist who would not tolerate noisy patrons or cigarette smoke during her performances, Dearie attracted a loyal and cult-like circle of fans.

Lisa Keller

Death Avenue. Nickname given to several New York City avenues where the New York Central Railroad tracks ran at street level, resulting in high pedestrian fatalities and consistent public outcry. Between the mid-nineteenth century and 1913, when the train line was finally buried underground, 10th Avenue, Fourth Avenue, and 11th Avenue were all christened Death Avenue in turn.

Elizabeth L. Bradley

debtor's prison. The attic of the old city hall served as a debtor's prison in colonial New York City until the New Gaol, with three stories and a basement, was built on Chambers Street in 1755. Under colonial and early state law, debtors could often be imprisoned on a creditor's unproven suspicion that they were hiding assets. Once in prison, debtors were forced to rely on family, friends, and private charity for their upkeep. Most prisoners were desperately poor workers who fell victim to the panics of the time: in some years, half owed less than $10 and several owed less than $1. There were also some merchants, among them William Duer, the largest financial speculator of the 1790s. In later years, especially after 1810, debtors were often allowed to post bond and live on the "limits," an area that eventually extended south of 14th Street to the tip of Manhattan. In 1784 the state legislature permitted insolvent debtors to be freed from future obligations if consent was obtained from the creditors who represented three-fourths of their debt; the quota was changed to two-thirds in 1813. From 1801 to 1803 state insolvency law was superseded by federal bankruptcy law, which allowed for voluntary (debtor-initiated) declarations, but this was for merchants and traders only. Women with debts of less than $50 were exempted from prison in 1811; debtors who were not freeholders and had less than $25 in assets were exempted in 1817 (the amount was increased to $50 in 1824). Eventually, reformers like Joseph Fay helped to convince the public that in the credit-driven economy insolvency was a consequence of misfortune rather than moral failure, and that imprisoning nonfraudulent debtors was impractical and unjust. In 1831 New York became the second state (after Kentucky) to forbid imprisonment for insolvency.

Peter J. Coleman, *Debtors and Creditors in America: Insolvency, Imprisonment for Debt, and Bankruptcy, 1607–1900* (Madison: State Historical Society of Wisconsin, 1974); James Ciment, "In the Light of Failure: Bankruptcy, Insolvency and Financial Failure in New York City, 1790–1860" (diss., City University of New York, 1992)

James Ciment

de Burgos, Julia (*b* Carolina, Puerto Rico, 17 Feb 1914; *d* New York City, 6 July 1953). Poet, journalist, and activist. Known as the Poet Laureate of Puerto Rico, she was a passionate literary talent of mixed heritage whose poems were critically acclaimed and published in every Spanish-speaking country. She moved to New York City in 1940 and worked as a journalist, marrying poet Armando Marín. After her divorce in 1947 de Burgos became depressed; in 1953 she collapsed on the street in Spanish Harlem and died of pneumonia. Because she was not carrying identification she was buried at the Hart Island potter's field. Her remains were eventually returned to Puerto Rico, where she was given a proper burial. Her social activism, born of her concern for equality for women and people of African and Latino descent, was evident in her poetry and journalism, as well as in her participation in the Négritude literary movement. Collector and poet Jack Agueros has translated and published her known poems and discovered hundreds of lost works, but her full body of work is yet to be unearthed. In East Harlem, Fifth Avenue at East 106th Street was named Julia de Burgos Boulevard in 2007.

Sharon Wilkins

DeCarava, Roy (*b* New York City, 9 Dec 1919; *d* New York City, 27 Oct 2009). Photographer. The only child of Elfreda Ferguson, a Jamaican immigrant and amateur photographer, he studied at a high school for textile studies, at the Cooper Union School of Art, and finally at the Harlem Community Art Center on 125th Street. After serving in the U.S. Army in World War II, DeCarava returned to New York City and became a leader in the street photography world, where photographers showcase subjects in public situations in a natural and candid manner. After becoming the first black photographer to win a prestigious Guggenheim Fellowship, he began to take photographs in Harlem. Meanwhile, he was mentored by the famous photographer Edward Steichen, who used DeCarava's pictures in the famous *Family of Man* exhibition at the Museum of Modern Art in 1955. Later, DeCarava began to specialize in photographing jazz musicians, such as Count Basie, Duke Ellington, Louis Armstrong, and Billie Holiday. DeCarava's first solo museum exhibition was at the Studio Museum in Harlem in 1969. He lived in the last decades of his life in the Bedford–Stuyvesant neighborhood of Brooklyn and taught for many years at Hunter College. At his death, he was widely recognized as one of the most important photographers of his generation. In 2006 he received the National Medal of Arts for his work.

Kenneth T. Jackson

Deckertown. Obsolete name of TRAVIS.

decorative arts. New York City became a center for the production of stylish silverware and household furnishings during the colonial era. Eighteenth-century craftspeople developed distinctive regional silver and furniture forms, including brandy-wine bowls and tankards; large, freestanding cupboards known as *kasten;* and serpentine-front, five-legged gaming tables. Émigré artisans continually brought new design concepts and patterns of workmanship to the city that complemented those of residents. As an international port and commercial center, the city had access to raw materials like mahogany and rosewood from the Caribbean and South America, Italian and native marbles, English and French furniture mounts and hardware, and English, European, and Asian textiles that gave local firms advantages over those of other regions well into the late nineteenth century. By the late eighteenth century the city's craftspeople were known nationally for the quality of their products. Prominent figures included cabinet- and chairmaker Thomas Burling (*fl* 1769–1802), whose clients included George Washington, and Robert Carter (*fl* 1783–1801), who led the cabinetmakers' contingent in the New York Federal Procession in 1788 to promote ratification of the Constitution.

In 1805 *Longworth's American Almanack* listed 66 cabinetmakers (including Duncan Phyfe, 1768–1854), 19 chairmakers, 15 carvers and gilders, 10 turners, and 23 upholsterers with shops in the city. Upholsterers traditionally performed services such as making curtains and draperies and hanging wall coverings, as well as providing fixed and removable furniture covers. The early nineteenth century saw an influx of French cabinetmakers led by Charles-Honoré Lannuier (*fl* 1803–19). According to the federal census of 1840, furniture manufacturers employed 793 workers in seven of the city's 17 wards; among these were the French-born cabinetmaker Alexander Roux (1813–86) and J. and J. W. Meeks (*fl* 1836–60). German-born craftspeople like John Henry Belter (1804–1863) entered the decorative trades in the middle decades of the nineteenth century.

Simultaneously, a new profession emerged: that of the interior decorator, who completed interiors after exterior construction was finished. Some architects, including Alexander Jackson Davis (1803–1892), designed furniture to complement specific commissions, such as his Gothic Revival designs for William Paulding's mansion, Lyndhurst, in Tarrytown, New York. One mid-century specialist was George Platt (1812–1873), who was praised by critic Andrew Jackson Downing. After the Civil War furniture manufacturers such as Pottier and Stymus, Leon Marcotte and Company, and Herter Brothers (*fl* 1864–1905) expanded their services and product lines to provide complete interiors. These firms were joined by others, including Sypher and Company, that also dealt in interiors, antiques, and decorative accessories, and the influential but short-lived firm of Associated Artists, formed by Louis Comfort Tiffany (1848–1933), needlework and textile designer Candace Wheeler (1827–1923), and two colleagues in 1879. These leading exponents of artful interiors gained patrons among the prominent and wealthy nationwide.

Two influential publications by New Yorkers further promoted interior design reform into the twentieth century. *The Decoration of Houses* (1897) by novelist Edith Wharton (1862–1937) and architect Ogden Codman (1863–1951) and *The House in Good Taste* by Elsie de Wolfe (Lady Mendl, 1865?–1950) called for simple, classical interiors, eschewing Victorian clutter. In the years surrounding World War I, recent émigré architects and designers such as Paul T. Frankl (1887–1958), Joseph Urban (1872–1933), and William Lescaze (1896–1969) introduced modern, functional European designs. The International style received its most concentrated publicity in an exhibition at the Museum of Modern Art in 1932. Industrial designers based in the city adapted streamlined functionalism to appliances and furnishings manufactured for national markets; among the best known were Raymond Loewy (1893–1986), Walter Dorwin Teague (1883–1960), and Russel Wright (1904–1976). Industrial and furniture designer Donald Deskey (1894–1989) employed the "art moderne" style in commissions for interiors such as those of Radio City Music Hall. Knoll International, organized by Hans Knoll in 1938, became a leading American and international manufacturer and distributor of furniture in modern and postmodern styles for the contract and residential markets with the contributions of Knoll's wife, Florence Knoll Bassett (*b* 1917).

The use of historic American styles paralleled the modern trend in twentieth-century interior design. The opening of the American Wing of the Metropolitan Museum of Art in 1924 stimulated the manufacture of reproductions of museum-quality antiques, as well as an interest in traditional interiors. Such interior designers and design firms as McMillen Inc. (founded by Eleanor McMillen Brown, 1890–1991), Mrs. Henry ("Sister") Parish II and Albert Hadley of Parish–Hadley Associates (*fl* 1962–94), and Mark Hampton (1940–1998) successfully applied updated traditional schemes to residential, civic, and commercial projects.

Modern traditionalism moved into the twenty-first century with designers including Alexa Hampton of Mark Hampton LLC, Mariette Himes Gomez, and Jamie Drake. For broader markets designer Ralph Lauren (*b* 1939) moved from clothing to environments for his customers, and entrepreneur and publisher Martha Stewart (*b* 1941) marketed lines of home furnishings based on her popular Martha Stewart Living franchise through discounters and department stores. The city's showrooms and custom workrooms continue to provide a broad spectrum of furnishings for metropolitan homes, while recent graduates of Pratt Institute, Parsons The New School for Design, and the New York School of Interior Design bring an artful New York sensibility to their arrangement.

See also FURNITURE and INTERIOR DESIGN.

Deborah Dependahl Waters

Deegan, William F. (*b* New York City, 29 Dec 1882; *d* New York City, 3 April 1932). Architect and political leader. He was educated at Cooper Union and served as a major in World War I. After the war he became active in the American Legion and in 1921 was named commander of New York State. A Democrat, he spent his political career in the Bronx. As an architect he worked for many important firms, including McKim, Mead and White; Post, Magnicke and Franke; and Starrett and Van Vieck. He was the president of the Bronx Chamber of Commerce, from which he resigned when the organization became critical of Mayor James J. Walker. Appointed commissioner of tenement housing in June 1928, he remained in office until his death. In 1930 Walker put him in charge of the Mayor's Committee on Receptions to Distinguished Guests. The Major Deegan Expressway in the Bronx, completed in 1956, is named for him.

Andrew Sparberg

de Forest, Lee (*b* Council Bluffs, Iowa, 26 Aug 1873; *d* Los Angeles, 30 June 1961). Engineer and inventor. He received his PhD in physics from Yale University in 1899 and moved to New York City in 1902. In 1906 he invented the Audion, a three-element vacuum tube consisting of a diode with an added grid that not only controlled the flow of electrons and oscillated radio waves, but also amplified them. This invention enabled him to make some of the earliest radio broadcasts (from a transmitter at Coney Island). However, it was with an arc transmitter, a conventional device not based on his Audion, that he engineered the broadcast of a performance by Enrico Caruso from the Metropolitan Opera in 1910. De Forest remained in New York City until 1925, residing on the Upper West Side (97th Street and Riverside Drive) and in the Bronx (1391 Sedgwick Avenue). A prolific writer, he was pessimistic toward television, transistors, and space travel, but predicted the use of microwave cooking in the home. He self-published his autobiography, *Father of Radio* (1949).

James A. Hijiya, *Lee de Forest and the Fatherhood of Radio* (Bethlehem, Pa.: Lehigh University Press, 1992); Maurice H. Zouary, *DeForest: Father of the Electronic Revolution* (New York: Authorhouse, 2000)

Val Ginter

de Forest, Robert (Weeks) (*b* New York City, 25 April 1848; *d* New York City, 6 May 1931). Philanthropist and housing reformer. A graduate of Yale College and Columbia Law School, he built a successful law practice and for 50 years was general counsel for the Central Railroad of New Jersey, becoming one of the wealthiest men in the United States. In 1882 he helped to found the Charity Organization Society, and in 1900 Governor Theodore Roosevelt named him chairman of the New York State Tenement Housing Commission, which drafted and sponsored the important housing law of 1901. He was then appointed the first commissioner of the city's Tenement House Department by Mayor Seth Low. De Forest served as president of the Russell Sage Foundation, the Welfare Council of New York City, Survey Associates, the National Housing Association, and the Metropolitan Museum of Art, to which he donated the American Wing. He lived at 7 Washington Square in Greenwich Village.

Kenneth T. Jackson

de Kooning, Willem (*b* Rotterdam, Netherlands, 24 April 1904; *d* East Hampton, N.Y., 19 March 1997). Painter. He moved to New York City in 1927, settled into a studio in Manhattan, and became acquainted with the artists John Graham, David Smith, and Arshile Gorky and the art student Elaine Fried, whom he later married. From 1935 he worked briefly in the mural division of the Federal Art Project sponsored by the Works Progress Administration. He later received other mural commissions in the city, including one for the Hall of Pharmacy at the World's Fair of 1939–40. His early paintings depict male figures during the Depression in ambiguous surroundings. At his first solo show (at the Egan Gallery in 1948) his black-and-white abstractions, which swiftly reverse and intermix form and space, firmly established his reputation. A central figure among the abstract expressionists, de Kooning lived and worked in the city until 1963, when he moved to Springs, Long Island.

Thomas B. Hess, *Willem de Kooning* (New York: Museum of Modern Art, 1968); Paul Cummings, Jörn Merkert, and Claire Stoullig, *Willem de Kooning: Drawings, Paintings, Sculpture* (New York: Whitney Museum of American Art, 1983)

Mona Hadler

Delacorte, George (Thomas, Jr.) (*b* New York City, 20 June 1894; *d* New York City, 4 May 1991). Publisher and philanthropist. He graduated from Columbia (BA 1913) and formed Delacorte Press in 1921, which published popular magazines and comic books. In 1942 he introduced Dell Books, pocket-sized paperbacks selling for 25 cents; between seven and 11 million were sold a year, despite shortages of materials during World War II. By 1945 Delacorte owned more than 200 magazines. He remained the chairman of Dell until he sold it to Doubleday for $35 million in 1976. With some of the proceeds from the sale he set up the Delacorte Fund to maintain and build public monuments in New York City. He also built Delacorte Theater in Central Park and renovated City Hall Park.

James E. Mooney

de Lancey, Stephen [de Lancy, Étienne] (*b* France, 24 Oct 1663; *d* New York City, 18 Nov 1741). Merchant. The son of a wealthy family, he moved to New York City in 1685, after the Edict of Nantes was revoked. He set up a mercantile business there, which prospered in part because of his connection through marriage to the Van Cortlandt family. De Lancey was also an alderman and a member of the state senate; his house at the corner of Queen (now Pearl) Street and Canal (now Broad) Street later became well known as Fraunces Tavern.

James E. Mooney

Delancey [de Lancey] **Square.** One of the oldest and most prominent open areas in colonial New York City, it existed in the 1760s. Located at what is now the area of Eldridge, Essex, Hester, and Broome streets, and referred to at the time as the Bowery, the vast common area was carved out of the eighteenth-century farm of the Delancey (de Lancey) family. In 1784 the property of the pro-British family was confiscated and sold off over a two-year period, raising $250,000 in revenue. In 1803 streets were ordered to be opened in this area.

Lisa Keller

Delanoy, Abraham, Jr. (*b* New York City, 1742; *d* Westchester County, N.Y., 1795). Painter. After working for the painter Benjamin West in London he returned to New York City in 1767 to become a portrait painter; he was unsuccessful and during the 1780s found work painting signs. Toward the end of his life Delanoy received commissions for portraits in New Haven, Connecticut. A few of his paintings are held by the New-York Historical Society, including some of the Beekman family.

James E. Mooney

DeLeon, Daniel (*b* Curaçao, 14 Dec 1852; *d* New York City, 11 May 1914). Activist and political leader. He worked for Henry George's mayoral campaign in New York City in 1886 and in 1890 joined the Socialist Labor Party (SLP); he became the editor of the party's newspaper, the *People,* in the early 1890s and dominated the party from the mid-1890s until the end of his life. DeLeon joined the Industrial Workers of the World in 1905, but was expelled in 1908 because he refused to repudiate political action as a primary strategy for working-class action. His disputes with union leaders and fellow socialists caused a split within the branch of the SLP in the city and led to the formation of the Socialist Party of America.

Glen Seretan, *Daniel DeLeon: The Odyssey of an American Marxist* (Cambridge, Mass.: Harvard University Press, 1979)

See also American Federation of Labor [AFL].

Melvyn Dubofsky

delicatessens. Food stores that sell such specialties as cured meats, pickled vegetables, flavored sodas, and seeded breads. The first delicatessens in New York City opened during the mid-nineteenth century and offered ethnic selections from central Europe, especially Germany. By the early twentieth century many delicatessens specialized in eastern European Jewish cuisine, and more than 60 were opened on the Lower East Side alone. "Appetizing stores" provided fish delicacies, in many instances prepared according to kosher laws, including lox, pickled herring, and whitefish, as well as salads, cheeses, bagels, and bialys. Such well-known enterprises as

Katz's Delicatessen, 205 East Houston Street, 1991. In World War II advertisements for the deli read, "Send a salami to your boy in the Army."

Zabar's, Barney Greengrass ("the Sturgeon King"), and Russ and Daughters helped to make bagels and lox a favorite Sunday breakfast. In 1936 there were more than 400 appetizing stores in the city, including 36 on the Lower East Side. Delicatessens remained popular after World War II and attracted customers from many ethnic backgrounds. In the early twenty-first century there are about 6000 delicatessens in the city; among the best-known are KATZ'S DELICATESSEN on Houston Street, the Second Avenue Kosher Delicatessen, the Carnegie Delicatessen, and the Stage Deli.

Jenna Weissman Joselit

Delineator. Magazine launched in New York City in January 1873 by the firm of E. Butterick. It initially contained only dressmaking patterns but by the 1890s also included fiction, nonfiction articles, and homemaking advice. Under the editorial direction of Theodore Dreiser (1907–10), Honore Willsie Morrow (1914–20), and Marie Mattingly Meloney (1921–26) it crusaded for women's equality before the law and for poor children. The most successful of Butterick's publications, it was merged with another, the *Designer,* in 1928. In 1937 it merged with the *Pictorial Review,* put out by Hearst Publications until January 1939.

Mary Ellen Zuckerman

Dell, Floyd (*b* Barry, Ill., 28 June 1887; *d* Bethesda, Md., 23 July 1969). Journalist and radical intellectual. Starting as a reporter in Davenport, Iowa, he moved on to the *Chicago Evening Post.* Dell's distinctly American and midwestern style of writing emerged when he was an editor for the *Post*'s "Friday Literary Review." In 1914 Dell, like a number of other midwestern writers, joined the literary and political scene that was Greenwich Village and began to write for the radical intellectual journal *The Masses,* a monthly journal run as a literary cooperative. While at *The Masses,* he worked with such luminaries as Lincoln Steffens, Max Eastman, Walter Lippmann, Upton Sinclair, Bill Haywood, Sherwood Anderson, John Reed, and Louis Untermeyer. In 1917 the crusading reformer Anthony Comstock virtually shut *The Masses* down, attacking Dell's sympathetic coverage of birth control pioneer Margaret Sanger as immoral and illegal. The federal government pressed charges against Dell and others, citing the Espionage Act. After two trials and no convictions, *The Masses* was forced into bankruptcy. Dell, along with Eastman, went on to found *The Liberator,* which became the spiritual successor of *The Masses.*

In 1918 Dell was drafted into the army, but because of his indictment under the Espionage Act, he was removed from service. Dell's work *King Arthur's Socks* was the first play preformed by John Reed's Provincetown Players, an experimental theater company, after their move to New York City. In 1926 Dell wrote *Love in Greenwich Village,* in which he described what he called the "Seventh Village" of writers and intellectuals. As a major force in New York City and American literary circles, Dell moved to Washington, D.C., in 1930 to work for the Federal Writers' Project. He remained there until his death.

Nathan Morgante

Dell Publishing Company. Firm of book and magazine publishers formed in New York City in 1920 by George T. Delacorte, Jr. It published "pulp" magazines exclusively for two decades, and during the 1930s was the world's leading publisher of comic books. In 1942 it introduced Dell Books, a line of small paperbacks that sold for 25 cents. It eventually opened Dial Press and Delacorte Press to publish hardcover books. In 1976 Dell Publishing Company was bought by Doubleday, reportedly for $35 million.

William H. Lyles, *Putting Dell on the Map: A History of the Dell Paperbacks* (Westport, Conn.: Greenwood, 1983)

Allen J. Share

Delmonico's. Restaurant. Originally opened in 1827 by the Swiss brothers Giovanni and Pietro Delmonico at 21 William Street as a confectioner, "Delmonico and Brother" served cakes, ices, and fine wines. In 1831 the small café expanded to 25 William Street to include a new restaurant specializing in Continental cuisine. Managed by their nephew Lorenzo, it became the best-known restaurant in the United States in the nineteenth century. In 1834 the Delmonicos opened a small hotel and a second restaurant at 76 Broad Street. After the William Street building was destroyed by the Great Fire of 1835, the Broad Street restaurant became the main location until a new, larger building was completed at 56 Beaver Street. Designed by James Brown Lord, the building, which became known as "The Citadel," cost $360,000 and featured two columns that supposedly were salvaged from the ruins of Pompeii. The Delmonicos opened restaurants in the financial district and at 23 Broadway, Fifth Avenue at 14th Street (the former Grinnell Mansion), 26th Street at Madison Square (in the Dodworth Studio Building), and Fifth Avenue and East 44th Street. The original Delmonico's closed in 1925, primarily as a result of Prohibition. In 1929 Oscar Tucci opened a restaurant called Oscar Delmonico's at the 56 Beaver Street location. In 1977 the Huber family opened another restaurant called Delmonico's at that location, which they operated until 1992. The building was left vacant until 1998, when the Bice Group opened another "Delmonico's," which continued to operate into the early twenty-first century.

The restaurant became famous for such culinary innovations as baked Alaska, eggs Benedict, chicken à la king, and lobster Newburg. Its private dining rooms were famous, and it was the first American restaurant to use tablecloths and to admit female diners. Patrons included Mark Twain, J. P. Morgan, Charles Dickens, Oscar Wilde, Henry Irving, Henry Ward Beecher, Theodore Roosevelt, and other presidents. One of the most popular and recognized restaurants in the city, Delmonico's was referenced in the works of Edith Wharton,

Delmonico's

Henry James, F. Scott Fitzgerald, and William Dean Howells.

Lately Thomas, *Delmonico's: A Century of Splendor* (Boston: Houghton Mifflin, 1967)

Betty Kaplan Gubert, Anne Epstein

Deloitte Touche Tohmatsu. Accounting firm, formed in 1895 by Charles Haskins and Elijah Watt Sells. Its offices were at 2 Nassau Street and the firm was soon influential in setting professional standards for accountants in New York State. In its early years the firm was commissioned to reorganize the accounting system of the federal government. In 1978 Haskins and Sells merged with a British firm, Deloitte and Company, and 11 years later merged again with Touche Ross. In the early twenty-first century Deloitte was the largest accounting firm in New York City, with about 7500 professionals at its offices at 2 World Financial Center in Manhattan.

de Mille, Agnes (*b* New York City, 24 Sept 1909; *d* New York City, 7 Oct 1993). Dancer and choreographer. She began her performing career as a concert dancer in the 1930s; her dramatic solos and duets led to her work for the popular stage and for ballet companies. Her innovative choreography for the dream ballet in the musical *Oklahoma!* (1943) was highly influential. She later worked on more than a dozen other Broadway musicals, was the first woman to direct on Broadway (*110 in the Shade,* 1963), and was the first American woman to lead a labor union (the Society of Stage Directors and Choreographers, 1965). De Mille's work reflects her belief that movement is as important as music and dialogue to the development of plot.

Barbara Barker

de Miranda, Francisco (*b* Caracas, 28 March 1750; *d* Cádiz, Spain, 14 July 1816). Revolutionary. During the American Revolution he fought as a captain with the Spanish forces against the British, whom he helped to defeat at Fort Pensacola, Louisiana, on 9 May 1781 and in the Caribbean. Inspired to seek freedom for South America from Spanish rule, in January 1784 he moved to New York City, where he met with Thomas Paine and several statesmen, including Governor George Clinton of New York, Robert Livingston, and Alexander Hamilton, to discuss plans for a revolt in Venezuela. He moved in July 1784 to Europe, where he spent the next 20 years in exile. He left London in October 1805 and returned in November to New York City, where he called on several friends, among them Rufus King, whom he had known in London; he also visited Philadelphia and Washington, D.C., where he met with Aaron Burr, James Madison, and Thomas Jefferson. After winning the tacit approval of the British and American governments for an expedition to Caracas, he returned to New York City on 23 December 1805, assembled a motley crew of 200 men, and set sail on the *Leander* on 2 February 1806 to meet other ships off Hispaniola. Their attacks on Venezuela were easily repulsed, and de Miranda soon returned to exile in Europe. While leading a rebellion in Venezuela in 1812 he was captured by the Spanish and taken to Spain, where he died in prison. He was the only man to take part in the American Revolution, the French Revolution, and the liberation of South America from Spanish rule.

Joseph F. Thorning, *Miranda: World Citizen* (Gainesville: University of Florida Press, 1952)

Kevin Kenny

Democratic Party. Political party formed in the early nineteenth century. After the first party system ended with the disintegration of the Federalist Party and the triumph of the Jeffersonian Republicans, a second national party system emerged in the 1820s and 1830s. Profiting from the political skills of Martin Van Buren, the Democratic Party in New York City and New York State became an important component of the second party system. It was challenged by the Workingmen's Party in the 1820s and 1830s and by the Whig Party after 1834. The most influential Democratic organization in the city was Tammany Hall, which predated the party itself (it was formed in the 1780s). The Democratic Party was challenged by a faction known as the Locofocos in 1835, leading to a re-formation of the party in 1837. As the city grew, the party became powerful by encouraging immigrants to become members. In the years before the Civil War its candidates lost several elections to the Whigs, who were often supported by nativists; a few Democratic leaders embraced nativism, but in general the Democratic Party remained sympathetic to immigrants, and its base of support among workers eventually allowed it to win most elections. During the

1850s and 1860s Fernando Wood was elected mayor of New York City with the support of Mozart Hall, an influential organization that he led. Differences of ethnicity, class, and religion led factions to develop within the party, among them Hunkers, Barnburners, Softs, Hards, and Swallowtails. The Democratic National Convention of 1868 was held at the new Tammany Hall on 14th Street near Third Avenue. Bitter battles erupted over Reconstruction and economic policy, and it was only after considerable debate that Governor Horatio Seymour of New York was nominated for the presidency; Seymour garnered many votes in the general election but lost to Ulysses S. Grant. Between 1872 and 1886 the mayoralty was controlled by the Swallowtails. The party survived a serious division in 1886, when the radical economist Henry George gained wide support in his mayoral campaign.

The consolidation of the five boroughs into one enormous city in 1898 brought a number of new Democratic organizations into metropolitan politics, in particular the political "machines" of Hugh McLaughlin in Brooklyn, Patrick J. Gleason in Long Island City, and John Y. McKane in Gravesend. From the 1920s the Pondiac Club, led by Edward J. Flynn, dominated in the Bronx, and in Queens during the interwar years Maurice Connolly controlled a powerful political machine that was riddled with scandal. The most important Democratic organization in the city remained Tammany Hall, which extended its reach to the outer boroughs under the astute guidance of Charles F. Murphy, its leader from 1902 until his death in 1924. Democratic politics during these years was almost exclusively dominated by the Irish. In the early twentieth century Tammany Hall gradually embraced reforms and sponsored such nationally known progressives as Alfred E. Smith and Robert F. Wagner (i), but corruption remained widespread, and the investigations led by Judge Samuel Seabury that ended the administration of Mayor James J. Walker sent Tammany into a decline that was never really reversed.

The Democrats in the 1930s were on the defensive, largely because of the success of Fiorello H. La Guardia. His election in 1933 to the first of three mayoral terms as a Republican with strong backing from Jews and Italians signaled a decline in the strength of the Irish, the most strongly Democratic ethnic group in the city. In 1949 Carmine DeSapio became the first non-Irish leader of Tammany Hall since William M. "Boss" Tweed, and La Guardia's supporters initiated civil service reforms that diminished the Democrats' powers of patronage. The indifference of Tammany Hall toward the New Deal enabled La Guardia and other Democratic organizations in the city, notably that of Flynn, to garner the largest share of federal support and largesse. Despite these difficulties the Democrats returned to power in 1945 and controlled the mayor's office for the next 20 years. Black democrats such as Adam Clayton Powell, Jr., Hulan E. Jack, and J. Raymond Jones became powerful figures in the party.

Tammany Hall was dealt a severe blow when Mayor Robert F. Wagner sided with a reform movement that forced DeSapio from office in 1961. Political machines further declined as the spread of television both helped immigrants assimilate into the American mainstream and allowed political candidates to more directly reach a large and diverse audience. This shift became evident during the mayoral campaign of 1965, in which Republican John V. Lindsay defeated Democratic candidate Abe Beame. The Democratic machine nevertheless retained considerable power in the outer boroughs, where in the 1970s strong organizations were developed by Meade Esposito in Brooklyn, Donald Manes in Queens, and Stanley Friedman in the Bronx. The most prominent Democrat in New York City in the 1980s was Mayor Edward I. Koch, who began his career as a reformer opposed to DeSapio. After his election in 1977, Koch became more conservative and reached an accommodation with the city's political machines, one result of which was a scandal that engulfed the Parking Violations Bureau during his third term. Many of his strongest critics were black Democrats; among them was David N. Dinkins, a liberal long associated with the Democratic organization in Manhattan, who defeated Koch in the Democratic mayoral primary in 1989.

The election of 1993, in which Rudolph W. Giuliani defeated Dinkins, marked the beginning of the longest period without a Democratic mayor in New York City—the longest such period since the rise of the Democratic Party. During this period, only Mark J. Green in 2001, who polled 47 percent to winner Michael Bloomberg's 50 percent, turned in a creditable showing among Democratic mayoral candidates. In 1997 Democratic candidate Ruth Messinger gained a mere 41 percent of the votes against the victorious incumbent, Giuliani, and in 2005 Republican incumbent Bloomberg had an easy victory against Democratic rival Fernando "Freddy" Ferrer, who obtained a mere 39 percent of the votes.

Despite the poor showing in mayoral contests, the Democratic Party in New York City remained otherwise strong in the early twenty-first century, holding almost all other important city positions and controlling the City Council; Democratic presidential candidates continued to amass overwhelming majorities in New York City, with New York City residents giving 75 percent of their votes to Al Gore in 2000, and 74 percent to John Kerry in 2004. In 2008 Barack Obama amassed landslide victories over John McCain in New York City, gaining 82.2 percent of the votes in city counties. In 2006 a New York City Democrat, Eliot Spitzer, regained the governor's office for his party for the first time in 12 years, but a sex scandal made his tenure in Albany a brief one. In 2008 U.S. Senator Hillary Clinton made the strongest bid for the presidential nomination by a New York Democrat since Franklin D. Roosevelt in 1944. But the continuing loss of mayoral races was an indication that New York City Democrats, riven by ethnic and racial divisions and the mixed success of their traditional liberal appeals, had somewhat lost their way in local politics. In 2007 there were 2,917,517 registered Democrats in New York City, representing 66 percent of all registered voters.

David Hammack, *Power and Society: Greater New York at the Turn of the Century* (New York: Russell Sage Foundation, 1982); Amy Bridges, *A City in the Republic: Antebellum New York and the Origins of Machine Politics* (New York: Cambridge University Press, 1984); John C. Walter, *The Harlem Fox: J. Raymond Jones and Tammany, 1920–1970* (Albany: SUNY Press, 1989); Chris McNickle, *To Be Mayor of New York: Ethnic Politics in the City* (New York: Columbia University Press, 1993); John H. Mollenkopf, *A Phoenix in the Ashes: The Rise and Fall of the Koch Coalition in New York City* (Princeton, N.J.: Princeton University Press, 1992)

Evan Cornog, Peter Eisenstadt

Democratic Republicans. New York State political coalition that formed in opposition to the ideals of Alexander Hamilton. It found its early support in the political organization of the former governor George Clinton, the wealthy landowner Robert Livingston, and upstate farmers. Although in the presidential election of 1789 the party won only 373 votes to the Federalists' 2342 in New York City, it gained a strong majority of the city's voters in the next decade, largely by appealing to artisans. Party leaders invited aspiring tradespeople to seek office as candidates and effectively advocated egalitarianism, tariff assistance to needy crafts, support of the French Revolution, and assistance to immigrants and the poor. The plurality that the Democratic Republicans won in the city in the presidential election of 1800 helped to elect Thomas Jefferson, and in the following years the party eclipsed the Federalists, who lost their majority on the Common Council. The Democratic Republicans then splintered: Aaron Burr, an important ally of Clinton and Livingston in 1800, formed his own ticket for the governorship in 1804; infighting occurred after the Embargo of 1808 between followers of DeWitt Clinton and of James Madison, whose headquarters were at Tammany Hall; and Clinton waged an independent campaign for the presidency in 1812 but continued to support the party. By the 1820s most members of the party were divided into two camps, one led by Andrew Jackson (who attracted supporters of Clinton), the other by John Quincy Adams (who attracted supporters of Madison).

Alfred Fabian Young, *The Democratic-Republicans of New York: The Origins, 1763–1797* (Chapel Hill: University of North Carolina Press, 1967)

Howard Rock

demonstrations. See Public order.

Demorest, Madame [née Curtis, Ellen Louise] (*b* Schuylerville, N.Y., 15 Nov 1824; *d* New York City, 10 Aug 1898). Businesswoman and philanthropist. She worked as a milliner and with her husband, William Jennings Demorest, built a fashion empire in New York City that included Madame Demorest's Fashion Emporium, Demorest's paper patterns, and the publications *Demorest's Illustrated Monthly Magazine* and *Mme. Demorest's Mirror of Fashions.* From 1860 to 1887 she operated an emporium successively at 473 Broadway, 838 Broadway, and 17 East 14th Street; it housed a dressmaking firm and from 1872 a pattern factory. Demorest turned her attention to philanthropy after 1876. She was a founding member of Sorosis, the first women's club in the nation. By the time of her retirement in 1883, Demorest's patterns had been largely supplanted by those of E. Butterick and Company.

Ishbel Ross, *Crusades and Crinolines: The Life and Times of Ellen Curtis Demorest and William Jennings Demorest* (New York: Harper and Row, 1963)

Wendy Gamber

Dempsey, Jack [William Harrison] (*b* Manassa, Colo., 24 June 1895; *d* New York City, 31 May 1983). Boxer. He first boxed in New York City in 1916. In 1919 he won the world heavyweight championship, which he twice defended in the city. On 14 December 1920 he knocked out Bill Brennan at Madison Square Garden in the 12th round, when he was well behind in scoring; and on 24 September 1923 he knocked out Luis Firpo at the Polo Grounds in the second round, after having been knocked out of the ring in the first. After losing the heavyweight title to Gene Tunney in 1926, he earned a rematch by knocking out Jack Sharkey at Yankee Stadium on 21 July 1927. After his retirement from the ring, he operated a well-known restaurant at Broadway and 49th Street. In 1934–35 he lived at the Ritz–Carlton at 112 Central Park South, and for a number of years he had an apartment at 145–46 Central Park West.

Randy Roberts, *Jack Dempsey: The Manassa Mauler* (Baton Rouge: Louisiana State University Press, 1979)

See also Boxing.

Steven A. Riess

De Niro, Robert (*b* New York City, 17 Aug 1943). Actor, director, and producer. Born to two artists in Greenwich Village, De Niro grew up in the Little Italy neighborhood of lower Manhattan. He attended the Little Red School House and Fiorello H. La Guardia High School on the Upper West Side before dropping out at age 13. Five years later, he began training with Stella Adler at the Actors Studio. He first appeared in the film *Greetings* (1968). The following year *The Wedding Party,* his first collaboration with director Brian de Palma, was released. De Niro's first mainstream recognition came with his critically acclaimed performance in *Bang the Drum Slowly* (1973). That same year he appeared in *Mean Streets,* the actor's first collaboration with director Martin Scorsese. The two worked together on several films set in New York City, including *Taxi Driver* (1976) and *Raging Bull* (1980). The first film he directed, *A Bronx Tale* (1993), was set on Arthur Avenue in the Belmont neighborhood. In 1988 De Niro formed Tribeca Productions to produce films in New York City both independently and for major studios. He opened the Tribeca Film Center in a former coffee factory at 375 Greenwich Street. Following the terrorist attacks of 11 September 2001, De Niro helped found the Tribeca Film Festival to revitalize New York City as a filmmaking center.

Anne Epstein

Dennett, Mary Ware (*b* Worcester, Mass., 4 Apr 1872; *d* Valatie, N.Y., 25 July 1947). Women's rights crusader and peace activist. She is best known for her advocacy of birth control and sex education. Her marriage to William Hartley Dennett ended in a sensational divorce trial in 1913, when he insisted that he continued to love both his wife and his mistress. During World War I, she worked for the American Union Against Militarism (the predecessor to the American Civil Liberties Union [ACLU]) in New York City. In 1915 she helped found the National Birth Control League, also in New York City, and led the organization until its collapse; she then formed the Voluntary Parenthood League in 1919. Dennett fought for an "open" birth control law, in contrast to Margaret Sanger's "doctor only" bill, which would likely have limited birth control access to wealthy women. Dennett's emphasis on constitutional rights rather than physicians' discretion made her a more radical figure than Sanger. In 1915 Dennett wrote the pamphlet "The Sex Side of Life" for her teenage sons. This was widely used by Young Men's Christian Associations and other social service organizations, even though the U.S. Post Office declared it obscene in 1922. "The Sex Side of Life" became the target of an obscenity prosecution in Brooklyn in 1929. The ACLU provided Dennett with free representation; she was convicted. After her conviction, the ACLU created the Mary Dennett Defense Committee, which created a rally at Town Hall on 21 May 1929. Dennett was vindicated by the U.S. Court of Appeals for the Second Circuit in 1930. The reversal of Dennett's conviction was an important step in undoing the censorship of artistic and educational works through obscenity law. The Court of Appeals wrote that if every publication that "might stimulate sex impulses" were to be considered criminally obscene, then "much chaste poetry and fiction, as well as many useful medical works" would be suppressed.

Constance Chen, *The Sex Side of Life: Mary Ware Dennett's Pioneering Battle for Birth Control and Sex Education* (New York: New Press, 1996); Martin H. Levinson, "Review of *The Sex Side of Life,*" *ETC: A Review of General Semantics* 54, 2 (Summer 1997), 257–8

Marjorie Heins

Denyse Wharf. Site of a ferry between Long Island and Staten Island established in 1742 by the Denyse family near the present-day Brooklyn tower of the Verrazano–Narrows Bridge. British forces assembled on Staten Island were shuttled here on 22 August 1776, the eve of the Revolutionary War Battle of Brooklyn.

Joseph Ditta

department stores. New York City became a mercantile center during the colonial period, and by the mid-nineteenth century the city was the largest market in the nation: it was the major seaport and financial center, had the largest population, and was the center of the needle trades and garment industry. Merchants and wholesalers from out of town came to New York City to purchase dry goods for distribution across the country, and women went there to shop. Whether of home manufacture or imported from Europe, consumer goods made the city a hub of retailing. A tourist guide informed prospective visitors in 1892 that "all America goes to New York for its shopping."

The forerunner of the department store was the dry-goods emporium, which sold fabrics and sheeting and a modest assortment of notions and ready-made items for women and children. In the decades after the Civil War merchants such as Rowland Macy and A. T. Stewart in New York, John Wanamaker in Philadelphia, and Marshall Field in Chicago took advantage of the new speed and regularity of railroad transport and telegraphic communication and transformed the dry-goods emporium. By facilitating production and distribution, they created the modern urban establishments known as department stores. Initially little more than enlarged, departmentalized dry-goods stores offering a limited assortment of merchandise, these establishments evolved into large mercantile palaces designed expressly for retailing. The department stores became mass-market distributors of goods ranging from furniture, jewelry, and glassware to books, toys, shoes, foodstuffs, and especially clothing for the whole family;

they also became the late-nineteenth-century symbol of every aspiring city.

The first generation of prominent American merchants (Macy, Stewart, and Wanamaker) was succeeded by one that included many German Jews; such entrepreneurs as Adam Gimbel, Herbert Marcus, Morris Rich, Abraham Abraham, Samuel and Jacob Lit, Isidor and Nathan Straus, and Fred and Ralph Lazarus moved the department store onto its modern foundations. Many of these stores continued to bear the names of their founders more than a century later.

With minor variations, dry-goods merchants in the late nineteenth century adopted similar business strategies to keep pace with the feverish growth of the department stores. In moving from a form of entrepreneurial capitalism, in which owners personally managed their stores, to an elaborate administrative structure modeled after that of large corporations, merchants were at the forefront of a new business culture that reorganized work along more efficient and bureaucratic lines. They sought to maintain a high volume of sales and rapid turnover of stock by keeping both prices and profit margins low. A one-price policy that prevented bargaining became a standard feature, as did a money-back guarantee. The heart of the store was the shopgirl: like the male clerk in the traditional dry-goods store, the female salesclerk became the typical employee of the modern department store. By the 1890s the largest stores in New York City, such as R. H. Macy and Siegel–Cooper, employed thousands of young, single, primarily working-class women. Mature women achieved a modicum of prestige as skilled sales personnel and were visible in management as buyers, floorwalkers, and cashiers.

The story of retail trade in New York City is one of constant geographical change. As the center of the population moved uptown, shopkeepers followed. During the eighteenth and early nineteenth centuries the city's many small specialty shops and general merchandise stores were clustered in the port area around Hanover Square, Exchange Place, and Pearl Street. By the mid-nineteenth century a burgeoning population had outgrown lower Manhattan, and the important commercial houses were centered at Broome, Grand, and Canal streets and near City Hall Park, just south of what was the finest residential section of the city. Broadway, which had an array of stores, hotels, restaurants, and theaters, became the principal thoroughfare for fashionable shopping and display. Rowland Macy, a newcomer to New York City, unwittingly brought about the next round of moves in 1858 when he opened a small dry-goods store on Sixth Avenue between 13th and 14th streets, well uptown from convenient shopping. In 1862 A. T. Stewart, the well-known merchant and proprietor of a uniquely successful dry-goods establishment on Broadway and Rector Street, followed Macy to the area above Washington Square and built a store covering an entire block front on Broadway between Ninth and 10th streets. Stewart's gleaming white, cast-iron palace, built expressly for retailing, was a spectacle in itself. Standing five stories tall, it had large display windows of French plate glass, a gas-lit interior, and a vast assortment of domestic and imported goods. Stewart's and the streets around it were reportedly filled with throngs of carriages and fashionable women taking part in a new, exciting consumer culture. For a short time A. T. Stewart was the largest, most innovative, and best-known dry-goods store in the United States.

By the late 1880s, as the population moved relentlessly uptown, virtually all the stores that made New York City the nation's shopping and fashion capital moved to the former residential area bounded by Broadway and Sixth Avenue between 10th and 23rd streets. The best-known included Arnold Constable; B. Altman; the Adams Company; Best and Company; Bonwit Teller; Brooks Brothers; Ehrich Brothers; Greenhut; Herns; Lord and Taylor; James McCreery; McCutcheon; R. H. Macy and Company; Hugh O'Neill's; Simpson, Crawford and Simpson; Stern Brothers; Tiffany and Company; and W. and J. Sloane. At the end of the century Siegel–Cooper (a Chicago emporium) rounded out this series of moves when it opened the largest and most flamboyant retail store in New York City on the block front between 18th and 19th streets on Sixth Avenue. The avenue between 14th and 23rd streets, known as the Ladies' Mile by 1900, with its spectacular architecture and extravagant mercantile displays, became the central location for retail trade for a generation of New Yorkers. Huge crowds were attracted to the big stores. At the opening in 1895 of James McCreery and Company, on the southwest corner of 23rd Street and Sixth Avenue, the owners boasted that 10,000 people could move comfortably within the store at one time. The following year Siegel–Cooper, which called itself the Big Store, attracted a crowd on opening day estimated at 150,000. The heyday of the large American department store was at hand and reflected a permanent change in American consumer habits. Shopping became a pastime that needed no justification: it provided the context for diverse forms of public and even cultural life and dwarfed all other activities, particularly for women. The department stores were for and about women, and merchants catered to them with service, magnificent displays, and low prices. Wealthy women mingled with the working class as almost everyone seemed to pour into the stores, if not to buy, then at least to look.

The supremacy of the Ladies' Mile as a shopping district was short-lived. R. H. Macy, the first store to move uptown just before the Civil War, was the first to move farther uptown in the early twentieth century. Pushed northward by changes on 14th Street and pulled by the developing subway and commuter rail service at 34th Street, it moved to its present location at Herald Square in 1904. In 1909 Gimbel Brothers, a firm that began in Philadelphia, followed Macy and opened a large retail establishment on Broadway between 32nd and 33rd streets. Over the years, however, Fifth Avenue came to be the principal thoroughfare for department stores and elegant shopping: in the years after Macy's move to Herald Square every major department store and specialty shop moved from Sixth Avenue, most of them to Fifth Avenue between 34th and 57th streets. By 1915 Lord and Taylor, B. Altman, and Arnold Constable had opened major stores on the avenue and anchored the new shopping district.

Not all the major department stores followed the movement of population up Manhattan Island; other retail districts took shape throughout the city. Bloomingdale's opened at 59th Street and Third Avenue in 1887, expanded the store west to Lexington Avenue, and has thrived at this original location. In Harlem, 116th and 125th streets became and have remained major shopping thoroughfares. And in Brooklyn, Abraham and Straus on Fulton Street was the retail flagship of the borough; for many residents the store was second in importance only to the Dodgers. In the Bronx, local shopping was centered at Fordham Road (the site of Loehmann's and Alexander's) and in the area commonly known as the Hub (around 149th Street and Third Avenue). And in Queens, retail districts took form along Jamaica Avenue by the 1920s and on Queens Boulevard during the 1960s, where both Macy's and Abraham and Straus opened stores.

Many of the best-known retail institutions in New York City went out of business during the 1970s, and the future of Fifth Avenue as the nation's premier and prestigious shopping street became unclear. Pressed on one hand by the arrival of high-end boutiques and European flagship emporiums on Madison Avenue between 57th and 72nd streets and on the other hand by the proliferation of discount chains and suburban shopping malls, Fifth Avenue had to reorient itself to a changing retail economy. Part of this change meant that surviving individual department stores became part of large conglomerates and often retained little individuality or luster. Among the more promising signs for Fifth Avenue were the expansion of both Bergdorf Goodman and Saks Fifth Avenue and the move in the spring of 1991 of Henri Bendel from 57th Street to Fifth Avenue. In the twenty-first century, the avenue remains a preeminent location for department store shopping in the world and a favored location for parades.

Elaine S. Abelson

De Peyster, Abraham (baptized New Amsterdam, 8 July 1657; *d* New York City, 3 Aug 1728). Colonial mayor. The son of a mercantile family from Amsterdam, he went to the Netherlands in 1675 to work in his family's firm, then returned to New Amsterdam in 1684 and was appointed to the city's Board of Aldermen the following year. A supporter of Jacob Leisler in 1689, he later joined the anti-Leislerians and was widely respected for his moderation in the bitter factional disputes of the day. Appointed mayor in 1691 by Governor Henry Sloughter, he remained in office until 1693, was appointed in 1696 to the council of Governor Richard Coote, the earl of Bellomont, and served briefly as acting governor in 1700. At the end of his life, De Peyster was one of the city's wealthiest merchants.

David William Voorhees

Deren [Derenkowsky], **Maya (Eleanora)** (*b* Kiev, Ukraine, 1917; *d* New York City, 13 Oct 1961). Filmmaker and writer. After immigrating to the United States in 1922, she lived in Syracuse, New York, and took an interest in union organizing and political writing. She settled in Manhattan in 1935. In 1940 she moved to Los Angeles with the Katherine Dunham Dance Company as a literary collaborator and assistant. She returned to New York City in 1943. The first film that she made by herself was *Witch's Cradle* (unfinished), shot during late summer with Marcel Duchamp in the surrealist gallery Art of This Century. Her studio on Morton Street became a magnet for the burgeoning intellectual and artistic life of New York City, which became an integral element in her subjective films *At Land* (1944), *A Study in Choreography for the Camera: Pas de Deux* (1945), and *Ritual in Transfigured Time* (1946). Deren focused public interest on personal, independent cinema through her writings, including *An Anagram of Ideas on Art, Form and Film* (1946), and popularized alternative exhibitions by renting the Provincetown Playhouse to screen films. She was awarded the first Guggenheim grant for creative work in motion pictures in 1946, and in 1947 began traveling to Haiti, where she continued her avant-garde film work with poetic experience, form, and ritual.

VeVe A. Clark, Millicent Hodson, and Catrina Neiman, *The Legend of Maya Deren: A Documentary Biography and Collected Works*, vol. 1, part 1, *Signatures (1917–1942)* (New York: Anthology Film Archives/Film Culture, 1984); Lauren Rabinovitz, *Points of Resistance: Women, Power and Politics in the New York Avant-garde Cinema, 1943–1971* (Urbana: University of Illinois Press, 1991)

Grai St. Clair Rice

de Salignac, Eugene (*b* Boston, 1861; *d* 1 Nov 1943, New York City). Photographer. Born to a French father and American mother, in 1900 he moved to Manhattan. By the age of 42 he was divorced and living in the West 20s, having begun a new career as a photographer for the city's Department of Bridges. From 1906 to 1934 he shot over 20,000 images of New York City and documented the creation of the city's modern infrastructure. One of his most iconic images was taken in 1914 of painters on the cables of the Brooklyn Bridge. Many of his images are held by the Museum of the City of New York.

Michael Lorenzini and Kevin Moore, *New York Rises: Photographs by Eugene de Salignac* (New York: Aperture, 2007)

Jessica Montesano

DeSapio, Carmine (Gerard) (*b* New York City, 10 Dec 1908; *d* New York City, 27 July 2004). Tammany Hall leader. Born in Greenwich Village, he became the first Italian and the youngest person to be named the head of the Democratic organization of New York County in 1949. He played a critical role in the elections of Mayor Robert F. Wagner (1953) and Governor W. Averill Harriman (1954) and tried to run the Democratic Party more openly than Tammany Hall traditionally had done. His success brought him national prominence and a reputation as an enlightened political boss. After his candidates for governor, state attorney general, and the U.S. Senate lost elections in 1958, a reform movement led by Herbert H. Lehman, Eleanor Roosevelt, and Wagner forced his removal from office in 1961. DeSapio's efforts to return to politics failed when he was defeated by Edward I. Koch in primary elections for Democratic district leaderships in 1963 and 1965.

Warren Moscow, *The Last of the Big-Time Bosses: The Life and Times of Carmine DeSapio* (New York: Stein and Day, 1976)

Chris McNickle

detective agencies. About the middle of the nineteenth century private detective agencies arose in New York City, where rapid growth was accompanied by an increase in criminal activity. The first agency in the United States was opened by George Relyea and two partners at 48 Centre Street; in the *National Police Gazette* (16 October 1845) the firm offered to conduct "both Criminal and Civil business [to find] all kinds of property . . . obtained by False Pretenses, Forgery, Burglary, or by any other dishonest means," with assurance that its agents were "always ready, at a moment's warning, to travel to any part of the United States." Relyea's offer to apprehend criminals in other cities and the frontier reflected a limitation of public law enforcement; although New York was one of the few cities with a police force, the jurisdiction of the force ended at the city limits, and criminals from other cities who fled there were not generally pursued. From the beginning, some of the real and rumored activities of detective agencies were met with widespread distrust; it was believed that detectives colluded with thieves to retrieve stolen property, a dim view was taken of their investigations on behalf of wealthy families into the backgrounds of suitors, and some critics blamed marital investigations for an epidemic of "sudden explosions in domestic life."

A branch of the Pinkerton National Detective Agency was formed in New York City in 1865. It distinguished itself and reassured its customers by refusing to work for rewards and by seeking the arrest and prosecution of those whom it apprehended; soon it was the leading agency in the nation. Private detectives were held in low repute, especially as agencies began to conduct espionage in the workplace (for example, using "spotters" on streetcars to catch conductors who kept, or "knocked down," the nickel fare). Employers regularly used private detectives to investigate the private lives of their workers, and it was reported that detectives sometimes rose to positions of leadership within unions to facilitate strike breaking. Detectives were also criticized for operating spurious voluntary societies such as the Association for the Suppression of Gambling (1851) and the Society for the Prevention of Crime (1880), which observed places of criminal activity, gathered the names of customers, and in some cases reported these names to employers. Pinkerton detectives sometimes assisted district attorneys and the police and at other times competed with them. In 1880 Inspector Thomas F. Byrnes opened a branch of the Police Department's detective bureau on Wall Street and announced in a letter to the business leaders of the financial district that he intended to offer services similar to those of Pinkerton. By the 1880s the word *Pinkerton* became a generic term for a private detective. Notable successes of Pinkertons included a raid led by Robert Pinkerton in 1882 on the office in New York City of the Kentucky State Lottery (recounted in the *New York Times* under the headline "The Police Not Needed"), the apprehending of Marm Mandelbaum in 1884, and the unexpected arrest in 1904 of the gang leader Monk Eastman, who tried to rob a drunken, wealthy young man being guarded by Pinkerton agents.

With the development of federal and state law enforcement agencies in the early decades of the twentieth century, the role of the private detective in crime investigation decreased. Pinkerton and its competitors were replaced in strike-breaking work in New York City by the agencies of Pearl L. Bergoff and others, which were nominally private detective agencies but seem to have done nothing but organize squadrons of thugs. After the New Deal curtailed this sort of activity, detective agencies increasingly focused on marital investigations; as early as 1912 the tracing of children hidden during custody disputes was mentioned as customary work. Private detectives remained active in business espionage. They also worked on corporate takeovers, often looking for incriminating information about a business or principal, seeking hints that a firm was willing to negotiate or back down, and sometimes simply investigating the real worth of a business. Landlords in New York City used private detectives to determine whether rent-controlled apartments were in fact their tenants' principal domiciles.

Frank Morn, *"The Eye That Never Sleeps": A History of the Pinkerton National Detective Agency* (Bloomington: Indiana University Press, 1982); William Parkhurst, *True Detectives: The Inside Stories of Today's Top Private Investigators* (New York: Jove, 1989; repr. with suppls., 1993)

Deutschlandle. Alternative name of KLEINDEUTSCHLAND.

de Valera, Eamon [Edward] (*b* New York City, 14 Oct 1882; *d* Dublin, 29 Aug 1975). Irish political activist. The son of an Irish mother and a Spanish father, he was born on East 43rd Street and christened at St. Agnes's Roman Catholic Church. He lived for two years in the city before moving to Ireland, where during the insurrection of 1916 he led Irish forces and was saved from execution only because he held both British and American citizenship. After escaping from a British prison in 1919, he traveled as a stowaway from Liverpool to New York City, where he began a tour of the United States to raise support for Irish independence. Dissatisfied with the terms of the Anglo–Irish Treaty, he led forces against those of the Irish parliament in the Irish Civil War (1922–23). Between 1932 and 1937 he led the Irish government. After drafting the constitution in 1937, de Valera served three terms as *taoiseach* (prime minister) and two as president of the Irish Republic.

T. Ryle Dwyer, *De Valera's Darkest Hour: In Search of National Independence, 1919–1932* (Dublin: Mercier, 1982); John Bowman, *De Valera and the Ulster Question, 1917–1973* (New York: Oxford University Press, 1989)

Kevin Kenny

Devery, William S. "Big Bill" (*b* New York City, *ca* 1855; *d* Queens, 20 June 1919). Chief of police. He worked as a bartender on the Bowery and then paid a bribe to Tammany Hall to become a policeman in 1878. Promoted to sergeant in 1884 and to captain in 1891, he soon obtained one of the most lucrative police jobs in the city, running the Eldridge Street Station in a well-known red-light district. Reportedly he told his men during his inaugural address: "If there's any gratin' to be done, I'll do it. Leave it to me!" Shamelessly corrupt, he had his aides approach saloon owners just before an election, promising protection if the ticket backed by Tammany Hall were elected. In addition to getting rich, he became chief of police in 1898. Although frequently exposed by Lincoln Steffens and other reformers, Devery was resilient. He never fined a policeman for breach of duty, only for getting caught. He lost his position when Seth Low defeated Mayor Robert A. Van Wyck in 1901, but he was still a rich man, dividing his time between a mansion on West End Avenue and a profitable real estate operation in Rockaway.

Kenneth T. Jackson

Devine, Edward T(homas) (*b* Union, Iowa, 6 May 1867; *d* Oak Park, Ill., 27 Feb 1948). Reformer, educator, and writer. In 1896 he became general secretary of the New York Charity Organization Society, a position he held until 1917. He also launched *Charities* (later called the *Survey*), a leading journal of social work. Under his guidance the society formed committees for tenement house reform and the prevention of tuberculosis and opened the New York Summer School of Philanthropy (1898, later the Columbia University School of Social Work). Devine directed the school from 1904 to 1907 and again from 1912 to 1917, and taught at Columbia University from 1905 to 1919. His published writings include *When Social Work Was Young* (1939). He lived at 542 West 112th Street.

Sandra Sidford Cornelius, "Edward T. Devine, 1867–1948: A Pivotal Figure in the Transition from Practical Philanthropy to Social Work" (diss., Bryn Mawr College, 1976)

Sarah Henry Lederman

De Vinne, Theodore Low (*b* Stamford, Conn., 25 Dec 1828; *d* New York City, 16 Feb 1914). Typographer and publisher of fine editions. He moved to New York City in 1848 and in 1850 became an apprentice to the printer Francis Hart, who engaged him as a partner in Francis Hart and Company in 1858. Under their direction the firm began printing *St. Nicholas Magazine* in 1872 and *Scribner's Monthly* in 1876. After Hart's death in 1877 De Vinne bought his share of the firm in 1883 and renamed the press after himself. An aesthetic conservative among Victorian printers, he argued for the simplification of title pages and condemned such fussy details as deckled edges. During a lecture at the Yale Club of New York he said, "I have given the best part of my life to the making of books that have been sold and read, and not rated as pieces of typographic bric-a-brac." De Vinne wrote many books on printing, including *The Invention of Printing* (1876), *Historic Printing Types* (1886), *The Practice of Typography* (1901–4; 4 vols., among them *A Treatise on Title-Pages*), and *Notable Printers of Italy in the Fifteenth Century* (1910).

Irene Tichenor, *No Art without Craft: The Life of Theodore Low De Vinne* (Boston: David R. Godine, 2005)

Melissa M. Merritt

Devoe and Raynolds. Firm of chemical manufacturers. Its origins date to 1754, when William Post began mixing, grinding, and importing pigments in a shop at his residence on Fletcher Street. Offices remained on the site for 100 years, and in 1798 the firm of Post and Sons was formed. It grew rapidly under two former clerks, F. W. Devoe and Charles T. Raynolds, and was reorganized several times during the 1850s. The offices moved in 1855 to 106 and 108 Fulton Street, a factory was built on Horatio Street, and other retail shops opened on Fulton, William, and Ann streets. For several decades the firm was the leading producer of paint in the United States, and by 1917 it had undergone a series of mergers. The factory on Horatio Street moved to Brooklyn in the 1920s, and the firm's headquarters moved to 44th Street and First Avenue in the 1930s. The firm made five major acquisitions by 1948, and in 1976 it was acquired by Grow Chemical (later the Grow Group), also based in New York City. Devoe paints remained popular in the metropolitan area.

The Colorful Years, 1754–1942: The Story of a Colonial Venture That Became an American Institution (New York: Devoe and Raynolds, 1942)

David B. Sicilia

Devoy, John (*b* Kill, County Kildare, Ireland, 3 Sept 1842; *d* Atlantic City, N.J., 29 Sept 1928). Irish nationalist. He was arrested and imprisoned for his revolutionary activities in Dublin in 1866. On his release in 1871 he emigrated to the United States and settled in New York City where he became one of the principal leaders of Clan na Gael, a secret Irish American society dedicated to the militant republican cause in Ireland. He later launched two weekly newspapers in New York City, the *Irish Nation* (1881–85) and the influential *Gaelic-American* (1903–28): its headquarters at 165 William Street served as a rendezvous site for revolutionary exiles. It was largely through his fund raising and organizational efforts in the United States that the militant nationalists were able to carry out the Easter Monday Rebellion (1916) in Ireland. Devoy wrote *Recollections of an Irish Rebel* (1929).

Desmond Ryan, *The Phoenix Flame: A Study of Fenianism and John Devoy* (London: A. Barker, 1937); William O'Brien and Desmond Ryan, eds., *Devoy's Post Bag, 1871–1928* (Dublin: C. J. Fallon, 1948, [1953])

John T. Ridge

Dewey, John (*b* Burlington, Vt., 20 Oct 1859; *d* New York City, 1 June 1952). Philosopher. He grew up in Burlington and after graduating from the University of Vermont earned a doctorate from Johns Hopkins University in 1884. After teaching philosophy and psychology at the University of Michigan he moved to the University of Chicago to become the head of the department of philosophy, psychology, and pedagogy. In 1904 he accepted a position at Columbia University and lived in New York City for the rest of his life, moving to 2880 Broadway in 1913, 125 East 62nd Street in 1927, 1 West 89th Street in 1939, and 1158

Fifth Avenue in 1945. One of his most important contributions was his theory of instrumentalism, which posited that the worth of any idea or moral value should be determined by its practical consequences rather than by reference to any transcendental source or standard. In keeping with these ideas he took active interest in many educational, social, and political issues throughout his career: he helped to form the New York Teachers' Union in 1916, the New School for Social Research in 1919, and the American Civil Liberties Union in 1920; took also part in the woman suffrage movement, worked with the Henry Street Settlement, and continued to develop his ideas about progressive democratic education. Criticized in some quarters for condoning the infringement of dissenters' civil rights during World War I, he supported many liberal causes over the next 40 years. In such books as *The Public and Its Problems* (1927) and *Liberalism and Social Action* (1935) he provided a model of social policy for educators, bureaucrats, reformers, and social workers. Dewey denounced the New Deal for being too conservative and called for a third party, but he opposed communism and all forms of political extremism. He retired in 1939 but remained intellectually active to the end of his life. On his 90th birthday 1500 dignitaries, colleagues, and friends gathered for a celebration at the Commodore Hotel. Among his most important works are *The Influence of Darwin on Philosophy* (1910), *Democracy and Education* (1916), and *Experience and Nature* (1925).

Kevin Kenny

Dewey, Melvil(le Louis Kossuth) (*b* Adams Center, N.Y., 10 Dec 1851; *d* Lake Placid, Fla., 26 Dec 1931). Originator of the Dewey Decimal System in libraries. After attending Amherst College he worked as a librarian there and in Boston, at the same time devising the decimal system of library classification that bears his name. He moved to New York City to become the librarian of Columbia College in 1883, and in 1887 he established at Columbia the School of Library Economy (later the School of Library Service), the first of its kind in the United States and the first at the university to admit women. He became the director in 1888 of the New York State Library in Albany. An advocate of simplified spelling, Dewey altered the spelling of his own first name.

Sarah K. Vann, ed., *Melvil Dewey: His Enduring Presence in Librarianship* (Englewood, Colo.: Libraries Unlimited, 1978)

Mary B. Bowling

Dewey, Thomas E(dmund) (*b* Owosso, Mich., 24 March 1902; *d* Miami, 16 March 1971). Prosecutor, governor of New York, and presidential candidate. After receiving his law degree from Columbia University he spent a few years in private practice before joining the U.S. attorney's office in 1931. Although a Republican, he was appointed special prosecutor in charge of the Investigation of Organized Crime in New York City by Governor Herbert H. Lehman, a Democrat. He earned national renown for successfully prosecuting the notorious crime syndicate MURDER INCORPORATED and many racketeers; his work and his colorful image inspired such films as *The Racket Busters*. He was elected district attorney of New York County in 1937 and, on the strength of his national reputation as a prosecutor, sought the Republican presidential nomination in 1940. This effort was unsuccessful, but in 1942 he was elected governor of New York State, an office he held for three consecutive terms. He received the Republican presidential nomination in 1944 but lost the election to Franklin D. Roosevelt; he received the nomination again in 1948 but lost to Harry S. Truman. After his third term as governor he resumed private law practice in 1955, becoming a partner of a venerable law firm on Wall Street that changed its name to Dewey, Ballantine, Bushby, Palmer, and Wood. Dewey lived from 1955 until the end of his life at 141 East 72nd Street.

Richard Norton Smith, *Thomas E. Dewey and His Times* (New York: Simon and Schuster, 1982)

See also LAWYERS.

Emery E. Adoradio

Dewey Arch [Dewey Triumphal Arch and Colonnade]. Temporary monument commemorating the victory of Commodore George Dewey (1837–1917) at Manila Bay during the Spanish–American War. Built of wood and staff (a mixture of straw and plaster), the 100-foot-tall (30.5-meter-tall) arch was erected in 1899 in Madison Square, where Broadway crosses Fifth Avenue, with colonnades stretching from 23rd to 25th streets. Designed by architect Charles R. Lamb (1860–1942) and sculptor Frederic W. Ruckstall (1853–1942), it was modeled on the Arch of Titus in Rome and featured sculptures by Daniel Chester French (1850–1931) and Karl Bitter (1867–1915). During his victory parade on 30 September 1899, Dewey did not actually pass under the triumphal arch. Many residents called for a permanent arch to be built at 59th Street and Fifth Avenue, or on Riverside Drive, because the existing arch location obstructed traffic. The city preserved it for one year, but Dewey failed to clinch the Democratic presidential nomination in 1900, and it became impossible to raise funds for a permanent arch. It was torn down in December 1900.

Kate Lauber

Dewhurst, Colleen (*b* Montreal, Canada, 3 June 1924; *d* South Salem, N.Y., 22 Aug 1991). Actress. She moved to New York City in 1946 to study acting at the American Academy of Dramatic Arts, and in 1952 made her debut on Broadway as a dancer in a revival of the Eugene O'Neill play *Desire Under the Elms*. In 1954 she met Joseph Papp while he was organizing the New York Shakespeare Festival, and they often collaborated, beginning with her portrayal of Katherine in his produc-

Dewey Arch, 1899, with Madison Square Garden in the background

tion of *The Taming of the Shrew* in Central Park in 1956. She also worked with the director José Quintero in a number of O'Neill's plays, earning critical acclaim for her portrayals of his powerful, tragic female characters. Dewhurst was the president of the Actors' Equity Association for two terms (from 1985). She was active in the unsuccessful fight to preserve the Morosco and Helen Hayes theaters on Broadway from being torn down to make way for the Marriott Marquis Hotel. She won two Tony Awards, four Emmy Awards, and two Obie Awards. She was married twice to actor and director George C. Scott.

Barbara Lee Horn, *Colleen Dewhurst: A Bio-Bibliography* (Westport, Conn.: Greenwood, 1993)

Amanda Aaron

DeWitt Clinton High School. Opened in 1897 as Boys' High School at 60 West 13th Street, it was the first public high school for boys in Manhattan. In 1900 it took its current name, and in 1929 it moved to Mosholu Parkway and 205th Street in the Bronx. The last public high school in the city to admit only boys, it became coeducational in 1983. In 2010 DeWitt Clinton High School had 4100 students. Well-known alumni of the school include the writers Lionel Trilling and James Baldwin, the actor Burt Lancaster, the playwright Neil Simon, and the politician Charles B. Rangel.

Erica Judge

de Wolfe, Elsie [Ella Anderson] (*b* New York City, 20 Dec 1865; *d* Versailles, France, 12 July 1950). Actress and decorator. She spent her childhood in the British Isles and was presented at the English royal court. In 1884 she returned to New York City and took up acting. A professional actress by 1890, she left the stage in 1905 to become a decorator, her reputation assured by her imaginative interior design at the Colony Club. Her book *The House in Good Taste* in 1913 helped her to become nationally known. From about this time she lived mostly in France, where she restored the Villa Trianon at Versailles and was widely considered one of the most influential arbiters of design.

James E. Mooney

Dewson, Molly [Mary Williams] (*b* Quincy, Mass., 18 Feb 1874; *d* Castine, Maine, 21 Oct 1962). Reformer. As the research secretary of the National Consumers' League from 1919 to 1924, she focused her efforts on the minimum wage. While serving as the civic secretary of the Women's City Club in 1924–25 she met Eleanor Roosevelt, who inspired her to take part in women's Democratic politics, first in the presidential campaign of Alfred E. Smith in 1928 and then in that of Franklin D. Roosevelt in 1932. From 1927 to 1932 she was the president of the New York Consumers' League, where she fought for better labor standards for women workers. From 1933 to 1937 she ran the Women's Division of the Democratic National Committee out of headquarters in New York City. Dewson remained active in political circles in the city until 1952, when she retired to Maine.

Susan Ware, *Partner and I: Molly Dewson, Feminism, and New Deal Politics* (New Haven: Yale University Press, 1987)

Susan Ware

Dial. Literary journal launched in 1880 and inspired by a transcendentalist journal of the same name published in Boston. Considered among the finest publications of its kind in the country, in 1898 it absorbed the *Chap-book*, a literary review based in Chicago. During the 1920s it published work by such members of the "lost generation" as Ezra Pound, Edna St. Vincent Millay, E. E. Cummings, and John Dos Passos, as well as by John Dewey, Jean Cocteau, and Bertrand Russell. Marianne Moore edited the *Dial* from 1925 until 1929, when it ceased publication.

William Wasserstrom, *The Time of the Dial* (Syracuse, N.Y.: Syracuse University Press, 1963)

David A. Balcom

Diallo, Amadou (*b* Sinoe, Liberia, 2 Sept 1975; *d* New York City, 5 Feb 1999). Police shooting victim. He was a West African immigrant living at 1157 Wheeler Avenue in the Bronx. On the night of 5 February 1999 four plain-clothes police officers from the Street Crimes Unit of the New York Police Department (NYPD) spotted Diallo and believed him to be the suspect in a series of rapes. When Diallo reached for his wallet, police assumed he was reaching for a gun, but Diallo was unarmed. They fired 41 shots, hitting him 19 times. The officers were indicted on several charges but were exonerated by a jury in Albany, New York, in early 2000. Diallo's shooting and the acquittal of the officers heightened racial tensions in New York City and led to several protests against the NYPD.

Nathan Morgante

Diamond District. Section of midtown Manhattan, near 47th Street between Fifth and Sixth avenues, that is the center of the retail and wholesale diamond trade in New York City. Dealers moved north to this area from two other locations, one near Canal Street and the Bowery that took shape in the 1920s, and the other surrounding the intersection of Nassau and Fulton streets, which was the first site of the Diamond Dealers Club (formed in 1931). The district grew in importance after Hitler's armies invaded the Low Countries: thousands of Jews fleeing the diamond centers of Antwerp (Belgium) and Amsterdam settled in New York City, and soon the diamond trade there was dominated by Orthodox Jews. The Diamond Dealers Club moved to 47th Street in 1941. Disputes between dealers are settled by the Diamond Dealers Club, which handles 80 percent of all the

"Diamond and Jewelry Way," 47th Street between Fifth and Sixth avenues, 1991

diamonds entering the United States. In the early twenty-first century the Diamond District maintained retail stores, jewelry exchanges, offices, and workshops where diamonds and other stones were cut, set, and prepared for sale.

Murray Schumach, *The Diamond People* (New York: W. W. Norton, 1981)

Janet Zapata

Dickens, Charles (John Huffam) (*b* Portsmouth, England, 7 Feb 1812; *d* Kent, England, 9 June 1870). Novelist. He made the first of his two visits to New York City in 1842 to give lectures, raise support for copyright laws, and record his impressions of the growing nation. He toured the city for a month, during which time he delivered impassioned readings and met with literary luminaries such as Washington Irving and William Cullen Bryant. On 14 February the Boz Ball (named after his pseudonym) was held in his honor at the Park Theatre and attended by 3000 members of the city's elite. Among the sites he visited were the Five Points, Wall Street, the Bowery, and the Tombs. He also marveled at the tirelessness of the city's fire brigade. On his return to England he wrote *American Notes* (1842) and *Martin Chuzzlewit* (1844), which criticized the city's dirty streets, cultural crudeness, and materialistic ideals. Part of this antagonism stemmed from his indignation over the lack of copyright laws and the pirating of his books in the United States. His description of New York City as a place where "a vast amount of good and evil is intermixed and jumbled up together" alienated many of his American readers. He returned to New York City in 1867 and read to large audiences at Steinway Hall on Broadway (on 22 occasions between 9 December and 20 April) and Plymouth Congregational Church in Brooklyn (four times between 16 and 21 January 1868). Commenting on the changes that had occurred in the city since his last visit, he declared: "Everything in it looks as if the order of nature were reversed, and everything grew newer every day, instead of older." At a banquet at Delmonico's on 18 April he promised that he would never again denounce America. Five days later he boarded a ship in New York Harbor and slipped out of the country, barely escaping capture by federal tax agents seeking a share of the proceeds from his lecture tour.

Sidney P. Moss, *Charles Dickens' Quarrel with America* (New York: Whitson, 1984); Fred Kaplan, *Dickens: A Biography* (New York: William Morrow, 1988); Jerome Meckier, *Innocent Abroad: Charles Dickens's American Engagements* (Lexington: University Press of Kentucky, 1990)

Robert Sanger Steel

Dietrich, Marlene [Marie Magdalene] (*b* Berlin, 27 Dec 1901; *d* Paris, 6 May 1992). Actress. Brought up in an upper-middle-class Prussian home, she shortened her name and embarked on an acting career at age 18. She became an international star after the director Josef von Sternberg chose her for the lead role in *The Blue Angel* (1930), in which she played a seductive cabaret singer named Lola Lola. During the 1930s she cultivated her image as a sultry, sophisticated femme fatale, known for her smoky voice and given to wearing men's clothing. She became an American citizen in 1939 and during World War II entertained Allied troops across Europe and North Africa. In 1951 she moved into an apartment at 933 Park Avenue. In 1967 she made her debut on Broadway, appearing in sold-out one-woman shows at the Lunt-Fontanne and Mark Hellinger theaters. In 1972 she moved to Paris and retired from the public eye. Dietrich made 37 films.

Donald Spoto, *The Blue Angel: The Life of Marlene Dietrich* (New York: Doubleday, 1992)

Robert Sanger Steel

Dillon, Read. Firm of investment bankers formed in New York City in 1832 as a partnership called Carpenter and Vermilye; it became Vermilye and Company in the 1860s. The sale of Civil War bonds established the reputation of the firm, which in 1905 was renamed after its principal partner, William A. Read. It had offices in four American cities and London and was known for underwriting bonds issued by New York City, as well as stocks and bonds of railroads and other industries. Clarence Dillon became the leading partner after World War I; in 1921 the firm took its current name. The firm gained an international reputation through its reorganization of the Goodyear Tire and Rubber Company (1921), its acquisition and refinancing of Dodge Brothers, and its underwriting of foreign bonds. From the 1930s the financing of petroleum and gas pipelines accounted for a large part of its business, as did the underwriting of state and municipal bonds (including those to finance the Triborough Bridge in 1937). The firm was a subsidiary of the Travelers Corporation from 1986 to 1991, when the Travelers sold its interest to Baring Brothers and Company, of London. The company's headquarters were at 535 Madison Avenue until 1997 when the company was bought by Swiss Bank Corporation (SBC), and later SBC was bought by UBS. From 2000 to 2007 UBS's international hedge fund division was Dillon Read Capital Management.

Robert Sobel, *The Life and Times of Dillon Read* (New York: Truman Talley/Dutton, 1991)

Mary E. Curry

DiMaggio, (Giuseppe Paolo) Joseph, Jr. (*b* Martinez, Calif., 25 Nov 1914, *d* Hollywood, Fla., 8 March 1999). Hall of Fame baseball player. The son of a fisherman, DiMaggio became a legend during his years with the New York Yankees and an American folk hero after his baseball career ended. (He is mentioned in Simon and Garfunkel's song "Mrs. Robinson," Madonna's song "Vogue," and Ernest Hemingway's novel *The Old Man and the Sea.*) When he had a 56-game hitting streak in 1941—a record that still stands—a hit song, "Joltin' Joe DiMaggio," was a popular recording of the day and a tribute to DiMaggio's achievement. Baseball player Ted Williams called DiMaggio "the greatest all-around player I ever saw." The Yankee Clipper, as DiMaggio was called, played his entire career (13 years) with the Yankees. He had a lifetime batting average of .325, hit .300 or better in 11 seasons, won two batting titles, and knocked in more than 100 runs nine times. He was voted American League Most Valuable Player three times and played on nine World Championship teams. He was named Greatest Living Player in a 1969 poll to celebrate baseball's 100th anniversary. In 1977 he was the first athlete to be awarded the Presidential Medal of Freedom, the nation's highest civilian award. Two of his brothers became major leaguers: Dom with the Boston Red Sox and Vince with the Pittsburgh Pirates. His marriage to Marilyn Monroe in 1954 created a media frenzy; they divorced within a year.

Frank Dyer

Dime Savings Bank. Savings bank formed in 1859 as the Dime Savings Bank of Brooklyn. It focused on small, individual depositors rather than large depositors and businesses. It changed its name to the Dime Savings Bank of New York in 1970, converted from a state to a federal charter in 1983, and became publicly owned in August 1986. Its headquarters were at 589 Fifth Avenue in 1994, when Dime purchased Anchor Savings Bank in one of the largest savings and loan mergers in history, executed under the leadership of Brooklyn native Richard D. Parsons, who later became the CEO of Time Warner. In 2002 Dime merged into Washington Mutual, a Seattle-based financial services company.

Leslie Gourse

Dine, Jim (*b* Cincinnati, Ohio, 16 June 1935). Artist associated with the pop art and neo-dada movements. Dine arrived in New York City at the age of 23 after graduating from Ohio State University. As a part of the avant-garde art scene, Dine's visual and performance works were first shown in New York City during "happenings" at the Judson Gallery at the Judson Memorial Church in Greenwich Village in 1959. His painting style blends found objects, collage, and vigorous brushstrokes reminiscent of abstract expressionism. In the early twenty-first century Dine continued to maintain a studio in New York City. A retrospective of his first 10 years in New York City, entitled *Walking Life: 1959–1969,* was presented in 1999 at the Guggenheim Museum.

Anne Epstein

Dinizulu, Nana (Yao Opare) (*b* Augusta, Ga., 20 Nov 1930; *d* Camden, N.J., 10 Feb 1991). Musician, dancer, and Akan priest. During the 1940s he formed Dinizulu and His African Dancers, Drummers and Singers, a troupe devoted to the music and dance of western and southern Africa. The group performed at the World's Fair of 1964–65 and annually at Cooper Union. In 1967 Dinizulu established Bosum-Dzemawodzi, a traditional African religious organization based on the Akan tradition, and in the following year in Jamaica, Queens, he opened Aims of Modzawe, an African cultural center, which later became the Dinizulu Center for African Culture and Research. Dinizulu was the chief priest of the traditional Akan religion in the United States.

Sule Greg C. Wilson

Dinkins, David N(orman) (*b* Trenton, N.J., 10 Oct 1927). Mayor. A graduate of Howard University and Brooklyn Law School, he served with the U.S. Marine Corps in Korea and entered private law practice on his return to the United States. He was a founding member in 1963 of the organization 100 Black Men and was elected to the New York State Assembly from Harlem in 1966. Dinkins was appointed chair of the Board of Elections (1972–73) and city clerk (1975–85). In 1985 he was elected borough president of Manhattan. In 1989 he defeated Mayor Edward I. Koch in the Democratic mayoral primary, and in the general election, with substantial backing from racial minorities and liberal whites, narrowly defeated Rudolph W. Giuliani to become the city's first black mayor. During the campaign Dinkins had supported wage increases for municipal employees and aid to the homeless, but in the early years of his administration he was forced by fiscal constraints to modify some of his proposals. In 1991 he implemented a crime reduction program called Safe Streets, Safe City: Cops and Kids that expanded the city's police force. His term was also marked by racial and ethnic tension: the boycott of a Korean grocer by blacks in Flatbush, tensions between Hasidim and blacks in Crown Heights, tensions between Dominicans and the police in Washington Heights, and a racially charged protest by the police in Manhattan in 1992. In 1993 he was defeated by Giuliani in his attempt to win a second term. The next year Dinkins became a professor in the practice of public affairs at Columbia University, and he continued to teach there in the early twenty-first century. In 2002 the Oral History Research Office and the Rare Book and Manuscript Library at Columbia launched the David N. Dinkins Archives and Oral History Project.

Martin Shefter

David N. Dinkins, 1990

Dion and the Belmonts. Popular vocal group from the 1950s. The group was named for its lead singer, Dion DiMucci, and the Belmonts, a Bronx trio composed of Carlo Mastrangelo, Freddie Milano, and Angelo D'Aleo that was named after the singers' neighborhood street, Belmont Avenue. Formed in 1957, the quartet achieved fame with the hits "I Wonder Why," "A Teenager in Love," and "Where or When." In 1960 Dion and the Belmonts split amicably; DiMucci opted to do solo records, and the Belmonts reverted to a trio. The group reunited briefly for a 1972 Madison Square Garden concert.

Andrew Sparberg

DiPalo's Fine Foods. Italian gourmet food store. Located at 200 Grand Street, it opened in 1925 at 206 Grand Street in lower Manhattan. The store sells cheeses, meats, olive oils, and other gourmet foods, many imported directly from Italy. It makes its own mozzarella and ricotta cheeses on site. As of 2010 Lou (Luigi) DiPalo, fifth-generation co-owner, continued to operate the neighborhood institution.

Jessica Montesano

diphtheria. Epidemics of diphtheria, typically a disease of childhood once called throat distemper, were reported in New York City as early as 1745. Because diphtheria blocks the upper airway with pseudomembranous tissue resulting from the body's inflammatory process, victims frequently suffocated until methods of intubation were developed in the late 1880s. More vexing to physicians was the ability of diphtheria to create a toxin that circulates throughout the body, worsens the inflammation in the throat, blocks normal heart function, and often causes death four to six weeks after the initial attack. The discovery of the diphtheria anti-toxin in 1890 provided an antidote to the long-term deadly effects of diphtheria bacilli. The New York City Department of Health was instrumental in developing municipal public health laboratories that both produced reliable, standardized quantities of anti-toxin and performed culture diagnoses for physicians in the city beginning in 1893. This work was largely the result of the famed bacteriologist and public health official Hermann M. Biggs and his assistant William H. Park. The incidence of diphtheria among schoolchildren in New York City began to fall with these and other public health efforts that continued into the 1930s, but the development of the diphtheria vaccine in 1936, and its subsequent widespread and safe use among children, led to the rapid demise of the disease. This dreaded disease is now completely avoided by children in the city who are properly immunized against it.

John Duffy, *A History of Public Health in New York City*, 2 vols. (New York: Russell Sage Foundation, 1968–74); Evelynn M. Hammonds, *Childhood's Deadly Scourge: The Campaign to Control Diphtheria in New York City, 1880–1930* (Baltimore: Johns Hopkins University Press, 1999)

directories. For a discussion of residential and business directories in New York City see City directories.

Disciples of Christ. The first congregation of the Disciples of Christ in New York City was formed after members of the First Baptist Church and the Ebenezer Baptist Church merged in 1810; they became affiliated with the Disciples of Christ after its formation in 1832 by members of the Christian Churches (1804) and the Churches of Christ (1809), who favored a return to primitive, apostolic Christianity. After merging with another congregation of Disciples of Christ, the congregation in the city was renamed the Central Christian Church. It occupied a building at 142 West 81st Street from 1910 until 1945, when it moved to a neo-Gothic church (erected 1909) at 1010 Park Avenue near 85th Street and changed its name to Park Avenue Christian Church; in the early twenty-first century it was the oldest continuous Disciples of Christ congregation in the city.

Winfred Ernest Garrison, *Religion Follows the Frontier: A History of the Disciples of Christ* (New York: Harper and Brothers, 1931); N. Eugene Tester, "Schisms within the Disciples of Christ, 1809–1909" (thesis, Northern Illinois University, 1969)

Kevin Kenny

discothèques. See Dance halls and discothèques.

distilling. The history of distilling in New York City is discussed in the entry Brewing and Distilling.

district attorneys. Officials responsible for prosecuting crimes and ensuring legal procedure in New York City according to state laws. Each of the city's five counties has one district attorney and a large staff of appointed assistant district attorneys, who present evidence and prosecute on behalf of the state. Cases include street, white-collar, and organized crime; district attorneys conduct investigations that lead to prosecution and also handle appeals.

During colonial times the prosecution of crimes was chiefly the responsibility of appointed lawyers; there was also a grand jury modeled after an English institution intended to check the tenacity of lawyers engaged as prosecutors by the king. The prosecutorial power of the state was limited in 1735 when a jury in the colony of New York refused to indict John Peter Zenger on charges of seditious libel. During the nineteenth century a state penal code was developed that provided a framework for prosecution. A lavish courthouse built as a public project by William M. "Boss" Tweed became known for expenditures far beyond its budget and for cases argued there in the late nineteenth century by such figures as William Travers Jerome. Until the 1930s the district attorney's office was mainly the preserve of a few politicians and their patrons: district attorneys were elected with the support of local political machines, and they chose assistants not so much for their legal skills as for their political loyalties. Women worked as "confidential secretaries," or "C-girls," who were valued for their ability to "file and forget"; the highest position open to women law graduates was that of paralegal.

The current office of district attorney, which exists for each of the boroughs, came into existence in 1935, when Governor Herbert Lehman named Thomas E. Dewey deputy assistant district attorney in New York County. He prosecuted rackets cases and investigated extortion rings, prostitution, gambling, and corruption in organized labor and government. He was formally elected to the office in 1937. Among the cases he prosecuted were those connected to crime boss "Lucky" Luciano and Tammany Hall boss Jimmy Hines. Public fascination with the activities of the office reached a peak in the late 1930s: Dewey's dramatic encounters with organized-crime figures inspired such films as *The Racket Busters* and *Smashing the Rackets* (both 1938). Frank S. Hogan succeeded Dewey in 1941, and he served for 32 years, until his resignation in 1974. Under his direction the Criminal Courts Building opened at 100 Centre Street in 1941. Its design was widely seen as a reflection of the rational and ordered approach to law enforcement of the late 1940s: covering two blocks, the building was designed by Harvey Wiley Corbett to house the courts, the city jail, and the offices of the district attorney; its soundproof walls and many entrances and office suites were intended to prevent unethical dealings. Women were employed as prosecutors from the late 1960s, and in 1981 Elizabeth Holtzman became the first woman in the city to be elected district attorney (in Kings County).

Robert Morgenthau became district attorney in 1974 and stayed until his retirement in 2009. He reorganized the office, including starting early screening of felony cases by assistant district attorneys. He created numerous special units, including a trial division, a sex crimes unit, a family violence and child abuse bureau, an investigation division, a labor racketeering unit, an official corruption unit, a witness aid and services unit, a community affairs unit, and other areas dealing with gangs, identity theft, and firearms. New York City's conviction rate rose from 73 percent in 1974 to about 90 percent in the early twenty-first century. In the early twenty-first century, more than 450 prosecutors worked for the district attorney of New York County.

Emery E. Adoradio, Meghan Lalonde

Ditmars/Steinway. Neighborhood in northwestern Queens of about 200,000 people, lying within Astoria and bounded to the north by Bowery Bay, to the east by La Guardia Airport, to the south by 23rd Avenue, and to the west by the East River. Older residents refer to the neighborhood as Steinway, after the piano maker Steinway and Sons, which bought a tract of 400 acres (160 hectares) along the northwestern shore of Queens between 1870 and 1873 and during the next decade built a spacious factory and a town with a church, library, kindergarten, and public trolley line. Unlike other factory towns, Steinway was not exclusively for workers; the firm treated it as a real estate investment, selling land and houses to the highest bidder, and eventually employees counted for less than one-third of the inhabitants. Nevertheless, the town set its clocks by the factory whistle. After the Interborough Rapid Transit line was extended to Ditmars Avenue in 1917, the area attracted many people who worked in Manhattan, as well as newlyweds (mostly Italians and Greeks) seeking their own apartments. Much of the main street, Astoria Boulevard, was destroyed to make way for the Grand Central Parkway, which provided approach to the Triborough Bridge (1936). Many Greeks moved to the area after World War II, and by the 1980s they made up the largest Greek community in the world outside Greece. According to the 2000 census, Greeks and Italians are still the largest demographic groups in the area; and into the twenty-first century, people from Colombia and Bangladesh are the third and fourth largest demographic groups in Steinway.

Richard K. Lieberman and Janet E. Lieberman, *City Limits: A Social History of Queens* (Dubuque, Iowa, Kendall/Hunt, 1983); Vincent Seyfried, *300 Years of Long Island City, 1630–1930* (Hicksville, N.Y.: Edgian Press, 1984)

Richard K. Lieberman

Ditmas Park. Section of Flatbush, Brooklyn, known for its freestanding Victorian homes. Although many areas of Victorian Flatbush are commonly referred to as Ditmas Park, the historic boundaries are Dorchester Road to the north, Newkirk Avenue to the south, Ocean Avenue to the west, and East 16th Street to the east. The area was rural until the

Argyle Road in Ditmas Park

late nineteenth and early twentieth centuries when the creation of Prospect Park, the completion of the Brooklyn Bridge, and improvements in transportation led to construction in the vicinity. Developer Lewis Pounds purchased a portion of the farm owned by the Van Ditmarsen family and developed it into a residential community. In a short time he built a large number of Colonial Revival–style, Tudor Revival–style, and bungalow homes. Pounds monitored the quality and character of the houses, which were quickly inhabited by prestigious families. By the 1920s, however, many of the area's wealthy residents had moved to more distant suburbs, and some Ditmas Park homes became boardinghouses or multi-family homes. Residents sought protection for the structures, and Ditmas Park was designated a New York City historic district in 1981. In the twenty-first century Ditmas Park attracts many young people and artists, and it is well known for its popular restaurants.

Maurita Baldock

Dock, Lavinia Lloyd (*b* Harrisburg, Pa., 26 Feb 1858; *d* Chambersburg, Pa., 17 April 1956). Nurse. She moved to New York City to attend the Bellevue Hospital School of Nursing in 1884 and in 1896 took up residence at the Henry Street Settlement on New York City's Lower East Side. She remained there for 20 years, and while in residence at the settlement she helped shape the profession of nursing through the establishment of standards, licensure, regulations, and the creation of several important nursing professional organizations. She was also a cofounder and secretary of the International Council of Nurses. Dock was a determined crusader against venereal disease and an outspoken suffragist, feminist, and social reformer. A vocal supporter of the labor movement, she was an early member of the New York Women's Trade Union League. Dock wrote the first textbook of pharmacology for nurses, *Materia Medica for Nurses* (1890), as well as *Hygiene and Morality* (1910). She also authored (with others) the four volume *A History of Nursing* (1907–12) and *The History of the American Red Cross* (1922). She returned to Pennsylvania in 1922.

Janet W. James, *A Lavinia Dock Reader* (New York: Garland, 1985)

Karen Buhler-Wilkerson

Doctorow, E(dgar) L(aurence) (*b* New York City, 6 Jan 1931). Novelist. He grew up near the Grand Concourse, attended the Bronx High School of Science and Kenyon College (BA 1952), and worked as an editor for the New American Library and Dial Press (editor-in-chief 1964–69). His early writings include the satirical science fiction novel *Big as Life* (1966), in which two gigantic naked figures cause pandemonium in Manhattan as they loom over the Pan Am Building. He achieved greater recognition for his novels *The Book of Daniel* (1971), based on the trial of Julius and Ethel Rosenberg, and especially *Ragtime* (1975), which is set in New York City in the early twentieth century and includes fictional as well as historical characters. One of the characters in his novel *Billy Bathgate* (1989) is the organized-crime figure Dutch Schultz. Among Doctorow's other works set in New York City are the play *Drinks before Dinner* (1978) and the novel *World's Fair* (1985). The composer and lyricist team of Stephen Flaherty and Lynn Ahrens later adapted *Ragtime* into a musical, which opened on Broadway in 1998 and was nominated for 12 Tony Awards; it won Tonys for Best Featured Actress (Audra McDonald), Original Score, Book, and Orchestration.

Carol C. Harter and James R. Thompson, *E. L. Doctorow* (Boston: Twayne, 1990)

B. Kimberly Taylor, Naomi Wax

Doctors' Riot. A violent disturbance from 13 to 14 April 1788 in which 5000 rioters ransacked New York Hospital because they believed that medical students were stealing cadavers from cemeteries. See Riots.

documentary filmmaking. New York City became the hub of documentary filmmaking in the United States during the late nineteenth century. After the Edison Manufacturing Company shot the film *Herald Square* with its new portable camera in May 1896, single-shot films—called actualities—of the city's street life were taken frequently by Edison, the American Mutoscope Company, and the American Vitagraph Company. During 1896–97 Alexander Black and Henry Evans Northrop of the Brooklyn Institute of Arts and Sciences began to integrate short films into their lantern-slide lectures. By 1903 George Kleine was selling a standardized illustrated lecture, "Lights and Shadows of a Great City, New York," which included 61 lantern slides and nine films. Such programs routinely contained a reformist message about the dangers of city living. There were also numerous short travelogues of the city; *Around New York in 15 Minutes* was released early in 1905 by the firm of Paley and Steiner and showed views of Manhattan and Brooklyn. Although most fiction film production moved to Los Angeles during the second decade of the twentieth century, New York City remained the principal center for documentary filmmaking. Paul Strand and Charles Sheeler, young artist-photographers associated with Alfred Stieglitz and his gallery, completed *Manhatta* in 1921. In this eight-minute documentary with intertitles drawn from Walt Whitman's poetry, the filmmakers went beyond the simple depiction of the city and sought to convey the dynamism and grandeur of metropolitan living. Through distribution abroad the film helped to initiate a cycle of "city symphony" films, including Walther Ruttmann's *Berlin: Symphony of a Great City* (1927) and several short subjects about New York City, including Jay Leyda's *A Bronx Morning* (1930) and Irving Browning's *City of Contrasts* (1931).

With the onset of the Depression in the 1930s documentary filmmakers became increasingly concerned about urban social issues, and a group sympathetic to the political left soon gathered around the local branch of the Film and Photo League, making newsreels and short documentaries such as *May Day in New York, 1931* (1931), *New York Hoovervilles* (1932), and *Workers Struggle in New York* (1932–33). Most of these filmmakers were associated with Frontier Films, which produced *Heart of Spain* (1937), *People of the Cumberland* (1938), and *Native Land* (1942). Pare Lorentz, a film critic and advocate of the New Deal based in the city, made his classic documentaries *The Plow That Broke the Plains* (1936) and *The River* (1937) from offices and editing rooms in Manhattan. *The City* (1939), directed by Steiner and Willard Van Dyke with a commentary written by Lewis Mumford, was shown at the World's Fair of 1939–40 to rave reviews. During World War II the Army Signal Corps took over the Kaufman Astoria Studio (formerly Paramount Pictures) and used it to produce training and propaganda films. Some films of the Office of War Information were meant to portray ordinary Americans; *Window Cleaner* (Jules Bucher, 1945), for instance, follows the activities of a man who cleans the windows of the Empire State Building. After the war the city's documentary filmmakers survived by producing films for industry and nonprofit organizations, making films about the urban experience when possible. James Agee, Helen Levitt, and Janice Loeb made *The Quiet One* (1949) and *In the Street* (1952) about youths struggling to find their way in the city. For *On the Bowery* (1956) Lionel Rogosin had local alcoholics convey the despair of their daily lives. Stan Brakhage's *The Wonder Ring* (1956), Shirley Clarke's *Bridges Go Round* (1958), and D. A. Pennebaker's *Day Break Express* (1958) were more experimental and more celebratory of the city.

The postwar rise of television led to new documentaries made for broadcast by the news divisions of the Columbia Broadcasting System (CBS) and the National Broadcasting Company (NBC). Television stations needed portable 16-millimeter equipment that could shoot news footage with sound synchronized to image, and the resulting technology helped to inaugurate the cinema verité revolution in documentary of the early 1960s, yielding several unusual documentaries, including Clarke's *The Connection* (1960) and Jonas Mekas's *The Brig* (1964), which captured performances by the Living Theater. In New York City as elsewhere, documentary was the virtually exclusive province of whites and men until the late 1960s when the influence of the New York State Council on the Arts and the National Endowment for the Arts helped with its diversification. William Greaves, a black actor and filmmaker, made *Still a Brother: Inside the Negro Middle Class* (1968) in New York City for National Educational Television, exploring the changing consciousness and increasing militancy of black Americans. He became the executive producer of *Black Journal* (1968–70), a monthly news and public affairs program on public television that gave opportunities to a generation of young black documentary filmmakers such as Charles Hobson and St. Claire Bourne. A similar program called *Realidades,* launched in 1972 on WNET and aimed at the city's Latino community, was overseen by the documentary filmmaker Jose Garcia (*The Ox-Cart,* 1972).

Newsreel, a filmmaking group loosely affiliated with Students for a Democratic Society, was formed in 1967 by politically committed leftists. Its New York City branch made documentaries such as *Columbia Revolt* (1968), about the student strike at Columbia University, and *Community Control* (1968), about efforts to decentralize the city school system in Ocean Hill and Brownsville. Newsreel's focus shifted to minority filmmakers and subjects in 1972; the renamed Third World Newsreel, under the leadership of Christine Choy, made a series of films including *From Strikes to Spindles* (1975), about the city's Chinese community, and *Who Killed Vincent Chin?* (1989), with Rene Tajima. Other minority filmmakers made films about the communities in which they lived, including Bill Miles (*I Remember Harlem,* 1981), Warrington Hudlin (*Street Corner Stories,* 1977), Carlos DeJesus (*The Devil Is a Condition,* 1972), and Bienvenida Matias (*In the Heart of Loisida,* 1979, with Marci Reaven). At the same time female New Yorkers made films reflecting feminist concerns, including Barbara Kopple (*Harlan County, U.S.A.,* 1975), Mirra Bank (*Yudie,* 1974), Deborah Shaffer (*Chris and Bernie,* 1974, with Bonnie Freedman), Claudia Weil (*Joyce at 34,* 1973, with Joyce Copra), and Mira Nair (*So Far from India,* 1982).

The work of Brooklyn-born brothers Ken Burns (*Brooklyn Bridge,* 1982, and *The Statue of Liberty,* 1985) and Ric Burns, director of the exhaustive *New York: A Documentary Film* (1999–2003), an eight-part, 17½-hour series about the city's history, contributed to New York City's documentation on film. *9/11* (2002), a film by Jules and Gedeon Naudet, inadvertently documented the terrorist attacks of 11 September 2001; the brothers were working on a film about probationary firefighters when the attacks occurred, and they shot one of the few video recordings of the first plane hitting the North Tower.

Lewis Jacobs, ed., *The Documentary Tradition: From Nanook to Woodstock* (New York: Hopkinson and Blake, 1971); Erik Barnouw, *Documentary: A History of the Nonfiction Film* (New York: Oxford University Press, 1974); Stephen Mamber, *Cinema Verite in America: Studies in Uncontrolled Documentary Film* (Cambridge, Mass.: MIT Press, 1974); William Alexander, *Film on the Left: American Documentary Film from 1931 to 1942* (Princeton, N.J.: Princeton University Press, 1981)

Charles Musser

documentary photography. Some of the first documentary photographs from New York City were produced between 1885 and 1902 by the newspaper reporter Jacob A. Riis, who photographed dark alleys and rear tenement interiors on the Lower East Side to supplement his report on the problems of the poor and win support for his efforts to improve urban housing, education, health, and recreation. Lewis Hine soon used photography to examine many of the same issues. His studies of child labor led to nationwide reform, and his poignant portraits of immigrants at Ellis Island helped to erode cultural prejudices. In the 1920s the documentary film *New York the Magnificent* (1921; later known as *Manhatta*) was made by the photographers Paul Strand and Charles Sheeler. Documentary photography developed more fully during the 1930s when many photographers were employed by the Federal Art Project and other agencies of the Works Progress Administration to document social displacement across the nation. Under the auspices of the project Berenice Abbott in 1935 began the series "Changing New York" to document the character of the city; she adopted a straightforward, unsentimental approach to recording urban contrasts. Other photographers engaged to document buildings and inhabitants of the city included Ben Shahn (1935–38) and Walker Evans (summer 1938). From 1936 to 1951 the Photo League offered classes and lectures by masters in the techniques of documentary photography, including Hine and Abbott. Some members, including Sid Grossman (1913–55), Sol Libsohn (*b* 1914), Dan Weiner (1919–59), and Ruth Orkin (1921–85), made detailed studies of Harlem, Chelsea, and Park Avenue north and south.

During the 1960s and 1970s the role of photojournalism in social documentary expanded. Some photojournalists, including Bruce Davidson (*b* 1931) and Danny Lyon (*b* 1942), tried to understand their subjects thoroughly before photographing them. Davidson's photographic essay "East 100th Street" (1970) depicted the difficulty and isolation of life in Spanish Harlem. Others used their work less to influence social reform than to promote self-examination. Through seemingly careless, fragmentary images of daily life, Garry Winogrand (1928–84) and Lee Friedlander (*b* 1934) encouraged viewers to interpret for themselves the needs of urban residents. Diane Arbus's portraits of people usually considered abnormal lacked the compassion traditionally expected of a social documentary and introduced a nonhumanistic approach to documentary photography. During the 1980s and early 1990s Larry Clark (*b* 1943) and Nan Goldin (*b* 1953) exulted in the banality of contemporary urban life and also examined sexual and psychological relationships.

The terrorist attacks of 11 September 2001 on the World Trade Center provided material for contemporary documentary photographers: Joel Meyerowitz (*b* 1938) was granted unfettered access to Ground Zero within days after the attacks, resulting in an exhibition and a book, *Aftermath: The World Trade Center Archive.* Hunter College professor Reiner Leist's (*b* 1964) "Window" project captured the changes Leist observed through the window of his apartment on Eighth Avenue between 1995 and 2001; taken with a nineteenth-century full-plate camera, Leist's photographs show the hole in the city's skyline after the Twin Towers fell. In 2008 Magnum photographer Christopher Anderson documented the economic downturn on Wall Street, while others have focused on the ever-changing city. In a 2008 exhibit at the New York Public Library titled *Eminent Domain,* Zoe Leonard (*b* 1961) documented the gentrification of the Lower East Side, while Thomas Holton focused on contemporary family life in Chinatown by photographing the Lams, a family of five living in a two-room apartment on Ludlow Street.

David Featherstone, ed., *Observations: Essays on Documentary Photography* (Carmel, Calif.: Friends of Photography, 1984); Peter Bacon Hales, *Silver Cities: The Photography of American Urbanization, 1839–1915* (Philadelphia: Temple University Press, 1984)

See also Photojournalism.

Dale L. Neighbors

Dodd, Mead and Company. Book publisher founded in 1839 as Taylor and Dodd, after John S. Taylor and Moses Woodruff Dodd. In 1870 the firm became Dodd and Mead when Edward S. Mead and Dodd's son Frank gained control of the business. It was located at 506 Broadway from 1856 until it moved to 762 Broadway in 1870. In 1876 Bleeker Van Wagener became a partner and the firm took its final name. In its early years, the firm published British and religious titles, but it later expanded to popular fiction, poetry, essays, juvenile literature, and trade books. In 1895 it launched the *Bookman,* a renowned literary journal of its day. The firm published works by Leo Tolstoy, Joseph Conrad, H. G. Wells, Jerome K. Jerome, Max

Beerbohm, Agatha Christie, Maurice Maeterlinck, Anthony Trollope, and G. K. Chesterton. It also helped launch the careers of African American poet Paul Lawrence Dunbar and literary Nobel Prize winner Anatole France (née Jacques Anatole François Thibault). From 1902 to 1904 it published the *New International Encyclopedia,* a 17-volume work that was constantly reviewed and updated until 1931. From 1910 to 1941 the firm had offices at 449 Fourth Avenue. In 1930 it began publication of Allan Nevins's *American Political Leaders* series and in 1956 published Winston Churchill's *History of the English-Speaking Peoples.* The firm expanded through acquisition in 1934 and in 1941 moved to 432 Fourth Avenue. From the 1950s to the 1970s, the firm published anthologies of African American poetry, essays, and stories and made its final move in 1967 to offices at 79 Madison Avenue. The firm was purchased in 1981 by Thomas Nelson Publishers of Nashville, and in 1986 the Gamut Publishing Company acquired a majority interest in the company. In 1988 Dodd, Mead and Company was liquidated, and it ceased its publications in 1990.

Stephanie Miller

Dodge, David Low (*b* Brooklyn, Conn., 14 June 1774; *d* New York City, 23 April 1852). Businessman and founder of the New York Peace Society. His early childhood memories were of the violence and horror of the American Revolution, which he later described as "the confused noise of the warriors more ferocious than the beasts that prowl the forest." He grew up and started a successful dry-goods business and later became manager of Connecticut's first cotton mill in Norwich. He seemed to make money at everything he undertook, and this continued after 1802 when he moved to New York. There, he began his second career as a peace activist. According to his autobiography, this attitudinal shift came after a rash of highway holdups drove him to travel with a loaded pistol. One night he nearly shot an innocent innkeeper by mistake. Although he had served in a militia, he now began to question the contradiction between calling himself a Christian and carrying a weapon. In 1809 Dodge published a pamphlet that declared that no war, not even defensive war, was acceptable to a true Christian and that states that engaged in warfare were at best pagan and possibly even satanic. He supported his arguments with passages from the Gospels. The pamphlet sold out its 1000-copy press run in two weeks and developed a following out of which he formed the New York Peace Society, the first nonsectarian peace organization in U.S. history. The group remained silent about its opposition to the War of 1812 to avoid being accused of disloyalty, but once that conflict ended in 1815 the group became visible again. That year Dodge published his antiwar tract *War Inconsistent with the Religion of Jesus Christ,* a cogent and all-encompassing argument against war that included not only the moral and political perspective but considerable detail about the damage to business and economic interests caused by warfare. In 1827 at the age of 53, the self-made entrepreneur retired from business to devote himself full time to the cause of peace. He died in 1852. His son, William Earl Dodge (1805–83), also combined successful business activities with peace activism and is honored with a statue at the intersection of Broadway and Sixth Avenue.

Mark Kurlansky

Dodge, Grace H(oadley) (*b* New York City, 21 May 1856; *d* Bronx, 27 Dec 1914). Reformer. Born into a prominent family, she was educated primarily at home and attended finishing school in Connecticut. After returning to New York City she became active in several charities, including the industrial schools of the Children's Aid Society, and began working to make social reform more systematic and efficient. Her friend Louisa Lee Schuyler, who influenced many of her later efforts, encouraged her to join the State Charities Aid Association. In 1881 she formed a club for young women that by 1885 grew into the Association of Working Girls' Societies. She also helped to organize the Industrial Education Association in 1884 and was appointed by Mayor William R. Grace in 1886 as one of the first two women on the Board of Education. Instrumental in founding Teachers College in 1889, she served as its treasurer from 1892 to 1911.

Dodge was also active in the Young Women's Christian Association (YWCA). A unifying figure at a time when the organization was torn by competing factions, she was active in 1906 in re-forming it as the YWCA of the USA, and she was the first president of the national board, which was based in New York City. She took an interest in moral education and helped to form the New York Travelers Aid Society (1907) and the American Social Hygiene Association (1912).

Abbie Graham, *Grace H. Dodge: Merchant of Dreams* (New York: Woman's Press, 1926); Esther Katz, "Grace Hoadley Dodge: Women and the Emerging Metropolis, 1856–1914" (diss., New York University, 1980)

Nancy Marie Robertson

Dodge [née Mapes]**, Mary (Elizabeth)** (*b* New York City, 26 Jan 1830; *d* Onteora Park, near Tannersville, N.Y., 21 Aug 1905). Writer and editor. Influenced by her father, James J. Mapes, who emphasized literature during her childhood, she was friends with William Cullen Bryant and Horace Greeley, whose home in lower Manhattan was often the site of informal literary gatherings. In 1864 *Irvington Stories* (a collection of her short stories) was published. Her children's book *Hans Brinker; or, the Silver Skates* (1866) became one of her best-known works and has gone through many editions. In 1962 it was made into a movie, which was released on DVD in 2004. In the late 1860s Dodge worked as an associate editor of *Hearth and Home* alongside Harriet Beecher Stowe. As the editor of *St. Nicholas: Scribner's Illustrated Magazine for Girls and Boys* (a title she suggested) from 1873 until the end of her life, she influenced American juvenile literature. Her stories from *St. Nicholas* are compiled in two books, *Baby Days* (1876) and *Baby World* (1884). During her tenure the magazine published important work by Rudyard Kipling, Louisa May Alcott, and Mark Twain and became the most popular magazine of its kind in the country. Dodge also published her poetry and verse collections *Rhymes and Jingles* (1874) and *Poems and Verses* (1904).

Alice B. Howard, *Mary Mapes Dodge of St. Nicholas* (New York: J. Messner, 1943)

Meryl Cates, Michael Joseph

Dodgewood. A section of northwestern Bronx bounded to the north by West 245th Street, to the east by Arlington Avenue, to the south by West 243rd Street, and to the west by Palisades Avenue. The land was once owned by William E. Dodge, whose holdings extended as far north as Westchester County and as far west as the Hudson River. Two mansions owned by his family still stand. Many of the area's large estates were sold to institutions and developers during the 1920s and 1930s. The neighborhood is an exclusive area of winding lanes and fine homes.

John McNamara, *History in Asphalt: The Origin of Bronx Street and Place Names* (New York: Bronx County Historical Society, 1984); John McNamara, *McNamara's Old Bronx* (New York: Bronx County Historical Society, 1989)

John McNamara

Doe Fund. Organization working with homeless people in New York City to provide opportunities for self-sufficiency. Headquartered at 232 East 84th Street, it was established by George T. McDonald in 1990. Their "Ready, Willing & Able" program was the first residential paid work and training program for homeless people. In the early twenty-first century the program has had continuing success with many of its members in the workforce.

Jessica Montesano

Dollar Dry Dock Savings Bank. Savings bank formed on 5 February 1983 by the merger of Dry Dock Savings Bank and Dollar Savings Bank. Dry Dock Savings Institution was formed in 1848 by leading shipbuilders for their workers, at the corner of Fourth Street and Avenue C. It attracted mostly local, working-class customers until 1932, when it merged with U.S. Savings Bank and opened branches throughout the city, changing its name in 1949 to Dry Dock Savings Bank. It merged with New York Federal Savings and Loan Association in 1976. Dollar Savings Bank opened in 1890 at 2771 Third Avenue in Mott Haven. It merged with Fordham Savings Bank in 1932 and expanded throughout the Bronx in the 1930s and 1940s, opening branches in Fordham and Parkchester. In 1951 it erected a 10-story building for its headquarters on the Grand Concourse at Fordham Road. Among the many projects that it funded was Co-op City. The Dry Dock Savings Bank and Dollar Savings Bank merger created the fifth-largest mutual savings bank in the country and one of the most successful in the metropolitan area. It moved its headquarters from the city in 1983, and was bought by Emigrant Savings Bank in 1992 and liquidated in 1995.

Andrew Mills, *The Story of Dry Dock Savings Institution, 1848–1948* (New York: Dry Dock Savings Institution, 1948)

James Bradley

Dolphy, Eric (*b* Los Angeles, 20 June 1928; *d* Berlin, 29 June 1964). Saxophonist, flutist, and bass clarinetist. After moving to New York City in 1959 he played avant-garde jazz as a sideman with Ornette Coleman, John Coltrane, and Charles Mingus. He played piercing, angular solos on three instruments with equal facility and became known for an uncompromising, complex style characterized by the use of quarter-tones and other devices not usually associated with jazz. His recordings include *Out to Lunch* (1964) and *Last Date* (1964).

Vladimir Simosko and Barry Tepperman, *Eric Dolphy: A Musical Biography and Discography* (Washington, D.C.: Smithsonian Institution Press, 1971)

Marc Ferris

domestic pigeon. See Rock Pigeon.

domestic servants. Most servants in New Amsterdam were household slaves allowed to live independently in exchange for work and a fee. Conditions changed after the American Revolution when workers from the country and free blacks moved to the city and sought employment in domestic service. Between 1790 and 1810 most free black women in the city were servants; a third of free black men, presumably servants as well, lived in white households. A shortage of domestic help also led free blacks to move to the city during the 1820s, and servants' quarters became a regular feature of residences about this time. Women worked as ladies' maids, parlormaids, kitchen maids, cooks, laundresses, and governesses and men as chauffeurs, gardeners, butlers, and valets; days began with lighting the fires and preparing breakfast and ended with shutting the house for the night, usually after the employers had gone to bed. The work was undesirable owing to the long hours, low wages, and isolation associated with it, and many servants eventually left their households. Employers considered satisfactory servants difficult to find, and in 1825 a group of wealthy women established the New York Society for the Encouragement of Faithful Domestic Servants. Young women were often sexually abused by their employers and then dismissed if the abuse came to light; former servants accounted for a quarter of the city's prostitutes in 1839 and almost half in 1859. Irish immigrants competed increasingly with blacks for domestic work after 1845. In 1855 about 40 percent of blacks in the city, 26 percent of Irish immigrants, and 9 percent of all other immigrant groups worked as servants, who numbered 34,302 in Manhattan (including laundry workers) and 4,441 in Brooklyn. Women found factory work a more appealing alternative; in 1860 it paid $2 to $6 a week, compared with $3 to $4 a month for domestic service. In 1870 servants (including laundry workers) accounted for 55,044 workers in the city, or 16 percent of the working population, and for more than half of working women. The children of immigrants who worked as servants often found other kinds of employment; children of black servants had fewer opportunities and often became servants themselves.

In 1920 there were by some estimates about 115,000 servants in the city (excluding laundry workers), or 6 percent of the working population. The number may have been twice that, since many failed to report their incomes and occupations. As electric appliances were introduced during the 1920s, housework became easier. The number of servants from southern and eastern Europe declined after the National Origins Act of 1924 imposed strict immigration quotas. As wages plummeted during the Depression, the demand for domestic help grew, and the number of servants rose to 262,469 in 1930. Maids stood waiting for work on more than 200 street corners in the city to be engaged for the day and paid by the hour at cruelly low wages. The writers Ella Baker and Marvel Cooke posed as maids and published an exposé called "The Bronx Slave Market" for the *Crisis* in November 1935. In 1937 the Domestic Workers' Union became Local 149 of the Congress of Industrial Organizations; it had few members and little effect on wages and working conditions, and ceased operations in 1968. At the beginning of World War II, blacks from the South sought domestic work in the city and retained the custom of living apart from their employers; this arrangement became so common that apartment buildings ceased to include maids' quarters in the 1950s. When other kinds of work became abundant during the war, the number of domestic workers decreased, especially among men. In 1940 there were about 140,000; more than 90 percent were women and most were black. The number fell in 1950 to 79,533, or slightly more than 2 percent of the workforce. Employment agencies arranged for maids from Great Britain and the South to work in the city, and the Amsterdam Employment Agency (1947–84) at Amsterdam Avenue and 149th Street found employment for blacks. As daily and hourly work became more popular, employers and employees began to negotiate with each other.

After the Immigration and Nationality Act of 1965 (Hart–Celler Act) took effect in 1968, women from the Caribbean and Latin America accounted for most domestic workers in the city. They often obtained visas through employers and domestic service agencies but increasingly worked in the city illegally, resulting in artificially low estimates of the number of domestic workers. In 1980 only 25,500 people, mostly women and more than 70 percent nonwhite, reported themselves as private household workers. The demand for domestic workers was high during the following decades, owing in part to the number of women working outside the home. Wealthy families had live-in help; many middle-class families engaged part-time housecleaners. Employment agencies that provided foreign workers flourished, among them the Finnish Agency (opened in 1933); the Asian–American Placement Agency, which arranged employment for Filipinos; and several Polish agencies. West Indian and Hispanic immigrants made up the bulk of workers, including a large proportion of illegal immigrants. In the twenty-first century child-care workers, home attendants, and nurses' aides accounted for most full-time household employees. They had still not procured legal protection from abuse; as of early 2010 a state domestic worker bill of rights had not yet been passed.

Ruth Sergel, ed., *The Woman in the House: Stories of Household Employment* (New York: Woman's Press, 1938); Alana Erickson Coble, *Cleaning Up: The Transformation of Domestic Service in Twentieth Century New York City* (New York: Routledge, 2006)

Alana Erickson Coble

Domingo, W(ilfred) A(dolphus) (*b* Kingston, Jamaica, 1889; *d* New York City, 14 Feb 1968). Writer and political reformer. He moved to New York City in 1913. From 1917 to the early 1920s he wrote articles for the radical black publications the *Messenger,* the *Crusader,* the *Emancipator,* and the *Negro World* (which was aligned with Marcus Garvey), and he maintained close ties to such radical groups as the Socialist Party, the Universal Negro Improvement Association, and the African Blood Brotherhood. After returning to Jamaica at the onset of World War II, he was arrested by the colonial regime and accused of being an agent provocateur. On his release from prison in 1943 he returned to New York City, where he promoted Jamaican and Caribbean independence.

Harold Cruse, *The Crisis of the Negro Intellectual* (New York: William Morrow, 1967)

Calvin B. Holder

Dominican Academy. Catholic college preparatory school for girls at 44 East 68th Street. The building, a five-story mansion, was donated by Colonel Michael Friedsam, former president of the department store B. Altman and Company. The school was established in 1897. In 2010 the school's enrollment was 220.

Jessica Montesano

Dominicans. Before 1961 the number of Dominicans immigrating to the United States was relatively small, owing in large part to severe restrictions imposed from 1930 by the repressive regime of Rafael Trujillo. Between 1950 and 1960 some 10,000 Dominicans immigrated to the United States. The assassination of Trujillo in 1961 and the subsequent removal of restrictions led to a surge of immigration, as did the defeat of a popular revolt in 1965 and the ensuing occupation of the Dominican Republic by the United States. Economic and political uncertainty after the mid-1960s prompted a large number of Dominicans to flee. The number of Dominicans immigrating to the United States each year increased from 14,000 in the 1970s to more than 22,000 in the 1980s; undocumented immigration increased as well.

By the mid-1980s Dominicans had become more active in the political life of New York City and began to run for elective office, notably in Washington Heights. A new leadership arose out of community efforts to promote economic development, to work with government agencies, and to combat discrimination. At the same time Dominican culture began to exert a presence in New York City after years of near-invisibility. The music and dance of the meringue and bachata came to rival salsa in popularity, and some merengue groups based in the city reached a wide audience in the Dominican Republic.

In the early twenty-first century Dominicans were the largest foreign-born immigrant group in New York City. Over 18 percent of Dominicans who were then in the United States lived in the Bronx and Manhattan. They were among the city's most residentially concentrated immigrant groups. The neighborhoods with the largest numbers of Dominicans were Washington Heights, Hamilton Heights, Inwood, Highbridge, University Heights, Kingsbridge, Corona, Morris Heights, and Tremont. Famous Dominicans living in the city included baseball player Alex Rodriguez, actor Manny Perez, and musician Johnny Pacheco. The garment industry employed a large number of Dominicans. Other areas of employment included hotels, restaurants, and hospitals. Many Dominicans also owned and operated bodegas, garment shops, and nonmedallion, or "gypsy," taxicabs that served immigrant neighborhoods.

The Dominican Day Parade, begun in 1981, is held each August in conjunction with Dominican Restoration Day, which commemorates the restoration of the republic after its reannexation by Spain. Modeled on its Puerto Rican counterpart, the parade was first staged in Washington Heights and later moved to Manhattan.

Sherri Grasmuck and Patricia Pessar, *Between Two Islands: Dominican International Migration* (Berkeley: University of California Press, 1991)

Eugenia Georges

Domino Sugar Plant. Industrial sugar-refining complex on the Brooklyn shore of the East River immediately north of the Williamsburg Bridge at 292-314 Kent Avenue. It was designed by Theodore A. Havemeyer in the Romanesque Revival style for Havemeyers and Elder, a sugar-refining company founded by the German immigrant cousins William and Frederick Christian Havemeyer in lower Manhattan in 1807. Constructed from 1881–84, part of the brick refinery was destroyed by fire in 1882. The largest and most iconic structures are three separate buildings encompassing the Filter, Pan, and Finishing House, which rise 155 feet (47 meters), not including a very prominent chimney. Upon completion it was the largest sugar refinery in the world and one of five located on the waterfront of Brooklyn. The Domino brand name was introduced in 1901, although the company was called the American Sugar Refining Company (also known as the Sugar Trust) for most of the twentieth century; it was renamed the Domino Sugar Corporation in 1991. Raw sugar was delivered to the plant by ship until 1999, when the first stage of converting sugar to liquid was transferred to a Baltimore refinery. After that the liquid sugar was delivered to the plant by barge until its closing in 2004. The Community Preservation Corporation bought the refinery, which in the early twenty-first century was part of a $1.2 billion redevelopment plan by Rafael Viñoly Architects that included apartments and a park. The combined Filter, Pan, and Finishing House structures were designated a New York City Landmark in September 2007 and incorporated into the plan; the rest of the plant's buildings were not protected, including the iconic yellow Domino Sugar sign.

Norman J. Brouwer, Kate Lauber

Donaldson, Lufkin and Jenrette. Firm of investment bankers formed in New York City in 1959 by William Donaldson, Dan Lufkin, and Richard Jenrette. It was devoted to researching small growth companies before entering investment banking, merchant banking, institutional trading and research, investment management, and brokerage. The firm was bought by the Equitable Life Assurance Society for $440 million in January 1985, and revenues continued to increase after the

Domino Sugar Plant, 2009

stock market crash of October 1987. In 2000 Donaldson, Lufkin and Jenrette had its headquarters at 277 Park Avenue and employed about 11,000 people. It was acquired later that year by Credit Suisse for $11.5 billion. In the early twenty-first century Credit Suisse used the DLJ brand for its private equity operations.

Mary E. Curry

Dongan, Thomas (*b* Castletown, Ireland, 1634; *d* London, 14 Dec 1715). Colonial governor. He served in the French and English military forces before his appointment as governor of New York by James, duke of York, in 1682. During his tenure he encouraged religious toleration, sought to set up postal services between Nova Scotia and the Carolinas, and assessed the strength of the French in Iroquois country. He also approved the "Charter of Liberties" establishing representative government in the colony; this was nullified by James, and in 1688 Dongan was replaced as governor by Sir Edmund Andros. Despite anti-Catholic feelings after the English revolution of 1689, Dongan remained in New York until 1691, when he returned to England. He later became the second earl of Limerick.

Thomas Patrick Phelan, *Thomas Dongan, Colonial Governor of New York, 1683–1688* (New York: P. J. Kenedy and Sons, 1933)

James E. Mooney

Dongan Hills. Neighborhood in east central Staten Island (2009 pop. *ca* 15,000). It is one of the largest neighborhoods in the city in area, extending as far as Todt Hill to the north, Grasmere and South Beach to the east, Ocean Breeze and the South Beach Psychiatric Center to the south, and the Richmond County Country Club to the west. It is named for Thomas Dongan, an Irish aristocrat who was appointed governor of the province of New York in 1682 by the duke of York. As part of the appointment he was granted 5100 acres (2064 hectares) on the northern shore of the island, which he eventually enlarged to 25,000 acres (10,100 hectares), including all of the present neighborhood. The well-known architect Ernest Flagg moved to the area in 1889, purchased 12 acres (5 hectares) of land, and built a summer retreat called Stone Court that became St. Charles Seminary after his death in 1947. He built many structures on Staten Island, often using the serpentine stone common to its hills. The housing stock of the neighborhood is varied. The Billiou–Stillwell–Perrine House (1661) at 1476 Richmond Road is the third-oldest building in the entire city. In the early twenty-first century Dongan Hills included old and new mansions, blocks of one-family and multi-family houses, a city housing project called Berry House, and townhouses and condominiums. The principal commercial thoroughfares were Richmond Road and Hylan Boulevard. Dongan Hills is a station of Staten Island Rapid Transit.

John-Paul Richiuso

Donovan, William J(oseph) (*b* Buffalo, 1 Jan 1883; *d* Washington, D.C., 8 Feb 1959). Lawyer and government official. He graduated from Columbia Law School (LLB 1907), practiced law in Buffalo and New York City, and served in World War I, where he organized and led the 69th New York Volunteers (the "fighting 69th"). He was awarded the Medal of Honor, the Distinguished Service Cross, the Distinguished Service Medal, the National Security Medal, and three purple hearts. He is the only American ever to win the four highest medals that the U.S. Army awards. In 1922 he became an assistant attorney general of New York State. From 1921 to 1927 he served as a trustee of Columbia University. From 1924 to 1929 he was an assistant district attorney for the Justice Department, during which time he enforced Prohibition zealously. He mounted an unsuccessful campaign for the lieutenant governorship of the state as a Republican in 1932 and was a senior partner of the law firm Donovan, Leisure, Newton and Irvine. In 1941 President Franklin D. Roosevelt appointed him the Coordinator of Information (COI). In this position, he coordinated the intelligence efforts of the various branches of the military and civilian law enforcement agencies, including the army, navy, and Federal Bureau of Investigation. His headquarters were in New York City in room 3603 of Rockefeller Center. He is best known for having led the Office of Strategic Services (OSS) from 1942 to 1945, an outgrowth of his work as the COI. The OSS later became the Central Intelligence Agency. He also served as an assistant to Telford Taylor at the Nuremberg war crimes tribunal. In 1946 he became a member of the advisory committee to the New York City Cancer Committee, and in 1952 he became the director of the New York Cancer Committee. Later he resumed his law practice in Manhattan, and from 1952 to 1954 he was the American ambassador to Thailand. He was often known by the nickname "Wild Bill" Donovan.

Anthony Cave Brown, *The Last Hero: Wild Bill Donovan* (New York: Times Books, 1982); Richard Dunlop, *Donovan: America's Master Spy* (Chicago: Rand McNally, 1982)

Martin Ebon

Dorflinger, Christian (*b* Rosteig, Alsace [now France], 16 March 1828; *d* White Mills, Pa., 11 Aug 1915). Glassmaker. After receiving his training in Alsace, he opened a small operation known as the Concord Street Flint Glass Works (later the Long Island Flint Glass Works) in Brooklyn in 1850, where initially he made chimneys for oil lamps and bottles for druggists. He introduced cutting operations by 1854 and changed his specialty to fine-cut tableware. He opened a large factory on Plymouth Street (1858) and the Greenpoint Flint Glass Works (1860) before retiring in January 1863 because of ill health. Dorflinger later built a factory in White Mills, Pennsylvania, where he became known for producing some of the country's finest brilliant cut glass.

John Quentin Feller, *Dorflinger: America's Finest Glass, 1852–1921* (Marietta, Ohio: Antique Publications, 1988)

Alice Cooney Frelinghuysen

Dorsey, Tommy [Thomas] (*b* Shenandoah, Pa., 19 Nov 1905; *d* Greenwich, Conn., 26 Nov 1956). Bandleader. He played the trombone and in 1924 moved to New York City with his brother Jimmy (*b* Shenandoah, 29 Feb 1904; *d* New York City, 12 June 1957), a saxophonist; the brothers took part in many recording sessions with Bix Beiderbecke, Adrian Rollini, and Red Nichols, played with the orchestras of Jean Goldkette and Paul Whiteman, and formed a band in 1934 that achieved some success. In the following year their public quarrels led them to pursue separate careers. The Tommy Dorsey Orchestra, formed with 12 members of the Joe Haymes Orchestra, became one of the most popular bands of its time; it engaged such well-known soloists as the trumpeter Bunny Berigan and the drummer Buddy Rich, but is perhaps best remembered for its performances with Frank Sinatra between 1940 and 1942. The Jimmy Dorsey Orchestra also enjoyed widespread popularity and had sidemen such as Ray McKinley, Lee Castle, and Bobby Byrne. The brothers reunited as the Fabulous Dorseys in September 1953 and played together until Tommy's death. The Dorseys are best known for having popularized a brand of dance music that was influenced by jazz.

George T. Simon, *The Big Bands* (New York: Macmillan, 1967; 4th edn G. Schirmer, 1981)

Loren Schoenberg

Dos Passos, John (Roderigo) (*b* Chicago, 14 Jan 1896; *d* Baltimore, 28 Sept 1970). Novelist. He rented a studio apartment at 14A Washington Mews in 1922 and in 1924 lived briefly at 106–10 Columbia Heights and in Brooklyn Heights. A figure in bohemian literary circles, Dos Passos wrote the novel *Manhattan Transfer* (1925), which linked the chaos of the city with the aimlessness and confusion of modern life. In 1932 he lived at 214 Riverside Drive. He became increasingly disillusioned with communism after the Spanish Civil War and turned to patriotism and conservatism; some of his later writings were published in the *National Review.* His autobiography, *The Best of Times: An Informal Memoir,* was published in 1966. Dos Passos was also an artist, and in 2001, the Queens library featured a retrospective exhibition titled *The Art of John Dos Passos.*

Virginia Spencer Carr, *Dos Passos: A Life* (Evanston, Ill.: Northwestern University Press, 2004)

Lawson Bowling

Douai, (Karl Daniel) Adolf (*b* Saxe-Altenburg, Germany, 22 Feb 1819; *d* Brooklyn, 21 Jan 1888). Political activist and writer. He fled Germany for Texas after the revolution of 1848, but was driven out of the state for abolitionist agitation and made his way to New York City, where he organized a school, became the editor of the *New Yorker Demokrat,* and was an early leader of the kindergarten movement in the United States. In 1858 his work *Fata Morgana* won a prize as the best German American novel and he became a leader of the German Freethinkers' League. After taking over the German labor newspaper the *Arbeiter Union* (1868) he helped to launch the *Volks-Zeitung* (1878), a leading socialist newspaper that he also edited. He wrote a memoir, *Better Times* (1877).

Stanley Nadel

Doubleday. Firm of book publishers formed in 1897 as Doubleday and McClure by the magazine publisher S. S. McClure and Frank Nelson Doubleday, a vice president of his firm. Initially it operated from McClure's headquarters at 142 East 25th Street. In 1900 Doubleday formed a partnership with Walter Hines Page that became known as the firm of Doubleday, Page, with offices at 34 Union Square East. Pennsylvania Station was the site of the firm's first bookstore (1910), and within 20 years the firm had more than 25 stores and was one of the largest retail book operations in the country. After a merger with the firm of George H. Doran in 1927, the name was changed to Doubleday, Doran, and offices were moved to the Doran Building at 244 Madison Avenue. In 1938 the administrative, editorial, and sales departments were consolidated and moved to offices at 14 West 49th Street in Rockefeller Center. During the next few years the firm concentrated on inexpensive books for a wide audience. When it was renamed Doubleday and Company in 1946, it was the largest book publisher in the United States. By the mid-1970s the firm operated more than 15 book clubs, including the highly successful Literary Guild, and in 1980 it bought the New York Mets. From 1978 until 1994 former first lady Jacqueline Kennedy Onassis worked as an editor for Doubleday. In 1986 Doubleday was bought by the Bertelsmann Publishing Group for $475 million. In 1988 it formed the Bantam Doubleday Dell Publishing Group, which in 1998 became a division of Random House Inc. In the early twenty-first century Doubleday published the following imprints as Doubleday Broadway: Broadway Books, Harlem Moon, Currency, Doubleday, Doubleday Image, Doubleday Religious Publishing, Main Street Books, Morgan Road Books, Nan A. Talese, and Spiegel & Grau. The firm's offices are at 1745 Broadway.

John Tebbel, *A History of Book Publishing in the United States* (New York: R. R. Bowker, 1972–81), vol. 2, pp. 318–31; vol. 3, pp. 107–13, 527–33; vol. 4, pp. 105–17

See also Book publishing.

Allen J. Share

Douglas, Aaron (*b* Topeka, Kans., 26 May 1899; *d* Nashville, Tenn., 2 Feb 1979). Painter. After studying at the University of Nebraska he moved to New York City in 1924 at the urging of Charles Johnson (editor of the magazine *Opportunity: A Journal of Negro Life*). He fell under the influence of the German painter Winold Reiss, emulating the simplified black-and-white designs and flat patterns in his work, and became associated with the artists of the Harlem Renaissance. In 1924 he was the only black visual artist to attend the conference in New York City of publishers, editors, and black intellectuals that resulted in the publication of *Harlem: Mecca of the New Negro.* His illustrations appeared in Alain Locke's *The New Negro* (1925), Eugene O'Neill's *The Emperor Jones* (1926), and James Weldon Johnson's *God's Trombones: Seven Negro Sermons in Verse* (1927), and on the covers of *Opportunity,* the *Crisis,* and the radical arts journal *Fire!!: A Quarterly Devoted to the Younger Negro Artists* (1926). He also painted *Aspects of Negro Life* (1934) for the Countee Cullen branch of the New York Public Library (now the Schomburg Center for Research in Black Culture), a modernistic mural with several panels that was intended to symbolize the strength of the "New Negro." Douglas later studied at Columbia University and the Académie Scandinave in Paris and settled in Nashville, where he was the chairman of the art department at Fisk University until his retirement.

Edmund Gaither

Douglass, David Bates (*b* Pompton, N.J., 21 March 1790; *d* Geneva, N.Y., 21 Oct 1849). Engineer, architect. A graduate of Yale College (1813), U.S. Army engineer during the War of 1812, and West Point professor and government engineer and surveyor (1815–31), Douglass moved to Brooklyn (1831) to pursue civilian assignments. He designed the first building of the University of the City of New York (now New York University). Completed in 1835 on Washington Square, the massive Gothic structure was considered among the city's finest buildings; its spire was the highest point in Manhattan. Douglass conducted the first surveys for the Croton Aqueduct, planned its route, and designed many of its hydraulic features (1833–36); differences with Stephen Allen, head of the commission overseeing the project, resulted in Douglass's replacement as chief engineer before construction began. Douglass designed and oversaw development of Green-Wood Cemetery in Brooklyn (1838–41); his progressive design inspired the naturalistic landscaping of numerous other cemeteries and of Central Park.

Gerard Koeppel

Douglass, Frederick [Bailey, Frederick Augustus Washington] (*b* Maryland, 14 Feb 1818; *d* Washington, D.C., 20 Feb 1895). Abolitionist. Douglass escaped from slavery disguised as a sailor; he took a train from Maryland and on 4 September 1838 arrived in New York City a free man, before traveling on to Massachusetts. He grew to national stature as an ardent advocate for equality and social justice. Steadfast in his support for abolitionist causes, Douglass spoke frequently on the topic and also edited and published a series of antislavery papers. Both his speeches and written commentary remain relevant to contemporary social issues. Later in his career he became a diplomat, securing his place in history as a statesman and reformer. In 2008 the newly renovated Frederick Douglass Circle at the northwest corner of Central Park surrounded a statue of Douglass by Gabriel Koren and marked the gateway of Frederick Douglass Boulevard (Eighth Avenue at 110th Street). The monument is engraved with Douglass's own words: "The types of mankind are various. They differ like the waves, but they are one like the sea."

Diane Jones Randall

Douglaston. Neighborhood in northeastern Queens (2009 pop. *ca* 25,000), near the border with Nassau County. It was settled in 1656 by Thomas Hicks on a peninsula first called Little Madman's Neck. In 1796 Hicks's estate passed to Thomas Wickes, and later to Wynant Van Zandt, who in 1819 built an imposing white mansion (now the Douglaston Yacht Club). Much of the land was bought in 1835 by George Douglas, a Scot, whose son William P. Douglas, a vice commodore of the New York Yacht Club, donated a right-of-way in 1866 to the railroad, which named the station for him. The Douglas Manor Company promoted part of the area as residential from 1906. Among the well-known residents of the neighborhood were Ginger Rogers, Richard Dix, and Clifton Webb in the mid-1920s, and later the tennis player John McEnroe (who learned to play at the Douglaston Club) and the Chilean pianist Claudio Arrau. Although all of Douglaston is desirable and the neighborhood as a whole is the wealthiest community in Queens, the windy, hilly streets of Douglas Manor are particularly attractive. In 1997 the Landmarks Preservation Commission designated Douglas Manor as the Douglaston Historic District. With excellent schools, abundant shopping, and a parklike setting, Douglaston continued to thrive in the early twenty-first century.

Lester Leake Riley, *The Chronicle of Little Neck and Douglaston* (New York: Ledger Printing, 1936)

Vincent Seyfried

Dover. Name briefly applied to Old Town by the British.

Dow Jones and Company. Firm of financial publishers known colloquially as Dow Jones. Its origins go back to the 1882 launch in New York City of a stock bulletin by Charles Dow, Edward Jones, and Charles Bergstresser. In 1884 they published an index of 11 major stocks that eventually evolved into the Dow Jones Industrial Average and in 1889 began publishing the *Wall Street Journal.* In 1899 Jones sold his interest in the firm, and in 1902 the two remaining partners sold the firm to Clarence Barron, who launched *Barron's Weekly* in 1921. The firm underwent rapid expansion after World War II: the circulation of the *Wall Street Journal* increased sharply, other newspapers were acquired, and the *Journal* established an award-winning reputation for its investigative journalism, winning 33 Pulitzer Prizes by 2007. During the 1980s and 1990s the firm expanded into electronic retrieval services and online news services. The *Wall Street Journal* remains one of the country's most respected newspapers, but the company missed numerous opportunities to expand into television, cable, and other media. In 2007, with the newspaper industry in sharp decline, Rupert Murdoch's News Corporation made a $5 billion bid for the company. A bitter takeover battle ended 105 years of family control.

Jerry Martin Rosenberg, *Inside the* Wall Street Journal: *The History and the Power of Dow Jones and Company and America's Most Influential Newspaper* (New York: Macmillan, 1982); Lloyd Wendt, *The* Wall Street Journal: *The Story of Dow Jones and the Nation's Business Newspaper* (Chicago: Rand McNally, 1982)

George Winslow

Downing, Andrew Jackson (*b* Newburgh, N.Y., 31 Oct 1815; *d* southern Westchester County, 28 July 1852). Nurseryman, landscape gardener, and writer. His work *A Treatise on the Theory and Practice of Landscape Gardening* (1841) established him as an authority in the field. In the *Horticulturist* in August 1851 he outlined the advantages of a large, centrally situated park in New York City. His partner on several projects was Calvert Vaux. Downing's only known work in New York City was his design for the Cemetery of the Evergreens on the border between Brooklyn and Queens, a collaboration with the architect Alexander Jackson Davis. He also prepared an unexecuted design for the New York Crystal Palace.

Andrew Jackson Downing

He died when the steamboat *Henry Clay* burned on the Hudson River.

David Schuyler, *Apostle of Taste: Andrew Jackson Downing, 1815–1852* (Baltimore: Johns Hopkins University Press, 1996)

David Schuyler

Downing, Thomas (*b* Chincoteague, Va., Jan 1791; *d* New York City, 10 April 1866). Restaurateur. Born free in a slaveholding state, he arrived in New York City in 1819 and began to sell oysters. At the time, eating oysters was one of the city's most popular pastimes, and the business was conducted primarily by free black men. By 1830 Downing's Oyster House at the corner of Broad and Wall streets was well known for its famous patrons, including Charles Dickens and leading politicians of the day. Downing sent "very choice" oysters to Queen Victoria, who in return sent him a gold chronometer. In 1848 he became a founding trustee of the New York Society for the Promotion of Education among Colored Children. He campaigned for black suffrage in New York State, sponsored rallies against the Fugitive Slave Law, and protested the custom of segregation in public transit. He was also a friend and occasional traveling companion of Frederick Douglass. After Downing's retirement his son George took over the restaurant and continued the business until at least 1871, but by then the heyday of the oyster house in the city was already passing. Downing is buried in the St. Philip's Church section of Cypress Hills Cemetery in Brooklyn.

John H. Hewitt, "Mr. Downing and His Oyster House: The Life and Good Works of an African-American Entrepreneur," *New York History* (July 1993), 229–52

Kenneth T. Jackson

Downing Stadium. Open-air municipal sports stadium across the East River from Manhattan's 125th Street on Randalls Island from 1936 to 2003. It was known as Randalls Island Stadium from 1936 to 1938 and as Triborough Stadium from 1938 to 1955, before being renamed in honor of former Park Department recreational director John J. Downing. A project of the Works Progress Administration and Park Commissioner Robert Moses, construction of the 21,000-seat stadium was completed just in time for the July 1936 U.S. Olympic track and field trials, held to select the American team for the Berlin Olympics later that summer. Capacity crowds filled the stadium for the two-day event at which the African American sprinter and jumper Jesse Owens qualified for four Olympic events, paving the way for his memorable performance later that summer, when his success in winning four gold medals at the Berlin Olympics famously clashed with the political and racial intolerance in Nazi Germany. The stadium hosted numerous operas, concerts, track and field meets, international rugby, cricket, and soccer matches, Negro League baseball games, college and professional football competitions, as well as several political gatherings from the 1930s up until its demolition in 2003, when it was replaced by Icahn Stadium.

David White

Downtown Athletic Club. Private club organized on 10 September 1926 in New York City. On 1 October 1930 it moved into a 35-story building at 19 West Street. The club was perhaps best known as the body that awarded the Heisman Trophy each year to the most outstanding college football player in the United States. First given in 1935, the trophy was named for John W. Heisman, the club's first athletic director. The club peaked at 4500 members in the 1960s and began admitting women as members in 1978. After sustaining damage from the 11 September 2001 attacks, the club never reopened and declared bankruptcy in 2002. The building at 19 West Street was converted into a residential tower and reopened in 2005 as the Downtown Club.

Jessica Montesano

downtown Brooklyn. Neighborhood in northwestern Brooklyn, encompassing the Fulton Mall, Borough Hall and the civic center, Brooklyn Heights, and the area around Fulton Ferry and bounded to the north by the Brooklyn–Queens Expressway, to the east by Flatbush Avenue and the Flatbush Avenue Extension, to the south by Atlantic Avenue, and to the west by Cadman Plaza. The first European settlers in the area were Dutch farmers and tradespeople who occupied land near the East River in the seventeenth century and soon formed a village called Breuckelen near

Fulton Ferry. The introduction of reliable steam ferry service between Brooklyn and Manhattan in the second decade of the nineteenth century spurred the construction of mansions and blocks of row houses and apartment buildings. City Hall was designed in the Classical Revival style and completed in 1849 (it was renamed Brooklyn Borough Hall in 1898). By mid-century several private academies had opened in the area, including the Brooklyn Female Academy (1844), which was succeeded by the Packer Collegiate Institute (170 Joralemon Street). Later schools included the Brooklyn Collegiate and Polytechnic Institute (now in Bay Ridge); the Polytechnic Institute of New York (Jay Street); St. Francis College, which first offered classes in 1859 and later moved to Remsen Street; Brooklyn Law School (1901); Long Island University; and New York City Technical College (Jay Street). The building at 311 Bridge Street, formerly the First Free Congregational Church, became the home of the Bridge Street African Methodist Episcopal Church in 1854. The oldest black congregation in the borough, it remained on Bridge Street for 84 years before moving to Bedford–Stuyvesant. When the Brooklyn Bridge opened in 1883, traffic was rerouted to the area around Brooklyn City Hall, and hotels, theaters, businesses, and newspaper offices opened nearby; department stores and other businesses moved to Fulton Street, which became a prosperous commercial center. Office towers were built on Court Street during the 1920s. Public buildings, including headquarters for the Board of Education (Livingston Street) and for the Transit Authority, accounted for most construction in the years surrounding World War II. Retail suffered during the 1950s and 1960s. In 1977 ground was broken for the Fulton Mall, which became the site of more than 100 retail stores (including a branch of Abraham and Straus at 420 Fulton Street) and one of the largest urban shopping districts in the United States. An office tower was erected at Pierrepont and Court streets in the 1980s for the investment banking firm Morgan Stanley. In the early 1990s downtown Brooklyn became attractive to businesses seeking larger quarters and lower rents than those found in Manhattan. Construction began on MetroTech Center, an office park for research and technology bounded by Johnson Street, Flatbush Avenue, and Willoughby and Jay streets. By 2008 MetroTech had brought more than 6000 jobs to the area. Several local businesses were well known: Junior's (near the mall, at 386 Flatbush Extension on the corner of De Kalb Street) is famous for its cheesecake, and Gage and Tollner's (372 Fulton Street; building 1870, interior 1892) became the only restaurant in Brooklyn with an interior designated as a landmark. Unfortunately, the restaurant did not survive into the twenty-first century. The area around Borough Hall remains a bustling center of transportation and government offices. Stores along the Fulton Mall, Atlantic Avenue, and Court, Livingston, and Montague streets attract many shoppers.

Ellen Marie Snyder-Grenier

draft riots. Civil disturbance during the Civil War from 13 to 16 July 1863 in New York City, sparked by the first federal draft and a $300 exemption fee, almost a year's salary for the average worker. Democrats, including former mayor Fernando Wood, warned that Abraham Lincoln's Emancipation Proclamation of 1 January 1863, combined with the new conscription law, would let the rich stay home while white workingmen died on the front lines to free blacks who would come north and take their jobs. In a city with slums, inadequate sanitation, high infant mortality, and falling real wages, poor whites vented their rage by attacking government offices, Republican officials, and the city's 12,500 African Americans. The 200,000 Irish Americans and Irish immigrants in the city, a quarter of the population, included a majority of the working class. Many were influenced by Catholic archbishop John Hughes: the United States had given asylum to Irish refugees fleeing British oppression, and they would fight to preserve the Union, he said, but not to free the slaves. Irishmen had volunteered in large numbers early in the war and had suffered high casualties; Irish newspapers saw betrayal in Lincoln's shift to a radical Republican agenda of abolition and racial equality. Nonetheless, most of the Irish remained Unionists, including Colonel Robert Nugent of the 69th regiment, the assistant provost marshal general who supervised New York's draft lottery, and the city's numerous Irish police officers who helped quell the riots. Officials blundered by holding the first draft lottery on a Saturday, 11 July, giving workers Sunday, their one day of the week off, to examine the list of draftees in the newspapers, work up their anger, stockpile bricks, cobblestones, and other weapons, and organize a protest for the next drawing of names on Monday, 13 July. Early on Monday columns of laborers, including many women and children, streamed northward from lower Manhattan to Central Park, regrouped, and proceeded to the draft office at 46th Street and Third Avenue, which they burned to the ground, along with the entire block. After beating the police superintendent unconscious, the mob mauled and scattered contingents of soldiers and police as it barreled downtown in search of stockpiles of guns and ammunition. In addition to armories, stores, and the homes of the wealthy Republicans like Mayor George Opdyke, the rioters attacked black churches, homes, and individuals. Black men were lynched from lampposts and chased into the rivers, while the Colored Orphan Asylum on Fifth Avenue and 44th Street was burned to the ground. Abolitionists, including *Tribune* editor Horace Greeley and black clergyman Henry Highland Garnet, were particular targets. Democratic leaders and Catholic priests ventured into the streets to calm the mobs, and militia and federal troops fired into the crowds. Suspecting a Copperhead conspiracy to foment the riots as a fire-in-the-rear during Robert E. Lee's invasion of Pennsylvania, prominent Republicans called for martial law and a federal investigation. Order was gradually restored by 16 July, after five regiments of soldiers arrived from the battle at Gettysburg, which had been fought only two weeks earlier. After four days of looting, arson, and lynching, 5000 blacks

Lynching on Clarkson Street during the draft riots of 1863

had fled Manhattan, many to free black settlements like Weeksville in Brooklyn. The official death toll of 105 makes these riots the most lethal in American history, and the true figure is probably closer to 500. Instead of martial law and executions for treason, Lincoln chose to compromise with the city's Democratic machine. The draft resumed peacefully in August after Tammany Hall boss William M. Tweed created a $2 million public fund to pay the $300 fee for any draftee who claimed hardship. The draft riots represent the largest working-class rebellion in American history.

Iver Bernstein, *The New York City Draft Riots: Their Significance for American Society and Politics in the Age of the Civil War* (New York: Oxford University Press, 1990); Barnet Schecter, *The Devil's Own Work: The Civil War Draft Riots and the Fight to Reconstruct America* (New York: Walker and Company, 2007)

Barnet Schecter

Drake, Joseph Rodman (*b* New York City, 7 Aug 1795; *d* New York City, 21 Sept 1820). Poet and physician. A descendant of an established New England family, he lived in Hunts Point as a child. While studying medicine in New York City he met Fitz-Greene Halleck, with whom he published in the *New York Post* from March to July 1819 the "Croaker Papers," which lampooned prominent local figures and constituted his only work published during his lifetime. Although he practiced medicine in New York City, he is better known for his poems, especially "The Culprit Fay" (an extended romantic fable set in the Hudson Highlands) and "The American Flag," both included in the collection *The Culprit Fay and Other Poems,* published by his daughter in 1835. His poem "Bronx" (1835), a paean to his childhood home, includes the following lines: "Yet I will look upon thy face again, / My own romantic Bronx, and it will be / A face more pleasant than the face of men." Drake's early death from tuberculosis inspired Halleck's elegy "Green be the turf above thee." The cemetery on Hunts Point Avenue in South Bronx where he was buried was taken over by the City of New York in 1910; declared a public park, it was dedicated as Joseph Rodman Drake Park in 1915.

Frank Lester Pleadwell, *The Life and Works of Joseph Rodman Drake* (Boston: Merrymount, 1935)

James Bradley, Ormonde de Kay

Dr. Brown's Soda. Soda company. Founded in 1869, its first flavor was Dr. Brown's Cel-Ray Tonic, a mixture of seltzer, celery seed extract, and sugar. A uniquely kosher soda (cola did not become kosher until the 1930s), Dr. Brown's could be found at Jewish delis throughout New York City. The labels on the soda cans were developed in the 1970s by Herb Lubalin and taken from old prints of New York City icons to emphasize the brand's origins. The original soda can images showed the Brooklyn Bridge (Cel-Ray), the Statue of Liberty (cream soda), Grand Central Terminal (orange soda), an ice cream parlor (root beer), the Astor Hotel (ginger ale), and the Third Avenue elevated train, which was later changed to the Central Park Carousel (black cherry). In the twenty-first century Dr. Brown's is a brand owned by PepsiCo and continues to be sold.

Jessica Montesano

Dreier, Ethel Eyre Valentine (*b* Brooklyn, 21 Aug 1874; *d* Fort Salonga, N.Y., 15 Dec 1958). Reformer, sister of Katherine Dreier and Mary E. Dreier. Shortly after graduating from the Packer Collegiate Institute she became president of the Asacog Club (later the United Neighborhood Guild), one of the first settlement houses in Brooklyn. A local leader of the suffrage movement, she led the Women's Suffrage Party of Brooklyn from 1913 to 1917. She also was president of the New York Women's City Club (1924–30, 1932–36), actively promoted low-cost housing, and helped to organize the Brooklyn Garden Apartments. Her wide-ranging reform interests extended to good government movements and education. Dreier lived in Brooklyn until 1941, when she moved to Long Island.

Eileen K. Cheng

Dreier, Katherine (Sophie) (*b* Brooklyn, 10 Sept 1877; *d* Milford, Conn., 29 March 1952). Reformer and arts patron, sister of Ethel Eyre Valentine Dreier and Mary E. Dreier. She helped to establish the Little Italy Neighborhood House in Brooklyn and the Manhattan Trade School for Girls in 1903. In 1920 she formed the Société Anonyme to provide an exhibition space for work by dadaists and other modern artists, which she also promoted through lectures and writings. She wrote *Western Art and the New Era* (1923).

Linda Elsroad

Dreier, Mary E(lizabeth) (*b* New York City, 26 Sept 1875; *d* Bar Harbor, Maine, 15 Aug 1963). Labor activist, sister of Ethel Eyre Valentine Dreier and Katherine Dreier. Born to a middle-class German family, she was drawn into the New York Women's Trade Union League in 1899 by Leonora O'Reilly, one of its most influential members, and in 1906 was elected its president. During her tenure she was arrested for drawing public attention to police brutality against striking women workers in New York City. Although she built a reputation as one of the few middle-class reformers trusted by the working women in the league, she resigned in 1914 because of her belief that the league should be led by a worker. From 1911 to 1915 she served with Robert F. Wagner (i) and Alfred E. Smith on the New York State Factory Investigating Commission, formed after the Triangle Shirtwaist factory fire of 1911 to investigate conditions in factories and to frame laws regulating occupational safety and health. Dreier also led the city's Woman Suffrage Party during the second decade of the twentieth century.

Annelise Orleck

Dreiser, Theodore (Herman Albert) (*b* Terre Haute, Ind., 27 Aug 1871; *d* Hollywood, Calif., 27 Dec 1945). Novelist. The 12th of 13 children born to a poverty-stricken family, he spent a year at Indiana University (1889–90) and became a newspaper reporter in Chicago in 1892. In 1894 Dreiser read the philosophy of Herbert Spencer and came to believe that human beings are the helpless victims of instinct and social forces, a theme that underlies his writing. He moved to New York City in the same year and stayed at the Mills Hotel (now the Atrium) at 160 Bleecker Street, but financial limitations forced him to move to East End Avenue and then to 6 West 102nd Street in 1913. His first novel, *Sister Carrie* (1900), about a kept woman who becomes a successful actress, caused public controversy and was suppressed by its publisher, Frank Doubleday, which led Dreiser to suffer a nervous collapse. During the nine years after his recovery in a sanitarium, he became financially successful as the editor of several women's magazines, which enabled him to write his second novel, *Jennie Gerhardt* (1911). He followed this critical success with *The Financier* (1912) and *The Titan* (1914), two parts of a trilogy based on the life of the financier Charles T. Yerkes; *The Genius* (1915), a semi-autobiographical novel; *The Color of a Great City* (1923), a rhapsodic tribute to New York City; and *An American Tragedy* (1925), the story

Theodore Dreiser

of a man driven by his social ambitions and passion to commit murder, which became his most critically and commercially successful work. During this period he lived at 439 West 123rd Street (1906–14), 165 West 10th Street (1914–20), 16 St. Luke's Place (1922–23), 118 West 11th Street (1923), and 1799 Bedford Avenue in Bedford–Stuyvesant (1925). In January 1925 he rented an office at 201 Park Avenue South to finish writing *An American Tragedy,* the success of which allowed him to move to 200 West 57th Street. After a trip to Soviet Russia in 1927 he became a social reformer, writing pro-communist works such as *Tragic America* (1932). He lived in Suite 1454 of the Ansonia Hotel at 2101–19 Broadway from 1931 to 1935 and moved to Los Angeles in 1938, where he joined the Communist Party in the following year. Dreiser was the leading figure in the American Naturalist movement, known for his powerfully realistic descriptions of daily life and his exploration of social problems.

W. A. Swanberg, *Dreiser* (New York: Charles Scribner's Sons, 1965); Richard Lingeman, *Theodore Dreiser: At the Gates of the City, 1871–1907* (New York: G. P. Putnam's Sons, 1986)

Anthony Gronowicz

Drew, Daniel (*b* Carmel, N.Y., 29 July 1797; *d* New York City, 18 Sept 1879). Industrialist. Born in Putnam County and son of an upstate farmer, he first worked as a drover. In 1829 he moved to New York City, where he ran a successful cattle business. In 1834 he entered the steamboat industry, and in 1844 he formed Drew, Robinson and Company, a banking and brokerage house on Wall Street. He began an association in 1853 with the Erie Railroad, of which he was named a director in 1857. As the railroad's treasurer and controlling agent, he proceeded to manipulate its stock, and with his confederates Jay Gould and Jim Fisk he engaged Cornelius Vanderbilt in the notorious Erie War between 1866 and 1868. In 1867 he founded the Drew Theological Seminary in Madison, New Jersey. In 1870 Gould and Fisk turned on him, and Drew lost the remainder of his fortune after the Panic of 1873. He filed for bankruptcy in 1876 and spent his declining years at 3 East 42nd Street.

Clifford Browder, *The Money Game in Old New York: Daniel Drew and His Times* (Lexington: University Press of Kentucky, 1986)

Allen J. Share

Drexel Burnham Lambert. Investment bank formed in Philadelphia in 1940, composed of partners from the earlier firm started by Francis M. Drexel; its customers included some of the city's largest industrial firms. The name changed to Drexel Harriman Ripley in 1966, when the firm moved to New York City; to Drexel Firestone in 1970; to Drexel Burnham in 1973, after a merger with the firm of Burnham (a brokerage firm formed in 1935 by I. W. Burnham); and to its present form in 1976, after a merger with the Compagnie Bruxelles Lambert. During the 1970s and 1980s, Drexel's star trader, Michael Milken, pioneered the creation of "junk bonds," or high-yield bonds. Drexel became the leading firm in the junk bond market, fueling the buy-out mania and financing the high-profile hostile takeovers of the 1980s, all of which made it the most profitable firm on Wall Street at that time. After the stock market crash of 1987, the firm dismissed Milken for his role in an insider-trading scheme, and in 1990 it filed for bankruptcy protection after pleading guilty to mail and securities fraud and was charged $650 million in fines.

Connie Bruck, *The Predators' Ball: The Junk Bond Raiders and the Man Who Staked Them* (New York: Simon and Schuster, 1988)

Mary E. Curry

Dreyfus Corporation. Financial services company established in 1951. Headquartered at 200 Park Avenue, in 1957 it was the first mutual company to launch a retail advertising campaign. In 1994 the firm became a subsidiary of Bank of New York Mellon Asset Management. As of 2009 it managed about $280 billion in mutual funds and accounts.

Driscoll, Clara (*b* Tallmadge, Ohio, 15 Dec 1861; *d* Florida, 6 Nov 1944). Designer. After attending design school in Cleveland, she moved to a boardinghouse at 32 South Oxford Street in Fort Greene, Brooklyn, while she studied at the recently founded Metropolitan Museum Art School. By June 1888 she was employed at the Tiffany Glass Company. She left the following year to marry fellow boarder Francis Driscoll. As was then typical, Tiffany employed only unmarried women, so she ceased working there after her marriage. Upon her husband's death in 1892, she returned and was asked to manage the six female employees of Tiffany's newly established women's glass-cutting department. Within two years, she had 35 young women (the so-called Tiffany Girls) working under her. Over the next decade and a half, Driscoll supervised the execution of numerous Tiffany windows and mosaics; she was also the unacknowledged designer of most of Tiffany's lamps. For much of this time, she lived in a boardinghouse at 44 Irving Place in Manhattan, a short walk from her workplace. She left Tiffany in 1908 or 1909 to remarry. Although highly regarded by Tiffany, which in 1907 took Driscoll and another employee on a three-month sketching tour of Brittany, she was never publicly credited for her designs. Consequently, her contributions remained largely unrecognized until the early twenty-first century, when scholars discovered her letters.

Martin Eidelberg, Nina Gray, and Margaret K. Hofer, *A New Light on Tiffany: Clara Driscoll and the Tiffany Girls* (London: New-York Historical Society, in association with D. Giles, 2007)

Susan Kriete

Dr. Seuss [Geisel, Theodor Seuss] (*b* Springfield, Mass., 2 Mar 1904; *d* La Jolla, Calif., 24 Sept 1991). Illustrator and children's book author. After settling in New York City in the late 1920s Geisel worked for the humor magazine *Judge* as a writer and illustrator, taking the professional name Dr. Seuss. In 1928 Standard Oil hired him to draw advertising cartoons for an insecticide called Flit and Essolube 5-Star motor oil; his motor oil campaign featured characters named Karbo-Nockus and Moto-Raspus. He later wrote his first children's book, *And to Think That I Saw It on Mulberry Street* (1937), about a boy's walk down a New York City street. During World War II Geisel drew cartoons for *PM* magazine and then moved to Hollywood where he produced military training films and newsreels with Frank Capra. He remained in California, later publishing many books, including *The Cat in the Hat* (1957), and becoming arguably the most famous children's book author of the twentieth century.

Kate Lauber

Drug, Hospital and Health Care Employees Union. Labor union. An affiliate was formed in New York City in 1932 as LOCAL 1199.

drug abuse. Efforts to prohibit the sale and use of drugs in New York City began in the late nineteenth century, when the state enacted laws prohibiting the sale of opium and morphine without a physician's prescription. Small quantities could nevertheless still be included in patent medicines, which were not controlled by law, and opium and morphine, as well as heroin and cocaine, could also be obtained from out-of-state mail-order houses until the federal government passed the Pure Food and Drug Act (1906). Early attempts to control the use of cocaine were more successful than efforts to control opiates. Introduced in the United States during the mid-1880s, cocaine was a popular tonic often taken in a wine solution: it was also eaten, injected, sniffed in powder form, and sprayed into the nostrils. Some deaths and a much larger number of chronic users resulting from the uncontrolled, legal use of cocaine eventually gave it a reputation as a deadly, habit-forming drug. In 1907 a state law sponsored by Assemblyman Alfred E. Smith made cocaine obtainable only through a physician, marking the beginning of an attempt at control that culminated in the federal Harrison Act (1914). Gradually cocaine use declined to the degree that the Mayor's Committee on Drug Addiction reported in 1930 that cocaine addiction was no longer a serious problem in the city.

Drug treatment programs were developed partly in response to the growing use of heroin, which became popular among opiate users before World War I and by 1915 was responsible for more admissions to Bellevue Hospital than morphine was. The best-known treatment program in the city was administered at the Towns Hospital, opened by Charles B. Towns, an insurance salesman from the South who moved to New York City in 1907; the hospital treated addiction by administering powerful doses of drugs over three to four days, purging the body and thereby supposedly detoxifying and ending drug craving. In the second decade of the century, the work of Ernest Bishop led to a form of treatment in which heroin addicts were given long-term, stable doses of opium. This treatment proved controversial because of an increasing sentiment that drugs should not be used for any purpose; this debate culminated in a decision by the U.S. Supreme Court in 1919 that prohibited treatment programs relying on indefinite drug maintenance. Despite the disfavor in which drug maintenance was held, New York State had established a network of morphine-maintenance clinics in 1918. One such clinic opened in New York City, but the city's Health Department opposed maintenance and also concluded that these drug treatment programs were ineffective. The goal of drug abstinence remained the standard until after World War II, when Vincent Dole and Marie Nyswander of Rockefeller University persuasively argued that some opiate addicts require indefinite, stable doses of drugs: in their studies a number of habitual addicts were successfully treated with methadone, a synthetic opiate.

As drug use became more widespread during the 1960s, residential drug treatment programs within the city operated by Daytop, Odyssey House, and Phoenix House relied on drug-free techniques, among them intensive group therapy and efforts to instill individual responsibility; like methadone maintenance, this approach suffered from a sharp fall-off in the number of participants in the early stages of treatment. During the 1970s the first attempts were made to end the sale and use of drugs through law enforcement. Laws introduced by Governor Nelson A. Rockefeller and enacted in 1973 mandated minimum prison terms for offenses that earlier had been punishable only by probation. The law increased the number of drug offenders in prison but did not diminish the use of drugs. After cocaine regained popularity during the 1970s, its possession and sale became among the most frequently prosecuted offenses. Eventually cocaine came again to be perceived not as a recreational drug but as a dangerous one linked to violence, paranoia, and dependency, especially when a smokable form of cocaine known as "crack" surfaced in the mid-1980s. Crack had a much stronger effect on the body than cocaine ingested by sniffing and was available at lower cost. Fear of the effects of crack led to an increased emphasis on law enforcement that filled the courts and prisons with drug offenders. Attention shifted to intravenous drug users in the 1980s, when it became clear that AIDS was being spread rapidly by shared hypodermic needles. The casual use of drugs declined in the early 1990s, although the number of habitual users remained high: in the mid-1990s it was estimated that there were 500,000 drug addicts in New York City, including 200,000 heroin addicts.

In 1997 Mayor Rudolph W. Giuliani's administration ordered a crackdown on drug abuse in public spaces and specific problem neighborhoods, such as Washington Square Park, Times Square, northern Manhattan, the South Bronx, and southeast Queens. He supported increased education in public schools through the Drug Abuse Resistance Education (DARE) program. More funding enabled the criminal justice system to implement further drug rehabilitation programs for addicted inmates. Experts estimated that marijuana use during the late twentieth century far surpassed all other illegal drugs in numbers of users. During the early twenty-first century, New York City laws were tightened against marijuana use, possession, and trafficking in order to discourage the use of more harmful drugs like cocaine or heroin. Between 1997 and 2007 the New York Police Department sharply increased the number of marijuana-related arrests and received much criticism, particularly because minorities appeared to be targeted in the crackdown.

In the early twenty-first century, Mayor Michael Bloomberg's office increased funding for programs such as LIFENET, a hotline that connects citizens to thousands of resources for recovery. The Take Care New York campaign further educated the public about the dangers of drug abuse. Business improvement districts, which became widespread in the early twenty-first century, allocated money for campaigns to discourage and curtail drug use in public. In many cases these campaigns were very effective: Bryant Park, for example, had once been notorious for open drug abuse and dealing, but it was completely revitalized by a business improvement district.

David F. Musto, Penelope Gelwicks

Drumgoole, John Christopher (*b* Granard, Ireland, 15 Aug 1816; *d* New York City, 28 March 1888). Priest. He moved to New York City as a child and was apprenticed to a cobbler. He later taught Sunday school, became a sexton, and helped to run a small bookstore. When he was nearly 50 he began studying for the priesthood at St. Francis Xavier College and St. John's College in Fordham, and after his ordination in 1869 he was assigned to St. Mary's Church, where he had been a sexton. He soon focused on helping homeless boys, building the Mission of the Immaculate Virgin to provide a home for 2000 youngsters at a cost of about $1 million, which he raised in charitable contributions.

Katherine Kurz Burton, *Children's Shepherd: The Story of John Christopher Drumgoole* (New York: P. J. Kenedy and Sons, 1954)

James E. Mooney

dry dock district. Former neighborhood in lower Manhattan, bounded to the north by 12th Street, to the east by the East River, to the south by Houston Street, and to the west by Avenue B. The area was the site of many ship fitters and iron works during the mid-nineteenth century; in 1855 the Novelty Iron Works, the Secor Iron Works, Young and Cutter, and Cornelius H. Delameter (builder of the *Monitor*) were among the largest of these firms and employed more than 2000 workers among them. In 1848 the Dry Dock Savings Bank opened at 619 Fourth Street to serve dockworkers, mariners, and mechanics; it was liquidated in 1992. The district is now the location of the northern third of the East River Park and of the Jacob Riis Houses, public housing built in 1949.

Kenneth A. Scherzer

Duane, James (*b* New York City, 6 Feb 1733; *d* Schenectady, N.Y., 1 Feb 1797). Mayor. The son of an Irish-born merchant, he was a clerk in the law office of James Alexander before gaining admission to the New York bar in 1754. He was named attorney general of New York in 1767 and was a member of the De Lancey political faction until his marriage to Maria Livingston in 1759, when he joined the Livingston faction. Despite his reservations about independence, he served in the Continental Congress from 1774 to 1784. A staunch Federalist, he was appointed mayor by Governor George Clinton in 1784, becoming the first to hold the office after the British evacuation. During his tenure, which lasted until 1789, he was instrumental in the city's rapid recovery from the war but was unsuccessful in his efforts to keep the national capital in the city. From 1789 to 1794 Duane was the U.S. district judge for New York State. A street in lower Manhattan is named for him.

Edward P. Alexander, *A Revolutionary Conservative: James Duane of New York* (New York: Columbia University Press, 1938)

See also Courts, §§1, 3; and Coffeehouses.

David William Voorhees

Duane Reade. New York City drugstore chain. It was named for the location of its first facility, which opened in 1960 on Broadway between Duane and Reade streets. Going public in 1998 it expanded exponentially, often willing to move into less than ideal, and thus cheaper, locations. In 2010 it was purchased by Walgreens, a national pharmacy chain, for $618 million. At that time it had 150 stores in Manhattan and 229 overall in the city.

Margaret Latimer

Dubinsky, David (*b* Brest-Litovsk, Poland [now Brest, Belarus], 22 Feb 1892; *d* New York City, 17 Sept 1982). Labor leader. He immigrated to the United States in 1911 and began working as a garment cutter. In 1921 he became the general manager of the Amalgamated Cutters' Union, Local 10 of the International Ladies' Garment Workers' Union (ILGWU). After being elected vice president of the union in 1922 he helped it to avoid bankruptcy and defeat a strong communist bid for control. When he became president in 1932, the union had more than $1 million in liabilities and fewer than 40,000 members; with loans and frugal management, supported by the National Industrial Relations Act, he improved the union's finances and increased its membership. He secured many benefits for members, including a 35-hour workweek, expanded union health centers, retirement pensions, death benefits, and two large cooperative housing developments. Dubinsky later organized the Jewish Labor Committee, in 1934 became vice president of the American Federation of Labor (AFL), in the following year formed the Committee for Industrial Organization (CIO; later the Congress of Industrial Organizations) within the AFL, and raised funds for antifascists during the Spanish Civil War.

Dubinsky resigned from the executive council of the AFL in 1936, when it denounced the CIO as illicit and suspended its member unions, including the ILGWU. He kept the ILGWU independent of both federations until 1940, when it rejoined the AFL. With other union leaders in New York City he formed the American Labor Party to give Franklin D. Roosevelt an additional ballot line in the presidential election of 1936. In 1944 he abandoned the party, which he believed had become too leftist, and organized the Liberal Party. During World War II he foresaw a communist threat to labor unions in western Europe and formed the Free Trade Union Committee within the AFL. His long campaign against labor racketeering achieved success in 1957 when the AFL–CIO established a code of ethics. With Alex Rose of the United Hatters, Cap and Millinery Workers International Union he guided Liberals and helped to elect John V. Lindsay mayor of New York City (1965). Dubinsky retired in 1966. With A. H. Raskin he wrote *David Dubinsky: A Life with Labor* (1977).

Max D. Danish, *The World of David Dubinsky* (Cleveland: World, 1957); Robert D. Parmet, *The Master of Seventh Avenue: David Dubinsky and the American Labor Movement* (New York: NYU Press, 2005)

Robert D. Parmet

DuBois, John (*b* Paris, 24 Aug 1764; *d* New York City, 20 Dec 1842). Bishop. After being educated in Paris he was ordained on 22 September 1787. During the French Revolution he became a refugee, and in August 1791 he moved to Norfolk, Virginia. In 1794 he opened the first Catholic church in Frederick, Maryland. Near Emmitsburg, Maryland, he built a chapel in November 1805 where he eventually opened Mount St. Mary's Seminary, and he was made the director of Elizabeth Ann Seton's first convent when it opened in Emmitsburg in June 1809. He also rode circuit from Pennsylvania to Virginia and was affiliated with the Society of St. Sulpice from 1808 to 1826. His appointment as bishop on 29 October 1826 was soon contested by parishioners, who asserted that he had obtained it through undue influence, and he was forced to refute their charges in 1827. With contributions that he collected in Europe (1829–31) he built a seminary; this was uninsured and in 1834 was destroyed by fire. During the same year, lay trustees at St. Patrick's Cathedral on Mott Street refused to pay a priest whom he had appointed, and eventually they refused to pay him as well. In February 1838 he suffered a stroke that left him unable to continue the administration of the diocese. DuBois is buried beneath the doorstep of St. Patrick's Old Cathedral on Mott Street, apparently at his request, so that people might walk on him in death as they had wished to do in life.

Richard Shaw, *John DuBois, Founding Father: The Life and Times of the Founder of Mount St. Mary's College, Emmitsburg, Superior of the Sisters of Charity, and Third Bishop of New York* (Yonkers, N.Y.: United States Catholic Historical Society/Emmitsburg, Md.: Mount Saint Mary's, 1983)

Mary Elizabeth Brown

Du Bois, W(illiam) E(dward) B(urghardt) (*b* Great Barrington, Mass., 23 Feb 1868; *d* Accra, Ghana, 27 Aug 1963). Writer, poet, and civil rights leader. After teaching at Wilberforce and Atlanta universities he formed the Niagara Movement with other black activists in 1905 to protest racial oppression. The movement failed to win either a large following or adequate funds and was superseded in 1909 by the National Association for the Advancement of Colored People (NAACP), which appointed him its director of publicity and research in New York City and the editor of its monthly publication the *Crisis.* Du Bois organized the first Pan-African Congress in 1919 and three subsequent meetings to foster African development and self-determination. His advocacy of "voluntary segregation" as a means of achieving economic development for blacks during the Depression was widely opposed within the NAACP and led to his resignation in 1934. He then returned to Atlanta University but rejoined the association in 1944 to study the global black population. In the following year he was elected international president of the fifth Pan-African Congress (organized by George Padmore). A dispute with Walter White, executive secretary of the NAACP, led to his permanent resignation from the organization in 1948. He became vice chairman of the Council on African Affairs, led by Paul Robeson, and chairman of

W. E. B. Du Bois

the Peace Information Center in 1949 and in 1950 unsuccessfully ran for the U.S. Senate as the candidate of the American Labor Party from New York. During the campaign he was indicted along with other officers of the Peace Information Center for his failure to register as an agent of a foreign government (the center was circulating an appeal to ban nuclear weapons, which the U.S. Department of State considered Soviet propaganda); he was later tried and acquitted. In 1961 he joined the American Communist Party and moved to Ghana. Du Bois published 19 books (including five novels), edited almost two dozen works, and wrote poetry and plays as well as hundreds of articles. His residences in New York City included 650 Greene Avenue (before 1920), the Paul Lawrence Dunbar Apartments at 2594 Seventh Avenue (until 1934), 409 Edgecomb Avenue (1944–51), and 31 Grace Court in Brooklyn Heights (until 1962).

David Levering Lewis, *W. E. B. DuBois: Biography of a Race, 1868–1919* (New York: Henry Holt, 1993)

R. L. Harris, Jr.

Dubos, René (Jules) (*b* St. Brice, France, 20 Feb 1901; *d* New York City, 20 Feb 1982). Microbiologist and environmentalist. From 1927 to the end of his life he worked at the Rockefeller Institute for Medical Research (later known as Rockefeller University) where his discovery in 1939 of the soil-borne antibiotic polypeptide gramicidin paved the way for the commercial development of antibiotics. He also examined the effect of pollutants on the environment and successfully led an effort to clean up Jamaica Bay, dedicated in 1987 as the René Dubos Wildlife Preserve. His published writings include *So Human an Animal* (1968), winner of the Pulitzer Prize.

Renee D. Mastrocco

Duchamp, Marcel (*b* Blainville, France, 28 July 1887; *d* Neuilly-sur-Seine, France, 2 Oct 1968). Painter and sculptor. After his painting *Nude Descending a Staircase* (1912) provoked a controversy at the Armory Show (1913) in Manhattan, he moved in June 1915 to New York City where he was associated with the collectors Louise and Walter Arensberg, with whom he lived for several months at 33 West 67th Street, and took part in the dada movement; he remained in the city until 1918. Duchamp soon abandoned conventional painting and created sculpture from diverse found objects: a bicycle wheel, a snow shovel, a urinal. Between 1915 and 1923 he completed his most important work, *The Bride Stripped Bare by Her Bachelors, Even,* also known as *The Large Glass.* He returned permanently to New York City in 1942 and helped to mount the exhibition *First Papers of Surrealism.* Duchamp is regarded as the founder of conceptual art. The Museum of Modern Art owns examples of his work.

Anne d'Harnoncourt and Kynaston McShine, eds., *Marcel Duchamp* (New York: Museum of Modern Art/Philadelphia: Philadelphia Museum of Art, 1973)

Judith Zilczer

Duchin, Eddy [Edwin Frank] (*b* Cambridge, Mass., 1 April 1909; *d* New York City, 9 Feb 1951). Bandleader and pianist. He moved to New York City in 1928 to play with Leo Reisman's group at the Waldorf=Astoria. After three years he left to form his own orchestra, which performed regularly for members of fashionable society at the Central Park Casino. His radio program *Hour of Charm* was broadcast locally, and he played at many hotels. Duchin was known for his elegant image and sophisticated piano improvisations. His son Peter later organized a similar band in the 1960s.

Marc Ferris

Dudley, Edward R. (*b* South Boston, Va., 11 March 1911; *d* New York City, 8 Feb 2005). Attorney and public official. After serving as legal counsel to the governor of the U.S. Virgin Islands, he became in 1948 the first African American ambassador to Liberia. He was later a judge in the domestic relations court and the New York State Supreme Court and an administrative judge of the New York Criminal Court. From 1961 to 1964, Dudley was Manhattan Borough President.

Kathleen Benson

Duer, William (*b* Devonshire, England, 18 March 1747; *d* New York City, 7 May 1799). Financier and statesman. After settling in New York City in 1768, he set up a lumber firm north of Saratoga, New York. A delegate to the Provincial Congress in 1775 and the Continental Congress in 1777, on which he served on the Board of War, he was deputy adjutant general of Continental troops from New York and signed the Articles of Confederation. During the American Revolution he won supply contracts for both American and French soldiers from the army that allowed him to become wealthy. In 1776 he was appointed to the colony's Committee of Safety and the Committee for Detecting Conspiracies. Duer helped to form the Bank of New York in 1784, was an assistant secretary of the U.S. Treasury, and speculated in land and stocks. In 1786 he served in the state assembly. In 1792 he and Alexander Macomb tried to profit off of information he gained through his experience as assistant secretary to the Treasury by buying up stock of the Bank of New York in anticipation of its buyout by the Bank of the United States. This plan was sabotaged by the Livingston family of New York, who withdrew their massive savings from the Bank of New York, forcing interest rates to soar and Duer into debt. His imprisonment for debt in 1792 set off the first financial panic in New York City, which Alexander Hamilton, as the secretary of the Treasury, calmed by having the Treasury buy several hundred thousand dollars of securities to restore investor confidence. Duer was sent back to prison as a debtor and died there seven years later.

Robert Francis James, *"The King of the Alley": William Duer: Politician, Entrepreneur, and Speculator, 1768–1799* (Philadelphia: American Philosophical Society, 1992)

James E. Mooney, Henry Cooper

Duffy, Francis P(atrick) (*b* Ontario, 2 May 1871; *d* New York City, 26 June 1932). Priest. After receiving his education in Ontario, he was ordained on 6 September 1896 and became an American citizen on 7 June 1902. He taught at St. Joseph's Seminary from 1898 to 1912, edited the *New York Review* (1905–7), and moved to New York City to form the Church of Our Savior in the Bronx (1912–16). Appointed chaplain of the 69th Regiment in 1914, he served at the Mexican border (1916–17) and in France (1917–18). From 1920 to 1932 he was the pastor of Holy Cross, near which a statue of him was built in Times Square. Duffy is best known for his military assignments during World War I.

Jim Bishop and Virginia Lee Bishop, *Fighting Father Duffy* (New York: Vision, 1956)

Mary Elizabeth Brown

Dulles, John Foster (*b* Washington, D.C., 25 Feb 1888; *d* Washington, D.C., 24 May 1959). Statesman. The son of a distinguished Presbyterian pastor, he graduated from Princeton University in 1908 and attended the Sorbonne and later George Washington University. In 1911 he joined the law firm of Sullivan and Cromwell in Manhattan. Paid only $50 a week at the outset because he lacked a law degree, by 1920 he was a partner in the firm. He became its chief operating partner in 1927 and eventually was reported to be the highest-paid lawyer in New York City. From the 1920s he lived at 72 East 91st Street. A specialist in international finance, he settled bondholders' claims against the Kreuger match empire. He also was an adviser to the American delegation at the conference in San Francisco regarding the establishment of the United Nations, advised Thomas E. Dewey on foreign policy, and was the main architect of the peace treaty with Japan after World War II. As secretary of state under President Dwight D. Eisenhower, Dulles pursued policies of brinkmanship and massive retaliation that intensified tension during the cold war.

George J. Lankevich

dumbbell tenements. The predominant tenements erected for workers between 1879 and 1901, named for their shape and based on a design by James E. Ware calling for two tenements connected one behind the other by a hallway. Ware's design won a competition in 1878 (sponsored by the journal *Plumber and Sanitary Engineer*) to design a tenement for a lot measuring 25 by 100 feet (8 by 30 meters); it was widely adopted after New York State passed the Tenement House Law of 1879 requiring a window in every residential bedroom. Dumbbell tenements were usually five to seven stories tall and had 14 rooms on each floor, seven on each side from front to back, divided into two four-room apartments in front and two three-room apartments in back. The four apartments shared two toilets, and the windows in 10 of the 14 rooms opened onto an air shaft less than 5 feet (1.5 meters) wide formed by the indented hallway sections of abutting tenements. Enclosure on all sides made the shaft dark and airless, and it often became a garbage dump and a fire hazard. From the start the design was criticized for sacrificing the interests of tenants to those of landlords, builders, and real estate agents. Dumbbell tenements housed about two-thirds of the city's population, or 2.3 million people, by the time their construction was outlawed by the Tenement House Law of 1901. Existing dumbbell tenements continued to house tens of thousands of New Yorkers into the twenty-first century.

Roy Lubove, *The Progressives and the Slums: Tenement House Reform in New York City, 1890–1917* (Pittsburgh: University of Pittsburgh Press, 1962); Moses Rischin, *The Promised City: New York's Jews, 1870–1914* (Cambridge, Mass.: Harvard University Press, 1962)

Allen J. Share

DUMBO. Brooklyn neighborhood (2000 pop. 2500) bounded to the north by the East River, to the east by Bridge Street, to the south by the Brooklyn–Queens Expressway, and to the west by Main Street. The arc of the Manhattan Bridge is the spine above the area, hence the acronym DUMBO, for Down Under the Manhattan Bridge Overpass. Before the American Revolution, the Loyalist John Rapalje owned the land. In 1784 Comfort and Joshua Sands purchased it, and by 1787 they subdivided the tract into building lots for a village called Olympia. The horse-powered New Ferry began service from Main Street to Manhattan in 1795. The same proximity to Manhattan and the river that made Olympia an eighteenth-century summer retreat helped transform it into a nineteenth- and twentieth-century industrial center. Homes gave way to warehouses and factories that made boxes; tin cans for food, kerosene, and paint; paper packaging for coffee and sugar; and metal kitchenware, pasta, shoes, paint, and soap. Eliphalet W. Bliss made a machine that rolled metal into tin cans; here his company also built metal-molding machinery for others. Robert Gair, who invented a machine for making paper boxes, erected at least 10 factories in the area and pioneered the use of reinforced concrete in factory building after 1904. Gair also built a pier, a powerhouse, and a stable and connected his works by rails, tunnels, and bridges. The western part of the neighborhood was nicknamed Gairville. In the 1930s and 1940s industry began to leave. Houses and shops were demolished when the anchorage and support piers of the Manhattan Bridge were built (1909). Completion of the Brooklyn–Queens Expressway further isolated the area. In the 1970s artists rediscovered the neighborhood's stone-paved streets and factory lofts, some of which continued to house workshops. In 1981 developer David C. Walentas purchased the Gair complex. His plans for a shopping mall and hotel aroused opposition, but since the late 1990s he and other developers have carved housing out of old factories and built new apartment buildings. In 2001 the city and state began developing the waterfront as Brooklyn Bridge Park. DUMBO has been designated a state historic district; development and rising rents remain contentious issues among its artists, small manufacturers, newcomers, and developers.

Martha Reiss, *Fulton Ferry Landing, DUMBO, Vinegar Hill Neighborhood History Guide* (Brooklyn: Brooklyn Historical Society, 2001)

Cathy Alexander

Dun and Bradstreet. Financial rating service. Its precursor was formed in 1841 by Lewis Tappan to provide the credit ratings of retailers to wholesale merchants in New York City. In 1849 Tappan sold his interest in the agency to his brother Arthur Tappan and to Benjamin Douglass, who in 1854 purchased Tappan's interest, changed the name of the firm to B. Douglass and Company, and expanded it to a national scale. In 1855 John M. Bradstreet, the agency's strongest competitor, moved his headquarters from Cincinnati to New York City and began publishing credit ratings in a book that he made available by subscription. The service proved popular and was easily imitated by, among others, Robert Graham Dun, who purchased Douglass's business in 1858 and in the same year began publishing the *Mercantile Agency's Reference Book.* In 1930 Dun's firm absorbed the National Credit Office, and in 1933 it merged with Bradstreet's firm. In the 1990s Dun and Bradstreet restructured and spun off several of its companies, and since 2000 it has split into two companies, launched a new corporate brand called D&B, and moved its headquarters to suburban Short Hills, New Jersey.

Edward N. Vose, *Seventy-Five Years of the Mercantile Agency: R. G. Dun and Co., 1841–1916* (New York: R. G. Dun, 1916); Roy Anderson Foulke, *The Sinews of American Commerce: 100th Anniversary, 1841–1941* (New York: Dun and Bradstreet, 1941); James D. Norris, *R. G. Dun and Co., 1841–1900: The Development of Credit-Reporting in the Nineteenth Century* (Westport, Conn.: Greenwood, 1978)

James D. Norris

Dunbar, Paul Lawrence (*b* Dayton, Ohio, 27 June 1872; *d* Dayton, 9 Feb 1906). Poet and novelist. He first visited New York City in 1896 to give a series of poetry readings and lived briefly at 131 West Third Street in May and June 1899. His earliest works were poems, some in Afro-American dialect and others in standard English. He also wrote four novels, of which the first three dealt with white characters and the last with black characters and themes, like most of his short stories. Although Dunbar lived most of his adult life in Washington, D.C., he used New York City in such works as his short stories "Finding of Zach," "One Christmas at Shiloh," and "The Trustfulness of Polly," and the novel *The Strength of Gideon* (1900). Episodes from the novel *The Sport of the Gods* (1902) are set in the Banner Cafe in the Tenderloin. Central themes of his work were the false ideals of blacks and the adversities of northward migration and adaptation to the urban environment. Dunbar also wrote lyrics to the musicals of Will Marion Cook, including *In Dahomey* (1902). He was the first black writer to achieve national fame and a major influence on the writers of the Harlem Renaissance.

Tony Gentry, *Paul Lawrence Dunbar* (New York: Chelsea House, 1989)

George A. Thompson, Jr.

Dunbar Apartments. Cooperative apartment complex in Manhattan, financed by John D. Rockefeller, Jr., designed by Andrew J. Thomas, and consisting of six garden apartment buildings arranged in the shape of a horseshoe around a courtyard; it was built between 1926 and 1928 on a site bounded by 150th Street, Adam Clayton Powell Jr. Boulevard, 149th Street, and Frederick Douglass Boulevard. Named for the poet Paul Lawrence Dunbar, it was the first development of its kind built for blacks. Units of four, five, and six rooms were offered for a down payment of \$150 and \$50 a room. Among the amenities were a nursery and kindergarten, a playground, a club room for older boys, an athletic field, men's and women's clubs, vocational guidance for tenants, stores, and the Dunbar National Bank, the first large bank in Harlem to have a black manager and staff. Many tenants defaulted on mortgage and maintenance payments during the Depression, forcing Rockefeller to foreclose on the mortgage in 1936; he returned the equity to the tenants, who were allowed to remain as renters. Well-known residents included the poet Countee Cullen, the writer W. E. B. Du Bois, the actor Paul Robeson, the tap dancer Bill "Bojangles" Robinson, the labor leader

A. Philip Randolph, and the explorer Matthew A. Henson. The Dunbar Apartments were designated a city landmark in 1970.

Eric Wm. Allison

Duncan, Isadora (*b* San Francisco, Calif., 27 May 1878; *d* Nice, France, 14 Sept 1927). Dancer and choreographer. At the age of 10 she left school to conduct her own dance classes, and in 1896 she moved to New York City with her mother to pursue a stage career. She left for London in 1900 and developed an infatuation with Europe that lasted throughout her life. Inspired by Greek antiquity, she rejected ballet and introduced a distinctive style characterized by flowing movements and the use of translucent gowns. During 1914–15 she lived at 303 Fourth Avenue where she also ran a studio. Duncan became widely known during World War I for her sexually provocative dancing, her publicly noted liaisons, and her frequent criticism of conventional marriage. She lived at 118 West 57th Street during 1922–23. Her autobiography, *My Life,* was published in 1927.

Fredrika Blair, *Isadora: Portrait of the Artist as a Woman* (New York: McGraw–Hill, 1986)

Peter M. Rutkoff, William B. Scott

Duncan, John H(emenway) (*b* New Orleans, 1854; *d* Highland Beach, N.J., 18 Oct 1929). Architect. He grew up in Binghamton, New York, and in 1879 moved to New York City to begin his practice. He gained prominence by winning competitions for the Brooklyn Soldiers' and Sailors' Memorial Arch (1892) and for Grant's Tomb (1897), and later designed the Knox Building at 452 Fifth Avenue (1902), private houses at 7 West 54th Street (1900) and 16 East 67th Street (1905), and the twin structures at 16 and 18 East 71st Street (1911). Duncan's adherence to principles of classical architecture put him at odds with the styles prevailing after World War I.

Elliott B. Nixon

Dunham, Katherine (*b* Chicago, 22 June 1909; *d* New York City, 21 May 2006). Dancer, choreographer, and artistic director. She studied modern dance and ballet, attended the University of Chicago (MA, anthropology), and undertook fieldwork in Haiti and Jamaica. In New York City she formed a dance company in 1939 for which she did her own choreography, effecting an innovative fusion of Afro-Caribbean and European forms. The company was acclaimed worldwide and trained several hundred dancers. During the 1940s and 1950s she worked on Broadway and in Hollywood, and from 1945 to the mid-1950s she taught at the Dunham School of Dance in New York City. After her company disbanded in 1967, Dunham moved to East St. Louis, Illinois, where she opened the Performing Arts Training Center (now called the Katherine Dunham Centers for Arts and Humanities). In 1977 she opened the Katherine Dunham Museum and Children's Workshop there. She was the recipient of a Kennedy Center Honor's Award (1983) and the Samuel H. Scripps American Dance Festival Award (1987); in 1987 she was inducted into the Hall of Fame of the National Museum of Dance in Saratoga Springs, New York. In New York City Dunham directed a program of her works called "The Magic of Katherine Dunham" for the 1987–88 season of the Alvin Ailey American Dance Theater. Gaining international attention in 1992, she began a 47-day fast in her home in response to Haiti's political turmoil; she was 82 at the time. Dunham remained active and attended events through her final months until she died in her Manhattan home at the age of 96.

Katherine Dunham performing in a theatrical production of Tropical Revue

Ruth Beckford, *Katherine Dunham: A Biography* (New York: Marcel Dekker, 1979)

Meryl Cates, Brenda Dixon Gottschild

Dunlap, William (*b* Perth Amboy, N.J., 19 Feb 1766; *d* New York City, 28 Sept 1839). Painter and playwright. In 1784 he went abroad to study with painter Benjamin West. Captivated by theater in London, he returned to Manhattan to write plays, many of which were later produced. From 1796 to 1805 he managed the Old American Company, a position that gave him virtual control of theater in New York City but after several years left him bankrupt and fatigued. Although he remained a prolific writer, he derived most of his income after about 1810 from painting miniatures, portraits, and religious pictures such as *Christ Rejected* (1822) and *Death on the Pale Horse* (1824). An active member of the American Academy of the Fine Arts, he joined with Samuel F. B. Morse to found the National Academy of Design in 1826. Dunlap wrote *History of the American Theatre* (1832) and *History of the Rise and Progress of the Arts of Design in the United States* (1834).

Maura Lyons, *William Dunlap and the Construction of an American Art History* (Boston: University of Massachusetts Press, 2005)

Carrie Rebora Barratt

Dunne, Finley Peter (*b* Chicago, 19 July 1867; *d* New York City, 24 April 1936). Satirist. After working as an editor in Chicago he wrote commentaries in Irish dialect from 1893 as the reformist "Mr. Dooley." He moved to New York City in 1901 where his column appeared in the *New York Times,* the *American Magazine,* and *Collier's,* which he also edited. In perhaps his best-known piece he had Mr. Dooley describe his friend "Prisidint Tiddy Rosenfelt" and coined the line: "no matther whether th' constitution follows th' flag or not, th' Supreme Court follows th' iliction returns."

Elmer Ellis, *Mr. Dooley's America: A Life of Finley Peter Dunne* (New York: Alfred A. Knopf, 1941)

Michael Green

Dunton. Name formerly applied to a section of north central Queens south of the Long Island Rail Road between 127th Street and the Van Wyck Expressway. It was developed from 1889 as West Jamaica on the land of several farms acquired by Frederick W. Dunton, a nephew of Austin Corbin who was active in real estate. The name Dunton was adopted in 1890 by a vote of local residents, soon after which Dunton Park opened between Liberty and 109th avenues. Eventually the area became a model community of one-family houses. The population was predominantly German, Irish, and Italian, many of whom were Jewish. After World War I it was absorbed into Jamaica.

Vincent Seyfried

Durand, Asher B(rown) (*b* Jefferson Village [now Maplewood], N.J., 21 Aug 1796; *d* Jefferson Village, 17 Sept 1886). Painter. He was apprenticed to the engraver Peter Maverick in 1812 near Newark, New Jersey, and in

Asher B. Durand

1817 became Maverick's partner and moved to New York City. His reputation was secured by an engraving (1820–23) after John Trumbull's painting *The Declaration of Independence.* A member of the New-York Historical Society (1821) and the Bread and Cheese Club (1825), he helped to form the New-York Drawing Association (1825), the National Academy of Design (1826), of which he was the second president (1845–61), the Sketch Club (1827), and the Century Association (1847). After receiving a commission for a series of presidential portraits from Luman Reed in 1835, he was able to devote himself entirely to painting. A trip with Thomas Cole to the Adirondack Mountains in 1837 led him to turn to landscape painting; scenes of New York State and New England were his preferred subjects. He traveled to Europe (1840–41) and after Cole's death became the acknowledged leader of the Hudson River School. Inspired by writings of the English critic John Ruskin, he modified his picturesque style in the early 1850s with elements derived from studies of nature. In his "Letters on Landscape Painting" (1855), nine essays published in the periodical the *Crayon* that stated the theories of the Hudson River School, he argued that the faithful depiction of nature could reveal the presence of God. Durand retired to the village of his birth in 1869.

David B. Lawall, *Asher Brown Durand: His Art and Art Theory in Relation to His Times* (New York: Garland, 1977); Linda S. Ferber, ed., *Kindred Spirits: Asher B. Durand and the American Landscape* (London: The Brooklyn Museum in association with D Giles Limited, 2007)

Timothy Anglin Burgard

Durant, Will (*b* North Adams, Mass., 5 Nov 1885; *d* Los Angeles, 7 Nov 1981). Writer, philosopher, and historian. Raised in a religious family, Durant turned away from Christianity in 1905 and soon after became a reporter for the *New York Evening Journal.* He became a socialist and taught at New York City's experimental Ferrer Modern School, where he met his wife, Ariel. He received his PhD in philosophy from Columbia University in 1917 and went on to write a book of essays on thinkers from Plato to John Dewey called *The Story of Philosophy* (1926). The book sold over two million copies in three years. He and Ariel spent the next 50 years writing *The Story of Civilization*, an 11-volume history in which they attempted to encapsulate all of Western political, social, and intellectual history. The 11 books were widely read, and in 1968 Durant won the Pulitzer Prize. Durant divided his time between New York City and Los Angeles.

Nicholas Kelly

Durocher, Leo (*b* West Springfield, Mass., 27 July 1905; *d* Palm Springs, Calif., 7 Oct 1991). Baseball player and manager. He played second base and shortstop in the major leagues from 1925 to 1945, including stints with the Yankees (1925–29) and the Brooklyn Dodgers (1938–45). Durocher became the Dodgers' manager in 1939 and proved instantly successful, leading them to their first winning season in six years and to the National League title in 1941. An outspoken manager known for his fiery disposition, combative style, and the quotation "Nice Guys Finish Last," he feuded with the Brooklyn ownership and was fired mid-season in 1948. The New York Giants then hired him, and Durocher led them in 1951 to the National League title (after a one-game playoff against Brooklyn) and in 1954 to a World Series victory over the Cleveland Indians.

Ben Silk

Durst, Seymour B. (*b* New York City, 1913; *d* New York City, 19 May 1995). Real estate investor and developer. Born in Washington Heights, he attended Horace Mann School in Riverdale, the Bronx, and the University of Southern California (BA, accounting, 1935). In 1940 he joined his family's real estate firm, the Durst Organization, and became president in 1974 when his father died. The Durst Organization mainly developed the midtown area, both east and west; from 1965 to 1975 he owned or held options on about 10 acres (4 hectares) of midtown land. He was known for his criticism of government intervention in real estate. During the 1970s he founded, with the financier Irving Kahn, the New York City Job and Career Center to teach job skills to high school students. In the twenty-first century it was still performing these services. He had a passion for New York City history and collected books, maps, prints, and signs that eventually became the Old York Library, now at the Graduate Center of the City University of New York. He was featured among the Forbes 400 richest Americans in the years 1985 and 1991. In 1989 he established the National Debt Clock—a billboard-sized, constantly updating sign that shows a running total of the gross national debt—in Times Square at 43rd Street and Sixth Avenue (it was moved to Bryant Park in 2004). He lived in a townhouse on East 61st Street until his death.

Jessica Montesano

Duryea House. Historic house in Brooklyn. It was built about 1740 as a gabled, Dutch colonial farm cottage in the village of New Lots (now the neighborhood of East New York) soon after its site of 100 acres (40 hectares) was acquired by Christian Duryea, a Huguenot. Duryea's descendants retained ownership of the house until 1886. The last owner of the house, Frederick Eversley, died in 1982. At the time there were only about a dozen eighteenth-century farmhouses remaining in the city, and preservationists hoped to maintain the Duryea House by moving it to a public park nearby. However, before its transfer to the city could be negotiated, the house was destroyed by fire in November 1989.

Jonathan Kuhn

Dutch. The Dutch first came to what is now New York City in 1609 during an expedition commissioned by the Dutch East India Company and led by the English explorer Henry Hudson. He sailed into the harbor on 3 September and explored the river that would be named for him after the English took control of the region in 1664. A colony called New Netherland was formed in 1614 in the area between the Delaware and Connecticut rivers. Commercial activity was initially centered at Fort Orange (near what is now Albany). In 1621 the Dutch West India Company (WIC) was created by the States General of the Netherlands; its charter provided for 19 directors, minimal supervisions by the States General, and a monopoly on Dutch trade in a large area extending as far east as West Africa and as far north as Newfoundland. Because its domain was so vast the company virtually ignored New Netherland until 1624, when it sent about 30 families and some single men, mostly Protestant Walloons from the Spanish Netherlands, to set up farms. While most of the colonists were settled at Fort Orange, a few were settled near the mouth of the Delaware River and on Nutten Island (now Governors Island), and some of these were moved in 1625 to Manhattan Island, where they were joined in the following year by settlers fleeing attacks by Indians at Fort Orange. In 1626 Peter Minuit, the company's leading official, bought Manhattan from local Indians for blankets, cloth, metal goods, and trinkets then worth 60 guilders. The colonists near the Delaware were moved to Manhattan in June 1627.

Manhattan's harbor and strategic location soon made it the colony's main settlement. A temporary stockade at its southern tip was replaced by a permanent one of earth and stone that was named Fort Amsterdam by the company, and the settlement became known as New Amsterdam. Makeshift houses around the fort were gradually replaced by more substantial ones. Many were tall and narrow and designed in a traditional Dutch style with stepped gables, and some were built of brick that had been carried to the colony as ballast. The main streets included Tuyn Straet (Garden Street) and Hoogh Straet (High Street). Two canals were built at what are now Beaver and Broad streets, and swampland was drained, filled, and converted into farmland. The main occupations were farming, producing ships' stores, lumbering, and fur trading. A *ziekentrooster* (comforter of the sick) was sent to the colony in 1624 as a lay preacher, followed by another in 1626 and the ordained minister Jonas Michaelius in 1628, who organized the Reformed Church there, a forerunner of the Collegiate Church. Religious services were initially on the second story of an old mill until a crude wooden church was built; this was replaced in 1642 by a stone church that stood inside the fort and was named St. Nicholas Church after the patron saint of the Netherlands. Children were educated by the church until 1638, when the schoolmaster Adam Roelantsen was sent to the colony and opened a school that eventually became the Collegiate School. There were 200 colonists and about 30 houses by the end of 1626, and 270 colonists by 1628.

During the 1630s colonists built settlements on land that eventually became part of Staten Island, Brooklyn, Queens, and the Bronx. A temporary settlement in Staten Island took form as early as the 1630s. By the mid-1630s a few settlers lived in Breuckelen (the forerunner of Brooklyn, named after a village in the Netherlands); informal ferry service soon connected the settlement with New Amsterdam, and as farmland became available for settlement a number of villages were built, including Midwout (Flatbush) and Amersfoort (Flatlands). In 1639 land north of the Harlem River was settled by the Danish captain Jonas Bronck. Land in Queens was bought from Indians during the same year and later became the site of an English settlement called Flushing, after the port city of Vlissingen in the Netherlands. The colonial governors, later called directors-general, were appointed by the WIC and ruled solely according to its wishes. The governors' oppressive policies toward the Indians promoted discontent in the colony. This was especially true of the policies of Willem Kieft (1637–47), which led to several bloody encounters between Indians and settlers. Occasionally the colonists became sufficiently disgruntled that remonstrances and delegations were sent to the company's directors, and the States General requested that the basis of the colonial government be broadened. Such measures were largely ignored in New Amsterdam until the administration of Petrus Stuyvesant (1647–64) as governor general. In April 1652 he was instructed to form a municipal government modeled on those in the Netherlands. Early in the following year appointments were made for five *schepens* (aldermen), a *schout* (sheriff and city attorney), and two *burgomasters;* these officials met weekly, and objections to their decisions could be raised with the company's directors. Despite additional reforms the government was never truly representative: director-general Stuyvesant continued to exercise broad powers and chose his associates from among the heads of elite families.

New Amsterdam attracted few settlers. In 1653 a fortified wall was built between the Hudson and East rivers along the northern end of the town; a wagon road running alongside it later became known as Wall Street. A census taken in 1656 showed that the town had only 120 houses and about 1000 inhabitants. To increase the population, orphans and children from poorhouses were sent from the Netherlands in 1655 and 1659, and indentured servants were also sought. In addition to the Dutch there were Germans, English, Scandinavians, Walloons, French Huguenots, and African slaves. Among the religious groups in the town were Lutherans, Quakers, English Independents, Anabaptists, Catholics, and Jews. The official denomination was the Calvinism of the Reformed church, but the company urged tolerance for fear that bigotry might threaten trade and discourage immigration; religious toleration was almost a necessity. Sephardim fleeing persecution in Brazil first moved to the colony in 1654. Permission was given on 4 March 1658 to form a village called Nieue Haarlem north of New Amsterdam. The first permanent settlement on Staten Island, Oude Dorp (Old Town), was formed in 1661. The English soon considered New Netherland an impediment to English settlements to the north and south, and conflicts with the Dutch over boundaries and trade, especially on Long Island and in what is now Connecticut, led King Charles II to grant the colony to his brother James, the duke of York, in March 1664. Colonel Richard Nicolls was then sent to seize the colony, accompanied by four warships and hundreds of soldiers. On 28 August his force sailed into New Amsterdam and set up a blockade. The city was virtually defenseless: the walls of the fort were never intended to withstand attack by a fleet and lay in disrepair, less than one-third of the supply of gunpowder was usable, and enthusiasm for fighting was so low that only about 150 soldiers could be deployed. Although Stuyvesant was determined to resist, cooler heads prevailed and New Amsterdam formally surrendered on 8 September without a shot fired. The rest of New Netherland soon did the same. Fort Amsterdam and New Amsterdam were respectively renamed Fort James and New York City, and the English conquest was recognized by the Treaty of Breda (July 1667), which ended the Second Anglo–Dutch War.

Life changed little for the Dutch under English rule. By the terms of surrender they were given the same rights as English citizens. Dutch and English members of the upper class shared almost equally in the city's administration, and Dutch culture and institutions remained dominant. As there were few unmarried English women, intermarriage between the English and Dutch became common. Families often attended the Reformed church, which continued to conduct services in the Dutch language. Dutch families learned English, and merchants and traders began to adopt English customs. English rule was interrupted briefly in August 1673, when a Dutch naval force commanded by Cornelis Evertsen de Jonge and Jacob Benckes entered the harbor and forced the English garrison to surrender within a few days; the victors renamed the city New Orange, after the Dutch royal family, and soon recaptured other former Dutch settlements. The colony reverted to England by the treaty of Westminster (February 1674), ending the Third Anglo–Dutch War, and the name New York City was restored. The relationship between the Dutch and the English in the colony remained complex. The ascension of William of Orange to the English throne in February 1689 fostered greater cooperation between them, but divisions surfaced later that year, when the Dutch masses, resentful of English rule, supported Leisler's Rebellion, which was opposed by virtually all the English (as well as by Dutch merchants, officials, and clergymen). The rebellion was put down in 1691 but remained a divisive political issue in the city for years afterward.

In 1749 the Swedish botanist Peter Kalm wrote that the Dutch remained the largest segment of the population in both the city and the colony. The clergy of the Reformed church supported the patriots of the American Revolution, whom families such as the Van Cortlandts, the Frelinghuysens, the Rutgers, and the Schuylers aided. (George Washington referred to New York and New Jersey as his "loyal Dutch belt.") The first federal census (1790) showed that 80,000 Dutch immigrants and descendants of Dutch settlers lived within 50 miles (80 kilometers) of the city. But the number of Dutch immigrants decreased steadily after 1673 until the mid-nineteenth century, and the importance of Dutch culture gradually eroded as the city became more heterogeneous. The Dutch language was nonetheless common in the city until the end of the nineteenth century, and during legislative debates about a new state constitution in 1846 it was suggested that literacy in both English and Dutch be a requirement to vote. A number of Dutch families became members of the city's political and mercantile elite: the Van Cortlandts, Stuyvesants, Vanderbilts, and Van Rensselaers, and later the Roosevelts and Van Wycks. Between 1945 and 1965 about 80,000 Dutch immigrants moved to the United States, and many settled in New York City. More than 20,000 people in the city reported to be of Dutch ancestry in 2007.

No Dutch residential quarter was ever formed in the city, but Dutch customs were preserved in the work of such writers as James Fenimore Cooper, Harold Frederic, Charles Fenno Hoffman, David Murdoch, James Kirke Paulding, and Washington

Irving, whose 1809 mock epic *A History of New York* was supposedly written by Diedrich Knickerbocker, an eccentric antiquarian whose name was adopted by a school of writers, a hospital in Manhattan, a magazine, a hotel, a baseball team and a basketball team, and a brand of beer. The St. Nicholas Society was formed in 1835 and the Holland Society in 1885, which from 1922 published a historical quarterly, *De Halve Maen* (The Half Moon). From 1903 the Netherland Club of New York was a private association for professionals and executives, and the Queen Wilhelmina Chair in the history, language, and literature of the Netherlands was inaugurated in 1913 at Columbia University. In the early twenty-first century New York City had a number of well-preserved examples of Dutch colonial architecture, including Dyckman House in Inwood (the only farmhouse of its kind remaining in Manhattan), Voorlezer House (at Richmondtown Restoration), the Lefferts Homestead in Flatbush, the Wyckoff House in Sheepshead Bay, the Lent Farmhouse in Steinway, and the Cornelius Van Wyck House in Douglaston Manor.

Oliver A. Rink, *Holland on the Hudson: An Economic and Social History of Dutch New York* (Ithaca, N.Y.: Cornell University Press, 1986); Joyce D. Goodfriend, *Before the Melting Pot: Society and Culture in Colonial New York City, 1664–1730* (Princeton, N.J.: Princeton University Press, 1994); Janny Venema, *Beverwijck: A Dutch Village on the American Frontier, 1652–1664* (Albany, N.Y.: State University of New Press, 2003); Russell Shorto, *The Island at the Center of the World* (New York: Doubleday, 2004); Jaap Jacobs, *New Netherland: A Dutch Colony in Seventeenth-Century America* (Boston: Brill, 2005)

Thomas E. Bird, Gerald F. De Jong, Charles Gehring

Dutch Farms. Name used until about 1845 by CONCORD.

Dutch Hill. A shantytown on the East Side of Manhattan in the mid-nineteenth century, near the intersection of 39th Street and First Avenue. Like most squatter settlements of the time it was situated north of the built-up area of the city. The inhabitants were predominantly German and Irish immigrants. Many worked at the nearby Voorhis and Mott quarries. By the end of the Civil War the growth and northward movement of population made real estate in the area valuable, and the squatters were displaced.

Kenneth T. Jackson

Dutch Kills. Neighborhood in northwestern Queens, lying within Long Island City and largely occupied by Queens Plaza at the western end of the Queensboro Bridge. The area was an important road junction in the American Revolution, and the British set up camps there during their occupation of the city from 1776 to 1783. There were scattered farms during the nineteenth century. The hamlet joined Hunter's Point, Ravenswood, Astoria, and Steinway to form Long Island City in 1870. The name is still used locally, and there is a Dutch Kills Community Association.

Vincent Seyfried

Dutch Reformed Church. Original name of the REFORMED CHURCH IN AMERICA.

Dutchtown (i). Alternative name of KLEINDEUTSCHLAND.

Dutchtown (ii). Former neighborhood in northwestern Brooklyn, lying east of Williamsburg and mostly along Scholes Avenue, Meserole Street, and Montrose Avenue. It was settled in the early 1840s by German immigrants who were unwelcome in Williamsburgh, which was mostly Irish and English. The German Savings Bank opened in 1866 on Montrose Avenue, and St. John the Evangelist Lutheran Church was formed on Ten Eyck Street. There was also a local newspaper, the *Triangel*. Germans were eventually accepted in Williamsburgh and by the end of the nineteenth century were its dominant ethnic group.

James Bradley

Duyckinck, Evert A(ugustus) (*b* New York City, 23 Nov 1816; *d* New York City, 13 Aug 1878). Writer and editor. He was the son of a successful publisher and bookseller on Water Street in Manhattan who was in turn a descendant of Everett Duÿckinck, a painter and glazier who sailed to America from the Netherlands with the Dutch West India Company. In 1835 Duyckinck graduated from Columbia College; he studied law and was admitted to the bar, but never practiced. He belonged to the group known as "Young America," which espoused literary nationalism and campaigned for fairness in international copyright laws. He was acquainted with many of the great writers of the nineteenth century, including Herman Melville, Edgar Allan Poe, Washington Irving, and James Fenimore Cooper. Duyckinck also published works by Nathaniel Hawthorne and William G. Simms as the editor of the Library of American Books (1845–47) and by Charles Dickens, Thomas Carlyle, and Johann Wolfgang von Goethe as the editor of the Library of Choice Reading.

Mary B. Bowling

Dvořák, Antonín (Leopold) (*b* Nelahozeves, near Kralupy, Bohemia, 8 Sept 1841; *d* Prague, Czechoslovakia, 1 May 1904). Composer. In June 1891 he was invited to assume the directorship of the National Conservatory of Music in New York City by its founder Jeannette Thurber, and after accepting a two-year appointment he arrived in the city in September 1892. He lived with his family in a four-story building at 327 East 17th Street. In addition to teaching at the conservatory he composed several works while living in the city, including his symphony *From the New World* (also known as the *New World Symphony;* given its premiere at Carnegie Hall on 16 December 1893) and his Cello Concerto in B Minor (November 1894 to February 1895). He returned to Prague in 1895.

Dyckman House. Historic house in Manhattan, at 204th Street and Broadway in Inwood. It was built about 1785 by William Dyckman, a grandson of the Westphalian immigrant Jan Dyckman, who settled the area in 1661. The house was sold in 1868 but reacquired by the family in 1915, restored, and given to the city. It is made of fieldstone, brick, and white clapboard and has a typically Dutch gambrel roof. The summer kitchen at the south end may predate the rest of the house; the front and back porches were added in 1825. There are period rooms, including parlors and a colonial kitchen, as well as exhibits of artifacts from the area. Dyckman House is the last remaining farmhouse in Manhattan.

Bashford Dean and A. M. Welch, *The Dyckman House* (New York: Gilliss, 1916); *Historic Houses in New York City Parks* (New York: Department of Parks and Recreation/Historic House Trust of New York City, 1989)

Jonathan Kuhn

dyes. The manufacture of dyes is discussed in the entry PAINTS, DYES, AND VARNISHES.

Dyker Heights. Neighborhood in southwestern Brooklyn, bounded to the north by Eighth Avenue and 62nd Street, to the east by New Utrecht and 18th avenues, to the south by Gravesend Bay and Fort Hamilton, and to the west by Eighth Avenue and Fort Hamilton Parkway; it encompasses Dyker Beach Park on Gravesend Bay and the huge Dyker Beach Golf Course to its north. Once part of the town of New Utrecht, the area is often considered a section of Bay Ridge. It may have been named for two Van Dykes who helped to divide the land in 1719 or for the dikes used to drain and reclaim marshland that once covered most of the area. It remained largely rural into the early twentieth century when developers built a number of one- and two-family houses. Mansions along 11th Avenue afforded magnificent views of the Narrows and Gravesend Bay. A business district developed along 13th Avenue. In the twenty-first century the neighborhood is chiefly residential. Most of the housing consists of one-family detached houses, and the population is predominantly Italian; many families have lived there for four or five generations and put up elaborate, brightly lit lawn displays at Christmastime.

Ellen Marie Snyder-Grenier

Dylan, Bob [Zimmerman, Robert Allen] (*b* Duluth, Minn., 24 May 1941). Singer, songwriter, and one of the most influential figures in the history of rock music. While growing up in Minnesota, he taught himself the guitar and harmonica and played in rock bands as a teenager. In January 1961 he moved to Greenwich Village where he began performing at nightclubs and coffeehouses under his new surname, taken in honor of poet Dylan Thomas. His performances of traditional folk songs and original compositions, his unique "talkin' blues" singing style, and his witty monologues earned him a devoted following and contributed to the rise of Greenwich Village as a center of popular culture. In April 1961 he was the opening act for John Lee Hooker at Gerde's Folk City on MacDougal Street. A favorable review in the *New York Times* by Robert Shelton soon led to a contract with Columbia Records, for which Dylan recorded such influential protest songs as "Blowin' in the Wind," "A Hard Rain's A-Gonna Fall," and "Like a Rolling Stone." During his 12 years living in New York City (1961–73), his music evolved from acoustic folk to a more electric sound, inspiring such classic rock musicians as the Beatles and Jimi Hendrix and contributing to the rise of rock music as social and political commentary. An active supporter of human rights, he performed at the 1963 March on Washington for Jobs and Freedom and the Live Aid concert in 1985. In 2004 he wrote an autobiography of his time in New York titled *Chronicles: Volume One.* Also in 2004 *Rolling Stone* magazine ranked him the second greatest rock artist of all time, after the Beatles. In 2005 PBS showed the documentary film *No Direction Home: Bob Dylan,* a two-part miniseries directed by Martin Scorcese.

Robert Sanger Steel

E

Eagle Insurance Company. Firm of fire insurers. It was the first fire insurer in New York City organized as a stock company. Incorporated on 4 April 1806 with capital stock of $500,000, it assumed the fire insurance portfolio of the Union Insurance Company of New Jersey in 1813. (This was the first known reinsurance agreement in the United States.) Later in the century the firm was acquired by the Norwich Union Fire Insurance Society of Britain. In 1962 it became a subsidiary of Continental Insurance Companies, which acquired all the American business of Norwich Union; the firm was renamed the National Reinsurance Company to reflect its focus on property and casualty reinsurance.

Robert J. Gibbons

earthquakes and faults. Many geological faults transect the New York metropolitan region, and in New York City the faults tend to run from northwest to southeast. The major faults in New York City are distinctive because the fault zones are characterized by shattered rock that has weathered, disintegrated, and been washed away by water, leaving valleys where the faults are. In northern Manhattan the Dyckman Street fault valley is apparent where it transects the Fort Washington Ridge. There is another distinctive fault valley paralleling 155th Street. One of the most conspicuous fault valleys in the area is paralleled by 125th Street. Where this fault zone bisects the Manhattan Ridge, erosion has created the Manhattanville Valley, which has a depth of about 200 feet (60 meters) below sea level but is filled with glacial deposits to just slightly above sea level. There is also a fault zone running southeast from about 110th Street and Fifth Avenue to about 96th Street and the East River. The present course of the Bronx River appears to be partly controlled by a fault in the northern Bronx. This is particularly apparent in the New York Botanical Garden, where the river cuts through soft, highly metamorphosed mica schist of the Manhattan formation to create a beautiful gorge.

The ground beneath metropolitan New York City could be a major shear zone where landmasses slide past one another at the rate of about half an inch (13 millimeters) a year, with a strain similar to that along the San Andreas fault in California (although California is positioned on the boundary between two tectonic plates, whereas New York City rests near the middle of one plate). Records of the U.S. Geological Survey show that there is considerable seismic activity in western Long Island, Westchester County, and southwestern Connecticut. Most earthquakes in New York City have been barely perceptible (although the three most severe, in 1737, in 1783, and on 10 August 1884, are retrospectively estimated to have measured 5.0 on the Richter scale), but the strain that builds up along the shear zone is likely to be relieved by a stronger earthquake at some point.

Steven D. Garber

Eastchester. Neighborhood in the northeastern Bronx, bounded to the north by the city of Mount Vernon, to the east by Co-op City, to the south by Edenwald, and to the west by Wakefield. Anne Hutchinson built a house there in 1642 after fleeing Puritans in New England and was killed in the same year by Wiechquaesgeck Indians (the Hutchinson River is named for her). Thomas Pell claimed the area in 1654 as part of a purchase from the Siwanoy Indians and in 1665 sold a large part of it to 10 farmers of English stock. This area was called at first the Ten Farms and then the town of Eastchester, the center of which was just across the current city limit in what is now Mount Vernon. Colonial farmers raised livestock and then grew wheat; a miller, blacksmith, cobbler, and tailor also worked in the area, and boats delivered goods to and from Manhattan by way of the Hutchinson River once a week. During most of the American Revolution the area was occupied by British and Hessian forces and subjected to raids by irregular American troops. In 1797, when the Boston Road connected the town directly to the Harlem Bridge (now the Third Avenue Bridge), President John Adams temporarily governed the nation from the farmhouse of his daughter and son-in-law when an epidemic of yellow fever prevented him from traveling to a meeting of the Congress in Philadelphia.

Farmers in the nineteenth century provided fruit, vegetables, and dairy products for the local market. By the middle of the century the grandchildren of Elizabeth Ann Seton purchased an estate of 51 acres (21 hectares), part of which later became Seton Falls Park. In 1877 the town built on Dyre Avenue the Village of Eastchester School, later known as the Little Red Schoolhouse (now a city landmark). The 1890s saw the incorporation of Wakefield as a village. The incorporation of Mount Vernon as a city bisected the town: the need for a modern sewer system led residents of the southern part to favor annexation by New York City, which was accomplished in 1895. In 1912 the New York, Westchester and Boston Railway built a high-speed commuter line with a station at Dyre Avenue, and in 1937 the city purchased the right of way south of the border with Westchester County for the Dyre Avenue line of Interborough Rapid Transit. This and the construction in the 1950s of the New England Thruway and Bruckner Expressway drew people and businesses to the area. In the early twenty-first century the neighborhood remained industrial, with one- and two-family houses predominating. The population is ethnically diverse, with blacks, Italians, and Germans in the majority.

Stephen Jenkins, *The Story of the Bronx* (New York: G. P. Putnam's Sons, 1912); Lloyd Ultan, *The Beautiful Bronx, 1920–1950* (New Rochelle, N.Y.: Arlington House, 1979); John McNamara, *History in Asphalt: The Origin of Bronx Street and Place Names* (New York: Bronx County Historical Society, 1984)

Lloyd Ultan

East Concourse. Neighborhood in the west central Bronx, bounded to the north by Tremont Avenue, to the east by Webster Avenue, to the south by East 149th Street, and to the west by the Grand Concourse. Its name dates to the formation in 1969 of the East Concourse Neighborhood Action Committee and was later adopted by the City Planning Commission. The development of the area coincided with the construction of railroads in the late nineteenth century; much of the housing stock consists of apartment buildings erected at the time the subways were built between the world wars. The population in the early twenty-first century was predominantly Latino and African American.

Stephen A. Stertz

East Elmhurst. Neighborhood in north central Queens, bounded to the north by La Guardia Airport, to the east by Flushing Bay, to the south by Northern Boulevard, and to the west by 85th Street. It was developed in 1905 as a neighborhood of frame houses on lots measuring 40 by 100 feet (12 by 30 meters); those on the bluff overlooking the bay had private beaches. Before World War II the area was wholly residential, but proximity to the airport brought commercial development to Ditmars Boulevard. Early in the twenty-first century, the Bulova Watch Company and British Airways maintained offices in East Elmhurst.

Vincent Seyfried

Eastern Orthodox. New York City has many Eastern Orthodox churches, where people from eastern Europe, the Balkans, and the Middle East worship in different languages according to the customs of their homelands. These various Orthodox groups belong to one undivided Eastern Orthodox Church: all acknowledge the primacy of the Ecumenical Patriarch of Constantinople and adhere to the canons defined by the seven ecumenical councils under the Byzantine empire (330–1453). Their differences in the United States are jurisdictional and derive from historical circumstances. The two largest Eastern Orthodox groups in the United States are the Greek Orthodox Archdiocese of North and South America, which on its formation in 1921 established headquarters in New York City and continues to maintain them there, and the Orthodox Church of America, which had its headquarters in the city until the 1970s. Other Orthodox jurisdictions with national headquarters in New York City include the Bulgarian Eastern Orthodox Church Diocese of New York, the Patriarchal Parishes of the Russian Orthodox Church in the United States and Canada, and the Ukrainian Orthodox Church of America and Canada. Major Orthodox groups with churches in the city include the Serbian Orthodox Church, the Antiochian Orthodox Christian Archdiocese of North America, the Ukrainian Orthodox Church of the USA, the Romanian Orthodox Episcopate of America, the American Carpatho-Russian Orthodox Greek Catholic Diocese of the USA, and the Albanian Orthodox Archdiocese of America.

Eastern Orthodoxy was established in New York City by immigrants from eastern and southern Europe. Nicholas Bjerring began holding services in English in his home at 951 Second Avenue in Manhattan, where he set up a chapel with a sign above the entrance reading "Greek–Russian Church." The chapel was used by Russians, Greeks, Serbs, and Syrians until 1883, when the Russian government withdrew its financial support and the chapel was forced to close. During the next 10 years Greek immigrants in the city formed their own churches outside the Russian Orthodox hierarchy in the United States.

With the encouragement of Prince George of Greece, who visited the city in 1891, about 500 Greek immigrants later in the year formed the Hellenic Brotherhood of Athena to collect donations for a Greek church. Archimandrite Paisios Pherentinos was sent to New York City by the Holy Synod of Greece to celebrate the first divine liturgy of the Church of the Holy Trinity in January 1892. Regular church services were held in a Protestant church on West 53rd Street near Eighth Avenue in Manhattan; Pherentinos also performed services for Greek families residing in Coney Island and other parts of Brooklyn. In 1904 the church purchased its own building at 151–53 East 72nd Street. Disagreement within the church led to the establishment in 1893 of the Annunciation Church. The church purchased a building at 310 West 50th Street in 1915.

St. Nicholas Chapel, a Russian church formed in the early 1890s, flourished from 1896 under the leadership of Alexander Hotovitsky. In 1902 he succeeded in obtaining financial support from Russia for the establishment of St. Nicholas Cathedral at 15 East 97th Street, which became the center of the Russian Mission Diocese for North America. The Syro-Arabian Mission was formed by the Russian Orthodox Church in 1892 for Arabic-speaking Orthodox Christians in the city, and in 1895 a group of Syrian immigrants formed the Syrian Orthodox Benevolent Society; in the following year Archimandrite Raphael Hawaweeny formed the first Syrian Orthodox parish in the United States at 77 Washington Street in lower Manhattan, the center of the Syrian immigrant community. By 1900 about 3000 Syrian immigrants had settled in Brooklyn, and in 1902 Hawaweeny purchased a building at Pacific Street in Brooklyn and formed St. Nicholas Cathedral, now considered the mother parish of the United States Antiochian Archdiocese.

The headquarters of the Russian Church in the Americas were transferred from San Francisco to New York City in 1903. In the following year its bishop, Tikhon, attempted unsuccessfully to assert Russian ecclesiastic authority over the Greek Orthodox churches in New York City. The city's Arabic-speaking Orthodox Christians continued to acknowledge Russian jurisdiction, and there was a Serbian mission within the Russian Church. In 1904 Tikhon received permission from the Russian Holy Synod to raise Hawaweeny to the rank of bishop of Brooklyn, and in the following year he himself became the first Eastern Orthodox archbishop in the United States. The Greeks did not recognize the jurisdiction of the Russian hierarchy in New York City and remained without a bishop of their own until 1918.

The number of members of Greek and other Orthodox congregations in the city was estimated at 3500 by a Greek newspaper in 1895 (and at more than 1000 by the *New York Times* in January of the following year). These numbers increased markedly during the first decades of the twentieth century, as more immigrants from Russia, the Balkans, and the Middle East settled in New York City. A census in 1916 reported that the Greeks alone had four parishes and 22,000 communicants. World War I led to an increase in the number of Eastern Orthodox immigrants who settled in New York City and caused jurisdictional divisions that persisted into the 1990s. In Russia the Bolshevik Revolution led the Russian Church in the United States (the Metropolia) to declare itself autonomous in 1918. In the following year Ukrainian refugees also established an autonomous church in the United States. Although the successor to the Metropolia, the autonomous Orthodox Church of America, was recognized by Moscow in 1970, jurisdictional divisions persisted among other Russian Orthodox groups in the United States over relations with the patriarchate in Moscow. Similar jurisdictional divisions occurred within the Serbian, Bulgarian, Albanian, and Romanian churches after World War II, when the Soviet Union occupied most of Eastern Europe. These divisions were further complicated with the breakup of the Soviet bloc in the late 1980s and realignment of the Balkans and Eastern Europe in the subsequent decade.

The Greek Orthodox Church also went through a major transition in the late 1990s with the retirement of Archbishop Iakovos, who had led the church for 37 years. The jurisdiction of the American Church was dramatically reduced when in July 1996 the Ecumenical Patriarchate established three new metropolitantes in Canada, South America, and Mexico. Iakovos's successors have struggled to keep the remaining U.S. jurisdictions united during the transitions and new challenges of the twenty-first century. In 2003 the Direct Archdiocesan District was established to serve Eastern Orthodox parishes in the Greater New York area, upstate New York, Long Island, the western half of Connecticut, and Washington, D.C.; that year the district included 67 parishes served by 69 priests.

Miltiades B. Efthimiou and George A. Christopoulos, eds., *History of the Greek Orthodox Church in America* (New York: Greek Orthodox Archdiocese, 1984); C. G. Hatzidimitriou, "Church–Community Relations in the United States," *Greeks in English-Speaking Countries: Culture, Identity, Politics,* ed. Christos P. Ioannides (New York: Aristide D. Caratzas, 1997), 69–87

Constantine G. Hatzidimitriou

Eastern Parkway. Grand boulevard and scenic landmark in Brooklyn, designed in 1866 by Frederick Law Olmsted and Calvert Vaux. Stretching from Grand Army Plaza through Crown Heights to Ralph Avenue, it was the first six-lane parkway in the world. The broad median strips were built as promenades and equestrian paths, the side lanes as service roads for carriages. Some of the most spectacular nineteenth-century houses in Brooklyn, many on what has long been known as "Doctors' Row," line the thoroughfare. A large Tudor building at 770 Eastern Parkway is the world headquarters of the Lubavitch movement.

Kenneth T. Jackson

Easter parade. Informal procession held on Fifth Avenue on Easter. Begun after the Civil War as a fashion promenade, it was an extension of the weekly "church parade" and drew on European traditions of displaying new clothes, symbolic of new life, during an Easter Sunday walk, one of few activities considered acceptable under strict Sabbath laws. It took its current form in the 1880s. The parade began when the elite stepped out of such grand churches as St. Thomas Episcopal Church, the Fifth Avenue Presbyterian Church, and St. Patrick's Cathedral after the Easter Sunday service and strolled along "millionaire row" (Fifth Avenue in the fifties blocks) before visiting friends and having lunch at lavish hotels nearby. Milliners and dressmakers from all over the country, especially the Lower East Side, flocked to watch and make sketches of the participants' outfits; department stores produced copies for sale within weeks. At the turn of the century extravagant hats for women became the focus of the parade. Smaller Easter parades were held in other parts of the city, including Grand Street in Harlem, but the one on Fifth Avenue was the best known and became the subject of songs by George M. Cohan ("The Great Easter Sunday Parade," 1927) and Irving Berlin ("Easter Parade," 1933). In later years it attracted demonstrators promoting peace, church attendance, and animal rights; protesting unemployment and the commercialization of Holy Week; and appealing for amnesty for refugees and political prisoners. In the twenty-first century the Easter parade was known for exuberant bonnets covered with Easter eggs, bunnies, flowers, and other emblems of spring. A popular tourist event, it extends along Fifth Avenue from Rockefeller Center to Central Park.

William S. Walsh, *Curiosities of Popular Customs and of Rites, Ceremonies, Observances, and Miscellaneous Antiquities* (Philadelphia: J. B. Lippincott, 1898)

Barbara Kirshenblatt-Gimblett

East Flatbush. Neighborhood in northeastern Brooklyn (2009 pop. *ca* 95,000), bounded to the north by East New York Avenue, to the east and south by Kings Highway, and to the west by Nostrand Avenue; it was once called Rugby. Development began in the 1920s after Interborough Rapid Transit extended its subway to Utica Avenue and to Flatbush Avenue along Nostrand Avenue. Modest one- and two-family attached brick houses were built, and most of the residents were middle-class Jews and Italians. During the late 1960s white families were replaced by African Americans and immigrants from the Caribbean. East Flatbush in the 1980s drew immigrants from Jamaica, Haiti, Guyana, Trinidad and Tobago, Grenada, Barbados, St. Vincent and the Grenadines, and Panama. A medical complex stands on Clarkson Avenue that includes the Kings County Hospital (1831), Brooklyn State Hospital (1895), and the New York Downstate Medical Center (1950). In 2006 a portion of Church Avenue was renamed Bob Marley Boulevard. In the early twenty-first century the neighborhood remained predominantly West Indian.

Stephen Weinstein

East Harlem. Neighborhood in northern Manhattan. The boundaries are imprecise but correspond roughly to East 142nd Street, the East River, East 96th Street, and Park Avenue. The area was rural for much of the nineteenth century. By the 1860s a residential settlement developed north and east of 110th Street and Third Avenue. The extension of elevated railways to the area in 1879 and 1880 and the construction of the Lexington Avenue subway in 1919 transformed the neighborhood. By the mid-1880s most streets were lined with tenements, which initially housed poor German, Irish, and Jewish immigrants. Around 1917 the Jewish population was about 90,000, a community that, along with that of central Harlem (80,000), constituted the second-largest Jewish community in the United States, after the Lower East Side. From the 1880s there was an influx of Italians, who numbered 80,000 by 1930, and who lived in an enclave bounded by East 119th Street, the East River, East 99th Street, and Third Avenue. They sponsored local religious festivals such as that of Our Lady of Mount Carmel. By the 1930s Puerto Ricans began to move into the neighborhood.

Well-known residents in East Harlem included Mayor Fiorello H. La Guardia, who represented the area in the U.S. Congress from 1923 to 1933, calling Lexington Avenue and 116th Street his "lucky corner" and always holding rallies there on the eve of an election; Leonard Covello, a principal of Benjamin Franklin High School, known for his openness and his skill at resolving conflicts; and Vito Marcantonio, a radical who lived in the neighborhood all his life and achieved success by maintaining close relations with Italian and Puerto Rican constituents.

During the 1940s and 1950s, as many Italians moved away, Puerto Ricans became the dominant ethnic group, numbering 63,000 in 1950 after an influx during the late 1940s. They opened bodegas and botánicas (stores selling herbs and other items used in religious ceremonies), some of which stood in an area known as La Marqueta, an enclosed street market beneath the elevated railroad on Park Avenue between 111th and 116th streets. Many religious institutions were formed, ranging from Catholic to revivalist Protestant churches in storefronts. Musical traditions were preserved by small record companies and dance halls that provided a source of social cohesion. Although many Puerto Ricans moved to other parts of the city in the second half of the twentieth century, they maintained ties to the neighborhood, which continued to be known as El Barrio. Many public housing projects went up in the 1950s.

By the early twenty-first century, East Harlem was a racially diverse neighborhood in which more than one-third of the population was Puerto Rican and the rest included African Americans, Italians, and other groups. Poverty and unemployment rates remained high, but there were concerted efforts to improve the housing stock through public-private partnerships. The Museo del Barrio, which exhibits the art of Puerto Rican and other Latin American artists, is an important cultural center.

Virginia Sánchez Korrol, *From Colonia to Community: The History of Puerto Ricans in New York City, 1917–1948* (Westport, Conn.: Greenwood, 1983)

Michael Lapp

East Jamaica. Former name of Hillside.

Eastman, Crystal (*b* Marlborough, N.Y., 25 June 1881; *d* New York City, 8 July 1928). Reformer, sister of Max Eastman. A graduate of New York University Law School (1907), she drafted the first workers' compensation law in New York State in 1910. As the secretary of the American Union against Militarism she campaigned against the entry of the United States into World War I. To defend conscientious objectors, she formed the Civil Liberties Bureau with Roger Baldwin in April 1917; this eventually became the American Civil Liberties Union.

Blanche Wiesen Cook, ed., *Crystal Eastman on Women and Revolution* (New York: Oxford University Press, 1978)

Samuel Walker

Eastman, Max (Forrester) (*b* Canandaigua, N.Y., 4 Jan 1883; *d* Bridgetown, Barbados, 25 March 1969). Writer and editor, brother of Crystal Eastman. A pupil of John Dewey's at Columbia University, in 1912 he took over the periodical *The Masses,* which he transformed into the most important radical magazine of the age by recruiting the writers John Reed, Sherwood Anderson, and Carl Sandburg and the artists John Sloan and Art Young, whose political cartoons helped make the magazine widely known. After *The Masses* was suppressed by the federal government because of its opposition to World War I, he joined with his sister in 1918 to launch *The Liberator,* which was more overtly supportive of the Soviet Union. During a visit there in 1922 he allied himself with Leon Trotsky, and he became Trotsky's leading American sponsor after returning to the United States in 1927; this made him a pariah among the American left. Over the years he expressed growing disenchantment with the Soviet Union, to the point where he had mixed feelings about supporting it during World War II. His writings appeared in increasingly conservative publications (including *Reader's Digest* and, after the war, the *National Review*), and he defended Senator Joseph R. McCarthy. He remained a contributing editor of *Reader's Digest* to the end of his life. Eastman's residences in New York City included 118 Waverly Place (from 1909 to 1911 and again from 1916), 27 West 11th Street (from 1912), 12 East Eighth Street (from 1917), and 8 West 13th Street (for the last 25 years of his life).

Alexander Bloom

Eastman, Monk [Delaney, William; Osterman, Edward] (*b* Brooklyn, 1873; *d*

New York City, 26 Dec 1920). Career criminal. He first worked as a "bouncer" at New Irving Hall, a dance hall, and later became powerful in gambling and prostitution. From the late nineteenth century to the early twentieth he led the Eastmans, a predominantly Jewish gang based at Chrystie Street; his greatest rival was the Five Points Gang, a predominantly Italian gang led by Paul Kelly. Though he worked as a henchman for Tammany Hall, his violence forced them to disassociate themselves from him after a particularly bloody riot on the Lower East Side. He served 10 years in Sing Sing prison. After being freed he joined the military at age 44 and fought in World War I. Eastman was shot dead at 14th Street and Fourth Avenue by a Prohibition agent with whom he had engaged in bootlegging and drug dealing.

Robert W. Snyder

East New York. Neighborhood lying east of Brownsville and Canarsie on the eastern edge of central Brooklyn, bounded to the north by Atlantic Avenue, to the east by South Conduit Boulevard, to the south by Linden Boulevard, and to the west by Pennsylvania Avenue; it overlaps New Lots and is sometimes said to include the neighborhoods of Highland Park, Cypress Hills, Spring Creek, and City Line. Once part of the town of New Lots, the area remained largely rural until 1835 when a merchant from Connecticut named John Pitkin bought up land north of what is now New Lots Avenue; he named the area to suggest that it was the eastern end of New York City and built a shoe factory at Williams Street and Pitkin Avenue, but the panic of 1837 forestalled his plans for development. There was an influx of German immigrants at mid-century, and the Deutsche Evangelische St. Johannes Kirche (now Grace Baptist Church) was built in 1885 at 223 New Jersey Avenue. Growth accelerated after the opening of the Williamsburg Bridge in 1903 and the completion of a subway line to New Lots by Interborough Rapid Transit in 1922. By 1940 the northern section was densely populated with German, Italian, Russian, Polish, and Lithuanian immigrants. Urban renewal in Brownsville during the 1950s and 1960s led a large number of blacks to settle in East New York. Many whites left; decay set in as buildings were abandoned and absentee landlords neglected their properties. Unemployment increased and the area deteriorated. One of the first revitalization projects was the East Brooklyn Industrial Park (1980). Private houses were built under the auspices of the Council of East Brooklyn Churches, including Nehemiah Plan Homes, one-family row houses of two stories that became common along Blake Avenue. Other housing includes two-story detached and semidetached houses, a few apartment buildings, and multistory public housing. In the 1980s East New York attracted immigrants from the Dominican Republic (accounting for a quarter of the total), Jamaica (accounting for somewhat fewer), Guyana, Haiti, Honduras, Ecuador, Trinidad and Tobago, and Panama. The neighborhood in the early twenty-first century was mostly black and Latin American, with a small but growing number of Asians. The main commercial thoroughfares are Pitkin Avenue, New Lots Avenue, and Pennsylvania Avenue. Many residents consider New Lots and Spring Creek Towers part of their neighborhood.

Ellen Marie Snyder-Grenier

East River. Saltwater estuary, or tidal strait, that separates Manhattan Island and the Bronx from the western end of Long Island (Brooklyn and Queens) and connects Upper New York Bay on the south with Long Island Sound on the north. It is joined by the Harlem River about 8.5 miles (14 kilometers) north of the Battery. One of its tributaries is a short commercial waterway called Newtown Creek, which forms the natural boundary between Brooklyn and Queens. Although the river is navigable for its entire length of 16 miles (26 kilometers), its varying depth and narrowness subject it to strong tidal fluctuations.

The river is spanned by 10 bridges, of which the most notable is the Brooklyn Bridge (1883), the first bridge linking Long Island with Manhattan. Among the more picturesque bridges is the Hell Gate Bridge (1917), or New York Connecting Railroad Bridge, with its sweeping classic arch. Thirteen tunnels pass beneath the river. Where the strait narrows between Queens and the Bronx is Hell Gate, a formerly turbulent and formidable rocky channel that wrought havoc with shipping until it was cleared in 1876 by the Army Corps of Engineers. The name is a corruption of the Dutch *hellegat*, "passage to hell," named by Dutch explorer Adriaen Block in 1614. The piers along the East River on South Street in lower Manhattan were the city's major center of shipping until the beginning of the twentieth century. Along the East River are seven islands (from south to north): U Thant (Belmont), Roosevelt (with its burgeoning high-rise residential community and historic landmarks), Mill Rock, Wards and Randalls (connected by landfill), Rikers (with its notorious city prison), and South Brother and North Brother.

The river is also remembered as the site of the tragic burning and sinking of the excursion steamboat *General Slocum* in 1904, when the vessel, carrying passengers on a Lutheran church outing, caught fire in midstream and ultimately was beached on North Brother Island, with the loss of more than 1000 lives, mostly women and children. In the early twenty-first century plans were under way to install a field of hydropower turbines on the floor of the East River to harness the renewable energy generated by the tidal strait.

Gerard R. Wolfe

East Village. Neighborhood in lower Manhattan, bounded to the north by 14th Street, to the east by Avenue D, to the south by Houston Street, and to the west by the Bowery and Third Avenue. Principal thoroughfares include St. Mark's Place (Eighth Street), Second Avenue, and Avenue A; the heart of the neighborhood is Tompkins Square Park. Well-known landmarks include St. Mark's Church in the Bowery and Cooper Union (1859), a free institution of higher learning that contains the oldest auditorium in New York City.

The East Village was considered a part of the Lower East Side until the early 1960s, when many intellectuals, artists, musicians, and writers seeking cheap housing moved to the area from Greenwich Village. Radicalism in politics and art flourished, and the area became known for its poetry houses and bookshops (the Nuyorican Café, the Peace Eye Bookstore), saloons and bars (Phoebe's, Stanley's), theaters (the Fillmore East), jazz clubs (Slug's, the Five Spot), and restaurants

"Breaking Up on the Ice at New York: A View from the East River," Harper's Weekly, *8 February 1862*

(Paradox Macrobiotics, Orchidia Ukrainian Pizza). The neighborhood was also the home of the Annex Tavern, the Negro Ensemble Company, and several newspapers, including the *East Village Other* and *Rat*. The neighborhood declined in the 1970s, but important figures in punk rock, jazz, painting, and poetry nevertheless continued to live in the area, as did a large community of Ukrainians, who after a period of immigration in the 1970s grew in number to about 20,000. Conditions improved during the 1980s, when many art galleries exhibited the work of young artists like Keith Haring and Jean-Michel Basquiat, and the eastern part of the neighborhood (Avenues A to D) attracted recent immigrants from the Dominican Republic, China, the Philippines, the United Kingdom, Poland, and Japan. As gentrification led to an increase in rents, squatters occupied and renovated abandoned buildings; a squatters' movement emerged and riots occurred toward the end of the 1980s. In 1990 the police responded to complaints about drug dealing and filthy conditions in Tompkins Square Park by evicting the homeless and closing the park, which was met by marches and riots. The park reopened in 1992.

Since the 1990s rising real estate prices, a weak dollar attracting international purchasers, and low vacancy rates have changed the once-gritty neighborhood into a middle-class haven for professionals, students at New York University and Cooper Union, and tourists. New high-rise apartment buildings and dormitories have transformed the landscape. Notable closures have included CBGB, the home of punk rock, on the Bowery, and the Rapture Café on Avenue A. The Second Avenue Deli relocated from Ninth Street to 33rd Street. Much of the art gallery scene of the 1980s has relocated to Williamsburg in Brooklyn. Despite this, the neighborhood retains a lower middle-class character due to the hundreds of older tenements and public housing. Each year, the Howl Festival celebrates the life and art of Allen Ginsberg and other neighborhood artists, intellectuals, and musicians. St. Mark's Place has made a surprising transition from hipster center to the nightly destination of thousands of Asian students and young professionals who flock to its sushi, Chinese, and fusion restaurants.

Christopher Mele, *Selling the Lower East Side: Culture, Real Estate and Resistance in New York City* (Minneapolis: University of Minnesota Press, 2000)

Graham Hodges

East Village Other. "Underground" newspaper launched in October 1965 by Allen Katzman and others. Published at first monthly, then semimonthly, then (from 1968) weekly, the newspaper chronicled the counterculture of the 1960s, which in New York City was largely centered at St. Mark's Place. Its reporters, who made no pretense of objectivity, wrote extensively about the drug culture and about radical groups such as the Weathermen. Among those who were the subject of stories and interviews were the poet Allen Ginsberg, the artist Andy Warhol, and the comedian Dick Gregory. The newspaper was also known for running sexually explicit personal advertisements long before they became a feature of mainstream journalism. The *Other* ceased publication in February 1972.

Allen Katzman, ed., *Our Time* (New York: Dial, 1972)

Thomas M. Hilbink

East Williamsburgh. Obsolete name for a part of west central Queens lying south of Metropolitan Avenue and west of Fresh Pond Road, within Ridgewood and abutting Brooklyn. The area was farmland for most of the nineteenth century; development followed the opening of an important trolley depot in 1881 and of the terminus of the Myrtle Avenue elevated line in 1888. The name fell into disuse during World War I.

Vincent Seyfried

Ebbets Field. Ballpark in central Brooklyn that housed the Brooklyn Dodgers from 9 April 1913 to 24 September 1957. It was lined by Montgomery Street, McKeever Place, Sullivan Place, and Bedford Avenue. The ballpark was named for Charles Ebbets, who, as the Dodgers' owner, purchased the land in small parcels for roughly $100,000 beginning in 1905. By 1912 he had acquired enough to erect a concrete and steel facility seating 18,000 people. The capacity was later expanded to 31,497; its largest crowd was 41,209 for a doubleheader against the New York Giants in 1934. Night baseball was first held there on 15 June 1938. Known for its short foul lines (348 feet [106 meters] to left field and 297 feet [91 meters] to right), Ebbets Field hosted eight World Series, including the Dodgers' only title in Brooklyn in 1955. But by the late 1940s, the stadium had become structurally unsound. It was also constrained by its low capacity and narrow aisles. After disagreements with Robert Moses on where to build a new stadium, Dodgers owner Walter O'Malley threatened to move the Giants and Dodgers to California. In 1958 the team became the Los Angeles Dodgers. The ballpark was torn down in February 1960 and replaced by a housing development, the Ebbets Field Apartments. Only a plaque remains.

Joshua Robinson

Ebenezer Gospel Tabernacle. Church located at 225 Lenox Avenue at 121st Street and designed by architect Charles Atwood in the Gothic Revival style (1889–91). Originally Unitarian, it moved north from midtown Manhattan and was sold to Orthodox Jews when membership had dwindled by 1919, becoming Temple Chebra Ukadisha B'nai Israel Mikalwarie. By 1942 dwindling attendance led to another sale, and it became Ebenezer Gospel Tabernacle. In the twenty-first century the congregation was largely African Ameri-

Ebbets Field, 1920

can. The building was designated a landmark in 1971.

Sharon Wilkins

Echo z Polski. Weekly newspaper launched in New York City in 1863 as the first Polish-language periodical in the United States. A political organ of immigrants, it supported the Polish insurrection against Russia that began in January 1863. It ceased publication in 1865.

James S. Pula

Ecker, Frederick H(udson) (*b* Phoenicia, N.Y., 30 Aug 1867; *d* New York City, 20 March 1964). Real estate developer. During the first half of the twentieth century, he led the Metropolitan Life Insurance Company in expanding into real estate development. Under his direction the company in 1924 built Sunnyside, a residential development in Long Island City consisting of 2125 apartment units in 54 low-rise buildings; the development was exempt from property taxes for 10 years. Appointed the company's president in 1929 and its chairman in 1936, Ecker in 1940 oversaw the construction of Parkchester, a complex of more than 12,000 apartments for 35,000 residents in the northern Bronx. Completed in 1941, it was the largest development of its kind and served as a prototype for similar projects in San Francisco, Los Angeles, and Arlington, Virginia. He also promoted urban redevelopment in the 1940s with two major projects on the East Side of Manhattan—Stuyvesant Town and Peter Cooper Village—and with Riverton in Harlem.

Marquis James, *The Metropolitan Life: A Study in Business Growth* (New York: Viking, 1947)

Marc A. Weiss

Occupations of Citizens of New York City, 1855

Blacksmiths 2,611	Laundresses 2,563
Butchers 2,643	Lawyers 1,112
Cabinetmakers 2,606	Machinists 1,714
Carters and draymen 5,338	Masons and bricklayers 3,634
Clerks and accountants 13,807	Merchants 6,001
Confectioners 704	Milliners 1,585
Coopers 1,018	Peddlers 1,889
Dealers 1,025	Porters 3,052
Dressmakers 7,436	Sailors and mariners 4,717
Drivers 1,741	Servants 31,749
Engineers 867	Shipbuilders 1,146
Farmers 193	Shoemakers 6,745
Firemen 270	Stonecutters 1,755
Grocers 4,079	Tailors 12,609
Hatmakers 1,422	Teachers 1,268
Jewelers 1,099	Tobacconists 1,996
Laborers 19,748	Wine and liquor dealers 619

economy. Settled as a trading post by the Dutch, New York City evolved into the nation's major center of maritime trade and later of manufacturing. As manufacturing declined after World War II, the city's economy became dominated by financial and other producer services.

1. Colonial Period

The original settlement that was to become New York City was founded by the Dutch West India Company. In the early seventeenth century the company acquired the Hudson Valley and established a trading post, New Amsterdam, at the southern end of Manhattan Island, which had an excellent port accessible to the Atlantic Ocean as well as to a deep hinterland free of waterfalls and replete with furs. Stockholders were granted land with 16 miles (26 kilometers) of frontage on the Hudson River if they arranged for the passage and settlement of 50 people. Under this policy Dutch fiefdoms were soon established on both sides of the river up to the smaller Dutch settlement of Fort Orange (now Albany). One of the largest estates was that of the Rensselaer family, which lay along both sides of the river and covered more than 1100 square miles (2816 square kilometers). The Dutch West India Company was interested primarily in commerce, not settlement, and established a policy of tolerance that benefited a number of groups, including Jewish refugees from Brazil. The company also brought African slaves to the colony.

Estimated Labor Force Participation in New York City by Sex, Race, and Hispanic Origin, 1930–2000

	Female				Male			
	Hispanic	White	Black	Other	Hispanic	White	Black	Other
1930	N/A	30.8	57.8	25.9	N/A	86.6	92.1	94.6
1940	N/A	32.5	50.7	27.3	N/A	81.1	80.8	86.5
1950	N/A	33.0	47.5	N/A	N/A	79.0	76.0	N/A
1960	38.0[1]	38.3	49.0	N/A	78.7[1]	78.2	78.5	N/A
1970	35.7	42.2	46.1	50.5[2]	74.7	73.9	71.4	70.9[2]
1980	40.7	46.6	51.3	59.3	70.1	70.2	64.5	76.0
1990	48.6	52.2	59.6	61.0	71.8	71.1	67.3	76.5
2000	46.8	51.1	55.5	N/A	61.7	66.1	60.1	N/A

1. Puerto Rican birth or parentage.
2. Chinese only. Male and female participation rates are 80.6 and 37.3 for Japanese, 75.8 and 74.2 for Filipinos.
N/A = Not Available.
Note: Figures are based on civilian labor force (from 1950 exclusive of armed forces) both employed and unemployed, age 14 or older from 1930 to 1960 and age 16 or older from 1970 to 2000. Figures for 1930 are estimates based on the category Gainful Workers, defined as people who usually have an occupation.
Sources: U.S. Bureau of the Census, Census of Population 1930, 1940, 1950, 1960, 1970, 1980, 1990, 2000; Evelyn Mann and Joseph Salvo, *New York City's Labor Force, 1970–1990* (New York: City Department of Planning, 1986)
Compiled by Nathan Kantrowitz and Alex Poole

In 1653 a municipal charter made New Amsterdam officially a city. The city's charter was modeled after the charter of its namesake, with political power conferred upon burghers, rich merchants, and to a lesser extent craftsmen and small proprietors. The company-appointed governor, Peter Stuyvesant, considered himself the ruler of what to him was a company town. The burghers, however, thought otherwise, leading to friction and acrimony. The period after the charter saw rapid development of New Amsterdam. Cobblestone streets replaced dirt, brick houses replaced wooden, and tile roofs replaced thatched. New Amsterdam was a substantial, tidy, Dutch town by 1660.

During the early seventeenth century many farmers and craftsmen in New Netherland were lured by the abundant resources of the Hudson Valley into the fur trade. As private traders they competed with the Dutch West India Company, which held a monopoly over the trade until 1638. At that time the fur trade became concentrated in the hands of a few exporters in the colony and four large firms in Amsterdam that set high export duties. Those who identified their occupation as peltry exporting during the mid-seventeenth century were the wealthiest men in New Amsterdam. Increasing competition from the French and English in the fur trade weakened the position of New Amsterdam. The English further disrupted the Dutch trade by passing the Act of Trade and Navigation of 1651, an attempt to tie colonial trade to England. Competition for a diminishing supply of peltry caused the Dutch to reduce their investments in the fur trade in New Amsterdam. By the time of the English takeover in 1664, the Dutch had begun to redirect the colony's export trade from peltry to grain and to expand the reach of their market from Amsterdam and New England to the West Indies and southern Europe.

In 1664, faced by a superior English invading fleet, Stuyvesant surrendered New Amsterdam and all of New Netherland. The town was renamed New York, and a new charter was imposed on the population of about 1500. In the following years English, Huguenot, and German communities took root in the port and the number of black slaves increased. Trade, primarily with the Caribbean islands, remained the principal economic activity, and competition from other colonial settlements was stiff: the volume of the city's trade was less than half that of Charleston, South Carolina.

Trade with Amsterdam nevertheless remained lucrative for a few English and Dutch merchants. By the 1680s firm connections were also forged with London by English immigrant merchants, who vied with the Dutch merchants for control of the agricultural hinterlands of New Jersey, Connecticut,

Leading Manufacturing Industries in New York City and King's County in Selected Years, 1810–2002

	No. of Establishments	No. of Employees	Value of Products
NEW YORK CITY, 1810			
Sugar refining	1		$420,706
Rope walks	6		$387,200
Spirits	11		$301,838
Breweries	15		$259,908
Tanneries	9		$113,285
Tobacco and snuff	1		$36,500
Moroccan skins	—		$17,500
Naileries	4		$16,732
Hatteries	5		$12,750
Chocolate	1		$8,500
All other industries	11		$4,553
Total	64		$1,579,472
KING'S COUNTY, 1810			
Rope walks	4		$108,000
Spirits	2		$80,000
Tanneries	6		$18,811
Flaxen goods	—		$12,087
Woolen goods	—		$3,763
Cloths	—		$1,375
Moroccan skins	—		$700
Total	12		$224,736
NEW YORK CITY, 1860			
Garments	398	26,857	$22,320,769
Sugar refining	14	1,494	$19,312,500
Printing and publishing	154	4,025	$10,179,155
Furniture	223	3,570	$3,947,500
Boots and shoes	491	4,084	$3,869,058
Gas	2	2,020	$3,784,500
Provisions[1]	29	326	$3,676,305
Bread, bakery products	264	1,099	$3,325,993
Flour and meal	6	193	$2,612,500
Iron castings	42	1,924	$2,606,490
All other industries	2,752	44,612	$83,472,599
Total	4,375	90,204	$159,107,369
KING'S COUNTY, 1860			
Sugar refining	4	295	$3,794,000
Liquors	40	464	$3,360,943
Oil	16	312	$2,246,964
White lead	8	356	$2,129,500
Hats and caps	19	787	$1,632,456
Cordage	12	492	$1,390,196
Machinery[2]	20	921	$1,298,300
Ship and boat building	15	514	$1,263,475
Bread, bakery products	122	412	$1,139,845
Soaps and candles	5	47	$858,200
All other industries	771	8,158	$15,127,641
Total	1,032	12,758	$34,241,520
NEW YORK CITY, 1900			
Garments	8,266	90,950	$239,879,414
Sugar refining	12	3,075	$88,598,113
Printing and publishing	1,431	22,960	$78,736,099
Masonry, brick, and stone	383	10,236	$43,353,473
Slaughtering, meatpacking	52	1,932	$42,879,218
Foundry, machine products	589	19,560	$41,089,475

(*continued*)

Leading Manufacturing Industries in New York City and King's County in Selected Years, 1810–2002 (*Continued*)

	No. of Establishments	No. of Employees	Value of Products
NEW YORK CITY, 1900 (continued)			
Malt liquors	89	200	$39,105,837
Tobacco	1,841	20,519	$37,998,261
Bread, bakery products	1,966	10,915	$32,239,307
Carpentering	1,491	8,660	$26,061,584
All other industries	23,656	273,756	$701,408,000
Total	39,776	462,763	$1,371,348,781
NEW YORK CITY, 1940			
Garments	5,542	138,491	$962,274,953
Printing and publishing	689	10,544	$300,745,053
Furs	1,832	10,872	$150,682,842
Bread, bakery products	1,868	20,500	$139,833,679
Meatpacking, wholesaling	39	3,960	$119,291,496
Commercial printing	1,415	13,268	$80,131,125
Millinery	682	12,098	$61,568,375
Malt liquors	22	1,403	$58,703,356
Paints and varnishes	142	2,248	$42,294,445
Lithographing	174	5,622	$36,236,137
All other industries	14,246	293,660	$2,156,898,814
Total	26,651	512,666	$4,108,660,275
NEW YORK CITY, 1967			
Printing and publishing	4,251	136,400	$2,615,400,000
Garments	10,026	243,300	$2,544,600,000
Electronic equipment	772	46,400	$566,700,000
Chemical products	654	20,300	$479,100,000
Fabricated metal products	1,602	37,300	$406,500,000
Textile mill products	1,252	33,800	$347,000,000
Machinery	1,120	23,000	$313,500,000
Beverages	134	10,900	$255,700,000
Leather products	840	30,400	$248,700,000
Paper products	544	21,200	$234,400,000
All other industries	7,926	292,300	$2,234,000,000
Total	29,121	895,300	$10,245,600,000
NEW YORK CITY, 1987			
Printing and publishing	3,060	102,000	$11,524,900,000
Garments	3,119	78,400	$3,458,900,000
Chemicals	250	6,900	$913,300,000
Electronic equipment	309	15,600	$898,600,000
Jewelry, silverware	781	11,900	$720,600,000
Fabricated metal products	771	16,700	$705,900,000
Textile mill products	626	17,000	$502,300,000
Industrial machinery	514	10,800	$483,400,000
Paper products	245	10,700	$410,100,000
Furniture and fixtures	493	10,100	$395,100,000
All other industries	4,427	156,000	$4,529,700,000
Total	14,595	436,100	$24,542,800,000
NEW YORK CITY, 2002			
Manufacturing	3,523	58,920	$10,950,335,000
Apparel manufacturing	1,239	22,535	$3,783,232,000
Printing and related support activities	620	8,864	$1,309,866,000
Textile mills	177	4,723	$1,211,435,000
Textile product mills	60	1,501	$458,563,000
Food manufacturing	207	2,477	$383,392,000
Computer and electronic product manufacturing	73	1,457	$324,705,000

(*continued*)

and the Hudson Valley. Smuggling was widespread in New York City and its surrounding ports. Merchants actively smuggled in the West Indies, and many traded with forbidden areas or evaded payment of duties. During this period dry-goods wholesalers who traded primarily with English firms for manufactured goods consistently prospered. Grain exporters who traded with Lisbon and Madeira dealt with an unstable market that brought either great fortune or great loss. Traders in the West Indies were subject both to the volatility of Caribbean sugar, molasses, and bills of exchange and to the difficulty of predicting the size of exportable surpluses in grain, flour, and timber. The West Indies were the fastest-growing market for New York City.

By the eve of the American Revolution the population had reached 25,000 and the volume of trade in New York City had increased markedly, although it was not yet as large as that of Charleston, Boston, or Philadelphia. The port of Charleston handled tobacco, rice, and indigo, the most important colonial exports. Flour, dried fish, and wheat, the secondary exports, were shipped from ports in New England and the Middle Atlantic, including New York, Baltimore, and Philadelphia.

2. 1776 to 1865

British occupation during the American Revolution halted the early manufactures and disrupted commerce and retailing. Many of the wealthiest merchants were Loyalists, and the greater number of them left the city during the war, thereby providing opportunities for rising lesser merchants and for new immigrants. New Yorkers in the countryside, mostly patriots, developed economic liaisons with these merchants during the war. The two groups benefited from their alliance during the postwar reconstruction of the city, but the old antagonism between farmer and merchant arose in the debates over ratification of the Constitution and economic quarrels about prices, embargoes, and paper money.

The Port of New York grew in importance during the American Revolution. Although trade ceased in most other cities, it thrived in New York City owing largely to the British occupation. Further disruptions in trade during the War of 1812 left the city as the country's dominant port.

The first census of 1790 showed that after Philadelphia, New York was the second largest city in the nation, with 33,000 people. In that heyday of the sailing ship, 10 of the 11 largest cities in the United States lay on the East Coast. The only exception, Albany, had access to the Atlantic by means of the Hudson River. The early nineteenth century marked the rise of interior waterways as the cheapest means for transporting goods to market. New Orleans emerged as a rival to New York City after the Louisiana Purchase and the rapid settlement of Ohio, Indiana, and Illinois. The links of New Orleans to those areas along rivers helped to make its volume of foreign trade second only to that of New York City. That challenge to New York City's dominance of national export trade was countered by the state of New York, which financed and built the Erie Canal. Opened in 1825 the canal linked the Hudson River to Lake Erie, providing a route between the entire Great Lakes region and the city, which by 1830 handled 40 percent of the country's foreign trade. New York City's dominance was assured during these years by its ready access to markets and the interior and its concentration of mercantile and financial institutions. These features made it the only one of the nation's five largest cities suited for handling both imports and exports, and it soon determined the flow of imports, exports, and credit to and from the interior. During the two decades before the Civil War the use of interior waterways declined as railroads were built, leading to shifts within the hierarchy of American cities. Cincinnati, St. Louis, Pittsburgh, Louisville, and Buffalo grew rapidly and by 1850 were among the country's 12 largest cities. Chicago, which had a population of less than 5000 in the 1840s, was connected to New York City by rail in 1850, and by 1860 its population reached 100,000. The railroads were extended to the western plains, and a link built to New Orleans in 1859 threatened again to draw bulk exports from the West and Midwest away from New York City to the South. This was forestalled by the Civil War, which suspended trade between Chicago and New Orleans.

Leading Manufacturing Industries in New York City and King's County in Selected Years, 1810–2002 (*Continued*)

	No. of Establishments	No. of Employees	Value of Products
NEW YORK CITY, 2002 (continued)			
Chemical manufacturing	36	1,106	$284,752,000
Furniture and related products	117	2,029	$222,868,000
Electrical equipment, appliance, and component manufacturing	17	657	$204,129,000
Fabricated metal products	61	732	$93,163,000
Miscellaneous manufacturing	740	10,927	$2,309,692,000
Total	6,870	115,928	$21,536,132,000

1. Includes pork, beef, preserved fruits, and pickles.
2. Includes steam engines, hay, and cotton presses.
Source: U.S. Bureau of the Census, Census of Manufacturers
Compiled by James Bradley and Alex Poole

3. 1866 to 1969

Shortly before the Civil War, manufactured goods accounted for only 10 percent of the country's exports, with foodstuffs and raw materials accounting for most of the rest. The period after the Civil War saw the rise of manufacturing based primarily on coal and steel. Buffalo, Pittsburgh, Cleveland, Detroit, and Milwaukee served as transport points between the coal fields in Appalachia and the iron ore mines at the western end of Lake Superior. Accumulations of capital and labor and proximity to markets, port facilities, and rail links helped older cities to become manufacturing centers as well, among them New York City, Chicago, Philadelphia, and Baltimore. Unlike the new manufacturing centers, the older East Coast cities focused on goods tied to mass markets rather than sources of raw materials. In Manhattan, manufacturers specialized in finished and semifinished nondurable consumer goods such as apparel, refined sugar, printed materials, leather goods, and tobacco products rather than durable producer goods such as primary metals, machinery, and transportation equipment. The expansion of low-wage factory work led to a rise in immigration. The city's population rose rapidly from 0.8 million in 1860 to 3.4 million in 1900, and in that year more than one of three city residents were foreign born. Factory workers in the city accounted for 11 percent of the national total. After World War I foreign immigration was restricted, but expanding employment in manufacturing drew workers from the rural South and Puerto Rico. For many years New York City had far more manufacturing jobs than any other city in the world.

The city nevertheless remained more economically diversified than others. Factory work consistently accounted for a smaller share of the employment there than in Cleveland, Chicago, Pittsburgh, Detroit, and Buffalo. As the country's leading port and center of commerce, finance, and business services during the century after the Civil War, it also was attractive as a headquarters location for major corporations. Of the nation's 500 largest industrial corporations, 144 of them had their headquarters in New York City in 1957, little changed from the estimated total of 150 headquarters in 1917. Chicago, in second place as a headquarters center, was far

Occupations of the Labor Force of New York City in Major Industry Groups and in Occupation Groups (for employed people 16 years and older)

IN MAJOR INDUSTRY GROUPS
1900–1930

	1900	1910	1920	1930
Agriculture	10,134	10,836	7,709	7,574
Clerical	N/A	234,860	402,414	535,315
Domestic and personal service	206,215	333,954	306,290	448,838
Manufacturing	419,594	873,497	952,312	1,021,199
Professional service	60,853	127,395	168,037	254,852
Public service	N/A	40,913	60,875	68,149
Trade and transportation	405,675	530,887	1,097,064	851,532
Total	1,102,471	2,152,342	2,994,701	3,187,459

(continued)

Occupations of the Labor Force of New York City in Major Industry Groups and in Occupation Groups (for employed people 16 years and older) (*Continued*)

1940–2000

	1940	1950	1960	1970	1980	1990	2000
Agriculture, forestry, fisheries, mining	4,434	6,316	5,291	9,537	6,458	8,830	2,101
Construction	131,599	144,342	124,337	111,077	78,904	133,954	139,385
Manufacturing	746,466	916,911	869,354	657,054	507,103	371,843	217,602
Transportation	61,126	213,056	213,823	187,636	201,046	216,862	211,506[1]
Communications, public utilities	67,604	96,505	92,448	128,607	90,625	87,396	N/A
Wholesale trade	233,400	318,184	172,119	161,064	139,689	131,538	101,812
Retail trade	388,357	437,633	453,674	457,212	387,437	428,960	295,803
Finance, insurance, real estate	224,460	242,566	272,019	340,199	349,043	401,765	372,809[2]
Business and repair services	74,133	111,667	129,233	169,829	192,836	212,276	N/A
Personal, entertainment, recreation	336,883	281,809	195,383	187,218	150,374	181,047	272,210[3]
Professional and related services	247,816	292,112	334,134	600,679	673,270	925,056	390,956[4]
Education, health, and social services	N/A	N/A	N/A	N/A	N/A	N/A	765,905
Public administration	126,733	158,147	148,352	181,258	141,398	158,110	146,807
Information	N/A	N/A	N/A	N/A	N/A	N/A	173,594
Other services (except public administration)	N/A	N/A	N/A	N/A	N/A	N/A	187,335
Not reported	73,639	57,276	181,023	—	—	—	—
Total	2,716,650	3,276,524	3,191,190	3,191,370	2,918,183	3,257,637	3,277,825

IN OCCUPATION GROUPS

1940–2000

	1940	1950	1960	1970	1980	1990	2000
Professional, technical, and kindred workers	217,032	338,060	378,400	456,304	492,342	656,286	1,206,052[5]
Managers, officials, and proprietors	288,152	380,496[6]	294,525	307,592	333,259	440,000	—[7]
Clerical and kindred workers	770,804[8]	629,906	726,674	836,171	727,624	672,434	896,486[9]
Sales workers	N/A	253,305	239,702	260,648	261,811	335,477	—[10]
Craftsmen, foremen, and kindred workers	329,479	399,119	358,102	318,288	246,350	244,817	209,665[11]
Operatives and kindred workers	580,053	686,249	686,434	323,501	224,233	158,981	N/A
Private household workers	123,202	79,533	67,850	39,979	25,525	24,211	N/A
Protective service	N/A	N/A	N/A	61,667	65,645	89,619	N/A
Service workers (except private household)	346,264	341,593	352,433	326,586	335,188	407,144	608,383
Laborers (except farm and mine)	114,168	130,066	138,954	126,048	97,589	99,584	N/A
Farming, forestry, fishing	1,578	N/A	1,906	9,057	8,033	8,352	1,464
Transport and material moving	N/A	N/A	N/A	125,561	100,584	120,642	355,775[12]
Others	68,634	38,297	234,494	N/A	N/A	N/A	N/A
Total	2,068,562	2,896,128	3,479,474	3,191,402	2,918,183	3,257,547	3,277,825

Note: Dash denotes zero; N/A = Not Available.
1. 2000 value is for "Transportation and warehousing, and utilities."
2. Includes "Rental and leasing."
3. 2000 value is for "Arts, entertainment, recreation, accommodation, and food services."
4. 2000 value is for "Professional, scientific, management, administrative, and waste management services"; for the purpose of comparison, the year 2000 value below for "Education, health, and social services" can be combined with this value, making a total of 1,156,861 for these two categories for year 2000 that is comparable to the values for "Professional and related services" for the previous decades.
5. 2000 value is for "Management, professional, and related occupations."
6. Includes farm managers.
7. Included in above number for "Professional, technical, and kindred workers."
8. Includes sales workers.
9. Value is for "Sales and office occupations."
10. Included in above value for "Clerical and kindred workers."
11. Value is for "Construction, extraction, and maintenance occupations."
12. Value is for "Production, transportation, and material moving occupations."
Sources: U.S. Bureau of the Census, Census of Population 1910, 1920, 1930, 1940, 1950, 1960, 1970, 1980, 1990, 2000
Compiled by James Bradley and Lisa Keller

below New York City, with 54 headquarters in 1957.

By the middle of the twentieth century the city's population was nearly eight million, a peak it surpassed by 2000. It continued to be by far the largest city in the United States, but its attractiveness as a manufacturing site was diminished by its congestion, aging physical plants, and rising costs of land and labor. Furthermore, as the real costs of transporting goods declined, manufacturers became able to supply the city's large market without being based there. New York City's manufacturing employment hovered around one million during the 1950s and then began to decline. The number of corporate headquarters located in the city also declined beginning in the 1950s.

New York City's Largest Publicly Held Companies by Annual Revenue in 2007

Name	2007 Revenue (billions)	Industry	No. of Employees[1]
Citigroup	$157.33	Financial services	387,000
JPMorgan Chase	$116.35	Financial services	180,667
American International Group	$109.61	Insurance	116,000
Verizon Communications	$93.47	Telecommunications	234,971
Goldman Sachs Group	$87.97	Securities	30,522
Morgan Stanley	$85.33	Securities	48,256
Merrill Lynch	$62.68	Securities	64,200
Lehman Brothers Holdings	$59.00	Securities	28,556
MetLife	$52.98	Insurance	49,000
Pfizer	$48.21	Pharmaceuticals	86,600
Time Warner	$46.48	Entertainment and media	86,400
Hess	$31.71	Petroleum	13,300
American Express	$31.56	Financial services	67,700
Alcoa	$30.75	Alumina and aluminum products	107,000
News Corp.	$28.66	Entertainment and media	53,000
Philip Morris International	$22.80	Tobacco, food, and beverage products	75,500
Bristol–Myers Squibb	$19.35	Pharmaceuticals	42,000
Loews	$17.55	Holding company	21,700
Bear Stearns	$16.15	Securities	14,153
Time Warner Cable	$15.96	Cable television and telecommunications	45,600
Bank of New York Mellon	$14.78	Banking	42,100
CBS	$14.07	Entertainment and media	23,970
L-3 Communications Holdings	$13.96	Communication systems	64,600
Colgate–Palmolive	$13.79	Health and beauty aids	36,000
Viacom	$13.42	Film production and cable television	10,800

1. Number includes all employees, not just those in New York City.
Source: *Crain's New York Business*, 26 May 2008
Compiled by Frank Nestor

4. 1970 to 1977

New York City experienced a severe economic decline during the early 1970s. Employment there fell continuously from a 1969 peak of 3.8 million to 3.2 million. This job loss was coupled with population loss. Manufacturing jobs declined precipitously by 35 percent from 1970 through 1977. The decline had some national causes, including two recessions and the decline of manufacturing from New England through the Midwest, and some local causes, including the flight of manufacturing from old cities and the shift of port activity to New Jersey as containerized shipping made New York City's port facilities obsolete. The number of corporate headquarters in the city dropped from 128 in 1965 to 90 in 1975. These declines brought on a fiscal crisis in the city's government in 1975. Through the efforts of New York State, municipal labor unions, and the financial community, however, the federal government lent the city government what it needed to avoid bankruptcy. Severe belt tightening and a shedding of city functions led to the emergence of a fiscally sound city government by 1978. But more important was the return of a strong city economy after 1977.

5. 1978 to 2010

After 1977 New York City became a postindustrial city, with fewer blue-collar jobs and more professional, technical, and managerial jobs. At the nadir of the city's economy in 1977 there were still 500,000 manufacturing jobs, 17 percent of all employment in the city. But by 2006 manufacturing jobs were down to 106,000, only 3 percent of all employment. Employment expansion came in the producer service industries of information (publishing, broadcasting, and film production); finance and insurance; and professional, scientific, and technical services (law, accounting, advertising, business consulting, computer software, engineering, and architecture); and also in the advanced consumer service industries of education, health, arts, entertainment, and recreation. Such a postindustrial economy required a high proportion of workers with college or postgraduate education. In 2000 total employment in the city was 3.7 million, much recovered from the low in 1977. The shift in the composition of employment also partly explains the upscaling of retail and the march of gentrification well beyond Manhattan.

The population loss of the 1970s was recovered by 2000, and the city continued to be the largest in the nation. But some former economic strengths did not rebound. Los Angeles surpassed New York City as both the country's leading manufacturing center and its leading ocean port. Furthermore, television production moved from New York City to Los Angeles. Foreign immigration to New York City soared after 1965, and the 2000 census reported that one of three city residents was born abroad, the same ratio as in 1900. Unlike 100 years ago, however, most of the new immigrants were from the Caribbean, elsewhere in Latin America, and Asia.

Total employment in the city peaked in August 2008 at 3.8 million (although some official estimates put the number at 3.4 million) before the national recession hit. By January 2010, however, for every 50 city jobs in the private sector, two had been lost, and city unemployment stood at 10.4 percent. Nonetheless, New York City fared better than the nation as a whole during the economic downturn in the first decade of the twenty-first century.

Robert A. East, *Business Enterprise in the American Revolutionary Era* (New York: Columbia University Press, 1938); Matthew P. Drennan and Robert Cohen, *The Corporate Headquarters Complex in New York City* (New York: Conservation of Human Resources, 1977); Russell Shorto, *The Island*

Largest Female-Owned Companies in New York City by 2007 Revenue

Company	2007 Revenue (millions)	2007 New York City Employees	Year Founded	Address
J&R Music and Computer World	$360.0	650	1971	23 Park Row
Henegan Construction	$230.0	150	1959	250 West 30th St.
TransPerfect	$156.7	351	1992	3 Park Ave.
Carole Hochman Design Group	$150.0	165	1930	135 Madison Ave.
Loren Communications International	$128.0	275	1975	155 East 55th St.
Condal Distributors	$105.0	225	1968	551 Dupont St.
Ruder Finn	$93.5	231	1948	301 East 57th St.
Meadows Office Furniture	$93.5	60	1967	71 West 23rd St.
Chloé Foods	$80.0	500	2003	3301 Atlantic Ave., Brooklyn
ICP	$60.0	67	1989	20 Clifton Ave., Staten Island
Sharp Decisions	$53.3	234	1990	55 West 39th St.
I. G. Federal Electrical Supply	$48.4	58	1932	47-20 30th St., Long Island City
Kleinknecht Electric	$40.0	225	1916	252 West 37th St.
ACC Construction	$39.3	38	1984	6 East 32nd St.
Kleinberg Electric	$32.9	120	1979	437 West 16th St.
Big Apple Car	$28.0	195	1983	169 Bay 17th St., Brooklyn

Source: *Crain's New York Business*, 30 June 2008
Compiled by Frank Nestor

at the Center of the World (New York: Vintage Books, 2005)

Matthew P. Drennan

Ecuadorians. Ecuadorian immigration to New York City started in the early 1960s. By 2000 Ecuadorians were the sixth-largest foreign-born group in the city, and close to two-thirds of the city's Ecuadorian population lived in Queens. Ecuadorians in New York City in the early twenty-first century lived largely in Corona, Jackson Heights, Astoria, Woodside, Elmhurst, Bushwick, Sunset Park, Washington Heights, Soundview, and Melrose. Ecuadorian restaurants, clubs, and civic associations are concentrated in Jackson Heights, where the Comité Cívico Ecuatoriano, a nonpolitical association of humanitarian, athletic, and cultural groups, also has its headquarters. Many Ecuadorians, especially those from Guayaquil and other coastal areas, belong to groups affiliated with their hometowns and provinces in Ecuador. Each year about 100,000 Ecuadorians take part in the Semana Ecuatoriana, a weeklong festival in August at Flushing Meadow Park.

Graciela M. Castex

Edenwald. Neighborhood in the north central Bronx, bounded to the east by Seton Falls Park. It is named for an estate owned from 1900 to 1913 by John H. Eden near Boston Road, Light Street, and Connor Street. The land was the site of the Hebrew Orphan Asylum until it was acquired by New York City after World War II for a public housing project of 2039 units called the Edenwald Houses, centered at 229th Street and Laconia Avenue. In the early twenty-first century the population of the project and of the surrounding one-family houses was predominantly African American.

Lloyd Ultan

Ederle, Gertrude (Caroline) (*b* New York City, 23 Oct 1906; *d* Wyckoff, N.J., 30 Nov 2003). Swimmer. At age 12 she broke the world record for the women's 880-yard freestyle event; she broke many others during the early 1920s, including some held by men. A member of the New York Women's Swimming Association, in 1926 she became the first woman to swim across the English Channel, cutting nearly two hours from the previous record. When she returned to New York City, a ticker-tape parade was held in her honor. Born and raised on Amsterdam Avenue in Manhattan, she is also closely associated with Queens, where she appeared in the Aquacade show during the 1939 World's Fair; in 1978 the Aquacade pool (now demolished) was dedicated to her and renamed the Ederle Amphitheater. She lived in Flushing, Queens, for most of her adult life and taught deaf children to swim until her death. She is buried in Woodlawn Cemetery in the Bronx.

James E. Mooney

Edgemere. Neighborhood in southwestern Queens on the Rockaway Peninsula, lying roughly between Beach 32nd and Beach 56th streets. It was acquired in 1892 by Frederick J. Lancaster, who formed the Sea Beach Improvement Company in 1894 to sell beach and meadow property. The area was first called New Venice; the current name means "edge of the sea" in Anglo-Saxon. Lancaster built the Hotel Edgemere in 1895, which he operated until 1919, as well as several cottages. Edgemere declined in the 1960s and 1970s and became part of the Arverne Urban Renewal area. In the 1990s and first decade of the twenty-first century, the city announced repeated plans for new middle-class and luxury developments, but the pace of change slowed because of the recession that began in 2008.

Vincent Seyfried

Edgewater. Neighborhood in the eastern Bronx, lying on the northern shore of the Throgs Neck Peninsula and bounded to the north by Weir Creek, to the east by Eastchester Bay, and to the south and west by the Throgs Neck Expressway. Before European settlement the area was the site of a Siwanoy fishing village. By 1792 it was part of the property of Edward Stephenson, whose farm and woodlands accounted for most of Throgs Neck; in 1851 it was bought and developed as an estate by George Adee and named by his wife. The family sold the land in 1910 to Richard Shaw, who operated a stock farm and rented out parcels as campgrounds. Eventually the tents were replaced with year-round homes, in the 1930s still on rented land. In 1986 Edgewater made the transition from a summer community to a cooperative community, giving residents a chance to buy a stake in the neighborhood itself. The neighborhood in the early twenty-first century is sometimes known as the Park of Edgewater and has about 700 small houses along its narrow lanes. There are almost no businesses, and only one street leads into the neighborhood.

John McNamara, *History in Asphalt: The Origin of Bronx Street and Place Names* (New York: Bronx County Historical Society, 1984)

Gary D. Hermalyn

Edison, Thomas (Alva) (*b* Milan, Ohio, 11 Feb 1847; *d* West Orange, N.J., 18 Oct 1931). Inventor. In April 1869 he left his position as a telegraph operator in Boston for the Western Union Telegraph Company to pursue a career as an inventor in New York City. He lived in nearby Newark, New Jersey, and invented products under contract for a number of telegraph companies in New York City, including Western Union and the Gold and Stock Telegraph Company. Among his contributions to telegraphy were improvements to stock tickers and methods of sending multiple messages over a single wire. Early in 1876 he used the wealth he had acquired in telegraphy to build an independent laboratory in suburban Menlo Park, New Jersey, where he moved at the end of March 1876 with many of the men who had assisted him earlier. In his five years there he invented the phonograph, which was manufactured by the Edison Phonograph Company and made him internationally known; the carbon-button telephone transmitter, for which Western Union controlled patents that allowed it to compete with the Bell Telephone Company; and the first incandescent electric light and power system. He formed the Edison Machine Works to manufacture generators and Bergmann and Company to produce lamp fixtures and other components; lamps were made at the Edison Lamp Company in Harrison, New Jersey. The Edison Company for Isolated Lighting marketed small power plants for individual buildings, and the Edison Illuminating Company of New York City operated the first permanent commercial incandescent light and power station, which began operation around Wall Street in September 1882. The Edison Electric Light Company, formed by several investors in Western Union, including J. P. Morgan, was the parent company that supported Edison's inventive work. From the summer of 1881 Edison lived for two years at 24 Gramercy Park South in Manhattan, and he later purchased a large house in suburban West Orange, where he worked to the end of his life. In 1892 his electric and power companies were merged with the General Electric Company. Among his later inventions were storage batteries, improvements to the phonograph, motion pictures, and technology for the milling of ore and the production of cement.

Matthew Josephson, *Edison: A Biography* (New York: McGraw–Hill, 1959); Andre Millard, *Edison and the Business of Invention* (Baltimore: Johns Hopkins University Press, 1990)

See also LIGHT AND POWER and TECHNOLOGY.

Paul Israel

Edison Manufacturing Company. First indoor motion-picture studio in the United States. It opened in February 1901 at 41 East 21st Street. It was a glass-enclosed structure that relied on sunlight for filming but allowed for year-round production. From its convenient location at the edge of the city's entertainment district, the studio manager Edwin S. Porter made such films as *How They Do Things on the Bowery* (1902) and *The Miller's Daughter* (1905). Actors often worked in films during the day and on stage at night. The company began preparations in 1905 for a larger production facility at 2826 Decatur Avenue (near Bronx Park), which began operation in 1907 and was itself enlarged in 1909 to give Edison four production units in continuous operation. Films made in the Bronx include Porter's *Rescued from an Eagle's Nest* (1908), with D. W. Griffith, and *Vanity Fair* (1915), with Minnie Maddern Fiske. When Edison ceased film production in 1918, the studios were sold to the Lincoln and Parker Film Company; later they were operated by a number of small, short-lived companies. Converted to sound in 1930, the facility was occasionally used to make animated films, industrial films, and short subjects into the 1960s, when it was demolished.

Charles Musser, *Before the Nickelodeon: Edwin S. Porter and the Edison Manufacturing Company* (Berkeley: University of California Press, 1991)

Charles Musser

Ed Sullivan Theater. Theater on Broadway and 53rd Street in Manhattan, built by Arthur Hammerstein and opened in 1927 as Hammerstein's. The theater experienced financial hardship in its early years and in 1934 was converted into a casino and nightclub named the Billy Rose Music Hall. In 1949 the Columbia Broadcasting System (CBS) converted the building into a television studio, and as the set for the immensely popular *Ed Sullivan Show* it became the site of performances by Elvis Presley, the Beatles, and other musicians. In 1967 the theater took its current name. After Sullivan's program ended, the theater remained idle for many years until 1993, when it was renovated by CBS and became the venue for the *Late Show with David Letterman.*

James Bradley

education. See ADULT EDUCATION, BILINGUAL EDUCATION, CATHOLIC SCHOOLS, COLLEGES AND UNIVERSITIES, INDEPENDENT SCHOOLS, LAW SCHOOLS, MEDICAL SCHOOLS, PROGRESSIVE EDUCATION, and PUBLIC SCHOOLS, as well as entries on individual institutions and educators.

Educational Alliance. Settlement formed in 1889 at 197 East Broadway, funded and led by German Jews in New York City with the aim of educating eastern European Jewish immigrants on the Lower East Side and helping them to adapt to life in the United States. It operated a kindergarten and offered vocational and religious training as well as classes in theater, art, music, English, and citizenship. Many of the foreign-born students enrolled at the settlement later became prominent in the city, among them the broadcasting executive David Sarnoff, the philosopher Morris Raphael Cohen, the municipal official Anna M. Kross, the comedian Eddie Cantor, and the sculptor Chaim Gross. One of the leading members of the board of trustees was Julia Richman (1855–1912), the first woman and the first Jew to be appointed a district superintendent in the city school system. The public schools eventually adopted many of the programs of the settlement, notably its classes in English for foreigners and its "Peoples University," a series of free evening lectures presided over by a trustee of the alliance, Henry Leipziger (1854–1917), who also founded the Hebrew Technical Institute. The Educational

Educational Alliance, 2009

Alliance later expanded its facilities and programs to include a senior citizens' apartment building, two camps in upstate New York, a day-care center, a program for handicapped students at Public School 35 in Manhattan, and a branch on the West Side of Manhattan. In the early twenty-first century the organization served as many as 30,000 New Yorkers through more than 40 programs.

Selma Berrol

Egan, Edward (Michael) Cardinal (*b* Oak Park, Ill., 2 April 1932). Roman Catholic cardinal. After ordination in Rome (1957) he moved from Chicago's ecclesiastical administration back to Rome to obtain a doctorate in canon law (1964). He pursued further service in Chicago and then was appointed a judge of the Sacred Roman Rota (1971–85); auxiliary bishop of the Archdiocese of New York (1985) and vicar for education; bishop of Bridgeport, Connecticut (1988); archbishop of New York (2000); and cardinal (2001). He was in New York City during the terrorist attacks of 11 September 2001 and was called to Rome shortly thereafter. As archbishop he established clerical child sex abuse policies, "realigned" underutilized parish plants, promoted vocations, and founded the John Cardinal O'Connor residence for retired priests in the Riverdale section of the Bronx. He is a member of the Board of Trustees at the Catholic University of America and the Board of Governors at the Ave Maria School of Law. In 2005 Egan was one of the cardinal electors who participated in the papal conclave that selected Pope Benedict XVI. His resignation at age 75 as archbishop of New York took effect in 2009.

Mary Elizabeth Brown

Egbertville. Neighborhood in central Staten Island near the junction of Rockland Avenue and Richmond Road and surrounded by the Greenbelt. The area was called Morgan's Corner in 1838, and because of its predominantly Irish population it was later known as Tipperary Corners, New Dublin, and Young Ireland. It is now named for the Egberts, a family that farmed the area in the eighteenth century. The neighborhood attracted many Italian families during the 1930s and 1940s. A bucolic village of detached single-family houses, Egbertville witnessed the building of large single-family homes on its few remaining lots in the early twenty-first century. The JACQUES MARCHAIS MUSEUM OF TIBETAN ART is in Egbertville.

John-Paul Richiuso

egg cream. Confection made with chocolate syrup, milk, and seltzer water (but neither eggs nor cream), originally served in candy stores on the Lower East Side in the 1920s. According to one account the Yiddish actor Boris Thomashevsky originated it after sampling *chocolat et crème* during a tour of Paris. According to another the drink was first sold by Louis Auster (*d* 1955) in his candy stores at 92 Cannon Street and on East Third Street and Avenue D; he was said to have sold more than 3000 egg creams a day before his stores closed in the 1950s.

Jeffrey Kisselhoff, *You Must Remember This: An Oral History of Manhattan from the 1890s to World War II* (New York: Harcourt Brace Jovanovich, 1989)

Rachel Sawyer

Egyptians. Egyptian immigration to the Americas began in the nineteenth century, when Egypt still belonged to the Ottoman Empire. Immigration increased markedly in the 1960s with President Gamal Abdel Nasser's policy of forced nationalization and his encouragement of emigration as a means of controlling overpopulation; it was also encouraged by a change in U.S. laws in 1965 that eased the immigration of educated professionals. Most of the new immigrants were young, unmarried men with university degrees (often earned in the United States or Europe). In 1970 there were 7642 Egyptians in New York City, of whom 5587 were foreign born. From 1982 to 1987, 3004 immigrants from Egypt settled in the city, more than from any other Arab nation. The number of foreign-born Egyptians in New York City in 2000 exceeded 15,000, making it the 36th-largest group of its kind in the city. Most worked as craftspeople, petty traders, and laborers; almost all were men, and many would eventually return to Egypt.

Over time the Egyptian population has dispersed throughout the city, with concentrations in Bay Ridge and Astoria. New York City has two Coptic Christian churches: St. Mary and St. Antonios Coptic Orthodox Church at 606 Woodward Avenue in Ridgewood, and St. George's Coptic Church at 108 St. Edward Street in Fort Greene. The Islamic Anjumar Mosque at 36–07 30th Street in Long Island City was built with the support of about 300 Egyptian New Yorkers.

Erica Judge, John Lowe

Eidlitz, Leopold (*b* Prague, 29 March 1823; *d* New York City, 22 March 1908). Architect, brother of Marc Eidlitz, and father of Cyrus L. W. Eidlitz. He settled in New York City in 1843 and designed St. George's Church in Stuyvesant Square (1846–48, with Otto Blesch) and the southern wing of the Tweed Courthouse (1876–78). His religious and commercial work as well as his theoretical writings strongly influenced his contemporaries. Eidlitz wrote *The Nature and Function of Art, More Especially of Architecture* (1881).

Marjorie Pearson

Eidlitz, Marc (*b* Prague, 31 Jan 1826; *d* New York City, 15 April 1892). Building contractor, brother of Leopold Eidlitz. He moved to New York City in 1847, where he soon became the city's most prominent building contractor. His commissions, most of which were from the "400," the city's wealthiest residents, included the Metropolitan Opera House; the Broadway Tabernacle; the Eden Musée; a portion of the Astor Library; Steinway Hall; the mansions of J. P. Morgan, Otto Goelet, and Robert L. Stuart; and St. Vincent's, St. Francis, and Presbyterian hospitals.

Andrew Wiese

Eight, The. Stylistically diverse group of artists formed in New York City in 1907; its members were the urban realists Robert Henri, John Sloan, George Luks, William Glackens, and Everett Shinn; the romantic symbolist Arthur B. Davies; the impressionist Ernest Lawson; and the post-impressionist Maurice Prendergast. The group was formed after the hanging committee of the National Academy of Design rejected paintings by Shinn, Glackens, and Luks; Henri then resigned his membership in the academy and announced that he and seven other artists would hold an exhibition of their own in protest. The group was named The Eight by James Gibbons Huneker, a sympathetic critic; others less sympathetic called them "the revolutionary black gang" and "the apostles of ugliness." The Eight exhibited only once: 63 works were on view at the Macbeth Galleries (450 Fifth Avenue) from 3 to 15 February 1908 and were then sent on a tour of nine cities. Although only seven paintings were sold, The Eight surpassed their initial goal of deflating the National Academy by broadening the opportunities for other artists to exhibit their work: their success led to the 1910 Exhibition of Independent Artists and the Armory Show of 1913.

Bennard B. Perlman, *The Immortal Eight: American Painting from Eakins to the Armory Show, 1870–1913* (Westport, Conn.: North Light, 1979)

Avis Berman

Eighth Street Bookshop. Bookstore opened in 1947 by the brothers Elias and Ted Wilentz. It became well known during the 1950s and 1960s as a literary gathering place in Greenwich Village and had close ties to the beat writers and artists. In 1965 the shop moved from 32 West Eighth Street to larger quarters at 17 West Eighth Street, where under Elias Wilentz it became one of the nation's foremost bookstores. It closed in 1979 after Wilentz's retirement.

Sean Wilentz

Eighth Street Playhouse. Single-screen movie theater located at 52 West Eighth Street. Formerly the Film Guild Cinema, in 1930 Marin C. Ansorge bought the lease to have it become one of the first theaters to feature television programs. Most famous for its Friday and Saturday midnight screenings of *The Rocky Horror Picture Show,* a 15-year tradition that began in the 1970s, the theater also played independent films in the 1970s, hosted 3-D festivals in the 1980s, and featured various other themed festivals such as the Sleaze Film Festival. When the owner died in the mid-1980s, the theater was taken over by City Cinemas and eventually United Artists, both of which featured first-run movies. For a period it was an empty storefront and, in the early twenty-first century, a movie rental store, until it closed in 2007.

Jessica Montesano

Eisenhower, Dwight D(avid) (*b* Denison, Tex., 14 Oct 1890; *d* Washington, D.C., 28 March 1969). Thirty-fourth president of the United States. He graduated in 1915 from the U.S. Military Academy at West Point. After commanding the Allied forces in Europe during World War II, he returned to the United States in 1945 and was honored on 19 June with a ticker-tape parade along Broadway in lower Manhattan. In 1948 he declined offers from both the Democrats and the Republicans to seek the presidency of the United States in favor of one to become the president of Columbia University. He lived in the presidential mansion at 60 Morningside Drive during his tenure and retained his title after becoming the first supreme commander of the North Atlantic Treaty Organization (NATO) in 1950. During his time at Columbia, he founded the Institute of War and Peace Studies, which was renamed the Saltzman Institute of War and Peace Studies in 2003. In 1952 he attended a rally in his honor at Madison Square Garden, and after much prodding from friends and Republican officials became a candidate for the presidency; after his election he left Columbia in 1953.

Stephen E. Ambrose, *Eisenhower* (New York: Simon and Schuster, 1983–84)

Edward T. O'Donnell

Eisenstaedt, Alfred (*b* Dirschau, Germany [now Tczew, Poland], 6 Dec 1898; *d* New York City, 24 Aug 1995). Photojournalist. He studied in Berlin and in 1935 moved to the United States. In the following year the new magazine *Life* published the first of his photographs, beginning an association that lasted until 1972, when he continued to work at his studio in Rockefeller Center. Eisenstaedt's candid, naturalistic style is typified by his best-known photograph "Total Surrender," of a sailor and nurse embracing in Times Square on V-J Day in 1945. His work has been published in several collections, among them *Eisenstaedt: Remembrances* (1990). He was a longtime resident of Jackson Heights in Queens. Since 1999 Columbia University's School of Journalism has given an annual award for magazine photography in his name.

Lisa Gitelman

E. J. Korvette. Firm of retailers formed in 1948 by Eugene Ferkauf (*b* 1920). Its name was derived from the first initials of Ferkauf and his associate, Joseph Zwillenberg, and from the name of a Canadian submarine chaser known as the Corvette used during World War II. The firm began operations when Ferkauf opened a luggage shop with backing from his father on the second story of a building on East 46th Street in Manhattan. He sold his goods at a markup of 20 percent (half of what was customary) and later added to his inventory household appliances and jewelry, also sold at low prices. Loss leaders (products sold at a reduced price to attract customers), sold at a discount of 35 percent, drew crowds and lawsuits from competitors, which Ferkauf viewed as free advertising. Under his direction the firm achieved great success and helped to launch a revolution in discount retailing in the 1950s and 1960s; it registered $20 million in annual sales by 1952 from five stores, and over the next 12 years $622 million in total sales from eight stores. Efforts by other retailers to pressure manufacturers into refraining from doing business with Korvette were successfully countered by means of middlemen. After opening a new store on Fifth Avenue and another in Herald Square, the firm experienced organizational problems that probably stemmed from its rapid, enormous growth. In 1966 Ferkauf merged it with Spartan Industries, an apparel manufacturer, to increase sales and profits. He severed all ties with his stores in 1968 and left the firm entirely in the control of Charles Bassine, the chairman of Spartan. The new managers sought to change the emphasis of Korvette by selling goods of higher quality at higher prices, but a confused marketing strategy failed and the firm began selling its stores in 1980, filed for bankruptcy the next year, and soon discontinued its operations.

Isadore Barmash, *More Than They Bargained For: The Rise and Fall of Korvettes* (New York: Lebhar–Friedman, 1981)

Leslie Gourse, Kenneth T. Jackson

Elaine's. Restaurant on the Upper East Side at 1703 Second Avenue that became famous after the 1960s as a locus for the media elite to mingle. In the twenty-first century, hostess and owner Elaine Kaufman ran this neighborhood Italian establishment.

Jessica Montesano

El Barrio. Neighborhood on the East Side of Manhattan, also known as East Harlem and Spanish Harlem, bounded to the north by 125th Street, to the east by Franklin D. Roosevelt Drive, to the south by 96th Street, and to the west by Fifth Avenue. The population of the area was predominantly Italian until Puerto Ricans began moving there during the 1920s; after World War II it became a largely Puerto Rican enclave. During the early twenty-first century the Puerto Rican identity diminished as Latin Americans from other countries, primarily Mexico and the Dominican Republic, settled in the neighborhood. There are many churches, bodegas, substandard tenements, and large public housing projects in El Barrio. Several community organizations and settlement houses are active in local affairs, as are the Protestant, Evangelical, and Roman Catholic denominations; their activities include organizing demonstrations and influencing legislation to bring about social reform. In the twenty-first century gentrification is evident in upgraded housing, including renovated town houses, new condominium

Teatro Latino in El Barrio, 110th Street and Fifth Avenue, 1938

complexes, and middle-class cooperative apartments that have attracted an economically and ethnically diverse population. The main shopping thoroughfare is 116th Street; the East River Plaza shopping center at FDR Drive, anchored by several major retailers, opened in 2008. The Museo del Barrio on Fifth Avenue and 104th Street is a center of Latin American culture.

Donald Stewart, *A Short History of East Harlem* (New York: Museum of the City of New York, 1972)

Joyce Mendelsohn

elderly. Most elderly people in colonial New York City were cared for at home. Public care was first offered by the "deacons house" in New Amsterdam. The city's first almshouse, built in 1736 under English rule, had a number of elderly inmates. When a new almshouse was built in 1796 more than half of its 622 inmates were placed there because they were old, and the same was true of an almshouse opened in larger quarters in 1816 at Bellevue (26th Street and the East River). The first private institutions for the elderly included the Association for the Relief of Respectable Aged Indigent Females, which was organized in 1815 to prepare its residents for death; the association built a home on 20th Street in 1839. At mid-century the elderly population increased, leading many to believe that it was inappropriate to house the elderly with children, vagrants, the insane, and the retarded. In 1849 the city moved its public charities to Blackwell's Island (later Welfare Island, now Roosevelt Island); near its center elderly public charges lived in two stone buildings, one for men and the other for women, and worked at tailoring, broom making, and shoemaking if they were able. By 1855 people older than 60 accounted for almost 3 percent of the city's population. Almshouses opened in Brooklyn by 1870 and in Staten Island and Queens; the last one, completed in 1888 in Queens, had 49 elderly people among its 56 inmates. Paupers received public care at the lowest possible cost: they lived in dormitories with little privacy; were fed a bland diet of rice, oatmeal, beef, potatoes, cabbage, and turnips; and were punished for breaking rules. Residents of such private homes as the Presbyterian Home (1869), the Baptist Home of Brooklyn (1875), and the nonsectarian Isabella Heimath Home (1875) had slightly more privacy but could still be treated indifferently. By 1890 the Association for the Relief of Respectable Aged Indigent Females moved to 104th Street and concentrated on making the lives of its residents more pleasant.

Increasingly considered a public burden, the elderly poor were suspected of improvidence by such reformers as Josephine Shaw Lowell, director of the Charity Organization Society, who believed that the responsibility for care should fall on relatives and friends. Her views set off a debate about the relative merits of indoor relief (provided in an institution) and outdoor relief (provided in the home) that continued to the end of the century. Most residents of almshouses were foreign born, and in 1904 Charles C. Weisz of the city's Department of Charities sought to restrict immigration for those older than 50, arguing that they would become public charges. Between 1910 and 1920 public attitudes softened. More private institutions opened and the belief strengthened that the state should provide special care for the elderly. When the New York State Old Age Security Act was passed in 1930, the city had more than 300,000 elderly residents, accounting for 5.5 percent of its population. In 1938 the almshouse department was renamed the Department of Welfare, and the hospitals department took control of the facility on Welfare Island and another in Dongan Hills. The Bureau for the Aged of the Welfare Council of New York City reported in 1940 that these facilities and 88 private homes provided residential care for 12,000 people, were filled to capacity, and had waiting lists and that the Department of Welfare provided financial aid to about 55,000 people. The Department of Welfare was renamed the Department of Social Services in 1967; its Office of Aging became independent in 1975. In 1968 the city stopped operating a home for the elderly and instead provided referrals to private homes.

After an aging trend during the 1970s and 1980s the proportion of elderly in New York City declined slightly in the 1990s. In 2000 those 65 years old and older accounted for 12 percent of the total population citywide (12.7 percent in Queens, 12.2 percent in Manhattan, 11.5 percent in Brooklyn, 10.1 percent in the Bronx, and 11.6 percent in Staten Island). In the same year about 18 percent of the city's elderly had incomes below the poverty line.

Alana Erickson Coble

Eldridge, Roy [Little Jazz] (*b* Pittsburgh, 30 Jan 1911; *d* New York City, 26 Feb 1989). Trumpeter. He moved in 1930 to New York City, where he soon developed an innovative style influenced by saxophonists and characterized by rapid playing, long phrases, a wide range, and exuberance. From 1941 to 1943 he played with the Gene Krupa Orchestra, becoming one of the first African American trumpeters to play with a white band. The preeminent trumpeter of the swing era, he had long engagements at the Arcadia Ballroom, Kelly's Stables, Birdland, the Metropole, and Jimmy Ryan's. Eldridge lived in Hollis, in the borough of Queens, from 1956 until the end of his life.

Ira Berger

Eldridge Street Synagogue. Orthodox synagogue, occupying the first large-scale building constructed by eastern Europeans. It opened on the Lower East Side as Kahal Adas Jeshurun Anshe Lubz. Designed in 1887 by the firm of Herter Brothers, it became known for its rich woodwork, dozens of stained-glass windows, and the bright frescoes on its walls, contrasting sharply with the unornamented tenements of the surrounding neighborhood. In the years before World War I, the congregation had 800 members, including the banker Sender Jarmulowsky and the city's foremost distributor for delicatessens, Isaac Gellis. As the neighborhood changed, the congregation fell on hard times and the building decayed. The synagogue was designated a city landmark in the 1980s. In the early twenty-first century it was restored by the Eldridge Street Project.

Jenna Weissman Joselit

Eldridge Street Synagogue, 2009

Electchester. Limited-dividend nonprofit housing cooperative in Fresh Meadows, Queens, established in 1949 and built on the 103-acre (41.7-hectare) site of a former golf course. A favored project of the head of the International Brotherhood of Electrical Workers (IBEW), Harry Van Arsdale, Jr., it was one of the first postwar union-sponsored limited-equity cooperatives. It was developed by Local 3 of the IBEW and the Joint Industry Board of the Electrical Industry; its 2405 units were built over a period of years. First Housing (382 units) opened in 1951, followed by Second Housing (688 units) in 1955, Third Housing (181 units) in 1953, Fourth Housing (382 units) in 1954, and Fifth Housing (182 units) in 1966, which consisted of two 23-story high-rise apartment towers. Members of the IBEW had preference in obtaining apartments, and as recently as the mid-1980s about 90 percent of the residents had IBEW connections. In the early twenty-first century the cooperative was more diverse racially than it had been in its earlier years (about 55 percent white, 25 percent African American, and 15 percent Latino), and the percentage of its more than 5500 residents with IBEW connections was down to about 50 percent.

Peter Eisenstadt

Electric Bond and Share. Electric utility holding company formed by the General Electric Company in 1905 under the leadership of Sidney Z. Mitchell. Situated at 2 Rector Street, the firm became the largest in the United States during the mid-1920s, generating 14 percent of the country's electricity in 1929. Its subsidiaries eventually operated in more than half the states and several Latin American countries. Dismantled under the Public Utility Holding Company Act of 1935, it became a diversified investment firm and merged with Boise Cascade in 1969. Ebasco Services, the service division and a leading utility consulting firm, became a subsidiary of Enserch in 1976.

Sidney Alexander Mitchell, *S. Z. Mitchell and the Electrical Industry* (New York: Farrar, Straus and Cudahy, 1960)

John L. Neufeld

Electric Circus. Nightclub in Greenwich Village in the 1960s. It was the most elaborate of the various clubs located at 23 St. Marks Place. The Electric Circus was upstairs from the nightclub the Dom and replaced the Balloon Farm, where Andy Warhol had staged the mixed-media *Exploding Plastic Inevitable* events featuring the rock band Velvet Underground. When it opened in 1967 the Electric Circus secured the reputation of St. Mark's Place as the psychedelic capital of New York. The club's large dance floor and series of smaller rooms featured elaborate lighting effects, multimedia performances, circus acts, experimental theater, and early electronic music shows. The club closed in 1971.

Melissa Baldock

electricity. See Light and power for a discussion of the electrification of New York City.

Elephantine Colossus. Elephant-shaped hotel on Coney Island (James V. Lafferty, Jr., architect). Completed in 1884 and destroyed by fire on 27 September 1896, it was the largest of three such tin-skinned, wooden elephants in the United States (only *Lucy* survives at Margate, New Jersey; *The Light of Asia* at South Cape May was demolished in 1900). Though popular with tourists, it was never successful as a hotel and later housed souvenir and tobacco shops. It stood on a seamy stretch of Surf Avenue near West 12th Street, where illicit pleasures traded under the euphemism of "seeing the elephant."

Joseph Ditta

elevated railways [els]. The earliest form of rapid transit in the United States, developed in New York City in the second half of the nineteenth century. The need to move large numbers of people between southern Manhattan and the northern reaches of the city encouraged a search for a faster alternative to the streetcar. The first elevated line was constructed in 1867–70 by Charles Harvey and his West Side and Yonkers Patent Railway company along Greenwich Street and Ninth Avenue between Dey and 29th streets. Tracks were laid atop iron (and later steel) superstructures about 30 feet (9 meters) above the ground, and cars were pulled by a cable connected to a steam-powered generator at the terminus. Cables often broke, requiring passengers to descend from the tracks by ladder. Such problems kept ridership low, and in 1871 the effort failed. In the following year the firm was reorganized as the New York Elevated Railroad Company, and a number of productive innovations were introduced: steam locomotives (or "dummies") were employed to haul the wooden cars, stations were added, and the line was extended south to South Ferry and north to Ninth Street and then 30th Street; by 1878 the line ran up Ninth Avenue to 61st Street.

The success of the line encouraged the development of new lines. The Gilbert Elevated Railway, reorganized as the Metropolitan Elevated Railway, opened a line on Trinity Place, Church Street, West Broadway, and Sixth Avenue between Rector Place and Central Park in June 1878. The New York Elevated Railroad Company built a line on Third Avenue that opened in August 1878, and by the end of the year it had track running from South Ferry to 129th Street. In 1879 the Man-

Elevated railroad at Ninth Avenue and 100th Street. Stereograph by E. and H. T. Anthony and Company

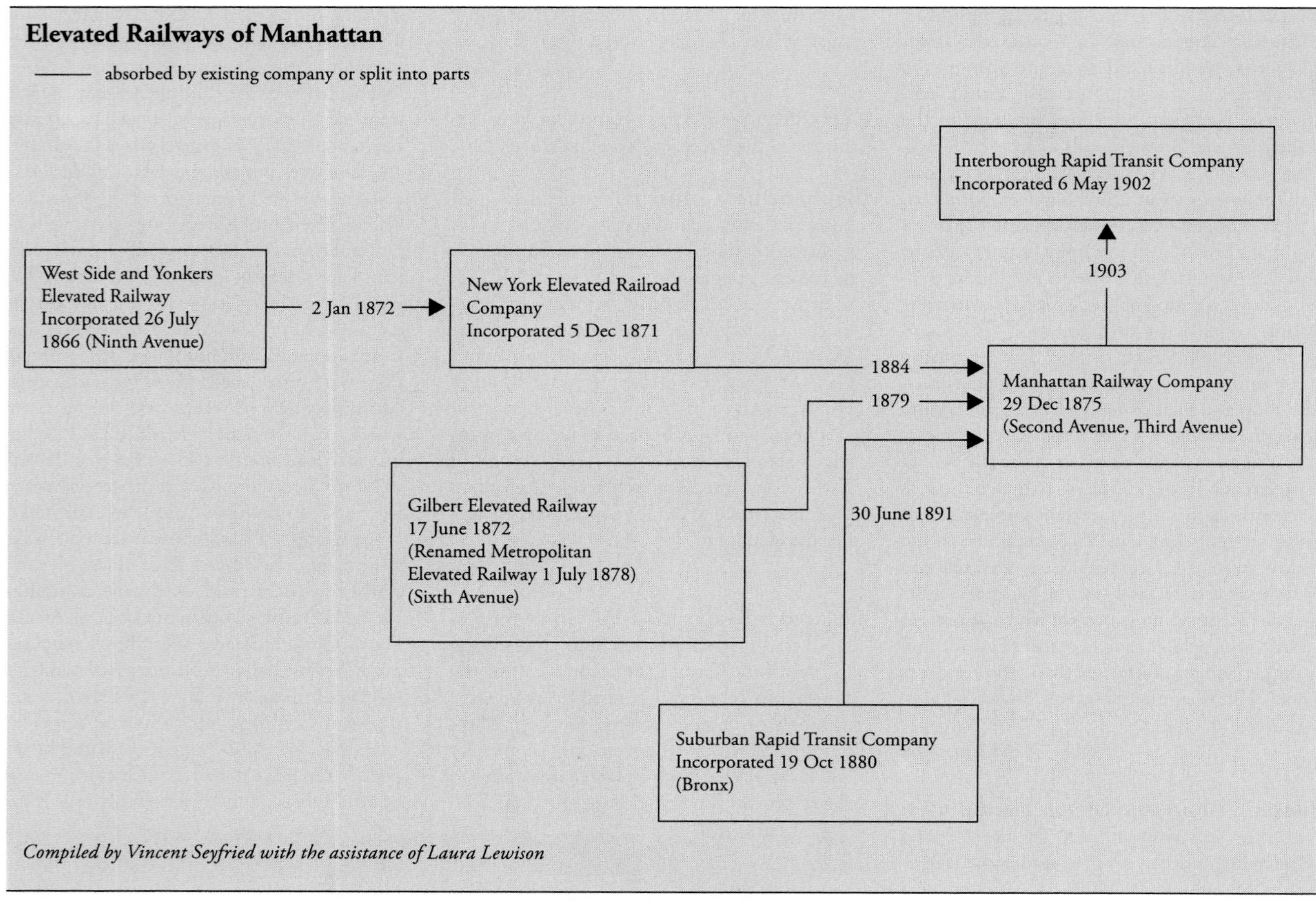

Compiled by Vincent Seyfried with the assistance of Laura Lewison

hattan Railway Company gained control of all the elevated lines in Manhattan and completed construction of the Second Avenue line, and on 1 March 1880 it opened the Second Avenue line between Chatham Square and 65th Street (extending it to 129th Street by 16 August). By 1880 the Third Avenue line was connected to Grand Central Depot and to the ferry terminal of the Long Island Rail Road on the East River at 34th Street. By 1881 the original Ninth Avenue line had been almost entirely rebuilt as a double-track line, extended north to 155th Street, and connected to the Sixth Avenue line by a track along 53rd Street and by another at Battery Place. The final phase of construction of elevated lines in Manhattan connected the Second Avenue and Third Avenue lines at Chatham Square (1882) and 129th Street (1891). The elevated trains were noisy and responsible for falling ash, oil, and cinder.

All further construction of elevated lines took place in the Bronx and Brooklyn, where most of the city's expansion around the turn of the century took place. Several steam-powered elevated lines went to northern Brooklyn, beginning with the Lexington Avenue line (1885). This fanned out from downtown and from the waterfront, where passengers could connect with ferries to Manhattan. The Suburban Rapid Transit Company was formed in March 1880, and between 1886 and 1902 it constructed a route that connected Manhattan (129th Street and Third Avenue) with the Bronx at Bronx Park, just north of Fordham Road. This line crossed the Harlem River on an iron drawbridge, ran on private right-of-way to 145th Street, and followed Third Avenue northward. Separate fares were required for passengers traveling between Manhattan and the Bronx. In 1891 the Manhattan Railway Company acquired control of Suburban and took over its operation. Through-service between the Bronx and Manhattan began in 1896 with a single five-cent fare, using the Suburban route north of 129th Street and the Second and Third Avenue lines south of it. Transfers between all four els in Manhattan were possible at South Ferry, and by using through-routing one could travel between lower Manhattan and the Bronx for five cents.

In Brooklyn by 1893 there were elevated lines along Myrtle Avenue, Lexington Avenue, Fulton Street, Broadway, and Fifth Avenue. From 1883 the New York and Brooklyn Bridge Railway operated cable-powered trains from Park Row in Manhattan to Sands Street in Brooklyn. By 1898 the various elevated companies in Brooklyn acquired trackage rights over the bridge and began through-service between boroughs. Large terminals were constructed at Park Row and Sands Street. In the suburban, semirural, and resort communities south of the city of Brooklyn, steam railroads originally built in the 1860s were incorporated into the elevated system in 1893–1900; these lines continued to run on the surface using trolley wire and were the precursors of the Brighton, Culver, Sea Beach, and West End lines. In 1899–1906 the Brooklyn Rapid Transit Company (BRT), which already ran streetcars, unified the various elevated companies of Brooklyn within a single network and replaced steam trains with multiple-unit electric trains (which used Frank J. Sprague's innovative system of electrification). Between 1900 and 1904 the Manhattan Railway instituted a number of changes: steam engines were retired in 1902–3, the Third Avenue line was extended to Fordham Road by 1901, and all lines were electrified. The Interborough Rapid Transit Company (IRT) constructed the first subway system from 1900 to 1904; in 1903 it acquired the Manhattan Railway Company to coordinate service on both systems. The first coordinated service between elevated railway and subway began in 1904, when the Westchester Avenue elevated from 149th Street to Bronx Park (180th Street) was constructed; both the Second Avenue elevated and the IRT subway used this route. In 1908 the BRT opened a

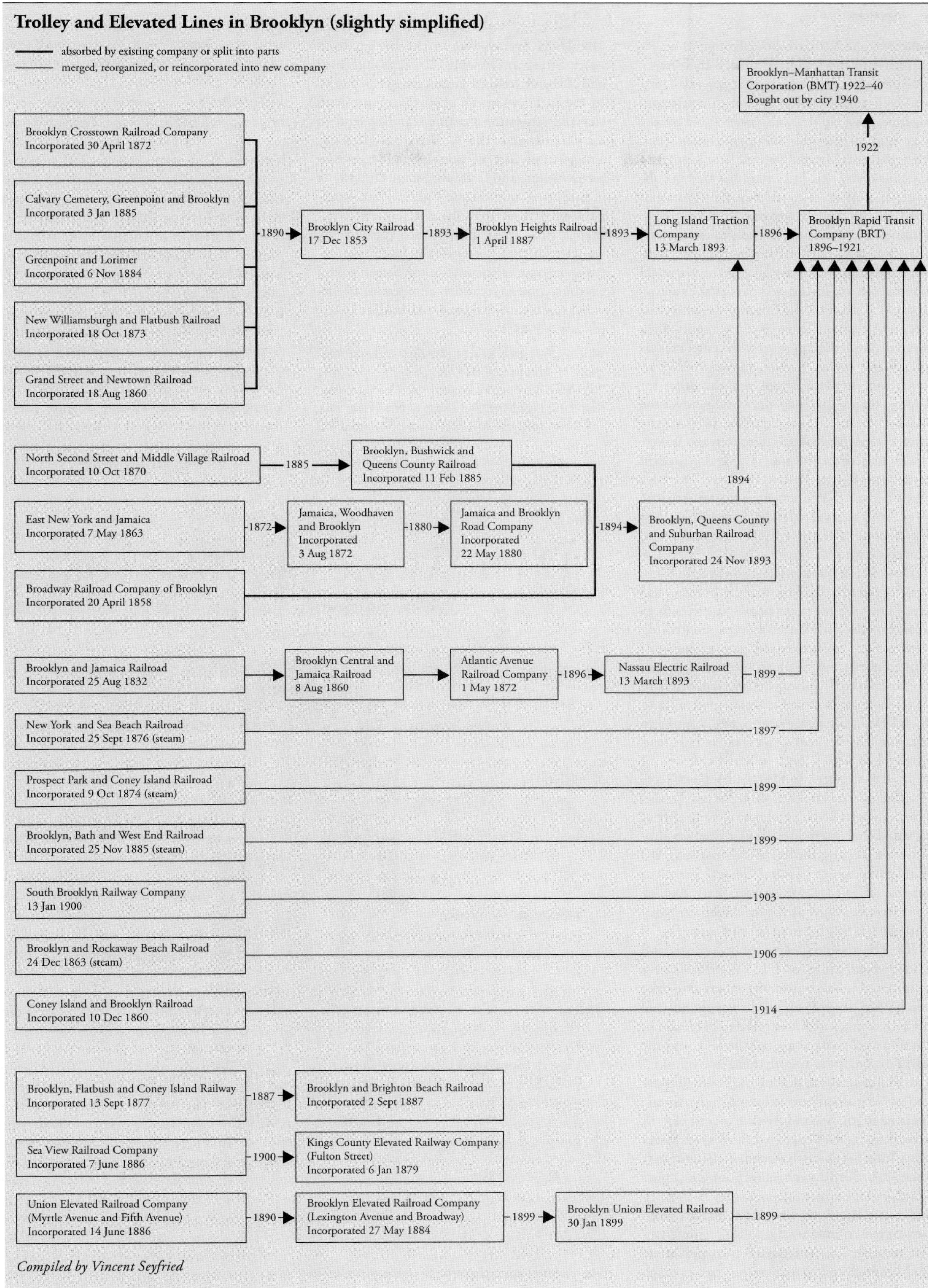

Trolley and Elevated Lines in Brooklyn (slightly simplified)
absorbed by existing company or split into parts
merged, reorganized, or reincorporated into new company
Brooklyn Crosstown Railroad Company Incorporated 30 April 1872
Calvary Cemetery, Greenpoint and Brooklyn Incorporated 3 Jan 1885
Greenpoint and Lorimer Incorporated 6 Nov 1884
New Williamsburgh and Flatbush Railroad Incorporated 18 Oct 1873
Grand Street and Newtown Railroad Incorporated 18 Aug 1860
1890
Brooklyn City Railroad 17 Dec 1853
1893
Brooklyn Heights Railroad 1 April 1887
1893
Long Island Traction Company 13 March 1893
1896
Brooklyn Rapid Transit Company (BRT) 1896–1921
1922
Brooklyn–Manhattan Transit Corporation (BMT) 1922–40 Bought out by city 1940
North Second Street and Middle Village Railroad Incorporated 10 Oct 1870
1885
Brooklyn, Bushwick and Queens County Railroad Incorporated 11 Feb 1885
East New York and Jamaica Incorporated 7 May 1863
1872
Jamaica, Woodhaven and Brooklyn Incorporated 3 Aug 1872
1880
Jamaica and Brooklyn Road Company Incorporated 22 May 1880
1894
Brooklyn, Queens County and Suburban Railroad Company Incorporated 24 Nov 1893
1894
Broadway Railroad Company of Brooklyn Incorporated 20 April 1858
Brooklyn and Jamaica Railroad Incorporated 25 Aug 1832
Brooklyn Central and Jamaica Railroad 8 Aug 1860
Atlantic Avenue Railroad Company 1 May 1872
1896
Nassau Electric Railroad 13 March 1893
1899
New York and Sea Beach Railroad Incorporated 25 Sept 1876 (steam)
1897
Prospect Park and Coney Island Railroad Incorporated 9 Oct 1874 (steam)
1899
Brooklyn, Bath and West End Railroad Incorporated 25 Nov 1885 (steam)
1899
South Brooklyn Railway Company 13 Jan 1900
1903
Brooklyn and Rockaway Beach Railroad 24 Dec 1863 (steam)
1906
Coney Island and Brooklyn Railroad Incorporated 10 Dec 1860
1914
Brooklyn, Flatbush and Coney Island Railway Incorporated 13 Sept 1877
1887
Brooklyn and Brighton Beach Railroad Incorporated 2 Sept 1887
Sea View Railroad Company Incorporated 7 June 1886
1900
Kings County Elevated Railway Company (Fulton Street) Incorporated 6 Jan 1879
Union Elevated Railroad Company (Myrtle Avenue and Fifth Avenue) Incorporated 14 June 1886
1890
Brooklyn Elevated Railroad Company (Lexington Avenue and Broadway) Incorporated 27 May 1884
1899
Brooklyn Union Elevated Railroad 30 Jan 1899
1899
Compiled by Vincent Seyfried

line over the Williamsburg Bridge as an alternative to the Brooklyn Bridge crossing.

Under the "dual contracts" project of 1913, the IRT and the BRT agreed to equip and operate new rapid transit lines built by the city and to rebuild many of the original elevated lines. In the Bronx, Brooklyn, and Queens many new lines were elevated in still-undeveloped outlying areas, saving costs and construction time compared to subway construction. The majority of these routes are still in everyday use in the early twenty-first century but are not elevated lines in the historical context; all are considered part of the subway system. Within the IRT elevated system, the Second Avenue, Third Avenue, and Ninth Avenue lines were equipped with center express tracks and many "hump" stations with two levels, one for local trains and the other for express trains. Two new drawbridges over the Harlem River connected these lines to the Bronx lines and enabled trains to reach Woodlawn (via Jerome Avenue, 1918) and Gun Hill Road and White Plains Road (via Webster Avenue, 1920). Tracks were also constructed over the Queensboro Bridge, providing access for Second Avenue trains to Astoria and Corona (1915–17).

Most of the elevated and surface lines belonging to the BRT and built before 1900 were now rebuilt with heavy-duty track to accommodate steel subway cars, permitting connections with new subways to be built along Fourth and Flatbush avenues in Brooklyn and along Broadway and Nassau Street in Manhattan; service was also extended to Richmond Hill, Jamaica, Astoria, and Corona in Queens. The elevated system reached its greatest level of use in 1921, when it carried 384 million passengers. In 1923 the BRT was reorganized as the Brooklyn–Manhattan Transit Corporation (BMT). After 1923 a number of elevated lines were abandoned because subways were being built parallel to them: the 42nd Street spur to Grand Central Terminal was closed in 1923, as were the Sixth Avenue spur between 53rd and 59th streets in 1924, and the East 34th Street spur in 1930.

The Depression decreased ridership, and under Mayor Fiorello H. La Guardia els were eliminated to raise property values along the tracks. The Sixth Avenue line was abandoned on 4 December 1938 and razed in 1939, and in June 1940 the city acquired the IRT and the BMT to facilitate the further removal of elevated lines, which during the following decades were abandoned along Ninth Avenue (11 June 1940), Second Avenue (north of 57th Street on 11 June 1940, south of 57th Street on 13 June 1942), Fifth Avenue in Brooklyn (1 June 1940), Third Avenue in Brooklyn (1 June 1940), Fulton Street (1 June 1940 and 29 April 1956), the Brooklyn Bridge (5 March 1944), Lexington Avenue (14 Oct 1950), Third Avenue between Chatham Square and 149th Street (12 May 1955), and Myrtle Avenue (4 Oct 1969). The Third Avenue line in the Bronx, from 149th Street to Gun Hill Road along Third and Webster avenues, closed on 29 April 1973. In the early twentieth century one pre-1904 elevated structure remains standing and in use—a portion of the "J" train (built in 1893), along Fulton Street, Brooklyn, between Alabama Avenue and Crescent Street. Brooklyn's Franklin Avenue shuttle right-of-way, originally an 1878 steam railroad to Coney Island, then a BRT/BMT pre-1904 elevated route, was rebuilt extensively in the late 1990s between Prospect Park and Fulton Street. About 70 route miles (113 route kilometers) of elevated rapid transit lines are still in daily use in New York City.

William Fullerton Reeves, *The First Elevated Railroads in Manhattan and the Bronx* (New York: New-York Historical Society, 1936); Alan Paul Kahn and Jack May, *The Tracks of New York*, vols. 2, 3 (New York: Electric Railroaders' Association, 1975, 1977); Robert Reed, *The New York Elevated* (South Brunswick, N.J.: A. S. Barnes, 1978); James Greller and Edward Watson, *The Brooklyn Elevated* (Hicksville, N.Y.: N.J. International, n.d. [?1985])

Erica Judge, Vincent Seyfried, Andrew Sparberg

elevators. The main mechanical means of moving vertically in New York City's tall buildings. Their beginnings in the city date back to 1853, when Elisha Graves Otis developed a device in his workshop in suburban Yonkers that would stop an elevator car with a severed cable from falling. Otis marketed his safety break aggressively and demonstrated it at New York City's Crystal Palace in 1854. Though Otis sold his first elevators to carry freight, elevators dedicated solely to passenger traffic soon followed, first in 1857 in the Broadway store of E. V. Haughwout and Company, and then elsewhere, most prominently in the Fifth Avenue Hotel, which

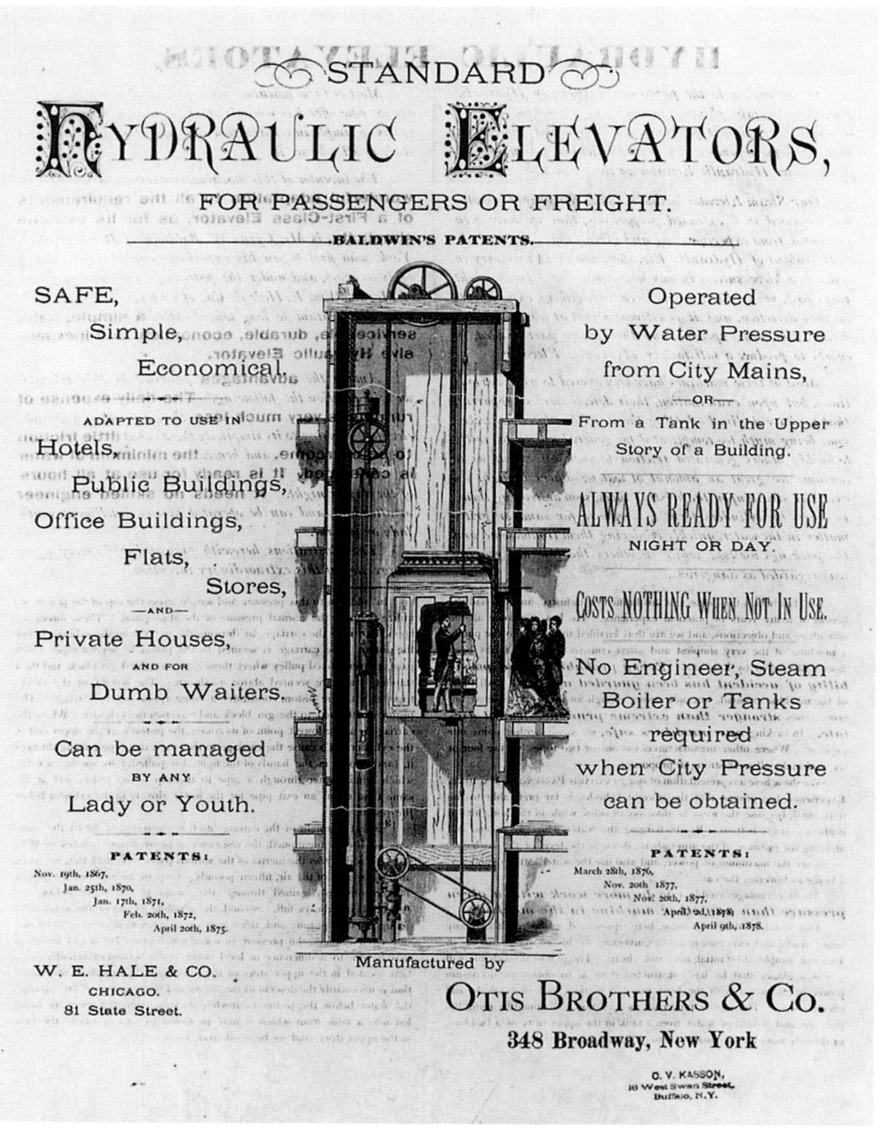

Otis Brothers advertisement for hydraulic elevators, 1878

opened in 1859 with an elevator designed by Otis Tufts. Elevators suddenly enabled architects and developers to construct buildings taller than four or six stories, increasing urban density.

As elevators became more common in the urban landscape, engineers continued to develop their technological capabilities. Elevators became taller and faster, especially after the shift from steam power to hydraulics in the 1870s, the introduction of electricity in the 1890s, and the introduction of the first gearless traction elevators in 1902. The first push-button elevator appeared in 1892, but it could manage only one trip at a time. Picking up multiple passengers and dropping them off at different floors remained impossible without elevator operators until about 1920, so all but the shortest buildings continued to rely on elevator operators until that time. Operators helped to develop the etiquette and social practices that evolved in elevators. They collaborated with passengers and building managers to create and enforce rules about facing the front of the elevator, taking off one's hat, whether to tip the operator, and so on. By the 1920s a new managerial focus on "service" encouraged managers to see operators as a valuable resource. They began to train operators to be friendly, to chat with passengers, and to allay fears about elevator travel. Though often demeaning, the social roles played by elevator operators helped them to build rapport with passengers that eventually led to leverage against their bosses. Operators built unions throughout the early twentieth century, but their first substantial victories did not come until the 1930s and 1940s, when they learned how to build solidarity with tenants and use it on the picket line and in labor arbitration. This was a short-lived victory; by the 1960s the higher cost of labor pushed New York City's building managers to install automatic elevators, displacing most operators. Those who remained, on expensive residential blocks and also scattered throughout the city, became institutions, well loved by their tenants and well protected by their union, Local 32B-32J of the Service Employees International Union.

In 1948 the Otis and Westinghouse companies began to sell the "Autotronic" and "Select-O-Matic" elevator systems, which automatically shifted traffic schedules over the course of the day. Elevator manufacturers have continued to experiment with new systems of traffic management. Milestones include the Elevonic 101 system released by Otis in 1979, which controlled elevators through microprocessors; the introduction of "fuzzy logic" in Japanese elevators in 1992; and the most recent generation of consoles that take reservations for specific floors and then direct passengers to specific elevators. This last innovation, called *destination dispatching,* mimics the abandoned role of the starter, returning the flow of elevator traffic to an earlier pattern; like all innovations in automatic elevators, it creates rules and algorithms that replicate patterns that operators and starters developed and practiced intuitively.

Grace Palladino, "When Militancy Isn't Enough: The Impact of Automation of New York City Building Service Workers, 1934–1970," *Labor History* 28, no. 2 (1987), 196–220; Jason Goodwin, *Otis: Giving Rise to the Modern City* (Chicago: Ivan R. Dee, 2001); Alisa Goetz, ed., *Up Down Across: Elevators, Escalators, and Moving Sidewalks* (London: Merrell Publishers, 2003); Patrick A. Carrajat, *The Past as Prologue: The History of the Elevator Industry in America, 1850–2001* (privately printed, 2005); Daniel Levinson Wilk, *Cliff Dwellers: Modern Service in New York City, 1800–1945* (diss., Duke University, 2005)

Daniel Levinson Wilk

Ellington, Duke [Edward Kennedy] (*b* Washington, D.C., 29 April 1899; *d* New York City, 24 May 1974). Bandleader, composer, and pianist. After a failed attempt to break into jazz in New York City in 1922, he returned in the following year to join the Washingtonians, led by the banjoist Elmer Snowden. A fellow sideman was the cornetist Bubber Miley, who was the first of the highly individual soloists with whom Ellington became associated. Later in 1923 the band began working at the Hollywood Club, on West 49th Street at Broadway. After Snowden left in 1924, Ellington took over as its leader, and until 1927 the band continued working regularly at the Hollywood (renamed the Kentucky Club in 1925). During this time the trombonist Tricky Sam Nanton joined the band, and Ellington recorded his first masterpiece, *Black and Tan Fantasy* (1927), written with Miley and featuring Miley's growling, "wa-wa" melody. The trumpeter Cootie Williams (who replaced Miley), the clarinetist Barney Bigard, and the saxophonists Johnny Hodges and Harry Carney brought new solo voices into the orchestra during its engagement from 1927 to 1931 at the Cotton Club (on Lenox Avenue at West 142nd Street). The setting was perverse—a pseudo-African "jungle" revue—but it stimulated Ellington, who brought forth jazz of a wide emotional and sonic palette and supplanted Fletcher Henderson as the foremost big-band leader in jazz.

Duke Ellington and his orchestra, 1923

In 1931 Ellington embarked on a lifetime of international touring, but he maintained his permanent residence in New York City, and his band often recorded and occasionally held engagements there, including brief returns to the Cotton Club in 1933 and 1937. Throughout his life he drew inspiration from the vitality of the city, a debt that he acknowledged most directly in the program notes to his composition *Harlem Air Shaft* (recorded in 1940). It was not Ellington but his protégé Billy Strayhorn who composed the well-known celebration of the city's transit system, *Take the "A" Train* (recorded in 1941), which became the band's theme song and was thus closely identified with its leader. In 1943 the orchestra broadcast on radio during its residency at the Hurricane Club (on Broadway and West 51st Street), and it performed at the Zanzibar (Broadway and West 49th Street) in 1945. Carnegie Hall was the venue for the premiere of several of Ellington's ambitious extended works in concerts given periodically between 1943 and 1951, and he first performed his *Second Sacred Concert* at the Cathedral of St. John the Divine in 1968. Ellington's addresses in the city included 381 Edgecomb Avenue (in the 1930s), apartment 4A at 935 St. Nicholas Avenue (1939–61), 400 Central Park West, his sister Ruth's apartment at 333 Riverside Drive (from 1961 until his death), and the Lincoln Towers, 140 West End Avenue.

Stanley Dance, *The World of Duke Ellington* (New York: Charles Scribner's Sons, 1970; repr. New York: Da Capo, 1981); James Lincoln Collier, *Duke Ellington* (New York: Oxford University Press, 1987); Mark Tucker, *Ellington: The Early Years* (Urbana: University of Illinois Press, 1991)

Barry Kernfeld

Elliott, Charles Loring (*b* Scipio, near Auburn, N.Y., 12 Oct 1812; *d* Albany, N.Y., 25 Aug 1868). Painter who studied art in Onondaga Hollow, New York, before moving to New York City in 1829. After training under John Quidor, he worked as an itinerant portraitist for 10 years. Competition from Henry Inman inspired him to hone his skills, and he gained a considerable reputation for fashionable portraiture, particularly of women. A prolific painter, he was a founder of the Century Association and belonged to the National Academy of Design. After Elliott's death his self-portrait at the National Academy of Design was draped in black and surrounded with more than 30 of his works.

Carrie Rebora Barratt

Ellis, Perry (Edwin) (*b* Portsmouth, Va., 30 March 1940; *d* New York City, 30 May 1986). Fashion designer. After receiving his master's degree in retailing from New York University in 1963, Ellis returned to his native Virginia where he began his fashion career as a buyer for the department store Miller and Rhoads. Singled out for his ability to predict which clothes would sell, he was recruited by the Vera Companies of Manhattan Industries in 1974. His talent at redesigning clothing earned him a chance to create his own line, and in 1978 he founded his eponymous clothing brand. Ellis's oversized look and offbeat sportswear designs broke away from the more conservative menswear designs of contemporaries such as Ralph Lauren and Calvin Klein. His talent earned him both financial success and fashion notoriety during the 1970s and 1980s, and his studio in New York City was famous for the creative freedom that it allowed young designers.

Anne E. Kornblut

Ellis Island. Island in Upper New York Bay, near the coast of New Jersey. Named for Samuel Ellis, who acquired the island in 1785, it was purchased from his heirs in 1808 by the State of New York and turned over to the federal government. For a time its fort and arsenal were used to defend the harbor; however, it is best known as the site of a federal immigration center, which, between its opening on 1 January 1892 and it closing in 1924, was the point of entry for more than 12 million immigrants, or 71 percent of all immigrants to the United States. The wooden buildings first used to house the immigration center were destroyed by fire in 1897; a fireproof replacement, designed in a French Renaissance style and trimmed with brick and limestone, was built by the local firm of Boring and Tilton and opened on 17 December 1900. Designed to accommodate as many as 500,000 immigrants a year, the new building became inadequate when the actual volume of immigrants each year was sometimes double this number. The government enlarged the island with landfill, from its original 3 acres (1.2 hectares) to 27.5 acres (11 hectares); added new wings and a third floor to the main building; and eventually erected 33 additional buildings. The heart of the center was a huge registry room where officials and health inspectors sought to deny entry to paupers, polygamists, people who were mentally defective, contract laborers, criminals, and people suffering from debilitating and contagious illnesses. More than 98 percent of the prospective immigrants gained entry, and 80 percent did so in fewer than eight hours. Once cleared, immigrants took a ferry to the Battery (about one-third of them settled in or near New York City) or a train to destinations throughout the country.

Congress in 1924 curtailed mass immigration and provided that those seeking entry would be screened in their countries of origin. This diminished the role of Ellis Island as an immigration center, and from that time it was used primarily to detain deportees. In 1954 the Immigration and Naturalization Service moved its offices to Manhattan, and Ellis Island was declared surplus property. The government tried to sell the island in the late 1950s, but lack of an adequate bid and public protest saved it from passing into private hands. In 1965 President Lyndon B. Johnson proclaimed the island a national monument to be run in conjunction with the Statue of Liberty by the National Park Service (NPS). Congress, however, declined to act on his request to appropriate funds for restoring the disused immigration facility as a historic site, and the facility deteriorated during the following years. In 1982 a commission formed by President Ronald Reagan set up a private foundation to collect corporate and individual donations for the repair and restoration of both Ellis Island and the Statue of Liberty. The project to restore Ellis Island began in 1984 with a budget of $160 million. The main building, restored to look as it did between 1918 and 1924 and housing a new museum of immigration, opened to the public in September 1990.

Ellis Island, 2009

Since the opening of the museum about two million people have visited Ellis Island annually. Further funding from the Statue of Liberty–Ellis Island Foundation and the labor of 12,000 volunteers from the Church of Jesus Christ of Latter-Day Saints (Mormons) enabled the NPS in 2001 to create the American Family Immigration Center, which provides public access to an automated database of millions of records of immigrants who passed through the facility. Visitors could enter only the main building, however, because the other structures had not been stabilized and there was no money or plan for their repair and restoration. The remaining buildings, mostly on the south side of the island, continued to deteriorate so badly that the National Trust for Historic Preservation placed them on its list of the 11 most endangered historic places. In 2001 the NPS signed an agreement with Save Ellis Island (SEI), another private nonprofit organization, for it to become the primary fund-raiser and partner to the NPS in "a program to preserve, rehabilitate, and enhance the South Side of Ellis Island." By 2007 most of the structures had been stabilized, and on 2 April, the NPS and SEI opened to visitors the restored Ferry Building, where they could view an exhibit titled *Future in the Balance: Immigrants, Public Health, and Ellis Island's Hospitals.*

Thomas M. Pitkin, *Keepers of the Gate: A History of Ellis Island* (New York: New York University Press, 1975); Harlan D. Unrau, *Ellis Island: Statue of Liberty National Monument, Historic Resource Study* (Denver: U.S. Department of the Interior, National Park Service, 1984); Barbara Blumberg, *Celebrating the Immigrant: An Administrative History of the Statue of Liberty National Monument, 1952–1982* (Boston: U.S. Department of the Interior, National Park Service, North Atlantic Regional Office, 1985)

Barbara Blumberg

Ellison, Ralph (Waldo) (*b* Oklahoma City, 1 March 1913; *d* New York City, 16 April 1994). Writer. Named after the American transcendentalist Ralph Waldo Emerson, he earned a scholarship through his trumpet playing in 1933 to Tuskegee Institute, where in 1936 he was introduced by the head of the music department to Howard University professor Alain Locke. Ellison set out for New York City after his third year, hoping to earn the wages to return to school in the fall. In Harlem, which Ellison would later recall as "overcrowded and exploited politically and economically," he took a series of odd jobs but ultimately began to focus on writing rather than art and music. Locke was in New York City while Ellison was staying at the Harlem Young Men's Christian Association and introduced the young intellectual to poet Langston Hughes, through whom he met novelist Richard Wright. In 1938 Ellison secured a job with the Federal Writers' Project researching folklore on "Negro culture." He remained on the project until 1942, when he began editing the journal *Negro Quarterly*. Though much of Ellison's writing was influenced by Marxism, by 1944 he had begun to question the dedication of communism to the black cause. Between 1943 and 1945 Ellison worked as a cook and baker on a merchant ship. During this period, he received a fellowship to begin his first novel, which was never published in its entirety.

During a 1945 trip to Vermont, Ellison first saw himself as an "invisible man," identified by others only as an embodiment of stereotypes and not as an individual. He worked on his novel *Invisible Man* for the next five years, interspersed with freelance jobs, before its publication in 1952; the following year it became a best seller and won the National Book Award. The novel is set largely in Harlem and ends with the Harlem riot of 1943. Ellison later taught at various academic institutions. During the 1960s he was criticized by some writers and political leaders for not being more active in the Black Power movement. He was also active in elite circles such as philanthropic boards and Manhattan's Century Club, an exclusive group that he lobbied hard to enter, strongly opposing the inclusion of women at the club. Ellison died of pancreatic cancer, leaving more than 2000 pages of an unfinished novel, which was published in 2010 as *Three Days before the Shooting*. He is buried in Trinity Church Cemetery in Washington Heights.

Garrett A. Felber

Elmhurst. Neighborhood in northwestern Queens (2000 pop. *ca* 100,000), bounded to the north by Roosevelt Avenue, to the east by Junction Boulevard, to the south by the Long Island Expressway, and to the west by railroad tracks (Conrail). Established in 1652 as Newtown, it was the administrative seat of the town of Newtown from 1683 to 1898, and was renamed in 1896 to avoid any association with the foul smells of Newtown Creek. The neighborhood became known for a fashionable housing development built north of the railroad station by the Cord Meyer Development Company between 1896 and 1910. Developments were added between 1905 and 1930 in adjoining areas, including Elmhurst Square, Elmhurst South, Elmhurst Heights, and New Elmhurst. After World War II Elmhurst evolved from an almost exclusively white, middle-class suburban community with a large Jewish and Italian population to the most ethnically diverse neighborhood in the city. By the 1980s immigrants from 112 different countries had settled there. Chinese immigrants accounted for one-fifth of the total, and there were large numbers as well from Colombia, Korea, India, the Philippines, the Dominican Republic, Ecuador, Pakistan, Peru, and Guyana. The neighborhood also had the first enclosed shopping mall in Queens (built in 1973). Three colonial churches are still used, two of which are known for their historic graveyards. The local subway station is Grand Avenue–Newtown. In the early twenty-first century Elmhurst was still considered the most ethnically diverse neighborhood in Queens.

Howard Arlington Northacker, *History of the First Presbyterian Church of Newtown at Elmhurst, New York* (New York: First Presbyterian Church of Newtown, 1927)

Vincent Seyfried

Elmhurst Hospital Center. Medical center and teaching hospital. The second-oldest institution in the municipal hospital system, it traces its origins to the establishment on the southern end of Blackwell's Island (now Roosevelt Island) of Island Hospital, which began as an infirmary for a prison nearby and grew into a general-care hospital for patients who could not be accommodated at Bellevue Hospital; the two hospitals were administratively separated in 1847. After a fire destroyed Island Hospital in 1858 prisoners confined on the island quarried granite there and erected a new structure. A stone from these years bearing the name of Island Hospital is now part of the southern facade of the hospital in Elmhurst. After a public outcry over filthy wards and poor care, the institution was renamed Charity Hospital in 1870 and its first medical superintendent was appointed. The hospital in 1875 opened a maternity ward, where its use of the new techniques of antisepsis made great progress against puerperal fever. In the same year the hospital opened a school of nursing, the fourth in the United States. Between 1910 and the 1930s the facility (now renamed City Hospital) grew from 742 beds to more than 1000. It was, however, impossible to reach by land until 1920, when an elevator connected Blackwell's Island to the Queensboro Bridge.

The need for expansion to serve the growing population of Queens led to the removal of City Hospital to 79-01 Broadway in 1957, at which time it was renamed City Hospital Center at Elmhurst. It became affiliated with the Mount Sinai School of Medicine in 1964 and took its current name in 1988. In the early twenty-first century the center had 531 beds and a wide range of outpatient services. It offered primary and specialty care to more than one million people in western Queens and was particularly well known for its emergency department, department of rehabilitation medicine, emergency psychiatric services, programs for patients with AIDS, and women's health services and for being a municipal acute care hospital with a skilled nursing unit.

Sandra Opdycke

El Morocco. Nightclub opened as a speakeasy in 1931 at 154 East 54th Street by John Perona. After the repeal of Prohibition, it became one of the most popular establishments in New York City. Known for its zebra-striped banquettes and glittering dark-blue ceiling, it attracted members of fashionable society, politicians, and entertainers. It moved to 307 East 54th Street in 1960. After Perona's death in 1961, a number of different owners closed and reopened the club several times. Although no longer an establishment of repute, it retained much of its original decor and ambiance until it closed in 1997.

Michael Batterberry and Ariane Batterberry, *On the Town in New York from 1776 to the Present* (New York: Charles Scribner's Sons, 1973)

Matthew Kachur

Elm Park. Industrial and residential area on the northern shore of Staten Island (2009 est. pop. 1500). Elm Park is bordered by Kill von Kull to the north, Port Richmond to the east, Mariner's Harbor to the west, and Forrest Avenue to the south. This part of Staten Island, along Richmond Terrace, was the earliest to industrialize. Nineteenth-century commercial enterprises included dye, varnish, brick, and chalk manufacturing works. The 1931 opening of the Bayonne Bridge linked Elm Park and its adjacent sections to the New Jersey industrial corridor, which includes Bayonne. Local children attend Public School 21. A substantial percentage of the school population is first-generation Latino.

Nancy V. Flood

Eloise. Children's book about a mischievous six-year-old girl named Eloise who lives at the Plaza Hotel. Written by actress Kay Thompson (*ca* 1903–98) and illustrated by Hilary Knight (*b* 1926), the book, fully titled *Eloise: A Book for Precocious Grown Ups,* was published in 1955 and became an instant success with both children and adults, selling more than 150,000 copies. "I am a city child," Eloise declares at the beginning of her story. "I live at the Plaza." Eloise and her pet dog and turtle have the run of the hotel, where she terrorizes the staff with her antics, such as ordering room service for one roast-beef bone, one raisin, and seven spoons with her signature line, "Charge it please and thank you very much." The character was rumored to have been based on Thompson's goddaughter Liza Minnelli, but Eloise more likely came from Thompson's nightclub act at the Plaza's Persian Room in 1954 when she would slip into character as a little girl during rehearsals, to great effect. Thompson, who lived rent-free at the Plaza, collaborated with Knight on *Eloise in Paris* (1957), *Eloise at Christmastime* (1958), and *Eloise in Moscow* (1959); a fifth book, *Eloise Takes a Bawth,* was scheduled for publication in 1964, but Thompson stopped publication (the book was finally published in 2002) and refused to allow any of the books to be republished during her life. Eloise became an iconic figure at the Plaza, and her portrait, painted by Knight, was hung in the hotel's Palm Court in 1957; after it was stolen during a fraternity party in 1960, Knight painted another one. As of the early twenty-first century the portrait remained in place, and Eloise fans continued to visit the famed hotel-dweller.

Kate Lauber

els. See Elevated railways.

Eltingville. Neighborhood in southwestern Staten Island (2009 pop. *ca* 20,000), bounded to the north by Greenridge, to the east by Great Kills, to the south by Lower New York Bay, and to the west by Annadale. The area was successively called South Side and Sea Side (1873), both after the name of its post office, before taking its current name, which recalls a family that settled the area in the early nineteenth century. The neighborhood was a wooded area where a largely Scandinavian population lived in small clusters of one-family houses until the completion in 1964 of the Verrazano–Narrows Bridge, which led to an influx from the Italian areas in Brooklyn, a sharp increase in the construction of one-family and multi-family houses and town houses, and a growth in commercial development along such streets as Hylan Boulevard. The population of Eltingville remained ethnically diverse in the early twenty-first century, with the Orthodox Jewish community increasing in size. The intersection of Richmond Avenue and Amboy Road is the oldest and most active commercial area and the site of a station of Staten Island Rapid Transit.

John-Paul Richiuso

Ely, Smith(, Jr.) (*b* Hanover, Morris County, N.J., 17 April 1825; *d* Livingston, N.J., 1 July 1911). Mayor. A prosperous merchant in New York City, he was elected as a Democrat to the state senate and twice to the U.S. House of Representatives during the 1870s, resigning after his appointment as mayor in 1877. He was reappointed in 1878 and was the commissioner of Central Park in 1897 and 1898.

Moses Sperry Beach, *The Ely Ancestry* (New York: Calumet, 1902), 219

James E. Mooney

Emerald Societies. Irish American fraternal societies organized according to occupation to engender Celtic pride. Music, particularly bagpipe bands, is a key component of the organizations. In the early twenty-first century the Grand Council of United Emerald Societies boasted more than 10,000 members and 25 affiliate societies, located predominantly in the the tri-state area. There are affiliate societies for employees of federal, state, and city agencies (including the police and fire departments) as well as for the utilities.

John J. Concannon

Emergency Medical Service. Principal provider of emergency medical care outside the hospital in New York City. It was formed in 1970 by the same legislation that established the New York City Health and Hospitals Corporation. From 1972 all employees dealing with patients were required to be eligible for state certification as emergency medical technicians (EMTs), with training in first aid, cardiopulmonary resuscitation, and emergency childbirth. The service inaugurated its own EMT training program in 1973; the first teams of EMTs began working in city ambulances in 1975; and the service was designated the coordinating agency for emergency medical care in New York City in 1977, with the authority to dispatch ambulances from both municipal and private hospitals. The service introduced a training program in 1984 for paramedics, who in addition to the training given to EMTs learn such procedures as reading electrocardiograms. Calls to the Emergency Medical Service are transmitted to the 911 emergency system of the Police Department; in response it dispatches basic life-support ambulances, staffed by two EMTs, and advanced life-support ambulances, staffed by two paramedics.

Andrea Balis

Emerson, Haven (*b* New York City, 19 Oct 1874; *d* New York City, 21 May 1957). Physician and public health official. As the commissioner of the Metropolitan Board of Health from 1915 to 1917 he expanded the health district plan to Queens and dealt effectively with the polio epidemic of 1916. From 1922 to 1940 he was the director of the DeLamar Institute of Public Health at Columbia University. He was among the first to advocate treating alcoholism as a disease and helped to form the American Heart Association. As the chairman for the American Public Health Association of the Committee on Control of Communicable Diseases he produced several influential reports, among them "Control of Communicable Diseases in Man" (1917). He lived for many years on the East Side of Manhattan.

Joseph S. Lieber

Emerson Hill. Neighborhood in northeastern Staten Island, bounded to the north by the Staten Island Expressway, to the east by Richmond Road, to the south by Dongan Hills, and to the west by Ocean Terrace. It occupies a site with one of the highest elevations in the city (300 feet [90 meters]) and affords views of the Narrows and New York Harbor. The history of the area is closely linked to the New England transcendentalists. From 1837 to 1864 it was the home of William Emerson, a judge of Richmond County from 1841 to 1843 whose house at the foot of the hill, called the Snuggery, was visited occasionally by his brother Ralph Waldo Emerson and from May to October 1843 by Henry David Thoreau, who worked as a tutor to Emerson's children. When fire destroyed the Snuggery in 1855, Emerson built a house on the hill that later became known as the Unger House. Iron was mined in the area in the middle of the nineteenth century, but declined by the 1870s. The hill was converted into a private community around 1930 by the real estate developer Cornelius G. Kolff, who gave it its current name. Only two roads lead to the enclave: Emerson Drive to the north and Douglas Road to the east. In the early twenty-first century Emerson Hill was a small, semiprivate community of fine one-family homes.

John-Paul Richiuso

Emery Roth and Sons. Architectural firm. Its founder, Emery Roth, Sr. (1871–1948), emigrated alone from Hungary at the age of 13; in 1893 he settled in New York City, where he worked as a draftsman until he bought an existing practice in 1898. The firm specialized in large residential buildings, particularly hotels and luxury apartments, among them the Ritz Tower (1926), the Beresford (1929), and the San Remo (1930). Roth's sons Julian and Richard were partners by the 1930s, and after World War II they became leading designers of office towers with highly functional, economical interiors. In both longevity and volume, Emery Roth and Sons ranks among the premier architectural firms in New York City.

Steven Ruttenbaum, *Mansions in the Sky: The Skyscraper Palazzi of Emery Roth* (New York: Balsam, 1986)

Carol Willis

Emigrant Savings Bank. New York City's only survivor of the nineteenth-century thrift movement still operating under its own name. In 1925 it was the largest savings bank in the United States. Depositors were overwhelmingly Irish for the bank's first century because of its close relationship with the Irish Emigrant Society (established 1841), a local group that handled remittances to Ireland. These de facto banking functions led the society, under the leadership of Gregory Dillon, a Catholic native of County Roscommon, and Joseph Stuart, a Presbyterian from County Armagh, to charter the Emigrant Industrial Savings Bank. It opened on 30 September 1850 at 51 Chambers Street, an address it maintained until 1969 when its headquarters moved to 5 East 42nd Street. Through the agency of Emigrant Savings Bank, Archbishop John Hughes financed a brick-and-mortar infrastructure for the rapidly expanding Catholic population, including a $400,000 mortgage for St. Patrick's (new cathedral). Emigrant's reputation as a Catholic bank was buttressed by its officers' charitable work. Emigrant's Test Books, transferred to the New York Public Library in 1995, are a rich source for Irish genealogy and social history. As of 2010 it operated 34 branches in the New York city metropolitan area.

Marion R. Casey, "Refractive History: Memory and the Founders of the Emigrant Savings Bank," *Making the Irish American: History and Heritage of the Irish in the United States,* ed. J. J. Lee and M. R. Casey (New York: New York University Press, 2006)

Marion R. Casey

Emmet, Thomas Addis (*b* Cork, Ireland, 24 April 1764; *d* New York City, 14 Nov 1827). Lawyer. He moved to New York City in 1804. Although he had extensive schooling and experience, his prominence in the Irish Rebellion against British rule in 1798 raised the suspicions of conservative Federalists in the city, who initially opposed his admission to the bar. Once accepted he quickly became what the jurist Joseph Story called "the favorite counsellor of New York." His most notable case was *Gibbons v. Ogden* (1824), in which he unsuccessfully defended before the U.S. Supreme Court the legality of the steamboat monopoly of New York State. He lived at 48 White Street.

Horace H. Hagan, *Eight Great American Lawyers* (Oklahoma City: Harlow, 1923)

Frederick S. Voss

Emmett, Dan(iel Decatur) (*b* Mount Vernon, Ohio, 29 Oct 1815; *d* Mount Vernon, 28 June 1904). Minstrel. With three other unemployed musicians he formed the Virginia Minstrels in February 1843 and presented the first American minstrel show in New York City, which inspired a nationwide obsession with the genre. Between 1858 and 1866 he composed and performed songs for Bryant's Minstrels, including "Blue Tail Fly" and "Turkey in the Straw." He is credited with writing "Dixie" ("Dixie's Land") for the minstrel stage in New York City in 1859, which was adopted by the Confederacy as its unofficial anthem; however, the authorship of the song has been and continues to be disputed.

Hans Nathan, *Dan Emmett and the Rise of Early Negro Minstrelsy* (Norman: University of Oklahoma Press, 1962; repr. 1977)

Robert B. Winans

Empire Blue Cross and Blue Shield. Private, nonprofit firm that provides health insurance in New York State, formed in 1973 by the merger of the Associated Hospital Service, or Blue Cross (1935), and the United Medical Service, or Blue Shield (1945). Soon after its formation it set up a health maintenance organization (Health Net) and implemented a hospital reimbursement system mandated by the state to contain the cost of inpatient care. During the mid-1990s the firm was one of few remaining nonprofit insurers in the United States to use "community rating," a system under which small group and individual customers with the same policy are charged the same premium regardless of how frequently they use medical services. It also continued to offer open enrollment, or guaranteed acceptance, to all applicants able to pay premiums, regardless of their medical status; state regulations helped to support this practice by controlling the rate of increase in hospital rates, thus reducing the gap between reimbursements paid by Blue Cross and Blue Shield and those paid by competing, profit-making insurers. In the early twenty-first century Empire Blue Cross and Blue Shield provided insurance to nearly five million Americans, most of them in New York City and its surrounding counties.

Robert A. Padgug

Empire Insurance Company. Insurance firm. Formed on 1 March 1925 as the Red Cab Mutual Casualty Company and renamed Empire Mutual Casualty in 1937, the firm took the name Empire Mutual Insurance Company in 1954, when its charter was broadened to permit underwriting property insurance as well as casualty insurance. It ceased underwriting in February 1977, when a financial examination by the state Department of Insurance showed its financial condition to be unsound. Under the control of the department, Empire was reorganized as a stock company on 1 January 1988 with offices at 122 Fifth Avenue. In 1998 it moved into the newly constructed Brooklyn Renaissance Plaza at 335 Adams Street.

Robert J. Gibbons

Empire State Building. Skyscraper on a site of 2 acres (0.8 hectare) on Fifth Avenue between 33rd and 34th streets. At 1250 feet (381 meters) in height, it culminated the commercial real estate boom of the 1920s and remained the world's tallest building until the 1970s. The project was a purely speculative venture for which construction costs were initially estimated at $50 million. The chief investors were the self-made millionaire John J. Raskob and the industrialist Pierre S. du Pont; Alfred E. Smith was the head of the corporation. Contracts for the project were signed in September 1929, only weeks before the stock market crash. The architectural firm of Shreve, Lamb and Harmon collaborated with structural and mechanical engineers and the general contractors Starrett Brothers and Eken to develop the design, guided throughout by the principle of maximum return on investment. Breaking records not only for height but for speed of construction, the entire operation was a spectacular demonstration of modern engineering and managerial efficiency. Demolition of the existing building on the site, the Waldorf-Astoria, began on 1 October 1929, and the first structural steel columns were set on 7 April 1930. At the peak of operations 3500 people were employed on construction, and in one 10-day period 14 stories were added to the frame. The job was completed 45 days ahead of schedule and $5 million under budget. Opening ceremonies were held on 1 May 1931 to wide acclaim, but leasing was slow during the Depression, and the building remained only half rented until after World War II, prompting some to call it the "Empty State."

Empire State Building, ca *1930*

On the foggy Saturday morning of 28 July 1945, a B-25 bomber crashed into the 79th story, killing 14 people but causing only minor damage to the structure. In 1953 a television antenna 200 feet (60 meters) tall was placed atop the structure; floodlighting of the upper stories was introduced in 1964. Usually described as 102 stories tall, the tower includes 85 stories of commercial and office space (2,158,000 square feet [200,665 square meters]) and an observation deck. A metal-and-glass "mooring mast" for dirigibles (used successfully only once, but immortalized by the 1933 film *King Kong*) added the equivalent of 16 stories. Admired for its majesty and fine proportions, the Empire State Building is visible from many parts of the city and dominates the skyline of midtown Manhattan. The American Civil Society of Engineers has named it one of the Seven Wonders of the Modern World. It was designated a National Historic Landmark in 1986. After the destruction of the World Trade Center in the 11 September 2001 terrorist attacks, the Empire State Building once again became the tallest building in New York City. A $550 million renovation, including $20 million to make the building more energy efficient, is expected to be finished in 2010.

Carol Willis, ed., *Building the Empire State* (New York: W. W. Norton, 1998)

Carol Willis

Encyclopedia of the Social Sciences. Encyclopedia in 15 volumes edited in New York City and published during 1930–35 by Macmillan, sponsored by the Social Science Research Council under the editorship of E. R. A. Seligman of Columbia University and Alvin Johnson of the New School for Social Research. The work was influential in legitimating a school of American social science premised on scientific rationalism, cultural pluralism, and democratic social reform. Contributors to the *Encyclopedia of the Social Sciences* included the philosophers John Dewey and Morris Raphael Cohen, the anthropologist Franz Boas, the economist Wesley Mitchell, the political scientist Harold Laski, and the historian Charles A. Beard.

Peter Rutkoff and William B. Scott, *New School: A History of the New School for Social Research* (New York: Free Press, 1986)

Peter M. Rutkoff, William B. Scott

Endicott and Company. Firm of lithographers. Formed in Baltimore as Endicott and Swett, it was moved to New York City in 1831 by George Endicott (1802–48), who by 1840 was joined by his brother William (circa 1817–51); in 1845 the firm was renamed G. and W. Endicott. The offices were at various locations during its early years and then successively at 59 Beekman Street (from 1846), 57 Beekman Street (1870–86), and 51 Cedar Street. The firm produced portraits, sheet music, membership certificates, views, and book illustrations and frequently worked for Currier and Ives. It became a leader in the industry in the mid-nineteenth century by engaging versatile painters and printers in an environment that encouraged work of high quality. The firm's artists included George T. Sanford (1815–48), John Penniman (1817–50), Francis D'Avignon (1813–after 1860), and Charles Parsons (1821–1910), a maritime specialist who began as an apprentice printer for the Endicotts and later became the head of the art department at Harper and Brothers. After the death of the brothers, George's widow, Sarah, and their son Francis took control of the business. Operations and products were standardized in 1851, and in the following year the firm was renamed Endicott and Company and began to cater to a mass market with prints of whaling, equine subjects, and later Civil War scenes. From 1886 to 1896 the firm was run by the second George Endicott, who renamed the firm after himself. Prints of New York City by Endicott and Company include "Park Hotel" (1834), "St. Thomas Chapel, Ravenswood (Queens)" (1839–40), two interior views of the U.S. Post Office on lower Broadway (1845), "View of the Ruins of the Great Fire" (1845), and "Harlem Bridge" (n.d.). The firm won awards for excellence in 1835, 1836, 1846, 1848, and 1856 at the annual American Institute Fair of New York City.

Wendy Shadwell

Engeman, William A. (*b* New York City, 1838; *d* Brooklyn, 11 Jan 1884). Businessman. As a young man he became wealthy by selling provisions to the Union army. After the Civil War he moved to Brooklyn, where he purchased undeveloped lots in Duck Hill, a section of Coney Island now known as Brighton Beach. By 1868 he owned 200 acres (80 hectares) of land on which he built the Ocean Hotel. He later sold much of his property and used the proceeds to introduce thoroughbred racing to Coney Island in 1879.

Stephen Weinstein

engineering. New York State was the birthplace of professional engineering in the United States. Civil engineering was first offered as an academic subject by the U.S. Military Academy at West Point in 1801, and degrees in the subject were first granted by Rensselaer Polytechnic Institute in 1835. On 5 November 1852 the first professional national engineering society, the Association of Civil Engineers (ASCE), was formed in New York City by 12 engineers led by Alfred W. Craven, chief engineer of the Croton Aqueduct Department. Often civil engineers engaged in public works met with conflict in the municipal bureaucracy: Craven argued that the authority for developing public works should rest with the experts in his office rather than with politicians, and in 1860 he was removed from office for insubordination by Mayor Fernando Wood. In 1865 the state legislature supported Craven by authorizing him to plan and manage the sewage system in Manhattan. The membership of the ASCE remained at 12 in

Footbridge suspended over construction on the Brooklyn Bridge, 1881

1867, but increased to 212 in 1871 and to 1090 in 1891. Around the turn of the century several other engineering societies were formed in New York City: the American Society of Mechanical Engineers (1880), the American Institute of Electrical Engineers (1884), and the Institute of Radio Engineers (1912). During these years the engineering profession became divided into factions, as the mining, mechanical, and electrical branches forged alliances with business and industry, while civil engineers continued to work on public projects. In 1894 Colonel George E. Waring, Jr., was appointed the street cleaning commissioner of New York City. A staunch environmentalist, he implemented changes relating not only to street cleaning but also to the water supply, sewerage, drainage, street paving, and household sanitation. The successful efforts of Craven and Waring to unify the administration of the city's public works were furthered during the first two decades of the twentieth century by Nelson P. Lewis, chief engineer of the Board of Estimate and Apportionment from 1902, who saw public works as the foundation of a comprehensive city plan that also provided for transportation and the street system, recreation facilities and public buildings, and a coordinated sanitary system. His efforts to unify engineering and planning culminated in 1921 in his work on the Regional Plan of New York and Its Environs, sponsored by the Russell Sage Foundation, which addressed the development of parts of New Jersey and Connecticut in addition to that of the city.

The trend toward integrating municipal services was reversed during the New Deal, when engineering efforts became administered by public authorities with specialized areas of jurisdiction: these included, in the field of transportation, the Triborough Bridge and Tunnel Authority, the New York City Transit

Authority, and the Port of New York Authority, and in sanitation, the Interstate Sanitation Commission. These divisions reflected the continued specialization of engineering in general, which persisted despite the efforts of some engineers in the city to unify the profession.

In the early twenty-first century engineering was taught at several institutions of higher learning in New York City, including the Fu School of Engineering at Columbia University (formed in 1864 as the School of Mines; given its current name in 1926), Cooper Union, and Polytechnic University, which merged with New York University in 2009.

Raymond H. Merritt, *Engineering in American Society, 1850–1875* (Lexington: University Press of Kentucky, 1969); Edwin T. Layton, *The Revolt of the Engineers: Social Responsibility and the American Engineering Profession* (Cleveland: Case Western Reserve University Press, 1971); Eugene P. Moehring, *Public Works and the Patterns of Urban Real Estate Growth in Manhattan, 1835–1894* (New York: Arno, 1981)

Joanne Abel Goldman

English. An English fleet took possession of New Netherland in 1664, sent by James, the duke of York (the future King James II, 1685–88). At the time New Amsterdam, the colonial capital, was inhabited by about 1500 people of Flemish, Walloon, French Huguenot, German, Danish, and Swedish background, most of whom spoke Dutch.

The concentration of the Dutch in New York City posed a threat to the English regime. When a Dutch fleet attacked the colony in 1673, the Dutch population welcomed the invaders and for 15 months supported a restoration of New Netherland. At the end of the war the States General again surrendered the colony to England, which restored its institutions for local and provincial government, including an elective assembly (briefly from 1683 to 1685; permanently after 1691). The city charter of 1686, granted by Governor Thomas Dongan, created a municipal government patterned after those of England, with an appointive mayor and an elective Board of Aldermen and Common Council.

The English population grew slowly, and the shortage of single English women in New York at the time led many unmarried English men to seek brides among the Dutch and the French. For a generation after the conquest the children of Englishmen who intermarried were often brought up in the Dutch Reformed Church, which was better organized in New York than the Church of England. Between 1677 and 1703, when about 5000 people lived in New York, the English share of the city's European population grew only from 20 to 25 percent, but at the same time the English assumed a disproportionate share of the highest offices and wealthiest occupations. Along with the French, the English dominated the Dock Ward near the East River, the city's richest neighborhood. Anglicans formed Trinity Church and installed William Vesey as its first rector on Christmas Day in 1697. Dutch families, particularly the wealthier ones, began learning English and taking other steps to help assimilate into the culture of the conquerors.

During the eighteenth century the English built cultural institutions to sustain their dominant position. William Bradford's weekly newspaper the *New York Gazette* became the first newspaper in the city in 1725, soon joined by John Peter Zenger's more contentious *New York Weekly Journal.* English-speaking religious denominations continued to grow and acquired greater autonomy; a Quaker meeting was formed in 1681, as were Baptist and Presbyterian congregations in 1716. From 1741 to 1758 a New Side (revivalist) Presbyterian Synod made New York City its headquarters. Among Anglicans, Trinity Church erected St. George's Chapel in 1752 and St. Paul's Chapel in 1766 (now the oldest public building in Manhattan). It also opened King's College in 1754. With the Anglican minister Samuel Johnson as its first president, King's graduated its first class in 1758; it was reopened as Columbia College after the American Revolution.

By the time of the American Revolution the city had 21,000 inhabitants, and the English were the dominant ethnic group in both numbers and influence. At the first federal census in 1790 the total population of the city was more than 33,000, exceeded in the United States only by Philadelphia; 74.2 percent of the total was of British origin, including the English (41.6 percent), Scots-Irish (14.9 percent), Irish (7.9 percent), Scots (7.5 percent), and Welsh (2.3 percent). The Dutch population had fallen to 16.5 percent of the total. In southern New York the Dutch constituted a majority (59 percent) only in Kings County, and there the English share of the population had risen to 31.5 percent.

The victory of the United States in the war made New York City and its surrounding communities more densely British than they had ever been. English immigration resumed soon after the war ended. Although most English immigrants assimilated easily, they encountered some of the same problems faced by other ethnic groups in New York City, as well as many of their own. During the War of 1812 the federal government imposed legal and physical restrictions on British citizens, and English merchants engaged in international trade were interned in an unprovisioned camp at Fishkill, New York. From 1834 to 1858 English immigrants accounted for a disproportionate share of the residents in Blackwell's Island Penitentiary and City Prison, Bellevue Hospital, the almshouse, and the lunatic asylum, sometimes twice as high as in the city as a whole. The St. George's Society, a club for upper-class professionals and merchants formed in 1770, attempted to aid English immigrants. Religious organizations formed by the British, such as the Salvation Army and the Young Men's Christian Association, also took root in the city and made efforts to assist the needy.

Throughout the nineteenth century many skilled workers and craftsmen emigrated from Great Britain. Textile workers, carpenters, and stonecutters often received better pay in New York City than they did at home. As passage across the Atlantic became cheaper and easier, the number of seasonal workers in New York City increased. At mid-century an estimated 800 English and Scottish bricklayers sailed to the city to work during the summer months. Prominent among English immigrants were architects such as Richard M. Upjohn and Thomas Adams, and landscapers such as Calvert Vaux, who designed much of Central Park. Women found work primarily as domestic servants and dressmakers.

Workers were assisted by groups such as the General Society of Mechanics and Tradesmen (1785), which in 1820 established a free school for the sons and daughters of deceased and indigent members, and in the following year added an apprentices' library. The society in 1833 began what were probably the first free lecture courses in New York City. In the 1820s and 1830s the English joined unions of carpenters, ship carpenters, typographers, printers, and bakers. The membership list of the New York Union Society of Journeymen House Carpenters in 1833–36 consists largely of English, Scottish, and Irish names. Fanny Wright, Robert Dale Owen, Thomas Skidmore, and George Henry Evans all helped to form the New York Workingmen's Party in 1829. In the 1830s several wealthy Englishmen formed a social club on Park Place, where they gathered for meals and games such as billiards, whist, chess, and checkers. The English in the city celebrated national holidays such as St. George's Day and (later) Queen Victoria's jubilees (1887, 1897). The city also had a number of pubs that served whiskey and porter, like the Richard the Third House, the Brown Jug Tavern, Luke Shaw's Eagle Porter House, and the Albion Hotel.

The English brought their sports as well, including English athletic equipment, regulations, gambling rules, sports magazines and newspapers, and sporting clothes. English immigrants created communities centered around sport that fostered the development of sporting clubs and associations. Two well-known cricket clubs in the city were the St. George Cricket Club (1838) and the New York Cricket Club (1844). The English wove into the cultural fabric of New York a love of sport and the human connections it can provide. English colonists introduced into New York such sports as ninepins, skittles, bowls, ball games, horse racing, fox hunting, rugby, soccer, and wrestling. After the American

Revolution, English immigrants were influential in introducing such sports as rowing, boxing, cricket, archery, croquet, track and field, tennis, badminton, polo, and yachting.

Most of those who emigrated from England in the nineteenth century were young and either Anglican or Methodist. They initially attended churches already existing in the city and later joined those built to sustain interest in Anglicanism, such as the Free Church of St. George the Martyr, founded in the 1840s. During the first half of the nineteenth century most of the English in New York City read American newspapers, only a few of which were devoted to English interests. Among those published in New York City were *The Albion; or, British, Colonial, and Foreign Weekly Gazette,* which catered to an educated readership and was published from the 1820s to the 1870s, and the *Anglo-American,* which focused on literary articles and news from England, and lasted only a few years in the 1840s. The *Old Countryman,* a newspaper aimed at the less educated and the working man, merged with another newspaper, the *Emigrant,* which ceased publication in the 1840s.

In 1855 the English were the third-largest ethnic group in the city (after the Irish and the Germans), and were represented in all city wards. The 16th ward, which extended along the Hudson River from 14th Street to 26th Street, had 1957 English immigrants, more than any other ward. The wealthy tended to live in Greenwich Village; laborers commonly lived in the northwestern wards of the city, or on the Lower East Side between Peck Slip and Catherine Street. The number of English immigrants in the city increased from 22,714 in 1885 to 35,907 by 1890, during which time they nevertheless declined as a proportion of the foreign-born from 7 percent to 5.5 percent and as a proportion of the total population from 3.6 percent to 2.4 percent. In Brooklyn the number of English immigrants also increased absolutely (from 12,611 in 1855 to 27,754 in 1890) and declined relatively. During the depression of 1893–97 and into the twentieth century, the number of English immigrants settling in New York City dropped sharply, and by 1920 they represented only 1.3 percent of the total population. English social institutions weakened, schools and churches opened their doors to other ethnic and religious groups, immigrants intermarried, and the group lost much of its distinctive character.

After 1920 women who immigrated to the United States from Britain outnumbered men. The War Brides Act of 1946 increased the number of English women entering New York City, and of the 58,259 English immigrants in the city in 1960, women accounted for 57 percent. The St. George's Society, which along with the British–American Chamber of Commerce is one of the few organizations catering to the city's English community, began accepting women as members in 1989.

Immigration laws increasingly favored the highly skilled and educated. In the 1970s many scientists, engineers, and especially physicians left England for the better opportunities and lower taxes available to them in New York City. In 2000, 28,996 immigrants entered the city from the United Kingdom, and the 2000 census showed that U.K. immigrants made up 2.7 percent of Manhattan's population, one of the city's five largest groups of foreign residents. The 2004 American Community Survey estimated 25,128 immigrants from the United Kingdom and 9205 from England.

Thomas J. Archdeacon, *New York City, 1664–1710: Conquest and Change* (Ithaca, N.Y.: Cornell University Press, 1976); Robert C. Ritchie, *The Duke's Province: A Study of New York Politics and Society, 1664–1691* (Chapel Hill: University of North Carolina Press, 1977); Joyce D. Goodfriend, *Before the Melting Pot: Society and Culture in Colonial New York City, 1664–1730* (Princeton, N.J.: Princeton University Press, 1992)

Juliana F. Gilheany, John M. Murrin

Environmental Defense Fund [EDF]. Environmental advocacy group formed in 1967 formerly known as Environmental Defense. It became one of the nation's leading watchdog organizations and pioneered the use of litigation, the courts, and policy research to focus public attention on strong environmental laws and their strict enforcement. The EDF grew out of the activities of the Brookhaven [New York] Town Natural Resources Committee in the mid-1960s. In later decades the EDF relocated to 257 Park Avenue South in New York City and became a national leader in environmental protection and standards enforcement in areas such as endangered species, the protection of fisheries, farm and food policy, public health, and global warming.

Marion Lane Rogers, *Acorn Days: The Environmental Defense Fund and How It Grew* (New York: Environmental Defense Fund, 1996)

Jared Day

E. P. Dutton. Book publisher. Opened in 1852 as Ide and Dutton, it was renamed E. P. Dutton and Company in 1858 when Edward Payson Dutton acquired full ownership of the business. In 1868 a branch office was opened at 726 Broadway in New York City, and the following year the firm's headquarters moved to 713 Broadway. E. C. Swayne, head salesman and European representative for the firm, arranged a partnership between the firm and the German printer Louis Nister, whose fine color illustrations increased the sales of Dutton's children's books and novelty items; Swayne became a partner in 1878. With 700 titles in its religious and juvenile lines alone, the firm moved in 1882 to 31 West 23rd Street. In 1906 the firm moved into mass-market publishing when it became the American publisher of Everyman's Library, a series of classic literature reprints. The company moved to 681 Fifth Avenue in 1911 and in 1913 expanded into educational publishing by acquiring the Thompson–Brown Company, a textbook publisher. Dutton died in 1923, leaving John Macrae and Henry Clapp Smith as trustees. In 1928 the two divided the firm, with Macrae remaining in publishing and Smith taking over the retail shop, which he renamed Dutton's. Macrae soon moved his operation back downtown to 300 Park Avenue South, near its former location.

Dutton published such authors as Van Wyck Brooks, Gore Vidal (who was briefly an editor in 1946), Maurice Herzog, Françoise Sagan, Jorge Luis Borges, and Aleksandr Solzhenitsyn and other writers from the Soviet Union. Children's books by such authors as A. A. Milne and Judy Blume were a mainstay. In 1962 the firm moved to 201 Park Avenue South. Under the direction of John (Jack) Macrae III in the 1970s, the firm changed owners several times; in 1975 it was sold to the Elsevier Publishing Company. Dutton made several acquisitions in the late 1970s and published such authors as Mickey Spillane, John Irving, Joyce Carol Oates, Lawrence Durrell, and Gail Sheehy. In 1978 it moved to 2 Park Avenue, and in 1981 it was purchased from Elsevier by the Dyson–Kissner–Moran Corporation. In 1986 it was acquired by the Penguin Group, where it currently operates as an imprint. Dutton and Penguin moved in 1990 to 375 Hudson Street.

Marjorie Harrison

Episcopalians. The Episcopal Church in America began as part of the Church of England and was therefore known as Anglican. In 1674 the first ministerial stipend was paid for Anglican services in New York City, and by 1686 the bishop of London probably had jurisdiction over Anglican churches in the colony of New York. In 1686 Governor Edmund Andros decreed that services according to the Book of Common Prayer should be held every Sunday and holy day, and that Communion should be administered regularly; he also provided for the licensing of members of the clergy and schoolteachers by the archbishop of Canterbury. Students preparing for ordination were tutored privately by senior clergy. In 1692 there were about 90 Anglican families in New York City and two Anglican congregations in the entire province. Trinity Church was formed by royal charter on 6 May 1697. Its first rector was William Vesey, an Anglican deacon and priest, and until 1700 its congregation met in the only Anglican church building in the province. In 1705 it received a farm of 62 acres (25 hectares) from Queen Anne. Ten congregations were formed in the province between 1700 and 1710, all supported by the Church of England. Anglican texts including the Book of Common Prayer were published in New York City as early as 1710. King's College was chartered under Anglican auspices in 1754 with the provisions that its presiding officer be an Anglican and that its chapel conform to the Anglican prayer book. By 1770 St. Paul's Chapel and St. George's Chapel also opened. Many Anglicans remained loyal to the Crown and fled the city after the American Revolution, among them Charles Inglis, the rector of Trinity Church from 1777 (he later became the first bishop of Nova Scotia). The first Anglican services in Brooklyn were held on Fulton Street in 1784. One of the church's most prominent members in the city was John Jay, later the first chief justice of the United States and the first president of the New York Society for the Promoting of the Manumission of Slaves (formed in 1785).

The church hierarchy expanded during the following years. At a convention in 1785 the New York Episcopal diocese was formed, and at another in 1786 Samuel Provoost was recommended for consecration as its first bishop, the ceremony taking place at Lambeth Palace Chapel in London in 1787. Among well-known Episcopalian laymen was James Duane, the first mayor after the war and a member of the vestry of Trinity Church. There were about 50 churches and 35 clergy members in New York State when Provoost retired in 1801. The General Theological Seminary (1817) was eventually built on land donated by Clement Clarke Moore. A black congregation, St. Philip's, was established in 1809. Benjamin Treadwell Onderdonk became bishop in 1830. The Seamen's Church Institute, a chapel aboard a ship moored on the East River near Pike Street, opened during his tenure. A supporter of the Oxford Movement, which called for a revival of High Anglican traditions, Onderdonk encountered resistance to the ordination of Arthur Carey, a student at the General Theological Seminary and an enthusiastic supporter of the movement; he waved aside complaints at Carey's ordination on 2 July 1843 on the grounds that they had already been heard and dismissed. Onderdonk was soon charged with licentiousness and immorality by his opponents, and after a trial on 2 January 1845 he was suspended by the presiding bishop; he was not replaced until 1852, when Jonathan Mayhew Wainwright, a supporter of Low Church traditions, was elected provisional bishop with right of succession. The diocese of western New York split off in 1838. About this time the painter Thomas Cole became active in the church and diocese, in part through his efforts to tie the work of the Hudson River School to noble moral and religious purpose.

The number of parishes increased in the mid-nineteenth century. The Oxford Movement inspired the formation of the churches of the Transfiguration, St. Mary the Virgin, and St. Ignatius and a revival of the Gothic style by such architects as Richard Upjohn (Trinity, Holy Communion, and Ascension churches) and James Renwick (Grace, Calvary, and St. James churches). The concept of a total community was introduced by William Augustus Muhlenberg, who formed the Church of the Holy Communion in 1844 and sponsored a sisterhood of deaconesses (1852) that expanded the scope of women's social ministries. St. Luke's Hospital, opened in 1850 on Fifth Avenue at 54th Street by Muhlenberg, was built around a three-story chapel. Most Episcopalians in the city remained neutral on the issue of slavery before the Civil War. An exception was William Jay, who challenged the rule that blacks could be approved for ordination but not admitted to the diocesan convention. His son John Jay, Jr., persuaded the diocese to admit St. Philip's into full membership in 1853. A women's ministry, the House of Mercy, was established at 86th Street and the Hudson River as a home for abandoned girls. It was taken over in 1863 by the Sisters of St. Catherine, who were allied with Muhlenberg and took lifetime vows, a habit, and monastic rule of life; they later became known as the Community of St. Mary. After Wainwright's death in 1854 Horatio Potter was elected provisional bishop of New York. He reconciled the factions divided during Onderdonk's tenure and proposed to build a cathedral in the city. About 1871 Edward A. Washburn, the rector at Calvary Church, and his assistant, William Graham Sumner, organized the Club, an association of the city's prominent Episcopal clergy. A number of women's orders were also formed, among them those of St. John the Baptist and St. Margaret. In 1881 the Order of the Holy Cross was established on the Lower East Side by James Otis Sargent Huntington. During the 1880s there were about 50 Episcopal churches in Manhattan. An elite organization for laity, the Church Club of New York (1887), sponsored a library, club rooms, and good works for the benefit of the poor. Seth Low, the president of Columbia University and a well-known reformer who later became mayor of New York City, led opposition to the governance of black congregations under a separate jurisdiction. Henry Codman Potter became the bishop of New York in 1887.

At the turn of the twentieth century, Sunday services were usually held at 10:30 a.m. and consisted of morning prayer, ante-Communion, a litany, and a sermon; baptisms were held immediately afterward, with Sunday school in the afternoon (marriages and funerals were generally held in homes). An evening prayer service that incorporated a sermon and music by a choir was common until the 1920s. Most churches had an altar made of wood, but with no cross upon it. Pews were usually subject to annual rental assessments, having been first sold at auction during construction. Music was provided by organists and small paid choirs. In 1903 David Hummel Greer, the rector of St. Bartholomew's, became the first regular bishop coadjutor. He became bishop of New York in 1908 after the death of Henry Codman Potter (bishop since 1887). The synod house, the bishop's house, the deanery (Ogilvie House), and a school were added to the Cathedral of St. John the Divine. Prominent Episcopalians in the city included the financier J. P. Morgan and Nicholas Murray Butler, president of Columbia. By 1913 the Seamen's Church Institute moved to a new building at 25 South Street, where each night it housed about 400 men. Trinity parish built the Chapel of the Intercession at 155th Street and Broadway in 1915. The diocesan conventions of 1917 and 1920 endorsed Prohibition; the one in 1920 proposed selecting women as delegates to diocesan conventions and candidates for vestries. Charles Sumner Burch was chosen to succeed Greer as bishop in 1919; during the same year the national headquarters of the Episcopal Church opened at 281 Fourth Avenue (they were later moved to 815 Second Avenue). Burch was succeeded in 1921 by the rector of Trinity Church, William Thomas Manning, who was rigidly orthodox and forbade the barefoot liturgical dance at St. Mark's Church in the Bowery, the use of Communion cups, and remarriage after divorce. In a sermon at the Cathedral of St. John the Divine in 1930 he attacked Judge Ben Lindsay's stance on divorce, prompting

Episcopal Bishops of the Diocese of New York

Samuel Provoost (1787–1801)
Benjamin Moore (1801–16)
John Henry Hobart (1816–30)
Benjamin Treadwell Onderdonk (1830–61; suspended from duties 1845–61)
Jonathan Mayhew Wainwright (provisional bishop 1852–54)
Horatio Potter (provisional bishop 1854–61, bishop 1861–87)
Henry Codman Potter (1887–1908)
David Hummel Greer (1908–19)
Charles Sumner Burch (1919–20)
William Thomas Manning (1921–46)
Charles Kendall Gilbert (1947–50)
Horace William Baden Donegan (1950–72)
Paul Moore, Jr. (1972–89)
Richard Frank Grein (1989–2001)
Mark Sean Sisk (2001–)

Lindsay to defend himself before the congregation of 3000. Initially Manning devoted himself to building the Cathedral of St. John the Divine, but he was forced to suspend his efforts in the face of financial difficulty and World War II (even the steel scaffolding was given over to the war effort). A strong supporter of women and blacks in the church, he escorted a locksmith to open a parish church that had been closed in a dispute over segregation. He also had an apartment in a slum dismantled and then reassembled in the cathedral for the congregation to see.

As membership waned, the church adapted to meet the changing needs of its parishioners. The membership of St. Bartholomew's, the largest congregation in the city, declined from 14,000 in 1926 to 2000 in 1930; that of Trinity, the smallest, declined from 1100 to 150. Under the episcopate of Horace William Baden Donegan from 1950, the diocese allowed women to serve on vestries (1957) and to be elected to diocesan convention (1958). Donegan also emphasized social work and with the sports announcer Red Barber erected a building to house the Episcopal City Mission Society. Other prominent Episcopalians at the time included Fiorello H. La Guardia, Franklin D. Roosevelt, and Thomas E. Dewey. James Albert Pike, a former Roman Catholic and agnostic, was a popular speaker and apologist for the Christian faith and the Episcopal Church as the chaplain of Columbia and dean of St. John the Divine. Samuel Shoemaker, the rector of Calvary Church, was known for his evangelism and helped to form Alcoholics Anonymous. The Community of the Holy Spirit, established during the late 1940s by Ruth Younger as a religious teaching order for women, opened St. Hilda's and St. Hugh's, a school at 619 West 114th Street. Paul Moore, Jr., bishop of New York from 1972, emphasized human rights, social action, and urban problems. Although he could not ordain them, he allowed five female deacons to take part in an ordination service on 15 December 1974; the ordination of women was allowed by the church in 1976. Moore also resumed construction of the cathedral in 1979. Harold L. Wright was elected the first black assistant bishop in 1974. Richard Frank Grein, bishop of New York from October 1989 until 2001, focused on community programs, evangelism, education, administrative restructuring, and relations with the Orthodox Church in Russia. In the early part of the twenty-first century, as many Episcopal parishes were attempting to split from their dioceses over disputes concerning human sexuality and to affiliate with foreign provinces of the Anglican Communion, the New York diocese remained remarkably stable under the leadership of Mark Sean Sisk (bishop from 2001), with little fragmentation or departure of those from either extreme.

James Elliott Lindsley, *This Planted Vine: A Narrative History of the Episcopal Diocese of New York* (New York: Harper and Row, 1984)

J. Robert Wright

Equality League of Self Supporting Women. Woman suffrage organization formed in 1907 in New York City by Harriot Stanton Blatch. In contrast to the genteel methods of other suffragist groups, it recruited wage-earning women and sought publicity through such tactics as street parades. It developed the militant, agitational style that led to votes for women in New York State in 1917. In 1910 the organization changed its focus to legislative lobbying and was renamed the Women's Political Union. Its strategies influenced the formation of the National Woman's Party.

Ellen Carol DuBois

Equal Rights Party. See Locofocos.

Equitable Building. Skyscraper at 120 Broadway in lower Manhattan. It was built from 1913 to 1915 as the headquarters for the Equitable Life Assurance Society of the United States by Ernest R. Graham and Associates. The building's volume was massive for its time, rising 40 stories with no setbacks, and covering the entire block bounded by Broadway, Cedar, Nassau, and Pine streets. It casts a 7-acre (2.8-hectare) shadow, making the streets below perpetually gloomy; this influenced the passage of the 1916 Zoning Resolution, which required setbacks for new buildings to allow sunlight to reach street level. The structure was designated a National Historic Landmark in 1978.

Caleb Smith

Equitable Building, 2009

Equitable Life Assurance Society of the United States. Insurance company formed on 26 July 1859 by Henry Baldwin Hyde and members of Manhattan's Fifth Avenue Presbyterian Church. The only financial product providing old-age security before the development of pensions, life insurance was then regarded as a form of philanthropy. ("Assurance" in the company's name suggests reliable payment of dividends.) The first president, William C. Alexander, was the son of the church's rector, and Alexanders were prominent in the company for many years. Hyde dominated Equitable until his death in 1899. Among his innovations were tontines (which worked like annuities), imaginative marketing, and a vigorous sales effort. By 1900 Equitable was one of the world's largest financial institutions, with agencies in 91 countries, more than $1 billion of insurance in force, and $40 million in annual premium income. Hyde held the majority interest in its shares. As the company and its assets were energetically wooed by bankers and stockbrokers, scandals broke out concerning financial self-dealing by officers and extravagant behavior by Hyde's son and heir, James Hazen Hyde. The 1905 Armstrong Committee investigations conducted by Charles Evans Hughes (later a New York governor, presidential candidate, and U.S. Supreme Court justice) left Equitable limping. The company converted from a stock company to one owned mutually by policyholders, ended its foreign business, and regained its reputation. Taking a chance, in 1910 it entered the new area of group insurance, which provided annuities for employees, and went on to dominate it. In the 1970s it introduced policies backed by the stock market and later acquired the investment firm Donaldson, Lufkin and Jenrette and the mutual fund specialist Alliance Capital. Suffering from declining capital due to fluctuating interest rates and poorly performing products, the company, under chief executive Richard H. Jenrette, was converted to a public corporation in 1992, returning to a stockholder-owned company. It then sold a majority interest to the French insurer AXA, of which it is a subsidiary.

Equitable has always had a large presence in New York City. Before computers were introduced in the 1960s, the company had as many as 10,000 employees, many of them female clerical workers recruited from city high schools who stayed with "Mother Equitable" for decades. When a prohibition against insurance companies' owning real estate other than their offices was eased in 1938, Equitable built the Clinton Hill and Fordham Hill apartment complexes in Brooklyn and the Bronx and financed a number of buildings, including the Time and Life Building on Sixth Avenue. The company's name is on four buildings in Manhattan. In 1870 Hyde built the company's headquarters at 120 Broadway. Designed by

George B. Post, this immense structure had some of the first elevators in an office building, allowing Hyde to create a pioneering upper-floor rental market for premium-priced offices above the company's own two floors. The building burned down in 1912 and was replaced by what was then the world's largest office building, the 40-story Equitable Building, owned by T. Coleman du Pont and designed by Ernest R. Graham (still standing). It cast such a long shadow over Trinity Church and the neighborhood that the city in 1916 passed a law mandating setbacks in upper floors. Later home offices owned wholly or in part by Equitable were at 393 Seventh Avenue (1924–61, architect Starrett and Van Vleck), 1285 Avenue of the Americas (1961–86, architect Skidmore, Owings and Merrill), and 787 Seventh Avenue (architect Edward Larrabee Barnes, 1986–96). The company and its parent, AXA, are at 1290 Avenue of the Americas.

John Rousmaniere, *The Life and Times of the Equitable* (New York: Equitable Companies, 1995)

John Rousmaniere

Erasmus Hall High School and Academy of the Arts. Public high school at 911 Flatbush Avenue in Brooklyn. Built as a private school for the children of Dutch farmers in 1787 and deeded to the City of Brooklyn in 1896, it was the first school to be chartered by New York State. The neo-Gothic structure was the first public school building in the United States to be designated a federal landmark. Four adjoining buildings were built around a central courtyard between 1905 and 1939, and the original building was restored in 1936, 1952, and 1987. Erasmus Hall is the second-oldest public school in the United States. In 1994 the campus split into three separate schools: Humanities, Science and Mathematics, and Business and Technology. In 2004 the school expanded to include the High School for Service and Learning and in 2006 the Academy for Hospitality and Tourism. Its alumni include chess player Bobby Fischer and entertainer Barbra Streisand.

B. Kimberly Taylor

Ericsson, John (*b* Värmland, Sweden, 31 July 1803; *d* New York City, 8 March 1889). Naval engineer. He studied in London from 1826 and pursued an interest in steam engines. About 1837 he met Captain Robert F. Stockton of the U.S. Navy, who became interested in his work on a steamship operated by a screw propeller. He moved to New York City in 1839 and oversaw the design and construction of the screw warship the *Princeton,* which Stockton had promoted. Later he developed "caloric" (hot-air) engines that proved unsuccessful for ship propulsion but were widely used for industrial purposes. At the Delamater Iron Works he built for the navy the revolutionary ironclad warship the *Monitor* (1861); its successful engagement against the Confederate ironclad the *Merrimack* brought him contracts for several similar vessels. From 1864 to 1889 Ericsson lived at 36 Beach Street.

Darwin H. Stapleton

Erie Basin. Man-made harbor in Brooklyn, built in the 1850s at the southern end of Red Hook by William Beard. By the late nineteenth century it was one of the most important shipping depots in the Port of New York, viewed as a terminus of the shipping network that included the Erie Canal. Grain shipped by barge from the Midwest accounted for most of the traffic. The basin contained several ship repair facilities, the largest of which was the Anglo-American Dry Docks. After it fell into disuse the facility was bought in 1958 by the Port of New York Authority. Early in the twenty-first century the nearby area found new life as a cruise port for the ocean liner RMS *Queen Mary 2* and other vessels as well as a site for large retail chain stores.

John J. Gallagher

Erie Canal. Canal completed in 1825 linking the Hudson River above Albany to Lake Erie at Buffalo. One of the greatest American engineering projects of the nineteenth century, it was a key factor in the emergence of New York City as the commercial capital of the United States. The Erie Canal was the first link between the Atlantic seaboard and the continental interior, breaching the Appalachian Mountain range at its single substantial gap, the Mohawk River Valley through central New York. The canal established New York City's virtual monopoly on nascent Great Lakes trade. The city quickly dominated the east–west movement of goods, people, and produce that Virginia and other especially southern rivals never accomplished and that Canada only approximated after the opening of the St. Lawrence Seaway (1959). Had the canal not immediately initiated permanent national commercial networks between the city and the interior, railroads might have made rivals of other seaboard cities during the 1830s. As it happened, parallel lines of first railroads and then highways reconfirmed the city's position as the center of American global trade.

It is ironic that no member of the city's large state legislative delegation voted for the canal's 1817 enabling law. The city's assembly members and senators, all Tammany Republicans, were driven by twin fears: that city taxpayers would be burdened with escalating costs for a project of uncertain practicability and only upstate benefit, and that a successful project would elevate its greatest advocate, populist Republican and Tammany antagonist DeWitt Clinton. The latter fear was sound. The longtime mayor, recently deposed by political opponents from the then-appointive office, was elected governor in a landslide two weeks after the enabling law was passed. "Clinton's Ditch" remains his enduring legacy. The canal was not Clinton's idea, however. A series of pseudonymous essays by a bankrupted pioneer grain merchant in a western New York newspaper (1807–8) launched serious consideration of the concept, prompting a state survey (1808) that proved it feasible. In 1810 a fellow state senator asked Clinton to give his influential support to a bill creating a canal commission to conduct detailed surveys and eventually oversee construction. Clinton was named to the commission, which was led for the next six years by Gouverneur Morris. Questions of design, funding, and popular support, plus the War of 1812, discouraged progress until December 1815, when Clinton, then holding no public office, revived the subject at a meeting of influential men at the City Hotel; the meeting produced a forceful memorial by Clinton addressed to the legislature and circulated throughout the state. A new commission was named (1816), with Clinton at its head; after detailed surveys, the start of construction was authorized (1817).

The canal was largely the work of upstate New Yorkers: country surveyors who taught themselves engineering; farmers, townspeople, and others along the canal line who contracted to build the canal in hundreds of short sections; and, in the later construction years, mostly Irish immigrants who provided the labor. A number of controversies arose during construction, but it was completed with relatively few delays, missteps, or budgetary crises. The canal was 363 miles (584 kilometers) long, with 83 locks to accommodate nearly 700 feet (213 meters) of level changes between the Hudson River and Lake Erie. It was only 40 feet (12 meters) wide at the surface, narrowing to 28 feet (8.5 meters) at a 4-foot (1.2-meter) depth; horses or mules pulled canal barges at 4 miles (6.4 kilometers) per hour. The course up the length of the Mohawk River Valley was through familiar territory; the next 200 miles (322 kilometers) to the nascent village of Buffalo was through sparsely settled country previously accessible only by notoriously rutted and often impassable roads.

New York City's greatest contribution during the construction period was financial. City-based merchants, banks, and other investors purchased most of the $7 million in state bonds that largely financed the project. The Bank for Savings, whose chief depositors were the city's working poor, eventually held $1 million in canal bonds; John Jacob Astor purchased more than $200,000 worth. Manhattan auction houses paid roughly $1.3 million to the canal construction fund through 1 to 2 percent duties on auction sales, the method of market entry then for nearly half of all imported goods. Less directly, city business interests contributed a significant share of canal tolls, which ultimately generated a $40 million profit for the canal before tolls were abolished (1883).

The slenderness of the waterway contrasts with its enormous effect, especially on New York City. Transportation costs between Buffalo and the city were reduced by up to 90 percent and transportation time from three weeks to eight days. The city's population, which had briefly declined in the early 1810s (largely because of restrictive national trade policies and war), nearly doubled during the canal construction years and quadrupled during the following 30 years. In 1815 the city handled less than one-fifth of U.S. exports and in 1860 well over one-third. In 1820 the city was a distant third to Baltimore and Philadelphia in flour exports; by 1827 it was the runaway leader. In 1821 (the first year of available statistics) the city handled just more than one-third of U.S. imports, and by 1860 more than two-thirds, with six times the imports as second-place Boston.

Although many factors influenced the city's rise as the nation's commercial capital, the canal was the most evident, in reality and perception; the successful ongoing construction of the canal in 1822 inspired the first editorial reference to New York as "a mighty and flourishing empire." Clinton eloquently and accurately predicted the canal's effect on the city a year and a half before the canal was completed: "That city will in the course of time become the granary of the world, the emporium of commerce, the seat of manufactures, the focus of great monied operations, and the concentrating point of vast, disposable, and accumulating capitals, which will stimulate, enliven, extend, and reward the exertions of human labour and ingenuity, in all their processes and exhibitions; and, before the revolution of a century, the whole island of Manhattan, covered with habitations and replenished with a dense population, will constitute one vast city."

Clinton's Ditch was enlarged to 70 feet (21.3 meters) wide and 7 feet (2.1 meters) deep during 1836–62 and was replaced by the current 12-foot-deep (3.7-meter-deep) broad canal for motorized vessels from 1905 to 1918. Used now almost exclusively for pleasure boating, the Erie Canal remains a historical link to the city's rise.

Robert G. Albion, *The Rise of New York Port, 1815–1860* (New York: Charles Scribner's Sons, 1939); Ronald E. Shaw, *Erie Water West: A History of the Erie Canal, 1792–1854* (Lexington: University Press of Kentucky, 1966); Evan Cornog, *The Birth of Empire: DeWitt Clinton and the American Experience, 1769–1828* (Oxford: Oxford University Press, 1998)

Gerard Koeppel

Ernst, Morris (Leopold) (*b* Uniontown, Ala., 23 Aug 1888; *d* New York City, 21 May 1976). Lawyer. His family moved to New York City when he was two years old and lived on the Lower East Side before moving to the Upper East Side. He attended Horace Mann High School in Riverdale. In 1913 he passed the bar and two years later cofounded the New York City law firm Greenbaum, Wolff and Ernst with which he was associated until his death. In 1917 he helped found the National Civil Liberties Bureau, later known as the American Civil Liberties Union (ACLU). He was one of two general councils for the ACLU from 1929 to 1954. Many of the cases he argued defended literary and artistic freedoms. His most famous case was in 1933 when he successfully defended James Joyce's *Ulysses* from being censored in the United States. He was a friend of Presidents Franklin D. Roosevelt, Harry Truman, and Herbert Hoover as well as of New York governor Herbert Lehman. He served on the New York State banking board from 1933 to 1945. He died in his home at 2 Fifth Avenue.

Jessica Montesano

Ernst and Young. Accounting firm. It was formed in 1989 by the merger of Ernst and Whinney (1906), founded and based in Cleveland, and Arthur Young (1894), founded in Chicago and based in New York City. The new firm was almost immediately embroiled in the savings and loan crisis, and ultimately was required to pay some $204 million in a civil suit and $400 million to the federal government. Despite these early troubles Ernst and Young grew into one of the largest public accounting firms in the world, with more than 130,000 employees worldwide. By 1992 it was performing more audits of publicly held, multinational companies than any other accounting firm and it was also active in the diverse branches of management consulting. Its company headquarters were at 5 Times Square in the early twenty-first century.

Chad Ludington

espionage. As the communications center of the United States, New York City became associated with espionage at the time of the American Revolution. Nathan Hale spied on British forces in Harlem. The Culper ring, a successful operation conducted on behalf of General George Washington in 1777, was named for the aliases of its members Abraham Woodhull (Samuel Culper, Sr.) and Robert Townsend (Samuel Culper, Jr.) and led by Major Benjamin Tallmadge, a local businessman who traveled about Manhattan listening to the conversations of British soldiers and observing activities on the docks; a network of couriers conveyed messages to Washington's headquarters by way of Long Island and Connecticut. The Culper ring employed invisible ink (known as sympathetic stain) and a code that assigned the numbers 711 to Washington, 727 to New York City, and 728 to Long Island. It operated undetected until the end of the war.

During World War I German saboteurs infiltrated a terminal of the Lehigh Valley Railroad on Black Tom Island, in New York Harbor near Jersey City, New Jersey, that stored ammunition intended for the Russian army. On the night of 30 July 1916 they exploded 34 carloads of munitions and 11 carloads of high explosives (totaling 1066 tons [967 metric tons]), causing $14 million in damages and killing seven people. Later in the war the United States employed the skills of the cryptologist Herbert O. Yardley. After the war Yardley established a secret office that did public business as the Code Compilation Company but worked principally for the State Department under the name the American Black Chamber; its offices were successively in a brownstone building at 3 East 38th Street in Manhattan, at 141 East 37th Street, and at 52 Vanderbilt Avenue. Over the years Yardley's staff broke the codes of Argentina, Brazil, China, Costa Rica, Cuba, the Dominican Republic, El Salvador, France, Germany, Great Britain, Japan, Liberia, Mexico, Nicaragua, Panama, the Soviet Union, and Spain. On 31 October 1929 Secretary of State Henry L. Stimson discontinued the operation on the grounds that "gentlemen do not read each other's mail." Yardley regarded this action as foolhardy and unjustified: he recounted the code-breaking activities in his book *The American Black Chamber* (1931) and spoke widely about his experiences.

Even before the United States entered World War II, Nazi Germany sought to gain strategic information and undertake sabotage. As early as 1937 a German American named Hermann Lang provided secret blueprints of the Norden bombsight to agents of a German espionage service called the Abwehr. The activities of German agents in the United States were monitored by the Federal Bureau of Investigation (FBI) with the cooperation of a German American double agent, William G. Sebold (also known as William G. Sawyers), who at the behest of the FBI set up the Diesel Research Company, with offices on 42nd Street; at the same time he maintained radio contact with the Abwehr in Hamburg from his home at Centerport, Long Island, using the call letters CQDXVW-2 and sending messages supplied by the FBI and army intelligence that skillfully combined information and misinformation. Lang's boastful account to Sebold on 7 March 1940 of his exploits with the Norden bombsight was monitored and recorded by the FBI, which on 30 July 1941 arrested Lang and about 30 other German spies. Sebold was the chief witness for the prosecution in the trial that followed; with the other convicted agents, Lang was given a prison sentence, and after the war he was deported to Germany. The attempts of the government to halt espionage and sabotage by what was known as the "fifth column" were depicted in the film *The House on 92nd Street* (1945).

The Nazi sabotage mission that came closest to doing damage in New York City was Operation Pastorius (1942), in which eight Germans in two groups of four, all with extensive experience in the United States, came across the Atlantic Ocean in the submarine U-202. They carried false identity papers, guns, explosives, and U.S. currency and were assigned to destroy bridges, railroad lines, and factories. On 14 June one group landed near Amagansett, Long Island, and took the Long Island Rail Road to Penn Station. The leader of the group, George Dasch, and Ernest Burger decided during dinner at the Waldorf-Astoria to divulge their mission to the FBI: Dasch went to Washington, D.C.; convinced the director of the FBI, J. Edgar Hoover, of his identity; and disclosed that the second group of saboteurs was to land in Florida. The authorities then apprehended Dasch's conspirators—Richard Quirin and Heinrich Heinck near Amsterdam Avenue and 75th Street in Manhattan, and Burger at the Governor Clinton Hotel. All eight men were tried by a secret military tribunal in Washington, D.C., and on 12 August Quirin and Heinck were executed with the four members of the second group. After serving prison sentences Dasch and Burger were pardoned in 1948 and returned to Germany. It was during World War II that the Office of Strategic Services was formed. Many Americans who played important roles in its early days were associated with New York City, among them William J. Donovan, its first director, and William Casey, who later served as the director of the Central Intelligence Agency.

The Soviet Union engaged in espionage in New York City as early as the 1920s, often conspiring with American communists and others sympathetic toward them; a prominent courier and eventual defector was Whittaker Chambers. Of several espionage rings operated by the Soviet Union toward the end of World War II, the one based in New York City was the largest and most effective. Organized by Anatoly Yakovlev, nominally a vice consul, the network functioned from 1944 to 1946. It included the German physicist Klaus Fuchs, who worked at Columbia University and was instrumental in developing the atomic bomb. The network may also have included Julius and Ethel Rosenberg, who were executed for treason in 1953. In Brooklyn the master spy Rudolf Abel worked undercover from 1950 to 1957. The United Nations soon provided a cover for espionage: many members of its secretariat were nationals of the Soviet Union and its allies, and even countries with which the United States had no diplomatic relations maintained missions in New York City. The Soviet Union was also able to conduct espionage from its mission at 136 East 67th Street, from its compound in suburban Glen Cove, Long Island, and from its 19-story residence in Riverdale in the Bronx, which had antennas on its rooftop and was well situated for wireless interception.

In 1996 FBI Special Agent Earl Edwin Pitts was arrested and charged with conspiracy to commit espionage for Russia and the former Soviet Union. He had worked in FBI foreign counterintelligence investigations in the bureau's New York City office from January 1987 to August 1989. Among other offenses, the FBI stated that Pitts had turned over a secret list of all Soviet officials in the United States with their known or suspected posts in Soviet spy agencies during his five-year relationship with the KGB. Pitts's association with the Russian surveillance organization was traced back to a meeting at the New York Public Library between him and Aleksandr V. Karpov, a high-level Russian official. Pitts pleaded guilty in 1997 and was sentenced to 27 years in prison.

Martin Ebon

Esposito, Meade (*b* Brooklyn, 1907; *d* Manhasset, N.Y., 3 Sept 1993). Political leader. Educated in public schools, he was a bail bondsman when he began his rise to prominence in 1960 by defeating a Democratic leader in Canarsie, a neighborhood in southeastern Brooklyn. In 1969 he was elected chairman of the Democratic Party in Brooklyn, the largest county political organization in the United States. For many years he was the host to the famous and powerful at legendary political lunches at Foffe's restaurant in downtown Brooklyn. He played a major role in rallying party leaders behind Edward I. Koch's successful mayoral campaign in 1977. After retiring as county leader in 1983 he remained one of the state's most influential politicians until his indictment and conviction in 1987 for having made an illegal gift to Representative Mario Biaggi of the Bronx. Esposito was given a suspended two-year prison term and fined $500,000.

Kenneth T. Jackson

Esquire. Men's magazine. Founded in 1933 during the Great Depression, it was established by Arnold Gingrich and David Smart. It started off as a racy magazine for men but soon developed into a more cosmopolitan publication, with a focus on men's fashion. In the 1940s the magazine developed a reputation for its literary contributions from writers such as Ernest Hemingway and F. Scott Fitzgerald. During the 1960s it was in the forefront of New Journalism, featuring contributions from Tom Wolfe, Norman Mailer, Tim O'Brien, John Sack, and Gay Talese. From 1969 to 1976 Gordon Lish served as the magazine's fiction editor and became known as "Captain Fiction" because of the authors whose careers he assisted, including Raymond Carver, Richard Ford, and Cynthia Ozick. *Esquire* was sold by its original owners to Clay Felker in 1977, who sold it to 13–30 Corporation two years later. When 13–30 dissolved in 1986, the Hearst Corporation bought it. David Granger was named editor in chief in June 1997. In 2009 the magazine started the Daily Endorsement Blog, aimed at promoting one item in any category every day, including its first presidential endorsement (Barack Obama) in November 2008. In the early twenty-first century *Esquire*'s main offices were located in midtown Manhattan.

Benjamin Yakas

Essex Street Market. Market on Grand Street between Ludlow and Essex streets, opened in 1818. It soon closed and in 1836 was replaced by the Monroe Market. In 1940 the municipally owned Essex Street Retail Market was set up to replace open-air markets in the area, as part of Mayor Fiorello H. La Guardia's efforts to remove pushcarts and itinerant peddlers from the Lower East Side. It was run cooperatively by merchants until 1986. Its management was then turned over to a private developer who evicted several merchants and raised rents for others. In the early twenty-first century the Essex Street Market remained an example of a successful commercial space that caters to local residents and visitors.

Suzanne R. Wasserman

Estonians. An Estonian community took root in New York City during the 1890s, when immigrants founded the New York Estonian Evangelical Lutheran Church, began publishing the first Estonian-language newspaper, and formed the American Estonian Benefit Society (renamed the New York Estonian Society in 1910) in Harlem. Significant immigration resulted from the failed 1905 revolution against Russia. The revolution created polarization among Estonians in New York City, where many revolutionaries joined the Communist Party of America. After a brief independence, Estonia was forcibly incorporated within the Soviet Union from 1944 to 1991 and emigration was prohibited. The United States did not recognize the legality of the Soviet annexation of Estonia and continued to recognize Estonia's diplomatic mission located at Rockefeller Center.

Between 1948 and 1952 about 10,000 Estonian refugees moved to the United States, the majority from government and professional ranks. A third of them settled in New York City, and Estonian House, the beaux-arts terra-cotta building at 243 East 34th Street purchased in 1946 by the Estonian Education Society, became the center of Estonian life in the city. The Lexington Avenue Lutheran Church eventually grew to 3200 members, making it one of the largest Estonian religious organizations in the world. By the time of the collapse of the Soviet Union in 1991 and the reestablishment of Estonian independence, many of the Estonians in the city were working in business and banking or as attorneys, engineers, and educators. Even those who moved to the suburbs continued to look to New York City for Estonian-related activities. Since 1991 Estonian immigration to New York City has consisted mainly of younger people coming to study, to work, and to see the world. In 1992 the Sixth World Estonian Festival was held in the city, drawing thousands of compatriots from five continents. Estonians cooperated with New York Latvians and Lithuanians to form the Baltic Appeal to the United Nations (BATUN) in 1966 for the purpose of lobbying for the freedom of the Baltic states. The New York City metropolitan Estonian population in 1933 was estimated at 12,000; in 2008 the number was 3800. In 2005 the city itself had 1000 residents of Estonian descent.

Jaan Pennar, Tõnu Parming, and Peter P. Rebane, eds., *The Estonians in America, 1625–1975: A Chronology and Fact Book* (Dobbs Ferry, N.Y.: Oceana, 1975)

Marju Rink-Abel

Ethical Culture Fieldston School. Independent coeducational elementary and secondary day schools in Manhattan and the Bronx. Their origins may be traced to the opening by Felix Adler in 1877 of a free kindergarten sponsored by the Ethical Culture Society. The school added elementary grades in 1880 and tuition-paying students in 1890. Originally called the Workingmen's School, it became the Ethical Culture School in 1895. It expanded to include a high school by 1900, graduating its first class in 1905. In 1928 the Fieldston School, newly constructed on an 18-acre (7-hectare) campus in Riverdale, opened for students in grades seven to 12. The Fieldston Lower School was built in 1933 on the campus. In the early twenty-first century the name Ethical Culture Fieldston School refers to the Ethical Culture School at 33 Central Park West in Manhattan and the Fieldston Lower, Middle, and Upper Schools on Fieldston Road in the Bronx; the four divisions serve about 1700 students.

Richard Schwartz

Ethical Culture Society of New York. Religious humanist association formed in 1876 by Felix Adler, the rabbi of Temple Emanu-El in New York City and a leading exponent of Reform Judaism. The association was based on his philosophy of ethical idealism, a blend of Kantian ideas and social and pedagogical reform. It soon became a leading advocate of radical political and social reforms, including those aimed at workers, women, and the poor. Some of its first leaders opened the first settlement house in the country, the University Settlement (1886), as well as the Hudson Guild (1895) and the first Workingmen's School (1877), which became the Ethical Culture School. In the early twenty-first century the society belonged to the American Ethical Culture Union, which was recognized as a religion but supported no one theology, doctrine, or creed, instead upholding the philosophy that human life is of the utmost value and that improved social, interpersonal, and ecological relations are possible through dedication to the potential and betterment of human beings.

Horace L. Friess, *Felix Adler and Ethical Culture: Memories and Studies*, ed. Fannia Weingartner (New York: Columbia University Press, 1981)

Amie Klempnauer

Eugene M. Lang Foundation. Charitable organization formed in 1968 by Eugene M. Lang (*b* 16 March 1919), a native of New York City and the founder of the Refac Technology Development Corporation. The foundation focuses its efforts on educational institutions, in particular Eugene Lang College at the New School for Social Research. It also supports medical care and research and makes grants to about 75 educational, cultural, and social service organizations in the city. During the 1980s Lang offered to pay the college tuition of every member of a sixth-grade class at Public School 121 in East Harlem who completed high school, and he later paid for tutoring and other assistance to the students. By January 1989 his example had inspired 21 other New Yorkers to make similar commitments to disadvantaged elementary school students. Lang continues to focus his philanthropic efforts on education in the early twenty-first century.

Kenneth W. Rose

Eugenio María de Hostos Community College. Junior college of the City University of New York, opened in 1968 at 475 Grand Concourse in the Bronx as the first branch of the university deliberately placed in an economically depressed area. The school was a pioneer in bilingual education and developed a strong health sciences program in affiliation with several hospitals in New York City. It offers day care free of charge to its students. In 2010 the college enrolled about 4700 full- and part-time students.

Marc Ferris

Europe, James Reese (*b* Mobile, Ala., 22 Feb 1881; *d* Boston, 10 May 1919). Music director. He moved to New York City in 1903, where he made his reputation as a music director in black musical theater. In 1910 he formed the Clef Club, both a booking agency and an informal union for black musicians in New York City. He led a 100-piece orchestra drawn from the Clef Club at Carnegie Hall in 1912 in the first of several concerts of music by black composers, emphasizing art music to counteract the prevailing opinion that blacks could produce only ragtime. In 1914 he became the music director for the internationally famous white dance team of Vernon and Irene Castle, which brought him national prominence and engagements from members of fashionable society in New York City. In the same year he left the Clef Club to form a competing organization, the Tempo Club. During World War I he led the 369th Infantry military band, which was all black. At the height of his career, he was killed by a deranged member of his band.

R. Reid Badger, "James Reese Europe and the Prehistory of Jazz," *American Music* 7, no. 1 (spring 1989), 48–67

Edward A. Berlin

Evacuation Day. Date of the final departure of British military forces from the United States, 25 November 1783. The signing of the Treaty of Paris on 3 September signaled the end of the American Revolution. New York City was the last official post held by the British, and after a delay of several days they evacuated the city under the direction of General Guy Carleton at one o'clock in the afternoon of 25 November, ending more than seven years of occupation. Within the hour American forces commanded by Generals George Washington and George Clinton marched the length of Manhattan to the Battery. At Fort George the American flag replaced the British flag. Boisterous celebrations continued for the next 10 days, culminating in Washington's poignant farewell to his officers on 4 December at Fraunces Tavern; the last British warship left for England the next day from Staten Island. For more than a century, Evacuation Day was marked by martial parades, patriotic oratory, and banquets; its 100th anniversary was one of the great civic events of the nineteenth century in New York City. The holiday ceased to be observed after World War I because of its proximity to Thanksgiving and the decline of anti-English sentiment, except for a brief revival on the occasion of its bicentenary in 1983.

Robert I. Goler

Evans, George Henry (*b* Bromyard, England, 25 May 1805; *d* Granville, N.J., 2 Feb 1856). Editor and land reformer. He moved to the United States with his father and brother in 1820 and worked as a printer's apprentice in Ithaca, New York. He soon became an admirer of Thomas Paine's writings on free thought and moved to New York City, where he joined a circle of craftsmen sympathetic to Paine's ideas. Allied with Frances Wright and Robert Dale Owen, he became a spokesman for an important faction of the Workingmen's Party in 1829 and during the next decade edited several newspapers devoted to labor issues (including the *Working Man's Advocate*), defended the union movement, and took part in the Locofoco revolt within the Democratic

Party. After 1840 he concentrated on land reform, which he considered the only practicable solution to class injustice. Supported by such prominent labor leaders as Mike Walsh and John Commerford, he formed the National Reform Association in 1844, appealing to workers with the slogan "Vote Yourself a Farm," but gained only a small following. Undeterred, he promoted the cause until the end of his life. Evans's ideas later influenced such diverse political efforts as those culminating in the Homestead Act of 1862 and Henry George's campaign for a single tax during the 1880s.

Sean Wilentz

Evans, Walker (*b* St. Louis, 3 Nov 1903; *d* Old Lyme, Conn., 10 April 1975). Photographer. He lived in New York City in the late 1920s, and his career began there in 1930, when his photographs were published in *The Bridge,* an anthology of poems by Hart Crane. In 1932 his work was exhibited at the Julien Levy Gallery, and in 1938 a major exhibition of his photographs for the Farm Security Administration was mounted at the Museum of Modern Art (MoMA). A later exhibition at the museum (1966) featured photographs he had taken of subway riders in New York City in 1938 and 1941. Evans was a contributing editor at *Time* (1943–45) and an associate editor at *Fortune* (1945–65). A retrospective of his work appeared at MoMA in 1971.

Laura Gwinn

Evarts, William M(axwell) (*b* Boston, 6 Feb 1818; *d* New York City, 28 Feb 1901). Lawyer and statesman. He graduated from Yale College and attended Harvard Law School, and in 1841 he began practicing law in New York City, where he became one of the best-known members of the bar. A staunch Republican, he successfully represented President Andrew Johnson in his impeachment proceedings in 1868 and was rewarded by being appointed attorney general. He was president of the New York Law Institute and a founder and first president of the Association of the Bar of the City of New York. At the Geneva arbitration in 1871–72 he represented the United States in its claims against England for having plundered the *Alabama* during the Civil War. He provided legal counsel for the Republican Party in the disputed presidential election of 1876 and was appointed secretary of state by the eventual winner, President Rutherford B. Hayes (1877–81). In 1885 he was elected by the New York State legislature to the U.S. Senate; he was largely responsible for the passage of the Evarts Act of 1891, which created the federal court of appeals.

Chester L. Barrows, *William M. Evarts: Lawyer, Diplomat, Statesman* (Chapel Hill: University of North Carolina Press, 1941)

Elliott B. Nixon

Everard. Bathhouse at 28 West 28th Street. Built in 1890 by James Edward, it was very successful as a public bathhouse in the red-light and gambling district of the Tenderloin in the early 1900s. The building itself was four floors, with 150 rooms and 150 walk-in lockers. It boasted the world's largest steam room, was open 24 hours, and catered mainly to a homosexual clientele after the 1950s. On 25 May 1977 the building burned down, resulting in nine deaths.

Jessica Montesano

Everett House Hotel. Hotel formerly at 212 Fourth Avenue near Union Square, built in 1848. Named for the Massachusetts statesman Edward Everett, who spoke at Gettysburg along with Lincoln, it was an imposing, classically designed brick structure with large, elegant rooms and antique furniture. The Everett House Hotel was considered one of the finest of its time; England's King Edward VII, then Prince of Wales, stayed there, and William "Boss" Tweed had headquarters there. It went bankrupt in 1906; in 1908 the Everett Building was built on the site (designated a New York City landmark in 1988).

Shan Jayakumar

Evergood, Philip (*b* New York City, 26 Oct 1901; *d* Bridgewater, Conn., 11 March 1973). Painter. The son of the Australian painter Meyer Blashki, he studied at the Art Students League and the Educational Alliance in New York City. During the 1930s he worked for the Public Works of Art Project and the mural division of the Federal Art Project of the Works Progress Administration, for which he completed a mural at the Richmond Hill Library in Queens. As the president of the Artists' Union (elected in 1937) he worked for artists' rights and for permanent government sponsorship of the arts. Evergood painted in an expressionist style characterized by an agitated line, distortions of human anatomy, and bold primary colors. The Whitney Museum of American Art owns a large collection of his works, including *Lily and the Sparrows* (1939).

John I. H. Baur, *Philip Evergood* (New York: Harry N. Abrams, 1975)

Patricia Hills

Evergreens Cemetery. Nonsectarian cemetery on the Brooklyn–Queens border near east New York. Founded in 1849 as the Cemetery of the Evergreens, the 225-acre (91-hectare) burial ground is a fine example of a classic rural cemetery that is designed, maintained, and used both as a place of interment and as a picturesque park. It is the only cemetery on which the mid-nineteenth-century landscape architect Andrew Jackson Downing worked. The initial buildings, one of which still stands in the twenty-first century, were designed by Alexander Jackson Davis. Calvert Vaux, John Y. Culyer, Samuel Parsons, Jr., and Richard Schermerhorn, Jr., are among other architects and engineers who have worked on the Evergreens. The monuments include distinguished examples of important styles, including high Victorian, Gothic Revival, and zinc (also called white bronze).

The grounds, located high on Long Island's terminal moraine, are historic. On the eve of the Battle of Brooklyn, 10,000 British soldiers crossed this land at night and outflanked George Washington's Continental Army. The site was chosen as a cemetery for its beauty and sweeping views of Manhattan and Jamaica Bay, for its proximity to Williamsburg's German American population, and because it allowed development in both Brooklyn and Queens (by law, no more than 200 acres [81 hectares] could be used for a cemetery in any one county). After two decades as a nonprofit entity, the cemetery was reorganized in 1872 as the Evergreens Cemetery, a for-profit corporation. The largest stockholder was William R. Grace, a shipping and banking magnate and two-term mayor of New York. Grace family members and employees continued to serve as officers and trustees into the 1980s. (The Evergreens returned to nonprofit status in 1952.)

A wide variety of people are interred at the Evergreens. Besides remains transferred from the churchyards of Brick Presbyterian, St. Mark's in the Bowery, St. Ann's, Sands Street Methodist, and other prominent Manhattan and downtown Brooklyn churches, leaders of the German American community, white and black Civil War veterans, merchant seamen (the Seaman's Grounds is the cemetery's oldest section), and many Chinese Americans are buried there. During the height of the anti-Asian movement in the 1880s the Chinese government chose the Evergreens as its New York cemetery, and burials in the several Celestial Hill sections continue to this day. Interred there also are victims of the 1904 disaster of the steamship *General Slocum,* the Triangle Shirtwaist fire of 1911, the 1918–19 influenza pandemic, and the race riots of the 1980s (Michael Griffith and Yusef Hawkins, two men killed in race-related crimes, are buried at the Evergreens). Other graves include those of the painter Martin J. Heade; the pioneering animator Winsor McCay; the first world champion of chess, William Steinitz; and a long line of show business figures, including major African American stars, from the slave pianist "Blind Tom" Wiggins to Adelaide Hall, Bill "Bojangles" Robinson, and the saxophone genius Lester "Pres" Young.

By the year 2000 the Evergreens was almost filled, with 525,000 graves. The board of trustees limited burials in order to preserve land and "emphasize the role of the grounds as a park, a bird sanctuary, and an historic site." Old trees have been replaced, and historic graves and lots have received special attention. In 2007 the New York State Board of Historic Preservation recommended that the Evergreens Cemetery be added to the National Register of Historic Places.

John Rousmaniere, *Green Oasis in Brooklyn: The Evergreens Cemetery, 1849–2008* (Brooklyn: The Evergreens/Smith–Kerr, 2008)

John Rousmaniere

Everlast Sports Manufacturing. Firm of sporting goods manufacturers formed in 1917 by Jacob Golomb (1893–1951), who named it for a durable men's bathing suit that he invented in 1910 and sold on the Lower East Side. In 1919 Jack Dempsey wore gloves bearing the name of the firm when he won the world heavyweight championship, and in 1921 Everlast began mass-producing boxing equipment that earned a reputation for reliability and durability. In 1938 the firm moved to a large facility at 750 East 132nd Street in South Bronx. It began producing swimwear, T-shirts, and other apparel in 1983, a venture that it soon abandoned in favor of licensing its logotype to other manufacturers; in 1989 licensing fees exceeded $2 million. Everlast was able to endure a decline in the popularity of boxing because of its name recognition and steady sales in large department stores in New York City. Daniel Golomb, son of the founder, sold the company in 2000 to George Horowitz. In 2003 Everlast moved its factory to Missouri and in 2007 was bought by Sports Direct.

Elizabeth J. Kramer, Stephen A. Stertz

Ewing, Patrick (*b* Kingston, Jamaica, 6 Aug 1962). Basketball player. He moved to the United States at age 13 and enrolled at Georgetown University in 1981. Renowned for his ability to block shots, Ewing led Georgetown to three consecutive National Collegiate Athletic Association championships from 1983 to 1985, winning in 1984. Over that span he also helped his school win three Big East championships at Madison Square Garden. In 1985 he was drafted by the New York Knicks as the first selection of the National Basketball Association (NBA) draft and soon became a fan favorite. The Knicks struggled during Ewing's first two seasons but made the playoffs every year for the rest of his career in New York, which ended in 2000 when he was traded to the Seattle SuperSonics. Ewing never won a championship but made the NBA finals twice. In his 17-year professional career, Ewing made 11 all-star teams, tallied more than 24,000 points and 11,000 rebounds, and blocked nearly 3000 shots. In 2003 the Knicks retired Ewing's jersey number, 33, in a ceremony at Madison Square Garden.

David White

excursion boats. Recreational waterborne travel for residents of New York City began in the early nineteenth century on sailing sloops. These were joined after 1825 by steam-powered boats, which were larger and faster and therefore permitted longer pleasure trips. Steam towboats also came into use on holidays to take passengers to the Atlantic fishing grounds. Pressed by competition from the railroads, shipping companies turned increasingly to the excursion business and developed large, fast, luxurious ships that could accommodate as many as 5000 passengers. Converted river and coastal liners were operated independently and proved profitable on short runs. Low fares made it possible for working- and middle-class New Yorkers to enjoy excursions lasting a day or longer.

Popular destinations included various riverside "groves," or picnic grounds, as well as beaches, resorts, amusement parks, and historic locations. From the earliest days of steamboat travel passengers frequented the Elysian Fields (at Hoboken, New Jersey), West Point, Newburgh, and Poughkeepsie on the Hudson River, and Sandy Hook and Monmouth Beach on the New Jersey shore. By the mid-nineteenth century Kingston Point on the Hudson and Bergen Point and Long Branch on the New Jersey shore were well visited. In the years after the Civil War, Glen Island was developed on the East River, as were Iona Island on the Hudson; Rye Beach, Seacliff, and Great Neck on Long Island Sound; and Coney Island and Rockaway in New York Bay. Early in the twentieth century Bear Mountain, Verplanck Point, Indian Point, Excelsior Grove, Forest Grove, and Alpine Grove became popular destinations on the Hudson. Often barges were used, propelled by steamboats or tugboats. Both daytime and evening trips were popular, offered by such companies as the McAllister Lines, the Iron Steamboat Company, the Meseck Line, the Hudson River Day Line, the Circle Line, and the Wilson Line. Among the best-known boats were the *Plymouth Rock,* the *Great Republic,* the *General Slocum* (which burned in 1904), the *Mandalay,* the *City of Keansburg,* the *Bay Belle,* the *Alexander Hamilton,* and the *Dayliner.* The first regular tour around Manhattan Island was probably that offered by Captain John Roberts from 1908. Only two companies remained active by 1990: the Circle Line, offering half-day trips around Manhattan and special charters, and the Seaport Line at South Street Seaport, which in 1985 began operating for private parties the sidewheelers *Andrew Fletcher* and *DeWitt Clinton* for trips around the harbor, and John F. Kennedy's former presidential yacht, the *Honey Fitz.* In 1993 the *Andrew Fletcher* and the *DeWitt Clinton* were sold to operators outside New York City. In the early twenty-first century some large private yachts continued to offer various charter services such as dinner sailings.

Arthur G. Adams

executions. See Public executions.

Explorers Club. Professional society with the mission of "encouraging scientific exploration of land, sea, air, and space," founded in New York City in 1904. Members of the club have accomplished many "famous firsts," which include traveling to the North Pole, the South Pole, the summit of Mount Everest, the deepest point in the ocean, and the surface of the moon. The annual dinner, held in New York City, honors the world's top explorers and is known for exotic fare such as tempura-style tarantula, termite spring rolls, roasted rattlesnake, yak Wellington, and ostrich tartare. Individuals are not eligible for membership solely on the basis of travel experience, but must also have participated in at least one scientific expedition. However, supporters of the club's goals are invited to become Friends of the Explorers Club. In addition to its headquarters at 46 East 70th Street in Manhattan, where it hosts weekly lectures and public programs, the club has more than 30 domestic and international chapters.

Holly Cronin

Exxon. Huge petroleum refiner and retailer. Among its forerunners was the Standard Oil Company (Ohio), set up by John D. Rockefeller in 1870. The headquarters were moved to 26 Wall Street as Rockefeller sought to consolidate his control over the oil industry. The firm eventually became known as Standard Oil Company (New Jersey) to distinguish it from other firms in the Standard network. It soon became the country's largest industrial corporation. In 1911 the Standard Trust was divided by the U.S. Supreme Court into 33 components; Standard Oil Company (New Jersey) received the largest share of the properties but was prevented from achieving integration by World War I, which led to cooperation among the country's oil companies to supply petroleum products to the Allies. Led by Walter Clark Teagle from 1917, Standard Oil of New Jersey after the war bought a one-half interest in Humble Oil and Refining Company, a Texas firm that offered a large supply of domestic crude as well as many successful entrepreneurs. The firm restructured its management and in 1927 took the first steps toward becoming a holding company. The search for oil continued, and new sources were found in Canada, Venezuela, and Iraq. A complicated series of patent agreements with the German firm of I. G. Farbenindustrie was reached in 1929, and the two firms later set up a joint American study company to trade research information on coal, petroleum, and natural gas that might lead to the manufacture of cheap artificial rubber and toluene. In 1942 these activities were considered treasonable by a committee of the U.S. Senate led by Harry S. Truman. Standard Oil of New Jersey merged with Socony–Vacuum Oil in 1934 to form Standard–Vacuum, which took over operations in the eastern hemisphere and lasted until April 1960.

After the end of World War II, Standard Oil of New Jersey continued its global search for petroleum reserves. Esso Chemical was formed as a wholly owned affiliate devoted to research. Seeking relief from antitrust suits and a wider world market, Standard Oil of New Jersey took the name Exxon on 1 November 1972; Esso Chemical became Exxon Chemical in 1973. Exxon remained the largest industrial corporation in New York City during the following decades, a period that included the disaster of the *Exxon Valdez* in March 1989. On 27 August 1990 the firm moved its headquarters to Irving, Texas.

Ralph W. Hidy and Muriel E. Hidy, *History of Standard Oil Company (New Jersey)*, vol. 1, *Pioneering in Big Business, 1882–1911* (New York: McGraw–Hill, 1955); George Sweet Gibb and Evelyn H. Knowlton, *History of Standard Oil Company (New Jersey)*, vol. 2, *The Resurgent Years, 1911–1927* (New York: McGraw–Hill, 1956); Henrietta Larson, Evelyn H. Knowlton, and Charles S. Popple, *History of Standard Oil Company (New Jersey)*, vol. 3, *New Horizons, 1927–1950* (New York: Harper and Row, 1971); Bennett H. Wall, *Growth in a Changing Environment: A History of Standard Oil Company (New Jersey), 1950–1972, and Exxon Corporation, 1972–1975* (New York: McGraw–Hill, 1988); Daniel Yergin, *The Prize: The Epic Quest for Oil, Money, and Power* (New York: Simon and Schuster, 1990)

Bennett H. Wall

Exxon explosion. Explosion and fire that occurred the night of 6 December 1970 at the Exxon Corporation (then known as Humble Oil and Refining Company) Bayway oil refinery in Linden, New Jersey, 1 mile (1.6 kilometers) west of Arthur Kill, which separates New Jersey from Staten Island. The refinery was engulfed in fires and explosions that lasted for hours, creating 1000-foot-high (305-meter-high) flames that lit up night skies and shattered windows all across Staten Island. Seven workers were injured, but no one was killed. Although sabotage was originally suspected, subsequent investigation traced the cause to an overheated reactor in the refinery. On 20 March 1979 another, less serious, explosion occurred at the same Exxon refinery, also injuring seven workers and again causing broken window glass in Staten Island.

Andrew Sparberg

E-ZPass. Electronic toll collection system that tracks vehicles as they pass through collecting stations, enabling drivers to prepay toll fares without stopping at the tollbooth or opening a window. The system consists of a remote device the size of a deck of cards, which is placed on the windshield of the automobile, and an electric system in the tollbooth. First implemented in the Hudson River tunnels in the 1980s and then in the tri-state area, the program aimed to reduce congestion on some of the busiest roads in the United States. By 2000, 68 percent of cars traveling on weekdays in New York and 58 percent of cars traveling on weekends used E-ZPass. As of 2010 E-ZPass was compatible with similar systems throughout the Northeast.

Nicholas Kelly

F

Facade Law. Law signed on 27 February 1980 to protect pedestrians from falling masonry (amending chapter 27, section 129, of the New York Administrative Code). It was prompted by the death in the preceding year of a first-year student at Barnard College who was struck by masonry that fell from a building at Columbia University. The law requires that owners of buildings have the condition of facades examined by experts and submit reports of those examinations to the city's Department of Buildings. Despite fears by preservationists that the law would encourage owners to remove historic facades rather than repair them, a study in 1990 concluded that there had been widespread compliance and few instances of facade stripping.

Robert E. Meadows, *Historic Building Facades: A Manual for Inspection and Rehabilitation* (New York: Landmarks Conservancy, 1986)

Brooke J. Barr

Factory Investigating Commission. The enforcement of factory laws became the responsibility of agencies of New York State in the 1880s. The laws and agencies were largely ineffective until after a fire on 25 March 1911 in the top three stories of the 10-story Triangle Shirtwaist factory in New York City. Within minutes the fire claimed 146 young Jewish and Italian women, many of whom jumped to their deaths from the windows. This tragedy resulted in the formation of the New York State Factory Investigating Commission. Led by State Senator Robert F. Wagner (i) and Alfred E. Smith, speaker of the New York State Assembly, the commission also included three other legislators; Mary E. Dreier, president of the New York Women's Trade Union League; Samuel Gompers, president of the American Federation of Labor; and two representatives from business. It employed a paid staff, received voluntary help from such reformers as Frances Perkins, and focused its efforts on factories in New York City. Between 1911 and 1914 the commission made more than 60 recommendations covering all industrial conditions. It was held together largely by Wagner and Smith, who used their political power to ensure that most of the recommendations were adopted by the legislature: 56 recommendations became the basis of a comprehensive system of laws that replaced weak and disjointed ones enforced with varying degrees of effectiveness. The new code revised fire laws and provided for automatic sprinklers in buildings with seven stories or more, established a 54-hour week for women in factories, regulated the operation of dangerous machinery, set standards for lighting, ventilation, and washrooms, extended the regulation of homework, banned several industries from using tenement labor, and reorganized the state's Department of Labor, doubling the number of inspectors to 125 and establishing an industrial board empowered to issue regulations that had the force of law. A minimum-wage law for women and children was the only major proposal that was defeated. The commission's work was the pinnacle of progressive reform in the city and state and became the basis for other labor law during later years.

Richard Greenwald, *The Triangle Fire: The Protocols of Peace and Industrial Democracy in Progressive Era New York* (Philadelphia: Temple University Press, 2005)

Irwin Yellowitz

Factoryville. Name applied to the northwest corner of West New Brighton in Staten Island from the late nineteenth century to the 1930s. It was derived from the large factories that covered the area, including that of the New York Dyeing and Print Works. The center of the neighborhood lay at the foot of Broadway.

James Bradley

Fairchild Publications. Firm of magazine publishers. It was formed in 1892, when a peddler named Edmund Fairchild took over a failing trade newspaper devoted to the men's clothing business. The paper was eventually called the *Daily News Record* and included a small feature about women's wear: in July 1910 this became the separate publication *Women's Wear Daily,* now the liveliest and best known of several trade publications owned by Fairchild. Others include *Home Furnishings Daily, Golf Pro Merchandising, Footwear News, Supermarket News, Electronic News, Metalworking News, M,* a glossy publication edited by Clay Felker (the founder of *New York* magazine), and several business directories. The firm was bought by Capital Cities Communications in 1968. In 1991 its offices moved to 7 West 34th Street. In 1999 Fairchild Publications was sold by the Walt Disney Company to Advance Publications, the parent company of Condé Nast Publications.

Leslie Gourse

Fairmount. Neighborhood in west central Bronx, lying within Tremont and bounded to the east by Southern Boulevard and to the west by Crotona Park. It is named after the estate of Robert Cochran, built in 1854. A village that took shape near Southern Boulevard and extended westward along 175th Street was one of the three "mounts" that gave Tremont its name. The extension of the Third Avenue elevated line in the 1890s and trolley cars in the early twentieth century spurred development. By the 1930s Tremont Avenue was the main street, and the largely Jewish population lived in apartment buildings. The Cross Bronx Expressway cut through the area in 1955. In the late twentieth and into the early twenty-first century, the population was largely Latin American.

Lloyd Ultan

fairs and festivals. More than 100 fairs and festivals sponsored by religious, ethnic, civic, and educational organizations, and by tenants' councils, community school boards, and block associations, are held each year in New York City. Most take place between May and October and last from a few hours to a weekend or longer. The most common venues are streets from which traffic is blocked, plazas, and parks; often there are processions, as well as plays and puppet shows mounted on temporary stages, and vendors selling food, clothing, and other goods. The public is usually admitted free of charge, but some fairs and festivals are organized to raise money, and a few, such as the San Gennaro Festival, have become successful commercial enterprises. Some events draw as many as 100,000 spectators a day.

The earliest street festival in the city was organized in July 1884 by the Church of Our Lady of Mount Carmel at East 116th Street in Manhattan to celebrate religion and Italian culture; the event included a procession and was repeated annually into the early twenty-first century. Among the other important ethnic festivals in the city are those of the Chinese New Year in midwinter, which transforms Mott Street in Manhattan south of Canal Street into a colorful display of dragon dances and fireworks; the West Indian carnival and parade along Eastern Parkway to Prospect Park in Brooklyn, an extraordinary procession reminiscent of Mardi Gras that has been adapted to the calendar and climate of New York City by being held on Labor Day; the festival of Good Friday at Crotona Park in the Bronx, which begins with a procession at St. Joseph's Church on Bathgate Avenue and continues with a reenacted crucifixion; the festival of the Giglio, celebrated in midsummer in Williamsburg and in the Bronx along Water Place, which commemorates San Paolino's return to his people (the symbolic "lily" is a structure of wood, paint, and papier-mâché 85 feet, or 26 meters, tall that serves as a platform for a seated orchestra carried through the streets on the shoulders of 100 men); the ancient Korean harvest festival of Choo-Seok, staged on a Sunday in autumn at Flushing Meadow Park by worshippers wearing Korean garb and offering fruits and prayers at the ancestral altar, while dancers, singers, drummers, and wrestlers perform and compete in an immense open space encircled by booths where Korean food is served; the Ganesha Chathurthi celebration at the Bowne Street Hindu Temple in late summer, marked by the depositing of a statue in a body of water nearby; and the Native American Pow Wow, produced by the Thunderbird Dancers at the Queens Farm Museum, which brings together members of 25 Indian tribes from throughout the Americas.

Other fairs and festivals commemorate patriotic occasions. Independence Day and Evacuation Day (25 November) were celebrated as early as the eighteenth century. Reenactments of historic battles were part of celebrations marking the 100th anniversary of the Civil War (at Richmondtown Restoration in Staten Island, 1961) and the 200th of the United States (at Forest Park in Queens, 1976); these later became annual events. The centenary of the Statue of Liberty was celebrated in 1986. Among the festivals honoring the struggles for independence of other nations are the Ecuadorian Festival and Parade, the Greek Cypriots National Heritage Festival, Colombian Independence Day, and the Czechoslovak Festival.

The 1970s and 1980s saw a proliferation of local festivals, many of which continue today. Some are boroughwide, such as the Richmondtown Autumn Celebration in Staten Island (based on Old Home Day, begun in 1941), Bronx Week (1970), and Queens Day (1977). Neighborhood festivals in Brooklyn include the East New York Street Fair, the Midwood Mardi Gras, and Welcome Back to Brooklyn, along with the larger Atlantic Antic, Flatbush Frolic, and Seventh Heaven fairs (all begun in 1975). In Manhattan festivals in Murray Hill and Gramercy Park and the Plantathon rival larger and more prominent fairs on avenues and cross streets that draw several hundred thousand participants: the Ninth Avenue International fair, the Columbus Avenue fair, and the 52nd Street fair (all dating from the 1970s), and the Second Avenue fair, Third Avenue fair, Avenue of the Americas fair, and 42nd Street fair (all dating from the 1980s).

Cultural festivals on a more modest scale include the Annual Fence Show (each September in Staten Island), the Promenade Arts Exhibition (on weekends in May and October in Brooklyn Heights), the Columbus Park Chinatown Summer Cultural Festival (on Sundays in midsummer in Manhattan), and the Queens Ethnic Music and Dance Festival (in September). Grand cultural festivals in Manhattan are held in midtown: the Museum Mile fair (June), the Lincoln Center Out-of-Doors Festival (August), and the New York Is Book Country fair (September). Harlem Week in late August salutes achievement in entertainment and sports. Its organizers exhort New Yorkers: "You haven't done this town till you've done it uptown."

Mimi Gisolfi D'Aponte

Fairview Heights. Obsolete name for a neighborhood in northeastern Staten Island lying within Castleton Corners and bounded to the north by Victory Boulevard, to the east by Clermont Place, to the south by Holden Boulevard, and to the west by Bradley Avenue. The name appears in the *Atlas of the Borough of Richmond, City of New York from Official Records, Private Plans and Actual Surveys* (1898) but never became widely used.

John-Paul Richiuso

Fairway. Independent food retailer, known by the slogan "Like No Other Market," with two stores in Manhattan, one in Brooklyn, and one in Plainview, Long Island. The original location, at 74th Street and Broadway, was established in 1930 as a fruit and vegetable market and then expanded to encompass all types of retail food products. Fairway added new locations in 2000 (133rd Street and 12th Avenue in West Harlem, and Plainview). In 2005 a fourth Fairway market opened on Van Brunt Street in Red Hook, Brooklyn, in a former nineteenth-century coffee warehouse. Fairway is known for its cheeses, meat, fish, fruits, and vegetables.

Andrew Sparberg

Fall River Line. Overnight passenger and freight steamship service connecting New York City with Fall River, Massachusetts, and Newport, Rhode Island. It began service to Fall River in 1847, at a time when the lower Connecticut River had not yet been bridged and most traffic between New York City and southern New England moved by water across Long Island Sound, with rail connections from Fall River to Boston. From 1893 the route was dominated by the New England Steamship Company, a subsidiary of the New Haven Railroad. The line was served by such large and well-appointed ships as the *Pilgrim* (1883), the *Puritan* (1889), the *Priscilla* (1894), and the *Commonwealth* (1907). The *Priscilla* was known for its elegant Renaissance interiors. It slept 1500 passengers, carried 800 tons (725 metric tons) of freight, and was powered by a four-cylinder, double-inclined compound engine of 8500 horsepower with five boilers. The steamer measured 440 feet (134 meters) by 52 feet (15.8 meters). The opening of the Cape Cod Canal in 1916 allowed for more direct travel to Boston, but the Fall River service continued until 1937.

Roger Williams McAdam, *The Old Fall River Line* (Lincoln, R.I.: Mowbray, 1937; rev. 1972 as *Floating Palaces: New England to New York on the Old Fall River Line*)

Arthur G. Adams

family planning. The use of artificial contraceptives increased during the mid-nineteenth century across the country as well as in New York City among the middle and upper classes. By mid-century abortions ended about 20 percent of pregnancies in the city; one of the city's best-known abortionists was the English immigrant ANN TROW LOHMAN, known as Madame Restell. Many other methods of birth control existed but none was particularly effective. Opposition to birth control grew as doctors professionalized and conservative groups endorsed strict moral codes. By the twentieth century the notion of separating sexual activity from reproduction slowly became accepted, and efforts to legalize and promote contraception were centered in New York City. One of the first public advocates of contraception was the anarchist EMMA GOLDMAN, who advocated family planning as a means of countering economic and sexual exploitation of workers. These efforts were soon overshadowed by the work of MARGARET SANGER, who helped to coin the phrase "birth control" in 1914 and became the leader of the movement, opening the first birth control clinic in the country in Brownsville in 1916; she met with fierce opposition. In 1915 the suffragist and sex-education advocate MARY WARE DENNETT formed the National Birth Control League, an organization reorganized in 1918 as the Voluntary Parenthood League. Despite Sanger's willingness to seek legislation making physicians the sole distributors of contraceptives, the city's medical establishment was reluctant to endorse birth control. An exception was Robert L. Dickinson, a gynecologist in Brooklyn who in 1923 established the Committee on Maternal Health to conduct medical research on reproductive health issues, including birth control and abortion. In 1931 the New York Academy of Medicine finally endorsed the use of birth control on medical grounds. Physicians' right to acquire and distribute contraceptives was established by the U.S. Supreme Court in the case of *United States v. One Package* (1936), a challenge to federal bans on the importation of contraceptives that was brought by the Birth Control Clinical Research Bureau, a facility opened at 17 West 16th Street by Margaret Sanger in 1923. The bureau and the American Birth Control League merged to form the Birth Control Federation of America in 1939, renamed the Planned Parenthood Federation in 1942 (see PLANNED PARENTHOOD FEDERATION OF AMERICA, INC.).

In New York City, as in the rest of the country, access to family planning services remained limited at the end of the 1950s, largely because the Catholic Church opposed birth control and abortion. As late as 1957 municipally funded health centers in the city would not provide contraceptives or information about them, and none of the city's 17 birth control centers was housed in a public hospital; Planned Parenthood offered the only subsidized family planning services in the city. The unofficial ban on dispensing contraceptives in municipal hospitals was eased on 17 September 1958 by the Board of Hospitals, which allowed contraceptives to be used in cases where pregnancy jeopardized a woman's life. Birth control became fully incorporated into the city's health programs only after the U.S. Supreme Court legalized the distribution of birth control devices to married couples in 1965 and to unmarried individuals in 1972. Abortions continued to be performed, occasionally resulting in criminal prosecution, but in April 1970 New York State passed a liberal reform law that made abortion legal. Because New York City did not impose a residency requirement, its abortion clinics served thousands of women from across the country until the U.S. Supreme Court legalized abortion nationwide in the case of *Roe v. Wade* (1973). In 1999, Plan B, an emergency contraceptive also known as "the morning after pill," became available in the city by prescription only. After federal changes in legislation, in November 2006 New York City pharmacies began carrying Plan B over the counter, and it became available in 94 percent of the city's drugstores in less than a year; the city's Department of Health and Mental Hygiene began offering emergency contraceptives at each of its 10 sexually transmitted disease (STD) clinics for free and without parental consent. In the early twenty-first century a wide range of family planning services are offered in most New York City hospitals and in a network of family planning clinics administered by the city's Human Resources Administration, but these facilities continue to face serious challenges.

Linda Gordon, *Woman's Body, Woman's Right: A Social History of Birth Control in America* (New York: Grossman, 1976); James C. Mohr, *Abortion in America* (New York: Oxford University Press, 1978); James Reed, *From Private Vice to Public Virtue: The Birth Control Movement and American Society since 1830* (Princeton, N.J.: Princeton University Press, 1978)

Esther Katz

F and M Schaefer Brewing. Firm formed in 1842 by Frederick Schaefer and Maximilian Schaefer, immigrants from Wetzlar, Prussia; it was the city's first producer of lager beer. For its manufacturing process it imported bottom-floating yeasts from Germany and fermented them at low temperatures. After operating for many years near Grand Central Terminal, the firm moved to Brooklyn in 1915. It manufactured ice and near-beer during Prohibition, and while remaining under family control expanded after World War II by buying breweries in Baltimore and in Albany, New York. For a time after 1945 it produced the sixth-largest volume of malt beverages in the country. It opened a modern factory near Allentown, Pennsylvania, in 1972 and in the following year bought the brand name of Piels, a beer made in Brooklyn from 1883 to 1963. Schaefer was the country's seventh-largest brewer in 1975, when it suffered financial losses that forced it to close its production facilities in the city, including its brewery in Brooklyn in 1976.

Stanley Wade Baron, *Brewed in America: A History of Beer and Ale in the United States* (Boston: Little, Brown, 1962)

K. Austin Kerr

FAO Schwarz. Firm of toy and game retailers formed in 1863 in Baltimore by Frederick August Otto Schwarz, an immigrant from Westphalia who moved to New York City in 1870 to open the Schwarz Toy Bazaar at 765 Broadway. With his three brothers he built a prosperous business by drawing on the expertise of select toy manufacturers in Europe. In 1880 he moved to larger quarters at 42 East 14th Street, across from Union Square. He moved the store to two other locations in the city before eventually settling uptown at 745 Fifth Avenue in 1931. In 1963 the Schwarz family sold the company, which went through several owners. In 1986 the store moved across the street to 767 Fifth Avenue. Although the firm later opened 17 stores throughout the United States, the flagship emporium in New York City remained the best known, in part because of its prominent location and in part because it was shown in several films. One of these films, *Big* (1988), featured Tom Hanks and Robert Loggia performing "Heart and Soul" and "Chopsticks" on the store's giant floor keyboard. A children's bank was opened at the store in 1988 by the First Women's Bank. In 1996 it opened FAO Schweetz, a candy retailer. In 2001 it opened FAO Baby on Fifth Avenue. In 2003 FAO Inc. filed for Chapter 11 bankruptcy, emerging in late April of the following year. That same year Vendex sold its share in the company to the hedge fund D. E. Shaw. In 2009 the company was acquired by Toys "R" Us Inc. The firm is known worldwide for its large selection of distinctive and expensive merchandise.

F. A. O. Schwarz Toys through the Years (New York: Doubleday, 1975)

Frank Morrow

Fareynikte yidishe geverkshaftn. See United Hebrew Trades.

Farley, James A(loysius) (*b* Grassy Point, N.Y., 30 May 1888; *d* New York City, 9 June 1976). Political leader. After graduating from Packard Commercial School in 1906 he worked as a bookkeeper. He was a warden of the port, the president of the state athletic commission, and a state assemblyman before he opened a bookkeeping firm in 1926. The secretary and chairman of the state Democratic committee from 1928 to 1944, he played an important role in the election of Franklin D. Roosevelt to the presidency in 1932. From 1932 to 1940 he was both chairman of the Democratic National Committee and postmaster general. After opposing Roosevelt's bid for a third term, he left public life and became chairman of the export division of Coca-Cola, a position he held for 35 years. He wrote an autobiography, *Jim Farley's Story* (1948). In 1982 the General Post Office at 421 Eighth Avenue was named the James A. Farley Building in his honor.

John T. Casey and James Boules, *Farley and Tomorrow* (Chicago: Reilly and Lee, 1937)

James E. Mooney

Farley, John M(urphy) (*b* Newton-Hamilton, County Armaugh, Ireland, 20 April 1842; *d* New York City, 17 Sept 1918). Cardinal. After moving to New York City in 1864, he was ordained on 11 June 1870 and in the same year became an assistant at St. Peter's in New Brighton. He was John McCloskey's secretary from 1872 until 1884, when he became the pastor of the Church of St. Gabriel's in the East 30s (now defunct), a position he retained until 1902. His handling of a breach between the clergy and the hierarchy that began as a confrontation between Michael A. Corrigan and Edward McGlynn won him the admiration of archdiocesan priests: to resolve it he recognized clerics passed over for chancery positions by elevating them to the title of monsignor, a papal honor previously reserved for the chancery. From 1891 to 1902 he was the vicar general and president of the Catholic school board. Appointed an auxiliary bishop on 21 December 1895 and an archbishop on 15 September 1902, he opened Cathedral College (1903), authorized the *New York Review* (1905–7), and helped to finance and edit the *Catholic Encyclopedia* (1907–12). Under his auspices national parishes were first established in the city for Italian-speaking Albanians who practiced Oriental rites (Our Lady of Grace, 1907), for Lithuanians (Our Lady of Vilna, 1909), and for Slovenians (St. Cyril's, 1916). He welcomed into his archdiocese the motherhouse of the Catholic Foreign Mission Society of America (established at Maryknoll in New York City, 1911), was named a cardinal on 27 November 1911, introduced monthly retreats for the clergy, and instituted a system for supervising charitable work and parishes dominated by ethnic minorities (1912). When the United States entered World War I he helped to organize the National Catholic War Conference and promoted wartime charities within his see, even though his health was failing. Farley is buried beneath St. Patrick's Cathedral.

Mary Elizabeth Brown

Farmer, A. W. Pseudonym of Samuel Seabury.

farming. See Agriculture.

Farragut. Neighborhood in east central Brooklyn, bounded to the north by Cortelyou Road and Holy Cross Cemetery, to the east by Kings Highway, to the south by tracks of the Long Island Rail Road, and to the west by Brooklyn Avenue. The area was originally part of the town of Flatbush and is named for the Civil War admiral David G. Farragut. From 1925 to 1950 the population consisted largely of Jews and Italians, who lived in one- and two-family detached and semidetached houses built in the 1920s and 1930s. A number of apartment buildings were erected after World War II; Vanderveer Estates (1949–50), a middle-income complex of 59 buildings, houses 2500 families. Most of the new immigrants settling in Farragut in the 1980s were blacks from the Caribbean. More than a quarter were Haitian, and there were also a large number of immigrants from Guyana, Jamaica, Trinidad and Tobago, Barbados, Grenada, China, and the Soviet Union. In the early twenty-first century Church Avenue is the principal commercial thoroughfare.

Walter Thabit, *East Flatbush on the Threshold* (New York: New York City Department of Planning, 1969)

Elizabeth Reich Rawson

Farrar, Straus and Giroux. Firm of book publishers formed as Farrar and Rinehart in June 1929 by John Farrar, Frederick Rinehart, and Stanley M. Rinehart at 12 East 41st Street. Sales for the first month totaled $26, but by September the firm had earned $46,000. In 1946 the firm of Farrar, Straus was formed by Farrar and Roger W. Straus, Jr., with offices at 580 Fifth Avenue. Renamed Farrar, Straus and Young in 1951 and Farrar, Straus and Cudahy in 1955, it took its current name in 1964 after the editor Robert Giroux became a full partner. It bought Octagon Books in 1968 and Hill and Wang in 1971 and remained one of few independent publishers after resisting attempts by several corporations to take it over. Farrar, Straus and Giroux remained known for literary excellence: between 1945 and 1985 it published the work of 13 Nobel laureates, including Aleksandr Solzhenitsyn and T. S. Eliot. Farrar, Straus and Giroux was acquired by Verlagsgruppe Georg von Holtzbrinck of Stuttgart, Germany, in 1994. In the early twenty-first century the firm's corporate offices were located at 19 Union Square West.

Allen J. Share

Farrell, Eileen (*b* Willimantic, Conn., 13 February 1920; *d* Park Ridge, N.J., 23 March 2002). Classical vocalist. Farrell came to New York City in 1939 and found work with the radio chorus of the Columbia Broadcasting System (CBS). The following year the network gave the soprano her own program, "Eileen Farrell Presents," which lasted seven years. In 1946 she married a New York City police officer and began making appearances with symphony orchestras. At one time she held the record as the New York Philharmonic's most frequent soloist. One critic wrote of the "immense softness" of her voice. She performed at the Roxy Theater in Manhattan and was a member of the acclaimed Bach Aria Group. Her first opera performance was in 1956 in Mascagni's *Cavalleria Rusticana* in Tampa. Farrell's Metropolitan Opera debut came with a new production of Gluck's *Alceste* in 1960; she remained at the Met for five seasons. Throughout the 1960s and early 1970s she was a popular guest on many top television variety programs. From 1971 to 1980 she taught voice at Indiana University.

Brian Kellow

Farrell, Suzanne [Ficker, Roberta Sue] (*b* Cincinnati, Ohio, 16 Aug 1945). Dancer. She attended the School of American Ballet in 1960 and a year later joined New York City Ballet. While there Farrell received much attention from George Balanchine, who considered her one of his muses and the ideal ballerina of his style. He created many principal roles for her in such works as the *pas de deux* "Meditation" (1963) and his full-length ballet *Don Quixote* (1965). Praised for the silken quality of her movements, her daring, and her fluid response to music, she inspired much of Balanchine's later choreography, including the ballets *Variations* (1966) and "Diamonds," a section of *Jewels* (1967). In 1969 a dispute between Balanchine and Farrell caused her and her husband, the dancer and choreographer Paul Mejia, to leave New York City Ballet and join Maurice Béjart's Ballet du XXe Siècle in Brussels. She returned to Balanchine's company in 1975, however, after the two reconciled. He then choreographed a series of renowned works for Farrell, including *Chaconne* (1976), in which she was paired with the favored partner of her later years, Peter Martins; *Vienna Waltzes* (1977); *Davidsbündlertänze* (1980); and *Mozartiana* (1981). After retiring in 1989 Farrell wrote *Holding On to the Air: An Autobiography* (1990) with Toni Bentley. In 2000 she started her own company, Suzanne Farrell Ballet, which trains dancers in the Balanchine style.

Nancy Reynolds, *Repertory in Review: Forty Years of the New York City Ballet* (New York: Dial, 1977); Barnard Taper, *Balanchine: A Biography* (New York: Times Books, 1984)

Nancy Reynolds

Far Rockaway. Neighborhood in southeastern Queens (2000 pop. *ca* 35,000), toward the eastern end of the Rockaway Peninsula west of the border with Nassau County. Canarsee Indians named the area Reckouacky (probably meaning "place of our people"), from which the present name derives; they sold it in 1685 to John Palmer, who in turn sold it in 1687 to an inhabitant of Flushing, Richard Cornell. Until 1898 the area was part of the town of Hempstead. In 1809 Cornell's heirs divided the land into 46 parcels; these were acquired in 1833 by John L. Norton, who later sold them piecemeal. During the same year the area became a seaside resort after a hotel called the Marine Pavilion opened to serve those fleeing an outbreak of cholera in New York City. Before the hotel burned in 1864, it served many illustrious guests, including Henry Wadsworth Longfellow, Washington Irving, and Jonathan Trumbull. More hotels and summer boarding houses appeared after rail service was extended by the South Side Railroad in 1869 and the Long Island Rail Road in 1872. A lack of city services inspired a secession movement, and a bill to make Far Rockaway a separate city passed the state legislature in 1915 and 1917 before being vetoed by the mayor of New York City. The area remained a beach resort until 1956 when the subway reached Far Rockaway. In the 1960s and 1970s many old mansions became nursing homes, and high-rise apartments rose along the shore. In the 1980s new immigrants from Jamaica and Guyana moved there. There were also immigrants from El Salvador, Haiti, the Dominican Republic, Guatemala, and Afghanistan. As of the early twenty-first century nearly 25 percent of the population was Orthodox Jewish. The neighborhood remained dominated by lower middle-class and middle-class housing and struggled with above average crime rates and poor schools.

Vincent Seyfried

Fasanella, Ralph (*b* Brooklyn, 7 Sept 1914; *d* Yonkers, N.Y., 16 Dec 1997). Painter. After fighting in the Spanish Civil War and serving in the navy during World War II, he moved to 47 Grove Street in Greenwich Village and became an organizer for the Congress of Industrial Organizations. He taught himself painting at the age of 30 and became known for his compassionate depictions of ordinary people in New York City and of immigrant life. His paintings, which frequently depict the city's bridges, subways, and parks, are "primitive" yet detailed and symbolic. Representative examples include a series of two paintings called *Iceman Crucified.*

Patrick Watson, *Fasanella's City: The Paintings of Ralph Fasanella with the Story of His Life and Art* (New York: Alfred A. Knopf, 1973)

Betty Kaplan Gubert

fashion. During the early nineteenth century New York City became the fashion center of the United States. With access to the Great Lakes region afforded via the Hudson River, the city enjoyed an advantage over such port cities as Boston, Philadelphia, and Charleston, South Carolina. Tailors, furriers, jewelers, haberdashers, and milliners multiplied in the city as it developed into a distribution center. Dry-goods stores gave way to department stores that were so impressive that travelers from Europe often likened the shopping in the city to that of Paris and London. Retailers settled into the best residential areas, which continued to move north as homeowners sought more space and quiet. By the 1820s the most successful shops congregated at lower Broadway, where A. T. Stewart, widely recognized as the city's most innovative retailer, erected a "marble palace" to house his business in 1846. Other merchants opened shops nearby and followed Stewart when he moved in 1862 to even grander quarters, bounded by Broadway, Fourth Avenue, and Ninth and Tenth streets. Eventually an elaborate shopping district took shape: it ran from 14th to 23rd streets between Sixth Avenue and Broadway and was later known as the LADIES' MILE.

Custom-made clothing dominated the fashion industry in New York City until manufacturers in the 1850s introduced "ready-to-wear," mass-produced clothing inspired by uniforms sold to the U.S. Army and Navy. The first ready-to-wear garment was the men's business "uniform," consisting of a tailored frock coat and trousers. Ready-to-wear for women included easily fitted outerwear articles such as mantles and capes that appeared in exclusive stores in New York City during the late 1850s, but in general women's ready-to-wear clothing did not become popular until women began wearing simpler clothing. Articles of women's clothing that resembled menswear in style such as shirtwaists (tailored blouses), walking skirts, and jackets were produced as ready-to-wear in the 1860s, inspired in part by the movement for women's rights. Unsized clothing patterns first appeared in fashion magazines in the early 1850s; sized patterns introduced in 1864 made it possible for amateur seamstresses and women working at home to produce fashionable clothes tailored to the wearer. By the 1890s most women owned an outfit consisting of a shirtwaist, jacket, and skirt. Sold separately, these items were suited to the development of retail catalogues, or wish books, which became popular in the 1870s and offered a multitude of ready-to-wear clothing.

A distinctly American style emerged in the 1890s. The "Gibson girl," a healthy, sporty image depicted by the illustrator Charles Dana Gibson, helped to define the fashions of New York City as natural and becoming, in contrast to the imposing artificiality of fashions from Paris. As early as the 1920s supporters of fashions made in America like Dorothy Shaver, vice president of Lord and Taylor, added designer labels to American clothing in an effort to counter the perception that clothing made in New York City was copied from French styles. Among the many successful designers working in the city during the 1930s were Claire McCardell, Charles James, Valentina, Lilly Daché, Nettie Rosenstein, Elizabeth Hawes, Germaine Monteil, Jessie Franklin Turner, Tom Brigance, and Clare Potter. During the 1940s New York City residents produced 125,000 designs a year. Their output was notable for its diversity: it included haute couture, ready-to-wear of high quality (known as "couture-caliber"), tailored coats and suits, inexpensive house dresses, and sportswear. Much innovation in fashion occurred during World War II, when the fashion industry was cut off from the influence of Paris and freer to promote native design. The core of the fashion district at the time was the intersection of 57th Street and Fifth Avenue, with most department stores on Fifth Avenue and specialty stores selling primarily custom-made clothes and accessories off Fifth and Madison avenues in the 1950s and 1960s. The district saw the closing of several of its department stores during the 1960s and 1970s.

In the late 1970s New York City emerged as an international fashion capital rivaling Paris and Milan. The city became the base for such leading designers as Halston, Bill Blass, Geoffrey Beene, Perry Ellis, and Donna Karan, and fashion shows increased in number and importance. The fashion world was ravaged, however, in the 1980s and early 1990s by the AIDS epidemic, which claimed the lives of several leading figures.

Another important force in reinforcing the city's influence as a fashion center is the large number of fashion publications published there, notably the trade newspaper *Women's Wear Daily* and the magazines *Vogue* and *Harper's Bazaar.* In addition, New York City became the home to several of the leading fashion design programs in the world including Parsons The New School for Design (1896) and the Fashion Institute of Technology (1944). These programs educated designers who were on the cutting edge of fashion, including Donna Karan, Calvin Klein, Tom Ford, and Michael Kors. In 1993 the industry event FASHION WEEK moved to Bryant Park and established a biannual, spectacular exhibition of contemporary designers in New York City. That same year the Fashion Center Business Improvement District, a not-for-profit corporation, was established to promote New York City's apparel industry and to improve the quality of life and economic vitality of Manhattan's garment district. In the early twenty-first century development along the High Line park inspired several fashion houses to relocate to the meatpacking district and Chelsea neighborhoods in Manhattan. These designers, including Diane von Furstenberg, and their interest in the area helped to reaffirm New York City's prevalence as a leader in high fashion.

Caroline Rennolds Milbank, Anne Epstein

Fashion Group International. Nonprofit professional organization of women in the fashion industry and related fields, formed in 1930 by Edna Wollman Chase of *Vogue;* Carmel Snow of *Harper's Bazaar;* Virginia Pope of the *New York Times;* the designers Claire McCardell, Lilly Daché, Edith Head, and Adele Simpson; and the cosmetics executives Elizabeth Arden and Helena Rubinstein. Eleanor Roosevelt served on the advisory board. The organization soon set up a placement bureau for the unemployed and also became an advocate for women working in fashion and related industries. The organization maintains a library, awards scholarships to fashion and merchandising schools, provides career counseling services, and supports environmental awareness programs and breast cancer research. In addition to the headquarters in New York City there are 44 regional groups throughout the United States and the world. In 2010 the Fashion Group International had more than 6000 members.

Phyllis Barr

Fashion Institute of Technology [FIT]. Public institution founded by Mortimer C. Ritter and Max Meyer in 1944 to create "the

Fashion Institute of Technology, 2009

MIT for fashion industries." Ritter, Meyer, and other apparel manufacturers organized the Educational Foundation for the Fashion Industries, which instigated a charter for fashion design and technology education in New York City. Originally located at 225 West 24th Street at the High School for Needle Trades (later renamed the High School of Fashion Industries), the college offered only design and scientific management degrees to its 100 students. In 1957 FIT became the second State University of New York community college, and in the late 1970s it offered four-year and then graduate curricula. In 1967 the school founded a museum, which currently holds 50,000 garments and accessories. In the 1970s it moved to its current location in the heart of the garment district, at Seventh Avenue and 27th Street, where it occupies a full city block and eight buildings. In 2007 it expanded to offer undergraduate and graduate degrees for 43 fashion-based majors, including design, pattern making, photography, and business, and it enrolled over 10,000 students. Its courses present students with real-world situations and equipment for programs such as jewelry, toy, and interior design. Graduates from FIT include fashion moguls Calvin Klein, Rebecca Moses, Bob Abajan, and Norma Kamali.

Stephanie Miller

Fashion Week. Biannual event founded in 1943 by fashion publicist Eleanor Lambert. Press Week, as it was originally called, publicized American designers who had previously worked in the shadow of the Parisian fashion scene. After American designers gained renown during the mid-twentieth century, they began producing individual shows at private spaces around New York City. In an effort to consolidate the shows for greater exposure, in 1993 Fern Mallis, former executive director of the Council of Fashion Designers of America, founded 7th on Sixth at Bryant Park. In fall 2010 Fashion Week moved from Bryant Park to Damrosch Park at Lincoln Center.

Kate Lauber

Father Divine [Baker, George] (*b* Hutchinson's Island, Ga., *ca* 1879; *d* Merion, Pa., 10 Sept 1965). Preacher. He worked part-time as a Baptist preacher and moved to Brooklyn before settling in Sayville, New York, where he formed the Peace Mission Movement, which provided meals for hungry members during the Depression. In 1933 he moved the organization to Harlem and it gained thousands of followers. He soon opened 200 centers in New York City and in Philadelphia, where he made his headquarters from 1942. Father Divine issued the publication *New Day* to promote his views; he supported celibacy and the use of cash in business transactions and inveighed against welfare, tobacco, liquor, and profanity. After his death, his wife, Mother Divine, succeeded him as the leader of the movement.

Robert Weisbrot, *Father Divine and the Struggle for Racial Equality* (Urbana: University of Illinois Press, 1983)

James E. Mooney

Father Knickerbocker. Pen name of WASHINGTON IRVING.

fauna. A wide range of animal species thrives in the diverse habitats of New York City. The waters off the city support more than 75 species of finfish, including the Mummiching (*Fundulas hetroclitus*) and the Bluefish (*Pomatomus saltatrix*), an aggressive carnivore and popular game fish. Young Bluefish, called "snappers," are common in the inlets and bays in summer and rely on such estuaries as New York Harbor for their growth. Birds such as terns (Common, Least, and Roseate) and gulls (Laughing, Black-backed, Bonaparte, Ring-billed, and Herring) are found along the coasts. Marsh islands and coastal dunes along the shore support Black Skimmers, Oystercatchers, and Brown Pelicans. Piping Plovers (considered threatened under the Endangered Species Act), which remain in the area from mid-March until early September and raise their chicks along the tidal wrack lines, make slight depressions in the sand to use as nests. Patches of Saltwater Cordgrass (*Spartina alterniflora*) and Seatmeadow Cordgrass (*Spartina patens*) harbor many animals. Coastal ecosystems abound with Mugwort, Sweet Clover, and Reedgrass (*Pharargmites australis*), an especially valuable plant to wildlife: its roots are the preferred food of muskrats, and its dense stems provide cover for pheasants. In the summer, nesting Red-winged Blackbirds are often seen flying in these areas hunting for insects. Waterbirds like the Canvasback, Scaup, Pintail, and Mallard live around freshwater bodies such as East Pond in the Jamaica Bay Wildlife Refuge, Clove Lake on Staten Island, and Alley Pond in Queens, which attracts nesting passerine (songbirds) like warblers (among them the Blue-winged Warbler).

The Norway Rat (or Brown Rat) was carried to North America by European settlers and is found throughout the city's sewer system; it is a choice food of Barn Owls. Other mammals in the city include the Raccoon, the Gray Squirrel, the Opossum, and several species of bat, among them the Hoary, Red, and Silver-haired bats and the Little Brown Myotis. Efforts are being made to restore the Hempstead Plains, grasslands not unlike the Western prairies that once stretched from eastern Brooklyn through Queens, Nassau, and Suffolk counties (only 19 acres [8 hectares] survived development, all in Nassau). In Brooklyn the National Park Service retards the growth of woody vegetation through mowing and fires, allowing the return of such grassland animals as Grasshopper Sparrows, Short-eared Owls, Meadowlarks, Upland Sandpipers, Meadow Voles, and White-footed Mice.

Unusual species living in the city include Monk Parakeets in Brooklyn and a band of Black-tailed Jack Rabbits inhabiting the grounds of John F. Kennedy International Airport in Queens; both probably escaped from shipments at the airport in the mid-twentieth century. A Florida Manatee named Chessie turned up in the East River in 1995, and Humpback Whales have been stranded on New York beaches. The North American Beaver, a species deeply embedded in New York's early economic development, returned in 2007 after being hunted almost to extinction during the heyday of the fur trade. The lone male beaver building a home on the Bronx River—the first sighted in New York in 200 years—was nicknamed "José" after U.S. Representative José E. Serrano of the Bronx, who has directed millions of dollars toward the environmental revitalization of the river.

See also AMPHIBIANS AND REPTILES, BIRDS, BUTTERFLIES, COCKROACHES, OYSTERS, and PALE MALE.

John T. Tanacredi

Fauset, Jessie Redmon (*b* Camden, N.J., 27 April 1882; *d* Philadelphia, 30 April 1960). Novelist, editor, and poet. The first black woman to graduate from Cornell University, she taught for almost 20 years at DeWitt Clinton High School in the Bronx and edited the *Crisis* (a publication of the National Association for the Advancement of Colored People) and a monthly magazine for black children. Her home in Harlem was an important literary salon during the Harlem Renaissance. Fauset published four novels between 1924 and 1933, and her poems have been collected in anthologies.

Carolyn Wedin Sylvander, *Jessie Redmon Fauset, Black American Writer* (Troy, N.Y.: Whitston, 1981)

See also HARLEM RENAISSANCE.

James E. Mooney

FDR Drive. Controlled-access highway running along the east side of Manhattan Island from the financial district to Harlem. Built under the direction of Robert Moses during the administration of Mayor Fiorello H. La Guardia and named for President Franklin D. Roosevelt, it was planned as a link in a projected circumferential belt parkway. Much of the landfill on which it is constructed consists of the rubble of buildings from London destroyed during World War II by the Luftwaffe's blitz. Convoys of ships returning

FDR Drive, 1940

from Great Britain carried the broken masonry in their holds as ballast.

Kenneth T. Jackson

Federal Archives Building. Office and residential building at 641 Washington Street in Manhattan. It stands 10 stories tall and fills the block bounded by Washington, Christopher, Barrow, and Greenwich streets. The brick building was built in 1892–98 by Willoughby J. Edbrooke in the Romanesque Revival style as a federal appraisers' warehouse, where customs agents weighed and tested samples of imports to determine customs duties. In 1938 the building was remodeled into office space for use by the federal archives. The federal government abandoned the building in 1976, and in 1982 it was again renovated for commercial and residential use. It was designated a landmark on 15 March 1966.

Brooke J. Barr

federal courts. See Courts, §3.

Federal Hall. Name given to two buildings successively occupying the same site at Wall and Nassau streets in lower Manhattan. The first, constructed in 1699 as the second city hall of the colony of New York, was remodeled in 1788 by Pierre L'Enfant and was the site of George Washington's inauguration on 30 April 1789. The second, now known as Federal Hall National Memorial, was designed by Ithiel Town and Alexander Jackson Davis in 1834 and erected in 1842. It is best known for the monumental statue of Washington by John Quincy Adams Ward that stands before it (1883). The building is one of the finest examples in New York City of Greek Revival architecture. Broad steps lead from Wall Street to a portico of eight Doric columns 32 feet (10 meters) high, which support an architrave with 16 triglyphs crowned by a plain triangular pediment. The northern face of the building (on Pine Street) also has a portico. Inside is a light-filled rotunda; the walls of the building are 5 feet (1.5 meters) thick.

The building was used successively as the custom house for the Port of New York (1842–62), as a subtreasury after the Customs Service moved to larger quarters at 55 Wall Street, as a branch of the Federal Reserve Bank (1920–25), for various federal offices (1925–55), and as a museum of the National Park Service (from 1955).

Mollie Keller

Federalist. Series of 85 essays advocating ratification of the Constitution of the United States. Seventy-seven of the essays were published in the newspapers the *Independent Journal* and the *New York Packet* between October 1787 and August 1788; these and eight others were included in a book entitled *The Federalist* published in New York City in 1788 by J. and A. M'Lean. The essays were written by Alexander Hamilton (nos. 1, 6–9, 11–13, 15–17, 21–36, 59–61, and 65–85) and John Jay (nos. 2–5 and 64), both natives of New York City, and James Madison (nos. 10, 14, 18–20, 37–58, and 62–63), a Virginian then living in the city, and were all signed with the pseudonym "Publius." The authors addressed the essays to "the People and State of New York," whose support for the Constitution they considered indispensable to the success of the new federal union. The essays were widely read and discussed and have been reprinted many times. They are regarded not only as an important Federalist document but also as a great work of political philosophy.

Edward Millican, *One United People: The Federalist Papers and the National Idea* (Lexington: University Press of Kentucky, 1990)

Edward T. O'Donnell

Federal Hall, 2009

Federalist Party. Political party of the late eighteenth and early nineteenth centuries. Taking coherent shape between the ratification of the U.S. Constitution in 1788 and the presidential election of 1792, it sought to maintain close ties with Great Britain and was sympathetic to commercial and manufacturing interests. The party became powerful in New York City during the 1790s, owing to the prominence of its leaders, Alexander Hamilton and John Jay, and property restrictions on voting; it declined because of Thomas Jefferson's election in 1800, the souring of relations with Britain after 1805, the expansion of suffrage, and the arrogance and insensitivity of its leaders, who too often tried to command the deference rather than win the support of the city's voters. The party lost control of the Common Council when voting laws were made more liberal in 1804, but regained control briefly in 1806 and again in 1809 as the city suffered the effects of the Embargo Act of 1807, which was endorsed heavily by Jefferson. Bolstered by the unpopularity of the War of 1812, it retained the majority until 1815, except in 1813 when the council was evenly divided between Federalists and Republicans. The party nominated Rufus King of New York for vice president in 1808 and for president in 1816, and supported DeWitt Clinton in 1812. It eventually disintegrated nationwide and ceased to exist in the city by 1820.

Evan Cornog

Federal Reserve Bank of New York. One of 12 banks created by the Federal Reserve Act of December 1913. It opened for business in New York City on 16 November 1914 with a 20-year charter. Although the powers granted by the legislation were minimal by modern standards, the Federal Reserve System was designed to regulate the currency, control domestic credit, and prevent financial panics of the kind that had repeatedly afflicted the country. The potential dominance of New York in the system was offset by the other Federal Reserve banks, while the Federal Reserve Board, appointed by the president of the United States, was to countervail the influence of the commercial banks that owned the Federal Reserve banks. Nevertheless, the New York bank immediately became the most influential unit in the system; on its first day it accepted $99,611,670 in deposits from 479 commercial banks.

At the first board meeting of the New York Federal Reserve Bank, Benjamin Strong was elected its principal executive officer, or governor. A former president of Bankers Trust, Strong had assisted J. P. Morgan in containing the financial crisis of 1907 and had intimate knowledge of foreign money markets. His bank dominated Federal Reserve Board decisions and purchased government securities for the other 11 banks. In 1916 the New York bank began accepting the gold reserves of foreign nations, and it coordinated much of the financing of World War I. Afterward, Strong implemented the system's adoption of open market operations as a principal instrument of monetary policy; he developed successful stabilization policies and facilitated Great Britain's return to the gold standard. By 1927 the Federal Reserve Bank of New York was the world's preeminent central bank, and all its units were granted charters of indefinite duration.

The Federal Reserve Bank of New York operated at 62 Cedar Street until 1924, when its permanent headquarters at 33 Liberty Street were completed. Designed by Phillip Sawyer and occupying a full city block, the stone building was modeled after a Renaissance Florentine palace and reaches five stories below street level to the bedrock of Manhattan Island. Designated a city landmark in 1965, its vaults hold 25 to 30 percent of the world's monetary gold reserve. The bank's principal offices are still located in this building, but some of its staff and operations were relocated to a high rise on Maiden Lane in the late 1970s.

Strong died in October 1928 and his successor, George Harrison, had to confront the stock market crash of 1929 and deepening Depression. The New York bank was unable to implement effective countercyclical measures, and monetary policy shifted to Washington, D.C.; the Banking Act of 1935 created a new board of governors, with individual bank leaders designated as presidents. The Federal Reserve Bank of New York remains the largest and most active unit of the Federal Reserve System and is uniquely influential in the development and implementation of monetary policy. It occupies a permanent seat on the Federal Open Market Committee and executes committee policy by buying and selling government securities for all the Federal Reserve banks and by conducting operations in foreign currency markets. It also performs standard Reserve Bank functions by lending to depository institutions, supervising banks, collecting checks, managing payments systems, and serving as fiscal agent for the federal government. Since George Harrison, it has had a number of distinguished presidents, including Allan Sproul (1941–56), Alfred Hayes (1956–75), Paul Volcker (1975–79), E. Gerald Corrigan (1985–93), and William J. McDonough (1993–2003).

Lester Chandler, *Benjamin Strong* (Washington, D.C.: Brookings Institution, 1958); Charles Belfore, *Monuments to Money: The Architecture of American Banks* (Jefferson, N.C.: McFarland & Co., 2005); Bernard Shull, *The Fourth Branch: The Federal Reserve's Unlikely Rise to Power and Influence* (Westport, Conn.: Praeger, 2005)

George J. Lankevich, Bernard Shull

Federation of Jewish Philanthropies. An agency formed in 1917 by 54 Jewish charitable organizations to consolidate their fund raising. During its first campaign it collected $200,000 more than its individual member organizations had done in 1915. To avoid conflicts the agency excluded religious educational organizations; in 1942 it absorbed a parallel organization in Brooklyn. By the late 1960s funds raised for Jewish agencies in Queens, Nassau, Suffolk, and Westchester counties reached $22 million. In 1974 the federation combined its fund-raising activities with those of the United Jewish Appeal.

Jean Ulitz Mensch

Feehan, William M. (*b* Queens, 29 Sept 1929; *d* New York City, 11 Sept 2001). Firefighter. He grew up in Jackson Heights, Queens. After graduating from Saint John's University in 1952, he joined the army and served in the Korean War. He joined the Fire Department in 1959, starting as a probationary firefighter, and steadily rose in rank, becoming the first person in the history of the department to hold every rank. He was appointed deputy fire commissioner in 1992 and served briefly as acting fire commissioner in 1993. After 1993 Feehan retained his position as deputy fire commissioner until 11 September 2001 when he raced to the World Trade Center from Fire Department headquarters in Brooklyn Heights after the terrorist attacks. Along with his close friend, Chief of Department Peter J. Ganci, Feehan directed rescue operations until the collapse of the South Tower took his life.

Max Seppo

Feiffer, Jules (Ralph) (*b* Bronx, 26 Jan 1929). Cartoonist and writer. As a child in the Bronx during the Depression he was influenced by comics and radio programs; he soon imitated master cartoonists' work and at an early age produced his own comic books. From 1946 he worked as an assistant to the syndicated cartoonist Will Eisner, with whom he produced "The Spirit" from 1949 to 1952, a popular cartoon carried by the *New York Daily Compass,* the newspaper of the Progressive Party. Feiffer attended the Pratt Institute in Brooklyn from 1947 to 1951. He wrote the book *Munro* while serving in the army from 1951 to 1953, followed by *Passionella* and *Sick, Sick, Sick,* none of which he was able to publish. Seeking to arouse interest in these works, he offered his services gratis to the *Village Voice,* which published his weekly comic strip of social and political satire. This became nationally syndicated in 1959; *Sick, Sick, Sick* was published during the same year and *Passionella* in 1960, and *Munro* was eventually made into an animated film by Al Kouzel and Gene Deitch that won an Academy Award.

His play *Little Murders* had its premiere on Broadway in 1967 but closed after seven performances; it reopened in 1969 under the direction of Alan Arkin at the Circle in the Square and won an Obie Award and an Outer Circle Drama Critics award. In 1971 he adapted *Little Murders* for the screen and wrote the screenplay for *Carnal Knowledge* (directed by Mike Nichols). He next completed a dramatization of "Hold Me," a comic strip he had produced in 1962, for the American Place Theater in 1977 and the screenplay for Robert Altman's *Popeye* in 1980. In 1985 he won a Pulitzer Prize for editorial cartooning. Feiffer's many books include *The Great Comic Book Heroes* (1965, edited by E. L. Doctorow), the cartoon novel *Feiffer on Nixon: The Cartoon Presidency* (1974), *Tantrum* (1979), and *Ronald Reagan in Movie-America* (1988). In addition to politics he also bases his work on the struggles of individuals in modern urban society. He lives in Manhattan.

Grai St. Clair Rice

Feinberg Law. Statute passed by the New York state legislature in 1949, requiring the state Board of Regents to list organizations it found to be subversive and to disqualify from public school employment any member of a listed organization. A product of the Red Scare that dominated American political life after World War II, the law mandated strict enforcement of existing statutes that barred from employment any school employee who advocated the overthrow of the government by "force, violence or any unlawful means." A 1953 amendment extended the law to state universities; the same year, the Board of Regents listed the Communist parties of the United States and of New York State as subversive organizations. Three years later, the regents required employees to sign a "Feinberg Certificate" declaring that they were not Communist Party members, and that if they had ever been, they had communicated that fact to the president of the state university.

Two suits were brought in New York State courts challenging the law; among the plaintiffs were the New York City Teachers' Union, individual teachers, parent–teacher associations, taxpayers, and Communist Party leaders. Initially, both courts (one of them in Kings County) struck down the law as a violation of the rights to free speech and due process; but in 1952 the U.S. Supreme Court reversed those decisions and upheld the law. (New York City math teacher Irving Adler was the lead plaintiff.) It was another 15 years before the Supreme Court overruled the *Adler* case and invalidated the Feinberg Law in *Keyishian v. Board of Regents,* a suit brought by five teachers at the State University of New York at Buffalo. Recognizing that "our Nation is deeply committed to safeguarding academic freedom, which is of transcendent value to all of us and not merely to the teachers concerned," the Court said that the First Amendment "does not tolerate laws that cast a pall of orthodoxy over the classroom."

Adler v. Board of Education, 342 U.S. 485 (1952); *Keyishian v. Board of Regents,* 342 U.S. 485 (1967); *Lederman v. Board of Education,* 196 Misc. 873 (Supreme Court of New York, 1949)

Marjorie Heins

Feld Ballet. Ballet company. Formed in 1974 by Eliot Feld, it gave the premieres of his own ballets and performed others by George Balanchine, Bronislava Nijinska, and David Parsons. Efforts begun in 1982 with the Board of Original Ballets Foundation to raise funds for a permanent home led to the renovation of an old movie theater, renamed the Joyce Theater. The company made its European debut at the Festival International de Danse in Paris and was featured on the public television series *Dance in America.* The New Ballet School, opened by Feld in 1978, offered free training to talented students in the public schools. After expanding in the 1990s to include a full academic curriculum and partnership with the New York City Department of Education, the school changed its name to NYC Public School for Dance, but it is commonly known as Ballet Tech. As of 2010 the school was located at 890 Broadway and had enrolled 17,240 students throughout its history.

Peter Maguire

Feldman, Morton (*b* Brooklyn, 12 Jan 1926; *d* Buffalo, N.Y., 3 Sep 1987). Composer. He grew up in Brooklyn where he worked for his family's textile business and began playing music at age eight. He graduated from New York's High School for Music and Art. In 1950, while attending a concert by the New York Philharmonic, Feldman met John Cage, who influenced his musical style. Feldman was part of the New York School of composers, which included Cage, Earle Brown, David Tudor, and Christian Wolff. His music was experimental and minimalist, inspired by New York City's abstract expressionist painters including Jackson Pollock and Mark Rothko, for whom Feldman named his 1971 composition *Rothko Chapel.* At the age of 47, he ended his nine-to-five job in New York City's garment industry to accept a teaching position at the University of Buffalo. His other works include *String Quartet II* (1983), which was more than six hours long and did not receive a full performance until 1999 when it premiered, in full, at Cooper Union in Manhattan.

Max Seppo

Felt, James (*b* New York City, 29 June 1903; *d* New York City, 4 March 1971). Real estate developer and public official. He graduated from the Wharton School in 1924, worked in real estate for his father, Abraham Felt, and in 1932 established his own firm, which dealt primarily in building management, tenant relocations, and the assembly of land packages for large development projects. As the chairman of the New York City Planning Commission from 1 January 1956 to 22 December 1962, he devised a master plan for the rezoning of New York City and conducted a major urban renewal study that called for the rehabilitation of older buildings, despite strong opposition from Robert Moses. In 1961 he urged Mayor Robert F. Wagner (ii) to form the Mayor's Committee for the Preservation of Structures of Historic and Esthetic Importance, the predecessor to the Landmarks Preservation Commission. His projects as a developer included Stuyvesant Town and Peter Cooper Village.

Brooke J. Barr

feminism. New York City became a center of feminist activism after the Civil War. The women's club Sorosis was formed in 1868 by the writer Jane Cunningham Croly in response to the decision of the New York Press Club to bar women; it provided an intellectual and social forum for women and was one of the first organizations of its kind in the country. During the same year Elizabeth Cady Stanton and Susan B. Anthony organized the National Woman Suffrage Association, which held conventions during the 1870s that provided platforms for advocates of women's rights, including the radical orator Victoria Woodhull. During the Progressive era the number of women's associations in the city increased rapidly. Among those formed were the Consumer's League (1891), the National Consumer's League (1899), the New York Federation of Women's Clubs (1895), the New York Women's City Club (1915), and a branch of the Woman's Peace Party (1915). The New York Women's Trade Union League (1903) took part in the shirtwaist strike of 1909–10 and protested the Triangle Shirtwaist fire of 1911. Women established many of the 82 settlement houses open in the city in 1911, including the College Settlement (1889) and the Henry Street Settlement (1893), which was directed by Lillian Wald. The issue of woman suffrage led to the formation of several local societies: the Woman Suffrage Party, the Equality League of Self Supporting Women, the New York City Equal Suffrage League, the New York Collegiate Suffrage League, and the Progressive Union for Woman Suffrage, which organized the first suffrage parade in 1908. Heterodoxy, a feminist discussion group, was formed by 25 women in 1912. Margaret Sanger published the magazine *Woman Rebel* in 1914 and in 1916 opened the country's first birth control clinic, in Brownsville in Brooklyn. The pacifist Crystal Eastman and the anarchist Emma Goldman were also prominent figures in the struggle for feminist goals in New York City.

During the 1920s such national organizations as the League of Women Voters (1920) and the National Federation of Business and Professional Women's Clubs (1919) opened branches in the city. In 1935 Mary McLeod Bethune organized the National Council of Negro Women at a Young Women's Christian Association in Harlem. Even as feminism declined nationally between the 1920s and the 1950s, the city remained a center for professional women in such fields as publishing, journalism, advertising, and retailing and attracted female college graduates seeking employment.

During the feminist revival of the 1960s the city became known as a stronghold for women's liberation. Such groups as New York Radical Women, New York Radical Feminists, and the Redstockings were formed late in the decade and grew rapidly. The news media covered feminist demonstrations, among them the invasion of McSorley's Old Ale House (which refused admission to women until 1970) and protests at the offices of national publications. Feuds within the local branch of the National Organization for Women (1966) also received widespread publicity. On 26 August 1970 thousands of women joined the Strike for Equality, a march to celebrate the 50th anniversary of woman suffrage. *Ms.* magazine was launched in the city in 1972. Local feminist leaders included Betty Friedan, president of the National Organization for Women from 1966 to 1970; Gloria Steinem, editor of *Ms.;* and the writers Kate Millett, Robin Morgan, and Susan Brownmiller. In the 1980s and 1990s, feminists in the city supported reproductive rights and economic equality, and strove to end sexual harassment and violence against women. These campaigns continued into the twenty-first century. Local colleges and universities, which founded women's studies programs and research centers, endorsed feminist goals. Among educational resources available since the 1970s are the Tamiment Library at New York University, whose collections include the archives of the New York chapter of NOW; the Feminist Press at the City University of New York, which publishes books by and about women; and Barnard College's annual conference on "The Scholar and the Feminist."

See also Woman suffrage.

Nancy Woloch

fencing. The distinction of New York City as the unrivaled center for the sport of fencing in the United States dates back to 1754, when a Dutchman named John Rievers opened a physical-education school that offered fencing lessons in lower Manhattan, near the corner of Stone and Whitehall streets. Fencing first began to emerge as a popular sport in the United States in the late 1840s, inspired by the *Turnvereine,* the German gymnastic societies, which had integrated fencing into their exercise regimens. The city's first fencing club, or *salle,* opened in 1874 at Broadway and West 43rd Street; its enterprising owners, a French fencing master named Regis Senac and his son Louis, soon emerged as U.S. fencing's earliest advocates. Their illustrated handbook *The Art of Fencing* was a best seller across the country. The Senacs owed much of their commercial success to the celebrity quotient of some of their clients, who included members of such prominent New York City families as the Vanderbilts, the Astors, and the Pierpont Morgans. By the turn of the twentieth century as many as 75 fencing establishments had sprung up around the city. The New York Athletic Club (NYAC), founded in 1868 on Central Park South, hired the elder Senac as its first fencing instructor. The NYAC's biggest local rival, the Fencers Club, founded in Manhattan in 1883, set out to become a mecca for top-ranked fencers and coaches; now situated on West 29th Street, it remains the best known of the country's oldest continuously operating salles. Fencing's rising popularity was demonstrated in 1893 when a crowd of more than 20,000 filled Madison Square Garden to watch an international meet featuring saber fencers on horseback.

The sport's long-standing racial and gender barriers were slow to fall, with traditionalists arguing that some fencing events were "unladylike." Virtually all of the city's high-level fencing facilities were accessible only to well-to-do white men, including officers of U.S. fencing's first governing body, the Amateur Fencers League of America (AFLA). The AFLA was established in New York City in 1891 by a group of New York fencers who had broken away from the Amateur Athletic Union in a dispute over rules for the national championships. A year later the first AFLA-sponsored national championship was held in Manhattan. (The AFLA continued to oversee the sport until 1981, when it was reorganized, relocated, and renamed the United States Fencing Association.) Although most of the yearly international fencing tournaments were held in Europe, New York City was the established venue for one of the most prestigious, the Martini and Rossi Challenge (later called the Wilkinson Sword Challenge). College-level fencing in the United States came under one roof in 1898, when a group of former Columbia University fencers founded the Intercollegiate Fencing Association. Women got a national fencing championship of their own with the creation in 1929 of the National Intercollegiate Women's Fencing Association (NIWFA), which oversees the oldest collegiate championships for women in any sport. One of its cofounders, New York University fencer Julia Jones (later Jones Pugliese), was the first NIWFA foil champion. In 1956 she became the first American woman to coach a collegiate fencing team, leading New York University and later Hunter College (where she spent 36 years) to a record number of AFLA and NIWFA championships. A lifelong New Yorker, she also had the distinction, at the 1970 World University Games, of being the first woman to coach a U.S. team at an international competition.

The popularity of fencing in twentieth-century New York City was greatly influenced by two events. One was the city's decision, at the height of the Depression, to offer fencing lessons in the public schools, thereby making public schools a de facto farm system that supplied talented young fencers to collegiate fencing powerhouses like Columbia University, New York University, City College, and St. Johns University. (It is widely believed that the decades-long dominance of New York collegiate fencing was never the same after fencing was dropped from the public school curriculum in the 1970s.) The second factor was immigration, which brought successive waves of European fencing masters to the United States. They arrived with new fencing techniques and strenuous conditioning programs that helped American fencers win international competitions. Some of the most notable immigrants included the Italian champion Aldo Nadi, who taught in New York City from 1935 to 1943; Michel Alaux, who was awarded the title Maître d'Armes by the New York Fencers Club in 1956 and was its head fencing master until 1974; Csaba Elthes, who moved to New York City from Hungary soon after the 1956 uprising there; and Giorgio Santelli, an Italian-born Olympic saber fencer (and Nadi's former Olympic teammate). Santelli's father, who had coached the Hungarian Olympic team, turned down an offer to become the chief fencing coach at the NYAC—and sent his son in his place. Santelli's subsequent accomplishments as coach for the Fencers Club, New York University, Columbia University, and five U.S. Olympic teams helped cement the reputation of his fencing school, Salle Santelli, as the country's leading producer of championship fencers. The school was near the Avenue of the Americas in Greenwich Village and also housed George Santelli Inc., the largest U.S. supplier of fencing equipment. It is estimated that by the time of his death in 1985, Santelli had taught 8000 people how to fence.

The AFLA's all-white membership was finally broken, briefly, in the 1930s by Violet Barker, a young African American woman who had begun taking fencing lessons at the Harlem Young Men's Christian Association. Barker had won a non-AFLA women's foil tournament, and her prize included complimentary membership in the AFLA. A short time later, however, at her first official AFLA competition, she was turned away by the organizers, who told her that blacks were not welcome. When she showed them her membership card and protested that she was in fact an AFLA member, one of the league officials told her "not anymore," and tore up her card. Barker never fenced again. In the early 1960s Uriah Jones moved to New York City from Connecticut looking for more advanced fencing instruction but had difficulty finding a fencing academy that would teach a black man. Santelli took him in as a student, however, and in 1968 Jones became the first African American to compete as a member of a U.S. Olympic fencing team and in 1971 to win an AFLA national fencing championship. Peter Westbrook of New York University, a protégé of Csaba Elthes who won a bronze medal at the 1984 Olympics, likened Jones's entry into fencing to that of Jackie Robinson's into baseball. Westbrook, a six-time Olympian, founded the Peter Westbrook Foundation in 1991 in New York City, which promotes fencing and academic success among inner-city youth. Before Westbrook, the best Olympic finish for an American fencer had come at the Rome Games in 1960 when Albert Axelrod, a Fencers Club member who had learned to fence at Stuyvesant High School in Manhattan, won the bronze medal in foil.

In 1988 the United States Fencing Association sanctioned the first national championship event in women's saber, a triumph for leading proponents of the event such as Salle Santelli's Denise O'Connor, a two-time Olympic foil fencer who later coached the women's team at Brooklyn College, and Ruby V. Watson, an African American fencer from Brooklyn who was nationally ranked in saber, foil, and épée. New York City is still the prime destination for world-class fencers and fencing masters from abroad; New Yorkers typically represent 50 to 60 percent of every U.S. Olympics fencing team. The city's reputation as the capital of American fencing seems likely to endure.

Aldo Nadi, *The Living Sword: A Fencer's Autobiography* (Sunrise, Fla.: Laureate Press, 1995); Richard Cohen, *By the Sword: A History of Gladiators, Musketeers, Samurai, Swashbucklers and Olympic Champions* (New York: Modern Library, 2002)

David Pitt

Ferber, Edna (*b* Kalamazoo, Mich., 15 Aug 1885; *d* New York City, 7 April 1968). Novelist and playwright. She achieved early success with her short stories about a traveling saleswoman who sold petticoats in the Midwest, and she also worked as a reporter. On the advice of her publisher she moved in 1912 to Manhattan. With George V. Hobart she adapted her stories for the stage; their dramatization *Our Mrs. McChesney* opened on Broadway in 1915 and ran for 151 performances. She became an occasional member of the Algonquin Round Table and an increasingly prolific writer. She received the Pulitzer Prize for her novel *So Big* (1924). Her novel *Show Boat* (1926) was the basis for the musical of the same name by Jerome Kern. Ferber's sentimental realism, strong female characters, and wit are most effective in the plays she wrote with George S. Kaufman, especially those, like *Dinner at Eight* (1932) and *Stage Door* (1936), that satirize metropolitan life. She wrote two memoirs, including *A Peculiar Treasure* (1939). She lived in the 1920s at 50 Central Park West, in the early 1930s at the Hotel Lombardy (111 East 56th Street), from 1934–38 at 791 Park Avenue, and from about 1950 to the end of her life at 730 Park Avenue.

Brenda Wineapple

Fermi, Enrico (*b* Rome, 29 Sept 1901; *d* Chicago, 28 Nov 1954). Physicist. In 1933 he formulated a theory of beta decay based on the neutrino. After winning the Nobel Prize for physics in 1938 he moved to New York City and joined the physics department at Columbia University, where he worked with H. L. Anderson on nuclear fission. He remained at Columbia until 1945. Fermi was an important figure in the Manhattan Project, which developed the atomic bomb.

James E. Mooney

Ferraro, Geraldine A(nne) (*b* Newburgh, N.Y., 26 Aug 1935). Politician. She became a teacher and lawyer (1961–74) and then Queens County assistant district attorney (1974–78) and representative of New York's ninth congressional district (1979–85). She ran unsuccessfully for vice president in 1984 (with Walter Mondale as the Democratic presidential candidate), the first woman nominated by a major political party to that office, and also for the Democratic nomination for U.S. senator from New York in 1992 and 1998. President Bill Clinton appointed her to the U.S. delegation of the U.N. Commission on Human Rights (1993–96). She wrote *Ferraro: My Story* (1985), *Changing History: Women, Power, and Politics* (1998), and *Framing a Life: A Family Memoir* (1998). Her papers are at Marymount Manhattan College.

Rosemary Breslin and Joshua Hammer, *Gerry!: A Woman Making History* (New York: Pinnacle, 1984)

Mary Elizabeth Brown

ferries. Because it is built largely on islands, New York City depended on ferries before it had bridges and tunnels. American Indians had been crossing local waterways with rafts and canoes for centuries when European settlers first made organized crossings of the East River in 1642. In 1661 the Netherlands Council granted a ferry charter to William Jansen for a route from Manhattan to Communipaw (now in Jersey City), New Jersey. Charters for other routes soon followed.

Early vessels were scows propelled by oars and sails, until small sloops and a distinctive sailing vessel called a periauger became dominant during the eighteenth century. The first steam ferry, the *Juliana,* began service in 1811 from Hoboken to Vesey Street under the direction of Colonel John Stevens. In the following year Robert Fulton and Robert R. Livingston established another service across the Hudson River, between Cortlandt Street and Powles Hook, with the *Jersey* and the *York.* Routes from Manhattan to Brooklyn across the East River were inaugurated successively by Fulton and William Cutting (from Beekman's Slip, 1814), by the South Ferry (from Whitehall Street to Atlantic Street, 1836), and by the Hamilton Ferry (from the Battery to Hamilton Avenue, 1846). By 1854 the Union Ferry Company had consolidated a dozen competing lines and was making 1250 crossings a day at a standard fare of two cents. Williamsburgh, for example, was served by six steam ferries leaving Peck Slip every 10 minutes during the working day and Grand Street every five minutes. By 1860 the various East River ferries were carrying almost 33 million passengers a year (about 100,000 each working day), and by 1870 about 50 million a year. Indeed, the folk wisdom of the time held that when there was fog in the harbor, half the business population of New York City would be late for work.

The early boats were catamarans with center paddle wheels. They were double-ended to obviate turning at terminals and to accommodate horse-drawn vehicles as well as passengers on foot. Later single hulls and side paddle wheels became the normal arrangement until the introduction in 1899 of the double-ender the *Bergen,* which by 1920 became the standard. Eventually, diesel power replaced steam on all local routes.

During the nineteenth century ferry services came largely under the control of railroad companies: ferries from Staten Island to Perth Amboy, New Jersey, and Whitehall Street were run by the Baltimore and Ohio; from Communipaw to Liberty Street and West 23rd Street by the Jersey Central; from Powles Hook to Cortlandt, Desbrosses, and West 23rd streets by the Pennsylvania Railroad; from Pavonia, New Jersey, to Chambers and West 23rd streets by the Erie Railroad; from Hoboken to Barclay, Christopher, and West 23rd streets by the Lackawanna Railroad; from Weehawken to Cortlandt and West 42nd streets by the West Shore–New York Central Railroad; and from Edgewater,

Ferry Routes of New York City

MANHATTAN–NEW JERSEY

	Manhattan Terminal	*New Jersey Terminal*	*Operator(s)*
Paulus Street Ferry (1812–1949)	Cortlandt Street	Jersey City (Exchange Place)	Pennsylvania Railroad
Hoboken Ferry (1821–1967)	Barclay Street	Hoboken (Delaware, Lackawanna, and Western Depot)	Hoboken Ferry
Christopher Street Ferry (1838–1955)	Christopher Street	Hoboken (Delaware, Lackawanna, and Western Depot)	Hoboken Ferry
North Weehawken Ferry (1859–1902)	West 42nd Street	Slough's Meadow	Weehawken Ferry 1859–72; New York Central Railroad 1872–1902
Pavonia Ferry (1861–1958)	Chambers Street	Jersey City (Erie Depot)	Erie Railroad
Desbrosses Street Ferry (1862–1930)	Desbrosses Street	Jersey City (Exchange Place)	Pennsylvania Railroad
Communipaw Ferry (1864–1967)	Liberty Street	Jersey City (Central Railroad of New Jersey Depot)	Jersey Central Railroad
Erie Ferry (1868–1942)	West 23rd Street	Jersey City (Erie Depot)	Erie Railroad
34th Street Ferry (1880–83)	West 34th Street	Jersey City (Exchange Place)	Pennsylvania Railroad
Weehawken Ferry (1884–1959)	West 42nd Street	Weehawken (West Shore Depot)	New York Central Railroad
West Shore Ferry (1885–1959)	Cortlandt Street	Weehawken (West Shore Depot)	New York Central Railroad
Upper Ferry (1886–1942)	West 14th Street	Hoboken (14th Street)	Hoboken Ferry
Edgewater Ferry (1888–1950)	125th Street	Edgewater	Riverside and Fort Lee Ferry 1888–1943; Electric Ferries 1943–50
West 13th Street Ferry West (1891–1901)	13th Street	Jersey City (Harsimus Cove)	Pennsylvania Railroad
Pennsylvania Ferry (1897–1910)	West 23rd Street	Jersey City (Exchange Place)	Pennsylvania Railroad
Royal Blue Line Ferry (1897–1905)	Whitehall Street	Jersey City (Central Railroad of New Jersey Depot)	Jersey Central Railroad
West New York Ferry (1902–22)	West 42nd Street	West New York	New York Central Railroad
Jersey Central Ferry (1905–41)	West 23rd Street	Jersey City (Central Railroad of New Jersey Depot)	Jersey Central Railroad
Lackawanna Ferry (1905–47)	West 23rd Street	Hoboken (Delaware, Lackawanna, and Western Depot)	Hoboken Ferry
Englewood Ferry (1905–42)	Dyckman Street	Englewood	New York and Englewood Ferry Corp.
Electric Ferry (1926–43)	West 23rd Street	Weehawken (Baldwin Avenue)	Electric Ferries
Weehawken–Port Imperial Ferries (1986–)	West 39th Street/South Ferry	Weehawken (Port Imperial)	New York Waterway
Weehawken–Lincoln Harbor Ferry (1991–)	West 39th Street	Weehawken (Lincoln Harbor)	New York Waterway
Hoboken Ferry (1989–)	Battery Park City	Hoboken	New York Waterway
Colgate–Palmolive Ferry (1994–)	Battery Park City	Jersey City (Exchange Place)	New York Waterway
Liberty Science Center Ferry	Battery Park City	Jersey City (Liberty Science Center)	New York Waterway
Port Liberté Ferry (1994–)	South Ferry	Jersey City (Port Liberté)	Chris's Bay Bus; New York Waterway
Monmouth County Ferry (1989–)	Wall Street	Highlands/Atlantic Highlands	Express Navigation
Edgewater to West 39th Street, Manhattan (2007–)	Midtown/West 39th Street	Edgewater Ferry Landing	New York Waterway
Hoboken, New Jersey, to Pier 11, Wall Street	Pier 11, Wall Street	Hoboken	New York Waterway
Newport Ferry (2006–)	Midtown/West 39th Street	Jersey City (Newport)	New York Waterway
Liberty Harbor Marina, New Jersey, Ferry	Pier 11, Wall Street	Jersey City (Liberty Harbor Marina)	New York Waterway
Belford, New Jersey, Ferry	Pier 11, Wall Street, and World Financial Center	Belford	New York Waterway

(*continued*)

Ferry Routes of New York City (*Continued*)

BROOKLYN–NEW JERSEY

	Brooklyn Terminal	*New Jersey Terminal*	*Operator(s)*
Brooklyn Annex Ferry (1877–1910)	Fulton Street	Jersey City (Exchange Place)	Pennsylvania Railroad
Annex Ferry (1885–*ca* 1900)	Fulton Street	Jersey City (Erie Depot)	Pennsylvania Railroad
Atlantic Annex Ferry (1929–35)	Atlantic Avenue	Jersey City (Exchange Place)	Pennsylvania Railroad

BRONX–NEW JERSEY

	Bronx Terminal	*New Jersey Terminal*	*Operator(s)*
Steamer Maryland Ferry (1876–1912)	Port Morris	Jersey City (Harsimus Cove)	New York, New Haven and Hartford Railroad

MANHATTAN–STATEN ISLAND

	Manhattan Terminal	*Staten Island Terminal*	*Operator(s)*
Staten Island Ferry (1816–)	Whitehall Street	St. George	Staten Island Rapid Transit 1816–1905; City of New York 1906–
Stapleton Ferry (1909–13)	Whitehall Street	Stapleton	City of New York

BROOKLYN–STATEN ISLAND

	Brooklyn Terminal	*Staten Island Terminal*	*Operator(s)*
Brooklyn and Richmond Ferry [69th Street Ferry] (1912–64)	69th Street	St. George	Brooklyn and Richmond Ferry 1912–39; Electric Ferries 1939–54; City of New York 1954–64
New York Bay Ferry (1924–26)	39th Street	St. George	City of New York

MANHATTAN–BROOKLYN

	Manhattan Terminal	*Brooklyn Terminal*	*Operator(s)*
Fulton Ferry (1814–1924)	Fulton Street	Fulton Street	Union Ferry Company 1814–1922; City of New York 1922–24
Navy Yard Ferry (*ca* 1825–68)	Jackson Street	Hudson Avenue	Navy Yard Ferry Co.
Broadway Ferry (i) (1836–1909, 1911–18)	Roosevelt Street	Broadway	Williamsburg Ferries 1836–1909; Brooklyn and Manhattan Ferry 1911–18
South Ferry (1836–1942)	Whitehall Street	Atlantic Avenue	Union Ferry Co. 1856–1922; City of New York 1922–42
Houston Street Ferry (1842–1918)	Houston Street	Grand Street	Nassau Ferry Co.
Catharine Street Ferry (*ca* 1850–1912)	Catharine Street	Main Street	Union Ferry Co.
Broadway Ferry (ii) (1851–1909; 1921–33)	Grand Street	Broadway	Williamsburg Ferries 1851–1909; City of New York 1921–33
Wall Street Ferry (1852–1912)	Wall Street	Montague Street	Union Ferry Co.
[name unknown] (1853–59)	Roosevelt Street	Bridge Street	Union Ferry Co.
Greenpoint Ferry (1853–1933)	East 23rd Street	Greenpoint Avenue	Greenpoint Ferry 1853–1921; City of New York 1921–33
10th Street Ferry (1853–1914)	East 10th Street	Greenpoint Avenue	Greenpoint Ferry Co.
Hamilton Ferry (1856–1942)	Whitehall Street	Hamilton Avenue	Union Ferry Co. 1856–1922; City of New York 1922–42
Williamsburg Ferry (*ca* 1859–1909)	Grand Street	Grand Street	Williamsburg Ferries
Broadway–23rd Street Ferry (1885–1909; 1911–18)	East 23rd Street	Broadway	Williamsburg Ferries 1885–1909; Brooklyn and Manhattan Ferry 1911–18
South Brooklyn Ferry (1887–1938)	Whitehall Street	39th Street	New York and South Brooklyn Ferry and Transportation Co. 1887–1906; City of New York 1906–38
Uptown Ferry (1901–9)	East 42nd Street	Broadway	Williamsburg Ferries
Williamsburg Express Ferry (1988)	Whitehall Street	Kent Avenue	City of New York

(*continued*)

Ferry Routes of New York City (*Continued*)

	Manhattan Terminal	*Brooklyn Terminal*	*Operator(s)*
Bayridge Ferry (1989–)	Wall Street	Bay Ridge	Express Navigation
Far Rockaway to Brooklyn Army Terminal to Pier 11, Wall Street (2008–)	Riis Landing	Pier 11, Wall Street	New York Water Taxi
Red Hook to Wall Street	Pier 11	Beard Street	New York Water Taxi
To Hunter's Point, East 34th Street, Pier 11 Wall Street, Fulton Ferry Landing, Williamsburg (2008–)	Fulton Ferry Landing	Pier 11, Wall Street	New York Water Taxi
MANHATTAN–QUEENS			
	Manhattan Terminal	*Queens Terminal*	*Operator(s)*
Astoria Ferry (1843–1918, 1920–36)	East 92nd Street	Astoria	New York and East River Ferry Co. 1843–1918; City of New York 1920–36
Calvary Cemetery Ferry (1851–53)	East 23rd Street	Long Island City (Penny Bridge)	Trustees of St. Patrick's Cathedral
Annex Ferry (1859–1907)	James Slip	Hunter's Point	Long Island Rail Road
Hunter's Point Ferry (1859–1925)	East 34th Street	Hunter's Point	Long Island Rail Road
[name unknown] (1886–1918)	East 99th Street	College Point	New York and College Point Ferry Co.
[name unknown] (1927–36)	East 34th Street	Long Island City (Borden Avenue)	East 34th Street Vehicular Ferry Co.
La Guardia Airport Ferry (Delta Water Shuttle) (1990–)	East 34th Street/Wall Street	La Guardia Airfield	Harbor Shuttle
Far Rockaway to Brooklyn Army Terminal to Pier 11, Wall Street (2008–)	Far Rockaway	Pier 11, Wall Street	New York Water Taxi
To Hunter's Point, East 34th Street, Pier 11 Wall Street, Fulton Ferry Landing, Williamsburg (2008–)	Fulton Ferry Landing	Pier 11, Wall Street	New York Water Taxi
BRONX–QUEENS			
	Bronx Terminal	*Queens Terminal*	*Operator(s)*
[name unknown] (1910–17)	Clason Point	College Point	Twin City Ferry Co.
[name unknown] (1921–39)	Clason Point	College Point	City of New York
BROOKLYN–QUEENS			
	Brooklyn Terminal	*Queens Terminal*	*Operator(s)*
Rockaway Ferry (1925–37)	Flatbush Avenue	Jacob Riis Park	City of New York
STATEN ISLAND–NEW JERSEY			
	Staten Island Terminal	*New Jersey Terminal*	*Operator(s)*
Perth Amboy Ferry (1867–1963)	Tottenville	Perth Amboy	Staten Island Railway 1867–1948; Sunrise Ferries 1948–63
Bergen Point Ferry (1876–1962)	Port Richmond	Bayonne	Port Richmond and Bergen Point Ferry Co. 1876–1937; Electric Ferries 1937–45; Port Richmond Ferry Co. *ca* 1946–*ca* 1948; Kill van Kull Ferry Co. and others *ca* 1948–*ca* 1962
Howland Hook Ferry (1896–1961)	Howland Hook	Elizabethport	New Jersey and Staten Island Ferry Co. 1896–*ca* 1932; Sunrise Ferries *ca* 1932–61
Carteret Ferry (1916–29)	Linoleumville	Carteret	Carteret Ferry
OTHER ISLAND FERRIES			
	Manhattan Terminal	*Island Terminal*	*Operator(s)*
Governors Island Ferry (*ca* 1870–)	Whitehall Street	Governors Island	U.S. Army *ca* 1870–1965; U.S. Coast Guard 1965–

(*continued*)

Ferry Routes of New York City (*Continued*)

	Manhattan Terminal	*Island Terminal*	*Operator(s)*
Ellis Island Ferry (1892–1954)	Whitehall Street	Ellis Island	U.S. Immigration and Naturalization Service
[name unknown] (1929–*ca* 1936)	East 116th Street	Wards Island	New York State Department of Mental Hygiene
	Bronx Terminal	*Island Terminal*	*Operator(s)*
[name unknown] (1923–*ca* 1969)	East 134th Street	North Brother Island	City of New York
Hart Island Ferry (1923–)	City Island	Hart Island	City of New York
Rikers Island Ferry (1923–69)	East 134th Street	Rikers Island	City of New York
MANHATTAN–YONKERS			
	Manhattan Terminal	*Yonkers Terminal*	*Operator(s)*
Yonkers to West 39th Street, World Financial Center (Battery Park City), and Wall Street Pier 11 (2009–)	World Financial Center (Battery Park City), Pier 11, Wall Street	Yonkers Recreation Pier	New York Water Taxi

New Jersey, to West 125th Street and from Staten Island to Elizabeth, New Jersey, and Bayonne, New Jersey, by the Public Service Railways. Many smaller routes were also served. Other routes were served by independent operators and by government agencies: on the East River by the Williamsburg Ferry and the Brooklyn Union Ferry, across the Narrows and the Hudson River by the Electric Ferry Company, across the Kill van Kull and the Arthur Kill by Sunrise Ferries, to Staten Island and various harbor islands by the City of New York, and to Ellis Island and Governors Island by the federal government.

The opening in 1883 of the Brooklyn Bridge dealt a severe blow to the commuter ferry in New York City. Manhattan was soon connected with the Bronx, Queens, and Brooklyn by bridges and tunnels that were accessible in all weather and carried many more vehicles than ferries could. By 1925 all commercial ferry lines across the East River had stopped operating. Among the ferries made obsolete by new bridges were one from College Point in Queens to Clason Point in the Bronx (by the Bronx–Whitestone Bridge, 1939) and another from St. George, Staten Island, to the foot of 69th Street in Bay Ridge, Brooklyn (by the Verrazano–Narrows Bridge, 1964). Ferry lines connecting Manhattan to New Jersey proved more durable: the longest-lived, run by the Lackawanna Railroad, lasted until 1967. Some lines survived: the Staten Island Ferry; a ferry between City Island and Hart Island run by the city; and a ferry between South Ferry in Manhattan and Governors Island run by the U.S. Coast Guard for service members and their families.

Periodic attempts to revive private commuter ferry service began in the early 1980s, in part because of increasing traffic congestion and environmental concerns. Among the routes that were introduced were ones from Weehawken to Pier 78 (on West 38th Street), from Hoboken (operating out of the old Lackawanna Railroad slip) to the Battery Park City Terminal at the World Financial Center, from La Guardia Airfield to Pier 11 on the East River at the foot of Wall Street, and from Roger Avenue in Jamaica Bay at Inwood, Queens, to Pier 11 (served by a modified hovercraft capable of running at 40 knots). Most of the new routes were popular with commuters, and during several severe storms during 1992–93 only ferries remained in service when tunnels were flooded.

The role of ferries grew exponentially after the terrorist attacks of 11 September 2001. They were used to move thousands of people out of downtown Manhattan, and when businesses reopened, for several years they replaced the Port Authority Trans-Hudson Corporation (PATH) commuter trains to and from New Jersey. In 2002 New York Water Taxi began service in an iconic, 74-passenger, yellow vessel connecting Fulton Ferry Landing in Brooklyn, Pier 11, the Battery, Chelsea Piers, and West 42nd Street in Manhattan. In 2007 five private companies ran ferries between points in Manhattan and landings in Brooklyn, Queens, New Jersey, Yonkers, and Haverstraw, New York.

Raymond Baxter and Arthur G. Adams, *Railroad Ferries of the Hudson, and Stories of a Deckhand* (Woodcliff Lake, N.J.: Lind, 1987); Brian J. Cudahy, *Over and Back: The History of Ferryboats in New York Harbor* (New York: Fordham University Press, 1990)

See also PORT OF NEW YORK.

Arthur G. Adams

Ferriss, Hugh (*b* St. Louis, 12 July 1889; *d* New York City, 29 Jan 1962). Architectural illustrator. After attending Washington University he moved to New York City in 1912 and worked in the office of Cass Gilbert. From 1915 he worked as a freelance artist, preparing illustrations for newspapers and magazines and perspective renderings for architects. Inspired by his interest in the city and his belief in the inspirational power of images, he made futuristic drawings of an ideal skyscraper city that were the basis of several exhibitions in the 1920s and were later published in the book *The Metropolis of Tomorrow* (1929). Ferriss was an officer to several professional organizations and a consultant on the design teams of the World's Fair of 1939–40 and the United Nations headquarters. He is best known for romantic charcoal drawings of the city's skyscrapers. In 1953 he published *Power in Buildings,* which contained drawings of major works of American engineering and architecture since 1929. His rooftop studio at Park Avenue and 40th Street was an aerie from which he drew inspiration.

Carol Willis

Ferry Point Park. Public park in the Bronx, near the entrance to the Bronx–Whitestone Bridge. In 1668 the land was recorded as the property of Micah Spicer, and it was farmed during the next two centuries. A ferry terminal stood on the site in the nineteenth century. The land was purchased around 1850 by the shipping magnate Augustus diZerega and the tobacco manufacturer Jacob Lorillard, who in turn sold it to the Catholic House of the Good Shepherd in 1916. In 1937 the site was converted into a park and given its current name. In 1998 the city granted Ferry Point Partners the rights to build a golf course designed by Jack Nicklaus on the site. The project fell through around 2001, leaving tons of landfill but no golf course. As of 2010 a new project was under way to turn unused land into a community area with sports fields as well as a waterfront promenade featuring a beach and picnic areas.

John McNamara, *McNamara's Old Bronx* (New York: Bronx County Historical Society, 1989)

John McNamara

festivals. See FAIRS AND FESTIVALS.

Fiduciary Trust Company International. Money management firm formed in 1931 by two lawyers from New York City, Grenville Clark and Elihu Root. In reaction against the excesses of banking during the 1920s, the two resolved that their firm would neither make commercial loans nor underwrite any securities. They also aimed to advertise as little as possible, a policy that the firm has maintained. Fiduciary Trust invests globally. In the early twenty-first century it had more than $10 billion under management for more than 1600 individuals and families and more than 200 corporations.

Chad Ludington

Field, Cyrus W(est) (*b* Stockbridge, Mass., 30 Nov 1819; *d* New York City, 11 July 1892). Industrialist. He made his fortune in the paper business and with a group of wealthy associates formed the New York, Newfoundland and London Telegraph Company to undertake the laying of the first telegraph cable between the United States and Great Britain; he formed a similar company in 1854 in London. The initial line was completed in 1858 and worked for only three weeks. He pursued the project until a permanent cable was laid in 1866 from Ireland to Newfoundland (extended by land lines to New York City). Between 1877 and 1879 he built the elevated railway system on Third Avenue. Field lived in a mansion on the northeast corner of Lexington Avenue and 21st Street in Gramercy Park.

Samuel Carter III, *Cyrus Field: Man of Two Worlds* (New York: G. P. Putnam's Sons, 1968)

Paul Israel

Field, David Dudley (*b* Haddam, Conn., 13 Feb 1805; *d* New York City, 13 April 1894). Lawyer. A prominent and controversial member of the city's Bar Association for 60 years, he was best known for his efforts to codify the law: he drafted a code of civil procedure that was adopted by New York State in 1848. He also represented Jay Gould and Jim Fisk in their efforts to save the Erie Railroad from takeover attempts by Cornelius Vanderbilt and August Belmont (1868–69) and defended William M. "Boss" Tweed in civil and criminal trials (1873–78). Field's draft of a penal code for New York State was enacted after many alterations in 1881.

Daun Van Ee, *David Dudley Field and the Reconstruction of the Law* (New York: Garland, 1986)

See also LAWYERS.

James D. Folts

Fields, C(lara) Virginia (*b* Birmingham, Ala., 6 Aug 1945). Civil rights activist, politician, and educator. A social worker and strong advocate for education and civil rights who marched with Dr. Martin Luther King, Jr., she served as a district leader and chair of Manhattan Community District 10. She became the first African American woman from Manhattan elected to the City Council. Fields was Manhattan borough president from 1998 to 2005.

Celedonia Jones

Fieldston. A privately owned neighborhood in the northwestern Bronx, bounded to the north by 250th Street, to the east by Manhattan College, to the south by Manhattan College Parkway, and to the west by the Henry Hudson Parkway. The land was once an estate of 250 acres (100 hectares) purchased in 1829 by Major Joseph Delafield, who named it after his family seat in England. At the beginning of the twentieth century the Delafield family developed it for housing. Lots were laid out along the contours of the rugged terrain rather than according to the grid adopted in other parts of the city. The name Delafield Woods was used for a while during the first quarter of the twentieth century; game was abundant and deer were seen until 1908. After the Interborough Rapid Transit subway along Broadway was extended to 242nd Street, the first house was completed in 1911. During the 1920s houses in the Tudor style were built, many designed by Dwight J. Baum, a local resident. Manhattan College, run by the Christian Brothers, moved to the area from Harlem after a land purchase in 1922. Mayor Fiorello H. La Guardia lived in the neighborhood during his later years. Several private schools also established themselves in the area, including the Fieldston School, Horace Mann Preparatory School, and the Riverdale Country Day School. Fieldston's residents pay a fee for services offered by the city in areas such as sewers and additional services such as snow and leaf removal. Known for its trees, large houses, and rural ambience, Fieldston was one of the wealthiest neighborhoods in the city in the early twenty-first century.

Lloyd Ultan and Gary Hermalyn, *The Bronx in the Innocent Years, 1890–1925* (New York: Harper and Row, 1985)

Gary D. Hermalyn

Fierstein, Harvey (Forbes) (*b* Brooklyn, 6 June 1954). Playwright and actor. The son of a handkerchief manufacturer, he grew up in Brooklyn and attended high school and studied art in Manhattan. He performed in cabarets on the Lower East Side, often as a female impersonator, and was well known for his portrayal of Ethel Merman. At age 22 he wrote an autobiographical one-act play that was produced off Broadway; he played the leading role of Arnold Beckoff. This play and two others completed in 1981 became *Torch Song Trilogy,* which ran on Broadway for three years and in 1983 won Tony Awards for best actor and best play. His musical *La Cage aux Folles* (1983), which he wrote while riding the subway to work, also won a Tony Award. In the early twenty-first century Fierstein undertook a number of film and television projects. In 2008 Fierstein was nominated for the Drama Desk Award for Outstanding Book of a Musical for *A Catered Affair.*

Janet Frankston

Fifteenth Street Meeting House. Quaker house of worship on 15 Rutherford Place and

Fieldston, 246th Street and Delafield Road, 1992

East 15th Street. It was founded in 1885 by the Hicksites, a branch of the Religious Society of Friends (Quakers). In the early twenty-first century the meeting house ran traditional Quaker worship sessions, a homeless shelter, and an art program.

Max Seppo

Fifth Avenue. Manhattan's showcase avenue, it is synonymous with upscale retailing, expensive residences, and important religious and secular institutions. Stretching for 6.75 miles (10.9 kilometers) between Washington Square and 142nd Street, Fifth Avenue divides cross streets between east and west. New York University anchors the south end; the Flatiron Building and Madison Square at 23rd Street announce the avenue's entrance to midtown. Between 34th and 59th streets venerable retail stores (such as Lord and Taylor [1826], Saks Fifth Avenue [1924], Tiffany's [1837], and Bergdorf Goodman [1901]) share the avenue with the Empire State Building, the New York Public Library, St. Patrick's Cathedral, Rockefeller Center, and St. Thomas Church. Former Fifth Avenue stores now out of business include B. Altman, Franklin Simon, Arnold Constable, Best, and Bonwit Teller. Between 59th and 110th streets along Central Park was, a century ago, the domain of luxurious mansions and town houses; in 2009 exclusive apartments shared Fifth Avenue with the Hotel Pierre, Temple Emanuel-El, the Church of Heavenly Rest, Mount Sinai Hospital, and a multitude of museums—the Frick Collection; Metropolitan Museum of Art; Solomon R. Guggenheim Museum; Cooper-Hewitt, National Design Museum; Jewish Museum; Museum of the City of New York; and El Museo del Barrio. North of 110th Street, Fifth Avenue remains residential in the twenty-first century, with hilly Marcus Garvey Park interrupting it between 120th and 124th streets.

Ronda Wist, *On Fifth Avenue, Then and Now* (New York: Carol Publishing Group, 1992)

Andrew Sparberg

Fifth Avenue Coach Lines. Firm of bus operators. Formed in 1885, it ran horse-drawn buses on Fifth Avenue between Washington Square and 89th Street. In 1905 it began the first successful motorbus operation in the United States, retiring all its horse-drawn buses in 1908. The firm demonstrated that single- and double-decker buses could be durable, urban mass transit vehicles. As New York City grew during 1900–30, bus routes were extended northward to Harlem and Washington Heights along Riverside Drive, upper Seventh Avenue, St. Nicholas Avenue, and Broadway and eastward over the Queensboro Bridge to Jackson Heights. After forming the New York City Omnibus Corporation as a subsidiary in 1926, the firm purchased New York Railways, the dominant streetcar operator in Manhattan, and converted the streetcars to buses between February 1935 and August 1936. Double-decker bus service ceased in 1953. The firm acquired the Surface Transportation Corporation in 1956, assuming its five bus routes in Manhattan and its entire system in the Bronx. In 1962 Fifth Avenue was purchased by a group of investors led by Harry Weinberg, whose efforts to discharge some unionized employees to reduce costs promptly caused a strike on 1 March. As a result of the strike the city acquired the firm's buses and garages by legal condemnation on 22 March, and the routes were taken over by the Manhattan and Bronx Surface Transit Operating Authority, itself part of the New York City Transit Authority.

Andrew Sparberg

Fifth Avenue Hotel. Hotel on Fifth Avenue between 23rd and 24th streets (opposite Madison Square), built by the developer Amos Eno from 1856 to 1858. Initially far from the hotel district, it was known as Eno's folly but soon became popular for its luxuriousness. It occupied a six-story building with a colonnade at the entrance and had fireplaces in every bedroom, private bathrooms, and elegant public rooms; it was also the first hotel in the city with elevators, which were steam-operated and known as the "vertical railroad." The hotel, at the time the largest in the world, could accommodate 800 guests, and a staff of 400 provided some of the best service in the city. Within a few years most of the city's grand hotels moved into the surrounding blocks. The hotel was the headquarters of the state Republican Party and contained an office of the Republican boss Thomas C. Platt, an architect of consolidation; a corridor off the lobby where he met petitioners seeking favors became known as the amen corner. By the turn of the century fashionable neighborhoods moved north, and in 1908 the Fifth Avenue Hotel was closed and demolished. It is commemorated by a plaque on its former site.

Harold Foote Gosnell, *Boss Platt and His New York Machine* (Chicago: University of Chicago Press, 1924); Nathan Silver, *Lost New York* (Boston: Houghton Mifflin, 1967); Oliver E. Allen, *New York, New York* (New York: Atheneum, 1985)

Eric Wm. Allison

Fifth Avenue Presbyterian Church. Church at Fifth Avenue and 55th Street, formed in 1875 by a congregation organized in 1808 on Cedar Street. Its first minister, John Brodhead Romeyn (1808–25), a moderator of the Presbyterian General Assembly, gave the church its reputation as the "cathedral church of Presbyterianism." Later ministers at the church included John Hall (1867–96), John Sutherland Bonnell (1935–62), and Bryant Kirkland (1962–87). Among the institutions formed under their leadership were the Duane Street Mission (1836–1913); the Romeyn Chapel on East 14th Street (1858–1904), which enrolled more than 800 children in its Sunday school; and a Chinese Sunday school (to 1909).

A Noble Landmark of New York: The Fifth Avenue Presbyterian Church, 1808–1958 (New York: Fifth Avenue Presbyterian Church, 1960)

David Meerse

Fifth Avenue Vietnam Peace Parade Committee. Committee that organized marches in New York City nearly every spring and autumn between 1965 and 1973 to protest the Vietnam War. Its headquarters were at 5 Beekman Street and later at 17 East 17th Street and 156 Fifth Avenue. Several marches drew hundreds of thousands of participants,

Fifth Avenue, 2009

including one on 15 April 1967 at which Martin Luther King, Jr., spoke. In 1967 the committee gathered 70,000 signatures to force a referendum on ending the war immediately and shifting funds from the military to schools, hospitals, and programs for the poor. It also organized "Stop the draft week," a series of protests at the Whitehall Street Induction Center on 4–8 December 1967.

Jonathan D. Bloom

52nd Street. A street between Fifth and Sixth avenues known for its jazz clubs during the 1930s and 1940s. Also called Swing Street, it was lined with Victorian brownstones that were used as speakeasies during Prohibition and converted to restaurants and nightclubs after its repeal in 1933. Clubs such as the Onyx, the Famous Door, Jimmy Ryan's, the Three Deuces, the Downbeat, Hickory House, and Kelly's Stable featured the big bands of Count Basie and Woody Herman and such soloists as the pianists Art Tatum and Fats Waller, the singer Billie Holiday, the trumpeter Roy Eldridge, and the violinist Stuff Smith. The clubs attracted racially mixed audiences and provided a fertile environment for improvisation. By 1943 such innovative bebop musicians as Charlie Parker, Miles Davis, Bud Powell, and Dizzy Gillespie had shifted their attention from Harlem to 52nd Street because of its greater opportunities for money and exposure; after riots erupted in Harlem that same year white customers increasingly favored clubs in midtown. The clubs of 52nd Street eventually lost popularity because of the unscrupulous practices of some owners, the association of jazz with drugs, harassment by the police, and an increase in real estate values as skyscrapers began to crowd midtown Manhattan. Jazz districts took shape around Times Square in the late 1940s and later in Greenwich Village. Several clubs opened on Broadway, among them the Royal Roost (1674 Broadway, 1946), Bop City (1619 Broadway at 49th Street, 1948), and Birdland (on Broadway just north of 52nd Street, 1949). By January 1950 Jimmy Ryan's was the only club still offering live music on 52nd Street. During the following years the street was dominated by striptease houses, and in the 1960s large office buildings replaced the brownstones.

Arnold Shaw, *The Street That Never Slept: New York's Fabled 52d Street* (New York: Coward, McCann and Geoghegan, 1971)

Ira Berger, Marc Ferris

Filipinos. Most people from the Philippines who settled in New York City after the 1920s were either soldiers assigned to local military installations such as Governors Island or farmworkers who moved from the western United States to seek employment. The Filipino Social Club of Brooklyn was formed in 1928. More Filipinos moved to the city after World War II, but their numbers remained small; this group included the children of earlier immigrants and students. The third and largest phase of Filipino immigration to the city began in the 1960s, as local hospitals actively recruited Filipino doctors and nurses; Filipino accountants, engineers, and teachers were also in demand. Others fled the Philippines as political refugees during the dictatorship of Ferdinand Marcos (1971–81). Filipinos during these years assimilated into the American mainstream and were not as visible as other immigrant groups. Most were familiar with American culture because of the former status of the Philippines as an American colony (1898–1946) and spoke English in addition to their native language (Tagalog). There were 43,229 people of Filipino ancestry in the 1990 census, and almost 50,000 in 2000. The most common occupation among Filipinos in the city was nursing, and in many local hospitals Filipino nurses came to constitute the majority of the nursing staff.

The largest concentration of Filipinos in New York City is in Queens, especially Woodside, Jackson Heights, and Elmhurst. More than 90 percent of the Filipinos are Roman Catholic, and they practice religious rituals such as the Flores de Mayo (also called the Santa Cruzan) and the block rosary (or Santo Niño). Other Catholic churches that offer services for Filipinos include St. Francis de Sales Church, Holy Innocents Roman Catholic Church, the Church of St. Agnes, and the Church of the Blessed Sacrament in Manhattan; and St. Sebastian's Roman Catholic Church, St. Michael's Church, and Immaculate Conception Church in Queens. There are several Filipino newspapers in the city, and television stations include GMA Pinoy TV, GMA Life, the Filipino Channel, Filipino on Demand, and MYX. The annual Philippine Independence Day Parade usually takes place the first Sunday of June.

Ronald T. Takaki, *Strangers from a Different Shore: A History of Asian Americans* (Boston: Little, Brown, 1989)

Chibu Lagman, Noël Shaw

Fillmore East. Theater on Second Avenue between Sixth and Seventh streets, converted in 1968 into a venue for rock concerts. Bill Graham, a rock impresario who had also opened the Fillmore West in San Francisco, operated it. The club, known as "the church of rock and roll," featured up-and-coming artists, including Joe Cocker, Jimi Hendrix, Janis Joplin, and Neil Young as well as the members of the Grateful Dead, the Incredible String Band, the Jefferson Airplane, Pink Floyd, Country Joe and the Fish, and Procol Harum. An in-house production company called the Joshua Light Show mounted elaborate light shows during the performances. The audiences at the Fillmore East were known for rowdiness. Famous live performances were recorded there, including the Allman Brothers' classic *At Fillmore East*. The theater closed in 1971 because of Graham's discontent with the commercialization of the music scene.

Nicholas Kelly

filmmaking. Filmmaking had its origins just outside New York City, when Thomas Edison worked in suburban Orange, New Jersey, from 1888 to 1893 with his staff of experimenters, notably William Kennedy Laurie Dickson. In early 1894 Dickson and the cameraman William Heise initiated regular commercial production at the Black Maria studio next to Edison's laboratory. They made 35-millimeter films, ranging in length from 50 to 150 feet (15 to 45 meters), that were meant for exhibition in the peephole kinetoscope. Charles E. Chinnock, a former employee of Edison, probably made the first motion picture film in what became New York City itself, in November 1894; he built a camera and made films for exhibition in his own, somewhat larger version of the kinetoscope. His first film, shot on the rooftop of 1729 St. Marks Avenue in Brooklyn, was of a boxing match between Robert T. Moore and James W. Lahey. Short films of dancing girls, a cockfight, and other subjects followed, all made in imitation of Edison's work. Early filmmaking in New York City was also pursued by other former associates of Edison: from May 1895 Woodville Latham and his sons Otway and Gray produced pictures for their eidoloscope projector at 35 Frankfort Street in Manhattan; Dickson by the spring of 1896 had become a part owner and the chief cameraman for the American Mutoscope Company; and Charles Webster and Edmund Kuhn formed the International Film Company and were in production by October 1896. After the Edison company completed the construction of a portable camera in May 1896, its staff members shot scenes of everyday life (*Central Park, Elevated Railway Station, 23rd Street,* and *Shooting the Chutes*). Within a short time they were using a makeshift studio on the rooftop of 43 West 28th Street.

New York City quickly became the center of the American film industry, a position it retained until World War I. Many early film companies were short-lived; the three principal producers before 1906 were the Edison Manufacturing Company, the American Mutoscope Company (later renamed the American Mutoscope and Biograph Company), and the American Vitagraph Company (its production entity was known from 1905 as the Vitagraph Company of America). After a proliferation of storefront theaters from late 1905 through 1906, film production expanded rapidly. The Kalem Company was formed in early 1907 with offices at 31 West 24th Street. Kalem along with Edison, Biograph, Vitagraph, two European producers with offices in New York City (Pathé and Méliès), and three producers from Chicago and Philadelphia formed the Motion Picture Patents Company in New York City in late 1908. The company intended to control all film production in the United States, but these plans failed. Carl Laemmle's Independent Moving Picture Company and the New York Motion Picture Company were making films in the city and area by 1909. They were followed in 1910–11 by the Yankee Film Company, the Champion Film Company, Reliance, Solax, Rex, Atlas, Thanhouser, Powers, and Nestor. All had offices in New York City, though many had studios in the outer boroughs, in Yonkers and New Rochelle in Westchester, and in Coytesville, Jersey City, and Fort Lee in New Jersey. Several united to form the Universal Film Manufacturing Company in 1912.

In the same year Adolph Zukor, Edwin S. Porter, and Daniel Frohman formed the Famous Players Film Company, with offices on West 26th Street, to make feature films of three or more reels (one hour or more in length). These initially featured well-known theatrical stars in filmed adaptations of their stage hits: James O'Neill in *The Count of Monte Cristo* (1912), James Hackett in *The Prisoner of Zenda* (1913), and Minnie Maddern Fiske in *Tess of the D'Urbervilles* (1913). William Fox expanded into filmmaking in 1914, producing *A Fool There Was* (1914) with Theda Bara and *Regeneration* (1915), directed by Raoul Walsh: both offered exterior scenes shot in New York City. In 1913 the vaudeville impresario Jesse Lasky, Samuel Goldfish (later known as Samuel Goldwyn), and Cecil B. DeMille formed the Jesse L. Lasky Feature Play Company. All New Yorkers, the three followed a growing trend by establishing production studios in California. They acquired some of David Belasco's employees (notably the lighting designer Wilfred Buckland) and film rights to his plays, which resulted in such productions as *The Girl of the Golden West* (1914) and *The Warrens of Virginia* (1915).

Film producers in New York City seeking better weather and new locales began sending small companies of actors and staff to California, Florida, and Cuba for winter shooting. Biograph, for example, sent a company to Los Angeles in January 1910. By 1912 Bison and Keystone (both owned by the New York Motion Picture Company), Nestor, Selig, Kalem, and Pathé had permanent production units based in Los Angeles, and Hollywood was the dominant production center by 1915, though executive offices remained in New York City. Production in the city continued, but a coal shortage in the winter of 1918–19 forced most remaining production units to move to the West Coast and encouraged the further consolidation of operations.

Some production then returned to New York City, where creative personnel sometimes felt more at home. Norma Talmadge returned from the West Coast in 1917 and with her husband and producer, Joseph Schenck, opened a studio at 320 East 48th Street where *The Song of Love* was filmed in 1924. By 1920 William Randolph Hearst had converted Sulzer's Harlem River Park and Casino at 127th Street and Second Avenue into the Cosmopolitan studio, which turned out pictures featuring his mistress, the comedian Marion Davies (*The Restless Sex* [1920] and *When Knighthood Was in Flower* [1922]), and *Humoresque* (1920), set on the Lower East Side. Fox opened a studio in May 1920 on West 55th Street in Manhattan, where Pearl White and Allan Dwan worked briefly. In September of the same year the Famous Players–Lasky Corporation (forerunner of Paramount) opened a new studio in Astoria (see KAUFMAN ASTORIA STUDIOS) where Gloria Swanson made nine films, including *Manhandled* (1924). In 1922 the city's share of American production stood at 12 percent, compared with 84 percent for Hollywood. Hearst and Davies shifted operations to the West Coast in 1924; in 1927 the Astoria Studio temporarily closed, as did the Biograph studio (which had been operated for several years by First National); and Talmadge retired soon after the arrival of sound. Independent filmmakers producing pictures for specific ethnic or racial groups remained. The Lower East Side nurtured the production of Yiddish films (for example *Broken Hearts* [1926], directed by Maurice Schwartz), and Harlem became a center for the production of African American films. Oscar Micheaux had a business office in the city by 1922 while he shot much of *Body and Soul* (1924, with Paul Robeson) and *The Exile* (1930) in Fort Lee. Avant-garde films were also made occasionally, beginning with *Manhatta* (1921), inspired by Walt Whitman and directed by Charles Sheeler and Paul Strand.

Sound at least temporarily revived filmmaking in New York City. By 1926 the Fox Film Corporation was conducting sound experiments at its studio in the city, which was also the base of Fox Movietone News (begun in 1927). The heavy dependence of feature filmmaking on sound stages reduced some of the advantages of Hollywood (notably its weather), and New York City was closer to actors and directors who worked on Broadway. Paramount converted the Astoria Studio to sound; its first talking feature appeared in 1929. Most films were adaptations of Broadway plays and musicals or vehicles that tested young talent from the stage. Perhaps this was one reason why the critic Harry Potamkin called for a "New York school" of filmmaking in December 1929; *Applause* (1929), made by Rouben Mamoulian, director of the Theatre Guild, and two experimental films were somewhat wistfully offered as evidence. Feature filmmaking in New York City had virtually ceased by 1937, a year in which not a single feature was shot there in its entirety, according to the *Film Daily Year Book*. Astoria was producing only shorts and inserts for Hollywood pictures. Even an independent Yiddish production of the late 1930s such as *Dem Khazns Zundl* (The Cantor's Son, 1937) could not be counted because extensive exteriors were shot in Pennsylvania, New Jersey, and Long Island. Among the very few films of the period made entirely in the city were films with African American casts such as *Moon over Harlem* (1939, directed by Edgar G. Ulmer) and *Murder on Lenox Avenue* (1941). By the late 1930s most experienced technicians had moved to Hollywood. Although Mayor Fiorello H. La Guardia tried to induce makers of films to return east in 1939, the war ended his efforts before any noticeable success.

New York City nonetheless remained a center of documentary activity (see DOCUMENTARY FILMMAKING), a strength that was reinforced during the war when the Army Signal Corps took over Astoria Studio and made it the headquarters for its extensive filmmaking operations. Many Hollywood film people did return to New York City in uniform. Meanwhile, important structural changes were occurring in the industry that ensured a different future for American filmmaking. In 1938 the federal government sued Paramount Pictures for monopolistic practices, among them the exclusion from their theaters of independently produced films. The case broke up the vertically integrated film industry and facilitated independent production. With tax laws further encouraging this trend, the number of independent producers increased rapidly after 1945. The production of feature films that were relatively close to the mainstream returned to the city with such pictures as *The House on 92nd Street* (1945), *Miracle on 34th Street* (1947), and *Naked City* (1948). Radio-Keith-Orpheum (RKO) built a studio on 134th Street and Park Avenue just after the war; the Hollywood producer David O. Selznick used it for *Portrait of Jennie* (1948). At the same time the city after World War II became the most important center of avant-garde filmmaking in the world. The arrival of Hans Richter and other Europeans contributed to this prominence, as did the activities of Maya Deren, who made her own films (beginning with *Meshes of the Afternoon* [1943]) and was associated with the Film Artists Society (1953, renamed the Independent Film Makers Association in 1955), the Creative Film Foundation (1955), and the film society Cinema 16 (1947–63), which educated several generations of cineastes in experimental and art film.

The rise of television and the continued strength of the theater supported the revival of filmmaking in New York City, providing training for technicians as well as early opportunities for such directors as Elia Kazan and Sidney Lumet. Kazan moved back and forth between filmmaking in Hollywood and theatrical directing in New York City, until *On the Waterfront* (1954), which was shot in suburban Hoboken and on a small stage at the old Vitagraph studio in Brooklyn. Lumet's first film, *Twelve Angry Men* (1957, with Henry Fonda), was shot at the old Famous Players studio on West 26th Street. Both were the work of the cinematographer Boris Kaufman, who helped train a generation of cinematographers in the city.

In the early 1950s the tradition of social realism associated with documentary film gave way to underground films—bizarre sexual extravaganzas by Ron Rice, Ken Jacob, George and Mike Kuchar, and especially Jack Smith. The movement was brought to public prominence by the success of Andy Warhol's *The Chelsea Girls* (1966) and fragmented amid the political activism of the late 1960s: the members of New York Newsreel made agitational political films (such as *Columbia Revolt* [1968]), while other filmmakers forged a school of severely aestheticist "structural" films (beginning with Michael Snow's *Wavelength* [1967]) that bore a kinship with minimalist painting and sculpture. This independent film culture was sustained by many institutions, of which four were especially important: the journal *Film Culture* (first appearing in January 1955), which initially emphasized the European art cinema but by the end of the decade had committed itself to the American avant-garde; the New American Cinema Group, an organization formed to promote independent film production; the Filmmakers' Cooperative, a nondiscriminatory distribution agency run by and for filmmakers; and the Anthology Film Archives, a permanent collection of the "monuments of cinematic art" opened in 1970. A central role in all of these was played by Jonas Mekas, an émigré from Lithuania who also made a series of "diary films" (beginning with *Diaries, Notes and Sketches (Walden)* [1968]).

In the 1950s and 1960s old studios were refurbished: the Biograph Studio in the Bronx became the Gold Medal Studio, where Kazan shot *A Face in the Crowd* (1957). The Famous Players studio, renamed the Production Center Studios, was used for such films as Lumet's *Long Day's Journey into Night* (1961) and Mel Brooks's *The Producers* (1967). A garage across from the old Cosmopolitan Studio was converted into the Filmways Studio, used for shooting Burt Balaban and Stuart Rosenberg's *Murder Incorporated* (1960), Francis Ford Coppola's *The Godfather* (1971), and Woody Allen's *Annie Hall* (1977). These small and in many ways outdated facilities closed in the late 1970s and were essentially replaced by the newly renovated Astoria Studio, reopened in November 1975 and renamed the Kaufman Astoria Studios in 1982. Elsewhere, unexpected structures were converted to provide sound stages: the Silver Cup Studios in Long Island City, for example, were an old bakery converted into 13 stages that opened in 1983; and the Chelsea Piers studio was built in 1988 on an abandoned pier at 23rd Street and the Hudson River.

As a growing number of television series were made on the West Coast, feature filmmaking in New York City was to an extent sustained by Madison Avenue, which was creating increasingly sophisticated television advertisements in the 1960s and 1970s. Television commercials provided technical expertise, temporary work for people working in films, and a chance to break into the business for others. Mayor John V. Lindsay set up the Mayor's Office of Film, Theater and Broadcasting in May 1966 to facilitate citywide production. It offered greater police cooperation while centralizing and simplifying the issuing of permits for location shooting.

Independent features continued to be made by New Yorkers such as Robert Frank (*Pull My Daisy* [1959]), Shirley Clarke (*Cool World* [1965]), Robert Downey (*Putney Swope* [1969]), and John Cassavetes (*Husbands* [1970]). In the late 1960s and early 1970s a new generation of filmmakers emerged that was fiercely committed to New York City: Woody Allen (*Take the Money and Run* [1969], *Hannah and Her Sisters* [1986], *Shadows and Fog* [1992], *Bullets over Broadway* [1994]), Martin Scorsese (*Mean Streets* [1973], *Taxi Driver* [1976], *King of Comedy* [1982]), and Paul Mazursky (*Next Stop, Greenwich Village* [1976]). Others such as Milos Forman (*Ragtime* [1981]) also worked extensively in the city, as did younger filmmakers such as Spike Lee (*She's Gotta Have It* [1986], *Do the Right Thing* [1989]). In the 1970s the avant-garde was revitalized by feminists, notably Yvonne Rainer, and members of racial minorities. Production was also pursued by a band of small-time but determined independents such as John Sayles (*The Brother from Another Planet* [1984]), Jim Jarmusch (*Stranger Than Paradise* [1984]), Amos Poe (*Alphabet City* [1982]), Raul Ruiz (*The Golden Boat* [1990]), Charles Lane (*Sidewalk Stories* [1991]), Todd Haynes (*Poison* [1991]), and Hal Hartley (*Trust* [1991]). Filmmakers often engaged issues of particular urgency to the city, notably the politics of race, violence, and American identity. The late 1980s saw something of a revival of the avant-garde, with Super-8 film and video figuring prominently.

Many productions spend a few days of location shooting in the city while shooting studio scenes in Los Angeles or Europe. According to the Mayor's Office of Film, Theater and Broadcasting, each year during the 1980s from 61 to more than 100 feature films were shot at least in part in the city. Between November 1990 and May 1991 the Hollywood studios boycotted New York City in a labor dispute with local unions. This along with a weak economy and overproduction opened the 1990s on a note of uncertainty, but by mid-decade feature filmmaking returned to the city, with films by Ang Lee (*The Wedding Banquet* [1993]), Brian De Palma (*Carlito's Way* [1993]), and Wayne Wang (*Smoke* [1995]).

After the terrorist attacks of 11 September 2001, Robert De Niro, Jane Rosenthal, and Craig Hatkoff founded the TRIBECA FILM FESTIVAL to spur the economic and cultural revitalization of lower Manhattan. The festival grew out of De Niro's Tribeca Film Center, the first commercial space in Tribeca dedicated to housing film, television, and entertainment companies, founded in 1989. The Tribeca Film Festival and Center focus on assisting filmmakers to reach the broadest possible audience and promoting New York City as a major filmmaking center. In 2005 the New York State Film Production credit program went into effect. The program, which offered studios tax credits from the city and state for up to 35 percent of production costs, used its initial $690 million to generate more than $2.6 billion in state and local taxes and directly brought 2500 jobs to New York City by 2008. New York City remains a filmmaking center into the twenty-first century, with many films, including *Cruel Intentions* (1999), *Spider-Man* (2002), and *The Devil Wears Prada* (2006), filmed on location in the city and featuring city landmarks.

Richard Koszarski, *The Astoria Studio and Its Fabulous Films: A Picture History with 227 Stills and Photographs* (New York: Dover, 1983); Richard Alleman, *The Movie Lover's Guide to New York* (New York: Harper and Row, 1988); J. Hoberman, *Bridge of Light: Yiddish Film between Two Worlds* (New York: Museum of Modern Art, 1991); James Sanders, *Celluloid Skyline: New York and the Movies* (New York: Alfred A. Knopf, 2001); Richard Koszarski, *Hollywood on the Hudson: Film and Television in New York from Griffith to Sarnoff* (Piscataway, N.J.: Rutgers University Press, 2008)

Charles Musser, David James

financial printing. The printing of bonds, stock certificates, prospectuses, annual reports, proxy mailings, Securities and Exchange Commission registration statements, public-offering circulars, and state and federal disclosure forms. The first printers catering to the needs of New York City's financial community were established during the colonial period, among them Bowne and Company, formed in 1775 by Robert Bowne. Aided by proximity to the financial center on Wall

Street, the city's financial printing business prospered throughout the nineteenth century and most of the twentieth, eventually dominated by a few major firms; joining Bowne were Sorg Printing (1820), Francis Emory Fitch (1886), Charles P. Young and Company (1902), and Pandick Press (1923). Later in the twentieth century, however, rapid changes in both financial markets and information technology caused turmoil. A boom in mergers and acquisitions during the 1980s along with the emergence of new types of complex financing prompted an increased demand for financial printing services, attracting competitors such as R. R. Donnelly, a large Chicago-based commercial printer, as well as new startup firms. Overall, sales rose to new highs, but profits dwindled as competition drove down prices and technological advances required new capital investments. Old typesetting machines had to be scrapped in favor of computer-based typesetting equipment. Added strains came with both the stock and bond market crashes of 1987 and the advent of new electronic systems for filing, disseminating, and exchanging financial documents. By 1990 Sorg, Charles P. Young, and Pandick were all forced into bankruptcy; financial printing had become a global business no longer centered in New York City.

Owen D. Gutfreund

Finch College. Women's college in Manhattan. It began in 1900 as a finishing school for young women run from a small apartment at 635 Madison Avenue by Jessica Garetson Cosgrave (1871–1949), a writer, feminist, and editor of the Sunday supplement of the *New York World.* In 1904 she opened the Finch School for Girls at 61 East 77th Street, naming it for her first husband, William Finch. She opened an elementary school in 1916 at 170 East 70th Street called the Lenox School to prepare students for Finch, which in the same year moved to 52 East 78th Street. The school received a state charter in 1937, becoming Finch Junior College, and was one of the most famous finishing schools in the nation; in 1952 it became a four-year college offering bachelor's degrees in arts and sciences. It suffered financially in the mid-1970s and closed in 1976, the buildings razed to make way for an Orthodox Jewish school. Notable alumnae of Finch College include Tricia Nixon, daughter of President Richard Nixon; the actresses Suzanne Pleshette and Arlene Francis; and the rock star Grace Slick.

James Bradley

Fine, Reuben (*b* Bronx, 11 Oct 1914; *d* New York City, 26 March 1993). Psychoanalyst and chess player. Born into a poor family, he graduated from City College in 1932 and won the world chess championship in 1938. One of the most feared players at the Marshall and Manhattan chess clubs in New York City, he was the finest "speed" player in the United States. He won eight of the 13 international competitions in which he took part and tied for second in most of the others, and also won seven U.S. Open tournaments between 1932 and 1941. During World War II he withdrew from competitive play, earned a doctorate in psychology, and set up a successful practice as a lay analyst in New York City, where he lived for most of his life. He was director of the New York Center for Psychoanalytic Training and the founder and first president of the Division of Psychotherapy and the Division of Psychoanalysis of the American Psychological Association. Fine's published writings include *The Psychology of the Chess Player* (1967) and *The Healing of the Mind: The Technique of Psychoanalytic Psychotherapy* (1971; 2nd edn 1982).

Kenneth T. Jackson

Fine Arts Federation. Arts council formed on 18 April 1895 by the American Institute of Architects, the Municipal Art Society, the National Sculpture Society, the Society of Beaux-Arts Architects, and five other organizations of artists and civic reformers; incorporated in October 1897. The stated purpose of its founders was to "ensure united action by the Art Societies of New York in all matters affecting their common interests, and to foster and protect the artistic interests of the community." The first president was the noted architect, critic, and writer Russell Sturgis. In cooperation with other organizations and the architect John M. Carrère, the federation was instrumental in establishing the Art Commission of the City of New York in 1898, and it later assumed responsibility for submitting the names of prospective members to the mayor. In 2010 the federation had 22 member organizations.

Michele H. Bogart, *Public Sculpture and the Civic Ideal in New York City, 1890–1930* (Chicago: University of Chicago Press, 1989)

Margot Gayle

Finley, John H(uston) (*b* Grand Ridge, Ill., 19 Oct 1863; *d* New York City, 7 March 1940). Educator and journalist. After earning a BA from Knox College (Galesburg, Illinois) he did graduate work in social science at Johns Hopkins University and moved to New York City, where he worked for the State Charities Aid Association in the 1890s. He was president of Knox College from 1892–99 and taught at Princeton University from 1900 to 1903, when he became president of City College of New York. During his decade in office the college became a major institution dedicated principally to educating male students from the lower middle class. Many were the sons of recent immigrants, and a large number were Jews, whom he welcomed in spite of the rampant anti-Semitism of the time. In 1905 he oversaw the moving of the main campus to a complex of Gothic Revival buildings in upper Manhattan designed by George B. Post. Finley left New York City in 1913 to become the state education commissioner but returned in 1920 to join the *New York Times;* for two decades he composed many of the lighter items on the editorial page and became a minor celebrity in the city's cultural life.

Marvin E. Gettleman, *An Elusive Presence: The Discovery of John H. Finley and His America* (Chicago: Nelson-Hall, 1979)

Marvin E. Gettleman

Finns. Until the late nineteenth century most of the Finns who settled in New York City were sailors. The Finnish Seamen's Mission, the first Finnish religious organization in the city, was formed in 1887 by Emil Panelius. According to the federal census, the city had 9845 inhabitants of Finnish extraction in the city in 1900. Finns established communities in Bay Ridge in Brooklyn, on and around Fifth Avenue between 115th and 136th streets, and along Eighth Avenue near Sunset Park in Brooklyn, a neighborhood that was named Pukin Maki (Goat Hill) by its residents and came to be known as Finntown. Men worked as tailors, goldsmiths, silversmiths, watchmakers, carpenters, and masons, and many women as domestic servants. The Finnish Aid Society Imatra, formed in 1890 with the aim of furthering Finnish culture in the city, built its own hall at 740 40th Street in Brooklyn. In the same year the socialist political organization the Workers' Club Imatra (no. 15) was formed in Manhattan and set up headquarters at 2056 Fifth Avenue in a building known as Fifth Avenue Hall (where the Socialist Party nominated Eugene V. Debs for the presidency in 1920). The club joined in 1906 with other Finnish socialist groups in the United States to form the Finnish Federation of the Socialist Party and later became more heavily involved in the American labor movement. The newspaper *New Yorkin Uutiset,* which launched in 1906 and ceased publication in 1996, united the local Finnish community. Finns also established athletic clubs, choral groups, temperance societies, libraries, and social and cultural clubs.

In 1916, 16 Finnish families built a four-story cooperative apartment building in Brooklyn and named it Alku I (Beginning I). It was soon followed by two cooperative garages and a cooperative shopping complex containing a pool room, a restaurant, a meat market, a bakery, and a grocery. The success of this project helped to further the acceptance of the cooperative movement throughout the United States. The number of Finns living in New York City reached 20,043 in 1930, after which time Finnish immigration to the United

States slowed. Fifth Avenue Hall was sold in 1955; the proceeds were used to support the newspaper *Raivaaja* (Pioneer). The Workers' Club Imatra, which after several changes came to be known as the Finnish American League for Democracy, closed in 1974. As of 2010 about 3000 Finns lived in the New York City metropolitan area. Current Finnish organizations include the New York Finnish Lutheran Congregation, located at 83 Christopher Street, and the American-Scandinavian Foundation, located at 58 Park Avenue.

Katri Ekman, Corrine Olli, and John B. Olli, *A History of Finnish American Organizations in Greater New York, 1891–1976* (New York: Greater New York Finnish Bicentennial Planning Committee, 1976)

Erica Judge

Fiorello H. La Guardia High School of Music and Art and Performing Arts. Public high school opened in 1936 in upper Manhattan as the High School of Music and Art by Mayor Fiorello H. La Guardia. Admission was based on competitive auditions and the evaluation of portfolios. The enrollment was at first 250 students but eventually grew to about 2000. Benjamin M. Steigman was the first principal (1936–59). In 1961 the school absorbed the High School of Performing Arts (an annex of the Metropolitan Vocational High School, opened in 1947 on West 46th Street in the theater district). Through efforts begun by the city planning commissioner Robert Moses the school moved in 1984 to a new building behind Lincoln Center, directly across the street from the Library and Museum of the Performing Arts; it took its current name in 1989. The school is considered a model for other high schools of the arts throughout the United States. The High School of Performing Arts on 46th Street was the setting for the film and the television series *Fame*.

Benjamin M. Steigman, *Accent on Talent: New York's High School of Music and Art* (Detroit: Wayne State University Press, 1964)

Bernard Hirschhorn

firearms. Guns arrived in New Amsterdam with Dutch settlers in the seventeenth century and have been part of the fabric of the city ever since, including a period during the nineteenth century when Manhattan gun dealers made the city the number one entrepot in the country for the small arms trade. Given the stringent regulation of guns in the city in the twenty-first century, it is a surprise to many to learn that the National Rifle Association was founded in New York City in 1871 and even ran a rifle range at Creedmore in Queens until the 1890s.

During the first years of settlement, Dutch "trade guns" were exchanged for furs with American Indians, and the British continued this tradition. There are extensive records of freemen and apprentices working as gunsmiths, stockmakers, armorers, and locksmiths as well as in other gun-related trades throughout the first two centuries of settlement. During the Revolutionary War a wide variety of guns were brought to the city from France, Britain, and Germany, and Committee of Safety muskets were made in the city. During the 1600s and 1700s artisans, often sole proprietors, made guns from imported and sometimes domestic parts. After the Revolution, the roots of many of New York City's large gun dealing "houses" were evident in businesses started by families such as the Moores, Coopers, Wolfes, and others.

In the first decades of the nineteenth century, gun selling underwent a transition that is evident in the work of Joseph Finch, who operated a shop from 1799 to 1825. By the 1830s and 1840s Smith and his peers were overtaken by dealers who imported mass-produced guns from overseas and from large domestic producers, especially those along the Connecticut River valley, and then sold them globally. By mid-century, a thriving gun dealer district was evident on Maiden Lane and on nearby blocks on Pearl Street and Broadway, an area remembered as "the great store center" by gun dealer Adam W. Spies. Gun sellers included manufacturers and importers, hardware stores (the phrase "hardware, cutlery and guns" is often found in historical documents), secondhand dealers, and even elite shops like Tiffany and Company, which by 1862 was proudly advertising "Military Wares" in city directories. Keeping pace with the expanded market, gun advertising moved from manufacturers' notices in newspaper classifieds and trade cards in the early century to elaborate illustrated broadsides and advertisements in city directories and magazines, culminating in lavish catalogs by the last few decades of the century.

Samuel Colt opened a New York City office at 155 Broadway in 1836 as an outlet for his Paterson, New Jersey, manufacturing operation. But Colt's revolver was not an icon then, and for most of the three decades before the Civil War the pepperbox (a multiple-barreled revolver) was the most popular handgun in New York City and everywhere else. Colt's resurrected company in Hartford, Connecticut, eventually became so powerful that he made his city dealers (whom he called "the Allies") sign exclusive distribution contracts including price controls from at least 1860 to 1873. After the Civil War New York City's dealers looked for markets outside of the United States, while domestic sales focused on cheap pocket pistols that were marketed with a wide range of brand names for the first time, including American Boy, Bang Up, Conqueror, Defiance, Little Giant, My Friend, and Tramps Terror. During the last decades of the century, guns were also marketed in elaborate catalogs, alongside "novelties," with the cheapest pistols selling for less than $1.

The most famous "New York City" shooting—that between Alexander Hamilton and Aaron Burr in 1804—actually took place in nearby Weehawken, New Jersey, and the parties used English-made flintlocks borrowed from Hamilton's brother-in-law. Particularly grisly killings, whether by axe, knife, or gun, were always covered in the papers, and it was not uncommon for them to note the use of guns in self-defense during "riots." Surprisingly, given the domestic violence caused by people armed with guns in the twentieth century, during most years of the nineteenth century, New Yorkers were more likely to kill each other with edged weapons rather than with guns. The notorious exceptions were the 1863 draft riots, during which gun violence was more prevalent. Indeed, in the wake of the riots, a report issued by Metropolitan Police Board president Thomas Acton noted that "the practice of carrying concealed deadly weapons by the violent and vicious classes of the city has become common." The city passed its first laws to require a permit to carry a pistol in the 1870s, and in 1911 the state enacted the Sullivan Law, probably the most stringent handgun control law in the country, requiring a person to have a permit to both purchase and carry a gun.

The twentieth century saw increasing levels of gun violence in urban areas, and New York City was no exception, as advances in production, marketing, and sales inevitably led to greater gun use. In the decades following passage of the Sullivan Law, authorities began to seriously enforce laws that controlled or banned concealed weapons. For most years in the century, with the exception of a period from the 1940s through the early 1960s, homicides by guns exceeded those by edged weapons. Violent crime rates and gun use spiked in the 1980s and early 1990s. The New York City Police Department estimated that there were two million illegal guns in circulation in the city during 1993, a year in which more than 1500 people were shot to death.

City gun ownership and use in violent crimes has fallen drastically since the 1990s for a number of reasons, including the end of the crack cocaine epidemic, the deployment of more police officers who better target gun crimes, and an improved economy. Because New York City has some of the most restrictive, expensive, and lengthy gun licensing requirements in the country, the vast majority of guns seized by authorities are from out of state. The city's most recent effort to target illegal guns has been to sue out-of-state gun dealers whom the city argues do not abide by federal firearms laws and whose guns have ended up in New York. This combination of structural changes and police tactics reduced the number of people shot to death to fewer than 300 in 2008. At the same time the city has become a difficult place for law-abiding citizens to own guns, and the police note that 92 percent of those who have applied for gun permits or permit renewals since 1994 have been denied.

Eric H. Monkkonen, *Murder in New York City* (Berkeley: University of California Press, 2001); H. J. Swinney, *The New York State Firearms Trade,* Vol. 5: *New York City* (Rochester: Rowe Publications, 2003)

Eric Wakin

fireboats. Ships that are equipped with firefighting equipment. The first in New York Harbor was put into service as early as 1800 and consisted of a hand pumper mounted on a barge run by 12 volunteers. Between 1867 and 1875 a privately owned steam-propelled "floating engine," the *John Fuller,* was rented by the Fire Department. Recognizing that New York was handling more shipping than all the other harbors in the United States combined, the department obtained its own vessel, the *William F. Havemeyer,* in 1875. With the consolidation of the two cities in 1898, Brooklyn added its two marine units to the three already in service in New York City at the time. The most powerful fireboat in the world, the *Firefighter,* went into service in 1938.

Fireboats were the first units in the Fire Department to be equipped with two-way radios (1937). They helped land-based units fight fires aboard ships at dock, including the SS *Normandie* (1942) and the aircraft carrier USS *Constellation* (1960), and other fires onshore, such as the Hoboken pier fire (1900), which killed 400 and destroyed the North German Lloyd docks; the Black Tom naval ordnance depot explosion in Jersey City (1916); and Brooklyn's Furman Street warehouse fire (1935).

During World War II fireboats undertook the dangerous mission of scuttling the ammunition-laden freighter *El Estero,* which exploded amid other ships carrying high-octane aviation fuel at a pier in Jersey City on 14 April 1943. The massive explosion was similar to the incident that destroyed the port of Halifax, Nova Scotia, in 1917. The *Firefighter* and the *John J. Harvey* were lashed to the freighter, which they towed away from the populated shore into deeper water. Similarly, the oil tankers *Alva Cape* and *Texaco Massachusetts* were separated by fireboats after colliding and catching fire in 1966, as were the tankers *Sea Witch* and *Esso Brussels* in 1974. After the terrorist attacks of 11 September 2001, the entire force of Fire Department boats, augmented by the retired, restored, and civilian-run fireboat *John J. Harvey,* supplied the only water available for operations at Ground Zero for three days.

The only fire protection on the water for the entire Port of New York, fireboats are directed by officers trained both as firefighters and marine engineers and often fight fires involving highly volatile cargo with the potential for enormous damage and loss of life. The city's fireboats frequently respond to alarms in Westchester County along the shore of Long Island Sound and along the western bank of the Hudson River as far south as Perth Amboy, New Jersey. They also are used in public celebrations and to greet incoming ships.

In 1975 the fireboat fleet was reduced from 10 to five units. Despite pressing concerns about the deterioration of aging oil refineries and storage tanks, toxic waste dumps along the shoreline, increasing numbers of liquefied natural gas tankers unloading in the harbor, and the use of Staten Island as a home port by the U.S. Navy, little attention was paid to augmenting the aging fireboat fleet until the increase in local and international passenger traffic in the harbor during the 1990s prompted a new look. In 2007, after an international design competition, bids for two new fireboats were awarded. In response to the threat of possible terrorist attacks like those of 11 September 2001, the new boats will be equipped to monitor chemical, biological, radiological, nuclear, and explosive agents (C-BRN), and they will have the ability to pump 50,000 gallons per minute. One of these fireboats, the *Three Forty Three,* was named in honor of the 343 New York City firefighters who lost their lives on 11 September 2001 at the World Trade Center.

Donald J. Cannon

fire escapes. Metal steps enclosed by railings installed on the exterior faces of multistory buildings to allow people to leave during an emergency. Throughout the seventeenth and eighteenth centuries New York City's residences consisted primarily of single-family homes, so fire escapes were not needed. By the early nineteenth century, however, multiple-unit TENEMENTS began to be seen in Manhattan, which were designed to accommodate larger numbers of immigrant families. From the 1820s this type of building became increasingly popular; by 1863 tenements housed more than 60 percent of the Manhattan population in more than 15,000 structures. Tenements were overcrowded, and fire safety was virtually nonexistent. The single interior stairwell was typically open (unenclosed) from the basement to the top floor, allowing a fire on a lower floor to quickly spread to the top of the building and block the only means of escape. Such a fire would sometimes force occupants to jump from upper-floor windows. This was the case on 2 February 1860 in a six-story tenement at 142 Elm Street. Despite heroic efforts by volunteer firefighters, 10 people died. Although this tragedy exposed deficiencies of a single-exit stairwell, it did not immediately lead to regulatory changes. It would take several more years and many fatal fires before the first Tenement House Law was enacted in 1867. The new regulations called for a secondary means of egress, presumably fire escapes, on tenement houses. In 1868 the city's Superintendent of Buildings issued specific design patterns for construction of fire escapes. These regulations were applied to existing and new tenements. The earliest fire escapes were essentially vertical ladders that were difficult to descend. Revisions to the Tenement House Law in 1901 required a stair angle of no more than 60 degrees, making the fire escape easier to climb down. This became the common zig-zag stair pattern found on most extant tenements. Despite such improvements, regulations called for narrow 20-inch-wide (51-centimeter-wide) steps that were only 6 inches (15 centimeters) deep, making a quick exit difficult. Even with these modest regulatory improvements, fire escapes, which were exposed to the elements year round, were poorly maintained. Furthermore, as more modern types of building construction evolved, complaints about their unsightliness grew. Tenants used them as extra storage space, and burglars used them to gain access to apartments. A 1968 revision to the city's building code banned fire escapes on new buildings. Long a part of the urban landscape, fire escapes have been used as a place for romance and a place to sleep outdoors on hot summer nights; these uses were enshrined in popular culture, for instance, in Leonard Bernstein's musical *West Side Story* (1957; 1961 film version) and Alfred Hitchcock's film *Rear Window* (1954).

Glenn P. Corbett

Fire escape, 2009

firefighting. Firefighting in New York City has evolved from a period of leather buckets and volunteers, through technological changes and political upheaval, to the challenges presented by modern-day skyscrapers, including the 110-story World Trade Center twin towers, which collapsed on 11 September 2001 after terrorists flew jetliners into them.

Hook-and-ladder company outside its headquarters in lower Manhattan, 1891

1. The Seventeenth and Eighteenth Centuries: Noisemakers and Sober Men

During colonial times all able-bodied men were required to help extinguish fires. In 1648 Governor Peter Stuyvesant hired fire wardens to cite the owners of poorly maintained wooden chimneys, the principal fire hazard in the city. In 1658 nighttime "rattle watch" was established, in which men patrolled the city with loud noisemakers that they sounded in the event of fire. The English established strict codes for the design and maintenance of chimneys and required every house and business to have leather fire buckets at hand.

Throughout the seventeenth century, fires were uncommon in the city because of the slow rate of development and the predominance of brick in construction. As the city grew larger and more populous after 1700, brick and stone proved too costly for most residents, and the risk of fires increased as wood became the favored construction material. The Common Council recognized the increased danger of fire and imported two Newsham hand pumpers from London in 1731. A volunteer force of 30 "strong, able, discreet, honest, and sober men" was appointed in 1737 by the General Assembly. The efficiency of this force proved crucial in controlling several fires, particularly during the "Negro plot" of 1741, marked by the burning of Fort George. By 1770 the city had eight engines and a force of 170 men. During the American Revolution, firefighting became a chaotic, improvised affair undertaken by members of the Royal Navy and local residents. Two major fires occurred during the war: the first, in 1776, was actually a series of fires probably caused by arson that destroyed nearly 500 houses in what is now the Lower West Side (more than one-third of the city), and the second consumed 64 houses near Cruger's Wharf along the East River in 1778. In 1785 Brooklyn residents voted to provide for a volunteer force of one company employing a captain and five men. On 19 March 1787 the Fire Department of the City of New York was reorganized by a special act of the state legislature, which appropriated funds for a chief engineer and six subordinates, to be appointed by the Common Council. There were few fires during the decades after the Revolution: only five broke out in 1795, and the annual total never exceeded 10, although there was a large fire in the "coffeehouse district" in 1796. In 1799 the Manhattan Company became the first of several private companies authorized to provide a steady supply of water to supplement existing supplies, which were drawn from rivers, cisterns, wells, natural springs, and primitive pumps. A makeshift fireboat was first employed in New York Harbor in 1800 to protect the increasingly vital waterfront. The number of fires increased annually from a low point of six in 1800, as development intensified and shoddily built wood-constructed neighborhoods expanded northward.

2. The Nineteenth Century: Reform and Development

During the early years of the nineteenth century, new volunteer companies were established to fill the growing need for greater protection. By 1810 three hook-and-ladder companies and 34 engine companies were staffed by 1005 volunteers. Riveted hose was introduced in 1808, replacing leaky hand-stitched hoses. After its incorporation in 1816 the Village of Brooklyn elected its first chief engineer to lead 35 firefighters assigned to three companies. That same year, the New York City Common Council encouraged enlistment in fire companies by offering to exempt veteran firefighters from jury duty and service in the militia. However, the Fire Department during these years was poorly organized: the role of the chief engineer was not clearly defined, and for a time civilian members of the Common Council were empowered to direct men and equipment during fires. Volunteers lacked coordinative leadership and control at the scenes of fires, and

Fire Commissioners of New York City

John J. Scannell, 1898–1901
Thomas Sturgis, 1902–3
Nicholas J. Hayes, 1904–5
John H. O'Brien, 1906
Francis J. Lantry, 1906–8
Hugh Bonner, 1908
Nicholas J. Hayes, 1908–9
Rhinelander Waldo, 1910–11
Joseph Johnson, 1911–13
Robert Adamson, 1914–17
Thomas J. Drennan, 1918–26
John J. Dorman, 1926–33
John J. McElligott, 1934–40
Elmer Mustard, 1940
John J. McElligott, 1940–41
Patrick J. Walsh, 1941–45
Frank J. Quayle, 1946–50
George P. Monaghan, 1950–51
Jacob Grumet, 1951–53
Edward F. Cavanagh, 1954–61
Edward Thompson, 1962–64
Martin Scott, 1964–65
Robert O. Lowery, 1966–73
John T. O'Hagan, 1973–78
Augustus Beekman, 1978–80
Charles J. Hynes, 1980–82
Joseph E. Spinnato, 1982–87
Joseph F. Bruno, 1987–90
Carlos M. Rivera, 1990–93
William M. Feehan, 1993
Howard Safir, 1994–96
Thomas Von Essen, 1996–2001
Nicholas Scoppetta, 2002–2009
Salvatore Cassano, 2010–

water supplies, inadequate at best, usually froze in winter. Firefighting methods were crude, often involving spectacular rescues, exterior "surround and drown" tactics, and the tearing down of adjacent buildings. Some firefighters were accused of drunkenness, theft, and failure to answer alarms, and some companies earned a reputation for brawling rather than firefighting. By 1834 insurance companies formed a paid salvage unit, known as the Fire Patrol, which rushed to fires in order to save whatever property it could. Some New Yorkers attributed the severity of the Great Fire of December 1835 to the negligence of the volunteer companies and called for a force of paid professionals.

The largest fire since 1776 occurred in Chatham Square in 1811 as more than 100 buildings burned. To address the need for a reliable source of water, a water reserve on Chambers Street near City Hall was authorized at that time. A serious fire occurred in 1821 at Crane's Wharf, followed by an outbreak of yellow fever in 1822. An increase in the water supply for both firefighting and drinking occurred during this period, but not at a pace to keep up with the increase in population. The Common Council authorized the construction of an additional water supply for fighting fires in 1829 at 13th Street and the Bowery, which was becoming the densest part of the city. The stone tower, 44 feet (13 meters) in diameter and 27 feet (8 meters) high, held an iron tank that contained more than 300,000 gallons of water that connected to iron pipes that fed the water to 30 fireplugs; there were also 50 cisterns in strategic locations.

Between the 1830s and the early 1860s, volunteer firefighting companies played a central role in city politics. Although many men joined companies to prove their courage and skill, others recognized that membership in a

Last surviving fire tower in New York City, Mount Morris Park, ca 1905

Major Fires within the Current Boundaries of New York City, 1741–2006

Date	Fire
18 March 1741	Fort George: Governor's house, barracks, and chapel destroyed.
21 Sept 1776	Great Fire of 1776: One-third of city affected, 492 houses destroyed.
3 Aug 1778	Cruger's Wharf: 64 houses destroyed.
9 Dec 1796	Coffee House Slip below Front St. between Murray Wharf and the Fly Market: 50 houses destroyed.
18 Dec 1804	Second Coffee House Fire, in area surrounding Wall and Pearl streets: 40 houses destroyed.
19 May 1811	Great Fire of 1811, in area surrounding Chatham St.: One firefighter killed, 102 houses destroyed.
24 Jan 1821	Crane's Wharf, Front St.: 31 houses destroyed.
18 May 1828	Bowery Theater, at Bayard St.: Two people killed, 25 to 30 buildings destroyed.
30 Apr 1833	Greenwich Village, in area surrounding Hudson and Greenwich streets: 90 to 100 buildings destroyed.
12 Aug 1835	Fulton, Nassau, and Ann streets: Five people killed, 35 houses destroyed.
16–17 Dec 1835	Great Fire of 1835, at Wall, Broad, and South streets: 20 blocks destroyed (600–700 buildings).
23 Sept 1839	National Theater, Leonard and Church streets: The theater, a school, and three churches destroyed.
5 Oct 1839	Water, Pearl, and Fletcher streets: Entire blocks affected, probably more than 100 buildings destroyed.
19 July 1845	Great Fire of 1845, at Broad St., Exchange Place, and William St.: 30 people killed, 300 buildings destroyed.
9 Sept 1848	Henry, Pineapple, Sands, and Washington streets, Brooklyn: Seven blocks of buildings destroyed, including three churches, two newspapers, and a post office.
5 Feb 1850	5–7 Hague St., Queens: Explosion kills 64 people.
10 Dec 1853	Offices of Harper and Brothers, Franklin Square: 16 buildings destroyed.
25 Apr 1854	Jennings, 231 Broadway: 11 firefighters killed.
5 Oct 1858	Crystal Palace, 42nd St. and Fifth Ave.: Building destroyed.
2 Feb 1860	Tenement on Elm St.: 20 people killed.
13–16 July 1863	Draft riots: Fires citywide, 43 buildings destroyed.
5 Dec 1876	Brooklyn Theater, 313 Washington St.: 295 people killed.
31 Jan 1882	World Building, Park Row and Nassau St.: 12 people killed.
22 Aug 1891	Taylor Building, Park Row: 61 people killed.
6 Feb 1892	Hotel Royal, Sixth Ave. and 40th St.: 28 people killed.
17 March 1899	Windsor Hotel, 565 Fifth Ave.: 33 people killed.
4 Nov 1902	Madison Square Garden: 15 people killed.
15 Jun 1904	*General Slocum* burns: 1021 people killed.
25 May 1911	Triangle Shirtwaist factory, Washington Place and Greene St.: 146 people killed.
6 Jan 1912	Equitable Life Assurance Building, 120 Broadway: Six people killed.
13 Sept 1919	20 acres (8 hectares) lying within area bounded by Sutton, Norman, and Greenpoint avenues, Greenpoint: 30 oil tanks destroyed.
29 Jan 1931	Lincoln Arcade, Broadway between 65th and 66th streets. Eight people injured, nine firefighters injured. Building destroyed.
13 July 1932	Coney Island residential area, 178 buildings destroyed.
1 Aug 1932	Ritz Tower Hotel: Seven firefighters killed.
18 Aug 1941	SS *Panuco,* Pier 27, Brooklyn: 41 people killed.
9 Feb 1942	SS *Normandie:* One person killed, 128 injured, ship destroyed.
24 Dec 1943	Lodging house, 437–439 West 42nd St.: 18 people killed.
17 Jan 1946	Staten Island Ferry, Battery: Three people killed, many injured, ferry house destroyed.
11 Dec 1946	Knickerbocker Ice Plant, 184th St. and Amsterdam Ave.: 37 people killed.
3 Dec 1956	Luckenbach Steamship Lines: Nine people killed.

(*continued*)

Major Fires within the Current Boundaries of New York City, 1741–2006 (*Continued*)

4 Apr 1956	Artificial-flower factory, 4065 Third Ave., Bronx: Six firefighters killed.
16 July 1956	Wanamaker Building: 187 firefighters injured, building razed.
14 Feb 1958	Elkins Company, 137 Wooster St.: Two firefighters and four members of a fire patrol killed.
19 Mar 1958	SGS Textile Printing Co., 623 Broadway: 24 people killed.
19 Dec 1960	USS *Constellation,* Brooklyn Navy Yard: 50 people killed.
10 May 1962	Mill Basin: Largest quantity of oil ignited since 1919 Greenpoint fire.
3 Oct 1962	Telephone company, 213th St. and Broadway: 23 people killed.
26 Oct 1962	Sefu Soap and Fat Co., 44–15 56th Road, Queens: Six firefighters killed.
17 Oct 1966	6 East 23rd St.: 12 firefighters killed.
13 Jan 1967	Explosion in Queens: Four city blocks destroyed.
8 Jan 1968	232–236 Johnson St., Brooklyn: 13 people killed.
18 July 1968	115–155 Mexico St., Queens: 11 people killed.
3 Feb 1969	595 Fifth Ave.: 11 people killed.
19 Dec 1969	31 Covert St., Brooklyn: 11 people killed.
10 Feb 1973	Gas tank explosion, Staten Island: 40 people killed.
24 Oct 1973	Puerto Rican Social Club, Bronx: 25 people killed.
25 Mar 1990	Happy Land Social Club, 1959 Southern Blvd., Bronx: 87 people killed.
8 Sept 1991	Staten Island Ferry Terminal: 20 injured.
25 Mar 1994	62 Watch St.: Three firefighters killed.
17 June 2001	Long Island General Supply Store: Three firefighters killed.
11 Sept 2001	World Trade Center: 2749 people killed, including 343 firefighters.
2 May 2006	Greenpoint, Brooklyn, former rope factory: 14 firefighters injured.

Sources: New York City Fire Department, http://nyc.gov/html/fdny/html/home2.shtml; *New York Times* (various)
Compiled by Meghan Lalonde, Edward T. O'Donnell, and Alex Poole

FDNY fire truck, 2009

fire company was often the first step in a political career (as it was for seven mayors elected after 1835). Foremen gained recognition, status, and financial rewards, legal and illegal. One of the best-known foremen was William M. "Boss" Tweed, who formed Americus Engine Company 6 on Henry Street in 1848 and became the boss of Tammany Hall. He won the loyalty of many fire companies, and saloons owned by firefighters soon became associated with the Tammany organization. In 1838 and 1841 the Common Council tried to remove the Fire Department from politics by reorganizing it, but the department continued to be dominated by Tammany Hall and was increasingly racked by violence, rioting, and sabotage.

The Fire Department also became enmeshed in the ethnic, religious, and class divisions that marked the city during the 1840s, and rivalries between companies grew so violent as to impair firefighting. During the 1850s Tweed's engine company was one of the most notorious. Embezzlement also became a serious problem. Of more than $240,000 approved by the council between 1835 and 1861 for the purchase of new equipment, only about $100,000 was spent as intended: the rest made its way to Tammany Hall or was pocketed by corrupt foremen. Faced with an increasingly disorganized department, chief engineer Alfred Carson (1848–57) regularly railed against the Common Council for failing to deal with the problems of the department. As long as the council was dominated by Tammany Hall, Carson's criticisms were ignored, except by those who sought to remove him. In February 1857 Carson was narrowly defeated by Harry Howard, who was supported by Tammany Hall and those who opposed any further structural or technological reform of the volunteer system. Despite negative publicity, however, the volunteer fire department enjoyed the support of the working class, and companies celebrated their affiliations in poems, plays, and songs. The iconic figure of "Mose the Fireman" was portrayed hundreds of times in the play *A Glance at New York* beginning in 1848.

The mid-nineteenth century introduced increasingly numerous, complex, and deadly firefighting challenges, including 300 buildings destroyed in the Broad Street district (1845), a major conflagration in downtown Brooklyn (1848), a warehouse fire and collapse killing 11 volunteer firefighters (1854), the burning of the New York Crystal Palace (1858), and the death of 20 residents in an Elm Street tenement fire (1860). Such threats of large fires led to more reform efforts and improved technology. A primitive telegraphic fire alarm system was authorized in December 1847, and by the summer of 1851 the city's fire headquarters were linked, though unreliably, to the city's fire bell towers. In 1854 Alfred E. Baker was hired by a consortium of insurance companies to investigate arson cases as the first fire marshal of the city. In 1859 insurance companies presented firefighting volunteers with their first two steam-powered fire engines.

Fire companies in the city were instrumental in both exacerbating and controlling the draft riots of July 1863. On 13 July, after the names of about 50 conscripts had been drawn, members of Black Joke Engine Company set fire to the office of the marshal for the ninth district on Third Avenue and 47th Street and prevented anyone from extinguishing it, setting the riots in motion. By the following day, however, most companies in the city, including the Black Joke, were patrolling their neighborhoods, fighting rioters, and protecting property. In letters to local newspapers, business leaders and railroad owners praised the fire companies for their vigilance.

By the mid-1860s the close ties between Tammany Hall and the volunteer companies and rising losses from fires led to renewed demands for a full-time paid professional fire department. In the spring of 1865 the state legislature replaced the volunteer companies with the Metropolitan Fire Department (MFD), a paid force of 700 exclusively under the direction of a board of commissioners. The shift to a professional department led to improvements in firefighting techniques. By early 1866 steam engines, horses, and a telegraph system were in service in downtown Manhattan. Efficiency improved after General Alexander T. Shaler, president of the board of fire commissioners (1867–70), reorganized the department according to a military model in which specialization, discipline, and merit were encouraged by a system of daily advisory orders, trials for disobedience, and ranks (the ranks of captain and lieutenant remained in use into the twenty-first century, as did such terms as battalion). By 1870 the MFD had extended service to the suburban districts north of 86th Street and in 1874 assumed responsibility for the West Bronx after it was annexed by New York City. Between 1867 and 1875 a private steam-propelled "floating engine," the *John Fuller,* was leased to the department. Locked-door fire alarm boxes were set up in the streets, and instructional classes began in 1869. The MFD soon won the praise of businesses, newspaper editors, and the public as losses due to fire plummeted. In 1869 the editor of the *New York Herald* established the James Gordon Bennett Medal, an award still presented yearly for the most outstanding act of heroism on the part of a member of the Fire Department.

The MFD was replaced in 1870 with the Fire Department of the City of New York (FDNY), retaining most of Shaler's organizational innovations. A school for foremen (company officers) opened in 1878. During the same period, new techniques and equipment for fighting fires were gradually introduced, including "interior attacks"; taller ladders; steam engines with greater pumping pressure; the first fireboat, the *William F. Havemeyer;* keyless alarm boxes; and telephones. After a fire at the offices of the *New York World* in 1883, a School of Instruction, the forerunner of the present-day Fire Academy, was established. Despite attempts by

Number of Firefighters in New York City, 1737–2008

Year	Number	Year	Number
1737	30	1905	2,157
1742	44	1910	4,332
1761	75	1915	5,026
1786	300	1920	6,767
1793	367	1925	6,969
1796	383	1930	7,587
1800	600	1935	7,452
1810	1,005	1940	11,631
1823	1,215	1946	10,357
1835	1,500	1950	11,348
1840	1,300	1955	12,226
1850	1,898	1960	13,280
1855	2,925	1965	13,991
1860	4,227	1970	14,855
1865	3,421	1975	14,773
1870	599	1980	12,832
1875	748	1985	13,017
1885	943	1990	12,769
1890	1,028	2007	11,544
1895	1,113	2008	11,275
1900	1,386	2009	11,213

Source: New York City Fire Department, http://www.nyc.gov/html/fdny

Twenty Worst Fires in New York City Based on Mortality, 1898–Present

	Date	Place	No. Dead
1	11 Sept 2001	World Trade Center	2749
2	15 Jun 1904	*General Slocum*	1021
3	5 Dec 1876	Brooklyn Theater, 313 Washington St.	295
4	25 May 1911	Triangle Shirtwaist Co., Washington Pl. and Greene St.	146
5	25 Mar 1990	Happy Land Social Club, 1959 Southern Blvd., Bronx	87
6	5 Feb 1850	5–7 Hague St., Queens	64
7	22 Aug 1891	Taylor Building, Park Row	61
8	19 Dec 1960	USS *Constellation,* Brooklyn Navy Yard	50
9	18 Aug 1941	SS *Panuco,* Pier 27, Brooklyn	41
10	10 Feb 1973	Gas tank explosion, Staten Island	40
11	11 Dec 1946	Knickerbocker Ice Plant, 184th St. and Amsterdam Ave.	37
12	17 March 1899	Windsor Hotel, 565 Fifth Ave.	33
13	6 Feb 1892	Hotel Royal, Sixth Ave. and 40th St.	28
14	24 Oct 1973	Puerto Rican Social Club, Bronx	25
15	19 Mar 1958	SGS Textile Printing Co., 623 Broadway	24
16	3 Oct 1962	Telephone company, 213th St. and Broadway	23
17	2 Feb 1860	Tenement on Elm St.	20
18	4 Nov 1902	Madison Square Garden	15
19	8 Jan 1968	232–236 Johnson St., Brooklyn	13
20	31 Jan 1882	World Building, Park Row and Nassau St.	12
20	17 Oct 1966	6 East 23rd St.	12

Note: Includes areas after 1898 consolidation.

Sources: New York City Fire Department, http://nyc.gov/html/fdny/html/home2.shtml; *New York Times* (various)

Compiled by Lisa Keller

Richmond firehouse, 2009

some politicians to interfere with funding and appointments, the introduction of civil service in 1884 helped to increase professionalism and keep the department out of politics. Responding to the deaths of more than 350 people in tenement fires during the 1890s, the FDNY joined the movement for housing reform. During the last ten years of the nineteenth century, the area served by the FDNY more than doubled. In 1895 the East Bronx was annexed to the city, and with consolidation in 1898, the FDNY absorbed the fire departments of the City of Brooklyn and of several communities in Queens.

3. The Twentieth Century and into the Twenty-First: Modern Challenges

Firefighting challenges and improvements continued at the turn of the twentieth century. The burning of the excursion steamship *General Slocum* in June 1904 killed more than 1000 passengers. When a fire at the Triangle Shirtwaist Company in 1911 killed 146 people, the FDNY helped to draft legislation to improve the safety and working conditions at factories. Working conditions for firefighters also improved during this period. Until 1919 all firefighters were required to remain on continuous duty save for two meal periods each day. Officers received 14 days of vacation annually, firefighters 10 days. After the Uniformed Firefighters Association (UFA) was formed in 1919, two platoons worked in split shifts, allowing firefighters to spend more time at home. Volunteer fire departments continued to operate in outlying sections of Brooklyn, Queens, and Staten Island until the 1920s, when many were taken over by the paid department. A few independent volunteer departments remained in operation into the twenty-first century, including one in Breezy Point.

A fire at the headquarters of Equitable Insurance in 1912 demonstrated the growing need for more effective methods of fighting fires in buildings taller than 10 stories. Gasoline-powered fire apparatus began to replace horse-drawn equipment in 1907, with the changeover completed by 1922. A fire alarm system was installed with a headquarters in Central Park and 1831 keyless boxes. FIREBOATS continued to be modernized during the 1930s as the first two-way radios were introduced in 1937, and the most powerful fireboat in the world, the *Firefighter,* began operation in 1938.

After major brush fires swept suburbanizing Staten Island during the spring of 1963, the FDNY assigned more companies there and installed larger mains. Twelve firefighters were killed in October 1966 when the floor of a building on 23rd Street in Manhattan collapsed in the worst disaster in the history of the FDNY before the terrorist attacks of 11 September 2001. In the mid-twentieth century the number of fire alarms increased sharply, from 62,021 in 1950 to 398,867 in 1975. The FDNY faced severe challenges during the 1970s, known as the War Years. After unsuccessful negotiations for higher salaries, the UFA called a strike on 6 November 1973. It lasted only five and a half hours, but all participants were fined after the courts ruled that the strike had violated the Taylor Law, which forbids public employees from striking. In 1975 budget cuts reduced the FDNY by 32 fire companies, and the fireboat fleet was also reduced. To distribute the workload more equitably between the busiest areas (with as many as 7000 runs a year) and the slowest (about 1500 a year), the FDNY introduced reassignments, interchanges, and supplementary squads. At the same time new technologies continued to improve its efficiency. Voice-activated street alarm boxes of the Emergency Reporting Service (ERS) replaced older pull boxes beginning in 1971, and a computer-assisted dispatching system in 1977 resulted in faster response times. (By 2007 the average time between an incoming alarm and the arrival of the first unit on the scene was only four minutes citywide.) Tower ladders, more efficient engines, and a super pumper unit were purchased. Hazardous materials units were formed when traditional tactics were found to be dangerous in fighting chemical fires and fires in buildings made of new materials. By the 1980s the number of alarms peaked and then began to decline, with 96,089 fires in the city in 1990. Affirmative action laws contributed to more opportunities in the FDNY for African Americans, Latinos, and women; 42 women joined the force in 1980 after a lengthy but successful class-action suit.

Before 11 September 2001 about 800 firefighters of the MFD and FDNY had been killed in the line of duty, but on that day 343 members of every rank—including First Deputy Commissioner William M. Feehan, Chief of Department Peter Ganci, and Chaplain Mychal Judge—died when the twin towers of the World Trade Center collapsed after being struck by terrorist-controlled jetliners. Within hours of the disaster thousands of firefighters, emergency workers, and paramedics from New Jersey, Long Island, Connecticut, and suburban counties to the north raced into New York City to help their comrades. In the aftermath of the 9/11 disaster private corporations and public agencies contributed many pieces of replacement apparatus. One, an engine donated by the state of Louisiana after 9/11 that served Brooklyn as Engine 283, was sent back to that state in 2005 to help residents of New Orleans after Hurricane Katrina, along with 660 members of the FDNY, including the New York City Urban Search and Rescue Team, the FDNY Disaster Assistance Response Team, the FDNY Incident Management Team (IMT), communications and support personnel, and members of the FDNY Counseling Services Unit. The engine remained in New Orleans as that city struggled to rebuild.

In 2002 the FDNY recorded 82 civilian fire fatalities, the lowest total since 1927. Between 9/11 and December 2007, 13 additional firefighters lost their lives in the line of duty. In 2008 the FDNY reported it had 11,275 active firefighters in the five boroughs.

Terry Galway, *So Others Might Live: A History of New York's Bravest: The FDNY from 1700 to the Present* (Jackson, Tenn.: Basic Books, 2002); David Von Drehle, *Triangle: The Fire That Changed America* (New York: Atlantic Monthly Press, 2003); Glenn P. Corbett and Donald J. Cannon, *Historic Fires of New York City* (Mount Pleasant, S.C.:

Fire hydrant, 2009

Arcadia, 2005); Marion Fontana, *A Widow's Walk: A Memoir of 9/11* (New York: Simon and Schuster, 2005); Gary Urbanowicz, Michael Boucher, and Frederick Melahn, Jr., *The Last Alarm: The History and Tradition of Supreme Sacrifice in the Fire Departments of New York City* (Evansville, Ind.: M.T. Publishing, 2007)

Donald J. Cannon

First Bank of the United States. Federal bank. Proposed by Alexander Hamilton, it was formed with capital assets of $4.7 million in Philadelphia in 1791 as a fiscal agent of the federal government and a commercial bank. It had eight branches, including one on what is now Pearl Street in Manhattan that opened on 1 April 1792 with assets of $1.8 million. The larger allotment of capital to Philadelphia was greatly resented by the branch in New York City, which was often unable to meet customers' demands, and the bank's deflationary policy of demanding the redemption of state notes was fiercely opposed by other banks in the city, including the Bank of New York. One of the most avid foes of the First Bank was John Jacob Astor, who offered to lend his own money to the federal government as an incentive not to renew the bank's charter, which was rescinded by Congress in 1811.

John T. Holdsworth, *First Bank of the United States* (Philadelphia: University of Pennsylvania Press, 1910)

James Bradley

First Baptist Church. Church at 265 West 79th Street in Manhattan, near Broadway. It began as a branch of the New Jersey Scotch Plains Baptist Church before incorporating under its own name in 1762. The church was situated in lower Manhattan until it moved to 39th Street and Park Avenue during the pastorship of Thomas Anderson (1862–78). The current building, designed by George Keister, was constructed in 1894 on a diagonal to the street, breaking the regularity of the city's grid plan. The structure has a unique stained-glass roof and two unequal towers rising on either side of the entrance, the taller one representing Christ as the head of the church and light of the world and the smaller deliberately left incomplete, a symbol of the wait for the return of Christ.

Aileen Laura Love

First Houses. Complex of eight four- and five-story buildings, each containing 123 apartments, on Third Street and Avenue A in Manhattan. It opened for tenants in December 1935 as the first completed project of the New York City Housing Authority and the first municipally built public housing project in the United States. The project began when the chairman of the housing authority, Langdon Post, sought to hasten the transfer of funds promised by the head of the U.S. Public Works Administration, Secretary of the Interior Harold Ickes, by accepting Vincent Astor's offer of a long-term, low-interest mortgage on a group of deteriorated "old law" tenements on the Lower East Side. Bernard Baruch provided a loan that allowed the authority to buy other buildings on the block. A refusal by the owner of the buildings, Andrew Muller, to sell prompted the authority to sue; the decision that slum clearance was a public purpose for which the authority could use eminent domain was reaffirmed by the New York State Court of Appeals in *New York City Housing Authority v. Muller* (1936). Laborers funded by the Works Progress Administration built the First Houses from designs by Frederick Ackerman, technical director of the housing authority. They demolished every third building on the block, thus making room for landscaped courtyards that allowed for cross-ventilation in the apartments, and renovated the remaining structures. They then built playgrounds, indoor recreation rooms, laundry rooms, and a health clinic. The First Houses were designated a landmark by the city in 1974.

Robert A. M. Stern, Gregory F. Gilmartin, and Thomas Mellins, *New York 1930: Architecture and Urbanism between the Two World Wars* (New York: Rizzoli, 1987)

Rosalie Genevro

First National City Bank (of New York). Commercial bank later known as Citibank.

First Presbyterian Church, Brooklyn. Church formed in 1822 on Cranberry Street. It was the site of a celebration when Brooklyn was incorporated as a city in 1834. The church moved in 1846 to 124 Henry Street, where its congregation actively supported abolitionists. Important contributions to church music were made by its pastor Charles S. Robinson (1860–76), author of 15 collections of hymns, and its organist and choirmaster Raymond H. Woodman (1880–1941). Under Philip Elliott (1931–61) the congregation initiated the Heights Fellowship (1949–52) to promote internationalism, ecumenism, and racial harmony, an effort that was continued by Paul Smith in the late 1980s.

David Meerse

First Presbyterian Church in Jamaica. Church at 89-60 164th Street in Queens, formed in 1662 by the oldest continuous Presbyterian congregation in the United States. The congregation first met in a stone building erected in 1699 at Jamaica Avenue and Union Hall Street (used by the British as a military prison during the American Revolution). The second church building was completed in 1813 and moved to 164th Street in 1920. In honor of Andrew Magill, who served as pastor for 34 years, the Magill Memorial Building was built in 1923 to provide Sunday school rooms and church offices.

David Meerse

First Shearith Israel Graveyard. Cemetary and historic site at 55 St. James Place. Interred in this graveyard are members of the First Shearith Israel Synagogue, the first Jewish congregation in America, buried between 1684 and 1828. Opened in 1684, it is in fact the second Jewish graveyard in New York, replacing the original graveyard the congregation used from 1656 to 1684; the location of the original site is unknown. The graveyard is a New York Historical Site.

Ben Silk

fiscal crisis. See Budget.

Fischer, Bobby [Robert James] (*b* Chicago, 9 March 1943; *d* Reykjavík, Iceland, 17 Jan 2008). Chess player. He moved to Brooklyn in 1948. Fischer's sister Joan bought him his first chess set at the candy store located below their apartment. At age eight he started taking lessons at the Brooklyn Chess Club. He came to prominence as a childhood prodigy, challenging the nation's leading players at the Manhattan Chess Club and the Marshall Chess Club and winning the U.S. Open at the age of 13. By 15 Fischer was a grandmaster. After dropping out of Erasmus Hall High School in Brooklyn to pursue a career in chess, he won a string of matches in the late 1960s with unprecedented ease, and in 1972 he defeated Boris Spassky for the world championship in Reykjavík, Iceland. A moody and temperamental player, he then retired suddenly from tournament chess and led a reclusive life in Los Angeles. In 1992 he reemerged to defeat Spassky in a tournament in Montenegro and Serbia, which was under a United Nations embargo at the time. As a result Fischer found himself facing federal charges and never returned to the United States, ultimately moving to Iceland. He is widely regarded as the greatest American chess player in history.

Frank Robert Brady, *Profile of a Prodigy: The Life and Games of Bobby Fischer* (New York: D. McKay, 1965)

Marc Ferris

Fish, Hamilton (*b* New York City, 3 Aug 1808; *d* Garrison, N.Y., 7 Sept 1893). Governor, U.S. senator, and secretary of state. A graduate of Columbia College (1827), he was admitted to the bar in 1830. He practiced law in New York City and became active in politics as a Whig. He served in the House of Representatives from 1843 to 1845; as lieutenant governor of New York from 1848 to 1849; as governor from 1849 to 1850; and as U.S.

senator from 1851 to 1857. A moderately antislavery member of the Senate, he joined the emerging Republican Party during his term. He actively campaigned for Abraham Lincoln's election to the presidency in 1860 and supported the Union effort in various capacities during the Civil War. Fish served as secretary of state under President Ulysses S. Grant from 1869 to 1877. In this capacity, he helped secure peaceful outcomes to several foreign policy challenges, including American neutrality in the face of the Cuban insurrection; the negotiation of the Treaty of Washington, which settled the *Alabama* claims with Great Britain and other lingering disputes; and the settlement of the *Virginius* dispute with Spain. In later years, he spent much time at his house in Stuyvesant Square and remained active in civic affairs, including as chairman of the Board of Trustees of Columbia University.

Frank Scaturro

Fish, Nicholas (*b* New York City, 28 Aug 1758; *d* New York City, 20 June 1833). Banker. A son of Jonathan and Elizabeth Sackett Fish and a member of a wealthy mercantile family, he became a close friend and political ally of Alexander Hamilton. In 1793 he was appointed revenue supervisor for the district of New York by President George Washington, a position that he held until 1801. He married Elizabeth Stuyvesant in 1803. As a Federalist alderman he led the opposition to Tammany Hall on the Common Council in 1806–17. He also invested in real estate and bank stocks and was president of the Butchers' and Drovers' Bank (elected 1831), chairman of the Board of Trustees of Columbia University (1824–32), and an active member of St. Mark's Episcopal Church in the Bowery. Fish's home on Stuyvesant Street was a favorite haven for Federalist leaders. His eldest son was the governor, senator, and secretary of state Hamilton Fish.

Elaine Weber Pascu

Fish, Preserved (*b* Portsmouth, R.I., 3 July 1766; *d* New York City, 23 July 1846). Whaling captain and merchant. He worked as a merchant in New Bedford, Massachusetts, before moving to New York City. There he formed a partnership in 1815 with his cousin Joseph Grinnell, also a merchant from New Bedford, with whom he sold whale oil and then acquired ships and organized packet lines to Liverpool and London. He retired from the firm in 1826 and succeeded Stephan Allen as president of the Tradesmen's Bank in 1829. Active in politics, he was a leader of the free trade movement in New York City and a prominent Jacksonian Democrat who joined the Whig Party during the specie crisis of 1837. Born a Quaker, Fish became an Episcopalian during the last years of his life.

Elaine Weber Pascu

Fisher, Avery (*b* Brooklyn, 4 March 1906; *d* New Milford, Conn., 26 Feb 1994). Executive and philanthropist. An amateur violinist, he graduated from New York University in 1929 and then worked in the publishing business for almost 15 years while in his spare time building his own radio sets, amplifiers, tuners, and speakers. In 1937 he formed his first company, Philharmonic Radio, which he sold in 1945. He then formed a second, Fisher Radio, which entered the high-fidelity market with a line of premium components and remained at the forefront through its technical innovations. In 1956 it offered the first transistorized amplifier, and in 1958 it brought out the first stereo radio-phonograph. Fisher counted many musicians among his friends and frequently invited groups of them to his apartment on Park Avenue for evenings of chamber music. In 1969 he sold his company to devote himself to philanthropy. His most public gift was an endowment fund to Lincoln Center that supports the Avery Fisher Prize, a gift of $25,000 to an American instrumentalist. Philharmonic Hall was renamed Avery Fisher Hall in 1973 after he donated $10.5 million to Lincoln Center for the Performing Arts.

Kenneth T. Jackson

Fisher, William August. See Abel, Rudolf.

fishing. See Commercial fishing and Sport fishing.

Fisk, Jim [James, Jr.] (*b* Bennington, Vt., 1 April 1834; *d* New York City, 7 Jan 1872). Prominent financier. He opened a brokerage house on Broad Street in 1865 that was promptly driven into bankruptcy by the deflation that followed the Civil War. In 1866 he regained prosperity by serving as the agent in the sale of Daniel Drew's Stonington Steamboat Line. With Drew's help during the same year he formed the brokerage firm of Fisk and Belden on Wall Street, which enabled him to develop close ties to Jay Gould. Both he and Gould were brought onto the Erie Railroad Board of Directors in 1867 by Drew, and in March 1868 the three began their struggle with Cornelius Vanderbilt for control of the railroad. In July Fisk became the general manager and controller, Gould the president and treasurer; within three months they issued $23 million in watered stock. When Drew and other stockholders obtained an injunction against them, William M. "Boss" Tweed interceded and influenced the judge to place the railroad under Fisk's and Gould's receivership. In the autumn of 1869 the two conspired with Abel R. Corbin, President Ulysses S. Grant's brother-in-law, to corner the gold market. After Grant released the federal gold reserves on 24 September (known as Black Friday), Fisk lost money but Gould sold short and made a fortune. Together they bought Pike's Opera House at Eighth Avenue and 23rd Street, where they built plush offices for the Erie; Fisk also mounted stage productions there and at Brougham's Theater (on West 24th Street) and the Academy of Music (on 14th Street) and launched the largest ferry on the Hudson River, which he named for himself. He was well known for his flamboyant style. On 6 January 1872 he was fatally shot by Edward S. "Ned" Stokes in the Grand Central Hotel in a dispute over the actress Helen Josephine "Josie" Mansfield.

W. A. Swanberg, *Jim Fisk: The Career of an Improbable Rascal* (New York: Charles Scribner's Sons, 1959); John Steele Gordon, *The Scarlet Woman of Wall Street: Jay Gould, Jim Fisk, Cornelius Vanderbilt, the Erie Railway Wars, and the Birth of Wall Street* (New York: Weidenfeld and Nicolson, 1988)

Allen J. Share

Preserved Fish, ca *1830*

FIT. See Fashion Institute of Technology.

Fitzgerald, F(rancis) Scott (Key) (*b* St. Paul, Minn., 24 Sept 1896; *d* Hollywood, Calif., 27 Dec 1940). Novelist and short-story writer. He moved to New York City in 1919, took a one-room apartment at 200 Claremont Avenue, and worked for an advertising agency in order to save enough money to marry Zelda Sayre. His first novel, *This Side of Paradise,* published in 1920, articulated the new morality of the "flaming youth" of that era. That same year he and Zelda moved into the Biltmore Hotel, on East 43rd Street. The couple soon became known for their drunken antics at scandalous parties in such luxury hotels as the Algonquin, the Knickerbocker, and the Plaza, a mirror of the excess that Fitzgerald both romanticized and criticized in his novels *The Beautiful and the Damned* (1922) and *The Great Gatsby* (1925). In 1924 the couple moved to Paris and the French Riviera, where they became part of the "lost generation" of disillusioned American expatriates that included Ernest Hemingway and Gertrude Stein. After Zelda was institutionalized with schizophrenia (1930), her husband's career declined; his novel *Tender Is the Night* (1934) was poorly received, and his attempt at a Hollywood screenwriting career in 1937 failed.

Anthony Gronowicz

5 Boroughs Ice Cream. New York City–based ice cream company founded by Scott and Kim Myles in Astoria, Queens. Inspired by an ice cream maker they received as a wedding gift, the couple experimented at home with various flavors before starting their company in the early twenty-first century. Each flavor aims to "capture the essence of gritty Gotham" and draws upon a particular neighborhood for its theme—flavors include Jackson Heights Mangodesh, Staten Island Landfill, and South Bronx Cha Cha Chocolate, among others. Most ingredients are locally produced, though the ice cream is made upstate in Boonville, New York.

Michael C. Repka

Five Points. Former neighborhood in Manhattan, lying in the sixth ward near Mulberry Bend. It was named for the proximity of five streets: Mulberry Street, Anthony (now Worth) Street, Cross (now Mosco) Street, Orange (now Baxter) Street, and Little Water Street (now defunct). The area was swampy and abutted a large pond known as the Collect (now Foley Square); the pond was filled in as a public works project in 1808, and for a few years it was the site of a well-kept neighborhood surrounding Paradise Square. About 1820 the fill began to sink and the area became foul-smelling. Buildings sank and crumbled, and prosperous residents left. Decaying houses, taverns catering to sailors, and shacks remained along the narrow, unpaved streets. A brewery built in 1792 and once known throughout the northeast for its Coulter beer became rundown and was soon the most squalid and dangerous establishment in the neighborhood. The building was subdivided in the 1830s, and parts of it earned such nicknames as "murderers' alley" and "den of thieves." Some of the residents were freed blacks; destitute Irish immigrants moved in, and soon the neighborhood had an Irish population that was exceeded in size only by that of Dublin.

Filthy conditions left the population vulnerable during the epidemics of the nineteenth century. During an outbreak of cholera in 1832 a third of all the cases reported in the city occurred in the sixth ward. The neighborhood was so disreputable that it attracted the interest of many personages from abroad, including Charles Dickens, who visited in 1842 and wrote in his *American Notes* (1842) of the conditions that he saw: alleys filled with knee-deep mud, free-roaming pigs, rotting houses, women sleeping on the floor. By mid-century the neighborhood was ruled by infamous Irish gangs, each several hundred strong: among these were the Plug Uglies, the Dead Rabbits, and the Roach Guards. Abraham Lincoln visited the area in 1860, and the city tried unsuccessfully to improve it. During the 1880s the journalist and reformer Jacob A. Riis called attention to its wretched conditions, prompting a campaign by the city to eliminate the neighborhood. The city acquired and condemned most of the tenements between 1887 and 1894 and later built Mulberry Bend Park (renamed Columbus Park in 1911). Eventually courthouses covered the area, part of which now lies in Chinatown.

Jacob Riis, *How the Other Half Lives* (New York: Charles Scribner's Sons, 1890); Tyler Anbinder, *Five Points: The 19th-Century Neighborhood That Invented Tap Dance, Stole Elections and Became the World's Most Notorious Slum* (New York: Plume, 2002)

Michele Herman

Five Points Gang. Street gang formed in the 1890s. It was led by the former prizefighter Paul Kelly (Paolo Antonini Vaccarelli) and was predominantly Italian; a subgroup called the James Street Gang was led by Johnny "the Brain" Torrio. By some estimates there were 1500 members. Like earlier nineteenth-century gangs, the Five Points Gang used force on behalf of corrupt politicians and businessmen. Involved mostly in illegal enterprises in lower Manhattan, it had as its major rival the Eastmans, a gang led by Monk Eastman that was predominantly Jewish. Kelly made his headquarters at the New Brighton Dance Hall on Great Jones Street. By 1915 business had slowed and the influence of the gang was diminished. Several members later became prominent in organized crime during Prohibition, including Torrio, Al Capone, Lucky Luciano, and Frankie Yale.

Robert W. Snyder

Five Points Mission. Mission formed in 1844 by the Ladies' Home Missionary Society of the Methodist Episcopal Church. By 1850 the society sponsored temperance meetings, a charity day school, and a mission chapel. At first the mission was based in a former saloon at the corner of Cross and Little Water streets. In 1852 it purchased and demolished the "old brewery," an infamous tenement on Cross Street (now Park Street) and constructed in its place a chapel, a parsonage, a schoolhouse, a bathing room, and dwellings for poor families. The Five Points House of Industry at 155 Worth Street, run by the minister Lewis M. Pease, separated from the mission in 1854. Both institutions moved out of the area in the 1890s.

Peter J. Wosh

Flagg, Ernest (*b* Brooklyn, 6 Feb 1857; *d* New York City, 10 April 1947). Architect. In 1882–83 he designed the floor plans for cooperative apartment buildings at 121 Madison Avenue and 245 Fifth Avenue (the Knickerbocker), on which he collaborated with the architect Philip K. Hubert. He was then retained to work on the mansion of Cornelius Vanderbilt, a cousin by marriage whom he so favorably impressed with his work that Vanderbilt sponsored his architectural studies at the École des Beaux-Arts in Paris from 1888 to 1889. On his return to New York City in 1891 he set up an architectural practice and promptly won a competition to design St. Luke's Hospital on Amsterdam Avenue at 113th Street. In his article "The New York Tenement House Evil and Its Cure" (pub-

Five Points, 1827 (from Valentine's Manual, *1855)*

Ernest Flagg's Singer Building from Liberty Street, ca *1905–10*

lished in *Scribner's* in 1893) he ascribed the dark, airless quality of tenements to the small size of the lots on which they were built (25 by 100 feet [8 by 30 meters]) and advocated combining lots to allow for buildings at least 100 feet square (about 9.3 meters square); this became a standard with the passage of the Tenement House Law of 1901. He designed model tenements for the City and Suburban Homes Company (at 68th and 69th streets on Amsterdam Avenue) and model hotels intended for the working class, for the banker and philanthropist Darius Ogden Mills. He also built the Singer Building (1908) at Broadway and Liberty Street; at 612 feet (186.5 meters) this structure was at the time the tallest building in the world, and its construction set off a debate about the effects of skyscrapers and the availability of light and air in New York City. Later he advocated setbacks and the use of only one-quarter of a lot for tall towers. Among his other notable buildings in New York City were Oliver G. Jennings's mansarded residence at 7 East 72nd Street and his own country house, Stone Court, in Dongan Hills, in Staten Island. Flagg's offices were at 35 Wall Street until 1912, when he moved to 109 Broad Street. About 1906 he built a residence for himself at 109 East 40th Street, and in 1918 he moved his office to 111 East 40th Street. His published writings include *Small Houses: Their Economic Design and Construction* (1922).

Alana Erickson Coble

Flammersburg. Former name of a neighborhood in north central Queens, lying in the southern half of College Point and bounded to the north by 15th Avenue, to the east by 130th Street, to the south by 23rd Avenue, and to the west by 119th Street. It was originally a parcel of 141 acres (57 hectares) bought from the Stratton family in 1851 by John A. Flammer, who divided it into 800 lots. In 1870 the neighborhood became part of College Point.

Vincent Seyfried

Flatbush. Neighborhood in central Brooklyn bounded to the north by Parkside Avenue, to the east by Nostrand Avenue, to the south by Avenue H, and to the west by Coney Island Avenue. Settled in 1652 as one of the six original towns of Brooklyn, it was situated in the center of the area known as Midwout (middle woods). Its name derives from the Dutch word *vlackebos* (wooded plain). The area remained rural until the 1880s, when it was made ripe for development by the opening of the Brooklyn, Flatbush and Coney Island Railroad (2 July 1878) and the impending annexation by the City of Brooklyn (1894). Henry A. Meyer, a local grocer, was the first to initiate large-scale construction. Germania Land and Improvement Company laid a grid across 65 acres (26 hectares) of land formerly occupied by the potato farm of the Vanderveers and built rows of Queen Anne cottages. Acres of farmland quickly became well-planned communities, and by 1910 the area had been transformed into a fashionable suburb that comprised such subdivisions as Vanderveer Park, Ditmas Park, Fiske Terrace, Albermarle–Kenmore Terrace, Manhattan Terrace, Matthews Park, Slocum Park, East Flatbush, Rugby, Wingate, Farragut, Erasmus, Beverley Square East, Beverley Square West, Caton Park, Midwood Park, and Yale Park.

After the opening in 1920 of the Brighton Beach subway line, large apartment buildings were erected along Ocean Avenue as far south as Kings Highway. Many of these new buildings were occupied by Jews from Williamsburg, Brownsville, and the Lower East Side. In these years the neighborhood was the site of Ebbets Field, where the Brooklyn Dodgers played from 1913 to 1957. The attention that the team drew helped to make Flatbush an exemplar of the city in the popular mind, and the characteristic patois of its white, middle-class residents became widely known as Brooklynese (a distinction also ascribed to Greenpoint). In the decades following World War II the Jewish population was largely supplanted by a Caribbean one and by immigrants from Pakistan, Afghanistan, Cambodia, Korea, Central America, and the former Soviet Union. Haitians accounted for about one-third of all immigrants settling in the neighborhood, which attracted about one-quarter of all Haitians who moved to the city. There were also a large number of immigrants from Jamaica, Guyana, Trinidad and Tobago, Grenada, Panama, Barbados, St. Vincent and the Grenadines, China, Pakistan, and the

Flatbush, Albemarle Road, 1991

Dominican Republic. On the whole Flatbush adapted well to its growing ethnic diversity, but it also had its share of difficulties. In the early twenty-first century it remained predominantly African American with Arabs and Mexicans along the western edge of Coney Island Avenue.

In the early twenty-first century Flatbush had 3500 one- and two-family houses and more than 30,000 apartments. Notable buildings in the neighborhood include the Flatbush Reformed Dutch Church, at Flatbush and Church avenues (the present structure is the third on the site and was built in 1798; the first was built by order of Peter Stuyvesant); the Erasmus Hall Museum, in the courtyard of Erasmus Hall High School opposite the church (originally Erasmus Hall Academy, opened in 1787 by the Flatbush Reformed Dutch Church and made a public school in 1896); Flatbush Town Hall at 35 Snyder Avenue (1875); and Loew's King on Flatbush Avenue near Beverly Road (1929), a grand movie theater. Newkirk Plaza, between Newkirk and Foster Avenues, was one of the city's first commercial revitalization projects in 1977. Prominent residents of the neighborhood have included the entertainer Barbra Streisand, football coach Joe Paterno, singer Barry Manilow, and chess champion Bobby Fischer. The main thoroughfare is Flatbush Avenue.

Elizabeth Reich Rawson, *Brooklyn Neighborhoods and How They Grew* (New York: Brooklyn Historical Society, 1987) [exhibition catalogue]; Adina Back and Francis Morrone, *Flatbush Neighborhood History Guide* (Brooklyn, N.Y.: Brooklyn Historical Society, 2008)

Elizabeth Reich Rawson, John Manbeck

Flatiron Building. Office building at the intersection of Broadway and Fifth Avenue at 23rd Street. Formally known as the Fuller Building, the Flatiron Building was erected in 1902 by Chicago architect Daniel H. Burnham. The building's nickname, and the name by which it is most commonly referred, Flatiron, is derived from the triangular shape of the building's plot, which is reminiscent of a pressing iron. Standing 20 stories tall with a rusticated limestone facade on a steel frame, the building remains a symbol of the early skyscraper era. The two wide expanses of the building flanked by Broadway and Fifth Avenue come to a point at a 6-foot- (1.8-meter-) wide northern apex on 23rd Street. Among those unfamiliar with the possibilities of steel-cage construction, the building's tendency to appear as nothing more than a flat wall from certain angles at first fostered a fear that it could very easily topple over. Far more people, however, made a pilgrimage to the building, making it one of the city's most popular tourist destinations in the early twentieth century. From the observation lounge on the top floor, visitors were offered a sweeping and then-unprecedented view of the city. Sightseers also remarked that from the north the building resembled a ship sailing up the avenue. The intersection at the building created unusual wind patterns, and young men would gather in throngs to watch as the wind whipped up and around the skirts of women walking by. Occasionally the spot became so congested that police would have to break up the gathering crowds, giving birth to the phrase "Twenty-Three Skidoo." Iconic depictions of the building by Edward Steichen and Walter Gropius helped to establish the building in the popular imagination.

Seth M. Scheiner, Joe Piscina

Flatiron Building, ca 1905

Flatiron district. Neighborhood in Manhattan, lying between Chelsea and Gramercy Park and bounded to the north by 23rd Street, to the east by Park Avenue, to the south by 14th Street, and to the west by Sixth Avenue. Named for the Flatiron Building on 23rd Street, the area was a flourishing commercial district during the late nineteenth and early twentieth centuries. It was known especially for elegant hotels, shops, and restaurants along Sixth Avenue between 14th and 23rd streets, later called the Ladies' Mile (designated a historic district in 1989). The neighborhood became a popular place to live in the late 1960s when artists, especially photographers, moved into its many inexpensive lofts. Since the 1980s the Flatiron district has acquired a reputation for fashionable cafes, restaurants, and nightclubs; interesting shopping; and a varied housing stock.

James Bradley, Andrew Sparberg

Flatlands. Neighborhood in southeastern Brooklyn (2009 pop. *ca* 27,000), bounded to the north by Flatlands Avenue, to the east by Paedergat Basin, to the south by Avenue U, and to the west by Flatbush Avenue. The name is also applied to the larger area that made up the seventeenth-century town called New Amersfoort by the Dutch and Flatlands by the British, and that includes the present neighborhoods of Marine Park, Mill Basin, Bergen Beach, Georgetown, Canarsie, East Flatbush, and Starrett City. In this vicinity the terminal moraine of Long Island meets the marshes of Jamaica Bay; the rich soil in the area attracted Canarsee Indians, who called the land Keskachauge. In 1636 the land was bought by Jacob van Corlear, Andries Hudde, Wolfert Gerritsen van Couwenhoven, and Wouter van Twiller, the governor of New Netherland. Under their auspices settlements were built near what became Beverly Road and Utica Avenue and near Kings Highway and Flatlands Avenue. The settlements together formed New Amersfoort in 1647, named after a city on the River Eem in the province of Utrecht. Couwenhoven built a plantation near the site on Kings Highway where the Flatlands Dutch Reformed Church was later built. By 1651 Governor Peter Stuyvesant had acquired a large plot in the town, and he granted residents local rule in 1661. Farming was the primary occupation. Colonists grew corn, squash, beans, and tobacco and fed their cattle salt hay; fishermen harvested clams in Jamaica Bay. Slaves accounted for about 20 percent of the population and were an important part of the economy until New York State abolished slavery in 1827. In the 1830s the population was about 700, making Flatlands one of the two smallest towns in the county.

The area grew rapidly after the Brooklyn City Railroad Company initiated horsecar service in 1875 to Kings Highway along the recently opened Flatbush Avenue, providing transportation to downtown Brooklyn. After the Flatbush Avenue streetcars were electrified in 1893, new suburban houses attracted a more diverse population. In 1896 the town was one of the last in the county to be annexed by the City of Brooklyn. Growth continued between 1900 and World War II. Interborough Rapid Transit was extended to the junction of Flatbush and Nostrand avenues, providing service to Manhattan in less than an hour. But the neighborhood was not served by the many transit lines leading to Coney Island and was only transformed by the automobile. Kings Highway, the major east-west artery in southern Brooklyn, stretched beyond Flatbush Avenue in the early 1920s, and two-family brick row houses with garages soon covered fields throughout the town.

House and barn built in Dutch Colonial style in Flatlands, 1900

After World War II much of the remaining open land in southeastern Brooklyn was covered by the neighborhoods of Mill Basin, Bergen Beach, and Georgetown, which were some of the last in Brooklyn to be developed according to a suburban model. The only industrial section was developed in the late 1960s on the northeastern edge of the neighborhood near Canarsie. During the 1980s the neighborhood and its environs attracted immigrants from Jamaica, Haiti, and Guyana, but for the most part the population remained Jewish, Italian, and Irish. The Flatlands Dutch Reformed Church on King's Highway and several eighteenth-century farmhouses, among them the Stoothoff–Baxter–Kouwenhoven house on East 48th Street and the Coe house on East 34th Street, remain from the colonial period.

Maud Dillard, *Old Dutch Houses of Brooklyn* (New York: Richard R. Smith, 1945)

Stephen Weinstein

Flatlands Dutch Reformed Church. Church formed on 9 February 1654 by order of Peter Stuyvesant in New Amersfoort, on a site now at the intersection of King's Highway and East 40th Street. The original building was an octagonal structure covered with spruce shingles that stood until 1794. The site is now occupied by the third church erected there, a building in the Greek Revival style constructed in 1848. The church is surrounded by maple trees and a seventeenth-century cemetery. Designated a landmark by the city in 1973, it was badly damaged by fire in 1977 and rebuilt in the following year.

Stephen Weinstein

Fleet Week. Week during which the U.S. Navy, U.S. Marine Corps, and U.S. Coast Guard dock active military ships in a variety of major cities. Since 1984 New York City has hosted one of the nation's largest Fleet Weeks when ships dock at various piers in the boroughs. It usually coincides with the week of Memorial Day and includes a variety of activities such as tours of visiting ships, lectures, and competitions. Nearly 4000 personnel participate across all five boroughs, volunteering with local community outreach organizations and visiting popular New York City attractions.

Anne Epstein

Fleetwood. Neighborhood in the southwestern Bronx centered at Morris Avenue and 165th Street. From 1870 to 1899 it was the site of Fleetwood Park Racetrack, a trotting track with a circumference of 1 mile (1600 meters) that was attended by such personages as Ulysses S. Grant, John D. Rockefeller, and the newspaper publisher Robert Bonner. After the track was closed, streets were cut through, row houses and apartment buildings erected, and shops opened. The population was at first Irish and Jewish and in the 1960s became largely black and Latino.

Lloyd Ultan

Fleischer, Nat(haniel S.) (*b* New York City, 3 Nov 1887; *d* New York City, 25 June 1972). Sportswriter and publisher. He graduated from City College of New York in 1908 and went to work as a teacher in the public schools. Between 1912 and 1929 he worked for several different newspapers in New York City, including the *Press,* the *Sun,* and the *Telegram,* and in 1922 he launched a boxing magazine called the *Ring.* As the editor of the publication he improved the image of boxing and advocated equal rights for blacks who practiced the sport. Fleischer continued to publish the *Ring* until the end of his life. He wrote *50 Years at Ringside* (1958).

Randy Roberts

Fleischmann Yeast Company. A company formed in 1868 by Charles and Maximilian Fleischmann, two brothers from Vienna. They skillfully promoted German compressed yeast at the Centennial Exposition in Philadelphia. Their showcase outlet, a bakery and café on Broadway at 10th Street, became a fashionable stop for shoppers along the Ladies' Mile. Raoul H. Fleischmann (1885–1969) worked in the Fleischmann family bakery (1907–11) and its successor, the General Baking Company (1911–25), before joining the F-R Publishing Company (1925–69), publishers of the *New Yorker.* The firm's compressed yeast revolutionized home breadmaking in the United States. In 1979 Fleischmann Yeast was acquired by Standard Brands.

Bradford Garnett

Flexner, Abraham (*b* Louisville, Ky., 13 Nov 1866; *d* Falls Church, Va., 21 Sept 1959). Medical educator, brother of Simon Flexner. From 1908 to 1912 he worked for the Carnegie Foundation for the Advancement of Teaching. In 1910 the foundation published his report *Medical Education in the United States and Canada,* which proved influential in modernizing physician training in North America. In 1913 he joined the staff of the General Education Board of the Rockefeller Foundation, where he was successively assistant secretary (1913–17), secretary (1917–25), and director of the Division of Studies and Medical Education (1925–28). In these positions Flexner secured tens of millions of dollars for the advancement of scientific medical education.

Thomas Neville Bonner, *Iconoclast: Abraham Flexner and a Life in Learning* (Baltimore: Johns Hopkins University Press, 2002)

Allen J. Share

Floating Hospital. Waterborne hospital established in 1866. It operated only during the warmer months until it began year-round service in 1975. The hospital cruised the Hudson River providing preventive care, health education, and other services to medically underserved groups. The Floating Hospital lost its dock space in lower Manhattan to recovery efforts after the terrorist attacks of 11 September 2001. In 2004, unable to find dock space accessible to the public, the Floating Hospital Corporation sold the ship that had served as the Floating Hospital since 1977, the *Lila Acheson Wallace.* In 2006 the Floating Hospital reopened in Long Island City as a land-based facility with 10 exam rooms.

Andrea Balis

flora. The grasses, flowers, shrubs, and trees growing throughout New York City only remotely resemble the varieties that grew there before European settlement. Many species were brought to the area by colonists, some purposely and others accidentally. A number spread to surrounding areas, sometimes crowding out native species, and a few carried diseases that proved devastating, among them the Dutch elm disease and the chestnut blight, which was introduced by a tree from Europe planted in Central Park. A dominant characteristic of plants in the city is their ability to survive highly acidic rain, a high degree of salinity, and air polluted by ozone, sulfur dioxide, and carbon monoxide; many of those from outside the region are also immune to local viruses and bacteria. Like the ecosystems in other cities, those of New York City grow and change. Many of its plants are found in other cities nearby, including Philadelphia, Newark (New Jersey), and New Haven and Hartford (Connecticut). The Autumn Olive (*Elaeagnus unbellata*), a species native to Asia, is used for reclamation planting because it grows profusely and can withstand extreme drought, salinity, and temperature. Its tart red berries provide food for Bobwhite Quail, Cedar Waxwings, robins, starlings, White-throated Sparrows, and Hermit Thrushes throughout the autumn and early winter. Birches such as the Gray Birch (*Betula populifolia*) are among the first to grow in cleared areas. Another species that thrives in sunny areas is the Black Cherry (*Prunus serotina*), which produces clusters of fragrant white flowers in May and berries that provide food for songbirds in late summer; mature trees range in height from 40 to 100 feet (12 to 30 meters) and have dark, rough outer bark. These trees are soon outgrown by others more tolerant of shade. Other common species in the metropolitan area are the Eastern Red Cedar (*Juniperus virginiana*), the Cottonwood (*Populus deltoides*), the American Holly (*Ilex opaca*), and the Red Maple (*Acer rubrum*). The Salt-spray Rose (*Rosa rugosa*) produces beautiful blossoms from May to October. Its rosehips are a rich source of vitamin C and were eaten in preserves by colonists to prevent scurvy in winter. Mugwort and Sweet Clover grow in salt marshes, often in the wake of construction, as does Reedgrass (*Phragmites australis*), which forces out other marsh grasses but provides a source of food and cover for some wildlife.

Steven D. Garber, *The Urban Naturalist* (New York: John Wiley and Sons, 1987)

Steven D. Garber, John T. Tanacredi

Floral Park. Neighborhood straddling Queens and Nassau County near the intersection of Jamaica Avenue and Little Neck Parkway. It was established around 1870 between Tulip and Carnation avenues in Nassau County and originally named Hinsdale after the chief counsel of the Long Island Rail Road, Elizur B. Hinsdale. The name was changed in 1890 to honor John Lewis Childs, who had opened a large commercial nursery in the area during the 1880s. The neighborhood extended northward into Queens after World War II, when the extension of Hillside Avenue as far east as the county line stimulated housing development between the county line and Little Neck Parkway on land that had long been used for farming. Floral Park remained in the early twenty-first century a community of modest one-family homes.

Vincent Seyfried

Flower Fifth Avenue Hospital. Teaching hospital in Manhattan. It was formed in 1890 as the Flower Free Surgical Hospital at 450 East 64th Street by administrators of the Homoeopathic Medical College of New York (later New York Medical College), who sought greater training opportunities for their students. The hospital had financial support from a prominent businessman and Democratic politician, Roswell P. Flower. Later the hospital and the college together were known as the New York Homoeopathic Medical College and Flower Hospital (1908) and as the New York Medical College and Flower Hospital (1936); a merger in 1938 with the Fifth Avenue Hospital at 105th Street formed an institution known as the New York Medical College, Flower and Fifth Avenue Hospitals. The hospital remained in the city after the college moved to Westchester County in 1972, but financial reverses in the late 1970s brought it near bankruptcy. In 1978 the Roman Catholic archdiocese of New York took over both the college and the hospital, which was converted in the following year from an acute-care facility into the Terence Cardinal Cooke Nursing Home.

Sandra Opdycke

Flower Market. Located at 28th Street and Sixth Avenue since the 1890s, the market is a cluster of wholesale and retail flower shops. In the mid-nineteenth century flowers were sold directly by local growers at markets. Later in the nineteenth century third-party agents were added as wholesale commission merchants. Manhattan's first flower district was around East 34th Street at the East River in the 1870s and relocated to Sixth Avenue between 26th and 29th streets by the end of the nineteenth century. The market is most active in the early morning, starting as early as 4 a.m. In 1999 the Flower Market Association of New York City was formed and headquartered at 120 West 28th Street. In the twenty-first century the Flower Market was composed of approximately 45 businesses and had estimated annual gross sales of $100 million.

Jessica Montesano

Floyd Bennett Field. First municipal airport in New York City. Built on 1500 acres (600 hectares) of reclaimed marshland in Jamaica Bay and dedicated in 1930 by Mayor James J. Walker, it was named for the pilot who flew Admiral Richard Byrd over the North Pole in 1926. Enlarged in 1936 by the Works Progress Administration, it was used by such aviators as Howard Hughes, Laura Ingalls, and John Glenn. Because of its location one hour away from central Manhattan, it never attracted more than one commercial airline flight a day, and its importance was so diminished after La Guardia Airfield opened in 1939 that in 1942 it was sold to the navy. As Naval Air Station New York it performed a vital function during the U-boat offensive of 1942 by providing air cover for convoys embarking from the Port of New York; the Naval Ferry Squadron based there delivered thousands of aircraft to the fleet from factories on Long Island. In 1972 the field was taken over by the National Park Service, which as of 2007 operated the field as part of the Jamaica Bay Unit of the Gateway National Recreation Area, displaying an old hangar and restored airplanes to the public.

Joseph F. Meany, Jr.

Flushing. Neighborhood in north central Queens, bounded to the north by Bayside Avenue, to the east by the Clearview Expressway, to the south by Union Turnpike, and to the west by Flushing Meadows–Corona Park. It was established by English settlers who received patents for it from Governor Peter Stuyvesant in 1654. The name is a corruption of Vlissingen, a village in the Netherlands. The area was desirable for its woodlands, freshwater, and salt hay. After the arrival of English Quakers in 1657 Stuyvesant sought to renege on earlier promises of religious toleration, prompting freeholders and Quakers in the nearby area to issue the Flushing Remonstrance, one of the earliest documents proclaiming religious freedom in America. Quakers bought land in 1692 for a meetinghouse, which now stands on Northern Boulevard. One of the first nurseries in the country, the Linnaean Gardens, opened in 1737 just north of Northern Boulevard. The nursery industry flourished throughout the nineteenth century, shipping fruit trees and ornamental trees and shrubs across the nation. After the Battle of Long Island in 1776 Flushing was occupied by British troops until 1783. The tolerance of the Quakers attracted a number of African Americans in the early nineteenth century, of whom the best known was Lewis Latimer, an electrical inventor who worked with Thomas Edison. The year 1843 saw the publication of a newspaper and the opening of the Flushing Institute, a secondary school for boys that eventually enrolled students from the southern United States, Central and South America, and Europe. Fast, direct rail service to New York City was provided from 1854. Flushing Town Hall was completed in 1864 (now a cultural center and a city landmark). Development accelerated after the Civil War as many wealthy New Yorkers built elegant houses. From the 1890s until World War I the

Floyd Bennett Field, 2009

Trustees of Flushing Village, 1887

neighborhood expanded to the east and south and new sections opened up to residential development, including Ingleside, Murray Hill, Broadway–Flushing, Bowne Park, Kissena, and Queensborough Hill. Flushing became a commuter suburb after trolley lines were extended (1888–99) and the Long Island Rail Road was electrified. Flushing High School opened in 1875, making it the oldest in the city; the 1915 building was designated a landmark in 1991.

Apartments were built in the 1920s, and the character of the area changed after subway service was introduced with a five-cent fare in 1928. After World War II apartments displaced entire blocks of houses, and during the 1960s many Japanese, Chinese, and Koreans settled in the neighborhood. Downtown Flushing acquired more urban characteristics. It attracted many immigrants during the 1980s; about 20 percent were Chinese (primarily from Taiwan) and 20 percent Korean, with others from India, Colombia, Afghanistan, Guyana, the Dominican Republic, Pakistan, the Philippines, and El Salvador. During the 1990s the older establishments like Alexander's department store closed and the commercial core saw the growth of Asian mini-malls. Beyond Main Street, blocks of one-family houses remained, interspersed with schools, churches, and well-kept cemeteries and parks. To protect the suburban character of their neighborhood, residents of Broadway–Flushing (north of Northern Boulevard) gained listing on the National Register of Historic Places in 2007 but could not obtain local designation as a historic district. The Landmarks Preservation Commission also declined to designate the Waldheim section.

Historic buildings include the Bowne House (1661) at 37-01 Bowne Street, the oldest surviving house in Queens; the Kingsland House on 37th Avenue, built about 1785, a rare example of English architecture (relocated to Weeping Beech Park in 1968); the Voelker Orth Museum, an 1890s home turned into a museum in 2003; the 1905 Flushing Armory; and RKO Keith's Flushing Theater (1928), a movie palace designed by Thomas Lamb, partially protected by landmark designation but vacant since the mid-1980s. In the heart of the neighborhood at Roosevelt Avenue and Main Street is an extensive network of Asian banks and businesses. There are several large Buddhist houses of worship and a large and ornate Hindu temple. Historic churches include St. George's Episcopal (1854); Bowne Street Community Church, with windows by Louis Comfort Tiffany (1892); and the Macedonia African Methodist Episcopal Church, founded 1811. The many nurseries that once flourished in the area are gone, but some of the trees raised in them survive, notably in Kissena Park; and the Queens Botanical Garden, founded as part of the 1939 World's Fair and established at its current location on Main Street before the 1964 World's Fair, continues the tradition. The historic weeping beech planted by Samuel Bowne Parsons in 1847 died in 1997, but several descendants survive in Weeping Beech Park.

Vincent Seyfried, Jeffrey A. Kroessler

Flushing Meadows–Corona Park. Public park in north central Queens, bounded to the northeast and east by Flushing, to the south by Kew Gardens and Forest Hills, to the west by Elmhurst, and to the northwest by Corona. It is the second-largest park in the city, with an area of 1255 acres (508 hectares). After the local American Indian tribe, the Matinecocks, had been pushed out, European settlers harvested the seafood and marsh grasses there, but the area remained largely natural. After New York's consolidation in 1898, rail lines were extended into the area, landfill was deposited in the tidal wetland to the north, and a river from Flushing Bay was blocked. The area was given over to industrial use and waste dumping: one ash heap reached a height of nearly 100 feet (30 meters) and became popularly known as Mount Corona. Known originally as Flushing Meadow Park, the park became the site of two world's fairs (1939–40, 1964–65), both largely the inspiration of Robert Moses. The fairs caused the addition of several features to the landscape: these included from the first fair a lake, a boathouse, paths, plantings, and the New York City Building (the temporary headquarters of the United Nations from 1946 to 1950 and later the Queens Museum); and from the second fair the Unisphere (a large steel globe and the centerpiece of the fair), Shea Stadium (1964, the former home stadium of the New York Mets), a public marina at Flushing Bay (1964), Space Park (later the New York Hall of Science), the Singer Bowl (from 1976 Louis Armstrong Stadium at the National Tennis Center), and the Winston Churchill Pavilion (a geodesic structure designed by R. Buckminster Fuller, from 1968 an aviary at the Queens Zoo). In 1967 the World's Fair Corporation returned the park to the city. The New York Zoological Society later redesigned and rebuilt the Queens Zoo, which reopened in 1992. In 1997 the 23,000-seat Arthur Ashe Stadium, the largest outdoor tennis venue in the world, opened in the park and replaced Louis Armstrong Stadium as the featured site of the US Open. In 2009 the baseball stadium Citi Field opened, replacing Shea Stadium as the home of the New York Mets.

The Flushing Meadow Improvement: Official Publication of the City and State (New York: Department of Parks, 1936–39)

Jonathan Kuhn

Flushing Remonstrance. Declaration of religious liberty, drawn up and approved at a town meeting in Flushing and dated 27 December 1657. The document was a reminder to Governor Peter Stuyvesant that the Patent of Flushing (1645) offered "liberty of conscience" to settlers. It was inspired by an order from Stuyvesant, a strict Calvinist, forbidding all colonists to allow Quakers into their homes and imposing a large fine of 50 guilders, with half the money going to any informer. The Flushing Remonstrance is sometimes regarded as the "first declaration of independence" and as a forerunner of the First Amendment. The

The Unisphere in Flushing Meadows–Corona Park, 2009

document itself is now held by the New York State Library in Albany.

Jeanne Field Spallone

Flynn, Edward J(oseph) (*b* Bronx, 22 Sept 1891; *d* Ireland, 18 Aug 1953). Party leader. He earned a bachelor's degree and a law degree at Fordham University and was elected a state assemblyman (1918–21) and sheriff of Bronx County (1922–25). As the leader of the Democratic organization in Bronx County from 1922 he maintained a reputation for honesty and a commitment to liberal policies. He was also an adviser to Franklin D. Roosevelt during Roosevelt's tenure as governor of New York and later as president. While serving as city chamberlain (1925–28), secretary of state of New York State (1929–40), and chairman of the Democratic National Committee (1940–44), Flynn was one of the most influential politicians in New York City. Flynn wrote a memoir, *You're the Boss* (1947).

See also Bronx, §2.

Chris McNickle

Flynn, Elizabeth Gurley (*b* Concord, N.H., 7 Aug 1890; *d* Moscow, 5 Sept 1964). Activist and political leader. After moving with her family to New York City in 1900 she attended Public School 9 in the South Bronx and Morris High School, leaving before graduation to become one of the few female organizers of the Industrial Workers of the World. She quickly became known as a strike leader, civil rights advocate, and extraordinary orator. She helped form the American Civil Liberties Union in 1920; in 1940 she was expelled from its board of directors for her membership in the Communist Party. Convicted of sedition under the Smith Act in 1952, she served three years in federal prison before being released in 1957. At her death she was the national chair of the Communist Party.

Martha Foley

F. Marquand. Former name of Black, Starr and Frost.

Fokine, Michel [Fokin, Mikhail (Mikhailovich)] (*b* Saint Petersburg, 23 April 1880; *d* New York City, 22 Aug 1942). Dancer and choreographer. He received his early ballet training at the Imperial School of Ballet in St. Petersburg and joined Sergei Diaghilev's Ballets Russes in Paris in 1909. He taught in New York City from 1919 and in 1923 settled there with his family, where he taught a generation of American dancers and restaged the better known of his more than 60 ballets. Fokine's influential choreographic principles helped to make ballet a serious theatrical form rather than mere entertainment. His book *Fokine: Memoirs of a Ballet Master* was published in 1961.

Dawn Lille Horwitz, *Michel Fokine* (Boston: Twayne, 1985)

Barbara Barker

Foley, James A. (*b* 1883; *d* New York City, 11 Feb 1946). Legislator and surrogate. He served in the state legislature (1907–19), where with Alfred E. Smith and Robert F. Wagner he guided the effort of the "new Tammany" to rewrite the state's labor laws after the Triangle Shirtwaist fire. In 1919 he was chosen Democratic leader of the state senate, which he left to become a surrogate in Manhattan (1920–46). In 1946, he was elected to lead Tammany Hall but resigned immediately, pleading ill health. He was urged to run for mayor and the U.S. Senate, but he declined to leave the probate bench. Foley was a nationally respected authority on the law of estates and an influential delegate to the state constitutional conventions of 1915 and 1938. He lived at 243 East 17th Street.

Frank Vos

Foley Square. Intersection of Duane, Lafayette, Center, and Pearl streets north of City Hall in Manhattan, and by extension the surrounding area. Much of the land once lay beneath the waters of the Collect, a pond drained and completely covered over by 1811; the area soon after became the site of one of the city's most notorious slums. In later years a number of municipal, state, and federal buildings were built around the square, including the New York County Court House (1926) and the U.S. Court House (1936), renamed for Thurgood Marshall in 2003. The square is named for Thomas F. Foley (1852–1925), a saloonkeeper and politician associated with Tammany Hall.

Linda Elsroad

folk and ethnic dancing. At the beginning of the twentieth century, officials in New York City promoted European folk dancing as a "wholesome" alternative to increasingly popular ragtime dances. The city's most evangelistic supporter of European folk dances was Elizabeth Burchenal, an employee of the Board of Education who worked with the Playground Association of America and set up after-school programs for girls from 1911. In 1915 the English Folk Song and Dance Society opened a branch in New York City; the society sent May Gadd, an English dance instructor, to New York City in 1927. She became director of the society in 1937 and remained in office for 46 years. During her tenure the society, which she renamed the Country Dance and Song Society of America to reflect her interest in Appalachian dances, sponsored seasonal festivals that regularly attracted hundreds of dancers and established folk dance clubs at local high schools and colleges, including Brooklyn College, Barnard College, and the Juilliard School; she also worked with the choreographer Agnes de Mille on the dance steps for the musicals *Oklahoma!* and *Brigadoon.* The New York Folk Festival Council, formed in 1931 and based at 222 Fourth Avenue, presented annual events in public parks, including a festival in May 1934 in Prospect Park that attracted 20,000 participants and spectators.

A leader in ethnic dance in the city was Asadata Dafora, who moved to New York from Freetown, Sierra Leone, in 1929, formed Shogola Olobo in 1932 and the African Dance Troupe in 1935, and wrote the dance opera *Kykunkor,* which opened at the Unity Theatre on East 23rd Street in April 1934. Dafora also provided choreography for *Bassa Moona,* which premiered in 1937 at the Majestic Theatre in Brooklyn and was staged at the Daly Theatre in Manhattan. In 1940 Mary Ann and Michael Herman formed the Community Folk Dance Center, which inspired so many imitators that John Martin, the dance critic for the *New York Times,* discontinued his weekly listing of folk dance events for lack of space. The Hermans had several changes of residence before moving in 1951 to 108 West 16th Street. There they opened Folk Dance House, maintained a costume collection and reference library, and conducted classes full-time. Although the building was demolished in 1969, they continued to teach and to present traditional folk-dance programs at St. Vartan's Armenian Church at 630 Second Avenue. In 1980 they moved to Long Island. Their contemporary La Meri also helped draw public attention to ethnic dancing during the 1940s. After settling in New York City in 1939, she formed a partnership with the dancer and choreographer Ruth St. Denis, with whom in May 1940 she opened the School of Natya at 66 Fifth Avenue. La Meri also led the Ethnologic Dance Center, which she moved in 1943 to 110 East 59th Street.

Several dancers overcame cultural prejudice, racism, and censorship in working to gain acceptance for the folk dances of the southern hemisphere. Katherine Dunham, a figure most closely associated with modern dance, launched the "anthropological" dance movement. After her local debut at a "Negro Dance Evening" at the 92nd Street Y in 1937, she moved her troupe to the city in 1939 and accepted the directorship of the New York Labor Stage. In 1945 she opened the Dunham School of Dance and Theater on West 43rd Street, which specialized in Afro-Caribbean dance; the school lasted until the mid-1950s. The Trinidadian anthropologist and dancer Pearl Primus also invigorated ethnic dance in the city during the 1940s. After a 10-month engagement at Café Society in 1943 she made her debut at the Belasco Theater the following year. Throughout her career she maintained a connection to the city through her School of Primal Dance (1961) at 17 West 24th Street and her teaching position at Hunter College. The Haitian dancer Jean-Léon Destine presented traditional Afro-Haitian dances in the 1940s and specialized in *vodun* dance. Perhaps best known for his short film *Witch Doctor,* he taught in Manhattan into the 1990s. The Philippine Dance Company of New York was formed in 1943 by Bruna Seril; led from 1969 by Reynaldo Alejandro, it achieved popularity and undertook national and international tours while maintaining a regular performance schedule in the city.

Early in the twenty-first century ethnic dance troupes representing every region of the globe remained based in New York City. Institutions that supported folk dancing included the McBurney Young Men's Christian Association (YMCA) at 215 West 23rd Street and the 92nd Street Y, which offered instruction in Israeli dancing.

Betty Casey, *International Folk Dancing U.S.A.* (New York: Doubleday, 1981); Simon J. Bronner, *Old-Time Music Makers of New York State* (Syracuse, N.Y.: Syracuse University Press, 1987)

Marc Ferris

folk music. Songs from England, Ireland, Scotland, and Africa were sung during the colonial period in public gatherings, homes, and workshops in New York City. Mariners at South Street in the first half of the nineteenth century devised many kinds of ballads and sea chanteys from songs of British and African origin. At mid-century Irish, English, and Scottish balladeers performed regularly on the stage, and their songs became popular in taverns. Songs were often published as broadsides to assure wide distribution. At the end of the century German, Swedish, and other immigrants organized choral societies that preserved their folk songs, some of which were later adapted for the vaudeville stage. In the early twentieth century blues songs were introduced in the city by blacks from the rural South.

Members of the Industrial Workers of the World often sang as they picketed during the early twentieth century, and folk music became an important vehicle for political expression during the 1930s: the Popular Front, a movement loosely associated with the Communist Party, spread its ideas through folk music. At the same time many folk musicians took up residence in New York City, including Leadbelly (Huddie Ledbetter, 1885–1949), a singer, songwriter, and blues guitarist from Louisiana who moved to the city in 1935 after his work came to the attention of Library of Congress folklorists John A. Lomax and his son Alan Lomax; Woody Guthrie, who sang about farmers displaced during the Dust Bowl of the 1930s; and Pete Seeger, who adopted the ballads and banjo styles of the southern Appalachian mountains. All three performed traditional songs and their own material and were associated with the bohemian culture of Greenwich Village, making the city a center for a new kind of folk music.

Between 1941 and 1942 the Almanac Singers were organized by Seeger, Guthrie, Lee Hays, and Millard Lampell. The group's members lived in a loft known as Almanac House at 130 West 10th Street and performed for drives organized by the Congress of Industrial Organizations and antifascist functions sponsored by the Popular Front. The group included several musicians who became well-known soloists: Burl Ives, Cisco Houston, Bess Lomax, and Earl Robinson. In the years after World War II Greenwich Village remained a center of folk music, and sing-alongs were often held in Washington Square despite the objections of city authorities. The radical group People's Songs was formed about this time, but it was less influential than earlier groups owing to the conservative political climate after the war. From the late 1940s to the early 1950s the Weavers became immensely successful for their arrangements of topical folk songs from around the world, and their song "Good Night, Irene" (1950) sold two million copies, an unprecedented number for a folk song.

During the 1950s and 1960s folk music was revived by Seeger and a new generation of singers, many of whom had been influenced by the civil rights movement and the student left. Two of the best known were from Brooklyn: Dave Van Ronk played the blues; and Elliot Charles Adnopoz, who took the name Ramblin' Jack Elliott, played in Guthrie's style and traveled west. The most influential folksinger was Bob Dylan, an admirer of Guthrie who moved to New York City in 1961 and performed original and traditional songs, accompanying himself on acoustic guitar and harmonica. He performed throughout the city before gaining public recognition. By the mid-1960s he turned to an electric style influenced by rock-and-roll. Judy Collins and the group Peter, Paul and Mary were among many folksingers who lived in the city during the 1960s and sang about the civil rights and antiwar movements. They first performed for small audiences at clubs in Greenwich Village such as Gerde's Folk City on West Third Street, and their records were later sold internationally. Irish folk music was revived in Ireland and the United States by the Clancy Brothers and Tommy Makem. The Pennywhistlers performed folk songs from Eastern Europe and the Balkans.

As radicalism declined in the 1970s so did the political importance of folk music, but solo folksingers accompanied by guitar continued to be popular in New York City. Indian folk music was performed in such celebrations as the Divali festival, as was *taiko* drumming during Japanese cherry blossom festivals. The rhumba, popular in Latin American neighborhoods, was introduced in nightclubs by well-known performers like Tito Puente and Celia Cruz. In the 1980s the Ethnic Arts Center and the World Music Institute supported performances by a range of international folk artists, and the Eagle Tavern on West 14th Street in Manhattan became a center for Irish folk music; in Greenwich Village musicians established Speakeasy's, a cooperative cafe on MacDougal Street where singers and songwriters performed topical songs and traditional folk music. In the early twenty-first century small venues in the city continued to showcase folk music, including the tiny Postcrypt Coffeehouse in the basement of St. Paul's Chapel at Columbia University, which was founded in 1964.

R. Serge Denisoff, *Great Day Coming: Folk Music and the American Left* (Urbana: University of Illinois Press, 1971); Jerome L. Rodnitzky, *Minstrels of the Dawn: The Folk-Protest Singer as Cultural Hero* (Chicago: University of Chicago Press, 1976)

Barbara L. Tischler

Folks, Homer (*b* Hanover, Mich., 18 Feb 1867; *d* New York City, 13 Feb 1963). Reformer. He moved to New York City in 1893 and in the same year was appointed by Louisa Lee Schuyler as the secretary of the State Charities Aid Association, a private organization that monitored public welfare institutions. In 1898–99 he served on the first Board of Aldermen of New York City and worked to reform municipal building codes. As the city's commissioner of public charities (1902–3) he opened the first municipal hospital for tuberculosis, on Blackwell's Island. He also prevailed on the state legislature to pass the Public Health Law (1913) and the Public Welfare Law (1929). He was a member of the New York State Public Health Council (1913–49). In 1921 he was instrumental in opening the East Harlem Health Center, the first neighborhood health center in New York City; its success led the city's public health department to take charge of it, and by 1944 the department operated 14 other centers in the city. During the Depression of the 1930s Folks advised President Franklin D. Roosevelt on welfare. He resigned from the State Charities Aid Association in 1947.

Sarah Henry Lederman

Follin, Miriam. See Leslie, Miriam.

food. New Yorkers enjoy a greater variety of food and drink than most other Americans because of the city's size, its status as a port, and its many immigrant groups. Manhattan was a center of the rum trade during the colonial period and had four rum distilleries in 1770. During the nineteenth century seafood was so abundant that lobsters were an everyday item, oysters were common at large fish houses, and caviar from the Hudson was served without charge by saloons. Much of the seafood destined for American markets passed first through Fulton Market in New York City, enabling local retailers and restaurant owners to take the freshest fish. Even salmon caught in the Pacific Northwest was typically shipped to New York City for sale, then back again to Portland (Oregon) and Seattle. With the arrival of large numbers of German immigrants in the 1840s New York City became an important center of brewing. In 1877 the Hell Gate brewery, established by the German immigrant George Ehret, was the largest brewer in the United States, and by 1879 there were 78 breweries in Manhattan and 43 in Brooklyn. Much of the demand for seafood and other products resulted from the fondness of New Yorkers for dining out. The grand dining RESTAURANTS of the late nineteenth century and the hotel restaurants of the early twentieth served native fish with a European flair. Among the dishes created or popularized in the city were lobster Newburg, sole Marguery, and baked Alaska (served at Delmonico's); crabmeat Remick (at the Plaza Hotel); clams Casino (by Julius Keller at Narragansett Pier); vichyssoise (at the rooftop garden of the Ritz–Carlton Hotel by Louis Diat); and chicken Divan (at Divan Parisien on East 45th Street). A number of popular mixed cocktails also originated in New York City, including the Bloody Mary (first served at the King Cole Bar in the St. Regis Hotel by the Parisian bartender Ferdinand "Pete" Petiot and known as the "red snapper"); the Manhattan (at the Manhattan Club in 1874 to honor the election of Governor Samuel J. Tilden); the Bronx, made up of gin, sweet vermouth, and orange juice (at the Waldorf Hotel in 1906 by the bartender Johnnie Solon); the Christy girl, made with peach brandy, gin, and grenadine (at the Sherry–Netherland Hotel); the gibson, named for the illustrator Charles Dana Gibson (at the Players); sangria (at the Spanish Pavilion during the World's Fair of 1964–65); and the kamikaze, a drink of lemon juice, lime juice, Cointreau, and vodka (at Les Pyrénées by Tony Lauriano in 1972).

In many neighborhoods of New York City elegant French and Italian restaurants are found alongside Korean grocers, pizzerias, Greek diners, soda shops, delicatessens, and Chinese markets. Many popular foods were created by immigrants who adapted their traditional recipes according to what was available in the United States. Italian dishes made in this fashion included veal parmigiana, clams Posillipo, spaghetti and meatballs, veal Marsala, Italian cheesecake, and spaghetti alla Caruso (all adaptations of Neapolitan or Sicilian dishes), pizza (originally poor people's food in Naples), pasta primavera (made with fettuccini noodles and vegetables by Sirio Maccioni, the owner of Le Cirque), and the hero sandwich. A large number of the foods associated with American Jews originated in New York City and were at first unknown to Jews in Europe and the Middle East, including bagels, blintzes, knishes, lox, Danish pastries, cheesecake, the Reuben sandwich, and egg creams, a confection sold at candy stores made with chocolate syrup, milk, and seltzer (but neither eggs nor cream). American Jews also popularized seltzer (called *belchwasser* or Jewish champagne and drunk as a remedy for dyspepsia), the bottled chocolate drink Yoo-Hoo, and the coffee-flavored soda Manhattan Special. Other ethnic foods originated or popularized in the city include the hot dog (by Nathan Handwerker of Nathan's at Coney Island); the English muffin (by Samuel Bath Thomas sometime after 1880); London broil (in restaurants throughout Manhattan); chocolate fondue (at the Chalet Suisse in 1956 by Konrad Egli); negimaki, a dish of beef rolls and scallions with soy sauce (at the restaurant Nippon by its owner Nobuyoshi Kuraoka in 1959); and eggs Benedict. Although most of these foods were well liked, immigrants also created a market for such exotic items as squid, mussels, salt cod, tripe, brains, heart, kidneys, chilies, cilantro, broccoli, and leeks.

Since the 1980s a surge of Latin American immigration has led to neighborhoods whose markets and eateries cater specifically to the recently arrived locals. In Queens, Brooklyn, and the Bronx one will easily find stores selling Salvadoran specialties like *pupusa* (stuffed masa cake), Cuban pork sandwiches, Peruvian rotisserie chickens, and Haitian *fritaille* (fried foods). In the late 1990s immigration from the various states once called Yugoslavia resulted in large numbers of Albanians, Serbs, Croatians, and Montenegrins bringing their homeland foods to the city, from Dalmatian *pasticada* (stuffed beef cooked in wine and spices) to steak à la Zagreb (breaded veal stuffed with ham and cheese), Albanian *corba* (a rice and lemon soup), *ematur* (an almond cake), and *kungull me kos* (battered and fried morsels of squash with garlic-yogurt sauce).

Many of the most popular American candies and confections were first made in New York City (see CONFECTIONERS), including Tootsie Roll (named by Leo Hirschfield for his daughter) and Chunky (named by Philip Silverstein for his granddaughter). The German immigrant Henry Heide sold more than 350 brands of candy from his shop in the city, among them Jujubes, Jujyfruits, Red Hot Dollars, Chocolate Sponge, Mexican Hats, Parlay bars, and Turkish Taffy. Yogurt became popular throughout the United States after Daniel Carasso and Joe Metzger began producing it under the name Dannon at a small factory in the Bronx. The ice-cream sandwich and a soft ice cream called frozen custard were introduced in the city, which was also the headquarters of two important makers of "premium" ice cream, Häagen-Dazs and Sedutto's.

The principal wholesale food market for the city, at Hunts Point in the Bronx, is the largest produce market in the world. It sells more than $1 billion worth of produce yearly and handles 50 to 60 percent of the nearly four billion pounds (1.8 billion kilograms) of fruit and vegetables consumed annually in greater New York.

Peter Benes, ed., *Foodways in the Northeast* (Boston: Boston University Press, 1984); Peggy Katalinich, *Foods of Long Island* (New York: Harry N. Abrams, 1985)

See also BAKERIES, BREWING AND DISTILLING, COMMERCIAL FISHING, DAIRYING, KOSHER FOODS, MEATPACKING, and SOFT DRINKS.

John F. Mariani

football. The first organized football game in New York City was played in 1870 when Rutgers College defeated Columbia University by a score of 6 to 3. New York University

A football game at the Polo Grounds during the first half of the twentieth century

Professional Football Teams in New York City

Name and Years Active	League
Brickley's Giants (1921)	NFL
New York Giants (1925–)	NFL
Brooklyn Horsemen (merged with Brooklyn Lions; 1926)	AFL
Brooklyn Lions/ Brooklion Horsemen (for last three games of the season; 1926)	NFL
New York Yankees (1926)	AFL
New York Yankees (1927–28)	NFL
Staten Island Stapletons (1929–32)	NFL
Brooklyn Dodgers (1930–43)	NFL
Brooklyn Tigers (1936)	AFL
New York Yankees (1936–37)	AFL
New York Yankees (1940)	AFL
New York Americans (1941)	AFL
Brooklyn Tigers (1944)	AFL
Brooklyn Dodgers (1946–48)	AAFC
New York Yankees (1946–49)	AAFC
New York Bulldogs/ New York Yanks (1949/1950–51)	NFL
New York Titans/ New York Jets/New York Jets (1960–62/ 1963–69/1970–)	AFL/AFL /NFL
New York Stars (1974)	WFL
New York Knights (1988)	AFL*
New York CityHawks (1997–98)	AFL*
New York Dragons (2001–)	AFL*

NFL = National Football League, AFL = American Football League, AAFC = All-American Football Conference, WFL = World Football League, AFL* = Arena Football League. A slash indicates that a team changed its name or league.

first played organized football in 1873. From the earliest days, games between local colleges were overshadowed by games between out-of-town schools that played in New York to attract more fans. As early as the 1880s Princeton and Yale played annually in the city on Thanksgiving Day, and in the 1890s crowds of more than 30,000 attended their games at the Polo Grounds. During the 1920s, games between the college football powerhouses Army and Notre Dame created the most excitement.

Brickley's Giants, which played only two games in 1921 as part of the National Football League (NFL) before disbanding, was the city's first major professional team. A new NFL team called the New York Giants was formed in 1925 by Tim Mara. The following year Red Grange, a recently graduated collegiate football star, and his agent Charles Pyle asked permission from Mara and the NFL to form another team in New York City. When the request was denied, they created the first of four organizations known as the American Football League (AFL). Among the teams in the new league was the first of five teams called the New York Yankees, which played in Yankee Stadium, and another called the Brooklyn Horsemen, which played four games before merging with the Brooklyn Lions of the NFL (the new team finished the season as the Brooklion Horsemen); the first AFL ceased operations after one year. The NFL soon established several more teams in the city, including the New York Yankees (1927–28), the Staten Island Stapletons (1929–32), and the Brooklyn Dodgers (1930–44), owned first by Dan Topping (who in 1939 acquired a controlling interest in the baseball Yankees and in 1946–48 owned the New York Yankees of the All-America Football Conference).

College football in New York City had its heyday during the interwar years, though it never generated the enthusiasm that it did elsewhere. New York University played its best football from 1926 to 1928. Led by Ken Strong, the team lost only four games in three seasons. In 1934 Columbia pulled a major upset by defeating Stanford by a score of 7 to 0 in the Rose Bowl. The team used a play called the KF-79 in which the quarterback, Cliff Montgomery, made a series of handoffs and fake handoffs to the halfbacks. From 1935 to 1937 the Fordham University Rams were known for their vaunted defensive line called the seven blocks of granite, which included Vince Lombardi and Alex Wojciechowicz. During the 1930s the Rams played a number of memorable scoreless games against the powerful University of Pittsburgh. In 1936 Fordham did not surrender a touchdown until the last game of the season, when its loss to New York University by a score of 7 to 0 ended its chances of playing in the Rose Bowl. On 25 October 1947 Columbia pulled off another remarkable upset by ending Army's 32-game winning streak.

Professional football teams proliferated during the late 1930s to the early 1950s, though many of them were short-lived: in the second AFL the Brooklyn Tigers (1936) and the New York Yankees (1936–37); in the third AFL the New York Yankees (1940) and the New York Americans (1941); in the All-America Football Conference the New York Yankees (1946–49) and the Brooklyn Dodgers (1946–48), who were absorbed by the Yankees after three losing seasons; and in the NFL a team called successively the New York Bulldogs (1949) and the New York Yanks (1950–51). The New York Titans, an original member of the fourth AFL (formed in 1960), became the New York Jets in 1963. In January 1969, the Jets, led by quarterback Joe Namath, defeated the Baltimore Colts in Super Bowl III by a score of 16 to 7. Often considered the greatest upset in the history of professional football, the Jets' victory gave instant credibility to the AFL, leading to its merger with the NFL the following year. The New York Stars of the World Football League played only six home games at Downing Stadium on Randalls Island in 1974 before disbanding. The Jets and the Giants remained the city's two main professional football teams into the twenty-first century. Though the Giants and the Jets moved to Giants Stadium in New Jersey in 1974 and 1983, respectively, both franchises retained the New York designation in their names. The Giants won the Super Bowl in 1987 and 1991. The Giants also won the Super Bowl in 2008, defeating the New England Patriots. In the final decades of the twentieth century, two Arena League Football teams, the New York Knights (1988) and the New York Cityhawks (1997–98), played their home games for a short time at Madison Square Garden.

New York City has also had several enduring rivalries between high school teams, such as that between De Witt Clinton High School and the High School of Commerce (now Louis D. Brandeis High School) and in Brooklyn between Erasmus Hall and Manual Training High School (now John Jay High School). Sid Luckman played for Erasmus Hall before his career at Columbia and with the Chicago Bears, and Yankee baseball great Lou Gehrig played football for Commerce.

Seven members of the Pro Football Hall of Fame were born in New York City: players Art Donovan (Bronx), Sid Luckman (Brooklyn), and John Mackey (Manhattan); owners Tim Mara (Manhattan), Wellington Mara (Manhattan), and Dan Reeves (Manhattan); and coach Vince Lombardi (Brooklyn).

Joseph A. Horrigan

Forbes, Malcolm (Stevenson) (*b* Brooklyn, 19 Aug 1919; *d* Far Hills, N.J., 24 Sept 1990). Publisher. He grew up in suburban Englewood, New Jersey, and attended Princeton University (AB 1941). In 1946 he joined the staff of *Forbes,* a fortnightly business magazine launched by his father, and from the mid-1960s he was its publisher, president, editor in chief, and sole owner. He was also a Republican state senator in New Jersey (1952–

58) and the unsuccessful Republican gubernatorial candidate in New Jersey in 1957. In his later career he became well known as a devotee of motorcycle riding and hot-air ballooning, as a collector of Fabergé eggs and historical artifacts and memorabilia, and as the host of lavish parties (several aboard his yacht and one in Morocco). For all his flamboyance and flair for publicity, Forbes was a shrewd businessman whose publishing concerns flourished under his management. He died of a heart attack at age 70.

Christopher Winans, *Malcolm Forbes: The Man Who Had Everything* (New York: St. Martin's, 1990)

B. Kimberly Taylor

Ford, George B. (*b* Clinton, Mass., 1879; *d* New York City, 13 Aug 1930). Architect and urban planner. After studying architecture at the École des Beaux Arts in Paris, he joined the New York City firm of George B. Post in 1907. He lectured on city planning at Columbia University from 1911–14, helped to author New York City's first zoning ordinance (passed in 1916), and in 1925 founded the journal *City Planner.* Concurrently, he volunteered his services to the Red Cross in France during World War I and headed up postwar reconstruction efforts there. During the 1920s he served as consultant to the Regional Plan Association of New York and was named its director in 1930 (succeeding the first director, Thomas Adams). His appointment was cut short by his death later that year of post-operation complications.

Susan Kriete

Ford, Patrick (*b* Galway, Ireland, 12 April 1837; *d* New York City, 23 Sept 1913). Journalist. In 1846 he moved to Boston with his parents, and after working in the printing office of William Lloyd Garrison's journal the *Liberator* he enlisted in the Union Army. He later settled in Charleston, South Carolina, before moving to New York City, where in 1870 he launched the weekly newspaper *Irish World* (renamed *Irish World and American Industrial Liberator* in 1878), soon the most important publication of its kind in the United States. Ford supported Irish nationalism, the right to strike, woman suffrage, the eight-hour day, the income tax, abolishing monopolies, insuring federal greenbacks, and nationalizing land in the United States and in Ireland, where he hoped that such a program would become a means for gaining independence. After the Land League was formed in Ireland in 1879 he oversaw the formation of 2500 similar organizations throughout the United States. A powerful voice in city politics, he supported such figures as Edward McGlynn and Henry George, a mayoral candidate in 1886. Ford lived at 350 Clermont Avenue in Brooklyn.

Kevin Kenny

Ford, Whitey [Edward Charles] (*b* Queens, 21 Oct 1928). National Baseball Hall of Fame pitcher. He was called "Whitey" for his blond hair, "Slick" for his craftiness on the mound, and "Chairman of the Board" for his ability to remain calm under pressure. He joined the New York Yankees in 1950, spent 1951–52 in the U.S. Army during the Korean War, rejoined the Yankees in 1953, and for the next 17 years was one of the premier pitchers in baseball. His lifetime record of 236 wins and 106 losses gave him the best winning percentage (.690) of any twentieth-century pitcher. He led the American League three times in wins and twice in earned run averages and shutouts. In 1961 he won the Cy Young Award in addition to being voted Most Valuable Player in the World Series; he was the starting pitcher in the World Series eight times. He was elected to the Hall of Fame in 1974. In 1987 the Yankees dedicated a plaque to Ford at Yankee Stadium in Monument Park. It reads: "One of the greatest pitchers ever to step on a mound."

Frank Dyer

Ford Foundation. Philanthropic organization. For decades the nation's largest, it was chartered in Detroit in 1936 to further charitable ends and to save the Ford family from having to sell the Ford Motor Company to pay the taxes on the estates of Henry Ford and his son Edsel. Until 1950 the foundation granted about $1 million a year to charities in greater Detroit. In that year the foundation's assets increased markedly when it was bequeathed 88 percent of the company's stock. A five-member study committee was then appointed by Henry Ford II to make plans for expanding the foundation; entities soon formed as a result included the Fund for the Advancement of Education, the Fund for Adult Education (a pioneer in educational television), and the Fund for the Republic. The foundation also set up research and policy organizations such as Resources for the Future and the Council on Library Resources. From 1951 to 1953 the foundation had its headquarters in Pasadena, California, home of its first president, Paul G. Hoffman. When Hoffman was succeeded by H. Rowan Gaither, a lawyer from San Francisco, offices were consolidated in New York City, and the foundation built a new building near the United Nations. In 1955 the foundation sold most of its stock and granted $642.6 million in proceeds to private colleges and universities, hospitals, and medical schools. From 1956 to 1965 the foundation was led by Henry T. Heald, a former president of New York University; during his tenure the foundation continued to support higher education (especially business and engineering) and expanded its arts program (it granted $80 million to symphony orchestras). Along with other foundations it was a target of congressional investigations during the 1950s (prompted by allegations of support for subversive activities, financial self-dealing, and undue accumulation of assets) and of inquiries during the 1960s that led to the Tax Reform Act. Its support of civil rights, minority voter registration, and other liberal causes led to boycotts of products of the Ford Motor Company. The foundation was criticized by the teachers' unions for its role in assisting school decentralization in New York City in 1967, which touched off a bitter strike.

In New York City the foundation supported educational, arts, and social service institutions ranging from Lincoln Center to the Vera Institute of Justice. In 1968 it established the Fund for the City of New York to improve the city's public services. McGeorge Bundy, a former national security adviser, was president of the foundation for 13 years from 1965, during which the foundation played a prominent role in civil rights, community development in inner cities, and environmental research and advocacy. In 1977 the foundation severed its ties to the Ford company and family. Franklin A. Thomas, a foundation trustee who became president of the foundation in 1979, focused on domestic poverty, problems of refugees and immigrants, and leadership in state government. By 2007 the foundation had distributed more than $530 million in grants.

The Ford Foundation occupied a brick-and-glass structure at 321 East 42nd Street designed by Kevin Roche and John Dinkeloo. Completed in 1967, the building has an enclosed courtyard with trees and greenery and is among the most elegant works of architecture in the city. As of 2008 the foundation headquarters was located at 320 East 43rd Street.

Dwight MacDonald, *The Ford Foundation: The Men and the Millions* (New York: Reynal, 1956; rev. New Brunswick, N.J.: Transaction, 1989); Richard Magat, *The Ford Foundation at Work: Philanthropic Choices, Methods, and Styles* (New York: Plenum, 1979); Francis X. Sutton, "The Ford Foundation: The Early Years," *Daedalus* 116, no. 1 (winter 1987), 41–91

Richard Magat

Fordham. Neighborhood in the northwestern Bronx, centered at the intersection of Fordham Road and the Grand Concourse and bounded to the north by Kingsbridge Road and East 194th Street, to the east by Fordham University and Webster Avenue, to the south by 183rd Street, and to the west by the Harlem River; to the north is Lehman College and to the south Bronx Community College, which occupies the former uptown campus of New York University. During the seventeenth century a few houses stood near what is now the intersection of Bailey Avenue and Kingsbridge Road, and a nearby ford across the Harlem River was the only direct crossing to the Bronx from Manhattan. A parcel of 3900 acres (1580 hectares) extending from the ford to the eventual site of the High Bridge and lying between the Harlem and Bronx rivers

Tiebout Avenue steps in Fordham

was granted in 1671 by Governor Francis Lovelace to the Dutch settler Jon Arcer (John Archer), who named it Fordham Manor after Saxon words meaning "houses by the ford (or wading place)." The first bridge from the Bronx to Manhattan, the King's Bridge, opened in 1693 a short distance from the ford. After Arcer's death the manor was divided into small farms. Claimed mostly by the British but raided by both sides during the American Revolution, the area was the site of many skirmishes between British and Continental troops that devastated local farms. It remained rural until the mid-nineteenth century. In 1841 the New York and Harlem Railroad was extended to a street that later became Fordham Road, and near the station St. John's College, a Roman Catholic college that later became Fordham University, was built. Edgar Allan Poe moved in 1846 to a small cottage, his last home, near what became Poe Park.

The neighborhood grew tremendously after rapid transit was extended from Manhattan. The Third Avenue elevated line was extended to Fordham Plaza in 1901; the Jerome Avenue elevated line opened in 1918, and the Grand Concourse subway in 1933. Between 1900 and 1950 a shopping district developed on Fordham Road, which became the largest in the borough and included Alexander's department store. Many five-story walk-up apartment buildings and six-story buildings with elevators were erected, a large number of which remained standing in the first decade of the twenty-first century. Most residents from the 1920s on were middle-class and working-class Jews, Irish, and Italians who had moved from crowded sections of Manhattan, and often they were the children and grandchildren of immigrants. The neighborhood became known for its outstanding schools, including the Bronx High School of Science. From the 1950s many older residents moved to the suburbs, and by 1980 much of the population consisted of Puerto Ricans, other Latin Americans, and blacks, many from the South Bronx. In the following years large-scale housing abandonment of the sort that had occurred in the South Bronx was forestalled, in part through the efforts of the Northwest Bronx Community and Clergy Coalition. From the 1980s many of the new immigrants settling in Fordham and its environs were Dominican; in the early twenty-first century there was an influx of Mexicans. Although the neighborhood has many problems, its apartment buildings are for the most part well maintained, as are its few one- and two-family houses. In 2001 the old Alexander's department store was refurbished and several new stores moved in, and retail sales continued to grow. The Fordham Road Business Improvement District was created in 2005. Fordham remains a vital area, best known for its shopping district and as the site of Fordham University.

Harry C. W. Melick, *The Manor of Fordham and Its Founder* (New York: Fordham University Press, 1950)

Peter Derrick

Fordham Preparatory School. Jesuit high school for boys on East Fordham Road in the Bronx, opened in 1841 as part of St. John's College (now Fordham University). Initially a boarding school, it lacked its own principal until 1921, and in the following years it became a day school. In 1970 it formed its own board of trustees and split off from the university, moving to a building on the east side of the university campus in 1972. The student enrollment in 2010 was 950.

Gilbert Tauber

Fordham University. Roman Catholic institution opened in 1841 as St. John's College by Bishop John Hughes in Fordham Manor. The first president was John McCloskey, later archbishop of New York. Unable to staff the school or support it financially, Hughes transferred control to the Society of Jesus in 1846, the year in which the first bachelor's degree was awarded. Until 1855 the Jesuits maintained a seminary at the school. The college opened a medical school and a law school in 1905 and in 1907 took its current name and established Fordham University Press. Later it opened the School of Pharmacy (1912), the School of Sociology and Social Service (1916), the School of Business Administration (1920), and the School of Education (1938). The law school moved successively to 42 Broadway in lower Manhattan, 20 Vesey Street, 140 Nassau Street, the Woolworth Building (where it remained for 30 years), and 302 Broadway (1943). The university became widely known for its athletic programs; from 1935 to 1937 the football team achieved great success with a defensive line known as the "seven blocks of granite" that included Vince Lombardi. In 1955 the university became part of the project to develop Lincoln Center, and in the early 1960s several divisions including the law school moved to a new campus bounded by 62nd Street, Amsterdam Avenue, 60th Street, and Columbus Avenue. When the university created St. Thomas More College in 1964, it became coeducational; in 1969 it came under the control of a lay board of trustees. As of 2010 Fordham had more than 16,000 undergraduate and graduate students in more than 70 academic programs at 10 schools and colleges. Two archbishops of New York graduated from Fordham: John Cardinal Farley (1867) and Francis Cardinal Spellman (1911).

Robert I. Gannon, *Up to the Present: The Story of Fordham* (Garden City, N.Y.: Doubleday, 1967)

Bernadette McCauley

Forest City Ratner. Commercial real estate development company. Established in 1985, the Brooklyn-based company is headquartered at One MetroTech Center and is a subsidiary of Forest City Enterprises. Notable projects include the completed New York Times Building and New York Mercantile Exchange as well as the Atlantic Yards Project in Brooklyn.

Jessica Montesano

Forest Hills. Neighborhood in central Queens, bounded to the north by the Long Island Expressway, to the east by Flushing Meadows–Corona Park, to the south by Union Turnpike, and to the west by Junction Boulevard and disused track of the Long Island Rail Road (the former Rockaway Beach line). It occupies what was once farmland owned by Frederick D. Backus, George Backus, and Horatio N. Squires, of which 600 acres (243 hectares) in the area then known as Whitepot were bought in 1906 by the Cord Meyer Development Company. The area was named Forest Hills for its proximity to Forest Park, and its streets were assigned names arranged in alphabetical order from Atom (75th Avenue) to Zuni (63rd Drive). The company installed utilities and under the direction of George C. Meyer engaged architects like Robert Tappan and William Patterson to design elegant one-family houses, which were built from 108th Street to 112th Street and between Queens Boulevard and 67th Road; some lots were donated for schools and churches. The Long Island Rail Road opened a station in Forest Hills on 5 August 1911, enabling residents to commute to Manhattan in 30 minutes. The trolley along Queens Boulevard inaugurated service on 27 August 1913 from 71st Avenue to Second Avenue in Manhattan, and Queens Boulevard was widened during the early 1920s. Development hastened after these improvements were made: in 1922 the Queens Valley Golf Club was laid out on 17.5 acres (7 hectares) of land, and by the end of 1924 there were 340 houses. Construction began on apartments along Queens Boulevard, including the Kelvin (1928) and the Livingston, Georgian, and Portsmouth (all 1929). Between 1927 and 1930 the population increased from 9500 to 18,207. Land along Queens Boulevard was excavated by the city in 1931 for the Independent subway, which opened to Union Turnpike on 31 December 1936 and transformed the part of Forest Hills northeast of Queens Boulevard. Additional apartment buildings were constructed and many stores opened to accommodate the growing population (32,500 in 1940). In the six decades after World War II some private houses were razed to build apartments, and the neighborhood became largely middle class, Jewish, and Italian.

The West Side Tennis Club (founded 1892) moved from Manhattan to Forest Hills Gardens in 1914 and built a 13,000-seat stadium in 1923; the club hosted the national tennis championship (since 1968 the US Open) from 1915 to 1977. Forest Hills in the early 1970s was the scene of a bitter dispute between middle-class homeowners and advocates of low-income housing. The controversy received national attention and helped to launch the political career of Mario M. Cuomo, a local lawyer who negotiated a compromise that largely defused the tensions. No open land remained in the mid-1990s, and only northern Forest Hills and sections near Queens Boulevard retained one-family houses on individual

Map of Forest Hills, drawn by Charlie Seewald

lots rather than large apartment buildings. Many new immigrants settled in Forest Hills during the 1980s, especially Bukharian Jews from Central Asia and Iranians. In the early twenty-first century the suburban Cord Meyer area north of Queens Boulevard suffered from the loss of mature trees, the paving of yards, and the demolition of historic houses for significantly larger replacements.

Vincent Seyfried

Forest Hills Gardens. Housing development in central Queens, bounded to the northeast by Burns Street and to the southeast by Union Turnpike; the southwestern boundary is irregular and runs roughly parallel to Burns Street. The planned community consisted of about 800 Tudor style homes and buildings. The land was originally part of an area formerly known as Whitepot and was later included in a parcel of 600 acres (243 hectares) bought in 1906 by Cord Meyer, who in 1908 sold a section below Queens Boulevard to Margaret Slocum Sage, the benefactor of the Russell Sage Foundation. On 142 acres (57 hectares) the landscape architect Frederick Law Olmsted, Jr., planned a Garden City development in the style of an English village, with a green, a railroad station, an inn, and 1500 houses designed by the architect Grosvenor Atterbury. A brick-paved square shaded by trees was built in front of the railroad station, with a town clock, arched passageways, and garden apartments built to resemble a row of country inns. Narrow, winding roads discouraged through traffic and provided room for large front gardens. Between February and May 1910 streets were laid out between Continental and Ascan avenues, and during the summer of the same year houses of varied height and design were erected using the new techniques of steel framing and concrete construction. The high price of land and construction drove the rents to $12 a month in 1910, a prohibitive amount for those with moderate incomes. Many elegant brick houses were built between 1910 and 1917, and in 1916–17 luxury houses were built in Greenway Terrace that sold for about $20,000; the Russell Sage Foundation built others by private contract. In 1912 the inn, a garage, and a country club were opened. The post office began service in 1914, and 10 acres (4 hectares) of land were sold to the West Side Tennis Club, where the U.S. Open tennis championship was contested until 1977 (the well-known tennis stadium opened on 10 August 1923). The Church-in-the-Gardens was built in 1915, followed by the Church of Our Lady Queen of Martyrs (dedicated on 28 May 1916). Several well-known figures lived in Forest Hills Gardens during these years, including Helen Keller, Dale Carnegie, Mayor John F. Hylan, the entertainer Fred Stone, and the sculptor Adolph A. Weinman. In 1922 the Forest Hills Gardens Corporation, an organization of property owners, bought the common areas. The first apartment building, the Forest Arms, was erected in 1924. Development ceased with the entry of the United States into World War II, and in the years following the war only about 25 houses were built; by the mid-1960s the last lots were finally developed. There were about 4500 inhabitants in 1970. Streets, parks, sewers, distinctive streetlights, and traffic lights are owned and maintained by the corporation, which preserves the residential character of the neighborhood. Until the mid-1970s, homes were sold with restrictive covenants, discriminating against Jews, blacks, and working-class people. In the 1980s a number of new immigrants settled in Forest Hills Gardens and its environs, mostly from Iran, India, the Soviet Union, and Israel. In the twenty-first century Forest Hills Gardens real estate remained desirable and expensive.

Vincent Seyfried

Forest Park. Public park in Queens, bounded to the north by Myrtle Avenue and Union Turnpike, to the east by Park Lane, to the south by Park Lane South, and to the west by Cypress Hills Cemetery. It occupies 535 acres (217 hectares) of hilly terrain and was once known as the Brooklyn Forest because of its acquisition in 1895 by the City of Brooklyn. In 1896 the firm Olmsted, Olmsted and Eliot designed a plan for the park, which was executed around the turn of the century. A golf course, originally of nine holes, opened in 1901; the clubhouse (1905), designed in a Dutch Colonial Revival style by the firm of Helmle, Huberty and Hudswell (which also designed the Williamsburgh Savings Bank), now houses the offices of the park's administrator. The park was ravaged in 1912 by a chestnut blight and for a time was used for lumbering; about the same time greenhouses were set up to grow plants for parks throughout the city. Popular carousels by the highly regarded designer Daniel Muller were added in 1918 (destroyed by fire in 1966) and 1972. Jackson Pond was used for fishing and ice skating before being filled in. The Interborough Parkway between Brooklyn and Queens was built through the park in 1935. Forest Park features ballfields, tennis courts, a band shell (on the site of an earlier bandstand and concert grove), a memorial field called Victory Field, a monument to World War I known variously as the Richmond Hill Doughboy and My Buddy, and an enclosed area in which model airplanes may be flown.

Jonathan Kuhn

Forrest, Edwin (*b* Philadelphia, 9 March 1806; *d* Philadelphia, 12 Dec 1872). Actor. He made his debut in New York as Othello in July 1826, then performed often in the Park and Bowery theaters. From 1839 to 1850 he owned and lived in a townhouse at 436 West 22nd Street. In 1849 his rivalry with the English actor William Charles Macready culminated in the bloody Astor Place Riot. After his divorce in 1851 he returned to Philadelphia but continued to act in New York City. In 1853 he appeared as Macbeth at the Broadway Theatre; the engagement lasted four weeks, an unprecedented run. He played Hamlet at Niblo's Garden in 1860 and gave his final performance in New York City in February 1871. Known for his commanding physique and powerful voice, Forrest was the first American-born actor to achieve an international reputation.

Don B. Wilmeth

Fort Amsterdam. The name of a fort erected by the Dutch in lower Manhattan, and by

Fort Amsterdam

extension one of several names sometimes applied to the entire settlement of New Amsterdam. The fort was a four-sided structure at the foot of Broadway, opposite Marketfield, Stone, and Bridge streets, near the eventual site of the U.S. Custom House. Unimpressive even by the standards of the seventeenth century, it was unable to protect the Dutch against a British fleet that appeared in the harbor in the late summer of 1664. On 2 September, without loss of life, Governor Peter Stuyvesant surrendered both fort and city.

Kenneth T. Jackson

Fort Apache. Nickname for the 41st police precinct of New York City, which had its station at Simpson Avenue south of 167th Street in the South Bronx and covers the neighborhoods of Hunts Point and Crotona Park East. The nickname became used when drugs, crime, and arson severely damaged the surrounding area during the 1960s and 1970s. The crime rate declined sharply in the 1990s, and in 1993 the precinct moved to a new precinct house a few blocks away. In 1997 the original precinct house became the new headquarters for Bronx detectives. A 1981 movie called *Fort Apache, The Bronx* starred Paul Newman.

Tom Walker, *Fort Apache* (New York: Avon Books, 1976); Jill Jonnes, *South Bronx Rising: The Rise, Fall, and Resurrection of an American City* (New York: Fordham University Press, 2002)

Evelyn Gonzalez

Fort Greene. Neighborhood lying at the foot of the Manhattan Bridge in northwestern Brooklyn (1990 pop. *ca* 40,000), bounded to the north by the East River, to the east by Vanderbilt Avenue, to the south by Atlantic Avenue, and to the west by Flatbush Avenue. The first European settler (and the first Italian in Brooklyn) was Peter Caesar Alberti, who from 1639 operated a tobacco plantation near Wallabout Bay. The area is named for Nathaniel Greene, a Revolutionary War general who oversaw the construction of Fort Putnam in 1776 on a hill overlooking the bay (the fort survived the Battle of Long Island but was abandoned during Washington's retreat). Between 1776 and 1783 thousands of captured Americans were held in prison ships moored in the bay. Overcrowding, contaminated water, starvation, and disease led to the deaths of nearly 12,000 Americans, whose corpses were interred in shallow graves along the sandy shore. Soon uncovered by the wind and tides, their remains were visible for years. In 1808, they were gathered and placed in a crypt located near the intersection of Hudson Avenue and York Street.

On the site of the tobacco plantation a shipyard opened in 1791, followed by the Brooklyn Navy Yard in 1801. During the 1840s a growing number of free blacks settled and found skilled work in shipbuilding, and by 1870 more than half the black population of Brooklyn lived in the area; many Irish, German, and English immigrants also lived there. In 1848 Frederick Law Olmsted and Calvert Vaux designed Washington Park, which covered 30 acres (12 hectares) of land and had cobblestone walks meandering under chestnut trees; it was later renamed Fort Greene Park. An austere Doric column called the Prison Ship Martyrs' Monument was erected in the park in 1908 and dedicated by the president of the United States. Shipbuilding remained the economic mainstay of the neighborhood until the navy yard closed in 1966. The population became ethnically and economically mixed, and several housing projects were built by the New York City Housing Authority for tenants of low and middle income.

The neighborhood has many types of buildings, including Second Empire brownstones and neo-Greco, Romanesque Revival, Queen Anne, and nineteenth-century Italianate town houses; in 1978 Fort Greene was designated a Historic District. Buildings that became landmarks include the original Hanson Place Baptist Church (1860), which served the Underground Railroad; the Lafayette Avenue Presbyterian Church (1862); the Brooklyn Academy of Music (1908); and the Williamsburgh Savings Bank, the tallest building in Brooklyn (1929).

The 1980s saw an influx of black and white professionals who were attracted by the proximity of the neighborhood to Manhattan and by brownstones that cost less than in other parts of the city. In the mid-1990s several well-known black artists and musicians lived in the neighborhood, and the population was about two-thirds black, a quarter white, and a tenth Latin American. Early in the twenty-first century, the neighborhood continued to gentrify as property values rose, more affluent families bought homes, and crime rates fell.

Barbara Habenstreit, *Fort Greene, U.S.A.* (Indianapolis: Bobbs–Merrill, 1974)

Judith Berck

Fort Greene, 2009

Fort Hamilton. A fort in Bay Ridge, Brooklyn. It is one of the oldest continuously garrisoned federal posts in the United States. Named for Alexander Hamilton, it stands on the site of an early Dutch blockhouse and of Fort Lewis, an earth and timber work that helped to deter British attack during the War of 1812. The structure was built between 1825 and 1831 as the first granite fort in the harbor. A decade after its construction the post engineer, Captain Robert E. Lee, supervised expansion of the gun platform and improvements to the water battery, Fort Lafayette. During the Civil War volunteer regiments trained at Fort Hamilton, and Fort Lafayette became a prison for captured Confederates. The post commander during the first months of the war was Abner Doubleday (called by some the inventor of baseball), who was later a hero at Gettysburg. A ship barrier across the Narrows assisted Fort Hamilton and its sister forts on Staten Island in protecting the harbor against Confederate raiders. Fort Hamilton also provided troops to help quell the draft riots of July 1863.

Rifled artillery made vertical-walled masonry fortifications obsolete after the Civil War. The last decades of the nineteenth century brought a new generation of long-range guns that were not removed from Fort Hamilton until the years surrounding World War II.

Fort Hamilton

Antiship artillery was replaced by antiaircraft artillery, itself removed in 1954 when Nike missiles began 20 years of protecting New York City. Fort Hamilton was a major embarkation and separation center during the two world wars. Early in the twenty-first century it was the home of a recruiting command and the Military Entrance and Processing Station for New York City. Fort Hamilton then supported more than 200 reserve and National Guard units, and as the only active army post in the metropolitan area, it did work once performed by several installations.

The name Fort Hamilton sometimes refers to the immediately surrounding civilian community as well, although less so than formerly. During most of the nineteenth century the fort had no chapel and depended on nearby churches that integrated it into the community. St. John's Episcopal Church, known as the "church of the generals," baptized Lieutenant Thomas "Stonewall" Jackson (later to achieve Civil War fame), and Robert E. Lee was one of its vestrymen. Many Irish or German Catholic soldiers helped put up the first building for nearby St. Patrick's Church. The neighborhood also had several saloons just off post that catered to soldiers. What remained of the civilian neighborhood in the early 1960s was diminished by the construction of approaches for the Verrazano–Narrows Bridge.

Russell S. Gilmore

Fort Hill. Neighborhood in northeastern Staten Island, lying within and near the center of New Brighton at an elevation of 210 feet (64 meters). The name recalls the earthen redoubts built by the British at the time of the American Revolution. During the second half of the nineteenth century the estate of Daniel Low occupied the hill. Eventually the estate was divided and sold in pieces. Fort Hill in later years underwent a resurgence, as young families restored houses to their former condition. In the early twenty-first century it remained a residential area of fine one-family houses, many of which are still owned by descendants of wealthy families who lived in the area during the late nineteenth and early twentieth centuries.

John-Paul Richiuso

fortifications. The defense of New York Harbor began with the city's founding. One of the first actions the Dutch settlers took was to erect Fort Amsterdam on a site now occupied by the former U.S. Custom House at the foot of Broadway in Manhattan. Soon after, they built small blockhouses at strategic points such as the Narrows. When the colony changed hands in 1664, England altered little in the city's defenses except the name of Fort Amsterdam (which became successively Fort James, Fort William, Fort Anne, and Fort George). But during the first half of the eighteenth century additional guns at the shore near the old fort created a redoubtable defense in the area still called the Battery. Effective antiship fortifications spread beyond Manhattan during the American Revolution, and at the same time American engineers built the city's only important nonmaritime forts. In preparation for the Battle of Long Island they built earthworks at various points on Manhattan, Governors Island, and eastern Long Island. The line of defenses behind which the defeated patriots took refuge, to include Fort Greene, Fort Putnam, and Fort Box, was imposing enough to deter General William Howe from immediate attack and permit Washington's retreat across the East River. The triumphant British returned to maritime concerns, and during their seven-year occupation of the city they built the first defenses at the Narrows capable of stopping ships.

In the nineteenth century improved technology made it possible to engage an enemy ever farther out on the water. Later defenses therefore lay in rings progressively more distant from the original settlement. The first half of the century was a time of massive masonry forts, only one of which, Castle Clinton, remains in Manhattan. The rapid expansion of New York City destroyed the early nineteenth-century Red Fort (or North Fort) within a generation; the White Fort (Fort Gansevoort) did not last much longer. The State of New York built Castle Clinton between 1807 and 1811, as tension with England appeared to be building toward another war. (Militarily unneeded by 1823, the fort became Castle Garden during 1823–55, the immigrant station during 1855–90, and the New York Aquarium during 1896–1941, before being returned to its appearance as a fort by the U.S. National Park Service.) Governors Island nearby still bears defenses of the same period: Fort Jay (called Fort Columbus, 1806–1904), Castle Williams, and South Battery. Fort Wood, which is now the sub-base of the Statue of Liberty, also stood ready for the War of 1812. The federal government began Fort Hamilton at the Narrows in 1825 and the earliest surviving defense on Fort Wadsworth in Staten Island in 1847. At mid-century the federal government also undertook a never-completed granite work 10 miles (16 kilometers) south at Sandy Hook, New Jersey, to replace Fort Gates, which dated from the War of 1812. Fort Hancock later rose on the same sand spit, which was too important a site to ignore. Until the dredging of the Ambrose Channel early in the twentieth century, Hancock offered the first shot at an enemy ship nearing the main entrance to New York Harbor.

At the East River entrance to the harbor, army engineers in 1856 completed Fort Schuyler (now the home of the State University of New York Maritime College). Later they began Fort Totten across Long Island Sound at Willets Point. The treacherous waters of Hell Gate provided natural protection against an enemy fleet under sail; the paired forts were intended to deal with steamships. The granite work at Willets Point, like the one at Sandy Hook, became obsolete before it was finished. At the turn of the century, however, when equipped with new long-range guns, Fort Totten emerged as the chief protector of the back entrance to New York Harbor, with reinforcement from Fort Schuyler and Fort Slocum, just south of New Rochelle on Long Island Sound.

Similar long-range guns armed Fort Hancock, rearmed forts Hamilton and Wadsworth, and pushed first-line defenses to dots of land beyond the eastern tip of Long Island, 100 miles (160 kilometers) from the city. Battleships also had been improved, but new batteries were more than a match for them. By the mid-1920s Fort Tilden in the Rockaways covered a 30-mile (50-kilometer) fan of ocean with two of the most powerful coast artillery guns ever made, 16-inch (40.6-centimeter) rifles firing a projectile as heavy as a small automobile. Later, interlocking fire was provided by a similar battery completed during

World War II on the Navesink Highlands near Fort Hancock.

In the 1920s the development of aircraft brought another dimension to the defense of New York City, with bases at both Fort Hamilton and Miller Field, just south of Fort Wadsworth. The navy built Rockaway Naval Air Station (now Jacob Riis Park), from which the first airplane to fly the Atlantic took off in 1919. After a decade as the city's first municipal airport, Floyd Bennett Field became a naval air station in 1941. Warplanes brought a new defensive mission to the harbor forts. In 1922 the 62nd Coast Artillery at Fort Totten set up the prototype antiaircraft installation. During World War II Fort Totten served as the antiaircraft headquarters for the Eastern Defense Command, coordinating guns throughout New York and New Jersey for the city's protection. Nike antiaircraft missiles replaced antiaircraft guns in 1954 and stood guard for the next 20 years. In 1990 the navy began construction of its controversial homeport at Stapleton on Staten Island. Many believed that busy and congested New York Harbor was no place for nuclear-armed vessels, but the argument soon became moot because with the end of the cold war the homeport closed in August 1994. Although no longer based in New York City, the navy, along with the air force, continues to provide for its security; both services would expect to detect enemies and engage them far at sea.

Henry M. Allen, *Historic Forts of New York State* (Auburn, N.Y.: n.pub., 1957); Russell S. Gilmore, *Guarding America's Front Door: Harbor Forts in the Defense of New York City* (New York: Publishing Center for Cultural Resources, 1983); Emanuel Raymond Lewis, *Seacoast Fortifications of the United States: An Introductory History* (Washington, D.C.: Smithsonian Institution Press, 1970; repr. Annapolis, Md.: Naval Institute Press, 1993)

Russell S. Gilmore

Fort Schuyler. A fort in the Bronx, almost directly beneath the Throgs Neck Bridge at the eastern end of Pennyfield Avenue. It was built between 1833 and 1838 to defend New York City against a possible naval attack from Long Island Sound, complementing Fort Totten on Willets Point in Queens on the opposite shore. Never used in battle and all but abandoned between 1878 and 1934, the fort remains an outstanding example of nineteenth-century military architecture: the interior court, known as St. Mary's Pentagon, is particularly impressive. The fort is now part of the campus of the Maritime College of the State University of New York. Visitors may visit a maritime museum within the fort or walk along the ramparts and enjoy a fine view of the northern shore of Long Island.

Kenneth T. Jackson

Fort Totten. A fort at Willets Point in Bayside in Queens. Begun in 1862, it was intended to be the strongest of the nation's system of seacoast fortifications, with five tiers of heavy guns. Work ceased in 1864 when fighting during the Civil War made it plain that vertical-walled masonry forts had become obsolete. The post saw use as a training ground for volunteer units from New York City during the war and afterward was the site of a major military hospital with 5000 beds. After the Civil War the fort housed the Engineer School of Application, and it later became the maritime mine center for the U.S. Army. Engineers also did important developmental work with searchlights and other technical coast defense equipment. Many distinguished engineer officers served at the fort, as well as the young medical officer Walter Reed, later famous for his work on yellow fever. In 1898 the fort was given its current name, after General Joseph Totten (1788–1864). By the turn of the century a new generation of antiship guns in small dispersed batteries, along with the electric mines perfected at Fort Totten, made for a powerful seacoast defense. The fort lost some of this equipment during World War I when guns were shifted to less secure portions of the U.S. coast and to Europe. The mission after World War I became largely one of air defense, which had been assigned to coast artillery as a new specialty. As World War II neared, the fort became the site of the first antiaircraft radar installation on the East Coast. After the war it continued as an administrative and training center for antiaircraft artillery, and when Nike missiles replaced the large sky-sweeping cannon in 1954, it became a nerve center for antiaircraft missiles for several years. In 1963 the secretary of defense announced the end of active service for the fort, and in 1967 it became a subinstallation of Fort Hamilton. Five reserve units based at Fort Totten were activated in Vietnam, and 29 during the Gulf War. The fort continued to provide military housing into the twenty-first century, and the huge 77th Reserve Command kept it involved in the nation's military efforts. In 2008 the park opened as part of the New York City Parks and Recreation system complete with visitors' center at a total cost of $1.3 million.

Russell S. Gilmore

Fort Tryon Park. Public park in Manhattan, bounded to the east by Broadway, to the south by several streets including West 190th, and to the west and north by Riverside Drive. It contains high, wooded ground once inhabited by the Wiechquaesgecks; until the late seventeenth century Dutch settlers called it Lange Bergh (Long Hill). During the American Revolution Hessian and British troops seized a colonial outpost there and named the battlements after Sir William Tryon, the last English governor of the colony of New York. Many prominent citizens built mansions on the heights during the nineteenth century, including C. K. G. Billings, whose mansion was bought by John D. Rockefeller, Jr., in 1917; however, it burned down in 1925. In 1927 Rockefeller sought to build a park on the property and engaged as its designer Frederick Law Olmsted, Jr. (son of a designer of Central Park), whose plan retained the entrance arch and several other rustic features of the estate. The city accepted the park as a gift in 1931, and the plan was completed in 1935. In 1938 the Cloisters opened in the park as a showcase for the medieval art collection of the Metropolitan Museum of Art. The promenades of the Cloisters facing the Palisades in New Jersey and the Hudson River provide some of the most striking views in Manhattan.

Jonathan Kuhn

Fort Schuyler, 2009

Fortune. Business magazine, founded in February 1930 by the publisher Henry R. Luce, who had founded *Time* magazine in 1923. It was marketed to the wealthy classes, despite the recent stock-market crash. It combined articles by highbrow literary writers and upscale business advertisements. By 1937 the magazine had more than 400,000 subscribers. *Fortune* devoted a whole issue to New York City, thereby promoting its advertisers' exhibits. Starting in July 1955 it published yearly lists of the largest industrial corporations in the United States, called the "Fortune 500." The magazine began biweekly publication in January 1978. Among the distinguished literary and political figures who have written for the magazine are Ernest Hemingway, Carl Sandburg, James Thurber, Bernard Baruch, Sidney Hook, Felix Frankfurter, and Adlai Stevenson. In the early twenty-first century *Fortune*'s headquarters were in the Time–Life Building at Rockefeller Center, 1271 Sixth Avenue.

Marjorie Harrison

Fortune, T(imothy) Thomas (*b* Marianna, Fla., 3 Oct 1856; *d* Philadelphia, 2 June 1928). Journalist. He moved in 1881 to New York City and worked as a printer for the *Weekly Witness.* Later that year he helped to publish the *Rumor,* a weekly newspaper that soon became the *New York Globe,* later working as an editor for the *Freeman* (1884–87) and as a reporter and editorial writer for the *Sun.* As an editor he consistently attacked racism and bigotry and advocated militant radicalism to secure civil rights, and in 1887 he initiated a movement to organize the National Afro-American League. As the editor of the *New York Age* during 1889–1907 he offered a position to Ida Bell Wells Barnett, who had been forced to flee Memphis for denouncing lynchings in the *Memphis Free Speech.* He was eventually influenced by his friend Booker T. Washington to assume a more conservative view of race relations. In 1907 financial and personal problems forced him to sell his interest in the *New York Age* to Fred R. Moore; Washington became a silent partner. Fortune struggled during his remaining years as a writer for various black publications.

Emma Lou Thornbrough, *T. Thomas Fortune: Militant Journalist* (Chicago: University of Chicago Press, 1972)

Sandra Roff

Fortune Society. Nonprofit organization dedicated to re-entry assistance for exprisoners. Formed in November 1967 to promote prison reform, the name was inspired by John Herbert's play about prison life, *Fortune and Men's Eyes* (1967), produced by David Rothenberg at the Actor's Playhouse in Greenwich Village. (The play was a shock to the public conscience about how prisoners and ex-prisoners are treated, which inspired a series of lectures by Rothenberg and two ex-prisoners, Pat McGarry and Clarence Cooper.) The Fortune Society publicizes prison conditions and advocates for prison reforms. Staffed primarily by ex-prisoners, it provides ex-prisoners with counseling and housing assistance. Many workers wear their old prison uniforms at the store, which sells goods made by ex-convicts and distributes informational materials. The society believes in an open-door policy to encourage at-risk youth and ex-prisoners to seek help, and it offers transitional residence housing and beds for treatment. One-third of the members of the Board of Directors were at one point prisoners or had substance-abuse problems.

Jessica Montesano

Fortunoff. Firm of jewelry, silverware, and housewares retailers, formed in 1922 at 561 Livonia Avenue in Brooklyn by the Russian immigrant Max Fortunoff (1896–1987) and his wife, Clara (1902–86). The firm built its reputation by underselling its competitors. In 1957 it began selling jewelry. Although the main store was moved in 1964 to suburban Westbury, Long Island, outlets were opened in Manhattan at 154 East 57th Street in 1969 and at 681 Fifth Avenue in 1979. Operating in New York, New Jersey, Connecticut, and Pennsylvania, it was acquired in 2008 by Lord and Taylor. Fortunoff filed for bankruptcy in 2009, and the Fortunoff and Mayrock families, who had owned the company, purchased the property, trademark, and brand name.

Leslie Gourse, Kenneth T. Jackson

Fort Wadsworth. For many decades the oldest continually staffed military reservation in the United States. Located beneath the Verrazano–Narrows Bridge at Bay Street and Wadsworth Avenue on Staten Island, it commanded the Atlantic approaches to New York Harbor. A fortification occupied the site as early as 1663, and the British controlled the installation throughout the American Revolution. On Evacuation Day in 1783 the captain of a warship of the Royal Navy, angered by the jeers of onlooking rebels, fired a shot at the fort that was probably the last of the war. New York State built a fort on the same site during the War of 1812; this was replaced by the present structure in 1847. The installation was renamed in honor of Brigadier General James S. Wadsworth in 1865, soon after he was killed in action during the Battle of the Wilderness in the Civil War. Decommissioned in the early 1990s, Fort Wadsworth is now part of the Gateway National Recreation Area.

Kenneth T. Jackson

Fort Washington Collegiate Church. Church located at Fort Washington Avenue and 181st Street. The redbrick church began as an outreach mission of the West End Collegiate Church. Built in 1909, the youngest of Manhattan's four collegiate churches embodies the teachings and history of the Collegiate Church of New York, the oldest Protestant church corporation in the United States (established 1628). The brick and timber building with stone trim stands on landscaped grounds surrounded by a fieldstone wall and iron fence. Inside, simple wood beams and rafters frame the ceiling. Until the adjoining parish house was built, worshippers probably entered from 181st Street and Colonel Robert Magaw Place, named for the American commandant of Fort Washington before its November 1776 surrender to the British.

Cathy Alexander

Fort Wadsworth, 2009

Forty Thieves. A corrupt group of members of the Board of Aldermen who extorted money from city contracts, franchises, and legislation at a time of expansive development in the early 1850s. One of its members was William M. Tweed, who learned methods of corruption that he later perfected as Boss Tweed.

Neal C. Garelik

Forverts. Yiddish-language daily newspaper launched in 1897, published at 173–75 East Broadway by the Forward Association and known variously as the *Jewish Daily Forward.* At its peak it was among the most widely read newspapers in the country, with a circulation of more than 200,000 in 1924. Under Abraham Cahan from 1901 to 1951 it espoused the cause of democratic socialism, supported the Jewish labor movement, especially trade unions, and published stories and serialized works by such writers as Sholem Asch, Abraham Reisin, Isaac Bashevis Singer, and Zalman Shneor. One of its most popular columns, the "Bintel Brief" (Bundle of letters), offered advice on a variety of topics. The 10-story Forverts Building was completed in 1911 and stood at the center of "Yiddish Newspaper Row" along East Broadway. During the 1920s the Forward Association financed the Yiddish-language radio station WEVD. The newspaper moved north in 1972; the building on the Lower East Side was designated a city landmark. *Forverts* became a weekly newspaper in the 1980s and introduced an English-language edition in 1990. Because of decreasing circulation, it launched a Russian-language edition in 1995, written in a distinct Jewish, yet secular voice. Although the Russian-language edition was sold in 2004, Yiddish circulation has increased in the twenty-first century because of the proliferation of Yiddish language courses at various universities.

Mordecai Soltes, *The Yiddish Press: An Americanizing Agency* (New York: Teachers College, Columbia University, 1924; repr. 1950); Charles A. Madison, *Jewish Publishing in America: The Impact of Jewish Writing on American Culture* (New York: Sanhedrin, 1976)

Seth Kamil

Fosdick, Harry Emerson (*b* Buffalo, N.Y., 24 May 1878; *d* Bronxville, N.Y., 5 Oct 1969). Minister and writer. He first gained fame as the pastor of the First Presbyterian Church in New York City from 1918. His status as a Baptist and as a liberal in the conflict between fundamentalists and modernists in the 1920s, as well as his much publicized sermon "Shall the Fundamentalists Win?" (1922), led to an effort by William Jennings Bryan and others to oust him from his pulpit for heresy. The issue twice went before the General Assembly of the Presbyterian Church before Fosdick resigned in 1925. Soon after, John D. Rockefeller, Jr., offered to finance a new interdenominational church where Fosdick's thousands of followers could hear him preach each Sunday. The result was the construction of Riverside Church between 120th and 122nd streets in Morningside Heights. Fosdick remained there until his retirement in 1946. An early supporter of birth control and of Alcoholics Anonymous, he was also a professor at Union Theological Seminary from 1915 to 1946.

Kenneth T. Jackson

Fosse, Bob [Robert Louis] (*b* Chicago, 23 June 1927; *d* Washington, D.C., 23 Sept 1987). Choreographer and director. He began dancing in musical comedies at an early age and after serving in the navy, where he worked on his performance technique, moved to New York City and studied at the American Theater Wing. A constant presence on Broadway, he won Tony Awards for many of his musicals, including *Sweet Charity* (1966), which follows the life of a dancer in New York City. In 1972 he received an unusual triple honor when he was awarded a Tony Award for *Pippin,* an Academy Award for *Cabaret,* and an Emmy Award for *Liza with a "Z."* While on Broadway he also choreographed *How to Succeed in Business without Really Trying* (1961), *Chicago* (1975), *Dancin'* (1978), and the films *Lenny* (1974) and *All That Jazz* (1979).

Kevin Boyd Grubb, *Razzle Dazzle: The Life and Work of Bob Fosse* (New York: St. Martin's, 1989); Martin Gottfried, *All His Jazz: The Life and Death of Bob Fosse* (New York, 1990)

Meryl Cates, James E. Mooney

Foster, George G. (*b ca* 1814; *d* Philadelphia, 16 April 1856). Reporter and satirist. He became one of the first professional city reporters while working for the *New York Tribune* in the 1840s under the direction of Horace Greeley. His experiences at the newspaper led him to write urban sketches that were collected and published as *New York in Slices* (1849) and *New York by Gas-light* (1850); these were widely read and with the collections *Fifteen Minutes around New York* (1853) and *New York Naked* (1854) provide a rather sensational but insightful portrait of the city. Foster also wrote a novel, *Celio; or, New York Above-ground and Under-ground* (1850).

Stuart M. Blumin

Foster, Stephen (Collins) (*b* Lawrenceville [now in Pittsburgh], 4 July 1826; *d* New York City, 13 Jan 1864). Songwriter. After publishing his first song in 1844 he wrote "Oh Susanna!" which became extremely popular, and negotiated one of the first composer's royalty contracts from the publishing firm of Firth and Pond in New York City. He lived at 97 Greene Street during 1860–61 and for some time at 6 Greenwich Street. Many of his songs were introduced by E. P. Christy's Minstrels, including "Camptown Races" and "Old Folks at Home (Swanee River)." Among his later compositions were "My Old Kentucky Home" and "Jeannie with the Light Brown Hair"; his last was "Beautiful Dreamer." Foster suffered from alcoholism and died penniless at Bellevue Hospital in Manhattan.

Catherine Owens Peare, *Stephen Foster: His Life* (New York: Henry Holt, 1952)

David J. Weiner

foundations. In the early twenty-first century New York City is home to 5740 of the roughly 72,000 grant-making foundations in the United States, including nine of the 50 largest by assets. Foundations based in the city account for 14 percent of the assets of all American foundations ($83,706 million of $614,656 million) and 13 percent of annual grants ($5,196 million of $39,004 million). If the 26 suburban counties that surround the city are included, the metropolitan region has about 10 percent of the foundations and 20 percent of the assets of all American foundations. Before 1900 the legal climate was hostile toward foundations, and the courts sometimes overturned bequests, such as one by Samuel J. Tilden that eventually led to the formation of the New York Public Library. The climate for foundations improved when the city's political leaders recognized that foundations could be used as instruments for influencing public policy and alleviating social ills, and during the first three decades of the twentieth century many of the foundations in the city were formed.

Among the foundations in New York City are such large, well-known ones as the Ford Foundation, the Carnegie Corporation of New York, the Rockefeller Foundation, the Commonwealth Funds, the Andrew W. Mellon Foundation, the Open Society Institute, the New York Foundation, the Henry Luce Foundation, and the Atlantic Philanthropies. They have full-time professional staffs and governing boards, with most members unconnected to the families that established the foundations. The most common type of foundation in New York City as elsewhere is the smaller family foundation, which generally does not have a full-time staff and is governed by a board consisting of family members, colleagues, and friends; an example is the Albert Kunstadter Family Foundation, run from an apartment on Fifth Avenue, which has assets of $1 million and supports programs in education, the arts, and international affairs. Many early female philanthropists from New York City chose not to put their names on their foundations, such as Margaret Olivia Sage (the Russell Sage Foundation), Anna Harkness (the Commonwealth Fund), and Anna McCormick Blaine (the New World Foundation). The tradition continues, for example, with Abigail Disney and her husband Pierre Hauser, who named their foundation the Daphne Foundation, and Helen LaKelly Hunt, who named her foundation the Sister Fund. Corporate foundations in New York City range from those on the scale of the Pfizer Foundation (assets of $350 million) and the Goldman Sachs Foundation ($260 million), to such small ones as the Fisher Brothers Foundation ($350,000), the Morris Levine Key Food Stores Foundation (formerly Key Food Stores Foundation, Inc.; $75,000), and the Robert Bowne Foundation, funded by the oldest continuously operating business in the city.

Operating foundations fund their own programs but make few or no grants to other organizations; prominent examples include the Century Foundation, which publishes studies in communications, economics, and international affairs; the Russell Sage Foundation, which focuses on economic and social research; and the Frick Collection, which operates the museum of the same name. Another type, community foundations, receive their funds from many donors rather than a single founder, family, or corporation and grant funds for a wide range of cultural, charitable, and civic activities in one geographic area; the New York Community Trust is the second largest such foundation in the United States, with assets of just over $2 billion (following the Tulsa Community Foundation, $3.1 billion). Some foundations are intended at the outset to last only a certain number of years because of their donors' belief that the funds will do the most good if expended over a fixed period: the Field Foundation, a leader in support of civil rights, discontinued operations in 1989 after 49 years; the Aaron Diamond Foundation (1991 assets of $80 million) was set up in 1955 and expired in 1996; and Atlantic Philanthropies is due to close its doors in 2016. The Altman Foundation, founded in 1913 by a New York City businessman, is one of the oldest continuous foundations in the country. The Wallace Foundation has its headquarters in the city and is involved with educational and cultural programs; the Robin Hood Foundation helps fight poverty in New York City.

Because of intermittent congressional scrutiny beginning in the 1950s, foundations began to work together more closely to foster public accountability. The New York Regional Association of Grantmakers (1979) has 285 members and an annual budget of $1.7 million. In 1991 it established City Connect, which links grant makers and city officials who have common interests. In 2001 it partnered with the Coalition for New Philanthropy to encourage African American, Latino, and Asian American donors. The Foundation Center, headquartered in the city, maintains databases on grant makers and grants and publishes directories and other materials on philanthropic giving. Other organizations group together foundations with similar interests, among them Grantmakers in Health, Women in Foundations / Corporate Philanthropy, Funders Concerned about AIDS, and the Agenda for Children Tomorrow, a project of the New York Community Trust, the Foundation for Child Development, and the United Way. Among the larger foundations in the New York City area in 2000, 173 gave $3 billion in grants, led by the Starr Foundation ($130 million), Ford Foundation ($89.4 million), and Andrew W. Mellon Foundation ($89.4 million).

In the twenty-first century about 37 percent of the money granted by foundations in New York City goes to recipients in the city, more than half by the nine largest foundations. New York–based foundations have historically invested more resources in the public policy arena and civil rights movements than their counterparts in other parts of the country. Small as well as large foundations support social change. The New York Women's Foundation, for example, worked to secure passage of the New York State Anti-Trafficking Act in 2007. With support from 14 foundations, the Campaign for Fiscal Equity filed a successful lawsuit claiming that the underfunding of New York City schools denied students their constitutionally protected right to quality education.

In the twenty-first century the proportion of foundations based in New York City has declined as huge foundations have been formed in other parts of the country. Furthermore, the stock market collapse of 2008 reduced the endowments of foundations and, consequently, their support of nonprofit organizations. Among those hardest hit was the Starr Foundation, which held 15.5 million shares of the ailing American International Group. A major recipient of donations from the financial community, Citymeals-on-Wheels, canceled a $2 million program.

Waldemar A. Nielsen, *The Big Foundations* (New York: Columbia University Press, 1972); Robert H. Bremner, *American Philanthropy* (Chicago: University of Chicago Press, 1960; rev. 1988); Steven Lawrence and Leslie A. Marino, *New York Metropolitan Area Foundations: A Profile of the Grantmaking Community* (New York: Foundation Center, 2002)

See also PHILANTHROPY.

Richard Magat

foundlings. The abandonment of infants was a growing problem in New York City during the nineteenth century. Motivated by poverty or shame, parents left their infants in public places or took them to city officials, who placed them in foster care if they were nursing and otherwise in almshouses. Some children were taken in by private arrangement at "baby farms," which were usually run by women. Because these operations could turn a profit only by severely limiting children's care, they eventually became notorious for infanticide.

Jacob A. Riis, Sister Irene and Her Foundlings *(New York Foundling Society, 1888)*

By the 1850s institutions were organized for children younger than two who could not be cared for in existing orphanages or adopted through the "orphan train" method of the Children's Aid Society (by being sent west). Wet nurses could leave their own infants at Nursery and Child Hospital (1854) while they worked. The Sisters of Charity ran the New York Foundling Hospital (1869) to receive illegitimate infants and thus preserve the reputation of women and families. The New York Infant Asylum (1865, reorganized 1872) accepted pregnant women as well as women nursing their own infants (these were also required to nurse foundlings). The Randall's Island Infant Hospital opened in 1869 as a publicly supported institution for the care of foundlings; by 1896 a controversy over high death rates there led reformers to develop a system of supervised foster care. The last infants were removed from Randalls Island in 1905, and the hospital was later demolished to make way for the Triborough Bridge.

Elsie Essmuller Vignec, *Children of Hope: Some Stories of the New York Foundling Hospital* (New York: Dodd, Mead, 1964)

Mary Elizabeth Brown

foundries. See METAL FOUNDING AND METALWORKING.

Four Corners. Neighborhood in north central Staten Island. The area was known as Centreville until the 1870s, when a new post office was named Castleton–Four Corners for the crossing of Manor Road, running north to south, and Victory Boulevard, running east to west (now the site of the main post office of the borough). In the mid-nineteenth century the Constanz Brewery was built on Manor Road just south of Victory Boulevard; it later became a shopping center. The intersection retained the name Four Corners; the surrounding area gradually became known as Castleton Corners. Businesses line both sides of Victory Boulevard. In the early twenty-first century the area remained an upscale commercial district.

Marjorie Johnson

Four Seasons Restaurant. Famous upscale eatery in the Seagram Building at 99 East 52nd Street and Park Avenue. It opened on 20 July 1959 and was designed by Ludwig Mies van der Rohe and Philip Johnson; the latter reportedly ate there every day. The Four Seasons is known for its expensive cuisine and massive indoor plants that change with the seasons; artwork by Pablo Picasso, Jackson Pollock, and Joan Miró; and its four seasons logo. In 1989 it became the second restaurant in New York City to be designated a landmark interior.

Stephanie Miller

Fourth Avenue. Former name of Park Avenue South and Book Sellers Row; see PARK AVENUE.

Fox, Richard Kyle (*b* Belfast, 12 Aug 1846; *d* Red Bank, N.J., 14 Nov 1922). Journalist. He settled in New York City in 1874 and within one year became the managing editor of the *National Police Gazette,* which he purchased in 1877. For 45 years he published the *Gazette* as a lurid 16-page magazine that included news of sports, crime, and the stage as well as sensational columns such as "Noose Notes," detailing executions, and "Crimes of the Clergy." Fox printed extensive news about prizefighting and helped to popularize pit and combat sports. He wrote *Prize Ring Champions of England from 1719 to 1889* (1889).

Randy Roberts

Fox Hills. Neighborhood in northeastern Staten Island, bounded to the west and north by Vanderbilt Avenue, to the east by Tompkins Avenue and the tracks of Staten Island Rapid Transit, and to the south by Steuben Street. The name was first used in the 1870s by Henry Meyer for his estate, but in the 1890s the area was known as Park Hill. The first 18-hole golf course in Staten Island was opened there in 1900 and was the site of championships until 1935. During World War I the largest army hospital in the nation was built in four months; the buildings were used during World War II as a military training base and as a camp for prisoners of war. Residential development accelerated after 1950. Early in the twenty-first century the area included immigrants from India, Liberia, China, and Jamaica. The Park Hill Apartments on Vanderbilt Avenue dominate Fox Hills.

Harlow McMillen

fox hunting. Fox hunts were first held in the metropolitan area in colonial times. Large packs of hounds were owned in the 1760s by James de Lancey and Lewis Morris; these were combined soon after de Lancey returned from a trip to England with horses and foxhounds. A hunt that became known as the Riding Hunt was organized by John Evers, de Lancey's hunting manager, and held weekly in what are now the Bronx, Brooklyn, and Queens. A few small packs of hounds were used in hunts in Manhattan, and in 1781 the proprietor of the King's Head Tavern in Brooklyn advertised a hunt in order to assemble a festive gathering of drinkers. In 1812 Cato's Tavern, which stood at what is now Third Avenue and 52nd Street, was the headquarters for the Belvidere Hunt. By 1822 all the hunts in Manhattan had been moved to Long Island and Westchester. An effort to revive fox hunting was made in 1856, when the Brooklyn Hunt was launched, but it was discontinued at the outbreak of the Civil War. The last fox hunt in the area was the Queens County Hunt, sponsored in 1877 by Frank Griswold, who imported a pack of Irish hounds for the event.

James E. Mooney

Foxhurst. Nineteenth-century estate in what is now the south central Bronx, on the Hunts Point Peninsula and bordering the Bronx River between what are now Farragut Street and East Bay Avenue. The estate was on a triangular parcel owned by H. D. Tiffany, a son-in-law of William Fox. George Fox, founder of the Quakers, apparently preached there in 1672. Revolutionary records describe the thick forest of Fox Woods. By 1900 Foxhurst had become a groomed estate surrounded by several dairy farms. The land is now occupied by the Hunts Point Terminal Market.

John McNamara, *History in Asphalt: The Origin of Bronx Street and Place Names* (New York: Bronx County Historical Society, 1984); John McNamara, *McNamara's Old Bronx* (New York: Bronx County Historical Society, 1989)

John McNamara

Frank, Jerome N(ew) (*b* New York City, 10 Sept 1889; *d* New Haven, Conn., 13 Jan 1957). Judge. Of German Jewish background, he graduated from the University of Chicago (1909) and University of Chicago Law School (1912) and practiced in Chicago. He joined the firm of Chadbourne, Stanchfield and Levy in Manhattan in 1928. One of President Franklin D. Roosevelt's "Brain Trust," he was counsel for the Agricultural Adjustment Administration (1933–35) and then Secretary of the Interior Harold Ickes; appointed to the Securities and Exchange Commission in 1937, he succeeded William O. Douglas as chairman in 1939. President Roosevelt appointed him to the U.S. Court of Appeals for the Second Circuit in 1941. He upheld the contempt conviction of defense lawyers for 11 communists tried under the Smith Act in 1950 (*U.S. v. Sacher*) and the conviction of Julius and Ethel Rosenberg. Overturning the contempt conviction of a union official in 1956, he wrote, "An overzealous prosecutor's heaven may be everyone else's hell." Frank expounded "legal realism" in *Law and the Modern Mind* (1930); other writings include the isolationist *Save America First* (1938), *Confessions of an Ex-isolationist* (1941), *If Men Were Angels* (1942), *Fate and Freedom* (1945), *Courts on Trial* (1949), and *Not Guilty* (1957). He lived at Riverside Drive and 84th Street.

Jeffrey A. Kroessler

Frank, Waldo (David) (*b* Long Branch, N.J., 25 Aug 1889; *d* White Plains, N.Y., 9 Jan 1967). Novelist and critic. He worked for a series of newspapers and magazines, including the *New York Times,* the *New Yorker,* and the *New Republic.* Influenced by the transcendentalist ideals of Walt Whitman, he launched the literary magazine *Seven Arts* (1916), which ran for only 12 issues, at which point the critic turned to novel writing. Frank is best known for more than 20 works of fiction, essays, criticism, and travel writing.

Casey Nelson Blake, *Beloved Community: The Cultural Criticism of Randolph Bourne, Van Wyck Brooks, Waldo Frank, and Lewis Mumford* (Chapel Hill: University of North Carolina Press, 1990)

James E. Mooney

Frankenthaler, Helen (*b* New York City, 12 Dec 1928). Painter. She studied with Rufino Tamayo while attending the Dalton School. After studying at the Art Students League and graduating from Bennington College in 1949 she returned to New York City and belonged to a circle of artists and poets that included Larry Rivers and John Ashbery. In 1952 she painted her acknowledged masterpiece, *Mountains and Sea.* She married the painter Robert Motherwell in 1958 (they later divorced). A member of the second generation of abstract expressionists, Frankenthaler invented the "soak-stain" technique of paint application, applying thinned pigment onto an unprimed, unsized canvas, giving the effect of watercolors, but more vivid. In 1963 she abandoned oil paints in favor of acrylics, working on larger, simpler, and more geometric pieces. The Whitney Museum of American Art held a retrospective of her work in 1969 that solidified her reputation. This was followed by exhibitions at the Metropolitan Museum of Art (1973) and the Museum of Modern Art (1989).

Stephen Weinstein

Frank Leslie's Illustrated Newspaper. First weekly news magazine in the United States, launched in 1855 by Frank Leslie. It covered international, national, and local news, the arts, and sports, often taking a sensational approach to stories of murder and disaster. A folio format provided ample room for both factual and fictional treatments of the lives of the wealthy (and occasionally the poor), often illustrated by lavish wood engravings. The magazine was especially noted for its pictures of the Civil War and Spanish–American War. Sold by Leslie's widow in 1889, it continued under various names until 1922.

Bud Leslie Gambee, *Frank Leslie and His Illustrated Newspaper, 1855–1860* (Ann Arbor: University of Michigan, Department of Library Science, 1964)

See also Leslie, Frank.

Robert Stinson

Franklin D. Roosevelt Boardwalk. Boardwalk in Staten Island bordering South and Midland beaches.

Franklin Furnace. Archive and exhibition space founded in 1976 by the performance artist Martha Wilson. Originally located at 112 Franklin Street in Tribeca, it housed the nation's largest collection of publications produced by artists, encompassing more than 12,000 items dating from 1960 to the present. Among its holdings were early works by Red Grooms, Claes Oldenburg, Jim Dine, and Gilbert and George, as well as publications submitted by artists worldwide whose work is suppressed for political reasons. After the New York City Fire Department closed the organization's headquarters in Tribeca (1990), the archive sought partnerships with institutions around the city to display up-and-coming avant-garde artwork. It merged its collection of post-1960 internationally published artists' books with the Museum of Modern Art in 1993 and became a virtual institution in 1998, shifting its focus to preserving performances and other forms of time-sensitive art through digital media. In 2006, the organization received a grant from the National Endowment for the Humanities to publish online records of the first 10 years of its installments and exhibitions.

Carol V. Wright

Franklin Simon. Firm of women's clothing retailers, formed in 1902 by Franklin Simon (*b ca* 1864; *d* 1934), who had worked for the retail firm of Stern Brothers since 1878. It operated a store at Fifth Avenue and 38th Street and then at 33 West 34th Street, where it remained prominent for decades. Simon enabled his employees to attend classes in his store and offered scholarships to New York University. After his death the firm was sold in 1936 to the Atlas Corporation, which in turn sold it to the City Stores Company in 1947. When this company filed for bankruptcy in 1979, Franklin Simon went into liquidation and its stores in 12 states ceased to operate.

Leslie Gourse, Kenneth T. Jackson

Franklin Square. Name of St. George's Square after 1817.

fraternal organizations. In New York City during the eighteenth and nineteenth centuries, fraternal organizations both secret and open were formed along geographic, ethnic, religious, and political lines. These organizations provided not only an outlet for social activity but often disability and death benefits for members and their families. The city's oldest and most influential fraternal group was the Freemasons, formally organized in 1730 and often an object of mistrust and hostility: a challenge to the Masons appeared on 26 November 1737 as a letter to the editor of the *New York Gazette,* and the famous anti-Masonic social and political movement that spread to the city in 1827 drove the order underground for 10 years. Several offshoots of Masonry had their beginnings in the city, and some became nationwide organizations: these included the Ancient Arabic Order of Nobles of the Mystic Shrine, formed in 1870 by two Freemasons, Walter Fleming and the actor Billy Florence; the Order of the Amaranth, formed in June 1873 by James B. Taylor as a recreational, less ritualistic organization for members of the Order of the Eastern Star, or female Masons; and the Independent Order of Odd Fellows, often regarded as the "poor man's Masons," which opened a lodge in Brooklyn in 1822. Orders based on national, ethnic, and religious origins were organized by Scotsmen (the St. Andrews Society, 1756), Germans (the German Society, 1756, and a secret society known as the German Order of Harugari, 1847), Irishmen (the Friendly Sons of St. Patrick, 1784, and the secret society the Ancient Order of Hibernians, 1836, intended to safeguard Catholic churches from hostile mobs), Englishmen (the St. George's Society, 1786), and free blacks (the African Society, 1795), who were barred from other orders. It has been estimated that 50 black organizations emerged between 1800 and 1860, including the New York African Society for Mutual Relief (1810), the Brooklyn African Woolman Benevolent Society (1831, named after John Woolman, a Quaker from New Jersey), the Abyssinian Daughters of Esther Association (1839), and the Boyer Lodge of Prince Hall Freemasonry (1842). The first racially integrated lodge was the Philomethan Lodge of the Odd Fellows, formed in 1843 by members of the Philomethan Literary Society (itself formed in 1829 by Henry Simpkins and Eli Hazzard and based at its own hall on Duane Street) and chartered by the Odd Fellows' governing body in Britain. Another integrated group, the Independent Order of Good Samaritans and Daughters of Samaria (1847), promoted abstinence from alcohol. In 1848 the 24 black Odd Fellows groups in Brooklyn and Manhattan counted almost 2000 members. Jewish fraternal organizations formed during these years included B'nai B'rith (1843), intended to promote education and improve the image of Jews, the Free Sons of Israel (1849), B'rith Abraham (1859), and the United Order of True Sisters (1846), formed by Henrietta Bruckman. In opposition to the fraternal orders of immigrants stood a virulently nativistic organization called the American Brotherhood (1844).

The period between the Civil War and the Depression marked the heyday of the city's fraternal organizations, which at any one time numbered at least 300. Among the secret societies with branches in the city were the Knights of Pythias (1868) and the National Grange, which had 45 wholesale merchants and sewing machine manufacturers as members. In 1866 Charles S. Vivian and a group of actors organized the Benevolent and Protective Order of Elks in the city to circumvent the state's Sunday dry law; the group was chartered in 1868 and gained chapters nationwide. During the last quarter of the nineteenth century and the first quarter of the twentieth, many mutual-aid societies were formed by immigrants, especially by Jews (such as Ahvas Israel, 1890, and the Workmen's Circle, 1900, which in 1918 had 250 branches and 25,000 members). Hundreds of smaller groups known as Landsmanshaftn were organized according to the European and Russian villages from which their members originated: examples include the Independent Grodno Sick Support Society and the Independent Kurlander Benevolent Society, which served perhaps a million New Yorkers before World War I. Greek fraternal organizations in the city included the Brotherhood of Athena (1891), which at its peak had 450 members, and a long-lasting group called the Panhellenic Union, organized in the basement of Holy Trinity Church at 1521–22 East 72nd Street in 1907. Nativist groups such as the Order of the American Union (1873) continued to flourish, and the Ku Klux Klan formed a chapter in the city that held regular meetings at the Chelsea Hotel; the hotel was near the Masonic Temple at 71 West 23rd Street, and the Klan may have infiltrated the Masons, a charge that was heatedly denied at the time. Among the city's other fraternal organizations were the Daughters of the American Revolution (1890), the predominantly Catholic groups the Knights of Columbus (1891) and the Order of Sons of Italy (1905), and the Knights of Liberty (1923), a group opposed to the Ku Klux Klan and led by Andrew J. Padon. In 1929 the city had 351 Masonic lodges.

The Depression was a watershed for the city's fraternal organizations, as the New Deal made the benefits offered by most voluntary associations superfluous. Many organizations established hospitals and foundations as a means of maintaining their sense of purpose. Most of the smaller groups disappeared, and those that lasted had difficulty recruiting new members. In 1930 the Masons lost ownership of their lavishly ornamented Level Club at 253 West 73rd Street, completed in 1927 at a cost of $4.3 million and celebrated by a huge parade up Fifth Avenue; the club was converted into condominiums in 1983. In 1937 the Shriners foreclosed on Mecca Temple, built in 1924 at 131 West 55th Street (later saved from demolition by the city and renamed the City Center of Music and Drama). Fraternal organizations suffered further after World War II, by which time many New Yorkers viewed the rituals practiced by secret societies as old-fashioned. Membership in the Masons declined from its peak of 134,786 in 1957 to 34,765 in 1990 (in 186 lodges), and the Knights of Pythias fared little better: although membership increased briefly when veterans joined after the war, it declined as residents of the city moved to the suburbs, and the Pythians were forced to relinquish what was once an elaborate symbol of their power, the ornate Pythian Building at 135 West 70th Street (built in 1926, remodeled into condominiums in the 1980s). The Boyer Lodge of Prince Hall Freemasonry took part in civil rights struggles in the 1960s and had as members such prominent figures as Adam Clayton Powell, Sr., Adam Clayton Powell, Jr., Arthur Schomburg, Julius A. Archibald, and Percy E. Sutton, but it, too, lost members in the following decades. In the early twenty-first century, service groups such as the New York Rotary Club (1909) and the Lions Club (1928) remained active.

Michael R. Weisser, *A Brotherhood of Memory: Jewish Landsmanschaftn in the New World* (New York: Basic Books, 1985)

Marc Ferris

Fraunces, Samuel (*b* ?West Indies, *ca* 1722; *d* Philadelphia, 1795). Innkeeper. He moved to New York City in the early 1750s, was granted a tavern license in 1756, and operated taverns there and in Philadelphia over the next 30 years. A member of Trinity Church, he married Elizabeth Dalley and had eight children. He is most often associated with FRAUNCES TAVERN in New York City. First known as the Queen Charlotte (after the young bride of George III), it assumed its proprietor's name after the outbreak of the American Revolution. Fraunces prepared meals in the English style and was renowned for his elegant desserts. He remained in New York City during most of the American Revolution and after independence was cited for his efforts to aid American prisoners of war by Congress, which awarded him $2000. After the Revolution he belonged with his son Andrew to the Columbian Order, or Tammany Society. Appointed steward of President Washington's household in New York City, he followed the president to Philadelphia in 1790. He left him in 1794 to assume the ownership of the renowned Tun Tavern in Philadelphia but died the next year; he was buried in Philadelphia at Christ Church.

Robert I. Goler

Fraunces Tavern. Meeting hall and inn built in 1719 at the corner of Queen Street (now Pearl Street) and Canal Street (now Broad Street). The building was used first as a private home and then as a public house for several decades before being purchased in 1762 by Samuel Fraunces, a West Indian who had moved to New York City from the Caribbean in the early 1750s. First known as the Queen Charlotte (after the young bride of George III), it assumed its proprietor's name after the outbreak of the American Revolution. The tavern was strongly associated with the cause of American independence: it was the site of the initial meeting in 1768 of the New York Chamber of Commerce and of meetings of the Sons of Liberty and the provincial congress. George Washington bade farewell to his officers there in 1783, and in 1785 the building became one of the first to be occupied by offices of the federal government when New York City was the national capital: it housed the Department of Foreign Affairs, the Department of the Treasury, and the Department of War. The tavern increasingly catered to a working-class clientele in the nineteenth century, although the New York Yacht Club did meet there after being organized in 1844. Run down and damaged by fire, the building was purchased in 1904 by the Sons of the Revolution, who rebuilt and restored it in the Colonial Revival style. It reopened in 1907 with a restaurant and the Fraunces Tavern Museum. The museum now occupies four connecting buildings and focuses on the history of New York City in the eighteenth century. The entire block housing the museum is listed on the National Register of Historic Places. In 1975 Fraunces Tavern was the target of a bomb attack that killed four persons, for which responsibility was claimed by the Fuerzas Armadas de Liberación Nacional.

Fraunces Tavern, 2009

Kym S. Rice, *Early American Taverns: For the Entertainment of Friends and Strangers* (Chicago: Regnery Gateway, 1983)

Robert I. Goler

Fraye Arbeter Shtime. Yiddish-language anarchist newspaper, launched in 1890 by the Pioneers of Liberty. It was published on the Lower East Side and chronicled anarchism in the United States and abroad. During Saul Yanovsky's editorship (1899–1919) it ceased to focus on insurgency and instead advocated libertarian schools, unions, and workers' co-operatives. It held annual conferences on anarchism in the city and with *Mother Earth,* a journal published by Emma Goldman, sponsored a celebration at Carnegie Hall of Peter Kropotkin's 70th birthday in 1912. Eventually it consisted mostly of historical essays and tributes to anarchist heroes, although it continued to provide commentary on contemporary issues. *Fraye Arbeter Shtime* was the longest-lived publication of its kind in the country when it ceased publication in 1977.

David A. Balcom

Fredericksz, Cryn (*fl* 1625–35). Engineer and surveyor. He was engaged by the Dutch West India Company to lay out the settlement of New Amsterdam and moved there in 1625 with diagrams for fortifications, houses, streets, a mill, a church, a school, and a hospital that had been drawn up in the Netherlands. Across from Bowling Green at the southern end of Manhattan he staked out a site for what became Fort Amsterdam, which was completed in 1635 in a style typical of the period; it was flanked by four bastions and had walls made of brick on the inside and battered earth and sod on the outside. His plan called for about a dozen streets stretching about a mile (1.6 kilometers) in total length. The first to be laid out was the Broad Way, which ran about a quarter of a mile (400 meters) to the northern edge of the settlement at Wall Street; Pearl Street marked the eastern boundary, Greenwich Street the western boundary. These streets are nearly all that remains of Fredericksz's plan.

Jonathan Aspell

Freedomland. Amusement park opened in July 1960 on 205 acres (83 hectares) in the eastern Bronx between the Hutchinson River Parkway and the New England Thruway. Advertised as the world's largest outdoor entertainment center and as the city's answer to Disneyland, it was created by C. V. Wood at a cost of $65 million. The park's seven theme areas represented various parts of the United States and were roughly arranged in geographic order. Visitors could ride horse-drawn streetcars in "Little Old New York," climb aboard a stage coach in "The Great Plains," and travel between "Chicago: 1871" and "San Francisco: 1906" in an old-fashioned train. Unsuccessful from the start, the park closed after the 1964 season, citing competition from the 1964 World's Fair in Queens. The site is now occupied by Co-op City and shopping centers.

Gary D. Hermalyn, Benjamin Hemric

Freedom National Bank. Commercial bank formed in Harlem by Dunbar McLaurin in 1964. The first deposits were solicited door to door by McLaurin, who appointed the baseball player Jackie Robinson to the board of directors. The bank sought to end the practice of redlining—that is, denying banking services to residents of certain, usually racially determined, areas—by providing capital to black entrepreneurs. Between 1977 and 1981 assets grew 234 percent, but debts and infighting among the directors led federal regulators to close Freedom National Bank in November 1990.

James O. Drummond

Freedom's Journal. First African American newspaper in the United States. It was launched in New York City as a weekly in March 1827, with John B. Russwurm and the Presbyterian clergyman Samuel E. Cornish as editors. Originally it served as a vehicle for answering the racist attacks on African Americans made by editors of various New York City newspapers. After Russwurm moved to Liberia in 1829, the newspaper ceased publication in March of that year. In May Cornish tried to continue publication under the name the *Rights of All,* but that paper folded in less than a year.

Sandra Roff

Free Expression Policy Project [FEPP]. Organization, founded in 2000, that provides research and advocacy on issues relating to free speech, copyright, and media democracy. Its main areas of interest involve restrictions on expression in publicly funded institutions such as libraries, museums, schools, universities, and arts and humanities agencies; measures including Internet filters or rating systems that restrict access to digital information; inequalities in the intellectual property system such as restrictive copyright laws; widespread issues of media democracy; and censorship of controversial art, information, and ideas directed at adolescents and children. FEPP was founded by Marjorie Heins, a lawyer and First Amendment scholar who formerly directed the Art Censorship Project of the American Civil Liberties Union. FEPP began as a project of the National Coalition against Censorship and later became part of the Brennan Center for Justice at New York University. It became independent in 2007.

Christopher M. Finan

Freeman, Frank (*b* Hamilton, Ont., 1861; *d* Montclair, N.J., 13 Oct 1949). Architect. He lived in Brooklyn and designed a variety of buildings there in the Romanesque Revival tradition during the last decade of the nineteenth century. His skill and versatility were displayed in the Hotel Margaret in Columbia Heights (1889, demolished), the Behr House, 82 Pierrepont Street (1890), the Bushwick Democratic Club (1892, demolished), the Brooklyn Fire Headquarters on Jay Street

FREEDOM'S JOURNAL.

"RIGHTEOUSNESS EXALTETH A NATION."

BY JNO. B. RUSSWURM. NEW-YORK, FRIDAY, MARCH 14, 1828. VOL. I.—NO. I.

THE COLORED AMERICAN.

SAMUEL E. CORNISH, EDITOR. New-York, Saturday, May 13, 1837.

Left *John B. Russworm,* right *Samuel E. Cornish, and mastheads of* Freedom's Journal *("Righteousness Exalteth a Nation"), 14 March 1828, and the* Colored American, *13 May 1837*

(1892), the Eagle Warehouse and Storage Company on Cadman Plaza East (1893–94), and the Brooklyn Savings Bank at Pierrepont and Clinton streets (1893–94, demolished).

Marjorie Pearson

Freeman's Journal. Weekly newspaper launched in 1840 by James White and John White and named after a moderate nationalist newspaper in Ireland. It emphasized the rights of Irish Catholics on both sides of the Atlantic and in 1841 was renamed the *Freeman's Journal and Catholic Register.* Bought in 1842 by Bishop John Hughes, it was the official publication of the Catholic Church in New York City until it was sold in 1844 to James A. McMaster. Its circulation rose from 4500 in 1846 to 16,000 by 1854. The editors supported the brand of nationalism promoted by Daniel O'Connell but opposed such extreme nationalist movements as Young Ireland and Fenianism as well as most American reform movements, especially abolitionism. The *Freeman's Journal* ceased publication in 1918.

Kevin Kenny

Freemasons [Masons]. Members of a secret male fraternal organization formed in the seventeenth century by English stonemasons' guilds. They use an elaborate system of visual symbols evoking items associated with stonemasonry, including aprons and compasses. The organization gained wide acceptance throughout the British colonies; the English Grand Lodge appointed Daniel Coxe the first provincial grand master of New York, New Jersey, and Pennsylvania in 1730, and a Masonic branch was formed in New York City in 1739. In 1787 the lodges in New York City and New York State declared themselves independent of their obligations to the British. Robert R. Livingston, grand master of New York State between 1784 and 1801, administered the first presidential oath at Federal Hall on 30 April 1789 to George Washington, a Mason from 1752 who used for the occasion the Bible of the St. John's Lodge no. 1. There were 10 lodges in the city by the end of the eighteenth century, and in 1802 the members began construction of their own building. A wide range of artifacts and prints from the early decades of the republic bearing Masonic images may have contributed to the Classical Revival in the nineteenth-century United States. Suspicions that Freemasonry was a mysterious sect that was above the law were intensified by the abduction and murder in upstate New York in 1826 of William Morgan, who was preparing to publish a report disclosing the secrets of Masonry, and led to the formation of the Anti-Masonic Party in 1828 in Utica, New York. Although membership in Masonic lodges in the city declined by 85 percent during the decade after Morgan's disappearance, Masons continued to occupy powerful positions in politics and society. In 1930 the Masons lost ownership of their lavishly ornamented Level Club at 253 West 73rd Street, completed in 1927 and celebrated by a huge parade up Fifth Avenue; the club was converted into condominiums in 1983. Local membership in the Masons declined after World War II, from a peak of 134,786 in 1957 to 34,765 in 1990 (in 186 lodges). As of 2010 the lodge in Manhattan was located at 71 West 23rd Street. Well-known Masons in New York City have included DeWitt Clinton, John Jacob Astor, Theodore Roosevelt, Irving Berlin, George M. Cohan, Fiorello H. La Guardia, Al Jolson, Harry Houdini, and Paul Whiteman.

Herbert T. Singer and Ossian Lang, *New York Freemasonry: A Bicentennial History, 1781–1981* (New York: Grand Lodge, 1981)

Marc Ferris, Robert I. Goler

Frémont, John C(harles) (*b* Savannah, Ga., 21 Jan 1813; *d* New York City, 13 July 1890). Explorer, senator, and businessman. After exploring the West and representing California in the U.S. Senate (1850–51), he moved in 1855 to New York City with his wife, Jessie; they settled at 56 East Ninth Street the following year when he became interested in seeking the presidency of the United States. He was the first presidential nominee of the Republican Party in 1856 but was soundly defeated in the general election by James Buchanan. After the Civil War Frémont bought a brownstone mansion at what is now 21 West 19th Street and invested heavily in railroads; however, poor decisions resulted in the loss of his fortune within a few years. He moved in 1873 to a cottage on Staten Island called the Esplanade, where he wrote his memoirs. From 1878 to 1883 he was governor of the Arizona Territory. Frémont was always seeking to regain his fortune and maintained a residence at 49 West 29th Street in Manhattan until the end of his life.

Allan Nevins, *Frémont, Pathmarker of the West* (New York: Appleton–Century, 1939)

James Bradley

French. The French presence in New York City dates to the 1620s, following the petition of Jean de Forrest, a French Huguenot who settled in the Netherlands in 1621, requesting permission to establish a settlement in America. The grant was authorized in 1624, and in May a group of French Huguenots arrived in Manhattan, where they reinforced the garrison built by the Dutch. The colony attracted many more Huguenots from the Netherlands, including the first colonial governor, Peter Minuit. Over time an increasing number of French merchants and skilled craftspeople settled in New Amsterdam. Steven de Lancey (born Étienne de Lancy), one of the most successful merchants, acquired enough wealth to build a large home and trading house, now known as Fraunces Tavern; he also presented the city with its first clock. Early progress in the colony was disrupted by conflict among the Netherlands, England, and France, and by the 1740s the English defeated the French and had taken their holdings in North America. The English governors of Manhattan nonetheless continued to welcome religious dissenters from France. Although the French prospered under British rule, many joined the growing movement against it, among them John Jay, Henry Laurens, Elisam Boudinot, Paul Revere, and James Bowdoin. During the American Revolution France supported the American colonists and contributed crucial engineering and military expertise, soldiers, and money; French Americans throughout the colonies also contributed strongly to the effort.

Some emigrated after the French Revolution in 1789, and in 1814 Joseph Bonaparte bought extensive acreage in upstate New York for a residence for his brother, the emperor Napoleon. Between 1816 and 1818 the emperor's nephew Joseph Napoleon built several large houses in New York City for his art collection and to provide a possible refuge for the emperor. In 1839 these holdings became the initial endowment of Fordham University. Unlike their counterparts in upstate New York (in New Paltz and other towns), New England, and Louisiana, French Americans in New York City in the early nineteenth century became assimilated into American society and gave up their language, churches, and schools. Few groups and institutions worked to preserve French culture.

In the city French architects designed several buildings during the nineteenth century. Joseph François Mangin collaborated in the design of City Hall (1802) and designed several other buildings, including the original St. Patrick's Cathedral on Mott Street (1809); Jenika de Feriet built a lavish home in 1824, the Hermitage, just outside New York City in what is now the Bronx. The French architectural influence became even more pronounced during the late nineteenth century, when Richard Morris Hunt returned to the city after studying at the École des Beaux-Arts. His ideas of design were reflected in the exuberant Renaissance style of such public buildings as the New York Public Library (begun in 1895) and Grand Central Terminal (begun in 1903), both designed by the French American architect John M. Carrère. The principles of the École des Beaux-Arts were also visible in private châteaux built in a wide range of styles: François I (the Rhinelander–Waldo mansion [1895], 72nd Street and Madison Avenue), belle époque (the Burden mansion [1905], Fifth Avenue at 91st Street), neo-French classical (the Duke mansion [1911], Fifth Avenue and 78th Street), Louis XVI (the

Frick mansion [1910], Fifth Avenue at 70th Street), and French Renaissance (the Arts Institute [1891], 57th Street). The best-known example of belle époque sculpture is the Statue of Liberty, presented to the United States by France in 1883 in honor of the 100th anniversary of the ending of the American Revolution, designed by Frédéric Auguste Bartholdi, built by French engineers and artists, and installed in 1886. French ideas and styles also had a strong effect on painting and lithography, in part because many studios were led by Americans who had studied in Paris (John Vanderlyn and Samuel F. B. Morse in the 1820s, and later John Singer Sargent and William Morris Hunt, brother of the architect), and in part because several gifted painters from France and French territories settled in the United States (among them John James Audubon, who landed in New York City in 1804, and Anthony Imbert, who in 1824 opened the first lithography studio in Manhattan). During the early twentieth century the techniques of French post-impressionists, Fauvists, and cubists were learned by many American painters and received wide exposure at the Armory Show (1913). A large number of French artists, including Marcel Duchamp, Fernand Léger, and Marc Chagall, taught in the United States during the first half of the twentieth century at such institutions as the New School for Social Research. French musicians, writers, philosophers, and art historians also contributed to the direction of American art during these years.

Authentic French cuisine was introduced in the United States at the French pavilion of the World's Fair of 1939–40. Soon after, Henri Soulé, maître d' at the restaurant of the pavilion, opened a lavish French restaurant called Le Pavillon on East 55th Street that inspired others in the city to open French restaurants as well as cooking schools, notably the French Culinary Institute. Several well-known French Americans have shaped American fashion and especially haute couture, including Coco Chanel, Lilly Daché, and Pauline Trièrge.

The French-speaking community is served by a number of cultural and educational institutions. Two of long standing, the Alliance Française (1898) and the French Institute (1911), merged in 1971; the combined organization (French Institute Alliance Française [FIAF]) later dedicated Florence Gould Hall, an auditorium where French works are often featured. The city is also the place of publication of the weekly newspaper *France-Amérique.* Among those of French origin who have lived for extended periods in New York City are the historian Jacques Barzun, the philosopher Jean-Paul Sartre, and the anthropologist Claude Lévi-Strauss. More than 60,000 people reported French ancestry in 2007.

Abigail Mellen

French, Daniel Chester (*b* Exeter, N.H., 20 April 1850; *d* Stockbridge, Mass., 7 Oct 1931). Sculptor. After achieving national acclaim as a sculptor he became a central figure from 1900 to 1917 in the cultural affairs of New York City, where he made many public sculptures: *Peace* for the temporary Dewey Arch (1899, destroyed); the Richard Morris Hunt Memorial (1901, Fifth Avenue at 70th Street); *Justice, Power, and Study* for the appellate courthouse (1900, Madison Avenue at 24th Street); *DeWitt Clinton, Alexander Hamilton,* and *John Jay* for the U.S. Chamber of Commerce (1902, removed); *Alma Mater* (1906, Columbia University); *Four Continents* for the U.S. Custom House (1907, Bowling Green); *Greek Epic, Lyric Poetry,* and *Religion* for the Brooklyn Institute of Arts and Sciences, where he also supervised the entire sculptural program (1908, Eastern Parkway); *Manhattan* and *Brooklyn* for the Manhattan Bridge (1916, Brooklyn Museum); and *Power and Wisdom* for a temporary victory arch commemorating World War I (1919, destroyed). The first sculptor on the city's Art Commission, he was also a delegate to the Fine Arts Federation, a member of the New York City Improvement Commission formed by Mayor George B. McClellan in 1904, and a trustee and director of the department of sculpture at the Metropolitan Museum of Art. For much of his life he lived both in New Hampshire and in New York City in a house that he bought in 1888 at 125 West 11th Street. Known as the "dean of American sculptors," French expressed the civic aspirations of the elite in blandly earnest public works.

Michael Richman, *Daniel Chester French: An American Sculptor* (New York: Metropolitan Museum of Art, 1977); Michele H. Bogart, *Public Sculpture and the Civic Ideal in New York City, 1890–1930* (Chicago: University of Chicago Press, 1989); Michele H. Bogart, *The Politics of Urban Beauty: New York and Its Art Commission* (Chicago: University of Chicago Press, 2006)

Michele H. Bogart

Sculpture at the U.S. Custom House by Daniel Chester French

French, Fred(erick) F. (*b* New York City, 1883; *d* Hammersly Hills, N.Y., 30 Aug 1936). Real estate developer. Using investment capital from individual investors who purchased equity shares in his projects, he built several apartment buildings and office towers in Manhattan. In 1925 he began work on Tudor City, a complex of 12 buildings containing 3000 apartments and 600 hotel rooms. Situated at 42nd Street near the East River and surrounded by slaughterhouses, electricity generators, and tenement buildings, this was the largest development of its kind in the city at its completion in 1928. In 1934 he built Knickerbocker Village, a housing complex for more than 1600 families financed as a limited-dividend project by the federal Reconstruction Finance Corporation and built on a site cleared of tenement buildings on the Lower East Side; this was one of the country's first urban redevelopment projects subsidized publicly and built and owned privately. French was one of the city's most innovative developers of the 1920s and early 1930s.

Marc A. Weiss

French Connection. Criminal drug cartel in the 1960s and early 1970s, so called from a 1962 Brooklyn case in which the New York City Police Department (NYPD) intercepted heroin hidden in a car shipped from Marseilles, France; arrested the principals, including two French nationals; and seized the heroin before it was sold. In 1972 authorities learned that large quantities of seized heroin from the 1962 and subsequent cases were stolen from the NYPD's property rooms. Approximately $70 million worth of confiscated drugs disappeared back into the streets; the stolen heroin was replaced with white flour. A 1969 book about the 1962 case (Robin Moore, author) was titled *The French Connection,* as was a 1971 Academy Award–winning motion picture starring Gene Hackman, a fictionalized account of the same case.

Andrew Sparberg

French flats. Name for five- and six-story apartment buildings without elevators erected in New York City from the 1860s, such as the Stuyvesant Apartments on East 19th Street (1869). The style of building was a French innovation. By the 1880s the term was applied to buildings of eight to 10 stories with elevators; the city's building department used it for all "first-class" apartment buildings. The name went out of fashion in the 1890s as apartments became common.

Alana Erickson Coble

Fresh Air Fund. Charitable organization that provides two-week summer vacations for children from disadvantaged communities in New York City. Participants are selected on the basis of financial need and are often from low-income communities that receive public assistance. The fund was formed in 1877 by the Reverend Willard Parsons, a minister at a small parish in Sherman, Pennsylvania, who provided 60 children from New York City tenements with country vacations for the summer. Later the same year he turned management over to the *New York Tribune,* which relinquished control on facing bankruptcy in 1962. The fund became independent in 1967. By 2007 the Fresh Air Fund had provided vacations for more than 1.7 million children between the ages of six and 18. In 2008 private individuals generated 75 percent of the fund's total income. It also offers a Career Awareness Program. The fund has headquarters in midtown Manhattan and operates five camps on Sharpe Reservation, a facility of 3000 acres (1200 hectares) in Fishkill, New York. In 2009 an estimated 10,000 children participated in Fresh Air Fund programs.

Alana Erickson Coble

FreshDirect. Online grocery delivery service based in Long Island City. FreshDirect was started in 2002 by Jason Ackerman, a former investment banker, and Joe Fedele, a cofounder of Fairway Market. The online grocer offers more than 3000 organic, local, and kosher products and prepared foods from New York City chefs. As of 2008 FreshDirect had filled more than six million orders for more than 250,000 customers.

Anne Epstein

Fresh Kills Landfill. Once the largest landfill in the world, Fresh Kills covers 2200 acres (890 hectares) of Staten Island. It was opened in 1948 as part of an effort to fill marshy areas around the city for large-scale public works projects like parks and highways. The landfill was meant to accept waste for only three years, but it quickly became a key part of the city's solid waste disposal plan; by the early 1970s it was receiving half of New York City's garbage. By 1987 close to 29,000 tons were tipped at Fresh Kills every day, and the landfill employed 650 full-time workers. By the mid-1990s it was so large that it was visible from space. In 1995 the Environmental Protection Agency estimated that it was generating almost 2 percent of the world's methane gas. In the twenty-first century that gas is being extracted, bottled, and sold for heating fuel. In March 2001 a barge delivered the last load of trash to the landfill's approximate total accumulation of 110 million tons, and for the first time in its history New York City had nowhere within its own borders to put its garbage. On 12 September 2001 the landfill was reopened for 10 months as the staging area for the search, investigation, and recovery effort that followed the terrorist attacks of the day before. Material left from the investigation has been placed on Fresh Kills' highest point, overlooking Manhattan. That location is slated to become a September 11th memorial when Fresh Kills is transformed into the city's largest park, three times the size of Central Park. The 30-year-long process began in 2003.

Robin Nagle

Fresh Meadows. Housing development in central Queens (2000 pop. 13,366). In 1923 the area became the site of a golf course at the intersection of Fresh Meadow Lane and Nassau Boulevard, planned by Benjamin C. Ribman of Brooklyn, that eventually became the site of major tournaments. On 1 April 1946 land near the intersection of Horace Harding Boulevard and 188th Street was bought by the New York Life Insurance Company for a residential development; Voorhees, Walker, Foley and Smith was the architectural firm and the George A. Fuller Company the general contractor. Construction began in 1946 and was completed in 1949. Called by many a "model urban community," the development was praised by the critic Lewis Mumford as "perhaps the most positive and exhilarating example of community planning in the country." New York Life sold it in 1972 to Harry B. Helmsley for $53 million, and soon afterward a tenants' association maintained that Helmsley had reduced services and was planning to develop the remaining open spaces. Tenants and owners reached a settlement in 1982 and relations became largely amicable. At first the population was almost exclusively white, prompting a discrimination suit in 1983 by the Legal Defense Fund of the National Association for the Advancement of Colored People (NAACP) that was successful. The area gradually become more diverse, with a growing population of blacks, Chinese, Japanese, Koreans, and Indians. Fresh Meadows remains a small town within the city. The Japanese School of New York opened in the neighborhood in 1975 as the city's first Japanese-language day school.

Patricia A. Doyal

Friars Club. Social club. Formed in 1904 by press agents in New York City, it attracted vaudeville, burlesque, and later film and television performers, many of whom could not gain admittance to more elite clubs such as the Players and the Lambs. The club adopted monastic terms for its officers, including its president (the abbot) and vice president (the dean), as well as for its clubhouse (the monastery). It undertook philanthropic works and staged social gatherings, including "frolics," "roasts," man-of-the-year awards, and testimonial dinners. The frolics, held yearly between 1908 and 1929 and featuring performances by such figures as Al Jolson and George M. Cohan, were held in New York City and then taken on tour. The roasts, which began as strictly private affairs, were filmed from the 1970s and broadcast on Dean Martin's television program. On 26 April 1960 Mayor Robert F. Wagner (ii) renamed Times Square "Friars Square" for a week to honor the humanitarian and civic efforts of the club; Duffy Square was similarly renamed for a week in 1974 on the occasion of the club's 70th anniversary. In June 1988 the club voted to admit women as members. In the early twenty-first century the main headquarters were at 57 East 55th Street.

Tina Margolis, "A History of Theatrical Social Clubs in New York City" (diss., New York University, 1990)

Tina Margolis

Frick, Henry Clay (*b* West Overton, Pa., 19 Dec 1849; *d* New York City, 2 Dec 1919). Industrialist. While still in his 20s, Frick recognized that the Bessemer steelmaking process would greatly increase the demand for coke (a coal product), and with several associates he began to purchase soft-coal lands in western Pennsylvania and to build coke ovens. By the time he was 30 he had become a millionaire. In 1881 he benefited from an exchange of shares in his mines and coke ovens for shares in the iron and steel mills owned by Andrew Carnegie; by 1889 Frick was in charge of the operations of Carnegie Brothers and Company. As president and then chairman of the board of Carnegie Steel (1889–1900) he oversaw the growth of the concern into the largest producer of steel in the world. In 1900 he moved to New York City, where he began building a magnificent mansion at 1 East 70th Street at Fifth Avenue (completed in 1914). The following year he became a member of the board of directors of the U.S. Steel Corporation, formed by J. P. Morgan. An avid collector of painting and sculpture, particularly of the Italian Renaissance, Frick bequeathed his mansion, his art collection, and an endowment of $15 million to the City of New York. The mansion is now the Frick Collection art museum.

George Harvey, *Henry Clay Frick, the Man* (New York: Charles Scribner's Sons, 1928)

Allen J. Share

Frick Collection. Museum on the Upper East Side of Manhattan. Opened in 1935, the Frick contains the collections of the industrialist Henry Clay Frick and is housed in his former mansion at 1 East 70th Street, designed by Thomas Hastings. The exhibitions include European paintings, mainly from the Renaissance to the end of the nineteenth century; important collections of small, classically inspired bronzes; Renaissance and eighteenth-century French furniture; Limoges enamels; prints and drawings; and Chinese and French porcelains. The museum has paintings by El Greco, Johannes Vermeer, Rembrandt, J.-A.-D. Ingres, Pierre-Auguste Renoir, Titian, Giovanni Bellini, John Constable, Jean Fragonard, Thomas Gainsborough, Frans Hals, William Hogarth, Hans Holbein the Younger, Piero della Francesca, J. M. W. Turner, Jan van Eyck, and James McNeill Whistler. A reference library contains some 750,000 photographs and slides and 174,000 books and catalogues.

George B. M. Harvey, *Henry Clay Frick: The Man* (New York: Charles Scribner's Sons, 1928); *The Frick Collection: An Illustrated Catalogue* (Princeton, N.J.: Princeton University Press, 1968–82); Bernice Davidson, Edgar Munhall, and Nadia Tscherny, eds., *Paintings from the Frick Collection* (New York: Harry N. Abrams, 1990)

Carol V. Wright

Friend, Charlotte (*b* New York City, 11 March 1921; *d* New York City, 13 Jan 1987). Medical researcher. She earned a bachelor's degree at Hunter College in 1944 and a doctorate in bacteriology at Yale University in 1950. While working at the Sloan–Kettering Institute in 1956 she discovered a virus that causes leukemia in mice, a breakthrough in cancer research. She continued her research at the Mount Sinai School of Medicine from 1966 and in 1971 published an important paper on a technique for making cancer cells revert to normal development patterns. A member of the National Academy of Sciences, Friend received many awards and worked to further the interests of women in science.

Barbara J. Niss

Friendship House. Catholic settlement house established in 1938 at 34 West 135th Street in Manhattan by the Russian émigrée Catherine De Hueck. Before settling in New York, De Hueck opened the first Friendship House in Toronto in 1930. It was dedicated to providing aid and education for blacks, and all funding was from donations. The house offered instruction in reading, writing, religion, sports, and art, as well as employment referrals, lectures, and religious instruction. When possible it paid college tuition for black students. Across from the main building De Hueck rented four stores that were used to collect donations, distribute clothing, and provide space for various activities. The organization also supported a youth group, a Catholic lending library, and a reading room. In 1949 Friendship Houses opened in Washington (D.C.), Chicago, Portland (Oregon), and Shreveport (Louisiana). Friendship House in New York City closed in 1957.

Bernadette McCauley

Friends Seminary. Elementary and secondary coeducational private school. Opened in 1786 on Pearl Street in lower Manhattan as the Friends Institute by the New York Monthly Meeting of the Religious Society of Friends, the school moved in 1826 to Elizabeth Street and in 1860 to Stuyvesant Square. In 1964 a new building was added on 16th Street, adjacent to the school and the Friends Meeting House. Although Quakers account for only about 3 percent of the student body and faculty, the educational outlook of Friends Seminary reflects its Quaker heritage, requiring four years of community service, and has a meetinghouse among its facilities.

Richard Schwartz

Fuchs, Klaus [Emil Julius] (*b* Russelsheim, Germany, 29 Dec 1911; *d* Dresden, East Germany, 28 Jan 1988). Physicist. After fleeing Germany in 1933 he earned his PhD in physics at the University of Bristol in England. In 1941 he began working on the British atomic bomb program and two years later came to Columbia University to work on the Manhattan Project. In 1944 he was transferred to the Los Alamos National Laboratory in New Mexico, and by 1950 he was found guilty of leaking information to the Soviet Union about U.S. nuclear weapon capabilities and atomic secrets of the United States and Britain.

Jessica Montesano

Fugazy [Fugazzi], **Luigi V.** (*b* ?Liguria, Italy, *ca* 1839; *d* New York City, 6 Aug 1930). Businessman. He moved to New York City in 1869 and was well established by the time a large number of Italians settled in the city in the late nineteenth century. Fugazy became wealthy and powerful through padrone services, a bank, a steamship agency, and an employment office. He also organized mutual-benefit societies, urged Italians to take part in American politics, and developed ties with Tammany Hall. His son Humbert and grandson William were well known locally as promoters of sporting events.

Mary Elizabeth Brown

Fuller, (Sarah) Margaret (*b* Cambridge, Mass., 23 May 1810; *d* near Fire Island, N.Y., 19 July 1850). Journalist. In her youth she was influenced by the New England transcendentalists. From 1844 she lived in New York City with the family of Horace Greeley and wrote for his newspaper, the *New York Tribune*. Her articles covered a wide range of subjects, including prison reform, immigration, prostitution, slavery, and literature. In 1846 the newspaper sent her to Europe, where she became the first American woman to be a foreign correspondent. She lost her life aboard the steamer *Elizabeth* on her return voyage.

Paula Blanchard, *Margaret Fuller: From Transcendentalism to Revolution* (New York: Delacorte, 1978); Charles Capper, *Margaret Fuller: An American Romantic Life* (New York: Oxford University Press, 1992)

See also Literature, §1.

Thea Arnold

Fulton, Robert (*b* Little Britain [now Fulton Township], Lancaster County, Pa., 14 Nov 1765; *d* New York City, 24 Feb 1815). Inventor, engineer, and painter. He grew up in Lancaster and briefly attended school there before turning to drawing, painting, and mechanics, and becoming an accomplished gunsmith. At the age of 17 he went to Philadelphia where he spent four years painting portraits and landscapes. After studying painting in England he became engrossed in the principles of undersea warfare, mechanically propelled ships, and canals. He designed and tested naval weaponry for the French and the British before meeting the American minister to France, Robert R. Livingston of New York City, who agreed to finance his experiments in steamboat technology and contracted with him to construct a steamboat to ply the Hudson River between New York City and Albany, New York. After landing in New York City in December 1806 he constructed the *North River Steamboat* at the shipyard of Charles Brown(e) in Manhattan. On 17 August 1807 the vessel, powered by a Watt steam engine, began service on the Hudson as the first commercially successful passenger steamboat in the world. Eventually he secured a monopoly on steamboat operations in New York State. Fulton also designed a steam naval vessel for the defense of New York Harbor during the War of 1812, as well as other ships and ferryboats. His last home was at 1 State Street. The *North River Steamboat* became known by its

Self-portrait of Robert Fulton after Elizabeth Emmet, ca *1815. Fulton copied Emmet's portrait but added the exploding boat in the background, a reference to the destruction of the brig* Dorthea *by his diving boat off Deal, England, on 15 October 1805*

popular name the *Clermont* only after his death.

Elaine Landau, *Robert Fulton* (New York: F. Watts, 1991)

See also PORT OF NEW YORK.

James E. Mooney, Darwin H. Stapleton

Fulton Ferry [Fulton Landing]. Historic district in northwestern Brooklyn lying at the bottom of the bluffs of Brooklyn Heights at the foot of Fulton Street and bounded to the north by the East River, to the east by Main Street, to the south by Front and Doughty streets, and to the west by Furman Street. Transport from the area to Manhattan was offered as early as 1642 by sailboats and rowboats for hire. The Fulton Ferry Company began regular steam ferry service in 1814 and by 1872, steam ferries made 1200 crossings daily. During the nineteenth century the waterfront around the ferry dock became a bustling mercantile center, and huge warehouses were built in the surrounding streets to accommodate commercial transport; there was also industry and a residential section. After the Brooklyn Bridge was completed in 1883 the number of ferry passengers declined and in 1924 service was discontinued. The only ferry service remaining is the New York Water Taxi. Most of Fulton Street was renamed Cadman Plaza West. Many industrial buildings were later converted to housing: the Eagle Warehouse and Storage Company (28 Fulton Street; 1893) is a residential condominium; the building of the Brooklyn City Railroad Company (8 Cadman Plaza West; 1861) houses the Old Fulton Street apartments; and the Empire Stores (53–83 Water Street; built in sections in 1870 and 1885) and the Tobacco Inspection Warehouse (25–39 Water Street) are part of the Empire Fulton Ferry State Park. A converted barge moored at the Fulton Ferry pier is the site of a chamber music series called Bargemusic and offers superb views of the river. The River Café, a popular gourmet restaurant, and the Brooklyn Ice Cream Factory share the address 1 Water Street. Grimaldi's Pizza, a famous pizza parlor, is also located nearby at 19 Old Fulton Street.

Elizabeth Reich Rawson

Fulton Fish Market. Wholesale fish market formerly located on the shore of the East River two blocks south of the Brooklyn Bridge. It originally consisted of stalls in a corner of the Fulton Market (1822) that were used until fish dealers moved across South Street to a shed along the river in 1831. A permanent building was erected on that location, between Beekman and Fulton streets, in 1869. Initially most fish sold there were delivered by fishing schooners and sloops. By the late nineteenth century the use of refrigeration and express railroads allowed fish to be delivered from all parts of the United

Fulton Ferry and South Street, ca 1898. Manhattan terminal of the Fulton Ferry (designed by John Kellum) at lower right; Fulton Fish Market in center; Brooklyn Bridge in background

Fulton Fish Market, ca 1937

Fulton Fish Market

States and Canada and sometimes from abroad. A freshwater fish market developed near Peck Slip, catering primarily to Jewish customers. The market became the largest in the country and one of the largest in the world, and remained so into the 1990s. As the shipping industry moved away from the South Street district and general produce markets moved to the west side of Manhattan, the fish market took over the former Fulton Market west of South Street and most of the old brick buildings in the neighboring blocks. Fishing boats stopped landing their catch at the market in the late 1970s but occasionally tied up there to wait out bad weather. The slip behind the market between Piers 17 and 18 was eliminated in 1985 with the creation of a new Pier 17 accommodating a three-story shopping and eating mall. One of the last working areas of the waterfront in Manhattan and the last important vestige of outdoor wholesale markets until its close in November 2005, the Fulton Fish Market remained busy from midnight until 9 a.m., its streets choked with refrigerator trucks from all over the continent and the vans of local retailers. The city made efforts to move the fish market to other locations for four decades in order to create more modern facilities and end the influence of organized crime. An early plan to move to Hunts Point in the Bronx died in the city's financial crisis of the 1970s. During the 1980s work was begun on a "Fish Port" at Erie Basin in south Brooklyn, but this was also eventually abandoned. More stringent standards for refrigerating and handling fish adopted in the 1990s made the facilities on South Street too costly to upgrade. Finally, a 400,000-square-foot (37,000-square-meter) fully refrigerated indoor facility was built at the Hunts Point Food Distribution Center in the Bronx at the cost of more than $86 million, and the Fulton Fish Market moved to the New Fulton Fish Market at Hunts Point on 14 November 2005. Thirty-seven seafood wholesalers operated there in 2008, supplying retailers, supermarkets, and restaurants around the country. As in the old location on South Street, hours of operation are from midnight to 9 a.m. Two early twentieth-century buildings at the old Fulton Fish Market on the shore of the East River stood empty in 2008, awaiting demolition or adaptive reuse.

Norman J. Brouwer

Fun City. A mildly derisive nickname for New York City, coined and popularized by the newspaper columnist Dick Schaap, who was inspired by a remark made by Mayor John V. Lindsay during a severe transit strike in 1966: "I still think it's a fun city."

Gerald Leonard Cohen

Fund for the City of New York. Charitable organization formed in 1968 by the Ford Foundation. Its major focus is a management information program, under which staff members work with government agencies to improve accountability and assess performance. It also makes grants to advocacy groups and cash-flow loans to nonprofit recipients of government contracts. In the early twenty-first century it continued to promote efforts to improve the functioning of government and nonprofit organizations.

Kenneth W. Rose

furniture. Roughly hewn furniture of cheap construction was made before 1660 in New Amsterdam. In the second half of the eighteenth century the market for furniture expanded from a regional to an international scope. Artisans made chairs, tables, sideboards, and other furniture, largely in the American Chippendale style. Outstanding makers of furniture such as Andrew Gautier, Gilbert Ash, and Thomas Burling enabled the city to surpass Philadelphia in the quality, and probably also in the quantity, of furniture produced. As early as 1795 cabinetmakers shipped 5000 Windsor chairs from the city to the West Indies, and by the 1820s furniture was also being shipped to the southern United States and South America. The growing demand for furniture led to the demise of the traditional system of manufacture, in which a master cabinetmaker engaged in all aspects of production and trade, and to increased specialization: about this time independent firms engaged in chairmaking and upholstering. Growth also led to conflicts between master cabinetmakers and journeymen. In 1802 an organization of masters attempted to issue a new list of rates for piecework, leading to a strike by angry journeymen.

Furniture making reached its height in the city during the first half of the nineteenth century. Shops for the elite produced elaborately carved mahogany pieces that English visitors conceded were superior to the best found in London. The famous shops of Duncan Phyfe and Honoré Lannuier at the beginning of the century attracted skilled workers with high wages, as did that of John Henry Belter in the 1850s. At the same time more than 4000 poorly trained workers known as "botches" assembled cheaply made furniture in auction, or "slaughter," shops. In Little Germany such shops used an extensive division of labor to produce furniture for mass markets. The predominantly German employees of these shops earned $5 to $6 a week, about one-third what workers earned in shops of the first rank.

In the two decades before the Civil War about 85 percent of all furniture made in New York City was sold outside the city, and an increasing amount was sent to the West and California. Few economies of scale existed among manufacturers of either cheap or high-quality furniture: 80 to 100 workers were employed in the best shops, which in the 1860s included those of Edward Hutchings on Broome Street and Alexander Roux nearby on Mercer Street, but often fewer than 50 workers were employed in the many auction shops. In the 1870s workers in auction shops began organized protests against low wages, and by 1873 the German Cabinetmakers' Association had 4000 members, making it the largest German union in the city and enabling it to stand at the forefront of the movement for an eight-hour workday. The slow decline of the furniture industry in New York City began in the 1870s when Cincinnati and later Grand Rapids, Michigan, became major manufacturing centers, depriving the city of its western trade. Although New York City gradually lost the market for cheap furniture, it continued to lead the nation in the manufacture of custom-made and high-grade "imperial" furniture. Small shops remained concentrated in what is now SoHo, where they produced fashionable artistic pieces and employed highly skilled Italian workers who in 1919 could make $4.80 a day, twice the wage of the average worker in the trade. By 1925 the 384 furniture shops in the city employed only 10,402 workers, fewer than in Chicago or Grand Rapids, but the value of furniture produced exceeded that of all other cities at $71.8 million. Despite its tenacity, the industry faced increasing handicaps throughout the twentieth century, especially in the form of rising rents. High-grade work began to leave the city for factories in Grand Rapids and North Carolina (although showrooms were often maintained in Manhattan), and the firms that remained tended to rely on repair work to stay in business. Employment in furniture declined steadily as a proportion of the city's workforce from the 1920s into the early twenty-first century.

The Furniture Industry (New York: Merchant's Association of New York, 1919); Nancy McClelland, *Duncan Phyfe and the English Regency, 1795–1830* (New York: William R. Scott, 1939)

See also DECORATIVE ARTS and INTERIOR DESIGN.

Richard Stott

furs. The fur trade in New Netherland was conducted by private Dutch merchants until 1615 when a charter guaranteed to the New Netherland Company exclusive fur trading rights in the colony. The Dutch West India Company acquired these rights in 1621. Fur trading required a delicate balance among producers and distributors of wampum (small shell beads that Indians used as money, known as "mother of the beaver trade"), Indian suppliers, and merchants on both sides of the Atlantic, but because peltry was a source of quick profits and a substitute for scarce currency, settlers from many backgrounds scrambled to join the fur trade. Although beaver dominated the market, otter, mink, and muskrat skins were also exported. During the 1650s French and English competition for pelts forced Dutch traders to diversify into other exports; payment to merchants in New Amsterdam took the form of specie, which resulted in the devaluation of wampum and led to bidding wars between Indian suppliers and private traders. The fur trade was again hurt in the late 1660s when a shift in fashion preferences in England and Europe away from beaver hats and collars resulted in a glut of peltry. English merchants responded to these trends by trying to regulate furs. Although some merchants argued that the fur trade should be left open to competition, regulations were intermittently imposed until 1701 when a Treaty of Neutrality with French Canada and the Iroquois made it possible to reestablish an open trade policy.

Disputes in the colony over the fur trade continued over the next few decades, as English merchants dominated the market and tried to regulate it. Many merchants bypassed the New York City market entirely and established direct ties with traders in and around Albany; others, defying the British to the end of the colonial period, traded independently along the Hudson River and smuggled fur pelts across the Canadian border. These offenses were regularly mentioned as a menace to the imperial government in New York City throughout the 1750s and 1760s, even though the fur trade had long since become insignificant to the economy of Great Britain.

By the early nineteenth century New York City was the site of a thriving wholesale fur market. Most operations were small. A key figure in the fur business was John Jacob Astor, a resident of New York City who made attempts beginning in 1808 to control the fur trade in the Far West. He remained active as a trader until 1834. Both the city's wholesale market and a lively retail trade were on the Lower East Side by the end of the century, reflecting the heavy concentration there of German and first-generation eastern European Jewish merchants and fur workers.

Following the uptown move of the garment industry, the fur market moved to a compact area on the perimeter of Chelsea by 1922, occupying the blocks between 25th and 31st streets and between Sixth and Eighth avenues. This district became the locus for a skilled, highly differentiated, and labor-intensive business with a distinct eastern European culture: ethnic restaurants, a synagogue, and the steam baths in the old Pennsylvania Hotel were as much a part of the district as the racks of skins and bolts of silk for linings that moved through the streets. The business was characterized by militant unionism as well. After World War II charges of communist affiliation nearly destroyed the Fur and Leather Workers Union, an offshoot of the Fur Workers' Union (formed in 1849).

The fur business reached its peak in the city during the 1940s and 1950s. Decentralization, manufacturing competition from Asia (notably from Korea and later China), and an aging of the first generation of merchants whose American-educated children were not interested in the fur business caused a sharp decline in the number of shops and workers in the city. Greek merchants appeared to take the place of the Jews. Fur retailers during the 1970s and 1980s sought to broaden the market, seeking in particular to appeal to the new group of young working women by emphasizing relatively low-priced fur coats that were ready made rather than custom made. The effort met with some success, and from 1977 to 1986 retail sales of furs in the United States tripled. By the late 1980s, however, the fur business suffered from a worsening U.S. economy, increasing competition from foreign companies, the highly visible tactics of the animal-rights movement, and the growing popularity of synthetic furs. Between 1979 and 1989 the number of fur manufacturers and wholesalers in New York City declined from 800 to about 300, and employment declined from 3600 to 1900.

Although a distinct fur district is only faintly evident in the twenty-first century, New York City has remained the center of the highly specialized fur industry in the United States. There is no longer any fur manufacturing in the city, nor is there a union presence, but retail sales are strong, trade organizations such as the Fur Information Council of America and the Associated Fur Manufacturers maintain offices in the city, and a number of trade periodicals are still published there. Few Jewish firms are still in business; Greeks and Koreans dominate the trade.

Philip S. Foner, *Fur and Leather Workers Union: A Story of Dramatic Struggles and Achievements* (Newark, N.J.: Nordan, 1950); Thomas Elliot Norton, *The Fur Trade in Colonial New York, 1686–1776* (Madison: University of Wisconsin Press, 1974)

Elaine S. Abelson, Cathy Matson

fusionism. In politics, coalitions of political parties and factions. This became a means of circumventing political machines during the 1840s in New York City, and after the Civil War fusionism became the principal strategy for those who sought political reform. Republicans, reform Democrats, and nonpartisan civic organizations repeatedly united to defeat mainstream candidates (almost always Democrats). Municipal reforms successfully backed by fusion movements included the introduction of the secret ballot, the rescheduling of city elections to odd-numbered years (so as not to coincide with state and national elections), and changes in the civil service. Fusion campaigns elected reform candidates such as Seth Low (1901), Fiorello H. La Guardia (1933), and John V. Lindsay (1965), but fusionists suffered from their rejection of the "spoils system," an inability to maintain party structures, a tendency for lawyers and other professionals within their administrations to tire quickly of governance, the Democratic practice of painting fusionists as elitists hostile to the working class, and the splintering of fusion coalitions by national elections.

Peter Field

F. W. Woolworth Company. Firm of retailers often referred to as Woolworth's. It was formed as a five-and-dime store in 1879 in Lancaster, Pennsylvania, by Frank Winfield Woolworth, who later took on his brother Charles Sumner Woolworth as a partner. A pioneer in retail, Woolworth's was one of the first stores with fixed prices and allowed customers to browse among wares lying out on display instead of keeping all items behind the counter. In 1886 Frank Woolworth moved the company's headquarters to a small office in New York City at 104 Chambers Street in order to cut out wholesalers and deal directly with manufacturers. In 1896 he opened his first store in the city at 17th Street and Sixth Avenue. He planned window displays and designed the red store front himself. In 1911 Frank and Charles incorporated the F. W. Woolworth Company to bring together the 596 affiliated stores. The chain became successful by selling necessary articles cheaply, and when its corporate headquarters moved into the newly erected WOOLWORTH BUILDING in New York City, the tallest building in the world at the time, it had more than 1000 stores in North America. Woolworth's remained in business into the 1990s, by which time it had lost much of its market share to other chain retailers. In 1997 the company began to focus on sporting goods, reinvented its corporate identity as Venator Group, and moved corporate headquarters to 112 West 34th Street. In 2001 the firm changed its name to Foot Locker Inc.

See also WOOLWORTH, F. W.

James E. Mooney

G

Gaelic Athletic Association of Greater New York [NYGAA]. Athletic association. Formed in 1914, it consists of members from 62 clubs that compete in traditional sports. The association arranges and oversees championship matches in Gaelic football, hurling, and camogie (women's hurling), which together are known as the Games of the Gael, and also offers instruction in these games to Irish American youths.

John J. Concannon

Gaelic Park. Park in the Bronx at 240th Street and Broadway. The land was acquired in 1926 by two members of the Gaelic Athletic Association of Greater New York (NYGAA), which in 1928 began using the site for Irish football and hurling events. In the late 1930s the owners went bankrupt, and the land was taken over by the city (it eventually passed to the Metropolitan Transit Authority). John O'Donnell leased the park on behalf of the NYGAA in 1941 and with his family maintained the park's stadium, playing field, bar, and ballroom. After a series of disputes with the association, the family ended its involvement with the park. In 1991 Manhattan College leased the land and has since renovated it to host its lacrosse, soccer, and softball teams. Gaelic Park and its games played an important role in the social life of several generations of Irish immigrants.

George Winslow

Gage and Tollner. Restaurant in downtown Brooklyn, opened in 1879 on Fulton Street by Charles Gage. The following year Eugene Tollner became a partner, and in 1882 it moved to 374 Fulton Street. The restaurant was well known for its varied preparations of oysters, clams, scallops, and lobster and for its interior: the main dining room was 100 feet (30 meters) long and had mahogany tables (seating 220), walled mirrors, brocaded velvet, and gaslit chandeliers of cut glass. Both the interior and exterior were designated landmarks by the city. Gage and Tollner was owned by the Dewey family for 68 years until its sale in 1988 to Peter Aschkenasy. The restaurant closed in 2004 after 125 years of operation.

Stephen Weinstein

Gaine, Hugh (*b* Belfast, Ireland, 1726/27; *d* New York City, 25 April 1807). Newspaper publisher. Although penniless when he arrived in New York City in 1745, he founded and published the *New York Mercury* in 1752 (later called the *New York Gazette*) and became the most successful newspaper publisher in the city before the American Revolution; he also worked as a merchant in cosmetics. A founding member of the Friendly Sons of St. Patrick, he was an original trustee of the New York Society Library, the first lending library in the city.

Alfred Lawrence Lorenz, *Hugh Gaine: A Colonial Printer-Editor's Odyssey to Loyalism* (Carbondale: Southern Illinois University Press, 1972)

See also Book publishing, Booksellers, and Printing.

William McGimpsey

Gallatin, (Abraham Alfonse) Albert (*b* Geneva, Switzerland, 29 Jan 1761; *d* Astoria [now in Queens], 12 Aug 1849). Diplomat and banker. He married Hannah Nicholson, daughter of Commodore James Nicholson, in 1793 and was secretary of the treasury from 1801 to 1814 under Presidents Thomas Jefferson and James Madison. About 1810 he formed a close association with the financier and fur trader John Jacob Astor, and after retiring from service as a diplomat to France (1816–23) and Great Britain (1826–27) and moving to New York City (1827), he was persuaded by Astor to become the first president (1831) of the National Bank of New York City, a predecessor of Manufacturers Hanover. Although the bank remained small, Gallatin exercised great influence in financial matters during the 1830s and was instrumental in encouraging banks in New York City to resume specie payments during the banking crisis of 1837. He maintained a series of residences in the city until 1837, when he settled permanently at 57 Bleecker Street. In several published writings during the 1830s and 1840s he stressed that only gold and silver could serve as acceptable national currencies and that issues of banknotes must be strictly limited. Active in the political, intellectual, and cultural life of the city, he was a founding trustee of New York University (1827), a founder and the first president of the American Ethnological Society (1842), and a president of the New-York Historical Society (1843). He also published extensively on American Indian languages. During the last years of his life Gallatin denounced American participation in the Mexican–American War and urged reconciliation with Great Britain regarding competing claims over the Oregon Territory. He died at the home of his daughter Frances Stevens and is buried at Trinity Cemetery in lower Manhattan.

Henry Adams, *The Life of Albert Gallatin* (Philadelphia: J. B. Lippincott, 1879); Raymond Walters, Jr., *Albert Gallatin: Jeffersonian Financier and Diplomat* (New York: Macmillan, 1957)

G. Kurt Piehler

Gallo, Joe (Joseph) [Crazy Joe] (*b* Brooklyn, 7 April 1929; *d* New York City, 7 April 1972). Gangster and racketeer. With his brothers Lawrence and Albert he was part of a prominent Brooklyn organized crime family in the 1950s and was allegedly responsible for the 1957 barbershop assassination of crime boss Albert Anastasia. In 1961 Gallo was convicted of extortion and served 10 years in New York State prisons. Shortly after his parole, he was alleged to have orchestrated the June 1971 Columbus Circle shooting of another crime figure, Joseph Colombo, the leader of the Italian American Civil Rights League. In April 1972, celebrating his birthday with family members and a bodyguard, Gallo was fatally shot at Umberto's Clam House on Mulberry Street in Little Italy, in apparent retaliation for the Colombo shooting; the murder was never solved.

Albert A. Seedman and Peter Hellman, *Chief!* (New York: Arthur Fields, 1974)

Andrew Sparberg

gambling. Betting on shuffleboard, billiards, cards, and other games was common in all social classes in colonial New York City, as it was in Boston, Philadelphia, and Charleston. Often it enlivened gatherings in taverns, coffeehouses, and private homes where people sought diversion from the day's work. In the mid-eighteenth century lotteries were introduced from England and used by churches, public corporations, and the city government to raise money for charitable causes and public works. During the 1790s most forms of securities trading were considered gambling. At this time "policy" became widespread, especially among the poor, who wagered on one to four numbers from a list of 12 in a lottery drawing.

During the 1830s, when the city became the largest in the nation, its rapidly growing and affluent population sought new diversions. The demand for gambling increased despite concerns about public morality heightened by many scandals in lotteries during the first two decades of the nineteenth century and despite bans by the state legislature on lotteries in the 1830s and gambling halls and other public gambling places in the 1840s. Professional gamblers were soon linked to city politics and popular entertainment, thus creating the basis for organized crime. New card games were developed. One of the first was faro, introduced in the city in the 1840s: by placing chips or money on a cloth embossed with a suit of cards, players bet on which card would appear next from a deck turned facedown in a dealing box. Faro was the most popular card game of chance in the city during the nineteenth century because of its speed and because the odds were more favorable to the bettor than in any other card game, even though operators cheated in many ways. From 1835 gamblers opened posh "hells," forerunners of modern casinos, in choice locations along Broadway from 24th Street to the Battery. By the 1860s there were about 100 hells; wealth and connections to government allowed the proprietors to operate quite openly.

The introduction of horse racing, baseball, and boxing provided opportunities for gamblers, who built racetracks, helped to arrange matches, and offered betting services. John Morrissey, a boxer popular among Irish workers, helped to build the first major racetrack in the United States at Saratoga Springs, New York (1864), and became the most important gambler in the city. Shortly after the Civil War he developed the first off-track betting system in the city, in which results from Saratoga were relayed by telegraph to a partner's "poolroom"; eventually fans could bet on sporting events anywhere in the country and receive the results almost immediately. Off-track betting and bookmaking were developed during the 1870s and soon became commonly operated around the city.

Although gambling was technically illegal the city's gamblers conducted their business openly, shielded from arrest by their money, political influence, and tight organization. Some professional gamblers formed ties with the heads of political machines, such as Big Tim Sullivan, a leader of Tammany Hall who was elected to the U.S. Congress and the state senate; others held political office in the wards where they maintained their operations. The public's acceptance of gambling encouraged shrewd entrepreneurs. Between 1909 and 1920 Arnold Rothstein built a gambling empire and became nationally known after allegedly rigging the outcome of the World Series of 1919. About this time some of the first prominent black gamblers in the city made their careers during the transformation of Harlem into a predominantly black neighborhood. Jose Enrique Miro, William Brunder, Big Joe Ison, and others introduced numbers games there in the 1920s, in which players bet on a single randomly generated number between zero and 999 and got paid 600 times their bet if the number "hit." Black numbers operators rose to political prominence. Several whites, including Dutch Schultz, also made money in Harlem by taking black operators as partners.

In the mid-twentieth century gambling was changed by the introduction of the telephone and the legalization of some forms of betting. By taking bets over the telephone, bookmakers made betting more convenient and obviated poolrooms and other public venues where they risked arrest. In 1939 voters ratified an amendment to the state constitution to legalize parimutuel betting at racetracks, which was taxed by the state. The revenues were so great that the city also levied a tax on track betting after World War II. The state legislature gradually undercut the municipal tax, prompting the city to seek other ways of earning income from gambling. After a decade of debate, off-track betting was introduced in 1971 but failed to produce as much revenue as expected; surcharges on winnings imposed later decreased payoffs and led bettors to continue betting with illegal bookmakers. In 1966 the legislature introduced a state lottery, which led to the decrease in the prevalence of numbers betting and became one of the largest in the nation after the state made drawings more frequent, introduced a range of games, and increased the value of prizes.

Three-card monte on the beach at Coney Island, 1866

Mayor Fiorello H. La Guardia destroying a slot machine, ca *1935*

In the early twenty-first century underground casinos and card rooms continue to operate, as does the occasional three-card monte dealer on the street. Churches and other nonprofit groups also raise money by holding large-scale bingo games and raffles, which although illegal are tolerated by the authorities.

David R. Johnson

gangs. The first street gangs in New York City were formed at the end of the eighteenth century by journeymen and apprentices free of their masters' control outside their workshops. These single young men organized loosely structured groups associated with neighborhoods, streets, and trades. Gangs harassed pedestrians and sometimes fought with each other over territory. By the Jacksonian period there were many gangs, attracting members from the trades least affected by industrialization and sometimes from volunteer fire companies. Such groups as the Chichesters, composed mainly of apprentice and journeymen butchers, survived for many years and maintained a hierarchical membership of older leaders and young followers. Gangs were especially popular on the Bowery, where gang members built self-esteem by taking part in pursuits outside the workplace such as brawling, carousing, going to the theater, and target shooting. Many wore long sideburns (called soap locks) and distinctive clothing, emblems of the male culture of the Bowery that became widely known through stories about the "B'hoy," a character depicted in the penny press and the popular theater. As neighborhoods in the city became divided along class lines, gangs congregated in saloons that increasingly became political as well as social institutions. During elections their allegiance was sought after by officeholders; they stole ballot boxes, intimidated supporters of rival candidates, and voted "early and often." Violence escalated during the 1840s as economic depression and an influx of Irish immigrants spurred a power struggle between native-born and immigrant groups. Gangs such as the Spartan Association, led by the radical Democrat Mike Walsh, fought with fists, clubs, and guns.

Irish immigrants changed the structure of gangs. When they moved to the city they often transferred to the gangs their allegiance to factions and secret societies in Ireland. In Irish working-class wards such gangs as the Dead Rabbits defended their neighborhoods against outside forces ranging from temperance advocates to rival gangs like the nativist Bowery Boys. But gangs also fed conflict within communities, and during the mid-nineteenth century neighborhoods were often divided according to unstable alliances that sometimes erupted into violence.

After the Civil War Tammany Hall united many gangs into political clubs run by district leaders. At the same time gangs became increasingly segregated by age, as district leaders sponsored "social clubs" for teenagers. Gangs remained tied to their ethnic groups but also became efficient political tools, frequently providing a link among politicians, gambling, and prostitution. By the turn of the twentieth century adult gang members were often small-time organized-crime figures engaged in citywide racketeering. Increasingly, gangs exacerbated class conflict within ethnic communities: during strikes over unionizing the garment trades on the Lower East Side, local *shtarkes* (sluggers) were hired by both Jewish manufacturers and union organizers.

During the Progressive era reformers identified gang membership as a form of juvenile delinquency. Similar analyses were made in the 1950s, when conflicts among white, black, and Latin American gangs aroused widespread concern, and the popularity of gangs was attributed to economic deprivation, psychological disorders, and a breakdown of social institutions. Widespread violence between black and Latin American gangs declined during the 1960s, a decline variously attributed to youth politics, the military draft, and drug addiction. Gang violence resumed in the early 1970s, when it spread from the South Bronx to the other boroughs. In 1975 the police identified 275 gangs with 11,000 members; estimates in the mid-1980s ranged from 4300 to 40,000 members.

In 1994 a Gang Task Force was formed to help deal with the problem of gangs in city jails. The Gang Intelligence Task Force came into being in 1996 to collect information and monitor gang members; it then became the Gang Intelligence Unit and subsequently the Intelligence Unit. In the twenty-first century the New York City Police Department succeeded in reducing gang violence, and gangs in the city were less powerful than they were in Los Angeles, Chicago, Houston, and other large U.S. cities. Some of the gangs in the early twenty-first century were the Ghost Shadows; the Jamaican Posse; and Sex, Money, Murda.

Anne Campbell, *The Girls in the Gang: A Report from New York City* (New York: Basil Blackwell, 1984)

Joshua Brown, Lisa Keller

Gansevoort Farmers' Street Market. Open-air farmers' market established in 1884, covering a little more than 2 acres (0.8 hectare) and bounded to the north by Little West 12th Street, to the east by Washington Street, to the south by Gansevoort Street, and to the west by West Street. Its use was restricted by law to farmers and gardeners, most of whom drove to the city daily from Long Island and New Jersey to sell their produce to peddlers and retailers. In 1887 the city widened Gansevoort Street to allow more vendors in the area. By 1926, with property in the area gaining in value, the city moved to close the farmers' market, and the transformation of the area into a meatpacking and meat distribution center began. In the twenty-first century the old market is part of the larger MEATPACKING DISTRICT in the city.

Suzanne R. Wasserman

Garbo [Gustafson], **Greta (Lovisa)** (*b* Stockholm, 18 Sept 1905; *d* New York City, 15 April 1990). Actress. While studying acting in Stockholm, she met the Swedish director Maurice Stiller, who took her to Hollywood in 1925; there she signed a contract with Metro–Goldwyn–Mayer. After appearing in silent films she gave memorable performances in the film version of Eugene O'Neill's *Anna Christie* (1930), *Ninotchka* (1939, her first comedy), *Grand Hotel* (1932), and *Camille* (1936), for which she won the New York Film Critics Award. After retiring in 1941 Garbo remained largely in seclusion in New York City. She lived at 2 Beekman Place (in the 1930s), the Ritz Tower, and the Campanile, 450 East 52nd Street. Garbo was known for her glamorous appearance and husky voice.

Leslie Gourse

García Rivera, Oscar (*b* Mayaguez, Puerto Rico, 6 Nov 1900; *d* Mayaguez, 1969). Politician. The first Puerto Rican elected to public

Gansevoort Farmers' Street Market

office in the continental United States, he moved to New York City in 1925. Initially, he worked for the Boorum and Pease Binder factory and then in the City Hall Postal Office. An active participant in the Postal Clerk's Union of America, he promoted union membership and advocated for better working conditions. He earned an undergraduate degree from Columbia University and received a law degree from St. John's College in 1930, among the college's first graduating class. With backing from the American Labor Party, the Republican Party, and the City Fusion Party he challenged Tammany Hall and was elected a state assemblyman from Manhattan in 1937, representing the 17th Assembly District. In public office until 1940, he supported civil rights legislation, civil service reform, child labor reform, workers' rights, and hot meals in public schools. He provided pro bono service for those in need of legal counseling in Puerto Rican neighborhoods and worked to increase voter registration, educational programs, and labor reform. In 2002 the East Harlem "Hellgate" post office was renamed the Oscar García Rivera Post Office.

René Torres Delgado, *El primer legislador puertorriqueño en Nueva York: Oscar García Rivera* (San Juan: Colección Hipatia, 1979)

Virginia Sánchez Korrol

Garden Bay Manor. Neighborhood in northwestern Queens, bounded to the north by 19th Avenue, to the east by 81st and 82nd streets, and to the south by Grand Central Parkway; it is the easternmost part of Ditmars and abuts the Marine Air Terminal. The name was coined by the original developers. Most of the apartments are in the garden style.

Vincent Seyfried

Garfield, John [Garfinkle, Jacob Julius] (*b* New York City, 4 Mar 1913; *d* New York City, 21 May 1952). Actor. He grew up on Rivington Street on the Lower East Side; then moved to Brownsville, Brooklyn; and finally settled in the Bronx. He was placed in a school for difficult children and was introduced to boxing to channel his aggression and to speech and drama classes to help with his stammer. In 1932 he made his Broadway debut and two years later joined the Group Theatre. He was one of the first actors to set up his own production company and was noted for his progressive thinking when he insisted that Canada Lee, a black actor, be featured in his famous film *Body and Soul* (1947). He also stared in *Four Daughters* (1938) and *The Postman Always Rings Twice* (1946). He is considered the predecessor of "Method" actors like Marlon Brando and James Dean.

Jessica Montesano

Garibaldi, Giuseppe (*b* Nice, France, 4 July 1807; *d* Caprera, Italy, 2 June 1882). Soldier, political leader, and founder of modern Italy. New York City was a brief stop in Garibaldi's global military and political career. Escaping the Roman republic's collapse in 1849, he slipped into the United States via Staten Island on 30 July 1850. He lived and worked with the compatriot and inventor Antonio Meucci at the latter's candle works until resuming his original profession, seafaring. He sailed for Peru in 1851, returned to New York in 1853, and left the United States permanently that November for England. In 1888 New York City's Italian American community placed Giovanni Turini's statue of Garibaldi in Washington Square Park. His home on Staten Island, which is now the Garibaldi–Meucci Memorial Museum, 420 Tompkins Avenue, is part of the Garibaldi Memorial, which was dedicated in 1907 to mark 100 years since his birth.

Jasper Godwin Ridley, *Garibaldi* (New York: Viking, 1974)

Mary Elizabeth Brown

Garibaldi Memorial, ca *1900*

Garinagu [Garifuna, singular]. Afro-Caribbean people forcibly exiled to Belize, Honduras, Nicaragua, and Guatemala during the late eighteenth century. According to immigration records the Garinagu may have arrived in New York City as early as 1925. After World War II Garinagu men, working for the U.S. Merchant Marines, migrated with their families in large numbers. The peak period of migration was the 1960s, following amendments to the U.S. Immigration and Nationality Act and the devastation caused by Hurricane Hattie in Central America. By the early twenty-first century more than 10,000 Garinagu, mainly from Honduras, had settled in areas of Brooklyn, Manhattan, and the southern Bronx, where they interact with African American and Latino populations yet maintain their unique Garifuna language and traditional family ties.

Emilyn L. Brown

garment district. Section of Manhattan dominated by the garment industry, located in the 30s between Madison and Eighth avenues. The area took shape during the late nineteenth century and soon became the country's leading center of garment production. Initially concentrated in tenements on the Lower East Side, the garment business gradually moved north and west as garment manufacturers were driven by law from residential buildings into lofts and increasingly required fancy showrooms for marketing. The district centered on Madison Square by 1910, but the garment trades were forced out by the Fifth Avenue Association during the following decade as the area became fashionable for shopping. In 1920 two sites along Seventh Avenue between 36th and 38th streets were developed by the Garment Center Realty Company, an association of 38 large manufacturers of women's clothing, which soon revitalized an area formerly known as the Tenderloin. By 1931 the garment district had the largest concentration of apparel manufacturers in the world and lay in the heart of Manhattan near hotels, the main retail district, and important railroad terminals in an area bounded by 42nd Street, Sixth Avenue, 30th Street, and Ninth Avenue. Traffic crowded Sixth, Seventh, and Eighth avenues, and along the side streets trucks delivered material and loaded finished garments carted through traffic on hand trucks by "push boys." At noon thousands of workers, mostly im-

Handcarts and clothing racks on Seventh Avenue, early 1990s

migrants from eastern and southern Europe, made their way through the streets to local cafeterias and lingered to smoke before resuming work at one o'clock. After World War II the garment district remained essentially in place, though by the 1980s a large amount of production had returned to lower Manhattan, especially to Chinatown and the Lower East Side.

Allen J. Share

garments. The shift from custom-made to ready-made clothing in the United States during the Industrial Revolution was stimulated by the growth of the middle class and a large increase in foreign-born labor. As the chief port of entry for immigrants to the United States, New York City became the nation's leading center of garment production by the mid-nineteenth century. Irish and German workers entered the garment trade in the 1840s; Germans introduced the practice of home manufacturing to the garment industry. Aided by Elias Howe's invention of the sewing machine in 1846, apparel was the fastest-growing industry in New York City from 1830 to 1860; in 1858 it employed 32,000 workers.

Most German Jewish immigrants who settled in New York City in the mid-nineteenth century went to work in the thriving secondhand clothing trade of Chatham Street, in an area popularly called Jerusalem. They were less common than many other immigrant groups in the prestigious ready-made trade of the Bowery and lower Broadway. Women predominated in the ready-made trade, men (who were usually paid more) in the custom trade. By the 1870s technology and immigration brought about the displacement of both women and skilled men: unskilled male newcomers readily learned to use the foot-powered sewing machine, and men were more adept than women at handling a newly invented heavy cutting knife (1875) that supplanted conventional shears. Women were further displaced in the 1870s by men from Germany and Austria-Hungary who worked for substandard wages. Women who remained in the late nineteenth century worked in three kinds of shops: the inside shop, operated by a manufacturer using his own employees; the home shop, where workers assisted by family members assembled goods brought home from the factory; and the outside shop, operated by a contractor who received an assignment from a manufacturer and used either factory or home labor.

Unregulated industrial homework in unsanitary conditions became characteristic of lower Manhattan, among not only Germans but also Irish and Italians. Contractors enjoyed a competitive advantage because the cost of home labor was minimal. Despite long hours, filth, and low pay, newcomers from Europe often worked additional time so that they could afford to send for family members still in Europe. Economic distress and religious persecution of Jews in Russia during the early 1880s led to a flood of immigrants into New York City; most were working in the garment trade soon after their arrival and were sympathetic toward unionism and socialism.

The first wave from southern Italy, known as *contadini,* or peasants, immigrated in the 1880s. Italian men with experience in the garment trades frequently found work in custom tailoring; those without experience became sewing-machine operators and pressers. By 1900 Italian women who were experienced home manufacturers monopolized home garment finishing in New York City, making four to five cents an hour; single Italian women were more likely to work outside the home than those who were married. The Italian sewing-machine operators and pressers were nonunionized and charged little, enabling them to become the leading ethnic group in the needle trades by the 1930s.

Jews from Russia and Poland who immigrated after 1903 to escape pogroms were more highly skilled than their predecessors. Many were members of the Jewish Labor Bund, formed in 1897 to promote socialism and cultural nationalism. Working conditions worsened with the development of the "task" system, under which teams of workers employed by a contractor were paid not by the hour but for a set amount of work, which nevertheless was to be completed within a specified time. Contractors often added to the daily workload, and the workday could last as long as 18 hours. The influx of immigrants spurred marked growth between 1880 and 1900, particularly in women's apparel: employment rose from 11,696 to 83,739. In the 1880s alone makers of women's apparel increased by 226.2 percent, makers of men's apparel by 117.8 percent.

Led by cutters of ladies' garments, Jewish garment workers in New York City began to organize unions during the 1880s. Socialist intellectuals formed the United Hebrew Trades to promote unionism, and by 1900 representatives of seven unions formed the International Ladies' Garment Workers' Union (ILGWU). In the following year the United Cloth Hat and Cap Makers of North America was formed at a convention. During its first decade the ILGWU struggled for survival, but during 1909–10 it was revitalized by successful strikes of shirtwaist workers and cloak makers; the cloak makers' walkout ensured the adoption of the "Protocol of Peace," which provided for the resolution of disputes between labor and management and the protection of workers' health. In 1911 a fire at the Triangle Shirtwaist Company in Greenwich Village took 146 lives, shocking the public and persuading the state legislature to enact 36 new labor laws within three years. The victory of the cloak makers in 1910 encouraged fur workers to organize a strike in 1912 that led to the founding the following year of the International Fur Workers' Union of the United States and Canada. In 1914 Jewish and Italian workers in the men's clothing trade withdrew from the United Garment Workers of America and formed the Amalgamated Clothing Workers of America.

Garment workers' unions were riven by conflicts during the 1920s, as communists challenged socialists for control of the needle trades. By the 1930s the communists won over the furriers. Extortion and racketeering were widespread in the garment industry during the first half of the twentieth century, and organized-crime figures worked for both labor and management. Among the best known were Benjamin "Dopey Benny" Fein, Jacob "Little Augie" Orgen, Arnold Rothstein, Louis "Lepke" Buchalter, and Jacob "Gurrah" Shapiro. Neither Thomas E. Dewey, the special prosecutor during the 1930s, nor other prosecutors in later years were able to eliminate the criminal element.

In addition to enjoying a ready pool of immigrant workers, the garment industry in New York City benefited from the proximity of textile mills in Massachusetts, New Jersey, and upstate New York. The industry prospered and moved uptown, following the growth of the city and new transportation patterns; gradually a new garment center took shape on the West Side, extending north from 34th to 40th streets and west from Sixth to Ninth avenues. Apparel manufacturers moved into buildings with showrooms. In the 1920s women began wearing dresses rather than skirts and blouses, a change that increased the importance of merchandising and gave rise to the jobber, who designed garments to be manufactured under contract and later sold them to retailers. In the knit outerwear trade, jobbers were sometimes called converters, a term that in the industry as a whole usually referred to those who obtained raw fabric for conversion into finished products. Apparel firms also depended on credit, especially to produce seasonal lines; among the more important lenders were factors, or "textile bankers," who used accounts receivable as security to finance manufacturing. Although merchandise continued to be sold in Manhattan, the availability of highways and trucks made it feasible to move production to cheaper locations in Brooklyn, New Jersey, and Connecticut. The city's share of the nation's employment in women's apparel declined from 62 percent in 1914 to 41 percent in 1939. The federal government banned industrial homework in 1942.

After World War II new production sites were set up in the South, Southwest, and West. Unskilled labor in these areas manufactured low- and medium-priced garments and new lines of casual wear. Easy-care finishes and improved cotton fabrics revolutionized the industry. Garment firms consolidated, making the small firm an anachronism. From the 1950s the quest for cheap labor moved much garment production to Hong Kong, South Korea, Taiwan, mainland China, and Japan, and later to Africa, eastern Europe, and Latin America. Meanwhile Jews and Italians in the industry were displaced by blacks and Puerto Ricans. After the Immigration Act of 1965 ended quotas based on national origin, the apparel trade attracted large numbers of Dominicans and Chinese: manufacturing expanded greatly in Chinatown, and by 1985 more than 16 percent of the city's garment workers were Chinese.

A large pool of exploitable, undocumented immigrants, stiff competition from imports, and lax enforcement of labor standards because of budget cuts brought about a return of the sweatshop in the 1970s and 1980s. In 1984 the U.S. Department of Labor rescinded its ban on homework in six of the nation's seven apparel-related industries. Women's clothing was the exception. In 1987 there were an estimated 3000 sweatshops and 30,000 home apparel workers in New York State. By 1990 low-priced imports controlled 60 percent of the domestic market. Although apparel remained a leading manufacturing industry in New York City, in 1993 it employed only 86,000 workers, 53,600 fewer than in 1980.

The Garment Industry Development Corporation, established in 1984 by labor and management with municipal and state funds, assists garment manufacturers in New York City with marketing, management education, and training programs. It sometimes works in cooperation with the Fashion Institute of Technology, opened in 1944 to train workers and managers. The continued vitality of this enterprise is borne out by prominent designers and companies with headquarters and some production in the city: among them are Bill Blass, Oscar de la Renta, Marc Jacobs, Donna Karan, Ralph Lauren, Nicole Miller, and Vera Wang. In 2007 companies based in New York City accounted for annual sales of $47 billion and maintained 5400 showrooms.

Manufacturing, however, continued to decline: garment industry employment in the city fell by 39.6 percent between 2001 and 2005. The terrorist attacks on the World Trade Center of 11 September 2001 had a devastating effect on manufacturing in Chinatown. One hundred of more than 250 factories in the area in 2000 disappeared, and Chinatown's share of garment manufacturing was halved to less than 10 percent by 2005. Rising rents and real estate values, as well as imports and police security restrictions, compounded the difficulties. By the early twenty-first century there were only 1900 apparel manufacturing jobs in Chinatown and 22,900 in New York City.

Roger Waldinger, *Through the Eye of the Needle: Immigrants and Entrepreneurs in New York's Garment Trades* (New York: New York University Press, 1986); Nancy L. Green, *Ready-to-Wear and Ready-to-Work: A Century of Industry and Immigrants in Paris and New York* (Durham, N.C.: Duke University Press, 1997); Xiaolan Bao, *Holding up More Than Half the Sky: Chinese Women Garment Workers in New York City, 1948–92* (Urbana: University of Illinois Press, 2001); Margaret M. Chin, *Sewing Women: Immigrants and the New York City Garment Industry* (New York: Columbia University Press, 2005); Daniel Soyer, ed., *A Coat of Many Colors: Immigration, Globalization, and Reform in New York City's Garment Industry* (New York: Fordham University Press, 2005)

Robert D. Parmet

Garnet, Henry Highland (*b* New Market, Md., 23 Dec 1815; *d* Monrovia, Liberia, 13 Feb 1882). Abolitionist. Born into slavery, at age nine he fled his owner's plantation with his father, mother, and older sister. The family eventually settled in New York City, where Garnet found work as a cabin attendant aboard a ship. In 1829 his sister was captured by slave hunters and then detained by local authorities and tried as a fugitive slave (she was released after several days). To avoid capture he hid at a friend's home on Long Island, where he remained for two years as an indentured farm laborer. He later studied at African Free School no. 1, on Mulberry Street, and at the High School for Colored Youth. Garnet completed his education in 1840 at the Oneida Institute in Whitesboro, New York, and became a minister and political activist. At the Negro Convention of 1843 in Buffalo, New York, he delivered a speech addressed to slaves in the South, declaring, "Let your motto be resistance! resistance! resistance!" Soon the most important and militant black abolitionist in New York City, Garnet was known internationally by 1850, made speeches throughout the northern and western states, and traveled to Europe as a representative of the abolitionist movement. After joining the United Presbyterian Church of Scotland he worked as a missionary in Jamaica from 1852 to 1855 and in 1856 became pastor of the Shiloh Presbyterian Church in New York City, where he eulogized such abolitionist martyrs as John Brown, held antislavery meetings, and urged blacks to support the Liberty and Free Soil parties, stressing in his sermons that slavery would not be ended by moral suasion alone. His strong support for the Civil War inspired hundreds of blacks from the city to enlist in the Union army; he himself recruited blacks for the army and became a chaplain for black troops. At President Abraham Lincoln's invitation he delivered a speech before the U.S. House of Representatives on 22 September 1864, the second anniversary of the Emancipation Proclamation. Garnet returned to the Shiloh Presbyterian Church after the war and in 1881 accepted an appointment as the U.S. diplomatic minister to Liberia.

Thelma Foote

Garth, David (Lawrence) (*b* Brooklyn, 5 March 1930). Political consultant. He worked in television in the late 1950s as a sports producer and in 1960 co-chaired the Adlai Stevenson campaign committee for the Democratic presidential nomination with Eleanor Roosevelt. In 1965 he was the principal adviser to John V. Lindsay's successful mayoral campaign, in which he used television, radio, and other media to great effect: his election techniques are widely regarded as having inaugurated the modern era of political campaigning in New York City. He then became one of the city's most successful and sought-after political media strategists, leading Lindsay's successful reelection campaign (1969) as well as the mayoral campaigns of Edward I. Koch (1977, 1981, 1985, 1989) and Rudolph W. Giuliani (1993). Garth was also the media strategist in Governor Mario M. Cuomo's unsuccessful campaign for a fourth term in 1994. His firm, the Garth Group, is at 1 West 67th Street in Manhattan.

James Bradley

Garvey, Marcus (Mosiah) (*b* St. Ann's Bay, Jamaica, 17 Aug 1887; *d* London, 10 June 1940). Black nationalist. After travel in Central America and a year in England, Garvey settled in 1914 in Kingston, Jamaica, where he formed the Universal Negro Improvement Association (UNIA). A devout Catholic and a disciple of Booker T. Washington, he sought to instill black pride through industrial training of the sort offered by the Tuskegee Institute and through Christian missionary work in Africa. He moved to the United States in 1916 and the following year settled in Harlem, where he formed a branch of UNIA that proved short-lived. In June he gave a fiery speech at a rally for the Colored Liberty League that gained him prominence. Over the next two years the emphasis of his politics changed from racial accommodation to black pride and Africanism, and UNIA became a powerful group with hundreds of chapters in the United States and Africa. To finance his movement and encourage black enterprise he formed a shipping firm, the Black Star Line, which launched its flagship, the *Frederick Douglass,* in November 1919 and acquired two other ships in 1920. That same year he undertook a plan to have black Americans colonize Africa and began negotiations with the government of Liberia. In the years following he sent funds as well as equipment and engineers to that country. By 1922 UNIA was foundering, the Black Star Line was being mismanaged and was soon to be bankrupt, and the Liberian government withdrew its colonization agreement. Garvey was then sent to prison on federal charges of mail fraud that were undeniably motivated by politics. After his release in 1927 he was deported to Jamaica.

Edmund David Cronon, *Black Moses: The Story of Marcus Garvey and the Universal Negro Improvement Association* (Madison: University of Wisconsin Press, 1955)

Greg Robinson

Marcus Garvey at Liberty Hall in Harlem, 1920

Gashouse District. Former name for a neighborhood on the East Side of Manhattan, bounded to the north by 27th Street, to the east by the East River, to the south by 14th Street, and to the west by Park Avenue South. A number of gas tanks were built near the East River in 1842; they leaked and emitted a foul stench that pervaded the area, which was initially populated mostly by Irish immigrants. A group of young toughs known as the Gashouse Gang terrorized the neighborhood until order was imposed by a police officer known as Clubber Williams. Germans and Jews moved in after the Civil War, Italians during the late nineteenth century. The popular culture of the district and the sashaying antics of its young women inspired Safford Waters's tremendously popular song "The Belle of Avenoo A" (1895). Several hospitals were built in the area: the Lying-In Hospital for indigent women (1822; later converted into luxury housing but maintaining a small museum), Columbus Hospital on 19th Street (1892; initially patronized by Italian immigrants and known as the Cabrini Medical Center [closed in 2008]), Willard Parker Hospital for Contagious Diseases, the New York Post Graduate Medical School and Hospital, and the New York Skin and Cancer Hospital. Most of these facilities were later replaced by the Beth Israel Hospital complex. During and after World War I Slovaks moved to the neighborhood, which was considered part of the Lower East Side. Most residents lived in old-law tenements; public baths on 23rd Street and Avenue A were the only bathing facilities for many. Lodging sponsored by the city for homeless men stood on 25th Street, and the first building of the American Society for the Prevention of Cruelty to Animals opened on 24th Street. The northern end of the neighborhood was the site of the largest enclave of Armenians in New York City. Some gas tanks remained in operation until after World War II. In 1947 and 1948 the tenements east of First Avenue, along with the remaining gashouses, were replaced by Stuyvesant Town and Peter Cooper Village. The working-class character of the neighborhood changed as the housing was upgraded during the 1970s and 1980s. The northern section of the area became largely Indian in the late 1980s.

Harriet Davis-Kram, Andrew Sparberg

gas lighting. System of public lighting introduced in New York City in 1823. The New York Gas Company was initially given exclusive rights to lay gas pipe in the streets of Manhattan below Grand, Sullivan, and Canal streets, but as the city grew, so did the gas franchises and gas lines, and by 1847 contracts had been awarded for lines stretching up to 42nd Street. Over the course of the nineteenth century, franchises vied for control of the New York City market, and in 1884 the New York, Manhattan, Harlem, Metropolitan, Municipal, and Knickerbocker gas light companies combined to form the Consolidated Gas Company of New York, now known as Consolidated Edison.

Alexander Lurkis, *The Power Brink: Con Edison, a Centennial of Electricity* (New York: Icare Press, 1982)

Elizabeth L. Bradley

gated communities. Residential enclaves that are enclosed with gates and sometimes have guardhouses. Although such communities are common in the American South and West, they are rare in the New York City area, unless one argues that apartment buildings with 24-hour door attendants are essentially gated communities. Those of the more traditional variety in New York City include Breezy Point in Queens, and Sea Gate, Bay Front Estates, and Mill Harbor condominiums in Brooklyn. There are dozens of such communities in the city suburbs, including two that are famous—Llewellyn Park in West Orange, New Jersey, and Tuxedo Park in Rockland County, New York.

Kenneth T. Jackson

Gates, Frederick Taylor (*b* Maine, N.Y., 2 July 1853; *d* Phoenix, 6 Feb 1929). Philanthropic administrator and businessman. As the administrator of John D. Rockefeller's philanthropic endeavors he helped to advance medical research and strengthen colleges of medicine in the United States during the opening decades of the twentieth century. He envisioned, planned, and organized the Rockefeller Institute for Medical Research and was president of its board of trustees from 1901 until his death. Gates was also the chairman of the General Education Board of the Rockefeller Foundation (1905–12) and director of the foundation (1907–17).

Allen J. Share

Gates, Horatio (*b* Essex, England, 26 July 1727; *d* New York City, 10 Jan 1806). General. After serving as an officer in the British army for 25 years, he moved to Virginia in 1772. Asked by George Washington to serve as an officer in the Continental army at the outbreak of the American Revolution, Gates was the commanding general at the Battle of Saratoga in upstate New York. There his stunning defeat of 10,000 British troops under the command of General John Burgoyne marked the turning point in the war and made him a national hero; some members of the Continental Congress wanted him to succeed Washington as the head of the entire American army. In 1790 he moved to New York City from his estate in Virginia and married the daughter of a wealthy merchant. Their home in the city, set on an estate of 90 acres (36 hectares), stood at what is now 24th Street and Second Avenue. At the end of the 1790s he opposed the Federalist hold on local politics, and in 1800 he won a seat in the state assembly as a Democratic Republican with the backing of the Tammany Society. Gates is buried in an unmarked grave at Trinity Cemetery.

James S. Kaplan

Gates, John Warne (*b* near Turner Junction, Ill., 8 May 1855; *d* Paris, 9 Aug 1911). Financier and speculator. During the 1880s he made a fortune in the manufacture of barbed wire, and through various mergers he formed the American Steel and Wire Company (later Republic Steel), which was eventually sold to J. P. Morgan and the U.S. Steel Trust. Known to New Yorkers as "Bet a Million" Gates, he won and lost millions of dollars in the stock market and the commodity exchanges. He generally tried to rig deals in his own favor but did not always succeed. He also wagered thousands of dollars on horse races and card games and in casinos; purportedly he once bet on which raindrop would be the first to trickle down a windowpane. When in New York City Gates lived in a lavish suite at the Waldorf-Astoria.

George A. Thompson, Jr.

Gateway National Recreation Area. Recreation area created in 1972 under the auspices of the National Park Service, one of the first areas of its kind designated in a large metropolitan region. It is composed of 26,000 acres (10,530 hectares) distributed among three units: Jamaica Bay and Breezy Point in southeastern Brooklyn and southern Queens (bordering John F. Kennedy International Airport), the shoreline of eastern Staten Island, and Sandy Hook in New Jersey. In its eastern section lies the Jamaica Bay Wildlife Refuge, accessible by Cross Bay Boulevard. Opened in 1953 by Robert Moses and Herbert Johnson, the recreation area attracts more than 300 species of nesting and migrating birds to 9155 acres (3708 hectares) of protected wetlands; the site also sustains a butterfly garden. The area includes Floyd Bennett Field in Brooklyn, the first municipal airfield in the city; Fort Tilden in Breezy Point; the Rockaway Naval Air Station; and the playing fields and oceanfront beach of Jacob Riis Park. The section of the recreation area in Staten Island overlooks Lower New York and Raritan bays and encompasses Great Kills Park (originally an Algonquin site, now a recreational fishing area), Crookes Point (a habitat for plants and small animals), and Miller Field (formerly a hydroplane airport for the U.S. Air Corps). Sandy Hook features Sandy Hook Lighthouse, the oldest operating lighthouse in the United States (originally built to protect the outer harbor and regulate the shipping lanes); Fort Hancock; ocean dunes; and a rare holly forest. The recreation area conducts programs in historical and environmental education.

Rachel Shor

Gayle [née McCoy]**, Margot** [Sarah Margaret] (*b* Kansas City, 14 May 1908; *d* New York City, 28 Sept 2008). New York's "queen of cast-iron architecture" and advocate of landmarks preservation. In 1945 she moved to New York City and took a job as a scriptwriter at the Columbia Broadcasting System (CBS), where her interest in public clocks developed. In 1953 Gayle was named the public relations director for the City Department of Commerce and joined the Democratic Party effort as state committee woman and Manhattan district leader. In 1957 she organized the Village Neighborhood Committee to restore the clock at the JEFFERSON MARKET COURTHOUSE and to save the monument, which is now a public library, from the auction block. In 1961 the courthouse officially became a landmark, and in 1965 Gayle helped establish the LANDMARKS PRESERVATION COMMISSION, in direct response to the demolition of Penn Station. Around 1968 Gayle turned her attention to cast-iron buildings and became known for carrying around a magnet to illustrate the presence of iron in a building's structure. In 1970 she founded the Friends of Cast-Iron Architecture in an effort to save SoHo from the freeway plan, which failed in 1971. Two years later SoHo was designated as the SoHo Cast Iron Historic District. Between 1975 and 1992 Gayle wrote a weekly column for the *Daily News*. She worked with such New York icons as Jane Jacobs, E. E. Cummings, and Lewis Mumford, while also forming the Friends of the City's Historic Clocks and the Victorian Society of America. She lived on the Upper East Side until her death.

Cecilia Magnusson

Gay Men's Health Crisis [GMHC]. Not-for-profit, volunteer-supported, and community-based organization dedicated to supporting people with acquired immune deficiency syndrome. It was formed in 1981 by six gay men, including the author Larry Kramer. The same year, the organization established the first AIDS hotline using a volunteer's answering machine. The first GMHC offices were located in the Chelsea neighborhood on West 22nd Street in Manhattan. The New York City AIDS Walk, first held in 1986, has benefited GMHC for more than 20 years and is the largest private AIDS fund-raising event in the world, raising more than $5.8 million in 2006. GMHC continues to provide social services and legal assistance to those infected with the human immunodeficiency virus (HIV) or AIDS as well as acting as a leader in developing comprehensive prevention education programs. The organization serves more than 15,000 men, women, and families who are living with or are affected by HIV/AIDS in New York City, and advocates for scientific, evidence-based public health solutions for hundreds of thousands of people worldwide.

Anne Epstein

Gaynor, John P(lant) (*b* Ireland, 1826; *d* San Francisco, 1889). Architect. He moved to the United States in 1849, opened an office in Brooklyn in 1851, and established himself as a designer of commercial buildings with cast-iron facades in New York City in 1856–62. The best known of these was erected in 1856 at 490

Broadway for the retailer E. V. Haughwout. Like the Halsey Building (1856, demolished) on Fulton Street in downtown Brooklyn, it was patterned after Andrea Sansovino's library in Venice. The iron components of Haughwout's and Halsey's buildings were cast by Daniel Badger's Architectural Iron Works and illustrated in its catalogue.

Marjorie Pearson

Gaynor, William J(ay) (*b* Oriskany, N.Y., 2 Feb 1848; *d* on shipboard, 10 Sept 1913). Mayor and judge. In 1873 he settled in Brooklyn, where he worked as a journalist before becoming a lawyer and entering public affairs. Known as a reformer, he won election as a justice of the state supreme court in 1893 and reelection in 1907. During his terms he made contributions to libel and slander law and won respect for his protection of individual rights. In 1909 he won the Democratic mayoral nomination with the support of Charles F. Murphy, the boss of Tammany Hall, in response to citywide calls for reform. After winning a three-way election he formed a moderately progressive government. Soon after gaining office he appointed a number of officials without connections to Tammany Hall, eliminated "no-show" positions, and instituted fiscal reforms. After barely escaping an assassination attempt in August 1910, he became irascible and engaged in serious feuds; the rest of his term was marked by corruption in the police department and unsuccessful efforts to obtain a new city charter and win municipal ownership of the subways. Denied renomination by Tammany Hall in 1913, Gaynor declared his candidacy for reelection with support from reform groups but soon fell ill and died. He is remembered as one of the city's most independent mayors.

Mortimer B. Smith, *William Jay Gaynor: Mayor of New York* (Chicago: Henry Regnery, 1951); Lately Thomas, *The Mayor Who Mastered New York: The Life and Opinions of William J. Gaynor* (New York: William Morrow, 1969)

Robert F. Wesser

Gay Rights Bill. Bill amending the city's Human Rights Law that prohibits discrimination in housing, employment, and public accommodations on the basis of sexual orientation. A similar bill introduced before the City Council on 6 January 1971 by council members Carter Burden and Eldon Clingan was the first of its kind proposed in the United States. Before its eventual passage the bill was defeated in committee every year except 1974, when it became the first bill in the history of the City Council to pass out of committee and be defeated by a full vote of the council. The measure was reintroduced each year before being redrafted by Thomas B. Stoddard. It passed on 20 March 1986 by a vote of 21 to 15; following testimony on behalf of the community by leaders Stoddard and Virginia Apuzzo, it was signed into law on 2 April by Mayor Edward I. Koch.

Lee Hudson, Joan Nestle

gays. Because of its huge population, New York City in the late nineteenth century provided a degree of anonymity that allowed a gay subculture to develop, chiefly within a large population of transient, unmarried men who often lived in unsupervised rooming houses and maintained few ties to their families. By the 1890s gay life was centered on the Bowery, Manhattan's largest working-class entertainment district; several saloons and dance halls popular among gays there were called "degenerate resorts." By the 1920s there were a number of gay enclaves. The best known was in Greenwich Village, where speakeasies and tearooms attracted gays from Brooklyn, the Bronx, Queens, and Staten Island and from the rural United States, as well as heterosexuals wishing to observe gay culture. Among the most popular gathering places in the mid-1920s were Paul and Joe's restaurant on Sixth Avenue and the Black Rabbit, a speakeasy on MacDougal Street run by Eva Kotchever, a lesbian from Poland; these closed after attacks by neighbors and the police.

Harlem was also an important center of gay life, especially during Prohibition. Such clubs as Smalls' Paradise and the Clam House were popular, as were smaller speakeasies unknown to heterosexuals. Gay black social clubs organized the city's largest drag (transvestite) balls, some of them held in the Savoy Ballroom and the Rockland Palace. The largest of these balls was the Hamilton Lodge Ball, which at the height of its popularity in the 1930s attracted 8000 participants and observers. Several figures of the Harlem Renaissance were prominent in the community. There was also an enclave in Times Square, little known by heterosexuals, where gay theater workers met in tearooms, restaurants, and streets. By the time of World War II the men's bar at the Astor Hotel (Broadway and 47th Street) was known nationally by gay sailors as a place to meet gay civilians while passing through the city. Many composers, poets, and playwrights drawn to the city by its cultural offerings became central figures in the gay world.

During World War II men on their way to Europe discovered gay culture in New York City, and afterward many returned to the city to settle. Gay bars opened, and enclaves formed on the East Side and West Side and in Brooklyn Heights and Jackson Heights; an especially large one developed along the Third Avenue elevated line, near the "bird circuit," a strip of bars that included the Golden Pheasant and the White Swan. As gays became more numerous and visible, they also came under more frequent attack by political leaders and the police: during the decade after the war, thousands of men were arrested on homosexual charges each year, and most gay bars remained in operation only a short time before being closed by the police or the state liquor authority, which prohibited bars and restaurants from serving homosexuals. Resistance to such measures was organized by a few gays and lesbians during the 1950s. A local chapter of the Mattachine Society formed in 1955 was the largest gay-rights organization in the United States by 1960. Under the leadership of Dick Leitsch, its president from 1965, the group adopted a militant stance: it defended men who had been arrested on morals charges by maintaining that they had been entrapped, and protested against the policing of gay bars. With the support of favorable court rulings, the group achieved considerable success by 1967.

Gay bars nonetheless continued to be raided by the police. After a riot broke out in June 1969 when patrons and passersby resisted a raid on the Stonewall Inn on Christopher Street, the Gay Liberation Front was organized by young activists. The group was soon superseded by the Gay Activists Alliance and Radicalesbians, which led demonstrations against Mayor John V. Lindsay and institutions considered hostile to gays, including the American Psychological Association (which classified homosexuality as a psychological disorder). The Lambda Legal Defense Fund and the National Gay Task Force were formed in 1973 in New York City to promote gay rights and became prominent nationwide. Groups in the city fought for a municipal gay-rights bill to protect gays and lesbians against discrimination in housing and employment; bills were introduced annually from 1971, but one was not passed until 1986 and not until 2002 were the protections extended explicitly to transgender individuals. Gay institutions prospered during the 1970s as the threat of police harassment diminished. Bars, discothèques, and bathhouses increased in number and operated openly; and gay choruses, athletic leagues, political associations, theater companies, and other organizations were formed. The gay press also flourished in the 1970s and 1980s: periodicals issued in the city included *Come Out!* (1969), *Christopher Street* (1976), and *New York Native*. The New York City Lesbian and Gay Community Services Center, opened in a renovated school building on West 13th Street in 1984, provided offices for several major organizations and meeting facilities for more than 200 others.

During these years the gay community was ravaged by AIDS, a lethal illness identified in the early 1980s. At first most victims were gay men and the disease was largely ignored, but as the number of deaths rose, the country panicked. In response to discrimination against people with AIDS, gays turned increasingly to activism. When the city was slow to allocate funds for such services as AIDS education, a group of men including the playwright Larry Kramer formed the Gay Men's Health Crisis (GMHC) in 1981 to press for more government services, support those stricken by the disease, and distribute condoms and educational materials in bars. The crisis exacerbated violence against gays, whom many blamed for the epidemic. In response to several vicious attacks in 1980 the New York City Gay and Lesbian Anti-Violence Project was formed by a group in Chelsea. Under the leadership of David Wertheimer (1985–89) it expanded its staff, organized programs to help the police and social workers respond to assaults against gays, and made "queer bashing" a public issue for the first time. At the same time older organizations, including the Lambda Legal Defense Fund, grew rapidly. Virulent attacks by the press (particularly the *New York Post*) on gays and people with AIDS in the mid-1980s led to the formation of the Gay and Lesbian Alliance against Defamation (GLAAD) in 1985.

The AIDS crisis, the conservative policies of President Ronald Reagan, and the decision of the U.S. Supreme Court to uphold anti-sodomy laws in *Bowers v. Hardwick* (1986) inspired increased activism and widespread support for organizations devoted to AIDS and gay issues. After the Gay Rights Bill was passed in New York City in 1986, gays demanded rights commensurate with those accorded to heterosexuals, including joint health insurance, visitation rights, and housing rights. Although the rate of infection with AIDS decreased in the late 1980s as gays became educated about preventive measures, the disease continued to ravage the community: 10,000 New Yorkers had died of it by 1987 and 20,000 by 1991. The crisis led to a resurgence of militant gay organizations, among them the AIDS Coalition to Unleash Power (ACT UP), formed by Kramer in 1987, and several of its offshoots, such as Queer Nation, which organized "kiss-ins" and "queer nights" at clubs frequented by heterosexuals, led marches on the homes of accused gay bashers, and distributed militant gay literature throughout the city.

A few successes were achieved during the early 1990s. The New York State Court of Appeals ruled in *Braschi v. Stahl Associates* (1989) that the right of succession to a rent-controlled apartment accrued to the longtime partner of a gay man who had died, as it would have to a legal spouse; at the urging of activists the state then extended similar rights regarding rent-stabilized apartments. In 1993 gay couples were granted the right to register with the city as domestic partners, and demands for domestic partner benefits were confirmed in January 1994. Gay voters played a crucial role in David N. Dinkins's narrow victory in the mayoral election in 1989 and also helped to elect a number of sympathetic judges and other public officials. Deborah Glick, the first openly lesbian state legislator, was elected from a district that included Chelsea and Greenwich Village in 1990, and Tom Duane, a well-known activist, became the first openly gay candidate elected to the City Council in 1991. In 2006 Christine Quinn became the first openly gay speaker of the New York City Council.

Eric Garber, "A Spectacle in Color: The Lesbian and Gay Subculture of Jazz Age Harlem," in *Hidden from History,* ed. Martin Bauml Duberman et al. (New York: New American Library, 1989); George Chauncey, *Gay New York: Gender, Urban Culture, and the Makings of the Gay Male World, 1890–1940* (New York: Basic Books, 1994)

See also AIDS, Lesbians, and Stonewall Riots.

George Chauncey, Jr.

GE. See General Electric.

Geddes, Norman Bel [Geddes, Norman Melancthon] (*b* Adrian, Mich., 27 April 1893; *d* New York City, 8 May 1958). Designer. After noticing a 1918 magazine article in which Otto H. Kahn was quoted saying that millionaires should give money to support struggling artists, Geddes sent the prominent banker a telegram asking for enough money to move him and his family from Los Angeles to New York City, where he wanted to work in theatrical design. He received $400 the next day. In New York, Kahn secured a position for Geddes at the Metropolitan Opera where he supervised the design of costumes and scenery for about 100 productions and became known for his innovative stage lighting. Beginning in 1927 he focused his efforts on industrial design, designing commercial products such as vacuum cleaners, yachts, automobiles, and trains; he also received commissions for the Futurama exhibit of General Motors at the World's Fair of 1939–40, the Hayden Planetarium (1935), and about 30 theaters worldwide. Geddes wrote an autobiography, *Horizons* (1932). He died of a heart attack in the University Club at 1 West 54th Street in Manhattan.

Jennifer Davis Roberts, *Norman Bel Geddes: An Exhibition* (Austin: University of Texas, 1979)

James E. Mooney

Gehrig, (Henry) Lou(is) (*b* New York City, 19 June 1903; *d* New York City, 2 June 1941). Hall of Fame baseball player. He was born of German descent at 309 East 94th Street in the Yorkville neighborhood of Manhattan and attended the High School of Commerce and then Columbia College, where he played briefly for the Lions. Signed by the Yankees in 1923, he played 2130 consecutive games beginning on 1 June 1925 (a major league record); his durability as a player earned him the nickname the "Iron Horse." His career ended in 1939 when he was found to have the incurable degenerative disease amyotrophic lateral sclerosis (now often called Lou Gehrig's disease). He retired after a now famous farewell speech at Yankee Stadium on 4 July 1939 (now Lou Gehrig Appreciation Day) when he told his tens of thousands of adoring fans that he regarded himself as the "luckiest man on the face of the earth." Later he was appointed to the New York City Parole Commission and served on it during the last months of his life. His last home was at 5204 Delafield Avenue in Fieldston in the Bronx. Most observers agree that Gehrig was the greatest first baseman in the history of baseball and that along with Babe Ruth, he was part of a one-two punch that has never been rivaled. His funeral was at Grace Episcopal Church in Riverdale; he is buried at Kensico Cemetery in suburban Westchester County.

Eleanor Gehrig and Joseph Durso, *My Luke and I* (New York: Thomas Y. Crowell, 1976); Ray Robinson, *Iron Horse* (New York: W. W. Norton, 1990)

Lawrence S. Ritter

Geisel, Theodor Seuss. See Dr. Seuss.

Geneen, Harold (Sydney) (*b* Bournemouth, England, 22 Jan 1910; *d* New York City, 21 Nov 1997). Business executive. He moved to the United States in 1911, took U.S. citizenship in 1918, and graduated from New York University in 1934. After serving in executive positions at Raytheon, Bell and Howell, and Jones and Laughlin, he became president in 1959 of International Telephone and Telegraph Corporation (ITT). For the next two decades he oversaw an aggressive policy of diversification that transformed the quiet telecommunications company into a wide-ranging conglomerate: among the firms it acquired were Avis (automobile rentals), Sheraton Hotels, and Hartford Insurance. One of his most controversial initiatives was an attempted takeover in 1965 of the American Broadcasting Company (ABC), which was blocked by the federal government. Geneen resigned as president and chief executive officer of ITT in 1972 but stayed on the board until 1977.

Robert Schoenberg, *Geneen* (New York: W. W. Norton, 1985)

Owen D. Gutfreund

General Electric [GE]. Industrial and financial conglomerate. Initially known as the Edison Electric Light Company, it was formed in 1878 in suburban Menlo Park, New Jersey, by Thomas Edison to support research on incandescent lighting and was funded by J. P. Morgan. It opened a power station on Pearl Street in Manhattan in 1882, the first functional one in the country, and enjoyed success producing lamps and other electrical supplies. In 1892 it ceased to be controlled by Edison, whose bankers arranged a merger with a competitor, the Thomson–Houston Company of Lynn, Massachusetts. Renamed the General Electric Company, the firm became the largest of its kind; its most important rival was the Westinghouse Electric Company. General Electric opened the first industrial research laboratory in the country in 1900, in the backyard barn of scientist Charles Steinmetz, and diversified by developing new products and buying other firms (it eventually made aerospace products and sold real estate). In 1956 it moved its headquarters from Schenectady, New York, to a famous art deco skyscraper at 51st Street and Lexington Avenue that bears its name (the GE Building). The firm maintained its headquarters at 570 Lexington Street until August 1974, when it moved its corporate offices to suburban Fairfield, Connecticut. Under the direction of John F. Welch in the 1980s it concentrated its efforts in technology, services, and manufacturing. In 1986 it bought RCA (including the National Broadcasting Company [NBC], the leading television network at the time) and 80 percent of the firm of Kidder, Peabody, which it liquidated in 1994. In 2001 Welch named Jeffrey Immelt as his successor. In 2002 the company acquired the Telemundo Communications Group Inc., and in 2004 it merged with Vivendi Universal Entertainment, resulting in the company NBC Universal, with General Electric owning 80 percent of it. In 2009 GE and the media company Comcast agreed to a joint venture in which Comcast would gain a 51 percent share of NBC Universal.

Peter A. Coclanis

General Slocum. An excursion vessel that burned on 15 June 1904, resulting in the worst disaster in New York City in the twentieth century and one of the worst in all of maritime history. Named for a Civil War general, the ship was launched in Brooklyn in 1891. Built of wood, it could accommodate 2500 passengers on three open decks. Its coal-fired boilers, built in Hoboken, New Jersey, turned two side paddle wheels. On the day of the fire the vessel had been chartered to take the congregation of St. Mark's German Lutheran Church on its annual picnic outing to the northern shore of Long Island. The church, on East Sixth Street just east of Second Avenue, was in the thriving community known as Kleindeutschland, which surrounded Tompkins Square on the Lower East Side. The *General Slocum* departed from the East Third Street pier at 9:40 a.m. and began moving up the East River past Blackwell's (now Roosevelt) Island. At 9:56 a.m. fire was discovered under the door of a forward cabin. Captain William Van Schaick, 68 years old, who in the preceding year had been given an award for safely transporting 35 million passengers, did not learn of the fire for at least seven minutes. By that time the ship had entered the treacherous waters of Hell Gate; because of a strong tide under its stern, a stiff breeze over its bow, and rocks on either side, there was no room to maneuver. Flames enveloped the forward part of the ship, and the half-rotted canvas fire hoses burst under the force of water. Most of the 1331 passengers onboard were women and children unable to swim. The captain realized that he would need to beach the vessel to save passengers, but because of the racing current and the rocks below, he decided to continue northward for another 1.5 miles (2.4 kilometers) to North Brother Island.

General Slocum Memorial (1906), 2009

Although the ship was equipped with more than 2500 life jackets, they proved useless because the canvas had rotted and the cork filler had crumbled. Meanwhile, the intense heat kept dozens of nearby vessels from getting sufficiently close to assist. Fewer than 15 minutes after smoke was first seen, the *General Slocum* lay a smoldering wreck on North Brother Island, and at least 1021 people were dead. The funerals lasted more than a week, and one of the processions from St. Mark's Church to the Lutheran Cemetery in Queens involved 156 hearses and stretched for almost a mile.

An investigation revealed that the Knickerbocker Steamboat Company, owner of the *General Slocum,* had never replaced the original lifebelts and hoses and that the first mate had not trained the crew in emergency procedures. The exact cause of the fire was not determined. Captain Van Schaick was convicted of neglect of duty and sentenced to 10 years in prison, but he was pardoned by President William Howard Taft after three and a half years at Sing Sing. Kleindeutschland did not recover. Partly as a result of the tragedy, its German residents moved uptown to Yorkville on the Upper East Side, Jewish families replaced them, and St. Mark's Church became an Orthodox synagogue. An organization of survivors of the *General Slocum* inaugurated an annual commemoration at the Lutheran Cemetery in Queens.

Edward T. O'Donnell, *Ship Ablaze: The Tragedy of the Steamboat* General Slocum (New York: Broadway Books, a Division of Random House, 2003)

Kenneth T. Jackson

General Society of Mechanics and Tradesmen. Organization formed in 1785 in New York City by 22 artisans to promote the political and financial interests of craftspeople in the United States. Its members fought for protective tariffs and formed the Mechanics Bank to help meet the credit needs of artisans. The society also built a series of impressive meeting halls and established a reputable school and a widely used apprentices' library. To ambitious members such as Stephen Allen the organization offered opportunities for public service that led to political careers. The General Society of Mechanics and Tradesmen currently remains active at its landmark building at 20 West 44th Street, purchased in 1899 with the help of Andrew Carnegie. Having experienced a renaissance at the beginning of the twenty-first century, it modernized its library and organized its archives.

Howard Rock

General Theological Seminary. Episcopal seminary at 175 Ninth Avenue (near 21st Street) in Manhattan, formed by John Henry Hobart, Theodore Dehon, and William White and sponsored by the church's general convention; founded in 1817, it is the oldest Episcopal seminary in the United States. Classes began with two professors teaching six students at St. Paul's Chapel in the spring of 1819. In 1820 the classes were moved to New Haven, Connecticut, and St. Mark's Library was opened in New York City by John Pintard. The first graduation was held in 1822, and the seminary then moved back to New York City.

The first professor of biblical languages at the seminary was Clement Clarke Moore, who taught from 1821 to 1850 and donated the current site, known as Chelsea Square, that became the campus by 1827; the first building, now known as the West Building, was erected in a Gothic Revival style between 1832 and 1836. During the 1830s and 1840s the campus was the American center of the Oxford Movement, which called for the revival of High Anglican traditions. A number of graduates of the seminary formed churches west of the Mississippi River. The seminary received permission to grant degrees in 1869 and conferred the Bachelor of Sacred Theology degree from 1876. Under Eugene Augustus Hoffman, a dean (1879–1902) and major benefactor, it expanded rapidly, adding the quadrangle, most of the grounds, and the library and other buildings and establishing professorships and endowments. It awarded the doctorate from 1881 and honorary degrees from 1885. By the end of Hoffman's tenure there were nearly 150 students and 13 full-time faculty members. The Chapel of the Good Shepherd (1885–88), a monument to the Hoffman family, was built in an English Collegiate Gothic style with a bell tower 161 feet (50 meters) tall and bronze doors designed by J. Massey Rhind; it was consecrated by the presiding bishop John Williams on 31 October 1888.

The seminary continued to expand after the turn of the twentieth century. In 1926 it introduced a tutorial system to supplement classroom instruction. The main front building was added in 1960. Women were admitted as full-time students in the Master of Divinity program in the autumn of 1971. Student marriages during the academic year were allowed from the autumn of 1972; in the same year the faculty issued a statement supporting the ordination of women, the first by an Episcopal seminary in the United States. Over faculty objections the trustees voted in 1978 to sell a Gutenberg Bible donated by Hoffman. After considering several alternatives, they voted in 1982 not to move the seminary to a new site, and extensive renovations were undertaken in the 1990s. From the 1950s into the 1990s the average enrollment ranged from 140 to 160. By the mid-1990s about 7000 students had enrolled since the school began.

In addition to the three-year Master of Divinity program, the General Theological Seminary offers a two-year Master of Arts program, a Master of Sacred Theology program, and a Doctor of Theology program (with a specialty in Anglican studies); it also operates the Center for Christian Spirituality, the Center for Jewish–Christian Studies and Relations, and a summer school. St. Mark's Library has more than 240,000 volumes. Its rare-book vault was damaged by fire in September 1993, but the library is still known as the finest theological library in the Episcopal Church. Under the leadership of Ward Ewing (dean from 1998), the Desmond Tutu Education Center was opened on 11 September 2007 in the context of a major international conference on "Reconciliation at the Roundtable."

Powel Mills Dawley, *The Story of the General Theological Seminary: A Sesquicentennial History, 1817–1967* (New York: Oxford University Press, 1969); Timothy A. Boggs, *Through the Gates into the City: A Metropolis, a Seminary and a Chapel* (New York: General Theological Seminary of the Episcopal Church, 2007)

J. Robert Wright

General Trades' Union. Citywide organization formed in 1833 by delegates from nine trades. It was responsible for a surge of militancy in labor between 1833 and 1836. The union espoused first the moderate criticisms of corrupt, greedy aristocrats by Ely Moore, a politician connected with Tammany Hall, then by 1835 the more pointed attacks of the chair maker John Commerford on "capital," which by his definition included not only aristocrats but also master artisans. Commerford's views were shared by many journeymen delegates, and even sympathetic small masters were denied membership in the council. Delegates were elected by the many craft unions formed in the mid-1830s, which also set up complex procedures and ad hoc committees to approve and govern strikes, ensure democratic debate and participation, handle grievances, and collect funds. One of the union's achievements was sponsoring parades and lively public celebrations of Independence Day. Female craftworkers were not accepted as equals by many members, who hoped that their own efforts against exploitation would allow women to return to domestic life; nonetheless, some journeymen pledged support to women on strike. Although the union shared with the Locofoco Democrats a hostility to the Second Bank of the United States, it abstained from formal endorsements and maintained political independence to avoid the kind of demise suffered by the Workingmen's Party in 1829–30. The General Trades' Union reached the height of its influence during a wave of strikes in 1836 but disbanded when the trade union movement was ravaged by the panic of 1837 and the subsequent depression.

Walter Hugins, *Jacksonian Democracy and the Working Class: A Study of the New York Workingmen's Movement, 1829–1837* (Stanford, Calif.: Stanford University Press, 1960); Sean Wilentz, *Chants Democratic: New York City and the Rise of the American Working Class, 1788–1850* (New York: Oxford University Press, 1984)

Iver Bernstein

gentrification. The process of older neighborhoods being renovated and rebuilt, followed by more affluent people moving in and usually forcing older, less affluent residents to leave. This is the reverse of the prevailing process of urban neighborhood change, which involves the sequential reuse of residential housing by progressively lower income groups. As older neighborhoods become more rather than less attractive to outsiders—either because of a new appreciation for prewar construction, proximity to mass transit, or lower crime rates—families with more financial resources than the current inhabitants move into an area and bid up the price of renting or buying real estate. In New York City after 1970—in neighborhoods like the Upper West Side, Chelsea, the meatpacking district, Park Slope, Fort Greene, SoHo, and Bedford–Stuyvesant—gentrification became a common, even predominant, experience as the suburbs lost status relative to the city. In the early twenty-first century, as the region recovered from the terrorist attacks of 11 September 2001 and as more professional families chose to remain in the city even after they had children, recent college graduates who could not afford Manhattan's priciest precincts began to flock to Harlem north of Central Park or Fort Greene and Williamsburg in Brooklyn, where they could find cheaper rents, a dynamic street life, and numerous entertainment options. Older residents of such areas felt pushed out by the newcomers.

Kenneth T. Jackson

geographical features. New York City's geographical features of general interest include its highest and lowest natural points and its land area, which varies from year to year depending on erosion, dredging, and development.

The city's total land area is approximately 303 square miles (785 square kilometers), the exact area varying with annual landfill and erosion. Queens makes up nearly one-third of that, at 110 square miles (285 square kilometers), with Brooklyn the second largest borough at 72 square miles (187 square kilometers), followed by Richmond (Staten Island) at 56 square miles (144 square kilometers), the Bronx at 42 square miles (109 square kilometers), and Manhattan, the smallest borough, at 23 square miles (60 square kilometers). The landmass is just one-fourth the size of New York Harbor, whose area of approximately 1200 square miles (3108 square kilometers) consists of the lower Hudson; the Harlem and East rivers; the Upper and Lower Bay; and the bays, kills, canals, and creeks that drain into them. The total length of the shoreline is approximately 1000 miles (1609 kilometers, or the approximate straight-line distance from New York to Savannah, Georgia), of which about 650 miles (1046 kilometers) is navigable waterfront. The natural, average depth for most of New York Harbor before dredging was approximately 20 feet (6.1 meters). Beginning in the early 1800s the city and federal governments have almost always been at work creating and maintaining some 240 miles (386 kilometers) of deep-water channels by dredging to the depth of the largest vessels, ranging from 30 feet (9.1 meters) to 50 feet (15.2 meters) in the early twenty-first century.

The city's highest natural point is at the top of Todt Hill in Staten Island. At 409.8 feet (125 meters) above sea level, it is the highest spot on the Atlantic Coast of the United States south and west of Maine. Outside Staten Island, the highest natural point in the city is the 284.5-foot hilltop in the Fieldston section of the Bronx, near Grosvenor and Iselin avenues and 250th Street. Manhattan's highest point is a matter of dispute. For many years it was believed to be in Fort Tryon Park, near the flagpole, at an elevation above sea level of 260 feet (79 meters). In fact, it is in Bennett Park, the site of the Revolutionary War compound called Fort Washington, at 183rd and Pinehurst streets. A schist outcropping there peaks at 265 feet (80.7 meters). The highest point in Queens, at 258.2 feet (78.7 meters), is in the Glen Oaks neighborhood on a busy service road on the parkway's south side, near the Towers Country Club. Brooklyn's highest point is in the northeast corner of Green-Wood Cemetery, above the intersection of 20th Street and Seventh Avenue, at an elevation of 220 feet (67.1 meters). The lowest natural point in the city's history very likely was the bottom of the freshwater pond called the Collect, with a maximum depth of 60 feet (18.2 meters). The Collect was filled in by 1811 and the site is now a park on Centre Street near Foley Square. Humans have dug as deep as 800 feet (244 meters) below sea level to build tunnels for transit and water supply in the city.

New York Panorama (New York: Pantheon, 1984) (originally published as *The WPA Guide to New York City* [1939])

See also GEOLOGY.

John Rousmaniere

geology. The New York City area owes its unique and diverse history to the geological processes that for more than a billion years have reshaped and altered its physical environment. Among the evolutionary phenomena that have changed the face of the North American continent were the formation and subsequent destruction of ancient mountain ranges (orogenies), their simultaneous erosion and sedimentation, and the shifting and colliding of the continental landmasses that changed the shape, direction, and size of its waterways. In more recent geologic times the forces of glaciation have altered the landscape dramatically while revealing evidence of its former geologic history.

1. Features

The Manhattan prong, a narrow projection extending down the east side of the Hudson Valley to the southern tip of Manhattan, dates to the time of the Grenville Orogeny (1000 million B.P.). Most of the rocks of New York City are generally believed to date from two later mountain-building events, the Taconian Orogeny of the Ordovician period (500 million to 430 million B.P.) and the Acadian Orogeny of the Devonian period (395 million to 345 million B.P.). During these events great compressive force bearing on accumulated sediments caused deep strata of rock to be tilted, folded, and raised; the result in the metropolitan area was a bedrock of igneous and highly metamorphosed rocks that now supports the skyscrapers of Manhattan. Before metamorphosis, successive sedimentary layers of such materials as graywacke sandstone, chert, dolomitic limestone, and sandy shale accumulated.

The topography of New York City results primarily from the different rates of erosion of rock formations that differ in hardness, and secondarily from the effect of the glaciers on what are now Brooklyn and Queens. There remain in New York City three basic formations of rock from the ancestral mountains, arranged in layers overlying the sediments presumed to date from before the Grenville Orogeny and tilted to the southwest along an axis roughly parallel to Long Island. The oldest formation is Fordham gneiss, named for its prominent distribution in Fordham. It is composed largely of quartz, orthoclase feldspar (in which quartz is found in distinct bands, sometimes with bands of hornblende), and biotite mica. Fordham gneiss is readily recognizable by its light to very dark gray color, displaying folded and distorted bands of foliation planes (layering). It is believed that the gneiss dates from the Precambrian period (more than 1000 million to 570 million B.P.). The second formation is known as Inwood marble, or Inwood dolomite, for the area at the northern tip of Manhattan where

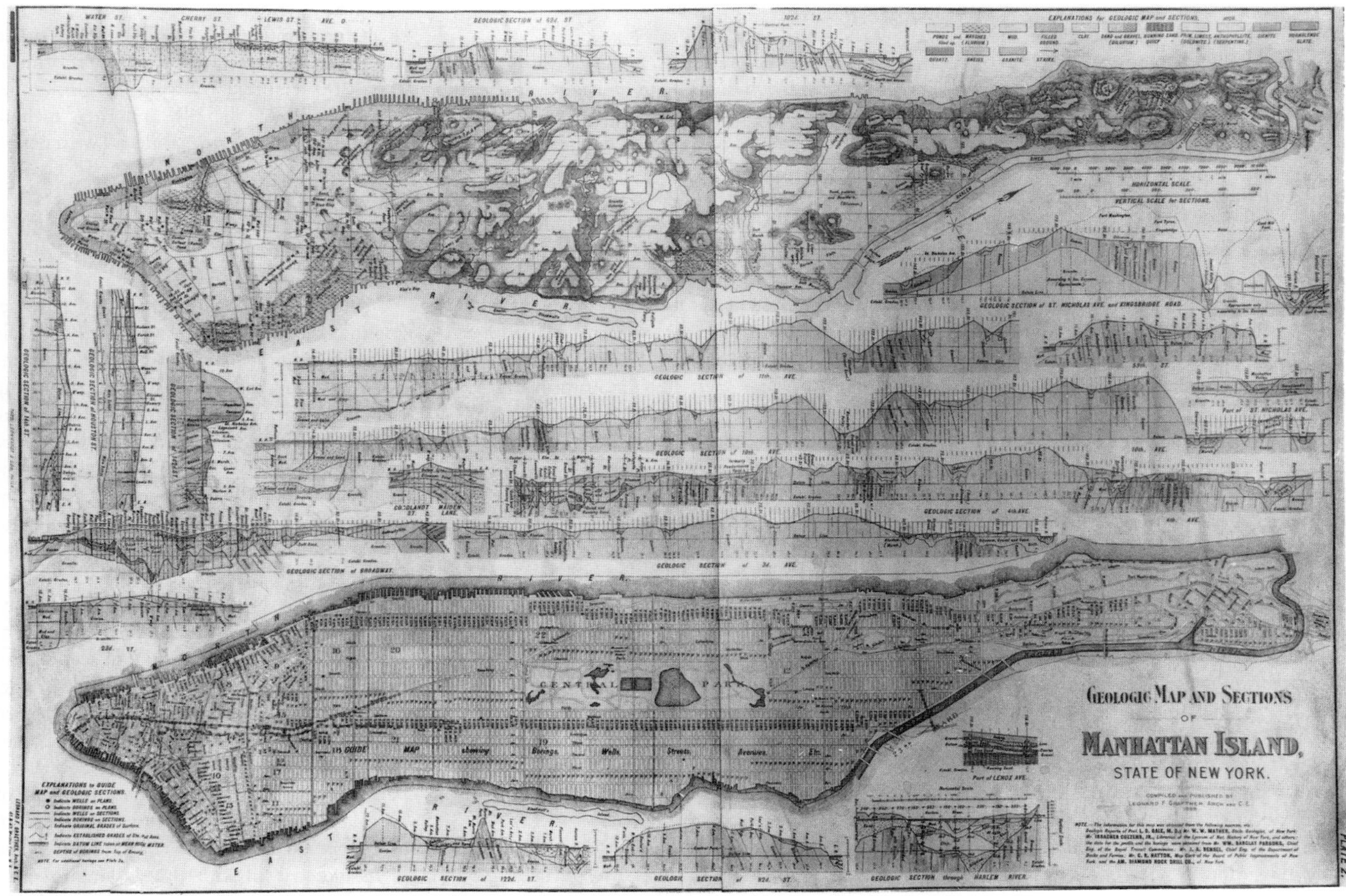

Geological map and sections of Manhattan, 1898

it has many prominent outcrops. It overlies the Fordham gneiss and may therefore be assumed to be a younger formation. Composed primarily of calcium and magnesium carbonate, the marble is almost white and coarsely grained, but prolonged weathering often causes it to disintegrate. Unlike the gneiss, it is unfoliated. Before metamorphosis Inwood marble was probably a dolomitic sandstone. Because Inwood marble is much less hard than gneiss, it is more vulnerable to erosion and appears only in low-lying areas, its height having been reduced far more quickly; it is visible at ground level in the flat plain of Harlem and as far north as Spuyten Duyvil. The third formation, and the youngest, is the predominant one on Manhattan Island: the ubiquitous mica schist of the Manhattan formation (see MANHATTAN SCHIST). Light gray in color but weathering to a blackish brown, it is easily recognizable by its tiny, glistening flakes of muscovite mica as well as widely distributed bands of foliation. It is composed almost entirely of quartz and plagioclase feldspar. Mica schist is highly durable and has long been a favored building material, as may be seen from such structures as the older buildings of City College of New York. Outcrops of the schist are widely distributed in Central Park, along Riverside Drive, at Coogan's Bluff (overlooking the site of the former Polo Grounds), in the Fort George and Fort Tryon ridges, in Inwood Hill Park (where schist and Inwood marble are interlayered with bands of hornblende schist), and along the Cross Bronx Expressway near the Harlem River and Alexander Hamilton Bridge.

Where the Fort George and Fort Tryon ridges merge at about 181st Street to form the Manhattan Ridge, the spine of mica schist continues south, past St. Nicholas Heights to about 125th Street, where it dips suddenly under the Manhattan Valley and rises again as Morningside Heights. The ridge then slopes gently down to the surface at 96th Street; on its west side outcrops are evident in Riverside Park as far south as 72nd Street. No further exposures of mica schist occur south of Central Park, although the formation is not far beneath the surface except at Washington Square, where it plunges several hundred feet before rising again near Chambers Street to about 40 feet (12 meters) below the surface. Above this bedrock is a conglomeration of loose boulders, gravel, sand, clay, soil, and former vegetation called regolith, much of it left behind by the later glaciers.

During the late Paleozoic period (250 million B.P.) the topography of what is now New York City was undergoing dramatic changes, as the Earth's crust drifted slowly but constantly across the surface of the planet. During the Mesozoic era (225 million to 65 million B.P.) the Atlantic continents drifted together to form a gigantic landmass named Pangaea in 1915 by the German meteorologist Alfred Wegner, who based his theory on the complementarity of the coastlines of the Atlantic continents and the similarity of rock formations on either side of the ocean (to the extent of containing some of the same fossils). When the continents again moved apart, the Earth's crust was uplifted, while other tectonic plates sank beneath the sea to create deep ocean trenches. The uplifted sediments slowly eroded and over time were steadily deposited to form the backbone of what are now the shoreline beaches. The beaches of Brooklyn, Queens, and the rest of Long Island well illustrate the deposition of sands and gravel of beaches eroded upland, as well as the effects of wave action and glaciation.

In Van Cortlandt Park in northern Bronx there is yet another rock formation, the Yonkers granite, an igneous rock that was formed below the surface by intense heat. It intruded into the Fordham gneiss as super-hot magma and slowly cooled without being exposed to the atmosphere, until erosion did its work. Resembling gneiss and frequently called granitic gneiss, it is composed of quartz, mica, and a pink feldspar called microcline. Another small formation that intruded into the Fordham gneiss is Ravenswood grandiorite. Of varying shades of gray, it contains quartz, feldspar, and hornblende, with garnets giving it a mottled appearance. It is found in an area of 6 square miles (15.5 square kilometers) of Ravenswood in northwestern Queens along the East River.

One of the more unusual rock formations distributed widely on Staten Island is serpentinite, a rock that when exposed to the atmosphere has a reddish-brown hue caused by iron oxide. This colorful rock was much favored by the Indians, who used it to carve the bowls of their pipes. A dramatic light green outcrop of serpentinite, directly across the Hudson from midtown at a bluff called Castle Point on the campus of the Stevens Institute of Technology in Hoboken, was described in 1609 in the journal of Henry Hudson's first mate, Robert Juet, as a "mountain that resembled a silver myne"; there is a small, similar outcrop along 11th Avenue in the West 50s of Manhattan.

Manhattan is marked by a series of faults, which are fractures caused by the movement of one mass of rock against another. The fault lines are easily recognizable as valleys that cut across the ridges of mica schist and form deep depressions or hollows. Examples include a fault at Dyckman Street that bisects the Manhattan Ridge, and another that runs parallel to 155th Street. The most prominent fault is near the Lorillard snuff mill in the New York Botanical Gardens, where the Bronx River once carved its way through the faulted rocks to create a narrow gorge.

The topography of New York City underwent important changes in late geological times during the Ice Age. Beginning about 1.5 million B.P., during the Pleistocene epoch, the Earth's climate cooled and glaciers were eventually formed that covered much of the northern hemisphere. On the North American continent the ice sheet extended as far south as the lower Midwest, covering northern Pennsylvania and New Jersey and reaching the Atlantic seacoast at what is now New York City. Four ice sheets advanced and retreated during the Pleistocene epoch; the Wisconsin was the most extensive and moved in a series of brief advances and retreats for about 60,000 years, covering all the area now making up New York City. The Wisconsin had a thickness of 2000 feet (600 meters) and carried with it giant boulders, rocks, gravel, sand, and particles of clay, which it left in a deposit called till. So immense were its powers that it deposited huge rocks from the New England Upland on Long Island. In Central Park the force of the glacial advance is evident from the many boulders scattered throughout, some weighing many tens of tons; these boulders, called erratics, remained after the ice withdrew. The action of the glacier also affected the huge outcrops of mica schist, which were gouged by other rocks dragged by the glacial ice and worn smooth by fine particles of sand. A huge outcrop of mica schist adjacent to the carousel in Central Park was rounded by the grinding effect of the overriding ice mass, giving it a steep, rough "down-glacier" side and a smoothly polished and striated "up-glacier" side. Other vestiges of the ice sheet are deep, steep-sided indentations called kettles that were formed when enormous chunks of ice broke off from the glacier, became buried by the till, and then melted; occasionally the kettles would fill with runoff or rainwater and become ponds. In Queens many kettles varying in depth from a few feet to more than 100 feet are prominent features of Alley Pond Park, Forest Park, and Highland Park.

Of the many remnants of the last Ice Age, about 12,000 to 14,000 B.P., the most visible is the Harbor Hill moraine, a continuous ridge of boulders, gravel, and sand marking the southernmost limit of the advance of the Wisconsin Ice Sheet. It extends the entire length of Long Island, forming a line of prominent bluffs and hilly terrain from Orient Point along the northern shore through Nassau and Queens counties, where the moraine forms the heads of Hempstead Harbor, Manhasset Bay, Little Neck Bay, and Flushing Bay. The moraine derives its name from the highest elevation on Long Island (391 feet, or 120 meters), at Harbor Hill, near Roslyn. The ridge, or terminal moraine, then marks the route of the Grand Central Parkway and passes through Alley Pond, Cunningham, and Forest parks. It forms a very visible escarpment in Highland Park, near the border of Brooklyn and Queens, providing a commanding view of its outwash plain as far as Jamaica Bay, 5 miles (8 kilometers) to the east. This level stretch of coastal lowland was formed by rushing streams of melting ice pouring from the glacier, which deposited a thick layer of stratified and sorted sediments. In Brooklyn the moraine follows Bushwick Avenue, Eastern Parkway, Crown Heights, Prospect Park, Park Slope, and Bay Ridge; near the Verrazano–Narrows Bridge it crosses into Staten Island, where it rises 410 feet (125 meters) at Todt Hill, the highest point on the Atlantic Coast between Maine and Florida, before crossing into New Jersey and then northern Pennsylvania. One dynamic event caused by the terminal moraine during the Late Pleistocene blocked the Narrows as well as the exit flows of many rivers, causing extensive parts of Manhattan and Queens to be submerged under two new lakes. Lake Hudson, which was situated approximately along the present Hudson River as far north as Haverstraw and may have been joined to Lake Hackensack near Elizabeth, New Jersey, inundated the lowland sections of Manhattan Island. Connected to it was Lake Flushing, which engulfed broad areas of northern Queens and Nassau County. These lakes remained for thousands of years, long enough for about 8 feet (2.4 meters) of glacial clay to accumulate in sections of Manhattan Island, where extensive clay deposits now overlay strata of sand and gravel in the Harlem and Inwood lowlands. Peat beds also were deposited in the postglacial sands of lower Manhattan. The postglacial climate created a swampy environment that supported many varieties of flora and fauna; paleontologists have unearthed the trunks of several common juniper trees from the late Pleistocene epoch in lower Manhattan; the skeletons of wooly mammoths, giant bison, saber-toothed tigers, hairy tapirs, a ground sloth, a giant mastodon, and a prehistoric horse (discovered in 1926 during excavations for the Independent Subway at 134th Street and St. Nicholas Avenue); and human remains and artifacts radiocarbon-dated to 3690 B.P.

In the postglacial period the North Atlantic coastline became tilted downward, with the shoreline southeast of New York City uplifting and the shoreline northeast subsiding. As a result the sea submerged the valleys of many coastal rivers, which became known as drowned valleys; among these were the valleys of the Delaware, the Connecticut, and the Hudson, which once extended eastward into the Atlantic Ocean, 120 miles (193 kilometers) to the edge of the Continental Shelf. The Hudson, a fjord or estuary rather than a river, remains tidal as far as Troy, 140 miles (225 kilometers) north of New York City. As a result of the glaciers many of the city's other waterways are also estuaries, including the East River, the Harlem River, Spuyten Duyvil, the Kill van Kull, and the Arthur Kill, as is Long Island Sound, which was once a river flowing easterly.

The many miles of New York City shoreline are continually altered by the ocean, in a recurring cycle of erosion and deposition. Because the downward slope of the coastal plain is gradual, the sands build up quickly to form an underwater bar parallel to the shoreline. Over time the bar rises above the surface, forming a barrier beach or barrier island. Behind this barrier the trapped seawater becomes a lagoon, which water flows into and out of through tidal inlets. An example of such a lagoon is Jamaica Bay, which over the years became for the most part a saltwater marsh that is now a refuge for sea birds. The bay contains a number of marshy islands called hassocks, formed by the buildup of sand, and its tides are governed by Rockaway Inlet; Rockaway Peninsula and Atlantic Beach nearby are barrier beaches developed over many years.

Annual weather cycles strongly affect the buildup and erosion of the barrier beaches. Violent winter storms and occasional autumn hurricanes attack the shore and erode the beach, interrupting the normal cycle in which beach sands are deposited and washed away, and at times even breaching the barrier beaches and carving new tidal inlets into the lagoon. Because the line of breakers runs from northeast to southwest and therefore approaches the beach obliquely, sand picked up by the backwash of the surf is moved southwest when it is redeposited. This action, called beach drifting, accounts for the yearly movement of hundreds of thousands of cubic yards of sand toward the western end of each barrier beach and has been only partially stemmed by the construction of huge rock jetties along the Rockaway and Coney Island beaches.

2. Scholarship

A number of scientific institutions in New York City have made important contributions to the study of geology. Research in geology at Columbia University began in its School of Mines (est. 1864), where the faculty included the noted paleontologist John Strong Newberry. After the department of geology dissociated from the School of Mines, Columbia continued to produce many eminent geologists, including the structural geologist Walter Bucher, the geomorphologists Armand Lobeck and Arthur Strahler, the igneous petrologist S. J. Shand, and Rhodes Fairbridge, widely known for his study of changes in sea level. The Lamont–Doherty Earth Observatory (est. 1949) in Palisades, New York, affiliated with Columbia, was important in developing the theory of plate tectonics in the early 1960s and assembling distinguished scientists such as Bruce Heezen and Marie Tharp, topographers of the ocean floors; Maurice Ewing, a geophysicist and the director of Lamont during the development of plate tectonics; and Lynn Sykes, a geophysicist and seismologist whose work on transform faults in the late 1960s helped to validate the theory of plate tectonics. Another important institution in the city is the American Museum of Natural History, known for its resources in mineralogy, meteoritics, and paleontology. Among those associated with the museum is Niles Eldredge, a paleontologist who with Stephen J. Gould developed the theory of punctuated equilibrium in 1972. The Geological Section of the New York Academy of Science, established in 1827, remains an important forum for professional geologists.

Christopher J. Schuberth, *The Geology of New York City and Environs* (New York: American Museum of Natural History, 1968); *Geological Highway Map, National Bicentennial Edition, Northeastern Region* (Tulsa, Okla.: American Association of Petroleum Geologists, 1976); Chet Raymo and Maureen E. Raymo, *Written in Stone* (Chester, Conn.: Globe Pequot, 1985); Bradford D. Van Diver, *Roadside Geology of New York* (Missoula, Mont.: Mountain, 1985); William L. Neuman, *Geologic Time* (Denver: U.S. Geological Survey / U.S. Government Printing Office, 1991)

Gerard R. Wolfe (§1), Frank Morrow (§2)

George, Henry (*b* Philadelphia, 2 Sept 1839; *d* New York City, 29 Oct 1897). Economist and reformer. After leaving school in Philadelphia at age 14, he learned typesetting and in 1858 moved to San Francisco, where he worked as a reporter and writer and at times lived in poverty. In his book *Progress and Poverty* (1879) he posited that tragic human deprivation was widespread because a few rich landowners were reaping an ever-increasing profit from the natural bounty of the land, the fruits of human labor, and invested capital, a situation he believed was contrary to natural law. The book was the most influential American economic treatise of the nineteenth century and made him internationally known. His single-tax movement sought the "abolition of all taxes on industry and the products of industry" as well as consumers and advocated the financing of government by a heavy tax on land. At the time, the prospect of relying on a land tax alone was feasible: spending by localities and states was already financed overwhelmingly by property taxes, and the system could have been restructured to shift the tax burden from buildings and other manufactured assets to land. George also wished to abolish the tariff as an obstacle to free trade. In 1880 he moved to New York City because of its importance in national affairs. He lectured in Ireland, England, Scotland, and Australia, where he championed human freedom and condemned oppressive government, socialism, monopoly, corruption, and the misery caused by industrialization in U.S. cities. His book *Protection or Free Trade* (1886) articulated his view of the benefits of international free trade for human well-being. In 1886, at the urging of labor leaders, he waged an independent campaign for the mayoralty of New York City. His candidacy was opposed by Tammany Hall and Catholic leaders (Edward McGlynn, a priest who outspokenly supported him, was directed to remain silent and was later excommunicated for disobeying), but he enjoyed considerable support among the Irish, who were impressed by his backing of the Irish Land League and of American labor rights. After a bitter campaign during which George's views were often misrepresented, the Democratic candidate, Abram S. Hewitt, received 90,552 votes, George 68,110, and the Republican candidate, Theodore Roosevelt, 60,435, in what is often considered the most dramatic mayoral election of the nineteenth century in New York City. Although George's followers believed that the election was rigged, fraud could not have accounted for the large differences in the votes tallied.

In 1887 George launched a weekly newspaper called the *Standard* (published at 25 Ann Street) and with several labor unions formed the United Labor Party. After abandoning plans to build a national labor party, he helped form local clubs in support of the single-tax movement. During the presidential campaigns of 1884, 1888, and 1892 he supported Democratic candidates and had some success in spreading his views about the benefits of free trade. He also advocated that churches take a more active role in reducing poverty. Although his health was poor and his book *The Science of Political Economy* unfinished, in 1897 he agreed again to seek the mayoralty of New York City. The campaign proved exhausting, and he died four days before the election; the funeral procession was the longest since that of Abraham Lincoln. Most academic economists of George's day disagreed with him, but in the late twentieth century there was a renewed interest in his views among economists. George lived at various addresses in Manhattan and Brooklyn and maintained an office at 16 Astor Place (from May 1886).

Charles A. Barker, *Henry George* (New York: Oxford University Press, 1955); Jacob Oser, *Henry George* (Boston: Twayne, 1974)

C. Lowell Harriss

George Cromwell Recreation Center. See Cromwell Recreation Center.

Georgetown. Neighborhood in southeastern Brooklyn, lying north of Mill Basin and bounded to the north by Avenue K and Bergen Avenue, to the east and south by Avenue N, and to the west by Ralph Avenue. It was developed in the mid-1960s as Georgetowne Greens, a suburban community with a shopping center and other amenities. Initially it covered a large tract of landfill at Ralph Avenue and Avenue L; the streets were paved and had curbs and sidewalks, and the housing consisted of two-family houses with brick fronts standing on large landscaped lots with driveways. Developers lost interest in the venture after Mayor John V. Lindsay proposed to build Harborville, a Mitchell–Lama housing project of 900 units on an adjacent lot of 32 acres (13 hectares) owned by the city. The proposal was defeated after intense local protest and forestalled further development of Georgetowne Greens, where the existing houses were sold. Developers bought the remaining land and built attached and semidetached three- and four-family houses. As of the early twenty-first century the neighborhood was middle class with large Italian and Jewish populations. The main commercial district is the Georgetown Shopping Center on Ralph Avenue between Avenues K and L.

Elizabeth Reich Rawson

George Washington Bridge. Steel cable, double-decked bridge spanning the Hudson River between 179th Street in Manhattan and Fort Lee, New Jersey. Designed by Othmar H. Ammann and built and operated by the Port of New York Authority, it opened in 1931

George Washington Bridge, looking toward New Jersey from Manhattan, 2009

as the longest suspension bridge in the world. The span connects Westchester County and New England to New Jersey and the rest of the United States; it is the only bridge across the Hudson in New York City. In 1922–25 Ammann led a campaign for a vehicular bridge at 179th Street; his efforts were crucial in persuading the Port Authority to undertake the project and to hire him as bridge engineer. Influenced by the Brooklyn Bridge, he planned to sheathe the towers in granite, but as the Depression cut into the agency's revenues, Ammann agreed to leave the steelwork exposed. The graceful silhouette of the George Washington Bridge belies its enormous weight. Designed to carry light-rail and vehicular traffic, the bridge has a main span of 3500 feet (1068 meters) and is constructed of 141,000 tons of steel. The upper deck of the bridge is suspended 212 feet (64.6 meters) above the Hudson River from four cables, each 4 feet (1.2 meters) in diameter; the cables are strung through the tops of the towers and fastened to huge anchorages in Fort Washington Park in New York City and the Palisades in New Jersey. The lower level of the bridge, also designed by Ammann, was added in 1962 to accommodate the increase in traffic crossing the Hudson, which in the early twenty-first century exceeds 54 million (eastbound) vehicles each year. The architect and designer Le Corbusier once described the bridge as the most beautiful in the world.

David P. Billington, *The Tower and the Bridge: The New Art of Structural Engineering* (New York: Basic Books, 1983)

Rebecca Read Shanor, Jameson W. Doig

George Washington Bridge Bus Station. Bus station opened in January 1963 at Broadway and 178th Street in Manhattan by the Port of New York Authority to replace several small terminals near 168th Street and Broadway. Its construction coincided with the addition of a lower deck on the George Washington Bridge and new expressway connections to the bridge, to which the station is connected by ramps. The station is used primarily by people commuting between Manhattan and suburban Bergen and Passaic counties (in New Jersey) and Rockland County (in New York); the facility has underground links to the 175th Street subway station for service to midtown and lower Manhattan. The station has never been as popular as the Port Authority Bus Terminal, but its proximity to local bus services makes it useful for travelers destined to or from upper Manhattan and the Bronx. On a typical weekday, approximately 15,000 passengers and 730 buses flow in and out of the station; in 2008, approximately 7.5 million passengers were accommodated on about 332,000 bus trips.

Andrew Sparberg

German American Bund. Anti-Semitic organization headquartered in New York City that flourished between 1936 and 1939 with about 8000 to 10,000 members, most of them immigrants. It distributed anti-Semitic tracts, held rallies and parliamentary exercises throughout the Northeast, and opened a compound, Camp Nordland, in Sussex County, New Jersey. Its leader, Fritz Kuhn (1896–1951), was a devotee of Adolf Hitler who encouraged German Americans to protect themselves against the sort of discrimination they had experienced during World War I by embracing anti-Semitism, German ethnic supremacy, and American patriotism. Investigations by government officials led the city commissioner to issue subpoenas in 1939 to the entire membership, including Kuhn and all known local leaders, as well as two tailors who had supplied the group's military uniforms. The German American Bund ceased operations after Kuhn was imprisoned for embezzlement, and its headquarters in the city were shut down by the federal government on 16 December 1941.

Jacqueline Lalley

Germania Life Insurance Company. Original name of the GUARDIAN LIFE INSURANCE COMPANY OF AMERICA.

Germans. German immigrants were present in New Amsterdam during its earliest years of settlement. Peter Minuit, who established the colony in 1626, was himself a native of the German town of Wesel am Rhein. Among those who followed him were Johann Ernst Gutwasser, the settlement's first Lutheran minister (1656–59), and the merchant Jacob Leisler, who arrived in 1660. In 1710 about 150 of the nearly 2150 Palatine Germans who fled to America during the War of the Spanish Succession settled in Manhattan. One of those who stayed was the young John Peter Zenger, who later became well known as a printer and publisher. In the 1790 census there were 2500 Germans; the city had two German Lutheran churches, a German Reformed church, a Moravian church, and a German Society. The first German neighborhood and commercial center in New York City took shape during the 1820s southeast of City Hall in the area extending from Pearl Street to Pine Street.

By 1840 more than 24,000 Germans lived in the city, and during the following 20 years a mass transatlantic migration brought another 100,000 who were fleeing land shortages, unemployment, famine, and political and religious oppression. In the 1840s new German immigrants settled in an area east of the Bowery and north of Division Street in the 10th and 17th wards. It extended to within sight of the East River along Avenue D in the 11th ward and reached the river in the 13th. Known variously as Kleindeutschland, Dutchtown, Little Germany, and Deutschlandle, the neighborhood was the major German American center in the United States for the rest of the century, with more than one-third of the city's German American residents. Other German American neighborhoods took form directly across the East River in Williamsburg (connected to Kleindeutschland by ferries at Houston Street and Grand Street) and across the Hudson in Hoboken, New Jersey. In 1860 there were more than 200,000 Germans in New York City, accounting for one-quarter of the city's total population and making it the first large immigrant community in U.S. history that spoke a foreign language. Natural increase and the arrival of 70,000 immigrants expanded the city's German population to more than 370,000 by 1880 when New York would have ranked as the third largest city in the German Empire. New German settlements were established in Yorkville around Third Avenue and 86th Street and across the East River in Queens, where Steinway and Sons built a piano factory and company town in the 1870s. The southern part of Kleindeutschland, which had older buildings and was more crowded, was resettled by more recent Jewish immigrants from central Europe by the 1880s and became known as the Lower East Side.

Germans were more religiously diverse than most immigrant groups. The early German settlers, who were predominantly Calvinists, were later joined by Lutherans and in the nineteenth century by Catholics from southwestern Germany. Catholics and Jews formed their own subcommunities within the city's German neighborhoods. Adherents of free thought, an outgrowth of the German Enlightenment, ranged from crusading atheists to members of small congregations with beliefs similar to those of Unitarians; freethinkers had their own churches, Sunday schools, "antirevivals," and holidays and were well known for the social events they organized for nonreligious Germans in the city. Germans were also active in the Ethical Culture Society of New York, formed in 1876 by Felix Adler, which continued the German tradition of free thought into the twenty-first century. Religious intolerance was strong among the city's German Protestants during the 1840s and 1850s, when some of them joined American nativist movements that agitated against immigrants and Catholics. Some German American Catholics were equally fervent, denouncing Martin Luther and the Protestant "heresy" on the 400th anniversary of his birth (1883). The struggle between the German Reformation and Counter-Reformation was less intense in New York City than in Germany because of the secularism of the city's artisans, intellectuals, and merchants. Many of the more religiously inclined Germans either fled the city for the churches of Brooklyn or headed for more congenial settlements in the Midwest. This secularism also tended to mute anti-Semitism among Germans. Although some

Germans in Brooklyn attacked a Jewish funeral procession in 1849, other instances of anti-Semitism in New York City were rare until the 1930s. German Jews were in fact integrated into the larger German society on all social levels, from the criminal gangs to the financial elite.

Those who emigrated from the fragmenting German states during the mid-nineteenth century often arrived in Manhattan with little national identity. Differences in dialect, politics, cuisine, and other aspects of regional culture left many unable to identify with immigrants who were from other parts of Germany. Kleindeutschland was made up of smaller neighborhoods of Swabians, Bavarians, Hessians, Westphalians, Hanoverians, and Prussians, and immigrants generally married within their subgroups. Voluntary associations were organized around hometown loyalties, sometimes unintentionally but in most cases purposefully (as Landsmannschaften). In 1862 the Swabians held a regional festival known as the Cannstätter Volksfestverein, an event that gave rise to other ethnic institutions such as a weekly newspaper in the Swabian dialect and *Volksfestvereine* organized by Bavarians (1874), Plattdeutschen (1875), and even Liechtensteiners. These regionally based networks promoted ethnic identities that competed with a larger German American identity well into the 1920s.

Regional ties were the basis of many associations, but they could not account for the multitude of businesses, sickness-and-death-benefit societies, social clubs, political organizations, and other groups that formed when Germans banded together. Fraternal orders such as the Freemasons, the Druids, the Independent Order of Odd Fellows, the Foresters, and the Redmen were joined by German American orders like the Hermannssöhne, the Harugari, the Vereinigte Deutscher Bruder, and B'nai B'rith. By the early 1870s the Harugari alone had 62 lodges with almost 7000 members in the metropolitan area. Among the most conspicuous German associations in the city were singing societies, which held concerts and sponsored large choral festivals. The Deutscher Liederkranz and the Arion Gesangverein became elite clubs after the Civil War; other German choral groups were identified with middle- and working-class Germans in the city. German musicians predominated in the New York Philharmonic Orchestra and provided it with most of its directors, including Leopold Damrosch, an early director of the Männergesangverein Arion. Damrosch soon founded the Oratorio Society, became the director of the Philharmonic, and rescued the failing Metropolitan Opera by introducing a full season of German repertory. Under the direction of his son Walter Damrosch and the management of Heinrich Conried, the Metropolitan became one of the world's greatest opera companies, with a staple of German operas and a largely German audience. Many of the cultural organizations received support from German business leaders, notably Otto H. Kahn, one of the leading philanthropists of the period.

German immigration led to the establishment of many breweries. George Ehret, who opened the Hell Gate brewery in 1866, was the largest brewer in the United States in 1879; the eighth-largest was Jacob Ruppert, also of New York City. In 1877 Manhattan had 78 breweries and Brooklyn had 43. Germans often congregated at beer halls, beer gardens, saloons, and other places where beer was sold. Some of the halls had stages where German theater was performed, and many had meeting rooms that were used by singing societies, lodges, clubs, unions, and political organizations. The large and often elaborately decorated beer halls were the pride of the German neighborhoods. When the city grew too hot for indoor entertainment during the summer, many Germans enjoyed picnics and festivals near suburban Hoboken, New Jersey, and at an elaborate beer garden in Jones's Wood. May festivals as well as music, gymnastic, and sharpshooting festivals attracted tens of thousands of celebrants during the mid-nineteenth century. The most prominent sponsor was Turngeminde, an organization formed by radical artisans. Strengthened and radicalized by an influx of exiles after the failed revolution of 1848, the group organized the Turnverein to promote physical conditioning, German culture, nationalism, and the abolition of slavery.

In the nineteenth century Germans formed numerous socialist political associations, including the Workers' League, the Kommunisten Klub, the First International, and the Socialist Labor Party. Germans were also prominent in the labor movement, and under their leadership in 1872 the New York Eight Hour League organized a strike of more than 100,000 workers. Germans later helped to form the American Federation of Labor, in which Adolph Strasser and Samuel Gompers were prominent, and the Knights of Labor. Although thousands of Germans joined radical unions and socialist organizations, in electoral politics they remained firmly in the Democratic Party. German American politicians like Anton Dugro, Philipp Merkle, and Magnus Gross formed their own organizations within the party, at first allied with Captain Isahia Rynders's faction in support of Mayor Fernando Wood. When Wood fell out with Tammany Hall and set up his own organization, the Germans remained loyal to him and were the key to his electoral victory in 1858. The abolitionist cause did draw German radicals into the Republican Party in the late 1850s, and a few remained in the party until the end of the century, but an anti-German riot in 1857 by the Metropolitan Police, sponsored by Republicans, weakened German ties to the party.

The undisputed leader of the German Democrats by the early 1860s was Oswald Ottendorfer, owner of the popular newspaper the *Staats-Zeitung*. During the next 30 years he led a number of coalitions dedicated to reform and opposed to Tammany Hall. His German Democratic Union Party helped to elect Mayor Charles Godfrey Gunther in 1863. After the organization of William M. "Boss" Tweed eclipsed the German Democrats in the late 1860s, Ottendorfer formed a German independent citizens' organization in the campaign against the Tweed Ring in 1871. Although he helped William F. Havemeyer to win the mayoralty in 1872, Ottendorfer was defeated when he himself sought it in 1874 and his German reform party collapsed.

The German population in New York City reached 748,882 in 1900, partly as a result of consolidation. There were also 133,689 Austrians in the city, almost all of German ethnicity. Although many institutions remained in Kleindeutschland into the early twentieth century, Yorkville surpassed the old neighborhood in importance, and Astoria in Queens and New Jersey grew increasingly popular, especially among the American-born and the prosperous. Deaths among German-born immigrants and the migration of their children to the suburbs reduced the population of German Americans in the city to 584,838 by 1920, but the numbers again increased when about 98,500 Germans fled the economic and political disorder of their country between the end of World War I and 1930.

Germans continued to shape the city's politics for many years. A local chapter of the National German-American Alliance (1901) was especially influential. The strength of the German American community in the city was undermined during World War I as George Sylvester Viereck and other Germans who advocated neutrality were labeled enemy agents and subjected to governmental repression. German-language courses were eliminated from the public schools and German-language works from the Metropolitan Opera; hamburgers became "liberty sandwiches" and sauerkraut became "liberty cabbage." German immigrants sought to restore their sense of ethnic pride during the interwar years, but these efforts were soon disrupted by the Nazi movement and another round of wartime hostility. German Americans made their activities less conspicuous; associations still met and Steuben Society parades were still sponsored, but active assertions of German culture and attempts at collective political action were stifled. The Turnverein became a meeting place for American Nazi activists in the 1930s and was affiliated with a front organization of the German American Bund. The close ties among Germans between Jews and Christians was ruptured by an anti-German boycott organized by Jewish war veterans and by an anti-Jewish boycott that followed.

In the mid-twentieth century many refugees of World War II settled in the metropolitan area, especially in Washington Heights in Manhattan, but they increasingly chose to live outside the city. The end of mass migration and a move to Long Island and New Jersey helped bring about the decline of Yorkville as a German American center in the 1960s and 1970s, leaving Astoria as the only neighborhood in New York City with an identifiable German presence in the 1980s. In 2000 there were approximately a quarter of a million New Yorkers of German ancestry.

Helmut F. Pfanner, *Exile in New York: German and Austrian Writers after 1933* (Detroit: Wayne State University Press, 1983); Stanley Nadel, *Little Germany: Ethnicity, Religion and Class in New York City, 1845–1880* (Urbana: University of Illinois Press, 1990)

Stanley Nadel

German Society of New York. Immigrant aid society formed in 1784 as a social organization and led by Baron von Steuben in 1785–94. It began to assist German immigrants in the 1830s and from 1843 arranged free medical care, helped to find friends and relatives, and provided employment services; it also published the pamphlet *Ratgeber für Auswanderer* (1833) and fought for equitable immigration laws. The president of the society became a member of the state Board of Commissioners of Emigration in 1847. The society continues to provide services for German immigrants into the twenty-first century.

Stanley Nadel

Gerritsen Beach. Neighborhood in southeastern Brooklyn, lying near Marine Park on a peninsula and bounded to the north by Avenue U, to the east by Gerritsen Avenue, to the south by Plum Beach Channel, and to the west by Shell Bank Creek and Knapp Street; it is bisected from west to east by the Gotham Avenue Canal. The neighborhood was named for Wolfert Gerrittsen, who in the early seventeenth century built a house and mill on Gerritsen Creek (now part of Marine Park); the mill was destroyed by fire about 1931. Until the early twentieth century the area remained undeveloped except for a few squatters' bungalows at the foot of Gerritsen Avenue. The firm of Realty Associates began building a middle-class summer resort there in 1920, and the southwest corner of Gerritsen's Meadow was soon covered by one-story bungalows with peaked roofs and no backyards. The popularity of this first venture spurred further growth. Some bungalows were made suitable for year-round habitation, two-story houses with backyards were built, and within a decade there were 1500 houses. Gerritsen Avenue is the main thoroughfare, and the population has long been mostly of Irish, German, and Italian descent. The area north of the canal, called New Gerritsen by local residents, is lined with stores and brick houses. The area south of the canal retains the character of a small fishing village and is a popular station for party boats. The volunteer fire department, which began operation in 1921 when the population began to grow, has headquarters at 32 Seba Avenue and may be the only remaining organization of its kind in Brooklyn. In the early twenty-first century Gerritsen Beach remains a tightly knit community of working-class families, many of whom have lived in the area for generations.

Elizabeth Reich Rawson

gerrymandering. The process of drawing the boundaries of election districts in unconventional shapes in order to achieve a favorable outcome for one party or group in an election. District lines are changed to spread out opposition votes among many districts or to concentrate minority votes within a limited number of districts. The New York State Constitution requires that districts be redrawn every 10 years; the majority leaders of both houses control this process. Several politicians in recent years have presented legislation that would give minority parties more power in the redistricting process. In New York City those who support reform in the redistricting process argue that it would increase competition in elections, allowing a wider variety of issues to be addressed. A number of politicians and community leaders, however, support gerrymandering on the grounds that creating districts that group minorities gives them better political representation.

John Mollenkopf, *A Phoenix in the Ashes: The Rise and Fall of the Koch Coalition in New York City Politics* (Princeton, N.J.: Princeton University Press, 1992)

Briana Dema

Gershwin, George [Gershvin, Jacob] (*b* Brooklyn, 26 Sept 1898; *d* Beverly Hills, Calif., 11 July 1937). Composer, brother of Ira Gershwin. The son of Jewish immigrants from Russia, Gershwin grew up on the Lower East Side of Manhattan. He was educated in New York City public schools and received only rudimentary training in music. After two years at the High School of Commerce, he dropped out and found work at age 16 as a song plugger in Tin Pan Alley. After a summer orchestration class at Columbia University, Gershwin began private music lessons. When he was 19 he wrote his first successful song, "Swanee" (1919) (lyrics by Irving Caesar). His next song, "I'll Build a Staircase to Paradise" (included in George White's *Scandals* of 1922), was his first collaboration with his brother Ira, who wrote the lyrics with Buddy DeSylva. The brothers were notable for their musical inventiveness and sophisticated lyrics including *Lady, Be Good!* (1924), which features the song "Fascinating Rhythm." In 1931 he wrote *Of Thee I Sing,* with scripts by George S. Kaufman and Morrie Ryskind and lyrics by Ira Gershwin. It was hugely popular and became the first musical to win Pulitzer Prize. His *Rhapsody in Blue* (1924) premiered at New York's Aeolian Hall. He also wrote *Concerto in F* (1925) for piano and orchestra, *An American in Paris* (1928), and the opera *Porgy and Bess* (1935). Gershwin's reputation rests on his skillful melding of popular and classical genres. He drew on the conventions of European concert music, the Jewish folk tradition, the music of Tin Pan Alley and Broadway, and elements of ragtime, jazz, and blues; his works are marked by syncopated rhythms, chromatic harmonies, and singable melodies. New York City inspired many of his works, including a one-act opera, *121st Street* (1925), and the songs "I'm Something on Avenue A" (1925), "Harlem River Chanty" (1925), "New York Serenade" (1928), "Harlem Serenade" (1929), "New York Rhapsody" (1931), "Union Square" (1933), and "There's a Boat Dat's Leaving Soon for Old New York" (1935). Gershwin died in 1937 from complications following surgery to remove a brain tumor. Thousands lined the street outside his funeral at Temple Emanu-El at 65th Street and Fifth Avenue in Manhattan. Mayor Fiorello H. La Guardia was a pallbearer. Gershwin is buried in Mount Hope Cemetery in suburban Hastings-on-Hudson, New York.

Edward Jablonski, *George Gershwin* (New York: G. P. Putnam's Sons, 1962); Robert Kimball and Alfred Simon, *The Gershwins* (New York: Atheneum, 1973); Charles Schwartz, *Gershwin: His Life and Music* (Indianapolis: Bobbs–Merrill, 1973)

Nicholas E. Tawa

Gershwin, Ira [Gershvin, Israel] (*b* New York City, 6 Dec 1896; *d* Beverly Hills, Calif., 17 Aug 1983). Lyricist, brother of George Gershwin. Born at the corner of Hester and Eldridge streets, he attended Townsend Harris High School and City College. His first successful musical was *Lady, Be Good!,* a collaboration with his brother that opened at the Liberty Theatre on 1 December 1924. He wrote lyrics for many other songwriters, among them Harold Arlen ("Let's Take a Walk around the Block," 1934) and Vernon Duke ("I Can't Get Started," which was included in Florenz Ziegfeld's *Follies* of 1936). With Kurt Weill he collaborated on *Lady in the Dark* (1941), which played for 467 performances at the Alvin Theatre, and on *The Firebrand of Florence* (1945), Weill's only failure on Broadway. He moved to California in 1936 but retained strong ties to New York City and wrote several works set there, including the play *Park Avenue* (1946), as well as lyrics for the film *The Barkleys of Broadway* (1949), with Fred Astaire and Ginger Rogers. Among Gershwin's residences in the city were 91 Second Avenue (in 1910), 316 West 103rd Street (from 1926), 125 East 72nd Street, and 33 Riverside Drive.

Robert Kimball and Alfred Simon, *The Gershwins* (New York: Atheneum, 1973)

Marc Ferris

Gertz. Firm of retailers. In 1911 Benjamin and Ida Gerts began selling candy and newspapers from a small shop at 162-10 Jamaica Avenue in Jamaica, Queens, that became successful during World War I. In the 1920s they expanded their sales to include stationery and desk equipment for offices. Their business developed into a chain of stores known as B. Gertz, and in 1933 they constructed a five-story building on the site of the original store. After Benjamin Gerts's death in 1933, his four sons and a son-in-law took over the business, which grew during the Depression until it was sold in 1941 to the Allied Corporation by the brothers, the last of whom died in 1957. No members of the family took part in operating the seven stores that remained. The store in Jamaica closed in 1981. Gertz was renamed Stern's in the last step of a merger of two divisions of the Allied Stores Corporation on 1 March 1983.

Leslie Gourse

Gibbons v. Ogden. U.S. Supreme Court case of 1824 (22 U.S. 1) that determined the unconstitutionality of a steamship monopoly sanctioned by the state of New York. In 1798 the New York State Legislature had granted exclusive steamboat rights between New York City and New Jersey to Robert Fulton and Robert Livingston, giving the two men control over licensing other boat operators. In 1813 they licensed Aaron Ogden to run a ferry service between New York City and New Jersey. Facing competition from a rival ferry service authorized by the federal government and run by Thomas Gibbons, Ogden successfully filed for a state injunction that barred Gibbons's ferry from New York waters. Gibbons appealed the decision of the state court all the way to the Supreme Court, which ruled in his favor on the basis of its interpretation of article I, section 8 of the Constitution, or the commerce clause. The Constitution, according to the Court led by Chief Justice John Marshall, gave Congress complete control over all interstate commerce. Coupled with other decisions by the Marshall Court, the ruling strengthened the power of federal over state government. The issue of state versus federal power held vast implications for the development of national infrastructure and the debate on slavery. The ramifications of the ruling also led to the further development of the Port of New York and a rapid national increase in steamboat commerce and travel.

David White

Gibran, (Gibran) Kahlil [Khalil] (*b* Bcharre, Lebanon, 6 Jan 1883; *d* New York City, 10 April 1931). Poet and painter. He settled in Boston with his mother and siblings in 1895 and moved in 1911 to New York City, where he took up residence in the Studio Building at 51 West 10th Street. In 1914 he had his first exhibition of paintings at the Montross Galleries; he became known for his portraits of Sarah Bernhardt, William Butler Yeats, and John Masefield. Gibran wrote in both Arabic and English for the city's flourishing Syrian press. In 1920 he joined with 10 other Syrian-Lebanese émigré writers to form the literary circle al-Rabitah al-Qalamiyya (the Pen League), which greatly influenced Arabic poetry. His first book was *The Madman: Parables and Poems* (1918); he is best known for *The Prophet* (1923), which by the turn of the twenty-first century had sold 11 million copies. Gibran wrote of love, beauty, and the problems of life with a mystical, philosophic vision that proved immensely appealing. He lived in the Studio Building until his death.

Barbara Young, *This Man from Lebanon: A Study of Kahlil Gibran* (New York: Alfred A. Knopf, 1945); Kahlil Gibran and Jean Gibran, *Kahlil Gibran: His Life and World* (New York: New York Graphic Society, 1974)

Ashbel Green, Paula Hajar

Gibson, Althea (*b* Silver, Clarendon County, S.C., 25 Aug 1927; *d* East Orange, N.J., 28 Sept 2003). Tennis player. She grew up in New York City, learned to play tennis at public courts on 155th Street in Harlem, and began playing amateur tennis in the 1940s. With help from the boxer Sugar Ray Robinson, she became the black girls' singles tennis champion of New York State at age 15. In 1950 Gibson was the first African American allowed to play in both the American and English championships and later the first African American player to be generally recognized as a world champion. In 1957 and 1958 she won both the American singles championship at Forest Hills and the English championship at Wimbledon; she also played on the team that won the Wightman Cup. Upon her return to New York City after winning Wimbledon in 1957, Gibson was greeted with a ticker-tape parade and an official welcome at City Hall. She was named the Associated Press Female Athlete of the Year in both 1957 and 1958 and retired soon thereafter. Her autobiography, *I Always Wanted to Be Somebody,* was published in 1958. The following year she played exhibition tennis matches in conjunction with the Harlem Globetrotters basketball team. During these years she lived on Central Park West; later she became a professional golfer and moved to suburban East Orange, New Jersey, where she cofounded the charitable Althea Gibson Foundation to help urban youth develop tennis and golf skills and became involved with New Jersey state athletics.

Leslie Gourse

Lithograph by Charles Dana Gibson, ca 1916

Gibson, Charles Dana (*b* Roxbury [now in Boston], Mass., 14 Sept 1867; *d* New York City, 23 Dec 1944). Illustrator. He entered the Art Students League at age 16 and studied there for two years. Initially unsuccessful in finding employment, he was engaged by the editor John Ames Mitchell to work for *Life* in 1886, and for 30 years his works appeared in the magazine weekly. In 1890 he developed a character known as the Gibson Girl, a chic young woman representing a late nineteenth-century ideal of American womanhood; he introduced a companion for her, Mr. Pipp, in 1898. Many of his drawings for the magazine were published in elegant collections, and in 1903 he charged $1000 for each drawing. Gibson had quarters in the Carnegie Studios and was president of the Society of Illustrators.

Fairfax Davis Downey, *Portrait of an Era as Drawn by C. D. Gibson: A Biography* (New York: Charles Scribner's Sons, 1936)

James E. Mooney

giglio. A tapering, multi-tiered tower, lifted and carried through the streets by about 125 men as part of four related feasts celebrated by Italian Catholics in Greater New York. The name is Italian for lily. The feast has its roots in written texts and oral legends about St. Paulinus (354–431) that relate the story of his imprisonment for the sake of the people of Nola in Campania, Italy, and his welcome with lilies when he returned. The giglio is derivative of the gigantic, ephemeral structures paraded in the civic and religious pageants and spectacles of Europe during the Renaissance and the Counter-Reformation. Immigrants from Nola introduced the feast to New York City in 1903 in Williamsburg, Brooklyn. The feast in East Harlem of St. Anthony of Padua was begun in 1918 by immigrants from Brusciano, near Nola. Similar ones for St. Paulinus were begun in Astoria and Fairview–Cliffside, New Jersey, in the 1930s. The feast in Harlem was last held in 1971 and later moved to Pelham Bay. The giglio is constructed of brightly painted papier-mâché attached to a wooden lattice frame. In 1966 an aluminum frame was introduced in Brooklyn. Giglio builder Romualdo Martello (1903–88) was known for his technical innovations and the sheer beauty of his designs. The annual Williamsburg celebration is considered one of the most spectacular religious festivals in the United States.

Joseph Sciorra

Gilbert, Cass (*b* Zanesville, Ohio, 24 Nov 1859; *d* Brockenhurst, England, 17 May 1934). Architect. He studied at the Massachusetts Institute of Technology for a year and traveled in Europe before moving to New York City, where he worked as a draftsman for McKim, Mead and White for a year; he then moved to Minnesota and after becoming successful there opened an office in New York City. He won a competition to design the U.S. Custom House at Bowling Green (1907). Among his next commissions were the Union Club and the Woolworth Building on Broadway, which incorporated terra-cotta facing in a neo-Gothic style over a steel frame and attracted public attention that helped to secure his election as president of the American Institute of Architects in 1908. In New York City he later designed the U.S. Courthouse and the New York Life Insurance Building; his design for the George Washington Memorial Bridge called for masonry covering steel piers and was rejected because of its expense. A president of the National Academy of Design and the National Institute of Arts and Letters and a founder of the Architectural League of New York, Gilbert worked without partners throughout his career. The largest collection of his materials is held by the New-York Historical Society. His memoirs, *Cass Gilbert: Reminiscences and Addresses,* were published in 1935.

James E. Mooney

Gilbert, C(harles) P(ierrepont) H. (*b* New York City, ?1861; *d* Pelham Manor, N.Y., 25 Oct 1952). Architect. He designed many opulent residences for wealthy New Yorkers and popularized the château-like François I style and the mansarded beaux-arts style from the 1890s to the 1920s. Among his clients were Isaac Fletcher (2 East 79th Street, 1897–99), F. W. Woolworth (Fifth Avenue and 80th Street, 1899, demolished), Joseph R. Delamar (233 Madison Avenue, 1902–5), and Felix Warburg (1109 Fifth Avenue, 1906–8). With the architect J. A. Stenhouse, Gilbert designed a house for Otto H. Kahn (1 East 91st Street, 1913–18). He also designed a group of lavish houses at Riverside Drive and 72nd Street (1899–1901).

Marjorie Pearson

Gilder, Richard Watson (*b* Bordentown, N.J., 8 Feb 1844; *d* New York City, 18 Nov 1909). Editor. Brought up in Flushing, he was an associate editor of *Scribner's Monthly Magazine* from 1870 to 1881 and the editor of *Century Illustrated Monthly Magazine* from 1881 to 1909. He published Mark Twain, Henry James, and William Dean Howells, along with many other important but lesser-known figures. His reputation for being overly Victorian and priggish, partly due to his having rejected Stephen Crane's *Maggie: A Girl of the Streets* on the grounds that it was not in good taste, is belied by his longtime editorial and personal support of Walt Whitman. Gilder was the secretary of a committee to raise funds for construction of the Washington Square Arch. As the chairman of the New York Tenement House Commission in 1894 he revealed that Trinity Church owned slums. His first home at 103 East 15th Street was a popular meeting place for artists, writers, and intellectuals; in 1888 he moved to 13 East Eighth Street. Between 1875 and 1885 Gilder also published 16 volumes of poetry.

Arthur John, *The Best Years of the Century: Richard Watson Gilder, Scribner's Magazine, and the Century Magazine, 1870–1909* (Urbana: University of Illinois Press, 1981)

George A. Thompson, Jr.

Gillespie, Dizzy [John Birks] (*b* Cheraw, S.C., 21 Oct 1917; *d* Englewood, N.J., 6 Jan 1993). Trumpeter, composer, and bandleader. In 1937 he moved to New York City, where he performed in Teddy Hill's Orchestra. Two years later he was playing in Cab Calloway's big band (1939–41), which put him at the vanguard of a new style, bop, in informal sessions at Minton's Playhouse, on West 118th Street. In 1943–44 he led a small group at the Onyx, on 52nd Street, also known as Swing Street, and then toured with the singer Billy Eckstine's bop big band, which included the alto saxophonist Charlie Parker. In 1945 the two made the first mature bop recordings and performed at New York Town Hall. Although not as accomplished a musician as Parker, Gillespie redefined the speed and harmonic sophistication of jazz trumpeting and composed several definitive bop themes. He also became known for his inimitable appearance (usually sporting sunglasses, a beret, and a goatee, with his trumpet bent upward at a 45-degree angle) and for his antic behavior (though he avoided drugs, the downfall of Parker and many other boppers). After an unsuccessful attempt to form a big band, he resumed leading small groups. His second big band, the Dizzy Gillespie Orchestra (1946–50), established Afro-Cuban jazz, a blend of big-band orchestration, bop improvisation, and three rhythmic streams: swing, bop, and Afro-Cuban. Later he mainly led small groups, but he also toured with the Giants of Jazz, which included the pianist Thelonious Monk (1971–72), and when finances allowed he worked again with big bands, such as the United Nations Superband (from 1988). With Al Fraser he wrote *To Be, or Not . . . to Bop: Memoirs* (1979). Until his death he performed at such New York clubs as Monroe's Uptown House, the Village Gate, and the Blue Note. He is buried in the Flushing Cemetery in Queens.

Donald L. Maggin, *Dizzy: The Life and Times of John Birks Gillespie* (New York: Harper Entertainment, 2005)

Barry Kernfeld

Gilmore, Patrick S(arsfield) (*b* Ballygar, Ireland, 25 Dec 1829; *d* St. Louis, 24 Sept 1892). Bandmaster. After a successful career in Boston, he moved to New York City in 1873 to assume leadership of the 22nd Regiment Band of the New York National Guard, a 65-piece ensemble that he transformed during the next 20 years into the nation's only touring brass band. Gilmore began a series of concerts on Saturday evenings at the 22nd Regiment Armory on 14th Street, and in May 1875 he leased and remodeled the Hippodrome, where he conducted celebrated daily concerts in spring and autumn that occasionally attracted 10,000 spectators; the venue became popularly known as Gilmore's Concert Garden. He was renowned for concerts that incorporated church bells, anvils, cannon, and hundreds of musicians. Toward the end of his career, he gave regular performances at Manhattan Beach. His last concert in the city was on 30 May 1892. Gilmore lived at 61 West 12th Street in Manhattan. Among his best-known compositions is "When Johnny Comes Marching Home Again" (1863).

Marwood Darlington, *Irish Orpheus: The Life of Patrick S. Gilmore, Bandmaster Extraordinary* (Philadelphia: Olivier–Maney–Klein, 1950)

Marc Ferris

Gilpin's Gold Room. Original name of the New York Gold Exchange.

Gilroy, Thomas F(rancis) (*b* Sligo, Ireland, 3 June 1839; *d* Queens, 1 Dec 1911). Mayor. He played a central role in the revival of Tammany Hall under John Kelly and Richard Croker in the years after William M. "Boss" Tweed fell from power. In 1892 Gilroy was elected mayor in an agreement with Democratic merchants who favored the presidential candidacy of Grover Cleveland. Like other Tammany leaders of the time, he advocated limited city government, low taxes, and public improvements. In 1894 Gilroy declined to seek reelection when merchants who had supported him two years earlier shifted to "reform." After watching Croker consolidate his control over Tammany Hall, he retired from politics in 1897 to concentrate on his real estate and banking investments.

David C. Hammack

Gilsey House. Hotel opened in April 1871 on Broadway at 29th Street. An elaborate structure of seven stories designed in a Second Empire style by Stephen Hatch for the developer Peter Gilsey, it was built of marble and cast iron from Daniel D. Badger's foundry. The hotel closed in 1911, and the building became used for light manufacturing. In 1980 it was converted into luxury cooperative apartments and is now a city landmark.

Leslie Dorsey and Janice Devine, *Fare Thee Well: A Backward Look at Two Centuries of Historic American Hostelries* (New York: Crown, 1964)

Margot Gayle

Gimbel's. Firm of retailers. It was operated in New York City from 1909 by two sons of Adam Gimbel, a peddler from Bavaria who in 1842 had opened a store in the frontier territory of Vincennes, Indiana; the brothers opened stores in Milwaukee (1887) and Philadelphia (1894) before building a lavish store in 1910 in Herald Square, one block from Macy's. Under the direction of Bernard Gimbel (1885–1966), a grandson of the founder, the firm became well known for its forceful advertising and promotion and particularly for its fierce competition with Macy's. Discounters eventually made Gimbel's unprofitable, and in 1986 its outlets at 86th Street and Lexington Avenue and at 33rd Street and Sixth Avenue were sold to real estate developers by BAT Industries, the British parent company of the firm. The Herald Square site later became a vertical shopping mall.

Leslie Gourse

Ginsberg, (Irwin) Allen (*b* Newark, N.J., 3 June 1926; *d* New York City, 5 April 1997). Poet and activist. He graduated from Columbia University in 1948. In 1956 he published *Howl and Other Poems,* the first of more than 40 books of poetry that made him a central figure in the beat movement in New York City, along with Jack Kerouac, William S. Burroughs, and Herbert Huncke. A dedicated antiwar activist and spokesman for the counterculture in the 1960s, he campaigned for homosexual rights in the 1970s. His book *Fall of America* won the National Book Award in 1972, and in the same year he was elected to the American Academy and the Institute of Arts and Letters. In 1986 he joined the faculty of Brooklyn College. Ginsberg died in 1997 of liver cancer and complications of hepatitis. He is buried in a family plot in Gomel Chesed Cemetery, one of a number of Jewish cemeteries near the city lines of Elizabeth and Newark, New Jersey. Best remembered today for his combination of poetry and political activism, Ginsberg is honored annually by the Howl Festival of Arts in the East Village. Several collections of his poetry and photographs have been published since his death.

Jane Kramer, *Ginsberg in America* (New York: Random House, 1969); Barry Miles, *Ginsberg: A Biography* (New York: Simon and Schuster, 1989)

See also Beats.

Graham Hodges

Ginsburg, Ruth Bader (*b* Brooklyn, 15 March 1933). Supreme Court justice. Born Joan Ruth Bader, she graduated from Cornell University in 1954. She attended Harvard Law School and later transferred to Columbia Law School, where she graduated tied for first in her class in 1959. She became a law clerk to Judge Edmund L. Palmieri of the Southern District of New York. Between 1961 and 1963, Ginsburg worked for the Columbia Law School Project on International Procedure, a project dedicated to comparative law. She taught at Rutgers University Law School from 1963 until 1972, when she became the first woman to earn tenure at Columbia Law School. In 1972 she became the first director of the American Civil Liberties Union's Women's Rights Project. In that capacity, she argued six cases before the U.S. Supreme Court, advocating heightened scrutiny of legal classifications based on gender. In 1980 President Jimmy Carter appointed Ginsburg to serve on the U.S. Court of Appeals for the D.C. Circuit. In 1993 President Bill Clinton appointed Ginsburg to the U.S. Supreme Court. Among her most prominent opinions on the Court was her majority opinion in *United States v. Virginia* (1996), which struck down the Virginia Military Institute's male-only admissions policy.

Frank Scaturro

Giovannitti, Arturo (*b* Campobasso, Italy, 7 Jan 1884; *d* Bronx, 31 Dec 1959). Writer and political leader. After moving to the United States at age 17 he studied theology, traveled throughout the country, and later preached the "propaganda of the deed" for the Italian Socialist Federation and the Industrial Workers of the World; he was also the editor of *Il Proletario* from 1911. After taking part in the mill strike in Lawrence, Massachusetts, he was charged with murder in the death of a striker but was acquitted in November 1912. While awaiting trial he wrote the book *Arrows in the Gale,* which included "The Walker," his best-known poem. A charismatic figure, he formed the Anti-Fascist Alliance (1923) and was an organizer for the International Ladies' Garment Workers' Union and a member of the Italian Labor Education Bureau. A collection of his poetry was published in 1962.

George J. Lankevich

Girl in the Red Velvet Swing. See Nesbit, Evelyn Florence.

Girl Scouts of the USA. Organization for girls formed in 1912 in Savannah, Georgia, by Juliette Gordon Low (1860–1927), intended to instill confidence and character in girls and to encourage them to become involved in their communities. The first troop was formed in New York City in the following year, and the organization moved its headquarters to 17 West 42nd Street in Manhattan in April 1916. A local chapter, the Girl Scout Council of Greater New York, was established in 1940. In 2008 this chapter had 21,085 members and more than 1700 community-based troops, along with a Girl Scout Service Center in each borough. The national headquarters of the Girl Scouts are at 420 Fifth Avenue.

James Bradley

Girls' High School. Original name of Wadleigh High School.

Gish, Lillian (*b* Springfield, Ohio, 14 Oct 1893; *d* New York City, 27 Feb 1993). Actress. She won a small part in the stage production of *Convict's Stripes* in Ohio (1902) before moving to New York City, where she danced in a production featuring Sarah Bernhardt in 1910. She appeared in silent films directed by D. W. Griffith, among them *Birth of a Nation* (1915), *Broken Blossoms* (1919), and *Orphans in the Storm* (1922). Renowned for her delicate beauty, she agreed to make six motion pictures for $1 million, a record for the time; she also had a distinguished career on Broadway in such productions as Chekhov's *Uncle Vanya* (1930), *Hamlet* (1936), and Ted Mosel's *All the Way Home* (1960). Among her last films was Robert Altman's *A Wedding* (1978). For many years she lived at 430 East 57th Street.

Janet Frankston

Giuliani, Rudolph (Rudy) W(illiam Lewis) (*b* Brooklyn, 28 May 1944). Mayor. He attended Catholic schools in Long Island and Brooklyn. At Manhattan College he considered entering the priesthood but instead went to New York University Law School, graduating in 1968. After working as a law clerk and an assistant U.S. attorney, he changed his registration in 1975 from Democrat to Independent and took a job as associate deputy attorney general in the administration of President Gerald R. Ford. He left in 1977 to work in private practice. He changed his party registration again in December 1980 to Republican and in 1981 was named an associate attorney general of the United States. He first came to national attention after being appointed U.S. attorney for the southern district of New York in 1983, from which office he aggressively pursued prominent Wall Street figures for insider trading. He also won several highly charged political corruption cases involving politicians close to then New York City Mayor Ed Koch.

In 1989 Giuliani ran for mayor of New York City as a Republican against Manhattan Borough President David Dinkins, who had unseated three-term Democratic incumbent Ed Koch in that party's primary and was running to be the city's first black mayor. The election was the closest in city history, with Giuliani losing by just 47,080 votes out of 1,899,845 cast. Running again in 1993 Giuliani eked out a margin of 53,367 votes, aided by several racially charged incidents under Mayor Dinkins. Giuliani was the first Republican mayor to take office since John Lindsay in 1965. His first term was marked by a turnaround in the city's fortunes: the crime rate fell and welfare rolls were reduced. Taxes and city payroll were both cut even as revenue rose. He also successfully took on organized crime at the Fulton Fish Market, at the Javits Center, and in commercial solid waste removal. Contentious relations with his own appointees, however, hampered the term; most notably, Police Commissioner William Bratton left his position after a 1996 *Time* magazine cover story gave Giuliani the credit for the drop in crime, and Schools Chancellor Ramon Cortines resigned following several years of personally charged criticism from the mayor.

In 1997 Giuliani easily won reelection against Democratic Manhattan Borough President Ruth Messinger, becoming the first Republican to win a second term as mayor since Fiorello H. La Guardia in 1941. The crime rate and welfare rolls continued to decline, but his popularity also declined significantly, in part because of a series of high-profile incidents involving the police and excessive force. Giuliani also partially undid the city payroll and spending reductions of his first term. In 1999 he considered a 2000 run against Hillary Clinton for the U.S. Senate but decided against it in the midst of a series of personal disclosures, including his diagnosis of prostate cancer and his impending divorce. Giuliani's popularity and reputation were revived, however, by his response to the terrorist attacks of 11 September 2001. He emerged as the face of New York City's resilience, leading *Time* to dub him "America's Mayor." He oversaw the early days of the cleanup, and although prohibited by term limits from running for a third term as mayor, he used his renewed popularity to endorse Republican mayoral candidate Michael Bloomberg, which proved crucial in Bloomberg's narrow victory.

After leaving office Giuliani founded a security consulting business, acquired and later sold an investment banking firm, and joined the Texas-based law firm Bracewell and Patterson, renamed Bracewell and Giuliani when he became a partner. In 2008 Giuliani ran unsuccessfully in the Republican presidential primary, losing to Republican Senator John McCain.

Fred Siegel, Harry Siegel

Glackens, William James (*b* Philadelphia, 13 March 1870; *d* Westport, Conn., 22 May 1938). Painter. He was trained in drawing at the Pennsylvania Academy of Fine Arts in Philadelphia before moving to New York City, where he worked as an illustrator for *McClure's Magazine*, the *New York World*, and the *New York Herald*. After traveling to Paris in 1895 Glackens began to dabble in oil painting that depicted contemporary life and soon became a regular participant in the Pennsylvania Academy's annual exhibit. He became a cofounder of the group of painters later known as the Ashcan School or The Eight, which included Robert Henri, John Sloan, George Luks, Everett Shinn, Ernest Lawson, Maurice Prendergast, and Arthur B. Davies. Influenced heavily by the impressionist style he encountered in Europe, Glackens concentrated on painting urban life as a social commentary on modernism within the city. According to Glackens, he "sought beauty and found it where conventional eyes saw ugliness."

James E. Mooney

Glad Tidings Tabernacle. Pentecostal church at 416 West 42nd Street, formed in 1907 by Marie Burgess (1880–1971). It was led by Burgess until 1909, when she was joined by her husband, Robert Brown (1872–1948). The tabernacle affiliated with the Assemblies of God Church in 1916 and in 1921 moved to 325 West 33rd Street. It sponsored missions throughout the city, evangelical rallies, and a radio ministry. Marie Burgess Brown remained the pastor until her death. In the twenty-first century Glad Tidings Tabernacle was located at 20 Murray Street.

William C. Kostlevy

Glaser, Milton (*b* 26 June 1929). Graphic designer. He attended Manhattan's High School of Music and Art and graduated from Cooper Union in 1951. After a Fulbright Scholarship in Bologna, Italy, he returned to Manhattan and in 1968 founded *New York Magazine* with Clay Felker where Glaser served as president and design director until 1977. In 1974 he opened Milton Glaser, Inc., a design firm, at 207 East 32nd Street. In 1976 New York State commissioned him to design a logo for it and the famous "I ♥ NY" was created. Since 1961 he has been an instructor and board member at the School of Visual Arts, and in the early twenty-first century is on the Board of Directors at Cooper Union.

Jessica Montesano

Glass, Philip (*b* Baltimore, 31 Jan 1937). Composer. He studied at the Juilliard School in the late 1950s and worked in Paris and India with Ravi Shankar and Allah Rakha in the mid-1960s. Soon he composed his first musical productions for the theater. When he returned to New York City in 1966 he moved into a loft on Bleecker Street and formed the Philip Glass Ensemble, a group of instrumentalists and singers that performed at art galleries and museums. In 1974 he gave his first major concert of his own works in the United States at Town Hall. *Einstein on the Beach*, a collaboration with the performance artist Robert Wilson, was staged at the Metropolitan Opera in 1976; the premiere of *Akhnaten* was given at the New York City Opera in 1984. His music, often considered minimalist, is repetitive, harmonically static, and highly rhythmic. He has also produced rock concerts. During the 2007–8 season, the Metropolitan Opera produced *Satyagraha* (1980), the New York City Ballet performed *Glass Pieces* (1983), with music by Glass and choreography by Jerome Robbins, and Glass and his ensemble performed *Powaqqatsi* (1988) at Brooklyn's Prospect Park.

Wim Mertens, *American Minimal Music: La Monte Young, Terry Riley, Steve Reich, Philip Glass* (New York: Broude, 1983)

Barbara L. Tischler

glassmaking. The first glassmaking operation in New York City was that of Evert Duÿcking, which opened as early as the mid-seventeenth century and probably manufactured window glass. Other glasshouses made windowpanes and bottles. Fine glass tableware was made from 1820 by Richard and John Fisher and John L. Gilliland, who opened the Bloomingdale Flint Glass Works (also called the New York Glass Works), a factory known for its plain and cut flint and colored glass until it closed in 1840. Brooklyn became the local center for fine glass production after Gilliland formed his own firm in 1823, the Brooklyn Glass Works (later the Brooklyn Flint Glass Works); it specialized in richly cut and colored glass, lamps, and chandeliers as well as pressed glass and made the globes for the city's gaslights. With Boston and Pittsburgh, New York City was one of the country's primary centers for glassmaking by the 1830s. The first important stained-glass studio was that of William Jay and John Bolton in Pelham, New York: its windows for St. Ann and the Holy Trinity Church (1843–48) in Brooklyn were one of the first extensive programs of stained glass in the country. The Brooklyn Glass Works became known internationally after winning a medal at London's Crystal Palace Exposition of 1851. From about 1860 the number of factories in the city declined as glassmaking factories were opened elsewhere,

The Bloomingdale Flint Glass Works of John and Richard Fisher near the Hudson River on West 47th Street, ca *1837*

especially west of the Allegheny Mountains near abundant sources of coal. Christian Dorflinger, one of the city's best-known glassmakers, opened a factory in White Mills, Pennsylvania. The Brooklyn Glass Works was taken over by Amory Houghton and his son and moved to Corning, New York, in 1868.

After 1865 glass factories in Brooklyn turned to the manufacture of decorative globes and shades for lamps. After Dorflinger retired, his works in Greenpoint, which employed immigrants and stressed handwork, changed ownership several times. It remained in operation until the 1940s as part of the Gleason–Tiebout Company and was known for the innovative etching techniques used for its light fixtures. During the second half of the nineteenth century the city's stained-glass makers became the foremost in the country. As the demand rose for stained glass in churches, public buildings, and private homes, the number of studios increased, many of them opened by German and English craftspeople, among them Charles Booth. Most made windows from sheets of colored glass that were painted with enamels and fired to achieve shading and modeling. In the late 1870s Louis Comfort Tiffany invented marbleized glass with gradations of color, texture, and density that could be used to achieve details with little or no paint. He bought sheets of colored and opalescent glass from various sources in and near the city, including the Thill and Heidt glasshouses in Brooklyn, until he built his own factory in Corona in 1893; there he developed vessels blown from his marbleized glass known as Favrile that made him internationally known. The glass industry became increasingly mechanized owing to a number of technological advances and was centered in enormous factories requiring large amounts of capital. Their size alone made them unsuitable for the densely populated city, and the number of glassmaking firms in Brooklyn declined from 12 in 1880 to six in 1909 and four in 1919.

After a period of decline, interest in glassmaking revived in 1962, when technology was introduced to allow the production of glass in small studios. In 1977 the New York Experimental Glass Workshop opened in Manhattan as the city's first studio devoted to glassmaking; it was eventually renamed UrbanGlass and moved into the former site of the Strand Theatre at 647 Fulton Street in Brooklyn, where artists continued to work and teach in the early twenty-first century.

Joshua Brown and David Ment, *Factories, Foundries, and Refineries: A History of Five Brooklyn Industries* (New York: Brooklyn Educational and Cultural Alliance, 1980)

Alice Cooney Frelinghuysen

Glatshteyn, Yankev (*b* Lublin, Poland, 20 Aug 1896; *d* New York City, 19 Nov 1971). Writer and critic. He arrived in New York City in 1914 and joined with Aaron Glanz (A. Leyeles) and N. B. Minkoff in establishing the Inzikhistn (Introspectivists), a modernist literary circle that dominated the American Yiddish avant-garde during the 1920s and 1930s. Best known as a poet, he was celebrated for his linguistic virtuosity, formal daring, and vivid imagery. Glatshteyn wrote 10 volumes of poetry over five decades in addition to several novels and many essays on Yiddish and world literature.

Janet Hadda, *Yankev Glatshteyn* (Boston: Twayne, 1980)

Jeffrey Shandler

Gleason, Jackie [Herbert John] (*b* Brooklyn, 26 Feb 1916; *d* Fort Lauderdale, Fla., 24 June 1987). Actor. He performed on Broadway as a young man and began a film career with a part in *Navy Blues* (1941). Gleason later won awards for his roles in the motion pictures *The Hustler* (1961) and *Gigot* (1962). On television he became well known for portraying comic characters in such series as *The Life of Riley* and *Cavalcade of Stars;* his best-known role is that of Ralph Kramden, a bus driver from Bensonhurst (Brooklyn), in *The Honeymooners,* a hit series during the 1950s that was filmed at the Adelphi Theater on 54th Street. Gleason won a Tony Award in 1959 as best actor for his performance in *Take Me Along.*

James Bacon, *How Sweet It Is: The Jackie Gleason Story* (New York: St. Martin's, 1985)

James E. Mooney

Gleason, Teddy [Thomas William] (*b* New York City, 8 Nov 1900; *d* New York City, 26 Dec 1992). President of the International Longshoremen's Association (ILA). He left school in the seventh grade and as a teenager followed his father and grandfather onto the docks. Over the years he worked as a checker, billing clerk, dockhand, truck loader, and timekeeper. By 1932 he was dock superintendent. During the Depression he was blacklisted by stevedoring companies and steamship lines because of his union activities. To support his family, he worked in a sugar factory during the day and sold hot dogs at Coney Island at night. He was elected president of the ILA in 1963 and served six consecutive four-year terms, retiring in 1987. In 1963 Gleason opposed the proposal by the administration of President John F. Kennedy to sell surplus wheat to the Soviet Union; he relented when it was agreed that half of the grain ships would be American. When the administration of President Lyndon Johnson reneged on the deal, Gleason began a dockworkers' boycott of the Soviet-bound wheat, which he called off after eight days. He was responsible for winning a guaranteed annual income that allowed hundreds of union members to collect $32,000 a year for doing no work after containerization eliminated their jobs.

Frank Dyer

Glendale. Neighborhood in west central Queens, bounded to the north by railroad tracks (Montauk division, Long Island Rail Road), to the east by Woodhaven Boulevard, to the south by cemeteries, and to the west by Fresh Pond Road. It originally consisted of farms and was developed in 1869 by John C. Schooley, a real estate agent from Jamaica, who reportedly named it after his birthplace in Ohio. He laid out streets and sold lots priced at $300 and measuring 25 by 100 feet (8 by 30 meters). The South Side Railroad was extended to the area in 1867 and opened a station at 73rd Place. Development increased after Myrtle Avenue on 23 May 1893 was given service by steam dummy (a horsecar or trolley car powered by a small steam engine). Until World War I farms were sold and laid out in blocks of row houses and one-family houses. Family shops opened along Myrtle Avenue, which from the 1890s until about 1920 was enjoyed for its picnic parks. After 1905 silk ribbons, matches, and airplanes were manufactured in the area, and in the 1920s studios there produced silent films. A large German population in the 1930s worked in local breweries and textile factories. The largest employer in the 1940s was Atlas Terminal, a large group of factories. In the 1980s the neighborhood attracted a number of immigrants from Romania, Yugoslavia, and Poland, as well as from China and the Dominican Republic. In the early twenty-first century the neighborhood remained a generally middle-class, tightly knit community.

Vincent Seyfried

Glenn L. Curtiss Airport. Original name of La Guardia Airport.

Glen Oaks. Neighborhood in eastern Queens, bounded to the north by Grand Central Parkway, to the north and east by Nassau County, to the south by Hillside Avenue, and to the west by Grand Central Parkway and the Creedmoor Psychiatric Center. Some areas have a postal address in Floral Park or Bellerose. Part of the town of Flushing, the area was the site of William K. Vanderbilt's estate, of which 167 acres (67 hectares) were bought in 1923 by the Glen Oaks Golf Club; the clubhouse stood on the highest point in Queens. In 1944 the Gross–Morton Company bought 175 acres (70 hectares) along Union Turnpike and with a $24 million Federal Housing Authority loan built Glen Oaks Village, a garden apartment complex of 2904 units in 134 two-story buildings in the colonial style. Unlike earlier garden apartment complexes, Glen Oaks has garages and parking behind the buildings. Many of the original residents were veterans of World War II. A shopping center was erected in the same style on Union Turnpike. Originally rental property, the complex became a cooperative in 1981. The 400-unit Parkwood Estates, another garden apartment complex, was built in the 1950s, as were dozens of one- and two-family houses. North Shore Towers, three apartment buildings of 33 stories each, was built between 1971 and 1974 on the remaining portion of the golf course. In addition to Creedmoor, the neighborhood is the site of Long Island Jewish and Hillside hospitals and the Queens County Farm Museum. The Glen Oaks branch of the Queens Borough Public Library opened in 1956 and has collections in Gujarati, Hindi, Malayalam, and Urdu.

Jeffrey A. Kroessler

Glickman, Marty [Martin] (*b* Bronx, 14 Aug 1917; *d* New York City, 3 Jan 2001). Sportscaster. A star football and track performer at Syracuse University, he was chosen for the U.S. Olympic team for the 1936 games in Berlin. On the eve of the 400-meter relay, Glickman and teammate Sam Stoller were replaced in the event, told by team officials that because they were Jewish, a victory would embarrass the Nazi hosts and Hitler. In 1998 the president of the U.S. Olympic Committee, citing "great evidence of anti-Semitism" in the Berlin games, presented Glickman with a plaque "in lieu of the gold medals" he was not able to win. Meanwhile, Glickman became a sportscaster and had a long and distinguished career, best known as the voice of the New York Knicks and the New York Giants. He also was the voice for the New York Jets, did pregame and postgame shows for the Brooklyn Dodgers and the New York Yankees, and was the announcer for Yonkers raceway. Glickman is enshrined in the Basketball Hall of Fame, the American Sportscasters Hall of Fame, and the New York Sports Hall of Fame.

Frank Dyer

Globe and Commercial Advertiser. Daily evening newspaper. It was launched on 9 December 1793 by Alexander Hamilton and others as a Federalist organ called the *American Minerva,* with Noah Webster as its editor. On 2 October 1797 it changed its name to the *Commercial Advertiser,* becoming known for its muckraking style in the late nineteenth century and the early twentieth under the editor Henry J. Wright. It was renamed the *Globe and Commercial Advertiser* on 1 February 1904 and was commonly known and sold by newsboys as the *Globe.* In 1923 it was bought by the newspaper magnate Frank Munsey, who merged it a week later (on 4 June) with the *Sun.*

George Britt, *Forty Years, Forty Millions: The Career of Frank A. Munsey* (New York: Farrar and Rinehart, 1935)

Michael Green

God Box. See Interchurch Center.

Goddard, Paulette [Levy (Levee), Pauline Marion Goddard] (*b* Queens, 3 June 1911; *d* Ronco, Switzerland, 23 April 1990). Actress. After beginning her career in New York City with a part in the revue *No Foolin'* (1926), she moved to Hollywood in 1931 and played bit parts in various films until Charlie Chaplin cast her in *Modern Times* (1936). She became one of the most popular film stars of the 1940s and appeared in more than 40 films, including *The Cat and the Canary* (1939), *The Great Dictator* (1940), and *Hold Back the Dawn* (1941). In the 1950s her popularity waned and she performed only rarely. A longtime friend of New York University and its former president John Brademas, Goddard bequeathed her entire estate of more than $20 million to the institution.

Sara J. Steen

Goddard Institute for Space Studies. Government institute at 112th Street and Broadway, founded in 1961 by Robert Jastrow; it is affiliated with the National Aeronautics and Space Administration (NASA). The institute is based in New York City because of its close links to local colleges and universities (notably Columbia University and the City University of New York), as well as to four high schools. Its research emphasis is on atmospheric science, especially global warming. In the early twenty-first century about 160 people worked there.

Godfrey, Arthur (Morton) (*b* New York City, 31 Aug 1903; *d* New York City, 16 March 1983). Television and radio personality. He received his first radio training on a submarine while in the U.S. Navy from 1920 to 1924. Following his discharge he worked a range of jobs and joined the Coast Guard in 1927, appearing on the radio for the first time in Baltimore. Godfrey freelanced and worked for the National Broadcasting Company in Washington, D.C., in the 1930s before moving to New York City in 1941. In 1945 he began airing his own half-hour morning show for Columbia Broadcasting System radio and gained national attention for his emotional live coverage of President Franklin D. Roosevelt's funeral procession. He got started on television in 1948 with *Arthur Godfrey's Talent Scouts,* a program that helped launch the careers of emerging entertainers like Tony Bennett and Lenny Bruce, and *Arthur Godfrey and His Friends.* Sometimes introduced as "the Old Redhead," Godfrey became nationally famous; his trademarks included inventing his own sales pitches, joking about his sponsors' products, and sometimes playing the ukulele on air. Lung cancer forced Godfrey to retire in 1959; his surgery was front-page news across the country. He attempted a comeback in the 1960s but failed to regain his former popularity.

Ben Silk

Godkin, E(dwin) L(awrence) (*b* Moyne, Ireland, 2 Oct 1831; *d* Brixham, England, 21 May 1902). Writer and editor. After receiving his education in Ireland and England he worked for two years from 1853 as a war correspondent in the Crimea. He then moved to New York City where he became the editor of the weekly journal the *Nation* and made it one of the most respected publications of its kind. With Carl Schurz he edited the *New York Evening Post* from 1881, becoming the editor in chief when Schurz withdrew. He was sympathetic to the Mugwumps, Republicans who opposed political machines and mistrusted organized labor. In a style marked by a keen sense of humor he wrote on Tammany Hall and many other subjects and was highly influential in the press. Godkin retired in 1900. Among his published writings are *Problems of Modern Democracy* (1896) and *Tendencies of Democracy* (1898).

William M. Armstrong, *E. L. Godkin: A Biography* (Albany: State University of New York Press, 1978)

See also INTELLECTUALS and PARTISAN PRESS.

James E. Mooney

Goethals Bridge. Steel cantilevered bridge spanning the Arthur Kill between Howland Hook in Staten Island and Elizabeth, New Jersey. Designed by the engineer Alexander Waddell and named for the Panama Canal's chief engineer, General George W. Goethals, it opened to traffic on 29 June 1928, the same day as the Outerbridge Crossing (also designed by Waddell). The two bridges provided the first crossings for motor vehicles between Staten Island and the mainland. The structure has a span of 672 feet (205 meters), a length of 7109 feet (2168 meters), and a clearance above water of 135 feet (41 meters). For many years it carried little traffic, but since the opening of the Verrazano–Narrows Bridge in 1964, which provided a direct route from New Jersey to Long Island, it has been heavily trafficked and construction of a twin span near the Goethals has been considered.

Rebecca Read Shanor, Jameson W. Doig

Goethals Bridge, 1937

Goethe-Institut. German cultural institute. Located at 1014 Fifth Avenue, the Goethe-Institut has a gallery, library, book center, and program center. One of the smallest museums in New York City, it hosts cultural exchange programs, helps connect Americans with German resources both in the United States and in Germany, and has courses for learning or teaching German. The Goethe-Institut New York is the regional coordinator of the 10 institutes in North America. In the twenty-first century it continues to operate the gallery and expand its cultural programs.

Jessica Montesano

Goetz, Bernhard Hugo (*b* New York City, 7 Nov 1947). Vigilante. He became famous for a widely publicized act of vigilantism that occurred on 22 December 1984 involving Goetz, a 37-year-old Caucasian electronics engineer, and four African American youths who asked him for money aboard the No. 2 subway near the Chambers Street station. Goetz drew a handgun, for which he did not have a license, and fired at the youths, hitting all four. Indicted for attempted murder, he became the focus of an international debate over self-defense and public safety. Although many observers believed he was a hero who had fought back against urban crime, others saw him as a depraved vigilante, possibly motivated by racism, whose use of force was disproportionate to the danger he faced. At a celebrated trial in June 1987 Goetz was acquitted of attempted murder, found guilty only of illegal possession of a handgun, and sentenced to a year in prison and five years' probation. He served eight months at Rikers Island. One of the four youths, Darrel Cabey, was paralyzed and brain-damaged as a result of the shooting. Cabey filed a civil suit against Goetz and in April 1996 was awarded $43 million in damages; Goetz filed for bankruptcy. Goetz later turned to politics, running unsuccessful campaigns for mayor in 2001 and public advocate in 2005. Some Goetz supporters continue to honor him for bringing attention to urban crime and lowering the New York City crime rate.

Robert Sanger Steel

Gold, Michael [Granich, Itzok] (*b* New York City, 12 April 1893; *d* San Francisco, 14 May 1967). Journalist and essayist. The son of poor immigrants, he grew up on the Lower East Side and attended New York University and Harvard University briefly before working for *The Masses.* Between 1914 and 1917 he published his first articles in *The Masses* and was also associated with the Provincetown Players. To protect himself during the Red Scare of 1919–20 he adopted the name Michael Gold after a Civil War veteran whom he admired. In 1920 he became an editor of the *Liberator,* which was formed after the federal government suppressed *The Masses.* He was the editor from 1928 to 1933 of the *New Masses,* a publication devoted to proletarian literature, which he defined as literature written by workers and dealing with workers' issues (he considered most other kinds of literature to be crippled by bourgeois idealism). From 1933 Gold was a columnist for the newspaper the *Daily Worker* (1924–57). His best-known work was *Jews without Money* (1930), an account of life on the Lower East Side.

James D. Bloom, *Left Letters: The Culture Wars of Mike Gold and Joseph Freeman* (New York: Columbia University Press, 1992)

Kevin Kenny

Gold and Stock Telegraph Company. Firm incorporated in August 1867 at 18 New Street to promote the first stock ticker, adapted from the printing telegraph invented by Edward Calahan and installed in 1868 at the New York Stock Exchange. Initially the firm served only brokers from the New York Stock Exchange, but it soon expanded its business to other exchanges throughout the United States. The Western Union Telegraph Company acquired the firm in May 1871 and continued to operate it as a subsidiary. It controlled most of the important printing telegraph patents and well into the twentieth century was the leading supplier of market reports and private-line printing telegraphs, which provided communication for banks, linkages between courthouses and lawyers' offices, and private lines connecting homes, offices, and factories. Gold and Stock Telegraph ceased operations in 1962.

Merchants' Telephone Exchange: List of Subscribers (New York: Gold and Stock Telegraph Company, 1880)

Paul Israel

Goldberg, Rube [Reuben Lucius] (*b* San Francisco, 3 July 1883; *d* New York City, 7 Dec 1970). Cartoonist. Born into a prosperous family, he moved to New York City in 1907 to work as a sports cartoonist for the *Evening Mail.* He produced widely syndicated single-frame cartoons and comic strips; his strip *Boob McNutt* ran for 20 years. When his popularity diminished in the 1930s, he turned to political cartooning with a conservative slant. Goldberg's best-known cartoons depict machines that use absurdly complicated means to accomplish simple tasks; his contraptions incorporate dripping water, falling coconuts, bursting balloons, and startled monkeys. He won the Pulitzer Prize for editorial cartooning in 1948, and the National Cartoonists Society created an award called the Reuben in his honor. Goldberg lived in the Brentmore, at 88 Central Park West, until 1963; his last home was at 169 East 69th Street.

Peter C. Marzio, *Rube Goldberg: His Life and Work* (New York: Harper and Row, 1973)

George A. Thompson, Jr.

Golden Gloves. See New York Golden Gloves.

Goldman, Emma (*b* Kaunas, Lithuania, 27 June 1869; *d* Toronto, 14 May 1940). Anarchist. She joined the radical movement in New York City in 1890 and dominated it until her deportation in 1919. From 1903 to 1913 she lived at 210 East 13th Street, where in 1906 she began publishing *Mother Earth,* a journal of political and cultural articles far ahead of their time. A believer in the emancipation of women physically and intellectually, she was perhaps best known as an advocate of birth control and sexual relations outside marriage. She was arrested for criticizing militarism and opposing American entry into World War I, for which she was imprisoned on Ellis Island. With hundreds of other immigrants deemed "dangerous radicals," she was deported to the Soviet Union. A critic of the Bolshevik regime, she wandered through Europe for the rest of her life. In exile she continued to speak out for anarchist causes.

Martha Foley

Goldman Sachs. Firm of investment bankers. It began as a firm of dealers in commercial paper formed in New York City in 1869 by Marcus Goldman, a German immigrant. Samuel Sachs became a partner in 1882, and by 1885 the firm was given its current name. A brokerage was added in the 1890s, and after 1900 the firm underwrote securities, primarily in consumer goods. Sidney J. Weinberg became a partner in 1927 and a senior partner in 1930. Under the direction of Gustave L. Levy, who joined the firm in the 1930s, the trading department undertook risk arbitrage. There were 13 partners by the mid-1940s. During the 1990s, under the leadership of Robert Rubin and Stephen Friedman, the firm bought a 50 percent stake in Rockefeller Center before selling its shares to Tishman Speyer in 2000. Goldman Sachs went public in 1999, and senior partner Henry Paulsen become chairman and CEO. The most successful firm of its kind, Goldman Sachs maintains more than 30 offices around the world. Its divisions specialize in investment banking, fixed-income and equities securities sales, trading and arbitrage, investment management, currency and commodities, and a broad range of other financing and investment services.

The firm's headquarters at 85 Broad Street were damaged in the terrorist attacks of 11 September 2001, and city officials subsequently pressed for the firm to open offices in the new Freedom Tower. In April 2005, however, Goldman Sachs announced that it would build its own $2 billion, 43-story headquarters in the last open commercial site in Battery Park City, assisted by $1.6 billion in tax-exempt Liberty Bonds from the state and the city. This financial incentive composed almost 20 percent of the federal government's $8 billion tax-free financing slated for New York City's post-9/11 redevelopment. Public response to the plan's financing was critical, although proponents noted that Goldman Sachs's presence near Ground Zero was essential to the area's future. In return for financing, the firm agreed to keep 9000 of its employees and significant trading operations in lower Manhattan and to create 4000 new jobs by 2019. During the global financial crisis that began in 2007, Goldman Sachs received billions of dollars in federal loan guarantees without which it might not have remained solvent.

Mary E. Curry

golf courses. In the late 1990s there were 16 golf courses in New York City, of which 14 had 18 holes and two had nine holes (the number of courses was up to 21 a decade later). The first municipal golf course in the United States, at Van Cortlandt Park, was designed by Tom Bendelow in 1895. Another of his designs, Forest Park Golf Course, opened the following year in Queens and became known for its rugged terrain. In the Bronx, Mosholu Golf Course (1914) opened in Van Cortlandt Park, and Pelham Bay Golf Course (1921) and Split Rock Golf Course (1928) opened at Pelham Bay Park, where they shared an art deco clubhouse. Two private clubs, Clearview Golf Course (1925) and Douglaston Golf Course (1927), were developed in Queens by Willie Tucker, and a Spanish-style clubhouse at Douglaston was designed by Clifford Wendehack, the well-known clubhouse architect of the 1920s. The three public courses in Staten Island are Silver Lake Golf Course (1927); La Tourette Golf Course (1928), which has a par of 72 and is considered the city's most challenging course; and South Shore Golf Course (1929). The clubhouse at La Tourette, once a residence, is a municipal landmark. La Tourette, Silver Lake, Split Rock, Dyker Beach Golf Course in Brooklyn (1928), and Kissena Park Golf Course in Queens (1933, the city's shortest course at 4642 yards [4245 meters], with a par of 64) were developed by the architect John R. Van Kleek. The city's longest course, Marine Park Golf Course (6736 yards [6159 meters]), was designed in Brooklyn in 1962 by Robert Trent Jones. The Towers private golf course is open only to residents of the North Shore Towers in Queens, and the Richmond County Country Club course in Staten Island is also private. A nine-hole course on Governors Island for military personnel stationed there closed in 1996. There are also two "pitch and putt" courses (in Flushing Meadows–Corona Park and Gateway National Park). In the 1980s the Department of Parks and Recreation turned the operation of golf courses over to outside operators. In 2000 Mayor Rudolph Giuliani added $13 million to the city's budget for installing better irrigation on the courses and other improvements.

Christina Plattner

Golfus, Emil R. See Abel, Rudolf.

Gompers, Samuel (*b* London, 27 Jan 1850; *d* San Antonio, Tex., 13 Dec 1924). Labor leader. He immigrated to the United States in 1863 and settled in New York City, where he worked as a cigar maker. In 1873 he organized the United Cigarmakers, which joined the Cigar Makers' International Union as Local 144 in 1875. As the head of the union's constitutional committee during the 1880s he introduced several measures that helped revitalize the organization. Conflicts between the Cigar Makers' International Union and the Progressive Cigarmakers arose in the 1880s and culminated in the formation of the

Samuel Gompers

American Federation of Labor. Elected president of the federation, Gompers endorsed the mayoral candidacy of Henry George, launched by a coalition of unions in 1886, and was an adviser to the Social Reform Club, which promoted workers' compensation, union labels, and collective bargaining. While testifying at state assembly hearings on production in tenements and conditions in sweatshops, he urged legislators to enact stricter factory codes. In his later years he spoke at several rallies organized by garment workers and helped settle disputes involving teamsters (1910), furriers (1912), and transit workers (1916). Gompers wrote *Seventy Years of Life and Labor: An Autobiography* (1925). He lived at 371 East Fourth Street.

Melvin Dubofsky, *When Workers Organize: New York City in the Progressive Era* (Amherst: University of Massachusetts Press, 1968); Stuart Bruce Kaufman, *Samuel Gompers and the Origins of the American Federation of Labor, 1848–1896* (Westport, Conn.: Greenwood, 1973); Harold Livesay, *Samuel Gompers and Organized Labor in America* (Boston: Little, Brown, 1978)

Ronald Mendel

Good Government Clubs. Organizations formed in the 1890s by the City Club of New York at the behest of the reformers Edmond Kelly and R. Fulton Cutting. Their aim was to mobilize the city's business and professional communities against Tammany Hall, which derided their members as "goo-goos." There were 24 clubs by 1894, when they were influential in securing the election of the fusion mayoral candidate William L. Strong.

Bernard Hirschhorn

Goodhue, Bertram Grosvenor (*b* Pomfret, Conn., 28 April 1869; *d* New York City, 23 April 1924). Architect. He moved to New York City in 1884 to work in the firm of Renwick, Aspinwald and Tucker. He formed a partnership with Ralph Adams Cram and Frank W. Ferguson, moving with them to Boston in 1891 and returning to New York City to run the firm's office there from 1903 to 1913. With Cram and Ferguson he designed St. Thomas Church at Fifth Avenue and 53rd Street (1905–13), his best-known neo-Gothic work. He also oversaw the design of the Church of the Intercession at the Trinity Cemetery on Broadway (1910–14). Tension within the firm, especially with Cram over the construction of the Cathedral of St. John the Divine, led Goodhue to open his own firm in 1914 in the Jackson Building on 47th Street, which he ran as an atelier. There, apprentices including Clarence Stein, Raymond Hood, and Wallace K. Harrison helped design such distinctive churches as St. Vincent Ferrer on Lexington Avenue (1914–18). A member of the Century Club from 1911, he won the commission for St. Bartholomew's Church on Park Avenue (1917–19), which incorporated a memorial portal commissioned by the Vanderbilts and designed by Stanford White. Goodhue blended neoclassical and modern styles in later designs, such as that for Convocation Tower, an office tower and religious complex planned for Madison Square; presentation drawings by Hugh Ferriss were shown at the 36th Annual Exhibition of the Architectural League of New York in 1921.

Richard Oliver, *Bertram Grosvenor Goodhue* (Cambridge, Mass.: MIT Press, 1983)

Edward A. Eigen

Goodhue, Jonathan (*b* Salem, Mass., 21 June 1783; *d* New York City, 24 Nov 1848). Commission merchant and shipping magnate. He arrived in New York City in 1807 and organized Goodhue and Company, a commission house on South Street. In 1813 he married Catharine Rutherford Clarkson, member of a prominent New York City family, and moved to 33 Whitehall Street in Manhattan. With Pelatiah Perit, who joined the firm in 1819, he used his commercial connections to the British banking house of Baring Brothers to gain control of the famous Black Ball Line of packet ships to Liverpool in 1834. Goodhue was an adherent of the Whig Party and a leader of the free trade movement. Like other prominent merchants he was a director of several banks and insurance companies and a supporter of humanitarian causes.

Robert Greenhalgh Albion, *Square-Riggers on Schedule: The New York Sailing Packets* (Princeton, N.J.: Princeton University Press, 1938)

Elaine Weber Pascu

Goodman, Benny [Benjamin David] (*b* Chicago, 30 May 1909; *d* New York City, 13 June 1986). Clarinetist and bandleader. He first played in New York City in 1928 with Ben Pollack at the Park Central Hotel and with Red Nichols and His Five Pennies. As a studio musician he took part in recording sessions, radio broadcasts, and other performances, including Broadway productions of George Gershwin's *Strike Up the Band* (1927) and *Girl Crazy* (1930). Goodman formed a big band in 1934 that soon attracted a wide audience and helped broaden the popularity of jazz. He used arrangements by other bandleaders, including Fletcher Henderson, and engaged such well-known players as the trumpeters Bunny Berigan and Harry James, the drummer Gene Krupa, and the pianist Jess Stacy; with the addition in 1936 of the pianist Teddy Wilson and the vibraphonist Lionel Hampton, his quartet became the first racially mixed group in popular music. He often performed in the Manhattan Room of the Hotel Pennsylvania. An appearance at the Paramount Theater in March 1937 led to such chaos by more than 21,000 enthusiastic fans that the event became known as the Paramount Riot. Goodman's performance at Carnegie Hall on 16 January 1938 demonstrated the adaptability of dance music to the concert hall. That same year he recorded Mozart's Clarinet Quintet with the Budapest Quartet and commissioned Béla Bartók to write *Contrasts.* In 1947 Goodman commissioned clarinet concertos from Aaron Copland and Paul Hindemith. For many years he maintained an apartment at 200 East 66th Street.

D. R. Connor, *Benny Goodman: Listen to His Legacy* (Metuchen, N.J.: Scarecrow, 1988)

Loren Schoenberg

Goodyear, Charles (*b* New Haven, Conn., 29 Dec 1800; *d* New York City, 1 July 1860). Inventor. Best known for inventing vulcanized

Charles Goodyear's rubber goods store (left) near the intersection of Grand Street and East Broadway, ca *1878*

rubber, he carried out some of his most important experiments in New York City. After encountering rubber for the first time in 1834, he moved to New York City to conduct experiments, working at various times on Bank Street and in Staten Island. After a number of failures he left the city in 1837, but he returned in 1840 for about a year to refine his successful sulfur-and-heat process later known as vulcanization. Goodyear spent little time in the city thereafter.

Robert M. Quackenbush, *Oh, What an Awful Mess: A Story of Charles Goodyear* (Englewood Cliffs, N.J.: Prentice Hall, 1980)

Robert Friedel

Goose Creek. Former fishing colony in southwestern Queens, lying along the cross-bay railroad line on the northernmost island in Jamaica Bay. It began as a few fishers' shacks built on piles along the shore and was first served by the railroad in 1888. About this time it became known for its weakfish, and in 1899 there were six clubhouses, two saloons, and a hotel. By 1903 there were more rowboats for hire than at any other fishing station in the bay, and Goose Creek was frequented by anglers from other parts of the city who traveled there by train to spend the day. Fishing and the harvesting of shellfish were stopped by the gradual pollution of Jamaica Bay, especially after a sewage treatment plant opened in Jamaica in 1914; angling was banned by the city in 1916. Although the fishing stations ceased to operate, the railroad continued to stop on schedule until the end of the summer of 1932.

Vincent Seyfried

Goosepatch. Name formerly applied to New Brighton.

Gorham Manufacturing. Firm of silversmiths, formed in 1865. Its predecessor was a silver manufactory opened in 1831 by Jabez Gorham (1792–1869). Based in Providence, Rhode Island, the firm opened wholesale showrooms in Maiden Lane in Manhattan in 1859 and adopted the English sterling standard of .925 fine silver in 1868. It aggressively marketed its sterling and electroplated wares, ecclesiastical goods, and bronzes through trade catalogues, retail and wholesale showrooms in Manhattan, and exclusive retail distributors nationwide. The firm moved its salesrooms to Broadway and 19th Street in 1883. Later it commissioned the firm of McKim, Mead and White to design a building at 390 Fifth Avenue for its retail operation, which moved there in 1905. In 1929 the retail store merged with Black, Starr and Frost to become Black, Starr and Frost–Gorham (from 1940 Black, Starr and Gorham). The combined shop operated at various addresses until 1962.

Charles H. Carpenter, Jr., *Gorham Silver, 1831–1981* (New York: Dodd, Mead, 1982)

Deborah Dependahl Waters

Gorky, Arshile [Adoian, Vosdanig] (*b* Khorkom, Vari Hayotz Dzore, Armenia, 15 April 1904; *d* Sherman, Conn., 21 July 1948). Painter. A refugee from the massacre of the Armenians during World War I, he settled in New York City in 1925 and became an instructor at the Grand Central School of Art in 1926. His masterly early work *The Artist and His Mother,* painted in the city between 1926 and 1936, is based on a photograph taken in Armenia. Originally influenced by Paul Cézanne and Pablo Picasso, he later became involved with the surrealists; the rich fluidity of line and complexity of association in his mature works is in part due to their influence. In 1935 Gorky joined the mural division of the Federal Art Project of the Works Progress Administration. In addition to works executed for the project, he painted the mural *Man's Conquest of the Air,* installed at the World's Fair of 1939–40 and now lost. In 1945 he had a show at the Julien Levy Gallery in New York City, for which the surrealist André Breton wrote an essay titled "The Eye Spring: Arshile Gorky." Under stress from medical and emotional problems, Gorky took his own life.

Ethel K. Schwabacher, *Arshile Gorky* (New York: Macmillan, 1957); Diane Waldman, *Arshile Gorky, 1904–1948: Retrospective* (New York: Harry N. Abrams/Solomon R. Guggenheim Foundation, 1981); Jim M. Jordan and Robert Goldwater, *The Paintings of Arshile Gorky: A Critical Catalogue* (New York: New York University Press, 1982)

Mona Hadler

gospel music. Style of vocal music having its roots in the expressive singing and impassioned call-and-response of the Sanctified and Spiritualist black Pentecostal churches. Its earliest exponents came to prominence in Chicago and Philadelphia in the 1930s. During these years a number of gospel groups performed regularly in New York City, including three from Virginia: the Selah Jubilee Singers, the Norfolk Jubilee Singers, and the Golden Gate Jubilee Quartet, who cultivated a secular following and performed at such venues as Barney Josephson's Café Society. Sister Rosetta Tharpe introduced gospel at the Cotton Club in 1939. By the 1940s several leading gospel soloists had moved to New York City, of whom one of the best-known was Clara Hudman Ghelston Brock, better known as "the Georgia Peach," a powerful contralto who originally performed with male quartets; unlike most female vocal soloists, who were Pentecostal, she was a Baptist. As the Church of God in Christ became the largest black Pentecostal denomination, its local branches became the leading venues for gospel concerts. The best-known was Washington Temple in Brooklyn; the wife of its pastor, Bishop F. D. Washington, was the gospel singer Madame Ernestine B. Washington, known as "the Songbird of the East." A forceful performer with a gritty voice, she exemplified the spiritual power of the Sanctified Church. Other soloists who performed at Washington Temple were two evangelists from Texas, Madame Emily Bram and Sister Jessie Mae Renfro. Another important figure, Madame Marie Knight, came to prominence at a Spiritualist church and performed for 10 years in a duo with Tharpe. Gospel soloists such as Madame Washington were eclipsed in popularity during the 1950s by male and female gospel groups, who usually wore choir robes and were accompanied by pianos and organs. The outstanding groups in the city included the Daniels Singers (led by Becky Moss Burroughs), Professor Charles Taylor and the Gospel All Stars (led by Ella Mitchell), and the Herman Stevens Singers (led by Dorothy McLeod). In later decades choirs of 50 and more became the major performing ensembles. Several were based in Manhattan and Brooklyn, among them the Washington Temple Choir, led by Timothy Wright.

The city also became known for elaborate gospel concerts staged in local churches. In 1951 Mahalia Jackson sang gospel at Carnegie Hall, and in 1961 Langston Hughes's *Black Nativity,* with Marion Williams and Professor Alex Bradford, became the first gospel musical to be presented Off Broadway. Later musicals included *Your Arms Too Short to Box with God* (1976) and *Mama I Want to Sing* (1980). Between 1954 and 1969 the Apollo Theater frequently presented gospel "caravans," weeklong concert series that became legendary. The enthusiastic audiences at the Apollo effectively transformed the venue into a church: programs sometimes ran so long that the intervening films had to be canceled, and nurses were on hand to minister to overwrought members of the audience. Among the performers who evoked the strongest responses were the Clara Ward Singers (led by Williams), the Soul Stirrers (led by Sam Cooke), the Davis Sisters (led by Ruth Davis), the Pilgrim Travelers (led by Kylo Turner), the Caravans (led by Inez Andrews and Shirley Caesar), the Nightingales (led by Julius Cheeks), the Raspberry Singers (led by Carl Hall), and the Swan Silvertones (led by Claude Jeter), as well as Bradford and the Reverend James Cleveland.

Anthony Heilbut, *The Gospel Sound: Good News and Bad Times* (New York: Simon and Schuster, 1971); Irene V. Jackson, *Afro-American Religious Music: A Bibliography and a Catalogue* (Westport, Conn.: Greenwood, 1979)

Anthony Heilbut

gospel tourism. Tourism to African American churches during regular worship services, mainly in Harlem. Since the 1980s foreign tourists (predominantly from Europe and Japan) have attended worship services at many Harlem churches on organized bus tours or in small groups. Tourists are drawn variously by an affinity for gospel music, curiosity about black American worship, or media representations of each. The phenomenon grew steadily throughout the 1990s, and by 2008, 1000 tourists were coming to Harlem in buses each Sunday morning, filling pews in several dozen churches. Some, such as First Corinthian Baptist Church and Abyssinian Baptist Church, receive more than 100 such visitors weekly.

Rowan Moore Gerety

Gotham. Popular nickname for New York City meaning "goat town" (Anglo-Saxon). Washington Irving applied the term to New York City in his satirical piece *Salmagundi* (1807). One legend has it that fifteenth-century residents of the village Gotham in Nottinghamshire, England, successfully feigned insanity to avoid paying taxes to King John. Hence Gotham came to mean "wise fools." Although Irving seems to have used the name sardonically to suggest a city of self-important but foolish people, the pejorative connotations were gradually lost.

Irving Lewis Allen

Gotham Book Mart. Former bookshop in Manhattan, opened by Frances Steloff on 3 January 1920 at 128 West 45th Street. It moved in 1923 to 51 West 47th Street and in 1946 to 41 West 47th Street, where it remained until 2006. It emphasized twentieth-century literature and had an inventory of 250,000 new, used, and out-of-print books and some 50,000 magazines. Singled out for its uniqueness by literary figures such as Arthur Miller and John Updike, it was called the most celebrated bookshop in New York City by the *New Yorker* in 1988. Nonetheless, the business fell upon hard times, and in July 2003 the Gotham Book Mart's building was sold for $7.2 million to Boris Aranov, owner of the adjacent building. In an effort to keep the store going, friends of Gotham owner Andreas Brown, who had bought the business and the building from Steloff in 1967, leased Brown a building at 16 East 46th Street in 2004. Brown could not keep the business profitable, however, and it closed in 2006.

W. G. Rogers, *Wise Men Fish Here: The Story of Frances Steloff and the Gotham Book Mart* (New York: Harcourt, Brace and World, 1965)

Allen J. Share

Gotham Court. "Model tenement" opened in 1850 by the Quaker philanthropist Silas Wood to provide housing for the poor. Situated in Manhattan on the block bounded to the north by Oak Street, to the east by Roosevelt Street, to the south by Cherry Street, and to the west by New Bowery (now St. James Place) and Franklin Square, the complex consisted of two rows of six tenements, each of five stories, standing back to back and facing two mews at 34 and 38 Cherry Street. Each of the 144 apartments in the complex was divided into a living room of 14 by 10 feet (4 by 3 meters) and a bedroom of 14 by 7 feet (4 by 2 meters). Shortly after it was occupied, the complex became notorious for overcrowding, filth, and crime. During the 1890s it was criticized by such reformers as Jacob A. Riis, and in 1895 Gotham Court was demolished under the Tenement House Law. The Governor Alfred E. Smith Houses now occupy the site.

Kenneth A. Scherzer

Gotham Court, 38 Cherry Street, ca *1885–90. Photograph by Richard Hoe Lawrence*

Gotti, John (*b* Bronx, 27 Oct 1940; *d* Springfield, Mo., 10 June 2002). Organized crime boss. He grew up in Sheepshead Bay, Brooklyn, and dropped out of school in eighth grade. His early crimes included hijacking, bookmaking, and burglary. In 1967 the Federal Bureau of Investigation arrested him and his accomplices while they were trying to steal a truck from John F. Kennedy International Airport. His headquarters were in the Ravenite social club on Mulberry Street in Manhattan's Little Italy and in the Bergin Hunt and Fish Club in Queens. Dubbed the "Dapper Don" by the press, Gotti became infamous when he took over the Gambino crime syndicate in 1985 by having its leader, Paul Castellano, murdered in front of Sparks Steak House on East 46th Street in Manhattan. Several juries, on account of juror intimidation, bribery, and the use of police informants, failed to convict him of serious charges three times between 1987 and 1990. He was finally convicted in 1992 on a number of charges, including Castellano's murder, with the help of testimony from fellow mobsters and police audiotapes on which he bragged about ordering the murder; he was sentenced to life in federal prison. He died in prison of throat cancer after 10 years.

Jesse Drucker

Gottlieb, Adolph (*b* New York City, 14 March 1903; *d* New York City, 4 March 1974). Painter. He grew up in New York City and during the early 1920s studied at the Parsons School of Design and the Art Students League. In 1935 he helped to form The Ten, a group dedicated to expressionist and abstract art. He was a leading figure in the abstract expressionist movement, also called the New York School, especially in its early stages during the 1940s; with Mark Rothko and Barnett Newman he publicly articulated its major themes in 1943 in a letter to Edward Alden Jewell, a critic for the *New York Times.* Gottlieb lived mainly in Brooklyn until 1956 and did not associate closely with other abstract expressionists. His best-known works are *Pictographs* (1941–51), *Grids and Imaginary Landscapes* (1951–57), and *Bursts* (1957–74).

Eileen K. Cheng

Gottschalk, Louis Moreau (*b* New Orleans, 8 May 1829; *d* Rio de Janeiro, 18 Dec 1869). Pianist and composer. After 1853 New York City was his home. A virtuoso, Gottschalk attracted popular and elite audiences. As America's first composer honored in Europe and North and South America, he wrote romantic works and also compositions inflected with African American and Afro-Caribbean folk themes, anticipating the birth of ragtime decades later. His works include *Bamboula* (1846–48), *The Banjo* (1854–55), *The Last Hope* (1854), and *A Night in the Tropics* (1858–59). He died at age 40 after contracting malaria on his travels in South America. He is buried in Green-Wood Cemetery.

S. Frederick Starr, *Bamboula! The Life and Times of Louis Moreau Gottschalk* (New York: Oxford University Press, 1995)

See also Clare, Ada (McElhenney).

Cathy Alexander

Gould, Jay [Jason] (*b* Roxbury, N.Y., 27 May 1836; *d* New York City, 2 Dec 1892). Financier and speculator. After moving to New York City he worked briefly as a leather merchant at 39 Spruce Street during 1859–60. He speculated and invested in railroads, and in 1860 he formed the brokerage house of Smith, Gould and Martin on Wall Street. With Daniel Drew and Jim Fisk he battled Cornelius Vanderbilt during the late 1860s to control the Erie Railroad, which he pillaged with the connivance of the railroad directors Peter B. Sweeny and William M. "Boss" Tweed. After the death of Fisk and the overthrow of the Tweed Ring, Gould lost control of the railroad in 1872, and he then used a fortune estimated at $25 million to invest in railroads in the West. He later owned the newspaper the *New York World* (1879–83) and the New York Elevated Railroad Company. On his death his fortune was estimated at $77 million. Despite his wealth Gould was shunned by fashionable society: he was blackballed by the New York Yacht Club, and Mrs. William Astor excluded him from her celebrated "400" list of those invited to be a part of her circle.

Maury Klein, *The Life and Legend of Jay Gould* (Baltimore: Johns Hopkins University Press, 1986); John Steele Gordon, *The Scarlet Woman of Wall Street: Jay Gould, Jim Fisk, Cornelius Vanderbilt, the Erie Railway Wars, and the Birth of Wall Street* (New York: Weidenfeld and Nicolson, 1988)

See also Western Union Company.

Allen J. Share

government and politics. The government of New York City is older than that of the United States and of most other American jurisdictions. Its political history has been spirited, contentious, and convoluted, encompassing such diverse figures as DeWitt Clinton, William M. "Boss" Tweed, Theodore Roosevelt, Fiorello H. La Guardia, and Nelson A. Rockefeller.

1. Colonial Period

The Dutch city of New Amsterdam, renamed New York City in 1664, continued as capital of the colony of New York under the

English Governors of New York, 1664–1775

	Appointed
Richard Nicolls (*b* 1624; *d* 28 May 1672)	8 Sept 1664
Colonel Francis Lovelace (*b ca* 1621; *d* 10 May 1686)	17 Aug 1667
Major Edmund Andros, Knight (*b* 6 Dec 1637; *d* Feb 1714)	10 Nov 1674
Anthony Brockholles, Commander in Chief (*d* 1723)	16 Nov 1677
Sir Edmund Andros	7 Aug 1678
Anthony Brockholles, Commander in Chief	13 Jan 1681
Colonel Thomas Dongan (*b* 1634; *d* 14 Dec 1715)	27 Aug 1682
Sir Edmund Andros	11 Aug 1688
Francis Nicholson, Lieutenant Governor (*b* 12 Nov 1655; *d* 5 March 1728)	9 Oct 1688
Jacob Leisler (*b* 1640; *d* 16 May 1691)	3 June 1689
Colonel Henry Sloughter (*d* 23 July 1691)	19 March 1691
Major Richard Ingoldsby, Commander in Chief	26 July 1691
Colonel Benjamin Fletcher (*b* ?1640; *d* 1703)	30 Aug 1692
Richard Coote, Earl of Bellomont (*b* 1636; *d* 5 March 1701)	13 April 1698
John Nanfan, Lieutenant Governor (*d* 1706)	17 May 1699
Earl of Bellomont	24 July 1700
William Smith, as eldest Councilor present (*b* 2 Feb 1655; *d* 18 Feb 1705)	5 March 1701
John Nanfan, Lieutenant Governor	19 May 1701
Edward Hyde, Viscount Cornbury (*b* 1661; *d* 1 April 1723)	3 May 1702
John, Lord Lovelace (*d* 6 May 1709)	18 Dec 1708
Peter Schuyler, President of the Council (*b* 17 Sept 1657; *d* 19 Feb 1724)	6 May 1709
Richard Ingoldsby, Lieutenant Governor	9 May 1709
Peter Schuyler, President of the Council	25 May 1709
Richard Ingoldsby, Lieutenant Governor	1 June 1709
Gerardus Beekman, President of the Council (*b* 1653; *d* 10 Oct 1723)	10 April 1710
Brigadier Robert Hunter (*d* March 1734)	14 June 1710
Peter Schuyler, President of the Council	21 July 1719
William Burnet (*b* March 1688; *d* 7 Sept 1729)	17 Sept 1720
John Montgomerie (*d* 30 June 1731)	15 April 1728
Rip van Dam, President of the Council (*b ca* 1660; *d* 10 June 1749)	1 July 1731
Colonel William Cosby (*b ca* 1690; *d* 10 March 1736)	1 Aug 1732
George Clarke, President of the Council (*b* 1676; *d* 12 Jan 1760)	10 March 1736
Admiral George Clinton (*b ca* 1686; *d* 10 July 1761)	2 Sept 1743
Sir Danvers Osborne, Baronet (*b* 17 Nov 1715; *d* 12 Oct 1753)	10 Oct 1753
James de Lancey, Lieutenant Governor (*b* 27 Nov 1703; *d* 30 July 1760)	12 Oct 1753
Sir Charles Hardy, Knight (*b ca* 1716; *d* 18 May 1780)	3 Sept 1755
James de Lancey, Lieutenant Governor	3 June 1757
Cadwallader Colden, President of the Council (*b* 17 Feb 1688; *d* 28 Sept 1776)	4 Aug 1760
Major General Robert Monckton (*b* 24 June 1726; *d* 21 May 1782)	26 Oct 1761
Cadwallader Colden, President of the Council	18 Nov 1761
Major General Robert Monckton	14 June 1762
Cadwallader Colden, Lieutenant Governor	28 June 1763
Sir Henry Moore, Baronet (*b* 7 Feb 1713; *d* 11 Sept 1769)	13 Nov 1765
Cadwallader Colden, Lieutenant Governor	12 Sept 1769
John Murray, Earl of Dunmore (*b* 1732; *d* 5 March 1809)	19 Oct 1770
William Tryon (*b* 1729; *d* 27 Jan 1788)	9 July 1771
Cadwallader Colden, Lieutenant Governor	7 April 1774
William Tryon	28 June 1775

Compiled by Edward T. O'Donnell

English. In 1665 the first English governor, Richard Nicolls (1664–68), issued the Duke's Laws, setting forth legal and governmental codes promulgated by the Duke of York, named proprietor of the colony by his brother Charles II. They made no provision for an elected assembly, which would have been dominated by the Dutch. Municipal government consisted of a mayor, four aldermen, and a sheriff appointed by the governor. In 1686 Governor Thomas Dongan (1682–88) granted a revised charter that divided the city into six wards: the North, East, West, South, and Dock wards, and an Out ward of farms to the north. The charter also called for a common council composed of a mayor and a recorder appointed by the governor, as well as an alderman and an assistant alderman elected from each ward. These officers also served as advisers to the Mayor's Court. The recorder provided legal counsel to the Mayor's Court as well as to the council, over which he presided when the mayor was absent. The colony of New York was divided into 12 counties in 1683, of which four and part of a fifth make up the modern New York City: New York (Manhattan), Kings (Brooklyn), Richmond (Staten Island), Queens, and southern Westchester (the Bronx).

When in 1685 the Duke of York ascended to the throne as James II, New York became a royal colony whose governor and 12-man advisory council were thereafter appointed by the king. The governor worked and lived in a fort at the southern tip of Manhattan (named successively Fort James, Fort William, Fort Anne, and Fort George), where British troops were stationed to provide for the city's defense. In addition, the Admiralty, the Treasury, and the War Office each had areas of jurisdiction in the colony. As a major port New York City was vulnerable to attacks by the French and the Spanish, and cannon were mounted in the area now known as the Battery. In 1696 the city's commerce came more directly under the aegis of the Board of Trade and the Treasury, which were empowered to enforce the Navigation Acts.

After England's Glorious Revolution of 1688–89 New Yorkers divided into supporters and opponents of Jacob Leisler, a militia captain chosen to lead the colony in the power vacuum created by the absence of Lieutenant Governor Francis Nicholson. In 1691 King William and Queen Mary named Colonel Henry Sloughter governor and instructed him to hold elections for a permanent legislative assembly. The 18 men elected met at a tavern until they acquired a chamber at City Hall in 1704. Throughout the colonial period New York County was allotted four representatives, whereas each of the other counties sent no more than two. City and colony politics were highly partisan, with factions forming around economic interests, religious groups, and leading families. About one-third of the assemblymen belonged to patrician families and one-third to the upper middle class; the rest were small farmers, shopkeepers, and artisans. Only merchants were elected to the assembly from the city during the colonial years. They used their influence to establish legislative standards for the quality and packing of flour, beef, pork, wood products, and skins produced upriver. Assemblymen customarily resided in their own districts. They were expected to be men of property and standing, but because land was available and status fluid they were socially more diverse than their counterparts in England. The vote was extended to men 21 years of age and older whose land was valued at £40 or produced 40*s.* in annual income, or who held freemen's status in New York City or Albany. Electoral participation exceeding 50 percent of the eligible voters was rare until the 1760s.

In 1696 the king created the Lords Commissioners of Trade and Plantations, also called the Board of Trade. This select group of administrators had broad power to monitor colonial trade, advise the king on the appointment of colonial governors, examine and occasionally disallow provincial laws, write instructions for incoming governors, and propose legislation for the colonies. Merchants in New York City sent representatives to England and encouraged fellow merchants in London and Bristol to protest decrees harmful to colonial trade. They also collaborated with influential friends in England to circumvent decisions of the Board of Trade, which gradually lost power to the secretary of state.

The eighteenth century often saw the governor and the colonial assembly compete for preeminence. Some royal governors, including Benjamin Fletcher (1692–98), Edward Hyde (1701–8), Viscount Cornbury (1702–8), William Cosby (1732–36), and George Clinton (1743–53), deemed the colonies lesser branches of the empire ("twigs belonging to the main Tree," according to Cornbury). They firmly enforced the trade laws and pressed the assembly for defense appropriations. Like the Whig governors Richard Coote, Earl of Bellomont (1698–1700), Robert Hunter (1710–19), and Henry Moore (1765–69), they also cultivated the support of a local "court party" to which they awarded patronage, land grants, judicial positions, and provisioning contracts.

Leaders in the city were often members of prominent families, including the DeLanceys, Morrises, Philipses, Beekmans, Livingstons, and Van Cortlandts. After 1730 elections were frequently contested by members of rival families, generating popular participation as ordinary voters found themselves in a position to choose between elite candidates. Merchants and the wealthy dominated both the mayoralty and the Common Council, which monitored the movement of visitors, regulated markets and set the price of bread, and sought to control such persistent problems as free-roaming hogs. The Common Council also included a number of artisans and shopkeepers, whose presence broadened city government and spurred public interest in elections.

In 1731 Governor John Montgomerie put into effect the last city charter of the colonial period, which provided for a seventh ward, Montgomerie, to the northeast. The charter prescribed few other changes and remained in effect until 1776, when the city fell to the British.

2. Federal Period to World War II

At the end of the American Revolution municipal authority was centered in the Common Council, which represented a small electorate of property owners. For several years the state appointed and removed mayors whenever party control changed: Major Richard Varick was removed after 12 years in office when control changed in Albany in 1803; DeWitt Clinton was removed from office in 1809 but returned the next year. The city's growth and complexity stimulated efforts to create a system more responsive to popular will and freer from interference by the state legislature. In 1804 members of Tammany Hall persuaded the legislature to enfranchise men who rented property and to adopt the paper ballot; by the 1820s the legislature removed all property qualifications for white men. The Common Council gained authorization to select its own mayor in 1821, ending the removal of mayors at the whim of the legislature. In 1830 the state fundamentally altered Montgomerie's charter by dividing the Common Council into a board of aldermen and a board of assistant aldermen and by making the mayor a distinct official with the power to veto actions of the council. A state constitutional amendment enhanced the mayor's independence in 1833 by providing for his direct popular election. When the first mayoral election was held in 1834, more than 35,000 voters took part.

In the 1840s the Common Council organized a professional police force, improved the paving and lighting of streets, completed the Croton water system, and expanded social services. To administer these and other municipal functions 10 city departments were formed in 1849 that were eventually subdivided into bureaus, of which all but the police department were led by elected officials. Voters chose from an overwhelming number of candidates because the amended charter rescheduled city elections to the same time as state and national elections. This confusion benefited ward caucuses, which elected delegates for party conventions. Ward meetings were small and easily manipulated by ambitious politicians, a point later emphasized by Theodore Roosevelt when he charged that

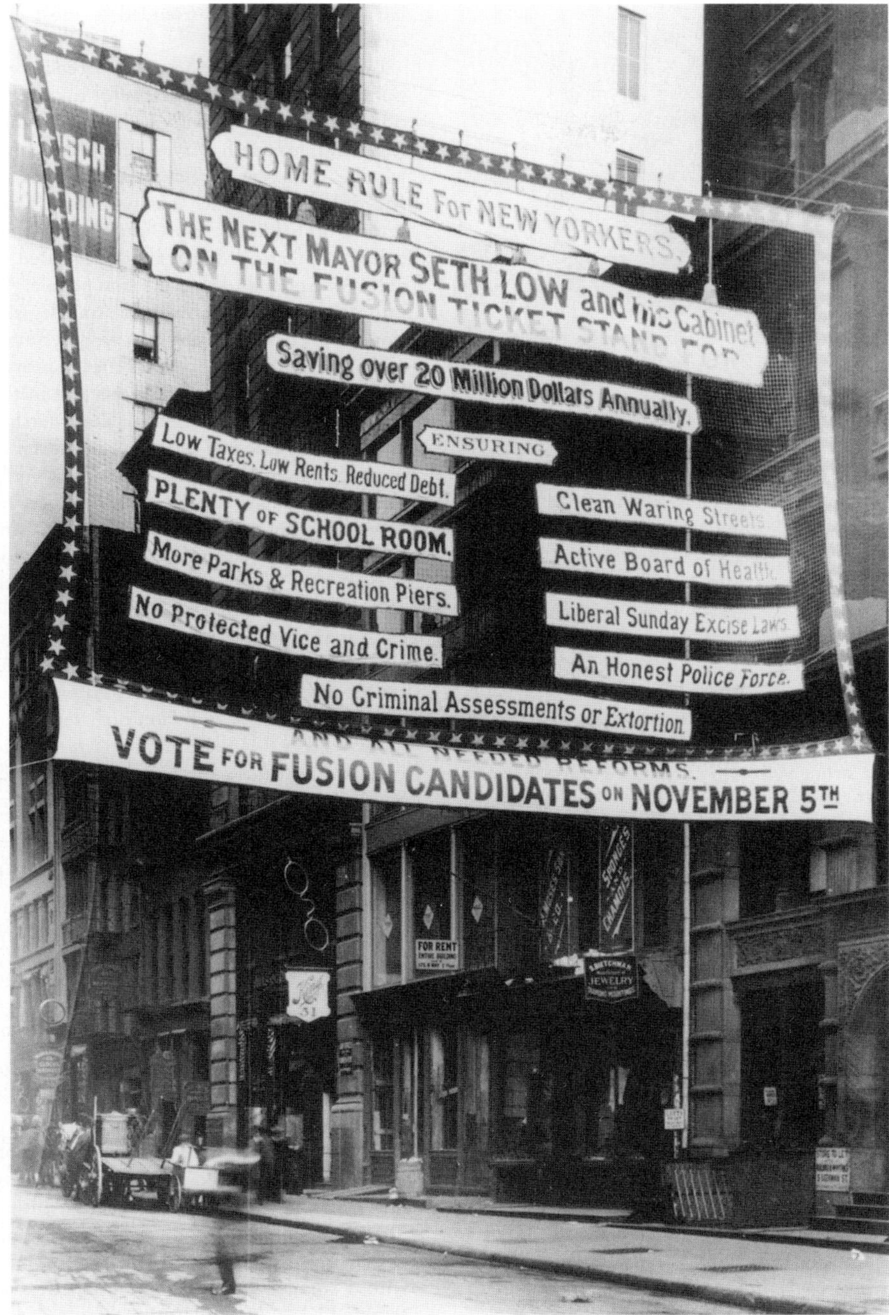

Campaign banner for Seth Low in Maiden Lane, 1891

two-thirds of the ward meetings were held in saloons and discouraged the involvement of respectable men. In 1853, after the corruption of the council had earned it the nickname the "Forty Thieves," the state enacted a new charter that restructured the municipal legislature into two distinct boards of aldermen and councilmen. Twenty-two aldermen were elected from the wards and 60 council members were elected by districts drawn to counter the influence of wards. The new charter further restrained the aldermen by giving the mayor a veto over legislation, eliminating the aldermen's role as city judges and transferring the council's control of the police to the mayor and two other elected officials.

In 1857 the state legislature issued a charter to separate municipal and state elections by moving those for municipal offices from November to December. The charter empowered the mayor to appoint city inspectors and the heads of the street department and the Croton Aqueduct; the finance and law departments remained under the comptroller and corporation counsel, both elected. Other measures in the charter of 1857 exposed the long partisan conflict between the strong Democratic forces of the city and the Republicans in the state legislature. As a check on the city, the state transformed the county Board of Supervisors, which consisted of the mayor and city officials, into an independently elected body made up of an equal number of Republicans and Democrats. The charter also merged the police forces of New York City, Brooklyn, and their suburbs into one department to be appointed by a state commission. These measures encouraged Mayor Fernando Wood in 1861 to propose that New York City secede from the state and establish itself as a "free city." Subsequent mayors protested the state's tendency to meddle in city affairs through state-appointed commissions for fire, park, and public health. To resist interference by the state, Tammany Hall consolidated its influence over the city's immigrant population, especially the Irish, who were once excluded from the organization. Politicians aligned with Tammany Hall began to establish power bases in elected posts such as those of county sheriff and city chamberlain, an office created in 1832 to oversee the city's surplus funds. By the late 1860s Tammany Hall, led by William M. "Boss" Tweed, induced the legislature by means of bribes to enact a new charter that abolished the state commissions and returned police and other municipal functions to the city. Despite its tainted origins the charter brought about a favorable reorganization of city government by establishing 10 executive departments to manage parks, public health, buildings, the police force, and other services, and gave the mayor the power to appoint the heads of these departments. The charter strengthened the mayor's veto power, which could now be overridden only by a three-fourths vote of the council; at the same time his authority was limited by the terms of the council offices, which were longer than his own. In the charter the legislature also unified the government of the city and county by abolishing the New York County Board of Supervisors, on which Tweed himself had sat since its formation in 1857.

After the fall of the Tweed Ring the legislature signed a new charter in 1873 that replaced the bicameral council with a board of aldermen: six of its 21 members were elected. In addition the charter created the Board of Estimate and Apportionment, consisting of the mayor, the president of the Board of Aldermen, and two other officials. Responsible for reviewing the budgets of city departments, the board eventually became a powerful influence in both the executive and the legislative branches of government. The charter was amended in 1884, when the state extended its civil service law to the city, eroding the control of Tammany Hall over patronage. These changes did not prevent the return to power of Tammany Hall, first under John Kelly (1872–86) and then under Richard Croker (1886–1902). To win important elections Tammany Hall often aimed to satisfy an influential minority of reform-minded Democrats

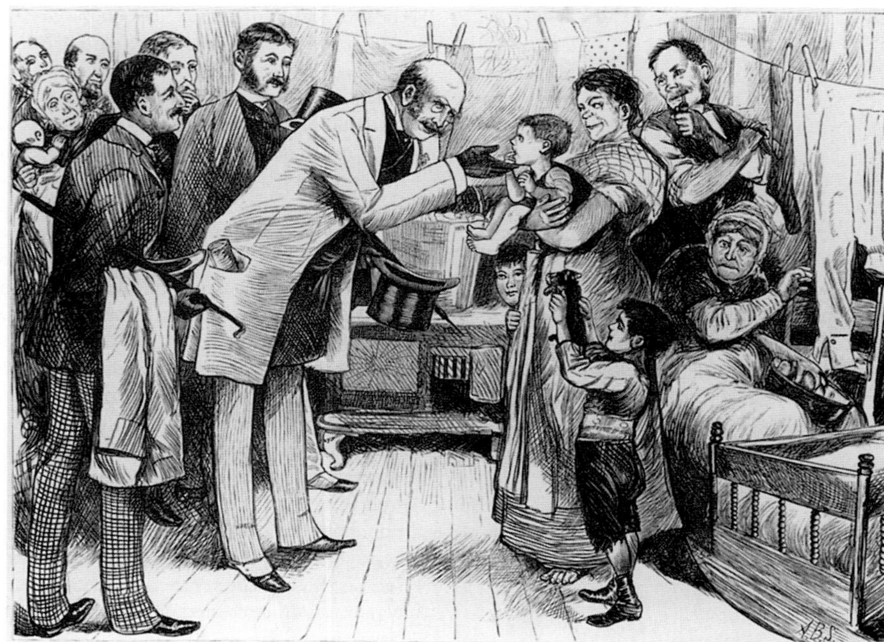

"The Canvass of a 'Swell' Candidate for Political Honors in a Tenement District," from Frank Leslie's Illustrated Newspaper, *19 November 1881*

sympathetic toward business. Threatened by a coalition of Republicans, reformers, and angry workers in 1886, it engineered the election of Abram S. Hewitt, a wealthy businessman and reformer. In the 1880s the legislature passed 390 acts concerning the city, a number that was sharply reduced after a constitutional amendment in 1894 gave the mayor the power to veto such acts.

In 1896 the legislature responded to the demands of business leaders and reformers to consolidate Manhattan, Brooklyn, Queens, the Bronx, and Staten Island into Greater New York. When the new charter took effect in 1898, each of the five counties became a borough of the new city: the population of New York City more than doubled, to nearly 3.5 million, in large part because Brooklyn had grown into the fourth largest city in the United States since its incorporation in 1834. Although much of the middle class in Brooklyn was resistant to consolidation, its business leaders believed that the change would promote development and reduce taxes. Seth Low, the Republican mayor of Brooklyn in the early 1880s, was eventually elected mayor of the consolidated city. The charter of 1897 preserved the power of the boroughs by allowing each of them to elect a president responsible for local administration of streets and other public works. Although officials such as sheriffs, judges, clerks, and registrars continued to work for the county, most positions were taken over by the new city government. Legislative power was centered in a two-house municipal assembly, and judicial functions in a municipal court of 23 districts. The mayor (whose term was extended from two years to four) retained a strong veto, which could be overridden only by a five-sixths vote of the assembly; the mayor also retained control over the executive departments, except for the finance department, which continued to be led by an independently elected comptroller. The charter weakened the mayor by barring him from a second consecutive term. The Board of Estimate and Apportionment, which prepared an annual budget for the city that could be decreased but not increased by the municipal assembly, acquired the power to control the granting of franchises to public services. Reformers hoped that consolidation would make the government more efficient and dilute the power of Tammany Hall. Greater efficiency was at least partly realized, but the influence of Tammany Hall persisted: the first mayor elected after consolidation was Robert A. Van Wyck, a tool of Tammany Hall who led one of the most corrupt administrations in the city's history. The legislature amended the charter in 1901 to reduce the mayor's term from four years to two and to increase the power of the borough presidents by giving them a prominent place on the Board of Estimate. Another amendment at this time transformed the bicameral assembly into a single board of aldermen with 73 members (reduced to 67 in 1916 and 65 in 1921). The first mayor to be affected by the shortened term was Low, a reformer who led one of the city's most effective administrations. When Low sought reelection in 1903, he was defeated by George B. McClellan, who enjoyed the backing of Charles Francis Murphy (the leader of Tammany Hall from 1902 to 1924) and Big Tim Sullivan (a powerful ward boss on the Bowery). Under McClellan civil service was extended to most city employees.

Tammany Hall during the Progressive era nominated reform Democrats for important offices, including Mayors William J. Gaynor (1910 until his death in 1913) and John Purroy Mitchel (1910–17). By the 1920s it was led by Mayor James J. Walker, who with the district leaders of Tammany Hall forged what they called a "practical democracy" dedicated to aiding the poor and the common people. An indirect result of his efforts was state legislation supported by Governor Alfred E. Smith and Senator Robert F. Wagner that improved housing and working conditions and in the process laid the foundation for a partnership between the state and the city. The charter of 1901 survived for more than 30 years with only one major change: an amendment to the state constitution in 1923 that formed a new, two-house municipal assembly, consisting of the Board of Aldermen and the borough presidents. Among the assembly's expanded powers was that of making amendments to the city charter that were not in conflict with the state constitution. Fiorello H. La Guardia, the Fusion Party candidate, defeated Tammany Hall in 1933 and as mayor from 1934 to 1945 initiated profound changes in the politics and government of the city. Backed by federal money provided under the New Deal, La Guardia carried through an ambitious program of public works that won him as much support from business and labor as Tammany Hall had commanded earlier. His "little New Deal" assigned many of the functions of government to permanent entities staffed by professionals, such as new college campuses (which later became the City University of New York) and municipal hospitals. In 1936 reformers crafted a new charter, which was notably clearer and shorter than that of 1901. It further augmented the power of the mayor, who was now allowed to appoint a deputy mayor in charge of routine executive duties. The charter abolished the office of city chamberlain and replaced the Board of Aldermen with a smaller, unicameral council. It also established a city planning commission charged with drafting a master plan for the city, preparing public works programs, and issuing zoning guidelines. Amendments to the charter could be made by petition of 50,000 qualified voters. Tammany Hall was weakened considerably by these measures, as well as by the adoption of proportional representation in the City Council in 1937 (which benefited minority parties at the expense of the Democrats), and by the further growth of the merit system. The length of the mayor's term reverted again to four years with the adoption of the charter of 1936.

3. After World War II

After 1945 the Democratic organizations in the Bronx and Brooklyn played an increas-

Members of the U.S. House of Representatives Elected from Districts All or Partly within the Current Boundaries of New York City

William Floyd (Democratic Republican) 1789–91 (Brooklyn, Queens, Staten Island)
John Laurence (Federalist) 1789–93 (Manhattan, Westchester)
Thomas Tredwell (Federalist) 1791–95 (Brooklyn, Queens, Staten Island)
Philip Van Cortlandt (Democratic Republican) 1793–1809 (Westchester)
John Watts (Federalist) 1793–95 (Manhattan)
Jonathan N. Havens (Democratic Republican) 1795–99 (Brooklyn, Queens)
Edward Livingston (Democratic Republican) 1795–1801 (Manhattan)
John Smith (Democratic Republican) 1800–1804 (Brooklyn, Queens, Staten Island)
Samuel L. Mitchell (Democratic Republican) 1801–4 (Manhattan), 1810–13 (Manhattan, Staten Island)
Joshua Sands (Federalist) 1803–5 (Brooklyn, Staten Island), 1825–27 (Brooklyn)
George Clinton, Jr. (Democratic Republican) 1804–9 (Manhattan, Brooklyn, Staten Island)
Samuel Riker (Democratic Republican) 1804–5, 1807–9 (Queens)
Gurdon Mumford (Democratic Republican) 1805–11 (Manhattan, Brooklyn, Staten Island)
Eliphalet Wickes (Democratic Republican) 1805–7 (Queens)
William Denning (Democratic Republican) 1809–10 (Manhattan, Staten Island)
Jonathan Fisk (Democratic Republican) 1809–11 (Westchester)
Ebenezer Sage (Democratic Republican) 1809–15, 1819–20 (Queens, Staten Island)
William Paulding, Jr. (Democratic Republican) 1811–13 (Manhattan, Staten Island)
Pierre Van Cortlandt (Democratic Republican) 1811–13 (Westchester)
Egbert Benson (Federalist) 1813 (Manhattan)
Pierre Denoyelles (Democratic Republican) 1813–15 (Westchester)
John Lefferts (Democratic Republican) 1813–15 (Brooklyn, Staten Island)
Jotham Post, Jr. (Federalist) 1813–15 (Manhattan)
William Irving (Democratic Republican) 1814–19 (Manhattan)
Henry Crocheron (Democratic Republican) 1815–17 (Staten Island)
George Townsend (Democratic Republican) 1815–19 (Queens, Brooklyn, Staten Island)
Jonathan Ward (Democratic Republican) 1815–17 (Westchester)
Peter H. Wendover (Democratic Republican) 1815–21 (Manhattan)
Caleb Tompkins (Democratic Republican) 1817–21 (Westchester)
Henry Meigs (Democratic Republican) 1819–21 (Manhattan)
Silas Wood (Democratic Republican) 1819–29 (Queens, Brooklyn, Staten Island)
James Guyon, Jr. (Democratic Republican) 1820–21 (Staten Island)
Churchill C. Cambreleng (Democrat) 1821–39 (Manhattan)
Cadwallader D. Colden (Federalist) 1821–23 (Manhattan)
John J. Morgan (Democratic Republican) 1821–25, 1834–35 (Manhattan)
Jeremiah H. Pierson (Democratic Republican) 1821–23 (Westchester)
Joel Frost (Crawford Republican) 1823–25 (Westchester)
Peter Sharpe (Adams–Clay Republican) 1823–25 (Manhattan)
Jacob Tyson (Crawford Republican) 1823–25 (Brooklyn, Staten Island)
Jeromus Johnson (Jacksonian) 1825–29 (Manhattan)
Gulian C. Verplanck (Jacksonian) 1825–33 (Manhattan)
Aaron Ward (Democrat) 1825–29, 1831–37, 1841–43 (Westchester)
John J. Wood (Jacksonian) 1827–29 (Brooklyn, Staten Island)
Henry B. Cowles (Adams Republican) 1829–31 (Westchester)
Jacob Crocheron (Democrat) 1829–31 (Brooklyn, Staten Island)
James Lent (Democrat) 1829–33 (Queens)
Campbell P. White (Democrat) 1829–35 (Manhattan)
John T. Bergen (Democrat) 1831–33 (Brooklyn, Staten Island)
Abel Huntington (Jacksonian) 1833–37 (Queens)
Cornelius W. Lawrence (Democrat) 1833–35 (Manhattan)
Dudley Selden (Democrat) 1833–34 (Brooklyn, Staten Island)
Isaac B. Van Houten (Democrat) 1833–35 (Manhattan)
Charles G. Ferris (Democrat) 1834–35 (Manhattan)
Samuel Barton (Democrat) 1835–37 (Manhattan)
Gideon Lee (Democrat) 1835–37 (Manhattan)
John McKeon (Democrat) 1835–37 (Manhattan)
Ely Moore (Democrat) 1835–39 (Queens)
Edward Curtis (Whig) 1837–41 (Westchester)
Josiah Ogden Hoffman (Whig) 1837–41 (Brooklyn, Staten Island)
Thomas B. Jackson (Democrat) 1837–41 (Brooklyn, Staten Island)
Gouverneur Kemble (Democrat) 1837–41 (Manhattan)
Abraham Vanderveer (Democrat) 1837–39 (Manhattan)
James De La Montanya (Democrat) 1839–41 (Brooklyn, Staten Island)
Moses H. Grinnell (Whig) 1839–41 (Manhattan)
James Monroe (Whig) 1839–41 (Queens)
Joseph Egbert (Democrat) 1841–43 (Manhattan)
Charles G. Ferris (Democrat) 1841–43 (Manhattan)
Charles A. Floyd (Democrat) 1841–43
James I. Roosevelt (Democrat) 1841–43 (Westchester)
Fernando Wood (Democrat) 1841–43, 1863–65, 1867–81 (Manhattan)
Joseph H. Anderson (Democrat) 1843–47 (Westchester)
Hamilton Fish (Whig) 1843–45 (Brooklyn, Staten Island)
Moses G. Leonard (Democrat) 1843–45 (Manhattan)
William B. Maclay (Democrat) 1843–49, 1857–61 (Queens)
Henry C. Murphy (Democrat) 1843–45, 1847–49 (Manhattan)
J. Phillips Phoenix (Whig) 1843–45 (Queens)
Selah B. Strong (Democrat) 1843–45 (Manhattan)
William W. Campbell (American) 1845–47 (Brooklyn, Staten Island)
John W. Lawrence (Democrat) 1845–47 (Manhattan)
William S. Miller (American) 1845–47 (Manhattan)
Henry Seaman (American) 1845–47 (Manhattan)
Thomas Woodruff (American) 1845–47 (Queens)
David S. Jackson (Democrat) 1847–48 (Westchester)
Frederick W. Lord (Democrat) 1847–49 (Manhattan)
William Nelson (Whig) 1847–51 (Westchester)
Henry Nicoll (Democrat) 1847–49 (Manhattan)
Frederick A. Tallmadge (Whig) 1847–49 (Manhattan)

(*continued*)

Members of the U.S. House of Representatives Elected from Districts All or Partly within the Current Boundaries of New York City (*Continued*)

Horace Greeley (Whig) 1848–49 (Manhattan)
David A. Bokee (Whig) 1849–51 (Manhattan)
George Briggs (Whig) 1849–53, 1859–61 (Queens, Manhattan)
James Brooks (Whig) 1849–53, 1863–66, 1867–73 (Manhattan)
John A. King (Whig) 1849–51 (Brooklyn, Staten Island)
J. Phillips Phoenix (Whig) 1849–51 (Manhattan)
Walter Underhill (Whig) 1849–51 (Queens)
Obadiah Bowne (Whig) 1851–53 (Brooklyn)
John G. Floyd (Democrat) 1851–53 (Manhattan)
H. Hobart Haws (Whig) 1851–53 (Queens, Brooklyn, Staten Island)
Abraham P. Stephens (Democrat) 1851–53 (Westchester)
Thomas W. Cumming (Democrat) 1853–55 (Westchester)
Francis B. Cutting (Democrat) 1853–55 (Manhattan)
James Maurice (Democrat) 1853–55 (Queens, Brooklyn, Staten Island)
Jared V. Peck (Democrat) 1853–55 (Westchester)
William M. Tweed (Democrat) 1853–55 (Manhattan, Brooklyn)
Hiram Walbridge (Democrat) 1853–55 (Manhattan)
William Walker (Democrat) 1853–55 (Manhattan)
Michael Walsh (Democrat) 1853–55 (Manhattan)
John Wheeler (Democrat) 1853–57 (Manhattan)
Thomas Child, Jr. (Whig) 1855–57 (Manhattan)
Bayard Clarke (Whig) 1855–57 (Westchester)
John Kelly (Democrat) 1855–58 (Manhattan)
Guy R. Pelton (Whig) 1855–57 (Manhattan)
James S. T. Stranahan (Whig) 1855–57 (Brooklyn)
William W. Valk (American) 1855–57 (Queens, Brooklyn, Staten Island)
Abram Wakeman (Whig) 1855–57 (Manhattan)
Thomas R. Whitney (American) 1855–57 (Manhattan, Brooklyn)
Horace F. Clark (Democrat) 1857–61 (Manhattan)
John Cochrane (Democrat) 1857–61 (Manhattan)
John B. Haskin (Democrat) 1857–61 (Westchester)
John A. Searing (Democrat) 1857–59 (Queens, Brooklyn, Staten Island)
Daniel Sickles (Democrat) 1857–61, 1893–95 (Manhattan)
George Taylor (Democrat) 1857–59 (Brooklyn)
Elijah Ward (Democrat) 1857–59, 1861–65, 1875–77 (Manhattan)
Thomas J. Barr (Democrat) 1858–61 (Manhattan)
Luther C. Carter (Republican) 1859–61 (Queens, Brooklyn, Staten Island)
James Humphrey (Republican) 1859–61 (Brooklyn)
Frederick A. Conkling (Republican) 1861–63 (Manhattan)
Isaac C. Delaplaine (Democrat) 1861–63 (Manhattan)
Edward Haight (Democrat) 1861–63 (Westchester)
James E. Kerrigan (Democrat) 1861–63 (Manhattan)
Moses F. Odell (Democrat) 1861–65 (Brooklyn)
Edward H. Smith (Democrat) 1861–63 (Queens, Brooklyn, Staten Island)
William Wall (Republican) 1861–63 (Manhattan)
Benjamin Wood (Democrat) 1861–65, 1881–83 (Manhattan)
John W. Chanler (Democrat) 1863–69 (Manhattan)
Anson Herrick (Democrat) 1863–65 (Manhattan)
Martin Kalbfleisch (Democrat) 1863–65 (Brooklyn)
William Radford (Democrat) 1863–67 (Westchester)
Henry J. Stebbins (Democrat) 1863–64 (Queens, Staten Island)
Dwight Townsend (Democrat) 1864–65 (Queens, Staten Island)
Teunis G. Bergen (Democrat) 1865–67 (Brooklyn)
William A. Darling (Republican) 1865–67 (Manhattan)
James Morgan Humphrey (Democrat) 1865–66 (Brooklyn)
Morgan Jones (Democrat) 1865–67 (Manhattan)
Henry J. Raymond (Republican) 1865–67 (Manhattan)
Stephen Taber (Democrat) 1865–69 (Queens, Staten Island)
Nelson Taylor (Democrat) 1865–67 (Manhattan)
William E. Dodge (Republican) 1866–67 (Manhattan)
John W. Hunter (Democrat) 1866–67 (Brooklyn)
Demas Barnes (Democrat) 1867–69 (Brooklyn)
John Fox (Democrat) 1867–71 (Manhattan)
John Morrissey (Democrat) 1867–71 (Manhattan)
William H. Robertson (Republican) 1867–69 (Westchester)
William E. Robinson (Democrat) 1867–69, 1881–85 (Brooklyn)
Thomas E. Stewart (Republican) 1867–69 (Manhattan)
Hervey C. Calkin (Democrat) 1869–71 (Manhattan)
Samuel S. Cox (Democrat) 1869–73, 1873–85, 1886–89 (Manhattan)
Clarkson N. Potter (Democrat) 1869–75, 1877–79 (Westchester)
Henry A. Reeves (Democrat) 1869–71 (Queens, Staten Island)
John G. Schumaker (Democrat) 1869–71, 1873–77 (Brooklyn)
Henry W. Slocum (Democrat) 1869–73 (Brooklyn)
Smith Ely, Jr. (Democrat) 1871–73 (Manhattan)
Thomas Kinsella (Democrat) 1871–73 (Brooklyn)
William R. Roberts (Democrat) 1871–75 (Manhattan)
Robert B. Roosevelt (Democrat) 1871–73 (Manhattan)
Dwight Townsend (Democrat) 1871–73 (Queens, Staten Island)
Samuel S. Cox (Democrat) 1873–85, 1886–89 (Manhattan)
Thomas Creamer (Democrat) 1873–75, 1901–3 (Manhattan)
Philip S. Crooke (Republican) 1873–75 (Brooklyn)
John D. Lawson (Republican) 1873–75 (Manhattan)
David B. Mellish (Republican) 1873–74 (Manhattan)
Henry J. Scudder (Republican) 1873–75 (Queens, Staten Island)
Stewart L. Woodford (Republican) 1873–74 (Brooklyn)
Simeon B. Chittenden (Republican) 1874–81 (Brooklyn)
Richard Schell (Democrat) 1874–75 (Manhattan)
Archibald M. Bliss (Democrat) 1875–83, 1885–89 (Brooklyn)
Abram S. Hewitt (Democrat) 1875–79 (Manhattan)
Edwin Meade (Democrat) 1875–77 (Manhattan)

(*continued*)

Members of the U.S. House of Representatives Elected from Districts All or Partly within the Current Boundaries of New York City (*Continued*)

Henry B. Metcalfe (Democrat) 1875–77 (Queens, Staten Island)
N. Holmes Odell (Democrat) 1875–77 (Westchester)
Benjamin Willis (Democrat) 1875–79 (Manhattan)
James Covert (Democrat) 1877–81, 1889–95 (Queens, Staten Island)
Anthony Eckhoff (Democrat) 1877–79 (Manhattan)
David Dudley Field (Democrat) 1877 (Manhattan)
Anson G. McCook (Republican) 1877–83 (Manhattan)
Nicholas Muller (Democrat) 1877–81, 1883–87, 1899–1902 (Manhattan)
Alexander Smith (Democrat) 1877 (Westchester)
William Vedeer (Democrat) 1877–79 (Brooklyn)
Edwin Einstein (Republican) 1879–81 (Brooklyn)
Waldo Hutchins (Democrat) 1879–85 (Westchester)
Levi P. Morton (Republican) 1879–81 (Manhattan)
James O'Brien (Democrat) 1879–81 (Manhattan)
Daniel O'Reilly (Democrat) 1879–81 (Brooklyn)
Perry Belmont (Democrat) 1881–88 (Queens, Staten Island)
P. Henry Dugro (Democrat) 1881–83 (Manhattan)
Peter P. Mahoney (Democrat) 1885–89 (Brooklyn)
Truman A. Merriman (Democrat) 1885–89 (Brooklyn)
Joseph Pulitzer (Democrat) 1885–86 (Manhattan)
William G. Stahlnecker (Democrat) 1885–93 (Westchester)
Egbert L. Viele (Democrat) 1885–87 (Manhattan)
Lloyd S. Bryce (Democrat) 1887–89 (Manhattan)
W. Bourke Cockran (Democrat) 1887–89 (Manhattan)
Amos J. Cummings (Democrat) 1887–89, 1889–94, 1895–1902 (Manhattan)
Ashbel P. Fitch (Democrat) 1887–93 (Manhattan)
Francis B. Spinola (Democrat) 1887–91 (Manhattan)
Steven V. White (Republican) 1887–89 (Brooklyn)
John M. Clancy (Democrat) 1889–95 (Brooklyn)
Edward J. Dunphy (Democrat) 1889–95 (Manhattan)
Frank T. Fitzgerald (Democrat) 1889 (Manhattan)
Thomas F. Magner (Democrat) 1889–95 (Brooklyn)
John H. McCarthy (Democrat) 1889–91 (Manhattan)
John Quinn (Democrat) 1889–91 (Manhattan)
Charles H. Turner (Democrat) 1889–91 (Manhattan)
William C. Wallace (Republican) 1889–91 (Manhattan)
David A. Boody (Democrat) 1891 (Brooklyn)
Alfred C. Chapin (Democrat) 1891–92 (Brooklyn)
W. Bourke Cockran (Democrat) 1891–95, 1904–9, 1921–23 (Manhattan)
John R. Fellows (Democrat) 1891–94 (Manhattan)
Joseph J. Little (Democrat) 1891–93 (Manhattan)
Franklin Bartlett (Democrat) 1893–97 (Staten Island, Manhattan)
John H. Graham (Democrat) 1893–95 (Brooklyn)
Joseph C. Hendrix (Democrat) 1893–95 (Brooklyn)
William Ryan (Democrat) 1893–95 (Westchester)
Lemuel E. Quigg (Republican) 1894–95 (Manhattan)
Isidor Straus (Democrat) 1894–95 (Manhattan)
Charles G. Bennett (Republican) 1895–99 (Brooklyn)
Benjamin Fairchild (Republican) 1895–97, 1917–19, 1921–23, 1923–27 (Bronx)
Israel F. Fischer (Republican) 1895–99 (Brooklyn)
James R. Howe (Republican) 1895–99 (Brooklyn)
Denis M. Hurley (Democrat) 1895–99 (Brooklyn)
Philip B. Low (Democrat) 1895–99 (Manhattan)
George B. McClellan (Democrat) 1895–1903 (Manhattan)
Richard C. McCormick (Republican) 1895–97 (Queens, Staten Island)
Henry Clay Miner (Democrat) 1895–97 (Manhattan)
Richard C. Shannon (Republican) 1895–99 (Manhattan)
William Sulzer (Democrat) 1895–1912 (Manhattan)
James J. Walsh (Democrat) 1895–96 (Manhattan)
Francis H. Wilson (Democrat) 1895–97 (Brooklyn)
John M. Mitchell (Democrat) 1896–99 (Manhattan)
Joseph M. Belford (Republican) 1897–99 (Queens, Staten Island)
Thomas J. Bradley (Democrat) 1897–1901 (Manhattan)
Edmund H. Driggs (Democrat) 1897–1901 (Brooklyn)
John H. G. Vehslage (Democrat) 1897–99 (Staten Island, Manhattan)
William L. Ward (Republican) 1897–99 (Westchester)
William A. Chanler (Democrat) 1899–1901 (Manhattan)
Bertram T. Clayton (Democrat) 1899–1901 (Brooklyn)
John J. Fitzgerald (Democrat) 1899–1917 (Brooklyn)
Jefferson M. Levy (Democrat) 1899–1901, 1911–15 (Manhattan)
Mitchell May (Democrat) 1899–1901 (Brooklyn)
Daniel J. Riordan (Democrat) 1899–1901 (Manhattan), 1906–23 (Staten Island, Manhattan)
Jacob Ruppert, Jr. (Democrat) 1899–1907 (Manhattan)
Townsend Scudder (Democrat) 1899–1901, 1903–5 (Queens, Staten Island)
John Q. Underhill (Democrat) 1899–1901 (Bronx)
Frank E. Wilson (Democrat) 1899–1905, 1911–15 (Brooklyn)
Oliver H. P. Belmont (Democrat) 1901–3 (Manhattan)
Henry Bristow (Republican) 1901–3 (Brooklyn)
William H. Douglas (Republican) 1901–3 (Manhattan)
Henry M. Goldfogle (Democrat) 1901–15, 1919–21 (Manhattan)
Harry A. Hanbury (Republican) 1901–3 (Brooklyn)
George H. Lindsay (Democrat) 1901–13 (Brooklyn)
Cornelius A. Pugsley (Democrat) 1901–3 (Bronx)
Frederic Storm (Republican) 1901–3 (Queens, Staten Island)
Montague Lessler (Republican) 1902–3 (Staten Island, Manhattan)
Edward Swann (Democrat) 1902–3 (Manhattan)
Robert Baker (Democrat) 1903–5 (Brooklyn)

(*continued*)

Members of the U.S. House of Representatives Elected from Districts All or Partly within the Current Boundaries of New York City (*Continued*)

Edward M. Bassett (Democrat) 1903–5 (Brooklyn)
Charles T. Dunwell (Republican) 1903–8 (Brooklyn)
Joseph A. Goulden (Democrat) 1903–11 (Manhattan, Bronx)
Francis B. Harrison (Democrat) 1903–5, 1907–13 (Manhattan)
William Randolph Hearst (Democrat) 1903–7 (Manhattan)
Ira E. Rider (Democrat) 1903–5 (Manhattan)
Francis E. Shober (Democrat) 1903–5 (Manhattan)
Timothy D. Sullivan (Democrat) 1903–6 (Staten Island, Manhattan)
William S. Bennet (Republican) 1905–11, 1915–17 (Manhattan)
William M. Calder (Republican) 1905–15 (Brooklyn)
William W. Cocks (Republican) 1905–11 (Queens, Staten Island)
Charles B. Law (Republican) 1905–11 (Brooklyn)
J. Van Vechten Olcott (Republican) 1905–11 (Manhattan)
Herbert Parsons (Republican) 1905–11 (Manhattan)
Charles A. Towne (Democrat) 1905–7 (Manhattan)
George E. Waldo (Republican) 1905–9 (Brooklyn)
Charles V. Fornes (Democrat) 1907–13 (Manhattan)
William Willett (Democrat) 1907–11 (Manhattan)
Otto G. Foelker (Republican) 1908–11 (Brooklyn)
Michael F. Conry (Democrat) 1909–17 (Manhattan)
Steven B. Ayres (Democrat) 1911–13 (Manhattan, Bronx)
Henry George, Jr. (Democrat) 1911–15 (Manhattan)
John J. Kindred (Democrat) 1911–13 (Manhattan)
Martin W. Littleton (Democrat) 1911–13 (Queens, Staten Island)
John P. Maher (Democrat) 1911–21 (Brooklyn)
Thomas G. Patten (Democrat) 1911–17 (Manhattan)
William C. Redfield (Democrat) 1911–13 (Brooklyn)
Richard Young (Republican) 1911–13 (Brooklyn)
Lathrop Brown (Democrat) 1913–15 (Queens, Staten Island)
Henry Bruckner (Democrat) 1913–17 (Manhattan, Bronx)
Jacob A. Cantor (Democrat) 1913–15 (Manhattan)
John F. Carew (Democrat) 1913–29 (Manhattan)
Walter M. Chandler (Republican) 1913–19, 1921–23 (Manhattan)
Harry H. Dale (Democrat) 1913–19 (Brooklyn)
Peter J. Dooling (Democrat) 1913–21 (Manhattan)
Daniel J. Griffin (Democrat) 1913–17 (Brooklyn)
George W. Loft (Democrat) 1913–17 (Manhattan)
Herman A. Metz (Democrat) 1913–15 (Brooklyn)
James H. O'Brien (Democrat) 1913–15 (Brooklyn, Queens, Staten Island)
Woodson R. Oglesby (Democrat) 1913–17 (Bronx)
Denis O'Leary (Democrat) 1913–14 (Queens, Staten Island)
Charles P. Caldwell (Democrat) 1915–21 (Queens, Staten Island)
Michael F. Farley (Democrat) 1915–21 (Manhattan)
Joseph V. Flynn (Democrat) 1915–19 (Brooklyn)
Reuben L. Haskell (Republican) 1915–19 (Brooklyn)
Frederick C. Hicks (Republican) 1915–23 (Queens, Staten Island)
G. Murray Hulbert (Democrat) 1915–18 (Manhattan, Bronx)
Meyer London (Socialist) 1915–19, 1921–23 (Manhattan)
Frederick W. Rowe (Republican) 1915–21 (Brooklyn)
Isaac Siegel (Republican) 1915–23 (Manhattan)
Oscar W. Swift (Republican) 1915–19 (Brooklyn, Queens, Staten Island)
George B. Francis (Republican) 1917–19 (Manhattan)
Fiorello H. La Guardia (Republican) 1917–19, 1923–33 (Manhattan)
Daniel C. Oliver (Democrat) 1917–19 (Manhattan, Bronx)
Thomas F. Smith (Democrat) 1917–21 (Manhattan)
Christopher Sullivan (Democrat) 1917–41 (Manhattan)
William E. Cleary (Democrat) 1918–21, 1923–27 (Brooklyn)
John J. Delaney (Democrat) 1918–19, 1931–48 (Brooklyn)
Jerome F. Donovan (Democrat) 1918–21 (Manhattan, Bronx)
Anthony J. Griffin (Democrat) 1918–35 (Manhattan, Bronx)
Thomas H. Cullen (Democrat) 1919–44 (Brooklyn)
James V. Ganly (Democrat) 1919–21 (Bronx)
John B. Johnston (Democrat) 1919–21 (Brooklyn)
John MacCrate (Republican) 1919–20 (Brooklyn)
Richard F. McKiniry (Democrat) 1919–21 (Manhattan, Bronx)
David J. O'Connell (Democrat) 1919–21, 1923–30 (Brooklyn, Queens, Staten Island)
Herbert C. Pell (Democrat) 1919–21 (Manhattan)
Joseph Rowan (Democrat) 1919–21 (Manhattan)
Nathan D. Perlman (Republican) 1920–27 (Manhattan)
Lester D. Volk (Republican) 1920–23 (Brooklyn)
Martin C. Ansorge (Republican) 1921–23 (Manhattan, Bronx)
Charles G. Bond (Republican) 1921–23 (Brooklyn)
Michael J. Hogan (Republican) 1921–23 (Brooklyn)
John Kissel (Republican) 1921–23 (Brooklyn)
Ardolph L. Kline (Republican) 1921–23 (Brooklyn)
Warren I. Lee (Republican) 1921–23 (Brooklyn)
Ogden L. Mills (Republican) 1921–27 (Manhattan)
Andrew N. Peterson (Republican) 1921–23 (Brooklyn, Queens, Staten Island)
Albert B. Rossdale (Republican) 1921–23 (Manhattan, Bronx)
Thomas J. Ryan (Republican) 1921–23 (Manhattan)
Robert L. Bacon (Republican) 1923–38 (Queens, Staten Island)
Loring M. Black (Democrat) 1923–35 (Brooklyn)
Sol Bloom (Democrat) 1923–49 (Manhattan)
John J. Boylan (Democrat) 1923–38 (Manhattan)
Emmanuel Celler (Democrat) 1923–73 (Brooklyn)
Samuel Dickstein (Democrat) 1923–45 (Manhattan)
George W. Lindsay (Democrat) 1923–35 (Brooklyn)
John J. O'Connor (Democrat) 1923–39 (Manhattan)
Frank Oliver (Democrat) 1923–34 (Bronx)
Anning S. Prall (Democrat) 1923–35 (Staten Island, Manhattan)

(*continued*)

Members of the U.S. House of Representatives Elected from Districts All or Partly within the Current Boundaries of New York City (*Continued*)

John F. Quayle (Democrat) 1923–30 (Brooklyn)
Charles I. Stengle (Democrat) 1923–25 (Brooklyn)
Royal H. Weller (Democrat) 1923–29 (Manhattan, Bronx)
Andrew L. Somers (Democrat) 1925–49 (Brooklyn)
Patrick J. Carley (Democrat) 1927–35 (Brooklyn)
William W. Cohen (Democrat) 1927–29 (Manhattan)
James M. Fitzpatrick (Democrat) 1927–49 (Bronx)
William I. Sirovich (Democrat) 1927–39 (Manhattan)
William F. Brunner (Democrat) 1929–35 (Queens, Staten Island)
Joseph A. Gavagan (Democrat) 1929–43 (Manhattan, Bronx)
Ruth S. B. Pratt (Republican) 1929–33 (Manhattan)
Martin J. Kennedy (Democrat) 1930–45 (Manhattan)
Matthew V. O'Malley (Democrat) 1931 (Brooklyn, Queens, Staten Island)
Stephen A. Rudd (Democrat) 1931–36 (Brooklyn, Queens, Staten Island)
James J. Lanzetta (Democrat) 1933–35, 1937–39 (Manhattan)
Theodore A. Peyser (Democrat) 1933–37 (Manhattan)
William B. Barry (Democrat) 1935–46 (Queens, Staten Island)
Charles A. Buckley (Democrat) 1935–65 (Bronx)
Edward W. Curley (Democrat) 1935–40 (Manhattan, Bronx)
Marcellus H. Evans (Democrat) 1935–41 (Brooklyn)
Vito Marcantonio (Republican, American Labor) 1935–37, 1939–51 (Manhattan)
James A. O'Leary (Democrat) 1935–44 (Staten Island, Manhattan)
Joseph L. Pfeifer (Democrat) 1935–51 (Brooklyn)
Richard J. Tonry (Democrat) 1935–37 (Brooklyn)
Bruce Barton (Republican) 1937–41 (Manhattan)
Eugene J. Keogh (Democrat) 1937–67 (Brooklyn, Queens, Staten Island)
Donald L. O'Toole (Democrat) 1937–53 (Brooklyn)
James H. Fay (Democrat) 1939–41, 1943–45 (Manhattan)
Leonard W. Hall (Republican) 1939–51 (Queens, Staten Island)
M. Michael Edelstein (Democrat) 1940–41 (Manhattan)
Walter A. Lynch (Democrat) 1940–41 (Manhattan, Bronx)
Joseph C. Baldwin (Republican) 1941–47 (Manhattan)
Louis J. Capozzoli (Democrat) 1941–45 (Manhattan)
James J. Heffernan (Democrat) 1941–53 (Brooklyn)
Arthur G. Klein (Democrat) 1941–45 (Manhattan)
William T. Pheiffer (Republican) 1941–43 (Manhattan)
Kenneth F. Simpson (Republican) 1941 (Manhattan)
Thomas F. Burchill (Democrat) 1943–45 (Manhattan)
Ellsworth B. Buck (Republican) 1944–49 (Staten Island, Manhattan)
John J. Rooney (Democrat) 1944–74 (Brooklyn)
James H. Torrens (Democrat) 1944–47 (Manhattan, Bronx)
James J. Delaney (Democrat) 1945–47, 1949–78 (Queens, Staten Island)
Henry J. Latham (Republican) 1945–58 (Queens, Staten Island)
Adam Clayton Powell (Democrat) 1945–67, 1969–71 (Manhattan)
Peter A. Quinn (Democrat) 1945–47 (Bronx)
Benjamin J. Rabin (Democrat) 1945–47 (Bronx)
Leo F. Rayfiel (Democrat) 1945–47 (Brooklyn)
James A. Roe (Democrat) 1945–47 (Queens, Staten Island)
Frederic R. Coudert (Republican) 1947–59 (Manhattan)
Jacob K. Javits (Republican) 1947–54 (Manhattan)
Gregory McMahon (Republican) 1947–49 (Queens, Staten Island)
Abraham J. Multer (Democrat) 1947–67 (Brooklyn)
Robert J. Nodar, Jr. (Republican) 1947–49 (Queens, Staten Island)
David M. Potts (Republican) 1947–49 (Bronx)
Robert Tripp Ross (Republican) 1947–49 (Queens, Staten Island)
Leo Isacson (American Labor) 1948–49 (Bronx)
L. Gary Clemente (Democrat) 1949–53 (Queens, Staten Island)
Isidore Dollinger (Democrat) 1949–59 (Bronx)
Louis B. Heller (Democrat) 1949–54 (Brooklyn)
Edna F. Kelly (Democrat) 1949–69 (Brooklyn)
Christopher C. McGrath (Democrat) 1949–53 (Bronx)
James J. Murphy (Democrat) 1949–53 (Staten Island, Manhattan)
T. Vincent Quinn (Democrat) 1949–51 (Queens, Staten Island)
Franklin D. Roosevelt, Jr. (Democrat) 1949–55 (Manhattan)
Victor L. Anfuso (Democrat) 1951–53, 1955–63 (Brooklyn)
Sidney A. Fine (Democrat) 1951–56 (Bronx)
Albert H. Bosch (Republican) 1953–60 (Queens)
Francis Dorn (Republican) 1953–61 (Brooklyn)
Paul A. Fino (Republican) 1953–68 (Bronx)
Lester Holtzman (Democrat) 1953–61 (Queens)
John H. Ray (Republican) 1953–63 (Staten Island, Brooklyn)
Irwin Davidson (Democrat) 1955–56 (Manhattan)
Herbert Zelenko (Democrat) 1955–63 (Manhattan)
James C. Healey (Democrat) 1956–65 (Bronx)
Leonard Farbstein (Democrat) 1957–71 (Manhattan)
Alfred E. Santangelo (Democrat) 1957–63 (Manhattan)
Ludwig Teller (Democrat) 1957–61 (Manhattan)
Seymour Halpern (Republican) 1959–73 (Queens)
John V. Lindsay (Republican) 1959–65 (Manhattan)
Jacob H. Gilbert (Democrat) 1960–71 (Bronx)
Joseph P. Addabbo (Democrat) 1961–86 (Queens)
Hugh L. Carey (Democrat) 1961–74 (Brooklyn)
William F. Ryan (Democrat) 1961–72 (Manhattan)
Benjamin S. Rosenthal (Democrat) 1962–83 (Queens)
John M. Murphy (Democrat) 1963–81 (Staten Island, Brooklyn; Staten Island, Manhattan)
Jonathan B. Bingham (Democrat) 1965–83 (Bronx)
James H. Scheuer (Democrat) 1965–73 (Bronx)
Lester L. Wolff (Democrat) 1965–81 (Queens)
Theodore R. Kupferman (Republican) 1966–69 (Manhattan)

(*continued*)

Members of the U.S. House of Representatives Elected from Districts All or Partly within the Current Boundaries of New York City (*Continued*)

Frank J. Brasco (Democrat) 1967–75 (Brooklyn)
Bertram L. Podell (Democrat) 1968–75 (Brooklyn)
Mario Biaggi (Democrat) 1969–88 (Bronx)
Shirley B. Chisholm (Democrat) 1969–83 (Brooklyn)
Edward I. Koch (Democrat) 1969–77 (Manhattan)
Bella Abzug (Democrat) 1971–77 (Manhattan)
Herman Badillo (Democrat) 1971–77 (Bronx)
Charles B. Rangel (Democrat) 1971– (Queens, Manhattan, Bronx)
Elizabeth Holtzman (Democrat) 1973–81 (Brooklyn)
Frederick W. Richmond (Democrat) 1975–82 (Brooklyn)
Stephen J. Solarz (Democrat) 1975–93 (Brooklyn)
Leo C. Zeferetti (Democrat) 1975–83 (Brooklyn)
Robert Garcia (Democrat) 1977–89 (Bronx)
S. William Green (Republican) 1977–93 (Manhattan)
Ted Weiss (Democrat) 1977–92 (Manhattan)
Geraldine A. Ferraro (Democrat) 1979–85 (Queens, Staten Island)
John LeBoutillier (Republican) 1981–83 (Queens, Staten Island)
Guy V. Molinari (Republican) 1981–89 (Staten Island, Bronx, Manhattan; Brooklyn, Staten Island)
Gary L. Ackerman (Democrat) 1983– (Queens)
Major R. Owens (Democrat) 1983–2007 (Brooklyn)
Edolphus Towns (Democrat) 1983– (Brooklyn)
Thomas J. Manton (Democrat) 1985–99 (Queens, Staten Island)
Charles E. Schumer (Democrat) 1981–99 (Brooklyn)
Alton R. Waldon, Jr. (Democrat) 1986–87 (Queens, Staten Island)
Floyd H. Flake (Democrat) 1987–97 (Queens, Staten Island)
Eliot L. Engel (Democrat) 1989– (Bronx)
Nita M. Lowey (Democrat) 1989– (Bronx, Queens) (as of 2003 representative's district no longer in city boundaries)
Susan Molinari (Republican) 1990–97 (Staten Island, Brooklyn)
José E. Serrano (Democrat) 1990– (Bronx)
Jerrold L. Nadler (Democrat) 1992– (Manhattan, Brooklyn)
Carolyn B. Maloney (Democrat) 1993– (Manhattan, Queens)
Nydia M. Velázquez (Democrat) 1993– (Brooklyn, Manhattan, Queens)
Gregory W. Meeks (Democrat) 1998– (Queens)
Joseph Crowley (Democrat) 1999– (Queens, Bronx)
Anthony D. Weiner (Democrat) 1999– (Brooklyn, Queens)
Yvette D. Clarke (Democrat) 2007– (Brooklyn)
Michael E. McMahon (Democrat) 2009– (Staten Island, Brooklyn)

Source: Kenneth C. Martis, *The Historical Atlas of United States Congressional Districts, 1789–1983* (New York: Free Press, 1982)
Compiled by James Bradley

ingly important role in the political process. The 1945 mayoral election was won by William O'Dwyer, a former judge and district attorney in Brooklyn. Formed at a time when Tammany Hall was under the sway of the organized-crime figure Frank Costello, his administration was marked by graft and corruption. When O'Dwyer resigned in the first year of his second term to become ambassador to Mexico, Vincent R. Impellitteri succeeded him as acting mayor. In a special election held in 1951 Impellitteri failed to win the support of the Democratic organization, which regarded him as incompetent, but won election as an independent. He was unable to win the organization's support for a full term in 1953: the head of Tammany Hall, Carmine DeSapio, designated instead Robert F. Wagner, the borough president of Manhattan. Wagner's victories in 1953 and again in 1957 strengthened the Democratic organization. During his tenure he recognized and negotiated with municipal employees' unions, and with Robert Moses he used federally funded urban renewal and public housing programs to reshape the city. Wagner perceived the growing importance of black voters and the strength of the reform movement in the Democratic Party, and he repudiated DeSapio when he sought reelection in 1961. County leaders who believed that Wagner's indecisiveness and a number of minor scandals made him a liability supported Arthur Levitt in the Democratic primary, but Wagner won a bitter primary with support from the municipal employees' unions and political advice from Alex Rose (head of the Liberal Party) and J. Raymond Jones (the black district leader from Harlem whom he later helped to defeat DeSapio to become New York County Democratic Party leader); after defeating Louis Lefkowitz, the Republican candidate, in the general election, he replaced all the Democratic county leaders except Charles A. Buckley of the Bronx. Despite his accomplishments Wagner failed to build a political base beyond the regular Democratic organizations, in part because he concentrated on consolidating support from the public employees' unions and securing federal funds for constituencies who had traditionally supported him; the increasing militancy of the civil rights movement and protest in the neighborhoods also undermined his power. In 1965 expenditures driven to some extent by the wage demands of municipal employees rose faster than revenues, causing the first of several increasingly difficult fiscal crises in the city. Wagner announced that he would not seek a fourth term when private polls showed that he could not win.

In Wagner's place the Democrats nominated the city comptroller, Abraham Beame, who had come up through the Brooklyn county party organization; the Republicans sought to revive the alliance of liberal Republicans and reform Democrats that had elected La Guardia by nominating Representative John V. Lindsay; angered by the nomination of Lindsay, William F. Buckley, Jr., offered himself as the nominee of the Conservative Party. With support from Governor Nelson A. Rockefeller, Alex Rose, and the garment unions, Lindsay won the election with 43.3 percent of the vote. In office he employed policy analysis and modern management tools, supported new neighborhood-based city agencies, and expanded the budget with state and federal aid; he was buffeted, however, by community protests, strikes by public employees, conflict over community school decentralization, and chronic fiscal difficulty. In attempting to win reelection in 1969 he lost the Republican nomination to a conservative, John J. Marchi; in the general election Marchi competed for the same votes with the Democratic candidate, Mario Procaccino, also a conservative, and Lindsay won by a narrow margin as the nominee of the Liberal Party with support from city employees (who had received generous wage settlements), liberal Democrats, Jews, blacks, and Puerto Ricans. The election of 1969 marked the decline of the political club and the increasing importance of the candidate and

Presidential Election Returns for New York City, 1836–2008 (by County 1836–96, including Kings, Queens, Richmond, and Westchester; by Borough 1900–2008)

(Excludes some minor-party candidates; name and party of winning candidate are in boldface.)

1836	**Martin Van Buren (Democrat)**	William H. Harrison (Whig)
New York	17,469	16,348
Kings	2,321	1,868
Queens	1,654	1,399
Richmond	649	649
Westchester	3,009	1,749
Totals	25,102	22,013

1840	Martin Van Buren (Democrat)	**William H. Harrison (Whig)**
New York	21,936	20,959
Kings	3,157	3,293
Queens	2,550	2,522
Richmond	861	903
Westchester	4,354	4,083
Totals	32,858	31,760

1844	**James K. Polk (Democrat)**	Henry Clay (Whig)
New York	28,296	26,385
Kings	4,648	5,107
Queens	2,751	2,547
Richmond	1,063	1,049
Westchester	4,412	4,258
Totals	41,170	39,346

1848	Lewis Cass (Democrat)	**Zachary Taylor (Whig)**
New York	18,975	29,070
Kings	4,881	7,511
Queens	1,310	2,444
Richmond	860	1,099
Westchester	2,146	4,112
Totals	28,172	44,236

1852	**Franklin Pierce (Democrat)**	Winfield Scott (Whig)
New York	34,280	23,122
Kings	10,624	8,491
Queens	2,903	2,209
Richmond	1,324	1,147
Westchester	5,283	4,033
Totals	54,414	39,002

1856	**James Buchanan (Democrat)**	John C. Frémont (Republican)	Millard Fillmore (American)
New York	41,913	17,771	19,924
Kings	14,174	7,846	8,651
Queens	2,394	1,886	2,523
Richmond	1,550	736	947
Westchester	4,600	4,450	3,641
Totals	64,631	32,689	35,686

1860	Stephen Douglas (Democrat)	**Abraham Lincoln (Republican)**
New York	62,482	33,290
Kings	20,599	15,883
Queens	4,391	3,749
Richmond	2,370	1,408
Westchester	8,126	6,771
Totals	97,968	61,101

(*continued*)

Presidential Election Returns for New York City, 1836–2008 (by County 1836–96, including Kings, Queens, Richmond, and Westchester; by Borough 1900–2008) (*Continued*)

1864	George B. McClellan (Democrat)	**Abraham Lincoln (Republican)**
New York	73,709	36,681
Kings	25,726	20,838
Queens	5,400	4,284
Richmond	2,874	1,564
Westchester	9,355	7,607
Totals	117,064	70,974
1868	Horatio Seymour (Democrat)	**Ulysses S. Grant (Republican)**
New York	108,316	47,748
Kings	39,838	27,711
Queens	6,388	4,973
Richmond	3,019	2,221
Westchester	11,667	9,642
Totals	169,228	92,295
1872	Horace Greeley (Democrat)	**Ulysses S. Grant (Republican)**
New York	77,814	54,676
Kings	38,108	33,368
Queens	5,655	6,082
Richmond	2,541	2,728
Westchester	11,112	10,233
Totals	135,230	107,087
1876	Samuel J. Tilden (Democrat)	**Rutherford B. Hayes (Republican)**
New York	112,621	58,776
Kings	57,557	39,125
Queens	9,994	6,971
Richmond	4,338	2,884
Westchester	12,054	9,574
Totals	196,564	117,330
1880	Winfield Hancock (Democrat)	**James A. Garfield (Republican)**
New York	123,015	58,776
Kings	61,062	51,751
Queens	10,391	8,151
Richmond	4,815	3,291
Westchester	11,858	11,367
Totals	211,141	133,336
1884	**Grover Cleveland (Democrat)**	James G. Blaine (Republican)
New York	133,222	90,095
Kings	69,264	53,516
Queens	10,367	8,445
Richmond	5,135	3,164
Westchester	12,525	11,286
Totals	230,513	166,506
1888	Grover Cleveland (Democrat)	**Benjamin Harrison (Republican)**
New York	162,735	106,922
Kings	82,507	70,052
Queens	12,683	11,017
Richmond	5,764	4,100
Westchester	14,948	13,799
Totals	278,637	205,890
1892	**Grover Cleveland (Democrat)**	Benjamin Harrison (Republican)
New York	175,267	98,967
Kings	100,160	70,505

(*continued*)

Presidential Election Returns for New York City, 1836–2008 (by County 1836–96, including Kings, Queens, Richmond, and Westchester; by Borough 1900–2008) (*Continued*)

1892 (*Continued*)	**Grover Cleveland (Democrat)**	Benjamin Harrison (Republican)	
Queens	15,195	11,704	
Richmond	6,122	4,091	
Westchester	16,088	13,436	
Totals	312,832	198,703	
1896	William Jennings Bryan (Democrat)	**William McKinley (Republican)**	
New York (includes present Bronx)	135,624	156,359	
Kings	76,882	109,135	
Queens	11,980	18,694	
Richmond	4,452	6,170	
Totals	228,938	290,358	
1900	William Jennings Bryan (Democrat)	**William McKinley (Republican)**	
Manhattan and Bronx	181,786	153,001	
Brooklyn	106,232	108,977	
Queens	14,747	12,323	
Staten Island	6,759	6,042	
Totals	309,524	280,343	
1904	Alton B. Parker (Democrat)	**Theodore Roosevelt (Republican)**	
Manhattan and Bronx	189,712	155,003	
Brooklyn	111,855	113,246	
Queens	18,151	14,096	
Staten Island	7,182	7,000	
Totals	326,900	289,345	
1908	William Jennings Bryan (Democrat)	**William H. Taft (Republican)**	
Manhattan and Bronx	160,261	154,958	
Brooklyn	96,756	119,789	
Queens	20,342	19,420	
Staten Island	6,831	7,401	
Totals	284,190	301,568	
1912	**Woodrow Wilson (Democrat)**	William H. Taft (Republican)	Theodore Roosevelt (Progressive)
Manhattan and Bronx	166,157	63,107	98,985
Brooklyn	109,748	51,239	71,167
Queens	28,044	9,201	14,951
Staten Island	8,437	3,035	3,771
Totals	312,386	126,582	188,874
1916	**Woodrow Wilson (Democrat)**	Charles E. Hughes (Republican)	
Manhattan	139,547	111,926	
Brooklyn	125,625	119,675	
Bronx	47,870	40,338	
Queens	31,350	34,670	
Staten Island	8,843	7,204	
Totals	353,235	313,813	
1920	James Cox (Democrat)	**Warren G. Harding (Republican)**	Eugene V. Debs (Socialist)
Manhattan	135,249	275,013	46,049
Brooklyn	119,612	292,692	45,100
Bronx	45,471	106,038	32,823
Queens	35,296	94,360	6,143
Staten Island	9,373	17,844	712
Totals	345,001	785,947	130,827

(*continued*)

Presidential Election Returns for New York City, 1836–2008 (by County 1836–96, including Kings, Queens, Richmond, and Westchester; by Borough 1900–2008) (*Continued*)

1924	John W. Davis (Democrat)	**Calvin Coolidge (Republican)**	Robert LaFollette (Progressive)
Manhattan	183,249	190,871	86,625
Brooklyn	158,907	236,877	100,721
Bronx	72,840	79,583	62,212
Queens	58,402	100,793	28,210
Staten Island	15,801	18,007	3,702
Totals	489,199	626,131	281,470
1928	Alfred E. Smith (Democrat)	**Herbert Hoover (Republican)**	
Manhattan	317,227	186,396	
Brooklyn	404,393	245,622	
Bronx	232,766	98,636	
Queens	184,640	158,505	
Staten Island	28,945	24,985	
Totals	1,167,971	714,144	
1932	**Franklin D. Roosevelt (Democrat)**	Herbert Hoover (Republican)	Norman Thomas (Socialist)
Manhattan	378,077	157,014	23,946
Brooklyn	514,172	192,536	50,509
Bronx	281,330	76,587	31,247
Queens	244,740	136,641	14,854
Staten Island	36,857	21,278	2,009
Totals	1,455,176	584,056	122,565
1936	**Franklin D. Roosevelt (Democrat)**	Alfred Landon (Republican)	
Manhattan	517,134	174,299	
Brooklyn	738,306	212,852	
Bronx	419,625	93,151	
Queens	320,053	162,797	
Staten Island	46,229	22,852	
Totals	2,041,347	665,951	
1940	**Franklin D. Roosevelt (Democrat)**	Wendell Willkie (Republican)	
Manhattan	478,153	292,480	
Brooklyn	742,668	394,534	
Bronx	418,931	198,293	
Queens	288,024	323,406	
Staten Island	38,307	38,911	
Totals	1,966,083	1,247,624	
1944	**Franklin D. Roosevelt (Democrat)**	Thomas E. Dewey (Republican)	
Manhattan	509,263	258,650	
Brooklyn	758,270	393,926	
Bronx	450,525	211,158	
Queens	292,940	365,365	
Staten Island	31,502	42,188	
Totals	2,042,500	1,271,287	
1948	**Harry S. Truman (Democrat)**	Thomas E. Dewey (Republican)	Henry A. Wallace (Progressive)
Manhattan	380,310	241,752	106,509
Brooklyn	579,922	330,494	163,896
Bronx	337,129	173,044	106,762
Queens	268,742	323,459	42,409
Staten Island	30,442	39,539	2,779
Totals	1,596,545	1,108,288	422,355
1952	Adlai Stevenson (Democrat)	**Dwight D. Eisenhower (Republican)**	
Manhattan	446,727	300,284	
Brooklyn	656,229	446,708	

(*continued*)

Presidential Election Returns for New York City, 1836–2008 (by County 1836–96, including Kings, Queens, Richmond, and Westchester; by Borough 1900–2008) (*Continued*)

	Adlai Stevenson (Democrat)	**Dwight D. Eisenhower (Republican)**	
1952 (*Continued*)			
Bronx	399,477	241,898	
Queens	331,217	450,610	
Staten Island	28,280	55,993	
Totals	1,861,930	1,495,493	
	Adlai Stevenson (Democrat)	**Dwight D. Eisenhower (Republican)**	
1956			
Manhattan	377,856	300,004	
Brooklyn	557,655	460,456	
Bronx	343,823	257,382	
Queens	318,723	466,057	
Staten Island	19,644	64,233	
Totals	1,617,701	1,548,132	
	John F. Kennedy (Democrat)	Richard M. Nixon (Republican)	
1960			
Manhattan	414,902	217,271	
Brooklyn	646,582	327,497	
Bronx	389,818	182,393	
Queens	446,348	367,688	
Staten Island	38,673	50,356	
Totals	1,936,323	1,145,205	
	Lyndon B. Johnson (Democrat)	Barry Goldwater (Republican)	
1964			
Manhattan	503,848	120,125	
Brooklyn	684,839	229,291	
Bronx	403,014	135,780	
Queens	541,418	274,351	
Staten Island	50,524	42,330	
Totals	2,183,643	801,877	
	Hubert H. Humphrey (Democrat)	**Richard M. Nixon (Republican)**	George Wallace (American Independent)
1968			
Manhattan	370,806	135,458	12,958
Brooklyn	489,174	247,936	33,563
Bronx	277,385	142,314	21,950
Queens	410,546	306,620	44,198
Staten Island	34,770	54,631	9,112
Totals	1,582,681	886,959	121,781
	George McGovern (Democrat)	**Richard M. Nixon (Republican)**	
1972			
Manhattan	354,326	178,515	
Brooklyn	387,768	373,903	
Bronx	243,345	196,754	
Queens	328,316	426,015	
Staten Island	29,241	84,686	
Totals	1,342,996	1,259,873	
	Jimmy Carter (Democrat)	Gerald R. Ford (Republican)	
1976			
Manhattan	337,438	117,702	
Brooklyn	419,382	190,728	
Bronx	238,786	96,842	
Queens	379,907	244,396	
Staten Island	47,867	56,995	
Totals	1,423,380	706,663	
	Jimmy Carter (Democrat)	**Ronald Reagan (Republican)**	John Anderson (Independent)
1980			
Manhattan	275,742	115,911	38,597
Brooklyn	288,893	200,298	24,341
Bronx	181,090	86,843	11,286

(*continued*)

Presidential Election Returns for New York City, 1836–2008 (by County 1836–96, including Kings, Queens, Richmond, and Westchester; by Borough 1900–2008) (*Continued*)

1980 (*Continued*)	Jimmy Carter (Democrat)	**Ronald Reagan (Republican)**	John Anderson (Independent)
Queens	269,147	251,333	32,566
Staten Island	37,306	64,885	7,055
Totals	1,052,178	719,270	113,845
1984	Walter F. Mondale (Democrat)	**Ronald Reagan (Republican)**	
Manhattan	379,521	144,281	
Brooklyn	368,518	230,064	
Bronx	223,112	109,308	
Queens	328,379	285,477	
Staten Island	44,345	83,187	
Totals	1,343,875	852,317	
1988	Michael S. Dukakis (Democrat)	**George H. W. Bush (Republican)**	
Manhattan	385,675	115,927	
Brooklyn	363,916	178,961	
Bronx	218,245	76,043	
Queens	325,147	217,049	
Staten Island	47,812	77,427	
Totals	1,340,795	665,407	
1992	**Bill Clinton (Democrat)**	George H. W. Bush (Republican)	H. Ross Perot (Independent)
Manhattan	416,142	84,501	27,689
Brooklyn	411,183	133,344	33,014
Bronx	225,038	63,310	15,115
Queens	349,520	157,561	46,014
Staten Island	56,901	70,707	19,678
Totals	1,458,784	509,423	141,510
1996	**Bill Clinton (Democrat)**	Bob Dole (Republican)	
Manhattan	394,131	67,839	
Brooklyn	432,232	81,406	
Bronx	248,276	30,435	
Queens	372,925	107,650	
Staten Island	64,684	52,207	
Totals	1,512,428	339,537	
2000	Al Gore (Democrat)	**George W. Bush (Republican)**	
Manhattan	449,300	79,921	
Brooklyn	497,468	96,605	
Bronx	265,801	36,245	
Queens	416,967	122,052	
Staten Island	73,828	63,903	
Totals	1,629,536	398,726	
2004	John Kerry (Democrat)	**George W. Bush (Republican)**	
Manhattan	526,765	107,405	
Brooklyn	514,973	167,149	
Bronx	283,994	56,701	
Queens	433,835	165,954	
Staten Island	68,448	90,325	
Totals	1,828,015	587,534	
2008	**Barack Obama (Democrat)**	John McCain (Republican)	
Manhattan	572,126	89,906	
Brooklyn	603,525	151,872	
Bronx	338,261	41,683	
Queens	447,906	145,898	
Staten Island	79,311	86,062	
Totals	2,041,129	515,421	

was one of the first elections in which television and political consultants played a dominant role.

In the early 1970s New York City faced a large budget deficit that was aggravated by increased borrowing and a sharp downturn in the economy. Lindsay declined to run for a third term in 1973 and was succeeded by Beame, the city's first Jewish mayor. By 1975 the financial crises finally led bankers to refuse to extend further credit to the city. The state formed two new agencies, the Municipal Assistance Corporation and the Emergency Financial Control Board, to restructure the city's debt and exert control over budgets and wage settlements. To stabilize finances the state agencies caused the city to reduce its payroll by 60,000 employees, obtained increased aid from the state, secured loan guarantees from the federal government, and persuaded the custodians of public employees' pension funds to invest in municipal bonds. Charter reform in 1975 gave formal status to community boards (developed by Wagner in the 1950s when he was borough president of Manhattan). In 1977 Beame was viewed as a weak candidate for reelection, even though he retained backing from the county Democratic organizations, and in the primary election he drew many opponents, including Representative Herman Badillo, Percy Sutton (former borough president of Manhattan), Mario M. Cuomo, and Representative Edward I. Koch, a reform Democrat from Greenwich Village who advocated fiscal discipline and emphasized his support for the death penalty and his opposition to public unions. Koch narrowly finished first, won a runoff election against Cuomo, and won the general election by soliciting support from minority leaders and from the county Democratic organizations.

In his reelection victories in 1981 and 1985 Koch redefined the Democratic political base along more conservative lines by assembling a coalition of white Catholics and Jews as well as a few Latinos and blacks. A steady improvement in the city's economy also strengthened his position. During his third term he was politically damaged by corruption in city agencies (uncovered by U.S. Attorney Rudolph W. Giuliani) and by racial antagonism, which many observers thought he worsened with undiplomatic and sometimes hostile comments about various black leaders. The economic downturn of 1989 also threatened the city's budget, which had doubled since the beginning of his tenure. The success of the Democratic presidential candidate Jesse Jackson in New York City during a primary election in 1988 enabled Koch's opponents to coalesce around David N. Dinkins, borough president of Manhattan, who had close ties to both black regular Democrats and the white reform movement. Dinkins defeated Koch in the Democratic mayoral primary in 1989 with nearly unanimous support from black voters (who had replaced Jews as the largest

New York City Mayoral and City Agencies

Name	Year Established
Administrative Justice Coordinator, Office of	2006
Administrative Trials and Hearings, Office of	1979
Adult Education, Mayor's Office of	2006
Advisory Committee on the Judiciary	2002
Aging, Department for the	1973
Anti-Graffiti Task Force, Mayor's	1995
Board of Elections	1900
Brooklyn Public Library	1896
Buildings, Department of	1936
Business Integrity Commission	2001
Campaign Finance Board	1988
Chief Medical Examiner, Office of	1918
City Clerk	1625
City Employee's Retirement System	1920
City Marshals, Mayor's Committee on	1980
City Planning Commission	1936
City University of New York	1847
Citywide Accountability Program	2001
Citywide Administrative Services, Department of	1996
Citywide Event Coordination and Management, Office of	2007
Citywide Health Insurance Access, Office of	N/A
Civil Service Commission	N/A
Commission to Combat Police Corruption	1995
Community Affairs Unit (Community Assistance Unit)	1951
Conflicts of Interest Board (formerly Board of Ethics)	1988 (1959)
Consumer Affairs, Department of	1968
Contract Services, Office of	1988
Correction, Department of	1895
Cultural Affairs, Department of	1968
Design and Construction, Department of	1999
Design Commission	1898
Domestic Violence, Mayor's Office to Combat	2001
Economic Development Corporation	1991
Economic Opportunity, Center for	2006
Education, Department of	2002
Emergency Management, Office of	1996
Empowerment Zone, New York	1996
Environmental Coordination, Office of	N/A
Environmental Protection, Department of	1978
Equal Employment Practices Commission	1997
Family Justice Center	N/A
Film, Theatre, and Broadway, Mayor's Office of	1974
Finance, Department of	N/A
Fire Department	1898
Fund to Advance New York City, Mayor's	1994
Health and Hospitals Corporation	1969
Health and Mental Hygiene, Department of	1866
Homeless Service, Department of	1993
Housing Authority	1934
Housing Preservation, and Development, Department of	1977
Human Resources Administration/Department of Social Services	1966
Human Rights, Commission on	1955
Immigrant Affairs, Office of	2003
Independent Budget Office	1996
Information Technology and Telecommunications, Department of	N/A
Intergovernmental Affairs, Mayor's Office of	N/A
Investigation, Department of	1873
Juvenile Justice, Department of	1979
Labor Relations, Office of	1967
Landmarks Preservation Commission	1965
Law Department	1849

(*continued*)

New York City Mayoral and City Agencies (*Continued*)

Name	Year Established
Loft Board	1982
Management and Budget, Office of	1933
Mayor's Office	1665
NYC TV	2003
Operations, Office of	1977
Parks and Recreation, Department of	1934
Payroll Administration, Office of	1936
People with Disabilities, Office for	N/A
Police Department	1845
Police Pension Fund	1857
Probation, Department of	N/A
Public Design Commission (formerly Art Commission)	1898
Queens Library	1896
Records, Department of	1977
Rent Guidelines Board	1969
Sanitation, Department of	1881
School Construction Authority	1988
Small Business Services, Department of	N/A
Special Enforcement, Office of	2006
Sports Commission	1986
Standards and Appeals, Board of	1916
Staten Island Growth Management Task Force	2003
Tax Commission	N/A
Taxi and Limousine Commission	1971
Transitional Finance Authority	1997
Transportation, Department of	1977
TSASC, Inc.	1999
United Nations Consular Corp and Protocol, Commission for the	1997
Veteran's Affairs, Mayor's Office of	1987
Voter Assistance Commission	1989
Water Board	1985
Water Finance Authority, New York City Municipal	1985
Women's Issues, Commission on	1975
Workforce Investment Board	2003
Youth and Community Development, Department of	1996

Source: NYC.gov, Office of the Mayor, http://www.nyc.gov
Compiled by Frank Nestor

component of the Democratic electorate), the municipal employees' unions, and white reform Democrats. The Republican and Liberal candidate, Giuliani, attracted many defectors among Democratic voters, but Dinkins narrowly won the general election with support from black voters, Latin Americans, white liberals, and a minority of white ethnic Democrats to become the first black mayor in the city's history. The election took place at a time when the charter was being amended yet again, in response to a decision by the U.S. Supreme Court that effectively abolished the Board of Estimate. The new charter transferred some of the board's powers to the mayor (such as that of granting contracts) and others to the City Council (such as those concerned with land use). Dinkins's success as a candidate was quickly overshadowed by a renewed fiscal crisis, conflict between blacks and Koreans in Flatbush and between blacks and Orthodox Jews in Crown Heights, and a perception of increasing street crime.

In 1993 Giuliani again challenged Dinkins for the mayoralty, this time narrowly prevailing and overwhelmingly won reelection in 1997 against the liberal Democratic candidate, Ruth Messinger, who had been Manhattan Borough President. The Giuliani years were marked by changes in policing practices that reduced violent crime in the city, although that period was also marked by several instances of police brutality, including the assault on Abner Louima, a Haitian immigrant, in the 70th Precinct of Brooklyn. The Giuliani administration also reduced welfare caseloads and required able recipients to work for their benefits. Although the late stage of his administration was marked by health problems and a nasty and public divorce, many lauded his leadership of the city in the wake of the attacks of 11 September 2001 on the World Trade Center.

Those attacks occurred on the day when the Democratic mayoral primary was slated to choose a nominee between the white liberal Mark Green, a former public advocate, and Fernando Ferrer, Bronx Borough President and the city's senior Puerto Rican elected official. Although Ferrer received strong support from African American leaders and ran first in the delayed primary election, he did not clear the 40 percent hurdle. Running to Ferrer's right, Green managed to win a close runoff to face a newcomer, Republican Michael R. Bloomberg, a recently converted Democrat who had built Bloomberg Communications into a multibillion-dollar corporation. With Democratic voters deeply divided over Green's nomination and voters' concern for restoring the city's economy and security following the events of 9/11, Bloomberg spent his own funds to narrowly win the 2001 mayoral election with an electoral coalition reminiscent of those which supported Mayors Giuliani and Koch.

Mayor Bloomberg proved to be a highly able steward of the city, which enjoyed economic recovery, continued declines in the crime rate during his first administration, and less racial animosity than had characterized the Giuliani administration. He also introduced many technological innovations, such as a 311 telephone system to improve citizen access to public services. In 2005 he prevailed easily over Democratic nominee Ferrer, once more spending a record amount in his victory. The second Bloomberg administration was characterized by mayoral control over the New York City public school system, many zoning and development decisions designed to promote market rate housing and office construction, and an innovative effort to reduce poverty. The mayor was thwarted by the state legislature, however, over introducing congestion pricing to the Manhattan traffic system. After the two-term limit of the city charter was extended in 2008, Bloomberg ran in 2009 for a third term, citing that the city required a leader with experience in finance and business because of the financial crisis and recession of 2008–9; he won the election on 3 November 2009.

I. N. Phelps Stokes, *The Iconography of Manhattan Island, 1498–1909, Compiled from Original Sources and Illustrated by Photo Intaglio Reproductions of Important Maps, Plans, Views and Documents in Public and Private Collections* (New York: Robert H. Dodd, 1915–28; repr. New York: Arno, 1967); Sidney I. Pomerantz, *New York: An American City, 1783–1803: A Study of Urban Life* (New York: Columbia University Press, 1938; 2nd edn Port Washington, N.Y.: I. J. Friedman, 1965); Patricia U. Bonomi, *A Factious People: Politics and Society in Colonial New York* (New York: Columbia University Press, 1971); Jerome Mushkat, *Tammany: The Evolution of a Political Machine, 1789–1865* (Syracuse, N.Y.: Syracuse University Press, 1971); Robert A. Caro, *The Power Broker: Robert Moses and the Fall of New York* (New York: Alfred A. Knopf,

1975); Edward K. Spann, *The New Metropolis: New York City, 1840–1857* (New York: Columbia University Press, 1981); Hendrik Hartog, *Public Property and Private Power: The Corporation of the City of New York in American Law, 1730–1870* (Chapel Hill: University of North Carolina Press, 1983); Martin Shefter, *Political Crisis, Fiscal Crisis: The Collapse and Revival of New York City* (New York: Basic Books, 1985); Joyce D. Goodfriend, *Before the Melting Pot: Society and Culture in Colonial New York City, 1664–1730* (Princeton, N.J.: Princeton University Press, 1992); John Mollenkopf, *A Phoenix in the Ashes: The Conservative Politics of Economic Boom in New York, 1977–1989* (Princeton, N.J.: Princeton University Press, 1992)

Patricia U. Bonomi (§1), Edward K. Spann (§2), John Mollenkopf (§3)

Governors Island. An island in Upper New York Bay. It is a half-mile (1 kilometer) southeast of Manhattan and across Buttermilk Channel from Brooklyn; it covers 172 acres (69 hectares) of land and is legally part of Manhattan. Known as Pagganck by local Canarsee Indians, it was sighted by Giovanni da Verrazano in 1524, and in 1624 it was the site of the original settlement of the Dutch West India Company. The newcomers moved to Manhattan in 1625. In 1637 Wouter van Twiller, the second governor general of the company, reportedly bought the island from the Indians for two axe heads, a string of beads, and some iron nails. The name was changed to Nooten Eylandt (Nut Island), and in 1664 under British occupation, they changed it transliterally to Nutten Island. In 1698 the colonial legislature set the island aside "for the benefit and accommodation of His Majesty's governors" (hence the island's name), whereupon Lord Cornbury had a villa in the Georgian style built as his official residence. At the outbreak of the American Revolution

Fort Jay, 2009

Governors Island, 2009

in 1776, patriots led by General Israel Putnam fortified and held the island until it was bombarded by British Admiral Richard Howe's warships. It then remained in British hands until 1783.

Construction was begun on Fort Jay after peace was restored in 1794. Work on the fort proceeded slowly, even with the voluntary participation of students from Columbia College; it was finally completed in 1808. In anticipation of another war with England, an imposing semicircular fort of red sandstone called Castle Williams was built from 1807 to 1811 under the direction of Colonel Jonathan Williams, chief of the Army Corps of Engineers; however, no shot was ever fired at an enemy from its three tiers of cannons. The island was officially part of New York State until 1800 when it was acquired by the federal government. During the Civil War the island became a recruiting depot and Castle Williams became a prison for Confederate officers. A headquarters and an administrative center for the U.S. Army were installed after the war.

In the 1890s, dredging from the excavation of the Fourth Avenue Subway (now the Lexington Avenue line) and the Brooklyn–Battery Tunnel was used to enlarge the island, adding 103 acres (41.7 hectares). On 20 September 1909 Wilbur Wright took off from Governors Island in his *Flyer* for a flight around the Statue of Liberty and Grant's Tomb. In the following year Glenn Curtis landed on the island after a successful flight in three segments from Albany, New York, to win a prize of $10,000 offered by Joseph Pulitzer, publisher of the *New York World*. The island performed several vital functions during World War I as a training center for pilots, as the post that carried out the seizure of all German ships in the harbor (the first overt American action of the war), and as a supply depot and major point of embarkation for troops bound for France. On 30 June 1966 the army turned the island over to the Coast Guard for use as the headquarters of the Eastern Area and of the Third Coast Guard District, whose primary duties were operating a training center and a base for search-and-rescue operations, providing aids to navigation, performing safety inspections, supervising ice-breaking operations, and organizing drug interdiction. The population of the island at that time was approximately 1600 members of the U.S. Coast Guard and their families. The Coast Guard closed its facilities and all personnel were relocated in 1996.

Since the departure of the military, the northern part of island has been designated as both a National Historic Landmark and a New York City historic district. Similarly designated are five buildings: the Governor's House (completed 1708, formerly the post commander's residence), Fort Jay, Castle Williams, South Battery (1812; formerly the officers' club), and the Admiral's House (1840, formerly the commanding general's house). Within the tree-lined historic district are fine examples of pre–Civil War arsenal buildings, Civil War–era housing, Victorian and Romanesque Revival residences, and early twentieth-century neoclassical architecture. When it closed officially in 1966, Governors Island was the oldest continuously operated military post in the United States.

In 1988 the island was the venue for a meeting between President Ronald Reagan and Soviet Premier Mikhail Gorbachev. In 2003 the Governors Island Preservation and Education Corporation, an agency overseen by the city and state, was designated to take responsibility for the planning, redevelopment, ongoing operations, and promotion of tourism, conferences, and cultural arts facilities for 150 acres (61 hectares) of the island. The remaining 22 acres (9 hectares) were assigned to the National Park Service to be the Governors Island National Monument. A number of plans have been put forward for possible use of the island. Governors Island is open to the public from May to October.

Edmund Banks Smith, *Governors Island: Its Military History under Three Flags, 1637–1922* (New York: Valentine's Manual, 1923); Ann L. Buttenwieser, *Governor's Island: The Jewel of New York Harbor* (Syracuse, N.Y.: Syracuse University Press, 2009)

Gerard R. Wolfe

Gowanus. Neighborhood in northwestern Brooklyn, bounded to the north by Baltic Street, to the east by Fourth Avenue, to the south by 14th Street, and to the west by Smith Street. The area was settled by the Dutch about 1640. The population increased sharply with the construction in the 1840s of the Gowanus Canal, which provided jobs for most residents. In the late nineteenth century it was a busy if sometimes rowdy neighborhood: in a section 12 blocks long on Smith Street were 23 taverns and many rooming houses catering to transients, mostly sailors and laborers. In the twentieth century the neighborhood calmed. Smith Street, the principal commercial thoroughfare, was lined with family shops and large furniture outlets, notably J. Michaels (founded 1886). A small Italian enclave lay to the east of the canal around Carroll Street, centered at Our Lady of Peace Roman Catholic Church and known until 1993 for Monte's Venetian Room, an Italian restaurant. Landmarks in the neighborhood include the tallest subway viaduct in New York City (on the F line at Smith and Ninth streets, with a clearance above the canal of 87.5 feet [26.7 meters]) and the Carroll Street Rail Bridge (1889), one of the few retractile bridges remaining in the United States. As of the early twenty-first century Gowanus remained a hub of industry and manufacturing, while its namesake canal struggled in recent years with environmental problems and the consequences of the decline of the shipping industry.

Georgia Fraser, *The Stone House at Gowanus* (New York: Witten and Knitner, 1909)

John J. Gallagher

Gowanus Canal. Artificial waterway in Brooklyn, extending from Hamilton Avenue to Douglass Street. A creek running roughly the same course, named for Gouwane, sachem of the Canarsees, was enlarged in the late 1840s by Edwin C. Litchfield. By 1884 the creek had been transformed into an industrial watercourse 5700 feet (1870 meters) long and 100 feet (30 meters) wide, with a depth in high water to 15 feet (4.5 meters). The canal greatly aided the commercial and residential development of Red Hook. By the late nineteenth century the canal was lined with industrial

Gowanus Canal, 2009

enterprises, including coal, lumber, brick, and stone yards; foundries; paint and ink factories; electroplating shops; flour, plaster, and paper mills; and an early purveyor of household heating and cooking gas (groups of young hoodlums who preyed on the many sailors and other transients in the area became known as the gashouse gangs). The canal was called an open cesspool by the *Daily Eagle* (14 July 1893). Because tides were ineffective in ridding the northern end of the channel of pollutants, a flushing tunnel 6250 feet (1905 meters) long was built connecting it to Buttermilk Channel. The canal declined during the early 1960s with the move toward containerized shipping. The flushing tunnel was inactive for several years and then restored to operation in 1989, at which time the canal was only a partly used waterway lined with stone, gravel, and concrete yards; some foundries; and petroleum storage facilities. Volunteer organizations such as the Urban Divers Estuary Conservancy (founded in 1998) and the Gowanus Dredgers Canoe Club (founded in 1999) used the canal for recreational purposes. In the early twenty-first century the Gowanus Canal Community Development Corporation, a nonprofit neighborhood preservation organization, was working on the revitalization of the Gowanus Canal area. In 2010 it was designated a Superfund clean-up site, with anticipated costs of $300 million to $500 million for the 10-year project.

John J. Gallagher, Matthew Kachur

Goya Foods. Firm of food importers formed in 1936 as Unanue, Inc., on Duane Street in lower Manhattan by Don Prudencio Unanue and his wife, Carolina Casal, Spanish immigrants from Puerto Rico. Initially it imported only Spanish olives, olive oil, and canned sardines for sale in bodegas throughout the city, but it soon offered dozens of other products, including beans, rice, coffee, condiments, spices, and frozen foods. It started using the name Goya for its foods in 1936 and bought its first factory in Brooklyn in 1958. Its foods became popular outside the Latin American community and were introduced in supermarkets and specialty stores. As competition increased the firm undertook aggressive advertising campaigns, adopting the motto "Si es Goya, tiene que ser bueno" ("If it's Goya, it has to be good"). In the early twenty-first century Goya Foods offered more than 1000 products, which were distributed from centers in Seville, Chicago, Miami, Tampa (Florida), Secaucus (New Jersey), and Bayamon (Puerto Rico). Owned and operated entirely by the Unanue family, the firm in 2005 had sales of more than $750 million and employed 2500 workers. Goya's headquarters have been in suburban Secaucus, New Jersey, since 1974.

James O. Drummond

G. P. Putnam's Sons. Firm of book publishers. Its origins may be traced to a partnership between John Wiley and George Palmer Putnam; when the two partners separated in 1848, Putnam took over the literary titles and established a firm under his own name at 155 Broadway. After nearing bankruptcy Putnam reopened the firm with his son George Haven Putnam in 1866 as G. P. Putnam and Son, which became G. P. Putnam's Sons in 1872 after two more of Putnam's sons joined the firm and Putnam himself died. Highly regarded during Putnam's lifetime, the firm moved to 200 Madison Avenue in 1961. With the purchase of Berkley Publishing in 1966 the firm acquired a mass-market paperback subsidiary. G. P. Putnam's Sons was itself taken over by the Music Corporation of America (MCA) in 1975, and the British publisher Penguin Group, part of Pearson PLC, purchased Putnam's in 1996.

See also Book publishing.

Eileen K. Cheng

Grace, William R(ussell) (*b* Cove of Cork [now Cóbh], Ireland, 10 May 1831; *d* New York City, 20 March 1904). Businessman and mayor. Soon after moving to Peru in 1851, he entered the guano trade with the firm of Bryce Brothers, in which he was a partner by 1854. He moved his headquarters to 110 Wall Street in Manhattan in 1866 and founded his own firm, W. R. Grace and Company. In the following years he built a fortune from trade between North America and the western coast of South America. He soon joined with other reform Democrats in challenging Tammany Hall, the Manhattan Democratic political machine. Grace became the first Catholic mayor of New York City in 1880 and was reelected in 1884.

Lawrence A. Clayton

Grace Church. Episcopal church on Broadway and 10th Street, occupied from 1846 by a congregation organized in 1808 at Broadway and Rector Street. The building is a graceful structure of white limestone designed by James Renwick, Jr., in a decorated Gothic Revival style. Its entrance is framed by a handsome memorial porch, and its eastern chancel window is filled with English stained glass. The rectors of the church have been influential in the branch of American Episcopalianism known as the Low Church. Under the rector Henry Codman Potter (1868–83) a magnificent marble spire was added to the church, and Grace Memorial House was built as a nursery. In keeping with Potter's desire to minister to the poor, Grace Chapel at 132 East 14th Street was rebuilt in 1876 and used as a community center offering English-language classes and other educational programs for immigrants. Potter's successor, William R. Huntington (1883–1909), retained Potter's emphasis on community work by running a mission house on the Lower East Side and expanding the operation on 14th Street into what became known as Grace Chapel Settlement. In 1977

Grace Church, 2009

Grace Church was designated a National Historical Landmark. In the early twenty-first century the church continued its charitable tradition: it maintained a shelter for homeless men on the side of the church facing Fourth Avenue as well as several missions overseas.

Peter J. Wosh

Gracie, Archibald (*b* Dumfries, Scotland, 25 June 1755; *d* New York City, 11 April 1829). Merchant. He arrived in New York City in 1784 and in the following year married Esther (Hetitia) Rogers, sister of the prominent merchants Moses, Nehemiah, and Henry Rogers. He established a firm in Virginia before settling permanently in New York City in 1793. A leading commission merchant and shipowner, he served on the directing boards of banks and insurance companies and was a close associate of Alexander Hamilton and Rufus King. He was also a vice president of the Chamber of Commerce (1800–25) and president of the St. Andrew's Society (1818–23). In 1798 he purchased property at Horn's Hook, near what is now East 88th Street, where he constructed his summer home, Gracie Mansion. Delays in collecting spoliation claims for shipping losses incurred during the Napoleonic Wars led to his financial ruin and the sale of the mansion in 1823. It became the official residence of New York City mayors during the administration of Fiorello H. La Guardia.

Elaine Weber Pascu

Gracie Mansion. The mayor's official residence, overlooking the East River at 88th Street and East End Avenue in Carl Schurz

Park. Built in two phases between 1799 and 1811 at Horn's Hook as the country home of Archibald Gracie, probably by the carpenter Ezra Weeks, it was one of several residences in upper Manhattan that afforded refuge from the noise and disease of the city. Among the many visitors were Washington Irving and Napoleon's brother, Joseph Bonaparte. Gracie sold the house in 1823. In 1853 land adjacent to the house was subdivided into lots; the land surrounding the house was designated a city park after Avenue B (now East End Avenue) was extended northward to East 83rd Street in 1876. The house remained a private residence until it was taken over by the parks department in 1896, which used it until 1923. It housed the Museum of the City of New York from 1924 to 1932. After being restored by the city, the house reopened as a museum in 1936. At the urging of the parks commissioner Robert Moses, it became the official mayoral residence in 1942. Susan Wagner, wife of Mayor Robert F. Wagner, lobbied to create an addition to the house for receptions and dinners. Designed by architect Mott B. Schmidt, the Wagner wing was completed in 1966, after Susan Wagner's death. Mayor Edward I. Koch established the Gracie Mansion Conservancy in 1981, which initiated a major restoration during 1983–84. In 2002 Mayor Michael R. Bloomberg, who lived elsewhere, restored the house and used it for ceremonies, meetings, and tours.

Mary C. Black, *New York City's Gracie Mansion: A History of the Mayor's House* (New York: J. M. Kaplan Fund, 1984); Ellen Stern, *Gracie Mansion: A Celebration of New York City's Mayoral Residence* (New York: Rizzoli International, 2005)

Mary Beth Betts

Gracie Square. Neighborhood on the Upper East Side of Manhattan (2000 pop. *ca* 27,000), lying along East End Avenue (Avenue B) in Yorkville and bounded to the north by 92nd Street, to the east by the East River, to the south by 79th Street, and to the west by York Avenue (Avenue A). It was once the site of the country estates of the Astor, Gracie, Rhinelander, and Schermerhorn families. Except for a few small developments such as Henderson Place (1882) and City and Suburban Homes (1901–13), the area consisted of brownstones, tenements, and light industry until luxury apartment buildings were erected in the 1920s; the Chapin and Brearley schools also opened about this time. Construction began on East River Park in 1876 (renamed Carl Schurz Park in 1911). The elevated John H. Finley Walk was built over the FDR Drive in 1941. Since 1942 the mansion of Archibald Gracie (1799) has been used as New York City's official mayor's residence. The parabolic-arch-shaped Municipal Asphalt Plant (1944), which stands at the northern edge of the neighborhood, was incorporated as a recreational facility into the Asphalt Green Sports and Art Center in 1982. The population is affluent; well-known residents have included Vincent Astor, Madame Chiang Kai-shek, Robert Moses, and Gloria Vanderbilt.

Mary C. Black, *New York City's Gracie Mansion: A History of the Mayor's House* (New York: J. M. Kaplan Fund, 1984)

Val Ginter

graffiti. Form of art, or vandalism, produced by writing names, numbers, or other images on various types of property, often public. Little attention was paid to graffiti in New York City until 1970, when a Greek American teenager from Washington Heights named Demetrius (last name unknown) wrote "Taki 183," his nickname and street address, or "tag," on hundreds of subway cars and walls throughout the city. Although it was not the first such display, thousands of people saw his tag, and soon scores of other teenagers were imitating it. In 1971 the *New York Times* reported in the article "Taki 183 Spawns Pen Pals" that removal of tags cost 80,000 total hours of labor and $300,000 in that year alone. By 1972 there was a flourishing subculture based on this activity, with its own jargon, informal organizations, and rules of conduct. "Bombings," a term used to describe the covering of as many surfaces as possible, began occurring across the city and especially the subway system; the budget of the New York City Transit Authority for removing graffiti rose from $250,000 in 1970 to more than $1 million a few years later. As soon as trains went back into service clean, they were bombed again, mocking the effort to obscure the graffiti and creating a sign of official failure. An anti-graffiti media attack was planned with the slogan "Make your mark in society, not on it."

The problem became so acute that in 1972 City Council president Sanford Garelik proposed a monthly "Anti-Graffiti Day" during which New Yorkers could volunteer to clean up graffiti. RCA Records canceled a full-page advertisement for an album by Lou Reed in the *Village Voice* that had drawn complaints from the Metropolitan Transportation Authority (MTA) and the Parks, Recreation, and Cultural Affairs Administration for its depiction of a man spray-painting Reed's name on a subway car. The MTA experimented with several cleaning solvents such as DWR (Dirty Word Remover) and Klout; they either proved ineffective or were so corrosive that subway car manufacturers threatened to void their warranties unless use of the solvents was discontinued. In October 1972 Mayor John V. Lindsay formed the city's first anti-graffiti task force, and a new law banned the carrying of open spray paint cans in public facilities without a permit, increasing the maximum fine from $25 to $500 and the maximum prison term from 10 days to three months. The MTA reported that graffiti could be seen on nearly all 7000 cars in the subway system. Official reports linked increases in crime to graffiti, and increased arrests did not seem to deter graffiti writers.

During the 1970s there was some support for the notion that graffiti was street art. Hugo Martinez, a sociology student at City College, formed United Graffiti Artists (UGA) in 1972 to promote graffiti as an art form. The first exhibition of members' work was held in December at Eisner Hall at City College, and by early 1973 many intellectuals considered such

Graffiti on a building in Long Island City, Queens, 2008

work "radical chic." Members of the UGA showed 20 canvases at the Razor Gallery in SoHo and won commissions from Twyla Tharp to paint backdrops during performances of her production *Deuce Coupe.* In autumn of 1973 the Museum of Modern Art held a slide show of murals painted on buildings (with their landlords' permission). To the disgust of many, Norman Mailer published a meditative essay on the creative power of graffiti, "The Faith of Graffiti," in 1974. At the height of the graffiti art movement such members of the UGA as "Phase2," "T-Rex 131," and "Bama" commanded as much as $3000 a canvas. The National Organization of Graffiti Artists was formed in July 1974 by Jack Peslinger, a director of Off-Broadway theater, but its members never achieved the financial success of their counterparts in the UGA. Interest in graffiti art declined after 1975, when the art season opened with an exhibition of such work at the Artist Space in SoHo. In October 1977 the Transit Authority erected an enormous subway car wash in the Coney Island yard that for an annual cost of $400,000 drenched cars in a solution of petroleum hydroxide. Known by graffiti artists as the "final solution," the "buff," and the "orange crush" (for the defoliant Agent Orange), the wash was effective in quickly removing graffiti from the cars.

Interest in graffiti art surged during the 1980s. Keith Haring and Jean-Michel Basquiat (then known as Samo) became widely known; Haring's work at that time sold for as much as $350,000. Several films explored ties between graffiti art, hip-hop music, and inner-city culture. David Ahearn's film *Wild Style,* featuring the graffiti artist Lee Quinones and the musician and artist Fred Brathwaite (also known as Fab Five Freddy and later as Freddy Love), opened to critical acclaim in March 1983 as part of the New Directors / New Film Series at Lincoln Center. In 1984 Henry Chalfant, long a supporter of graffiti art, helped to produce the documentary *Style Wars* for the Public Broadcasting System. Timothy Hutton played the lead role in *Turk182* (1985), a commercial motion picture about a graffiti artist. In 1980 the Transit Authority launched its "graffiti enhancement program," in which more than 200 painters were employed to cover graffiti on subway cars with quick-drying white paint; graffiti artists simply painted over the white surfaces, and the program was declared a failure in the autumn of 1980.

Mayor Edward I. Koch, an outspoken opponent of graffiti, introduced a $1.5 million program to build fences and provide guard dogs for the Corona Yard in September 1981. In 1982 the MTA was given $22.4 million to fence in all train yards. Razor wire atop the fencing replaced the use of guard dogs, which had drawn criticism for being excessive and brutal. The city's anti-graffiti policies were called into question by the arrest on 15 September 1983 and subsequent death of Michael Stewart, an alleged graffiti artist. The incident generated accusations of police brutality (Stewart was black, the arresting officers white).

In 1984 Transit Authority chairman David Gunn ordered all cars with graffiti removed from service, and during his tenure the amount of graffiti in the subways decreased quickly. A 1985 law banned sales of spray paint and broad-tipped markers to minors, with a fine of $500. During the same year $6.3 million was awarded to transit workers with health problems stemming from exposure to fumes from cleaning solvents. But in the 1990s the Transit Authority reported an increase in the amount of graffiti on its trains, the number of "hits" having doubled in 1990 to 46,000, and the anti-graffiti task force was reconvened after a hiatus of 18 months. The authority spent $1.4 million replacing scratched plastic windows between January 1990 and June 1992, and in 1992 it announced a plan to spend $24.3 million to equip all buses and subway cars with scratch-resistant glass. It also explored such strategies as issuing night-vision goggles to the transit police, while community groups used video cameras to catch graffiti artists in the act. As the city became more orderly and as crime declined after 1992, graffiti became far less visible in the five boroughs. In June 2006, however, the Brooklyn Museum and the Martinez Gallery mounted a show of graffiti artists.

Craig Castleman, *Getting Up: Subway Graffiti in New York* (Cambridge, Mass.: MIT Press, 1982); Jim Dwyer, *Subway Lives: 24 Hours in the Life of the New York City Subway* (New York: Crown, 1991)

Brenda Edmands, Meghan Lalonde

Graham, Martha (*b* Allegheny, Pa., 11 May 1894; *d* New York City, 1 April 1991). Dancer and choreographer. She grew up in southern California and from 1916 trained under Ruth St. Denis and Ted Shawn. In 1923 she moved to New York City, where she initially danced in the exotic dance tradition of her mentors but quickly developed an independent style stripped of ornamentation. During the early 1930s she founded a dance company for women and formalized her dance techniques of contraction and release to classical themes. Her early works of choreography, *Lamentations* (1930) and *Primitive Mysteries* (1931), were characterized by a stark simplicity, structural tautness, and mythic overtones. In 1926 she opened a studio on Fifth Avenue between 12th and 13th streets, where she worked closely with the accompanist and composer Louis Horst, her intellectual adviser and the publisher of the journal *Dance Observer.* During the summers of 1936–41 she taught dance with Doris Humphrey, Hanya Holm, and Charles Weidman at the Bennington College School of Dance in Vermont; there she met the classically trained dancer Erick Hawkins, who became the first male member of her company. At the same time she provided choreography for several distinctly American works, including *Frontier* (1935; sets by Isamu Noguchi), *American Document* (1938; featuring Hawkins), *Letter to the World* (1940), and *Appalachian Spring* (1944; featuring Hawkins and Merce Cunningham, music by Aaron Copland), in which she explored the roots of the American cultural experience and drew on her deep interest in religion and psychology. After 1944 Graham continued to work in the three dance styles that she explored early in her career: the abstract, the mythic, and the American. She continued in particular to explore themes derived from Greek mythology and Freudian psychology. More than 40 of her dancers became choreographers and company directors, notably Hawkins, Cunningham, Sophie Maslow, and Anna Sokolow.

Elizabeth Kendall, *Where She Danced* (New York: Alfred A. Knopf, 1979); Ernestine Stodelle, *Deep Song: The Dance Story of Martha Graham* (New York: Schirmer–Macmillan, 1984)

Peter M. Rutkoff, William B. Scott

Graham–Windham Services to Families and Children. Child welfare organization formed in 1977 by the merger of the Graham Home and Windham Children's Services. Established in 1806 by Isabella Graham, it is the oldest nonsectarian child-care agency in the United States. It has helped an estimated 6000 children and families each year through adoption programs, foster boarding homes, group homes, family day care, preschool and day-care centers, a family service center, a mental health clinic, and a residential campus and school. In the early twenty-first century its headquarters are at 33 Irving Place.

Phyllis Barr

Gramercy Park. Neighborhood on the East Side of Manhattan, bounded to the north by 23rd Street, to the east by Third Avenue, to the south by 18th Street, and to the west by Park Avenue South. Dutch settlers once called the area Krom Moerasje (little crooked swamp); the name was changed to Gramercy by the English. The land was bought from a descendant of Peter Stuyvesant, Samuel Ruggles, who drained the swamp, laid out streets in an English style around a private park (1831; Lexington Avenue between 20th and 21st streets), and offered 66 lots for sale. The park was opened to Union soldiers during the draft riots of 1863, the only occasion when nonresidents were allowed inside. Some of the first residents included Valentine Mott, the chief medical officer of the Union army and the founder of Bellevue Hospital and New York University Medical School; George Templeton Strong; and James Harper, mayor, whose ornate "mayor's lights" still adorn his former residence at 4 Gramercy Park West. Some of the oldest luxury apartments in the city were built in 1884 at the southeast corner of the park

4 Gramercy Park West, home of Mayor James Harper from 1847 to 1869

(they were advertised as French flats to distinguish them from tenements). Residents and Republican legislators defeated several proposals by the city after 1890 to cut a road through the park, and by the 1920s many of the original townhouses had been replaced by high-rise apartment buildings. Lexington Avenue between 14th and 20th streets was renamed Irving Place for Washington Irving, who never lived in the area but often visited a nephew who lived at Lexington Avenue and 17th Street.

The neighborhood became less fashionable after the extension of the Third Avenue elevated line (26 August 1878) and the onset of the Depression in the 1930s. From the 1940s many of the remaining nineteenth-century townhouses were remodeled and converted into apartments, and several became private clubs, including 16 Gramercy Park (the Players, formed by Edwin Booth), 15 Gramercy Park (the National Arts Club, once owned by Samuel J. Tilden), and 3 Gramercy Park (the Nederlander Club). A Quaker meetinghouse on Gramercy Park South became the Brotherhood Synagogue. Many artists, writers, and performers lived in the neighborhood, including George Bellows, Robert Henri, Eugene O'Neill, O. Henry, David Graham Phillips, Ida Tarbell, Nathanael West, and Ludwig Bemelmans; other well-known residents have included Theodore Roosevelt; Eleanor Roosevelt, who was baptized at Calvary Episcopal Church at the northwestern edge of the park; Stanford White, who lived where the Gramercy Park Hotel now stands; and Elsie de Wolfe, who with White developed the field of interior design and lived in the Washington Irving house (southwest corner of 17th Street and Irving Place). The neighborhood again became fashionable from the 1970s onward into the twenty-first century; the park remains private and looks much as it did in the early nineteenth century.

Stephen Garmey, *Gramercy Park: An Illustrated History of a New York Neighborhood* (New York: Routledge, 1984); Carole Klein, *Gramercy Park: An American Bloomsbury* (Boston: Houghton Mifflin, 1987)

Harriet Davis-Kram

Gramercy Park Hotel. Hotel located at 2 Lexington Avenue on the north side of Gramercy Park. Designed by Robert T. Lyons and built by the famous developer brothers Bing and Bing, it opened in 1925. The site had been the home of architect Stanford White. The hotel's bar was infamous as a watering hole to artists, writers, and musicians. Several notable people have been associated with the hotel, including Humphrey Bogart, who was married there; S. J. Perelman, who lived there; and Babe Ruth, who frequented the bar. In 2003 the hotel was sold to designer Ian Schrager, who redid it with artist Julian Schnabel as a luxury boutique hotel; the lobby exhibits modern art by artists such as Andy Warhol, Jean-Michel Basquiat, and Richard Prince.

Gramercy Park Hotel, 2009

Jessica Montesano

Grand Army Plaza (i). Oval plaza constructed in 1870 by Frederick Law Olmsted and Calvert Vaux as an approach to Prospect Park in Brooklyn, which they designed. Originally called Prospect Park Plaza, it was renamed in 1926 in honor of the Civil War's Union army. The plaza is the site of a triumphal arch 80 feet (24 meters) high designed by John H. Duncan (1892). The arch is adorned with a four-horse bronze chariot group (1898) and sculptures on its southern facade (1901), both by Frederick MacMonnies. A fountain was designed by Egerton Swartwout north of the arch in 1932, and a bust of President John F. Kennedy by Neil Estern was installed in 1965. In between stands the Bailey Fountain, completed in 1932 and adorned with bronze figures of Neptune and Tritons. The perimeter of the plaza is lined with apartment buildings.

Elliott B. Nixon, Stephen Weinstein

Grand Army Plaza (ii). Plaza at the southeast corner of Central Park, between 58th and 60th streets, bisected by Central Park South. Its southern half includes the Plaza Hotel (1907). The northern half features a statue of General William T. Sherman by Augustus Saint-Gaudens (1907).

Ben Silk

Grand (Boulevard and) Concourse. Thoroughfare in the western Bronx, and by extension the streets on either side of it. It extends for 4.5 miles (7.5 kilometers) between 138th Street and Mosholu Parkway, and north of 161st Street it has 11 lanes with a total width of 182 feet (55 meters), two tree-lined dividers, and broad sidewalks. It was conceived by the engineer Louis Aloys Risse in 1870 and built between 1902 and 1909. An important innovation was the use of grade separations at the major cross streets, which allowed the traffic on the street to flow unimpeded by directing the crosstraffic beneath it through underpasses. The concourse extended only as far south as 161st Street until 1927, when it came to include a newly widened portion of Mott Avenue. It

Grand Army Plaza (i), ca *1905–10*

soon became the main parade route for the borough, the site of its government, and the axis of an important shopping and entertainment district. Elegant apartment buildings were erected that offered cross ventilation, large rooms, and uniformed door attendants and attracted the wealthiest inhabitants of the Bronx. Among those who lived in the area were Mayor Joseph V. McKee, the opera singer Roberta Peters, the popular singer Eydie Gorme, the comedian Milton Berle, the baseball players Babe Ruth and Charlie Keller, the filmmakers Stanley Kubrick and Garry and Penny Marshall, and the novelist E. L. Doctorow. After World War II the population aged; children of local residents moved to the suburbs and in time were replaced by middle-class blacks and Latin Americans. Many synagogues were converted to churches; one became the Bronx Museum of the Arts. By 1990 a perceptible number of Koreans and Cambodians had moved to the area near Fordham Road. Notable buildings along the Grand Concourse include Public School 31 (1899) at 144th Street, the Bronx General Post Office (1937) at 149th Street, the Mario Merola Bronx County Building (1934) at 161st Street, and the Edgar Allan Poe Cottage (circa 1812) at Kingsbridge Road.

Lloyd Ultan, *The Beautiful Bronx, 1920–1950* (New Rochelle, N.Y.: Arlington House, 1979); Gary Hermalyn and Robert Kornfeld, *Landmarks of the Bronx* (New York: Bronx County Historical Society, 1989)

Lloyd Ultan

Grand Central Terminal. Major railroad terminus in midtown Manhattan. From the earliest days of railroads in New York City locomotives hauled their cars as far into the city as was allowed, and with them came noise and dirt. In 1854 the Common Council forbade their operation south of 42nd Street, a boundary well north of the settled part of the city, and horses were used to haul the cars to their destinations farther downtown. By 1869 Cornelius Vanderbilt controlled all the railroads into the city, and he engaged the architect John B. Snook to design a "head house" at Fourth Avenue and 42nd Street, which opened in 1871 as Grand Central Depot. The facility was never successful: it was in a constant state of rearrangement and enlargement, trains could exit only in reverse, and despite its name the depot was really in the hinterlands, an area that the city's horsecar lines had reached only recently. Shortly after the depot was built, Vanderbilt began to lower the many tracks below street level, first in a roofed-over deep cut and then in a tunnel that began at 96th Street and fanned out at 57th Street to a width of 41 tracks on the upper level and 26 on the lower.

In 1889 the city demanded that the railroads either electrify their operations or move out

Perspective view of the proposed entrance to the Grand Boulevard and Concourse, East 161st Street and Mott Avenue, 1895

Grand Central Terminal, 1930s

Grand Central Terminal, 2009

of the city altogether. A proposal to build a new depot was advanced by William Wilgus, the chief engineer responsible for submerging the tracks and electrifying the lines as far north as Mott Haven in the Bronx. He also proposed to raise revenues by selling and leasing the air rights over the tracks, between Madison and Lexington avenues from 42nd to 50th streets, to allow for the construction of office and apartment buildings. A limited competition for the design was won by the firm of Reed and Stem, which devised a system for separating automobile, pedestrian, train, and subway traffic by using ramps to route Park Avenue around the terminal on viaducts. Whitney Warren of the architectural firm of Warren and Wetmore designed the beaux-arts facade at 42nd Street as a triumphal triple archway facing south, allowing for a dramatic approach from Park Avenue. Sculpture is integral to the design rather than ornamental: above the entrance, monumental statues of Minerva, Mercury, and Hercules in a pediment nearly 50 feet (15 meters) tall surround a clock with a diameter of 13 feet (4 meters). The interior of this terminal is dramatic: behind the main waiting room at the south entrance is the Main Concourse, a vast, vaulting space 120 feet (36 meters) wide, 375 feet (114 meters) long, and 125 feet (38 meters) high, surmounted by a blue ceiling painted to resemble a starlit sky. At the west end a grand staircase allows visitors to descend to the lower level; among the concessions there is the Oyster Bar, a popular restaurant that serves more than 1000 dozen oysters a day.

Because Grand Central Terminal is situated on a prime parcel of midtown real estate, its architectural integrity has occasionally been threatened by commercial development schemes. One advanced in 1960 would have divided the waiting room into four horizontal stories, with bowling alleys on the upper three. Soon after this proposal was put forward, Grand Central Terminal was designated a landmark. This status came to be resented by the owner, the Penn Central Railroad, because it empowered the Landmarks Preservation Commission to reject such proposals as one to build a 54-story tower over the waiting room. A suit to have the landmark status revoked failed on the grounds that the city had the right to protect its architectural heritage.

In the 1990s several major restoration projects cleaned up decades of grime from the station and revitalized it. Layers of dirt were removed from the ceiling, allowing an astrological mural originally made in 1912 and replaced in the 1930s to be seen again. More than 100 retail stores and restaurants were created. A new access area, Grand Central North, was added in 1999, connecting it to 47th and 48th streets.

Grand Central Terminal, owned by the Metropolitan Transportation Authority, has 44 platforms with 67 tracks, covering 48 acres (19.4 hectares). It has 10 underground stories with infrastructure. A planned expansion in 2011 would connect it to the Long Island Rail Road, which currently goes to Penn Station, and would add more tracks. The terminal houses the Metro-North Commuter Railroad, which connects the city to the New York counties of Westchester, Putnam, and Dutchess and Connecticut counties of Fairfield and New Haven. It also is a terminus for numerous subway lines. More than 125,000 commuters and half a million pedestrians pass through it daily.

Deborah Nevins, ed., *Grand Central Terminal: City within the City* (New York: Municipal Art Society, 1982); Kurt Schlichting, *Grand Central Terminal: Railroads, Architecture and Engineering in New York* (Baltimore, Md.: Johns Hopkins University Press, 2001)

James E. Mooney, Lisa Keller

Grand Hyatt. Hotel on 42nd Street in Manhattan, immediately to the east of Grand

Central Terminal. Opened as the Hotel Commodore (1919; Warren and Wetmore, architects), it continued in operation under its original name until 1976, when co-developers Donald Trump and the Hyatt Corporation used the structural shell of the building to create the Grand Hyatt. The new hotel opened in 1980 as a luxury convention hotel with 1400 rooms. It has a facade of reflective glass sheathing and a space-frame cocktail lounge that forms a canopy over the main entrance. The hotel underwent a $65 million renovation in 2004 and 2005, which included the redesign of 1311 guestrooms; the addition of amenities such as wireless, high-speed Internet access; and the construction of several new meeting spaces, including the new Manhattan Ballroom at the lobby level.

May N. Stone

Grand Prospect Hall. Reception hall designed by Ulrich J. Huberty and built in 1892 by entrepreneur John Kolle as a "temple of music and amusement." Located at 263 Prospect Avenue in Park Slope, Brooklyn, the 140,000-square-foot (13,006-square-meter) French Renaissance–style palace is four stories high with a grand ballroom and garden space. It was the first commercial building in Brooklyn to have electric lights. Victorian society once held court there; in the early twenty-first century it can be rented for weddings and other celebrations.

Jessica Montesano

Grand Union Hotel. Hotel on the southeast corner of Park Avenue and 42nd Street. Designed in 1872 by the architect Edward Schott, its exterior had a mansard roof and reflected the Second Empire style of the Grand Central Depot across the street. The hotel was run on the European plan (in which meals are not included in the price of a room), and its restaurant became popular with politicians. The hotel closed on 2 May 1914 and was demolished for construction of the Interborough Rapid Transit subway and the Pershing Square Building.

Val Ginter

Graniteville. Neighborhood in northwestern Staten Island, lying between Port Richmond and Bulls Head and bounded to the north by Forest and East Richmond avenues, to the east by the Martin Luther King Expressway, to the south by the Staten Island Expressway, and to the west by South Avenue. Once known as Bennett's Corners and then as Fayetteville, it was renamed for quarries operated from the 1840s to about 1896 to extract trap rock from the geological formation that includes the Palisades. From about the turn of the twentieth century until the 1940s there were many Italian and Greek dairy and truck farms in the area. The largest local employer until the end of World War II was the Unexcelled Fireworks Company, which made munitions in a plant consisting of 167 buildings; the Weissglass Dairy stood at the northwestern edge of the neighborhood along Forest Avenue. The land is covered by town houses and one- and two-family houses along new streets. Moore Catholic High School stands at the southern edge of the neighborhood. Baron Hirsch Cemetery, one of two large Jewish cemeteries in the borough, contains 50,000 graves and covers 80 acres (32 hectares) of land along Richmond Avenue, the major north-south thoroughfare. Little of the original grass and marshlands remains for development or conservation.

Harlow McMillen

Grant, Hugh J(ohn) (*b* New York City, 1852; *d* New York City, 3 Nov 1910). Mayor. The son of a West Side Democratic tavern keeper, he attended public schools, spent two years at Manhattan College, studied in Germany for a year when he was 16, and then returned to the city to attend St. Francis Xavier and Columbia Law School. Rising through Irish American fraternal organizations, he avoided an 1882 scandal involving bribes from streetcar operators and became the sheriff of New York County in 1885. Tammany support and Mayor Abram S. Hewitt's reputation for bigotry against Irish and other immigrants helped him win the race for mayor in 1888; he won reelection in 1890. Grant favored limited government, low taxes, and public investment in streets, sewers, water lines, and fire stations. He also sought to have the city build a harness racetrack. He did not seek reelection in 1892. Defeated by William L. Strong in an 1894 attempt to regain office and having lost control of Tammany Hall to Richard Croker, he left politics in 1897 to focus on real estate investments.

David C. Hammack

Grant, Madison (*b* New York City, 19 Nov 1865; *d* New York City, 30 May 1937). Lawyer and political activist. He attended private schools in New York City and received a BA from Yale College (1887) and an LLB from Columbia Law School (1890). He lived on Park Avenue and spent most of his life in the city, where he helped to form the New York Zoological Society (1895), of which he was secretary (1895–1924) and president (1925–37). One of the most influential nativists of his time, he sought to restrict immigration on the basis of ethnicity. Through his writings he promoted the idea that immigrants from southern Europe were inferior to those from northern and western Europe and would destroy the country by eroding cultural values and reducing national achievement; he was especially hostile toward Jews. As vice president of the Immigration Restriction League from 1922 he played an important role in the passage of the Immigration Act of 1924, which reduced the number of immigrants allowed to enter the country while increasing the proportion from northwestern Europe. Grant's published writings include *The Passing of the Great Race* (1916), *The Founders of the Republic on Immigration, Naturalization and Aliens* (with C. S. Davison, 1928), *The Alien in Our Midst* (with Davison, 1930), and *The Conquest of a Continent* (1933).

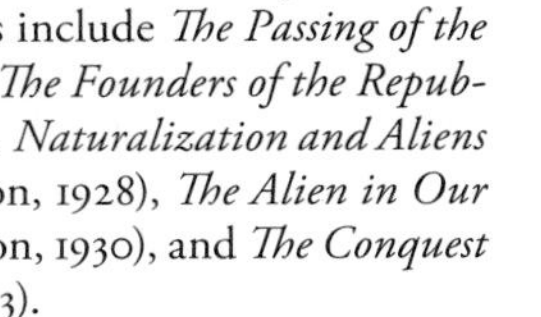

Walter Friedman

Interior of the Grand Union Hotel

Grant, Ulysses S(impson) [Hiram Ulysses] (*b* Point Pleasant, Ohio, 27 April 1822; *d* Mount McGregor, N.Y., 23 July 1885). Commander of the Union armies in the Civil War and 18th president of the United States. He graduated from the U.S. Military Academy at West Point in 1843 and won repeated victories in the West before President Abraham Lincoln made him commander of all Union armies during the Civil War. He became the country's first full general in 1866 and secretary of war in 1867. He was elected president in 1868 and again in 1872. He moved to New York City permanently in 1881. After an initial stay in the Fifth Avenue Hotel, Grant purchased a brownstone house at 3 East 66th Street and invested his money in the banking firm of Grant and Ward, a partnership formed between Ferdinand Ward and the former president's son, Ulysses, Jr. Ward turned out to be a swindler who engaged in fraudulent practices that caused the collapse of the firm in May 1884, leaving Grant in substantial debt. Soon afterward, Grant decided to write his memoirs to support his family but several months later was diagnosed with inoperable cancer of the throat. Grant moved with his family to a cottage at Mount McGregor, New York, in the Adirondacks about five weeks before he died. He nonetheless finished his memoirs, *Personal Memoirs* (1885–86), and they remain one of the most widely acclaimed works of its genre and restored the Grant family's wealth. Grant was buried in New York City on 8 August 1885. GRANT'S TOMB, a national memorial at Riverside Drive and West 122nd Street, occupies a site donated by Mayor William R. Grace and houses the remains of Grant and his wife, Julia Dent Grant.

Frank Scaturro

Grant City. Neighborhood in southeastern Staten Island (2009 pop. *ca* 4800), lying at the foot of Todt Hill and bounded to the west and north by Richmond Road and Jefferson Avenue, and to the east and south by Hylan Boulevard. Until after the Civil War the area was known as Frenchtown for its French population; it was renamed for President Ulysses S. Grant by a builder, John C. Thompson. About the turn of the twentieth century hotels and picnic grounds were clustered around the station of Staten Island Rapid Transit at the center of the neighborhood. Semler's Hotel (1910) was a local landmark until it was demolished in 1965 and replaced by the Grant City Apartments, a complex of 305 units on Lincoln Avenue. Ballfields were added before World War I. Many houses in the ranch and Cape Cod styles were built after World War II; they account for much of the housing, along with older houses built after the Civil War and bungalows from the turn of the twentieth century. In the early twenty-first century Grant City remained a closely knit residential community where small family stores and businesses line the streets near the railroad station.

Harlow McMillen

Grant's Tomb. Monument near the intersection of Riverside Drive and West 122nd Street in Manhattan, the final resting place of President ULYSSES S. GRANT and his wife, Julia Dent Grant. As the result of an offer to the family from Mayor William R. Grace, the remains of President Grant were at first placed in a temporary vault in Riverside Park. The Grant Monument Association, formed shortly after Grant's death in 1885, raised about $600,000 from more than 90,000 donors for the construction of a permanent tomb on the site of the vault. The association adopted a design proposed by the architect John H. Duncan, which was influenced by such famous mausoleums as those of Mausolus at Halicarnassus, Hadrian, and Napoleon, as well as the Garfield Memorial. On 27 April 1897, the 75th anniversary of Grant's birth, the tomb was dedicated in a ceremony attended by his widow and President William McKinley. The state of New York declared the day a holiday, and about one million people witnessed the dedication proceedings. Julia Grant was interred beside her husband in 1902. For many years Grant's Tomb was one of the most celebrated buildings in the nation, and it remained unsurpassed in popularity among the city's attractions through World War I. The Grant Monument Association continued to administer the site until 1959, when it was taken over by the National Park Service. During the years that followed, the monument was afflicted with desecration and neglect. These conditions came to public attention during the 1990s, and the federal government conducted a restoration of the monument in time for its centennial in 1997. The monument is a neoclassical granite structure 150 feet (45 meters) tall. Among its elaborate features are Doric columns, a domed rotunda, and allegorical relief sculptures symbolizing aspects of Grant's life. On the exterior of the structure two figures representing Victory and Peace support Grant's epitaph, "Let Us Have Peace." The interior of the tomb is made of Lee and Carrara marble from Italy; within its center crypt are twin sarcophagi containing the remains of Grant and his wife. Grant is the only president buried in New York City, and his tomb is the second-largest mausoleum in the western hemisphere.

Frank J. Scaturro, *President Grant Reconsidered* (Lanham, Md.: University Press of America, 1998)

Frank Scaturro

Grapevine. Nineteenth-century tavern where the popular expression "I heard it through the grapevine" reputedly originated. Housed in a wooden 1830s structure at the corner of Sixth Avenue and West 11th Street, the Grapevine was a popular gathering place for Greenwich Village artists, actors, and politicians. The building was demolished in 1915.

Valerie Paley

graphic design. New York City became the capital of graphic design in the United States just before 1900. For many years it was virtually an anonymous activity, practiced by printers as an extra service to their customers and by art service studios. In 1914 the American Institute of Graphic Arts (AIGA) was formed in the city. The New York Art Directors Club,

Grant's Tomb (designed by John H. Duncan), 2009

formed in 1921, became the largest organization of editorial and advertising art directors in the United States. The term *commercial art* was introduced about this time to refer to a wide range of graphic arts and crafts, including typography, advertising design, and package design. In the 1950s and 1960s the field of graphic design grew with extraordinary speed, owing partly to the need of large corporations to forge distinctive identities.

In part because of its many magazines, book publishers, and advertising agencies, New York City also became the home of a large number of graphic design firms. Some of these firms offer a wide range of design services, while others specialize in such areas as corporate annual reports and retail packaging. Among the firms of longest standing are those of Milton Glaser, the Pushpin Group, Chermayeff and Geismar, Pentagram, Vignelli Associates, and Gipps, Balkind and Frankfurt; important younger firms include Smollan Carbone, Drentell Doyle, Doublespace, and Alex Isley Associates. The AIGA issues the quarterly critical journal the *AIGA Journal of Graphic Design,* and several trade publications are based in the city, notably *Print* (bimonthly), *U&lc* (Upper and lower case; published by the International Typeface Company), *Art Direction, Graphic Design U.S.A.,* and *Graphis.* Many schools and workshops in New York City offer training in the graphic arts, including the Art Students League on 57th Street, the National Academy of Design on Fifth Avenue, the Robert Blackburn Printmaking Workshop at 55 West 17th Street, the Pratt Institute in Brooklyn (offering undergraduate and graduate degrees in advertising and graphic design), the School of Visual Arts, the Parsons School of Design, Cooper Union (which houses the Herb Lubalin Study Center for training in typography), and the Fashion Institute of Technology, a branch of the State University of New York that offers courses in communication arts and advertising. Graphic design exhibitions are mounted at the Herb Lubalin Study Center and the galleries of the AIGA, the International Typeface Company, the School of Visual Arts, the Art Directors Club, the Shirley Goodman Resource Center at the Fashion Institute of Technology, the Museum of American Illustration (maintained by the Society of Illustrators), and Parsons The New School for Design.

Steven Heller

Grasmere. Neighborhood in southeastern Staten Island, bounded to the north by the Staten Island Expressway, to the east and south by Hylan Boulevard, and to the west by the tracks of Staten Island Rapid Transit. It lies at the southern end of Clove Valley and is bisected from north to south by Clove Road and from west to east by Fingerboard Road. During the nineteenth century the area was the site of Sir Roderick Cameron's estate, and it was named for the village in the Lake District in England. The Durkee Manufacturing Company made marine hardware from the 1920s to 1951 in a plant on Clove Road. An estate of the Goggi family on Hylan Boulevard became the Academy of St. Dorothy in 1932. Two privately owned ponds are surrounded by houses on rolling land: Brady's Pond, the only freshwater pond within the city limits fit for swimming, and Cameron's Pond. Nearby, the Stonegate Condominiums were built on Fingerboard Road, as were the Elb Gardens apartments on Clove Road. The *Staten Island Advance,* the only daily newspaper in the borough, opened a publishing plant on Fingerboard Road in 1960. The Carmelite Sisters in 1973 opened the Carmel Nursing Home, the only Roman Catholic nursing home in the borough. Staten Island Rapid Transit has a station in Grasmere. In the early twenty-first century the neighborhood had a growing condominium market that was supported by the area's close proximity to the Verrazano–Narrows Bridge, which links Staten Island to the rest of the city.

Harlow McMillen

Grasso, Dick (Richard A.) (*b* Jackson Heights, N.Y., 1946). Businessman. Chairman and chief executive of the New York Stock Exchange from 1995 to 2003, he was involved in a 1999 controversy when he met at the exchange with members of the Revolutionary Armed Forces of Colombia (FARC), which is considered a terrorist organization. In 2003 the exchange board voted him out of his position after another controversy over his nearly $190 million compensation package. In 2004 Attorney General Eliot Spitzer sued him for repayment of the package; four years later, the appellate court ruled in Grasso's favor.

Jessica Montesano

Gravesend. Neighborhood in southern Brooklyn (2000 pop. 77,691), adjacent to Bensonhurst, Coney Island, and Sheepshead Bay; bounded (roughly) on the north by Avenue P, the east by Coney Island Avenue, the south by the Belt Parkway, and the west by Stillwell Avenue. One of the six original towns of Kings County, Gravesend was the only colonial American settlement founded by a woman, Lady Deborah Moody, who in 1643 led a group of English religious dissenters to the community she planned around a square bisected by McDonald Avenue and Gravesend Neck Road. A formal patent dated 19 December 1645 granted the shareholders autonomy to govern and worship; Gravesend thus became an early haven for persecuted Quakers. Although Gravesend is home to the oldest surviving cemetery in New York City (established circa 1650), its name has no relation to burial grounds: either Lady Moody named it for Gravesend, England (which means "at the end of the grove"), or Willem Kieft, director general of New Netherland when the town was founded, suggested it be named for his birthplace, s'Gravenzande (which means "count's strand" in Dutch).

Gravesend, 2009

The area remained mostly farmland until the period 1862–79, when five steam railroads (later electrified) opened to serve nearby racetracks and the resort hotels on Coney Island. The city of Brooklyn annexed Gravesend in 1894, which led to the extension of streets and public amenities; this in turn spurred drastic development. The bulk of the neighborhood's building stock was completed by 1930, and until the early 1990s it housed a population almost exclusively Italian American. Recent immigrants have come from Mexico, Central and South America, Asia, the Middle East, and countries of the former Soviet Union. A large Syrian Jewish enclave is centered on Ocean Parkway.

Eric J. Ierardi, *Gravesend: The Home of Coney Island* (Charleston, S.C.: Arcadia, 2001)

Joseph Ditta

Gray, Spalding (*b* Barrington, R.I., 5 June 1941; *d* New York City, *ca* 10 Jan 2004). Actor, screenwriter, and playwright. After studying literature at Emerson College in Boston, he moved to New York City in 1967 to work in underground theater. Along with Elizabeth LeCompte he created a trilogy of semiautobiographical plays called *Three Places in Rhode Island,* which ran at the Performing Garage from 1975 to 1978. Out of this process Gray began to develop solo monologues, the first of which was *Sex and Death to the Age 14.* His collaboration with LeCompte led to their founding in 1975 the Wooster Group, an experimental theater company. Gray appeared in several movies; his experiences in Southeast Asia working on the 1984 film *The Killing Fields* inspired the monologue *Swimming to Cambodia* (1984), which won an Obie Award and was later made into a 1987 film with the same title. In June 2001 he suffered severe injuries in a car crash. After the accident Gray experienced bouts of depression, and in January 2004 he disappeared. On 7 March 2004 police pulled his body from the East River; investigators determined his death was most likely a suicide. In 2005 his final monologue was published with the title *Life Interrupted: The Unfinished Monologue.*

Sarah Wansley

Graziano, Rocky [Barbella, Thomas Rocco] (*b* New York City, 1 Jan 1921; *d* New York City, 22 May 1990). Boxer. He grew up on the Lower East Side and began boxing professionally in 1942 while absent without official leave from the army. Graziano's boxing style was that of a street brawler, and his pugnacious, hard-hitting technique and ability to take a punch captivated the public and made him one of the most popular champions ever. He is best known for his three middleweight championship fights with Tony Zale. He lost the first bout held at Yankee Stadium in 1946, won the rematch in Chicago on 16 July 1947, and lost the rubber match in 1948. After retiring in 1952 with a record of 67 wins, 10 losses, and six draws, he became a television comedian and wrote his autobiography, *Somebody Up There Likes Me.* In 1991 he was inducted into the International Boxing Hall of Fame.

Steven A. Riess

Great Atlantic and Pacific Tea Company [A&P]. Firm of food retailers. Formed as a partnership in 1859, it initially had one tea shop on Vesey Street but later became the first major chain of grocery stores in the country and the largest enterprise of its kind in the world, operating more than 15,000 stores by 1929. For many years it was controlled by the Hartford family, and although it declined somewhat after World War II, it remained the largest retailing firm in the country until 1965. After suffering a number of setbacks in the late 1960s and 1970s, it was bought in 1979 by a German firm, the Tengelmann Group. In 1986 it bought the Shopwell–Food Emporium and Waldbaum grocery chains. In the mid-1990s A&P was the largest grocery chain in New York City and the fourth-largest in the country. A&P was losing money in the late 1990s and turned unprofitable at the turn of the twenty-first century. In 2008 A&P bought Pathmark, which made it the number-two grocery retailer in the New York City metropolitan area as well as in Philadelphia.

Richard S. Tedlow, *New and Improved: The Story of Mass Marketing in America* (New York: Basic Books, 1990)

Peter A. Coclanis

Advertisement for the Great Atlantic and Pacific Tea Company

Greater Bethel African Methodist Episcopal Church. Denominational church commissioned in 1819 by Richard Allen, founder of the Bethel African Methodist Episcopal (AME) church in Philadelphia. After the first annual AME conference in New York (1820), William Lambert, former trustee with AME Zion in New York City, formed Greater Bethel AME in a converted schoolhouse in lower Manhattan. Greater Bethel and other AME churches expanded rapidly over the next few decades, and with the advent of the Civil War they provided direct aid to southern blacks, funded educational facilities, and established missions in the Caribbean and Africa. The church moved to the southeast corner of Malcolm X Boulevard and West 123rd Street in 1901 into the landmarked building that formerly housed the Harlem Library (1981–92; Edgar K. Bourne, architect).

Emilyn L. Brown

Greater Central Baptist Church. Located at 2152 Fifth Avenue, it ministers to a well-established, largely African American congregation in central Harlem.

Sharon Wilkins

Greater New York. Term that had a specific meaning in the late nineteenth century and gradually acquired a more general one. In the years before and immediately after the consolidation of New York City in 1898, it referred to the five boroughs of the city as newly defined: the Bronx, Brooklyn, Manhattan, Queens, and Staten Island. Over the years the term came to acquire a broader sense, connoting also the nearby suburbs of Westchester County, Long Island, New Jersey, and Connecticut. Greater New York was defined as a

Front (left) and back (right) of promotional material for the Great Atlantic and Pacific Tea Company

31-county region in three states with a population of more than 22 million as of 2000.

Kenneth T. Jackson

Greater New York Hospital Association. Nonprofit organization formed in 1904 as an advocacy group for hospital superintendents in New York City. After it absorbed the Hospital Conference of the City of New York and the Hospital Council of Brooklyn in 1937 it became the sole voice of nonprofit hospitals in the city. Among its first projects in this new role was an effort to obtain more funds from the city to provide care for indigent patients. In the twenty-first century it represents nearly 300 hospitals in the metropolitan area and supports research and education, particularly in the areas of finance, health economics, and organization and management.

Brian Greenberg

Greater New York Savings Bank. Savings bank incorporated in Brooklyn in May 1897 by a group of business leaders led by Charles J. Obermayer. Its name referred to the forthcoming consolidation of New York City. The bank first occupied quarters in Park Slope at Seventh Avenue and First Street, which it soon outgrew. It merged with the Guardian Savings Bank in 1908, City Savings Bank of Brooklyn in 1964, and Flatbush Savings Bank in 1970. It became publicly owned in 1987 and later opened four branches on Long Island. It was located at One Penn Plaza in 1997, when it was purchased for $293 million by the Astoria Federal Savings and Loan Association.

Stephen Weinstein

Great Fire. The fire of 16–17 December 1835 caused more damage to property than any other event in the history of New York City. It destroyed more than 20 square blocks of mostly wooden buildings bounded by Wall and Broad streets, Coenties Slip, and the East River. Every fire company in Manhattan and many from Brooklyn, Long Island, New Jersey, and other areas responded to the alarm, but their efforts were hampered by inadequate water supplies, primitive equipment, and bitterly cold temperatures that froze water pipes and leather fire hoses. Most of the fire was subdued on 18 December by 1900 firefighters, including 400 from Philadelphia. Losses in the pier, warehouse, and commercial districts were estimated at $20 million to $40 million; the volume of claims forced 23 of the 26 fire insurance companies in the city to declare bankruptcy. The Great Fire led to demands for the reorganization of the volunteer force or its replacement with a paid one, and for the introduction of horse-drawn engines equipped with steam pumps. The cause of the fire was never determined.

Donald J. Cannon

Great Kill. Name used until the 1880s for a neighborhood in Manhattan, bounded to the north by 57th Street, to the east by Sixth Avenue, to the south by 35th Street, and to the west by the Hudson River. It was named for a river of the same name that flowed from the Hudson into Manhattan along what is now West 41st Street. The Dutch word *kille* means riverbed. The river running through the area was 4640 meters long. From the early eighteenth century to the late nineteenth the area was the site of the Great Kill Farm, a large estate owned by various members of the Hopper family. William F. Havemeyer lived near what is now Columbus Circle during the 1850s and 1860s. By the 1880s the Great Kill had been filled in and apartment buildings had replaced many houses.

James Bradley

Great Kills. Neighborhood in southeastern Staten Island (2009 pop. *ca* 26,000), occupying 2.5 square miles (6.5 square kilometers) bounded to the north by Arthur Kill Road, to the east by Corbin Avenue, to the south by Great Kills Harbor, and to the west by Robinson Avenue. Great Kills Park and Crookes

View of the Great Fire of 1835 from the top of the Bank of America, Wall and William streets

Point form a hook of land that shields most of the harbor from the Atlantic Ocean. The shoreline area was known as Clarendon and the inland area as Newtown until the two were combined under the name Gifford's, after the local commissioner and surveyor of roads Daniel Gifford; the current name was adopted in 1865. The neighborhood was relatively unaffected by the opening in 1964 of the Verrazano–Narrows Bridge and remains spacious, with mostly middle- and upper-middle-class homes. Sycamore Street and its environs are covered by zoning laws that limit the size of new buildings and the construction of town houses. Amboy Road is a main commercial street, with many restaurants and stores.

Stanford M. Forrester

Great Migration. Long-term movement of blacks from the South to the urban North. It transformed New York City and other northern cities between 1900 and the mid-twentieth century. Earlier, relatively small groups of blacks had settled in southern Manhattan and in midtown in neighborhoods such as the Tenderloin district, San Juan Hill, and Hell's Kitchen. Beginning in the 1890s, however, they began moving north in larger numbers, and in Manhattan they soon concentrated in west and central HARLEM, moving the city's black population from 60,666 in 1900 to approximately 327,000 by 1930. While southerners made up most of the migrants, the islands of the Caribbean also contributed to the growth of New York City's black population, especially the British islands of Barbados, Jamaica, and Trinidad, and in 1930 one-sixth of the city's black population was foreign born.

By 1905 black migrants began to settle in Harlem, which offered a soft housing market in an uptown neighborhood designed and built for middle-class whites. Over the next 20 years the existing black population joined thousands of newcomers in Harlem, which became the nation's largest black urban center and its most famous cultural mecca. Other neighborhoods in the southern Bronx and the Bedford–Stuyvesant section of Brooklyn also opened up to black migrants. What had been in the nineteenth century a largely marginalized population in New York City emerged by the 1930s as a powerful force in the city's political, economic, and cultural life.

Gilbert Osofsky, *Harlem: The Making of a Ghetto, Negro New York, 1890–1930* (New York: Harper, 1963); James N. Gregory, *The Southern Diaspora: How the Great Migrations of Black and White Southerners Transformed America* (Chapel Hill: University of North Carolina Press, 2005)

Jared Day

Great North Side. See NORTH SIDE.

Greatorex [née Pratt], **Eliza** (*b* Manor Hamilton, Ireland, 25 Dec 1820; *d* Paris, 9 Feb 1897). Painter and etcher. She moved to New York City about 1840 and soon after married the musician Henry W. Greatorex. After his death in 1858 she began to produce oil paintings, drawings, and etchings and became known for scenes of New York City. One of her most successful series of etchings was *Old New York from the Battery to Bloomingdale* (1875). In 1869 she became the first woman elected an associate of the National Academy of Design.

Wendy Shadwell

Great Road. See BOSTON POST ROAD.

Great Square. See DELANCEY SQUARE.

Great Trees. Unusually beautiful, strange, or old trees nominated by city residents. The first Great Tree search was conducted by the Department of Parks and Recreation in 1985. An updated guide was published in 2000 that included 105 specimens, such as a 150-foot tall Tulip tree in Riverdale with a room-sized hollow space in its trunk.

Kate Lauber

Greeks. New York City is the home of one of the largest Greek communities in North America. The first Greek immigrant to New York City on record was Basil Constantin, who settled in the city in July 1844. By 1855 several Greek merchants in the city imported currants and exported cotton and wheat as part of international trading firms. They also acted as representatives of the Greek government: Demetrius N. Botassi, who moved to New York City in 1856, was the Greek consul general for more than 58 years. Perhaps the first Greek student in New York City was Christodoulos M. L. Evangelides, who graduated from Columbia College in 1836; welcomed into the homes of prominent New Yorkers, he was the subject of a poem by William Cullen Bryant. In 1857 the Peleponnesos opened as the first Greek restaurant in the city and the forerunner of a business in which thousands of Greek immigrants eventually distinguished themselves. In 1880 the Greek population of the city was nevertheless only 69. The first of many Greek flower shops opened in 1885.

Until about 1910 most Greek immigrants were men from rural areas. Those who were married sent for their wives and children from Greece when they felt financially secure; the unmarried often brought brides back from Greece. Some young Greek boys seeking to immigrate to the United States fell victim to an exploitative practice similar to that maintained by the Italian *padrones*: systematically recruited by go-betweens in Greece who arranged for their passage in return for a period of work as bootblacks or peddlers, once in the United States young Greeks were often crowded into unsanitary living conditions and forced to work long hours at low wages in order to discharge their obligation.

Strong family ties, fervent Greek nationalism, hard work, and upward mobility became characteristic of Greek immigrants of New York City. They worked at the docks, sold flowers and fruit, and shined shoes. Their community was concentrated in lower Manhattan around Madison and Fulton Streets, where men shared single rooms. Greeks entered the American middle class rapidly; for the most part they did not choose careers as wage earners but instead quickly sought to open shops or buy pushcarts. In 1873 a former sailor named Hatzikiris saved enough money to form the Greek-American Confectionery Company, which eventually supplied candy to retailers throughout the East Coast. Worsening economic conditions in Greece caused the number of immigrants to increase sharply after 1891: there were 15,979 Greek immigrants to the United States between 1890 and 1900, of whom at least 1309 settled in New York City, and by some estimates nearly one in four Greek males between ages 15 and 45 immigrated to the United States between 1900 and 1915. In 1891 about 450 members of the Brotherhood of Athena (the first Greek fraternal society in the city) raised funds to establish the Church of the Holy Trinity, the first Greek Orthodox church in the city and only the third in the United States. Through the efforts of Solon Vlasto, president of the Brotherhood of Athena, on 6 April 1893 the Greek flag was flown in honor of Greek Independence Day over City Hall and over Reiner Hall (475 Pearl Street), from which a crowd of 300 Greeks marched to Broadway by way of Chambers Street. This was the beginning of the grand Greek Independence Day Parade, which has become an annual event along Fifth Avenue and was televised, live, for the first time in 2007. Vlasto also launched the Greek-language newspaper *Atlantis* in 1894 (it began daily publication in 1904 and remained in operation until 1972), which maintained a politically conservative stance to which the *National Herald* offered a liberal alternative from 1915. From 1904 a number of shipping lines scheduled service from the southern Greek port of Patras to New York City.

A survey of Manhattan businesses owned by Greeks in 1909 recorded 151 bootblack parlors, 113 florists, 107 lunchrooms and restaurants, 70 confectioneries, 62 retail fruit stores, and 11 wholesale produce dealers. In 1911 there were at least 24 Greek fraternal organizations in the city, and the first Greek-language parochial school opened in the Bronx. By one estimate the Greek population of New York City was 20,000 in 1913; in 1920 the figure for the United States was more than 400,000. Unlike other immigrants the Greeks did not live in concentrated ethnic quarters or ghettos but were scattered throughout the boroughs, with some areas of concentration near the original settlement at Madison Street on the Lower East Side, along Sixth Avenue in the West 30s, along Second and Third avenues in the 20s and 30s, and in Brooklyn. After World War I most Greek immigrants settled along Eighth Avenue between 14th and 45th streets. The English language spoken in the city combined with the Greek language of the immigrants to produce something of a dialect during the period of mass immigration. Early Greek-language films and sound recordings were made in New York City, and radio programs were first broadcast in the 1930s.

Like other immigrants from southern Europe, Greek Americans suffered from the nativist movements of the interwar period. Their long Greek names and heavily accented English made them identifiable targets for employment discrimination and other forms of prejudice. Greek business owners were hurt when their competitors spread rumors accusing them of dishonesty and of operating establishments with unsanitary conditions. The Greeks of New York City fought back through their fraternal and business organizations, stressing to their members the importance of assimilation, American values, and U.S. citizenship. Greek immigrants enrolled in English-language and civics courses in record numbers so that they might send for relatives still in Greece. In New York City in the 1920s Greeks joined the fur and hotel workers' unions in significant numbers and became active in the labor movement. The Depression years were the high points of Greek American labor and communist activity, an activity that steadily declined after World War II. The federal census of 1940 recorded 53,300 Greek Americans living in New York City, of whom 53.6 percent had been born in Greece. Between 1948 and 1965 special refugee legislation allowed about 70,000 Greeks to enter the United States, supplemented by thousands of professionals seeking higher education or having a specialty that was in demand. In New York City, unlike in other American cities, immigrants continued to outnumber the children of immigrants. The steady flow of new immigrants strengthened the ethnic character of the community but did not weaken the tendency toward assimilation. The Maidman Playhouse Off-Broadway became the first Greek theater in New York City in 1963. Between 1966 and 1971 about 15,000 Greek immigrants settled in the United States each year under new legislation that favored prospective immigrants with relatives already living in the United States. The number eventually stabilized at about 9000 a year and remained at this level to the end of the 1980s. Although a large number of Greeks also moved illegally to New York City during this period, most eventually found their way into the mainstream and became productive citizens.

After 1965 Astoria in Queens became the dominant center of Greek immigrant settlement in New York City and the home of the largest number of Greek-owned shops and community organizations, including a Greek-American Homeowners Association. A sizable number of Greek Americans also settled in Washington Heights in Manhattan and Bay Ridge in Brooklyn. In all these neighborhoods Greek immigrants often bought two-family houses with apartments that they could rent out to tenants. Immigration in the 1970s and 1980s differed in several important respects from that of earlier years: entire families often immigrated together, and immigrants were better educated, better off financially, and more familiar with urban life than their forerunners had been. Many Greek immigrants opened restaurants offering Greek food and music aimed at customers who were not Greeks but rather members of other ethnic groups. They also popularized the gyro sandwich, which found its way into restaurants throughout the city. By the 1990s few Greek immigrants Anglicized their names. Increased opportunity and a higher standard of living in Greece decreased the number of immigrants to the United States during the late 1980s, a trend clearly in evidence in Astoria. Many children of older immigrants left New York City for the suburbs of Long Island, where Greek churches reported marked increases in membership.

Greek organizations in New York City remained dedicated to fraternal, professional, educational, social, and religious purposes. The Hellenic American Neighborhood Action Committee (1972) provides services to youth, immigrants, and the elderly, including health services, employment counseling, family counseling, and English-language instruction; it receives public funds and maintains offices throughout the city. More than 100 hometown and regional organizations maintain ties to a particular Greek village or region and distribute newspapers and newsletters throughout the country. New York City is also the headquarters of the Greek Archdiocese of North and South America. In addition to the *National Herald,* now the only Greek-language daily newspaper with a national circulation, there are several local Greek weeklies and the monthly Greek-language magazine *Nea Iorke* (1947). New York City remains a capital for the production of Greek films, music recordings, and radio and television programs. In politics, history was made in 2000 with the election of Michael N. Gianaris to the New York State Assembly 36th district, which includes Astoria. Although George Delis had been appointed district manager of Community Board One (one of 59 community boards, it is involved in land use, budgeting, and service deliveries) in 1977 and held this position for 30 years, the Gianaris race was the first time that a Greek American was elected to public office in New York City.

Theodore Saloutos, *The Greeks in the United States* (Cambridge, Mass.: Harvard University Press, 1964); Michael Contopoulos, *The Greek Community of New York City: Early Years to 1910* (New York: Aristide D. Caratzas, 1992)

Constantine G. Hatzidimitriou

Greeley, Horace (*b* Amherst, N.H., 3 Feb 1811; *d* Pleasantville, N.Y., 29 Nov 1872). Newspaper editor and political leader. He moved to New York City in 1831 and took lodgings at 168 West Street in Greenwich Village, where he lived until 1832. He began his career as an editor for the *New Yorker* in 1834 but soon turned to political pursuits. At the request of such Whig leaders as Thurlow Weed, in 1838 he began to edit the *Jeffersonian,* a weekly newspaper in Albany, New York. He then edited the *Log Cabin,* the leading Whig newspaper of the presidential campaign of 1840. In 1841 he launched the *New York Tribune,* the first daily Whig newspaper in New York City. Its editorial and financial success enabled Greeley to influence public opinion nationwide and disseminate his political views, which were an amalgam of Whig tenets and social radicalism. He was a staunch advocate of protectionism, abolitionism, and the Homestead Act. He also called for reform at the local level, and his social and political activism was linked to his experiences in the city. He lived at 63 Barclay Street during 1842–43, in a house on the Upper East Side between 48th and 49th streets from 1844 to 1850, and at 35 East 19th Street from 1850 to 1853. His opposition to nativism threw him into conflict with the conservative faction of the city's Whig organization. The poverty and suffering that he saw aroused his sympathy for the plight of laborers, leading him to endorse such measures as workers' cooperatives and unions, the 10-hour workday, and Associationism, an American version of Fourierism.

As the Civil War undermined his credibility, he was criticized especially for hesitating to support President Abraham Lincoln's reelection in 1864 and for pursuing peace activities during the last two years of the war. He gradually lost control of the *Tribune,* and his influence in national politics declined as competition from other newspapers increased. In 1872 he received the presidential nomination of the Liberal Republicans and was soundly defeated by General Ulysses S. Grant after a vituperative and abusive campaign. He returned to the *Tribune,* of which he had only nominal control, and died shortly afterward at a sanatorium. Many prominent political figures, including Grant and Salmon P. Chase, attended his funeral in New York City. Statues of Greeley stand in Herald Square and outside City Hall, as well as in suburban Chappaqua in Westchester County, where he maintained a weekend and summer home.

Glyndon G. Van Deusen, *Horace Greeley: Nineteenth-Century Crusader* (Philadelphia: University of Pennsylvania Press, 1953)

Eileen K. Cheng

Green, Andrew Haswell (*b* Worcester, Mass., 6 Oct 1820; *d* New York City, 13 Nov 1903). Lawyer, public official, and preservationist. Admitted to the bar in 1844, he practiced law with Samuel J. Tilden. He served on the Board of Education for six years beginning in 1855 (including three as president) and was president and comptroller of the Central Park Commission from 1857 until 1871 (when he assumed emergency duties as city comptroller during a fiscal and political crisis that was occasioned by the machinations of William M. "Boss" Tweed and that eventually led to Tweed's imprisonment). It was largely at Green's initiative that the state legislature granted to the commission the authority to revise the plan of the city west and north of the park. In 1868 he recommended in a report issued by the commission that the many municipalities and unincorporated areas in southern Westchester, Kings, Queens, and Richmond counties be consolidated with Manhattan to form a single municipality comprising what are now the five boroughs. After making many requests to the legislature over the following 20 years, he was appointed president of the Consolidation Inquiry Committee, and as a member of a new commission consisting principally of the mayors of the affected municipalities he helped to draft the Consolidation Law in 1895, which was enacted in 1897 and took effect on 1 January of the following year. Although best known as the father of consolidation he also played an important role in the formation of the New York Public Library, chartered in 1895 when the library bequeathed by Tilden was combined with the existing Astor and Lenox libraries: as an executor of Tilden's estate he negotiated a settlement with the heirs according to which the new institution received $2 million, and he successfully argued that the new library should have a circulation department in addition to a reference department. He remained a trustee of the library to the end of his life. As a preservationist he worked to safeguard City Hall, the Palisades, and Niagara Falls; was a commissioner of the Niagara Reservation during its first 20 years (the last 15 as its chairman); and persuaded the state legislature in 1895 to form the American Scenic and Historic Preservation Society, which he later led. He was fatally wounded by a deranged gunman at Park Avenue and 40th Street.

Andrew Haswell Green

John Foord, *The Life and Public Services of Andrew Haswell Green* (Garden City, N.Y.: Doubleday, Page, 1913); Harry Miller Lydenberg, *History of the New York Public Library: Astor, Lenox and Tilden Foundations* (New York: New York Public Library, 1923)

Seymour Durst

Green [née Robinson]**, Hetty** [Henrietta Howland] (*b* New Bedford, Mass., 21 Nov 1834; *d* New York City, 3 July 1916). Financier. The only child of a wealthy New Bedford whaling family, she was taught business and finance by her father and grandfather from an early age. In 1865 her father and maternal aunt died, leaving Green an inheritance of nearly $10 million, some of which she did not receive until the resolution of a trial in 1871 concerning her alleged falsification of her aunt's will, a battle that she eventually lost after five years in court. Green lived in and around New York City and spent her professional life managing and increasing this inheritance, making herself almost certainly the wealthiest woman in the United States. She invested millions in real estate and corporate and municipal bonds, established herself as a money lender, and acquired vast property holdings when loans failed to be repaid. Green added to her fortune in the panic of 1907, lending to corporations when banks all but stopped making loans. She received widespread media coverage; newspapers reported changes in her interest rates and published editorials about her. The majority of this coverage was critical; newspapers called Green the "Witch of Wall Street" and often described her as greedy and stingy. She is remembered as much for these qualities as for her financial prowess; the *Guinness Book of World Records* declared her the "World's Greatest Miser." Indeed, she and her two children moved between boarding houses in New York and New Jersey and received medical aid from free clinics rather than pay for health care. Unlike her fellow Gilded Age tycoons, Green never publicly donated money to charity. She left her family an estate valued at more than $100 million upon her death.

Ben Silk

Greenbelt. Group of seven public parks in Staten Island, covering about 2500 acres (1000 hectares) near the center of the borough. The land was acquired by the city in stages beginning in 1964. Robert Moses planned to clear it to make way for a freeway between the Outerbridge Crossing and the Verazzano–Narrows Bridge. In 1982 the city formally designated the park under its current name. The park is primarily a nature preserve that supports a large number of plant and animal species, including more than 50 species of birds. It has about 28 miles (45 kilometers) of trails. Beneath its upland hills, near the entrance of Reed's Basket Willow Swamp Park, is an ancient formation of serpentinite bedrock that is covered by stones, boulders, clay, and sand left by the Wisconsin glacier. The Greenbelt offers programs in environmental science and is a popular venue for hiking and bird-watching.

Ben Silk

Greenberg, Clement (*b* New York City, 16 Jan 1909; *d* New York City, 7 May 1994). Art critic. Born in the Bronx, he attended the Art Students League in 1925 before obtaining a bachelor's degree from Syracuse University; from 1936 he worked as a civil servant in New York City. He began writing art criticism for the *Partisan Review,* where he was editor from 1940 to 1942 and published his seminal pieces "Avant-Garde and Kitsch" (1939) and "'American Type' Painting" (1955). From 1942 to 1949 he was art critic for the *Nation;* he also wrote for *Arts Digest* and the *New Leader* and was an editor at *Contemporary Jewish Record* (later *Commentary*) from 1944 to 1957. His relationship with the *Nation* soured after he wrote a letter accusing editor Julio Alvarez del Vayo of writing Soviet propaganda; editor-in-chief Freda Kirchwey refused to print the accusation, and the *New Leader* ran the letter instead, resulting in a libel suit. Greenberg was known for his support of abstract expressionists in New York City, including Jackson Pollock and Barnett Newman, and for his theory of modernism, which advocated the precedence of formal elements such as colors and shapes over representational subjects. He became one of the most influential postwar American art critics; he wrote the monographs *Joan Miró* (1948), *Matisse* (1953), and *Hans Hofmann* (1961) and published an anthology of his criticism, *Art and Culture* (1961). In the late 1960s Greenberg's ideas fell out of fashion. Although he never regained the dominance he once held over the art world, his criticism remained significant into the early twenty-first century. *Collected Essays and Criticism,* a four-volume compilation of his work, was published from 1986 to 1993.

Kate Lauber

Green Book. Pocket-sized, paperback directory published annually by the New York City's Department of Citywide Administrative Services. It was first published in 1918 and was known as the Green Book because of the color of its cover; it became officially known as the Green Book in 1984. In more than 500 pages it lists addresses and telephone numbers of officials and government agencies; describes commissions, boards, committees of the City Council, terms of office, departmental responsibilities, and court jurisdictions; and provides a brief chronology of important dates in the city's history, as well as such facts about the city as the assessed value of its property and a timetable for its budget.

Eric Wm. Allison

green buildings. Buildings that use more resource-efficient and sustainable modes of construction, maintenance, and operation. New York City's first comprehensive green building project was a series of renovations to the historic Schermerhorn Building at 380 Lafayette Street in 1992. The Department of Design and Construction (DDC) formed the Office of Sustainable Design (OSD) in 1997. The city's first green construction project was a renovation of the Natural Resources Defense Council building in 1998. The next year, 4 Times Square, developed by the Durst Corporation and designed by Fox and Fowle architects, became the first green skyscraper in North America. That same year the OSD published DDC's *High Performance Building Guidelines,* which helped introduce sustainable design to the entire city. The planned Freedom Tower; World Trade Center Office Towers 2, 3, and 4; and World Trade Center Memorial and Memorial Museum are set to achieve Leadership in Energy and Environmental Design (LEED, the Green Building Rating System) Gold certification. In 2005 the city enacted Local Law 86, requiring most city-owned and city-funded buildings to achieve LEED Silver certification. As of 2010 New York City maintained dozens of residential, commercial, and educational green buildings.

Jessica Montesano

Greenfield. Name applied to Parkville in Brooklyn until 1870. The opening of the Coney Island Plank Road between Brooklyn and Coney Island in 1850 led to the development of the area in the following year, along with that of the adjacent neighborhood of Windsor Terrace. The land was purchased in 1851 and 1852 from the Tredwell and Ditmas families by the United Freeman's Association (freed slaves) and totaled about 114 acres (46 hectares). William Taylor built the first house in the area on Foster Avenue in 1852. Streets were laid out at an angle to the north-south grid; the first houses were built in 1853. The oldest section lies between Windsor Terrace and Kensington and consists mainly of frame houses and six-story apartment buildings constructed in the early twentieth century.

Stephen Weinstein

Greenfield, Elizabeth Taylor (*b* Natchez, Miss., ?1817; *d* Philadelphia, 31 March 1876). Classical musician. Born into slavery, she became a prominent, and most likely the first, African American singer to appear on the classical music stage in New York City, where she made her debut at Metropolitan Hall on 31 March 1853. Dubbed the "Black Swan" by journalists, she was nearly laughed off the stage by a hostile and outraged white audience, who were prevented from rioting only by the presence of a massive turnout of police. Her insistence upon performing in a hall where "colored" people were not allowed in turn evoked public criticism from a group of African American clergymen, who asked that she perform again free for black music lovers who had been excluded. Reviews, generally unfavorable, focused on the unusually broad range of her untrained voice, which covered more than three octaves. Reviewers' primary objection was to the lower notes, which were found "unfeminine." Greenfield went to England for more training but ran out of money and had to return to the United States. She opened a studio in Philadelphia, where she was active in the local music scene until her death.

A Brief Memoir of the "Black Swan," Miss Elizabeth Greenfield, the American Vocalist (London: 1853)

Jean Ashton

Greenmarket. Farmers' markets program run by New York City's Council on the Environment operating in each of the five boroughs. The first two markets opened in 1976 at 59th Street and Second Avenue and at Union Square Park on 14th Street and Broadway. During the 1980s Union Square Park was refurbished with the market as its focal point, making it one of the most recognizable markets of the initiative, a distinction it retained in the early twenty-first century, when the program operated 45 markets citywide, including 27 in Manhattan and 10 in Brooklyn. The market at Union Square attracts thousands of customers daily and is open year round. Some markets operate seasonally or only one day per week with low volume. All the vendors are producers of their own farmed goods.

David White

Greenpoint. Neighborhood in northwestern Brooklyn covering a triangular parcel of 946 acres (383 hectares) and bounded to the north and east by Newtown Creek, to the south by the Brooklyn–Queens Expressway and North Seventh Street, and to the west by the East River. The Dutch acquired the area in 1638 from Keshaechqueren Indians and named it for a grassy expanse that extended into the East River. By the early nineteenth century it was a farming area sparsely populated by the descendants of Pieter Praa, a Dutch Huguenot. Neziah Bliss, an ironworker who moved to the area in 1832, soon surveyed lots and in 1838 opened a turnpike to Astoria and Williamsburgh. Between 1840 and 1860 the neighborhood became an industrial center. Two ferry lines during the 1850s offered the first convenient access to the East Side of Manhattan. Flourishing industries included printing, pottery, petroleum and gas refining,

Greenpoint, 2009

glassmaking, and iron making. Shipbuilding developed along the East River: leading firms included the Continental Iron Works, which built the ironclad ship the *Monitor* of Civil War fame, and the Astral Oil Works, founded by Charles Pratt and merged with the Standard Oil Company in 1874. Streets were named for people, places, and items important to industry. Most of the population was Dutch, English, or Irish until the 1880s, when immigrants from Poland, Russia, and later Italy settled in the area to work in the factories and warehouses lining Kent Avenue, West Street, and Newtown Creek. According to tradition the neighborhood was the place of origin of the dialect known as Brooklynese (a distinction also ascribed to Flatbush). To provide workers with decent housing Pratt built the Astral Apartments on Franklin Street between India and Java streets in 1886 alongside rows of brick houses that lined Milton and Noble streets west of Manhattan Avenue. During the first half of the twentieth century shipbuilding, manufacturing, and warehousing gradually diminished, and the industries of Greenpoint declined after World War II. During the 1950s there was a marked increase in the number of Poles, who made the neighborhood the center of the city's Polish community and accounted for about half of all the immigrants who settled there in the 1980s. Others came from Puerto Rico, Guyana, the Dominican Republic, Colombia, Ecuador, China, and Pakistan. Two bridges, Kosciuszko and Pulaski, honor Polish heroes.

The main commercial district of Greenpoint lies along Manhattan Avenue, and restaurants and bakeries serve kielbasa, Polish dumplings, and flan. The oldest church is the Episcopal Church of the Ascension (1853). The Church of the Transfiguration (Russian Orthodox), dominated by onion-shaped cupolas, stands at North 12th Street and Driggs Avenue; the Church of St. Stanislaus Kostka (Roman Catholic) on Humboldt Street has the largest Polish congregation in Brooklyn. In the northern section Italians annually take part in a 10-day celebration of the Feast of Our Lady of Mount Carmel, in which men compete for the honor of carrying a tower called the *giglio* through local streets. McCarren Park stands on the former site of the Bushwick Creek between Berry and Leonard streets; Monsignor McGolrick Park on Nassau Avenue contains a monument commemorating the *Monitor.* Among famous Greenpointers are actors Mae West and Mickey Rooney and author Henry Miller. The McCarren Pool, which closed in 1984, was a site of popular concerts until 2008; the New York City Parks Department has said it will rebuild it. The neighborhood's industrial past reappeared in 1978 when oil that had been leaking since the 1940s and 1950s was found in Newtown Creek; the spill is considered to be the nation's largest. Cleanup of the area continues into the twenty-first century. Growth resulted in residential conversion of industrial buildings in 1986 and the rezoning of the waterfront in 2005.

Greenpoint-Williamsburg: An Industrial Study (New York: Department of City Planning, 1987)

Stephen Weinstein, John Manbeck

Greenpoint Glass Works. Glass factory established on the Brooklyn waterfront in 1860. Christian Dorflinger (1828–1915), a French immigrant, operated several smaller factories before buying the Greenpoint property on Commercial Street near Newtown Creek. There he erected a plant with four times the capacity of his previous glassworks. He built dock facilities for receiving raw materials and shipping finished products, and in accord with French tradition built housing for the elite glassblowers whom he brought from France. The successful firm had a reputation for quality and efficiency, with products ranging from kerosene lamp chimneys to Mary Todd Lincoln's table service for the White House. By the mid-1860s Dorflinger had left Brooklyn for Pennsylvania. The factory was leased to various firms, which continued under the Greenpoint Glass Works name while manufacturing decorative vases and globes and chimneys for oil, gas, and electric lights. In 1905 the Gleason–Tiebout Company, makers of glass for gas and electric lighting, bought the property.

William L. Felter, *Historic Green Point: A Brief Account of the Beginning and Development of the Northerly Section of the Borough of Brooklyn, City of New York, locally known as Green Point* (Brooklyn, N.Y.: Green Point Savings Bank, 1918); Joshua Brown and David Ment, *Factories, Foundries, and Refineries: A History of Five Brooklyn Industries* (Brooklyn, N.Y.: Brooklyn Educational and Cultural Alliance, 1980)

See also Glassmaking.

Cathy Alexander

Green Point Savings Bank. Savings bank opened on 11 January 1869 and originally situated at the corner of Franklin and Oak streets, moving several times before building its own headquarters on the corner of Manhattan Avenue and Calyer Street in 1907. After buying the Home Savings Bank in 1931 it became one of the most successful savings banks in the city, and by 1990 was its second-largest. The bank was acquired by North Fork Bancorporation in 2004.

William L. Felter, *Historic Green Point* (New York: Green Point Savings Bank, 1918)

James Bradley

Greenridge. Neighborhood in south central Staten Island, lying near the intersection of Arthur Kill Road and Richmond Avenue. The area was once called Marshland and in colonial times was a Huguenot settlement, where the Huguenots built their first church in America (it was burned down by Native Americans). In 1776 during the Revolution, the English army's 17th Lancers made camp at this location. The name changed to Greenridge in 1876. It consisted mostly of fields and woods until one- and two-family houses were built in the 1960s. Al Deppe's, a popular restaurant from the 1920s to the 1960s, once drew patrons from throughout the borough. At the intersection of Arthur Kill Road and Richmond Avenue is the Greenridge Plaza Shopping Center. The Staten Island Mall is across the Fresh Kills Bridge on Richmond Avenue and Richmond Hill Road.

Harlow McMillen

Greenwich House. Social service agency and arts organization located on Barrow Street in Greenwich Village. It opened in 1902 to serve the then primarily immigrant population. Social reformers such as Mary Kingsbury Simkhovitch, Jacob A. Riis, Carl Schurz, and Felix Adler joined together to improve living situations and ease the transition into American society in what was the most densely populated neighborhood in Manhattan. As a settlement house, the agency focused on housing initiatives and on creating New York City's first neighborhood association, the Greenwich Village Improvement Society. Greenwich House also started music and pottery schools, with its arts curricula being molded by such varying names as Eleanor Roosevelt, Jackson Pollock, and Kirk Douglas. In 1921 the house opened a nursery school. In 1942 an after-school program began, and 20 years later an outpatient drug-counseling center was established. In the early twenty-first century Greenwich House continued to serve more than 7500 people per year through programs ranging from its Parole Treatment Program to the AIDS Mental Health Project.

Anne Epstein

Greenwich Village. Neighborhood, also referred to as "the Village," in lower Manhattan (2000 pop. *ca* 100,000), bounded to the north by 14th Street, to the east by Fourth Avenue and the Bowery, to the west by the Hudson River, and to the south by Houston Street (though its whose borders have been blurred by the ever-growing SoHo and NoHo neighborhoods). The area was once a marshland studded by a few hills that was known as Sapokanican to the Canarsee Indians who camped and fished there; it fed a meandering trout stream called the Manetta (an Indian term meaning "devil water"; later known as Minetta Brook). By the 1630s Dutch settlers had advanced 2 miles (3 kilometers) north into the remote province, then called Noortwyck, to clear pastures and plant crops. Wouter van Twiller, second director general

Greenwich Village
0 500 1,000 Feet
0 100 200 300 Meters
© 2009 Identity Map Company by Jackson & Danniel Maio, NYC
N
Hudson River
Pier 46
Pier 45
Hudson River Park
W 14 Street
W 13 Street
Little W 12 Street
W 12 Street
W 11 Street
W 10 Street
W 9 Street
W 8 Street
E 14 Street
E 13 Street
E 12 Street
E 11 Street
E 10 Street
E 9 Street
E 8 Street
Ninth Avenue
Eighth Avenue
Seventh Avenue South
Sixth Avenue (Avenue of the Americas)
Fifth Avenue
Fourth Avenue
University Place
Broadway
Astor Pl
Hudson Street
Greenwich Avenue
Greenwich Street
Washington Street
West Street
Gansevoort Street
Horatio Street
Jane Street
Bethune Street
Bank Street
Perry Street
Charles Street
Charles Lane
Christopher Street
Barrow Street
Morton Street
Leroy Street
Clarkson Street
Pat LaFrieda Lane
W Houston Street
West Houston Street
King Street
Varick Street
Carmine Street
Downing Street
Bleecker Street
Grove Street
Bedford St
Commerce St
St. Luke's Place
Jones Street
Cornelia Street
W 4 Street
Waverly Place
Waverly Pl
Washington Pl
Washington Place
Charles St
Jane Jacobs Way
Washington Square Park
Washington Square South
W 3 Street
Minetta Lane
MacDougal Street
Sullivan Street
Thompson Street
West Broadway
Wooster Street
Greene Street
Mercer Street
Crosby Street
Lafayette Street
Bond Street
Prince Street
Jackson Square
Abingdon Square
Sheridan Square Gardens
Christopher Park
Father Demo Square
Winston Churchill Square
Father Fagan Park
St Vincent's Hospital
PS 41
Jefferson Market Library
Washington Square Village
Silver Towers
NYU Bobst Library
NYU Law School
Judson Memorial Church
Kimmel Skirball Center
St Luke in the Fields
Greenwich Village Middle School
Film Forum
Coles Sports Center
Washington Mews
Hudson Park Library
James J. Walker Ballfield
Dapolito Recreation Center

of New Amsterdam, found the fertile basin bordering Minetta Brook ideal for cultivating tobacco, and he claimed extensive acreage near it for his personal plantation, Bossen Bouwerie ("farm in the woods"). After the English conquest of New Amsterdam in 1664 the settlement evolved into a country hamlet, first designated Grin'wich in records of the Common Council in 1713. Richmond Hill, a three-story colonnaded mansion built by Major Abraham Mortier in 1767, exemplified the stylish architecture of the rural estates. Freed African slaves also farmed parcels of land in this sparsely populated district, establishing an independent community near what are now Minetta Lane and Thompson Street that endured to the end of the nineteenth century.

Greenwich Village survived the American Revolution as a pastoral suburb. Commercial activity after the war was centered near the edge of the Hudson, where fresh produce markets drew traffic from downtown. Sightseers attracted by its salutary climate and seeking to escape the commotion of the city often traveled the length of Greenwich Street. In the 1780s the city purchased on the site of a drained swamp at what is now Washington Square Park a parcel of 8 acres (3 hectares) for use as a potter's field (closed in 1826) and public gallows. At the foot of Christopher Street stood Newgate Prison from 1797 to 1829. Efforts to preserve the crooked colonial lanes were mounted as early as the second decade of the nineteenth century, when a coalition of residents prevailed on the Common Council to modify the grid plan of 1811. As a result much of the district was exempted from the rigid symmetry that dictated the development of Manhattan north of Houston Street. The comparative seclusion of the area began to erode during yellow fever and cholera outbreaks in 1799, 1803, 1805, and 1821. Those seeking refuge fled north to the wholesome backwaters of the West Village (one of the oldest quarters of Greenwich Village, bounded by Greenwich Avenue, Christopher Street, and West Street), triggering the construction of temporary housing as well as banking offices. During an especially virulent epidemic in 1822 many who had intended to remain in the area only temporarily chose instead to settle there permanently, increasing the population fourfold between 1825 and 1840 and spurring the development of markets and businesses. Speculators subdivided farms, leveled hills, rerouted Minetta Brook, and undertook landfill projects.

Blocks of neat row houses soon accommodated middle-class merchants and tradespeople. From 1820 a more affluent residential development emerged to the east near Broadway; rows of imposing, marble-trimmed town houses lent dignity to the newly planned blocks of Bond and Great Jones Streets, LeRoy Place (on Bleecker Street west of Broadway), and Lafayette Place, which encompassed the uniform elegance of Colonnade Row. Another fashionable area of redbrick town houses developed around Washington Square Park at the foot of Fifth Avenue. The crowning addition to this urban plaza was a triumphal arch of Tuckahoe marble designed by Stanford White, erected in 1892. New York University erected buildings on the east side of Washington Square starting in 1836; and the neighborhood soon became the site of art clubs, private picture galleries, learned societies, literary salons, and libraries, including the large Astor Library (1854) on Lafayette Place. Fine hotels, shopping emporia, and theaters also proliferated along Broadway between Houston Street and 14th Street. At the close of the nineteenth century, German, Irish, and Italian immigrants moved into Greenwich Village to work at the breweries, warehouses, and coal and lumber yards near the Hudson. As the housing stock deteriorated, older residences were subdivided into cheap lodging hotels and multiple-family dwellings or were demolished for higher-density tenements. Plummeting real estate values and incomes and the shabbiness of the area prompted nervous retailers and genteel property owners to move uptown.

Greenwich Village at the turn of the twentieth century was a quaintly picturesque and ethnically diverse backwater. By the beginning of World War I it was widely known as a bohemian enclave with secluded side streets, low rents, and a tolerance for radicalism and nonconformity. Although most residents were members of the conservative working class or of a vestigial upper class, attention increasingly became focused on artists and writers noted for their boldly innovative work: books and irreverent "little magazines" were published by small presses, art galleries exhibited the work of the avant-garde, and experimental theater companies blatantly ignored the financial considerations of Broadway. In 1913 residents of the neighborhood figured prominently in the Paterson Strike Pageant and the Armory Show. A growing awareness of its idiosyncrasies helped to make Greenwich Village an attraction for tourists, who could easily reach Washington Square by the Fifth Avenue Coach Line, and Sheridan Square after it became a station of Interborough Rapid Transit in 1917–18; the neighborhood became still more accessible after Seventh Avenue South was cut through and Sixth Avenue was extended south of Carmine Street. Entrepreneurs provided amusements ranging from evenings in artists' studios to bacchanalian costume balls that they promoted as "pagan romps," as well as candlelit tea rooms, novelty nightclubs, bizarre boutiques, counterfeit artists' garrets, and burlesque revues. During Prohibition local speakeasies attracted patrons from uptown. The insularity of the neighborhood was further eroded by a number of public works projects, including subway excavations in the West Village and the widening of older streets to accommodate more traffic. Decrepit row houses were remodeled into "artistic flats" for the well-to-do, and rents increased during the 1920s by 140 percent and in some cases by as much as 300 percent. In 1926–27 luxury apartment towers began to be built at the northern edge of Washington Square.

The stock market crash of 1929 halted new construction. A number of steps were taken to alleviate the hardships caused by the Depression. The Washington Square Outdoor Art Show was inaugurated in 1932 to exhibit and promote sales of the work of local artists and continued to be held semiannually. Society sculptor Gertrude Vanderbilt Whitney opened a museum dedicated to modern American art on West Eighth Street in 1931. The New School for Social Research, on West 12th Street since the late 1920s, inaugurated the University in Exile in 1933. Urban renewal in Washington Square South resulted in the demolition of many nineteenth-century structures and helped to inspire a movement for historic preservation. A plan by Robert Moses to carve a roadway through Washington Square was defeated in the early 1950s, as were aggressive efforts to expand by New York University.

Greenwich Village was a center for the Beat movement in the 1950s (see Beats). Writers, painters, actors, musicians, and dissidents, many from San Francisco, moved into the southern and eastern portions of the neighborhood. Galleries became concentrated along Eighth Street, coffeehouses on MacDougal Street, and storefront theaters on Bleecker Street, and "happenings" and other unorthodox artistic, theatrical, and musical events were staged at the Judson Memorial Church on Washington Square South. In 1955 the weekly newspaper the Village Voice emerged as a champion of the city's growing Off-Broadway theater. Efforts at historic preservation were strengthened by "down-zoning" changes enacted in 1961 (the same year Jane Jacobs's *The Death and Life of Great American Cities,* one of whose protagonists was Greenwich Village, was published) and by the designation in 1969 of a contiguous Greenwich Village historic district that protected more than 2035 structures and encompassed most of the West Village from Sixth Avenue to Hudson Street. A large homosexual community centered at Christopher Street benefited from the tolerance of local residents but was also subject to occasional harassment by the police. A confrontation between the police and patrons of the Stonewall Inn on Christopher Street in 1969 culminated in a riot known as the Stonewall Rebellion, which is regarded as having marked the beginning of the nationwide movement for gay and lesbian rights.

In the 1970s and 1980s Greenwich Village became a rallying place for antiwar protesters (where several safe houses used by the Weather Underground were located) and for activists mobilized by the AIDS epidemic, which struck the neighborhood with particular force. The neighborhood's St. Vincent's Catholic Medical Center (170 West 12th Street), founded in 1849, was one of the first hospitals to address the AIDS crisis in the 1980s and has since had one of the more renowned treatment centers for human immunodeficiency virus in the nation.

Preservationists helped to halt construction of a new highway, Westway, and enlisted public support for protecting the waterfront, exempted from earlier landmark designation. Many old commercial buildings, such as the Manhattan Refrigerating Company and Bell Laboratories, were converted into residences. The neighborhood also gained notoriety as an outpost of the city's drug and music culture, home to such institutions as Jimi Hendrix's Electric Lady sound studios, which opened in 1968 at 52 West Eighth Street. Despite the presence of this provocative culture, Greenwich Village remained an attractive residential neighborhood for professionals and families. Tourists continued to patronize the neighborhood's bars, discothèques, art galleries, bookshops, and Italian groceries, as well as the Joseph Papp Public Theater on Astor Place, and to take part in walking tours sponsored by many individuals.

Washington Square Park remains a forum for soap-box oratory, demonstrations, fashion parades, and impromptu performances of jazz, folk, rock, and rap. The annual Halloween Parade and the Gay Pride March draw thousands of participants and spectators. Because of the high real estate costs, the area is no longer home to the struggling artists that inhabited it in the mid-twentieth century, but rather to a large number of celebrities and other affluent families; nonetheless, the Village still maintains a strong communal identity reminiscent of its Bohemian past.

Caroline F. Ware, *Greenwich Village, 1920–1930* (Boston: Houghton Mifflin, 1935); *Greenwich Village Historic District Designation Report* (New York: Landmarks Preservation Commission, 1969); Edmund T. Delaney and Charles Lockwood, *Greenwich Village: A Photographic Guide* (New York: Dover, 1976); Terry Miller, *Greenwich Village and How It Got That Way* (New York: Crown, 1990); Jan Seidler Ramirez, *Within Bohemia's Borders: Greenwich Village, 1830–1930* (New York: Museum of the City of New York, 1990)

Jan Seidler Ramirez

Green-Wood Cemetery. Nonsectarian, not-for-profit, 478-acre (193-hectare) cemetery and crematory in Brooklyn, occupying a site overlooking New York Harbor. It was established in 1838 by prominent New Yorkers who saw a need for burial space outside of overcrowded Manhattan churchyards. The original design was by David Bates Douglass, who was also responsible for the Croton Aqueduct with strong assistance from Almerin Hotchkiss, who later designed Bellefontaine Cemetery in St. Louis and Chippiannock Cemetery in Rock Island, Illinois. Modeled after Père Lachaise Cemetery in Paris and Mount Auburn Cemetery in Cambridge, Massachusetts, Green-Wood was designed as a rural retreat where visitors could escape the difficulties of urban living. In an 1849 essay Andrew Jackson Downing wrote that, of America's rural cemeteries, Green-Wood was "the largest and unquestionably the finest . . . grand, dignified and park-like." Green-Wood became fashionable after the body of DeWitt Clinton was moved there from Albany and a large bronze memorial by sculptor Henry Kirke Brown was commissioned. The natural beauty of the cemetery, its design, its elaborate monuments, and the prominence of those buried there soon made Green-Wood a popular tourist destination. Its success inspired a competition to design a "Central Park" for New York City, with Calvert Vaux and Frederick Law Olmsted submitting the winning plan.

In 2006 Green-Wood was designated a National Historic Landmark. Its Gothic Revival entrance (1861) at Fifth Avenue and 25th Street, designed by Richard Upjohn and Sons,

Green-Wood Cemetery, 1852

Entrance to Green-Wood Cemetery, 2009

is a New York City landmark. Green-Wood contains nearly 7000 trees, including many rare specimens. Among its nearly 600,000 permanent residents are political leaders Seth Low and William M. Tweed; inventors Peter Cooper, Elias Howe, and Samuel F. B. Morse; artists Asher B. Durand, William Merritt Chase, George Catlin, John Kensett, George Bellows, Eastman Johnson, John George Brown, Philip Evergood, and Jean-Michel Basquiat; stained-glass competitors Louis Comfort Tiffany and John La Farge; composers Leonard Bernstein, Fred Ebb, and Louis Moreau Gottschalk; newspaper publishers Horace Greeley and James Gordon Bennett; actors Frank Morgan (*The Wizard of Oz*) and Laura Keene; abolitionist Henry Ward Beecher; lithographers Nathaniel Currier and James Merritt Ives (the men behind the firm Currier and Ives); many Civil War generals, including Henry W. Halleck and Henry W. Slocum; and more than 3000 Civil War veterans.

Richard J. Moylan

grid plan. Far-reaching plan approved by the state legislature of New York in 1811, also known as the Commissioners' Plan. Devised by a commission made up of the political leader Gouverneur Morris, the surveyor Simeon De Witt, and the lawyer John Rutherford, it established a basis for the orderly sale and development of land in Manhattan between 14th Street and Washington Heights by laying out a rectangular grid of streets and property lines without regard for topography. Twelve numbered avenues, each 100 feet (30 meters) wide, ran north and south. In the interior, Third, Fourth, Fifth, and Sixth avenues were 920 feet (280 meters) apart; along the riverfronts the avenues were closer together, in expectation of greater development. The signature of the plan was its 155 cross streets placed only 200 feet (60 meters) apart, producing a grid of about 2000 long, narrow blocks. Convinced that simple rectangular houses and lots were best, the commissioners avoided the addition of circles, ovals, and other features like those used by Pierre L'Enfant in his plan for Washington, D.C. The commission was instructed by the legislature to lay out streets and public squares of sufficient dimension to provide "free and abundant circulation of air" for public health. They provided small parks in the interior of the island at 53rd, 66th, 77th, and 120th streets and several large public spaces: one of 26 acres (11 hectares) uptown for a reservoir, another of 54 acres (22 hectares) on the Lower East Side for a wholesale market complex, and a third of 275 acres (111 hectares) extending from 23rd to 34th streets and from Third to Seventh avenues for a military training ground, or "parade" (which it was hoped would eventually become a central park).

The grid plan of 1811 was repeatedly altered because it lacked the support of a formal planning commission. Union, Tompkins, Stuyvesant, and Madison squares were added, as were Lexington and Madison avenues to bisect the long blocks between Third and Fifth avenues. More disruptive changes occurred with the elimination of the two large spaces provided for the market and militia. When plans for a park downtown were forestalled, the street plan was altered to allow for the extension of Fourth, Fifth, and Sixth avenues south to 14th Street, and for the extension northward of Broadway. The angled course of Broadway later made possible the development of such areas as Times Square. Despite these changes the basic plan for most streets and blocks survived and continued to dominate the city's development. The one great exception was the building of Central Park in the late 1850s. Later modifications were made along the riverfronts, notably at Riverside Park.

Edward K. Spann, "The Greatest Grid: The New York Plan of 1811," *Two Centuries of American Planning,* ed. Daniel Schaffer (Baltimore: Johns Hopkins University Press, 1988), 11–39

See also STREETS AND HIGHWAYS and HOUSE NUMBERING AND STREET NAMING.

Edward K. Spann

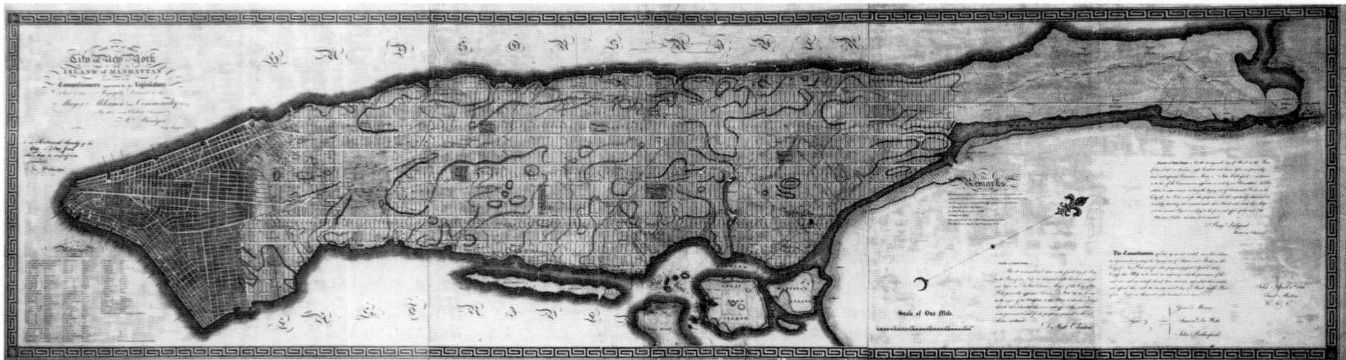

Commissioners' map of New York City, 1811

Grinnell, Minturn and Company. Shipping firm formed in New York City in 1815 as Fish and Grinnell by Preserved Fish (1766–1846?) and Joseph Grinnell (1788–1885), formerly merchants in New Bedford, Massachusetts. It became Fish, Grinnell and Company when Grinnell's brothers Henry Grinnell (1799–1874) and Moses H(icks) Grinnell (1803–77) became partners. After Fish and Joseph Grinnell retired and Henry Grinnell's brother-in-law Robert Bowne Minturn (1805–66) joined the firm, it was reorganized as Grinnell, Minturn and Company (1833) and became one of the city's great shipping firms. Its swallowtail flag flew over more than 50 vessels, including regular packet lines to Liverpool and London and the famous clipper the *Flying Cloud.* All three partners were officers of banks and insurance companies and were prominent in civic and philanthropic affairs. Henry Grinnell supported polar expeditions and was a founder of the American Geographical and Statistical Society, of which he became president. Minturn helped to establish organizations that aided immigrants and the poor in New York City and contributed to St. Luke's Hospital; he was both a president of the Union League Club and a member of the original Central Park Commission, as was Moses H. Grinnell, who was also president of the local Chamber of Commerce (1847, 1849–52) and the New England Society (1843–54). A close friend of Daniel Webster, Moses H. Grinnell became active in politics and in 1838 won election to U.S. Congress as a Whig. He later became a Republican, served on the Union Defense Committee at the outbreak of the Civil War, and in 1869 was appointed collector of the Port of New York by President Ulysses S. Grant. Among the junior partners in the firm was Franklin H. Delano, who married Laura Astor, daughter of William Backhouse Astor.

Allan Nevins, ed., *The Diary of Philip Hone, 1828–1851* (New York: Dodd, Mead, 1927); Robert Greenhalgh Albion, *The Rise of New York Port, 1815–1860* (New York: Charles Scribner's Sons, 1939)

Elaine Weber Pascu

Griscom, John Hoskins (*b* ?New York City, 14 Aug 1809; *d* 28 April 1874). Physician and public health official. He began a private practice in New York City in 1836. Appointed city inspector in 1842, he wrote the influential report *The Sanitary Condition of the Laboring Population of New York* (1845). During the following years he became a leader in the movement for public health and sanitation reform. Among the measures that he advocated was the establishment of a powerful, professionally staffed board of health that would systematically collect vital statistics and other data. Griscom was a founding member of both the New York Academy of Medicine and the New York Medical and Surgical Society. He was also a physician at New York Hospital from 1843 until about 1870.

Charles E. Rosenberg and Carroll Smith-Rosenberg, "Pietism and the Origins of the American Public Health Movement: A Note on John H. Griscom and Robert M. Hartley," *Journal of the History of Medicine and Allied Sciences* 23 (1968), 16–35

Allen J. Share

grocers. Most food in colonial New York City was sold by vendors in public markets. One of the first such markets opened on Pearl Street in lower Manhattan in 1656; more elaborate ones also opened but eventually were superseded by small shops. As the population grew during the first half of the nineteenth century, more specialized shops sold produce, baked goods, meat, fish, dairy products, spirits, coffee, or tea. In 1882 James Butler opened a grocery store on Second Avenue; he had 200 stores that grossed $15 million annually and 1100 stores by 1934. Chain grocery stores were introduced in the first decades of the twentieth century, and the most important ones had their own warehouses, distribution networks, and manufacturing plants by the 1920s. In August 1930 the King Kullen Grocery Store was opened by Michael J. Cullen at 171st Street and Jamaica Avenue in Queens. Considered by many the first supermarket in the country, it had ample parking and was large and well stocked with a wide assortment of foods. It kept costs low by furnishing its stores sparsely and having customers serve themselves. Other stores adopted Cullen's methods and transformed the retail food industry, which operated with lower margins and higher turnover than formerly and became more efficient and profitable. Supermarkets also took advantage of improvements in food processing, packaging, preservation, and distribution. By the 1940s most large chains such as A&P had adopted Cullen's methods. After World War II there was fierce competition in the city among such large chains as A&P, D'Agostino, Daitch, Pathmark, Pioneer, and Waldbaum. As their marketing techniques became increasingly sophisticated, supermarkets came to rely less on display advertising in newspapers and more on circulars and broadcast advertising. There were also several large cooperative and independent supermarket groups, as well as small-scale convenience stores, "mom and pops," and bodegas, the last of which began to gain popularity in the 1970s as a growing influx of Hispanic immigrants began to open individually owned small grocery stores, often with signature red and yellow awnings. Several gourmet grocery stores have opened in recent decades: Dean and Deluca (1977), Whole Foods (2001), and Trader Joe's (2006). In the early twenty-first century supermarkets accounted for about 63 percent of retail food sales in New York City.

Richard S. Tedlow, *New and Improved: The Story of Mass Marketing in America* (New York: Basic Books, 1990), 182–258

Peter A. Coclanis

Grolier Club. Club formed in 1884 by nine business and cultural figures who were collectors of books and prints. Named for the sixteenth-century French bibliophile Jean Grolier, its purpose was to encourage "literary study and the arts of the book." During its first century the club had more than 3000 members, mounted more than 600 imaginative exhibitions on diverse topics, published about 150 books, and held a large number of lectures and symposia in its impressive clubhouses. The first of these was in rented quarters; the second was built for the club at 29 East 32nd Street and is a designated landmark. The present building, designed by Bertram Grosvenor Goodhue, a member of the club, was completed in 1917 at 47 East 60th Street and enlarged in 1984.

James E. Mooney

Grosset and Dunlap. Firm of book publishers formed in 1898 as Dunlap and Grosset, a bookshop at 11 East 16th Street, by Alexander Grosset and George T. Dunlap. The name was changed to Alexander Grosset and Company when Dunlap left in 1899, and then to Grosset and Dunlap on his return in the following year. The first books published were pirated editions of Rudyard Kipling, most of which were already in the public domain because they had been republished earlier by other firms. In the first decade of the twentieth century the firm began the practice of reissuing the paperbound books of other publishers in hardcover form and managed to sell the new hardcover editions at prices not much higher than those of the original paperbound editions. This innovation made it one of the leading reprint publishers in the United States. In 1903 it moved its offices to 52 Duane Street, and in 1907 it expanded into children's books by purchasing the firm of Chatterton and Peck, thus acquiring the rights to the Rover Boys series by Edward Stratemeyer, which sold more than five million copies; it later published popular children's series based on the characters Tom Swift, the Bobbsey Twins, the Hardy Boys, and Nancy Drew.

In 1910 the firm moved its offices and manufacturing operations to 518 West 26th Street and opened a retail shop on 26th Street and Broadway (moved in 1916 to 1140 Broadway). It introduced such techniques as selling books at newsstands, drugstores, and department stores; made extensive use of retail displays and posters; and was among the first publishers to coordinate the publication of popular novels with the release of their film versions. When Grosset died in 1934, Dunlap became president of the firm, which in 1939 moved to 1107 Broadway. In 1945 the firm joined with the Curtis Company, a nationwide book distributor, to form the paperback publisher Bantam Books, of which it became the sole owner in 1964. Grosset and Dunlap and Bantam were acquired in 1968 by the National General Corporation, which in 1974 sold Grosset to Filmways and Bantam to IFI International. In 1978 Grosset and Dunlap ranked third in hardcover sales and remained an important publisher of children's books, but in the next few years sales declined markedly. The firm was sold to the Putnam Publishing Group in 1982. In 1996 the Putnam Group was acquired by the Penguin Group. The offices are at 345 Hudson Street.

See also Book publishing.

Marjorie Harrison

Ground Zero. Term used to refer to the site of the World Trade Center after the terrorist attacks of 11 September 2001 (see September 11). It was first used in print by a *New York Times* reporter in 1946 writing of the nuclear bombs that destroyed Hiroshima and Nagasaki at the end of World War II.

Group Theatre. Experimental theater group formed in 1931 by Harold Clurman, Cheryl Crawford, and Lee Strasberg, members of the Theatre Guild. Modeled on the Moscow Art Theatre and influenced by the teaching methods of Konstantin Stanislavsky, it was intended to be a permanent acting company with a repertory that would involve more than aesthetics—it would create a tradition of common values. Initial members included Stella Adler, Clifford Odets, J. Edward Bromberg, Sanford Meisner (later a director and acting teacher), and Morris Carnovsky and Franchot Tone of the Theatre Guild; the first directors were Clurman, Crawford, and Strasberg. The initial production was Paul Green's play *The House of Connelly.* Under Strasberg's direction and the auspices of the Theatre Guild, the play was well received at its premiere at the Martin Beck Theatre on 23 September 1931. Others who soon became members were Adler's brother Luther Adler, Margaret Barker, Phoebe Brand, Lee J. Cobb, Frances Farmer, Jules Garfield (later known as John Garfield), Elia Kazan, Ruth Nelson, and Art Smith; Sylvia Sidney and Jane Wyatt performed occasionally, and Boris Aronson often designed sets. They developed a style of acting called "the Method." Members were paid whether or not they performed and regardless of the size of their parts. During its leanest year, 1932–33, the group even rented a 10-room walk-up apartment on West 57th Street. There was also talk of opening a restaurant.

Critics applauded the group's innovative approach, and they introduced more than 20 new American plays by the most influential writers of the day, including Maxwell Anderson (*Night over Taos,* 1932, 48th Street Theatre), John Howard Lawson (*Success Story,* 1932, Maxine Elliot Theatre; *Gentlewoman,* 1934, Cort Theatre), Green and Kurt Weill (*Johnny Johnson,* 1936, 44th Street Theatre), Irwin Shaw (*Quiet City,* 1938, Belasco Theatre, score by Aaron Copland; *The Gentle People,* 1939, Belasco Theatre), and William Saroyan (*My Heart's in the Highlands,* 1939, Guild Theatre). The most important playwright was Odets, whose first play, *Awake and Sing!,* was performed in 1935 at the Belasco Theatre. He achieved critical success with *Waiting for Lefty,* a one-act play inspired by a strike of the city's taxi drivers in 1934. On its opening night at the Civic Repertory Theatre, 6 January 1935, the audience rose to its feet chanting "Strike! Strike!" as the main character, a strike leader, called to his workers. Within months the play was performed by leftist groups nationwide and by the Group Theatre in London, where it was an overwhelming success. The production was also an important example of the kind of cooperation between actors and the audience that the company sought to inspire.

The Group Theatre earned critical and commercial success with Odets's *Golden Boy* (1937, Belasco Theatre). In 1937 Strasberg and Crawford resigned, disheartened by the defection to Hollywood of such members as Clurman, Tone, Garfield, and Odets. The actor Bobby Lewis briefly ran the Group Theatre School (or Studio) in 1937–38 and Clurman soon returned. Despite its many successes, the Group Theatre never made enough money to establish a permanent company. Among its last productions were Shaw's *Retreat to Pleasure* (1940, Belasco Theatre, directed by Clurman) and Odets's *Rocket to the Moon* (1938, Belasco Theatre) and *Night Music* (1940, Broadhurst Theatre). Odets's *Clash by Night* (1941, Belasco Theatre, directed by Strasberg) is sometimes identified as the last production by the Group Theatre, but it was produced by Billy Rose with only two of the company's actors, and the name of the Group Theatre was deleted from the playbill. In 1941 the Group Theatre ceased operations.

Harold Clurman, *The Fervent Years: The Story of the Group Theatre and the Thirties* (New York: Alfred A. Knopf, 1945); Cindy Adams, *Lee Strasberg: The Imperfect Genius of the Actors Studio* (Garden City, N.Y.: Doubleday, 1980); Elia Kazan, *A Life* (New York: Alfred A. Knopf, 1988); Wendy Smith, *Real Life Drama: The Group Theatre and America, 1931–1940* (New York: Alfred A. Knopf, 1990)

Grove Press. Firm of book publishers formed in 1948 on Grove Street by John Balcomb and Robert Phelps and purchased in 1951 by Barnet Rosset. It initially published reprints of the classics but early on began to acquire the rights to foreign works, including those of Samuel Beckett, Marguerite Duras, Jean Genet, André Gide, Eugène Ionesco, and Alain Robbe-Grillet. During the 1950s and early 1960s it published banned works of D. H. Lawrence and Henry Miller over which it fought and won important obscenity cases. It also published the *Evergreen Review* from 1957 to 1973. Grove Press was acquired in 1985 by Ann Getty, who was later joined by George Weidenfeld. In the early 1990s the firm merged with the Atlantic Monthly Press.

Montana Katz

Grymes Hill. Neighborhood in northeastern Staten Island, overlooking Upper New York Bay and bounded to the northwest by Victory Boulevard, to the east by Richmond Road and Van Duzer Street, to the south by the Staten Island Expressway, and to the west by Clove Road. It is one of three hills in the northern half of the borough and is bisected by Howard Avenue. Major George Howard bought the hill in 1830, and in 1836 it became the home of Mme. Suzette Grymes, the widow of the first governor of Louisiana; Jacob Vanderbilt also lived in the area during the nineteenth century. Horrmann Castle was built about this time. The mansion of William Greene Ward, a general in the Civil War, and that of the Cunard family became the campus of Wagner College in 1918. Notre Dame Academy opened in 1903 on the Wendt estate. In 1938 Notre Dame College bought the estate of John H. Gans, a shipping tycoon, and had a campus on the premises until 1971, when the land was taken over by the Staten Island branch of St. John's University. In the 1980s there was a modest settlement of immigrants from India, Korea, the Philippines, Honduras, and Yugoslavia. Housing developments in Grymes Hill include apartment buildings overlooking Silver Lake and the 12-story Sunrise Towers Condominiums facing the Staten Island Expressway. In the early twenty-first century much of the neighborhood remains generally upper middle to upper class and white.

Harlow McMillen

Guardian Angels. Volunteer crime-fighting organization of young men and women, formed by Curtis Sliwa (*b* New York City, 1954) in February 1979 as the Magnificent 13 subway safety patrol. Members adopted a uniform of T-shirts and red berets and rode the subways to deter crime, making citizen's arrests when necessary. The group took its current name by September of that year, and membership eventually exceeded 1000. The organization caused debate between those who cited improvements in community empowerment and safety and others critical of vigilantism. In 1995 group member Gabriel Hatcher founded CyberAngels, an online "neighborhood watch" and Internet safety education program. In the early twenty-first century the Guardian Angels has more than 100 chapters in the United States and abroad and makes its headquarters at 717 Fifth Avenue.

James Hawkins, *The Guardian Angels* (Hillside, N.J.: Enslow, 1983); Dennis J. Kenney, *Crime, Fear and New York City Subways: The Role of Citizen Action* (New York: Praeger, 1987)

Grai St. Clair Rice

Guardian Life Insurance Company of America. Firm of insurers formed on 10 July 1860 as the Germania Life Insurance Company to sell life insurance to German-speaking customers. The principal figure behind its formation was Hugo Wesendonck (1817–1900), a former member of the Frankfurt Parliament and a participant in its rump session who had fled Germany to escape a death sentence and settled in New York City as a political refugee in December 1849. He recruited for the Board of Directors a distinguished group of German-born New Yorkers that included the financier and diplomat August Belmont, the publisher Oswald Ottendorfer, the brewer Maximilian Schaefer, and the financier Joseph Seligman; he was also the first president of the firm (1860–97). The largest single holder of the firm's initial stock was his brother Otto Wesendonck, better known as a friend and benefactor of the composer Richard Wagner. With the onset of World War I, any identification with Germany became a distinct disadvantage: the firm ceased writing policies in Europe in December 1917 and on 1 March 1918 abandoned its original name in favor of its current one. Stock owned by German citizens was seized by the federal government and auctioned off in 1919. In the early twenty-first century the firm had its headquarters at 7 Hanover Square in downtown Manhattan.

Anita Rapone, *The Guardian Life Insurance Company, 1860–1920: A History of a German–American Enterprise* (New York: New York University Press, 1987)

Theresa Collins

Guggenheim, Meyer (*b* Langnau, Switzerland, 1 Feb 1828; *d* Palm Beach, Fla., 15 March 1905). Businessman and philanthropist. He moved to Philadelphia in 1848 and worked with his father Simon Guggenheim as a peddler of stove polish. Meyer later became wealthy as a lace and embroidery retailer, a coffee importer, and an investor in railroads, mining, and smelting. He gave equal partnership to his sons, Isaac, Daniel, Murry, Solomon, Benjamin, Simon, and William. In 1888 Meyer moved to New York City, where he lived at 36 West 77th Street and invested in a smelting firm, Guggenex. He amassed a fortune in copper, tin, gold, diamonds, nitrates, and rubber. Among the many charities he supported were The Mount Sinai Hospital and the New York Botanical Garden. His granddaughter Peggy became an important patron of modern art, Solomon conceived the Guggenheim Museum, and Simon was elected to the U.S. Senate from Colorado.

George J. Lankevich

Guggenheim, Peggy [Marguerite] (*b* New York City, 26 Aug 1898; *d* Composampiero, Italy, 23 Dec 1979). Art collector. After spending nearly 20 years abroad, learning about avant-garde art in Paris and establishing the Guggenheim Jeune, a gallery for modern art in London, she returned to New York City in 1941. A year later, she opened the Art of This Century gallery at 30 West 57th Street, which featured contemporary European and American artists such as Jackson Pollock, Mark Rothko, and Robert Motherwell until the gallery closed in 1947. After 1946 Guggenheim returned to Europe, where she established the Peggy Guggenheim Collection, housed in the Palazzo Venier dei Leoni in Venice, Italy. Her collection, which contained more than 260 works, exhibited cubist, surrealist, and abstract expressionist art and was one of the few galleries in Europe that included significant amounts of work by American artists. She bequeathed her holdings, estimated at $30 million, to her uncle's Solomon R. Guggenheim Foundation, with the proviso that the Peggy Guggenheim Collection in Venice remained intact. Her memoirs include *Out of This Century: Confessions of an Art Addict* (1946).

Stephanie Miller

Guggenheim Museum. See Solomon R. Guggenheim Museum.

guidebooks. Guides to New York City reflect continuously changing attitudes toward the city, as well as stages in its growth. The city's rise to commercial preeminence after the War of 1812 was confirmed by the appearance of competing guidebooks for visiting merchants published by A. T. Goodrich (1818) and Edmund M. Blunt (1828). Some guides for commercial visitors began to specialize according to trade; commercial and professional directories replaced several early guides. By 1860 New York City had grown so complex and its population was so large (more than 800,000) that general guidebooks found a market with local residents as well as business visitors. *Appleton's New York City and Vicinity Guide* provided thorough, brief accounts of places and institutions through a series of editions from 1849 to the 1890s; it was widely imitated. *King's Handbook of New York City: An Outline, History and Description of the American Metropolis* (1891 and later), edited by Moses King (1853–1909), offered a profusely illustrated, comprehensive guide to the city; its companion, *Views of New York* (1896; in later editions *Views of New York and Brooklyn*), was perhaps the most complete early portfolio of photographic views of the city. Population growth also inspired a new kind of guide, intended to provide a sense of moral order. George G. Foster's *New York by Gas-Light* (1850; repr. 1990), perhaps the first work of this kind, aimed at rural and small-town Protestants who confronted new ethical dilemmas and a loss of community in the new metropolis. After the Civil War many works created a "moral map" of the city, identifying areas plagued by crime, vice, and political corruption and populated by immigrants or the newly wealthy, and assigning degrees of moral "light" and "darkness" to each; a notable example is James D. McCabe, Jr.'s *Light and Shadows of New York Life; or, Sights and Sensations of the Great City* (1868). Churchmen responded with such guides as *The Catholic Churches of New York City* (1878) by John Gilmary Shea and *Handbook of Sociological Information with Especial Reference to New York City* (1894) by William Howe Tolman and William Hull; following the lead of businessmen, professional social workers transformed such guides into the comprehensive annual *Charities Directory.*

Nostalgic works on old landmarks, old streets, and "old New York" in general became popular in the 1880s, when the then-250-year-old city was beginning to develop its modern skyline. The first guides designed not so much for the business traveler or resident as for the tourist included Robert Shackleton's illustrated *Book of New York* (1917) and *Rider's New York City: A Guide for Travellers* (1916). By the 1920s tourists supported distinct guides to architecture, sculpture, art, and literature. Jacob A. Riis's *How the Other Half Lives* (1890) and Hutchins Hapgood's *The Spirit of the Ghetto: Studies of the Jewish Quarter of New York* (1902) served not only as works of social analysis but also as guides to immigrant neighborhoods. By the 1930s members of minority groups and immigrants were writing descriptions of their own communities for a general audience, such as James Weldon Johnson's *Black Manhattan* (1930) and Konrad Bercovici's *Around the World in New York* (1938), which provided an account of every ethnic neighborhood in the city. The new, more inclusive sensibility influenced the *New York City Guide* (1939), prepared by the Writers' Project of the Works Progress Administration, one of few general guidebooks to note the locations of union halls and famous strikes and to provide sympathetic and full descriptions of middle- and lower-income neighborhoods. Kate Simon's *New York Places and Pleasures* (4 edns, 1959–71) emphasized authenticity and gave detailed descriptions of streetscapes, little-known neighborhoods, museums, and commercial establishments, and the *AIA Guide to New York City* (1967; 3rd edn 1988), edited by Norval White and Elliot Willensky, earned a reputation as a comprehensive guide to architecture; both remained popular into the twenty-first century, as did Gerald R. Wolfe's *New York: A Guide to the Metropolis: Walking Tours of Architecture and History* (1975; 2nd edn 1994).

Almost all the guidebooks of the 1980s, 1990s, and 2000s were designed for the tourist and consumer, such as *New York in Flashmaps* (1991) and R. S. Wurman's more complete *NYC Access* (1991), which detail the location, opening times, and cost of museums, shops, restaurants, theaters, and other amusements. Many fields have specialized guidebooks, including *Museums in New York, Secret New York, Kids' Guide to New York City,* and *The Audubon Guide to Finding Birds.* Guides to restaurants are published by the *New York Times,* Seymour Britchky, and Zagat; among the guidebooks to landmarks and historic sights are the Green Guides published by Michelin (1968–) and the *Blue Guide New York* (1983; 2nd edn 1991) by Carol von Pressentin Wright. One of the more unusual guides to the city is *Permanent New Yorkers: A Biographical Guide to the Cemeteries of New York* (1987), by Judi Culbertson and Tom Randall.

Other important historical guides to the city include I. N. Phelps Stokes's *The Iconography of Manhattan Island, 1498–1909* (1915–28; repr. 1967), John Atlee Kouwenhoven's *The Columbia Historical Portrait of New York* (1953), Moses Rischin's *The Promised City: New York's Jews, 1870–1914* (1962), and Nathan Silver's *Lost New York* (1967; repr. 1982).

David C. Hammack

Guinan, Texas [Mary Louise Cecilia] (*b* Waco, Tex., 12 Jan 1884; *d* Vancouver, Canada, 5 Nov 1933). Nightclub manager. After a career as a bronco rider and vaudeville performer she moved in 1923 to New York City, where illegal nightclubs flourished during Prohibition. In the subsequent year she opened the El Fay Club with backing from the organized-crime figure Larry Fay, and during the following decade she managed more than a dozen nightclubs in midtown. She became known for her flamboyant personality; her wardrobe of huge hats, ermine wraps, and garish jewelry (one bracelet had 586 diamonds); and her colorful speech (she greeted her customers with "Hello, suckers!" and originated the phrase "Give the l'il girl a great big hand"). Her nightclub troupes included such well-known performers as Ruby Keeler and Clare Luce. Guinan is buried in Calvary Cemetery in Queens.

Louise Berliner, *Texas Guinan, Queen of the Night Clubs* (Austin: University of Texas Press, 1993)

Warren Sloat

Gulf and Western. Industrial firm that later became Paramount Communications.

Gulick, Luther (Halsey, III) (*b* Osaka, Japan, 17 Jan 1892; *d* Greensboro, Vt., 10 Jan 1993). Reformer. He received a PhD in political science from Columbia University (1920). From 1921 to 1961 he led the Institute of Public Administration in New York City, and President Franklin D. Roosevelt appointed him to the Committee on Administrative Management, which issued a report in 1937 that inspired a comprehensive reorganization of the federal government. He was also the executive director of the Committee on Management Survey (1950–52) formed by Mayor William O'Dwyer to plan the reorganization of the city government, the city administrator (1954–55), and a member of the State Commission on Governmental Operations of the City of New York (from 1959).

Bernard Hirschhorn

Gun Hill. Neighborhood in the northwestern Bronx, lying within the neighborhood of Norwood and centered on Gun Hill Road between Jerome Avenue and the Bronx River. The name dates to the Revolutionary War, when the Americans dragged cannons to the area from the Battery for safekeeping; the cannons were spiked by Tories and took 11 months to repair. Gun Hill Road, an old Indian trail, was used from the colonial period onward as a vital artery to the King's Bridge. The northernmost part of the area was used for dairy farming in the nineteenth century before being purchased in 1863 as the site of Woodlawn Cemetery. In 1912 Montefiore Hospital opened as a home for tubercular patients on the crest of the hill at Bainbridge Avenue. The completion in 1917 of the Woodlawn line of Interborough Rapid Transit along Jerome Avenue led to the construction of apartment buildings in the 1920s that attracted many Jewish and Irish residents. In the 1980s African American and Latin American families began moving into the neighborhood.

John McNamara, *History in Asphalt: The Origin of Bronx Street and Place Names* (New York: Bronx County Historical Society, 1984)

Elizabeth Beirne

Gunther, Charles Godfrey (*b* New York City, 7 Feb 1822; *d* New York City, 22 Jan 1885). Mayor. The son of wealthy German immigrants, he was a successful merchant in New York City. Through wealth and friendships he became active in the Democratic Party; he helped to form the Democratic Union Club and was a member of the Young Men's Democratic Committee and the president of the almshouse governors in the city. He failed to win election as mayor in 1861 but succeeded in 1863 and served until 1866. His victory demonstrated the independent power of the German Union Democratic Party, which assembled a reform coalition and established itself as a force in Manhattan politics. After briefly concentrating on business as a railroad executive, he unsuccessfully sought a seat in the state senate. He is buried at the Green-Wood Cemetery in Brooklyn.

Stephen D. Engle

Guston [Goldstein], **Philip** (*b* Montreal, 27 July 1913; *d* Woodstock, N.Y., 7 June 1980). Painter. A self-taught artist who began painting at the age of 14, he completed a number of politically charged works during the Great Depression and moved to New York City in 1936 as an artist under the Works Project Administration. He, alongside Mark Rothko, Adolph Gottlieb, and Robert Motherwell, was a member of the New York School, which was dedicated to contemporary art, particularly Guston's specialty of abstract expressionism in and around New York City during the 1940s and 1950s. As abstract expressionism gained notoriety within the city, Guston was featured in solo and group exhibitions at the Solomon R. Guggenheim Museum and the Jewish Museum in the mid-1960s. In 1965 he helped establish the New York Studio School for Drawing and Painting. Concerned with what he saw as the power of the New York art critics to influence art and painting, in the late 1960s Guston made an abrupt change in genres, from painting largely abstract pieces to figurative works that portrayed domestic items such as light bulbs, shoes, cigarettes, and clocks. In 1970 the New York Marlborough Gallery featured an exhibition of his figurative paintings, which signified his irreversible conversion to the genre of figurative art. His later compositions often portrayed enigmatic hooded figures, bearing similarity to one of his early paintings, *Conspirators* (*ca* 1930), which depicts a member of the Ku Klux Klan.

Joanna Weber, *Philip Guston: A New Alphabet, the Late Transition* (New Haven: Yale University Art Gallery, 2000)

Stephanie Miller

Guthrie, Woody [Woodrow Wilson] (*b* Okemah, Okla., 14 July 1912; *d* New York City, 3 Oct 1967). Folksinger and songwriter. He grew up in Oklahoma and moved to New York City in 1940, where folk music had become well established. From the early 1940s he performed in barrooms and union halls and at political rallies and marches. He served in the U.S. Merchant Marines from 1943 to 1945 and after World War II returned to the city, where he lived in Coney Island. He wrote and adapted more than 1000 songs, many of which are about the struggles of the poor in the United States, the labor movement, and the hardships of the Dust Bowl and the Depression. One of his best-known songs is

"This Land Is Your Land"; he also wrote *Songs to Grow On* for children. After 15 years of affliction with Huntington's chorea he died at Creedmoor State Hospital in Queens. Guthrie was perhaps the most important figure of his day for folksingers of later generations, especially Bob Dylan, who emulated his music and his personal style; the folk music centered in Greenwich Village during the mid-1990s also had its origins in Guthrie's work. He lived at various locations in New York City: in 1940–41 at 130 West 10th Street in Manhattan, in 1942 at 148 West 14th Street, in 1942–43 at 74 Charles Street, in 1943 at 3755 Cypress Avenue in Brooklyn, in 1943–50 at 3520 Mermaid Avenue in Coney Island, in 1950–52 at Beach Haven Apartments (at 59 Murdoch Court in Gravesend), and from 1952 to the end of his life at 15913 85th Street in Howard Beach. He wrote the memoir *Bound for Glory* (1943).

Henrietta Yurchenko, *A Mighty Hard Road: The Woody Guthrie Story* (New York: McGraw–Hill, 1970); Joe Klein, *Woody Guthrie: A Life* (New York: Alfred A. Knopf, 1980)

Barbara L. Tischler

Guy, Francis (*b* Lorton, England, 1760; *d* Brooklyn, 1820). Painter. Trained as a tailor and dyer of fabrics, he came to America in 1795 and established a silk-dyeing business in Baltimore, Maryland. He picked up landscape and seascape painting and about 1817 moved to Brooklyn and settled in a house on Front Street. In the last months of his life, in 1819 and early 1820, Guy placed his easel near an upstairs window and produced two streetscapes titled *Winter Scene in Brooklyn*. One is now in the collection of the Brooklyn Museum. Besides providing true-to-life images of his neighbors (one is seen slipping on the ice), the paintings show old Brooklyn and New York City before the financial, economic, and immigration booms of the 1830s and 1840s transformed them permanently into cities. He was buried in the churchyard of the Sands Street Methodist Church (whose steeple can be seen in the far distance of the painting). After the church was sold to make way for the Brooklyn Bridge, his remains were transferred to the Evergreens Cemetery in Bushwick.

John Rousmaniere

Guyanese. Emigration from the South American state of Guyana to the United States was on such a small scale until the late 1960s that the Immigration and Naturalization Service did not keep separate statistics for it. The annual number of documented Guyanese immigrants rose to about 2000 in the early 1970s and about 10,000 in the 1980s and early 1990s. In 1980 there were 32,000 Guyanese in New York City. About 73,000 Guyanese were admitted for legal residence in the 1990s, during which undocumented immigrants were estimated to be as high as 210,000 to 250,000. Emigrants from Guyana of Chinese and Indian descent moved to the city to escape discrimination by the government of Forbes Burnham, which took power in 1964 and was largely controlled by Guyanese of African descent. By the early 1990s Guyanese of Indian origin accounted for 65 percent of the Guyanese community in the city and about half of recent immigrants; this group included mostly Hindus and some Muslims, who settled in Indian neighborhoods near the Grand Concourse, in Jamaica and Richmond Hill, and along Euclid and Crescent avenues in Brooklyn. The rest of the community was of African descent, mostly Methodist, Anglican, and Catholic, and lived in neighborhoods with other West Indian groups along Atlantic Avenue and to the south toward Foster Avenue and Flatbush Avenue in Brooklyn. The two groups have little contact in New York City. Many Guyanese professionals were among the immigrants; those unable to obtain permanent resident status and recertify in their professions often worked as domestic servants and in service industries and manufacturing. In 2000 Guyanese accounted for the third largest group of newcomers to New York City, with more than 130,000 people. Large communities existed in Richmond Hill (more than 30,000), Morris Heights, and Woodhaven.

Graciela M. Castex

Gypsies [Roma]. A name commonly but inaccurately applied to the Roma, or Romani, a people of Indian descent. The details of their ancestry and the time of their exodus toward the West (believed to be about A.D. 1000) remain unclear. The first specific reference to Gypsies in New York City was in the *New York Times* of 8 July 1852 noting that two Gypsy brothers from England arrived in the city in 1851. The first large-scale Gypsy migration from Europe was that from Serbia in the 1890s, which was brought about by government restrictions there on nomadism. Gypsies circumvented U.S. immigration laws by identifying themselves by their nationality rather than as Gypsies, and Gypsies from each European country tended to live in the same areas as other immigrants from the same country. Many settled at first with other Balkan immigrants on the Lower East Side, in an area bounded by First and Ninth streets, Avenue A, and the East River. After World War I large numbers of Gypsies from the Austro–Hungarian Empire settled initially on Fifth, Sixth, and Ninth streets on the East Side before leaving for Chicago and elsewhere during the 1920s. Gypsies moved to New York City from other parts of the United States after various relief programs were put into effect during the 1930s, and from Hungary after the revolution of 1956. In the 1970s and 1980s Muslim Gypsies from southern Yugoslavia settled in the Bronx, and in the early 1990s a sharp increase in attacks on Gypsies in eastern Europe brought growing numbers of refugees to the city. Gypsies in Greater New York are descended principally from liberated slaves and are known as the Vlax Roma; during the first four decades of the twentieth century most Vlax Roma in Manhattan belonged to the Kalderash, an ethnic division of the Gypsies concentrated in Russia. The Machvaya Vlax, from Serbia, settled in Brooklyn but after World War II moved into Manhattan in increasing numbers. The Lovari Vlax, from Hungary, settled for the most part in Newark, New Jersey.

Rena Gropper, *Gypsies in the City: Culture Patterns and Survival* (New York: Darwin, 1975); Ian F. Hancock, *The Pariah Syndrome: An Account of Gypsy Slavery and Persecution* (Ann Arbor, Mich.: Karoma, 1987)

Ian Hancock

Gyp the Blood [Horowitz, Harry] (*b* 1889; *d* Ossining, N.Y., 13 April 1914). Gangster and leader of the infamous Lenox Avenue Gang. Despite his small size, Horowitz was vicious and violent, supposedly willing to break a man's back over his knee on a two dollar bet. On 15 July 1912, Horowitz and three members of his gang murdered gambler Herman "Beansie" Rosenthal outside the Metropole Hotel at 147 West 43rd Street in Manhattan, allegedly at the request of New York City Police Detective Lieutenant Charles Becker. The case received sensational coverage in William Randolph Hearst's newspapers. This incident is said to have been the first use of a get-away car, a gray Packard. Horowitz was convicted of murder and executed at Sing Sing prison.

Anne Epstein

H

Häagen-Dazs. Ice cream brand concocted by Polish-born Reuben Mattus (1912–94). As a youth in the Bronx he delivered his mother's homemade ices and ice cream to local retailers. In 1936 Mattus married Rose Vesel, who would later develop the marketing of Häagen-Dazs. In the late 1950s Reuben created an ice cream with more butterfat and less air than the product then typically sold in supermarkets. He gave it a meaningless, foreign-sounding name. Häagen-Dazs ice cream went on sale in three flavors: vanilla, chocolate, and coffee. Daughter Doris opened the first Häagen-Dazs scoop shop in Brooklyn Heights in 1976. In 1983 Pillsbury bought the business for $70 million; Häagen-Dazs is now owned by General Mills.

Cathy Alexander

Hadassah. Women's volunteer organization formed in 1912 at Temple Emanu-El in New York City by Henrietta Szold and others to provide public health nursing in Palestine. It is the oldest and largest women's Zionist organization in the world. In 1913 it sent two nurses to Palestine to open a maternity center in Jerusalem, and in 1934 it founded Youth Aliyah to rescue German youths (of whom 4300 made their way to Palestine by the end of the war). Hadassah is committed to health care, Jewish education, and women's issues. It operates a teaching hospital and medical school affiliated with the Hebrew University in Jerusalem, as well as many clinics throughout Israel. At its headquarters in Manhattan the organization maintains an extensive film library documenting its projects and publishes *Hadassah* magazine. In the early twenty-first century Hadassah had more than 300,000 members, including 10,000 in New York City.

Donald Miller, "A History of Hadassah New York" (diss., New York University, 1968); Marlin Levy, *Balm in Gilead: The Story of Hadassah* (New York: Schocken, 1973); Carol B. Kutscher, "The Early Years of Hadassah: 1912–1921" (diss., Brandeis University, 1976)

Jean Ulitz Mensch

Hagstrom Map Company. Company founded in 1916 in New York City by Andrew G. Hagstrom (1890–1977). It began with maps of the neighborhoods and boroughs of newly consolidated Greater New York and ultimately offered atlases, American city street guides, pocket maps, and New York City specialty maps, including the first complete map of the New York City Rapid Transit System and "How to Get In and Out of New York by Automobile." In the early twenty-first century Hagstrom is part of the Langenscheidt Publishing Group, a major publisher of maps in the United States.

Elizabeth L. Bradley

Haight, Charles C(oolidge) (*b* New York City, 17 March 1841; *d* Garrison, N.Y., 8 Feb 1917). Architect. The son of a rector at Trinity Church, he undertook many architectural commissions for clients associated with the church during the last quarter of the nineteenth century. His most notable designs include the midtown campus of Columbia University (1874–84, demolished), the quadrangle of the General Theological Seminary in Chelsea (1883–1902), the New York Cancer Hospital (1884–86, 1889–90) at 455 Central Park West, Trinity School (1894) at 139 West 91st Street, and a series of warehouses for the Trinity Church Corporation near Canal Street. In his later years Haight designed the neo-Gothic Second Battalion, 105th Field Artillery Armory, in the Bronx (1910).

Marjorie Pearson

Haitians. During the Haitian revolution from 1791 to 1803, as many as 4000 whites, free blacks, and slaves fled St.-Domingue (now Haiti) and settled in New York City. Some settled at once in the city, while others went first to other countries (especially France) or to other colonies, including Jamaica, Trinidad, and Cuba. Although many Haitians had hopes of returning soon to Haiti to reclaim their property, after several years a few set up their own shipping businesses or opened boardinghouses, and some worked in shops owned by French businessmen who had fled to the city during the French Revolution. Most Haitians, however, did not speak English and could obtain only menial employment. The city gave shelter and financial aid to white refugees, about 300 of whom lived without charge in a government house on Vesey Street until they could move to their own quarters. This aid was not extended to black refugees.

During the first half of the nineteenth century, the Haitian population became well established in Manhattan. Many Haitians met after Sunday Mass at St. Peter's Church, 16 Barclay Street, to renew their friendships and discuss recent events in Haiti. On 10 August 1801 about 20 Haitian refugees led by Marcel Sam attempted to stage a riot to liberate Haitian slaves in the custody of Jeanne Mathusine Droibillan Volunbrun. Their efforts were aborted and they were arrested and each sentenced to 60 days in jail, despite legal aid provided by the Manumission Society. The best-known and most widely respected immigrant of the period was Pierre Toussaint, a former slave who became a professional hairdresser to upper-class women and children. With money from his business he supported the widow of his former master, bought freedom for other slaves, gave to Catholic charities, and helped orphaned, homeless, disabled, and sick people from many ethnic backgrounds. By 1850 a second generation of Haitians integrated into the social and economic life of the city. As marriages to blacks from different backgrounds became more common, Haitians lost some of their ethnic distinctness. By the turn of the twentieth century, political unrest and the *kako* (guerrilla) movement in Haiti resulted in much of the Haitian business and political elite, including Haitians of Syrian and Lebanese origin, fleeing to New York City.

Immigration increased during the U.S. occupation of Haiti (1915–34). Between 1916 and 1945 the Haitian community in New York City was notable for its diversity. Much of it was in Harlem and included students on scholarship at Teachers College who were expected to return to Haiti after completing their studies; business leaders who had lost their holdings to the kakos; and writers and artists attracted to the literary explosion of the Harlem Renaissance. In Harlem, liberals and Marxist politicians found a place where they could express their nationalist ideas and their discontent with the U.S. occupation. Some Haitians supported the Universal Negro Improvement Association (UNIA), the organization behind the "back to Africa" movement initiated by Marcus Garvey. Among its leaders were several Haitians, including Elie Garcia, who led a delegation of UNIA members to Liberia in 1920 and later became the secretary of the Black Star Line; and the activist Jean-Joseph Adam, who served as secretary and interpreter for a UNIA delegation to the League of Nations in Geneva in October 1922. One of the most influential Haitian activists in the city was Jacques Roumain, who lived in Harlem from 1939 to 1941, during which time he befriended black writers and activists in the Communist Party and participated in several important literary and political events; he was himself a communist and often discussed his ideas and projects with his friends Paul Robeson and Ralph Ellison at the home of Louise Thompson.

Between the two world wars, Haitian immigrants in Harlem were largely middle and upper class. Some formed Utilités d'Haïti, a firm that became very successful through importing Haitian goods into the U.S. market. They also organized several clubs, including Solidarité, the Club Aristocrate, the Club l'Arc-en-ciel, and the Club Clair de Lune, where they could reflect on their country, collect funds for various causes, and form social bonds that lessened the pain of racism. Even after the U.S. occupation in Haiti ended, Haitian political organizations continued to flourish in Harlem. One of these, the Association Démocratique Haïtienne, organized a memorial service for Roumain in May 1945.

From 1957 to 1986 most Haitian immigrants in New York City were political refugees who had fled the brutal dictatorships of François and Jean-Claude Duvalier. More than 34,000 Haitians moved to the city between 1983 and 1989, and the influx continued into the twenty-first century as political life in Haiti became chaotic and violence erupted in the streets there. Most who left during this time settled in Brooklyn, Manhattan, and Queens, with concentrations in Crown Heights, East Flatbush, the Upper West Side, and Cambria Heights. In these neighborhoods families opened many restaurants, barbershops, garages, grocery stores, record shops, bakeries, and various retail stores that catered to the Haitian population, often extending credit and speaking French or Creole during transactions. From the 1950s many Haitian women worked as domestics or in child care. A number of radio stations, television programs, and newspapers began to supply the Haitian community with information about events in New York City, in other Haitian communities overseas, and in Haiti itself. *Haïti-Observateur,* established in 1971 in the city, was the first weekly newspaper for Haitian émigrés. It developed a large distribution network in the United States, Canada, and France and was introduced in 1986 in Haiti itself, where it entered into competition with established local newspapers. *Haïti-Progrès* was first published in New York City in 1981, and more recently the Brooklyn-headquartered weekly newspaper *Haitian Times* published its first issue on 27 October 1999.

In 1986 many Haitians living in the city celebrated in the streets to mark the collapse of the government of Jean-Claude Duvalier. The community was also highly visible on 20 April 1990, when 100,000 Haitians blocked traffic in Brooklyn and lower Manhattan to protest the U.S. Food and Drug Administration's recommendation that blood banks reject donations from Haitian immigrants, who were presumed to be at a disproportionately high risk of carrying AIDS. At the same time Haitians with U.S. citizenship became active in government and politics: some were appointed to municipal agencies and others sought elective office at the city and state levels. On 24 April 2007, Mathieu Eugene, founder and executive director of Youth for Education and Sport, became the first Haitian American to be elected to the New York City Council, representing the 40th district in Brooklyn, which includes Crown Heights. Some city-based political organizations are affiliated with political parties in Haiti and lend financial and logistical support to candidates there. Likewise, candidates who vie for the Haitian office of the presidency campaign in Haitian American neighborhoods in search of financial contributions.

Haitian American hometown associations have served as engines of development for their respective villages because they sponsor projects (hospitals, schools, community buildings) in such Haitian localities. Hometown associations such as the Organization for the Development of Lascahobas, Comité de Support pour la Commune de Miragoâne, Solidarite Jacmelienne, Fraternité Valléenne, Association des Amis de Belle-Anse, Les Amis des Enfants de Lascahobas, and Organization for the Advancement of the Island of La Gonave actively collect funds to finance ongoing projects beneficial to their villages. While the activities of these organizations remain influenced by the homeland, community service centers such as the Haitian Centers Council, Flatbush Haitian Center, Haitian-Americans United for Progress, and Bedford Haitian Community Center attend to the needs of people in local neighborhoods.

The Catholic Church, a potent force in the Haitian American community, operates parish-based charitable organizations. Father Guy Sansaricq, born in Haiti in 1934, served for 22 years (1971–93) as a parochial vicar at Sacred Heart Parish in Cambria Heights and later as pastor at St. Jerome's Church in Brooklyn (1993–present). Pope Benedict XVI appointed him auxiliary bishop of Brooklyn on 6 June 2006. Haitian American Protestant churches, which provide social services and places of worship to their brethren, have contributed much to the community. Evangelical Crusade of Fishers of Men, which started in Brooklyn in 1973, is a leading example.

Two alleged cases of police brutality stunned the Haitian community in recent years. Members of the New York Police Department (NYPD) arrested Abner Louima, a 30-year-old Haitian American resident of Queens, after an incident at the Rendez-Vous nightclub on Brooklyn's Flatbush Avenue on 9 August 1997. The officers brought him to the 70th precinct station house. While handcuffed, he was taken to the bathroom of the facility and sodomized with a toilet plunger by two policemen. With a ruptured intestine and bruises over his body, he spent many weeks in a hospital and at home recuperating. On 27 February 1998 the court found five officers who participated in this ordeal guilty on several counts. The second case involved Patrick M. Dorismond, a 26-year-old unarmed and off-duty Haitian American security guard, who was shot by an undercover NYPD police officer while waiting in midtown Manhattan for a taxi on 16 March 2000. Amidst much protest from the larger African and Caribbean community, which declared the incident one of racism, a grand jury investigation concluded that this was an accidental shooting.

In January 2010 Port-au-Prince in Haiti was devastated by an earthquake. As the New York City Haitian community struggled to respond to the tragedy, Governor David A. Paterson and Mayor Michael R. Bloomberg in February announced the creation of the New York Haitian Earthquake Family Resource Center at the National Guard Armory at 1579 Bedford Avenue to provide daily reports on relief efforts; offer various legal services and grief counseling; and provide access to telephones and computers.

Michel S. Laguerre, *American Odyssey: Haitians in New York City* (Ithaca, N.Y.: Cornell University Press, 1984)

Michel S. Laguerre

Halberstam, David (*b* New York City, 10 April 1934; *d* Menlo Park, Calif., 23 April 2007). Author and journalist. Raised in the Bronx, he covered the civil rights movement for the *New York Times* during the 1960s. He also reported on the Vietnam War and won a Pulitzer Prize in 1964 for his work. Later in his career he shifted his focus to sports writing. He published several novels throughout his career, including *The Best and the Brightest* (1960), *The Next Century* (1991), and *Playing for Keeps* (1999). A lifelong New Yorker, he lived on the Upper West Side. He died in an automobile crash in the San Francisco area.

Jessica Montesano

Hale, Nathan (*b* Coventry, Conn., 6 June 1755; *d* New York City, 22 Sept 1776). Soldier and spy. After graduating from Yale College in 1773, he taught school for two years. He enlisted in the Connecticut militia as a lieutenant in 1775 and quickly rose to captain. Following the British victory in the Battle of Long Island in August 1776, Hale was selected for Knowlton's Rangers, a scouting unit headed by Colonel Thomas Knowlton, and volunteered to penetrate the British camp as a spy. He headed out in mid-September and was captured in Huntington, Long Island, on 21 September. He confessed to the British commander, General William Howe, that he had been spying and was hanged in Manhattan the next morning, probably at the intersection of what is now Third Avenue and East 66th Street. The words he is purported to have said before being hanged—"I only regret that I have but one life to lose for my country"—made him a hero of the American Revolution. A statue of Hale by Frederick MacMonnies was placed in City Hall Park in 1893.

Henry Phelps Johnston, *Nathan Hale 1776: Biography and Memorials* (New Haven: Yale University Press, 1916); George Dudley Seymour, *Documentary Life of Nathan Hale* (New Haven: privately printed, 1941)

Richard E. Mooney

Hale House Center. Facility for drug-addicted children at 152 West 122nd Street in Manhattan. It was opened in 1969 by Mother

(Clara M.) Hale (1905–92) to care for the infant of a drug addict and was later expanded and managed by Hale and her daughter Lorraine E. Hale, a physician. A building at Manhattan Avenue and 113th Street was converted into temporary housing for reunited families in 1985, and during the same year Mother Hale was honored by President Ronald Reagan. Preferring foster homes to group homes, municipal agencies in October 1989 stopped sending children to Hale House, but the center continued to provide residential child care for children younger than five and expanded its programs to include education. Lorraine Hale was forced to resign in 2001 after being indicted for misappropriating more than $1 million. Subsequent leadership restored the organization's finances and reputation.

Alana Erickson Coble

Half Moon Hotel. Located at West 29th Street and the Boardwalk on Coney Island, it was built in an effort to change Coney Island's image from a honky-tonk day trip destination to a classier seaside resort. The 16-story, 400-room Spanish Colonial style building was among the largest in Coney Island during the 1920s and 1930s. Billed as "the only New York City hotel on the Atlantic," the Half Moon served as a popular tourist destination despite being far from the principal amusement areas located toward the eastern end of the peninsula. The hotel gained a different kind of notoriety in 1941 when mobster-turned-informant Abe Reles fell to his death from a police-guarded sixth-floor room the night before he was to testify against high-ranking Mafia figures and members of Murder Incorporated. During World War II the navy used the building as a hospital, and after the war it became a civilian hospital. In 1954 it was converted into a nursing home by the Metropolitan Jewish Geriatric Center. The building was demolished in 1995 to make way for senior citizen housing on the site.

Ben Silk

Hall, A(braham) Oakey (*b* Albany, N.Y., 26 July 1826; *d* New York City, 7 Oct 1898). Mayor. He was district attorney of New York City as a Whig and then as a Republican during the 1850s. In 1862 he joined the Democratic Party and became an ally of William M. "Boss" Tweed. As mayor from 1868 to 1872 he became entangled in the scandals of the Tweed Ring and was twice indicted for corruption. Although he was eventually exonerated, his career was ruined, and he chose exile in London. Hall later returned to the United States.

Croswell Bowen, *The Elegant Oakey* (New York: Oxford University Press, 1956)

Jerome Mushkat

A. Oakey Hall

Hall, Cornelius A(loysius) (*b* Staten Island, 1889; *d* Staten Island, 5 March 1953). Borough president. Unlike most of his predecessors, who were mostly Republicans, he was an independent Democrat. During the 1930s he served as the commissioner of public works in Staten Island. As borough president of Staten Island from 1945 to 1953, Hall saw the Staten Island Ferry Terminal to completion in 1951.

Andrew Wiese

Hall, George (*b* New York City, 21 Sept 1795; *d* Brooklyn, 18 April 1868). First mayor of Brooklyn. A painter and glazier by trade, he belonged to the Temperance and Whig parties. He served as mayor for one year after the adoption of the municipal charter in 1834. After the city was enlarged by the annexation of Williamsburgh and Bushwick, he was elected in 1855 to a two-year term to the same office.

Ellen Fletcher

Hallett's Cove. Small settlement in northwestern Queens near the ferry landing at the foot of Astoria Boulevard. It was the site of one of Queens' earliest settlements, by Jacques Bentyn in 1638, who soon abandoned it. William Hallett, Sr., received this area as a land grant for 161 acres in 1652 from the Dutch. On 20 May 1721 Joseph Hallett donated some of his family's land to found the first local school. His family persists to this day, operating the Hallett Funeral Home in Flushing. The first ferry service from Manhattan to Long Island was from Horne's Hook (86th Street) to Hallett's Cove. Stephen A. Hasley wrote a resolution that in 1839 renamed the town Astoria, hoping that the town would enjoy the patronage of John Jacob Astor.

Vincent Seyfried, Henry Cooper

Hall of Fame for Great Americans. Monument in the Bronx, established to honor well-known Americans and dedicated on 30 May 1901 by Henry Mitchell MacCracken, president of New York University. It occupies a semicircular vaulted colonnade 630 feet (190 meters) long behind the Hall of Languages (1894), Gould Memorial Library (1899), and the Cornelius Baker Hall of Philosophy (1912) on the former campus of New York University. The first monument of its kind in the country, it relied on the public and an expert panel to choose its members. The first 29 members were honored with tablets designed by Tiffany Studios, and in 1907 the first of 97 busts was installed. In February 1966 the site was entered in the National Register of Historic Places. It fell under the jurisdiction of the City University of New York after the campus was taken over by Bronx Community College in 1973. Renovations costing $3 million were completed in 1985, but the last installation of a bust was that of Franklin Delano

The Hall of Fame for Great Americans, ca 1910, with the domed roof of Gould Memorial Library (designed by McKim, Mead and White) in the background

Roosevelt in 1992, and in the early twenty-first century the Hall of Fame remains financially troubled and largely ignored by the public.

George J. Lankevich

Hall of Records. Name until 1962 of the building at the corner of Chambers and Centre streets now known as the SURROGATE'S COURT.

Halloween Parade. Nation's largest public Halloween celebration. Officially titled New York's Village Halloween Parade and commonly known as the Greenwich Village Halloween Parade, it has occurred annually on Halloween night (October 31) since 1973 along a route that begins on Spring Street and runs straight up Sixth Avenue to 21st Street. It attracts approximately two million onlookers and 60,000 marchers dressed in creative costumes. The parade began when Ralph Lee, a Greenwich Village puppeteer and mask maker, planned a pageant for neighborhood children and their friends who marched from house to house. He eventually won a *Village Voice* Obie Award for his work with the event. Beginning in 1975, a local organization, Theater for the New City, took over the event to present the puppet show and parade on a larger scale. After 1979 Jeanne Fleming acted as the parade's artistic and producing director. By the twenty-first century it had grown into a nationally known event, respected for its contribution to the artistic and imaginative culture of New York City and providing a place for visual and performance artists to showcase their works.

Anne Epstein

Halpern, Moyshe-Leyb (*b* Zolochev, Galicia [now in Ukraine], 2 Jan 1886; *d* New York City, 31 Aug 1932). Poet. He immigrated to the United States in 1908 and soon had his first poems published in the Yiddish press in New York City. He led an itinerant and impoverished life and remained a largely independent figure among the Yiddish literati, though he was associated with the circle of writers known as the Yunge. In his two collections of verse, *In Nyu-york* (1919) and *Di goldene pave* (The Golden Peacock, 1924), he displays a distinctively direct and unsentimental voice capable of both lyric and imaginatively probing modern verse.

Ruth R. Wisse, *A Little Love in Big Manhattan* (Cambridge, Mass.: Harvard University Press, 1988)

Jeffrey Shandler

Hamburg–American Line. Firm of transatlantic shippers formed as the Hamburg-Amerikanische Paketfahrt Aktien-Gesellschaft (HAPAG) in Hamburg in 1847. It initially operated three copper-bottomed sailing ships including the *Deutschland,* which had a capacity of 220 passengers and first sailed for New York City on 15 October 1847. Monthly service between Hamburg and the city was offered from 1848; the average westbound sailing time was 41 days. The firm commissioned its first steamship, the *Borussia,* in 1856 and soon bought others because they were larger, safer, faster, and more comfortable than sailing ships. The finest ones, including the *Fürst Bismarck,* the *Augusta Victoria,* the *Normannia,* and the *Columbia* weighed at least 10,000 tons, had at least 13,000 horsepower, and could cross the Atlantic in as few as seven days. By 1897 HAPAG had opened lines to the Caribbean and South America and was the largest steamship company in the world. The largest and fastest ships were reserved for the American line, which had its offices at 37 Broadway and its main docking facilities in Hoboken, New Jersey. It provided service from Hamburg to Cherbourg, France, and Southampton, England, before docking in New York City and was crucial in encouraging immigration because it offered relatively inexpensive transatlantic fares. The line carried an average of 34,466 passengers a year from Hamburg to the city during the 1860s, 90,889 during the 1880s, and 60,041 during the 1890s. As the number of Germans immigrating to the United States declined before the turn of the twentieth century, southern and eastern Europeans accounted for an increasing number of the firm's passengers. HAPAG and its rival, North German Lloyd of Bremen, provided passage for a quarter of the European immigrants moving to the United States during 1906–7, and on its ships alone 150,633 emigrants sailed to New York City in 1907. Its largest steamships were admired throughout the world, among them the *Imperator* (1912), which registered 52,000 tons, had six decks, and carried 3,849 passengers. When much of the German merchant marine was seized by British and U.S. forces during World War I, the pride of the line, the *Vaterland* (1914), became an American troop carrier and was renamed the *Leviathan.* The Hamburg–American Line resumed service during the 1920s and in 1934 combined its resources with North German Lloyd at the insistence of the Nazi government, operating under the name HAPAG–Lloyd Union; service was suspended during the 1940s. After resuming operations separately in the 1950s the firms merged in 1969. In 1998 HAPAG–Lloyd was acquired by TUI AG, a German-based tourism company. The conglomerate runs an airline, offers round-the-world cruises, and has a fleet of more than 140 container ships.

Kevin Kenny

Hamill, Pete (*b* Brooklyn, 24 June 1935). Journalist and author. The oldest of seven children of Irish immigrants, he attended Regis High School in Manhattan but left there at age 16 to work in the Brooklyn Navy Yard. He later served in the U.S. Navy and used the G.I. Bill of Rights to study painting and writing in Mexico. He attended the Pratt Institute and then worked as a graphic designer until 1960, when he got a job at the *New York Post.* He eventually served as editor of both the *Post* and the *New York Daily News* and wrote short stories, television and movie scripts, and novels, many of which are set in either Brooklyn or Manhattan. His nonfiction book *Downtown: My Manhattan* (2004) is about his "love affair" with New York. He has lived in Brooklyn for decades.

Frank Dyer

Hamilton, Alexander (*b* Nevis, British West Indies, 11 Jan 1755; *d* New York City, 12 July 1804). Secretary of the treasury and revolutionary leader. He settled in New York City in 1772 and studied at King's College (now Columbia University). When the American Revolution began he organized a city artillery company; later he was a lieutenant colonel on George Washington's staff. His marriage to Elizabeth Schuyler (1780) connected him to one of the state's most powerful families. He was a delegate to the Continental Congress in 1782–83. From 1783 to 1790 he lived at either 57 or 58 Wall Street. As a prominent lawyer, he successfully defended the British merchant Joshua Waddington in a case (1784) that helped establish the principle of judicial review. That same year he helped to form the Bank of New York (1784). A forceful advocate of a strong central government, he was a delegate to the Constitutional Convention in 1787 and a leader in the successful campaign to secure ratification of the Constitution in New York. To this end he wrote at least 51 papers in the *Federalist.* Under the new federal government, Hamilton served as the first secretary of the treasury (1789–95). During his tenure he supported policies that aided the growth of New York City as a financial center. In 1795 he returned to practice law in the city. In 1800 he began construction in Harlem of his country home, the Grange (now called the Hamilton Grange National Memorial). Active in Federalist politics as the leader of a wing opposed to John Adams, he helped to launch the *New York Evening Post* in 1801 to further his views. As a strong opponent of Aaron Burr, he helped thwart Burr's candidacy for the U.S. presidency in 1800 and for the governorship of New York in 1804. He lost his life in a duel with Burr in Weehawken, New Jersey, on 11 July 1804, and is buried in the graveyard of Trinity Church.

Broadus Mitchell, *Alexander Hamilton* (New York: Macmillan, 1957–62); Harold C. Syrett, ed., *The Papers of Alexander Hamilton* (New York: Columbia University Press, 1961–87); Julius Goebel, Jr., and Joseph H. Smith, eds., *The Law Practice of Alexander Hamilton* (New York: Columbia University

Press, 1964–81); Ron Chernow, *Alexander Hamilton* (New York: Penguin, 2004)

See also Abolitionism.

Barbara A. Chernow

Hamilton Beach. Neighborhood in southwestern Queens, lying on a narrow peninsula separated from the eastern edge of Howard Beach by Hawtree Creek basin and bounded to the east by the Rockaway transit line and John F. Kennedy International Airport. Developed about 1926, it had a station on the Rockaway line of the Long Island Rail Road that closed in October 1955; municipal subway service began in 1956. In the mid-1990s Hamilton Beach lacked sewers and municipal sanitation service and had the only volunteer fire department in Queens. It has fewer than a dozen streets, which lie barely above the level of Jamaica Bay and flood easily. Nearly half the inhabitants are Irish and Catholic. Access to the area is provided by a wooden bridge from 102nd Street and a pedestrian bridge from 163rd Avenue. In the early twenty-first century new houses were being built, but the neighborhood remained tightly knit and multigenerational.

Vincent Seyfried

Hamilton Grange. Historic house in St. Nicholas Park in Harlem Heights. A country residence commissioned by Alexander Hamilton, who named it after his family's ancestral home in Scotland, it was designed in the Federal style by John McComb, Jr., an architect of City Hall, and stood 9 miles (14 kilometers) from town at the time it was built. The estate was completed shortly after Hamilton's death in 1804 and remained in the family until 1834. After a succession of owners the house was given to St. Luke's Episcopal Church in 1889 and was moved two blocks south to Convent Avenue and 141st Street. It was acquired in 1924 by the American Scenic and Historic Preservation Society and in 1933 opened as a public museum; its operation was taken over in 1962 by the National Park Service. In 2008 the house was moved again to St. Nicholas Park.

Hamilton Grange National Memorial: Report (Washington: U.S. Government Printing Office, 1988)

Jonathan Kuhn

Hamilton Grange, 2009

Hamilton Heights. Neighborhood on the West Side of Manhattan, lying between Washington Heights and Morningside Heights and bounded by 135th Street to the south, 155th Street to the north, Edgecombe Avenue to the east, and the Hudson River to the west; it includes the Hamilton Heights–Sugar Hill historic district and is considered part of West Harlem. The neighborhood is named for Alexander Hamilton, who once owned much of the area and spent the last two years of his life in what is now the Hamilton Grange National Monument. Most of the housing dates from the extension of elevated and subway lines to the neighborhood in the late nineteenth and early twentieth centuries. This fairly elegant housing became less desirable to whites in the 1930s and 1940s as the African American population rose. The brownstone revival of the 1960s and 1970s led to a new movement of middle-class African Americans to the area. In the 1980s a large number of Latin Americans settled in the neighborhood; almost three-quarters of all the immigrants who moved there were Dominican, as smaller numbers arrived from Jamaica, Ecuador, Haiti, and China. In the early twenty-first century the demographics were continually in flux but remained largely African American and Latin American. One of the highest hills in Hamilton Heights slopes up from the Hudson River at 155th Street and contains the cemetery and mausoleum of Trinity Church. The campus of City College of New York lies along Convent Avenue between 132nd and 140th streets, and atop the North River Wastewater Treatment Plant, Riverbank State Park towers over the Hudson River from 137th Street to 145th Street.

See also Sugar Hill and Hamilton Grange.

Lisa Gitelman, Holly Cronin

Hamilton Square. One of the five open spaces provided for on the decisive 1811 Commissioners' Plan, it was bounded by 66th and 68th streets and Third and Fifth avenues. Its 18 acres (7.3 hectares) were laid out in 1807 from former common land taken over by the city known as the Dove lots. Two large ovals, constituting the square, were bordered by 28 building lots, 14 on each side. For several years the lot owners and the city argued as to whether the square was to be public or private. The 1807 agreement called for a private square, but the 1811 plan called for a public one, with lots of a different size and position. The dispute was resolved in 1813 when the city agreed to refund the original lot owners their purchase price plus interest (dating back to 1811). In 1837 the square was rented out as pasture land to the Commissioner of the Almshouse, Bridewell, and Penitentiary. In the 1840s the square was slated to change in character when the city gave the Washington Monument Association a plot of land to build its long-desired monument. A huge ceremony and military parade was staged on 4 July 1847, attended by the New York State governor, to celebrate the laying of the monument's foundation. The project was never completed because of a lack of money. In 1865 a large portion of the square was regraded to became a parade ground for the New York State National Guard; some portions of it were given to charitable institutions and other portions were sold off and divided into 152 building lots. The area between Fourth and Fifth avenues was discontinued in 1867 and the remainder closed in 1868 for street expansion.

Lisa Keller

Hammacher Schlemmer. High-end housewares and electronics store. Opened in 1848 at 209 Bowery by German immigrants, it published its first catalogue in 1881. In 1926 it moved to 147 East 57th and added luxury housewares to its inventory. It was the first store to introduce a pop-up toaster (1930), electric razor (1934), steam iron (1948), microwave oven (1968), telephone answering machine (1968), and cordless telephone (1975).

Jessica Montesano

Hammels. Former name of a section of Rockaway Beach in southeastern Queens, lying on the Rockaway Peninsula around Beach 85th Street. It began as four or five boardwalks that ran from the bay to the ocean. A hotel, the Eldert House, was kept by Garret Eldert and faced the bay on the east side of what is now Beach 85th Street; in August 1869 it was leased to Louis Hammel of Elm Park on Staten Island. The railroad ran within a few paces of the hotel after a trestle was extended across the bay in 1880; a railroad station was then built, and trains carried thousands of visitors annually. A dock in front of the hotel, Fifth Landing, was a regular stop for boats of the Iron Steamboat Company carrying day visitors from Manhattan. In later years hotels on the bay declined as resorts along the shore attracted most beachgoers. Hammels was incorporated with Hollands into the Village of Rockaway Beach in 1897. A large housing project, Hammel Houses, was built in 1955.

Vincent Seyfried

Hammerstein, Oscar (*b* Stettin, Prussia [now Szezcin, Poland], 8 May 1846; *d* New York City, 1 Aug 1919). Opera impresario, grandfather of Oscar Hammerstein II. After immigrating as a penniless teenager to the United States and settling in New York City, he made a fortune in the tobacco business by inventing machines for the manufacture of cigars and launching a trade journal. He later designed and built theaters, first in Harlem and then in midtown. With profits from the Victoria, a vaudeville house managed by his son Willie, he financed the Manhattan Opera Company, which opened in 1906 in a theater that he built on West 34th Street west of Eighth Avenue. His company posed a challenge to the Metropolitan Opera. It had a well-trained orchestra and chorus, leading soloists, and an adventuresome repertory: it not only mounted fine productions of the standard works but also gave the American premieres of Richard Strauss's *Elektra* and Claude Debussy's *Pelléas et Mélisande.* After three seasons of extravagant spending and the rejection of subsidies from wealthy members of fashionable society, he was obliged to sell his interests to the Metropolitan. Hammerstein designed all his theater buildings, which were praised for their impressive interiors and excellent acoustics; none survives.

George A. Thompson, Jr.

Hammerstein, Oscar (Greeley Glendinning), II (*b* New York City, 12 July 1895; *d* Doylestown, Pa., 23 Aug 1960). Librettist and lyricist, grandson of Oscar Hammerstein. Born on East 116th Street, he attended Columbia University and collaborated on operettas and musical comedies with Rudolf Friml and Jerome Kern. His most important contribution to the creation of the modern musical was *Show Boat* (1927, music by Kern), in which for the first time plot was a central element and the songs developed the characters. During the 1930s he worked primarily in Hollywood. He returned to Broadway with *Oklahoma!* (1943), the first in a series of collaborations with Richard Rodgers that included such successful works as *Carousel* (1945), *State Fair* (1945, film), *South Pacific* (1949), *The King and I* (1951), *Flower Drum Song* (1958), and *The Sound of Music* (1959), as well as several failures. His residences in New York City included buildings at Central Park West and 87th Street (1911), 509 West 121st Street (1917), 1067 Fifth Avenue (1930–31), and 157 East 61st Street (during the 1940s).

George A. Thompson, Jr.

Hammett, (Samuel) Dashiell (*b* St. Mary's County, Md., 27 May 1894; *d* New York City, 10 Jan 1961). Writer. At the age of 19 he began working for a detective agency, which later would provide material for his writing. He contracted tuberculosis during World War I and began writing detective novels, short stories, and mysteries. In 1923 his short story "Arson Plus" was published in *Black Mask* crime magazine. Some of his best-known works include *The Maltese Falcon* (1930) and *The Thin Man* (1934). In 1946 he was elected president of the New York Civil Rights Congress. He died at Lenox Hill Hospital.

Jessica Montesano

Hammond, John (*b* New York City, 15 Dec 1910; *d* New York City, 10 July 1987). Music producer. Born into the wealthy Vanderbilt family, Hammond grew up in Manhattan and from a young age was interested in music. He played both violin and viola but stopped to become a record producer at the age of 20. He discovered and produced records of several talented performers, including Fletcher Henderson, Bessie Smith, Billie Holiday, Charlie Christian, Teddy Wilson, and Count Basie. Hammond is known for integrating the music business by both breaking the color line among musicians and widening the listening audience. In 1938 and 1939 he organized a series of concerts known as Spirituals to Swing at Carnegie Hall. After a personal hiatus, be began working again, this time for Columbia Records, and in the 1960s and 1970s he launched the recording careers of Aretha Franklin, Bob Dylan, and Bruce Springsteen, believing the political singers showed the same vibrancy as the jazz singers of decades past. He also wrote a memoir, *John Hammond on Record* (1974).

Jessica Montesano

Hammons, David (*b* Springfield, Ill., 24 July 1943). Performance artist, conceptual artist, and sculptor. Through his artwork, he probes the black experience in America, embraces "dirty" materials that evidence human use, and dissects symbols and stereotypes. Before arriving in New York City from Los Angeles in 1974 he created a series of "body prints" by greasing and imprinting his body on chalked board. In New York City he relies on the city as the source and setting of his art. Scavenging Harlem for bones, coal, hair, wine bottles, and bottle caps, Hammons fashions ephemeral works in public spaces. Some performances, such as his 1983 *Bliz-aard Ball Sale* of snowballs in Cooper Square, subsist only as photographs. Sponsored by the Public Art Fund in 1986, he outfitted five poles with basketball hoops, patterned them with bottle caps, and erected the piece in Cadman Plaza Park, Brooklyn. Despite the elusive nature of his work, Hammons is featured in the permanent collection of the Museum of Modern Art. The P.S.1 Contemporary Art Center hosted a retrospective of his politically and racially charged work in 1990.

David Hammons, *David Hammons: Rousing the Rubble* (Cambridge, Mass.: MIT Press, 1991)

Clare Richfield

Hampton, Lionel (Leo) (*b* Louisville, Ky., 20 April 1908; *d* New York City, 31 Aug 2002). Bandleader and vibraphonist. He began his career as a drummer in Chicago and later Los Angeles. After a suggestion from Louis Armstrong, Hampton recorded playing the vibraphone, becoming the first jazz musician to do so. In November 1936 he moved to New York City to play in Benny Goodman's quartet, becoming part of one of the first racially integrated groups in jazz. Hampton lived at the Doris E. Brooks Houses on 137th Street, where he would continue to live for more than 30 years. After forming his own band in 1940, Hampton had many best-selling hits, including "Sunny Side of the Street" and "Flying Home." His virtuosity on the vibraphone was legendary and made him one of the most important figures of the jazz "swing" era of the 1930s and 1940s. Outside the music world, Hampton became an active proponent of low-income housing, founding the Lionel Hampton Development Corporation, which he partially self-funded. He built a complex of 350 apartments called the Lionel Hampton Houses at Eighth Avenue and 131st Street in 1971, and seven years later constructed the Hampton Houses on St. Nicholas Avenue and 130th Street. In addition to working as a musician and real estate developer, Hampton is well known in New York City for his longstanding involvement in Republican politics. He wrote *Hamp: An Autobiography* (with James Haskins, 1989). Hampton continued playing and leading bands until his death. He is buried in Woodlawn Cemetery in the Bronx.

Ira Berger

Hand, (Billings) Learned (*b* Albany, N.Y., 27 Jan 1872; *d* New York City, 18 Aug 1961). Jurist. He graduated from Harvard University (1893) and Harvard Law School (1896) and practiced in Albany, moving to New York City in 1902 and joining the firm of Gould and Wilkie (1904). In 1909 President William Howard Taft appointed him to the U.S. District Court for the Southern District of New York. A supporter of Theodore Roosevelt in 1912, he unsuccessfully ran for chief judge of the New York State Court of Appeals on the Progressive Party ticket. Appointed to the Federal Court of Appeals for the Second Circuit (1924), he rose to senior judge in 1939 when Martin T. Manton resigned. During his tenure the court upheld the constitutionality of the Smith Act (1950). His age prevented his elevation to the U.S. Supreme Court by President Franklin D. Roosevelt, but he was called "the tenth justice." He retired on 15 May 1951 but continued to take on special assignments. He wrote more than 2000 opinions, including the Aluminum Company of America antitrust case, stating that Congress "did not condone 'good trusts' and condemn 'bad' ones; it forbad all" (1945); *Masses Publishing Co. v. Patten* (1917), sustaining the First Amendment right to send antiwar leaflets through the mails (overturned by the Second Circuit); and *United States v. Coplon* (1950), overturning an espionage conviction because the Federal Bureau of Investigation obtained evidence illegally. Hand gained national attention with his "The Spirit of Liberty" address at "I Am an American Day" in Central Park (21 May 1944). He lived at 142 East 65th Street.

Gerald Gunther, *Learned Hand: The Man and the Judge* (New York: Alfred A. Knopf, 1994)

Jeffrey A. Kroessler

Handy, W(illiam) C(hristopher) (*b* Florence, Ala., 16 Nov 1873; *d* New York City, 28 March 1958). Composer, cornetist, and music publisher. A self-taught cornetist, he was widely known as a performer and composer by the late 1890s. He moved in 1918 to New York City, where he established the Pace and Handy Music Company as the leading publisher of music by African American artists. During the Harlem Renaissance he lived on Strivers' Row. Handy's practice of incorporating syncopated rhythms into popular music earned him the nickname "father of the blues." He wrote more than 150 songs, including "Memphis Blues," "St. Louis Blues," and "Yellow Dog Blues," as well as the book *Father of the Blues: An Autobiography* (1941).

Harry A. Ploski and James Williams, eds. and comps., *Reference Library of Black America*, vol. 3 (Detroit: Gale Research, 1990)

Cynthia Copeland

Hansberry, Lorraine (*b* Chicago, 19 May 1930; *d* New York City, 12 Jan 1965). Playwright. The daughter of African American activists, she left the University of Wisconsin in 1950 for New York City, where she took writing classes at the New School for Social Research and worked as an associate editor of *Freedom,* a radical black newspaper published by Paul Robeson. She achieved success on Broadway in 1959 with her play *A Raisin in the Sun*, which depicts a black family struggling to leave a slum of Chicago for a better neighborhood and was the first play produced on Broadway by a black woman. Hansberry became the first black and the youngest American to receive the New York Drama Critics' Circle Award. In 1964 she produced her next and last play about white intellectuals in Greenwich Village, *The Sign in Sidney Brustein's Window*, with the help of her former husband, Robert Nemiroff. Hansberry died of cancer at age 34 and is buried in Bethel Cemetery in Croton-on-Hudson, New York. Among her posthumous works are *To Be Young, Gifted and Black* (1969), adapted from her letters, essays, and other writings, and *Les Blancs* (1970), about an African leader caught between the conflicting demands of his tribal traditions and modernity. A musical called *Raisin*, based on *A Raisin in the Sun*, was staged in 1973.

Lorraine Hansberry, 1959

Julius Lester, introduction to *"Les Blancs": The Collected Last Plays of Lorraine Hansberry*, ed. Robert Nemiroff (New York: Random House, 1972)

E. G. Hill

HAPAG–Lloyd. Shipping firm formed by the merger of the Hamburg–American Line and the North German Lloyd Steamship Lines.

Hapgood, Hutchins (*b* Chicago, 21 May 1869; *d* Provincetown, Mass., 18 Nov 1944). Journalist. As a reporter from 1897 at the *New York Commercial Advertiser* (later the *New*

Happy Land Building, 2009

York Globe) he practiced the "personal journalism" championed by his city editor Lincoln Steffens and was introduced to the Lower East Side by his fellow reporter Abraham Cahan. A collection of his vividly written articles about the lives of Jewish immigrants was published in 1902 as *The Spirit of the Ghetto: Studies of the Jewish Quarter in New York*. Hapgood also described the Bowery and its residents and worked for other newspapers in New York City, including the *Morning Telegraph* and the *Evening Post,* before turning his attention to radical causes, an interest encouraged by his having taken part in discussions of anarchism, the labor movement, and Freudian psychology at the salon of Mabel Dodge. After World War I his career stagnated and he worked infrequently. In 1935 he exposed Theodore Dreiser's anti-Semitism in the *Nation*. Historian Moses Rischin described *The Spirit of the Ghetto* as "devoid of stereotype or sentimentality, sympathetic yet sober and realistic, intimate yet judicious and restrained." Hapgood's other published writings include *Types from City Streets* (1910) and an autobiography, *Victorian in the Modern World* (1939).

Moses Rischin, Introd. to *The Spirit of the Ghetto*, by Hutchins Hapgood (Cambridge, Mass.: Harvard University Press, 1967), vii–xxxvi

Allen J. Share, Stephen Weinstein

happenings. Artistic events of the late 1950s and 1960s that combined drama, music, the visual arts, and written texts and were at least partially improvised. Both the term and the earliest such event are attributed to Allan Kaprow, who presented "18 Happenings in Six Parts" in a loft at the Reuben Gallery on lower Fourth Avenue in the autumn of 1959. Frequently these impromptu spectacles included the audience, breaking down the distinction between viewer and art object. Their structure was inspired by the composer John Cage, whose seminars at the New School for Social Research drew many of the artists who made happenings in the city. Happenings were staged at diverse venues: by Kaprow in an abandoned brewery in the Bronx and in the courtyard of a derelict hotel in Chelsea, and by others in various lofts, art galleries, and public spaces. Claes Oldenburg staged his "Washes" in a swimming pool at Al Roon's Health Club and other happenings in his storefront on East Second Street.

Michael Kirby, *Happenings: An Illustrated Anthology* (New York: E. P. Dutton, 1965)

Kathleen Hulser

Happy Land fire. Arson fire on 25 March 1990 at the Happy Land Social Club at 1959 Southern Boulevard in East Tremont in the Bronx where 87 people died. It was started by Julio Gonzalez, who after a quarrel with his female companion, Lydia Feliciano, splashed gasoline through the front door of the club (its only exit) and set the gasoline afire. Feliciano, who worked at the second-floor club, and four others survived the fire, but all the patrons inside were trapped and died within minutes from smoke inhalation. The club had been temporarily shut in 1988 for a variety of fire code violations, including a lack of fire exits, sprinklers, and emergency lights, but reopened soon after. In September 1991 Gonzalez was convicted of all charges connected with the crime and sentenced to 25 years to life in prison. In terms of fatalities, the Happy Land fire is one of the worst fires in the city in the past 50 years, exceeded only by the 2001 destruction of the World Trade Center.

Rachel Sawyer

Happy Land Monument (dedicated in 1995), 2009

Harcourt Brace. Firm of book publishers formed as Harcourt, Brace and Howe at West 47th Street on 29 July 1919 by Alfred Harcourt, Donald Brace, and Will D. Howe. Harcourt and Brace were both graduates of Columbia University and former employees of the publishers Henry Holt and Company. Ellen Knowles Eayres, Harcourt's secretary and later his wife, also played an important role in the company. The firm published *Main Street* (1920) by Sinclair Lewis, who had encouraged Harcourt to open his own firm: the book became its first best seller. Howe concentrated on textbook publishing; in 1921 he left the firm (which was consequently renamed Harcourt Brace and Company), and his efforts were continued by S. Spencer Scott. In the following years the firm acquired the list of Brewer, Warren and Putnam (1932) and the entire firm of Reynal and Hitchcock (1948). After Harcourt resigned as president in 1942, the firm was led successively by Brace (to 1948), Scott (to 1954), and William Jovanovich, who had joined the firm as a textbook salesman and editor in 1947. In 1960 Harcourt Brace, now with publicly traded stock, merged with the World Book Company and was renamed Harcourt, Brace and World. In the following year Jovanovich began the first imprint arrangement in U.S. publishing by issuing books with Kurt and Helen Wolff, formerly of Pantheon. The firm moved to its own 27-story building at 757 Third Avenue in 1963 and in the following year had sales of more than $451 million (compared with $8 million in 1954). It acquired majority interests in the Canadian branch of Longmans, Green; in the English firm Rupert Hart-Davis (which ultimately was sold off); and in Grune and Stratton (1968) and Academic Press (1969). In 1970 the firm took the name Harcourt Brace Jovanovich, and in 1973 it purchased Pyramid Publications, which was renamed Jove Books and sold in 1978; it also acquired the History Book Club and the Instructor Book Club. In an effort to diversify, the firm acquired agriculture and business magazines, insurance companies, and television stations, as well as the profitable Sea World marine parks (1976), a purchase that met with some skepticism. The firm moved its trade department in 1982 from New York City to San Diego and in 1984 opened a newly constructed corporate headquarters in Orlando, Florida. It bought Holt, Rinehart and Winston from the Columbia Broadcasting System in 1986, thus strengthening its positions as one of the largest publishers of elementary, secondary, and college textbooks in the United States and a world leader in medical and scientific books and journals. To prevent a hostile takeover by the British press magnate Robert Maxwell in 1987, Jovanovich took on $2.6 billion in debt, a controversial tactic. In 1989 his son Peter became president and chief executive officer of the firm. To reduce its huge debt, the firm sold its four Sea World parks and two other parks for $1.1 billion in 1989. John S. Herrington, a former secretary of energy, replaced the elder Jovanovich as chairman of the board in 1990. In 1991 Peter Jovanovich recommended a sale to the General Cinema Corporation. Harcourt Brace Jovanovich had more than 11,000 employees in 1990 and recorded $1.8 billion in sales. In 1992 it changed its name to Harcourt Brace and in 2007 was sold to Houghton Mifflin and renamed again as Houghton Mifflin Harcourt. Its offices were at 15 East 26th Street.

See also Book publishing.

Marjorie Harrison

hard-boiledness. The stereotype of the "hard-boiled" New Yorker expresses fundamental differences between New York City and smaller places. It identifies the New Yorker as brash, rude, tough, and cynically indifferent or sometimes hostile to the fate of others, but at the same time sophisticated, streetwise, and able to survive amid the pressures and dangers of city life.

The stereotype exists primarily in oral culture and may be traced back at least as far as the 1840s through popular literature, journalism, and entertainment. In Benjamin Baker's play *A Glance at New York in 1848* the actor Francis Chanfrau portrayed Mose the Bowery B'hoy, a combative workingman from the East Side. Mose, ruthless stock speculators and "confidence men," shrewdly independent newsboys, and remorseless prostitutes were depicted in novels and urban sketches written in the 1840s and 1850s by Ned Buntline, George G. Foster, and others. Once established, all these types continued to embody popular conceptions of the skills and attributes necessary to navigate the perils of big-city life. Some popular authors, including the novelist Horatio Alger after the Civil War and later the short-story writers O. Henry, Damon Runyon, and Ring Lardner, softened the outlines of the hard-boiled stereotype with elements of sentimentality and humor. Others, who wrote fiction and nonfiction about the city in the realist tradition, made no such compromises. In works like Stephen Crane's *Maggie: A Girl of the Streets* (1896) and Jacob A. Riis's *How the Other Half Lives* (1890) survival in the city's worst neighborhoods depends on the toughness and cynical indifference that form the grim core of the hard-boiled stereotype. Toughness and cynicism are central as well to a new popular genre of the twentieth century, the hard-boiled American detective story. This genre, which found its voice in the early 1920s in *Black Mask,* a magazine published in New York City, features a private detective who is both at war with the corruption and other stern realities of the metropolis and embedded within them, and who, like the earlier characters of Foster and Buntline, is able to prevail largely because he is an insider who knows how the evil city works. Numerous other detective stories of the hard-boiled genre featured cynical, tough, and fiercely independent protagonists whose grit and savvy helped them solve murders and navigate the big city, usually New York City, Chicago, or Los Angeles, written by the likes of Ross Macdonald, Mickey Spillane, and Walter Mosley.

Vaudeville, which flourished in New York City as nowhere else, built on the brashness and toughness of Mose the Bowery B'hoy and other traditional types to fill out the character of the "wiseguy" or "wiseacre" and to establish the wisecrack as the characteristic form of humor of the hard-boiled New Yorker. Tough, worldly Jewish women such as Sophie Tucker and Fanny Brice and such Irish American performers as James Cagney helped to give this kind of humor specific ethnic dimensions, and, more importantly, to build ethnicity into the hard-boiled stereotype in ways that reinforced the city's distance from rural and small-town America. Like Chanfrau before them, Cagney, Brice, and other vaudeville performers spoke in a distinctive accent that contributed to the image of the New Yorker as brash, cynical, and severe.

Stuart M. Blumin

Hardenbergh, Henry J(aneway) (*b* New Brunswick, N.J., 6 Feb 1847; *d* New York City, 13 March 1918). Architect. He designed such luxury hotels as the first Waldorf–Astoria at Fifth Avenue and 33rd Street (1893 and 1897; demolished), the Manhattan Hotel at Madison Avenue and 42nd Street (1896; demolished), and the Plaza Hotel at Fifth Avenue and 59th Street (1905–7). Each was dominated by a prominent mansard roof with gabled dormers. Under the patronage of Edward S. Clark, Hardenbergh was an early developer of the Upper West Side: he planned such structures as the Dakota at Central Park West and 72nd Street (1880–84) and two block fronts of houses on West 73rd Street (1879–80, 1882–85).

Marjorie Pearson

Harding, J. Horace (*b* Philadelphia, 31 July 1863; *d* New York City, 4 Jan 1929). Banker. In 1883 Harding joined his father-in-law's firm, C. D. Barney and Company, and soon became a senior partner. Respected for his financial acumen, he directed the New York, New Haven and Hartford Railroad Company, the New York Municipal Railways System, the American Beet Sugar Company, and the Bronx Gas and Electric Company. He was also the final trustee in closing the firm of Jay Cooke and took part in many corporate mergers and reorganizations. Harding supported a plan of the Long Island State Park Commission in the 1920s to build a scenic parkway from Queens to Lake Ronkonkoma in Nassau County (now the Northern State Parkway), and he also urged the construction of a highway from Shelter Rock Road in Nassau County to Queens Boulevard in Elmhurst to improve access to his country club; the road was named Horace Harding Boulevard after his death.

Alana Erickson Coble

Hare Krishnas. Members of the International Society for Krishna Consciousness, a religious society based on Hindu ideals formed in New York City by Swami Prabhupada in 1966. The society draws on traditions of *bhakti* (devotion) and the worship of Krishna, a popular god considered an incarnation of Vishnu, a member of the Hindu Trinity. Hare Krishnas often wear saffron robes and dance and chant in the street, and men shave their heads; they seek to spread their ideas to others, often by distributing written materials on the street and offering free vegetarian food. The society has headquarters in West Virginia and chapters worldwide, including one on Schermerhorn Street in Brooklyn.

Raymond Brady Williams, *Religions of Immigrants from India and Pakistan: New Threads in the American Tapestry* (Cambridge: Cambridge University Press, 1988)

Madhulika S. Khandelwal

Haring, Keith (*b* Kutztown, Pa., 4 May 1958; *d* New York City, 16 Feb 1990). Artist and social activist. After moving to New York City to study at the School of Visual Arts, he became a part of the burgeoning street art and independent artist community. He organized exhibitions and performances at Club 57, the underground club in the basement of an East Village church, and other alternative venues to exhibit the art he and other artists, such as Kenny Scharf and Jean-Michel Basquiat, had created. In 1980 Haring began using blank advertising panels in subway stations to make drawings in white chalk. His various artworks, accessible and familiar, quickly became iconic. The "subway drawings" and pop culture symbols Haring created, such as his "radiant baby," earned the prolific artist international recognition, which in 1982 culminated in the first of his more than 100 solo exhibitions at the Tony Shafrazi Gallery. In 1986 he opened the Pop Shop at 292 Lafayette Street to sell merchandise bearing his art (closed in 2005). Haring created many public works in New York City and globally, including the *Crack Is Wack* mural (1986) on the FDR Drive and a mural made in honor of the 100th anniversary of the Statue of Liberty (1986). Through the Keith Haring Foundation, established in 1989, he gave support to AIDS-related organizations until he died at the age of 31.

Cecilia Magnusson

Harkness Ballet. Dance company formed in 1964 by socialite Rebekah Harkness (1915–82), and originally located in a limestone town house at 4 East 75th Street. Harkness, a benefactress of Robert Joffrey's ballet troupe (founded 1956), funded the international tours of Joffrey's company until 1964, when she and Joffrey had a falling out. Harkness broke with his troupe to form the Harkness Ballet, modeled after the St. Petersburg Ballet School, with Lawrence Rhodes as its first principal dancer. Harkness purchased and renovated the Colonial Theater in 1972, on 63rd and Broadway, renaming it the Harkness Theatre. Despite its prestige, the Harkness Ballet company disbanded in 1975.

Cecilia Magnusson

Harlan, John M(arshall) (*b* Chicago, 20 May 1899; *d* Washington, D.C., 29 Dec 1971). Supreme Court justice. Grandson and namesake of a Supreme Court justice, he graduated from Princeton University (1920), followed by three years as a Rhodes Scholar at Balliol College, Oxford. He earned his law degree at New York Law School (1925). Early in his New York City legal career, he alternated between private practice and service as a prosecutor under the U.S. attorney for the Southern District of New York. He also helped prosecute municipal corruption as a special assistant attorney general for New York. In the 1930s he built a reputation as one of Manhattan's top litigators. During World War II he served as chief of the operational analysis section of the Eighth Air Force. He gained national prominence after the war. In 1951 he became chief counsel to the New York State Crime Commission, which investigated the influence of organized crime on state government. President Dwight D. Eisenhower appointed him to the U.S. Court of Appeals for the Second Circuit in 1954 and to the U.S. Supreme Court the following year. Widely respected for his judicial craftsmanship, Harlan dissented from several of the activist decisions of the Warren Court.

Frank Scaturro

Harlem. Neighborhood in Manhattan, bounded to the north by the Harlem River, to the east by Fifth Avenue, to the south by 110th Street (Central Park North), and to the west by Morningside and St. Nicholas avenues; it includes Bradhurst, Strivers' Row, Manhattanville, Hamilton Heights, and Sugar Hill. The area was settled by Dutch farmers who named it Nieuw Haarlem, and because of its remoteness from settled areas of New York City, it remained a largely autonomous village for many years. During the eighteenth and nineteenth centuries it was known as Northern Manhattan, and 86th Street was sometimes considered its southern boundary. Many prominent families had estates there in colonial times, including the de Lanceys, the Bleekers, the Rikers, and the Hamiltons. At Harlem Heights in 1776 the Continental army defeated British troops advancing to the city. The population was 203 in 1790. During the 1840s and 1850s the farmland became unproductive so many farms were deserted and taken over by Irish squatters. Transport to the city was provided by horse-drawn streetcar lines and a steamboat that ran during the summer from 125th Street to Peck Slip.

During the 1880s elevated railroads were extended along Second, Third, Eighth, and Ninth avenues, encouraging development over the next 25 years. Initially the most dramatic changes occurred in adjoining neighborhoods: tenements were built in East Harlem and apartment buildings on the Upper West Side. As the population rose the neighborhood became predominately German; much of the housing consisted of brownstones. The boundaries of the neighborhood were generally placed at 155th Street, the East River, 110th Street, and Morningside and St. Nicholas avenues. Attractive "new law" tenements and spacious apartment buildings with elevators were erected between 1898 and 1904 when subway lines were extended along Lenox

Harlem, 1798, drawing by Archibald Robertson

Avenue. Oscar Hammerstein opened the Harlem Opera House in 1889 in the hope that middle-class families would move to the area in large numbers. This did not happen, but the neighborhood did attract a large number of eastern European Jews, who settled between 110th and 125th streets to avoid or escape from the tenements of the Lower East Side. About this time blacks first moved to the neighborhood, where they found better housing, a more attractive environment, and less racism and violence than in other parts of the city; most settled near 135th Street. Such organizations as the West Side Improvement Association tried to exclude blacks but had little effect, as tenants willing to pay full rent for vacant apartments were highly sought after by real estate agents. Between 1904 and 1908 the Afro-American Realty Company of Philip Payton was especially active in encouraging black tenants to move into the neighborhood. In 1914 the St. James Presbyterian Church moved to Harlem from West 51st Street. Several black churches were formed in Harlem or moved there: the Abyssinian Baptist Church (1923), Canaan Baptist Church, St. Philips Episcopal Church (formed 1818, moved to Harlem 1911), and St. Martin's Episcopal Church (formed 1928). Powerful black fraternal lodges and social clubs also developed.

At its height in 1917 the Jewish population in Harlem was 80,000; when combined with that of East Harlem (90,000), it made up the second-largest Jewish neighborhood in the United States, after the Lower East Side. The most important institution was probably the Institutional Synagogue, formed in 1917 by Rabbi Herbert S. Goldstein. Other highly influential congregations included Temple Israel, Ohab Zedek, Shaare Zedek, and Anshe Chesed, along with scores of storefront synagogues. The neighborhood declined during World War I owing to severe overcrowding, and after 1920 most Jews moved to newer neighborhoods on the West Side and in the Bronx, Brooklyn, and Queens. By 1930 the Jewish population had declined to about 5000. All the large synagogue buildings were sold to Christian churches during the 1920s and 1930s.

Between 1920 and 1930 the number of African Americans in Harlem increased by 120,000 (to more than 200,000), while the number of whites decreased by an equivalent amount. Most of the new black residents were from the American South; others were from other parts of New York City (such as San Juan Hill) and the Caribbean. Blacks from throughout the nation were soon attracted to the area by economic opportunities and a flourishing cultural life. Langston Hughes, Countee Cullen, Zora Neale Hurston, and other writers launched a literary and artistic movement known as the HARLEM RENAISSANCE; distinctive styles of painting were forged by Romare Bearden, William H. Johnson, and Richmond Barthé; black theater and dance flourished; and comedians such as Jackie "Moms" Mabley and "Pigmeat" Markham performed their routines at the APOLLO THEATER. Late in the second decade of the century James P. Johnson, Fats Waller, and Willie "the Lion" Smith helped to popularize Harlem stride, a vibrant form of early jazz piano, and jazz continued to flourish in the neighborhood for the next quarter-century. Fletcher Henderson, Duke Ellington, Chick Webb, and many other leaders performed big-band jazz at nightclubs in Harlem, and many famous jazz musicians lived in the neighborhood, among them Louis Armstrong, Coleman Hawkins, Bessie Smith, Ethel Waters, and the tap dancer Bill "Bojangles" Robinson. In the early 1940s the innovative style of jazz called bebop was developed at local clubs by Charlie Parker, Dizzy Gillespie, and Thelonious Monk. Critics such as Carl Van Vechten popularized the spirited musical and cultural life of Harlem and helped to attract a large white clientele, who patronized both segregated clubs such as Connie's Inn and the COTTON CLUB and integrated ones such as the Apollo Theater, Smalls' Paradise, and the Savoy Ballroom. The local branch of the Young Men's Christian Association became a meeting place for black intellectuals, writers, and artists. During this period Harlem became known not only as a neighborhood, but as a symbol of black cultural success and independence.

Harlem was also a center of black economic and political life. For the middle third of the twentieth century the neighborhood was the site of some of the most successful businesses owned by blacks, among them the Carver Savings and Loan Association; the United Mutual Life Insurance Company; several funeral homes, law firms, and medical practices; and two well-known newspapers, the *Amsterdam News* and the *New York Age*. From the efforts of such nationally known figures as labor leader A. Philip Randolph and scholar-activist W. E. B. Du Bois, to those of blacks in the local Democratic and Republican Party clubs, Harlem blacks during the 1920s and 1930s helped blacks attain federal, state, and city government offices and pushed government officials to embrace civil rights policies. In the 1920s Marcus Garvey, a Jamaican immigrant, became the first leader of a mass black nationalist movement in the United States with the foundation of the Universal Negro Improvement Association; although by 1930 the movement had largely ended, Harlem remained a fertile ground for black nationalism. The Communist Party, forthright in its opposition to segregation, also attracted a large following in Harlem during the 1930s.

Despite the onset of the Great Depression, the nightlife for which the neighborhood was known continued to thrive at the Rockland Palace Ballroom and the Savoy Ballroom. Yet, as was the case in previous years, this notoriety masked the profound hardships the community faced. The Depression devastated Harlem's local economy. Although blacks continued to settle in the neighborhood, the rents remained high and apartments were subdivided into ever smaller units. At one point the population density in the neighborhood was more than twice that of the city as a whole. The economic distress contributed to a new political assertiveness, directed in particular at local stores that depended on black customers but had no black employees. Using the slogan "Don't buy where you can't work," the National Urban League initiated a boycott against chain stores operated by whites. In the summer of 1934 more than 19,000 families were on relief; the unemployed gathered at the TREE OF HOPE (near the Lafayette Theatre) to touch its trunk. A riot broke out in March 1935 when a black youth who had been caught stealing a penknife in a department store on 125th Street was incorrectly rumored to have been beaten to death; a restless crowd smashed windows and looted stores along the street, and businesses lost millions of dollars. The riot brought government attention to Harlem's economic problems and helped strengthen partnerships between the city's political leaders, local celebrities, and Harlem's church leaders, including Father Divine; Adam Clayton Powell, Sr., of the Abyssinian Baptist Church; and George W. Becton. Yet the community's underlying problems remained unaddressed in several fundamental ways, and this would not be the last riot to occur in the neighborhood.

World War II compelled blacks to fight abroad for rights they were denied at home. Despite the symbolic boxing victories of heavyweight champion Joe Louis (who defeated Nazi Germany's boxing champion Max Schmeling), the armed forces remained segregated, and the playwright Loften Mitchell articulated the views of many blacks when he spoke out against military service. Blacks were excluded from working in the munitions industry until late 1941, when Randolph effected a change in policy by threatening to march on Washington, D.C. After a white police officer shot a black soldier in Harlem during a dispute, a riot broke out on 1 August 1943, and an angry crowd overturned automobiles and burned many businesses. This riot led to a continuation of the government–community partnership that had existed since the 1935 riot and helped local black politicians reach higher positions of power. Adam Clayton Powell, Jr., in 1944 won a seat in the House of Representatives, where he enjoyed a long, successful, and controversial career. J. Raymond Jones, known as the "Harlem Fox," became a district leader in 1945 and was an influential figure in local and national Democratic Party politics into the 1960s. Hulan E. Jack was elected the first black borough president of Manhattan in 1953. A more militant brand of politics was espoused by the charismatic leader Malcolm X in the 1960s.

In the postwar period the population of Harlem suffered a steady decline caused by crime, heroin addiction, and other social problems. The role of the neighborhood as the center of black cultural life in the city was eclipsed by Greenwich Village, where several black jazz musicians lived, and other areas such as Bedford–Stuyvesant. Despite the civil rights demonstrations, protests, and boycotts against segregation that occurred in the neighborhood during the 1960s, there were two more riots in 1964 and 1965 (and another in 1977) due to the longstanding problems of poverty, racial injustice, and poor relations between the police and the community. In the 1970s and 1980s, as the public schools failed to prepare students adequately, the number of high school graduates declined. The unemployment rate among young working-class blacks consistently exceeded 30 percent, and many families were headed by poor single mothers, a good number of them teenagers. The incidence of tuberculosis, AIDS, and cancer was astoundingly high: in 1990 the *New England Journal of Medicine* reported that men in Harlem had a lower life expectancy than their counterparts in Bangladesh.

Despite the limited and mixed record of government agencies in facing these challenges, black leaders from Harlem continued to be involved in government during the final decades of the twentieth century and into the opening years of the twenty-first. Charles B. Rangel, a local black politician, defeated Powell for his seat in the House of Representatives in 1970, beginning a decades-long congressional career that has helped shape Democratic politics and government policy in both Harlem and Washington, D.C. Other leaders whose early careers in Harlem's Democratic Party organizations subsequently led to major offices included David N. Dinkins, who was elected the first black mayor of New York City in 1989, and David A. Paterson, who became the first black governor of New York State in 2008.

The architectural record of Harlem is rich and varied. Although neglected residential buildings bear witness to the community's painful present, other architecture in Harlem recalls the neighborhood's proud heritage. The Morris–Jumel Mansion (1765) is one of the few remaining buildings in Manhattan predating the American Revolution, and the High Bridge (1837–48), originally part of the Croton Aqueduct, is the oldest remaining bridge connecting Manhattan to the Bronx. Coogan's Bluff, at West 155th Street, was the site of the Polo Grounds, home of the baseball team the New York Giants. The residences of the elite of black Harlem may be seen at the Dunbar Apartments (1928), on Strivers' Row on West 139th Street, and in Sugar Hill at 155th Street and Edgecombe Avenue. Despite its difficulties, Harlem has several thriving cultural institutions, including the Studio Museum of Harlem; the National Black Theatre; the Schomburg Center for Research in Black Culture, one of the most important research institutions of its kind; and the Dance Theatre of Harlem, one of the premier ballet companies in the nation.

A development boom in Harlem began in the 1990s and continued into the first decade of the twenty-first century as major renovations were undertaken on dozens of buildings north of 110th Street and east of Morningside Park. In addition, new luxury apartment houses became particularly common between 110th and 125th streets in central Harlem. Preliminary census figures in 2010 indicated that for the first time in almost a century, African Americans no longer constituted a majority of the population.

Claude McKay, *Harlem: Negro Metropolis* (New York: E. P. Dutton, 1940; repr. New York: Harcourt Brace Jovanovich, 1968); Allon Schoener, ed., *Harlem on My Mind: Cultural Capital of Black America, 1900–1968* (New York: Random House, 1968); Gilbert Osofsky, *Harlem: The Making of a Ghetto, 1890–1930*, 2nd edn (New York: Harper and Row, 1971); Jeffrey S. Gurock, *When Harlem Was Jewish, 1870–1930* (New York: Columbia University Press, 1979); Ronald H. Bayor, John L. Jackson, Jr., *Harlemworld: Doing Race and Class in Contemporary Black America* (Chicago: University of Chicago Press, 2001)

Jeffrey S. Gurock, Calvin B. Holder, Durahn A. B. Taylor, Kenneth T. Jackson

Harlem Commonwealth Council. Urban development corporation formed in 1967 with an initial grant of $400,000 from the Office of Equal Opportunity. Its organizers included Kenneth Marshall of the Metropolitan Applied Research Center; Billy Rolle of the United Block Association; Marshall England of Haryou–Act; Preston Wilcox, a professor at Columbia University; and Roy Innis, director of the Congress of Racial Equality. The council financed a study by Columbia of the feasibility of supporting business and industry in Harlem and, despite negative conclusions, began operations, securing federal grants of nearly $1 million by 1968 under the direction of Donald Simmons. Under James H. Dowdy the council in the following year formed alliances with businesses in New York City that led to the establishment and refurbishment of several businesses in Harlem, including the Acme Foundry, the Schultz Company, Nigel Contracting and Construction, and Ben's Lumber Yard. The diversified holdings of the Harlem Commonwealth Council, particularly in real estate, have enabled it to attract a number of popular franchises to the area. In the early twenty-first century the council also has an incentive scholarship and internship program to promote careers in health care and a New Ventures Program that offers training for business entrepreneurs.

Emilyn L. Brown

Harlem Hellfighters. Popular name of the 369th Regiment of the New York National Guard and the 15th Regiment, New York National Guard. It was formed in 1913 as the 15th Regiment and during World War I served with the 16th and 161st divisions of the French

The Harlem Hellfighters marching over a bridge in Harlem, 1919

army, being redesignated the 369th U.S. Infantry. All the enlisted men were black and most of its officers white. By the end of World War I the 369th had served 191 days in combat, longer than any unit in the American Expeditionary Force. The first two Croix de Guerre awarded to any Americans went to Corporal Henry Lincoln Johnson and Private Needham Roberts of the 369th, and the unit also earned the Croix de Guerre as a unit citation. Equipped by the French, the unit was not subject to American segregation policy despite the American headquarters' request to the contrary. The unit's band, led by the composer James Reese Europe, helped to introduce jazz to France during its tours of the nation. The unit returned home on 17 February 1919 to New York City, where more than one million people attended its welcoming parade. The troops, led by the Harlem Hellfighters marching band, paraded from Madison Square up Fifth Avenue, then across 110th Street and north on Lenox Avenue. During the year following the homecoming, the 369th built its first armory (at 142nd Street and Fifth Avenue), which remained in use into the early twenty-first century. From 1936 to 1940 Colonel Benjamin O. Davis, Sr., commanded the unit; he later became the first black American general. In 1940 the unit was mobilized for war, redesignated the 369th Coast Artillery (Anti-Aircraft), and sent to Hawaii, where it was known as Hooper's Troopers (after its commanding officer, Colonel Chauncey Hooper). It was renamed the 369th and 870th Anti-Aircraft Artillery Battalions in 1943 and in 1945 saw combat at Okinawa. The 15th Regiment of the New York Guard, under Colonel Woodruff Chisum, served stateside. In 1950 the 369th was mobilized for stateside active duty in the Korean War. It later became a field artillery group and (in 1974) the 369th Transportation Battalion. In 1990–91 two companies of the 369th and its headquarters detachment served in the Persian Gulf, earning a Meritorious Unit Citation, with the 15th New York Guard replacing it at home.

Emmettt J. Scott, *Scott's Official History of the American Negro in the World War* (Chicago: Homewood, 1919); Arthur W. Little, *From Harlem to the Rhine: The Story of New York's Colored Volunteers* (New York: Covici Friede, 1936)

Eleanor Hannah, Yarema Hutsaliuk

Harlem Hospital Center. Currently administered by the New York City Health and Hospitals Corporation, it opened in 1887 in a house on East 120th Street to accommodate patients awaiting transfer to facilities on Wards and Randalls islands. It also served as an emergency branch for Bellevue Hospital. In 1907 the hospital moved to 506 Lenox Avenue, where it gradually developed a full range of medical services. Louis T. Wright joined the outpatient department in 1920 as the first black physician to serve in a hospital in New York City and was named director of surgery after 23 years of service. The hospital's national reputation for trauma care was tested in 1958 when it successfully treated Martin Luther King, Jr., after he was stabbed during a visit nearby. It formed an affiliation with the College of Physicians and Surgeons of Columbia University in 1962, and its residency program became one of the largest training programs for physicians of color. The hospital shared in many of the financial difficulties of the municipal health-care system during the 1960s and mid-1970s; its 50-year-old nursing school closed in 1977 for budgetary reasons, and the widespread poverty in Harlem placed special burdens on its community health clinics. As of 2010 it had 272 beds in addition to a sickle cell anemia center, a burn unit, and more than 11 clinics in Harlem.

Aubre de L. Maynard, *Surgeons to the Poor: The Harlem Hospital Story* (New York: Appleton–Century–Crofts, 1978)

Sandra Opdycke, Eric Hollingsworth

Harlem Renaissance. Literary and artistic movement that reached its high point between 1925 and the onset of the Depression in 1929. Writers and artists traveled to Harlem from throughout the United States to take part in the movement (Countee Cullen was its only important exponent who grew up in Harlem), not because it represented a single style or aesthetic but rather because it offered them the chance to become part of a vibrant community. Although the point at which the Harlem Renaissance began is open to debate, it is agreed that an important early influence was W. E. B. Du Bois's book *The Souls of Black Folk* (1903), which advanced the thesis that black American consciousness is composed of warring African and American influences. In 1917 the white playwright Ridgely Torrence staged his *Three Plays for the Negro Theatre*, which for the first time on stage depicted African American characters with sympathy and depth. The Jamaican immigrant Claude McKay responded to widespread rioting against blacks in 1919 with his defiant sonnet "If We Must Die," and in 1921 the popular all-black musical *Shuffle Along* by Noble Sissle and Eubie Blake brought authentic African American comedy, music, and dance back to the Broadway stage after more than a decade of exclusion. Jean Toomer's *Cane* (1923), a hybrid of prose, poetry, and drama, set new standards of accomplishment for modernist black writers.

These developments took place at a time when many northern industrial centers were expanding dramatically. Unstable real estate conditions in Harlem before World War I enabled African Americans fleeing harsh conditions in the South to settle in the neighborhood, which at the time was populated mainly by German Jews. A diverse community developed that included both blacks who had lived in other parts of New York City for generations and a large number of newcomers from the Caribbean. Religious institutions played a prominent role in the community, notably the Abyssinian Baptist Church on 138th Street and St. Philip's Protestant Episcopal Church on 133rd Street; the weekly newspapers the *New York Age* and the *Amsterdam News* were also important, as was the local branch of the New York Public Library, which sponsored lectures and was the intellectual center of the neighborhood. Despite the relative freedom enjoyed by African Americans in New York City, many were frustrated by high rents, crowded living conditions, and unemployment. The proposed remedies ranged from black nationalism, advocated by groups such as Marcus Garvey's Universal Negro Improvement Association, to eventual integration into American society, the goal of the National Association for the Advancement of Colored People (NAACP) and the National Urban League. As this debate continued, blacks regarded themselves as no longer needing to be subservient but aggressively urbane. Several publications played an important role in defining the militant, self-assertive image of what came to be called the "New Negro," among them the *Crisis* (1910), published by the NAACP and edited by Du Bois (later assisted by the novelist and literary editor Jessie Redmon Fauset) and *Opportunity* (1923), published by the National Urban League and edited by the sociologist Charles S. Johnson. Fauset, Johnson, the poet and diplomat James Weldon Johnson, and the aesthete Alain Locke advocated a genteel black art that would combat racism by proving that African Americans were "civilized." With the backing of Charles Johnson, Locke in 1925 compiled and edited a special issue of the monthly periodical the *Survey Graphic* titled "Harlem: Mecca of the New Negro." In the same year Locke expanded and published this material as *The New Negro: An Interpretation*, in which he called on black American artists to enhance their racial consciousness by studying African art and emulating its styles and themes.

Locke helped many visual artists to acquire patrons, such as Mrs. R. Osgood Mason (known as "Godmother") and the William E. Harmon Foundation (formed in 1922 by William Elmer Harmon, a millionaire from Ohio). The Julius Rosenwald Fund and the General Education Board also supported black artists and writers. Carl Van Vechten, author of the best-selling novel *Nigger Heaven* (1926), introduced many writers to potential patrons, and a literary contest organized by *Opportunity* culminated in an awards dinner on 1 May 1925 where African American writers and intellectuals met white authors and editors from leading magazines and publishing houses; a result was the publication of the books of poetry *Color*, by Cullen (1925, Harper and Brothers), and *The Weary Blues*, by Langston Hughes (1926, Alfred A. Knopf). Fiction soon replaced poetry as the dominant literary form of the Harlem Renaissance. From 1924 novels were published by writers such as Walter White (*Fire in the Flint* [1924]), Fauset (*There Is Confusion* [1924]), McKay (*Home to Harlem* [1928]), Nella Larsen (*Quicksand* [1928]), Wallace Thurman (*The Blacker the Berry* [1929]), Hughes (*Not without Laughter* [1930]), Cullen (*One Way to Heaven* [1931]), and Arna Bontemps (*God Sends Sunday* [1931]).

The Harlem Renaissance was marked by vigorous debate over literary tradition, folk culture, political responsibility, and sexual freedom. Cullen and McKay modeled their work on traditional literary forms; Zora Neale Hurston and Hughes championed black folk expression, including jazz, blues, and common speech. Du Bois insisted that African American writers had an obligation to be propagandists for their race; Thurman and others pursued bohemian ideals that were largely divorced from issues of race. Locke believed that black artists must draw on African models to create a uniquely black art; others believed that the work of black artists was not essentially different from that of white artists, only that its development had been blocked by racial discrimination.

Among the painters associated with the Harlem Renaissance were Aaron Douglas, William H. Johnson, Palmer Hayden, and Malvin Gray Johnson. Douglas became known for his illustrations in Locke's *The New Negro* and James Weldon Johnson's *God's Trombones: Seven Negro Sermons in Verse* (1927), and for the covers of *Opportunity* and the *Crisis*. For the Countee Cullen branch of the New York Public Library (now the Schomburg Center for Research in Black Culture) he executed a stylized, multipanel mural titled *Aspects of Negro Life* (1934) intended to symbolize the strength of the "New Negro." William H. Johnson began his career in Paris and settled in Harlem in 1929, where he persuaded Locke to become his American agent. At first influenced by expressionism and later by primitivism, he was known for his treatment of southern religious and folkloric themes. Hayden moved to New York City in 1919 to study art at Cooper Union and at the urging of Locke treated African subjects in such paintings as *Fétiche et Fleurs* (1926) and *Nous Quatre à Paris* (1930). He lived in Paris for five years (1927–32) but continued to exhibit his works in New York City. During his later career he painted images of rural black life. Malvin Gray Johnson (1896–1934) studied at the National Academy of Design and became known for his interpretations of black genre themes and Negro spirituals. Although he was not African American, the German artist Winold Reiss also was strongly associated with the Harlem Renaissance and influenced the work of Douglas. He was commissioned to illustrate "Harlem: Mecca of the New Negro" and to produce (with Douglas) a series of portraits titled "Harlem Residents and the 'New Negro': The Young Leaders of the Harlem Renaissance" (1925). The painter Archibald John Motley, Jr., did not live in New York City, but an exhibition of his work at the New Gallery in 1928 was well received by both critics and artists. The most important sculptor of the Harlem Renaissance was Augusta Savage. After studying with George Brewster at Cooper Union she won a scholarship to study in France in 1923, but the invitation was later revoked because of her race. In 1930 she went to Europe on a grant from the Julius Rosenwald Fund and produced such works as *Gamin*, a bust of her young nephew that captured the exuberance of young artists in Harlem. She opened the Savage Studio of Arts and Crafts in Harlem in 1932 and worked to create opportunities for younger artists. Her heroic sculpture *The Harp* adorned the entrance to the Contemporary Arts building at the World's Fair of 1939–40. Three other sculptors were associated with the Harlem Renaissance although New York City was not their home. Meta Warrick Fuller (1877–1968) was born in Philadelphia, studied in Paris, and eventually settled in Framingham, Massachusetts. Her sculpture *Ethiopia Awakening* symbolized the restoration of African heritage to a high place in black American consciousness. Sargent Johnson (1887–1967) lived in San Francisco, but his works were shown annually in New York City at the exhibitions of the Harmon Foundation. In pieces such as *Chester* (1931) and *Copper Mask* (1935), which were heavily influenced by African art, he aimed to portray the natural beauty and dignity of blacks to a black audience. Richmond Barthé, who was born in Mississippi in 1901, studied at the Art Students League and the Art Institute of Chicago. His elegant sculptures of dancers, such as *Feral Benga* (1935), and his busts of West Indian and black American men and women embodied the sensuous, racial themes favored by many artists of the Harlem Renaissance. The photographer James VanDerZee, who was born in Lenox, Massachusetts, in 1886, maintained a studio in Harlem and documented the lives of its residents. His black-and-white portraits of subjects ranging from Marcus Garvey and the heiress A'lelia Walker to African American fraternities and funerals constitute the most complete visual record of Harlem in the period. The role of music in the Harlem Renaissance was important and at the same time peripheral: artists and writers heard jazz singers, instrumentalists, and bandleaders such as Bessie Smith, Louis Armstrong, Fletcher Henderson, and Duke Ellington at the Cotton Club, Smalls' Paradise, and the Renaissance Casino, but musicians were not normally associated with the goals of the movement.

Perhaps the most dramatic change wrought by the Harlem Renaissance was the sense that black artists gained by being part of a group linked by ethnic pride, political activism, and a shared cultural lineage. This sensibility was fostered by collective exhibitions such as those sponsored by the Harmon Foundation, which showed the work of leading black artists from Harlem and across the nation. At the same time there was debate about how much freedom artists and writers really enjoyed given their reliance on white patronage, a reliance made necessary by the failure to sustain independent African American cultural institutions. Among such institutions that were unsuccessful were *Fire!!: A Quarterly Devoted to the Younger Negro Artists* (1926), a magazine launched by Thurman and other writers that proclaimed radical intentions but appeared only once; the magazine *Harlem* (1928), also edited by Thurman; the Harlem African Art Museum; and the Salon of Contemporary Negro Artists. By 1930 the Harlem Renaissance was in sharp decline, but important work continued to be produced, notably novels by Hughes, Bontemps, Thurman, Hurston, and George Schuyler. The racially based riot that rocked Harlem in 1935 marked the definitive end of the movement.

A rich collection of materials related to the Harlem Renaissance was amassed by the bibliophile Arthur Schomburg and is now part of the Schomburg Center for Research in Black Culture.

Alain Locke, ed., *The New Negro: An Interpretation* (New York: Albert and Charles Boni, 1925); Nathan I. Huggins, *Harlem Renaissance* (New York: Oxford University Press, 1971); David Levering Lewis, *When Harlem Was in Vogue* (New York: Alfred A. Knopf, 1981); Arnold Rampersad, *The Life of Langston Hughes*, vol. 1, *1902–1941: I Too Sing America* (New York: Oxford University Press, 1986); Bruce Kellner, ed., *The Harlem Renaissance: A Historical Dictionary for the Era* (Westport, Conn.: Greenwood, 1987)

Edmund Gaither, Arnold Rampersad

Harlem Renaissance [Rens]. Professional basketball team. Created in 1923 by Robert L. Douglass, a native of St. Kitts and a former professional basketball player, the Harlem Rens, as they came to be known, were one of the first and most successful all-black traveling professional basketball teams in the country. The team name came from the Renaissance Casino and Ballroom in Harlem, where the team often played. Formed before the Chicago-based Harlem Globetrotters, the Rens competed against both black and white teams and in 1934 won 88 straight games. Between 1932 and 1936, the Rens won 473 games and lost only 49. In 1963 the entire team was inducted into the Naismith Memorial

Basketball Hall of Fame. The members included Charles T. "Tarzan" Cooper, John "Casey" Holt, Clarence "Fats" Jenkins, James "Pappy" Ricks, Eyre "Bruiser" Satch, William "Wee Willie" Smith, and William J. "Bill" Yancey.

Frank Dyer

Harlem River. Navigable tidal strait about 8 miles (13 kilometers) long between Manhattan and the Bronx, connecting the East River with Spuyten Duyvil Creek and the Hudson River. Its course was changed in 1923 when the Harlem River Ship Canal was cut through huge rock outcroppings between Inwood and Marble Hill in northern Manhattan, leaving Marble Hill attached to the Bronx. Six swing bridges, one lift bridge, and three arch bridges span the river, among these the High Bridge at East 173rd Street, built with massive stone arches in 1837–48 to carry the Croton Aqueduct system.

Harlem River: Its Use previous to and since the Revolutionary War (New York: J. D. Torrey, 1857)

Gerard R. Wolfe

Harlem River and Manhattan Bridge. Original name of the Washington Bridge.

Harlem River–Bronx State Park. Original name of Roberto Clemente State Park.

Harlem River Houses. Public housing complex opened in October 1937, nationally recognized for its attractive design. Bounded by West 151st Street to the south, West 153rd Street to the north, Macombs Place to the west, and Harlem River Drive to the east, the development contains 574 apartments in four- and five-story buildings. One of two New York City projects built by the Public Works Administration (PWA) during the New Deal (the other was Williamsburg Houses in Brooklyn), Harlem River Houses was intended specifically for African Americans. In a rare twist on the usual outcome of "separate but equal" policies, the complex was immediately recognized as architecturally superior to most federally subsidized housing produced for white occupancy during this era, and indeed, has been rated as one of the best designed U.S. public housing projects ever built.

Archibald Manning Brown, a society architect, racial liberal, and talented manager, led the seven-member architectural team, which included John Louis Wilson, the first African American graduate of Columbia University's School of Architecture. Team member Horace Ginsbern, with his pre-Depression experience designing garden apartment houses on the Grand Concourse in the Bronx, is thought to have been responsible for the perimeter-hugging layout, which creates for the passerby the impression of conventional New York City apartment buildings. Thus, the complex fits into its surroundings, unlike most large-scale public housing. The interior of the project reflects the classical architectural training of most of the team. The large central court, with its formal layout, London plane trees, benches, and cobbled walks, is reminiscent of a European park.

Harlem River Houses, 2009

While the architectural collaboration was important, the successful outcome can also be credited to the fact that the project originated in the PWA's experimental housing program early in the New Deal. This program aimed at creating appealing housing for a wide section of the population, not just the poor. Thus, Harlem River Houses benefited from a relatively generous budget and high aspirations for quality. By contrast, later public housing, with rare exceptions (many of them in New York City), became the bottom of a two-tier system that included for the upper tier generous tax subsidies for single-family houses. Community pressure was an equally important factor. Initially the city did not plan to build in Harlem, even though federal money was available, and African Americans were acknowledged to be the worst hit of all New Yorkers by the housing crisis of the Great Depression. The only suitable undeveloped parcel available in Harlem was owned by the Rockefeller family, which demanded a price double what federal guidelines for land acquisition allowed. Mass protests, outreach to the media, and appeals to public officials, coordinated by the Consolidated Tenants' League of Harlem, ultimately pushed the city to acquire the site by condemnation. In the twenty-first century Harlem River Houses continued to provide a quality living environment.

Gail Radford

Harlem River Ship Canal. Waterway connecting the Hudson and Harlem rivers. Work began in 1826, with the purpose of promoting

Harlem River Ship Canal, Third Avenue Bridge at 130th Street, ca *1905; Mott Iron Works is in the background to the right*

more efficient commercial shipping to Long Island Sound from the Hudson River and the system of barge canals crisscrossing upper New York State. In 1895 the first section was completed, making it possible for ships to circumnavigate Manhattan for the first time, and also separating Marble Hill from the rest of Manhattan. The entire project was completed in 1938.

Gary Hermalyn, "The Harlem River Ship Canal," *Bronx County Historical Society Journal* 20 (1983), 1–23

Gary D. Hermalyn

Harlem Savings Bank. Original name of the Apple Bank for Savings.

Harlem Square. One of the five open spaces provided for on the 1811 Commissioners' Plan. It was bounded by Sixth (Lenox) and Seventh avenues and 117th and 121st streets and consisted of 20 acres (8 hectares). It was discontinued in 1836 by the same act that established Mount Morris Square, which ran from 124th to 120th streets and Fourth to Sixth avenues.

Lisa Keller

Harlem YWCA. Branch of the Young Women's Christian Association (YWCA), formed in 1905. It met in rented rooms on West 63rd Street before following the city's black community north to Harlem, moving in 1913 to two rented buildings on West 132nd Street and in 1919 to a newly constructed building at 137th Street and Lenox Avenue. Housing a large cafeteria, reception and meeting rooms, classrooms, offices, a gymnasium, a swimming pool, showers, a laundry, and locker rooms, the new building was the best-equipped YWCA with a black membership in the United States. Later additions included an adjacent residence hall (1926) with a capacity of more than 200 and an annex to the administration building (1932). The construction of the annex was funded by John D. Rockefeller, Jr., a longtime supporter of the YWCA and of the Harlem branch in particular. In its earliest years the Harlem YWCA emphasized religious concerns: it sponsored vesper services and Bible study and admitted as members only women who were also members in good standing of evangelical Protestant churches. Participation was extended in 1912 to nonevangelicals and non-Christians. In addition, the organization held monthly public meetings at prominent churches in the city, where a musical program was followed by an educational address, often dealing with such issues as woman suffrage, antilynching legislation, U.S. involvement in World War I, education, and civil rights legislation. Speakers over the years included Ida B. Wells, Mary McLeod Bethune, Lucy Laney, T. Thomas Fortune, Bishop Alexander Walters, Mary Church Terrell, Madame C. J. Walker, and Booker T. Washington. Perhaps the greatest contribution of the Harlem YWCA to the life of black New Yorkers was its trade school, which trained women to become domestic servants, seamstresses, secretaries, beauticians, and nurses. For young girls there were team sports, after-school programs, a club called the Girl Reserve, and a camp in the Catskills, Fern Rock. The Harlem YWCA closed after the fiscal crisis that beset New York City during the 1970s.

Judith Weisenfeld

Harmonie Club. Social club formed in 1852 as the Harmonie Gesellschaft, a select German Jewish counterpart to the other social clubs in New York City; it took its current name in 1893. The club distinguished itself by having German as its official language and by hanging the kaiser's portrait in its hall for many years. In 1906 a clubhouse designed by Stanford White was constructed at 4 East 60th Street; the Harmonie Club was the first men's club in the city to admit women to dinner.

James E. Mooney

Harper, James (*b* Newtown [now in Queens], 13 April 1795; *d* New York City, 27 March 1869). Mayor and businessman. With his brother John Harper he formed the publishing firm of J. and J. Harper and Brothers in 1817. In 1844 he was elected mayor as the nominee of the American Republican Party with Whig and Democratic support; during his term he lived at 50 Rose Street. A reformer, he advocated frugal government, limits on city services, low taxes, and social controls. His most noteworthy achievement while in office was the formation of the Municipal Police, or Night and Day Watch, one of the nation's earliest organized police forces. He returned to his publishing house in 1845 and worked there to the end of his life. He lived at 4 Gramercy Park from 1847 until his death from a carriage accident in Central Park.

Jerome Mushkat

HarperCollins. Firm of book publishers formed in 1817 as a printing firm by the brothers James and John Harper called J. and J. Harper at the corner of Front and Dover streets in Brooklyn. It soon began publishing books as well as printing them, and after the founders' younger brothers Fletcher Harper and Joseph Wesley Harper joined the firm in the 1820s, it became the largest book publisher in the United States. In 1833 it changed its name to Harper and Brothers and moved into two buildings on Cliff Street, which eventually expanded as far as Pearl Street. By the early 1850s the firm occupied a number of five-story buildings, employed several hundred people, and handled all aspects of book publishing, from editing to sales. The firm had become the world's largest publisher when a fire on 10 December 1853 destroyed its facility at 333 Pearl Street; it then moved to a fireproof building on Franklin Square where a distinctive circular iron stairway became known as the "stairway to literary fame" because of the many major English and American writers published by the firm, including Charles Dickens, Anthony Trollope, Herman Melville, Edgar Allan Poe, Mark Twain, William Dean Howells, and the Brontë sisters. The firm also launched the literary and intellectual journal *Harper's New Monthly Magazine* (1850); the politically oriented *Harper's Weekly* (1857), which published Dickens's *A Tale of Two Cities,* Wilkie Collins's *The Woman in White,* George Eliot's *Middlemarch,* and Thomas Hardy's *The Return of the Native,* as well as illustrations by Winslow Homer and Thomas Nast; *Harper's Bazar* (1867), a magazine for women eventually sold to William Randolph Hearst (who amended the spelling to *Harper's Bazaar*); and *Harper's Young People* (1879, later renamed *Harper's Round Table*). At its high point during the 1880s the firm had nearly 800 employees and more than 4000 titles in print. The difficult economic climate of the 1890s forced it into receivership, and it procured an $850,000 loan from the financier J. P. Morgan and was reorganized. It continued to publish well-known writers in the early twentieth century, including James Thurber, E. B. White, Aldous Huxley, John Dos Passos, and Presidents William Howard Taft and Woodrow Wilson. In 1913 it sold one million copies of Lew Wallace's *Ben-Hur* (1880) to Sears Roebuck, the largest single sale of a book in history.

The firm ceased printing its own books in 1923, reorganized the ownership of its stock, and moved its offices to 49 East 33rd Street; in the following decades it branched out into religious books, bibles, textbooks, and books for young people. Twenty-one members of the Harper family spanning three generations worked for the firm until 1944, including James W. Harper, the first in the family to attend college (at Columbia University). Cass Canfield, who joined the firm in 1924, was its president from 1931 to 1945, chairman of the board from 1945 to 1962, and then director emeritus. In 1962 Harper and Brothers merged with Row, Peterson, and Company to become Harper and Row. During the 1960s Canfield recruited managers with financial experience such as Winthrop Knowlton and Brooks Thomas in an effort to keep the house independent as many publishers were bought up by corporate conglomerates. To this end he sold a large share of stock in the firm in 1965 to the Minneapolis Star and Tribune Company, owned by John Cowles, Jr., which had earlier bought *Harper's Magazine;* Cowles became chairman of the board at Harper and Row in 1968 and later was chairman of its executive committee. The firm moved its offices to 10 East 53rd Street in 1972. In 1974 it suffered a 17-day strike by 320 of its employees in New York City, the first strike in the modern history of book publishing; there was also a weeklong strike in 1977 by 240 employees. Under the presidency of Winthrop Knowlton, Harper and Row acquired a number of other publishers, including Basic Books (1969), Thomas Y. Crowell (1977), and J. B. Lippincott (1978). It was itself acquired in 1987 by the News Corporation, led by Rupert Murdoch. In 1989 the firm acquired the textbook publisher Scott, Foresman. It took its current name in June 1990 after forming an affiliation with William Collins, a British publisher also owned by the News Corporation. In the early twenty-first century HarperCollins is one of the leading English-language publishers worldwide; its imprints and divisions in the United States published about 1600 titles a year, and a large children's division published books by Maurice Sendak, Shel Silverstein, Margaret Wise Brown, and Laura Ingalls Wilder. Its New York City offices are at 10 East 53rd Street.

Joseph Henry Harper, *I Remember* (New York: Harper and Brothers, 1934); Eugene Exman, *The House of Harper: One Hundred and Fifty Years of Publishing* (New York: Harper and Row, 1967)

See also Book publishing.

Marjorie Harrison

Harper's Magazine. Launched as *Harper's New Monthly Magazine* in 1850 by the New York City firm of Harper and Brothers, it was intended to educate the general public while whetting its appetite for books published by Harper. The magazine contained articles on topics ranging from science to travel as well as reprints of fiction by such well-known English writers as Charles Dickens, William Makepeace Thackeray, Anthony Trollope, Edward Bulwer-Lytton, and George Eliot. It included work by American writers as early as 1851 and stressed American contributions after the Civil War. Among its features were a humor section titled "The Editor's Drawer" and such columns as George William Curtis's "The Editor's Easy Chair" and William Dean Howells's "The Editor's Study," which was introduced in 1886 and ran for six years. The magazine attracted such artists as Winslow Homer, Frederic Remington, Edwin A. Abbey, and John Singer Sargent. It appealed to educated middle-class families and became one of the most successful and influential magazines in the country's history. In 1900 it reached the peak of its success, was renamed *Harper's Monthly Magazine*, and published a 50th-anniversary issue that included pieces by Howells, Stephen Crane, Owen Wister, Mark Twain, and Theodore Dreiser. Adapting to changing tastes, during the next few years it stressed science, history, biography, and criticism over fiction and focused on current affairs after World War I. In 1925 it took its current name, changed its format, and became a magazine of ideas and editorial comment. It focused on politics, sociology, science, and economics during the 1950s and published William Styron's *The Confessions of Nat Turner* and Norman Mailer's *Armies of the Night* in the late 1960s. The magazine experienced financial troubles in the following decades and periodically sought a new identity under a succession of editors. In 1962 it merged with Row, Peterson and Company and later was acquired by the Minneapolis Star and Tribune Company. In 1984 the John D. and Catherine T. MacArthur Foundation and the Atlantic Richfield Company formed the Harper's Magazine Foundation, which publishes the magazine into the twenty-first century. In 2000 it was redesigned, and several old features were brought back. Also in the twenty-first century the magazine created several online blogs.

Frank Luther Mott, *A History of American Magazines*, vol. 2, *1850–1865* (Cambridge, Mass.: Harvard University Press, 1938), 383–405; Edward E. Chielens, ed., *American Literary Magazines: The Eighteenth and Nineteenth Centuries* (New York: Greenwood, 1986), 166–71

Alice Fahs

Harrigan and Hart. Team of comedians. Its members were the Irish musical comedy performers Ned (Edward) Harrigan (1845–1911) and Tony Hart (1855–91), who formed a successful partnership between 1871 and 1885. Harrigan wrote most of their material, including 33 plays that depicted life in New York City, particularly on the Lower East Side, where he was brought up. Although many of his plays such as the famous series on the "Mulligan Guards" centered on Irish immigrants, other ethnic groups such as Germans, Jews, Italians, and blacks were also treated sympathetically. Harrigan continued writing plays after the dissolution of his partnership with Hart and also owned several theaters in New York City.

Ely Jacques Kahn, *The Merry Partners: The Age and Stage of Harrigan and Hart* (New York: Random House, 1955); Richard Moody, *Ned Harrigan: From Corlear's Hook to Herald Square* (Chicago: Nelson–Hall, 1980)

John T. Ridge

Harriman, Edward H(enry) (*b* Hempstead, N.Y., 25 Feb 1848; *d* Arden, N.Y., 9 Sept 1909). Financier and railroad magnate, father of New York Governor W. Averell Harriman and E. Roland Harriman. In 1870 he became a stockbroker and bought a seat on the New York Stock Exchange. He was involved in the reorganization of rail lines, and he later became the director of both Union Pacific Railroad (1897) and South Pacific Railroad (1901). In 1902 he worked with J. P. Morgan, J. D. Rockefeller, and others to form the Northern Securities Company, a railroad trust that the Supreme Court dissolved two years later. Harriman funded a scientific expedition to Alaska in 1899. Harriman State Park in Bear Mountain, New York, is named for him.

Lloyd J. Mercer, *E. H. Harriman, Master Railroader* (Boston: Twayne, 1985)

Mary E. Curry

Harriman, E. Roland (*b* New York City, 24 Dec 1895; *d* Arden, N.Y., 16 Feb 1978). Businessman and philanthropist, son of Edward H. Harriman and brother of W. Averell Harriman. He graduated from Yale University in 1917 and in the same year married Gladys Fries, daughter of a manufacturing chemist with interests in the South. He was a founding partner in 1927 of the banking firm of Harriman Brothers and Company. Its successor, Brown Brothers Harriman and Company (1931), was for many years the only large commercial bank in the United States owned and operated by a partnership instead of a corporation. In 1950 he was named by President Harry S. Truman to succeed General George C. Marshall as chairman of the American Red Cross, a position to which he was reappointed to seven more three-year terms by Presidents Dwight D. Eisenhower, John F. Kennedy, Lyndon B. Johnson, and Richard M. Nixon. He also served for 23 years as chairman of the Union Pacific Railroad and even longer as president and chairman of the Boys' Club of New York, founded by his father in 1876. In his philanthropic activity Harriman advanced the principle that "a trustee should either work, give, get or get out." He maintained a home in Manhattan but regarded his primary residence as his estate in Arden, New York, where he was a leading patron of harness racing and the founder of the U.S. Trotting Association.

Kenneth T. Jackson

Harriman, W(illiam) Averell (*b* New York City, 15 Nov 1891; *d* Yorktown Heights, N.Y., 26 July 1986). Governor and investment banker, son of Edward H. Harriman and brother of E. Roland Harriman. He attended Yale University and was named to the board of the Boys' Club, an organization that his father had founded. By 1913 he was a director of the Union Pacific Railroad. In 1922 he formed W. H. Harriman and Company (later Brown Brothers Harriman) and became a successful investment banker. A Republican in his early career, he supported the Democratic presidential candidacy of Alfred E. Smith in 1928 and in 1933 was named chairman of the Emergency Reemployment Campaign in New York City by President Franklin D. Roosevelt. As the American ambassador to the Soviet Union from 1943 to 1946, he assiduously cultivated a relationship with Nikita Khrushchev. He sought the Democratic presidential nomination in 1952, losing to Adlai E. Stevenson, and in 1954 he was elected governor of New York. After again being defeated for the Democratic presidential nomination by Stevenson in 1956, he sought reelection as governor in 1958 and was defeated by Nelson A. Rockefeller by 450,000 votes. On President John F. Kennedy's behalf he negotiated a limited but important nuclear-test-ban treaty with the Soviet Union in 1963. The W. Averell Harriman Institute for Soviet Studies at Columbia University is named for him.

Randy Abramson, *Spanning the Century: The Life of W. Averell Harriman, 1891–1986* (New York: William Morrow, 1992)

Marjory Potts

Harrington, (Edward) Michael (*b* St. Louis, 24 Feb 1928; *d* Larchmont, N.Y., 31 July 1989). Writer and political activist. In New York City he edited the *Catholic Worker* and soon became a leading participant in the political culture of the leftist intelligentsia. Within a few years he shifted from Catholic radicalism to anticommunist democratic socialism, cultivating ties with labor unions and liberal politicians and opposing groups that he felt did not understand the dangers of totalitarianism, including Stalinists and the founders of Students for a Democratic Society. He succeeded Norman Thomas as chairman of the Socialist Party in 1968. Despite his ardent anticommunism he increasingly battled elements within the party that supported the U.S. intervention in Vietnam and rejected any collaboration with the New Left. In 1972 he resigned from the party, joining with other former members in the following year to form the Democratic Socialist Organizing Committee (DSOC). In 1982 he engineered its merger with the New American Movement, a group oriented toward the New Left, to form the Democratic Socialists of America, with headquarters in New York City. For many years Harrington taught at Queens College. The most influential of his many books, *The Other America* (1962), describes the plight of those untouched by the economic boom in the United States after World War II.

Loren J. Okroi, *Galbraith, Harrington, Heilbroner: Economics and Dissent in an Age of Optimism* (Princeton, N.J.: Princeton University Press, 1988)

Richard Yeselson

Harris, Elisha (*b* Westminster, Vt., 5 March 1824; *d* Albany, N.Y., 31 Jan 1884). Public health official. He worked with Stephen Smith to improve sanitary conditions in New York City; their efforts led to the passage of the Metropolitan Health Act of 1866, which established the first effective health board for the city. He was the first registrar of records for the Metropolitan Board of Health (1866–69) and organized the first free public vaccination program for smallpox in 1869. Toward the end of his career he held several important posts: sanitary superintendent of the city (1869–70), registrar of vital statistics (1873–76), and original member of the New York State Board of Health (1880).

Joseph S. Lieber

Harrison, Hubert Henry (*b* St. Croix, Danish West Indies, 1883; *d* New York City, 1927). Political activist. He moved in 1900 to New York City, where he worked as a laborer during the day and studied at night. In 1909 he joined the Socialist Party, for which he wrote theoretical articles such as "Socialism and the Negro" (1912). In these he argued for the primacy of the black struggle in the socialist cause, and he became well known as a lecturer and soapbox orator. In 1914 he left the socialists, whom he saw as racist. He organized the Liberty League of Afro-Americans in June 1917, which was the first militant group of the "New Negro" movement, and in its newspaper, the *Voice,* he called for organizing labor, armed defense against lynch violence, federal action to protect civil rights, and socialism. When the league disbanded soon after, Harrison briefly rejoined the Socialist Party, edited the radical black periodical the *New Negro,* and led the Colored National Liberty Congress, which advocated laws against lynching. In 1920 he joined the Universal Negro Improvement Association, led by his former disciple Marcus Garvey, and he briefly edited its newspaper, *Negro World.* Dissatisfied with Garvey's plans to establish colonies of American blacks in Africa, he attempted to organize a Liberty Party to work for civil rights. He took U.S. citizenship in 1922 and became a lecturer for the New York Public Library, for which he helped to organize the Schomburg Center for Research in Black Culture. He formed a group in 1924 called the International Colored Unity League that proved short-lived and supported the creation of a black separatist state in the South. Harrison wrote two books of essays, *The Negro and the Nation* (1917) and *When Africa Awakes* (1920).

Theodore G. Vincent, *Black Power and the Garvey Movement* (Berkeley, Calif.: Ramparts, 1971)

Greg Robinson

Harrison, Wallace K(irkman) (*b* Worcester, Mass., 28 Sept 1895; *d* New York City, 2 Dec 1981). Architect. He moved in 1916 to New York City, where he was a draftsman for McKim, Mead and White and also worked in the atelier of Harvey Wiley Corbett and the firm of Bertram Grosvenor Goodhue. He developed a style that incorporated classical and space-age motifs in such structures as the Trylon and Perisphere at the World's Fair of 1939–40 and the main terminal at La Guardia Airport (1964). He helped to form the firm of Harrison, Fouilhoux and Abramovitz, which was responsible for many of the city's distinctive skyscrapers; with Raymond M. Hood he designed Rockefeller Center. Among Harrison's best-known buildings are the United Nations (1953) and Lincoln Center for the Performing Arts (1966).

Victoria Newhouse, *Wallace K. Harrison, Architect* (New York: Rizzoli, 1989)

Edward A. Eigen

Harrisville. Obsolete name of SANDY GROUND.

Harry N. Abrams. Firm of book publishers formed in 1950 by Harry N. Abrams as the first American publisher devoted solely to books about art. It began its operations at a time when the American market for art books was limited, restricted in particular by the inferior quality and prohibitive cost of American color reproduction. By opening an office in Amsterdam in 1953 the firm was able to take advantage of European expertise and technology, and it became the first publisher to issue art books of high quality in large quantities and at moderate prices for the U.S. market. The firm was acquired in 1966 by the Times Mirror Company, and Abrams left to set up a new firm, Abbeville. In 1997 the company was purchased by La Martinière Group of Paris.

Eileen K. Cheng

Harsenville. Former neighborhood on the Upper West Side of Manhattan, bounded to the north by 81st Street, to the east by Central Park West, to the south by 68th Street, and to the west by the Hudson River. It was named after Jacob Harsen and his family, who moved to the area in 1763 and built a large farm there; such prominent families as the de Lanceys, the Dyckmans, and the Somerindycks owned farms nearby. In 1803 Harsenville Road was built through what later became Central Park. A Dutch Reformed church was formed by the Harsens in 1805. The rural character of the area changed when schools, churches, a post office, shops, and saloons were built during the 1830s and 1840s. In the 1860s Mayor Fernando Wood lived at 77th Street and 11th Avenue (now West End Avenue). The Dutch Reformed church was eventually demolished, and Harsenville Road was torn up to make way for Central Park. By the 1880s the Upper West Side was developed and the former name of the neighborhood fell into disuse.

James Bradley

Hart, Kitty Carlisle [Conn, Katherine] (*b* New Orleans, La., 3 Sept 1914; *d* New York City, 17 April 2007). Arts administrator and actress. She studied at the Royal Academy of the Dramatic Arts and made her acting debut in 1932 under the stage name Kitty Carlisle. In 1933 she appeared in two films with Bing Crosby, but *A Night at the Opera* (1935) with the Marx Brothers made her famous. After marrying the playwright Moss Hart in 1946 she continued to act for several years and was a regular panelist on the television quiz show *To Tell the Truth* from 1956 to 1977. She was named the head of the state conference on women by Governor Nelson A. Rockefeller in 1966, a vice chairwoman of the New York State Council on the Arts in 1971, and the head of the council in 1976 (reappointed in 1982). She became best known as a prominent member of fashionable society and perhaps as the most well-known advocate for the arts in New York State and city. For more than 50 years Hart lived in an 11-room apartment at 32 East 64th Street in Manhattan. She continued to perform around the city until her death, often taking the stage at Feinstein's at the Regency Hotel. She is buried next to her husband in Ferncliff Cemetery in suburban Hartsdale, New York.

Rohit T. Aggarwala

Hart, Lorenz (Milton) (*b* New York City, 2 May 1895; *d* New York City, 22 Nov 1943). Lyricist. He grew up in Harlem and graduated from the Columbia University School of Journalism in 1917. His first important musical was *Dearest Enemy,* written with Richard Rodgers and performed at the Knickerbocker Theatre in 1925; the show included "Where the Hudson River Flows," one of his many songs inspired by New York City. He enjoyed a long partnership with Rodgers, whose romantic music he underpinned with wry and often cynical lyrics. During the last decade of his life, Hart lived at 320 Central Park West. In 1943, the last year of his life, he moved to the Delmonico at 502 Park Avenue and 59th Street.

Samuel Marx and Jan Clayton, *Rodgers and Hart: Bewitched, Bothered, and Bedeviled* (New York: G. P. Putnam's Sons, 1976)

Marc Ferris

Hart, Moss (*b* New York City, 24 Oct 1904; *d* Palm Springs, Calif., 20 Dec 1961). Playwright and musical theater director. He was born and raised in a tenement at 74 East 105th Street. After studying at Columbia University Hart produced his first successful Broadway play with George S. Kaufman, *Once in a Lifetime* (1930). Over the following years Kaufman and Hart collaborated on several Broadway hits, including *You Can't Take It with You* (1936) and *The Man Who Came to Dinner* (1939). After his split with Kaufman, Hart continued to write Broadway plays, although directing became a major occupation. Hart married actress Kitty Carlisle in 1946. Hart also wrote screenplays, producing *Gentlemen's Agreement* in 1947, for which he was nominated for an Oscar. He won the Tony Award for best director in 1957 for *My Fair Lady,* adapted from George Bernard Shaw's *Pygmalion* in 1956. His book *Act One: An Autobiography* (1959) was a best seller. Hart directed *Camelot* in 1960, his final show. He died of heart failure and is buried at Ferncliff Cemetery in suburban Hartsdale, New York.

Meghan Lalonde

Hart–Celler Act. See Immigration and Nationality Act of 1965.

Hart Island. Island in Long Island Sound, site of the largest potter's field in the United States. Originally known as Spectacle Island and Little Minnefords and now sometimes called Hart's Island, it is situated just northeast of City Island and is part of the Bronx. Acquired by Oliver de Lancey of West Farms in 1774 and later owned by the Haight and Rodman families and by John Hunter, the 101-acre (41-hectare) island has housed Confederate prisoners; yellow fever, tuberculosis, and psychiatric patients; city inmates; and a Nike missile base. It was bought by the City of New York in 1869, and the first interment was Louisa Van Slyke, an orphan who died in that year at Charity Hospital. About 850,000 people, all of them unclaimed and many of them unidentified, are now buried three deep in unmarked, mass graves. A granite cross erected in 1902 bears the inscription "He Calleth His Children by Name." At one time inmates from the Reformatory Prison on the island buried the dead; the task is now handled by prisoners from Rikers Island who volunteer and are paid a stipend for the approximately 1500 annual burials. The only access is by a ferry run by the Department of Corrections from Fordham Street on City Island. Hart Island is not open to the public, although visits are allowed for relatives of those buried there. In 2006 Manhattan artist Melinda Hunt, while working on a documentary film about the island, filed a Freedom of Information request for access to burial records, and in 2007 the Department of Corrections released about 50,000 handwritten records from 1985 to 2007. As part of her Hart Island Project, she has set up a Web site that provides a history of the island and an online database with information regarding who is buried there; in 2010 it had records from 1980 to 2008. Older burial records are kept by the Department of Corrections and the Municipal Archives, although thousands were lost in a fire in the 1970s.

Kenneth T. Jackson

Hartley, Robert M(ilham) (*b* Cockermouth, England, 17 Feb 1796; *d* New York City, 3 March 1881). Philanthropist. After moving to New York City from England he opened a mercantile firm. Inspired by evangelical Protestantism, he retired to direct the New York City Temperance Society; he later became one of the city's most influential philanthropists as the general agent of the Association for Improving the Condition of the Poor from 1843 to 1876. Although he denounced indiscriminate charity and distinguished between the "worthy" and "unworthy" poor, he also recognized the evils of slum environments and focused the efforts of the association on public health and housing reform. Hartley helped to form the Society for the Relief of the Ruptured and Crippled.

See also Dairying.

Marilyn Thornton Williams

Harugari. Fraternal order formed in New York City in 1847 by Philipp Merkle to promote German language and culture and the ideals of "friendship, affection, and humanity." Most of its members were artisans or skilled workers, and the group maintained close ties to the labor movement. By 1873 the order had 62 lodges with about 7000 members in the metropolitan area. Although Harugari suffered a decline in membership during the next decade, it recovered and continued operating into the twentieth century.

Stanley Nadel

Harvard Club. Club formed in 1865 for people associated with Harvard University who live or work in New York City. Its landmarked clubhouse at 27 West 44th Street was designed by the firm of McKim, Mead and White and constructed in phases from 1893 to 1915. Of neo-Georgian design with dark-red "Harvard" brick, it is a handsome building inside and out, and its great Harvard Hall (1905) is one of the most impressive interior spaces in the city. The club has dining rooms of various types and sizes, a library and reading room, and accommodations for squash and other indoor activities.

James E. Mooney

Harvey, George (Brinton McClellan) (*b* Peacham, Vt., 16 Feb 1864; *d* Dublin, N.H., 20 Aug 1928). Newspaperman and businessman. He worked for a newspaper in Vermont before moving to New York City, where he joined the staff of the *New York World;* he became its editor in 1891. After a few years he left to work on Wall Street, where he made a fortune. In 1899 he bought the *North American Review,* naming himself its editor; he took over *Harper's Weekly* in 1901. A strong supporter of Woodrow Wilson's presidential candidacy in 1912, he later opposed Wilson's Fourteen Points and endorsed Warren G. Harding in the election of 1920. Appointed ambassador to London during the 1920s, Harvey also edited the *Washington Post* and wrote a biography of Henry Clay Frick that was published in 1928.

Willis Fletcher Johnson, *George Harvey: "A Passionate Patriot"* (Boston: Houghton Mifflin, 1929)

James E. Mooney

HARYOU–ACT. Comprehensive antipoverty program launched in 1964. It combined the efforts of two organizations: Harlem Youth Opportunities Unlimited (HARYOU), inspired by psychologist Kenneth Clark and funded in 1964 with grants of $100,000 from the city (made by Mayor Robert F. Wagner) and $230,000 from the House Committee on Education and Labor (the result of efforts by Representative Adam Clayton Powell, Jr.); and Associated Community Teams (ACT), established by the President's Committee on Juvenile Delinquency. The two groups differed in their methods, with HARYOU focusing on education, job training, and lobbying and ACT inclined toward rent strikes and the organizing of neighborhood boards. HARYOU–ACT achieved some success before ceasing operations in 1968, and its emphasis on community initiatives and youth programs proved influential.

Herbert Krasny, *Beyond Welfare: Poverty in the Supercity* (New York: Holt, Rinehart and Winston, 1966)

Emilyn L. Brown

Hasidim. Adherents of a mystical, revivalist form of Judaism that is inspired in part by the kabbalah and that celebrates various aspects of everyday life, frequently with song and dance. During the early twenty-first century more than 100,000 Hasidic Jews lived in New York City, mostly in the Brooklyn neighborhoods of Borough Park, Williamsburg, and Crown Heights. Hasidism was founded in eighteenth-century Poland by Israel ben Eliezer, a rabbi known as the Baal Shem Tov. The Hasidic migration to New York City occurred mostly after World War II; the majority were Hungarian or Polish Jews. In the Hasidic community adherence to Jewish law and practice pervades every aspect of life, as everything is holy or potentially holy. All children attend yeshiva (Jewish religious school), marry only other Hasidim, and have restricted interaction with non-Hasidim. Hasidic Jews have large families, contributing to the growth of the community. The primary languages spoken by Hasidim are Yiddish, Hungarian, and English; Hebrew is reserved for prayer. The largest Hasidic sects are the LUBAVITCHERS, the SATMARS, and the Bobov; others include the Ger, the Belz, the Tzelem, the Stolin, and the Papa. Tensions among Hasidim stem from differences over doctrine and leadership; there is also conflict with other residents of Brooklyn, especially racial minorities, over such issues as the construction of schools, housing, and police protection. Hasidim have been successful in political lobbying due to the fact they vote as a bloc.

Nicole Marwell, *Bargaining for Brooklyn* (Chicago: University of Chicago Press, 2007)

Jessica Montesano

Hassam, (Frederick) Childe (*b* Dorchester [now in Boston], Mass., 17 Oct 1859; *d* East Hampton, N.Y., 27 Aug 1935). Painter. After settling in New York City in 1889, he opened a studio on Fifth Avenue and 17th Street and joined the Society of American Artists. Hassam frequented the Players Club, where he met Julian Alden Weir and other artists with whom he formed the group known as Ten American Painters in 1898. He worked in an impressionist style and painted many street scenes of New York City, including *Fifth Avenue in Winter* (1899). In 1913 he displayed his work at the Armory Show. Hassam divided his time during the last 40 years of his life between East Hampton, Long Island, and his studio on West 57th Street in Manhattan.

Stephen Weinstein

Hastings. Name used from 1664 to 1683 for NEWTOWN.

Haswell, Charles Haynes (*b* New York City, 1809; *d* New York City, 12 May 1907). Political figure, civil engineer, and New York historian. He was a member of the Common Council and Board of Corrections and a trustee of the Brooklyn Bridge; at his death at age 98 he was believed to be the oldest living member of Tammany Hall. At the age of 23 he built one of the first practical steam-powered launches. As the first engineer in chief of the U.S. Navy from 1836 to 1852, he lobbied for steam propulsion and iron construction against the firm opposition of the senior officer corps. He was more successful introducing the use of sacrificial zinc slabs to protect marine steam boilers and ships' bottoms from galvanic action. After being forced out of the navy for political reasons, Haswell served as U.S. surveyor of steamers, built steam engines for the Russian navy, and managed challenging civil engineering projects, including laying foundations for many New York City buildings. For many years he was the chief measurer of the New York Yacht Club. Haswell's entertaining and generally reliable memoir of antebellum New York, *Reminiscences of New York by an Octogenarian, 1816–1860* (1896), is a chronology of important and trivial events. The author said his aim was "to reveal New York as it actually was near eighty years ago, not to maintain 'the dignity of history.' "

John Rousmaniere

hatting and millinery. The hatting and millinery industries became concentrated in New York City in the early nineteenth century. The styles of men's and women's hats were set in the city, which was the center for fashion in the United States. One of the first prominent men's hatters was Charles Knox, who began his career as an apprentice for Leary and Company, a firm on Broad Street in which he eventually became a foreman. At the age of 19 he opened a small shop in 1838 that became known as "the hole in the wall" at 110 Fulton Street; he later moved successively to 128 Fulton Street and 212 Broadway. Competition arose about this time among the many small firms in the city making men's silk and beaver hats and led in 1850 to the "battle of the hatters," waged by Knox, John Genin, and Nicholas Espenscheid. In 1857 Robert Dunlap, an apprentice to Knox who had been denied a raise, opened his own business at 577 Broadway and became the most formidable competitor of Knox, with whom he dominated the hatting trade in the city by the 1870s; he eventually opened a large factory at 60 Nostrand Avenue in Brooklyn. In the 1870s Knox's firm was reorganized by his son Edward M. Knox, who opened a "business palace" beneath the Fifth Avenue Hotel at Madison Square. The Knox Hat Company opened two large factories in the 1890s in Brooklyn, at 340 Fulton Street and at the corner of Grand and St. Mark's avenues; its hats were sold throughout the United States, France, Germany, and South America. In 1919 it merged with Dunlap's firm. In addition to hat manufacturing, New York City became the national center for hat importing and jobbing.

Like hatting, millinery (the making of women's hats) was a business conducted by small firms that competed intensely with each other; many retail shops were run by women and employed five people or fewer. Prominent wholesale millinery manufacturers in the city in the late nineteenth century and the early twentieth included Hill Brothers, Ridley and Sons, and John Miles. Retail millinery offered unusual opportunities in business for women, and a few, including Lilly Daché, ran successful enterprises into the 1950s and 1960s. By the start of the twenty-first century the number of firms had declined because fewer men and women wore hats.

Robert R. Updegraff, *The Story of Two Famous Hatters* (New York: Knox Hat Company, 1926); *Rebuilding an Industry: The History of the Eastern Women's Headwear Association* (New York: Eastern

Women's Headwear Association, n.d. [1951]); David Bensman, *The Practice of Solidarity: American Hat Finishers in the Nineteenth Century* (Urbana: University of Illinois Press, 1985)

Wendy Gamber

Havemeyer, Henry O(sborne) (*b* New York City, 18 Oct 1847; *d* Commack, N.Y., 4 Dec 1907). Businessman. He was the son of Frederick C. Havemeyer, Jr., and made most of the deals that permitted his family to control the sugar industry. Ruthless and astute, he was the chief architect of the Sugar Trust (1887), which declined after his death. A building at Columbia University and a street in the heart of Williamsburg are named for the family.

James Bradley

Havemeyer, William F(rederick) (*b* New York City, 12 Feb 1804; *d* New York City, 30 Nov 1874). Businessman and mayor. The son of the sugar refiner William Havemeyer (1770–1851), he was born at 31 Pine Street. In 1828 he formed a partnership with a cousin in the sugar business, which he left in 1842 to enter local politics. A Democrat and a member of Tammany Hall, he was elected mayor nonconsecutively in 1845 and 1848 largely based on his reputation as a sound financial manager with integrity. After leaving office he resumed his career in business and then made a triumphant return to politics in 1872 when the scandals of the Tweed Ring prompted him to seek the mayoralty as a Republican. His independent style was not suited to the political patronage system of the time, however, and he lost the election.

J. C. Havemeyer, *Life, Letters and Addresses of John Craig Havemeyer* (New York: Fleming H. Revell, 1914)

James Bradley

Hawkins, (Cornelius) Connie (*b* Brooklyn, 17 July 1942). Basketball player. While a teenager in Brooklyn he was recognized as a great basketball player with an original and acrobatic playing style. Hawkins earned a scholarship to the University of Iowa but was subsequently kicked off the team and banned from the National Basketball Association (NBA) because of his association with notorious fixer Jack Molinas, despite never having played a collegiate game. Hawkins played first with the Harlem Globetrotters, then in the American Basketball Association and the American Basketball League. In 1969 the NBA lifted its ban and he joined the Phoenix Suns. His NBA career came to an end in 1975 with a career average of 16.5 points and 8.0 rebounds per game. Hawkins was inducted into the NBA Hall of Fame in 1992.

Cecilia Magnusson

Hawkins, Edler Garnet (*b* New York City, 13 June 1908; *d* Princeton, N.J., 13 Dec 1977). Minister and civil rights leader. He attended Bloomfield College in New Jersey (AB 1935) and Union Theological Seminary in Manhattan (BD 1938). As the pastor of St. Augustine Presbyterian Church in the Bronx from 1938 to 1970, he was noted for establishing a church youth ministry and for confronting racism within the church. Hawkins helped to form the national Commission on Church and Race of the Presbyterian Church and in 1964 became the first black elected moderator of the General Assembly of the United Presbyterian Church in the United States. He spent the later years of his career, from 1970 to 1977, as a professor of theology at Princeton Theological Seminary.

David Meerse

Hawkins, Erick [Frederick] (*b* Trinidad, Colo., 23 April 1909; *d* New York City, 23 Nov 1994). Dancer, choreographer, and artistic director. In New York City he studied at the School of American Ballet and danced with the American Ballet (1935–37) and Ballet Caravan (1936–39). In 1938 he became the first male member of the modern dance company of Martha Graham, eventually becoming her dance partner and husband. By 1951 his associations with Graham ended and he formed his own company. He evolved an innovative choreographic style based on smooth, unhurried, meditative movement, reflecting his interest in Buddhist philosophy and American Indian culture.

Brenda Dixon Gottschild

Sugar refinery of Havemeyer and Elder in Williamsburg, ca *1860*

Hayden, Palmer (Cole) (*b* Wide Water, Stafford County, Va., 1890; *d* New York City, 18 Feb 1973). Painter. After serving in World War I he moved to New York City in 1919 and studied art at Cooper Union and at the Boothbay Art Colony in Maine. At the urging of Alain Locke he painted marine subjects and then African subjects (*Fétiche et Fleurs,* 1926). In 1927 he went to Europe, but he continued to exhibit his works in New York City with the encouragement of the Harmon Foundation and to explore African American subjects (*Nous Quatre à Paris,* 1930). He returned to New York City in 1932 and for the next decade concentrated on characterizations of rural black life. As his works became better known many blacks criticized his caricatured figures as being too close to prevalent white stereotypes of blacks.

Edmund Gaither

Hayden Planetarium. Named after Charles Hayden, financier and philanthropist, the structure was built in 1935 as part of the American Museum of Natural History at 79th Street and Central Park West. Its centerpiece, a Zeiss projector, was used in programs to show the movements of stars, the rising and setting of the sun and moon, and the precession of the equinoxes. During World War II the U.S. Army and Navy used the planetarium as an instruction center for courses on celestial navigation. Exhibits of rockets, satellites, and astronautics were added in the 1950s. With the advent of laser technology the planetarium offered dramatic programs on black holes and supernovas in the 1980s, using special photography, synthesized sound and music, and a Zeiss VI Star projector. The original Hayden Planetarium ceased to exist in January 1997, but in February 2000 it reopened after being rebuilt with significant improvements, including the installation of a customized Zeiss Mark IX Star projector as a part of the American Museum of Natural History's Rose Center for Earth and Space.

Ronald Rainger

Hayes, Helen [Brown, Helen Hayes] (*b* Washington, D.C., 10 Oct 1900; *d* Nyack, N.Y., 17 March 1993). Actress. At the age of

Helen Hayes, 1977

eight she moved to New York City and won her first role on Broadway as a mime in Victor Herbert's *Old Dutch,* which opened at the Herald Square Theatre on 22 November 1909. After her success in Norma Besant's *Coquette* (1927), she appeared in hundreds of productions, becoming best known for playing the leading roles in *Caesar and Cleopatra* (1925), *Mary of Scotland* (1935), and *Queen Regina* (1935). During a career of more than 60 years on the stage she won three Tony Awards; she also won Academy Awards for her performances in *The Sin of Madelon Claudet* (1931) and *Airport* (1970). Often called the "first lady of American theater," Hayes was president of the American Theater Wing and the American National Theater Academy and directed women's activities for the March of Dimes. In 1983 the Little Theater on West 44th Street was renamed in her honor.

Janet Frankston

Hayes, Patrick (Joseph) (*b* New York City, 20 Nov 1867; *d* Monticello, N.Y., 4 Sept 1938). Catholic cardinal. Ordained on 8 September 1892, he graduated from Catholic University (1894) and was at the Church of St. Gabriel in the East 30s (now defunct) from 1894 to 1902. He was secretary to John Farley before becoming the chancellor and president of Cathedral College (1903–14). On 24 November 1917 he was appointed bishop ordinary to the chaplains of the U.S. Army and Navy; on 10 March 1919 he was appointed an archbishop. He signed the Bishops' Program of Social Reconstruction (1919), endorsed Irish independence but not violent revolution (1919–20), and promoted temperance but not Prohibition. In 1920 he launched the first fund-raising campaign for the Catholic Charities, an organization with which he remained closely associated. After his election as a cardinal on 24 March 1924 he remained active in workers' issues, encouraged the activities of the Catholic Worker movement begun by Dorothy Day and Peter Maurin and the Catholic Trade Union in his archdiocese, sponsored the Catholic Industrial Conference in 1933, and gave seminars to his clergymen in labor ethics (1937–38). In 1940, the cornerstone was laid for Cardinal Hayes High School in the Bronx, which as of 2010 remained at 650 Grand Concourse. Hayes is buried beneath St. Patrick's Cathedral.

John Bernard Kelly, *Cardinal Hayes: One of Ourselves* (New York: Farrar and Rinehart, 1940)

Mary Elizabeth Brown

Haynes, George Edmund (*b* Pine Bluff, Ark., 11 May 1880; *d* New York City, 8 Jan 1960). Civil rights reformer. He took part in the Association for the Protection of Colored Women (1905), the Committee for Improving the Industrial Conditions of Negroes in New York (1906), and the Committee on Urban Conditions among Negroes (1910); was a founder of the National Urban League (1911); and became the first black graduate of the New York School of Philanthropy (later the School of Social Work of Columbia University; 1910) and the first to receive a PhD from Columbia (in economics; 1912). Later he taught black history and social work at City College of New York (1951–59). Haynes stressed interracial cooperation. He wrote *The Negro at Work in New York City: A Study in Economic Progress* (1912).

Samuel Kelton Roberts, "Crucible for a Vision: The Work of George Edmund Haynes and the Commission on Race Relations, 1922–1947" (diss., Columbia University, 1974)

Thea Arnold

Hayworth, Rita [Cansino, Margarita Carmen] (*b* Brooklyn, 17 October 1918; *d* New York City, 14 May 1987). American actress, dancer, and model. Born to Spanish-born flamenco dancer Eduardo Cansino and English/Irish American Ziegfeld girl Volga Haworth, she began performing with her parents at age six in a vaudeville act called "The Dancing Cansinos." The family left Brooklyn for California when Rita was still a teenager. After being discovered in a Tijuana nightclub and changing her name to Hayworth (adding a *Y* to her mother's maiden name), she eventually became famous as a pin-up girl and for her roles in such movies as *Gilda* (1946) and *The Lady From Shanghai* (1948). After a successful career in Hollywood, Hayworth returned to New York City and lived the remainder of her life in the San Remo apartment building on Manhattan's Upper West Side. She suffered from early-onset Alzheimer's disease; the Rita Hayworth Gala for the Alzheimer's Association is held annually in New York City and Chicago. The American Film Institute ranks her as one of the greatest stars of all time.

Caleb Smith

HBO. See Home Box Office.

health. See Hospitals, Mental health, Occupational health, Public Health, and individuals and institutions relating to health care in New York City.

Health Insurance Plan [HIP]. Nonprofit health maintenance organization formed in 1944 under Mayor Fiorello H. La Guardia for the benefit of municipal workers and other middle-income wage earners. Organized and regulated under the state health code, it offers medical and hospital services through a network of more than 50 physician groups in the metropolitan region. In 2004 it opened its corporate headquarters at 55 Water Street in lower Manhattan. In 2010 HIP had about 1.4 million members in New York, Massachusetts, and Connecticut.

Robert A. Padgug

Hearst, William Randolph (*b* San Francisco, 29 April 1863; *d* Beverly Hills, Calif., 4 Aug 1951). Newspaper publisher and political leader. In 1887 he became the proprietor of the *San Francisco Examiner,* which was owned by his father, a millionaire mining entrepreneur and U.S. senator. After making a success of the *Examiner,* Hearst moved to New York City in 1895 and purchased the *New York Morning Journal.* In the following years, the heated competition between his now-evening paper, the *New York Journal,* and Joseph Pulitzer's *New York World* gave rise to what was known as "yellow journalism," a spectacular, often sensationalized, always reader-friendly form of daily journalism. By focusing on Spanish atrocities in Cuba, Hearst and his fellow New York City publishers helped to mold public opinion against Spain, contributing to the country's drift toward the Spanish–American War in 1898. He considered his "new journalism" an answer to the needs of a democratic society, and in daily newspapers selling for one cent he offered expanded sports coverage and illustrations, introduced comic strips such as "The Katzenjammer Kids" (1897), and covered events ignored by the "elite" press, especially workers' issues. The circulation of his newspapers exceeded one million by 1900, and in 1901 he renamed the morning edition the *American* and the evening edition the *Journal.*

After the turn of the twentieth century, Hearst used his newspapers to advance his political career. He was elected to two terms in the U.S. Congress (1903–7) from the 11th district in Manhattan. In 1905 he sought the mayoralty as a member of the Municipal Ownership League but lost to George B.

McClellan, Jr., the candidate backed by Tammany Hall, in a disputed election; in 1906 he unsuccessfully sought the governorship as a Democrat. He remained a force in New York State and City politics for another 20 years, though he never again held elective office. After establishing a reputation as a Tammany opponent, he made peace with the regular Democratic organization and was a major ally of Mayor John F. Hylan, who was elected in 1917 and reelected in 1921. He was an early and vocal opponent of U.S. intervention in World War I.

By 1922 Hearst's publishing empire included 20 daily newspapers, two wire services, the colossal King Features Syndicate, and half a dozen magazines, most of which were published in New York City. He was one of the first newspaper publishers to expand his media empire into film, newsreels, and radio. Though an initial supporter and contributor to the campaign of Franklin D. Roosevelt, he turned against Roosevelt in the mid-1930s and became a conservative opponent of the New Deal. Hearst, who wrote his own editorials, alienated many of his readers with his stridently anti-Roosevelt comments. Circulation fell at his newspapers, though his personal spending continued to climb. In 1937 his empire came close to bankruptcy; he recovered control of it only after World War II. After his death in 1951, his media empire included two newspapers in New York City: the *Journal-American* and a tabloid, the *Mirror.*

W. A. Swanberg, *Citizen Hearst: A Biography of William Randolph Hearst* (New York: Charles Scribner's Sons, 1961); David Nasaw, *The Chief: The Life of William Randolph Hearst* (Boston: Houghton Mifflin, 2000)

Robert F. Wesser

Hearst Building and Tower. Located at 300 West 57th Street and Eighth Avenue in Manhattan, the original six-story, 40,000-square-foot (3700-square-meter) design was completed in 1928 by publisher William Randolph Hearst and architect Joseph Urban at a cost of $2 million. The building was intended to house Hearst's 12 magazines. From its completion in 1929 the building remained largely unchanged, and in 1988 the Landmark Preservation Commission designated it a city landmark. With this designation came many obstacles for the addition of the tower, which the Hearst Board of Directors began discussing in 1997. The plans were finally approved with the contingency that the original stone facade be left intact. The tower, designed by architect Norman Foster, opened in 2006 and was the first skyscraper to rise from the city landscape after the terrorist attacks of 11 September 2001. It was also the first "green" commercial building in New York City to win the Gold award from Leadership in Energy and Environmental Design (LEED). The tower added an additional 46 stories to the preexisting stone facade and employed an unconventional diagonal-grid (diagrid) framing pattern that required 20 percent less steel than a conventionally framed skyscraper would have used; 90 percent of the steel used also contained recycled material. The building was designed with a number of environmental considerations, including heat-conductive limestone flooring and cooling systems that use rainwater collected on the roof. The building uses 26 percent less energy than a typical structure of its size and was awarded a gold designation by the United States Green Building Council. Owned by the Hearst Corporation, the building is the international headquarters for a number of publications worldwide, including *Cosmopolitan* and *Esquire.* The estimated cost for the completion of the tower was $500 million.

Hearst Building and Tower, 2009

In 2006 the tower earned the Emporis Skyscraper Award as the best skyscraper completed that year.

See also Green buildings.

Meghan Lalonde

Hearst Magazines. Division of the Hearst Corporation with headquarters at 959 Eighth Avenue in Manhattan. It traces its origins to 1903 when William Randolph Hearst began publishing *Motor.* In the following years he acquired *Cosmopolitan* (1905), *Good Housekeeping* (1911), and other periodicals. Hearst Magazines became known for its diverse output, which it achieved in part by testing new magazines through sales of the first issue at newsstands rather than in costly direct-mail packages sent to potential consumers. Over the years its publications came to include *Colonial Homes, Country Living, Esquire, Harper's Bazaar, House Beautiful, Redbook, Smart Money, Town and Country,* and *Marie Claire.*

Melissa M. Merritt

Heartland Village. Neighborhood in west central Staten Island, bounded to the north by Rockland Avenue, to the east by Forest Hill Road, to the south by Richmond Hill Road, and to the west by Richmond Avenue. It is part of Community District 2. A middle-class residential area with a suburban character, it had its origins as a single development designed and built in the southeastern section of New Springville in 1968–71. The original development consisted of detached and semi-detached one-family houses of two and three stories, with built-in garages and underground utility connections. The area adjoins the Staten Island Mall (1973) and centers on Public School 69 and Intermediate School 72 (1975).

Charles L. Sachs

Hebrew Free Loan Society. Nonprofit organization that grants interest-free loans on a nonsectarian basis with the goal of fostering economic self-sufficiency. It was formed in 1892 at the Wilner Synagogue on Henry Street by 11 Russian Jewish immigrants who began with working capital of $95. By the early twenty-first century the society had lent more than $200 million to nearly 860,000 borrowers. Its offices are at 675 Third Avenue.

The Poor Man's Bank (New York: Hebrew Free Loan Society, 1943)

Joyce Mendelsohn

Hebrew Immigrant Aid Society [HIAS]. International service for Jewish immigrants and refugees, formed in New York City on 16 March 1909 by the merger of the Hebrew Sheltering Society (1889), dedicated to helping eastern European Jews, and the Hebrew Immigrant Aid Society (1902), formed to provide traditional burial for Jewish immigrants who died on Ellis Island. Initially a modest organization with an annual budget of less than $10,000, during its first decade it helped immigrants to gain legal entry into the United States, obtain work and schooling, and find relatives. Its facilities included an information office at 229 Broadway that in 1912 had more than 150,000 visitors. During the same year the service helped survivors of the *Titanic,* received nearly 15,000 immigrants (and provided shelter for more than 3000), and oversaw an English translation of its Yiddish-language bulletin, published under the auspices of the Connecticut Daughters of the American Revolution. By 1914 the service had a national membership and international affiliations. During and after World War II it opened offices to help refugees and displaced persons. It took its current name in 1954 after merging with the United Service for New Americans and the migration department of the American Jewish Joint Distribution Committee, consolidating all American Jewish refugee services. In 1965 the world headquarters moved from Lafayette Street to 200 Park Avenue South. HIAS was especially active during the Hungarian revolution in 1956; the Middle Eastern crises of 1956, 1967, and 1973; and the Iranian revolution in the early 1980s. It was one of the first aid agencies that went into Iraq in 2003 after the invasion of that country. In the early twenty-first century HIAS headquarters were at 333 Seventh Avenue in Manhattan. The board of directors has included such influential members as Louis Marshall, Jacob Schiff, Oscar Straus, Cyrus Sulzberger, and Stephen S. Wise.

Mark Wischnitzer, *Visas to Freedom: The History of HIAS* (Cleveland: World, 1956); Irving Howe, *World of Our Fathers* (New York: Harcourt Brace Jovanovich, 1976)

Michael N. Dobkowski, Allen J. Share

Hebrew Mutual Benefit Society. Burial and mutual aid association formed in 1820 by several members of Shearith Israel who broke away in 1825 to found B'Nai Jeshurun. The society established temporary quarters in Washington Hall at 533 Pearl Street, where it adopted a constitution in 1826. Organized to aid the needy, visit the sick, help new immigrants, and assist in burials, the society opened its membership to all Jews in 1845. In the mid-1990s it reimbursed medical expenses and provided funerals and graves in suburban Hastings, New York, and Washington Cemetery in Brooklyn.

Joyce Mendelsohn

Hebrew Union College–Jewish Institute of Religion. Rabbinical school formed in 1950 by the merger of the Jewish Institute of Religion (1922) of New York City and Hebrew Union College (1875) of Cincinnati. In 1979 it moved to 1 West Fourth Street and became affiliated with New York University. The campus in New York City is one of four in the United States and Israel. A cantorial school, the School of Sacred Music, is also under its auspices.

Samuel E. Karff, ed., *Hebrew Union College–Jewish Institute of Religion at One Hundred Years* (Cincinnati: Hebrew Union College Press, 1976)

Marc Ferris

Heck [née Ruckle], **Barbara** (*b* Ballingrane, County Limerick, Ireland, 1734; *d* Augusta, near Prescott, Ont., 17 Aug 1804). A founder of Methodism. She moved to New York City on 11 August 1760 with her family. Dismayed at what she considered signs of spiritual poverty, including her brother's indulgence in card playing, in 1766 she formed the city's first Methodist congregation with her cousin Philip Embury. This initially consisted of five members and met in Embury's home on Augustus Street; it later built Wesley Chapel (now John Street United Methodist Church). Considered by many the "mother of American Methodism," Heck later moved to Canada and helped to establish Methodism there.

Garwood Lincoln Caddell, *Barbara Heck: Pioneer Methodist* (Cleveland, Tenn.: Pathway, 1961)

Charles Yrigoyen, Jr.

Hecker, Isaac (Thomas) (*b* New York City, 18 Dec 1830; *d* New York City, 22 Dec 1888). Writer, editor, and religious leader. As a youth he worked in his father's bakery and took part in a number of religious movements including Methodism, Unitarianism, Mormonism, and transcendentalism; he was also briefly a member of the political movement known as the Locofocos. Religious stirrings and the writings of the German Romantics led him to seek fulfillment and social purpose in communitarian ventures at Brook Farm and the Fruitlands in Massachusetts. Dissatisfied with his experiences there, he looked to Orestes A. Brownson as a mentor and in 1844 converted to Catholicism and joined a congregation known as the Redemptorists; he was ordained in 1847 and spent several years on a mission circuit devoted to immigrants. He later sought to open a center in New York City devoted to the conversion of American-born non-Catholics. After his plan was rejected by his superiors he and three other Redemptorists formed a congregation known as the Missionary Priests of St. Paul the Apostle (Paulists). To advance the congregation's work he launched two monthly periodicals, the *Catholic World* (1865) and the *Young Catholic* (1870), and formed the Catholic Publication Society (1866, now Paulist Press). Hecker wrote *Questions of the Soul*

(1855), *Aspirations of Nature* (1857), and *The Church and the Age* (1887).

Vincent F. Holden, *The Yankee Paul: Isaac Thomas Hecker* (Milwaukee: Bruce, 1958)

Robert Emmett Curran

Heeney, Cornelius (*b* County Offaly, Ireland, 1754; *d* Brooklyn, 3 May 1848). Merchant and state legislator. After immigrating to the United States in 1784, he made a fortune selling furs in New York City, and at one time was partnered with John Jacob Astor in the fur trade. He gave large sums of money to his parish church, St. Paul's on Barclay Street, as well as Old St. Patrick's Cathedral, its school, and its orphanage. He also donated the land for the second Catholic church in Brooklyn, St. Paul's, and for the orphanage and industrial school that adjoin it. With the soapmaker Andrew Morris, he donated the property that became the site of the present St. Patrick's Cathedral on Fifth Avenue. The second Roman Catholic in the state legislature, he served from 1818 to 1822. He was instrumental in establishing a branch of the Sisters of Charity in New York City, and in 1820 he became the patron and guardian of a fatherless 10-year-old boy from Brooklyn, John McCloskey, who later became the second archbishop in New York City and the first cardinal in the United States. After the Great Fire of 1835 destroyed his mercantile establishment, he chose not to rebuild and instead retired to his house and farm in Brooklyn, where he continued his philanthropic work. In 1845 he formed the Brooklyn Benevolent Society, to which he left a bequest enabling it to distribute more than $2 million to the poor and homeless of Brooklyn.

John J. Concannon

Heins and LaFarge. Firm of architects founded by George Lewis Heins (1860–1907) and Christopher Grant Lafarge (1862–1938). It designed a number of religious and public buildings in New York City that were distinguished by their Guastavino tile vaulting. In 1891 the firm won a competition for executing the Byzantine–Romanesque design of the Cathedral of St. John the Divine; the choir, crossing, and two side chapels were built between 1892 and 1911, when the firm was replaced by Ralph Adams Cram. Heins and LaFarge also drew the plans for the administration building (1899) and six animal houses (1910) at the New York Zoological Gardens in the Bronx, and for the underground stations and control houses of the city's first subway system (1901–4).

Marjorie Pearson

Heisman Trophy. Annual award presented in December to the most outstanding player in college football for the season. It is named in honor of John Heisman, a former athletics director of the Downtown Athletic Club (DAC) and college football player and coach who died in 1936 (in 1935 it was known as the DAC trophy). The trophy, which is more than 1 foot (30.5 centimeters) tall and weighs more than 25 pounds, is in the mold of a football player carrying the ball under one arm, with his other extended to ward off potential tacklers. It was sculpted by Frank Eliscu and modeled after Ed Smith, who played at New York University in the early 1930s. The DAC presented the trophy at an annual dinner at its club at 19 West Street in Lower Manhattan from 1935 until 2000. The DAC's building was damaged during the terrorist attacks of 11 September 2001, and the award was presented at the New York Marriott Marquis in Times Square that year. In 2002 the DAC declared bankruptcy; the Yale Club has presented the award in subsequent years at a series of midtown locations, including the Nokia Theatre in Times Square beginning in 2005.

David White

Heiss, Carol (*b* New York City, 20 Jan 1940). Figure skater. She grew up in Queens and in 1953 placed second to skating great Tenley Albright in her first appearance at the U.S. Figure Skating Championships. Heiss remained in Albright's shadow for the next three years, placing second at the national championships each year and at the 1956 Olympic Games. She defeated Albright for the first time at the 1956 World Figure Skating Championships, her first of five consecutive world championship titles. Heiss also earned the gold medal at the 1960 Olympic Games at Squaw Valley, in California.

David White

Held, John, Jr. (*b* Salt Lake City, 10 Jan 1889; *d* Belmar, N.J., 2 March 1958). Illustrator. He began his career in New York City in 1912 designing streetcar posters and advertisements for Wanamaker's department store. During the 1920s he became known for his absurd but forgiving caricatures of "flappers"; his comic strips "Rah Rah Rosalie" and "Margy" and other work appeared in such magazines as *Judge, Life,* the *Smart Set, Liberty, Vanity Fair, Harper's Bazaar,* and the *New Yorker.* He later turned away from illustrating to write novels and short stories, work with watercolors, and make wash drawings of animals. In 1939 he exhibited several bronze sculptures of horses at the Bland Gallery in New York City.

Shelley Armitage, *John Held, Jr., Illustrator of the Jazz Age* (Syracuse, N.Y.: Syracuse University Press, 1987)

Michael Joseph

heliports. Facilities for helicopter take-offs and landings, created by the city in the 1950s. Small heliports were maintained by the police department at the Battery and on 34th Street at the East River, and from 1953 by the Port of New York Authority at its bus terminal on Eighth Avenue; the first sizable facility opened at the foot of Wall Street in 1953. Service from commercial airports to a heliport atop the new headquarters of Pan American Airways began on 22 December 1965 after much controversy. The service proved unprofitable and was suspended in 1968. New York Airways used larger helicopters when it resumed service to the same site on 1 February 1977, but on 17 May the landing gear of a helicopter collapsed, killing four passengers and a passerby. After service was moved to a rooftop heliport near the World Trade Center, another helicopter crashed at Newark Airport on 18 April 1979, and service ceased altogether. In 1981 a new company, New York Helicopter Airways, began airport service from the eastern end of 34th Street, in what represented perhaps the final concession that heliports were not compatible with the area that needed them most: central Manhattan. In the twenty-first century there were three main public heliports: Pier 6 and FDR Drive, West 30th Street and 12th Avenue, and 34th Street and FDR Drive.

Paul Barrett

Heller, Joseph (*b* Brooklyn, 1 May 1923; *d* East Hampton, N.Y., 12 Dec 1999). Novelist. The son of Russian immigrants, he grew up in Coney Island, attended New York University (AB 1948) and Columbia University (MA 1949), and taught writing at City College. He drew on his experiences as a bombardier during World War II in his novel *Catch-22* (1961), an absurdist, antiwar black comedy that became a best seller and was made into a popular film (1970); Heller wrote most of the novel at 390 West End Avenue. His later writings include the novels *Something Happened* (1974), *Good as Gold* (1979), and *God Knows* (1984), as well as an account of his battle with Guillain–Barré syndrome, *No Laughing Matter* (1986), written with Speed Vogel. Heller's circle of friends in Manhattan included Mel Brooks, Zero Mostel, and Mario Puzo; he lived on the Upper West Side but later moved to East Hampton, New York.

B. Kimberly Taylor

Hell Gate and Hell Gate Bridge. Body of water running across a narrow strait between Astoria, in Queens, and Wards Island, connecting the East River with Long Island Sound, and the bridge spanning it. The name *Hell Gate* is a corruption of the Dutch *Hellegat* ("passage to hell"). The waterway was hazardous to navigation because of its powerful tides and many rocky outcroppings. The narrow channel's treacherous waters were described by Adriaen Block, who made the first reported passage in 1612. In 1780 the British frigate *Hussar* ran aground and sank in the channel while carrying gold and silver for military paymasters in New York City (its treasure is still sought after by divers), and dozens of other ships had sunk by the time the U.S. Army Corps of Engineers in 1876 blasted out most of the dangerous underwater rocks by setting off what was then the world's largest explosion ever detonated. The channel was later widened and deepened, but remains difficult to navigate.

One of two bridges spanning the waterway is the New York Connecting Railroad Bridge, commonly known as the Hell Gate Bridge, which joins the Bronx and Queens and provides a direct rail link between New England and New York City. Completed in 1917 from plans by engineer Gustav Lindenthal and architect Henry Hornbostel, it is one of the finest steel arch bridges in the world. It is said that the picturesque Hell Gate Bridge was the model for Australia's Sydney Harbour Bridge. The Robert F. Kennedy Memorial Bridge nearby, designed by engineer Othmar H. Ammann, opened in 1936 and connects Manhattan, the Bronx, and Queens. Both bridges pass over Wards Island and Randalls Island, which were once separated by a shallow tidal creek called Little Hell Gate.

Description of the Government Works at Hell Gate (New York: n.pub., 1873)

Gerard R. Wolfe

Hellman, Lillian (*b* New Orleans, 20 June 1907; *d* Vineyard Haven, Mass., 30 June 1984). Playwright. She grew up in Manhattan, where she spent most of her life, aside from brief stays in Hollywood and suburban Westchester County. She lived from 1911 to 1925 at 330 East 95th Street and during the late 1930s at the Hotel Élysée (56–60 East 54th Street). A communist sympathizer and apologist for Stalinism, she became well known for her contemptuous testimony in 1952 before the House Un-American Activities Committee, leading her to be blacklisted in Hollywood. Her reputation revived during the 1970s when she published three volumes of memoirs, but she was harshly criticized by many liberal anticommunists, who accused her of distorting history. From 1970 to 1984 her principal residence was 630 Park Avenue. Hellman's published writings include the plays *The Children's Hour* (1934), *The Little Foxes* (1939), and *Watch on the Rhine* (1941), and the memoirs *An Unfinished Woman* (1969), *Pentimento* (1973), and *Scoundrel Time* (1976), which vividly depict her romantic liaison with the writer Dashiell Hammett and the turbulence of the 1950s.

Doris V. Falk, *Lillian Hellman* (New York: Ungar, 1978)

Lawson Bowling

Hellmann's Mayonnaise. Mayonnaise brand that was born in 1905 when recent German immigrant Richard Hellmann opened a delicatessen on the Upper West Side at 490 Columbus Avenue. In several dishes he featured his wife's recipe for mayonnaise, which became so popular that he sold it individually and eventually opened a factory for jarring mayonnaise in 1912. Hellmann lived in New York City until his death in 1971.

Jessica Montesano

Hell's Kitchen. Obsolete term for an area of the West Side of Manhattan that is now called Clinton and Midtown West, bounded to the north by 59th Street, to the east by Eighth Avenue, to the south by 30th Street, and to the west by the Hudson River. In colonial times most of the area was covered by forest and farmland. At the end of the eighteenth century the Hopper family owned the land north of the Great Kill (which met the Hudson at what is now 42nd Street); land south of the Great Kill to what is now 32nd Street was covered by the Glass House Farm, which contained a glass-bottle factory. During the first half of the nineteenth century these properties were divided into lots; a railroad station opened at 11th Avenue and 30th Street in 1851, and soon there were slaughterhouses, warehouses, lumberyards, factories, and tenements throughout. The Irish were the largest ethnic group, but Scots, Germans, and African Americans also lived there. By the end of the Civil War the area was one of the worst slums in the city, known for such notorious gangs as the Gophers. The name Hell's Kitchen was perhaps taken from that of a gang formed in the area in 1868 or was adopted by local police during the 1870s. An African American enclave in the northern part of the neighborhood became facetiously known as San Juan Hill. The Ninth Avenue elevated line was extended about this time. Greeks and eastern Europeans joined the Irish in the area after 1900, followed by African Americans from the South and Puerto Ricans in the 1940s. After the 1950s other immigrant groups moved there, along with a community of actors and artists, who were initially attracted by the close proximity of the theater district, the Actors Studio on West 44th Street, and the huge Manhattan Plaza apartment buildings on West 42nd Street that was built in the 1970s to house artists.

Several public works projects were undertaken during the 1930s, including the West Side Highway, the Lincoln Tunnel, the New York Central Railroad West Side Improvement Project, and the Port Authority Bus Terminal. Many families were displaced and tenements destroyed at this time, and Paddy's Market, a well-known pushcart market, was forced to move in 1938 from the area under the Ninth Avenue elevated line between 38th and 42nd streets; the elevated line closed in 1940. After two teenage boys were killed in gang wars in 1959, local organizations sought to improve the image of the neighborhood by calling it Clinton (after DeWitt Clinton Park, between 52nd and 54th streets west of 11th Avenue). During the 1960s, with the decline of the ocean liner, much of the waterfront and the piers were abandoned, and most of the housing in the northern section was demolished to make way for Lincoln Center and related developments. The creation of a Special Clinton District (SCD) in 1974 blocked changes for almost 20 years by trying to preserve the low-density nature of the neighborhood and requiring special permits for any construction. In the 1980s efforts were accelerated to renovate the neighborhood as a fashionable

Hell's Kitchen, Ninth Avenue

area, and a series of high-profile convictions reduced the influence of the Irish gang the Westies. The neighborhood slowly lost its warehouses, Irish bars, and ramshackle tenements as it became trendy during the 1990s and the early years of the twenty-first century; the booming economy and intensified demand for residential and commercial spaces led to gentrification. Zoning rules were relaxed after 2001, and the building boom in the neighborhood resulted in many large-scale projects, including the Hearst Tower at Eighth Avenue and 56th Street. Many buildings were converted to cooperatives and condominiums; television studios producing such shows as Comedy Central's *Daily Show* moved into the area; and cruise ships returned to docks on the West Side. The Intrepid Sea-Air-Space Museum, aboard an aircraft carrier from World War II docked at Pier 86 on West 46th Street, was opened in 1982 and became a popular tourist attraction; it was closed for renovations in 2006 and reopened in 2008. In the early twenty-first century the neighborhood features a wide array of cultural attractions, such as the Alvin Ailey American Dance Theater, CBS Broadcast Center, and Sony Music Studios. The area is also famous for its many restaurants and the numerous international food stores lining Ninth Avenue. The rough-and-tumble reputation of the neighborhood was celebrated in popular culture, notably in the ballet "Slaughter on Tenth Avenue" (from the musical *On Your Toes* [1936]) and the musical *West Side Story* (1957).

Lisa Keller, George Winslow

Helmsley, Harry B(rakmann) (*b* New York City, 4 March 1909; *d* Scottsdale, Ariz., 4 Jan 1997). Real estate developer. He grew up in the Bronx. With Leon Spear, a manager of properties in the garment district, he formed Helmsley–Spear in 1955. The firm became the city's largest in the business, and in 1961 it bought the Empire State Building in a complicated leaseback arrangement with the Crown family of Chicago (the owners of the building) and the Prudential Insurance Company (the owners of the land). As a partner of Lawrence Wien, Helmsley bought several valuable office buildings and hotels, including the Fisk and Lincoln buildings and the Plaza Hotel. Later in the 1960s he bought Wien's financial interest in the Empire State Building as well as several of the city's leading real estate brokerage and property management firms; he then erected the Pfizer Building and 1 Penn Plaza. In 1969 he bought the Furman–Wolfson real estate trust for $165 million, thus gaining ownership of 30 large buildings in New York City, Chicago, and Los Angeles. In 1972 he divorced his first wife of 32 years and married one of his employees, Leona Roberts; she became the president of the Harley and Helmsley Hotels, a subsidiary of Helmsley–Spear that bought and refurbished 21 hotels in the city, including the Villard Houses (renamed the Helmsley Palace) and the Harley (renamed the Helmsley). By the 1980s the Helmsleys' real estate assets were valued at more than $1 billion. The couple was indicted for tax evasion and mail fraud in 1988; he was declared incompetent to stand trial, but she was convicted of evading $1.2 million in federal taxes.

Richard Hammer, *The Helmsleys: The Rise and Fall of Harry and Leona* (New York: New American Library, 1990)

Lisa Gitelman, Marc A. Weiss

Helmsley [Roberts; née Rosenthal], **Leona (Mindy)** (*b* Marbletown, N.Y., 4 July 1920; *d* Greenwich, Conn., 20 Aug 2007). Hotel and real estate executive. She worked in real estate for several years before marrying billionaire Harry B. Helmsley in 1972. As the president of Harley and Helmsley Hotels, a subsidiary of his firm that managed 21 hotels in New York City, she became widely known for a series of advertisements that portrayed her as an exacting supervisor intolerant of the slightest imperfections in hotel furnishings. Indicted for tax evasion in 1988, she was convicted of evading $1.2 million in federal taxes and sentenced to four years in prison after a celebrated trial at which many disgruntled employees testified about the Helmsleys' financial dealings and about construction work done on their mansion in suburban Greenwich, Connecticut. One witness quoted her as having said that "only the little people pay taxes." In her will, she left $12 million to her dog.

Richard Hammer, *The Helmsleys: The Rise and Fall of Harry and Leona* (New York: New American Library, 1990)

Henderson, Fletcher (Hamilton, Jr.) [Smack] (*b* Cuthbert, Ga., 1 Dec 1897; *d* New York City, 29 Dec 1952). Bandleader, arranger, and pianist. After settling in New York City he toured with the singer Ethel Waters (1921–22) and recorded accompaniments for blues singers. At the Roseland Ballroom (on Broadway at West 51st Street) he led an innovative big band from 1924 that included the cornetist Louis Armstrong (1924–25), the tenor saxophonist Coleman Hawkins, and the arranger Don Redman. Until the late 1920s this was acclaimed as the best jazz band in New York City, but Henderson was indifferent to success. The membership changed often and in 1934 the group disbanded. His own arrangements, including *King Porter Stomp,* were crucial to the great popularity of Benny Goodman's big band in 1935. From 1936 he resumed working as a leader, except for a period as a staff arranger for Goodman.

Walter C. Allen, *Hendersonia: The Music of Fletcher Henderson and His Musicians: A Bio-Discography* (Highland Park, N.J.: Walter C. Allen, 1973)

Barry Kernfeld

Henderson, Skitch [Lyle Russell Cedric] (*b* Birmingham, England, 27 Jan 1928; *d* New Milford, Conn., 1 Nov 2005). Pianist, conductor, and composer. He started playing the piano at the age of four under the tutelage of his aunt. After playing in roadhouses in the Midwest, including a 1937 MGM tour with Judy Garland, he moved to New York City to conduct the National Broadcasting Company (NBC) Symphony Orchestra. After World War II he worked as a music director for NBC radio, including for *The Philco Hour with Bing Crosby* (1948–55); Crosby allegedly gave Henderson the nickname "Skitch" for his remarkable ability to quickly transcribe music. Switching over to NBC television, he led the band for both *The Tonight Show* (1962–66) and *The Today Show.* He also released hundreds of recordings, including a groundbreaking version of George Gershwin's *Porgy and Bess,* for which he won a Grammy Award in 1963. In 1983 he founded the New York Pops Orchestra, a nonprofit orchestra that specializes in American pop music; he served as both director and conductor of the orchestra until his death.

Sarah Wansley

Hennock, Frieda (Barkin) (*b* Kovel, Poland [now Ukraine], 27 Dec 1904; *d* Washington, D.C., 20 June 1960). Attorney and public official. She attended Morris High School in the Bronx and graduated from Brooklyn Law School in 1924. From 1926 to 1948 she worked as a criminal and corporate lawyer in New York City. She was appointed commissioner of the Federal Communications Commission by President Harry Truman in 1948. She was the first female commissioner and served until 1955; during her tenure she successfully lobbied for the agency to set aside permanent educational stations for public broadcasting.

Jessica Montesano

Henri, Robert [Cozad, Robert Henry] (*b* Cincinnati, 25 June 1865; *d* New York City, 12 July 1929). Painter and teacher. Brought up in the western United States, he studied at the Pennsylvania Academy of the Fine Arts in Philadelphia and later in Paris. After returning to Philadelphia he became the teacher of the young painters John Sloan, George B. Luks, William Glackens, and Everett Shinn, all of whom followed him to New York City after he moved there in 1900. He taught at the New York School of Art from 1902 to 1908 and then opened his own school. Rejecting impressionism and the genteel styles of painting favored by traditionalists, he urged the National Academy of Design to include the work of young realist painters in its annual shows. With Sloan in 1908 he organized an exhibition at the Macbeth Galleries of The Eight, which stirred controversy for its celebration of unconventional styles and its depictions of urban, working-class life. Henri's best-known works include *Laughing Child* (1907). His lecture notes and talks were published as *The Art Spirit* in 1930.

William Innes Homer, *Robert Henri and His Circle* (Ithaca, N.Y.: Cornell University Press, 1969)

Patricia Hills

Henri Bendel. Firm of specialty retailers. In 1896 Henri Bendel (*b* Lafayette, La., 1858; *d* 1939) opened a small millinery shop at 10 Bond Street, which he moved to 67 East Ninth Street in the following year, to Fifth Avenue in 1906, and to 10 West 57th Street during World War I. The firm operated a number of boutiques that sold hats, women's clothing, perfumes, cosmetics, and home furnishings. The elegant, imaginative store window designs set the standard for other designers. The retailing firm The Limited, Inc. (later renamed Limited Brands) bought Bendel in 1985. In 1991 its main department store moved to a building at 712 Fifth Avenue, with three-story windows designed by the French glass designer René Lalique.

Leslie Gourse, Kenneth T. Jackson

Henry Holt and Company. Firm of book publishers, formed in 1866 in New York City by Henry Holt and Frederick Leypoldt as the firm of Leypoldt and Holt; in 1873 it became Henry Holt and Company when Holt became the sole owner. The firm published literary works and a highly regarded list of books by prominent nineteenth-century American scientists and social scientists. It was also a leading publisher of poetry (notably that of Robert Frost) and of textbooks. In 1960 the firm strengthened its educational division by merging with Rinehart and Company and John C. Winston Company to form Holt, Rinehart and Winston. The new firm was acquired in 1967 by the Columbia Broadcasting System (CBS), which in 1985 sold its trade division of the company to the German firm Verlagsgruppe Georg von Holtzbrinck. The new trade house formed by this transaction reassumed the name Henry Holt and Company. CBS sold the school and college departments, still known as Holt, Rinehart and Winston, to Harcourt Brace Jovanovich in 1986. In the 1990s Henry Holt had offices at 115 West 18th Street in Manhattan; in the early twenty-first century, the Macmillan group of publishers, of which Henry Holt is a part, had relocated to the Flatiron Building at 175 Fifth Avenue.

See also Book publishing.

Eileen K. Cheng

Henry Street Settlement. Settlement house. It had its beginnings in the work of Lillian Wald and Mary Brewster, who from 1893 provided nursing care at home for the indigent on the Lower East Side. Their work was financed by Betty Loeb and her son-in-law, the financier Jacob Schiff. As other nurses joined them, their need for larger quarters led them to move in 1895 to a building at 265 Henry Street that became known as the Henry Street Settlement. Within a decade of its founding more than 20 nurses worked for the settlement, which was the first institution of its kind to have a visiting nurse service. They lived in the neighborhoods where they worked and by the turn of the twentieth century attended to 4500 patients, made 35,035 home visits and 3542 convalescent visits, and gave 28,809 first-aid treatments. Their nursing services were available throughout the city from 9 a.m. to 6 p.m., seven days a week. Patients were usually visited daily or as often as needed; night nurses, cleaning, and laundry were provided for the gravely ill. The nurses ran convalescent homes and first-aid stations, where they treated burns, infections, and injuries. In some sections of the city they provided assistance 24 hours a day to women in childbirth and held health conferences for the mothers of infants. The settlement had 46 residents by 1911, of whom 41 were women. By 1913 it occupied seven houses serving the Lower East Side and had branches in uptown Manhattan and the Bronx. Its citywide visiting nurse service made 200,000 home visits, and settlement clubs for boys, girls, and mothers had 3000 members and 25,000 participants in various programs.

The settlement operated a dance school where national and folk dances were revived, a playground (one of the first in the nation), a gymnasium, debating clubs, literary societies, a kindergarten, a savings and loan fund, and a cooperative food store. The year 1915 marked the opening of the Neighborhood Playhouse (now at 340 East 54th Street). This became the first theater in the United States to present a play by a black author with a black cast before a racially integrated audience (*Rachel,* by Angelina Weld Grimké), and by the 1920s the playhouse was a leading experimental theater. Wald retired in 1933, when the staff included 265 nurses. The nursing service, which achieved independent status in 1944, moved to 107 East 70th Street and became known as the Visiting Nurse Service of New York. In its first century of operation the settlement saw the ethnic composition of the Lower East Side change from eastern and central European to mostly Asian and Hispanic. The building on Henry Street was designated a National Historic Landmark in 1989. In the early twenty-first century the Henry Street Settlement occupied 20 sites, had a budget of more than $30 million, and served 60,000 people a year.

Karen Buhler-Wilkerson

Henry Street Settlement, 2009

Henson, Jim (James) Maury (*b* Greenville, Miss., 24 Sept 1936; *d* New York City, 16 May 1990). Puppeteer, television producer, and filmmaker. He moved with his wife to New York City in 1963 where he began to produce shows with fictional puppet characters he called Muppets. He introduced the concept of portraying puppets on television with the puppeteer working off screen. In 1968 Henson began collaboration on *Sesame Street,* a television program with both live actors and Muppets that dominated children's public television for several decades. Kermit, a green frog Muppet, was Henson's signature creation, and Henson brought him along for most television appearances and interviews. Henson continued to make films and television shows and appearances for his Muppets until his sudden death from complications related to pneumonia. A large public memorial service, which included numerous musical performances by Muppet characters, was held for him at the Cathedral of St. John the Divine in upper Manhattan.

David White

Henson, Matthew Alexander (*b* Charles County, Md., 8 Aug 1866; *d* New York City, 9 Mar 1955). First African American to set foot on the North Pole on 6 April 1909. He later became the first African American member of the Explorers Club, despite being previously excluded, and once worked at the American Museum of Natural History. After his North Pole expedition, Henson worked in a garage in Brooklyn while Commander Robert E. Perry, with whom Henson made the voyage, received numerous accolades for the exploration. African American politician Charles Anderson wrote to President William Taft in 1913 and arranged for Henson's civil service appointment at the New York Customs House. He worked there as a messenger boy for more than 20 years. He was buried at Woodlawn Cemetery in the Bronx after being denied burial rights at Arlington National Cemetery in Washington, D.C., but in 1988 his remains were moved, with those of his wife, to Arlington.

Kathleen Benson

Hepburn, Katharine (Houghton) (*b* Hartford, Conn., 12 May 1907; *d* Old Saybrook, Conn., 29 June 2003). Actress. She made her debut on Broadway under the name Katherine Burns in *Night Hostess* in September 1928 before appearing in November under her own name in *These Days* at the Cort Theatre. After working as an understudy and acting in many plays that closed quickly, she had her first long run in *The Warrior's Husband* at the Morosco Theater in 1932, in which she played an Amazon warrior and made her entrance bounding down stairs with a stag over her shoulders. The exuberance and success of this performance won her a contract with Radio–Keith–Orpheum (RKO) for George Cukor's film *A Bill of Divorcement* (1932). While filming *Woman of the Year* in 1941 she began a relationship with the married Spencer Tracy, which lasted until he died in 1967; she made nine motion pictures with him. One of her most explicitly feminist works, *Adam's Rib* (1949, with Tracy), was shot in New York City. In 1962 she appeared in the film adaptation of Eugene O'Neill's *Long Day's Journey into Night* (1962), directed by Sidney Lumet, which was rehearsed on Second Avenue and shot in a house on City Island. Hepburn received Academy Awards for her films *Morning Glory* (1933), *Guess Who's Coming to Dinner* (1967, with Tracy), *The Lion in Winter* (1968), and *On Golden Pond* (1981). Her autobiography *Me: Stories of My Life* was published in 1991. For many years Hepburn lived at 244 East 49th Street in the Turtle Bay neighborhood of Manhattan. After her death that block was renamed Katharine Hepburn Place in her honor.

Katharine Hepburn

Garson Kanin, *Tracy and Hepburn: An Intimate Memoir* (New York: Viking, 1971); Christopher Andersen, *Young Kate: The Remarkable Hepburns and the Childhood That Shaped an American Legend* (New York: Henry Holt, 1988)

Grai St. Clair Rice

Herald Square. Section of midtown Manhattan, centered at the intersection of Sixth Avenue, 34th Street, and Broadway and encompassing Greeley Square. The area is named for the *New York Herald*, which from 1895 to the 1920s had its headquarters in a two-story, arcaded Italianate building on 35th Street designed by the firm of McKim, Mead and White. It became the heart of the Tenderloin area during the 1870s and 1880s after the Sixth Avenue elevated line was built, and it was known for theaters, dance halls, seafood restaurants, hotels like the Herald Square Hotel and the McAlpin Hotel, and the Manhattan Opera House. The dry-goods firm of R. H. Macy bought and razed the opera house in 1901 and in 1902 opened its flagship department store. Other stores that moved to the area included Gimbel's, Saks Fifth Avenue, and Ohrbach's, making it a major shopping area. In the early twenty-first century only Macy's remained. In the center of the square is the Bennett Clock, named for James Gordon Bennett, Jr., publisher of the *Herald*.

Michele Herman

View of Herald Square, north from 34th Street along Broadway, 1904. The Sixth Avenue elevated railway is to the right; in the background the New York Times *building is under construction*

Herbert, Victor (August) (*b* Dublin, 1 Feb 1859; *d* New York City, 26 May 1924). Composer. He studied the cello and composition in Germany and moved to New York City in 1886 with his wife, Therese, a noted Viennese opera singer. He was a founder of the New York String Quartet and formed an orchestra for light music that came to be highly regarded. From 1898 to 1904 he conducted the Pittsburgh Symphony; he was also a guest conductor of the New York Philharmonic Society. Among his symphonic compositions are two cello concertos (1885, 1894) and the tone poem *Hero and Leander* (1901). In his mid-30s he began writing operettas, a genre at which he excelled: *Babes in Toyland* (1903), *Mlle Modiste* (1905), *The Red Mill* (1906), and *Naughty Marietta* (1910) were all successfully produced in New York City. He also wrote one grand opera, *Natoma* (1911), and a one-act opera, *Madeleine* (1913), and in 1916 composed music for the film *The Fall of a Nation*. Among his finest songs are "Kiss Me Again" (1905), "In Old New York" (known also as "The Streets of New York," 1906), "Ah, Sweet Mystery of Life" (1910), "I'm Falling in Love with Someone" (1910), and "Italian Love Song" (1910). He wrote almost 40 operettas, known for their memorable tunes, adept orchestrations, full-sounding textures, resourcefully manipulated harmony and rhythm, and waltz and march meters reflecting his European background. Although the tonal polish of Herbert's songs made him the most popular composer of his day in New York City, his melodies have extended ranges, demanding leaps, and chromatic alterations that make them more difficult to sing than most music from Tin Pan Alley.

Edward N. Waters, *Victor Herbert: A Life in Music* (New York: Macmillan, 1955)

Nicholas E. Tawa

Hernández, Victoria (*b* Aguadilla, Puerto Rico, 1897; *d* Trujillo Alto, Puerto Rico, 1998). Entrepreneur. A pioneer businesswoman, she was critical in the development of the city's Latin music industry. She arrived in New York City in 1919 with her brothers, Jesús and Rafael (a composer). Her first store, Almacenes Hernández, was El Barrio's first Latin music record store; it opened in 1927 at 1735 Madison Avenue but soon moved to 1724 Madison to provide a backroom for Victoria's piano lessons and Rafael's composing. Victoria became an intermediary between musicians and recording labels, among them Victor and Decca Records. She managed tours and bookings for Cuarteto Victoria, Rafael's group, and promoted her own record label, Hispano. Her second music store, Casa Hernández, at 786 Prospect Avenue in the South Bronx, opened in 1941, selling records and musical instruments on one side and women's dresses on the other. She married Gabriel Oller, who was noted for founding the Spanish Music Center in East Harlem and the Dynasonic record label.

Ruth Glasser, *My Music Is My Flag: Puerto Rican Musicians and Their New York Communities, 1917–1940* (Berkeley: University of California Press, 1995)

Virginia Sánchez Korrol

Herrmann, Bernard (*b* New York City, 29 June 1911; *d* North Hollywood, Calif., 24 December 1975). Composer. His family lived at 214 East 15th Street; he attended DeWitt Clinton High School, graduated from New York University, and studied at the Julliard School. In 1933 he conducted the first concert of the New School's New Chamber Orchestra, and the next year he began working as a staff conductor at Columbia Broadcasting System (CBS). By 1943 he was the chief conductor of the CBS Symphony Orchestra. During that time he lived at 325 East 57th Street. He was best known for his scores of all of Alfred Hitchcock's films, notably *Psycho* (1960), *The Man Who Knew Too Much* (1956), and *Vertigo* (1958). He composed scores for television, radio shows, theater, and movies that included *Citizen Kane* (1941; his first film), *Cape Fear* (1962), and *Taxi Driver* (1976; his last film).

Steven C. Smith, *A Heart at Fire's Center: The Life and Music of Bernard Herrmann* (Berkeley: University of California Press, 1991)

Jessica Montesano

Herter Brothers. Firm of furniture manufacturers and interior decorators, formed in 1864 by Gustave Herter (1830–98) of Stuttgart, Germany, and his half-brother Christian (1839–83). Its predecessor was a shop at 48 Mercer Street opened in 1851 by Gustave, who moved to the city in 1848, reportedly worked for the firm of Tiffany, Young and Ellis, and had brief partnerships with Auguste Pottier and Erastus Bulkley. The shop expanded to 547 Broadway and produced furniture, architectural woodwork, and decorations for banks and private residences in the city between 1858 and 1864. Christian joined the firm after studying in Stuttgart and possibly in Paris before moving to the city in 1859. In the years after the Civil War, Herter Brothers became known nationwide for the craftsmanship and innovative designs of its furniture. Christian acquired his brother's interest in the firm in 1870, and under his direction from 1870 to 1883 it became known for suites of furniture in an Anglo-Japanesque style commissioned by such customers as the financiers Jay Gould and Mark Hopkins. The last and most important commission he accepted was the design and interior decoration of William H. Vanderbilt's house at Fifth Avenue and 51st Street (1879–82); among the pieces he created for it was a mother-of-pearl inlaid rosewood library table (now in the Metropolitan Museum of Art). After he withdrew, the firm continued under William Baumgarten until 1891 and William Gilman Nichols until it ceased operations in 1906.

Katherine S. Howe, Alice Cooney Frelinghuysen, Catherine Hoover Voorsanger, et al., *Herter Brothers: Furniture and Interiors for a Gilded Age* (New York: Harry N. Abrams, in association with the Museum of Fine Arts, Houston, 1994)

Deborah Dependahl Waters

Herts and Tallant. Firm of architects. Established by Henry Beaumont Herts (1871–1933) and Hugh Tallant (1869–1952), it was best known for innovative theater designs. Herts and Tallant's first work was for socially progressive institutions, including the Harmonie Club (1898) and the Aguilar Library (1899). The firm was introduced to the theater world by Herts's sister, Alice Minnie Herts, an early director of the Educational Alliance who later established the pioneering Children's Educational Theater. Combining beaux-arts aesthetics and modern design principles with such technical innovations as cantilevered balconies, the firm's designs for theaters were nationally celebrated. Among these were the New Amsterdam Theatre (1903), the most important example in the city of art nouveau; the New Lyceum Theater (1903), in an ornate beaux-arts style; the New German Theater, in collaboration with art nouveau poster artist Alfonse Mucha (1908; demolished); and the Brooklyn Academy of Music (1908), featuring unprecedented terra-cotta decoration. After the partnership between the two men ended in 1911, Herts alone designed the home of the New York Giants baseball team, the Polo Grounds (1911; demolished); other theaters, including the Shubert (1913) and the Booth (1913); several synagogues; and Yeshiva University (1928).

Peter L. Donhauser

Heschel, Abraham J(oshua) (*b* Warsaw, 11 Jan 1907; *d* New York City, 23 Dec 1972). Rabbi, theologian, and author. He was born to a distinguished Hasidic family and received his doctorate in philosophy from the University of Berlin in 1933. In 1940 he fled the Nazis and moved to the United States, where he taught at Hebrew Union College in Cincinnati. He moved in 1945 to New York City and joined the faculty of the Jewish Theological Seminary of America, where he remained for 27 years (living at 425 Riverside Drive). Later he became one of the best-known and most widely respected Hasidic scholars and also worked to bring about greater ecumenism between different branches of Judaism and between Jews and Christians. In 1964 he risked the anger of Jews by meeting with Pope Paul VI, as a result of which the second Vatican Council issued the statement *Nostra Aetate* condemning anti-Semitism and affirming the enduring validity of Judaism. In the following year Heschel became the first rabbi to receive a visiting professorship at Union Theological Seminary. He was also active politically and spoke repeatedly against racism and the Vietnam War. In 1965 he marched with Martin Luther King, Jr., in Selma, Alabama, and he was also a chairman of Clergy Concerned about Vietnam. Heschel wrote more than 20 books, among them *God in Search of Man: A Philosophy of Judaism* (1955).

John C. Merkle, *The Genesis of Faith: The Depth Psychology of Abraham Joshua Heschel* (New York: Macmillan, 1985); Donald J. Moore, *The Human and the Holy: The Spirituality of Abraham Joshua Heschel* (New York: Fordham University Press, 1989)

Edward T. O'Donnell

Heterodoxy. Women's luncheon and lecture club formed in Greenwich Village in 1912 by the former Unitarian minister Marie Jenney Howe. Over the years it enlisted 110 known members, including the social reformer Crystal Eastman; the suffragist Inez Millholland Boissevain; the schoolteacher and activist Henrietta Rodman; the anarchist Rose Strunsky; the socialist, peace activist, and suffragist Katherine Anthony; the lawyer and theatrical producer Helen Arthur; the novelist and playwright Ida Wylie; the novelist and teacher Helen Hull; the suffragist and prison reformer Paula Jakobi; and the writer and radio commentator Mary Margaret McBride; as well as Elisabeth Irwin, director of the Little Red School House in Greenwich Village; S. Josephine Baker, director of the New York City Bureau of Child Hygiene; and the writer Mabel Dodge, who described the members as "unorthodox women . . . who did things and did them openly." The group met every other Saturday in local restaurants to discuss controversial topics. In 1915 Edith Lees, wife of Havelock Ellis, spoke to the club, as did Gertrude Stein and Alice B. Toklas in 1934. Although most members were feminists, the club welcomed women regardless of their politics, background, or sexual orientation. It remained active until 1940.

Judith Schwarz, *Radical Feminists of Heterodoxy: Greenwich Village, 1912–1940* (Lebanon, N.H.: New Victoria, 1982)

Jan Seidler Ramirez

Hewitt, Abram S(tevens) (*b* Haverstraw, N.Y., 31 July 1822; *d* New York City, 18 Jan 1903). Mayor and industrialist. He graduated from Columbia College in 1842 and in 1845 opened an iron mill in Trenton, New Jersey, with Edward Cooper, a classmate whose father, the industrialist Peter Cooper, financed the operation. He produced a variety of new iron and steel products and invested in many firms, often serving on their boards. In 1855 he married Peter Cooper's daughter Sarah and began supervising the construction of the Union for the Advancement of Science and Art (later known as Cooper Union); he was chairman of its board of trustees until 1903. Influenced by Samuel J. Tilden, he began his political career as a Democrat and was active in the campaign against William M. "Boss" Tweed. He was elected to five congressional terms beginning in 1874 and was chairman of the Democratic National Committee in 1876 during Tilden's presidential campaign (when Peter Cooper mounted a rival campaign as the candidate of the Greenback Party). Backed by Tammany Hall in 1886, he was elected mayor in a dramatic campaign against the radical economic reformer Henry George and Theodore Roosevelt, the future president. Once in office he struggled to achieve his long-sought goals to unify business, labor, and taxpayers and to end corruption, improve municipal services (particularly rapid transit), and help the poor. In 1886 Hewitt ended his association with Tammany Hall after a dispute over patronage, and he was defeated for reelection. He remained active in philanthropic affairs and business to the end of his life.

Allan Nevins, *Abram S. Hewitt, with Some Account of Peter Cooper* (New York: Harper and Brothers, 1935)

Jerome Mushkat

High Bridge. Oldest of the great bridges in New York City, spanning the Harlem River at 173rd Street. It was built between 1837 and 1848 to bring water to the city from the reservoirs of the Croton Aqueduct system to the north. The original High Bridge was Roman in conception, and many artists portrayed its massive stone arches. In the early 1920s a single span of steel replaced the stone piers in the riverbed because they interfered with navigation. A pedestrian walkway, closed since 1960, offered a fine view of the entire area. The High Bridge Watch Tower on the Manhattan side of the bridge is a state landmark. The bridge was closed in 1970, but in 2007 Mayor Michael Bloomberg announced that it would be restored and reopened and set aside about $65 million for the project; in 2010 the New York City Parks Department awarded a $4 million contract to Lichtenstein Consulting Engineers to design the renovation.

Kenneth T. Jackson

Highbridge. Neighborhood in the southwestern Bronx, bounded to the north by the Cross Bronx Expressway, to the east by Jerome Avenue and the Edward L. Grant Highway, to the south by East 161st Street, and to the west by the Harlem River; it is about six blocks wide and 10 blocks long and lies northwest of Yankee Stadium. The area is named for the High Bridge (the oldest extant bridge in New York City) built across the Harlem River between 1837 and 1848 to carry water from the Croton Aqueduct to Manhattan. It was rural and in the mid-nineteenth century became a resort, accessible by river steamer and favored by many residents of Manhattan. Bridges to Manhattan for railroads and other vehicles were built during that time, but development accelerated after 1900 with the introduction of rapid transit service. The Jerome Avenue elevated line (1918) included a spur connection to the Ninth Avenue elevated line that passed directly through the area; the Grand Concourse subway (1933) had a stop nearby at 161st Street. During these

View of High Bridge from the Bronx to Manhattan at 174th Street, ca *1900*

years many five-story walkup apartment buildings and six-story buildings with elevators were erected. By 1940 the rapidly growing population consisted mostly of middle- and working-class descendants of Irish and Jewish immigrants. During the 1950s and 1960s the New York City Housing Authority built several high-rise apartment buildings overlooking the Harlem River. Many residents moved to the suburbs, and the population became predominantly African American and Latino. Scores of apartment buildings were abandoned by landlords during the 1970s as arson fires ravaged the area and the population declined; from the 1980s on the area stabilized, and some of the older housing was refurbished. In the early twenty-first century many new immigrants from Africa moved into the community.

Peter Derrick

Highland Park. Neighborhood in east central Brooklyn, bounded to the north by the border with Queens County, to the east by Force Tube Avenue, to the south by Liberty Avenue, and to the west by Pennsylvania Avenue; it is nearly coextensive with Cypress Hills, which is bounded to the east by Eldert Lane and to the south by Atlantic Avenue. It is named for a park of 141 acres (57 hectares) at its northern edge, which in the twenty-first century has been left to return to a natural state and is now one of few natural urban forests. The neighborhood was developed in the second half of the nineteenth century and by the 1890s was a large suburb. It was neglected by the 1970s, and Jamaica Avenue was lined with abandoned houses and empty lots. During the 1980s the neighborhood and its environs attracted many immigrants from Guyana, the Dominican Republic, and Jamaica. By 2000 the population was largely black, with a smaller number of Latin Americans, Italians, and other whites. Most of the housing in the area consisted of one- and two-family detached houses, along with some apartment buildings. Fulton Street and Jamaica Avenue are the main thoroughfares.

Ellen Marie Snyder-Grenier

High Line. Section of the former West Side Line elevated freight railroad, from Gansevoort Street to West 34th Street running 13 miles (21 kilometers) mostly along 10th Avenue. The West Side Line was used starting in 1847 to transport goods to and from the west side harbor on the street level. In 1929 the city elevated the tracks to its present 30-foot (9-meter) height, and it opened in 1934. By the 1960s the High Line was seldom used, and it was abandoned in 1980. The tracks became overgrown until the 1990s when neighborhood activists formed Friends of the High Line. The city-owned space was saved from demolition and in 2006 construction began for turning the High Line into an urban park and promenade. In June 2009 the first section opened, from Ganesvoort Street to 20th Street.

Jessica Montesano

High Line, 2009

High School of Music and Art. Original name of Fiorello H. La Guardia High School of Music and Art and Performing Arts.

highways. See Brooklyn–Queens Expressway, FDR Drive, Streets and highways, and West Side Highway.

Hill and Knowlton. Public relations firm established in Cleveland in 1927 by John W. Hill, who in 1933 formed a partnership with Donald Knowlton. The firm opened a branch in New York City in 1938. During the mid-1940s Hill reorganized the firm and moved its headquarters to New York City. It later became a subsidiary of the firm J. Walter Thompson. Hill and Knowlton was the largest public relations agency in the United States until 1984. After acquiring the third-largest agency, Carl Byoir and Associates, in 1986 it was again the largest firm in its field, with combined revenues of more than $125 million. Some of its clients have included the American Heart Association, the government of Kuwait, the tobacco industry, and the Catholic Church in America. In 2010 its headquarters were at 909 Third Avenue in Manhattan.

John W. Hill, *The Making of a Public Relations Man* (New York: David McKay, 1963)

Alan R. Raucher

Hillcrest. Neighborhood in central Queens, lying mostly in Jamaica and partly in Flushing and bounded to the north by Union Turnpike, to the east by Jamaica Estates, to the south by Hillside Avenue, and to the west by 164th Street. It was developed on 200 acres (80 hectares) of land in the spring of 1909 by William F. Wyckoff, who formed the Hillcrest of Jamaica Company. After the first two sections were prepared along Union Turnpike, development was hastened by the incorporation on 9 March 1910 of the Jamaica–Hillcrest Company under the direction of Bryan L. Kennelly. In succeeding months the company paved streets north of Hillside Avenue; installed gas, water, and electricity; and built houses ranging in price from $6500 to $12,000. Lots were sold at auction from 1910 to 1915, and by 1913 there were 60 houses. Further development was aided by the growth of Jamaica Estates. The opening of the elevated line along Jamaica Avenue in 1918 brought Hillcrest within the five-cent fare zone. The sale of houses in the northern section increased after Grand Central Parkway opened in 1933. By World War II Hillcrest had become densely built up with comfortable one-family houses. It became more ethnically diverse during the 1970s. About one-fifth of the immigrants who settled in the area in the 1980s were from Guyana; others were from Haiti, China, India, and Colombia. As of the early twenty-first century Hillcrest had developed a substantial Orthodox Jewish population.

Vincent Seyfried

Hillman, Sidney (*b* Zagare, Russia, 1887; *d* New York City, 10 July 1946). Labor leader. A refugee of the revolution of 1905 in Russia, he devoted himself to the labor movement. In 1914 he moved to New York City, where he became the first president of the Amalgamated

Clothing Workers of America, which challenged the timidity, nativism, and craft elitism of the men's clothing trade union affiliated with the American Federation of Labor (AFL). For this he earned the enmity of Samuel Gompers, president of the AFL, but gained the support of such progressive reformers as Louis D. Brandeis, Lillian Wald, Florence Kelley, and Fiorello H. La Guardia, who were impressed with his commitment to "industrial democracy" and the "new unionism." Hillman became known as the country's foremost "labor statesman" for introducing a new method of collective bargaining and innovations such as unemployment insurance, the union bank, and affordable cooperative housing. He worked closely with Governor Franklin D. Roosevelt and his aides, including Felix Frankfurter, Frances Perkins, and Rexford Tugwell. A ready supporter of the New Deal, he was appointed to the National Industrial Recovery Board by President Roosevelt, who relied on his political advice about labor and social welfare legislation. Hillman recognized the unique opportunity of the situation and with John L. Lewis formed the Committee for Industrial Organization (CIO; later renamed the Congress of Industrial Organizations) to introduce unionism to American heavy industry. He carefully built a relationship between the CIO and the Democratic Party and in New York City helped to form the American Labor Party, which proved more effective than the local Democratic machine in mobilizing the electorate. After a strike at Woolworth's department store in 1937, he helped to form the Department Store Workers Organizing Committee. During World War II he established the Political Action Committee of the CIO, which strengthened the alliance between the Democratic Party and the labor movement that endured for a quarter-century. At his death Hillman was recognized as a leader of both the national labor movement and the anti-fascist coalition abroad.

Steve Fraser

Hillquit, Morris (*b* Riga, Latvia, 1 Aug 1869; *d* New York City, 7 Oct 1933). Lawyer and political leader. He moved to New York City in 1886 and built a law practice by working closely with garment workers' unions. A leader of the Socialist Party of America (SPA), he sought election to the U.S. House of Representatives five times. He won 22 percent of the vote in the mayoral election of 1917 and sought the mayoralty again in 1933. Hillquit sought to preserve the SPA and the spirit of socialism in the city in the face of challenges from communism and the New Deal.

Norma Fain Pratt, *Morris Hillquit: A Political History of an American Jewish Socialist* (Westport, Conn.: Greenwood, 1979)

Melvyn Dubofsky

Hillside. Neighborhood in east central Queens east of Jamaica, bounded to the north by Hillside Avenue, to the east by 184th Street, to the south by Jamaica Avenue, and to the west by 175th Street. During the 1870s and 1880s it was variously called East Jamaica and Rockaway Junction (after the branch-off of the Rockaway line of the Long Island Rail Road at 178th Street). The developers of the Jamaica Estates extended 178th Street to the railroad; at their urging the railroad opened a station on 15 May 1911 named Hillside for its location at the foot of the terminal moraine below Hillcrest and Jamaica Estates. The name was also given to a group of houses built on surrounding streets between 1922 and 1924 but eventually became disused.

Vincent Seyfried

Hine, Lewis (Wickes) (*b* Oshkosh, Wis., 26 Sept 1874; *d* Hastings-on-Hudson, N.Y., 4 Nov 1940). Photographer. He moved to New York City in 1900 to teach nature study at the Ethical Culture School, where, given a camera as a teaching aid, he later offered classes in photography. One of his first projects at the school was a sympathetic depiction of immigrants at Ellis Island, which inspired him to seek commissions from social agencies; eventually he left the school to pursue a career in social documentation. In 1907 he was made the official photographer for a pioneering sociological study that was published as *The Pittsburgh Survey* (1910–13). Later he became a staff photographer for the National Child Labor Committee, which had its headquarters in New York City. Between 1907 and 1916 his work appeared in exhibitions, periodicals, and brochures sponsored by supporters of child labor laws. After working for a year in the Balkans for the Red Cross (1918–19) he returned to the city to find that social photography was no longer in great demand, and so he produced what he called "work portraits" of workers in various industries. In 1930 he was commissioned to document the construction of the Empire State Building, but throughout the rest of the decade he was employed only occasionally, mainly by the Tennessee Valley Authority, the Rural Electrification Agency, and the Works Progress Administration. Shortly before his death a retrospective exhibition of his photographs at the Riverside Museum briefly revived interest in his work, which treated working-class subject matter with warmth of feeling and visual force. Monographs of his work include *Men at Work: Photographic Studies of Modern Men and Machines* (1932; 2nd edn, enlarged, 1977).

Judith Mara Gutman, *Lewis W. Hine and the American Social Conscience* (New York: Walker, 1967); Daile Kaplan, *Lewis Hine in Europe: The Lost Photographs* (New York: Abbeville, 1988)

Naomi Rosenblum

Hines, Gregory (Oliver) (*b* 14 Feb 1946, New York City; *d* 10 Aug 2003, Los Angeles). Tap dancer and actor. He began his dance training early in life, studying alongside his brother Marcus with celebrated Broadway choreographer Henry LeTang from the age of three. At the age of six Gregory appeared with his brother at the Apollo Theater in Harlem with their song and dance act "The Hines Brothers." His Broadway debut came two years later in a 1954 production of *The Girl in Pink Tights* at the Mark Hellinger Theatre. Hines received Tony nominations for his Broadway roles in *Comin' Uptown* (1980), *Sophisticated Ladies* (1981), and *Eubie!* (1992) and won the award for Best Actor in a Musical for *Jelly's Last Jam* (1992). Hines's 1989 performance at Carnegie Hall alongside tap-dance greats like Jimmy Slyde, Arthur Duncan, Steve Condos, and the up-and-coming Savion Glover did much to repopularize the art form in the United States after decades of relative obscurity. Hines became involved in film as well, acting alongside his brother in 1984's *The Cotton Club*—a film set in the 1930s at the popular Manhattan jazz club. Hines was posthumously inducted into the Tap Dance Hall of Fame in 2004.

Patrick Barrett

Hines, James J. (*b* New York City, *ca* 1876; *d* Long Beach, N.Y., 26 March 1957). Politician. A former blacksmith, he became the Democratic leader in 1912 of the 11th assembly district (consisting of Morningside Heights and southwestern Harlem). Although a member of Tammany Hall, he often opposed the reigning boss, Charles F. Murphy. By the mid-1930s he was the most powerful politician in Manhattan, known for his success as a "fixer" and his public friendships with judges and organized-crime figures alike. Hines was eventually prosecuted by Thomas E. Dewey, district attorney of Manhattan, for protecting a numbers racket controlled by Dutch Schultz. He was convicted in 1939 and imprisoned; the case helped to make Dewey a national figure.

Frank Vos

Hinsdale. Name applied to Floral Park from about 1870 to 1890.

HIP. See Health Insurance Plan.

hip-hop and rap. Popular and primarily urban form of music in which one or more performers chant rhyming verses in counterpoint to a highly rhythmic musical accompaniment, usually recorded. Hip-hop evolved in the mid-1970s in the Bronx and other urban centers and became closely associated with African American residents of New York City. Rap, a variant of spoken-word poetry performed against a particular rhythm, is an integral component of hip-hop and also developed closely in association with African American residents of the city. Hip-hop had many antecedents: patter by Jamaican disc jockeys at open-air parties, between and during musical selections (a practice known as *toasting*); a longstanding black convention of verbal sparring called *the dozens*, characterized by insults and braggadocio; and a tradition in black poetry of consciously evoking jazz, the blues, and popular music in language and orthography, a tradition that comprehends the poetry of Langston Hughes and Sterling Brown; of African American writers such as Amiri Baraka, who from the late 1950s read or improvised texts to musical backing; and of the improvised, militant, black-power declarations of the group the Last Poets in Harlem during the late 1960s.

Hip-hop flourished during the 1970s at parties that resembled the rent parties held in Harlem before the Depression. Using several turntables and recordings by such musicians as James Brown and George Clinton, disc jockeys (DJs) devised elaborate, layered musical patchworks that provided a backing for rapping and dancing. Among the techniques that they mastered was *scratching*, a sound effect created by moving a record clockwise and counterclockwise while the stylus is held against it. At the same time there developed a highly rhythmic, acrobatic form of movement known as *break dancing*. Rap soon evolved from a live genre to a recorded one, as recordings were made of rappers performing over other recordings. Some of the first widely popular rap recordings were made by musicians from New York City, including the Sugarhill Gang ("Rapper's Delight" [1979]) and Grandmaster Flash and the Furious Five ("The Message" [1982]). Although rap began as a true popular music that used inexpensive, widely available resources, it eventually became more complex and increasingly dependent on synthesizers and other sophisticated equipment, particularly with the integration of rap, rhythm, and melody typical of hip-hop. In the mid-1980s the popularity among white audiences of rap songs like "Rock Box" (1984) by Run-D.M.C. made large record companies recognize that rap had commercial potential. As commercial interests changed the nature of rap, the form moved from the streets and small clubs into large commercial venues; eventually, adulterated forms of rap found their way into broadcast advertising. The New York City–based Beastie Boys, a trio of white rappers, achieved high popularity with these new audiences. Def Jam Recordings, started by Rick Rubin and Russell Simmons, emerged as one of the first hip-hop music labels, promoting mostly New York City acts including the Beastie Boys and Run-D.M.C. Simmons became hip-hop's first major entrepreneur, launching a clothing line, Phat Farm. His forays into commercial ventures would be subsequently emulated by rappers Puff Daddy (Sean Combs) and Jay-Z (Sean Carter). In the early 1990s a number of prominent rap musicians continued to be associated with New York City, including LL Cool J (James Todd Smith), Big Daddy Kane (Antonio Hardy), KRS-One (Lawrence Krishna Parker), Rakim (Rakim Allah), and the groups Public Enemy and A Tribe Called Quest. The primary city radio station to emerge was WBLS but was later surpassed by WQHT, more popularly known as Hot 97. During this period, mix tapes—cassette tapes often releasing songs from an artist's upcoming album, unreleased songs, or exclusive freestyles—were a unique part of the New York City music scene. DJs Tony Touch, Doo Wop, Kid Capri, DJ Clue, and countless others were entrenched in the promotion of city artists.

During the mid- to late 1990s, despite New York City hip-hop undergoing an artistic and commercial golden era, the media focused on the beginning of a feud with West Coast artists who claimed that Los Angeles had supplanted New York City as the center of the industry. This rivalry led to the murder in 1997 of the celebrated rapper The Notorious B.I.G. (Christopher Wallace), who had been raised in Bedford–Stuyvesant. His best friend and producer, Puff Daddy (who later changed his moniker to Diddy), became the guardian of his legacy, and his record label, Bad Boy Records, remained a commercial force for years. Perhaps the most dominant commercial hip-hop entity of the 1990s was the Wu-Tang Clan, a collection of rappers from Staten Island who released a string of successful group and solo albums. Other important hip-hop acts from this period included Brooklyn-born Jay-Z, whose moniker was taken from his local subway lines; his rival Nas (Nasir bin Olu Dara Jones), who was raised in the Queensbridge housing projects; Bronx-raised Big Pun (Christopher Rios), who was one of the preeminent Latino rappers; and the rappers of the highly regarded independent label Rawkus Records, including Mos Def (Dante Smith) and Talib Kweli (Talib Kweli Greene). This successful era in hip-hop came to an end, however, after the murder of The Notorious B.I.G.; Big Pun's death from a heart attack (2000); the dissolution of many longstanding acts in the 1990s, such as A Tribe Called Quest (disbanded 1998; reunited in 2006 for a tour); and Jay-Z's initial retirement in 2003. Despite several mainstream acts retaining popularity, such as 50 Cent (Curtis Jackson III), and the underground popularity of political rapper Immortal Technique (Felipe Andres Coronel), New York City's dominance in the industry was challenged early in the twenty-first century by the rise of southern rap in cities such as Atlanta, Georgia.

Gene Santoro, Janos Marton

Hippodrome. Theater on the east side of Sixth Avenue between 43rd and 44th streets. It opened in 1905 and was built by Frederick Thompson and Elmer S. Dundy, who had also created Luna Park on Coney Island. Called the largest theatrical structure in the world,

Hippodrome, ca 1910

it had an auditorium with 5300 seats and a vast projecting stage with two circus rings and a large elliptical water tank. The exterior of the building was distinguished by two corner towers, each supporting a sparkling globe outlined in electric lights. The Hippodrome was well known as the site of theatrical extravaganzas, performances by dancing elephants, boxing matches, operas, and appearances by Annette Kellerman, the "million dollar mermaid." It closed in 1939.

Rebecca Read Shanor

Hirschfeld, Abraham (*b* Tarnow, Poland, 20 Dec 1919; *d* New York City, 9 Aug 2005). Successful real estate developer and unsuccessful politician. He moved to Palestine in the 1930s before coming to New York City with his family in the 1950s. His first endeavor was as a real estate developer with the building of numerous open-air parking garages. Hirschfeld also held part ownership in the Vertical Club, the Hotel Pennsylvania, and the Crowne Plaza Hotel at Times Square. He quickly developed his image as an influential New Yorker with an eccentric reputation. In 1993 he briefly took over the bankrupt *New York Post,* firing longtime editor Pete Hamill and publishing several controversial issues before relinquishing control. Hirschfeld was found not guilty of tax fraud in 1996 and at the trial's conclusion proposed to offer each juror $2500. Four years later he was sentenced to three years in prison for a plot to kill a business partner. Hirschfeld also ran for numerous political offices, garnering a wealth of publicity and creating a stir with his "Honest Abe" campaigns. He rarely collected more than 1 percent of the popular vote. His political efforts included campaigns for U.S. Congress, New York State comptroller, state lieutenant governor, and Manhattan borough president, among other offices.

David White

Hirschfeld, Al(bert) (*b* St. Louis, 21 June 1903; *d* New York City, 20 Jan 2003). Caricature artist. In 1925 he began an association with the *New York Times,* where his pen-and-ink caricatures of personalities in the performing arts appeared as frequently as four times a week throughout his career. He also displayed his work at the Whitney Museum of American Art, the Museum of Modern Art, the Metropolitan Museum of Art, and various galleries; published several anthologies; designed postage stamps; and wrote Broadway shows with S. J. Perelman and others. Hirschfeld's work is characterized by a distinctive, spare style that combines long, sweeping lines, intricate curves, and extensive cross-hatching. Early in his career he began concealing the name of his daughter Nina in his drawings; the number of times that her name appears is given near his signature. Hirschfeld worked on the top floor of his town house in the East 90s and was a regular at the opening nights of Broadway shows. He received two Tony Awards for his drawings of theater personalities, who knew that a Hirschfeld caricature meant they had made it on Broadway.

Sara J. Steen

Hispanics. See Latinos/Hispanics.

Hispanic Society of America. Nonprofit organization dedicated to preserving and displaying the art and culture of Spain and Portugal, formed in 1904 by the philanthropist Archer Milton Huntington (1870–1955), son of the railroad magnate Collis P. Huntington. It maintains a free museum and reference library at its headquarters on Audubon Terrace in Manhattan, which it first occupied in 1908. The collection was largely assembled by Huntington, and its works range from prehistory through the periods of Roman and Moorish domination to the twentieth century; it includes paintings by such artists as Goya, El Greco, Velázquez, Luís de Morales, Joaquín Sorolla y Bastida, and Francisco de Zurbarán, as well as sculptures, works of decorative art, and a collection of Spanish ceramics that is considered the foremost in the United States. In 2010 the library held several thousand manuscripts and more than 200,000 early and modern books, as well as prints, photographs, and maps. The exterior of the building was designed by Huntington's cousin Charles Pratt Huntington and conforms to the neoclassical style of

Headquarters of the Hispanic Society of America, ca *1940s*

Audubon Terrace as a whole. The skylit interior of the main gallery, finished in elaborately worked, dark red terra-cotta, suggests a courtyard of the Spanish Renaissance.

A History of the Hispanic Society of America, Museum and Library, 1904–1954, with a Survey of the Collections (New York: Hispanic Society of America, 1954)

Carol V. Wright

Hiss, Alger (*b* Baltimore, Md., 11 Nov 1904; *d* New York City, 15 Nov 1996). Lawyer and U.S. government official. A graduate of Harvard Law School, he entered government service with the Agricultural Adjustment Administration in 1933; in 1936 he joined the State Department and became an adviser at international conferences during World War II. In 1947 he become president of the Carnegie Endowment for International Peace. In 1948 Whittaker Chambers, a magazine editor and former Communist Party courier, accused Hiss before the House Un-American Activities Committee of helping to transmit confidential governmental documents to the Soviets before World War II. Hiss denied the charges and would continue to do so until his death. Under the statute of limitations he could not be tried for espionage, but a grand jury indicted him in December of 1948 on two counts of perjury. After two trials, Hiss was convicted in 1950 and received a five-year prison term. His trial created great controversy, many believing that the Federal Bureau of Investigation tampered with evidence to secure a conviction. Hiss was released from prison in 1954, his term shortened for good conduct. He wrote *In the Court of Public Opinion* (1957) in which he maintained his innocence. Unable to practice law, Hiss worked for many years as a stationery and printing salesman in New York City and lived in Manhattan. In 1967 the New School for Social Research hired him to give a series of lectures on the New Deal. His son, Tony Hiss, became a staff writer for the *New Yorker.* He died at Lenox Hill Hospital in New York City.

Andrew Sparberg

historical societies. See Bronx County Historical Society, Brooklyn Historical Society, New-York Historical Society, and Staten Island Historical Society.

historic preservation. Early efforts to preserve monuments of the colonial and Federal eras in New York City began in the last quarter of the nineteenth century, in opposition to what Walt Whitman described as "the pull-down-and-build-over-again spirit." Hamilton Grange was moved to a new site (1889) and Fraunces Tavern was reconstructed on its original site (1907) by the architect William Mersereau for the Sons of the Revolution. During the expansion of the municipal

Historic Districts of New York City

District	Year Designated
Brooklyn Heights (Brooklyn)	1965
Sniffen Court, Murray Hill (Manhattan)	1966
Turtle Bay Gardens, Turtle Bay (Manhattan)	1966
Charlton–King–Vandam, Greenwich Village (Manhattan)	1966
Gramercy Park (Manhattan)	1966, extended 1988
St. Nicholas, Harlem (Manhattan)	1967
Macdougal–Sullivan Gardens, Greenwich Village (Manhattan)	1967
Treadwell Farm, Upper East Side (Manhattan)	1967
Hunters Point, Long Island City (Queens)	1968
St. Mark's, East Village (Manhattan)	1969, extended 1984
Greenwich Village (Manhattan)	1969, extended 2006
Henderson Place, Yorkville (Manhattan)	1969
Mott Haven (Bronx)	1969
Cobble Hill (Brooklyn)	1969, extended 1988
Jumel Terrace, Hamilton Heights (Manhattan)	1970
Chelsea (Manhattan)	1970, extended 1981
Stuyvesant Heights, Bedford–Stuyvesant (Brooklyn)	1971
Mount Morris Park, Harlem (Manhattan)	1971
Central Park West–West 76th St., Upper West Side (Manhattan)	1973
Riverside Drive–West 105th St., Upper West Side (Manhattan)	1973
Park Slope (Brooklyn)	1973
SoHo–Cast Iron District, SoHo (Manhattan)	1973
Carroll Gardens (Brooklyn)	1973
Boerum Hill (Brooklyn)	1973
Carnegie Hill, Upper East Side (Manhattan)	1974, expanded 1993
Hamilton Heights (Manhattan)	1974, extended 2000
Stuyvesant Square (Manhattan)	1975
South St. Seaport (i) (Manhattan)	1977
Fulton Ferry (Brooklyn)	1977
Central Park West–West 73rd and 74th Sts., Upper West Side (Manhattan)	1977
Metropolitan Museum, Upper East Side (Manhattan)	1977
Albemarle–Kenmore Terraces, Flatbush (Brooklyn)	1978
Brooklyn Academy of Music, Fort Greene (Brooklyn)	1978
Fort Greene (Brooklyn)	1978
Fraunces Tavern Block Financial District (Manhattan)	1978
Audubon Terrace, Washington Heights (Manhattan)	1979
Prospect Park South, Flatbush (Brooklyn)	1979
Prospect Lefferts Gardens (Brooklyn)	1979
Longwood, Pueblo de Mayaguez (Bronx)	1980, extended 1983
Upper East Side (Manhattan)	1981
Ditmas Park (Brooklyn)	1981
Clinton Hill (Brooklyn)	1981
Morris High School, Morrisania (Bronx)	1982
West End–Collegiate, Upper West Side (Manhattan)	1984
New York City Farm Colony–Seaview Hospital, Willowbrook (Staten Island)	1985
Riverside Dr.–West 80th–81st Sts. (Manhattan)	1985
Morris Ave., Tremont (Bronx)	1986
Tudor City, Turtle Bay (Manhattan)	1988
West 71st St., Upper West Side	1989
Riverside–West End Ave., Upper West Side (Manhattan)	1989
Ladies' Mile, Flatiron District (Manhattan)	1989
South St. Seaport (ii)	1989
Central Park West, Upper West Side (Manhattan)	1990
Riverdale (Bronx)	1990
Greenpoint (Brooklyn)	1991, amended 200
Tribeca West (Manhattan)	1991
Tribeca East (Manhattan)	1991

(*continued*)

Historic Districts of New York City (*Continued*)

District	Year Designated
Tribeca North (Manhattan)	1992
Tribeca South (Manhattan)	1992, extended 2002
African Burial Ground and City Hall (Manhattan)	1993
Jackson Heights (Queens)	1993
Ellis Island (Manhattan)	1993
Clay Avenue, Morrisania (Bronx)	1994
Mott Haven East, Mott Haven (Bronx)	1994
Bertine Block, Mott Haven (Bronx)	1994
St. George–New Brighton (Staten Island)	1994
Governors Island (Manhattan)	1996
Stone St. (Manhattan)	1996
Vinegar Hill (Brooklyn)	1997
Douglaston (Queens)	1997
Herdenbergh–Rhinelander (Manhattan)	1998
East 17th St.–Irving Place (Manhattan)	1998
Fort Totten (Queens)	1999
NoHo (Manhattan)	1999, extended 2008
Stockholm St. (Queens)	2000
Madison Square North (Manhattan)	2001
Hamilton Heights–Sugar Hill Northeast (Manhattan)	2001
Hamilton Heights–Sugar Hill Northwest (Manhattan)	2002
NoHo East (Manhattan)	2003
Gansevoort Market (Manhattan)	2003
Murray Hill Extension (Manhattan)	2004
St. Park's Avenue–Stapleton Heights (Staten Island)	2004
Douglaston Hill (Queens)	2004
Fieldston (Bronx)	2006
Weehawken St. (Manhattan)	2006
Crown Heights North (Brooklyn)	2007
Manhattan Ave. (Manhattan)	2007
Sunnyside Gardens (Queens)	2007
Faber Pencil Factory (Brooklyn)	2007
DUMBO (Brooklyn)	2007
Fiske Terrace–Midwood Park (Brooklyn)	2008
West Chelsea (Manhattan)	2008
Alice and Agate Courts (Brooklyn)	2009
Fillmore Place (Brooklyn)	2009
Audubon Park (Manhattan)	2009
Prospect Heights (Brooklyn)	2009

Source: New York City Landmarks Preservation Commission, http://www.nyc.gov/html/lpc/html/home/home.shtml

government, City Hall was protected, as were a few historic houses such as the Morris–Jumel Mansion and Dyckman House in upper Manhattan and the Bartow–Pell and Van Cortlandt mansions in the Bronx. The advent of the Works Progress Administration (WPA) in 1935 provided opportunities for artists, architects, and historians to record the city's historic monuments. Berenice Abbott produced *Changing New York* (1939), the Historic American Buildings Survey commissioned a collection of drawings that documented Federal and Greek Revival architecture in New York City, and the WPA published its well-known *New York City Guide* (1939).

The enormous scope of the projects undertaken by Robert Moses aroused public sentiment in favor of historic preservation in New York City. The Municipal Art Society, a public-interest advocacy and educational group dedicated to preservation, encouraged this interest in the 1950s when it sponsored architectural walking tours and compiled information on the city's notable structures that was eventually published in Alan Burnham's *New York Landmarks* (1963). State legislation allowing municipalities to set up landmark commissions was initiated by Albert Bard in 1956; by 1961 New York City revised its zoning, and Platt and Harmon Goldstone (on behalf of the Municipal Art Society) urged James Felt, chairman of the City Planning Commission, to implement aesthetic zoning as a means of preserving noteworthy structures. Instead, Felt helped persuade Mayor Robert F. Wagner to form the Mayor's Committee for the Preservation of Structures of Historic and Esthetic Importance in 1962, and separate legislation was drafted in 1965 to establish a permanent Landmarks Preservation Commission.

Many notable buildings were lost and historic neighborhoods eroded in New York City before legal means were devised to halt their destruction. Pennsylvania Station was demolished in 1963–64, as were the château-like Brokaw mansions on Fifth Avenue at 79th Street in 1965; both events helped galvanize public opinion in favor of historic preservation. The Brooklyn Heights Association tried to protect buildings from demolition by petitioning for designation of the neighborhood as a National Historic Landmark and as a historic district; landmark status was achieved after Wagner signed the Landmarks Preservation Commission bill. In 1966 the National Historic Preservation Act established the National Register of Historic Places. Historic preservation was further encouraged during the 1970s by changes in federal law that allowed income tax credits for federally certified preservation and restoration work.

By 1968 James Marston Fitch established at Columbia University the nation's first professional program in the restoration of historic architecture. The Municipal Art Society formed two related organizations in the 1970s: the Historic Districts Council, which joins representatives from designated historic districts to discuss preservation and advocate new historic districts; and the New York Landmarks Conservancy, a nonprofit entity that administers a revolving fund for restoration projects and offers technical advice on preservation matters.

The 1980s and 1990s saw challenges to the landmarks law in New York City and in particular to the commission's regulatory jurisdiction over Grand Central Terminal (1978) and St. Bartholomew's Church on Park Avenue (1991). Each case went to the U.S. Supreme Court, which upheld the landmarks legislation and affirmed the regulation of historic places as a valid part of the city's land-use policy. Despite the rulings the commission remained controversial: some critics believed that historic status should be granted only to individual buildings and that by designating entire neighborhoods the commission was defeating the intent of zoning; others contended that historic preservation inhibited development and was too costly. In the 1980s several religious organizations sought exemption from the landmarks law on the grounds that it interfered with their missions, as a result of which the Landmarks Conservancy set up a sacred properties fund to help religious organizations maintain, restore, and repair their properties.

As of 2010 the Landmarks Preservation Commission had designated 1250 individual landmarks, 110 interior landmarks, 10 scenic landmarks, and 100 historic districts, totaling 25,000 buildings in the five boroughs. These included distinctive residential neighborhoods such as Greenwich Village and the Upper West Side in Manhattan, Cobble Hill and Park Slope in Brooklyn, and a section of Riverdale in the Bronx. Any proposed demolition or new construction within a historic district was subject to review and approval by the commission. Several groups with interests in specific types and periods of architecture help to educate their members and the public about historic preservation through lectures, walking tours, and publications; among these are the Victorian Society, the Friends of Cast Iron Architecture, and the Friends of Terra Cotta.

Harmon H. Goldstone and Martha Dalrymple, *History Preserved: A Guide to New York City Landmarks and Historic Districts* (New York: Simon and Schuster, 1974); *Guide to New York City Landmarks* (New York: John Wiley and Sons, 4th ed. 2008); Barbaralee Diamonstein-Spielvogel, *The Landmarks of New York: An Illustrated Record of the City's Historic Buildings* (New York: Harry N. Abrams, 1988; repr. New York: Monacelli, 2005)

Marjorie Pearson

Historic Richmond Town. Historic site and outdoor museum in Richmond Creek Valley in Staten Island, near the geographic center of the borough and bordered by Latourette Park to the north and Richmondtown to the east. It was formerly known as Richmondtown Restoration. The site covers 25 acres (10 hectares) of land that were once the county seat and 75 acres (30 hectares) of Richmond Creek, an estuary of the Fresh Kills. Of its 28 historic buildings, 11 are on their original sites, including Voorlezer's House (1696), believed to be the oldest extant schoolhouse in the country; the Third County Courthouse (1837), now a visitor's center; and the office of the county clerk and surrogate (1848, 1886, 1912), now the Historical Museum. On the shores of the Fresh Kills are the sites of Richmond Mill and various farm buildings. During the 1960s, 11 other historic buildings were moved to the site to prevent their destruction, including the Britton Cottage (1677, 1765, 1800) and the Guyon–Lake–Tysen House (1740, 1820), both from New Dorp. The Jacob Crocheron House (1820) was moved from Woodrow in 1988. About 15 buildings are restored and open to the public, and others are undergoing restoration. Guided tours and interpretive programs illustrate the development of the village and the daily life of its residents. Changing exhibitions display the permanent collections and contemporary topics. Historic Richmond Town is administered by the Staten Island Historical Society, and its land and buildings are owned by the city, which provides operational assistance through its department of cultural affairs.

Barnett Shepherd

histories. The first serious attempt to trace the history of New York City was William Smith's *History of the Province of New-York* (London: Thomas Wilcox, 1757; rev. Philadelphia: Mathew Carey, 1792). Drawn from primary sources, this narrative gave particular attention to the early years of English control. Writers of the period such as Cadwallader Colden criticized the book because of the author's sympathies with the Whigs. Apart from reprints of Smith's book and collections of documents, historical writing on New York after the American Revolution typically consisted of chapters in descriptive books such as Samuel L. Mitchell's *The Picture of New-York* (New York: I. Riley, 1807), the work that inspired Washington Irving's satiric *History of New York* (Philadelphia: Inskeep, Bradford, 1809). In the mid-nineteenth century the first extended treatments of the city's history were Daniel Curry's *New York: A Historical Sketch of the Rise and Progress of the Metropolitan City of America* (New York: Carlton and Phillips, 1853), David T. Valentine's *History of the City of New York* (New York: G. P. Putnam, 1853), Mary L. Booth's *History of the City of New York* (1861 and later editions), and William L. Stone's *History of New York City from the Discovery to the Present Day* (New York: E. Cleave, 1872). With the exception of Joel T. Headley's *The Great Riots of New York, 1712 to 1873* (New York: E. B. Treat, 1873), the histories of this period stressed material progress, with little attention to social unrest and political corruption. Other laudatory interpretations of the city's history were written in the last quarter of the nineteenth century, including Benson J. Lossing's *History of New York City* (New York: Perine, 1884), Charles B. Todd's *The Story of the City of New York* (1888), and Martha Lamb's *History of the City of New York: Its Origin, Rise, and Progress* (A. S. Barnes, 1877–80; rev. Cosimo Classics, 2005). R. S. Guernsey's *New York City and Vicinity during the War of 1812–15* (New York: C. L. Woodward, 1889–95) was recognized as one of the earliest works devoted to a specific historical period.

As New York City evolved into a world metropolis, historians increasingly combined hope for continued progress with a nostalgic celebration of simpler times. Works expressing this more complex vision of the city were popular during the 1920s; among them were Charles Hemstreet's *The Story of Manhattan* (New York: Charles Scribner's Sons, 1901), William T. Bonner's *New York: The World's Metropolis* (New York: R. L. Polk, 1924), and Sarah M. Lockwood's *New York* (New York: Doubleday, Page, 1926). Henry C. Brown wrote several historical volumes during the Depression, including *The Story of Old New York* (New York: E. P. Dutton, 1934). After World War II the manners and mores of the city were recorded by such writers as Frank Weitenkampf in *Manhattan Kaleidoscope* (New York: Charles Scribner's Sons, 1947) and Lloyd R. Morris in *Incredible New York: High Life and Low Life of the Last Hundred Years* (New York: Random House, 1951). John A. Kouwenhoven wrote a careful pictorial history titled *The Columbia Historical Portrait of New York* (Garden City, N.Y.: Doubleday, 1953); Benjamin A. Botkin, editor of *New York City Folklore* (New York: Random House, 1956), and Bayrd Still, editor of *Mirror for Gotham: New York as Seen by Contemporaries from Dutch Days to the Present* (New York: New York University Press, 1956), collected many useful sources.

Academic examinations of the political and social history of New York City proliferated from the mid-twentieth century. Among the most widely read were Charles Garrett's *The La Guardia Years: Machine and Reform Politics in New York City* (New Brunswick, N.J.: Rutgers University Press, 1961), Moses Rischin's *The Promised City: New York's Jews, 1870–1914* (Cambridge, Mass.: Harvard University Press, 1962), Robert A. Caro's *The Power Broker: Robert Moses and the Fall of New York* (New York: Alfred A. Knopf, 1974), Charles Lockwood's *Manhattan Moves Uptown: An Illustrated History* (Boston: Houghton Mifflin, 1976), Thomas J. Archdeacon's *New York City, 1664–1710: Conquest and Change* (Ithaca, N.Y.: Cornell University Press, 1976), Thomas Kessner's *The Golden Door: Italian and Jewish Immigrant Mobility in New York City, 1800–1915* (New York: Oxford University Press, 1977), Edward K. Spann's *The New Metropolis: New York City, 1840–1857* (New York: Columbia University Press, 1981), Amy Bridges's *A City in the Republic: Antebellum New York and the Origins of Machine Politics* (New York: Cambridge University Press, 1984), Thomas Bender's *New York Intellect: A History of Intellectual Life in New York City, from 1750 to the Beginnings of Our Own Time* (New York: Alfred A. Knopf, 1987), Joshua Freeman's *In Transit: The Transport Workers Union in New York City, 1933–1966* (New York: Oxford University Press, 1989), Kessner's *Fiorello H. La Guardia and the Making of Modern New York* (New York: McGraw-Hill, 1989), Richard Plunz's *A History of Housing in New York City: Dwelling Type and Social Change in the American Metropolis* (New York: Columbia University Press, 1990), and Roy Rosenzweig and Elizabeth Blackmar's *The Park and the People: A History of Central Park* (Ithaca, N.Y.: Cornell University Press, 1992). General mass-market histories written during this period included Susan E. Lyman's *The Story of New York: An Informal History of the City* (New York: Crown, 1964) and Oliver E. Allen's *The Tiger: The Rise and Fall of Tammany Hall* (Cambridge, Mass.: Da Capo Press, 1993).

Neighborhoods, boroughs, and special topics about the history of New York City are discussed in Pamela Jones's *Under the City Streets: A History of Subterranean New York* (Holt, Rinehart and Winston, 1978), John G. Bunker's *Harbor and Haven* (1979), Jill Stone's *Times Square* (Macmillan, 1982),

David W. McCullough's *The Great Bridge: The Epic Story of Building the Brooklyn Bridge* (New York: Simon and Schuster, 1983), Stephen Garmey's *Gramercy Park: An Illustrated History of a New York Neighborhood* (Balsam Press, 1984), Jill Jonnes's *South Bronx Rising: The Rise, Fall, and Resurrection of an American City* (New York: Fordham University Press, 2002), and James Trager's *Park Avenue* (New York: Atheneum Books, 1989). Robert A. M. Stern's historical surveys of New York City architecture cover the nineteenth through the twenty-first centuries: *New York 1880* (Monacelli, 1999), *New York 1900* (Rizzoli, 1983), *New York 1930* (Rizzoli, 1987), *New York 1960* (Monacelli, 1995), and *New York 2000* (Monacelli, 2006). Oral histories of the city include Jeff Kisseloff's *You Must Remember This: An Oral History of Manhattan from the 1890s to World War II* (San Diego, Calif.: Harcourt Brace Jovanovich, 1989).

In the twenty-first century Edwin G. Burrows and Mike Wallace tackled the city's story in the comprehensive *Gotham: A History of New York City to 1898* (New York: Oxford University Press, 2000), and Kenneth T. Jackson and David S. Dunbar created the historical anthology *Empire City: New York through the Centuries* (New York: Columbia University Press, 2005). In *The Island at the Center of the World: The Epic Story of Dutch Manhattan and the Forgotten Colony That Shaped America* (New York: Vintage, 2005), Russell Shorto chronicled the early Dutch colony in New York, highlighting its ethnic diversity and narrating the power struggle between Peter Stuyvesant and a little-known lawyer named Adriaen van der Donck. In *The Big Oyster* (New York: Random House, 2007), Mark Kurlansky framed the city's history through its early role as the oyster capital of the world.

Harold Eugene Mahan

Hobart, John Henry (*b* Philadelphia, 14 Sept 1775; *d* Auburn, N.Y., 12 Sept 1830). Episcopal bishop. He helped to form the General Theological Seminary (1817) and many parishes and missions. Between 1816 and 1830 he was the bishop of the Episcopal Diocese of New York and the rector of Trinity Church on Wall Street. Known for his quick temper and iron hand, he wrote many books and took as his motto the phrase "Evangelical Truth and Apostolic Order." His proposal for a cathedral on Washington Square (1828) was later realized as the Cathedral of St. John the Divine.

J. Robert Wright

Hoffman, Dustin (Lee) (*b* Los Angeles, 8 Aug 1937). Actor. He moved to New York City in 1958, lived on the Lower East Side, and made his debut on Broadway in 1961. In the following years he worked Off Broadway in productions of the American Place Theatre (1964–66) and the Circle in the Square (1967). After becoming widely known for his role in Mike Nichols's film *The Graduate* (1967) he continued to live and work at intervals in New York City, where he appeared in productions of Murray Schisgal's *Jimmy Shine* (1968–69), Arthur Miller's *Death of a Salesman* (1984), and *The Merchant of Venice* (1989). He has appeared in many popular films, including *Rain Man* (1988), *Wag the Dog* (1997), and *Mr. Magorium's Wonder Emporium* (2007), and he remains active in film and television roles.

Hoffman Island. Small artificial island off the eastern shore of Staten Island, just to the north of Swinburne Island. Built in 1872 on Orchard Shoals, it has an area of 11 acres (4.5 hectares) and is named for John T. Hoffman (mayor of New York City 1866–68, governor of New York State 1869–71). In the 1900s it housed a quarantine station used to isolate arriving immigrants suspected of having infectious diseases; for a time during World War II it was the site of a training facility of the U.S. Merchant Marine, as well as the anchorage of an antisubmarine net that extended across the entrance to the harbor. In the early twenty-first century the island is part of the GATEWAY NATIONAL RECREATION AREA and is closed to visitors—except for large colonies of nesting wading birds.

Gerard R. Wolfe

Hofstadter, Richard (*b* Buffalo, N.Y., 6 Aug 1916; *d* New York City, 24 Oct 1970). Historian. After receiving his BA from the University of Buffalo in 1936, he moved to New York City to enroll in the graduate history program at Columbia University. He became active in the city's radical movement and joined a unit of the Communist Party at Columbia in 1938, but he had little interest in activist politics and left the party after a year. He taught part time at Brooklyn College and then full time at City College in the spring of 1941. His book *Social Darwinism in American Thought* (1944) became a classic work in American social history; in 1946 he joined the history department at Columbia, where in 1959 he became the DeWitt Clinton Professor of American History. By the time of his death from leukemia he was widely recognized as the most important and influential historian in the United States. Hofstadter's published writings include *The American Political Tradition and the Men Who Made It* (1948), as well as *The Age of Reform* (1956) and *Anti-Intellectualism in American Life* (1963), both of which won Pulitzer prizes.

David S. Brown, *Richard Hofstadter: An Intellectual Biography* (Chicago: University of Chicago Press, 2006)

James Bradley

Hogan, Frank (Smithwick) (*b* Waterbury, Conn., 17 Jan 1902; *d* New York City, 2 April 1974). District attorney. After receiving his law degree from Columbia University in 1928 he worked for a private firm; he was later part of a two-man firm that became one of few of its size to survive the Depression. In 1935 he joined Thomas E. Dewey in a special investigation of organized crime, and after Dewey was elected district attorney of New York County in 1937, Hogan became his administrative assistant. With Dewey's endorsement, his own nomination for the office of district attorney was arranged in 1941 by the major political parties, perhaps largely because he had no strong political sympathies; he easily won the election and retained the office for 32 years. He preserved the nonpartisan character of the office established by Dewey (whose reforms he expanded), emphasized the judicial nature of prosecution, and used discretion in seeking indictments, thus helping to establish a model for prosecution used throughout the country. Throughout the United States he was known as "Mr. District Attorney."

Barry Cunningham, *Mr. District Attorney* (New York: Mason/Charter, 1977)

Emery E. Adoradio

hogs. Swine roamed the streets of Manhattan for more than two centuries, from the days of Dutch colonial rule through the mid-nineteenth century. It was common for New Yorkers to set their hogs loose to forage on trash; in many ways they acted as unofficial garbage collectors, but not everyone appreciated their presence and efficiency. In the 1650s Peter Stuyvesant repeatedly complained that the animals were destroying the foundation of New Amsterdam's fortifications. Stuyvesant called for soldiers to shoot all loose hogs, but his plans were quashed by public outcry. As the city grew during the eighteenth and nineteenth centuries, the hogs' infractions seemed to multiply. Not only did they uproot pavement and forage where they were not welcome, but they also blocked traffic, knocked down pedestrians, sullied ladies' skirts, and attacked children who approached their piglets. By the nineteenth century hog owners tended to come from poor and working-class families, and they relied on their animals as a source of income and protein. Most of the complaints against swine were lodged by wealthier residents who hoped that the city would evolve into a more sanitary and civilized one. Municipal leaders tried to control the unruly hogs by fining and indicting owners, establishing pounds, and legalizing hunting on the streets. For the most part, however, attempts at clearing the streets of swine were unsuccessful. Early in his term as mayor, Cadwallader D. Colden (1818–21) hired hog catchers to collect the animals and take them to the almshouse where they would be served for dinner. The hog catchers were met with riots led by working-class women and men who came out to protect their property. Other hog riots occurred in 1826, 1830, and 1832 when the city renewed its efforts at enforcing antihog ordinances. It would not be until 1849, when widespread panic over a cholera epidemic led to increased attention to public health and sanitation, that free-roaming hogs would be effectively banned from the streets. Penned hogs would be permitted in the more rural areas of the city until real estate development eventually caught up. In 1859, for instance, a ban was placed on all penned hogs south of 86th Street. Up until that point pig pens and associated offal boiling establishments were common as far south as 50th Street. The enforcement of this ordinance led to the "Piggery Wars" during which police and health inspectors raided the properties of hog owners, destroyed pens, and impounded the animals. With this ordinance, even hog owners north of 86th Street needed licenses to keep their livestock. Restrictions continued to increase as the population and development of the city expanded. In the early twenty-first century prospective hog owners must seek permits from the Board of Health.

Hendrik Hartog, "Pigs and Positivism," *Wisconsin Law Review* (July/August 1985), 899–934

Catherine McNeur

Holiday, Billie [Fagan, Eleanora] (*b* Philadelphia, 7 April 1915; *d* New York City, 17 July 1959). Singer. The daughter of the guitarist Clarence Holiday, she began singing in nightclubs and bars in Harlem by the early 1930s. After gaining the attention of John Henry Hammond she made her first recording in 1933 with Benny Goodman; during the 1930s she made recordings with small groups that included the pianist Teddy Wilson and several members of Count Basie's band, among them Lester Young, who gave her the nickname Lady Day. In 1937–38 she toured with the bands of Basie and Artie Shaw and also sang at nightclubs in Harlem. She later obtained long-term engagements at Café Society in Greenwich Village and as the principal performer at such nightclubs on 52nd Street as Kelly's Stables and the Onyx Club. Her impeccable timing, burnished tone, and profoundly expressive delivery made her the most important jazz singer after Louis Armstrong. Throughout her career she fought racism: she made critical remarks and was occasionally arrested for taking part in disputes after white nightclub patrons insulted her and attacked her companions. Her song "Strange Fruit" (1939) became well known at Café Society and was one of the first popular songs denouncing the treatment of blacks. At the height of her career she lived at 286 West 142nd Street. Heroin addiction and trouble with the police led her cabaret license to be revoked in 1949, and in the following years she performed less frequently, though she made several memorable appearances at Carnegie Hall. From 1957 Holiday lived at 26 West 87th Street. Her autobiography, *Lady Sings the Blues* (1956), indicts racism, ill-conceived drug policies, and hypocrisy.

Billie Holiday

Robert G. O'Meally, *Lady Day: The Many Faces of Billie Holiday* (New York: Little, Brown, 1991)

Douglas Henry Daniels

Holiness and Pentecostal churches. The Holiness movement began in New York City when the Methodist sisters Sarah Worrall Lankford and Phoebe Worrall Palmer developed a doctrine that united the perfectionism of the 1830s with Methodist ideas of Christian perfection (or "entire sanctification") as a religious experience following conversion. From 1835 Lankford held Tuesday meetings for women in the home at 54 Rivington Street that she shared with her sister and brother-in-law. Palmer took over these meetings by the late 1830s and after 1839 opened them to men. They became popular and were moved to 23 St. Mark's Place and then to 316 East 15th Street in 1871; they were still being held as late as 1914. During the 1830s Palmer helped to organize the Five Points Mission, which consisted of a home, a school, a workroom, and a chapel. Offshoots of the Holiness movement formed outside Methodism. One known as Oberlin perfectionism began in the city under Charles G. Finney, pastor of the Chatham Street Chapel (1832–35) and the Broadway Tabernacle (1836–37). His *Lectures to Professing Christians* were delivered at the Broadway Tabernacle in 1837 and serialized in the *New York Evangelist*. Another strand of perfectionism developed after prayer meeting revivals of 1857–59 that began in a Dutch Reformed church on Fulton Street and quickly spread to cities across the United States, Canada, and Great Britain. One of its most important exponents was William E. Boardman, a Presbyterian minister who often attended Palmer's Tuesday meetings and wrote *The Higher Christian Life* (1858), a widely circulated treatise that united Methodistic and Oberlin perfectionism.

The prayer meeting revival led to the formation of the Antioch Baptist Church at 264 Bleecker Street by the minister John Quincy Adams. It operated a press and bookstore and circulated the *Christian*, a monthly publication dedicated to advancing the gospel of Holiness. The movement also found adherents among several small Methodist splinter groups. The Wesleyan Methodist Connection (now Wesleyan Church) was organized in 1843 by Methodist Episcopal Church abolitionists and from 1844 to 1852 had its national headquarters, a publishing house, and a church on King Street. After attending Palmer's meetings during the 1860s and experiencing entire sanctification, Amanda Smith (1837–1915) gave sermons in a number of the city's black churches. Congregations of the Free Methodist Church were formed in Manhattan and Brooklyn during the 1860s and worked extensively among the city's poor. In 1860 Jane Dunning, a Free Methodist laywoman, became the superintendent of the Providence Mission at 329 West 37th Street, which served the black community. One of her converts, Jerry McAuley, organized the Water Street Mission in 1872; its principal financial sponsor was Joseph Mackey, editor of the *United States Dry Goods Reporter*. The mission also issued a newsletter edited by the Free Methodist pastor J. S. Bradbrook. During these years the Salvation Army was formed and through its rescue work became the best-known exponent of Holiness. In 1881 the Christian and Missionary Alliance Church was founded in the city by A. B. Simpson, a pastor of the Thirteenth Street Presbyterian Church from 1879 to 1881 who also oversaw a missionary training school, a home for faith healing, a mission board, an interdenominational mission publication, and the evangelical Gospel Tabernacle.

By the 1880s resistance mounted against Holiness teaching in a number of churches, including the Methodist Episcopal Church. One of the first new denominations was the Church of God Reformation Movement (1881), founded by Daniel Sidney Warner. Later known as the Church of God (Anderson), it began a ministry in the city under Charles James Blewitt in 1897. The ministry of the Church of the Nazarene was begun in the city by William Howard Hoople, son of a prominent leather merchant. He and Charles BeViev opened a mission at 123 Schenectady Avenue in Brooklyn on 4 January 1894 that was soon organized into the Utica Avenue Tabernacle. A second congregation was formed on Bedford Avenue in 1895 and a third in the following year; the three congregations merged into the Association of Pentecostal Churches of America on 31 March 1896.

Pentecostalism developed after 1900 as an offshoot of the Holiness movement; it emphasized glossolalia, or "speaking in tongues," as evidence of the "baptism of the Holy Spirit." After a manifestation of glossolalia in 1901 the Holiness evangelist Charles F. Parham sent Marie Burgess to work in a Holiness mission at 416 West 42nd Street in New York City in 1907 and to spread his teachings concerning spirit baptism. There she met and married Robert Brown, with whom she formed the Glad Tidings Tabernacle. The Church of God (Anderson) moved to rented quarters at 2450 Grand Avenue in 1906 and by 1908 added a missionary home and chapel. In 1907 the Association of Pentecostal Churches of America united with the Church of the Nazarene to form the Pentecostal Church of the Nazarene, which took the name Church of the Nazarene in 1919 to dissociate itself from Pentecostalism. As early as 1908 Pentecostal ministries were launched among Italians by the evangelist Peter Ottolini.

A number of black Pentecostal and Holiness churches opened after an influx of black workers into New York City from the South during World War I. In 1919 R. C. Lawson formed a congregation of the Refuge Churches of Our Lord in Harlem (renamed the Church of Our Lord Jesus Christ of the Apostolic Faith in 1931). During the 1920s and 1930s congregations of the predominantly black Church of God (Spreading Gospel), Churches of God in Christ, and United Holy Church were established. Glad Tidings Tabernacle was the largest Pentecostal church in New York City by the 1920s, giving rise to congregations in a number of the city's ethnic communities. Ivan Voronaev, a Russian Baptist pastor, opened the first Russian Pentecost Church in the city after being introduced to Pentecostalism by the Browns in 1920. Another was Hans R. Waldvogel, who in 1925 took over a struggling German Pentecostal mission, the Ridgewood Pentecostal Church at 815 Seneca Avenue, and transformed it into a thriving congregation that eventually led to the formation of other congregations throughout the metropolitan area. A Finnish church was organized during the 1920s, and the Salvation Army was highly successful in its mission work among Swedish immigrants in Brooklyn. Pentecostal evangelism was also taken up by Puerto Ricans who settled in the city during the 1920s. One of the first pastors, Juan Lugo, began his ministry in Greenpoint in 1929.

From the 1930s a number of Pentecostal leaders became prominent. One of the most important was Mother Horn, who opened the Mount Calvary Assembly Hall of Pentecostal Faith Church in Brooklyn in 1930. She later established a second church in the old Olympia Sports Club in Harlem, which became her headquarters, and broadcast a radio program. Under Charles Manuel ("Sweet Daddy") Grace (1881–1960) the United House of Prayer for All Nations on the Rock of the Apostolic Faith Church provided low-income housing and employment in church industries. During the 1930s a Spanish-speaking congregation was organized by Francisco Olazabel as the Bethel Christian Church; it became the Assembly of Christian Churches and made its headquarters in the city in 1939. After failing to succeed his father as the general overseer of the Church of God of Prophecy, Homer A. Tomlinson (1894–1968) formed the Church of God (Queens, New York) in 1943. In 1954 he traveled to more than 100 countries to proclaim his reign as "King of the World." He also sought the U.S. presidency as the candidate of the Theocratic Party. After Tomlinson's death the church moved its headquarters to Huntsville, Alabama. The converted organized-crime figure and drug addict Billy Roberts opened the Soul Saving Station in Harlem in 1940. By 1973 it had 11,000 members, took the name Soul Saving Station for Every Nation Crusaders of America, and had ties to the Pentecostal Holiness Church.

New churches took shape after World War II. By 1950 there were eight Church of God (Anderson) congregations in the city. A ministry known as Teen Challenge was organized in 1958 in Brooklyn by David Wilkerson, an Assemblies of God minister whose work with young drug addicts gained attention through his book *The Cross and the Switchblade* (1963; made into a motion picture of the same name in 1970). The Bible Church of Christ was formed in 1961 by Roy Bryant, as was the House of Our Lord Church in Brooklyn by the activist pastor Herbert Daughtry. In 1975 the Church of the Nazarene bought the clubhouse of the Lambs in Times Square and under Paul Moore and Sharon Moore focused its efforts on performing artists as well as the homeless in Times Square and Hell's Kitchen. George Baker, known as Father Divine, established the Father Divine Peace Mission in Harlem during the 1930s, which became known for its service to the poor, claims of faith healing, teachings on racial equality, and strict moral code. In 1942 it moved its headquarters to Philadelphia. Reverend Ike used the media extensively to promote his doctrine of material prosperity as the leader of the United Christian Evangelistic Association, which made its headquarters in Washington Heights. Brooklyn Tabernacle, led since 1971 by Jim Cymbala, is noted for its Grammy Award–winning 300-voice Brooklyn Tabernacle Choir directed by Cymbala's wife, Carol. The church also operates a downtown learning center that includes an adult literacy program and programs for children and senior citizens.

Charles Edwin Jones, *A Guide to the Study of the Pentecostal Movement* (Metuchen, N.J.: Scarecrow, 1983); Charles Edwin Jones, *Black Holiness: A Guide to the Study of Black Participation in Wesleyan Perfectionist and Glossolalic Pentecostal Movements* (Metuchen, N.J.: Scarecrow, 1987)

William C. Kostlevy

Holland House. Hotel at 276 Fifth Avenue, on the southwest corner of 30th Street. Designed by the architects George Edward Harding and William Tyson Gooch as a reproduction of the Earl of Holland's mansion in London, it opened in 1891 and was run on the European plan (in which meals are not included in the price of the room). The 11-story hotel had Gorham silver, Royal Worcester china, and Wilton carpeting and was said to be the most luxurious hotel in New York City until the Astoria was added to the Waldorf (1897). A unique feature of the hotel was the Herzog Teleseme, an electromechanical indicator with which guests could dial any one of 140 services from their rooms. The Holland House closed with the onset of Prohibition and was converted into an office building. In 2003 the lobby and facade were restored and other aspects of the building updated. Many of the hotel's opulent furnishings were incorporated into a 1920s commercial renovation of the former Mark Twain home in Hartford, Connecticut.

Val Ginter

Hollands. Neighborhood in south central Queens, lying on the Rockaway Peninsula around Beach 92nd Street. It was originally a parcel of 65 acres (26 hectares) along Beach 92nd Street bought for $350 in 1855 by Michael P. Holland, Sr., who had operated a hotel in Jamaica in the 1840s and 1850s and who opened a hotel on his newly acquired property in 1857. After his death, his wife and his son, Michael P. Holland, Jr., speculated in real estate and operated the hotel, which was destroyed by fire on 9 April 1883 and later rebuilt. For 20 years the younger Holland was influential in Rockaway and initiated many improvements; he also operated Third Landing on the bay, the local point of embarkation for passengers of the Iron Steamboat Company. Hollands was incorporated with Hammels into the Village of Rockaway Beach in 1897. The extension of railroad service to Rockaway stimulated intensive development, and hundreds of hotels, boardinghouses, and bathing pavilions were built along the beaches. In 1924 Cross Bay Boulevard opened for traffic, with a terminus at Beach 94th and Beach 95th streets. The Hollands subway station stands at Beach 90th Street.

Vincent Seyfried

Holland Tunnel. Double-tubed, underwater vehicular tunnel spanning the Hudson River between Canal Street in lower Manhattan and Jersey City, New Jersey. It was built over seven years by the Port of New York Authority and named after its engineer Clifford M.

Holland, who died before its completion. When it opened in 1927 it was the longest underwater tunnel in the world, measuring 8557 feet (2610 meters) and having a maximum depth of 93 feet (28.4 meters). The greatest challenge in building the tunnel was the design of a ventilating system that would remove exhaust-filled air from the underground tubes and bring in fresh air. About 2000 tests were conducted to determine the amount of exhaust gases that would be produced and their effect on drivers. In the final stages of investigation an experimental tunnel was built to study the best method of ventilation: this study resulted in an innovative system in which fresh air is drawn from outside through four ventilating buildings and blown by fans into a duct under the tunnel roadway. The air is released through narrow slots above the curb and dilutes the exhaust gases, which are drawn out through an exhaust duct in the ceiling of the tunnel. The ventilating system of the Holland Tunnel became the model for other underwater tunnels in New York City and around the world. In 1993 it was designated a National Historic Landmark. Traffic volume in 2007 in both directions was about 34.7 million vehicles. In the early twenty-first century it is operated by the Port Authority of New York and New Jersey.

Rebecca Read Shanor

Holliday [Tuvim], **Judy** (*b* New York City, 21 June 1921; *d* New York City, 7 June 1965). Actress. She graduated from Julia Richman High School in Manhattan in 1938 and began working as a backstage switchboard operator for Orson Welles's Mercury Theater. She then joined with Betty Comden, Adolph Green, John Frank, and Alvin Hammer to form a cabaret troupe called the Revuers, which performed in nightclubs such as the Village Vanguard and on radio from the autumn of 1938 until 1944. In 1945 she made her debut on the stage in *Kiss Them for Me*. She replaced Jean Arthur in the role of Billie Dawn in the play *Born Yesterday* in 1946, which ran for almost four years and made her widely known; she also appeared in the film version of the play in 1950, winning an Academy Award for Best Actress. Her performance as the dim-witted Doris Attinger in the motion picture *Adam's Rib* (1949) was also highly regarded. Holliday's liberal leanings caught the attention of the Senate Internal Security Subcommittee, which called her to testify in 1952, and her career suffered as a result; Garson Kanin later said of her appearance before the committee that no one was "more steadfast or less craven." She began rebuilding her career with the motion picture *It Should Happen to You* (1954) and appeared in the play *Bells Are Ringing* (1956) in a role written for her by Comden and Green, winning a Tony Award for her performance. Her last major film, a version of the play, was shot in 1960. Holliday died at the age of 43 of breast cancer and is buried at Westchester Hills Cemetery in suburban Hastings-on-Hudson, New York.

Gary Carey, *Judy Holliday: An Intimate Life Story* (New York: Seaview, 1982); Will Holtzman, *Judy Holliday* (New York: G. P. Putnam's Sons, 1982)

Allen J. Share

Hollis. Neighborhood in central Queens, bounded to the north by Grand Central Parkway, to the east by Francis Lewis Boulevard, to the south by Hollis Avenue, and to the west by 184th Street. It was established in 1885 by Frederick W. Denton, a nephew of Austin Corbin, who was a supervisor of Jamaica Town and a promoter of the Bicycle Railroad in East Patchogue, Long Island. He planned to name the area Woodhull after a general who was captured by a British detachment in 1776 at what is now 197th Street and Jamaica Avenue, but to avoid confusion with another Woodhull in Steuben County he named it instead after his own birthplace in New Hampshire. A railroad station was built during the summer of 1885. A tollgate on the Hempstead and Jamaica Turnpike at Jamaica Avenue and 186th Street was used until 4 October 1895. Carpenter's Tavern (1710), the site of General Woodhull's capture, was replaced by housing in 1921. The neighborhood grew slowly as fine Victorian houses were erected along Woodhull Avenue between 188th and 198th streets. The extension of electric streetcar service in May 1897 attracted developers of upper-middle-class houses: in 1906 Hollis Park Gardens was built between 192nd and 195th streets between Jamaica and Hillside avenues, and many similar developments went up during the next 20 years. The growing demand for housing stimulated the construction in 1921 of blocks of row houses, concentrated between Jamaica and Hillside avenues. By World War II no open land remained and Hollis was a commuter suburb. After 1955 the ethnic composition changed south of the railroad, and by 1980 the population was 80 percent black and Latin American. During the following decade the neighborhood attracted immigrants from Guyana, Haiti, China, India, and Colombia. In the mid-1990s Hollis was a middle-class community of well-kept, one-family houses, with fewer than half a dozen high-rise apartment buildings. The pioneering hip-hop group Run-D.M.C. came out of Hollis in the 1980s, and the Hollis Hip-Hop Museum opened in Hollis Famous Burgers in 2009.

Vincent Seyfried

Holliswood. Neighborhood in east central Queens, bounded to the north by Grand Central Parkway, to the east by Francis Lewis Boulevard, to the south by Hillside Avenue, and to the west by 188th Street. It was a hilly and heavily wooded area north of Hollis when it was promoted as a site for upper-middle-class housing in 1905 by the Grenoble Realty Company. Because the area was isolated and far from means of transport, the sale of lots was slow and in 1918 the plan failed. As the need for housing grew during the 1920s, interest in development renewed and many houses were built. Growth slowed during the Depression but revived after World War II. Haitian, Chinese, and Indian immigrants settled in the neighborhood and its environs during the 1980s. In the early twenty-first century Holliswood remained an area of winding streets and irregular parcels; its many trees and elegant houses with large yards made it one of the most attractive neighborhoods in Queens. Governor Mario Cuomo and his family lived in Holliswood.

Vincent Seyfried

Hollyer, Samuel (*b* London, England, 1826; *d* New York City, 29 Dec 1919). Engraver. He moved to New York City in 1851 and was commissioned by several publishing companies. His best-known work consists of more than 140 historical engravings of New York City that he produced from 1901 to 1912. His winter residence was at 430 West 23rd Street. In the early twenty-first century his work was in the permanent collection at the Metropolitan Museum of Art, the Museum of the City of New York, and the New-York Historical Society.

S. Markham and J. Gotwals, *Guide to Samuel Hollyer's Old New York Views, 1901–1912* (New York: New-York Historical Society, 2003)

Jessica Montesano

Holm, Hanya (*b* Worms, Germany, 3 March 1893; *d* New York City, 3 Nov 1992). Choreographer. She settled in New York City in 1931 and opened a branch of the Wigman School, named for the German modern dancer Mary Wigman. In 1936 she opened her own school in the city and developed a form of dance that combined Wigman's tradition of expressionism with her own gift for abstract design. Holm provided choreography for the musical comedies *Kiss Me Kate* (1948) and *My Fair Lady* (1956). She retired from teaching in 1967 but continued to work with the Nikolais Dance Theater.

Walter Sorell, *Hanya Holm: The Biography of an Artist* (Middletown, Conn.: Wesleyan University Press, 1969)

Peter M. Rutkoff, William B. Scott

Holt, John (*b* ?1721; *d* New York City, 30 Jan 1784). Newspaper publisher and printer for the patriot cause. A merchant, postmaster, and former mayor, he came to New York City from Williamsburg, Virginia, to further learn the printing trade from James Parker. Holt's association with Parker's printing and postal empire as lessee and partner was marred by financial disagreements as he published Parker's newspaper and subsequently, beginning in 1766, his own *New-York Journal, or General Advertiser.* The printer of choice for the New York Sons of Liberty, he issued many anti-British broadsides and Whiggish pamphlets that circulated throughout the colonies. Although appointed state printer in 1777, Holt suffered the hardships of Revolutionary wartime printers, fleeing both the occupation of New York City and the British burning of Kingston, his place of exile. He continued sporadically his *New-York Journal* in Poughkeepsie and returned to New York City just as the British were evacuating to begin the *Independent New-York Gazette.* His widow continued the newspaper and marked his grave in St. Paul's churchyard with a distinctive printer's tombstone.

Mariam Touba

Holt, Rinehart and Winston. Publishing house; see Henry Holt and Company.

Holy Cross Armenian Apostolic Church. The oldest Armenian Apostolic Church in New York City, located at 580 West 187th Street. It opened on Epiphany, or "Armenian Christmas," 6 January 1929. In 2004 it celebrated its 75th anniversary of serving the once-thriving Armenian community in Washington Heights. It remains best known as the site where, on 24 December 1933, stunned parishioners saw Armenian zealots fatally stab Archbishop Leon Touryan at the altar during his Christmas Eve service, precipitating a division of the Armenian Apostolic Church of America into two churches, an administrative split that persisted into the twenty-first century.

Harold Takooshian

Holy Trinity Cathedral of the Ukrainian Autocephalous Orthodox Church in Exile. Cathedral at 117–85 South Fifth Street in Williamsburg, Brooklyn, built in 1906 as the main branch of the Williamsburg Trust Company by the architectural firm of Helmle and Huberty, which also designed the boathouse in Prospect Park. The building is an opulent terra-cotta temple in the Roman Revival style inspired by the World's Columbian Exhibition of 1893. It was the main branch of Williamsburg Trust until 1911. The bank was dissolved by the U.S. Supreme Court in 1922, and the building stood vacant for some time. After remodeling it housed the Magistrate Court of the Fifth District from 1928 and became a cathedral in the mid-1960s.

Brooke J. Barr

Holy Trinity Lutheran Church. Congregation founded during an 1868 split from St. James Lutheran Church; it was one of the few English-speaking Lutheran congregations in New York City (most were German-speaking). Originally housed at 47 West 21st Street, its home in the twenty-first century at 3 West 65th Street was built from 1902 to 1904 and designed by Schickel and Ditmars; the building is known for its copper steeple. In 1938 the St. James congregation rejoined Holy Trinity, which is famous for its Sunday evening Bach Vespers, a series begun during the church's centennial in 1968.

Kate Lauber

Home Box Office [HBO]. National cable television service launched in New York City in November 1972. It initially had headquarters in the Time Warner Building (50th Street and Sixth Avenue) before moving in 1983 to 1100 Avenue of the Americas. The first successful venture of its kind, by the early twenty-first century it provided service to 30 million customers in the United States. Its programs, sold in more than 150 countries, include motion pictures, documentaries, comedy programs, and sports broadcasts. It has produced several acclaimed series, including *Sex and the City* (1998–2004), which essentially made New York City a character, and *The Sopranos* (1999–2007), a mob drama that took place in suburban New Jersey. In the early twenty-first century HBO's parent company is Time Warner.

Janet Frankston

Homecrest. Neighborhood in southwestern Brooklyn, bounded to the north by Avenue U, to the east by East 21st Street, to the south by Avenue W, and to the west by Ocean Parkway. The area was originally farmland in the town of Gravesend and was developed after 1900, when it was advertised as "Homecrest by the Sea." Residents could walk to the shore in 10 minutes and reach Manhattan by train in 30. Large one-family Victorian houses on landscaped double lots had the latest modern conveniences. In the first decade of the twenty-first century the population was diverse and included large numbers of Chinese, Russians, Koreans, Italians, Israelis, Egyptians, and Lebanese. The quiet streets of Homecrest are lined with trees and modest one- and two-family brick houses, one-story bungalows, town houses, and low-rise apartment buildings. The main commercial district lies along Avenue U, and there is additional shopping along Coney Island Avenue.

Elizabeth Reich Rawson

Home Insurance Company. Firm of insurers incorporated in 1853. It grew steadily and became licensed throughout the United States as a provider of property and casualty insurance. It lobbied for more stringent fire and building codes along with standardized fire-fighting equipment in the late nineteenth and early twentieth centuries. It was also a pioneer in licensing agencies across the United States and in Canada. It was purchased in 1991 by TVH Acquisition Corporation. In 2010 Home Insurance had total assets of $6.7 billion, about 5000 employees, and was the 23rd largest property and casualty insurer in the country. Its headquarters were at 59 Maiden Lane.

Claude M. Scales III

homelessness. Shelter for the homeless poor in New York City dates from the late seventeenth century when some churches rented a building for emergency lodging. In 1734 the city erected a "house of correction, workhouse and poorhouse" whose residents were referred to as "family." But organized charity devoted itself chiefly to disciplining the unruly poor. A few experimental projects aside, private shelters targeted "wild children" and women

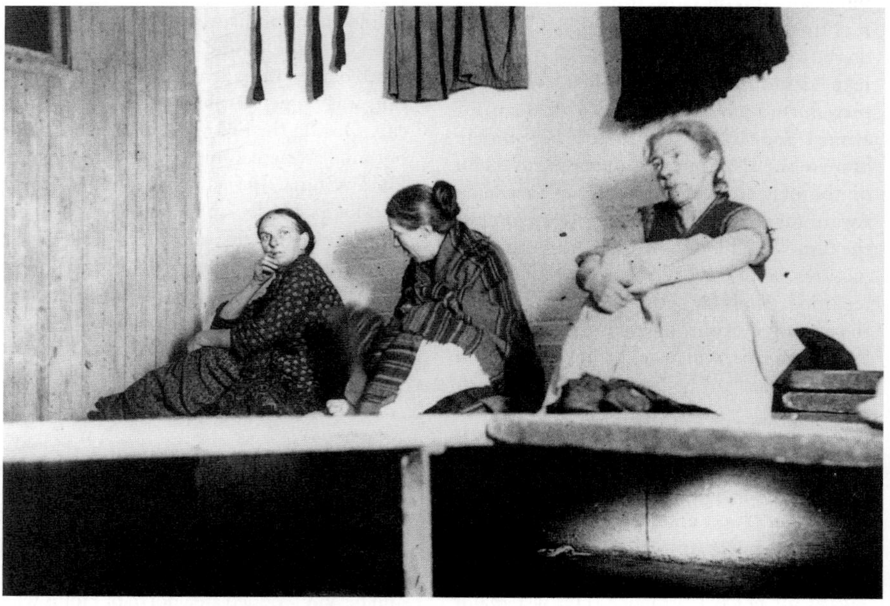

Homeless women at a temporary shelter attached to the 30th Street police station, ca 1885–90

of the streets. In 1857 the police formalized longstanding practice and required each precinct to designate a station house for lodging "vagrant and disorderly persons" overnight. Soon notorious for the crush of disreputable humanity they housed, such "night refuges" did offer stranded citizens an alternative to the almshouse. This practice of offering the "soft side of a plank" to homeless people inaugurated an enduring policy of deterrence and improvisation. Demand mounted with economic downturns and declined when police aggressively enforced vagrancy statutes.

After the Civil War evangelical "rescue missions" opened. During tough times citizens' groups organized food, fuel, and clothing drives for the poor, drawing criticism from advocates of "scientific charity" for "indiscriminate" almsgiving. The 1886 Municipal Lodging House Act empowered the city to operate homeless shelters but excluded women, children, the elderly, and the infirm. In 1893 the Charity Organization Society opened a Wayfarer's Lodge where guests paid for their stay by chopping wood. Similar "work tests" were later adopted (if erratically enforced) by public shelters. In February 1896, at the urging of reformer Jacob A. Riis, the police station houses were abruptly closed, stranding thousands until a barge moored in the East River was pressed into service as a floating shelter. Other makeshifts followed until 1909 when the first Municipal Lodging House opened at 438 East 25th Street, boasting the latest amenities, nearly 1000 beds, and separate dormitories for women and children.

Virtually from the start, routine need for housing outstripped capacity, and the city's homeless resorted to "sleeping rough" under bridges and in parks, saloons, waiting rooms, churches, public toilets, and the subways. When demand surged, the city lodged men on steamboats and piers along the East River, on Ellis Island, in jails, and even in the morgue. Tainted by corruption under Tammany Hall, the Municipal Lodging House enjoyed a brief renaissance after 1914 under reformist superintendent Stuart Rice. He managed a "hybrid institution" saddled with the task of providing emergency respite for temporarily jobless men and rehabilitating those with crippling disabilities.

Extraordinary measures to deal with homelessness were taken during the Great Depression. Two "annexes" opened in the early 1930s, with nearly 4000 beds between them. Facilities like the Salvation Army's Gold Dust Lodge were limited to men of the "better" classes. In 1935 a women's shelter was added and two work camps opened north of the city. By June, the city sheltered a record 21,000 people, including transient families, but night censuses still found thousands sleeping in the streets, subways, and parks. Shantytowns, some with hundreds of residents, cropped up in Riverside Park and Central Park and along the East River. World War II soon mobilized all available labor, and only the elderly and disabled were left behind; by 1944 public shelters lodged fewer than 800 men.

The postwar men's shelter census was swollen by returning veterans, who joined the seedy retirement community of elderly white men along the stretch of flophouses, missions, and rough taverns known as the Bowery. Some 8000 men found cheap lodging there. Most paid their own way, relying on pensions, panhandling, and casual labor or wiping auto windshields. Small knots of men pooled earnings for bottles of wine and repaired to street corners and vacant lots. Occasional police sweeps disrupted the routine, but a more serious threat came from "jackrollers" who preyed on the unwary or the stupefied. Missions continued to ply soup and sermons. The city's "Muni" on East Third Street housed 600 men until 1964; when its dormitories closed, scores slept in the lobby. Others found their way to jails and hospitals. Only a few dozen typically slept outdoors. Shelter was not their defining problem, and sociologists took to calling them "disaffiliated." Even those claiming steady income and lodging had shrugged off the usual ties that bind—work, family, and community—and showed little interest in forging new ones.

Beginning in the early 1960s thousands of long-term patients were discharged from state psychiatric facilities, some without secure housing. Unused to living on their own, they were easily exploited by unscrupulous landlords. As neighborhoods "gentrified," cheap housing (such as single-room occupancy hotels, or SROs) disappeared, rarely to be replaced. Demand at public shelters grew during the 1970s and clientele changed. First-time shelter users were more likely to be young minority men, and by mid-decade severe mental illness rivaled alcoholism as the signature affliction of homeless men. Capacity at the missions and flophouses topped out; the overflow slept in the "Big Room" on East Third Street. Women competed for 47 beds at a nearby shelter on Lafayette Street. Both facilities regularly turned applicants away. Visible homelessness seeped into the urban landscape.

In October 1979 Robert Hayes, a young corporate lawyer, filed *Callahan v. Carey,* a class-action suit charging state and city defendants with violating obligations toward the indigent needy. An initial ruling in the state supreme court recognized a de facto right to shelter for men (soon extended to women), and the first new public facilities in 40 years opened that winter. In August 1981 *Callahan* was settled by a consent decree affirming a right to shelter (defined as "clean bedding, wholesome food and adequate security and supervision"), setting minimal standards for its provision and providing for regular monitoring of conditions. The Legal Aid Society sought and won protection for homeless families in protracted litigation (*McCain v. Koch*) beginning in 1984.

Throughout the 1980s shelter rolls swelled while thousands of homeless people remained on the streets. Pressured by the courts, vocal advocacy, and the prospect of lost federal funds, Mayor Edward I. Koch expedited conversion of tax-foreclosed properties into affordable housing, reclaiming some 20,000 units between 1987 and 1990. Progress slowed under Mayor David N. Dinkins and then ground to a standstill under Mayor Rudy Giuliani, with the exception of "supported housing" developed (with the state) for people with disabilities. His administration intensified policing of the street-dwelling homeless under "quality-of-life" auspices, fought bitterly with advocates, and moved unsuccessfully to make shelter conditional on compliance with facility rules.

Irregularly honored in practice, an unconditional right to shelter was repeatedly upheld by a judiciary skeptical of bureaucratic discretion. But in 2003 a New York State appellate court reversed precedent and ratified "reasonable standards," requiring residents to make supervised progress to exit public shelter. Failure to comply could result in formal eviction proceedings. These proved rare in practice and, contested by the Legal Aid Society, patently ineffective. But informal threats of expulsion may have persuaded untold numbers to leave. A 2003 settlement in *McCain* ensured that homeless families would have housing even if they refused specific placements. This inaugurated a two-year moratorium on litigation; conflict resolution was vested in a Special Masters Panel. With its

Hooverville in Queens, 1932

prodding, substantive reforms in processing homeless family applicants were implemented. When the panel's term expired, oversight authority reverted to the court. Three years later, in September 2008, the city reached a settlement with Legal Aid that ended court supervision and recognized a constitutional right to shelter for homeless families, and all court orders were vacated.

The administration of Mayor Michael R. Bloomberg made concerted efforts to install a corporate mentality, with accountability its watchword, in civil service terrain. Bureaucracies were enjoined to cooperate as problem solving required, policy was explicitly to be coupled to empirical evidence, and progress in meeting stated goals posted. In 2004, after broad-based consultation, an ambitious plan was announced to reduce street homelessness and shelter rolls by two-thirds in five years. Needs assessment became more rigorous and street outreach better coordinated. Shelter diversion efforts (inquiring into viable alternatives) were matched by aggressive insistence that residents begin to make arrangements to leave a shelter as soon as they arrive. Dubious makeshifts (short-term rental assistance, assisted doubling up, referral to substandard boarding homes) were enacted to further reduce shelter demand. At the same time, a bold program to develop affordable housing—165,000 units in 10 years—was unveiled. As of mid-2008, progress had been uneven. Reaching across bureaucratic divides had shown success, especially with criminal justice and foster care. Visible street homelessness had declined. The census in shelters for singles dropped, but the number of homeless families (most with children) climbed to historic highs (more than 9500) in October 2007. Progress in developing supported housing slowed. Credit markets tightened, fueling anxiety about Bloomberg's housing plan. By late 2007 40 percent of units promised had financing, almost all of them existing units "preserved" as affordable. Funding for new construction remained uncertain.

Nels Anderson, *The Homeless in New York City* (New York: Welfare Council, 1934); Howard Bahr, *Skid Row: An Introduction to Disaffiliation* (New York: Oxford University Press, 1973); Kenneth Kusmer, *Down and Out, On the Road* (New York: Oxford University Press, 2002); Kim Hopper, *Reckoning with Homelessness* (Ithaca, N.Y.: Cornell University Press, 2003)

Kim Hopper

Home Life Insurance Company. Firm of insurers formed by several prominent residents of Brooklyn, including A. A. Low and John T. Stranahan (1808–98), a former congressman. It opened headquarters at the corner of Court and Joralemon streets on 1 May 1860, as well as a branch on Wall Street. The headquarters moved in 1870 to Manhattan and in 1892 to a new building at 256 Broadway designed by the firm of Napoleon Le Brun and Sons (this was among the tallest buildings in the world when it opened). The firm introduced guaranteed insurability for prospective policyholders and offered business insurance, pension planning, and life insurance plans that helped families to pay college tuition. Its headquarters moved in 1987 to 75 Wall Street. In 1990 Home Life had assets of $14 billion and $45 billion of policies in force. In 1992 it merged with Phoenix Mutual Life Insurance Company of Hartford, Connecticut.

James Bradley

homeopathy [homoeopathy]. System of medical treatment in which small doses of medicines are administered that produce symptoms similar to those of the disease being treated, thus inducing the body to heal itself. It originated in the work of the German physician Samuel Hahnemann and was introduced in the United States by Hans Burch Gram (1786–1840), who began practicing medicine in New York City in 1825. Gram's efforts led to the formation in 1835 of the New York Homoeopathic Society and in 1841 of the New York Homoeopathic Physicians' Society. In 1844 homeopaths in the city were instrumental in forming the American Institute of Homoeopathy; the Homoeopathic Medical College of New York opened in 1860 (known from 1869 as the New York Homoeopathic Medical College). The number of homeopaths in the city grew from 115 in 1860 to nearly 1000 by the turn of the century. Among the most prominent were Timothy F. Allen (1873–1902), William Tod Helmuth (1833–1902), Samuel Lilienthal (1815–91), and George S. Norton (1851–91). Several publishers in the city issued works about homeopathy, including Boericke and Runyon, William Radde and Son, Hahnemann Publishing House, and Chatterton.

Having failed in their attempt in 1857 to have half the beds at Bellevue Hospital set aside for homeopathic practice, homeopaths in 1863 organized the New York Medical College for Women, one of only two institutions of its kind in the world. The first class of six was admitted in 1866; a hospital for women and children was added a few years later, and the whole institution was called the New York Medical College and Hospital for Women. This remained in operation until 1918 when the trustees decided to close the hospital and admit the remaining women to the Homoeopathic Medical College of New York, which until then had admitted only men. The opening of Hahnemann Hospital in 1869 at Lexington Avenue and 67th Street was followed by that of the New York Homoeopathic Surgical Hospital in 1874. In 1875 the two institutions merged and one hospital building on Wards Island was set aside for homeopathy. By 1900 there were more than 100 homeopathic clinics, dispensaries, and hospitals in the city; these included Hahnemann Hospital and the Laura Franklin Free Hospital for Children at 17 East 111th Street, formed in 1886 by Franklin Delano and his wife (these two combined in 1922 to form the Fifth Avenue Hospital at 105th Street, advertised as the first hospital in the world to contain only rooms for individual patients rather than wards), as well as Flower Hospital, Metropolitan Hospital, Harlem Homoeopathic Hospital, and Ward's Island Homoeopathic Hospital. In 1936 the New York Homoeopathic Medical College renamed itself the New York Medical College, marking the end of a long period of influence of homeopathy in the city.

Interest in homeopathy revived during the early 1970s amid growing dissatisfaction with the U.S. health system. By offering an alternative to the aggressive, highly technical methods of conventional medicine, homeopathy won new followers attracted by its emphasis on health, natural medicines, and treating the whole person rather than the diseased organ. The National Center for Homeopathy, offering information and referral, opened in 1974 in Alexandria, Virginia; in 2007 its listing of homeopathic practitioners included 15 in New York City.

Leonard P. Wershub, *One Hundred Years of Medical Progress: A History of New York Medical College, Flower and Fifth Avenue Hospitals* (Springfield, Ill.: Charles C. Thomas, 1967); Martin Kaufman, *Homoeopathy in America: The Rise and Fall of a Medical Heresy* (Baltimore: Johns Hopkins University Press, 1971); Phillip A. Nicholls, *Homoeopathy and the Medical Profession* (London: Croom Helm, 1988)

Francesco Cordasco

Homeport–Stapleton. U.S. Navy base in Staten Island. The name refers to a strategy called *homeporting*, according to which vessels are dispersed among many ports as a safeguard against catastrophic losses that can result if a fleet is concentrated in only a few ports. The base opened in 1990 to provide a berth for battleships, destroyers, cruisers, and reserve frigates. It included a technologically advanced pier measuring 1410 feet (430 meters) by 90 feet (27.5 meters), with large maintenance buildings nearby. More than 4000 uniformed personnel working at the base were housed at Fort Wadsworth and elsewhere in Staten Island and Brooklyn. As part of a nationwide policy to reduce and reallocate military spending, the federal government closed Homeport–Stapleton in 1994. In 2009 the city announced plans for a $150 million joint private-public redevelopment, with 800 residential housing units and retail stores and a new waterfront esplanade.

Barnett Shepherd

Homer, Winslow (*b* Boston, 24 Feb 1836; *d* Scarborough, Maine, 29 Sept 1910). Painter. After fulfilling an apprenticeship at the age of 21 in the Boston lithography firm of J. H. Bufford, he moved to New York City and

Winslow Homer, The New Year *(1869)*

attended night school at the National Academy of Design. In 1859 he moved to 128 East 16th Street. During the first years of the Civil War he was sent to sketch scenes of the front, which were published in *Harper's Weekly.* After returning to the city he concentrated on war paintings and was elected to the National Academy of Design; his work was shown at a number of exhibitions there. Homer lived in a studio at 51 West 10th Street during the 1870s and in another at Washington Square North and University Place from 1882 until 1884, when he moved to Prout's Neck, Maine.

Gordon Hendricks, *The Life and Work of Winslow Homer* (New York: Harry N. Abrams, 1979); Nicolai Cikovsky, *Winslow Homer* (New York: Harry N. Abrams, 1990)

James E. Mooney

home rule. Legal term for local autonomy. The concept of home rule emerged in the nineteenth century in opposition to legal doctrines that treated cities as inferior creatures of their states, possessing only those powers expressly delegated to them and subject to the plenary power of the states to alter, reduce, or abolish local authority. Home rule affirms the power of local governments to legislate regarding local matters, and limits the power of states to displace local decisions.

The constitution of New York State first provided a measure of home rule for New York City in 1894. The current home rule provision, article IX, was adopted in 1963. Among other provisions it prohibits the state from adopting special laws concerning the property, affairs, or government of New York City, except at the city's request. (There is no comparable restriction on general laws, by which the state may exert its authority over municipal matters.) Article IX also grants the city and other local governments the authority to adopt and amend local laws relating to local "property, affairs, or government," as well as other specifically enumerated local matters, including the "government, protection, order, conduct, safety, health, and well-being of persons or property" within the locality, as long as the local laws are not inconsistent with the state constitution or general laws.

Home rule has generally been effective in enabling local governments to take the initiative and legislate with respect to local matters without having to obtain express permission from the state government. It does not, however, provide the city with much legal protection from interference by the state legislature. The New York State Court of Appeals has held that the legislature may act by special law with respect to local "property, affairs, or government" without a request from the city "if the subject be in a substantial degree a matter of state concern . . . though intermingled with it are concerns of the locality" (*Adler v. Deegan,* 1929, concurring opinion of Chief Judge Cardozo). The court has also found that the property, affairs, and government of New York City are often matters of state concern. It has sustained special state laws regulating the city's multiple dwellings, mandating that a specific percentage of the city's budget be devoted to education, and displacing city residency requirements for municipal employees. Home rule also does not apply to local finances. Local governments in New York State depend on the legislature for the power to tax. Local spending, borrowing, taxing, and lending are subject to tight constitutional restraints and may be further restricted by the legislature. In the twenty-first century these restrictions continued to thwart the city's own current initiatives; for instance, in 2008 the New York State Legislature did not approve a New York City proposal to implement congestion pricing, a proposal to charge cars and trucks a fee to enter Manhattan south of 86th Street.

Richard Briffault

Hondurans. The first Honduran immigrants to New York City were Garifuna, natives of an area along the Caribbean coast of mixed African, American Indian, and European ancestry who spoke a Creole language unrelated to Spanish. Garifuna from Honduras played an important role in the early 1960s in organizing hospital workers in Local 1199. Many Hondurans settled near Southern Boulevard and Van Cortlandt Park in the Bronx, and in Flatbush and near Pennsylvania Avenue in Brooklyn, where Garifuna from other Central American countries also lived. In 1980 the federal census counted 9500 Hondurans in the city, and during the next decade at least 11,000 more became legal residents. Meanwhile, the Honduran consulate estimated in 2000 that the metropolitan area included 70,000 Hondurans. During war and upheaval in Central America from the late 1970s to the early 1990s Honduran mestizos of Spanish and Indian descent settled in the city, especially along Pennsylvania Avenue. A few were professionals; most were single, lacked permanent resident status, and worked in manufacturing and service industries. Racial discrimination and lack of documentation severely limited opportunities for Garifuna, who formed civic groups in Brooklyn. Hondurans accounted for most of the 87 victims of a fire at the Happy Land Social Club on Southern Boulevard in the Bronx in 1990. More than 32,000 foreign-born in New York City alone reported Honduran ancestry in the 2000 census.

Graciela M. Castex

Hone, Philip (*b* New York City, 25 Oct 1780; *d* New York City, 5 May 1851). Businessman, mayor, and diarist. The son of a woodworker, he became wealthy in an auction business that he formed with his brothers in 1797, and in 1821 he retired to pursue his artistic, cultural, and political interests. He served two terms as an assistant alderman and in 1825 was chosen by the Common Council for a one-year term as mayor, during which he presided over the opening of the Erie Canal and entertained the Marquis de Lafayette. After losing much of his fortune in the panic of 1837, he returned to work; President Zachary Taylor eventually appointed him as naval officer for the district of New York. Hone is best known for his diary, in which he wrote about political events and the social life of the city's elite from 1826 until his death.

Allan Nevins, ed., *The Diary of Philip Hone, 1828–1851* (New York: Dodd, Mead, 1927)

See also U.S. Customs Service.

Evan Cornog

Hood, Raymond M(athewson) (*b* Pawtucket, R.I., 21 March 1881; *d* Stamford, Conn., 15 Aug 1934). Architect. After studying at the École des Beaux-Arts and working for Henry Hornbostel in Pittsburgh, he moved to New York City in 1914. With John Mead Howells he entered a competition to design the Chicago Tribune Building in 1922; their submission, a plan for a neo-Gothic tower, won the first prize of $50,000. Hood then designed a number of innovative skyscrapers in New York City, among them the American Radiator Building at 40 West 40th Street (1924, renamed the American Standard Building and now the Bryant Park Hotel), which he modeled after a medieval spire, clad in black brick and gold terra-cotta ornament and illuminated at night. Further experiments with color and pattern culminated in the Daily News Building at 220 East 42nd Street (1930, with J. M. Howells), with a facade of bold vertical stripes of white brick and dark window bands, and the McGraw–Hill Building at 330 West 42nd Street (1931), sheathed with blue-green terra-cotta tiles. A member of the team that designed Rockefeller Center, he was largely responsible for the RCA Building and the concept of roof gardens. Hood was highly successful at persuading clients that his unusual ideas would return profits and gain wide publicity.

Walter H. Kilham, Jr., *Raymond Hood, Architect: Form through Function* (New York: Architectural Book Publishing, 1973)

Carol Willis

Hook, Sidney (*b* New York City, 20 Dec 1902; *d* Stanford, Calif., 12 July 1989). Philosopher. He grew up in Williamsburg in Brooklyn and studied with Morris Raphael Cohen at the City College of New York and with John Dewey at Columbia University. He joined the faculty at New York University in 1927, remaining there until 1972. Although initially an advocate of communism and a supporter of the communist presidential candidate in 1932, by 1934 he was a tenacious anticommunist who believed that Josef Stalin had betrayed the principles of socialism. After publishing *Towards the Understanding of Karl Marx* (1933) and *From Hegel to Marx* (1936) Hook was widely accepted as the preeminent American scholar of Marxism. During the 1930s he sought to counter the appeal of the Popular Front, and in 1939 he organized the Committee for Cultural Freedom to emphasize the similarities between Stalinism and fascism; in 1949 he became the primary organizer and first leader of the American Committee for Cultural Freedom. Often near the center of intellectual controversies in the city and the nation, Hook was a proponent of philosophical pragmatism. He considered scientific thought the primary avenue to truth, argued vigorously for a definition of academic freedom that excluded communists, and supported nuclear deterrence, vigilance during the cold war, and an active welfare state. In 1987 he published the memoir *Out of Step: An Unquiet Life in the Twentieth Century.*

Paul Kurtz, ed., *Sidney Hook and the Contemporary World: Essays on the Pragmatic Intelligence* (New York: John Day, 1968)

Terry A. Cooney

Hook Creek. A tributary of Jamaica Bay and by extension a neighborhood in the southeast corner of Queens, on a narrow neck of land fronting the bay on three sides. It is surrounded by marshes and consists of fishing shacks and boating supply outlets on three short streets. The neck is bisected by Rockaway Boulevard, a heavily traveled artery that gives access to the Rockaway Peninsula. Before 1920 the boulevard was a narrow turnpike road impassable during exceptional tides, and a trolley company that owned the road provided the sole access outside of the neighborhood. The Department of Parks and Recreation manages two natural areas nearby: Hook Creek Marsh and the Idlewild Park Preserve.

Vincent Seyfried, Jeffrey A. Kroessler

Hoover, Herbert (Clark) (*b* West Branch, Iowa, 10 Aug 1874; *d* New York City, 20 Oct 1964). Thirty-first president of the United States. After a successful career in business, he was later the secretary of commerce under Presidents Warren G. Harding and Calvin Coolidge. As the Republican presidential candidate in 1928, he made one of his most successful campaign speeches at Madison Square Garden; he defeated the Democratic nominee, Alfred E. Smith, by a large margin. Unable to end the Depression, he failed to win reelection in 1932 against Franklin D. Roosevelt. He moved to New York City in 1934, took up residence in suite 31A of the Waldorf–Astoria Towers, and remained active in public life. In 1947 he was chosen by President Harry S. Truman to lead the Commission on the Organization of the Executive Branch, a bipartisan effort to streamline a federal government that had grown immense during the New Deal and the war. Known as the Hoover Commission, it had headquarters in Washington, D.C., but was effectively run from Hoover's office: he wrote most of the recommendations, and most were adopted. After being reappointed in 1953 by President Dwight D. Eisenhower, Hoover remained in charge of the commission until 1955. For the last 30 years of his life Hoover lived at the Waldorf–Astoria.

George H. Nash, *The Life of Herbert Hoover* (New York: W. W. Norton, 1996)

Edward T. O'Donnell

Hoovervilles. See Shantytowns.

Hopedale. Name formerly applied to a hamlet south of Queens Boulevard and north of Union Turnpike where an inn called Hopedale Hall once stood. The Long Island Rail Road opened a station there in July 1875 and a depot in October; the Maple Grove Cemetery opened in the same year only a quarter of a mile (400 meters) away. After a railroad station opened there in May 1879, the Hopedale station closed and the hamlet dwindled. The name last appears on a map from 1886.

Vincent Seyfried

Hopkins, Harry (Lloyd) (*b* Sioux City, Iowa, 17 Aug 1890; *d* New York City, 29 Jan 1946). Public official. After moving to New York City in 1912 he worked at a settlement, Christodora House, and at the Association for Improving the Condition of the Poor; these experiences led him to believe that unemployment was the chief cause of poverty. In October 1931 he was appointed by Governor Franklin D. Roosevelt as the executive director of the Temporary Emergency Relief Association for New York State, and under his leadership the association provided work for thousands of residents of New York City. After Roosevelt was elected to the White House, Hopkins successively led the Federal Emergency Relief Administration, the Civil Works Administration, and (from 1935) the Works Progress Administration.

George T. McJimsey, *Harry Hopkins: Ally of the Poor and Defender of Democracy* (Cambridge, Mass.: Harvard University Press, 1987)

Sarah Henry Lederman

Hopper, Edward (*b* Nyack, N.Y., 22 July 1882; *d* New York City, 15 May 1967). Painter and printmaker. He studied painting with William Merritt Chase, Robert Henri, and Kenneth Hayes Miller at the New York School of Art and worked initially as an illustrator and commercial artist; in the early years of the twentieth century he lived in a studio at 53 East 59th Street. After travels abroad in 1906–7 and 1909 he took part in the Exhibition of Independent Artists in 1910. From 1913 until his death he lived and worked at 3 Washington Square North; he exhibited frequently at the MacDowell Club (1912–18) and the Whitney Studio Club (1920–25). Hopper's cityscapes and interior scenes evoke the anonymity and isolation of modern life. The Whitney Museum of American Art owns the largest collection of his works.

Gail Levin, *Edward Hopper: The Art and the Artist* (New York: W. W. Norton/Whitney Museum of American Art, 1980); Gail Levin, *Hopper's Places* (New York: Alfred A. Knopf, 1985)

Judith Zilczer

Horace Mann School. Private elementary and secondary school opened in Manhattan in 1887 by Nicholas Murray Butler, who, with the encouragement of Frederick A. P. Barnard (then president of Columbia University), had studied the educational theories of Horace Mann and others in Berlin. The school emphasized the training of public school teachers. In the early twenty-first century Horace Mann–Barnard Elementary School and the Horace Mann School (high school) were located on an 18-acre (7.3-hectare) plot in the Bronx and enrolled more than 1700 students.

Richard Schwartz

Horne, Lena (Calhoun) (*b* New York City, 30 June 1917; *d* New York City, 9 May 2010). Dancer, singer, and actress. Born in Brooklyn, she left school at age 14 and became a dancer at the Cotton Club in Harlem at 16. She met Cab Calloway, Duke Ellington, and Billie Holiday at the club and later performed on Broadway, in nightclubs, and had brief engagements with the orchestras of Noble Sissle and Charlie Barnet. In 1941 she had a seven-month engagement at the Café Society in Greenwich Village during which she became well known as a singer. She was the first African American signed to a long-term studio contract, one of the first African American women to successfully work on both sides of the color line, and (in the mid-1940s) the highest-paid African American actor in the country. Her biggest hit was the musical *Stormy Weather* (1943), in which she starred alongside some of her former Cotton Club colleagues. In her many films Horne acted in roles that were not stereotypical, becoming one of the first African American actresses to do so; her career was nonetheless held back because of prevailing racial attitudes, particularly in the South, where her scenes were edited out of some films. In 1957 she had an engagement of unprecedented length at the Waldorf–Astoria and made her Broadway debut in the musical *Jamaica,* which ran for a year and a half. She made a comeback in 1981 in *Lena Horne: The Lady and Her Music,* a one-woman show that remained on Broadway for a year and won a Tony Award. For many years she lived in the Apthorp apartment building on Manhattan's Upper West Side.

Lena Horne with Cab Calloway

Donald Bogle, *Brown Sugar: Eighty Years of America's Black Female Superstars* (New York: Harmony, 1980); James Haskins and Kathleen Benson, *Lena: A Personal and Professional Biography of Lena Horne* (New York: Stein and Day, 1984)

Ira Berger

Horney [née Danielsen], **Karen** (*b* Hamburg, 16 Sept 1885; *d* New York City, 4 Dec 1952). Psychiatrist. After studying in Germany and living for two years in Chicago she moved to New York City in 1934, entered private practice, and until 1941 taught at the New School for Social Research. A critic of classical Freudianism, she argued in *The Neurotic Personality of Our Time* (1937) that social forces rather than psychosexual dynamics are responsible for personality disorders. She helped to form the Association for the Advancement of Psychoanalysis, taught at the American Institute for Psychoanalysis, edited the *American Journal of Psychoanalysis,* and wrote both scholarly and popular works. From the 1970s Horney's work received greater attention because of its feminist implications. She lived at 240 Central Park South.

Jack L. Rubins, *Karen Horney: Gentle Rebel of Psychoanalysis* (New York: Dial, 1978); Bernard J. Paris, *Karen Horney: A Psychoanalyst's Search for Self-Understanding* (New Haven: Yale University Press, 1994)

Mary Elizabeth Brown

Horowitz, Vladimir [Gorovitz, Vladimir (Samoliovich)] (*b* Kiev, Ukraine, 1 Oct 1903; *d* New York City, 5 Nov 1989). Pianist. After leaving the Soviet Union in 1925 he performed for several years in the major cities of Europe and made a sensational American debut on 12 January 1928 at Carnegie Hall, playing Tchaikovsky's Piano Concerto no. 1 with the New York Philharmonic under Sir Thomas Beecham. He soon took up residence in New York City and in 1933 married Wanda Toscanini, daughter of the conductor Arturo Toscanini. From 1944 he lived on East 94th Street near Fifth Avenue. An idiosyncratic and often reluctant performer, he retired from the concert stage from 1953 to 1965 and again from 1969 to 17 November 1974, when he gave the first piano recital ever held at the Metropolitan Opera House. Horowitz's technique was supremely virtuosic; his performances often provoked controversy because of a tendency toward overly romantic gestures and a less-than-literal view of the written score. His repertory emphasized the late nineteenth century and the early twentieth, especially the music of the Russians Modest Mussorgsky, Alexander Scriabin, Sergei Rachmaninoff, and Serge Prokofiev. He played few large works of Mozart and Beethoven and seemed better suited to work on a smaller scale by Domenico Scarlatti and Muzio Clementi.

Glenn Plaskin, *Horowitz: A Biography* (New York: William Morrow, 1983); Harold C. Schonberg, *Horowitz: His Life and Music* (New York: Simon and Schuster, 1992)

Barbara L. Tischler

horse racing. The beginning of thoroughbred horse racing in the metropolitan area dates to 1665 when Governor Richard Nicolls established the Newmarket Track at Salisbury Plain in what is now suburban Hempstead, Long Island; there, races were contested for a silver cup over a course 2 miles (3.2 kilometers) long. The first track in what is now New York City was the Church Farm Course (probably in lower Manhattan), where from 1725 to 1753 the New York Subscription Plate was awarded. The sport continued during the American Revolution, which made it anathema to virtuous patriots who later banned it as aristocratic and immoral. The ban was repealed in 1820, and the Union Course opened on Long Island in the following year and became the scene of great match races, beginning with one between Eclipse and Sir Henry in 1823 before a crowd estimated at 60,000, and ending with another between Fashion and Peytona in 1845 before a crowd that was even larger. By this time thoroughbred racing was being surpassed in popularity by harness racing, which gained favor in the 1820s because the standardbred horses used in this sport were cheaper and more useful than thoroughbreds: Lady Suffolk, the winner of more than $35,000 in purses, began her racing career after pulling a butcher's cart. Races were originally spontaneous events along Third Avenue and Harlem Lane and were made more structured by the New York Trotting Club (1825), which built a course in Centerville, Long Island. As thoroughbred racing continued to suffer, virtually destroyed by the depression of 1837 and the westward migration of the breeding business, harness racing prospered: by 1860 there were seven trotting tracks in the metropolitan area, including the Fashion Course in Newtown (1854). The breeding of standardbreds by then could be expensive, especially if owners wanted to compete with rich rivals like Cornelius Vanderbilt.

Thoroughbred racing enjoyed a renaissance under the auspices of the American Jockey Club, formed in 1865 by Leonard Jerome, August Belmont, and William R. Travers. Jerome built Jerome Park in Fordham (now the Bronx), which became a lavish, upper-class resort. The track staged dashes and handicap races, offered large purses, and in 1871 introduced parimutuel betting, which failed to supplant auction-pool gambling and was abandoned. The feature event at the track was the Belmont Stakes (1867), a race 1-3/8 miles (2.2 kilometers) long that eventually became the final event of the Triple Crown. The locus of racing shifted in 1879 to Coney Island, where William Engeman built the proprietary

Horse racing at Union Course, Long Island, 1845

Brighton Beach racecourse, which was followed in 1880 by the elite Sheepshead Bay Track of the Coney Island Jockey Club and in 1885 by Mike and Philip Dwyer's Gravesend Track. Engeman and the Dwyers were entrepreneurs seeking large, plebeian audiences. In 1889, when Jerome was closed to make way for a reservoir, the Westchester Racing Association replaced it with a new, opulent resort, Morris Park Racetrack, in what is now the eastern Bronx. Its track was 1-3⁄8 miles (2.2 kilometers) long, and the grandstand, seating 15,000, was the largest in the country. The growing popularity of racing led to the construction of four more tracks in or adjacent to New York City: Aqueduct Racetrack (1894), Jamaica Racetrack (1903), Empire City Racetrack in Yonkers (1900), and Belmont Park in Elmont, Long Island (1905), built to replace Morris Park at a cost of $2.4 million.

Racetracks within the Present Boundaries of New York City

Union Course, Queens, 1821–51
Centerville (Eclipse) Course, Queens, 1830–59
National (Fashion), Queens, 1854–56
Jerome Park, Bronx, 1866–89
Brighton Beach, Brooklyn, 1879–1908
Sheepshead Bay, Brooklyn, 1880–1910
Gravesend, Brooklyn, 1886–1910
Morris Park, Bronx, 1889–1904
Aqueduct, Queens, 1894–1956, 1959–
Empire City, Bronx, 1900–1942
Jamaica, Queens, 1903–59

From the 1880s the principal form of gambling at the tracks was bookmaking, which in 1887 was banned outside the tracks. The betting element tied the sport intimately to machine politicians and organized crime and made racing a prime target of moral reformers. Elite horse enthusiasts in the city led by August Belmont responded by establishing the Jockey Club in 1894 to develop national standards for the sport. This became an adjunct of the new State Racing Commission (1895) and was recognized as the arbiter of the American turf. Nonetheless, opposition continued, and in 1910 progressive reformers halted racing. It resumed in 1913, employing oral betting to circumvent the law, and the prestigious events formerly staged in Brooklyn shifted to Belmont Park.

American racing thrived after World War I, and New Yorkers enjoyed the exploits of horses like Man o' War, yet local racing was held back because only oral betting with bookmakers affiliated with John Cavanagh was permitted at the tracks. Off-track gambling flourished under men like Arnold Rothstein, and bootleggers like Big Bill Dwyer emerged as the owners of out-of-town tracks. In 1940 parimutuel betting was legalized, leading to greater profits at the thoroughbred tracks and the establishment of harness racing at Roosevelt Raceway on Long Island (1940) and Yonkers Raceway (1950). Racing became the leading American spectator sport in the 1950s, but locally it was troubled by aging facilities and the state's relatively large "take" from the parimutuel pool (eventually raised to 17 percent). The nonprofit New York Racing Association established in 1956 to reinvigorate the sport took over all the tracks, closing Jamaica, rebuilding Aqueduct, and spending $30.7 million in 1968 to refurbish Belmont. By the twenty-first century the association was mired in corruption charges and had fallen into bankruptcy; under a deal with the state in 2008, its franchise to operate the tracks at Aqueduct, Belmont, and Saratoga Springs was renewed for 25 years, and the association was expected to work under an overhauled board of trustees and a new oversight board appointed by the governor. The state offered a bailout package of $105 million, which would be recouped by new video lottery terminals installed at Aqueduct, expected to bring in $400 million annually.

William H. P. Robertson, *The History of Thoroughbred Racing in America* (New York: Prentice Hall, 1964); Melvin L. Adelman, *A Sporting Time: New York City and the Rise of Modern Athletics, 1820–1870* (Urbana: University of Illinois Press, 1986); Steven A. Riess, *City Games: The Evolution of American Urban Society and the Rise of Sports* (Urbana: University of Illinois Press, 1989)

Steven A. Riess

horses. Powerful, bulky horses were introduced to New Amsterdam by Dutch settlers for carrying heavy loads and operating gristmills and sawmills. In the 1660s finer-boned horses were imported by English colonists, who in 1665 opened a racetrack on Long Island to encourage the development of faster breeds. By the nineteenth century horses had become entrenched in city life: while trotting along the broad, straight roads of Manhattan and carriage rides in Central Park were popular activities among the wealthy, horses served all classes of city residents. Big workhorses hauled goods from arriving ships and pulled omnibuses and horsecars in the earliest forms of mass transit. Private broughams and barouches filled the streets; horse-drawn, double-decker stagecoaches ran on Fifth Avenue, and hacks and two-wheeled hansom cabs were available for hire throughout the city. New York City had the heaviest concentration of horse-drawn vehicle and component manufacturers in the country by 1850, led by such manufacturers as Brewster and Company. In 1831 a horse-drawn omnibus, the first of its kind in the United States, offered regular service on a route along Broadway. In 1833 the *New York Journal* established an express service to obtain news quickly from Washington, D.C., and the South; its two dozen horses covered the 227 miles (363 kilometers) between Washington and the city in 20 hours. Horses were widely used in firefighting after 1860, as well as in the growing industrial sections, where breweries were known for their wagons pulled by enormous draft horses. During the 1860s and 1870s horses were so essential to the city that many were overworked: the average lifespan of a streetcar horse in New York City was about four years, and horses were often housed in crowded, dirty garages. In 1872 an equine virus killed 200 horses a day, shutting down transportation and delivery operations. Horses also contributed to urban problems: in a city with no systematic street-cleaning, each horse produced between 15 and 35 pounds of manure a day, plus one quart of urine. The smell could be overpowering, and the resulting flies spread disease. If an overworked draft horse died on the street, its heavy body was often left in place to decay or was dumped into the river. People also complained about the noise that , horses' iron-shod hooves made on cobblestone streets. Advancing technology, rather than municipal action, solved these problems. At the turn of the century streetcars were electrified, automobiles became more common, and horse-drawn omnibuses were replaced by motorized buses (although for a few years, starting in 1900, automobiles were banned because they frightened horses). The last horsecar ran on West Street in Manhattan until 1918. Between 1910 and 1920 the number of horses in New York City declined from 128,000 to 56,000.

Horses continued to draw hansom cabs for tourists around the southern part of Central Park in the early twenty-first century, although the cabs provoked criticism from animal-rights activists, who prevailed on the city to impose limits on the number of hours that horses could work, especially in hot weather. Some called for carriage horses to be banned altogether, especially after the deaths of two horses in 2006 and an audit the following year showing questionable practices by the carriage industry. Recreational riding continued in the city's parks, although the Claremont Riding Academy on the Upper West Side, the last public stable in Manhattan, closed in 2007. The police department maintained its mounted unit at Pier 76 on Manhattan's West Side; officers were also stationed at Pelham Bay Park, Fresh Meadows, Coney Island, and the First Precinct in lower Manhattan. The mounted unit in 2008 included 120 riders and 80 horses, plus a second troop with 30 riders and 28 horses.

See also Horse racing, Stables, and Streetcars.

James O. Drummond, Kate Lauber

Horsmanden, Daniel (*b* Purleigh, England, 4 June 1694; *d* Flatbush [now in Brooklyn], 23 Sept 1778). Judge. He studied law in England and by 1731 had a practice in New York City. In 1744 he published an account of the "Negro plot" of 1741. A supporter of the Livingston political faction, he was appointed recorder, supreme court judge, and admiralty judge. In 1747 he lost these offices during a time of political change and was nearly sent to debtors' prison. After regaining favor he was again made a judge during the 1750s and a chief justice during the 1760s.

James E. Mooney

horticulture. The Dutch who settled in America in the seventeenth century had a sophisticated understanding of horticulture and planted many gardens and orchards throughout New Amsterdam. One of the many orchards that they planted on Staten Island was raided by Indians in 1655 during a conflict known as the Peach War. In 1737 the first commercial nursery in America opened in what is now Flushing and soon offered fruit trees, shrubs, and ornamental plants. In the 1750s in what later became Queens the Newtown Pippin was developed into a prime apple for the London market. Several other new varieties of plants were grown in the country's first greenhouse, built in 1764 by James Beekman near what is now 51st Street and First Avenue in Manhattan.

The Elgin Botanical Garden, established in 1801 by David Hosack, a professor of botany and medicine at Columbia College, was the first public botanical garden in the United States, covering 20 acres (8 hectares) of land on a site now occupied by Rockefeller Center. Its gardener, the taxonomist Frederick Pursh, helped to identify plants brought back from the Lewis and Clark expedition. During the 1830s a nursery was opened in Brooklyn by a gardener of Belgian descent named Andrew Parmentier, and through the efforts of the Prince Nursery of Flushing the Isabella grape, found growing in Brooklyn Heights, became the most popular edible grape in the United States (until it was supplanted in the 1850s by the Concord grape). Many new plants were introduced to New York City with the opening of Central Park in 1858, including the Japanese maple, transported from Japan by Commodore Matthew C. Perry and grown by Samuel Bowne Parsons in his nurseries, one of which, Kissena Nurseries, became the site of Kissena Park.

Horticulture thrived in New York City between 1880 and 1940. Wealthy New Yorkers who owned large suburban estates planted elaborate gardens, usually cared for by English-trained gardeners. One of these was Thomas H. Everett, who started working at the New York Botanical Garden in 1932, eventually becoming its senior horticulture specialist, and was the author of the *New York Botanical Garden Illustrated Encyclopedia of Horticulture* (1980–82). This same period saw the planting of the first flowerbeds in the city's parks. In 1891 Nathaniel Lord Britton, a professor of botany at Columbia, and his wife, Elizabeth Knight Britton, an expert on lichens, campaigned for the establishment of the New York Botanical Garden, designed by Calvert Vaux, John Charles Olmsted, and John R. Brinley at the northern end of Bronx Park along East Fordham Road. Among the many conservatories built in the city at this time was the one in Central Park (1899). The Horticultural Society of New York (1902) sponsored the first New York Flower Show, and in 1910 the Brooklyn Botanic Garden, designed by Olmsted Brothers and Harold apRhys Caparn, opened next to the Brooklyn Museum along Washington and Flatbush avenues.

During the Depression flowerbeds disappeared from the parks, and the park department after 1934 called for the destruction of all but three greenhouses. The great gardens on the outskirts of the city were also lost as suburban neighborhoods developed. A modest rebirth occurred after World War II, and in 1965 Wave Hill, an estate in Riverdale with gardens and a greenhouse, became a city park; about the same time the Queens Botanical Garden moved to a site adjoining Flushing Meadow Park. The city acquired Sailors' Snug Harbor on Staten Island and its gardens and greenhouses in 1972, and after a lapse the New York Flower Show was revived in 1985. The most visible addition to plant life in the city was made by the arrival of impatiens, an Indonesian species used in flower borders throughout the city.

See also Botanical Gardens.

Henry Hope Reed

Hosack, David (*b* New York City, 31 Aug 1769; *d* New York City, 22 Dec 1835). Physician. After attending Columbia he graduated from Princeton in 1789, studied medicine in the colonies and abroad, and in 1795 became a professor of botany and medicine at Columbia. In 1804 he was the attending physician at the duel between Aaron Burr and Alexander Hamilton. He resigned from Columbia in 1811 to take a position at the College of Physicians and Surgeons; he later held annual lectures and was influential in forming Bellevue Hospital. Hosack launched the *American Medical and Philosophical Register,* published a number of books, and helped to organize the New-York Historical Society.

Christine Chapman Robbins, *David Hosack, Citizen of New York* (Philadelphia: American Philosophical Society, 1964)

See also Public health.

James E. Mooney

hospitals. In the eighteenth and the early nineteenth centuries New York City had only a few hospitals. The almshouse infirmary opened in 1736, followed by New York Hospital in 1771. New York Hospital was generously supported by the Dutch gentry, and many of its trustees were descendants of the earliest Dutch settlers. Other medical facilities in the city included the Lying-In Hospital, which was organized after the yellow fever epidemic of 1798. Bellevue Hospital grew out of the almshouse infirmary: a separate institution from 1819, it was among the first public institutions to respond effectively to the medical needs of the rapidly increasing dependent and poor. Kings County Hospital, which like Bellevue had begun as an almshouse infirmary, opened in Flatbush in

New York Hospital, 1869

1831, and Brooklyn City Hospital was incorporated in 1845 under the auspices of the Brooklyn Association for Improving the Condition of the Poor. By the beginning of the Civil War there were 12 more hospitals, including St. Vincent's Hospital (1849), opened by the Sisters of Charity; the Jews' Hospital (1855, later renamed Mount Sinai Hospital); and St. John's Hospital (1861), the first hospital in Queens. Other charity hospitals with ethnic and religious affiliations included the French Hospital, Methodist Episcopal Hospital, Norwegian Lutheran Deaconesses' Home and Hospital (later the Lutheran Medical Center), Beth Israel Hospital (later the Beth Israel Medical Center), Swedish Hospital, and the German Hospital (later Lenox Hill Hospital). Although they drew patients from all economic levels, these institutions served mostly the poor: members of the upper and middle classes were generally cared for in their homes.

Hospitals of the period offered warmth, shelter, regular meals, and minimal nursing, often provided in spartan surroundings. Because antisepsis was not widely practiced until late in the nineteenth century, hospital care and particularly surgery carried a higher risk of infection than home care did. Several children's hospitals were formed during these years, as was the Home for the Relief of Aged Indigent Black Persons, which later became Lincoln Hospital. Homoeopathic institutions expanded, and maternity hospitals were established to provide for unwed mothers. In less settled areas like Blackwell's Island and Staten Island a number of special hospitals sponsored by local business leaders and members of the clergy were built for those suffering from tuberculosis and other contagious diseases, and from mental disorders.

Many hospitals of the late nineteenth century operated on minimal budgets, often in private brownstones or small buildings, and treated "respectable" working-class patients who were wary of the stigma attached to the large charity hospitals. These neighborhood hospitals faced difficulty as increasingly rigorous medical standards raised the cost of providing care and as patients began using the expanding public transit system to move to outlying communities. Facilities with fewer than 50 beds lasted for an average of only five years, and by 1910 most of the smallest neighborhood hospitals closed. The larger ones expanded and new ones opened, steadily increasing the number of hospital beds in the city. By 1908 the State Charities Aid Association reported that there were 63 general hospitals in New York City, of which 26 were in Manhattan and 23 in Brooklyn.

The municipal hospital system in New York City underwent many changes in organization during the late nineteenth century. In 1875 hospitals for contagious diseases were transferred to the new Department of Health isolation facilities on Blackwell's (now Roosevelt) Island, and by the turn of the century mental hospitals and prisons also were placed under separate jurisdiction. Bellevue and its dependent facilities Gouverneur Hospital, Harlem Hospital, and Fordham Hospital were removed from the Department of Charities in 1902 and became governed by a separate board of trustees. The old charities department (renamed the Department of Public Welfare) retained control of the municipal facilities in Brooklyn, and the Department of Health directed those in Queens and the institutions for contagious diseases.

Private, nonprofit hospitals that survived into the twentieth century adopted antiseptic procedures that sharply reduced mortality rates after surgery. Large hospitals like Bellevue, Mount Sinai, New York, Lenox Hill, St. Luke's Hospital, and Presbyterian Hospital expanded their X-ray departments and clinical laboratories. Physicians increasingly encouraged their well-to-do patients to use the modern facilities, which became the focus of the new "scientific medicine"; between 1890 and 1905 the use of all hospital services increased by 85 percent. Although most new medical knowledge pertained to the classification of illness rather than its treatment, and although maternal death rates in the city's hospitals remained high into the 1930s, physicians and patients alike placed a great deal of trust in medical science, of which the modern hospital became a powerful symbol.

Private hospitals in New York City received much of their funding from the state until 1894, when state assistance to hospitals was banned. The city then began making fixed per capita grants to the hospitals in recognition of their services to the poor. In 1908 Comptroller Bird S. Coler instituted a new system under which patients had to be certified as destitute before the hospital was reimbursed by the city for their care. Although total city outlays increased, they lagged far behind rising costs, and by 1921 reimbursement by the city represented only 10 percent of the revenue of private nonprofit hospitals, with donations accounting for about 20 percent and patients' fees 69 percent (compared with 38 percent in 1911). One-third of patients who paid a fee were in private rooms; the rest were in "pay wards," where they were excused from the housekeeping chores that were performed by convalescent patients who did not pay. Hospitals also developed graduated rate structures, sought increased municipal support for the charity care they provided, and advertised their private accommodations.

Free-standing dispensaries that had provided care during the nineteenth century fell victim to the same increasing specialization and technology that had brought an end to small neighborhood hospitals and were gradually replaced by outpatient departments. By 1926 the outpatient department at Bellevue, the city's largest, served an average of 900 patients a day. Physicians found it increasingly difficult to sustain their practices independently of a hospital; as the hospital became more important to doctors, they in turn became more important to the hospital. At St. Luke's–Roosevelt Hospital, New York Hospital, and many others, trustees for the first time permitted doctors to charge private patients for hospital visits and accepted more physicians as visiting staff: the proportion of practitioners with admitting privileges at hospitals rose from one-third in 1908 to one-half in 1926.

The Department of Hospitals was formed in 1929 to administer all 20 municipal hospitals and health institutions and to inspect and license private health-care facilities. By 1930 there were about 125 hospitals in New York City, with a total of about 30,000 beds. Only a few hospitals had a daily census of more than 250 patients: Bellevue, Lincoln, St. Luke's, Mount Sinai, New York Hospital, New York Long Island College Hospital, and New York Post-Graduate Hospital (later University Hospital). Presbyterian Hospital and New York Hospital joined with Columbia and Cornell medical schools to establish the city's first modern medical centers.

The nature of hospital care in New York City as elsewhere changed dramatically when nursing became professionalized. Before the late nineteenth century patients were tended by poorly paid and untrained workers or by fellow convalescent patients who were required to assist with ward tasks in exchange for care. An exposé in the early 1870s at Bellevue Hospital led the social reformer Louisa Schuyler to mobilize support for the Bellevue Training School for Nurses. Opened in 1873, the school was the first of hundreds in the United States designed according to the teachings of Florence Nightingale. Nearly every sizable hospital in New York City soon opened a "Nightingale school," and for more than half a century hospital wards were staffed primarily by nursing students, who worked long hours for little pay while most graduate nurses took private-duty assignments. Graduate nurses became numerous in hospitals only during the Depression, when the number of private-duty assignments dwindled.

During the 1930s entire wings of private rooms stood empty and the demand for charity care soared. Of the city's more than 30,000 hospital beds, half were in private institutions that relied extensively on fees from patients. A few hospitals closed, but most simply reduced their number of beds and looked to the city for assistance. The city reimbursed private hospitals more than $5 million for care to the indigent in 1933 and $6.4 million by 1940. Municipal hospitals also were hurt by the financial crisis of the 1930s, but their physical plants were improved with the help of funds from the Works Progress Administration and the Public Works Administration.

Professionalism in the Department of Hospitals increased during the tenure of S. S. Goldwater, formerly the nationally respected administrator of Mount Sinai Hospital, and the department's budget rose steadily from $17 million in 1934 to $36 million in 1945. Many more positions in the department came under civil service protection, new laboratory facilities were constructed, physicians in municipal outpatient departments earned salaries for the first time, maternity services and equipment were modernized, and a blood bank was established.

Public and private hospitals experienced soaring admissions during the decade following World War II: in 1948 the city reported an average occupancy rate of 102 percent in

Brooklyn City Hospital, ca *1850*

municipal facilities. The power and prestige of modern medicine were strongly reinforced by the new "miracle" sulfa drugs, penicillin, and the tetracyclines, which eliminated many of the most feared diseases, permitted more difficult surgery, and sharply cut maternal mortality rates. As health benefits became a recognized issue for collective bargaining, Blue Cross and other hospital insurance systems that had begun in the 1930s expanded rapidly. In 1945 Mayor Fiorello H. La Guardia introduced the Health Insurance Plan of Greater New York (HIP), which was made available to city residents and workers earning less than $5000 a year; employers paid half the cost of coverage. By 1947 more than 110,000 members were enrolled in the plan, and New York City was considered a leader in the national effort to make hospital care more widely available to those who had long been excluded because of the high cost of private care and the stigma of wards.

During the postwar years private hospitals reopened wings closed during the Depression; they renovated old buildings and built new ones. The federal government expanded its veterans' hospitals in the city, and the municipal hospital system launched an ambitious renovation campaign. By 1968 the city had about 65,000 beds in 145 hospitals, of which 80 were nonprofit, 18 were municipal, and 47 were federal or proprietary. About one-quarter of the city's hospitals had more than 500 beds (compared with 7 percent of the hospitals in 1924). Subsidized care was made available for the poor and elderly in 1965 with the passage of Medicare and Medicaid. Within a year these programs accounted for more than half the income received by hospitals in New York City and 86 percent of the income received by municipal hospitals. Medicare in particular enabled many people to afford private hospitals, but a large number of Medicaid patients as well as the uninsured remained in the public system. As a result the municipal hospitals continued to face shortages and understaffing even though they experienced a decline in their number of patients. Calls for a reorganization of the Department of Hospitals led to its replacement in 1970 by a new agency, the New York Health and Hospitals Corporation.

In the late 1950s and early 1960s powerful unions were organized by nonprofessional hospital workers, who for the most part were poorly paid women and members of racial minority groups. Local 1199 gained its first formal recognition at Montefiore Hospital in 1958 and in the following year led a bitter and ultimately successful strike against seven private hospitals. Meanwhile the Association of Federal, State, County and Municipal Employees gained ground in municipal hospitals. By 1970 collective bargaining was well established in the municipal hospital system and in most private hospitals. Several studies during these years demonstrated wide racial disparities in local hospitals: in 1964 the Department of Health found that whites accounted for 78 percent of the patients in private, nonprofit hospitals but only 26 percent of those in municipal hospitals, and that the proportion of patients with health insurance ranged from 80 percent among whites to 40 percent among blacks and 25 percent among Puerto Ricans. These inequities were accompanied by a growing animosity toward hospitals in New York City: in low-income neighborhoods such as Bedford–Stuyvesant and the South Bronx, local hospitals were condemned and even occupied by residents.

In the decades after 1965 a growing number of lawyers, insurers, social workers, bioethicists, and particularly patients claimed a role in health-care decisions that until then had been left to physicians. At the same time the escalating cost of medical care led to governmental efforts to control costs, many focused on reimbursement rates for hospitals. State legislation in the late 1970s and the formation in 1983 of the federal Diagnosis-Related Group (DRG) system constrained hospitals by making external funding conditional on an increasing number of requirements; as the economy worsened, many hospitals reduced the number of beds for the first time since the Depression and consolidated to reduce administrative costs. By 1983 the number of general hospitals had fallen to 70 and the number of beds to 35,000. The financial crises of the early 1990s exacted a particularly heavy toll on the municipal hospital system of New York City. Repeated rounds of layoffs, cutbacks, and hospital closings led to demonstrations and strikes by hospital staff. An unusually high number of deaths in municipal emergency rooms in 1991 drew intense public scrutiny and caused the director of the Health and Hospitals Corporation to resign and the mayor to request a special investigation of the municipal system by the New York Academy of Medicine.

The growing cost of hospital stays during the late twentieth and early twenty-first centuries led to a prolonged effort by government regulators and managed-care companies to control the growth of hospitals, to limit the number of beds in the city, and to lower reimbursement rates and the average hospital stay. It was assumed that limiting the availability of inpatient services and lowering public payments would force the institutions to be more efficient, thereby lowering overall costs. During this period some of the smaller hospitals closed, while major medical schools and larger institutions merged. In the mid-1990s Mount Sinai and New York University merged two of the city's most important medical centers in an ill-fated effort to broaden their range of services and to improve through combined efficiency. That same year Presbyterian Hospital and New York Hospital combined as the New York–Presbyterian Hospital. Similarly, Long Island Jewish and Beth Israel attempted to merge. In parallel moves, the Catholic hospital system began a series of mergers and closures in an effort to compete for better-insured patients, who often sought out care in the larger hospitals that had direct relationships with the prestigious medical schools of the city. Some of these mergers were successful, but others fell apart as goals and interests of the medical staffs, trustees, and administrations of the new facilities conflicted.

As the number of hospital beds in the city declined, so did the number of patients. Between the late 1980s and the late 1990s the number of inpatients declined from about 30,000 to 20,000 patients a day. This occurred despite the growing population of elderly in the city. As baby boomers reached retirement age some worried that pressure would increase for inpatient services and for the vast array of procedures now available. Hip and knee replacements, angioplasty and various heart-related procedures, new cancer treatments, and a general growing demand for services for the elderly forebodes a crisis in the early twenty-first century. Despite a century-long opposition to a national health insurance system, many hospital administrators expect that there will be a greatly increased role for federal financing and governance of the city's and the nation's institutions.

David Rosner, *A Once Charitable Enterprise: Hospitals and Health Care in Brooklyn and New York, 1885–1915* (Cambridge: Cambridge University Press, 1982); Leon Fink and Brian Greenberg, *Upheaval in the Quiet Zone: A History of Hospital Workers' Union, Local 1199* (Urbana: University of Illinois Press, 1989); Sandra Opdycke, *No One Was Turned Away: The Role of Public Hospitals in New York City since 1900* (New York: Oxford University Press, 1999)

Sandra Opdycke, David Rosner

New York City's Largest Hospitals by 2007 Operating Expenses

Name	Operating Expenses (millions)	No. of Employees	No. of Certified Beds	Address
New York–Presbyterian Hospital	$2,859.6	17,723	2,242	525 E. 68th St., Manhattan
Montefiore Medical Center	$2,193.0	11,353	1,122	111 E. 210th St., Bronx
Memorial Sloan–Kettering Cancer Center	$1,511.5	6,220	514	1275 York Ave., Manhattan
Mount Sinai Hospital	$1,253.3	8,155	1,406	1 Gustave L. Levy Pl., Manhattan
Beth Israel Medical Center	$1,210.5	6,535	1,106	First Avenue at 16th St., Manhattan
New York University Medical Center	$1,076.1	6,574	1,033	550 First Ave., Manhattan
St. Luke's–Roosevelt Hospital	$1,060.7	5,565	1,046	1000 10th Ave., Manhattan
Maimonides Medical Center	$831.0	5,162	705	4802 10th Ave., Brooklyn
St. Vincent Catholic Medical Center of New York*	$660.8	4,897	662	170 W. 12th St., Manhattan
Bellevue Hospital	$629.1	4,704	912	462 First Ave., Manhattan
Staten Island University Hospital	$613.0	4,729	785	475 Seaview Ave., Staten Island
Kings County Hospital Center	$608.6	4,866	700	451 Clarkson Ave., Brooklyn

*In 2010 St. Vincent's faced possible closure because of financial difficulties.
Source: *Crain's New York Business*, 24 March 2008
Compiled by Frank Nestor

Hospital Saturday and Sunday Association. Original name of the UNITED HOSPITAL FUND.

Hostos Community College. See EUGENIO MARÍA DE HOSTOS COMMUNITY COLLEGE.

Hotel des Artistes. Elegant apartment building at 1 West 67th Street in Manhattan, between Central Park West and Columbus Avenue. Designed by George Mort Pollard, it opened in 1918. The apartments were intentionally designed without kitchens; instead, residents ordered meals by telephone from the Café des Artistes on the ground floor, and these were sent up by dumbwaiter. The idea was for residents to be able to dine in style without the bother of having a cook in residence. The system did not last, but after the café opened to the public, it flourished and became known as one of the most romantic and fashionable restaurants in Manhattan. The café closed in 2009. Among the many famous residents of the hotel have been Rudolph Valentino, Isadora Duncan, Noël Coward, Zasu Pitts, Fanny Hurst, William Powell, and Norman Rockwell.

Kenneth T. Jackson

Hotel Employees and Restaurant Employees International Union. Labor union formed in 1891 and originally affiliated with the American Federation of Labor (AFL). Its numerous locals in New York City lost strength during Prohibition when thousands of skilled restaurant positions were eliminated and craft-oriented locals of chefs and waiters proved ineffective in organizing unskilled workers at cafeterias and lunch counters. In 1934 independent industrial unions conducted a two-month strike against the city's hotels; this was unsuccessful but inspired a movement to merge the independent locals with those of the AFL. After an investigation led by Thomas E. Dewey in 1936, three local officers of the AFL were convicted of complicity in a labor racket organized by Dutch Schultz, allowing the former leaders of the independents to be elected to lead the restructured locals.

In the mid-1990s the union had two principal locals in New York City, Local 6 and Local 100. Local 6 was chartered in 1938 to represent hotel housekeeping, laundry, and food and beverage workers. To accommodate such employees as electricians who belonged to different unions, the New York Hotel Trades Council was formed to coordinate collective bargaining. Most of the city's hotels were unionized by 1946. Between 1947 and 1950 the international union expelled officials from three locals for their leftist politics. A decline in restaurant employment from 1972 led to the consolidation of 10 specialized restaurant locals into Local 100. In the mid-1990s Local 6 represented 19,000 employees in 149 hotels and motels and 50 private clubs. In 2004 the Hotel Employees and Restaurant Employees International Union merged with the Union of Needletrades, Industrial and Textile Employees to form UNITE HERE.

Matthew Josephson, *Union House, Union Bar: The History of the Hotel and Restaurant Employees and Bartenders International Union, AFL-CIO* (New York: Random House, 1956); Morris A. Horowitz, *The New York Hotel Industry* (Cambridge, Mass.: Harvard University Press, 1960)

Gilbert Tauber

Hotel Knickerbocker. Hotel opened by John Jacob Astor in 1906 on the southeast corner of Broadway and 42nd Street. It was designed in the French Renaissance style by the architects Martin and Davis, Bruce Price, and Trowbridge and Livingston. It became known for its many publicly displayed works of art: in the main barroom hung Maxfield Parrish's mural *Old King Cole*, later moved to the St. Regis Hotel. The building was converted to office space in 1920, was known as the Newsweek Building from 1940 to 1959, and was renovated to be a textile showroom building in 1980. The building was sold in 1998 to SL Green and renovated for mixed use. In 2005 SL Green sold the building to Sitt Asset Management, which sold it quickly at a large profit to Istithmar World. Originally Istithmar planned to build on an empty plot next to the old hotel and combine the two buildings into a five-star hotel, but it abandoned the idea. Although street-level stores were still doing well in 2010, 235,000 square feet (21,832 square meters) of the existing building were listed as available for sale at that time.

May N. Stone, Meghan Lalonde

Hotel Martinique. Hotel at 32nd Street and Broadway in Manhattan, designed in a French Renaissance style with a mansard roof by Henry J. Hardenbergh and built in 1897. It was enlarged in 1910–11 and for many years was known as a glamorous meeting place with ornate dining rooms and nightly entertainment. The hotel gradually fell into disrepair and by 1980 was being used as temporary housing for the homeless. In 1989 the Martinique was acquired by Harold Thurman, a Long Island real estate developer, who turned it into a Holiday Inn in 1996.

Chad Ludington

Hotel Pennsylvania. See New York's Hotel Pennsylvania.

hotels. In the colonial period inns (also called taverns) were typically remodeled private houses. The first building in the United States to be erected specifically for use as a hotel was probably the City Hotel (begun in 1794) on the west side of lower Broadway between Thames and Cedar streets. Until the early 1840s it was the city's principal site for prestigious social functions and concerts; the hotel was demolished in 1849. Luxury hotels began to appear in New York City by the mid-nineteenth century: John Jacob Astor erected the Astor House on Broadway between Barclay and Vesey streets in 1834–36. Farther uptown at Madison Square, the Fifth Avenue Hotel (1859, six stories) had a marble facade and provided a setting for important social events. Many of the finer establishments featured the European plan (without meals included in the cost of the room) rather than the more common American plan. Most of the hotels built in the 1870s and 1880s were undistinguished, but during the prosperous 1890s larger and more luxurious hotels reached heights of as much as 17 stories, employed steel construction, and had telephones, electric lighting, and improved elevators. Residences at each end of the fashionable shopping district on Fifth Avenue were replaced with stylish hotels: at the southeast corner of Central Park were the original Plaza Hotel (1890),

Hotel Bertholdi

the Hotel Savoy (1892), and the New Netherland Hotel (1893); and between 33rd and 34th streets stood the WALDORF–ASTORIA (1893–97), which consisted of two conjoined hotels with about 1300 guest rooms and 40 public rooms. Two innovative hotels of a very different character were designed by Ernest Flagg to provide inexpensive accommodations to single working men: Mills House no. 1 (1896–97) at 160 Bleecker Street and Mills House no. 2 (1896–98) at Rivington and Chrystie streets.

After the turn of the twentieth century the wealthy found it fashionable to live in fine hotels for either the winter or the entire year. The new Plaza Hotel (1907; Hardenbergh) was built on the site of the identically named former hotel in Manhattan. Apartment hotels, which had first appeared in the late nineteenth century, were popular during this period. Most of them catered to the middle class and were situated in the western part of midtown or on the Upper West Side, now more easily accessible because of the subway. Several popularly priced tourist hotels opened in Times Square. In the second decade of the twentieth century huge facilities were erected near the city's new railroad complexes to accommodate middle-class travelers. These hotels were grandly decorated, affordable, convenient, and functional and provided business services and such modern amenities as a bathroom with every bedroom. The first was the Hotel McAlpin (1912, 1500 rooms) near Pennsylvania Station. The architectural firm of Warren and Wetmore designed the Ritz–Carlton Hotel (1910), the Vanderbilt Hotel (1912), the BILTMORE HOTEL (1913), and the Hotel Commodore (1919, 2000 rooms), next to Grand Central Terminal; over the years the firm shifted its emphasis from Edwardian elegance to modern convenience. In 1919 NEW YORK'S HOTEL PENNSYLVANIA (McKim, Mead and White) opened near Pennsylvania Station as the largest hotel in the world, with 2200 rooms.

Grand Union Hotel

The Standard, 2009

After World War I some commercial hotels were added near the railroad stations, but most were constructed around Times Square. Among several moderately priced hotels built on Lexington Avenue was the Shelton Hotel (1924, Arthur Loomis Harmon), intended as a clubhouse for bachelors; the building represented a skillful application to skyscraper design of the city's zoning laws of 1916. The ST. GEORGE HOTEL in Brooklyn, expanded in 1930, had 2632 rooms and was the largest hotel in the five boroughs, while the second Waldorf–Astoria on Park Avenue (1931, Schultze and Weaver) became one of the most luxurious hotels in the world. The postwar building boom had produced an excess of hotel accommodations, and 30 years passed before construction resumed in anticipation of the World's Fair of 1964–65. The first motor inns were opened on the West Side of Manhattan, and some new hotels were erected in midtown, including the first giant convention hotels: the Americana Hotel (1962) on Seventh Avenue between 52nd and 53rd streets and the NEW YORK HILTON (1963) on Sixth Avenue between 53rd and 54th streets. Older establishments found themselves threatened by declining occupancy rates, and as high-speed travel shortened the length of business trips and lessened the need for hotel accommodations, many hotels closed or were taken over by large chains.

During the 1980s and 1990s thousands of expensive hotel rooms were added in the city. Most of the new facilities were in midtown (the Marriott Marquis Hotel in Times Square, 1985), though some were farther downtown (the New York Vista Hotel, 1981, and the Hotel Millennium, 1991, near the site of the World Trade Center). To meet requirements for the preservation of historic structures, the Helmsley Palace (1980, later renamed the NEW YORK PALACE) on Madison Avenue incorporated sections of the Villard Houses at its base, and the Embassy Suites Hotel (1990) and the Hotel Macklowe (1990) near Times Square incorporated landmark theaters. Sometimes older structures were redesigned to lower construction costs: examples include the Grand Hyatt (1980), which used the steel structure of the Hotel Commodore, and the much smaller Morgans Hotel (1984) and Plaza Athenee (1984) on the East Side.

The hotel market declined after the terrorist attacks of 11 September 2001 but rebounded in subsequent years as foreign investors entered the market, buying into the Plaza, the New York Palace, the Essex House (renamed the Jumeirah Essex House), and the Hotel Pierre (renamed the Taj Pierre). Some hotels, like the Plaza and the Stanhope, converted a portion of their rooms to condominiums, recalling turn-of-the-century apartment hotels. In the early twenty-first century, despite a national economic downturn, New York City's hotels remained relatively buoyant because of international tourists. The city had more than 73,000 hotel rooms with 85 percent occupancy and an average daily room rate of $294 in the first half of 2008, compared with the national average of 61 percent occupancy and a daily room rate of $107.

May N. Stone

Hotel Theresa. Hotel 13 stories tall at Seventh Avenue and 125th Street in Harlem, designed with white brick and terra-cotta facing by George Blum and Edward Blum. Initially the tallest building in Harlem, it opened in 1913 on the busiest thoroughfare in the neighborhood during a period of rapid growth, and at first it did not admit blacks. The hotel was popular for its double-height penthouse dining room, with views of the Palisades and Long Island Sound. It was bought in 1937 by Love B. Woods, a black businessman who ended its policy of racial discrimination; in the same year Joe Louis held a celebration there after winning the world heavyweight boxing title. In the following years the hotel became known as the "Waldorf of Harlem"; it thrived as the fashionable gathering place of prominent figures and also housed such important cultural institutions as the Organization of Afro-American Unity (led by Malcolm X) and the March Community Bookstore (run by A. Philip Randolph). The hotel attracted international attention in 1960 when President Fidel Castro of Cuba moved his entourage there from downtown Manhattan during a visit to the United Nations; while at the hotel he met with Nikita S. Khrushchev, premier of the Soviet Union, and Gamal Abdel Nasser, president of Egypt. In 1966, after years of deterioration, the Hotel Theresa was bought by an investment group and converted into a modern office building, the Theresa Towers, which continues to house many community organizations. It was designated as an official landmark in 1993.

Amanda Aaron

Harry Houdini in a packing box, 1914. From Houdini: His Life Story *(1928)*

Houdini, Harry [Weiss, Ehrich] (*b* Budapest, 6 April 1874; *d* Detroit, 31 Oct 1926). Magician. Born to Hungarian immigrants, he performed as a trapeze artist before learning the art of illusion. He moved to New York City with his father in 1886 and briefly worked as a necktie cutter, and at 16 he changed his name in honor of the French magician Jean-Eugène Robert-Houdin. In 1894 he married Wilhelmina Rahner, who became his assistant. He achieved moderate success during the 1890s by entertaining audiences in beer halls, theaters, and dime museums. In 1900 he embarked on a four-year tour of Europe during which he amazed audiences by extricating himself from a variety of shackles, ropes, handcuffs, prison cells, and locked containers. He was an international star by the time he returned to New York City, where he began performing elaborate stunts. On one occasion he freed himself after being shackled in chains, locked in a box, and submerged in the East River; on another he escaped from a straitjacket while suspended, head down, high above Broadway. From 1916 to 1923 he exhibited his skills in several motion pictures, including *The Master of Mystery* and *The Grim Game.* He lived for several years at 305 East 69th Street, and from 1904 until the end of his career in a brownstone at 278 West 113th Street, which he fitted with an oversized bathtub so that he could practice his underwater tricks. Although Houdini loved illusion, he despised mediums and mind readers. In 1908 he wrote *The Unmasking of Robert-Houdin,* which exposed his former idol as a faker. His other published writings are *Handcuff Secrets* (1907) and *A Magician among the Spirits* (1924). He is buried in Machpelah Cemetery in Queens.

Harold Kellock, *Houdini: His Life Story* (New York: Harcourt, Brace, 1928); Ruth Brandon, *The Life and Many Deaths of Harry Houdini* (London: Secker and Warburg, 1993)

Robert Sanger Steel

House, Edward (Mandell) (*b* Houston, Tex., 26 July 1858; *d* New York City, 28 March 1938). Businessman and presidential adviser. After meeting Woodrow Wilson, then governor of New Jersey, at the Hotel Gotham in New York City in 1910, House became Wilson's close friend and most trusted adviser. For the next few years House lived in New York City, where he solicited the support of businesspeople during Wilson's presidential campaign in 1912 and his first term as president. Known as Wilson's "silent partner," he played a vital role in securing the support of Wall Street for Wilson's financial legislation, particularly the Federal Reserve Act. He was also an adviser to Mayor William J. Gaynor. House died in his apartment on East 68th Street. He was often known as Colonel House (the title was honorary).

James Bradley

Houseman, John [Haussmann, Jacques] (*b* Bucharest, 22 Sept 1902; *d* Malibu, Calif., 31 Oct 1988). Actor and director. He directed *Four Saints in Three Acts* in 1934 and collaborated with Orson Welles on productions for the Federal Theatre of the Works Progress Administration. In 1937 the two founded the Mercury Theater in New York City, and the following year broadcast a radio dramatization of H. G. Wells's "The War of the Worlds," which many listeners mistook for a report of a Martian invasion. He returned to Broadway several times during his career and at the age of 66 helped to establish the school of drama at Juilliard. In 1972 he formed the Acting Company, of which he served as artistic director. The John Houseman Theater opened on West 42nd Street in 1986. Houseman wrote *Run Through: A Memoir* (1972), *Front and Center* (1979), and *Final Dress* (1982).

JillEllyn Riley

house numbering and street naming. The need to identify buildings with numbers did not occur in New York City until the American Revolution, when British occupying forces numbered houses in order to keep an eye on residents. Even then, however, the same number might be found on two or more buildings on the same street, the numbers sometimes reversed direction, a few streets had similar names, and many were not identified with street signs. The only reliable indicator of location in the city was a system of distance markers laid out in the 1760s, radiating from the corner of Nassau and Wall streets. In 1793 the New York Common Council's Street Committee imposed universal house numbering and the use of street signs. Breaking with the traditional British and French system of running numbers down one side of the street and back on the other, the Street Committee adopted a policy, also used in Philadelphia, of alternating odd and even numbers on the uptown and downtown sides of the street. Determining which sides of the twisting streets were, in fact, uptown and downtown was a challenge, as was getting owners to post tin signboards once city workers marked the numbers with chalk. There were many absent, mistaken, and duplicated house numbers.

Identifying streets and houses was potentially simplified in 1811 when the Commissioners of Streets and Roads imposed the rectilinear grid on Manhattan. The plan reveals a concern for practicality, as do the commissioners' decision to give the streets and avenues logical, progressive names: the streets from First to 155th and the avenues from First to 12th, with the Lower East Side avenues running from A to D (the exception was Broadway). This simple, orderly, and predictable arrangement was soon compromised by the addition of two named avenues between Third and Fifth Avenues: Lexington (honoring the Revolutionary War Battle of Lexington) and Madison (for former President James Madison). Renaming became more aggressive between 1880 and 1900 when all the avenues on the Upper West Side and one on the East Side were given appealing or historic names, such as Riverside Drive and Park and Amsterdam avenues, to encourage real estate development. Similar efforts to have street numbers replaced with memorable names of American heroes, states, or Indian tribes were unsuccessful.

In 1825 the *New-York Evening Post* asked, "Is it not a reproach to the public authorities of New York that neither are the great majority of houses designated by numbers, not one in ten of the streets pointed out by name to the passing stranger?" This complaint was still being voiced 30 years later by newspapers, citizens, and particularly publishers of city directories, whose livelihood depended on street numbers and who went so far as to assign numbers of their own. Compounding the confusion, the city assigned numbers not to all lots but only to existing houses, which meant that every time a new house went up in a formerly vacant lot, a new number had to be issued for all the buildings on the street. "He who goes to bed at No. 50 in his street, may wake up the next morning at No. 100," the *Evening Post* commented in 1839. To encourage a semblance of order, the Common Council mandated that numbers be changed only near or on May 1, the city's traditional "moving day" when leases expired.

At first, house numbers on the cross streets ran continuously across the width of the island, from river to river. In 1838 the city map was divided into half along Fifth Avenue, already known as "the Middle Road" because it was the center of the three oldest straight avenues (Fourth, Fifth, and Sixth); Fifth Avenue became the starting point for house numbers running both east and west on the cross streets. In 1861 the city began distributing house numbers evenly on these streets using what was known as the Philadelphia (where it originated) system. One hundred house numbers were assigned to most cross-town blocks, odd numbers on the north side and even numbers on the south. Between Fifth and Sixth Avenues, for example, the numbers were (and remain) between 1 and 100 West; between Seventh and Eighth they were between 201 and 300 West. The problem of Central Park on the West Side was solved in 1886 when house numbers began at 1 at Central Park West, instead of 301. The system applied on the East Side except at the two, narrow non–Commissioners' Plan avenues, Madison and Lexington, where the interval was 50 numbers.

Into the twentieth century, however, house numbering continued to be a point of contestation and neglect. In 1921, for instance, the U.S. postmaster general came to New York City from Washington, D.C., to lecture city officials on their obligation to help the mail get delivered expeditiously. (A *Times* headline ran, "Postmaster General says That If Farmers Can Do It So Can Big Towns.") It was a half century before serious attempt was made to rationalize house numbers on the avenues, where no two numbers appeared near the same cross street. New York City Postmaster Albert Goldman proposed numbering Manhattan's avenues using the standard-interval Philadelphia system during the 1930s. The number "45-1 Fifth Avenue" would go on the first building on the avenue above 45th Street, and so on. The advantages seemed obvious to Goldman. The city's daily seven million pieces of mail would be delivered without the time-consuming requirement of correcting addresses (a chore costing an estimated $250,000 annually), and New Yorkers and tourists would no longer be delayed finding their destinations. The proposal gained strong support from the Manhattan borough president and from other governmental and citizens groups—with the exception of the Fifth Avenue Association, a powerful business organization, whose merchant members complained that the proposed system would impose an undue burden by requiring them to purchase new stationery. With that, the new idea died. However, at least a standard for locating house numbers was agreed on, although that standard was contradictory. Above Eighth Street, from Fifth Avenue across the avenues to the East River, the east sides would have odd numbers and the west sides even numbers, while from Sixth Avenue to the Hudson, the east sides would have even numbers and the west sides odd numbers. This odd-even, East Side–West Side pattern was reversed south of Washington Square, where the benchmark was West Broadway.

Outside Manhattan, the other boroughs had their own street and house numbering traditions. The most radical change was made in the 1920s by Queens when it unified its 60 villages and 2500 roads with a version of the Philadelphia system. Addresses included not only the house number but also the nearest avenue and street, whose names had been changed to numbers. The address "37-69 103rd Street" indicates that on 103rd Street, house number 69 is between 37th and 38th avenues. Some Queens communities, however, declined to rename their streets, and there was plenty of confusion because roads, drives, places, and lanes interposed between the west-east running avenues and the north-south running streets. The solution was to give them the same numbers; therefore, Queens has a 71st Avenue, 71st Crescent, 71st Drive, 71st Place, 71st Road, and 71st Street.

One historic and current pattern in street and house identification is the vanity address—the special name or number sought by people who feel entitled to special status. In the 1820s some residents preferred the use of "place" or "square" to merely "street." In 1870 the avenue now called West Broadway, which runs south from Washington Square Park, was known as South Fifth Avenue. Boss William M. Tweed owned land there and decided the addresses would be more prestigious if they started at number 1 at the park and increased as they advanced south. After Tweed's fall, the avenue was renamed and the numbers were reversed to the usual pattern. In the twentieth century, vanity addresses were sought by groups wishing to highlight themselves or one of their leaders. The city responded by providing a street honorific, called a "co-naming," that was posted below the actual street number. Juan Pablo Duarte Boulevard (on St. Nicholas Avenue between 162nd and 193rd Streets) honors a founder of the Dominican Republic, and Seminary Row (West 122nd Street between Amsterdam and Claremont Avenues) passes by Jewish and Union Theological Seminaries. Many places or streets are named for individuals. Manhattan's York Avenue is named for Sgt. Alvin York, a World War I hero, and there are Herman Melville Place (104 East 26th Street) and Duke Ellington Boulevard (106th Street west of Broadway). Such honorifics can be controversial, however, as groups and neighborhoods haggle over who deserves co-naming. In 2007 the City Council approved co-namings in boroughs outside Manhattan for 64 people, many of them victims of or first responders to the terrorist attacks of 11 September 2001.

In the 1960s and afterward, "plaza" and "square" were revived to produce unique and often out-of-sequence addresses, including 1 Chase Manhattan Plaza in the financial district and Penn Plaza near Pennsylvania Station. Such addresses were issued by the government to help keep companies from leaving the city. According to the Manhattan Borough President's Topographical Bureau, approximately 100 address changes were made for these and similar reasons every year during the 1980s. The ancient wish to signify real or desired prestige through a house number continued into the twenty-first century, when many companies enjoyed avenue addresses even though their entrances were on side streets.

Henry Hoffmann, "Changed House Numbers and Lost Street Names in New York of the Early Nineteenth Century and Later," *New-York Historical Society Quarterly Bulletin*, vol. 21, no. 3 (1937), 67–92; Sarah Kershaw, "Meet Me at 60th and 60th," *New York Times,* 15 Dec 2000; John Tauranac, *Manhattan Block by Block: A Street Atlas* (New York: Tauranac Maps, 2000, rev edn); Christopher Grey, "History Lessons by the Numbers," *New York Times,* 7 Nov 2008; Reuben S. Rose-Redwood, "From Number to Name: Symbolic Capital, Places of Memory and the Politics of Street Renaming in New York City," *Social and Cultural Geography* 9:4 (June 2008), 431–52

John Rousmaniere

House Sparrow. A bird about 6 inches (15 centimeters) long: the male is white and chestnut and has a large black throat patch and a gray head; the female is dull brown and has a pale stripe over the eye. The bird was introduced to the New York City metropolitan area in the early 1850s from Europe and soon became well established. By the 1890s its population had reached a peak: during the summer of 1892 Frank Chapman reported seeing about 4000 bathing in one small pool in Central Park. One of the most widely distributed land birds in the world, it lives in the city year round and has as many as three broods a year, laying from four to six eggs in each clutch between late March and mid-August in birdhouses, in holes in trees and buildings, and less often in bulky, domed stick nests in trees.

John Bull

housing. New York City's diverse housing—ranging from mansions for the wealthy to slums for the poor—and dense population made it the first vertical city in the world. Construction of new dwellings could not keep pace with the rapid population growth the city experienced from the mid-nineteenth century onward. Residential and commercial spaces in the city were rarely separate, and in the late twentieth century much commercial space began to be converted to residential use. New York City was the first American city to construct PUBLIC HOUSING and provide subsidies for middle-class housing.

The New Amsterdam row house of the late seventeenth century was a typical city dwelling. It consisted of narrow multistory dwellings squeezed into lots 25 feet (8 meters) wide. It had a raised basement where the kitchen was located, a parlor, and an upper story, sometimes with dormer windows, for sleeping. The roofs had the characteristic Dutch steep pitch, and the more costly were decorated with orange tiles and crow-stepped gambrels. At the front of the building was a stoop, from a Dutch word meaning step or platform, which included a staircase and landing outside the door to the parlor. The building was usually entered through a passage under the stoop; the stoop itself was used only on special occasions. Lower stories could be converted into a shop or restaurant, rooms rented out when extra income was needed, or the building converted into apartments. The Dutch farmhouse, the other common housing type of New Amsterdam, was a single-story open barn of heavy timber, with clapboard siding and a steep-pitched or sometimes gambrel-pitched loft, and a second-story door at the gabled end.

In the late seventeenth and eighteenth centuries, the British built symmetrical, redbrick residences of two and three stories. They were timber-framed and clad in masonry, with ornate sashes and linteled doorways. By the early nineteenth century New York City's prosperous classes lived in Georgian and Federal row houses; they were built of brick and wood and stood 18 to 20 feet (5.5 to 6 meters) wide and two stories tall, with pitched roofs and dormer attics where the servants usually lived. Poor and working-class residents of the city lived on narrow streets and back alleys, in jerry-built one- and two-story wooden structures with workshops on the ground floor and living quarters on the second floor or in the attic. Housing patterns were set by the 1811 Commissioners' Plan, which formed a grid that accommodated developers' preferences for lots of standard dimensions (25 feet [8 meters] wide and 100 feet [30 meters] deep).

Between 1820 and 1860 an influx of European immigrants to lower Manhattan pushed the city's wealthy residents north. Increasing population resulted in higher residential prices; high costs and lack of inexpensive housing resulted in overcrowding in poor areas. South of Canal Street in the 1830s mansions, churches, and breweries were converted to low-rent, multiple residences called rookeries, where families lived in cramped, dark, airless apartments. Rookeries provided the model for TENEMENTS, cheaply constructed buildings that contained small, uncomfortable apartments. In the 1830s and 1840s tenements dominated the area between Fulton Street and Corlear's Hook on the Lower East Side and to the west, in the notorious Five Points neighborhood. Density and the absence of fresh water and sewage systems resulted in cholera epidemics in 1832, 1849, 1854, and 1866. By mid-century thousands of people bunked in boardinghouses, or "crib joints," along the Bowery, and upward of 18,000 lived in quarters below street level.

During the Civil War housing reformers inspected the hygienic and fire-safety conditions of some 15,000 tenements and succeeded in having rudimentary fire and sanitary codes enacted. The Tenement House Law of 1867 was enacted to improve conditions. From 1879 the "dumbbell" design of architect James E. Ware was intended to raise hygienic standards by providing ventilation and light for interior rooms. In Brooklyn and Williamsburg fire codes were less restrictive and the population was sparser; a tradition of narrow house fronts in downtown Brooklyn spread across South Brooklyn as well, spurring the development on narrower lots of row houses only two rooms deep. In Brooklyn the philanthropist

Captain John Schenck House, built ca *1656 at what became Avenue U and East 63rd Street in Flatlands,* ca *1900*

Alfred T. White built low-rent housing for the "worthy poor," based on the "model tenement" experiments of such philanthropists as Silas Wood; he developed the Home Buildings (1877) and the Tower Buildings (1879) in Brooklyn Heights, incorporating interior courtyards that offered tenants more sunlight than Manhattan tenements. To the east and southeast of these developments lay the Navy Yard, or "Jungle," where three-story, wooden houses with rear buildings and outdoor privies were crowded together.

By the mid-nineteenth century wealthy Manhattan residents had migrated uptown, expanding the upper-class housing stock by moving to 14th Street, 34th Street, Fifth Avenue, and eventually the Central Park area by the end of the century. The A. T. Stewart House on Fifth Avenue and West 34th Street (1869), occupying six lots, was emblematic of the new uptown MANSIONS for the very wealthy. Previously the affluent had occupied Federal and Greek Revival row houses, made of redbrick or wood, two or three stories tall, with shallow basements, slope-roofed attics, and dormer windows. As the middle class and upper middle class expanded, BROWNSTONES became the preferred dwellings. The more prosperous the owner, the more ornate and tall the building became, often reaching five stories with as many as 20 rooms. Brownstone construction in Washington Square and Gramercy Park during the 1840s increased their popularity throughout the city.

It also became fashionable, especially for young married couples, to live in the better boardinghouses and hotels, such as Astor House (1836) and the lavish St. Nicholas Hotel (1853). By the 1870s and 1880s the new luxury APARTMENTS with concierge services, known as FRENCH FLATS, became popular among the upper classes. The five-story Stuyvesant (1869) and the 10-story Dakota (1884) resembled châteaux, with suites of several rooms and servants' quarters. Gilsey House (1871) and other hotels on Broadway between Madison and Herald Squares offered comparable suites and concierge services; the Apthorp apartments (1908) were also luxurious. The advent of the first mechanical elevator in 1858 and its increased usage by the 1870s helped propel the popularity of apartments and encourage the construction of taller buildings. In 1870 Haight House used a steam elevator to assist residents in reaching its five floors. Stevens House on Broadway and West 26th–27th streets (1872) was considered visionary for the time as one of the tallest residential buildings in New York City, with eight stories; it later became a hotel. The Vancorlear was the first to use water hydraulic elevators when it opened in 1880. Another innovation in New York City housing was the 11-story Chelsea Hotel (1884), one of the first COOPERATIVES, which meant it was owned, not rented, by the occupants. High-rise buildings with elevators became the most popular mode of housing for the middle classes during the late nineteenth century; one example of this are the Central Park Apartments (Spanish Flats) (1883), consisting of eight 10-story buildings with extremely large apartments (up to 8000 square feet [743 square meters]) on Central Park South. By 1900 elevators became electrically run and further popularized tall buildings. High-rise residences spread above 59th Street around Central Park; the Ansonia, on Broadway and West 72nd Street, was the largest building of its kind in 1904 and was typical of luxury construction, with its grand architecture and large courtyard.

In 1901 there were upward of 83,000 rookeries, frame houses, and dumbbell tenements in New York City, of which 60,000 had been built since the Tenement House Law of 1879. Half the city's population lived in buildings with six or more families, and less than one-fifth lived in one-family houses. The Tenement House Law of 1901 required fire escapes and separate privies for each family in already existing, or "old law," tenements; prohibited inside rooms without windows and required 12-foot (4-meter) side courts and backyards for all buildings constructed according to the "new law"; made it uneconomical to install air shafts and build on lots 25 feet (8 meters) wide, leading to the development of lots 40 to 50 feet (13 to 15 meters) wide; and created the Tenement House Department, which pressured the landlords of old law buildings to comply with the code by installing fire escapes, cutting open inside rooms, and replacing unsanitary privies. The new law encouraged the construction uptown of solid, well-lit, six-story buildings containing apartments (known as flats) that had dumbwaiters, cooking ranges, and hot running water catering to the emerging middle class. The extension of the subway to Washington Heights, Brownsville, and Morrisania led to the introduction of improved tenements in developing neighborhoods. Henry Morgenthau's American Real Estate Company developed flats near subway stations in Washington Heights and South Bronx. The city zoning law of 1916 protected owners of apartment buildings from commercial and industrial developers, but it did not protect racial and ethnic minorities. Housing covenants barred Jews from apartment buildings on Park Avenue and blacks from those surrounding Harlem.

The expansion of housing in the early twentieth century significantly benefited both middle and working classes, for whom multiple-dwelling buildings became the preferred mode of residence. From 1905 to 1908 70,000 apartments were built in northern Manhattan and 30,000 in the Bronx. Many of these contained stylish flats with large rooms, parquet floors, and bathrooms with tubs, renting for $5 to $6 a room per month. Construction of apartment buildings expanded greatly during the 1920s in response to favorable legislation, continued high demand, and reformist measures. The state legislature enacted emergency controls for unreasonable rent increases in 1920 as well as a 10-year tax abatement for developers of apartments. In 1922 insurance companies gained the right to invest in housing projects, provided the rents charged were limited. In 1926 the Limited Dividend Housing Companies Law significantly helped expand low-income housing, with provisions to use eminent domain to gain land for building and the right to grant tax abatements to LIMITED-DIVIDEND HOUSING companies that built apartments renting for $12.50 a room or less. Worker-sponsored housing projects benefited from this legislation; some examples are the Amalgamated Housing Corporation, the United Workers Cooperative, and the Workers Cooperative Colony, formed by socialists. The Amalgamated was among the largest housing sponsors of this kind.

As New York City transit routes were extended through the outer boroughs, residential construction boomed. Rows of art deco apartment buildings were erected along the Grand Concourse, as were luxury apartment buildings along Riverside Drive and on Central Park West; one example of this is the Beresford (1929), designed by Emery Roth with three Baroque projections at the top. Tax incentives encouraged the construction of Spanish-Moorish flats on and around Northern Boulevard in Jackson Heights (the Metropolitan Life Insurance Company built Spanish Gardens, a complex of 2125 units designed by Andrew Thomas), and garden apartments were built along Queens Boulevard and Pelham Parkway. Progressive builders worked closely with reformers to incorporate design improvements into the Multiple Dwellings Law of 1929, which mandated larger courtyards, basic plumbing, and fire-resistant construction and imposed bulk and setback requirements for high-rise residences. This boom produced close to half a million apartments during the 1920s, almost a third of the city's multiple dwellings by 1930. In the outer boroughs 106,384 one-family and 111,662 two-family dwellings were constructed in this period. The garden apartment became a favored style, which meant green spaces, courtyards, and less building coverage on the sites; the majority were built in the outer boroughs, especially Queens. The first such garden apartment was the Greystone (1918), built in Queens on 79th Street and Northern Boulevard (another Greystone was built in the Bronx in 1929). This era also marked the rise of the modern development corporation, which oversaw all phases of building construction and management. One of the first was the Queensboro Corporation, formed by Edward A. MacDougal in 1909, which built walkup apartments on a mass scale in Jackson Heights and Corona. Foreseeing the effect of subway expansion, MacDougal developed 325 acres (132 hectares) of Queens farmland into middle-class housing. The Bronx witnessed similar developments aimed at its middle-class Jewish population.

The Depression devastated private construction, causing builders and mortgage firms to seek relief from state and federal authorities. The Reconstruction Finance Corporation invested in Knickerbocker Village (1934), a limited-dividend project that cleared slums on the Lower East Side, and supported federal insurance for home mortgages provided by the Federal Housing Administration. In order to answer the demand for low-income housing, the fledgling New York City Housing Authority in 1936 completed the First Houses, a 123-unit development on the Lower East Side. The housing authority accepted existing racial and income divisions, building the Harlem River Houses (1937) for African Americans. In 1938 lobbying efforts by the Citizens Housing Council led to approval of article 18 of the state constitution, authorizing comprehensive city planning, slum clearance, and urban redevelopment. The Williamsburg and Queensbridge Houses were completed in 1940. The housing authority sheltered 40,000 people by 1941. Limited government subsidies caused planners to construct spartan, high-rise buildings like the 10-story East Harlem Houses (1941).

This new legislation also resulted in the construction of working- and middle-class housing complexes. The Metropolitan Life Insurance Company built Parkchester, with 42,000 residents (1940), and Stuyvesant Town, for 20,000 (1943); the latter was facilitated by Robert Moses's use of eminent domain and tax-subsidy provisions of the Redevelopment Companies Law of 1943. In central Queens the City Planning Commission developed Forest Hills, the parkways around the World's Fair of 1939–40, and the Independent subway, reviving the speculative construction of semi-detached houses and row houses. William Gutterman developed Kew Gardens Hills with houses that were 18 feet (5.5 meters) wide, had six or more rooms and built-in garages, and sold for $5990; when working-class buyers hesitated to buy, he added finished basements with "Kentile" floors and faucets that mixed hot and cold water. During World War II the Lanham Act (1940) increased government subsidies for projects like the Wallabout (1941) and Fort Greene (1944) houses (for shipyard workers and navy dependents in the area surrounding the Brooklyn Navy Yard), and for Quonset villages housing 30,000 residents at several sites (including Flushing Meadow Park and Manhattan Beach).

The New York City Housing Authority built 75,000 units during the 1950s and became the landlord to 500,000 low-income tenants. A combination of Moses's influence, the use of title I of the Housing Act of 1949, and a $215 million bond issue transformed the Lower East Side with the addition of 10-, 12-, and 14-story projects named for Governor Alfred E. Smith, Fiorello H. La Guardia, Lillian Wald, and Bernard Baruch; the Taft, Jefferson, and Wagner complexes were built in East Harlem; and low-rent units across Brownsville and South Bronx were erected. This funding was also used to build housing for the staffs of Columbia University and New York University, as well as 28,000 units renting for $25 to $75 a room, and enabled the garment unions' consortium and the United Housing Foundation to build cooperative projects like the Hillman Houses on the Lower East Side and Penn South in midtown. Moses encouraged the investment of savings banks in Parkway Village in Kew Gardens and of New York Life Insurance in the award-winning development Fresh Meadows, middle-income apartment buildings at Trump Village (1964; 3800 units) in Brighton Beach, and at Lefrak City (1967; 5000 units) near the Long Island Expressway.

The extensive use of public funds to subsidize housing lasted well into the 1970s. Federal programs such as the war on poverty, the Municipal Loan Program, and philanthropic groups such as the Bedford Stuyvesant Restoration Corporation extended urban renewal to the city's ghettos. The Mitchell–Lama Act subsidized middle-income projects like Co-op City (1968–70) in the Bronx, where 15,500 units rented for $20 a room, and added 138,849 units by the 1970s. In 1968 the legislature authorized the construction of Battery Park City, a complex of 5000 middle-income apartments, the same year it chartered the Urban Development Corporation (UDC) to override zoning rules and expedite the construction of middle-income housing. The UDC built 32 projects, including Twin Parks in the Bronx and the cooperative apartments on Roosevelt Island, with mortgage subsidies that eventually endangered the state's credit. Neighborhood initiatives resulted in the construction of 33,000 units in the early 1970s by church groups with mortgage subsidies from the Model Cities program. Soaring mortgage and labor rates slowed the construction of private, medium-rent housing from 20,000 units a year in the early 1960s to fewer than 5000 late in the decade. Buildings were abandoned at a staggering rate (an estimated 200,000 apartments were lost from 1960 to 1975) and were subject to arson. Neighborhoods in the South Bronx, Central Harlem, and Bushwick became uninhabitable. In 1973 the federal government ordered a moratorium on new public housing development. Local groups led the charge to reclaim apartments in the South Bronx; by 1981 some 112,000 units had reverted to the city after being transferred to tenant owners when managers failed to collect adequate rents from their neighbors. NEHEMIAH PLAN HOMES, an organization initiated by East Brooklyn Congregations in 1982, built more than 2300 houses on vacant land and became a national model for low-income homeownership.

In the 1980s market-rate housing dominated. Helmsley–Spear offered cooperative ownership plans to tenants in Tudor City and Parkchester in 1978, and during the 1980s landlords converted nearly 320,000 rental apartments to cooperative ownership. The pressure to build high-priced housing eliminated two-thirds of the city's 150,000 single-room occupancy units (SROs) by the late 1980s, and there was considerable new construction in Hell's Kitchen (which became known as Clinton) and along upper Broadway. Low-income residents were often displaced as new laws favored developers building market-rate apartments. The supply of high-end new apartments peaked during the economic recession of the late 1980s; at the same time the homeless population was rising. Housing costs soared in the 1990s, and formerly undesirable neighborhoods went through gentrification with the accompanying rise of home prices. The city depleted its subsidies for affordable housing and sold off many city-owned buildings and land to private developers.

In the twenty-first century residential prices had risen to an all-time high by the middle of the first decade. Luxury buildings were developed in areas that never would have been considered suitable previously, and condominiums became one of the most popular housing types; unlike cooperatives, condominiums did not require residents to gain approval of building members or cooperative boards. Rezoning of many areas resulted in new high-rise developments with considerably more square footage as well as thousands of housing units in areas that were formerly designated for manufacturing or low-rise structures. The selling of air rights from neighboring buildings allowed for additional floor area in new construction. Inclusionary housing ZONING, a new trend, allowed developers to build low-income housing in return for more square footage in other, more expensive areas. For the first time in 10 years, affordable housing was funded heavily by tax credits and multiple financial sources, leading to public-private partnerships; this was encouraged by Mayor Michael Bloomberg, who supported increased low-income housing. Government programs failed to keep up with the costs entailed in constructing low-income housing, so incentives were offered to increase private-sector investment. Not-for-profit housing organizations, tapping into shrinking public funding, developed supportive housing aimed at assisting the formerly homeless, single mothers, and the chronically ill; these buildings also contained social services to assist residents. In the early twenty-first century apartments in multiple-dwelling buildings remain the most common mode of housing in New York City; of approximately three million occupied dwellings in the city in 2005, more than two-thirds were apartments.

Anthony Jackson, *A Place Called Home: A History of Low-Cost Housing in Manhattan* (Cambridge, Mass.: MIT Press, 1976); Richard Plunz, *A History of Housing in New York City: Dwelling Type and Social Change in the American Metropolis* (New York: Columbia University Press, 1990)

See also Dumbbell tenements, Homelessness, and Row houses.

Lisa Keller, Joel Schwartz

Hoving, Thomas (Pearsall Field). (*b* New York City, 15 Jan 1931; *d* Manhattan, 10 Dec 2009). Author and museum director. Son of a successful businessman who later became chairman of Tiffany and Company, he attended various prep schools and earned a bachelor's degree and doctorate from Princeton University. He worked at the Cloisters from 1959 to 1965, when he became parks commissioner for Mayor John V. Lindsay. He created the "Happenings," building-sized banners in Central Park for the public to paint. Hoving ran the Metropolitan Museum of Art from 1967 to 1977; he is credited with boosting attendance and expanding the museum's collections with acquisitions such as the Temple of Dendur, but he is also sometimes criticized for his perceived lack of concern for professional and artistic integrity. After leaving the Met he wrote numerous books, including his memoir *Making the Mummies Dance: Inside the Metropolitan Museum of Art* (1993) and *Art for Dummies* (1999).

Ben Silk

Howard Beach. Neighborhood in southwestern Queens (2000 pop. 28,121), bounded to the north by the Belt Parkway, to the east by 102nd Street, to the south by Jamaica Bay, and to the west by 78th Street. It was established in the 1890s by William J. Howard, a glove manufacturer in Brooklyn who operated a goat farm on 150 acres (61 hectares) of meadowland near Aqueduct as a source of skins for kid gloves. In 1897 he bought more land and filled it in, and during the following year he built 18 cottages and opened a hotel near the water, which he operated until it was destroyed by fire in October 1907. He gradually bought more land and in 1909 formed the Howard Estates Development Company; he dredged out Stillwell Basin (later Shellbank Canal) and used the dredgings for fill on the meadows. By 1914 Howard had reclaimed 500 acres (200 hectares) of land, built several streets, laid out mains for water and gas, and built 35 houses priced between $2500 and $5000. A railroad station (opened in April 1913) and a post office were given the name Ramblersville; a casino, a beach, and a fishing pier were added in 1915. The railroad station and the post office took the name Howard Beach on 6 April 1916, and during 1916–17 more bungalows and cottages were built and several streets were paved. In 1922 a group of investors took over the development and sold lots for about $690 each.

The demand for more housing during the 1920s stimulated development and the construction of dozens of houses each year; there were 510 private houses at the end of 1935. In 1933 all street names were replaced by numbers to conform to the system used in the rest of Queens. After a fire destroyed the trestle across the bay, the Long Island Rail Road terminated service to Howard Beach in October 1955; subway service was inaugurated on 28 June 1956 from a station at 159th Avenue. During the 1950s a development called Rockwood was built in a large area west of Cross Bay Boulevard; cooperatives and condominiums were built in the 1980s. Howard Beach attracted a large Italian American population. It was home to several organized crime figures, notably John Gotti and Joey Massino. Tennis player Vitas Gerulaitis grew up there. The geographical isolation imposed by the bay, the airport, and the parkway gives the neighborhood a strong sense of community and local pride.

Vincent Seyfried, Jeffrey A. Kroessler

Howe [Horenstein], **Irving** (*b* Bronx, 11 June 1920; *d* New York City, 5 May 1993). Editor and critic. He grew up in a poor neighborhood in the eastern Bronx and joined the Young People's Socialist League at age 14. During the late 1930s he attended City College of New York, where he became a leading Trotskyist activist and took part in rallies for many social causes; he later abandoned communism and embraced democratic socialism. After fulfilling military service he returned to the city and from 1948 to 1952 wrote literary and cultural criticism for *Time.* During the 1950s he taught at universities outside the city, and in 1954 he launched the magazine *Dissent.* He returned to the city in 1963 to join the English department at Hunter College, where he remained until 1986. He remained politically active as a lecturer, writer, and member of the Democratic Socialists of America and continued to edit *Dissent.* Howe's published writings include *World of Our Fathers* (1975), a poignant account of Jewish life in New York City that was a bestseller and won many awards, and *A Margin of Hope: An Intellectual Autobiography* (1982).

James Bradley

Howell, James (*b* Bradford, Wiltshire, England, 16 Oct 1829; *d* Brooklyn, 27 Jan 1897). Mayor of Brooklyn. An iron founder by trade, he was elected the 19th mayor of Brooklyn and served two consecutive terms (1878–81). His tenure was marked by retrenchment because of the effects of the financial crisis of 1873, but he did oversee the late stages of construction of the Brooklyn Bridge and was a trustee for the project.

Ellen Fletcher

Howells, William Dean (*b* Martins Ferry, Ohio, 1 March 1837; *d* New York City, 11 May 1920). Novelist and literary critic. Although he originally gained fame in Boston, where he was the editor of the *Atlantic Monthly* and wrote several novels, the best-known of which is *The Rise of Silas Lapham* (1885), he moved permanently to New York City in 1888, a shift that was given as evidence that Manhattan had become the intellectual capital of the United States. He took an apartment in an old house overlooking Livingston Place and wrote several novels reflecting his disillusionment with a society that he saw as crippled by social and economic ills: *Annie Kilburn* (1888) was pro-labor and *A Hazard of New Fortunes* (1890) chronicled the "frantic panorama" of competitive life in the city. In the early 1890s he rented an apartment at 241 East 17th Street, and in 1895 he moved to one overlooking Central Park, where he wrote articles in support of such authors as Leo Tolstoy, Henrik Ibsen, Émile Zola, and Stephen Crane. Howells became the first president of the American Academy of Arts and Letters in 1908 and remained active in controversial social and political causes. He lived the last 10 years of his life at the Hotel St. Hubert, at 120 West 57th Street.

Kenneth S. Lynn, *William Dean Howells: An American Life* (New York: Harcourt Brace Jovanovich, 1970)

See also Literature.

Anthony Gronowicz

Howland Hook. Neighborhood in northwestern Staten Island, lying at the confluence of the Arthur Kill and the Kill van Kull; the Goethals Bridge (1928) stands at its southern edge. The neighborhood is also called Holland Hook, after Henry Holland, one of the representatives for Staten Island in the colonial assembly of New York. Ferries ran from the area to Elizabeth, New Jersey, between 1736 and 1961. In the mid-1990s Howland Hook was mostly industrial, the site of both the United States Lines container port, the largest facility of its kind in New York City, and Port Ivory, a disused plant and port of Procter and Gamble that was once the largest employer in the borough. In 1995 the city began dredging the harbor to reopen the ports to commercial activity. In 2007 Mayor Michael Bloomberg initiated a project to link the Staten Island Railroad to the national network in New Jersey. It now serves as one of four sites to transport solid waste out of the city. Wetlands protected by the state account for some of the land.

Harlow McMillen

Hudson, Henry (*b* England; *d* after 23 June 1611). Explorer. He dedicated his life to finding a passage to China through North America. After unsuccessful voyages in 1607 and 1608 he made his third attempt in the early spring of 1609. With backing from the Dutch East India Company he set sail with a crew of 18 from Amsterdam on the *Halve Maen;* icebergs north of Norway and the threat of mutiny led him to seek shelter along the North American coast, and on 2 September he dropped anchor in the lower bay of what became New York Harbor, which he explored in small boats for 10 days. He then sailed up the Hudson River (which he named) to the site of what became Albany, taking small boats as far as what became Troy, New York. Hudson made his last voyage in 1611; after he discovered Hudson's Bay and claimed it for England, his crew mutinied and cast him adrift. A statue of Hudson stands atop a tall shaft in Henry Hudson Park in Spuyten Duyvil.

Noel Bertram Gerson, *The Magnificent Adventures of Henry Hudson* (New York: Dodd, Mead, 1965)

James E. Mooney

Hudson River. Bordering the western edge of New York City, it is one of the most important waterways in the world. As an extension of the Atlantic Ocean the Hudson River is technically an estuary, but because it results from glacial scouring, it is also referred to as a fjord. From its source in upstate New York at Lake Tear of the Clouds in the Adirondacks, the river flows for 315 miles (507 kilometers) in a generally southerly direction to Upper New York Bay. It is navigable for ocean vessels as far north as Troy, New York; tidal for 154 miles (248 kilometers) as far north as Troy; and saline for about 60 miles (97 kilometers) as far north as Newburgh, New York, depending on seasonal rain runoff. The river is the boundary between New York State and New Jersey for 17 miles (27 kilometers). At its southern end it is known as the North River, and at its mouth it is 4400 feet (1340 meters) wide. The river traverses one of the oldest geological regions in the United States. For millions of years before the retreat of the last glacier, the Wisconsin Ice Sheet, it extended another 120 miles (193 kilometers) into the Atlantic to the edge of the Continental Shelf, but the rising seawater flooded the old river course, thus contributing to the navigability of the river. Despite years of pollution the river is rich in marine life. In the 1970s and 1980s strict controls on the dumping of toxic waste and strong efforts by environmentalists improved the quality of the water and enabled many varieties of fish to reestablish themselves, including striped bass, herring, sturgeon, and shad.

The Hudson was an important trade route for the Algonquin tribes, especially in its lower valley. The first European to see the river was the Florentine navigator Giovanni da Verrazano, who in 1524 sailed up the river for François I of France, for whom he claimed the land. In the following year the harbor was visited by Esteban Gomez, a Portuguese mariner sailing under the Spanish flag who named the river Rio de San Antonio. In 1609 the Englishman Henry Hudson, sailing for the Dutch East India Company, explored the river as far north as Albany in search of a passage to Asia. He provided an extensive report on the "Great River to the North," many details of which were chronicled in the log of his first mate, Robert Juet. The river was a major trade route for the early Dutch and English colonists and later was crucial during the American Revolution. Control of the river was vital for the survival of the rebellion, and one-third of all the battles were fought along its shores. The capture near Tarrytown, New York, of British Major John André, who had the plans for the fortress at West Point hidden in his boot, probably saved the American cause. In 1807 Robert Fulton inaugurated the era of steam navigation when he piloted his *North River Steamboat* (later known as the *Clermont*) up the Hudson. Traffic on the river reached its peak in the mid-nineteenth century when the Delaware and Hudson Canal and the Erie Canal were opened, but it declined when railroads were built on both sides of the river. The striking beauty of the river, particularly along the Palisades and in the Hudson Highlands, inspired literary works by Washington Irving and the paintings of the Hudson River School.

William Bertrand Fink, *Getting to Know the Hudson River* (New York: Coward-McCann, 1970); Tom Lewis, *The Hudson: A History* (New Haven: Yale University Press, 2005)

Gerard R. Wolfe

Hudson River

Hudson River lines. The business of transporting passengers by water from New York City to Albany, New York, and other points up the Hudson River developed after the first voyage of Robert Fulton's steamship the *North River Steamboat* in 1807 and was profoundly altered by two developments in the early nineteenth century. Intense competition was spurred by the ruling of the U.S. Supreme Court in *Gibbons v. Ogden* (1824) that the official monopoly on steam travel in the waters of New York held by Fulton and Robert R. Livingston was unconstitutional, and improvements in the design of ships reduced the time needed to travel to Albany. In 1832 the major operators of day lines formed a quasi-monopoly called the Hudson River Steamboat Association, which later evolved into the Hudson River Day Line under unified management. Night services began in 1832 with the sailings of the *James Kent*; service to Albany was offered by the People's Line Association from 1835. Among the ships sailing the Hudson during this period were the *Isaac Newton* (from 1846), the *Alida* (1847), and the *New World* (1848). From 1856 the Citizen's Line offered service to Troy, New York.

After the Hudson River Railroad reached Albany in 1851, people traveled by sail and steam less often for business and more often for recreation. Traffic was greatest between 1860 and 1920; among the best-known ships of this period was the *Mary Powell*, a sidewheel steamer known as the "speed queen of the Hudson." Built in 1861 it was powered by a vertical beam engine and ran a daily round trip of 180 miles (290 kilometers) between Kingston and Manhattan. Remodeled in 1903 for excursion service, it ran on the Hudson River Day Line until 1917 and then was retired and dismantled. Other ships serving this route included the *St. John* (1864), the *Dean Richmond* (1865), the *Drew* (1866), and the *Adirondack* (1896).

In 1902 the night services were combined when the Hudson Navigation Company was formed by Charles Wyman Morse. The company operated under various names until 1939, although it was generally known as the Hudson River Night Line. In the early twentieth century the Hudson was served by such ships as the *C. W. Morse* (1903), the *Hendrick Hudson* (1906), the *Robert Fulton* (1909), and the *Washington Irving* (1913). The largest steamship was the *Berkshire* (in service from 1913 to 1937). Built by the New York Shipbuilding Company (Camden, New Jersey), the ship measured 422 feet (129 meters) by 50 feet (15 meters) and was powered by a vertical beam engine with a cylinder of 85 inches (2.15 meters) and a stroke of 12 feet (3.66 meters). The *Berkshire* provided night service between New York City and Albany. The *Alexander Hamilton* (1924) was the last operating sidewheel steamer on the Hudson River Day Line. Designed by J. W. Millard and built by the Bethlehem Shipbuilding Corporation of Maryland, it measured 349 feet (106 meters) by 77 feet (23 meters) and had a triple-expansion inclined engine and feathering sidewheels. The retirement of the *Alexander Hamilton* in September 1971 ended a long tradition of steam-powered travel on the Hudson. Although the Hudson River Day Line was disbanded in 1949, the *Dayliner* was put into service in 1972, and successor companies continued regular sailings up the Hudson River until 4 September 1989.

Donald C. Ringwald, *Hudson River Day Line: The Story of a Great American Steamboat Company* (Berkeley, Calif.: Howell–North, 1965); Arthur G. Adams, *The Hudson through the Years* (Westwood, N.J.: Lind, 1985)

Arthur G. Adams

Hudson River Park. Narrow, 5-mile-long (8-kilometer-long) park on Manhattan's West Side, located between Battery Park and 59th Street. In 1998 the signing of the Hudson River Park Act created the Hudson River Park Trust to oversee the design, construction, and maintenance of the largest construction of open space in Manhattan since the completion of Central Park. Supported by city and state governments and supplemented by lease agreements with private tenants including Chelsea Piers, the Hudson River Park Trust also operates the only designated urban marine sanctuary in New York City. Although it is composed of four unique and separately designed segments, the park design is unified by regulations concerning esplanade paving, railings, and light poles, as well as the bike path built as part of the redevelopment of the West Side Highway. The bikeway and boating opportunities, educational activities, and community events including free movies during the summer months have helped make the park one of the most popular recreation sites on the West Side.

Anne Epstein

Hudson River Railroad. Freight railroad chartered in 1846, merged in 1869 with the New York and Harlem Railroad to form the New York Central and Hudson River Railroad.

Hudson River School. School of landscape painting that flourished between 1825 and 1870; the name, which appeared in print in 1879, was probably first used during the 1870s pejoratively by artists and critics who promoted European styles of painting and supported the Society of American Artists (1877–1906) as an alternative to the more conservative National Academy of Design. A sketching tour up the Hudson River to the Catskill Mountains by Thomas Cole and the purchase of several of his landscapes by John Trumbull, William Dunlap, and Asher B. Durand in the same year are considered to mark the school's beginning. Members subscribed to concepts of the sublime, the beautiful, the picturesque, and associationism articulated in the writings of such influential European critics as Edmund Burke (1729–97), William Gilpin (1724–1804), Sir Uvedale Price (1747–1829), and Archibald Alison (1757–1839). Cole was the first artist to treat the American landscape as a metaphor for the new nation. New York City was the center of the school, which was often called the "native," "American," or "New York" school. Many members had studios in the Tenth Street Studio Building (1857–1956) and belonged to such societies as the Sketch Club (1827–69) and the Century Association (formed in 1847). Their works were bought by art galleries in the city such as Williams, Stevens, Williams and Company, and Goupil and Company (formed in 1846, reorganized as M. Knoedler and Company) and by patrons such as Jonathan Sturges and Robert Leighton Stuart. Several influential periodicals including the *Crayon* (1855–61) were published in the city, where a number of institutions promoted the works of the school, among them the American Academy of the Fine Arts (1802–42), the National Academy of Design (formed in 1826), and the American Art Union (1838–52).

Although most members of the school traveled and worked in Europe, they often chose the Hudson River as a subject for their works and also used it as a route to sketching sites in the Catskills, the Adirondacks, and the mountains of New England. Durand became the acknowledged leader of the school after Cole's death. He articulated its theories in "Letters on Landscape Painting," nine essays published in the *Crayon* in 1855 and based in part on the argument that the faithful depiction of nature reveals the presence of God. Cole's pupil Frederic E. Church sought to evoke cosmic truths by blending art and science in landscape paintings of grand scale; he became known internationally as the foremost American landscape painter for paintings that he completed after travels in North

Jasper F. Cropsey, Castle Garden *(1851)*

America, South America, Europe, and the Near East. Such artists as John Frederick Kensett, Martin Johnson Heade (1819–1904), and Jasper F. Cropsey (1823–1900) painted smaller landscapes in a "luminist" style characterized by the careful study of light and atmosphere. They explored concepts of humanity's relation to nature and God and sought to represent the direct experience of a spiritual presence in nature by rendering their subjects with perceptual intensity.

The decline of the Hudson River School was brought about by the Civil War, which permanently altered Americans' perceptions of their country and its landscape; the influence of European academic training; the popularity of French Barbizon art and impressionism among American collectors; and a new emphasis on decorative design inspired by a movement in Britain. Although a few leading members remained popular into the early twentieth century, the school by the 1880s was widely viewed not as a contemporary force in American art but rather as a historic movement that had established an American tradition of landscape painting.

John K. Howat, *American Paradise: The World of the Hudson River School* (New York: Metropolitan Museum of Art, 1987); Kenneth Myers, *The Catskills: Painters, Writers, and Tourists in the Mountains, 1820–1895* (Yonkers, N.Y.: Hudson River Museum of Westchester, 1987); Angela Miller, *The Empire of the Eye: Landscape Representation and American Cultural Politics, 1825–1875* (Ithaca, N.Y.: Cornell University Press, 1993); Linda S. Ferber, *Nature and the American Vision: The Hudson River School at the New-York Historical Society* (New York: New-York Historical Society and Rizzoli, 2009)

Timothy Anglin Burgard

Hudson Square [St. John's Park]. One of the oldest squares in New York City, shown on both the 1787 Taylor–Roberts and 1800 Goerck–Mangin plans. It originally extended from North Moore to Laight Streets between Varick and Hudson Streets. By 1807 the southern boundary had been moved a block north to Beach Street. Owned by Trinity Church, the square was intended to be private and serve adjacent homes. It took more than 20 years for the lots to be sold and homes erected, as the church encountered stiff opposition to its plan to sell 99-year leaseholds. Eventually, 64 lots around the square were sold, with owners retaining exclusive rights to the use of the square under an unusual arrangement: if they failed to maintain it, the square was to be ceded to the city for public use. During these decades numerous improvements were made, including the addition of gaslight, creation of curbstones and streets around the square, the addition of fencing, and the planting of extensive vegetation. By 1827 it had become quite fashionable, and its alternative name, St. John's Park, was in use. Trinity Church maintained the right, with the consent of two-thirds of the lot owners, to sell the land, and did so in 1866 for $1 million to Cornelius Vanderbilt's Hudson River Railway Company. Construction of a railroad freight depot began in 1867 with the cutting down of 200 trees, which marked the end of the square. The land later became part of the approach to the HOLLAND TUNNEL.

Lisa Keller

Hudson Yards. The term refers to a large area bounded by the Hudson River, Eighth Avenue, 28th Street, and 43rd Street. Since the mid-nineteenth century, transportation facilities, starting with railroad yards and steamship piers, have dominated the area. The New York Central Railroad (NYCRR) and its successors operated the West 30th Street yards, a large freight facility between West 30th and 34th streets running from 10th Avenue to the Hudson River. This rail yard was part of the NYCRR's West Side rail route, which extended from Manhattan's northern tip to approximately Canal Street and was the principal conduit for New York City's consumer food items until 1967 when new wholesale food distribution markets opened at Hunts Point in the Bronx. The rail access also accounted for the industries and warehouses that originally characterized the Hudson Yards area. The Lincoln Tunnel, originally opened in 1937, improved truck access; the Port Authority Bus Terminal, first opened in 1950 and expanded twice afterward, added another large transportation facility. After World War II the NYCRR and its successors lost Manhattan freight customers until the final freight train ran in 1980. By then the West 30th Street yards had been virtually abandoned. Two major public projects were built in the Hudson Yards during the 1980s: the Jacob Javits Convention Center (opened in 1986) between West 34th and West 38th streets west of 11th Avenue, and the West Side Yard of the Metropolitan Transit Authority Long Island Rail Road (LIRR) (opened in 1987) between 30th and 33rd streets west of 10th Avenue on the old NYCRR yard site. Included in the latter was a tunnel connecting the old NYCRR West Side route to Penn Station, allowing Amtrak trains between Manhattan and upstate New York cities to use Penn Station instead of Grand Central Terminal.

Hudson Yards, 2009

In 2005, the area was rezoned from manufacturing to commercial and residential, making it possible for the site to accommodate as many as 13,500 units of housing and 24 million square feet of office space. Reduced demand for commercial occupancy after the 2008–10 economic downturn meant that the approval and building process was slower than expected.

Andrew Sparberg

Hughes, Charles Evans (*b* Glens Falls, N.Y., 11 April 1862; *d* Barnstable, Mass., 28 Aug 1948). New York governor, Supreme Court justice, and politician. He graduated from Brown University in 1881 and from Columbia Law School in 1884. He attracted public notice as the chief counsel on the Stevens Gas Commission (1905), which investigated utility practices in New York City, and as the counsel for the Armstrong Commission (1905–6), which mounted an inquiry by the state into insurance fraud. His findings led to unprecedented legislation to prevent corruption. In 1906 he was elected governor of New York; during his term he helped to formulate one of the most effective workers' compensation laws in the nation. He was appointed to the U.S. Supreme Court in 1910 and held his seat until 1916. He resigned to become the Republican candidate for president. Defeated by Woodrow Wilson he resumed private practice until 1921 when he was appointed secretary of state. Reappointed to the Supreme Court by Herbert Hoover, he met some of his greatest challenges as its chief justice from 1930 to 1941; he guided the court as it voided crucial aspects of the New Deal and incurred the anger of many liberals. Largely because of his efforts the court salvaged its credibility and blunted President Franklin D. Roosevelt's plans to fashion a court sympathetic to the legislation of the New Deal. Hughes lived from 1886 to 1888 at 110 East 81st Street, for one year beginning in December 1888 at 129 East 62nd Street, from 1893 to 1905 on West End Avenue and 75th Street, and from 1917 to 1921 at 32 East 64th Street.

Merlo J. Pusey, *Charles Evans Hughes* (New York: Columbia University Press, 1963)

Frederick S. Voss

Hughes, Ellen [Mother Mary Angela] (*b* Annaloghan, County Tyrone, Ireland, *ca* 1806; *d* New York City, 5 Sept 1866). Nun. The sister of Archbishop John Hughes, she immigrated to the United States in 1818 and became a member of the Sisters of Charity in Maryland in 1825. She moved to New York City in 1846 and helped to establish the Sisters of Charity of Mount St. Vincent. Instrumental in the charity's early work, she opened St. Vincent's Hospital in 1849 and served as its superior until 1855, the year she became mother general of the Sisters of Charity of Mount St. Vincent.

Bernadette McCauley

Hughes, John (Joseph) (*b* Annaloghan, County Tyrone, Ireland, 24 June 1797; *d* New York City, 3 Jan 1864). Archbishop. In 1820 he entered Mount St. Mary's Seminary near Emmitsburg, Maryland, where he supported himself as a gardener. He was ordained for the Diocese of Philadelphia on 15 October 1826 and appointed a coadjutor for the Diocese of New York on 7 January 1838. After John DuBois suffered a stroke in 1838, Hughes was put in charge of the diocese and in 1839 was given the title of apostolic administrator. His efforts to foster Catholic unity were complicated by the strength of ethnic loyalties. During his tenure he authorized a German parish staffed by diocesan clergy (St. Nicholas, 1833), a German parish staffed by clergy from a religious order (Most Holy Redeemer, 1844), a French parish (St. Vincent de Paul, 1840), and an Italian parish (Church of St. Anthony of Padua). In 1839 he toured Europe to seek funds and staff; he interested several religious orders in the city's mission, including the Ladies of the Sacred Heart (1841), the Sisters of Mercy (1846), and the Christian Brothers (1853). He also devoted himself to fighting anti-Catholicism. Arguing that Protestantism was being furthered by the Public School Society (a private organization that provided free education for poor children), he asked the state to give Catholics a share of the tax revenues that supported the society. When the legislature rejected his proposal, he urged Catholics to vote for a slate of candidates who endorsed it (29 October 1841). They received few votes, but the fear of Catholic voting power led the legislature to introduce a public school system, to which Hughes responded by building parochial schools.

Appointed bishop on 20 December 1842, Hughes strengthened his authority by transferring ownership of parish property from lay corporations to a corporation in which the bishop was the principal trustee. He organized parishioners in 1844 to guard their churches against nativist rioters. In 1846 he laid the basis for Fordham University by placing St. John's College under the auspices of the Jesuits; during the same year he organized a diocesan community of sisters after the Sisters of Charity of St. Vincent de Paul informed him that the rules of their order prevented them from fulfilling his wishes to care for boys. When the archdiocese was formed on 19 July 1850, Hughes was appointed archbishop, and he soon began the construction of St. Patrick's Cathedral. Although he favored religious liberty for Ireland, he did not endorse the anti-British nationalist movement Young Ireland or the violent movement for independence. In 1861–62 he toured Europe as Abraham Lincoln's unofficial representative to promote the cause of the Union. Hughes last appeared in public on 17 July 1863, at Governor Horatio Seymour's request, to address participants in the city's draft riots. His remains were moved to St. Patrick's Cathedral in 1883.

Richard Shaw, *Dagger John: The Unquiet Life and Times of Archbishop John Hughes of New York* (New York: Paulist, 1977)

Mary Elizabeth Brown

Hughes, (James Mercer) Langston (*b* Joplin, Mo., 1 Feb 1902; *d* New York City, 22 May 1967). Poet and playwright. After graduating from high school in Cleveland, Ohio, Hughes spent a year in Mexico with his father, briefly attended Columbia University, and worked in the United States and abroad. He won a poetry award sponsored by *Opportunity: A Journal of Negro Life* in 1925, and in the following year all his poems were published by Alfred A. Knopf as *The Weary Blues.* He earned his BA from Lincoln University in Pennsylvania in 1929 and then devoted himself entirely to writing. In his work he depicted the lives of black characters, often in the voice of the fictional character Simple. His play *Mulatto* (1935) ran on Broadway for two years; he also wrote songs and was a member of the American Society of Composers, Authors and Publishers. He won a Guggenheim Fellowship in 1935 and during World War II wrote radio scripts and toured with the United Service Organizations (USO), often reading selections from his work. From 1942 to 1947 he lived at 634 St. Nicholas Avenue. He taught creative writing at Atlanta University in 1947 and was poet-in-residence at the University of Chicago Laboratory School in 1949. His last home was at 20 East 127th Street in Harlem (from 1948). During the last decade of his life he devoted himself to poetry collected in *The Panther and the Lash* (1967), which he dedicated to Rosa Parks. Among Hughes's works are the autobiographies *Big Sea* (1940) and *I Wonder as I Wander* (1956), and the book *The Sweet Flypaper of Life* (1955), which was well received for its humor and optimism.

Langston Hughes

Arnold Rampersad, *The Life of Langston Hughes* (New York: Oxford University Press, 1986–88)

James E. Mooney

Huguenot. Neighborhood in southwestern Staten Island, bounded to the north by Poillon Avenue, to the east by Hylan Boulevard, to the south by Foster Avenue, and to the west by Woodrow Road; it is bisected by Huguenot Avenue. The area was settled during the seventeenth and eighteenth centuries by Huguenots who built a church of native serpentine rock that was still standing in 2009. The area was called Bloomingview during the nineteenth century and before being renamed for a station of Staten Island Rapid Transit near the intersection of Amboy Road and Huguenot Avenue. The clean, sandy beaches in the area attracted vacationers, and in the early twentieth century several resorts opened, including the 100-room Terra Marine Hotel; John Kaltenmeier's Hotel stood near the railroad station. A miniature steam railway ran along Richmond Beach, where a boardwalk 20 feet (6 meters) wide was built; eventually the beach became the site of St. Joseph by-the-Sea High School. Streets were laid out in the 1930s; development increased after Richmond Parkway opened in the 1970s, connecting the Outerbridge Crossing with the center of the island. Residences in Huguenot range from undistinguished row houses to opulent estates. In the early twenty-first century the neighborhood is the site of Intermediate School 7 (Bernstein), Intermediate School 75 (Paulo), and Tottenville High School. Small ponds of glacial origin are still found in the wooded sections remaining in eastern Huguenot.

Harlow McMillen

Huguenots. The first permanent European settlement in the metropolitan area was formed in Manhattan by a group of Walloons sponsored by the Dutch West India Company in 1624. Huguenot refugees from the Netherlands and from Germanic states accounted for many of the colonists who moved to New

Amsterdam in the following years; among them were Peter Minuit and the Bayard, Delanoy, and Delavall families. Harlem was settled in 1637 by the Walloon brothers Hendricus and Isaac DeForest and also became a Huguenot center. In 1650 Huguenots accounted for about one-fifth of the population of New Amsterdam. Before the 1680s most French Calvinists moved to New York City after staying for a time in Protestant European countries. A number of refugees fled directly to the city after King Louis XIV of France made a policy of eradicating Calvinism that culminated in the revocation of the Edict of Nantes in 1685; many of these refugees were merchants and craftspeople from the seaport of La Rochelle, the province of Aunis, and the Isle of Ré. Jacob Leisler, a German-born merchant with Huguenot roots, was the city's agent for settling the refugees, and from 1687 he bought land for them in Westchester County in what is now New Rochelle, New York. He later was the leader of Leisler's Rebellion and was executed in 1691. From 1658 to 1663 Harlem was the site of a French congregation under the ministry of Michel Cipierre. Pierre Daille moved to the city in 1682 and organized the first French congregation, which conducted services in Fort James and became defunct in the mid-1690s. Another congregation formed under Pierre Pieret in 1687 erected a French church on Petticoat Lane, the first in the city; it was replaced in 1704 by a stone building known as l'Église du St. Esprit at Church and Pine streets.

The toleration of ethnic and cultural diversity in the city led to the rapid assimilation of the Huguenots, and by the early eighteenth century such Huguenot merchants as Stephen de Lancey, Peter Jay, and Gabriel Laboyteaux were among the city's leaders. Huguenot craftspeople were also distinguished, especially such silversmiths as Bartholomew Le Roux, Simeon Soumaine, and Peter Quintard. Huguenots accounted for about 11 percent of the city's population by 1703, but after 1720 lost their independent religious identity: most became affiliated with other denominations, especially the Anglican Church. In 1804 l'Église du St. Esprit became an Episcopal church; in the early twenty-first century it continued to serve French-speakers. The Huguenot Society of America, formed in New York City in 1883, is dedicated to preserving Huguenot history.

Thomas J. Archdeacon, *New York City, 1664–1710: Conquest and Change* (Ithaca, N.Y.: Cornell University Press, 1976); Jon Butler, *The Huguenots in America: A Refugee People in New World Society* (Cambridge, Mass.: Harvard University Press, 1983)

David William Voorhees

Doris Humphrey, center, *with Edith Orcutt, Katherine Litz, Letitia Ide, Miriam Raphael, Ada Korvin, Beatrice Seckler, and Joan Levy in* New Dance *(1935)*

Humphrey, Doris (*b* Oak Park, Ill., 17 Oct 1895; *d* New York City, 29 Dec 1958). Dancer and choreographer. She studied at Ruth St. Denis's dance school Denishawn until 1928, when she rejected exotic art dancing and opened up her own studio in New York City with Charles Weidman. While lecturing on modern dance at the New School for Social Research during 1931–40 she formed a circle of modernists in Greenwich Village that included the dance critic John Martin and the composers Aaron Copland and Henry Cowell. She articulated the idea that dance is the art of movement rather than pageantry, costume, or theatrical effects in the experimental dances *Water Study* (1928), *Life of the Bee* (1929), *Drama of Motion* (1930), and *The Shakers* (1931). Because of severe arthritis she retired from dancing in 1946, but she continued to teach in her studio in New York City. In 1951 Humphrey joined the faculty of the Juilliard School of Music, where in 1955 she founded the Juilliard Dance Theater. She wrote *An Artist First: An Autobiography* (1972).

Peter M. Rutkoff, William B. Scott

Huncke, Herbert (*b* Greenfield, Mass., 9 Jan 1915; New York City, 8 Aug 1996). Writer, street hustler, and subculture icon who gave the beat literary movement and generation its name. Raised in Chicago, at age 13 he began using drugs and traveling around the country, often earning money by having sex with older men. In 1939 he hitchhiked to Times Square in New York City, where he lived most of his life. In 1946 the researcher Alfred Kinsey approached Huncke at the Angle Bar at 42nd Street and Eighth Avenue to interview him about his sex life with men and hired him to find other interviewees for his study of human sexual behavior. Huncke became friends with the writer William Burroughs and recruited him for the Kinsey study. Burroughs introduced Huncke to the writers Allen Ginsberg and Jack Kerouac, who were then undergraduates at Columbia University. Huncke became the group's guide to drugs and the underworld of Times Square. He described this group as "beat," or tired and beaten down, and Kerouac soon began to use the word to describe the entire literary movement. The beat writers lauded Huncke for his unaffected and stream-of-consciousness writings, many of which were never published. He showed up as a prominent character in Burroughs's novel *Junkie* and Kerouac's *On the Road.* Ginsberg referenced him countless times in his poetry. Huncke served in the merchant marine during World War II and spent much of the 1950s in prison for various drug-related crimes, but he remained an unrepentant drug addict all his life. He published a series of memoirs but relied on famous friends like Ginsberg, Patti Smith, and Jerry Garcia to keep him housed, clothed, and fed. He lived out his last years in the Chelsea Hotel, where he died at the age of 81.

Benjamin Schafer, ed., *The Herbert Huncke Reader* (New York: William Morrow, 1997)

Breanne Scanlon

Huneker, James Gibbons (*b* Philadelphia, 31 Jan 1857; *d* New York City, 9 Feb 1921).

Critic. He taught piano at the National Conservatory in New York City and wrote for the *New York Recorder* (1891–95) and the *Morning Advertiser* (1895–97). He then began a long association with the *Sun* (1900–17), for which he wrote criticism on music, art, literature, and the theater. He also worked for the *New York Times* as a foreign correspondent (1912–14) and music critic (1918–19). Huneker wrote more than 20 books on music and other topics, including a study of New York City called *New Cosmopolis* (1915) and a novel about artists in the city, *Painted Veils* (1920).

Arnold T. Schwab, *James Gibbons Huneker, Critic of the Seven Arts* (Stanford, Calif.: Stanford University Press, 1963)

See also Intellectuals and Little magazines.

Hungarians. The first Hungarians arrived in New York City after the unsuccessful Hungarian Revolution of 1848–49. The great revolutionary Louis Kossuth visited the city to muster support for his cause in December 1851, and he was greeted with rousing receptions. Manhattan's most notable Hungarian émigré after mid-century was Imre Kiralfy, a producer and choreographer who with his brother Bolossy staged some of the city's most popular music and dance numbers of the period. Joseph Pulitzer, the reporter and newspaper owner who founded the Columbia School of Journalism, was also from Hungary.

Hungarians were a prominent part of the European immigration movement in the late nineteenth century. About 10,000 Hungarians settled in Manhattan in the 1870s, mostly on Second Avenue between First and 10th streets and between 55th and 72nd streets. The largest period of Hungarian settlement in New York City was 20 years beginning in 1890: by 1910 the federal census counted 76,625 people of Hungarian origin in Manhattan and Brooklyn, and other estimates ranged as high as 110,000. Hungarian churches, synagogues, restaurants, nightclubs, newspapers, and businesses flourished, mostly in lower Yorkville but also in parts of the Lower East Side.

Those who identified themselves as Hungarians before World War I included many ethnic Slovaks, Romanians, Ruthenians, and Croatians from the Austro-Hungarian Empire. After the war many of the city's Hungarian-speaking residents were from Czechoslovakia, Austria, and Yugoslavia. Most of the city's Hungarians were Roman Catholic and Eastern Orthodox, though a large number were Protestant and Jewish. Hungarian Jews tended to identify more with their national origin than other eastern European Jews. Gypsies also contributed significantly to Hungarian music, dance, and literature.

Immigration declined after World War I, and the center of New York City's Hungarian community became Yorkville, in the upper 70s and lower 80s from Second Avenue to the East River, between the area's Czech and German communities. Hungarian neighborhoods also formed in the Bronx, Brooklyn, and Queens. In the area surrounding Second Avenue and 79th Street stood Hungarian churches, stores, butcher shops, and restaurants. By 1940 the city's Hungarian population surpassed 123,000, making it the largest Hungarian community in the United States. During this period there were eight Hungarian daily, weekly, and monthly newspapers in the city.

In the 1980s only a few hundred immigrants from Hungary settled in New York City, but many of the 5440 immigrants from Romania were believed to be of Hungarian ancestry. After the collapse of the Eastern bloc governments in 1989, thousands of Hungarians settled in the city, mostly in Queens (especially Ridgewood, Glendale, Long Island City, and Astoria); again, many of these immigrants were from Romania. Some gravitated to the old Hungarian neighborhood in Yorkville, though gentrification made this area too expensive for newcomers. In the mid-1990s several Hungarian institutions could still be found in Yorkville. The American Federation for Hungarian Education and Literature (also called Hungarian House) occupied two row houses on East 82nd Street, offering a library and other resources, and Puski–Corvin Magyar Konyveshaz remained the city's lone Hungarian bookstore. Weekly Hungarian newspapers included such established publications as *Amerikai Magyar Nepszava* (American Hungarian People's Voice [1899]) and the *Hungarian Word* (1902), as well as *Szabdsag* (Liberty [1991]). According to the 1990 federal census 75,721 New Yorkers described themselves as being at least partly of Hungarian origin.

Prominent New Yorkers of Hungarian descent have included the magician Harry Houdini; the pediatrician Béla Schick; the composer Sigmund Romberg; the fencer Giorgio Santelli; the religious leader Stephen S. Wise; the composer Béla Bartók, who fled Hungary after the Nazi invasion and lived in the city from 1940 to 1945; two of Bartók's disciples, the composer Tibor Serly and the pianist Gyorgy Sandor; the sculptor Karl Illava, who created the War Memorial on Fifth Avenue and 67th Street; the architect Emery Roth; the quarterback Joe Namath; the actor Tony Curtis; and Congressman Ted Weiss, who represented the Upper West Side from 1977 to 1992. In 2009 about 50,000 New Yorkers claimed Hungarian ancestry.

James Bradley

Hunt, Richard Morris (*b* Brattleboro, Vt., 31 Oct 1827; *d* Newport, R.I., 31 July 1895). Architect. He was the first American trained at the École des Beaux-Arts in Paris. After studying and traveling in Europe, he moved to New York City in 1855 and in 1858 designed the Tenth Street Studios, where he introduced the French atelier system. Among those who worked with him there were such painters of the Hudson River School as Frederic E. Church. Hunt developed a lively, eclectic style and with such apprentices as William R. Ware, Frank Furness, and George B. Post designed several public buildings, including the Presbyterian Hospital on Madison Avenue (1872, commissioned by James Lenox), mansions (among them one commissioned by William K. Vanderbilt at Fifth Avenue and 52nd Street, 1882), commercial structures such as the Tribune Building (1883), and the pedestal for the Statue of Liberty (1886). A member of the Century Club, he formed the American Institute of Architects, led the Municipal Art Society, and was a trustee and architect of the Metropolitan Museum of Art (1902). In 1898 a monument was erected in his honor by the Municipal Art Society at Fifth Avenue and 70th Street facing the Lenox Library (1870), one of many commissions that he received from the Astors, Vanderbilts, and Lenoxes. None of the mansions Hunt designed along Fifth Avenue and few of his public buildings survive.

Paul R. Baker, *Richard Morris Hunt* (Cambridge, Mass.: MIT Press, 1980)

Edward A. Eigen

Hunter, Alberta (Memphis, Tenn., 1 April 1895; *d* New York City, 17 Oct 1984). Singer and songwriter. After a singing career in Chicago, she moved to New York City in 1922, when Paramount Records recorded her composition "Down Hearted Blues," later made famous by Bessie Smith. Hunter performed on Broadway, in London, and with the United

Alberta Hunter

Service Organizations (USO) until 1956, when she left the entertainment industry to study nursing at the Young Women's Christian Association in Harlem. She then worked as a licensed practical nurse for 20 years at Goldwater Memorial Hospital but resumed her career as a performer in 1977 after being introduced to Barney Josephson, the owner of the Cookery, a restaurant and jazz club in Greenwich Village. In recognition of her success in the entertainment industry, Hunter received the Mayor's Award of Honor for Arts and Culture in 1983.

Frank C. Taylor with Gerald Cook, *Alberta Hunter: A Celebration in Blues* (New York: McGraw–Hill, 1987)

Val Ginter

Hunter College. College of the City University of New York. It began in 1869 as the Normal and High School for the Female Grammar Schools of the City of New York, renamed in the following year the Normal College of the City of New York and in 1914 Hunter College (after its first president, Thomas Hunter). From its inception the college operated a model school where prospective teachers could gain practical experience. The college held its first classes in rented space at Broadway and Fourth Street; a neo-Gothic building opened at 68th Street and Lexington Avenue in 1873. Overcrowding during the 1920s led to the opening of extension centers in Queens and Brooklyn (the Brooklyn Collegiate Center of Hunter College in the building of the Chamber of Commerce at Court and Livingston streets [1926]) and of a satellite campus in 1931 in northern Bronx (now Lehman College). By 1925 the college also offered evening classes at the freshman level open to all female high school graduates. After a fire at 68th Street the college operated temporarily out of rented space at 2 Park Avenue before opening a larger, modern building at 68th Street and Park Avenue in 1940; the repaired original structure became the home of Hunter High School. Two new towers were built during the presidency of Donna Shalala (1980–87). The college admitted only women until 1964, and as late as 1986 women received 74 percent of its undergraduate degrees and an even larger proportion of its master's degrees. In the twenty-first century Hunter College enrolled more than 21,000 students; its main campus remained at 659 Park Avenue. The college also operated two campus schools at 94th Street and Park Avenue for gifted children from pre-kindergarten to high school.

Samuel W. Patterson, *Hunter College: Eighty Five Years of Service* (New York: Lantern, 1955)

Selma Berrol

Hunter College High School. Secondary school founded in 1869 as the Female and Normal High School to prepare women for teaching through a combined high school and college program. One year later the institution changed its name to the Normal College of the City of New York, and in 1903 the secondary school and college were separated. In 1914 both the high school and college were renamed in honor of Thomas Hunter, the schools' first president, and in 1974 the school admitted its first male students. The school is publicly funded. Admission to the laboratory school for intellectually gifted students is determined by competitive examination in the sixth grade for its six-year secondary school program from grades seven to 12. Students must be residents of New York City to attend. The school has moved several times and has been located at 93rd Street and Amsterdam Avenue, 234 West 109th Street, 320 East 96th Street, 930 Lexington Avenue, and 466 Lexington Avenue. Since 1977 it has been at 94th Street between Park and Madison avenues and occupies the former Squadron A, Eighth Regiment Armory designed by John R. Thomas. The building is in the style of a medieval French fortress with square towers and round turrets with the facade facing Madison Avenue designated as a landmark in 1966. In the twenty-first century approximately 1200 students are enrolled. Notable alumni include soprano Martina Arroyo, writer Audre Lorde, and poet Diane di Prima.

Dianna Ng

Hunters Point. Neighborhood in northwestern Queens, lying within Long Island City; it is bounded to the north by 45th Avenue and abuts the East River and Newtown Creek. The land was owned in colonial times by Jacob Bennett, and after his death in 1817 it belonged to a parcel including all of Long Island City given over to his son-in-law George Hunter. The estate was sold after Hunter's death in 1825 to Jeremiah Johnson, a real estate agent from Brooklyn acting for Eliphalet Nott, the president of Union College in Schenectady, New York. In 1853 Nott engaged the developers Jonathan Crane and Charles Ely to lay out Hunters Point, and during the summer of the same year sand hills were leveled and swamps filled in. A map from 1858 shows only a few streets: 47th to 54th avenues, Vernon Boulevard, and Fifth Street. Development hastened after railroad service was extended by the Flushing Railroad (1854) and the Long Island Rail Road (1861); visitors and commuters traveled there, and hotels, saloons, and stores were soon built around the ferry terminal at Borden Avenue. St. Mary's Roman Catholic Church on Vernon Boulevard opened in 1869; the current church dates from 1887. Oil refineries and factories for varnish, ceramic pipe, and cooperage were active along the waterfront, where ships from Europe docked regularly. The Steinway Tunnels under the East River at Hunters Point were begun by William Steinway in 1892 as a trolley line. After several setbacks they opened in 1907 as the first connection between Manhattan and Queens, but they were not used regularly until being converted for subways in 1915 (now the No. 7 line).

The area became less popular as a residential neighborhood after the Queensboro Bridge opened in 1909 and industrialization increased. Local industry declined gradually after World War II. One block of row houses dating from the 1870s (45th Street between 21st and 23rd avenues) was designated a historic district in 1968. Public School 1, an 1892 Long Island City elementary school, was converted to artists' studios in 1976; in 2000 it became an affiliate of the Museum of Modern Art. Built across from the Queens County Court House (1876, rebuilt 1908), the 48-story Citicorp Building (1989) is the tallest building in New York City outside of Manhattan. In 1984 an ambitious plan was adopted for the development of the waterfront, but construction proceeded slowly. By 2002 an estimated 3300 industrial jobs were concentrated in 90 businesses, and the city encouraged other economic uses. In 2001 37 blocks were rezoned for high-density development, and in 2004 another rezoning, the Hunters Point Subdistrict, enlarged the commercial district around the Citicorp Building and facilitated additional residential construction. The massive Pennsylvania Railroad power plant near the waterfront was clumsily transformed into residences.

Jeffrey A. Kroessler, Vincent Seyfried

Huntington [née Hyatt], **Anna** (*b* Cambridge, Mass., 10 March 1876; *d* Redding, Conn., 4 Oct 1973). Sculptor. She studied sculpture in Boston and in 1902 moved to New York City to study at the Art Students League with Hermon MacNeil. She worked privately with Gutzon Borglum, whose expertise in equestrian sculpture was a formative influence. In 1906 she went to Paris for further training; there her sculpture of Joan of Arc on horseback won an honorable mention at the Paris Salon of 1910 (a full-sized bronze replica was installed at Riverside Drive and 93rd Street in 1918). In 1923 she married the railroad heir Archer Milton Huntington, founder and director of the Hispanic Society of America, for which she executed the bronze sculptures *El Cid Campeador* (1927, Hispanic Society Courtyard) and *José Martí* (1958–59, Central Park South and Sixth Avenue). She became the first female artist elected to the American Academy of Arts and Letters (1932), which mounted a major retrospective of her work (1936). Huntington was also a collector and advocate of contemporary American sculpture. Much of her private collection was installed at Brookgreen Gardens, the coastal estate in South Carolina that she purchased with her husband in 1930. She remained active as a figurative sculptor well into her 90s.

Doris E. Cook, *Woman Sculptor: Anna Hyatt Huntington, 1876–1973* (Hartford, Conn.: D. E. Cook, 1976)

Jan Seidler Ramirez

Huntington, Daniel (*b* New York City, 14 Oct 1816; *d* New York City, 18 April 1906). Painter and galvanizer of artists in New York City. He was principally a portraitist inspired to paint allegorical and didactic subjects, such as *Mercy's Dream* (1841), which he painted after a trip to Europe with Henry Peters Gray. In 1849 a group of leading artists and writers in New York City organized a show of his work at the Art Union Buildings. He attracted many prominent patrons during the 1850s, and after the Civil War he became the leading portraitist of the upper class in New York City. Huntington was president of both the National Academy of Design (1862–70, 1877–80) and the Century Association (1879–95) and a founder of the Metropolitan Museum of Art, of which he was a vice president in 1871–74 and 1876–1903.

Carrie Rebora Barratt

Hunts Point. Neighborhood in the southwestern Bronx (2000 pop. 46,824), bounded to the north by Westchester Avenue and the Bronx River, to the east by the Bronx River, and to the west by Prospect Avenue; it is bisected by the Bruckner Expressway and contains the residential neighborhood of Longwood. The area was once part of West Farms in lower Westchester County and was covered by large estates. It was annexed to New York City in 1874 and was developed with apartment buildings after a subway line to Manhattan was extended in 1904. During the following decades the population was predominantly Jewish along with a few German, Irish, and Italian immigrants; later it became largely black and Puerto Rican. During the 1960s, with housing deteriorating, businesses closing, and many white residents leaving for the suburbs, the neighborhood was beset by poverty, drugs, crime, arson, and abandoned buildings. In the mid-1960s, the city built the Hunts Point Terminal Market along the shores of the East and Bronx rivers to rehouse the antiquated produce markets of lower Manhattan. The largest produce market in the United States, the market was run by the city until 1986 when it came under the control of a merchants' cooperative. Neighborhood conditions improved during the 1990s as crime decreased; community organizations refurbished older apartment buildings and built many new units of owner-occupied row houses; and artists converted industrial lofts into housing and studio space.

Evelyn Gonzalez, *The Bronx* (New York: Columbia University Press, 2004)

See also Hunts Point Food Distribution Center.

Evelyn Gonzalez

Hunts Point Food Distribution Center [Hunts Point Market]. Largest food distribution center in the world. Covering 329 acres (133 hectares) of land jutting into the East River at the southern tip of the Bronx, it opened in 1967 as the central wholesale market for produce for the city, replacing the Washington Market in lower Manhattan. The distribution center, commonly called the Hunts Point Market, is actually three separate markets: the New York City Terminal Produce Cooperative Market, the Hunts Point Cooperative Market (joined 1974), and the new Fulton Fish Market (joined 2005). The first two are the world's biggest wholesalers in produce and meat, respectively, and the fish market is the largest wholesale fish market outside of Japan. The city owned the market until 1986, at which time the wholesale merchants themselves began to cooperatively own and operate it.

In the early twenty-first century the Hunts Point Distribution Center was distributing food to more than 30 million people in the Greater New York City area and beyond; it is a gigantic supermarket for the region. Much of the fresh food in restaurants and grocery stores, including produce, fish, and meat, passes through the wholesale market. The meat section has 1 million square feet (92,903 square meters) of refrigerated space, with more than 50 wholesalers. The revenues of the Terminal Produce Market surpass $2 billion annually; each year more than three billion pounds of fruits and vegetables are distributed to small groceries and restaurants. The Fulton Fish Market cost $80 million to build and covers 450,000 square feet (41,806 square meters) of space; its yearly revenue exceeds $1 billion.

Other food distributors and food service companies are also housed at Hunts Point. Many of the market companies are small, family-owned businesses, with some tracing their roots back to the original Washington Market. More than 25,000 people work at 800 businesses there, including food wholesalers, distributors, and processing businesses. Among the buyers are between 1500 and 1800 independent green grocers; restaurant owners pay purveyors to purchase goods. Produce is trucked in from almost every state across the country and arrives by air from more than 50 foreign countries.

Suzanne R. Wasserman

Hurok [Gurkov], **Sol(omon Israelovich)** (*b* Pogar, Russia, 9 April 1888; *d* New York City, 5 March 1974). Impresario. He moved to New York City from Russia in 1906 nearly penniless and for a while sold hardware and notions and took odd jobs, saving what money he could. In 1911 he arranged concerts for labor organizations and workers' clubs; in 1915 he became the manager of a series of Sunday evening concerts at the New York Hippodrome that featured such artists as Mischa Elman, Anna Pavlova, and Alma Gluck. For more than five decades he presented some of the world's most distinguished orchestras, concert artists, ballet and theater companies, and folk ensembles. He sponsored the first American performances of several groups from the Soviet Union, including the Bolshoi Ballet and the Moiseyev Dance Company. On 26 January 1972 his offices at 56th Street and Sixth Avenue were firebombed, killing one employee and injuring 13. His life was the subject of the motion picture *Tonight We Sing* (1953). Hurok wrote *Impresario: A Memoir* (1946) and *S. Hurok Presents: A Memoir of the Dance World* (1953).

Harlow Robinson, *The Last Impresario: The Life, Times, and Legacy of Sol Hurok* (New York: Viking, 1994)

See also American Ballet Theatre.

Allen J. Share

Hurston, Zora Neale (*b* Notasulga, Ala., 7 Jan 1891; *d* Fort Pierce, Fla., 28 Jan 1960). Novelist. She attended Howard University and Barnard College, where she studied cultural anthropology with Franz Boas. A prominent figure of the Harlem Renaissance who called herself the "queen of the Niggerati," she worked and socialized with such figures as Langston Hughes, Carl Van Vechten, and Alain Locke. Her first published work of fiction was the short story "Drenched in Light"

Zora Neale Hurston

(later retitled "Isis"), which appeared in 1925 in *Opportunity;* her novel *Their Eyes Were Watching God* (1937) is generally considered her most accomplished work. She lived in New York City until 1949, first on 131st Street and then West 66th Street. For most of her life she had financial difficulties, and she died impoverished and unrecognized. Her work became the subject of renewed interest during the 1980s.

Mary Lyons, *Sorrow's Kitchen: The Life and Folklore of Zora Neale Hurston* (New York: Charles Scribner's Sons, 1990)

Thea Arnold

Hussar. British frigate. The ship struck Pot Rock and sank near Hell Gate in November 1780. Reports that the *Hussar* carried gold to pay the British army led to a number of salvage attempts into the twentieth century. The exact location of the wreck is unknown.

Hutchinson [née Marbury], **Anne** (*b* Alford, England, 1591; *d* near Pelham Bay [now in the Bronx], 1643). Religious leader. She settled in Boston to seek religious freedom and under the instruction of the Puritan divine John Cotton began teaching groups of women in her home. Her concept of the indwelling of the Holy Spirit was treated as antinomian heresy that threatened the moral structure of the colony. After her claim to direct revelations of the Spirit was repudiated by Cotton, she was excommunicated, tried, and banished in 1637. With her husband William Hutchinson she formed a community in Rhode Island; his death in 1642 and growing religious controversy led her to move with her children to a riverbank in Dutch territory adjoining Pelham Bay (near what is now the Boston Road Bridge). Soon after, she and all but one of her children were killed in an Indian raid. The river was named in Hutchinson's honor, as was the parkway that later ran along it.

Elizabeth Ilgenfritz, *Anne Hutchinson* (New York: Chelsea House, 1991)

Eileen W. Lindner

Huxtable (née Landman), **Ada Louise** (*b* New York City, 14 March 1921). Architecture writer and critic. She graduated from Hunter College in 1941 and was a curatorial assistant for architecture and design at the Museum of Modern Art from 1946 to 1950. For the next three years she was a contributing editor to *Progressive Architecture and Art in America* before being named the first architecture critic at the *New York Times*, a position she held from 1963 to 1982. She was awarded the first Pulitzer Prize for distinguished criticism in 1970. In the twenty-first century she continued to write architectural pieces for newspapers and to publish books.

Jessica Montesano

H. W. Wilson Company. Print and Web resource company. Founded by Halsey William Wilson in 1898, it was a product of Morris and Wilson, a company that Wilson and his college roommate established in 1889 as a book-selling business at the University of Minnesota. Morris sold his share of the company to Wilson, and as Wilson found difficulty with restocking books, having to look through individual publisher's guides, he had the idea to create a comprehensive catalogue of new books that remained current each year; this led to the *Cumulative Book Index.* In 1911 he moved his business to suburban White Plains, New York, and six years later to its permanent home in the Bronx at 950 University Avenue. The company expanded adjacent to its original location in 1929. In the twenty-first century the company publishes several indexes and reference guides, including the *Readers' Guide to Periodical Literature* (1901), which are known as the "green books" in libraries nationwide; *Book Review Digest* (1905); and most recently the *General Science Index* (1978). It also has several online reference databases.

Jessica Montesano

Hyde, Edward, Viscount Cornbury (*b* England, 28 Nov 1661; *d* London, 31 March 1723). Colonial governor. A first cousin to Mary II and Queen Anne, he was appointed royal governor of both New York and New Jersey, taking up residence at the fort in New York City in May 1702. An experienced military officer (colonel of the royal regiment of dragoons), he strengthened New York City's defenses during Queen Anne's War, placing some 38 cannon at the Battery. While initially calming the fevered politics of New York Colony, he eventually faced a rising opposition in New Jersey, and later New York. Led by Lewis Morris (1671–1746), a skilled politician and propagandist, his opponents charged him with financial malpractice (subsequently disproved) and transvestism (on hearsay alone). When replaced as governor in December 1708, he was arrested for debt by local creditors. He returned to England in 1710 on acceding to the title third earl of Clarendon. After successfully defending his administration and reputation, he was appointed to high offices by Queen Anne and became a leader of the House of Lords. His wife, Katherine O'Brien (1673–1706), died in New York City and is buried in Trinity Church Yard.

Patricia Bonomi, *The Lord Cornbury Scandal: The Politics of Reputation in British America* (Chapel Hill: University of North Carolina Press, 2000)

James E. Mooney

Hylan, John F(rancis) (*b* Hunter, N.Y., 20 April 1869; *d* New York City, 12 Jan 1936). Mayor. While working as a motorman on an elevated line and attending law school he became friendly with John McCooey, who later became the Democratic boss of Kings County. After serving in several judicial positions in Brooklyn (1906–17) he was proposed as a mayoral candidate by McCooey and William Randolph Hearst. Supported by Tammany Hall, he defeated the incumbent, John Purroy Mitchel, in 1917 and was reelected in 1921. He inveighed against the "transit interests" but was widely considered Hearst's puppet and a man of minimal ability; he nonetheless won the admiration of Fiorello H. La Guardia. Hylan lost the Democratic mayoral primary in 1925 to James J. Walker, who later named him a justice of the Children's Court. Hylan Boulevard in Staten Island is named in his honor.

John F. Hylan, 1920

See also SUBWAYS.

Frank Vos

Hynes, Charles J(oseph) [Joe] (*b* Brooklyn, 28 May 1935). Kings County district attorney and author. After receiving a BA and law degree from St. John's University, he entered public service. In the 1970s he led the rackets bureau of the Brooklyn district attorney's office and served as special state prosecutor to investigate nursing home fraud. In 1980–82 he was New York City's fire commissioner. Governor Mario M. Cuomo named Hynes special state prosecutor for the city criminal justice system in 1985 and two years later named him special prosecutor in the HOWARD BEACH case concerning the death of Michael Griffith, a black man whom whites chased onto the Belt Parkway. Hynes then wrote an account, *Incident at Howard Beach: The Case for Murder* (1990), with Bob Drury. In 1989 Hynes won the first of five terms as Kings County (Brooklyn) district attorney. He also ran unsuccessfully in Democratic primary contests for New York State attorney general in 1978 and 1994 and for governor in 1998.

His district attorney's office is no stranger to controversy. Early in Hynes's tenure, the prosecution of a racial-bias crime involving the death of an Orthodox Jewish student in Crown Heights and a police corruption scandal were both turned over to federal prosecutors amid controversy. Hynes has voiced opposition to the death penalty but has demanded it in a number of cases. His gun policy included cash-for-weapons buyback programs, jail for those arrested with a loaded firearm, and no plea bargaining in cases involving illegal firearms. In the early twenty-first century, Hynes took on the Brooklyn Democratic organization, winning convictions against its chairman, Clarence Norman, Jr.

Hynes pioneered social-services strategies against crime. He established the Crimes Against Children Bureau, the School Advocacy Bureau and Truancy Reduction program, and the ComALERT program to support those on parole or probation. He also developed the Domestic Violence Bureau and the Family Justice Center, which are housed together so that victims of domestic abuse receive services under a single roof. His Drug Treatment Alternative-to-Prisons program became a model for similar efforts nationwide. In 2007 he published a novel, *Triple Homicide.*

Cathy Alexander

I

Iakovos, Archbishop [Coucouzis, Demetrios A.] (*b* Imbros, Greece, 29 July 1911; *d* Stamford, Conn., 10 April 2005). Religious leader. Coucouzis took the name Iakovos on becoming a priest in 1940, shortly after moving to the United States. He served at the Cathedral of the Holy Trinity in New York City before becoming archbishop of the Greek Orthodox Archdiocese of North and South America (headquartered at 8–10 East 79th Street; now the Greek Orthodox Archdiocese of America). In 1959 he became the first Orthodox leader to meet with a pope in 350 years, and in 1965 he marched with Dr. Martin Luther King, Jr., in Selma, Alabama. He retired in 1996.

Kate Lauber

IATSE. See International Alliance of Theatrical Stage Employees and Moving Picture Machine Operators of the United States and Canada.

IBEW. See International Brotherhood of Electrical Workers.

IBM. See International Business Machines.

Icahn Stadium. Track and field stadium located on Randalls Island across the East River from 125th Street in Manhattan. It opened in 2005 on the site of the former Downing Stadium, which was torn down in 2003. The facility cost $42 million to construct and was paid for by private and public funding in equal amounts. It hosts high school, college, and professional meets throughout the track season as well as free youth sports programs for children from Harlem and the South Bronx. The stadium has seating for 5000, and its modern Mondo surface track made it one of the fastest tracks in the nation in the first decade of the twenty-first century; Jamaican sprinter Usain Bolt broke the 100-meter world record on it in May 2008 before he won three gold medals and reset the world record at the Beijing Olympics that summer.

David White

ice harvesting. The harvesting of ice from rivers became an important part of the economy of New York City after Frederic Tudor in 1805 arranged a profitable shipment to Martinique of ice weighing 130 tons (118 metric tons). Shipments from the Port of New York to the American South, the Caribbean, and Asia increased in number from five in 1816 with a total weight of 1200 tons (1088 metric tons) to 363 in 1856 with a total weight of 146,000 tons (132,400 metric tons). A number of firms supplied ice to local residents, including the Knickerbocker Ice Company (1855), the Washington Ice Company, and the New York City Ice Company. Most households maintained deep wells to preserve their supply, which they stored in large blocks insulated by sawdust and hay to minimize melting. By 1882 the Knickerbocker Ice Company was the city's largest ice firm, with storage facilities at West 43rd Street, West 20th Street, Bank Street, 432 Canal Street, Delancey Street, East 33rd Street, 92nd Street, and East 128th Street. The city's annual consumption of ice was estimated at nearly 1.9 million tons (1.7 million metric tons), some of which was sold by icemen from 1500 horse-drawn carts. Icemen were often Italian immigrants who became known for the colorful manner in which they peddled their goods. The winter harvesting season offered a supplemental income for 15,000 to 20,000 farmers who cut, dragged, and delivered ice from the Hudson River and lakes upstate to icehouses on riverbanks. In 1896 Charles W. Morse (1856–1933), an ice magnate from Maine, acquired control over most of the city's large-scale ice operations, which he incorporated

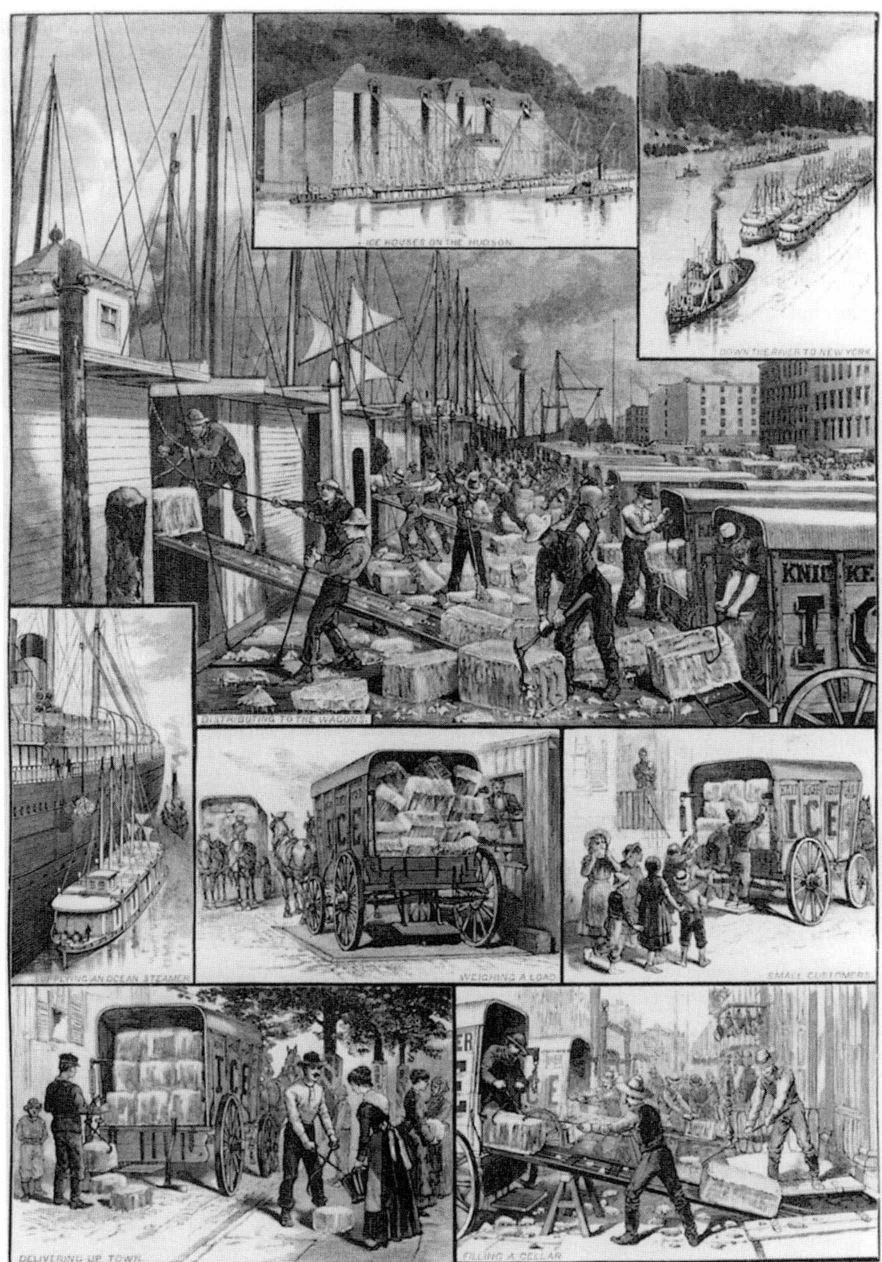

Illustration for "Ice Industry of New York," Harper's Weekly, *30 August 1884*

as the American Ice Company. His trust became the target in 1899 of antitrust proceedings by New York State that also implicated Mayor Robert A. Van Wyck and Richard Croker, who owned large amounts of stock in the company. Instead of contesting the charges, Morse moved his operations to Chicago, which as the center of the nation's meatpacking business was its largest ice market. The growing availability of refrigeration crippled the ice trade by the 1920s, but at least 90 firms continued to harvest and deliver ice until World War II.

Richard O. Cummings, *The American Ice Harvests: A Historical Study in Technology, 1800–1918* (Berkeley: University of California Press, 1949)

Marc Ferris

ice hockey. Ice hockey was first played in New York City in the late nineteenth century, when the best-known team was the St. Nicholas Athletic Club, an amateur team that regularly defeated teams from Canada. The first professional team was the New York Americans, which entered the National Hockey League (NHL) in 1925; it changed its name to the Brooklyn Americans to attract fans but suspended operations on 28 September 1942. The New York Rangers, formed in 1926, won the Stanley Cup in 1928, 1933, 1940, and 1994. During the 1970s the Greenleafs won four consecutive Metro Junior championships. Other teams in the city have included the Rovers, the Slapshots, and two members of the World Hockey Association—the Raiders (1972) and the Golden Blades (1973–74). As of the early twenty-first century a few city schools fielded competitive ice hockey teams and, in addition to extensive youth and adult programs at Chelsea Piers, New York City was home to a growing number of recreational programs for adults, and a handful of well-respected and affordable community youth programs had become well established; these included the Riverbank State Park Rangers, Ice Hockey in Harlem at Central Park's Lasker Rink, and the Coney Island–based New York Stars, all of which emphasized character building and academic success in addition to physical fitness, fun, and teamwork.

See also Ice skating.

James Duplacey, Holly Cronin

ice skating. City planners opened the first organized ice-skating rink in the United States in New York City in 1858, at the southeast corner of Central Park. Skating soon became popular among members of the upper and middle classes, who bought thousands of skates every year, ranging from cheaply made models to expensive imports from England and Germany. Conover and Walker, a hardware store at 474 Broadway, was one of the first businesses to sell imported skates, and Alexander Macmillan at 702 Broadway was the city's foremost skate manufacturer. Macmillan's iron and steel skates cost between $13 and $30; many New Yorkers fashioned homemade wooden skates for much less. City officials at first segregated the pond in Central Park by sex, but one intrepid female skater infiltrated the men's rink in 1860, and in 1870 separate areas for men and women were eliminated; the participation of women in ice skating helped to remove barriers that excluded them from other sports.

As the popularity of skating increased, members of the upper class formed clubs and opened private rinks. The New York Skating Club, formed in January 1863 with 150 members, stressed the gracefulness of the sport and organized events at some of the many ponds on the East Side of Manhattan, including the Fifth Avenue Pond (between Fifth and Madison avenues and 57th and 59th streets) and Beekman's Ponds (between Fifth and Third avenues and 57th to 65th streets). Brooklyn also had many sites for skating, including Union Pond in Williamsburg and Washington Pond at Fifth Avenue and Third Street. The stockbroker Leonard Jerome flooded a pond for skating at his famous racetrack in the Bronx in 1870, but by then interest in skating had waned. After it revived toward the end of the century the St. Nicholas Rink opened in December 1895 at 66th Street and Ninth Avenue, and the New York Skating Club was re-formed as the New York Skate Club in December 1916. Indoor rinks opened during the 1920s, the most popular of which was the opulent Iceland Rink at 304 West 50th Street, which featured an orchestra, a restaurant, lockers, and annual ice carnivals and pageants. After World War II skaters patronized such private facilities as Skyrink, on the 16th story of a building at 450 West 33rd Street, but this had closed by the 1990s.

Despite the disappearance of ponds throughout the metropolitan area, ice skating continued to thrive through the construction of numerous public and private rinks. New York City is home to the outdoor rink at Rockefeller Center, which opened on Christmas Day 1936 and is probably the most famous skating rink in the world. Also often featured in films set in New York City is the picturesque, pond-shaped Wollman Memorial Rink in southeastern Central Park, built in 1949 with funds donated by Kate Wollman in memory of her parents. Named in her honor, the Kate Wollman Rink in Brooklyn's Prospect Park opened in 1961, having been built under the auspices of Parks Commissioner Robert Moses. After four decades serving millions of skaters, Prospect Park launched a campaign to replace its rink with a state-of-the-art year-round facility, Lakeside Center, which is slated for completion in 2011. The Lasker sisters sponsored the controversial 1966 construction of the Lasker Rink and Pool overlooking the Harlem Meer in northern Central Park. In the early 1990s Central Park's two rinks were purchased by the developer Donald Trump, who revitalized the ice surfaces and took over management of the newly coined Trump Wollman and Trump Lasker facilities. Completed in 1991, Riverbank State Park on the Hudson River at 145th Street features a covered full-size ice hockey rink that is frequently used for public skating sessions. In 1994 work began on a pair of indoor hockey rinks named the Sky Rink at Chelsea Piers, which remained Manhattan's only year-round skating facility in 2009. Beginning in 2006 Citibank sponsored the Pond at Bryant Park, a free rink in midtown that is popular during the holidays but ends the skating season early to make way for late-January Fashion Week festivities in the park. During

Skating in Central Park

the early twenty-first century ice skating continued to increase in popularity, as evidenced by the 2008 revival of Seaport Ice at South Street Seaport and launch of the Polar Rink, a synthetic skating surface at the American Museum of Natural History. In 2009 work began on restoring Greenpoint, Brooklyn's McCarren Park Pool, a section of which will serve as an outdoor ice rink during the winter season.

Marc Ferris, Holly Cronin

Idlewild International Airport. Name used from 1948 to 1963 for JFK International Airport.

ILGWU. See International Ladies' Garment Workers' Union.

Illustrated Daily News. Original name of the Daily News.

Il Progresso Italo-Americano. Daily Italian-language newspaper. It was launched in 1880 in Little Italy by Carlo Barsotti to publish news of interest to Italian immigrants. Its circulation reached 400,000 during the 1930s and 1940s, owing to the prominent role of Italy in world affairs. After several changes of ownership in the early 1980s, the newspaper became embroiled in a labor dispute with its employees, 40 of whom left to launch a competing daily newspaper called *Oggi*. *Il Progresso* ceased publication in 1988.

Leslie Gourse

Imagine. See Strawberry Fields.

Imbert, Anthony (*b* France, ?1794; *d* New York City, 21 Aug 1834). Lithographer. He probably arrived in the city in 1824, established one of the first lithography firms in the United States at 79 Murray Street, and produced a large amount of lithography of high quality. Early in his career he made lithographs of various fine-art images. Two of his most notable works were Cadwallader D. Colden's *Memoir* (1826), which depicted the opening ceremonies at the Erie Canal and contained illustrations by several artists, and Alexander Jackson Davis's *Public Buildings* (1827), the poor sales of which prompted Imbert to produce cheaper, popular works for a middle-class audience, including sheet music, portraits, caricatures, and notably a series of prints titled "Life in New York."

Wendy Shadwell

immigration, 1624–1900. New York City has long been the premier immigrant city in North America: settled as a Dutch and later a British colony; transformed by millions of Irish, Germans, Italians, Jews, and others in the nineteenth and the early twentieth centuries; and transformed again after World War II by immigrants from the Caribbean, Latin America, the Middle East and, especially, Asia.

The first European settlers in what was then known as New Amsterdam were Walloons, Romance-speaking settlers of Germanic and Celtic origin, who went there in 1624 under the sponsorship of the Dutch West India Company. During the next few decades French Huguenots, Dutch, English, and Germans joined them. Supported by liberal Dutch policies toward immigration, New Amsterdam soon became the most culturally diverse European colony in North America. In 1643, when the population was about 500, a French Jesuit identified 18 languages spoken in the city. By the 1680s, after New Amsterdam had become the British colony of New York, the governor noted that there were "religions of all sorts, one church of England, several Presbiterians and Independents, Quakers and Anabaptists of Severall sects, [and] some Jews." The latter arrived from the West Indies as well as from Europe in the last decades of the seventeenth century. The colony was also shaped by ethnic and class conflicts, such as Leisler's Rebellion (1689–91), led by a German-born merchant who championed Dutch artisans and small shopkeepers against the local aristocracy of English and Dutch landlords and merchants.

As the city became the leading port in the nation late in the eighteenth century, it grew rapidly and remained culturally and ethnically diverse. The proportion of Africans rose steadily (reaching a peak of 20.9 percent by 1746), and slave rebellions broke out in 1712 and 1741. At the first census (1790), the city was the second largest in the colonies (after Philadelphia): of its 33,131 inhabitants, most were of English or Dutch descent; slightly less than one-third were Scottish, Irish, or both; and many of the rest were German, French, or Welsh. Some immigrants, such as Alexander Hamilton, who was born in the West Indies, came to seek their fortune in New York not from Europe but from the Caribbean and South America.

By the early nineteenth century economic conditions in much of northern and western Europe led increasing numbers to leave their homelands: population increased, depressions recurred, families subdivided their farms for younger generations into plots too small for subsistence, larger farms run as businesses replaced small ones, and factories replaced handcraft workshops. Crop failures and other agricultural crises became a constant affliction: for example, British land policies in Ireland and a devastating potato famine from 1845 to 1847 led to severe hardship. Revolutions and religious persecution also led to emigration. And countless young men and a few women left their native lands in search of adventure.

The opening of the Erie Canal in 1825 and the growth of New York City as a major world seaport and center for manufacturing created a tremendous need for labor. Between 1815 and 1915, about 33 million people moved to the United States from all over the world, three-quarters of them through the Port of New York. Irish and German Catholics made up the greatest numbers, and their presence in a city that was still strongly Protestant and Anglo-Saxon led to conflicts over temperance, city government, and the religious orientation of public education. Nativism, strongly influenced by anti-Catholicism, became an organized political movement. Led by such figures as Butcher Bill Poole, gangs of nativist brawlers fought often with Irish gangs like the Plug Uglies and the Dead Rabbits. In response, Catholic immigrants organized under the leadership of Bishop (later Archbishop) John Hughes, who opposed nativists with stinging oratory and shrewd political tactics. Class and racial animosity reached a peak during the draft riots of 1863. Protest by Irish immigrants against the inequities of the new Civil War conscription law soon unleashed longstanding hostilities toward both the wealthy and poor African Americans. About 119 people were killed, including 11 African Americans; most of the other victims were rioters.

Almost half of all employed immigrants worked in the clothing industry or as manual laborers, servants, cooks, waiters, and household help. Irish immigrants arrived with less money than most other groups, and larger numbers of them took unskilled work or became domestic servants. About two-fifths of all employed immigrants worked as craftspeople or in factories. Germans and other immigrants had been cabinetmakers, jewelers, tailors, shoemakers, bakers, and carpenters in their native countries, and some used capital that they had brought with them or accumulated to open their own shops, which often catered to their own ethnic group. Intense economic rivalry existed within immigrant groups as well as between immigrant groups and the native-born. Often Irish workers competed with African Americans for employment on the waterfront. In the late 1830s and 1840s Irish and German workers were accused of undercutting the wages of American-born laborers, and the recruitment of immigrants as strikebreakers led to violent clashes. Some immigrants helped shape the labor movement by joining American trade unions or forming their own. During the 1850s German labor leaders instilled in the labor movement a militant class consciousness and supported radical and socialist unions.

In the 1850s about two million immigrants moved through the Port of New York. Although most soon traveled to other parts of the country, others settled in the city because they found work or could not afford to travel any farther. Those who stayed often moved to the lower wards close to the docks, factories, foundries, and older immigrant neighborhoods, where they sought work, shelter, and kinship. In the area south of 14th Street they crowded into cellars, tiny apartments, and newly built tenements. New immigrant neighborhoods took shape: the central and lower wards near the southeastern tip of Manhattan were largely Irish; Kleindeutschland, or Little Germany, lay along the East River between 14th and Grand streets; and there were enclaves of English, Scots, Welsh, Dutch, Jews, French, Italians, Scandinavians, and Latin Americans. But all immigrant neighborhoods were heterogeneous: different nationalities often lived on the same street. In the 1850s a few people left the lower wards for Williamsburg and other parts of Brooklyn, upper Manhattan, and Hoboken, New Jersey. Immigrant neighborhoods often became slums owing to overcrowding, poverty, and the lack of basic services such as sewers and running water; the Five Points was the most notorious slum in the nation. Tuberculosis, pneumonia, and scrofula afflicted many immigrants, and epidemics of cholera, typhoid, and typhus occurred frequently, especially in the poorest neighborhoods. An inefficient city government, insufficient garbage and sewage removal, and an inadequate public health system were unprepared to respond to these problems. Consequently, immigrants suffered much higher rates of disease and death than did the American-born.

Immigrants at South Ferry, ca *1900*

Immigrant neighborhoods had strong social networks, often formed in fraternal organizations, saloons, firehouses, political clubs, music halls, military companies, benevolent societies, beer gardens, theaters, sporting clubs, and churches. German and Irish immigrants supported the Democratic Party largely because it was opposed to nativism, temperance, and Sunday blue laws. In return for their support, Tammany Hall (the Democratic Party organization in Manhattan) offered them work, food, shelter, minor political offices, and camaraderie. Through membership in fire companies and gangs the Irish became politically powerful and by the 1860s controlled Tammany Hall. By the last quarter of the nineteenth century the Irish and the Germans had become well established in the economic and political life of the city.

After 1855 the city created an official immigration entry center at Castle Garden, an unused fortification off the southern tip of Manhattan. A new entity, the New York State Board of Commissioners of Emigration, initiated procedures at Castle Garden, eliminating most of the exorbitant charges and fraudulent practices that had troubled earlier immigrants. Few restrictions on entering the United States existed, although over the decades nativists tried to increase the residency requirement for naturalized citizenship from five years to either 14 or 21. The open-door policy began to shift with the Chinese Exclusion Act of 1882, which barred Chinese laborers from entering the United States and prevented those already in the country from becoming citizens.

By mid-century New York City was the largest city in the western hemisphere. Its population stood at 622,924 in 1855 and included immigrants from most nations of the world, who accounted for more than half the total: 175,735 residents were from Ireland, 95,986 from Germany, 32,135 from Great Britain, and 21,790 from other countries including France, Prussia, Poland, Italy, and Canada.

A second phase of immigration began in the late 1880s, as Russian and Polish Jews as well as southern Italians, Greeks, Poles, Hungarians, Romanians, Bohemians, and others from southern and eastern Europe fled changes similar to those that had beset northern and western Europe in the first half of the century. In addition to dramatic increases in the population, worldwide competition in agricultural production, and the economic displacement wrought by industrialization, a blight ravaged vineyards in southern Italy and led thousands of farm laborers and tenants to leave the land for cities. As European states removed restrictions on emigration, millions left. Political upheaval and religious persecution forced out others, such as the millions of Jews who fled pogroms in eastern Europe and the Russian Pale of Settlement.

Between 1880 and 1919 more than 23 million people immigrated to the United States, and of these, 17 million entered through New York City. Russian Jews and Italians made up the two largest groups. Unlike many immigrants of previous years who had moved to farmlands or smaller towns, most who immigrated during this period settled in cities, including five of six Russian Jews and three of four Italians, and a large number remained in New York City, where opportunities for employment were plentiful. As the largest port in the nation, the city provided employment along the waterfront. It was also a center for light manufacturing and supported a huge garment industry, in which immigrants, especially Jews and Italians, often found work. Families sewed garments at home, and young

Foreign-Born Population within the Present Boundaries of New York City by County, in Absolute Numbers and as a Percentage of Total Population, 1860–1890

	New York		Kings		Queens		Westchester		Richmond	
1860	386,345	47	109,077	39	14,090	25	27,823	27	8,575	33
1870	419,094	44	153,811	36	19,075	25	37,344	28	10,113	30
1880	478,670	39	188,312	31	22,001	24	23,710	21	10,961	28
1890	639,943	42	272,895	32	35,146	27	38,392	26	14,779	28

Source: U.S. Bureau of the Census

Compiled by James Bradley

Italian and Jewish women worked in sweatshops and small factories, supervised by Italian and Jewish foremen and tailors. Two-thirds of Jewish immigrants were skilled laborers (compared with 20 percent of other groups) and practiced trades such as butchery, carpentry, shoemaking, and tailoring. The expansion of the city's infrastructure also led to a demand for construction workers and manual laborers. Although immigrant workers were frequently exploited, most were upwardly mobile and remained in the city.

The struggle of immigrant workers in the garment industry helped shape the U.S. labor movement in the early twentieth century. The International Ladies' Garment Workers' Union had only 2000 members in 1909, when more than 15,000 shirtwaist makers, most of whom were young Jewish and Italian women, went on strike in more than 500 factories. The strike lasted for four months and galvanized the union movement; in 1910 between 50,000 and 70,000 Jewish and Italian tailors in the cloak-making industry went on strike, eventually securing the union shop. The abuse of workers in sweatshops became a matter of public concern after a fire at the Triangle Shirtwaist factory (see Triangle Shirtwaist fire) in 1911 killed 146 women, mostly young immigrants. The fire and labor strikes helped stimulate interest in the union movement.

Immigrants of the late nineteenth century usually settled in ethnic neighborhoods. A "little Italy" took form in the area of Mulberry Street and another near East 110th Street, and a sprawling Jewish neighborhood covered previously German sections of the Lower East Side, which became a district of theaters, foreign-language newspaper publishers, dancehalls, churches and synagogues, nickelodeons, saloons, coffeehouses, and ethnic and religious festivals. These immigrant neighborhoods forged ethnic identities out of disparate regional ties. It was here, not in Italy, for example, that Sicilians, Calabrese, and Neapolitans began to see themselves as Italians. Tens of thousands of immigrants soon moved to the expanding working-class neighborhoods of upper Manhattan, the Bronx, and Brooklyn (accessible by the Brooklyn Bridge after 1883). About this time a Chinatown evolved in lower Manhattan, but it remained small and predominantly male owing to the Chinese Exclusion Act, which prevented men who had previously settled in the United States from bringing wives to join them.

An immigration gateway opened on Ellis Island in 1892. Although the United States still welcomed most immigrants, over the next decade the federal government put in place additional restrictions, including replacing the New York Board of Emigration with federal jurisdiction, enforcing regulations that made steamship companies responsible for returning passengers rejected by U.S. inspectors, and adding additional excluded categories, such as polygamists, people suffering from contagious diseases, and anarchists and other political radicals.

Many Americans were alarmed by immigration during the late nineteenth century. Because some believed that current immigrants were more difficult to assimilate than earlier immigrants had been, they introduced formal programs of Americanization. In addition to academic subjects, the New York City's public schools taught punctuality, the value of hard work, and the superiority of the "American way." Fearing that their traditions would be undermined, some immigrants sent their children to parochial schools or to classes taught in their native language. Settlement houses such as the Henry Street Settlement and Greenwich House, in addition to attempting to eradicate some of the worst conditions in immigrant neighborhoods, also initiated assimilation programs. In response to such programs a few immigrants abandoned their own culture while others held firmly to it, but by the second generation an amalgamation with American culture had occurred. Vaudeville performers, songwriters of Tin Pan Alley, and operators of nickelodeons were often immigrants or the children of immigrants, and by introducing popular entertainment of an ethnic character they gained national audiences.

Robert Ernst, *Immigrant Life in New York City, 1825–1863* (New York: Columbia University Press, 1949); Sidney I. Pomerantz, *New York: An American City, 1783–1803: A Study of Urban Life* (New York: Columbia University Press, 1938; 2nd edn 1965); Thomas Kessner, *The Golden Door: Italian and Jewish Immigrant Mobility in New York City, 1880–1915* (New York: Oxford University Press, 1977); David M. Reimers, *Still the Golden Door: The Third World Comes to America* (New York: Columbia University Press, 1992)

Carol Groneman

immigration, 1900–present. At the turn of the twentieth century the ethnic makeup of New York City's population became increasingly diverse and large. In 1907 the number of immigrants was almost twice what it had been in 1882, and since then the proportion of all immigrants from northern and western Europe had declined from 87 percent to 19 percent. Immigrants in the city made up 41 percent of the total population in 1910, a peak for the rest of the century. Growing numbers of young men (sometimes called "birds of passage") moved to the United States to work for a few years before returning to their native countries, which about 20 to 30 percent of Italian, Hungarian, Greek, and Slavic immigrants did each year. Smaller numbers of Chinese lived in isolation in Chinatown; only 6321 were recorded in 1900.

Local politics began to take recent immigrants into account. Irish Democrats retained control of the patronage system and with other political operators recognized the advantages of gaining the support of the new immigrants, whose votes were soon sought by the Republican, Socialist, and Socialist Labor parties and by various reform coalitions. Although Irish Democrats continued to dominate Tammany Hall, during the first decade of the century the Lower East Side was presided over by Jewish district leaders, assembly and city representatives, and local judges.

Nearly 40 percent of the city's population was foreign born in 1920, and immigrants and their children made up a majority of the city's people. Russian Jews, the largest foreign-born group, numbered 480,000; there were 391,000 Italians, almost as many as the Irish-born and German-born combined. Half to two-thirds of the southern Italians and two-thirds of the Slavs living in the city in 1920 were women, suggesting that families from southern and eastern Europe were moving to the United States to settle permanently.

Like others before them, immigrants of the early twentieth century were blamed for poverty, filth, disease, and crime in the slums. They were also subjected to social theories of race fashionable at the turn of the century: it was argued that nationalities possessed different traits, and that Anglo-Saxon characteristics risked being overwhelmed by southern and eastern European ones, which were considered inferior. The results of this hostility were new laws and policies to restrict the incoming migrants. In 1907 a gentleman's agreement was negotiated by the U.S. Department of State to end direct immigration between the United States and Japan. During World War I the government played to fears of "mongrelization" as a means of strengthening national solidarity.

German Americans were hurt by pressure to end what was called hyphenated Americanism, and their culture was weakened from attacks by the government and such campaigns as one to rename sauerkraut "liberty cabbage" during the war. But some intellectuals and writers in the city tended to esteem immigrants. Horace Kallen endorsed cultural pluralism and argued that compulsory assimilation was inconsistent with American democracy. Randolph Bourne wrote that immigrants could forge a dynamic federation of cultures in the United States. Israel Zangwill argued that immigrants should abandon their native characteristics and join forces to create a superior American nationality; his play *The Melting Pot* enjoyed a long run in the city in 1909, although the metaphor of its title was later criticized as assimilationist.

A depression after World War I, the Red Scare, and the fear of an influx of immigrants led to the passage of laws restricting immigration. Quotas were set in proportion to the size of each country's contribution to the total population of the United States in 1920. As finally put into place in 1929, a limit of 150,000

Selected Countries of Birth of the Foreign-Born Population of the Cities of New York and Brooklyn, 1855–1890, and of New York City, 1900–2000

	1855	1860	1870	1880	1890	1900	1910	1920	1930
Africa	50	24		111	213	357			
Asia[1]	75	89		48	208	925			
Australia		64		253	474	484			987
Austria[2]	376	533	3,078	5,371	28,686	71,427	190,237	126,739	127,169
Belgium	223	252		723	819	1,221		3,467	
Canada	4,586	5,694	7,307	11,367	14,295	21,926	26,072	25,271	39,622
Central America[3]				29	183	920			
China				870	2,548	6,080			
Cuba				2,073		2,011		2,815	
Czechoslovakia[4]				8,223	8,233	15,005		26,437	35,318
Denmark	439	532		1,910	3,334	5,621	7,989	9,092	11,096
England[5]	35,324	34,697	45,275	49,988	62,400	68,836	78,135	71,404	78,003
Europe[6]				211	4,325	223			
Finland						3,733	7,409	10,240	13,224
France	7,326	6,940	10,306	11,846	12,937	14,755	18,265	23,020	23,285
Germany	116,691	135,883	191,328	218,821	305,521	322,343	278,114	194,154	237,588
Greece			49	78	301	1,309	8,038	21,455	27,182
Hungary			591	4,182	12,885	31,516	76,625	64,393	59,883
India			47	125	185	250			
Ireland	232,488	218,477	280,219	277,409	275,156	275,102	252,662	203,450	192,810
Northern Ireland									27,821
Italy	1,039	1,067	3,019	13,411	49,514	145,433	340,765	390,832	440,250
Japan			5	21	164	311			
Lithuania									
Mexico	81	111	86	168	218	282			
Netherlands	971	1,059	2,011	2,848	2,011	2,608	4,191	4,750	5,335
Norway	351	355	673	1,767	6,448	11,387	22,280	24,500	38,130
Poland	1,276	1,357	2,602	9,521	8,646	32,873		145,679	238,339
Portugal	224	153	146	191	169	277			
Romania						10,499	33,584	38,139	46,750
Russia/ Soviet Union[7]	163	369	1,224	4,760	52,187	155,201	484,189	479,797	442,431
Scotland	11,085	9,318		13,365	18,569	19,836	23,115	21,545	38,535
South America[8]	221	238	307	570	721	995		5,742	14,268
Spain	501	527	682	1,048	1,413	1,491		10,980	13,992
Sweden	745	788	2,663	6,042	16,394	28,320	34,950	33,703	37,267
Switzerland	1,153	1,085	2,845	5,514	6,355	8,371	10,450	9,233	9,895
Syria[9]								4,485	8,696
Turkey[10]	41	34	54	98	303	1,401	9,855		15,115
Wales	1,273	907		1,254	1,475	1,686	1,778	1,510	1,903
West Indies[11]	1,465	719	943	1,407	3,439	3,856	5,990	5,907	13,032
Yugoslavia[12]								5,271	6,450

1. East and Southeast Asia, excluding China and Japan
2. Within present boundaries
3. Excluding Mexico
4. Within boundaries as of 1990 (includes Czech Republic and Slovakia in 2000)
5. Including Wales 1870, 1950; including Wales, Scotland, and Northern Ireland 2000
6. Excluding nations individually enumerated

1940	1950	1960	1970	1980	1990	2000
		13,029	23,578			92,435
5,107	31,977		42,459	122,410		229,210
		1,374				3,860
145,106	124,256	84,389	28,024	26,263	11,877	6,700
3,888			3,681			
40,345	35,860	29,034	20,545	15,874	13,919	17,318
			150,093			245,142
		19,789	37,348	60,824	162,682	207,914
		28,567	63,043	46,880	42,286	26,030
26,884	31,030	27,767	21,523	26,884	30,130	8,628
8,905	6,707		2,760			
63,115	53,614	40,769	29,748	22,364	17,996	28,996
5,757	41,009		14,173			124,443
11,245	8,891		3,452			
19,696	20,461	19,016	15,514			12,386
224,749	185,467	152,502	98,336	60,749	38,886	27,708
28,593	29,815	28,882	35,000	42,080	31,241	29,805
62,588	51,968	45,602	31,717	21,457	13,849	11,144
			5,032	21,880	42,367	68,263
150,325	141,723	114,163	68,778	41,354	29,853	22,604
21,501	3,085		6,604	1,409		
409,489	344,115	281,033	212,160	156,413	96,339	72,481
			7,843	9,549	12,433	19,415
7,475	15,005	15,089	13,599	11,367	6,584	
2,973	3,234		3,514			122,550
5,608	5,571		3,693			2,455
30,750	25,552	18,532	10,229			
194,163	179,878	168,960	119,604	78,135	65,184	65,999
2,676			3,040	4,678	3,581	2,718
40,655	29,409	24,784	21,165		17,566	19,280
395,696	314,603	204,821	117,363	88,415	79,701	81,408
33,292	26,405	19,615	11,683	6,408		
12,429	38,295		71,429	153714		410,048
13,583		10,528	10,694		8,834	7,836
28,881	20,424	11,705	6,140	2,962		2,421
8,551	7,151		3,930			
8,598			2,185			5,191
17,663		11,803	10,069		6,561	9,026
1,296			763	444		
13,344		36,152	36,834			830,119
6,475	6,736	12,399	16,491	21,419	20,364	19,535

7. Figures for 1855–1910 and 2000 are for Russia; those for 1920–90 are for Soviet Union

8. Including Central America 1930–50

9. Including Palestine 1930–40

10. Including Greece 1855

11. Including Cuba 1890, 1910, 1940

12. Within boundaries as of 1990

Compiled by James Bradley and Andrew A. Kryzak

was imposed for all countries outside the western hemisphere. The law discriminated against Jews, Italians, and other southern and eastern European immigrants and ensured the continued exclusion of Asians. Italy, which had sent more than 200,000 people annually in the first decade of the twentieth century, had a quota just under 6000. Of the Asians, only Filipinos were allowed to come, but during the 1930s they too were restricted.

During the 1920s those immigrants already in the city began to assimilate into American culture while establishing neighborhoods and communities often based on race and ethnicity. Many new neighborhoods and ethnic enclaves remained intact until the late 1940s, including the Grand Concourse in the Bronx, which was settled largely by Jews. The islands of Jamaica and Barbados and other parts of the West Indies were unaffected by the restrictive legislation: as colonial possessions of Great Britain they fell within its generous quota rather than under quotas of their own. Between 1900 and 1930 more than 150,000 West Indians immigrated to the United States, and almost half settled in New York City; in the 1920s they accounted for a quarter of the black population of Harlem. West Indians contributed much to the Harlem Renaissance and new political movements such as that led by Marcus Garvey. During these years many African Americans from the South also moved to the city.

By the 1930s Italians were a political force in the city and helped to elect Fiorello H. La Guardia to the mayoralty. Women became the majority of immigrants about this time. The Depression led to a decline in immigration: during the entire decade of the 1930s only half a million people moved to the United States, fewer than during the 1830s, and of these some later returned to their homelands. New York City was the destination of almost one-third of those who moved to the United States during the Depression, and a quarter of the immigrants of the 1930s were Jews fleeing Nazism. Immigration all but ceased during World War II but resumed afterward. Frequent airplane flights were offered between the city and Puerto Rico, the natives of which had been citizens of the United States since 1917; in the 1950s the number of island-born Puerto Ricans in the city rose from 190,000 to 430,000.

During World War II many African Americans moved to the city, and after 1945 they were followed by displaced Germans, Italians, Poles, Greeks, and Jewish survivors of the Holocaust. Under the auspices of some programs refugees were to be dispersed throughout the country, but many, especially Jews, wished to stay in the city. About one-quarter of the immigrants who were admitted under the displaced persons acts of 1948 and 1950 remained there. Special laws for displaced

Foreign-Born Population of New York City by Borough, in Absolute Numbers and as a Percentage of Total Population, 1900–2000

	Manhattan		Brooklyn		Queens		Bronx		Staten Island		Total	
1900	850,884[1]	41	355,697	37	44,812	29	N/A	N/A	18,687	28	1,270,080	37
1910	1,104,019	47	571,356	35	79,115	28	148,935	34	24,278	28	1,927,703	40
1920	922,080	40	659,287	32	111,676	24	266,971	36	31,533	27	1,991,547	35
1930	641,618	34	868,770	34	266,150	25	477,342	38	39,520	25	2,293,400	33
1940	540,197	28	767,638	28	276,588	21	460,476	33	35,121	20	2,080,020	28
1950	461,102	23	630,526	23	288,197	18	373,894	26	30,487	16	1,784,206	23
1960	374,698	22	516,349	20	335,623	20	306,592	21	25,428	11	1,558,690	20
1970	307,630	20	456,636	17	416,887	21	229,210	20	26,695	9	1,437,058	18
1980	348,581	24	530,973	24	540,818	29	215,313	18	34,514	10	1,670,199	24
1990	383,866	26	672,659	29	707,153	36	274,793	23	44,460	12	2,082,931	28
2000	452,440	29	931,769	38	1,028,339	46	385,827	29	72,657	16	2,871,032	36

1. Includes the Bronx.
N/A = Not Available
Source: U.S. Bureau of the Census
Compiled by James Bradley

persons and refugees also permitted the immigration of Italians and Greeks.

Puerto Ricans were the largest Latin American group in the city after 1945, but later other Latin Americans also became numerous. The largest number of Latinos to arrive from South America were Colombian professionals and members of the middle class in the 1950s in the face of escalating violence in the Colombian countryside. Cubans fled their homeland after Fidel Castro's rise to power in 1959, and although most settled in the Miami, Florida, area, several thousand came to New York City. They were followed by Dominicans, Salvadorans, and Guatemalans, especially after 1960, who were fleeing poverty and violence due to the civil wars in their nations. Pressured by political turmoil and economic difficulties in the Middle East, Arabs and Israelis also moved to New York City after 1960.

Immigration to the city changed dramatically after the passage of the IMMIGRATION AND NATIONALITY ACT OF 1965 (the Hart–Celler Act), which ended discrimination based on national origin: equal quotas of 20,000 were set for each country in the eastern hemisphere, but the immediate family members of U.S. citizens were exempt from the quotas. Greeks and Italians benefited from the law, and about one-third of Greek and Italian immigrants to the United States between 1965 and 1975 settled in New York City; there were also Eastern European refugees of communist regimes, including Czechs who fled the failed revolution against Soviet domination in 1968. Most Irish immigrants were unable to prove that their reason for seeking to immigrate was political, occupational, or family-related (as required by the new law), and they were further disinclined to leave Ireland because of its improved economic conditions. However, after the late 1970s economic woes once again afflicted Ireland; as a result, after 1980 many Irish came on temporary permits and then became undocumented immigrants when their visas expired.

The new limits on immigration from the western hemisphere did have an effect on Latin Americans and peoples from the Caribbean. However, the exemption for immediate family members of U.S. citizens enabled many from the western hemisphere to come to the United States. Then in 1986 Congress granted an amnesty for nearly three million undocumented immigrants, and in 1990 the legislators passed a new immigration law that increased immigration by 35 percent. As a result, immigration increased to the United States from Jamaica, Trinidad and Tobago, St. Vincent, Grenada, Barbados, Panama, Guyana, and other parts of the Caribbean. Nearly half of all West Indian immigrants settled in New York City. Some were descendants of immigrants from the Indian subcontinent who had settled in the Caribbean as contract workers, but most were English-speakers of African descent; there was also a large group of Haitians, who spoke French and Creole. The Hart–Celler Act also permitted more immigration from African nations, but most Africans lacked family networks in the 1970s in the United States, and few qualified for entry. Nonetheless, a small but growing number of Egyptians, Ethiopians, South Africans, Nigerians, and Senegalese settled in the city after 1965, and by the late 1980s they accounted for a few thousand inhabitants. Immigrants from nearly all parts of South Asia, East Asia, and the Middle East moved to the United States after 1965. The largest group was the Chinese; others included an increasing number of well-educated Indians and Filipinos, as well as Koreans, many of whom were doctors or greengrocers. Indochinese refugees also made their way to the city, although only 20,000 settled there, as did some Pakistanis.

Immigrants accounted for only 18 percent of the city's population in 1970 (the lowest figure in years), after which about 80,000 settled there annually. Although the total population of the city declined by 800,000 between 1970 and 1980, the number of immigrants rose by about 250,000, or 16 percent. Civil war, violence, and poverty in Central America after 1970 led thousands to move to the city. Some Peruvians, Uruguayans, Ecuadorans, Argentinians, and Portuguese-speaking Brazilians left their homelands to seek better economic opportunities. From the mid-1970s more than 90,000 refugees of political turmoil and repression moved to the city from Cuba, Haiti, Vietnam, Cambodia, Poland, Romania, Afghanistan, Central America, and elsewhere; the number would have been greater had it not been for restrictive emigration policies. For most of the 1970s Soviet Jews had difficulty receiving permission to emigrate and those who succeeded usually settled in Israel. By 1981, when the Soviet government virtually ceased to grant exit visas, about 100,000 Soviet Jews had settled in the United States, most in New York City. The fundamentalist revolution in Iran in 1979 also led to large-scale emigration.

Of the many immigrants living in New York in 1980, about 80 percent were from Asia, the Caribbean, and Latin America. Dominicans constituted the largest group, followed by Jamaicans, Chinese, Haitians, Italians, Trinidadians, Colombians, Ecuadorians, Soviet Jews, and Guyanese. More than half the Asians in the city in 1980 were Chinese. In the following decade the Chinese population, estimated at 300,000, was concentrated in three Chinatowns: the oldest around Canal Street on the East Side of Manhattan, another in Flushing (Queens), and the third near Bay Ridge (Brooklyn). The temporary collapse of the Polish labor movement Solidarity in 1981 led Poles to immigrate to the United States. After 1975 emigration from Greece and Italy declined, but the 1980s saw the settlement in the city of a few thousand Greeks and Italians who were on the whole better educated and more highly skilled than their forerunners at the turn of the twentieth century had been. The number of unauthorized immigrants rose as economic and political pressures encouraged emigration from countries that had long waiting lists for legal admission to the United States. Between 1980 and 1990 the population of the city grew by a quarter of a million; much of the increase was accounted for by immigrants, including some who were unauthorized but nonetheless were willing to be counted.

In 1980 immigrants made up 24 percent of the population of the city (most having settled there after 1965). Factories that formerly provided employment for native-born workers now employed immigrants, even though manufacturing declined in the 1970s. Dominicans and Chinese opened small factories or became subcontractors in the garment industry, and as more labor was needed, shops and homework became common. Other immigrants found work providing services as nurses' aides, household workers, and beauticians. Grocery stores, restaurants, and other small businesses owned by immigrants served ethnic communities and provided work for family members whose inability to speak English hampered their search for employment elsewhere. Several immigrant groups came to be associated with one type of business or service: often, Indians operated newsstands, Jamaicans worked as nurses' aides, and Dominicans owned bodegas. Work in households and in personal service was often taken by women recently settled in the United States and particularly by those who had emigrated alone. About 20 percent of immigrants who settled in the city after 1965 worked in the professions.

Immigration by Soviet Jews rose dramatically after the Soviet government in 1988 lifted its ban on exit visas, and in the following years thousands of Soviet Jews moved to New York City. More than three-quarters of Dominican immigrants who moved to the United States settled in the city, most of them in upper Manhattan. In the 1990s it was estimated that immigrants accounted for about one-third of the population; the number of illegal immigrants was estimated at 400,000. The Chinese were concentrated on the Lower East Side and in other Chinese neighborhoods, but most of those who moved to the city after 1965 were spread throughout the boroughs. West Indians, Soviets, Italians, Poles, and some Chinese (mainly from Hong Kong) settled in Brooklyn, Latin Americans and Irish in the Bronx. Queens had the largest immigrant population, with neighborhoods of nearly every nationality, the principal ones being Chinese, Korean, Indian, Greek, and Colombian.

Immigrants from more than 100 nations lived in the city by 1990, and immigration continued to rise at a rate somewhat higher than that of the preceding decade. In 2005 nearly 2.9 million immigrants accounted for more than 36 percent of the city's population. Dominicans replaced Italians as the largest foreign-born population, and immigrants and their children made up a majority of New York City's people. The children of immigrants comprised a majority in the city's schools, and immigrants themselves were vital to the city's economy. New York City contained more than eight million people according to the revised 2000 census, the highest official figure ever for the city's population. It reached 8,213,839 in 2005. However, the actual figure could easily be greater because of the undercounting of the population. The largest number of immigrants were Latinos and English-speakers from south of the border, but more than 600,000 Asians lived in the city in 2005. Black immigrants accounted for nearly one-third of the city's African Americans.

The boroughs of Queens and Brooklyn were particularly attractive to the newcomers, and Queens was probably the most diverse urban area in the world, with Koreans, Indians, Dominicans, Columbians, Irish, West Indians, and Guyanese living there. The Chinese, for example, settled in Manhattan's Chinatown, but also in the Flushing section of Queens. Chinese numbers also increased in the Sunset Park area in Brooklyn. West Indians were especially prominent in Brooklyn as were Russians in the southern section of Brooklyn. Even Staten Island, the whitest borough, received many immigrants after 1990. For example, a small group of Liberian refugees lived there after 2000.

After 1990 relatively new groups also settled in the city. Africans had only a small presence before 1990, but roughly 100,000 lived there in 2000, although some were undocumented street merchants and were missed by the census. The Mexican population also grew quickly after 1990, numbering only 20,000 in 1980 but growing to 60,000 in 1990. The census picked up nearly 200,000 Mexicans in 2000, and their numbers grew rapidly after that.

The heterogeneity of the city permitted immigrants to mingle easily. In a city where 121 languages were spoken, there were ethnic churches, political associations, social organizations, cultural events, festivals and parades, events, shops, and restaurants for every ethnic group, and dozens of foreign-language newspapers, magazines, and television and radio stations.

Languages Spoken in New York City Homes

Language	Estimated Population
English only	3,981,767
Spanish or Spanish Creole	1,883,804
Chinese	381,506
Russian	193,563
French (including Creole, Patois, Cajun)	174,140
Italian	109,817
Other Indic languages	94,737
Korean	82,620
Yiddish	82,089
Hebrew	60,069
Greek	59,192
Polish	57,288
African languages	55,912
Tagalog	51,258
Arabic	49,264
Urdu	46,904
Other Indo-European languages	44,203
Other Asian languages	33,925
German	23,686
Serbo-Croatian	23,223
Hindi	23,012
Japanese	22,071
Portuguese or Portuguese Creole	18,435
Other Slavic languages	15,825
Persian	11,772
Vietnamese	8,966
Other Pacific Island languages	8,962
Hungarian	8,631
Gujarathi	8,414
Armenian	4,909
Thai	3,792
Scandinavian languages	3,756
Other West Germanic languages	3,389
Other and unspecified languages	3,116
Mon-Khmer, Cambodian	2,991
Other Native North American languages	429
Laotian	383

Notes: The data indicate languages spoken by those five years old and older and are based on a 2006 total population of 7,637,820. English, as well as the language shown, may or may not be spoken in the home.
Source: U.S. Census Bureau, *American Community Survey* (2006)
Compiled by Frank Nestor

Nathan Glazer and Daniel Moynihan, *Beyond the Melting Pot,* 2nd edn (Cambridge, Mass.: MIT Press, 1970); Robert A. Orsi, *The Madonna of 115th Street: Faith and Community in Italian Harlem, 1880–1950* (New Haven: Yale University Press, 1990); Frederick M. Binder and David M. Reimers, *All the Nations under Heaven: A Racial and Ethnic History of New York City* (New York: Columbia University Press, 1995); Daniel Soyer, *Jewish Immigrant Associations and American Identity in New York, 1880–1939* (Cambridge, Mass.: Harvard University Press, 1997); Nancy Foner, *From Ellis Island to JFK: New York's Two Great Waves of Immigration* (New Haven: Yale University Press, 2000)

David M. Reimers

Immigration and Nationality Act of 1965 [Hart–Celler Act]. U.S. legislation that reopened the door to mass immigration, making New York City more multicultural and diverse than it had ever been. Cosponsored by Senator Philip Hart (D-Mich.) and Congressman Emanuel Celler (D-N.Y.), and signed by President Lyndon Johnson in front of the Statue of Liberty, it and its subsequent amendments ended the national origins quota system that had been in place since 1924 and otherwise made it easier for people to immigrate to the United States. Shortly after the act passed, 18 percent of New York City's population was foreign-born; by 2000 the percentage had climbed to 39 percent. Throughout the 1980s and 1990s roughly 100,000 newcomers from abroad settled in the city annually. In 1940 people of European origin constituted 95 percent of the city's residents; by 1990 they accounted for less than half. Latinos, blacks (including 500,000 from the Caribbean), and Asians in 1990 made up the majority of the city's population.

The first immigrants benefiting from the law's family reunification preferences were southern and eastern Europeans. Under the old national origins quotas 308 Greeks could enter yearly; between 1965 and 1975, 3000 Greeks settled in the city annually. Astoria, Queens, became a thriving Greek neighborhood. After that, as economic conditions in Europe improved, European immigration dwindled, and immigration from Asia, Latin America, and the Caribbean burgeoned. Before the act only 2000 from all of Asia were permitted entry annually and 100 people a year from the newly independent West Indian nations. Under the law's preference for immigrants with needed skills and occupations, thousands of Asian and Caribbean medical workers, engineers, and other technically skilled professionals arrived in New York City. More than half of the interns at the city's municipal hospitals were Asian immigrants in the mid-1970s. Having established themselves, these newcomers were soon able, under the family reunification preferences, to send for spouses, minor children, parents, and thousands of other relatives. The city's Chinese population grew from 33,000 in 1960 to 300,000 in 1990. Manhattan's Chinatown engulfed neighboring Little Italy and the Jewish Lower East Side, while new Chinese neighborhoods sprang up in Queens and Brooklyn. In 1990, 80 foreign-language and ethnic newspapers were published in New York City, half of them started after 1970. Koreans operated 90 percent of the city's fruit and vegetable stores; Latino, Asian, and Caribbean women labored in its garment factories. In the opening years of the twenty-first century heavy and still more diverse immigration into New York City continued.

David M. Reimers, *Still the Golden Door: The Third World Comes to America* (New York: Columbia University Press, 1992); Leonard Dinnerstein and David M. Reimers, *Ethnic Americans: A History of Immigration* (New York: Columbia University Press, 1999); Center for Immigration Studies, "Three Decades of Mass Immigration: The Legacy of the 1965 Immigration Act," September 1995, http://www.cis.org/articles/1995/back395.html

See also IMMIGRATION 1900–PRESENT.

Barbara Blumberg

Impellitteri, Vincent R(ichard) (*b* Isnello, Sicily, 4 Feb 1900; *d* Bridgeport, Conn., 29 Jan 1987). Mayor. Elected president of the City Council as the candidate of the Democratic and American Labor parties in 1945 and of the Democratic Party alone in 1949, he became the acting mayor of New York City after the resignation of Mayor William O'Dwyer in 1950. Although he lost the Democratic nomination for mayor in a special primary election later that year, he won the general election as the candidate of the Experience Party, becoming the first person elected mayor of New York City without the support of a major party. His administration was accused of incompetence, corruption, and links to organized crime, and he lost the Democratic mayoral primary in 1953 to Robert F. Wagner (ii). He was named a criminal court judge in 1954.

Warren Moscow, *The Last of the Big-Time Bosses: The Life and Times of Carmine DeSapio* (New York: Stein and Day, 1971)

Chris McNickle

IND. See INDEPENDENT SUBWAY SYSTEM.

Independent. Weekly newspaper launched on 7 December 1848 by the Congregationalist leaders Leonard Bacon, Joseph P. Thompson, and Richard S. Storrs and published until 13 October 1928. Among the leading contributors was Henry Ward Beecher. In the 1860s the newspaper was transformed from a denominational voice against slavery into a radical advocate of equality, abolition, and reform. This change was brought about by its owner, Henry Chandler Bowen, and by Beecher, Joshua Leavitt, and especially the women's rights advocate Theodore Tilton. The newspaper suffered during the scandalous breach between Tilton and Beecher that shook Congregationalism in the 1870s; Bowen then became the sole editor and renewed its emphasis on religion, but by continuing to publish the leading American poets, he also maintained its literary appeal.

Vincent R. Impellitteri, 1951

Mariam Touba

Independent Network News [INN]. Television news service that provided national and international news to television stations unaffiliated with the major networks during the 1980s. Formed by the New York City television station WPIX in 1980, the service produced a half-hour national newscast called *USA Tonight* as well as 35 to 40 news stories each day for local stations. INN programming aired on stations reaching about 90 percent of American homes in the mid-1980s, but the creation of the Fox television network in 1987 reduced the number of independent stations. With a dwindling number of potential customers, INN shut down in 1990.

George Winslow

Independent Order of Odd Fellows [IOOF]. Secret, ritualistic fraternal organization formed in 1819. Columbia Lodge no. 1 in Brooklyn was chartered in 1822, and in 1863 the order owned a large hall at the corner of Baxter and Grand streets. By 1924 there were 25,248 members in New York City in 157 lodges. Membership was increased by veterans of World War II to 29,978 in 1950 but declined in the following years. The IOOF offers insurance for members and their families and supports heart research, a summer camp for children with cancer, and the Rebekah Rehab and Extended Care Center at the Odd Fellows Life Community (formerly United Odd Fellow and Rebekah Home) at 1072 Havemeyer Avenue in the Bronx, which provides residencies and food service deilvery programs to senior citizens and participants of the program.

Marc Ferris

independent schools. In addition to public and parochial schools, New York City has a large number of independent or "private" schools that provide a secular education. The independent schools are nonprofit, governed by a board of trustees, and primarily supported by tuition, charitable contributions, and endowment income. The Dutch opened the Collegiate School (1628), now the oldest independent school in the United States. Other early independent schools include

Trinity School (1709) and Columbia Grammar and Preparatory School (1764), opened during British rule, and Friends Seminary (1784). In 2008 there were 35 independent schools providing comprehensive or secondary education, with a total enrollment of 20,000; about one in six students at these schools received some form of financial assistance. (Another 27 independent schools provided elementary education to 7000 students.) About two-thirds of the independent schools in the city date from between 1880 and 1930, a time of considerable advancement in both private and public education, and two-thirds are coeducational; most of the rest are for girls. Some retain religious affiliations to promote moral development and ethical values. Several private schools have been established to serve the needs of the city's foreign and professional children, such as the Professional Children's School (1914) and the Lycée Français de New York (1935). Most of the schools are on the Upper East Side and Upper West Side of Manhattan. The independent schools in the city are generally noted for high academic standards, small classes, faculty members with advanced degrees, large libraries, and a focus on individual academic achievement and civic responsibility. Some require their students to take part in community service programs, and nearly all offer advanced placement college courses, study abroad, athletics, student publications, and instruction in the performing and fine arts. All but a few graduates of the independent schools attend four-year colleges, often in the Ivy League. Nearly all the independent schools in New York City belong to the Independent Schools Admissions Association of Greater New York and the National Association of Independent Schools.

Well-known independent schools in New York City include the Alexander Robertson School (1789), the Packer Collegiate Institute (1845), Polytechnic Preparatory Country Day School (1854), Brooklyn Friends School (1867), the Ethical Culture Fieldston Schools (1878), the Dwight School (1880), the Brearley School (1884), Staten Island Academy (1884), Horace Mann School (1887), the Spence School (1892), the Nightingale–Bamford School (1906), the Riverdale Country School (1907), the Birch Wathen Lenox School (1916), the Dalton School (1919), Elisabeth Irwin High School (1921), Saint Ann's School (1965), and the Anglo-American International School (1980).

Gerard Koeppel

Independent Subway System [IND]. Third underground railway system in New York City. It was conceived by Mayor John F. Hylan, who dominated transit politics during his two terms in office (1918–25) and who denounced the existing Interborough Rapid Transit (IRT) and Brooklyn Rapid Transit (later Brooklyn–Manhattan Transit, or BMT) as corrupt monopolies that ignored the needs of the people. The New York City Board of Transportation adopted a basic plan for the new system on 9 December 1924, and the first subway began service on 10 July 1932 as part of the Eighth Avenue line, which was supplemented during the next eight years by four other lines: the Fulton Street, the Brooklyn–Queens crosstown, the Queensboro, and the Sixth Avenue. Because the IND had to compete with both the IRT and the BMT, its routes were confined primarily to built-up areas where heavy traffic could be generated. Except for the Queensboro line and a segment of the Eighth Avenue line that extended to Washington Heights, the IND did not reach far into the outskirts of the city. Unlike the first two subway systems, the IND had little effect on residential expansion. In June 1940 it merged with the IRT and the BMT to form a unified system. The Sixth Avenue line, completed on 15 December 1940, was the last addition to the IND.

Clifton Hood

India House. Luncheon club in the financial district, founded in 1914 by Willard Straight and other businesspeople in international trade. From 1921 it has occupied a three-story Italianate brownstone at 1 Hanover Square built between 1851 and 1854 by Richard Carman. It was renovated in 1914 and 1924, and the Marine Room was added to contain a notable collection of maritime objects and Oriental art. Formerly the building was the headquarters of the Hanover Bank, the New York Cotton Exchange (1870–85), and W. R. Grace and Company (1885–1913). The current name was adopted after a merger in 1988. In 2005 the India House Club and the Poulakakos family renovated the building, and it received a Lucy G. Moses Preservation Award from the New York Landmarks Conservancy. The building was declared a New York City landmark in 1965 and a National Historic Landmark in 1977.

Elliott B. Nixon

India House, ca 1900

Indians. Colonial traders were among the first South Asians in New York City. During the early twentieth century, several thousand Indians moved to the United States, mostly settling on the West Coast, where they worked on railroads and farms. New York City was the destination of a few students, professionals, and businesspeople. During the first half of the twentieth century many Indians in the United States promoted the cause of Indian independence from Britain. A few well-educated Indians settled in the city after the passage of the Luce–Celler Act (1946), which allowed Indians to be naturalized and set an annual immigration quota of 100. In the following decades Indians of the upper middle class who were well connected in American society formed a network of organizations to extend these rights. The India League of America, formed in New York City by the importer Jagjit Singh, campaigned ceaselessly for the political rights of Indians in the United States.

From the 1950s the number of Indian students increased, and after completing their education many remained and began careers, as did many representatives of the Indian government after finishing assignments at such institutions as the United Nations. The Sikh community grew and opened *gurudwaras* (temples), as well as the Sikh Cultural Society. Most immigrants during these years were men; women who settled in the city usually did so as wives, although there were a few female students and professionals. Indians were concentrated in Manhattan and organized a wide range of cultural activities. Some of the most important sponsors were student clubs such as the Indian Students Association of Columbia University. Renowned artists, particularly classical musicians and dancers, performed regularly in the city, and film screenings at Columbia and public theaters were also popular. Traditional Indian foods became available in a few specialty stores. The city's few Hindus emphasized domestic prayers and held small private gatherings for group worship. Christian congregations conducted services in English, Urdu, Malayalam, Tamil, and Hindi. Common languages such as Urdu were used in Muslim religious gatherings. Indian Jews sometimes celebrated holidays with Jews of other ethnic backgrounds; they also held separate observances incorporating traditional Indian food and dress and recitations of religious texts.

After the Immigration and Nationality Act of 1965 was passed, immigration from India increased tremendously: by the end of the decade they numbered several thousand in the United States. Most of these new immigrants were physicians, engineers, scientists, scholars, accountants, architects, bankers, and merchants; many chose to live in New York City, where they settled in neighborhoods in Queens. Several Indian professionals in 1970 launched the newspaper *India Abroad*, aimed at the widely spread expatriate population. After 1970 about 20,000 South Asians, many Indian, moved to the United States each year. Some were businesspeople who opened travel and insurance agencies, groceries, or clothing stores. Jackson Heights became a commercial center after the Sam and Raj appliance store opened there on 74th Street in 1976; by 1990 there were about 100 stores selling items ranging from groceries to saris and jewelry. Immigrants also found work as taxi drivers, autoworkers, cashiers, newsstand operators, and toll takers.

As their numbers increased, Hindus rented spaces to hold public religious services, and in 1976 a temple in a South Indian style was built in Flushing. The Geeta Temple soon opened in Elmhurst and moved to larger quarters in 1983. In 1972 the Sikh Cultural Society dedicated a large gurudwara in Richmond Hill. In 1989 the first Global Convention of Overseas Indians was held in the city, drawing Indian leaders from India, Africa, Europe, North America, and the Caribbean. In 2000 Indians ranked 14 of the top 20 foreign-born groups in New York City, and about two-thirds of them lived in Queens.

Maxine P. Fisher, *Indians of New York City: A Study of Immigrants from India* (New Delhi: Heritages, 1980)

Madhulika S. Khandelwal

Indian Village. Leafy, residential neighborhood of single-family homes in the east Bronx bounded on the north by Pelham Parkway, the south by Morris Park Avenue, the east by the grounds of Jacobi Medical Center, and the west by Narragansett Avenue. The streets are named for Indian tribes: Seminole, Choctaw, Pawnee, and Narragansett. Most of the houses were built during the 1930s. Historically home to many Bronx politicians, the neighborhood escaped the turmoil the South Bronx experienced during the 1970s and 1980s. Real estate taxes are relatively low, and the homes are mainly on 50-by-100-foot (15.3-by-30.5-meter) lots. Residents are predominantly Italian, but also Jewish and Irish, with a growing number of Asians, especially Indian and Chinese hospital personnel because of its proximity to the Albert Einstein College of Medicine of Yeshiva University, its hospital, and the Jacobi Medical Center. The name Indian Village has been used by real estate agents since the 1980s, but people who live there usually say they live in the Bronx, unlike residents of another Bronx neighborhood, Riverdale, who say that they live in Riverdale. Politically the area is conservative but elects both Republicans and Democrats.

Karen Markoe

Industrial Workers of the World [IWW]. Federation formed in 1905 to organize destitute workers throughout the United States, including textile workers in the Northeast. In New York City the IWW drew many of its members from among Jewish and Italian immigrants working in the garment trade. It supported the principle that labor organizations could regulate society and the economy, without formal state and political institutions (anarcho-syndicalism) and often used militant tactics. The members were popularly known as Wobblies. During 1911–12 Elizabeth Gurley Flynn, Joseph Ettor, and Arturo Giovannitti, leaders of the organization in New York City, led a strike of hotel and restaurant workers that was ultimately unsuccessful but disrupted service at some of the city's finest establishments and became known as one of the most tumultuous efforts of its kind before World War I. An even better-known strike was one by silk workers in Paterson, New Jersey, organized in 1913 by such IWW leaders as Flynn and "Big Bill" Haywood with the support of such intellectuals as Mabel Dodge, John Reed, and Max Eastman. The Paterson Pageant, a dramatization of the strike, was proposed by Reed during a soirée held in Greenwich Village by Dodge and attended by Haywood; the pageant was later staged at Madison Square Garden. The Paterson strike itself failed, and the alliance between IWW leaders and Greenwich Village intellectuals disintegrated. After 1913 the IWW focused its efforts on workers in the West, but it retained a residual influence among both clothing workers and cultural rebels in the metropolitan area.

Patrick Renshaw, *The Wobblies: The Story of Syndicalism in the United States* (Garden City, N.Y.: Doubleday, 1967); Melvyn Dubofsky, *We Shall Be All: A History of the IWW* (New York: Quadrangle, 1969); Steve Golin: *The Fragile Bridge: Paterson Silk Strike, 1913* (Philadelphia: Temple University Press, 1988)

Melvyn Dubofsky

influenza. Influenza, commonly known as the flu, was named for a sixteenth-century Italian explanation of its presumed cause: the influence of the stars or occult astral bodies. It is a viral infection that visits New York City and almost everywhere else in the United States annually, generally during the late autumn and winter. In most cases the result is a cold, cough, fever, and achiness, but those with serious underlying medical problems can become seriously ill and even die after infection with the influenza virus. About every eight to 18 years the virus mutates so significantly that pandemic outbreaks erupt. One historian of medicine estimates that about 86 influenza pandemics occurred worldwide between the years 1173 and 1874. Relatively few influenza epidemics have occurred in New York City, although influenza was recognized in Manhattan as early as 1789. Perhaps the most serious outbreak of the flu was the worldwide pandemic of 1918, which took the lives of about 12,000 New Yorkers. In the 2009–10 flu season New Yorkers were vaccinated against H1N1, or "swine flu," which had been particularly virulent and deadly earlier in 2009 worldwide.

John Duffy, *A History of Public Health in New York City* (New York: Russell Sage Foundation, 1968, 1974); A. C. Crosby, *The Forgotten Pandemic: The Influenza of 1918* (Cambridge: Cambridge University Press, 1989)

Howard Markel

Ingleside. Former name of a section to the east of downtown Flushing in north central Queens, bounded to the north by Northern Boulevard, to the east by Utopia Parkway, to the south by Kissena Park, and to the west by Murray Street, Sanford Avenue, and Kissena Boulevard. It was assembled and laid out by the Realty Trust Company of New York between 1893 and 1899; building lots had frontage of 40 feet (12 meters), 50 feet (15 meters), and 60 feet (18 meters). From 1896 to 1898 many elegant houses priced from $4000 to $6000 were built. After the line for the Flushing–Jamaica trolley was extended through Ingleside in 1899, the value of property rose sharply. In 1908 Ingleside became one of the first developments to have sewers installed on all streets. A demand for housing increased during the 1920s, and one-family houses were built.

Vincent Seyfried

Inman, Henry (*b* Utica, N.Y., 20 Oct 1801; *d* New York City, 17 Jan 1846). Portrait painter. He began an apprenticeship in 1814 with John Wesley Jarvis and in 1821 opened his own studio on Vesey Street. With a former student, Thomas Seir Cummings, he formed a partnership in 1824 and was granted many commissions for miniatures and portraits; both artists served as officers at the National Academy of Design. Inman lived in Philadelphia from 1831 until 1834, when a commission to paint four mayoral portraits for City Hall brought him back to New York City. He attracted a large number of prestigious commissions during the last years of his life. Inman was honored by colleagues and patrons with a memorial exhibition at the American Art-Union, the first retrospective of one artist's work in the United States.

William H. Gerdts and Carrie Rebora, *The Art of Henry Inman* (Washington, D.C.: National Portrait Gallery, Smithsonian Institution, 1987)

Carrie Rebora Barratt

INN. See Independent Network News.

Inner City Broadcasting. Communications corporation formed in 1971 in New York City by Percy E. Sutton, a former borough president of Manhattan, through the purchase of the radio stations WLIB-AM and WLIB-FM (now WBLS-FM). During the 1970s WBLS developed a style of programming, aimed at listeners between the ages of 18 and 34, known as "urban contemporary," which made it one of the most popular radio stations in the city and was widely imitated. Inner City expanded when it purchased radio stations in Los Angeles and Detroit. Its subsidiaries included Inner City America Music (ICAM), Apollo Entertainment Television (AET), and Inner City Cable Corporation, formed for joint cable ventures in Detroit, Philadelphia, and Washington, D.C.; it also retained partial ownership of Queens Inner Unity Cable Television Systems. In 1982 it bought the Apollo Theater, which it sold in 1991. In 2002 it ran into legal trouble for trying to buy broadcasting rights to *Showtime at the Apollo* in a bidding war with Heritage Networks that started in 1998. In 2005 it sold off its last cable investment, refocusing on its radio stations. In 2006 WLIB switched from a mainly talk format to playing gospel music.

Laura Gwinn

insignia. See Seal of the City of New York.

Institute of Musical Arts. Original name of the Juilliard School.

Institute of Public Administration. Private organization formed in 1906 as the Bureau of City Betterment of the Citizens Union to monitor the government of New York City at the departmental level. In 1907 it became the Bureau of Municipal Research, led by the reformers William H. Allen, Henry Bruère, and Frederick A. Cleveland. Its first administrative survey, *How Manhattan Is Governed* (1907), led to an improved budget system, and its social surveys resulted in more effective social service programs. In 1911 it opened the Training School for Public Service in New York City and began sending staff members to other cities to help improve the work of their governments. Luther Gulick succeeded Charles A. Beard as the director of the bureau in 1921, and in the same year the bureau and its training school were merged to form the National Institute of Public Administration. The organization took the name Institute of Public Administration (IPA) in 1931, in part to reflect the international scope of its work, and Gulick became its president and chairman. The IPA ceased operations early in the twenty-first century after a century of work in the field of public administration and municipal reform. The organization's legacy lives on through a graduate fellowship at New York University named for its longtime head, Luther Gulick.

Luther Gulick, *The National Institute of Public Administration: A Progress Report* (New York: National Institute of Public Administration, 1928); Jane S. Dahlberg, *The New York Bureau of Municipal Research: Pioneer in Government Administration* (New York: New York University Press, 1966)

Bernard Hirschhorn

Institute for Social Research. Experimental school founded as the Institut für Sozialforschung in 1923 at the University of Frankfurt and moved to Columbia University in 1934 as Hitler came to power in Germany. Its members included the philosophers Walter Benjamin, Max Horkheimer, Herbert Marcuse, Theodor Adorno, Franz Neumann, and Otto Kirchheimer, who studied the relationship between contemporary society, culture, and politics through the lens of critical theory, an interpretation of Marxism influenced by the philosophy of Georg Wilhelm Friedrich Hegel. Members of the institute later fused the tradition of radical social critique with the psychological perspectives of Sigmund Freud in works like Adorno's *The Authoritarian Personality* (1950) and Marcuse's *Eros and Civilization* (1955). The institute returned to Frankfurt in 1951.

Martin Jay, *The Dialectical Imagination: A History of the Frankfurt School and the Institute for Social Research* (Boston: Little, Brown, 1973)

Peter M. Rutkoff, William B. Scott

Institute Park. Former name of a park in northwestern Brooklyn, lying on a triangular parcel bounded to the north by Eastern Parkway, to the east by Washington Avenue, and to the south and west by Flatbush Avenue. Institute Park took its name from the Brooklyn Institute of Arts and Sciences (1897), now known as the Brooklyn Museum. The museum shares the site with the main branch of the Brooklyn Public Library and the Brooklyn Botanic Garden.

Elizabeth Reich Rawson

insurance. See Life insurance; Property and liability insurance; and Reinsurance.

intellectuals. Before the American Revolution, intellectual endeavor in New York City was undertaken mostly by doctors, lawyers, and merchants who belonged to clubs and literary and scholarly societies, visited museums, and subscribed to periodicals. The work of these men was often ambitious. Cadwallader Colden, a graduate of the medical faculty at the University of Edinburgh and the lieutenant governor of the colony (1761–76), was an amateur physicist who wrote *The History of the Five Indian Nations* (1727), one of the first ethnographic studies. William Livingston launched the Whig magazine the *Independent Reflector* (1752–53) and in 1754 was instrumental in forming the New York Society Library and King's College (later Columbia University). As New York became a commercial center many discerned its potential as an intellectual center, although it remained overshadowed by Philadelphia until the beginning of the nineteenth century. Some of its best-known thinkers were Alexander Hamilton and John Jay, who with James Madison wrote the *Federalist* (1787–88). The leading intellectual circle of the late eighteenth century was the Friendly Club (1793–98), formed by the painter and art historian William Dunlap and the physician Elihu Hubbard Smith.

The life of the mind flourished during the first half of the nineteenth century. The American Academy of Fine Arts was formed in 1801, the New-York Historical Society in 1804, and the Literary and Philosophical Society in 1814. The leading societies had quarters in the New York Institution of Learned and Scientific Establishments (1816). Members usually were amateurs with many talents, among them Samuel Latham Mitchill, Washington Irving, Samuel F. B. Morse, and Albert Gallatin. De Witt Clinton was the president of both the Literary and Philosophical Society and the American Academy of Fine Arts, and the vice president of the New-York Historical Society. The best-known literary clubs were the Bread and Cheese, formed by James Fenimore Cooper in 1821, and the Sketch Club (1827), which became the Century Club in 1846.

Thinkers from the working class criticized various urban problems and particularly disparities of wealth. Inspired by Thomas Paine, they denounced property and privilege and argued that the value of goods and services should be determined by the labor necessary to produce and perform them. Cornelius Blatchly maintained in *An Essay on Common Wealths* (1822) that landlords, merchants, and bankers unfairly enriched themselves through the efforts of laborers. Thomas Skidmore, an English immigrant who wrote *The Rights of Man to Property* (1829), demanded that the egalitarian promise of the American Revolution be extended to the economic realm and called for an end to property rights and other inherited privileges. George Henry Evans, editor of the *Workingmen's Advocate,* urged that land be given to those who settled in the West. In his *Political Writings* William Leggett called for an end to privilege and monopoly and presented a scheme of equal rights and open competition that was adopted by the Locofocos of the Democratic Party. In an abandoned church on Broome Street the Scottish radicals Frances Wright and Robert Dale Owen opened the Hall of Sciences in 1829, an institute for workers that was extant until 1831; they later introduced the idea of communitarian socialism, which was revived in the 1840s by Albert Brisbane. The ideas he presented in the manifesto *The Social Destiny of Man* (1840) gained the support of Horace Greeley, the powerful editor of the *New York Tribune* and a supporter of trade unionism, women's rights, and abolitionism. The University of the City of New York (later New York University), the first tuition-free institution in the city, opened in 1831. The German Utopian socialist Wilhelm Weitling became well known in the late 1840s for tracing communism to primitive Christianity.

By mid-century newspaper editors were prominent intellectual figures, and newspapers and magazines gradually gained in influence. Edgar Allan Poe and Margaret Fuller were among the first professional journalists, and Greeley and William Cullen Bryant, the editor of the *Evening Post,* helped to shift the focus of intellectual life toward print media. Rather than belong to the Century Club, Walt Whitman and Herman Melville took part in a nationalist literary movement led by Evert A. Duyckinck and known as "young America"; they also contributed to the *Democratic Review,* a journal edited by John O'Sullivan, who believed that literature should play a vital role in shaping the nation's democratic culture. Publishing was the fastest-growing business in the city between 1840 and 1860, and by the 1860s New York was the national center of journalism. *Harper's Weekly* began publication in 1857 and the *Nation,* another weekly newspaper, followed in 1865. By the 1870s many doubted the city's ability to accommodate its many European immigrants (especially poor Irish Catholics), to whom some intellectuals attributed the rise of political machines and municipal corruption. The corruption of William M. "Boss" Tweed's government was denounced by George William Curtis, editor of *Harper's Weekly,* and E. L. Godkin, editor of the *Nation,* as the inevitable result of giving power to immigrants and workers; a fear that empowering former slaves would have similar results led them to abandon their commitment to Reconstruction and instead oppose any federal intervention in the South.

As Godkin predicted, the foremost question of the late nineteenth century became the relation between labor and capital; many intellectuals in the city sided with labor. During the 1870s the Marxists Friedrich Bolte, Friedrich Sorge, and Karl Speyer offered cogent critiques of social relations under capitalism, and German radicals played a central role in the International Workingmen's Association. The writer William Dean Howells took issue with the widespread condemnation of the anarchists arrested for rioting at the Haymarket in Chicago in 1886, who he believed were denied the right of public expression. Henry George, the author of *Progress and Poverty* (1879), urged that all profits from land ownership be taxed and redistributed. His mayoral candidacy in 1886 was supported by the Irish radicals Edward McGlynn, a Catholic priest, and Patrick Ford, editor of the *Irish World and American Industrial Liberator* (1870); both were instrumental in forming the American Land League, an organization dedicated to land reform and Irish independence that was also supported by John Devoy, a leading Irish nationalist.

Institutions of higher education, until 1890 unimportant for most professions and marginal to the intellectual life of the city, expanded at the urging of those who believed that New York needed at least one great university if it was to gain an international reputation. Between 1895 and 1905 Columbia University and New York University reorganized their professional schools and introduced graduate programs. During their terms as Columbia's president, Seth Low (1890–1901) and Nicholas Murray Butler (1902–45) transformed it into a nationally renowned university, where the newest methods of research and graduate training were introduced by such figures as John Burgess and William Dunning.

The most important intellectual circles were those that developed in Greenwich Village. James Gibbons Huneker led a bohemian group based in cafés and saloons between Union Square and Tompkins Square and during the 1890s irreverently attacked the elite. The Progressive theorists Walter Lippmann and Herbert Croly began publishing the *New Republic* in 1914, and intellectuals like Randolph Bourne, Horace Kallen, and John Dewey articulated a philosophy rooted in the democracy and heterogeneity of city life. Novelists wrote works of social realism that drew on Progressive reforms. Prominent women included the feminists Charlotte Perkins Gilman, Harriot Stanton Blatch, and Rebecca Harding Davis, the reformer Lillian Wald, and the social activists Crystal Eastman, Margaret Sanger, and Emma Goldman. Abraham Cahan edited the *Jewish Daily Forward,* a Yiddish-language socialist newspaper, and also wrote *The Rise of David Levinsky* (1917), a novel about immigrants' assimilation. In pre–World War I Greenwich Village, Mabel Dodge Luhan sponsored a literary salon, Alfred Stieglitz opened a gallery, Eugene O'Neill formed the Provincetown Players, and Goldman and Big Bill Haywood presented radical ideas in lectures. *The Masses,* a socialist journal in decline, was revitalized by a group that included Bourne, John Reed, Max Eastman, Floyd Dell, and Louise Bryant: under their direction it became an eclectic journal of socialism, feminism, and radical art that captured the exuberance of the Village. Because it opposed the entry of the United States into World War I the magazine was denied postal privileges by the federal government and eventually ceased publication.

After 1917 radical intellectuals focused on assessing the impact of the Bolshevik Revolution and gauging theories of progressivism, liberalism, and social engineering on the basis of evidence offered by the Soviet Union. In 1918 Max Eastman began the journal *The Liberator,* which was more doctrinaire than *The Masses* and less art oriented. A few radical writers sought to preserve the established link between art and politics, among them Michael Gold and Joseph Freeman, who worked together for *The Liberator* until its cessation in 1924, and in 1926 formed the *New Masses,* a magazine of proletarian literature. To encourage young working-class writers they formed John Reed clubs across the country: the chapter in New York City, dominated by the radical young critics William Phillips and Philip Rahv, became the most influential. However, for most intellectuals during the 1920s, modernism replaced radicalism. Some of the first studies of American modernism were *Axel's Castle* (1939) and *The Triple Thinkers* (1938; revised and enlarged 1948) by Edmund Wilson, editor of the *New Republic.* Although intellectuals from throughout the country continued to move to Greenwich Village, they generally eschewed politics; others sought to escape America altogether by moving to Paris.

At the onset of the Depression the attitudes of the 1920s seemed self-indulgent, and interest in politics revived among intellectuals. Wilson wrote about the impact of the Depression in *The American Jitters: A Year of the Slump* (1932) and about the evolution of socialist theory in *To the Finland Station* (1940). The *New Masses* became a forum for renewed interest in the union of art and politics, and the *Nation* and the *New Republic* moved further to the left. Malcolm Cowley, who lived in Paris and Greenwich Village in the 1920s, replaced Wilson as the literary editor of the *New Republic,* joined the Communist Party, and drafted "Culture and Crisis" (1932), a statement supporting the communist presidential candidate William Z. Foster and enlisting writers in the cause of revolution; the statement was signed by 52 leading intellectuals. Artists, writers, and critics joined radical parties and gave a political slant to their work.

In 1933 Phillips and Rahv persuaded Freeman to help sponsor a new literary magazine. *Partisan Review,* launched in the spring of 1934, had a communist orientation devoted to proletarian literature. In spite of their hopes for the potential success of proletarian art, the editors eventually doubted the quality of much of it and had misgivings about the role of intellectuals and critics in the radical art movement. They suspended publication of the magazine from 1936 until 1937, when it was revived with an independent editorial position and four additional editors: F. W. Dupee, Dwight Macdonald, George L. K. Morris, and Mary McCarthy. From this time until the entry of the United States into World War II the magazine enjoyed its greatest success. It attracted leftist writers representing a wide range of views, among them Wilson, Wallace Stevens, Lionel Trilling, Sidney Hook, and James T. Farrell; several others published their first work there, among them Delmore Schwartz, Saul Bellow, John Berryman, and Elizabeth Bishop. The magazine also sought to revive the literary reputations of modernist writers by embracing a new conception of radical art known as revolutionary modernism, which asserted that a radical "sensibility" was as important as a political consciousness, and the avant-garde could steer the world toward socialism. This position permitted harmonious relations between the proletarian writer and the critic, who became essential for identifying the radical insights of writers of both the Left and the Right. It was applied to writers as diverse as Dostoyevsky, Kafka, Eliot, Dreiser, Hemingway, and André Malraux. A similar relationship between artist and critic was adopted in the visual arts.

The call for the formation of the Popular Front against fascism after 1935 led to a political shift among radicals. The League of American Writers of the Popular Front aimed to broaden the base of the radical art movement by uniting the Left and the liberal Center. The term "people" replaced "workers," and the works of Whitman and Emerson were studied in addition to those of European radicals. The Popular Front collapsed after the Nazi-Soviet Pact of 1939, and the entry of the United States into World War II forced the literary Left to think in national rather than ideological terms. Anti-Stalinist radicals supported the Allies; Alfred Kazin's *On Native Grounds* (1942) exemplified the patriotism of younger critics and writers by interpreting American literature of the nineteenth century and the early twentieth as progressive and distinctly American.

About this time a number of intellectuals moved from Europe to New York to escape fascism, among them Isaac Bashevis Singer, Hans Morgenthau, Hannah Arendt, Marc Chagall, W. H. Auden, and Bertolt Brecht. By the end of the war their ideas and those of other intellectuals in the city dominated American thought; writers associated with *Partisan Review* were especially influential. Scholars abandoned radicalism for liberal anticommunism and articulated new ideas about criticism. Trilling, a Columbia professor and the preeminent American literary critic of the time, wrote *The Middle of the Journey* (1947), a novel about the intellectual and political odyssey of his generation, and *The Liberal Imagination* (1949), in which the theories of Marx were supplanted by those of Freud as tools of literary analysis. Among those who influenced his work was Reinhold Niebuhr, a teacher at Union Theological Seminary who identified human "darkness" in Nazism and Stalinism and questioned the perfectibility of humankind. Arendt further linked bolshevism and fascism by equating the totalitarianism of the Left with that of the Right. According to the sociologist Daniel Bell and others, ideology ended with the war and was replaced by a rough consensus among intellectuals who accepted the welfare state, decentralized power, a mixed economy, and political pluralism. Sociological studies by Bell and his colleague Seymour Martin Lipset suggested that class antagonism was becoming secondary to pluralism on the one hand and concerns for personal status on the other. At Columbia Richard Hofstadter wrote that American history should be analyzed not according to conflict-based theories but rather by understanding a kind of "mute organic consistency." The American Jewish Committee sponsored *Commentary,* a general-interest magazine that became more like *Partisan Review:* under the editorship of Elliot Cohen it offered political and literary analysis and discussion of modern Jewish identity. Those holding to democratic socialism, like the critic Irving Howe and the art historian Meyer Schapiro, helped to publish the magazine *Dissent.*

Intellectuals became nationally prominent and worked mostly in universities. No institution was more prominent than Columbia, which attracted Trilling, Dupee, Bell, Lipset, Hofstadter, Schapiro, and Niebuhr, as well as the critics Mark Van Doren and Richard Chase and the historian Jacques Barzun. Despite the emphasis on consensus and intellectual harmony, underground arts movements grew during the 1950s. During the late 1940s the beat movement developed from friendships among a number of writers, including Allen Ginsberg, Jack Kerouac, and William Burroughs. Many of its proponents lived in Greenwich Village, and the movement gained wider recognition after the publication of Ginsberg's *Howl* (1956) and Kerouac's *On the Road* (1957). Beat literature was considered subversive for its rejection of the social conformity and materialistic visions of the postwar years. These values were also rejected by a number of black writers who formed a literary movement inspired by black history: in the novel *Invisible Man* (1952) Ralph Ellison examined black history of the early twentieth century, ending with the radical and racial movements in Harlem during the 1930s. The Living Theater, formed in 1947 by Julian Beck and Judith Malina, rebelled against the conventions of Broadway. Young figurative painters were challenged by the abstract expressionism of Jasper Johns and Robert Rauschenberg and by the literal realism of the pop artists Andy Warhol, Roy Lichtenstein, and James Rosenquist. Columbia sociologist C. Wright Mills, whose work was not generally accepted in the academy, argued in *White Collar* (1951) and *The Power Elite* (1956) for a continuation of radical analysis based on American themes.

During the 1960s notions of intellectual harmony were shattered. As the civil rights movement unfolded in the South, frustration and rage were evident in the work of the novelist James Baldwin and by the playwrights Lorraine Hansberry (*Raisin in the Sun,* 1959) and LeRoi Jones (*The Dutchman, The Slave,* and *The Toilet,* 1964). The work of such artists as Ginsberg, Warhol, and the Living Theater gained popularity, and young radicals found Mills's arguments compelling (some were incorporated by the activist Tom Hayden into the Port Huron Statement, the manifesto of Students for a Democratic Society). After becoming the editor of *Commentary* in 1960, Norman Podhoretz sought to infuse it with a new intellectual and political spirit: he published provocative articles on foreign policy along with excerpts of *Growing Up Absurd* (1960), a stinging criticism of education by Paul Goodman. (Podhoretz later steered the magazine back toward the center and eventually to the right.) During a newspaper strike in 1963 the *New York Review of Books* was begun by Jason Epstein, Barbara Epstein, and Robert Silvers. Once jokingly called the "New York Review of each other's books" by Hofstadter, it took up the cause of the New Left. The Vietnam War, racial and ethnic conflicts (especially those fomented by the teachers' strike of 1968), and perceived excesses of the counterculture caused deep rifts in political and cultural life. William F. Buckley, Jr., launched the *National Review,* a conservative journal, in 1965. In universities intellectuals who had become prominent after the war confronted the student movement. A strike at Columbia in 1968 engulfed Trilling, Dupee, Bell, Fritz Stern, and Hofstadter and split old friendships and alliances. Accusations flew among journals and editors: Rahv and Howe battled over politics of the Left, *Partisan Review* offended many former contributors by supporting the literary counterculture, and *Commentary* criticized the *New York Review* for publishing leftist material, particularly a detailed cover illustration of a "Molotov cocktail."

By the 1970s intellectuals in the city were divided into several groups. Neoconservatism drew political essayists such as Podhoretz, Buckley, and Irving Kristol, and others like

Hilton Kramer, an art critic for the *New York Times* who later edited the *New Criterion.* Former members of the New Left took academic posts and revitalized journals of the Left, among them the *Nation,* which returned to its leftist perspective under the editorship of Victor Navasky. Women in the metropolitan area were active in the feminist movement, which gained a national following partly because of the popularity of *Ms.,* a magazine edited by Gloria Steinem. The materialistic outlook of the 1980s gave a primacy to business matters and conservative ideas, which were discussed in the *Wall Street Journal,* the *Public Interest,* and *National Review,* while specialized audiences turned to new magazines such as the literary journal *Grand Street.* In the mid-1990s *Commentary, Dissent,* the *New York Review,* and other major magazines of opinion continued to be published in the city but lacked the urgency and influence that they had enjoyed in earlier times. In 2003 the *Partisan Review* folded after 68 years. By 2009, Web-based blogs and publications were gaining in influence as new forums for intellectual discourse.

Henry F. May, *The Enlightenment in America* (New York: Oxford University Press, 1976); Alexander Bloom, *Prodigal Sons: New York Intellectuals and Their World* (New York: Oxford University Press, 1986); Thomas Bender, *New York Intellect: A History of Intellectual Life in New York City from 1750 to the Beginnings of Our Own Time* (New York: Alfred A. Knopf, 1987)

Alexander Bloom, Kevin Kenny

Interborough Rapid Transit Company [IRT]. Operator of the first subways in New York City. The company was formed on 10 July 1902 by August Belmont, a wealthy financier who in 1900 formed the Rapid Transit Subway Construction Company to build and equip his publicly owned subway. The IRT opened on 27 October 1904, running from City Hall up the East Side of Manhattan to Grand Central Terminal, then west along 42nd Street to Times Square, and up Broadway through the Upper West Side. At 96th Street it divided into two branches that continued to the Bronx, one terminating at Van Cortlandt Park and the other at Bronx Park. The IRT was the first subway in the world to have separate express and local tracks in each direction. The IRT stimulated the residential growth of the Upper West Side, Harlem, northern Manhattan, and the Bronx. The express trains reached speeds as great as 40 miles (64 kilometers) an hour, making them the world's fastest form of urban mass transit at the time.

In December 1905 Belmont acquired his major competitor, the Manhattan Railway Company, which operated the island's elevated lines. Meanwhile the IRT continued to expand, building an extension from Manhattan to Brooklyn in 1908. In 1913 the IRT joined with another competitor, the Brooklyn Rapid Transit Company, thereby increasing the length of its system from 296 to 619 single-track miles (476 to 996 single-track kilometers).

The IRT was profitable until World War I, but was crippled by postwar inflation. It survived the 1920s only by deferring maintenance and cutting wages, and it entered bankruptcy in August 1932. After taking office in 1934 Mayor Fiorello H. La Guardia sought to bring the private subway companies under public ownership, but his efforts were delayed by opposition from Democrats in the state legislature until June 1940, when the IRT became part of the city's transit system.

Clifton Hood

Interchurch Center. Nineteen-story office building for religious organizations at 475 Riverside Drive in Manhattan (at 120th Street), opened in 1960 with funds largely provided by John D. Rockefeller, Jr. The building is popularly known as the God Box. The governing board intended the center to be a visible symbol of ecumenical Christian unity that would house administrative offices of the National Council of Churches, several mainline Protestant and Orthodox denominations, and various interfaith agencies. The center did not attract support from the more conservative and evangelical churches. As Protestant denominations moved their offices out of New York City in the 1980s, the center rented more of its space to educational, nonprofit, and social service agencies.

Peter J. Wosh

interior design. In the United States interior design was centered in New York City when it was a fledgling field dominated by a few society decorators, and it remained so as it

Interchurch Center, 2009

evolved into a profession with thousands of trained practitioners. Elsie de Wolfe, generally regarded as the first professional interior decorator, was neither an architect nor a craftsperson but instead a provider of supervisory design services. She began working about 1905 and by 1913 had a successful practice catering to millionaires. In 1909 she decorated a "showcase" house with the architect Ogden Codman, author with Edith Wharton of *The Decoration of Houses* (1897); among their influential innovations was the replacement of the front stoop with an entrance at ground level and a small flagstone courtyard. Nancy McClelland (*d* 1959) inaugurated a decorating department at a branch of Wanamaker's in 1913, the first ever opened in a department store. Ruby Ross Wood (1880–1950), a disciple of de Wolfe, launched an influential design practice. In 1924 Eleanor McMillen (later Eleanor McMillen Brown) formed a full-service firm under her own name that employed draftspeople, designers, and craftspeople who worked in diverse styles from many periods. Dorothy Draper (1889–1969) became the first woman who was not an architect to focus on nonresidential design: she played an important role to the end of the 1950s in developing partnerships with architects that eventually led to the evolution of such specialties as contract design and space planning. The New York School for Fine and Applied Arts (later the Parsons School of Design) placed a greater emphasis on interior design under the leadership of Frank Alvah Parsons from 1905 to 1930, and the New York School of Interior Design was formed in 1916. As decoration began to encompass some elements of architecture and the applied arts, magazines on interior design spread nationwide the innovative designs of New York City.

The field underwent another expansion in the 1950s and 1960s as specialties emerged in office landscaping, color theory, lighting design, and acoustical design, and by the 1970s in store design, display design, and environmental psychology. The term *interior designer* came into widespread use in contrast to the more limited *interior decorator*. Among the professional bodies formed were the Interior Design Educators Council (1962), to establish education standards, and the National Council for Interior Design Qualifications (1972), to administer examinations and accredit degree programs. In 1975 the National Society of Interior Designers (1957) merged with the American Institute of Interior Designers (formerly the American Institute of Decorators) to form the American Society of Interior Designers.

C. Ray Smith, *Interior Design in Twentieth-Century America: A History* (New York: Harper and Row, 1987)

See also Decorative arts and Furniture.

Owen D. Gutfreund

International African Arts Festival. Four-day cultural event held annually in Brooklyn. Originally known as the African Street Carnival when it began in 1971, it is the largest Afrocentric event of its kind in the United States. Planned as part of commencement exercises by the Uhuru Sasa School (then at 10 Claver Place) and its parent organization, the East, the festival was too large to be held at Claver Place by 1975 and moved to Boys' and Girls' High School at Fulton Street and Schenectady Avenue. It took the name African Street Festival in 1986 and became a nonprofit organization. Russell D. Clown, Mama Kuumba, Sun Ra, the Weusi Kuumba Troupe, and the Dinizulu African Drummers, Dancers, and Singers became some of the regular performers. In 2008 the International African Arts Festival attracted about 75,000 people and more than 300 vendors of African food, clothing, art, crafts, and literature.

Sule Greg C. Wilson

International Alliance of Theatrical Stage Employees and Moving Picture Machine Operators of the United States and Canada [IATSE]. Labor union formed in New York City by stagehands in 1893. It later included such theatrical workers as carpenters, electricians, property crew, and ushers as well as motion picture projectionists and other film, radio, and television employees. As the entertainment business evolved, the great variety of craftspeople working in it led to many jurisdictional disputes with other unions. In 1995 it took on the name International Alliance of Theatrical Stage Employees and Moving Picture Technicians, Artists and Allied Crafts in the United States, its Territories and Canada. In the early twenty-first century IATSE had around 109,000 members.

Martha S. LoMonaco

International Brotherhood of Electrical Workers. Labor union. Its branch in New York City, Local 3, was chartered by the American Federation of Labor in 1900 and soon became powerful. Under the leadership of Harry Van Arsdale, Jr., it won the first pension funded by an employer, a five-hour day, and cooperative housing. In 1962 it reserved 1000 apprenticeships for members of ethnic minorities. In 1965 it organized the city's taxi drivers. Local 3 remained the principal representative of electrical workers in the city in 2007. Apprentices are required to earn either an associate or a bachelor's degree in labor studies from Empire State College.

Colin J. Davis

International Brotherhood of Teamsters. Union formed in 1901. The Teamsters set up the Joint Council of New York City soon after their founding. This council united all the branches of the Teamsters in New York City and was composed mostly of cartmen and later of truckers: it supported regulation of the business and the exclusion from it of African Americans. Eventually the union launched a drive to enroll members engaged in other trades, including taxi drivers, private carters, and warehouse workers. By 1955 the Joint Council of New York City was the largest Teamster organization in the country, with 123,000 members belonging to 60 locals in greater New York. The Teamsters gained an unsavory reputation in the early 1960s because of racketeering scandals, mishandling of pension funds, and links to organized crime, with corruption in the national union mirrored locally in New York City. In 1992 Ron Carey was elected president on a platform promising to sell the union's limousines, luxury jets, and condominiums, cut his own salary from $225,000 to $125,000, and banish the mob from the union's national health insurance plan. In 2007 Anthony Rumore was indicted by federal authorities on charges of using union labor for personal benefit.

Graham Hodges

International Business Machines [IBM]. Firm of electronic data-processing equipment manufacturers, incorporated on 16 June 1911 in New York City as the Computing-Tabulating-Recording Company (C-T-R). It set up offices in 1914 in a few small rooms on Broad Street; as sales grew, the company moved to Broadway. In 1924 the firm took its present name. The earliest products were tabulating devices that allowed increasingly complex calculations; these were most useful for accounting functions, notably those connected with establishing the Social Security program in the 1930s. The firm also introduced the first electronic typewriter that enjoyed wide commercial success. In 1938 the headquarters were moved to 590 Madison Avenue. During World War II the firm's accounting machines kept track of personnel and war equipment, and its plants produced war material such as control instruments, Browning automatic rifles, bombsights, and paper for war bonds. It introduced its first large-scale calculator, the automatic sequence controlled calculator (ASCC), in 1944. In the following year the Watson Scientific Research Laboratory (named for the president of the firm, James J. Watson, Sr.) was dedicated at Columbia University. Another important technical innovation was the IBM 701, the first large vacuum-tube computer (1952). In later years IBM worked in such diverse fields as navigational systems for spacecraft, personal computers, and superconductivity. Although the firm moved its corporate headquarters to suburban Armonk, in Westchester County, in 1964, it remained one of the largest corporate tenants in New York City. In 1983 a new and substantially larger building replaced the existing one on Madison Avenue. In the early twenty-first century, its New York City offices were at 650 Fifth Avenue.

Shan Jayakumar

International Center of Photography. Museum and school opened in 1974 by the photojournalist Cornell Capa. It is the only institution in a major U.S. city devoted to exhibiting, teaching, and collecting photography. The center has two facilities in New York City, the museum at 1130 Sixth Avenue at 43rd Street and the school at 1114 Sixth Avenue. It sponsors about 20 exhibitions each year that reflect a commitment to "concerned photography," typified by the liberal, humanistic work of Robert Capa, Werner Bischof, and David Seymour ("Chim"); it also exhibits avant-garde photography, retrospectives of modern masters, and fashion and advertising photography, and it circulates its materials around the world. The center sponsors lectures, workshops, and documentary and experimental video programs and offers a master's degree in conjunction with New York University. In the early twenty-first century its permanent collection contains about 100,000 prints.

Anne H. Hoy

International Design Center. Complex of several buildings in the former Dutch Kills Industrial Bank in Long Island City, in Queens, occupied predominantly by showrooms for interior furnishings. Developed between 1981 and 1986 by Lazard Realty, it was planned by the firm of I. M. Pei and designed by Gwathmey Segal Associates and Stephen Lepp Associates. The oldest buildings were erected in 1914 by Michael J. Degnon, who also built the Sunnyside railroad yards and the subway tunnel between Manhattan and Steinway, Queens. Former tenants of the buildings include the American Chicle Company, American Eveready, and Bucilla. In its heyday, showroom tenants included Herman Miller and Knoll North America. Architects and designers, among them Stanley Tigerman, Thad Hayes, Mario Botta, and James Wines of SITE, designed inventive showrooms for the center's tenants. The Design Center was virtually empty by the early 1990s, with many of its firms having migrated back to Manhattan. The last showroom was closed by 1998, and the Design Center was replaced by the Queens Atrium Corporate Center, an office complex.

Ann L. Buttenwieser

International Exhibition of Modern Art. See Armory Show.

International Fur and Leather Workers Union. Labor union formed in 1913, one year after fur and leather workers in New York City led a strike and won a shorter workweek and paid holidays. Conflict grew within the union between 1917 and 1927, as members became dissatisfied with unresponsive leaders and as criminal elements sought to stifle dissent. Ben Gold, who managed the New York Joint Council and the Needle Trade Workers Industrial Union, became a central figure during this period when he coordinated a successful drive to weaken the influence of Louis "Lepke" Buchalter and other racketeers. The union entered the Congress of Industrial Organizations (CIO) in 1937, merged with the National Leather Workers Association in 1939, and began building new locals and securing sizable wage increases during World War II. In 1947 the union's leadership opposed U.S. policy toward the Soviet Union, and it left the CIO in 1950 in anticipation of being expelled. After Gold's conviction on perjury charges, the union merged in 1955 with the Amalgamated Meat Cutters and Butcher Workmen.

Philip Foner, *The Fur and Leather Workers Union: A Story of Dramatic Struggles* (Newark, N.J.: Nordam, 1950); Bert Cochran, *Labor and Communism: The Conflict That Shaped the American Unions* (Princeton, N.J.: Princeton University Press, 1977); Harvey Levenstein, *Communism, Anticommunism and the CIO* (Westport, Conn.: Greenwood, 1981)

Ronald Mendel

International House. Residence and meeting place near Columbia University for foreign graduate students at 500 Riverside Drive in Manhattan. It was opened in 1924 by Harry Edmonds, a leader in the Christian student movement, with the aid of John D. Rockefeller. The International House has inspired the establishment of more than 60 similar facilities worldwide. It can accommodate over 1000 residents.

Elliot S. Meadows

International Ladies' Garment Workers' Union [ILGWU]. Labor union organized in New York City in 1900. It consisted at first of Jewish immigrants and drew many Italian immigrants during its first two decades. In its early years the union led successful strikes of shirtwaist workers (1909) and cloakmakers (1910). The cloakmakers' strike led the Joint Board of Sanitary Control to establish guidelines for hygiene and safety in the workplace and helped to create the "Protocol of Peace," which provided for the resolution of disputes between labor and management and the protection of workers' health; the union opened a health center in 1914. During the 1920s an attempted communist takeover led to intense conflict among members, and a disastrous strike by cloakmakers nearly destroyed the union. By this time Jewish men, who initially had made up a majority of the union's members, were outnumbered by young Jewish women and members of other ethnic groups. In 1932 David Dubinsky became president of the union, which from the following year benefited from the labor policies of President Franklin D. Roosevelt. The union organized its 150,000 members, repaid its loans, and in 1935 helped to form the Committee for Industrial Organization (CIO) within the American Federation of Labor (AFL); the CIO was later suspended by the AFL and became an independent group called the Congress of Industrial Organizations, which the ILGWU refused to join. In 1936 members of the union were instrumental in forming the American Labor Party in New York City; many eventually abandoned the party because of its increasingly leftist positions and formed the Liberal Party, with which the union was closely allied for 25 years. By the time Dubinsky retired in 1966 the ILGWU had grown to more than 450,000 members and had $571 million in assets. Having forsaken its socialist goals, it focused on securing benefits for its members, including health coverage, recreational facilities, a 35-hour work week, retirement pensions, death benefits, and low-cost housing. From 1945 the union's ethnic composition continued to change as blacks, Puerto Ricans, Asians, and others entered the industry and Jews and Italians found other forms of work. During the late 1960s membership declined and the garment industry was increasingly driven overseas. Under Sol C. Chaikin (1977–86) and Jay Mazur (1986–95) the ILGWU fought problems arising from the growing employment of illegal aliens, the return of industrial homework in New York City and elsewhere, worsened working conditions, and declining membership (less than 150,000 in 1993). With the garment trades in distress, in 1995 the ILGWU merged with the Amalgamated Clothing and Textile Workers Union to form UNITE, the Union of Needletrades, Industrial and Textile Employees, with Jay Mazur as president. Bruce Raynor, who became president in 2001, continued in that office in 2004 when UNITE merged with the Hotel Employees and Restaurant Employees International Union to form UNITE HERE, with 440,000 members. The ILGWU had returned to the AFL in 1940, and in 1955 become part of a new AFL-CIO formed by the merger of the AFL with the Congress of Industrial Organizations. In 2005 UNITE HERE and six other unions broke away from the AFL-CIO to form a new federation, Change to Win, aimed at reversing organized labor's decline in membership and increasing workers' wages.

Louis Levine, *The Women's Garment Workers* (New York: B. W. Huebsch, 1924); Benjamin Stolberg, *Tailor's Progress: The Story of a Famous Union and the Men Who Made It* (Garden City, N.Y.: Doubleday, Doran, 1944); Leon Stein, ed., *Out of the Sweatshop: The Struggle for Industrial Democracy* (New York: Quadrangle, 1977); Gus Tyler, *Look for the Union Label: A History of the International Ladies' Garment Workers' Union* (Armonk, N.Y.: M. E. Sharpe, 1995)

Robert D. Parmet

International Rescue Committee. Relief organization formed by Albert Einstein to rescue refugees of Hitler's regime and help "victims of racial, religious, and ethnic persecution and oppression, as well as people uprooted by war, violence, and famine to survive and rebuild their lives." It opened its first office at 11 West 42nd Street on 24 July 1933. Volunteers operating out of a hotel room in Marseilles, France, rescued more than 2000 refugees, among them the philosopher Hannah Arendt and the artists Marcel Duchamp and Max Ernst. In the following years the committee provided assistance during crises in Hungary (1956), Cuba (1959), Czechoslovakia (1968), Bangladesh (1971), Kurdistan (1991), and Iraq (2007). Its main offices are located at 122 East 42nd Street, from which it operates relief programs in Africa, Asia, Europe, the Middle East, and Central America, as well as domestic refugee resettlement programs in cities nationwide. George Rupp became its president in 2002.

Jesse Drucker

International Telephone and Telegraph [ITT]. International conglomerate formed in New York City in 1920 as a holding company for several Caribbean telephone companies. Its founder, Sosthenes Behn (1882–1957), intended for it to be an international counterpart to American Telephone and Telegraph. The firm acquired several Latin American and European telephone systems and after World War II shifted the focus of its acquisitions to electronics firms. Between 1959 and 1972, CEO Harold Geneen stabilized ITT's finances and transformed the firm into a true conglomerate: among the businesses that he acquired were Sheraton Hotels, the Hartford Insurance Company, and the lumber firm Rayonier. ITT was based in New York City from 1930 to 1995: at 67 Broad Street (1930–61); 320 Park Avenue (1961–90); and 1330 Sixth Avenue (1990–95). Beginning in 1989, the firm divested its telecommunications business, and in 1995 it split into three independent companies: ITT Corporation, which was focused on the hotel and gaming businesses and later (1997) merged with the White Plains, New York–based Starwood Hotels and Resorts; ITT Hartford, which became a stand-alone insurance operation, Hartford Financial Services Group, and continued operations in Hartford, Connecticut; and ITT Industries, a manufacturing, engineering, and defense technology firm that changed its name back to ITT Corporation in 2006 and is now based in suburban White Plains.

Robert Sobel, *ITT: The Management of Opportunity* (New York: Truman Talley, 1981)

Rohit T. Aggarwala

International Workingmen's Association. International labor organization. It was formed in London on 28 September 1864 by French and British labor leaders under the guidance of Karl Marx and supported trade unions and legislative campaigns for an eight-hour workday. After the Civil War it gained influence in New York City, and in 1868 Section 1 of the International Workingmen's Association was formed from the General German Workingmen's Association, a group of German craftsmen and reformers in the city who adhered to the ideas of Marx and Ferdinand Lassalle. The section played a fundamental role in the trade union movement of the late 1860s by collecting strike funds, compiling labor statistics, helping to organize black workers, and providing leaders such as Friedrich Sorge, Adolph Douai, Friedrich Bolte, and Conrad Kuhn. Section 12, formed in 1871, was dominated by middle-class land reformers and antimonopolists such as John Commerford, Lewis Masquerier, and William West. Another member was Victoria Woodhull, a flamboyant champion of equal rights for women who became influential in the organization by leading a memorial procession through the city for French Communards executed in 1871 and by reporting on labor affairs in *Woodhull and Claflin's Weekly* (financed by Cornelius Vanderbilt, a friend of her sister Tennessee Claflin). Her feminism was dismissed as a diversion from the issues of labor and wages by Sorge, Bolte, and other members of Section 1, who viewed the members of Section 12 as middle-class interlopers lacking in sympathy for the working classes. Sorge sought to deny admission to sections unless at least two-thirds of their members were wage earners; West argued that only the middle class had the "experience and the intelligence" required for the success of the labor movement. This conflict led the association to divide in late 1871. The Hague Congress of 1872 gave its blessing to Sorge's faction, and the general council was moved to New York City and placed under his authority. Members of Section 12 held their own assembly in Philadelphia and formed a competing International Workingmen's Association, which incorporated the land reformers' yearnings for a simple rural society and was sought out by the New York Workingmen's Assembly in 1872–73. By the mid-1870s the International Workingmen's Association was nearly extinct in Europe owing to government repression and had been weakened in the United States because it raised the specter that open class warfare in the manner of the Paris Commune might spread across the Atlantic. It ceased functioning in 1876 after the movement for an eight-hour workday was defeated.

David Montgomery, *Beyond Equity: Labor and the Radical Republicans, 1862–1872* (New York: Alfred A. Knopf, 1967)

Iver Bernstein

Interstate Park. Name applied to Bellaire when it was first developed in 1899.

Interview Magazine. Cultural magazine. Started by pop artist Andy Warhol and John Wilcock in 1969, it was initially dedicated to the cult of celebrity, which fascinated Warhol, and featured cutting-edge graphics alongside interviews of celebrities. These interviews were edited and designed in an eccentric style similar to Warhol's own books. At its start, copies of the magazine were handed out among "in-crowds" in New York to gain interest and attract new readers. Toward the end of his life, Warhol withdrew from overseeing the magazine day-to-day, and it became more conventionally written and edited under Bob Colacello following Warhol's death in 1987. The magazine's emphasis thereafter was on the fashion world and the fashion elite. In the beginning of the twenty-first century, the magazine was published by Brant Publications and was composed of 30 percent features and 70 percent advertisements.

Benjamin Yakas

Intrepid Sea, Air, and Space Museum. Decommissioned World War II aircraft carrier that was converted into a museum docked at Pier 86 on the West Side of Manhattan. Launched in 1942 at a cost of $44 million, the *Intrepid* was 900 feet (275 meters) long and carried more than 100 aircraft and 3000 personnel through the many campaigns of the Pacific War against the Japanese navy. The carrier was modernized in 1954 and, after serving in the Korean and Vietnam wars, was scheduled in 1976 to be scrapped. To save and renovate the *Intrepid,* a foundation was formed in 1978 by Zachary Fisher, a builder and philanthropist. Opened in August 1982, the museum recounts the history of the ship, which is a federal landmark, and has a collection of aircraft, from early wooden flying machines to supersonic jet fighters. Alongside the carrier the museum also displays a historic diesel-powered submarine and the Concorde, the world's fastest commercial airliner.

Ann L. Buttenwieser

investment banking. Form of banking that meets the needs of business and government for long-term capital. An important function of investment bankers is to originate, underwrite, and distribute new issues of securities, which may then be traded on organized securities exchanges or over the counter. Although investment banking, commercial banking, and securities trading are distinct functions, some notable financial firms in New York City have engaged in more than one, and the city has long been an international leader in all three.

Securities trading in the city began with the refinancing in 1790 of debts incurred during the American Revolution. In the early years of the nineteenth century there was some trading in the stock of private firms (principally banks and insurers), and new issues of stock were still sold by subscription. The beginnings of investment banking date to the second decade of the nineteenth century, when some new issues were bought in large blocks by financiers who then resold them at a profit. Among the first to engage in this practice was John Jacob Astor, who with two other wealthy merchants contracted in 1813 with the federal government to take over and distribute for a commission the unsubscribed portion of a war loan of $16 million. From 1815 the states made several large offerings of securities to finance transportation enterprises such as the Erie Canal. The source of much of the demand for these government securities was Europe, where investment capital had accumulated. Several private banking houses in New York City organized the transfer to Europe of U.S. securities before the Civil War: the firm known from 1826 to 1848 as Prime, Ward and King, formed in 1790 as a brokerage, dealt in foreign exchange by the 1820s and enjoyed close ties to Baring Brothers, a leading merchant banking house in Britain that distributed new issues of federal and state bonds to European investors; Winslow, Lanier and Company, formed in 1849, specialized in negotiating U.S. railway securities and helped to make New York City the center of this important field of investment banking; and the firm of August Belmont was the agent in the United States for the Rothschilds.

The Civil War brought an unprecedented volume of government debt issues to financial markets in the United States, with lasting effects on investment banking. The firm of Jay Cooke in Philadelphia introduced the practice of offering federal war bonds to small retail customers throughout the nation, and several firms in New York City built retail investment banking businesses as Cooke's agents. A second effect of war finance was the establishment of banking houses by German immigrants who earlier had settled in the United States and prospered as merchants. The firm of J. and W. Seligman, formed in New York City in 1862, soon opened branches through family contacts in several U.S. and European cities. The Seligmans dealt extensively in government debt, of which they sold $200 million in Germany during the war. Other prominent banking houses established during the Civil War era by Germans were Kuhn, Loeb and Company (1867), M. Goldman (1869, predecessor of Goldman Sachs), and Lehman Brothers (1868). A third group of private banking houses that appeared in the city during the 1860s were firms with origins in New England, called Yankee firms, of which the most prominent were the houses of J. P. Morgan and Levi P. Morton. The Yankee firms also depended for their success on affiliations or other close ties with banking houses in Europe.

Legislation passed during the Civil War made possible the rise of national banks. These were commercial banks, but a few of the larger ones in New York City developed a business in investment banking as well. Foremost among these was the First National Bank, formed in 1863, which dealt as an investment banker in government war bonds and under the leadership of George F. Baker was a leading investment bank by the end of the century. In the 1890s National City Bank under James Stillman also became a major investment bank. The keys to the success of the national banks in investment banking were not European contacts but rather large corporate accounts and balances of U.S. banks held as reserves in New York.

After the Civil War the focus of investment banking shifted from government finance to railroad finance. The large financial requirements of the railroads and the greater risks of dealing in securities of corporations rather than governments led to innovations in investment banking. The long-standing practice among financiers of forming cooperative syndicates to bid for and buy securities was extended after the Civil War to the sale of securities. Even more important was the formation in 1870 of the first underwriting syndicate: bankers belonging to such a syndicate made a commitment to purchase at an agreed price and resell any portion of a corporate issue that could not be sold by the corporation itself. Because the bankers were assuming a greater risk, they became more active in managing the affairs of the issuing corporations. Investment bankers in New York City had a decided edge in organizing and managing syndicates because of the development of money and capital markets there, and leaders such as Morgan, Baker, Stillman, and Jacob Schiff of Kuhn, Loeb wielded great power. From the 1890s to World War I the emphasis in investment banking shifted gradually from railroads to industrial companies and public utilities, and from bonds to common stocks. Leading bankers in the city became active in managing the industrial and utility corporations, much as they had done with the railroads. Allegations that investment bankers had formed a so-called Money Trust to control finance and industry were investigated by a committee led by Representative Arsène Pujo. The findings issued by the committee in 1913 had little immediate effect on federal legislation, but states began to enact "blue sky" laws regulating securities dealing.

World War I forced the belligerent powers of Europe to turn to the United States to borrow money, buy war supplies, and sell accumulated financial assets. Huge loans to Britain, France, and other nations were made by syndicates led by the firm of J. P. Morgan, which also became the purchasing agent for the British and French governments. The massive transfer of money and financial assets from Europe made the United States a creditor nation, and New York City eclipsed London as the leading financial center in the world. After the United States entered the war in 1917, the federal government raised money through four "liberty" loans and a "victory" loan, amounting to $21.5 billion in two years. Investment bankers and commercial bankers participated in purchasing and distributing the bonds. As they had done during the Civil War, the bankers sold to small savers as well as to the wealthy individuals and institutional investors who were their traditional customers. During the 1920s syndicates led by firms in New York City originated and distributed numerous corporate stock and bond issues as well as foreign securities.

The stock market crash of 1929 and the worldwide depression that followed focused public attention on weaknesses in financial arrangements in the United States and on dubious practices in banking. From 1933 a series of new federal laws began to regulate investment banking. The Glass–Steagall Act (1933) mandated a separation of commercial banking (the lending and taking of deposits) from investment banking (securities underwriting and trading). As a consequence J. P. Morgan chose to remain in commercial banking, while some of its partners left to form the investment bank of Morgan Stanley. Other federal laws of 1933 and 1934 required prior registration of public offerings of securities, full disclosure of all material facts, and the regulation of stock market trading by a new federal agency, the Securities and Exchange Commission. Investment banking did not recover from the Depression until the economic expansion of the 1950s. World War II had little effect on it because the legislation of the 1930s allowed commercial banks to continue originating and dealing in government debt: corporate finance was the area left to investment banking under the Glass–Steagall

Act. The leading investment banks in New York City, such long-established houses as Morgan Stanley, Goldman Sachs, Dillon Read, and Kuhn, Loeb, were protected by law from the competition of commercial banks. They organized, led, and managed major corporate underwriting syndicates and counseled leading corporations.

By the 1960s growth and structural change brought newer firms to prominence. An increase in the number of individual shareholders gave a competitive advantage to retail firms such as Merrill Lynch that could distribute shares widely. At the same time pension funds and mutual funds accounted for a growing share of securities holdings, and firms such as Salomon Brothers and Donaldson, Lufkin and Jenrette made a specialty of serving such institutional customers. There was also a change in the geography of investment banking, as many of the largest firms moved from lower Manhattan to midtown. The 1970s and 1980s were a period of inflation, disruptions in the supply of oil, fluctuations in interest rates and exchange rates, increased volatility in securities markets, and the return of the United States to the status of an international debtor. The regulatory system put in place during the 1930s began to unravel. Soaring interest rates in the 1970s stimulated financial innovation: money market mutual funds, introduced by retail investment firms such as Merrill Lynch, offered interest rates well above the regulated ones paid by commercial banks and thrift institutions and gained a large amount of invested funds at their expense. In 1975 the federal government ended the long-standing tradition of fixed brokerage commissions, which led to competitive fees and to the liquidation or merger of several investment firms. The last quarter of the century witnessed considerable deregulation of financial services that included ending regulated interest rates, permitting nationwide banking, and repealing the Glass–Steagall separation of commercial and investment banking.

Competition, consolidation, and a shift from partnership to corporate organization were trends that affected the issuing and underwriting sector of investment banking in the 1980s and 1990s. Large, well-capitalized investment banks often could underwrite large issues by themselves: syndicates of many firms were needed neither to share risks and profits, because the larger firms could hedge their risks in financial futures and options markets, nor for distribution, because issues could be placed with the large institutional investors around the world. The repeal of the Glass–Steagall Act in 1999 allowed commercial banks to underwrite and trade in securities, making investment banking more competitive. It also led to the emergence of huge financial conglomerates such as Citigroup and JPMorgan Chase, which operate across a broad range of financial services, including investment banking.

Another development that began in the 1980s was a wave of corporate mergers, hostile takeovers, and leveraged buyouts in which publicly held companies were taken private. Often these maneuvers were financed by what became known as junk bonds, which were of low grade and offered high yields. During the 1990s and early twenty-first century, specialized private-equity firms such as the Carlyle Group, Kohlberg Kravis Roberts (KKR), and Blackstone gathered pools of capital from pension funds, endowment funds, and wealthy individuals and institutionalized the buyout innovations of the 1980s. Investment bankers on Wall Street thus became principals of companies rather than merely financiers of them, much as investment bankers had taken large roles in corporate affairs a century earlier. Still another development of recent decades was the securitization of mortgages and other traditional forms of financial assets. In the past lenders would hold such assets until the borrowers repaid the loan. With securitization, traditional assets become collateral standing behind new issues of financial obligations; they gain liquidity from being tradable in financial markets. These innovative developments brought unprecedented attention to investment banking as a profession, and salaries, bonuses, and profits from buyout deals and securitizations rose dramatically.

The so-called globalization of banking and financial markets around the turn of the twenty-first century entailed both opportunities for Wall Street's investment bankers and threats to them. On the one hand, since they were the most innovative and experienced banks, they branched out from their New York City base to become leading firms in older international financial centers such as London and Frankfurt, and newer ones such as Tokyo and Shanghai. On the other hand, the rise of financial centers outside of the United States threatened to erode the position New York City held as the preeminent international financial center from 1914 to the early twenty-first century. In late 2008 Wall Street was in turmoil as a subprime mortgage crisis led to the failure or reorganization of many investment banks, including Morgan Stanley and Goldman Sachs voluntarily becoming bank holding companies and the total collapse and dissolution of Lehman Brothers. Nonetheless, the city remained the world's leading stock exchange and the global center of investment banking. Perhaps the twenty-first century will see new challenges to Wall Street from Hong Kong, Shanghai, Singapore, and London, but Manhattan will likely remain a major money center in the future.

Vincent P. Carosso, *Investment Banking in America: A History* (Cambridge, Mass.: Harvard University Press, 1970); George P. Baker and George David Smith, *The New Financial Capitalists* (Cambridge: Cambridge University Press, 1998)

Richard Sylla

Inwood. Neighborhood at the northern tip of Manhattan, bounded to the north and east by the Harlem River, to the south by Fairview Avenue and Fort George Hill, and to the west by the Hudson River. Broadway is the principal north-south avenue and bisects Inwood; principal east-west streets are Dyckman and 207th. The area is thought to have been the site of Peter Minuit's purchase of Manhattan from the Indians in 1626. In the nineteenth century estates were built in the hilly western section, which was never leveled. During the early twentieth century tenements went up in the flat eastern section after Interborough Rapid Transit (IRT) extended its subway in 1906; apartment buildings for

Inwood Heights, 1913

middle-class tenants proliferated after the Eighth Avenue subway's "A" train opened in 1932. In 1923 Columbia University opened Baker Field, an athletic complex west of Broadway at 218th Street. In 1984 Columbia University built Lawrence A. Wien Stadium for football at Baker Field, and Columbia-Presbyterian Hospital opened a branch in 1988 at 220th Street. In the early 1990s New York City Parks Department rebuilt the boat marina on the Hudson River at the foot of Dyckman Street. In 1992 Guillermo Linares became the first Dominican elected to public office in the United States when he won a seat representing Inwood on the City Council. Large sections of parkland in the neighborhood include Inwood Hill Park, which covers 196 acres (79 hectares) and contains the last remnant of primeval forest in Manhattan. Inwood is also the site of the Dyckman House (circa 1785), the last Dutch farmhouse in the borough. The population in 2009 of Inwood and of Washington Heights to its south was 200,000, mostly Latin American, and in the twenty-first century, more affluent families became markedly more visible.

Michele Herman

IOOF. See Independent Order of Odd Fellows.

Ira Haupt and Co. Brokerage firm. Established in 1928, it was most famous for the 1963 salad-oil swindle and subsequent bankruptcy. After its founder died in 1962, the firm was run by new, young managers eager to expand, and it was under that leadership that the firm accumulated more than $24 million in debt from its commodity customer, Allied Crude Vegetable Oil Refining Corporation (which was $150 million in debt). The New York Stock Exchange agreed to set up a $12 million fund to pay for customer losses, the firm was suspended from trading, and in 1964 an involuntary petition of bankruptcy was filed against the company.

Jessica Montesano

Iranians. Iranians in New York City are a diverse group that includes Persians, Turks, Kurds, Armenians, and Assyrians. Shi'ite Muslims, who constitute the majority of the population in Iran, are relatively less numerous in the city. There is a large Jewish population (by some estimates accounting for one-third to one-half of the total) and small numbers of other Iranian religious minorities: Christians, Zoroastrians, and Baha'is. The federal census of 2000 reported 8506 Iranians living in the city, but community estimates put the number closer to twice that many. The first Iranians in New York City, a small group of diplomats, merchants, and students, arrived in the 1920s and 1930s. By the 1970s the community grew substantially, profoundly affected by the 1979 Iranian revolution that overthrew the U.S.-backed monarchy of Shah Mohammad Reza Pahlavi (1910–80). Affluent families, many connected to the shah's regime, as well as other refugees came to New York City in great numbers. After the revolution, Iranian businesses in the city extended beyond the traditional carpet, garment, and jewelry enterprises. The *Iranian Yellow Pages Directory* for Greater New York, first published in 1984, reflected the vibrant economic life of the community. The annual Persian Day Parade (begun in 2003) draws thousands, many second- and third-generation Iranian Americans, to Madison Avenue in midtown Manhattan. Showcasing the cultural heritage of Iran and the contributions of the community in the United States, the parade coincides with *Nowruz,* the Iranian New Year, which falls on the first day of spring in March. In 2006 Mayor Michael Bloomberg proclaimed 19 March "Persian *Nowruz* Day" in recognition of the importance of the holiday. Because Greater New York is home to the second largest concentration of Iranians in the country (following California), the city has historically been a major center for Iranian cultural and political activities, including events protesting U.S. support for the shah in the 1960s and 1970s, opposition to U.S. military intervention in Iran after the U.S. invasion of Iraq, and censorship of the Islamic Republic for human rights violations as seen by the community's outcry against President Mahmoud Ahmadinejad's 2007 visit to New York City. Recently, Iranians in the city have joined national efforts by such groups as the National Iranian American Council and the Iranian American Political Action Committee for a greater voice in U.S. politics by hosting fund-raising events for electoral candidates and organizing lobbying efforts.

Leyli Shayegan

Iraqis. Iraqis in New York City are scattered across the five boroughs, with clusters in the Bronx, Bay Ridge, and Staten Island. The 2000 census showed that 957 New Yorkers identified as Iraqi or of Iraqi descent, but the number is probably closer to three times that. The reasons for emigration have varied: starting in the 1930s and 1940s Christian and Jewish Iraqis came to the United States for economic reasons; in the 1960s students came to attend medical school. But perhaps the most important stimulus for Iraqi immigration to the United States was the U.S. blockade of Iraq starting in 1990; 30,000 Iraqis were resettled in the United States, with a small percentage, mostly Shia Muslims, coming to New York City. Shi'ites worship at the Al-Khoie Center in Queens and at the Ahl Al-Bayt Mosque on Fulton Street in Brooklyn. Another Iraqi religious group are the pacifist Mandeans, many of whom have settled in Queens. The 1950s saw an economically motivated influx of Iraqi Jews, from both Baghdad and Israel. Many Iraqi Jews, who are active in the electronics, jewelry, and clothing industries, belong to Congregation Bene Nahharayim on Midland Parkway in Jamaica Estates. A well-known Iraqi Jewish musician is the *oud* player Hakki Obadia, who, with the Syrian American drummer Eddie Kochak, helped to develop the Amer-aba (American Arab) style of music. Another high-profile person of Iraqi Jewish heritage is Ella Shohat, feminist professor of multicultural studies at New York University. The proportion of professional Iraqi New Yorkers is high compared with Iraqis in other U.S. cities; many are physicians. For decades, the most high-profile Iraqi American in New York City was activist M(ohammad) T. Mehdi (1926–98), whose lifelong mission was to present to U.S. audiences an Arab perspective on Middle Eastern issues.

Paula Hajar

Ireland Mill. Former name of Queensborough Hill.

Irish. New York City has one of the largest concentrations of Irish in the world and has been since the nineteenth century a major destination for Irish immigrants.

1. Colonial and Early National (Pre-Famine) Periods

In the 1720s Irish indentured servants, clerks, and soldiers came to New York City as trade between the United States and Ireland increased. Flaxseed and finished linen goods were shipped between New York City and Dublin, Belfast, and Londonderry, much of it in the hands of Irish mercantile houses such as Greg, Cunningham and Company, which opened local branches in the city. An annual parade in honor of the patron saint of Ireland, Patrick, dates to as early as 1762 (see St. Patrick's Day Parade) even though the eighteenth-century New York Irish were a diverse population of English-speaking Anglicans, Huguenots, Quakers, Presbyterians, and Methodists. Catholics were not permitted official freedom of worship until 1784, thus relatively few Gaelic-speaking Irish settled in the city.

Some of the city's most successful merchants during the eighteenth century were Irish, including William Constable, Cornelius Heeney, Dominick Lynch, Daniel McCormick, James McEvers, John McVickar, Robert Ross Waddell, and Hugh Wallace. During the American Revolution Irish patriots could be found in equal numbers to Irish Loyalists. James Duane, mayor of New York City from 1784 to 1789, was the son of an Irishman who emigrated in 1700; and George Clinton, the first governor of New York State (1777–95) and uncle of DeWitt Clinton, was the son of an immigrant who left County Longford in 1729. The repeal of the Alien and Sedition Acts cleared the way for Irish exiled after the Irish Rebellion of 1798, several of whom emerged as community leaders: attorneys Thomas Addis Emmet and William Sampson; Dr. William James MacNeven; and journalist Thomas O'Connor, who became coeditor in 1814 of Edward Gillespy's the *Shamrock or, Hibernian Chronicle* (1810), New York's first Irish American newspaper.

In 1816 there were 12,000 Irish in the city; but in the 1830s about 200,000 Irish arrived at the Port of New York, predominantly Catholic and unskilled. Organizations such as the Society of the Friendly Sons of St. Patrick (1784) and the Irish Emigrant Society of New York (1841) were formed to help them. In September 1850 the Emigrant Industrial Savings Bank opened at 51 Chambers Street. Its predominantly Irish depositors used the bank to finance the emigration of relatives and friends for the remainder of the nineteenth century. Emigrants' officers and trustees were also intimately involved in the politics of immigration reform: Gregory Dillon (1782–1854), Andrew Carrigan (1804–72), and especially John E. Develin (1820–88) helped birth the state Commissioners of Emigration (1847) that led to the establishment of the immigration station Castle Garden in 1855 as well as emigrant care facilities on Wards Island. From 1825 the leading Irish newspaper in the city was the *Truth Teller,* a weekly that was succeeded in 1857 by the *Tablet,* published by the Sadlier brothers, whose firm (established 1832) also brought out religious books and moral fiction for the Irish market.

The Catholic Church in the United States grew with the increased numbers of Irish Catholic emigrants. The first Catholic elementary school opened at St. Peter's in 1800, New York City was raised to a see (bishopric) in 1808, and St. Patrick's on Mott Street became the city's first Catholic cathedral when it opened in 1815; from 1817 it operated a free school for girls. St. James's Church on Jay Street was opened in 1823 to serve Brooklyn's Irishtown. St. Joseph's in Greenwich Village opened in 1833; it is the oldest extant Catholic church building in Manhattan. An estimated 50,000 non-Catholic Irish lived in New York City in 1860. Periodic confrontations between Protestant and Catholic Irish, which stemmed from complex political and cultural attitudes rather than merely religious differences, were called Orange–Green or Orange Riots. The earliest account is of an attack by Irish Catholics living on the outskirts of the city in Greenwich Village that took place when Irish Protestants marched through the neighborhood on 12 July 1824 to commemorate William of Orange's victory at the Battle of the Boyne (1690).

Nativist swings in popular opinion led to acts against the city's Irish that ranged from discrimination in hiring (typified by "No Irish" phraseology) to religious persecution such as the burning of St. Mary's Church on Grand Street in 1831. The fraternal Ancient Order of Hibernians was founded in May 1836 to help counter anti-Irish prejudice. St. Vincent's Hospital and the House of Mercy (both 1849), were set up to meet the needs of Irish Catholics as well as to counter the proselytism accompanying Protestant charity. As increasing numbers of Irish joined the Catholic clergy, Bishop John Hughes led efforts to obtain state funds for private schools between 1839 and 1842. The rejection of these requests and the overwhelming financial obligations of an immigrant church meant that only about 50 percent of Catholic children were educated in parochial schools during the 1840s, a figure reduced by more than half just 30 years later; the remainder attended ward schools. The Jesuits opened two Catholic colleges, St. John's in Fordham (1841) and St. Francis Xavier (1847) on West 16th Street, both of which attracted young Irish American men who wished to train in the professions. A third, Manhattan College (1849), was run by the Christian Brothers. Manhattanville (1841) and the College of Mount St. Vincent (1847) were established by the Society of the Sacred Heart and the Sisters of Charity, respectively, to educate Irish American women.

By 1844 an estimated 80,000 to 90,000 Catholics, most of whom were Irish, worshiped in 15 parishes on Manhattan Island. Sts. Peter and Paul, the first of architect Patrick Keely's (1816–96) oeuvre of more than 500 Catholic churches, opened in Williamsburg in 1846, and the Diocese of Brooklyn was spun off from New York in 1853. Consequently, Calvary Cemetery in Queens (1848) and Brooklyn's Cemetery of the Holy Cross (1849) give New York City the distinction of having the largest Irish burial grounds in the world.

2. Peak Immigration

Many newly arrived Irish immigrants, particularly those who were refugees from the Irish Potato Famine of the 1840s, lived in the crowded and cheap tenements of the fourth and sixth wards, with blacks and Chinese as neighbors. As early as 1855 the Irish made up a quarter to a half of the total population in 16 of the city's 22 wards, and more than one-quarter of the population in both Manhattan and Brooklyn had been born in Ireland. Institutions like the Convent of Mercy (Brooklyn, 1862), Catholic Protectory (1863), New York Foundling Asylum (1869), Mission of the Immaculate Virgin (1871), and Angel Guardian (Brooklyn, 1899) were established for women and children, who were most vulnerable to the effects of the unemployment and poverty that many newly arrived Irish faced. Municipal charity, especially that dispensed by the Bellevue Almshouse, helped families get through rough periods.

By 1855 about 86 percent of the city's laborers and 74 percent of its domestic servants were from Ireland. Irish women were also well represented among laundresses and nurses, and more than half of the city's blacksmiths, weavers, masons, bricklayers, plasterers, stonecutters, and polishers were Irish-born men. At mid-century more than 11,000 Irish men and women worked as dressmakers, seamstresses, furriers, hatters, shoemakers, and tailors. Many were employed by Irish entrepreneurs such as Daniel Devlin, Charles Knox, Hugh O'Neill, and A. T. Stewart, men who were part of the city's commercial elite, as were wholesale grocer James Olwell, hardware merchant Felix Ingoldsby, and banker Joseph Stuart. On a smaller scale, businesses such as carting concerns, groceries, and saloons created an Irish middle class as early as the 1850s. Across the East River, 63 percent of all agricultural laborers in Kings County in 1860 were Irish.

With the increase in the city's Irish population, the number of Irish organizations also grew. They met, among other places, at Hibernian Hall and Montgomery Hall, both on Prince Street, which were also the headquarters for several militia companies, such as the Irish Volunteers (1871); for the 69th Regiment (the Irish Brigade, which served with distinction during the Civil War); and for the Convention of Irish Societies, the first coordinating organization for the St. Patrick's Day Parade. One of the most enduring forms of organization was the county society, based on place of origin in Ireland; the earliest known in New York City was the Sligo Young Men's Association (1849). The county societies provided disability and death benefits to members and fostered social and employment networks. They banded together in 1904 under the rubric of the United Irish Counties Association (UICA) to coordinate their events. As a result, chain migration operated quite specifically in New York City: Cork, Kerry, Galway, and Clare emigrants, for example, went to Manhattan, while Donegal, Mayo, Leitrim, and Longford people gravitated to Brooklyn.

Irish nationalism thrived in New York City, which became the headquarters for U.S. support of Irish political causes (see Irish Republicanism). The Fenian Brotherhood and the Clan na Gael dominated revolutionary activities during the second half of the nineteenth century. Newspapers in the city such as the *Irish Citizen* (1867), the *United Irishman* (1885), and the *Gaelic American* (1903) were edited by exiled Irish political leaders. Other forms of nationalism included campaigns for land reform in Ireland spearheaded by Patrick Ford's *Irish World* (1878); the cultivation of the Irish language and the study of Irish literature, history, and music, which were the focus of the monthly bilingual magazine the *Gael,* published in Brooklyn from 1881 to 1904; and sports, particularly Gaelic football and hurling, after the formation of the Gaelic Athletic Association (GAA) of New York in 1914. One of the most visible annual activities of the New York Gaelic Society was its *Feis Ceoil agus Seanachas,* a festival of music, dance, and song for which musician Victor Herbert dedicated his "Irish Rhapsody" in 1892. An alternative expression of Irish identity was membership in the Orange Order, a fraternal group of Protestants who opposed Irish political independence. There were Orange lodges in New York City from the middle of the nineteenth century that revived the tradition of marching on 12 July, leading to serious disturbances in 1870 and 1871 that resulted in deaths and injuries; as late as 1890, 1000 Orangemen assembled in Jones's Wood to mark the bicentenary of the Battle of the Boyne.

In politics the Irish in New York City were influenced by anti-alien, anti-Irish, and anti-Catholic party platforms. Once suffrage was extended in 1827, men like labor radical Mike Walsh (1815–59) aspired to political careers, as did self-made millionaire George Law (1806–81), a second-generation Irish Protestant who was briefly a favorite of the Know-Nothing Party in 1856. Immigrants were especially courted by politicians associated with Tammany Hall, and as early as 1844 an estimated 90 percent of enfranchised Irish Catholics in New York City voted Democratic. Their vehement opposition to the Republican implementation of the military draft in 1863, as well as to emancipation, escalated into the largest civil disturbance in U.S. history (see Draft Riots). But the Irish did not come to dominate Tammany Hall until the 1870s when John Kelly (1822–86) took over as its leader after the Tweed Ring fell from power. A succession of Irish bosses then made the local Democratic organization the most famous urban political machine in the United States.

Tammany Hall was behind the election in 1880 of the city's first Irish Catholic mayor, the businessman William R. Grace, and prepared men such as Alfred E. Smith, James A. Farley, and Robert F. Wagner for state and national politics. By 1900, when 22 percent of the city was Irish by birth or descent, the Friendly Sons of St. Patrick was dominated by men connected with Tammany Hall. The Irish benefited the most from employment on public works projects and made important inroads into the civil service (notably the police and fire departments, the post office, the courts, and the transit system).

The Irish influence was felt culturally through entertainment, language, and sports. One of the most famous blackface minstrel troupes was the Bryant Brothers (Dan, Neil, and Jerry O'Brien), who introduced the song "Dixie" to New York City and the United States in 1859. Tyrone Power and Barney Williams portrayed stage Irishmen as loquacious, devil-may-care buffoons, a caricature that was increasingly resented by both Irish and Irish Americans. Edward Harrigan and Tony Hart between 1873 and 1885 were the first to portray the New York Irish realistically through songs such as "The Babies on Our Block." Tin Pan Alley composer Ernest R. Ball (1878–1927) was one of many who wrote songs capitalizing on Irish sentimentality; famous songs include "Mother Machree" (1910), "When Irish Eyes Are Smiling" (1912), "Too-Ra-Loo-Ra-Loo-Ral (That's an Irish Lullaby)" (1914), and "Little Bit of Heaven, Sure They Call It Ireland" (1914). George M. Cohan's "Yankee Doodle Dandy" became an anthem of Irish American patriotism. Traditional Irish music and dance was performed by entertainers such as the champion jigger Kitty O'Neil (1852–93) and virtuoso piper Patsy Touhey (1865–1923). In motion pictures, the image of the Irish in New York City was depicted by the likes of Dion Boucicault and Chauncey Olcott. Pat O'Brien became the typical Irish priest or policeman, and James Cagney the typical Irish tough.

Irish language words—such as *baloney, slugger, growler, goon, fluke, cop,* and *by golly*—seeped into the urban vernacular via stage, sports, and the underworld. In sports, County Mayo produced heavyweight champion Gene Tunney (1897–1978) and policeman Martin Sheridan (1881–1918). The Irish American Athletic Club operated from 1897 to 1914 at Celtic Park at 43rd Street in Woodside, Queens.

More than 275,000 Irish were settled in New York City in 1890; with consolidation in 1898, it became the most Irish place in the world.

3. The Twentieth Century and Beyond

By the start of the twentieth century New York City's Irish community was well-established. St. Patrick's Cathedral at Fifth Avenue and 50th Street was consecrated in 1910. The Friendly Sons of St. Patrick, the Catholic Club (1871), and the American Irish Historical Society (1896) attracted prominent men. Fathers James Driscoll, John F. Brady, and Francis P. Duffy were censured for modernism in their bimonthly *New York Review* (1905–8). Father Duffy (1871–1932) was demoted to parish work, but history remembers him as the chaplain of New York's Fighting 69th (165th Infantry Regiment) during World War I.

The Irish worked in the docks, railroad yards, and factories of Chelsea and Hell's Kitchen but began to move to Brooklyn, particularly around the navy yard, in Greenpoint and Williamsburg, and after 1890 in the ninth ward near Prospect Park and in Flatbush, Sunset Park, and Bay Ridge. Irish settlements in Queens on the eve of World War I included Long Island City, Astoria, Woodside, Sunnyside, and Rockaway Beach; in the Bronx Irish parishes were common in Mott Haven, Melrose, Morrisania, Highbridge, Fordham, and Kingsbridge.

An upsurge in Irish immigration to the city during the 1920s supported the newspaper the *Irish Echo* (1928), and the demand for Irish records and radio broadcasts increased. The music consisted predominantly of dance standards orchestrated into a hybrid Irish American style; nevertheless, some traditional musicians, such as the fiddler Michael Coleman (1889–1945) from County Sligo, made dozens of recordings for various New York City labels. Irish-born parents made a special effort to expose their American-born children to traditional culture through formal lessons with "professors" like fiddler James Morrison (1893–1947) and dancing master James McKenna (1885–1977). The success of an annual UICA *Feis* (cultural festival) beginning in 1932 led to a demand for the advice of the city's Irish in establishing similar music and dance festivals around the country. From 1928 the GAA leased land at Broadway and 240th Street in the Bronx for a stadium; at the height of its popularity the park drew as many as 6000 spectators for Sunday sports events. Most Irish county associations were able to field football teams, hurling teams, or both in New York City and recruited Irish Americans only when immigration from Ireland slowed. The only All-Ireland (Gaelic) football championship played abroad took place at New York City's Polo Grounds on 14 September 1947 to mark the centenary of the Great Famine.

In 1930 nearly 250,000 men and women of Irish birth still lived in the city, the majority in northern Manhattan neighborhoods and the southern Bronx. Many people maintained close ties with Ireland, where most nationalist movements, ranging from constitutional to militant republicanism, had New York City equivalents. Through secret negotiations the Clan na Gael and John Devoy (1842–1928, a revolutionary nationalist in the city since the 1870s) played an important role in the events preceding the Irish rebellion of Easter 1916. Eamon de Valera (1882–1975), head of Sinn Fein (the new Irish republican political party), who was born at Lexington Avenue and 51st Street, used New York City as his base to raise money and support for the recognition of Irish independence during 1919–20. About half the members of the Transport Workers Union (TWU) during the 1930s were Irish-born men who translated Irish republican sympathies into support for unionism. During the 1930s and 1940s the Irish of New York City juggled not only the left-wing radicalism of Mike Quill (1905–66) and the TWU but the right-wing anticommunism of the Christian Front and the conservative leadership of Francis Cardinal Spellman. During World War II the American Friends of Irish Neutrality was formed by Paul O'Dwyer (1907–98) to counter British propaganda in the United States that sought to pressure Ireland into compromising its neutrality; the American League for an Undivided Ireland made New York City its national headquarters in 1947.

The city's second-generation Irish remained substantial even as numbers declined: 423,758 in 1910 dropped to 228,373 in 1960, still a larger population than any place in Ireland. Civil service and municipal employment remained popular with immigrants; a building boom meant much work in construction; and the longshoremen's, transit, "sandhog," and carpenters' unions were heavily Irish. Many firms were known to favor Irish employees: supermarket chains like Butlers, Reeves, and A&P; restaurants such as Schrafft's and Stouffer's; airlines like Aer Lingus and Trans World Airlines (TWA); and New York Telephone, Con Edison, and Metropolitan Life.

New York City's population of people of Irish birth or parentage was 450,000 in 1950, mainly in neighborhoods at the city limits. An active social center was the Irish Institute Building on West 48th Street (1952). During the following decade the city's Irish residents began to organize along occupational lines through Emerald Societies, in which employers ranging from the Fire Department, transit police, and the courts to the Department of Education and communications workers were represented. During the early 1980s there were more than 40 such groups, overseen by a Grand Council of United Emerald Societies (1975), but by 2007 this number had shrunk to 25 with about 10,000 members.

Irish aldermen, assemblymen, and state senators were common until the 1930s when Mayor Fiorello H. La Guardia restructured city government and changed its ethnic character. Even then Edward J. Flynn and Frank V. Kelly ran the Democratic organizations in the Bronx and Brooklyn for many years. After the administrations of Mayor William O'Dwyer (born in Ireland) and Robert F. Wagner, Jr. (partly of Irish descent), there followed a long period, extending into the 1990s, during which the number of Irish municipal officeholders declined. Nevertheless, the city still sent Irish Americans such as Daniel P. Moynihan, Robert F. Kennedy, John J. Rooney, Hugh L. Carey, and William F. Ryan to serve in Congress. After immigration reform, only 7500 new Irish immigrants settled in the city between 1965 and 1980, but in the early 1980s an estimated 20,000 to 40,000 or more undocumented Irish settled in New York City. They tended to work as housekeepers, nannies, waiters and waitresses, bartenders, doorkeepers, and day laborers. Woodside in Queens and Woodlawn in the Bronx were strong Irish enclaves. Catholic Charities opened an Irish Outreach Office, the Irish Immigration Reform Movement (IIRM) opened the Emerald Isle Immigration Center, and the city published a *Guide for Irish Immigrants* (1989). In the late 1980s the IIRM began a national campaign to increase the number of visas allotted to Ireland as a means of reducing the volume of illegal immigration; 48,000 visas were allotted to the Irish under the Immigration Act of 1990. The *Irish Voice* newspaper was launched in 1987 to cater to the city's newest Irish immigrants. The Irish Lobby for Immigration Reform once again took up the cause of the undocumented Irish in 2005. The Irish Northern Aid Committee was formed to assist victims of violence in Northern Ireland, including political prisoners and their families, but repeatedly battled charges of illegal gun running. The voice of New York Irish republicanism from 1972 was the *Irish People.*

From the 1970s a heightened focus on Irish identity led to the formation of new cultural organizations, such as the Irish Arts Center (1972), the New York Irish History Roundtable (1984), and the Irish Repertory Theatre (1988). New York University created Glucksman Ireland House in 1993, and within a decade it had become one of the premier Irish and Irish American studies programs in the United States; in 1997 New York University began collecting for the Archives of Irish America. The city's St. Patrick's Day Parade remains a demonstration of Irish ethnic and religious pride more than two centuries after the first march, drawing 150,000 participants and millions of spectators from several generations on the sidelines as well as via television; controversy exists, however, over its exclusion of gays and lesbians. New York City writers of Irish ancestry include Jimmy Breslin, Elizabeth Cullinan, Pete Hamill, Alice McDermott, Peter Quinn, and Terence Winch. Irish theater in the city has included the Abbey Theatre's 1911 *Playboy of the Western World,* Brian Friel's *Dancing at Lughnasa* (1992), Martin McDonagh's *The Beauty Queen of Leenane* (1998), and Conor McPherson's *The Seafarer* (2007). After a 1996 Radio City Music Hall debut, *Riverdance* had 600 performances on Broadway during 2000–1. The sesquicentennial of the Great Famine was marked in New York City with a unique quarter-acre reproduction of the Irish landscape in Battery Park City; its unveiling was delayed until 2002 by the terrorist attacks of 11 September 2001.

Many New York City Irish left for the suburbs after World War II. The federal census of 1980 found that 647,733 New Yorkers claimed Irish birth or descent; in 1990 that number was 535,846. According to the 2006 American Community Survey, 441,726 New Yorkers claimed Irish or Scotch Irish ancestry, only 5 percent of all New Yorkers. In 2000 the greater metropolitan area had 2.7 million people of Irish ancestry, accounting for 8 percent of all such in the United States.

Richard C. Murphy and Lawrence J. Mannion, *The History of the Society of the Friendly Sons of Saint Patrick in the City of New York 1784–1955* (New York: Friendly Sons of Saint Patrick, 1962); Ann M. Shea and Marion R. Casey, eds., *The Irish Experience in New York City: A Select Bibliography* (Syracuse, N.Y.: Syracuse University Press, 1995); Ronald H. Bayor and Timothy J. Meagher, eds., *The New York Irish* (Baltimore, Md.: Johns Hopkins University Press, 1996); Linda Dowling Almeida, *Irish Immigrants in New York City, 1945–1995* (Bloomington: Indiana University Press, 2001); Mary C. Kelly, *The Shamrock and the Lily: The New York Irish and the Creation of a Transatlantic Identity, 1845–1921* (New York: Peter Lang, 2005); J. J. Lee and Marion R. Casey, eds., *Making the Irish American: History and Heritage of the Irish in the United States* (New York: New York University Press, 2006)

Marion R. Casey

Irish Advocate. Weekly newspaper launched in 1893 by John C. O'Connor, an Irish immigrant. It was popular for its homey tone and format and its articles about Irish American leaders and organizations. It relied heavily on reprinted material and voluntary contributions, and most of its readers were regular subscribers. Unlike its competitors the newspaper did not take strong editorial positions on Irish causes. When O'Connor died in October 1946 the newspaper was taken over by his daughters, Pearl and Elise, and his son, James. The *Advocate* ceased publication in April 1989.

John J. Concannon

Irish-American. Weekly newspaper launched in New York City in 1849 by Patrick Lynch, Edward Cole, and Patrick Meehan and edited by Lynch and from 1857 by Meehan. It became the most popular publication of its kind in the city during the 1850s and 1860s, reaching a circulation of 20,000 in 1854 and 40,000 by 1861. The newspaper was successful partly because it endorsed a moderate brand of Irish nationalism and thus maintained an uneasy truce with the Catholic Church. (Its short-lived competitors, the *Nation* [1848] and the *Citizen* [1854], were strongly opposed by Bishop John Hughes for urging armed struggle against British rule in Ireland.) Increasing competition from the *Irish World* eventually forced it to narrow its scope. Like many other Irish publications, the *Irish-American* was opposed to reform movements, especially abolitionism. It ceased publication in 1915.

William Leonard Joyce, *Editors and Ethnicity: A History of the Irish American Press, 1848–1883* (New York: Arno, 1976)

Kevin Kenny

Irish Brigade. Brigade composed of the 63rd, 69th, and 88th regiments of the New York Infantry (together with the 116th Pennsylvania

Infantry and the 28th Massachusetts Infantry) during the Civil War. The Irish Brigade recruits and their families earned their citizenship fighting for the Union. Recruiters initially targeted the Irish population in New York City because of its vast size—almost 25 percent of the city's population was Irish. After the midpoint of the Civil War, however, the membership of the brigade became less Irish. Set themes were used in the recruitment of soldiers. Initial popular enthusiasm for the war was sustained and fueled by skilled charismatic Irish leaders, including the former 1848 Young Ireland revolutionary Thomas Francis Meagher. Meagher persuaded New York's governor to grant state backing for the Irish Brigade in October 1861. Recruiters also appealed to Irish nationalism; natural Irish fighting ability; support of the Constitution, democracy, and the Union; and acceptance into American society, which nativists had challenged. Some soldiers enlisted for patriotic reasons. They were eventually paid for their services by the New York State bounty, the county bounty, and the federal bounty. The three regiments were organized in the New York City area from 7 August 1861 and shipped out to Washington, D.C., by Christmas. All three regiments fought together. General Meagher resigned on 14 May 1863; subsequently, they were led by four officers: colonels Richard Byrnes and Patrick Kelly, and generals Robert Nugent and Thomas A. Smyth. The brigade fought in approximately 30 battles. Antietam (17 September 1862), Fredericksburg (13 December 1862), and Gettysburg (1–3 July 1863) were the most famous; Fredericksburg was its worst defeat. Over the course of the Civil War, approximately 1000 soldiers were killed in action from the 7000 who fought for the Irish Brigade.

David Power Conyngham, *The Irish Brigade and Its Campaigns* (New York: William McSorley and Company, 1867; repr. New York: Fordham University Press, 1994); William Corby, *Memoirs of Chaplin Life: Three Years in the Irish Brigade with the Army of the Potomac*, ed. Lawrence A. Kohl (New York: Fordham University Press, 1992); Phillip Thomas Tucker, ed., *The History of the Irish Brigade* (Fredericksburg, Va.: Sergeant Kirkland's Museum and Historical Society, 1995)

Marion Archer Truslow

Irish Echo. Weekly newspaper launched in New York City in 1928 by Charles Connolly, a printer of Irish background. It covered events in Ireland but gave greater attention to local news of the Irish in the city. In the 1980s the newspaper broadened its coverage to include Irish American activities outside New York City. Its headquarters were at 11 Hanover Square in the early twenty-first century.

John T. Ridge

Irish Hunger Memorial. Public art. At Vesey Street and North End Avenue, this park, dedicated 16 July 2002, commemorates the Irish famine and migration (1845–52). Brian Tolle's design recalls past famines and encourages visitors to reflect on present-day and future hunger. From the east, the memorial is a replica of an Irish hillside; it rests on a giant tilted foundation. The memorial entranceway on the west side passes through this limestone and glass base, inscribed with quotations about hunger and accompanied by readings on an audio track. Outside, on the hillside, the path ascends through a ruined Irish cottage and a landscape dotted with Irish stones and flora to the summit overlooking New York Harbor.

Irish Hunger Memorial, 2009

Cathy Alexander

Irish Institute. Philanthropic society formed in 1948 by Paul O'Dwyer to promote cultural endeavors in the United States and Ireland; it was incorporated on 11 December 1950. The institute bought a four-story building at 326 West 48th Street in 1952 that was used as a headquarters by many Irish organizations until it was sold in 1982. From the proceeds of this sale the institute gave financial support to the first scholarly history of the Irish in New York City, published by Johns Hopkins University Press (1995).

Marion R. Casey

Irish Nation. Weekly publication launched in 1882 by John Devoy to promote militant Irish Republicanism. It soon became the foremost publication of its kind. For a time it promoted the "new departure" policy formulated during the late 1870s by Devoy, Michael Davitt, and Charles Stewart Parnell, which sought to unite three movements: those devoted to armed-force Republicanism, peaceful constitutional change, and reform of the system of landowning and tenanting in Ireland. After returning to a more militant stance during the 1880s and declaring that insurrection was the only means to achieve independence, the *Irish Nation* failed in 1886. Its causes were taken up by the *Gaelic American* (1903), which remained under Devoy's direction until his death.

Kevin Kenny

Irish Republicanism. Ideas about Irish Republicanism were introduced to New York City by such political exiles as Thomas Addis Emmet and William Sampson, veterans of the unsuccessful Irish uprising of 1798 who advocated forming an Irish republic. During the nineteenth century the city became the national center of Irish nationalism in the United States. In 1858 the Fenian Brotherhood (named for a mythical band of warriors) was formed there by John O'Mahony, an exile after the rebellion of 1848, as an affiliate of the Irish Revolutionary Brotherhood (IRB), formed in Dublin by James Stephens. There were Fenian circles in the Union army and navy, and by 1865 the Fenians had 250,000 followers, many of them veterans of the Civil War. An Irish Republican government in exile modeled on the American government was set up in Philadelphia and supported by Fenians in New York City, who provided American money and manpower to the government in exile and also to Fenian insurrectionaries in Ireland. In the years after the Civil War a dissident Fenian faction sought to provoke a war with England by invading Canada, in the belief that with England at war an insurrection in Ireland might succeed and would in any event be certain to receive American support. On 12 April 1866 the dissidents tried to seize the island of Campobello, New Brunswick, off the coast of Maine; American troops dispersed them and the British and American navies intercepted a shipment of arms. After landing in New York City on 10 May, Stephens denounced the policy of attacking Canada, ousted O'Mahony, and called for restricting armed conflict to Irish soil. Another attack on Canada was nonetheless mounted on 1 June by Col. John O'Neill, who crossed the border with 800 men and defeated a Canadian militia company before retreating to Buffalo, leaving 12 Canadians dead and 40 wounded, and eight Fenians dead and 20 wounded. Another attack was mounted on June 7 from St. Albans, Vermont, by a thousand Fenians.

The Fenian organizations in both the United States and Ireland nearly collapsed after their plans for an insurrection were discovered by police informants; there were only scattered rural uprisings on 5–6 March 1867. Many Irish Republicans went into exile in New York City, and in 1867 the Republican organization Clan na Gael was formed there by Jerome C. Collins. On 25 May 1870 O'Neill led a foray into Canada that according to the *New York Times* attracted 30,000 Fenians from the city. However, only a few hundred appeared at the border, and they were easily repulsed by the 13,000 Canadian troops who met them. After Jeremiah O'Donovan Rossa and John Devoy were released from prison on condition of permanent exile in 1871 they moved to New York City, where they were met by Democrats and Republicans seeking to win the Irish vote: Tammany Hall reserved a suite for them at the Astor House (which they refused), and William M. "Boss" Tweed was the grand marshal of a parade in their honor. Under Devoy's leadership the Clan na Gael quickly became the most powerful Republican organization on either side of the Atlantic; by the late 1870s it had about 10,000 members and overshadowed the Fenians. In 1877 a seven-member council known as the Joint Revolutionary Directory was formed to bind it to the IRB. The city's Fenians, led by O'Donovan Rossa after 1877, adopted increasingly extreme policies, among them establishing a "skirmishing fund" to wage guerrilla warfare against the British Empire. They also paid the Irish-born inventor John Phillip Holland $23,000 to build a submarine that could cross the Atlantic and engage the powerful Royal Navy. The *Fenian Ram* was 31 feet (9.5 meters) long and designed for a three-man crew. After being launched in the Hudson River in May 1881, it made frequent runs beneath New York Harbor, diving to depths as great as 60 feet (18 meters) and remaining below the surface for as long as an hour, but was never put to its intended use.

Assuming that England would eventually be drawn into a war, the Clan na Gael continued sending money to Ireland for arms, and in 1916 a brief uprising was staged. The Anglo-Irish Treaty of 1922 was widely considered unsatisfactory, because although it established an independent Irish republic it left six mainly Protestant counties in the north of Ireland under British control, leading the IRB to launch a campaign to achieve their incorporation. During the late 1960s the issue was taken up by the Irish Republican Army, which used violent tactics supported by American groups such as the Irish Northern Aid Committee (Noraid).

During the 1980s and early 1990s much attention focused on the case of Joe Doherty, who in 1981 escaped from a jail in Belfast before standing trial for killing a British soldier. After making his way to New York City he was arrested at Clancy's Bar on Third Avenue near 56th Street in June 1983 by agents of the Federal Bureau of Investigation working undercover. A federal judge ruled in 1984 that Doherty should not be extradited because his crime was political. The federal government then sought to deport him as an illegal alien; he remained in prison while seeking an appeal. In 1988 the attorney general of the United States ruled that Doherty could be deported to Britain. The Board of Immigration appeals later held that the ruling should be reviewed. Doherty's case became an issue in the mayoral election of 1989: the Republican candidate, Rudolph W. Giuliani, was the U.S. attorney in charge of prosecuting him; the Democratic candidate, David N. Dinkins, called for granting him political asylum. Doherty's petition for asylum was denied in 1992, by which time he had spent nine years in detention without having been convicted of any crime. In February of that year, he was deported to Northern Ireland, where he remained in jail until 1998 when he was released under the terms of the Good Friday Agreement.

Kevin Kenny

Irish World and Industrial Liberator. Weekly newspaper launched as the *Irish World* in 1870 by Patrick Ford; it was renamed in 1878. Like its predecessors the newspaper was devoted to Irish nationalism, but it also supported workers' movements and such causes as feminism, the eight-hour workday, the right to strike, abolishing monopolies, the income tax, insuring greenbacks, and nationalizing land in the United States and in Ireland where Ford hoped that such a policy would lead to independence. The *Irish World and Industrial Liberator* became the most important newspaper of its kind in New York City and during the 1880s had a national circulation of 35,000. It ceased publication in 1951.

Kevin Kenny

IRT. See Interborough Rapid Transit Company.

Irving, Washington (*b* New York City, 3 April 1783; *d* Sunnyside, N.Y., 28 Nov 1859). Essayist and short-story writer. He grew up at 128 William Street in lower Manhattan, and in 1802 his family moved nearby to a building at Ann and William streets. He wrote for the *Morning Chronicle* and with James Kirke Paulding produced the humorous journal *Salmagundi* during 1807–8. *A History of New York* (1809), a collection of satirical essays published under the pen name Diedrich Knickerbocker, was his first well-known work. He then moved to Europe, remaining there 17 years, during which time two collections of his stories were published: *The Sketch Book of Geoffrey Crayon, Gent.* (1819–20), which included "Rip van Winkle" and "The Legend of Sleepy Hollow," and

Washington Irving

Bracebridge Hall (1822). On his return to the United States he published *A Tour on the Prairies* and other works about the frontier. In 1836 he moved from Colonnade Row in the city to Irvington, in nearby Westchester County. He visited the city frequently, staying at his nephew's house at 46 East 21st Street.

Lewis G. Leary, *Washington Irving* (Minneapolis: University of Minnesota Press, 1963)

James E. Mooney

Irving House. Hotel opened in 1848 at 281 Broadway in Manhattan, occupying the entire west side of the block front between Chambers and Reade streets on the former site of A. T. Stewart's dry-goods emporium. Managed by Daniel D. Howard, it had several well-known guests, among them the Swedish soprano Jenny Lind (during her first U.S. tour, September 1850) and the Hungarian revolutionary Louis Kossuth (December 1851). Commercial tenants included a druggist, a hatter, a tailor, and a bookshop. In September 1852 Howard was succeeded by William H. Burroughs as the manager of the hotel, which by the spring of 1856 was no longer in business. Author James Grant Wilson, in *The Memorial History of the City of New-York* (1893), identifies Irving House as the "granite building" at 273 Broadway in which the printer Samuel Adams was slain by John Caldwell Colt in 1841.

Joel Honig

Isaacs, John (*b* 30 Jan 1915, Panama City, Panama; *d* 26 Jan 2009, Bronx). Basketball player. His family emigrated to New York City when he was five, and he was the point guard at Textile High School in Manhattan. In 1936 he signed his first professional contract, with Bob Douglas, founder of the Harlem Renaissance Big Five basketball team and commonly referred to as the Father of Black Basketball. Isaacs quickly became the star of the team and was nicknamed the Wonder Boy. Also known as the Rens, the eight-player, all-black 1939 team won the first-ever World Professional Basketball Championship in Chicago. Its other players were Puggy Bell, Clarence "Fats" Jenkins, Eyrie "Bruiser" Saitch, Charles "Tarzan" Cooper, William "Wee Willie" Smith, Zach Clayton, and William "Pop" Gates. By 1943 the great Renaissance teams had disappeared and Isaacs joined another all-black team, the Washington Bears. For over 50 years, he also taught basketball to children at the Madison Square Boys and Girls Club in the Bronx.

Jessica Montesano

Isaacs, Stanley M(yer) (*b* New York City, 27 Sept 1882; *d* New York City, 12 July 1962). City councilman, borough president, and civic leader. He graduated from Columbia College and New York Law School and led the campaign for enactment of the State Multiple Dwelling Law of 1929, which mandated improvements in tenement housing. A leader of the liberal wing of the Republican Party, he was borough president of Manhattan from 1938 to 1941 and oversaw the completion of the East River Drive (now the FDR Drive). He was elected to the City Council from the Upper East Side in 1941 and remained a member to the end of his life, serving as minority leader of the council and often as its only Republican. He was also the president of United Neighborhood Houses, an organization of settlement houses.

Edith S. Isaacs, *Love Affair with a City: The Story of Stanley M. Isaacs* (New York: Random House, 1967)

Mary B. Bowling

Islam. See Islamic Cultural Center of New York, Muslims, and Nation of Islam.

Islamic Cultural Center of New York. First building in New York City designed specifically as a mosque. It was established at 1 Riverside Drive in 1963, and its site at 1711 Third Avenue was purchased three years later by the governments of Kuwait, Saudi Arabia, and Libya. Skidmore, Owings and Merrill designed the 21,000-square-foot (1951-square-meter) mosque; Swanke Hayden Connell designed the 130-foot (39.6-meter) minaret. One of the most striking religious structures in the city, the Islamic Cultural Center is oriented toward Mecca, necessitating a 29-degree slant from Manhattan's street grid. The first service was held in 1991; in 1999 it was the site of a service for Amadou Diallo. In the early twenty-first century the mosque attracts 4000 worshippers weekly to Friday night services.

Kate Lauber

Island Hospital. Hospital on Blackwell's Island, a forerunner of Elmhurst Hospital Center.

Israelis. The Israelis in New York City generally moved to the United States after the Six Days' War of 1967 and consisted mostly of sabras seeking professional opportunities. These immigrants were attracted by the American emphasis on personal success; there were also Israelis originating from Muslim countries who moved to the city to escape economic and social discrimination. Israeli immigrants usually settled in predominantly Jewish neighborhoods in Brooklyn and Queens; Borough Park became a popular destination for the Orthodox, Queens for secular Ashkenazim. Immigration increased again after the Yom Kippur War of 1973.

In the 1980s many Israeli emigrants of Sephardic origin opened garment retailing firms, diamond and jewelry factories, electronics stores, and taxicab, automobile, and moving services. Afternoon schools for Israeli children were opened in Queens and in Brooklyn (Etgar and Nitsan) as was a communal Israeli club in the Central Queens Young Men's–Young Women's Hebrew Association (YM-YWHA) in Forest Hills. Israeli immigrants usually identified with national secularism, traveled often between New York and Israel, and did not form communal organizations or join American Jewish ones. In the early years of the twenty-first century, Israeli newspapers and a local Hebrew-language newspaper, *Israel Shelanu,* enjoyed a wide audience. More than 23,000 New Yorkers reported Israeli ancestry in 2007.

Moshe Shokeid, *Children of Circumstances: Israeli Emigrants in New York* (Ithaca, N.Y.: Cornell University Press, 1988)

Hadassa Kosak

Italians. New York Harbor was explored in 1524 by Giovanni da Verrazano, an Italian employed by François I of France. During the next few centuries the small Italian population in the area included such well-known figures as Lorenzo da Ponte, who wrote librettos for several of Mozart's operas before moving in 1805 to New York City, where he later became the first professor of Italian language and literature at Columbia College (later Columbia University). From the 1820s to the 1850s a few Italian political refugees lived in Staten Island, among them Giuseppe Garibaldi. The Archdiocese of New York formed a national parish for Italians in Greenwich Village in 1866.

Fewer than 20,000 Italians lived in New York City in 1880, but between 1899 and 1910 about 1.9 million people from southern Italy moved to the United States. About 77 percent were landless farmers fleeing rural poverty. By 1900, 220,000 Italians lived in the city and by 1910, 545,000; many later returned to Italy. Before World War I women and girls often worked in the garment trade, while men worked in construction. About 4000 Italian laborers worked on the Lexington Avenue subway, and many others dug tunnels, paved streets, and laid down subway track elsewhere in the city. Tens of thousands of Italians were employed in manufacturing. Some craftspeople, especially tailors and barbers, opened shops, and entrepreneurs became street vendors and bootblacks; professionals were fewer in number. By the time of World War I, immigrants had sent about $750 million back to Italy.

The largest Italian enclaves in the city were formed before the turn of the twentieth century on the Lower East Side and in Greenwich Village. Other large Italian neighborhoods were in East Harlem in Manhattan and Williamsburg and Greenpoint in Brooklyn. Immigrants from the same Italian town often settled together, preserving their dialects and customs and forming mutual aid societies that helped members in the event of illness or death. The Sons of Italy was formed as a union of mutual aid societies in 1905. Because Italians competed with better-established immigrant groups for work, they were considered a threat to labor solidarity and encountered hostility in unions. They were nonetheless active in the labor movement, and Italian women and girls accounted for a large segment of the International Ladies' Garment Workers' Union. Some Italians gravitated toward anarchism and such radical movements as the Industrial Workers of the World. In 1913 the anarchist Carlo Tresca first published the newspaper *L'Avvenire* in the city; it was suppressed, and its successor, *Il Martello,* was repeatedly confiscated.

Within the Catholic Church Italians came into conflict with the Irish. Parish churches often refused to sponsor Italian religious festivals, which continued to be held by Italian societies. In ethnically mixed parishes Italians were often relegated to the church basement to worship, as American Catholics rejected Italian brands of faith that sometimes incorporated elements of folk religion. Among the second generation, family and community events were held in the parish church, and many children attended the parish school. Italians were slow to move into municipal politics: of more than half a million Italians in the city in 1911, only 15,000 voted. Neglected by Irish politicians who governed the city through the Democratic Party, Italian immigrants remained loyal to patrons in their own neighborhoods.

Italian racketeers formed crime syndicates that together made up La Cosa Nostra, which was modeled on secret societies in Italy but took shape as an American Mafia with bootlegging operations during Prohibition; it later became an arm for illegal gambling, loansharking, pornography, drug smuggling, and labor racketeering. The influence of wealthy Mafiosi helped some Italian politicians to gain power. In 1931 Al Marinelli became the first Italian district leader in Tammany Hall, reportedly installed by the racketeer Lucky Luciano, who mistrusted the Irish Democrats in charge of city government.

After World War I the number of Italian immigrants settling in the city declined sharply. Nevertheless, by 1930 the more than one million people of Italian descent in New York City accounted for 17 percent of the city's population, the highest concentration of Italians in the United States. During the 1930s as many as 110,000 Italians lived east of Lexington Avenue between 96th and 116th streets and east of Madison Avenue between 116th and 125th streets. Working-class families improved their standard of living and spoke English as provincial loyalties dissipated and immigrant societies declined. By the 1930s more Italians had skilled work than previously, and a class of proprietors developed. Among the large ventures were clothing factories and construction firms, including a building supply firm owned by Generoso Pope that was the largest of its kind in the country.

The Republican Party and radicalism provided a route to city government for many Italians excluded from Tammany Hall, where Irish Americans dominated. Fiorello H. La Guardia was elected mayor in 1933 for the first of three terms with the support of the Republican and American Labor parties. In addition to guiding reforms during the Depression, he helped Italians gain political prominence; his protégé Vito Marcantonio, a radical from East Harlem, held a seat in Congress from 1935 to 1937 and from 1939 to 1951. Other radicals included Tresca and Peter Cacchione, a communist who held a seat on the City Council from 1941 to 1947. Pope became influential and widely known as the publisher of *Il Progresso Italo-Americano*, the city's major Italian-language newspaper, and in the 1930s sought to form a coalition of Italian Democrats.

By the 1940s Frank Costello had become a major power in Tammany Hall. Another was Carmine DeSapio, who broke with the Irish Democrats and became a district leader in Greenwich Village in 1939 and the county leader of Manhattan in 1949; a cover story in *Time* in 1956 called him "America's most celebrated boss." The political ascendance of the city's Italians was also reflected in the special mayoral election of 1950, contested by Vincent R. Impellitteri, Ferdinand Pecora, and Edward Corsi. The dispersion of the Italian population to the suburbs eventually undermined clubhouse politicians like DeSapio, who was defeated in an election for a district leadership in 1961 by a reform club that included among its members Edward I. Koch.

The city's Italian Americans demonstrated a capacity for political activism during the 1960s and 1970s, inspired in part by the black pride movement. The Italian American Civil Rights League gave expression to ethnic resentment among Italians during the late 1960s and early 1970s; its rally on "Unity Day" at Columbus Circle in June 1971 drew thousands of protesters angered by stereotypical images of Italians. Volunteers formed groups that became part of a new social and political network. The Congress of Italian-American Organizations was organized to procure social services and community development funds after a report in 1975 revealed that only 15 percent of Italian households below the poverty line were receiving public assistance. The Calandra Institute at the City University of New York was formed to promote the interests of Italian students whose levels of education lagged behind those of other ethnic groups in the city. The American Italian Historical Association was established in Manhattan, as was the Italian Academy for Advanced Studies in America at Columbia University. The National Organization of Italian-American Women, formed in Manhattan in 1980, sought to provide a network for women in business and other professions. One of the first members was Geraldine A. Ferraro, a congresswoman from Queens who in 1984 became the first woman nominated by a major party for national office. Meade Esposito led a powerful Democratic coalition in Brooklyn until his retirement during Koch's third term as mayor. Peter Vallone of Queens became speaker of the City Council, and John J. Marchi served in the state senate from the 1950s into the 1990s. Mario M. Cuomo lost an election for the mayoralty to Koch in 1977 but later became governor. Rudolph W. Giuliani, who was born in Flatbush in 1944 and became a federal attorney famous for prosecuting organized-crime figures, received overwhelming support from Italian American voters in the mayoral election of 1989, which he narrowly lost to David N. Dinkins; Giuliani defeated Dinkins in 1993 and was reelected to a second term in 1997.

In 1980 more than one million people of Italian descent made up the largest national group in New York City, accounting for one-seventh of the total population. Perhaps two million people of Italian descent lived in the suburbs of New York City. About two-thirds lived in Brooklyn and Queens, although about 40 percent of the population of Staten Island was Italian owing partly to the opening of the Verrazano–Narrows Bridge in 1964. The demographic shift to the outer boroughs reflected a more middle-class character. Of those employed in the city, 40 percent had administrative, retail, and technical occupations, and 40 percent were blue-collar workers and laborers (26 percent of construction workers in the city were Italian), while 10 percent were professionals, mostly elementary- and secondary-school teachers. The poverty rate for Italians in 1980 was 9.7 percent, well below the rate of 12.9 percent for all whites in the city.

By 2000 about 700,000 Italians remained in the city, accounting for 9 percent of the population. This can partly be attributed to the fact that Italians have the highest rates of home ownership in the city among the foreign-born. Besides the 150,000 Italians living in Staten Island and in the small suburban enclave of Howard Beach in Queens, the largest concentration of Italians in 2000 was in Bensonhurst, although it registered a 30 percent decline for the 1990s to 60,000.

Italian social life in the city continues to revolve around ethnic family values, which may account for low divorce rates, for the small numbers of elderly Italians in group homes and of working mothers with young children, and for the persistent presence of Italians in the metropolitan area. Notwithstanding the long and distinguished tenure of Francis J. Mugavero as the archbishop of the Brooklyn and Queens archdiocese, still relatively few Italians are in the clergy and local Catholic church hierarchy. Despite successful federal prosecutions, five organized-crime syndicates, or "families," maintain operations in the city (see Organized crime).

Several institutions are dedicated to Italian culture in the city, including the Casa Italiana, home of the Italian Academy for Advanced Studies in America at Columbia University, and the John D. Calandra Italian American Institute of Queens College. The city is known for gourmet Italian and family-style Italian American cuisine; some maintain that the first pizzeria in the city was Gennaro Lombardi's, opened on Spring Street in Manhattan in 1905 (see Pizza). This food culture is the centerpiece of the commercialized Little Italy Historic District in lower Manhattan. Contemporary Italy is also represented in the migration of Italian home-design firms to SoHo. Important ongoing traditions include the annual parade on Columbus Day and the San Gennaro Festival on Mulberry Street in September.

Leonard Covello, *The Social Background of the Italo-American Schoolchild* (Leiden, Netherlands: E. J. Brill, 1967); Thomas Kessner, *The Golden Door: The Italian and Jewish Immigrant Mobility in New York City, 1880–1915* (New York, Oxford University Press, 1977); Donald Tricarico, *The Italians of Greenwich Village: The Social Structure and Transformation of an Ethnic Community* (New York: Center for Migration Studies, 1984); Robert A. Orsi, *The Madonna of 115th Street: Faith and Community in Italian Harlem, 1880–1950* (New Haven: Yale University Press, 1985)

Donald Tricarico

ITT. See International Telephone and Telegraph.

Ives, Charles (Edward) (*b* Danbury, Conn., 20 Oct 1874; *d* New York City, 19 May 1954). Composer. As a student at Yale University he conducted experiments with unresolved dissonance that left his teacher Horatio Parker nonplussed. Ives moved to New York City after his graduation in 1898 and with several colleagues from Yale lived in a series of apartments, each nicknamed "Poverty Flat," at 317 West 58th Street (to 1901), 65 Central Park West (1901–7), and 34 Gramercy Park (to 1908). As the organist at Central Presbyterian Church (1900–1902) he took part in 1902 in the premiere of his cantata *The Celestial Country,* one of his few compositions to receive a public performance while he lived in the city. After his marriage to Harmony Twichell in 1908 the couple lived at 70 West 11th Street (to 1911), 118 Waverly Place (1911–12), and 29 West 11th Street (1914–15). During these years his music became increasingly dense and dissonant and was for the most part ignored. He sustained his musical career by working in life insurance, first at the Mutual Insurance Company and then as a partner with Julian Myrick in the firm of Ives and Myrick, which at his instigation introduced a new form of annuity. He bought a house in West Redding, Connecticut, in 1912 but continued to spend winters in New York City; from 1917 to 1926 he lived at 120 East 22nd Street. After a heart attack in 1918 Ives retired from the insurance business, and his productive years as a composer ended about the same time. From 1926 he lived at 164 East 74th Street.

Ives's music reflected his determination to overturn what he saw as the primly genteel conventions of the concert music of his day, as well as his deep affection for the secular and religious music of nineteenth-century America. He used polyrhythms and polytonality before many other composers did, and his works contain many allusions to hymn tunes, military marches, patriotic songs, and ragtime. New York City figured in such compositions as the orchestral works the *General Slocum* (1904) and *Central Park in the Dark* (1906) and the songs "Romanzo di Central Park" (1900) and "Ann Street" (1921). He achieved public recognition toward the last years of his life and was awarded the Pulitzer Prize in 1947 for his Symphony no. 3, an honor that he derided as being one of the "badges of mediocrity."

Frank Rossiter, *Charles Ives and His America* (New York: Liveright, 1975)

Barbara L. Tischler

IWW. See Industrial Workers of the World.

J

Jack, Hulan E(dwin, Sr.) (*b* St. Lucia, British West Indies, 23 Dec 1906; *d* New York City, 19 Dec 1986). Harlem politician and public official. After entering Democratic politics in the 1930s he was elected in 1940 to represent Harlem in the state assembly, from which he resigned when he was elected borough president of Manhattan in 1953. Jack was the first black borough president in New York City and the highest-ranking black elected official in the country during the 1950s. In 1957 he was elected to a second term, toward the end of which he was indicted and convicted for accepting an illegal gift valued at $4500. In 1960 he resigned his office in disgrace. His conviction was bitterly criticized by many blacks, who accused the city government of racial discrimination. In 1968 he reentered politics, again winning election to the state assembly; he served one term. Jack was indicted for conspiracy and conflict of interest in 1970 by the federal government, which accused him of using improper means to promote certain products at groceries in Harlem; he was later convicted and sentenced to three months in prison. Toward the end of his life he was a political consultant to the conspiracy theorist Lyndon H. LaRouche, Jr.

Calvin B. Holder, "The Rise and Fall of the West Indian Politician in New York City, 1900–1988" (New York: Medgar Evers College, Caribbean Research Center, 1991)

Calvin B. Holder

Jackson Heights. Neighborhood in northwestern Queens, bounded to the north by Astoria Boulevard, to the east by 94th Street and Junction Boulevard, to the south by Roosevelt Avenue, and to the west by the Brooklyn–Queens Expressway. It consisted originally of farmland rising 65 feet (19 meters) above the surrounding lowlands in the sparsely populated area of Trains Meadows. The land was bought in 1908 by a syndicate of bankers and real estate agents called the Queensboro Realty Company, led by Edward A. MacDougal; Justice P. Henry Dugro was an agent. After the Queensboro Bridge opened in 1909 the area became more attractive to developers, and by the end of 1910 the syndicate had acquired 350 acres (140 hectares) of land. It prevailed on the city to close Trains Meadow Road and lay out streets in a regular grid pattern numbered consecutively (First Street became the present 54th Street). The neighborhood was named for Jackson Avenue (now Northern Boulevard). As part of the Dual Contract, the Interborough Rapid Transit Company (IRT) and the Brooklyn and Manhattan Transit Company (BMT) built what is now the Flushing line, for which Roosevelt Avenue was specially laid out. The elevated line opened in May 1917 with four stations in Jackson Heights: 74th Street, 82nd Street, Elmhurst Avenue, and Junction Boulevard. The Queensboro Corporation encouraged the Fifth Avenue Coach Company to initiate direct service with double-decker buses to Jackson Heights in 1922.

The first apartment building was erected at 82nd Street and Northern Boulevard in 1911, and by 1912 there were 8 miles (13 kilometers) of paved streets with sidewalks, curbs, and gutters and 5 miles (eight kilometers) of sewers. During the next 20 years Queensboro Realty engaged prominent architects to design two-family houses and especially the apartment buildings for which the neighborhood became known, many bordering the street on two sides and separated from each other by a communal garden; there was also a golf course and a community center. An innovator in urban housing, the corporation offered cooperative apartments as early as 1920 and semidetached houses known as garden apartments from 1923; it also practiced exclusionary policies aimed at Jews, Catholics, and African Americans. The neighborhood had 3600 residents in 1920. Suites of two to seven rooms in apartment buildings were rented for $90 to $200 a month in 1928. By the beginning of the Depression the entire tract had been built up except the northern section near Astoria Boulevard and the eastern section near Junction Boulevard: these areas as well were gradually developed during the 1930s. The population increased during the 1930s from 44,000 to 54,290, in part because of the opening of the Independent (IND) subway to Roosevelt Avenue on 19 August 1933. A large number of immigrants settled in Jackson Heights in the 1980s, especially from Colombia, China, and the Dominican Republic and to a lesser extent from India, Ecuador, Korea, Guyana, Peru, Cuba, and Pakistan. The neighborhood also became home to the largest Argentinian community in New York City. In 1993 the Landmarks Preservation Commission designated a large portion of the neighborhood a historic district, preserving the historic architecture. After the murder of Julio Rivera, a gay man, by skinheads in 1990, the gay residents organized, and since 1993 Jackson Heights has been the site of the Queens Pride parade and festival along 37th Avenue.

Vincent Seyfried, Jeffrey A. Kroessler

Jacobi, Abraham (*b* Hartum, Westphalia [Germany], 6 May 1830; *d* Bolton Landing, N.Y., 10 July 1919). Physician. After completing his medical training in Germany, he was imprisoned for taking part in the revolution of 1848; on his release he moved to New York City, taught at the College of Physicians and Surgeons, and practiced medicine for 66 years, focusing his efforts on caring for the poor. He served a term as president of the American Medical Association in 1912 and was twice elected president of the American Pediatric Society. Among his many concerns was teaching hygiene in schools, which he believed would slow the spread of tuberculosis among children. He was married to Mary Putnam Jacobi.

Rhoda Truax, *The Doctors Jacobi* (Boston: Little, Brown, 1952)

James E. Mooney

Jacobi (née Putnam), **Mary Corinna** (*b* New York City, 31 Aug 1842; *d* New York City, 10 June 1906). Physician and suffragist. The daughter of the New York City publisher G. P. Putnam, she grew up in the suburbs of New York City, received an MD from the Female Medical College of Pennsylvania in 1864, and became a leading physician. She devoted herself to the welfare of children and to improving the status of women in medicine. With her husband, Abraham Jacobi, she was active and influential in the suffrage movement. During 1871–89 she taught at the Women's Medical College of the New York Infirmary for Women and Children, and in 1872 she founded the Women's Medical Association of New York City, serving as its president from 1874 to 1903.

Rhoda Truax, *The Doctors Jacobi* (Boston: Little, Brown, 1952)

Kathryn Kish Sklar

Jacobi Medical Center. Municipal hospital complex in the Bronx, formerly known as the Bronx Municipal Hospital Center. A teaching affiliate of the Albert Einstein College of Medicine of Yeshiva University, it is composed of two hospitals on the same campus, on Pelham Parkway and Eastchester Road. One hospital, opened on 15 September 1954, is named for Nathan B(ristol) Van Etten (1866–1954), who maintained a family practice in the Bronx for more than 60 years, was president of the American Medical Association, and later became known for his work with communicable diseases. This hospital was originally intended for tuberculosis patients but was later converted to general care. The second hospital, opened on 1 November 1955, is named for Abraham Jacobi (1830–1919), an internationally renowned professor of pediatrics in New York City and a president of the American Medical Association. The facility was primarily the work of Marcus Kogel, who, as the city's commissioner of hospitals, oversaw its design and construction. Jacobi Center has periodically suffered from the same financial constraints as the rest of the municipal system, but it has also won distinction for its burn unit, trauma center, and day-care center for children with AIDS (the first in the nation) and its departments of neurology, newborn intensive care, and acute psychiatry. Jacobi Hospital had 470 beds as of 2010.

Jesse Drucker, Sandra Opdycke

Jacob K. Javits Convention Center. Public convention complex in Manhattan bounded by 38th Street, 11th Avenue, 34th Street, and 12th Avenue. It has 1.8 million square feet (167,220 square meters) of floor space contained under a vast frame and tinted-glass canopy and was commissioned by the New York State Urban Development Corporation from the firm of I. M. Pei in 1979 to replace the outmoded Coliseum on Columbus Circle. Designed by a team under James Ingo Freed, it can accommodate six events simultaneously and 85,000 visitors in various halls and more than 100 meeting rooms. The center opened in 1986 at a cost of $500 million, $125 million over budget; the overrun was soon recovered in earnings from conventions. The number of visitors increased each year and by 1990 reached three million. In the mid-1990s it was estimated that the center accounted for nearly 2 percent of the city's economy. In the early part of the twenty-first century, however, convention experts reported that, because the center was much smaller than similar venues in Las Vegas, Chicago, New Orleans, and Atlanta, New York City could not compete for the largest meetings. Moreover, excessive labor costs made it unattractive to national convention planners.

Carol Willis

Jacob Ruppert Brewery. Brewery founded in the Yorkville area of Manhattan in 1867 by the German immigrant Jacob Ruppert and occupying the blocks between 90th and 93rd streets, and Second and Third avenues. It was among the oldest operating breweries on the island of Manhattan, and in the years before World War I Ruppert products dominated the American beer market. Under the management of former congressman and New York Yankees owner "Colonel" Jacob Ruppert, Jr., who succeeded his father in 1915, the brewery manufactured the Ruppert, Knickerbocker, Ruppiner, and Jacob Ruppert Ale brands. Knickerbocker beer, in particular, was known to many as the official beer of the New York Giants and for the image of "Father Knickerbocker" on its label and in its advertisements. In 1963 Ruppert Brewery was purchased by the developer Marvin Kratter, who closed the Yorkville plant in 1965 and sold the Ruppert name and recipes to the Brooklyn-based Rheingold Brewery. In 1976 the plant became the site of the present-day Ruppert and Yorkville Towers apartment complex, designed by Davis, Brody and Associates.

Maureen Ogle, *Ambitious Brew: The Story of American Beer* (Orlando, Fla.: Harcourt, 2006)

Elizabeth L. Bradley

Jacobs [née Butzner], **Jane** (*b* Scranton, Pa., 4 May 1916; *d* Toronto, Canada, 25 April 2006). Urban theorist. At age 20 she moved to New York City with a high school diploma and stenographer's training. While holding a string of secretarial jobs, she wrote freelance articles on urban life for *Vogue* and *Harper's Bazaar.* Following two years of classes at Columbia University, she worked in the New York City headquarters of the Office of Wartime Information and later the Overseas Information Agency from 1943 to 1952. She lived in Brooklyn Heights and on Washington Square, and in 1947 she and her husband, architect Robert H. Jacobs, purchased a former candy store at 555 Hudson Street.

In 1952 Jacobs took a job at *Architectural Forum,* where her work included reviewing some of the massive public housing developments and other urban renewal projects then under way. There she was influenced by William Kirk, of Union Settlement in East Harlem, and his ideas about how neighborhoods function. With a 1958 grant from the Rockefeller Foundation, Jacobs expanded such insights for her first book, *The Death and Life of Great American Cities* (1961), in which she combined a damning analysis of simplistic planning orthodoxy with her observations, particularly from the streets of New York City, of the rich complexity of urban life. Jacobs identified four "generators" of civic vitality: short blocks, density, diverse uses, and a variety of buildings (by age and type). She also described her efforts to defeat Robert Moses's plan for a lower Manhattan expressway to route a traffic artery through Washington Square.

Over the course of 1961–62, Jacobs organized her West Village neighbors to defeat a plan targeting the area for slum clearance, confronting Mayor Robert Wagner and City Planning Commission chairman James Felt. The Committee to Save the West Village successfully opposed the urban renewal project, cultivating Congressman John Lindsay as an ally. (As mayor, Lindsay later supported the group's efforts to build affordable housing along Washington Street.) Jacobs also led a coalition (including both Tammany Hall boss Carmine De Sapio and reformer Ed Koch of the Village Independent Democrat) against a proposed expressway along Broome Street. Eventually credited with thereby preserving SoHo's architecture, Jacobs fought multiple incarnations of the "crosstown expressway." She was even charged with inciting a riot at one 1968 hearing. Also critical of the Vietnam War, she was arrested (along with Allen Ginsberg, Susan Sontag, and Benjamin Spock) during a sit-in at the Whitehall Street Draft Center in 1967. The following year, in order to protect her sons from the U.S. military draft, Jacobs moved her family to Toronto, Canada, where she published seven more books and remained active in local and national politics. In addition to overturning prevailing ideas about urban policy and planning, Jacobs left legacies in New York City by helping to preserve neighborhoods like SoHo and Greenwich Village.

Jacob K. Javits Convention Center, 2009

Christopher Klemek, *Block By Block: Jane Jacobs and the Future of New York* (Princeton, N.J.: Princeton Architectural Press, 2008)

Christopher Klemek

Jacques Marchais Museum of Tibetan Art. Museum at 338 Lighthouse Avenue in Staten Island, opened in 1947. It contains the Asian art collection of Jacques Marchais (née Edna Koblentz, 1890–1948), who lived nearby and ran an art gallery on Madison Avenue, and is built to resemble a Tibetan monastery. The art is largely religious, with pieces ranging from elaborate, jewel-encrusted figures of deities to humble devotional objects made of human and animal bone.

Carol V. Wright

Jahn's. Chain of ice cream parlors. John "Papa" Jahn opened the first one in 1897 at Alexander Avenue and 138th Street in the Bronx. Papa soon added outlets in Jamaica, Richmond Hill, and Flushing in Queens for his three children, Elsie, Frank, and Howard, respectively. The chain then further expanded in the Bronx, on Long Island, and in Florida. The parlors became well known for such extravagant dishes as the Kitchen Sink, a gargantuan portion of ice cream, fruit, and syrups that served eight. In 2006, the only remaining Jahn's, at 81-04 37th Avenue in Richmond Hill, was still decorated with Frank Jahn's paintings of New York City, a nickelodeon, gas lamps, and a soda fountain, evoking nostalgia for the era of the ice cream parlor.

Stephen Weinstein

jails. The correctional facilities in New York City are technically jails rather than prisons because only a few of the inmates are serving time after having been convicted of crimes. The first jail in the city was opened in 1625 when the Dutch set aside dungeons in Fort Amsterdam to confine "Indians" and those who had been convicted of crimes. The Stadt Huys, the first city hall, erected in 1642 on the corner of Pearl Street and Coenties Slip, contained a jail in addition to courts, a tavern, and a school. In 1704 a jail for felons and debtors was installed in the basement of City Hall, then at the northern end of Broad Street. Because of overcrowding and poor conditions, a new jail was built in 1759 in an adjacent field. This building served as the city prison until 1775, when the Bridewell was constructed. During the American Revolution the British used both the old and the new jails as military prisons. One of their first provost marshals was Captain William Cunningham, who became infamous for the suffering that he caused prisoners. After the war the Bridewell again functioned as a city jail. A state prison opened in 1797 in Greenwich Village for convicts sentenced to terms of three years or more. The Bridewell was converted into a debtor's jail in 1816, when a city penitentiary was installed in an almshouse at the Bellevue Establishment (26th Street and First Avenue). The penitentiary was the first prison to use the "stepping wheel," a mill wheel driven by prisoners that was a form of punishment that also exploited the prisoners as a source of cheap labor. In 1832 the city established the Department of Charities and Corrections, and in 1836 a penitentiary opened on Blackwell's Island, allowing the jail at Bellevue to become reserved for female inmates. The Halls of Justice, later known as the Tombs, was constructed in 1838, at which time the Bridewell was converted into the Hall of Records.

In 1825 a philanthropic organization called the Managers of the Society for the Reformation of Juvenile Delinquents in the City of New York opened the House of Refuge as a reform institution that would "prevent pauperism and [the] committing of crime" by young men and women. Situated at Madison Square Park on the grounds of a former arsenal, this facility of 4 acres (1.6 hectares) consisted of remodeled army barracks and originally housed six girls and three boys. The refuge was moved successively to the site of the Bellevue Fever Hospital (1839) and to a parcel of 10 acres (4 hectares) on Wards Island (1850) before being exchanged in 1851 for 30 acres (12 hectares) of land on Randalls Island, where separate buildings were built for girls and boys. In 1884 the city acquired an island of 87 acres (35 hectares) in the East River from the Ryker family to use as a prison farm. A separate department of correction was formed in 1895 with jurisdiction over five prisons, nine jails, and three prison farms.

The city's largest jail facility is Rikers Island, which has 10 units with a combined capacity of more than 17,000 inmates. The city also operates the Manhattan Detention Complex (the Tombs) and a jail barge in the Bronx that opened in 1992. The Brooklyn Detention Complex, closed in 2003, reopened in 2008 after renovations. Jails that once operated in Queens, the Bronx, and a former Brooklyn Navy Yard brig are now closed. So are two former Staten Island ferry boats and two British prison barges that were put into service during the early 1990s when a crack epidemic and aggressive policing swelled the jail population beyond capacity. In 2003 in an attempt to merge the Departments of Corrections and Probation, Mayor Michael Bloomberg

Prisoners on Blackwell's Island, ca *1885–90*

City jail, 1940

appointed Martin F. Horn commissioner of both agencies.

Joseph P. Viteritti

Jamaica. Largest and most densely populated neighborhood in central Queens. It was first inhabited by Jameco, or Yamecah, Indians, whose name means *beaver* in Algonquian; they lived on the northern shore of Jamaica Bay and along Beaver Stream and Beaver Pond (filled in 1906). English colonists from Massachusetts and eastern Long Island moved to the area in 1656 and secured a patent for the land from the Dutch government, which named the area Rustdorp (rest town). It soon became the seat of Queens County; the court and the county clerk's office were established there, and executions were carried out around Beaver Pond. After the English took control in 1683, the area became the seat of the Town of Jamaica, which included all the land south of what are now the Interborough and Grand Central parkways. In the mid-eighteenth century horse races were held around the pond. The area was heavily Tory during the American Revolution and was occupied from 1776 to 1783 by British troops, whose huts lay in the foothills north of Hillside Avenue. It was incorporated as a village in 1814. Rail service to New York City provided by the Long Island Rail Road began in 1836. A farmhouse owned by the Smith family was acquired by Rufus King, who built a mansion nearby, King Manor (now the landmark King Mansion), which became part of Kings Park; his son John Alsop King, elected governor of New York State in 1856, also lived there.

After the Civil War Jamaica grew rapidly: the population was 780 in 1875, 3922 in 1880, 6500 in 1898, and 58,200 in 1910. A number of landmark churches were built, and horsecar service began in 1866, followed in 1888 by the opening of an electric trolley line. Development increased further after an elevated line (the Brooklyn–Manhattan Transit) was extended in 1918 along Jamaica Avenue; the low fare (five cents) enabled people to live there and work in the city. A branch line of the Jamaica "el" was built to connect with the Long Island Rail Road in South Jamaica, offering direct service over Jamaica Bay to the Rockaways (the branch was abandoned in the late 1920s). Jamaica Avenue became known throughout central Queens for its department stores, and between 1920 and 1940 parcels along the avenue between 160th and 168th streets had the highest relative assessed valuations in Queens County (in relation to their frontage). Among the notable structures on the avenue was Loew's Valencia (1929), a movie palace in the Spanish Baroque style, now the Tabernacle of Prayer. The avenue was also the site of the first modern supermarket, King Kullen, opened by Michael J. Cullen in 1930 (later converted to the machine shop for Thomas Edison Vocational High School). Connections to the rapid transit lines of Manhattan, Brooklyn, and the Bronx were provided by the Independent subway, which opened in Jamaica on 24 April 1937. By 1940 there were five theaters and one nightclub.

After World War II Jamaica gradually declined as young people moved to Nassau County. Stores lacking adequate parking lost customers to shopping malls in Elmhurst and other suburbs, and the two largest department stores, Macy's and Gertz, left the neighborhood, and service on the Jamaica el was cut back several stations from the 168th Street terminal. After 1960 the ethnic composition of the area changed rapidly, and by 1980 its population was predominantly black and Latin American. The Greater Jamaica Development Corporation was formed to plan several developments, including York College, an 11-story office of the U.S. Social Security Administration, a pedestrian mall on 165th Street, a subway extension along Archer Avenue, and a farmers' market; it also planned the restoration of King Manor and its surrounding park. During the 1980s and 1990s Jamaica attracted many different immigrant groups, of which one-fifth was from Guyana and many of the rest from Haiti, China, India, Colombia, Jamaica, the Philippines, the Dominican Republic, and Pakistan. Vast redevelopment efforts were in the planning stages and some were under way in 2010.

Gerard R. Wolfe

Jamaica Bay. Shallow tidal wetland of about 20 square miles (50 square kilometers) between Brooklyn and Queens, consisting of grassy marshes sheltered from the Atlantic Ocean by Rockaway Peninsula. It forms a large part of the Gateway National Recreation Area. Within it are dozens of islands, of which only the largest, Broad Channel, is inhabited. On the northern half of this island is the Jamaica Bay Wildlife Refuge, which has two freshwater ponds and a remarkable number of shorebirds and is the largest urban refuge in the United States built on landfill wholly within the boundaries of a city.

Before the arrival of the Dutch, the bay was a favorite fishing and hunting ground for the Canarsee and Rockaway Indians. It was sparsely settled until 1880, when the New York, Woodhaven, and Rockaway Railroad built a wooden trestle 5 miles (8 kilometers) long across the bay to connect the Rockaways to the rest of Queens. The bay became increasingly polluted by expanding industry along the shores and by two sewers, one in Canarsie (1886), which drained New Lots, and one in Jamaica (1914). In 1916 fishing and swimming were banned by the Board of Health, and all the summer resort hotels closed. The opening in the mid-1920s of the Cross Bay Boulevard made Broad Channel accessible to automobiles and further development. After a fire in 1950 destroyed the wooden railroad trestle, the Metropolitan Transportation Authority acquired the property and rebuilt the line, connecting it to the subway system in 1953, maintaining a station at Broad Channel. In the 1980s efforts to clean up the waters achieved considerable success. The Jamaica Bay Wildlife Refuge has become a popular destination for bird lovers and those seeking "refuge" from the busy city.

The Future of Jamaica Bay (New York: Department of Parks, 1938)

Gerard R. Wolfe

Jamaica Estates. Neighborhood in east central Queens, bounded to the north by Union Turnpike, to the east by 188th Street, to the south by Hillside Avenue, and to the west by Home Lawn Street. It was a tract of 503 acres (200 hectares) bought by the Jamaica Estates Company in 1907 and developed beginning in April 1908; backers included Timothy L. Woodruff, the lieutenant governor of New York State and the chairman of the Republican State Committee; Michael J. Degnon, builder of the Belmont Tunnel and a contractor for the municipal subways; Edward Grant, the comptroller of the City of New York; and many bankers. The development was designed as a "residential park" in which the streets were laid out to fit the contours of the land and only detached, one-family houses with an attic and two stories were built; it also included an elegant entrance with a stone gatehouse on Hillside Avenue. During the next 20 years many houses occupying at least three lots were built, the least expensive costing $6000. Grand Central Parkway was laid out through Jamaica Estates in the 1920s but was landscaped to blend with the neighborhood. In December 1929 the deed restrictions expired and the Jamaica Estates Association was formed to preserve the character of the neighborhood; the only apartment buildings allowed were along Hillside Avenue. In the early twenty-first century there are about 1700 houses of various styles, shaded by trees on 88 square blocks. Many of the inhabitants are doctors, lawyers, and political figures.

Vincent Seyfried

Jamaica Hills. Neighborhood in east central Queens (2000 pop. *ca* 13,900), bounded to the north by the Grand Central Parkway, to the east by Homelawn Street (Jamaica Estates), to the south by Hillside Avenue, and to the west by Parsons Boulevard (Briarwood); it lies along a terminal moraine extending the length of Long Island. Named for its hilly terrain, the area was developed during the 1920s and 1930s after subway lines were extended to Jamaica. After 1965 the population, which had large Jewish and Greek components, became ethnically more diverse. Almost 25 percent of the new immigrants who settled in the neighborhood and its environs during the 1980s were from Guyana; many others were from Jamaica, the Dominican Republic, Colombia, El Salvador, China, and Haiti. Beginning in the 1990s large numbers of newcomers from Bangladesh and Pakistan arrived. Meanwhile, the traditionally older, one-family frame houses and newer two- and three-family attached brick houses began to be supplemented by larger one- and two-family homes. A few apartment buildings stand near Hillside Avenue. To the north of Jamaica Hills are Queens Hospital Center and St. John's University, and to the south, the main commercial section of Jamaica.

Andrew Sparberg

Jamaica Hospital. Nonprofit hospital in Jamaica at 89th Avenue near the Van Wyck Expressway, opened in a small house by a group of women in 1891 to provide emergency care for local residents. It added an operating room and several more wards in 1899 and an orthopedic clinic in 1916 in response to the polio epidemic. The hospital had no male board members until 1920. The growth in population that followed the opening of the subway along Jamaica Avenue led to the building of a new facility in 1924 with 123 beds. From 1950 until the late 1970s the hospital underwent further expansion, adding dental services and a nursing home. A major program of renovation and new construction was initiated in 1987. As of 2010 Jamaica Hospital had 431 beds.

Sandra Opdycke

Jamaicans. The first period of Jamaican immigration to the United States on a large scale began shortly after 1900 and ended in the 1920s. By 1930, 55,000 foreign-born blacks lived in New York City, an estimated half of them Jamaican. Jamaicans maintained an important presence in Harlem during the 1920s; they included Marcus Garvey, the black nationalist leader of the Universal Negro Improvement Association, and the poet and novelist Claude McKay, a leading figure in the Harlem Renaissance. Amendments to the Immigration and Nationality Act in 1965 brought about a second and much larger influx: according to Census Bureau figures the number of Jamaican immigrants in New York City increased from 11,160 in 1960 to slightly more than 160,000 in 2005, when they were the third largest immigrant group in the city.

Jamaicans who moved to New York City early in the century generally lived in Harlem and Bedford–Stuyvesant; post-1965 immigrants have settled along with other English-speaking West Indians principally in central Brooklyn, especially in Crown Heights, Flatbush, East Flatbush, and Canarsie–Flatlands. Large numbers have also settled in northeast Bronx (Wakefield and Williamsbridge) and southeast Queens, especially Laurelton, Springfield Gardens, and St. Albans. Jamaicans have found work mainly in the service sector: many Jamaican women work in health care as nurses and nurses' aides, in private households as child-care workers and attendants to the elderly, and in sales and office positions; men are found in a variety of jobs such as security guards, construction workers, janitors, and carpenters. Jamaicans have low rates of self-employment, although there are a number of Jamaican-owned businesses, including restaurants, bakeries, travel agencies, and record stores. Some Jamaican men operate vans that compete with the public transportation system.

Jamaicans in New York City often set themselves apart socially and culturally from African Americans although they also identify with African Americans on the basis of shared experiences of racial discrimination. The national identity that they have striven to maintain is frequently subsumed by a larger West Indian identity, one perhaps made inevitable by a common linguistic and cultural background: with other English-speaking West Indians, Jamaicans often attend churches rather than form congregations of their own, belong to groups in the workplace and to neighborhood associations, and take part in the West Indian American Day Parade every Labor Day in Brooklyn. There is no locally published Jamaican newspaper in New York City, although an edition of the *Jamaican Weekly Gleaner* intended for North America enjoys wide circulation. About a dozen Jamaican alumni associations, composed of graduates of various high schools and colleges on the island, exist in the New York City area.

Reggae, dance hall, and other forms of Jamaican popular music have earned a large following among youth from a variety of racial and ethnic backgrounds. Prominent New Yorkers of Jamaican origin include Colin L. Powell, former U.S. secretary of state, who was born to Jamaican parents and grew up in the Bronx; Una Clarke, born in Jamaica and City Council member from 1991 to 2001; and her American-born daughter, Yvette Clarke, elected to the U.S. House of Representatives in 2001.

Philip Kasinitz, *Caribbean New York: Black Immigrants and the Politics of Race* (Ithaca, N.Y.: Cornell University Press, 1992); Nancy Foner, ed., *Islands in the City: West Indian Migration to New York* (Berkeley: University of California Press, 2001)

Nancy Foner

Jamaica Pass. Obsolete name of BROADWAY JUNCTION.

Jamaica Racetrack. Thoroughbred racetrack in Queens, opened on 27 April 1903 by the Metropolitan Jockey Club with 15,000 people in attendance. It had 9000 grandstand seats, costing $2 each, as well as field space costing 75 cents. Access was mainly by the Long Island Rail Road and local trolley lines. The oval track, 1 mile (1.6 kilometers) in circumference, was well drained and very fast. Jamaica was the least prestigious track of its time: the ambience was rather modest, and the large crowds were raucous, loud, and loyal. The attendance of 64,670 on Memorial Day 1945 was a state record. Facilities deteriorated over time, and the track closed on 1 August 1959.

Steven A. Riess

James, Charles [Boucheron, Charles; James, C. Haweis; James, C(harles) B. H.; Boucheron] (*b* Sandhurst, England, ?1905/6; *d* New York City, 23 Sept 1978). Fashion designer. The son of a British army officer and an American mother, he began his career at the age of 18 as a milliner in Chicago under the name Boucheron before moving to New York City in 1938 to design hats and dresses for his select clientele. Between 1929 and 1940 he moved freely between the United States and Europe, gaining inspiration from legendary designers such as Paul Poiret and Christian Dior. In 1940 he settled in New York City, where he opened a custom-order shop. His reputation as a daring and innovative designer attracted such influential and fashionable customers as Mrs. William Randolph Hearst, Jr.; he also designed the salon of Elizabeth Arden. As his career progressed James's contentious and eccentric character destroyed many relationships, including that with Arden, and he spent years engaged in contractual disputes while his customers waited for their orders. He retired in 1958 to lecture at the Rhode Island School of Design and the Pratt Institute and spent the last years of his life in the Chelsea Hotel. James is especially noted for having successfully combined European classical tradition and American individualism. Many of his designs, including his "Taxi" dresses of the 1920s and 1930s and his grand ball dresses of the 1940s and 1950s, are now held at the Smithsonian Institution and the Fashion Institute of Technology.

Anne E. Kornblut

James, Henry (Jr.) (*b* New York City, 15 April 1843; *d* London, 28 Feb 1916). Novelist. Born at 21 Washington Place, he lived in Europe and in Albany, New York, before moving with his family to West 14th Street. In 1855 he left for Europe, visiting New York City infrequently in the following years, including a stay of about six months at 111 East 25th Street in 1875 and visits to Edith Wharton's sister-in-law at 21 East 11th Street in 1904 and 1911. His novel *Washington Square* (1881) explored the morals of the upper class in the city. After 20 years abroad, James traveled across the United States in 1904–5; the resulting book *The American Scene* (1907) focused on New England and New York City, criticizing the city for its materialism and loss of manners. Only a few years later, however, in 1911, he described New York City as "a very extraordinary and terrific and yet amiable place," admitting that he felt "a sneaking kindness for its pride and power."

Jeff Finlay, Dianna Ng

James Beard Cooking School. Cooking school at 167 West 12th Street established in 1955. When it opened, the chef and writer JAMES BEARD taught classes in the kitchen of his own house in Greenwich Village. A year after Beard's death in 1985, the James Beard Foundation, of which the cooking school is now a part, was founded to honor the legacy of Beard, who is considered the father of American gastronomy.

Jessica Montesano

James McCreery. Dry-goods shop opened in 1837. It catered to wealthy women and built its reputation on service and on its stock of imported fabrics and dress materials, particularly silk. Like other stores it moved uptown in stages: from Canal Street, to Broadway and 11th Street, to what became its most prestigious address, the southeast corner of West 23rd Street and Sixth Avenue. For more than two decades its gleaming marble building marked the northern edge of the shopping district. By the end of the nineteenth century it was considered the most elegant establishment of its kind. When the shopping district moved farther uptown during the first decade of the twentieth century, McCreery's moved to 34th Street; it ceased to be popular after World War II and closed in 1954.

Elaine S. Abelson

J. and W. Seligman. Firm of investment advisers. It began operations on 1 May 1864 as a merchant banking firm with headquarters at 59 Exchange Place and branches in San Francisco, New Orleans, London, Frankfurt am Main, and Paris. The founders were eight brothers from a Bavarian Jewish family who immigrated to the United States between 1837 and 1842; worked as peddlers, shopkeepers, merchants, and importers; and during the Civil War supplied the Union army with clothing and sold federal securities in Europe. The firm, which raised capital for the city, its transit system, the nation's railroads, and the Panama Canal, was for many years under the control of the family, the members of which were prominent civic leaders. After Joseph Seligman's death the firm was run successively by his brother Jesse Seligman and his son Isaac Newton Seligman. From 1907 to 1919 it was based at its own building at 1 William Street (later occupied by Lehman Brothers and then by Banca Commerciale Italiana). In 1937 the last partner belonging to the family retired and the firm developed a specialty in investment fund advisement. After a leveraged buyout in January 1989 control passed to a group led by William C. Morris. In 2008 Ameriprise Financial bought the firm for an estimated $440 million, and the new manager became RiverSource, an Ameriprise subsidiary. In the twenty-first century its headquarters were at 100 Park Avenue.

Ross L. Muir and Carle J. White, *Over the Long Term: The Story of J. & W. Seligman and Co.* (New York: J. and W. Seligman, 1964); Stephen Birmingham, *Our Crowd: The Great Jewish Families of New York* (New York: Harper and Row, 1967)

Theresa Collins

Japanese. Japanese immigrants came to New York City during the last quarter of the nineteenth century and constituted a small, predominantly male, middle-class population. In 1876 six Japanese businessmen arrived in the city to establish trade between Japan and the United States in wholesale and retail goods (primarily silk). During the following 20 years Japanese businessmen continued to enter the city and some became permanent residents, though large-scale Japanese immigration continued to be limited by American and Japanese efforts to restrict entry. In 1890–91 there were 600 Japanese in the city, more than half of whom lived in Brooklyn and worked at the Brooklyn Navy Yard. In the mid-1890s the number of Japanese began to increase, rising to more than 1000 in 1900, with 90 percent employed in domestic work. In 1897 the first Japanese newspaper, a short-lived weekly, was published by a Japanese college student in Brooklyn. As the number of Japanese grew, church and social groups arose to meet their needs. The Japanese Christian Institute (1899) was the first of several organizations that offered room and board to Japanese immigrants and businessmen, and in 1907 Toyohiko Campbell Takami formed the Japanese Mutual Aid Society, a community welfare group; from this evolved the Japanese Association of New York (1914), sponsored by the Japanese government, which in addition to offering support for immigrants kept track of their numbers (its totals often differing considerably from those of the federal census). A number of newspapers were launched during these years, including the *Japanese American Commercial Weekly, Nyuyoku jiho* (1904–10), and the semiweekly *Nyuyoku shimpo* (from 1911 until the outbreak of World War II).

The naval directives of 1907 increased the regulations on employment of aliens and led the Brooklyn Navy Yard to discharge large numbers of Japanese workers. This caused much of the Japanese community to move to Manhattan in search of new employment: by 1909 most of the 3000 Japanese in the city lived there. In 1908 Japan and the United States reached a "gentlemen's agreement" concerning immigration: as a result Japan issued two types of passport—one for skilled or unskilled laborers, the other for nonlaborers such as students, merchants, businessmen, and professionals, who were required to have a middle school education or its equivalent—and all Japanese citizens in the United States were required to register at Japanese consular offices. During the first 15 years of the twentieth century 75 percent of those registered at the city's Japanese consulate held passports for nonlaborers: of these, one-fifth were from urban areas. Passport records suggest that many Japanese who visited New York City on temporary visas as students or businessmen chose to remain in the city permanently, even though many failed to finish school or succeed at business.

Although racism was not as violent in the East as it was on the Pacific Coast, many Japanese were consigned to work as laborers because of anti-Japanese sentiment. The Japanese population in the city was 4652 in 1920, and about 75 percent were domestic workers in 1921. Most of the rest worked at semiskilled or unskilled jobs in small businesses such as amusement concessions at Coney Island. The Japanese were isolated from white European immigrants and scattered in areas such as southern Manhattan, 123rd Street, and downtown Brooklyn; some lived on large estates on Long Island. During the period from 1924 to 1952, when the National Origins Act was enforced and Japanese emigrants were excluded from the United States, the Japanese population in the city hovered between 2500 and 2900.

After the outbreak of World War II all Japanese organizations were forced to cease operations, and during the war a number of their leaders and other Japanese were detained at Ellis Island. The population at large was not interned, as was the case on the West Coast, but many immigrant businesses failed amid a general hostility toward the Japanese. In the years following the war the Japanese Association of New York, Japanese Christian churches, and Japanese Buddhist temples were revived, and several new organizations were formed, such as the Japanese American Citizens League, Japanese American Help for the Aging, and the Japanese American United Church. The *Nyuyoku nichibei* was launched as a weekly newspaper with sections in Japanese and English. By 1950 the number of Japanese in the city increased to more than 3800 as Japanese Americans who had been interned in the western United States resettled in the East. A small influx from Japan began after 1952 and strengthened in 1965 when the Immigration Act abolished quotas on Japanese immigration. The number of Japanese in the city stood at about 14,000 in 1970 and about 21,000 in 1980, of whom 17,000 were Japanese born. In 1990 the total population was 16,828, of which 12,837 were Japanese born. Although the number of Japanese immigrants in the city steadily increased during this period, it declined as a percentage of total Asian immigration. In 2000 the Japanese population numbered 26,419, mostly located in Manhattan.

Prominent Japanese in New York City have included the art critic Sadakichi Hartmann, the bacteriologist Hideyo Noguchi, the sculptor Isamu Noguchi, the chemist Jokichi Takamine, the ministers Ernest Atushi Ohori, Sojiro Shimizu, and Alfred Saburo Akamatsu, and the lawyers George Yamaoka and G. Gentoku Shimamoto.

Mitziko Sawada, *Tokyo Life, New York Dreams: Urban Japanese Visions of America, 1890–1924* (Berkeley: University of California Press, 1996)

Mitziko Sawada

Japanese American Association. Community organization formed in 1914 as the Japanese Association of New York. Inspired by similar organizations in the western United States, it sought to fight racism, help Japanese immigrants in their dealings with government, and obtain financial support from Japan. The association originally drew most of its members from the Japanese Mutual Aid Society, and until 1940 it conducted periodic censuses at the request of the Japanese consulate. The racial makeup and activities of the association caused it to be perpetually under surveillance by the Federal Bureau of Investigation from 1920 to 1942, and with the onset of World War II the government closed its offices and confiscated its files. The association was revived in 1945 under the New York American Committee for Japan Relief and for the next few years worked closely with the postwar Licensed Agency for Relief in Asia. In 1953 it reverted back to its original name, the Japanese American Association, and into the twenty-first century has expanded its social programs to include aid for the elderly in the tri-state area, scholarships, sports leagues, and language workshops for Japanese and Japanese Americans.

Mitziko Sawada

Japan Society. Nonprofit organization in Manhattan, formed in 1907 to promote cultural understanding between the United States and Japan. It occupies a building at 333 East 47th Street designed by Junzo Yoshimura that has an outdoor garden. The society sponsors lectures and discussions on cultural, educational, and public affairs; film programs; concerts of traditional and contemporary Japanese music; and language courses. An art gallery opened in 1971 was the first in the nation devoted exclusively to Japanese art; it exhibits traditional and modern works from private and institutional collections throughout the world. In 2007 the society celebrated the 100th anniversary of its founding.

Carol V. Wright

Jarmulowsky's Bank. Savings bank catering to Jewish and Italian immigrants on the Lower East Side, opened in 1873 by Sender Jarmulowsky. Made wealthy when the bank prospered, Jarmulowsky donated money to the building fund for the Eldridge Street Synagogue and to many other local charities. In 1912 the bank moved to a newly completed 12-story building at 54–58 Canal Street; after Jarmulowsky's death later in the year his sons managed the bank until World War I, when depositors troubled by rumors of insolvency and eager to send money to relatives in Europe demanded payment in gold. The state banking superintendent closed the bank in August 1914 after discovering that it had $654,000 in assets and $1,703,000 in liabilities; mobs of angry depositors gathered outside the bank the next day and in front of the Jarmulowskys' home at 393 Fort Washington Avenue a month later. The family managed to escape over adjacent rooftops, but one of the founder's sons was later indicted and convicted for mismanagement. Many depositors recovered only a small portion of their savings. In the early twenty-first century the bank building was used by garment manufacturers.

Edward T. O'Donnell

Jarvis, John (*b* England, 1780; *d* New York City, 12 Jan 1840). Painter. In 1785 his family moved from England to Philadelphia where he became an apprentice to the engraver Edward Savage from 1796 to 1801. He moved to New York City in 1802 and painted portraits in collaboration with Joseph Wood. He is best known for several full-length depictions of heroes of the War of 1812 that he painted for City Hall.

Janet Frankston

Javits, Jacob K(oppel) (*b* New York City, 18 May 1904; *d* Palm Beach, Fla., 7 March 1986). Senator and state attorney general. Born on the Lower East Side, he represented the Upper West Side from 1947 to 1955 as a Republican in the U.S. Congress, where he supported legislation on civil rights, health, and social welfare. He served as attorney general of New York State during 1955–57. As a U.S. senator for New York (1957–81) he sponsored the War Powers Resolution (1973) and the Pension Reform Act (1974). He unsuccessfully sought election to a sixth term in 1980. A prominent spokesman for liberal Republicanism, Javits represented New York in the U.S. Senate longer than anyone before him. The Jacob K. Javits Convention Center was named for him in 1984. He wrote *Javits: The Autobiography of a Public Man* (1981).

Lee R. Hiltzik

Jay, John (*b* New York City, 12 Jan 1745; *d* Bedford, N.Y., 17 May 1829). Chief justice of the United States and governor. A graduate of King's College (1764; now Columbia University), he was Robert R. Livingston's law partner and married Sarah Livingston, the daughter of William Livingston. In 1773 he served on a royal commission that determined the boundary between New York and New Jersey. A delegate to both continental congresses, he became a strong supporter of the American cause only after the Declaration of Independence was adopted. During the war he helped draft New York State's first constitution (1777), served as the state's first chief justice (1777–79), was president of the Continental Congress (1778), and played an important role in negotiating the peace treaty with Britain (1783). Although secretary for foreign affairs (1784–89), he argued eloquently for adoption of the new Constitution in his *Federalist* essays. During these years he lived at 133 Broadway. He became the first chief justice of the United States (1789–95) and later negotiated a treaty with Britain (1794) that ended British occupation of the Northwest Territory and resolved trade and navigation issues. He served two terms as governor of New York (1795–1801) before retiring. His later years were spent in Bedford in nearby Westchester County. Jay was also a president of the American Bible Society.

Frank Monaghan, *John Jay: Defender of Liberty against Kings and Peoples* (New York: Bobbs–Merrill, 1833; repr. Salem, N.H.: Ayer, 1972); Walter Stahr, *John Jay* (London: Hambledon and London, 2005)

See also Abolitionism; Coffeehouses; and Livingston, Brockholst.

Barbara A. Chernow

jaywalking. Urban expression referring to crossing the street outside of the regulated crosswalk lines. It was first used in the *Chicago Tribune* in 1909 and stemmed from a combination of the words *jay*, a rural person unfamiliar with the city streets, and *walk*. Although jaywalking is illegal in North America, it is commonplace in many cities, including New York City, which has a high density of pedestrian traffic and relatively slow pace of automobiles. During the infancy of Mayor Rudolph Giuliani's Broken windows policy, the first tickets for this "infraction" were issued, but into the twenty-first century, jaywalking shows no signs of abating in the metropolis.

Cecilia Magnusson

jazz. The initial prominence of New York City on the jazz scene came not through musical innovation, but rather through what would become historic recordings of artists from elsewhere in the country. The first jazz recording, after black coronetist Freddie Keppard declined an offer for fear of imitation, was by a white group from New Orleans, the Original Dixieland Jass Band, in 1917. A second pinnacle recording was blues singer and vaudevillian Mamie Smith's "Crazy Blues," which sold an incredible 75,000 copies during its first month in Harlem alone. Despite these early recordings, however, in the early 1920s New Orleans remained the home of jazz and Chicago its prominent musical center.

Meanwhile, Harlem was home to an outgrowth of ragtime playing called stride, developed by the "Father of Stride Piano" James P. Johnson, his protégé Fats Waller, and other pianists such as Willie "the Lion" Smith and Luckey Roberts. Composer, arranger, and bandleader James Reese Europe returned from World War I in France with his 369th Infantry Band and Bill "Bojangles" Robinson as regimental drum major and marched ceremoniously up Fifth Avenue and along Harlem's arterial thoroughfare, 125th Street, in 1919.

One symbol of jazz's shift from Chicago to New York City was the move of prodigal coronetist and singer Louis Armstrong in 1924. Though he was married to King Oliver's pianist, Lil Hardin, it was largely at her urging that Armstrong moved on his own to New York City and joined pianist Fletcher Henderson's band. In the city he recorded with blues singers Gertrude "Ma" Rainey and Bessie Smith, both of whom had capitalized on the clamor for blues vocalists after the success of Mamie Smith's records. A significant concert in the development of jazz and New York City's prominence was Paul Whiteman's Aeolian Hall concert that same year. The self-proclaimed "King of Jazz," Whiteman set out "to make a lady out of jazz," and the concert, titled an "Experiment in Modern Music," began with a rendition of the Original Dixieland Jass Band's popular 1917 success "Livery Stable Blues" and ended with the premier of George Gershwin's "Rhapsody in Blue," with Gershwin himself at the piano. That year also saw the move of pianist and composer Duke Ellington and his Washingtonians to New York City and their full-time tenure at the Kentucky Club (later known as the Hollywood Club).

During the latter 1920s increased Prohibition enforcement in Chicago, further exacerbated by the 1929 St. Valentine's Day Massacre, combined with New York City's preeminence in the recording and broadcasting industries to result in a surge in the popularity of New York City swing bands and dance clubs. Whites-only clubs such as the Cotton Club (at Lenox Avenue and 142nd Street), whose lavish revues featured Ellington as a headliner starting in 1927, and the Roseland Ballroom (at 51st Street and Broadway) drew young listeners dancing the Lindy Hop, Charleston, and jitterbug. The integrated Savoy Ballroom (at Lenox Avenue and 140th Street) frequently featured orchestra battles during the height of the swing era (about 1935 to 1946), most famously between Benny Goodman's orchestra and the house band, led by drummer Chick Webb, and again the following year by the Count Basie Band. The popularity of swing led to the national stardom of many white leaders such as Goodman, Artie Shaw, Tommy Dorsey, and Glenn Miller. Though black bandleaders such as Ellington, Cab Calloway, Count Basie, and Jimmy Lunceford gained notoriety as well, others such as Teddy Wilson and Benny Carter struggled, and Fletcher Henderson sold compositions to Goodman and eventually disbanded his own group and joined the clarinetist as an arranger and sometime pianist. Carnegie Hall on West 57th Street provided the setting in 1938 for efforts to "dignify" jazz at concerts, one organized by Goodman and another, titled "From Spirituals to Swing," by the record producer and talent scout John Hammond. Sandwiched between these events was an all-day outdoor concert given by 32 leading big bands at Randalls Island called "Carnival of Swing"; the performance, which drew an audience of nearly 25,000, is regarded as the first jazz festival. By 1939 an estimated 200 "name" bands toured the country, employing more than 3000 jazz musicians, most of whom used New York City as their mainstay.

Though big bands gained notoriety for their dancing appeal, small groups formed under the leadership of popular swing artists. From 1935 to 1941 Ellington made more than 140 small-group recordings, and in 1936 Goodman led a small integrated group composed of pianist Teddy Wilson, vibraphonist Lionel Hampton, and guitarist Charlie Christian. In addition to Goodman's quartet, the Count Basie Ensemble, Tommy Dorsey's Clambake Seven, Bob Crosby's Bob Cats, Chick Webb

Rose Jazz Center, 2009

and His Little Chicks, Artie Shaw and His Gramercy Five, and Woody Herman's Woodchoppers all represented smaller group efforts by popular big band leaders. New York City's 52nd Street, known as Swing Street or "the street that never sleeps," featured small-group performances in clubs such as the Onyx (home to Art Tatum's Spirits of Rhythm), the Famous Door (hosting the likes of Count Basie and Ben Webster), the Three Deuces (featuring a young Dizzy Gillespie), and Kelly's Stable, where saxophonist Coleman Hawkins, home from a five-year stay in Europe, developed his improvisational style on the classic "Body and Soul," famously captured on Hawkins's 1939 recording session for Victor records. During these years singer Billie Holiday also recorded with myriad groups, her colleagues forming a virtual catalogue of soloists of the swing era. However, it was her partnership with former Basie sideman saxophonist Lester Young that produced some of the most memorable recordings of her early career.

The early 1940s saw a coalescing of several factors that irrevocably changed the course of jazz music, driving it away from the mainstream and toward a more eclectic niche market. Although Ellington's annual concerts beginning in 1943 at Carnegie Hall were well received and Stan Kenton's big band became immensely popular, Harlem was again the site of a dramatic musical innovation. Minton's Playhouse on West 118th Street and Clark Monroe's Uptown House on West 134th Street were the site of after-hours jam sessions (beginning after the 4:00 a.m. official wartime curfew at which nightclubs were required to close); most notably, these sessions involved Charlie Christian, pianists Thelonious Monk and Bud Powell, drummers Kenny Clarke and Max Roach, and perhaps most importantly alto saxophonist Charlie Parker and the trumpeter Dizzy Gillespie. Coinciding with what has been argued to be both a musically and racially separatist movement was a recording ban by the musicians' union that lasted from 1942 to 1944. What emerged in 1945 with releases by the movement's foremost innovators, Gillespie and Parker, was a musical form that was more jagged, dissonant, and frenetic than its earlier counterpart. Taking its name from Gillespie's own composition, the new music became known as "bebop."

Whether bebop was in fact revolutionary, or rather a logical extension of the developments from the swing period, has been a subject of much debate. Perhaps because of the same conditions that bred bebop, or rather as a reaction to the nascent movement, the 1940s saw a revival of Dixieland music (or "New Orleans" music to those who believed that the term "Dixieland" referred to the Mason–Dixon Line that had separated the North and South). Legendary New Orleans trumpeter Bunk Johnson had long been out of the music business, but he was found, fitted with false teeth, and disingenuously promoted as Louis Armstrong's tutor. Though initially available to New Yorkers only through recordings, the revival arrived in the city during 1945–46 when Johnson and clarinetist George Lewis played the Stuyvesant Casino on Second Avenue. Along the same lines, a similar style emerged at Nick's (on Seventh Avenue South, and later West 10th Street), referred to loosely as Dixieland, Chicago jazz, and Nixieland (after the club). Also flourishing at Jimmy Ryan's, Eddie Condon's, the Central Plaza, and the Metropole—many located in the vicinity of Swing Street—the jazz scene in New York City during this period was diverse. However, factions arose not only between the so-called "moldy figs," critics who favored traditional jazz, and progressives, but also between musicians of the older generations such as Armstrong who saw themselves primarily as entertainers, and young, serious players like Miles Davis and Charlie Parker. Gillespie, brandishing a bent trumpet bell, horned-rimmed glasses, and a dynamic personality, remained the exception rather than the rule for most beboppers.

Often thought of as the antithesis of the bebop movement, "cool jazz"—also known as

West Coast jazz—grew out of bop in both its musical concepts and some of its key figures. Though the style is usually identified with California and the softer, lilting sounds of Stan Getz, Gerry Mulligan, and Shorty Rogers, all of these musicians grew up on the East Coast. Ultimately, cool jazz received its name from a 1949 album by Miles Davis and Gil Evans titled "Birth of the Cool." Davis, having left Charlie Parker's bop group in 1948, had fallen in with a group of musicians hanging around Evans's 55th Street apartment. Evans had proved himself adept at arranging bop standards such as "Donna Lee" and "Anthropology," but it was Davis who finally brought together the nonet composed of six winds (trumpet, trombone, French horn, tuba, and alto and baritone saxophone) and a three-piece rhythm section. The group appeared at the Royal Roost (Broadway and 47th Street), alternating sets with Count Basie, in 1949 and 1950. Another popular New York City group of the cool period was the Modern Jazz Quartet (MJQ), which cultivated a large college-age following doing tours of concert halls and schools across the country.

In New York City, as well as in Chicago, Philadelphia, and Detroit, the residual effects of bebop remained largely unphased by the cool movement. The hard-hitting, polyrhythmic drumming of Art Blakey, Philly Joe Jones, and Max Roach ushered in what became known as "hard bop." Blakey, along with pianist Horace Silver, formed the Jazz Messengers in 1954, a group that would act as a training ground for young jazz musicians spanning nearly 45 years. The group was originally assembled as a 17-piece all-Muslim big band, simply called the Messengers, for a gig at Small's Paradise. Blakey had adopted the name Adbullah Ibn Buhaina and, along with trumpeter Barrymore Rainey, organized a group of New York jazz musicians in 1947 using Blakey's Harlem apartment as a Muslim mission. Outgrowing the space, the group reportedly exceeded 100 members (12 of whom were musicians) and moved its headquarters to 30th Street. The movement toward Islam in jazz was not specific to Blakey's group; Dizzy Gillespie's band had also spawned a number of converts, including Liaqat Ali Salaam (Kenny Clarke), Yusef Lateef (Bill Evans), and Talib Dawud (Alfonso Nelson Rainey). Other notable members of the Ahmadiyya Movement in Islam included pianists Ahmad Jamal and McCoy Tyner. Charlie Parker is remembered by various Muslim names and as having practiced Islam for the latter period of his life.

By the mid-1950s the geographic core of New York City jazz had shifted. Though Birdland, named after Charlie "Bird" Parker, at Broadway and 52nd Street still thrived, the jazz alley of 52nd Street had largely been replaced by clubs in Greenwich Village, such as the centrally located Village Vanguard (at Seventh Avenue and West 11th Street), which

Jazz musicians in Washington Square Park, 2009

would later become a rite of passage for young musicians recording live sets. Other downtown havens included the Half Note, featuring musicians such as Lennie Tristano, John Coltrane, and Charles Mingus; Slugs Saloon (on East Third Street), which boasted hard-bop musicians Art Blakey, Freddie Hubbard, and Lee Morgan; the Village Gate (on Bleecker Street), also a popular recording spot; and the Five Spot, where progressives like saxophonist Ornette Coleman and pianist Cecil Taylor enjoyed extended residencies. In addition to the breakthrough playing of Coleman and Taylor, bop innovator Thelonious Monk brought a quartet featuring a maturing John Coltrane on tenor sax to the Five Spot in 1957. Through both his tenure with Monk and his time as a Miles Davis sideman, Coltrane forged a new sound first in hard bop, then modal jazz, and eventually became a leader in the free jazz movement.

Coltrane had played with Davis at the Audubon Ballroom (on Broadway between 165th and 166th streets) during the early 1950s, replacing alto saxophonist Jackie McLean. However, alongside his contemporary Sonny Rollins, Coltrane was reportedly outmatched, and it was not until after his stint with Monk that he rejoined Davis successfully in 1958. The following year he made two pinnacle recordings: *Kind of Blue* (as a sideman in Davis's quintet) and *Giant Steps* (as a leader of his own quartet). By 1960 Coltrane was leading his own group full time; he opened at the Jazz Gallery with Steve Khun, Pete LaRoca, and Steve Davis as his rhythm section but quickly replaced Khun with McCoy Tyner, and by 1962 he brought in bassist Jimmy Garrison and drummer Elvin Jones in what would later be referred to simply as "the quartet." Even as Coltrane moved into more discordant sounds and unconventional instrumental combinations, he rivaled Miles Davis with some of the most popular groups of the mid-1960s.

Following the trend southward, the New York City loft scene emerged in lower Manhattan near the small theaters, cafes, and performance spaces that had been hotbeds during the 1960s. Loft performances were a more informal setting void of alcohol and with low admission costs. Cecil Taylor, Archie Shepp, Albert Ayler, Marion Brown, Don Cherry, Sunny Murray, and Roswell Rudd all played significant roles in the scene. Along with Ornette Coleman, who started a space called Artists House below his residence on Prince Street, saxophonist Sam Rivers opened Studio Rivbea in 1971 (on Bond Street), which lasted until 1978. Another characteristic of the loft was its response to the hierarchy of power in the jazz business (with mostly white, nonmusicians occupying the administrative positions); loft venues managed and operated by musicians also included Ali's Alley (Rashied Ali), Ladies' Fort (Joe Lee Wilson), and the Brook (Charles Tyner). The loft community also put together small festivals to counteract larger, mainstream events such as the Newport Jazz Festival, which had moved to New York City in 1972 after a riot in Rhode Island the previous year.

Following the fusion movement with popular Miles Davis–led groups and Wayne Shorter's Weather Report, trumpeter Wynton Marsalis emerged in the 1980s as the new face of jazz. Established clubs such as Birdland, which underwent a revival in 1986 and eventually settled on West 44th Street, and the Village Vanguard (still in its original location) were joined by clubs like the Blue Note (on West Third Street) and Fat Tuesday's (on Third Avenue at 17th Street). Modern jazz had already become synonymous with New York City; however, the introduction of jazz concerts at Lincoln Center led to the reification of a particular type of jazz in the city's aesthetic. In 1988 the Lincoln Center Jazz Orchestra, a repertory big band, was established, and Jazz at Lincoln Center began in 1991. Jazz in the 1990s saw a resurgence of talented young musicians, summarily referred to as the young lions, led by saxophonist Joshua Redman (son of avant-garde tenor Dewey Redman); trumpeters Roy Hargrove, Nicholas Payton, and Terrell Stafford; pianists Eric Reed and Brad Mehldau; drummer Brian Blade; and bassist Christian McBride. Removed from the setting of the Lincoln Center jazz program and the neoclassicism of the young lions, in the early twenty-first century freer forms of jazz are performed at the annual summer Vision Festival and newer venues such as saxophonist John Zorn's performance space, The Stone, which sought to reinvent the loft scene by not serving beverages and giving all revenue to performers.

Garrett A. Felber

J. C. Penney. Firm of retailers, formed in 1902 in Kemmerer, Wyoming, by the dry-goods merchant James Cash Penney (1875–1971). It made its headquarters in New York City in 1914 but was popular mostly in small towns and rural areas. During the 1980s it became more competitive by diversifying and opening suburban outlets that sold more expensive, brand-name clothing. The firm moved its headquarters to Dallas in 1988. As of 2005 it was the third largest retailer in the country.

Peter A. Coclanis

Jefferson, Thomas (*b* Shadwell, near Charlottesville, Va., 13 April 1743; *d* Albemarle County, Va., 4 July 1826). Third president of the United States. He arrived in New York City on 21 March 1790 to become the first secretary of state of the United States. Because housing was scarce he lodged at the City Tavern, on the west side of Broadway between Cedar and Thames streets, before moving early in June to a small house at 57 Maiden Lane. As secretary of state he administered a staff of five and an annual budget of $7961 (which included his own salary of $3500) and was a trusted adviser to President George Washington; he coordinated diplomatic efforts abroad, organized the first patent office (but did not patent his own inventions), submitted a report to Congress on uniform weights and measures, and effected a compromise with Alexander Hamilton and James Madison whereby the federal government assumed state debts in return for having a permanent capital established on the shores of the Potomac. With Madison he left the city on 1 September 1790 for Virginia. A street in lower Manhattan is named for Jefferson, and a statue of him stands at Columbia University. In a letter to William Short (8 September 1823) Jefferson described New York City as "a cloacina of all the depravities of human nature."

Dumas Malone, *Jefferson and His Time* (Boston: Little, Brown, 1951)

Joyce Mendelsohn

Jefferson Market. Market opened at Greenwich Lane and Sixth Avenue in 1833 by request of residents of the ninth ward. A country market was added in 1836 for fishers, hucksters, and poulterers, and the Jefferson Courthouse, designed by Calvert Vaux and Frederick Clarke Withers, was erected nearby in 1877. By 1913 the market was primarily a retail operation, its prices often higher than those offered by local stores. In 1929 it was replaced by the Women's House of Detention.

Suzanne R. Wasserman

Jefferson Market Courthouse. National historic landmark in Greenwich Village, completed in 1877. It stands at the southwest corner of 10th Street and Sixth Avenue on the former site of a public meat and produce market for which it is named. The market, which opened on 5 January 1833 and had a wooden fire watchtower with a bell weighing 9000 pounds (4100 kilograms), was razed in 1873 by the Board of Aldermen to make way for a civic complex of redbrick structures that in addition to the courthouse included a new market, a firehouse, and a small jail. The architects Frederick Clarke Withers and Calvert Vaux designed a colorful structure in the High Victorian Gothic style with pinnacles and gables, distinctive stone carvings, stained-glass windows, a patterned slate roof, and a tower 172 feet (52 meters) tall with a four-faced illuminated clock, a huge bell, and space for a fire watch, crowned by a pyramidal roof. In a national poll of architects in 1885 the courthouse was voted one of the 10 most beautiful buildings in the United States. The third district civil court met on its second floor, the second district police court on its first. By 1929 only women's cases were tried in the courthouse and the other buildings of the complex were replaced by the Women's House of Detention, an 11-story building of tan brick for which Mayor James J. Walker broke ground in October. After the district court system was overhauled in 1945, the courthouse fell vacant in 1946; it temporarily housed the U.S. Census Bureau and then the Police Academy Annex, but it proved ill suited for government purposes and was scheduled to be sold at auction in 1959. Although the city had no preservation law at the time, the vigorous efforts of community groups in 1960 persuaded Mayor Robert F. Wagner and James Felt, chairman of the City Planning Commission, to withdraw the courthouse from sale and provide funds for its conversion by the New York Public Library into a much-needed branch. Renovated by Giorgio Cavaglieri, the Jefferson Market Library opened on 27 November 1967. After another neighborhood campaign the Women's House of Detention was demolished in 1973 and the site was landscaped as a garden adjacent to the library. The courthouse is recognized as an outstanding example of adaptive reuse.

Thomas F. De Voe, *The Market Book: A History of the Public Markets of the City of New York* (New York: Burt Franklin, 1970; repr. New York: Augustus M. Kelley, 1862); Francis R. Kowsky, *The Architecture of Frederick Clarke Withers and the Progress of the Gothic Revival* (Middletown, Conn.: Wesleyan University Press, 1980)

Margot Gayle

Jefferson Market

Jefferson School of Social Science. School formed in 1944 by the merger of two earlier adult communist schools in New York City, the Workers School (1923–44) and the School for Democracy (1942–44). The latter originated after the Rapp–Coudert state legislative investigation of left-wing professors at the city's municipal colleges resulted in the dismissal in 1941 of 60 faculty members and administrators by the Board of Higher Education. New York governor Herbert H. Lehman stopped the dismissals after the Nazi armies invaded the Soviet Union on 22 June 1941. Meanwhile, the Communist Party had created the School for Democracy to employ the ousted college teachers. When the Soviet Union began to prevail against Hitler, the party embraced patriotism and adopted the name Jefferson School. The school was part of an attempt to persuade Americans that after the war Russia and the United States would continue a close alliance.

Financed by such "rich rebels" as Frederick Vanderbilt Field, the school occupied a renovated nine-story former warehouse at Sixth Avenue and 16th Street in lower Manhattan. The director, Howard Selsam, a former tenured philosophy professor at Brooklyn College, and his assistant, David Goldway, a former City College of New York English teacher (both victims of the Rapp–Coudert purge), had earlier administered the School for Democracy and continued running the

Jefferson School from 1944 to 1956. By 1947 Doxey Wilkerson, former editor of the *People's Weekly World* in Harlem, joined the Jefferson School as director of curriculum. Most of the students came from the offices and light industries of the New York City region.

The central pedagogical task at the Jefferson School was to teach Marxism, but it was a "softer" version than at the earlier Communist Party schools. The basic course, Science of Society (the equivalent of Principles of Communism at the Workers School), emphasized coexistence. Marc Blitzstein, Eli Seigmeister, and Pete Seeger taught music; the cartoonist Ad Reinhart and Moses and Raphael Soyer taught art; Annette Rubinstein taught literature; Dashiell Hammett taught mystery writing; historian Herbert Aptheker taught African American history; and Eleanor Flexner taught women's history. Into the 1950s the cold war weakened the communist schools, and the Subversive Activities Control Board insisted that the school confess that it was an agent of the Soviet Union. Selsam and the others denied the charge, but after a legal struggle, the Jefferson School closed its doors in 1956.

Marvin E. Gettleman, "'No Varsity Teams': New York's Jefferson School of Social Science, 1943–1956," *Science and Society* 66 (Fall 2002), 336–59

See also McCarthyism, Communism, and New York Workers School.

Marvin E. Gettleman

Jehovah's Witnesses. Millenarian religious group formed in 1872 by Charles Taze Russell (1852–1916) whose beliefs are based solely in the teachings of the Bible and first-century Christianity. In 1909 the group established its headquarters at 25 Columbia Heights in Brooklyn and changed its name to the Watch Tower Bible and Tract Society. Russell believed that Christ had returned spiritually in 1874 and would soon begin a thousand-year reign on earth along with 144,000 people who were "sealed" to share his power. He asserted that this millennial age could not be fully realized until "satanic" forces were annihilated (including all Christian churches and the nations of the world). After Russell's death in 1916 Joseph F. Rutherford became the leader of the group, previously known as the International Bible Students. The current name was adopted in 1931. Rutherford emphasized the publication of periodicals and tracts; vigorous door-to-door proselytizing, in which all adherents of the faith were expected to take part; and the acquisition of buildings known as Kingdom Halls, which functioned in place of churches. Under Rutherford's direction, male followers refused to fight in World War I, which led to the first of many controversial court cases; others involved the refusal by Witnesses to recite the Pledge of Allegiance, their virulent anti-Catholicism, and their aversion to such medical protocols as blood transfusions. Nathan Knorr succeeded Rutherford as the group's leader in 1942. Some followers tired of waiting for the long-expected return of Christ and defected from the movement in the mid-1970s. After Knorr's death in 1977 he was succeeded in turn by Frederick Granz (1977–92), Milton Henschel (1992–2000), and Don A. Adams (2000–present) as president. In the mid-1990s the Jehovah's Witnesses claimed to have 40,000 to 80,000 adherents in New York City. The group maintained its international headquarters in Brooklyn and had extensive real estate holdings in Brooklyn Heights. It was governed by a group of nine officials, all male, chosen by existing members of the council. The Witnesses published two periodicals, *The Watchtower Announcing Jehovah's Kingdom,* first published in 1879, with a circulation of 37 million in 174 languages, and *Awake!,* with a circulation of 36 million in 82 languages. It also published a textbook in 2005, *What Does the Bible Really Teach?,* designed for use in home Bible study, available in 189 languages and selling more than 99 million copies. The religion claimed a worldwide membership of more than seven million early in the twenty-first century.

M. James Penton, *The Apocalypse Delayed: The Story of Jehovah's Witnesses* (Toronto: University of Toronto Press, 1988); Paul K. Conkin, *American Originals: Homemade Varieties of Christianity* (Chapel Hill: University of North Carolina Press, 1997)

Charles H. Lippy, Meghan Lalonde

Jennings [Graham], **Elizabeth** (*b* New York City, 1830; *d* New York City, 1901). Early civil rights activist and African American schoolteacher who won a landmark court decision that helped desegregate New York City's public transit system. On Sunday 16 July 1854 she tried to board a horse-drawn streetcar on Chatham Street in lower Manhattan. Late for church where she played the organ, Jennings and her friend Sarah Adams hailed the first car they saw. Repelled by the conductor, Jennings insisted she had the right to ride. A fight ensued that ended with both black women being tossed from the car. In an act of defiance, Jennings jumped back on the car and was brutally beaten by the conductor, driver, and a police officer. Outraged, the African American community rose to her defense. Led by her abolitionist father, Thomas L. Jennings, the Black Legal Rights Association was formed to battle discrimination. It was the first case for Chester A. Arthur, an attorney from the firm of Culver, Parker, and Arthur. The trial took place in Brooklyn Supreme Court before Judge William Rockwell. Citing a new law that made railway companies responsible for the acts of their employees, the Third Avenue Railway was sued for $500. Against all odds, Arthur, the future twenty-first president of the United States, won. On 22 February 1855 an all-white male jury awarded Jennings $250 in damages. Judge Rockwell declared, "Colored persons if sober, well-behaved and free from disease, [have] the same rights as others." After the Jennings victory, several test cases followed ending desegregation on city transportation. Jennings' activism didn't end there. She was a member of the Female Literary Society of New York, which raised money to free slaves and established the first kindergarten for black New Yorkers. In 2006 New York City renamed the corner of Park Row and Spruce Street (originally Chatham) Elizabeth Jennings Place.

Jerry Mikorenda

Jennings, Thomas L. (*b* Manhattan, 1791; *d* 11 February 1859). Inventor, businessman, and civil rights leader. He was the first African American granted a patent from the United States. A tailor and clothier by trade, Jennings began experimenting with chemicals to remove stains at the request of his customers. On 3 March 1821, he received U.S. patent 3306X for a process called "dry scouring," a forerunner of dry cleaning. Jennings used the wealth from his invention for social change. In 1827 he, along with several other black business leaders, established Freedom's Journal, the nation's first African American newspaper. He was a champion of the anti-colonialization movement and a founder of many early civil rights organizations such as the Wilberforce Society, the New York African Society for Mutual Relief, the Phoenix Society, the New York Vigilance Committee, and the Black Legal Rights Association. Jennings was also a key member of the first three national conventions of the People of Color and trustee of the Abyssinian Baptist Church. In his eulogy to Jennings in the *Anglo-African* newspaper, Frederick Douglass called him "a noble man" who led an "active, earnest and blameless life."

Jerry Mikorenda

Jerome, Jennie (Jeanette) [Lady Randolph Churchill] (*b* Brooklyn, 9 Jan 1854; *d* London, 9 June 1921). Socialite and mother of Winston Churchill. In 1899 the *New York Times* described her as "the most brilliant and beautiful American woman in England" and as a "politician, a musician, an editor, a writer, an artist in dress, and a notable amateur actress." She was the daughter of New York financier and sportsman Leonard Jerome, for whom the Bronx's Jerome Avenue and Jerome Park Reservoir are named. She was born at what is now 197 Amity Street in the Cobble Hill neighborhood of Brooklyn; a plaque at 426 Henry Street in Brooklyn falsely claims that as the location of her birth in addition to incorrectly listing her birth date. She married Lord Randolph Churchill in 1874 and spent the rest of her life overseas. According to legend, she was responsible for inventing the Manhattan cocktail, commissioning it for a party in October 1874 celebrating the newly elected governor of New York State, Samuel J. Tilden, a friend of her late father. This story, however, is false, as Lady Churchill was in England during that month, giving birth to the future prime minister of Great Britain. Her association with the cocktail most likely comes from the fact that the Manhattan Club later occupied a house once owned by her father at Madison Avenue and 26th Street, across from Madison Square Park.

Anne Sebba, *American Jennie: The Remarkable Life of Lady Randolph Churchill* (New York: W. W. Norton, 2007)

Anne Epstein

Jerome, Leonard Walter (*b* Pompey, N.Y., 3 Nov 1817; *d* Brighton, England, 4 March 1891). Financier. He graduated from Union College, practiced law, and was a consul in Trieste before moving to New York City in 1855 where he made and lost several fortunes on Wall Street. An avid sportsman, he helped to organize the American Jockey Club, built a racetrack at Jerome Park, and was known as a yachtsman and four-in-hand driver. For many years he was the principal owner of the *New York Times* and supported the arts. He also financed the construction of Jerome Boulevard from Jerome Park to the Harlem River. Toward the end of his life Jerome spent much time in England, where he is remembered as the grandfather of Winston Churchill.

Anita Leslie, *The Remarkable Mr. Jerome* (New York: Henry Holt, 1954)

James E. Mooney

Jerome, William Travers (*b* New York City, 18 April 1859; *d* New York City, 13 Feb 1934). Lawyer. Elected district attorney of New York County in 1901, he prosecuted some of the best-known criminal cases of the time, including those involving Abraham Henry Hummel, Charles F. Dodge, and Harry Thaw (who fatally shot the architect Stanford White). Although he had gained the office partly through family connections, he soon proclaimed his distaste for the nepotism and political favoritism of Tammany Hall. His tenacity in prosecuting public officials earned him an appointment to a committee led by State Senator Clarence Lexow that uncovered corruption in the city's police department; he also became a leading member of reformist groups and successfully campaigned for office as a member of the Fusion Party.

Richard O'Connor, *Courtroom Warrior: The Combative Career of William Travers Jerome* (Boston: Little, Brown, 1963)

Emery E. Adoradio

Jerome Park. Neighborhood in the northwestern Bronx, bounded to the northeast by Mosholu Parkway, to the east by Jerome Avenue, to the south by Kingsbridge Road, and to the west and northwest by Sedgwick Avenue. The area was part of the Bathgate estate in the nineteenth century until it was purchased by the stock speculator Leonard Walter Jerome (the maternal grandfather of Winston Churchill), who opened the Jerome Park Racetrack. The track closed in 1889 to make room for the Jerome Park Reservoir, and the eastern half of the property was ultimately used as the site for DeWitt Clinton High School, the Bronx High School of Science, Harris Park, Hunter College in the Bronx (now Lehman College), Walton High School, and a local elementary school. In 1917 the Kingsbridge Armory, one of the largest armories in the world, was built at Kingsbridge Road and Jerome Avenue. The residential area south of the reservoir and west of the armory consists mostly of five- and six-story apartment buildings constructed in the 1920s for Irish and Jewish families attracted by the Lexington Avenue line of Interborough Rapid Transit. In later years the neighborhood became increasingly Latin American. The buildings along Kingsbridge Road have shops and restaurants at street level.

Lloyd Ultan

Jerome Park Racetrack. Thoroughbred racetrack opened on 25 September 1866 by Leonard Jerome and the American Jockey Club on the Bathgate estate in Fordham in what is now the Bronx. It was a fashionable, elite course, and its opening marked the revival of thoroughbred racing in the metropolitan area. The track occupied 230 acres (93 hectares) and had outstanding facilities, including a clubhouse comparable to luxury hotels. Innovations included handicapping, claiming races, races for two-year-olds, and parimutuel betting. The track also popularized sprint races and staged annual stakes events, beginning with the Belmont Stakes in 1867, which was run there until 1890. The track closed in 1889 to make way for the Jerome Park Reservoir, temporarily reopening in 1891 for the races of the Monmouth Park (New Jersey) Racing Association.

Steven A. Riess

Jesup, Morris K(etchum) (*b* Westport, Conn., 21 June 1830; *d* New York City, 22 Jan 1908). Philanthropist. He moved to New York City about 1838 and became a banker as a young man; after retiring in 1884 he devoted himself to dozens of religious and cultural institutions in the city. Jesup was the president of many organizations, including the Young Men's Christian Association (1872–75), the Five Points House of Industry (1873–1908), the New York City Mission and Tract Society (1881–1903), the American Museum of Natural History (1881–1908), and the New York State Chamber of Commerce (1899–1907). He lived at 197 Madison Avenue with his wife, Maria DeWitt Jesup, who was also active in charity and reform work.

William Adams Brown, *Morris Ketchum Jesup: A Character Sketch* (New York: Charles Scribner's Sons, 1910)

Alana Erickson Coble

jewelry. During the eighteenth century a few jewelers in New York City worked in small workshops and foundries, and by 1795 a small jewelry district had taken shape at Maiden Lane. A number of retail jewelers worked on lower Broadway in the first half of the nineteenth century, including Marquand and Paulding (now Black, Starr and Frost), Tiffany and Company, and later Starr and Marcus. Larger pieces of jewelry set with gemstones became popular after the Civil War, as the nation prospered and manufacturing techniques improved and with the discovery of gold and silver in the West and diamonds in South Africa. Between 1860 and 1890 the value of jewelry production increased from $2.5 million to $5.6 million. The new fashions largely reflected European tastes. By the turn of the twentieth century platinum was widely used, and jewelry in the Edwardian style was in great demand. The firms of E. M. Gattle, Theodore A. Kohn, Charlton, Dreicer, and Udall and Ballou flourished, and the French firm of Cartier opened a branch in New York City in 1909. Dreicer introduced new ways of cutting diamonds, and Raymond C. Yard, who had worked at Marcus and Company, the foremost American art nouveau jeweler, founded his own firm, which specialized in finely crafted jewelry with precious stones.

Electricity and new machinery enabled emerging manufacturing jewelers to keep up with the demand for fashionable platinum and diamond jewelry. Prominent manufacturing jewelers included Jacob Mehrlust; Walter P. McTeigue; the firm of Oscar Heyman Brothers, which produced jewelry for leading retailers; Julius Wodiska, an innovator in platinum jewelry; and William Scheer, a supplier of more than half the fine jewelry in the United States. The geometric configurations of Parisian art deco were highly influential in the 1920s, and in the 1930s gold jewelry set with large, colored gemstones was popularized by Paul Flato and his designer Fulco di Verdura, who formed his own company in 1939. The same year marked the opening of a branch of Van Cleef and Arpels in New York City and of the World's Fair, where Tiffany; Black, Starr and Frost–Gorham; Udall and Ballou; Marcus; and Cartier contributed displays at the House of Jewels. Exuberant, figural jewelry with colored gemstones was made in the 1940s by the independent jewelers David Webb, Seaman

Schepps, and John Rubel; the latter made jewelry for Van Cleef and Arpels before opening his own business. Harry Winston specialized in large gemstones and exhibited such well-known items as the Jonker and Hope diamonds. In the 1950s marketing became the key for the survival of the retail jeweler. Branches opened throughout the country and abroad, appealing to a wide clientele, and houses such as Black, Starr and Frost were acquired by large conglomerates. In the early twenty-first century Harry Winston's company was still hailed by celebrities and jewelry collectors, residing in prime retail space on Fifth Avenue along with other luxury jewelers like Tiffany and Cartier. A huge percentage of diamonds for U.S. consumers passed through the famed diamond district on 47th Street between Fifth and Sixth avenues before reaching retail stores across the country. Jewelers and jewelry repair companies competed side by side in a bazaar-like atmosphere of bartering and haggling for precious stones and settings made of gold, silver, and platinum.

Penny Proddow and Debra Healy, *American Jewelry: Glamour and Tradition* (New York: Rizzoli, 1987); Dorothy T. Rainwater: *American Jewelry Manufacturers* (West Chester, Pa.: Schiffer, 1988)

Janet Zapata

Jewett murder. Notorious crime committed in New York City on 10 April 1836. The victim was Helen Jewett (*b* Augusta, Maine, June 1813), a witty and literate woman who read poetry and literary magazines and who had worked for about a year as a prostitute in Manhattan. She was murdered late at night with an axe in a brothel at 41 Thomas Street. Circumstantial evidence showed that Jewett's companion, Richard P. Robinson, a 19-year-old shop clerk, was the murderer. Great public interest surrounded the sensational trial. Some observers were outraged by the openness and extent of prostitution in the city; others found Robinson an appealing character. The state presented a weak case, and Robinson was acquitted. Most historians believe he was guilty.

Marilynn Wood Hill, *Their Sisters' Keepers: Prostitution in New York City, 1830–1870* (Berkeley: University of California Press, 1993); Patricia Cohen Cline, *The Murder of Helen Jewett: The Life and Death of a Prostitute in Nineteenth Century New York* (New York: Knopf, 1999)

George A. Thompson, Jr.

Jewish Board of Guardians [Jewish Board of Family and Children's Services]. Volunteer agency formed on 23 April 1921 by the merger of the Jewish Prisoners Aid Society (1893), the Jewish Protectory and Aid (1902), Jewish Big Brothers (1907), and Jewish Big Sisters (1913) to combat juvenile delinquency. Some of its first facilities were the Lakeview Home for unwed mothers, donated by Mrs. Joseph Proskauer, and the Hawthorne–Cedar Knolls reform school, built by Jacob Schiff. During the 1920s the agency shifted its focus to educational improvement, and under Mortimer Schiff it built a summer camp. Camp therapy was introduced during the 1930s, and the Madeline Borg centers opened based on the "quick response" approach to crisis intervention. In 1978 the Jewish Board of Guardians merged with the Jewish Family Services, and they became the Jewish Board of Family and Children's Services. Under the direction of Doris Rosenberg in 2007 the organization had 600 volunteers working in 80 programs that accommodated more than 45,000 people a year. Its offices are at 120 West 57th Street.

George J. Lankevich

Jewish Child Care Association. Successor to the Hebrew Benevolent Association (1822), formed in 1942 by the merger of 19 organizations dedicated to children's welfare, including an orphanage (1860) and the Hebrew Sheltering Guardian Society (1879). Under the direction of Mary Boretz from 1918 to 1945, it introduced foster home care and help for neglected children. In the 1990s it offered services to help Soviet Jews adjust to life in New York City. In the early twenty-first century the Jewish Child Care Association serves 12,000 people, offering day care, a kinship foster home program, and adoption placement. It runs outpatient mental health clinics and the Pleasantville Cottage School, a suburban residential treatment center for children. Its headquarters are at 120 Wall Street.

George J. Lankevich

Jewish Defense League. Organization formed in 1968 by a small group of Orthodox Jews led by Meir Kahane of Brooklyn. During its first two years it taught self-defense and organized street patrols and neighborhood watches. The league became an advocate for Soviet Jews and by 1972 called for the large-scale immigration of Soviet Jews to Israel. It also took a militant stance on Israeli defense and toward Palestinian refugees. In the early 1970s it was connected to several terrorist attacks, mainly in New York City and Washington, D.C., against Soviet interests in the United States. In 1975 Kahane was convicted of planning to kidnap a Soviet diplomat and bomb the Iraqi embassy, for which he served a year in prison. The Federal Bureau of Investigation linked the group to the 1985 bombing that killed the regional director of the American–Arab Anti-Discrimination Committee, Alex Odeh. On 5 November 1990 Kahane was assassinated in Manhattan by an Egyptian-born U.S. militant who was later found to be complicit in the 1993 bombing of the World Trade Center. In 1994 Baruch Goldstein, a charter member of the league, murdered 29 Palestinians praying in a mosque in Hebron. In 2004 the group split in two over the appointment of Bill Maniaci as chairman.

Janet L. Dolgin, *Jewish Identity and the Jewish Defense League* (Princeton, N.J.: Princeton University Press, 1977)

Michael N. Dobkowski

Jewish Guild for the Blind. Charitable organization formed in 1914 as the New York Guild for the Jewish Blind to provide care and support for the Jewish blind in their homes. The organization opened a home for poor Jewish children in 1919 in suburban Yonkers, New York, and later added residential services there for adults. In 1923 it moved to its own building in Manhattan at 172 East 96th Street; by this time it offered programs in sports, music, and handicrafts. The guild moved in 1944 to larger quarters at 1880 Broadway. After World War II it added programs for the multiply disabled. The Guild School for children and teenagers with visual, developmental, psychiatric, and orthopedic disabilities opened in 1951. After the guild began offering services to people of all faiths, it adopted its current name in 1960 and in the following year opened the first psychiatric clinic in the country specializing in problems associated with blindness. Since 1971 and into the twenty-first century its headquarters are at 15 West 65th Street.

Sandra Opdycke

Jewish Institute of Religion. Rabbinical and cantorial school founded in 1922 next to the Free Synagogue at 30 West 68th Street by Stephen S. Wise to train Reform rabbis and promote research and community service. It emphasized free inquiry, social reform, and Zionism and under Wise's direction launched the *Jewish Institute Quarterly* (1924–30) to report on social issues. Financial difficulties led Wise to negotiate a merger in 1950 with Hebrew Union College in Cincinnati, forming Hebrew Union College–Jewish Institute of Religion.

George J. Lankevich

Jewish Labor Committee. Group formed on 25 February 1934 in New York City to represent Jewish workers with ties to the AFL–CIO. Initially it focused on rescue efforts and resistance to the Nazis in Europe; in the 1940s it joined with B'nai B'rith, the American Jewish Committee, and the American Jewish Congress to become an important Jewish defense organization. After the 1950s it became active in a wide range of concerns, including civil and human rights, social justice, efforts to help Soviet Jews, labor politics in Israel, and cultural activities. During the 1950s and 1960s it advocated for civil rights for minorities in the United States and equal rights for Jews living in the Soviet Union. The Jewish Labor Committee is known for its liberal, secular views; in the twenty-first century its headquarters are at 25 East 21st Street.

Michael N. Dobkowski

Jewish Museum. Museum at 1109 Fifth Avenue in Manhattan, formed in 1904 by a gift of books and ceremonial objects to the Jewish Theological Seminary by Judge Meyer Sulzberger. On 8 May 1947 it moved to its current site, formerly the mansion of Felix M. Warburg. The museum expanded to an adjacent building in 1963 and renovated its entire facilities in 1993. The Jewish Museum is the largest and most comprehensive institution of its kind in the world. Its permanent collection includes more than 26,000 paintings, sculptures, drawings, photographs, artifacts, ceremonial objects, and other items documenting 4000 years of Jewish life and culture.

Jewish Theological Seminary. Seminary opened by Sabbato Morais (1823–1897) in 1887 on West 19th Street to train Conservative rabbis and preserve traditional Judaism in the United States. It foundered when only eight students enrolled (one of whom became the chief rabbi of the British Empire), and after a reorganization it moved in 1902 to quarters at 531 West 123rd Street donated by Jacob Schiff. Its new president was Solomon Schechter, a leading scholar and rabbi from Europe who engaged Mordecai Kaplan to set up a teachers' institute (1909), promoted Zionism, and established the United Synagogue of America (1913). The seminary attracted some of the best faculty in the world, established a rigorous curriculum, and inspired its students to see Judaism as an "evolving religious civilization" with important ties to the United States. During Cyrus Adler's tenure as president (1915–40) the library was expanded, and a museum of ceremonial objects opened in 1929 (later moved to the Jewish Museum). In 1930 the seminary moved to a building at 3080 Broadway designed by the firm of Gehron, Ross, Ashley. Under Louis Finkelstein (1940–72) it became known internationally, introduced interfaith study, and opened an institute for training cantors (1952) and a graduate division (1969). The library, which contained 70,000 volumes, was destroyed in a fire in 1966; a new one was dedicated in 1983. As chancellor (1972–86) Gerson Cohen admitted women as candidates for ordination and strengthened ties to Israel. In the early part of the twenty-first century, no longer operating solely to train future rabbis, the Jewish Theological Seminary was made up of five schools: the Albert A. List College of Jewish Studies, the Graduate School, William Davidson Graduate School of Jewish Education, the Rabbinical School, and the H. L. Miller Cantorial School and College of Jewish Music. A national center of Conservative Judaism, Jewish Theological Seminary had approximately 100 faculty members and 700 students. The seminary had an arrangement with Columbia University that allowed students from either institution to cross-register with the other.

Elliot N. Dorff, *A Living Tree: The Roots and Growth of Jewish Law* (Albany: State University of New York Press, 1988)

George J. Lankevich

Jews. In September 1654, 23 Jewish refugees from Brazil, who had been loyal to the Dutch authorities there, sought asylum in New Amsterdam. Upon arrival, they met up with several co-religionists from Holland who were considering the possibility of a permanent settlement in the young city. Governor Peter Stuyvesant tried to deny the newcomers the right to settle, arguing that they were theological opponents of Christianity and deceitful usurers, and possibly would become a public charge upon the fledgling community. The Dutch West India Company, however, ignored his protest and decided that Jews could live there as long as they did not constitute a financial burden on the developing society. But the group did not last long, and over the next decade or so, all but two of the original Jewish settlers left New Amsterdam after facing difficulties in establishing themselves economically.

Permanent signs of Jewish communal life began to appear in the 1670s and 1680s. By 1693 a map of the city indicated the presence of a "Jews' Synagogue," although it is likely that services were held in private quarters at that time. In 1654 the first congregation, Shearith Israel, today known as the Spanish–Portuguese Synagogue, rented in lower Manhattan; it built its first synagogue at Mill Street in 1730. In 1776 the city had the second largest Jewish community in the colonies (the largest being in Charleston, South Carolina). Most Jews in New York City were patriots, and many served in the Continental army during the American Revolution. In 1789, when Gershom Mendes Seixas of Shearith Israel took part in President George Washington's inauguration with a dozen Christian religious leaders, Jews accounted for less than 1 percent of the national population. During the eighteenth and nineteenth centuries most Jews moving to the United States were Ashkenazim, and their first New York City congregation, Congregation B'nai Jeshurun, was formed by Ashkenazi immigrants in 1825. About this time Mordecai Manuel Noah was appointed high sheriff of New York City; he became well known as a proponent of a plan called *Ararat* to resettle oppressed Jews from overseas in northern New York State. The fraternal organization B'nai B'rith was formed in 1843 on Essex Street on the Lower East Side.

In 1850 nearly one-third of the 50,000 Jews in the United States lived in New York City. Most had fled deprivation and persecution in central Europe; many were peddlers, storekeepers, craftspeople, and laborers, and some eventually became wealthy manufacturers and financiers. There were 15 synagogues of different groups at that time, reflecting varying styles of worship imported from European locales; by 1859 there were 27 synagogues, as well as 40 fraternal organizations for education and mutual aid. The Jews' Hospital opened in 1852 (renamed Mount Sinai Hospital in 1866). Several Jewish newspapers were printed in the city, including the *Asmonean* (1849–58), the *Jewish Messenger* (1857–1902), and the *Hebrew Leader* (1859–74). Distributed throughout the country, these publications provided a forum for protesting the mistreatment overseas of Jews. Several Jewish figures in the city gained national reputations through the newspapers; among the most notable were Jacques Judah Lyons, Isaac Bondy, Samuel Isaacs, Morris Raphall, Samuel Adler, Sampson Simson, and Henry Hendricks.

As proponents of acculturation, central European Jewish immigrants and their children adapted their religious practices to blend with American life. Reform Judaism predominated, although there were also some traditional synagogues. Temple Emanu-El, Temple Rodef Sholom, Temple Anshe Chesed, Shearith Israel, and B'nai Jeshurun were among the most important synagogues uptown. During the late nineteenth century a wealthy Jewish elite took shape; among its members were Jacob Schiff, Isidor Straus, Nathan Straus, Oscar Straus, Adolph Lewisohn, Louis Marshall, Felix Warburg, and Joseph Seligman. Oscar Straus and Seligman entered American political life, Seligman as a confidant of President Ulysses S. Grant and Straus as the first Jewish cabinet member in the Theodore Roosevelt administration.

Between 1880 and 1915 about 1.4 million Jews fleeing intermittent pogroms and constant economic discrimination in eastern Europe made the city their home. By 1915 Jews accounted for more than a quarter of the city's population. Between 1880 and 1890 three of four Jewish immigrants to the city settled on the Lower East Side where most lived in overcrowded walk-up tenements of five stories. Initially many immigrants were peddlers or found work in the garment and tobacco industries or in construction. By 1890 Jews from eastern Europe were the largest group, and eastern European Orthodoxy predominated. Many eastern European Jews

Russ and Daughters Appetizers, 2009

worshipped in *landsmanshaft* synagogues, transitory congregations established by immigrants from the same town seeking to preserve their local traditions. As late as 1917 most Jews in the city worshipped in about 800 small synagogues formed by immigrants. Eventually a number of these congregations prospered and adapted to American life. A few of the best-known synagogues on the Lower East Side were Beth Hamidrash Hagadol (Norfolk Street), Kehal Adath Jeshurun (Eldridge Street), Ohab Zedek Congregation (Norfolk Street), and the First Roumanian–American Congregation (Rivington Street). During the first quarter of the twentieth century about 37,000 Sephardim moved to the city. Most were from Turkey and the Balkan countries and spoke Judeo-Spanish; some were from Greece, and others spoke Judeo-Arabic and were mostly from Syria. They settled in their own enclaves on the Lower East Side where they formed support groups along with religious institutions patterned on those in their native cities; they also sponsored Judeo-Spanish theater and newspapers, among them *La America* and *La Vara.*

Rabbis from eastern Europe were dismayed at their lack of control over many aspects of religious life and at the difficulty of preserving Orthodoxy. Disaffection was particularly marked among the children of immigrants. Many Jews wished to maintain a kosher diet, but there was no authority for inspecting kosher foods. To address these problems the Association of the American Orthodox Hebrew Congregations was formed in 1887 and undertook a search for a rabbi to lead the older generation back to the Torah, inspire the younger generation to maintain the faith, and introduce order into the kosher food industry, which was often corrupt. During the same year Rabbi Jacob Joseph of Vilna (Lithuania) accepted the post, which he retained until his death in July 1902. His efforts ultimately failed because he lacked ecclesiastical authority to enforce his edicts. Within a week of his death the Union of Orthodox Rabbis of the United States and Canada was formed in the city to continue his efforts nationally. In 1898 a group of more acculturated Orthodox Jews founded the Union of Orthodox Jewish Congregations of America to address the problems of religious disaffection by integrating Jewish traditions into modern life. At their Modern Talmud Torahs, or communal afternoon schools, they used the pedagogic methods of John Dewey to present traditional teachings with social sensitivity to this country's mores. They also organized synagogues for families who spoke both Yiddish and English and had modern and traditional concerns. The Jewish Endeavor Society during the first decade of the century and Young Israel after 1910 organized such congregations. Mordecai Kaplan, a young rabbi, worked with both organizations and later led the Reconstructionist movement. These experiments in integrating Judaism into American life soon became models for Conservative, modern Orthodox, and Reform synagogues throughout the country. These Americanized Orthodox groups also cooperated closely with the Jewish Theological Seminary. Jacob Schiff and Louis Marshall offered financial support to traditional groups if they agreed to promote Judaism in the most American manner. These alliances eventually led to the formation in 1909 of the Kehillah (Jewish Community of New York) in response to allegations by Thomas Bingham, the New York City police commissioner, of widespread crime among Jewish immigrants. The group included acculturated immigrants and the German Jewish elite and ultimately addressed not only criminality but anti-Semitism, philanthropy, Jewish education, and employment. It also tried to supervise more closely the production of kosher foods.

The influx of poor Jews in the city caused social tension. Many reports studied health, housing, education, employment, crime, and mortality in Jewish neighborhoods and concluded that overcrowding had to be eliminated. To this end recommendations were made to build the Brooklyn, Manhattan, and Williamsburg bridges; to set aside land for public parks; and to provide better housing. The work of such social reformers as Hutchins Hapgood, Norman Hapgood, Lincoln Steffens, and Jacob A. Riis helped to ensure that the recommendations were carried out even though Riis and other reformers doubted whether Jews were committed to assimilation. Others considered Jewish immigrants a threat to American culture and unrestricted immigration. Partly because they feared for their own position in the city, German Jews in 1901 formed the Industrial Removal Office, which resettled more than 100,000 Jews in other parts of the United States during the next decade and a half. For those remaining in the city they developed a network of social welfare organizations to encourage assimilation: the United Hebrew Charities was their advocate on Ellis Island; the Hebrew Technical Institute, the Young Women's Hebrew Association, and settlement houses like the Educational Alliance urged them to learn English and be productive workers. Many Jewish neighborhoods had a strong socialist culture rooted in traditions of European radicalism that were exacerbated by the immigrants' anger at their exploitation in the United States. The best-known socialist newspaper, the Yiddish-language *Vorwert,* founded in 1897 was instrumental in spreading socialism even as its editor, Abraham Cahan, worked to assimilate immigrants. By World War I it boasted a daily circulation in excess of 100,000. Three other mass-circulation Yiddish dailies, the *Yiddishes Tageblatt* (1885), the *Morgen Zhurnal* (1902), and the *Tag* (1914), represented other viewpoints. The Arbeiter Ring, a socialist fraternal organization formed in 1892, was vital to the development of radicalism.

By the turn of the century German Jews were well established in politics. As a Russian–Polish enclave took shape on the Lower East Side, Jews, known for being independent, became a recognized force in politics. In presidential elections between 1888 and 1912 no party won the eighth assembly district in downtown Manhattan twice in a row. By the turn of the century Jewish votes were sought by Republicans supporting Theodore Roosevelt and by Democrats in Tammany Hall, who had often opposed Jews' efforts to gain access to political power and the city's payroll. In 1900 Henry Goldfogle, a resident of the Lower East Side chosen by Tammany Hall, became the first Jewish congressman to represent the area. Socialism flourished as Jewish labor unions became powerful, especially after 1900, when the International Ladies' Garment Workers' Union, the Amalgamated Clothing Workers, and the United Hebrew Trades developed a large membership. After 1905, following a failed Russian revolution, there was an influx of young immigrants more ideologically committed to socialism. Many of them were aligned with the Bund (the Jewish Labor Alliance of Poland and Lithuania). Efforts at organizing unions at about this time were marked by violence and divisive strikes, but in 1910 Jewish unionists and their bosses set a precedent for collective bargaining in the United States when with the aid of Schiff, Marshall, and Louis D. Brandeis they fashioned the "Protocol of Peace" that ended a massive strike by cloakmakers. In 1904 Moritz Graubard was elected to the state assembly on the Republican ticket; in 1906 Samuel Koenig, a Hungarian Jew, was elected secretary of state of New York as a Republican. Despite popular support for their causes, few radicals were elected to government, largely because of divisions between the American Socialist and Socialist Labor parties. The American Socialist Party also lost the votes of Jewish immigrants because of its stance against unrestricted immigration. It was not until 1914 that Meyer London, who repudiated his party's platform on immigration, capitalized on temporary disaffection with Tammany Hall to become the first socialist congressman from the Lower East Side. Many immigrants lost sympathy for radicalism during the seven years that they were required to maintain residency before qualifying to vote.

Even before World War I Jews began leaving the Lower East Side for Yorkville, central Harlem, Williamsburg, and Brownsville. Poorer Jews moved to cramped quarters in East Harlem. By the time of World War I more than 100,000 Jews lived in each of the new neighborhoods, and 325,000 lived on the Lower East Side, where some blocks had a density of 1000 people per acre (2500 people per hectare). After the Bolshevik Revolution and the formation of the American Communist Party the city became a national center of radical politics. Jews accounted for nearly 30 percent of the city's total population in 1920, the highest percentage until that time and for decades after. By the 1920s the focus of Jewish life in the city had shifted from the Lower East Side to upper Manhattan, Brooklyn, the Bronx, and Queens; these neighborhoods ranged from upper middle class to working class and until the 1950s included the Grand Concourse, Fordham, Tremont, Morrisania, Jamaica, Astoria, Jackson Heights, and the Rockaways. Although the Kehillah was dismantled in 1922, its founding principle of blending Judaism into American life continued to influence Jewish educators and community workers, and the Bureau of Jewish Education and the New York Federation of Jewish Philanthropies (both formed under its auspices) remained in operation. Prosperous Sephardim often moved to Harlem, the Grand Concourse, and New Lots, and eventually Sephardic neighborhoods were established in Bensonhurst, Flatbush, and Forest Hills. Washington Heights began attracting German Jewish refugees in the years preceding World War II.

Although the children of Jewish immigrants suffered during the Depression, their economic distress was mitigated by their having risen in the prior decade out of blue-collar jobs into more stable white-collar and skilled occupational pursuits. Jewish working-class neighborhoods, however, were sites of both spontaneous and organized rent strikes when poor people were evicted from their homes. This era of social strife and dislocation also witnessed the growth of a community of intellectuals that included scholars such as Irving Howe and Alfred Kazin, who opted for radicalism. With ideas that germinated while they were students at City College of New York, they and other students joined the Socialist and Communist parties. But most Jews put their political faith in the Democratic or Republican parties, displaying a particular affection for Franklin D. Roosevelt as New York governor and later as president. They backed the New Deal policies and locally supported the popular Mayor Fiorello H. La Guardia.

After World War II a large segment of the native-born population moved to the burgeoning suburbs of Greater New York. Their exodus, however, did not decrease the Jewish population of the city. As of 1957 approximately two million Jews lived in the five boroughs, meaning that one of four New Yorkers was Jewish. They worked as teachers, social workers, small businesspeople, and professionals. They were joined by new Jewish immigrants to the city, many of whom were survivors of the Holocaust. Although these newcomers possessed a variety of religious values, including some who had lost all connection with religious life, a significant number were deeply committed Orthodox Jews. Hasidic refugees in particular made up a major new segment of Brooklyn enclaves in Williamsburg and Boro Park.

Beginning in the 1960s Sephardim moved to the city from North Africa and the Middle East, especially Morocco and Egypt. The 1960s and 1970s saw the continued transformation of Jewish neighborhoods, with the population of established neighborhoods in the Bronx and Brooklyn decreasing. Liberal politics became more divided as blacks and Latinos conflicted with Jews over the distribution of political power. One of the bitterest conflicts was a public school strike in 1968 that pitted the United Federation of Teachers, which was heavily Jewish, against black advocates of community control of schools. The

Kramer's Kosher Poultry Market

strike ended in a limited victory for the advocates of community control, and along with debates over affirmative action and support for Israel, it influenced many Jews away from cooperation with an increasingly militant black leadership. For a period during the late 1960s and early 1970s, Jews practiced their own brand of extreme militancy. Under Rabbi Meir Kahane, the Jewish Defense League often used violent methods both to defend co-religionists in confrontations with other American racial groups and to protest Soviet treatment of Jews. More temperate Jewish voices, such as those of the Student Struggle for Soviet Jewry and the New York Council on Soviet Jewry, articulated revulsion against anti-Semitism in the Soviet Union.

During the 1970s and 1980s the city's Jewish population declined, with 1.1 million living in the city in 1981. Increases in wealth among Jews, an upsurge in citywide crime, and urban turmoil accelerated the move to suburbia and the Sun Belt. By 1991 the Jewish population was still estimated at just over one million, but by 2002, for the first time in close to a century, the Jewish population of the five boroughs dipped below one million. Surveys indicated that 972,000 Jews still lived in New York City, a 5 percent decrease since 1991. These numbers would have declined further if not for the continuing immigration of Jews from the former Soviet Union, most of whom settled initially in Brooklyn's Brighton Beach. Many Jews leaving New York City moved to Westchester, Nassau, and Suffolk counties.

A Jewish community study of 2002 estimated that 456,000 Jews lived in Brooklyn, most in the neighborhoods of Borough Park, Bensonhurst, Flatbush, Sheepshead Bay, Canarsie, and Midwood (which included a large concentration of Syrian Jews). New Jewish enclaves were growing in Park Slope and Brooklyn Heights. Most of the 186,000 Jews in Queens lived in Forest Hills, Kew Gardens, Flushing, Kew Garden Hills, and Hillcrest. About a quarter million Jews lived in Manhattan, nearly half on the Upper West Side and Upper East Side; there were between 25,000 and 30,000 on the Lower East Side and a large number in Washington Heights. Of the 45,000 Jews in the Bronx, most lived in the growing neighborhoods of Riverdale, Van Cortlandt, and Kingsbridge; many Jews also lived in Co-op City and the neighborhoods along Pelham Parkway. About 42,000 Jews lived in Staten Island, many in large enclaves near Richmond Avenue and Victory Boulevard.

Most Jews in New York City are solidly middle class and well-educated; however, there continue to be significant numbers of economically disadvantaged Jews in the city. In 2002 it was estimated that one in five Jewish households lived below generally accepted levels of poverty. Although many New York Jews do not maintain a strong connection to Jewish religious life, the city has more facilities for observant Jewish living—such as synagogues, schools, ritual baths, and kosher food stores—than any other place outside Israel. Most Jews are committed to the survival of Israel and are dedicated to helping endangered Jews around the world: a 2002 study showed that 92 percent of those Jews surveyed were deeply concerned about the fate of the Jewish state, and 86 percent said that it was important to help fellow Jews who were oppressed. Helping to raise Jewish consciousness are the many national and international organizations with their headquarters in New York City, including the American Jewish Committee, the American Jewish Congress, the World Jewish Congress, and the Anti-Defamation League of B'nai B'rith; the several Zionist organizations include the United Jewish Appeal, Israel Bonds, Hadassah, and the Jewish National Fund. The city also has several facilities for training modern American rabbis: a branch of the Hebrew Union College–Jewish Institute of Religion (Reform) in Greenwich Village, the Jewish Theological Seminary (Conservative) and the new Yeshiva Chovevei Torah (Orthodox, established in 2000) in Morningside Heights, and the Rabbi Isaac Elchanan Theological Seminary of Yeshiva University (Orthodox) in Washington Heights. Hasidic yeshivas and others espousing more insular forms of Orthodoxy are found mostly in Jewish sections of Brooklyn and Queens. The Center for Jewish History in Greenwich Village—a partnership between the American Jewish Historical Society, the YIVO Institute for Jewish Research, the Leo Baeck Institute, the Yeshiva University Museum, and the American Sephardi Federation—opened in 2000 and provides a study center, exhibition space, and document depository. Other institutions with comparable missions are the longstanding Jewish Museum on the Upper East Side and the Museum of Jewish Heritage, a "living memorial to the Holocaust," which opened in 1997 in Battery Park City.

Hyman B. Grinstein, *The Rise of the Jewish Community of New York, 1654–1860* (Philadelphia: Jewish Publication Society of America, 1945); Moses Rischin, *The Promised City: New York's Jews, 1870–1914* (Cambridge, Mass.: Harvard University Press, 1962); Irving Howe, *World of Our Fathers* (New York: Harcourt Brace Jovanovich, 1975); Deborah Dash Moore, *At Home in America: Second Generation New York Jews* (New York: Columbia University Press, 1981); Marc D. Angel, *La America: The Sephardic Experience in the United States* (Philadelphia: Jewish Publication Society, 1982)

Marc D. Angel, Jeffrey S. Gurock

JFK International Airport. Airport in southeastern Queens on the shores of Jamaica Bay. Planned during the administration of Mayor Fiorello H. La Guardia, the project was transferred to the Port of New York Authority in 1948, over the objections of Robert Moses (who favored placing it under his newly created New York Airport Authority). Opened 1 July 1948 as New York International Airport (informally, Idlewild Airport), it was 15 miles (24 kilometers) from mid-Manhattan and unusually large for the time (1100 acres [445 hectares], later expanded to 4930 acres [1995 hectares]). Its configuration was unique: because the airlines had demanded that runways be laid out in every possible direction to allow for shifting winds, the center of the airport was occupied by terminals and parking lots. These alone covered more area than the entire expanse of La Guardia Airport, until then the city's principal airfield. Idlewild was the point of origin for the first jet service provided by a U.S. carrier, when a Boeing 707 of Pan American Airways flew to London on 26 October 1958. It was also the first airport at which airlines were encouraged to build their own terminals; some that resulted were of real architectural distinction, including those of Pan American Airways, Northwest Airlines, United Airlines, and Eero Saarinen's terminal for Trans World Airlines. The airport took its current name in 1963. Later it saw the first service by "jumbo" jet (again by Pan American) and reluctantly accommodated the supersonic airplane, the Concorde. During the 1970s JFK became the busiest cargo airport in the world, with a cargo center of 344 acres (139 hectares) serving 57 all-cargo airlines; by 2006 the cargo area had expanded to 1700 acres (688 hectares). Measured by numbers of travelers, JFK was the busiest airport in the New York City region through most of the 1990s; in 2006 airlines at JFK carried more than 42 million passengers.

George Scullin, *International Airport: The Story of Kennedy Airport and U.S. Commercial Aviation* (Boston: Little, Brown, 1968); James Kaplan, *The Airport* (New York: William Morrow, 1994); Jameson W. Doig, *Empire on the Hudson* (New York: Columbia University Press, 2001), chs. 11 and 12

Paul Barrett, Jameson W. Doig

J. Levine Company. Bookstore at 5 West 30th Street in Manhattan, between Fifth Avenue and Broadway. It was opened by the family of a *Sofer,* or holy scribe, who moved to the Lower East Side from Lithuania in 1905. Once the largest manufacturer of Torah covers and ark curtains in the United States (which it began manufacturing in 1920), by the early twenty-first century the company had remained in the family for four generations and expanded its business to a variety of Judaica, including through its Web site, which offers for sale art, books, gifts, and videos, among other things.

Kenneth T. Jackson

J. M. Kaplan Fund. Charitable organization formed in 1945 by Jacob M. Kaplan (1891–1987), founder of the Welch Grape Juice Company and its owner from 1940 to 1958. Kaplan led the fund until 1977, when he was succeeded by his daughter, Joan K. Davidson. The fund donates exclusively to projects in New York State. In New York City it has been active in the arts, landmark preservation, social welfare, parks beautification, and civil liberties. It took part in the successful effort to save Carnegie Hall in 1960 and in the development of South Street Seaport, and has supported the New School for Social Research, Westbeth Artists' Housing, Mobilization for Youth (on the Lower East Side), the Association for Union Democracy, the Green Guerillas, and the Coalition for the Homeless. It has also supported greenmarkets in the city, the revitalization of 42nd Street, various clothing drives, and museum exhibitions. In the early twenty-first century the organization also focused on supporting neighborhood parks and libraries as well as on historic preservation in lower Manhattan.

Kenneth W. Rose

Joffrey, Robert [Anver Bey Abdullah Jaffa Kahn; Anver Joffrey] (*b* Seattle, 24 Dec 1928; *d* New York City, 25 March 1988). Dancer and choreographer. He trained with Mary Ann Wells before moving in 1949 to New York City, where he studied ballet and modern dance and taught at the High School of the Performing Arts (1950–55). In 1952 he began providing choreography for ballets, galas, industrial shows, musicals, and operas (for the National Broadcasting Company and the New York City Opera), and in the following year he formed the American Ballet Center (now the Joffrey Ballet School). His first company, the Robert Joffrey Theatre Ballet, which began touring on 2 October 1956 with six dancers, grew slowly until it obtained support in 1962 from Rebekah Harkness for expansion, workshops, and international tours. In 1964 Harkness took over the company contracts to organize the Harkness Ballet. With Gerald Arpino (1923–2008) Joffrey formed the Robert Joffrey Ballet in 1965; in the following years he increasingly devoted himself to administration while Arpino took over much of the choreography, which became characterized by athleticism and eroticism. The company stressed ballets intended to appeal to youth, including Joffrey's *Astarte* (1967), which was backed by a rock score and used innovative film technology; Arpino's sleek, ritualistic work *Trinity* (1971); and Twyla Tharp's first ballet, *Deuce Coupe* (1973). It also offered revivals of modern classics by Kurt Jooss (*The Green Table*), George Balanchine, Léonide Massine (*Parade*), Frederick Ashton, Bronislava Nijinska, and Vaslav Nijinsky, notably *Le Sacre du printemps* (1987). Although financial problems limited new productions and the size of the company, Joffrey encouraged experimental choreographers like Tharp, Oscar Araiz, and Laura Dean. The company was in residence at the City Center from 1966 to 1982. A small training company called Joffrey II was formed in 1970, and an affiliate was set up in Los Angeles in 1983.

George Dorris

John Finley Walk. Promenade along the western bank of the East River between 63rd Street and 125th Street in Manhattan, including an elevated section at Carl Schurz Park. At the suggestion of Stanley M. Isaacs, borough president of Manhattan, it was named in 1940 for John H. Finley, an editor of the *New York Times*, president of City College, and education commissioner of New York State who reportedly had often walked the perimeter of Manhattan.

Owen D. Gutfreund

John F. Kennedy International Airport. See JFK International Airport.

John Jay College of Criminal Justice. College of the City University of New York. Its forerunner was a police science program leading to an associate degree, begun in 1955 under the auspices of the Police Academy and the City College School of Business. The program was broadened soon after to offer courses of study leading to bachelor's and master's degrees and in 1965 was taken over by the College of Police Science, then newly formed. John Jay College opened in 1967 in rented space at 315 Park Avenue South and moved in 1973 to 59th Street between Ninth and 10th avenues. The college offers undergraduate programs leading to bachelor of arts and bachelor of science degrees in fields related to criminal justice and fire science, as well as five similar programs leading to an associate degree. Graduate programs on the master's and doctoral levels are also available. As of 2010 the school enrolled 14,000 students, taught by a faculty of around 1000 men and women. Although the college at its inception attracted many members of the police and fire departments seeking advancement, in later years most of its students were recent graduates of high schools in New York City.

Selma Berrol

John Reed Club. Social club formed in New York City in 1929 by artists and writers close to the Communist Party and named after the journalist and revolutionist John Reed. Its members included the cartoonist William Gropper (1897–1977). The club was inspired by the Prolecult movement in the Soviet Union and soon launched chapters in 10 other cities. The artists in the club organized exhibitions and opened an art school in New York City in which the instructors included Louis Lozowick (1892–1973) and Raphael Soyer. By 1936 the club had disbanded in accordance with efforts by the Communist Party to encourage more nonsectarian and broad-based groups such as the American Artists' Congress.

Patricia Hills, *Social Concern and Urban Realism: American Painting of the 1930s* (Boston: Boston University Art Gallery, 1983)

Patricia Hills

John Jay College of Criminal Justice, 2009

Johns, Jasper (*b* Augusta, Ga., 15 May 1930). Artist. The only son of a failed farmer, he grew up with relatives in rural South Carolina. After serving for two years in the Korean War, he settled in New York City in 1952 and befriended Robert Rauschenberg, already an accomplished artist, with whom he worked part time designing window displays for Tiffany and Bonwit Teller. During the ensuing years he turned his back on abstract expressionism and began depicting commonplace objects with biographical connections to his own life in paintings such as *Flag* (1955), *Target with Four Faces* (1955), and *Gray Numbers* (1959). He came to prominence in 1958 when the gallery impresario Leo Castelli gave him a one-man show that laid the basis for both pop art and minimalism. During the 1960s and 1970s he delved into the crosshatch movement and continued to explore new ways to blur the distinctions between art and everyday life; one of his sculptures, *Painted Bronze* (1960), depicts two beer cans. In 1977 he exhibited more than 200 of his works in a retrospective at the Whitney Museum. *The Seasons*, an autobiographical series of paintings that was acclaimed as a turning point in his career, was shown by Castelli in 1987. The Catenary series of prints begun by Johns in the late 1990s incorporates many autobiographical themes, including flags, family photos, and a Halloween costume the artist wore as a child. The Metropolitan Museum of Art purchased its first piece by Johns, *White Flag,* in 1998, a testament to his enduring legacy as a classic artist, and the Museum of Modern Art owns more than 400 of his works. In 1999 Lincoln Center's proposed selling of its publicly displayed piece *Numbers 1964* evoked such a negative public reaction that the center eventually revoked its proposal. Johns's paintings consistently set records for the highest prices paid for the work of a living artist.

Robert Sanger Steel

Johnson, Alvin (Saunders) (*b* Homer, Neb., 18 Dec 1874; *d* Upper Nyack, N.Y., 7 June 1971). Educator. He studied economics at Columbia University and in 1919 helped to found the New School for Social Research as an experimental institute that combined social research with adult education. As its director from 1922 to 1963 he built the school into a thriving institution by replacing the permanent faculty with visiting lecturers and broadening the curriculum to include courses in literature, music, philosophy, psychology, and art. Johnson was also an editor of the *Encyclopedia of the Social Sciences* and the *Yale Review.* In 1933 he organized the University in Exile, a forerunner of the graduate faculty at the New School, which provided an academic sanctuary for refugee scholars from Nazi Germany. Johnson wrote *Pioneer's Progress* (1952).

See also New School.

Peter M. Rutkoff, William B. Scott

Johnson, Charles Spurgeon (*b* Bristol, Va., 24 July 1893; *d* Louisville, Ky., 27 Oct 1956). Sociologist and educator. He received a doctorate in sociology from the University of Chicago and moved to New York City in 1921 to work at the National Urban League. As the executive director of its Department of Research and Investigations, he investigated the social and economic conditions of urban and rural African Americans. From 1922 he edited the league's monthly journal *Opportunity,* giving special attention to issues relating to black migration. His published writings include *Shadow of the Plantation* (1934) and *Collapse of Cotton Tenancy* (1935). In 1928 Johnson left the league for Fisk University, becoming its first black president in 1946; he remained there until his death.

Nancy J. Weiss, *The National Urban League, 1910–1940* (New York: Oxford University Press, 1974)

See also Harlem Renaissance.

Seth M. Scheiner

Johnson, (Jonathan) Eastman (*b* Lovell, Maine, 29 Jul 1824; *d* New York City, 5 Apr 1906). Artist. The leading genre painter in New York City during the 1860s and 1870s, Johnson exhibited regularly at the National Academy of Design, belonged to the Century Club and the Union League Club, and was a founding trustee of the Metropolitan Museum of Art. The son of a government official, Johnson settled permanently in New York City in 1858. Fame came in 1859 when he exhibited *Negro Life at the South* (New-York Historical Society) at the National Academy of Design; elected as an associate, in 1860 he became a full academician. During the Civil War he followed the Union troops in search of genre subjects and also painted many pictures sympathetic to slaves and freedmen, such as *The Freedom Ride* (Brooklyn Museum). Summers spent on Nantucket during the 1870s provided new subjects of rural work and leisure, but about 1880 he turned toward full-time portraiture and painted many important New Yorkers, such as Bishop Henry C. Potter, Frederick A. P. Barnard, William Evarts, William H. Vanderbilt, John D. Rockefeller, Jay Gould, and Presidents Grover Cleveland and Benjamin Harrison.

Teresa A. Carbone and Patricia Hills, *Eastman Johnson: Painting America* (New York: Brooklyn Museum of Art in association with Rizzoli International Publications, 1999)

Patricia Hills

Johnson, James P(rice) (*b* New Brunswick, N.J., 1 Feb 1894; *d* New York City, 17 Nov 1955). Pianist and composer. He played his first professional engagement in Far Rockaway in 1912 and later performed at rent parties and clubs in New York City; he began recording in 1921. He was the principal creator of Harlem stride, an early style of jazz piano that was more loose and improvisational than classic ragtime, its immediate forebear. His best-known compositions include "Carolina Shout" (1918), the anthem of Harlem stride; the phenomenally popular song "Charleston" (1923); "Runnin' Wild" (1923); "If I Can Be with You" (1926); and "Keep Shufflin' " (1928). He also wrote a blues opera, *De Organizer* (1940), in collaboration with Langston Hughes, and several concertos and other classical compositions, among them *Yamekraw* for piano and orchestra (1928).

Scott E. Brown, *James P. Johnson: A Case of Mistaken Identity*/Robert Hilbert, *A James P. Johnson Discography, 1917–1950* (Metuchen, N.J.: Scarecrow/Institute of Jazz Studies, 1982–86)

Kathy J. Ogren

Johnson, James Weldon (*b* Jacksonville, Fla., 17 June 1871; *d* Wicasset, Maine, 26 June 1938). Educator, author, songwriter, and civil rights activist. Educated at Atlanta University in Atlanta, Georgia, he became the first African American admitted to the Florida bar. He collaborated with his younger brother J. Rosamond Johnson as a songwriter, and in 1899 the brothers wrote "Lift Every Voice and Sing," which became known as the Negro National Anthem. In 1902 Johnson moved to New York City, where he joined his brother at the Marshall Hotel on West 53rd Street, a black-run establishment that was a national hub for African American artists and performers. James and Rosamond teamed up with producer Bob Cole in a trio that authored some 200 popular songs, librettos, and comic operas. One of these songs, "The Congo Love Song" earned the Johnson brothers some $13,000 in royalties. In 1906 Johnson was appointed U.S. consul to Puerto Cabello, Venezuela, though he was soon transferred to Corinto, Nicaragua, where he finished his most famous book, *The Autobiography of an Ex-Colored Man.* The novel was published anonymously in 1912 and soon fell out of print, but in 1927 it was republished by Alfred Knopf to wide acclaim.

Upon returning to New York City in 1914, Johnson began a campaign for equal rights as an editorial writer at the *New York Age* and worked as a field secretary for the National Association for the Advancement of Colored People (NAACP). Starting in 1920 he served as the NAACP's general secretary for 10 years, during which time he released anthologies of black poetry and spirituals. Johnson was central to the campaign for the unsuccessful Dyer Anti-Lynching Bill: his arguments undercut the myth that lynching was used exclusively as retaliation for interracial rape, drawing attention to black women and white victims of lynching, and he galvanized anti-lynching campaigns throughout the South. In 1925 this work earned him the NAACP's Spingarn Medal for outstanding achievement by an African American. Johnson devoted his later years almost exclusively to writing, publishing a history of the Harlem Renaissance (*Black Manhattan,* 1930), an autobiography (*Along This Way,* 1933), and a philosophical appeal for integration (*Negro Americans, What Now?,* 1934). He died in an automobile accident. More than 2500 people attended his funeral in Harlem, which was followed by his burial at Green-Wood Cemetery in Brooklyn.

Rowan Moore Gerety

Johnson, Philip (Cortelyou) (*b* Cleveland, 8 July 1906; *d* New Canaan, Conn., 25 Jan 2005). Architect. He graduated from Harvard University in 1930 and then became associated with the Museum of Modern Art, where he directed the architecture department from 1932 to 1934. With Henry-Russell Hitchcock he organized the polemical exhibition on the International style in 1932 that introduced avant-garde European architecture to Americans. In 1943 he returned to Harvard for a degree in architecture. Among his first works was his own "Glass House" in suburban New Canaan, Connecticut (1949). He resumed his directorship at the Museum of Modern Art from 1946 to 1954 and in 1964 designed its sculpture garden and East Wing addition. During the 1960s he accepted large commissions nationwide, especially from colleges and other cultural institutions; those in the city included the New York State Theater at Lincoln Center (1964, with Richard Foster), several buildings for the Washington Square campus of New York University, and the interior of the restaurant the Four Seasons (1959, in the Seagram Building), later designated a landmark. After entering a partnership with John Burgee (*b* 1933) in 1967 he focused on large commercial projects. He shocked many with his conversion to postmodernism in his design for the American Telephone and Telegraph Building at 550 Madison Avenue (1984, headquarters of Sony from 1991): its masonry cladding and "Chippendale" top marked a nostalgic revival of historical forms and ornament in skyscrapers of the 1980s. His other commissions include a castle-like office tower at 33 Maiden Lane (1986) and another at 885 Third Avenue (1986), known informally as the Lipstick Building because of its color and shape.

Carol Willis

Johnson, (William) Samuel (*b* Guilford, Conn., 14 Oct 1696; *d* Stratford, Conn., 6 Jan 1772). Minister and first president of King's College (later Columbia University). Early in his tenure at the college he became embroiled in a controversy with William Livingston, a Presbyterian who with others advocated a nonsectarian college; Johnson contributed essays against the plan to the *New-York Mercury* and the *New-York Gazette.* During the years leading to the American Revolution he supported the controversial plan to have bishops in the colonies. A prolific author of works of theology and Berkelian philosophy, Johnson wrote *Ethics, Elementa, or the First Principles of Moral Philosophy* (1746).

David C. Humphrey, *From King's College to Columbia, 1746–1800* (New York: Columbia University Press, 1976); Peter N. Carroll, *The Other Samuel Johnson* (Rutherford, N.J.: Fairleigh Dickinson University Press, 1978)

Phyllis Barr

Johnson, William H(enry) (*b* Florence, S.C., 18 March 1901; *d* Central Islip, N.Y., 13 April 1970). Painter. He moved to New York City in 1921 to study at the National Academy of Design and spent the summers of 1923–26 in Provincetown, Massachusetts. His early works included still lifes and portraits in an academic realist style. In 1926 he went to Paris and became influenced by the work of expressionists and European modernists such as Chaim Soutine. On returning to New York City in 1929 he moved to Harlem, became associated with the Harlem Renaissance, and hired Alain Locke as his American agent. In the following year he went back to Europe; he remained in Denmark, Norway, and Sweden until 1939 when he returned to the United States and was commissioned by the Works Progress Administration. Johnson painted religious scenes and war themes in a primitivist style. Hospitalized for the last two decades of his life, he died in obscurity and was brought to the public's attention when his work was the subject of a 1992 retrospective at the Studio Museum in Harlem.

Novae: William H. Johnson and Bob Thompson (Los Angeles: California Afro-American Museum Foundation, 1990)

Edmund Gaither

Johnson and Higgins. Firm of insurance brokers formed in 1845 as Jones and Johnson by Walter Restored Jones, Jr., and Henry W. Johnson. It took the name Johnson and Higgins in 1854 when Jones left the firm and A. Foster Higgins joined it. During the early years the firm specialized in the adjustment of claims and the brokerage of marine insurance. During the late nineteenth century it gradually became engaged in the brokerage of fire insurance, a field that grew because of increasing urbanization and fires in Chicago (1871) and Boston (1872). The firm opened branch offices in several U.S. cities and in 1899 changed its form of organization from a partnership to a privately held corporation, with all shares held by employees. During the early twentieth century it adjusted claims from the Baltimore fire of 1903, the San Francisco earthquake of 1906, and the sinking of the *Titanic* in 1912. It also provided marine and nonmarine insurance to the federal government during both world wars. After World War II it offered new services to an expanding market, and Johnson and Higgins became the largest privately held insurance brokerage firm in the world. The company merged with Marsh and McLennan in 1997 and the name disappeared from the masthead.

Claude M. Scales III

John Street United Methodist Church. First Methodist church in the United States. Erected in 1768 (dedicated 30 October) on the site of the former Wesley Chapel at 44 John Street, it has been the site of sermons by many well-known Methodist leaders, including Francis Asbury. African Americans were members of the church since its founding, but in 1796, faced with discriminatory practices within the church and among the white clergy, African American sexton Peter Williams and fellow African American congregants left the church and formed the Mother African Methodist Episcopal Zion Church. The John Street Church was rebuilt in 1818 and 1841 and renovated in 1975. It has an active congregation and a museum of portraits and artifacts.

Francis Bourne Upham, *The Story of Old John Street Methodist Episcopal Church* (New York: Cathedral, 1932)

Kathleen Benson, Celedonia Jones, Diane Jones Randall, Sharon Wilkins, Charles Yrigoyen, Jr.

John Wiley and Sons. Firm of book publishers formed by Charles Wiley in 1807 as a bookshop on Reade Street. By 1814 it published reprints of works by European authors. After the shop moved to 3 Wall Street its back room, known as the "Den," became a gathering place for intellectuals. The firm was beset by financial troubles and on Wiley's death in 1826 was taken over by his son John, who in 1824 formed a partnership with George Long; renamed Wiley and Long, it moved to 22 Nassau Street. George Palmer Putnam joined the firm in 1836, and Long left it in 1840; the firm then became known as Wiley and Putnam, with a branch in London established by Putnam. During this period the firm published the Library of American Books, a series dedicated to American writers both popular and unknown, including Nathaniel Hawthorne, Herman Melville, and Edgar Allan Poe. When Putnam returned from London in 1847 he dissolved his partnership with Wiley, who from that time concentrated on scientific and technological publications, an area in which the firm became preeminent by the end of the Civil War. Wiley's son Charles Wiley became a partner in 1865, as did his son William H. Wiley in 1875; the firm took its current name in 1876. In 1902 Major Wiley, then head of the firm, was elected to the first of three terms as a congressman from New Jersey. The first women joined the firm as a result of the labor shortage occasioned by World War I. During the 1920s the firm began to expand into fields other than engineering and science.

In the mid-1990s John Wiley and Sons maintained its role as a global publisher of print and electronic products, specializing in scientific and technical books and journals, professional and consumer books and subscription services, and textbooks and educational materials for colleges and universities. W. Bradford Wiley II, great-great-great-grandson of the founder, was the chairman of the firm, which had its corporate headquarters and main editorial offices at 605 Third Avenue and subsidiaries in the United States, Canada, Europe, Asia, and Australia; he retired in 1993 and died in 1998. The company became listed on the New York Stock Exchange in 1995, and since 2002 its headquarters have been located in suburban Hoboken, New Jersey.

See also Book publishing.

Marjorie Harrison

Jolson, Al [Yoelson, Asa] (*b* Srednik, Russian Empire [Lithuania], 26 May 1886; *d* San Francisco, 23 Oct 1950). Singer. After emigrating from Russia and working in circuses, minstrel shows, and vaudeville, he appeared on Broadway in the musical *La Belle Paree* (1911). He became well known during the next 14 years for his robust, emotional singing style and energetic clowning. After the 1920s he performed mostly in motion pictures and on radio, appearing in the starring role of the *Jazz Singer,* the first talking motion picture, or "talkie." Jolson moved to an apartment at 36 West 59th Street in 1922 and during the 1920s kept a suite at the Ritz–Carlton (374 Madison Avenue).

Jones, J(ohn) Raymond (*b* St. Thomas, U.S. Virgin Islands, 1899; *d* New York City, 9 June 1991). Political leader. In the early 1920s he formed the Carver Democratic Club, which later became the most important black political organization in New York City, and he was in the vanguard of black Democrats who took control of elective politics in Harlem during the late 1930s. A district leader for much of the period from 1945 to 1967, Jones served on the City Council from 1962 to 1967 and became the county chairman with Manhattan Democrats in the mid-1960s. Under his leadership the Carver Democratic Club promoted the careers of such influential black politicians as Representatives Charles B. Rangel and Adam Clayton Powell, Jr. (his political rival in Harlem after World War II); Percy E. Sutton, borough president of Manhattan; the federal judges Constance Baker Motley and James Watson; Robert C. Weaver, secretary of housing and urban development; Basil Paterson, secretary of state of New York; and Mayor David N. Dinkins. Jones was a brilliant strategist sometimes known as the "Harlem Fox."

John C. Walter, *The Harlem Fox* (Albany: State University of New York Press, 1989); Calvin B. Holder, "The Rise and Fall of the West Indian Politician, 1900–1988" (New York: Medgar Evers College, Caribbean Research Center, 1991)

Calvin B. Holder

Jones's Wood. Name given in the nineteenth century to an undulating, wooded, and sparsely populated tract in Manhattan occupying about 160 acres (65 hectares) roughly between Third Avenue and the East River from 66th Street to 75th Street. Named after the country seat of the Jones family, it was proposed as the site of a public park in 1844 by William Cullen Bryant in an editorial in the *New York Evening Post.* In 1851 the state legislature authorized the city to acquire a portion of the land for this purpose, but opposition arose at once, and in 1854 the authorization was repealed. Nevertheless, Jones's Wood remained popular as a pleasure ground frequented by private clubs, church groups, benevolent societies, and labor unions for organized excursions, sporting events, picnics, socials, and festivals; it was especially favored by the city's German population. The grounds held amateur shooting galleries, bowling alleys, beer halls, and outdoor dancing stands as well as the Jones's Wood Hotel (occupying the old Provoost Mansion) and the Coliseum, a large structure seating 14,000 designed in 1874 by the architectural firm of Kastner and Beach. The northward development of Manhattan brought about the eventual demise of the area. In 1894 fire destroyed some 11 acres (4 hectares) of the neighborhood, including the Coliseum.

Joy M. Kestenbaum

Joplin, Scott (*b* northeastern Texas, 1868; *d* New York City, 1 April 1917). Composer. He spent his early career mostly in Missouri. His "Maple Leaf Rag" (1899) brought him to national prominence, and he became known as the "king of ragtime writers." He moved to New York City in the summer of 1907 in an unsuccessful effort to find a producer for his still unfinished opera *Treemonisha* (1911). He remained there for the rest of his life, having more than 20 works published during that decade, including the opera. Joplin became closely associated with the city's leading African American vaudevillians and had business contacts with such major figures in music publishing as Irving Berlin. During the half-century after his death Joplin was largely forgotten, although "Maple Leaf Rag" was retained in the jazz repertory. He was rediscovered during the 1970s, receiving both critical and popular acclaim. His opera was finally produced; selections of his music used in the film *The Sting* (1973) won an Academy Award in 1973; a piano recording of his rag "The Entertainer" (1902) won a Grammy Award for "best pop instrumental"; and recordings of his music became best sellers in both popular and classical categories. In 1976 he was posthumously awarded a special bicentennial Pulitzer Prize for *Treemonisha.* When he died in 1916, he was living in a Harlem brownstone at 163 West 131st Street. He is buried in St. Michael's Cemetery in East Elmhurst in Queens.

James Haskins, with Kathleen Benson, *Scott Joplin* (Garden City, N.Y.: Doubleday, 1978); Edward A. Berlin, *King of Ragtime: Scott Joplin and His Era* (New York: Oxford University Press, 1994)

Edward A. Berlin

Jordanians. Jordanians began settling in New York City during the 1960s. The early immigrants were mostly Christians and tended to be overshadowed by the much larger (circa 13,000) and politically vibrant Jordanian community in suburban Yonkers. The first generations of New York City Jordanians owned automobile repair shops and real estate agencies, as well as small tobacco, stationery, and grocery stores. The later generations entered the professions, particularly law and medicine. In the 2000 census 897 Jordanians were counted in the five boroughs, though community estimates put the real number at almost 3000.

Paula Hajar

Josephson, Barney (*b* Trenton, N.J., *ca* 1902; *d* New York City, 29 Sept 1988). Nightclub owner. In December 1938 he opened Café Society at 2 Sheridan Square in Greenwich Village, one of the first racially integrated nightclubs under white ownership. During its first four years the club presented such boogie-woogie pianists as Pete Johnson, Meade "Lux" Lewis, and Albert Ammons, helping to inspire a vogue for the genre that spread nationwide. In 1940 he opened Café Society Uptown at East 58th Street, which like its counterpart downtown presented such performers as Billie Holiday, Lena Horne, Sarah Vaughan, and Zero Mostel. Josephson enjoyed great success until 1947 when his brother Leon, an acknowledged communist, was cited for contempt by the House Un-American Activities Committee. Vilified by such newspaper columnists as Walter Winchell and Lee Mortimer, he was compelled to sell his clubs. He then opened a restaurant called the Cookery at University Avenue and Eighth Street, where from 1969 he again presented music. The best-known performer at the Cookery was the blues singer

Alberta Hunter, who sang there from 1977 until her death in 1984.

Marc Ferris

Journal of Commerce. Daily newspaper launched in 1827 by Samuel F. B. Morse, who intended it to promote moral virtues in licentious New York City. Based at the Merchant's Exchange Building on Wall Street, it sold for six cents a copy. The newspaper soon discarded its pietistic agenda and focused more on finance, particularly international trade and transportation. Under the editorship of Gerard Hallock (*d* 1865) it expanded, merging with the *New York Gazette and General Advertiser* in 1840. During the Civil War the newspaper gained much notoriety when it was critical of Abraham Lincoln's "war on the South," and on one occasion it printed details of Union military strategy. In 1861 a federal grand jury found the newspaper "disloyal," and the government subsequently refused to provide it with postal services. A settlement was reached when Hallock stepped down. In 1927 the *Journal of Commerce* was bought by the Ridders, who owned several newspapers in New York City, and it remained part of the Knight–Ridder chain into the 1990s before it became part of the Commonwealth Business Media group. After many years on Wall Street the newspaper moved to the World Trade Center in 1991. The offices were located in nearby Newark, New Jersey, in the early twenty-first century.

James Bradley

Joyce Theater. Theater founded in 1982 by Eliot Feld and Cora Cahan as an alternative to the high-rent, full-sized theaters or downtown loft spaces available for dance companies during the 1970s. Located at 175 Eighth Avenue, it was originally the Elgin Theater but was converted into a 472-seat performance space by architect Hugh Hardy. Since 1982 more than 200 dance companies have performed for an annual audience of 140,000 patrons; it is known as the theater "created by dancers for dance." The theater hosts a wide array of performance genres, including flamenco, modern, ballet, and tap dancing. In 1996 it expanded to oversee the Joyce SoHo at 155 Mercer Street, which is dedicated to the performance of works by new and emerging choreographers.

Stephanie Miller

Jozef Pilsudski Institute of America for Research in the Modern History of Poland. Research institute formed in 1943 at 180 Second Avenue in Manhattan. It maintains a research library and archives on Polish history since 1863, publishes books, sponsors lectures, and promotes research. In the early twenty-first century it remains at its original location and is an active research center for modern Polish history.

James S. Pula

J. P. Morgan. Merchant bank. Formed in 1843 by George Peabody as George Peabody and Company, the bank helped to develop the railroads in the United States. J(unius) S(pencer) Morgan (1813–90) became a partner in 1854, and on Peabody's retirement in 1864 he took control of the firm, which he renamed J. S. Morgan and Company, in London. Dabney, Morgan, and Company, the firm's affiliate in New York City at 53 Exchange Place, was managed by his son J. P. Morgan, who in 1871 became a partner in Drexel, Morgan. This firm, allied with the bank Drexel and Company and strongly connected to European banks, soon became one of the most prosperous investment banks in the United States, important in both government and railroad finance. In 1873 it helped to refinance the Civil War debt by underwriting federal bonds worth $1.4 billion. Its headquarters were set up at 23 Wall Street during the same year. From 1875 the firm became the engine of the Morgans' enterprises. It was the main underwriter of stock and bond issues for the railroads and controlled several important reorganizations, including that of the Northern Pacific Railroad Company. After 1890 the firm undertook more corporate financing, and in 1895 it rescued the federal government during a gold shortage; in the same year it was renamed J. P. Morgan and Company. The firm was also the primary underwriter in the mergers that formed General Electric in 1892, U.S. Steel in 1901, and International Harvester in 1902.

Assisted by his partners Henry P. Davison, George Perkins, and Charles Coster, J. P. Morgan became the central figure in national finance. He helped to limit bank failures during a panic in 1907 by permitting his firm to act as a sort of central bank. This action raised concern over the power of the country's largest banks, and Morgan became the primary target of an investigation conducted in 1912 by Representative Arsène Pujo into reported perfidies of the "money trust." Although exonerated, Morgan was distressed by the proceedings and died soon after. In 1913 the architectural firm of Trowbridge and Livingston erected a new building at 23 Wall Street that dominated the financial district (it was designated a landmark in 1965). Under the direction of Morgan's son J. P. Morgan, Jr. (1867–1943), the firm ceased to function as a central bank after the formation of the Federal Reserve System and focused increasingly on investment banking in Asia, Latin America, and western Europe; it remained the preeminent investment bank in the United States. Morgan himself was overshadowed by several partners, among them Dwight Morrow, Russell Leffingwell, and Thomas W. Lamont, the chairman after 1943.

Headquarters of J. P. Morgan at Wall and Broad Streets, ca 1900

During the Great Depression in the 1930s the firm ceased to dominate national finance. The Glass–Steagall Act (1933), passed in part to separate Morgan's interests, forced banks to choose between underwriting and lending. The firm then became a commercial bank, and its investment services were taken over by its former partners, who established the firm of Morgan, Stanley in 1935. The firm of J. P. Morgan was incorporated as a commercial bank in 1940; its partnership was dissolved in 1941 and it became a publicly held company. Prosperous after World War II, it merged in 1959 with the Guaranty Trust. Its bank subsidiary, Morgan Guaranty, became a leader in international trade and in financing industries that developed in the United States after the war, among them defense contracting and the manufacture of plastics and airplanes. J. P. Morgan and Company was incorporated in 1969 as a one-bank holding company for Morgan Guaranty, which remained among the largest and strongest firms of its kind in the United States, catering exclusively to commercial clients. In 1990 it became the first commercial bank allowed by the Securities and Exchange Commission to engage in limited investment banking. In the 1990s J. P. Morgan and Company transformed itself almost entirely into an investment bank and operated in that capacity until its acquisition by the Chase Manhattan Bank in 2000.

Ron Chernow, *The House of Morgan: An American Banking Dynasty and the Rise of Modern Finance* (New York: Atlantic Monthly Press, 1990)

See also Investment banking.

Susan Aaronson, Tao Tan

JPMorgan Chase and Company. One of the largest commercial banking organizations in the United States, formed when Chase Manhattan Corporation bought J. P. Morgan and Company in 2000. In the twenty-first century it has more than 3000 offices in 17 states and is headquartered in New York City; JPMorgan Chase also operates in more than 70 countries, making it a leader in global financial services. The bank, officially known as JPMorgan Chase Bank, National Association, is involved in investment banking, consumer and business financial services, asset management, investment, and wealth management. It is also the second largest issuer of MasterCard and Visa credit cards in the United States.

The Chase National Bank of the City of New York, founded in 1877, evolved into today's giant in large part by combining with significant institutions beginning in the 1920s and continuing to the recent past. The merger of Chemical Banking Corporation with Chase Manhattan Corporation in 1996 created the largest banking organization in the country. The new entity made Chase the leader in New York consumer banking and syndicated lending. Morgan Guaranty Trust Company moved into investment banking beginning in 1980; in addition to traditional lending, it underwrote stock and bond issues and gave advice on mergers. The merger of Morgan and Chase propelled the combined firm into the front ranks of banking; indeed, JPMorgan Chase became the world leader in syndicate lending and derivatives. The promise of retail banking attracted JPMorgan Chase to acquire Chicago-based Bank One in 2004, and in the New York City metropolitan area Chase solidified its presence by acquiring 339 additional offices from the Bank of New York in 2006.

Benjamin J. Klebaner

Judd, Donald (Clarence) (*b* Excelsior Springs, Mo., 3 June 1928; *d* New York City, 12 Feb 1994). Sculptor. After serving in the army during the Korean War, he earned a BA in philosophy at Columbia University and studied painting at the Art Students League. He returned to Columbia in the late 1950s for graduate study in art history with Meyer Schapiro and Rudolf Wittkower. By the 1960s he was one of the foremost American artists and a leading figure in the minimalist movement. His writings helped to identify a new generation of artists and to lift the art world in New York City out of the doldrums of second-generation abstract expressionism and away from what he saw as tired European aesthetic conventions. For most of his active career Judd had a studio in a cast-iron building in SoHo. In 1996, out of stipulations in his will, the Judd Foundation was created in New York City and Marfa, Texas; in the early twenty-first century the Manhattan location is at 101 Spring Street.

Kenneth T. Jackson

Judge. Humor magazine launched by several cartoonists from *Puck,* including James Albert Wales. First issued on 29 October 1881, it sold for 10 cents and became known for its political themes and full-page, brightly colored chromolithographic cartoons of leading political figures. Among its features was a series depicting the "Judge," a character drawn on the inside cover who attacked corruption and disparaged immigrants, especially Jews. Under Isaac M. Gregory the magazine became a publication of the Republican Party. It strongly supported William McKinley in the presidential election of 1896, in part through Grant Hamilton's "full dinner pail" cartoons. Circulation rose to 85,000 before the turn of the twentieth century. After the magazine's publisher was reorganized as the Leslie–Judge Company in 1909, James Lee became the editor and trod a politically independent course, choosing such topics of general humor as women's organizations and popular poets and producing holiday issues. In 1922 the magazine merged with *Leslie's Weekly* and under new direction added crossword puzzles, contests, a man-about-town column called "Judge, Jr.," and a subtitle, "The Nation's Perpetual Smileage Book." By 1923 it sold for 15 cents and circulation peaked at 250,000. It attracted such popular writers as Stephen Leacock, S. J. Perelman, Walter Trumbell, and Stephen Vincent Benét and such cartoonists as Oliver Herford and Theodor Seuss Geisel (who later wrote children's books as Dr. Seuss). During the Depression circulation declined, leading the publisher to reduce the price to 10 cents and publish only monthly from July 1932. In 1937 the magazine was reorganized under Harry Newman, who changed the subtitle to "The National Magazine of Humor, Politics and Satire," raised the price to 25 cents, and sought to make the content more sophisticated; *Judge* nonetheless declined in popularity and ceased publication in 1949.

Walter Friedman

Judge, Mychal [Michael] **F.** [Robert Emmet], **OFM** (*b* Brooklyn, 11 May 1933; *d* New York City, 11 September 2001). Priest and first official victim of the terrorist attacks of 11 September 2001 on the World Trade Center. Robert Emmet Judge took the name Michael when he entered the Franciscan Order of Friars Minor 13 August 1954 and changed the spelling to Mychal about 1986. Ordained 25 February 1961, he first served in St. Francis of Assisi Church at 135 West 31st Street during 1969–70, returning in 1986. His ministry to paralyzed police officer Steven McDonald developed into a partnership that made three peacemaking trips to Northern Ireland (1998–2000). He became a New York Fire Department chaplain in 1992. The first officially recorded victim of the World Trade Center attack, he had just completed the last rites for Daniel Suhr when hit by debris from the South Tower that was blown into the North Tower lobby. Shannon Stapleton of Reuters photographed his body being carried by firefighters to St. Peter's Church at 22 Barclay Street. Edward Cardinal Egan presided over his funeral 15 September, which thousands attended. He is interred at Holy Sepulchre Cemetery, Totowa, New Jersey. Permanent memorials include the renaming of 31st Street between Sixth and Seventh avenues, an annual Walk of Remembrance, and a bench at the TWA Flight 800 International Memorial at Smith Point County Park on Fire Island, as he was among those who responded to that airline crash.

Michael Ford, *Father Mychal Judge: An Authentic American Hero* (New York: Paulist, 2002)

Mary Elizabeth Brown

Judson Dance Theatre. Avant-garde dance collective. It evolved from a dance composition class with choreographer Robert Dunn and included Yvonne Rainer, Lucinda Childs, Alex and Deborah Hay, James Waring, Trisha Brown, Steve Paxton, Carolee Schneeman, Judith Dunn, David Gordon, and Elaine Summers, and others. Some of the dancers also studied with Merce Cunningham, and their work was influenced by avant-garde composer John Cage. Judson Memorial Church, located at 55 Washington Square South, provided the dancers with its meeting room as a public performance space, and the collective presented its first performance, *A Concert of Dance,* on 6 July 1962. Because of the collective's egalitarian structure, its style was eclectic, and its work expanded the traditional definition of dance. The collective existed through 1964, producing 20 performances and influencing postmodern American dance in the decades that followed.

Sally Banes, *Democracy's Body: Judson Dance Theatre, 1962–1964* (Durham, N.C.: Duke University Press, 1993)

Kate Lauber

Judson Memorial Church. Baptist church at 55 Washington Square South in Manhattan, formed in 1890 by Edward Judson, pastor of the Berean Baptist Congregation. In 1892 it moved into a building designed by the firm of McKim, Mead, and White in the Romanesque Revival style and constructed of yellow Roman brick and limestone. This structure, a city, state, and federal landmark, is regarded as an architectural masterpiece, well known for its marble relief by Augustus Saint-Gaudens and stained-glass windows by John La Farge. Judson and his parishioners established a durable tradition of social activism, sponsoring cooking and sewing classes, a health center, and employment services. The church continued to advocate liberal reforms into the next century. In the 1960s its minister, Al Carmines, led a radical arts ministry, sponsoring modern dance and experimental music performances in the church's auditorium. Politically, the church supported abortion rights, the peace movement, and gay and lesbian rights, and later donated space for trials of an experimental AIDS drug.

Aileen Laura Love

Judson Poets' Theatre. Theater formed in 1961 by members of the arts program at Judson Memorial Church in Greenwich Village. Led by the church's assistant pastor, Al Carmines, and its director, Lawrence Kornfeld, the theater has presented an eclectic repertory ranging from plays by Strindberg, Gertrude Stein, and Sam Shepard to avant-garde musicals and performance events. Integral in the development of Off-Off-Broadway theaters, several plays and musicals went on to find commercial and television audiences. The Judson Poets' Theatre essentially ended in 1982 after Carmines suffered a brain aneurysm. The theater program briefly revived during 1991 through 1992.

D. S. Moynihan

Juilliard School. Conservatory of music chartered in 1904 as the Institute of Musical Art by Frank Damrosch, with an endowment of $500,000 from James Loeb. Based on the European model and intended for American music students of the highest caliber, the school was planned for 150 students but within a year of its opening in October 1905 had nearly 500, who attended classes at the Lenox Mansion, a six-story brownstone at 53 Fifth Avenue at 12th Street. The early faculty included such prominent figures as the violinists Franz Kneisel and Leopold Auer, the flutist Georges Barrère, the singer Georg Henschel, the composer Rubin Goldmark, the theorist Percy Goetschius, and the pianists Carl Friedberg, Josef Lhévinne, Rosina Lhévinne, Olga Samaroff-Stokowski, Alexander Siloti, and Ernest Hutcheson (president of the school from 1937 to 1945). The school moved in 1910 to 120 Claremont Avenue in Morningside Heights. The Juilliard Musical Foundation, formed in 1919 by a bequest of $20 million from the textile magnate August D. Juilliard and enlarged by a bequest of $10 million from Frederick A. Juilliard, oversaw the establishment in 1924 of the Juilliard Graduate School, which largely duplicated the offerings of the Institute of Musical Art; the two schools merged in 1926 to form the Juilliard School of Music (name abbreviated to its current form in 1968), which soon began to accept students from abroad, in part to compete with the Curtis Institute in Philadelphia. In 2007, 25.8 percent of Juilliard's students came from outside the United States, with especially strong representation from Korea, Canada, China, Japan, Israel, Taiwan, and the former Soviet states.

From 1945 the school was led by the composer William Schuman, who oversaw the formation of the Juilliard String Quartet, the adoption of a basic-musicianship curriculum called "Literature and Materials of Music" that became widely imitated, and the establishment in 1951 of a dance division that numbered among its faculty Martha Graham, Agnes de Mille, and Antony Tudor. Schuman resigned in 1962 to become president of Lincoln Center. Under his successor Peter Mennin the school in 1968 opened a drama division led by John Houseman. In 1969 the school became a part of Lincoln Center—where it moved into a five-story complex encompassing several theaters and concert halls, an extensive music library, and set and costume shops for staged productions—and in 1970 opened the Juilliard Opera Center. Joseph Polisi became the president of the school in 1984. The study of jazz was introduced in 2001. A major building renovation and expansion was completed in 2010 and included the addition of 40,000 square feet (3716 square meters) of space.

Juilliard is generally regarded as the leading conservatory of music in North America. It enrolls some 800 students and offers artist diplomas and the degrees of bachelor of music, bachelor of fine arts (in drama and dance), master of music, and doctor of musical arts; it also has an active precollege division. Prominent members of the faculty have included Bessie Schönberg (dance), Michael Kahn (drama), and Wynton Marsalis, Milton Babbitt, and the members of the Juilliard String Quartet (music). Well-known students have included Itzhak Perlman, Leontyne Price, Paul Taylor, Richard Rodgers, Renée Fleming, and Kevin Kline.

Frank Damrosch, *Institute of Musical Art, 1905–1926* (New York: Privately printed, 1936); Andrea Olmstead, *Juilliard: A History* (Champaign: University of Illinois Press, 1999); Maro Chermayeff and Amy Schewel, *Juilliard* (New York: Harry N. Abrams, 2003)

James M. Keller

Jujamcyn Theaters. Entertainment enterprise formed in 1956 by Virginia and James Binger; the name is derived from the names of the Bingers' children: Judy, James, and Cynthia. The firm owns and operates five Broadway theaters and has produced such shows as *M. Butterfly, Grand Hotel, Into the Woods, The Secret Garden,* and *Angels in America.* In 1984 it inaugurated the Jujamcyn Award to recognize outstanding contributions by a resident theater. After James Binger's death in 2004 (Virginia died in 2002) the group was sold to Rocco Landesman, Jujamcyn's longtime producer and president.

Robert Seder

Julia (y Arcelay), Raul (Rafael Carlos) (*b* San Juan, 9 March 1940; *d* Manhasset, N.Y., 24 Oct 1994). Actor. He moved to New York City in 1964 and in 1971 won renown as Proteus in a modern, musical version of *Two Gentlemen of Verona* presented by the New York Shakespeare Festival. He then played the title role in *Othello* and appeared in plays by George Bernard Shaw, Noël Coward, Jean-Paul Sartre, and Harold Pinter, as well as Broadway musicals. He frequently took time away from the stage to act in films, notably *Kiss of the Spider Woman* (1985) and *The Addams Family* (1991), but he lived in Manhattan and regarded New York City as his home. Julia was active in political and social causes, including the Hunger Project.

Kenneth T. Jackson

Jumel [née Brown; Bowen], **Elizabeth** [Eliza] (*b* Providence, R.I., 1775; *d* New York City, 22 July 1865). Adventuress. Known for her beauty, she was reportedly the madam of a French bordello in her youth and later a prostitute in Providence. She lived with the wine merchant Stephen Jumel in his mansion at Whitehall and Pearl streets for a number of years before marrying him. In 1810 she received as a gift from him the house of Roger Morris, which had been George Washington's headquarters during the battle for Manhattan in 1776. Rejected in the city's social circles, she moved with her husband to France in 1815, where they were well received. She returned to New York City without her husband but then rejoined him in France. She moved back to New York City in 1826 with his power of attorney, sold his property, and kept the proceeds. After Jumel died penniless, she married former vice president Aaron Burr, from whom she sought a divorce in 1834 after he misused the Jumel fortune; the divorce was granted on the day of his death in 1836. Jumel was reportedly the wealthiest woman in North America at mid-century.

Leonard Faulkner, *Painted Lady: Eliza Jumel* (New York: E. P. Dutton, 1962)

See also Morris–Jumel Mansion.

James E. Mooney

Jumel, Stephen (*b* Bordeaux, France, *ca* 1754; *d* New York City, 22 May 1832). Wine merchant. The son of a French merchant family, he moved to New York City in 1795 and formed a partnership with Jacques Desobry. During the trade embargo of 1807–9 he

The mansion of Stephen Jumel

found ways to conduct business that earned large profits. He was also known for marrying the stunning Eliza Brown, for whom in 1810 he purchased Roger Morris's house (Washington's former headquarters) in upper Manhattan. With her he moved to France in 1815. She returned to the city to gain his wealth, and he returned to destitution.

James E. Mooney

Junior's, 2009

Junior's. Restaurant opened by Harry Rosen in 1950 at the corner of DeKalb and Flatbush avenues in Brooklyn. Situated across the street from the Brooklyn campus of Long Island University, it was a temporary classroom when a fire damaged a campus building in 1968, as well as a meeting place for the faculty during their strike in 1979. It was renovated after it burned in a fire in 1981 and in the early twenty-first century is still known for its sandwiches, cheesecake, large portions, extensive menu, reasonable prices, and the many condiments placed on its tables.

Marjorie Harrison

K

Kahal Adas Jeshurun Anshe Lubz. Original name of the ELDRIDGE STREET SYNAGOGUE.

Kahane, Meir (Martin David) (*b* New York City, 1 Aug 1932; *d* New York City, 5 Nov 1990). Rabbi and political activist. He grew up in Brooklyn and as a youth became an ardent Zionist. After earning degrees from Brooklyn College, New York Law School, and New York University he became a rabbi at the Howard Beach Center, remaining there for two years before moving to Israel. He returned to the city in 1967, became a rabbi in Rochdale Village, and wrote a regular column for the *Jewish Press.* The eruption of anti-Semitism during a teachers' strike in 1968 inspired him to form the JEWISH DEFENSE LEAGUE, a militant organization devoted to Jewish rights; he encouraged his followers to use violence, was often accused of vigilantism, and was jailed repeatedly for taking part in anti-Soviet demonstrations and for encouraging the use of explosives. He moved back to Israel and was elected to the Knesset after waging a campaign in which he advocated expelling Palestinians from the occupied territories. On one of his many visits to New York City he was assassinated by an Egyptian-born U.S. citizen who was acquitted of homicide but later convicted for involvement in the 1993 bombing of the World Trade Center.

Robert I. Friedman, *The False Prophet: Rabbi Meir Kahane* (New York: Lawrence Hill, 1990)

James E. Mooney

Kahn, Ely Jacques (*b* New York City, 1 June 1884; *d* New York City, 5 Sept 1972). Architect. After graduating from Columbia University Architecture School in 1907, he spent four years at the École des Beaux-Arts in Paris, where he met prominent architects such as William Van Alen, future designer of the Chrysler Building. In 1919 he became a partner at Albert Buchanan's firm, which by 1930 became Kahn Architects and then in 1940 Kahn and Jacobs. While teaching at Cornell University and providing much of the inspiration for Ayn Rand's *The Fountainhead,* Kahn participated in numerous important New York City projects, including the Bergdorf Goodman Store Building (1927), 2 Park Avenue (1928), the Film Center Building (1929), and the Squibb Building (1929), all works consistent with Kahn's polychromatic art deco style. His firm later turned to a more modernist style, especially as skyscrapers became the symbol of American modernity, as seen in his project at 1407 Broadway (1950). Kahn also did work on the Municipal Asphalt Plant (1944), several New York City synagogues, and the New York Stock Exchange (1956). Kahn and Jacobs closed in 1973.

Cecilia Magnusson

Kahn, Otto H(ermann) (*b* Mannheim, Germany, 23 Feb 1867; *d* New York City, 29 March 1934). Financier and arts patron. Born to a family of merchant bankers, he settled in New York City in August 1893 and in January 1896 married Addie Wolff; her father, Abraham Wolff, was an elder partner at Kuhn, Loeb and Company and arranged for him to join the firm in January 1897. He soon emerged as an expert in railroad finance and as a spokesman for both his firm and the conservative sensibilities of Wall Street. His accomplishments in finance were, however, overshadowed by his extraordinary patronage of the arts; more than anyone of his generation he promoted the arts as a worthy object of philanthropy (he once told Mayor John F. Hylan that a piano in every house would deter more crime than a policeman on every doorstep). His energetic chairmanship of the Metropolitan Opera from 1908 to 1931 secured its status as a nonprofit entity, and he helped to make the city an indispensable destination on the American tours of many influential European theater and dance companies, including Sergei Diaghilev's Ballets Russes, Jacques Copeau's Théâtre du Vieux Colombier, Konstantin Stanislavsky's Moscow Art Theatre, and Max Reinhardt's Repertory Company. Kahn also supported the Washington Square Players (later the Theatre Guild), the Provincetown Players, and the New Playwrights Theatre, as well as many individual artists and writers, among them Hart Crane (during his writing of *The Bridge).* Kahn's mansion at 1 East 91st Street is a landmark and was purchased by the Convent of the Sacred Heart in 1934.

Otto H. Kahn

John Kobler, *Otto the Magnificent: The Life of Otto Kahn* (New York: Charles Scribner's Sons, 1988)

Theresa Collins

Kalbfleisch, Martin (*b* Vlissingen, Netherlands, 8 Feb 1804; *d* Brooklyn, 12 Feb 1873). Mayor of Brooklyn. He studied chemistry and settled in New York City in 1826. In 1835 he opened a color works in Harlem that he moved to Greenpoint in 1842; as the Brooklyn Chemical Works this became one of the most important chemical firms in the United States. Kalbfleisch was the last supervisor of Bushwick in Brooklyn (1852–54), served as a Brooklyn alderman (1855–61), and was mayor of Brooklyn for nearly seven years (1861–63, 1868–71). He was elected to the U.S. Congress as a Democrat and served from 1863 until 1865. He remained active in politics until the end of his life.

Ellen Fletcher

Kalman [née Berman]**, Maira** (*b* Tel Aviv, Israel, 15 Nov 1949). Author, illustrator, and designer. As a child she immigrated to New York City with her family and lived at the Hotel Monterey on 94th Street and Broadway. She attended New York University, where she met her future husband and collaborator, TIBOR KALMAN, with whom she founded in 1979 M&Co., a graphic and product design company whose products continue to be sold at the Museum of Modern Art in the early twenty-first century. She wrote *Stay Up Late* (1987), a book of illustrated song lyrics that featured her characteristic design of primitive-looking characters in bright colors. The books that followed, including the series on "Max" the dog and *Next Stop Grand Central* (2001) (based on her murals in Grand Central Terminal), revealed her childlike, witty, and colorful passion for words and for New York City. Kalman has contributed several illustrated covers to the *New Yorker* (most famously, her 2001 cover "New Yorkistan") and published *Fireboat: The Heroic Adventures of the John J. Harvey* (2002) about the terrorist attacks of 11 September 2001 and an illustrated version of E. B. White and William Strunk's *Elements of Style* (2005). Her work has been exhibited in the Children's Museum of Manhattan and the Julie Saul Gallery in lower Manhattan. In the early twenty-first century she lives in Greenwich Village.

Cecilia Magnusson, Meghan Lalonde

Kalman, Tibor (*b* Budapest, 6 Jul 1949; *d* San Juan, Puerto Rico, 2 May 1999). Social activist and designer. He fled the Soviet repression in Hungary at age seven to settle in suburban Westchester County with his family. At New York University he became an active member of the Students for a Democratic Society and dropped out to support communists for Cuba. His work doing window displays for the Student Book Exchange at New York University so impressed the owner that he was hired as the first creative director of what would become Barnes and Noble. In 1979 Kalman cofounded the graphic and product design company M&Co with his wife MAIRA KALMAN, whom he married in 1967. While M&Co. was growing with such clients as the Museum of Modern Art, Kalman was renowned for allegedly turning down clients whose ideas he deemed toxic to the public. The United Colors of Benetton hired him to run *Colors* magazine and promote the clothing company's message about multiculturalism and social activism. In 1989 M&Co. designed the "Red Square" building at Houston Street and Avenue A, whose roof, decorated with an enormous original "askew" clock and a statue of Lenin, can be seen from afar. In 1993 he designed, for the 42nd Street Redevelopment Authority, the EVERYBODY billboard featured at the foot of the construction of the new Condé Nast Building at 42nd Street and Broadway. Kalman believed that design could be the catalyst for real change, and his self-proclaimed "contraryism" earned him the titles of "perverse optimist" and "bad boy of graphic design." He lived with his wife in Greenwich Village.

Michael Beirut and Peter Hall, *Tibor Kalman, Perverse Optimist* (New York: Princeton Architectural Press, 2000)

Cecilia Magnusson

Kane Street Synagogue. Conservative synagogue formed in Brooklyn in the 1850s by a largely Dutch and Bavarian congregation. It was originally known as the Boerum Schule and had quarters near Brooklyn Borough Hall before moving to Cobble Hill in 1905. The synagogue was a charter member of the United Synagogues of America. At one time its membership included the family of composer Aaron Copland. The synagogue is reputed to be the oldest in Brooklyn.

Jenna Weissman Joselit

Kaplan, Mordecai M(enahem) (*b* Svencionys, Lithuania, 11 June 1881; *d* Bronx, 8 Nov 1983). Rabbi and theologian. After moving to the United States with his family in 1890 he was ordained in 1902 at the Jewish Theological Seminary, where in 1909 he was appointed dean of the Teachers Institute. He formed the Society for the Advancement of Judaism in 1922 and was the leading exponent of Reconstructionism, a branch of Judaism that views the faith as an "evolving religious civilization" in which cultural elements are as important as theological and legal ones. A teacher at the Jewish Teachers Seminary for 50 years, Kaplan influenced generations of rabbis, whom he urged to apply scriptural and rabbinical texts imaginatively to contemporary issues.

Emanuel Goldsmith, Mel Scult, and Robert M. Seltzer, *The American Judaism of Mordecai M. Kaplan* (New York: New York University Press, 1990)

Thomas E. Bird

Karan [Faske], **Donna (Ivy)** (*b* New York City, 2 Oct 1948). Businesswoman and fashion designer. Educated at the Parsons School of Design, Karan worked as an assistant to Anne Klein and later served as the head of Klein's design team until 1984. In 1984 she and her husband Stephen Weiss cofounded the Donna Karan collection, which focused on using comfortable fabrics for elegant and fashionable women's clothing. In 1989 she started a women's sportswear line, DKNY (Donna Karan New York) and in 1992 began a menswear collection. Eventually she expanded her company to include accessories, beauty products, eyewear, and home furnishings. In 2001 the company was acquired by Moët Hennessy Louis Vuitton, but Karan remained chairwoman and designer in charge. The Donna Karan International headquarters are at 550 Seventh Avenue. Her collection is available in self-standing stores as well as upscale department stores throughout the United States, Middle East, Asia, and Europe.

Stephanie Miller

Käsebier [née Stanton], **Gertrude** (*b* Fort Des Moines [now Des Moines], Iowa, 18 May 1852; *d* New York City, 13 Oct 1934). Photographer. She developed a strong interest in photography while studying portrait painting at the Pratt Institute in Brooklyn. From 1897 she photographed subjects in natural poses against a plain background, a rebellion against the painted backdrops and elaborate furniture used by photographers such as Napoleon Sarony. Working in successive studios on and near Fifth Avenue, she soon became one of the best-known photographers in New York City, admired for her portraits of figures such as the architect Stanford White and the painter Arthur B. Davies, and for her timeless images of motherhood. Alfred Stieglitz featured her work in the first issue of *Camera Work* (1903) as well as in various exhibitions at the Photo-Secession galleries. After breaking with Stieglitz in 1912 she aligned herself with Clarence H. White and the Pictorial Photographers of America. Her activity dwindled after World War I. In 1929 she was the subject of a retrospective exhibition at the Brooklyn Institute of Arts and Sciences (now the Brooklyn Museum).

W. I. Homer, ed., *A Pictorial Heritage: The Photographs of Gertrude Käsebier* (Wilmington: Delaware Art Museum, 1979); Barbara L. Michaels, *Gertrude Käsebier: The Photographer and Her Photographs* (New York: Harry N. Abrams, 1992)

See also PHOTOGRAPHY.

Barbara L. Michaels

Katz's Delicatessen. Delicatessen established by a Russian immigrant family on the Lower East Side in 1888. Located at the south-

Katz's Delicatessen, 2009

west corner of Houston and Ludlow streets, it re-created the flavors of Europe and continued a tradition of meat preparation and preservation predating refrigeration. During World War II Katz's encouraged customers to "send a salami to your boy in the army," a slogan that continues in the establishment's signage. In the 1989 romantic comedy movie *When Harry Met Sally*, Meg Ryan's famous fake-orgasm scene took place in the restaurant. In 2007 Katz's Delicatessen served 5000 pounds of corned beef, 2000 pounds of salami, and 12,000 hot dogs every week.

Kenneth T. Jackson

Kaufman, George S(imon) (*b* Pittsburgh, Pa., 16 Nov 1889; *d* New York City, 2 June 1961). Playwright, essayist, director, and screenwriter. After his dismissal from the *Washington Times* he moved to New York City in 1913, where he lived at 241 West 101st Street and worked as a drama critic and columnist for several newspapers, including the *New York Tribune* and the *Evening Mail.* In 1917 he became the drama editor of the *New York Times,* a position he held until 1930. His reviews were well known for their wit; he once wrote that Raymond Massey, an impersonator of Abraham Lincoln considered overbearing by many, would not be satisfied until he had been assassinated. From 1921 he lived in an apartment at 200 West 58th Street. Quoted as having said that it was good to have company when locked in a room with a blank piece of paper, he almost always wrote in collaboration with others. With Marc Connelly he wrote the play *Dulcy* in 1921; the two continued to collaborate until 1924. He also worked with fellow members of the Algonquin Round Table, among them Edna Ferber, with whom he wrote *Royal Family* (1927), *Dinner at Eight* (1932), and four other plays. With Morrie Ryskind he wrote several comedies for the Marx Brothers (including *The Cocoanuts* [1925] and *Animal Crackers* [1928]), as well as *Of Thee I Sing,* which opened at the Music Box Theatre on 26 December 1931 and was the first musical to win a Pulitzer Prize. On his own he wrote the play *Butter and Egg Man* (1925). He lived at 158 East 63rd Street from 1929 until 1932, when he moved to 14 East 94th Street. About this time he began working with Moss Hart (1904–61), with whom he wrote *Once in a Lifetime* (1930), *You Can't Take It with You* (1936), and *The Man Who Came to Dinner* (1939), which opened at the Music Box on 16 October 1939 and ran for 739 performances. Screen rights to most of his plays were bought by studios in Hollywood where he eventually worked on such films as the Marx Brothers' *A Night at the Opera* (1935); he later directed *Guys and Dolls* (1950) and wrote *The Solid Gold Cadillac* (1953) with Howard Teichmann. Kaufman married the actress Leueen MacGrath, with whom he wrote *Silk Stockings* (1955). He moved to 410 Park Avenue during the mid-1940s and to 1035 Park Avenue about 1950, where he remained until the end of his life.

Scott Meredith, *George S. Kaufman and His Friends* (New York: Doubleday, 1974)

Walter Friedman

Kaufman, Irving R(obert) (*b* New York City, 24 June 1910; *d* New York City, 1 Feb 1992). Federal judge. He attended Fordham University (LLB 1931) and in 1949 became the youngest federal judge in the United States when President Harry S. Truman appointed him the chief judge of the U.S. Court of Appeals for the Second Circuit. He became widely known in April 1951 when he sentenced Julius and Ethel Rosenberg to death for espionage. In 1961 he issued the first order to desegregate an elementary school in the North (in suburban Westchester County), and in the following decades he wrote several opinions in which he took a broad view of the First Amendment. He retired in 1987 but was designated a senior judge and remained active on the bench nearly to the end of his life.

B. Kimberly Taylor

Kaufman Astoria Studios [KAS]. Motion-picture studio opened in 1920 by the Famous Players–Lasky Corporation at 35th Avenue between 34th and 37th streets in the neighborhood of Astoria, Queens, just across the East River from the company's headquarters in Manhattan. Between 1921 and the time Famous Players–Lasky became known as Paramount Famous Lasky in 1927 (it was renamed Paramount Pictures in 1936), about one-quarter of its films were made there; the rest were made in Hollywood. After being adapted for the production of motion pictures with sound by Western Electric in 1929, the facility was renamed Eastern Studios Inc. The proximity of the studio to Broadway was of benefit to Paramount, which produced such films there as the musical *Heads Up* (1930) by Richard Rodgers and Lorenz Hart. The Marx Brothers made their jump from Broadway to the screen at the studio, filming *The Cocoanuts* (1929) and *Animal Crackers* (1930) there. The production of feature films in Astoria diminished during the mid-1930s and virtually ceased by 1937, though the studio continued to be used for short subjects, "second-unit" work for films made in Hollywood, and Paramount News. In 1942 the U.S. Army took control of the studio, which it renamed the Signal Corps Photographic Center, and began producing and editing wartime films (*A World at War* [1943]; *Autobiography of a Jeep* [1943]); the army continued to use the studio to produce educational and training films until the 1960s. In 1975, as Kaufman Astoria Studios, the studio reopened for the production of commercial feature films: among the many films made there in the following years were Sidney Lumet's *The Wiz* (1977), Bob Fosse's *All That Jazz* (1979), and Woody Allen's *Radio Days* (1987). The studio was designated a landmark in 1978 and in 1988 became the site of the MUSEUM OF THE MOVING IMAGE, while continuing its commercial operations. It has been a home to production for the television series *Sesame Street* (1969–) and *The Cosby Show* (1984–92) and the films *Glengarry Glen Ross* (1992), *Scent of a Woman* (1992), and *The Bourne Ultimatum* (2007). In the early twenty-first century the studio continued to attract filmmakers with six stages, recording studios, a lighting and grip company, and postproduction facilities.

Richard Koszarski, *The Astoria Studio and Its Fabulous Films* (New York: Dover, 1983)

Charles Musser

Kavookjian, Haik (*b* near Istanbul, 20 Aug 1875; *d* New York City, 26 April 1977). Businessman and activist. In 1896 he fled Turkey and after arriving in New York City founded the Bingham Photo Engraving Company (1915), amassing a fortune as it became the largest firm of its kind in the city. He became the head of the Photo Engravers Board of Trade, founded or led half a dozen Armenian cultural and educational organizations, and financed the construction of St. Vartan Armenian Cathedral (1968, 34th Street and Second Avenue), headquarters of the Eastern Diocese of the Armenian Apostolic Church of North America.

Harold Takooshian

kayaking and canoeing. New York City's many creeks, ponds, and rivers—not to mention its immense bay—was long navigated by American Indians in canoes and kayaks before the arrival of Dutch and English settlers. Easy for one person to launch and handle, fast and seaworthy, and at home in waters both shoal and deep, these small boats have remained important in the area. After the Civil War their admirers began to organize. The New-York Canoe Club, founded in 1871 at New Brighton, Staten Island, included both paddled and sailing canoes and ran races for many years. Sailing canoes (sometimes called "poor man's yachts") were popular and raced out of Staten Island, Gravesend Bay in Brooklyn, City Island in the Bronx, and several clubs on the shores of the Hudson River above 90th Street. New York City's sailing canoe racing launched the careers of two founders of American yachting and sailing: William Picard Stephens, a canoe designer, journalist, and historian; and Thomas Fleming Day, who edited the influential canoeing and boating magazine the *Rudder* from 1890 for almost 30 years. Reportedly the longest recorded canoe trip in history began at New York City in 1936 and ended 16 months later at Nome, Alaska. In 1927, 1931, and afterward, canoeists raced around Manhattan (in replicas of war canoes in 1967); beginning in 2006 this 27-mile (43.5-kilometer) marathon was called the Mayor's Cup Race and attracted as many as 94 competitors. In the 1990s and early 2000s kayaking and canoeing reached new popularity in the city on the 160 miles (258 kilometers) of urban waterways known as the New York City Water Trail. More than two dozen launching ramps were built and maintained by the Department of Parks and Recreation, which also established safety rules for kayakers and canoeists. Several organizations loan out sea kayaks and canoes. Among them is the Gowanus Dredgers Canoe Club in Brooklyn, which was awarded the Municipal Arts Society Certificate of Merit in 2006 for its efforts to reclaim the Gowanus Canal. Another is the Downtown Boathouse, which, with one clubhouse in Tribeca and two others in the city, claimed 30,000 trips in 2004. Other kayaking clubs are located on the Harlem River at Inwood.

William Picard Stephens, *Traditions and Memories of American Yachting* (Brooklin, Maine: WoodenBoat, 1989); John Rousmaniere, "The Inevitability of Skipper Day," *WoodenBoat,* May/June 2006

John Rousmaniere

Kazan, Abraham E(li) (*b* Russia, 1889; *d* New York City, 21 Dec 1971). Real estate developer. He moved to New York City from Russia and initially operated the credit union for the Amalgamated Clothing Workers of America. His first development, the Amalgamated Houses near Van Cortlandt Park in the Bronx, was financed with a long-term mortgage from the Metropolitan Life Insurance Company, municipal property tax abatements under a new state limited-dividend housing law, and additional funds from the *Jewish Daily Forward* and the Amalgamated Bank (owned by the Amalgamated Clothing Workers of America). The houses opened in 1927, and Kazan became president of the Amalgamated Housing Corporation. In 1951 he formed the nonprofit United Housing Foundation, which during the 1960s used vacant land to build Rochdale Village in Queens and Co-op City, a housing development of 15,372 units on a site of 300 acres (120 hectares) in the northeastern Bronx. Kazan led efforts to build limited-equity cooperative housing and became one of the city's foremost developers of low- and middle-income housing, producing more than 33,000 apartment units in six decades.

Kenneth G. Wray, "Abraham E. Kazan: The Story of the Amalgamated Houses and the United Housing Foundation" (thesis, Columbia University, 1991)

Marc A. Weiss

Kazan [Kazanjioglou], **Elia** (*b* Constantinople [now Istanbul], 7 Sept 1909; *d* New York City, 28 Sept 2003). Director, actor, and teacher. With his family he moved to New York City in 1913 and lived briefly on West 136th Street. After earning an AB from Williams College (1930) and attending the Yale School of Drama (1930–32) he returned to the city and joined the Group Theatre (1931–41), with which he acted in Clifford Odets's *Waiting for Lefty* and directed Robert Ardrey's *Casey Jones* and *Thunder Rock*. He also worked with several groups associated with the political left, including the Theatre of Action, the Federal Theatre Project, the League of Workers Theatre, and the Theatre Union. During the 1940s he first achieved critical acclaim on Broadway with Thornton Wilder's *The Skin of Our Teeth* (1942, Plymouth Theatre) and Arthur Miller's *All My Sons* (1947, Coronet Theatre) and *Death of a Salesman* (1949, Morosco Theatre). His most successful collaborations were with Tennessee Williams: *A Streetcar Named Desire* (1947, Barrymore Theater), *Camino Real* (1953, Martin Beck Theatre), *Cat on a Hot Tin Roof* (1955, Morosco Theatre), and *Sweet Bird of Youth* (1959, Martin Beck Theatre). In 1945 he directed his first motion picture, *A Tree Grows in Brooklyn*. With Cheryl Crawford and Robert Lewis he formed the Actors Studio in 1947 and engaged several of its graduates in his productions, including Marlon Brando, James Dean, Julie Harris, and Eli Wallach. He directed several films in the following years that were well received: *A Streetcar Named Desire* (1951), *On the Waterfront* (1954), *East of Eden* (1955), and *Splendor in the Grass* (1961). In 1952 he testified about his association with the Communist Party before the House Un-American Activities Committee and in his own defense took out a full-page advertisement in the *New York Times* on 12 April. With Robert Whitehead he led the Repertory Theater of Lincoln Center from 1962 to 1965, and he directed its production of Miller's *After the Fall* (1962). Kazan gradually became disenchanted with both plays and films and increasingly devoted himself to writing novels, which include *The Arrangement* (1967) and *Beyond the Aegean* (1994). In 1999 he received an Academy Award for lifetime achievement.

Kazin, Alfred (*b* Brooklyn, 5 June 1915; *d* Manhattan, 5 June 1998). Literary critic. He grew up in Brownsville and as an undergraduate at City College (graduated 1935) wrote book reviews for the *New York Times* and the *New York Herald Tribune*; he also worked closely with Malcolm Cowley at the *New Republic* and earned an MA from Columbia University (1938). In 1935 he began work on his book *On Native Grounds: An Interpretation of Modern American Prose Literature* (1942), for which he conducted research at the New York Public Library and which brought him recognition as an authority on American literature and culture. He also wrote for the *Partisan Review*, held editorial positions at *Fortune* and the *American Scholar*, and taught at New York University, Hunter College, and the City University of New York. At a time when most critics looked to Europe for artistic standards, Kazin proclaimed himself a socially and politically aware "literary radical" who dealt with American culture on its own terms and wrote from his own experiences. The city was often the subject of his writings. *A Walker in the City* (1951), written in a studio on Pineapple Street in Brooklyn Heights, describes his childhood in Brooklyn. *Starting Out in the Thirties* (1965) is an account of his work as a young man, including his years under Cowley. *New York Jew* (1978) addresses the fascination and fear that the city holds for him. In 1996 he was presented with the inaugural Truman Capote Lifetime Achievement Award for excellence in literary criticism.

Richard Cook, *Alfred Kazin: A Biography* (New Haven: Yale University Press, 2007)

Naomi Wax

Keens Chophouse. Restaurant at 72 West 36th Street in Manhattan. Originally part of the select actors' club the Lambs, it became an independent establishment in 1885, catering to the actors, playwrights, and producers who worked at the theaters around Herald Square. Regular patrons joined the Keens Chophouse Pipe Club, which for a lifetime fee of $5 provided diners with their own long-stemmed clay pipes. Catalogued and stored in racks above the tables, the pipes were always at the ready for anyone who called for his "clay" after dinner. Over the years the club grew to include more than 50,000 members, including Babe Ruth, Will Rogers, Enrico Caruso, and Douglas MacArthur. Keens remained an all-male preserve until 1901, when the actress Lillie Langtry sued the restaurant. She won, and the Langtry Room was named in her honor. In the early twenty-first century Keens is the only remaining structure from the old Herald Square theater district and continues to operate as a restaurant, pub, and bar serving its famous mutton chops.

Kenneth T. Jackson

Keens Chophouse, 1917

Keller, Helen (Adams) (*b* Tuscumbia, Ala., 27 June 1880; *d* Westport, Conn., 1 June 1968). Writer, lecturer, and philanthropist. At the age of 19 months she lost her hearing and sight as a result of an unexplained illness. Accompanied by her lifelong "teacher" Anne Sullivan, Keller traveled to New York City in 1894 to improve her speech at the Wright–Humason School on 76th Street and became acquainted with many members of fashionable society, including John Burroughs and Mark Twain. While attending Radcliffe College she was a frequent visitor to the city; she moved in 1917 to a house at 7111 112th Street in Forest Hills in Queens. During the following years she made several appearances with Sullivan in vaudeville acts, including one at the Palace Theatre in 1920. In 1938 she left the city to live in suburban Westport, Connecticut. Keller's published writings include two autobiographical works, *The Story of My Life* (1901) and *Midstream* (1928), and *My Religion* (1926), about the teachings of Emanuel Swedenborg.

Elizabeth J. Kramer

Kelley, Florence (*b* Philadelphia, 12 Sept 1859; *d* New York City, 17 Feb 1932). Reformer. A member of an elite family from Philadelphia and the daughter of a powerful Republican congressman, she graduated from Cornell University in 1882 and became a prominent Progressive reformer. She moved to New York City in 1886. After a stint in Chicago, Kelley returned to New York City in 1899 as the head of the National Consumers' League, a position she held until her death. Through this organization, she fought at the state and federal levels for woman suffrage, a minimum wage for women, and other social legislation. Kelley lived in the Henry Street Settlement on the Lower East Side of Manhattan. In addition to her work with the National Consumers' League, Kelley helped found the New York Child Labor Committee and the National Association for the Advancement of Colored People (NAACP) in 1909.

Josephine Goldmark, *Impatient Crusader: Florence Kelley's Life Story* (Urbana: University of Illinois Press, 1953; repr. New York: Greenwood, 1976); Kathryn Kish Sklar, *Florence Kelley and the Nation's Work: The Rise of Women's Political Culture, 1830–1900* (New Haven: Yale University Press, 1995)

Kathryn Kish Sklar

Kellor, Frances (Alice) (*b* Columbus, Ohio, 20 Oct 1873; *d* New York City, 4 Jan 1952). Social scientist and reformer. She earned a law degree from Cornell University in 1897, studied sociology at the University of Chicago, and moved to New York City in 1905. In 1908 she was appointed to the New York State Commission on Immigration. She was a founder of the National Urban League and in 1910 became the first woman to lead the New York Bureau of Industries and Immigration. In her published writings Kellor analyzed female workers, black Americans, crime, unemployment, and immigration.

John Recchiuti

Kellum, John (*b* Hempstead, N.Y., 27 Aug 1809; *d* Hempstead, 24 July 1871). Architect. He began his career as a carpenter and became an architect several years after settling in Brooklyn in 1841. Initially he worked with Gamaliel King, who was active in local business and political circles and designed the Brooklyn City Hall (1846–51, 209 Joralemon Street; now Borough Hall), the Kings County Courthouse (1865, demolished), commercial buildings in Brooklyn and Manhattan including Kings County Savings Bank (1868, 135 Broadway), and such churches as St. Paul's (1838, Court and Congress streets, Brooklyn), the Twelfth Street Reformed Church (1869, Brooklyn), and the Sullivan Street Methodist Church (1860, West Fourth Street, Manhattan). From 1850 the firm of King and Kellum had a varied practice. It received a commission for the Friends Meeting House (1859, 28 Gramercy Park South; later Brotherhood Synagogue) but was best known for its commercial cast-iron architecture, beginning with the Cary Building (1857, Chambers and Church streets). Kellum's independent career began in 1859 with a commission from A. T. Stewart for a new cast-iron department store (1859–62, 1867–68, demolished), which became nationally renowned. Other designs for Stewart, his most important client, included a mansion (1864–69, demolished), the innovative cast-iron Working Women's Hotel (1869–78, later the Park Avenue Hotel; demolished), and the suburb of Garden City, Long Island (1869–71). Among his commercial buildings were the Mutual Life Insurance Company (1863–65, demolished), Steinway Pianos (1863–64, demolished), the New York Stock Exchange (1864–65, demolished), the New York Herald (1865–67, demolished), Tiffany's (1869, 15th Street and Union Square East; later the Amalgamated Bank), McCreery's Store (1869, Broadway and 11th Street; converted into apartments), lofts with cast-iron facades in SoHo, and cast-iron ferry terminals on the East River. His only large public commission was the New York County, or "Tweed," Courthouse (1861–71, 52 Chambers Street).

Deborah S. Gardner, "The Architecture of Commercial Capitalism: John Kellum and the Development of New York, 1840–1875" (diss., Columbia University, 1979)

Deborah S. Gardner

Kelly, John ["Honest John"] (*b* New York City, *ca* 1822; *d* New York City, 1886). Political boss. Self-taught and ambitious, he became an alderman in 1852. In 1854 he was elected to the U.S. House of Representatives, where he vigorously attacked the Know-Nothings. In 1858 he became sheriff of New York County. He left Tammany Hall in 1868 to protest the Tweed Ring but returned in 1871 as a reformer, and between 1872 and 1886 he became the organization's first Irish Catholic boss. He quashed other Democratic factions in the city and established party discipline by tightly controlling patronage. In 1876 he was elected comptroller of New York City. He supported and then opposed Samuel J. Tilden and tried to block Grover Cleveland's presidential nomination. During his tenure Kelly transformed Tammany Hall from a ring into a political machine.

See also Tammany Hall.

Frank Vos

Kennedy, Joseph P(atrick), Sr. (*b* Boston, 6 Sept 1888; *d* Hyannis, Mass., 18 Nov 1969). Financier, father of John F. Kennedy and Robert F. Kennedy. After a successful career as a financier and as a film producer in Hollywood, he moved with his family to 252nd Street and Independence Avenue in Riverdale in 1927; in the following year he bought a mansion at 294 Pondfield Road in Bronxville, New York, and he also lived briefly in the 1920s at the Gramercy Park Hotel, 2 Lexington Avenue. He campaigned actively for Franklin D. Roosevelt in the presidential campaign of 1932, and from 1934 to 1935 he was the head of the Securities and Exchange Commission, which had been recently formed to regulate the securities markets. In 1941 he sold his house in suburban Bronxville and for the rest of his life lived in Washington, D.C., and Hyannisport, Massachusetts. The firm of Joseph P. Kennedy Enterprises managed the Kennedy family fortune at 100 East 42nd Street in Manhattan.

Doris Kearns Goodwin, *The Fitzgeralds and the Kennedys* (New York: Simon and Schuster, 1987)

Edward T. O'Donnell

Kennedy, Robert F(rancis) (*b* Brookline, Mass., 20 Nov 1925; *d* Los Angeles, 6 June 1968). U.S. attorney general, senator, and presidential candidate. The third son of Joseph Kennedy, Sr., he lived from 1927 to 1929 at 5040 Independence Avenue in the Riverdale section of the Bronx. In 1961 he was named attorney general of the United States by his brother, President John F. Kennedy. He resigned from office in 1964, moved to an apartment at United Nations Plaza in Manhattan, and in November was elected to the U.S. Senate from New York. As a senator he supported liberal social programs and institutions, among them the Bedford Stuyvesant Restoration Corporation, which sought to revitalize a poor neighborhood by achieving cooperation between business and community leaders. In March 1968 he entered the race for the

Democratic presidential nomination but was assassinated after winning the primary election. The ROBERT F. KENNEDY MEMORIAL BRIDGE was named for him in 2008.

Arthur Schlesinger, Jr., *Robert F. Kennedy and His Times* (Boston: Houghton Mifflin, 1978)

Edward T. O'Donnell

Kennedy Airport. See JFK INTERNATIONAL AIRPORT.

Kensett, John Frederick (*b* Cheshire, Conn., 22 March 1816; *d* New York City, 14 Dec 1872). Painter. In the 1820s and 1830s he trained and worked as an engraver in New Haven, Connecticut; New York City; and Albany, New York. After studying art in Europe from 1840 he returned in 1847 to New York City, where he was elected to the National Academy of Design (1849), the Century Association (1849), the Sketch Club (1854), and the Union League Club (1863). His landscapes and paintings of coastal scenes from these years employ a "luminist" style characterized by a sensitive rendering of light and atmosphere, and associate him with the second generation of the Hudson River School. His dramatic series of paintings from 1872 are often referred to as the "Last Summer's Work." Kensett was a president of the Artists' Fund Society, a member of the National Art Commission (1859), chairman of the Metropolitan Fair Art Committee (1864), and a founding member and trustee of the Metropolitan Museum of Art (1870).

John K. Howat, John Paul Driscoll, et al., *John Frederick Kensett: An American Master* (New York: Worcester Art Museum/W. W. Norton, 1985)

Donna Ann Grossman

Kensington. Neighborhood in west central Brooklyn bounded to the north by Caton Avenue, to the east by Coney Island Avenue, to the south by Avenue H, and to the west by McDonald Avenue; it is bisected by Ocean Parkway. Part of the original Dutch Town of Flatbush and a section of Parkville, it was settled in 1737 and colonized by Dutch farmers. It remained rural until 1850 when the Coney Island Plank Road opened. Development accelerated after Ocean Parkway was completed in 1876. The middle section of Parkville became Kensington after the turn of the twentieth century. Much of the housing stock was built in the 1920s and consists of detached single-family homes, brick and brownstone row houses, and six-story apartment buildings. In the 1980s Kensington and its environs attracted immigrants from China, the former Soviet Union, Bangladesh, Poland, Indonesia, Turkey, Mexico, Ireland, Haiti, Guyana, the Dominican Republic, and Jamaica. Orthodox Jews moved over from crowded Borough Park, and a Muslim community grew near Coney Island and Foster avenues. A commercial district lies along Church Avenue where the semiannual Church Avenue Fair is held, with additional retail outlets on Ditmas, 18th, and McDonald avenues. Kensington Stables (1930) remains the only stable for horseback riding in Prospect Park. In 2000 the population was more than 45,000; the neighborhood remains middle class and racially integrated.

Kensington, 2009

Nanette Rainone, ed., *The Brooklyn Neighborhood Book* (Brooklyn, N.Y.: Fund for the Borough of Brooklyn, 1985)

John J. Gallagher, John Manbeck

Kent, James (*b* Putnam County, N.Y., 31 July 1763; *d* New York City, 12 Dec 1847). Jurist. After being educated at Yale College he worked as a lawyer. A Federalist, he was appointed recorder of New York City in 1797 and presided over the court of general sessions; he became a justice on the state supreme court in 1798, its chief justice in 1804, and chancellor of the Court of Chancery in 1814. In these positions Kent wrote opinions that helped to shape common law and equity law nationwide. After retiring in 1823 he lived in Manhattan and wrote *Commentaries on American Law* (1826–30), which earned him the nickname the American Blackstone.

John T. Horton, *James Kent: A Study in Conservatism* (New York: D. Appleton–Century, 1939)

See also LAWYERS.

James D. Folts

Kent, Rockwell (*b* Tarrytown, N.Y., 21 June 1882; *d* Plattsburgh, N.Y., 13 March 1971). Painter, printmaker, and political activist. He studied architecture at Columbia University and realist painting under Robert Henri and Kenneth Hayes Miller. An opponent of the National Academy of Design, he championed progressive artists and in 1911 organized an independent exhibition at the Society of Beaux-Arts Architects in New York City. He drew inspiration from the wilderness of Newfoundland, Greenland, and Alaska to develop an austere, symbolic style of landscape painting. He also illustrated an edition of Shakespeare and completed a mural, *The Power of Electricity,* for the World's Fair of 1939–40. His ties to the Communist Party led to the revocation of his passport by the State Department, which he contested; the decision was ultimately overturned by the U.S. Supreme Court. In 1967 he received the Lenin Peace Prize. Kent donated his collection of drawings to Columbia University.

David Traxel, *An American Saga: The Life and Times of Rockwell Kent* (New York: Harper and Row, 1980); Fridolf Johnson, ed., *Rockwell Kent: An Anthology of His Works* (New York: Alfred A. Knopf, 1982)

Judith Zilczer

Kerensky, Alexander (Feodorovich) (*b* Simbirsk [now Ulyanovsk], Russia, 4 May 1881; *d* New York City, 11 June 1970). Revolutionary leader. He was prime minister of the Russian Provisional Government in 1917 before the Bolshevik takeover. Forced into exile, he lived in western Europe until 1940, when he immigrated to the United States and settled in New York City. For the last three decades of his life he lectured extensively. From his apartment on Riverside Drive, Kerensky wrote profusely on his revolutionary experiences; his published writings include *Russia and History's Turning Point* (1965) and *The Kerensky Memoirs* (1966).

Richard Abraham, *Alexander Kerensky: The First Love of the Revolution* (New York: Columbia University Press, 1987)

Paul Robert Magocsi

Kerik, Bernard B. (*b* Newark, N.J., 4 Sept 1955). Police commissioner. He served between 21 August 2000 and 31 December 2001 under Mayor Rudolph W. Giuliani and directed the New York Police Department during the terrorist attacks of 11 September 2001; before that he was corrections commissioner. President George W. Bush nominated Kerik to be U.S. secretary of homeland security on 3 December 2004; a week later Kerik withdrew his nomination when it was revealed he employed an undocumented housekeeper. Subsequently he encountered a slew of legal problems in 2006 and 2007, including a guilty plea to two ethics violations that occurred during his New York City government employment, resulting in a large fine. In 2010 he pled guilty to eight felony charges and was sentenced by a federal court judge to four years in prison.

Andrew J. Sparberg

Kern, Jerome (David) (*b* New York City, 27 Jan 1885; *d* New York City, 11 Nov 1945). Composer. He lived at 411 East 56th Street until his family moved to Newark, New Jersey, in 1897. He received a thorough education in music at the New York College of Music and in Germany. After working on Broadway as a song plugger and rehearsal pianist he moved to London to adapt English musicals for performance on Broadway. His first hit song was "How'd You Like to Spoon with Me?" (1905). He returned to New York City and lived in an apartment at 107 West 68th Street in 1907, then achieved his first success on the stage with *The Red Petticoat*

(1911). After a brief move farther uptown in 1912 he occupied 226 West 70th Street, his last residence in New York City; he lived there until 1915, when he moved to suburban Bronxville, New York. His most outstanding and influential score was that for *Show Boat* (1927), a musical with book and lyrics by Oscar Hammerstein II based on a novel written by Edna Ferber in 1926. Its songs, including "Ol' Man River," "Can't Help Loving Dat Man of Mine," "Why Do I Love You?," and "Bill," combined European operetta with an American vernacular that included folk ballad, syncopated dance, and the music of Tin Pan Alley. *Show Boat* greatly influenced younger composers on Broadway, including George Gershwin, Richard Rodgers, and Cole Porter, who admired its distinctively American plot and integration of narrative and characterization. Kern wrote more than 70 scores for screen and stage, some in collaboration with Hammerstein, Guy Bolton, and P. G. Wodehouse, and more than 900 songs, including "Smoke Gets in Your Eyes" (from his musical *Roberta,* 1933, made into a film in 1935), "They Didn't Believe Me" (1914), "Look for the Silver Lining" (1920), "The Song Is You" (1932), and "All the Things You Are" (1940). At least two of his songs were inspired by places in New York City: "Nestin' Time in Flatbush" (1917) and "Bojangles of Harlem" (1936).

Gerald Martin Bordman, *Jerome Kern: His Life and Music* (New York: Oxford University Press, 1980)

Nicholas E. Tawa

Kerouac, Jack [Jean-Louis] (*b* Lowell, Mass., 12 March 1922; *d* St. Petersburg, Fla., 21 Oct 1969). Novelist. He moved to New York City at age 17 and spent a year at the Horace Mann School before attending Columbia University on a football scholarship. In 1944 he met William Burroughs and Allen Ginsberg, then a student at Columbia; the three formed the nucleus of the group of writers that became known as the Beats. Kerouac described his life in New York City in *The Town and the City* (1950), *Lonesome Traveler* (1960), and *Vanity of Duluoz* (1969). In April 1951 he wrote a draft of his best-known novel, *On the Road* (published 1957), in an apartment at 454 West 20th Street in Manhattan. Kerouac lived at intervals from 1952 to 1963 at 94-21 134th Street in Queens and in 1953 at 501 East 11th Street in Manhattan.

Ann Charters, *Kerouac: A Biography* (San Francisco: Straight Arrow, 1973); Tom Clark, *Jack Kerouac: A Biography* (New York: Harcourt Brace Jovanovich, 1984)

Ann Charters

Keteltas affair. New York City political scandal of 1796 that facilitated the rise to power of the Jeffersonian Democratic Republicans. The controversy arose when the Federalist alderman Gabriel Furman ordered that two allegedly insolent ferrymen should be whipped and jailed without the right to counsel or the right to testify in their own defense; the Republican attorney William Keteltas then demanded that the state assembly remove Furman from office. When the assembly later absolved Furman, Keteltas condemned it for "flagrant abuse of rights" and was jailed for contempt. Along with many poor craftsmen and laborers, Jeffersonians berated the Federalists for the incident, which they saw as evidence of Federalist disregard for the middle and poorer classes.

Alfred F. Young, *The Democratic–Republicans of New York: The Origins, 1763–1797* (Chapel Hill: University of North Carolina Press, 1967)

Howard Rock

Kew Gardens. Neighborhood in central Queens, bounded to the north by the Interborough Parkway and Queens Boulevard, to the east by Kew Gardens Road, to the south by Myrtle Avenue, and to the west by Forest Park. Much of the area was acquired in 1868 by Albon P. Man, who developed Richmond Hill to the south, chiefly along Jamaica Avenue, while leaving undeveloped the hilly land to the north. Maple Grove Cemetery on Kew Gardens Road opened in 1875. A station for mourners opened in October, and trains stopped there from mid-November. The station was named Hopedale, after Hopedale Hall, a hotel at what later became Queens Boulevard and Union Turnpike. In the 1890s the executors of Man's estate laid out the Richmond Hill Golf Course on the hilly terrain south of the railroad. This remained in use until it was bisected in 1908 by the main line of the Long Island Rail Road, which had been moved 600 feet (180 meters) to the south to eliminate a curve. The golf course was then abandoned and a new station was built in 1909 on Lefferts Boulevard on the site of spring-fed Crystal Lake. Man's heirs Alrick Man and Albon Man, Jr., decided to lay out a new community and called it at first Kew and then Kew Gardens after the well-known botanical gardens in England. The architects of the development favored English and neo-Tudor styles, which predominated in many sections into the twenty-first century. In 1910 the property was sold piecemeal by the estate, and during the next few years streets were extended, land graded, and water and sewer pipes installed. The first apartment building was the Kew Bolmer at 80-45 Kew Gardens Road, erected in 1915; a clubhouse followed in 1916 and a private school in 1918. Where Lefferts Boulevard crosses over the railroad, it was lined with shops in the manner of the Ponte Veccio in Florence. In 1921 the Homestead Hotel at the railroad station opened for resident guests, who paid $40 a week for a room and bath with meals and $85 a week for two rooms and bath with meals (later an assisted living residence). The Kew Gardens Inn opened in 1920 at Queens Boulevard and Kew Gardens Road; it became a hospital in 1940 and was demolished in 1982. Elegant one-family houses were built in the 1920s, as were apartment buildings such as Colonial Hall (1921) and Kew Hall (1922) that numbered more than 20 by 1936. Several Broadway and film stars lived in Kew Gardens during the 1920s.

In July 1933 Grand Central Parkway opened from Kew Gardens to the edge of Nassau County; this road was extended in 1935 as the Interborough (now Jackie Robinson) Parkway to Pennsylvania Avenue in East New York. Because the parkways used part of the Union

Passengers boarding a morning train at the Kew Gardens Station of the Long Island Railroad, ca *1920s*

Turnpike roadbed, no houses were sacrificed. The greatest change was wrought by the opening of the Independent subway along Queens Boulevard to Union Turnpike on 31 December 1936; four months later the subway was extended to Jamaica. Residents could then reach Manhattan and Brooklyn 24 hours a day for five cents. The immediate effect was to stimulate the construction of larger apartment buildings like Kent Manor and high-rise buildings along Queens Boulevard, and the last vacant land disappeared. In 1941 Queens Borough Hall opened on Queens Boulevard; Frederick MacMonnies's statue *Civic Virtue,* derided as "Fat Boy" by Mayor Fiorello H. La Guardia, was moved from City Hall Park to Queens Boulevard at that time. The Queens Criminal Courthouse opened in 1961. A large community of Jewish refugees from Germany took shape during World War II. In 1964 the neighborhood received a measure of unwanted notoriety when a bar manager named Kitty Genovese was murdered before 38 witnesses, none of whom came to her aid, though contrary to popular belief several did contact the police. The incident focused attention on the growing crime problem in New York City and the increasing insularity and apathy of its residents. The neighborhood attracted new immigrants after 1965 from China, Afghanistan, Israel, the Soviet Union, India, Colombia, and Korea; about 2500 Iranian Jews arrived after the Iranian revolution of 1979. In the 1990s and early twenty-first century the neighborhood lost several historic houses to demolition or unsympathetic alteration, prompting the Kew Gardens Civic Association to seek designation as a historic district.

Vincent Seyfried

Key Food. Cooperative chain of supermarkets formed in 1937 by a group of independent grocers in Brooklyn who hoped that by joining forces they would lower their expenses and compete with growing national chains like the Great Atlantic and Pacific Tea Company (A&P). The original outlet was at Second Avenue and 45th Street in Sunset Park. By 2008 Key Food operated nearly 160 stores in the New York City metropolitan area, most in the five boroughs. The warehouse is in the Brooklyn Terminal Market at Avenue D and East 89th Street in East Flatbush, and the corporate headquarters is located in Staten Island.

Stephen Weinstein

KeySpan Energy Corporation. Energy company, formerly Brooklyn Union Gas Company. It renamed itself after deregulation of the natural gas industry in the 1990s. By 2007 the corporation had merged with other companies to become New York State's largest electricity provider, the nation's fifth-largest supplier of natural gas, and the largest gas utility operator in the Northeast, serving 2.6 million customers in New York, Massachusetts, and New Hampshire. In August 2007 National Grid, a utilities company based in the United Kingdom, finalized the $11.8 billion debt-takeover and cash acquisition of KeySpan, whose name will gradually be replaced with that of National Grid.

Cathy Alexander

Kheel, Theodore W. (*b* Brooklyn, 9 May 1914). Lawyer and political appointee under numerous New York City mayors and U.S. presidents. He was most well known as a labor mediator and negotiator. After completing an undergraduate law program at Cornell University in 1937, he served as an attorney on the National Labor Relations Board, as the executive director of the National War Labor Board, and as the head of the Labor Relations Division in New York City early in his career. Kheel established himself as a preeminent labor negotiator with his role in ending the East Coast Longshoremen's Strike of 1962, the New York City newspaper strikes of 1961–63, and nationwide railroad strikes in 1964. The *New York Times* labeled him the most influential peacemaker in New York City during the second half of the twentieth century. His clients included the National Football League, the *New York Times,* and the AFL–CIO. As a public advocate, Kheel repeatedly backed improvements of New York City's public transportation while calling for limitations on commuter automobile traffic and highway building.

David White

Kidd, Captain [William] (*b* Greenock, Scotland, *ca* 1645; *d* London, 23 May 1701). Pirate and privateer. He went to sea early in life. When war broke out between France and England in 1688, he received from the governor of the English colony of Nevis a commission as a privateer, empowered to harass and plunder enemy shipping in times of war. He then attacked and plundered French ships and colonies until the members of his crew abandoned him, taking with them his ship and treasure (most were pirates who preferred piracy to war). He acquired another ship and during an unsuccessful pursuit of his former crew landed in New York City in time to aid the forces sent to end Leisler's Rebellion. His alliance with the new government worked to his advantage, and he profited from the friendship of such rich and powerful residents of the city as Robert Livingston. In 1691 he married the wealthy widow Sarah Bradley Cox Oort, with whom he moved to what is now 119–21 Pearl Street and bought a pew in Trinity Church. A summer home, called Saw Kill, stood near the East River at what is now 74th Street.

In 1695 Kidd embarked on a trading voyage to London in the hope of obtaining a royal privateering commission. When he left London in the following year he had a commission to hunt pirates, along with financial backing from the leaders of the Whig government, an alliance that he owed to the intervention of Livingston and the newly appointed governor for New York and Massachusetts, Richard Coote, Earl of Bellomont. He sailed to New York City, enlisted more men for a crew, and set out for the Indian Ocean. But instead of hunting pirates he turned pirate himself, capturing five ships off the coast of India before heading for Madagascar. By the time he sailed for home, the East India Company had set the English government against him, and when he met with Coote in Boston he was arrested and sent to England. His well-publicized and highly political trial ended in his conviction and hanging. Only a small part of Kidd's reputedly large treasure was ever recovered by authorities, and a popular belief that the rest remains buried has inspired searches ranging from the Indian Ocean to New York City.

Harold T. Wilkins, *Captain Kidd and His Skeleton Island: The Discovery of a Strange Secret* (London: Cassell, 1935); Dunbar M. Hinrichs, *The Fateful Voyage of Captain Kidd* (New York: Bookman, 1955); Robert C. Ritchie, *Captain Kidd and the War against the Pirates* (Cambridge, Mass.: Harvard University Press, 1986)

Robert C. Ritchie

Kilgallen, Dorothy (Mae) (*b* Chicago, 3 July 1913; *d* New York City, 8 Nov 1965). Journalist and television personality. She wrote for the *New York Evening Journal* (later the *Journal-American*) from 1931 until her death. She flew on and reported from the first around-the-world journey using commercial airliners (1936). Starting in 1938 she wrote the newspaper's syndicated column "The Voice of Broadway." Kilgallen covered many notable events: the trials of Bruno Hauptmann, Sam Shepard, and Jack Ruby; Nikita Khrushchev's U.S. tour; and the coronation of Queen Elizabeth II. She also did radio and in 1950 appeared as a panelist during the premiere telecast of *What's My Line?*—a game show on which panelists guessed contestants' occupations. For the rest of her life she was a regular on the weekly program, which had almost 10 million viewers in 1952.

Lee Israel, *Kilgallen* (New York: Delacorte Press, 1979)

Cathy Alexander

Kill van Kull. Tidal strait roughly 3 miles (5 kilometers) long and 1000 feet (300 meters) wide that separates Staten Island and Bayonne, New Jersey, connecting Upper New York Bay with Newark Bay. It is traversed by the Bayonne Bridge, and at its western end is Shooters Island. The Kill van Kull is one of the busiest waterways in New York Harbor, used by oil tankers and container ships bound for Port Newark and Port Elizabeth in New Jersey.

Gerard R. Wolfe

Kimball, Francis (*b* Kennebunk, Maine, 24 Sept 1845; *d* New York City, 20 Dec 1919). Architect. Known as a theater designer, he moved to New York City in 1879 to refurbish the Madison Square Theatre and later built the Casino Theatre at Broadway and 39th Street (1882). In 1890 he designed the Montauk Club in Brooklyn in a Venetian neo-Gothic style and after working with the English architect William Burges was inspired to use a French neo-Gothic style for the Rhinelander Mansion on Madison Avenue (1899). With George Thompson he built a tower for the Manhattan Life Insurance Building at 60–80 Broadway (1892), which was the first skyscraper in the city with a frame made entirely of steel. Kimball also designed the tower of the United States Trust Company (1907).

Edward A. Eigen

King, Moses (*b* London, 1853; *d* New York City, 13 June 1909). Publisher. He moved to New York City in 1881 and established the Moses King publishing house at 34 West 33rd Street, which he ran until his death. His publishing company was known for its guidebooks including *King's Handbook of New York City* (1893), its accompanying *King's Photographic Views of New York* (1895), and *Notable New Yorkers.* He died in his home at 2 West 88th Street.

Jessica Montesano

King, Rufus (*b* Scarborough, Maine, 24 March 1755; *d* New York City, 29 April 1827). Lawyer, senator, and diplomat. He represented Massachusetts at the Constitutional Convention and earned a reputation as a strong nationalist and gifted orator. After moving to New York City he was appointed to the first U.S. Senate; as minister to Great Britain (1796–1803) he intervened to prevent Irish political exiles from receiving asylum in the United States. In 1805 he purchased on Jamaica Avenue in Queens land and a house (see KING MANOR). He later served again in the Senate (1813–25) and again as minister to Britain (1825–26); he was also the Federalist candidate for the vice presidency in 1804 and 1808 and an unofficial candidate for the presidency in 1816, and he sought the governorship of New York in 1816. King's role in the politics of New York City was circumscribed by hostility from Irish voters who resented his earlier role in suppressing Irish immigration. Although he opposed the declaration of war in 1812, his patriotic response in raising money for the city's defense won him respect as a Federalist elder statesman long after his party ceased to be a political force. King was an early member of the New-York Historical Society, a warden of Trinity Church, a trustee of Columbia College, the first president of the Queens County Society for the Promotion of Agriculture and Domestic Manufactures, and an instrumental supporter of Grace Church in Jamaica, where he is buried in the churchyard. King Street in Manhattan was named for him in 1807. His eldest son, John A. King, was governor of New York (1857–59), and a second son, Charles, was the editor of the *New-York American* (1823–45) and president of Columbia College (1849–64).

Rufus King

Robert Ernst, *Rufus King: American Federalist* (Chapel Hill: University of North Carolina Press, 1968)

Mariam Touba

King Manor. Historic house at 153rd Street and Jamaica Avenue in King Park in Jamaica, Queens, built as a farmhouse in a Dutch style between 1733 and 1755. It was bought in 1805 by Rufus King, a signer of the U.S. Constitution, who oversaw the remodeling and expansion of the house. Among the additions were a three-story structure with a gambrel roof and a Greek Revival portico. The house remained with King's heirs until 1896, was deeded to the city in 1898, and later became a museum with many furnished period rooms. After an extensive exterior and interior renovation that restored the manor to its early-nineteenth-century appearance, the museum reopened to the public in 1994.

Jonathan Kuhn

King Manor, 2009

King Model Houses. See STRIVERS' ROW.

Kingsborough Community College. Junior college of the City University of New York, opened in 1963 at 2001 Oriental Boulevard in Brooklyn, on a campus of 67 acres (27 hectares) at the eastern tip of Coney Island. It offers a highly regarded program in marine and fisheries technology, as well as programs in environmental health and science and in print journalism and broadcast technology. In the early twenty-first century Kingsborough served approximately 30,000 students per year.

Marc Ferris

Kingsbridge. Neighborhood in the northwestern Bronx, bounded to the north by Mosholu, to the east by Broadway, to the south by Marble Hill, and to the west by the hills of Spuyten Duyvil. It is named for the King's Bridge, the first bridge connecting Manhattan with the mainland, built by Frederick Philipse in 1693 over Spuyten Duyvil Creek at what is now Kingsbridge Avenue and 230th Street. A strategic area and the site of frequent battles during the American Revolution, it

Kingsbridge, ca *1900*

was largely farmland until the 1860s, when the Johnson Iron Foundry along the banks of Spuyten Duyvil Creek made munitions for the Union army. Increasing migration into the area was stimulated by the construction of the Seventh Avenue subway line by Interborough Rapid Transit in 1908. In 1913 the Church of the Mediator (Episcopal) was consecrated on Kingsbridge Avenue at 231st Street; St. John's Church (Catholic) was built next door to the south. In the early twenty-first century residents of the blocks immediately surrounding Broadway were mostly Dominican, yet the rest of the neighborhood was of largely mixed ethnicity; 231st Street and Broadway was the center of the commercial district, which included restaurants and a movie theater. The housing stock consists of one-family houses and interspersed five- and six-story apartment buildings dating from the 1920s, as well as a few high-rise apartment buildings from the 1950s and 1960s.

Lloyd Ultan

King's College. Original name of Columbia University.

Kings County. One of the five counties of New York City, coextensive with the borough of Brooklyn.

Kings County Hospital Center. Municipal hospital in Brooklyn, administered by the New York City Health and Hospitals Corporation. It began in 1831 as a one-room infirmary in the town of Flatbush that expanded in 1837. In 1929 Mayor James J. Walker approved funds to construct a new complex. Built in 1931, this complex covered an entire block along Clarkson Avenue between New York and Albany avenues. The institution continued to expand, establishing affiliates in Bedford–Stuyvesant and East New York. In 1956 the hospital formed an affiliation with the Downstate Medical Center (renamed the Health Science Center in 1986), a medical school of the State University of New York. The hospital encountered financial and other problems in the 1980s and 1990s, notably a controversy surrounding its treatment in 1991 of Yankel Rosenbaum, a victim of the riots in Crown Heights whose death was attributed to a stab wound that had gone unattended at the hospital. This incident and others led to a series of investigations and calls for the hospital to be privatized. In the early twenty-first century the hospital had more than 600 beds and was undergoing a $500 million rebuilding and modernization campaign — the largest in the history of the New York City Health and Hospitals Corporation.

James Bradley

King's Highway. See Boston Post Road.

Kingsland, Ambrose C(ornelius) (*b* New York City, 24 May 1804; *d* New York City, 13 Oct 1878). Mayor. In 1820 he opened a dry-goods store with his brother that soon expanded into international trade. The business flourished as an importer of sperm oil, and it also acquired and operated whaling vessels. Nominated for the mayoralty by the Whig Party in 1851, Kingsland defeated his Democratic opponent, Fernando Wood, because of divisions within Tammany Hall. The election was the first held under a new municipal charter forced on the city by a state legislature dominated by Whigs, which diminished the powers of the mayor and increased those of a bicameral city council. The limitations imposed by the charter helped to make Kingsland an ineffective mayor: during his tenure police officers were appointed by aldermen, nearly autonomous city departments were riddled with corruption, and the members of the city council, known as the Forty Thieves, ran the city for their own profit. His main achievement was his endorsement of the plan to build Central Park. He failed to be renominated after one two-year term, and he returned to his business, now called A. C. Kingsland and Sons, which expanded into trade with Great Britain, China, and the East Indies. Kingsland never again held elective office, but he remained active in the Whig Party during its final years, was a commissioner of the Croton Aqueduct, and served on the Chamber of Commerce.

Melvin G. Holli and Peter d'A. Jones, eds., *Biographical Dictionary of American Mayors, 1820–1980: Big City Mayors* (Westport, Conn.: Greenwood, 1981)

Rohit T. Aggarwala

Kingsland House. Historic house at 14335 37th Avenue in Flushing, Queens. It was built by Charles Doughty circa 1785 and named for his son-in-law Joseph King, a British sea captain who bought it in 1801. The house has two and a half stories, a gambrel roof, a split front door in the Dutch style, and a columned front porch. It was twice moved because of development: in 1923 to a site formerly occupied by a stable after being displaced by a proposed subway extension, and in 1968 to property once owned by the nurseryman Samuel Parsons, near a weeping beech that he planted in 1847. In 1968 the house became the headquarters of the Queens Historical Society, which sponsors exhibitions there.

Jonathan Kuhn

Kips Bay. Neighborhood on the East Side of midtown Manhattan (2009 pop. *ca* 9500), bounded to the north by 34th Street, to the east by the East River, to the south by 27th Street, and to the west by Third Avenue. It is named for Jacobus Kip, who in the mid-seventeenth century owned a large farm extending to a bay of the East River. Among the affluent and influential residents during the nineteenth century were Horace Greeley and Francis Bayard Winthrop. In 1878 and 1880, respectively, elevated railways were constructed along Third and Second avenues, which caused many of the old estates to be replaced by tenements. The Second Avenue Elevated was razed in 1942; the Third Avenue line was razed in 1956. Beginning in the 1960s large apartment buildings and complexes were built, including Kips Bay Plaza (1965), which contains the first exposed concrete structures in the city. Hospitals have dominated Kips Bay for more than a century, including Bellevue Hospital and New York University Medical Center. A large variety of shops and restaurants run along Second and Third avenues.

James Bradley, Andrew Sparberg

Kiralfy, Imre (*b* Pest [now in Budapest], 1 Jan 1845; *d* Brighton, England, 27 April 1919). Choreographer and producer. With his brother Bolossy Kiralfy (*b* Pest, 31 Jan 1847; *d* London, 6 March 1932) he made his debut in New York City in 1869 at the head of a family troupe that performed Hungarian and Slavic dances. In the 1870s and 1880s the brothers became important producers of musical spectacles in the city: their productions used large contingents of dancers, elaborate scenery, and special effects to illustrate biblical and historical themes. These productions eventually grew too large for ordinary stages and were moved to outdoor amphitheaters in Staten Island and the New Jersey Palisades. From 1886 the brothers worked separately: Imre moved to London, and Bolossy produced shows for exhibitions,

Advertisement for Imre Kiralfy's "Columbus and the Discovery of America" at the Barnum & Bailey Greatest Show on Earth, 1891

circuses, and world's fairs in New York City, London, and on the Continent.

Barbara Barker

Kirstein, Lincoln (*b* Rochester, N.Y., 4 May 1907; *d* New York City, 5 Jan 1996). Arts patron. While a student at Harvard University (BS 1930) he launched the literary magazine *Hound and Horn* and formed the Harvard Society for Contemporary Art, a forerunner of the Museum of Modern Art in New York City. In 1933 he invited the Russian dancer and choreographer George Balanchine to New York City, and the two formed the School of American Ballet and several ballet companies, including the American Ballet, the American Ballet Caravan, Ballet Society, and the New York City Ballet (1948). Kirstein was also the president of the School of American Ballet and the general manager of the New York City Ballet until 1989. His published writings include *Dance* (1935) and *Thirty Years: Lincoln Kirstein's the New York City Ballet* (1978), an account of his partnership with Balanchine. In 1984 President Ronald Reagan presented him with a Presidential Medal of Freedom for his contribution to the arts. Before his death he donated his dance history collection of papers, art, and other materials to the New York Public Library for the Performing Arts.

Martin Duberman, *The Worlds of Lincoln Kirstein* (New York: Knopf, 2007)

Montana Katz

Kissinger, Henry (Alfred) (*b* Fürth, near Nürnberg, Germany, 27 May 1923). Diplomat. He fled Nazi Germany with his parents in August 1938 and settled in an apartment on Fort Washington Avenue in Washington Heights. While attending George Washington High School he worked in a factory downtown that made bristles for shaving brushes. After graduating in 1941 he enrolled in the business school of City College of New York on 23rd Street. He was drafted by the army in 1943 and after his military service transferred to Harvard University, where he began his career in foreign policy. He was the national security adviser to President Richard M. Nixon (1969–73) and secretary of state under Nixon and President Gerald R. Ford (1974–77). Kissinger Associates, an international consulting firm, was formed in the early 1980s with headquarters at Park Avenue and 51st Street. Kissinger won the Nobel Peace Prize in 1973.

Bernard Kalb and Marvin Kalb, *Kissinger* (Boston: Little, Brown, 1974); Walter Isaacson, *Kissinger: A Biography* (New York: Simon and Schuster, 1992)

James Bradley

Kitchen (Center for Video, Music, Dance, Performance, Film and Literature). Performing arts center and organization. Founded by Woody and Steina Vasulka in 1971, the Kitchen provides emerging and established artists opportunities to create and present new work. It opened as a video art center in the unused kitchen of the Mercer Arts Center and soon offered live performances as well as music in its presentations. In 1974 the Kitchen was incorporated as a nonprofit organization and moved to a SoHo facility. During the next 10 years it attracted more artists and gained a larger audience. The center also added dance and film to its repertoire. In 1985 the Kitchen moved to its new and permanent home at 512 West 19th Street in Chelsea, which houses an administrative space, a media services department, and two of the largest black box theaters in the country. It opened a SoHo annex in 1994, the Kitchenette, which presents daily video exhibitions. Throughout 2000 the Kitchen hosted four national symposia with the support of the Ford Foundation. Each symposium offered panels and open discussions about the crossroads of art and technology, as well as having performances realized through technologies. The Kitchen presents more than 100 live performances a year, has a touring program, and takes part in occasional television projects. Many artists have worked with the organization, including Philip Glass, Laurie Anderson, Bill T. Jones, Eric Bogosian, David Byrne, Jenny Holzer, Cindy Sherman, Robert Mapplethorpe, Trisha Brown, and Meredith Monk. The Kitchen's Archive Project is an ongoing effort to preserve, catalogue, restore, and modernize its archival collection of audiotapes and videotapes, which dates to 1972 and contains early work by some of these artists.

Joan Acocella

Kitt, Eartha (Mae) [Keith, Eartha Mae] (*b* North, S.C., 17 Jan 1927; *d* Weston, Conn., 25 Dec 2008). Actress and singer. At age eight she moved to Harlem to live with her aunt (whom Kitt believed was her biological mother). Because of the abusive environment there, Kitt chronically ran away from home. She attended the High School of Performing Arts but dropped out to work in a Brooklyn factory. As a teen she tried out for the Katherine Dunham Dance Company on a dare; she was invited to join it and through it toured the world during the late 1940s. In her early 20s she performed in Paris nightclubs but eventually moved back to New York City and performed at the Village Vanguard and was cast in the Broadway show *New Faces of 1952*. Several best-selling albums followed, including her 1953 hit song "Santa Baby." Throughout her career Kitt worked on the stage, in film, and on television; she was nominated for two Tony Awards for her work in *Timbuktu!* (1978) and *The Wild Party* (2000). In December 2004 she appeared as the Fairy Godmother in the New York City Opera's production of *Cinderella*. In 2006 she costarred in the Off-Broadway musical *Mimi le Duck*. She was known for her purring singing voice and was often characterized as a "sex kitten." Even into her final years she continued to play cabarets and give other live performances in New York City and abroad.

Jessica Montesano, Penelope Gelwicks

Kitty Genovese murder. Controversial incident that occurred in Kew Gardens in the early morning of 13 March 1964 when Kitty Genovese (*b* 1935), the manager of a bar, was stabbed to death as her repeated screams for help were ignored by 38 witnesses. Winston Moseley, a business machine operator, was convicted of the murder and received the death penalty, which was later commuted to life imprisonment. The case led to many discussions of urban anonymity and of inaction in the face of violent crime.

A. M. Rosenthal, *Thirty-eight Witnesses* (New York: McGraw–Hill, 1964)

Robert W. Snyder

Klein, Anne [Golofski, Hannah] (*b* New York City, 1923; *d* New York City, 19 March 1974). Fashion designer. Born in Brooklyn, she attended Girls' Commercial High School and won a scholarship to the Traphagen School of Fashion in New York City (1937–38). In 1938 she began work as a sketcher on Seventh Avenue and then in 1948 she moved to Junior Sophisticates. In 1963 she opened her own company on Seventh Avenue and began designing lines of modern, practical clothes aimed primarily at young women.

Caroline Rennolds Milbank

Klein, Calvin (Richard) (*b* Bronx, 19 Nov 1942). Fashion designer. He was born and raised in the Bronx and attended the High School of Art and Design on Second Avenue and East 59th Street and the Fashion Institute of Technology at Seventh Avenue and 27th Street. Later, he served an apprenticeship in a coat and suit house in Manhattan. In 1968 he opened a coat business with Barry Schwartz and in the following year became president of a firm bearing his name. The success of his coats prompted him to expand his designs to include sportswear and eventually fragrances, eyewear, swimwear, lingerie, and a fashionable line of men's and women's clothing sold under the marque "cK." Klein won several awards for men's and women's fashions, including America's Best Designer in 1993. His company was bought in 2003 by Phillips–Van Heusen Corporation.

Anne E. Kornblut

Kleindeutschland. Former neighborhood on the Lower East Side of Manhattan, bounded to the north by 16th Street, to the east by the East River, to the south by Division and Grand streets, and to the west by the Bowery; it was also known as Little Germany, Deutschlandle, and Dutchtown. A German enclave took form there in the 1830s and 1840s near what was then the northeastern edge of the city. Immigrants from various German regions often settled together, and the population grew to hundreds of thousands. Kleindeutschland was a vital cultural center for two generations of German immigrants and became the foundation of the Jewish neighborhood that took form on the Lower East Side at the end of the nineteenth century.

Stanley Nadel

Kleindeutschland, 1914; George Ehret's restaurant and café at 130–32 Third Avenue, just north of 14th Street

Kleinfeld Bridal. Bridal salon. It began in 1941 when the Kleinfeld family invested $600 to open a fur shop at 8206 Fifth Avenue in Bay Ridge, Brooklyn. Over the following decades the shop employed local seamstresses and salespeople as it evolved into a wedding gown emporium. In 1990 it was sold to a French investor and suffered a decline until 1997 when Gordon Brothers Group, a Manhattan investment firm, bought the business, saved it from bankruptcy, and resold it in 1999 to Ronald Rothstein, Mara Urshel, and investor and actor Wayne Rogers. In 2005 co-owners Rothstein and Urshel opened Kleinfeld Bridesmaids' Loft at 270 West 38th Street in Manhattan and moved the bridal shop from its original Brooklyn location to Manhattan at 110 West 20th Street.

Holly Cronin

Kline, Ardolph L(oges) (*b* Sussex County, N.J., 21 Feb 1858; *d* New York City, 13 Oct 1930). Mayor. He was a colonel in the Spanish–American War, an unsuccessful candidate for sheriff, and an alderman from 1904 until his appointment as acting mayor in late 1913. After working as a tax commissioner between 1914 and 1918 he won a seat in the U.S. Congress in 1920 as a Republican; he returned to New York City after being appointed a local agent for the U.S. Shipping Board.

James E. Mooney

Kline, Franz (Joseph) (*b* Wilkes-Barre, Pa., 23 May 1910; *d* New York City, 13 May 1962). Painter. He studied painting in Boston, Paris, and London before moving to New York City in 1938, where he became known for woodcuts, watercolors, and oil paintings executed in a realistic mode. His work was shown at outdoor exhibitions in Washington Square and won awards from the National Academy of Design. He led the Painters' Club with Willem de Kooning. By 1950 he worked primarily on large canvases using black paint applied with wide house-painting brushes. A leader of the abstract expressionist movement, he taught at the Pratt Institute from 1953. A number of his works were shown in an exhibition at the Museum of Modern Art in 1955 and in a traveling exhibition in 1958–59. Kline had a studio on West 14th Street.

Fielding Dawson, *An Emotional Memoir of Franz Kline* (New York: Pantheon, 1967)

James E. Mooney

Knapp Commission. Investigative body with five members formed in May 1970 by Mayor John V. Lindsay to examine allegations of corruption in the New York City Police Department. Its formation followed an exposé in April 1970 in the *New York Times* alleging that certain police officers received millions of dollars a year in illegal payments from drug dealers, bookmakers, businesspeople, and organized crime. The central figure in the investigation was Frank Serpico, a police detective who with a few colleagues between 1967 and 1970 gathered extensive evidence of corruption in the department, in particular the collection of payoffs from owners of small businesses; he divulged the evidence to the *New York Times* only after repeatedly failing to elicit a response from the police leadership or city hall. The chairman of the commission, Whitman Knapp, and his chief investigating counsel, Michael Armstrong, conducted an investigation that lasted two years and held hearings that produced three stinging reports. The last of these attacked city officials for failing to investigate charges of misconduct by the police and alleged that more than half of all police officers were corrupt. Serpico's battle against corruption was recounted in Peter Maas's book *Serpico* (1973) and a 1973 movie of the same name starring Al Pacino. While the Knapp Commission produced some reforms, many of the same problems continued; and in 1992 Mayor David Dinkins was forced to create the Mollen Commission, which issued a 1994 report on police corruption.

George Winslow

Knickerbocker. Surname of the historian who narrated Washington Irving's satirical *History of New York* (1809), as well as a number of Irving's Hudson River Valley stories, including "Rip Van Winkle" (1820) and "The Legend of Sleepy Hollow" (1820). Although Irving borrowed the name Knickerbocker from an actual, Dutch-descended family in Schagticoke, New York, his narrator, Diedrich Knickerbocker, was a creation of pure fiction, whose nostalgic, ornery, and sometimes ribald portraits of the Dutch settlers of New Amsterdam and their modern-day descendants brought Irving fame in the United States and abroad. After the commercial and critical success of Irving's New York writings, the term Knickerbocker quickly became shorthand for a quintessential New Yorker and was taken up by a number of literary ventures, including Lewis Gaylord Clark's *Knickerbocker Magazine* (1833–65), and by a variety of social and commercial organizations. These included the first-ever baseball team, the Knickerbocker Base Ball Club (1842); the Knickerbocker Club on Fifth Avenue (1871); and insurers, banks, ice manufacturers, and steamship companies. In the late nineteenth century Father Knickerbocker became the symbol for Manhattan in the struggle for consolidation with Miss Brooklyn and the less-populated outer boroughs. In the twentieth century Irving's historian was invoked by New York's first basketball team, popularly known as the New York Knicks; he was the mascot of the official beer of the New York Giants, Knickerbocker Beer; and he graced the Hearst newspapers as the name of New York's preeminent, syndicated gossip columnist, Cholly Knickerbocker. At the beginning of the twenty-first century the term Knickerbocker could still be found on streets, restaurants, and dry cleaners in New York City, but the connection to Irving's original fiction had mostly been lost.

Elizabeth L. Bradley

Knickerbocker Base Ball Club. Group formed on the East Side of Manhattan in 1842 that played a game believed to be the precursor of modern baseball; the rules of the game were standardized by Alexander J. Cartwright and several other team members in 1845. In the autumn of 1845 members of the club competed against each other in Manhattan before moving to the Elysian Fields in Hoboken, New Jersey. They lost the first game that they played against another team, the New York Club, in June 1846. During the late 1850s the members helped to form the National Association of Base Ball Players. In the face of a growing tendency toward professionalism and commercialism in baseball, the Knickerbockers remained an amateur social and athletic club until they disbanded in the mid-1870s.

George B. Kirsch

Knickerbocker Club. All-male social club formed in quarters on Fifth Avenue in 1871 by 18 members of the Union Club who had reservations about admissions policies and other changes being made there. Among its founders were Alexander Hamilton (grandson of the secretary of the treasury), John Jacob Astor, Moses Lazarus, and August Belmont. Originally the group met at Delmonico's with an exclusively white tie dress code. The first clubhouse opened in 1872 near Union Square. In 1875 members interested in driving four-horse teams formed a subgroup known as the Coaching Club. In 1915 the club moved to a building at Fifth Avenue and 62nd Street designed by William Adams Delano of the firm of Delano and Aldrich. In the early twenty-first century the club had several hundred members.

James E. Mooney

Knickerbocker Fire Insurance Company. Name used from 1846 by the United Insurance Company of the City of New York.

Knickerbocker Magazine. Literary journal launched in 1833 by Samuel Langtree. It advanced the ideas of the Knickerbocker Group, which consisted mainly of Whigs from New England who sought to create a national literature and make New York City a literary center. The magazine became the first well-respected literary periodical in the United States after it was taken over by Lewis Gaylord Clark in 1834. To make it competitive with English publications (which were cheaper in New York City than in London), Clark sought to infuse it with a distinctively American flavor. He used no reprints but did not object when its contents were reprinted by others; as a result the literary pieces he published were soon circulated nationally. Among those who wrote for the magazine were Henry Wadsworth Longfellow (who published his first poems in it), Francis Parkman (whose *Oregon Trail* was published serially in 1847), William Cullen Bryant, James Fenimore Cooper, Fitz-Greene Halleck, Nathaniel Hawthorne, Washington Irving, and John Greenleaf Whittier. The magazine declined with the Knickerbocker Group after 1850; never profitable, it ceased publication in 1865.

Jeff Finlay

Knickerbocker Village. Lower Manhattan apartment complex, bounded by Cherry, Market, Catherine, and Monroe streets. It is a group of 12-story buildings surrounding inner gardens and contains 1600 apartments. Knickerbocker Village replaced a notorious slum called the Lung Block because of its high incidence of tuberculosis cases. Fred F. French, a noted real estate developer, constructed the buildings in 1933–34; it was one of the first limited-profit housing developments in New York City and used federal New Deal funds for some of its financing. Julius and Ethel Rosenberg, who were executed as spies in 1953, lived in the building at 10 Monroe Street, and it was there, in apartment 11E, that Ethel allegedly typed David

Greenglass's notes from Los Alamos. In the early twenty-first century Knickerbocker Village continues to be a desirable middle-class enclave.

Andrew Sparberg

Knight, Hilary (*b* Hempstead, N.Y., 1 Nov 1926). Artist and children's book illustrator, best known for creating the character Eloise with author Kay Thompson. In 2009 he donated to the New York Public Library his papers, which include sketches, layouts, correspondence, and research.

Knights of Columbus. Roman Catholic fraternal order. The first local unit within what is now New York City was Brooklyn Council no. 60 (formed 23 Sept 1891), followed by the Long Island Chapter (Brooklyn, 19 Jan 1897), New York Council no. 124 (Manhattan, 12 May 1895), the New York Chapter (12 Dec 1899), and the Staten Island Chapter (13 Oct 1913). In its early years the organization overcame a fear by local bishops that their ecclesiastical authority would be undercut. During the Spanish–American War it began a tradition of attending to members of the armed services. Later it organized blood-donation campaigns and sports programs for youths, promoted spiritual activities, and articulated Catholic opinion on social issues. The Long Island and Staten Island chapters raise funds for programs for handicapped children offered by the Catholic Charities; the New York Chapter does the same for the Foundling Hospital. In 1944 the New York Chapter became the holder of the permit for the Columbus Day Parade.

Mary Elizabeth Brown

Knights of Labor, District Assembly 49. Labor union, formed in 1869 in Philadelphia as a union of skilled garment workers; the full name was Noble and Holy Order of the Knights of Labor. Seeking to transcend divisions of occupation, race, and sex, the union later extended membership to all "producers," which included most workers (although not lawyers, bankers, or liquor dealers). District Assembly 49 was formed in 1882 and had about 60,000 members, accounting for most of the Knights in New York City and Brooklyn; it was perhaps the most influential assembly in the national organization, which in 1886 had 700,000 members. Unlike the national leadership, the local one, known as the home club, rejected trade unionism because it considered craft unions a regressive form of organization destined to be replaced by mixed assemblies based on producerism. It nonetheless sought and gained the affiliations of the city's trade unions, which also belonged to their own international unions. Cooperation between the assembly and the unions eventually disintegrated, owing largely to jurisdictional disputes that arose when District 49 encouraged local unions to leave their international organizations for exclusive membership in the Knights. In 1886 a conflict erupted between the district assembly and the Cigar Makers' International Union (CMIU) that fractured the labor movement in the city. After locking out 15,000 workers in January, the United Cigar Manufacturers Association canceled its contract with the CMIU in February and signed another one for lower wages with the Cigarmakers' Progressive Union, a rival organization supported by District 49, which negotiated to have its own label used on cigars rather than that of the CMIU. During the spring and summer the CMIU exerted its influence in the trade to force employers to renegotiate its contracts, and in August the Cigarmakers' Progressive Union itself voted to join the international union rather than meet the ultimatum of District 49 to merge with the Knights.

Despite these divisions the district worked with the craft unions to promote the mayoral candidacy in 1886 of Henry George, a social reformer nominated by the newly formed Independent Labor Party. District 49, however, weakened, largely through the efforts of Samuel Gompers, who opposed dual unionism and undertook a national speaking tour to excoriate the Knights. It remained in operation into the 1890s, forming an alliance with the socialist Daniel DeLeon in 1894 that was short-lived, but it never again challenged the tenets of American trade unionism.

Stuart B. Kaufman, *Samuel Gompers and the Origins of the American Federation of Labor, 1848–1896* (Westport, Conn.: Greenwood, 1973)

Richard Yeselson

Knopf, Alfred A. (*b* New York City, 12 Sept 1892; *d* Purchase, N.Y., 11 Aug 1984). Book publisher. He graduated from Columbia University in 1912 and in 1915 founded his own publishing firm, Alfred A. Knopf Inc., at 220 West 42nd Street. The firm published in a variety of areas, emphasizing history, music, and quality fiction. Knopf became known for introducing the works of foreign writers to American readers and for raising the standards of book design. Willa Cather, H. L. Mencken, John Hersey, and Joseph Conrad were among the authors whom Knopf published and considered good friends. He also published the *American Mercury* along with Mencken from 1924 to 1934. He sold his firm to Random House in 1960, but Alfred A. Knopf Inc. continued as a separate imprint, and Knopf remained active in its oversight into the final years of his life. In early 2009 the Knopf Publishing Group merged with Doubleday Publishing Group to form the Knopf Doubleday Publishing Group.

See also Book publishing.

Eileen K. Cheng, David White

Koch, Edward I(rving) (*b* New York City, 12 Dec 1924). New York City mayor (1978–90). A leading Democratic reformer during the 1950s and 1960s, he defeated Manhattan Democratic leader Carmine DeSapio in the 1963 and 1965 primary elections for the Democratic district leadership of Greenwich Village. In the 1977 primary election, he opposed Mayor Abraham D. Beame and several other candidates for the Democratic mayoral nomination. After narrowly topping the field in the first round of the Democratic primary, he defeated Mario M. Cuomo in a runoff and went on to win the general election by advocating fiscal discipline and emphasizing his support of the death penalty for capital crimes and his opposition to public unions. Koch developed a conservative Democratic political base by winning the votes of most white Catholics and Jews and of a smaller proportion of Latinos and African Americans. Koch helped to restore financial stability to the city during his first mayoral term, and he was reelected in 1981 as the candidate of both the Democratic and Republican parties. A few weeks into his second term he decided to seek the governorship when Governor Hugh L. Carey declined to seek reelection. He lost a bitterly fought primary election to Cuomo after an interview was published in which he had spoken disparagingly of upstate New York. In 1985 Koch became only the third mayor since the consolidation of Greater New York in 1898 to win a third term. But after this election his political reputation suffered because of an economic crisis, racial turmoil, and a scandal in the Parking Violations Bureau in which his ally Donald Manes was embroiled. Koch's attempt to win a fourth term failed when he was defeated in the 1989 Democratic primary by David N. Dinkins.

Koch was a colorful personality who provoked strong emotions. He frequently attacked

Edward I. Koch, 1987

political pieties and sometimes endorsed Republican candidates. His supporters found his outspokenness and independence refreshing, and his frequently shouted signature question "How'm I doing?" gave him an air of unpretentiousness. But liberals complained that he was given to intemperate statements on foreign policy, the United Nations, and other issues beyond his purview. For most of his mayoralty he enjoyed support on newspaper editorial pages. Among his many books, *Mayor* (1984), published while Koch was in office, became a best seller, and for the next 20 years reporters continued to seek his comments on major events of the day.

John Mollenkopf, *A Phoenix in the Ashes: The Rise and Fall of the Koch Coalition in New York City Politics* (Princeton, N.J.: Princeton University Press, 1992)

Martin Shefter

Kolkin, Lucille Gewirtz (*b* New York City, 1919; *d* New York City, 27 Aug 1997). Shipyard worker and activist. Raised in Bensonhurst, Brooklyn, and educated at Hunter College, class of 1938, she was one of the "Rosie the Riveter" workers in military facilities during World War II. At the Brooklyn Navy Yard (formally called the United States Naval Shipyard) for almost two years she worked the night shift as a mechanic in the shipfitting shop, fabricating and laying out metal structural components for battleships and other vessels under construction or repair. By early 1945 almost 4700 women were working at the yard. Kolkin's letters and other papers provide an intimate view of daily life in the navy yard, including the physical demands of the job, the camaraderie among female employees, and discriminatory treatment of black workers, whom she counseled. When her husband was assigned to a California station, she followed him west. After the war they lived in Brooklyn and Manhattan. She worked for many years for the National Opinion Research Center, studying the outcomes in people's lives related to health care, education, and employment. She was active in the civil rights and anti–Vietnam War movements and at Penn South, a cooperative housing complex built by the International Ladies' Garment Workers' Union. Kolkin's papers are collected at the Brooklyn Historical Society.

Jennifer Egan, "Reading Lucy," *Brooklyn Was Mine,* ed. Chris Knutsen and Valerie Steiker (New York: Riverhead Books, 2008), 21–32

John Rousmaniere

Koreans. About 10,000 Koreans entered the United States before the Immigration Act of 1924 barred the entry of Asians. Of the few who initially settled in New York City, many were Protestants, students, or political refugees; they banded together to protest the Japanese takeover of the Korean peninsula. In 1920 they established the New York Korean Church, the first Korean church in the city, near Columbia University. The sanctuary became a center for anti-Japanese political activities and counted among its members students at Columbia who later became prominent political leaders after Korean independence. After the Korean War there was an influx of students from South Korea. Most of these stayed after finishing their studies and many became influential business leaders, Protestant ministers, publishers of Korean-language newspapers, and leaders of such important organizations as the Korean Association of New York, an umbrella organization representing all Koreans in the metropolitan area. The number of immigrants increased after the Immigration and Nationality Act of 1965 allowed the reunion of families. The new immigrants settled throughout the city but were concentrated in Flushing, Jackson Heights, and Elmhurst—all in Queens. After achieving success, most moved to the suburbs; these patterns prevented Koreans from gaining a sizable electoral influence anywhere in the city. Koreans attained solidarity by organizing religious, professional, recreational, business, family, and alumni associations, as well as informal clubs. Among the most important were revolving credit associations known as *kye,* which provided business capital and money for consumer goods. These were derived from traditional cooperatives designed to promote mutual assistance, friendship, and goodwill.

Owing largely to community self-help networks, Koreans acquired more small businesses than most other groups of immigrants did (in 1991 Koreans in the metropolitan area ran about 10,000 small businesses). Many bought greengroceries, retail fish stores, and dry-cleaning stores. Often these were in predominantly African American neighborhoods, drawing protest from some blacks who sought to retain control of their communities. In 1979 a few organizations distributed anti-Korean leaflets and picketed Korean shops. Racial tensions rose in 1988 when a Korean greengrocery in Brooklyn was driven out of business by a black boycott. Another boycott of two Korean groceries on Church Avenue in Brooklyn began in January 1990 and attracted national attention.

According to the Korean American Small Business Service, 70 percent of employed Koreans in the metropolitan area worked in Korean businesses in 1986, and such important associations as the Korean Produce Retailers Association, the Korean Seafood Association, and the Korean Dry Cleaners Association provided group insurance, tax guides, legal services, and seminars to members. The most comprehensive services were offered by the Korean Produce Retailers Association, which sponsored the first *Chusok* festival of thanksgiving in 1982. In later years the festival was held annually at Flushing Meadow Park in Queens on a Sunday in October (and on the 15th of the eighth lunar month in Korea). In 1967 *Hangkook Ilbo,* a Korean-language daily newspaper in South Korea, began to publish an edition based in New York City.

From the 1970s immigrants were drawn mainly from the elite of such South Korean cities as Seoul and Pusan. According to a survey by the *Hangkook Ilbo* in 1987 most Korean immigrants moved to the city with their families; 89 percent of Korean householders were married and lived with their spouses, 74 percent had completed college in Korea, and 96 percent were employed (as were 80 percent of the spouses). The presence of two and often three generations in the household was important to the economic success of many Koreans, nearly half of whom eventually moved to the suburbs. The federal census of 2000 recorded 90,896 Koreans living in the five boroughs, 70 percent of which live in Queens. The total figure for Koreans in the metropolitan area was placed at 210,000 by the Korean Foreign Ministry the same year. From 1990 to 2000 the Korean community in New York City grew by 30 percent. In 2000 Koreans ranked 12th in foreign-born groups, with more than 70,000 new immigrants. Flushing was home to one of the largest concentrations of Koreans in the city.

According to a survey by *Hangkook Ilbo* 63 percent of the population attended Protestant churches, mostly Presbyterian, which were important social centers. In the metropolitan area in 1991 there were 390 Korean Protestant churches, 15 Korean Catholic churches, and 11 Buddhist temples. Early in the twenty-first century the Korean news media remained a vital source of cohesion in the Korean community. In addition to *Hangkook Ilbo* these included local editions of three Korean-language newspapers based in Seoul (*Joong Ang Ilbo, Chosun Ilbo,* and *Sae Gae Ilbo*), three weekly newspapers, three radio stations, and two television stations.

Illsoo Kim, *New Urban Immigrants: The Korean Community in New York* (Princeton, N.J.: Princeton University Press, 1981), 181–225

See also Koreatown.

Illsoo Kim

Koreatown. Neighborhood and business district roughly from 32nd Street to 35th Street, between Broadway and Fifth Avenue, also known as K-Town. In the late 1970s Korean textile and apparel wholesalers clustered around 32nd Street because of cheap rents, proximity to the garment district, and high foot traffic. In the early 1980s Korean-owned businesses grew because Korean merchants who shopped at wholesalers' showrooms created a demand for Korean restaurants and amenities. By the late 1980s 32nd Street was dominated by Korean businesses. In the twenty-first century the area caters mostly to second-generation Korean Americans, young people, and tourists. The area is also distinguished by storefronts on multiple levels, much like the Korean capital of Seoul. A street sign above the intersection of 32nd Street and Broadway reads "Korea Way."

Jessica Montesano

Berenice Abbott, Chicken Market *(1937), 55 Hester Street*

Kosciuszko Bridge. Truss bridge of steel and reinforced concrete spanning Newton Creek between Brooklyn and Queens, near but unconnected to Kosciuszko Street. Opened on 23 August 1939 as the Meeker Avenue Bridge on the former site of Penny Bridge (an old drawbridge), it was renamed in 1940 in honor of the Polish patriot and Revolutionary War general Tadeusz Kosciuszko. At first part of the Brooklyn–Queens Connecting Highway, it later became part of the Brooklyn–Queens Expressway, providing rapid access between the Midtown Tunnel and the Williamsburg Bridge. The bridge has a maximum span of 300 feet (91.5 meters) and a maximum height of 125 feet (38.1 meters), and the approaches are steep. These factors, plus the narrow 11-foot lanes, lack of shoulders, and huge traffic load carried every day, make the Kosciuszko Bridge a particularly hazardous stretch of expressway. The bridge is operated by the New York State Department of Transportation.

Andrew Sparberg

Kosciuszko Foundation. Polish American cultural and educational institution formed in New York City in 1925. It was named in honor of Tadeusz Kosciuszko, who designed the fortress at West Point and was instrumental in the American victory in Saratoga, New York, during the American Revolution. The foundation provides scholarships to Americans of Polish heritage, supports exchanges of students and scholars between the United States and Poland, publishes books, and operates summer sessions for Americans to study at Polish universities. It also promotes Polish culture in American society through the sponsorship of exhibits, concerts, publications, and film festivals. The Kosciuszko Foundation has its offices at 15 East 65th Street in Manhattan.

James S. Pula

kosher foods. Food that conforms to dietary rules of the Jewish religion. The production of matzo, or unleavened bread, in New York City expanded rapidly during an influx of Jewish immigrants between 1880 and 1920. Most matzo bakeries were on the Lower East Side, including that of Horowitz Brothers and Margareten, which had factories on East Fourth Street; Meyer London's Matzos Bakery on Bayard Street; and the Finsilver Matzoth Baking Company on Pitt Street. Soon the slaughtering and meatpacking industry in the city also expanded to accommodate a rising demand for kosher meat. The wholesale value of kosher food increased 70 percent between 1900 and 1909, and by 1916 kosher meat retailers in the city reached $50 million in sales. The number of butcher shops selling kosher meat increased from 1500 in 1902 to 7500 in 1930; some of the largest kosher butchers and meat wholesalers were the firms of Isaac Gellis on Essex Street and S. Ershowsky and Brothers on East Houston Street. By 1934 there were about 12,000 kosher food processors and dealers, with annual sales of more than $200 million. Because demand for kosher food was large, kosher certification remained problematic for decades. The first efforts at regulation were made at the turn of the century by Rabbi Jacob Joseph of the Association of the United Hebrew Congregation. Later efforts continued to provoke controversy, including those of the New York Kehillah between 1910 and 1920, the Union of Orthodox Jewish Congregations in the 1920s, and the Kashruth Association in the 1930s.

Disputes over prices resulted in several "kosher meat riots." The most severe occurred in May 1902, when butchers in the city closed their shops after packers raised the cost of kosher meat. A settlement was reached, but many customers still considered prices too high and organized a citywide boycott. Similar incidents took place in 1910, 1929, and 1937. Resentment arose when the power to regulate the kosher food business was given to the federal government by the National Industrial Recovery Act (NIRA) of 1933, and in 1934 a suit was brought by the Schechter

Samstein's Kosher Meat & Poultry Market

Brothers, kosher poultry wholesalers in Brooklyn convicted of violating the Live Poultry Code: NIRA was ruled unconstitutional by the U.S. Supreme Court in the case of *Schechter Poultry Corporation v. United States* (1935). In the 1940s the Union of Orthodox Jewish Congregations and the Kosher Law Enforcement Bureau (1944) became the primary monitors of the kosher food business. The numbers of dealers and manufacturers in the city declined during the following decade, as kosher products were introduced by large food producers. Eventually, most kosher food was bought by non-Jews, who recognized that such food was associated with high standards. In the 1980s the largest firm of matzo bakers was that of Aron Streit (1924) on Rivington Street in Manhattan; matzo was also made by Horowitz Brothers and Margareten, which maintained a factory in Queens, and by many small firms in Borough Park in Brooklyn. Glatt kosher food, prepared according to more stringent standards than other kosher food, was at first sold mostly in Williamsburg, Borough Park, and other neighborhoods in Brooklyn but later spread to the other boroughs. Many kosher restaurants in the city in the twenty-first century offer not only traditional kosher foods but kosher versions of Chinese, Italian, and other types of cuisine. The city also has a number of kosher wine distributors, including the Royal Corporation in Brooklyn, the makers of Kedem, Monfort, and Bartenura wine.

Harold P. Gastwirt, *Fraud, Corruption and Holiness: The Controversy over the Supervision of Jewish Dietary Practice in New York City* (Port Washington, N.Y.: Kennikat, 1974)

James Bradley, Hadassa Kosak

Kosinski [Lewinkopf], **Jerzy (Nikodem)** (*b* Łódź, Poland, 14 June 1933; *d* New York City, 3 May 1991). Novelist and photographer. After earning a master's degree in history and another in political science at the University of Łódź he became a doctoral candidate in sociology at the Polish Academy of Sciences (1955–57). He arrived in New York City on 20 December 1957 and in the following months worked as a parking lot attendant, taxi driver, paint scraper on excursion boats, chauffeur, and cinema projectionist. He wrote a number of nonfiction works (the first two published under the pseudonym Joseph Novak), including *The Future Is Ours, Comrade: Conversations with the Russians* (1960), and in 1965 he became a U.S. citizen. His works of fiction include *The Painted Bird* (abridged edn 1965, complete edn 1970), *Steps* (1968, National Book Award), *The Devil Tree* (1973), and *The Hermit of 69th Street* (1988). He also adapted two of his novels for the screen (*Being There*, 1971; *Passion Play*, 1979) and won prizes for his photographs, which were exhibited in many countries. Kosinski gathered material for his books by prowling the streets of New York City and other cities, sometimes in disguise.

Norman Lavers, *Jerzy Kosinski* (Boston: Twayne, 1982); Paul R. Lilly, Jr., *Words in Search of Victims: The Achievement of Jerzy Kosinski* (Kent, Ohio: Kent State University Press, 1988); Tom Teicholz, ed., *Conversations with Jerzy Kosinski* (Jackson: University Press of Mississippi, 1993)

Allen J. Share

Kossuth, Louis [Lajos] (*b* Monok, Hungary, 16 Sept 1802; *d* Turin, Italy, 20 March 1894). Revolutionary. After leading the failed Hungarian revolution of 1848 he fled Hungary as it was occupied by Russian troops, and in 1851 he embarked on a seven-month tour of the United States to seek support for Hungarian independence. He landed at Staten Island on 5 December and was greeted with an elaborate procession and public reception. The following day a crowd of thousands attended Mayor Ambrose C. Kingsland's reception for him at Castle Garden and the Battery, where he was saluted with cannon fire before proceeding up Broadway by carriage, cheered by tens of thousands of spectators. A municipal banquet was held in his honor on 11 December at the Irving House (Broadway and Chambers Street), and he was also given receptions at Columbia College and Plymouth Church in Brooklyn before leaving the city for Philadelphia on 23 December. News of his visit to New York City dominated the city's newspapers for the entire month, and his ideas influenced "young America," a Romantic nationalist literary movement led by Evert A. Duyckinck and John O'Sullivan. The wide-brimmed, soft felt hats that he often wore became fashionable among young men, and long cloaks known as Kossuths were worn into the 1860s. On 15

March 1928 an audience of 25,000 attended the dedication of a bronze statue erected in his honor at 113th Street and Riverside Drive, including a delegation of 520 Hungarians who had traveled to the city for the occasion.

Donald S. Spencer, *Louis Kossuth and Young America* (Columbia: University of Missouri Press, 1977)

Kevin Kenny

Koufax, Sandy [Braun, Sanford] (*b* Brooklyn, 30 Dec 1935). Baseball pitcher. From 1962 through 1966 he was the most dominating pitcher in the history of baseball: his record was 111–34; he pitched four no-hitters, including a perfect game in 1965; he led the National League in earned run average each year; he was named Most Valuable Player (MVP) in 1963; and he won three Cy Young Awards (1963, 1965, 1966). He led the National League in wins three times, in strikeouts four times, and in shutouts three times, and he was twice voted MVP of the World Series. Koufax, whose parents divorced when he was three years old, grew up in Borough Park, Brooklyn, and moved to suburban Long Island after his mother remarried; Sandy took the surname of her new husband. After he finished ninth grade the family returned to Bensonhurst, Brooklyn, where Koufax attended Lafayette High School. He received a bonus to sign with the Brooklyn Dodgers in 1955. Despite the blazing speed of his fastball, Koufax struggled with control problems during his early years with the Dodgers. He was so uncertain of his future in baseball that he enrolled in Columbia University, which offered night courses in architecture. But he eventually found his control, worked his way into the starting rotation, and produced an incredible career. Plagued by traumatic arthritis in his left elbow, Koufax retired after the 1966 season. He was the youngest player (at age 36) ever elected to the National Baseball Hall of Fame.

Sandy Koufax with Ed Linn, *Koufax* (New York: Viking Press, 1966)

Frank Dyer

Kramer, Larry (Lawrence D.) (*b* Bridgeport, Conn., 25 June 1935). Gay rights activist, playwright, and novelist. After graduating from Yale University in 1957, he moved to New York City where he worked for the William Morris Agency, Columbia Pictures, and later, United Artists. In 1978 he published his first novel, *Faggots*. After spending time in London and Hollywood, Kramer returned to New York City in the early 1980s as the AIDS epidemic was beginning to make national news. In 1982 Kramer and five others started the Gay Men's Health Crisis (GMHC), a volunteer-supported AIDS resource hotline that has grown into the largest AIDS-related nonprofit organization in the United States. In 1985 Kramer's autobiographical play *The Normal Heart* opened at the Public Theater. Kramer's increasing discontent with GMHC inspired him to form AIDS Coalition to Unleash Power (ACT UP), a radical activist group committed to direct action to end the AIDS crisis. In 1989 Kramer led ACT UP members in a takeover of the trading floor of the New York Stock Exchange and a disruption of a Sunday mass at St. Patrick's Cathedral. Kramer also publicly complained about the *New York Times* and Mayor Edward Koch, both of whom he believed facilitated the spread of the human immunodeficiency virus (HIV) and AIDS by remaining silent on the issue. *The Destiny of Me*, the sequel to *The Normal Heart*, won two Obie Awards and was nominated for a Pulitzer Prize in 1993. Following a liver transplant in 2001 Kramer continues to be one of the most controversial and recognizable voices in the AIDS movement. He lives in New York City and suburban Connecticut.

Anne Epstein

Krapp, Herbert J. (*b* New York City, 21 Feb 1886; *d* Stuart, Fla., 16 Feb 1973). Architect. After working for the firm of Herts and Tallant he formed his own practice and became the principal architect for the Shubert and Chanin organizations, which dominated Broadway theater between the two world wars. He specialized in designing functional theaters on limited sites, with excellent acoustics and sightlines and restrained ornamental designs. Krapp was the most prolific architect of legitimate theaters on Broadway. Of his 21 theaters in New York City, many remain prominent in the twenty-first century.

See also Theater architecture.

Anthony W. Robins

Krasner, Lee [Krassner, Lenore] (*b* Brooklyn, 27 Oct 1908; *d* New York City, 19 June 1984). Painter. The daughter of Russian immigrants, she entered the Women's Art School of Cooper Union in 1926 (graduating in 1929) and became active in the art world of New York City during the 1930s. She worked on the Federal Art Project of the Works Progress Administration from 1934 (the poet Harold Rosenberg was a fellow assistant in 1935), studied with Hans Hofmann in 1937, and exhibited her work with the American Abstract Artists in 1940. Her cubist abstractions made her a well-known figure in the avant-garde. She married Jackson Pollock in 1945, and with him she moved in the same year to Springs, Long Island. She continued to spend winters in New York City at various addresses until she purchased an apartment at 180 East 79th Street. Between 1945 and 1949 she completed her "little image" paintings, abstract expressionist works in which she perfected her own version of Pollock's "all-over" composition. During the 1950s she incorporated collage into her work, creating bold, innovative paintings that represent a high point in her career. She had her first solo exhibition in 1951 at the Betty Parsons Gallery; with her nephew Ronald Stein she executed in mosaic a mural commissioned for the Uris Building (completed in 1959).

Barbara Rose, *Lee Krasner: A Retrospective* (Houston: Museum of Fine Arts/New York: Museum of Modern Art, 1983)

Mona Hadler

Kreischerville. Name applied until 1927 to Charleston.

Kuhn, Conrad (*fl* 1866–72). Labor leader. He was president of the cigarmakers' union (1866–72) and helped to organize the Association of United Workers (1868), a German labor council that sponsored the *Arbeiter Union*, the first daily German labor newspaper in New York City. Under his leadership the German unions became the most active participants in the city's labor movement, taking the lead in strikes for an eight-hour workday in 1872. Kuhn delivered the major address of the campaign, which helped to attract more than 100,000 city workers to the strike. His career as a labor leader ended when the movement was crushed and he was blacklisted.

Stanley Nadel

Kuhn, Loeb and Company. Firm of investment bankers. It was formed as a private bank in 1867 by Abraham Kuhn and Solomon Loeb, German immigrants who owned dry-goods stores in Indiana and Ohio; the first offices were at 31 Nassau Street. Jacob Schiff became a partner in 1875 and was a senior partner by 1885. Under his leadership the firm raised capital in Europe for American industry and refinanced almost every important railroad in the country, including the Pennsylvania, the Louisville and Nashville, and the Baltimore and Ohio. It also worked with Edward H. Harriman on the reorganization of the Union Pacific Railroad. A number of partners were added in the late nineteenth century, including Abraham Wolff, Felix Warburg, Paul Warburg, and Otto H. Kahn. During a struggle for control of the Northern Pacific Railroad in 1901, Schiff advised Harriman, and J. P. Morgan advised his rival James J. Hill, leading to the formation of a holding company called Northern Securities that was declared an illegal combination by the U.S. Supreme Court in 1904. Paul Warburg retired in 1914 to become the first president of the Federal Reserve Bank of New York. Unlike many other investment banks, Kuhn, Loeb remained small during the 1920s.

It specialized in railroad and industrial issues until the 1940s, when public sealed bidding became required for railroad securities. By the mid-1970s the firm's capital was becoming depleted, and in 1977 the partners agreed to merge with Lehman Brothers to form Lehman Brothers Kuhn Loeb.

Ken Auletta, *Greed and Glory on Wall Street: The Fall of the House of Lehman* (New York: Random House, 1986)

Mary E. Curry

Ku Klux Klan [KKK]. The name of three past and present secret societies, first formed in 1866 and revived in 1915 and in the years after World War II. The second of these was the largest, gaining nationwide influence and millions of members between 1921 and 1925 when it was especially strong in Indianapolis, Denver, Portland (Oregon), Chicago, Detroit, Atlanta, Memphis, and Dallas; it also achieved some success in New York City. Lloyd P. Hooper, KKK "grand goblin," set up headquarters at the Hotel Embassy in March 1921 and oversaw an initiation as early as 10 June. In July a local unit, or klavern, was formed in Brooklyn, and in September one began meeting in the Bronx as the American Civic Association. According to C. Anderson Wright, a defector from the KKK, 21 klaverns were operating in New York City in December 1922. Many members were inspired by the anti-Catholic and anti-Semitic ideology of the local newspaper the *American Standard.* A typical diatribe declared, "To receive into your home Roman Catholics, to give them employment in your office, is to put your home and your office at the mercy of the Roman Catholic system." Even so, William Joseph Simmons, "imperial wizard" of the KKK, described New York City as "the most un-American city of the American continent" and Columbia University as the "least American of all schools."

The KKK made stronger inroads into the suburbs, especially Yonkers in Westchester County and Stamford, Greenwich, and Bridgeport in Connecticut. On Long Island it won elections in 1923 in Islip, Babylon, Oyster Bay, and Brookhaven, and in 1924 it took temporary control of the Suffolk County Republican Committee. In New Jersey the state headquarters were in West Hoboken, and the order won many adherents in Newark, Paterson, and Elizabeth. At the Democratic National Convention at Madison Square Garden in 1924, the KKK was a particularly divisive issue. After 1925, however, the group collapsed in the New York City area, as in much of the rest of the country. It did maintain a shadowy existence in the South for the remainder of the century, but it would never again gain a substantial following in the New York region.

Kenneth T. Jackson, *The Ku Klux Klan in the City* (New York: Oxford University Press, 1967)

Kenneth T. Jackson

Kunitz, Stanley (*b* Worcester, Mass., 29 July 1905; *d* New York City, 14 May 2006). Poet. He graduated summa cum laude in 1926 from Harvard College and earned an MA in English from Harvard the following year. He worked as editor for the H. W. Wilson Company in New York City until he was drafted in 1943. In 1950 he was appointed director of the poetry workshop at the New School for Social Research. At Wilson Company Kunitz served as editor of the Wilson Library Bulletin and as coeditor for *Twentieth Century Authors.* His poems began to appear in various magazines, including *Poetry, Commonwealth,* the *New Republic,* the *Nation,* and the *Dial.* In 1985 Kunitz founded Poets House in the city, one of the most important poetry centers in the nation. Its collection of 45,000 poetry books includes almost everything published after 1990, as well as audio and video recording of poetry readings; it also sponsors extensive poetry readings in the city. He was an adjunct professor at Columbia University from 1967 to 1985. He published more than 12 books of original poems in his lifetime, including *Selected Poems: 1928–1958,* which won the Pulitzer Prize for poetry in 1959. His collection *Passing Through: The Later Poems, New and Selected* won the National Book Award in 1995; he published until he was 100 years old. Kunitz' honors included a National Medal of Arts (1993), the Bollingen Prize (1987) for lifetime achievement in poetry, the Robert Frost Medal (1998), and Harvard's Centennial Medal (1992). He served two terms as Consultant in Poetry for the Library of Congress, one term as Poet Laureate of the United States, and one term as the New York State Poet. His style transformed over the decades, from highly philosophical and intellectual writings to more personal and disciplined narratives, and from strict iambic pentameter meters to free prosody rooted in the rhythm of speech. Kunitz influenced many twentieth-century poets, including James Wright, Mark Doty, and Louise Glück.

Benjamin Yakas

Kunstler, William (Moses) (*b* New York City, 7 July 1919; *d* Manhattan, 4 Sept 1995). Lawyer. The son of a physician, he grew up in Manhattan and attended DeWitt Clinton High School. A decorated World War II veteran, he earned his law degree from Columbia University in 1948 and established a practice in Greenwich Village. During the 1960s he defended Freedom Riders, the Catonsville Nine, and the Chicago Eight. In the Chicago Eight case verbal jousts with Judge Julius Hoffman led to contempt citations, but Kunstler never served a day in jail; ultimately, conspiracy convictions against seven defendants were voided. Kunstler also defended the black activists Stokely Carmichael and H. Rap Brown, American Indian militants, Martin Luther King, and Adam Clayton Powell. His 1965 challenge to the legitimacy of Mississippi's congressional delegation led him to found the Center for Constitutional Rights (1966).

For more than 20 years Kunstler was Manhattan's most controversial attorney. He was present at the Attica prison revolt in 1971; filed suit on behalf of Tompkins Square squatter-protesters; successfully defended Larry Davis, accused of attempting to murder police officers; defended African American youths who allegedly accosted and then were shot by subway vigilante Bernard Goetz; and defended the youth convicted of attacking a jogger in Central Park in 1989. In the 1990s he participated in the defense of the World Trade Center bombers and argued that "black rage" explained murders on the Long Island Railroad. On the national scene he represented Washington, D.C., mayor Marion Barry against drug charges and argued successfully before the Supreme Court that burning an American flag was "symbolic speech" protected by the First Amendment. Kunstler used public relations as well as the law to defend those on the fringe of society. He wrote *Beyond a Reasonable Doubt* (1961), a study of the Chessman trial, and *The Case for Courage: Stories of Ten Famous Attorneys* (1962).

George J. Lankevich

Kurds. After the failure of the Kurdish revolution in Iran in 1975 the U.S. Department of State was responsible for resettling about 700 Kurds to the United States, some of whom took up residence in New York City. In time, some sent for relatives, and by the early 1990s the community in the city numbered about 2000. The city's Kurds are nationals of Iraq, Iran, Syria, and Turkey; they are overwhelmingly male and maintain a low profile. Many work in engineering, some in medicine and business. Most live around the far reaches of Ocean Parkway and Coney Island Avenue in Brooklyn; others live in various parts of Queens. The Kurdish Library, established in a brownstone in Brooklyn in 1986 by Vera Beaudin Saeedpour, is a center for the study of Kurdish history, culture, and contemporary affairs. It was an important source of information during the Kurdish refugee crisis that followed the Gulf War in 1991.

Marc Ferris

Kushner, Tony (*b* New York City, 16 July 1956). Playwright and activist. Born in Manhattan, he and his family relocated to Lake Charles, Louisiana, when he was two years old. Kushner returned to New York City to study medieval history at Columbia University and received a master's degree in theater directing from New York University. His works include *A Bright Room Called Day* (1985), *Hydriotaphia* (1987), *Slavs!* (1995), *Homebody/Kabul* (2001), and the musical *Caroline, or Change* (2002). He is most well known for his two-part play *Angels in America: A Gay Fantasia on National Themes* (Part One: *Millennium Approaches* [1990]; Part Two: *Perestroika* [1992]). Set primarily in New York City, the play examines challenges faced by Americans at the end of the twentieth century. Kushner's tackling of the AIDS epidemic, the rising conservative movement, religion, and sexuality in his plays has put him at the forefront of contemporary drama. He is also outspoken regarding gay and lesbian rights, conflicts in the Middle East, and other civil rights issues. He has received a Pulitzer Prize for Drama, an Emmy Award, two Tony Awards, three Obie Awards, an Oscar nomination, a Spirit of Justice Award from the Gay and Lesbian Advocates and Defenders, and a Cultural Achievement Award from the National Foundation for Jewish Culture. In 2003 Kushner married his longtime partner, magazine editor Mark Harris. Their wedding announcement was the first homosexual union featured in the "Vows" column of the *New York Times*.

Anne Epstein

L

labor. New York City became a national center of labor activity in colonial times. Among the first labor conflicts were slave insurrections in 1712 and 1741. Three craft strikes were recorded before 1788, and in 1794 a group of journeymen printers formed the Franklin Typographical Society, the city's first permanent association of wage earners. A citywide labor movement did not begin until the presidency of Andrew Jackson. Journeymen, small masters, and radicals banded together to form the Working Men's Party (1829–31), which sought egalitarian political and social reforms and briefly had many supporters among the electorate. After its demise the city's craft unions organized the General Trades' Union, a confederation that between 1833 and 1836 joined with various unaffiliated unions (including several led by women) in carrying out nearly 40 strikes to combat declining wages and working conditions. In 1834 it led efforts to form the National Trades' Union, the country's first organization uniting workers in different cities. The panic of 1837 crushed this national movement and abetted a nativism during the 1840s that divided unions and forced many to cease operations; a few survived the decade and undertook new efforts, ranging from George Henry Evans's land reform movement to the Subterranean Democracy of the Bowery, an insurgent faction within the Democratic Party spearheaded by radical Mike Walsh. After the late 1840s the city's workforce grew enormously and soon came to consist largely of immigrants from Ireland and Germany and their children. Labor advocates disagreed over whether and how to organize immigrants, especially the unskilled, and over forming relationships with the city's political parties, especially the Democrats, who aggressively fought for the immigrants' support. Compounded by ethnic and cultural tensions, these questions defined debates over the relative merits of craft unionism, industrial unionism, and broader political action. Immigrants, especially Germans, offered ideas about organizing that confirmed the city's importance as a center of activism. In 1850 the labor movement regained its strength through several bitter strikes and the formation of the Industrial Congress, a coalition of unionists, reform groups, and intellectuals that lasted until 1852.

Efforts to organize intensified as industrialization accelerated. As early as 1850 the city was the most productive manufacturing center in the United States and an attractive location for the needle trades, printing, and other industries. During the Civil War alone its trade unions undertook more than 90 strikes, mainly for higher wages to offset rising prices. Despite these shows of solidarity, deep divisions remained. As the number of whites increased with immigration, blacks accounted for a dwindling share of the workforce and were subjected to worsening discrimination: this reached a crisis during the draft riots of 1863, when crowds of white workers who had gathered to protest the draft swept through the city terrorizing black residents. Although denounced by labor leaders, the incident long remained a source of bitterness.

Labor won several important victories during the last decades of the nineteenth century. In 1872, 100,000 workers in the building trades waged a successful three-month strike for the eight-hour day. Nearly every major labor organization was well represented in the city, notably the socialist International Workingmen's Association, which had its headquarters there, the Knights of Labor, and several individual craft unions. Such prominent editors as John Swinton and Patrick Ford launched newspapers devoted to labor issues. In 1882 a group of Irish American workers joined with union delegates and German American socialists to form the Central Labor Union (CLU). Employing boycotts and such measures as the observance of Labor Day in 1882, it eventually included more than 200 groups and maintained friendly relations with its chief rivals, most importantly the Knights of Labor. After a court ruling against a boycott in 1885, the CLU and other groups focused on fielding candidates for political office: they chose the reformer Henry George to run in the mayoral election of 1886. His campaign, based in part on instituting a single tax on land, nearly prevailed and seemed to presage even broader political activity, but the movement collapsed owing to dissent among labor leaders and the timely introduction of state reforms.

After George's defeat the labor movement took a more conservative course. Skilled craft unions dominated; the most important leader in the city was Samuel Gompers, who had become well known as an organizer for the Federation of Organized Trades and Labor Unions in 1881. Initially a supporter of the CLU, he grew wary of focusing on political elections and organizing poor, unskilled workers, especially immigrants. In 1886 conflicts led to the rapid decline of the Knights of Labor and the formation of the American Federation of Labor (AFL), which represented only a fraction of the country's workers but under Gompers's leadership became the leading labor confederation, largely through its emphasis on organizing craft workers. About this time a large influx of immigrants settled in the city from southern and central Europe and Russia, leading to sharp ethnic antagonism among these groups and with longer-established ones. By the early twentieth century the new immigrants launched their own activist movement centered in the needle trades. The International Ladies' Garment Workers' Union (ILGWU) was formed as an affiliate of the AFL, and locals proliferated. Helped in their efforts by such reform groups as the Women's Trade Union League, the unions staged strikes that gradually changed the industry: one of the most successful, the "uprising of the thirty thousand," was led by young Jewish and Italian women and resulted in important gains. Radicalism in the labor movement was revived by a Yiddish-speaking milieu of socialists, anarchists, and reformers on the Lower East Side, the base of such important publications as Abraham Cahan's newspaper *Vorwerts.* Italians and other immigrants also formed radical circles, and the cause of labor was championed by a number of other groups, including settlement house workers, writers in Greenwich Village for such publications as the *Masses,* and the Socialist Party.

World War I marked a change in the fortunes of the labor movement nationwide. The political Left was put on the defensive by a general reaction against radicalism. Disagreements over whether to support the Bolshevik Revolution broke out among labor leaders, ending in thuggery and gunfights during the mid-1920s. Hostile government investigations into several unions, especially in the building trades, produced a sordid picture of widespread graft and racketeering. After the war many employers sought to reverse the gains of labor by taking part in an aggressive "open shop" campaign. Several unions survived, notably those in the garment trades, and the conservatism of the AFL was challenged by Sidney Hillman, president of the Amalgamated Clothing Workers of America (ACWA). Hillman called for grouping workers along industry rather than craft lines and also introduced a form of collective bargaining, sometimes called "industrial democracy," that invited workers to settle disputes on the shop floor; his ideas were well received and became known as "new unionism." Under Hillman the ACWA also offered unemployment insurance, low-cost housing for members in Manhattan and the Bronx, and group health care and opened the Amalgamated Bank, which provided workers with low-interest credit. By the late 1920s the city's labor movement was nonetheless severely weakened. The Depression brought more serious problems, as even unions that had remained relatively strong suffered enormous losses. The ACWA lost 50,000 members between 1929 and 1933, and wages fell to between 40 and 50 percent of what they had been before the Depression. Earlier abuses returned, and labor leaders struggled to preserve their gains and combat sweatshops, destructive competition, and the movement of businesses to rural areas.

Important Strikes in the History of New York City

DATE	PARTICIPANTS	NUMBER OF WORKERS (ESTIMATED)	OUTCOME
1677	Cartmen	12	Strikers held in contempt of court. First criminal prosecution for a strike in the colonies.
1684	Cartmen		Fined for violation of the law.
7 April 1741	Bakers		Prosecuted as criminal conspiracy.
May–June 1833	Journeymen carpenters		Wage increase. General Trades Union of the City of New York (GTU) founded 14 Aug 1833.
Feb 1836	Tailors		National Guard called in. Twenty journeymen tailors indicted for illegal combination, denied right to unionize. Largest protest meeting in United States to date (30,000 participants). Call for new political party.
15 July 1850	Tailors	2,000	First time in history of United States that worker is killed in a trade dispute. Few concrete gains. Cooperative Union of Tailoring Estates founded.
1886	Various		Many workers win 8- or 10-hour day.
Jan 1887	Longshoremen		Wages and benefits cut. One year after strike not one longshoremen's organization left in Port of New York.
11 Feb 1887	Knights of Labor District Assembly 49		
20 July 1899	Newsboys, bootblacks		Wage increase.
7–11 March 1904	Amalgamated Association of Street and Electric Railway Employees (AASERE), Brotherhood of Locomotive Firemen (BLF), Brotherhood of Locomotive Engineers (BLE)		Defeated. Open shop.
24 Nov 1909–15 Feb 1910	International Ladies' Garment Workers' Union (ILGWU)	30,000	Higher wages, better conditions, 52-hour work week.
7 July–2 Sept 1910	International Ladies' Garment Workers' Union (ILGWU)	60,000	"Protocol of Peace." 50-hour work week, overtime pay, 10 legal holidays, compulsory arbitration, joint labor–management board. Foundations laid for long, stable unionism.
Nov 1910	Brooklyn Boot and Shoe Workers	3,000	Defeated. No concessions.
18 March 1911	Industrial Workers of the World, Local 168		
7 May 1912	Hotel Workers Industrial Union	18,000	A few contracts signed.
21 June 1912	Industrial Workers of the World		
28 June 1912	United Hebrew Trades	9,000	Union recognition, 49-hour week, overtime pay, 10 paid holidays, ban on home work, permanent board of arbitration, joint board of sanitary control. Almost complete unionization of fur industry.
16 April 1916	International Ladies' Garment Workers' Union (ILGWU)	60,000	Full representation of ILGWU, binding two-year contracts, standard collective bargaining agreements.
4 Aug–27 Sept 1916	Amalgamated Association of Street and Electric Railway Employees (AASERE)		No concrete gains.
7 Aug 1919–6 Sept 1919	Actors' Equity Association (AEA)	3,000	Secured unpaid rehearsal time, closed shop, strict eight-performance week. Membership in Actors' Equity reaches 14,000, creating a stable union in theater.

(*continued*)

Important Strikes in the History of New York City (*Continued*)

DATE	PARTICIPANTS	NUMBER OF WORKERS (ESTIMATED)	OUTCOME
July 1932	Amalgamated Clothing and Textile Workers (ACTW)	30,000	Decline of ILGWU in New York City is arrested.
Aug 1932	Amalgamated Clothing and Textile Workers (ACTW)	15,000	Strengthens ILGWU on East Coast.
6 Feb–12 March 1934	Taxi drivers		Violence, destruction of property, eventual wage increase.
10–21 March 1941	Transportation Workers Union (TWU)		Wage increase.
3–19 Oct 1945	International Longshoremen's Association (ILA)	35,000	Wage gains, improved working conditions, challenge to Joseph P. Ryan's control of union.
1959	Local 1199		
7–8 Nov 1960	United Federation of Teachers (UFT)	5,000	Collective bargaining agreement promised. Challenge to Condon–Waldin Act against public employee strikes.
12 April 1962	United Federation of Teachers (UFT)	20,000	Wage increase. Violation of Condon–Waldin Act begins era of public employee strikes.
6 Dec 1962–31 March 1963	International Typographical Union (ITU)	20,000	Small wage increase, new technology allowed. *Mirror* ceases publication after strike displaces 1,400 employees.
2 Jan–1 Feb 1965	Social Service Employees Union (SSEU)	8,000	Salary increase, welfare fund for educational purposes, caseload reductions, end to "midnight" raids on welfare recipients.
1–13 Jan 1966	Transportation Workers Union (TWU)	35,000	Wage increase, fare increase.
Jan 1968	Uniformed Sanitationmen's Association (USA)		Binding arbitration, large pay increase.
9 Sept 1968	United Federation of Teachers (UFT)	54,000	Strike leaders jailed. Teachers allowed back into classrooms in Ocean Hill–Brownsville.
18–25 March 1970	United Federation of Postal Clerks (UFPC), National Postal Union (NPU)	57,000	Wage increase, full health benefits, locally based wages, amnesty for striking workers. Postal Reorganization Act requires collective bargaining on all issues and binding arbitration.
14–19 Jan 1971	Patrolmen's Benevolent Association (PBA)	25,000	Salary increase, prosecutions under Taylor Law, police unions strengthened.
June 1971	American Federation of State, County and Municipal Employees (AFSCME)	8,000	Public disapproval, union fined.
Dec 1971–1972	Communication Workers of America (CWA)		
1991	Employees of *Daily News*		British publisher Robert Maxwell buys the newspaper on 15 March and settles with union leaders on 31 March. Thirty-five management workers are laid off.
1–10 April 1992	National Hockey League's Player Association (NHLPA)		Season expanded to 84 games, each team required to play two games in non-NHL cities, and players received increases in playoff bonuses and control over the free agency system.
12 Aug 1994–2 April 1995	Major League Baseball Players Association (MLBPA)		Revenue sharing among teams from a luxury tax to slow payroll growth of high-revenue teams. Shortened 1995 season.

(*continued*)

Important Strikes in the History of New York City (*Continued*)

DATE	PARTICIPANTS	NUMBER OF WORKERS (ESTIMATED)	OUTCOME
4–19 Aug 1997	International Brotherhood of Teamsters (IBT)	185,000	Most UPS workers (UPS is a member of the Teamsters) received benefit increases. Raised initial pay for part-time workers, 10,000 part-time jobs converted to full-time positions, existing part-timers to fill five-sixths of new full-time positions. UPS remained in IBT's pension plan.
15 June 1999–26 Feb 2001	International Longshoremen's Association Local 1814	284	Defeated. Domino Sugar eliminated 110 jobs and workers received a three-year contract giving a one-time 5% raise in addition to the workers' average weekly base pay of about $600.
1 May–Oct 2000	Commercial actors of the Screen Actors Guild (SAG), American Federation of Television and Radio Artists (AFTRA)	135,000	Steady increase over three years in the maximum flat fees paid to actors in cable commercials in exchange for unlimited ad use. Advertisers to employ union actors in Internet commercials, though specifics unclear.
5–23 Aug 2000	International Brotherhood of Electric Workers, Communications Workers of America	86,000	Reduced overtime for Verizon Communications customer service representatives and an overtime cap for other union employees. Those performing jobs in more than one language received a raise. Wage and benefit increase, stock options, and greater job security.
7–11 March 2003	Broadway musicians, as part of the American Federation of Musicians Local 802	325	Minimum number of musicians required in Broadway's 13 largest theaters lowered by about 25% for the next decade.
20–22 Dec 2005	Local 100 of the Transport Workers Union (TWU), Local 726 (Staten Island), Local 1056 (Queens) of the Amalgamated Transit Union against the Metropolitan Transportation Authority (MTA)		No change in pension plan and some workers received a refund for prior pension contributions. Steady annual salary increases for the next three years and Martin Luther King, Jr., Day is a paid holiday. Improved disability insurance and maternity benefit. Contract expiration date changed to 15 January. Workers to contribute 1.5% of their overall gross pay toward health care coverage with no cap on percentage increase. District courts fined TWU $2.5 million, and Local 100 president Roger Toussaint stayed in prison for three days.
5 Nov 2007–12 Feb 2008	Writers Guild of America, East (WGAE), Writers Guild of America, West (WGAW)	More than 12,000	Writers to receive residuals, payments for subsequent airings of a show and for programs streamed on the Internet. WGA to have a form of jurisdiction over digital programming. A short period remained during which studios may air shows on the Internet for promotional purposes without writer compensation.
10–28 Nov 2007	Broadway stagehands, as part of the Theatrical Protective Union Number One (Local One) of the International Alliance of Theatrical Employees	350	More flexibility in dismissing stagehands during load-in, the period when a production is loaded into a theater, as long as there is a daily minimum of 17stagehands on duty. Extension of the continuity call to two hours before or one hour before and after a performance; those who work after earn double the pay. Union members received an annual raise higher than 3.5%.

Change came with the election of President Franklin D. Roosevelt and Mayor Fiorello H. La Guardia. Organized labor was greatly strengthened by the Wagner Act (1935), introduced by Senator Robert F. Wagner. The act was among the most progressive pieces of labor legislation ever enacted at the national level: it guaranteed the right to collective bargaining, allowed free speech in advocating unionism, and gave unions and their members the right to protest unfair labor practices and seek redress of grievances through the National Labor Relations Board. In 1936 the Congress of Industrial Organizations (CIO) was formed to compete with the AFL; it borrowed and extended innovative practices of the new unionism. During the same year its branch in the city gave institutional support to Roosevelt by organizing the American Labor Party, which delivered votes to him as well as to La Guardia and Governor Herbert H. Lehman. Encouraged by a sympathetic government and the increasing militancy of workers (often led by members of the Communist Party), several local affiliates of the CIO, including the United Textile Workers and the United Electrical Workers, organized workers in manufacturing. La Guardia, a Republican supporter of Roosevelt, publicly backed labor and in the first few years of the New Deal alone provided more than 200,000 jobs for the city's unemployed. He also supported the right to collective bargaining and the right to strike (although not for municipal workers). Such figures as Hillman and David Dubinsky, president of the ILGWU, served on several government boards and were influential in elections throughout the New Deal. Although overshadowed in politics somewhat by the CIO, the AFL retained as members most of the city's organized workers, counting largely on its unions in the building trades for its strength. In response to successes of the CIO, a few unions in the AFL, including the ILGWU and the International Brotherhood of Electrical Workers, organized factory workers according to the industrial model of the CIO; otherwise there was little overlap between the two organizations. Several leaders of the AFL in the city who were not entirely opposed to industrial organizing eventually held the highest positions in organized labor. One was George Meany, president of the State Federation of Labor and later the AFL.

Unions prospered with the return of economic stability during World War II. A precedent for civil service unions was set by the Transport Workers Union of America, which despite its small size enforced contract provisions made when the city took over public transit in 1940. By 1945 labor groups in the city were firmly allied with the Democratic Party. New problems arose after the war, when an influx of black workers from the South and immigrants from the Caribbean coincided with the flight of manufacturers from the city. Because of personal differences and its committed anticommunism, the AFL remained divided from the CIO until 1955, when Meany orchestrated a merger of the two groups to form the AFL–CIO. From the mid-1950s municipal unions made important gains. Under Mayor Robert F. Wagner they won the right to organize, and in 1958 Executive Order 49 gave many of them the right to collective bargaining. The transport workers brought the city to a halt with a 12-day strike in 1966; strikes during the next three years by social workers and sanitation workers led to the passage of the Taylor Law (1967), which outlawed strikes by municipal employees. The most divisive conflict of the time was the teachers' strike of 1968 in Ocean Hill and Brownsville, which marked a turning point in race relations in the city (see Teachers' unions). After 13 teachers and six other school employees were transferred by the Ocean Hill–Brownsville school board, a strike by the United Federation of Teachers (UFT) was

New York City's Largest Local Unions by Number of Members

Name	2007 Members	2006 Assets (millions)	Year Founded	Address
1199SEIU United Healthcare Workers East	295,000	$64.4	1932	310 West 43rd St., Manhattan
UFT Local 2	150,000	n.d.	1960	52 Broadway, Manhattan
SEIU Local 32BJ	85,000	$28.4	1934	101 6th Ave., Manhattan
Transport Workers Union Local 100	39,975	$44.3	1934	80 West End Ave., Manhattan
IBEW Local Union 3	30,677	$32.1	1888	158-11 Harry Van Arsdale, Jr. Ave., Flushing, Queens
UNITE HERE Local 6	25,000	$13.7	1938	709 8th Ave., Manhattan
New York City Patrolmen's Benevolent Association	24,000	n.d.	1894	40 Fulton St., Manhattan
IBT Local 237	22,914	$4.1	1951	216 West 14th St., Manhattan
UFCW Local 1500	21,856	$27.7	1951	221-10 Jamaica Ave., Queens Village, Queens
Professional Staff Congress AFT Local 2334	20,956	$6.9	1972	61 Broadway, Manhattan
AFTRA-NY Local	20,619	n.d.	1937	260 Madison Ave., Manhattan
OPEIU Local 153	18,556	$0.8	1945	265 West 14th St., Manhattan
AFSCME Local 1549	18,000	n.d.	1964	125 Barclay St., Manhattan
RWDSCU Local 1549	14,000	$49.0	1925	97-45 Queens Blvd., Rego Park, Queens
Committee of Interns and Residents SEIU Local 1957	12,500	$4.6	1957	520 8th Ave., Manhattan
Council of School Supervisors and Administrators	11,903	$11.8	1968	16 Court St., Brooklyn
LIUNA Local 300 Mail Handlers	11,468	$1.2	1972	401 Broadway, Manhattan

Source: *Crain's New York Business*, 20 Aug 2007

Compiled by Frank Nestor

called by their controversial leader Albert Shanker. The UFT and the Afro-American Teachers Association squared off over the issue of community control of schools, trading charges of racism and anti-Semitism. Shanker was sentenced to 15 days in prison for defying a court injunction; the strike ended after the teachers were reinstated, but the experiment with local control was reduced, straining relations between the UFT and some black community groups well into the 1990s.

In the following years labor gained strength on only a few fronts. Under the direction of Victor Gotbaum, the American Federation of State, County, and Municipal Employees (AFSCME), the largest representative of municipal employees, launched an ambitious unionization drive, aided by the expansion of municipal government and service industries. By the early 1970s the power base of District Council 37 of AFSCME shifted from motor vehicle operators, most of whom were white men, to hospital, clerical, and administrative workers, most of whom were black women. Workers became more militant, and divisions formed over such ideologically charged issues as the Vietnam War and support for undemocratic regimes in Latin America, which were favored by the conservative building trades unions but not by those in the public sector (AFSCME was the only union on the executive council of the AFL–CIO that regularly opposed Meany in his support for the war). The municipal unions became important power brokers in city politics by contributing money and organizers to electoral campaigns, but they were vulnerable to budget cuts during times of austerity: in negotiations prompted by the fiscal crisis in 1975 they accepted reductions in wages and benefits and agreed to invest pension funds in municipal bonds to keep the city from bankruptcy.

The strength of unions diminished again during the 1980s, when the city and state cut their budgets, hostility toward labor took root under Presidents Ronald Reagan and George Bush, and the economy slowed late in the decade. Building trades unions focused on retaining control of large projects and became more vulnerable than ever to cancellations of plans for new office buildings. They did manage to remain strong beyond their numbers: although representing less than one-fifth of the city's organized workforce, the building trades unions held most of the major political positions open to labor leaders, controlling the Central Labor Council and the State Federation of Labor, two influential partners in the coalition that helped elect Governor Mario M. Cuomo in 1982.

According to a survey in 1988, more than 30 percent of its regular workforce was unionized, while in the same year the corresponding figure for the United States as a whole was 16.8 percent. Some unions sought to expand their jurisdiction, among them the IGLWU, which competed with others to represent the city's office workers. Militant unionism returned with a strike of workers at the *Daily News* in 1991. Early in the twenty-first century New York City remained a stronghold for labor. One of the largest and most active labor organizations was the New York City Central Labor Council (NYCCLC), whose 1.3 million members included 400 local unions representing teachers, truck drivers, operating engineers, nurses, construction workers, electricians, firefighters, retail workers, janitors, train operators, bakers, and many others.

Joshua Freeman, *In Transit: The Transit Workers Union in New York City, 1933–1966* (New York: Oxford University Press, 1989); Richard J. Attenbaugh, *Education for Struggle* (Philadelphia: Temple University Press, 1990)

See also Child labor, Maritime unions, and Occupational health.

Kerry Candaele, Sean Wilentz

Laconia. Name formerly applied to a section of Williamsbridge lying between the Boston Road and Wakefield in the northwestern Bronx. Originally named Laconia Park, it was a real estate development built in the late 1880s on the estates of William Blodgett and Marmaduke Tilden.

John McNamara, *History in Asphalt: The Origin of Bronx Street and Place Names* (New York: Bronx County Historical Society, 1984)

Gary D. Hermalyn

Ladies' Mile. Name retrospectively applied to a shopping district along Broadway and Sixth Avenue and between 14th and 23rd streets that took form in the mid-nineteenth century as wealthy residents of lower Manhattan moved north. The anchor of the district was the store of R. H. Macy, which opened in 1858 at Sixth Avenue and 14th Street, near wealthy customers who lived on Fifth Avenue. During the next 20 years other stores followed, marking off a district between the stores of A. T. Stewart at Ninth Street and Stern Brothers at 23rd Street. The retailers of the Ladies' Mile occupied cast-iron palaces of different styles, and their display windows were designed to imitate those of Europe. Some of the most elegant stores were those of Lord and Taylor, B. Altman, and Arnold Constable. The opening of the Sixth Avenue elevated line in 1878 provided convenient access for customers throughout the city. Spurred by the construction of the Flatiron Building (1902–3), commercial establishments such as publishers and booksellers gradually replaced the residences on Fifth Avenue, and by the time of World War I the Ladies' Mile had been abandoned by department stores for sites farther north. During the 1990s and early years of the twenty-first century, the area experienced a strong commercial revival, and crowds once again thronged the sidewalks of what was once the nation's preeminent shopping district.

La Farge, John (*b* New York City, 31 March 1835; *d* Providence, R.I., 14 Nov 1910). Painter. Born near Washington Square in Manhattan, he attended St. John's College (now Fordham University) and Mount St. Mary's in Maryland; he completed his artistic training in France. He settled near Washington Square and produced drawings for *Riverside Magazine.* He became known for his murals at the Church of the Incarnation, St. Thomas's Church (burned 1905), and the Church of the Ascension and also for his thousands of stained-glass windows. La Farge had a studio at 51 West 10th Street.

H. Barbara Weinberg, *The Decorative Work of John La Farge* (New York: Garland, 1977)

James E. Mooney

Lafayette, Marquis de [Du Motier, Marie Joseph Paul Yves Roch Gilbert] (*b* château of Chavaniac, Auvergne, 6 Sept 1757; *d* Paris, 20 May 1834). Statesman. He first visited New York City from 4 August to 8 August 1784. On his return to the city on 11 September he was given a banquet by officers of the Continental Army at Capes Tavern, and during receptions by municipal officials and Mayor James Duane on the following day he was presented with the "freedom of the city" in a golden box. He left the city on 15 September, returned three months later, and before his departure on 21 December was escorted to his frigate by a select committee, honored with a parade and artillery salute, and presented with a farewell ode. Lafayette returned to the city on 14 August 1824 for a six-day visit that included a "triumphal procession" to City Hall, a reception by the mayor, and a state banquet on 16 August. During another visit from 5 September to 14 September a performance of *Lafayette; or, The Hero of Olmutz* was given at the Park Theatre on 9 September, the Lafayette Museum at 11 Park Street was illuminated on 13 September, and the next evening a "grand fete" and reception at Castle Garden drew 6000 guests. Lafayette stayed in the city again for three days beginning on 20 September. He made his last visit from 3 July to 14 July 1825. On 4 July a reception for him at City Hall was followed by performances at the Park Theatre and Castle Garden. He remarked that he was greatly impressed by the "prodigious progress" of the city. Samuel F. B. Morse was commissioned to paint a full-length portrait of Lafayette to hang in City Hall; Walt Whitman, then six years old, later recounted that Lafayette had picked him up and kissed him while visiting Brooklyn.

J. Bennett Nolan, *Lafayette in America Day by Day* (Baltimore: Johns Hopkins University Press, 1934)

Allen J. Share

Lafayette Theatre. Theater in Harlem, opened in 1912. From 1915 to 1932, when there were few serious roles for blacks on Broadway, it was the venue for various black stock com-

Lafayette Theatre

panies, most known by the name the Lafayette Players. Under the leadership of a white director, A. C. Winn, they presented a range of one-act plays and adaptations of lightweight successes from Broadway. The Lafayette became the most celebrated theater in Harlem, and many members of the Lafayette Players gained recognition as serious dramatic actors. From 1935 to 1939 the theater was the headquarters in Harlem of the Federal Theatre Project of the Works Project Administration and housed productions including *Voodoo Macbeth,* directed by Orson Welles. After being abandoned in the late 1930s, the theater was used temporarily as a church. While being restored as the New Lafayette, it was destroyed by fire in 1968.

E. G. Hill

Lafever, Minard (*b* near Morristown, N.J., 1797; *d* 1854). Carpenter, draftsman, and writer. He moved to New York City in 1828 and in the following year published a builder's guide, *The Young Builder's General Instructor,* the first in a popular series that helped to disseminate the Greek Revival style throughout the United States. The Old Merchant's House (1832) and St. James Roman Catholic Church (1837), both in Manhattan, include details from his handbooks. During his later career he designed Gothic Revival buildings in Brooklyn, including the Church of the Saviour (1844), Holy Trinity Protestant Episcopal Church (1847), and Packer Collegiate Institute (1854), his final commission.

Jacob Landy, *The Architecture of Minard Lafever* (New York: Columbia University Press, 1970)

Val Ginter

La Guardia, Fiorello (Raffaele) H(enry) [Enrico] (*b* New York City, 11 Dec 1882; *d* New York City, 20 Sept 1947). Mayor and congressman. He was born at 177 Sullivan Street in lower Manhattan and brought up in the American West, where his father, Achille, was a bandmaster in the U.S. Army. He studied law at New York University and was admitted to the bar in 1910. In 1916 he became the first Italian American elected to the U.S. Congress; he was a Republican opposed to Tammany Hall who represented a working-class district in lower Manhattan. While holding office he commanded U.S. air forces on the Italian–Austrian front during World War I. By the end of the 1920s he led a progressive minority in the House of Representatives that fought against Prohibition, racism, and the prevailing economic doctrine of laissez faire. His ideas won increasing acceptance during the Depression and eventually helped shape the recovery and relief programs of the New Deal. After a brief tenure as president of the city's Board of Aldermen (1920–21), he was reelected to Congress in 1922; there he sponsored the Norris–La Guardia Act, which prohibited injunctions in labor disputes. In 1932 he lost his seat to James Lanzetta in the Democratic landslide that elected Franklin D. Roosevelt to the presidency.

Fiorello H. La Guardia, 1942. The mayor was well known for reading comic strips over the radio. One newspaper wrote that his popularity was attributable to his "lusty mugging and robust histrionics."

La Guardia turned to municipal politics and was elected mayor in 1933 as a Fusion candidate (see Fusionism), helped by the investigations that forced Mayor James J. Walker from office, the city's financial troubles, and the Depression. He disclaimed loyalty to the Fusion Party, became known for his aggressive political leadership, and was suspicious of those who threatened his power. Recognizing upon taking office that the city was divided into haphazardly administered political fiefdoms and had inadequate social and health services, he modernized and centralized its government, consolidated departments, and eliminated unnecessary borough and county offices. He was frustrated by what he considered a hostile press and saw radio broadcasting as a means of reaching the people directly: in what became the best-remembered act of his mayoralty, he gave a dramatic reading of the comic strip *Dick Tracy* during a newspaper strike on 8 July 1945. He assumed a larger role than preceding mayors had done by taking up local needs not with the Board of Aldermen or the state but with the White House: he persuaded President Roosevelt to grant billions of dollars in funds to the city for the construction of bridges, tunnels, reservoirs, sewer systems, parks, highways, schools, hospitals, health centers, and airports. For the first time in the city's history it had a unified transit system and could provide public housing for its poor and training and subsidies for its artists. As president of the U.S. Conference of Mayors for nearly a decade, La Guardia led a national coalition that fought for a generous federal urban policy. In the spring of 1941 Roosevelt appointed him director of the Office of Civilian Defense, a position he assumed while seeking a third term as mayor. After war broke out he could no longer balance both tasks, and in February 1942 he resigned from his position in Washington, D.C. After leaving office at the end of 1945 he served briefly as the director general of the United Nations Relief and Rehabilitation Administration.

La Guardia provided honest, inspired, impassioned leadership. He embodied some contradictions: although he enjoyed a reputation as a civil libertarian, he cracked down on gamblers, closed burlesque houses, and used his powers of "garbage collection" to rid newsstands of sexually explicit magazines. He also failed to consider the long-term effect of his progressive policies, and by the time he left office, New York City was plagued with debt, facilities too expensive to maintain, and a rapidly growing bureaucracy. La Guardia's residences in New York City included 39 Charles Street (1914 or 1915–21), 1852 University Avenue in Riverdale (1921–early 1930s), 23

East 109th Street (1929–32), 1274 Fifth Avenue (1933–42), Gracie Mansion (which became the official mayoral residence during his third term as mayor, 1942–45), and 5020 Goodridge Avenue in Riverdale (from 1945). He is buried in Woodlawn Cemetery in the Bronx.

Thomas Kessner, *Fiorello H. La Guardia and the Making of Modern New York* (New York: McGraw-Hill, 1989)

See also Buses, Civil service, Government and politics, Markets, and No Deal Party.

Thomas Kessner

La Guardia Airport. Airport in north central Queens, adjacent to Long Island Sound, opened in 1929 as North Beach Airport and in 1939 renamed New York Municipal Airport–La Guardia Field (commonly known as La Guardia Airport). Development of the airport was promoted by Mayor Fiorello H. La Guardia, an enthusiastic advocate of aviation. Though it had poor soil and obstructing buildings, the site offered easy access to planned highways. The field was stabilized and expanded with funds from the federal Works Progress Administration, and by the early 1940s it covered 558 acres (226 hectares), including 17 million cubic yards (13 million cubic meters) of landfill from Rikers Island and from subway excavations. Experts thought that trans-Atlantic travel might require refueling at sea, so La Guardia Airport originally included a seaplane station, a circular structure 144 feet (41 meters) high; although soon abandoned, the station remained intact into the twenty-first century.

In order to attract airlines from competing Newark Airport, Mayor La Guardia negotiated below-cost landing fees. Then, in an effort to make the airport self-sustaining, he insisted that spectators pay to be admitted to the observation deck (a policy that proved lucrative). He also persuaded banks, hairdressers, gift shops, and other businesses to set up concessions along the walkways to airline gates, correctly estimating that these would be used by passengers en route to their flights, generating rental income for the airport. The flooding and collapse of several runways in the 1940s led many to believe that the airport would never be suitable for large postwar aircraft, but new landing-field technology permitted the runways to be lengthened and reinforced so that all but the largest commercial aircraft could be accommodated. It seemed unlikely in the early postwar years that the airport could sustain itself economically, and in 1947, over the objections of Commissioner Robert Moses (who favored placing the field under his newly created New York Airport Authority), Mayor William O'Dwyer and the Board of Estimate ceded control to the Port of New York Authority, which was thereafter in charge of modernizing and operating the airport. Air-cargo service was at first a mainstay of the airport but later declined in importance. Between 1950 and 1990, measured by passenger traffic, La Guardia was by turns the leading airport in the New York City metropolitan region and the second after John F. Kennedy International Airport. Since the early 1990s it has regularly trailed both Kennedy and Newark airports in passenger volume. Even so, in 2008 it served 26 million travelers, seven times the number served in 1950. More than 9000 people worked at La Guardia in 2008.

See also Aviation.

Paul Barrett, Jameson W. Doig

La Guardia Airport, 1941

Air traffic control tower at La Guardia Airport, 2009

La Guardia Community College. Junior college of the City University of New York, opened in 1971 in Long Island City in Queens. It is the only community college in the city that requires internships for graduation. The college oversees two high schools on its campus, and its division of continuing education offers programs in Astoria, Harlem, and Chinatown and on the Upper East Side. In the early twenty-first century La Guardia enrolled more than 14,000 students.

Marc Ferris

La MaMa Experimental Theatre Club. Off-Off-Broadway theater and cultural organization. Presenting mainly new works by international artists, it was founded in 1961 by Ellen Stewart and originally located at 321 East Ninth Street. Now housed at 74A East Fourth Street in the East Village, La MaMa operates three theaters—The First Floor Theatre, The Club, and The Annex—as well as an art gallery and a six-story studio building containing rehearsal spaces. One of the first Off-Off-Broadway theaters to support a full-time resident company, La MaMa figured centrally in the growth of Off-Off-Broadway theater, providing a place for new playwrights to stage their work and acting as a center for the counterculture artistic movements of the 1960s and 1970s. Since its founding, La MaMa has also had a multinational and multicultural focus, seeking to bring to the fore the work of artists from around the world. Artists that have worked with La MaMa include Romanian-born director Andrei Şerban and composers Elizabeth Swados and Philip Glass. Other artists whose development was fostered at La MaMa include actors Robert De Niro, Al Pacino, Bette Midler, Diane Lane, and Harvey Fierstein and playwrights Sam Shepard, Lanford Wilson, and Caryl Churchill. The archives of La MaMa, kept by Stewart since 1961, provide one of the most extensive collections of primary source material of the Off-Off-Broadway theater movement that played so important a role in the development of modern American drama.

Patrick Barrett

La Marqueta. Indoor market in El Barrio, under the Park Avenue viaduct of the Metro-North Commuter Railroad between 111th and 116th streets. Built as part of Mayor Fiorello H. La Guardia's program to eliminate push-carts, it opened in 1936 and became known as the "life of East Harlem." The number of vendors declined in the 1960s, and from the mid-1970s the complex fell into disrepair, leading Mayor Edward I. Koch to talk of refurbishment. In 1990 the city dissolved its contract with the firm responsible for the market, La Marqueta Development Associates, for failing to begin renovations. The area outside the market became a greenmarket in 1994, and in the early twenty-first century vendors continued to sell at both the greenmarket and indoor space. The city continued negotiating with the Harlem Community Development Corporation about renovation plans.

Melissa M. Merritt

Lamb, Thomas W(hite) (*b* Dundee, Scotland, 1871; *d* New York City, 26 Feb 1942). Architect. He designed more than 300 movie theaters in New York City and around the world, including the Regent Theater (1913, seating 1800), now on Adam Clayton Powell Jr. Boulevard at 116th Street. With a facade modeled after that of the Doges' Palace in Venice, the Regent is generally considered the first true movie palace. He also designed many theaters for Marcus Loew, the leading movie theater operator in the city, with whom he was associated from 1908. His work for Loew included Loew's State Theatre (1921, seating 3300; demolished) at the headquarters of the company in Times Square and such exotic venues as the Pitkin Theatre (1929) in Brooklyn and the 175th Street Theatre (1930, seating 3560) in upper Manhattan. He also designed several legitimate stage theaters, including the Cort Theatre (1912) and the Hollywood Theater (1929; now the Mark Hellinger Theatre) on Broadway, the theater used by Warner Brothers to show its first "talkies," and the Albee Theatre in downtown Brooklyn (1925, seating 3200; demolished).

Anthony W. Robins

Lambs. Social club for people in the performing arts formed in 1874 by five actors at Delmonico's restaurant. It was named after a club of the same name in London that honored the essayist Charles Lamb and his London salon of the nineteenth century. The members met at various restaurants around Union Square before moving to rented quarters at 34 West 26th Street. The club was situated for generations at 134 West 44th Street in the theater district. The architect and club member Stanford White, who had been responsible for the alterations to a clubhouse at 70 West 36th Street, was asked to design a new clubhouse, which was completed just in time for the Christmas Gambol of 1904. White's portrait was placed in the position of honor in the Grille, the spiritual center of the club. The present address is 3 West 51st Street. Members of the Lambs take part in monthly "Lambastes," four annual stage productions in their theater, and the Lambs Foundation, which supports classes for actors. The club steward is called the Shepherd, the membership the Flock, and the clubhouse the Fold. Members of the Lambs include Fred Astaire, Irving Berlin, George M. Cohan, and W. C. Fields.

James E. Mooney

Lamont, Thomas (William) (*b* Claverack, N.Y., 30 Sept 1870; *d* Boca Grande, Fla., 2 Feb 1948). Journalist, financier, and diplomat. He moved to New York City in 1893 to work as a reporter for the *New York Tribune.* After two years he left to form the consulting firm of Lamont, Corliss, which soon became prominent on Wall Street and helped him to become treasurer of the Bankers Trust Company (1903–9), vice president of First National Bank (1909–11), and a partner in the firm of J. P. Morgan and Company (1910–48). He and his wife, Florence, rented Franklin D. Roosevelt's house on East 65th Street until 1921 when they bought a townhouse at 107 East 70th Street. He owned the *New York Evening Post* (1918–22) briefly and the *Saturday Review of Literature* (1922–38). By the 1920s he was one of the city's most powerful financiers, overshadowing even J. P. Morgan, Jr. A well-known diplomat, Lamont represented the United States at the peace talks in Paris in 1919 and helped to formulate the Dawes Plan for German reparations in 1924.

James Bradley

La Motta, Jake [Giacobbe] (*b* New York City, 10 July 1921). Boxer. He grew up on the Lower East Side of Manhattan and in Philadelphia and moved to the Bronx in the late 1930s. From the beginning of his professional boxing career in 1941, La Motta's aggressive, brawling style made him a popular fighter, and he was soon considered one of the best middleweights in the world. Known as the Bronx Bull, he fought frequently at Madison Square Garden, which was the site of two of his six bouts with Sugar Ray Robinson and where he deliberately lost to Billy Fox in 1947, resulting in a temporary suspension from boxing. He became the middleweight champion of the world in 1949 but lost the title to Sugar Ray Robinson in 1951. La Motta retired in 1954 and is still considered to have been one of the greatest middleweights in the history of the sport. He wrote *Raging Bull: My Story* (1970) and was portrayed by Robert De Niro in Martin Scorsese's Academy Award–winning motion picture *Raging Bull* (1981).

James Bradley

landfill. During the seventeenth century Manhattan was bounded to the north by the North River, which ran along sections of Greenwich and Washington streets and what are now 10th, 11th, and 12th avenues; the southern boundary was the high-water mark, which on the East River was at Pearl and Cherry streets and First Avenue. Large coves and inlets pierced Corlear's Hook and East 12th, 25th, and 90th streets. Landfill was first added by the Dutch, who excavated canals, filled in swamps for building sites, and built piers into the East River that became foundations for new land when commerce expanded under English rule. The charter of Governor Thomas Dongan (1686) gave to the city all state-owned land under water between low and high tide. Streets were elongated and new blocks built according to the British grid pattern. Just before the American Revolution development began along the shoreline of the East River in Brooklyn, and industries moved to landfill between Fulton Street and Atlantic Avenue. Atlantic Basin, which was modeled after British and European ports, pushed new blocks into Buttermilk Channel. During the first half of the nineteenth century more land was added in the East River to accommodate facilities for the Port of New York, the busiest port in the nation; beyond this area, longer docks were built for large new sailing and steam-powered ships. With dredgings from the Erie Basin in Brooklyn, Red Hook was transformed from an island into a peninsula. Market spoil and debris from fires and demolished buildings were used to build several blocks between Greenwich and West streets and between Vesey and Liberty streets. Land was added to eastern Staten Island, southern Brooklyn, and lower Manhattan to build fortifications along New York Bay, and the northern shore of Staten Island was also expanded.

Most maritime-related landfill was complete by the Civil War; the next phase of landfill created municipal facilities, highways, and parks. Industrial materials were deposited in swamps to provide land for building. During the late nineteenth century the Brooklyn Ash Removal Company extended northern Queens by depositing coal ash from Manhattan in Flushing Bay. Abundant and cheap, ash was also dumped along RANDALLS ISLAND to form a bridge to Wards Island. At the turn of the century excavations from the Interborough Rapid Transit Company's subways provided cheap fill for one of the city's largest landfills—the extension of GOVERNORS ISLAND southward into New York Bay—and for moving RIVERSIDE PARK westward into the Hudson. An ambitious landfill program was begun in the 1930s and carried out mainly by Robert Moses during the following 20 years. Garbage, ash, earth from excavations for highways and buildings, and sand from the Rockaways were used in filling in parts of New York and Jamaica bays, wetlands, and rivers to build parks (Ferry Point, Soundview, Dreier Offerman, Marine, Owls Head, Spring Creek, East River, Flushing Meadows, and Fresh Kills), highways (the Brooklyn–Queens Expressway, Henry Hudson Parkway, and East River and Franklin D. Roosevelt drives), and beaches (South, Orchard, and Oakland). The Port of New York Authority filled in parts of Flushing and Jamaica bays to enlarge La Guardia and Idlewild (now John F. Kennedy) airports.

After 1960 development on new land was increasingly opposed by those concerned for the environment. The expansion of Idlewild Airport was halted largely because of efforts by supporters of the Jamaica Bay Wildlife Refuge. Gaps were filled between several piers in south Brooklyn to build a staging area for containerized cargo shipments. In 1974 the construction of Waterside, a housing complex on pilings, added a block to the edge of the East River between 25th and 30th streets. Dredgings from the harbor and earth excavated from the site of the World Trade Center provided the fill between Battery Park and Harrison Street for what in the 1980s became BATTERY PARK CITY. Plans for an extension of several blocks into the Hudson between Harrison and West 34th streets were part of the proposal for Westway, a large-scale development incorporating a highway and a park that was canceled in 1990. In the early twenty-first century, landfill accounted for 33 percent of the land in lower Manhattan and a large portion of the city's shoreline.

Ann L. Buttenwieser, *Manhattan Water-Bound: Planning and Developing Manhattan's Waterfront from the Seventeenth Century to the Present* (New York: New York University Press, 1987)

Ann L. Buttenwieser

land grants. See AMERICAN INDIANS.

Landmarks Preservation Commission. Public body formed in 1965 to identify and protect landmarks and historic districts; the law establishing it amended section 534 of the New York City Charter and title 25, chapter 3, of the Administrative Code. The formation of the commission was inspired by the rapid growth in building after World War II and the loss of such valued structures as Pennsylvania Station. Designations of structures at least 30 years old are made on the basis of aesthetic, architectural, cultural, and historic significance to the city, state, or nation. In 1973 jurisdiction was extended to interiors customarily open to the public and to scenic landmarks on property owned by the city. Designations are preceded by public hearings and reviewed by the City Council. Once a designation has been made, alterations to a protected feature are prohibited without the prior approval of the commission. The mayor appoints the full-time, paid head of the commission and 10 part-time, unpaid commissioners, all of whom serve three-year terms. The commission must include three architects, one historian, one city planner or landscape architect, one real estate agent or developer, and one resident from each of the five boroughs. It is supported by a paid professional staff. In 1978 the U.S. Supreme Court upheld the constitutionality of the landmark preservation law in a notable case concerning Grand Central Terminal. By the early twenty-first century the commission had granted landmark status to more than 25,000 buildings, which included 1200 individual landmarks, 110 interior landmarks, 10 scenic landmarks, and 92 historic districts in all five boroughs.

Brooke J. Barr

landsmanshaftn. Associations formed by Jewish immigrants from eastern Europe. The members of each one had the same town of origin, and often one town was represented by several landsmanshaftn, reflecting political, religious, and generational divisions among its former residents. From the 1880s the landsmanshaftn provided members with health and death benefits, loans, and help in securing employment and housing. Before the turn of the twentieth century most landsmanshaftn were religious congregations or lodges of larger fraternal orders; later, independent mutual-aid associations and branches of radical orders became more numerous, but the older groups survived as well. Although most groups were exclusively for men, some women's and mixed groups were also formed. After World War I landsmanshaftn provided large sums of money as well as technical assistance to the beleaguered Jewish communities of eastern Europe. In 1938 the groups numbered nearly 3000, with a total membership of about half a million. After World War II they absorbed many survivors of the Nazi persecution and published memorial books (or *yizker-bikher*) to record for posterity the local history and folklore of former Jewish towns. There were never many American-born members of the landsmanshaftn, and as the immigrant generation vanished, so did most of the associations.

Michael R. Weisser, *A Brotherhood of Memory: Jewish Landsmanshaftn in the New World* (New York: Basic, 1985); Hannah Kliger, ed., *Jewish Hometown Associations and Family Circles in New York: The WPA Yiddish Writers' Group Study* (Bloomington: Indiana University Press, 1992)

See also FRATERNAL ORGANIZATIONS.

Daniel Soyer

Landsteiner, Karl (*b* Vienna, 14 June 1868; *d* New York City, 26 June 1943). Nobel Prize–winning immunologist and physician. In Vienna he worked with a group of scientists who discovered the polio virus in 1908. In 1900 he identified and classified the human blood groups A, B, AB, and O, a discovery that allowed for successful blood transfusions. Affiliated with New York City's Rockefeller Institute for Medical Research (now Rockefeller University) from 1922 to 1943, he was awarded the Nobel Prize in medicine in 1930.

Renee D. Mastrocco

Lane Bryant. Firm of women's clothing retailers. It began as a private dressmaker's shop in the apartment on Gouverneur Street of Lena Bryant (1879–1951), a Lithuanian immigrant widowed in 1900 and the mother of a young son. She designed what was probably the first maternity dress in the United States by attaching an accordion-pleated skirt to the bodice of a dress with an elastic band, and as a result she was overwhelmed with customers. In 1905 she moved to 38th Street near Fifth Avenue, specializing initially in maternity clothes and later in clothes for larger women. About this time she reportedly signed her name as Lane Bryant inadvertently when opening a bank account for her growing business and decided not to correct the euphonious error. Her firm evolved into a large and successful operation and in 1947 modernized its store at 455 Fifth Avenue. After surviving many changes in retailing, it was bought by the firm the Limited in 1982.

Leslie Gourse, Kenneth T. Jackson

Lansky, Meyer [Suchowljansky, Maier] (*b* 4 Grodno, Russia [now Belarus], July 1902; *d* Miami, 15 Nov 1982). Organized-crime figure, notable for adopting a corporate model

Meyer Lansky, ca 1936

to organize and consolidate organized crime in New York City. His family immigrated in 1911 to the Lower East Side of Manhattan. Lansky began his criminal career in gambling, smuggling, burglaries, and bootlegging during Prohibition, later becoming involved in pornography, prostitution, drug smuggling, and extortion. Along with Benjamin "Bugsy" Siegel, he headed the infamous Bugsy–Meyer Mob, one of the most vicious gangs of its time. In 1931 Lansky and his longtime associate (and member of the Italian Mafia) Charles "Lucky" Luciano formed The Commission—the governing body of the Italian Mafia in the United States, composed of representatives of New York City's Five Families. Later in the decade he became one of the founders of the National Crime Syndicate, a multiethnic crime syndicate whose influence Lansky, not known for his modesty, claimed to be "bigger than U.S. Steel." As head of Murder Incorporated (a term coined by *New York World–Telegram* reporter Harry Feeney), Lansky masterminded many well-known mob killings, including that of "boss of all bosses" Salvatore Maranzano in 1931.

Lansky considered himself a patriot, allegedly breaking up a number of pro-Nazi gatherings and working with the Office of Naval Intelligence's Operation Underground to identify German spies in the United States during World War II. But throughout this time his exploitative mob activities continued and even expanded. By the 1940s he had gambling and prostitution operations in Florida, New Orleans, and Cuba, as well as in Siegel's Flamingo Hotel in Las Vegas. Fearing pending prosecution on charges of tax evasion, the aging Lansky tried in 1970 to relocate to Israel, claiming the right to do so under the Law of Return, which allowed Jews the right to migrate to Israel and gain citizenship. Under pressure from the U.S. government, Israeli prime minister Golda Meir intervened personally to force the mobster's deportation from the country. Arrested upon arrival in Miami, he was tried in 1974 on numerous counts but managed to escape conviction. Lansky died in his home in Miami.

See also Organized crime.

Patrick Barrett

Lapchick, Joe [Joseph Bohomiel] (*b* Yonkers, N.Y., 12 April 1900; *d* Monticello, N.Y., 10 Aug 1970). Basketball coach. He was a player with the Original Celtics in New York City before serving from 1936 to 1947 as the head coach of St. John's College (later St. John's University); during his tenure the team appeared seven times in the National Invitation Tournament (NIT), which it won in 1943 and 1944. From 1947 to 1956 he coached the New York Knickerbockers, compiling a record of 326 wins and 247 losses. He was again the head coach at St. John's from 1956 to 1965, during which his teams twice more won the NIT. For his entire career at St. John's his record was 334 wins and 130 losses. In 1973 St. John's and the Basketball Hall of Fame began awarding the annual Joe Lapchick Award to the outstanding collegiate basketball player in the country.

Albert Figone

Lasker, Mary Woodward (*b* Watertown, Wis., 1902; *d* Greenwich, Conn., 23 Feb 1994). Philanthropist. She moved to New York City in 1923. In 1942 she and her husband, Albert Davis Lasker, established the Lasker Foundation, donor of the annual Albert Lasker Awards for outstanding contributions to medical research. She was also a leader in urban beautification efforts in the city and once donated 300 Japanese cherry trees to the United Nations.

Kenneth T. Jackson

Latimer, Lewis (Howard) (*b* Chelsea, Mass., 8 Sept 1848; *d* New York City, 11 Dec 1928). Inventor associated with the development of the telephone and electric lighting. The son of fugitive slaves, he served in the U.S. Navy during the Civil War and learned drafting while working for a firm of patent solicitors in Boston. In 1876 he drew the plans for Alexander Graham Bell's telephone and helped Bell to prepare and submit the patent application before a rival inventor. In 1880 the inventor Hiram Maxim, who founded the U.S. Electric Lighting Company in the borough of Brooklyn, hired Latimer as a mechanical draftsman. There he became familiar with electric incandescent lighting and supervised the installation of street lighting in New York City as well as in Philadelphia and Montreal. In 1884 he was hired by Thomas Edison, Maxim's archrival, as chief draftsman, patent investigator, expert witness, and director of the company library for Edison Electric Light Company (now General Electric Company) at 65 Fifth Avenue in Manhattan. At Edison's encouragement, Latimer wrote and illustrated one of the earliest scientific books on electric lighting (*Incandescent Electric Lighting*, 1890). In 1918 he was named one of 28 charter members of the distinguished Edison Pioneers, a group credited with creating the electrical industry; he was the only African American among the charter members. Latimer's other inventions include the train water closet (1874), an apparatus for cooling and disinfecting (1886) that was used in hospitals, the safety elevator (1894), and locking racks for hats, coats, and umbrellas (1896) that were used in restaurants, hotels, and office buildings. The house where the Latimer family lived at 64 Holly Avenue in Flushing, Queens, was moved in 1988 to 34-41 137th Street and opened as a historic house museum.

Winifred Latimer Norman and Lily Patterson, *Lewis Latimer, Scientist* (New York: Chelsea House Publishers, 1994)

See also Light and power.

Joyce Mendelsohn

Latin Americans. See Latinos/Hispanics.

LatinoJustice PRLDEF. Civil rights organization founded in New York City by attorneys Jorge Batista, Victor Marrero, and César Perales in 1972 as the Puerto Rican Legal Defense and Education Fund. Its stated mission is to protect the civil and human rights of Puerto Ricans and other Latinos. The organization's first lawsuit, *Aspira v. New York City Board of Education* (1974), resulted in the Aspira Consent Decree, which promoted bilingual education and the employment of Spanish-speaking teachers throughout the city's school system. This ground-breaking legislation became the model for other cities with large Latino populations. In 1986 two successful class-action suits against the New York City Police Department resulted in minority-outreach recruitment programs, changes in testing, and increased promotion and career advancement. The group advocated for equal housing opportunities in Williamsburg (1976). It filed the case of *Housing Justice Campaign v. City of New York* in 1988, an unsuccessful attempt to block plans to sell city property to private developers. The Voting Rights project (1991) and litigation in numerous districting and redistricting cases ensured Latino representation in political elections. LatinoJustice PRLDEF supports amnesty, legalization, and citizenship for undocumented immigrants and protects the rights of day workers throughout the Northeast.

Gabriel Haslip-Viera et al., eds., *Boricuas in Gotham: Puerto Ricans in the Making of Modern New York City* (Princeton, N.J.: Markus Weiner, 2004)

Virginia Sánchez Korrol

Latinos/Hispanics. People from Spain and its possessions have been present in what is today New York City since the earliest times of European colonization. The first historically significant reference is the arrival in New Amsterdam in 1654 of a small group of Sephardic Jews from the former Dutch colony of Recife, Brazil, who founded the Spanish and Portuguese Synagogue (Congregation Shearith Israel). New York's Spanish-language population remained very small until the mid-nineteenth century, when the United States expanded trade in Latin America and the Caribbean. Between 1845 and 1870, according to the U.S. Census Office records, the number of Manhattan and Brooklyn residents who were originally from Cuba and the West Indies, Mexico, Central and South America, and Spain grew more than seven times, from 508 to 3605—with a majority of Cubans, other Spanish-language Caribbeans, and Spaniards among them. In 1880 the city's total Spanish-language population jumped to 5294, and 10 years later it had reached 5994.

This demographic group continued to expand after the Spanish–American War (1898), when the United States acquired Puerto Rico and increased its influence in the Caribbean.

The first Latino immigrants included many exiled political leaders fighting for the independence of Cuba and Puerto Rico from Spain, among them Félix Varela (1788–1853), Cirilo Villaverde (1812–94), José Martí (1853–95), Ramón Emeterio Betances (1827–98), and Eugenio María de Hostos (1839–1902). Cuban-born Varela, a Roman Catholic priest, was arguably the most important Latino exile living in New York City during the first half of the nineteenth century. A prolific writer, theologian, and philosopher, he was also the publisher of *El Habanero,* an influential Spanish-language periodical. In 1837 Varela was appointed vicar general of the Diocese of New York; he played a central role in the efforts of the Catholic Church to provide shelter and aid to new arrivals from Europe, particularly during the wave of Irish immigrants of the 1840s. Cirilo Villaverde was a former secretary to Narciso López, the leader of a failed Cuban insurrection against Spain, and the author of *Cecilia Valdés* (1882), widely regarded as a classic of Cuban literature. His wife, Emilia Casanova de Villaverde (1832–97), was an important community activist and political writer. Author, poet, and political chief of the expeditionary force that started the second war for Cuban independence, José Martí, "the Apostle of Cuba," is one of the towering figures of Spanish-language literature; he died shortly after leaving New York City, where he spent the last 15 years of his life and wrote most of his works. Betances was the organizer of the Cry of Lares (Grito de Lares), a frustrated revolt against Spanish rule of Puerto Rico in 1868; for that reason he is remembered as the Father of Puerto Rican independence. The philosopher, sociologist, and educator Eugenio María de Hostos was, along with Martí and Varela, one of the major intellectual personalities of nineteenth-century Latin America. Another important figure of this period was Arturo Alfonso Schomburg (1874–38). Schomburg migrated to New York City from Puerto Rico at age 17 and became involved in the Puerto Rican section of the Cuban Revolutionary Party; although primarily known as one of the seminal promoters of black culture, his legacy as an Afro-Caribbean Latino intellectual (or Afro-Borinqueño, as he used to call himself) is being increasingly acknowledged.

The political, social, and cultural activism of these men and women continued into the first decades of the twentieth century, with many civic and political organizations concerned with different issues affecting Latinos in the United States. Among the most successful of those early associations were the socialist, anarchist, and nationalist (Puerto Rican) labor organizations, especially those connected with the cigar industry; already by 1893, one of those groups had created a "populist committee" that became active in the city's electoral politics. Tobacco trade-union leaders Luisa Capetillo (1879–1922) and Bernardo Vega (1885–1965) documented in their memoirs those community-building struggles.

In 1900 half of the more than 7500 Latinos living in New York City came from the Caribbean. Many arrived with entrepreneurial skills and opened boardinghouses and small businesses that catered to newcomers. Family-owned tobacco factories were one of the staples; there were nearly 500 of them on the Lower East Side and in Chelsea. Other businesses included restaurants, bodegas, and *botánicas,* stores that sold items such as herbs, religious statues, and candles. In 1923 the *Guía Hispana,* a guide to commercial and professional services offered by Latinos, listed 275 businesses and 150 professionals, including physicians, dentists, and lawyers. Working-class Latinos were in turn concentrated in Harlem, Chelsea, Yorkville, the West Side, and the Lower East Side of Manhattan, as well as in the Columbia Street and Navy Yard districts of Brooklyn.

By 1920 the city's Latino population reached 41,094. Spaniards constituted the majority, with 14,659 nationals, or 35 percent of the total, but 10 years later they were surpassed by Puerto Ricans, who for several decades became synonymous with the city's Latinos. Already accounting for 18 percent in 1920, Puerto Ricans increased their share to 40.7 percent in 1930, 46 percent in 1940, and 81 percent by 1960, their historical peak. Some of those who left Puerto Rico were political exiles, but most were escaping its troubled economy. Their migration accelerated with the island's worsening economic and social crises during the Depression, postwar expansion in the United States, and industrialization efforts in Puerto Rico—the so-called Operation Bootstrap—during the 1950s. By 1990 New York City's Puerto Rican population had declined to 50 percent, as greater numbers of people began leaving the city for the suburbs and other parts of the country, and by 2000, although still constituting the dominant group, it represented only 35 percent of the Latino population of the city.

The number of Latinos from other countries increased after the Cuban Revolution (1959) and the Dominican civil war (1965), and even more significantly with the huge immigrant wave that started to arrive in the United States from Latin America in the late 1970s. New York City's Latino population grew from 1,202,281 in 1970 to 1,406,024 in 1980, to 1,783,511 in 1990, and to 2,2160,554, or one-third of the city's entire population, in 2000. In 2009 Dominicans constituted the second-largest group, followed by Mexicans, Ecuadorians, Colombians, and people from every other country in South and Central America. This population spread itself all over the city, creating new Latino enclaves, such as those of Washington Heights (Dominicans) and Jackson Heights (Colombians and other South Americans), but also moving into well-established Latino neighborhoods, sometimes altering their previous ethnic makeup; the clearest example of the latter trend is the presence of Mexicans in the traditionally Puerto Rican El Barrio (East Harlem).

Latino immigrants became active in political organizations in the 1890s, including the Caribe Democratic Club, the Hispanic-American Democratic Club, the Puerto Rican and Hispanic League, and the Federation of Puerto Rican Democratic Clubs. In the late 1920s the Republican Party supported the candidacies of two Puerto Rican politicians, Rafael Bosch (for the state assembly) and Victor Fiol Ramos (for the City Council). Latinos made their first strong effect on the city's elections during the reform period of the late 1930s and early 1940s. Mayor Fiorello La Guardia and Representative Vito Marcantonio, whose congressional district in East Harlem included El Barrio, encouraged Latinos to take part in politics and supported the successful candidacy of Oscar García Rivera, a Puerto Rican state assemblyman from East Harlem (1937, 1939). During the late 1940s and 1950s Latino politicians, most of them Puerto Ricans, were appointed to district leadership positions and supported for political office by the Democratic Party.

The 1960s saw the birth of a more activist brand of politics. Groups such as the Young Lords, the Puerto Rican Student Union, and the Puerto Rican Socialist Party addressed issues such as housing, education, health, and civil rights. They also heightened the political awareness of the younger generation and provided models for greater political assertiveness. By the late 1960s Puerto Rican and other Latino politicians entered the political establishment. Mayor Robert F. Wagner (1953–65) had opened up city government to Latinos, appointing Herman Badillo and others to high posts in his administration. Wagner's successor, John V. Lindsay (1966–73), also reached out to Latinos. With the support of reform Democrats, Badillo was elected the first Puerto Rican congressional representative in 1970. (In 1978 he was replaced by another Latino, Robert García, who held office until 1990.) Badillo's success and the changes within the Democratic and Republican parties during the 1970s and 1980s led to more support for other Puerto Rican and Latino candidates. Many entered politics at the most local level, successfully running for positions on community school boards; examples are Adriano Espaillat, the first Dominican to be elected to the New York State Assembly, and the commissioner of the Mayor's Office for Immigrant Affairs, Guillermo Linares. Other Latino political leaders from New York City include members of Congress Nydia Velázquez and José Serrano; U.S. senator for New Jersey Robert Menéndez (born in New York City to Cuban immigrants); former Bronx borough presidents Fernando "Freddy" Ferrer and Adolfo Carrión, Jr., the latter first director of the newly created White House Office of Urban Affairs Policy; New York State Assembly members Carmen E. Arroyo, Luis M. Diaz, Ruben Diaz, Jr., Félix Ortiz, José Peralta, Philip P. Ramos, José Rivera, Naomi Rivera, Peter M. Rivera, and José M. Serrano; state senators Rubén Díaz, Pedro Espada, Hiram Monserrate, and Congressman Serrano's son José Marco Serrano, who in 2004 won his seat over 26-year Republican incumbent Olga Méndez; City Council members María del Carmen Arroyo, Maria Baez, Julissa Ferreras, Sara M. González, Margarita López, Melissa Mark-Viverito, Migue Martínez, Rosie Méndez, Diana Reyna, Joel Rivera, and Sonia Sotomayor.

Roberto E. Villareal and Norma G. Hernández, eds., *Latinos and Political Coalitions* (New York: Greenwood, 1991); Rodney E. Hero, *Latinos and the U.S. Political System* (Philadelphia: Temple University Press, 1992); *Latin American Music* (Redlands, Calif.: Libros Latinos, 1992); Gabriel Haslip-Viera and Sherrie L. Baver, *Latinos in New York: Communities in Transition* (Notre Dame, Ind.: University of Notre Dame Press, 1996); Claudio Iván Remeseira, ed., *Hispanic New York: A Sourcebook* (New York: Columbia University Press, 2010)

Gabriel Haslip-Viera, Clara Rodríguez, David L. González, Claudio Iván Remeseira

Latin Quarter. Nightclub opened in 1942 by Lou Walters. The three-story building at 200 West 48th Street was formerly called the Great White Way, Cotton Club, Palais Royal, and Palais d'Or. The restaurant and nightclub featured nightly shows and live music, including acts by Frank Sinatra, Mickey Rooney, Patti Page, and Mae West. The first year it opened the club grossed more than $1.5 million and attracted tens of thousands of patrons. In the next 10 years the club grossed more than $10 million and was visited by more than five million people. Walters sold the club in 1958 but returned to manage it in 1965 until its closing in 1969. In 1966 a well-publicized strike of chorus girls began with a walkout, the 28 girls demanding overtime pay, a welfare fund, and basic sanitation requirements; the strike lasted four nights. In the late 1960s it was the only nightclub that featured a chorus line. A month later chorus girls held another strike, and this time caused the building to be boarded up. Since the club officially closed, several reincarnations have opened around the same location. The term *Latin Quarter* also refers to the glamour of New York City's nightclub era. In 2003 a popular reincarnation opened at 511 Lexington at 48th Street. A year later a fight during rap artist Ja Rule's holiday party ended in a fatal shooting outside the club. Former New York Giants wide receiver Plaxico Burress accidentally shot himself in the leg while at the nightclub in 2008.

Jessica Montesano

latitude and longitude. The latitude of New York City measured from Central Park is 40° 47' N, and the longitude is 73° 58' W.

Latter-Day Saints. See Mormons.

Latvians. Latvians started to arrive in New York City during the second half of the nineteenth century, seeking political freedom and better living conditions. Mostly members of the working class, they formed the New York Latvian Society (*Ņujorkas Latviešu Biedrība*) in 1893. The first Latvian-language Lutheran church service in New York was held at the end of the 1890s, and a permanent parish with its own minister was established in the 1930s. This church, after a reorganization in 1946, became and has remained a core ethnic and national institution, performing many of the same functions as the Latvian Society had earlier.

In 1900 about 400 Latvians lived in New York City, but this number increased substantially after the repressions in the Baltic provinces following the failed 1905 Russian Revolution. After the Bolshevik Revolution of 1917 and Latvia declaring independence in 1918, a few returned to Latvia and some to the Soviet Union, but by 1931 the Latvian population of New York had grown to 8000. New York Latvians became a stable, low-key community, directing their efforts toward education, national heritage, language, and religion. The community boasted a newspaper, choirs, an orchestra, youth clubs, literary groups, and amateur theater performances—mostly under the umbrella of the Latvian Society. It also founded a credit union, whose principal practical benefit was insurance for burial expenses. The community supported Latvian independence by lobbying for de jure recognition by the U.S. government and sending contributions to welfare organizations. The first congress of the American National Latvian League was held in New York City in 1919; a Latvian Chamber of Commerce opened in 1938.

World War II contributed to an increase in the number of Latvian immigrants in New York City, first as the Baltic states came under military occupation in 1940, and then soon after the end of the war when Latvia was annexed by the Soviet Union. These latter immigrants were admitted as political refugees and materially assisted by Latvian Relief, Inc.; they found their first jobs primarily in construction and as building superintendents. They had a strong national orientation, and many of them regarded their presence in the United States as temporary. Immigrants during the 1950s included a large number of artists, performers, writers, educators, and political and religious leaders. Some of the earlier institutions continued, but overlap with the previous cohort of Latvian immigrants was rather limited. The annual Loyalty Day parade, however, was a central event, as well as the performance of Latvian songs, music, and folk dances to larger audiences at fairs, parades, and festivals, as well as exhibits of Latvian art. As a principal center of Latvians in the country, New York City has also been the locus of publishing for many Latvian periodicals, magazines, and books.

In 1960 the U.S. Census recorded 16,688 individuals in New York City who claimed Latvian ancestry; this number dropped to 8885 in 1970 and 3777 in 2000, but the total of self-identified Latvians in the surrounding counties of three states was approximately 12,000 at the beginning of the twenty-first century.

During the 1990s and into the twenty-first century, Latvians in New York City ceased to be a colony of exiles and became an organized ethnic community of first- to third-generation Latvian Americans. Children and young people find they have to cope with Latvian as a second language. The strongest and most durable cultural activities of the Latvian community are the New York Latvian Concert Choir (founded in 1975); meetings of various fraternities and sororities; schools and summer camps; and large gatherings at midsummer's night (*Jōņ diena*), National Independence Day, and Christmas. The regaining of Latvian independence in 1991 brought a new mission to the New York City Latvian community as they provided humanitarian help, financial aid, and professional skills for rebuilding the country.

Several Latvian women have distinguished themselves in New York City: artist Vija Celmins is well represented in the Museum of Modern Art; actress Laila Robins is seen frequently on Broadway and in films; soprano Maija Kovaļevska made her debut with the Metropolitan Opera debut in 2006; and runner Jelēna Prokopčuka won the New York City Marathon in 2005 and 2006.

M. Kārklis et al., *The Latvians in America, 1640–1973: A Chronology and Fact Book* (Dobbs Ferry, N.Y.: Oceana, 1974); V. V. Sīmanis, ed., *Latvia* (St. Charles, Ill.: The Book Latvia, 1984); *Ņujorkas Latviešu Evaņģeliski Luteriskā Draudze, 1896–1998* (New York Latvian Evangelical Lutheran Parish, 1896–1998) (New York: Hatco, 2000)

Sigurd Grava

Lauder, Estée [née Mentzer, Josephine Esther] (*b* Queens, 1 July 1906?; *d* New York City, 26 April 2004). Businesswoman, considered the "cosmetics queen." She grew up on Hillside Avenue in the neighborhood of Corona in Queens. In 1924 she began selling skin creams that her chemist uncle, John Schatz, developed in Brooklyn. She married Joseph Lauder in 1930 and formed the Estée Lauder Company in 1946. In 1948 she secured counter space in Saks Fifth Avenue and from there achieved fame for her trademark personal selling approach. In 1953 she introduced her first fragrance, the tremendously successful Youth Dew, a bath oil that doubled as a perfume. Lauder believed in the value of promoting her products with free samples and invented the concept of providing gifts with purchases. She is also known for marketing her brands by featuring a single fashion model as the "face of Estée Lauder" in advertisements. In 1965 she introduced a men's line, Aramis. She moved her corporate headquarters to the General Motors Building on Fifth Avenue near Grand Army Plaza and the Plaza Hotel in 1968, and by 1982 her business was the largest privately held cosmetics firm in the world. Among the Estée Lauder brands are Clinique, Prescriptives, Origins, La Mer, Aveda, and the New York–based Bumble and Bumble. Both of Lauder's sons, Leonard and Ronald, worked for the company, as have her grandchildren, notably William P. Lauder, who became president and chief executive officer in 2004. Lauder retired in 1994.

Holly Cronin

Laurel Hill. Small industrial neighborhood in northwestern Queens, lying between Long Island City and Maspeth and bounded to the north by the Long Island Expressway, to the east by 58th Street, to the west by Laurel Hill Boulevard, and to the south by Maspeth Creek. It was originally the farm of Edward Waters and was bought in 1853 by Jacob Rapalye, who renamed it and built an imposing mansion on high ground between 44th and 46th streets on 55th Drive; his son August Rapalye lived there until 1890. After the Civil War the South Side Railroad cut a track through the property, with a stop at Penny Bridge over Newtown Creek. Later, F. Haberman's National Enameling and Stamping Company built plants on the banks of Newtown Creek that poisoned the air with corrosive fumes. The farmland behind the mansion was sold in the 1880s for development as the village of Laurel Hill to cater to travelers and visitors to the Calvary Cemetery, one of the oldest and largest cemeteries in the United States. The Phelps Dodge copper refining plant, which was built in addition to the National Enameling and Stamping Company, opened on Newtown Creek in 1920 but closed in 1983; the polluted site remained vacant for decades. Early in the twenty-first century the area remains commercial and industrial, with a few private houses scattered throughout. The Long Island Expressway and the Calvary Cemetery isolate Laurel Hill, to which access is provided only on the side near Maspeth.

Vincent Seyfried, Jeffrey A. Kroessler

Laurelton. Neighborhood in southeastern Queens, bounded to the north by Francis Lewis Boulevard, to the east by Laurelton Parkway, to the south by 147th Avenue, and to the west by Springfield Boulevard. In 1906, 300 acres (120 hectares) just east of Springfield Gardens at the junction of the Atlantic and Montauk divisions of the Long Island Rail Road were acquired by William H. Reynolds, a former state senator, who incorporated the Laurelton Land Company to develop the tract. In January 1907 the company paid $8000 for an elegant railroad station just east of 222nd Street, which opened in April 1907. Lots were priced from $500 to $750 and sold in parcels of three; only one-family houses costing at least $4000 could be built. A few expensive houses costing between $5500 and $17,500 were constructed during the next 10 years, after which Reynolds abandoned Laurelton to develop Long Beach. As the demand for housing rose during the 1920s Laurelton revived and became the site of many more middle-class houses. In 1928 the grounds of the golf club were developed as blocks of houses in a Spanish style with tile roofs. In 1935 Laurelton Parkway, connecting Southern Parkway and the Belt, opened over old millponds. Predominantly Jewish from the 1940s and 1950s, Laurelton attracted middle-class African Americans from Springfield Gardens in the following decades. During the 1980s Laurelton drew many immigrants from Jamaica (almost half of all immigrants settling in the neighborhood), Haiti, Guyana, and Trinidad and Tobago, and by the twenty-first century the population was 70 to 80 percent black. The houses were mostly well-maintained English Tudors and Spanish stuccos; a garden club planted the malls.

Vincent Seyfried

Lauren [Lifshitz]**, Ralph** (*b* Bronx, 14 Oct 1939). Fashion designer. He grew up in the Bronx, graduating in 1957 from DeWitt Clinton High School. At age 16 his brother Jerry changed his last name from Lifshitz to Lauren; Ralph followed suit. Although he had a lifelong interest in design, he began his career on the business side of fashion, working during the day as both a salesman at Brooks Brothers and a buyer for Allied Stores while taking business classes at night at City College. In 1967 his creativity prompted Beau Brummell Neckwear to ask him to create his own line of men's ties, which he named Polo. In 1968 he founded Polo Fashions and Polo Men's Wear, expanding his designs to include men's clothing, shoes, and luggage. He later established a marque of women's clothing, Ralph Lauren (1971), and designed costumes for the film *The Great Gatsby* (1973). By the mid-1980s Polo Fashions had reached $600 million in sales, and Lauren's salary reportedly exceeded $15 million. In 1986 he restored the Rhinelander Mansion on Madison Avenue, creating a boutique featuring his fashions. A leading exponent of a traditional, "Ivy League" style characterized by aristocratic simplicity, Lauren has likened his approach to that of Coco Chanel. Although he has earned many fashion awards, including several Coty awards, his success as a designer has been more popular than critical.

Anne E. Kornblut

lawn bowling. Dutch pastime popular in New York City from the 1620s when matches were held in the area at the southern end of Broadway now known as Bowling Green. It was very popular in the early eighteenth century but virtually disappeared during the nineteenth. Lawn bowling was revived in the 1920s by the New York Lawn Bowling Club, which constructed two 15,000-square-foot (1393.5-square-meter) bowling greens at 69th street in Central Park. In the twenty-first century the club continued to operate and bowl at the two greens annually from May through November.

James Weir Greig, *The Game of Bowling on the Green, or Lawn Bowls* (New York: American Sports Publishing, 1904)

Laura Lewison

Lawrence, Cornelius Van Wyck (*b* Flushing [now in Queens], 18 Feb 1791; *d* Flushing, 20 Feb 1861). Mayor. He moved to New York City in 1812 and worked in business before his election to the House of Representatives as a Jacksonian Democrat in 1832. In 1834 he became the first directly elected mayor of New York City when he defeated the Whig candidate Gulian C. Verplanck by 174 votes; he remained in office until 1837. Lawrence also directed several corporations and was collector of New York from 1845 to 1849.

James E. Mooney

Lawrence, Jacob (*b* Atlantic City, N.J., 7 Sept 1917; *d* Seattle, Wash., 9 June 2000). Painter. He moved to Harlem at seven years of age with his mother and siblings in 1924. During the Great Depression, Lawrence trained under Henry Bannarn and Charles Alston in the Harlem Art Workshop, a project of the Works Progress Administration. He became famous for his *Migration* series, a set of 60 small paintings depicting the movement of African Americans from the rural South to the industrial cities of the North during the first decades of the twentieth century. Lawrence completed the series before he turned 23 and after months of research at the library of the Schomburg Center for Research in Black Culture. The series catapulted him to national fame almost immediately when it was published in *Fortune* magazine in 1941, the same year that Lawrence became the first African American artist to be included in the permanent collection of the Museum of

Modern Art. Lawrence continued painting throughout his life, and eventually became a professor of art at the University of Washington. The mosaic *New York in Transit,* his last public work, hangs in the Times Square subway station.

Rowan Moore Gerety

law schools. Legal training during the eighteenth century was usually completed by an apprenticeship that lasted as long as seven years. Students paid a fee and served an attorney in return for instruction in the principles and practice of law; they copied, drafted, and filed documents and read legal treatises and textbooks. Such an apprenticeship was required well into the nineteenth century. Efforts to establish more formal training were undertaken by James Kent, whose lectures on law at Columbia College in 1794 and 1795 became the basis for his *Commentaries on American Law.* Benjamin Butler opened the city's first law school in 1838 at the University of the City of New York (now New York University), but it closed after a year. During the Jacksonian era efforts were made to abolish the stringent controls on admission to the bar that fostered elitism. The New York State constitution of 1846 abolished the training requirement and allowed any male citizen 21 years or older to practice law after passing a public examination. Although self-directed reading became an acceptable means of preparation, apprenticeships continued to predominate and were eventually replaced by "clerkships," in which students were sometimes paid for their services. Admission to the bar solely on the basis of office study was allowed until the 1970s. In 1858 law schools were established by both New York University and Columbia. They were supported almost entirely by tuition. To compete with clerkships they adopted lower admissions standards (applicants did not need a high school education), set a curriculum oriented toward the practice of law, and scheduled classes at times convenient for working students. Lessons were based on textbooks, treatises, lectures, and recitations.

The late nineteenth century saw the establishment of higher standards and the expansion of the city's law schools. In 1871 the state court of appeals was empowered to set requirements for admission to the bar. Under Theodore W. Dwight during the 1870s and 1880s the Columbia College School of Law became one of the country's two largest law schools and an important influence on the city's bar. Before 1890 the law school at New York University seldom had more than 75 students. After the first woman was admitted to the state bar in 1886, the university cooperated with the Women's Legal Education Society to introduce a special one-year course in 1890. Women were also admitted to the regular law school for the first time that year, and the first women graduated in 1892. The growth of law schools, the development of the typewriter and stenography, and the introduction of women to clerical work led to the decline of clerkships. More students went to law school after 1894 with the introduction of a uniform written bar examination that emphasized academic skills, and between 1889 and 1899 enrollments rose in New York City from 600 to about 1800. Under Seth Low, who became president of Columbia in 1890, the law school adopted policies similar to those introduced at Harvard Law School by Christopher Columbus Langdell during the 1870s. Columbia raised its admissions requirements, broadened the curriculum, adjusted the schedule to discourage students from working, and added a third year of study. Columbia also adopted the "case method" of legal instruction developed at Harvard, which focused on the written opinions of judges. Columbia became exclusive and rigorous, and enrollment declined.

In response to Low's reforms many faculty and students left Columbia in 1891 to form New York Law School, which became known for its focus on practice, its lax admissions, and its flexible class schedule, as was the case with the first night school, Metropolis Law School, which was chartered in the same year and merged with New York University in 1895. Enrollments continued to rise and new schools opened that focused on practice, among them Brooklyn Law School (1901), Fordham University School of Law (1905), and St. John's University School of Law (1925). Like New York University and New York Law School, these attracted immigrants and a small but increasing number of women, and enrollments increased between 1910 and the late 1920s. By 1928 there were almost 11,000 law students in the city. These developments, especially the enrollment of immigrants, provoked a reaction by the bar. In the mid-1920s the New York State Bar Association sought to prevent students without the equivalent of two years of college education from studying law in school or an office; the state court of appeals adopted such a rule in 1927, which went into effect in 1929. At the same time most schools adopted admissions and curricular policies similar to those of Columbia and Harvard. In 1928 only Columbia was approved by the Section of Legal Education of the American Bar Association among all law schools in New York City. But by 1938 New York Law School was the only school in the city without approval. The new policies and the Depression reduced enrollments by half between 1928 and 1938, and World War II exacerbated conditions. New York Law School closed during the war.

Enrollments quickly returned to their previous level after the war. During the late 1940s and 1950s legal education became standardized according to the model set by the exclusive schools. Institutions in the city improved their facilities, expanded their faculty, raised entrance requirements, and reformed their curricula. Enrollments rose in the 1970s because more women and ethnic minorities were attracted to the profession. The Benjamin N. Cardozo School of Law at Yeshiva University opened in 1976, followed by the City University of New York Law School at Queens College in 1983. In 2010 New York City was home to eight law schools: Benjamin N. Cardozo School of Law, Brooklyn Law School, Columbia University Law School, City University of New York School of Law, Fordham University School of Law, New York Law School, New York University School of Law, and St. John's University School of Law.

Paul M. Hamlin, *Legal Education in Colonial New York* (New York: New York University, Law Quarterly Review, 1939); Robert B. Stevens, *Law School: Legal Education in America from the 1850s to the 1980s* (Chapel Hill: University of North Carolina Press, 1983)

James A. Wooten, Meghan Lalonde

lawyers. The legal profession grew slowly in colonial New York City, where initially property law and debt collection accounted for most legal work. Between 1695 and 1769 there were 49 practicing lawyers, many of them poorly trained. Preparation for a career in law consisted of an apprenticeship of as long as seven years with a lawyer. The profession was not well regarded until the 1730s, when commerce expanded rapidly and the demand for skilled lawyers increased. Commercial and maritime law grew in importance, and on the eve of the American Revolution, lawyers were few but well established. Among the most important were the editors of the *Independent Reflector* (1752–53): William Smith, Jr., William Livingston, and John Morin Scott, who was also a leader of the Sons of Liberty. Many other leaders of the legal community opposed the Revolution.

After the war such men as Alexander Hamilton, John Jay, and Aaron Burr became active in national politics, and a career in law became a path to social, economic, and political success. By the early nineteenth century lawyers were prominent in the city; these included Thomas Addis Emmet and William Sampson, who sought to codify the law and simplify the process for admission to the bar, and the legal scholar James Kent. Under the new state constitution of 1846 the systems of apprenticeship and judicial appointment were abolished: male citizens 21 and older were allowed to practice law after passing a public examination, and judges were elected by popular vote. A code of civil law was drafted by David Dudley Field, a lawyer in the city who believed that undue complexity made the law inaccessible to everyone outside the profession. Usually known as the Field Code, it

Largest Law Firms in New York City, 2008

Firm	Year Founded	Number of Attorneys (estimated)	Address
Skadden, Arps, Slate, Meagher, and Flom	1948	2,251	4 Times Square, Manhattan
White and Case	1901	2,205	1155 Avenue of the Americas, Manhattan
Dewey and LeBoeuf	1909	1,455	1301 Avenue of the Americas, Manhattan
Weil, Gotshal, and Manges	1931	1,359	767 5th Ave., Manhattan
Orrick, Herrington, and Sutcliffe	1863	1,076	666 5th Ave., Manhattan
Cleary Gottlieb Steen, and Hamilton	1946	1,000	1 Liberty Plaza, Manhattan
Shearman and Sterling	1873	870	599 Lexington Ave., Manhattan
Simpson Thacher, and Bartlett	1883	869	425 Lexington Ave., Manhattan
Proskauer Rose	1899	784	1585 Broadway, Manhattan
Davis Polk and Wardwell	1849	774	450 Lexington Ave., Manhattan
Debevoise and Plimpton	1931	772	919 3rd Ave., Manhattan
Wilson Elser Moskowitz Edelman, and Dicker	1979	752	150 East 42nd St., Manhattan
Sullivan and Cromwell	1879	748	125 Broad St., Manhattan
Paul, Weiss, Rifkind, Wharton, and Garrison	1875	732	1285 Avenue of the Americas, Manhattan
Fried, Frank, Harris, Shriver, and Jacobson	1971	675	1 New York Plaza, Manhattan
Willkie Farr and Gallagher	1888	669	787 7th Ave., Manhattan
Milbank, Tweed, Hadley, and McCloy	1866	657	1 Chase Manhattan Plaza, Manhattan
Cadwalader, Wickersham, and Taft	1792	610	1 World Financial Center, Manhattan
Cravath, Swaine, and Moore	1819	554	Worldwide Plaza, 825 8th Ave., Manhattan
Thelen, LLP*	1924	553	875 3rd Ave., Manhattan
Kaye Scholer	1917	530	425 Park Ave., Manhattan
Chadbourne and Parke	1902	481	30 Rockefeller Plaza, Manhattan
Schulte Roth and Zabel	1969	481	919 3rd Ave., Manhattan
Kelley Drye and Warren	1893	378	101 Park Ave., Manhattan
Epstein Becker and Green	1973	372	250 Park Ave., Manhattan
Kramer Levin Naftalis and Frankel	1968	372	1177 Avenue of the Americas, Manhattan
Stroock and Stroock and Lavan	1876	357	180 Maiden Lane, Manhattan
Hughes Hubbard and Reed	1888	334	1 Battery Park Plaza, Manhattan
Cahill Gordon and Reindel	1919	287	80 Pine St., Manhattan
Kasowitz, Benson, Torres, and Friedman	1993	286	1633 Broadway, Manhattan

*Dissolved October 2008

Source: *National Law Journal* (2008)

Compiled by Frank Nestor

simplified civil law by combining the practice of common law and equity and was adopted by the state assembly in 1848. During the next 25 years it became the basis of civil codes in 24 states.

The influence of trial lawyers in the city increased during the nineteenth century and reached a pinnacle about the 1880s. The partners William F. Howe and Abe Hummel became well known for their spectacular success in defending clients charged with arson, murder, or involvement in organized crime. William M. Evarts defended President Andrew Johnson in his impeachment trial in 1868 and was appointed attorney general of the United States (1868–69). Perhaps the best-known trial lawyer in the city was Charles O'Conor, who led the prosecution against William M. "Boss" Tweed in the early 1870s. Joseph Choate continued to try cases into his 80th year in 1912. In 1870 the Association of the Bar of the City of New York was formed by fewer than 500 of the 4000 lawyers practicing in the city; Evarts was president from 1870 to 1880. A private club, it sought to protect the profession for the elite. Its members blamed the reforms of 1846 for a decline in professional standards, called for more rigorous ethics and training, and were prominent in fighting corruption in municipal government during the 1870s. Among them were Samuel J. Tilden, a vice president of the association who as chairman of the Democratic Party in New York State (1866–74) investigated the Tweed Ring, and James C. Carter, who helped to prosecute Tweed. Carter also led the opposition to proposals for codification in the 1870s and 1880s, which many lawyers in the city (especially those of the bar association) considered an encroachment on the legal profession by government. Field defended Tweed after members of the bar association rejected his offer to work for the prosecution.

During the 1870s the importance of business law increased with the number of large public corporations. The firms of Cravath (now Cravath, Swaine, and Moore), which moved to the city in 1854, and Shearman and Sterling (1873) opened offices on Wall Street and made innovations that were soon widely imitated. Cravath was among the first to focus on offering advice to corporate clients in such areas as financial management and the prevention of lawsuits. It also introduced the "Cravath system," adopted by many firms by 1900, in which not only partners, associates, and clerks but also law students working in the firm were paid a salary beginning at $30 a month. By the 1890s business law and especially corporate law dominated the practices of many lawyers, who spent less time in court than formerly and often worked as associates and partners in large corporate firms such as those on Wall Street, the most powerful in the city.

A degree in law rather than a clerkship soon became the prerequisite for a career as a lawyer. Columbia Law School became increasingly rigorous and exclusive; many of its graduates found work in the city's most prominent firms, which employed mostly white Republican Protestant men from the upper middle class. A number of them eventually had careers in government, including Elihu Root, secretary of war under presidents William McKinley and Theodore Roosevelt, and John W. Davis, the Democratic presidential nominee in 1924. Members of religious or ethnic minorities were employed by some corporate firms including Cravath, where William D. Guthrie, a Roman Catholic, and Charles M. Da Costa, a descendant of West Indian Jews, were important figures. A few firms employed mainly Catholics or Jews, among them Proskauer Rose Goetz and Mendelsohn (1875). Women were allowed to practice law in New York State in 1886 and were admitted by New York University Law School from 1890; Melle Titus, who enrolled there in 1891, was the first woman in the city to graduate from law school and become a lawyer. The university also sponsored the Women's Legal Education Society, which offered an introductory course in law for women. A number of LAW SCHOOLS opened in the city during the first decades of the twentieth century: Brooklyn Law School in 1901, Fordham University School of Law in 1905, and St. John's University School of Law in 1925. Legal education became more accessible to women, immigrants, and workers, especially through classes offered at night, and women were first admitted to Columbia in 1927. But corporate law remained largely the preserve of the elite.

Lawyers became well known for their roles in reforms undertaken during the first two decades of the twentieth century. Charles Evans Hughes was a member of the Stevens Gas Commission (1906), which investigated the practices of utility companies in the city, and became known nationally as the counsel for the Armstrong Commission in its investigation of insurance fraud (1906–7); he served as governor of New York (1907–10), sought the presidency as a Republican in 1916, and was chief justice of the United States from 1930 to 1941. Samuel Untermyer led a congressional investigation of the Wall Street banking system in 1912. Some of the best-known public interest lawyers were women, most of them graduates of the New York University Law School. Among them were Crystal Eastman (graduated 1907), a feminist and labor activist who formed the American Civil Liberties Union with Roger Baldwin in the city in 1920, and Dorothy Kenyon, an advocate of civil liberties and one of several women lawyers who worked for Mayor Fiorello H. La Guardia. Helen L. Buttenwieser (graduated 1936) was employed by Cravath, Swaine, and Moore and joined the New York City Bar Association in 1937, the first year it accepted women as members. One of the first women to work as an associate in a corporate firm, she was also well known for her work in civil liberties. Prominent trial lawyers during these years included Samuel Leibowitz, who defended the Scottsboro Boys during the 1930s, and William J. Fallon.

The legal profession in the city strengthened in the years before and after World War II. Lawyers were needed during the Depression to work for the government and handle an unprecedented number of bankruptcies. As a federal prosecutor appointed to investigate organized crime in the city, Thomas E. Dewey in the mid-1930s gained 72 convictions on racketeering charges in 73 cases brought against restaurateurs, poultry producers, bakers, and truckers; he was later elected to three terms as governor of New York and nominated for the presidency by the Republicans in 1944 and 1948. Two important organizations formed in the city were the National Lawyers Guild (1937), which played an important role in drafting and implementing New Deal policies, and the Legal Defense and Educational Fund of the National Association for the Advancement of Colored People (NAACP) (1939). The number of immigrants and children of immigrants becoming lawyers grew rapidly. Among them was La Guardia, who worked while attending law school at New York University before being elected mayor in 1933. Ferdinand Pecora, a graduate of the same law school, was counsel to the U.S. Senate in its investigation of banking (1934–35), which led to the formation of the Securities and Exchange Commission; he later became a justice of the Supreme Court of New York. Corporate firms continued to grow after World War II and reached the height of their strength in the 1950s and 1960s, when most opened offices in plush modern buildings on and near Park Avenue. They drew their clients from among the largest domestic and international corporations and formed a network unmatched in wealth and power that exerted considerable influence on national legislation. Several members of the city's corporate firms became national public figures, including John Foster Dulles, Henry L. Stimson, John McCloy, and Cyrus Vance. The 1960s saw a rapid increase in the number of African Americans and women employed as lawyers in the city. During the late 1960s students at New York University formed the Women's Rights Committee, which helped to make several important scholarships available to women. They also formed the National Conference of Law Women, which successfully fought sex discrimination in admissions to law school and in employment. A prominent legal activist in the city during the 1970s was Florynce Kennedy, who was known for her confrontational style. Radical causes were also taken up by such lawyers as William M. Kunstler and Arthur Kinoy. Most of the country's radical law organizations established their base in the city, such as the Center for Constitutional Rights.

Changes in the practice of law during the 1970s and 1980s led the city's legal profession to expand rapidly. Aggressive strategies for mergers and acquisitions were developed by Joseph Flom of Skadden, Arps, Slate, Meagher, and Flom and his colleague Marty Lipton; their approach was soon adopted by such leading firms as Cravath, Swaine, and Moore, Shearman and Sterling, and Sullivan and Cromwell. Arranging or preventing hostile takeovers became lucrative for these firms, and to reduce rising legal costs some large corporations expanded their own legal departments. Tort litigation increased after the U.S. Supreme Court ruled in 1977 that lawyers could advertise their services. Plaintiff lawyers often won enormous damages for their clients and earned contingency fees averaging 33 to 40 percent. Between the early 1970s and 1990 the number of lawyers in the city increased from 30,000 to more than 60,000, and by 1980 women accounted for 40 percent of the student body at New York University, more than ever before. In 1990 Conrad K. Harper became the first African American president of the bar association. By the same year the five largest firms in the city each employed at least 400 lawyers in the metropolitan area and offered starting salaries of at least $83,000. In 2007 the average salary for lawyers in New York City was $205,000, including bonuses. In July of the same year, 10,907 law students took the New York Bar exam, an increase of over 20 percent from 2000, and a record 70.6 percent passed the exam.

In 2006, according to the New York State Office of Court Administration, there were 74,425 practicing lawyers in New York State registered with the New York State Bar Association; by the end of 2008 the total exceeded 93,000, and the New York State Board of Law Examiners expected numbers to continue to increase. According to the 2008 *National Law Journal,* the five largest law firms in the city (ranked by number of attorneys) were Skadden, Arps, Slate, Meagher, and Flom; White and Case; Dewey and LeBoeuf; Weil, Gotshal, and Manges; and Orrick, Herrington, and Sutcliffe.

George Whitney Martin, *Causes and Conflicts: The Centennial History of the Association of the Bar of the City of New York, 1870–1970* (Boston: Houghton Mifflin, 1970); Karen Berger Morello, *The Invisible Bar: The Woman Lawyer in America, 1638 to the Present* (New York: Random House, 1986); Michael J. Powell, *From Patrician to Professional Elite: The Transformation of the New York City Bar* (New York: Russell Sage Foundation, 1988)

Kevin Kenny, Meghan Lalonde

Lazard Frères. Firm of investment bankers. Formed as a dry-goods company in New Orleans in 1848 by Alexandre Lazard, Simon Lazard, and Élie Lazard, it became a firm of bankers in the 1850s and opened offices in San Francisco (1851), Paris (1852), and London (1870); an office was opened in New York City in 1880 by Simon Lazard and his cousin Alexandre Weill. Under the direction of André Meyer from the 1950s to the 1970s, the firm became known for arranging mergers and acquisitions. Its general partner Felix Rohatyn oversaw the restructuring of the city's debt and finances during the fiscal crisis of the mid-1970s and served for nearly 20 years as the chairman of the Municipal Assistance Corporation. Under the direction of its senior partner, Michel David-Weill, the firm took part in the buyout of RJR Nabisco in 1989, the merger in the same year of Time Inc. and Warner Communications, and the acquisitions in the 1990s of McCaw Cellular by American Telephone and Telegraph, Snapple by Quaker Oats, and Paramount by Viacom. In the mid-1990s Lazard Frères remained small and exclusive and was devoted primarily to financial advising, but after it joined with its international branches in forming Lazard LLC in 2000, it became a publicly held company in 2005.

Mary E. Curry

Lazarsfeld, Paul F(elix) (*b* Vienna, 13 Feb 1901; *d* New York City, 30 Aug 1992). Sociologist. After earning his doctorate in mathematics in 1925 from the University of Vienna, he accepted a Rockefeller Fellowship in the United States in 1933 and in 1940 moved to Columbia University, where he remained for the rest of his career. In 1945 he became the director of Columbia's Bureau of Applied Social Research, and his widespread use of surveys as an analytical tool helped make opinion polling a scientific endeavor. In 1952 he was elected president of the American Sociological Association. His work on unemployment and consumer behavior and his careful methodological advances transformed social research worldwide.

Kenneth T. Jackson

Lazarus, Emma (*b* New York City, 22 July 1849; *d* New York City, 19 Nov 1887). Poet. She was educated by private tutors and began publishing poetry in her early teens. A number of her poems were published in *Scribner's Monthly* and *Lippincott's Magazine,* and her father published her poems in book form, a copy of which was sent to author Ralph Waldo Emerson, with whom Emma corresponded for many years. Her 1883 poem "New Colossus" was inscribed on a bronze plaque and mounted on the pedestal of the Statue of Liberty in 1903; it ends with the famous lines: "Give me your tired, your poor, / Your huddled masses yearning to breathe free, / The wretched refuse of your teeming shore. / Send these, the homeless, tempest-tost to me, / I lift my lamp beside the golden door!" In reaction to the Russian pogroms against Jews in the early 1880s and the expulsion of Jews from Russia's Pale of Settlement, Lazarus became involved in Jewish affairs, arguing for the creation of a Jewish homeland and working with the Hebrew Immigrant Aid Society. She is buried in the Beth-Olom Cemetery in Brooklyn.

Sarah Brafman

LDCs. See Local development corporations.

Leake and Watts. Orphanage and social service agency founded in 1831 by John Watts with money from the estate of his friend John George Leake. Leake, a New York lawyer, stipulated that his money fund a home for the "maintenance and education" of orphans regardless of their nationality or faith. The Leake and Watts Orphan House moved to its current location at the Cathedral of St. John the Divine in 1843 in a Greek Revival building designed by Ithiel Town in what is now Morningside Heights. The agency provided shelter, discipline, and academic and industrial training for boys, and later girls, until the age of 15, when they were entrusted to a relative or indentured out. In 1888 Leake and Watts sold its property to the Cathedral of St. John the Divine. The orphanage moved to a 30-acre (12-hectare) farm in Yonkers with grounds designed by Frederick Law Olmsted. In the twentieth century Leake and Watts changed its concentration from orphans to neglected children. The agency established a social services department and began offering foster care. In 2008 Leake and Watts Services in Yonkers and the Bronx provided various services for children and families of the New York metropolitan area. The old Leake and Watts building, overlooking Morningside Park, is now known as the Town Building, named for its architect. The oldest surviving structure in Morningside Heights, it is on the grounds of the Cathedral of St. John the Divine.

Maurita Baldock

leather. See Shoes, boots, and leather.

Lebanese. See Syrians and Lebanese.

Lebanon Hospital. Private hospital in the Bronx, incorporated in 1890 and opened in 1893 with 50 beds in a disused Ursuline convent on the corner of Westchester Avenue and 151st Street. It originally served Jewish immigrants. In 1894 a school of nursing was added. A new building opened in 1932 on the Grand Concourse; another completed in 1943 at the intersection of 173rd Street, Mount Eden Parkway, and Selwyn Avenue was used by the army until 1946. The hospital merged in 1962 with Bronx Hospital to form the Bronx–Lebanon Hospital Center.

Tina Levitan, *Islands of Compassion* (New York: Twayne, 1964)

Andrea Balis

Lebow, Fred (*b* Arad, Romania, 3 June 1932; *d* New York City, 9 Oct 1994). Founder of the New York City Marathon. He fled Romania during the Nazi occupation of World War II and finally immigrated to New York City in the 1960s. He attended the Fashion Institute of Technology in Manhattan and became a well-known figure in the garment district. Lebow's love of running led him to join other enthusiasts and create the first New York City Marathon in 1970, funding the entire production himself for $300. The first race was held entirely within Central Park and had just 127 runners and 53 finishers; few in the city even knew the marathon was taking place. Over the course of the next decades Lebow proved a tireless promoter and marketer of the running movement and the marathon, even wearing running shoes to all of his business meetings. By 1976 the race had grown into a corporately sponsored five-borough event, with thousands of runners and spectators in addition to much media attention. Lebow was instrumental in turning exercise, running, and more specifically marathons from an activity of the highly dedicated and talented few into one of the masses. In 1992, even though he had been diagnosed with brain cancer, Lebow ran and completed the New York City Marathon for the first time. The stretch of 89th Street between Madison and Fifth avenues is named Fred Lebow Way, and a statue of Lebow stands just inside the east 90th Street entrance of Central Park. In the early twenty-first century the New York Road Runners organization, which Lebow directed, continues to operate the New York City Marathon, which now has more than 40,000 finishers each year.

See also Running.

David White

Le Brun, Napoleon (Eugene Henry Charles) (*b* Philadelphia, 2 Jan 1821; *d* New York City, 9 July 1901). Architect. He studied architecture with Thomas U. Walter and worked in Philadelphia for about 20 years before moving in 1864 to New York City, where he used a Romanesque style for the Church of the Epiphany, a French Gothic style for the Episcopal Church of St. Mary the Virgin (West 46th Street), and an imitation of the Dutch Renaissance style for the engine house in Old Slip near the foot of Wall Street, the Home Life Insurance building on Broadway, and firehouses at East 67th Street. Le Brun's office building for the Metropolitan Life Insurance Company at Madison Square received an award from the American Institute of Architects.

James E. Mooney

Le Cirque. French restaurant. Located at 151 East 58th Street on the ground floor of the Bloomberg corporate headquarters, it is in its third incarnation. Owner Sirio Maccioni first opened Le Cirque in 1974 at 60 East 65th Street. In 1997 he relocated the restaurant to the New York Palace Hotel at 455 Madison Avenue and temporarily changed its name to Le Cirque 2000. In 2004 it closed for two years before Maccioni reopened Le Cirque at its current location. With a dining room ceiling designed to look like a large circus tent, it is internationally famous for its delicate, expensive, and decadent food.

Jessica Montesano

L'Eco D'Italia. Italian-language daily newspaper launched in New York City in 1849 by Giovanni Francesco Secchi de Casali (*b* Piacenza, Italy, 1818), a revolutionary in exile who arrived in New York City in 1843. The newspaper favored Italian unification and for many years was an important chronicle of Italian American news. Although largely supplanted after 1880 by *Il Progresso Italo-Americano,* it continued to appear at irregular intervals until 1896.

Francesco Cordasco

Lederberg, Joshua (*b* Montclair, N.J., 23 May 1925; *d* New York City, 2 Feb 2008). Geneticist, microbiologist, and educator. He grew up in Washington Heights and attended Stuyvesant High School. While an undergraduate and medical student at Columbia University he discovered how to conduct genetic crosses in bacteria, a finding that became one of the foundations of modern biotechnology and molecular biology. He received his doctorate from Yale University in 1947 and joined the faculty at the University of Wisconsin in the same year. In 1958 he was awarded the Nobel Prize in medicine for his work in genetics, which stemmed from his research at Columbia and Yale. He later served as the first chairman of the department of genetics at Stanford University medical school from 1959 to 1978. In 1978 he returned to New York City to assume the presidency of Rockefeller University, a post he held until 1990 when he became University Professor Emeritus and Raymond and Beverly Sackler Foundation Scholar.

Ledger, Heath(cliff Andrew) (*b* Perth, Australia, 4 April 1979; *d* New York City, 22 Jan 2008). Actor. He got his start in Australian movies before moving to the United States in 1998. He starred in several movies before he won an Academy Award nomination for his role in the 2005 film *Brokeback Mountain.* Ledger lived in Boerum Hill, Brooklyn, until 2007. Ledger was found dead from an accidental drug overdose at his home at 421 Broome Street in SoHo.

Anne Epstein

Lee, Spike [Shelton Jackson] (*b* Atlanta, Ga., 20 March 1957). Film director, writer, and actor. In 1959 he moved with his parents to the Fort Greene area of Brooklyn where his childhood experiences offered him perspectives on race and class that he later explored in many of his films. He attended John Dewey High School before leaving for Morehouse College in Atlanta. Lee returned to New York City in 1979 and enrolled at the Tisch School of the Arts at New York University. His final film project, *Joe's Bed–Stuy Barbershop: We Cut Heads,* earned him several awards and recognition in the industry. Lee's first feature-length film was *She's Gotta Have It* (1986), which traced the romances of an African American woman from Brooklyn. Budgeted at just $175,000, the movie earned more than $7 million and was recognized at the Cannes Film Festival as the best production by a new filmmaker. The film's success allowed Lee to open his own production company, 40 Acres and a Mule Filmworks, at 124 DeKalb Avenue in Brooklyn. He continued to portray racial and class tensions in New York City with his later films. *Do the Right Thing* (1989) examined the struggles between Italians and African Americans in the Bedford–Stuyvesant section of Brooklyn. As with a number of his works Lee also acted in the film, playing its main character, a pizza delivery boy torn between the worlds of his Italian employers and his African American community. Lee intended to encourage an open discussion on race, but many critics believed that the film advocated violence. Lee's views on race and violence were again displayed with his biographical film *Malcolm X* (1992). As his career progressed, many mainstream film critics were more accepting of Lee, viewing his movies as efforts to promote racial harmony through the expression of an often harsh reality. But many of his films, such as *Summer of Sam* (1999), which explored the serial killings and racial tensions during the summer of 1977 in New York City, and *Bamboozled* (2000), a portrayal of black minstrel shows, still evoked controversy. Lee is also known as an avid sports fan; he has frequently expressed admiration for his idol, the African American Brooklyn Dodger baseball great Jackie Robinson, and became well known during the 1990s for sitting courtside at Madison Square Garden and taunting opposing players who competed against his beloved New York Knicks.

David White

Offices of 40 Acres and a Mule, 2009

Lefcourt, Abraham E. (*b* Birmingham, England, 1877; *d* New York City, 13 Nov 1932). Real estate developer. He began developing lofts and warehouses in 1910 and by 1924 owned property worth more than $10 million, including more properties than any other landowner in the area bounded by 39th Street, Broadway, 35th Street, and Eighth Avenue; his Lefcourt Clothing Center, a building of 27 stories at 275 Broadway, became the anchor of the new garment district, where he was soon a leading developer. During the 1920s he also erected several tall office buildings in Manhattan and some of the first large apartment buildings and hotels in Newark, New Jersey. Lefcourt expanded into finance, forming the Lefcourt Normandie National Bank in 1928; many of his enterprises declared bankruptcy during the Depression.

Marc A. Weiss

Lefferts Homestead. Historic house on Flatbush Avenue near Empire Boulevard in Prospect Park. It was built as a farmhouse in a Dutch style between 1777 and 1783 by Peter Lefferts, a lieutenant in the Continental Army and later a judge on the county court and a delegate to the Constitutional Convention. The house has a gambrel roof and front and back porches, and its rooms are arranged symmetrically. It once stood on Flatbush Avenue near Maple Street, then was moved to Prospect Park after Lefferts's descendants deeded the house to the city in 1918. Lefferts Homestead is one of the few houses of its style remaining in Brooklyn.

Jonathan Kuhn

LeFrak, Samuel (*b* New York City, 12 Feb 1918; *d* New York City, 16 April 2003). Real estate developer. In 1905 his grandfather and father established a modest company in New York City, mainly building tenements on the Lower East Side, that became the LeFrak Organization. Involved in the family business from childhood, Samuel became its president in 1948. While he was in charge during the postwar construction boom, the firm built some 150,000 middle-income houses and apartments in the New York City metropolitan area. Among the best known are LeFrak City, an immense complex of 18-story buildings with 5000 apartments in Queens; the first tower of Battery Park City in downtown Manhattan (after which LeFrak withdrew from the project); and the 10,000-apartment Newport complex in Jersey City. Dubbed "a Donald Trump for the middle class" by the *New York Times,* LeFrak initially scorned government funding but eventually built the first project under New York's Mitchell–Lama program, which provided subsidies to developers of low- and middle-income housing.

Susan Kriete

LeFrak City. Housing development in Rego Park in Queens (2000 pop. *ca* 14,000), covering 40 acres (16 hectares) and bounded to the north by 57th Avenue, to the east by 99th Street, to the south by the Long Island Expressway, and to the west by Junction Boulevard. It was built between 1960 and 1968 as a complex offering "total facilities for total living" for working- and middle-class tenants by the LeFrak Organization, led by the prominent developer Samuel LeFrak. Twenty towers of 18 stories each have a total of 5000 apartments with one to three bedrooms; there are also playgrounds between buildings, three tennis courts, a swimming pool, 2800 outdoor parking spaces, a public garage with 750 spaces, a security service, a post office (Elmhurst branch), two office buildings with 500,000 square feet (46,500 square meters) of space in which the main tenant is the New York City Department of Environmental Protection, and 325,000 square feet (30,000 square meters) of retail space. The development also offers several organizations for tenants and senior citizens. In the 1980s LeFrak City had a period of instability with a changing population, but by 1991 a turnaround was achieved with an influx of Russian and other immigrants. The immigrant experience has acted as a unifying factor for residents, and management has made major renovations since 1996.

James O. Drummond

Legal Aid Society. The country's oldest and largest nonprofit free legal service organization. It was established in New York City in March 1876 as the Deutscher Rechtsschutz Verein to provide legal advice to German immigrants. German merchants, eager to facilitate the assimilation of immigrants, formed the society at the suggestion of Edward Salomon, a former governor of Wisconsin, in a meeting on Wall Street. Charles K. Lexow, a graduate of Columbia Law School (1875), was engaged by the society on 31 March and earned $1000 for a year's work; early causes of the society dealt with citizenship, seamen's rights, and child labor. During Arthur von Brieson's 26-year tenure as president (1890–1916), the society ended German sponsorship (1896) and extended its services to all poor people. Legal Aid offered competent defense work provided by a paid legal staff and developed a much-praised system of case assignment. In 1916 the society handled 41,646 cases, or 40 percent of all legal-aid cases in the nation. Charles Evans Hughes succeeded Brieson and expanded membership even as he fostered the Volunteer Defenders Committee (Rockefeller Lawyers) to defend the indigent. President Harrison Tweed between 1936 and 1945 drew idealistic young lawyers to the staff. In 1962 the society's juvenile division pioneered representation before family court, but criminal defense became the organizational priority after the federal government assumed legal services for the poor that same year, and after the U.S. Supreme Court required states to appoint lawyers for defendants unable to pay legal fees (*Gideon v. Wainwright*, 1963). In 1966 a contract negotiated with Mayor John V. Lindsay allowed the society to remain a private institution that received public funds, an arrangement that became the model for the federal Legal Services Corporation.

To improve services for clients, the Legal Aid Society fought to upgrade detention facilities, establish lawyer–client conference rooms, increase reimbursement rates for court-appointed attorneys, and improve treatment for prisoners suffering from mental illness. A bitter strike in 1982 forced New York City to briefly consider a public defender system, but the plan was rejected as impractical. Societal pressure encouraged the city to act on the problem of homelessness, and it won higher shelter allowances for welfare recipients. However, the organization was embarrassed by its defense of clients charged with drug dealing; these clients received representation because they claimed to have no assets. By the 1990s the Legal Aid Society survived budget cuts imposed by Mayor Rudolph W. Giuliani and emerged as a stronger representative of the poor. In 2006 it mobilized 850 lawyers, 600 staff, and about 1000 volunteers to settle 275,000 cases.

George Whitney Martin, *Causes and Conflicts: The Centennial History of the Bar Association of the City of New York* (Boston: Houghton Mifflin, 1970); Michael J. Powell, *From Patrician to Professional Elite: The Transformation of the New York City Bar Association* (New York: Russell Sage Foundation, 1988); David T. Wasserman, *A Sword for the Convicted: Representing Indigent Defendants on Appeal* (Westport, Conn.: Greenwood, 1990)

See also Lawyers.

George J. Lankevich

Le Gallienne, Eva (*b* London, 11 Jan 1899; *d* Weston, Conn., 3 June 1991). Actress, director, writer, and producer. She moved to New York City in 1915 and in 1926 formed the Civic Repertory Theater (on 14th Street west of Sixth Avenue), which for six seasons until 1933 presented classic plays at low prices and supported an acting school. There she took the role of Peter Pan, in which she was the first actress to appear to fly, and presented *Alice in Wonderland,* which she adapted for the stage with Florida Friebus.

Martha S. LoMonaco

Legal Momentum. Legal advocacy organization. Formerly named NOW Legal Defense and Education Fund, it was formed in 1970 in New York City by the National Organization for Women (NOW), from which it remains distinct. It administers legal, educational, and public information programs aimed at achieving equality for women in schools, the courts, the workplace, and the family. The organization's interests include issues about sexual harassment, reproductive rights, violence against women, and pension reform. The organization acquired its new name in 2004; in the early twenty-first century its headquarters are located at 395 Hudson Street in Manhattan.

Leggett, William (*b* New York City, 30 April 1802; *d* New Rochelle, N.Y., 29 May 1839). Political writer. He first gained public attention in 1829 for his editorials in the *Evening Post,* edited by William Cullen Bryant, a supporter of President Andrew Jackson. In 1834 he was temporarily put in charge of the newspaper and quickly adopted a radical stance. Believing that the division between monopolists and workers was growing, Leggett called for political reforms to remove all economic privilege and legal favoritism. His views, delivered in an unsparing, vitriolic style, pushed well beyond the conventional boundaries of egalitarian principle (he was called an agrarian by his opponents) and inspired dissenting Democrats who in 1835 seceded to form the Equal Rights Party in New York City (nicknamed the Locofocos by their enemies). Leggett's health failed as the movement began; he regained sufficient strength late in 1836 to launch another newspaper, the *Plaindealer,* and to endorse the abolition of slavery. After his death he was considered a martyred hero among the city's radical Democrats until the Civil War, when he faded into obscurity.

Sean Wilentz

Lehman, Herbert H(enry) (*b* New York City, 28 March 1878; *d* New York City, 5 Dec 1963). Governor, brother of Irving Lehman. He was the son of Mayer Lehman, a German immigrant who after settling in the United States in 1849 made a fortune in textiles and finance and helped to found the investment banking firm of LEHMAN BROTHERS. In his early career he was lieutenant governor of New York State under Governor Franklin D. Roosevelt and chairman of the finance committee of Alfred E. Smith's presidential campaign in 1928. Elected governor as a Democrat in 1932, 1934, and 1936 and again in 1938 with the endorsement of the American Labor Party (after the term of office had been extended to four years), he initiated and signed legislation pertaining to labor relations, the minimum wage, and unemployment insurance. Between 1942 and 1946 he was the director of the United Nations Relief and Rehabilitation Agency. Although he lost a race for a seat in the U.S. Senate in 1946, he won a special election in 1949 and was reelected to a full term in 1950. During his tenure he fought for liberal social policies and challenged the accusations of Senator Joseph R. McCarthy against alleged communists. With Eleanor Roosevelt and Thomas Finletter he began a reform movement in 1959 that led in 1961 to the ouster of Carmine DeSapio from Tammany Hall. He then retired from politics and dedicated himself to more than 25 philanthropic causes with which he had been associated throughout his life. He received the Presidential Medal of Freedom, the nation's highest peacetime medal. Lehman College in the Bronx, Lehman Hall at Barnard College, and the Lehman Center for American History at Columbia University are among the many facilities and institutions named in his honor.

Chris McNickle

Lehman Brothers. Global investment banking, securities, and asset management firm. Initially it was a mercantile goods company, formed in 1850 in Montgomery, Alabama, by three German immigrants, Henry, Emmanuel, and Mayer Lehman. In 1868 Mayer and Emmanuel Lehman left the South to form a cotton brokerage firm in New York City at 133–35 Pearl Street. In 1870 the firm helped to form the New York Cotton Exchange, becoming the first company to trade commodities futures. It had an underwriting partnership from 1908 to 1926 with Goldman Sachs and Company. For many years the firm was run by members of the Lehman family; the most influential were Philip Lehman (1861–1947), who supervised the firm's entrance into investment banking, and Robert Lehman (1891–1969), the senior partner from 1926 to 1969. It made several innovations in investment banking during the 1930s, introducing among other services "private placements," a system for matching prospective corporate borrowers with corporate investors such as insurance companies.

Lehman Brothers merged with its powerful rival Kuhn, Loeb in 1977 but was weakened by internal conflicts and was acquired in 1984 by Shearson, the retail brokerage unit of American Express, and renamed Shearson Lehman Brothers. Its headquarters moved in 1985 to the World Financial Center at Vesey Street in Manhattan. In May 1994 American Express divested itself of the firm, which became an independent, publicly owned corporation again named Lehman Brothers. The firm initially struggled, but under the leadership of Chief Executive Officer Richard S. Fuld transformed itself into a global investment bank, growing well beyond its initial strengths in bonds. In 2003 Lehman Brothers acquired the investment advisory firm Neuberger Berman, adding more than $200 billion to its portfolio of assets under management.

On 11 September 2001 Lehman Brothers's global headquarters offices in 3 World Financial Center were severely damaged by falling debris from the terrorist attack against the World Trade Center; more than 6500 employees were displaced. The firm quickly recovered, building a new trading floor in New Jersey within 48 hours and relocating its businesses to more than 40 temporary locations in New York City, including the entirety of the Sheraton Manhattan Hotel. In October 2001 Lehman Brothers purchased a just-built 32-story building at 745 Seventh Avenue from rival Morgan Stanley and moved in April 2002. In August 2007 the firm closed BNC Mortgage, its subprime lender, and eliminated more than 1000 jobs because of poor market conditions. In 2008 Lehman Brothers faced an unprecedented loss from the subprime mortgage crisis and eventually filed for bankruptcy and dissolved the same year, precipitating a global economic crisis.

See also INVESTMENT BANKING.

James Bradley, Tao Tan

Lehman College. College of the City University of New York. It began in 1931 as an extension of Hunter College at Bedford Park Boulevard West in the Bronx. When separated from Hunter in 1968 it was named after Herbert H. Lehman, former governor of New York and a U.S. senator. In the 1970s the campus underwent a rapid expansion during which a Center for the Performing Arts was added. In 1990 a branch campus opened in Hiroshima, Japan, funded by Japanese sponsors who were impressed with the college's program in English as a second language. In the early twenty-first century the college enrolled more than 10,000 graduate and undergraduate students, full and part time. Lehman grants bachelor of arts, bachelor of science, bachelor of fine arts, and master's degrees.

Selma Berrol

Leisler's Rebellion. Term used to refer to political unrest from 1689 to 1691 in the province of New York after the Glorious Revolution in England. Colonial politics were thrown into disarray after the overthrow of King James II in 1688 and the subsequent downfall of the Dominion of New England, which included New York. After the New York City militia rebelled and seized Fort James on 31 May 1689, a committee of safety was formed, and from 27 June a convention of representatives from East Jersey and all counties in New York except Albany governed the province. On 28 June the convention chose Jacob Leisler (1640–91), a captain of the militia and a successful German-born merchant, to become "captain of the fort," and on 16 August it made him the chief military commander. Leisler led a militantly anti-Catholic faction that supported the claims of William of Orange to the English throne. The city government, however, remained in the hands of appointees of James II until September, when the provincial convention called for elections in which Peter Delanoy became the mayor. After the arrival of several ambiguously addressed royal letters, Leisler assumed the title of lieutenant governor and dissolved the convention on 16 December. The city became bitterly divided over this and other of his actions. He further antagonized his opponents by making summary arrests of alleged "papists," and he alienated a number of his supporters through his tax policies. In May 1690 the city was the site of an intercolonial conference organized by Leisler, the first of its kind, to plan a military and naval expedition against Canada. This was undertaken in the summer of 1690 but ended without success. Leisler then faced increasingly vocal resistance. In January 1691 former city officials returned from exile with the arrival of a contingent of English regulars commanded by Richard Ingoldsby. Leisler's refusal to surrender the fort to Ingoldsby and a violent battle between pro- and anti-Leislerians for control of the city led the new royal governor, Henry Sloughter, to arrest Leisler and many of his sympathizers after he took control on 17 March. At the urging of such opponents as Nicholas Bayard, Leisler was tried for treason and tortured and executed on 16 May with an associate, Jacob Milborne. Leisler's Rebellion was the most divisive conflict in colonial New York and helped to develop the bitter factionalism that shaped city politics for several decades.

Jerome R. Reich, *Leisler's Rebellion: A Study of Democracy in New York, 1664–1720* (Chicago: University of Chicago Press, 1953); Thomas J. Archdeacon, *New York City, 1664–1710: Conquest and Change* (Ithaca, N.Y.: Cornell University Press,

1976); Robert C. Ritchie, *The Duke's Province: A Study of New York Politics and Society, 1664–1691* (Chapel Hill: University of North Carolina Press, 1977); Charles Howard McCormick, *Leisler's Rebellion* (New York: Garland, 1989)

David William Voorhees

Lennon, John (Winston Ono) (*b* Liverpool, England, 9 Oct 1940; *d* New York City, 8 Dec 1980). Singer and songwriter. He was a founding member of the Beatles, for which he and Paul McCartney wrote songs including "Help," "Revolution," "Strawberry Fields," and "Lucy in the Sky with Diamonds." He married the performance artist Yoko Ono in 1969 and moved with her to New York City in 1971 after the Beatles disbanded; the two lived at the St. Regis Hotel (2 East 55th Street) in 1971–72 and recorded a number of songs, among them "The Dream Is Over," "Woman," and "Imagine." They lived at the Dakota at 1 West 72nd Street, where they also had an office and a studio on the ground floor. Lennon was a peace activist during the Vietnam War; his activism resulted in a deportation attempt by the administration of President Richard Nixon in 1972. Among Lennon's last songs was "(Just Like) Starting Over," which he recorded shortly before his assassination in front of the Dakota. Mark David Chapman pleaded guilty to the murder and remained in prison as of 2010. A garden in Central Park named Strawberry Fields is dedicated to Lennon's memory.

John Robertson, *The Art and Music of John Lennon* (New York: Carol Publishing, 1991)

James E. Mooney

Lenox Hill. Neighborhood on the East Side of Manhattan, bounded to the north by East 77th Street, to the east by Lexington Avenue, to the south by East 60th Street, and to the west by Fifth Avenue. The farm of Robert Lenox once covered 30 acres (12 hectares) bounded by what became East 74th Street, Fourth Avenue, East 68th Street, and Fifth Avenue; the hill for which the neighborhood is named stood at what is now 70th Street and Park Avenue. A parcel bounded by what are now East 68th Street, Third Avenue, East 60th Street, and Fifth Avenue was named Hamilton Square and set aside as public space in 1807. At his death in 1840 Lenox left his estate to his son James, who donated land on Fourth Avenue between East 71st Street and East 69th Street for Union Theological Seminary and Presbyterian Hospital. The area attracted several charitable and religious institutions during the 1860s, when fashionable New Yorkers lived below 59th Street: the German Dispensary (1868; later renamed Lenox Hill Hospital) on East 77th Street off Fourth Avenue; the Normal School (later Hunter College), Hahnemann Hospital, and Mount Sinai Hospital in Hamilton Square; the Lenox Library (1877) at Fifth Avenue and East 70th Street; and the Seventh Regiment Armory (1879) on Fourth Avenue at East 66th Street. In the 1880s elegant town houses lined the side streets, and lavish mansions along Fifth Avenue faced the newly completed Central Park; Fourth Avenue, renamed Park Avenue in 1888, became a grand boulevard known for its handsome residences after the New York Central Railroad was electrified (1907) and placed entirely underground (1913). Multimillion-dollar cooperative apartments in these luxury buildings erected between 1910 and 1920 are highly coveted. Lenox Hill is served by Lexington Avenue, a thoroughfare of shops and restaurants, and Madison Avenue, known for its boutiques, art galleries, and luxury hotels. The Whitney Museum of American Art, the Asia Society, and the Frick Collection are major cultural attractions in the area.

James Trager, *Park Avenue* (New York: Atheneum, 1990)

Joyce Mendelsohn

Lenox Hill Hospital. Hospital on the Upper East Side of Manhattan. It opened in 1868 as an offshoot of the German Dispensary, a facility opened at 132 Canal Street in 1857 to serve Germans on the Lower East Side. Known as the German Hospital and Dispensary of New York, the hospital was a private facility that occupied a site at 8 East Third Street. But these facilities became overcrowded and plans were made to build new ones at 77th Street and Fourth (now Park) Avenue (formerly the Robert Lenox farm). A corporation led by Carl Gottfried Gunther (later the mayor) was formed; its members included the pediatrician Abraham Jacobi, the gynecologist Emil Noeggerath, the surgeon Ernst Krackowizer, the ophthalmologist Herman Althof, the publishers Anna Ottendorfer and Oswald Ottendorfer, and the newspaper editor Carl Schurz. Initially the hospital served mostly indigent patients. During the 1860s it stood next to a swamp and across from the stables of the New York Cab Company. Most of the patients were from Yorkville, a growing German neighborhood east of Park Avenue. After World War I the neighborhood became fashionable as open railroad tracks along the avenue were covered and elegant houses were built. The first private pavilion opened in 1901; the hospital took its current name in 1918, and after 1949 a number of beds became semiprivate. After World War II the inpatient and outpatient facilities expanded to fill the block bounded by 77th Street, Lexington Avenue, 76th Street, and Park Avenue. In 2001 the hospital added the sponsorship of the Manhattan Eye, Ear and Throat Hospital to its roster of services. In 2006 the hospital opened a new cardiac care center and radiology center, and in 2007, a new emergency department.

See also Hospitals.

Ann L. Buttenwieser

Lenox Library. See Libraries and New York Public Library.

Lenya, Lotte [Blamauer, Karoline (Wilhelmine)] (*b* Vienna, 19 Oct 1898; *d* New York City, 27 Nov 1981). Actress and singer. After becoming well known in Berlin for her performances in the theatrical works of her husband, Kurt Weill, she fled with him from Nazi Germany and arrived in New York City on 10 September 1935; they lived at the St. Moritz Hotel (50 Central Park South) before moving to an apartment at 231 East 62nd Street. After her husband's death in 1950 she continued to appear on stage and in films. She won a Tony Award for her portrayal of Jenny the prostitute in a production by the Theatre de Lys of *The Threepenny Opera,* which ran for 2611 performances between 1954 and 1961. During these years she divided her time between her home in Rockland County and several apartments on the East Side, the last at 404 East 55th Street. Lenya later appeared as Fräulein Schneider in the Broadway production of *Cabaret*, which from 1966 through 1969 ran for 1165 performances at the Broadhurst Theatre.

Donald Spoto, *Lenya: A Life* (Boston: Little, Brown, 1989)

Marc Ferris

Leo Baeck Institute. Independent nonprofit center formed in 1955 and devoted to the political, economic, social, and cultural history of German-speaking Jews to the time of the Nazis. It provides annual research fellowships; presents exhibits; sponsors lectures, international symposia, and monthly faculty seminars; and publishes books, lectures, and exhibition catalogues as well as *Library and Archives News* (two to three times a year), the *LBI News* (occasionally), a yearbook, and a quarterly bulletin. Its building at 15 West 16th Street houses a library containing, in the early twenty-first century, more than 70,000 volumes, periodicals, and serials; more than 30,000 photographs; and a collection of prints, drawings, paintings, and sculptures. The institute also has an extensive archive of unpublished manuscripts and memoirs.

Allen J. Share

Leonard, Benny [Leiner, Benjamin] (*b* New York City, 7 April 1896; *d* New York City, 18 April 1947). Boxer and referee. He grew up on the Lower East Side and became a professional boxer in 1911 under a pseudonym because of the opposition of his parents. Under the management of Billy Gibson he won the world lightweight championship by knocking out Freddy Welsh on 28 May 1917 in New York City. He retired as champion in 1925 after several memorable defenses, although financial troubles inspired a brief return to the ring in 1931. Leonard compiled a record of 88 wins, five losses, and one draw (with 115 fights declared no decision). He was elected to the Boxing Hall of Fame and is generally regarded as one of the best lightweight fighters in the history of boxing.

Steven A. Riess

Lerner, Max (*b* Minsk, Russia, 20 Dec 1902; *d* New York City, 5 June 1992). Political scientist, writer, and journalist. He immigrated to the United States in 1907, attended Yale University and Washington University in St. Louis, and received his PhD from the Robert Brookings School of Economics and Government. An adherent of the political Left who for a time advocated economic planning through "democratic collectivism," he edited the *Nation* in the 1930s and the newspapers *PM* and the *Star* in the 1940s, was a contributing editor of the *New Republic* and the managing editor of the *Encyclopedia of the Social Sciences,* and from 1948 until his death wrote a syndicated column for the *New York Post.* He also taught at several colleges and universities, among them Sarah Lawrence College, near his home in suburban Westchester County. Lerner's published writings include *It Is Later Than You Think: The Need for a Militant Democracy* (1938), *Ideas Are Weapons: The History and Uses of Ideas* (1939), *The Mind and Faith of Justice Holmes* (1943), *Actions and Passions: Notes on the Multiple Revolution of Our Time* (1949), *America as a Civilization* (1957), and *The Age of Overkill* (1962), as well as modern editions of works by Aristotle, Machiavelli, Adam Smith, Alexis de Tocqueville, and Thorstein Veblen.

John Recchiuti

Lesbian Herstory Archives. World's largest collection of materials relating to lesbians, founded in New York City in 1973 by the Lesbian Herstory Educational Foundation and opened to the public in the following year. The archives receive more than 1000 visitors a year; the foundation publishes a newsletter, maintains a Web site giving a virtual tour of the holdings, and has microfilmed for library use its periodical and subject files collections. In addition to a reading room, the archives have a museum and art gallery and space for readings and performances. While the materials in the collection are international in scope, they are richest in New York City's lesbian communal history. In the early twenty-first century the archives are located at 484 14th Street in Park Slope, Brooklyn.

Lee Hudson, Joan Nestle

lesbians. In 1665 the Duke of York included in the laws governing what later became New York City the capital offense of sodomy, defined as "unnatural lusts of men with men and women with women." This "buggery" law remained in effect until 1797, when the death penalty for the offense was abolished. By 1890 lesbians (scornfully referred to as *tribadists,* or sexual perverts) were documented as part of the city's criminal culture: mannish women were often found among the "social undesirables" who gathered nightly in the Bowery at the Artistic Club, the Slide, and Walhalla Hall, and at Paresis Hall on Fourth Avenue. Theories about women who had lost their true womanly nature abounded; throughout the 1890s speakers at conferences in the city such as the International Medico-Legal Congress of 1893 recommended hysterectomies as a cure. Frequent references to practitioners of tribadism suggest that the city had a large lesbian population. When a farcical play called *A Florida Enchantment* by A. C. Gunter opened on Broadway in April 1896, critics reviled it for its presentation of a masculine woman who cursed, smoked a cigarette, and tried to seduce all the other women onstage. Although the play did not depict lesbianism directly (the female character swallowed magical seeds to change her sex), it clearly implied that lesbianism and the liberation of women were linked. In 1899 a special investigative committee questioned Mayor Robert A. Van Wyck about his knowledge of lesbian meeting places. Some lesbians survived by "passing," or living their public and sometimes private lives disguised as men. The most famous passing woman of the nineteenth century was Murray Hall, who masqueraded as a man for more than 25 years and was a respected politician in the thirteenth senatorial district and an important member of Tammany Hall. She was married twice to women who did not reveal her secret, and because of her disguise was able to register and vote many years before women were enfranchised. She died of breast cancer after refusing to see a doctor, even when the pain in her chest was unbearable. The *New York Times* wrote in her obituary (19 January 1901) that "she even had a reputation as a man about town, a bon vivant, and all around good fellow."

In 1912 a group of female writers, activists, journalists, health reformers, socialists, and advocates of "free love" formed Heterodoxy, a club for "unorthodox" women that met for biweekly lunches in Greenwich Village until 1940. At least 24 of the club's 110 known members were lesbians. Among those who often visited the club were Edith Lees, the wife of Havelock Ellis, and Gertrude Stein and Alice B. Toklas. Some lesbians became part of the city's social elite, such as Elsie de Wolfe and her companion Elisabeth Marbury. In 1922 a lesbian character was featured in Sholem Asch's Yiddish drama *The God of Vengeance;* after the play moved uptown from Greenwich Village it was quickly closed and the entire cast was arrested. *The Captive,* a play by the French writer Édouard Bourdet about the breakup of a marriage by the wife's lesbian suitor, opened on Broadway on 29 September 1926. According to local newspapers hundreds of female couples attended each performance, and local florists sold large quantities of violets, symbolic in the play of the lesbian character. As part of Mayor James J. Walker's campaign against vice, the police joined with religious groups and John S. Sumner, secretary of the New York Society for the Suppression of Vice, to close the play on obscenity charges and arrest its star, Helen Mencken. On 6 April 1927 the New York State legislature passed the Padlock Law forbidding the presentation of any work depicting "sex perversion" onstage; this law remained in effect until 1967. A complaint by Sumner in December 1929 prompted the police to remove Radclyffe Hall's novel *The Well of Loneliness* from all bookstores, and in February of the following year a local judge ruled the book obscene in a trial that kept the theme of lesbianism on the front page of the *Times.* A higher court later reversed the opinion. Less controversially, from 1926 to 1933 lesbian actress, producer, and director Eva Le Gallienne founded and ran the first New York City repertory theater, her critically acclaimed Civic Repertory Theater in the Village on 14th Street.

From the 1920s lesbians gathered at bars and dinner clubs such as Tony Pastor's and Howdys, an exotic bar where lesbians, bohemians, and tourists watched the lesbian performers Blackie and Bubbles Kent impersonate men. This tradition of male impersonation continued during the next two decades at Club 82 on East Fourth Street and later at the 81 Club nearby. After the northward migration of blacks during World War I, Harlem became a cultural mecca for young black lesbians. In the 1920s and well into the 1930s lesbians there congregated at rent parties where performers sang "sissy man" and "bull dagger" blues; a well-known hostess was A'lelia Walker, the daughter of the entrepreneur and social activist Madame Walker. Other clubs featured lesbian entertainers such as Gladys Bentley, Moms Mabley, and Ma Rainey; literary gatherings attracted such poets as Gladys May, Casely Hayford, Mae V. Cowdery, Georgia Douglas Johnson, and Angelina Weld Grimké. Lesbians in Harlem were not safe from police raids and intimidation by the vice squad: in 1922 the lesbian activist Mabel Hampton was arrested at an all-women's party and sent to the reformatory in Bedford Hills for two years on a charge of prostitution. Hampton served as an air raid warden in her Harlem community during World War II, one of many lesbians in military or national service.

The public lesbian social life of Harlem continued into the 1930s and 1940s, with "drag" balls, yearly trips up the Hudson, and dances. Mona's, a bar in midtown, became a gathering place for lesbians in the 1940s. By the following decade bars catering openly and exclusively to lesbians proliferated in Greenwich Village, among them the Pony Stable, Laurel's, Swing Rendezvous, Bagatelle, Seven

Steps, Bohemia, Kookie's, Gianni's, the Three, and the Sea Colony on Abingdon Square. Dancing with a partner of the same sex was illegal, and women who did not wear at least three pieces of women's clothing were periodically arrested for transvestism. There was an uneasy collaboration between the vice squad, the police, and the organized crime figures who often owned and managed the bars. The Sea Colony had a back room for dancing equipped with a red light that flashed on when the police arrived each week to collect their bribes—but often the police did not leave after the money was exchanged, and many lesbians reported being beaten and sexually assaulted.

Lesbians in Greenwich Village referred to the Women's House of Detention, a redbrick building on the corner of Sixth Avenue and Eighth Street, as the "country club." During the 1950s it became the scene of public displays of affection as women on the street called up to their incarcerated girlfriends. The prison was considered an embarrassment by city officials and closed in the early 1970s. From the 1950s working-class lesbians met in Riis Park on the weekends to play softball and enjoy the beach. A more established community catered to artistic, affluent lesbians in the beach town of Cherry Grove on Fire Island, where Janet Flanner and others rented summer homes; police raids in both communities were common. Barbara Gittings in 1958 formed a local chapter of the Daughters of Bilitis, the first incorporated membership organization for lesbians in the city. Intimidation and harassment by the Federal Bureau of Investigation and other authorities occurred frequently, and for fear of being exposed most members used only their first names or pseudonyms. Shortly after Ruth Simpson moved the Daughters of Bilitis to its own loft on Prince Street, internal disagreements led the group to disband.

The city subjected lesbians to raids, entrapment, verbal abuse, and physical threats into the early 1960s. The last raid on a lesbian bar reported in the newspapers was in March 1964: on a Friday night the police entered Mary Angela's on Seventh Avenue South and took away 43 women in police vans with barred windows. Charged with disorderly conduct and disturbing the peace, they were held overnight and forced to walk a gauntlet of jeering officers the next morning. The judge dismissed the case when a detective was unable to identify the women who he alleged had been dancing together at the bar. In 1964 Rene Cafiero, Nancy Garden, and other lesbian members of the New York League for Sexual Freedom demonstrated in front of the U.S. Army Building against the exclusion of homosexuals from the military. Lesbians took part in the first protest sponsored by a gay-rights organization when the Mattachine Society picketed the United Nations on 16 April 1965 to protest the Cuban government's imprisonment of homosexuals in labor camps. One first-person account in the *Village Voice* credited a lesbian with having instigated the STONEWALL RIOTS (28 June 1969), in which gay men and lesbians resisted a police raid on the Stonewall Inn in Greenwich Village, an event considered by many as having begun the lesbian and gay liberation movement. New lesbian bars opened during the 1970s, such as Bonnie and Clyde's, Ariel, and the Dutchess in Greenwich Village, and Peaches and the Sahara uptown. In addition several restaurants catered only to women, among them Mother Courage on the Hudson River, the Women's Coffeehouse, and Bonnie's, and women's bookstores opened in Greenwich Village (Djuna Books) and on 92nd Street and Amsterdam Avenue (Womanbooks). Dances for women only were held monthly at the Woman's Center and bars were no longer the most popular place for lesbians to meet.

Lesbians belonged to the Gay Liberation Front (1969–70) and the Gay Activists Alliance (1970–74), which met in a disused firehouse on Wooster Street, but because men dominated these organizations, the women soon grew restless and formed their own group, the Lesbian Liberation Committee. In 1971 a group of lesbians including Ginny Vida and Nath Rockhill formed the Lesbian Feminist Liberation, an organization that provided social alternatives to the bars. A group of lesbians and gay academicians met in 1972 to form the Gay Academic Union, the first national organization that aimed to integrate lesbian and gay studies into the college curriculum and to represent the concerns of lesbian and gay teachers and students; the union encouraged the work of such lesbian theorists as Karla Jay, Esther Newton, Julia Penelope, and Catherine Stimpson and helped form the Center for Lesbian and Gay Studies (CLAGS) at the Graduate School of the City University of New York. Other groups included Women against Rape, Gay Women's Alternative, and Radicalesbians, which published the most influential lesbian document of the 1970s, a four-page pamphlet titled "The Woman-Identified Woman." Several books with lesbian themes reached a wide readership: *Sappho Was a Right-On Woman* (1972) by Barbara Love and Sidney Abbott, *Lesbian Nation* (1973) by Jill Johnston, and *Rubyfruit Jungle* (1973) by Rita Mae Brown, set in New York City. The LESBIAN HERSTORY ARCHIVES, formed in 1973 and opened to the public in the following year in the apartment of Joan Nestle and Deborah Edel in Manhattan, became the largest archive of its kind in the world.

Political gains were achieved in the early 1970s by the Gay Activists Alliance, the Lesbian Feminist Liberation, the New York Political Action Committee, and the Study Group and by such activists as Meryl Friedman, Martha Shelley, Kitty Cotter, and Blue Lunden. Council members Carter Burden and Eldon Clingan introduced the first gay-rights bill in the country before the City Council on 6 January 1971 (not passed until 20 March 1986). Cafiero and Dallice Covello in 1972 were the first openly lesbian delegates to the national convention of a major political party (as supporters of the Democratic candidate George McGovern). The Coalition for Lesbian and Gay Rights, formed in 1977, was led by Eleanor Cooper and Betty Santoro. Salsa Soul Sisters, the first social and political organization in the United States exclusively for lesbians from racial minority groups, was formed in September 1974 by Dolores Jackson; now known as African-American Wimmin United for Social Change, in the early twenty-first century it meets weekly at the Lesbian, Gay, Bisexual, and Transgender Community Center on 13th Street in Manhattan. Black lesbians who became prominent in the city during these years included the poets Audre Lorde, Jewelle Gomez, Cheryl Clarke, Pat Parker, and Sapphire; the performers Storme DeLarverie, Edwina Lee Taylor, and Pamela Sneed; and the community leaders Betty Powell, Joyce Hunter, Candace Boyce, Sandra Lowe, Joan Gibbs, and Marjorie Hill. Lesbian activists served on the city's Commission on the Status of Women, among them Jean O'Leary (1975), Charlotte Bunch, and Vida (1980–91). The first openly lesbian candidate for public office was Virginia Apuzzo, who unsuccessfully sought a seat in the New York State Assembly in 1978. From 1986 the first openly lesbian judges, Mary Bednar, Joan Lobis, Marcy Kahn, Karen Burstein, and Roz Richter, were appointed to the city's civil, criminal, and family courts, and the Office for the Lesbian and Gay Community, the first of its kind in the United States, was formed in 1989 by Mayor Edward I. Koch, who appointed a lesbian director, Lee Hudson. A community liaison position created by the New York Police Department was filled by Detective Vanessa Ferro, and Jacquelyn Shaffer and later Katie Doran served as community liaison in the district attorney's office of Manhattan with liaison Liz Garro in the Brooklyn district attorney's office.

In 1990 Deborah Glick became the first openly lesbian candidate to win election to the state assembly. In 1993 gay and lesbian couples were granted the right to register with the city clerk as domestic partners, expanding benefits from the first domestic partnership registry for city employees established in 1989. Also in 1993 city employees received medical benefits for domestic partners, ending a long lawsuit against the Board of Education that included two lesbian plaintiffs, Ruth Berman and Connie Kurtz.

From the mid-1990s to 2007 there were more than 400 political, social, and religious organizations for lesbians in New York City, ranging from Queer Nation, the Pink Panthers, and Dyke Action Machine to Las Buenas Amigas, Asian Lesbians of the East Coast, and We Wah and Bar Chee Ampe, a group for lesbian and gay American Indians. Jewish lesbians attended Congregation Beth Simchat Torah, a predominantly gay and lesbian synagogue on Bethune Street with a lesbian rabbi, Sharon Kleinbaum. The city also supported several early lesbian publications, of which the best known were *Womenews, Sappho's Isle, Visibilities,* and the lesbian separatist publication *Tribade.*

Domestic partnership gains peaked in 1998 with the passage of legislation codifying previous executive orders and the Board of Education case by extending benefits and services—such as health care, welfare fund benefits, and bereavement—to partners of city employees. In 2005, by executive order, Mayor Michael Bloomberg began a program to extend insurance coverage to domestic partners for private city vendors, although a later attempt in 2006 to convert that effort into law by the City Council was invalidated in court.

The "marriage movement" was replacing domestic partnership efforts in the early twenty-first century, propelled by increasing numbers of couples with children, couples with one partner seeking immigration rights, and aging couples. Receiving spousal rights, including more than 1100 spousal benefits, required a revision of state and federal relationship law. In 2002 lesbian City Council member Christine Quinn, later elected majority speaker in 2006, joined with lesbian council member Margarita Lopez and others to cosponsor a successful bill to recognize gay marriages from other jurisdictions. In April 2007 Governor Eliot Spitzer introduced legislation legalizing same-sex marriage and extending the rights of civil marriage to protect same-sex partners and their children. It passed the New York State Assembly in June 2007. In September 2007 the courts ruled that New York must recognize out-of-state marriages of public employees for pension disbursement.

Judith Schwarz, *Radical Feminists of Heterodoxy: Greenwich Village, 1912–1940* (Lebanon, N.H.: New Victoria, 1982); Kaier Cartin, *We Can Always Call Them Bulgarians* (Boston: Alyson, 1987); Joan Nestle, *A Restricted Country* (Ithaca, N.Y.: Firebrand, 1988); Lillian Faderman, *Old Girls and Twilight Lovers* (New York: Penguin, 1991); Steve Hogan and Lee Hudson, *Completely Queer: The Gay and Lesbian Encyclopedia* (New York: Henry Holt, 1998)

Lee Hudson, Joan Nestle

Lescaze, William (*b* Geneva, Switzerland, 27 March 1896; *d* New York City, 9 Feb 1969). Architect. After training in Switzerland he moved to New York City in 1923 and opened a firm with George Howe in 1929 (Howe and Lescaze). One of the first proponents of the International style in the city, he submitted a plan for a "tower in the park" housing development between Chrystie and Forsyth streets (1931) that was shown at the International Exhibition at the Museum of Modern Art in 1932; he designed the Williamsburg Houses in Brooklyn (Public Works Administration, 1938) in a similar style. Sleek modern lines characterize Lescaze's designs for the Aviation Building at the World's Fair of 1939–40 and a number of retail outlets and private houses, including his town house at East 48th Street (1933), as well as renovations he made to the lobby and Egyptology library of the Brooklyn Museum.

Lorraine Welling Lanmon, *William Lescaze, Architect* (Philadelphia: Art Alliance Press/Cranbury, N.J.: Associated University Presses, 1987)

Edward A. Eigen

Leslie, Frank [Henry Carter] (*b* Ipswich, England, 21 March 1821; *d* New York City, 10 Jan 1880). Magazine publisher. He became a skilled news illustrator in London, using the pseudonym Frank Leslie to conceal his trade from his disapproving father. In 1848 he settled in New York City, where he worked as a wood engraver and illustrator for several publications and in 1854 published the *Illustrated News* with P. T. Barnum. A more successful venture was *Frank Leslie's Lady's Gazette of Fashion and Fancy Needlework,* launched in the following year as the first in a series of magazines bearing his name; later in the year he began publishing *Frank Leslie's Illustrated Newspaper,* the first weekly news magazine in the United States and an enormous success. Leslie attacked the "swill milk" interests of the city in 1858: he inveighed against the use of distillery refuse as animal feed and published graphic pictures of diseased cows. But in general his publications refrained from taking political stands and were neutral during the Civil War. During his career Leslie published about 40 periodicals in English and German, most of which emphasized humor, crime, gossip, and fiction of interest to women and children. The depression of the 1870s hurt his business, which after his death was restored to profitability by his second wife, Miriam Follin Squier.

Frank Luther Mott, *A History of American Magazines,* vol. 1, *1741–1850* (New York: D. Appleton, 1930); Budd Leslie Gambee, Jr., *Frank Leslie and His Illustrated Newspaper, 1855–1860* (Ann Arbor: Department of Library Science, University of Michigan, 1964)

Robert Stinson

Leslie [Squier; née Follin], **Miriam** [Leslie, Frank] (*b* New Orleans, 5 June 1836; *d* New York City, 18 Sept 1914). Magazine publisher. She was born into a wealthy family who moved to New York City when she was 14 years old. She edited *Frank Leslie's Chimney Corner* (1865) and *Frank Leslie's Lady's Journal* (1871) and married Leslie in 1874. On his death in 1880 she assumed control of his business, which was still suffering from the depression of the 1870s, and restored it to profitability. She herself took the name Frank Leslie in 1881. After a brief marriage in 1891 to Oscar Wilde's brother Willie Wilde, she resumed her career in journalism, then leased some of her publications, sold others, and worked as a writer and lecturer. Leslie left an estate valued at $2 million to the woman suffrage movement.

Madeline B. Stern, *Purple Passage: The Life of Mrs. Frank Leslie* (Norman: University of Oklahoma Press, 1953)

Robert Stinson

Letterman, David (*b* Indianapolis, 12 April 1947). Comedian and entertainer. He attended Ball State University (graduating in 1969), worked as a weatherman in Indianapolis and as a comedian in Los Angeles, and then moved to New York City. He appeared frequently as a guest host of Johnny Carson's *Tonight Show* and then in 1980 became the host of his own daytime program for the National Broadcasting Company (NBC); he moved to a nighttime program, *Late Night with David Letterman,* in 1982. During the following years he became known for a wry, irreverent, and self-deprecating humor, replete with topical references to New York City, that proved especially popular with young adults. It was widely assumed that he would become the host of the *Tonight Show* on Carson's retirement, and the decision by NBC to choose another host instead prompted Letterman to move to the Columbia Broadcasting System (CBS) in 1993. For his program, the *Late Show with David Letterman,* CBS renovated the Ed Sullivan Theater on Broadway and 53rd Street. In 1991 Letterman started his own production company, Worldwide Pants, which produces his show and several others. In the twenty-first century Letterman continues to host the *Late Show;* he renewed his contract in 2009 through the fall of 2012.

Lever House. Skyscraper at 390 Park Avenue in Manhattan between 53rd and 54th streets. Designed by Gordon Bunshaft, a partner in the firm of Skidmore, Owings and Merrill, and completed in 1952 as the headquarters for the soap manufacturer Lever Brothers, it was the first glass skyscraper on Park Avenue. The building's stunning geometry of metal and glass prompted architects to reconsider traditional skyscraper design, and within a decade of its construction it had inspired numerous imitations in New York City and around the world. The building has 24 stories atop a horizontal slab supported by columns. It is encased in a blue-green skin of glass banded

Lever House, 2009

in stainless steel. At night the skyscraper takes on a crystalline beauty and seems to float above Park Avenue. Lever House was designated a city landmark in 1982.

Rebecca Read Shanor

Lewisohn, Leonard (*b* Hamburg, Germany, 10 Oct 1847; *d* London, 5 March 1902). Industrialist. He arrived in Manhattan in 1865 and opened an importing business at 251 Pearl Street. In 1867 he formed a partnership with his brothers Julius Lewisohn and Adolph Lewisohn (1849–1938). The three purchased a copper mine in 1879 that was the first of several profitable mining ventures; they also acquired smelting firms and virtually controlled the industry until successfully challenged by the Guggenheims in 1900. Lewisohn was a prominent contributor to the Jewish Theological Seminary. His daughters Irene and Alice in 1915 organized the Neighborhood Playhouse of Henry Street Settlement at 466 Grand Street, an early promoter of experimental theater.

Stephen Birmingham, *Our Crowd: The Great Jewish Families of New York* (New York: Harper and Row, 1967)

Joyce Mendelsohn

Lewisohn Stadium. The stadium of City College of New York, between West 136th and West 138th streets and Convent and Amsterdam avenues. Built at the instigation of John H. Finley, president of the college from 1903 to 1913, it was named after the philanthropist Adolph Lewisohn (*b* Hamburg, *ca* 1849; *d* New York City, 17 Aug 1938), who donated $50,000 for construction and presented the stadium to the college on 29 May 1915. The stadium was designed by Arnold W. Brunner as a half-oval of reinforced concrete with 24 tiers of seats below a row of 64 Doric columns. It seated 6000 and had standing room for 1500. The stadium was best known as the site of reasonably priced orchestral concerts presented each summer from 1918 to 1966. It was demolished in 1973.

Laura Lewison

Lexow, Rudolf (*b* Schleswig–Holstein [now part of Germany], 10 Jan 1821; *d* Brooklyn, 16 July 1909). Editor and novelist. He immigrated to the United States and settled in New York City after the revolution of 1848. In 1852 he founded the *Criminal Zeitung und Belletristisches Journal,* which became a leading German American newspaper and literary journal under his editorship (circulation reached 20,000 in 1855 and more than 70,000 in the 1880s). His published writings include the novels *Amerikanische Criminal-Mysterien oder das Leben der Verbrecher in New-York* (1854) and *Annies Prüfungen* (1860), and histories of the revolution of 1848 and the U.S. Civil War. One of his sons was Clarence Lexow, a state senator who investigated municipal corruption during the 1890s.

Stanley Nadel

Lexow Committee. Legislative committee impaneled between 1894 and 1895, named for and chaired by State Senator Clarence Lexow of the sixteenth and later twenty-third districts. With some help from Charles H. Parkhurst's City Vigilance League, the committee uncovered and exposed a system of corruption in the police force including vice operations, rigged elections, and physical brutality. These were the result of endemic cronyism and political patronage as well as a high turnover rate within the police force. The result was the defeat of Tammany Hall in the municipal elections that year and the election of reformer Mayor William Strong. The Police Parade was also canceled that year, and Theodore Roosevelt took over as police commissioner, instituting extensive reform efforts throughout the police department.

Joseph P. Viteritti

liability insurance. See Property and liability insurance.

Liberal Party. Statewide political party formed in New York City in 1944. Former members of the American Labor Party who had become disaffected by its left-wing stance made up most of the initial membership; the principal organizers were Alex Rose and David Dubinsky. The party evolved into a reformist group largely controlled by Rose that sometimes nominated its own candidates for public office and at other times provided a second line on the ballot to a liberal Democrat or Republican. In the 1940s and 1950s it promoted rent control and consumer protection laws, and in the 1960s it took part in a suit for congressional reapportionment favorable to urban areas, a suit eventually upheld by the U.S. Supreme Court. Later it opposed the Vietnam War and called for the impeachment of President Richard M. Nixon after the Watergate scandal. A high point for the party was marked in 1969 when it was the vehicle for the reelection of Mayor John V. Lindsay, who had been denied renomination by the Republican Party. With the end of the Vietnam War the party declined in membership and influence, especially after Rose's death in 1976. The party's fortunes revived in 1993, when it endorsed the Republican mayoral candidate Rudolph W. Giuliani: he received 62,469 votes on the Liberal line, more than the 53,581 votes by which he defeated the Democratic incumbent, Mayor David N. Dinkins. Mayor Giuliani appointed Fran Reiter, the party's state chairman, to the position of deputy mayor for planning and community relations. The Liberal Party is believed to be the longest-standing third party in the United States. In early 1994 there were 26,704 registered Liberals in New York City, representing 0.8 percent of all registered voters. In 2008 the party's headquarters were at 391 Park Avenue South in Manhattan.

Chad Ludington

Liberator. Radical journal. It was founded by Max Eastman, his sister Crystal Eastman, and Floyd Dell in 1918, a year after their journal *The Masses* was forced to shut down as a result of being censored by the postal service. A spiritual successor to *The Masses,* the *Liberator* advocated for racial equality, socialism, birth control, and women's rights and against the jingoistic prowar mass media. The *Liberator* was run by the same politically active writers and artists from *The Masses* and published stories about international socialist movements with pro-Soviet leanings. Within 10 years the magazine had transformed into a reflexively uncritical vessel of the Communist Party and was renamed the *Worker's Monthly.* This resulted in an exodus of the former *Masses* editors, who went on to launch the *New Masses,* which was published until 1948.

Nathan Morgante

libraries. New York City has more than 1000 libraries and multibranch library systems. The first libraries in the city were private collections, some of substantial size by the eighteenth century. The earliest known nonprivate library, a small deposit of books in Trinity Church, existed by 1698; there were a few other small library enterprises early in the eighteenth century. The first institutional library of consequence was the New York Society Library, founded in 1754 during a period of cultural awakening and modeled on the Library Company of Philadelphia established by Benjamin Franklin in 1731. For many years the New York Society Library, a subscription, or social, library (charging a membership fee), was an enclave for the city's elite. Many of its first directors were also founders in 1754 of King's College (later Columbia University), which had a library by 1757. The bookseller Garret Noel in 1763 opened the first for-profit lending library and reading room in the city, the third in the colonies, and from 1797 to 1804 Hocquet Caritat operated the best commercial lending library in eighteenth-century North America. Several specialized libraries also began in the late eighteenth century and the early nineteenth, notably at the New-York Historical Society, Union Theological Seminary, New York Hospital, and the New York Academy of Medicine.

Additional social libraries appeared in the early nineteenth century, several of them for the education and moral improvement of urban workers. Among the best known was the Mercantile Library Association of New York, organized by merchants' clerks in 1820; it later was transformed into a general subscription library. The General Society of Mechanics and Tradesmen in 1820 opened the Apprentices' Library, a free institution that eventually developed a large collection of general literature; in 1972 it became a subscription library. An apprentices' library organized in Brooklyn in the 1820s was the predecessor of the Brooklyn Mercantile Library, which began in 1857 and was later converted into the Brooklyn Library, a general subscription library that merged with the Brooklyn Public Library in 1902. Other social libraries in outlying areas were the Harlem Library (1825), the Washington

Columbia University library, ca *1895*

New York City Public Library Systems, 2008: New York Public Library (Manhattan, Bronx, and Staten Island), Brooklyn Public Library, and Queens Public Library

NEW YORK PUBLIC LIBRARY (NYPL), MANHATTAN

Library	Address
58th Street	127 East 58th St.
67th Street	328 East 67th St.
96th Street	112 East 96th St.
115th Street	203 West 115th St.
125th Street	224 East 125th St.
Aguilar	174 East 110th St.
Andrew Heiskell Braille and Talking Book Library	40 West 20th St.
Bloomingdale	150 West 100th St.
Chatham Square	33 East Broadway
Columbus	742 10th Ave.
Countee Cullen	104 West 136th St.
Donnell Library Center	20 West 53rd St.
Early Childhood and Resource Center	66 Leroy St.
Epiphany	228 East 23rd St.
Fort Washington	535 West 179th St.
George Bruce	518 West 125th St.
Hamilton Fish Park	415 East Houston St.
Hamilton Grange	503 West 145th St.
Harlem	9 West 124th St.
Hudson Park	66 Leroy St.
Humanities and Social Sciences	5th Ave. at 42nd St.
Inwood	4790 Broadway
Jefferson Market	425 Avenue of the Americas
Kips Bay	446 3rd Ave.
Macomb's Bridge	2650 Adam Clayton Powell, Jr. Blvd.
Mid-Manhattan Library[1,2,4]	455 5th Ave.
Morningside Heights	2900 Broadway
Muhlenberg	209 West 23rd St.
Mulberry	10 Jersey St.
New Amsterdam	9 Murray St.
New York Public Library for the Performing Arts[2]	40 Lincoln Center
Ottendorfer	135 2nd Ave.
Riverside	127 Amsterdam Ave.
Roosevelt Island	524 Main St.
St. Agnes	444 Amsterdam Ave.
Schomburg Center for Research in Black Culture[2]	515 Malcolm X Blvd.
Science, Industry, and Business Library (SIBL)[2]	188 Madison Ave.
Seward Park	192 East Broadway
Terence Cardinal Cooke–Cathedral	560 Lexington Ave.
Tompkins Square	331 East 10th St.
Washington Heights	1000 St. Nicholas Ave.
Webster	1465 York Ave.
Yorkville	222 East 79th St.

NEW YORK PUBLIC LIBRARY (NYPL), BRONX

Library	Address
Allerton	2740 Barnes Ave.
Baychester	2049 Asch Loop North
Belmont	610 E. 186th St.
Bronx Library Center[1]	310 East Kingsbridge Rd.
Castle Hill	947 Castle Hill Ave.
City Island	320 City Island Ave.
Clason's Point	1215 Morrison Ave.

(*continued*)

Heights Library (1868), and several libraries in Queens.

The first privately endowed, independent, free public reference library in the United States, the Astor Library, was formed in New York City in 1848 by the will of John Jacob Astor and incorporated in 1849. Opened in 1854, the Astor Library ranked among the foremost libraries in the country in the scope and quality of its collections. During the years preceding the Civil War the Cooper Union for the Advancement of Science and Art and the Young Men's Christian Association offered free reading rooms to the public, Charles Loring Brace opened a reading room for the uplift of the poor, and the Maimonides Library of the Jewish fraternal organization B'nai B'rith operated a public circulating collection that survived until 1906. New York City was also the site in 1853 of the earliest known librarians' convention: 82 librarians and other interested men met to discuss library development and plans for a librarians' association.

By 1876 there were some 90 small collections in clubs, academies, asylums, schools, and other organizations in the city. Among these was another endowed free reference library, the Lenox Library, a collection of Americana, Bibles, and rarities incorporated by James Lenox in 1870. The major academic library in the city was at Columbia, which by 1876 ranked ninth in holdings in the United States. The librarian at Columbia from 1883 to 1889 was Melvil Dewey, a founder of the modern library profession. At Columbia he began the first institution to educate librarians, the School of Library Economy (1887), which in defiance of college policy enrolled women. Owing in part to this conflict Dewey left Columbia for Albany, New York, to become the secretary of the University of the State of New York and the director of the State Library. He took with him the library school, which was reconstituted as the New York State Library School. In 1926 it combined with the New York Public Library (NYPL) Library School (1911) to form the School of Library Service of Columbia University. These schools operated distinguished programs, and the library science library at Columbia was renowned until the dissolution of the School of Library Service in 1992. In the early twenty-first century Pratt Institute, Long Island University, and Queens College offered graduate degrees in library science.

Between the 1870s and 1890s several free lending libraries were established under private auspices, some independent and some operated by agencies such as settlement houses. Many of these libraries eventually received municipal appropriations and from 1892 received state aid; to get these funds several subscription libraries were converted into free public libraries. The most prominent free libraries were three multibranch systems (all later consolidated with NYPL): the New York Free Circulating Library (1878, incorporated

New York City Public Library Systems, 2008: New York Public Library (Manhattan, Bronx, and Staten Island), Brooklyn Public Library, and Queens Library (*Continued*)

Library	Address
Eastchester	1385 East Gun Hill Rd.
Edenwald	1255 East 233rd St.
Francis Martin	2150 University Ave.
Grand Concourse	155 East 173rd St.
High Bridge	78 West 168th St.
Hunt's Point	877 Southern Blvd.
Jerome Park	118 Eames Pl.
Kingsbridge	280 West 231st St.
Melrose Beach	910 Morris Ave.
Morrisania	610 East 169th St.
Morris Park	985 Morris Park Ave.
Mosholu	285 East 205th St.
Mott Haven	321 East 140th St.
Parkchester	1985 Westchester Ave.
Pelham Bay	3060 Middletown Rd.
Riverdale	5540 Mosholu Ave.
Sedgwick	1701 Martin Luther King, Jr. Blvd.
Soundview	660 Soundview Ave.
Spuyten Duyvil	650 West 235th St.
Throg's Neck	3025 Cross Bronx Expressway Extension
Tremont	1866 Washington Ave.
Van Cortlandt	3874 Sedgwick Ave.
Van Nest	2147 Barnes Ave.
Wakefield	4100 Lowerre Pl.
Westchester Square	2521 Glebe Ave.
West Farms	2085 Honeywell Ave.
Woodlawn Heights	4355 Katonah Ave.
Woodstock	761 East 160th St.
NEW YORK PUBLIC LIBRARY (NYPL), STATEN ISLAND	
Dongan Hills	1617 Richmond Rd.
Great Kills	56 Giffords Ln.
Huguenot Park	830 Huguenot Ave.
New Dorp	309 New Dorp Ln.
Port Richmond	75 Bennett St.
Richmondtown	200 Clarke Ave.
St. George Library Center[1]	5 Central Ave.
South Beach	21–25 Robin Rd.
Stapleton	132 Canal St.
Todt Hill–Westerleigh	2550 Victory Blvd.
Tottenville	7430 Amboy Rd.
West New Brighton	976 Castleton Ave.
QUEENS LIBRARY (QBPL), QUEENS	
Arverne	312 Beach 54th St.
Astoria	14-01 Astoria Blvd.
Auburndale	25-55 Francis Lewis Blvd.
Baisley Park	117-11 Sutphin Blvd.
Bayside	214-20 Northern Blvd.
Bay Terrace	18-36 Bell Blvd.
Bellerose	250-06 Hillside Ave.
Briarwood	85-12 Main St.
Broad Channel	16-26 Cross Bay Blvd.
Broadway	40-20 Broadway
Cambria Heights	218-13 Linden Blvd.
Central Library	89-11 Merrick Blvd.

(*continued*)

1880); the Aguilar Free Library (1886), formed by German American Jews to aid assimilation by eastern European Jewish immigrants; and the Cathedral Library (1887), sponsored by the Roman Catholic Archdiocese and from 1893 open to the public. In Brooklyn the Pratt Institute ran a free public library from 1888 to 1940, and a few communities in the Bronx, Queens, and Staten Island also had small libraries. But New York City did not have the central, tax-supported, municipal library common by the late nineteenth century in many other U.S. cities and commensurate with its status as the nation's largest city and cultural metropolis. Efforts to establish such a library had foundered.

Events beginning in the early 1890s culminated in not one but three public library systems shortly after New York City was consolidated in 1898: the Brooklyn Public Library, the Queens Borough Public Library, and NYPL. The key impetus was the founding of NYPL in 1895 as a privately endowed free public reference library, the result of a merger of the Astor Library, the Lenox Library, and the Tilden Trust, a legacy of Governor Samuel J. Tilden. The city agreed to build and maintain a central building in Manhattan for the new institution, and in 1901, under pressure from municipal officials seeking to systematize tax-supported library service, NYPL began to assume responsibility for local circulating library service in Manhattan, the Bronx, and Staten Island; Brooklyn and Queens kept their own recently founded library systems. Andrew Carnegie provided funds in 1901 to construct branch library buildings throughout the city; in turn the municipality contracted to provide annual maintenance for public library service in addition to sites for the Carnegie branches (which were eventually absorbed by NYPL). Public libraries were thus firmly established as essential public services. Although substantial state aid was forthcoming after 1950, the Brooklyn and Queens Borough public libraries and NYPL branch system depended mainly on municipal funds. The wide-ranging research collections of NYPL, among the world's largest, remained for the most part privately supported.

The branch system of NYPL initially overshadowed the other two public libraries, but by the mid-twentieth century the Brooklyn Public Library had become an important institution, and the Queens Borough Public Library grew into a major system, with the highest circulation of any municipal library in the United States. The years after World War II saw substantial growth in municipal library service: by 2008 there were more than 200 public library branches citywide. The three systems serve the city's diverse population with projects to promote literacy and teach English as a second language, and special programs and services for children, residents of nursing homes, the blind and physically handicapped,

New York City Public Library Systems, 2008: New York Public Library (Manhattan, Bronx, and Staten Island), Brooklyn Public Library, and Queens Library (*Continued*)

Library	Address
Corona	38-23 104th St.
Court Square	25-01 Jackson Ave.
Douglaston/Little Neck	249-01 Northern Blvd.
East Elmhurst	95-06 Astoria Blvd.
East Flushing	196-36 Northern Blvd.
Far Rockaway	1637 Central Ave.
Flushing[1]	41-17 Main St.
Forest Hills	108-19 71st Ave.
Fresh Meadows	193-20 Horace Harding Expressway
Glendale	78-60 73rd Pl.
Glen Oaks	256-04 Union Turnpike
Hillcrest	187-05 Union Turnpike
Hollis	202-05 Hillside Ave.
Howard Beach	92-06 156th Ave.
Jackson Heights	35-51 81st St.
Kew Gardens Hill	72-33 Vleigh Pl.
Langston Hughes	100-01 Northern Blvd.
Laurelton	134-26 225th St.
Lefferts	103-34 Lefferts Blvd.
Lefrak City	98-30 57th Ave.
Long Island City	37-44 21st St.
Maspeth	69-70 Grand Ave.
McGoldrick	155-06 Roosevelt Ave. (off Northern Blvd.)
Middle Village	72-31 Metropolitan Ave.
Mitchell–Linden	29-42 Union St.
North Forest Park	98-27 Metropolitan Ave.
North Hills	57-04 Marathon Pkwy.
Ozone Park	92-24 Rockaway Blvd.
Peninsula	92-25 Rockaway Beach Blvd.
Pomonok	158-21 Jewel Ave.
Poppenhusen	121-23 14th Ave.
Queensboro Hill	60-05 Main St.
Queensbridge[3]	10-43 41st Ave.
Queens Village	94-11 217th St.
Ravenswood[3]	35-32 21st St.
Rego Park	91-41 63rd Dr.
Richmond Hill	118-14 Hillside Ave.
Ridgewood	20-12 Madison St.
Rochdale Village	169-09 137th Ave.
Rosedale	144-20 243rd St.
St. Albans	191-05 Linden Blvd.
Seaside	116-15 Rockaway Beach Blvd.
South Hollis	204-01 Hollis Ave.
South Jamaica	108-41 Guy R. Brewer Blvd.
South Ozone Park	128-16 Rockaway Blvd.
Steinway	21-45 31st St.
Sunnyside	43-06 Greenpoint Ave.
Whitestone	151-10 14th Rd.
Windsor Park	79-50 Bell Blvd.
Woodhaven	85-41 Forest Pkwy.
Woodside	54-22 Skillman Ave.
BROOKLYN PUBLIC LIBRARY (BPL), BROOKLYN	
Arlington	203 Arlington Ave.
Bay Ridge	7223 Ridge Blvd.
Bedford	496 Franklin Ave.
Bedford Learning Center	496 Franklin Ave.

(*continued*)

the homebound, and the homeless. The public libraries supply state-subsidized library service and educational programs to prison inmates in all five boroughs. At times city officials have considered consolidating all the public libraries, but studies indicated that few advantages would result. Although they have cooperated in some ways, the three systems remain distinct.

The public libraries support the city's educational systems, public and private, by serving legions of students from the elementary level to the graduate and professional, especially when the schools have weak libraries or none at all (as was true of public elementary schools until the 1960s). With the opening of the Mid-Manhattan Library of NYPL in 1970, New York City finally had the very large, central, college-level lending collection commonly available in other cities (in 2008 the Mid-Manhattan Library was sold and the main research library reconfigured to include circulating materials). Columbia University remains the city's predominant academic library. Strong in most subjects, it has extensive holdings in law, health sciences, East Asian studies, business, architecture, social welfare, rare books, and manuscripts. One of the great collections in education (founded in 1887) is at Teachers College. The main library of New York University (1835) was considerably strengthened for research purposes by the opening in 1973 of the Elmer Holmes Bobst Library and Study Center, which includes the Avery Fisher Center for Music and Media (1986) and resources for the study of American radicalism and the labor movement. In 1961 the Graduate School and University Center of the new City University of New York was organized; at its headquarters, opposite the central building of NYPL, the school developed a collection in aid of graduate study but not a comprehensive research library.

The advent of hundreds of specialized libraries in New York City was a twentieth-century phenomenon that followed the city's progress as a center of the visual and performing arts, communications, finance, advertising, medicine and science, international affairs, law, design, commerce, and corporate management. World-renowned collections in the performing arts developed at the New York Public Library for the Performing Arts at Lincoln Center. In the visual arts the Metropolitan Museum of Art houses important collections, dating from 1880, of books, slides, and photographs; the Frick Art Reference Library (1920) encompasses the fine arts of western Europe and the United States; the Museum of Modern Art Library covers art after 1880; and NYPL has art, picture, fine print, and photograph collections. A premier collection of prints, drawings, rare books, and manuscripts is at the Pierpont Morgan Library, incorporated in 1924 as an endowed public reference library.

The libraries and information centers in banking and investment houses in the finan-

New York City Public Library Systems, 2008: New York Public Library (Manhattan, Bronx, and Staten Island), Brooklyn Public Library, and Queens Library (*Continued*)

Library	Address
Borough Park	1265 43rd St. at 13th Ave.
Brighton Beach	16 Brighton First Rd.
Brooklyn Heights	280 Cadman Plaza West
Brower Park	725 St. Marks Ave. at Nostrand Ave.
Brownsville	61 Glenmore Ave. at Watkins St.
Bushwick	340 Bushwick Ave. at Seigel St.
Business Library	280 Cadman Plaza West
Canarsie	1580 Rockaway Pkwy.
Carroll Gardens	396 Clinton St.
Central Library[1]	Grand Army Plaza
Central Library Learning Center	Grand Army Plaza
Clarendon	2035 Nostrand Ave.
Clinton Hill	380 Washington Ave.
Coney Island	1901 Mermaid Ave.
Coney Island Learning Center	1901 Mermaid Ave.
Cortelyou	1305 Cortelyou Rd.
Crown Heights	560 New York Ave.
Cypress Hills	1197 Sutter Ave.
DeKalb	790 Bushwick Ave.
Dyker	8202 13th Ave.
Eastern Parkway	1044 Eastern Pkwy.
Eastern Parkway Learning Center	1044 Eastern Pkwy., 2nd Floor
East Flatbush	9612 Church Ave.
Flatbush	22 Linden Blvd.
Flatbush Learning Center	22 Linden Blvd.
Flatlands	2065 Flatbush Ave.
Fort Hamilton	9424 4th Ave.
Gerritsen Beach	2808 Gerritsen Ave.
Gravesend	303 Ave. X
Greenpoint	107 Norman Ave.
Highlawn	1664 West 13th St.
Homecrest	2525 Coney Island Ave.
Jamaica Bay	9727 Seaview Ave.
Kensington	410 Ditmas Ave.
Kings Bay	3650 Nostrand Ave.
Kings Highway	2115 Ocean Ave.
Leonard	81 Devoe St.
Macon	361 Lewis Ave.
Marcy	617 DeKalb Ave.
McKinley Park	6802 Fort Hamilton Pkwy.
Midwood	975 East 16th St.
Mill Basin	2385 Ralph Ave.
New Lots	665 New Lots Ave.
New Utrecht	1743 86th St.
Pacific	25 4th Ave. at Pacific St.
Paerdegat	850 East 59th St.
Park Slope	431 6th Ave.
Red Hook	7 Wolcott St.
Rugby	1000 Utica Ave.
Ryder	5902 23rd Ave.
Saratoga	8 Thomas S. Boyland St.
Sheepshead Bay	2636 East 14th St. at Ave. Z
Spring Creek	12143 Flatlands Ave.
Stone Avenue	581 Mother Gaston Blvd.
Sunset Park	5108 4th Ave.
Ulmer Park	2602 Bath Ave.
Walt Whitman	93 Saint Edwards St.

(*continued*)

cial district constitute an informal library network for the financial community, which is also served by the Business Library of the Brooklyn Public Library. In the health sciences major resources include the collections of universities and medical centers, and the great public reference library of the New York Academy of Medicine, a node in the national system of access to biomedical information. Other notable science collections are at the Chemists' Club, the New York Botanical Garden, and the American Museum of Natural History. The Science, Industry, and Business Library of NYPL, a facility consolidating the public library's collections and services in scientific and economic fields and employing the latest electronic technology, opened in the former B. Altman Building in 1996.

New York City has nearly 100 libraries in law firms and associations, courts, and law schools. The Dag Hammarskjöld Library at the United Nations has important holdings in international affairs. Major local history collections are at the New-York Historical Society and the Brooklyn Historical Society (founded in 1863 and until 1985 known as the Long Island Historical Society). The City Hall Library, a source of information on municipal affairs, was initiated by urban reformers in 1913 as the Municipal Reference Library and operated by NYPL from 1914 to 1967, when it reverted to the city. The New York City–based American Geographical Society transferred its library to the University of Wisconsin at Milwaukee in 1978; the Map Division of NYPL remains a rich geographical resource. The Parks Library at the Arsenal in Central Park holds the correspondence from Robert Moses's tenure as parks commissioner. Research collections reflecting the city's ethnic and religious diversity began to develop in the 1890s, when the library of the Jewish Theological Seminary and the Jewish and Slavonic Divisions of NYPL were established. The Schomburg Center for Research in Black Culture, a division of NYPL, dates to the mid-1920s. Collections relating to eastern European Jewish culture are at the YIVO Institute for Jewish Research (1925) and to German-speaking Jewry at the Leo Baeck Institute (1955). The library of the Center for Migration Studies on Staten Island (1964) is strong in Italian American materials; that of the Hispanic Society of America (1904) documents the culture of Spanish- and Portuguese-speaking peoples. The Museum of the American Indian (1916) transferred its library in 1930 to the Huntington Free Library and Reading Room in the Bronx; the American Museum of Natural History has American Indian materials.

Although informal understandings have long existed among the city's libraries, formal cooperative arrangements date from after World War II. Biomedical libraries established the Medical Library Center of New York in 1959 for cooperative storage and service. NYPL, Columbia University, Yale University,

New York City Public Library Systems, 2008: New York Public Library (Manhattan, Bronx, and Staten Island), Brooklyn Public Library, and Queens Library (*Continued*)

Library	Address
Washington Irving	360 Irving Ave.
Williamsburgh	240 Division Ave.
Windsor Terrace	160 East 5th St. at Fort Hamilton Pkwy.

1. Main or central library that is the largest in the borough.
2. Research library that houses an in-depth collection in one or several subjects.
3. Family Literary Center by appointment only.
4. Flagship library of and the largest library in the entire NYPL system.

Sources: Web sites of the New York Public Library, Brooklyn Public Library, and Queens Library

Compiled by Frank Nestor

and Harvard University in 1974 formed the Research Libraries Group, a consortium that later became national in scope. New York State has been a strong proponent of interlibrary cooperation in the public interest, and in its interlibrary loan system a number of the city's libraries serve as referral resources. Several hundred libraries of all types belong to the New York Metropolitan Reference and Research Library Agency, formed in 1964 under a state program of support for reference and research library resource systems. In the early twenty-first century, these and other local, regional, and national library networks in which New York City libraries take part were active in the application of new technology to enhance library resources and services.

George Watson Cole, "Early Library Development in New York State (1800–1900)," *Bulletin of the New York Public Library,* Nov–Dec 1926 [repr. New York: New York Public Library, 1927]; Frank L. Tolman, "Libraries and Lyceums," *History of the State of New York,* ed. Alexander C. Flick, vol. 9, *Mind and Spirit* (New York: Columbia University Press, 1937), 47–91; Robert B. Downs, *Resources of New York City Libraries: A Survey of Facilities for Advanced Study and Research* (Chicago: American Library Association, 1942); Cornelia Marwell, ed., *Library Resources in New York City: A Selection for Students* (New York: School of Library Service, Columbia University, 1979)

See also Archives.

Phyllis Dain

Library and Museum of the Performing Arts. Former name of the New York Public Library for the Performing Arts.

licensing. In the seventeenth and eighteenth centuries licensing in New York City was concerned mostly with examining and sealing weights and measures, inspecting food, and regulating markets. In the nineteenth century licensing vastly expanded to include transportation, peddling, selling flammable items (such as gunpowder, charcoal, and kindling wood), and operating establishments catering to the public (boardinghouses, junk shops, and so on). The Bureau of Licenses was established in 1904 after a state investigation uncovered a notorious operation on the Lower East Side in which businesses posing as employment agencies were steering young women, mostly immigrants, to prostitution and other illegal enterprises. The bureau was given regulatory jurisdiction over only employment agencies, and reformers called for one centralized municipal department to oversee all the city's licensing duties. The Department of Licenses was formed as a result in 1914, although some licensing responsibilities remained with other municipal entities. The new department had as its purpose to regulate businesses and other operations so as to protect consumers, public health, and public safety. It had licensing jurisdiction over places of entertainment (theaters, cinemas, and cabarets), hacks and truck drivers, and businesses that were potential outlets for stolen property (junk dealers, pawnbrokers). But the office's first commissioner, George H. Bell (1878–1965), was actually less a consumer advocate than a self-appointed guardian of the city's morals. During his tenure (1914–17) he worked with the National Board of Censorship to ensure that no films shown in New York City depicted crime, lewdness, or even slapstick. In 1916 the department closed down 20 film productions and threatened to revoke the license of any theater that showed Margaret Sanger's film about birth control. Bell even demanded that hurdy-gurdy players have their instruments in tune before they could receive a license. After Bell left office the department issued a growing number of licenses (117,884 in 1924, compared with 29,157 in 1914), and it continued to censor the entertainment business well into the 1930s. In 1922 it shut down a play titled *The Demi-Virgin,* an action eventually overturned by the New York State Court of Appeals. Later Mayor Fiorello H. La Guardia worked with the department to close down burlesque houses. When shows did resume, it was only under the commissioner's strict supervision.

During the 1950s the Department of Licenses focused more on business regulation, and licensing responsibilities became more diffused: by 1960 it issued less than 13 percent of the 833 types of licenses distributed by 24 municipal agencies. In 1968 New York City consolidated the Department of Markets and its weights and measures division with the Department of Licensing. In 1969 Mayor John V. Lindsey created the New York City Department of Consumer Affairs (DCA), and the City Council passed the first municipal Consumer Protection Law. The new department expanded licensing responsibilities, implemented education programs, and focused on consumer protection. By the time of the city's fiscal crisis in the mid-1970s politicians increasingly resorted to licensing fees to raise revenue, to the great resentment of the business community. An underground economy took shape to circumvent the licensing requirements, a phenomenon that sometimes had baleful consequences. In 1990, 87 people were killed in a fire at the Happy Land Social Club in the Bronx, an unlicensed operation that did not meet the city's fire protection codes. During the 1990s there were many calls for a reform of the city's licensing apparatus, which was increasingly seen as unfair and burdensome to small businesses. In 1994 Mayor Rudolph W. Giuliani created a task force to elimi-

New York City Driver's Licenses on File, 2009

County	Male	Female	Total
Bronx	242,440	179,830	422,270
Kings	494,772	367,081	861,853
New York	389,874	324,414	714,288
Queens	587,395	452,208	1,039,603
Richmond	153,353	141,664	295,017
New York City	1,867,834	1,465,197	3,333,031

Source: New York State Department of Motor Vehicles

Compiled by Andrew A. Kryzak

nate some of the unnecessary and antiquated licensing requirements still in place. The city withdrew from licensing and regulating a number of activities affecting small businesses. Some activities, such as laundries, masquerade balls, and small movie theaters, lacked consumer complaints and financial support, while others, such as beauty parlors, were regulated by the state. The Giuliani administration also used existing licensing laws to enforce its 1997 quality of life campaign, shutting down illegal nightclubs using a 1926 law requiring bars and clubs to have a cabaret license in order for three or more people to dance.

In the early twenty-first century the Department of Consumer Affairs licensed more than 70,000 businesses in 55 industries, including parking garages, laundries, cigarette dealers, home improvement contractors, pawnbrokers, employment agencies, debt collection agencies, and sidewalk cafes. In 2006 Mayor Michael Bloomberg broadened the agency's mission by placing it in charge of the Office of Financial Empowerment, an antipoverty department focused on increasing financial stability for New Yorkers with low incomes, including financial counseling. Technological advancements allowed approximately one-third of industries regulated by the DCA to submit applications for new licenses online, and permitted nearly all industries to renew licenses over the Internet. The department's Web site handled consumer complaints, as did the city's telephone hotline, 311. In 2008 the DCA investigated 7600 consumer complaints and recovered $8.4 million in restitution for New Yorkers through mediation and enforcement efforts.

Janos Marton, James Bradley

Lichtenstein, Roy (*b* New York City, 27 Oct 1923; *d* New York City, 29 Sept 1997). Painter. He attended Benjamin Franklin High School, studied with Reginald Marsh at the Art Students League, and in 1940 left the city to attend the School of Fine Arts at Ohio State University (MFA 1950). He then moved to Cleveland to work as an engineering draftsman, and in 1951 he had his first one-man show in New York City, at the Carlebach Gallery. By the early 1960s he was associated with the pop art movement, and his works were exhibited at the Leo Castelli Gallery and other venues. He moved his studio in 1965 to 26th Street in Manhattan and in the following year to the Bowery. Lichtenstein's best-known works are large paintings in the style of comic strips, in which the subject's thoughts are often revealed in an accompanying "thought bubble."

Chad Ludington

Liebling, A(bbott) J(oseph) (*b* New York City, 18 Oct 1904; *d* New York City, 28 Dec 1963). Journalist. Born on the Upper East Side and raised in Manhattan and Far Rockaway, Liebling studied at Dartmouth College and graduated from the Columbia School of Journalism in 1925. He worked at various newspapers and lived in France before joining the *New Yorker* in 1935; there he wrote articles on boxing, horseracing, food, and New York City and covered World War II as a foreign correspondent. In his column "Wayward Press," Liebling made his name as a media critic by describing the press as a crooked circus and making statements like "People everywhere confuse what they read in the newspapers with news," and "The function of the press in society is to inform, but its role in society is to make money." A strong critic of the House Un-American Activities Committee, Liebling befriended Alger Hiss. He wrote books on topics ranging from politics to food, of which he was a connoisseur, and published collections of his columns. In 2002 *Sports Illustrated* named his book *The Sweet Science* (1956) the best sports book ever written. Liebling lived at 45 West 10th Street.

Raymond Sokolov, *Wayward Reporter: The Life of A. J. Liebling* (New York: Harper and Row, 1980)

Ben Silk

Liebmann Breweries. Original name of Rheingold Breweries.

Liederkranz of the City of New York. German singing society formed in New York City in 1847. Formerly known as Deutscher Liederkranz der Stadt New York, it was led after mid-century by Oswald Ottendorfer and the piano maker William Steinway, who in 1867 raised the initiation fee to $50 and the annual dues to $24. Despite the expensive fee and dues for that time, the society continued to grow and by 1869 had more than 1000 members. It built its own quarters on Fourth Street in 1863; when the city's wealthier German Americans later moved uptown, it built a new and far more sumptuous Liederkranz Halle on East 58th Street in 1881. Membership declined after World War II, and the society moved to its present location in the former Henry Phipps town house at 6 East 87th Street.

History of the Liederkranz of the City of New York, 1847 to 1947, and of the Arion (New York: Drechsel, 1948)

Stanley Nadel

Lienau, Detlef (*b* Uetersen, Denmark [now Schleswig–Holstein, Germany], 17 Feb 1818; *d* New York City, 29 Aug 1887). Architect. He received his training in Germany and France and in 1848 immigrated to the United States. Highly regarded by his contemporaries, he introduced the French Second Empire style and the mansard roof to New York City when he designed the Hart Schiff house at 32 Fifth Avenue (1850–52, demolished). Other influential works by Lienau include the houses of William and Edmund H. Schermerhorn, at 49 and 45–47 West 23rd Street (1859 and 1868–70, demolished), and a row of marble-fronted houses designed as an ensemble for Rebecca Colford Jones, at Fifth Avenue at 55th Street (1868–70, demolished).

Marjorie Pearson

Lievre, Eugen (*fl* 1848–60). Political activist and hotel owner. A German immigrant, he bought the Shakespeare Hotel at the corner of Duane and William streets in Manhattan in 1848 and made it a center of social activities for Germans. He was a member of the Befreiungsbund, a group formed by the utopian communist leader Wilhelm Weitling in 1847–48, and allowed many German radicals to use his hotel as a meeting place throughout the 1850s; their activities were depicted in a play by Max Cohnheim. He later sold the hotel and opened the Hôtel Hansa in Hoboken, New Jersey.

Stanley Nadel

Life. Weekly magazine. Published in New York City by Time Inc. beginning in November 1936, it was the nation's first popular "picture weekly" and perhaps the most widely read U.S. periodical in the mid-twentieth century. *Life* presented striking visual summaries of the news; a staff of highly skilled photographers used new cameras that allowed for more candid and action shots. Although editor-in-chief Henry R. Luce insisted that *Life* readers frequently be "educated" with lavish essays on history and culture, he never wanted the magazine to take itself too seriously. It regularly offered layouts of young women in bathing suits as well as such features as "*Life* Goes to the Movies." Although initially unaffected by the coming of television, *Life* could not overcome rising production costs during the 1960s. Late in the decade the magazine began deemphasizing pictures in favor of longer essays. At the same time television news, through the greater use of satellite transmission and videotape, improved its capacity to offer visual representations of breaking stories, which had once been *Life*'s strength. *Life* ceased publication in December 1972. Subsequent attempts by Time to revive *Life* as a monthly and a newspaper supplement were unsuccessful.

Loudon Wainwright, *The Great American Magazine* (New York: Knopf, 1986)

See also Magazines.

James L. Baughman

life insurance. Life insurance has been important to New York City since colonial underwriters sold the first short-term policies for travelers embarking on hazardous journeys, and the Presbyterian Synod offered clergy policies financed largely by church members. As well as offering financial protection for survivors, life insurance was already considered a form of investment in the 1790s, when the New York Insurance Company organized a contributory fund, called a tontine, which grew as members of the pool died and eventually reverted to the last survivor. The Tontine Coffee House was built in 1792 at Wall and Water streets. More modern insurance appeared in the early nineteenth century when whole-life policies (as opposed to policies for finite terms) were financed with level premiums and sold in the city. A charter for the New York Life Insurance and Trust Company was granted in 1830 to William Bard, who assembled $1 million in capital and set up a network of sales agents throughout New York State. The 1837–42 depression made such money raising difficult and spurred the formation of mutual companies, which required little capital and offered policyholders a share in profits and ownership.

Four of the city's (and country's) most successful life insurers appeared between 1841 and 1868. The Nautilus Insurance Company was founded as a marine and fire insurer in 1841 to fill the large hole left by the bankruptcies of most of the city's property insurers due to the great fire of 1835. Nautilus began selling life policies in 1848 and a year later was renamed New York Life Insurance Company. The Mutual Life Insurance Company of New York was chartered in 1842 and its sales increased steadily. The Equitable Life Assurance Society was formed in July 1859 by Henry Baldwin Hyde, backed by fellow members of the Fifth Avenue Presbyterian Church. The first president, William Alexander, was the brother of the church's minister. Equitable and, later, other insurers sold an annuity policy called a deferred dividend (or tontine) contract, which became extremely popular for its offer of both death claim protection and future earnings for survivors. The fourth insurer, Metropolitan Life Insurance Company, founded in 1868, began by selling policies to members of a German-speaking association and specializing in low-cost industrial (also called debit) life insurance, with small weekly premiums collected at customers' homes. New York insurers developed statistical methods for evaluating risk.

Fierce competition for clients and numerous financial scandals stirred up public demand for regulation. In 1849 the first insurance law in New York State required that no firm could be established in the city or Kings County with less than $100,000 in capital. A decade later New York became the first state to establish a department regulating insurers. Because many of the country's largest life insurers were based in Manhattan, New York insurance law became the national standard. Several companies, meanwhile, expanded abroad. The Germania Life Insurance Company had offices in Germany and agents in the Caribbean and Central America in the 1860s, and Equitable's global network was so vast that the company boasted, "The sun never sets on the Equitable." (Those and other companies later closed their non-U.S. offices, yet the country's largest insurer in the late twentieth century, New York–based American International Group [AIG], grew from a seedling insurance company established in Shanghai, China, in 1919 by Cornelius Van Der Starr.)

These were big institutions. In 1900, when 50 cents of every dollar of family savings was in a life insurance or annuity policy, the only financial institution in the world that was larger than Equitable, Mutual Life, or New York Life was the Bank of England. This growth left the companies with the problem of finding suitable investment vehicles. Sensitive to their size and potential effect on financial markets, regulators did not permit insurers to buy securities until the 1880s. Insurers established trust companies as investment entities that became closely allied with Wall Street; J. P. Morgan and Company sold almost $39 million in securities to a subsidiary of New York Life.

As they helped build the securities markets, insurers developed commercial real estate, most notably their impressive home offices (headquarters buildings) in Manhattan, where more than 1000 employees were working to process the thousands of documents that poured in every day. The demand for clerical workers made these companies some of the first to depend on large numbers of women staff. Equitable and other insurers had close relationships with one or two high schools, many of whose female graduates arrived every year to work in the vast rooms of desks and mechanical calculators. Some of these home offices are still standing, among them the massive buildings of Metropolitan Life and New York Life on Madison Square and the Equitable Building at 120 Broadway—one of six home offices that the company has occupied in Manhattan (four of which are still standing).

Concern about financial abuses climaxed in a scandal that began at Equitable in 1905 and spread through the industry. State senator William Armstrong formed the Legislative Insurance Investigating Committee, whose chief counsel, Charles Evans Hughes, traced a pattern of collusion, stock manipulation, and excess pay to executives. When insurers were forced to sever their ties with financial intermediaries, Wall Street lost some of its largest clients. Partially to recoup their image, insurance companies became active in social work. A welfare division was organized at Metropolitan Life in 1909 by Lee Frankel, a sociologist, through whose efforts a free visiting nurse service for policyholders was established in the city.

New types of life insurance—most notably group insurance—were developed. In 1918 the Teachers Insurance and Annuity Association (TIAA) was formed in New York City as a nonprofit corporation by the Carnegie Foundation for the Advancement of Teaching to provide inexpensive insurance and pension benefits for college teachers. In 1938 regulators permitted life insurers to invest heavily in real estate. By 1947 Metropolitan Life had built one large apartment complex, Parkchester, in the Bronx and another in Manhattan, Peter Cooper Village–Stuyvesant Town, with 11,250 apartments and 25,000 residents on First Avenue between 14th and 20th streets. Equitable financed developments with a total of 2400 apartments at Fordham Hill, the Bronx, and Clinton Hill, Brooklyn.

In 1953 the 18 life insurers based in the city had more than $90 billion in life insurance in force and more than $25 billion in assets. With competition from Wall Street, banks offering money-market funds and other investments, and other new investment vehicles, life insurance lost some of its glow in the 1970s. A wave of deregulation allowed insurers to diversify into commercial real estate, the securities business, and other ventures. A race for assets left several companies troubled. Equitable was heavily burdened by the high cost of billions of dollars' worth of guaranteed investment contracts that it had sold to pension plans. The company was demutualized and a majority of its shares were sold to the French insurer AXA. At the end of the twentieth century, the large companies that had once dominated the business retrenched significantly but still maintained a strong hold on the country's annuity and pension businesses. The life insurance companies continued to maintain a strong presence in the city. In 2006 Metropolitan Life attempted to develop Stuyvesant Town into luxury apartments, and the company's name was on the tall former Pan American Airlines building towering over Grand Central Terminal.

Terence O'Donnell, *History of Life Insurance in Its Formative Years* (Chicago: American Conservation, 1936); J. Owen Stalson, *Marketing Life Insurance: Its History in America* (Cambridge, Mass.: Harvard University Press, 1942); Morton Keller, *The Life Insurance Enterprise, 1885–1910: A Study in the Limits of Corporate Power* (Cambridge, Mass.: Harvard University Press, 1963); John Rousmaniere, *The Life and Times of the Equitable* (New York: Equitable, 1995)

Jack Blicksilver, John Rousmaniere

light and power. In the early nineteenth century in New York City, gas manufactured from coal replaced oil burned in street lights and domestic lamps. The first gas company in the city, the New York Gas Light Company, was incorporated by the state legislature on 26 March 1823 at the behest of the banker Samuel Leggett and others. It obtained a 30-year exclusive franchise from the city that gave it the right to lay underground gas pipes in the area south of Grand Street (which at the time encompassed most of the city); it also constructed a gas works at the corner of Hester Street and Rhynders (now Centre) Street, on what is now the Lower East Side. This monopoly proved politically controversial and was criticized by the Workingmen's Party in 1829. The Manhattan Gaslight Company was formed in the following year, and the competition between the two companies led to a reduction in the price of gas. The rivalry ended in 1833, when the city awarded the Manhattan Gaslight Company an exclusive franchise for all territory north of Grand Street, allowing each company to prosper for a time by serving its own territory. Other gas companies were formed over the next few decades under the General Gas-Light Company Act of 1848. In August 1878 one of these, the Knickerbocker Gas Light Company, sharply reduced the price of gas, triggering a price war that proved so unsettling to the industry that all the companies in the city agreed in 1880 to pool a portion of their revenues, a prelude to a later consolidation. Also by this time the threat of competition from electricity had appeared.

On the evening of 20 December 1880 the Brush Electric Light Company demonstrated electric arc street lights in New York City for the first time, illuminating Broadway from 14th to 26th streets. The following year the company was granted permission by the Gas Commission to erect more street lamps along Broadway, extending to 34th Street; it also built the city's first central electric station at 133 West 25th Street. After providing street lighting free of charge for six months, the Brush Electric Illuminating Company received a contract from the city, and in the following years it erected electric stations at West and Bank streets, 48–50 Washington Street, and 204 Elizabeth Street. For the next several years the Gas Commission, composed of the mayor, controller, and public works commissioner, parceled out street lighting contracts to various electric light and gas companies.

Arc lighting was quickly superseded in importance by incandescent electric lighting. The Edison Electric Illuminating Company of New York was incorporated on 17 December 1880 and was awarded a franchise by the Board of Aldermen on 19 April 1881; the board overrode the veto of Mayor William R. Grace, who believed that the compensation being offered by Edison's company for tearing up the streets and installing wires was inadequate. On 3 May 1881 the board again overrode Grace's veto in awarding franchises to both the Brush Electric Illuminating Company and the United States Illuminating Company. All three companies were given the right to serve Manhattan south of 136th Street, a huge area given their limited technical and financial capabilities. On 4 September 1882 the Edison Electric Illuminating Company commenced operation of its first direct current generating station at 257 Pearl Street, initiating the modern era of electricity.

Concerted efforts were made over the next two decades to encourage competition and stimulate the spread of electrification: 28 political subdivisions in what is now New York City granted at least 92 franchises for the provision of electricity. Of the 25 franchises awarded in Manhattan, all but one included the right to serve the entire island. The city's gas companies responded to the potentially devastating competition from electric light and power, as well as from a new rival, the Equitable Gas Light Company formed by William Rockefeller and others in 1882, by consolidating: on 10 November 1884 the New York, Manhattan, Harlem, Knickerbocker, Metropolitan, and Municipal gaslight companies merged to form the Consolidated Gas Company of New York. The Mutual Gas Light Company, not part of the merger, was later absorbed by Consolidated. Public outrage at the consolidation led the state senate to appoint an investigating committee, which determined that the gas companies had made excessive profits. In 1886 the state legislature passed a bill reducing the price of gas from $1.75 to $1.25 per 1000 cubic feet (28 cubic meters). Consolidated Gas next sought to gain control over its rivals in the electric lighting business: in 1890 it absorbed the United Electric Light and Power Company, which used a Westinghouse alternating current system and which had recently taken over the Brush Electric Illuminating Company.

Consolidated Gas was continuously threatened with new competition in the gas business. The Standard Gas Light Company under the direction of Russell Sage received valuable rights from the state legislature, and in 1897 the New Amsterdam Gas Company was formed with the support of J. P. Morgan from the merger of the Equitable Gas Light Company, the New York and East River Gas Company of Long Island, and several other firms. A rate war that broke out in 1899 among Consolidated, Standard, and New Amsterdam ended in the following year when Consolidated absorbed the other two, thus again gaining nearly complete control of the gas business in Manhattan and major portions of the rest of the city (except Brooklyn; see Brooklyn Union Gas Company). It later acquired the New York and Queens Gas Company (1913) and New York Mutual Gas (1922).

Consolidated Gas also initiated the restructuring of the electric-utility industry in New York City at the beginning of the twentieth century. Anthony N. Brady, William C. Whitney, and others formed a syndicate that purchased the Block Lighting and Power Company, the Borough of Manhattan Electric Company (formerly the Excelsior Steam Power Company), the North River Electric Light and Power Company, and the Mount Morris Electric Light Company and formed the New York Gas and Electric Light, Heat and Power Company. This company in 1899 absorbed Edison's original company, the Edison Electric Illuminating Company of New York. This company and United Electric Light and Power supplied nearly all the electricity used in Manhattan and the Bronx. By 1901 Consolidated Gas, led by Harrison E. Gawtry, had gained controlling interests in both electric companies, thus gaining near-monopoly control over both gas and electricity in much of the city.

Consolidated Gas and the electric companies under its control met with frequent challenges. In 1902 Mayor Seth Low charged the companies with price gouging. A 1905 investigation, for which Charles Evans Hughes was chief counsel, caused adverse publicity for Consolidated Gas and recommended a reduction in the price of gas. In the same year a state law created a Commission of Gas and Electricity, but granted it limited powers, which were challenged in court. In 1907 Hughes, then governor, proposed and subsequently signed legislation establishing one of the first state public service commissions in the United States: one of two district commissions was given jurisdiction over the city, including the authority to set rates and regulate capital structures.

Demand for electricity increased markedly between 1900 and 1935. While gas came to be used exclusively for cooking and heating, demand for it also continued to grow. Consolidated Gas expanded under the direction of George B. Cortelyou, acquiring the New York and Queens Electric Light and Power Company (1913), Bronx Gas and Electric (1921), and Brooklyn Edison (1928), and in 1936 it officially changed its name to Consolidated Edison (Con Edison). After World War II, Con Edison successfully converted from manufactured gas to natural gas (1951–56) and purchased Staten Island Edison (1952), three power plants owned by the transit authority (1959), and the Consolidated Telegraph and Electric Subway Company (1960). The only company to stave off acquisition by Con Edison was the Long Island Lighting Company. By the 1960s Con Edison provided electricity to all of New York City except the Rockaways; gas to Manhattan, the Bronx, and part of Queens; and steam to part of Manhattan. It also served most of Westchester County.

Concerns about plant safety and the environment made it difficult for Con Edison to maintain sufficient generating capacity in the 1960s and 1970s, and as a result the city was beset by a series of major power blackouts. Controversy dogged the company. A number of construction projects were abandoned, including a 1000-megawatt nuclear plant at Ravenswood in Queens (1962) and a 2000-megawatt pumped-storage hydroelectric plant at Storm King Mountain in Cornwall on Hudson (1963). Con Edison was hard hit by the oil embargo of 1973–74. Of three nuclear plants (all at Indian Point, up the Hudson from New York City in Buchanan), one was sold in 1974 and another was shut down. As of 2007 the remaining plant was in the process of its license renewal, but this was controversial as the "Riverkeeper" organization and numerous local officials cited environmental and national-security concerns. Federal energy legislation of the mid-1990s led to a restructuring of the electric utility industry. Encouraged by the New York State Public Service Commission, Con Edison began selling off generating capacity and prepared for consumer choice. In the early twenty-first century Con Edison owned less than 10 percent of its total generating capacity, but remained one of the largest distributors of electricity and energy-related products in the state, with nearly 15,000 employees and $27 billion in assets.

Leonora Arent, *Electric Franchises in New York City,* Columbia University Studies in History, Economics and Law, vol. 88, no. 2 (New York: Columbia University, 1919); Alexander Lurkis, *The Power Brink: Con Edison: A Centennial of Electricity* (New York: Icare, 1982); Joseph A. Pratt, *A Managerial History of Consolidated Edison, 1936–1981* (New York: Consolidated Edison, 1988)

William J. Hausman

lighterage. Movement of freight by large flat-bottomed barges called lighters. Lighterage became a major enterprise early in the history of New York City: there were no land crossings of the East River until 1883 or of the Hudson until 1908, and even then the crossings did not accommodate freight railroad cars. Lighter fleets consisting of barges, as well as tugboats, were formed to carry cargo within the port. A barge was usually a wooden scow of 90 by 30 feet (27 by 9 meters) that had a shed overhanging most of the deck to protect the cargo and a cabin at one end to house the captain and sometimes his family. The largest fleets were operated by railroad companies between large freight facilities along the shore of the Hudson River in New Jersey and smaller Manhattan terminals, some of which had hundreds of barges and tugboats. During the 1930s barges were gradually replaced by trucks that used the Holland and Lincoln tunnels and the George Washington Bridge. The last barge operating in the harbor, which carried bagged coffee from Brooklyn to Hoboken, New Jersey, ceased operation in the 1980s.

See also Port of New York.

Norman J. Brouwer

Lighthouse. Nonprofit vision rehabilitation agency, the largest in the United States. It was formed in 1905 by the sisters Winifred and Edith Holt, who from the preceding year had operated the Ticket Bureau for the Blind from their home at 44 East 78th Street to help the visually impaired attend musical performances. The agency was incorporated in 1906 as the New York Association for the Blind, Inc. The Holts adopted European instructional methods to help the blind become self-supporting. They established a program to teach skills to the blind in their homes, organized the first formal census of blind people in New York City, opened the Bourne Workshop (becoming Lighthouse Industries in 1951), persuaded the Board of Education to accept blind students in public schools, published the first Braille magazine for children, and opened the summer camp River Lighthouse for blind adults at Cornwall-on-Hudson, New York. Winifred Holt successfully argued for a state law requiring vision screening for newborns, a procedure that significantly reduced the incidence of blindness among children. The work of the Lighthouse led in 1908 to the formation of the National Society to Prevent Blindness. In 1913 President William Howard Taft dedicated a new building for the Lighthouse at 111 East 59th Street.

During the 1920s the Lighthouse introduced special classes for blind children and opened a new camp for blind girls in Waretown, New Jersey; other facilities for children were added to River Lighthouse during the 1940s. In 1951 a branch of the Lighthouse was established in Queens, and Lighthouse Industries moved to a large factory at 36-20 Northern Boulevard in Long Island City. Other branches were added in Westchester County (1961), Staten Island (1977), and Dutchess County (1985). The Child Development Center of the Lighthouse (later renamed the National Center for Vision and Child Development) opened in 1964. Later the Lighthouse expanded several programs to help the growing elderly population; it offered programs for the partially sighted, many of whom were elderly, and helped to form the National Center for Vision and Aging in 1984 to make vision problems among the elderly more widely known. In 1990 the organization adopted its popular name, the Lighthouse, as its official name. In 2004 its headquarters building was renamed the Sol and Lillian Goldman Building.

See also Blindness.

Sandra Opdycke

Lighthouse Hill. Neighborhood in central Staten Island, bounded to the north by Forest Hill Road, to the east by Rockland Avenue, to the south by the base of a hill in Richmondtown, and to the west by Latourette Golf Course. It lies in the hills that run northeast toward Upper New York Bay. Named for the Staten Island Lighthouse (1907), it is also called Richmond Hill. At the southern end stands Latourette Mansion, built in the 1830s and now the clubhouse of the Latourette Golf Course. Fine houses line the streets along the crest of Lighthouse Hill to the golf course. The northern section, called Meisner Hill, is the site of the Eger Health Care Center of Staten Island. At the northwestern edge is the Greenbelt, a large area of forest crisscrossed by remains of farmers' stone walls.

Harlow McMillen

lighthouses. Reefs and shifting sandbars often caused shipwrecks in the winding channels leading to the Port of New York during the eighteenth century, prompting merchants to organize a lottery in 1764 to pay for the construction of a stone lighthouse at the entrance to Lower New York Bay near the outer end of Sandy Hook, New Jersey. Early lighthouses were powered by oil lamps and candles. In Britain in 1772 William Hutchinson developed the use of reflectors to magnify oil and candle light; this advance spread rapidly. The federal government assumed responsibility for lighthouses in 1789. Increased traffic during the 1820s led to the construction of lighthouses on Fire Island and the heights of Navesink, New Jersey, and to the installation of a lightship anchored off Sandy Hook, the first device of its kind in the United States. From the 1880s lighthouses were built in Lower New York Bay;

Lighthouse on North Brother Island, ca *1880–90*

Sands Point Lighthouse, 1884

another was the Robbins Reef Lighthouse in Upper New York Bay off Bayonne, New Jersey, operated for almost 30 years by Kate Walker, a widow who brought up two children there. The first electric arc lamp in the United States was introduced in 1898. After Ambrose Channel was opened in 1908 to provide a deeper and more direct route to the port, the lightship at Sandy Hook was replaced. Lighthouses were automated in the 1950s. The last lightship in Ambrose Channel was replaced in 1967 with a light on a platform supported by four legs screwed into the ocean floor; this was one of the last manned lights when it was automated in 1988.

Lilienthal, Max (*b* Munich, 16 Oct 1815; *d* Cincinnati, 5 April 1882). Rabbi. He earned a doctorate in philosophy at the University of Munich at age 16 and became well known in Europe before moving to New York City in 1845. Soon elected the principal rabbi of three congregations, he stressed the separation of church and state and supported ecumenism, becoming the first rabbi to deliver sermons to Christian congregations in New York City. In 1855 he moved to Cincinnati, where he was involved with the Union of American Hebrew Congregations and was a professor at Hebrew Union College.

David Philipson, *Max Lilienthal, American Rabbi: Life and Writings* (New York: Bloch, 1915)

James E. Mooney

Lily Pleasure Club. Original name of University Settlement.

Limelight. First nightclub to be located in a former church. The Episcopal Church of the Holy Communion was a 12,000-square-foot (1115-square-meter) Gothic Revival sanctuary, designed by Richard Upjohn, that was built between 1844 and 1853 at the northeast corner of Sixth Avenue and 20th Street. With declining membership and resources, the church sold the space in 1983 to Peter Gatien, who promptly turned it into a popular dance club. Following a notorious murder committed there in 1996, the club was closed but reopened sporadically during the 1990s. Gatien faced a number of legal problems including tax evasion, to which he pled guilty. Limelight reopened as the Avalon in 2003 but was later closed.

Kenneth T. Jackson

limited-dividend housing. Private housing for limited profit developed in New York City in the mid-nineteenth century to increase the availability of housing for low- and middle-income tenants. The first such project, the Workingmen's Home (1855, designed by John W. Ritch), was built for black families as a philanthropic enterprise by the Association for Improving the Condition of the Poor; of the many similar projects that followed, the largest was sponsored by Alfred T. White in Brooklyn between 1877 and 1890. Eventually White's Improved Dwellings Company housed almost 500 families at rents well below the market level. In return, tenants were expected to follow a moral canon that prescribed religion and forbade alcohol. Like others who followed, White focused his efforts on the "deserving poor," families on the threshold of the middle class.

Limited-dividend firms such as William Field and Son added innovative features to subsidized housing during the late nineteenth century. In designing the Home, Tower, and Riverside buildings (1877–90) for White, the firm employed designs developed in England and sought to provide shared garden space. Other projects were built by the Improved Dwellings Association in Manhattan and Charles Pratt in Brooklyn. The City and Suburban Homes Company (1896) maintained tenements of high quality on the Upper East Side through its subsidiaries, New York Avenue Estate and First Avenue Estate; by 1915 it owned almost 3000 apartments in Manhattan and another 250 in Brooklyn, and it remained one of the largest philanthropic organizations in the United States until the New Deal. Smaller limited-profit companies included the New York Fireproof Tenement Company (1899); the Open Stair Dwellings Company (1910), which built the Mesa Verde in Jackson Heights (1926, Henry Atterbury Smith); and the City Housing Corporation (1924), which planned the low-density development Sunnyside (1924, Clarence S. Stein, Henry Wright, Frederick Ackerman).

The construction of limited-dividend housing was stimulated when the state legislature in 1922 passed a law permitting life-insurance companies to invest in it. The Metropolitan Life Insurance Company soon built a large development in Brooklyn with more than 2000 units (1924, Andrew Thomas). In 1926 the law was amended to encourage the participation of labor unions and workers' cooperatives. The result was affordable housing that was remarkably well built, including the Amalgamated Estate in the Bronx (1927) and Grand Street Housing on the Lower East Side (1930), both sponsored by the Amalgamated Clothing Workers and designed by the firm of Springsteen and Goldhammer. Other notable limited-dividend efforts included the Workers Cooperative Colony in the Bronx (1927, Herman J. Jessor), Thomas Garden Apartments in the Bronx (1928, Andrew Thomas), and the Phipps Garden Apartments in Queens (1928, Stein). After the limited-dividend law was

Limelight, 2009

further amended, Metropolitan Life built Parkchester in the Bronx (1940, Richmond H. Shreve) and Peter Cooper Village (1947, Gilmore D. Clarke) and Stuyvesant Town (1949, Clarke) in Manhattan. The years following World War II saw the development of more projects by insurers, notably at Fresh Meadows by New York Life Insurance (1949, Vorhees, Walker, Foley and Smith) and at Fordham Hill in the Bronx by Equitable Life Assurance (1949, Leonard Schultz).

The Limited-Profit Housing Companies Law of 1955 (known as Mitchell–Lama) further expanded limited-dividend development. Many of the housing projects built during the two following decades were financed by Mitchell–Lama mortgages and tax exemptions, in return for which landlords agreed to accept limited rents. The best-known middle-income projects of these years were Penn Station South in Manhattan (1962, Jessor), Co-op City in the Bronx (1968–70, Jessor), Starrett City in Queens (1976, Jessor), Riverbend in Manhattan (1967, Davis, Brody), and 1199 Plaza in Manhattan (1974, Hodna/Stageburg). Mitchell–Lama was eventually terminated because of inflation during the mid-1970s, rent increases, and tenant strikes. In later years the principles of limited-dividend housing were adopted by such nonprofit entities as the Urban Development Corporation (1968), the Battery Park City Authority (1966), and local development corporations. By the 1980s most of this activity had been subdued. In 2007, however, a significant revival of the limited-divided strategy reemerged with the proposal to build below-market rental housing for teachers and educators in the Bronx, financed by the city's Teachers' Retirement System and the New York City Housing Development Corporation. The origins of this project harked back to the limited-dividend housing laws of the 1920s, when a shortage of affordable apartments was endemic to New York City housing production.

James Ford, *Slums and Housing* (Cambridge, Mass.: Harvard University Press, 1936); Richard Plunz, *A History of Housing in New York City: Dwelling Type and Social Change in the American Metropolis* (New York: Columbia University Press, 1990)

Richard Plunz

Limited-Profit Housing Companies Law. See Mitchell–Lama.

Limón, José (Arcadia) (*b* Culiacán, Mexico, 12 Jan 1908; *d* Flemington, N.J., 2 Dec 1972). Dancer and choreographer. He immigrated to the United States at the age of seven, moved to New York City at 20 to study painting, and learned modern dance at the studio of Doris Humphrey and Charles Weidman. In 1947 he formed his own company,

José Limón in Day on Earth *by Doris Humphrey*

which became the first to tour internationally under the auspices of the U.S. Department of State. He also taught at the Juilliard School in New York City. Limón's style was lyrical yet powerful. He emphasized human dignity and worth in such works as *The Moor's Pavane, Emperor Jones, Missa Brevis,* and *The Traitor.* His company continued to operate at 307 West 38th Street in the early twenty-first century.

Margaret Latimer

Lincoln, Abraham (*b* near Hodgenville, Ky., 12 Feb 1809; *d* Washington, D.C., 15 April 1865). Sixteenth president of the United States. He first visited New York City as a Whig congressman from Illinois on 9 September 1848 accompanied by his wife, Mary, and sons, Robert and Edward, en route to speaking engagements in Massachusetts. Lincoln and Mary returned to the city as tourists after visiting Niagara Falls on 29 July 1857.

In late 1859 the Young Men's Central Republican Union, political activists opposed to the presidential aspirations of New York senator William H. Seward, invited Lincoln (and others) to speak at Plymouth Church in Brooklyn for a $200 honorarium as part of a series introducing western politicians to the eastern elite. Lincoln accepted, arriving after crossing the river from Jersey City by ferry on Saturday, 25 February 1860, registering at the Astor House on Broadway between Barclay and Vesey streets. Here he first learned that he would speak two days later not in Brooklyn but at the newly opened Cooper Union in Manhattan. After visiting the offices of the antislavery *New York Independent,* Lincoln attended Sunday services at Plymouth Church on 26 February and heard a sermon there by Rev. Henry Ward Beecher. On 27 February he toured Broadway and sat for a photograph at Mathew Brady's temporary photography gallery at 643 Broadway at Bleecker Street. The photograph subsequently was widely copied, helping introduce Lincoln to the American public. That evening, 1500 people crowded Cooper Union's Great Hall to hear Lincoln deliver the most important speech of his political career to date—capped by his memorable "right makes might" conclusion opposing slavery. Lincoln later attended supper in his honor at the Athenaeum Club on Fifth Avenue at 17th Street, then went to the offices of the *New York Tribune* on Newspaper Row to proofread typeset galleys of his oration. The next day, four local publications—the *Tribune,* the *Times,* the *Herald,* and the *Post*—printed the entire speech, accompanied by lavish praise. The triumph helped launch Lincoln's presidential campaign; three months later he won the Republican nomination (though he never secured a single delegate from New York State). After leaving for a New England speaking tour on 28 February, Lincoln returned to Manhattan on 11 March 1860. Later that day he attended worship services at both Beecher's church in Brooklyn and the Universalist Church in Manhattan, took tea at Hiram Barney's home on Union Square, and visited the main post office. He also toured the House of Industry in the notorious Five Points slum, where he gave an impromptu inspirational talk to resident orphans. That November, Lincoln won election to the presidency, securing the state's electoral votes though he received barely 30 percent of the popular count in New York City.

Lincoln returned to the city as president-elect on 19 February 1861 en route to his inauguration in Washington, D.C., again taking up residence at the Astor House, from whose balcony he gave a speech after parading down Broadway in an open carriage from the train station on 30th Street between Ninth and 10th avenues. The next day, after breakfast at Moses Grinnell's mansion on Fifth Avenue and 14th Street, he was guest of honor at a reception in the Governor's Room at City Hall, hosted by pro-Confederate mayor Fernando Wood. Lincoln spoke there briefly, then again outdoors from the balcony to crowds below. He later attended a performance of Verdi's *Ballo in Maschera,* causing a sensation at intermission when crowds recognized him. He refused an invitation to P. T. Barnum's American Museum, but his family did visit.

New York City remained anti-Republican throughout the Lincoln presidency. Though the city provided troops for the war effort and housed one of the first pro-Lincoln Union League Clubs, it also erupted in violent anti-administration draft riots in July 1863. Lincoln feared for a time that his son Robert, en route to Washington from Harvard, was caught in the maelstrom. Opposition notwithstanding, First Lady Mary Lincoln spent many days in New York City during the war vacationing and shopping. She redecorated the White House with many furnishings she bought in the city.

President Lincoln passed through the city unannounced on 24 June 1862 en route to a secret war strategy conference with retired general Winfield Scott at West Point. He returned to Washington, D.C., through the city the following day as he headed back to Washington. Lincoln rejected invitations to speak in the city in both 1862 and 1864. On 18 May 1864 he authorized the shutdown of the *New York World* and the *New York Journal of Commerce,* and the arrest of their editors and publishers, for printing a spurious presidential proclamation declaring a new draft. Three days later he lifted suspension of their publication. The *World* violently opposed his reelection campaign, printing scurrilous racist cartoons and a book alleging that he favored racial equality. Lincoln again fared poorly in New York City on election day but eked out another statewide victory on 8 November 1864.

Unpopular in New York City in life, the martyred Lincoln returned triumphantly in death on 24 April 1865, honored at a funeral procession from Desbrosses Street to City Hall Park attended by hundreds of thousands of admirers. He lay in state in an open coffin on the second floor of City Hall from 1 p.m. until the following day at noon, when his body was taken on toward his burial in Illinois. Lincoln was lauded by the city's ministers, priests, and rabbis at Easter and Passover services and deified in worshipful popular prints issued by the city's engravers and lithographers. New York City's image-makers, who had attacked the living Lincoln as often as they honored him, contributed more than any others to spur his transfiguration into national sainthood.

Harold Holzer

Lincoln Center for the Performing Arts. Performing arts complex, housing 12 resident arts organizations on a 16.3-acre (6.6-hectare) campus on the Upper West Side of Manhattan bounded by 66th Street, Columbus Avenue, 62nd Street, and Amsterdam Avenue. The project was envisioned with the help of John D. Rockefeller III in 1954 when the Metropolitan Opera, the New York Philharmonic, and the Juilliard School each needed new facilities. The following year Robert Moses identified the neighborhood known as San Juan Hill as a prime candidate for urban renewal. Construction began on 14 May 1959, and over the next decade the buildings were completed: Philharmonic Hall (renamed Avery Fisher Hall in 1973), the New York Public Library for the Performing Arts, the Metropolitan Opera House, the Juilliard School, and the Lincoln Center Theater (housing what eventually became the Vivian Beaumont and Mitzi E. Newhouse theaters) became the first buildings to open on the campus. Lincoln Center later became home to the Chamber Music Society of Lincoln Center, the Film Society of Lincoln Center, Lincoln Center Presents, Lincoln Center Theater, the New York City Ballet, the New York City Opera, the New York Philharmonic, and the School of American Ballet. In October 2004 Jazz at Lincoln Center opened six blocks south in the Time Warner Center at Columbus Circle. During the following decades Lincoln Center became nationally and internationally known through features such as the Mostly Mozart Festival and broadcasts of concerts on public radio and television. In 2006 Lincoln Center embarked on the massive 65th Street Redevelopment Project, which included renovations and construction on Alice Tully Hall (completed 2009), the Julliard School (substantially completed 2009), and the outdoor fountain and plaza areas (Revson fountain opened 2009, along with other plazas, pools, and terraces). In July 2008 philanthropist David H. Koch announced plans to donate $100 million over 10 years to the renovation and maintenance of the New York State Theater. In recognition of this gift, the theater was renamed in his honor. Lincoln Center remains one of the leading cultural institutions in the United States, with more than half a million visitors each year.

Marc Ferris, Anne Epstein

Lincoln Medical and Mental Health Center. Municipal hospital at 234 East 149th Street in the Bronx, administered by the New York City Health and Hospitals Corporation. It began as the Colored Home, a residential facility for elderly blacks at First Avenue between 64th and 65th streets in Manhattan that was opened in 1839 by the Society for the Relief of Worthy Aged Colored Persons. After moving to the Bronx in 1898 the institution was renamed Lincoln Hospital and Home of the City of New York in 1902 and opened to patients of every race, although the home and the nursing school continued to be designated for blacks. In 1925 Lincoln had 345 ward beds, a number of private rooms, a maternity department, a dispensary for outpatients, and an ambulance service. It became part of the municipal hospital system in 1927 under the direction of the city's Department of Public Welfare, and the home was formally closed. The Lincoln School for Nursing continued to operate and was renamed the Lincoln School for Practical Nurses in the 1960s, but it too finally closed during the early 1970s. In 1976 the hospital moved to 234 East 149th Street, where it was increasingly strained by the city's fiscal limitations and the severe needs of its community. The hospital became renowned for its substance-abuse division (which offered acupuncture and herbal remedies among its treatments), its designation as a New York State Regional Trauma Center, and its 100 ambulatory clinics. The mental health facilities at Lincoln, provided through its department of psychiatry, include inpatient and outpatient units for adults, a clinic for children, a substance abuse clinic, and a day-treatment program for adolescents run in collaboration with the Board of Education. In the early twenty-first century Lincoln provided more than 300 beds and annually had more than 380,000 clinic visits, more than 140,000 emergency room visits, and more than 2000 births.

Douglas Crawford McMurtrie, *Our Old Folks, Being an Account of the Work of the Lincoln Hospital and Home* (New York: Lincoln Hospital and Home, 1914)

Sandra Opdycke

Lincoln School. Progressive school of Teachers College opened in 1917 by Abraham Flexner, who forged a curriculum that avoided traditional subjects in favor of "project units" focusing on such topics as the daily life of the Hudson River and the history of boats (third grade), foods (fourth grade), land transportation (fifth grade), and books through the ages (sixth grade). The school moved in 1922 to 123rd Street and Morningside Avenue and in 1940 merged with the Horace Mann School to become the Horace Mann–Lincoln School. When Teachers College withdrew its financial support for the school and ultimately closed it in 1948, parents won in court the right to open the New Lincoln School as an independent venture on 110th Street. The new school moved to East 77th Street in 1976 and merged with the Walden School in 1988. The Walden–Lincoln School closed in 1991; the building was purchased by the Day School.

Levi Thomas Hopkins and James E. Mendenhall, *Achievement at Lincoln School: A Study of Academic Test Results* (New York: Teachers College Press, 1934)

Alfonso J. Orsini

Lincoln Square. Neighborhood on the Upper West Side of Manhattan. Named for the public square formed by the intersection of Broadway and Columbus Avenue between 65th and 66th streets, it is known as one of the most prominent arts and cultural centers in New York City. The Lincoln Square Business Improvement District officially stretches from Columbus Circle at 58th Street, Broadway to 70th Street, and Columbus Avenue from 60th to 68th streets. The area was originally referred to as San Juan Hill because of its large population of Puerto Rican immigrants. The neighborhood's tenement houses provided the setting for the movie *West Side Story;* these buildings were razed after the film's production as part of Robert Moses's urban renewal projects of the late 1950s. In addition to the Lincoln Center for the Performing Arts, the neighborhood is also home to the ABC television studios, Fordham University's Lincoln Center campus, and the Fiorello H. La Guardia High School of Music and Arts and Performing Arts.

Anne Epstein

Lincoln Theater. One of the earliest venues to allow African Americans to perform. It was home to the Anita Bush Players, a black theatrical troupe that performed there before World War I. For a time Fats Waller was the theater's resident organist. Since the 1960s the building, located at 58 West 135th Street in Harlem, has been occupied by the Metropolitan A.M.E. Church.

Sharon Wilkins

Lincoln Tunnel. Vehicular tunnel under the Hudson River. It is the busiest such facility in the world, connecting midtown Manhattan (West 30th–42nd streets) and Weehawken, New Jersey (where roadways lead to the New Jersey Turnpike, N.J. Route 3, and U.S. Routes 1 and 9). Built and operated by the Port Authority of New York and New Jersey, it was constructed in three stages between 1934 and 1957 and was the world's first three-tube, six-lane underwater tunnel. The central tube opened 22 December 1937 (length: 8216 feet [2506 meters]); the north tube opened 1 February 1945 (7482 feet [2282 meters]); and the south tube opened 25 May 1957 (8006 feet [2442 meters]). Approximately 40 million vehicles used the Lincoln Tunnel in 2006 (150,000 per average weekday). Traffic can be adjusted for either a 3/3 or 4/2 directional mode, depending on demand. Air quality is monitored from adjacent ventilating buildings.

The Lincoln Tunnel is a key mass transit link, with direct ramps into the Port Authority Bus Terminal. Since 1970 a 2.5-mile (4-kilometer) Exclusive Bus Lane (XBL) on the New Jersey side has allowed commuter buses (from New Jersey, upstate New York, and Pennsylvania) a route into the tunnel bypassing regular traffic. Each weekday between 6 and 10 a.m., approximately 1700 buses carrying 62,000 commuters use the XBL; annually this represents 419,000 buses and more than 18 million passengers.

G. M. Rapp and A. H. Baker, *Lincoln Tunnel: The Field Measurement and Study of Stresses* (New York: Port of New York Authority, 1937)

Rebecca Read Shanor, Andrew Sparberg

Lind, Jenny (Johanna) (*b* Stockholm, Sweden, 6 Oct 1820; *d* Worcestershire, England, 2 Nov 1887). Opera singer. An acclaimed soprano from a young age, she became internationally renowned after her performance in *Der Freischutz* at the Swedish Royal Opera in 1838. P. T. Barnum invited the "Swedish nightingale," as she was known, to the United States in 1850, where she gave 93 large-scale concerts across the country. Her first two U.S. performances were given as charity concerts in New York City on 11 and 13 September 1850 at the Castle Garden Theater in lower Manhattan; the sold-out performances were met with huge crowds and adulation. She earned more than $250,000 from the two-year tour, then returned to Europe, where she became known as a philanthropist and professor of voice at the Royal College of Music in England.

Benjamin Yakas

Lindbergh kidnapping. Bruno Richard Hauptmann, the convicted kidnapper of the 20-month-old son of the aviator Charles A. Lindbergh and Anne Morrow Lindbergh, lived in the Bronx (at 1279 East 222nd Street). The abduction occurred on 1 March 1932 at the Lindberghs' home in suburban Hopewell, New Jersey. On 2 April John F. Condon, a retired school principal who had offered to intercede in a letter published in the *Bronx Home News,* met twice with the kidnapper in St. Raymond's Cemetery in the Bronx, the second time delivering $50,000 in ransom. On 12 May 1932 the infant's body was found in a grave just a few miles from his parents' home. Hauptmann was arrested in September 1934 after trying to spend some of the marked ransom money at a filling station in Flemington, New Jersey. He maintained his innocence until he was executed on 3 April 1936, and his wife fought to clear his name until her death on 10 October 1994.

Jim Fisher, *The Lindbergh Case* (New Brunswick, N.J.: Rutgers University Press, 1994); Lloyd C. Gardner, *The Case That Never Dies: The Lindbergh Kidnapping* (New Brunswick, N.J.: Rutgers University Press, 2004)

Walter Friedman

Linden Park. Disused name for Dongan Hills.

Lindenthal, Gustav (*b* Brno [now in Czech Republic], 21 May 1850; *d* Metuchen, N.J., 31 July 1935). Engineer and architect. Educated at polytechnic institutes in Brno and Vienna, he immigrated to the United States in 1874 and designed bridges in Pittsburgh before opening an engineering firm in New York City. He was the commissioner of the New York City Department of Bridges in 1902–4, during which time he prepared plans for the Manhattan Bridge (later redesigned by Leon Moisseiff), completed the Williamsburg Bridge, directed the reconstruction of the Brooklyn Bridge, and designed the Queensboro Bridge. Many consider his greatest work to be the Hell Gate Bridge (1917), the longest bridge in the world at the time of its completion. Lindenthal hoped to build a bridge across the Hudson River, but his plan of 1921 for a colossal suspension bridge between 57th Street in Manhattan and New Jersey was rejected in favor of Othmar H. Ammann's plan for the George Washington Bridge. Lindenthal is sometimes referred to as the "dean" of American bridge engineers.

Rebecca Read Shanor

Lindenwood. Large housing complex in southwestern Queens, centered at 153rd Avenue and 88th Street in Howard Beach, just west of the junction of the Belt Parkway and Conduit Boulevard. At one time the entire area was marshland along Spring Creek, the waterway forming the boundary between Brooklyn and Queens. The area was reclaimed in 1952–53, and the complex was then erected. Seventeen six-story buildings in Empire Gardens stand north of 155th Avenue; south of 155th Avenue lies Lindenwood Gardens, which has 40 clusters of two-story garden apartments. There are 24 more clusters between 84th Street and 79th Street.

Vincent Seyfried

Lindsay, John V(liet) (*b* New York City, 24 Nov 1921; *d* Hilton Head, S.C., 19 Dec 2000). Mayor and congressman. A graduate of Yale College and Yale Law School and a Navy veteran of World War II, he made his mark representing Manhattan's East Side "Silk Stocking" district from 1959 to 1965. In Congress he stood out as a liberal Republican supporter of civil rights and the Great Society. He ran for mayor in 1965 as a fusion Republican–Liberal and defeated Democrat Abraham Beame and Conservative Party candidate and journalist William F. Buckley.

On Lindsay's first day in office, the city's transit workers shut down the subways. His attempt to create a Civilian Complaint Review Board to monitor the police was defeated at the polls. Lindsay instituted a number of administrative reforms of city government, created the city's first income tax, and named

John V. Lindsay, 1966

Thomas Hoving as parks commissioner with a mandate to revitalize and democratize the city's parks. However, his bid to reorganize the transportation system under city control failed when the state created the Metropolitan Transportation Authority. In 1967 President Lyndon Johnson named Lindsay vice chairman of the National Advisory Commission on Civil Disorders, also known as the Kerner Commission.

In New York City, middle- and working-class whites, especially those living outside of Manhattan, became increasingly disillusioned with the mayor. Crime rose dramatically, racial tensions increased, and city services deteriorated. An attempt to grant minorities community control over their schools led to controversy in the Ocean Hill–Brownsville section of Brooklyn and three subsequent citywide teacher strikes in 1968. The controversy drove a wedge between blacks and whites, especially the largely Jewish teachers' union, and stymied any further education reform.

Lindsay lost the Republican nomination for mayor in 1969 to Staten Island state senator John Marchi. Instead, he ran in November on the Liberal Party line against Marchi and Democrat Mario Procaccino. Lindsay won by a plurality of votes with a coalition of liberal whites, minorities, and young people. He left the Republican Party in 1971. During his second term, Lindsay encountered more problems, including a fight over a public housing project in Forest Hills, Queens, and a police corruption scandal. An increasingly weak economy during his second term, combined with high levels on municipal spending and dubious accounting tricks, helped set the stage for the city's near bankruptcy a few years later. In 1972 he ran for the Democratic nomination for president, but fared poorly. On his return to New York City, Lindsay's popularity declined and he did not run for reelection in 1973.

After his mayoralty, Lindsay practiced law and published a novel as his reputation took a beating in the aftermath of the 1975 fiscal crisis. He made one last attempt at public office, running for the Democratic Senate nomination in 1980, but lost to Liz Holtzman. After that, he largely dropped out of public view. In his later years, he suffered severe health problems.

Republican Rudolph Giuliani modeled his 1989 and 1993 mayoral campaigns after Lindsay's 1965 fusion campaign; however, Giuliani's policy priorities differed greatly from Lindsay's. Though lauded for his advocacy of civil rights, Lindsay was unable to stem New York City's decline during the 1960s and 1970s.

John V. Lindsay, *The City* (New York: W. W. Norton, 1969); Barry Gottehrer, *The Mayor's Man* (Garden City, N.Y.: Doubleday, 1975); Vincent J. Cannato, *The Ungovernable City: John Lindsay and His Struggle to Save New York* (New York: Basic, 2001); Charles Morris, *The Cost of Good Intentions: New York City and the Liberal Experiment, 1960–1975* (New York: W. W. Norton, 1980)

Vincent J. Cannato

Lindy Hop [jitterbug]. New York state dance. Originating in Harlem during the late 1920s, the Lindy Hop was rooted in African rhythms and popular contemporary dances such as the Charleston, the Texas Tommy, the two-step, and the breakaway. It is traditionally danced to swing or big-band music and performed socially by couples. The dance contains a common set of steps but also emphasizes improvisational movement. Partners may separate at arm's length for part of a step, several steps, or separate entirely, allowing both dancers to display their technical and musical skills. Many credit "Shorty" George Snowden, an influential dancer, for naming the Lindy Hop after the aviator Charles A. Lindbergh in the late 1920s. Dancer Frankie Manning developed a more horizontal, elongated, and smoother style of the dance that became popular and in 1935 created the first Lindy airstep or aerial, which involves one dancer of a pair being guided through the air by the other. Aerials became one of dance's most exciting and recognizable characteristics. The Lindy Hop was especially prevalent at such Harlem nightclubs as the Alhambra, the Renaissance, and the Savoy. Herbert "Whitey" White, a Savoy bouncer, started and managed a Lindy Hop performance troupe called Whitey's Lindy Hoppers, composed of young dancers, including Manning, Norma Miller, Leon James, and Al Minns. These Lindy Hoppers and others competed in contests held at the Savoy, the Apollo Theater, and at the annual Harvest Moon Ball competition in Madison Square Garden.

After 1935 the Lindy Hop became known as the jitterbug. In the late 1930s dance schools started teaching the Lindy Hop to the public. With this surge in interest, White booked shows throughout the city and internationally until World War II. His Lindy Hoppers showcased ensemble choreographed routines with acrobatic airsteps and expressive solos at nightclubs, on Broadway, and at the 1939 World's Fair Hall of Music. They also performed in several movies, including the Marx Brothers' *A Day at the Races* (1937) and *Hellzapoppin'* (1941), the latter featuring what many consider the best Lindy Hop routine on film. After World War II the dance diminished in popularity. Throughout the 1960s and 1970s dance companies such as the Mama Lu Parks Dancers and the Pepsi Bethel Authentic Jazz Theater continued to perform the Lindy Hop even with the emergence of new popular dance forms. During the 1980s the Lindy Hop became the subject of renewed interest around the world, which inspired the formation of the New York Swing Dance Society and its performance company, the Big Apple Lindy Hoppers. Numerous movies featured the Lindy Hop, including *Malcolm X* (1992), for which Manning served as a consultant. The dance's reemergence in New York City culture was also the subject of documentaries. In 1999 the Broadway show *Swing!* (1999) contained several Lindy Hop routines and was a Tony Award nominee. During Memorial Day weekend in 2009 thousands of Lindy Hoppers came to the city to celebrate Frankie Manning's 95th birthday with dances, performances, and tributes.

Frank Nestor

Lindy's. Restaurant opened in 1921 by Leo Lindemann at 1626 Broadway between 49th and 50th streets. In 1930 Lindemann opened a second Lindy's at 1655 Broadway on the northwest corner of Broadway and 51st Street. The restaurants were known for their sandwiches, sturgeon, herring, cheesecake, and wisecracking waiters. They were immortalized by the writer Damon Runyon, who changed the name to Mindy's in his short stories. The original restaurant closed in 1957, followed by the second in 1969. In the early twenty-first century the name was still used by a chain of restaurants operated by the Riese Organization.

Matthew Kachur

Linoleumville. A company town in Travis, Staten Island, in the late nineteenth century and the early twentieth.

Lion's Head. Greenwich Village pub and restaurant. A hangout for journalists, writers, actors, and musicians, it opened as a coffeehouse on Charles Street in the mid-1960s but was best known while at 59 Christopher Street in Sheridan Square until it closed in 1996.

Margaret Latimer

Lippmann, Walter (*b* New York City, 23 Sept 1889; *d* New York City, 14 Dec 1974). Journalist. He graduated from Harvard University and became well known for his early works *A Preface to Politics* (1913) and *Drift and Mastery* (1914). After working as an associate editor of the *New Republic* (1914–21), he published *Public Opinion* (1922), in which he expressed fears about the abuse of stereotypes by political leaders and the inability of the masses to understand complex political issues. In 1931 he became a syndicated columnist for the *New York Herald Tribune,* beginning an association that lasted for 30 years. Lippmann's politics were unpredictable—he supported and then opposed Franklin D. Roosevelt, Dwight D. Eisenhower, John F. Kennedy, and Lyndon B. Johnson—but he was consistent in his skepticism about American democracy. His residences in New York City included 121 East

Walter Lippmann

79th Street (as a youth), 46 East 80th Street (1902–17), 785 Madison Avenue (1919–23), 50 Washington Mews (1923–26), 39 Fifth Avenue (from 1926), 245 East 61st Street (1929–37), 1021 Park Avenue (from 1966), and the Lowell Hotel at 28 East 63rd Street (1970–73).

Alexander Bloom

LIRR. See Long Island Rail Road.

Lispenard Swamp. Former wetland, irregularly shaped and roughly bounded to the north by Spring Street, to the east by Wooster Street, to the south by Duane Street, and to the west by Greenwich Street. In 1730 Anthony Rutgers, the owner of an adjoining farm, proposed to drain the swamp if it were granted to him. His offer was accepted, and in 1733 he built a drain and a bridge across the swamp at what later became Greenwich Street. The area was later called Lispenard Swamp or Lispenard Meadows, after Rutgers's son-in-law Leonard Lispenard, who lived nearby at what is now the intersection of Hudson and Desbrosses streets.

Gilbert Tauber

Litchfield, Edwin C(lark) (*b* Delhi, N.Y., 21 Jan 1815; *d* Aix-les-Bains, France, 1885). Lawyer and businessman. As a lawyer he specialized in railroads, and with his older brother Electus B. Litchfield he was active in building street railways, developing the Gowanus Canal in Brooklyn, and investing in large tracts of land, including a part of the Cortelyou farm that later became the central part of Park Slope. In addition he was active in the planning of Prospect Park. He and his wife were connoisseurs of the arts and left an important collection of European works. His mansion, Litchfield Villa, called Grace Hill after his wife's surname, is now the Brooklyn headquarters of the Department of Parks and Recreation.

John J. Gallagher

Litchfield Villa. Historic house in Brooklyn, at Prospect Park West between Fourth and Fifth streets. It was built between 1853 and 1857 as a country residence for Edwin C. Litchfield, an attorney, railroad financier, and real estate speculator who invested in land in Brooklyn from the 1850s. Designed in an Italianate style by the distinguished architect Alexander Jackson Davis, it was called Grace Hill by the Litchfield family. The house was incorporated into Prospect Park and in 1892 was made the headquarters of the parks department of Brooklyn; it received a two-story addition in 1911. In the 1940s the stucco exterior and imitation stone facade were removed. The villa is notable for its size, square tower, and rich detailing. Carriage houses and a stable are nearby.

Jonathan Kuhn

literary agents. The rise of the literary agent in England and the United States coincided with the growth of the literary marketplace in the early nineteenth century. The Scottish émigré James Lawson arrived in New York City in 1815 and worked with authors such as William Cullen Bryant, James Kirke Paulding, Edgar Allan Poe, and John Greenleaf Whittier; he made contacts with publishers and editors by doing them small favors and did not charge authors a fee for his services. Park Benjamin, best known as the editor of *Brother Jonathan,* established an informal agency in the city in the 1840s. By the 1860s his advertisements announced that for $10 he would give advice on a manuscript, and if the work appealed to him, he would recommend it to a publisher. Writers were also assisted in their dealings with publishers by the Atheneum Bureau of Literature (1878), the New York Bureau of Literary Revision (1882), the Writer's Literary Bureau (1887), and the Author's League of America (1912), which later came to include the Authors Guild and the Dramatists Guild. With the passage of the International Copyright Act in 1891, the need for agents grew. Between 1892 and 1898 Paul Revere Reynolds (1864–1944) represented a number of leading British publishers in New York City, as well as such English authors as H. G. Wells and Joseph Conrad and (from 1895) the American authors Stephen Crane, Ellen Glasgow, and Frank Norris. Reynolds's authors paid him 10 percent of the money they earned on sales of their books but had no contracts with him. Before the turn of the twentieth century many of the leading agents were women: Flora May Holly (1868–1960), who began as an editorial assistant at the *Bookman* in the mid-1890s and by the end of the decade had established a literary agency at 156 Fifth Avenue, worked with authors like Gertrude Atherton, Noël Coward, and Theodore Dreiser, edited romances and detective stories to make them more salable, and at her home held regular gatherings for literary figures; Elisabeth Marbury (1856–1933) represented many French dramatists and the dramatic works of English authors like George Bernard Shaw and Oscar Wilde; and Alice Kauser began as an employee of Marbury and later opened her own agency. Notwithstanding the objections of publishers like Henry Holt, who maintained that agents were ruining publishing, in the 1930s literary agents became increasingly important in placing manuscripts with book and magazine publishers, and women continued to be strongly represented in the field. Ann Watkins, a leading agent in the 1940s, built her business on knowing the preferences of editors; Elizabeth Nowell of the Maxim Lieber Agency shaped Thomas Wolfe's drafts into magazine-length segments; and Helen M. Strauss in 1944 became the first literary agent to work at the William Morris Agency, where later Berta Kaslow also worked. Other important literary agents included Harold Ober, who edited some of F. Scott Fitzgerald's magazine pieces, Elizabeth McKee of the Harold Matson Company, Bernice Baumgarten of Brandt and Brandt, Alan C. Collins and Edith Haggard of the Curtis Brown Agency, Bertha Lausner, and Andrew Wylie.

James Hepburn, *The Author's Empty Purse and the Rise of the Literary Agent* (London: Oxford University Press, 1968); James L. W. West III, *American Authors and the Literary Marketplace since 1900* (Philadelphia: University of Pennsylvania Press, 1988)

Marc H. Aronson

Literary Digest. Weekly periodical of news, art, and politics, launched in New York City in 1890 by Isaac Kauffman Funk (1839–1912), a southern clergymen and a founder of Funk and Wagnalls Publishing Company. It was one of the first publications to take extensive public opinion polls, and it accurately forecast the results of the presidential elections of 1924 and 1928. By 1927 it had a circulation of more than 1.5 million, a figure surpassed only by the *Saturday Evening Post.* The publication received unwelcome notoriety in 1936 when it predicted that the Republican presidential candidate Alfred M. Landon would defeat President Franklin D. Roosevelt, a prediction that proved embarrassingly inaccurate when Roosevelt was reelected in a landslide. This along with the ascendancy of *Time* and *Newsweek* irrevocably damaged the fortunes of *Literary Digest,* which merged with *Time* in 1938.

James Bradley

literature. New York City became a literary center in colonial times, and in the twenty-first century it remains the world's largest literary marketplace.

1. To 1900

The first literary description of Manhattan was written by Giovanni da Verrazano about his exploration of the surrounding waterways in 1524. Translated, it read: "After a hundred leagues we found a very agreeable place between two small but prominent hills. . . . The people . . . dressed in birds' feathers of various colors, and they came toward us joyfully, uttering loud cries of wonderment." One of the first poets in New Amsterdam was Jacob Steendam, a clerk for the Dutch West India Company who sent "The Complaint of New Amsterdam to Her Mother" to the Netherlands for publication in 1659, followed by "The Praise of New Amsterdam" in 1661. Freedom of the press in the colonies was first established in New York in 1735 by the trial of John Peter Zenger, editor of the *New-York Weekly Journal,* who had been charged with libel for attacking Governor William Cosby but acquitted by a colonial court. Philosophers and polemicists of the American Revolution were some of the first writers in English in the city, which had a strong faction of militant revolutionaries as well as the largest Tory population in the colonies. One well-known political satirist in the city was Philip Freneau, who wrote such poems as "American Liberty" and "Libera Nos Domine." During a varied career that included a stint as the captain of a privateer during the war, he focused on lyrical poetry, which became his best-known work. Under the name Publius, the statesmen Alexander Hamilton, John Jay, and James Madison wrote 85 essays in 1787 and 1788 urging the ratification of the Constitution; these were published in the city's newspapers and collected as the FEDERALIST, the country's first literary classic.

After the Revolution New York City grew popular as the setting for works of fiction. Susanna Rowson, a writer from New England, based her novel *Charlotte Temple: A Tale of Truth* (1791) on a story from the city; it went through 200 editions and was unequaled as a best seller until the publication in 1852 of Harriet Beecher Stowe's *Uncle Tom's Cabin.* The yellow fever epidemic of 1798 provided material for such Gothic novels as *Arthur Mervyn* (1799) by Charles Brockden Brown, who moved to the city from Philadelphia and boarded with the critic and playwright William Dunlap. From 1809 installments of the satiric *History of New York* by Washington Irving were published as a hoax under the pseudonym Diedrich Knickerbocker by the *New York Evening Post;* the entire collection was later published as a book about New Amsterdam, *A History of New York from the Beginning of the World to the End of the Dutch Dynasty,* and became the first work of American fiction known abroad. The name *Knickerbocker* became a nickname for a New Yorker and was adopted by a group of writers seeking to develop a national literature from the 1820s. One of the movement's principal exponents was James Fenimore Cooper, who in 1821 published *The Spy,* a novel based on a story told to him by John Jay. By 1825 the Cooper Club, or the Lunch, included, besides Cooper, such literary men as Dunlap, Fitz-Greene Halleck, the poet William Cullen Byrant, the inventor Samuel F. B. Morse, the publisher Charles Wiley, and James Kent, author of the *Commentaries on American Law* (1826–30). The Knickerbockers looked to the local landscape as a source of national pride and set much of their writing in woods, fields, rivers, prairies, and mountains. The first American sea novel, *The Pilot* (1823), was written by Cooper, who had served in the navy and sought to improve on Sir Walter Scott's *The Pirate.*

The growth of newspaper publishing from the 1830s helped to make the city the nation's publishing capital by the 1840s, attracting some of the most important writers of the day. As a young man Walt Whitman worked for the *Aurora* in Manhattan and for several newspapers in Brooklyn, including the *Brooklyn Eagle,* which he edited during 1846–47. After booksellers refused *Leaves of Grass,* he published it himself in 1855. He called himself "manhattanese" and wrote of New York City in the poem "Mannahatta." After visiting the city in 1831 to publish his third book of poetry, Edgar Allan Poe settled there in 1844 to become the editor of the *Broadway Journal.* During the same year he wrote a series of letters about the city for the *Columbia Spy* in Pennsylvania. He extolled the natural beauty of the area but at the same time predicted that "in some thirty years every noble cliff will be a pier, and the whole island will be densely desecrated by buildings of brick, with portentous *facades* of brown-stone." Poe later based his book *The Mystery of Marie Rogêt* on a Manhattan murder. He was known as one of the city's best literary critics and by the end of his life had edited five magazines and made contributions to 30 more.

Writers were lured by the city's burgeoning publishing industry. Margaret Fuller arrived from Cambridge, Massachusetts, in 1844 to become book review editor for the *Tribune,* soon gaining recognition as a literary critic as well. In 1845 she published *Woman in the Nineteenth Century,* one of the emerging feminist movement's most influential works. She also wrote exposés on local hospitals and prisons. On leaving for Europe in 1846 she wrote that 20 months in New York City "have presented me with a richer and more varied exercise for thought and life, than twenty years could in any other part of these United States." Herman Melville was born on Pearl Street and grew up in the city until he went to sea. He returned in 1845 to write about his adventures as a sailor in the Marquesas and Tahiti in *Typee* (1846) and *Omoo* (1847). During these years he sought out such writers as Irving and William Cullen Bryant and enjoyed spirited evenings with Evert A. Duyckinck, who wrote the *Cyclopaedia of American Literature* (1855) and worked as an editor for the publishers John Wiley and G. P. Putnam. Between 1847 and 1850 Melville wrote *Mardi, Redburn,* and *White-Jacket* and began *Moby-Dick.*

After mid-century a number of writers rose to prominence from the newly fashionable area north of Washington Square. As a boy in the late 1840s Henry James visited at his grandmother's house on Washington Square North and heard Poe's stories from his elder brother William. The younger James spent most of his life in Europe and returned only sporadically, but he would mine his New York City background among the city's elite in the novel *Washington Square* (1881) and other works. His lifelong friend Edith Wharton was born at 14 West 23rd Street into a similar social milieu. As a child she read the collected works of Irving, an old family friend, and while living on Madison Avenue as a young woman she published some of her first poems in *Scribner's, Harper's,* and the *Century.* In 1883 Emma Lazarus wrote her sonnet "The New Colossus," which in 1903 was inscribed on a plaque and placed inside the pedestal of the Statue of Liberty. By 1888 when William Dean Howells took an apartment in Stuyvesant Square, the country's literary center had shifted from Boston to New York City. Howells called for a new realism and strove for it in *A Hazard of New Fortunes* (1890), which he wrote while working as a columnist for *Harper's New Monthly Magazine.* Considering the city the only one that belonged to the whole country, he often depicted it as a place of limitless opportunity where capitalists and revolutionaries and the rich and the poor coexisted. By the turn of the twentieth century New York City's thriving literary community and book publishing industry drew writers from all over the country, including Mark Twain, who at the height of his popularity lived at Fifth Avenue and 10th Street.

During the last decade of the nineteenth century themes of disillusionment dominated literary works produced in the city. In *How the Other Half Lives* (1890), Jacob A. Riis reported on the dire conditions in New York City's immigrant neighborhoods. His work influenced Lincoln Steffens, who moved to the city from San Francisco in 1892, and Stephen Crane, who wrote the first draft of *Maggie: A Girl of the Streets* (1893) before he ever saw the Bowery. Crane lived with friends in a studio at the Art Students League on East

23rd Street, where he wrote *The Red Badge of Courage* (1895). The building was also the setting of Howells's novel *The Coast of Bohemia* (1893). Theodore Dreiser arrived in Greenwich Village in 1895, and several years later he moved to the then sparsely settled West Side, which was the setting for *Sister Carrie* (1900), the nation's first "city novel." Themes characteristic of the country's rapidly growing urban environments—such as alienation, materialism, mechanization, the breakdown of tradition, and the conflict between the artist and society—would preoccupy novelists in the following decades. In 1893 S. S. McClure, a publisher from Illinois, launched *McClure's Magazine,* assembling a staff of writers that included Steffens, Ida Tarbell, William Allen White, Ray Stannard Baker, and Frank Norris, who on moving to the city from San Francisco in 1898 commented, "Of all the ambitions of the Great Unpublished, the one that is strongest, the most abiding, is the ambition to get to New York." McClure infused muckraking with art and authority and named Willa Cather, a teacher in Pittsburgh, the managing editor of the magazine. William Sydney Porter, who made his fame as O. Henry, found the heart of the city in the Tenderloin, an area of bars, dance halls, brothels, and gambling houses that had grown up along Sixth Avenue between 14th and 47th streets. Only a year after his arrival, he was producing a story a week for the *Sunday World.*

2. After 1900

Literature in New York City took new paths after the turn of the twentieth century. As the city grew northward, row houses and elegant apartment buildings drew better established and more prosperous writers to the West Side. Among them were Ellen Glasgow, Sara Teasdale, Edna Ferber, Marc Connelly, and later Sinclair Lewis and Fanny Hurst. The apartment boom of the early 1900s created vacancies that enabled hundreds of African Americans who were living in the Tenderloin and San Juan Hill, as well as African American elite, to move to what had once been the farming village of Nieuw Haarlem. In 1910 W. E. B. Du Bois moved to the city from Atlanta to edit the *Crisis,* the first magazine devoted to the work of black writers. James Weldon Johnson, whose groundbreaking novel *The Autobiography of an Ex-Colored Man* was published in 1912, moved to Harlem from the neighborhood of artists and writers around West 53rd Street in 1914. He wrote that New York City "sits like a great witch at the gate of the country, showing her alluring white face and hiding her crooked hands and feet under the folds of her wide garments constantly enticing thousands." Du Bois and Johnson were in the vanguard of the gathering of black writers and artists who would create the Harlem Renaissance. Meanwhile, Greenwich Village was becoming an "American bohemia," as Max Eastman, editor of the influential publication *The Masses,* described it. *The Masses* was among the first of the literary journals and little magazines that thrived there between 1910 and 1920 and quickly became a focus of Village intellectual life. Many writers came to prominence as contributors to publications in Greenwich Village. The *Smart Set* was taken over in 1914 by George Jean Nathan and H. L. Mencken, for 15 years one of the most authoritative voices in American letters. Mencken wrote a column for the magazine, and as one of its editors he published work by Eugene O'Neill, F. Scott Fitzgerald, and James Joyce. From about 1915 a number of writers in the city were associated with the Provincetown Players, including Steffens, John Reed, O'Neill, Dreiser, Edna St. Vincent Millay, Walter Lippmann, and John Dos Passos. About 1916–17 writers whom Gertrude Stein called the "lost generation" first moved to Greenwich Village, which according to Malcolm Cowley was attractive for its literary culture, cheap living, and welcoming environment for young writers. Among them were Hart Crane, Edmund Wilson, Matthew Josephson, and E. E. Cummings. The literary journal *Others* published some of the first work by William Carlos Williams, Wallace Stevens, and Marianne Moore. *Seven Arts,* a publication that lasted for only a year in 1917, engaged Waldo Frank and Van Wyck Brooks as editors and published O'Neill's first short story, Sherwood Anderson's Winesburg stories, and Claude McKay's *Harlem Dancer* (printed under the pseudonym Eli Edwards); the magazine also published work by Dos Passos, D. H. Lawrence, S. N. Behrman, Robert Frost, Carl Sandburg, Amy Lowell, and Stephen Vincent Benét. On the Lower East Side, a number of newspapers were important venues for fiction writers. The editor of the *Jewish Daily Forward,* Abraham Cahan produced a novel, *The Rise of David Levinsky* (1917), while publishing the work of Sholem Aleichem, Sholem Asch, I. J. Singer, and Isaac Bashevis Singer. On East 13th Street in her one-room apartment, Emma Goldman produced *Mother Earth,* which published the work of Johan August Strindberg and Henrik Ibsen.

Stylish literary entertainments were the hallmark of such magazines as the *Smart Set,* the *American Mercury,* and *Vanity Fair,* which included on its staff Dorothy Parker, Robert Benchley, and Robert E. Sherwood; the three ate lunch together every day at the Algonquin Hotel and formed the core of what was later called the Algonquin Round Table. The *Little Review,* a magazine begun in Chicago by Margaret Anderson, moved to the city in 1917 and accepted experimental fiction and poetry by such writers as Hart Crane and Djuna Barnes. Its editors gave James Joyce's *Ulysses* its first printing, in installments from 1918 to 1920, and were fined $100 in an obscenity suit brought by John S. Sumner, head of the New York Society for the Suppression of Vice. The foremost little magazine was the *Dial,* a publication founded by Fuller and Ralph Waldo Emerson in Cambridge, which moved to New York in 1917. By 1920, under Scofield Thayer and J. Sibley Watson, Jr., it was a monthly devoted to the "best of European and American art, experimental and conventional," in the words of Moore, its editor from 1925 until it ceased publication in 1929.

The 1920s saw the flourishing of a literary aesthetic rooted in the vast array of experiences provided by the growing city. Inspired in part by James, Wharton wrote of the elite of Washington Square during the Gilded Age in *The Age of Innocence* (1920, Pulitzer Prize). Fitzgerald's *This Side of Paradise* (1920) set a tone for what Wilson called "jazz-age romanticism." In *The Bridge* (1930) Hart Crane celebrated the Brooklyn Bridge as a symbol of the beauty made possible by a fusion of art and technology. In *Manhattan Transfer* (1925) Dos Passos depicted city life as a panorama of disparate lives and voices. Fitzgerald's *The Great Gatsby,* Dreiser's *An American Tragedy,* and Lewis's *Arrowsmith* were also published in 1925. Other writers portrayed the places they came from: Cather wrote about Nebraska; Sherwood Anderson about Ohio; and Thomas Wolfe, who arrived in 1923, about North Carolina. Boni and Liveright, one of the newer publishing firms that joined the nineteenth-century houses, published works by Sigmund Freud, Dreiser, O'Neill, Sherwood Anderson, George Moore, Gertrude Atherton, Robinson Jeffers, Henrik Van Loon, and Rose Macaulay and also founded the Modern Library, a series that sold more than 300,000 copies a year of works by such renowned writers as Freud, William Faulkner, Anderson, Ernest Hemingway, O'Neill, Cummings, and Hart Crane. Another important house was Alfred A. Knopf, which published Mencken, Nathan, and Cather.

The literary world of the city became increasingly fashionable from the mid-1920s. The *New Yorker* magazine began publication in 1925 and published writers such as E. B. White, James Thurber, and Dwight Macdonald. Other well-known critics and editors of these years included Cowley and Josephson, the editors of *Broom,* an international magazine of the arts, and Mark Van Doren, literary editor of the *Nation.* Wilson took over as literary editor of the *New Republic* in 1928 and was succeeded in 1929 by Cowley, who made the magazine a literary force; he often wrote the lead reviews himself and was admired by such writers as Alfred Kazin, who began his career as a reviewer for the magazine. John O'Hara arrived in New York City from Pottsville, Pennsylvania, in 1927 and documented the city's high life in some of his short stories and in his novel *Butterfield 8,* named for the telephone exchange for the fashionable East Side. Beginning in 1928 he wrote more than 200 stories for the *New Yorker.* His first novel, *Appointment in Samarra,* was published in 1934, and he went on to write 11 more as well as a stage adaptation of his short story collection *Pal Joey* while living in the city.

The Harlem Renaissance reached its height during the 1920s and 1930s. Some of its most important figures were Charles Johnson, editor of *Opportunity* (the magazine of the National Urban League); Jessie Redmon Fauset, editor of the *Crisis;* and Alain Locke. Zora Neale Hurston moved to Harlem and won a prize for a story in *Opportunity;* she later became an anthropologist and wrote the novels *Jonah's Gourd Vine* (1934) and *Their Eyes Were Watching God* (1937). Rudolph Fisher, who moved to New York City to study bacteriology and pathology at the Columbia College of Physicians and Surgeons, became a radiologist, ran a hospital, and also wrote *The Walls of Jericho* and *The Conjure Man Dies,* the first mystery dealing entirely with black characters. In 1925 Fauset, Locke, and Charles Johnson produced the landmark anthology *The New Negro,* which included work by Fisher, Hurston, Countee Cullen, Arna Bontemps, Wallace Thurman, Nella Larsen, and Jean Toomer. The white critic and photographer Carl Van Vechten published *Nigger Heaven* in 1926, and in 1928 McKay's *Home to Harlem* became a best seller. In 1937 Richard Wright moved to Harlem to edit a short-lived literary magazine, *New Challenge.* The publication of his collection of stories *Uncle Tom's Children* (1938) won him national recognition and a Guggenheim Fellowship and influenced many minority writers to turn to social realism in the 1940s. Ralph Ellison, who came to Harlem after three years at the Tuskegee Institute, was introduced to Wright by Langston Hughes. The two novelists became literary friends and Ellison read the pages of Wright's classic *Native Son* (1940) as Wright wrote it. Ellison considered the Harlem of the late 1930s and early 1940s both a haunting "ruin" and a place of liberation and light; the neighborhood became the setting for his novel *Invisible Man* (1952). Harlem of the same era was also used by James Baldwin as the setting for his novel *Go Tell It on the Mountain* (1953).

The vibrancy and contrasts of life in the city continued to inspire and intrigue writers in the 1930s. Dashiell Hammett finished writing *The Maltese Falcon* there in 1930, and Lillian Hellman achieved success with the plays *The Children's Hour* (1934) and *The Little Foxes* (1939). Henry Roth wrote of a childhood spent on "snug, homogeneous, orthodox 9th Street" and in Harlem in *Call It Sleep* (1934). *Esquire* was launched in 1933 by Arnold Gingrich and in its first issue included pieces by Hemingway, Dos Passos, Hammett, and Erskine Caldwell. An immediate success, the magazine published Fitzgerald's *The Crack-up* in three installments in 1936. Describing the city during these years, John Steinbeck wrote: "All of everything is concentrated here, population, theater, art, writing, publishing, importing, business, murder, mugging, luxury, poverty. It is all of everything. It goes all night. It is tireless and its air is charged with energy." White marveled at the city's variety: "I am twenty-two blocks from where Rudolph Valentino lay in state, eight blocks from where Nathan Hale was executed, five blocks from the publisher's office where Ernest Hemingway hit Max Eastman on the nose, four miles from where Walt Whitman sat sweating out editorials for the *Brooklyn Eagle,* thirty-four blocks from the street Willa Cather lived in when she came to New York to write books about Nebraska." For Thomas Wolfe the city aroused fascination but also feelings of "naked homelessness, rootlessness, and loneliness." His books *Of Time and the River* (1935), *The Web and the Rock* (1939), and *You Can't Go Home Again* (1940) were edited meticulously by Maxwell Perkins of Scribner's. For John P. Marquand the city was an "indefinable combination of triumph, discouragement and memories" and provided the setting for the novels *So Little Time* (1943) and *Point of No Return* (1949). His work was also edited by Perkins, as was that of Fitzgerald, Hemingway, and Caldwell.

The 1940s saw another generation of writers emerge in the Village. Djuna Barnes settled at Patchin Place after a number of years in Paris, where she had published *Nightwood* (1936). After winning a Rockefeller Fellowship and moving to New York City in 1939, Tennessee Williams found work waiting on tables and reciting poetry; by the 1940s his plays, among them *The Glass Menagerie* (1944) and *A Streetcar Named Desire* (1947), were being produced on Broadway. James Agee arrived in 1932 and worked for *Fortune* magazine; in 1939 he took a job with *Time* magazine where he became a noted film critic while writing *A Death in the Family* (1957, published posthumously). Anaïs Nin left Paris for New York City (she had spent her childhood in a West Side brownstone), where she published *Winter of Artifice* (1939) and *Under a Glass Bell* (1944). William Styron arrived from North Carolina in 1947, took a writing class at the New School taught by Hiram Haydn, and finished *Lie Down in Darkness* (1951) at age 26. Columbia University became another literary center where Van Doren, winner of the Pulitzer Prize for poetry in 1940, taught such students as John Berryman, Thomas Merton, Herb Gold, Allen Ginsberg, and Jack Kerouac. His brother Carl Van Doren, also a literary editor of the *Nation* and a teacher at Columbia, urged Kazin to write his critical work *On Native Grounds: An Interpretation of Modern American Prose Literature* (1942). Lionel Trilling succeeded Van Doren as the preeminent literary figure at Columbia.

In the late 1930s and 1940s, a group of Jewish writers, many of them from families of immigrants in Brooklyn, became well-known critics. Among them were Kazin; Irving Howe, editor of *Dissent;* Norman Podhoretz, editor of *Commentary;* and Delmore Schwartz. In 1937 *Partisan Review* was launched by Philip Rahv and William Phillips and soon became a focus for these writers and others, including Dwight Macdonald (editor of the publication from 1937 to 1943), F. W. Dupee, Mary McCarthy, Harold Rosenberg, Meyer Schapiro, and Lionel Abel. Schwartz's story "In Dreams Begin Responsibilities" was published to great acclaim in the first issue. The early stories of another Brooklynite, Bernard Malamud, appeared in *Partisan Review* and *Commentary.* His first and best-known novel, *The Natural,* was published in 1952; his second, *The Assistant* (1957), drew on Malamud's childhood in Brooklyn. *The Fixer* (1966) won the Pulitzer Prize for fiction as well as a National Book Award. In 1953 Saul Bellow made his *Partisan Review* debut with a translation of Isaac Bashevis Singer's "Gimpel the Fool." Bellow, a Canadian who moved to New York City, made it the setting of his novels *The Victim* (1947), *Seize the Day* (1956), *Herzog* (1964), *Mr. Sammler's Planet* (1969), and *Humboldt's Gift* (1975). By the 1950s many of these writers were concentrated on the West Side. As Podhoretz wrote, "One of the longest journeys in the world is the journey from Brooklyn to Manhattan." The sociologist, cultural critic, and novelist Paul Goodman described life in New York City in the 1940s and 1950s in his tetralogy *The Empire City: A Novel of New York.* His nonfiction *Growing Up Absurd* made him famous in the 1960s.

In the 1940s, while some writers were leaving Brooklyn, others were arriving or returning. For five years a house in Brooklyn Heights was shared by *Harper's Bazaar* literary editor George Davis, Carson McCullers, W. H. Auden, the theatrical designer Oliver Smith, and Jane and Paul Bowles; Wright also lived there briefly while writing *Native Son.* In a duplex in Brooklyn Heights, Norman Mailer wrote *The Naked and the Dead* (1948) upstairs and Arthur Miller wrote *All My Sons* (1947) in the lower unit. Miller bought another house in the neighborhood where he wrote *Death of a Salesman* (1949, Pulitzer Prize) and *A View from the Bridge* (1955, Pulitzer Prize), a work set in Red Hook. In 1957 Truman Capote rented a basement apartment in Brooklyn Heights, where he wrote *Breakfast at Tiffany's* (1958) as well as the "nonfiction novel" *In Cold Blood* (1966).

After World War II the *New Yorker* became a more literary publication under editor William Shawn, who created a tradition of excellence in nonfiction reporting and writing.

John Hersey's *Hiroshima* (1946) was the first in a series of influential books that began life as articles in the magazine; others included Rachel Carson's *Silent Spring* (1963) and Jonathan Schell's *The Fate of the Earth* (1982). The magazine was also known for profiles and other pieces by A. J. Liebling, Lillian Ross, Joseph Mitchell, and Capote.

In the 1950s the low rents of the East Village drew many of the writers who would come to be known as the BEATS. Ginsberg moved to an apartment on East Seventh Street in 1951; he was joined there in 1953 by William Burroughs, who wrote *Junkie* under the pseudonym William Lee. The year 1957 saw the publication of Ginsberg's poem "Howl" in the *Evergreen Review* as well as Kerouac's *On the Road.* Kerouac visited New York City often and wrote *The Subterraneans* (1958), a novel based on the beats' life there. A younger generation of writers followed, among them LeRoi Jones (Amiri Baraka), Hubert Selby, Gilbert Sorrentino, Robert Creeley, and Diane Di Prima, who with Alan Marlowe opened the American Theatre for Poets. This theater produced Di Prima's one-act plays and those of Jones, Robert Duncan, Frank O'Hara, and Michael McClure, as well as dance programs and "happenings." Poetry readings were often given at Cafe le Metro and St. Mark's Church in the Bowery. The magazine *Umbra* attracted many black writers, including Jones, Larry Neal, Ishmael Reed, Toni Cade, and Nikki Giovanni. Among the most prominent poets of what became known as the New York School were John Ashbery and James Schuyler. Ashbery won all three major American poetry awards, the Pulitzer, the National Book Award, and the National Book Critics Circle Award, in 1975 for his *Self-Portrait in a Convex Mirror.* Schuyler was awarded the Pulitzer Prize in 1981 for his collection *The Morning of the Poem.*

During the 1950s the West Side came to be associated with a group of thinkers and writers that included Podhoretz, Howe, Kazin, Susan Sontag, Jason Epstein, Barbara Epstein, Murray Kempton, and Elizabeth Hardwick. As a 15-year-old at North Hollywood High School in California, Sontag had discovered *Partisan Review* on a newsstand and determined that someday she would write for it. When she arrived in New York City in 1959, she was thrilled—"All I could think was New York! New York!" she wrote. Her dream was realized in 1961 when she persuaded Phillips to let her write a review for the magazine around the same time that her first novel, *The Benefactor,* was accepted by Farrar, Straus and Giroux. The *Paris Review* moved to the city in 1959, and during the 1960s George Plimpton's apartment on East 72nd Street became one of the city's liveliest literary salons, the only one, according to the journalist Gay Talese, that regularly drew together Hellman, Mailer, Macdonald, Styron, James Jones, Irwin Shaw, Philip Roth, Jack Gelber, Peter Matthiessen, Terry Southern, John Marquand, Jr., and Blair Fuller.

During the newspaper strike of 1963, when they were having dinner together, Robert Lowell, Elizabeth Hardwick, and Jason and Barbara Epstein conceived the idea for the *New York Review of Books,* which became an important West Side intellectual forum. Under founding editors Robert B. Silvers and Barbara Epstein, the fortnightly *Review* became and remains one of the country's most influential literary publications. Also in 1963 *Esquire* devoted an entire issue to literature that included many writers based in New York City. The offerings of *Esquire* and the *New Yorker* led to a new brand of novelistic journalism in such works as Mailer's *Armies of the Night* (1968, Pulitzer Prize) and *The Executioner's Song* (1979, Pulitzer Prize) and Tom Wolfe's *Kandy-Kolored Tangerine-Flake Streamline Baby* (1965) and *The Right Stuff* (1979). Elements of fiction and journalism were also combined by E. L. Doctorow in *Ragtime* (1975). His *World's Fair,* which won the National Book Award in 1985, and *Waterworks* (1994) were also set in New York City. By the 1970s the city teemed with an array of literary talent. Puerto Rican writers replaced Jewish writers in describing the city's immigrant experience. Piri Thomas, whose *Down These Mean Streets* had been published in 1967, joined Miguel Algarín, a poet and Rutgers professor, in founding the NUYORICAN POETS CAFE. Drawing on the Puerto Rican *trova* tradition, the Nuyoricans believed that poetry should be heard live and held weekly POETRY SLAMS.

The feminist movement and the increased presence of women in the publishing field led to the publication of more works by women. Among them were Kate Millett's feminist classic *Sexual Politics* (1970) as well as critical works by Elizabeth Janeway, Elizabeth Hardwick, and Barbara Ehrenreich. Novels such as Erica Jong's *Fear of Flying* (1973) and Judith Rossner's *Looking for Mr. Goodbar* (1975) explored the sexual side of feminist liberation. Other female writers living in New York City in the 1970s included the poets Adrienne Rich, June Jordan, and Ntozake Shange, whose play *for colored girls who have considered suicide/when the rainbow is enough* (1975) was produced first Off-Broadway and later moved to the Booth Theatre. Bronx native Grace Paley, who had been publishing short stories since the 1960s, came to prominence with her collection *Enormous Changes at the Last Minute* (1974), and from 1986 to 1988 she was New York State's first official state author. Cynthia Ozick, who also grew up in the Bronx, published essays and short stories and the novella *The Shawl,* which appeared in the *New Yorker* in 1980. Laurie Colwin, whose first story was published in the *New Yorker,* published several collections and two novels in the 1970s and 1980s. Paula Fox recorded the paranoia of Brooklyn life in her novel *Desperate Characters* (1970).

The disruptions and anomie of the 1980s, as New York City suffered from a crack epidemic and racial unrest, were reflected in Tom Wolfe's novel *Bonfire of the Vanities* (1989). Jay McInerney's *Bright Lights, Big City* (1984) described more upscale cocaine use. Mark Helprin's acclaimed *Winter's Tale* (1983) dealt with the city in the early 1900s and toward the end of the century. A number of gay writers, most notably Edmund White and Andrew Holleran, began meeting in a group they called the Violet Quill. Holleran's *Dancer from the Dance* (1978) and White's *Caracole* (1985) and *The Beautiful Room Is Empty* (1988) chronicled gay life in New York City. At the end of the decade Cuban American Oscar Hijuelos's *The Mambo Kings Play Songs of Love* (1989), which described immigrant life in Spanish Harlem, became the first novel by a Latino to win the Pulitzer Prize for fiction. Richard Price's *The Wanderers* (1974) was an evocation of his childhood in the Bronx housing projects; *The Clockers* (1992), a tale of lower-echelon crack dealers, brought him fame in the 1990s. In 1988 Joan Didion, who had said "Goodbye to All That" on leaving New York City 20 years earlier, returned to the city with her husband, John Gregory Dunne. His sudden death in late 2003 was the impetus for *The Year of Magical Thinking,* which won a National Book Award.

The 1980s also saw the influence of postmodernism in the stories of Donald Barthelme and the novels of Don DeLillo. Although he had been writing novels in the 1970s, DeLillo first received widespread acclaim for *White Noise,* which won the National Book Award in 1985. *Underworld,* partly set in New York City and published in 1997, took the post-nuclear world with its attendant terror and absurdity as its subject and established DeLillo as a major novelist of his generation. *Cosmopolis* (2003) uses the one-day odyssey across Manhattan in a stretch limo of a multibillionaire asset manager to treat themes of greed, violence, and alienation. The book is dedicated to Brooklyn writer Paul Auster, who created his own brand of postmodernism, blending absurdism and elements of crime fiction. He gained renown for the *New York Trilogy,* three books published sequentially and issued as one volume in 1987. A Flatbush writer, Jonathan Lethem, won a National Book Critics Circle Award for *Motherless Brooklyn* in 1999, which was followed by another Brooklyn novel, *The Fortress of Solitude,* in 2003. Between 1999 and 2006, Kevin Baker published three historical novels about New York City—*Dreamland*

(1999), *Paradise Alley* (2002), and *Strivers Row* (2006)—known as the *City of Fire* trilogy. Although she did not live in the city, Nobel Prize–winner Toni Morrison set her 1992 novel *Jazz* primarily in the Harlem of the 1920s. From the late 1980s through the turn of the century, Deborah Eisenberg published five books of distinguished short stories and won three O. Henry Awards. Michael Cunningham won the Pulitzer Prize and the PEN/Faulkner Award for *The Hours,* which was set partly in the city. His *Specimen Days: A Novel* (2006), invoking Walt Whitman's spirit and autobiography of the same name, portrayed the city in three different times, including 150 years into the future. Jhumpa Lahiri, whose book of short stories *Interpreter of Maladies* won the Pulitzer Prize, moved to New York City and set her 2003 novel *The Namesake* there.

Susan Edmiston and Linda D. Cirino, *Literary New York: A History and Guide* (Boston: Houghton Mifflin, 1976; rev. edn Layton, Utah: Gibbs Smith, 1991); Philip Lopate, ed., *Writing New York: A Literary Anthology* (New York: Library of America, 1998)

See also Book publishing, Magazines, Little magazines, and individual authors, publications, and publishing houses.

Susan Edmiston

Lithuanians. Lithuanians first moved to New York City in large numbers during the second half of the nineteenth century; many were socialists and other revolutionaries fleeing a failed uprising against Russian domination in Lithuania and Poland. From the 1880s to 1914 a new majority consisted of farmers and unskilled workers who found employment in shipyards, manufacturing, and the garment industry. The newspapers *Lietuwiszka Gazieta* (Lithuanian Gazette, 1879–80) and *Unija* (Unity, 1884–85) were short-lived because of financial difficulties and internal editorial conflicts. The prosocialist newspaper *Lietuwizskasis Balsas* (the Lithuanian Voice, 1885–89; Jonas Sliupas, publisher) stressed the importance of Lithuanian heritage and called for the formation of a national Lithuanian organization. Soon after, the Lithuanian Alliance of America (1886–) was begun in Pennsylvania; it survived internal conflicts between clerics and communists and moved to New York City where it became a fraternal and mutual benefit society and published the periodical *Tevyne* (Motherland, 1889–). Catholics accounted for much of the population and formed several churches: St. Mary of Angels (1894), St. George (1905), and the Annunciation of the Blessed Virgin (1914) in Brooklyn; Our Lady of Vilnius (1905) in Manhattan; and the Church of the Transfiguration (1908) in Queens. The Roman Catholic Alliance issued the publication *Garsas* (the Sound, 1917–30). Liberals and moderates rallied around the privately run newspaper *Vienybe* (Unity, 1911–) and formed the Lithuanian National League in Brooklyn, which was associated with the Lithuanian Alliance of America. Under Antanas Bimba, editor of *Laisve* (Liberty, 1911–87), communists who supported the government in Moscow joined the Communist Party of America and launched a number of publications: *Darbas* (Labor, 1919–20) of Local 54 of the Amalgamated Workers Union, *Kommunistas* (1920–21), *Kova* (the Struggle, 1920–22), *Tiesa* (the Truth, 1922), *Sviesa* (Light, 1933–40), and *Siuvejas* (the Tailor, 1934). Communists who opposed Moscow published *Darbininku Tiesa* (Worker's Truth, 1922) and *Nauja Gadyne* (New Era, 1931–43). After World War I, New York City became an international center of efforts for Lithuanian independence.

Many Lithuanians lived in Williamsburg in Brooklyn before World War II and later moved to the suburbs, especially Long Island and New Jersey. During the world's fairs of 1939–40 and 1964–65 thousands of folk singers, hundreds of folk dancers, and dozens of choirs took part in the Lithuanian Days organized by local groups. The independence movement in the city intensified with the annexation of Lithuania by the Soviet Union in 1940. The years after the war saw an influx of refugees opposed to communism; they formed a number of professional organizations, youth groups, and the Committee for a Free Lithuania (1951–). The Franciscan Fathers, based in Brooklyn, offered comprehensive social and cultural programs and also issued the publications *Aidai* (Echoes, 1950– ; since 1992 *Naujasis Židinys–Aidai*, or New Fireplace–Echoes), devoted to Lithuanian art, science, and politics, and *Darbininkas* (the Worker, 1955–2006). Local groups sponsored courses in Lithuanian language and culture at Fordham University (1957–69) and opened the Lithuanian Citizens Club in Queens and the Lithuanian Cultural Center (1974–) in Brooklyn, which amassed materials for extensive archives. Manyland Books, a publisher of works in Lithuanian and English, also opened in the city.

In the early twenty-first century Lithuanians in New York City number between 10,000 and 12,000, forming the largest Baltic community in New York City and the second-largest Lithuanian one in the United States (after Chicago). Most live in central Brooklyn and in Woodhaven, Richmond Hills, and Jamaica in Queens. More than 90 percent are Catholic; the rest include a few evangelical Lutherans. Well-known Lithuanians in the city have included the writer and publisher Jonas Valaitis, the tennis player Vitas Gerulaitis, the composer Elizabeth Swados, and the film critic and producer Jonas Mekas.

Algirdas M. Budreckis, *The Lithuanians in America, 1651–1975: A Chronology and Fact Book* (Dobbs Ferry, N.Y.: Oceana, 1975)

Vladimir Wertsman

Little, Jacob (*b* 1796/7; *d* 1865). Speculator. During the 1830s he became the most prominent figure on Wall Street by developing innovative techniques for manipulating the price of stocks, especially those of railroad and canal companies. Because he specialized in making prices fall, he was known as "the great bear of Wall Street," but he was equally adept at making prices rise: in 1834 he drove the price of the Morris Canal and Banking Company from $10 to $185 in less than two months. Little's schemes were not always successful, and after declaring bankruptcy three times he was effectively ruined by the crash of 1857 and died in poverty.

George Winslow

Little Africa. Name given to several black communities in New York City. It was first applied to what became the Five Points, an area composed of land grants made to Africans in 1659 by the Dutch West India Company. This area, adjacent to the Collect, was also known as Stagg Town and remained a mostly African American area until the mid-nineteenth century. It was the original site of the Abyssinian Baptist Church, opened on Worth Street in 1808 by free Anglo-Africans and Ethiopian sailors. The African Burial Ground was part of this community. Toward the end of the eighteenth century many African Americans settled in the Greenwich Village area now bounded to the north by Bleecker Street, to the east by Mercer Street, and to the west by Thompson, Sullivan, MacDougal, and Carmine streets. It had been given to 11 Africans, including Big Manuel, in 1644 by the Dutch West India Company and was a buffer for the Dutch colony against local Indians, who repeatedly destroyed Europeans' farms. Abyssinian Baptist Church moved to this new Little Africa by the 1850s, first to Thompson Street and then to Waverly Place. The enclave eventually included the African Grove Theatre, an independent branch of the Young Men's Christian Association, and many businesses. During the 1890s the name Little Africa was also applied to the area near Broadway and Harrison streets in Williamsburg, Brooklyn.

Seth M. Scheiner, *Negro Mecca: A History of the Negro in New York City, 1865–1920* (New York: New York University Press, 1965); M. A. Harris, *A Negro History Tour of Manhattan* (New York: Greenwood, 1968)

Sule Greg C. Wilson

Little Church around the Corner. See Church of the Transfiguration (ii).

Little Germany. Alternative name of KLEINDEUTSCHLAND.

Little Italy. Neighborhood in lower Manhattan, bounded to the north by Houston Street, to the east by Mulberry Street, to the south by Canal Street, and to the west by Broadway. Italians first settled in the Five Points during the 1850s, and efforts to set up a Roman Catholic parish for Italians began in 1858; the Church of St. Anthony of Padua was formed in 1866 by Franciscans of the Province of the Immaculate Conception, and its current Romanesque church at 153–57 Sullivan Street was dedicated on 10 June 1888. *Il Progresso Italo-Americano,* an Italian-language daily newspaper, was launched in the neighborhood in 1880 by Carlo Barsotti. The parish of the Church of the Transfiguration (formerly Zion Episcopal Church) at 25 Mott Street was largely Italian by the 1880s, and a chapel that later became the Church of Our Lady of Pompeii opened at 25 Carmine Street on 8 May 1892. By the 1920s the neighborhood was roughly bounded to the north by West Fourth Street and Houston Street, to the east by the Bowery, to the south by the Five Points and Canal Street, and to the west by Greenwich Village (which also had a large Italian settlement). Genoans, Calabrians, Neapolitans, and Sicilians settled in an area bounded by Houston Street, the Bowery, the Five Points, and Broadway; Piedmontese, Tuscans, and Neapolitans settled in an area bounded by West Fourth Street, West Broadway, Canal Street, and the Hudson River. Immigrants from southern Italy first celebrated the Feast of San Gennaro along Mulberry Street about 1926.

In later years Little Italy diminished in size. The parish of the Church of the Transfiguration had become largely Chinese by the 1950s, and much of Little Italy was absorbed by Chinatown after 1968. In the mid-1990s the western boundary of Little Italy continued to recede as Chinatown expanded. The neighborhood remains well known for the spot (129 Mulberry Street) where in 1972 the organized-crime figure Joey Gallo was shot to death during a family dinner, and for its bakeries (including the Parisi Bakery on Mott Street and Ferrara Bakery on Grand Street). Geographic pressure from the north and the east (from Nolita and the growing, gentrified Lower East Side, respectively) had by the early twenty-first century essentially pushed Little Italy's borders to Mulberry Street between Canal and Spring streets. As a result, the Little Italies in the other four boroughs became more important hubs for Italian-descended New Yorkers, even as tourists continued to flock to Mulberry Street in lower Manhattan.

John Horace Mariano, *The Italian Contribution to American Democracy* (Boston: Christopher, 1921)

Mary Elizabeth Brown

little magazines. Literary and political magazines devoted to work deemed unacceptable by publications of general circulation. Their name, which became popular about the time of World War I, came into use because the magazines rarely paid their contributors. The first little magazine in New York City was *M'lle New York* (1895–99), edited by Vance Thompson but dominated by its iconoclastic associate editor James Gibbons Huneker, the leader of a bohemian circle near Union Square. Printed on buff paper and illustrated in black and pink, it had an air of fin de siècle decadence tempered by the philosophy of Oscar Wilde and Friedrich Nietzsche, and it poured scorn in equal measure on the city's literary elite and the notion of democratic culture. There were few little magazines from the time *M'lle New York* ceased publication until the "little renaissance" after 1910, when many magazines were published in Greenwich Village by intellectuals in revolt against conventional aesthetic, moral, and political standards. The editors delighted in outraging public taste and were willing to lose money to do so. Although a few of the magazines became popular, most had 1000 subscribers or fewer and survived for less than a year. In addition to unknown writers, they often published the most distinguished writers in the United States and Europe.

New York City soon became the national center of little magazines. Among the best-known were *The Masses* (1911–17), which focused on art and radical politics and was edited by Max Eastman from 1912; the *Pagan* (1916–22), which published such poets as Malcolm Cowley and Hart Crane; *Seven Arts* (1916–17), which published criticism by Waldo Frank, Van Wyck Brooks, and Randolph Bourne; and the *Quill* (1917–29). Among the less successful were *Rongwrong* (1917), the *Lyric* (1917–19), and several magazines published by Angelo Bruno. The *Little Review* began publication in Chicago in 1914 and in 1917 moved to New York City, where it published work by Ezra Pound, William Butler Yeats, T. S. Eliot, and Wyndham Lewis; after issuing James Joyce's *Ulysses* in serial form, the editor Margaret Anderson and assistant Jane Heap were prosecuted and fined, and the magazine moved to Paris in 1922.

Little magazines reached the height of their influence during the 1920s and 1930s. *Contact* (1920–23; 1932) published critical essays and poetry by William Carlos Williams, Robert McAlmon, E. E. Cummings, and S. J. Perelman. The *Dial* (1920–29) issued the work of Eliot, Pound, Cummings, Yeats, Marianne Moore, and D. H. Lawrence. Under the direction of Samuel Roth *Two Worlds* (1925–27) also published poetry as well as some of the first sections of Joyce's *Finnegans Wake* and engaged Pound as a contributing editor. *Fire!!: A Quarterly Devoted to the Younger Negro Artists* (1926), the most important little magazine of the Harlem Renaissance, was overseen by Wallace Thurman with Langston Hughes and Zora Neale Hurston. Like *The Masses* and the *Liberator*, the *New Masses* dealt with politics, satire, and aesthetics under the direction of Joseph Freeman (1926–28) and Michael Gold (1926–33); after 1933 it abandoned the little magazine format by turning away from art and the avant-garde and focusing exclusively on politics. A number of magazines were launched in the 1930s: the *Miscellany* (1930–31), *Fifth Floor Window* (1931–32), the *American Spectator* (1932–37), *Blast* (1933–34), the *Greenwich Villager* (1933–34), the *Latin Quarterly* (1933–34), *Manhattan Poetry Parade* (1936), and *Acorn* (1938). *Twice a Year* (1938) published articles on the arts and work by new writers and staunchly defended civil liberties. *Partisan Review,* launched in 1934, was sympathetic to the political Left and soon became one of the most important literary journals in the country, publishing work by leading American and European writers. The little magazines of the early 1940s included *Vice Versa* (1940–42), which published new poetry and inveighed against established journals; *Decisions* (1941–42), a magazine dedicated to defending democracy, especially against Nazism, that published essays and poetry by Thomas Mann, W. H. Auden, and Somerset Maugham; *VV* (1942), which was devoted entirely to the plastic arts and promoted surrealism and psychology; and *Politics* (1944–49), edited by Dwight Macdonald. After World War II the influence of little magazines declined. Many left the city to become affiliated with universities.

Frederick J. Hoffman et al., eds., *The Little Magazine: A History and Bibliography* (Princeton, N.J.: Princeton University Press, 1946); Arthur F. Wertheim, *The New York Little Renaissance* (New York: New York University Press, 1976); Elliot Anderson and Mary Kinzie, eds., *The Little Magazine in America: A Modern Documentary History* (Yonkers, N.Y.: Pushcart, 1978); Abby Arthur Johnson and Ronald Maberry Johnson, *Propaganda and Aesthetics: The Literary Politics of Afro-American Magazines in the Twentieth Century* (Amherst: University of Massachusetts Press, 1979)

Kevin Kenny

Little Neck. Neighborhood in the northeast corner of Queens, bounded to the north by Little Neck Bay, to the east by Nassau County, to the south by Grand Central Parkway, and to the west by 247th Street. It was originally inhabited by Matinecock Indians, a tribe of the Algonquin nation. With what is now Douglaston it was assigned in 1663 by the Dutch to Thomas Hicks, Thomas Ellison, and John Ellison; Richard Cornell soon settled there as well. During the American Revolution the area remained Loyalist but was despoiled by the thievery of Hessian and British soldiers. Zion Episcopal Church was dedicated in 1830. The best-known resident in the nineteenth century was Bloodgood H. Cutter, a wealthy eccentric known as the Long Island Farmer Poet. In the 1850s and 1860s oystermen operated more than a dozen sloops and schooners at the foot of Old House Landing Road (now Little Neck Parkway) to supply clams and oysters to the surrounding population. The Old House was destroyed by fire on 31 May 1865; the railroad was extended to the area in the following year. Beers's map of 1873 shows Little Neck as a hamlet of 23 houses, a hotel, and a church at the intersection of Northern Boulevard and Little Neck Parkway. In 1906 the Rickert–Finlay Company laid out Westmoreland south of the railroad station, and in the following year Marathon Park was laid out just to the west. Waverly Hills was developed in 1908 south of Northern Boulevard between Little Neck Parkway and the Nassau line, followed by Little Neck Hills in 1914 between Browvale Lane and Little Neck Parkway. A large tract to the west between Browvale Lane and Douglaston Parkway was promoted as Douglaston Hills in 1924.

Vincent Seyfried

Little Red School House. Private elementary and secondary school opened by Elisabeth Irwin on East 16th Street in 1921 as an experiment in progressive education. The intellectually rigorous school stressed learning through experience, play, and self-expression and eschewed tests and grades. It was sponsored by the Public Education Association and was at first part of the city's public school system. Mayor John F. Hylan's hostility toward the school led to the condemnation of its first site, and the school was forced to move to Public School 61 and then to Public School 41 on Greenwich Avenue. In 1932 the Depression and a withdrawal of private funds led to attempts to close the school by the city's Board of Superintendents, but parents raised enough money to keep it open as a private school on 196 Bleecker Street. Students in the secondary grades of the Little Red School House attend the Elisabeth Irwin School, which occupies a building at 40 Charlton Street purchased in 1941. Irwin died in 1942, and the directorship passed to Randolph B. Smith, who led the institution for the next 25 years. In the early twenty-first century about 500 students were enrolled in kindergarten through 12th grade.

Agnes De Lima, *The Little Red School House* (New York: Macmillan, 1942)

Alfonso J. Orsini

Little Review. Literary journal launched in Chicago in 1914 and moved in 1917 to New York City, where it was published from a basement office on West 14th Street. Under the leadership of its editor Margaret Anderson and her assistant Jane Heap, it sponsored experimental fiction and poetry. From March 1918 to 1920 it published James Joyce's *Ulysses* in installments, which led to the editors' conviction on charges of pandering obscenity and the destruction of four offending issues by the U.S. Post Office. The journal moved to Paris in the 1920s and ceased publication in 1929.

Margaret C. Anderson, *My Thirty Years' War: An Autobiography* (New York: Covici, Friede, 1930)

Jan Seidler Ramirez

Livermore, Jesse L(auriston) (*b* Shrewsbury, Mass., 26 July 1877; *d* New York City, 28 Nov 1940). Speculator. Brought up on a farm in Massachusetts, he began speculating in stocks as soon as he left school and became a millionaire before his 30th birthday. An expert in selling stocks short, he declared bankruptcy in 1915 but soon recovered and became one of the most famous speculators on Wall Street before the Depression by working with other large speculators to manipulate stock prices. In one of his largest deals he made more than $10 million by speculating on a fall in the price of wheat; at another time he increased the price of shares in the grocery firm Piggly Wiggly by 50 points in one day. He did not recover from his fourth bankruptcy, in 1934, because the reforms of the New Deal outlawed stock market manipulation. In 1940 he published a book about his investment techniques called *How to Trade in Stocks.*

Paul Sarnoff, *Jesse Livermore, Speculator-King* (New York: Investors' Press, 1967)

George Winslow

Living City. Interactive Web site devoted to the history of New York City's public health system. Focused on the period after the Civil War and through the end of World War I, it provides an extensive collection of primary documents on the city's battles to stem the ravages of infectious disease. Included are both professional and popular primary materials illustrating the effect of disease on New York City's population. The annual reports of the New York City Department of Health, illustrations from popular magazines such as *Frank Leslie's Illustrated Newspaper,* and photographs from a variety of sources provide a rich repository for both scholars and the general public. Developed by the Center for the History and Ethics of Public Health at Columbia University, the project was funded by a grant from the National Science Foundation in 2001.

"The Living City," Web site, http://www.livingcityarchive.org

Molly Rosner

Livingston. Neighborhood in north central Staten Island, bounded to the north by the Kill van Kull, to the east by the Snug Harbor Cultural Center, to the south by Castleton Avenue, and to the west by West New Brighton. It was developed as Elliotville in the 1840s by Samuel MacKenzie Elliot, a prominent eye surgeon who treated such well-known literary residents as George William Curtis, Sidney Howard Gay, and Francis George Shaw. The name was changed when the railroad established a station on the northern shore in the Livingston homestead. The city operates Walker Park here, a recreation area with tennis courts and playing fields that draws many visitors.

Marjorie Johnson

Livingston, Edward (*b* Clermont, N.Y., 28 May 1764; *d* Rhinebeck, N.Y., 23 May 1836). Statesman, brother of Robert R. Livingston. After attending schools along the Hudson and graduating from Princeton College in 1781 he studied law, was admitted to the bar, and won election to Congress as a Democrat in 1794, serving until 1801. In that year he received simultaneous appointments as mayor and as U.S. attorney for the New York District. While in office he contracted yellow fever; on recovering he learned that municipal funds had been stolen by an aide and assumed responsibility by repaying the city with all his property. He then moved to New Orleans to rebuild his career but was troubled by debts for the next 24 years. After resolving his financial problems he returned to New York City. He later served in the U.S. Senate from Louisiana and was secretary of state under President Andrew Jackson.

William B. Hatcher, *Edward Livingston: Jeffersonian Republican and Jacksonian Democrat* (Baton Rouge: Louisiana State University Press, 1940)

James E. Mooney

Livingston, (Henry) Brockholst (*b* New York City, 26 Nov 1757; *d* Washington, D.C., 19 March 1823). Justice of the U.S. Supreme Court and son of William Livingston. A member of one of the most influential families in New York City, he was an officer in the Continental army during the American Revolution and a secretary to his brother-in-law, John Jay, during a mission to Spain. His intrigues against Jay there caused bitterness between the two men that inspired Livingston's anti-Federalist politics in the 1790s and his opposition to Jay's campaigns for the governorship of New York. Livingston was a lawyer who in 1802 became a judge on the Supreme Court of New York State. As a justice of the U.S. Supreme Court from 1807 until his death, he abandoned anti-Federalism for a brand of conservative nationalism compatible with the views of Chief Justice John Marshall.

Frederick S. Voss

Livingston, Philip (*b* Albany, N.Y., 15 Jan 1716; *d* New York City, 12 June 1778). Merchant and statesman. After graduating from Yale College in 1737, he became an importer in New York City, where he lived in a town house on Duke Street; he also had a country house in Brooklyn Heights. A member of the state assembly, he attended the first and second continental congresses and signed the Declaration of Independence. In New York City he helped to organize King's College (now Columbia University), New York Hospital, the New York Society Library, the Chamber of Commerce, and the first Methodist church in the colonies. He was also the president of the St. Andrew's Society, the city's oldest benevolent institution.

James E. Mooney

Livingston, Robert R(obert) (*b* New York City, 27 Nov 1746; *d* Clermont, Columbia County, N.Y., 26 Feb 1813). Jurist and diplomat, brother of Edward Livingston. After studying at King's College (now Columbia University) he became a law partner of John Jay, served as the recorder of the City of New York, and later was a delegate to the Continental Congress. As chief judge of the Court of Chancery of New York State (1777–1801) he administered the presidential oath of office to George Washington on the steps of Federal Hall. During the peace negotiations with Britain he was secretary for foreign affairs (1781–83). He became active in Republican politics because of his opposition to Alexander Hamilton's economic policies and because his family had received little patronage from the Federalists. As Thomas Jefferson's minister to France (1801–4) he conducted negotiations that led to the Louisiana Purchase. Livingston was also interested in agriculture and steamboat navigation. He supported the experiments of Robert Fulton that led to the launching of the *North River Steamboat* in 1807, and he used his influence to secure a monopoly for himself and Fulton on steamboat operations in New York State.

Clare Brandt, *American Aristocracy: The Livingstons* (Garden City, N.Y.: Doubleday, 1986)

Barbara A. Chernow

Livingston, William (*b* Albany, N.Y., 30 Nov 1723; *d* Elizabethtown, N.J., 25 July 1790). Writer and political leader. He graduated from Yale in 1741 and moved to New York City, where he established himself as a leading lawyer. With William Smith, Jr., and John Morin Scott he wrote and published one of the first American magazines, the *Independent Reflector* (1752–53), a lively periodical that opposed efforts by the Anglican Church to establish a colonial episcopacy and to gain control over a proposed institution eventually established as King's College (later Columbia University). He also worked with Smith to publish in 1752 and 1762 the first digest of the laws of provincial New York, covering the period from 1691 to 1756. Until a political reversal in 1768 he was active in politics in New York City; he then moved to New Jersey, where he was later governor for 14 years.

Dorothy Rita Dillon, *The New York Triumvirate: A Study of the Legal and Political Careers of William Livingston, John Morin Scott, William Smith, Jr.* (New York: Columbia University Press, 1949; repr. New York: AMS, 1968)

Barbara A. Chernow

Living Theatre. Theater company formed in 1946 by Judith Malina, a former pupil of the director Erwin Piscator, and her husband, Julian Beck, in an artist's loft on Wooster Street in Manhattan. It began by producing poetic dramas but eventually developed an improvisational style in works such as *The Connection* (1959), about drug addiction, and *The Brig* (1963), about life in the U.S. Marines. In 1963 the theater was closed for nonpayment of taxes and the company went abroad after the brief imprisonment of Malina and Beck, where it created works of an increasingly political and confrontational nature. The company returned to the United States in 1968. The Becks moved to Brazil in 1970 but were later expelled for their controversial theatrical activities and returned to the United States. After Beck's death in 1985, Hanon Reznikov filled his role as codirector of the company. The company has always been a vocal advocate for the Lower East Side neighborhood, and in 2006 the Living Theatre signed an extended lease for a space in a new residential development located at 21 Clinton Street, the company's first permanent home since 1993. Malina continued to act in and direct performances as late as 2007. Reznikov died in May 2008.

Edwin Milson and Alvin Goldfarb, *Living Theatre: An Introduction to Theatre History* (New York: McGraw–Hill, 1983)

D. S. Moynihan

local development corporations [LDCs]. Nonprofit corporations that provide affordable housing, deliver social services, offer planning assistance in low- and middle-income neighborhoods, and work to improve commercial districts by encouraging public and private investment; they are also known as community development corporations. The first LDC in the city, the Bedford Stuyvesant Restoration Corporation, was formed in Brooklyn in 1966 with political support from Senators Robert F. Kennedy and Jacob K. Javits and technical assistance from the Pratt Center for Community Improvement. Like many of its counterparts elsewhere, the corporation was an outgrowth of programs devised to combat juvenile delinquency, such as Mobilization for Youth, Harlem Youth Opportunities Unlimited, and the Gray Areas program of the Ford Foundation. During its first two decades the corporation built and renovated 1600 dwellings, assisted 1700 homeowners and 130 businesses, and created 16,000 jobs. In 1966 Senators Kennedy and Javits sponsored an amendment to the Economic Opportunity Act that created the Special Impact Program, which provided federal funding for LDCs.

LDCs devoted to urban renewal were set up during the 1970s and 1980s in response to housing abandonment and arson in the South Bronx, Harlem, and other neighborhoods. Groups such as the Banana Kelly Community Improvement Association and the South East Bronx Community Organization, led by Father Louis Gigante, renovated and managed apartment buildings and constructed owner-occupied housing for low-income families in the Bronx. These corporations received technical assistance from the Urban Homesteading Assistance Board (1975) and additional support from the Association for Neighborhood and Housing Development (1974). Private financial intermediaries were established to complement and support the activities of LDCs. The Community Preservation Corporation, formed in 1974 at the behest of David Rockefeller, pooled resources from more than 50 commercial banks, savings banks, and life insurance companies in New York City to finance 26,000 new and renovated apartments. The Local Initiatives Support Corporation (1979), a project of the Ford Foundation, and the Enterprise Foundation, formed by the developer James Rouse in 1982, created the New York Equity Fund in 1989 to attract corporate investment for rental housing through a federal program providing tax credits for the development of low-income housing.

Although reductions in federal urban spending weakened LDCs during the 1980s, many groups maintained and expanded their activities with increased municipal, state, and private funds. In Williamsburg the St. Nicholas Neighborhood Preservation Corporation invested $30 million to develop more than 600 housing units. The New York City Housing Partnership, formed in 1982 as an affiliate of Rockefeller's New York City Partnership, worked with LDCs to finance and sell new housing to middle-income families. To strengthen the local economy, LDCs assisted merchants in neighborhood commercial areas and built urban industrial parks. In 1982 they began to manage business improvement districts (BIDs), authorized by the state legislature to raise funds for revitalizing commercial and industrial areas. By 1992 20 BIDs were operating in Manhattan and the outer boroughs. The expertise of LDCs and their intermediaries became increasingly important to the management of such city and state initiatives as the municipal housing plan (1986), a 10-year program providing $5 billion for housing.

LDCs in New York City are nationally recognized in neighborhood revitalization and urban redevelopment. The Nehemiah Plan, initiated by East Brooklyn Congregations in 1982, has built more than 2900 town houses on vacant land and is a national model for low-income homeownership. Charlotte Street in the South Bronx, once a stark symbol of inner-city decay visited by Presidents Jimmy Carter and Ronald Reagan, is the site of Charlotte Gardens, a cluster of 92 one-family houses.

Neal R. Peirce and Carol F. Steinbach, *Corrective Capitalism: The Rise of America's Community Development Corporations* (New York: Ford Foundation, 1987)

John T. Metzger

Local 1199 (1199SEIU United Healthcare Workers East). World's largest local union and part of the Service Employees International Union (SEIU). It was formerly a chapter of the Drug, Hospital and Health Care Employees Union, founded in New York City in 1932 by pharmacists and drugstore workers. It first successfully organized nonprofessional hospital workers in 1958 under the leadership of Leon J. Davis at Montefiore Hospital in the Bronx. On 8 May 1959 about 3500 hospital workers began a strike against seven large private hospitals in New York City that lasted 46 days. This unprecedented action ended when both sides agreed that labor relations in the hospitals would be supervised by a quasi-public agency, the Permanent Administrative Committee. The committee was successfully challenged in 1962; the local began organizing professional and technical workers in 1963, and in the same year it won the right to collective bargaining under provisions of the state's labor relations act. In 1965 it was granted the power to represent workers throughout New York State, won a contract in 1968 that for the first time secured a minimum salary for workers of $100 a week, and in 1973 began to organize registered nurses. During this era the union gained recognition for its diverse membership and its commitment to civil rights. An initial attempt by the national union to merge with SEIU in the early 1980s prompted the local to declare itself independent. Internal disputes persisted until 1988, when Dennis Rivera became its president. Rivera oversaw the local's 1998 incorporation into SEIU and a tremendous growth in membership as it integrated smaller SEIU chapters and conducted new organizing drives. In addition to collective bargaining for its 300,000 members along the East Coast, 1199 utilizes its substantial budget to lobby and make political endorsements across party lines.

Eric Robinson

Locke, Alain [Arthur] **(LeRoy)** (*b* Philadelphia, 13 Sept 1885; *d* New York City, 9 June 1954). Philosopher, writer, and educator. He graduated from Harvard in 1907 with a degree in philosophy and in 1910 moved to Germany to study at the University of Berlin. Locke returned to the United States in 1913 and began a 40-year tenure at Howard University in Washington, D.C. He earned a PhD in philosophy from Harvard in 1918. In the mid-1920s he became increasingly involved with a growing Harlem elite of writers, critics, and artists, editing *Survey Graphic,* a collection of fiction, poetry, essays, and dramas including contributions from James Weldon Johnson, W. E. B. Du Bois, Arthur Schomburg, and Walter White. Fired from Howard in 1925 as part of an administrative effort to increase the number of white faculty members, Locke was reinstated in 1927 under a new president. He published *The New Negro,* a collection of writings including his own influential essay by the same title that announced the new consciousness of the Harlem Renaissance. Locke was named president of the American Association for Adult Education in 1945, chaired conferences and editorial boards, and taught at both the New School for Social Research and City College before retiring from Howard in 1953.

Garrett A. Felber

Locofocos [Equal Rights Party]. Egalitarian faction of the Democratic Party formed in the autumn of 1835. It began as a group opposing the nomination of a slate of candidates at a meeting of Tammany Hall; party regulars managed the meeting so as to nominate their slate before the opposition could gain control. The regulars then fled, extinguishing the gaslights as they left. The opposing group proceeded with the meeting by candlelight, using matches called locofocos. The name was later applied derisively by Democrats allied with Tammany Hall and eventually adopted by the dissidents themselves. The Locofocos drew some members from the former Workingmen's Party and were sympathetic to workers and labor unions, but they focused primarily on restoring Thomas Jefferson's standards to the Democratic Party. They opposed monopolies (particularly chartered banks and transportation companies) and supported Martin Van Buren's plan for an independent treasury. In the mid-1830s it appeared that the group might hold the balance of power between the Democrats and their newly formed competitors, the Whig Party and the Native American Democratic Association. After Van Buren brought about a reconciliation with Tammany Hall, the Locofocos disbanded; the result was a stronger and less conservative Democratic organization in the city.

Leo Hershkowitz, "The Locofoco Party of New York: Its Origins and Career, 1835–1837," *New-York Historical Society Quarterly* 46 (1962), 305–29; Amy Bridges, *A City in the Republic: Antebellum New York and the Origins of Machine Politics* (Cambridge: Cambridge University Press, 1984)

Evan Cornog

Locust Point. Neighborhood in the northeastern Bronx (2004 est. pop. 450) on a peninsula in Throgs Neck facing Long Island Sound. It is named for the indigenous locust-wood trees, which because of their resistance to rot were esteemed by early settlers. The area was called Horse Neck in 1667 and later Locust Island, for it was cut off from the mainland during high tide. In 1848 local landowner John Wright built a causeway to the mainland. The present name prevailed when the land was subdivided in 1910, after which summer bungalows were replaced by permanent houses. In 1961 an approach to the Throgs Neck Bridge was built on the eastern edge of the neighborhood.

John McNamara, *McNamara's Old Bronx* (New York: Bronx County Historical Society, 1989)

John McNamara

Loeb, Jacques (*b* Prussia, 7 April 1859; *d* New York City, 11 Feb 1924). Physiologist. He moved to the United States in 1891 and joined the Rockefeller Institute for Medical Research in 1910. During his years at the institute he was known as a champion of the mechanistic conception of life. He conducted research in artificial parthenogenesis and protein chemistry and was the editor of the *Journal of General Physiology.*

Philip J. Pauly, *Controlling Life: Jacques Loeb and the Engineering Ideal in Biology* (New York: Oxford University Press, 1987)

Lee R. Hiltzik

Loehmann's. Firm of clothing retailers. It began in 1921 when Charles Cord Loehmann became a co-owner of his mother's store in Brooklyn; he was in charge of retail sales until 1931, when he opened his own store, Charles C. Loehmann, to sell annual surplus stock of women's apparel manufacturers. The firm took its current name in 1964, opened a chain of stores, and became known throughout the New York City metropolitan area for the fine quality and low prices of its merchandise. It opened headquarters in the Bronx in 1968 and became a division of the Associated Dry Goods Corporation of New York in 1983. In 2006 Loehmann's was taken over by Dubai Investment Group for $300 million and had stores in 17 states.

James E. Mooney

Loesser, Frank (Henry) (*b* New York City, 29 June 1910; *d* New York City, 26 July 1969). Composer. The son of German immigrants, he grew up on West 107th Street and attended City College. As a self-taught piano player he wrote songs in Tin Pan Alley, including

"Heart and Soul," a perennial favorite of neophyte pianists. In 1936 he moved to the West Coast, and while in the service during World War II he wrote the hit song "Praise the Lord and Pass the Ammunition." He soon returned to New York City, where he wrote the score for *Where's Charley?* (1948), an adaptation of a British stage comedy. His best-known musical, *Guys and Dolls,* based on Damon Runyon's stories of amiable ne'er-do-wells in New York City, opened at the 46th Street Theater in November 1950 and achieved great success for its flawless integration of book and song. His later works include *The Most Happy Fella,* given its premiere in 1956, and *How to Succeed in Business without Really Trying* (1961), a spoof of corporate life that won a Pulitzer Prize. After Loesser's death a number of his musicals were given popular revivals.

Thomas M. Hilbink

Loews Corporation. Diversified holding company, formed in 1911 by Marcus Loew (1870–1927) as Loew's Theatrical Enterprises, an entertainment firm with holdings in New York City ranging from vaudeville theaters to nickelodeons. The firm responded to the increasing popularity of motion pictures by opening several movie theaters in the city between 1915 and 1920. It became nationally known in 1924 when it bought Metro Pictures and merged it with Goldwyn Pictures and Louis B. Mayer Pictures to form Metro–Goldwyn–Mayer (MGM), a Hollywood studio that soon dominated the film industry. During the 1920s and 1930s Loews built dozens of lavish movie theaters throughout the city, most having elegant interiors and distinctive terra-cotta ornaments. After antitrust suits forced it to relinquish MGM, the firm was bought in 1946 by Laurence and Preston Tisch, who then bought a number of hotels including the McAlpin and the Belmont–Plaza. During the 1960s and 1970s Loews diversified, acquiring the tobacco manufacturer Lorillard (1968), the insurance firm CNA Financial Corporation (1974), and the watchmaker Bulova (1977); it sold its movie theaters in 1985 (although they continued to use the name Loews as of the early twenty-first century) and in the following year bought nearly 25 percent of the stock in the Columbia Broadcasting System. In the early twenty-first century the corporation continued to operate CNA and its hotel chain, as well as several energy subsidiaries.

James Bradley

Loew's Paradise. Huge movie theater built in 1929 in the Bronx on the Grand Concourse and 188th Street. Designed by John Eberson and built at a cost of $4 million, the theater had a lavish auditorium (seating 4200) and a lobby resembling a Spanish patio. Loew's Paradise was divided into four theaters in the 1980s, and it closed in the early 1990s. Renovated and reopened in 2005, it was used mostly for special events in the early twenty-first century.

David Nasaw

lofts. Before the 1970s the term *loft* was applied to multistory buildings used for light manufacturing, storage, or showrooms. After the 1970s it came to refer to spacious, stylish apartments without traditional rooms, usually in renovated commercial buildings. While most lofts remain residential in nature, others are used solely as event spaces and galleries.

Most lofts were constructed between the 1870s and 1930, first in lower Manhattan near port facilities and later in midtown. Typically, lofts were built as adaptable space and rented by the story; the structure could support heavy loads with unpartitioned interiors and high ceilings. Windows are large, but the deep interior space lacks natural light and is thus undesirable for offices. Facades are often ornamented, especially in the central business district, but lobbies are spare and there are more elevators for freight than for passengers.

The most famous loft district in New York City is SoHo, where many six- to eight-story buildings were erected during the 1870s and 1880s for light manufacturing and storage. Cast iron was used for facades, but the main load-bearing structure remained masonry until metal skeletal construction was approved by the building code in 1888. After the 1890s lofts of 12 stories and more proliferated, especially south of 14th Street, where the garment industry concentrated after laws were passed to regulate sweatshops and restrict work at home. Between 1910 and 1914 more than 200 lofts were constructed, most of them on cross streets in the area between 23rd and 34th streets and Fifth and Sixth avenues. These buildings rose 20 or more stories, and cast shadows over sidewalks and buildings below. Thousands of workers spilled onto the fashionable avenues during lunch hour, leading local merchants to join reformers in calling for regulation. This movement led to the passage of a zoning law in 1916 that restricted the height and bulk of buildings and banned light industry near Fifth Avenue. The volume of construction increased again during the 1920s in the new garment district west of Sixth Avenue between 34th and 42nd streets. Zoning requirements shaped these buildings into forms that stepped back at upper levels, and the vogue for art deco inspired a rich variety of ornament; showrooms were an important feature in these buildings. After reaching a peak in 1931, the amount of loft space in Manhattan decreased, mirroring the decline of the manufacturing sector.

The conversion of lofts into residences began in the 1950s, when artists seeking low rents and large spaces set up studios in old commercial structures. In violation of codes, many inhabited their comfortless quarters and petitioned to legalize occupancy, a change approved for certain areas in 1968. This proved the first step in the gentrification of former manufacturing districts such as SoHo and TRIBECA. Later, lofts became fashionable for the well-to-do; expensive shops and galleries began to drive out older businesses. In 1980 the City Planning Commission adopted a policy designed to maintain some zones for manufacturing while allowing for more conversions into residences. The 1982 Loft Law established the New York City Loft Board to regulate the conversion of loft spaces from commercial/manufacturing use to residential use with regard to zoning and building codes.

By the early twenty-first century city planning officials had essentially given up on the protection of manufacturing districts in Manhattan, reasoning that the factories that had decamped first to the southern United States and later to Asia and Latin America were not coming back to New York City, no matter what inducements the city could offer. Thus, in 2010 former warehousing and manufacturing districts in WILLIAMSBURG, GREENPOINT, and the MEATPACKING DISTRICT, for example, were being converted to residential use.

Sharon Zukin, *Loft Living: Culture and Capital in Urban Change* (Baltimore, Md.: Johns Hopkins University Press, 1982)

Carol Willis, Kenneth T. Jackson

Logue, Edward J(oseph) (*b* Philadelphia, 7 Feb 1921; *d* Martha's Vineyard, 27 Jan 2000). Urban planner. After serving as the head of the New Haven Redevelopment Agency and the Boston Redevelopment Authority, he was persuaded by Governor Nelson A. Rockefeller of New York to become the head of the Urban Development Corporation on its formation in 1968. Under his leadership (to 1975) the corporation planned and constructed major projects throughout the Empire State, including several "new towns." In New York City its most important project was Roosevelt Island. Logue was later president of the South Bronx Development Organization (1978–85) and the president of his own development company, Logue Boston.

I. Steen

Lohman, Ann Trow (*b* Painswick, England, 1812; *d* New York City, 1 April 1878). Abortionist. She moved from England to New York City in 1831 and by the end of the decade advertised in local newspapers and directories as Madame Restell, "female physician and professor of midwifery." She lived first on Chambers Street and from 1864 in a four-story brownstone at 52nd Street and Fifth Avenue, where she provided women with contraceptives, abortions, and help with deliveries and in arranging clandestine adoptions. She was vilified in several sensationalistic tracts as the "wickedest woman" in New York City and imprisoned on Blackwell's Island. She took her own life on the eve of another trial; Anthony Comstock, secretary of the New York Society for the Suppression of Vice, called her suicide a "bloody ending to a bloody life." The size of her estate was estimated at between $600,000 and $1 million.

Clifford Browder, *The Wickedest Woman in New York: Madame Restell, the Abortionist* (Hamden, Conn.: Archon, 1988)

Allen J. Share

Lombardi, Vince(nt Thomas) (*b* Brooklyn, 11 June 1913; *d* Washington, D.C., 3 Sept 1970). Football coach. He played football at Fordham University as part of the defensive line known as the "seven blocks of granite" (1934–36). In 1947 he coached the freshman team at Fordham, for which he installed the "T" formation, and in the following year he coached the varsity offense. Lombardi worked for five seasons as an assistant coach at the U.S. Military Academy in West Point before joining the coaching staff of Jim Lee Howell with the New York Giants in 1954. Given complete control of the Giants' offense, he helped them in 1956 to win their first championship in 18 years. He later became the legendary head coach of the Green Bay Packers (1959–67), who under his leadership won the first two Super Bowl games ever played.

Michael O'Brien, *Vince: A Personal Biography* (New York: William Morrow, 1987)

Joseph A. Horrigan

Lombardi's. First pizzeria in New York City and the country, established in 1905 at 53 Spring Street. It began as an Italian grocery store in 1897 operated by Gennaro Lombardi and remained a family business until 1984, when it closed. Known for its thin-crust pizza cooked in coal ovens, it was reopened in 1994 by a childhood friend of Lombardi's grandson and moved a block from its original location to 32 Spring Street, where it remained in the early twenty-first century.

Jessica Montesano

Lombardo, Guy [Gaetano Albert] (*b* London, Ont., 19 June 1892; *d* Houston, 5 Nov 1977). Bandleader. He made his debut in New York City with his band the Royal Canadiens in 1929 at the Roosevelt Hotel Grill Room, where he performed each winter for the next 33 years. His well-known New Year's Eve celebrations were broadcast first on radio and then on television by the Columbia Broadcasting System until 1976. Lombardo performed at Carnegie Hall in 1969 and owned Lombardo Music Company, a publishing firm at 1619 Broadway.

Herndon Booton, *The Sweetest Music This Side of Heaven: The Guy Lombardo Story* (New York: McGraw–Hill, 1964)

Marc Ferris

London, Meyer (*b* Russia, 29 Dec 1871; *d* New York City, 6 June 1926). Lawyer and political leader. He moved in 1888 to New York City, where he built a career as an attorney for garment workers' unions and became an active member of the Socialist Party of America. In 1914 he became the first socialist candidate elected to the U.S. House of Representatives from New York State, winning reelection in 1916 and 1920. London was killed in an automobile accident.

Harry Rogoff, *An East Side Epic: The Life and Work of Meyer London* (New York: Vanguard, 1930)

Melvyn Dubofsky

London Terrace. Apartment complex in Manhattan, erected in 1930 between 23rd and 24th streets and Ninth and 10th avenues. It contains 1670 apartments in 14 buildings of 16 stories each, and at the time of its construction it was one of the largest developments of its kind in the world. The complex includes a block-long private garden, a swimming pool, a solarium, shops, and banks. The name is derived from that of a fashionable row of four-story town houses built in 1845 on the same site by Alexander Jackson Davis, and at first the management sought to evoke associations with Britain by having the doormen wear the uniforms of London bobbies.

Sandra Opdycke

Long Island City. Neighborhood in northwestern Queens, bounded to the west and north by the East River; to the east by Hazen Street, 49th Street, and New Calvary Cemetery; and to the south by Newtown Creek. It encompasses several smaller neighborhoods: Hunters Point, Ravenswood, Astoria, Steinway, Dutch Kills, Blissville, and Sunnyside. Before 1853 most of the low-lying area flooded easily, and in colonial times there were few roads or settlers. During the American Revolution the British army camped along what is now 39th Avenue and its continuation through the railroad yards in Sunnyside. In 1837 the farm of the Hunter family was sold to two developers, Neziah Bliss and Eliphalet Nott, who in 1853 leveled sand hills and laid out streets. Terminals were built for the Flushing Railroad (1854) and the Long Island Rail Road (1861), and a ferry to Manhattan offered service from 1859. Hunters Point began to industrialize during the Civil War, and in 1869 a street railway connected it with Astoria. In May 1870 Long Island City became an incorporated municipality, the fourth within the current boundaries of New York City (after New York City itself, Brooklyn, and Williamsburgh); for much of the late 1880s and 1890s Patrick J. Gleason was its feisty and influential mayor. The Steinway family in 1870 erected a plant on the East River at what is now Steinway Street and laid out Steinway Village, which became heavily German. In the 1870s and 1880s large oil refineries, lumber yards, and factories for asphalt, ceramic pipe, barrels, tinware, and light manufacturing were built in Hunters Point, where schooners and sailing ships delivered raw materials and carried finished products from docks along the shore; in later years chemical and glass factories and gas plants lined the shore to Astoria. Between 1874 and 1880 swamps were drained and the land filled in to a depth of 10 to 30 feet (3 to 9 meters) to end flooding. The notorious Hell Gate Reef, a deadly trap for ships, was dynamited in 1876 and again in 1885. Construction began on the Steinway Tunnel but was delayed by an explosion on 28 December 1892.

The roads and ferries and proximity to commercial waterways attracted additional manufacturers in the 1900s. In 1905 the Pennsylvania Railroad, parent company of the Long Island Rail Road, erected a large plant on Second Street to electrify its suburban routes (the power plant was transformed into residences in 2008), and from 1908 to 1910 it laid out the yards in Sunnyside. The Steinway Tunnel was finally completed in 1907, but wrangling with the City of New York over valuation delayed its opening until 1915. After the Queensboro Bridge opened in 1909, new streets were laid out, blocks of houses were built, and land values rose; inland development was especially intense. Michael J. Degnon completed Degnon Terminal, a complex of wharves, railroad sidings, and factories on Dutch Kills in 1913. In 1914 the first apartment building was constructed in Astoria, and aircraft parts were produced in the neighborhood during World War I. Interborough Rapid Transit extended elevated lines to Astoria and to Corona along Queens Boulevard in 1917, and the five-cent subway fare stimulated further growth; during the 1920s the last open land in Astoria was developed. During a time when the local economy was severely affected by the Depression, the Independent subway reached to the neighborhood in 1933, and the Triborough Bridge opened in 1936. The manufacture of aircraft parts revived during World War II; the Steinway piano factory turned out gliders.

Long Island City underwent marked changes after the war. Many of the large factories closed, and some were converted to other uses: in 1983 the Silvercup Bakery became the Silvercup Studios, used for video production. In 1985 factories on Thomson Avenue (Adams Chewing Gum, Eveready Batteries, and Sunshine Biscuits) became the International Design Center, a complex of showrooms for furniture and interior design firms; the venture lasted only a few years. La Guardia Community College took over the disused factories of the White Motor Company and the Equitable Bag Company. The residential population grew as older apartments and factories were refurbished as living spaces. Early in the twenty-first century Long Island City remained the most heavily industrialized area in Queens County, with railroad yards, the Queens–Midtown Tunnel, one end of the Queensboro Bridge, and blocks of factories in its lower reaches. North of the bridge and Northern Boulevard were private homes, apartments, and commercial buildings; the housing in Astoria consisted almost entirely of apartments interspersed with older private houses, many of them attached. A high-rise residential complex on the waterfront from Newtown Creek to 45th Avenue was proposed in 1984 as part of the Hunters Point Redevelopment Project and approved in 1990. The Citicorp Building (1989) on Jackson Avenue rose to 48 stories and became the tallest building in New York City outside Manhattan. After rezoning by the Department of City Planning in 2001 and 2004, the area attracted new high-rise residential and commercial development, especially around Bridge Plaza and in Hunters Point.

Vincent Seyfried

Long Island City High School. Original name of WILLIAM CULLEN BRYANT HIGH SCHOOL.

Long Island Historical Society. Original name of the BROOKLYN HISTORICAL SOCIETY.

Long Island Rail Road [LIRR]. Railroad connecting Manhattan and Brooklyn to Queens, Nassau, and Suffolk counties. Primarily a commuter route for most of its history, it is the third-oldest railroad in the United States and the only one still using its original name. The first train ran on 18 April 1836 between Brooklyn and Jamaica (Queens). The route was designed to connect New York City to Boston (passengers rode to Greenport, New York, and then took a ferry to Connecticut) and was built through the sparsely populated center of the island rather than through the villages along the shore. Tracks were extended to Hicksville in 1837, to Hempstead in 1838, and to Greenport in 1844. Inadequate freight and passenger traffic led the LIRR to declare bankruptcy in 1850, and it did not recover until several branches were built, including those to Northport (1868), Sag Harbor (1870), and Port Jefferson (1873). Competitors also arose; the LIRR absorbed all of them by the end of the nineteenth century, most notably the South Side Railroad and the Flushing, North Shore and Central Railroad, achieving a virtual land transportation monopoly on Long Island.

In 1900 the Pennsylvania Railroad (PRR) purchased the LIRR to take advantage of the LIRR's rights to build a Manhattan terminal. The result was the huge complex of tunnels between Queens, Manhattan, and New Jersey, as well as Pennsylvania Station, all completed in 1910. Beginning on 26 July 1905 the LIRR began using newly developed multiple-unit (MU) electric trains between Flatbush Avenue (Brooklyn) and Rockaway Park (Queens); the fast and frequent service spearheaded development of residential communities in Queens and Nassau counties. By 1930 MU electric service covered most of Queens and had reached Hempstead, Babylon, Long Beach, West Hempstead, Far Rockaway, Whitestone, Port Washington, and East Williston. Beginning in the 1920s, competition in the form of subway extensions (Queens) and new highways cut into the LIRR's passenger and freight traffic, while New York State refused to allow fares to increase between 1918 and 1947. In Queens, the Whitestone branch was abandoned in 1932; the Rockaway Beach branch south of Ozone Park was abandoned in 1950 after a trestle fire and sold to New York City in 1952 for inclusion into the subway system, which occurred in 1956. The LIRR entered bankruptcy on 2 March 1949 and suffered two major collisions in 1950 (one in Kew Gardens, Queens, on 22 November) that killed more than 100 people. Bankruptcy ended on 12 August 1954 when New York State passed legislation that gave the railroad special corporate status for 12 years due to the essential nature of its service. In January 1966 the PRR sold the LIRR to New York State, which initiated improvements that continued into the twenty-first century. The same year, after being placed under the direction of the newly formed Metropolitan Transit Authority, a fleet of 770 M1 model electric cars replaced all pre–World War II rolling stock; electric train service was extended from Mineola to Hicksville and Huntington (1970) and between Hicksville and Ronkonkoma (1988) to encompass 90 percent of LIRR customers. Reverse signaling was installed between Pennsylvania Station and Jamaica and on the Port Washington branch. Major construction projects included new yards in Manhattan just west of Penn Station and at Ronkonkoma; two large and modern rolling stock repair facilities in Queens; and a new train control facility just west of Penn Station that is shared with Amtrak. A fleet of 174 M3 model electric cars was added during 1985–87. Tracks, the third rail (the rail that supplies electric current), signals, communications systems, and station platforms and stairs were continually renewed and replaced.

In the early twenty-first century the LIRR operated about 350 miles (560 kilometers) of track and was the largest commuter railroad in the United States, carrying about 100,000 regular commuters every weekday and thousands more during off-peak periods, including to and from Long Island beaches and resorts during summer months. More than half of 730 daily weekday trains enter Penn Station through two tunnels; Flatbush Avenue (Brooklyn) and Hunters Point Avenue (Long Island City) are also LIRR New York City terminals. Except for the Port Washington branch, all passenger routes pass through Jamaica station, which has eight passenger tracks serving its five platforms plus additional bypass and lay-up tracks. The Main line extends 95 miles (150 kilometers) from Penn Station to Greenport. Branches east of Jamaica include lines to Babylon, Montauk, Port Jefferson, Oyster Bay, Port Washington, Hempstead, West Hempstead, Long Beach, and Far Rockaway. The Bay Ridge branch, which is for freight only, connects Glendale (Queens) with Brooklyn's waterfront. LIRR's Penn Station facilities were totally rebuilt during 1990–94; Jamaica station was rebuilt

Trains of the Long Island Railroad at Atlantic and Fifth avenues in Brooklyn, ca *1895–1910*

Long Island Rail Road

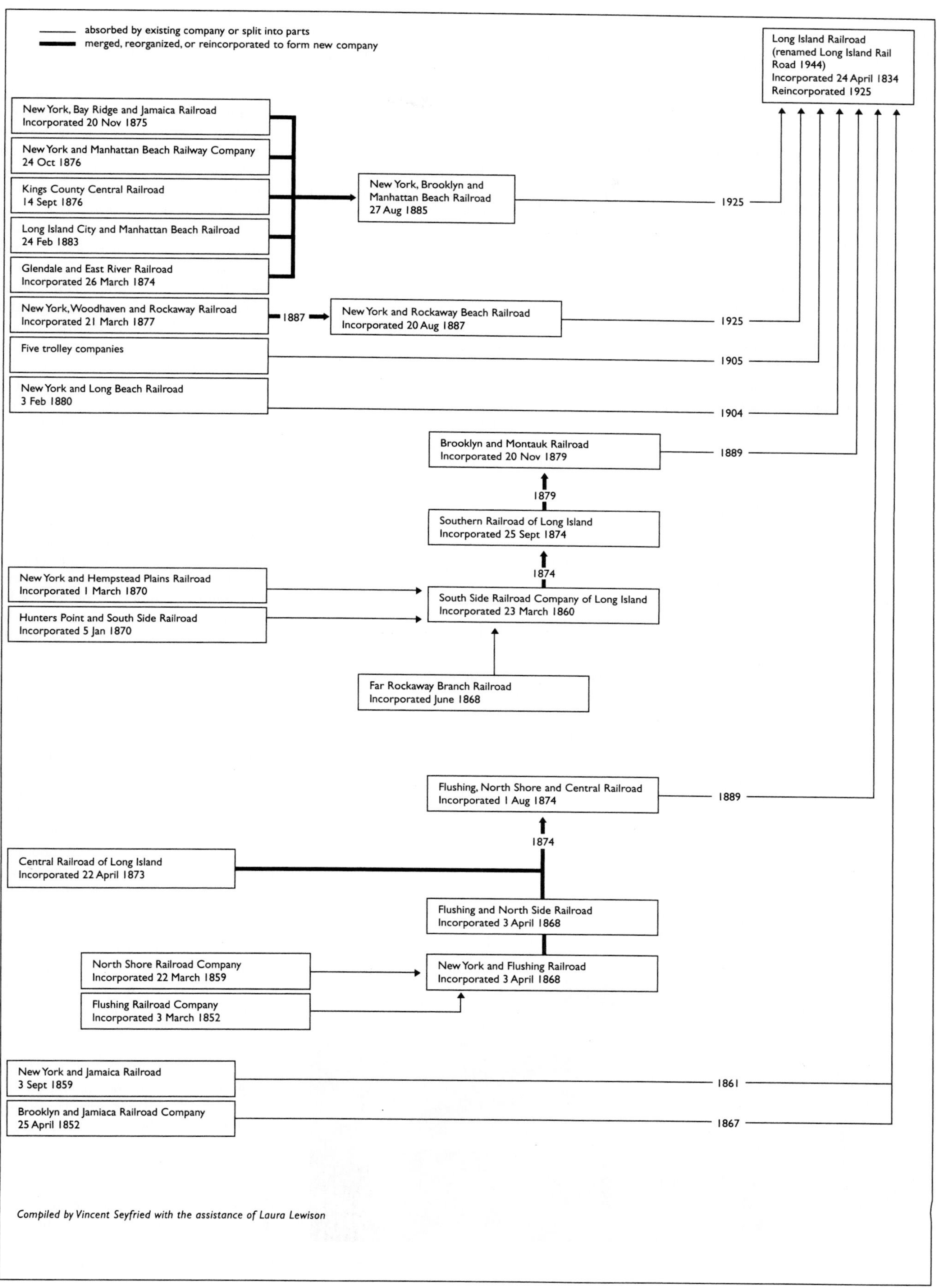

Compiled by Vincent Seyfried with the assistance of Laura Lewison

during 2000–2006 and included a new AirTrain rail connection to John F. Kennedy International Airport; Woodside station, a key interchange with the No. 7 subway, was totally rebuilt in 1999. Work to rebuild Flatbush Avenue and its adjacent subway stations was completed in 2009.

By 2000 a new diesel train fleet of 134 C3 bi-level cars and 46 locomotives replaced all older equipment; 23 of the locomotives were equipped to use third-rail power in order to provide direct service between Penn Station and branches without electrification. During 2003–6 the M1 model electric cars were all replaced by 836 new M7 cars. In 2008 work was under way on the East Side Access project, the most significant LIRR project since Penn Station's opening. When completed, LIRR trains will serve Manhattan's East Side via the 63rd Street tunnel lower level and new deep-level tunnels terminating at a new station beneath the existing Grand Central Terminal.

See also Railroads.

Vincent Seyfried, Andrew Sparberg

Long Island University. Private university established in Brooklyn in 1926; the name was adopted at the outset because Brooklyn belongs geographically to Long Island. The impetus for opening the school was a recommendation by a committee formed in 1925 by the incoming mayor, James J. Walker, at the request of Representative Emmanuel Celler of Brooklyn. Ralph Jonas, chairman of the committee and president of the Brooklyn Chamber of Commerce, pledged half a million dollars for the new university. The university opened in downtown Brooklyn on a site of 22 acres (9 hectares). In 1928 it launched one of the first academic honors programs in the United States, and in the following year it formed an affiliation with the Brooklyn College of Pharmacy (absorbed in 1979 as the Arnold and Marie Schwartz School of Health Sciences). William Zeckendorf, the real estate developer for whom the downtown campus is named, was elected to the university's board of trustees in 1942 and eventually became its chairman. The university dedicated campuses on Long Island in Brookville (1954, the campus of C. W. Post College) and Southampton (1963) and smaller ones in Suffolk County (1959, now at Brentwood), Dobbs Ferry in Westchester County (1975), and Rockland County (1980), as well as administrative offices in Greenvale, Long Island. Many students are the first in their families to attend college. Degrees are offered in the liberal arts, the sciences, business, public administration and information sciences, communications, the visual and performing arts, education, and health sciences. In the early twenty-first century Long Island University has a combined undergraduate and graduate enrollment of more than 31,000 students; of these, almost 12,000 are associated with the Brooklyn campus.

Elliot S. M. Gatner, "Long Island: The History of a Relevant and Responsive University, 1926–1968" (diss., Teachers College, Columbia University, 1974)

Marjorie Harrison

longitude. See Latitude and longitude.

Long Neck. Name applied to Travis during the Civil War.

longshoremen. Dock workers. A strike in 1836 was the first documented indication that longshoremen in New York City were organizing. They soon formed benevolent societies and unions such as the Alongshoremen's United Benefit Society (1853) and the Longshoremen's Union Protective Association (LUPA, 1866). By 1874 hourly rates rose as high as 40 cents for day work and 80 cents for night work, but hours were so irregular that longshoremen typically earned only $12 to $13 a week. After a pay cut in 1874, thousands of LUPA members went on strike, but their efforts failed and the union was crippled. In 1887 the ocean and maritime associations of the Knights of Labor were crushed after 50,000 members organized a strike in sympathy with 150 longshoremen in the city and coal handlers in Newark. Loading and unloading ships remained low paying and dangerous well into the twentieth century. A congressional investigation for the U.S. Industrial Commission in 1912 showed that longshoremen on the West Side hauled cargo for as many as 20 hours a day, at times carrying sacks of sugar, coffee, and other commodities weighing as much as 350 pounds (160 kilograms).

The system invited corruption. Hiring was done in "shape-ups" at each pier head, where bosses chose a few men for a day's work from hundreds of applicants. Discrimination, kickbacks, loan-sharking, and racketeering were common. Conditions on the waterfront became notorious under Joseph Patrick Ryan, president of the Atlantic District of the International Longshoremen's Association (ILA) from 1918 until after World War II. He forged sweetheart contracts with employers and enforced them on his own union workers, using convicts paroled into his custody. After Ryan was elected the ILA's president-for-life in 1943, exposés by Malcolm Johnson in the *New York Sun* and the efforts of the Jesuit priest John M. Corrigan encouraged workers to engage in wildcat strikes. This corrupt world was depicted in the Elia Kazan film *On the Waterfront* (1954) starring Marlon Brando. Governor Thomas E. Dewey formed the New York Crime Commission in 1951, Ryan was expelled from office, and the New York–New Jersey Waterfront Commission took over and replaced shape-ups with government-run hiring halls. The American Federation of Labor revoked the ILA's charter and formed the International Brotherhood of Longshoremen (IBL), but the ILA survived and the IBL ceased operations in 1959.

After containerization was introduced in the 1950s, the job of unloading ships that once required 25,000 workers every day in the port could be handled by just 2000 to 3000 men. Much of that cargo was landed in New Jersey, leaving New York City's piers empty for the first time in a century as the number of positions on the waterfront in the city and New Jersey declined from 48,000 in the 1950s to 12,000 in the mid-1980s. Important benefits for longshoremen were won by Thomas

Long Island University, 2009

(Teddy) Gleason, president of the ILA from 1963 to 1987. In 2001 the ILA suffered a major setback when the Waterfront Commission for the first time allowed a stevedoring company to assign members of its laborers' union to unload ships at Port Newark instead of hiring longshoremen.

Charles Larrowe, *Shape-up and Hiring Hall: A Comparison of Hiring Methods and Labor Relations on New York and Seattle Waterfronts* (Berkeley: University of California Press, 1955); Allen Raymond, *Waterfront Priest* (New York: Henry Holt, 1955); William DiFazio, *Longshoremen, Community, and Resistance on the Brooklyn Waterfront* (South Hadley, Mass.: Bergin and Garvey, 1985)

Joe Doyle, John Rousmaniere

Longwood. Neighborhood in the southwestern Bronx (2000 pop. 21,891), bounded to the north by Westchester Avenue, to the east and south by Southern Boulevard, and to the west by Prospect Avenue. It is part of the neighborhood of Hunts Point. During the nineteenth century the area was part of the town of West Farms. It received its name from one of many large estates: part of this estate, which occupied what is now the western part of the neighborhood, was acquired in the 1870s by S. B. White and renamed Longwood Park. Just before 1900 a few town houses were built on a section of the former estate that later became a landmarked district in 1980. After the subway reached the area in 1904, the rest of the estates were subdivided and apartment buildings were erected. The population remained predominantly Jewish until blacks and Puerto Ricans moved in during the 1950s. In the 1960s and 1970s drugs, crime, and housing abandonment threatened the neighborhood, but through historic district status, affordable housing programs, and community efforts, much of the neighborhood was rebuilt and refurbished from the 1980s on.

Evelyn Gonzalez, *The Bronx* (New York: Columbia University Press, 2004)

Evelyn Gonzalez

Loral Corporation. Firm of electronics and aerospace equipment manufacturers, formed in 1948 in the Bronx by William Lorenz and Leon Alpert. In the mid-1960s its offices moved to Manhattan. The firm won several lucrative contracts with the U.S. Air Force in the late 1960s and early 1970s and excelled in providing advanced electronics equipment and aerospace technology. It became a member of the New York Stock Exchange in 1963. In 1996 Lockheed Martin acquired Loral's defense electronics and systems integration business, and the remaining units regrouped to form Loral Space and Communications, Inc., a satellite communications company. In 2002 Loral paid a $14-million fine to the U.S. State Department for alleged involvement with a failed Chinese rocket launch, which the company neither confirmed nor denied. As of 2006 Loral was one of the nation's leading defense contractors, with sales of nearly $8 billion.

James Bradley

Lord and Taylor. Firm of retailers that began in 1826 as a small dry-goods shop on Catherine Street. Its owners were Samuel Lord and his junior partner George Washington Taylor, who retired from the business in 1852. The shop moved successively to the corner of Grand and Chrystie streets (1853), where it became known as the city's "fashion emporium," and to a five-story marble building on Broadway that became the focus of the Ladies' Mile (1860). Lord's clerk and his eldest son, John T. Lord, became partners in the firm; when the Lords retired after the Civil War, younger members of the family succeeded them. Lord and Taylor moved in 1872 to a building at Broadway and 20th Street that was the first in New York City to have an iron frame. After the panic of 1873 the firm was taken over by Edward P. Hatch, who annexed a building nearby that made Lord and Taylor the first retailer on Fifth Avenue. A store opened in 1914 on Fifth Avenue between 38th and 39th streets and became the principal retail facility. Dorothy Shaver, who joined the firm in 1924, became the first woman ever to lead a major American retailer when she was elected president in 1945. She greatly enhanced the reputation of the store and made it the leading supporter of American fashion designs throughout the world. In 2006 NRDC Equity Partners LLC bought Lord and Taylor from Federated Department Stores. In the early twenty-first century the company had 47 stores nationwide.

Leon A. Harris, *Merchant Princes: An Intimate History of Jewish Families Who Built Great Department Stores* (New York: Harper and Row, 1979); Joseph Devorkin, *Great Merchants of Early New York: "The Ladies' Mile"* (New York: Society for the Architecture of the City, 1987)

Laura Gwinn

Lorillard. See P. Lorillard and Company.

Lotos Club. Literary club formed in 1870. Initially based at 2 Irving Place, it moved successively to 21st Street in 1876, 46th Street in 1893, West 57th Street in 1910, and 5 East 66th Street in 1947. This location, designed by Richard Howland Hunt about the turn of the twentieth century as a private home, remains the clubhouse early in the twenty-first century. Nicholas Murray Butler, president of Columbia University, became the club's president in 1923. Women were first admitted in 1976. The club offers lodging and meals, monthly exhibitions, special dinners for mayors, literary evenings, art exhibitions, musical recitals, and lectures on public affairs; it is one of the oldest literary clubs in the country.

James E. Mooney

lotteries. Lotteries became popular in the early days of colonial America and subsequently played an important role in the development of a variety of legal educational and financial institutions as well as illegal organizations and crime groups in New York City. In 1611 the financially pressed Virginia Company held a lottery to fund the Jamestown colony. The New York State Assembly passed its first legislation regulating lotteries in 1721. In New York City receipts from lotteries were put to diverse purposes: protection of the city against attacks by the French and Indians (1746), education, repairs for City Hall (1761), a church in Brooklyn (1774), the American Revolution, relief for Loyalist refugees (1781), and a poorhouse (1795). Between 1797 and 1817, 16 lotteries in New York State raised $217,400 for canals, schools, roads, churches, and public works. Lotteries also played an important role in the development of the city's financial system. Many pioneers in banking and finance, such as John Thompson, founder of the First National Bank of New York and Chase National Bank, began their careers by selling lottery tickets, and in the early nineteenth century stockbrokers on Wall Street sold more lottery tickets than securities. The profitability of lotteries for their sponsors in addition to several scandals led to widespread criticism; in 1833 and 1834

Colony of New-York

New-York, Light House, and Publick Lottery.

Anno 1763. [No. 2070—]

THE Possessor of this Ticket, if drawn a Prize, shall by Virtue of a Law of this Colony, be intituled to the Prize so drawn, subject to Fifteen per Cent Deduction.

L

Lottery ticket, 1763

legislation was introduced outlawing lotteries. In the 1840s and 1850s John Frink and Reuben Parsons popularized poor people's "casinos," and the NUMBERS, or policy, racket became an important source of profits for organized crime. In 1876 it was reported that more than 33 agencies sold more than a million illegal lottery tickets each year in New York City. A syndicate of gamblers based in New York City also sold tickets of the Louisiana Lottery Company nationwide between 1868 and 1892.

In 1964 New Hampshire became the first state to once again offer a legal lottery game, and in 1967, in part to compete with the numbers racket and in part to raise funds for education, New York State established a lottery that eventually expanded to include games of many types. In the 2006–7 fiscal year, state-run lotteries brought in more than $6.65 billion in revenues and contributed nearly $2.36 billion statewide to education, with $1.12 billion allotted to New York City.

George Winslow

Louima, Abner (*b* Thomassin, Haiti, 1966). Haitian immigrant brutally assaulted by New York City police. He moved to New York City in 1991. On 9 August 1997, 30-year old Louima visited Club Rendez-Vous in East Flatbush in Brooklyn and became involved in a fight outside the club. Police from the 70th Precinct arrived, and a confrontation resulted in which one of the officers was punched and Louima was arrested. Louima was beaten by officers with fists, nightsticks, and police radios and was raped with a plunger in the bathroom of the police station, causing severe internal injuries requiring surgery. The incident provoked outrage among minority communities throughout the city. On 29 August 1997, an estimated 7000 demonstrators marched on City Hall and the 70th Precinct station house where the attack took place. The march was dubbed Day of Outrage against Police Brutality and Harassment. The subsequent criminal trial led to the imprisonment of Officers Justin Volpe, Charles Schwarz, Thomas Bruder, and Thomas Wiese. Volpe was sentenced to 30 years in prison without the possibility of parole; Schwarz was sentenced to 15 years; Bruder's and Wiese's convictions were later reversed on grounds of insufficient evidence. Louima's civil suit against the city resulted in a settlement of $8.75 million, the largest police brutality settlement in New York City history.

Benjamin Yakas

Lovelace, Francis (*b* Hurley, England, *ca* 1621; *d* Oxford, England, 1675). Colonial governor. He was appointed the second governor of New York State in 1668 by the duke of York. As governor, Lovelace raised taxes and improved infrastructure. In 1673 he was in Massachusetts planning a postal route between New York City and Boston when the Dutch recaptured the colony of New Amsterdam, ending his term as governor. The duke of York blamed Lovelace for the loss of his colony. In 1674 he confiscated Lovelace's home, a plantation on Staten Island, and locked Lovelace in the Tower of London, where he died.

Max Seppo

Low, A(biel) A(bbot) (*b* Salem, Mass., 7 Feb 1811; *d* Brooklyn, 7 Jan 1893). Merchant and father of Seth Low. Born at a time when ambitious merchants were abandoning New England for opportunities in New York, he moved to Brooklyn in 1829 with his father. In 1840 he completed a visit to Canton and sought to dominate trade with China by building fast clipper ships, beginning with the *Houqua* in 1844. The swiftness of his ships the *Samuel Russell,* the *Oriental,* and the *Surprise* allowed him to buy fresh tea in Canton later than his competitors, at low prices, and sell it in the United States earlier, at high prices. At the peak of his career in 1849 he moved his firm into new quarters on Burling Slip in lower Manhattan. In the following year one of his ships was the first to ply the newly opened route from China to London, thus making slower ships obsolete. When trade with China declined in the 1860s he dedicated himself to other pursuits, becoming president of the New York Chamber of Commerce and of a private school in Brooklyn; he retired from business in 1887. Low's house stands at 3 Pierrepont Place in Brooklyn Heights, and the building occupied by his business is at 167–71 John Street in Manhattan, at South Street Seaport.

Helen Augur, *Tall Ships to Cathay* (New York: Doubleday, 1951)

Ellen Fletcher

Low, Seth (*b* Brooklyn, 18 Jan 1850; *d* Bedford Hills, N.Y., 17 Sept 1916). Mayor and educator, son of A. A. Low. Educated at Brooklyn Polytechnic Institute and Columbia College (AB 1870), he undertook legal studies that he later abandoned to enter his father's business, the trading company A. A. Low and Brothers. In 1881 he was elected mayor of Brooklyn as a reformist Republican, after two Republican candidates withdrew in his favor. During his two two-year terms he achieved de facto home rule and implemented civil service and public school reforms. His sympathy for the mugwumps in 1884 and his hostility to patronage did not sit well with regular Republicans, and he decided not to seek reelection in 1885. A trustee of Columbia College beginning in 1881, he became its president in 1890. During his tenure the college promoted graduate education, absorbed several professional schools, and formed an affiliation with Barnard College. He was chiefly responsible for having Columbia move in 1897 from 49th Street to Morningside Heights, and he financed the centerpiece of the new campus, Low Memorial Library (named for his father). At the same time he helped to draft the charter for a consolidated New York City, and in 1897 he campaigned in the first election in which its mayoralty was at stake, losing to Robert A. Van Wyck, a Democrat backed by Tammany Hall. He prevailed in a second attempt for the mayoralty, defeating the Democratic candidate E. M. Shephard in 1901 after a campaign in which he advocated reform and spending for capital improvements. He failed to win reelection in 1903, losing to George B. McClellan, Jr., a Democrat supported by Tammany Hall who attacked Low's enforcement of blue laws (restricting the sale of goods on Sunday) and his purported Republican partisanship. In 1914 he resigned his trusteeship at Columbia in a dispute involving what he believed was the right for non-Christian groups to have access to the university's St. Paul's Chapel. Low retired to Bedford Hills, where he organized a farmer's cooperative, mediated labor disputes, and was chairman of the Board of Trustees of the Tuskegee Institute, the New York Chamber of Commerce (which his father had also led), and the committee on cities of the New York State Constitutional Convention of 1915.

Benjamin R. C. Low, *Seth Low* (New York: G. P. Putnam's Sons, 1925); Gerald Kurland, *Seth Low: The Reformer in an Urban and Industrial Age* (New York: Twayne, 1971)

Harold S. Wechsler

Lowell, Josephine Shaw (*b* West Roxbury [now in Boston], Mass., 16 Dec 1843; *d* New York City, 12 Oct 1905). Social worker, reformer, and philanthropist. The wife and sister of Union officers, she was widowed at age 20. She later became interested in conditions in poorhouses and jails of New York State. She joined a county visiting committee of the State Charities Aid Association, for which she helped to write a report on a poorhouse near her home in Staten Island: she was appalled at the conditions there, where men, women, children, vagrants, alcoholics, the insane, and the mentally challenged were crowded together with minimal care. Lowell believed that intermingling of this sort would lead to hereditary pauperism, perpetual dependence, and a negative attitude toward work. In 1876 she became the first female commissioner of the State Board of Charities, and for 13 years she worked to open separate reformatories for women, move the mentally challenged and the insane to separate institutions, exclude children from jails, and ensure that overseers of poorhouses were paid a salary rather than according to the number of people lodged each night. Under her leadership the board in 1882 formed the Charity Organization Society of the City of New York to reduce waste and duplication; she remained associated with the society until her death. In 1886 she led an effort to form the Working Women's Society (later the Consumers' League), which advocated a code of working conditions for young women employed in retail stores and urged customers to boycott stores that refused to honor it. During a bitter depression in the winter of 1893–94 she formed the East Side Relief Work Committee, which initiated such employment projects as street cleaning and the whitewashing of tenement buildings. She was also active in the mayoral campaign of 1894 in which the candidate endorsed by Tammany Hall was defeated. About 1884 Lowell wrote *Public Relief and Private Charity.*

Jane Allen

Lowenstein, Allard K(enneth) [Allard Augustus] (*b* Newark, N.J., 16 Jan 1929; *d* New York City, 14 March 1980). Lawyer and congressman. Active in the civil rights and antiwar movements, in 1968 he was a leading supporter of the presidential candidacy of Senator Eugene J. McCarthy and fervently opposed President Lyndon B. Johnson. Although he mounted seven campaigns for Congress in and around New York City, he was elected only once (in Long Island in 1968). He joined the law firm of Layton and Sherman. He was fatally shot in the firm's Rockefeller Center office by a former colleague.

Richard Cummings, *The Pied Piper: Allard K. Lowenstein and the Liberal Dream* (New York: Grove, 1985); William H. Chafe, *Never Stop Running: Allard Lowenstein and the Struggle to Save American Liberalism* (New York: Basic Books, 1993)

Lisa Gitelman

Lower East Side. Neighborhood in Manhattan, bounded to the north by 14th Street, to the east by the East River, to the south by Fulton and Franklin streets, and to the west by Pearl Street and Broadway; it includes the East Village, Chinatown, Little Italy, Tompkins Square, Astor Place, and the housing development Knickerbocker Village. Some of the first settlers in the area were free black farmers who moved to the Bouwerie, or Dutch farms. After smaller plots were consolidated into larger ones during the seventeenth century, much of the area was covered by James de Lancey's farm, which was confiscated and sold after the American Revolution. An enclave of craftsmen developed around the large pond known as the Collect at the intersection of Baxter, Worth, and Park streets and later became known as the Five Points. The first tenements in the city were erected near Corlear's Hook in 1833, and Irish immigrants settled in the northern section along the Bowery. Kleindeutschland, a German enclave, developed north of Houston Street in the 1840s. The 1880s saw an influx of Italians, Jews from eastern Europe, Russians, Romanians, Hungarians, Ukrainians, Slovaks, Greeks, and Poles. One of the largest ethnic enclaves was a Jewish one that in 1920 had a population of 400,000. The Yiddish theater flourished along Second Avenue between Houston Street and 14th Street. Pushcart vendors sold inexpensive clothing and ethnic food on Orchard Street and household items on Grand Street.

The burgeoning population found housing in the many tenements built in the area after 1850. The neighborhood remained a prototypical big-city slum, despite such attempts at mandating improvements as the introduction of dumbbell tenements in 1878 and reforms in 1901 that led to the construction of "new law" tenements with improved sanitary conditions and more comfortable living space. Conditions in the area were decried by reformers such as Jacob A. Riis, author of *How the Other Half Lives* (1890); attempts to ameliorate them led to the formation of service and welfare organizations such as the Educational Alliance and a number of settlement houses, the best known of which were the University Settlement and the Henry Street Settlement. In 1936 the First Houses at Third Street and First Avenue became the first housing project built by the city's housing authority. This and subsequent efforts to replace tenements with city housing had at best a mixed record in attacking the underlying causes of poverty on the Lower East Side.

In the early 1900s the neighborhood became known for its artists and its radical politics. Anarchism, capitalism, socialism, and communism were widely discussed on the streets and in newspapers such as the *Jewish Daily Forward* and *Morgen Freiheit,* which also reported news and gossip. Performances from many cultures were given at the Henry Street Playhouse (opened in 1915), and several important entertainers grew up in the area, among them Eddie Cantor, George Gershwin, Ira Gershwin, Irving Berlin, Jimmy Durante, Al Jolson, and the Marx Brothers. Alfred E. Smith and Big Tim Sullivan were among the best-known political figures. Tens of thousands of immigrant families settled in the neighborhood despite unprecedented overcrowding and poverty.

The neighborhood became the first racially integrated section of the city after World War II, when thousands of blacks and Puerto Ricans moved there. As the Spanish-speaking population increased, the area sometimes came to be referred to as Loisida, derived from the phonetic spelling of the original name as pronounced by Spanish-speakers. Poets, writers, and musicians found social tolerance and cheap food and housing in the northern section, which became the center of the beat movement; Fourth Avenue was soon the site of many secondhand bookstores. By the 1960s most Jewish and eastern European residents had moved out of the neighborhood, which in the following decade was beset by persistent poverty, crime, drugs, and abandoned housing. The area stabilized to some degree during the 1980s, and its inexpensive housing attracted venturesome students and members of the middle class, as well as immigrants from China, the Dominican Republic, the Philippines, the United Kingdom, Poland, Japan, Korea, India, and Bangladesh. In its southern reaches the Lower East Side became heavily Chinese.

As with its neighbor, the East Village, the Lower East Side saw increased gentrification beginning in the 1990s when older tenements

Lower East Side, Orchard Street between Stanton and Rivington streets, 1991

New York Public Library, Seward Park Branch in the Lower East Side, 2009

were cleared and expensive apartment buildings took their place. The opening of the New Museum at 235 Bowery in late 2007 reflected the change from skid row to middle class as surely as did the appearance of a Whole Foods supermarket on Houston Street near the Bowery. Farther east, posh restaurants jostled for room with nightclubs. Orchard Street, once filled with cheap clothing stores, featured high-end restaurants, bars, and fashionable boutiques. A bit of the old days continued at the rock club the Bowery Ballroom on Delancey Street and the Mercury Lounge on Houston Street. Several high-end hotels opened in the district. One development diverging from such upscale trends was the growth of Chinatown into the Lower East Side, thereby resurrecting the traditional immigrant quality of the neighborhood. The Lower East Side Tenement Museum charts the demographic and cultural changes of the neighborhood.

Moses Rischin, *The Promised City: New York's Jews, 1870–1914* (Cambridge, Mass.: Harvard University Press, 1962); Irving Howe, *World of Our Fathers: The Journey of the East European Jews to America and the Life They Found and Made* (New York: Harcourt Brace Jovanovich, 1975); Thomas Kessner, *The Golden Door: Italian and Jewish Immigrant Mobility in New York City, 1880–1915* (New York: Oxford University Press, 1977); Stanley Nadel, *Little Germany: Ethnicity, Religion, and Class in New York City, 1845–1880* (Urbana: University of Illinois Press, 1990)

Graham Hodges

Lower East Side Tenement Museum. Museum at 97 Orchard Street in Manhattan, founded in 1988 by Ruth J. Abram and Anita Jacobson. Situated in the heart of what was the most crowded neighborhood in the world about 1910, it represents the nation's first effort to preserve a tenement. The building itself dates to 1863, making it a rare example of a structure that predated virtually every housing law in the United States. The two lower stories were used for commercial purposes; each of the four upper stories was divided into four apartments of three rooms each. Even though the building itself occupied 68 feet (20.7 meters) of a lot that was 88 feet (26.8 meters) deep, the largest rooms in the apartments were only 12 by 11 feet (3.7 by 3.4 meters), and the bedrooms were 8 feet (2.4 meters) square. Thus each apartment totaled only about 325 square feet (30 square meters), within which as many as 15 people might have lived, some of them lodgers taken in to supplement family income. For more than four decades the building provided no running water, no flush toilets, and no electric lights, and most of its rooms lacked windows. Although the so-called dumbbell tenement law of 1879 required that every room have an opening to the outside, the law did not apply to existing buildings, and thus residents of 97 Orchard Street continued to live in primitive circumstances. About 1905 running water and flush toilets were finally installed as a result of the tenement law of 1901. The building was condemned as a residence in 1932, and the upper floors were sealed until 1988. In 1994 the tenement rooms were opened to the public, by which time the museum was scattered over three locations, featuring a gallery, a theater, an archive, and a full program of walking tours, plays, multimedia shows, and exhibitions. By 2008 the museum had expanded to an adjacent building.

See also Tenements.

Kenneth T. Jackson

Lower Manhattan Development Corporation [LMDC]. Joint city–state agency charged with coordinating the redevelopment of lower Manhattan after the terrorist attacks of 11 September 2001 (see September 11). The agency supported the creation of a master plan, helped fund the planned memorial and museum, provided funds to help residents and businesses that had suffered as a result of the attack, and supported the creation of infrastructure that would help rebuild the downtown area. Created in November 2001 by Governor George Pataki as a subsidiary of the Empire State Development Corporation, the Lower Manhattan Development Corporation (LMDC) was initially funded by $2 billion of Community Development Block Grants from the U.S. Department of Housing and Urban Development; Congress appropriated an additional $750 million to the agency for the repair of damaged utilities and $33 million for aid to firms that lost employees in the 9/11 attacks. John C. Whitehead, a former head of Goldman Sachs, was the agency's first chairman, presiding over a 16-member board appointed by Governor Pataki and Mayor Rudolph W. Giuliani.

The LMDC's primary responsibility was to oversee and allocate funds for the rebuilding of the 16-acre (6.5-hectare) World Trade Center (WTC) site in coordination with the Port Authority of New York and New Jersey, the site's owner, and the many federal, state, and city agencies involved in the rebuilding. In 2002 the LMDC solicited designs for the site in an open competition. In February 2003, of seven semifinalists, the LMDC chose to see designs from two firms—Rafael Viñoly's THINK and Studio Daniel Libeskind—and voted in favor of the THINK design. This selection was overruled by Governor Pataki in favor of Libeskind's plan, titled *Memory Foundations.* The Libeskind master plan called for a spiral of five office towers arranged in ascending height around a memorial on the footprints of the former twin towers, with one central tall building called the Freedom Tower. Silverstein Properties, which had obtained a 99-year lease on the building just months before the attack, chose architect David Childs of Skidmore, Owings and Merrill to redesign the building, which was renamed One World Trade Center. He brought in other architects to design his other three buildings, including the Richard Rogers Partnership, Maki and Associates, and Lord Norman Foster. The LMDC also held design competitions for the National September 11 Memorial and Museum and chose Michael Arad and Peter Walker's design, *Reflecting Absence.*

In addition to the WTC site, the LMDC allocated funds for development and renewal projects throughout the whole area south of Houston Street, which was most affected by the 9/11 attack and its aftermath. These outlays included $237 million in subsidies to downtown renters and condominium owners to encourage residents to return to lower Manhattan; $250 million to the WTC Memorial Foundation; $220 million toward waterfront improvements on both the East and Hudson rivers; and $38 million toward renovation of the Fulton Corridor Revitalization Program. In 2007 Governor Eliot Spitzer appointed Avi Schick (then president of the Empire State Development Corporation) as chairman of the LMDC and David Emil, former owner of the restaurant Windows on the World, as president.

By 2006 the LMDC had allocated the entirety of its $2.7 billion appropriation toward WTC rebuilding, business and residential support, park development, and cultural programs in lower Manhattan. Its final disbursement plan for the remaining $162 million of the Community Development Block Grants and an additional $9.5 million was approved by the Department of Housing and Urban Development in July 2007 and amended in January 2009.

Andrew A. Kryzak, Lisa Keller

Lower New York Bay. Principal waterway leading into New York Harbor, bounded by the curving arm of Sandy Hook, New Jersey, by Rockaway Point in Queens, by Coney Island and southwestern Brooklyn, by the eastern shore of Staten Island, and by Raritan Bay. The bay follows the preglacial route of the Hudson River. Several dredged channels lead into the harbor: the largest of these is Ambrose Channel, which has a depth of about 40 feet (12 meters), a width of 2000 feet (600 meters), and a length of 7 miles (11.5 kilometers) and extends as far north as the Narrows.

At the entrance to Lower New York Bay is Ambrose Light Station, operated by the National Data Buoy Center and anchored to the seafloor off Sandy Hook. The facility, which has been rebuilt several times, originally replaced the Ambrose Lightship, which served as the main navigational aid to the harbor entrance from 1823 to 1957, until a permanent Texas Tower was installed. The tower has been struck at least twice by passing ships, the most serious incident occurring in 1996 when it was rammed by a Greek oil tanker, causing such severe damage to the station that despite three years of repairs, the entire station had to be replaced and moved a short distance; it is now located approximately 7.5 miles (12 kilometers) off Sandy Hook. (It was later found that at the time of the collision the light had not been working.) The facility is now automated; its 60,000 candle-power light is visible for 18 miles (29 kilometers).

Gerard R. Wolfe

Loyalists. Loyalists, also called Tories, were American supporters of Great Britain during the War of Independence. In New York City Loyalists played a particularly important role. As early as the Stamp Act (1765), some inhabitants of the city began to distance themselves from the protest against the policies of the British Parliament. Disturbed by the violent tactics employed by New York City's Sons of Liberty, some more moderate New Yorkers had no desire to follow the Sons or their leader, Isaac Sears. When Parliament in 1767 created new taxes on Americans, the Townshend duties, the merchants of New York City knew what they had to do. In 1769 they took control of the committee created to enforce a boycott of British goods, elbowing the Sons of Liberty out of their former leadership of the protest movement in the city. When Parliament dropped all the Townshend taxes except that on tea, the New York merchants agreed in 1770 to resume importing British products (except for the still-taxed tea), causing fury among the Sons of Liberty. Their outrage was matched by that of the other colonists, who thought the actions of the New York City merchants bordered on betrayal. The city's reputation as an unpatriotic place had already been established.

Events moved rapidly. After Parliament passed the Tea Act (1773), New York City's merchants continued to steer a moderate course, while Massachusetts went in the opposite direction with the Boston Tea Party (1773). When Parliament punished Boston with the Intolerable Acts (1774), New York City's merchants called for what became known as the First Continental Congress (1774). Meanwhile, New York City's Tory newspaper publisher, James Rivington, continued to print the British side, creating still more suspicion about the city's allegiance. Furthermore, in January 1775 other Loyalists in Newtown and Jamaica, Queens County, publicly supported the British. However, the biggest shock to other Americans in January 1775 came when New York's colonial assembly, led by a member from the city, James DeLancey, repudiated both the Congress and the renewed trade boycott. The assembly was seen as a stronghold of Loyalism.

Although the battles of Lexington and Concord in April 1775 led to the collapse of New York's colonial government, Loyalism continued to surface in both Queens County and Staten Island. In November 1775 the people of Queens—encouraged by Tory lieutenant governor Cadwallader Colden and his son David, both of whom lived in Flushing—soundly rejected joining a rebel New York provincial congress. In retaliation, some Queens Tories were arrested. Staten Islanders also voted to ignore the rebel government, and gave in only after threats. Secretly some Staten Islanders did what sabotage they could.

Rivington also was silenced in November 1775 when Sears and some allies seized his printing press and took it out of the colony. At the same time Sears kidnapped the Reverend Samuel Seabury, a Loyalist writer of pamphlets, from his parish in southern Westchester, which is now the Bronx. Seabury, a minister of the Church of England (the Episcopal Church), had, with the other Episcopal clergy, preached allegiance to George III and encouraged their congregations in their loyalty. Most of the Tories in the Bronx, Queens, and Staten Island appear to have been worshipers in the Church of England. In contrast, mostly Dutch Kings County—today's Brooklyn—had few Loyalists.

The displays of Loyalist strength dismayed other Americans and hurt the city's reputation. New York City seemed even more Tory when the rebel government based in Manhattan acted less than heroic. A British warship, the *Asia,* had entered New York harbor in

May 1775. Frightened that the ship's powerful broadsides might devastate the city, New York's leaders permitted the ship to buy food supplies. Making the situation appear even more suspicious, New Yorkers continued to keep in touch with their Tory governor, William Tryon, currently in exile on a merchant ship in the harbor.

In this case the suspicions were justified. A former Tory servant of Tryon's, James Brattle, sent the governor excellent intelligence obtained while working for a leading patriot. Tryon also tried and failed to set up a Tory sanctuary on Bedloe's Island. Only in April 1776 did New York's leaders finally stop the flow of information to their old governor.

The presence of Loyalists in Manhattan and its environs should have been an important advantage to the British when they conquered the area in 1776. Although it has been estimated that only 6 percent of Manhattan was Loyalist, the outer boroughs had good numbers of Tories. In fact, a Queens Tory's geographic knowledge of the terrain helped the British army win the Battle of Long Island on 27 August 1776.

Nonetheless, the British squandered the potential advantages presented by New York City's Loyalists. When, on 2 July 1776, the redcoats landed in Staten Island, the Tories welcomed them until some of the soldiers started raping women. When the British army swept through the Bronx during October 1776 Loyalists had to endure as much pillaging as their neighbors. Tories in Manhattan and Queens soon learned how arbitrary and corrupt the British military occupation could be. The mayor of New York City, David Mathews, a leading Loyalist, was accused of embezzlement. James Rivington grew so disenchanted with the British occupation that he sent secret information to the rebels.

Because New York City stayed in British hands during the entire Revolution, it became a safe place for Loyalists who fled their homes elsewhere in the colonies. Because of the destruction of many buildings by two fires, in 1776 and 1778, housing was scarce. Loyalists had to endure crowding, dirty streets, and a crime wave. Nor did the rebels forget to punish New York City's Tories. Confiscation of Loyalist property occured after the British departed in 1783. Another New York law, the Trespass Act (1783), sought to punish Tories who had used the property of patriots and resulted in a host of lawsuits.

Some Loyalists, fearing for their safety, left with the British. Others stayed and took their chances. Within a few years, resentment against them lessened, and legal discrimination against Tories had mostly disappeared by the end of the 1780s.

Alexander C. Flick, *Loyalism in New York during the American Revolution* (New York: Columbia University Press, 1901); Bernard Mason, *The Road to Independence: The Revolutionary Movement in New York, 1773–1777* (Lexington: University of Kentucky Press, 1966); Philip Ranlet, *The New York Loyalists*, 2nd edn (Lanham, Md.: University Press of America, 2002)

Philip Ranlet

Loyola High School. Secondary school at 980 Park Avenue in Manhattan, between 83rd and 84th streets. Founded in 1900 as a Catholic boys' school by the Society of Jesus, it became coeducational in 1973. In the early twenty-first century the enrollment is about 200. Prominent figures who have attended the school include Mayor Robert F. Wagner, Jr., and Wellington Mara, owner of the New York Giants. Loyola is the only independent coeducational Jesuit high school in the city.

Gladys Chen

Lubavitchers. Members of one of the largest Hasidic sects in the world, Chabad-Lubavitch, headquartered in CROWN HEIGHTS, Brooklyn. The sect was founded by Shneur Zalman (1745–1812) in eastern Europe in the late eighteenth century and named for the Russian town where it was based for more than 100 years. Yosef Yitzchak Schneersohn (1880–1950), the sixth rebbe, or spiritual leader, fled Warsaw during World War II and settled in Crown Heights in 1940. After the Holocaust, many Lubavitchers emigrated from eastern Europe and joined the rebbe, who was succeeded by his son-in-law, Menachem Mendel Schneerson (1902–1994). Lubavitchers were devoted to the seventh rebbe, and some believed him to be the messiah. He built an infrastructure for proselytizing—Lubavitch couples move from Crown Heights to locations around the world to win new converts of nonobservant Jews—that is unique to Hasidic sects. Most Lubavitchers speak Yiddish; men dress in black suits and black hats and women wear wigs or cover their heads. Children are educated in private religious schools (yeshiva). The location at 770 Eastern Parkway serves as the sect's global headquarters in Crown Heights, which in the early twenty-first century was nearly 80 percent black (mostly West Indian), with Lubavitchers densely settled in blocks adjacent to 770 and around Kingston Avenue, their commercial thoroughfare.

Lubavitchers' presence in Crown Heights has not been without problems. In response to dramatic demographic changes occurring in the neighborhood during the 1960s, they formed a controversial civilian neighborhood patrol called the Maccabees, which black residents accused of being a vigilante group; it was replaced by another patrol called Shmira. Many non-Lubavitch Jews, such as the Bobov Hasidim, left Crown Heights, despite being asked by their rabbis to stay. To strengthen the Lubavitchers presence in the neighborhood, Chevra Machazikei Hashchuna (Coalition to Strengthen the Neighborhood) was formed during the 1970s and obtained millions of dollars in government funds for development. The tensions between Lubavitchers and West Indians culminated in the 1991 Crown Heights riots when a car in the rebbe's motorcade accidentally killed a boy, Gavin Cato; a group of black men killed a visiting Hasid, Yankel Rosenbaum, in retaliation. Much effort was made to reconcile the two sides, although there have been some violent incidents in the early twenty-first century. After the seventh rebbe's death in 1994, many in Crown Heights have maintained their belief that he is the messiah despite denials from Lubavitch officials, a disagreement that continues in the early twenty-first century.

Kate Lauber

Luce, (Ann) Clare Boothe (*b* New York City, 10 April 1903; *d* Washington, D.C., 9 Oct 1987). Playwright and public official. She attended schools in Garden City and Tarrytown, New York, and edited the magazines *Vogue* and *Vanity Fair* from 1930 to 1935; she also wrote newspaper columns and such plays as *The Women* (1936), *Kiss the Boys Goodbye* (1938), and *Margin for Error* (1939), which were well received on Broadway. She lived at River House (435 East 52nd Street) from 1935 until 1938, when she moved to the Waldorf-Astoria Towers at 100 East 50th Street. In 1942 she was elected as a Republican to the U.S. House of Representatives, representing Connecticut until 1947. After serving as ambassador to Italy from 1953 to 1957 she was a consultant on foreign affairs to the White House during the 1970s and 1980s. Luce was married to the magazine publisher Henry R. Luce.

Wilfrid Sheed, *Clare Boothe Luce* (New York: E. P. Dutton, 1982); Joseph Lyons, *Clare Boothe Luce* (New York: Chelsea House, 1989)

James E. Mooney

Luce, Henry R(obinson) (*b* Tengchow [now P'eng-lai], China, 3 April 1898; *d* Phoenix, 28 Feb 1967). Magazine publisher. He was the son of missionaries and attended Yale University. With the financial backing of the families of Yale classmates, he and Briton Hadden launched TIME in New York City in March 1923, the first successful news magazine. When Hadden died in 1929, Luce assumed control of Time, Inc., and the company launched FORTUNE, a business monthly, the next year. Luce's greatest publishing venture was *Life* magazine, as he believed a market existed for an inexpensive picture weekly. Despite production problems, *Life* debuted in November 1936 and was one of the country's most-read magazines during the 1940s and 1950s. Luce insisted that his magazines favor what he dubbed, in a 1941 *Life* essay, "The American Century." He wanted the United States to abandon its traditional isolationism in favor of world leadership and promoted U.S. support of the nationalist Chinese government against first the Japanese and then Communist revolutionary forces. Luce encouraged the creation of the weekly SPORTS ILLUSTRATED in 1954, also based in New York City. Luce himself, however, remained ambivalent about publishing in the city. He toyed with relocating Time, Inc., operations and, on retiring in 1964, moved to Phoenix.

James L. Baughman, *Henry R. Luce and the Rise of the American News Media* (Boston: Twayne, 1987; rev. edn Baltimore, Md.: Johns Hopkins University Press, 2001)

James L. Baughman

Lüchow's. German restaurant opened in 1882 at 110 East 14th Street at Irving Place. The building was constructed in 1840, when the neighborhood was still residential, but by the late nineteenth century it was at the southern edge of the thriving Gashouse District. The restaurant was almost adjacent to the Academy of Music and became especially popular among figures in the entertainment world. Jan Ignace Paderewski and Enrico Caruso were frequent patrons, and in 1914 Victor Herbert founded the American Society of Composers, Authors and Publishers in the restaurant. The songwriter Gus Kahn wrote "Yes, Sir, That's My Baby" in one of its rooms. The décor was reminiscent of a German beer hall, polka bands played constantly, and the waiters wore lederhosen year round. In June 1982 Lüchow's moved uptown to a site near Times Square. The change was not successful and the restaurant closed in 1984.

Kenneth T. Jackson

Luciano, Lucky [Charles; Ross, Charles; Lucania, Salvatore] (*b* Lercara Friddi, Sicily, 11 Nov 1896; *d* Naples, Italy, 26 Jan 1962). Gangster. He moved to New York City at the age of nine, living on First Avenue near 14th Street in Manhattan. During his teens he became a member of the Five Points Gang and became a bootlegger during Prohibition; after that he became involved in the prostitution business. He worked closely with gangsters Louis "Lepke" Buchalter and Arnold Rothstein. In 1936 he was found guilty of running a prostitution ring and sentenced to 30 to 50 years in Sing Sing Prison. He was deported in 1946 to Italy, where he resumed his criminal career. Luciano conformed to the popular image of an organized-crime leader: he favored custom-made shirts and sleek cars and bore facial scars from a beating he had received in the gang wars. He called the older generation of criminals "mustache Petes" and allied himself with younger, more energetic gangsters, such as Meyer Lansky and Bugsy Siegel. In the late 1920s he lived at the Barbizon–Plaza Hotel, 101 West 57th Street; under the alias Charles Ross he lived from 1933 to 1936 in suite 39D of the Waldorf–Astoria Towers at 100 East 50th Street. Although he never returned to New York City after he was deported, he is buried in St. John's Cemetery in Queens.

See also ORGANIZED CRIME.

Warren Sloat

Luckman, (Sidney) Sid (*b* Brooklyn, 21 Nov 1916; *d* Miami Beach, Fla., 5 July 1998). Football player. After graduating from Erasmus Hall High School in Brooklyn, he attended Columbia University (BA 1938) after meeting head coach Lou Little at Baker Field during a Columbia football game. Unlike many of the 40 colleges that recruited him, Columbia did not offer him a scholarship. Nonetheless, Luckman worked several odd jobs to afford his education and remain close to his family in Brooklyn. At Columbia he played left halfback from 1936 to 1938, running, passing, punting, and kicking extra points while calling signals on offense and playing safety on defense. He was an All-American quarterback and led the team to key upset wins over both Army and Yale during his senior year. After becoming the first overall pick of the National Football League (NFL) draft in 1939, Luckman went on to spend 12 seasons with the Chicago Bears and became the NFL's first successful "T-formation" quarterback. He led the Bears to championships in 1940, 1941, 1943, and 1946. In 1943 the Chicago Bears played the first game at the Polo Grounds against the New York Football Giants; to honor his homecoming, it was declared Sid Luckman Day. That same year, Luckman was named the league's most valuable player. After retiring from the Bears, he became a successful businessman; coached part time with the Bears; became the head coach of the U.S. Merchant Marine Academy in Kings Point, New York; and worked as a quarterback coach at Columbia. He was inducted into the College Football Hall of Fame in 1960 and the Pro Football Hall of Fame in 1965. In 1994 Erasmus Hall, his high school alma mater, named its football field in his honor.

Frank Dyer, Meghan Lalonde

Ludwig, Daniel K(eith) (*b* South Haven, Mich., 24 June 1897; *d* New York City, 27 Aug 1992). Industrialist. The nephew of four captains on the Great Lakes, he bought a small boat at the age of nine, which he repaired and then leased at a profit. After finishing the eighth grade he left school to sell shipping supplies and at age 19 borrowed $5000 to finance his first business, converting steamers into freight barges to transport molasses and wood. He became wealthy after starting a tanker business, which he expanded even during the Depression; his primary corporate enterprise, National Bulk Carriers, was based in New York City, and he eventually extended his investments into wood products, oil, gas, coal, minerals, real estate, and agriculture. Named one of the country's two wealthiest men in 1976, he lost much of his fortune in a development venture in the Brazilian jungle during the 1970s. Ludwig spent the last years of his life in Manhattan and was known for his strolls through midtown and his solitary lunches.

Amanda Aaron

Luhan [née Ganson]**, Mabel Dodge** (*b* Buffalo, N.Y., 26 Feb 1879; *d* Taos, N.M., 13 Aug 1962). Writer and patron. Born into a wealthy Buffalo family and widowed in her 20s, she met her second husband, Edwin Dodge, in Paris. They returned to New York City in 1912 but then separated. She entered the New York City social scene with gusto in 1913 when she helped produce the Armory Show, where she distributed Gertrude Stein's book *Portrait of Mabel Dodge at the Villa Curonia,* introducing Stein to U.S. audiences. Luhan created a vibrant salon in her apartment at 23 Fifth Avenue, where intellectuals and radicals such as Alfred Stieglitz, E. A. Robinson, Lincoln Steffens, Emma Goldman, Walter Lippmann, Max Eastman, and Margaret Sanger gathered for "Evenings"—discussions of socialism, anarchy, birth control, and art. Luhan created a dance school for Elizabeth Duncan (sister of Isadora) in suburban Croton, New York, but she did not maintain a presence in the city as she had during her "Evenings." After her marriage to Russian painter Maurice Sterne and brief residence at 23 North Washington Square, in 1917 Luhan followed Sterne to Taos, New Mexico. There she created a thriving artists' colony, attracting Georgia O'Keeffe, D. H. Lawrence, and Martha Graham, among others. After divorcing Sterne, in 1923 she married a Pueblo Indian, Antonio Luhan, and lived with him in Taos until her death. She detailed her life in a four-volume memoir, *Intimate Memories* (1933–37).

Kate Lauber

Luks, George (Benjamin) (*b* Williamsport, Pa., 13 Aug 1867; *d* New York City, 29 Oct 1933). Painter. He studied art in Pennsylvania and Europe before moving in 1896 to New York City, where he worked as a cartoonist for the *New York World.* Luks was part of THE EIGHT, a group of artists who held an influential exhibition at the Macbeth Galleries (450 Fifth Avenue) from 3 to 15 February 1908. The Eight, especially Luks, were famous for their realistic depictions of street scenes in turn-of-the-century, working-class New York City. One of his most famous paintings is *Hester Street* (1905).

Max Seppo

Lumet, Sidney (*b* Philadelphia, 15 June 1924). Theater, film, and television director. He made his acting debut at the age of four at the Yiddish Art Theatre. As a child he worked in radio, on Broadway, and eventually in films, and after World War II he directed Off-Broadway plays. The first motion picture he directed was *12 Angry Men* (1957), starring Henry Fonda. His film adaptations of Broadway plays include *The Fugitive Kind* (1959) and *Long Day's Journey into Night* (1962). In the following decades he shot nearly all his films in New York City: the gritty urban locales of *The Pawnbroker* (1965) and *The Group* (1966) helped to establish his reputation as an exponent of the realist tradition. Lumet's works *Serpico* (1974), *Dog Day Afternoon* (1975), *Network* (1976), and *Prince of the City* (1981) all focus on New York City. In 1990 he directed *Q&A*, also set and filmed in the city. Lumet continued to make films set in New York in the early twenty-first century and in 2005 received an Academy Award for lifetime achievement.

Frank R. Cunningham, *Sidney Lumet: Film and Literary Vision* (Lexington: University Press of Kentucky, 1991)

Charles Musser

Lundy's [Lundy Brothers Restaurant]. Seafood restaurant and clam bar in Sheepshead Bay, Brooklyn, at the intersection of Ocean and Emmons avenues. It was opened in 1920 by (Frederick William) Irving Lundy. From 1934 it occupied a huge, two-story stucco building in the Spanish mission style that seated up to 2400 and where 220 waiters served as many as 5000 meals a day. The ambience evoked a time when Sheepshead Bay was a major fishing area. Lundy's declined because of the failing health of its owner and eventually closed in 1977. It was reopened in 1995 at its original location, at one-third its original size; it closed again in January 2007. A branch of Lundy's located at 50th Street and Broadway in Manhattan opened in 2001 but was short-lived.

Stephen Weinstein

Lung Block. Nickname for a block in lower Manhattan on the Lower East Side that became known in the early twentieth century as a breeding ground for tuberculosis. The name stems from the unhealthy conditions that marked the area and was coined by journalist Ernest Poole. The Lung Block became an early flash point between civic reformers and advocates for the poor, as one side sought to demolish and rebuild the block and the other attacked the condescending nature of the reformers. In 1933 the block was demolished to make way for Knickerbocker Village, an apartment complex for low- and middle-income workers.

Nathan Morgante

Lunt, Alfred (David) (*b* Milwaukee, 19 Aug 1892; *d* Chicago, 3 Aug 1977). Actor. During a performance of *A Young Man's Fancy* in 1919 he met Lynn (Lillie Louise) Fontanne (1892–1983), whom he married in 1922. The two appeared together in New York City and London in 27 plays, including Ferenc Molnár's *The Guardsman* (1924); Noël Coward's *Design for Living* (1933), which they also produced; and Friedrich Dürrenmatt's *The Visit* (1958), in which they gave their last performance. The Old Globe Theatre was renamed the Lunt–Fontanne Theatre in 1958. The couple lived at 130 East 75th Street from 1936 to 1950.

Sara J. Steen

Lutèce. Restaurant opened on 16 February 1961 at 249 East 50th Street in a pair of connected brownstones by André Surmain, with André Soltner as its chef. At the time the most lavishly decorated and expensive restaurant in the city, it was named for Lutetia, the Roman name for Paris. Soltner and his wife, Simone Soltner, became the sole proprietors in 1972, redecorating the three small dining rooms and the trellised country garden room with a more subdued decor. Many who filled the restaurant at lunchtime were associated with the United Nations nearby. Lutèce was noted for serving what many considered the finest French food in New York City and for its unintimidating ambience; would-be patrons had to reserve their tables one month in advance. In 2004 the restaurant closed almost 43 years to the day after it opened.

Marjorie Harrison

Lutheran Medical Center. Voluntary nonprofit hospital in Sunset Park, Brooklyn, founded in 1883 as the Voluntary Relief Society for the Sick and Poor among Norwegians in New York and Brooklyn by a Norwegian Lutheran deaconess and nurse, Sister Elisabeth Fedde (1850–1921). In 1892 it was incorporated as the Norwegian Lutheran Deaconesses' Home and Hospital. Over the years the hospital acquired a reputation for activism in efforts to revitalize the community. It merged in 1956 with the Lutheran Hospital of Manhattan and took its current name. In 1969 the hospital acquired an abandoned factory of American Machine and Foundry, which by 1977 was converted into a modern hospital. The Sunset Park Family Health Center Network, an ambulatory care branch, became the largest federally funded community health center in the United States. In 1986 Lutheran Medical Center won the first award for excellence in community service of the American Hospital Association. In 1993 it became a teaching affiliate of the State University of New York Health Science Center at Brooklyn. In the early twenty-first century Lutheran Medical Center had more than 500 beds and served a large number of immigrants in the neighborhoods of Bay Ridge, Sunset Park, and Park Slope.

Chad Ludington

Lutherans. Lutherans were among the Dutch settlers in New Amsterdam. They formed a congregation in 1649 but were unable to obtain a pastor. A Lutheran minister, Johann

St. John's Evangelical Lutheran Church, New Lots, Brooklyn, ca *1890*

Ernst Gutwasser, moved to the colony in 1656; his presence drew protest from the Dutch Reformed Church, and the Dutch government forced him to leave in 1659. The Dutch West India Company nonetheless refused to ban the practice of Lutheranism in private homes, a policy retained by the English after 1664. A permanent minister, Bernardus Arensius, was installed in 1671 and served the colony for 20 years. In 1676 the small congregation built a wooden church at the southwest corner of Rector Street and Broadway. Thirty Dutch Lutheran families lived in the city in 1695. Dwindling finances forced them to sell part of their church property in 1696 to Trinity Episcopal Church. Arensius's death in 1691 created a vacancy that was not filled until Andrew Rudman was installed in 1702; he was replaced after one year by Justus Falckner, the first Lutheran ordained in America.

In 1702 the growing number of German Lutherans in the city joined Trinity Church (now known as the Old Cattle Shed), which they attended until the congregation built another church out of stone in its place in 1729. Falckner's death in 1723 was followed by another long gap between pastors, which ended when Michael Christian Knoll arrived from Hamburg in 1732. The years between 1708 and 1722 saw an influx of Palatinate Germans; they tolerated services in Dutch for many years but by 1742 were sufficiently numerous that they asked Knoll to perform occasional services in German. A refusal by the Dutch to offer half of all services in German prompted the Germans to break away in 1749. In 1750 they built their own church on Frankfort Street, which was named Christ Church but became known as the Old Swamp Church. The Lutheran leader Henry Melchior Mühlenberg moved to the city in 1751, reconciling factions within Trinity Church and providing an English translation of the Augsburg Confession. In 1760 the city's congregations joined the Evangelical Lutheran Ministerium of Pennsylvania and Adjacent States. English was increasingly used for services, and in November 1771 Dutch was used for the last time at Trinity Church.

Trinity was destroyed by fire in 1776, and during the American Revolution its Tory minister fled, as did the minister of Christ Church, Frederick Mühlenberg. St. Matthew's Church took over the edifice and congregation of Christ Church in 1777. After the war the two congregations joined under the minister John Christopher Kunze, who helped to reorganize the New York Ministerium in 1785 as an entity separate from the Pennsylvania Ministerium and published the first Lutheran hymnal and prayer book in the city. He brought the Dutch and the Germans together in 1784, by which time there were at least 1000 Lutherans in New York City, and also advanced the use of the English language in German services. Hartwick Theological Seminary opened in 1797. The English Lutheran Church in the City of New York was formed during the same year and built Zion Church on Pearl Street; in 1810 the congregation became Episcopalian. A German–English Lutheran church, St. Matthew's, was built on Walker Street in 1822 (moved in 1868 to a new building at Broome and Elizabeth streets), and St. James Church was built by an English-speaking congregation in 1826.

Conflicts over doctrine began in 1839, when 1000 German immigrants passed through New York City, spreading confessional, fundamentalist beliefs. These immigrants and others formed an evangelical branch of the Lutheran Church that became known as the Lutheran Church–Missouri Synod. Lutherans in the city influenced by their beliefs opened Trinity Church at Ninth Street and Avenue B in 1843, and by 1918 there were 51 Missouri Synod churches in the metropolitan area. Because of a continuing shortage of ministers the Lutheran Church grew slowly. One observer estimated that there were 200,000 Lutherans in the city in 1836. After 1840, 10 churches were built in Manhattan, seven in Brooklyn, and one each in Strattonport (St. John's Church, 1855) and Port Richmond (St. John's Church). In 1865 there were 24 churches, among them the churches of St. Mark (1847, 327 Sixth Street) and St. John (1855, 81 Christopher Street), St. John's Church (1849, at Graham Avenue and Ten Eyck Street in Williamsburg), and St. Peter's Church (1862, 54th Street and Lexington Avenue). The first Swedish Lutheran church, Gustavus Adolphus, was built on East 22nd Street in 1865.

Seeking a stronger emphasis on evangelicalism, the New York Ministerium split from the national Lutheran General Synod in 1867 and helped to organize the General Council; a group of its English-speaking members formed a less evangelical organization, the New York Synod, and returned to the General Synod. Lutheran congregations grew along with the number of German and Scandinavian immigrants. In 1900 there were 97 churches, 60 of them German and German–English and 19 Scandinavian. They included Advent Lutheran Church (1897, Broadway and 93rd Street), Immanuel Church (1886, 88th Street), the Finnish Church (1890, 752 44th Street in Brooklyn), Bethany Church (1896, 582 Teasdale Place in the Bronx), Salem Church (1893, Long Island City), and St. Paul's Church (1899, West New Brighton). The Central Association of Lutheran Young People's Associations of the City of New York (1888), known as the Luther League, flourished nationally during the first half of the twentieth century. Efforts were made at consolidation, but Lutherans in the city like those nationwide remained divided. The General Synod and the General Council merged in 1918 with the United Synod in the South to form the United Lutheran Church in America (ULCA), with headquarters at 39 East 35th Street. In 1920 more than 160 ministers of various synods in all five boroughs served 110,430 Lutherans, who made up the second-largest Protestant body in New York City. St. Luke's Church was erected on West 46th Street in 1924, and Trinity Church in Long Island City was dedicated in 1927.

In 1940, 11 synodical bodies oversaw 205 churches: among these bodies were the United Lutheran Synod of New York (part of the ULCA, with 104 churches), the American Lutheran Church (German and Norwegian, five churches), the Augustana Synod (Swedish, 17 churches), the Missouri Synod (54 churches), the Norwegian Lutheran Church (13 churches), and the Finnish Synod (two churches). The American Lutheran Church absorbed three other synods in 1960 and the ULCA joined with another three in 1962 to form the Lutheran Church in America, which was based at 231 Madison Avenue. Declining attendance during the 1970s and 1980s led many churches to expand their offerings. St. Peter's Church, rebuilt as part of the Citicorp Building, sponsored a jazz vespers series. At Central Park West and 65th Street, Holy Trinity Church (congregation formed 1868; building erected 1903) sponsored a shelter for the homeless, a program for the emotionally disabled, and a nationally known series of Bach vespers. Most of the synods merged to form the Evangelical Lutheran Church in America in 1988; among those remaining independent was the Missouri Synod. In the early twenty-first century there were 181 Lutheran congregations in New York City, concentrated in Brooklyn and Queens.

Samuel Geiss Trexler, *Crusaders of the Twentieth Century: A Lutheran Story in the Empire State* (New York: Macmillan, 1926)

Alana Erickson Coble

Lycée Français de New York. Private dual-language school for students in pre-nursery through 12th grade. It opened in 1935 at the French Institute at 22 East 60th Street under Count Charles de Ferry de Fontnouvelle, the French Consul General in New York. It was established as an American institution with a French curriculum and French as the main language of instruction. Accredited by the French Ministry of National Education and by the New York State Association of Independent Schools, the school prepares its students for higher education in either French or American educational institutions. It is located at 505 East 75th Street and in 2007 enrolled 1050 students.

Stephanie Miller

Lying-In Hospital. Maternity hospital opened in 1799 by the Society of the Lying-In Hospital to provide medical care for poor women. It moved in 1892 to the Midwifery Dispensary on Broome Street and in 1894 to a mansion owned by Hamilton Fish on Second Avenue and 17th Street. An extensive new hospital was built on the site in 1902. The Lying-In Hospital formed an affiliation with the New York Hospital in 1928. When the New York Hospital–Cornell Medical Center opened in 1932, it absorbed the hospital as its obstetrics and gynecology division.

Adele A. Lerner

Lyons, James J(oseph) (*b* New York City, 12 Feb 1890; *d* New York City, 7 Jan 1966). Borough president. A successful leather-goods and shoe salesman with little interest in politics, he was designated the Democratic candidate for borough president of the Bronx in 1933 by the party leader Edward J. Flynn. His nonpolitical past made him an attractive candidate at a time when Judge Samuel Seabury was conducting investigations into political corruption. After his election he became known as a witty promoter of the Bronx who often used clever phrases and stunts: he once planted a flag of the Bronx in Marble Hill to claim the neighborhood from Manhattan. Reelected six times before retiring in 1961, he served on the Board of Estimate for 28 years, longer than any member before him.

Chris McNickle

Lying-In Hospital

Lyons Law. Municipal law enacted in 1937, sponsored by James J. Lyons, borough president of the Bronx. It required municipal employees to have been residents of the city for three years at the time of their appointment and to maintain a residence within the city limits. Because of personnel shortages in the areas of public health and education, by the late 1950s various city and state exemptions were passed that freed more than half the city's employees from its provisions. The law had also come under increasing attack as an example of provincialism. The Lyons Law was repealed in 1962 during the administration of Mayor Robert F. Wagner.

Matthew Kachur

M

MAC. See Municipal Assistance Corporation [MAC].

MacArthur, Douglas (*b* Little Rock, Ark., 26 Jan 1880; *d* Washington, D.C., 5 April 1964). General. After leading the Allied forces in the Southwest Pacific during World War II and being relieved of command by President Harry S. Truman on 11 April 1951 for insubordination, he was welcomed in New York City with a ticker-tape parade on 21 April. An unsuccessful presidential candidate in 1952, he accepted a position on the board of Remington Rand and moved to a suite in the Waldorf Towers in Manhattan, where he spent the last years of his life, and where his widow, Jean MacArthur, remained until her death in 2000. After his death MacArthur lay in state at the Seventh Regiment Armory.

D. Clayton James, *The Years of MacArthur* (Boston: Houghton Mifflin, 1985)

Andrew Wiese

Macdonald, Dwight (*b* New York City, 24 Mar 1906; *d* New York City, 19 Dec 1982). Writer. He graduated from Phillips Exeter Academy in 1924 and received his BA from Yale University in 1928. The following year he became an associate editor at *Fortune Magazine,* resigned in 1936, and edited the *Partisan Review* from 1937 to 1943. He left to begin his own journal, *Politics,* a small radical publication, in 1944 and was its editor for the next five years. He also wrote for the *New Yorker* and *New York Review of Books*. In the mid-1970s he taught at John Jay College in Manhattan. He lived on the Upper West Side.

Michael Wreszin, *A Rebel in Defense of Tradition: The Life and Politics of Dwight Macdonald* (1994)

Jessica Montesano

MacDowell, Edward (Alexander) (*b* New York City, 18 Dec 1860; *d* New York City, 23 Jan 1908). Composer. Born at 220 Clinton Street, where he lived until about 1876, he studied in France and Germany and then returned to New York City in 1896 to become the first professor of music at Columbia University; during these years he lived near 96th Street and Central Park West. He was president of the Society of American Musicians and Composers from 1899 to 1900, and a conductor and composer for the Mendelssohn Glee Club at Barnard College. After leaving the faculty in 1904 because of differences with the president of Columbia, Nicholas Murray Butler, he remained in New York City to teach privately. An accident with a hansom cab at Broadway and 20th Street in 1904 brought about his mental and physical decline. In 1905 a number of friends and admirers formed the MacDowell Club, which attracted 400 members. MacDowell was the first American composer to achieve renown in Europe. In his symphonic poems, piano sonatas, and two piano concertos he forged a distinctive American style influenced by his European contemporaries Johannes Brahms and Franz Lizst but by no means derivative of them.

Margery M. Lowens, "The New York Years of Edward MacDowell" (Ph.D. dissertation, University of Michigan, 1971)

Barbara L. Tischler

Macfadden, Bernarr [McFadden, Bernard Adolphus] (*b* near Mill Spring, Mo., 16 Aug 1868; *d* Jersey City, N.J., 12 Oct 1955). Writer and publisher. Without benefit of formal schooling he moved to New York City in 1894 to work as a health crusader and publisher and in 1899 launched a popular monthly magazine called *Physical Culture.* In later years his publications included the first confession magazine in the United States, *True Story* (1919), which made him a millionaire, *True Detective Mysteries* (1924), *Liberty* (which he acquired in 1931), and a tabloid newspaper, the *New York Evening Graphic* (1924). He also wrote and published more than 150 books on diet, fitness, and sex and sponsored an encyclopedia of physical culture. Macfadden reveled in publicity: he gave lectures, promoted "health homes," denounced alcohol and tobacco, accused the American Medical Association of being a self-interested monopoly, and advocated fasting, natural healing, and exercise. His frankness about nudity and his exhibitions of healthy bodies affronted moral censors.

Robert Ernst, *Weakness Is a Crime: The Life of Bernarr Macfadden* (Syracuse, N.Y.: Syracuse University Press, 1991)

Robert Ernst

Machito [Grillo, Raúl Frank] (*b* Tampa, Fla., 16 Feb 1909; *d* London, 15 April 1984). Bandleader. Although born in Florida, he grew up in Cuba, where he learned to play the piano and percussion and sing. In 1937 he settled in Manhattan; there he worked as a singer with Xavier Cugat's band and in 1940 formed his own band, the Afro-Cubans, with his brother-in-law Mario Bauzá as its music director. The band performed at the Park Palace Ballroom in Harlem and made many recordings. After serving in the U.S. Army during 1943–45 he returned to New York City, where his band gave weekly performances at La Conga Club that were broadcast nationwide. His work during the 1940s with saxophonists Charlie Parker and Flip Phillips and trumpeter Dizzy Gillespie proved highly influential in the evolution of Latin jazz. In later years Machito lived in the Bronx; toured the United States, Latin America, and Europe; and played at the Casa Blanca in Manhattan.

Chad Ludington

Mackerelville. Nineteenth-century neighborhood on the Lower East Side of Manhattan, lying near Avenue A south of 14th Street. It was named for its many fish businesses and fish peddlers. The population was mostly Irish and poor, and the neighborhood had some gangs and its share of crime. In the 1880s European Jews moved in after new tenements were built; Irish residents moved out and Mackerelville soon disappeared.

James Bradley

Macmillan. Communications conglomerate. It traces its origins to a bookshop opened at 53 Bleecker Street in 1869 by the English bookseller George Edward Brett as an American division of the London publisher Macmillan. The firm began its own publishing operations in 1886 and was incorporated as P. F. Collier and Son in 1898. Under Brett's son George Platt Brett revenues rose from $50,000 in 1890 to more than $10 million in 1935, and by 1920 sales of elementary, high school, and college textbooks accounted for about half the firm's income. In 1923 the firm moved to 60 Fifth Avenue, near 12th Street. It remained the largest publisher in the country from the 1930s until World War II, when it was surpassed by Doubleday. In 1934 Collier merged with Crowell Publishers to form Crowell–Collier. It became a publicly held company in 1950 and gained independence from the British division in 1952, absorbing the Free Press of Glencoe, Illinois, in 1961. During the 1960s the firm bought such operations as the Berlitz Language Schools, Uniforms by Ostwald (a manufacturer of uniforms for marching bands), the Katharine Gibbs secretarial schools, and the Brentano chain of bookstores. Headquarters shifted to 866 Third Avenue in 1966. After the parent company shortened its name to Macmillan in 1973, the publishing subsidiary became the Macmillan Publishing Company. In April 1984 it took over Scribner Book Companies. Macmillan was bought by Robert Maxwell of Maxwell Communication Corporation of Great Britain for $2.6 billion in November 1988. It later became part of the conglomerate Viacom. Maxwell died in 1991 and during subsequent bankruptcy proceedings Macmillan was broken up. Macmillan Publishers Limited of Great Britain, acquired by Verlagsgruppe Georg von Holtzbrinck in 1995, maintains a presence in New York City operating as Macmillan US, a group of publishing houses including Farrar, Straus and Giroux; Henry Holt and Company; W. H. Freeman and Worth Publishers; Palgrave Macmillan; Bedford/St. Martin's; Picador; Roaring

Brook Press; St. Martin's Press; Tor Books; and Bedford Freeman and Worth Publishing Group.

Charles Morgan: *The House of Macmillan (1843–1943)* (New York: Macmillan, 1944)

See also BOOK PUBLISHING.

Allen J. Share

Macombs Dam. Built in 1813 by Robert Macomb to power a mill on the Harlem River near a site now occupied by Yankee Stadium. It blocked boats sailing the river, and in 1838 residents of the riverbank led by Lewis G. Morris chartered a coal barge and paid the crew to break through the dam with axes. When the owners of the dam sued for damages, the New York State Court of Appeals ruled that the federal government had jurisdiction over navigable waterways and that the state should not have permitted the dam to be built. A park at the Bronx landing bears the name of the dam, as does the drawbridge built near the site.

Lloyd Ultan

Macombs Dam Bridge. Swing drawbridge spanning the Harlem River between 155th Street at Seventh Avenue in Manhattan and Jerome Avenue at 161st Street in the Bronx. Completed in 1896 as the third bridge on the site, it is named for Robert Macomb, who built a dam there in 1813. The bridge has a span of 408 feet (125 meters) and rises 29.2 feet (8.9 meters). In Manhattan a long approach viaduct descends from Edgecombe Avenue to Seventh Avenue. The bridge is well known to baseball fans as a link from Manhattan to Yankee Stadium. It is operated by the New York City Department of Transportation (NYCDOT) and carries approximately 40,000 vehicles per day. Between 1999 and 2004 the NYCDOT undertook a $145 million renovation of the Macombs Dam Bridge: the structure was repaired and repainted; the draw mechanism and electrical systems were reconditioned; the connecting truss bridge from Jerome Avenue on the Bronx side and the viaduct from West 155th Street on the Manhattan side were reconstructed; and the roadway decks on the bridge and connecting ramps were replaced.

Andrew Sparberg

Macy, Josiah (*b* Nantucket, Mass., 28 Feb 1785; *d* Rye, N.Y., 15 May 1872). Merchant and banker. Born to a prominent whaling and shipping family in Nantucket, he worked in virtually every aspect of the maritime trade. He began his career as a common sailor before becoming a ship's master and later the owner of a shipping and commissions business. He moved to New York City in 1815 to take part in the transatlantic "triangle trade," which carried slaves, cash crops, and manufactured goods between West Africa, the plantations of the Caribbean and the southern United States, and the manufacturing centers of Europe and the northeastern United States. One of the leading commercial shippers of his time, Macy operated a packet service that served Liverpool, England, and Charleston, South Carolina; owned a fleet of whaling vessels; directed the Tradesman's Bank; and managed a trading house in Manhattan. In the 1860s his firm entered the petroleum business; its refinery was purchased by the Standard Oil Company in 1872.

David A. Balcom, Andrew Wiese

Macy's. See R. H. MACY.

Macy's Thanksgiving Day Parade. This lavish annual holiday event started in 1924 and is sponsored by Macy's department store. It marks the unofficial start to the Christmas season with the arrival of Santa Claus at the parade's end. The original route began at 145th Street and Convent Avenue in Harlem and continued downtown 5.5 miles (8.9 kilometers), ending in Herald Square at 34th Street. The first parade featured clowns, floats, and marching bands as well as 25 live animals borrowed from the Central Park Zoo. The now famous large balloons appeared in 1927 as Felix the Cat, a dragon, an elephant, and a toy soldier. For two years, 1928 and 1929, the balloons were released at the end of the route. They floated for several days before they ran out of helium, and individuals who found the balloons could return them to Macy's for a $100 prize. This practice stopped, however, because of safety concerns. The parade has been held annually except during World War II; between 1942 and 1944 festivities were suspended partly because of an increased need for helium and other materials used to make the large balloons. By the beginning of the twenty-first century the parade drew more than three million spectators along the 2.5-mile (4-kilometer) course, which begins at 77th Street and Central Park West on Manhattan's Upper West Side. More than 44 million people watch the national television broadcast annually.

Anne Epstein

Mad Bomber. Popular name of George P. Metesky (*b* 2 Nov 1903; *d* Waterbury, Conn., 23 May 1994), who between 1940 and 1956 planted 33 homemade bombs throughout New York City, of which 23 detonated before being found; six of these caused injuries to a total of 15 people. Some targets were attacked more than once: Grand Central Terminal (five times), Pennsylvania Station (three times), Radio City Music Hall (twice), and the Port Authority Bus Terminal (twice). Metesky was 54 years old when arrested at his home in Waterbury, Connecticut, on 18 January 1957. A former employee of Consolidated Edison, he was disgruntled about the rejection of a claim for workers' compensation that he had filed in 1934. He was traced through a series of letters about the claim that he wrote to the *New York Journal–American* from 1956. Metesky served 17 years in an asylum for the criminally insane and was released in December 1974.

Rohit T. Aggarwala

Madden, Owney [Owen Victor] (*b* Leeds, England, 18 Dec 1891; *d* Hot Springs, Ark., 24 Apr 1965). Gangster, bootlegger, and entrepreneur. After his father died his family immigrated to Hell's Kitchen, where as leader of the Irish gang the Gophers Madden took the nickname "The Killer" and in 1915 was sent to Sing Sing for manslaughter. After his early release in 1923 Madden ran liquor into New

Macombs Dam Bridge, ca *1900*

York City from England and the West Indies and operated an illegal brewery. He owned several nightclubs, most notably the Cotton Club at 142nd Street and Lenox Avenue, and invested in world champion prizefighters. When Charles Lindbergh's son was kidnapped, Madden and other gangsters offered to track the baby down. In 1932 he returned to Sing Sing for a year for violating parole; after his release he moved to Arkansas and invested in gambling operations.

Kate Lauber

Madison Avenue. Major avenue in Manhattan between 23rd Street and 138th Street. Its width is 70 feet (21.4 meters) south of 42nd Street and 80 feet (24.4 meters) north of 42nd Street. Construction during the 1840s was called for because few lots were still available on large avenues, and because of the wide distance between Park Avenue to the east and Fifth Avenue to the west. In the last half of the nineteenth century the avenue became a residential street for the upper middle class, and it had some commercial establishments by the turn of the twentieth century; these extended as far north as 59th Street in 1910–30 and included such exclusive hotels as the Biltmore, the Roosevelt, and the Ritz–Carlton, as well as fashionable men's shops. After World War II the avenue became identified with the advertising business, although only two major agencies ever had their offices there (Young and Rubicam; and Batten, Barton, Durstine and Osborn). In the first decade of the twenty-first century, Madison Avenue was lined with fashionable shops and residences between 59th and 96th streets.

Martin Mayer, *Madison Avenue, USA* (New York: Harper and Brothers, 1958)

John Tauranac

Madison Avenue Presbyterian Church. Church located on Madison Avenue at 73rd Street. Established on the Lower East Side in 1834, it was first known as "the church in the swamp." Four years later, members of this congregation joined with members of the old Seventh Presbyterian Church to form the 11th Presbyterian Church of the City of New York. The church became known for its strict enforcing of religious laws, even punishing members for failing to attend services. In 1864 the congregation moved uptown to 55th Street between Lexington and Third Avenues. There it became the Memorial Presbyterian Church before moving to Madison Avenue and 53rd Street where it became the Madison Avenue Presbyterian Church. The church moved in 1899 to where it stands today.

Anne Epstein

Madison Square. Neighborhood on the East Side of Manhattan, centered at a park occupying 6.8 acres (2.75 hectares) that is bounded to the north by 26th Street, to the east by Madison Avenue, to the south by 23rd Street, and to the west by Broadway and Fifth Avenue. It was once part of the Parade, a tract of about 240 acres (97 hectares) set aside in 1807 for an arsenal, a barracks, and a potter's field; the tract was pared to 90 acres (36 hectares) and renamed for President James Madison in 1814. The playing field of the Knickerbocker Base Ball Club once stood at 27th Street and Madison Avenue. Soon all that remained of the original tract was the square, which opened on 10 May 1847 and was from the 1850s to the 1870s the center of an aristocratic neighborhood of brownstones where Theodore Roosevelt and Edith Wharton were born. Across from the western edge of the park an obelisk was erected in 1857 over the grave of General William J. Worth, who fought in the Mexican War. The luxurious Fifth Avenue Hotel opened nearby in 1859. The intersection of Madison Avenue and 26th Street was occupied

Madison Square with Metropolitan Life Insurance Building (designed by Napoleon Le Brun), 1910

successively by a depot of the New York and Harlem Rail Road, Barnum's Hippodrome (1873), the first Madison Square Garden (1879), and the second Madison Square Garden (1890, designed by Stanford White). About the turn of the twentieth century the area became a commercial district for toy, china, and insurance companies; in recent years, some of these buildings have been converted to apartments. Madison Square is known for several architecturally distinguished buildings, among them the Metropolitan Life Insurance Company Building, with its art deco skyscraper and campanile; the New York Life Insurance Company Building, topped with a gilded pyramid; and the Flatiron Building (1902), erected on a triangular lot at Broadway and 23rd Street. The Appellate Division of the New York State Supreme Court on Madison Avenue is adorned with a collection of fine sculptures. The Madison Square Park Conservancy was formed in 2003 to restore and revitalize the park and support its programs and maintenance.

Marcus Benjamin, *A Historical Sketch of Madison Square* (New York: Meridian Britannia, 1894)

See also SPORTS.

Joyce Mendelsohn

Original site of Madison Square Garden

Madison Square Garden (designed by Stanford White), ca *1900*

Madison Square Garden. Name used for four major indoor sporting and entertainment facilities in New York City. The first was a grimy, drafty structure opened by William Vanderbilt on 31 May 1879 at 26th Street and Madison Avenue, on a site used since 1874 by the impresarios P. T. Barnum and Patrick S. Gilmore. Vanderbilt emphasized sports, and his most popular athletic attraction was the boxing champion John L. Sullivan. After he razed the building in 1889 because it was losing money, officials of the Horse Show Association replaced it with one designed in a Moorish style by Stanford White, erected at a cost of $3 million. The second-tallest building in the city, it had the largest auditorium in the United States (seating 8000), a theater, a concert hall, apartments, a roof cabaret, and the city's largest restaurant, topped by Augustus Saint-Gaudens's *Diana*. The facility was the site of the horse show, the Westminster Kennel Club shows, bicycle races, long-distance footraces, boxing matches, physical culture exhibitions, and political rallies. Despite its popularity, it lost money: with a mortgage of $2 million and $20,000 in monthly operating costs, its rentals seldom brought in more than $1500 a day, and many days it went unrented. The F&D Real Estate Company purchased the structure in 1911 for $3.5 million, but it went bankrupt in 1916 when the New York Life Insurance Company foreclosed on the property.

Business turned around in 1920 when the promoter Tex Rickard leased the building for $200,000 a year for 10 years. The newly legalized sport of boxing was the key to the renewed success of Madison Square Garden, bringing in $5 million in five years; but other attractions were also important, including circuses, track meets, six-day bicycle races, and rodeos. The facility was the site in 1924 of the Democratic National Convention, which lasted 17 days. In 1925 the building was razed to make way for the new headquarters of the New York Life Insurance Company. Rickard raised $6 million for a new arena at 50th Street and Eighth Avenue, which opened on 28 November 1925 and was immediately profitable. Earnings surpassed $1 million in 1927, and the building remained profitable to the end of 1931 despite the Great Depression. New attractions included professional hockey (the New York Rangers) and the Ice Show. From 1931 to 1933 the journalist Ned Irish staged an annual college basketball tripleheader for charity: the event was so successful that in 1934 he scheduled six doubleheaders between local and national teams. Irish made Madison

Square Garden a renowned venue for basketball, especially after it became the site of the National Invitational Tournament in 1938. Yet the main attraction was still boxing, and 32 championship fights were staged between 1925 and 1945. The single largest crowd (23,306) was for the welterweight championship fight between Henry Armstrong and Fritzie Zivic on 17 January 1941.

After World War II Madison Square Garden was filled almost daily with crowds attending familiar attractions like the circus (which alone had 77 shows a year) and new ones like professional basketball (the New York Knicks). But the college basketball scandals of 1951 were a major setback, ending the popular intercollegiate doubleheaders; and the boxing business declined in the late 1950s because of antitrust violations, the influence of organized crime, and overexposure on television. The building had poor sightlines and lacked modern amenities, and in 1968 it was replaced by a new, circular complex atop Pennsylvania Station, costing $116 million, that had an arena seating 20,344 and a smaller facility called the Felt Forum.

In 1977 Madison Square Garden was purchased for $60 million by the conglomerate Gulf and Western (later renamed Paramount). Top ticket prices rose sharply, from $8.50 in 1970, to $45 in 1990, and more than $300 in 2009. In 1992 the facility underwent a renovation costing $200 million, during which 98 box suites were constructed, each renting for as much as $190,000. Madison Square Garden has its own cable television network that broadcasts Rangers and Knicks games. The New York Liberty, a basketball team of the Women's National Basketball Association, also made the Garden its home. As of 2009 plans were in place to renovate and modernize the Garden once again.

Joseph Durso, *Madison Square Garden: 100 Years of History* (New York, 1979)

Benjamin Yakas, Steven A. Riess

Mad magazine. America's longest running humor magazine launched in 1952 by Harvey Kurtzman and William M. Gaines, who had published a satirical comic book called *Tales Calculated to Drive You Mad: Humor in a Jugular Vein.* Published by E. C. Publications at 485 Madison Avenue, it lampooned advertisements and popular culture. In 1954 *Mad* adopted as its mascot the fictitious character Alfred E. Neuman, a freckle-faced boy with a moronic grin whose only pronouncement was "What, me worry?" The magazine thrived by perfecting an anarchic brand of humor closely associated with New York City and aimed largely at preadolescent males. It became known for its irreverent comic strips, parodies of films and television programs, and especially its "fold-ins," seemingly innocuous illustrations on the inside back cover that depicted something different and usually derisive when folded. In addition to its regular, monthly issues *Mad* publishes six special issues a year, as well as a large number of paperback anthologies. Since the late 1950s the *Mad* label has been applied to a variety of other media including audio recordings, an Off-Broadway production of *The Mad Show* featuring uncredited assistance from Stephen Sondheim, board and computer games, and the popular *MADtv* television show. *Mad* magazine is operated by DC Comics, a subsidiary of Warner Brothers Entertainment.

Maria Reidelbach, *Completely Mad: A History of the Comic Book and Magazine* (Boston: Little, Brown, 1991)

Patricia A. Perito

Madoff, Bernard L. (*b* New York City, 29 April 1938). Wall Street money manager who confessed to a $50 billion Ponzi scheme that was the largest financial fraud in U.S. history. He grew up in the Laurelton neighborhood of Queens and graduated from Far Rockaway High School in 1956 and then Hofstra University in 1960. As owner of Bernard L. Madoff Investment Securities he became adept at developing new trading technologies and was so respected for his financial acumen that he served three one-year terms as chair of NASDAQ, the major electronic exchange in the United States. Ultimately, his list of clients for his investment firm included some of the nation's most successful families. He was convicted on various counts of financial fraud in 2009 and sentenced to 150 years in prison. Madoff lived in a penthouse apartment on East 64th Street at Lexington Avenue; it was later sold as part of his assets in order to settle some of the massive debt.

Mafia. See Organized crime.

magazines. The first magazines in New York City were published by James Parker during the 1750s. These were followed in 1787 by Noah Webster's *American Magazine,* which ceased after a year, and *New-York Magazine* (1790–97), which published theater reviews, poetry, and a monthly listing of local events. By the 1790s the city was a national center of commerce, culture, and publishing, and the number of magazines increased. Nearly all publications at the time were plagued by financial problems and a chronic scarcity of contributors and readers; many new ones appeared after postal regulations were changed in 1794 to allow magazines to be sent through the mail. A number of these sought a national audience, often imitating British journals and even copying their material. The first American medical journal, the *Medical Repository* (1797–1824), was published quarterly in the city. Other specialized magazines appeared during the first decades of the nineteenth century, many of them devoted to such varied topics as science, literature, art criticism, politics, satire, and fiction. Charles Brockden Brown's *Monthly Magazine and American Review* (1799–1800) printed fiction, poetry, and articles about literature, science, and politics. One of the city's first women's magazines, the *Lady's Weekly Miscellany,* was published from 1805 to 1808. A journal of satire, *Salmagundi* (1807–8), was offered by Washington Irving, his brother William Irving, and James Kirke Paulding; *Analectic* (1813–21) was edited for its first two years by Washington Irving and solicited pieces from Paulding. One of the city's first religious magazines, the *Methodist Review,* was introduced in 1818 and was soon followed by the *New York Observer* (1823) and the *Methodist Christian Advocate* (1826). The weekly *Ladies' Literary Cabinet* (1819–22) was edited by Samuel Woodworth. Short-lived but important journals included the *American Monthly and Critical Review* (1817–19), the *Literary and Scientific Repository* (1820–22), and the weekly magazine *New-York Mirror* (1823–57; from 1823 to 1840 edited by Samuel Woodworth and Nathaniel Parker Willis, and published by George Pope Morris), which supported the Knickerbocker literary group and reported news of the elite.

By 1825 more magazines were published in New York City than anywhere else in the country. Innovations in printing between 1825 and 1850, especially the development of the cylinder press, helped the magazine business to grow rapidly, as did the expansion of literacy. Magazines for a general audience became common. The *New-York Review and Atheneum Magazine* (1825–26) was edited by William Cullen Bryant and Robert C. Sands and drew contributions from Fitz-Greene Halleck and Nathaniel Willis. The first magazine aimed at the city's African American population, *Freedom's Journal,* began publication in 1827. The country's first general sports magazine, *Spirit of the Times* (1831–1902), was introduced in the city by William Porter. There were also a number of religious magazines, such as the *New York Evangelist* (1832) and the *Church Review* (1848). Under Lewis Gaylord Clark the literary magazine the *Knickerbocker* (1833–65) published such writers as Paulding, Bryant, Sands, Willis, and James Fenimore Cooper, many of them writing about life in Manhattan. The *Ladies' Companion* (1834–44) of William Snowden received contributions from Edgar Allan Poe and Henry Wadsworth Longfellow. Political journals also appeared: the *Democratic Review* (1837–59), which moved to the city in 1841, printed political and literary pieces, including stories by Poe and Nathaniel Hawthorne. The *Mirror of Liberty* (1838–41), a magazine for African Americans, was edited by the abolitionist and civil rights leader David Ruggles. The literary and satirical journal *Arcturus* (1840–42) was published by the critics Cornelius Mathews and Evert A. Duyckinck. New specialized periodicals included the *American Agriculturalist* (from 1842), *Scientific American* (from

1845), and *American Whig Review* (1845–52). The weekly publication *Broadway Journal* (1845–46) offered literary criticism, political commentary, poetry, and reviews of art, theater, and music; it attracted such writers as James Russell Lowell and Poe, who edited the last issues. The *Home Journal* (from 1846; edited by Morris and Willis) was the most sophisticated publication for the home; renamed *Town and Country* in 1901, it continued into the twenty-first century. The *Congregationalist Independent* was published from 1848 to 1928.

The mid-nineteenth century saw a marked change in the city's magazines. Book publishers, growing in number and influence, issued magazines of their own, and the books and magazines often shared material. Harper and Brothers introduced *Harper's New Monthly Magazine* in 1850, followed by *Harper's Weekly* (1857) and *Harper's Bazar* (1867). An important rival was *Putnam's Monthly,* a magazine of literature and political commentary begun in 1853 by the firm of G. P. Putnam; one of its most popular features was "The World of New York," introduced in 1856. During the 1850s Frank Leslie began publishing some of the first illustrated magazines and newspapers. These provided news about international, national, and local events, accompanied by vivid and timely illustrations. *Leslie's Weekly* was especially thorough in its coverage of Manhattan. It undertook such ambitious projects as investigating Mayor Fernando Wood's activities and the events of Election Day in 1858, and leading a successful campaign against unsanitary conditions in dairies. One of the first trade publications was the *Hardware Man's Newspaper and American Manufacturer's Circular* (from 1855), later renamed *Iron Age.*

The panic of 1857 caused a number of magazines to fail, including the *Democratic Review* and the *New York Mirror.* The scholarly publication *Anglo-African Magazine* (1859–60) was edited and published by Thomas Hamilton. During the Civil War the issues of slavery, states' rights, and the tariff dominated many magazines; some such as *Leslie's Weekly* and *Harper's Monthly* lost their southern readership. Other hardships included the rising cost of paper and ink and competition from newspapers, which provided more immediate coverage of the war. The *Nation,* a journal of political commentary, was begun in 1865. Among new trade publications were the *Telegrapher* (1864–77), issued weekly, and the *Publishers' and Stationers' Weekly Trade Circular* (from 1872), which later became *Publishers Weekly,* the leading publication of the book trade.

In the decades after the Civil War, production technology improved and magazine publishers sought wider audiences and adopted aggressive marketing techniques. Subscription prices fell, advertising increased, and circulation rose. Some of the first figures to adopt new practices were in New York City, such as Frank Munsey, S. S. McClure, and the publishers of the women's magazines *McCall's* and the *Delineator.* Publications devoted to woman suffrage and other feminist issues appeared during these years, notably the *Revolution* (1868–72), edited by Susan B. Anthony, Elizabeth Cady Stanton, and George Trainor, and the more radical magazine *Woodhull and Claflin's Weekly* (1870–76). *Appleton's Journal* (1869–81) was issued by the book publisher D. Appleton, as was *Scribner's Monthly* (later renamed the *Century*) by Charles Scribner in 1870. Scientific, technical, and trade journals of the time included *American Garden,* which began publication in 1871 in Brooklyn, and *Popular Science Monthly* (1872). After the war the most influential religious magazines were published elsewhere, but a few appeared in the city. Some of the best-known were Henry Ward Beecher's *Christian Union* (1870–93, later renamed the *Outlook*) and the *Brooklyn Magazine* (1884–89) of Edward Bok and Frederic Colver, which printed Beecher's sermons.

Magazine vendor, ca *1935–40*

As early as 1880 publishers in the city produced a quarter of the country's magazines and two-thirds of those with a circulation of more than 100,000. Cheaper delivery by mail was made possible after postal rates for second-class mailings were reduced in 1885. Most magazines begun about this time, such as *Munsey's, McClure's, Cosmopolitan,* and *Everybody's,* appealed to the middle class and emphasized national politics, the economy, and social issues rather than articles on travel, history, literature, and the arts. Many of the city's magazines covered both local and national news. New publications that reported and analyzed contemporary events included the *Literary Digest* (1890–1938) and the *Review of Reviews* (1891–1937). The center of women's magazine publishing moved to New York City from Philadelphia, and the number of women's magazines grew as women, especially those in the middle class, sought advice about their role in society. The *Delineator, McCall's,* and the *Pictorial Review* began publication during the late nineteenth century, followed by the *Woman's Home Companion* and *Good Housekeeping* in the early twentieth. Fashion magazines like *Harper's Bazar* and *Vogue* grew with the emerging fashion industry. The *Smart Set* (1890) chronicled news of the city's elite; under the editorial direction of George Jean Nathan and H. L. Mencken it published literary reviews, essays, and satirical pieces. Bernarr Macfadden built an empire based on magazines about health and sex, starting with *Physical Culture* in 1899.

Early in the twentieth century a number of magazines, most of them published in New York City, became known nationally for their investigative reporting, termed "muckraking" by President Theodore Roosevelt. Articles on the country's social and economic problems appeared in *Collier's, Everybody's, Leslie's Monthly, Cosmopolitan, Pearson's, Scribner's,* the *Delineator,* and *Broadway,* attracting public attention and more subscribers. Some of the most ambitious efforts were undertaken by *McClure's* in January 1903 when it published articles on Standard Oil by Ida Tarbell, on the United Mine Workers by Ray Stannard Baker, and on corruption in Minneapolis by Lincoln Steffens, prefaced with an editorial piece by McClure. The early decades of the century saw the introduction of the *Crisis* (1910), the publication of the National Association for the Advancement of Colored People, and of the radical journals *The Masses* (1911) and the *New Republic* (1914), which with the *Nation* offered sharper criticism of society than most other magazines did. Under Frank Crowninshield *Vanity Fair* (1913–36) reported on cultural affairs. Increasingly supported by advertising, magazines began to conduct market research and use advertising agents, leading to the establishment of the first advertising agencies in the city. In 1914 the Audit Bureau of Circulation was organized to meet advertisers' demands for verified circulation figures. Advertising became even more influential after World War I, determining the size, distribution, and even the content of magazines. Macfadden introduced the first confession magazine, *True Story,* in 1919; it appealed to a wide audience and with a number of successful imitations flourished during the 1920s and 1930s. Other "pulps" devoted to adventure, mystery, Western themes, and romance also became popular, many of them produced by the firm of Street and Smith; science fiction pulps were introduced in the late 1920s.

Economic and cultural change in the decades between the world wars radically altered the magazine market. Two of the most successful publications were intended to give readers information quickly and easily: *Reader's Digest* (1922), begun by Lila and DeWitt Wallace in a basement in Greenwich Village and soon moved to Westchester County, and the news magazine *Time* (1923) of Henry R. Luce and Briton Hadden. The *American Mer-*

cury (1924) was edited by Nathan and Mencken and consistently debunked the middle class. The *New Yorker* (1925), edited by Harold Ross, began as a humor magazine and eventually took on a literary emphasis. A number of business publications were introduced during these years: *Tide* (1927) for advertisers and *Fortune* (1930) for businesspeople, both published by Luce, and *Business Week* (1929), published by McGraw–Hill. These were among the first trade magazines to maintain editorial standards as high as those of consumer publications. The year 1933 marked the introduction of *Newsweek,* by Thomas Martyn and Samuel Williamson, and of *United States News* (later *U.S. News and World Report*). As the country's most important intellectual center, New York City supported the *Partisan Review* (formed 1934), a magazine devoted to works of the avant-garde as well as those by European writers. Many publications suffered during the first months of the Depression when advertisers reduced their spending, and some were forced out of business, among them *Scribner's,* the *Review of Reviews,* and the *Century.* Hearst's empire, which owned *Good Housekeeping* and *Cosmopolitan,* faltered and ceased publishing the *Pictorial Review-Delineator* in 1939 owing to insufficient advertising revenues. The industry suffered further during World War II because of shortages of paper and consumer goods.

After the war magazines were forced to compete with television for audiences and advertising. The competition proved fatal for *Look, Life,* the *Saturday Evening Post,* and all the magazines published by Crowell–Collier, including *Collier's,* the *Woman's Home Companion,* and the *American.* During the 1960s postal rates and paper prices rose and advertising revenues declined. Publishers raised subscription prices and emphasized to prospective advertisers that magazines had more of an effect than television because people read them at their leisure, and that unlike television they had a secondary, "pass-along" audience. Competition from television also accelerated a trend toward specialization. Some general-interest magazines were transformed for a narrower audience. One of the most successful examples of this trend was *Cosmopolitan,* which under the direction of Helen Gurley Brown from 1965 aimed at aspiring single women. From the 1960s women's magazines sought to adjust to the changes wrought by the feminist movement, which inspired the politically oriented magazine *Ms.* and eventually more traditional magazines such as *Working Woman, Self, Lear's,* and *Victoria.* The introduction of ink-jet printing, selective binding, and computers allowed publishers to customize magazines for different readers. As television became the primary provider of entertainment, many magazines abandoned fiction and focused exclusively on news and information. The market for business publications outstripped that for consumer magazines: *Money, Fortune, Forbes, Crain's New York Business,* and *New York City Business* provided detailed coverage of financial and corporate activity, much of it centered in New York City.

Many publications were absorbed during the 1970s and 1980s by media conglomerates like Time–Warner and Thomson and Maxwell and became increasingly national in their focus. At the same time some publishers introduced publications for segments of the population that had been largely ignored, especially Latin Americans and gays. *Vanity Fair,* revived by Condé Nast in 1983, achieved great success under the direction of Tina Brown, who later moved to the *New Yorker.* The most successful magazines published in the city since the 1980s were devoted to money, diet, fitness and health, child-rearing, travel, the home (*HG, Metropolitan Home, Architectural Digest*), fashion (*Vogue, Harper's Bazaar, Women's Wear Daily, Esquire, GQ*), sex (*Penthouse*), and the magazine business itself (*Magazine Age*). In the twenty-first century New York City remains the center of the magazine industry in the United States.

Theodore Peterson, *Magazines in the Twentieth Century* (Urbana: University of Illinois Press, 1956); John William Tebbel and Mary Ellen Zuckerman, *The Magazine in America, 1741–1990* (New York: Oxford University Press, 1991)

See also LITTLE MAGAZINES.

Mary Ellen Zuckerman

magdalen societies. Charitable organizations formed to help prostitutes and lead them to respectability. The New-York Magdalen Society, the first organization of its kind in the United States, was formed on 1 January 1830 by John R. McDowall, a missionary of the American Tract Society working in the Five Points. With several wealthy women he opened a "house of refuge" for prostitutes in 1831. The society's first annual report accused genteel New Yorkers of frequenting prostitutes and caused an uproar, leading the members to close the house of refuge. Undeterred, McDowall called for a moral crusade in his tract *Magdalen Facts* (1832) and began publishing *McDowall's Journal,* which inspired middle- and upper-class women to launch a number of reform societies in local churches. These groups merged in May 1834 and became the New York Female Moral Reform Society under the direction of Lydia Andrews Finney, the wife of the evangelist Charles Grandison Finney. A new house of refuge opened on West 25th Street but did not become active, perhaps because its sponsors were unrealistic. In 1836 the society shifted its focus to preventing prostitution and doing charity work. Renamed the New-York Magdalen Asylum, the house of refuge moved in 1850 to East 88th Street and in 1893 to a building on West 139th Street with room for 125 persons.

Several magdalen homes were organized in the mid-nineteenth century. The House of Mercy at Inwood-on-the-Hudson (1850) was an important one that moved successively to East 86th Street and in 1891 to larger quarters on 206th Street. The House of the Good Shepherd, established in 1857 by five nuns of the Order of Our Lady of the Good Shepherd of Angers, was the largest home in the city (with a capacity of 500) and admitted women regardless of creed. The Florence Crittenton Mission for Fallen Women, which occupied a building on Bleecker Street near the Bowery, was well known and sought to reclaim prostitutes with lodging and nightly Gospel meetings. In 1866 the Midnight Mission opened at 208 West 46th Street; in 1891 St. Joseph's Night Refuge was founded on West 14th Street by Friends of the Homeless, which was among the first agencies to assume that women were driven to prostitution by poverty rather than moral weakness. St. Joseph's provided beds and meals for 3500 homeless women a year. Magdalen homes reached the height of their influence during the late nineteenth century. In the following decades prostitution came to be seen as a criminal activity, and by the 1950s the remaining magdalen homes abandoned moral reform and concentrated instead on providing shelter for unwed mothers.

Alana Erickson Coble

Magnum Photos. Photographic cooperative established in 1947 in New York City and Paris and owned by photographer-members. It seeks to allow independent photographers to work outside the conventions of magazine journalism by cultivating an "idiosyncratic mix of reporter and artist." Magnum's staff does not direct but assists photographers, and copyright is assigned to the author of an image rather than to the newspaper or magazine in which it is published. The agency provides photos to museums and galleries as well as for advertising and television.

Max Kozloff and Magnum Photographers, *New Yorkers: As Seen by Magnum Photographers* (Brooklyn: PowerHouse Books, 2003)

Holly Cronin

Mahan, Alfred Thayer (*b* West Point, N.Y., 27 Sept 1840; *d* Quogue, N.Y., 1 Dec 1914). Naval officer and historian. He is best known for his 1890 book *The Influence of Seapower upon History, 1660–1783,* which is based on lectures he researched and wrote while living in New York City. His thesis that naval superiority is the key to national power prompted naval buildups at home and around the world.

Susan Kriete

Mahler, Gustav (*b* Bohemia, Czech Republic, 7 July 1860; *d* Vienna, 18 May 1911). Conductor and composer. In 1875 he began studying at the Vienna Conservatory; he wrote his first symphony in 1888. He moved to Manhattan in 1907 and the next year became the conductor of the Metropolitan Opera for three years. In 1909 he also conducted for the New York Philharmonic Orchestra. He completed his final symphony, the Ninth, in New York City.

Jessica Montesano

Maidenform. Firm of intimate-apparel manufacturers, formed in 1922 by the dressmakers Ida Rosenthal and William Rosenthal with Enid Bissett. It was based at 36 West 57th Street in Manhattan and during its first year introduced the Maiden Form Brassiere, the first uplift brassiere. In 1927 the firm was renamed the Maiden Form Brassiere Company and moved to 245 Fifth Avenue. During the next decade it became one of the largest intimate-apparel manufacturers in the world. Known for its astute marketing, it ran original and inventive advertising campaigns, among them one based on the slogan "I dreamed . . . in my Maidenform bra," which lasted from 1949 to 1969. The headquarters were moved to 90 Park Avenue in 1964 and at the end of the twentieth century to New Jersey.

James Bradley

Mailer, Norman (Kingsley) (*b* Long Branch, N.J., 31 Jan 1923; *d* New York City, 10 Nov 2007). Novelist and journalist. He grew up in Brooklyn, attended Harvard University, and was an infantryman in World War II. In 1948 he published *The Naked and the Dead,* widely regarded as one of the most compelling novels about the war. In 1955 Mailer, along with friends Daniel Wolf and Edwin Fancher, founded the newspaper the *Village Voice*. His columns there and in *Esquire* constituted a new style of writing known as New Journalism. A 1957 essay from *Dissent,* "The White Negro," examined isolated peoples and the quest for an authentic life and was considered provocative at the time. His notable works include *An American Dream* (1965), set in New York City, and *Miami and the Siege of Chicago* (1968), an analysis of the 1968 Democratic and Republican conventions. Mailer won Pulitzer Prizes for *The Executioner's Song* (1979) and *The Armies of the Night* (1968), a personal history of antiwar protests that also won the National Book Award and the Polk Award. He directed experimental films in addition to writing more than 40 works of fiction and nonfiction. In 1969 he ran for mayor of New York City on a platform that advocated the city's secession as the 51st state. Mailer was a lifelong devotee of boxing and lived most of his life in Brooklyn Heights.

Leslie Gourse

Mainbocher [Bocher, Main (Rousseau)] (*b* Chicago, 9 Oct 1891; *d* Munich, 27 Dec 1976). Fashion designer. He began his career in Paris as a fashion artist in haute couture. When he returned to the United States he worked as an editor at *Harper's Bazaar* for several years before opening his own couture house in 1930. The best known of his many dresses was worn by Wallis Simpson during her wedding to the Duke of Windsor in 1937. His gold lamé lumberjack jacket and aproned evening dresses reflected his ability to juxtapose down-to-earth designs and ornate materials. From 1940 to 1971 Mainbocher was known for having one of the most elegant and expensive couture houses in New York City.

Caroline Rennolds Milbank

Maine (USS). Ship and patriotic symbol, whose sinking on 15 February 1898 helped precipitate the Spanish–American War. It was built at the Brooklyn Navy Yard and exploded off Havana, Cuba, killing 260. Although the cause probably was a fire in the coal bunker, most Americans believed that a Spanish mine sank the ship. William Randolph Hearst proposed a memorial to the *Maine* at a point overlooking the Narrows; this idea evolved into the towering, gilded, allegory-rich USS *Maine* Monument unveiled in 1913 at the southwestern entrance to Central Park, overlooking Columbus Circle. Displaying the names of the deceased, the monument was designed and built by H. Van Buren Magonigle and Attilio Piccirilli, who also created the Fireman's Memorial in Riverside Park at 100th Street. For decades, memorial services for the *Maine* were held there or in the nearby 122nd Regiment Armory on West 62nd Street. Services were often led by Monsignor John P. Chidwick, the ship's Roman Catholic chaplain at the time of the sinking, later rector of St. Agnes Church on East 43rd Street and president of St. Joseph's Seminary at Dunwoodie, in Yonkers. The *Maine* is also commemorated by a plaque at the Theodore Roosevelt Birthplace National Historic Site at 28 East 20th Street. A less celebratory memorial is at Evergreens Cemetery in Brooklyn, where William Anthony, a marine on the *Maine,* is buried. After the explosion Anthony, rather than jump ship to save himself, sought out Captain Charles D. Sigsbee to make his report "that the ship has been blown up and is sinking." Anthony enjoyed brief fame as a national hero but ended up living on the streets and committed suicide in Central Park in November 1899.

John Rousmaniere

Malamud, Bernard (*b* Brooklyn, 26 April 1914; *d* New York City, 18 March 1986). Novelist and short-story writer. The son of Russian immigrants who operated a small grocery store in Brooklyn, he grew up speaking both English and Yiddish. He attended Erasmus Hall High School and graduated from City College of New York in 1936. After college he wrote fiction in his spare time. His short stories were published in a number of magazines, including the *New Yorker, Harper's,* and the *Atlantic,* and he also contributed articles to the *New York Times*. During the 1950s and 1960s he became one of the leading figures in Jewish American letters through his novels *The Natural* (1952), *The Assistant* (1957), and *The Fixer* (1966, National Book Award and Pulitzer Prize) and the collection of short stories *The Magic Barrel* (1958, National Book Award), often drawing inspiration from his life in New York City. In addition to working as a writer Malamud taught at Erasmus Hall (1940–48), Harlem High School (1948–49), Oregon State College (1949–61), and Bennington College in Vermont (from 1961 until the end of his life).

Jeffrey Helterman, *Understanding Bernard Malamud* (Columbia: University of South Carolina Press, 1985); Harold Bloom, ed., *Bernard Malamud* (New York: Chelsea House, 1986); Edward A. Abramson, *Bernard Malamud Revisited* (New York: Twayne, 1993)

Allen J. Share

Malba. Neighborhood in north central Queens, bounded to the north by the East River (Powell's Cove), to the east by the Whitestone Expressway, to the south by 15th Avenue, and to the west by 138th Street. Its name is derived from the first letters of the surnames of the five founders, all residents of New Haven, Connecticut: George A. Maycock, Samuel R. Avis, George W. Lewis, Nobel P. Bishop, and David R. Alling. The land was acquired in 1883 by William Ziegler, president of the Royal Baking Powder Company; a subsidiary, the Realty Trust Company, developed 163 acres (66 hectares) in 1908 for boaters and anglers, and in the same year railroad service was extended. There were 13 houses by the time of World War I, and more than 100 were built in the 1920s. The railroad station closed in 1932. In 2009 Malba's 400 houses ranged in value from just under $1 million to nearly $5 million, with many purchased as tear-downs. The Malba Association attended to the interests of the homeowners, but they had not prevented the loss of many original houses to demolition and replacement by much larger homes.

Vincent Seyfried, Jeffrey A. Kroessler

Malbone Street wreck. Subway accident on 1 November 1918, the first day of a strike by workers of the Brooklyn Rapid Transit Company that led to the temporary employment of untrained dispatchers. During the evening rush, a train bound for Brooklyn on what is now the Franklin Avenue shuttle line jumped the track as it approached the Malbone Street station (now the Prospect Park station). Before crashing, the train reached a speed of more than 30 miles (48 kilometers) an hour on a downgrade ending in several curves where the speed limit was 6 miles (10 kilometers) an hour. The crash resulted in at least 93 deaths, although a conclusive casualty toll was never reached.

Brian Cudahy, *The Malbone Street Wreck* (New York: Fordham University Press, 1999)

George A. Thompson, Jr.

Malcolm [Melkonyan], **M(elkon) Vartan** (*b* Sivas, Turkey, 12 Sept 1883; *d* Sawyer's Island, Maine, 21 June 1967). Lawyer and activist. In 1895 he fled Sivas because of the massacre of the Armenians by the Turkish. He graduated from the University of Massachusetts in 1907, earned a law degree from Harvard University in 1910, and opened law offices at 32 Liberty Street in New York City in 1912, becoming a prominent business lawyer and a champion of the rights of immigrants, especially Armenian refugees. His work *The Armenians in America* (1919) helped to shape a consciousness of Armenian American history. With the anthropologist Franz Boas of Columbia University he was an expert witness in the case *United States v. Cartozian* (1925), in which some Asian immigrants were recognized as "free white persons" entitled to naturalization in the United States.

Harold Takooshian

Malcolm X [Shabazz, el-Hajj Malik el-; Little, Malcolm] (*b* Omaha, Neb., 19 May 1925; *d* New York City, 21 Feb 1965). Religious and political leader. One of seven children born to Earl and Louise Little, both disciples of Marcus Garvey, he was raised in Lansing, Michigan; moved to Boston to live with his half-sister Ella; and later moved to New York City. Malcolm spent substantial time in Harlem working for the New Haven Railroad and participating in petty crime between 1941 and 1943 before moving back to Boston where he was arrested in 1946 for larceny. Influenced by his siblings as well as personal writings from Elijah Muhammad, Malcolm converted to the Nation of Islam when paroled in 1952 and, as is customary within the religion, assumed the last name X to represent his lost original name. He became a leading figure within the sect, helping to establish more than 60 mosques across the country, most notably the important Mosque 7 in Harlem. He also initiated the periodical *Muhammad Speaks,* which began publishing in 1961. Malcolm X's ascendancy to the local Harlem spotlight was solidified in 1957 with the police beating of Johnson X Hinton, who received medical care only after Malcolm X organized a phalanx of men from Mosque 7 to surround the 28th Precinct Station House on West 123rd Street, demanding Hinton's release. As both temple minister at Mosque 7 and the national spokesman for the Nation of Islam, Malcolm X became a media figure, preaching the group's rhetoric of racial separatism, economic pragmatism, and political disengagement. However, following the growing incompatibility between the beliefs of Elijah Muhammad and Malcolm X, as well as internal strife within the Nation of Islam, Malcolm X was "silenced" by Muhammad in December 1963 for describing the assassination of President John F. Kennedy as a case of the "chickens coming home to roost."

Malcolm X broke with the group on 8 March 1964 and formed a new one, Muslim Mosque Incorporated, whose office was located in suite 128 of the Hotel Theresa. In June 1964 he formed the more middle-class political extension, the Organization of Afro-American Unity (OAAU); its offices were also at the Theresa, and the group held weekly meetings at the Audubon Ballroom on 166th Street and Broadway. Malcolm X, who had lived at 23-11 97th Street in East Elmhurst since establishing Mosque 7 in the early 1950s, was in the midst of an eviction battle with the Nation of Islam, who owned the property, when his house was firebombed early on the morning of 14 February 1965. While awaiting a court appeal and the repair of the house, Malcolm X and his family moved in with friends in Queens. He delivered his final public speech at Barnard College on the afternoon of 18 February to 1500 students and faculty of Barnard and Columbia University before being assassinated in the early afternoon of 21 February addressing an OAAU rally at the Audubon Ballroom. He left his wife, Betty Shabazz, and six daughters. *The Autobiography of Malcolm X* was coauthored with Alex Haley and published posthumously in November of that year.

Garrett A. Felber

Maltese. Emigrants from the Maltese islands began to settle in New York City during the early twentieth century, with the largest concentrations in Astoria. In the mid-1990s the number of Maltese in Queens was unknown; the number in New York State was estimated at 33,000. In 2010 more than 3500 people claimed Maltese ancestry in the city.

Antonia S. Mattheou

Mamma Leone's. Restaurant in Manhattan, opened as Leone's on 26 April 1906 on Broadway at 39th Street (near the Metropolitan Opera) by Luisa Leone (1873–1944), the wife of a wine merchant named Gerolamo Leone. The tenor Enrico Caruso was the first of many prominent customers. The restaurant moved shortly after World War I to 239 West 48th Street and in 1988 to 261 West 44th Street. After the death of Luisa Leone her sons Gene and Celestine gave the restaurant its familiar name. In 1959 Gene Leone sold it to Restaurant Associates. Mamma Leone's became the best-known Italian restaurant in New York City, although perhaps frequented more by tourists than by residents. In 1994 it closed.

Mary Elizabeth Brown

Mandel, Henry (*b* Russia, 1884; *d* New York City, 10 Oct 1942). Real estate developer. During the 1920s he erected office buildings, apartment buildings, and hotels throughout New York City, including the Pershing Square Building near Grand Central Terminal (1923, 27 stories), the Hearst Building at Columbus Circle, and the Brittany, Lombardy, and Tuscany hotels in Manhattan. In 1929 he razed tenements on a large site in Chelsea to build London Terrace, 14 buildings of 20 stories each containing 2000 apartments for middle-class workers. Mandel also built the luxurious Parc Vendome complex of 600 apartments on West 57th Street, completed in 1931.

Marc A. Weiss

Mandolin Brothers. Musical instrument store located at 629 Forest Avenue on Staten Island, specializing in vintage stringed instruments including mandolins, guitars, and ukuleles. It opened in 1971 and was immortalized in Joni Mitchell's "Song for Sharon," which begins "I went to Staten Island, Sharon / To buy myself a mandolin." Mitchell was not the only well-known client. George Harrison, Paul Simon, Paul McCartney, Bob Dylan, and Béla Fleck have all purchased various instruments from the store.

Anne Epstein

Manes, Donald R. (*b* Brooklyn, 18 Jan 1934; *d* Queens, 13 March 1986). Borough president. He began his career in 1957 as an assistant district attorney of Queens, an aide in the state legislature, and a city councilman (1965). Elected borough president of Queens in 1971, he worked to encourage economic development, decentralize city offices, and expand educational, athletic, and cultural facilities. In 1974 he sought the Democratic gubernatorial nomination, and in the same year he became chairman of the Democratic Party in Queens, a position that prepared him to serve as President Jimmy Carter's campaign chairman in New York City (1980). Two days after he was sworn in for his fourth term as borough president in 1986, his career collapsed when he attempted suicide. In the following weeks it was revealed that he stood to be indicted by federal and city prosecutors for having accepted bribes since 1979 from vendors seeking contracts with the Parking Violations Bureau. Manes resigned from office and took his own life a few weeks later. The scandal dominated the last years of the administration of Mayor Edward I. Koch and led to a law prohibiting government officials from holding party office.

Jack Newfield and Wayne Barrett, *City for Sale: Ed Koch and the Betrayal of New York* (New York: Harper and Row, 1988)

Nora L. Mandel

Mangin, Joseph François (*b* Châlons-sur-Marne [now Châlons-en-Champagne], France, 17 Dec 1764; *d* after 1818). Engineer and architect; co-designer of City Hall. He arrived in New York City (1794) after fleeing a slave rebellion in Santo Domingo (Haiti), where he had been mapping as a French army engineer. In 1795 Mangin was named engineer-in-chief of New York City's port and harbor fortifications and was appointed one of several city surveyors, effectively licensing him to conduct public and private surveys. In 1797 the city contracted with Mangin and Casimir Goerck (who soon died) to make the first official post-Revolution map of the city. After extensive surveys, Mangin produced the map in 1803, declaring that it "is not the plan of the City such as it is, but such as it is to be." The map, which idealized existing streets and projected new ones beyond the city limits, was rejected; nevertheless, Mangin's unwelcome but novel city planning led to the appointment (1807) of the state commission that devised Manhattan's eventual street grid.

Mangin was the lead designer of City Hall, a competition he entered and won with John McComb (1802). For reasons that are unclear (possibly involving the contemporaneous rejection of Mangin's city map), McComb alone was named architect for the construction (1803–12). This led to discrediting in succeeding generations of Mangin's role in the City Hall design, compounded by the erasure of Mangin's name from the original drawings by a McComb descendant in the 1890s. In 2003 Mangin was officially recognized as principally responsible for the French Renaissance design, a style unknown to McComb.

Mangin's other architectural credits include the Park Theatre, New York's first original-use playhouse (1795–98; destroyed by fire 1848); Newgate Prison, the state's first penitentiary, on the Hudson River at the foot of Christopher Street (1796–97; closed 1829, later demolished); the Manhattan Company reservoir, on Chambers Street (1800; demolished 1853); the second First Presbyterian Church, on Wall Street (1810; dismantled and removed to Jersey City 1844); and the first St. Patrick's Cathedral on Mulberry Street, the city's first Gothic Revival building (1809–15). Little is known of Mangin's life after 1818.

Gerard Koeppel

Manhattan. The smallest in area of the five boroughs making up New York City. It consists principally of the island of Manhattan, which extends about 13 miles (21 kilometers) from north to south and about 2 miles (3 kilometers) from east to west, surrounded by the Harlem River to the northeast and north, the East River to the east, Upper New York Bay to the south, and the Hudson River to the west. The borough of Manhattan is coextensive with New York County. In addition to the island of Manhattan it includes several smaller islands (among them Governors Island, Randalls Island, Wards Island, Roosevelt Island, and U Thant Island) and the neighborhood of Marble Hill, which is geographically part of the Bronx. Manhattan occupies about 22.6 square miles (58.5 square kilometers), or 7.1 percent of the entire city. It is the site of virtually all of the hundreds of skyscrapers that are the symbol of the metropolis, and it is also the oldest, densest, and most built-up part of the urbanized region. The population of Manhattan is ethnically, religiously, economically, and racially diverse. It grew from 33,000 in 1790 to 2.33 million in 1910, and then began a slow decline. A low point of 1.43 million was reached in 1980, after which the population again began to increase. By 2000 the number of its inhabitants was 1.54 million.

Uncertainty surrounds the origin of the name, which has been variously traced to the Munsee words *manahactanienk* ("place of general inebriation"), *manahatouh* ("place where timber is procured for bows and arrows"), and *menatay* ("island"). It is in any event the earliest known Munsee place name, appearing in 1610 as Manahatta on a map prepared by a Spanish spy in the English court where Henry Hudson was detained before his return to the Netherlands.

Manhattan was the second part of New York City (after Governors Island in 1624) to be settled by Europeans when the Dutch West India Company established a permanent outpost on the southeastern tip of the island in 1625. There they built Fort Amsterdam to defend the community, and from there the population slowly moved north. New Amsterdam fell to the British in 1664, who renamed

Financial district, lower Manhattan, with Hudson River and New Jersey in background, 2009

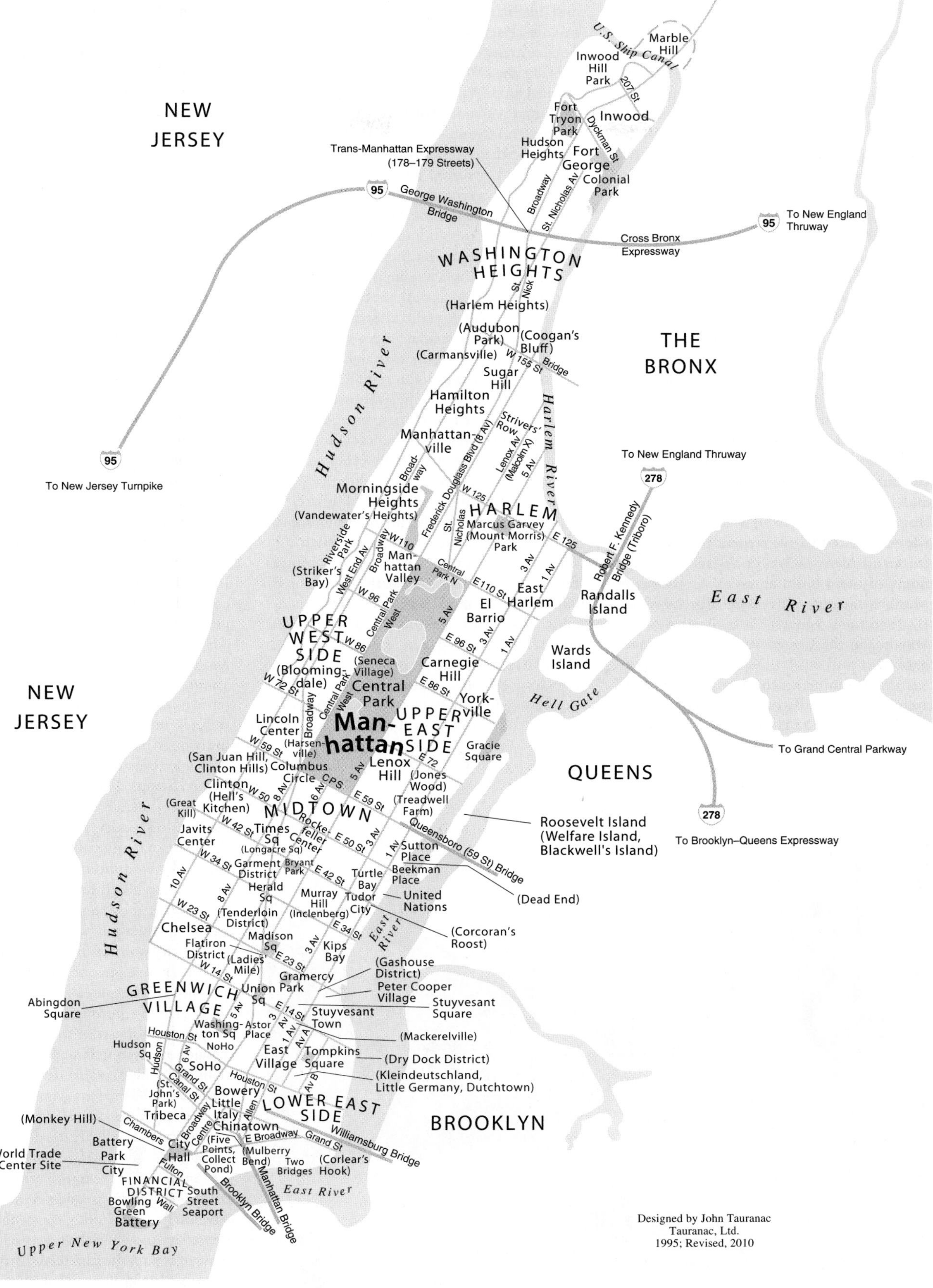

Designed by John Tauranac
Tauranac, Ltd.
1995; Revised, 2010

the settlement New York. Even though most of the island was well north of the area that the settlers occupied, from that time the city and the island of Manhattan were essentially the same until New York City in 1874 began annexing parts of what is now the Bronx.

Manhattan experienced significant population growth, economic growth, and political maturation during the first half of the nineteenth century, as New York City grew to be the nation's largest city and a center of U.S. commerce. The first waves of immigration to the city brought people from Ireland and Germany to Manhattan. During the Civil War merchants initially sought to make Manhattan a free city, independent of both North and South, so that it could continue its role as a commercial and manufacturing center. After a controversial draft for the Union army in 1863 that seemed especially to target the Irish, riots ravaged the island for four days and more than 100 people were killed (see DRAFT RIOTS). After the Civil War, the economy of the city surged. As it became an entrepreneurial and business capital, ambitious individuals from other countries and states—such as J. P. Morgan, John D. Rockefeller, Andrew Carnegie, and Henry Clay Frick—moved there, many of them building great MANSIONS on Manhattan, especially along Fifth Avenue. By 1900 approximately half of all the millionaires in the United States lived in Manhattan.

In the late nineteenth century Manhattan architecture was distinctive for its mansions for the very rich, its TENEMENTS for the poor, and its luxurious APARTMENTS for upper middle-class families. Some of the city's most notable architectural achievements are buildings like the Dakota or Ansonia, both located on the Upper West Side. Into the twenty-first century, the majority of Manhattan residents continue to live in multifamily dwellings.

Most of the streets of lower Manhattan are narrow and twisting, reflecting their having followed Indian paths or random trails. Everything north of Houston Street, however, became marked by a grid pattern after the state legislature passed an act in 1807 providing for the appointment of three commissioners to lay out the city's streets and avenues. The result was the GRID PLAN of 1811 (also known as the Commissioners' Plan), which imposed a kind of waffle-iron system on Manhattan that changed it irrevocably. The straight, right-angled street plan simplified surveying, minimized legal disputes over lot boundaries, maximized the number of lots fronting each thoroughfare, and stamped New York City with a standard plot of 25 by 100 feet (8 by 30 meters).

The physical organization of Manhattan is relatively simple. Twelve major avenues, each 100 feet (30 meters) wide, run north and south: the longest is 10th Avenue, reaching as far north as Fort George at the tip of the island, and the most elusive is 12th Avenue, which does not begin until 23rd Street. Four short avenues (A, B, C, and D) exist only on the Lower East Side. Because at the time of the Commissioners' Plan two diagonal thoroughfares, Broadway and the Bowery Road, were already in place and heavily used, they were left unchanged and their junction at 14th Street was set aside for Union Square. Intersecting the avenues at right angles and running east and west between the East River and the Hudson River are 220 consecutively numbered streets, most of them 60 feet (18 meters) wide. The exceptions are the streets that intersect Broadway as it crosses one of the avenues: 14th, 23rd, 34th, 42nd, 57th, 72nd, 86th, 96th, 106th, 125th, and 145th streets. These streets are 100 feet (30 meters) wide and are also the site of subway stations.

A notable feature of the Manhattan landscape is CENTRAL PARK, 843 acres (340 hectares) spanning the middle of the island framed by the Upper East Side, the Upper West Side, 59th Street to the south, and 110th Street to the north. The park is a masterpiece of American landscape architecture, designed by Frederick Law Olmsted and Calvert Vaux. Four "transverse roads" make it possible to cross the park by car or bus. Throughout its history, Manhattan has experienced a gradual evolution of public transportation from horse-drawn streetcars, to trolleys, to elevated trains. Many of these changes were contingent on the political climate of the day more than on pure economic interests or technological advances. In the twenty-first century Manhattan has a complex subway and bus system that is the most extensive and heavily used in the country.

Differences between Manhattan and the rest of New York City have sometimes been a source of friction. Manhattan is politically more liberal than the city's other boroughs as well as more affluent (in 2000 the median individual income was more than $70,000, the highest of any of the 3000 counties in the United States). Manhattan has also exerted a disproportionately large political influence in relation to the city as a whole and has been the home of many political leaders, including Alexander Hamilton, Theodore Roosevelt, Al Smith, Fiorello H. La Guardia, and William "Boss" Tweed of Tammany Hall. TAMMANY HALL was practically synonymous with powerful big-city political machines for more than a century and operated only in Manhattan and not in the outer boroughs. Despite its small size the borough is also the business and financial heart of the country, as well as a major international media and communications hub. The *New York Times* and *Wall Street Journal,* published in Manhattan, are read around the world, and all the major television networks have their headquarters in the borough.

Manhattan is the home of most of the institutions, buildings, and neighborhoods that have made New York City famous. The first university in Manhattan was King's College in what is now the financial district, founded in 1754. The college eventually changed its name to Columbia University and moved its campus to Morningside Heights. Other notable educational institutions in Manhattan

Manhattan was transformed from a low-density to a vertical city; this photo shows a city garden in 1890 at 89th Street and West End Avenue

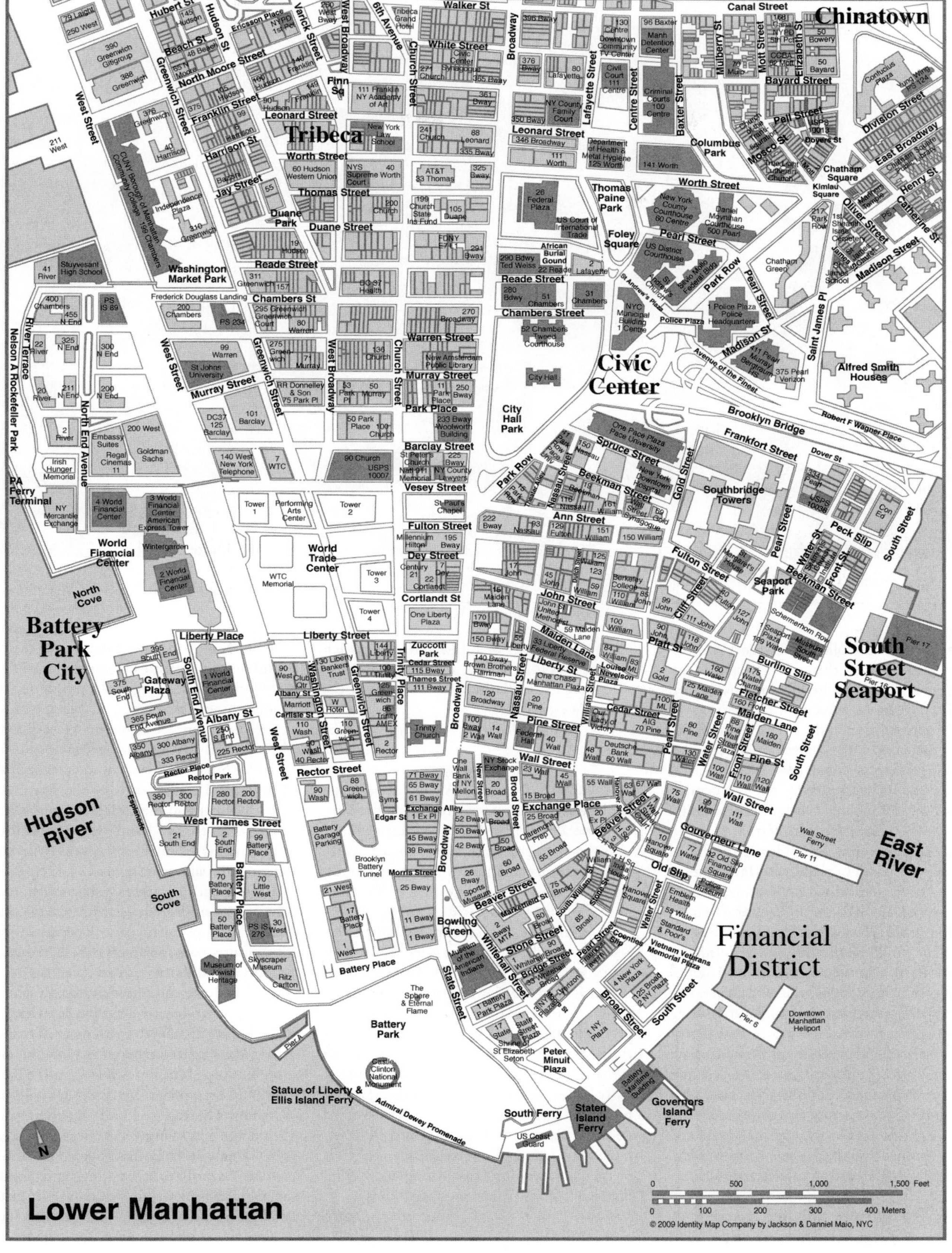
Lower Manhattan
Chinatown
Tribeca
Civic Center
Battery Park City
South Street Seaport
Financial District
Hudson River
East River
North Cove
South Cove
Walker St
Canal Street
Hubert St
Beach St
North Moore Street
Franklin Street
Leonard Street
Harrison St
Worth Street
Jay Street
Thomas Street
Duane Street
Reade Street
Chambers St
Chambers Street
Warren Street
Murray Street
Park Place
Barclay Street
Vesey Street
Fulton Street
Dey Street
Cortlandt St
Liberty Place
Liberty Street
Cedar Street
Thames Street
Albany St
Rector Street
Rector Place
West Thames Street
Battery Place
West Street
Hudson Street
Greenwich Street
Varick Street
West Broadway
6th Avenue
Church Street
Broadway
Lafayette Street
Centre Street
Baxter Street
Mulberry St
Mott Street
Elizabeth St
Bayard Street
Pell Street
Mosco St
Division Street
East Broadway
Chatham Square
Kimlau Square
Oliver Street
Catherine St
Henry St
Madison Street
Columbus Park
Thomas Paine Park
Foley Square
Pearl Street
Park Row
Police Plaza
Madison St
Saint James Pl
Avenue of the Finest
Alfred Smith Houses
Brooklyn Bridge
Robert F Wagner Place
Frankfort Street
Dover St
Spruce Street
Beekman Street
Gold Street
Nassau Street
Ann Street
John Street
Maiden Lane
Platt St
Pine Street
Wall Street
William Street
Pearl Street
Water Street
Front St
South Street
Peck Slip
Beekman Street
Burling Slip
Fletcher Street
Maiden Lane
Pine St
Wall Street
Gouverneur Lane
Old Slip
Exchange Place
Beaver Street
Broad Street
New Street
Trinity Place
Washington Street
South End Avenue
North End Avenue
River Terrace
Nelson A Rockefeller Park
Washington Market Park
City Hall Park
Duane Park
Finn Sq
Zuccotti Park
Bowling Green
Battery Park
Stone Street
Bridge Street
Whitehall Street
State Street
Peter Minuit Plaza
Statue of Liberty & Ellis Island Ferry
Admiral Dewey Promenade
South Ferry
Staten Island Ferry
Governors Island Ferry
US Coast Guard
Castle Clinton National Monument
World Trade Center
WTC Memorial
World Financial Center
Brooklyn Battery Tunnel
Downtown Manhattan Heliport
Wall Street Ferry
Pier 11
Pier 6
Pier 17
Pier A
Vietnam Veterans Memorial Plaza
Museum of Jewish Heritage
Skyscraper Museum
Ritz Carlton
Esplanade
PA Ferry Terminal
0 500 1,000 1,500 Feet
0 100 200 300 400 Meters
N
© 2009 Identity Map Company by Jackson & Danniel Maio, NYC

View of Manhattan Island looking north including the East River (right), 2009

include Barnard College, New York University, Cooper Union, the Juilliard School, City College of New York, and Union Theological Seminary. World-class cultural institutions in Manhattan include the Metropolitan Museum of Art, the American Museum of Natural History, the New-York Historical Society, Lincoln Center for the Performing Arts, the Metropolitan Opera, Carnegie Hall, and the Broadway theater district. In addition, the beaux arts–style New York Public Library is located in midtown Manhattan.

The skyline of Manhattan includes memorable buildings like the Fuller (or Flatiron) Building, the Woolworth Building, the Empire State Building, the Chrysler Building, the Time Warner Center, the Bank of America Tower, and hundreds of other skyscrapers displaying diverse architectural styles. Manhattan is also known for beautiful brownstone homes set close to the sidewalk, many of which have been declared landmarks or converted into multiunit apartment buildings. Because it has streets that are narrow by U.S. standards, buildings that are closely spaced and tall, and an enormous level of pedestrian and vehicular traffic, Manhattan often overwhelms visitors. Certainly it is unlike any other place in the United States, and in the world only Tokyo, Shanghai, and Hong Kong rival it for so much intensely concentrated activity in such a small area. Among the many famous neighborhoods in Manhattan are Chinatown, the Lower East Side, Greenwich Village, SoHo, Chelsea, Harlem, Morningside Heights, Little Italy, Yorkville, and the Upper West Side.

Kenneth T. Jackson, Penelope Gelwicks, Lisa Keller

Manhattan [cocktail]. Alcoholic beverage made with rye whiskey, vermouth, and bitters. It is generally stirred with ice and then strained into a cocktail glass with a cherry as a garnish. New York City financier J. P. Morgan drank one at the close of each trading day. There are several versions of the drink's origins. *Valentine's Manual of New York* states that the drink was "invented by a man named Black who kept a place 10 doors below Houston Street on Broadway" in the 1860s. Others attribute the name to the drink's dark color and its resemblance to New York City's dirty water late in the eighteenth century. Another popular myth is that the drink was created at the request of Lady Jennie Jerome for a party at the Manhattan Club in 1874 celebrating newly elected governor Samuel J. Tilden. This is unlikely, however, because of the fact that on the date of the party, Jerome was in England giving birth to her son, Winston Churchill.

Anne Epstein

Manhattan Beach. Neighborhood in southwestern Brooklyn lying on a peninsula at the eastern end of Coney Island and bounded to the north by Sheepshead Bay, to the east and south by the Atlantic Ocean, and to the west by Corbin Place. Originally known as Sedge Bank, it was developed in 1877 as a self-contained summer resort on 500 acres (200 hectares) of salt marsh by Austin Corbin's Manhattan Beach Improvement Company. During the resort's heyday the Manhattan Beach Hotel and the Oriental Hotel offered entertainment by band leaders Patrick S. Gilmore and John Philip Sousa (who commemorated the resort in his *Manhattan Beach March* [1893]). Several factors contributed to the decline of the resort early in the twentieth century: amusement parks opened in West Brighton, many parts of Brooklyn became suburban, and the three racetracks in the Town of Gravesend closed in 1910. Residential development began after 1907, when the Manhattan Beach Improvement Company divided its land north and east of the hotels into building lots for Irish and Italian Americans. In 1920 the St. Margaret Mary Roman Catholic Church was built for their needs. From the 1920s until 1942 Joseph P. Day's Manhattan Beach Baths occupied the beaches on the east and south, providing entertainment to subscribers. During World War II the federal government operated Maritime and Coast Guard training stations at the eastern end. Kingsborough Community College (1964) and Manhattan Beach Park (1955) now occupy the area. After the 1970s the large community of

Manhattan Beach Estates, ca *1900*

Soviet Jews in Brighton Beach extended into this neighborhood. In the early twenty-first century most of the population of Manhattan Beach lives in one-family houses and in modified bungalows on 20 tree-lined streets arranged in alphabetical order and named after places in England. Since 2000 many homes have been enlarged and the population has grown beyond 16,000. The neighborhood is quiet and has a few commercial establishments on Oriental Boulevard and West End Avenue. A pedestrian bridge (1882) still connects the communities of Manhattan Beach and Sheepshead Bay. In 1997 New York City's first Holocaust Memorial Mall was built at the end of Sheepshead Bay. In 2003 the Leon M. Goldstein High School for Sciences opened on the Kingsborough campus.

Nanette Rainone, ed., *The Brooklyn Neighborhood Book* (Brooklyn: Fund for the Borough of Brooklyn, 1985); Kenneth Jackson, John Manbeck, eds., *The Neighborhoods of Brooklyn* (New Haven: Yale University Press, 2d ed, 2004)

John Manbeck, Stephen Weinstein

Manhattan Beach Hotel. Summer resort hotel constructed in 1877 on the eastern end of Coney Island by the Manhattan Beach Improvement Company, a firm led by Austin Corbin. Designed by J. Pickering Putnam in the Queen Anne style, the hotel had 150 rooms on four stories and attracted upper-class customers of the sort who frequented Newport (Rhode Island) and Long Branch (New Jersey), among them August Belmont and Leonard Walter Jerome. The hotel offered entertainment ranging from displays of scenic fireworks to performances by John Philip Sousa, whose *Manhattan Beach March* (1893) is named for the resort. The Manhattan Beach Hotel was adjacent to the fashionable Sheepshead Bay racetrack and near two other racetracks; their closing in 1910 led to the demise of the hotel, which was razed in 1912.

Stephen Weinstein

Manhattan Bridge. Steel, two-level suspension bridge spanning the East River between Canal Street in Manhattan and Flatbush Avenue in Brooklyn. Designed by Leon Moisseiff and opened in 1909, it is often mistakenly attributed to Gustav Lindenthal, who submitted a plan for the bridge in 1903 that was rejected by city administrators. The entrance to the bridge on Canal Street is decorated by a grand arch and flanking colonnades designed by Carrère and Hastings. The bridge is 6855 feet (2091 meters) long, with a main span of 1470 feet (462.3 meters), and clears the East River at 135 feet (41.1 meters). The upper level has four lanes and a pedestrian walk; the lower level has three vehicular lanes and four subway tracks. The Manhattan Bridge stands north of the Brooklyn Bridge and south of the Williamsburg Bridge.

Rebecca Read Shanor

Manhattan Chess Club. Formed in 1877 by three dozen casual players who met regularly in the back room of a café in the Bowery. Its members included almost every American master of the next 100 years, including the world champions José (Raúl) Capablanca and Bobby Fischer. The club also played a major role in organizing such historic events as the first official chess World Championship match (1886) and the famous New York Tournaments of 1924 and 1927. The club remained active and met at Carnegie Hall at the end of the twentieth century. It was one of the oldest chess clubs in the United States before it closed in 2002.

The Manhattan Chess Club of the City of New York, Organized, 1877, Incorporated 1883 (New York: Manhattan Chess Club, 1894)

James Glass

Manhattan College. Private liberal arts college, opened by the Brothers of the Christian Schools in 1853 at 131st Street and Broadway in Manhattan as the Academy of Holy Infancy. After moving to Riverdale in the Bronx in 1923, the college added schools of engineering, business, and education and human services. It developed a cooperative arrangement with the College of Mount St. Vincent in 1964 and became coeducational in 1973. The college's athletic teams are nicknamed the Jaspers, after the college's first baseball coach, Brother Jasper of Mary (who according to school tradition invented the "seventh-inning stretch"). In the early twenty-first century about 3000 undergraduate students and 500 graduate students were enrolled.

Marc Ferris

Manhattan Bridge, 1910

Manhattan Company. Company formed in 1799 at 23 Wall Street, originally to provide water for New York City. Permitted to pursue other interests as a result of a clause in the charter that many attribute to Aaron Burr (one of the founders of the company), it opened a bank on 1 September 1799 that became an unexpected competitor of Alexander Hamilton's Bank of New York. By 1840 the company had ceased to function as a water utility, and the bank was one of the most important commercial banks in the city. The headquarters were at 40 Wall Street at the turn of the twentieth century, by which time the bank had attained national prominence. It later merged with and incorporated several local banks, including the Bank of the Metropolis (1871) in 1918 and the Merchants National Bank (1803) in 1920. In 1930 it had 78 branches throughout all five boroughs and carried deposits of $404 million. It merged with the Chase National Bank in 1955 to form the Chase Manhattan Corporation. In 2000 Chase Manhattan merged with JP Morgan to form JPMorgan Chase, and Manhattan disappeared from the corporate name.

Ann C. Gibson

Manhattan Eye, Ear and Throat Hospital. Private hospital chartered in 1869 as a clinic for the poor. First housed in a rented brownstone on East 34th Street, it moved to Park Avenue and 41st Street in 1881, by which time it was already nationally recognized, and to East 64th Street in 1906. A renovation in 1980 expanded the facilities to provide space for research and development in diagnostics and treatment. The hospital is the regional center for specialty care in ophthalmology, otolaryngology, and plastic and reconstructive surgery. It offers educational services and free screening for city residents. In 2000 the Manhattan Eye, Ear and Throat Hospital became a subsidiary of Lenox Hill Hospital.

Andrea Balis

Manhattan Institute for Policy Research. Nonprofit research and education organization formed in 1978 by Antony Fisher and William Casey (later the director of the Central Intelligence Agency). It is generally associated with conservative ideas but is nonpartisan and has attracted contributors and staff members from diverse political backgrounds. The institute studies issues such as choice in public education, the privatization of municipal services, and the limits of multiculturalism. It also publishes a quarterly magazine, *City Journal*, that is devoted to urban issues. The institute met with some success in the mayoral election of 1993, when Rudolph W. Giuliani espoused its proposals to reduce local business taxes, decentralize the public school system, assume a tougher stance toward homeless drug addicts, and privatize some municipal services. In the early twenty-first century the institute had about 30 staff members. Its offices are at 52 Vanderbilt Avenue in Manhattan.

Chad Ludington

Manhattan New York Temple. The 119th temple of the Church of Jesus Christ of Latter-day Saints (LDS), or Mormon church, it was initially constructed in 1976 as a stake center that included a visitors' center and chapel; it was designed by Schuman, Lichtenstein and Claman (later SLCE Architects). From 2002 to 2004 the church was transformed into a temple to accommodate the increasing number of Mormons in the city, which had tripled in the previous decade to more than 40,000. The temple occupies the top three floors, with a baptistry on the first floor, a meetinghouse, and offices on lower floors. LDS temples are used for special ceremonies and are open only to members of the church. A steeple with a 10-foot statue of the angel Moroni was added in the fall of 2004.

See also Mormons.

Kate Lauber

Manhattan Opera House. Opera house built by Oscar Hammerstein in 1906 in an effort to compete with the Metropolitan Opera by offering more affordable tickets. In 1911, in order to eliminate competition from the venue, the Metropolitan Opera bought Hammerstein's opera house, under the condition that he quit producing operas for 10 years. That same year, Lee and Jacob Shubert reopened it as a "combination" house, which featured vaudeville shows and concerts. In 1922 the building was purchased by the Ancient Accepted Scottish Rite of Free Masonry, which built the Grand Ballroom. The opera house is also known for its excellent acoustics; in 1926 Warner Brothers leased the building to record the soundtrack for *Don Juan*. In 1940 its name changed to the Manhattan Center in order to attract other events, such as trade shows, union meetings, and "big band" dances. It also housed radio broadcasts, recordings, and performances by artists such as Harry Belafonte, Leonard Bernstein, and Paul Robeson. The Unification Church purchased the building in 1976 and held religious meetings, cultural events, and music recordings. In 1986 the Manhattan Center Studios transformed the opera house into a state-of-the-art facility suitable for multimedia broadcasting as well as for corporate uses. It is located at 311 West 34th Street and seats approximately 3000 patrons.

Stephanie Miller

Manhattan Plaza. Apartment complex between 42nd and 43rd streets and Ninth and Tenth avenues, containing 1689 units in two buildings, one of 46 stories and the other of 45 stories. Designed by the firm of David Todd and built by Richard Ravitch, it was intended to provide market-rate housing for the affluent but was later reconceived as a subsidized facility for artists, actors, and musicians. The complex opened on 1 June 1977 and soon helped to revitalize the area. Prominent residents have included the jazz musician Charles Mingus and the playwright Tennessee Williams. In the early twenty-first century it houses about 3500. The Laurie Beechman Theatre opened in 1983 at the base of the building and seats about 120 at restaurant tables.

Jesse Drucker

Manhattan Project. Secret government effort to design a nuclear weapon during World War II. Formally known as the Manhattan Engineer District, the project, which ran from August 1942 to 1946, was overseen by Major General Leslie R. Groves and scientist J. Robert Oppenheimer. The Manhattan Project was so named because its first headquarters were located in lower Manhattan at 270 Broadway in a skyscraper that housed both the North Atlantic Division of the U.S. Army Corps of Engineers and the engineering firm Stone and Webster. Before the Manhattan Project was established, researchers at Columbia University were exploring ways to split an atom and harness the resulting energy. The cyclotron and laboratories were in Pupin and Schermerhorn Halls. At one point the Columbia football team was recruited to move thousands of pounds of uranium for experiments that resulted in the first nuclear reactor. Columbia also built a pilot plant in the former Nash Automobile Building at 3280 Broadway at 133rd Street to concentrate the uranium-235 isotope that was used in the first atomic bombs. Located on the 10th, 11th, and 14th floors of the Woolworth Building at 233 Broadway, the Kellex Corporation operated as an elaborate front for nuclear research. One of the more than 3700 employees of the company was Klaus Fuchs, later discovered to be a Soviet spy. The Baker and Williams Warehouses on West 20th Street between 10th and 11th avenues in Manhattan housed tons of radioactive materials. Another set of warehouses were located at 2377–2387 Richmond Terrace in Staten Island. In 1943 the Manhattan Project's headquarters moved to Oak Ridge, Tennessee, but several offices and administrators remained in New York City. The Madison Square Area Engineers Office was on the 22nd floor of a building at 261 Fifth Avenue at 29th Street in Manhattan. This office was responsible for securing and shipping various materials needed for making bombs. The Union Carbide and Carbon Corporation, formerly located at 30 East 42nd Street in Manhattan, operated the plant in Tennessee that turned uranium gas into bomb fuel.

Richard Rhodes, *The Making of the Atomic Bomb* (New York: Touchstone, 1986); Cynthia Kelley, ed., *The Manhattan Project* (New York: Black Dog and Leventhal, 2007)

Anne Epstein

Manhattan Psychiatric Center. State mental hospital. It began in 1899 as Manhattan State Hospital when the state of New York consolidated two hospitals on Wards Island that it had taken over in 1896 (one at the eastern end for men and the other at the western end for women). The new hospital had 4400 patients and was the largest psychiatric institution in the world; as admissions far outnumbered discharges, the hospital became overcrowded and inadequately staffed and its buildings deteriorated. A fire in 1923 that killed 22 patients and three attendants helped rouse public support for a bond issue to improve the safety of all state hospitals. In 1926 the hospital had 7000 patients. To prepare for the reversion of the land on which the hospital stood to the city in 1943, more than half the patients were moved in 1940 to other psychiatric hospitals. The city in turn donated the land to the state, and in 1955 the hospital moved into three new buildings on Wards Island.

During the 1960s the number of patients declined after the introduction of tranquilizers and antidepressants. With the decentralization of the state hospital system in December 1969, the hospital was divided into the Dunlap Manhattan Psychiatric Center, the Kirby Manhattan Psychiatric Center, and the Meyer Manhattan Psychiatric Center; the reversal of this policy in 1976 by the Department of Mental Hygiene of New York State led the centers to be consolidated in 1979 into the Manhattan Psychiatric Center, which in the same year became affiliated with New York University Medical Center. The center emptied one of its three buildings in 1981 and made it available to the Kirby Forensic Psychiatric Center, a specialized facility for mental patients who have had involvement with the criminal justice system. Although the center introduced several innovative programs during the 1970s and the 1980s, it was repeatedly criticized for inadequate staffing, minimal standards in its programs, and other problems. These complaints culminated in the case of *Doe v. Cuomo,* which was settled in 1988 with an agreement to increase the clinical staff at the hospital and expand its therapeutic programs. In the same year the center began the largest renovation project in the history of the state, according to which its buildings were gutted and completely refitted over the following 11 years. As of 2009 there were 509 beds.

Sandra Opdycke

Manhattan Savings Bank. Savings bank formed in 1942 by the merger of three banks chartered in the 1850s. The oldest of these, the Manhattan Savings Institution, was founded on 10 April 1850 at Constitution Hall (650 Broadway) by Mayor Ambrose C. Kingsland and Caleb S. Woodhull, a former mayor, to serve customers of modest means. Its offices were situated first at 648 Broadway before moving in 1855 to 644 Broadway. The two other banks, the Metropolitan Savings Bank and Citizens Savings Bank, also began in lower Manhattan with a similar purpose; all three institutions prospered during the late nineteenth and early twentieth centuries. After the merger the new bank set up headquarters at 754 Broadway, which moved in 1951 to 385 Madison Avenue. The Manhattan Savings Bank had 17 branches in New York City and Westchester County and $2.8 billion in deposits by 1990, when it was acquired by the Republic New York Corporation. The Manhattan Savings Bank name was no longer used after the 1999 merger of Republic New York Corporation and HSBC.

Chad Ludington

Manhattan schist. A metamorphic rock formed about 450 million years ago and found today on Manhattan Island. Washington, Hamilton, and Morningside Heights in northwestern Manhattan lie on top of a schist formation, which rises above the Harlem Valley to the east. It has been used as a building material in many Manhattan structures, such as St. Paul's Chapel (1766) and the original buildings of City College's upper Manhattan campus (1906). New York sidewalks often have a glittering appearance because Manhattan schist, which contains shiny flecks of mica, is used in the concrete mix. A common myth is that tall buildings in Manhattan are clustered in areas where schist lies close to the surface, but geology did not influence the location of Manhattan's skyscraper districts.

Caleb Smith

Manhattan School of Music. Conservatory opened in 1917 on the Upper East Side as the Neighborhood Music School by the philanthropist Janet D. Schenck, who served as its director until 1956. It took its current name in 1939 and in 1969 moved to 120 Claremont Avenue in Morningside Heights, the building formerly occupied by the Juilliard School. Under the direction of Schenck's successors, the conservatory developed programs in opera, accompanying, and jazz. The Manhattan School, which underwent a major physical expansion in 2001, enrolls more than 800 students and grants bachelor's, master's, and doctoral degrees in performance and composition.

James M. Keller

Manhattan State Hospital. Hospital that later became the Manhattan Psychiatric Center.

Manhattan Theatre Club. Manhattan-based nonprofit theater company incorporated in 1970. It has been recognized for premiering works by American playwrights such as Terrence McNally, Sam Shepard, Beth Henley, and John Patrick Shanley. It has also produced American premieres of foreign playwrights including Athol Fugard and Harold Pinter. In addition, the club administers an education program for New York–area students and teachers. Initially located on the Upper East Side, Manhattan Theatre Club moved in 1984 to the lower level of City Center on West 55th Street, where it has two performance spaces: Stage I, with 299 seats, and Stage II, with 150. In 2003 the company began to produce Broadway plays at the newly renovated 650-seat Biltmore Theatre at 261 West 47th Street (renamed the Samuel J. Friedman Theatre in 2008). Manhattan Theatre Club's productions have won several Pulitzer Prizes, as well as numerous Tony Awards, Obies, and Drama Desk Awards, among other honors.

Helen Graves

Manhattan Transfer. A defunct interchange station in Harrison, New Jersey. Opened in 1910 by the Pennsylvania Railroad, its original purpose was for changing steam locomotives to electric locomotives on trains bound for Pennsylvania Station in Midtown Manhattan via the railroad's new tunnels under the Hudson River. It also provided a stop where passengers could change between trains of the railroad's main line and those still bound for the old Exchange Place station in Jersey City and its ferry connection to Downtown Manhattan. The station later gave its name to a 1925 novel written by John Dos Passos, as well as to a popular singing group. It was closed in 1937 following the electrification of the Pennsylvania Railroad's main line to Philadelphia.

Brian J. Cudahy, *Rails Under the Mighty Hudson: The Story of the Hudson Tubes, the Pennsy Tunnels, and Manhattan Transfer* (New York: Fordham University Press, 2002)

Kenneth T. Jackson

Manhattan Valley. Neighborhood on the Upper West Side of Manhattan, bounded to the north by 110th Street, to the east by Central Park West, to the south by 100th Street, and to the east by Amsterdam Avenue. The name became popular in the 1960s and refers to the sloping of Manhattan Avenue, which runs north from 100th Street. From the time of its initial urbanization in the mid-nineteenth century, the area has consistently maintained a working-class character. Among its initial inhabitants were Irish immigrant squatters evicted in the 1850s from their homes to the east where the construction of Central Park was getting under way. With the opening of the Ninth Avenue Elevated line in 1878, the area, which was sufficiently distant from the downtown locus of New York urban life, became a convenient site for the location of asylums for the elderly and the poor. It was the original site of the New York Cancer Hospital (later moved and now known as the Memorial Sloan-Kettering Cancer Center). The original cancer hospital building with its distinctive towers is today part of an upscale condominium development on Central Park West. Although there are stirrings of gentrification along Central Park West and the classic row houses on Manhattan Avenue, much of the housing consists of "old law" tenements and public housing, including the Frederick Douglass Houses. The character of the area has been sustained in part due to active work by community-based groups such as the Manhattan Valley Development Corporation to upgrade and maintain the area's affordable housing stock.

Elliott Sclar

Manhattanville. Nineteenth-century village that flourished during the Industrial Revolution on what is now north of the the Upper West Side of Manhattan. Surrounded by open land and country residences, it was in the valley near the present intersection of 125th Street and Broadway. The community was the site of churches, a grade school, and Manhattan College (1815). A ferry terminus on the Hudson River, a mill, and a brewery contributed to a thriving enclave that had about 500 residents at mid-century. In the early twentieth century it was still a working port and a neighborhood filled with manufacturing establishments, warehouses, and some residences. The 125th Street elevated subway station was built on Broadway, and the Riverside Drive Viaduct was built at its parallel western edge. In the first decade of the twenty-first century Columbia University acquired 17 acres (7 hectares) of this west Harlem community north of 125th street as the site of a new $7 billion campus to be built in stages.

Karen E. Markoe

Mannes College of Music. Conservatory opened in 1916 on East 70th Street as the David Mannes Music School by the violinist David Mannes and his wife, the pianist Clara Damrosch. It moved in 1919 to East 74th Street and took its current name in 1953. In addition to bachelor's and master's degrees in music performance the school offers training in composition and theory (it is a noted bastion of Schenkerian musical analysis). The school moved to West 85th Street in 1984 and in 1989 became an independent division of the New School for Social Research. In 2010 it enrolled 295 students in its college division, 490 students in its preparatory division, and 350 students in its extension division. Notable graduates include the mezzo-soprano Frederica von Stade, the pianist Richard Goode, and the pianist and conductor Murray Perahia.

David Mannes, *Music Is My Faith* (New York: Privately printed, 1949)

James M. Keller

Manning, William Thomas (*b* Northampton, England, 12 May 1866; *d* New York City, 18 Nov 1949). Episcopal bishop. He moved to Nebraska with his family at age 16 and earned a bachelor of divinity degree in 1891 from the University of the South in Sewanee, Tennessee. After serving as a parish priest in California, Pennsylvania, and Tennessee he was assigned to Trinity Church in New York City, the wealthiest Episcopal parish in the country, of which he became rector in 1908. He was elected bishop of New York in 1921 and held the office until 1946; his diocese included not only Manhattan, the Bronx, and Staten Island but also seven counties north of New York City, consisting of more than 300 clergymen, 250 parishes and chapels, and 100,000 communicants. His priority was the construction of the Cathedral of St. John the Divine, on which he was consulted for every detail. He raised $13 million for the project, and despite a decrease in funds during the Depression, the nave and west front were completed by 1939. Frail and ascetic in appearance, Manning was noted for his conservative theology and strict interpretation of church tenets. As a dedicated High Churchman and a militant practitioner of his faith, he was often at the center of controversy, especially on such issues as remarriage after divorce and the rules of propriety in church services.

William Dudley Foulke Hughes, *Prudently with Power: William Thomas Manning, Tenth Bishop of New York* (New York: Holy Cross Publications, 1963)

Jane Allen

Man-o'-War Reef. Outcropping in the East River that later became Belmont Island.

Man Ray [Radnitsky, Emmanuel] (*b* Philadelphia, 27 Aug 1890; *d* Paris, 18 Nov 1976). Painter and photographer. He moved to Brooklyn with his family in 1897 and as a young man was influenced by the realist paintings of John Sloan and Robert Henri. In 1911 he began visiting "291," a gallery run by Alfred Stieglitz, who became his mentor. At the age of 26 he attended a salon organized by Walter Arensberg on West 67th Street, where he met Marcel Duchamp, who became a close friend for the next 50 years. He spent most of the rest of his life in Paris, where he was at the forefront of the Dadaist and surrealist movements and enjoyed a successful career as a commercial photographer.

Stephen Weinstein

Manship, Paul (*b* St. Paul, Minn., 24 Dec 1885; *d* New York City, 28 Jan 1966). Sculptor. He trained in New York City in 1905 and was then a fellow at the American Academy in Rome (1909–12). After his return he produced the bronze sculpture *Dancer and Gazelles* (1916) and other small-scale decorative sculptures for private homes and gardens. His major public commissions date to the 1930s, when he executed the Paul J. Rainey Memorial Gateway (1934) for the New York Zoological Park, the Prometheus Fountain (1934) for Rockefeller Center, and several large sculptural groups for the World's Fair of 1939–40. His sculpture style was typically archaistic, combining a naturalistic treatment of anatomy with stylized, linear details that revealed his admiration for Greek sculpture. Manship served terms as president of the National Sculpture Society (1939–42), vice president of the National Academy of Design (1942–48), and president of the American Academy of Arts and Letters (1948–54). Among his late works are the gates for the William Church Osborn Memorial Playground (1952) and the Children's Zoo (1961), both in Central Park. He lived at 319 East 72nd Street.

Harry Rand, *Paul Manship* (Washington, D.C.: Smithsonian Institution Press, 1989)

Susan Rather

mansions. From the eighteenth century onward the wealthy built large homes that reflected their wealth and status. The first mansion in New York City was the home of Stephen de Lancey, built in 1719 at 115 Broadway and converted into the Queen's Head Tavern in 1762. Country residences were built north of the city by wealthy families before the American Revolution, among them Whitehall, owned by Governor Peter Stuyvesant (destroyed by fire in 1715); the home of Nicholas Bayard near Grand, Broome, Crosby, and Lafayette streets in what is now SoHo (built 1735; demolished 1821); the Rutgers–Crosby mansion on Cherry Street (built 1754; demolished 1875); the Apthorpe mansion on the West Side (built 1764; demolished 1892); James Beekman's Mount Pleasant on the East Side (built 1763; demolished 1874); the Morris–Jumel Mansion in northern Manhattan (1765); and Richmond Hill, built in 1769 on the west side of Broadway for Abraham Mortier and later occupied by Aaron Burr and John Jacob Astor (moved in 1820 during the development of Charleton Street). Many well-known people stayed at the mansion of Captain Archibald Kennedy at 1 Broadway (1760), which became the Washington Hotel in 1830 and was demolished in 1882. Across Bowling Green from the Kennedy house stood Government House (1790), designed by John McComb as the Executive Mansion but never occupied by a president: it became a boarding house in 1798. A mansion built for Archibald Gracie in 1804 at Bridge and State streets was demolished in 1879.

Broadway remained the most fashionable street well into the Federal period. During the first half of the nineteenth century the only large house built in the city was that of John Cox Stevens at College Place, designed by Alexander Jackson Davis, built in 1846–47, and soon demolished. The first mansion on Fifth Avenue was a marble palace built by John Kellum for the businessman A. T. Stewart in 1864–69; it remained the wonder of the city until the death of Cornelius Vanderbilt in 1877, when members of his family decided to end their exclusion from society by building ornate houses along the west side of Fifth Avenue between 50th and 58th streets. There soon followed a frenzy of construction along Fifth Avenue that lasted from the 1880s to World War I and culminated in a mansion for Henry Clay Frick designed by the firm of Carrère and Hastings and built between 70th and 71st streets. Commissioned mostly by clients desirous of social status, the houses were designed in historical European styles and usually built of white stone; ornaments were often made by craftspeople who had moved to the city from Europe. The houses were rarely sold but rather left to the owner's heirs, who often had them demolished, especially during the mid-1920s when the construction of apartment buildings virtually guaranteed a fortune. Some of the mansions became consulates and museums, including those of Frick (now the Frick Collection) and Andrew Carnegie (now the Cooper–Hewitt Museum; for illustration see ANDREW CARNEGIE).

Mosette G. Broderick

Manteo Sicilian Marionette Theater. Theater devoted to *opera dei pupi,* a style of puppetry developed in Sicily during the early nineteenth century. The Manteo family of Catania, Sicily, opened the theater in Argentina about 1894 and moved to New York City in 1919. Using the "rod control" technique known in Roman times, the family built life-sized marionettes and opened a theater on the Lower East Side in 1923, later moving to nearby Little Italy. They performed Torquato Tasso's *Gerusaleme Liberata* and Ludovico Ariosto's *Orlando Furioso,* which was divided into 394 episodes that required 13 months of nightly performances to complete. In 1936 the entire season consisted of 56 episodes of *Orlando Furioso* performed in a 300-seat theater at 107 Waverly Place; admission was 25 cents. In the summer the theater toured the East Coast. After Agrippino Manteo's death the title of Papa Manteo passed to his son Miguel Manteo, who led the troupe until his death in 1989. Electricians by day, the family performed for the Festival of American Folklife at the Smithsonian Institution (1975), the World Puppetry Festival (1980), the American Museum of Natural History (1982), and the Staten Island Institute of Arts and Sciences. In the early twenty-first century the Manteo family lived in Staten Island, where their collection of Sicilian marionettes was one of only a handful in the United States. The family continues to perform for high schools and colleges in the metropolitan area.

Barbara Kirshenblatt-Gimblett

Mantle, Mickey (Charles) (*b* Spavinaw, Okla., 20 Oct 1931; *d* Dallas, 13 Aug 1995). Baseball player. Although born in Oklahoma, Yankee fans considered him the pride of New York City. A powerful switch-hitter, Mantle played his entire 18-year career with the New York Yankees, replacing the legendary Joe DiMaggio in center field. He was named Most Valuable Player (MVP) of the American League three times, played in 16 All-Star games, and was on seven World Championship teams. He hit 536 career home runs and still holds the record for most World Series home runs (18). An outstanding athlete in high school in Commerce, Oklahoma, Mantle was offered a football scholarship to the University of Oklahoma but instead signed with the Yankees after graduation for a reported bonus of $1,100. Several of his home runs remain the stuff of legend. He hit a 565-foot homer in Washington, D.C., in 1953, and in 1956 he missed hitting the ball out of Yankee Stadium by about 18 inches, with the ball hitting the top of the right field upper-deck facade. He and teammate Roger Maris were involved in a memorable duel in 1961 in pursuit of Babe Ruth's home run record. Maris broke Ruth's record with 61 homers that year, while Mantle hit 54. He retired in 1969 and was inducted into the National Baseball Hall of Fame in his first year of eligibility. Mickey Mantle's Restaurant and Sports Bar, on Central Park South, became a popular destination for baseball fans and tourists to New York City. Mantle was diagnosed with inoperable liver cancer in 1995 and admitted to years of alcohol abuse. He had a liver transplant that year, but died two months later at the age of 63.

Frank Dyer

Manton, Martin T(homas) (*b* New York City, 2 Aug 1880; *d* Fayetteville, N.Y., 17 Nov 1946). Convicted judge. He earned a law degree at Columbia University (1901) and formed the law firm of Cochran and Manton. President Woodrow Wilson appointed him to a federal judgeship (1916), then to the U.S. Circuit Court of Appeals for the Second Circuit (1918). In March 1928 he sat on the Federal Statutory Court, a special tribunal that ruled in favor of the Interborough Rapid Transit (IRT) raising the subway fare to seven cents; the U.S. Supreme Court reversed his ruling. He later oversaw the receivership of the IRT, but then Judge John M. Woolsey ruled that Manton's intervention had usurped the authority of the U.S. District Court for the Southern District of New York, which had jurisdiction over bankruptcy cases. Long rumored to be engaged in unethical conduct after suffering financial reverses during the Depression, Manton was investigated in 1938 by Manhattan District Attorney Thomas E. Dewey, who submitted a list of charges to the House Judiciary Committee. Manton resigned in January 1939 and was indicted by a federal grand jury in April for accepting loans and gifts of $186,146 from litigants in eight cases, most involving patent law. Convicted and fined $10,000, he served one year and seven months. He lived with his son in Fayetteville, New York, until his death.

Jeffrey A. Kroessler

Manufacturers Hanover. Commercial bank, formed in 1961 by a merger of Manufacturers Trust and the Hanover Bank, both of which had a long history in New York City. The origins of Manufacturers Trust can be traced to the founding in 1812 of the New York Manufacturing Company, a textile company with a charter authorizing banking activities. This bank gradually evolved into the Chatham and Phenix Bank, with which J. P. Morgan was associated. In 1932 Chatham and Phenix was absorbed by Manufacturers Trust, a Brooklyn bank founded in 1853. In 1950 Manufacturers purchased the Brooklyn Trust Company, which had been largely responsible for financing the construction of the Brooklyn Bridge. The Hanover Bank was founded in 1851 and grew from loans and investments made in the South and West after the Civil War. In 1912 it merged with Gallatin Bank, chartered in 1829 as the National Bank of the City of New York, funded largely by John Jacob Astor, and first led by Albert Gallatin, secretary of the treasury under Presidents Thomas Jefferson and James Madison. An act of Congress in 1965 allowed the merger of Manufacturers and Hanover to stand, despite a U.S. Department of Justice challenge that it violated antitrust laws. The new bank expanded during the 1960s and 1970s, but by 1979 it was excessively dependent on delinquent international loans. In 1992 a weakened Manufacturers Hanover Bank became a division of Chemical Bank under the parent company, the Chemical Banking Corporation, which acquired Chase Manhattan in 1996, took the Chase name, and merged with J. P. Morgan and Company in 2000.

Chad Ludington

Mapleton. Neighborhood in west central Brooklyn, bounded to the north by Washington Cemetery, to the east by 23rd Avenue, to the south by 63rd Street, and to the west by 17th Avenue. Once part of the Dutch Town of New Utrecht, Mapleton is now considered a subdivision of Borough Park, along with Blythebourne. The neighborhood stands on high ground and when first settled offered fine views of Lower New York Bay. It was a sparsely populated farming area until William Sugarman of the Alco Building Company developed Mapleton Park in 1907. In addition, extensions of the Sea Beach, West End, and Culver divisions of Brooklyn–Manhattan Transit between 1913 and 1919 transformed the community. Small apartment buildings and one-family houses were built by the firm of New Utrecht Improvement. In the early twenty-first century the population was primarily Jewish and Italian, with a growing number of Chinese.

Stephen Weinstein

Mapplethorpe, Robert (*b* Queens, 4 Nov 1946; *d* Boston, 9 March 1989). Photographer. He attended Pratt Institute from 1963 to 1970. After solo exhibitions at the Light Gallery (1976), the Holly Solomon Gallery (1977), and the Robert Miller Gallery, he achieved prominence and exhibited internationally. Mapplethorpe's work covered a wide range of subjects, including portraits, still lifes, and female nudes. His name is inextricably associated with his explicitly homoerotic male nudes, some of which caused a furor when they were included in an exhibition that received federal funds. He lived at 24 Bond Street in Manhattan. After his death from AIDS, Mapplethorpe's ashes were buried in Queens with his mother, who died shortly after him. Published collections of his photographs include *Robert Mapplethorpe: Photographs* (1978), *Lady: Lisa Lyon* (1983), *Robert Mapplethorpe: Certain People* (1985), and *Robert Mapplethorpe* (1988).

maps of New York City. The first engraved map that named New Amsterdam and Manhattan was included in Johannes de Laet's book *The New World* (1630); titled *Nova Anglia, Novum Belgium et Virginia + Bermuda majori mole expressa* (New England, New Netherland, and Virginia, and Bermuda Drawn on a Larger Scale), it was engraved by Hessel Gerritsz, official cartographer for the Dutch East India Company. Later maps showed development northward from the chaotic streets of lower Manhattan to the grid above 14th Street, which John Randel surveyed and mapped for the 1811 Commissioners Plan. After the Great Fire of 1835, engineer and surveyor William Perris began making fire insurance maps of Manhattan and Brooklyn that included streets, blocks, tax lots, and current use classifications, as well as previous land uses, roads, and natural features. Although Perris pioneered the form, many others published fire insurance maps of the city, including Bromley and Company, Hyde and Company, G. M. Hopkins, and most notably the Sanborn Map Company, which produced finely detailed maps from the late 1800s through the 1950s. The Sanborn maps and other historical maps of the city's natural features, such as the *British Headquarters Map* (circa 1782) and the *Sanitary and Topographical Atlas of the City and Island of New York* (1865) by Egbert Viele, were widely used by engineers, architects, planners, and historians in the early twenty-first century. For practical navigation, residents and tourists often relied on Internet sources such as Google Maps, which featured satellite images of the city.

See also Grid plan, Hagstrom Map Company, Sanborn fire insurance maps.

Kate Lauber

Mara, Tim(othy James) (*b* New York City, 29 July 1887; *d* New York City, 17 Feb 1959). Football executive. He was born on the Lower East Side, became a successful bookmaker (at the time a legal trade), and in 1925 bought the New York Giants of the National Football League (NFL) for $500. The team was financially unsuccessful in its first season until more than 70,000 spectators attended its last game, against the Chicago Bears at the Polo Grounds; this convinced Mara that professional football could succeed in New York. On four occasions his efforts to build a following for the Giants were threatened by leagues that sought to compete with the NFL: the American Football League nearly destroyed his team in 1926, two other leagues of the same name had franchises in New York City in 1936–37 and 1940–41, and the All-America Football Conference caused serious financial problems for the Giants in 1946–49. Mara's son Wellington was later the president of the team.

Joseph A. Horrigan

marble cemeteries. Two cemeteries in New York City built as early responses to early nineteenth-century health crises. Regular epidemics of cholera, yellow fever, diphtheria, typhus, and other contagious diseases were blamed in part on leeching of human remains into the water supply and on "miasmic vapors" rising from shallow graves. One solution was to build cemeteries with room-sized marble vaults 10 feet (3 meters) underground. The only public burial grounds in the city that were built this way were the New York Marble Cemetery (1830, 41½ Second Avenue) and the New York City Marble Cemetery (1831, 52–74 East Second Street). They were located in what was then the city's northern area, built of Tuckahoe marble by Perkins Nichols, and managed by the owners of the plots they contained. The city's first nonsectarian cemeteries open to the public, they were carefully landscaped and parklike, with memorial markers almost out of sight. They became well known when former president James Monroe was buried at New York City Marble Cemetery after his death on 4 July 1831; the only U.S. president to die in New York City, his remains were transferred to a Virginia cemetery in 1858. The cemeteries, which are both less than 450 feet (140 meters) in length, each contain no more than 300 graves, most of them of members of the city's upper and middle classes, including leading merchants, several mayors, and a large number of children who died during epidemics (approximately one-half the interments in New York Marble Cemetery's early years were remains of girls and boys younger than six). The marble cemetery plan quickly lost its appeal with the appearance of the rural cemetery movement in the 1840s. After a long period of poor maintenance in a declining neighborhood, both cemeteries recovered around the turn of the twenty-first century and were opened to visitors on some days of the year. Both had been designated New York

New York Marble Cemetery, 2009

City landmarks. New interments are made occasionally.

John Rousmaniere

Marble Collegiate Church. First Dutch Reformed church in North America, formed in 1628 by Jonas Michaëlius, the first ordained clergyman in New Amsterdam. It was at the center of several controversies during colonial times, especially after the English conquest of 1664, and issues of class, political loyalty, and language divided the congregation and diminished its influence. The church lost all four of its pastors immediately after the American Revolution. As a leader of the "chapel movement" during the nineteenth century, the church built chapels in impoverished and immigrant neighborhoods and eventually added social programs and English classes to aid assimilation. The struggling congregation of 200 was taken over in 1932 by Norman Vincent Peale, whose optimistic theology drew audiences of 4000 and more by the 1950s. The interior of the church, which features stained-glass windows designed by Frederick Wilson for Louis Comfort Tiffany in 1900–1901, was extensively restored in 1984.

A Monograph to Commemorate the Three Hundredth Anniversary of the Organization in 1628 (New York: Marble Collegiate Church, 1928)

Randall Balmer

Marble Hill. Neighborhood lying on a rocky mound overlooking the Harlem River and bounded to the north by West 230th Street, to the east by Exterior Street, and to the west by Johnson Avenue. Although situated on the landmass making up the Bronx, it belongs to New York County and is part of the borough of Manhattan for most administrative purposes. Its unique status derives from its history. Once part of the island of Manhattan, it was bounded by the Harlem River and Spuyten Duyvil Creek and connected to the mainland at 230th Street and Kingsbridge Avenue by the Kings Bridge (1693); the Farmers' Free Bridge (1759) was built to the mainland near Exterior Street. The neighborhood was the site of a marble quarry in the early nineteenth century. After June 1895 it was severed from Manhattan when the Harlem River Ship Canal was dug, and it became an island surrounded by the canal and Spuyten Duyvil Creek. Before World War I the creek was filled in, leaving Marble Hill part of the mainland, and for many years residents were listed in the telephone directories of both Manhattan and the Bronx. The neighborhood did not become populous until the subway was extended along Broadway to 225th Street. Apartment buildings erected in the 1920s and 1930s soon replaced most of the existing one-family frame houses. About this time a velodrome was built east of Broadway; in 1950 it became part of the site of the Marble Hill Houses, a low-income housing project that initially attracted many municipal employees. In the early twenty-first century the population was mostly black and Latin American, with a large Dominican community. The area is mainly residential.

Gary D. Hermalyn

Marble Palace. Nickname of the first department store in the world, a four-story structure situated on the southeast corner of Broadway and Reade Street and opened in 1846 as the dry-goods emporium of A. T. Stewart. The building was of Anglo-Italianate design and featured white Tuckahoe marble. Eventually the Marble Palace occupied the entire block, as far south as Chambers Street. It was the largest store in the world by the 1850s. In 1862 Stewart moved his store to Broadway and Ninth Street; the Marble Palace became the home of the *Sun* from 1919 to 1950 and became known as the Sun Building. It was bought by the city in 1970, which converted it into municipal offices. The building, at 280 Broadway, is a National Historic Landmark; it was extensively renovated during the late 1990s at a cost of $26 million.

Kenneth T. Jackson

Marcantonio, Vito (*b* New York City, 12 Dec 1902; *d* New York City, 8 Aug 1954). Congressman. He was born near East 112th Street in a predominantly Italian immigrant neighborhood and began his career in the early 1920s as an aide and protégé of Representative Fiorello H. La Guardia, who like him was a Republican sympathetic toward the left. After La Guardia was defeated by a Democrat in 1932 Marcantonio ran successfully for the seat in 1934, having gained the endorsement of La Guardia's organization, the City Fusion Party. Defeated in the Democratic landslide of 1936, he was reelected in 1938 as the candidate of the Republicans and the American Labor Party. A fiery speaker, he successfully broadened his support to include not only Italians but also African Americans and Puerto Ricans, who represented an increasing share of the voters in his district. He was a staunch supporter of civil rights, Puerto Rican independence, and the New Deal and embraced many policies of the American Communist Party, including its unpopular stand against war after the Soviet Union made its pact with Germany in 1939. As the cold war began he faced stiff opposition and was only narrowly reelected in 1948. As the mayoral candidate of the American Labor Party in the following year he won 13.8 percent of the vote across the city and a majority in East Harlem. He lost his seat in Congress in 1950, when the Democrats, Republicans, and Liberals sponsored a single candidate against him.

Gerald Meyer, *Vito Marcantonio: Radical Politician, 1902–1954* (Albany: State University of New York Press, 1989)

Maurice Isserman

Marchi, John J(oseph) (*b* Staten Island, 20 May 1921). Legislator. The son of Italian immigrants, he graduated from Manhattan College (1942), St. John's Law School (1949), and Brooklyn Law School (1953). He saw action as a Coast Guard officer during World War II. In 1956 he was elected to the state senate and quickly joined the Republican inner circle; he became chairman of the City of New York Committee (1963–72) and then of the powerful Senate Finance Committee (1973–88). During his career he supported measures to reinstate capital punishment. He defeated Mayor John V. Lindsay in the Republican primary in 1969, but in the general election he finished third behind Lindsay (Liberal) and Mario Procaccino (Democrat); in 1973 he was again the Republican mayoral nominee. In the early 1970s he risked his career by supporting the Lindsay administration's controversial South Richmond Plan prepared by the Rouse Company to guide development on the island, ultimately thwarted by opposition from the Conservative Party. During the fiscal crisis in 1975 he was a key player in passing the rescue package in Albany, New York. After the U.S. Supreme Court invalidated the Board of Estimate in 1989, Marchi became known as the Father of Secession. He introduced legislation to create a Charter Commission for Staten Island and served as chairman; in 1993 Staten Islanders voted to accept the proposed charter for an independent City of Staten Island by a two to one margin, but the movement died in the State Assembly. Marchi retired from the senate in 2006 as the nation's longest serving state legislator.

Jeffrey A. Kroessler, Barnett Shepherd

March of Dimes Birth Defects Foundation. Charitable organization formed in 1938 in New York City as the National Foundation for Infant Paralysis by President Franklin D. Roosevelt and Basil O'Connor, with the goal of fighting polio. It occupied offices in the Equitable Life Assurance Building at 120 Broadway and acquired the name March of Dimes after a national radio broadcast by the comedian Eddie Cantor, who urged listeners to send dimes for the organization to the White House. After polio vaccines were developed by Jonas Salk and Albert Sabin, the organization shifted its emphasis in 1958 toward fighting birth defects through research and education. The current name dates from 1979. Its headquarters are in White Plains, New York.

Montana Katz

marinas. Private boats were kept in undeveloped shoal coves and bays in the metropolitan area during the nineteenth century. After the New York Yacht Club was formed in 1884 other private boating facilities were soon provided.

79th Street Boat Basin, 2009

As parks commissioner, Robert Moses opened the first public marinas in 1937 at the 79th Street Boat Basin (with 80 moorings and 116 slips in the early twenty-first century) as part of a project known as the West Side Improvement; he added the World's Fair Marina in Flushing Bay in the early 1960s. Recreational boats may be stored and serviced for a fee at more than 40 public and private facilities with approximately 5600 slips in Manhattan, the East Bronx, North Queens, Staten Island, and Brooklyn.

Ann L. Buttenwieser

Marine Air Terminal. Facility completed in 1939 on the western end of La Guardia Airport to accommodate seaplanes. Designed by the architectural firm of Delano and Aldrich in the art deco style, it has a prominent circular waiting area decorated with a mural by James Brooks titled *Flight* (1940); at 12 feet (3.7 meters) high and 237 feet (72 meters) long, it is one of the largest murals created for the Works Progress Administration. The terminal now serves the passengers of intercity shuttle flights. Both the building and its interior have been designated historic sites by the New York City Landmarks Preservation Commission; it is also listed on the National Register of Historic Places.

Lisa Gitelman

Marine Midland Bank. Commercial bank formed in Buffalo in 1850 to finance the growing shipping trade along the Great Lakes. It had headquarters in New York City and Buffalo. In 1980 the Hongkong and Shanghai Banking Corporation (HSBC) purchased a 51 percent interest in Marine Midland, which it extended to full ownership in 1987. The bank continued to do business under the Marine Midland name until 1998, when it was rebranded HSBC Bank USA.

Gladys Chen

Marine Park. Neighborhood in southeastern Brooklyn bounded to the north by Flatlands Avenue, to the east by Flatbush Avenue, to the south by Avenue U, and to the west by Gerritsen and Nostrand avenues. Originally part of the Town of Flatlands (Dutch: Amersfoort), it is adjacent to a park of the same name occupying 798 acres (323 hectares) of New York City parkland, the largest park in Brooklyn, and 1024 acres (415 hectares) donated to the Gateway National Recreation Area. An archaeological dig revealed that the marshland had been used for hunting and fishing by the Keshawchqueren tribe. Dutch settlers continued to farm and established the first tidemill in North America, the Gerritsen gristmill (1688–1938). A parcel of 140 acres (57 hectares) was bought and donated in 1916 to the city for mandated use as a public park by the philanthropists Alfred T. White and Frederic B. Pratt and added to in 1920 by the family of William C. Whitney, who owned stables there. Although Mayor John F. Hylan resisted the gift in the 1920s, development of the park began in 1938 and in 1939 the recreation area opened. A wave of speculation ensued along Jamaica Bay, which the federal government planned to transform into a major port. Residential development increased during the 1930s after the completion of the Belt Parkway (Leif Ericson Drive), the extension of Flatbush Avenue south of Avenue U, and the opening of the Marine Parkway Gil Hodges Memorial Bridge to the Rockaways. Streets were laid out at an oblique angle to the grid of surrounding neighborhoods. Public transit was inadequate, and detached, single-family houses were built with driveways and garages so that owners could easily keep automobiles in the isolated neighborhood. The Marine Park Civic Association, formed in 1926, welcomed the middle-class residents, many of whom were civil servants. In 1970 the neighborhood was transformed by the opening of Kings Plaza, the first large shopping mall in Brooklyn. The section of the park south of Avenue U remained undeveloped except for a golf course in 1963 and the Gerritsen Creek Nature Trail. In 2000 the Salt Creek Nature Center opened. The Hendrick I. Lott House (1720 and 1800), recognized by the New York City Historic House Trust, lies in the middle of the neighborhood. Among the churches in the area are St. Thomas Aquinas Roman Catholic Church and St. Columba Roman Catholic Church. Most of the population is Italian, Irish, and Jewish with recently arrived Greeks and small groups of African Americans and Asians. A former resident of Marine Park is Joe Torre, longtime manager of the New York Yankees.

The Gerritsen Creek Nature Trail (New York: City of New York Parks and Recreation Natural Resources Group, 1989)

Stephen Weinstein, John Manbeck

marine pollution. Although pollution of the approximately 1200 square miles (3108 square kilometers) of water that fills New York Harbor and its estuaries has been a relentless problem throughout the city's history, it was not seriously addressed for centuries. In 1936 a frustrated Mayor Fiorello H. La Guardia observed that the city was still disposing of sewage the same way the Dutch had done 300 years earlier—by pouring it into the harbor. In New Amsterdam this was accomplished with open canals. Later, English colonists posted rows of slaves to pass tubs of waste to the river. In 1797 the Common Council ordered that sinks and drains be built at City Hall to prevent urine from overflowing from outhouses. Nearby, the Collect, a once-pristine pond where early settlers had fished and swum, had devolved into such "a very stink and common sewer" that the Common Council had it filled in by 1810.

There were few sewers in the city before the Croton Aqueduct opened in 1842, but as citizens stopped using local well water, the resulting rise of the water table made outhouses useless, and by 1852, 148 miles (238 kilometers) of sewers were spilling waste into the harbor. In the 1870s swimmers in the Hudson River found that it was unwise to jump in the water except at peak high tide. As criticism mounted over the pollution and stench, the state legislature passed a law in 1871 making dumping in the Harlem River, East River, or Upper Bay a misdemeanor. Garbage scows and barges were delegated to carry waste out into deep water outside Sandy Hook; however, it was discovered that many cargoes actually were dumped in the Upper Bay and even the rivers. A groundbreaking study of pollution in the harbor in 1907 by Daniel D. Jackson, sponsored by a business committee that included J. P. Morgan, reported that in the Queens estuary of Newtown Creek, the water seemed "almost a thick black oil" and was "coated with an oily scum." In 1909 the city conducted its first water-quality analysis at 12 survey stations in the harbor, but with little effect. The famous oyster beds stretching some 350 square miles (907 square kilometers) were shut down when the City Health Department in 1927 declared that local oysters were unsafe to eat. Miles out in the Atlantic, the bottom of the city's dumping grounds in the Hudson Canyon was without oxygen and any sign of life. Sewage was not the only pollution; in the late 1960s government watercraft picked up 24,000 tons of debris every year.

Efforts to control and mitigate sewage began during the 1930s, when 70 percent of the present-day wastewater system was constructed. During the 1960s the city's first large sewage treatment plant was built at Newtown Creek and work began on the North River Sewage Treatment Plant on the Hudson between 137th and 145th Streets (under Riverbank State Park). In 1977 the city established the New York City Department of Environmental Protection, and by 2008, 14 sewage plants were treating 1.8 billion gallons (6.8 billion liters) of wastewater a day. A sludge boat, the *Red Hook,* with a capacity of 1.2 million gallons (4.5 billion liters), was launched in early 2009 to collect sewage that would be transformed into dry fertilizer. As the city's 53 survey stations were reporting that bacteria levels were down and oxygen levels up, volunteer groups such as the Electric Oyster Project were working to open new oyster beds. But problems remained, including the flow of polychlorinated biphenyls (PCBs) and fertilizer runoff down the Hudson River from upstate factories and farms. Furthermore, rainstorms could double the normal daily flow of wastewater, overtaxing sewage treatment plants and causing untreated waste to pour into the harbor through the city's 450 combined sewer overflow locations. The improvement of the storm drainage system became one of the highest priorities of the Department of Environmental Protection in the early 2000s.

Robert Boyle, *The Hudson River: A Natural and Unnatural History* (New York: W. W. Norton, 1969); John Waldman, *Heartbeats in the Muck: History, Sea Life, and Environment of New York Harbor* (Guilford, Conn.: Lyons Press, 1999); Philip Lopate, *Waterfront: A Journey around Manhattan* (New York: Crown, 2004); New York City Department of Environmental Protection, "New York Harbor Water Quality Survey," http://nyc.gov/html/dep/html/news/hwqs.shtml

John Rousmaniere

Mariners Harbor. Neighborhood in northwestern Staten Island, bounded to the north by the Kill van Kull, to the east by the approach to the Bayonne Bridge, to the south by Forest Avenue, and to the west by the Goethals Bridge. The area was long associated with such maritime businesses as commercial fishing and oyster harvesting (curtailed in 1916 by pollution of the harbor), shipbuilding (at its height during World War II, notably at the Bethlehem Steel Shipyard), and boat repair. There are small businesses along Richmond Terrace, the main thoroughfare. The housing stock consists of older one-family houses, some attached housing, and two subsidized housing projects.

Marjorie Johnson

Maritime College. Specialized college within the 64-campus State University of New York (SUNY), located at historic Fort Schuyler in the Throgs Neck section of the Bronx on a spit of land between the East River and Long Island Sound. Maritime College dates from 1874 when it was called the New York Nautical Training School situated on the school ship *St. Mary's* moored in the East River. The college came ashore in 1938 when Fort Schuyler was modernized as a Works Progress Administration project. In 1948 the college joined the newly created SUNY. It is the oldest maritime college in the United States. In addition to academic buildings and dormitories, the training ship *Empire State VI* is berthed next to the campus, a vital laboratory for students who go to sea each summer. The college graduates both deck and engine merchant marine officers, as well as others headed for careers in the transportation industry. In 2010 there were over 1500 students, including those pursuing master's degrees.

Karen E. Markoe

maritime unions. Seamen in New York City first went on strike in 1802 seeking to increase their monthly wage from $10 to $14. They took part in a labor convention in 1850, and in 1895 offices were opened in the city by the International Seamen's Union (ISU), a national federation that included craft unions for deckhands, stewards, and engine room personnel, and such organizations as the Harbor Boatmen's Union of New York (chartered in 1907). The National Industrial Union of Marine Transport Workers, which was affiliated with the Industrial Workers of the World, opened a branch in the city in 1913 that by 1916 had 5000 members. In 1928 communists began organizing seamen into the Marine Workers Progressive League, reorganized in 1930 as the Marine Workers Industrial Union (MWIU); it competed with the Marine Transport Workers for recruits among unemployed seamen, who congregated around South Street and took lodging at the Seamen's Church Institute. The MWIU disbanded in 1935 to infiltrate the ISU, leading to two bitter strikes in 1936 and the formation of the National Maritime Union (NMU) in 1937. After gaining nearly all the members of the ISU, the NMU had nearly 100,000 members in 1945. Between 1947 and 1950 it was weakened by infighting between communists and their opponents that led to the expulsion of communist leaders (Joseph Curran, the founding president, remained in control); it was also challenged by the Seafarers International Union (SIU), formed in the city in 1938 by members of the Sailors' Union of the Pacific, who were opposed to the communists. The NMU and the SIU had contradictory racial policies: the NMU sought to end racial segregation in shipping on the East Coast, and the SIU barred blacks from working in the deck and engine room departments until the early 1950s. Both unions suffered terrible casualties in the Atlantic during World War II. Containerization, ships sailing under foreign registry, and the decline of passenger service diminished the NMU to 22,000 members by 1988, at which time it closed its headquarters in New York City and merged with District 1 of the Marine Engineers Benevolent Association. In 2001, NMU merged with the Seafarers International Union of North America. As of 2010 membership stood at about 11,700.

William Gottlieb, *This Is the NMU* (New York: William P. Gottlieb, 1956); Bruce Nelson, *Workers on the Waterfront: Seamen, Longshoremen, and Unionism in the 1930s* (Urbana: University of Illinois Press, 1989)

Joe Doyle

markets. The first regularly appointed marketplace in New Amsterdam occupied an area of vacant land between the warehouse of the Dutch West India Company and Fort Amsterdam. Known as Market Street or Market-Field, it was used by Indians and country people (called "strangers" by the colonists) to sell pelts, corn, and fish daily to local residents until 1641, when officials seeking to regulate the trade established a weekly market day. Because local farmers grew only tobacco, food shortages were common, and by 1650 on market day residents waited along the shore between Whitehall and Broad streets, known as the Strand, for farmers and Indians to arrive. The authorities responded by opening the first public market there in 1656; it was replaced by the Custom-House Bridge Market in 1675, which remained the primary market until it was razed in 1708. Officials established the first public meat market in 1658 after charges of corruption were leveled against the store of the Dutch West India Company. Known as the Broadway Shambles, it stood in front of Fort Amsterdam and was staffed by 12 "sworn butchers" authorized to slaughter all cattle within the city limits. By 1683 produce and meat could be sold every day, but unauthorized peddlers, or "hucksters," and residents were prohibited from transacting any sales outside the official markets, a rule that remained in place until 1841. Butchers paid a tax for the exclusive right to make sales in the markets.

Initially the Common Council recommended sites for new markets, and it designated several in 1691: the Broad Street Market, the Coenties Slip Fish Market, and the

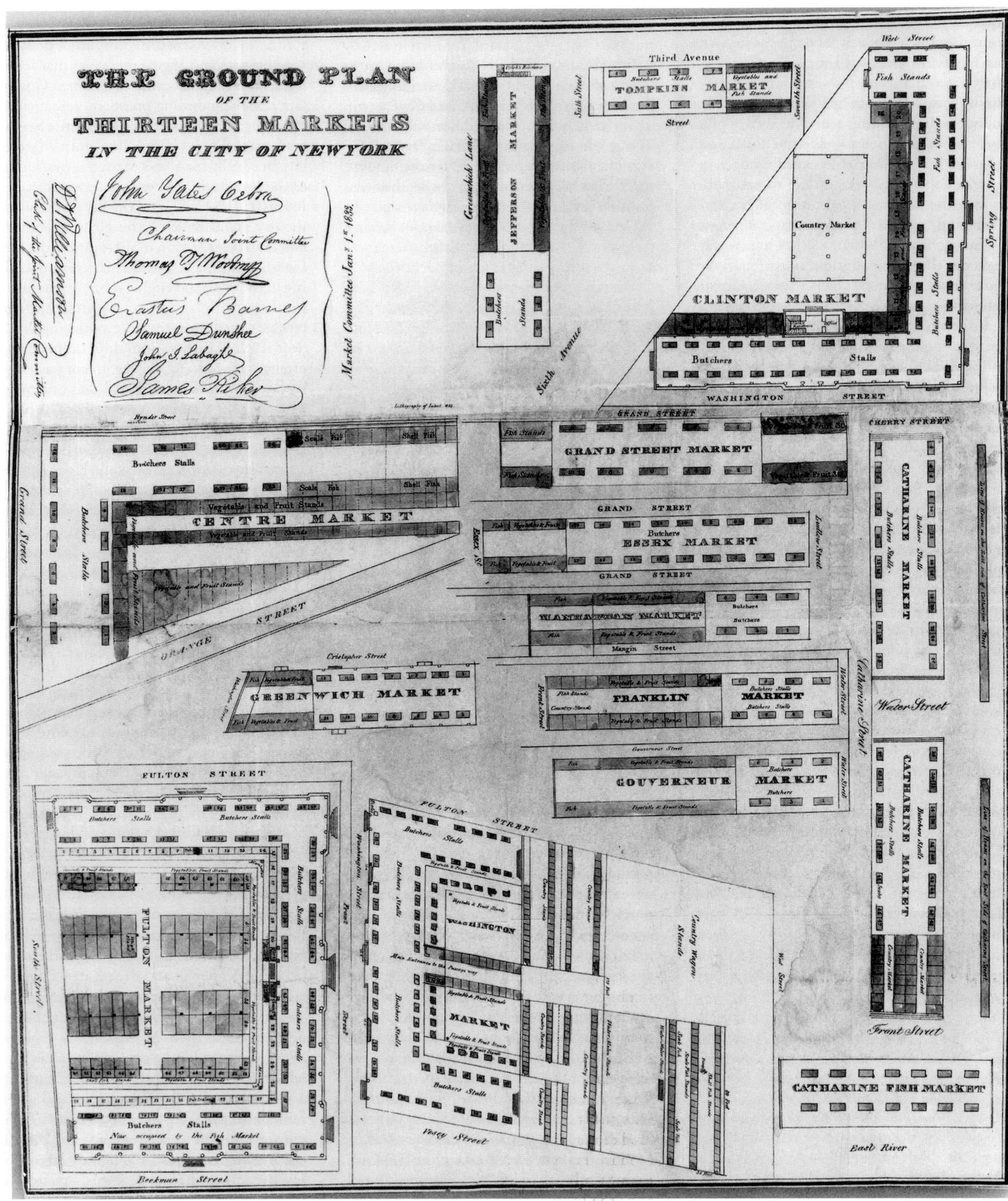

Anthony Imbert, Ground Plan of the Thirteen Markets in the City of New York

Old Slip Market, which sold only meat. Customs changed when the Fly Market was formed in 1699 in response to a petition by residents of Pearl Street. Similar arrangements were made elsewhere, and once neighborhoods were granted permission to build a market they often raised money for it by selling lottery tickets. Those built during the first half of the eighteenth century included the Wall Street Market, the Flatten Barrack Market, the Broadway Market, where trading between Indians and slaves was outlawed in 1740 for promoting "disease"; the White Hall Slip Market, built in 1746 on the former site of the Custom-House Bridge Market; the Exchange Market; and the Peck Slip Market, erected by residents of the wealthy neighborhood facing Water Street as the first brick market in the city. By mid-century a large volume of business was done at the Fly Market, which stood next to the ferry, attracting farmers from Long Island. It also functioned as a slave market. Overcrowded, filthy, and dilapidated by 1795, it closed in 1816 and was replaced by the Fulton Market.

Markets built during the second half of the eighteenth century included the Bear (or Hudson), Crown, Oswego, Catherine, and Spring Street markets; those built during the first half of the nineteenth included the Grand-Market Place and the Corlear's Hook (Grand Street), Collect, Greenwich, Goveneur, Washington, Fish, Centre, Essex, Franklin, Manhattan, Clinton, Tompkins, Jefferson, Monroe, and Harlem markets. Butchers were among the most influential figures in markets during these years; they wore high hats and long-tailed coats.

Corruption and graft abounded. Speculators known as "forestallers" took advantage of desperate farmers who could not find or afford stalls in the markets. During yellow fever epidemics in the late eighteenth century and the early nineteenth, butchers and farmers deserted the markets in the infected districts, leaving them vulnerable to unlicensed "shark" butchers.

Nicolino Calyo, The Butcher

The need for food increased rapidly as the local population and economy expanded after the Civil War. Perishables were delivered without regard for demand, quality, or price, and gluts became common. After four peddlers installed pushcarts on Hester Street in 1866, stationary open-air pushcart markets were set up in many parts of the city, used by peddlers and hucksters selling food surpluses; the best-known was one on the Lower East Side. An area near Gansevoort Street became a farmers' market in 1882, and in 1889 the West Washington Market was built for wholesaling, especially of poultry.

New York City markets were largely unregulated until 1900. By this time crops from nearby farms no longer met the city's needs. Produce was delivered by rail and steamship from all over the country and abroad. Upon delivery to New York City, produce was graded and distributed by shippers, commission merchants, wholesalers, and jobbers and often had to pass through several dealers before reaching the retailers. Secondary wholesale distributing points, or jobbers' markets, were at the Harlem Market and in Brooklyn at the Wallabout Market.

Corruption remained unchecked, and markets were also known for their filth and stench and for the street congestion that they caused. The city established a Pushcart Commission in 1905 and another one in 1912, which recommended that there be a wholesale terminal market in each borough; only one resulted, the BRONX TERMINAL MARKET, and not until 1929. One of few other changes was the formation of the Department of Markets in 1917, which eventually operated and supervised the city's wholesale markets, including the Bronx Terminal, Wallabout, West Washington, Gansevoort, and Fulton Fish markets.

The city had more than 50 open-air markets by 1923 and 15,000 peddlers in 1933, leading Mayor Fiorello H. La Guardia to make a number of controversial changes after 1934. Although many of the city's immigrants depended on peddling for a living, especially during the Depression, La Guardia abolished open-air pushcart markets. With federal funds the city erected several indoor municipal retail markets and banned all pushcarts after 1 December 1938. But high rents made stalls unprofitable for vendors, and the indoor markets soon languished. Later customers preferred the convenience of bodegas and supermarkets, and refrigeration obviated daily shopping.

The Hunts Point Market replaced the WASHINGTON MARKET as the city's wholesale food center in 1967. By 2008 it was the largest produce market in the world, selling more than $1 billion worth of produce yearly. In 2005 the FULTON FISH MARKET, which had opened on Fulton Street in 1822, relocated to Hunts Point. A farmers' market sponsored by GREENMARKET, a program of the nonprofit Council on the Environment, opened in Union Square in 1976 and eventually drew 20,000 regular customers. The Bronx Terminal Market became mainly a supplier of Latin American grocers who carted produce in pickup trucks.

By the end of the twentieth century, the city's indoor markets catered mostly to the poor, and a growing number of immigrants worked, like their predecessors, as peddlers. Early in the twenty-first century, New York City's Economic Development Corporation poured $1.5 million into renovating the ESSEX STREET MARKET. In a city increasingly segregated into the rich and the poor, the market stands as an example of a successful commercial space that caters to local residents and visitors alike.

Thomas F. De Voe, *The Market Book* (New York: Burt Franklin, 1862; repr. 1969); Suzanne R. Wasserman, "'The Good Old Days of Poverty': The Battle over the Fate of New York City's Lower East Side during the Depression" (diss., New York University, 1990)

See also GANSEVOORT FARMERS' STREET MARKET, HUNTS POINT FOOD DISTRIBUTION CENTER, and JEFFERSON MARKET.

Suzanne R. Wasserman

Marot, Helen (*b* Philadelphia, 9 June 1865; *d* New York City, 3 June 1940). Writer and reformer. She moved to New York City in 1902 to investigate child labor conditions for the Neighborhood Workers of New York City. In 1905 she led the school visiting committee of the Public Education Association of New York. As executive secretary of the Women's Trade Union League of New York (1906–13) she organized the shirtwaist strike of 1909–10. She wrote two books, *American Labor Unions* (1914) and *Creative Impulse in Industry* (1918), and was an editor of the radical newspaper *The Masses* (1916–17) and the journal *The Dial* (1918–19). Her home was at 206 West 13th Street.

Nancy Schrom Dye, *As Equals and as Sisters: Feminism, the Labor Movement, and the Women's Trade Union League of New York* (Columbia: University of Missouri Press, 1980)

Sarah Henry Lederman

Marquand and Company [Marquand and Paulding]. Firm of jewelers that later became BLACK, STARR AND FROST.

Marquis, Don(ald Robert Perry) (*b* Walnut, Ill., 29 July 1878; *d* Queens, 29 Dec 1937). Humorist, poet, and playwright. From 1913 to 1922 he wrote a popular newspaper column for the *New York Sun*, "The Sun Dial," in which he created fictional characters to represent typical city dwellers. Among these were Hermione, a dilettante from Greenwich Village; Clem Hawley, a heavy drinker critical of

Prohibition; Archy, a cockroach who wrote verse by jumping from one typewriter key to the next (his writings were always uncapitalized because of his inability to hold down two keys at once); and Mehitabel, an adventurous alley cat. In addition to his newspaper columns (reissued in several compilations, including *the lives and times of archy and mehitabel,* 1940), Marquis wrote poems, novels, short stories, and plays (the first and most successful of which was *The Old Soak,* 1922, in which Hawley is the main character).

Lynn Lee, *Don Marquis* (Boston: Twayne, 1981)

Patricia A. Perito

Marsalis, Wynton (Learson) (*b* New Orleans, 18 Oct 1961). Trumpeter and composer. A stand-out trumpet player during his youth, he enrolled in New York City's Juilliard School of Music in 1978 and remained in the city thereafter. In 1980 he joined Art Blakey's Jazz Messengers and subsequently played with several jazz luminaries, including Herbie Hancock, Dizzy Gillespie, and Sonny Rollins. As a bandleader he has released more than 30 recordings—mostly jazz, but several classical recordings as well. Marsalis is the only artist to have won Grammy Awards for both jazz and classical music in the same year—a success he achieved in 1983 and again in 1984. In 1997 Marsalis became the first musician to receive a Pulitzer Prize for jazz recording. Since 2004 he has been the artistic director of Jazz at Lincoln Center.

Michael C. Repka

Marsh, Reginald (*b* Paris, 15 March 1898; *d* Dorset, Vt., 3 July 1954). Painter and illustrator. The son of two wealthy expatriate American artists, he graduated from Yale Art School in 1920 and moved to New York City. He worked as a freelance cartoonist for the *Daily News* and the *New Yorker.* He also studied with John Sloan at the Art Students League, where he later taught from 1935 to 1954. Throughout the 1930s and 1940s Marsh sketched and painted subjects, often using watercolor, in places such as Harlem, the Bowery, 14th Street, burlesque halls and subways, and Coney Island and other local beaches. In 1937 he was commissioned for a large-scale project on the rotunda of the U.S. Custom House in lower Manhattan. He also famously illustrated John Dos Passos's *U.S.A.* trilogy (1945).

Marilyn Cohen, *Reginald Marsh's New York: Paintings, Drawings, Prints and Photographs* (New York: Whitney Museum of American Art/Dover, 1983)

Patricia Hills

Marshall, Louis (*b* Syracuse, N.Y., 1856; *d* Zurich, 1929). Lawyer and civic leader. The son of immigrants, he graduated from Columbia University Law School in 1877 and in 1894 became a partner in the firm of Guggenheimer, Untermyer and Marshall in New York City. He was a prominent member of the German Jewish elite and president of the American Jewish Committee from 1912 to 1929. Under his leadership the committee submitted legal briefs in cases concerned with religious freedom, fought against anti-Semitism, took part in Leo Frank's legal defense, and opposed restrictions on immigration. Marshall attended the peace conference in Paris and was instrumental in ensuring that guarantees of minority rights were written into the constitutions of all the newly created eastern European states. He was president of Temple Emanu-El and chairman of the board of the Jewish Theological Seminary.

Mortin Rosenstock, *Louis Marshall, Defender of Jewish Rights* (Detroit: Wayne State University Press, 1965)

Michael N. Dobkowski

Marshall, Thurgood (*b* Baltimore, Md., 2 July 1908; *d* Washington, D.C., 25 Jan 1991). Justice of the Supreme Court and civil rights lawyer. He began working in New York City in 1935 as a lawyer for the National Association for the Advancement of Colored People (NAACP) at 69 Fifth Avenue. After becoming the chief counsel of the association he settled in the city in 1938, living at 409 Edgecombe Avenue in Harlem. He worked with other NAACP leaders to plan the lawsuit that led to the overturning of racial segregation in public schools (*Brown v. Board of Education,* 1954). In 1955 he moved to Morningside Gardens on 123rd Street between Broadway and Amsterdam Avenue. He was nominated to the U.S. Court of Appeals for the Second Circuit by President John F. Kennedy in 1961 and left the city for Washington, D.C., in 1965, when he was named solicitor general by President Lyndon B. Johnson. Johnson then appointed him to the Supreme Court in 1967.

Michael D. Davis and Hunter R. Clark, *Thurgood Marshall* (New York: Birch Lane, 1992)

Thomas M. Hilbink

Marshall Chess Club. One of the oldest and most active chess clubs in the United States. Formed in 1915 by Frank J. Marshall, national chess champion from 1909 to 1936, it moved in 1931 to its own brownstone building at 23 West 10th Street, which it continued to occupy as of 2010. The club has sponsored several memorable events, including rounds of national championships and a tournament in 1956 in which Bobby Fischer defeated Donald Byrne in what became known as the "game of the century." Leading American players who have developed at the club include Reuben Fine, Arthur Dake, Larry Evans, Edmar Mednis, and Andrew Soltis.

Chess: The Game of the Ages (New York: Marshall Chess Club, 1932)

James Glass

marshals. Enforcement officers authorized under the New York City Civil Court Act (1962). Marshals are responsible for executing mandates of the Civil Court. They are appointed by the mayor to five-year terms and are unsalaried: their income consists of fees paid by the parties in court cases. By law, there can be no more than 83 marshals at a time; as of 2007 there were 44 marshalships.

Neal C. Garelik

Marsh and McLennan. Firm of insurance brokers founded in Chicago from the 1905 merger of agencies controlled by Henry W. Marsh and Donald R. McLennan. Marsh managed insurance for U.S. Steel and McLennan was an expert in railroad insurance; when the two joined forces they captured the insurance accounts for all major railroads in the Midwest and opened main offices in New York and Chicago. After years of growth, the company went public in 1962. In 1998 Marsh and McLennan obtained office space in floors 93 through 100 of One World Trade Center, an ultimately tragic move as 295 employees died during the terrorist attacks of 11 September 2001. In the aftermath, the company created Axis Specialty Limited, a global insurance and reinsurance company, to address industry cutbacks. In 2004 New York Attorney General Eliot Spitzer filed a civil suit against the company amidst concerns about price-fixing and conflicts of interest among insurance brokers. Chief Executive Officer Jeffrey Greenberg resigned as a result of the investigation and was replaced by Michael Cherkasky; after company reorganization, a settlement was reached in 2005. In 2010 the company's headquarters were at 1166 Avenue of the Americas.

Kate Lauber

Martí [y Pérez], **José** [Julián] (*b* Havana, 28 Jan 1853; *d* Dos Ríos, Cuba, 19 May 1895). Poet and revolutionary. He was educated in Havana, published his first poems by age 15, and launched the newspaper *La patria libre* at 16. For supporting Cuban nationalism during an uprising in 1868 he was imprisoned by Spanish authorities and deported to Spain, where he continued to write and earned a degree in law. He moved to New York City on 3 January 1880 and remained there for most of the next 15 years, working from his headquarters at 120 Front Street to end slavery and Spanish rule in Cuba. While in the city he was the editor of *Patria,* a Cuban nationalist weekly newspaper launched in 1892, and wrote poetic works such as *Versos sencillos* (1890–91); he also led the Partido Revolucionario Cubano in Brooklyn and helped to form La Liga (1890) to promote the rights of Cuban and Puerto Rican blacks. After leaving the city for the Caribbean on 31 January 1895 he outlined plans for a Cuban insurrection in the *Manifesto of Montecristo,* issued from Santo Domingo on 25 March. He led an expeditionary force to Cuba on 11 April and was killed while fighting the Spanish. An equestrian statue of Martí stands in Central Park.

Peter Turton, *José Martí, Architect of Cuba's Freedom* (London: Zed Books, 1986)

Kevin Kenny

Martin, Mary (*b* Weatherford, Texas, 1 Dec 1914; *d* Rancho Mirage, Calif., 3 Nov 1990). Actress. She attended school in Nashville and moved to New York City, where in 1938 she became known for singing "My Heart Belongs to Daddy" in Cole Porter's *Leave It to Me* on Broadway. After making several motion pictures in Hollywood she returned to the Broadway stage, where she performed in *South Pacific* (winning a Tony Award in 1949), *Peter Pan* (1954), and *The Sound of Music* (1959); she also toured with such productions as *Annie Get Your Gun* and *A Celebration of Richard Rodgers* and had many roles on television. Martin was known for the vivacity and precision of her performances. She wrote an autobiography, *My Heart Belongs* (1976). Her son, Larry Hagman, also became a film and television star.

Shirlee P. Newman, *Mary Martin on Stage* (Philadelphia: Westminster, 1969)

James E. Mooney

Martyrs' Monument. Memorial in Brooklyn's Fort Greene Park honoring the nearly 12,000 Americans who died aboard British PRISON SHIPS in nearby Wallabout Bay during the Revolutionary War. The idea for the memorial originated with the New York Tammany Society, one of whose early leaders, Benjamin Romaine, had collected the remains of the prison ship dead from the beaches of the bay. In 1808 the society mounted a "Grand Funeral Procession," long remembered as one of the great civic events of the early nineteenth century, in which the remains were deposited in a small wooden crypt overlooking the bay at Hudson Avenue and York Street. Despite repeated attempts to erect a more permanent marker, nothing of consequence happened until 1873, when the remains were moved again—this time to a more substantial stone crypt in Washington (now Fort Greene) Park, recently landscaped by Frederick Law Olmsted and Calvert Vaux. A new group, the Society of Old Brooklynites (1880), revived the campaign for a permanent memorial but failed to gain traction until the Daughters of the American Revolution (DAR) joined the effort in the 1890s. In 1902 Congress appropriated $100,000 to construct a monument, and the Martyrs' Monument Association, led by the DAR, chose a neoclassical design by Stanford White of the architectural firm McKim, Mead and White. Fort Greene Park was substantially renovated and the 1873 crypt incorporated into the base of a 148-foot (45-meter) Doric column (reputedly the tallest in the world) that is approached via a 100-foot-wide (30.5-meter-wide) granite staircase. Atop the column rests a bronze decorative lantern designed by the sculptor A. A. Weinman. Although its unveiling on 14 November 1908 was attended by a throng of appreciative spectators, the monument was badly neglected thereafter. A major repair program was completed in celebration of the monument's centennial in 2008.

Edwin G. Burrows

Martyrs' Monument, 2009

Marvel Comics. Firm of comic book publishers, formed in 1939 in New York City as Timely Publications. It introduced the characters the Human Torch and the Sub-Mariner in the same year, its "superhero" Captain America in 1941, and the Fantastic Four in 1961. The firm sought to distinguish itself from its competitor DC Comics by imbuing its superheroes with human frailties. Some of its most memorable characters were introduced in 1962, including the Incredible Hulk, Thor the Thunder God, and Spider-Man. It also developed the first African American superhero, the Black Panther, who first appeared with the Fantastic Four in 1966 and was given his own series in 1973. In 1971 the firm published an issue that focused on drug abuse (The Amazing Spider-Man Comics no. 96) without the seal of approval of the Comics Code (adopted in 1954), as a result of which the code was relaxed. Later publications by Marvel Comics include X-Men (1975), Marvel Graphic Novel (1982), a comic "album" based on the European model, and Epic Comics. In the twenty-first century, Marvel branched out into the motion picture industry, turning popular comics like Spider-Man, Iron Man, the Incredible Hulk, and Thor into successful films.

Will Jacobs and Gerard Jones, *The Comic Book Heroes* (New York: Crown, 1985); Mike Benton, *The Comic Book in America: An Illustrated History* (Dallas: Taylor, 1989); *The Marvel Comics Encyclopedia: The Complete Guide to Characters of the Marvel Universe,* rev. edn (New York: DK Publishing, 2009)

Patricia A. Perito

Marx Brothers. Team of comedians. Its members, all born in New York City, were Chico (Leonard) Marx (*b* 26 March 1886; *d* Beverly Hills, Calif., 11 Oct 1961), Harpo (Adolph) Marx (*b* 23 Nov 1888; *d* Hollywood, 28 Sept 1964), Groucho (Julius) Marx (*b* 2 Oct 1890; *d* Los Angeles, 19 Aug 1977), Gummo (Milton) Marx (*b* 23 Oct 1893; *d* Palm Springs, Calif., 21 April 1977), and Zeppo (Herbert) Marx (*b* 25 Feb 1901; *d* Palm Springs, 30 Nov 1979). Groucho was born at 239 East 114th Street; from 1895 to 1910 the family lived at 179 East 93rd Street. Some of the brothers attended Public School 86 on 96th Street; none graduated. Groucho began his career in show business at 15 as a singer in a vaudeville trio and was soon followed by Gummo. The two formed the Nightingales in 1907 with a female singer (soon replaced by a male singer) and in the following year were joined by Harpo. In 1910 the brothers moved to Chicago with their mother, Minnie Marx, who was also their manager; Chico had his own act in Pittsburgh before joining the others in 1912. Gummo, the "straight man" of the group, was drafted during World War I and replaced by Zeppo. The brothers toured the vaudeville circuit and won a performance at the Palace Theatre in 1915. After returning to New York City they appeared on Broadway in the phenomenally successful musical revue *I'll Say She Is!* (1924), in George S. Kaufman's *The Cocoanuts* (1925; film version, Astoria Studios, 1929), which satirized financial speculation in Florida, and in *Animal Crackers* (1928; film version, Astoria Studios, 1930), a satire by Kaufman and Morrie Ryskind of efforts by Jews to assimilate into genteel society. From 1924 to 1926 Groucho lived in an apartment building at Riverside Drive and 161st Street. The brothers signed a lucrative contract with Paramount Pictures in 1931 and moved to California. After Zeppo's retirement they returned to New York City in 1935 to film *A Night at the Opera* by Kaufman and Ryskind. The Marx Brothers perfected an anarchic brand of comedy that relied on physicality, rapid timing, and verbal repartee and came to be strongly associated with ethnic New York City. Each brother had a distinctive persona that varied little from one film to the next: Groucho portrayed a wiseacre and ne'er-do-well, Chico an Italian immigrant with an unorthodox style of playing the piano, and Harpo a frenetic harpist who never spoke. Off screen Harpo was an occasional member of the Algonquin Round Table.

Harpo Marx with Rowland Barber, *Harpo Speaks* (New York: Random House, 1961; rev. Freeway, 1974); Hector Arce, *Groucho* (New York: G. P.

Putnam's Sons, 1979); Wes D. Gehring, *The Marx Brothers: A Bio-bibliography* (New York: Greenwood, 1987); Groucho Marx and Richard J. Anobile, *The Marx Brothers Scrapbook* (New York: Harper and Row, 1989).

Charles Musser, David Nasaw

Mary Louis Academy. Catholic high school for girls at 176-21 Wexford Terrace in Jamaica Estates, opened in September 1936 and run by the Sisters of St. Joseph; it was named for the general superior of the order who chose the site, formerly the Adikes estate. Classes were held in the faculty convent (formerly the main house on the estate) until a new building was completed. An addition completed in 1956 doubled the size of the school. In the early twenty-first century about 1000 students are enrolled.

Gilbert Tauber

Marymount Manhattan College. College opened in 1936 on Fifth Avenue and 84th Street. One of six women's colleges in the United States founded by the Religious of the Sacred Heart of Mary (a Roman Catholic order formed in France in the mid-nineteenth century), it began as a junior college affiliated with Marymount College in Tarrytown, New York. In 1947 New York State granted the school a charter as Marymount Manhattan College and the school began offering a four-year liberal arts curriculum leading to a bachelor's degree. The college moved to its present site at 221 East 71st Street in 1948 and became independent of Marymount in Tarrytown in 1961. The main building was designated a city landmark; the Joseph C. Nugent Building was erected adjacent to it in 1975. The college first admitted men in 1989. In 2005, following its decision to confer an honorary degree on then Senator Hillary Rodham Clinton, an advocate of abortion rights, the college was compelled to sever its historic ties to the Catholic Church. Citing Pope John Paul II's 1990 *Ex corde Ecclesiae*, the apostolic constitution on Catholic universities, Edward Cardinal Egan, archbishop of New York, declared that the Catholic Church no longer recognized the school as a Catholic institution. In the early twenty-first century more than 2000 students were enrolled.

Katherine Kurz Burton, *Mother Butler of Marymount* (New York: Longmans, Green, and Company, 1944)

Matthew J. Brennan

Mary Powell. Sidewheel steamboat, built in 1861 by Michael S. Allison of Jersey City, New Jersey. Known as the "speed queen of the Hudson," it was 300 feet (91 meters) long and had a vertical-beam engine made by the firm of Fletcher Harrison and Company. Each day from Monday to Saturday between 1861 and 1912 the *Mary Powell* made a round trip of 180 miles (290 kilometers) from Rondout, New York, to Manhattan, where it docked at noon, and back to Rondout by 9 p.m. The ship earned a reputation for punctuality and safety under the exacting command of Absalom L. Anderson. It was later remodeled and used for various excursions by the Hudson River Day Line. It was retired in 1917 and dismantled, its whistle acquired by the steamboat *Robert Fulton*.

Donald C. Ringwald, *The Mary Powell* (Berkeley, Calif.: Howell–North, 1992)

Arthur G. Adams

Masliansky, Zvi Hirsch (*b* Slutsk [now in Belarus], 16 May 1856; *d* Brooklyn, 11 Jan 1943). Jewish preacher. A religious Zionist and a brilliant speaker whose rhetoric bridged the gap between traditional Jewish preaching and modern oratory, he was forced because of his political activities to flee Russia in 1895. He settled in New York City, where he became active in Zionist circles and gained enormous popularity as a speaker among eastern European Jewish immigrants. From 1898 he delivered a Yiddish sermon on Friday nights at the Educational Alliance, and in 1902 he helped to launch *Di yidishe velt,* a daily newspaper in Yiddish and English. Masliansky published several volumes of sermons and memoirs.

Daniel Soyer

Masons. See Freemasons.

Maspeth. Neighborhood in west central Queens (2009 pop. 53,000), bounded to the north by the Brooklyn–Queens Expressway, to the east by 69th Street, to the south by Metropolitan Avenue, and to the west by Newtown Creek and Brooklyn. It is named for the Mespat Indians, who inhabited the headwaters of Newtown Creek. Founded by the English minister Francis Doughty under Dutch authority, it was the first European settlement in Queens County (1642). It was attacked by Indians in 1643 and abandoned in 1644. Several roads were laid out during the eighteenth century. DeWitt Clinton, governor of New York State (1817–28), had a summer home at 56th Terrace and 56th Avenue, where he planned the Erie Canal. In 1847 St. Saviour's Church, designed by Richard Upjohn in the country Gothic style, was built on land donated by James Maurice; the Landmarks Preservation Commission declined to designate the church a landmark, and it was dismantled in 2008 (with the intent of it being rebuilt elsewhere). In 1852 Mount Olivet Cemetery was opened and development escalated: the population grew from 1449 in 1875 to 4300 in 1898. Fertilizer works and lumber yards grew up along the creek; inland were a linoleum plant and rope walks (long, narrow buildings where hemp was spun into rope). The eastern edge of Maspeth abutting Newtown Creek remained industrial and commercial, especially along Grand and Maspeth avenues. In 1925 German and Hungarian residents opened Metropolitan Oval, which in 2009 was the oldest soccer field in continuous use in the United States. In the early 2000s the population was still mostly Catholic, including Poles, Lithuanians, Germans, Irish, and Italians, with increasing numbers of Koreans, Puerto Ricans, Dominicans, and Greeks. The neighborhood remained solidly blue collar, with many sanitation workers, firefighters, truck drivers, factory workers, laborers, and small shopkeepers. The Long Island Expressway and a belt of cemeteries nearby isolated the northern section of Maspeth from northern and central Queens and kept it suburban; the side streets were lined with one-family detached houses. The 1898 Brinkerhoff School became Maspeth Town Hall, a community center, in the 1980s. Grand Avenue, the main shopping street, connects Brooklyn and Elmhurst.

Vincent Seyfried, Jeffrey A. Kroessler

Masses. Monthly magazine launched in 1911 as the reinvigorated descendant of an earlier muckraking socialist publication of the same name. It was published from offices situated first on Nassau Street and from June 1913 at 91 Greenwich Avenue. Edited by Max Eastman and his associate editor Floyd Dell, *The Masses* was organized under a system of collective ownership and editorship. It became known for its bold, powerful graphics, advocacy of class warfare, and relentless satire of bourgeois values. The magazine's opposition to World War I resulted in its suppression by federal censors, and it ceased publication in December 1917.

Rebecca Zurier, *Art for the Masses: A Radical Magazine and Its Graphics, 1911–1917* (Philadelphia: Temple University Press, 1988)

Jan Seidler Ramirez

Massine, Léonide [Miassin, Leonid (Fedorovich)] (*b* Moscow, 8 Aug 1895; *d* Cologne, 16 March 1979). Choreographer. He first visited New York City with the Ballets Russes in 1916, when ballet was virtually unknown in the United States. By the time of his third visit in 1933 ballet was popular, and Massine was widely known to American audiences. In Manhattan he joined Ballet Theatre in 1942 and provided choreography for a production in 1948 of *The Red Shoes*, in which he also danced. Believing that a ballet should incorporate art and music of high quality, he was as comfortable in the classical idiom as he was at creating choreography for the short features shown in movie theaters. Although his later works were too didactic for his audiences, such earlier ones as *Gaïeté Parisienne* and *Parade* are still performed regularly. Massine was a pivotal figure in the popularization of classical dance in the city. He wrote *My Life in Ballet* (1968).

Clarissa L. Bushman

Masterson, Bat [William Barclay] (*b* Iroquois County, Ill., 24 Nov 1853; *d* New York City, 25 Oct 1921). Peace officer, gambler, and newspaper reporter. After a career as a gunfighter and gambler in the West he moved to New York City in 1902, where he became a sportswriter and editor at the *Morning Telegraph.* At the time of his death he was the sports editor of the newspaper and secretary of the company. Masterson is buried in Woodlawn Cemetery in the Bronx.

Kenneth T. Jackson

Mathewson, Christy [Christopher] (*b* Factoryville, Pa., 12 Aug 1880; *d* Saranac Lake, N.Y., 7 Oct 1925). Baseball pitcher. After attending Bucknell University he played for the New York Giants, managed by John J. McGraw, from 1900 to 1916. Nicknamed "Big Six" after a well-known fire company in New York City, he was noted for his superb control and particularly for his "fadeaway" (screwball) pitch. During his career he won 373 games and lost only 188, compiling a lifetime earned run average of 2.13. He threw 80 shutout games, including three against Philadelphia in the World Series in 1905; won 20 or more games in 12 consecutive seasons; and won 30 or more games in four seasons. Religious and college-bred, he enjoyed a wholesome image and may have been a model for William Gilbert Patten's series of dime novels *Frank Merriwell at Yale.* He was treated like a son by the ruthless and controversial McGraw. Mathewson wrote *Pitching in a Pinch: Baseball from the Inside* (1912) and a play that opened on Broadway, *The Girl and the Pennant: A Base-ball Comedy on Four Acts* (1913). Exposure to poison gas during a training accident in World War I contributed to his death from tuberculosis. In 1936 he was one of five original members inducted into the Baseball Hall of Fame.

Ray Robinson, *Matty, an American Hero: Christy Mathewson of the New York Giants* (New York: Oxford University Press, 1993)

Jeffrey Scheuer

Matthews, Victoria Earle (*b* Fort Valley, Ga., 27 May 1861; *d* New York City, 10 March 1907). Journalist and reformer. Born into slavery, she moved to New York City in 1873 and worked sporadically for large daily newspapers such as the *New York Times,* the *New York Herald,* the *New York Age,* and the *New York Globe.* She is best known for having established the White Rose Industrial Association in 1897, a mission that offered employment advice to black female migrants, a kindergarten, a library, and classes in cooking, sewing, and black history. The association was at 86th Street in 1900 and later moved to 262 West 137th Street in Harlem. Matthews wrote *The Awakening of the Afro-American Woman* (1897).

Thea Arnold

Victoria Earle Matthews

Maurer, Louis (*b* Biebrich [now in Germany], 21 Feb 1832; *d* New York City, 19 July 1932). Lithographer and painter. He arrived in New York City in 1851 and worked briefly for the publisher Thomas Strong. He then spent eight years with Currier and Ives, joined Major and Knapp in 1860, and from 1872 to 1884 produced commercial lithography for his own firm, Maurer and Heppenheimer. A draftsman, illustrator, and printer, he specialized in figures and animals (especially horses): his series "Life of a Fireman" is one of his finest. Maurer was a central figure within printing circles for 80 years and lived his last 57 years at 404 West 43rd Street. His son Alfred H. Maurer (1868–1932) was a well-known painter in New York City.

Wendy Shadwell

Max's Kansas City. Restaurant, bar, and hangout for musicians, artists, writers, and politicians from 1965 until it closed in 1981. Two theories about the origin of the name come from the poet Joel Oppenheimer: the first that the name was related to a place described by fellow poet Max Finstein, and the other that the name referred to Kansas City strip steaks for their expensive nature and high quality. Max's was located at 213 Park Avenue South between 17th and 18th streets. Known for its back room featuring psychedelic burlesque shows, it drew a wide range of patrons, from Andy Warhol and Abbie Hoffman to Mel Brooks and Mick Jagger. Although the club became synonymous with sex, drugs, and rock and roll, owner Mickey Ruskin was also committed to fostering the careers of young artists and performers, including Robert Rauschenberg and Debbie Harry, who was a waitress at Max's before gaining fame with the band Blondie. Bruce Springsteen and Aerosmith both had their first New York City performances at Max's. After the original establishment closed in 1974, it reopened in 1975 as one of the birthplaces of punk rock, featuring The Ramones and The Misfits, among others, under the management of Tommy Dean Mills. Ruskin died in 1983 of a drug overdose at age 50. Max's closed again in 1981 but reopened briefly in 1998 at a new location on West 52nd Street. In 2001 his former girlfriend Yvonne Sewell-Ruskin established the Max's Kansas City Project in his memory to provide financial assistance to young artists in need.

Yvonne Sewall-Ruskin, *High on Rebellion: Inside the Underground at Max's Kansas City* (New York: Thunder's Mouth Press, 1998)

Anne Epstein, Meghan Lalonde

Maxwell, William Henry (*b* Stewartstown, Ireland, 5 March 1852; *d* New York City, 3 May 1920). Educator. After moving to the metropolitan region in 1874 he became the superintendent of schools for the City of Brooklyn and then the first superintendent of the public schools of New York City after consolidation (1898–1917). Faced with shortages of space and funds brought on by massive immigration in the early twentieth century, he initiated programs for immigrants and the poor, including kindergartens, recreation centers, courses in English, and vocational training. He was president of the National Education Association from 1904 to 1905; he also edited the *Educational Review.* Maxwell lived at Park Avenue and 59th Street.

Samuel Abelow, *Dr. William Henry Maxwell* (New York: Scheba, 1934)

Selma Berrol

Maxwell's Plum. Restaurant and bar in Manhattan, opened in April 1966 on First Avenue and 64th Street by Warner LeRoy. For many years the best-known "singles bar" in New York City, it was known for attracting large crowds and for its deliberately garish decor, which included Tiffany lamps, ornate mirrors, and large expanses of stained glass. At the peak of its popularity in the 1970s the restaurant served 350,000 meals a year. Business fell off sharply during the following decade, and the restaurant closed in July 1988.

Maybelline New York. Cosmetics brand originally launched in 1915 as Lash-Brow-Ine by New York chemist T. L. Williams, who created the "first modern eye cosmetic for everyday use." The product was modeled after a combination of Vaseline and coal dust that Williams found his sister, Maybel, using to darken and thicken her eyelashes. Renamed Maybelline Cake Mascara in 1917, it became an immediate local success in the metropolitan area, and the company expanded to include mail-order sales and began distributing products through drugstores and other retail outlets during the 1930s. In 1967 the company was acquired by Plough, and two years later its headquarters moved to Tennessee. In 1996, with acquisition by L'Oréal USA, the company's headquarters moved back to New York City and it became Maybelline New York in 2004.

Jessica Montesano

Mayflower Madam. Nickname given by tabloid newspapers in New York City to Sydney Biddle Barrows (b. 1952), who operated an escort service called Cachet at 307 West 74th Street from 1979 to 1984. She was arrested and prosecuted for promoting prostitution in 1984. She was so called for being a descendant of two original settlers of the Plymouth Colony, John Howland and William Brewster, as well as of Nicholas Biddle, president of the Second Bank of the United States (1823–36). Barrows pled guilty to the charge, and shortly after published *Mayflower Madam* (1986), a best-selling autobiography that was the basis of a television movie (1987) of the same name starring Candice Bergen. Barrows remained unapologetic about her business and lectured on her experiences; she also wrote several books on sexuality, including *Mayflower Manners: Etiquette for Consenting Adults* (1990), *Just between Us Girls: Secrets about Men From the Mayflower Madam* (1996), and *Getting a Little Work Done* (2000).

Timothy J. Gilfoyle

Maynard [née Cooper], **Joan Bacchus** (*b* Brooklyn, 29 Aug 1928; *d* Brooklyn, 22 Jan 2006). Historic preservationist and artist. She attended Bishop McDonnell Memorial High School, the Art Career School, Empire State College, and Columbia University. Maynard participated in the first Fulton Art Fair in Bedford–Stuyvesant in 1958; she was a commercial artist during the 1960s, working as an art director for McGraw–Hill and contributing to *Golden Legacy*, an illustrated magazine for young people about black history, and *Crisis*, the magazine of the National Association for the Advancement of Colored People. When remnants of the nineteenth-century black community of WEEKSVILLE were discovered by helicopter in 1968, Maynard became a founding member of the Society for the Preservation of Weeksville and Bedford–Stuyvesant History. She served as executive director from 1974 to 1999 and advocated for the restoration of the Hunterfly Road Houses for almost 40 years. Maynard worked to create a connection between the historical and contemporary black communities in the Weeksville area (present-day Bedford–Stuyvesant and Crown Heights); she especially strived to give children an active role in Weeksville's preservation. Maynard raised money from government and private sources and donated her own savings to the project, receiving numerous awards and accolades for her efforts, which were essential to the successful establishment of the Weeksville Heritage Center in 2005.

Kate Lauber

mayoralty. The first mayor of New York City was Thomas Willett, appointed by the English

Mayors of New York City since the Conquest of the City by the English in 1664

Mayor	Term
Thomas Willett	1665
Thomas Delavall	1666
Thomas Willett	1667
Cornelius Van Steenwyck	1668–70
Thomas Delavall	1671
Matthias Nichols	1672
John Lawrence	1673–74
William Dervall	1675
Nicholas De Meyer	1676
Stephanus Van Cortlandt	1677
Thomas Delavall	1678
Francis Rombouts	1679
William Dyre	1680–81
Cornelius Van Steenwyck	1682–83
Gabriel Minvielle	1684
Nicolas Bayard	1685
Stephanus Van Cortlandt	1686–88
Peter Delanoy	1689–90
John Lawrence	1691
Abraham De Peyster	1692–94
Charles Lodwik	1694–95
William Merrett	1695–98
Johannes De Peyster	1698–99
David Provost	1699–1700
Isaac De Reimer	1700–1
Thomas Noell	1701–2
Philip French	1702–3
William Peartree	1703–7
Ebenezer Wilson	1707–10
Jacobus Van Cortlandt	1710–11
Caleb Heathcote	1711–14
John Johnson	1714–19
Jacobus Van Cortlandt	1719–20
Robert Walters	1720–25
Johannes Jansen	1725–26
Robert Lurting	1726–35
Paul Richard	1735–39
John Cruger	1739–44
Stephen Bayard	1744–47
Edward Holland	1747–57
John Cruger, Jr.	1757–66
Whitehead Hicks	1766–76
David Matthews	1776–84
James Duane	1784–89
Richard Varick	1789–1801
Edward Livingston	1801–3
DeWitt Clinton	1803–7
Marinus Willett	1807–8
DeWitt Clinton	1808–10
Jacob Radcliff	1810–11
DeWitt Clinton	1811–15
John Ferguson	1815
Jacob Radcliff	1815–18
Cadwallader D. Colden	1818–21
Stephen Allen	1821–24
William Paulding	1825–26
Philip Hone	1826–27
William Paulding	1827–29
Walter Bowne	1829–33
Gideon Lee	1833–34
Cornelius Van Wyck Lawrence	1834–37
Aaron Clark	1837–39
Isaac L. Varian	1839–41
Robert H. Morris	1841–44
James Harper	1844–45
William F. Havemeyer	1845–46
Andrew H. Mickle	1846–47
William V. Brady	1847–48
William F. Havemeyer	1848–49
Caleb S. Woodhull	1849–51
Ambrose C. Kingsland	1851–53
Jacob A. Westervelt	1853–55
Fernando Wood	1855–58
Daniel F. Tiemann	1858–60
Fernando Wood	1860–62
George Opdyke	1862–64
C. Godfrey Gunther	1864–66
John T. Hoffman	1866–68
Thomas Coman (acting)	1868
A. Oakey Hall	1869–72
William F. Havermeyer	1873–74
Samuel B. H. Vance (acting)	1874
William H. Wickham	1875–76
Smith Ely, Jr.	1877–78
Edward Cooper	1879–80
William R. Grace	1881–82
Franklin Edson	1883–84
William R. Grace	1885–86
Abram S. Hewitt	1887–88
Hugh J. Grant	1889–92
Thomas F. Gilroy	1893–94
William L. Strong	1895–97
Robert A. Van Wyck	1898–1901
Seth Low	1902–3
George B. McClellan	1904–9
William J. Gaynor	1910–13
Ardolph L. Kline (acting)	1913
John Purroy Mitchel	1914–17
John F. Hylan	1918–25
James J. Walker	1926–32
Joseph V. McKee (acting)	1932
John P. O'Brien	1933
Fiorello H. La Guardia	1934–45
William O'Dwyer	1946–50
Vincent R. Impellitteri	1950–53
Robert F. Wagner	1954–65
John V. Lindsay	1966–73
Abraham D. Beame	1974–77
Edward I. Koch	1978–89
David N. Dinkins	1990–93
Rudolph W. Giuliani	1994–2001
Michael R. Bloomberg	2002–

(*continued*)

Returns of Mayoral Elections in New York City, 1834–1894

1834	
Cornelius Van Wyck Lawrence (Democrat)	17,576
Gulian C. Verplanck (Whig)	17,395
Others	18
Total	34,989
1835	
Cornelius Van Wyck Lawrence (Democrat)	17,696
Others	2,500
Total	20,196
1836	
Cornelius Van Wyck Lawrence (Democrat)	15,754
Seth Geer (Whig)	6,136
Alexander Ming, Jr. (Locofoco)	2,712
Samuel F. B. Morse (Native American)	1,497
Others	75
Total	26,174
1837	
Aaron Clark (Whig)	16,140
John I. Morgan (Democrat)	12,974
Moses Jacques (Locofoco)	3,911
Others	28
Total	33,053
1838	
Aaron Clark (Whig)	19,723
Isaac L. Varian (Democrat)	19,204
Richard Riker (Conservative)	395
Others	19
Total	39,341
1839	
Isaac L. Varian (Democrat)	21,072
Aaron Clark (Whig)	20,005
Others	36
Total	41,113
1840	
Isaac L. Varian (Democrat)	21,243
J. P. Phoenix (Whig)	19,622
Others	36
Total	40,901
1841	
Robert H. Morris (Democrat)	18,605
J. P. Phoenix (Whig)	18,206
Samuel F. B. Morse (Native American)	77
Others	45
Total	36,933
1842	
Robert H. Morris (Democrat)	20,633
J. P. Phoenix (Whig)	18,755
Thomas F. Field (Abolition)	136
Others	63
Total	39,587
1843	
Robert H. Morris (Democrat)	24,395
Robert Smith (Whig)	19,516
Others	73
Total	43,984
1844	
James Harper (Native)	24,606
Jonathan I. Coddington (Locofoco)	20,726
Morris Franklin (Whig)	5,207
Others	22
Total	50,561
1845	
William F. Havemeyer (Democrat)	24,183
James Harper (Native)	17,472
Dudley Selden (Whig)	7,082
Others	226
Total	48,963
1846	
Andrew H. Mickle (Democrat)	21,675
Robert Taylor (Whig)	15,111
William B. Cozzens (Native)	8,301
Others	757
Total	45,844
1847	
William V. Brady (Whig)	21,310
J. Sherman Brownell (Democrat)	19,877
E. G. Drake (Native)	2,078
Others	433
Total	43,698
1848	
William F. Havemeyer (Democrat)	23,155
William V. Brady (Whig)	22,227
Others	848
Total	46,230
1849	
Caleb S. Woodhull (Whig)	21,656
Myndert Van Schaick (Democrat)	17,535
Others	103
Total	39,294
1850	
Ambrose C. Kingsland (Whig)	22,546
Fernando Wood (Democrat)	17,973
Others	335
Total	40,854
1852	
Jacob A. Westervelt (Democrat)	33,251
Morgan Morgans (Whig)	23,719
Others	1,088
Total	58,058
1854	
Fernando Wood (Soft Shells–Hard Shells)	19,993
James W. Barker (Know Nothing)	18,553
Wilson G. Hunt (Reform)	15,386
Others	5,828
Total	59,760
1856	
Fernando Wood (Democrat)	34,860
Isaac O. Backer (American)	25,209
Anthony J. Bleecker (Republican)	9,654
James S. Libby (Bog Democrat)	4,764
James R. Whiting (Municipal Reform)	3,646
Others	84
Total	78,217
1857	
Daniel F. Tiemann (Independent)	43,216
Fernando Wood (Democrat)	40,889
Others	103
Total	84,208
1859	
Fernando Wood (Mozart Democrat)	29,940
William F. Havemeyer (Tammany Democrat)	26,913
George Opdyke (Republican)	21,417
Others	106
Total	78,376
1861	
George Opdyke (Republican)	25,380
C. Godfrey Gunther (Tammany Democrat)	24,767
Fernando Wood (Mozart Democrat)	24,167
Others	81
Total	74,395
1863	
C. Godfrey Gunther (Independent Democrat)	29,121
Francis I. A. Boole (Tammany Democrat)	22,597
Orison Blunt (Republican)	19,383
Others	65
Total	71,166
1865	
John T. Hoffman (Tammany Democrat)	32,820
Marshall O. Roberts (Republican)	31,657
John Hecker (Mozart Democrat)	10,390
C. Godfrey Gunther (Independent Democrat)	6,758
Others	77
Total	81,702

(*continued*)

Returns of Mayoral Elections in New York City, 1834–1894 (*Continued*)

Candidate	Votes
1867	
John T. Hoffman (Tammany Democrat)	63,061
Fernando Wood (Mozart Democrat)	22,837
William A. Darling (Republican)	18,483
Others	100
Total	104,481
1868	
A. Oakey Hall (Democrat)	75,109
Frederick A. Conkling (Republican)	20,835
Others	321
Total	96,265
1869	
A. Oakey Hall (Democrat)	65,568
Others	1,051
Total	66,619
1870	
A. Oakey Hall (Tammany Democrat)	71,037
Thomas A. Ledwith (Anti-Tammany Democrat)	46,392
Others	1,989
Total	119,418
1872	
William F. Havemeyer (Republican)	53,806
A. R. Lawrence (Liberal–Republican)	45,398
James O'Brien (Apollo Hall Democrat)	31,121
Total	130,325
1874	
William H. Wickham (Democrat)	70,071
Salem H. Wales (Republican)	36,953
Oswald Ottendorfer (Independent)	24,226
Others	443
Total	131,693
1876	
Smith Ely, Jr. (Democrat)	111,880
John Dix (Republican)	57,811
Others	552
Total	170,243
1878	
Edward Cooper (Republican)	79,986
August Schell (Democrat)	60,485
Others	2,793
Total	143,264
1880	
William R. Grace (Democrat)	101,760
William Dowd (Republican)	98,715
Others	1,827
Total	202,302
1882	
Franklin Edson (Democrat)	97,802
Allan Campbell (Republican)	76,385
Others	4,124
Total	178,311
1884	
William R. Grace (Independent)	96,288
Hugh J. Grant (Tammany Democrat)	85,361
Frederick S. Gibbs (Republican)	44,386
Others	1,300
Total	227,335
1886	
Abram S. Hewitt (Democrat)	90,552
Henry George (Labor Union)	68,110
Theodore Roosevelt (Republican)	60,435
Others	895
Total	219,992
1888	
Hugh J. Grant (Democrat)	114,111
Joel B. Erhardt (Republican)	73,037
Abram S. Hewitt (Citizens Democrat)	71,979
Others	13,643
Total	272,770
1890	
Hugh J. Grant (Democrat)	116,581
Francis M. Scott (Republican)	93,382
Others	7,846
Total	217,809
1892	
Thomas F. Gilroy (Democrat)	173,510
Edwin Einstein (Republican)	97,923
Henry Hicks (People's)	2,466
Others	12,250
Total	286,149
1894	
William I. Strong (Republican)	154,094
Hugh J. Grant (Democrat)	108,907
Others	11,315
Total	274,316

Sources: *Manual of the Corporation of the City of New York,* 1870 [for years 1834–70]; *The City Record* [for years 1872–94]

Compiled by James Bradley

governor Richard Nicolls in 1665. For a century and a half the mayor was appointed annually, first by the colonial governor and then by the governor of New York State. The early mayors had limited powers: they sat on the Common Council, where they were at best first among equals. During the nineteenth century the powers and responsibilities of the office fluctuated wildly through many charter revisions, but in general they increased. The mayor in 1820 became elected by the Common Council and in 1830 was given the power to veto the decisions of the council, of which he was no longer a member. When the first direct mayoral elections were held in 1834, the Democrat Cornelius Van Wyck Lawrence defeated Gulian C. Verplanck by 181 votes. In 1849 the mayoral term was extended to two years. Most mayors in the nineteenth century were businessmen, and the best-known ones, such as Philip Hone, William F. Havemeyer, and William R. Grace, are remembered more for their accomplishments out of office than in it. One of few dominant mayors during these years was Fernando Wood (1855–58, 1860–62). No head of Tammany Hall attained the office during the organization's long period of influence, which lasted until after World War II.

The mayor became the symbolic head of government at consolidation in 1898 but continued to operate under severe constraints for decades, especially regarding appointments and budgets: the newly created borough presidents' offices circumscribed the ability of the mayor to control the city's payroll, and other powers were now shared with a strengthened Board of Estimate. The mayoral term was extended to four years in 1905. The person chiefly responsible for defining the modern mayoralty was Fiorello H. La Guardia (1934–45), who by declaring his independence from political bosses and determinedly seeking publicity made himself the focus of power and attention throughout his long tenure. Mayoral power was further strengthened by reforms to the city charter in 1961 that gave mayors the authority to prepare the capital budget (formerly prepared by the City Planning Commission), to alter the operating budget (an authority formerly shared with the Board of Estimate), and to reorganize municipal offices (also formerly shared with the Board of Estimate). Reforms in 1975 encouraged decentralization within the executive branch by allowing commissioners greater discretion than previously in decisions about staffing and the budget, which had formerly been made by the central budget and personnel offices; mayors rarely implemented these reforms because they undermined mayoral control over the commissioners. The mayor's powers of appointment were slightly weakened in 1975 when approval by the City Council became necessary for some positions that had fallen entirely under mayoral jurisdiction, including several on the Municipal Arts Commission, the Board of Health, the Board of Standards and Appeals, the City Planning Commission, the Civil Service Commission, the Landmarks Preservation Commission, the Tax Commission, the Taxi and Limousine Commission, and

Returns of Mayoral Elections in New York City by Borough, 1897–2009

1897	Robert A. Van Wyck (Democrat)	Seth Low (Citizens Union)	Benjamin Tracy (Republican)
Manhattan and Bronx	143,666	77,210	55,834
Brooklyn	76,185	65,656	37,611
Queens	9,275	5,876	5,639
Staten Island	4,871	2,798	2,779
Total	233,997	151,540	101,863
Others, 44,230			
Total vote: 531,630			

1901	Seth Low (Fusion)	Edward M. Shephard (Democrat)
Manhattan and Bronx	114,625	88,858
Brooklyn	162,298	156,631
Queens	12,757	13,321
Staten Island	7,133	6,367
Total	296,813	265,177
Total vote: 561,990		

1903	George B. McClellan (Democrat)	Seth Low (Fusion)
Manhattan and Bronx	188,681	132,178
Brooklyn	102,569	101,251
Queens	17,074	11,960
Staten Island	6,458	6,697
Total	314,782	252,086
Others, 28,417		
Total vote: 595,285		

1905	George B. McClellan (Democrat)	William R. Hearst (Independent)	William M. Ivins (Republican)
Manhattan and Bronx	140,264	123,292	64,289
Brooklyn	68,778	84,835	61,192
Queens	13,228	13,706	7,213
Staten Island	6,127	3,096	4,499
Total	228,397	224,929	137,193
Others, 15,676			
Total vote: 606,195			

1909	William J. Gaynor (Democrat)	Otto T. Bannard (Fusion)	William R. Hearst (Independent)
Manhattan and Bronx	134,075	86,497	87,155
Brooklyn	91,666	73,860	49,040
Queens	17,570	11,907	15,186
Staten Island	7,067	5,040	2,806
Total	250,378	177,304	154,187
Others, 22,198			
Total vote: 604,067			

1913	John Purroy Mitchel (Fusion)	Edward E. McCall (Democrat)
Manhattan	131,280	103,429
Bronx	46,944	25,684
Brooklyn	137,074	77,826
Queens	34,279	20,097
Staten Island	8,640	6,883
Total	358,217	233,919
Others, 34,991		
Total vote: 627,127		

(*continued*)

Returns of Mayoral Elections in New York City by Borough, 1897–2009 (*Continued*)

1917	John F. Hylan (Democrat)	John Purroy Mitchel (Fusion)	Morris Hillquit (Socialist)
Manhattan	113,728	66,748	51,176
Bronx	41,492	19,247	30,374
Brooklyn	114,487	52,921	48,880
Queens	35,399	13,641	13,477
Staten Island	8,850	2,940	1,425
Total	313,956	155,497	145,332

Joseph Bennett (Republican), 56,438; Others, 20,586
Total vote: 691,809

1921	John F. Hylan (Democrat)	Henry H. Curran (Republican)	Jacob Panken (Socialist)
Manhattan	261,452	124,253	28,756
Bronx	118,235	34,919	21,255
Brooklyn	260,143	128,259	29,580
Queens	87,676	36,415	2,741
Staten Island	22,741	9,000	275
Total	750,247	332,846	82,607

Others, 31,242
Total vote: 1,196,942

1925

Democratic Primary	James J. Walker	John F. Hylan
Manhattan	102,835	27,802
Bronx	45,308	21,228
Brooklyn	65,671	60,814
Queens	28,203	32,163
Staten Island	6,321	12,197
Total	248,338	154,204

General Election	James J. Walker (Democrat)	Frank D. Waterman (Republican)	Norman Thomas (Socialist)
Manhattan	247,079	98,617	9,482
Bronx	131,226	39,615	11,133
Brooklyn	244,029	139,060	16,809
Queens	103,629	58,478	1,943
Staten Island	22,724	10,794	207
Total	748,687	346,564	39,574

Others, 26,272
Total vote: 1,161,097

1929	James J. Walker (Democrat)	Fiorello H. La Guardia (Republican)	Norman Thomas (Socialist)
Manhattan	232,370	91,944	37,316
Bronx	159,948	52,646	39,181
Brooklyn	283,432	132,095	71,145
Queens	166,188	75,911	24,807
Staten Island	25,584	15,079	3,248
Total	867,522	367,675	175,697

Others, 53,795
Total vote: 1,464,689

1932	John O'Brien (Democrat)	Lewis H. Pounds (Republican)	Morris Hillquit (Socialist)	Joseph McKee (write-in)
Manhattan	308,944	116,729	40,011	42,299
Bronx	181,639	48,366	68,980	50,212
Brooklyn	358,945	157,152	113,622	73,431

(*continued*)

Returns of Mayoral Elections in New York City by Borough, 1897–2009 (*Continued*)

1932 (cont.)	John O'Brien (Democrat)	Lewis H. Pounds (Republican)	Morris Hillquit (Socialist)	Joseph McKee (write-in)
Queens	176,070	105,068	24,981	61,648
Staten Island	30,517	16,586	2,293	6,782
Total	1,056,115	443,901	249,887	234,372

Others, 269,585
Total vote: 2,253,860

1933	Fiorello H. La Guardia (Republican–City Fusion)	Joseph McKee (Recovery)	John O'Brien (Democrat)
Manhattan	203,479	123,707	192,649
Bronx	151,669	131,280	93,403
Brooklyn	331,920	194,558	194,335
Queens	154,369	141,296	90,501
Staten Island	27,085	18,212	15,784
Total	868,522	609,053	586,672

Charles Solomon (Socialist), 59,846; Others, 81,309
Total vote: 2,205,402

1937	Fiorello H. La Guardia (City Fusion–Progressive–American Labor–Republican)	Jeremiah T. Mahoney (Democrat–Trades Union–Anti-Communist)
Manhattan	328,995	237,006
Bronx	272,322	166,805
Brooklyn	494,516	286,647
Queens	213,939	172,973
Staten Island	34,858	27,325
Total	1,344,630	890,756

Others, 64,834
Total vote: 2,300,220

1941	Fiorello H. La Guardia (City Fusion–United City–American Labor–Republican)	William O'Dwyer (Democrat)
Manhattan	298,225	227,717
Bronx	259,607	185,295
Brooklyn	439,856	348,048
Queens	166,364	259,239
Staten Island	22,249	33,876
Total	1,186,301	1,054,175

Others, 53,250
Total vote: 2,293,726

1945	William O'Dwyer (Democrat–American Labor)	Jonah J. Goldstein (Republican–Liberal–Fusion)	Newbold Morris (No Deal)
Manhattan	253,371	100,591	100,064
Bronx	227,818	95,582	88,404
Brooklyn	386,335	161,119	136,262
Queens	228,275	65,240	77,687
Staten Island	29,558	9,069	5,931
Total	1,125,357	431,601	408,348

Others, 71,385
Total vote: 2,036,691

1949	William O'Dwyer (Democrat)	Newbold Morris (Republican–Liberal–Fusion)	Vito Marcantonio (American Labor)
Manhattan	278,343	219,430	123,128
Bronx	254,014	185,248	82,386
Brooklyn	425,225	332,433	113,478

(*continued*)

Returns of Mayoral Elections in New York City by Borough, 1897–2009 (*Continued*)

1949 (cont.)

	William O'Dwyer (Democrat)	Newbold Morris (Republican–Liberal–Fusion)	Vito Marcantonio (American Labor)
Queens	270,062	200,552	34,677
Staten Island	38,868	18,406	2,957
Total	1,266,512	956,069	356,626

Others, 83,710
Total vote: 2,662,917

1950

	Vincent Impellitteri (Experience)	Ferdinand Pecora (Democrat–Liberal)	Edward Corsi (Republican)
Manhattan	246,608	214,610	102,575
Bronx	215,913	217,254	54,796
Brooklyn	357,322	362,246	113,392
Queens	303,448	129,223	99,225
Staten Island	37,884	12,018	12,384
Total	1,161,175	935,351	382,372

Paul L. Ross (American Labor), 147,578;
Others, 70,429
Total vote: 2,696,905

1953

	Robert F. Wagner (Democrat)	Harold Riegelman (Republican)	Rudolph Halley (Liberal–Independent)
Manhattan	236,960	147,876	84,532
Bronx	206,771	97,224	122,678
Brooklyn	339,970	183,968	175,537
Queens	207,918	208,829	80,548
Staten Island	31,007	23,694	3,809
Total	1,022,626	661,591	467,104

Clifford T. McAvor (American Labor), 53,045;
Others, 39,780
Total vote: 2,224,146

1957

	Robert F. Wagner (Democrat–Liberal–Fusion)	Robert K. Christenberry (Republican)
Manhattan	316,203	112,173
Bronx	316,299	96,726
Brooklyn	494,078	163,427
Queens	341,212	191,061
Staten Island	40,983	22,381
Total	1,508,775	585,768

Others, 129,511
Total vote: 2,224,054

1961

Democratic Primary

	Robert F. Wagner	Arthur Levitt
Manhattan	122,607	66,917
Bronx	78,626	47,885
Brooklyn	136,440	103,296
Queens	102,845	64,157
Staten Island	15,498	10,471
Total	456,016	292,726

General Election

	Robert F. Wagner (Democrat–Liberal–Brotherhood)	Louis J. Lefkowitz (Republican–Civic Action–Non-Partisan)	Lawrence E. Gerosa (Independent–Citizens Party)
Manhattan	265,015	174,471	36,893
Bronx	255,528	134,964	67,213
Brooklyn	396,539	251,258	105,232

(*continued*)

Returns of Mayoral Elections in New York City by Borough, 1897–2009 (*Continued*)

General Election (cont.)

	Robert F. Wagner (Democrat–Liberal–Brotherhood)	Louis J. Lefkowitz (Republican–Civic Action–Non-Partisan)	Lawrence E. Gerosa (Independent–Citizens Party)
Queens	290,194	243,836	99,987
Staten Island	30,145	31,162	12,279
Total	1,237,421	835,691	321,604

Others, 72,830
Total vote: 2,467,546

1965

Democratic Primary	Abraham D. Beame	Paul R. Screvane	William F. Ryan	Paul O'Dwyer
Manhattan	53,386	66,444	48,744	6,775
Bronx	66,064	54,260	16,632	5,976
Brooklyn	128,146	79,485	24,588	8,332
Queens	82,601	63,680	22,570	6,895
Staten Island	6,148	7,512	1,204	697
Total	336,345	271,381	113,738	28,675

General Election	John V. Lindsay (Republican–Liberal–Independent Citizen)	Abraham D. Beame (Democrat–Civil Service–Fusion)	William F. Buckley (Conservative)
Manhattan	291,326	193,230	37,694
Bronx	181,072	213,980	63,858
Brooklyn	308,398	365,360	97,679
Queens	331,162	250,662	121,544
Staten Island	37,148	23,467	20,451
Total	1,149,106	1,046,699	341,226

Others, 115,420
Total Vote: 2,652,451

1969

Democratic Primary	Mario Procaccino	Robert F. Wagner	Herman Badillo	Norman Mailer	James H. Scheuer
Manhattan	26,804	40,978	74,809	17,372	7,117
Bronx	50,465	33,442	48,841	4,214	10,788
Brooklyn	87,630	81,833	52,866	10,299	11,942
Queens	79,002	61,244	37,880	8,700	8,994
Staten Island	11,628	6,967	2,769	703	509
Total	255,529	224,464	217,165	41,288	39,350

Republican Primary	John J. Marchi	John V. Lindsay
Manhattan	12,457	44,236
Bronx	16,132	12,222
Brooklyn	33,694	20,575
Queens	40,469	26,658
Staten Island	10,946	3,675
Total	113,698	107,366

General Election	John V. Lindsay (Liberal–Independent)	Mario Procaccino (Democrat–Non-Partisan–Civil Service Independent)	John J. Marchi (Republican–Conservative)
Manhattan	328,564	99,460	61,539
Bronx	161,953	165,647	76,711
Brooklyn	256,046	301,324	152,933
Queens	249,330	245,783	192,008
Staten Island	16,740	19,558	59,220
Total	1,012,633	831,772	542,411

Others, 71,387
Total vote: 2,458,203

(*continued*)

Returns of Mayoral Elections in New York City by Borough, 1897–2009 (*Continued*)

1973

Democratic Primary	Abraham D. Beame	Herman Badillo	Mario Biaggi	Albert H. Blumenthal
Manhattan	45,901	73,676	17,830	41,906
Bronx	41,508	55,432	39,462	18,400
Brooklyn	96,621	57,836	48,352	31,913
Queens	73,520	33,990	45,992	28,960
Staten Island	8,912	2,902	7,524	2,062
Total	266,462	223,836	159,160	123,241

Democratic Primary Runoff	Abraham D. Beame	Herman Badillo
Manhattan	77,928	112,482
Bronx	97,415	86,482
Brooklyn	201,866	93,140
Queens	153,415	57,658
Staten Island	17,999	4,819
Total	548,623	354,581

General Election	Abraham D. Beame (Democrat)	John J. Marchi (Republican)	Albert H. Blumenthal (Liberal)	Mario Biaggi (Conservative)
Manhattan	158,050	45,803	101,117	17,882
Bronx	160,774	37,609	32,661	50,805
Brooklyn	321,477	73,776	60,340	51,713
Queens	283,474	90,942	66,059	60,490
Staten Island	37,355	28,445	5,120	9,096
Total	961,130	276,575	265,297	189,986

Others, 7,883
Total vote: 1,700,871

1977

Democratic Primary	Edward I. Koch	Mario M. Cuomo	Abraham D. Beame	Bella Abzug	Percy Sutton	Herman Badillo
Manhattan	49,855	25,056	23,507	54,591	34,742	26,895
Bronx	23,237	22,939	25,534	20,429	24,588	34,246
Brooklyn	49,894	55,439	62,921	37,790	42,215	28,838
Queens	51,515	56,719	44,342	33,623	28,286	8,961
Staten Island	5,747	10,335	7,306	4,286	1,366	868
Total	180,248	170,488	163,610	150,719	131,197	99,808

Democratic Primary Runoff	Edward I. Koch	Mario M. Cuomo
Manhattan	114,084	61,555
Bronx	69,230	55,017
Brooklyn	131,583	112,862
Queens	107,182	105,149
Staten Island	9,770	19,639
Total	431,849	354,222

General Election	Edward I. Koch (Democrat)	Mario M. Cuomo (Liberal)	Roy M. Goodman (Republican)
Manhattan	184,842	70,717	19,324
Bronx	116,436	75,754	6,102
Brooklyn	204,934	153,134	11,491
Queens	191,894	186,590	18,460
Staten Island	19,270	36,747	3,229
Total	717,376	522,942	58,606

Barry Farber (Conservative), 57,437; Others, 13,781
Total vote: 1,370,142

(*continued*)

Returns of Mayoral Elections in New York City by Borough, 1897–2009 (*Continued*)

1981	Edward I. Koch (Democrat–Republican)	Frank J. Barbaro (Unity)
Manhattan	189,631	56,702
Bronx	132,421	22,074
Brooklyn	261,292	48,812
Queens	275,812	31,225
Staten Island	53,466	3,906
Total	912,622	162,719

Others, 147,303
Total vote: 1,222,644

1985	Edward I. Koch (Democrat–Independent)	Carol Bellamy (Liberal)	Diane McGrath (Republican–Conservative)
Manhattan	170,198	41,190	17,491
Bronx	136,263	14,092	12,358
Brooklyn	246,748	29,256	25,738
Queens	246,854	25,098	36,032
Staten Island	62,163	3,835	10,049
Total	862,226	113,471	101,668

Others, 29,397
Total vote: 1,106,762

1989

Democratic Primary	David N. Dinkins	Edward I. Koch	Harrison J. Goldin	Richard Ravitch
Manhattan	151,113	96,923	6,889	17,499
Bronx	101,274	66,600	4,951	5,946
Brooklyn	170,440	139,268	9,619	13,214
Queens	113,952	129,262	5,857	9,443
Staten Island	11,122	24,260	1,493	1,432
Total	547,901	456,313	28,809	47,534

General Election	David N. Dinkins (Democrat)	Rudolph W. Giuliani (Republican–Liberal–Independent Fusion)
Manhattan	255,286	157,686
Bronx	172,271	99,800
Brooklyn	276,903	237,832
Queens	190,096	284,766
Staten Island	22,988	90,380
Total	917,544	870,464

Henry Hewes (Right-to-Life), 17,460; Ronald S. Lauder (Conservative), 9,271; Others, 85,106
Total vote: 1,899,845

1993	Rudolph W. Giuliani (Republican–Liberal)	David N. Dinkins (Democrat)
Manhattan	166,357	242,524
Bronx	98,780	162,995
Brooklyn	258,058	269,343
Queens	291,625	180,527
Staten Island	115,416	21,507
Total	930,236	876,896

George J. Marlin (Conservative–Right-to-Life), 15,926; Others, 65,945
Total vote: 1,889,003

1997	Rudolph W. Giuliani (Republican–Liberal)	Ruth Messinger (Democrat)
Manhattan	138,718	128,478
Bronx	81,897	102,979
Brooklyn	174,343	145,349

(*continued*)

Returns of Mayoral Elections in New York City by Borough, 1897–2009 (*Continued*)

1997	Rudolph W. Giuliani (Republican–Liberal)	Ruth Messinger (Democrat)
Queens	176,751	92,194
Staten Island	45,120	10,288
Total	615,829	479,288
Others, 21,241		
Total vote: 1,116,358		
2001	Michael R. Bloomberg (Republican–Independence)	Mark J. Green (Democratic–Working Families)
Manhattan	179,797	202,574
Bronx	80,597	102,280
Brooklyn	189,040	217,222
Queens	210,432	163,528
Staten Island	84,891	23,664
Total	744,757	709,268
Alan G. Hevesi (Liberal–Better Schools), 10,331; Others, 16,226		
Total vote: 1,480,582		
2005	Michael R. Bloomberg (Republican/Liberal–Independence)	Fernando Ferrer (Democrat)
Manhattan	197,010	120,813
Bronx	76,417	117,734
Brooklyn	209,723	140,282
Queens	202,116	107,086
Staten Island	67,827	17,304
Total	753,089	503,219
Thomas V. Ognibene (Conservative), 14,630; Others, 18,997		
Total vote: 1,289,935		
2009	Michael R. Bloomberg (Republican/Liberal–Independence)	William C. Thompson (Democrat)
Manhattan	159,837	118,651
Bronx	53,796	88,845
Brooklyn	153,739	175,691
Queens	162,933	127,646
Staten Island	55,161	24,036
Total	585,466	534,869
Stephen Christopher (Conservative), 18,013; Others, 16,454		
Total vote: 1,154,802		

Note: Primaries are included when they are critical in determining election outcomes.

the Environmental Control Board. Reforms to the charter in 1989 abolished the Board of Estimate and divided its powers between the mayor and the City Council: the budgeting powers of the council were increased, and the power to award contracts was assigned to the mayor.

The mayor of New York City is elected to a four-year term in years following national presidential elections. A limit of two terms was approved by referendum in 1993 and overturned in 2009. In addition to preparing and administering the operating and capital budgets, the mayor is responsible for collective bargaining with municipal unions and for appointing staff members, deputy mayors, and most commissioners of municipal agencies, as well as for appointing and funding special commissions. The mayor is assisted by a budget unit led by the director of the Office of Management and Budget, a management unit led by the director of the Office of Operations (which supervises the operations of municipal agencies), the Office of Labor Relations (which conducts collective bargaining on the mayor's behalf), and legislative liaison offices in Washington, D.C., and Albany, New York. In fiscal year 2008 the mayor's office had a budget of $86.9 million and 1005 full-time employees; the mayor is authorized by the city charter to receive a salary of $225,000 a year and has many perquisites, including a chauffeured limousine and quarters in Gracie Mansion, a residence owned by the city. Michael R. Bloomberg was elected in 2001 as the 108th mayor in the city's history, and he was reelected in 2005 and 2009. Bloomberg, a self-made billionaire, takes only $1 per year as salary and lives in his private residence rather than Gracie Mansion, which is used for public events.

Wallace Sayre and Herbert Kaufman, *Governing New York City: Politics in the Metropolis* (New York: Russell Sage Foundation, 1960); David Eichenthal, "Changing Styles and Strategies of the Mayor,"

Urban Politics New York Style, ed. Jewel Bellush and Dick Netzer (Armonk, N.Y.: M. E. Sharpe, 1990)

Charles Brecher

Mayor's Cup(s). Trophies awarded to sailors and, later, kayakers racing in New York waters. The initial Mayor's Cup race was conceived in 1967 by Peter Stanford, of South Street Seaport, with the aim of reintroducing sailboat racing to New York Harbor, where the sport once thrived. Held annually in autumn, the race typically attracted about 20 boats, including schooners and other traditional sailing yachts, as well as thousands of spectators. South Street Seaport last ran the race in 2005. In 2007 a new event for these boats, New York Classic Week, was introduced by the New York Harbor Sailing Foundation, with other trophies replacing the Mayor's Cup. In 2006 a new Mayor's Cup went into competition for the New York City Kayak Championship, using a 26.7-mile (43-kilometer) course circumnavigating Manhattan. The 2007 race had 98 paddlers from seven countries.

John Rousmaniere

Mays, Willie Howard, Jr. (*b* Westfield, Ala., 6 May 1931). Baseball player, considered among the best in modern history. In 1951 he became center fielder for the New York Giants and was National League Rookie of the Year; in 1954 he was Most Valuable Player as the Giants won the World Series; in 1955 he hit a league-best 51 home runs. After 1957 he moved with the Giants to San Francisco. Mays returned to New York City to finish his playing career with the Mets for the 1972–73 season. After retiring, he went on to coach the Mets until 1979. Career highlights include 660 home runs, 3283 hits, 12 consecutive Gold Glove Awards, and membership in the Hall of Fame.

Andrew Sparberg

McAdoo, William Gibbs (*b* near Marietta, Ga., 31 Oct 1863; *d* Santa Barbara, Calif., 1 Feb 1941). Lawyer, public official, and senator. He moved to New York City in 1892 to practice law on Wall Street. He organized and oversaw the construction of the first railroad tunnel under the Hudson River in 1904 and in the same year founded the Hudson and Manhattan Railroad, making sure that women who sold tickets earned the same pay as their male counterparts. An early supporter of Woodrow Wilson, as secretary of the treasury from 1913 to 1918 he played a critical role in establishing the Federal Reserve, set up the program known as "Liberty Loans," and introduced life insurance for members of the armed forces. After World War I he moved to California, and in 1924 he sought the Democratic presidential nomination; he led through much of the voting at the Democratic convention in Madison Square Garden but lost to John W. Davis. McAdoo later became a senator from California.

William McAdoo

John J. Broesamle, *William Gibbs McAdoo: A Passion for Change* (Port Washington, N.Y.: Kennikat, 1973)

Ashbel Green

McAllister, (Samuel) Ward (*b* Savannah, Ga., December 1827; *d* New York City, 31 Jan 1895). Lawyer and society figure. He moved to New York City at the age of 20 to be introduced in elite circles, later returning to Savannah, where he practiced law and became wealthy. After living in Europe and Newport, Rhode Island, for a few years he settled again in New York City, where by the late 1860s he helped to choose members for an select group known as the "four hundred," named for the number of guests who could be accommodated in Mrs. William Astor's ballroom. He reflected on his successes in this circle in the book *Society As I Have Found It* (1890).

James E. Mooney

McAneny, George (*b* Jersey City, N.J., 24 Dec 1869; *d* Princeton, N.J., 29 July 1953). Newspaperman and borough president. He was a correspondent for the *New York World* who supported initiatives to make government more efficient through reform of the civil service, formation of the Bureau of Municipal Research, and zoning and regional planning. As an assistant secretary of the New York Civil Service Reform Association during 1892–94 and its secretary during 1894–1902, he drafted new civil service rules. In 1908 he was a member of the committee that revised the city charter. Elected borough president of Manhattan on a fusion ticket (1910–13), he was president of the Board of Aldermen under the reform mayor John Purroy Mitchel (1914–17) and was the city's acting mayor for several months. During 1916–21 he was the executive manager of the *New York Times*. In later years McAneny led the Regional Plan Association (from 1930), was the city's sanitation commissioner and briefly its comptroller (in the early 1930s), and was chairman of the board of the Title Guarantee and Trust Company. He also helped to plan the World's Fair of 1939–40 and was active in the landmark preservation movement.

Richard Skolnick

McBride, Henry (*b* West Chester, Pa., 25 July 1867; *d* New York City, 31 March 1962). Art critic. After moving to New York City in 1889 to study art, he formed an art department for the Educational Alliance in 1900 and in the following year became the director of the School of Industrial Arts in Trenton, New Jersey. He made frequent trips abroad, often to Paris, where he became acquainted with Gertrude Stein and her circle. In 1913 he joined the *Sun* as an art writer and soon became its chief critic, a position he held until 1950. He also contributed to the *Dial* and to *Creative Art* (which he edited from 1930 to 1932), and he wrote a monthly column for *Art News* from 1950 to 1955. McBride wrote favorably about modern artists from Constantin Brancusi to Jackson Pollock. A collection of his essays, *The Flow of Art: Essays and Criticisms of Henry McBride*, was published in 1975.

Patricia Hills

McCall's Magazine. Women's magazine launched in 1873 by the tailor James McCall as *The Queen: Illustrating McCall's Bazar Glove-fitting Patterns*. Originally it supplied readers with new dressmaking patterns produced by James McCall and Company. In 1890 the firm became the McCall Publishing Company with George H. Bladworth as president. When James Henry Ottley took over in 1893, he increased the size of the magazine by adding a section of fiction and changed the title to *McCall's Magazine: The Queen of Fashion* (1897); circulation surpassed one million in 1908. Ottley sold the magazine in 1913, it underwent several changes in format, and circulation declined. Sections on home decoration, food, child care, and fashions were added to expand the readership, and by the 1970s the magazine tried to attract working women. In the 1990s the New York Times Magazine Group was the publisher, and in 2000 entertainer Rosie O'Donnell became editor-in-chief, relaunching the magazine in 2001 as *Rosie.* The magazine ceased publication at the end of 2002 after O'Donnell became concerned that the magazine did not reflect her editorial vision.

Mary Ellen Zuckerman, *A History of Popular Women's Magazines in the United States, 1792–1995* (Westport, Conn.: Greenwood Press, 1998)

Sandra Roff

McCarren, Patrick (Henry) (*b* East Cambridge, Mass., 18 June 1847; *d* Brooklyn, 23 Oct 1909). Political leader. A state senator, he ousted Hugh McLaughlin as the Democratic boss of Brooklyn with support from Tammany Hall after its candidates were successful in the municipal elections of 1903. Later he declared that he would "rather be a serf in Russia than a satrap of Tammany" and opposed Tammany Hall until the end of his life.

Frank Vos

McCarthy, Mary (Therese) (*b* Seattle, 21 June 1912; *d* New York City, 25 Oct 1989). Novelist. After graduating from Vassar College in 1933 she became a literary figure in New York City and a freelance writer for the *Nation* and the *New Republic.* She lived at 52 Gramercy Park North during the early 1940s and at 14 Henderson Place in 1944. After unintentionally becoming involved with a committee that defended Leon Trotsky, she became a steadfast anti-Stalinist, leading her to help reshape the *Partisan Review.* Her views were at the center of a literary feud during the 1970s with Lillian Hellman over Hellman's discussion in her memoirs of having been a communist sympathizer during the 1950s. McCarthy's published writings include the novels *The Group* (1963) and *Birds of America* (1971). She was married to Edmund Wilson.

Carol W. Gelderman, *Mary McCarthy: A Life* (New York: St. Martin's, 1988)

Lawson Bowling

McCarthyism. As the largest city in the nation, the center of its communications industry, and the home of the Communist Party of the United States and at least 40 percent of its members, New York City was profoundly affected by the repressive anticommunist ideology known as McCarthyism. Although the term was inspired by the anticommunist charges of Senator Joseph R. McCarthy of Wisconsin between 1950 and 1954, in New York City as elsewhere the climate in which McCarthyism flourished was in evidence at least a decade before the hearings began. During 1940–41 the Rapp–Coudert investigations by the state legislature into schools and colleges in the city led to the dismissal of about 60 faculty members. Anticommunist fervor diminished during World War II but resumed soon after. In 1949 the state legislature passed the Feinberg Law, which mandated the elimination of members of the Communist Party from public school and college faculties. The Board of Education administered the measure by engaging a separate staff to oversee the political investigation of its employees. Suspected communists were questioned in internal hearings before the counsel to the board and often forced to disclose the names of other alleged communists. More than 435 public school and college teachers in the city were discharged as a result of these hearings, as were most of about 50 others who were questioned in public by the Internal Security Subcommittee of the U.S. Senate and invoked the Fifth Amendment. Social workers, other municipal employees, and many U.S. citizens who worked for the United Nations were similarly persecuted, as political tests as a condition of employment became widespread.

The entertainment industry was an inviting target for McCarthyism. Blacklists were enforced by radio and television networks, their commercial sponsors, and advertising agencies, who feared retaliation from the political right if they did not comply. The book *Red Channels* (1950) included the names of 151 entertainers alleged to be subversive, only some of whom had ever belonged to the Communist Party. In 1951 and 1952 the House Un-American Activities Committee held several highly publicized hearings on the entertainment industry.

The federal courthouse in Foley Square in Manhattan was the site of the most important political trials of the McCarthy period. In 1949 the federal government prosecuted the 11 highest-ranking members of the Communist Party under the Smith Act (1940), which prohibited advocating the overthrow of the government; the U.S. Supreme Court upheld the conviction of the defendants. In the following year Alger Hiss, a former official in the U.S. Department of State, was convicted of perjury in Manhattan in connection with allegations that he had transmitted government documents to the Soviet Union. There was widespread skepticism regarding the motives of the prosecutors, the soundness of the evidence, and the fairness of the proceedings in Hiss's case, as there was in that of Julius and Ethel Rosenberg, charged with atomic espionage in 1950, convicted in 1951, and executed in June 1953. Although New York City had a reputation for liberalism, the violation of the civil rights of communists and former communists was generally tolerated.

Lawrence H. Chamberlain, *Loyalty and Legislative Action: A Survey of Activity by the New York State Legislature, 1919–1949* (Ithaca, N.Y.: Cornell University Press, 1951); David Caute, *The Great Fear: The Anti-communist Purge under Truman and Eisenhower* (New York: Simon and Schuster, 1978); Ellen W. Schrecker, *Many Are the Crimes: McCarthyism in America* (Princeton, N.J.: Princeton University Press, 1999)

Ellen W. Schrecker

McClellan, George B(rinton), Jr. (*b* Dresden, Saxony, 23 Nov 1865; *d* Washington, D.C., 30 Nov 1940). Mayor. Named for his father, the well-known Civil War general, he spent his childhood in several places, including New York City. After attending Princeton University and New York Law School he entered local politics in 1889 and later won election as president of the Board of Aldermen. For several terms beginning in 1894 he served with distinction in Congress. In 1903 he was persuaded to accept the Democratic mayoral nomination by the new boss of Tammany Hall, Charles F. Murphy, who sought to oust the fusion incumbent, Seth Low. McClellan was elected by a large majority and reelected in 1905 to a four-year term after a bitter contest with the newspaper publisher William Randolph Hearst. He ran an efficient, honest government that was praised even by his critics: he introduced an ambitious program of public works, fought to expand the subway system, and inaugurated a construction project in the Catskills to increase the city's water supply. After quarreling with Murphy over patronage and Murphy's support of Hearst for the governorship in 1906, McClellan retired from politics.

Robert F. Wesser

McCloskey, John (*b* Brooklyn, 10 March 1810; *d* Mount St. Vincent-on-Hudson [now in the Bronx], 10 Oct 1885). Cardinal. He moved to Manhattan in 1817 with his parents. After his father's death in 1820, he entered Mount St. Mary's Seminary near Emmitsburg, Maryland. In 1834 he became the first man born in the metropolitan area to be ordained to the secular (diocesan) priesthood. He was the pastor of St. Joseph's (now on Sixth Avenue) from 1837 to 1841, and from 1841 to 1847 he was the first president of St. John's College (now Fordham University). In 1847 he was appointed the first bishop of Albany, New York, a position he resigned to become the archbishop of New York in 1864. Although many Irish Catholics in the city supported Irish independence, he condemned Fenian violence in 1866. He endorsed Levi Silliman Ives's Catholic Protectory and John Christopher Drumgoole's Mission of the Immaculate Virgin and authorized the city's first permanent parishes for Italians (St. Anthony of Padua, 1859), Poles (St. Stanislaus, 1872), and blacks (St. Benedict the Moor, 1883). An attendee of the First Vatican Council (1869–70), he was elected the first American cardinal in 1875 and dedicated St. Patrick's Cathedral in 1879. His intervention in 1884 prevented the Italian government from confiscating the North American College in Rome, which the hierarchy in the United States supported financially and to which it sent seminarians for training. That same year he retired to Mount St. Vincent-on-Hudson. McCloskey is buried beneath St. Patrick's Cathedral.

John Cardinal Farley, *The Life of John Cardinal McCloskey, First Prince of the Church in America, 1810–1885* (New York: Longmans, Green, 1918)

Mary Elizabeth Brown

McCloy, John J(ay) (*b* Philadelphia, 31 March 1895; *d* Stamford, Conn., 11 March 1989). Lawyer, government official, and businessman. After earning an undergraduate degree from Amherst College in 1916 he graduated from Harvard Law School in 1921. He joined the firm of Cravath, De Gersdorff, Swaine and Wood in November 1924, often traveling to Europe on business. From the 1920s he specialized in corporate law, and he played an important role during the 1930s on behalf of the Bethlehem Steel Company in litigation resulting from the Black Tom explosion. In 1940 he became a consultant to Secretary of War Henry L. Stimson, and in April 1941 he was appointed assistant secretary of war. Toward the end of World War II he helped to plan the occupation of Germany and the trials for war crimes at Nuremberg. He resigned from the war department in November 1945 and joined the firm of Milbank, Tweed, Hope, Hadley and McCloy in New York City, leaving in February 1947 to become president of the International Bank for Reconstruction and Development. He returned to the United States in August 1952, was named chairman of Chase National Bank in January 1953, and oversaw its merger with the Bank of Manhattan Company in March 1955 to form the Chase Manhattan Bank, the second-largest commercial bank in the country. After his retirement from the bank in December 1960 he returned to private practice with Milbank, Tweed. During his career McCloy advised presidents from Franklin D. Roosevelt to Ronald Reagan.

Alan Brinkley, "Minister without Portfolio," *Harper's*, Feb 1983, pp. 30–46; Thomas Alan Schwartz, *America's Germany: John J. McCloy and the Federal Republic of Germany* (Cambridge, Mass.: Harvard University Press, 1991); Kai Bird, *The Chairman: John J. McCloy, the Making of the American Establishment* (New York: Simon and Schuster, 1992)

Allen J. Share

McClure, S(amuel) S(idney) (*b* County Antrim, Ireland, 17 Feb 1857; *d* Bronx, 21 March 1949). Magazine publisher. Educated in Illinois, he moved in 1885 to New York City where he formed a syndicate for newspaper features and in 1893 launched *McClure's*, one of the first mass-circulation magazines. In addition to sentimental fiction, the magazine published early work by Stephen Crane, Frank Norris, O. Henry, and Willa Cather; essays about scientific wonders, historical figures, art, and business; and the work of such prominent "muckrakers" as Ida M. Tarbell, Ray Stannard Baker (1901–6), and Lincoln Steffens, whose well-known series "The Shame of the Cities" appeared in 1902–3. McClure's penchant for articles on municipal corruption, trusts, labor unions, and the "white slave" trade stemmed from their marketability rather than any ethical commitment. He spent much of his time visiting foreign capitals in search of editorial material. His attempt to form a corporate conglomerate that would have included an insurance firm, a bank, a textbook publisher, and a model housing project prompted his staff to leave in protest in 1906, and his plans failed. After losing control of *McClure's* in 1912 he bought into the *Evening Mail* in 1915 as its editor-in-chief; embarrassed by the pro-German sympathies of the newspaper's principal owner during World War I, he sold his interest in 1917. He briefly regained control of *McClure's* in 1922 but failed to halt its decline; it ceased publication in 1929. McClure retired on a trust fund established by his former colleagues. He wrote *My Autobiography* (1914).

Peter Lyon, *Success Story: The Life and Times of S. S. McClure* (New York: Charles Scribner's Sons, 1963); Harold S. Wilson: *McClure's Magazine and the Muckrakers* (Princeton, N.J.: Princeton University Press, 1970)

Robert Stinson

McClure's Magazine. Periodical founded in 1893 by Samuel Sidney McClure. Known for its muckraking exposés, science articles, fiction, and half-tone illustrations, the popular 10-cent monthly had substantial literary and political influence in the first decade of the twentieth century. Ida Tarbell's "History of Standard Oil" and Lincoln Steffens's "Shame of the Cities" series put the magazine at the forefront of Progressive era journalism. The magazine also attacked municipal corruption and the Tammany Hall political machine. Fiction contributors included Rudyard Kipling, O. Henry, and Jack London.

Eric Robinson

McComb, John, Jr. (*b* New York City, 17 Oct 1763; *d* New York City, 25 May 1853). Architect. He built a lighthouse at Montauk Point, New York (1795), and also designed a country house for Alexander Hamilton known as the Grange (1801–2; moved in October 2009 from Convent Avenue near 141st Street into the northern end of St. Nicholas Park near Hamilton Terrace). On 4 October 1802 an entry he designed with Joseph François Mangin won a competition to design City Hall; he was appointed the sole architect in charge of construction on 22 March 1803, generating a controversy about whether he or Mangin was the principal designer. Other commissions included St. John's Chapel, formerly on Varick Street (1803–7), and Castle Clinton (1811–15), as well as engineering and surveying projects. As a city surveyor (1813–21) and as the street commissioner he planned streets, sewers, canals, and piers. McComb is often considered the city's most important architect of the Federal period.

Mary Beth Betts

McCooey, John (Henry) (*b* New York City, 18 June 1864; *d* Brooklyn, 21 Jan 1934). Politician. In 1909 he succeeded Patrick McCarren as the Democratic leader of Brooklyn, a position he held for 25 years. Under his direction the organization cooperated with Tammany Hall, long its enemy, to distribute patronage. In the mayoral primary election of 1925 he backed the incumbent mayor, John F. Hylan, but in the general election he shifted his support to the winner, James J. Walker. In 1932 he defused attempts by Tammany Hall to block Herbert H. Lehman's nomination for the governorship. A consummate politician known as "Uncle John," McCooey avoided controversy whenever possible. Although never elected to office, he remained on the public payroll from 1887 until 1930, when he retired as chief clerk of the Kings County Surrogate's Court.

Frank Vos

McDougall, Alexander (*b* Islay, Scotland, July/Aug 1732; *d* New York City, 9 June 1786). Soldier. After moving to New York City he commanded privateers during the Seven Years' War and in 1763 became a merchant. An avid

Alexander McDougall *by John Ramage, ca 1785. Miniature on ivory*

opponent of the Crown, he was jailed for libel, became a popular hero, and served on a committee of correspondence. During the American Revolution he rose to the rank of major general in the Continental Army and commanded the highlands along the Hudson. After a court-martial for insubordination he became more conservative, served in the national and state legislatures, helped organize the Bank of New York, and until the end of his life directed the New York State Society of the Cincinnati.

James E. Mooney

McEnroe, John (Patrick, Jr.) (*b* Wiesbaden, Germany, 16 Feb 1959). Tennis player. He grew up in Queens and lived successively in Flushing on Northern Boulevard and in Douglaston on Beverly Road, Rushmore Avenue, and Manor Road; he attended Trinity School in Manhattan. As an amateur with a powerful left-handed serve and volley, he won the US Open in Flushing in 1979, 1980, 1981, and 1984. McEnroe retired from professional tennis in 1992 but continued to live in New York City where he was an on-air personality and tennis commentator. He was inducted into the International Tennis Hall of Fame in 1999.

Joseph S. Lieber

McGlynn, Edward (*b* New York City, 27 Sept 1837; *d* Newburgh, N.Y., 7 Jan 1900). Radical priest. After attending public schools in New York City and the Urban College of Propaganda in Rome, he was ordained on 24 March 1860 and became associated with a group of liberal clergymen. During his tenure as pastor of St. Stephen's at 149–55 East 28th Street from 1866 to 1887 (the longest pastorate of his career), the parish had 20,000 members. Economic hardship caused by deflation in the late nineteenth century led McGlynn to study contemporary proposals for abolishing poverty. A supporter of the economic theories of Henry George and the Irish Land League, he came into the conflict with Archbishop Michael A. Corrigan that led to his excommunication on 4 July 1887; public protest inspired an investigation by the Vatican and his reinstatement in 1892. Although he refused to build a parochial school that he considered unnecessary, one did open at St. Stephen's in 1887. McGlynn was appointed by Corrigan to St. Mary's in Newburgh, New York, in 1894.

Stephen Bell, *Rebel Priest and Prophet: A Biography of Dr. Edward McGlynn* (New York: Devin-Adair, 1937)

Mary Elizabeth Brown

McGraw, John J(oseph) (*b* Truxton, N.Y., 7 April 1873; *d* New Rochelle, N.Y., 25 Feb 1934). Baseball manager. He played third base for the Baltimore Orioles from 1891 to 1900, helping the team to win three National League pennants and compiling a lifetime batting average of .334. From 1902 to 1932 he managed the New York Giants during their most successful years, winning 10 pennants and finishing second in the league 11 times. A diminutive man nicknamed "Little Napoleon" and "Black John," McGraw was tyrannical and abusive: he taunted players, berated umpires, and incited crowds. As both a player and a manager he was feared and widely hated but also respected for a cunning and pugnacious brand of baseball that stressed the bunt, the steal, the hit-and-run play, and sheer intimidation. Off the field he consorted with showmen and gamblers and attended college. He wrote a memoir, *My Thirty Years in Baseball* (1923; repr. 1974). Connie Mack, for many years the manager of the Philadelphia Athletics, said in 1927: "There has been only one manager and his name is McGraw."

Charles C. Alexander, *John McGraw* (New York: Viking, 1988); Joseph Durso, *Casey and Mr. McGraw* (New York: Sporting News, 1989)

Jeffrey Scheuer

McGraw–Hill. Firm of book, magazine, and multimedia products and information services. It was started in New York City in 1888 when James H. McGraw, a schoolteacher from upstate New York, acquired his first magazine, the *American Journal of Railway Appliances*. In 1909 he and John A. Hill, also a magazine publisher, formed the McGraw–Hill Book Company. When Hill died in 1917, McGraw changed the name to the McGraw–Hill Publishing Company and expanded its services. It later became one of the world's largest educational and professional book publishers, also issuing magazines such as *Business Week, Aviation Week and Space Technology, BYTE,* and *Architectural Record* and providing information services in finance (Standard and Poor's), construction (F. W. Dodge), and energy (Platt's). In 1930 the company commissioned Raymond M. Hood to design a new headquarters at 330 West 42nd Street. Designed in an art deco style and decorated with horizontal bands of blue and green terra-cotta, the building was among the first to use curtain-wall construction (the structure is partly supported by interior walls). McGraw–Hill opened its present headquarters in Rockefeller Center in 1972. It was designated a city landmark in 1990. In 2008 the company had about 4800 employees in New York City and had published books written or edited by 25 winners of the Nobel Prize.

Roger Burlingame, *Endless Frontiers: The Story of McGraw–Hill* (New York: McGraw–Hill, 1959)

See also Book publishing.

Donald S. Rubin

McGuire, Peter J(ames) (*b* New York City, 6 July 1852; *d* Camden, N.J., 18 Feb 1906). Labor leader. The son of Irish immigrants, he became the family's primary wage earner at the age of 11, when his father enlisted in the Union Army; he found work selling newspapers, shining shoes, cleaning stables, and running errands for the department store Lord and Taylor. After attending courses and lectures at Cooper Union he was apprenticed to a carpenter and later became a journeyman. He joined the labor movement out of concern about rising unemployment, horrendous working conditions, and attacks by the police on workers' rallies. A tireless organizer and talented speaker and writer, he traveled along the East Coast fighting for workers' rights and an eight-hour workday. In August 1881 he formed the United Brotherhood of Carpenters and Joiners; he also helped to establish Labor Day as a national holiday (1882) and to form the American Federation of Labor, of which he was the first secretary (1886). McGuire died in poverty and obscurity. He is remembered for his motto, "Organize, Agitate, Educate."

Mark Ehrlich, "Peter J. McGuire: The Story of a Remarkable Trade Unionist," *Carpenter,* March 1982; L. A. O'Donnell, "Peter J. McGuire, Architect of the House of Labor," *Irish Echo,* 2 Sept 1989

John J. Concannon

McIntosh, (William) Burr (*b* Wellsville, Ohio, 21 Aug 1862; *d* Hollywood, Calif., 28 April 1942). Actor. His theatrical career began in 1885 with his role in Bartley Campbell's *Pacquita* in Manhattan. In the 1900s he worked as a photographer and showed his work at his studio on West 33rd Street. Throughout his life he was in more than 50 films; his most active years were from 1914 to 1934. He was best known for his role in D. W. Griffith's *Way Down East* (1920).

Jessica Montesano

McKane, John Y(oung) (*b* County Antrim, Ireland, 10 Aug 1841; *d* Brooklyn, 5 Sept 1899). Political leader. He grew up in Sheepshead Bay and first held political office as a commissioner of common lands in Gravesend, where he was a powerful town supervisor from 1878 to 1893. He also served as the chief of police of Coney Island, which during his lenient tenure became known as a center of licentious behavior. His political career declined when politicians and businessmen in Brooklyn sought to annex Gravesend, regulate commercial amusements, and undertake suburban development for the middle class. After a celebrated trial for election fraud in 1893 McKane served five years in prison.

Stephen Weinstein

McKee, Joseph V(incent) (*b* 8 Aug 1889; *d* New York City, 28 Jan 1956). Acting mayor.

A Wall Street lawyer, he became president of the Board of Aldermen in 1926 through the Democratic organization of Edward J. Flynn in the Bronx. He became acting mayor on the resignation of Mayor James J. Walker in September 1932 and remained in office until December, striking a popular chord among citizens with demands for municipal economy and political reform (among other measures he reduced his mayoral salary from $40,000 to $25,000). Although not a candidate in the special election held on 8 November 1932 that was won by John P. O'Brien, he received 232,501 write-in votes. As the mayoral nominee of the Recovery Party in the regular election of the following year, he drew Democratic votes from O'Brien, thus facilitating the election of Fiorello H. La Guardia. A noted Roman Catholic layman after leaving office, McKee was sometimes known as Holy Joe.

Andrew Wiese

McKim, Charles Follen (*b* Isabelle Furnace, Pa., 27 Aug 1847; *d* St. James, N.Y., 14 Sept 1909). Architect. In 1867 he left the Lawrence Scientific School at Harvard University after a year to go to Paris to become an architect. Encouraged by his father, who planned to build a few suburban houses, he studied at the Atelier Daumet and the École des Beaux-Arts. In 1872 he settled in New York City and partnered with William Rutherford Mead; in 1879 the two joined with Stanford White to found McKim, Mead and White, which would become the most prominent architectural firm in the United States. During the 1880s he focused on introducing European styles to the United States and worked to build noble homes for the wealthy as well as museums, universities, hospitals, and libraries: he eventually became the principal designer of New York City's University Club and Harvard Club, as well as Columbia University's Morningside Heights campus. He built many houses in the city in styles ranging from Italian Renaissance to neo-Federal. Known for his precision, he looked to history to validate the details of his buildings, largely ignoring popular French styles and instead seeking inspiration in the styles of Italy and eighteenth-century America. He lived in New York City for most of his life, and most of his commissions were there and in Newport (Rhode Island), Boston, and later Washington, D.C. He led an austere personal life, renting rooms in row houses east and west of Fifth Avenue on 35th Street.

By the 1890s McKim was regarded as the dean of American architecture, admired in part because he devoted himself to architecture rather than family. In the late 1890s he became frail but nevertheless traveled to Europe, where he formed the American Academy in Rome and won the gold medal of the Royal Institute of British Architects in 1903. His reputation saved the firm from collapse after Stanford White's murder and the lurid publicity that followed, but McKim suffered a nervous breakdown from which he never recovered and died at the home of Mrs. Stanford White.

Charles Moore, *The Life and Times of Charles Follen McKim* (Boston: Houghton Mifflin, 1929); Leland M. Roth, *McKim, Mead and White* (New York: Harper and Row, 1983)

Mosette G. Broderick

McKim, Mead and White. Firm of architects. It started in 1872 as a loose partnership between Charles Follen McKim (1847–1909) and William Rutherford Mead (1846–1928); they were soon joined by William B. Bigelow, who was replaced on his retirement in 1879 by Stanford White (1853–1906). The firm operated from a small office at 57 Broadway, and during the next few years, following Bigelow's retirement, designed mostly resort and suburban houses in the metropolitan area; but after their Villard Houses (1882–83) at 451–57 Madison Avenue were widely acclaimed,

McKim, Mead and White, elevation of the waiting room at Pennsylvania Station

they received more commissions in the city, especially from wealthy business leaders for fine houses along and just off Fifth Avenue. Eventually assistants handled much of the drawing and site work, and during prosperous times the firm had almost 100 employees. It became known for the pronounced order of its designs, many based on Italian palazzos and Bostonian brick houses, and for its workmanship: McKim himself meticulously arranged for the dry-jointed walls of J. P. Morgan's library. The firm undertook refittings of existing houses for favored clients such as W. C. Whitney (1889–90 and 1898–1902). Other commissions included several apartment buildings erected as investments by insurance companies, row houses at Seventh Avenue and 139th Street (1891–92) for middle-class tenants designed for the contractor David H. King, and a few tenement buildings, including two remaining ones on West 83rd Street (1885–86) and at 359 West 47th Street (1886–87).

The firm designed a few commercial buildings during the 1880s but did not receive commissions for skyscrapers in the following decades, perhaps because its buildings were expensive to build. It built the Imperial Hotel at Broadway and 32nd Street (1889–94, demolished) and in the late 1880s converted the unoccupied Plaza apartment building into a luxury hotel. The firm entered several architectural competitions but initially lost most of them. White designed and invested in Madison Square Garden (demolished 1925). During the 1890s the firm received commissions for the campuses of Columbia University in Morningside Heights (McKim) and New York University on a hill in the Bronx (now Bronx Community College); in the 1890s and the early twentieth century it also designed buildings for the Century Association, the University Club, the Harvard Club, the Metropolitan Club, and the Harmonie Club. Many designs were executed in the "free classical" style, including the Judson Memorial Baptist Church (1888–96) at Washington Square, one of few churches designed by the firm. Other commissions for public buildings included the Brooklyn Museum (1893–1915) and the wings of the Metropolitan Museum of Art (1904–20) along Fifth Avenue (members of the firm supported the formation of art collections and often served on the boards of museums). In 1903 the firm built two tall showroom buildings on Fifth Avenue for the jewelers Gorham and Tiffany. Perhaps the best-known architectural firm of the late nineteenth century, McKim, Mead and White helped to transform New York City from a city of brownstone into one of white marble and tawny brick. In 1961 the name of the firm was changed to Steinman, Cain, and White, because of the death of its original principals. In 1971 it was renamed Walker O. Cain and Associates.

Leland M. Roth, *McKim, Mead and White* (New York: Harper and Row, 1983)

Mosette G. Broderick

McKinsey and Company. Firm of management consultants formed in Chicago in 1925 by the noted consultant James O. McKinsey. It quickly gained a reputation in both Chicago and New York City as a leader in its field and continued to flourish after McKinsey's death in 1937. In 2007 the firm had 44 offices in 22 countries and 2300 consultants. Its headquarters are at 55 East 52nd Street in Manhattan.

William B. Wolf, *Management and Consulting: An Introduction to James O. McKinsey* (Ithaca, N.Y.: New York State School of Industrial and Labor Relations, 1978)

McLaughlin, Hugh (*b* Brooklyn, 25 April 1823; *d* Brooklyn, 7 Dec 1904). Political leader. Originally a fishmonger, he worked as a master foreman at the Brooklyn Navy Yard and later became a millionaire through real estate speculation. He won election three times as register of Kings County (1861–67, 1871–73) and dominated politics in Brooklyn for almost half a century. Known as the "sage of Willoughby Street," he opposed Tammany Hall (led by William M. "Boss" Tweed, John Kelly, Richard Croker, and Charles F. Murphy during his career) and the incorporation of Brooklyn into New York City. McLaughlin is considered the founder of the Democratic organization in Brooklyn.

Frank Vos

McLoughlin Brothers. Firm of children's book publishers formed in 1858 by Edmund and John McLoughlin. Unlike the city's older publishers, it emphasized graphic vibrancy over literary taste and originality, issuing flashy inexpensive books in quantities without rival. Its success was confirmed after John McLoughlin adapted progressive color printing technology to produce some of the first chromoxylographs, chromotints, and chromolithographs. In 1870 the firm opened a factory for color printing in Brooklyn, the largest of its kind in the world. By 1894 a plant devoted to color lithography was added, employing a staff of 75 artists. After John McLoughlin's death in 1905, the firm was taken over by his sons James G. McLoughlin and Charles McLoughlin; it soon sank into mediocrity, and after Charles McLoughlin's death in 1920 it was sold to the firm of Milton Bradley in Springfield, Massachusetts.

Michael Joseph

McSorley's Old Ale House. Saloon long claimed to be the oldest continuous drinking establishment in New York City, located at 15 East Seventh Street. A large sign over its door reads "Established 1854"; however, that claim

McSorley's, 2009

has been questioned. McSorley's gained its fame through *New Yorker* writer Joseph Mitchell; his famous story "McSorley's Wonderful Saloon" first appeared in the magazine in 1940 and later in book form. Since then, the establishment has been celebrated in books, documentaries, city tour guides, and newspaper and magazine articles—all of which include the opening year of 1854. However, a 1995 *New York Times* article pointed to an amateur researcher whose work with old city maps and business directories, tax-assessment records, municipal archives, and census data led him to conclude that McSorley's Old Ale House opened later. The original owner, John McSorley, died in 1910, and his son Bill became the saloon operator. The childless Bill McSorley claimed that the ale house would die with him, but it continued after his death in 1938, eventually turning over to Dorothy Kirwan. Fears that she would make changes or renovations to the now historic place proved groundless. For the next 30 years she preserved the nineteenth-century ambience of sawdust-covered floors, potbellied stove, stained wooden tables, and Civil War memorabilia. She even refused to change the rule against admitting women, and the ale house remained for "men only" until 1970. McSorley's still sells only ale, and its old ambience and appearance remain—including the "Established 1854" sign over the entrance.

Joseph Mitchell, *McSorley's Wonderful Saloon* (New York: Grosset and Dunlap, 1943)

Richard McDermott

Mead, Margaret (*b* Philadelphia, 16 Dec 1901; *d* New York City, 15 Nov 1978). Anthropologist. After moving to New York City she graduated from Barnard College in 1923 and earned an MA in psychology (1924) and a PhD in anthropology (1929) from Columbia University. She studied with Franz Boas and Ruth Benedict and did cultural research in the South Pacific, conducting her most intensive fieldwork between 1925 and 1939. In 1926 she began a lifelong association with the American Museum of Natural History as an assistant curator in the department of anthropology; she rose to the rank of curator by 1964. The publication in 1928 of her first book,

Coming of Age in Samoa, brought her widespread acclaim. In 1940 she became a professor at Columbia, and in 1944 she formed the Institute for Intercultural Studies, a nonprofit organization that supported cultural research. She directed the Institute for Contemporary Culture at Columbia from 1948 to 1952 and was an adjunct professor there from 1954 until her death. She also lectured widely and wrote an autobiography, *Blackberry Winter: My Earlier Years* (1972). Her residences in New York City included 72 Perry Street (during the 1940s and early 1950s), 193 Waverly Place (in the 1960s), and the Beresford at 211 Central Park West (from 1966). The Hall of Pacific Peoples at the American Museum of Natural History includes an exhibit on her fieldwork, and the park surrounding the building bears her name. Mead is regarded as the most influential anthropologist of her generation.

Jane Howard, *Margaret Mead: A Life* (New York: Simon and Schuster, 1984); Lois W. Banner, *Intertwined Lives: Margaret Mead, Ruth Benedict, and Their Circle* (New York: Knopf, 2003)

Ira Jacknis

Meagher, Thomas Francis (*b* Waterford, Ireland, 23 Aug 1823; *d* Fort Benton, Mont., 1 July 1867). Lawyer and public official. After escaping from Tasmania, where he was serving a sentence of life imprisonment for his role in the Young Irelander Rebellion of 1848, he settled in New York City in 1852. He prospered as a lawyer and journalist and established himself as a leader among Irish immigrants. During the Civil War he commanded the Irish Brigade, which was built around a core of volunteers from the city. At the time of his death he was the acting governor of the Montana Territory.

John Paul Jones, *The Irish Brigade* (New York: R. B. Luce, n.d. [1969])

William D. Griffin

Meany, (William) George (*b* New York City, 16 Aug 1894; *d* Bethesda, Md., 10 Jan 1980). Labor leader. He lived in Harlem until the age of five, when his family moved to 695 East 135th Street in Port Morris. As a child he became interested in the union activities of his father, Michael Meany, the president of the Plumbers' Bronx Local no. 463. George left school at 14 and later attended trade school while working as a plumber's helper. After becoming a journeyman plumber he joined the union in 1916, winning election as a member of the local executive board in 1920 and as its business agent in 1922. Believing that membership in craft unions should be restricted, he zealously safeguarded his members' employment and also mastered the arcane contractual minutiae of the building trades. As the secretary from 1923 of the New York City Building Trades Council, he impressed labor leaders and politicians with his intelligence and deference. He was a vice president of the New York State Federation of Labor by 1932 and became its president in 1934. Through alliances with such powerful figures as Governor Herbert H. Lehman and Mayor Fiorello H. La Guardia he successfully pressed for legislation guaranteeing unemployment insurance and workers' compensation. He became the secretary-treasurer of the American Federation of Labor (AFL) in 1940, and its president in 1952, and in 1955, he oversaw the merger of the AFL with the Congress of Industrial Organizations to form the AFL–CIO, becoming the country's most important trade unionist even though he had never organized a shop union, taken part in a strike, or even walked a picket line. Meany was the first president of the AFL–CIO, a position he held until his retirement in 1979.

Joseph C. Goulden, *Meany: The Unchallenged Strong Man of American Labor* (New York: Atheneum, 1972)

Richard Yeselson

meatpacking. Meat was produced for local consumption in New York City from colonial times. Independent butchers bought animals from drovers or outlying stockyards and brought them to slaughter in the city, where they worked in "baulks," spaces in slaughterhouses containing a hoist, a table, and gutters. Built of wood, poorly lit and ventilated, and impossible to clean, they filled the surrounding streets with wastes and with the sounds of animals dying. Blood eventually flowed into ponds, streams, and rivers, and large waste pieces were carried away to dumping grounds or sold to tanners, soap and tallow makers, and sugar refiners. By 1656 the first measures regulating slaughterhouses were passed. Private slaughterhouses were banned in 1676 and replaced by a single public facility on Pearl Street north of Wall Street, where licensed butchers operated under controlled conditions. Additional public slaughterhouses were built at the outskirts of the city and moved northward as the city grew, to Peck Slip in 1696, Roosevelt and Water streets in 1720, the Bowery near the Bull's Head Tavern in 1850 (where a livestock market was set up near several small illegal slaughterhouses), Mulberry Street in 1776 (which became known as "slaughterhouse row" when private slaughterhouses opened there), and Moore and Water streets during the British occupation. Cattle were driven from Westchester and Putnam counties over the King's Bridge to the Bull's Head Market, and drovers stayed at the Dyckman House (circa 1784) at the northern end of Broadway. The public slaughterhouse, moved to Corlear's Hook near Jackson and Water streets in 1784, was abolished in 1790 in the face of opposition from butchers.

A meat industry developed in the city from 1791. The Bull's Head Market was moved in 1825 to a larger site near East 24th Street and Third Avenue, and when the local supply of livestock became inadequate, cattle were driven to the city from stockyards as far west as Ohio; the best-known drover was Daniel Drew. The drives increased in size until 1845, when they were superseded by rail transport. In 1848 the cattle market was moved to 44th Street. After large stockyards were built at railheads in New Jersey, the number of slaughterhouses increased along both sides of the Hudson River, especially on West Street in Manhattan. By the 1850s New York City

Stockyards on the East River below 46th Street, 1942

was the largest center of beef production in the country. Slaughterhouses were a major public health issue, and when the Board of Health adopted the first sanitary code in 1870, they became regulated and were banned outright between Second and 10th avenues. Large new companies like Schwarzchild and Sulzberger developed factories for slaughtering and processing meat: known as abattoirs after model public slaughterhouses near Paris, these were large buildings with improved sanitation. Animals were herded along ramps to the upper stories to be slaughtered and cleaned by teams of butchers working in long rows of baulks; meat was stored in ice rooms in the lower stories, and waste parts were processed by other workers. From the 1870s large quantities of fresh meat were shipped from the city to Europe in containers cooled with ice.

By 1877 the city designated an offal pier on West 38th Street, and there were four major abattoirs in the area: the Central Stockyard and Transit Company in Jersey City, New Jersey (established in 1874 by the Pennsylvania Railroad); the Manhattan Abattoirs on West 34th Street; the Butcher's Hide and Melting Association on East 44th Street; and the Union Stock Yard Abattoir on West 60th Street. There were also 52 small, private slaughterhouses, which became the focus of intense efforts at reform. In 1884–85 the Ladies' Health Protective Association led a campaign to replace slaughterhouses and rendering plants in the East 40s with abattoirs. The slaughter of poultry was forbidden in markets and restricted to licensed slaughterhouses in 1894, and in 1898 slaughtering in Manhattan was restricted to an area known as Abbatoir Center in the East 40s near the East River and to another area between 39th and 41st streets including Abattoir Place (39th Street) near the Hudson; slaughterhouses were also concentrated along Newtown Creek and in English Kills in Brooklyn. After refrigeration was improved in 1882, national companies based in the Midwest found that dressed meat was cheaper to send east than live animals. They built huge, efficient plants in the Midwest and forced eastern producers to go out of business or to relocate, but a growing demand for kosher meat, which could be kept no more than three days after being butchered, allowed meatpacking in New York City to survive.

About the turn of the century the "beef trust" of Chicago became widely resented. In 1902 the Ladies Anti-Beef Trust Association led consumer riots against kosher markets that passed on higher prices from wholesalers. A group of retail butchers organized the New York Butchers Dressed Meat Company to compete with midwestern meatpackers. An abattoir was built at West 39th Street and 11th Avenue by the company according to scientific standards of sanitation and efficiency. Opened in 1905, it was called the "model abattoir of the world" during a national debate following the publication of *The Jungle*, Upton Sinclair's critical novel about the meatpacking industry. The plant met new standards that were also adopted in the construction of abattoirs like Wilson and Company on the East Side (1906) and Joseph Stern and Sons on the West Side (1912). These plants were fireproof and had their own stockyards, power stations, rendering houses, transportation links, and cold-storage facilities for keeping meat until prices were favorable. Inside they were finished with impermeable, washable materials and equipped with elaborate plumbing, cooling, and ventilating systems and tracks for moving animal parts. The tasks of butchering were divided among as many as 24 employees.

In 1906 New York City had 240 sites for slaughtering cattle and hogs. Packers in the city produced the third-largest volume of dressed meat in the country during the 1920s and 1930s, but after World War II their share in the market declined as the cost of labor rose and the industry became increasingly dependent on trucking and new technology. At the same time more cold-storage plants were built in the metropolitan area. The slaughtering district on the East Side was cleared for United Nations Plaza in the late 1940s and the one on the West Side was closed by strikes around 1960. Meat dealers declined in number and in 2008 were concentrated around West 14th Street (the MEATPACKING DISTRICT) in Manhattan, Hunts Point in the Bronx, and the Brooklyn Coop Market.

Fred William Wilder, *The Modern Packing House: A Complete Treatise* (Chicago: Nickson and Collins, 1905); John Duffy, *A History of Public Health in New York City* (New York: Russell Sage Foundation, 1968, 1974)

Michael R. Corbett

meatpacking district. Area in lower west Manhattan, from the Hudson River to Greenwich Avenue, and from Bethune to 16th Street. In the nineteenth century the area was known as the Gansevoort Market and became the center for the city's slaughterhouses and wholesale meat trade. As the industry moved to different areas, the district became increasingly rundown and by the 1960s was infamous as a center for drugs and illicit sexual activity—particularly gay and transsexual. During the renaissance of the city in the 1990s the area was transformed into a high-end area appealing to young professionals, with luxury housing, boutique stores, and expensive restaurants. In 2009 fewer than 40 area businesses connected to the meatpacking industry remained. The Gansevoort Market Historic District was established by the New York City Landmarks Preservation Commission in 2003.

Lisa Keller

Medgar Evers College. College of the City University of New York, founded in 1970 to serve the Bedford–Stuyvesant area. It was named for Medgar Wiley Evers (1925–63), a civil rights leader. Representatives of the local community helped elect the college's first president. A liberal arts college, it offers associate and baccalaureate degrees in the fields of business; liberal arts and education; and science, health, and technology. In 2004 the school enrolled 4614 students. The main location is at 1650 Bedford Avenue, with a second location at 1150 Carroll Street.

Stephanie Miller

medical examiner. Until the early twentieth century there were 11 county coroners in what became the five boroughs of New York City, all of whom were elected. Reports in the press of their corruption and incompetence along with the efforts of reformers Richard S. Childs and Robert S. Binkerd led to an investigation in 1914 by Leonard M. Wallstein, the commissioner of accounts under Mayor John Purroy Mitchel. In the following year the state legislature replaced the system of elected coroners with a centralized medical examiner's office, the first of its kind in the nation. The chief medical examiner was required to be a skilled physician, pathologist, and microscopist and was to be appointed by the mayor. The Office of Chief Medical Examiner of the city of New York was established in 1918, pursuant to the New York State legislature's 1915 act creating it. The first person to hold the office was Charles Norris (1918–35), who was followed by Thomas A. Gonzales (1935–54), Milton Helpern (1954–73), Dominick DiMaio (1973–78), Michael Baden (1978–79), Elliot M. Gross (1979–87), Beverly Leffers (1987–88), and Charles S. Hirsch (1989–). A long-standing connection between the medical examiner's office and New York University was established in 1947, when the university acquired a parcel of land of 11 acres (5 hectares) between First Avenue and the East River and between 30th and 34th streets. The university agreed to donate a portion of the land for the construction of the Institute of Forensic Medicine, which came to house the medical examiner's office and the city morgue, and the city agreed in return to close the streets in the area and to transfer their title to the university; the medical examiner's office moved to 520 First Avenue in 1960. In addition the Department of Forensic Medicine at the New York University School of Medicine made it a policy to recruit faculty members from the Office of Chief Medical Examiner. The office was beset by controversy in 1985, when Gross was alleged to have produced misleading or inaccurate autopsy reports, some for people who had died while in police custody. The allegations led to federal, state, and city investigations that cleared Gross of willful wrongdoing. In the early twenty-first century, about

250 people work for the medical examiner's office throughout the five boroughs.

Bernard Hirschhorn, "Richard Spencer Childs: His Role in Modernization of Medicolegal Investigation in America," *American Journal of Forensic Medicine and Pathology* 4 (1983), 245–54

Bernard Hirschhorn

medical schools. Formal medical instruction began in New York City in the mid-eighteenth century by physicians who taught private courses in anatomy to supplement a three-year apprenticeship. The first formal medical school in North America was organized in 1767 with six faculty members by King's College (later Columbia College and then Columbia University). Like all medical schools for the next century it was affiliated with a college only so that it could award degrees, and it remained financially and administratively independent. Most physicians in colonial America continued to receive their training at hospitals rather than medical schools. Until the late nineteenth century medical students were required to complete two courses lasting four or five months, in addition to an apprenticeship with a physician. The medical school at King's College closed during the American Revolution and reopened in 1792. A second medical school, the New York College of Physicians and Surgeons, was opened in 1807 by the New York County Medical Society and in 1813 absorbed the medical school at Columbia. This medical school was independent until 1860 when it merged with Columbia College. Among the many other medical schools established before the mid-nineteenth century, only one survived for more than a few years: the Medical Department of the University of the City of New York (later New York University), formed in 1841.

As the apprenticeship system declined in New York City during the second quarter of the nineteenth century, new methods of clinical instruction supplemented medical lectures. The most important programs were developed at Bellevue Hospital, where a medical board composed of faculty members was formed in 1847. During 1855–60 the hospital added a teaching building and an amphitheater for lectures and surgical operations and took control of a city hospital on Wards Island that it used as a teaching facility. The Homoeopathic Medical College of New York opened in 1860, as did the Long Island College Hospital Medical School in Brooklyn. Bellevue Hospital Medical College (1861) was the first medical school in the United States tied closely to a large hospital.

Women were denied admission into medical schools until the opening in 1863 of the New York Medical College and Hospital for Women, which was homeopathic. A second medical school for women, the Women's Medical College of New York Infirmary, opened in 1865. A number of other short-lived medical schools were organized in New York City after the Civil War. After a fire destroyed the medical school at New York University in 1869, it was rebuilt opposite Bellevue Hospital to allow greater access to the hospital's clinical facilities. In 1882 Bellevue was divided into units for clinical instruction staffed by each of the three leading nonhomeopathic medical schools in the city. This period marked the beginning of the arrangement whereby faculty members at medical schools provided medical care at hospitals in return for being allowed to use hospital facilities for teaching and research.

Two postgraduate schools were organized in 1882 to train physicians in medical specialties: the New York Post-Graduate Medical School and Hospital, and the New York Polyclinic Medical School and Hospital. The College of Physicians and Surgeons merged with Columbia University in 1891. The merger in 1898 of the medical school at New York University with Bellevue Hospital Medical College to form the University and Bellevue Hospital Medical College (later renamed the New York University School of Medicine) was unacceptable to several faculty members of New York University, who later that year organized the Cornell University Medical College with the financial support of Oliver H. Payne. With gifts from William Vanderbilt the College of Physicians and Surgeons built the Vanderbilt Clinic and the Sloane Maternity Hospital in the 1880s. Fordham University added a medical school in 1905 (forced by financial troubles to close in 1921). Columbia in 1928 opened a medical center based at Presbyterian Hospital on the Upper West Side (with contributions from Edward Harkness and his mother), as did Cornell University Medical College and New York Hospital in 1932 in midtown (with contributions from Payne Whitney and others).

The admission of women to medical schools in the early twentieth century led to the closing of the two women's medical schools in New York City. The Homoeopathic Medical College of New York, which loosened its ties to homeopathy, became the New York Medical College and created a medical center on the Upper East Side with the Flower Free Surgical Hospital and later the Fifth Avenue Hospital. Medical education in New York City rose to national prominence largely because of the internship and residency programs offered in its municipal hospitals, and state licensing of physicians brought about the demise of less reputable schools; by the early 1920s almost all physicians took hospital internships immediately after graduating from medical school.

After World War II, New York State assumed a greater role in medical education. Evidence of discrimination against Jews and Italians in admission to medical schools prompted the state to enact laws prohibiting discrimination in 1948 and also led to the establishment of the Albert Einstein College of Medicine as part of Yeshiva University in the Bronx in 1955. In response to the growing shortage of physicians, the state in 1950 transformed Long Island College Hospital in Brooklyn into the State University of New York (SUNY) Downstate Medical Center (later renamed the SUNY Health Science Center at Brooklyn). It also granted annual subsidies to private medical schools in the city to help increase enrollment and developed programs to provide financial aid and to increase the number of African American and Spanish-speaking students. Among the most successful programs for racial minorities was one at the Sophie Davis School of Biomedical Education (1973, later part of the City University of New York), where two years of undergraduate education at the university were combined with education at an affiliated medical school.

Federal support of health research in the 1950s increased biomedical research in schools and research institutes in the city. Soon New York State was receiving more federal funds for health research than any state except California. Degrees were granted from 1954 by the Rockefeller Institute, an internationally renowned medical research laboratory (in 1965 renamed Rockefeller University). Both Rockefeller and the Memorial Sloan Kettering Cancer Center established joint teaching and research programs with Cornell University Medical College. In an effort to improve the quality of care in municipal hospitals, medical schools and their affiliated teaching hospitals in the early 1960s agreed to provide them with designated services. The early results were discouraging, and public officials, community leaders, and the press accused the participating medical schools and teaching hospitals of mismanagement, misuse of funds, and lack of commitment to improving the quality of care; in time, however, the affiliation agreements brought better results. The Mount Sinai School of Medicine was established in 1968 largely because the management at Mount Sinai Hospital believed that a medical school was needed to maintain the hospital's stature. The New York Medical College, which moved in part to suburban Valhalla, New York, in 1968, was purchased by the Archdiocese of New York in 1978 to improve the staffing of its hospitals.

In the twenty-first century the medical schools in New York City were important providers of health care. Two medical schools on Long Island, the SUNY Health Sciences Center at Stony Brook (1971) and the New York College of Osteopathic Medicine of the New York Institute of Technology in Old Westbury (1977), both used hospitals in New York City for clinical training.

James J. Walsh, *History of Medicine in New York: Three Centuries of Medical Progress* (New York:

National Americana Society, 1919); Kenneth M. Ludmerer, *Learning to Heal: The Development of American Medical Education* (New York: Basic Books, 1985); William G. Rothstein, *American Medical Schools and the Practice of Medicine: A History* (New York: Oxford University Press, 1987); Sandra Opdycke, *No One Was Turned Away: The Role of Public Hospitals in New York City since 1900* (New York: Oxford University Press, 1999)

Medina, Harold (Raymond) (*b* Brooklyn, 16 Feb 1888; *d* Westwood, N.J., 14 March 1990). Judge. He graduated from Princeton University (1909) and Columbia Law School (1912) and taught law at Columbia from 1915 to 1940. His private practice earned him $100,000 a year by 1947, when he accepted an appointment to the U.S. District Court for the Southern District of New York. In 1949 he presided over the nine-month trial of 11 communists indicted under the Smith Act, ending with their conviction and their lawyers sentenced for contempt of court. He served on the Circuit Court of Appeals for the Second Circuit from 1951 (succeeding Learned Hand) until he became a senior circuit judge in 1958; he retired in 1980. He wrote *Judge Medina Speaks* (1954) and *The Anatomy of Freedom* (1959). For many years he lived at 14 East 75th Street.

Jeffrey A. Kroessler

Meeker Avenue Bridge. Original name of the Kosciuszko Bridge.

Megalopolis. Term coined by the French geographer Jean Gottman, whose book *Megalopolis: The Urbanized Northeastern Seaboard of the United States* (1961) defined the corridor 600 miles (1000 kilometers) long between Boston and Washington, D.C., centered at New York City, and its 38 million residents as a new social, economic, and political entity. He credited the word to the ancient Greeks, who used it for a newly founded city intended to be their largest. According to Gottman the Megalopolis was the "richest, best-educated, best-housed, and best-serviced" urbanized region in the world.

Kenneth T. Jackson

Meiers Corners. Neighborhood in north central Staten Island, near the intersection of Victory Boulevard, Jewett Avenue, and Watchogue Road. It took shape early in the twentieth century as a transfer point for trolley lines along Victory Boulevard and Jewett Avenue. The neighborhood is named for Joachim Meier, who lived in the Martling–Cozine House, a stone house built before the American Revolution that survived into the 1980s. Small shops line Victory Boulevard, to the south of which is a residential area of small one-family houses. The population is largely white.

Marjorie Johnson

Meili, Trisha. See Central Park jogger.

Meisner, Sanford (*b* Brooklyn, 31 Aug 1905; *d* Sherman Oaks, Calif., 4 Feb 1997). Actor, teacher, director. In 1924 he received a scholarship to the Theatre Guild School of Acting. He remained with the guild until 1931, when he and others launched the Group Theatre, an artists' collective. In the Group Theatre, which lasted only a decade, Meisner performed more than a dozen roles and directed. Beginning in 1935 Meisner taught acting at the Neighborhood Playhouse School of the Theater; he was also head of the department from 1936 to 1959. After several years on the West Coast, he resumed his former position in the playhouse school from 1964 to 1990. Meisner's teaching emphasized spontaneity and living truthfully under the imaginary circumstances of the script; his students included David Mamet, Sydney Pollack, Gregory Peck, Grace Kelly, Peter Falk, Tony Randall, and Joanne Woodward.

Sanford Meisner and Dennis Longwell, *On Acting* (New York: Vintage Books, 1987); "Sanford Meisner," *Current Biography,* ed. Charles Moritz (New York: H. W. Wilson Company, 1992)

Cathy Alexander

Mellon Foundation. See Andrew W. Mellon Foundation.

Melrose. Neighborhood in the southwestern Bronx (2000 pop. 19,563), bounded to the north by the intersection of Brook and Park avenues, to the east by Brook Avenue, to the south by 149th Street, and to the west by Park Avenue; its center is a commercial area on 149th Street at a former transfer point between the subway and the Third Avenue elevated line. When the area was developed in the 1850s as a suburb for those who worked in Manhattan, the population was mostly German. The village was transformed into an urban neighborhood during the 1890s, when cheap rapid transit was provided by the Third Avenue elevated line. Development increased again after the subway was extended to the area in 1904. The site of beer gardens, German churches, and *Turnvereine* (German gymnastics associations), Melrose retained its German character until the 1940s. The commercial district around 149th Street, known as the Hub, was for the first half of the twentieth century the commercial and entertainment center of the Bronx, with theaters and several department stores, including the first Alexander's (1928). By then, the population also included Italians along Morris Avenue and some Russian Jews and Irish. During the 1960s and 1970s building abandonment, slum clearance, arson, drugs, and crime left behind a devastated urban landscape with a largely poor population. A small remnant of the Italian enclave remained until the 1970s. By the late 1990s community organizations had rebuilt the area with thousands of units of renovated apartments and new owner-occupied affordable housing, and in the early twenty-first century the neighborhood was thriving once again.

Jim Rooney, *Organizing the South Bronx* (Albany, N.Y.: State University of New York Press, 1995); Evelyn Gonzalez, *The Bronx* (New York: Columbia University Press, 2004)

Evelyn Gonzalez

Melville, Herman (*b* New York City, 1 Aug 1819; *d* New York City, 28 Sept 1891). Novelist. Although widely identified with seafaring and New England, he spent most of his life in New York City, which profoundly influenced his writing. He was born at 6 Pearl Street and lived as a child at 33 Bleecker Street (1824–28) and 675 Broadway (1828). From 1834 to 1845 he lived outside the city. After he returned and lived at 103 Fourth Avenue, he quickly wrote five novels, including the best-selling South Seas adventures *Typee* (1846) and *Omoo* (1847). After the cholera epidemic of 1849 he left for New England, where he wrote *Moby-Dick* (1851) and another masterpiece, "Bartleby the Scrivener" (1853), which is set in a New York City office. On his return to the city in 1863 he moved to 104 East 26th Street and went to work as a customs inspector on the piers at Gansevoort Street. In his spare time and retirement he wrote poetry, books, and stories that included *Billy Budd, Sailor.* In 1882 he was invited to join the Century Association, an artists' and writers' club, but declined because he felt he was too much of a hermit, though he was often seen on the streets and in the city's bookstores. Melville is buried at Woodlawn Cemetery in the Bronx.

Perry Miller, *The Raven and the Whale* (New York: Harcourt, Brace, 1956); Edwin Haviland Miller, *Melville* (George Braziller, 1975); Andrew Delbanco, *Melville: His World and His Work* (New York: Knopf, 2005)

Jeff Finlay, John Rousmaniere

Melvina. Former neighborhood in west central Queens. It was originally the farm of the Van Cott family and became one of the first real estate developments in Maspeth. On a map published in October 1852 by a real estate agent from New York City, John H. Smith, the area was shown as being bounded to the north by Maspeth Avenue and to the south by Flushing Avenue, and extending 257.5 feet (78.5 meters) on either side of 59th Street. There are

25 houses on Beers's map of 1873. Melvina was later absorbed by Maspeth.

Vincent Seyfried

Memorial Fund Association. Original name of the MILBANK MEMORIAL FUND.

Memorial Sloan–Kettering Cancer Center. Hospital established in 1884 as the New York Cancer Hospital, the first institution in the United States devoted exclusively to the care of cancer patients. It was originally situated at the corner of Central Park West and 106th Street. The hospital became the first in the country to use radiation therapy in 1904, only six years after the discovery of radium. It was renamed the Memorial Hospital for the Treatment of Cancer and Allied Diseases in 1917 and moved in 1937 to its present site on land donated by John D. Rockefeller bounded by 67th and 68th streets and First and York avenues. A laboratory devoted to cancer research and financed by two executives from General Motors, Alfred P. Sloan, Jr. (chairman of the company) and Charles F. Kettering, opened in 1945 as the Sloan–Kettering Institute; in 1960 the hospital took its current name. Experiments at the hospital during World War II into the effects of chemical warfare led to chemotherapy treatments for various types of cancer. In 1971 Congress designated the hospital the prototype of a comprehensive cancer center. In addition to superior research and treatment facilities, the hospital is known for attracting dedicated volunteers, most notably esteemed New York pianist George Feyer, who is remembered for his weekly concerts enjoyed by patients from 1961 until 1999. While maintaining strong institutional ties with Weill Medical College of Cornell University and Rockefeller University, the Sloan–Kettering Institute opened the independent Louis V. Gerstner, Jr., Graduate School of Biomedical Sciences in 2005. In 2006 the Mortimer B. Zuckerman Research Center, a 23-story research facility, was opened. In the early twenty-first century the center remained the world's largest private cancer facility and was ranked as one of the best cancer hospitals in the United States.

Andrea Balis, Michael C. Repka

Mendes, Henry Pereira (*b* Birmingham, England, 13 April 1852; *d* New York City, 20 Oct 1937). Rabbi. He led the Sephardic congregation of Manchester, England, before moving in 1877 to New York City, where he led Congregation Shearith Israel for 60 years. A man of broad culture, he was a rabbinic teacher and writer as well as a physician and helped to form the Jewish Theological Seminary, the Lexington School for the Deaf, and Montefiore Hospital. He was a founder and president of the Union of Orthodox Jewish Congregations, as well as an outspoken and active Zionist. He lived at 90 Central Park West.

David de Sola Pool, *An Old Faith in the New World: Portrait of Shearith Israel* (New York: Columbia University Press, 1955)

Marc D. Angel

mental health. In New York City the treatment of mental illness became a public responsibility in 1665 when a provincial law authorized towns within the colony of New York to share the cost of maintaining "distracted persons." For more than a century those who required public maintenance were confined in cellars, attics, strongrooms in poorhouses, and jails. Hospital care for the insane first became available in the state when New York Hospital began admitting mental patients in 1792, and by 1808 the hospital opened a separate lunatic asylum on its grounds, funded by the state legislature. Demand from communities throughout the state eventually exceeded the supply of beds, and most insane indigent people were forced to remain in local almshouses and jails. From the early 1820s reformers such as Thomas Eddy, treasurer of New York Hospital, advocated the new methods of "moral treatment" introduced in Europe, which stressed humane care of the mentally ill and cure rather than confinement. This approach required adequate space, comfortable surroundings, and trained staff, all of which were available from 1821 at Bloomingdale Asylum of New York Hospital, on Broadway and 116th Street (where Columbia University now stands).

In the mid-1820s most of the insane paupers at Bloomingdale and the almshouse were transferred to Bellevue Hospital, the city's largest municipal hospital. Repeated public complaints about overcrowding at Bellevue eventually led to the opening of a separate lunatic asylum with 164 beds on Blackwell's Island (1839), the first public mental hospital in New York State and the first municipal mental institution in the country. In Flatbush in Brooklyn the insane were placed in the county poorhouse, an arrangement that was criticized by the reformer Dorothea Dix during her state tour of asylums in 1844. The poorhouse was replaced by separate buildings for the insane on the same site in 1845 and 1855, each of which suffered from overcrowding and minimal staffing. When Charles Dickens visited the asylum on Blackwell's Island in 1842, he found it little better than the asylum in Brooklyn and noted its "lounging, listless, madhouse air." Each enlargement of the facilities was quickly followed by a flood of new admissions: in 1848 the asylum on Blackwell's Island held more than 400 patients. A separate building for women was added to the asylum in the same year and by 1860 the facility held 750 patients in appalling conditions. More than 80 percent of the asylum patients were foreign born at this time, compared with 45 percent of the city's total population. When the number of patients reached 1300, additional facilities were built on Wards Island (1871, later the Manhattan Psychiatric Center) and Hart Island (1878), but these rapidly became as grim and overcrowded as the facility on Blackwell's Island.

Periodic reforms did little to improve the conditions of the city asylums, which became infamous for bad food, frequent epidemics, graft-ridden administrations, and incompetent staffs that included convicts from the city prison. The reporter Nellie Bly tried to provoke change in the system by committing herself to the city asylum in 1887 and then writing the widely read series "Ten Days in a Mad-house." The only governmental action taken during the 1880s to improve asylums was a law empowering the State Board of Charities to deport alien and nonresident paupers who were insane. This power was later extended to the State Commission on Lunacy and resulted in thousands of deportations, with 1700 in 1912 alone. Growing complaints during the 1880s helped bring about the passage of the State Care Aid Act (1890), under which the insane were placed in state hospitals as space became available. Asylums in Manhattan and Brooklyn were taken over by the state and became state hospitals. In 1894 Bloomingdale Asylum, which had about 400 patients, moved from the city to larger quarters in suburban White Plains.

Organized psychiatric research was first conducted in the United States at the Pathological Institute of New York State Hospitals (1895). Initially the institute examined only morbid materials (cadavers, organs, and tissue samples), but in 1902 its new director Adolf Meyer moved the institute to Wards Island, where it became affiliated with the state hospital; in 1929 the institute moved to the Columbia–Presbyterian Medical Center. From 1909 the mental hygiene movement gave a new emphasis to finding a cure for mental illness. It was led by Clifford Beers, who described his own experiences as a mental patient in the widely read book *A Mind That Found Itself* (1908) and launched the National Committee for Mental Hygiene at the Manhattan Hotel. The movement stressed research, public education, and better institutional care, and the use of the term *mental hygiene* reflected a conviction that mental problems could be cured. Within 20 years similar societies were formed in 30 countries around the world. Child guidance clinics were set up for the mentally ill in 1919; community services for the mentally ill expanded during the 1920s; the city's Vocational Adjustment Bureau established its first workshop for the emotionally disturbed in

1925; and the New York Academy of Medicine persuaded the Board of Education to augment its services for emotionally disturbed children. The Payne Whitney Psychiatric Clinic opened at New York Hospital in 1932, and in 1944 a large after-care clinic was set up at the New York State Psychiatric Institute (the descendant of the Pathological Institute) to serve patients released from the many state hospitals in and around New York City. The term *mental health* was adopted in the late 1930s.

The growing acceptance of psychoanalysis had a strong effect on mental health care. Despite opposition from most psychiatrists in the United States, A. A. Brill (who first translated Sigmund Freud's work into English), Smith Ely Jelliffe, and others in New York City formed the New York Psychoanalytical Society in 1911, the second such organization in the United States. The city's psychoanalytic community, which grew rapidly during the 1920s, was split by several controversial issues, such as whether psychoanalysts should be required to be physicians and whether culture plays an important role in individual development; Karen Horney, Clara Thompson, William Silverberg, and others who stressed the importance of culture formed the Association for the Advancement of Psychoanalysis (1941), which later established the American Institute of Psychoanalysis as its teaching branch. Psychoanalytic treatment became sought after by the city's affluent residents. It exerted a profound influence on literature and the arts, and the psychoanalyst became a stock figure in accounts of neurosis and anxiety among the privileged.

Institutional services for the mentally ill expanded in New York City at the turn of the twentieth century, and by 1912 the Manhattan Psychiatric Center was the world's largest mental hospital, with more than 4500 patients. Another 1200 New Yorkers were cared for in other state hospitals. Admission rates rose abruptly during the 1920s, and the patient population included a growing number of children suffering from encephalitis. By the early 1930s more than 25,000 city residents lived in state institutions, occupying two-thirds of the beds in the system. During these years the state initiated various reforms and expanded facilities within the city (opening Creedmoor State Hospital in Queens), but it failed to accommodate the growing number of people needing care. Overcrowding continued, buildings deteriorated, and care remained primarily custodial. Local governments often referred the large population of dependent elderly people to the state-funded facilities, even if their primary problems were not psychiatric; by 1945 three-fifths of the patients at Manhattan Psychiatric Center were older than 60. In 1947 Albert Deutsch published his influential exposé of U.S. mental institutions, *The Shame of the States,* devoting one chapter each to Manhattan State Hospital and to the psychiatric unit at Bellevue.

The growing interest in community-based care for the mentally ill led the state legislature to pass the Community Mental Health Services Act in 1954, the first act of its kind in the United States. It called for local boards to develop community mental health programs, with state aid covering as much as 50 percent of the costs. The city's Department of Mental Health, Mental Retardation and Alcoholism Services was formed in 1955 as part of this effort. The trend toward community care was aided by the availability from 1955 of tranquilizers and antidepressants. In the mid-1950s state mental institutions, including those in New York City, experienced the first annual declines in their number of patients. A phase of construction of large state hospitals ended with the opening of Bronx State Hospital in 1955. When South Beach Psychiatric Center opened on Staten Island in 1974, community services were as much a part of its program as the care of inpatients. The pace of "deinstitutionalization" was quickened by a growing body of court decisions stressing patients' rights. Epidemiological studies in New York City in the early 1960s by Leo Srole and Bruce Dohrenwend supported the idea that mental illness and health were part of a continuum rather than discrete conditions and that the illness responded to varying kinds of treatment and was not necessarily disabling.

The 1970s and 1980s brought new challenges. Community mental health services strained to support the large number of patients newly released from state hospitals. Divisions among psychoanalysts continued, and by 1979 there were at least 11 training groups for psychoanalysis within Greater New York. By the early 1990s fiscal problems, jurisdictional disputes between state and city agencies, a shrinking job market, and drastic reductions in the city's stock of affordable housing made it difficult for the city to meet the needs of its mentally ill, many of whom were homeless and suffered from alcoholism and drug abuse. In 1991 the city's Department of Mental Health, Mental Retardation and Alcoholism Services supported 870 community programs (most provided under contract by voluntary agencies). Numerous other services were funded through charitable contributions, private insurance, and patients' fees. Early in the twenty-first century the city had more than 3000 licensed psychologists, about the same number of psychiatrists, and more than 12,000 social workers.

David M. Schneider and Albert Deutsch, *The History of Public Welfare in New York State, 1867–1940* (Chicago: University of Chicago Press, 1941); Norman Dain, *Concepts of Insanity in the United States, 1789–1865* (New Brunswick, N.J.: Rutgers University Press, 1964); John Duffy, *A History of Public Health in New York City* (New York: Russell Sage Foundation, 1968, 1974); Reuben Fine, *A History of Psychoanalysis* (New York: Columbia University Press, 1979); Gerald N. Grob, *Mental Illness and American Society* (Princeton, N.J.: Princeton University Press, 1983)

Sandra Opdycke

Mercantile Library Association. Organization formed by merchant clerks in 1820 that opened a circulating library in rented rooms

Clinton Hall at Astor Place and Lafayette Street, site of the Mercantile Library Association, ca *1890 (demolished 1890)*

at 49 Fulton Street in the following year. It accepted members from diverse backgrounds but allowed only merchant clerks to vote and hold office. In 1828 a number of its prominent members formed the Clinton Hall Association to raise funds and manage real estate acquired for a permanent library building, and in 1830 a new building called Clinton Hall opened to the public at the corner of Nassau and Beekman streets. The library moved in 1854 to the Italian Opera House at Astor Place. It became a cultural center that offered lectures and evening classes. Membership reached a peak of more than 12,000 in 1870, and the library's collection of 120,000 volumes made it the leading circulating library in the United States. The reading room had more than 400 newspapers and periodicals and 3000 reference works and was reportedly used by 1000 people a day in 1871. After the Opera House was demolished, a new Clinton Hall opened on the same site in 1891. In addition to the main library the association had a downtown office and seven branch libraries. Although the establishment of free public libraries led to a decline in membership, a new Clinton Hall opened in 1933 at 17 East 47th Street that included 230,000 volumes available to 3000 members. In 2009 the Mercantile Library was renamed the Center for Fiction. It continues to operate a circulating library with a reading room open to all subscribers; the collection's literary fiction collection includes approximately 75,000 titles from the past 100 years and 10,000 from the nineteenth century; it also has about 20,000 works of nonfiction relating to literature and maintains a writers' studio and offers a series of literary programs open to the public.

Fiftieth Anniversary Celebration of the Mercantile Library Association (New York: G. F. Nesbitt, 1871)

Elaine Weber Pascu

Mercer, Mabel (*b* Burton-on-Trent, England, 3 Feb 1900; *d* Pittsfield, Mass., 20 April 1984). Singer. In the 1920s she entertained expatriates such as F. Scott Fitzgerald and Cole Porter at Bricktop's renowned nightclub in Paris. After immigrating to the United States in the late 1930s she settled in New York City in 1941. She developed a large following for her performances in cabarets and nightclubs, becoming known as the "queen of the intimate supper clubs" for her flawless diction, elegance, and emotional sensitivity to lyrics, as well as for her attention to forgotten repertory. Her influence extended to many popular songwriters and singers, including Frank Sinatra.

Cynthia Copeland

Merchants Association of New York. Trade association. It was formed in 1897 by wholesale traders in an effort to attract dry-goods firms to New York City and assist those already there. After 1900 it developed into a powerful group with influence over governmental affairs. In 1942 it was renamed the Commerce and Industry Association of New York, and in 1973 it merged with the New York Chamber of Commerce. In 2002 the combined organization, known as the New York Chamber of Commerce and Industry, merged with David Rockefeller's New York City Partnership to form the PARTNERSHIP FOR NEW YORK CITY (ii).

Arnold J. Bornfriend, "The Business Group in Metropolis: The Commerce and Industry Association of New York" (diss., Columbia University, 1967)

Donald R. Stabile, Andrew A. Kryzak

Merchant's House Museum. Historic house at 29 East Fourth Street erected in 1832 by Joseph Brewster in a synthesis of the Federal and Greek Revival styles. Built in what was then a fashionable neighborhood, it was purchased in 1835 by Seabury Treadwell, who was retired from a successful career as a marine-hardware merchant, and was occupied by various members of the family for the next 98 years; his youngest daughter Gertrude is credited with having kept the contents of the household intact. Opened as a museum in 1936, the house contains an extensive collection of furnishings and personal items from the Federal and Victorian periods. For more than 20 years before his death in 1988, the architect Joseph Roberto worked to restore the house and bring it to public attention. A city landmark listed on the National Register of Historic Places, the Merchant's House Museum is New York City's only family home preserved intact, inside and out, from the nineteenth century.

Joyce Gold

Merchant's House Museum, 2009

Mercury Theater. Repertory company for classical drama formed in the autumn of 1937 by Orson Welles, then 22 years old, and John Houseman. Its first production was *Julius Caesar,* mounted in a theater at Broadway and 41st Street in an abbreviated, 90-minute version that was staged as an allegory of Europe under fascism. This and an all-black version of *Macbeth* and other productions were critically and popularly successful, but the company's commitment to repertory work and cheap tickets soon undermined its finances, and with the failure of Georg Büchner's *Danton's Death* in 1938–39, it was forced to close. The company made Welles nationally renowned, and he was offered a weekly radio program presenting adaptations of famous novels. Houseman and actors from the company took part in the program, which was often referred to as the Mercury Theater on the Air. Its rendition of H. G. Wells's *The War of the Worlds* (31 October 1938) caused panic across the nation when many mistook it for a news bulletin relating an invasion by Martians.

George A. Thompson, Jr.

Merkle, Philipp (*b* Rheinpfalz [now in Germany], 20 March 1811; *d* New York City, 3 May 1899). Political activist and minister. He studied theology at the University of Heidelberg before immigrating to the United States and settling in New York City in 1833. He was a Lutheran minister until 1835, when he organized and became the "speaker" of a congregation of freethinkers known as the German Universal Christian Church. In 1847 he helped to form the Harugari, the largest German fraternal order in America, which he led. A prominent figure among Germans in the Democratic Party, he held a series of patronage positions: appraiser of drugs for the federal government (appointed 1853), city excise commissioner (appointed 1878), and coroner (elected 1881).

Stanley Nadel

Merman [Zimmermann], **Ethel (Agnes)** (*b* Queens, 16 Jan 1908; *d* New York City, 15 Feb 1984). Singer and actress. She worked as a secretary while moonlighting as a singer at nightclubs. She was performing vaudeville at the Palace Theatre before she made her debut in the musical comedy *Girl Crazy* (1930) and began making short films in Astoria with Paramount Studios shortly after. During the next 40 years Merman performed on Broadway and became known for her powerful singing and good-humored acting in such shows as *Anything Goes* (1934), *Annie Get Your Gun* (1946), and *Gypsy* (1959). She moved to the Century Apartments at 25 Central Park West in 1933 and during the 1960s lived at the Park Lane Hotel at 36 West

Ethel Merman in Annie Get Your Gun, *1946*

59th Street and at the Berkshire Hotel at 21 East 52nd Street. She spent the last years of her life at the Hotel Surrey (20 East 76th Street).

Merrick [Margulois]**, David (Lee)** (*b* St. Louis, 27 Nov 1911; *d* London, 26 April 2000). Producer. In St. Louis he graduated from Washington University and worked as a lawyer. After settling in New York City in 1946 he began his career as a producer of plays and musicals; his most successful included *Fanny* (Harold Rome, 1954), *Gypsy* (Jule Styne and Stephen Sondheim, 1959), *Hello, Dolly!* (Jerry Herman, 1964), *Marat/Sade* (Peter Weiss, 1965), *Play It Again, Sam* (Woody Allen, 1969), and *42nd Street* (Gower Champion, 1980), at 3486 performances one of the longest-running shows on Broadway. He produced a revival of George Gershwin's *Oh, Kay!* in 1991. Merrick's astute management and shrewd use of publicity made him one of the most successful producers on Broadway, with more than 85 productions to his credit.

Howard Kissel, *David Merrick: The Abominable Showman: The Unauthorized Biography* (New York: Applause Books, 1993)

Martha S. LoMonaco

Merrifield, R(obert) Bruce (*b* Fort Worth, Tex., 15 Jul 1921; *d* Cresskill, N.J., 14 May 2006). Biochemist. Upon earning his PhD in chemistry from the University of California, Los Angeles, in 1949, he moved to New York City for a position at the Rockefeller Institute for Medical Research (later Rockefeller University). There Merrifield developed solid-phase peptide synthesis, a fast, efficient method for synthesizing certain types of amino acid chains. This became a fundamental technique in biochemistry and pharmacology and earned Merrifield the 1984 Nobel Prize in chemistry. He spent his entire career at Rockefeller University and continued his bench work until just before his death.

Eric Hollingsworth

Merrill Lynch, Pierce, Fenner and Smith. Firm of stockbrokers formed in the early 1940s through the merger of the firms Merrill Lynch (1915), Fenner and Beane (1916), and E. A. Pierce and Company (1927). Winthrop Smith, who worked for Merrill Lynch in the 1920s and for E. A. Pierce in the 1930s, was instrumental in arranging the merger; his name replaced that of Alpheus Beane in the name of the firm in 1958. Charles E. Merrill was the key figure in mapping the strategy of the firm, which emphasized service to middle-class investors and long-term investment in blue-chip securities. The firm maintained its headquarters in New York City and had more than 100 branch offices nationwide; it became the nation's most successful brokerage firm in the 1940s. At a time when brokerage suffered from a disreputable image, it introduced a number of innovations that later became widely imitated, including publication of an annual report, aggressive advertising, the preparation of research reports, and training for new brokers. Donald T. Regan, who enrolled in the training program at the end of World War II, became chief executive officer of the firm in 1971 before leaving to serve as President Ronald Reagan's secretary of the treasury and chief of staff. In 2007 Merrill Lynch, Pierce, Fenner and Smith was the largest brokerage firm in the United States, with more than 500 branches worldwide. It was acquired by Bank of America during the financial crisis in 2008.

Henry Hecht, ed., *A Legacy of Leadership: Merrill Lynch, 1885–1985* (New York: Merrill Lynch, 1985)

Edwin J. Perkins

Merton, Robert K(ing) (*b* Philadelphia, 5 July 1910; *d* New York City, 23 Feb 2003). Sociologist. He received his graduate education at Harvard University and began teaching at Columbia University in 1941, where he remained for the rest of his career and rose to the rank of university professor. In dozens of books and articles he defended sociology as a science capable of being tested by empirical evidence. He focused on "middle range theory," which explored everyday life, and coined the phrase "self-fulfilling prophecy." His many awards include a Guggenheim Fellowship (1962) and the Career Distinguished Service Award (1980) of the American Sociological Association. Merton's best-known works, *Social Theory and Social Structure* (1949) and *The Sociology of Science* (1973), are standards in the field.

Piotr Sztomka, *Robert K. Merton: An Intellectual Profile* (New York: St. Martin's, 1986)

Andrew Wiese

Merton, Thomas (*b* Prades, France, 31 Jan 1915; *d* Bangkok, 10 Dec 1968). Writer and theologian. He graduated from Columbia University (BA 1938, MA 1939), where he studied literature with Mark Van Doren and philosophy with Daniel Walsh; he also took part in communist activities and helped to produce a student humor magazine. On 16 November 1938 he converted to Catholicism in a ceremony in the parish of Corpus Christi, 531–35 West 121st Street. In 1939–40 he lived at 35 Perry Street. He entered the Trappist monastery of Our Lady of Gethsemani in Kentucky on 10 December 1941 and wrote poetry (including *Figures for an Apocalypse,* 1949), an autobiography (*The Seven Story Mountain,* 1948), meditations on Eastern mysticism (*Seeds of Contemplation,* 1949), and essays on war and peace.

Michael Mott, *The Seven Mountains of Thomas Merton* (Boston: Houghton Mifflin, 1984)

Mary Elizabeth Brown

Merzbacher, Leo (*b* Fürth [now in Germany], 1810; *d* New York City, 1856). Rabbi. He emigrated from Bavaria to the United States and in 1841 became the first professionally trained rabbi in New York City. He was a teacher for the German Orthodox congregation Rodeph Shalom and for Anshe Chesed, the earliest German congregation in the city. In 1845 he founded the Reform synagogue Temple Emanu-El. He was an organizer of the Independent Order of B'nai B'rith and is credited with having originated its name. Merzbacher published a revised prayer book in 1855 and is regarded as the first Reform rabbi in the United States.

Stanley Nadel

metal founding and metalworking. During the colonial period New York City became an important center for tinsmiths and coppersmiths, and later for iron founders. The early iron foundries were small operations (10 workers or fewer) that also wrought copper, brass, and tin. Wrought iron and cast iron were both produced at the New York Air Furnace (in the 1780s) and the Phoenix Foundry (by 1800), and in the early nineteenth century the growth of shipbuilding made iron founding a major industry. The Allaire Ironworks (opened by James P. Allaire in 1816) was the first of several huge foundries where boilers weighing several tons were constructed for the steamships of the 1820s and 1830s. The first ironworks to specialize in steam engines was that of Robert McQueen (a protégé of Robert Fulton), whose Columbian Foundry was one of the leading manufacturers in New York City (82 employees in 1820). By 1830 employment at Allaire reached 200. Other notable ironworks included the Novelty Ironworks (opened by Thomas Stillman in 1830), the Delameter Works (the only major ironworks on the Hudson River, opened in 1835), the Morgan Ironworks (1838), and the Cornell Ironworks (1847). But even operations like McQueen's were too small to build engines for the oceangoing vessels of the 1840s, and to obtain more space most of the large foundries and other firms that were connected to shipbuilding moved to sites along the East River. The industry was hurt by the depression of 1837, but the unprecedented prosperity of the late 1840s created a boom in shipbuilding and manufacturing and a vast expansion of the city's iron foundries. By 1850 the Novelty Works had 938 employees, the Allaire Works, 500 (up from 250 in 1847).

By the middle of the nineteenth century foundries that in some cases covered several city blocks became the subject of newspaper and magazine articles and even tourist attractions. The organization of these huge enterprises greatly impressed observers. *Harper's Magazine* described the Novelty Works in 1851 as resembling a "state or kingdom." At the top of these "kingdoms" were the proprietors, men like Allaire and Stillman whose knowledge and industriousness helped to make the East River one of the most advanced and technologically innovative centers for founding and machining in the 1850s. Laborers at ironworks worked in highly specialized departments, yet it was necessary for them to remain versatile because most large engines were custom-built, and parts cast or turned on lathes required extensive chipping and filing to achieve acceptable tolerances. The elite workers were molders and machinists, who accounted for about 50 percent of the workforce; in the 1850s these men received $10 to $12 weekly, about twice as much as their many semiskilled helpers. Foundries also employed blacksmiths, pattern makers, instrument makers, carpenters, and unskilled laborers. Many of the workers were immigrants from England (especially among molders and machinists), Ireland, and Germany, who often lived in the wards near the East River. Allaire, Novelty, and Morgan alone accounted for one-third of the 7770 metalworkers in the city in 1860. In 1863 7000 machinists closed the Novelty, Allaire, and Delameter ironworks in a strike for higher wages, and in the following year the Iron Molders' Union campaigned to prevent the manufacture of castings at the state prison in Sing Sing; but generally the mixture at ironworks of skilled and semiskilled employees thwarted unity, and a traditional coolness between molders and machinists limited the influence of each group on management and on fellow workers in the labor movement.

The Civil War marked the high point for the ironworks. Guns and warships were ordered, and the Delameter Ironworks built the ironclad *Monitor* (1861). The war obscured such problems as the spiraling price of land and the high cost of doing business in Manhattan, and when it ended most of the industry began to move to the Delaware River, where proximity to coal and other advantages made production cheaper. The Novelty Works closed in 1870, its machinery outmoded and its real estate on the East River too valuable for heavy industry. The Allaire Works failed during the depression of 1873, and its site on the river became a stable. Surviving businesses included tinsmiths, coppersmiths, and iron and brass foundries such as the Delameter works, which had 50 to 100 employees and flourished by doing repair work and custom architectural and ornamental ironwork as well as producing hardware for "modern conveniences" like indoor plumbing, central heating, and gas lighting. Firms like Daniel Badger's Architectural Ironworks (1846) that had begun specializing in moldings for cast-iron buildings before the war found themselves in the primary area of growth when the war ended. The Cornell works (1847), known as the "iron university," had plants on Centre and 26th Streets, which in 1870 produced 16,000 castings for the inner and outer walls of the new Tiffany Building on Union Square at 15th Street. But over time the costs of operating in the city doomed the foundries in Manhattan; some moved elsewhere, especially to New Jersey, but in most cases the huge fixed capital investment in buildings, cupolas, and air furnaces made moving economically unfeasible. By 1928 only five foundries remained in Manhattan, though several others continued to operate in Queens. Smaller metalworking firms exhibited a surprising vitality because of their ability to produce small batches of cast iron, wrought iron, and brass. The manufacturing census of 1920 counted 657 metalworking shops in the city, with 26,562 employees.

The military buildup brought on by the two world wars greatly increased the demand for metal production and benefited what remained of the industry. One of the five women who are the subject of the well-known documentary film *Rosie the Riveter* (1944) made shell casings in a machine shop in Manhattan. In 1954 there were 53,000 workers in the city producing fabricated metal products, including ornamental ironwork, heating and plumbing fixtures, and stamps and wire; at the same time only 7000 workers produced primary metals. During the following decades employment in metalworking declined, primarily because of rising rents. In the early twenty-first century metalworking in the city was scarce and limited to the outer boroughs.

John Leander Bishop, *A History of American Manufacturers from 1608 to 1860* (Philadelphia: Edward Young, 1868); Edward Ewing Pratt, *Industrial Causes of Congestion of Population in New York City* (New York: Columbia University, 1911; repr. AMS, 1968)

Richard Stott

Methfessel Institute. Original name of STATEN ISLAND ACADEMY.

Methodists. The first Methodist congregation in New York City was established in 1766 by Barbara Ruckle Heck and her cousin Philip Embury, Irish immigrants who settled in the city in August 1760. Distressed by what she considered signs of indifference to religion (including her brother's fondness for cards), Heck urged Embury to give sermons lest all "go to Hell together." She gathered a congregation of five that initially met at Embury's home on Augustus Street. A larger room was rented nearby, and a Methodist organization was formed and led by Embury and Thomas Webb, a British army captain. The congregation met in a sail-rigging loft on William Street from 1767 until Wesley Chapel was completed and dedicated at 44 John Street on 30 October 1768.

In the following years the city became one of the country's most important centers of Methodist activity. It was a base for such missionaries as Richard Boardman, Joseph Pilmoor, and Francis Asbury, who were sent to the colonies by John Wesley. Membership rose to about 200 by the eve of the American Revolution. Sermons were offered in Queens and Brooklyn as early as 1768 by Thomas Webb and on Staten Island in 1771 by Francis Asbury. By 1784, the year the Methodist Episcopal Church in America was organized in Baltimore, there were only 60 Methodists in New York City, but the number grew steadily in the following years. Churches opened in Queens in 1785, Staten Island in 1787 (Woodrow Church), and Brooklyn in 1794. In the early nineteenth century Wesley Chapel became known as the John Street Methodist Episcopal Church. Disaffected by discrimination there, black members under Peter Williams, James Varick, and Christopher Rush left to hold their own services in 1796, and in 1800 they erected their own building, Zion Church. A denomination was organized formally in 1821 and in 1848 was named the AFRICAN METHODIST EPISCOPAL ZION CHURCH.

Methodism expanded during the nineteenth century. A congregation of the African Methodist Episcopal church was organized in 1817 under William Lambert and eventually became the Bethel African Methodist Episcopal Church. By 1830 the Methodist Episcopal Church set up the Harlem Mission, which included all of Manhattan north of 23rd Street and became the site of some of the most influential congregations, including those of St. Paul, St. Andrew, Madison Avenue, and Park Avenue. Among the first churches in the Bronx were several opened between 1850 and 1865 on Willis Avenue and in Morrisania, Fordham, and Tremont. One of the first Methodist urban missions in the country was the Five Points Mission, opened in 1844 by the Ladies' Home Missionary Society of the Methodist Episcopal Church to provide housing, food, clothing, and Christian guidance for adults and children. From 1845 to 1879 the society also sponsored Bethel Ship, a mission for Scandinavian immigrants and sailors aboard a vessel docked in New York Harbor. In 1888 the Woman's Home Missionary Society of the Methodist Episcopal Church opened a shelter for "worthy female immigrants" near Battery Park; it moved to Greenwich Village in 1927 and became known as the Alma Mathews House, after its most prominent deaconess. The Madison Avenue congregation was renamed Christ United Methodist Church and moved to Park Avenue and 60th Street, where it became the city's best-known Methodist church under the nationally known minister Ralph W. Sockman from 1917 to 1961. In 1963 Methodists opened the Church Center for the United Nations on United Nations Plaza, a facility devoted to such ecumenical activities as seminars on world affairs.

In 1968 the Methodist Church united with the Evangelical United Brethren Church to form the United Methodist Church. In the twenty-first century two of the most important Methodist agencies are the General Board of Global Ministries and the General Commission on Christian Unity and Interreligious Concerns; both have offices in the Interchurch Center at 475 Riverside Drive in Morningside Heights.

Charles Yrigoyen, Jr.

MetroCard. Transit fare card introduced by the Metropolitan Transportation Authority (MTA) in 1994. By the end of 2003 all MTA New York City Transit buses and subways had discontinued tokens. The thin, plastic MetroCard stores cash value and is read by an electronic reader. Public acceptance of the card was slow but surged when free MetroCard transfers between subways and buses began in 1997. In 1998 MetroCards offered volume discounts and unlimited-ride seven- and 30-day passes. One-day unlimited ride passes also became available, as did paper single-ride MetroCards. In January 1999 the first MetroCard vending machines with computer touch screens went into service. In the twenty-first century the MTA has campaigned to get all riders to purchase MetroCards and has eliminated many of the sales booths and replaced them with vending machines.

Cathy Alexander

Metromedia. Brand name, privately held investment partnership, and management company. In addition to entertainment, its global interests and subsidiaries have included food and hospitality services, high technology, and telecommunications. Originally called Metropolitan Broadcasting Company, it was formed in 1958 when German-born entrepreneur John W(erer) Kluge bought from Paramount Pictures its interest in the broadcasting stations that had belonged to the defunct DuMont Broadcasting Corporation, among them WABD, which he renamed WNEW-TV. The firm took its current name in 1960 when its diversifications included out-of-home advertising and publishing. After Metromedia shifted its emphasis to ventures largely unrelated to radio and television, its broadcast group was purchased in 1986 for more than $4 billion by Australian media magnate Rupert Murdoch, owner of Twentieth Century Fox, who created Fox Broadcasting Company. In the early twenty-first century Metromedia Company has both domestic and international interests in restaurant chains, telecommunications, wireless cable and television, fiber-optic networks, and energy production.

Metromedia and the DuMont Legacy: W2XWV, WABD, WNEW-TV (New York: Museum of Broadcasting, n.d.)

Val Ginter

Metro-North Commuter Railroad. Subsidiary of the Metropolitan Transportation Authority (MTA), formed on 1 January 1983 and renamed MTA Metro-North Railroad in the mid-1990s. Using the former lines of the New York Central Railroad and the New York, New Haven and Hartford Railroad, Metro-North provides service between Grand Central Terminal and the Bronx, Connecticut, and Westchester, Putnam, and Dutchess counties. Under contract with New Jersey Transit it also provides service between Hoboken, New Jersey, and Orange and Rockland counties. In 2007 Metro-North had an operating budget of $464.3 million and 1783 employees and carried 265,949 passengers on an average weekday; the annual number was 80.1 million. It had 120 passenger stations, 1188 rail cars, and 735 miles (1178 kilometers) of track. Under the MTA capital program more than $5.5 billion was allocated between 1982 (when the lines were still being operated by Conrail) and 2009, and the number of riders increased as service improved.

Peter Derrick

Metropolitan. Former neighborhood in west central Queens, surrounding the intersection of Metropolitan and Flushing avenues in what is now Ridgewood and an area near Maspeth Creek. It was an unprosperous hamlet that was the site of a tollhouse for Flushing Avenue. The two main avenues were turnpikes from 1816 until about 1870. The name fell into disuse after World War I.

Vincent Seyfried

Metropolitan Baptist Church. Church at 151 West 128th Street in Manhattan. It occupies an arch-and-vault Romanesque Revival building originally owned by the Presbyterian

Riverdale station of Metro-North, 1992

church, designed by John R. Thomas and built in 1884. The church is a white stone edifice with orange granite columns at the entrance and a coned-roof side chapel. Its auditorium was built in 1890 under the design of Richard R. Davis. In 1912 the congregation of the Metropolitan Baptist Church was formed through the merger of the Zion Baptist Church and the Mercy Seat Baptist Church of Harlem. The members of the newly formed church originally worshipped at 45–47 West 134th Street. Under the leadership of W. W. Brown (1914–30) the church secured its present location and the congregation grew to more than 1000 members. Brown was a founder of the Baptist Negro Education Center, a cooperative between white and black Baptists. The church's social and political activism continued, especially in the 1960s when African American Baptist ministries helped support the civil rights movement. Metropolitan Baptist Church is a city, state, and federal landmark. It serves the local community, while its choir and gospel soloists attract an international audience.

Aileen Laura Love

Metropolitan Board of Health. Forerunner of the New York City Board of Health. After the end of the Civil War and the expectation of an outbreak of cholera in New York City, a group of city leaders joined with physicians from the New York Academy of Medicine to survey health conditions in Manhattan. What they found was frightening. Massive immigration combined with poorly maintained tenements, overflowing privies, spoiled food, and filthy streets to produce outbreaks of cholera, typhoid, yellow fever, and typhus. The report they produced, the Citizens' Association *Report on the Sanitary Condition of the City,* led to the establishment in 1866 of the first permanent municipal public health department in the United States, the Metropolitan Board of Health. It was initially responsible for providing sanitation, pure water, street cleaning services, garbage removal, and housing inspections as well as a host of other services to the residents of New York City, the city of Brooklyn, and Westchester and Long Island. Soon this regional Board of Health had become separate departments, identified with the then-independent cities of New York and Brooklyn. Headquartered on the Lower East Side, at 301 Mott Street, the board had 24 sanitary inspectors and 37 assistants, each with specific districts to regulate. Edward B. Dalton was the first Sanitary Superintendent. By its second year the board oversaw the construction of 4000 sewer connections, and the repair of 10,000 more. In addition to taking on issues of cleanliness the board closed 100 unsafe or unsanitary factories in its first year. This was a vast improvement over the early nineteenth century's disjointed and ineffective public health system. The *Code of Sanitary Ordinances and Laws Relating to the Metropolitan Board of Health* was published in 1867. This extensive list regulated the distribution and preparation of food and drink and the conduct of physicians and inspectors, and helped codify the terminology that would be used in issues relating to public health. The Board of Health also helped bring attention to poor living conditions on the Lower East Side.

James Joseph Walsh, *History of Medicine in New York,* vol. 3 (New York: National Americana Society, 1919); Charles E. Rosenberg, *The Cholera Years: The United States in 1832, 1849, and 1866* (Chicago: University of Chicago Press, 1987); David Rosner, ed., *Hives of Sickness: Public Health and Epidemics in New York City* (New Brunswick, N.J.: Rutgers University Press, 1995)

Molly Rosner

Metropolitan Club. Private club in Manhattan, founded in 1891. It occupies a building built in 1894 at the corner of Fifth Avenue and 60th Street overlooking Grand Army Plaza and Central Park. Commissioned by J. P. Morgan and designed by Stanford White, the building cost almost $2 million, a sum covered by the pledges of the 700 members originally enrolled, who included Morgans, Vanderbilts, Hamiltons, Cromwells, Browns, Whitneys, and Roosevelts. The lavish club has many dining rooms, a library, 34 bedrooms on the top floor, and a bowling alley in the basement. Membership is extended to both men and women. In the early twenty-first century there were about 1500 members.

Paul Porzelt, *The Metropolitan Club of New York* (New York: Rizzoli, 1982)

Thea Arnold

Metropolitan Council on Housing. Nonprofit tenants' advocacy group formed in 1959 by Jane Benedict, a supporter of rent control. Its forerunner was a coalition of neighborhood tenant advocacy groups formed in response to Title I of the Federal Housing Act of 1949, which required the U.S. Housing and Home Finance Administration to absorb more than half the costs incurred by private concerns in redeveloping residential properties in poor neighborhoods. Redevelopment accelerated under Robert Moses, who directed the Committee on Slum Clearance, and caused 100,000 New Yorkers to be driven from their homes by 1960. Owing largely to the efforts of the council, the Rent Stabilization Law was passed in 1969, limiting annual rent increases for housing built after 1947. Initially an important voice for public housing, the council eventually shifted its support to what it called "housing in the public domain," or housing owned publicly and controlled by tenants rather than private landlords.

Ronald Lawson, ed., *The Tenant Movement in New York City, 1904–1984* (New Brunswick, N.J.: Rutgers University Press, 1986)

Melissa M. Merritt

Metropolitan Hotel. Six-story hotel on the northeast corner of Broadway and Prince Street. Designed in the Italian palazzo style by the firm of Trench and Snook, it opened in 1852 as the second great luxury hotel in New York City (after the Astor House, 1836). The hotel had lavishly furnished public parlors and about 500 guest rooms, with hot and cold running water and steam heat provided throughout. The building also housed Niblo's Garden, an entertainment center consisting of a theater, ballroom, and refreshment room. The hotel and its garden complex were demolished in 1895.

May N. Stone

Metropolitan Life Insurance Company. Financial institution formed in New York City in 1863 when a group of Manhattan business leaders raised $100,000 to found the National Union Life and Limb Insurance Company headquartered on lower Broadway. It began selling "industrial," or workingman's, insurance in 1879. Millions of industrial policies were sold, usually for a fee of five or 10 cents a week collected at the policyholder's home. The firm moved its offices in 1893 to 1 Madison Avenue; the Metropolitan Life Tower, a well-known building, was completed in 1909, and in the same year the firm set up a welfare division to provide home nursing services to policyholders. A campaign begun by the firm in 1922 to provide affordable housing to city dwellers led to the construction of a large-scale housing project in Long Island City and of a complex of 11,000 apartments called Stuyvesant Town and Peter Cooper Village (1943). During the Depression the firm rehabilitated more than 7000 foreclosed farms and made loans to finance the construction of the Empire State Building and Rockefeller Center. It became the first life insurer to install a large-scale electronic data processing system in 1954. In the 1980s it acquired the Goldman Sachs Building near Wall Street and the Pan Am Building (200 Park Avenue, now known as the Met Life Building), the headquarters for the management of its wide-ranging real estate holdings. In the early 1990s Metropolitan Life had sales offices throughout the five boroughs and more than $130 billion in assets under management. In the fiscal year ending in 2008 its net income was $3.1 billion and it served more than 70 million customers worldwide.

Daniel May

Metropolitan Museum of Art. Art museum, known colloquially as the Met, located

Metropolitan Museum of Art, ca *1880*

on Fifth Avenue between 80th and 84th streets, formed in 1870 by members of the Union League Club, including John Jay, the poet William Cullen Bryant, William T. Blodgett, the lawyer Joseph H. Choate, the railroad executive John Taylor Johnston, Henry W. Bellows, and the painters John Frederick Kensett and Worthington Whittredge. It was proposed by Jay in Paris in 1865 as an educational institution and cultural monument for the city and the nation. The Board of Trustees, formed in 1870, included the founders as well as the painters Frederic E. Church and Eastman Johnson, the sculptor John Quincy Adams Ward, and the architects Russell Sturgis and Richard Morris Hunt. Johnston was elected the first president in 1870, and in the following year a site along Fifth Avenue was chosen, largely because of its proximity to Central Park. The first important collection, 174 European paintings (mostly Dutch and Flemish), was acquired in 1871 and helped the museum to become widely known. By levying a tax the city raised $500,000 for construction costs. Calvert Vaux was the architect and with Jacob Wrey Mould designed a small, redbrick building in a neo-Gothic style with a steel and glass roof reminiscent of that on the Crystal Palace in London (1851).

The museum was organized largely by George Fiske Comfort, founder of the College of Fine Arts at Syracuse University, who sought to provide enrichment, especially for workers, and drew up a detailed plan for establishing curatorial departments, a series of loan exhibitions, and lectures and school programs (his plan was later adopted by other American museums). A department of casts and reproductions was set up to provide copies of works unavailable for display. As early as 1883 a bequest was made to buy architectural casts, engravings, and photographs. The first director of the museum was the art collector Luigi Palma di Cesnola, elected in 1879. After a curator was appointed in 1882, followed by two others in 1889, the collection was divided into three departments: paintings, drawings, and prints; sculpture, antiquities, and objets d'art; and casts and reproductions (which lasted until the 1930s). The museum opened schools throughout the city that offered instruction in woodworking, metalworking, drawing and design, modeling and carving, carriage drafting, and plumbing; these closed in 1892 when the museum shifted its focus to the study and enjoyment of authentic works of art. In 1888 and 1894 Theodore Weston and Arthur Tuckerman made additions to the building. In 1895 Richard Morris Hunt designed a grand Beaux-Arts entry wing along Fifth Avenue.

The museum expanded rapidly into the twentieth century, adding to its holdings the Crosby Collection of musical instruments, the Marquand and Altman collections of paintings (mostly by Old Masters), and the Garland Collection of Asian porcelains. An estate of about $7 million was bequeathed to the museum by the manufacturer Jacob Rogers in 1901 and produced income that was used to buy books and works of art. One of the museum's most important benefactors was J. P. Morgan, who as president (1904–13) continued to expand the collections and the physical plant. Under his direction the museum acquired a magnificent collection of European art, and excavations begun in 1906 housed its first Egyptian artifacts. He also commissioned the firm of McKim, Mead and White to build a wing (completed in 1910) to house the collection of decorative arts and his own collection of medieval and Renaissance works, and to complete the wings (1926) flanking Hunt's Fifth Avenue facade. In 1909 the museum mounted the Hudson–Fulton exhibition, the first comprehensive examination of American art by a major museum. Attended by more than 300,000 visitors, the show commemorated the Dutch and American heritage of the city with Dutch and early American paintings and American industrial arts.

As the collections grew, the curatorial departments were subdivided into categories that reflected the evolution of art history. In 1924 the American wing opened, and American art became a separate department. The CLOISTERS, a museum of medieval art and architecture assembled by George Grey Barnard, became a branch of the Metropolitan Museum after it and Fort Tryon Park, a tract of 56 acres (23 hectares) surrounding it, were bought for the city by John D. Rockefeller in 1925. A larger building was erected to accommodate both the original collection and one donated by Rockefeller; designed by Charles Collens with Rockefeller and James Rorimer, an associate curator of decorative arts, the Cloisters opened in 1938 and incorporated the many architectural fragments assembled by Barnard in France. In 1929 the museum acquired an outstanding collection of French impressionist paintings from Louisine Havemeyer.

An unusual and unexpected gift to the museum in 1925, the largest up to that time, came from newspaper and magazine publisher Frank Munsey. It included several hundred acres near Manhasset, Long Island, which the museum developed into a "model" suburban community called Munsey Park, with homes based on traditional American designs. Real estate sales and other residuals of the bequest netted the museum more than $10 million by 1950.

For many years the museum rejected modern American and European art; in 1930 it refused Gertrude Vanderbilt Whitney's offer of her collection of American paintings and money to build a wing for it. After World War II the museum merged with the Whitney Museum of American Art and the Museum of Modern Art under the "three museum agreement," which collapsed largely because the administration of the Metropolitan rejected the tenets of modern art, especially abstraction. At the same time the museum in the 1940s even explored the possibility of moving entirely, an idea rejected by the parks commissioner, Robert Moses.

The focus of the museum changed after the war. Organizational changes were proposed by Francis Henry Taylor, the director during the 1940s, who first envisioned the Metropolitan as a series of many smaller museums within a single structure. He was followed in 1955 by Rorimer and in 1967 by Thomas P. F. Hoving, who sought to reshape the museum to serve a more diverse population. Hoving's style of administration often provoked controversy, and his somewhat cavalier attitude toward acquisitions led to an investigation by New York State into the practice of selling collections to raise purchasing funds. He enlarged the education department and opened a depart-

Metropolitan Museum of Art, facade on Fifth Avenue (designed by McKim, Mead and White), 1909

ment of community programs and a department of contemporary and twentieth-century art (1967). Exhibitions during his tenure such as *Harlem on My Mind* incorporated both social and artistic themes, and with the exhibitions *In the Presence of Kings* and *Tutankhamun* (1978) Hoving developed an approach, quickly dubbed "the blockbuster," that drew enormous audiences and was soon imitated by other museums. He also secured Robert Lehman's collection of European art, considered by many the finest private collection of its kind in the United States, and contracted with architects Kevin Roche John Dinkeloo and Associates to design six new wings. This "master plan" was completed in 1991 under the supervision of director Philippe de Montebello, Hoving's successor, and it is perhaps de Montebello's greatest legacy. The designs for galleries of European decorative arts, twentieth-century art, and Chinese and Japanese art; a roof sculpture garden; special exhibition spaces; and a new restaurant have expanded the Metropolitan into one of the largest and most comprehensive art museums in the western hemisphere.

After de Montebello became director in 1978, the museum's endowment increased substantially and major gifts of art came from Walter Annenberg, Florence and Herbert Irving, Muriel Kallis Steinberg Newman, and Jayne Wrightsman. Temporary exhibitions had both scholarly and popular appeal and reflected the museum's encyclopedic reach. At the same time, the museum sold reproductions of works displayed in the permanent collections and in such popular exhibitions as *The Vatican Collections, Van Gogh in St. Remy and Auvers, India!, Degas,* and *Vermeer and the Delft School.* In 2008 de Montebello retired and was replaced by Thomas P. Campbell, who at the time of his appointment was the curator in the Department of European Sculpture and Decorative Arts as well as supervising curator of the Museum's Antonio Ratti Textile Center.

A stain on the Metropolitan's reputation occurred in 2002 with the destruction of a rare Renaissance masterpiece, the free-standing marble sculpture *Adam* by Tullio Lombardo, when a poorly constructed pedestal on which the sculpture stood gave way. In the twenty-first century the museum owned more than two million objects. Its collection of Egyptian art is second only to the one in Cairo.

Winifred E. Howe, *A History of the Metropolitan Museum of Art* (New York: n.p., 1913 [vol. 1]/Columbia University Press, 1946 [vol. 2]); Calvin Tomkins, *Merchants and Masterpieces: The Story of the Metropolitan Museum of Art*, rev. 2nd edn (New York: Henry Holt, 1989)

Peter L. Donhauser

Metropolitan Opera. American opera company. Its first season in 1883 coincided with the opening at Broadway and 39th Street of the Metropolitan Opera House, a structure seating 3700 that was built when a number of wealthy New York City residents were unable to obtain boxes at the Academy of Music on 14th Street. Designed by J. C. Cady in a conservative Italian Renaissance style, the new building was criticized as a "yellow brick brewery" by James H. Mapleson, impresario at the Academy of Music, which eventually ceased operations because of the pressure of competition. The first season at the Metropolitan Opera was managed by Henry E. Abbey and consisted of standard Italian and French operas along with Wagner's *Lohengrin,* all sung in Italian. In the interest of economy the holders of boxes at the opera house consigned the next seven seasons to a company based in Germany and led successively by Leopold Damrosch and Edmond C. Stanton. The repertory again included Italian and French works and Wagner, now all sung in German (except in some tour performances) by such singers as Marcella Sembrich and Lilli Lehmann. In 1891–92 Abbey returned to the company with the European impresario Maurice Grau to mount Italian and French operas in their original languages. He continued as the manager until his death in 1896, which led to a reorganization under the leadership of Grau alone and to the cancellation of an entire season in 1897–98.

As the manager of the opera until 1903, Grau presented the singers Joanna Gadski and Antonio Scotti and signed a contract with Enrico Caruso, a mainstay of the company under Grau's successor Heinrich Conried (1903–8). Conried was responsible for a number of achievements, notably the unauthorized American stage premiere of Wagner's *Parsifal* (1903), which the composer's heirs failed to prevent by lawsuit; he retired in the face of ill health and some criticism. The financier Otto H. Kahn, one of the most loyal backers of Conried and the company, chose as the new manager of the opera house Giulio Gatti-Casazza, who introduced Emmy Destinn and Frances Alda, and later Lucrezia Bori, Claudia Muzio, Rosa Ponselle, Elisabeth Rethberg, Ezio Pinza, Lily Pons, Tito Schipa, Maria Jeritza, Giovanni Martinelli, Beniamino Gigli, Lauritz Melchior, Friedrich Schorr, Giuseppe De Luca, Lawrence Tibbett, Rose Bampton, and Grace Moore. The role of chief conductor of the company was filled by Arturo Toscanini (1908–15) and then Artur Bodanzky (1915–39), who later shared his responsibilities with Tullio Serafin and Ettore Panizza. Gatti-Casazza believed in novelties, a few of them durable, including the world premieres of Puccini's *La fanciulla del West* (1910) and *Il Trittico* (1918).

In the following decades the company acquired a broad appeal that belied its reputation as a bastion of wealth and snobbery: immigrants were eager to hear singers from their homelands, some of whom were immigrants themselves; the first regular radio broadcasts of performances were made in 1931, and a long-running sponsorship by Texaco of broadcasts on Saturday afternoons began in December 1940; and the Metropolitan Opera Ballet solidified its reputation as one of the most important ballet companies in the city. At the same time the company was buffeted by the Depression, and its very existence was threatened by 1935, when Gatti-Casazza retired. Plans to move the company to new quarters at Radio City (originally designed by Joseph Urban as an opera house), Rockefeller Center, or another location were deferred owing to a lack of funds. In time the company was placed on surer financial footing, owing in part to the formation in 1935 by Mrs. August Belmont (1878–1979) of the Metropolitan Opera Guild, which began issuing the magazine *Opera News* in December 1936. The company was also helped during these lean years by the introduction of two of the greatest Wagner singers of the century, Kirsten Flagstad and Lauritz

Metropolitan Opera House at Broadway and 39th Street, 1937

Melchior. Gatti-Casazza's successor as the manager of the company, Edward Johnson, was a former tenor who brought to the stage such well-known singers as Bidù Sayão, Jussi Björling, Zinka Milanov, Giuseppe Di Stefano, and Ljuba Welitsch, as well as an abundance of American talent: Jan Peerce, Helen Traubel, Risë Stevens, Leonard Warren, Eleanor Steber, Astrid Varnay, Richard Tucker, Dorothy Kirsten, and Robert Merrill. With World War II, the loss of some European artists was compensated for by such new residents as the singers Licia Albanese and Jarmila Novotná and the conductors Bruno Walter and Fritz Busch. The company was stable during the 1940s and enjoyed a remarkable esprit de corps. Johnson undertook few experiments in repertory, but he did introduce Benjamin Britten's *Peter Grimes* (1947–48) and Modest Mussorgsky's *Khovanshchina* (1949–50).

Rudolf Bing became the manager of the company in 1950 and initiated a shift in emphasis toward prominent conductors (Leonard Bernstein, Zubin Mehta) and stage directors (including some not usually identified with opera, such as Margaret Webster and Alfred Lunt). Although Bing disclaimed the "star system," he did avail himself of well-known singers dating from Johnson's tenure and introduced others of the same caliber: Cesare Siepi, Mario Del Monaco, Renata Tebaldi, Victoria de Los Angeles, Carlo Bergonzi, Nicolai Gedda, Leonie Rysanek, Birgit Nilsson, Mirella Freni, Joan Sutherland, Renata Scotto, and Montserrat Caballé. In 1955 he engaged the first black soloist with the company, the contralto Marian Anderson, who was followed by Leontyne Price and others. He also presented the world premieres of two operas by Samuel Barber, *Vanessa* (1958) and *Antony and Cleopatra* (1966), and of Marvin David Levy's *Mourning Becomes Electra* (1967). The premiere of *Antony and Cleopatra* marked the opening at Lincoln Center on 16 September 1966 of a new Opera House, designed by Wallace K. Harrison and built at a cost of $50 million. Important debuts were made on its stage, including those of Plácido Domingo (1966) and Marilyn Horne (1970). After Bing the company was managed successively by Schuyler Chapin (1972–75), who introduced the singers Kiri Te Kanawa and José Carreras, by Anthony Bliss (1975–85), who introduced José Van Dam, Tatiana Troyanos, Jessye Norman, and Samuel Ramey, and briefly by Bruce Crawford and then Hugh Southern. The conductor James Levine was then named artistic director and exerted a decisive influence. In the 1980s the Metropolitan discontinued its extensive national tours, a practice as old as the company itself. The assistant manager Joseph Volpe was named to the highest administrative position in the company in 1990–91. In 2006, Joseph Volpe retired, with Peter Gelb taking over the role of general manager.

Beginning in the early twenty-first century, the Metropolitan Opera has followed the popular trend of modernization of traditional operas. These productions tend to use symbolic stage design and modern costumes, such as the twentieth-century tuxedoes worn in the 2008 production of *Macbeth*. The Metropolitan Opera has expanded its audience by broadcasting its operas on the Public Broadcasting Service (PBS) and in movie theaters. In the 2007–8 season, PBS aired 14 full-length operas. In that same season, eight screenings of operas at the Met were shown at more than 100 theaters. The Metropolitan Opera also has its own radio station on Sirius Satellite Radio.

Gerald Fitzgerald, ed., *Annals of the Metropolitan Opera* (Boston: Metropolitan Opera Guild /G. K. Hall, 1989)

John W. Freeman

Metropolitan Transportation Authority [MTA]. Public authority created by the State of New York in 1968 to set policies and budgets for transportation agencies in the five New York City boroughs and seven suburban counties. Its board of directors has jurisdiction over the New York City Transit Authority, the Staten Island Rapid Transit Operating Authority, the Long Island Rail Road, Metro-North Railroad, the Metropolitan Suburban Bus Authority, and the Triborough Bridge and Tunnel Authority. During its first decade the authority improved commuter rail service and made plans to build subway lines to Queens and under Second Avenue; these projects were suspended in the mid-1970s owing to lack of funds. Richard Ravitch, who became chairman in 1979, focused instead on refurbishing existing facilities. In response to a decline in the number of transit passengers, the authority launched a series of large five-year capital programs, which have continued from 1982 to the present.

In the mid-1990s, MTA renamed all of its agencies (although the old names remained the legal ones), putting "MTA" in front of all of the names in order to better establish the fact that they are all governed by the MTA board. Thus, the New York City Transit Authority became MTA New York City Transit, and other agencies were renamed MTA Long Island Bus and MTA Bridges and Tunnels.

The MTA capital programs allotted more than $75 billion between 1982 and 2009, largely to restore safe and reliable transit service, representing the largest transit capital renewal effort in U.S. history. In 2003 MTA created the MTA Capital Construction Company to build major new projects, and in 2004, MTA Bus to operate formerly private express and local bus routes previously overseen by the city. In 2007 the operating budgets for all of the MTA agencies totaled $10.36 billion, and there were 67,457 employees. On an average weekday in 2007 MTA facilities were used by more than 8.3 million passengers and 854,000 motor vehicles. Under its 2005–9 capital program, MTA resumed construction of the Second Avenue subway and Long

Island Rail Road access to Grand Central Terminal.

Derrick, Peter: "Catalyst for Development: Rapid Transit in New York," *New York Affairs* 9.4 (1986), 27–59

Peter Derrick

Metrotech Center. Office and educational complex in downtown Brooklyn, bounded to the north by Tillary Street, to the east by the Flatbush Avenue Extension, to the south by Willoughby Street, and to the west by Jay Street. It comprises more than a dozen buildings on 10 blocks, with a total area of 16 acres (6.5 hectares). The aim of the project was to provide back-office space for businesses at prices lower than those prevailing in lower Manhattan. Construction started in 1986; the $100 million cost of the first buildings was borne by the city and by Polytechnic University, which renovated two buildings and built a third to house its Center for Advanced Technology in Telecommunications and its Dibner Library of Technology and Science. Among the firms that moved their headquarters to Metrotech were Brooklyn Union Gas and the Securities Industry Automation Corporation; other early tenants included operations centers for Chase Manhattan Bank (now JP Morgan Chase) and the now-defunct Bear, Stearns and Company. Other notable tenants in the early twenty-first century are National Grid (formerly Brooklyn Union Gas) and the Fire Department of New York's E-911 dispatch center. Metrotech was designed by the development firm of Forest City Ratner, with several architects taking part in the project. The firm of Ehrenkrantz, Eckstut, and Whitelaw designed and landscaped the open space, which includes a central commons of 3.3 acres (1.3 hectares). In the early 1990s the project was envisioned to reach 8.1 million square feet (750,000 square meters) of office space, but the original site offers roughly only 5.2 million square feet (480,000 square meters).

John Voelcker

Meucci, Antonio (*b* Italy, 13 April 1808; *d* Staten Island, 18 Oct 1889). Telephone inventor. He lived for a time in Havana, where in 1841 he saw electrified wires transmitting sound. He moved to Staten Island in 1850 and provided housing there for Italian political figure Giuseppe Garibaldi. In August 1870 Meucci is believed to have transmitted the human voice from a distance of 1 mile (1.6 kilometers) by using copper plait as a conductor, insulated by cotton. He called this device *telettrofono* and filed a patent caveat for the invention in 1871, which he could not afford to renew the following year. After reading an announcement in 1876 that Alexander Graham Bell had invented the telephone, Meucci sought legal redress but was hampered by poverty and his poor knowledge of English. Meucci's accomplishments are detailed at the Garibaldi–Meucci Museum at 420 Tompkins Avenue in Rosebank, Staten Island, where he is buried.

Giovanni Ermenegildo Schiavo, *Antonio Meucci: Inventor of the Telephone* (New York: Vigo, 1958)

Mary Elizabeth Brown

Mexicans. Mexicans in New York City and its surrounding suburbs numbered more than 500,000 in 2008, surpassing Dominicans in 2006 as the group giving birth to the largest number of babies in the city, according to the city's Planning Department. The state of Puebla accounts for 47 percent of Mexican migration to the city, with some 70 percent coming from the larger Mixteca region. The large majority of migrants are people of mixed European and Indian ancestry who speak Spanish, but an increasing number speak indigenous languages, including Mixteco, Zapoteco, and Nahuatl.

Between the 1940s and the late 1960s, the slow flow of migrants did not grow much. Then the political upheavals of 1968 pushed many young Mexican adults to move north, and the peso crisis of 1975–76 added to that push. The most recent flow of migrants to New York City can be traced to the economic crisis of the 1980s and following, as well as to two other factors: an increased demand for Mexican workers, whom employers regarded as hardworking and undocumented, hence quiescent; and the legalization program of the 1986 Immigration Reform and Control Act, which fostered an increase in family reunification during the early and mid-1990s. Parents who legalized their status in 1987–88 were able to gain permanent residency by the mid-1990s and bring their children to live with them legally. The undocumented relatives and friends of those moving to New York City often followed them, contributing to a large increase in the number of undocumented Mexicans in the city. This fast pace of Mexican immigration during the 1990s—the population tripled from 100,000 to 300,000 between 1990 and 2000—slowed during the first decade of the twenty-first century because the catalyst of family reunification was no longer there. The Mexican population in New York City is split between those who are in the country legally and those who have not had access to citizenship.

Mexicans in New York City are underrepresented among citywide elected representatives, partly because the Mexican population is spread out in six or seven concentrations, including East Harlem, South Bronx, Sunset Park and Brighton Beach in Brooklyn, Jackson Heights in Queens, and several neighborhoods in Staten Island. Hence, Mexicans are one of many groups in the many districts where they live and are entering an ethnic queue in politics that is already crowded with whites, blacks, Jews, Puerto Ricans, Dominicans, and some Asians already established in the political system. Educationally, Mexican youth in New York City confront serious challenges: among 16- to 19-year-old Mexicans, 47 percent are not attending and have not graduated from high school, compared with 22 percent for Puerto Ricans, 18 percent for African Americans, and 7 percent for whites (2000 census). Whereas 95 percent of 14-year-old Mexican American boys are in school, only 26 percent of 19-year-olds remain in the educational system. Such challenges contribute toward Mexican males entering a racialized underclass in the city and females becoming "urban ethnics." Youth who have gained legal status or citizenship tend to be more financially successful. Mexican community organizations have created mentorship and after-school programs to disseminate information and provide youth with a place to foster their educational aspirations. Asociación Tepeyac, the largest Mexican nonprofit organization in New York City, has made promoting education a primary goal. Other such organizations include the Mexican American Students Alliance, the Mexican Educational Foundation of New York, and the Mixteca Organization. The chancellor of the City University of New York (CUNY) has formed a Committee on Mexicans and Education in New York and is holding coordinated outreach with the Mexican community in all five boroughs. CUNY is also supporting other programs, such as Baruch College's Emerging Leaders program, which helps Mexican community leaders learn how to run nonprofit organizations.

Robert Smith, *Mexican New York: Transnational Worlds of New Immigrants* (Berkeley: University of California Press, 2006)

Robert Smith

Meyer [née Nathan]**, Annie (Florance)** (*b* New York City, 19 Feb 1867; *d* New York City, 23 Sept 1951). Philanthropist. She played a prominent role in founding Barnard College (1889), of which she was a lifelong trustee, and also helped writer Zora Neale Hurston attend it. Although opposed to woman suffrage, she was an ardent advocate for the civil rights of all minorities. Meyer was a prolific writer of essays, novels, short stories, letters to the editor, and plays (which include *The Dominant Sex* [1911] and *Black Souls* [1932]), several of which had short runs on and off Broadway. With her husband Alfred Meyer she supported numerous charitable, artistic, political, and civic causes.

Lynn D. Gordon

Meyer, Cord (i) (*b* Germany, 4 Dec 1823; *d* Maspeth [now in Queens], 10 June 1891). Businessman, father of Cord Meyer (ii). He immigrated to the United States as a boy and moved to suburban Maspeth, Long Island, in 1852. In 1873 he opened the Acme

Fertilizer Company, a factory on Newtown Creek where animal bones were burned to produce an ingredient necessary in sugar refining and fertilizer manufacture. Later he became a part owner of a profitable sugar refinery.

Vincent Seyfried

Meyer, Cord (ii) (*b* Maspeth [now in Queens], 9 Oct 1854; *d* Great Neck, N.Y., 14 Oct 1920). Businessman, son of Cord Meyer (i). He became the superintendent of his father's company, the Acme Fertilizer Company, when he was 20 years old and later entered into private banking with C. L. Rathbone and Company. In 1890 he formed the Cord Meyer Company and began to speculate in real estate. In Queens he developed the Elmhurst neighborhood on a large tract of land north of the village of Newtown, and in 1893 he formed the Citizens' Water Supply Company, a boroughwide utility of which he was president. Meyer became active in politics and was chairman of the Democratic State Committee in 1904–6. He created the Queens neighborhood of Forest Hills from farmland in 1906–10 and was active in its development. Meyer lived in suburban Great Neck, Long Island.

Vincent Seyfried

Michaëlius, Jonas (*b* Grootebroek, Netherlands, 1584; *d* after 1637). Minister. He was educated at the University of Leiden and set sail from Texel on 24 January 1628, landing on 7 April in New Amsterdam, where he became the first minister of the Dutch Reformed Church in North America; his first communion drew 50 Walloon and Dutch communicants. He is best known for a letter that he wrote about the colony on 11 August 1628 to colleagues in Amsterdam (published in 1904 as *Manhattan in 1628, as Described in the Recently Discovered Autograph Letter*); he found the climate "good and pleasant" but lamented the state of civil government, the barbarity of the natives, and the lack of provisions. Michaëlius left New Netherland in 1632. A message from the Assembly of Nineteen in 1637 to the Classis of Amsterdam, which had recommended his reappointment, contains the last known record of his name.

Randall Balmer

Middleburgh. Name used from 1652 to 1664 by Newtown.

Middletown (i). Neighborhood in the eastern Bronx, bounded to the north by Pelham Bay Park, to the east by Country Club, to the south by Tremont Avenue, and to the west by the Hutchinson River Parkway. Middletown Road was the route of General William Howe's march to Eastchester Bay in October 1776 that led to the Battle of Pell's Point. Large private estates covered most of the area into the early twentieth century, when the completion of the Lexington Avenue subway to Pelham Bay along Westchester Avenue spurred the development of one- and two-family houses and small apartment buildings. In the early twenty-first century the population included residents of Italian, Irish, and Greek descent; the Latino and African American population had increased. Most who live in the neighborhood consider themselves residents of Pelham Bay.

Gary D. Hermalyn

Middletown (ii). Neighborhood in Queens during the American Revolution and the early nineteenth century, lying within Long Island City and centered at the junction of Ridge Road (now 46th Street) and Newtown Avenue. It consisted of three or four houses and a one-room schoolhouse.

Vincent Seyfried

Middle Village. Neighborhood in west central Queens, bounded to the north by Eliot Avenue, to the east by Woodhaven Boulevard, to the south by Cooper Avenue and the Long Island Rail Road, and to the west by the Lutheran Cemetery. The population in 2000 was about 29,000. It began as a hamlet of families of English descent and was named for its location at the midpoint of the Williamsburgh and Jamaica Turnpike (now Metropolitan Avenue), which opened in 1816 and ran from Bushwick Avenue to Jamaica; the hamlet was established in the same year. In 1852 a Lutheran church in Manhattan bought several farms north and south of Metropolitan Avenue and opened a large cemetery, now Lutheran All Faiths Cemetery. Victims of the 1904 burning of the *General Slocum* were buried there. In 1854 a restaurant opened across the street catering to the funeral trade; it became Niederstein's in 1888 and remained popular until sold for development in 2005. The German population grew greatly after the Civil War. In 1879 the Roman Catholic diocese laid out St. John's Cemetery east of 80th Street. The Fresh Pond Crematory opened in 1901. The growth of Middle Village was limited by the cemeteries and by Juniper Swamp, which was filled in 1915, and it came to cater almost exclusively to visitors to the cemeteries. For years Metropolitan Avenue was lined with monument works, flower shops, small hotels, and saloons. Working farms in the outskirts along Dry Harbor Road and Caldwell Avenue lasted until World War I. In 1941 the Works Progress Administration transformed the former swamp into Juniper Valley Park. The need for housing in the 1920s spurred development, and blocks of one-family detached houses were built south of Metropolitan Avenue and around the park. After World War II the population became heavily Jewish and Italian, and Christ the King Catholic High School was built just east of the elevated station. A shopping mall was built on Metropolitan Avenue west of the Lutheran Cemetery. By the early 1990s a number of immigrants from Yugoslavia and the Balkans had moved to the area. Housing from the 1920s survived into the twenty-first century, with single-family homes selling for more than $500,000 in 2008.

Vincent Seyfried, Jeffrey A. Kroessler

Midland Beach. Neighborhood in east central Staten Island, lying southeast of Hylan Boulevard. By 1900 it was one of the finest

Yard shrine on Furmanville Road in Middle Village, 1992

summer resorts in the metropolitan area. Along with summer bungalows a pier was built to accommodate excursion boats carrying visitors from the other boroughs and New Jersey. Disastrous fires and ocean pollution contributed to the demise of the resort after World War II. The beach is administered by the parks department, which maintains baseball fields, picnic grounds, and parking areas nearby. The original bungalows have been insulated for year-round use, and many one-family houses have been built as far inland as Hylan Boulevard. Since 2000 many Russian immigrants have moved to the area. With the restoration of the Franklin Delano Roosevelt boardwalk and the creation of new restaurant facilities, the area has once again become a popular resort destination.

Marjorie Johnson

midtown. The center of Manhattan, roughly bounded to the north by 59th Street, to the east by Third Avenue, to the south by 34th Street, and to the west by Eighth Avenue. Beginning in the 1920s it became New York City's central business district, eclipsing lower Manhattan. This was in large part due to the presence of Grand Central Terminal and to numerous subway lines there. The eastern section is dominated by office buildings, among them the Empire State, Chrysler, Seagram, International Business Machines, American Telephone and Telegraph, and Helmsley buildings and the Met Life Building (200 Park Avenue, formerly the Pan Am Building). At the center of the neighborhood is Rockefeller Center and to the west the theater and garment districts. Other well-known buildings include St. Patrick's Cathedral, the New York Public Library, the Museum of Modern Art, and Carnegie Hall. Many hotels are situated in midtown, including the Plaza and the Waldorf=Astoria. Important intersections include Herald Square, Times Square, Grand Army Plaza, and Columbus Circle.

Elliott Sclar

midwifery. In colonial New York City most infants were delivered by midwives who lacked formal medical training but were required by law to take an oath promising good behavior, conscientious care, and equitable fees. Physicians took a strong interest in midwifery from the 1790s. Valentine Seaman, a surgeon from New York City, opened a school for midwives at the new maternity ward of the Almshouse (1798), and two other physicians from the city published manuals for midwives. From the mid-nineteenth century physicians sought to supplant midwives altogether: the New York County Medical Society voted against licensing midwives in 1860, and the New York Midwifery Dispensary (1890) limited its staff to medical students. The share of all deliveries made by midwives dwindled during the 1880s, but immigration in the 1890s brought to the city hundreds of European women who were formally trained in midwifery, which many immigrants saw as a traditional and respected profession. Despite the growing professionalization of medical care, midwives presided at 42 percent of the births in New York City in 1905.

An estimated 1000 midwives were in New York City in 1907, of whom only 4 percent had been born in the United States. Many physicians viewed midwives as ill-trained and of low character and associated midwifery with illegal and unsafe abortion practices. Even defenders of midwives agreed that they should be screened, trained, and licensed. The New York Committee for the Prevention of Blindness argued that midwives should be required to put silver nitrate in the eyes of newborns to prevent conjunctivitis; with its support Bellevue Hospital opened a free School for Midwives in 1911, the only such school in the United States operated by a municipality. In 1914 the health department established strict licensing requirements, allowing only midwives trained in certified schools to practice in the city. Bellevue was the only certified school in the United States.

By 1910 the number of licensed midwives working in New York City reached 1344, of whom 9 percent were American born. The New York Academy of Medicine passed a resolution supporting the education and registration of midwives in 1911, and in the following year one of the nation's foremost

Midtown Manhattan looking west, 2009

professors of pediatrics, Abraham Jacobi of New York City, spoke in favor of midwifery in his opening address as the president of the American Medical Association. Stricter regulation of midwives did little to silence the controversy over their qualifications raging in medical and popular journals from 1910 to 1930, and the midwives' lack of influence and funds put them at a disadvantage in the struggle against those seeking to eradicate their profession. A widely publicized study in 1933 by the New York Academy of Medicine inflamed the controversy by finding that of all the maternal deaths in the city during 1930–32, two-thirds had been preventable and physicians had been responsible for 61 percent of them and midwives for only 2 percent. The academy criticized physicians for excessive intervention during childbirth and maintained that the growing trend of hospital deliveries was accompanied by greater risk of infection. The report was passionately debated and criticized by the New York Obstetrical Society. At the same time the trend away from home deliveries by midwives and toward hospital deliveries by physicians continued; it accelerated as new hospital maternity wards opened, limits on immigration were imposed in 1924, and transportation from home to hospital improved. The proportion of childbirths in the United States taking place in hospitals increased from nearly 40 percent in 1935 to 50 percent in 1940, 90 percent in 1950, and 99 percent by the early 1970s.

Nurse midwifery was established as a profession about the time when traditional midwifery began to die out. First practiced by members of the Frontier Nursing Service in Kentucky in 1925, it was introduced in New York City by the Maternity Center Association (MCA), which opened a school of midwifery for registered nurses in Harlem in 1931. In the 1950s nurse midwives based at the MCA continued to deliver infants at home; in 1958 the training program moved to Downstate Medical Center–Kings County Hospital in Brooklyn, and increasingly the nurse midwife came to be seen as a member of the obstetrical team. During the 1970s interest in midwifery and home births revived as many expressed disillusionment with organized medicine, but in 1988 only 1500 nurse midwives were certified and practicing nationwide, of whom about 250 were in Greater New York. In 1992 the organization NYC Midwives played a key role in the successful passage of the New York State Professional Midwifery Practice Act. In 2000 NYC Midwives along with other chapters of the American College of Nurse Midwives formed the New York State Association of Licensed Midwives.

The Midwife in the United States (New York: Josiah Macy, Jr., Foundation, 1968)

Sandra Opdycke

Midwood. Neighborhood in south central Brooklyn (2004 pop. *ca* 170,000), bounded to the north by Avenue H and the campus of Brooklyn College, to the east by Flatbush Avenue, to the south by Avenue T, and to the west by Coney Island Avenue. Originally covered by thick forest, the area was named Midwout (middle woods) by Dutch settlers in 1652 and lay between the towns of Gravesend and Flatlands. It contains the communities of Nottingham (1923) and East Midwood (1910). The residence of Johannes Van Nuyse (1128 East 34th Street; also known as the Coe House) was begun in 1744 with additions made in 1793 and 1806. The Van Nuyse–Magaw residence was built in 1800 with an addition in 1803 (moved in 1916 to a site at 1041 East 22nd Street). The area remained largely undeveloped until apartment buildings and detached houses went up in the 1920s. At the same time the film industry established itself in the neighborhood. The Vitagraph company occupied a studio at Avenue M and East 14th Street and owned a warehouse in East Flatbush until 1925, when the company moved to Hollywood and the studio was taken over by Warner Brothers. In 1953 the National Broadcasting Company set up studios on the Vitagraph lot, from which it later broadcast major variety programs, soap operas, and the situation comedy *The Cosby Show.* The balance of the movie lot became Shulamith School for Girls (1962), a yeshiva. Entertainment figures associated with Midwood include the filmmaker Woody Allen, who graduated from Midwood High School, and the actress Marisa Tomei, who graduated from Edward R. Murrow High School. Senator Charles Schumer and U.S. Supreme Court Justice Ruth Bader Ginsburg also lived in Midwood.

With the arrival of subway transportation after 1920, the number of Jews of various backgrounds, notably Hasidim, increased markedly in the area. Some houses on smaller plots and apartment buildings were erected after World War II. The neighborhood declined during the 1970s as many residents moved to the suburbs and the commercial districts deteriorated. In the 1980s, however, new residents were drawn to the area by its quiet, middle-class ambience. These included a large Sephardic Jewish population and the largest settlement of Syrian Jews anywhere in the world. The biggest single group of new immigrants to Midwood during the decade were from the former Soviet Union; there were also large numbers from China, Haiti, Israel, Pakistan, Guyana, Jamaica, Iran, and India. In 1982 the Pakistani population built a mosque on Coney Island Avenue. The main shopping areas lie along avenues J and M, Kings Highway, and Flatbush, Nostrand, and Coney Island avenues. Midwood holds its annual Midwood Mardi Gras, a street fair, on Avenue M. Brooklyn College moved to the vicinity in 1937 and lies partially within Midwood and partially within Flatbush neighborhoods; the administration encourages community participation.

Kenneth Jackson, John Manbeck, eds., *The Neighborhoods of Brooklyn* (New Haven: Yale University Press, 2nd ed 2004)

Elizabeth Reich Rawson, John Manbeck

Mielatz, Charles (Frederick William) (*b* Brandenburg, Germany, 1864; *d* New York City, 2 June 1919). Artist. He came to the United States at the age of six, moved to New York City in the early 1880s, and produced his first etching in 1883. A pioneer of multiplate color etchings, throughout his life he produced etchings of landscapes, cityscapes, and historical scenes. Mielatz was a member of the New York Etching Club and the Brooklyn Society of Etchers. In 1904 he was one of the first etching teachers employed at the National Academy of Design and was the primary instructor of etching from 1906 until his death.

Jessica Montesano

Milbank Memorial Fund. Charitable organization formed as the Memorial Fund Association on 3 April 1905 by Elizabeth Milbank Anderson (1850–1921), who inherited nearly $10 million from her father, Jeremiah Milbank. The death of her young son from diphtheria led her to focus her philanthropic efforts on public health and child welfare: a gift of $150,000 to the Association for Improving the Condition of the Poor enabled the construction of the Milbank Memorial Baths, opened in 1904 on East 38th Street, which became a model for other public baths in the city. The *Milbank Quarterly,* begun in 1923, evolved into an international journal of health policy. In the 1930s and 1940s the fund developed programs in nutrition and mental health, and in the 1960s it shifted its focus toward professional education and training. New efforts over the following two decades included a fellowship program in epidemiology and clinical medicine, a program in occupational health, and the publication of the *Milbank Health Policy Reviews* (1988–89). In the early twenty-first century the organization was headquartered at 645 Madison Avenue.

Clyde V. Kiser, *The Milbank Memorial Fund: Its Leaders and Its Work, 1905–1974* (New York: Milbank Memorial Fund, 1975)

Kenneth W. Rose

milestones. Eighteenth- and nineteenth-century carved road markers. They measured distances from City Hall in Manhattan and the Bronx or to ferries and prominent locations in Brooklyn, Queens, and Staten Island. One such stone is displayed in the Luce Center of the New-York Historical Society.

Joseph Ditta

Milgram, Stanley (*b* New York City, 15 Aug 1933; *d* New York City, 20 Dec 1984). Social psychologist most widely known for his powerful laboratory experiments at Yale University (1960–65) that documented how 60 percent of average people would electrocute an unwilling stranger when ordered to do so by an authority figure in a lab coat. Except for his 13 years studying or teaching at Yale and Harvard University (1954–1967), he was an avid and lifelong New Yorker: he was born in the Bronx, graduated from Monroe High School (1950) and Queens College (BA 1954), and taught at the City University of New York Graduate Center (1967–84) in a Manhattan office overlooking West 42nd Street. In a 1970 essay Milgram defined the new field of "urban psychology," the scientific study of how big-city living affects the behavior, personality, values, and relationships of individuals. His collected writings, *Individual in a Social World* (1992), display his ability to reveal the unseen causes of interpersonal behavior with inventive methods.

Thomas Blass, ed., *Obedience to Authority: Current Perspectives on the Milgram Paradigm* (Mahwah, N.J.: Erlbaum, 2000); Thomas Blass, *The Man Who Shocked the World: The Life and Legacy of Stanley Milgram* (New York: Basic Books, 2004)

Harold Takooshian

military companies. See TARGET COMPANIES.

Mill Basin. Neighborhood in southeastern Brooklyn, lying along Jamaica Bay and bounded to the north by Avenue U and to the east, south, and west by the Mill Basin Inlet. Although Mill Basin proper is a peninsula, the area between Avenues U and T is now part of the Mill Basin neighborhood. Most business is conducted on Avenues U and T. The streets in Mill Basin proper are circular, and many homeowners dock their boats behind their property. The area was called Equandito (broken lands) by the local Canarsee Indians, who sold it in 1664 to John Tilton, Jr., and Samuel Spicer. During the seventeenth century it became part of Flatlands and tidal mills were built on it; the land was owned from 1675 by Jan Martense Schenck and between 1818 and 1870 by the wife of General Phillip S. Crooke. The Crooke–Schenck House, which stood at East 63rd Street, was dismantled in the early 1960s and reassembled at the Brooklyn Museum. Allegedly, members of the Schenck family were friends of the pirate Captain Kidd, and pirate treasure was reportedly found in Mill Basin as recently as 1920. The area retained its rural character until Robert L. Crooke built a lead-smelting plant in 1890. The Crooke Smelting Company was bought out by the National Lead Company, and Crooke sold the remainder of the land to the firm of McNulty and Fitzgerald, which erected bulkheads and filled in the marshes.

Until the early twentieth century the chief resources were the abundant crabs, oysters, and clams in Jamaica Bay. However, in 1906 the Flatbush Improvement Company bought marshland and engaged the firm of Atlantic, Gulf and Pacific to dredge creeks and fill in meadows. Eventually the parcel surrounding the basin had an area of 332 acres (135 hectares) and was fit for industrial development, and within a decade National Lead, Gulf Refining, and other leading firms engaged in heavy industry opened plants there. Atlantic, Gulf and Pacific bought the land in 1909 and built three large dry docks employing 1000 workers, but Jamaica Bay failed to attract a large volume of shipping. A project begun in 1913 and completed in 1923 to extend Flatbush Avenue to Rockaway Inlet provided an additional 2700 feet (823 meters) of dock facilities at the basin and a strip of land for a road across the marshes. In 1915 a channel was dredged to the main channel of Jamaica Bay, and a bulkhead and wharf were built on the mainland side of Mill Creek. By 1919 Mill Island, part of the larger Mill Basin area, was the site of at least six manufacturing and commercial concerns. During the late 1920s and 1930s the docks were rented to a number of small industrial firms. The Mill Basin neighborhood remained industrial for 30 years, but its further industrial development was hindered when plans for rail service to the rest of Brooklyn went unrealized. Residential development began after World War II when Atlantic, Gulf and Pacific sold to the firm of Flatbush Park Homes the land bounded to the north by Avenue U, to the east by East 68th Street and East Mill Basin, to the south by Basset Avenue, and to the west by Strickland Avenue and Mill Avenue. Primarily Irish, Italian, and Jewish residents built brick bungalows in the late 1940s and early 1950s on lots measuring 50 by 100 feet (15 by 30 meters). In 1963 the Alex Lindower Park was constructed between Strickland Avenue, Mill Avenue, and 60th Place. Mill Basin is now one of the most exclusive residential areas in Brooklyn. Beginning in the mid-1990s wealthy families moved in and built larger, luxury homes on the old lots. In the early twenty-first century Russian, Asian, and Israeli families have moved into the neighborhood.

Elizabeth Reich Rawson, Stephen Weinstein

Miller, Arthur (Asher) (*b* New York City, 17 Oct 1915; *d* Roxbury, Conn., 10 Feb 2005). Playwright. Born on West 110th Street to an affluent coat manufacturer, he moved with his family to the Flatbush section of Brooklyn. After the stock market crash of 1929 he attended James Madison High School, graduated from Abraham Lincoln High School in 1932, and became a member of the Federal Theatre Project in 1938. He married his college sweetheart, Mary Slattery, in 1940. During World War II, he worked the night shift at the Brooklyn Navy Yard to support his family. His first successful Broadway play, *All My Sons* (1947), received the Drama Critics Circle Award. He is best known for his play *Death of a Salesman* (1949), an exploration of the American myth of money and success that earned a Pulitzer Prize and a Tony Award. *The Crucible* (1953), a powerful account of the witch trials in Salem, Massachusetts, in 1692, is an allegory of the McCarthy era; *A View from the Bridge* (1955) recounts the story of a Sicilian American family in Red Hook. From 1956 to 1961 he lived at 444 East 57th Street and from 1962 to 1968 at the Chelsea Hotel at 222 West 23rd Street. In 1956 Miller left his first wife and married Marilyn Monroe; he later married photographer Inge Morath in 1962. He wrote an autobiography, *Timebends* (1988), and continued to write plays until his death.

Christopher Bigsby, *Arthur Miller* (London: Orion, 2008)

Robert Seder

Miller, Henry (Valentine) (*b* New York City, 26 Dec 1891; *d* Pacific Palisades, Calif., 7 June 1980). Writer and painter. Born in the Yorkville neighborhood, his family moved to 662 Driggs Avenue in Williamsburg, Brooklyn, where he spent his childhood. He briefly attended City College of New York. After spending much of the 1930s in Paris, Miller returned to the United States in 1940 to California where he wrote until his death. His most acclaimed works, originally banned in the United Sates, included *Tropic of Cancer* (1934), *Black Spring* (1936), and *Tropic of Capricorn* (1939).

Jessica Montesano

Miller Army Air Field. Former military base, now part of Gateway National Recreation Area in New Dorp, Staten Island. The field sits on farmland acquired by Cornelius Vanderbilt from 1836, which was inherited by his son George William Vanderbilt in 1885. On Vanderbilt's death in 1914 the farm passed to his heirs, and in 1919 the U.S. Army purchased the site, which is located on the water, for harbor defense. Completed in 1921, the airfield, named for World War I airman Captain James Ely Miller, became the base for the New York National Guard's 102nd Observation Squadron from 1923 through the 1930s. The only coastal defense air station in the eastern United States when constructed, Miller hosted test runs for Remington–Burnelli and Bellanca aircraft and was used by famed arctic pilots Richard Byrd and Floyd Bennett in the 1920s. During World War II the 102nd was activated and sent to Alabama; coastal defense fortifications were erected and the site became a supply depot for overseas shipping and a prisoner of war camp. During the 1950s Miller held Nike air defense missiles; in 1962 it became headquarters for the 11th Division of the U.S. Army Special Forces. In 1960 one of the planes involved in a collision over Staten Island crashed into Miller Field; 135 people died. The site was deactivated in 1969 and transferred to the National Park Service in 1973. As of the twenty-first century the Miller Army Air Field Historic District was home to an original double seaplane hangar, an old lighthouse, bicycle paths, and athletic fields.

Ben Silk

millinery. See Hatting and millinery.

Mill Rock. Uninhabited island in the East River about 1500 feet (457 meters) off East 96th Street, Manhattan, and the site of the only city park, Mill Rock Park, theoretically accessible by boat (at present it is not open to the public). The island is about 4 acres (1.6 hectares) in area and remains undeveloped. In 1885 Great Mill Rock Island and Little Mill Rock were joined to form the present Mill Rock. It owes its name to John Marsh, who in 1701 erected a mill there. At the outbreak of the War of 1812, a blockhouse mounted with two cannons was erected as part of a chain of fortifications to defend New York Harbor from attack by the British navy. In the late nineteenth century the Army Corps of Engineers manufactured explosives on the site to be used for blasting rocks from Hell Gate Channel. Mill Rock was deeded to the city in 1958.

Gerard R. Wolfe

Millrose Games. Annual winter track meet first held in 1908 and moved to Madison Square Garden in 1914. It initially was organized by the Millrose Athletic Association, which was itself formed by employees of Wanamaker's department stores; the name Millrose was that of Rodman Wanamaker's summer home. Over the years the meet became a prestigious event and was sometimes called the "indoor Olympics." Controversy attended the meet in 1950 when the judges reversed their ruling on the outcome of the mile race (the issue was not settled for nine months), and in 1955 when the running of the Wanamaker Mile resulted in both a world indoor record (by Gunnar Nielsen, 4:03.6) and a fierce shoving match. Among those who have taken part in the Millrose Games are Paavo Nurmi, Frank Shorter, Marty Liquori, Steve Scott, Eammon Coghlan, Carl Lewis, Mary Decker, Jackie Joyner–Kersee, Kenenisa Bekele, Gail Devers, and Maurice Green. The event, held annually in early February, continued to feature Olympic athletes at the Garden in the early twenty-first century with the men's Wanamaker Mile as the main attraction.

Robert Hillenbrand

Mills, C(harles) Wright (*b* Waco, Tex., 28 Aug 1916; *d* West Nyack, N.Y., 20 March 1962). Sociologist and social critic. After receiving a PhD in sociology from the University of Wisconsin (1942) he spent the summer of 1943 in Greenwich Village, where he started his association with left-wing intellectuals such as Daniel Bell, Dwight Macdonald, and Philip Rahv. In 1945 he began a lifelong association with Columbia University, serving as professor of sociology from 1945 until 1962. He was influential in the study of class, power, and social structure. *White Collar* (1951) was a scathing analysis of the new American middle class. In *The Power Elite* (1956), Mills coined the title phrase as he berated the concentration of power in America among corporate, political, and military leaders. In *The Sociological Imagination* (1959) he argued that sociologists should connect larger historical forces to the personal experiences of individuals. Influenced by Karl Marx and Max Weber, Mills believed that knowledge could bring about positive social change. He rejected academic pretension and assumed the role of public intellectual. His appeal to young radicals in "Letter to the New Left" (*New Left Review*, 1960) and his support for the Cuban revolution in *Listen, Yankee: The Revolution in Cuba* (1960) were deeply influential on the New Left movement, and his strident individualism—he often rode a motorcycle—made him an iconic figure. Mills lived for a time on 114th Street. He died of a heart attack at age 45 in suburban Nyack, New York.

Nicholas Kelly

Mingus, Charles (*b* Nogales, Ariz., 22 April 1922; *d* Cuernavaca, Mexico, 5 Jan 1979). Double bass player, pianist, and composer. He grew up in Los Angeles and became a virtuoso double bass player in the 1940s; from 1951 he lived at a series of addresses in New York City, including 5 Great Jones Street (in the mid-1960s) and Manhattan Plaza (for the last several years of his life). He composed ambitious works that melded such diverse influences as the lush orchestral textures of Duke Ellington's writing and the raw, emotionally charged music heard in many African American churches. He appeared frequently at the Five Spot, the Half Note, the Showplace, and the Village Vanguard. His most important recordings include *The Black Saint and the Sinner Lady* (1963) and *Meditations on Integration* (1964). Mingus redefined the role of the double bass soloist in the jazz ensemble and was probably the most ambitious composer of his generation to work in jazz. Much of his writing represented a radical departure from the jazz tradition, embracing atonality, extended forms, and an unusual degree of rhythmic freedom; yet he also created a body of compositions that in their hard-swinging directness hark back to the very roots of African American music.

Brian Priestley, *Mingus: A Critical Biography* (New York: Da Capo, 1984)

Peter Keepnews

mining. Deposits of iron ore in the serpentine hills of Staten Island were discovered by Dutch settlers, who gave the name Yserberg (iron hill) to what later became Todt Hill. Staten Island became an important center of mining and quarrying during the nineteenth century. The ore was exported and used primarily in blast furnaces; if screened, ground, and washed it could be used to produce red ochre paint. By the 1920s about 300,000 tons (272,000 metric tons) had been extracted, primarily from the mines at Todt Hill, Ocean Terrace, the Serpentine Road (Emerson Hill), and Jewett Avenue. Deposits of precious stones were reported in the hills but attempts to recover them were futile; the area eventually produced 80 tons (73 metric tons) of fibrous serpentine that was used as asbestos. From 1841 to 1896 granitelike rock was quarried from the secondary stratum of sandstone under the island and used to pave Whitehall Street, sections of Broadway, and Bowling Green in Manhattan, as well as the streets of Charleston, South Carolina. Hand-broken stone from Staten Island was used for paving the streets of Brooklyn, and tens of thousands of tons were sold for building foundations, docks, and sea walls. Gypsum was quarried on Staten Island as late as the 1960s.

Kevin Kenny

Minnesota Strip. Area on Eighth Avenue from Port Authority north about 10 blocks called the Minnesota Strip because it was reputed to be overrun with prostitutes from the Midwest. The first known usage of the term was in 1975. When the massive redevelopment of the Times Square area began in the 1990s, the name fell out of use.

Jessica Montesano

Minsky, Billy [Michael William] (*b* New York City, 1891; *d* Brooklyn, 12 June 1932). Impresario. He was a society reporter for the *World* before beginning his career in the theater, for a good part of which he worked with his brothers Abe (1881–1949), Herbert (?1892–1959), and Morton (1902–87). He produced shows with Abe at the National Winter Garden on East Houston Street (1913), which was owned by their father; at the Park Theatre on Columbus Circle (for one year beginning in 1922); again at the National Winter Garden (1923–24), where he installed a runway to give his patrons a closer look at the chorus girls; and at the Apollo Theatre (from 1924). In 1931 he staged one of the first burlesque shows on Broadway, at the Republic Theatre on 42nd Street. Minsky was a leading producer of burlesque in New York City and the greatest showman of all the impresarios in his family. His shows were noted for their freshness, the high caliber of their performances, and their risqué quality. The slim, attractive chorus girl was a mainstay of his productions.

Rowland Barber, *The Night They Raided Minsky's* (New York: Simon and Schuster, 1960); Morton Minsky and Milt Machlin, *Minsky's Burlesque* (New York: Arbor House, 1986)

William Green

minstrelsy. The American minstrel show has its roots in eighteenth-century theater. Beginning in the 1760s some British plays, regularly performed in New York City, included black characters, and from the 1790s to the 1830s an indigenous tradition of "Negro impersonators" in blackface presented caricatures of black music and dance between the acts of plays. The publication and frequent performance of humorous songs in black dialect indicated the increased popularity of "Ethiopian delineators" after 1815. Although Thomas D. "Jim Crow" Rice (1808–60) developed his famous blackface song-and-dance routine "Jump Jim Crow" in the Midwest in the 1820s, he was performing it by 1832 in New York City, where he later appeared frequently and introduced many of his blackface farces. By the early 1840s a number of white performers regularly presented blackface song and dance in theaters and circuses in New York City. In February 1843 at the Bowery Amphitheatre a troupe of four white men called the Virginia Minstrels offered the first full program entirely in blackface; they enjoyed wide popularity and helped to make blackface the first indigenous form of American popular entertainment. Their performances established the format and humorous content of early minstrel shows, as well as their core instrumentation (banjo, violin, tambourine, and bones). To the end of the antebellum period most innovations in minstrelsy took place in New York City, where strong competition forced performers to be inventive and allowed only the best ones to succeed. The conventions of the interlocutor and the endmen and the division of the show into three parts originated in the city and became standard throughout the country. Minstrelsy evolved into a form of popular entertainment that both appropriated and denigrated black culture and lampooned many elite cultural forms, including opera, theater, concert music, and dance.

The Ethiopian Serenaders were the leading resident company in New York City until their departure for a tour of England in 1846. In the same year E. P. Christy moved his group Christy's Minstrels to the city from Buffalo; they introduced songs by Stephen Foster and were the most prominent minstrel group in Manhattan until they disbanded in 1854. As demand increased, other troupes expanded and enjoyed long runs: when minstrelsy was at its height in the late 1840s and early 1850s four or five major minstrel companies often performed in the city throughout the season, and six or seven troupes had shorter engagements. Charlie White became prominent in minstrelsy in 1846 and enjoyed a long career as the leader of his own troupe (White's Serenaders), as a performer in other troupes and variety halls, and as a manager of theaters. The Buckley family moved to the city in 1848 and performed until 1858 as the New Orleans Serenaders; this group originated the operatic burlesque, which became a permanent feature of minstrelsy. George Christy left Christy's Minstrels in 1853 and joined Wood's Minstrels to form Christy and Wood's Minstrels. This group dominated minstrelsy in the city until it was eclipsed by Bryant's Minstrels, formed by Dan Bryant and his brothers in February 1858, which remained the most popular troupe in New York City until Bryant's death in 1875. In 1859 the Bryants introduced the song "Dixie" ("Dixie's Land") by Dan Emmett at a theater at 472 Broadway, and in 1863 they originated the practice of including parodies of contemporary plays and current events. The first resident minstrel company in Brooklyn made its debut in September 1862 at Hooley's Opera House, at Court and Remsen streets; Hooley's Minstrels and other minstrel shows appeared there for more than 15 years. Notable troupes of black minstrels, all of which were strictly traveling shows, began to appear in the mid-1850s but did not flourish until after the Civil War. The last company to dominate minstrelsy in New York City was the San Francisco Minstrels, which moved to the city in 1865 and continued to work there until 1883.

After the Civil War competition from variety shows and musical comedies pressured minstrel troupes to change their programs. By the late 1870s they incorporated more players, traveled nationwide, and put on lavish productions that included less blackface material and more elements from other forms of popular entertainment. By the end of the nineteenth century minstrelsy ceased to be nationally popular, although a few blackface artists such as Lew Dockstader worked in the city in the 1880s and 1890s, well-known traveling shows played regularly in New York City into the twentieth century, and blackface acts continued to have a place in vaudeville. The legacy of minstrelsy, though complex, was largely negative: it created and perpetuated derogatory stereotypes of blacks that endured for many decades.

George C. D. Odell, *Annals of the New York Stage* (New York: Columbia University Press, 1927–49); Robert C. Toll, *Blacking Up: The Minstrel Show in Nineteenth-Century America* (New York: Oxford University Press, 1974); Eric Lott, *Love and Theft: Blackface Minstrelsy and the American Working Class* (New York: Oxford University Press, 1993)

See also Black theater and Theater.

Robert B. Winans

Minton's Playhouse. Jazz club. Often considered the most important jazz club in the United States, it was opened in 1938 by the tenor saxophonist Henry Minton at 210 West 118th Street, on the first floor of the Hotel Cecil. It seated slightly more than 100 and had a clientele that was largely black. The club reached the peak of its popularity in 1940 and 1941 when it became known as the focus of an evolving style of jazz known as bop. At jam sessions on Monday evenings soloists such as the saxophonists Charlie Parker and Eddie "Lockjaw" Davis and the trumpeters Miles Davis and Dizzy Gillespie performed with the house band, which included the pianist Thelonious Monk, the drummer Kenny Clarke, and the double bass player Curly Russell. Following a period of decline in the 1950s Minton's closed in 1974 but reopened in 2006 under the name Uptown Lounge at Minton's Playhouse.

Marc Ferris

Minuit, Peter (*b* Wesel, Duchy of Cleves [now Germany], 1580; *d* at sea, 1638). Director general of New Netherland. He worked under William Verhulst in New Amsterdam until 1626, when he was appointed director general as Verhulst's replacement. After signing a treaty with local Indians that granted ownership of the colony to the Dutch West India Company, purportedly for the equivalent of $24, he sought to amalgamate isolated settlements to the north and south and established trade and diplomatic relations with the English settlement at Plymouth. A quarrel led him and the colonial secretary Johan van Remunde to be recalled to the Netherlands for examination; Minuit was dismissed but returned to the colonies to establish a Swedish settlement on the Delaware River, where he was appointed governor.

James E. Mooney

Miracle case. First Amendment lawsuit that originated in Manhattan and culminated in a Supreme Court decision striking down New York State's ban on "sacrilegious" movies. The case began in December 1950 when *The Miracle*, a 40-minute film by the Italian neorealist director Roberto Rossellini, opened at the Paris Theater on West 58th Street. The film is a religious parable featuring a dim-witted peasant woman who becomes pregnant when drunk and thinks it is a case of immaculate conception. She is mocked by villagers but escapes to a hilltop church where she experiences religious ecstasy after giving birth. Francis Cardinal Spellman, the powerful head of the New York Archdiocese, condemned the film as "a despicable affront to every Christian" and "a vicious insult to Italian womanhood" and asked the state Board of Regents, the body empowered to license movies for exhibition, to revoke the film's license. The board obliged, ruling the film sacrilegious, in violation of New York's censorship law. Joseph

Burstyn, the film's distributor, sued the board, and although he lost in the New York State courts, the U.S. Supreme Court ruled in 1952, in the case of *Burstyn v. Wilson,* that "sacrilege" is too vague a censorship standard to be permitted under the First Amendment. The Court said that trying to decide what qualifies as sacrilege sets the censor "adrift upon a boundless sea amid a myriad of conflicting currents of religious views, with no charts but those provided by the most vocal and powerful orthodoxies." The Court added that "it is not the business of government . . . to suppress real or imagined attacks upon a particular religious doctrine." Although it was not the end of film licensing in the United States, the case was a landmark on the road to artistic freedom and to upholding the separation of church and state.

Alan Westin, *The Miracle Case: The Supreme Court and the Movies* (Tuscaloosa: University of Alabama Press, 1961); John Cooney, *The American Pope: The Life and Times of Francis Cardinal Spellman* (New York: Times Books, 1984); Marjorie Heins, Free Expression Policy Project, "*The Miracle:* Film Censorship and the Entanglement of Church and State," Oct 2002, http://www.fepproject.org/commentaries/themiracle.html

Marjorie Heins

Misericordia Hospital. Former name of Our Lady of Mercy Medical Center.

Miss Spence's School for Girls. Original name of the Spence School.

Mitchel, John Purroy (*b* Fordham [now in the Bronx], 19 July 1879; *d* Lake Charles, La., 6 July 1918). Mayor. The son of Irish Catholic parents, he attended Columbia University and New York Law School. His work as a special investigator of municipal corruption won him recognition and election in 1909 as president of the Board of Aldermen on a fusion ticket. Soon his progressivism, administrative talents, and credentials as an independent Democrat captured the attention of President Woodrow Wilson, who appointed him collector of the Port of New York in 1913. Nominated later that year as the mayoral candidate of a fusion alliance, he defeated Edward E. McCall, who was aligned with Tammany Hall and supported by Charles F. Murphy. Known as the "boy mayor," at age 34 he was the youngest mayor to date. His term in office was marked by controversial reforms. He appointed able officials; was strongly supported by progressives who helped him to reorganize and restructure city government; reformed vice control, taxation, transit, and home rule with mixed success; and introduced a relief program for the unemployed that achieved little. Although energetic and idealistic, he often gave the impression of a gentleman overly solicitous to the wealthy. Mitchel antagonized many constituent groups, especially Germans, Irish, and the lower classes, with his support of a plan for vocational education, his revelation of mismanagement in the Catholic Charities, and his militant support for the Allies at the beginning of World War I. In 1917 the fusion movement collapsed and he was defeated for reelection by John F. Hylan, the candidate backed by Tammany Hall. Mitchel joined the air corps and was killed in a training accident. Much of his work was later praised as a precedent for Mayor Fiorello H. La Guardia's reforms. A small park along Broadway at West 116th Street was named for him, and in 1928 a monument in Central Park at East 90th Street was dedicated to him.

Edwin R. Lewinson, *John Purroy Mitchel: The Boy Mayor of New York* (New York: Astra, 1965)

Robert F. Wesser

Banner from John Purroy Mitchel's mayoral campaign as a fusion candidate

Mitchell, Joseph (*b* Fairmont, N.C., 27 Jul 1908; *d* New York City, 24 May 1996). Journalist. He worked for various New York City newspapers and most notably the *New Yorker* magazine. Known for his profiles of interesting New Yorkers, aspects of his work—including the long profile as a journalistic form, casual prose, and a little fictionalizing—anticipated and inspired nonfiction writers and the "new journalism" of the 1960s and 1970s. Mitchell was raised in a family of cotton and tobacco traders and attended the University of North Carolina from 1925 to 1929. In 1929 the *New York Herald Tribune* published an article he wrote about tobacco and offered him a job. Mitchell arrived in Manhattan in October 1929 in the midst of the stock-market crash and spent the Depression reporting for the *Herald Tribune,* the *World,* and the *World-Telegram.* His reportorial style included a judicial use of the first-person singular, understated narration, and lots of dialogue; he also had an ongoing fascination with certain subjects like food, saloons and gin mills, the waterfront and the harbor, and a Bowery theater ticket-taker named Mazie. In 1938 Mitchell published a collection of his reporting called *My Ears Are Bent,* and Harold Ross hired him as a staff reporter for the *New Yorker.* Especially after joining the *New Yorker,* Mitchell profiled small entrepreneurs and working-class entertainers, unusual communities like the Mohawk steelworkers of Brooklyn and the fishmongers of Fulton Fish Market, and various loudmouths and street-corner intellectuals. His last subject, Joe Gould, was a man who lived on the streets of Greenwich Village and claimed to be writing "An Oral History of Our Time." Some have seen irony in the fact that after profiling this "writer" who did not write, Mitchell stopped publishing himself. From 1965 until his death, he went to his office regularly, closed the door, typed, and threw the results of his labors into the trash. During these years, Mitchell received awards and volunteered his time to the South Street Seaport Museum, the New York City Landmarks Preservation Commission, and other organizations. His reputation grew among younger nonfiction writers, but more general popularity eluded him until 1992 when a collection of his writing called *Up in the Old Hotel* was published. In 2000 a movie version of Mitchell's book *Joe Gould's Secret* was released. In 2001 Pantheon reissued *My Ears Are Bent,* and since then Mitchell's reputation has continued to grow.

Joseph Mitchell, *Up in the Old Hotel* (New York: Pantheon, 1992); Joseph Mitchell, *My Ears Are Bent* (New York: Pantheon: 2001 [1938]); Raymond J. Rundus, *Joseph Mitchell: A Reader's and Writer's Guide* (New York: iUniverse, 2003)

Daniel Levinson Wilk

Mitchell, Sidney Z(ollicoffer) (*b* Dadeville, Ala., 17 March 1862; *d* New York City, 17 Feb 1944). Entrepreneur. He installed the first incandescent lighting system on a navy ship in 1883 while serving as a cadet at the U.S. Naval Academy in Annapolis, Maryland. After obtaining the Edison franchise for the Pacific Northwest and starting many lighting companies he moved in 1905 to New York City, where he presided over the Electric Bond and Share Company for 28 years. During the 1920s his utility stock holdings made him one of the wealthiest men in the world. He died at his home at 1010 Fifth Avenue.

John L. Neufeld

Mitchell–Lama [Limited-Profit Housing Companies Law]. Act passed in 1955 by the state legislature of New York, sponsored by Senator McNeil Mitchell and Assemblyman Alfred A. Lama and supported by Mayor Robert F. Wagner. It encouraged the construction of middle-income housing by authorizing mortgages backed by the state for 90 percent of the cost of eligible projects, as well as 20-year partial tax exemptions to builders. After 20 years developers had the option to exit the program by paying off their mortgage, relieving themselves of government oversight and forfeiting their tax breaks. The first city project built under Mitchell–Lama was the Ebbets Field Apartments, built on the site of the Brooklyn Dodgers' baseball stadium in Crown Heights. By the 1970s Mitchell–Lama had subsidized the construction of 138,849 units, including 15,500 at Co-op City (1968–70) in the Bronx. Because of inflation during the mid-1970s, rent increases, and tenant strikes at Co-op City, the program was terminated, and the Department of Housing and Community Renewal (DHCR) became responsible for managing the existing Mitchell–Lama developments. Later legislation dictated that if a project included rental units built before 1974, those units would be covered by rent stabilization after a buyout. For rental units built after 1974, developers could increase rents to reflect market rates. Owners of cooperative apartments would be able to individually sell their apartments at market prices although they would lose their tax abatements. The buyout clause in the original legislation anticipated the resolution of the city's housing crisis during the postwar years, but in the twenty-first century Mitchell–Lama housing remains desirable and applicants are often relegated to waiting lists, leaving legislators scrambling to preserve the remaining units. A total of 101 developments remain in use in New York City, comprising almost 46,000 units. Many developments have become eligible for buyout and developers had removed 26,000 units from the program by 2007. In November 2007 a new law closed a potential loophole allowing Mitchell–Lama property owners to immediately raise rents to market rate on pre-1974 apartments, and other bills circulated that included incentives for owners to remain in the program. In 2008, 6000 units in Starrett City, renamed Spring Creek Towers, were protected from deregulation following the sale of the 140-acre (56.7-hectare) Brooklyn development. Meanwhile, a September 2007 report by the New York State inspector general condemned DHCR oversight of Mitchell–Lama with charges of negligence and corruption in its applicant-selection procedures, prompting the agency to reexamine its policies pertaining to Mitchell–Lama.

Joel Schwartz

Mitchill, Samuel Latham (*b* North Hempstead, N.Y., 20 Aug 1764; *d* New York City, 7 Sept 1831). Statesman, physician, and scholar. After attending King's College (now Columbia) he earned a medical degree in Scotland in 1786 and eventually became the surgeon general of the New York State militia. In 1797 he began publishing the *Medical Repository,* the first professional medical journal in the United States, and he remained its principal editor for more than 20 years. He served for three terms in the state assembly and for 13 years in the U.S. House of Representatives and the U.S. Senate during the administrations of Thomas Jefferson and James Madison. A Quaker and a fiery nationalist, he believed that Americans were building a model government and advocated internal improvements at federal and state expense: he introduced the resolution authorizing the expedition of Lewis and Clark, urged the defense of the country against the Barbary pirates, and helped to form the federal Committee on Indian Affairs. He sought unsuccessfully to rename the country Fredonia and was certain that an American would find a cure for all diseases. As one of the first promoters of sanitary reforms he helped to form the Institute for the Deaf and Dumb and the College of Physicians and Surgeons, of which he was an officer. Called the "congressional dictionary" by Jefferson, he was the first professor of chemistry in the United States, one of the first American geologists (he wrote a geological survey of the Hudson River), and an innovator in education, associated with more than 85 national and international literary and scientific societies. Mitchill wrote *The Picture of New York* (1807), the city's first encyclopedia, and helped to form the New York Anti-Slavery Society.

Courtney R. Hall, *A Scientist in the Early Republic: Samuel Latham Mitchill, 1764–1831* (New York: Columbia University Press, 1934); Alan David Aberbach, *In Search of an American Identity: Samuel Latham Mitchill, Jeffersonian Nationalist* (New York: P. Lang, 1988)

See also Science.

Alan David Aberbach

Mobilization for Youth. Program launched in 1962 by a number of public and private agencies, including the Henry Street Settlement and the Columbia University School of Social Work, to prevent juvenile delinquency by improving economic opportunities for poor young men. It was led by a team of professional reformers under the direction of the social scientists James McCarthy and Winslow Carlton and influenced by such sociologists as Lloyd Ohlin and Richard Cloward, who argued in his book *Delinquency and Opportunity* (1960) that young men became delinquent out of frustration over lack of economic opportunity. The project received funds from the President's Commission on Juvenile Delinquency, the National Institute of Mental Health, the Ford Foundation, and the city. It began operations on the Lower East Side, where the staff provided advice about education, employment, drug rehabilitation, consumer fraud, and rent strikes; it also helped residents to obtain social services, a role it focused on almost exclusively after drawing political fire for its activism in August 1964. Mobilization for Youth was discontinued in 1972.

Joseph H. Helfgot, *Professional Reforming: Mobilization for Youth and the Failure of Social Science* (Lexington, Mass.: Lexington, 1981)

Alana Erickson Coble

molasses. See Sugar.

Mollen Commission. Special commission charged with investigating police corruption, formed after the arrest for cocaine trafficking on 7 May 1992 of six New York City police officers in suburban Suffolk County. Over the objections of Police Commissioner Lee P. Brown, Mayor David N. Dinkins appointed the panel on 25 June, with Milton Mollen, a former judge, as its chairman. On 27 September 1993 the commission began the city's first public hearings on police corruption in more than 20 years with Officer Michael Dowd as its star witness. After sensational testimony by Dowd and others about corruption and brutality in the Ninth Precinct in the East Village, the commission issued an interim report on 28 December 1993 that called the department "incompetent" in policing itself. In March 1994 three officers from the 73rd Precinct in Brownsville were charged with dealing drugs, usually while on duty. Ten days later three officers from the 30th Precinct in Harlem were caught on videotape while beating local residents and stealing drugs and cash. Eventually 11 more officers from the precinct were arrested as a new police commissioner, William J. Bratton, joined in the campaign to weed out corruption. The commission's final report was issued on 6 July 1994. Its central proposal was the creation of an independent commission, appointed by the mayor, that would be empowered to conduct its own investigations and to review efforts by the Police Department at eliminating corruption.

Kenneth T. Jackson

MoMA. See Museum of Modern Art.

Mondrian [Mondriaan], **Piet(er Cornelis, Jr.)** (*b* Amersfoort, Netherlands, 7 March 1872; *d* New York City, 1 Feb 1944). Painter. He was an important contributor to the De Stijl art movement (also known as neoplasticism), a movement founded in Holland in 1917; De Stijl artists used straight lines, largely rectangular forms, and a limited palette of primary colors plus black, white, and gray. After fleeing London in 1940 he moved to New York City, where he lived and worked at 353 East 52nd Street. Mondrian had one-man exhibitions at the Valentine Dusending Gallery in 1942 and again in 1943, when he moved to 15 East 59th Street. His few years in New York City had a profound effect on his later work. He abandoned the black lines of his earlier paintings in *New York City I* (1942), *Broadway Boogie-Woogie* (1943), and *Victory Boogie-Woogie* (1944, unfinished), which are imbued with the rhythmic vitality of the city. He is buried in Cypress Hills Cemetery.

Hans L. C. Jaffé, *Piet Mondrian* (New York: Harry N. Abrams, n.d. [?1970])

Monitor (USS). Ironclad warship that fought the Confederate ship CSS *Virginia* in the first battle between iron ships in history. The 172-foot (52-meter) ship was built at the Continental Iron Works factory in Greenpoint, Brooklyn, and at DeLamater Iron Works in Manhattan and outfitted at the Brooklyn Navy Yard in January 1862 during the Civil War. The ship was built by Swedish engineer John Ericsson in just over 100 days, and its novel design allowed the entire boat except for the revolving gun turret and pilothouse to be submersed underwater. It and the ironclad CSS *Virginia* met at the Battle of Hampton Roads near Norfolk, Virginia, on 9 March 1862. Neither ship suffered serious damage, but the battle was effectively a victory for the U.S. Navy, buoying Union morale and confidence in its navy and technological ingenuity. The *Monitor* sank later that same year in a storm off the coast of North Carolina. The ship is commemorated in the Greenpoint section of Brooklyn with a street named after it and a statue in Monsignor McGolrick Park. A statue of Ericsson holding a miniature of the *Monitor* is also located in Battery Park.

David White

Monk, Thelonious (Sphere) (*b* Rocky Mount, N.C., 10 Oct 1917; *d* Englewood, N.J., 17 Feb 1982). Pianist and composer. His family moved in 1922 to New York City, where he attended Stuyvesant High School. During the early 1940s he was the house pianist at Minton's Playhouse (at the Hotel Cecil on West 118th Street in Harlem), taking part in jam sessions that helped to lay the groundwork for the development of modern jazz. He made his first recordings as a leader in 1947. Because of his jagged, syncopated style, his music at first met with little acclaim. In 1951 police revoked his cabaret license after he took the fall in a drug bust (the drugs supposedly belonged to his friend, pianist Bud Powell), and for the next six years his public appearances in New York City were limited. His successful engagement in 1957 at the Five Spot Cafe on the Lower East Side eventually helped him to become widely known; *Time* published a cover story about him on 28 February 1964. Among the recordings that he made in New York City were two with a quartet at the Five Spot in 1958 and two others with a 10-piece ensemble (one at Town Hall in 1959, the other at Philharmonic Hall in 1963). He also performed frequently at the Five Spot, the Jazz Gallery, the Village Vanguard, and the Village Gate. For most of his life he lived at 243 West 63rd Street; the junction of West 63rd Street and West End Avenue was named Thelonious Sphere Monk Circle in 1983. Monk's unusual concept of harmony, daringly uneven rhythms, and use of whole-tone scales helped pave the way for the innovative style of jazz known as bop, although Monk himself was too idiosyncratic a musician to fit comfortably into this category or any other.

Peter Keepnews

Monkey Hill. Former neighborhood in lower Manhattan, lying near City Hall; its main streets were Park Row and Chambers, Rose, William, and Duane streets. For many years the most prominent landmark was the Rhinelander Sugar House on William Street, which was used as a prison by the British during the American Revolution. The neighborhood was affluent during the late nineteenth century. All the historical landmarks and brownstone houses were demolished in 1892 to make way for businesses, and the name Monkey Hill soon became disused.

"Last Days of Monkey Hill," *Sun,* 10 April 1892, p. 3

James Bradley

Monroe, James (*b* Westmoreland County, Va., 28 April 1758; *d* New York City, 4 July 1831). Fifth president of the United States. He lived in New York City during the Confederation Congress session of 1784–86. While in the city he met and married Elizabeth Kortwright, a member of a prominent family of merchants. On leaving the White House in 1825 he returned to Virginia, where he was plagued by ill health and financial difficulties. After the death of his wife he returned to New York City in October 1830 to live with his daughter and his son-in-law Samuel Gouverneur at the northeast corner of Lafayette and Prince streets. His funeral service on 7 July 1831 at St. Paul's Episcopal Church was followed by a procession up Broadway to the East Side, where he was buried in the New York City Marble Cemetery; at the time this was the most elaborate funeral ever held in the city. In 1858 Monroe's remains were reinterred in Richmond, Virginia.

George Morgan, *The Life of James Monroe* (New York: AMS, 1969); Harry Ammon, *James Monroe: The Quest for National Identity* (New York: McGraw–Hill, 1971)

Matthew Kachur

Monroe, Marilyn [Mortenson (Baker), Norma Jeane] (*b* Los Angeles, 1 June 1926; *d* Brentwood, Calif., 5 Aug 1962). Actress and model. Her career was launched when a photographer at *Yank* magazine encouraged her to apply to the Blue Book Modeling agency. She became one of their most popular models, landing a contract with 20th Century Fox in 1946 and changing her name to Marilyn Monroe. She married New York Yankees superstar Joe DiMaggio in 1954. That same year one of the most iconic images of Monroe was captured on Lexington Avenue at 52nd Street in front of the Trans-Lux Theater while she was filming a scene for *The Seven Year Itch:* hundreds of fans and photographers watched as the updraft from a subway grate blew her skirt into the air, angering DiMaggio, who also witnessed the event, and adding to their growing marital tensions. After divorcing DiMaggio, Monroe married New York playwright Arthur Miller in 1956; they lived at 444 East 57th Street before separating in 1960. After their divorce in 1961 Monroe entered the Payne Whitney Psychiatric Center on the Upper East Side but quickly transferred to the Columbia–Presbyterian Medical Center where she was hospitalized for depression for several weeks. In 1962 Monroe returned to New York City from California and sang "Happy Birthday" to President John F. Kennedy at Madison Square Garden while rumors circulated of an affair between the two. On 5 August 1962 she was discovered dead in her California home; the cause of death was determined to be "acute barbiturate poisoning" and an accidental overdose.

Sarah Churchwell, *The Many Lives of Marilyn Monroe* (New York: Metropolitan Books/Henry Holt, 2005)

Meghan Lalonde

Monroe's Uptown House. Jazz club at 198 West 134th Street, opened by Clark Monroe in the mid-1930s. Billie Holiday sang there for three months in 1937, and toward the end of the decade it was the site of important experiments in bop and of the first solo performances in New York City by the saxophonist Charlie Parker. A shift in the focus of bop toward 52nd Street prompted the club to move downtown in 1943, and it closed within the year. In December 1944 Monroe opened the Spotlite at 56 West 52nd Street, which lasted for about two years.

Marc Ferris

Montauk Club. Social club in Brooklyn, incorporated in 1889. It soon moved to a clubhouse in Park Slope designed by Francis H. Kimball on Eighth Avenue at Lincoln Place and Plaza Place. Inspired by the Gothic palaces of Venice and incorporating into its exterior and interior American Indian themes and depictions of American plants and animals, the building is one of the most distinctive in New York City. After its founding many of the club's members were actively involved in promoting consolidation of Brooklyn with Manhattan. Prominent members have included Charles Pratt, Richard Schermerhorn, and Edwin C. Litchfield. Since its inception the club has hosted many prominent figures, including Presidents Grover Cleveland, Herbert Hoover, Dwight D. Eisenhower, and John F. Kennedy.

James E. Mooney

Montefiore Medical Center. Private hospital in the northern Bronx. It was formed in 1884 as the Montefiore Home for Chronic Individuals by Jewish philanthropists to honor Moses Montefiore, a former sheriff of London. Initially the hospital was devoted to providing permanent care for poor, incurably ill Jews and had 25 beds in its ward at 84th Street and York Avenue (Avenue A) in Manhattan. The Board of Trustees was led by Jacob Schiff and the first chief of staff was Simon Baruch; among the physicians who volunteered their services were Bernard Sachs and Abraham Jacobi. The facility became nonsectarian in 1887 and moved in 1889 to Broadway between 138th and 139th streets. It bought a farm in exurban Bedford, New York, for tuberculosis patients in 1897 and moved in 1913 to its present site between Gun Hill Road and 210th Street, where its first private pavilion was opened; it became a teaching hospital in 1916 and opened a nursing school in 1922. The introduction of antibiotics after World War II prompted the hospital to shift its focus from long-term care to acute care. Under the leadership of Martin Cherkasky between 1950 and 1980 the sanitarium was sold and the facility in the Bronx became affiliated with several public and private hospitals, becoming the second largest medical center in New York. Under the leadership of Spencer Foreman (1986–2008), the center created more than 1000 inpatient beds in three hospitals, a biomedical research institute, community health care centers throughout the Bronx and nearby Westchester, rehabilitation and nursing home care, and outpatient services for the city jail on Rikers Island. Montefiore became affiliated with the Albert Einstein School of Medicine in 1963 and took its current name during the 1980s.

Montauk Club (designed by Francis H. Kimball), Lincoln Place and Eighth Avenue, Park Slope, 1900

Dorothy Levinson, *Montefiore: The Hospital as Social Instrument, 1884–1984* (New York: Farrar, Straus and Giroux, 1984)

Ann L. Buttenwieser

Montez, Lola [Gilbert, Marie Dolores Eliza Rosanna] (*b* Limerick, Ireland, 1818; *d* New York City, 17 Jan 1861). Courtesan and dancer. By 1846 Montez was the mistress of Ludwig I of Bavaria; her intervention in politics helped cause his abdication and her banishment in 1848. After touring the United States and Australia as a dancer, she spent the last years of her life in New York City, where she gave a small series of lectures. She died in a boarding house at 194 West 17th Street and was buried in Green-Wood Cemetery (as Mrs. Eliza Gilbert).

Helen Holdredge, *The Woman in Black: The Life of Lola Montez* (New York: G. P. Putnam's Sons, 1955)

Elliott B. Nixon

Monthly Review. Socialist magazine. Founded in New York City in the midst of the cold war by economist Paul Sweezy and social scientist Leo Huberman, it was initially funded by F. O. Matthiessen and operated out of Huberman's apartment. The magazine's first issue in May 1949 featured a story by Albert Einstein titled "Why Socialism?" In 1952 the Monthly Review Press, a book publishing arm, was formed. Like many other small independent magazines in the city, the *Monthly Review* struggled financially, subletting office space from the NATION in the late 1950s. The magazine attempted to expand globally, operating a London office from 1966 to 1983; however, its circulation remained small—never topping 12,000—and in the early twenty-first century was about 8500. In May 2006 a daily online magazine was established; in 2008 the magazine's headquarters remained in the city at 146 West 29th Street.

See also NEW LEADER, SOCIALIST PARTY OF AMERICA.

Kate Lauber

Montresor Island. Former name of RANDALLS ISLAND.

MONY. See MUTUAL LIFE INSURANCE COMPANY OF NEW YORK.

Moody [née Dunch], **Deborah, Lady** [Lady Moody] (*christened* London, 3 Apr 1586; *d* [probably] Gravesend [now in Brooklyn], between Nov 1658 and 11 May 1659). Colonist. The wealthy widow of a baronet, Lady Moody left England in defiance of an order from the Court of the Star Chamber that she curtail her visits to London and remain on her Wiltshire estate. She came to New England by 1639 and settled at Lynn, outside Boston, where her Anabaptist views conflicted with the tenets of the Salem Church. Rather than risk public censure she moved in 1643 to New Netherland where she founded Gravesend, the sole English town on the Dutch-dominated western tip of Long Island. A proponent of religious freedom, Moody harbored persecuted Quakers and possibly adopted their beliefs. At her death she left one of the largest private libraries in the New World. She was likely buried in the Gravesend Cemetery, but the exact location of her grave is lost. The house at 27 Gravesend Neck Road, known locally as Lady Moody's House, was probably built after her lifetime.

Victor H. Cooper, *A Dangerous Woman: New York's First Lady Liberty: The Life and Times of Lady Deborah Moody (1586–1659?)* (Bowie, Md.: Heritage Books, 1995)

Joseph Ditta

Moody's Investors Service. Bond-rating business, formed by John Moody in New York City in 1900. It has played an influential role in the financial markets by evaluating the credit worthiness of the bonds, notes, preferred stock, and short-term debt of corporations and government borrowers, assigning to each security a credit-quality rating that is then published, along with supplemental research. Moody's is, with Standard and Poor's, one of the two largest bond-rating services in the United States. It also publishes a wide range of other financial reports and has expanded worldwide operations to five continents; however, it still maintains its headquarters in Manhattan at 250 Greenwich Street in 7 World Trade Center.

Owen D. Gutfreund

"moon hoax." Deception perpetrated in a series of articles published in the *Sun* between 21 and 31 August 1835, which purported to describe the surface of the moon as seen by the astronomer Sir John Herschel through a giant telescope at the Cape of Good Hope. The descriptions in the articles of lakes, forests, animals, and flying "man-bats" on the moon caused a popular sensation in New York City. The hoax was exposed in early September by the *Journal of Commerce* and the *New York Herald,* which reported that the articles had been concocted by Richard Adams Locke, assistant editor of the *Sun.* The articles reportedly raised the circulation of the *Sun* to 19,000, the highest of any daily newspaper in the world; they were widely reprinted throughout the United States and inspired an article by Edgar Allan Poe in the *Sun* on 13 April 1844, which reported spuriously that balloonists had crossed the Atlantic Ocean in three days.

Richard Adams Locke, *The Moon Hoax* (New York: William Gowans, 1859)

Steven H. Jaffe

A VISIT FROM ST. NICHOLAS.

BY CLEMENT C. MOORE.

'Twas the night before Christmas, when all through the house
Not a creature was stirring, not even a mouse;
The stockings were hung by the chimney with care,
In hopes that St. Nicholas soon would be there;
The children were nestled all snug in their beds,
While visions of sugar-plums danced in their heads;
And mamma in her kerchief and I in my cap,
Had just settled our brains for a long winter's nap—

3

Clement Clarke Moore, A Visit from St. Nicholas *(1842)*

Moore, Clement Clarke (*b* New York City, 15 July 1779; *d* Newport, R.I., 10 July 1863). Writer and philologist. His father, Benjamin Moore, was the president of Columbia College, where Moore graduated as valedictorian in 1798. He grew up in a mansion just south of what is now 23rd Street between Ninth and 10th avenues on his family's estate, named Chelsea by his grandfather, Thomas Clarke. Moore's family had deep roots in New York City: his great-great-grandfather, Captain Samuel Moore, acquired an estate in present-day Newton, Queens, in 1652. Moore, who inherited slaves with his family's property, wrote an anonymous pamphlet in 1804 skewering President Thomas Jefferson for his racist views; he often published pieces in the *New York Evening Post* and wrote books and pamphlets on agriculture, religion, and government, compiling the *Compendious Lexicon of the Hebrew Language* in 1809. Moore was the founding warden of the CHURCH OF ST. LUKE-IN-THE-FIELDS and he also donated the land for the GENERAL THEOLOGICAL SEMINARY, where in 1821 he became the first professor of Greek, Hebrew, and Oriental languages. About 1830 he divided the Chelsea estate into lots for development; he later built a home at Ninth Avenue and 23rd Street.

Moore's most well-known piece of writing is the poem "A Visit from St. Nicholas" (popularly known as "The Night before Christmas"). An anonymous copy was published in the *Troy Sentinel* on 23 December 1823, although Moore was not acknowledged as the author until 1837; the poem appeared in his book *Poems* in 1844. In the late nineteenth century the family of Major Henry Livingston, Jr. (1748–1828), a Revolutionary War veteran from Poughkeepsie, New York, claimed that Livingston was the poem's true author. Moore's biographer Samuel White Patterson has maintained that Moore wrote the poem at age 24 as entertainment for his children, and despite doubts cast by Vassar professor Don Foster in 2000, modern scholars generally agree that Moore is the author. Moore is buried in Trinity Church Cemetery and Mausoleum in Washington Heights, and two city parks bear his name: one in Newton, Queens, and one at 22nd Street and 10th Avenue. The New-York Historical Society holds one of Moore's four handwritten copies of the poem.

Michael Joseph, Kate Lauber

Moore, Ely (*b* Belvidere, N.J., 4 July 1798; *d* Lecompton, Kans., 27 Jan 1860). Political leader. After completing an apprenticeship with a printer in New Jersey, he moved to New York City and married the daughter of a well-connected politician in Tammany Hall. He later engaged in land speculation and became a spokesman for the Democratic Party. His oratorical power and sympathy for the labor movement gained notice from the printers' union, which helped to elect him president of the newly formed General Trades' Union in 1833. A moderate in union politics, he edited a labor newspaper and delivered ceremonial speeches. In 1834 he won election as president of the National Trades' Union at its first convention and as a Democratic representative in the U.S. Congress, where he soon lost support from unions over a dispute concerning labor in state prisons. During his two terms in Washington he worked for various labor reforms while backing the pro-southern Jacksonian mainstream on sectional issues. Defeated for reelection in 1838, he spent the next dozen years serving political appointments and campaigning unsuccessfully for other elective offices. After briefly publishing a newspaper in New Jersey, Moore spent his final years as a special federal agent to the Indian tribes in Lecompton. He is best known as the first labor leader in Congress.

Sean Wilentz

Moore, Marianne (Craig) (*b* Kirkwood, Mo., 15 Nov 1887; *d* New York City, 5 Feb 1972). Modernist poet. After graduating from Bryn Mawr College in 1909, she taught at the Carlisle Indian Industrial School in Carlisle, Pennsylvania, for several years before moving to New York City, where from 1918 to 1929 she lived at 14 St. Luke's Place. In 1921 she published her first book, *Poems,* and began working at the New York Public Library; her book *Observations* (1924) won the Dial award. She was the acting editor of the *Dial* from 1925 until 1929, when she left to devote herself entirely to her own writing. From 1931 she lived at 260 Cumberland Street in Brooklyn. She won a Guggenheim fellowship in 1945 and in 1951 published *Collected Poems,* which won a National Book Award and the Bollingen and Pulitzer prizes. A devoted fan of the Brooklyn Dodgers, Moore was sometimes seen at home games wearing a tricorn hat and flowing cape. In addition to living for many years in Brooklyn, from 1966 until the end of her life she lived at 35 West Ninth Street in Manhattan.

Charles Molesworth, *Marianne Moore: A Literary Life* (New York: Atheneum, 1990)

James E. Mooney

Moore Catholic High School. School founded in 1962 by Francis Cardinal Spellman and the Presentation Sisters of Staten Island. It was certified by the state in 1966 as the Countess Moore High School. Originally a girls' school, it became coeducational in 1969 and adopted its current name in 1978. In the early twenty-first century the school, which is located at 100 Merrill Avenue in Staten Island, enrolled about 1000 students.

Kate Lauber

Moran, Edmond J(oseph) (*b* Brooklyn, 1896; *d* New Canaan, Conn., 15 July 1993). Tugboat and shipping entrepreneur. The grandson of Michael Moran, a mule driver on the Erie Canal who in 1860 founded the Moran Towing Corporation, he worked for 69 years in one of the nation's oldest and largest tugboat operations. Although the company expanded from Maine to Texas and inland to the Great Lakes and the Mississippi and Ohio rivers, the focus of its activity was the Port of New York. During World War II he served as a rear admiral, commanding the 160 tugboats that enabled Allied forces to carry out the D-Day invasion of France on 6 June 1944. He retired as chairman of Moran Towing in 1984.

Ben Silk

Moravian Church. The origins of the Moravian Church in what is now New York City date to 1742, when David Bruce was sent to preach to Moravians living in Manhattan, Staten Island, and Long Island. In the following decades services are thought to have been held in a schoolhouse at Egbertville. In response to a request for a full-time clergyman, the Moravian authorities in Bethlehem, Pennsylvania, sent Hector Gambold to Staten Island in 1763. The New Dorp Moravian Church was dedicated in December of that year on Richmond Road and remained standing into the early twenty-first century, when there were 10 Moravian churches in New York City (one in the Bronx, two in Brooklyn, two in Manhattan, one in Queens, and four in Staten Island).

Morgan, Edwin Denison (*b* Washington, Mass., 8 Feb 1811; *d* New York City, 14 Feb 1883). Governor and senator. He moved to New York City in 1836 after working as a clerk in his uncle's grocery store in Hartford, Connecticut. With Morris Earle and A. D. Pomeroy he opened a wholesale grocery, Morgan and Earle; this declared bankruptcy after a year, and so he went into business on his own as a grocer, banker, and broker. Soon one of the city's leading merchants, he was elected to the Board of Assistant Aldermen in 1849 and appointed its president. With the help of Solon Humphreys his firm, E. D. Morgan, handled more than $30 million in securities between 1858 and 1860. Elected to the state senate in 1850 as a Whig, he introduced the bill establishing Central Park, and in 1858 he won election as governor with the support of Thurlow Weed; in 1860 he was reelected by what was then the largest margin ever in a gubernatorial election in New York State. He worked in 1862 to direct the fortification of New York Harbor. In 1863 he was elected to the U.S. Senate. As the leader of the Republican National Committee from 1872 to 1876 he favored sound currency and civil service reform. At the end of his life Morgan had a fortune of $8 million; much of it was donated to charities in the city, including the Women's Hospital, Presbyterian Hospital, and the Eye and Ear Hospital.

Walter Friedman

Morgan, J(ohn) P(ierpont) (*b* Hartford, Conn., 17 April 1837; *d* Rome, 31 March 1913). Financier. The son of Junius Spencer Morgan, a successful merchant and banker, he was educated in Boston and Europe and moved to New York City in 1857 to work as an accountant. In 1861 he became an American agent of his father's firm, which was based in London. He was a member of Dabney, Morgan and Company from 1864 until 1871, when he became a partner in Drexel, Morgan and Company. In 1895 he reorganized Drexel as J. P. Morgan and Company, which became one of the most powerful banking houses in the world, nicknamed the "House of Morgan." Capitalizing on the rise of American industry in the 1870s, he began financing American companies with British funds. In the 1880s and 1890s he refinanced and restructured such leading American railroads as the Erie, the Southern, and the New York Central. By serving on the board of directors of many railroads and exerting a strong influence over their activities, he became one of the world's most powerful railroad magnates. He also reshaped American manufacturing by financing important mergers, including those that formed General Electric, American Telephone and Telegraph, International Harvester, and U.S. Steel. At the same time he helped to finance the federal government: during the depression of 1895 he provided $62 million in gold to relieve a currency crisis, and in 1907 he mobilized bankers in the city to avert a national financial collapse. Because of such displays of power, he aroused the enmity of progressive reformers and the distrust of the federal government. He was a target in 1912 of the investigation led by Representative Arsène Pujo into the "Money Trust," the elite group of tycoons who dominated the American economy, but he emerged unscathed.

Morgan was among the leading art and book collectors of his time. He helped found the Metropolitan Museum of Art, to which he donated many valuable paintings and sculptures. To house his vast collection of books he built the Morgan Library adjacent to his townhouse at 219 Madison Avenue, at 36th Street, where he lived from the early 1880s until his death; this became a public reference library in 1924. He also helped found the Young Men's Christian Association, was for decades the senior warden of St. George's Episcopal Church on Stuyvesant Square, and was a generous benefactor of many hospitals, schools, and churches in New York City.

Ron Chernow, *The House of Morgan: An American Banking Dynasty and the Rise of Modern Finance* (New York: Atlantic Monthly Press, 1990); Jean

Strouse, *Morgan: American Financier* (New York: Random House, 1999)

Robert Sanger Steel

Morgan, J(ohn) P(ierpont), Jr. (*b* Irvington-on-Hudson, N.Y., 7 Sept 1867; *d* Boca Grande, Fla., 13 March 1943). Banker. After graduating from Harvard College in 1889, "Jack," as his family called him, spent a year working in a Boston bank. In 1891 he joined his father's New York City firm, Drexel, Morgan and Company, becoming a partner in 1892. The firm was reorganized as J. P. Morgan and Company in 1895. In 1898 he became a partner in J. S. Morgan and Company, the London merchant bank founded by his grandfather in 1854.

Morgan returned to Wall Street in 1905 a staunch Anglophile, arranging to spend up to six months of each year in England. In 1909 his father's New York City bank and the Philadelphia affiliate, Drexel and Company, provided the capital for a new London partnership, Morgan, Grenfell and Company. The firm became the agent for British government purchases of war supplies in the United States in January 1915. That spring the firm made a similar arrangement with France. In the years prior to U.S. entry into World War I, Morgan made $1.5 billion worth of loans to the Allies. Over the course of the war, Morgan bought $3 billion worth of military supplies for the Allies. In February 1924 a record $150 million long-term loan to Japan was floated in the United States following the devastating earthquake in Tokyo and Yokohama. In all, from 1919 to 1933 Morgan underwrote almost $2 billion in railroad bonds and another $2 billion in bonds of American industrial corporations. He syndicated over half of the bonds issued for German reparations payments used in the Dawes Plan of 1924 and one-third under the Young Plan of 1929.

Following the death of his father in 1913, Morgan was made senior partner of the firm; he became chairman of the board when J. P. Morgan and Company incorporated in 1940, serving until his death. Morgan summarized his approach to business in a statement before the Pecora Congressional hearings in May 1933, saying, "At all times the idea of doing only first-class business, and that in a first-class way, has been before our minds." Morgan added 4000 books and manuscripts to the 19,000 acquired by his father. He turned his father's Morgan Library into a public research facility in 1924 and added an annex in 1928.

John Douglas Forbes, *J. P. Morgan Jr., 1867–1943* (Charlottesville: University of Virginia Press, 1981); Ron Chernow, *The House of Morgan* (New York: Grove Press, 1990)

Benjamin J. Klebaner

Morgan, Thomas Hunt (*b* Lexington, Ky., 22 Sept 1866; *d* Pasadena, Calif., 4 Dec 1945). Nobel Prize–winning biologist. In 1904 he joined the faculty at Columbia University, where his research on fruit flies confirmed that genes are carried on chromosomes and influence the expression of physical traits. His work provided the basis of transmission genetics and helped to establish Columbia as a leading center for biology. His books defined genetics as the foundation of cytology, embryology, and evolution. Morgan won the Nobel Prize for physiology or medicine in 1933.

Ronald Rainger

Morgan Library and Museum. Complex of buildings that occupies the east side of Madison Avenue between 36th and 37th streets. Established in 1924 as the Pierpont Morgan Library, the institution was first housed in a 1906 building commissioned by J. P. Morgan and designed by the firm of McKim, Mead and White. It now comprises the original library, a 1928 annex, a nineteenth-century brownstone, and a 75,000-square-foot (7000-square-meter) addition designed by Renzo Piano that was completed in 2006. At the conclusion of this expansion, the organization was renamed. The Morgan's initial collection was made up of those items owned by Morgan that were not donated to other institutions upon his death; however, acquisitions are ongoing. Its nearly 10,000 prints and drawings include a large group of etchings by Rembrandt, as well as works by Leonardo da Vinci and Albrecht Dürer. Prominent among the more than 1300 medieval and Renaissance manuscripts are the ninth-century Lindau Gospels and the Hours of Cardinal Alessandro Farnese. There are three Gutenberg Bibles in the collection of printed books, as well as a notable selection of children's and illustrated books. Among the literary and historical manuscripts are the only surviving manuscript of John Milton's *Paradise Lost*, the journals of Henry David Thoreau, and Charles Dickens's manuscript of *A Christmas Carol*. The Morgan's music holdings include the world's largest collection of Gustav Mahler manuscripts. The small art collection consists of many of Morgan's favorite objects, including Qing porcelain, a group of medieval pieces, and works by Hans Memling and Lucas Cranach. The Morgan also houses ancient Near Eastern manuscripts, seals, and tablets. In 2000 the Morgan launched a comprehensive online catalogue of its medieval and Renaissance manuscripts that will eventually make available approximately 75,000 images, representing every significant illustration in the collection.

See also J(OHN) P(IERPONT) MORGAN.

Helen Graves

Morgan's Corner. Name used about 1838 for EGBERTVILLE.

Morgan Stanley. Firm of investment bankers. Founded by Henry S. Morgan and bond expert Harold Stanley (1885–1963), who left J. P. Morgan and Company when it abandoned investment banking in favor of commercial banking to comply with the Glass–Steagall Act. Morgan Stanley opened on 16 September 1935 at 2 Wall Street; Stanley was president of the firm until 1941, when it was reorganized as a private partnership and he became a senior partner. The firm joined the New York Stock Exchange in 1942; it became publicly owned in 1985 and expanded globally through the twentieth century, merging in 1997 with Dean Witter, Discover and Co. During the terrorist attacks of 11 September 2001, 13 of the firm's employees died in its World Trade Center offices. In 2005 the firm returned to lower Manhattan, occupying a new building at One New York Plaza (its headquarters remained at 1585 Broadway). In late 2008, with Wall Street in turmoil as

Morgan Library and Museum, 2009

investment banks folded because of the subprime mortgage crisis, Morgan Stanley and Goldman Sachs voluntarily reorganized to become bank holding companies. Japanese commercial bank Mitsubishi paid $9 billion for a 21 percent stake in the firm to strengthen its standing.

Ron Chernow, *The House of Morgan: An American Banking Dynasty and the Rise of Modern Finance* (New York: Grove Press, 2001)

Kate Lauber

Morgen Freiheit. Yiddish-language daily newspaper. It was launched in April 1922 by the Jewish branch of the American Communist Party and published at 47 Chrystie Street. Under the direction of Moses J. Olgin it became known for its high journalistic standards and during the 1920s had a circulation of 23,000. By the late 1920s the newspaper had become affiliated with the Communist Party and adhered to the party line, lending support to the Arabs in the Palestinian riots of 1929 and to the pact between Hitler and Stalin. In 1970 *Morgen Freiheit* was published five times a week. It ceased publication in 1977.

Charles A. Madison, *Jewish Publishing in America: The Impact of Jewish Writing on American Culture* (New York: Sanhedrin, 1976)

Seth Kamil

Morgenthau, Henry, Jr. (*b* New York City, 11 May 1891; *d* Poughkeepsie, N.Y., 6 Feb 1967). Public official, father of Robert M. Morgenthau. Born at 211 Central Park West, he studied agriculture and published the *American Agriculturist.* In 1928 he was appointed chairman of the Agriculture Advisory Commission and commissioner of conservation by Governor Franklin D. Roosevelt; he led the Federal Farm Board and the Farm Credit Administration (1933) after Roosevelt was elected president and was his confidant. As secretary of the treasury from 1934 to 1945 he influenced postwar economic policy, establishing the International Monetary Fund and the International Bank for Reconstruction and Development, known as the World Bank.

John Morton Blum, *Roosevelt and Morgenthau* (Boston: Houghton Mifflin, 1972)

Neal C. Garelik

Morgenthau, Henry, Sr. (*b* Mannheim, Germany, 26 April 1856; *d* New York City, 25 Nov 1946). Businessman and philanthropist, father of Henry Morgenthau, Jr. After settling in Brooklyn with his family in 1865 he graduated in 1877 from Columbia Law School and amassed a fortune by developing real estate in northern Manhattan and the Bronx. A supporter of President Woodrow Wilson, he was the finance chairman of the Democratic National Committee (1912 and 1916) and the U.S. ambassador to Turkey (1913–16). He also helped to establish the American National Red Cross and Bronx House.

Neal C. Garelik

Morgenthau, Robert M(orris) (*b* New York City, 31 July 1919). District attorney, son of Henry Morgenthau, Jr. He graduated from Amherst College in 1941 and Yale Law School in 1948, and from 1961 to 1970 he served as the U.S. attorney for the Southern District of New York State. In 1962 he won the Democratic gubernatorial nomination but lost the general election to Governor Nelson A. Rockefeller. He ended a second candidacy for the governorship in 1970 after failing to win the nomination of the Liberal Party. A deputy mayor to John V. Lindsay (1970), he became the district attorney of New York County in 1975, a position he held until 2009, when he retired at the age of 90. He was known as a fair prosecutor and never recommended the death penalty.

Neal C. Garelik, Meghan Lalonde

Morgen Zhurnal. Yiddish-language morning newspaper. It was launched in 1901 by Jacob Sapirstein and published at 75–79 Bowery. It was the only daily morning newspaper of its kind and was popular for its large section of employment advertisements. The newspaper had an Orthodox and Republican bias. Circulation peaked at 111,000 in 1916. *Der Morgen Zhurnal* merged with *Der Yiddishe Tageblatt* in 1928 and with the daily newspaper *Der Tog* to form *Der Tog–Morgen Zhurnal* (1953–72).

Mordecai Soltes, *The Yiddish Press: An Americanizing Agency* (New York: Teachers College, Columbia University, 1924; repr. 1950)

Seth Kamil

morgues. The first morgue in New York City began operating on 21 June 1866 on the grounds of Bellevue Hospital at 26th Street near the East River. Built as a temporary storage facility for the bodies of unknown persons, it housed an autopsy room with four marble tables, a refrigeration room, two rooms for viewing the dead and holding religious services, and an administrative office. All bodies were photographed for identification and remained at the morgue for 72 hours or less, depending on their condition and the weather; they could be viewed only in the presence of the coroner, who gave written consent for their release to family members. Those that were not claimed were removed to the potter's field on Hart Island for burial. Clothing was exhibited for 30 days and stored for as long as a year to permit eventual identification; registration numbers of graves were also kept. Additional storage areas and a hospital museum were eventually added, and by 1897 the morgue received about 8000 bodies a year, of which about 250 were never identified.

In the mid-1990s the morgue was managed by the Office of Chief Medical Examiner of the City of New York and had a collection center in each borough. Autopsies were performed by the medical examiner's offices in Manhattan, Brooklyn, and Queens; the offices in Manhattan and Brooklyn performed autopsies for the morgue in Staten Island and for the one in the Bronx, which planned to open its own medical examiner's office. Autopsies in New York City are required in the event of many causes of death: homicide, suicide, poisoning, drug overdose, fatal accidents, and certain diseases; deaths occurring in hospitals, the workplace, police custody, and prisons; and deaths unattended by a physician. Autopsies are also performed on term fetuses that die at home and on the bodies of people who die while traveling to the city. Unidentified bodies remain in the city's morgues for about 14 days before burial on Hart Island.

Jane DeLuca

Mormons. Members of the Church of Jesus Christ of Latter-day Saints (LDS), popularly known as the Mormon church, a religious organization originally established in upstate New York in 1830 and later headquartered in Salt Lake City, Utah. In 1828 an upstate farmer named Martin Harris who was a neighbor of the church's first leader, Joseph Smith, Jr., came to New York City to seek expert advice regarding copies of characters found on gold plates that Smith said he had received from an angel. Harris met with Professor Charles Anthon of Columbia College, then one of the country's leading linguists. Anthon later denied authenticating the characters, but Harris came away from the meeting sufficiently encouraged that he mortgaged his farm to fund the first printing of the *Book of Mormon*, a critical event in the beginnings of the new faith. Smith himself subsequently visited New York City in 1832, where he marveled at the "truly great and wonderful" buildings and remarked on the city's international and ethnic diversity.

A permanent presence of Mormons in New York City began in 1837 when Parley Pratt established the first LDS congregation in Manhattan. New York City served as one of the church's headquarters in the eastern United States from that time on. In the nineteenth century, several important LDS newspapers and publications were printed in New York City, and as many as 90,000 European Mormons passed through its port on their way to the western United States. By the end of the nineteenth century many Mormons had begun to move to New York City to pursue education and careers. Joined by a substantial number of emigrant German Mormons, they soon represented one of the largest concentrations of Mormons in the eastern United States. In 1919 the church built one of its first chapels in the eastern United States in Brooklyn. In 1934 this growth was recognized with the formation of a church stake based in New York City. At its formation the New York stake was the only one east of Colorado and only the third formed outside the traditional areas of Mormon settlement in the western United States. The Mormon Pavilion at the 1964–65 New York World's Fair was subsequently moved to serve as the church in Plainview, New York. Much of the church's growth in New York City has been in the Latino community, both from proselytizing activity and from the immigration of Mormons from Latin America. Other important growth has come in immigrant communities from Africa and Asia and the continued migration of Mormons from other parts of the United States. As of 2007 there were 43 Mormon congregations in New York City, including 19 non-English language groups. A signal event for the church was the installation of the MANHATTAN NEW YORK TEMPLE in the early 2000s at Lincoln Square.

James W. Lucas

Morningside Heights. Neighborhood on the Upper West Side of Manhattan between 110th and 123rd streets. Historically farmland and country estates, during the eighteenth century the area was known both as Vandewater Heights, after a local landowner, and Harlem Heights because it overlooks Harlem. The battle of Harlem Heights was fought in 1776 in a buckwheat field near the site of Barnard College. The area began to be developed in the early 1800s, and the Bloomingdale Asylum for the Insane opened in 1818. In the 1890s the area became the home of the tomb of former President Ulysses S. Grant, the Episcopal Cathedral of St. John the Divine, and Columbia University, which was placed in a large new campus designed by McKim, Mead and White on the former asylum site. One last Bloomingdale building still stands in the early twenty-first century, just west of Low Memorial Library.

After construction began on the cathedral, the area was sometimes known as Cathedral Heights (other churches in the area include Riverside and Corpus Christi churches, and St. Paul's Chapel at Columbia). Some called it Columbia Heights. But the name that stuck was one borrowed from the park that was laid out in the 1880s at the foot of the east-facing cliffs, Morningside Park. Although Morningside Heights is widely considered to run from 125th to 110th Streets, historian Andrew S. Dolkart has defined it by the length of the Morningside Park cliffs that give it its name and that extend from 110th to 123rd Streets, where the subway leaves the tunnel to cross West Harlem (Manhattanville) on elevated tracks.

Another of its many nicknames is "the Acropolis of the New World," as the neighborhood is an educational center that includes Barnard College, the Bank Street College of Education, Teachers College, the Manhattan School of Music, and Union and Jewish Theological Seminaries. Many students and faculty members live in the area, which is noted for its many low- and medium-rise apartment buildings, restaurants along Broadway and Amsterdam Avenue, and bookstores. In 2008 the population of approximately 47,000 was ethnically and racially mixed and largely middle class. Efforts to have Morningside Heights declared a historic district began in 1996 and were ongoing in the early twenty-first century.

Christopher J. Schuberth, *The Geology of New York City and Environs* (Garden City: Natural History Press, 1968); Andrew S. Dolkart, *Morningside Heights: A History of Its Architecture and Development* (New York: Columbia University Press, 1998)

Michele Herman, John Rousmaniere

Morningside Park. A 30-acre (12-hectare) public park in northern Manhattan bounded to the north by 123rd Street, to the east by Morningside Avenue, to the south by 110th Street, and to the west by Morningside Drive. In 1867 Central Park Commissioner Andrew Haswell Green recommended establishing a park on the site because a steep ridge of Manhattan schist made it impractical to build there. Architects Jacob Wrey Mould and Calvert Vaux, and landscape architect Frederick Law Olmsted all contributed to the design and construction, which was completed in 1895. In 1968 Columbia University abandoned construction of a gymnasium in the park following weeks of student and community protests.

Caleb Smith

Morning Telegraph. Daily theatrical and racing newspaper, first published weekly as the *Sunday Morning Visitor* (from 12 May 1839) and the *Sunday Mercury Weekly* (from 27 October 1839 to November 1897). It covered horse racing intensively and featured columnists like Ben Hecht, Ring Lardner, and Walter Winchell. The newspaper reached its height under Moe Annenberg, who bought it in 1929 and waged a circulation war with the *Racing Form,* which he soon acquired. Publication ceased on 10 April 1972 due to rising costs and labor disputes, and the *Racing Form* took over the *Telegraph*'s features.

Steven A. Riess

Moroccans. Moroccan New Yorkers number somewhere between 5000 (per the 2000 census count) and 15,000 (per the community estimate). Their occupational profile has changed since the 1990s as Moroccan physicians, researchers, engineers, businesspeople, travel agents, and educators have come to Moroccan neighborhoods, including Atlantic Avenue and Bay Ridge in Brooklyn and Astoria's Steinway Street and Woodside in Queens. Moroccan culture has made its mark on the city's musical scene through the performances of Hassan Hakmoun, whose Gnawan dance recital music mixes West African rhythms with Arab and North African melodies, and jazz singer-songwriter Malika Zarra, whose fusion music also reflects Morocco's complex (Gnawan, Berber, Arabic, French) cultural richness. Moroccans are proud that their nation was the first in the world to seek diplomatic relations with the United States (1777). The American Moroccan Institute, a New York City–based think tank founded in 2003, sponsors panels and conferences among Moroccan ministers, American elected officials and diplomats, and professors from an array of universities.

Paula Hajar

Morris, Gouverneur (*b* Morrisania [now in the Bronx], 31 Jan 1752; *d* Morrisania, 6 Nov 1816). Political leader and diplomat, half-brother of Lewis Morris. He graduated in 1768 from King's College (later Columbia University), gained admission to the bar, and was a delegate to the provincial congress (1775–77) and the Continental Congress (1778–79). After being defeated for reelection he moved to Pennsylvania, from which he was elected to the Constitutional Convention in 1787. He purchased the land that is now Morrisania in the Bronx and soon after left for France, where he arrived in February 1789 and eventually served as the American ambassador (1792–94). After his return to the United States he lived at Morrisania, served in the

Gouverneur Morris

U.S. Senate (1800–1803), and was the chairman of the commission that recommended the construction of the Erie Canal (1810–13). He is buried in the graveyard of St. Ann's Episcopal Church in the Bronx.

Theodore Roosevelt, *Gouverneur Morris* (Boston: Houghton, Mifflin, 1888; repr. New York: AMS, 1981); Mary-Jo Kline, *Gouverneur Morris and the New Nation, 1775–1788* (Salem, N.H.: Ayer, 1978)

Barbara A. Chernow

Morris, Lewis (*b* Morrisania [now in the Bronx], 8 April 1726; *d* Morrisania, 22 Jan 1798). Signer of the Declaration of Independence, half-brother of Gouverneur Morris. The third and last lord of the manor of Morrisania, he was an active supporter of the patriot cause in 1775. He led the delegation to the provincial convention from Westchester and then served in the army (eventually attaining the rank of major-general) as well as the Continental Congress (1775–77). From 1777 to 1790 he was an intermittent member of the upper house of the state legislature. After the war he restored his estate, which had been plundered by the British. Morris is buried in the graveyard of St. Ann's Episcopal Church in the Bronx.

Barbara A. Chernow

Morris, Mark (*b* Seattle, 29 Aug 1956). Choreographer. After training in Seattle, he moved to New York City in 1976. With several dancers he formed the Mark Morris Dance Group (1980), which soon began touring and performing such works as *Gloria* (1981), *New Love Song Waltzes* (1982), *One Charming Night* (1985), *L'Allegro, il Penseroso ed il Moderato* (1988), and *Dido and Aeneas* (1989). By the end of the 1980s, he was widely recognized as the most important young choreographer of the decade. His insistent musicality, scabrous humor, and direct treatment of the sublime and the horrible made him controversial. His work draws on such disparate sources as the writings of Roland Barthes, the rock songs of Yoko Ono, eighteenth-century opera, and Indian ragas. Its musical inspiration and humanistic themes make his choreography closer to early and middle modern dance (Isadora Duncan, Doris Humphrey, Paul Taylor) than to the postmodern choreography of the generation preceding his. In 2001 the Mark Morris Dance Center opened in Brooklyn, becoming the company's first permanent headquarters in the United States. It is used as a rehearsal space for the dance community and as a school that offers dance classes to students of all ages. Morris has also received commissions from such companies as the American Ballet Theatre and the New York City Opera. In 2007 he directed and choreographed *Orfeo ed Euridice* for the Metropolitan Opera.

Joan Acocella

Morris, (Augustus) Newbold (*b* New York City, 2 Feb 1902; *d* New York City, 30 March 1966). Lawyer and public official. He graduated from Yale College (1925) and Yale Law School (1928) and was an assistant corporation counsel during 1934–35. A Republican from the East Side of Manhattan, he was a member of the Board of Aldermen (1935–37) and the president of the City Council (1937–45). In an attempt to continue Fiorello H. La Guardia's reforms he was the unsuccessful mayoral candidate of the No Deal Party in 1945. After two years on the City Planning Commission (1946–48) he again sought the mayoralty in 1949 as the candidate of the Republican, Liberal, and City Fusion parties but lost to the incumbent Democrat William O'Dwyer. In 1952 he was appointed by President Harry S. Truman to investigate corruption as a special assistant to the attorney general. He returned to city government from 1960 to 1965 as the parks commissioner.

Neal C. Garelik

Morris, Richard (*fl ca* 1662). Landowner, great-grandfather of Gouverneur Morris. In 1662 he settled on 2000 acres (800 hectares) of land in the southeastern Bronx. The vast estate was annexed to the city in 1874 and is now known as MORRISANIA. His son Lewis Morris II (1671–1746) was the first American-born chief justice of New York State (1715–33) and the first governor of New Jersey (1738–46), and his great-grandson Lewis Morris, Jr. (1726–98), was a judge, general, state senator, and signer of the Declaration of Independence.

Elizabeth Morris Lefferts, *Descendants of Lewis Morris of Morrisania* (New York: T. A. Wright, 1907); Lucy Dubois Akerly, *The Morris Manor* (New York: Order of Colonial Lords of Manors in America, 1916)

Neal C. Garelik

Morris, Richard B(randon) (*b* New York City, 24 July 1904; *d* New York City, 3 March 1989). Historian. He grew up in the Bronx and attended high school at Townsend Harris Hall in Manhattan. He attended City College (BA 1924) and Columbia University (MA 1925, PhD 1930). His preeminence as a colonialist was secured in 1946 when Columbia University Press published his book *Government and Labor in Early America*. He accepted a full professorship at Columbia in 1949 and gained a wider audience through articles in *American Heritage*, the *Saturday Review*, and the *New York Times Magazine*. His later works include *The Peacemakers: The Great Powers and American Independence* (1965, winner of the Bancroft Prize) and *Seven Who Shaped Our Destiny: The Founding Fathers as Revolutionaries* (1973). He officially retired in 1973 but continued to work on the campus almost daily as the editor of the papers of John Jay. Morris was president of the American Historical Association and the Society of American Historians, and he won the Bruce Catton Prize for Lifetime Achievement in the Writing of History. He lived in suburban Mount Vernon.

Allen J. Share

Morris, Robert H(unter) (*b* New York City, 15 Feb 1802; *d* New York City, 24 Oct 1855). Mayor. The grandson of Richard Morris, the second chief justice of the state supreme court of New York, he studied law and was an assistant district attorney for New York City (1827–33), a state assemblyman (1833–34), and a recorder for the City of New York (1838–41). He rose to prominence within the Democratic Party in 1840 after he uncovered an election scandal involving the Whigs. Nominated for the mayoralty by the Democrats, he was elected in 1841 and reelected in 1842 and 1843. He moved against the Whigs, who dominated the Common Council and were attempting to gain complete control of the city government, and called for a revision of the city charter to increase the mayor's executive powers. His proposals to reform the police were adopted. In 1844 the Democrats were defeated by the American Republicans, a nativist party led by James Harper. Morris became the postmaster for New York City in 1845 and in 1853 was elected a justice of the state supreme court from the first judicial district.

Edward Spann, *The New Metropolis: New York City, 1840–1857* (New York: Columbia University Press, 1981)

Edward T. O'Donnell

Morrisania. Neighborhood in the southwestern Bronx (2000 pop. 44,357), bounded to the north by the Cross Bronx Expressway, to the east by Crotona Park and Prospect Avenue, to the south by East 161st Street, and to the west by Claremont Park and Webster Avenue. From 1670 the land was the estate of the Morris family. In 1790 it was proposed as the site of the federal capital by Lewis Morris, owner of the estate and a signer of the Declaration of Independence. The area remained sparsely populated until Gouverneur Morris, Jr. (a grandson of Morris) allowed an extension of the railroad to be built in 1840 and sold a site adjacent to it for Morrisania Village in 1848. Those who first moved to the area worked in Manhattan, but soon the village had its own piano makers, German breweries, and construction industry. More settlements made along the rail line became the town of Morrisania in 1855, with the original village as its political center. In 1874 the town became part of the 23rd ward when it was annexed to New York City. The Third Avenue elevated line was extended to the area in 1887, offering regular service to Manhattan. Tenements replaced houses, and the neighborhood was already well established and urban by the time the subway was extended to its southeastern corner in 1904. By 1905 its population of 60,000 included Russian Jews, Germans, and some Irish and Italians. Morrisania remained the civic and social center of the borough until 1920, when its population reached 140,000. During the following decade many residents moved to modern housing in the northern sections of the Bronx. In the 1950s blacks and Puerto Ricans moved to Morrisania in large numbers, replacing the earlier white ethnic population. The total population declined during the 1960s and 1970s because of a cycle of drugs, crime, arson, and housing abandonment. The neighborhood was further destabilized by the construction of many super blocks of low-income, high-rise public housing and the demolition of the Third Avenue elevated line. The population rose from the late 1980s on because of new immigrants from Latin America, the Caribbean, and Africa. By the early twenty-first century community groups had renovated deteriorated apartment buildings and filled in vacant blocks with low-rise, owner-occupied affordable housing.

Joel Schwartz, "Community Building on the Bronx Frontier: Morrisania, 1848–1875" (Ph.D. diss., University of Chicago, 1972); Evelyn Gonzalez, *The Bronx* (New York: Columbia University Press, 2004)

Evelyn Gonzalez

Morris Heights. Neighborhood in the west central Bronx. It is centered at Dr. Martin Luther King Jr. Boulevard and bounded to the north by University Heights, to the east by Jerome Avenue, to the south by Highbridge, and to the west by the Harlem River. The land was acquired before the American Revolution by Richard Morris, second chief justice of New York State, and Lewis G. Morris and Fordham Morris raised prize cattle on the estate in the nineteenth century. A village took shape as a dock was built on the Harlem River in 1838 (the present site of Roberto Clemente State Park) and a railroad station was completed in 1866. Trolley lines leading to subways attracted an Irish and Jewish population to apartment buildings in the 1920s. After World War II these residents moved to the northern Bronx and the suburbs, and the neighborhood became predominantly black and Puerto Rican. During the 1980s it attracted many new immigrants, especially from the Dominican Republic (accounting for more than 40 percent of the total), Jamaica, and Guyana, and to a lesser extent from Honduras, El Salvador, Ghana, and Nigeria. Morris Heights is the site of a low-income housing project called the Sedgwick Houses. Hip-hop is said to have originated in the recreation room of 1520 Sedgwick Avenue.

Lloyd Ultan

Morris High School. First public high school in the Bronx, opened in 1897 as the Mixed High School and situated from 1904 at Boston Road and 166th Street. It was renamed successively after Peter Cooper and (in 1903) Gouverneur Morris. The building, a collegiate Gothic Revival structure designed by C. B. J. Snyder and completed in 1904, was constructed of colored brick with limestone and terra-cotta trim and arranged in a modified "H" plan that included a long, rectangular central block from which a central tower rose five stories. By 1925 five high schools opened as offshoots of the school. The interior, exterior, and surrounding avenues in the Morris High School Historic District have landmark status. Well-known graduates of the school include the industrialist Armand Hammer, the baseball player Hank Greenberg, the Nobel laureate Herman Muller, the dancing-school entrepreneur Arthur Murray, and General Colin L. Powell, chairman of the Joint Chiefs of Staff under Presidents George H. W. Bush and Bill Clinton and secretary of state under President George W. Bush. The school closed in 2005.

Gary Hermalyn, *Morris High School and the Creation of the New York City Public High School System* (New York: Bronx County Historical Society, 1993)

Rachel Shor

Morris–Jumel Mansion. Historic house in Manhattan, at Edgecombe Avenue near 160th Street in Harlem Heights. It was built in the Palladian style in 1765 for British army colonel Roger Morris and included a two-story portico with a pediment and an octagonal room to the rear. The commanding location of the mansion, overlooking the Harlem Valley and central Manhattan, made it strategically important in 1776 during the American Revolution, when it was occupied successively by George Washington and by British and Hessian militia. After the war the mansion was a roadside tavern, and in 1810 it became the residence of Stephen and Eliza Jumel, who decorated it in the French Empire style. ELIZA JUMEL, reportedly one of the wealthiest women in the nation, was widowed in 1832, then briefly married former U.S. vice president Aaron Burr, and lived in the house until her death in 1865. The city bought the house in 1903; in the following year the Washington Headquarters Association opened it as a period museum. In the twenty-first century the house is run by Morris-Jumel Mansion Inc.

William Henry Shelton, *The Jumel Mansion* (Boston: Houghton Mifflin, 1916); *Historic Houses in*

Morris High School (designed by C. B. J. Snyder), ca *1905–10*

Morris–Jumel Mansion, 2009

New York City Parks (New York: Department of Parks and Recreation/Historic House Trust of New York City, 1989)

Jonathan Kuhn

Morris Park (i). Neighborhood in the east central Bronx, bounded by Pelham Parkway, Parkchester, and Van Nest. From 1890 to 1913 the area was the site of Morris Park Racetrack, an elegant facility built by the businessman and horse fancier John A. Morris; the Belmont Stakes was run there until 1905, and an air show was held in 1908. After a fire destroyed the track in 1910, streets were cut through and 3019 lots were auctioned off. The neighborhood consists of small one-family houses and two- and three-story apartment buildings. Morris Park Avenue is the principal commercial thoroughfare, and Italians form the largest ethnic group.

Lloyd Ultan

Morris Park (ii). Former neighborhood in Queens. It was developed by the Long Island Improvement Company in 1884 in the area between 113th and 126th streets and between 101st and 89th avenues and was later extended as far south as Liberty Avenue. The name was taken from that of Morris Grove, a picnic park on Atlantic Avenue that had been in operation since the 1840s. Development was initially slow, and in 1890 a tract was acquired by William Ziegler, president of the Royal Baking Powder Company, who entrusted its development to Jere Johnson, a prominent real estate agent from Brooklyn. In 1892 Johnson incorporated the Morris Park Improvement Company and aggressively promoted the sale of lots and houses. A railroad station that opened at Morris Grove in July 1878 was moved to a park one block square on Lefferts Avenue and renamed Morris Park. In 1894 Morris Park was absorbed into the village of Richmond Hill; the railroad station closed in 1940.

Vincent Seyfried

Morse, Samuel F(inley) B(reese) (*b* Charlestown, Mass., 27 April 1791; *d* New York City, 2 April 1872). Inventor and artist. After working as an artist in London, Boston, and Charleston, South Carolina, he moved to New York City in 1823; he favored historical and classical subjects and supported himself and his family through portraiture. A founder of the National Academy of Design in 1826, he was its president until 1842. In 1832 he was appointed a professor of painting and sculpture at the University of the City of New York. While returning from a trip to Europe in that same year, he took part in shipboard conversations about electricity that eventually led him to design an electric telegraph system in his studio at the university. About this time he became involved in the anti-Catholic agitation of the Native American Democratic Association, and he was its unsuccessful mayoral candidate in 1836. With the help of the professor of chemistry Leonard Gale and the mechanic Alfred Vail, he made his telegraph operable between 1837 and 1838 and after several years obtained $30,000 from Congress to build an experimental line between Washington, D.C., and Baltimore. He devised a code of dots and dashes, expressed by short and long electric impulses, in which he sent the first message to Vail in 1844. Private telegraph companies began operating in 1846. Among his other interests was photography: after meeting Louis Daguerre in Paris in 1839 he made the first sun photographs in the United States by placing objects on chemically treated paper, which he then exposed to the sun. In later years he helped Peter Cooper and Cyrus W. Field to lay the first transatlantic telegraph cable. Morse's last home was at 5 West 22nd Street in Manhattan.

Samuel F. B. Morse

Edward Lind Morse, *Samuel F. B. Morse: His Letters and Journals* (Boston: Houghton Mifflin, 1914); Carleton Mabee, *The American Leonardo: A Life of Samuel F. B. Morse* (New York: Alfred A. Knopf, 1943); Paul S. Staiti, *Samuel F. B. Morse* (Cambridge: Cambridge University Press, 1989)

Paul Israel

Morton, Levi P(arsons) (*b* Shoreham, Vt., 16 May 1824; *d* Rhinebeck, N.Y., 16 May 1920). Governor. A successful businessman, he opened a bank on Wall Street in 1863 and was elected to the U.S. House of Representatives in 1878 and again in 1880, resigning during his second term after being appointed minister to France; in this capacity he oversaw the gift of the Statue of Liberty. After returning to the United States, he failed to win a seat in the U.S. Senate but became vice president to Benjamin Harrison in 1889. Elected governor of New York in 1895, he reformed the civil service and oversaw the consolidation of New York City. In 1897 Morton returned to his business, now called the Morton Trust Company, which was absorbed by the Guaranty Trust Company. He lived at 681 Fifth Avenue until 1911, when he moved his family to 998 Fifth Avenue (1912, McKim, Mead and White), becoming one of the first members of the city's elite to embrace apartment living.

Robert McNutt McElroy, *Levi Parsons Morton: Banker, Diplomat, and Statesman* (New York: G. P. Putnam's Sons, 1930)

James E. Mooney

Moses, Robert (*b* New Haven, Conn., 18 Dec 1888; *d* West Islip, N.Y., 29 July 1981). Planner and public official. He graduated from Yale College in 1909, attended Oxford University, and earned a PhD from Columbia University in 1914. His work for the city's bureau of municipal research was sufficiently admired by Governor Alfred E. Smith to gain him an appointment in 1924 as president of the state parks council and the Long Island State Park Commission. By 1930 he built 9700 acres (3900 hectares) of parks on Long Island, including the lido at Jones Beach, the Northern State Parkway, and the Southern Parkway. In 1934 he was made parks commissioner of New York City by Mayor Fiorello H. La Guardia and moved quickly to consolidate his power. He accepted generous perquisites instead of a salary, circumvented civil service rules that prohibited people from holding several public offices (eventually he held 12 at the state and municipal levels), and secured city funds to supplement those granted to work-relief projects under the New Deal: by 1936, 80,000 people were employed on his projects that included the refurbished Central Park Zoo, 255 playgrounds, 11 outdoor swimming pools, Orchard Beach and Jacob Riis parks, and parkways like the Interborough and the Laurelton. As head of the authorities that built the Triborough Bridge and the Marine Parkway Bridge, he used surpluses achieved from toll collections on the Triborough to build a circumferential highway network extending from the Henry Hudson Bridge in Manhattan to the Belt Parkway around Brooklyn (completed in 1940); he also sought to build a suspension bridge between the Battery and Brooklyn in 1939. Although his attempt failed he managed instead to gain control of a combined Triborough Bridge and Tunnel Authority and of the Brooklyn–Battery Tunnel.

In 1939 Moses tried unsuccessfully to have La Guardia place the New York City Housing Authority under the control of a board that would coordinate housing and recreation. He did obtain the mayor's support for his efforts to persuade the Metropolitan Life Insurance Company to invest in housing projects for middle-income tenants on the Lower East Side. After being appointed by La Guardia to the city's planning commission in late 1941, he used revenues from the Triborough Bridge to prepare a list of postwar projects, including highways, parks, hospitals, and housing. In 1943 he prevailed on the state legislature to grant tax relief to Metropolitan Life, as well as the authority, to clear slums to make room for Stuyvesant Town, a complex of 35 buildings containing 8756 residential units. Named the city's construction coordinator by Mayor William O'Dwyer in early 1946, Moses set out to rebuild the city for the modern automobile: he built the Brooklyn–Queens Expressway under the Heights Promenade, as well as highway loops, parking garages, and a civic center in downtown Brooklyn. He proposed similar roadways for lower Manhattan, including a crosstown artery at Broome Street. With state and federal road funds he elevated the Gowanus Expressway above Sunset Park and routed the Cross Bronx Expressway and the Brooklyn–Queens Expressway through blocks of tenements and apartment buildings. In 1946–47 he played a role in the process of choosing a site for the United Nations, which he at first planned to situate in Flushing Meadow but later helped to bring to Turtle Bay by negotiating with John D. Rockefeller, Jr.

Moses was insistent on replacing slums with public housing. He built spartan, 12- and 14-story structures on the Lower East Side and in Harlem, Morrisania, and Brownsville: the city's housing authority completed an average of one project every month from 1947 to 1949. As the head of the mayor's committee on slum clearance, he worked with private developers to exploit Title I of the Housing Act of 1949. He also oversaw a collaboration by New York University and Bellevue Hospital on a medical center at East 34th Street, reached by a crosstown expressway at 30th Street. He conceived other clearance projects for Corlear's Hook on the Lower East Side, Washington Square South, Manhattantown on West 97th Street, and half a dozen other sites that required removing thousands of residents to municipal projects in Brooklyn and the Bronx; 15,000 were displaced by Manhattantown alone, which along with Washington Square South prompted large protests. In the mid-1950s he made plans for Lincoln Center for the Performing Arts, Seward Park, and Penn Station South, where the United Housing Foundation sponsored cooperatives for middle-income residents. In 1955 he reached an agreement with the Port of New York Authority to add a lower deck to the George Washington Bridge (linked to the Henry Hudson Parkway) and to build the Staten Island Expressway and the Verrazano–Narrows Bridge. His use of Title I by 1959 added 16 projects containing 28,000 apartments to the city's housing stock, occupying a total area of 314 acres (127 hectares).

In the 1960s Moses increasingly clashed with those who advocated small-scale neighborhood life and historic preservation. He enraged residents of Greenwich Village with plans to run automobiles through Washington Square as well as residents of the East Side with parking lots in Central Park and his derisive attitude toward Joseph Papp's productions of Shakespeare. He resigned as parks commissioner and from the Mayor's Committee on Slum Clearance in 1960 to plan the New York World's Fair of 1964–65 and was forced from his state appointments by Governor Nelson A. Rockefeller in 1962. He left his last stronghold, the Triborough Bridge and Tunnel Authority, in 1968.

During 40 years as the master builder of New York City, Moses exerted an incalculable influence on the five boroughs and their nearby suburbs. He admired large structures and the automobile (although he himself never learned to drive) and hated slums. His projects affected every borough: he uprooted white-collar professionals in Washington Square and on the Upper West Side, relieved congestion in downtown Brooklyn, cut through the Bronx with the Cross Bronx Expressway, and built bridges and motorways that opened Queens and Staten Island to the masses. All told he built 13 vehicular spans and gave the city more superhighways than Los Angeles (416 miles, or 669 kilometers). From 1939 until his death he lived at 1 Gracie Terrace in Manhattan.

Robert A. Caro, *The Power Broker: Robert Moses and the Fall of New York* (New York: Alfred A. Knopf, 1974); Joel Schwartz, *The New York Approach: Robert Moses, Urban Liberals, and Redevelopment of the Inner City* (Columbus: Ohio State University Press, 1993); Hillary Ballon and Kenneth T. Jackson, eds., *Robert Moses and the Modern City: The Transformation of New York* (New York: W. W. Norton, 2007)

Joel Schwartz

Mosholu. Neighborhood in the northwestern Bronx, lying along Mosholu Avenue. It was a hamlet during the nineteenth century and was given the Algonquin name for Tibbett's Brook, which probably translates as "smooth stones" or "small stones"; there was a post office on the Albany Post Road and a wagon shop, a general store, a Methodist church, and a few houses. The population increased after Mosholu Parkway was planned in 1888 and the subway along Broadway was extended to 242nd Street in the early twentieth century. Later trolley and bus connections along upper Broadway led to the construction of a few one-family frame houses and brick houses. Many who live in Mosholu consider themselves residents of Riverdale.

Gary D. Hermalyn

Moskowitz [Israels; née Lindner]**, Belle** (*b* New York City, 5 Oct 1877; *d* New York City, 2 Jan 1933). Political strategist. Born to East Prussian immigrants in Harlem, she began her career in social reform and did settlement work at the Educational Alliance in 1900. She married the architect Charles Henry Israels in 1903 and shortly afterward joined the local chapter of the Council of Jewish Women, which sponsored her campaign to license dance halls in 1908–10. Her interest in reform eventually led her to campaign on behalf of the Committee of Fourteen, which fought prostitution, as well as for the Progressive Party, woman suffrage, and fusion candidates for offices in New York City.

Widowed in 1911, she married Henry Moskowitz in 1914. From 1913 to 1916 she was a labor mediator in the dress and shirtwaist trade, and in 1918 she mobilized women in support of the gubernatorial candidacy of Alfred E. Smith, who after his election appointed the Reconstruction Commission at her suggestion to plan the state's future. As the commission's executive secretary, Moskowitz appointed Robert Moses as its chief of staff and oversaw the publication of reports that formed the core of Smith's later legislative programs. She also helped Smith to promote a port authority, became the first publicity director of the Democratic State Committee, and managed Smith's campaigns for reelection and for the Democratic presidential nomination in 1928. Moskowitz belonged to the Democratic Union of Women and the Women's City Club and was a publicist for the Empire State Building: after 1928 she was responsible for having Lewis Hine photograph its construction.

Elisabeth Israels Perry, *Belle Moskowitz: Feminine Politics and the Exercise of Power in the Age of Alfred E. Smith* (New York: Oxford University Press, 1987; repr. Routledge, 1992)

Elisabeth Israels Perry

Moskowitz, Henry (*b* Huşi, Romania, 27 Sept 1879; *d* New York City, 17 Dec 1936). Reformer. He grew up on the Lower East Side, where he worked in settlement programs. In 1898 he was inspired by Lillian Wald and Felix Adler to work toward the formation of the Downtown Ethical Society (later called Madison House). A leader of movements against prostitution and in favor of the moderate labor reformers known as industrial pacifists, he supported the Progressive Party and in 1912 sought election to Congress from the twelfth district. In the same year he became president of the Municipal Civil Service Commission under Mayor John Purroy Mitchel. Later in his career Moskowitz supported Alfred E. Smith, of whom he wrote a biography with Norman Hapgood in 1928 (*Up From the City Streets: Alfred E. Smith*). His wife was Belle Moskowitz, whom he married in 1914.

Elisabeth Israels Perry

mosques. Muslim houses of worship and centers of Islamic communities. Although the first Muslims likely arrived in New York City as African slaves in the eighteenth century, it was not until 1907 that a group of European Muslim immigrants founded the American Mohammedan Society, the first Islamic community centered on a mosque. The group probably rented space until 1931, when they bought property on Powers Street in Williamsburg, Brooklyn. Powers Street remained the only known mosque in New York City until 1939, when Moroccan Sheik Daoud Ahmed Faisal founded the Islamic Mission of America, or Masjid Daoud, which still existed in the early 2000s in its original location at 143 State Street in Brooklyn Heights.

The number of Muslims in New York City increased rapidly during the last third of the twentieth century, and they rented former commercial and industrial spaces, brownstones, and shuttered schools for use as prayer halls, or they simply gathered in one another's apartments. By 1980 there were eight or nine mosques in the city; by 1991 that number had increased to 37, with 12 in Queens, 15 in Brooklyn, six in Manhattan, two in the Bronx, and two in Staten Island. By 1994 there were more than 70, and by 2009 more than 150, serving between 600,000 and 800,000 Muslim New Yorkers.

The city's first purpose-built mosque was constructed in 1983 by the Islamic Center of Corona, or Masjid Al-falah, at 42-12 National Street in Corona, Queens. The structure, with a modest dome and minaret, can accommodate up to 200 men in its main prayer space and has an adjacent women's prayer room hidden behind smoky glass as well as a funeral parlor in the rear. In 1991 the city's second dedicated mosque was built at 137–58 Geranium Avenue in Flushing by the Muslim Center of New York. This 18,600-square-foot (1728-square-meter) building provides space for up to 500 worshippers and also has a community hall, educational facilities, space for administrative offices, and two rental units. The most prominent mosque in New York City is the Islamic Cultural Center on 96th Street and Third Avenue in Manhattan. Completed in 1991, it was financed without the payment of interest by its local community as well as by the governments of Islamic member states of the United Nations, including Kuwait, Iran, Iraq, Saudi Arabia, Pakistan, and Turkey, with King Hassan II of Morocco contributing the interior furnishings. Architect Michael McCarthy of Skidmore, Owings and Merrill designed an edifice whose architecture favors no single nation's traditions. Rather, it stands as a landmark for all Muslims in the city, and its location on the border of the Upper East Side and East Harlem is a symbolic reminder of the two broad and distinct Muslim constituencies in the city: the immigrant and the African American (see Nation of Islam).

Most mosques in New York City, however, are fashioned out of converted space. In many instances, a mosque inhabits only part of its building, leaving the exterior mute to the particular life of the community within. It is important to note that a mosque is not merely a structure, but the center of an Islamic community, and thus it undertakes the many roles that any community center must assume. The purpose of a mosque is defined by more than a dozen functions, only one of which is the furnishing of a place for prayer. It must also provide for the housing of poor Muslims, the distribution of charity, the education of its members in both sacred and secular affairs, and the building of community generally. In keeping with this wide mission, 14 of New York City's mosques house accredited private schools, five of which offer secondary education.

In recent years, mosques have gained architectural character as the city's Muslim population has grown and become more rooted in place. Whereas most Islamic communities traditionally shied away from the attention drawn by decoration, long residence and integration within many neighborhoods have permitted mosques a sense of belonging to the wider city that is reflected in more distinctive architectural ornament. Although few buildings boast the prominence and scale of the Islamic Cultural Center, mosques have begun to reveal themselves to the outside world with modest domes, minarets, and Arabic script. Their facades reflect the continuing transition of New York City's Muslims from a private minority into a more public collective, communicating their members' increasing role in the life of the city.

Marc Ferris, "'To Achieve the Pleasures of Allah': Immigrant Muslims in New York City, 1893–1991," *Muslim Communities in North America*, ed. Yvonne Yazbeck Haddad and Jane Idleman Smith (Albany, N.Y.: State University of New York Press, 1994), 209–30; Edward Grazda and Jerilynn D. Dodds, *New York Masjid: The Mosques of New York City* (New York: PowerHouse Books, 2002)

See also Muslims.

Andrew A. Kryzak

Most, Johann (Joseph) (*b* Augsburg [now in Germany], 5 Feb 1846; *d* Cincinnati, 17 March 1906). Anarchist. His radical views and calls for the assassination of leaders led to his imprisonment throughout Europe. In December 1882 he left London for New York City, where he continued to produce his newspaper, *Freiheit,* from an office at 167 William Street and published *The Science of Revolutionary Warfare* (1885), a manual of terrorism recommending dynamite as the most appropriate means for waging class warfare. He also produced a number of anticapitalist plays at the German-language Thalia Theater (1896) at 46 Bowery and often took the leading roles; in *The Strike* (1901) he portrayed himself. A well-known public speaker, he toured the country and was arrested a number of times for publishing statements considered seditious and derogatory to the United States. Most spent three terms in prison on Blackwell's Island and was due to be deported under the Espionage Act when he died during a speaking tour.

Frederic Trautmann, *The Voice of Terror: A Biography of Johann Most* (Westport, Conn.: Greenwood, 1980)

Kevin Kenny

Mostel, Zero [Samuel Joel] (*b* New York City, 28 Feb 1915; *d* Philadelphia, 8 Sept 1977). Actor and comedian. From 1942 he worked as a stand-up comedian in Greenwich Village and became noted for a zany, exaggerated, improvisational style influenced by the Yiddish theater of the 1930s. During the McCarthy period he was blacklisted as a communist (1952–58); forced to take up painting to support his family, he rented a studio on 28th Street. His experiences during these years are depicted in Martin Ritt's film *The Front* (1976), in which he appeared. His acting career revived in the early 1960s and he won Tony Awards for his performances in the Broadway musicals *A Funny Thing Happened on the Way to the Forum* (1962) and *Fiddler on the Roof* (1964), often considered his best works.

Jared Brown, *Zero Mostel: A Biography* (New York: Atheneum, 1989)

Tina Margolis

Mother African Methodist Episcopal [AME] Zion Church. Founding congregation of the African Methodist Episcopal Zion Church and the oldest organized African American church in New York State. Mother AME Zion built its first permanent structure at 156 Church Street in 1800. The church was a link to the Underground Railroad, gaining enough prominence to be referred to as the Freedom Church. It is rumored that the church was the site where abolitionist and activist Sojourner Truth changed her name from Isabella Baumfree. In 1853 Mother AME Zion built a church in Seneca Village, later the site of Central Park. In 1914 it moved to a formerly Episcopal sanctuary at 151 West 136th Street; between 1923 and 1925 the church built its present structure at 146 West 137th Street. Membership increased from 300 to more than 1000 because of the efforts of the pastor, James W. Brown, who became a bishop in 1936. The James Varick Community Center, named for the denomination's first bishop, was built near the church in 1972. In the early twenty-first century the church occupies seven buildings, of which three were built and four were purchased; it continues to act as a hub for social reform and activism in the central Harlem community.

Dennis C. Dickerson

Mother Horn [Horn, Rosa Artimus] (*b* Sumter, S.C., 1886; *d* Baltimore, 11 May 1976). Religious leader. Building her reputation as a faith-healer in Georgia and Illinois, she was ordained a Pentecostal minister in Indiana. After forming a church in Evanston, Illinois, she moved to Brooklyn in 1926 and to Harlem in 1930, where she formed Mount Calvary Assembly Hall of the Pentecostal Faith Church at 400 Lenox Avenue. During the 1930s she became well known for her impassioned evangelical meetings at the church, which regularly attracted audiences of 3000 and were broadcast every Wednesday and Sunday by the radio station WHN. Several other stations along the eastern seaboard soon carried the program, and Horn eventually opened branches of her church in five cities.

Kevin Kenny

Motherwell, Robert (*b* Aberdeen, Wash., 24 Jan 1915; *d* Provincetown, Mass., 16 July 1991). Painter. He grew up in San Francisco and became noted for using black, white, and ocher in his paintings because of his love for the scenery of California. Influenced by Paul Cézanne and Henri Matisse, he traveled to France and formed connections with the European surrealists Marcel Duchamp, Max Ernst, and André Breton before settling in Greenwich Village in 1932. A leader with Jackson Pollock, Willem de Kooning, and Mark Rothko of the American abstract expressionist movement in the 1930s and 1940s, Motherwell was married to the painter Helen Frankenthaler and taught at Hunter College.

Leslie Gourse

Motley, Constance Baker (*b* New Haven, Conn., 14 Sept 1921; *d* New York City, 28 Sept 2005). Civil rights leader and judge. She was the ninth among twelve children born to immigrants from the British West Indies; her father was a Yale fraternity house chef. Her youthful protest against discrimination at a public beach brought her to the attention of local businessman and philanthropist Clarence Blakeslee, who funded her college education at Fisk University (1939–40) and New York University (1941–43). After graduating from Columbia Law School (1946) she worked for the National Association for the Advancement of Colored People Legal Defense Fund, cooperating with Thurgood Marshall and Jack Greenberg on landmark cases. She wrote the original complaint in the case *Brown v. Board of Education* (1954) and won nine of the 10 cases she argued before the U.S. Supreme Court; her pleadings achieved James Meredith's entry into the University of Mississippi (*Meredith v. Fair,* 1962), ended segregation in Memphis's restaurants (*Watson v. City of Memphis,* 1963), and reversed the convictions of African American students who had sat in at Birmingham lunch counters (*Gober v. City of Birmingham,* 1963). She also sat vigil in bombed churches, visited Martin Luther King, Jr., in jail in Birmingham in 1963, and with her family personally integrated a New York City apartment house (1961). Motley was the first African American woman to serve in the New York State Senate (1964) and the first female borough president of Manhattan (1965–66). On 25 January 1966 President Lyndon B. Johnson named her the first African American female district court judge in the Southern District of New York, a jurisdiction she subsequently administered as chief judge (1982) and later served as senior judge (1986). Her important legal decisions guaranteed prisoners due process rights (*Sostre v. McGinnis,* 1970), forced the law firm Sullivan and Cromwell to hire more female associates (*Blank v. Sullivan and Cromwell,* 1975), and protected copyright holders against quick-print reproduction of their writings without compensation or permission (*Basic Books v. Kinko's Graphics,* 1991). She wrote an autobiography, *Equal Justice under Law* (1988).

George J. Lankevich

Mott, Valentine (*b* Glen Cove, N.Y., 20 Aug 1785; *d* New York City, 26 April 1865). Physician and surgeon. He began his medical studies in 1804 at Columbia College (MD 1806). Because physicians in New York City at the time could acquire clinical experience mainly in prisons and almshouses under the supervision of largely corrupt politicians, he promptly left for London and Edinburgh. Upon his return to the city in 1809 he was offered the chair of surgery at Columbia. He remained there until 1826, when he resigned over disagreements with the administration. With a few associates he then founded Rutgers Medical College, which disbanded a few years later. He returned in 1830 to Columbia and then taught at the University Medical College. Mott was a champion of the poor and a proponent of the use of cadavers in surgical instruction, a notion then considered sacrilegious. He was a president of the New York Academy of Medicine, a fellow of the Imperial Academy of Paris and the Medical Society of London, and a Knight of Constantinople.

Shan Jayakumar

Mott Haven. Neighborhood in the southwestern Bronx (2000 pop. 49,031), bounded to the north by East 149th Street and St. Mary's Park, to the south by the Bronx Kill, to the west by the Harlem River, and to the east by the southeasterly continuation of East 149th Street and the East River. Developed in 1850 as an industrial village and as a suburb for people working in Manhattan by Jordan L. Mott, the owner of a nearby ironworks, it soon included the residential and industrial sections of North New York and Port Morris. After the Third Avenue elevated line was extended in 1886 it became a fashionable area with elegant new row houses, and the industrial section became a center of piano manufacturing. Germans and Jews settled throughout; Alexander Avenue was largely Irish and the northwestern section Italian. Despite a thriving commercial section and the convenience of new subways, by 1940 the piano industry had disappeared, the neighborhood was less affluent, and much of the old housing was scheduled for demolition under slum clearance programs. After 1950 the population became increasingly black and Puerto Rican, and many areas were rebuilt with low-income, high-rise public housing. The neighborhood suffered less housing devastation than other parts of the Bronx in the 1960s because of its mix of row houses (some owner-occupied) and its public housing for the poor. From the 1990s on, many of Mott Haven's row houses were bought and renovated by middle-class blacks. The area contains the Alexander Avenue Historic District, a thriving antique furniture retail center in its southernmost streets, and two historic churches, St. Ann's Episcopal Church (built in 1841 under the auspices of Gouverneur Morris, Jr.) and St. Jerome's Roman Catholic Church.

Evelyn Gonzalez, *The Bronx* (New York: Columbia University Press, 2004)

Evelyn Gonzalez

Mould, Jacob Wrey (*b* Chislehurst [now in London], 1825; *d* New York City, 14 June 1886). Architect. After immigrating to the United States he achieved immediate success in New York City for his polychromatic design of the All Souls Church, popularly called the "Church of the Holy Zebra," at Fourth Avenue and 20th Street (1853–55). Among the many structures he designed were several in Central Park with Frederick Law Olmsted and Calvert Vaux: Bethesda Terrace (1858–71), the Music Stand (1863–65, demolished), the Boathouse (1870–71, demolished), the Sheepfold (1870–71), the Stable (1870–71), and the Casino (1870–71, demolished). He also designed the initial buildings for the Metropolitan Museum of Art (1874–80) and the American Museum of Natural History (1874–77) and translated from Italian to English some librettos of Mozart's operas.

Marjorie Pearson

Mount Eden. Neighborhood in the west central Bronx, lying within Tremont. Named for Rachel Eden, who bought a hilly farm there in 1820, the area was farmland into the early decades of the twentieth century. During the 1920s and 1930s apartment buildings were built that were occupied mostly by wealthy Jews, and Bronx–Lebanon Hospital opened in 1942. After 1975 the population became mostly black and Latin American. Mount Eden Avenue and Mount Eden Parkway form the main thoroughfare. The novelist E. L. Doctorow grew up in the neighborhood.

Lloyd Ultan

Mount Hope. Neighborhood in the central Bronx, lying within Tremont along Tremont Avenue and bounded to the west by the Grand Concourse. The land once belonged to the Morris family and for many years was used for farming. In 1868 it became known as the Western Reserve. In the 1920s and 1930s a large number of Jews moved to five- and six-story apartment buildings in the area. By the early 1990s most of the inhabitants were black and Latin American. The neighborhood is the site of a public school, the Mount Hope School.

Lloyd Ultan

Mount Loretto–Mission of the Immaculate Virgin. Orphanage opened at 53 Warren Street in 1870 by Irish immigrant John Drumgoole as St. Vincent's Home for Homeless Boys of All Occupations, in response to the prevailing policy of children's aid groups of sending thousands of homeless Irish Catholic children (orphaned by Ireland's Great Potato Famine and then the Civil War) to western states in the late 1860s. In 1882–83 the orphanage expanded from its 10-story building at 80 Lafayette Street in Manhattan to Pleasant Plains on the southern shore of Staten Island, where Drumgoole founded a working farm called Mount Loretto. One of his innovations there was providing vocational training for the children. Drumgoole was ordained at the age of 52; at his death in 1888, the mission cared for 2000 children at Lafayette Street and Mount Loretto, which had become one of the largest farms in New York state. The mission continued to accommodate children throughout the twentieth century until large orphanages began to give way to foster homes and smaller facilities. Mount Loretto ended its city contracts for foster care in 1995. The mission began to focus on developmentally disabled children, especially those with autism, and in recent years has sought to serve only Staten Island rather than the entire city. In 2002 Mount Loretto began a partnership with the GRACE Foundation, a nonprofit advocacy group for families with autistic children, and continues to serve 1000 people daily with its various programs.

Nancy V. Flood

Mount Neboh Baptist Church. Church formed in 1937. The congregation originally met in the home of its first pastor and moved several times before it moved in 1980 to 1883 Adam Clayton Powell Jr. Boulevard at the corner of 114th Street. This building, which is the former home of Temple Ansche Chased and the Roman Catholic Church of Our Lady of the Miraculous Medal, is one of only two sanctuaries in New York City to have housed Jewish, Catholic, and Protestant congregations. Although currently a Christian house of worship, the building retains a skylight and stained-glass windows that depict traditional Jewish symbols.

Sharon Wilkins

Mount Olivet Baptist Church. Located at 201–203 Malcolm X Boulevard and 120th Street, the building was built by architect Arnold W. Brunner in 1907 for Temple Israel, a synagogue for German Americans. The largely African American Mount Olivet congregation, which had been founded in 1876 on West 26th Street, bought the building in 1925.

Sharon Wilkins

Mount Pleasant. Obsolete name for a neighborhood in northwestern Queens east of Maurice Avenue, just northeast of Maspeth. It appears only in the Beers's atlas of 1873 and on Beers's wall map of 1886. The land rises steeply from Maspeth Creek to a height of 132 feet (40 meters) above sea level; the hill is now traversed by 69th Street. As late as 1922 the area formed Maurice's Woods, a tract of 72 acres (29 hectares) donated to the Episcopal Church for a seminary by James Maurice, a former congressman; the tract is now covered by houses.

Vincent Seyfried

Mount Prospect. Hill on the terminal moraine in Brooklyn, just east of the intersection of Eastern Parkway and Flatbush Avenue. Before the Battle of Long Island (August 1776) it was used as an observation post by the American forces. In 1856 a reservoir was built on the site to supply the western part of the borough. The city took part of the land for a park in 1937 and designated the rest for the Brooklyn Central Library. The name inspired those of Prospect Park and Prospect Heights.

John J. Gallagher

Mount Sinai Hospital. Hospital incorporated in 1852 as the Jews' Hospital in the City of New York and opened on West 28th Street between Seventh and Eighth avenues in 1855. Initially it admitted only patients who were Jewish, but after treating a large number of Union soldiers during the Civil War it admitted patients regardless of their background, and in 1866 it took its current name. In 1872 the hospital moved from a building that held only 45 beds to much larger quarters on Lexington Avenue between 66th and 67th streets, where it opened a modern laboratory, a training school for nurses (1881–1971), an outpatient department, a house staff system, and specialty departments that included the first pediatrics department (1878) established in a general hospital and the first neurological service (1900) in a hospital in New York City. The site at Lexington Avenue was ideal at first, and the number of beds eventually expanded from 120 to 225, but the hospital was nevertheless unable to meet the demands of a rapidly growing city. In 1898 land was purchased at Fifth Avenue and 100th Street and a new hospital consisting of 10 buildings with 456 beds was completed in 1904. During the world wars Mount Sinai sponsored the Base Hospital no. 3 of the American Expeditionary Forces and the Third General Hospital of the U.S. Army, both composed of a core group of physicians and nurses from the hospital. Research assumed a larger role at 100th Street following World War I, and many medical contributions were made: 21 diseases, tests, instruments, and phenomena were named after physicians at the hospital, including

Crohn's disease, Tay–Sachs disease, the Shwartzman phenomenon, and the Rubin test. In 1910 postgraduate training of physicians began in conjunction with Columbia University, and in 1953 Mount Sinai was named a major affiliate of the university. The Mount Sinai Medical School received its first charter in 1963, became affiliated with the City University of New York in 1967, and opened in 1968. Authorized to grant the MD and the PhD, it was the first medical school in New York City after the Flexner Report (1910) to be developed by a hospital rather than a university. Now known as the Mount Sinai Medical Center, it is internationally recognized as one of the top teaching hospitals in the world, and as of 2007 it had 1171 beds and a permanent medical staff of nearly 1800.

Joseph Hirsh and Beka Doherty, *The First Hundred Years of the Mount Sinai Hospital of New York, 1852–1952* (New York: Random House, 1952); Janie Brown Nowak, *The Forty-Seven Hundred: The Story of the Mount Sinai Hospital School of Nursing* (Canaan, N.H.: Phoenix, 1981)

Barbara J. Niss

Mount Vernon Hotel Museum and Garden. Historic house at 421 East 61st Street in Manhattan, built as a carriage house in 1799. Along with 23 acres (10 hectares) of surrounding land, it was owned by Colonel William S. Smith and Abigail Adams Smith, daughter of John Adams. The building was converted in 1826 and for seven years was a fashionable day resort called the Mount Vernon Hotel. After purchasing the building in 1924, the Colonial Dames of America restored and furnished it, and in 1939 it opened as the Abigail Adams Smith Museum. In 2000 it was renamed the Mount Vernon Hotel Museum and Garden; it has nine period rooms, a collection of federal artifacts and furniture, and a garden in the eighteenth-century style. The building is one of few in the city constructed of Manhattan schist.

Linda Elsroad

movie theaters. The first movie theaters in New York City were opened in storefronts about the end of the nineteenth century. Nickelodeons became popular in the following decade and the city soon had hundreds of them. These began with little more than a projector, a screen, a piano, and camp chairs and slowly became decorated auditoriums. The nickelodeon took on some of the characteristics of the vaudeville hall and the stage theater and evolved into what became known as the movie palace. Early movie palaces included the Audubon Theatre and Ballroom (1912, seating 2368) at Broadway and West 165th Street and the Regent Theater (1913, seating 1800), now on Adam Clayton Powell Jr. Boulevard at 116th Street. Both designed by Thomas W. Lamb, the Audubon was owned by William Fox, founder of 20th Century Fox; the Regent was managed by Samuel "Roxy" Rothafel and featured a facade modeled after that of the Doge's Palace in Venice.

The American movie theater reached its peak during the 1920s as a luxurious and often exotic place. Theaters seating several thousand patrons offered weekly programs including not only motion pictures but vaudeville, organ recitals, orchestras, comedians, and magicians; they also served as civic centers for such events as high school graduation ceremonies. New York City had more than 1000 theaters, many concentrated in Times Square and others on the "subway circuit" in various neighborhoods. A small group of entrepreneurs came to control hundreds of theaters in regional and national circuits, including Fox, the vaudeville promoters B. F. Keith and E. F. Albee, and Marcus Loew, builder of the largest chain of theaters in the city. Rothafel managed only a few theaters, among them the Roxy Theater at 50th Street and Seventh Avenue, known as the "cathedral of the motion picture" (Walter Ahlschlager, 1927, seating 6000; demolished) and Radio City Music Hall at Rockefeller Center (Associated Architects, 1932). Showcase theaters were later built by such corporations as Paramount and Warner Brothers. The leading theater architects in the city were Lamb, John Eberson, C. Howard Crane, G. Albert Lansburgh, and the firm of Rapp and Rapp. Crane, Lamb, and Eberson began as architects of legitimate stage theaters; these and their early movie palaces relied on plaster ornamental designs in the Adam style. Three of Lamb's early movie theaters on Broadway, the Strand (1914, seating 3000; demolished), the Rivoli (1917, seating 2000; demolished), and the Capitol (1919, seating 5000; demolished), helped to make Times Square the focus not only of stage theaters but also of movie theaters. His later work, in a similar style, included the Loew's State (1921, seating 3300; demolished) at the headquarters of Loew's firm in Times Square and the Albee Theatre in downtown Brooklyn (1925, seating 3200; demolished).

Other architects stressed the exotic: theaters called the Rialto, the Tivoli, the Oriental, the Paradise, and the Valencia were designed in styles reminiscent of Baroque Spain, ancient Egypt, India, and the Far East. Rapp and Rapp designed theaters for Paramount and Loew's in a regal French manner, among them the Paramount Theater (1926, seating 3700; gutted) in the Paramount Building on Times Square and the Brooklyn Paramount (1928, seating 4100; converted) in the theater district of downtown Brooklyn. Crane's series of immense theaters for Fox included the Brooklyn Fox Theatre (1928, seating 4000; demolished), combining Baroque, South Asian, and art deco ornament; and the Roxy Theater, which combined elements from a variety of ancient Egyptian, Greek, and Roman sources. Eberson developed the so-called atmospheric theater: in place of a domed classical ceiling was a blue plaster surface on which cloudlike images were projected by a hidden machine; electric lightbulbs simulated stars, and the walls resembled the backdrops of a stage. His work included Loew's 72nd Street Theatre on the East Side of Manhattan (1932, seating 3200; demolished), designed in an extravagant southeast Asian style.

Among the largest and most elaborate movie palaces in New York City were five "wonder theaters" built for Loew's in 1929–30 in the major population centers outside midtown Manhattan: Brooklyn was served by the Kings Theatre in Flatbush (Rapp and Rapp, seating 3670), Queens by the Valencia Theatre on Jamaica Avenue (Eberson, seating 3550), the Bronx by the Paradise Theatre on the Grand Concourse at Fordham Road (Eberson,

Mount Vernon Hotel Museum, 2009

seating 3885), upper Manhattan by the 175th Street Theatre on Broadway (Lamb, seating 3560), and New Jersey by the Jersey Theatre in Jersey City (Rapp and Rapp, seating 3300). The Kings Theatre and the Jersey Theatre were French in style, the 175th Street Theatre was Oriental, the Valencia Theatre was Spanish, and the Paradise Theatre was Italian (its sources included Michelangelo's tombs for the Medici). There were various reasons for the explosion of exotic designs. The architectural settings of the theaters unquestionably added to the fantasy of moviegoing; the theater owner A. J. Balaban, who formed the firm of Balaban and Katz in Chicago and later operated the Roxy Theater, spoke of bringing the fabulous sights of the world to the masses. Moreover, movie palaces flourished at a time when historically derived styles were generally accepted, before eclecticism gave way to modernism.

During the Depression the building of large movie palaces ceased, and architects of smaller theaters turned from the extravagance of the 1920s to the abstract, streamlined styles of the 1930s. Eberson produced a series of small, modernistic theaters, including the Lane Theatre in Staten Island (1938, seating 600). After the advent of television in the 1950s, movie theaters no longer dominated urban entertainment. Through the twentieth century, enormous movie palaces seating thousands could no longer function economically and gradually fell victim to conversion and demolition. Smaller theaters presented independent and foreign films, including the 586-seat Paris Theater, which opened in 1948 on 58th Street near Fifth Avenue and showed mainly French films; in 2008 it remained one of the oldest art houses in the country and continued to show one movie per week. As giant theater multiplexes swept the country at the turn of the twenty-first century, New York City, despite losses like the single-screen Beekman Theater, which closed in 2005, remained a center of independent film. Theaters such as Film Forum on West Houston Street (1970), the Walter Reade Theater at Lincoln Center (1990), and BAM Rose Cinemas at the Brooklyn Academy of Music (1998) showed independent and avant-garde movies as well as revivals, while megatheaters on 34th and 42nd streets showed more commercial films. Movies were also shown on rooftops and in museums, universities, libraries, and parks around the city.

Ben M. Hall, *The Best Remaining Seats: The Story of the Golden Age of the Movie Palace* (New York: Clarkson N. Potter, 1961); David Naylor, *American Picture Palaces: The Architecture of Fantasy* (New York: Van Nostrand Reinhold, 1981); David Nasaw, *Going Out: The Rise and Fall of Public Amusement* (Cambridge, Mass.: Harvard University Press, 1999)

See also LOEWS CORPORATION, LOEW'S PARADISE.

Anthony W. Robins

Moving Day. The English custom of celebrating May Day led to the practice of signing leases on 1 May in New York City. In the nineteenth century, a chronic housing shortage and high rents led tenants in the city to move frequently in the hope of improving their situation; all trade ceased that day because the streets were filled with traffic. After the economic depression of 1873 ended, more housing was built and tenants gradually moved less often. Commercial leases are still effective on 1 May or (in keeping with the English tradition of paying land rents at Michaelmas) 1 October.

Alana Erickson Coble

Moynihan, Daniel Patrick (*b* Tulsa, Okla., 16 March 1927; *d* New York City, 26 March 2003). Senator, educator, and diplomat. He grew up in the Hell's Kitchen neighborhood of Manhattan, attended Tufts University (BA 1948, MA 1949, PhD 1961), and in 1965 was an unsuccessful candidate for the presidency of the New York City Council. He held various positions under Presidents John F. Kennedy, Lyndon B. Johnson, Richard M. Nixon, and Gerald R. Ford, including those of ambassador to India (1973–75) and ambassador to the United Nations (1975–76); he also taught at Harvard University, first as director of the Joint Center for Urban Studies at Harvard and the Massachusetts Institute of Technology (1966–69), and later as professor of education and urban politics (1969–73) and professor of government (1973–77). As the Democratic nominee for the U.S. Senate in New York in 1976, he defeated Senator James L. Buckley. Reelected in 1982, 1988, and 1994, he became chairman of the Senate Committee on Finance in 1993. His many books on politics, ethnicity, race relations, and poverty include *Beyond the Melting Pot: The Negroes, Puerto Ricans, Jews, Italians and Irish of New York City* (with Nathan Glazer, 1963).

Douglas E. Schoen, *Pat: A Biography of Daniel Patrick Moynihan* (New York: Harper and Row, 1979)

Lee R. Hiltzik

Mozart Hall. Political organization formed in 1858 by Fernando Wood after his expulsion from Tammany Hall. It was named for a building at the corner of Bleecker Street and Broadway in Greenwich Village. A force in city politics throughout the 1860s, the organization provided Wood with the popular support he needed to do battle with Tammany Hall. It was intended by him to be the true representative of the Democratic Party and of Irish and German immigrants. The most notable achievement of the organization was to secure school wards for Germans. More closely allied with Tammany Hall after the Civil War, Mozart Hall lost much of its power and disbanded in 1867.

James Bradley

Ms. Semimonthly magazine. Launched as a 30-page insert in the December 1971 issue of *New York* magazine, its first stand-alone issue appeared the following month in 1972. Founded by several women, including the activist Gloria Steinem and it first editor Letty Cottin Pogrebin, it began as a monthly publication that covered topics such as the domestic battering of women and alternatives to mastectomy, encouraged advertisements aimed at female readers, and broke with a long-standing policy among women's magazines by making relatively few references to its advertisers in its editorial pages. *Ms.* was sold to an Australian publisher in November 1987, which sold it in turn to Lang Communications in October 1989. In the early 1990s the magazine had a circulation of more than 100,000 and carried no advertising. Since 2001 the magazine has been published by the Feminist Majority Foundation, which is based in Los Angeles and in Arlington, Virginia.

Laura Gwinn

MTA. See METROPOLITAN TRANSPORTATION AUTHORITY.

MTA Arts for Transit. Program established in 1985 by the Metropolitan Transportation Authority (MTA) to install permanent and temporary works of art in the rapid-transit network. Projects include rotating exhibitions in select subway and regional rail stations, posters on trains featuring "Poetry in Motion" and transit-inspired artwork, and sculpture and mosaics installed as part of station renovations. Tom Otterness and Roy Lichtenstein are among the well-known artists whose work is featured in New York City's subway stations—at the 14th Street station under Eighth Avenue and in the Times Square station, respectively. Arts for Transit also manages Music Under New York, which oversees a diverse group of subway musicians.

Michael C. Repka

MTV [Music Television]. Cable television service based in New York City that spawned the popularity of music videos. Conceived by John Lack, an executive at Warner Amex Satellite Entertainment Company, it began showing videos 24 hours a day on 1 August 1981. The service quickly won the support of record companies, which saw it as a vehicle for promoting their artists, and of corporate sponsors eager to reach its youthful audience. It claimed 15 million subscribers by the end of its first year in operation. In 1985 the service was taken over by Viacom International, a media conglomerate that expanded the service worldwide. After the rise of competing outlets for music videos such as the Internet in the 1990s, MTV abandoned its original music format in favor of shows reflecting popular culture, such as reality programs and satirical comedies. Although this change sparked criticism, MTV remains one of the most popular television networks throughout the world. MTV studios are located at 1515 Broadway in Times Square.

Robert Sanger Steel

muckraking. Term coined by Theodore Roosevelt in 1906 to describe journalism that exposes corruption, exploitation, and health hazards; he likened its practitioners to the nameless character in John Bunyan's *The Pilgrim's Progress* who stared only at the muck with a rake in his hand and missed the sky above. The style of journalism to which he referred began about the turn of the twentieth century, when idealistic young writers from small cities and towns moved to New York City to build their careers. Their exposés were published in mass-circulation magazines such as *McClure's, Everybody's, Ladies Home Journal, Hampton's, Collier's,* and *Cosmopolitan.* In January 1903 an editorial in *McClure's* signaled the beginning of a journalistic movement that aspired toward social criticism, and the same issue contained installments of stories by Lincoln Steffens, Ida M. Tarbell ("History of the Standard Oil Company"), and Ray Stannard Baker ("Right to Work," about coal mining). Jacob Riis, a journalist and photographer, compiled *How the Other Half Lives* (1890), which exposed the condition of tenements in New York's Lower East Side and was one of the first publications of the Progressive era that sought social and political reform. Corruption was exposed in Tammany Hall in Steffens's series "The Shame of the Cities" (1902–3) and at the New York Life Insurance Company and the Equitable Life Assurance Society in Thomas Lawson's "Frenzied Finance" (1904). George Kibbe Turner's "Daughters of the Poor" (1909) focused on the practice of forcing immigrant girls into prostitution. During the Progressive era the muckrakers were distinguished by their numbers and the quality and extent of their research and investigations. They helped bring change to Wall Street in their attacks on big business and ultimately fueled national reforms for urban living conditions, medical patents, child labor laws, child prostitution, and women's rights.

Louis Filler, *The Muckrakers* (University Park: Pennsylvania State University Press, 1976); Rodger Streitmatter, *Mightier than the Sword: How the News Media Have Shaped American History* (Boulder, Colo.: Westview Press, 1997)

Robert Stinson, Meghan Lalonde

mugwumps. Reform-minded Republicans who in 1884 abandoned their party and presidential nominee James G. Blaine to support Democratic candidate Grover Cleveland. Mostly wealthy and well-educated lawyers and businessmen, mugwumps renounced corrupt political machines and excessive corporate power and advocated civil service reform, tariff reductions, and honest politics; they rejected Blaine because of his reputation for political immorality. Cleveland carried New York State in the election with the help of city-based mugwump support. Prominent New York City members included E. L. Godkin (editor of the *Nation*), George William Curtis (editor of *Harper's Weekly*), Carl Schurz, George Jones (owner of the *New York Times*), Thomas Nast, and Richard Watson Gilder. Most mugwumps realigned with the Republican Party in 1888 to support William McKinley's presidential candidacy. A corruption of the Algonquin word *maqquomp* (great man), the term *mugwump* referred to politicians who were indecisive and "sitting on the fence, with their mugs on one side and their wumps on the other."

Richard Skolnick, Joseph Breen

Muhlenberg, William Augustus (*b* Philadelphia, 16 Sept 1796; *d* St. Johnland [now in Kings Park], N.Y., 8 April 1877). Episcopal clergyman. He moved to New York City in 1828 and formed the Flushing Institute, an Episcopal boys' preparatory school. In 1846 he became the rector of the Church of the Holy Communion (Sixth Avenue and 20th Street), where he developed the practice of "evangelical Catholicism," an attempt to combine, in the Episcopal church, Protestant evangelicalism with traditional Catholic ritual and order. He wrote the proposal known as the "Muhlenberg Memorial" (1853), which called the Episcopal Church to greater evangelical and ecumenical commitment, planned and opened St. Luke's Hospital on Fifth Avenue between 54th and 55th streets (1858), and in 1870 organized St. Johnland, a utopian industrial community on Long Island.

Alvin Wilson Skardon, *Church Leader in the Cities: William Augustus Muhlenberg* (Philadelphia: University of Pennsylvania Press, 1971)

Allen C. Guelzo

Mulberry Bend. Former neighborhood in Manhattan, lying near the Five Points along Mulberry Street between Park and Bayard streets. A predominantly Italian area with many wretched tenements and liquor stores, it was known for some of the worst overcrowding in nineteenth-century New York City. In *How the Other Half Lives* (1890) Jacob A. Riis described Mulberry Bend as the most dangerous place in the city. In 1897 Mulberry Bend Park replaced buildings condemned on a parcel bounded by Bayard Street, Mulberry Street, Park Street, and Baxter Street; this was renamed Columbus Park in 1911.

Carol Groneman

Mulberry Street Boys. Name sometimes given to the Dead Rabbits.

Mullaly, John (*b* Belfast, 1835; *d* New York City, 1911). Reformer. He moved to New York City as a young man and began his career as a correspondent for the *New York Herald.* From 1857 to 1858 he was a secretary to Samuel F. B. Morse. He later became the editor of the Catholic newspaper *Metropolitan Record* (remaining for 14 years), worked for other newspapers, was the commissioner of health of New York City, and served on the Board of Tax Assessors. In 1881 he formed the New

Jacob A. Riis, Mulberry Bend *(ca 1888–89)*

York Park Association, which argued successfully for the creation of parks in what is now the Bronx. The city in 1888 acquired Van Cortlandt, Pelham Bay, Bronx, Crotona, and Claremont parks, as well as four parkways. Mullaly Park, dedicated in 1932, is bounded by Jerome Avenue, McClellan Street, River Avenue, and East 162nd Street in the Bronx. Mullaly wrote *The Milk Trade of New York and Vicinity* (1853) and *The New Parks beyond the Harlem* (1887).

Jonathan Kuhn

Mumford, Lewis (*b* Flushing [now in Queens], 19 Oct 1895; *d* Amenia, N.Y., 26 Jan 1990). Writer, urban planner, and critic. Raised on the Upper West Side of Manhattan, he graduated from Stuyvesant High School and then studied at City College, Columbia University, and the New School. His book *The Study of Utopias* appeared in 1922. For more than a decade until the mid-1930s he lived in the planned community of Sunnyside Gardens in Queens; however, he eventually became disgusted with the city and moved permanently north of Manhattan to Amenia, New York. For many years he was an architectural critic for the *New Yorker,* reviewing skyscrapers, housing plans, and urban renewal projects for the magazine. He was an adamant critic of congestion and overbuilding in New York City and wrote that midtown Manhattan had grown so crowded that architecture would cease to matter. His book *The City in History* (1961) won the National Book Award. During the 1960s and 1970s Mumford explored the theme of moral renewal in his writings. His autobiographical works include *Findings and Keepings* (1975) and *Works and Days* (1978).

Donald L. Miller, *Lewis Mumford: A Life* (New York: Weidenfeld and Nicholson, 1989); Robert Wojtowicz, *Sidewalk Critic: Lewis Mumford's Writings on New York* (New York: Princeton Architectural Press, 2000)

James E. Mooney, Anne Epstein

Municipal Archives. Archives that hold valuable records created or received in the course of transacting official city business. Among the materials held by the Municipal Archives in New York City are plans for the construction and alteration of the Brooklyn Bridge; the design drawings of Central Park and 150 other city parks; records of the Board of Education; papers of Robert Moses, commissioner of the Parks Department (1934–60); records of the Manhattan Buildings Department; property tax assessment ledgers from 1789 to 1980; district attorneys' case files and criminal court records from as early as 1684; mayoral records from 1849 to the present; petitions, minutes, and accounts of the legislative branch from as early as 1625; records of the towns in Queens, Richmond, Kings, and Westchester (Bronx) counties before consolidation in 1898; ledgers of nineteenth-century almshouse and charity hospitals; moving images and sound recordings from the municipal broadcasting system WNYC; vital records; and manuscript materials and photographs from the New York City unit of the Federal Writers' Project of the Works Progress Administration (1936–43). More than two million photographs in 45 collections are held by the archives, including images of every house and building in the five boroughs, taken during 1939–41 and 1983–89 by the city for property tax assessment purposes. The holdings of the Municipal Archives total 200,000 cubic feet (5,660 cubic meters). A public reference room is at 31 Chambers Street.

Kenneth R. Cobb

Municipal Art Society of New York [MAS]. Art society founded in 1893 by architect Richard Morris Hunt and a group of painters, sculptors, and art enthusiasts. Following the motto "To make us love our country, we should make our country lovely," this open-membership organization was an early and influential force in the national turn-of-the-century movement for civic beautification. MAS was the first among eponymous municipal art societies in Cincinnati, Cleveland, Chicago, Baltimore, Boston, and Philadelphia, which together gave rise to the "city beautiful" and civic art movements and also paved the way for the establishment of the fields of city planning and civic design (later known as urban design) and for city-planning departments. An aesthetic counterpart to the political municipal reform movement, MAS and the larger municipal art movement initially sought to promote civic values by placing exemplary sculpture and murals in public parks and buildings. The first project, described in 1894 as "the first attempt in America at municipal art," was appropriately a series of allegorical murals (later restored with MAS support) for the Criminal Courts Building on Centre Street, and was followed by efforts to establish the city's Municipal Art Commission in 1898. Apart from a number of public monuments and artworks, subsequent projects focused on the "useful art" of street furniture, street signs, and tree planting. Anticipating the organization's continued advocacy for improving city living conditions, by 1908 MAS joined the larger reform movement that sought to address traffic congestion and tenement crowding, sponsoring proposals for new bridges, tunnels, and beaux-arts style diagonal streets in 1911 and lobbying for the first zoning regulations in the nation, which were made law in 1916. From the 1950s to the 1970s MAS was similarly influential in the preservation movement, organizing walking tours and protests and lobbying for the Landmarks Law of 1965 and 1973 and the establishment of the LANDMARKS PRESERVATION COMMISSION. In the 1980s the organization once again became involved in large-scale planning issues, establishing a planning center to work with community groups and other organizations involved in the redevelopment of Penn Yards, Greenpoint, Williamsburg, Fresh Kills Landfill, Atlantic Yards, and, through the Metropolitan Waterfront Alliance, the larger city waterfront. In the early twenty-first century MAS continued to focus on the city streetscape, preservation, and city-planning issues.

Mel Scott, *American City Planning Since 1890* (Berkeley: University of California Press, 1969); William H. Wilson, *The City Beautiful Movement* (Baltimore: The Johns Hopkins University Press, 1989); Anthony C. Wood, *Preserving New York: Winning the Right to Protect a City's Landmarks* (New York: Routledge, 2007)

Peter L. Laurence

Municipal Assistance Corporation [MAC]. Public finance corporation formed by the New York State legislature in 1975 to cope with the fiscal crisis of New York City. Its first chairman, Felix G. Rohatyn, served for 18 years. The corporation monitors the city's finances and borrows money on its behalf. Because its bonds are guaranteed by a first lien on the revenues due the city from two state-authorized taxes (sales tax, stock transfer city), its debt is more secure than bonds issued by the city itself. This enabled MAC to borrow even when the city government was excluded from the capital market. When interest rates declined in the last decade of the twentieth and the early years of the twenty-first centuries, the corporation was able to refinance its securities, lowering its debt service obligations below the revenues generated by the two state taxes. To gain access to these surplus funds, the municipal government has been required by MAC to adopt various cost-savings measures and to invest in capital projects designed to strengthen the city's economy. Although MAC has continued to shape municipal financial policies in these ways, its influence declined after the city regained access to the capital market. MAC ceased functioning when its last bonds were retired in 2008.

Martin Shefter, *Political Crisis/Fiscal Crisis: The Collapse and Revival of New York City* (New York: Basic Books, 1985)

Martin Shefter

Municipal Building. Skyscraper at the intersection of Chambers and Centre streets. Its construction followed an architectural competition that the city sponsored in 1907–8 for a large office building to consolidate various agencies. Urged by Mayor George B. McClellan to enter, the firm of McKim, Mead and White won with a proposal for a classically detailed skyscraper—an irony given the fact that Charles Follen McKim disdained high-rise buildings as destroyers of civic beauty. The U-shaped structure was designed

Municipal Building at Chambers and Centre streets, ca *1914*

by a younger partner, William Mitchell Kendall (1856–1941), and adroitly placed on an irregular site bisected by Chambers Street and criss-crossed by underground transit connections. Completed in 1913, the 25-story block was surmounted by a central 15-story "wedding-cake" tower and adorned with Adolf A. Weiman's sculpture *Civic Fame.* It was designated a landmark in 1966. In the early twenty-first century the building housed more than 3000 city employees; about 28,000 people are married in the second-story wedding chapel every year.

Carol Willis

municipal courts. See Courts, §1.

Munsey, Frank A(ndrew) (*b* Mercer, Maine, 21 Aug 1854; *d* New York City, 22 Dec 1925). Publisher. After arriving in New York City in 1882 he launched the weekly children's magazine *Golden Argosy,* for which he wrote many stories relating the progress of a protagonist from poverty to wealth. Among his later magazines was *Munsey's* (first published 1889), a profitable monthly publication that sold for 10 cents a copy and provided funds for other enterprises, including a chain of grocery stores, banks in Baltimore and Washington, D.C., and various newspapers. The magazine was one of the first to have a mass circulation and to be driven by advertising; it printed lavishly illustrated articles on art, business, and European royalty as well as sentimental fiction, and avoided the "muckraking" that characterized its competitors. From 1901 to 1925 Munsey bought, merged, sold, and ruined a dozen newspapers, several of which were based in New York City. His more successful acquisitions included the *New York Press* (1912), which he made into an organ of support for Theodore Roosevelt's presidential candidacy, the *Sun* (1916, which absorbed the *New York Press* to obtain a franchise from the Associated Press), the *New York Herald* (1918, later merged with the *Sun*), the Paris edition of the *Herald* (1918), the *Telegram* (1918), the *Globe* (1923, merged with the *Sun*), and the *Evening Mail* (merged with the *Telegram*). In 1924 he attempted to buy the *New York Tribune* in the hope of merging it with the *Herald* but in the end sold the *Herald* to the owner of the *Tribune,* Mrs. Ogden Reid, who effected the same merger herself. During his career Munsey owned at least 17 newspapers, including daily publications in Boston, Philadelphia, Baltimore, and Washington, D.C. *Munsey's* ceased publication in 1929.

George Britt, *Forty Years, Forty Millions: The Career of Frank A. Munsey* (New York: Farrar and Rinehart, 1935); Frank Luther Mott, *A History of American Magazines,* vol. 4, *1885–1905* (Cambridge, Mass.: Harvard University Press, 1957)

Robert Stinson

murals. There were few murals in New York City before the late nineteenth century. A number with themes inspired by the Italian Renaissance were painted by John La Farge, who during the 1880s received mural commissions for the Union League Club House, the Vanderbilt Houses, and the Whitelaw Reid Music Room. His best-known mural was *Ascension of Our Lord* (1889) in the Church of the Ascension. With Edwin Blashfield and Kenyon Cox he formed the National Society of Mural Painters in 1893, which between 1895 and 1902 encouraged a number of muralists; most treated academic themes and were not innovative.

Murals were commissioned from Frederick Crowninshield, Will H. Low, George W. Maynard, Frank Fowler, D. Maitland Armstrong, and C. Y. Turner by the Waldorf–Astoria and from Edwin Abbey and Thomas W. Dewing by the Hotel Imperial and the Hotel Manhattan. Ten artists painted murals in the appellate courtroom of the Criminal Courts Building (1899). The Vanderbilts, the Huntingtons, and the Lewisohns were among the few families at the time who commissioned murals for their homes. The first two decades of the twentieth century saw more commissions, especially by banks, insurance companies, department stores, and courthouses.

Most private commissions were suspended during the Depression of the 1930s; exceptions included those for Rockefeller Center, where Radio City Music Hall was decorated with modernist murals painted by Stuart Davis and Yasuo Kuniyoshi and with photographic murals by Edward Steichen. In the adjoining RCA Building were photographic murals by Margaret Bourke–White and a fresco in the lobby by Diego Rivera (1931) that incorporated portraits of Lenin, Marx, and other communist leaders (destroyed in 1932 and replaced in 1937 with a mural by José María Sert that was less distasteful to Rockefeller). Most murals of the time were narrative. The New School for Social Research commissioned works from José Clemente Orozco and Thomas Hart Benton, whose mural *America Today* (1931) was later moved to the Equitable Life Assurance Center.

The success of Rivera, Orozco, and David Siqueiros inspired the federal government to sponsor a mural program in 1933. The Section of Fine Arts of the U.S. Department of the Treasury was responsible for many murals painted in the city, as was the Federal Art Project of the Works Progress Administration, which sponsored more than 200 murals in the metropolitan area between 1935 and 1943. These agencies provided unprecedented opportunities for artists and drew broad public attention to murals, which for the first time appeared in schools, hospitals, libraries, and prisons. Some works were abstract, but most were tailored to the institutions that made the commissions. Simple styles were favored over the allegorical ones used previously. Among the best-known muralists supported by the Federal Art Project in the city were Davis, Ilya Bolotowsky, James Brooks, Byron Browne, Philip Evergood, Arshile Gorky, Balcomb Greene, Philip Guston, Lee Krasner, Anton Refregier, and Moses Soyer. World War II saw the end of the New Deal projects, and eventually some murals painted under its auspices were destroyed. Everett Shinn completed several realist murals for the Oak Room of the Plaza Hotel in 1944, but for the most part private commissions declined.

Interest in large-scale outdoor murals revived during the late 1960s. A mural association called City Walls was formed by professional artists wishing to support artists financially; the first mural painted under its auspices was *East 9th Street Wall* (1967) by Allan d'Arcangelo. Others who received commissions included Jason Crum, Richard Anuszkiewicz, Nassos Daphnis, Tania, Robert Wiegand, and Mel Pekarsky. Another association, CITYarts Workshop (1968), organized projects carried out by amateurs and overseen by professional artists. The first mural that it sponsored was *Anti-drug* (1969) by Susan Kiok, followed by *Chinatown Today* (1973) and *Chi Lai Arriba* (1974) by Alan Okada, *Wall of Respect for Women* (1974) by Tomie Arai, and projects in Queens and Manhattan by J. Braun-Reinitz in 1990. *Trompe l'oeil* was made popular by Richard Haas, whose first mural in the city was painted outside a loft on Prince Street in SoHo in 1974; his later work included a series of storefronts along Mulberry Street and murals for Prospect Place in Brooklyn, a substation of Consolidated Edison at Peck Slip, Barney's clothing store, and a number of private residences. Large indoor works also became popular. One of the most striking, Roy Lichtenstein's *Mural with Blue Brushstroke* (1985), was painted five stories high in the lobby of the Equitable Life Assurance Center and is visible from the street.

CITYarts Workshop sponsored more than 250 new public artworks in its first 40 years. In addition, a number of murals from the 1930s were restored, including Brooks's *Flight* at the Marine Air Terminal of La Guardia Airport, a group of paintings at Harlem Hospital, Abraham Champanier's mural for Gouverneur Hospital (one panel is now at the New York Public Library at Lincoln Center), and abstract murals for the radio station WNYC and the Williamsburg Housing Project in Brooklyn. The Municipal Art Society began the Adopt-a-Mural project, through which 17 threatened public artworks out of the city's 430 murals in libraries, schools, and hospitals were selected to be saved. Following the terrorist attacks of 11 September 2001, many neighborhoods and community and municipal organizations sponsored murals commemorating the victims and the resilient spirit of New York City.

Eva Cockcroft, Jim Cockcroft, and John Weber, *Toward a People's Art: The Contemporary Mural Movement* (New York: E. P. Dutton, 1977); Greta Berman, *The Lost Years: Mural Painting in New York City under the Works Progress Administration's Federal Art Project, 1935–1943* (New York: Garland, 1978)

Greta Berman

Murder Incorporated. Nickname applied to an organization of criminals based in the Brownsville neighborhood of Brooklyn during the 1930s that carried out contract killings for a nationwide organized-crime syndicate. Its leaders included Lucky Luciano (the most powerful), Meyer Lansky, Joe Adonis, and Frank Costello; Louis "Lepke" Buchalter and Albert Anastasia, popularly known as the "lord high executioner," were in charge of operations. Estimates of the number of murders committed by the organization range from 400 to 1000. It disbanded in 1940 when a number of lower-level criminals were arrested: Abe "Kid Twist" Reles, a lieutenant in the organization, provided information to the district attorney that led to the prosecution and execution of Buchalter and several other members. But before Reles was able to testify against Anastasia, he fell to his death under mysterious circumstances from the window of the Half Moon Hotel in Coney Island on 12 November 1941; many observers felt that he had been murdered.

Burton B. Turkus and Sid Feder, *Murder, Inc.: The Story of "The Syndicate"* (New York: Farrar, Straus and Young, 1951)

See also Organized crime.

Warren Sloat

Murphy, Arthur H. (*b* New York City, 1868; *d* New York City, 6 Feb 1922). Political leader. Of Irish descent, he attended Ottawa University and in 1893 moved to the Bronx, where he opened a liquor, cigar, and real estate business. He served on the city's Board of Aldermen from 1903 to 1909, became a member of the general committee of Tammany Hall, and unsuccessfully sought the borough presidency of the Bronx in 1909. When the Bronx became a separate county in 1914, Murphy was elected its first Democratic leader, a position he held until his death. He cooperated with the leadership of Tammany Hall in Manhattan and had his own political club in his saloon near Bronx Borough Hall.

Gary Hermalyn and Laura Tosi, *Elected Public Officials of the Bronx since 1898* (New York: Bronx County Historical Society, 1989)

Stephen A. Stertz

Murphy, Charles F(rancis) (*b* New York City, 20 June 1858; *d* New York City, 25 April 1924). Political boss. Born in a tenement on the East Side, he became a horse-car driver and a successful saloon owner and political worker. He was named leader of the Gashouse District in 1892, and in 1897 Mayor Robert A. Van Wyck appointed him dock commissioner (the only salaried municipal position he ever held). Intelligent, taciturn, and somewhat straight-laced, he became the leader of Tammany Hall at a time (1902) when scandals and political defeat had severely damaged its authority. In 1903 he named Representative George B. McClellan, Jr. (son of the general), as a mayoral candidate and also recruited to the ticket two prominent reformers, the incumbent comptroller and aldermanic president.

They won easily. In 1905 his organization used fraudulent ballots to block William Randolph Hearst's mayoral candidacy. Murphy placed Mayors William J. Gaynor and John F. Hylan in office, as well as Governors John A. Dix, William Sulzer, and Alfred E. Smith. When Sulzer turned against Tammany Hall, Murphy had him impeached, a mistake that contributed to John Purroy Mitchel's victory in the mayoral election of 1913. Widely regarded as the most effective machine politician in the city's history, Murphy also launched and guided the careers of Senator Robert F. Wagner (i); Edward J. Flynn, a Democratic leader of the Bronx; and James A. Foley, a nationally respected probate judge. During his tenure Democratic legislators opposed Prohibition and passed progressive labor laws. Toward the end of his life he exerted considerable influence on national Democratic politics: he hoped to send Smith to the White House but died weeks before the Democratic National Convention met (and deadlocked) at Madison Square Garden. Murphy left an estate valued at more than $2 million, the sources of which remain unclear. For many years he lived at 305 East 17th Street.

Nancy J. Weiss, *Charles Francis Murphy, 1858–1924: Respectability and Responsibility in Tammany Politics* (Northampton, Mass.: Smith College Press, 1968)

Frank Vos

Murray, Arthur [Teichman, Arthur Murray] (*b* New York City, 4 April 1895; *d* Honolulu, 3 March 1991). Dancer and entrepreneur. Brought up in East Harlem, he developed a talent for ballroom dancing while a student at Morris High School in the Bronx. By the early 1920s he offered dance instruction kits by mail order: these contained detailed charts indicating where each dancer's feet should be placed and in which sequence. From the beginning he aimed at a clientele that was socially insecure. His first advertisement was headed "How I Became Popular Overnight" and ran in the magazine *True Story.* He based his business in Atlanta but used a mailing address in New York City to create a cosmopolitan image; he eventually broadened the business's scope from mail-order instruction to dance studios, which opened in 1928 in New York City and eventually numbered in the hundreds throughout the United States. From 1950 until 1960 he was the host of a "dance party" on television. Sales representatives working for his company were accused in 1960 of using high-pressure tactics to manipulate the lonely and the aged. Murray sold the company in the early 1960s.

George A. Thompson, Jr.

Murray, John (*b* Swatara Creek, Pa., 1737; *d* New York City, 11 Oct 1808). Merchant. He moved to New York City in his teens to set up an importing business with his brother, which by the time of the American Revolution owned more ships than any other firm in the colonies. During the British occupation he and other members of the Chamber of Commerce handled the internal affairs of the city, and after the war he was president of the Chamber of Commerce from 1798 to 1806. Murray also directed the Bank of New York and was active in such humanitarian causes as the Free School for Poor Children, the Humane Society, and prison reform. By the end of his life he had a fortune of $500,000 and valuable land in Murray Hill, named for him.

James E. Mooney

Murray Hill (i). Neighborhood on the East Side of Manhattan, bounded to the north by 40th Street, to the east by Third Avenue, to the south by 34th Street, and to the west by Madison Avenue. During colonial times the area was known as Inclenberg, named after an estate of 25 acres (10 hectares) occupied by Robert and Mary Murray. From the 1820s to the 1890s the tracks of the New York and Harlem Railroad ran at grade along Fourth Avenue; a tunnel was dug in the early 1850s to hide the trains from view and to prevent the need to pull cars up the hill. The Common Council ordered the addition of a grassy mall 40 feet (12 meters) wide at the center of Fourth Avenue between 34th and 38th streets. The avenue was named Park Avenue, and its gracious width and planted mall stimulated development. By the end of the nineteenth century such prominent families as the Belmonts, the Rhinelanders, the Tiffanys, the Havemeyers, the Phelpses, the Delanos, and the Morgans had brownstone mansions along Fifth and Madison avenues in the area. Many professional, political, and social clubs followed, including the Union League Club at 38 East 37th Street. The picturesque 71st Regiment Armory (1905; Clinton and Russell) on Park Avenue between 33rd and 34th streets was replaced in 1976 by Norman Thomas High School and an office tower at 3 Park Avenue. Murray Hill is the site of many clubs, churches, high-rise apartment buildings, and restaurants. Landmarks include the Morgan Library and Museum (1906; McKim, Mead and White; expansion 2006 by Renzo Piano) and town houses built in the early twentieth century, among them the ornate DeLamar Mansion (Madison and 37th Street), now the Polish Consulate, built to show up J. P. Morgan's house across the street.

Tales of Murray Hill (New York: Irving Trust, 1952)

Joyce Gold

Murray Hill (ii). Neighborhood in north central Queens, lying within Flushing near 150th and Murray streets south of Northern Boulevard. It was once owned by M. B. Parsons and M. A. Murray, and much of it was the site of King and Murray's Nursery. After the nursery closed, the area was developed in 1889 as Murray Hill, and a railroad station opened in April of the same year. Additional streets were laid out, and more than 200 lots were sold. During the next 25 years the sale of lots continued, and the developer built houses according to buyers' specifications. Early in the twenty-first century many single-family homes were being turned into two- or three-family homes, and an increasing proportion of residents were renters instead of owners; the Korean population in the neighborhood was increasing.

Vincent Seyfried

Murray Hill Hotel. Hotel on Park Avenue between 40th and 41st streets, completed in 1884 after plans by Stephen Hatch. It stood eight stories tall, including two ornamental towers, and had 600 guest rooms. In 1893 *King's Handbook of New York City* called the hotel "an establishment of the highest class." Its facade was of brownstone, granite, and redbrick, the interior furnished with red and white marble floors, burgundy and gold carmine upholstery, gilt-framed mirrors, and rococo walls. In its heyday the Murray Hill Hotel was patronized by Mark Twain, Senator George Hearst, Jay Gould, Diamond Jim Brady, and Presidents Grover Cleveland and William McKinley. It did not survive the redesigning of lower Park Avenue into a business district and was demolished in 1945–46 to make way for an office building.

Chad Ludington

Murray's Roman Gardens. Restaurant and hotel at 228–32 West 42nd Street in Manhattan. It opened after the 1907 remodeling of an 1872 building that began as a school before being transformed by McKim, Mead and White into the Percival, a bachelor apartment house. The architect, Henri Erkins, altered the exterior to resemble the Hôtel de Strasbourg in Paris and designed an exotic, mirrored interior, making it one of New York City's earliest theme restaurants. With the onset of Prohibition, the building's lower floors were occupied by Hubert's Museum and Heckler's Trained Flea Circus, while the lavish upper floors became a male brothel, eventually known as the Barracks, later closed because of the AIDS epidemic. The building was demolished in the late 1990s as part of the 42nd Street Development Project and replaced by Madame Tussaud's Wax Museum.

James Traub, *The Devil's Playground: A Century of Pleasure and Profit in Times Square* (New York: Random House, 2004)

Val Ginter

Murrow, Edward [Egbert] **R(oscoe)** (*b* Greensboro, N.C., 25 April 1908; *d* Pawling, N.Y., 27 April 1965). Broadcaster. He arrived in New York City in 1930 and worked from 1932 at the Institute of International Education on West 45th Street, where he helped scholars persecuted by the Nazis. In 1935 he joined the Columbia Broadcasting System

(CBS) at 485 Madison Avenue, and in 1937 he went to London to take charge of its European bureau. He organized the network's first news team in Europe and during World War II became well known for his radio reports, which were broadcast live from London rooftops during German bombing raids. After the war he returned to New York City, where he became a vice president at CBS in charge of news. Uncomfortable with his role as an executive, he returned to broadcasting in 1947 with the nightly radio series *Edward R. Murrow with the News.* At studios above Grand Central Terminal he joined with Fred Friendly as his coproducer in 1951 to begin the television series *See It Now,* which set the standards for television documentaries and contributed to the fall of Senator Joseph R. McCarthy. He also appeared on the television series *Person to Person* (1953) and *Small World* (1957, also produced with Friendly), and worked with Friendly on the series *CBS Reports* (1960), with Murrow as the reporter in the classic documentary *Harvest of Shame.* Increasingly distressed by the growing commercialism of television, Murrow left CBS in 1961 to become the director of the U.S. Information Agency, remaining until January 1964. His programs may be viewed at the Museum of Television and Radio.

Erik Barnouw, *A History of Broadcasting in the United States* (New York: Oxford University Press, 1967, 1970); A. M. Sperber, *Murrow: His Life and Times* (New York: Bantam, 1987)

A. M. Sperber

Muscular Dystrophy Association. Nonprofit organization formed in 1950 in New York City by a group of parents to advocate research into hereditary muscle-destroying disorders. In the same year its first branch was chartered in Flatbush, Brooklyn. On Labor Day of 1966 the association broadcast the first of many annual fund-raising programs on television, from the Americana Hotel on Sixth Avenue. In 1986 it was announced that researchers sponsored by the association had identified the gene that, when defective, causes the most common form of muscular dystrophy, Duchenne dystrophy. In the early 1990s the association sponsored weekly clinics at eight leading hospitals in New York City, at which patients received treatment from hospital staff; a coordinator from the association oversaw these services and in most cases also arranged for payment. The association continued to be funded almost entirely by private contributions and worked to cure 40 neuromuscular diseases, including nine kinds of muscular dystrophy. The headquarters was moved in January 1991 from 810 Seventh Avenue in Manhattan to Tucson, Arizona. As of 2007 there were more than 200 local offices nationwide in addition to 230 sponsored hospital-affiliated clinics.

Sandra Opdycke

Museo del Barrio. Museum at 1230 Fifth Avenue in Manhattan, between 104th and 105th streets. Founded in 1969 in a classroom in East Harlem, it is dedicated to preserving and documenting the art of Puerto Rico and Latin America. The museum maintains a permanent collection of paintings, sculptures, photographs, and other objects ranging from pre-Columbian times to the present and has a large number of folk materials, including an important group of *santos de palo* (carved and painted wooden figures of saints). The exhibition program emphasizes the work of contemporary Puerto Rican and Latin American artists, especially those working locally, as well as the folk heritage, history, and community life of the people of El Barrio.

Carol V. Wright

Museum Mile. Section of upper Fifth Avenue in Manhattan from 82nd Street to 105th Street. Named for the dense grouping of nine museums and other fine-art institutions, this section of Fifth Avenue is home to the Metropolitan Museum of Art (82nd Street), Goethe Institut New York/German Cultural Center (83rd Street), Neue Galerie New York (86th Street), Solomon R. Guggenheim Museum (89th Street), Alumni of the National Academy Museum and School of Fine Arts (89th Street), Cooper–Hewitt National Design Museum (91st Street), Jewish Museum (92nd Street), Museum of the City of New York (103rd Street), and El Museo del Barrio (104th Street). The Museum for African Art (to be located at 110th Street) was under construction in 2010.

Dianna Ng

Museum of Arts and Design. Museum opened in 1956 at 29 West 53rd Street as the Museum of Contemporary Crafts and focusing on collecting and exhibiting handmade objects of clay, glass, wood, metal, and fiber.

Museum of Arts and Design, the former Huntington Hartford Building, 2009

It moved to 40 West 53rd Street in 1986 and was renamed the American Craft Museum. In 2002 the museum again changed its name, calling itself the Museum of Arts and Design. The change was made to reflect the fluid boundaries between art, design, and crafts and to reflect a wider spectrum of interest. In 2008 it reopened at 2 Columbus Circle in a freestanding building designed in 1965 by Edward Durell Stone as Huntington Hartford's Gallery of Modern Art. The move tripled the amount of total space and doubled the amount of exhibition space, enabling the museum to display its permanent collection of jewelry, ceramics, metals, fiber, glass, paper, wood, and mixed-media objects as well as to mount temporary shows. Its new home also includes a store and space for educational programming.

Catherine J. Mathis

Museum of Chinese in the Americas. Museum founded in 1980 by Jack Tchen, Charlie Lai, and other Chinese American artists, historians, and students. It was founded to preserve the history and culture of the Chinese and their descendants in the West. It focuses on the Chinese diaspora throughout the western hemisphere through visual and audio exhibitions, school programs, and an extensive collection of Chinese American and Asian American archival documents. The museum is located at 215 Centre Street, with collections and a research center on Mulberry Street in Chinatown.

Stephanie Miller

Museum of Jewish Heritage. Opened on 15 September 1997 in Battery Park City, its collection has more than 15,000 artifacts, photographs, documents, and archival films. The museum is organized around the three themes of "Jewish Life a Century Ago," "The War against the Jews," and "Jewish Renewal." It has a registry of Holocaust survivors and serves as a living memorial to the Holocaust, both through its exhibits and its commemoration.

Jessica Montesano

Museum of Modern Art [MoMA]. Museum located at 11 West 53rd Street in Manhattan. The first exhibition was sponsored by museum founders Abby Aldrich Rockefeller, Mary Quinn Sullivan, and Lillie P. Bliss. Titled "Cézanne, Gauguin, Seurat and van Gogh," the show consisted of an initial gift of eight prints and one drawing. It opened in the Heckscher Building at 730 Fifth Avenue on 7 November 1929, nine days after the Wall Street crash. In 1932 the museum moved to a townhouse at its current address leased from John D. Rockefeller, Jr. A bequest from Bliss in 1934 formed the core of the permanent collection. By 1937 MoMA had outgrown the Rockefeller townhouse and in 1939 dedicated a new building designed by Philip L. Goodwin and Edward Durell Stone at the same location. In 1984 the museum underwent a massive renovation that nearly doubled its exhibition space, which was doubled again during another renovation project completed in 2006. The project, designed by Yoshio Taniguchi, features 630,000 square feet (58,530 square meters) of new and redesigned space, including an entire building dedicated to education and research. MoMA's collection holds 150,000 paintings, sculptures, drawings, prints, photographs, architectural models and drawings, and design objects, including some of the world's most widely recognized pieces of art, such as *The Starry Night* by Vincent van Gogh, *Water Lilies* by Claude Monet, and *Campbell's Soup Cans* by Andy Warhol. In addition, the museum also owns 22,000 films and other media-related documents. The museum's library contains 300,000 books, and the archives contain approximately 2500 linear feet (762 meters) of historical documentation. In January 2000 MoMA and the P.S.1 CONTEMPORARY ART CENTER in Long Island City, Queens, became affiliated, allowing for innovative opportunities for collaboration and outreach.

Anne Epstein, Sharon Zane

Museum of Jewish Heritage, 2009

Museum of Natural History. See AMERICAN MUSEUM OF NATURAL HISTORY.

Museum of Television and Radio. Former name of the PALEY CENTER FOR MEDIA.

Museum of the American Indian. See NATIONAL MUSEUM OF THE AMERICAN INDIAN.

Museum of the City of New York. Museum incorporated on 21 July 1923 to preserve the history of New York City, inspired by the Carnavalet in Paris and by city museums in London, Berlin, and Hamburg. At first confined to cramped quarters in Gracie Mansion, it mounted an exhibition at the Fine Arts Building on West 57th Street called "Old New York" (1926), characterized in the annual report of 1927 as an effort to describe the city's development in an arresting manner and "awaken in the schoolboy and immigrant an understanding and pride in his citizenship." The exhibition was so successful that supporters of the museum searched for new, more spacious quarters. A site along Fifth Avenue was donated by the city, and funds for a new building were raised by public subscription, although the trustees' original plans were drastically reduced after the stock market crash of 1929. A new building on Fifth Avenue at 103rd Street designed in the neo-Georgian style by Joseph H. Freedlander was dedicated on 11 January 1932. In subsequent decades several large collections were added, including the J. Clarence Davies Collection of more than 15,000 paintings, prints, and maps; the photographic collections of Percy Byron, Jacob A. Riis, and Berenice Abbott; the Harry T. Peters Collection of more than 3000 prints by Currier and Ives; and furnishings for period rooms donated by the Rockefeller family. Many costumes, theater pieces, and decorative objects were also acquired, and the museum became the first in the nation to set up a curatorial department for toys. The museum has one of the world's finest collections of objects relating to theater in the city; its holdings are strongest in objects from the nineteenth and early twentieth centuries. In 2006 the museum launched an $80 million renovation and expansion to accommodate its nearly 200,000 annual visitors. It completed the first stage of the renovation in fall 2009 with the opening of the 2800-square-foot (260-square-meter) James G. Dinan and Elizabeth R. Miller Gallery as well as a center devoted to preserving the museum's collections.

Rick Beard

Museum of the Moving Image. Museum of the history of film, television, and digital media. Opened to the public in 1988 on 35th Avenue at 37th Street in Astoria, Queens, the museum occupies a studio building on the former site of Astoria Studio (now Kaufman Astoria Studios), one of the nation's largest motion picture and television studios. The facility, built in 1920, served as a film production center for Paramount Pictures and, from 1942 through the 1960s, for the U.S. Army. It was listed on the National Register of Historic Places in 1978. The museum has a comprehensive collection of more than 130,000 moving-image–related artifacts, mounts artistic and innovative interactive exhibitions, provides educational and interpretative programs, and annually hosts more than 300 film screenings and dialogues with significant contributors to the field. A major expansion and renovation of the museum was under way in 2010.

Holly Cronin

museums. The number, quality, and variety of its museums has helped confirm New York City as the cultural capital of the United States. The first nonprofit educational museum in the city was the short-lived Tammany Museum, formed in 1790 to collect Americana including Indian artifacts for the Society of St. Tammany, the city's first cultural organization. Gardiner Baker (*d* 1798), a collector of zoological specimens, mechanical devices, and books, became keeper of the museum with the support of John Pintard, a merchant, philanthropist, and scholar. Exhibitions were held initially in the Wall Street Building formerly occupied by the federal government. Later renamed the American Museum, its collections expanded to include a live mountain lion, a preserved orangutan fetus, copper engravings, and a model of a Scottish threshing and winnowing machine; after the museum's scholarly emphasis was abandoned, the society turned it over to Baker to run as a private for-profit venture.

Art academies often housed collections (mostly plaster copies of classical sculptures) and mounted exhibitions of members' work. One of the first was the American Academy of the Fine Arts (1802); this was overshadowed from 1826 by the National Academy of Design, which continued to sponsor exhibitions into the early twenty-first century. Under the direction of Pintard the New-York Historical Society was chartered in 1804 as a library of national and local history and a meeting place for prominent men. Interest mounted to assemble a permanent collection devoted to science, leading to the formation of the Lyceum of Natural History in 1817 (destroyed by fire some years later). Small collections were assembled by individuals, cultural clubs, and literary and scientific societies.

In addition to public galleries, before the Civil War the city had several "dime" museums, which were dedicated to entertainment and showed curiosities for a fee. The best-known in the city was Barnum's American Museum, opened by P. T. Barnum at Broadway and Ann Street in 1841. It offered curiosities of both art and nature, such as jugglers, dioramas, the spurious "Feejee mermaid," and Charles Stratton, whom Barnum renamed Tom Thumb because he stood only 25 inches (63 centimeters) tall. Such presentations led the public to associate showmanship and theatricality with museums, and the distinction between dime museums and public galleries was sometimes blurred according to directors' tastes. Rigorous standards were upheld by the New York Gallery of Fine Arts, formed in 1844 as a permanent public art gallery around the private collection of Luman Reed. Acquired in 1858 by the New-York Historical Society, the collection was later augmented by such diverse objects as marble bas-relief sculptures from the palace of Sardanapalus at Nineveh (donated by James Lenox), a collection of Egyptian antiquities (donated by Henry Abbott), and John James Audubon's watercolor originals for the engravings used in *Birds of America* (1827–38). The collection rivaled some European galleries after Thomas J. Bryan and Louis Durr donated paintings by European masters. In 1846 a permanent art gallery was opened by the Brooklyn Institute (formerly known as

The Museum of the Moving Image, located at the site of the former Kaufman Astoria Studios, 2009

American Museum at City Hall Park, 1825

the Apprentices' Library). From its inception the Cooper Union for the Advancement of Science and Art, chartered in 1859 to provide free education for workers, included among its facilities a public art gallery free of charge; it opened the Museum for the Arts of Decoration at Astor Place in 1897.

Most of the city's museums were established by industrialists who amassed fortunes in the decades of prosperity after the Civil War. Advances in the natural sciences during the 1860s by such theorists as Charles Darwin, Thomas Huxley, and Charles Lyell inspired Albert Smith Bickmore, a naturalist trained at Harvard, to form the American Museum of Natural History. It was conceived as a partnership between the city, which erected the building and supplied funds for maintenance, and the trustees, who supported the collections, staff, and programs. Bickmore and a few associates used their own money to buy the first exhibitions, a collection of stuffed birds and mammals owned by the German Prince Maximilian zu Wied–Neuwied and originally housed at the Arsenal in Central Park. The museum opened in 1869 as an institution dedicated to research and public instruction in the natural sciences and ethnology. Collections there and at other natural history museums eventually included big-game trophies and entire families of monkeys, birds, insects, and plants.

In 1870 members of the Union League Club including John Jay (grandson of the chief justice) and William Cullen Bryant proposed a public art museum to promote education and social and moral betterment. To these ends the Metropolitan Museum of Art was incorporated by the state legislature, and the city raised $500,000 toward construction costs. The first collection consisted of American and European paintings formerly owned by William T. Blodgett, and in 1880 the museum opened its first building along Fifth Avenue in Central Park. During the late nineteenth century the Brooklyn Institute became the Brooklyn Institute of Arts and Sciences, which encouraged research and public education and founded a museum of art, natural history, and ethnology dedicated to assimilating immigrants. Its building, designed by McKim, Mead and White, was erected between 1895 and 1926. Renamed the Brooklyn Museum, it became known for its collections of Egyptian, African, pre-Columbian, American, and decorative art, which gradually took precedence over scientific collections. One of its branches was the Brooklyn Children's Museum, the first of its kind in the world. Opened in 1899, it mounted displays with materials for children to touch, arranged to emphasize relationships and accompanied by brief labels in large, readable type.

A number of wealthy patrons left large bequests during the early twentieth century to form and maintain museums. In 1901 the railroad magnate Jacob S. Rogers left $7 million to the Metropolitan Museum of Art, making it the wealthiest museum in the world. The collections of Benjamin Altman and J. P. Morgan, donated in 1913 and 1917, established it as a museum of international importance, with holdings eventually including musical instruments, arms and armor, and primitive art from around the world. In 1926 part of the medieval collection was installed at the Cloisters, a section of a Romanesque Benedictine monastery from southern France bought by John D. Rockefeller and reconstructed in Fort Tryon Park. Audubon Terrace in upper Manhattan became the site of the Hispanic Society of America, founded in 1904 as a free public museum and library for the study of Hispanic culture; the Museum of the American Indian, which opened in 1916 and was later taken over by the Smithsonian Institution; and the American Numismatic Society. A number of collections held in private residences became public museums, among them the Frick Collection of European paintings and sculptures, maintained in the former residence of the industrialist Henry Clay Frick on Fifth Avenue (designed by Thomas Hastings), and the Pierpont Morgan Library (renamed the Morgan Library and Museum), holding books and art formerly owned by Morgan and housed in his Renaissance mansion on East 36th Street (1906, McKim, Mead and White). The Museum of the City of New York, opened in the Gracie Mansion in 1923 to preserve local history, amassed fine examples of clipper ships, colonial portraits, furniture, toys, costumes, and fire engines; in 1932 it moved to Fifth Avenue at 103rd Street. The American Museum of Natural History added astronomy to its areas of study in 1937 with the gift of the Hayden Planetarium from the philanthropist Charles Hayden.

Several collectors took measures to preserve and promote the work of modern artists. The Whitney Studio and the Whitney Studio Club were founded by Gertrude Vanderbilt Whitney to display the work of young artists; her collection became the basis of the Whitney Museum of American Art (1930). The Museum of Modern Art was set up in 1929 to collect not only paintings and sculptures but also drawings, prints, photographs, films, stage designs, furniture, and work in architecture and commercial design. Its initial holdings were donated by Lillie P. Bliss. Abby Aldrich Rockefeller later donated part of her collection and with Mrs. Simon R. Guggenheim provided generous funds to buy avant-garde works by twentieth-century artists. The holdings of Solomon R. Guggenheim evolved into the Museum of Non-Objective Painting (1939, renamed the Solomon R. Guggenheim Museum in 1952), which occupied rented quarters before moving to a building on Fifth Avenue between 88th and 89th streets designed by Frank Lloyd Wright. The collections of the Museum for the Arts of Decoration were taken over by the Smithsonian Institution during the 1960s and installed in a mansion on Fifth Avenue (formerly owned by Andrew Carnegie) that became known as the Cooper–Hewitt Museum of Decorative Art and Design. Several museums opened during the mid-twentieth century, among them the Museum of Contemporary Crafts (1956, later renamed the Museum of Arts and Design), the Museum of American Folk Art (1963), the International Center of Photography (1974), and the Museum of Broadcasting (1975, later renamed the Paley Center for Media). Smaller institutions devoted to modern art often lacked permanent collections but offered educational programs to the public and opportunities for lesser-known artists to exhibit their work. The Bronx Museum of the Arts was formed in 1972 by the Bronx Council on the Arts to display traveling exhibitions from other museums and the work of local artists. Other popular exhibition spaces included P.S.1 Contemporary Art Center in Long Island City, Queens, and the New Museum of Contemporary Art, Artists Space, and Franklin Furnace in lower Manhattan.

Other museums were dedicated during this time to house collections of works by national, ethnic, and cultural groups, notably the Asia Society, the Japan Society Gallery, the Museum of Chinese in the Americas, the Jewish Museum, the Ukrainian Museum, the Museo del Barrio, the Studio Museum in Harlem, and the Jacques Marchais Museum of Tibetan Art. Historic houses throughout the city were also preserved, often through local efforts. Among those restored in Manhattan were the Abigail Adams Smith Museum, the Morris–Jumel Mansion, and the houses of William Dyckman, Frederick Van Cortlandt, and Seabury Treadwell (known as the Merchant's House Museum). More survived in the outer boroughs, including the Lefferts Homestead in Prospect Park; the Valentine–Varian House, which became the headquarters of the Museum of Bronx History, and Poe Cottage in the Bronx; the Queens Quaker Meeting House, a rare example of seventeenth-century architecture and one of the country's oldest places of worship, and the Louis Armstrong House Museum in Queens; and the Alice Austen House in Staten Island. Work also began on the restoration of 40 buildings from Richmondtown (see Historic Richmond Town), a project sponsored locally and directed by the Staten Island Historical Society to trace the development of a village from the seventeenth century to the nineteenth; the Snug Harbor Cultural Center, home to several museums, opened in the 1970s. Some museums in the city were established in unconventional places: the New York Transit Museum is housed underground in a 1936 subway station in Brooklyn, and the Intrepid Sea, Air, Space Museum is centered around a World War II aircraft carrier at Pier 86 in Manhattan.

During the late twentieth century some institutions sought new sources of funds and explored new systems of management. The Brooklyn Children's Museum became independent of the Brooklyn Museum in 1979 and provided a model for institutions in Manhattan and Staten Island. As natural habitats were destroyed and many species faced extinction, natural history museums reevaluated their practices and ceased to harvest specimens for display. In the early twenty-first century many museums expanded or moved to new spaces, such as the Queens Museum of Art, the American Museum of the Moving Image, the Museum for African Art, and the New Museum of Contemporary Art. New institutions opened, including the Rubin Museum of Art (1999), the Chelsea Art Museum (2002), the Lower East Side Tenement Museum (1988), the New York City Police Museum (1998), the New York City Fire Museum (1987), the Skyscraper Museum (1997), the Sports Museum of America (2008), the Museum of Jewish Heritage (1997), the

Members of New York City's Cultural Institutions Group, 2008

Name and Year Founded[1]	Address
American Museum of the Moving Image (1988)	Astoria Studios, 36-01 35th Ave., Astoria, Queens
American Museum of Natural History (1869)	Central Park West and 79th St., Manhattan
Bronx County Historical Society (1955)	2209 Bainbridge Ave., Bronx
Bronx Museum of the Arts (1971)	1040 Grand Concourse at 165th St., Bronx
Brooklyn Academy of Music (1861)	30 Lafayette Ave., Brooklyn
Brooklyn Botanical Gardens (1910)	1000 Washington Ave., Brooklyn
Brooklyn Children's Museum (1899)	145 Brooklyn Ave., Brooklyn
Brooklyn Museum (1823)	200 Eastern Pkwy., Brooklyn
Carnegie Hall (opened 1891)	57th St. and Seventh Ave., Manhattan
Flushing Town Hall[2] (1862)	137-35 Northern Blvd., Flushing, Queens
Jamaica Center for Arts and Learning (1972)	16-04 Jamaica Ave., Jamaica, Queens
Lincoln Center for the Performing Arts (1955)	132 West 65th St. or 70 Lincoln Center Plaza, Manhattan
Metropolitan Museum of Art (1870)	1000 Fifth Ave., Manhattan
Museo del Barrio (1969)	1230 Fifth Ave. at 104th St., Manhattan
Museum of the City of New York (1923)	Fifth Ave. at 103rd St., Manhattan
Museum of Jewish Heritage (1997)	36 Battery Place, Battery Park City, Manhattan
New York Botanical Garden (1891)	Bronx River Parkway at Fordham Road, Bronx
New York City Center (opened 1943)	130 West 56th St., Manhattan
New York Hall of Science (1964)	47-01 111th St., Corona, Queens
New York Shakespeare Festival (1954)	Delacorte Theater, Central Park West at 81st St., Central Park, Manhattan
New York State Theater (opened 1964): New York City Ballet and New York City Opera (1948 and 1943)	20 Lincoln Center Plaza, 63rd and Columbus Aves., Manhattan
P.S.1 Contemporary Art Center (1971)	22–25 Jackson Ave. at the intersection of 46th Ave., Long Island City, Queens
Queens Botanical Garden (1939)	43–50 Main St., Flushing, Queens
Queens Museum of Art (1972)	Flushing Meadows–Corona Park, Flushing, Queens
Queens Theater in the Park (1989)	Flushing Meadows–Corona Park, Flushing, Queens
Snug Harbor Cultural Center (1801)	1000 Richmond Terrace, Staten Island
Staten Island Botanical Garden (1977)	1000 Richmond Terrace, Staten Island
Staten Island Children's Museum (1974)	1000 Richmond Terrace, Staten Island
Staten Island Historical Society (1856)	441 Clarke Ave., Staten Island
Staten Island Museum (1881)	75 Stuyvesant Place, Staten Island
Staten Island Zoo(logical Society) (opened 1936)	614 Broadway, Staten Island
Studio Museum of Harlem (1967)	144 West 125th St., Manhattan
Wave Hill (1965)	675 West 252nd St., Bronx
Wildlife Conservation Society (1895)	2300 Southern Blvd., Bronx

1. Included are city-owned institutions that receive direct subsidies from the New York City Department of Cultural Affairs.

2. The Flushing Council on Culture and the Arts is located here and was founded in 1979.

Source: New York City Department of Cultural Affairs Web site, http://www.nyc.gov/html/dcla/html/home/home.shtml

Compiled by Frank Nestor

Museum of American Finance (1988), the Museum of Sex (2002), and the City Reliquary (2002), founded in Williamsburg by New York City firefighter Dave Herman. The city continued to support scores of museums even while the economic downturn of 2008 resulted in widespread concern about funding for cultural institutions.

Nathaniel Burt, *Palaces for the People: A Social History of the American Art Museum* (Boston: Little, Brown, 1977); Joel J. Orosz, *Curators and Culture: The Museum Movement in America, 1740–1870* (Tuscaloosa: University of Alabama Press, 1990); Deirdre Cossman, *Museums of New York City: A Guide for Residents and Visitors* (Yardley, Pa: Westholme, 2005)

Ella M. Foshay

music. See Bands, Choruses, Classical music, Folk music, Gospel music, Hip-hop and rap, Jazz, Music criticism, Opera, Ragtime, and Rock, as well as entries on individual figures and institutions.

musical instrument manufacture. The manufacture of lutes and violins in New York City was reported as early as the 1690s. During the eighteenth century the workshops were concentrated around South Street, and most instrument makers were immigrants who combined the manufacture of new instruments with the repair of older ones and the sale of imported instruments and music. After 1750 artisans such as Christian Claus (1789–99), Thomas Dodds (1785–99), and Archibald Whaites (1793–1816) frequently placed newspaper advertisements proclaiming their ability to make as many as a dozen kinds of instruments. On its introduction into the city in the 1770s the piano replaced the harpsichord as the standard keyboard instrument: although only two of the 21 instrument makers active in the city in the 1790s made pianos (most made wind and stringed instruments), within a decade an enormous demand for pianos led to a rapid expansion of the business. John Gelb, an organ builder from 1798, formed a business with his brothers Adam and William that made pianos until 1872. About 1800 many instrument makers and dealers moved to the area around the new City Hall, and by the 1820s instrument making was the city's fifth-largest industry, after shipbuilding, sugar refining, metalworking, and furniture making. At the same time the origin of instrument makers in the city changed from predominantly British in the 1820s to German and central European in the 1830s and 1840s. Most German-speaking workers entered the trade as journeymen but many later became shop supervisors, and some opened shops of their own. A census in 1855 found that 553 of the 836 instrument makers living in New York City were immigrants, and of these 58 percent were German. Some of the leading piano-making firms of the period included Dubois and Stodart (founded 1819), Bacon (1841), Hardman (1842), Haines (1851), Weber (1852), Mathusek (1857), Steck (1857), Behning (1861), Sohmer (1872), and Behr (1881). Other firms made violins (August and George Gemunder), flutes (E. Riley, A. G. Badger), woodwinds (Firth and Pond, 1848–65), and brass instruments (Schreiber Cornet Company, Stratton).

As pianists began to demand greater volume and tone from their instruments, piano makers experimented with various methods of reinforcing their pianos. The firm of Steinway and Sons, formed in 1853 by Heinrich E. Steinweg, patented a cast-iron piano frame in the 1850s that won a gold medal at the World's Fair in London in 1862. Steinway's success directed attention to the innovations of other artisans in New York City and led to the expansion of instrument shops, which required larger spaces and more craftspeople to manufacture pianos with cast-iron frames. The district where retail musical instrument shops were centered moved progressively northward, extending to Cooper Square in the 1850s and to 14th Street in the 1870s and 1880s; the expansion of the trade in the city continued unabated until the 1890s. According to the federal census of 1890 New York

Advertisement for Firth, Hall, and Pond, Pianoforte and Music Warehouse

City had 131 instrument firms employing 5958 craftspeople, who produced about $13 million worth of instruments.

In the late 1890s the city's instrument business suffered from a succession of technological and economic changes, despite which it expanded as far north as West 57th Street by about 1900. It initially benefited from the introduction of automated player pianos, but the benefit was soon offset by the increased popularity of phonographs and radios. Instrument making declined throughout the Depression, and during World War II many of the larger piano factories were requisitioned for the production of war materials (very few reopened). When Sohmer left the city in the early 1980s Steinway became the only remaining piano maker. In the early twenty-first century a few small ateliers in the city made wind, string, and percussion instruments of high quality. Among the best-known were the Gael Français Violin Workshop and Matt Umanov Guitars.

Nancy Groce, *Urban Craftsmen: Musical Instrument Makers in New York City* (New York: Pendragon, 1991)

Nancy Groce

musical theater. The first known musical theater performances in New York City were ballad operas such as *The Beggar's Opera* (London, 1728) by John Gay and Johann Pepush, presented by the Hallam Company at the New Theatre on Nassau Street in 1753. In 1796 the Old American Company performed the first important American musical comedy, *The Archers,* with libretto by William Dunlap and music by Benjamin Carr. The musical stage was dominated by English and European works well into the nineteenth century, but the number of American works grew by the 1840s. *A Glance at New York* (1848) depicted neighborhoods in the city and character types associated with them, including "Mose the Bowery B'hoy." American-themed burlesques became popular after John Brougham presented *Pocahontas; or, the Gentle Savage* (1855). Minstrel companies made regular visits by the 1850s, and several minstrel houses opened in the city. Musical productions increased rapidly after the Civil War. *The Black Crook* (1866) featured melodrama, spectacle, and ballet dancers clad in flesh-colored tights; it was an enormous success and inspired a number of imitations. Other extravaganzas combined elaborate settings with a burlesque of a literary work and were popular among the upper classes. One of the best-known was *Evangeline,* which opened in 1874 and toured until the end of the century. By the 1870s New York City was the country's most important center for musical theater.

After the triumphant premiere of *HMS Pinafore* by Gilbert and Sullivan in 1879, English comic opera dominated musical theater in the city until the turn of the twentieth century. Popular among upper-class audiences, it inspired such works as *Robin Hood* (1891), by the American composer Reginald De Koven. Minstrel shows were favored by immigrants and workers, as was vaudeville, which evolved after Tony Pastor transformed variety shows into family entertainment. At the Theatre Comique, Edward Harrigan and Tony Hart produced musical plays depicting life among Irish, Germans, and blacks in the city. As immigration reached a peak at the turn of the twentieth century the number of ethnic theaters increased, especially those for German and Yiddish speakers. Ethnic characters also became a mainstay in the Irish musicals of W. J. Scanlan and Chauncey Olcott, the "Fritz" musicals of J. K. Emmet, and the "Dutch" comedy burlesques of Weber and Fields. By the end of the nineteenth century there were a few works by African Americans, among them *The Origin of the Cakewalk; or, Clorindy* (1898) by Paul Lawrence Dunbar and Will Marion Cook. *The Passing Show* (1894) was produced by George W. Lederer, who declared it a "review" of the political, social, and theatrical events of the year. Based on the olio section of the minstrel show and on the vaudeville variety show, it was soon widely imitated in shows known as revues. The English comic opera *Florodora* (1900), a production in the style of Gilbert and Sullivan, ran for many years. The operettas of Victor Herbert, such as *Babes in Toyland* (1903) and *Naughty Marietta* (1910), were also highly successful. The urban settings and characters of Harrigan and Hart were brought up to date by George M. Cohan in such comedies as *Little Johnny Jones* (1904). In 1907 Florenz Ziegfeld produced the first of his annual *Follies,* a revue known for its comedians, dancers, singers, chorus girls, and elaborate scenery.

During World War I composers of musical comedies rejected European styles in favor of American ones. Ragtime was incorporated into a few songs on the musical stage and was widely adopted in musical comedy after Irving Berlin composed an entire score of modified ragtime for the revue *Watch Your Step* in 1914. Composer Jerome Kern and librettist Guy Bolton (later joined by P. G. Wodehouse) experimented with small casts, simple settings, and contemporary stories in musicals such as *Very Good Eddie* (1915) at the intimate Princess Theatre. More traditional operettas remained among the most popular forms, and a number were written for the American stage by composers trained in Europe, including Rudolf Friml (*Rose-Marie,* 1924) and Sigmund Romberg (*The Student Prince,* 1924). After the success of *Shuffle Along* (1921) by Noble Sissle and Eubie Blake, other musicals written and performed by blacks were presented during the early 1920s; they introduced new dance steps as well as early jazz, which supplanted ragtime. Later in the decade George and Ira Gershwin incorporated jazz-inspired music and satirical lyrics like those of W. S. Gilbert in a series of successful musicals culminating in *Of Thee I Sing* (1931), which won a Pulitzer Prize. Several productions of the songwriters Richard Rodgers and Lorenz Hart were highly successful, including *A Connecticut Yankee* (1927). One of the longest-running productions of the 1920s was *Good News* (1927), a musical by B. G. DeSylva, Lew Brown, and Ray Henderson about college life. Traditional and contemporary styles were blended in *Show Boat* (1927), a musical by Kern and Oscar Hammerstein II about a family of showboat performers from the 1880s to the 1920s.

The number of musicals produced in the city fell drastically after the stock market crashed in 1929, and many important figures in musical theater moved to Hollywood to make motion pictures. Broadway nonetheless saw some of its finest productions between 1929 and 1960. Cole Porter wrote insinuating melodies and clever lyrics for such musical comedies as *Fifty Million Frenchmen* (1929) and *Anything Goes* (1934), and a sophisticated style of topical revue was introduced by Arthur Schwartz and Howard Dietz in *The Little Show* (1929) and *The Band Wagon* (1931). Some writers and composers sought to explore the country's growing unrest in their work. *Johnny Johnson,* a musical with a strong anti-war message by Kurt Weill, was produced by the Group Theatre in 1936; *The Cradle Will Rock,* a musical by Marc Blitzstein dealing with conflicts between workers and capitalists, caused controversy in a production by Orson Welles's Mercury Theater in 1937. Social and political themes yielded to escapist ones during World War II. In 1943 Rodgers and Hammerstein produced *Oklahoma!,* a nostalgic operetta about cowboys and farmers in 1907 in the Oklahoma Territory. It enjoyed unprecedented popularity and was the first work of its kind to include a violent death onstage and a "dream ballet" (choreography by Agnes de Mille) to explain and enhance the dramatic action. Other "musical plays" by Rodgers and Hammerstein included *Carousel* (1945), *South Pacific* (1949), *The King and I* (1951), and *The Sound of Music* (1959).

Although some composers and lyricists sought to imitate Rodgers and Hammerstein, a more traditional style of musical comedy also flourished during the 1940s and early 1950s. Irving Berlin wrote the score for *Annie Get Your Gun* (1946), in which Ethel Merman played the character of Annie Oakley; other popular comedies included Frank Loesser's *Guys and Dolls* (1950), about Broadway gamblers and their girlfriends; *Wonderful Town* (1953), a depiction of life in Greenwich Village during the 1930s by Leonard Bernstein, Betty Comden, and Adolph Green; and *The Pajama Game* (1954) by Richard Adler and Jerry Ross, a story about personal and professional relationships in a pajama factory. In 1956 Alan Jay Lerner and Frederick Loewe adapted George Bernard Shaw's comedy *Pygmalion* into a musical, *My Fair Lady,* that had a record-breaking run. Their show helped to revive interest in operettas set in bygone eras; encouraged adaptations of other successful plays, novels, and motion pictures; and inaugurated the practice of using actors rather than singers for important roles. The story of Romeo and Juliet provided the inspiration for the musical *West Side Story* (1957) by composer Leonard Bernstein, librettist Arthur Laurents, lyricist Stephen Sondheim, and director Jerome Robbins. Jerry Bock and Sheldon Harnick wrote an ironic version of the European operetta in *She Loves Me* (1963) and in 1964 joined with Robbins to create *Fiddler on the Roof,* which soon became one of the country's most popular musicals. New subjects and settings were also used in a number of musical comedies, notably *Gypsy* (1959), a story based on the life of the stripper Gypsy Rose Lee; *How to Succeed in Business without Really Trying* (1961), a satire of the corporate world; *Cabaret* (1966), set in Berlin during the 1930s; and *Hair* (1968), which introduced rock music and nudity to Broadway.

During the early 1970s concern arose about the failure of Broadway to attract new artists and audiences. Revues based on songs by well-known composers and revivals of old productions predominated. Some of the few new works were created by Sondheim, whose shows were innovative and controversial: *Company* (1970), *Follies* (1971), *A Little Night Music* (1973), *Pacific Overtures* (1976), *Sweeney Todd* (1979), *Sunday in the Park with George* (1984), *Into the Woods* (1987), and *Passion* (1994). His early collaborations with the director Harold Prince, known as "concept musicals," were shaped around an idea or visual image rather than a libretto and score. In some musicals that followed this model the director and choreographer were the primary creative figures: examples include *Pippin* (1972) and *Chicago* (1975) by Bob Fosse and *A Chorus Line* (1975) and *Dreamgirls* (1981) by Michael Bennett. As production costs and ticket prices rose during the 1980s, some writers, performers, and producers preferred to work in the more relaxed environment of Off Broadway, Off Off Broadway, and regional theater. The most successful productions were often European or British: *Cats* (1981) and *The Phantom of the Opera* (1989) by Andrew Lloyd Webber played in London before being shown in New York City, and *Les Misérables* (1987) and *Miss Saigon* (1991) were presented by a team of French songwriters. In 1990 Tommy Tune used elements of the concept musical in *Grand Hotel,* his adaptation of a popular motion picture.

Rent opened Off Broadway in 1994 and became one of the longest-running musicals in history, moving to Broadway's Nederlander Theater in 1996. Like *Hair* had been in the 1960s, *Rent* was a rock musical for the 1990s: the show, about artists living in the Lower East Side during the AIDS epidemic in New York City, was also the first to offer inexpensive rush seats. Stage adaptations of films increased around the turn of the twenty-first century: adaptations of the Disney animated films *Beauty and the Beast* (1994) and *The Lion King* (1997) were lush productions and major Broadway successes. *The Producers* (2001), an adaptation of Mel Brooks's 1968 film, became a Tony Award–winning show, with record-breaking sales during its six-year run. The show pioneered the premium Broadway ticket with its extraordinarily high prices: most tickets were $100, and a company called Broadway Inner Circle began selling $480 VIP tickets several months after the show opened. *Hairspray,* adapted from the 1988 John Waters film, opened in 2002 with Harvey Fierstein playing Edna Turnblad. In the early twenty-first century many successful musicals began as Off-Broadway productions: *Avenue Q* (2003) was inspired by *Sesame Street; Spring Awakening* (2006), which was adapted from a controversial 1891 German play, continued the evolution of the rock musical; and *In the Heights* (2007), a musical set in New York City's Dominican neighborhood of Washington Heights, featured hip-hop and Latino music. Acclaimed revivals of *Gypsy* and *South Pacific* opened in 2008.

Cecil Smith and Glenn Litton, *Musical Comedy in America* (New York: Theatre Arts Books, 1950; rev. 1981); Allen Woll, *Black Musical Theatre: From Coontown to Dreamgirls* (Baton Rouge: Louisiana State University Press, 1989); Gerald Bordman, *American Musical Theatre: A Chronicle* (New York: Oxford University Press, 1978; 2nd edn 1992)

Margaret M. Knapp, Kate Lauber

MCA [Music Corporation of America]. Corporate conglomerate formed in 1924 in Chicago by Jules Stein. Begun as a talent agency, MCA booked popular big bands in New York City and in the 1930s was the largest musical talent agency in the United States; from 1945 it also booked performers for theater, films, and television. After the firm left the booking business in 1962 it grew under the leadership of Lew Wasserman into a diversified entertainment company with subsidiaries in television (WWOR-TV, channel 9, acquired in 1987), motion pictures (Universal Pictures), music (MCA Records), and book publishing (G. P. Putnam's Sons); it was also active in cable television and movie theaters through its ownership of 50 percent of the USA Network and Cineplex Odeon. In 1991 MCA was acquired by the Japanese electronics firm Matsushita Electric Industrial Company, which sold WWOR-TV. In 1995 Seagram Company Ltd. purchased 80 percent of MCA and renamed the television and film divisions Universal Studios, Inc., and the music divisions Universal Music Group. The following year, G. P. Putnam's Sons was sold to the Penguin Group. Geffen Records absorbed the remaining music divisions in 2003. As of 2009, MCA Nashville Records, the country music label, was the only remaining branch to maintain the MCA name.

George Winslow, Meghan Lalonde

music criticism. Reviews of the first concerts in New York City appeared in newspapers such as John Peter Zenger's *New-York Weekly Journal* (founded in 1733) and Hugh Gaine's *New-York Mercury* (founded in 1752). While early articles were unsigned, by the early nineteenth century they were signed and appeared in newspapers such as the *Evening Post,* the *Gazette and General Advertiser,* the *Herald,* the *Albion,* the *New-York Musical Journal,* and the *New-York Mirror.*

By the time the New York Philharmonic Orchestra began operations in 1842 the foundation for a circle of music critics had been laid by Henry C. Watson, an English writer whose reviews were published in *Albion,* the city's leading literary periodical at the time. William Henry Fry, a columnist for the *New York Tribune* between 1852 and 1863, campaigned for American music, often in effusive prose. His successor at the *Tribune* was Watson, followed in 1867 by John Hassard, who provided insightful reviews of Wagner's *Der Ring des Nibelungen* from Bayreuth in 1876. The late nineteenth century saw the rise of powerful critics in New York City, reflecting the city's growth as a cultural center, and the proliferation of its musical institutions. Music criticism appeared in the *Tribune,* the *New York Herald,* the *New York Times,* the *Sun,* and the *New York World,* the most widely read newspapers of the day, and in literary journals such as *Harper's* (1850–), *Scribner's Magazine* (1887–1900), and the *Dial* (1880–1929). Several publications dominated the musical press, including *Watson's Art Journal* (1864–1905), the *New York Figaro* (1881–1900), *Musical America* (1898–), the *Musical Observer* (1907–31), and the *Musical Quarterly* (1915–).

From 1880 until the 1920s the work of such critics as Henry T. Finck, Henry Krehbiel, William James Henderson, Richard Aldrich, and James Gibbons Huneker made the city the country's leader in music criticism. These critics had similar training, and their extensive knowledge won wide respect. Reports from the Bayreuth Festival in 1876 were cabled to the *New York Times,* the first transatlantic music criticism. Finck's enthusiastic reports from the festival for the *Tribune* helped to make Wagner popular in North America. Although often in disagreement with Finck, Krehbiel also gave favorable reviews of Wagner's work, as well as that of Brahms. As Hassard's successor at the *Tribune* from the mid-

1880s until his death in 1923, Krehbiel was known for his vivid prose style, but a growing conservatism hindered his understanding of such "modernists" as Stravinsky and Schoenberg. The *New York Times* gained authority in music criticism after engaging Henderson in 1887. A brilliant stylist with solid musical training, he shared Krehbiel's affinity for Wagner and Brahms and his distaste for the work of modernists like Debussy and Strauss. In reviews of such works as *Salome* he stressed moral value as an important criterion for music criticism. He worked for the *Sun* from 1902 until his death in 1937 and often gave lectures about music at the New York Musical College and the Institute of Musical Art. His successor at the *Times* was Aldrich, who was more open-minded but nevertheless opposed radical manifestations of modernism. Unlike his peers he wrote in a witty, entertaining style. Huneker, the youngest critic in the circle, wrote music, art, and drama reviews in turgid prose for the *Sun* from 1900 to 1912; he was the only critic active in the city before World War I who supported contemporary composers, including Strauss and Schoenberg.

A new group of critics came to prominence during the 1920s as their predecessors retired. Music in the city became divided between advocates of modern music and the conservatives, who saw the concert hall as a sort of museum. The conflict was carried into the city's press and its venerable musical institutions. During these years the League of Composers emerged as the leading defender of modern music and launched the important publication *Modern Music* (1924–46), which attracted prominent composers as contributors, among them Aaron Copland and Henry Cowell.

In the years between the world wars a more moderate approach was taken by Deems Taylor at the *World* (1921–25), Lawrence Gilman at the *Tribune* (1923–37), and Olin Downes at the *Times* (1924–55). They cultivated an elevated literary style like that of their predecessors, but except for Gilman they were usually more straightforward; they were also more likely to accept the modernism of Stravinsky, Bartók, and Prokofiev. Downes was the first major music critic in the city to adopt a simple and direct style aimed more at the average reader than the cultural elite. The most radical critic of the time was Paul Rosenfeld, who wrote for literary journals and *Modern Music* and was a supporter of the avant-garde composers Charles Ives, Edgar Varèse, and Wallingford Riegger.

Music criticism in the city changed after the appointment of Virgil Thomson as Gilman's successor at the *Herald Tribune* in 1940. A Francophile and himself a composer, Thomson was known for the wit, clarity, and depth of his reviews and became one of the country's leading voices in music criticism. On his retirement in 1954 he was succeeded by the musicologist Paul Henry Lang, who offered a scholarly perspective during his six-year tenure. After Downes's death in 1955 Howard Taubman served as the chief music critic for the *Times* until 1960. His replacement was Harold C. Schonberg, who dominated music criticism in the city for two decades and won a Pulitzer Prize in 1971 for reviews distinguished not only by wide-ranging expertise but also by fine literary craft.

Music critics were forced to adapt to the changing interests of their readers and to the exigencies of the newspaper industry in the decades after 1960. One of the city's few surviving daily newspapers, the *Times,* sought to expand its readership by offering reviews of jazz and rock; among its most versatile critics was John Rockwell, who worked in both classical and popular genres. On his retirement in 1980 Schonberg was succeeded by Donal Henahan, who was followed by Edward Rothstein in 1991, Bernard Holland in 1995, and Anthony Tommasini in 2000. The number of full-time critics at the *Times* gradually declined by 2008 to four (two for classical music, two for popular music), and the newspaper increasingly used freelance writers to cover important musical events.

The *New Yorker* became a dominant force in music criticism in 1972 when Andrew Porter began his 20-year tenure at the magazine. He often discussed several related events in a longer essay drawing on his extensive musical background and musicological inclinations. His reviews, known for their engaging style and incisiveness, tended to favor opera, contemporary music, and obscure or unknown works of the past. He was succeeded by Paul Griffiths in 1992 and Alex Ross in 1996, by which time coverage was reduced.

The *Village Voice* attracted such well-known jazz and rock reviewers as Robert Christgau and Gary Giddins, and *Rolling Stone* became a primary source for rock criticism. Despite the city's prominence as a musical center, music criticism in the first decade of the twenty-first century diminished and became increasingly the province of bloggers. Some critics maintained a parallel presence in print media and the blogosphere, with the latter providing a forum for extensive opinion-sharing by readers that often undercut the momentousness of the critics' own pronouncements.

Hermann Klein, *Unmusical New York: A Brief Criticism of Triumphs, Failures and Abuses* (London: J. Lane, 1910); Henry T. Finck, *My Adventures in the Golden Age of Music* (New York: Funk and Wagnalls, 1926); Barbara Mueser, "The Criticism of New Music in New York, 1919–1929" (diss., City University of New York, 1975); Mark N. Grant, *Maestros of the Pen: A History of Classical Music Criticism in America* (Boston: Northeastern University Press, 1998)

James Deaville

Muslims. It is probable that Muslims were among the Africans transported to New York City during the colonial period, and that Muslim sailors passed through the Port of New York. The first Islamic institution in the city was established by Alexander Russell Webb, a white journalist who converted to Islam while serving as the American consul to the Philippines (from 1887). After moving to New York City in 1893 he set up a missionary headquarters at 30 East 23rd Street and formed the Moslem World Publishing Company, which issued the periodicals *Moslem World: Dedicated to the American Islamic*

The Islamic Center at East 96th Street in Manhattan, 1992

Propaganda and *Voice of Islam.* Immigrants from Muslim countries arrived in New York City soon after the turn of the twentieth century. In 1907 Polish, Russian, and Lithuanian immigrants formed the American Mohammedan Society, which at its peak had about 400 members; the society worshipped at 108 Powers Street in the Williamsburg neighborhood from 1931. A tiny community of Druze (an offshoot of Islam) settled in the city before 1924. In 1939 Sheik Daoud Ahmed Faisal, born in Morocco and later a resident of the island of Grenada, opened the Islamic Mission of America on State Street in Brooklyn Heights. The group rented a former mansion at 143 State Street in Brooklyn that it purchased in 1947. A large number of Arab Muslims settled in the city after 1948.

By this time Islam had gained converts among the city's African Americans. Followers of Marcus Garvey were influenced by the Moorish Science Temple, formed in 1913 in Newark, New Jersey, and led by Noble Drew Ali. After the founder's death in 1929 the movement split, and some Moors in 1933 opened Temple no. 21 at Livonia Avenue in Brooklyn (later moved to 349 Bainbridge Avenue), which was probably the first black mosque in New York City. Members of the movement later opened temples no. 54 in Brooklyn, no. 72 in Manhattan, and no. 69 in the Bronx. African American conversions to Islam increased in number after the Nation of Islam, based in Chicago and led by Elijah Muhammad, opened Temple no. 7 at the Young Men's Christian Association in Harlem in 1946, and especially after it sent Malcolm X to Manhattan in June 1954 as the imam of Mosque no. 7, which was now situated at 102 West 116th Street. The Nation of Islam appealed to many African Americans because of its emphasis on black identity and empowerment, but some of its practices and tenets proved controversial, especially its exclusion of whites and its espousal of African American separatism and racial superiority.

More conventional Islamic traditions were maintained during the 1950s by representatives from Muslim countries to the United Nations. Under the auspices of the Pakistani League of America (formed in 1954) the Pakistani delegation sponsored ceremonies at Pakistan House (12 East 65th Street) and several local hotels during the feast marking the end of the holy month of Ramadan. In 1955 the Pakistanis joined with representatives from Indonesia, Egypt, and other Islamic countries to organize the Islamic Center of New York, based temporarily at Pakistan House and moved to 1 Riverside Drive in 1957. At Columbia University the first Muslim student organization in New York City was formed in 1956.

After a pilgrimage to Mecca in 1964 Malcolm X embraced Sunni Islam, severed his ties with Elijah Muhammad, and established a mosque at the Theresa Hotel on 125th Street and Seventh Avenue (now Adam Clayton Powell Jr. Boulevard). For a brief period his successor as the imam of Mosque no. 7 and as the spokesman in the city for the Nation of Islam was Louis Farrakhan. The assassination of Malcolm X in 1965 left the followers of the Nation of Islam irrevocably fragmented. A blast of dynamite ignited a fire that destroyed Mosque no. 7, which was rebuilt into a complex of stores, classrooms, and a prayer space in 1970. After it reopened Mosque no. 7 was also called Mosque no. 7A before being renamed Masjid Malcolm Shabazz in 1976 (a *masjid* is a place of prayer). Other mosques of the Nation of Islam in the city included Mosques no. 7B at 103-05 Northern Boulevard in Queens, no. 7C at 120 Madison Street in Brooklyn, and no. 7D at 2000 Morris Avenue in the Bronx (later moved to 960 Woodycrest Avenue). Muhammad was succeeded after his death in 1975 by his son Wallace D. Muhammad, who guided his followers away from racial confrontation and toward Sunni orthodoxy. The Nation of Islam then became divided into factions, with Farrakhan leading one adhering closely to the teachings of Elijah Muhammad.

Many mosques opened during these years, principally in African American neighborhoods. Several in Brooklyn were allied with Dar-ul-Islam (House of Islam), a Sunni group formed in 1963 by former members of the Islamic Mission of America; its principal place of worship was the Ya Sin Mosque, opened in 1967 at 52 Herkimer Street and later moved to 342 Van Siclen Avenue. After the federal government relaxed immigration restrictions in 1965, a large number of Muslim immigrants from around the world settled in the city. The Elmhurst Muslim Society, formed in 1969 by Pakistanis in the basement of an abandoned school building at 85-37 Britton Avenue, was also frequented by Muslims from Syria, Afghanistan, Egypt, Africa, and Bangladesh. In 1972 the Albanian-American Islamic Center of New York and New Jersey converted a former mansion at 1325 Albemarle Road in Flatbush into a mosque where Pakistani, Turkish, and Arab Muslims also worshipped. Pakistanis and Bangladeshis in 1976 opened the Islamic Center of Corona (Masjid al-Falah) at 101-03 43rd Avenue; it moved in 1983 to 42-12 National Street.

In the late twentieth century immigration from countries where Islam is dominant accounted for the growth in the city's Muslim population, including newcomers from Africa; parts of eastern Europe, Turkey, central Asia, the Middle East, the Indian subcontinent; most of Indonesia and Malaysia; and parts of China, the Philippines, and Latin America (especially Guyana). The *Minaret,* a fortnightly newspaper first published in 1974, and the Islamic Circle of North America, formed in Queens in 1971 to spread Islamic teaching throughout the continent, expanded their activities in the late 1980s. A group aligned with Dar-ul-Islam in 1983 opened the Masjid al-Muminun and a school at 1221 Atlantic Avenue in Bedford–Stuyvesant, which eventually ministered to about 40 families. In 1985 the United Muslims' Day parade was held in midtown Manhattan, beginning a practice repeated each year in September, and an Islamic radio program was launched on the radio station WNWK-FM. An organization of Latin American Muslims was formed by a Puerto Rican woman in 1987, and the Islamic Cultural Society in Manhattan sponsored frequent talks about Islam for American audiences at the United Nations and at Riverside Church.

Early in the twenty-first century the majority of the half million Muslims in New York City adhered to the Sunni tradition. Muslim organizations varied considerably in size and composition, from the overwhelmingly elderly American Mohammedan Society to the Islamic Mission of America, which had one of the most diverse congregations in the city. There were about 60 mosques in the city, most of which occupied basements, storefronts, or disused factories. The largest was the Mosque of New York of the Islamic Center of New York, planned over a period of almost 40 years, with most of its financing from Kuwaitis; it was designed by the firm of Skidmore, Owings and Merrill in a style incorporating both traditional elements (such as a minaret and dome) and modernist ones and opened in September 1991 at 96th Street and Third Avenue. Other well-known mosques and masjids in the city included the Masjid al-Farouq on Atlantic Avenue and the Islamic Community Center in Flatbush; a mosque at 137-64 Geranium Avenue in Flushing was being built by the Muslim Center of New York (a predominantly Pakistani organization). The city's Druze community, which consisted of about 500 families of refugees from the civil war in Lebanon, were served by the head of the Druze Council of North America (based in New Jersey). Islam remained an important force among African Americans, who accounted for 25 to 40 percent of all the Muslims in New York City.

Earle H. Waugh et al., eds., *The Muslim Community in North America* (Edmonton: University of Alberta Press, 1983); "Muslims in New York City," Middle East Institute, Columbia University, http://www.tc.columbia.edu/muslim-nyc/index.html

Marc Ferris, Janos Marton

Muste, A(braham) J(ohannes) (*b* Zierikzee, Netherlands, 8 Jan 1885; *d* New York City, 11 Feb 1967). Minister, labor leader, and peace activist. He grew up in Michigan and studied to become a Dutch Reformed minister. Eventually he moved to New York City, where his first pastorate was the Fort Washington Collegiate Church in Washington Heights. He opposed World War I and became a Quaker and pacifist. During the 1920s and 1930s he took part in efforts to form unions and establish training programs for textile workers. From 1921 to 1933 he directed Brookwood Labor College in Westchester County; he was instrumental in the formation of the radical organization of the American Workers Party. Muste renounced Marxism in 1936 for radical pacifism and returned to the city, where he settled with his family in the Bronx in an apartment complex of the Amalgamated Clothing Workers. For several years he worked at the Presbyterian "Labor Temple" at 14th Street and Second Avenue. As chairman of the Fellowship of Reconciliation (1940–53) he was instrumental in forming the Congress of Racial Equality (CORE) in 1942 and influenced the Gandhian education of such civil rights leaders as Bayard Rustin, James Farmer, Martin Luther King, Jr., and Coretta Scott King. After World War II he led many protests against the proliferation of nuclear arms, including acts of civil disobedience during air-raid drills. In 1956 he helped to launch *Liberation,* a monthly magazine of the New Left. Muste worked during the mid-1960s to organize some of the first large-scale protests against the Vietnam War and traveled to North and South Vietnam on peace missions in 1966 and 1967.

Nat Hentoff, ed., *The Essays of A. J. Muste* (New York: Simon and Schuster, 1967); Jo Ann Robinson, *Abraham Went Out: A Biography of A. J. Muste* (Philadelphia: Temple University Press, 1981)

Jonathan D. Bloom

mutual aid societies. Organizations formed by various ethnic, religious, and racial groups to give social and economic support to their members. They were especially active during the peak years of immigration to the United States in the late nineteenth century and the early twentieth, when they offered advice to immigrants seeking to adjust to life in the United States. Most of the societies provided members with some form of health and accident insurance for a small fee; almost all also ensured a decent burial by defraying expenses and providing mourners.

The Present Status of Mutual Benefit Associations (New York: National Industrial Conference Board, 1931)

See also FRATERNAL ORGANIZATIONS and LANDSMANSHAFTN.

Robert A. Slayton

Mutual Life Insurance Company of New York [MONY]. Firm of life insurers, formed in 1843 by Morris Robinson and Alfred S. Pell at 44 Wall Street. The first president was Robinson (1843–49), who introduced new methods of marketing and advertising, including door-to-door soliciting. By 1870 the firm had $242 million of policies in force and was the leading insurer in the country. It lost much of its market during the last quarter of the nineteenth century, when several companies introduced tontine plans and competition increased. In 1884 the firm bought headquarters at 34 Nassau Street. Under the direction of Richard McCurdy (1885–1905) it introduced a deferred dividend plan in 1885 that allowed dividends to be paid at the end of a specified period rather than only on the policyholder's death. An aggressive manager, McCurdy expanded the firm's agency force, strengthened its investment portfolio, and liberalized contracts. MONY was one of many life insurance firms in the city examined by the Legislative Insurance Investigating Committee led by State Senator William Armstrong in 1905; as a result of the committee's findings, most of the firm's executives, including McCurdy, resigned under pressure and were replaced by a group led by Charles A. Peabody (1905–27). Under Peabody's direction the firm expanded its investments in real estate in New York City: by 1943 property in the city accounted for 70 percent of its mortgage loans and 89 percent of its land holdings. The headquarters were moved in 1950 to Broadway between 55th and 56th streets. In 1990 MONY had about $63 billion of policies in force and assets of $23 billion and was the 14th-largest life insurance firm in the country. On 8 July 2004 MONY merged with AXA Financial, Inc.

Shephard B. Clough, *A Century of American Life Insurance: A History of the Mutual Life Insurance Company of New York, 1843–1943* (New York: Columbia University Press, 1946)

James Bradley

Muzak. Firm that offers background music to subscribers. It traces its roots in New York City to 1922, when George O. Squier, a retired army major-general, conceived of transmitting news, music, lectures, and advertising directly into private homes by means of electric wires. The result of his plan was Wired Radio Inc., out of which the Muzak Corporation was formed in 1934. By this time wireless radio was already widespread in American homes, and consequently Muzak concentrated on selling its prerecorded "functional music" to hotels and restaurants. In 1938 the firm introduced music for offices and factories that was intended to offset boredom and monotony in the workplace, and franchises were licensed throughout the United States. After World War II the firm moved from 151 West 46th Street to 229 Park Avenue South. Industrial psychologists in the 1950s promoted the virtues of music in the workplace, and President Dwight D. Eisenhower had Muzak installed in the White House. During these years Muzak began using FM radio side channels instead of direct wiring for transmitting its prerecorded programs. In 1966 Muzak moved into new headquarters at 100 Park Avenue South; there the firm remained until the mid-1980s, when it was purchased by Westinghouse. The firm's last location in New York City was at 888 Seventh Avenue. In 1986 Muzak was purchased by the Field Corporation of Chicago and moved to Seattle.

Chad Ludington

Myers, Myer (*b* New York City, 1723; *d* New York City, 12 Dec 1795). Silversmith and goldsmith. The son of Dutch Sephardic immigrants, he executed tableware as well as religious objects for both Jewish and Protestant congregations; his work was often characterized by rococo flourishes. He was also a merchant and land speculator and a leader of the synagogue Shearith Israel. During British occupation he was in patriotic exile in Philadelphia. In 1786 he was elected chairman of the Gold and Silver Smith's Society in New York City. Myers lived successively at 14 Pearl Street and 17 Pearl Street. Examples of his craft may be seen at the Metropolitan Museum of Art, the Museum of the City of New York, and the New-York Historical Society.

Jeanette W. Rosenbaum, *Myer Myers, Goldsmith, 1723–1795* (Philadelphia: Jewish Publication Society of America, 1954)

Robert I. Goler

Myerson [Grant], **Bess** (*b* New York City, 16 July 1924). Miss America and public official. Born in the Bronx, she became the first Jewish woman to win the Miss America pageant in 1945, the year she graduated from Hunter College. In the following decade she appeared on television variety and game shows and worked as a consumer adviser for several corporations. Beginning in the late 1960s she became involved in New York City politics and was appointed by Mayor John Lindsay as New York City's first commissioner of consumer affairs. Mayor Edward I. Koch appointed her cultural affairs commissioner in 1983. She was forced to resign in 1987 amid highly publicized allegations that she had given a municipal job to the daughter of Justice Hortense Gabel, the judge handling the divorce of her lover, Carl "Andy" Capasso; she was later acquitted of charges of conspiring to bribe Gabel. She was also the founder of the Museum of Jewish Heritage in New York City.

Jesse Drucker

N

NAACP. See National Association for the Advancement of Colored People.

Nabisco. Forerunner of the firm RJR Nabisco.

Namath, Joe [Joseph William] (*b* Beaver Falls, Pa., 31 May 1943). Football player. The son of Hungarian immigrants, he played football for the University of Alabama. In 1965 he signed an unprecedented three-year contract with the New York Jets worth $427,000 over the three years. He remained with the team as a quarterback for 12 years, during which he set many records for passing. In 1969 he fulfilled his own audacious prediction that the Jets would win the Super Bowl by leading his team to victory in Miami against the Baltimore Colts, who had been heavily favored. His flamboyant way of life and charismatic personality earned him the nickname "Broadway Joe" and made him one of the most popular and controversial athletes of his time. Namath retired from the game for six weeks in June 1969 after refusing to sell his share in the Upper East Side bar Bachelors III. His connection to the bar, located on Lexington Avenue, drew criticism because of its reputation as a hangout for gamblers. Namath finally succumbed to pressure from Commissioner Pete Rozelle, selling his share and reporting to training camp. While playing for the Jets he lived at 370 East 76th Street in Manhattan. In 1969 Namath received the Bronze Medallion, the highest award given to civilians by New York City. He was also inducted into the Pro Football Hall of Fame in 1985. Since 1977 he has continued to be a well-known figure as a sports announcer and through various acting roles.

Joseph S. Lieber

Narrows. Tidal strait separating Brooklyn from Staten Island and forming the main entrance into New York Harbor. It was formed during the last Ice Age. In 1524 Giovanni da Verrazano became the first known white man to enter the Narrows. In 1964 the Narrows was spanned by the Verrazano–Narrows Bridge, the largest suspension bridge in the world at the time, making Staten Island more accessible to other citizens of New York City.

Nassau Heights. An obsolete name for a part of northwestern Queens lying within Elmhurst south of Queens Boulevard and east of Grand Avenue. The name first appeared on a map of the Bretonniere farm published in December 1853 by its developer W. E. Caldwell; the farm occupied a parcel now bounded by the tracks of the Long Island Rail Road (northeast), 58th Avenue (southeast), 83rd Street (southwest), and 55th Avenue (northwest). On some maps the neighborhood extended as far south as Caldwell Avenue. The tract was slow to develop: streets were not laid out until 1896 and houses were not built until the 1920s.

Vincent Seyfried

Nast, Thomas (*b* Landau, now Germany, 27 September 1840; *d* Guayaquil, Ecuador, 7 December 1902). Political cartoonist. Nast moved to New York City as a boy, and attended the National Academy of Design. At age 15 he went to work as a draftsman for *Frank Leslie's Illustrated Newspaper.* After that he went to the *New-York Illustrated News,* and in 1861 joined *Harper's Weekly,* publishing more than 2200 cartoons for the magazine until he left in 1886. During the Civil War, Nast's pro-Union illustrations of battlefields and his caricature of those who favored compromise with the south led Lincoln to call Nast "our best recruiting sergeant." Nast's fame earned him ample work

HARPER'S WEEKLY
A JOURNAL OF CIVILIZATION

Vol. XVIII.—No. 888.] NEW YORK, SATURDAY, JANUARY 3, 1874. [WITH A SUPPLEMENT. PRICE TEN CENTS.

Th. Nast

CHRISTMAS-EVE—SANTA CLAUS WAITING FOR THE CHILDREN TO GET TO SLEEP.—[See Poem on Page 4.]

Thomas Nast's cover drawing for Harper's Weekly, *3 January 1874*

140 HARPER'S WEEKLY. [February 26, 1870.

"UNION IS STRENGTH."

DISTRIBUTION OF THE SECTARIAN FUND.

SECTARIAN BITTERNESS.

OUR COMMON SCHOOLS AS THEY ARE AND AS THEY MAY BE.—[See Page 141.]

Thomas Nast, "Our Common Schools as They Are and as They May Be," Harper's Weekly, *26 February 1870*

---

as a book illustrator—he illustrated 110 in his lifetime—but he continued to draw for *Harper's.* His political cartoons helped to bring down William "Boss" Tweed and his Tammany Hall regime—Tweed even tried to bribe Nast to change his subject matter—in part through his famous depiction of Tammany Hall as a bloodthirsty tiger. When Tweed fled imprisonment in 1875, it was a Nast cartoon that allowed officials in Vigo, Spain, to identify and detain him. Nast was the first cartoonist to portray the Republican Party as an elephant and the Democratic Party as a donkey. In his later years, Nast devoted himself increasingly to oil painting and book illustration, with the brief exception of the unsuccessful launch, in 1890, of an illustrated magazine *Nast's Weekly.* In 1902 Theodore Roosevelt appointed Nast general consul of the United States in Guayaquil, Ecuador, where he died the same year during an outbreak of yellow fever. He is buried in Woodlawn Cemetery in the Bronx.

James E. Mooney, Rowan Moore Gerety

Nathan, Maud (*b* New York City, 20 Oct 1862; *d* New York City, 15 Dec 1946). Reformer. A member of an established Sephardic Jewish family, she began a long career in charitable activity and social reform at the age of 17. Soon after her marriage to her first cousin she became a director at the nursing school of Mount Sinai Hospital, which her father-in-law had helped to found. Between 1890 and 1925 much of her attention was devoted to the Consumers' League of New York City, an organization of elite and working-class women that fought to improve women's working conditions. She was also a major force in the woman suffrage movement and worked for Theodore Roosevelt's Progressive presidential candidacy in 1912. She wrote a memoir, *Once upon a Time and Today* (1933).

Kathryn Kish Sklar

Nathan's. A hot dog stand on Surf Avenue in Coney Island, opened in 1916 by Nathan Handwerker, a former employee of the entrepreneur Charles Feltman. It became popular because of its low prices, garish architecture, and hectic ambience. The owners later licensed a franchising operation, which by 2008 had more than 1400 outlets around the world. Since it opened, the original stand has hosted the Nathan's Famous Fourth of July International Hot Dog Eating Contest, which receives national media coverage and draws thousands of spectators annually.

For illustration, see page 880.

Stephen Weinstein

Nation. Weekly magazine launched in 1865 to support the cause of former slaves after the Civil War. In its early years the editor was E. L. Godkin and the literary editor Wendell Phillips Garrison (son of William Lloyd Garrison). The magazine established itself as a consistent supporter of civil rights, civil liberties, and free expression. Until World War I it published only unsigned articles in the interest of nonpartisanship. In spite of its national focus the magazine often covered issues relevant to New York City, such as the corruption of the Tweed Ring, the policies of Robert Moses, and the revision of the municipal charter. Prominent contributors have included Harold Laski, Frederick Law Olmsted, and Freda Kirchwey, who edited, owned, and published the magazine from 1937 to 1955. In 1966, the magazine founded the Nation Institute to promote independent media. In the early twenty-first century the *Nation* remained the oldest continuously published weekly magazine in the United States, headquartered at 33 Irving Place in Manhattan.

Alan Pendleton Grimes, *The Political Liberalism of the Nation, 1865–1932* (Chapel Hill: University of North Carolina Press, 1953); Sara Alpern, *Freda Kirchwey: A Woman of "The Nation"* (Cambridge, Mass.: Harvard University Press, 1987)

Amanda Aaron

Nathan's, 2009

National Academy of Design. Organization formed on 14 January 1826 by Samuel F. B. Morse and others after unsuccessful attempts to merge the American Academy of the Fine Arts and the New York Association of Artists (also known as the Drawing Association). It limited its membership to artists and exhibited the work of living artists exclusively. In 1863 the academy erected a building designed by P. B. Wight at the corner of 23rd Street and Fourth Avenue. Despite its sympathy for contemporary art, the academy sustained criticism for becoming conservative; rebellious artists formed the rival Society of American Artists in 1877. The academy then suffered a decline in activity and respect, but toward the end of the century it rebounded and absorbed the Society of American Artists. The National Academy of Design, which continues to host an annual exhibition, currently operates an art school and museum at 5 East 89th Street, with a permanent collection that features the work of its members.

Thomas Cummings, *Historical Annals of the National Academy of Design* (New York: Kennedy Galleries, 1969)

Carrie Rebora Barratt

National Allied Publications. Original name of DC Comics.

National Archives–Northeast Region. One of 11 regional archives of the National Archives and Records Administration (NARA), located at 201 Varick Street and founded in 1950. It houses federal records from New York, New Jersey, Puerto Rico, and the Virgin Islands, which were stored at the Brooklyn Naval Supply Activities Depot until 1952, when they moved to 641 Washington Street in Manhattan. Reorganized in 1969 as the archives branch of the Federal Records Center–New York, the permanent records moved to Bayonne, New Jersey, in 1974. When NARA became an independent agency in 1985, the archives branch was made separate from the Federal Records Center and became the National Archives–New York Branch (later the National Archives–Northeast Region). In 1992–93 the archives moved to the federal building at 201 Varick Street in Manhattan. The facility is open to the public and contains microfilm readers and public-access computers for searching databases of NARA holdings. Its collections include significant manuscript materials related to New York City: photographs, maps, federal court proceedings, Custom House records, national census records (1790–1930), regional naturalization records (1790–1970s), and ship passenger lists for immigrants to New York City and other U.S. ports. It holds the records for the criminal case heard after the *General Slocum* disaster and provincial admiralty records dating from 1685. Often used by genealogical researchers, in the early twenty-first century the archives maintained more than 63,000 cubic feet (1800 cubic meters) of valuable material.

Donald R. McCoy, *The National Archives: America's Ministry of Documents* (Chapel Hill: University of North Carolina Press, 1978)

Kate Lauber, Robert C. Morris

National Association for the Advancement of Colored People [NAACP]. The National Association for the Advancement of Colored People (NAACP) was formed as a coalition between members of the Niagara Movement, led by W. E. B. Du Bois and William Monroe Trotter in 1905, and white liberals such as William English Walling, Mary White Ovington, and Oswald Garrison Villard (grandson of abolitionist William Lloyd Garrison). Following race riots in Springfield, Illinois, in 1908, the National Negro Conference was held in New York City in 1909, to refute scientific claims of racial inferiority and promote federal legislation against lynching, federal aid for public education, better public opinion of the Negro, and an organization to carry out these initiatives.

The organization was named in 1906 and incorporated in 1911. As its first officers, the committee named William English Walling as treasurer, Villard as executive secretary, and Du Bois the director of publicity and research. The first task of Du Bois was to establish *The Crisis: A Record of the Darker Races* (known commonly as *The Crisis*), the

National Academy of Design, 23rd Street and Fourth Avenue, ca *1885*

official organ of the organization, which had a circulation of more than 100,000 by 1920. The NAACP also focused early on overturning institutionalized racism and Jim Crow segregation through the courts. The group was influential in the 1915 case of *Guinn v. United States,* in which the Supreme Court outlawed Oklahoma's "grandfather clause," which had exempted white voters from requirements while disenfranchising blacks. Early efforts also resulted in a nationwide protest of D. W. Griffith's controversial 1915 film on the Ku Klux Klan, *Birth of a Nation,* leading to its ban in several cities.

The NAACP mounted a determined antilynching campaign between World War I and World War II, having sent secretary Walter White to Arkansas in 1919 to investigate the Elaine Race Riot in which as many as 200 African American tenant farmers were killed; White eventually oversaw the organization's study: *Thirty Years of Lynching in the United States.* The association also turned its attention to securing equal funding for black and white school systems and fighting segregation in public accommodations and transportation. The NAACP Legal Department, headed by Thurgood Marshall and Charles Hamilton Houston, led to the formation in 1940 of the NAACP Legal Defense Fund. The organization secured its greatest accomplishment in 1954, the case of *Brown v. Board of Education* in which the Supreme Court overturned the *Plessy v. Ferguson* decision, declaring "separate but equal" school segregation unconstitutional.

Although the NAACP lost primacy during the civil rights movement to Martin Luther King's Southern Christian Leadership Conference (SCLC), the Student Nonviolent Coordinating Committee (SNCC), and the Congress for Racial Equality (CORE), the NAACP helped push through initiatives like the Civil Rights Act of 1964, which ended the legal basis of public, educational, and employment discrimination. During the 1980s, the NAACP shifted its attention to economic development and the fight against poverty. In 1986, the organization moved its headquarters from New York City to Baltimore, but it ran into debt in the early 1990s, dismissing recently elected Benjamin Chavis in 1994. The latter part of the decade saw a return of financial stability to the organization and it launched a strong voter campaign in the 2000 presidential election. President George Bush refused an invitation to speak at the NAACP national convention in 2004, the first president to do so since Herbert Hoover, but addressed the convention two years later during midterm elections.

Garrett A. Felber

National Audubon Society. Wildlife conservation society. Its forerunner was formed in 1886 by George Bird Grinnell, editor of the magazine *Field and Stream,* to halt the destruction of the North American bird population by hunters and hat manufacturers. The group attracted more than 38,000 members during its first three months of operation, overwhelming Grinnell and leading him to disband it in 1888. Other Audubon societies were organized in 17 states by 1899; these were loosely connected through the magazine *Bird Lore,* launched in 1899 by Frank Chapman of the American Museum of Natural History, and the first national Christmas bird count, sponsored by Chapman in 1900. The state societies became part of the National Association of Audubon Societies for the Protection of Wild Birds and Animals in 1901; this organization played an important role in helping to pass the New York State Audubon Plumage Law (1910) and the federal Migratory Bird Treaty Act (1918). During the 1930s the association began supporting research on endangered birds. It took its current name in 1940 and during the 1960s focused on promoting such environmental protection laws as the Clean Air, Clean Water, Wild and Scenic Rivers, and Endangered Species Acts. In the early twenty-first century, the organization also focused its attention on global warming, preservation of the Arctic National Wildlife Refuge, and ecosystem restoration along the Great Lakes and Mississippi River. The National Audubon Society opened its first urban center in Prospect Park, Brooklyn, in 2002. In the early twenty-first century the society had over 500 local chapters. It has its national headquarters at 700 Broadway in Manhattan.

Eric Wm. Allison

National Black Theatre. Cultural arts organization. The current location at Fifth Avenue between 125th and 126th streets, Manhattan, opened in 1990, houses the National Black Theatre (NBT), which was founded by Dr. Barbara Tear in 1968. Her goal was to reeducate the black community, raising its consciousness and restoring the cultural traditions that she felt had been stripped away; NBT actors were "liberators" and plays were "revivals" or "rituals." This complex, built independently by the company, incorporates the Western Hemisphere's largest example of Yoruba sacred art.

Kathleen Benson

National Broadcasting Company [NBC]. The oldest permanent radio and television network in the United States, formed in 1926 by a group of highly influential businessmen representing the Radio Corporation of America (RCA), General Electric, and Westinghouse. It began radio broadcasts with a gala at the Waldorf–Astoria on 15 November. The network grew so quickly that by 1927 it began building permanent studios at 711 Fifth Avenue, and in time the amount of programming could not be accommodated on one network alone. The result was the creation of two separate entities: the Blue Network, which offered mostly cultural programs (music, drama, and commentary), and the Red Network, which specialized in comedy and light entertainment. The number of affiliates also increased, from 25 when operations began to 61 across the United States in 1931, by which time the network reported a net profit of $2,346,766. In the following year RCA, under the leadership of David Sarnoff, bought out General Electric and Westinghouse to become the sole owner. From the outset NBC featured popular vaudeville entertainers of the day on its broadcasts: Rudy Vallee, Fred Allen, Jack Benny, Ed Wynn, Eddie Cantor, Al Jolson, Groucho Marx, Bob Hope, Bing Crosby, Red Skelton, Edgar Bergen and Charlie McCarthy, and George Burns and Gracie Allen all had regular programs. The series *Amos 'n' Andy,* recorded in Chicago, secured the network's position as the most popular radio network in the United States. Sporting events and political speeches were also mainstays of its broadcast offerings. In spite of the Depression NBC enjoyed unabated success, and in 1931 it made plans to move into Rockefeller Center, then under construction in midtown Manhattan. By 1933 the division NBC News had been created by Lowell Thomas.

With the encouragement of Sarnoff NBC began experimental television broadcasts from the Empire State Building in 1932, and in 1939 it began its first regular television service with a broadcast of President Franklin D. Roosevelt opening the World's Fair. In 1941 the network obtained a commercial television license from the Federal Communications Commission (FCC) for WNBT-TV in New York City, which became the world's first commercial television station. Although the development of television was interrupted by World War II, radio continued to grow. In 1943 the FCC ruled that no organization could own more than one radio network. As a result NBC sold the weaker Blue Network, which eventually became the American Broadcasting Company (ABC). After the war the growth of television resumed, and many radio programs were adapted to the new medium. *Meet the Press,* begun as a radio program in 1945, moved to television in 1947 and eventually became the longest-running program in television history. The number of American homes equipped with television increased from 14,000 in 1947 to 175,000 in 1948. During the 1950s the radio division at NBC focused on news, sports, and public affairs programs, while the television division expanded its broadcast day beyond the afternoon and evening hours to include mornings as well. *Today,* begun in 1952, was the first morning program to offer news, human interest stories, and entertainment in a format that became widely imitated. NBC Television transmitted the first coast-to-coast color broadcast in 1953 and aired the first videotape in 1956, and in

1962 the Telstar communications satellite made it possible to relay live broadcasts from one continent to another almost instantaneously.

By the 1960s television was as much a part of American life as radio had been since the 1930s, and NBC was the leader in the burgeoning industry with programs such as *Rowan and Martin's Laugh-In* and *Star Trek*. But the popularity of radio was declining by the 1970s. Although the network succeeded in its efforts to revive NBC Radio, which became profitable by 1985, it decided in 1988 to sell eight of its nine radio stations, retaining only WNBC in New York City. In 1986 General Electric, one of the original part-owners of the network, purchased RCA for $6.3 billion, becoming the sole parent company of NBC. A 2004 merger with Vivendi Universal Entertainment created NBC Universal; General Electric maintained an 80 percent stake in NBC, which by the early twenty-first century had grown into a global media company through acquisition and expansion. In 2009 Comcast, a cable operator, announced that it would purchase NBC from GE, owning 51 percent to GE's 49 percent. The company's headquarters remained at 30 Rockefeller Plaza, where tourists gathered daily to watch the taping of the *Today* show.

Erik Barnouw, *A History of Broadcasting in the United States* (New York: Oxford University Press, 1966–70); Robert Campbell, *The Golden Years of Broadcasting: A Celebration of the First 50 Years of Radio and Television on NBC* (New York: Charles Scribner's Sons, 1976)

Chad Ludington

National City Bank of New York. Name used from 1865 by a bank later known as Citibank.

National Conference for Community and Justice. Organization formed in 1927 by Charles Evans Hughes, S. Parkes Cadman, and Roger W. Straus to combat bias, bigotry, and racism in the United States. Originally called the National Conference of Christians and Jews, the organization promoted tolerance and understanding among different races, religions, and cultures. In the 1980s it included Muslims in its interfaith programs. In the 1990s the name was changed to the National Conference for Community and Justice to reflect the growing diversity of the United States. In 2003 it launched a program to combat inequities in access to health care between different ethnicities and races. In addition to its national headquarters on 328 Flatbush Avenue, Brooklyn, the National Conference also operates 64 regional offices in 34 states and the District of Columbia.

National Consumers' League. Organization formed in New York City in 1898 by women active in the Consumers' League of New York City (1890). It had its headquarters in the Charities Building at 44 East 23rd Street. Under the innovative leadership of its first secretary general, Florence Kelley, the league quickly became an effective proponent of social and labor legislation to improve the working conditions of women and the health of mothers and infants, and to eliminate child labor. It gained members from the social elite, the middle class, and trade unions. By 1906 the league had more than 60 national affiliates. It published influential studies of exploitative working conditions, and its advisory board prepared an annual agenda that guided the efforts of local affiliates in state legislatures and state and federal courts. The league's influence diminished in the 1920s, and after Kelley's death in 1932 its offices were moved to Cleveland.

Kathyrn Kish Sklar, *Florence Kelley and the Nation's Work: The Rise of Women's Political Culture, 1830–1900* (New Haven: Yale University Press, 1995)

National Council of Churches of Christ in the USA [NCC]. Association formed in 1950 by the merger of the Federal Council of Churches and seven other interdenominational agencies. It made its headquarters at Riverside Drive and 120th Street in Manhattan and was influential in persuading members of the Rockefeller family to establish the Interchurch Center opposite Riverside Church and Union Theological Seminary. In 1952 it authorized the publication of the Revised Standard Version of the Bible. As of 2008, the council was the country's largest ecumenical agency, with 35 Protestant, Anglican, and Orthodox member organizations and a combined membership of more than 40 million persons. A vehicle for action, education, and service in the United States and abroad, it has sparked controversy for its public statements on such issues as civil rights and American foreign policy.

Eileen W. Lindner

National Council of Negro Women. Federation formed in New York City on 5 December 1935 by representatives of 29 black organizations at the Young Women's Christian Association (YWCA) on 137th Street in Harlem at the initiation of the educator Mary McLeod Bethune, an adviser to President Franklin D. Roosevelt. Its purpose was to coordinate the work of its members and to encourage black women to take part in government and politics, education, and business. As the leader of the council from 1957 into the early twenty-first century, Dorothy I. Height oversaw an expansion of its activities into such diverse fields as on-the-job training, preventing drug abuse and teenage pregnancy, and African relief. It moved its national headquarters to Washington, D.C., in 1942.

Tracey A. Fitzgerald, *The National Council of Negro Women and the Feminist Movement, 1935–1975* (Washington, D.C.: Georgetown University Press, 1985)

Larry A. Greene

National Debt Clock. A billboard-sized display of the current United States public debt. It was invented and sponsored by real estate developer Seymour Durst, who wanted to highlight the rising national debt. It was first installed on 42nd Street, close to Times Square, in 1989. In 2004, the clock was dismantled and replaced by an upgraded version and moved to 1133 Sixth Avenue. In 2008, the national debt exceeded $10 trillion for the first time, which led to plans for a third clock with extra numbers capacity. In the early twenty-first century the clock was run by Seymour's son Douglas, through the Durst Organization.

Benjamin Yakas

National Debt Clock, 2009

National Enquirer. Established in 1926 in New York City as the *Enquirer*, the magazine was started by William Randolph Hearst's protégé William Griffin. The publication was purchased by Generoso Pope, Jr., in 1952 for $75,000. He changed the magazine to a tabloid, and vastly increased circulation by featuring gory stories and various confessions. In 1957 it was renamed the *National Enquirer*, which became famous for stories related to sex, the grotesque, and the unusual. It later tried to clean up its image with less sensational stories. In 1969 the headquarters moved from New York to Florida.

Jessica Montesano

National Foundation for Infant Paralysis. Original name of the March of Dimes Birth Defects Foundation.

National Industrial Conference Board. Original name of the Conference Board.

National Institute of Public Administration. Former name of the Institute of Public Administration.

National Lampoon. Monthly humor magazine launched in April 1970 by Henry Beard, Douglas Kenney, and Robert Hoffman, graduates of Harvard University who had worked on the *Harvard Lampoon.* It was published in New York City by Matty Simmons and Leonard Mogel, owners of Twenty-First Century Communications. Known as the "Humor Magazine for Adults," it attracted such cartoonists and writers as Gahan Wilson, John Hughes, and Michael O'Donohue and aimed to ridicule everything and everyone, especially adolescents, popular culture, celebrities, and other magazines. Circulation peaked at 842,000 in 1974 and then declined, but it spawned many books, films, recordings, and plays, including the Off-Broadway show *Lemmings* (1973). In March 1990 the *National Lampoon* was bought by James P. Jimirro of J2 Communications, and in 1998 it ceased publication.

Al Sarrantonio, ed., *The National Lampoon Treasury of Humor* (New York: Simon and Schuster, 1991)

Walter Friedman

National Lead Industries. Former name of NL Industries.

National Memorial African Book Store. Bookstore at 2107 Seventh Avenue (at 125th Street) opposite the Hotel Theresa in Harlem. Run by Lewis H. Michaux, it operated from 1930 to 1974 and was known for its wide selection of books by black authors, for its art gallery, and for the many intellectuals who frequented the store. It faced what is now called African Square, a site where soapbox orators made speeches.

Sule Greg C. Wilson

National Museum of the American Indian. Museum founded in 1916 by George Gustav Heye (1874–1957), a wealthy engineer and financier, featuring objects that represent all the native peoples of the Americas. Also known as the Heye Foundation, the Museum of the American Indian opened to the public in 1922 on Audubon Terrace in Harlem. In 1926 a storage facility (called the research branch or annex) opened in the Pelham Bay section of the Bronx. While field collecting was extensive during the 1910s and 1920s, the museum was forced to radically retrench during the Depression. By the 1970s declining financial support and attendance led to protracted merger negotiations with the American Museum of Natural History. However, in 1989 the trustees decided to transfer the collections to the Smithsonian Institution, where they became the National Museum of the American Indian. The collection finally reached a total of about 890,000 objects. The museum gave up its original buildings in upper Manhattan and the Bronx. Its presence in New York State, called for by the articles of incorporation, is represented by the George Gustav Heye Center, which opened in the U.S. Customs House in lower Manhattan in 1994. In addition, the museum operates its main exhibit building on the Mall in Washington, D.C. (opened in 2004), and a Cultural Resources Center in Suitland, Maryland (opened in 2003). Its library, formerly a part of the Huntington Free Library in the Westchester Square area of the Bronx, was transferred to Cornell University in 2004.

Duane Blue Spruce, ed., *Spirit of a Native Place: Building the National Museum of the American Indian* (Washington, D.C.: National Museum of the American Indian/National Geographic Society, 2004)

Ira Jacknis

National Puerto Rican Forum. Organization devoted to improving the economic conditions of the Puerto Rican community. It was founded in 1957 by Antonia Pantoja and a cadre of professionals and activists, including Herman Badillo, to bring about social change. Its Puerto Rican Community Development Project, launched in the early 1960s, detailed a series of initiatives. Assuming a national focus in 1972, the organization redefined its mission from advocacy and research to service. The organization called upon the expertise of more than 60 organizations and community leaders and led to the conceptualization of ASPIRA, the educational agency for private- and public-sector leadership development; City University of New York's research center, the Centro de Estudios Puertorriqueños; and Boricua College. The forum sponsored small-business loans, community development, adult literacy, English-as-a-second-language courses, occupational placements, and an occupational language-training course. One of the largest agencies serving the Spanish-speaking population in the continental United States, it had offices in Manhattan, the Bronx, and Chicago. It partnered with federal, state, and city agencies to promote Welfare-to-Work programs, Wheels-to-Work programs, Technology Learning Centers, after-school programs, the Allied Health Services Academy, and the teacher-training program Maestros Excelentes. It published a quarterly newspaper, *El Foro,* and organized events and lectures. It closed in 2008.

Virginia Sánchez Korrol

National Railroad Passenger Corporation. See Amtrak.

National Review. Biweekly magazine launched in November 1955 in New York City by William F. Buckley, Jr., as a forum for conservative thought, both traditional and libertarian. It attracted contributions from such noted conservatives as Clare Boothe Luce and George F. Will, as well as disenchanted leftists such as John Dos Passos and Max Eastman, and was a respected journal by the early 1970s. The *National Review* continues to promote American conservative thought in the early twenty-first century.

John Chamberlain, *The National Review Reader* (New York: Bookmailer, 1957)

Lawson Bowling

National Rifle Association. Organization formed in New York City in 1871. There were several causes underlying its formation: the prominent role of the rifle in the Civil War; advocacy by William Connant Church, the influential editor of the *Army and Navy Journal,* of marksmanship training as practiced by Captain George Wood Wingate of the New York National Guard; and the Orange Riot of 1871, which revealed how inadequately members of the National Guard were trained. The association benefited from an increased interest in shooting skills among militia and professional soldiers after the Battle of Little Bighorn in 1876 and helped to make riflery an important sport in the 1870s and 1880s, though opposition to marksmanship practice in New York City forced the organization to move to Sea Girt, New Jersey. After failing to obtain federal funding or form a partnership with the army, it became moribund in 1892. It revived in 1901 and established headquarters in Washington, D.C. In conjunction with the State of New York, the association established the first set of hunting rules and safety regulations in 1949.

Russell S. Gilmore

National September 11 Memorial and Museum. Museum and memorial to commemorate the lives of those who died in the terrorist attacks of September 11, 2001, against the World Trade Center and the Pentagon, the worst terrorist attack committed on U.S. soil. The memorial is scheduled to be dedicated on 11 September 2011, the 10th anniversary of the attacks. Designed by Michael Arad and landscape architect Peter Walker and Partners, the outdoor memorial, titled *Reflecting Absence,* consists of a forested, horizontal plaza punctuated by two 1-acre (0.4-hectare) pools located in the original footprints of the twin towers of the World Trade Center. Waterfalls from all sides plunge 30 feet (9 meters) into the pool basins, which are centered by deeper waterfall drop-offs, or voids, symbolizing the loss of lives on 9/11, as well as a previous terrorist attack against the World Trade Center on 26 February 1993, when five people died. The combined names of the nearly 3000 victims of these attacks will be cut into bronze parapets bordering each pool and will include those who died in and near the twin towers, those who died at the Pentagon, those who died in the planes that hit the twin towers and the Pentagon, and those who died aboard a fourth plane that passengers downed in a field in Pennsylvania.

The memorial and museum, designed by the architectural firm of Davis Brody Bond, will connect the above-ground plane of the memorial with the subterranean cavity of the missing towers. A 2.5-story atrium will provide for the museum's security screening, and there will be an auditorium and a private chamber for the bereaved. A pair of monolithic tridents salvaged from a jagged piece of tower facade that remained standing after the attack will be displayed. There will also be a repository for unidentified and unclaimed victims' remains maintained by New York City's Office of the Chief Medical Examiner, to which there will be no public access. The museum's galleries, in the former footprint of the North Tower, will chronicle the events of 9/11, while the memorial exhibit will occupy the South Tower footprint, which will also contain classrooms and displays of commemorative response art. One of the items that will be on display is the "Last Column," a piece of steel removed from Ground Zero and made iconic by the memorial graffiti affixed to it by construction workers, first responders, and clean-up crews during the recovery operations. The museum is tentatively scheduled to open to the public by 2013.

Jan Seidler Ramirez

National Track and Field Hall of Fame. Founded in 1974, the National Track and Field Hall of Fame was located in Charleston, South Carolina, until 1983 and became a traveling exhibit before being shut down because of space limitations in Indianapolis in the mid-1990s. In 2000 New York City, with its newly refurbished world-class indoor track facility in Washington Heights, was selected over nine other cities as the new host for the hall of fame. The exhibit contains a 40-foot-long (12-meter-long) glass "wall of fame," listing the more than 200 inductees, as well as a theater, photo and display gallery, extensive memorabilia, and interactive exhibits about nutrition, training, the New York City Marathon, and how technology has changed the sport. Inductees born in New York City include Bob Beamon, Jim Beatty, John Carlos, Lillian Copeland, Harry Hillman, Charlie Jenkins, Abel Kiviat, Al Oerter, and Maren Seidler; coaches Bob Giegengack, Mel Rosen, and Joe Yancey; and administrator James Sullivan. Other inductees with connections to the city include Tom Courtney, a star runner at Fordham University in the 1950s; Larry Ellis, a coach at Jamaica High School in the 1950s and 1960s; and Matt McGrath, an Olympic hammer throw champion and Irish immigrant who was also a New York City policeman in the early twentieth century. Fred Lebow, founder of the New York City Marathon, is also a member, as are Bill Rodgers and Alberto Salazar, who combined to win the five-borough race every year from 1976 to 1982. The Armory Track and Field Center at 216 Fort Washington Avenue on 168th Street and Broadway has housed the National Track and Field Hall of Fame since 2004. In the early twenty-first century it was the only national sports hall of fame located in the city.

David White

National Tuberculosis Association. Original name of the National Lung Association, of which the New York Lung Association is an affiliate.

National Urban League. Social service and civil rights organization with headquarters in New York City. Formed on 16 October 1911 as the National League on Urban Conditions among Negroes, it resulted from the merger of the National League for the Protection of Colored Women (1906), the Committee for Improving the Industrial Condition of Negroes in New York (1906), and the Committee on Urban Conditions among Negroes (1910). The founders included both blacks and whites, notably Ruth Standish Baldwin, William Bulkley, Frances Kellor, and George Edmund Haynes. Reflecting the approaches of both the Progressive movement and Booker T. Washington, the league sought to further its goals through investigation, advocacy, negotiation, and education. It adopted its current name on 4 February 1920. The league set up local affiliates, including one in New York City, where it sponsored youth programs, health clinics, and adult education programs and sought to integrate unions and improve housing (often unsuccessfully). Through its national office it provided social welfare and employment services for black migrants to northern cities and worked to broaden employment opportunities for blacks. Activities increased under the direction of Whitney Young in the 1960s, when the league sought to mediate between civil rights groups and white legislative and business leaders. Over the years the National Urban League developed and supported such programs in New York as the Visiting Nurses, the Utopia Neighborhood Club, Big Brothers and Big Sisters, and the Juvenile Park Protective League. During the early twenty-first century, the league, under the direction of former New Orleans mayor Marc H. Morial, continued to work for community improvement and civil rights.

Guichard Parris and Lester Brooks, *Blacks in the City: A History of the National Urban League* (Boston: Little, Brown, 1971); Nancy Weiss, *The National Urban League, 1910–1940* (New York: Oxford University Press, 1974); Jesse Moore, Jr., *A Search for Equality: The National Urban League, 1910–1961* (University Park: Pennsylvania State University Press, 1981); Nancy Weiss, *Whitney M. Young, Jr. and the Struggle for Civil Rights* (Princeton, N.J.: Princeton University Press, 1989)

Cheryl Greenberg

Nation of Islam. Syncretic religion begun in 1930 by Wallace Fard Muhammad (sometimes referred to as W. D. Fard) in Detroit. The Lost-Found Nation of Islam — later known to the public as the Nation of Islam or simply the Black Muslims — drew on symbols, themes, and theology of Noble Drew Ali's Moorish Science Temple, traditional Islam, Marcus Garvey's Black Nationalism, and the Black Christian Church. Elijah Muhammad, born Elijah Poole, established Temple No. 2 in Chicago in 1932 and assumed control of the organization after a brief power struggle following Fard's mysterious disappearance in 1934. Fard was understood to be the personification of Allah with Muhammad as his messenger. When Muhammad was jailed for draft evasion from 1942 to 1946, his wife, Sister Clara Muhammad, became supreme secretary of the sect.

The emergence of the Nation of Islam in New York City came largely under the guidance of minister Malcolm X. Having become a full-time employee of the Nation in 1953, a year after his release from prison, Malcolm X spent much of 1954 sharing duties between Philadelphia Temple No. 12 and New York Temple No. 7, located at 102 West 116th Street, before taking over as full-time minister of the Harlem Temple that year. Though the Federal Bureau of Investigation lists a temple in Harlem (135th Street and Seventh Avenue) dating back to 1947, it was largely unorganized and had difficulty drawing members amid other more established Islam-based religious groups such as the Ahmadiyya Movement, Moorish Science Temple, and International Muslim Brotherhood. Speaking at the annual Savior's Day Convention in Chicago, which celebrates the birth of W. D. Fard, Malcolm X met a young Louis Walcott, who would later become known as Louis X (Farrakhan), minister of Temple No. 11 in Boston.

The Nation of Islam grew exponentially in the late 1950s, especially Harlem's Temple No. 7. In its vicinity, the Nation opened a Muslim restaurant, which functioned as the primary social space outside the temple, as well as business ventures such as the Shabazz Bakery. Following trips to Africa and the Middle East by both Malcolm X and Elijah Muhammad in 1959, Muhammad dictated that the temples be referred to as mosques, in one of the earliest indications of the group's move toward orthodoxy. A national paper, *Muhammad Speaks*, was formed in 1961 after a local pilot paper under the same name was initiated by Malcolm X. As a result of internal strife and his public comment that President John F. Kennedy's assassination was a "case of the chickens coming home to roost," Malcolm X was "silenced" by Muhammad in December 1963 and left the organization in March 1964. Louis Farrakhan assumed the position of head minister of Mosque No. 7 following Malcolm X's departure. After the assassination of Malcolm X on 25 February 1965 at the Audubon Ballroom (3940 Broadway), Mosque No. 7 burned down under suspicions that Nation of Islam members had killed the former national spokesman and minister. The mosque was soon rebuilt by architect Sabbath Brown at the site of the former Lenox Casino, now a Sunni Muslim congregation known as the Masjid Malcolm Shabazz.

Following Elijah Muhammad's death in 1975, the Nation of Islam underwent a transformation toward Sunni Islam under the direction of his son, Wallace Muhammad, and was renamed the World Community of al-Islam in the West in 1976, before finally becoming the Muslim American Society in 1985. The Nation of Islam, however, was rebuilt according to many of its original tenets in 1978 by Louis Farrakhan and his supporters, who reinstated the newspaper, renamed the *Final Call*. In 2000 both Muhammad and Farrakhan claimed reconciliation at the annual Savior's Day Convention. In the early twenty-first century Muhammad's Mosque No. 7, located at 106–8 West 127th Street, remained the organization's New York City headquarters.

See also Muslims.

Garrett A. Felber

nativism. During the nineteenth century most nativist violence in New York City was directed at Catholics. In one of the first incidents, which took place on Christmas night in 1806, a mob gathered outside St. Peter's Church and forced the Irish congregation to flee. In the mid-1830s violence against Irish immigrants increased, and the Native American Democratic Association was formed. The Whig Party, which had sought to attract immigrants in 1834, turned against them after attacks on Whigs by immigrants were publicized. Whig newspapers printed excerpts from *Six Months in a Convent* and *Awful Disclosures,* false accounts of sexual escapades among nuns that inflamed anti-Catholic sentiment. In the mayoral election of 1836, the Native American Democratic Association chose Samuel F. B. Morse as its candidate after Philip Hone declined; Morse received only one-tenth as many votes as the winning Democrat. A number of issues promoted by nativists remained important in political debate, especially temperance and the question of control over the public schools. The American Republican Party, formed in 1843, attracted nativists and promised reform at a time when dissatisfaction with government was widespread. In the elections of 1844 it nominated as its mayoral candidate the publisher James Harper, who gained the support of such influential Whig journalists as James Watson Webb and Thurlow Weed; Harper won the election, and the party also gained a majority on the Common Council.

During the next six years nativists retreated from politics and formed secret societies opposed to immigration, of which there were at least 60 in Manhattan and Brooklyn by 1852. Members of the Order of the Star-Spangled Banner were supposedly instructed to answer "I know nothing" to all questions about their organization; the term *Know Nothing* was apparently first applied as a political label to the nativists by the *New York Tribune* in November 1853. The Know-Nothings failed to elect a mayor in the city but became strong nationwide as dissatisfaction with the existing party system spread. In the city, nativism gained support among craftsmen and mechanics, who felt threatened economically and politically by the rising number of immigrants. Many nativists feared that Catholics would undermine the republic by answering to the Pope rather than the United States; others hoped that by reducing the rate of immigration, progress toward industrialization would be slowed or even halted. Most groups called for the exclusion of immigrants from appointive and elective office and advocated a waiting period of 21 years for citizenship.

The lasting effect of nativism was to strengthen the Democratic Party, which generally accepted immigrants. By 1855 the majority of the city's population was foreign born, and nativism ceased to be an important force in politics. A few candidates, including Mayor Abram S. Hewitt (1887–88), adopted a nativist stance later in the century, but generally enjoyed little success.

Amy Bridges, *A City in the Republic: Antebellum New York and the Origins of Machine Politics* (Cambridge: Cambridge University Press, 1984); Tyler Anbinder, *Nativism and Slavery: The Northern Know Nothings and the Politics of the 1850s* (New York: Oxford University Press, 1992)

Evan Cornog

Thomas Nast, "The American River Ganges: The Priests and the Children," Harper's Weekly, *30 September 1871*

NBC. See National Broadcasting Company.

Nederlander Organization. Second largest theater management firm in the United States, founded by David Nederlander, a jeweler from Detroit, in 1912 and developed by his son James. At one time the firm and its rival the Shubert Organization together owned about 70 percent of the theaters on Broadway. In the 1970s and 1980s rising costs and declining attendance forced the organization to produce fewer shows and rent out its theaters to concert producers and religious organizations; some of its theaters closed altogether. In the 1980s and early 1990s the Nederlander Organization fought attempts by preservationists to have theaters near Times Square designated as landmarks. As of 2010 the family-owned company operated several Broadway theaters: the Gershwin, Brooks Atkinson, Lunt–Fontanne, Marquis, Minskoff, Nederlander, Neil Simon, Palace, and Richard Rodgers theaters were all under Nederlander ownership.

Sara J. Steen

Nedick's. Chain of restaurants begun in the early 1920s at 27th Street and Broadway that made and sold orange drink. Known for its orange and white decor and its slogan "Good food is never expensive at Nedick's," the firm quickly expanded to more than 100 outlets in the five boroughs. During the 1950s it also opened outlets in Newark, New Jersey; Albany, New York; and Philadelphia, Baltimore, and Washington, D.C. The popularity of Nedick's was due to its quick and inexpensive menu: orange drink, coffee, and doughnuts, and later frankfurters in an effort to compete with successful chains such as Nathan's. During the 1970s growing national chains such as McDonald's and Dunkin' Donuts provided stiff competition, and after a concession that Nedick's operated at the Central Park Zoo was criticized in 1981 for the quality of its food and service, the firm ceased operations.

Robert Sanger Steel

Neel, Alice (*b* Colwyn, near Philadelphia, 28 Jan 1900; *d* New York City, 13 Oct 1984). Painter. After studying from 1921 to 1925 at the Philadelphia School of Design for Women (now Moore College of Art) she was briefly married to the Cuban artist Carlos Enriquez. In 1932 she settled in Greenwich Village, where she painted portraits of left-wing activists and intellectuals such as Kenneth Fearing and Joe Gould, and expressionist renderings of street scenes that conveyed a message of social protest. She moved to Spanish Harlem in 1938 and to West 106th Street in the late 1950s, just as interest in her work was reviving. Neel became notorious for her satirical portraits of artists, critics, and collectors. The Whitney Museum of American Art held an exhibition of her work in 1974, and in 1976 she was elected to the National Institute of Arts and Letters.

Patricia Hills, *Alice Neel* (New York: Harry N. Abrams, 1983)

Patricia Hills

Negro Ensemble Company. Theater company. Formed in 1967 with a grant from the Ford Foundation, it began as a repertory company of 14 and held workshops for actors and playwrights in St. Mark's Playhouse in the East Village; the actor and playwright Douglas Turner Ward was its artistic director. Although its repertory activities were discontinued in 1972 owing to a lack of funds, the directorate of the company continued to operate in a new location uptown. In its first 20 years the company staged more than 200 productions, including workshops. During this period plays presented by the company won four Obie Awards, two Tony Awards, and a Pulitzer Prize (*A Soldier's Play* by Charles Fuller, 1982). In 2005 the company, along with more than 400 New York City arts institutions, received part of a $20 million grant from the Carnegie Corporation. The Negro Ensemble Company celebrated its 40th anniversary in 2007.

Ellen Foreman, "The Negro Ensemble Company: A Transcendent Vision," *The Theatre of Black Americans: A Collection of Critical Essays,* ed. Errol Hill (New York: Applause Theatre Books, 1987), 270–82; Ron Howell, "The Negro Ensemble Company: 20 Years of Theatrical Excellence," *Ebony,* March 1987, pp. 90–98

See also THEATER, §6.

E. G. Hill

Negro Plot of 1741. An alleged conspiracy by slaves to burn New York City and murder its white inhabitants. The accusations were leveled in March 1741, after authorities discovered an interracial theft ring and illegal interracial meetings and implicated slaves in several fires and robberies. That some of the slaves were Spanish-speaking caused particular concern at a time when public attention was focused on the Anglo–Spanish War. Officials convened the provincial supreme court, which indicted more than 170 persons on charges of conspiracy based largely on hearsay and circumstantial evidence. Thirty-one blacks and four whites were executed, and more than 70 blacks and seven whites were banished from the city.

Thomas J. Davis, *A Rumor of Revolt: The "Great Negro Plot" in Colonial New York* (New York: Free Press, 1985); Jill Lepore, *New York Burning: Liberty, Slavery, and Conspiracy in Eighteenth-Century Manhattan* (New York: Vintage, 2006)

Cynthia A. Kierner

Nehemiah Plan Homes. Organization that builds two-story, one-family row houses for working-class and low-income families on land formerly owned by the city. It was conceived by the retired commercial builder and civic activist I. D. Robbins and launched by East Brooklyn Congregations, a nonprofit, community-based coalition of mostly black churches formed in 1982–83. It derives its name from the Old Testament prophet who was sent to rebuild Jerusalem. By 2008 the program had built about 2900 homes in East Brooklyn and the South Bronx.

Bernard Hirschhorn

Neighborhood Guild. Former name of UNIVERSITY SETTLEMENT.

Neighborhood Music School. Original name of the MANHATTAN SCHOOL OF MUSIC.

Neighborhood Playhouse. Theater company formed in 1915 by Alice and Irene Lewisohn to serve the large immigrant population of the Henry Street Settlement. The repertory of the amateur company reflected the diverse nature of the audience and included Japanese and Hindu dramas as well as works by George Bernard Shaw, Eugene O'Neill, and Leonid Andreyev. The troupe gradually became more professional, but the theater faced financial problems that finally forced it to close in 1927. The Neighborhood Playhouse School of the Theatre was founded in 1928; under the direction of Sanford Meisner, a member of the Group Theatre, it became an important training ground for young actors. Meisner stayed for 55 years, retiring in 1990, and became famous for the techniques of acting named after him. In 2009 the school, located at 340 East 54th Street, trained actors in a two-year certificate program and offered the Playhouse Juniors, for children in grades one through 12. Alumni include Sandra Bullock, Robert Duvall, Allison Janney, Steve McQueen, Gregory Peck, Mary Steenburgen, Eli Wallach, and Joanne Woodward.

Alice Lewisohn Crowley, *The Neighborhood Playhouse: Leaves from a Theatre Scrapbook* (New York: Theatre Arts Books, 1959)

D. S. Moynihan, Lisa Keller

neighborhoods. In New York City neighborhoods range widely in size and composition. Some cover a few square blocks and have only several hundred residents (such as Hook Creek in Queens and Emerson Hill in Staten Island); others take in large sections of boroughs (such as Flushing and Jamaica in Queens and Harlem in Manhattan). Most neighborhoods in the city have a generally recognized central district, but their boundaries are often difficult to define, especially if the population is transient and heterogeneous, the neighborhood is centrally situated, or the question of boundaries is politically sensitive. Some large neighborhoods encompass smaller neighborhoods: examples include Bedford–Stuyvesant and Williamsburg in Brooklyn and Morrisania in the Bronx. The number of neighborhoods in New York City is impossible to measure precisely but is more than 400.

The origin of neighborhoods in the city may be traced to the charter granted under Governor Thomas Dongan (1686), which divided lower Manhattan into six wards (North, South, Dock, East, West, and Out). Although the city was small, intimate, and unified, residentially there was some differentiation: in the poor areas, like the waterfront district of the Lower East Side, residents formed urban villages that were largely self contained; throughout the eighteenth century many residents lived and worked in the same house. The wards became more distinct as the markets, churches, and taverns of different ethnic groups gradually clustered in separate areas. Early in the eighteenth century ethnic communities took shape around local churches (Dutch in the North and West wards, English and Huguenots in the East and Dock wards). But for the most part the wards remained ethnically and economically diverse, and by the end of the century most ethnic groups had been assimilated (except for Jews and blacks, whose communities were isolated). The ethnic neighborhoods gave way to ones based on trade and class: by 1800 carters, coachmakers, and building artisans had become situated on inexpensive land north of Chambers Street, shipbuilding and maritime crafts in Corlear's Hook, printers in Franklin Square, and "nuisance" industries like brewing and tallow making in the sixth ward. Residents of Manhattan also maintained social ties and transacted business in an area extending west to

Newark and the Meadowlands in New Jersey, north to what is now Yonkers, and east to the borders of what is now Nassau County. During the early nineteenth century industrial districts were systematically developed along the advancing northern periphery of the city, and residential areas like Gramercy Park were designed after the Georgian private parks of London, with restrictive residential covenants and blocks of one-family housing for the wealthy.

The years before the Civil War saw enormous geographic mobility, which allowed the affluent to isolate themselves in residential enclaves and often made neighborhoods economically and racially segregated as well, with black residents concentrated in the fifth ward and especially the Five Points. Landowners dispersed to neighborhoods that were removed from those of their tenants; wealthy merchants who had previously resided in lower Manhattan sold their homes to expanding businesses and moved to newly fashionable districts like Madison Square and Fifth Avenue; and the middle- and upper-class inhabitants moved to new housing in uptown Manhattan, as old artisan neighborhoods like the West Side, the fifth ward, and the eighth ward were rebuilt as warehouse districts. "Moving Day," on 1 May of each year, became a mass ritual. During the late nineteenth century tenement neighborhoods were developed, including the Lower East Side, Hell's Kitchen (Irish), and Yorktown (German), each replete with ethnic saloons, churches, benevolent societies, and clubs.

Despite increased class division and the emergence of separate residential districts (much of the East Side north of 14th Street was primarily residential), neighborhood identities remained vague until late in the century, except at the extremes of the economic spectrum: New Yorkers did have a sense of the boundaries of notorious slums like the Five Points. Members of the working class continued to define neighborhoods by such local landmarks as alleyways and saloons. The awareness of neighborhoods became sharper in the 1850s and 1860s, when journalists and reformers focused their attention on the conditions of the slums, and sharper still after the Civil War.

In the outer boroughs many neighborhoods began as cities and towns that were eventually absorbed as the boroughs expanded. These included industrial communities (such as Williamsburg and Astoria), villages (Bushwick, Flatbush, and Morrisania), suburban resorts (Bensonhurst and Bayside), suburbs built between 1910 and 1940 for Italians, Jews, Poles, and other immigrants from the crowded tenements of Manhattan, many of whom continued to travel to Manhattan by subway to work (the Grand Concourse, Jackson Heights, and Greenpoint), and speculative building ventures for the middle class (Forest Hills and Rego Park before World War II, and Kew Gardens and Canarsie after the war). The most distinct neighborhoods tended to be those populated by racial and ethnic minorities and the working class, such as Canarsie and Bensonhurst.

Perceptions play a large role in shaping the evolution of neighborhoods: areas that are perceived as desirable tend to grow and prosper, which in turn makes them more desirable. At the same time the boundaries of a prosperous neighborhood inevitably expand, which serves the interests of residents of adjoining areas, of real estate brokers and speculators, and sometimes of government. A similar process works in reverse to the detriment of declining neighborhoods. Sometimes neighborhoods are renamed in an effort to improve their image: Yellow Hook became Bay Ridge in 1853 to avoid associations with the yellow fever epidemic of 1848–49, and Hell's Kitchen became Clinton after gang violence in the late 1950s. Oftentimes, these namings are pushed by the real estate industry to improve the attractiveness of a neighborhood. Sometimes these names stick, as with the "East Village," while others are mocked like "SoHa"(south of Harlem). The historic preservation movement, which took hold in the 1950s, focused attention on the architectural integrity of neighborhoods and led to the designation of historic districts. The methods developed by preservationists later helped community activists to prevent the "gentrification" of poor neighborhoods.

From the 1960s into the 1990s neighborhoods were prominent in political and social controversies. The bitter public school strike of 1968 in Ocean Hill and Brownsville revolved around the issue of community control, an issue that continues to affect the debate over community school and community planning districts. The mayoral candidacy in 1969 of the writer Norman Mailer employed the slogan "Power to the Neighborhoods." Although the idea of the neighborhood has considerable popular appeal in New York City, it betrays a longing for a sense of local community that may never have existed.

In the 1990s and in the early twenty-first century many neighborhoods around the city began to experience gentrification as the city's economic outlook improved. Former industrial neighborhoods like Williamsburg in Brooklyn became popular among young artists, and old immigrant neighborhoods such as the Lower East Side became havens for young professionals. Even neighborhoods that had become infamous for crime like Bedford–Stuyvesant began to see an influx of new, more well-off inhabitants. This has led to many conflicts, as long-time residents often feel that the new inhabitants are destroying the fabric of their community.

New York City Planning Commission, Plan for New York City, vol. 6 (Cambridge, Mass.: MIT Press, 1969); Elizabeth Blackmar, *Manhattan for Rent, 1785–1850* (Ithaca, N.Y.: Cornell University Press, 1989); Nan A. Rothschild, *New York City Neighborhoods: The Eighteenth Century* (San Diego: Academic, 1990); Kenneth A. Scherzer, *The Unbounded Community: Neighborhood Life and Social Structure in New York City, 1830–1875* (Durham, N.C.: Duke University Press, 1992)

Kenneth A. Scherzer

Neponsit. Neighborhood in southwestern Queens on the Rockaway Peninsula, bounded to the east by Adirondack Boulevard (Beach 142nd Street) and to the west by Beach 149th Street; Belle Harbor lies to the east and Jacob Riis Park to the west. The neighborhood began as a tract laid out in January 1910 by the Neponsit Realty Company, which first sold lots and houses in July 1911; houses costing less than $3000 were prohibited, as were hotels and stores. Unlike other areas in Rockaway the development was designed for year-round suburban living, the houses built of vitrified block and cement stucco for protection against fire and salt air. During the 1920s and 1930s the area became fully built up; in the early twenty-first century it remained a wealthy neighborhood where zoning laws narrowly restricted development to single-family homes. In 2003 the neighborhood made headlines when the Neponsit Health Care Center, a municipal nursing home, was closed and its residents evicted with several hours' notice.

Vincent Seyfried

Nesbit, Evelyn Florence (*b* Tarentum, Pa., 25 Dec 1884; *d* Santa Monica, Calif., 17 Jan 1967). Model and actress. In 1900 Nesbit moved to New York City, where she gained renown by posing for artists and photographers. She became a chorus girl in the Broadway musical *Floradora* (1901), where she captured the attention of architect Stanford White and Harry K. Thaw, heir to a Pittsburgh railroad fortune. White had an affair with Nesbit,

Evelyn Florence Nesbit

who eventually married Thaw. On 25 June 1906, at a performance of *Mamzelle Champagne* on the roof of Madison Square Garden, a building designed by White, Thaw shot White three times at close range, killing him instantly. The murder became known as the crime of the century and the 1907 trial was a media sensation. Thaw was eventually found not guilty due to temporary insanity and committed to the Matteawan State Hospital for the Criminally Insane. He divorced Nesbit in 1916. Nesbit published two memoirs and served as an adviser for the film story of her affair with White, *The Girl in the Red Velvet Swing* (1955).

Paula Uruburu, *American Eve: Evelyn Nesbit, Stanford White: The Birth of the "It" Girl and the Crime of the Century* (New York: Riverhead Books, 2008)

Kate Lauber

Neue Galerie New York. Museum located at 1048 Fifth Avenue on Museum Mile and founded in 2001 by art dealer Serge Sabarsky and art collector Ronald S. Lauder. The museum focuses on German and Austrian fine and decorative arts of the early twentieth century as well as artists who served as major influences on the expressionist movement. Its collection contains paintings, sculptures, works on paper, photographs, and objects of decorative art and includes works by Gustav Klimt, Egon Schiele, and George Grosz. The museum is located in a beaux-art mansion built by Carrère and Hastings in 1914 for William Starr Miller.

Dianna Ng

Nevelson, Louise [née Berliawsky, Leah] (*b* Kiev, Ukraine, 23 Sept 1899; *d* New York City, 17 April 1988). Sculptor. She arrived in New York City in 1920, but it took her several decades to establish a career. Her best-known work is made from discarded wooden objects she found in the streets of the city, assembled in compartments of large wall sculptures, typically painted in matte black, occasionally in white, and less often in gold. She was the first woman to make a reputation in the burgeoning field of public art, receiving commissions from civic agencies, corporations, and religious institutions. New York City has featured several of her public works: *Night Presence IV* (1972), at Park Avenue and 92nd Street; *Shadows and Flags* (1977), a group of seven sculptures at Louise Nevelson Plaza, a triangular space at the intersection of Maiden Lane, William Street, and Liberty Street (the first space in the city named for an artist); her largest relief, *Sky Gate New York* (1977–78), in the lobby of One World Trade Center (destroyed on 11 September 2001); and a group of white sculptures and reliefs in the Erol Beker Chapel of the Good Shepherd in St. Peter's Lutheran Church (1977), part of the Citicorp Center at Lexington Avenue and 54th Street. Her work was the subject of major exhibitions at the Whitney Museum of American Art in 1967, 1970, and 1980; at the Guggenheim Museum in 1986; and at the Jewish Museum in 2007.

Brooke Kamin Rapaport, ed., *The Sculpture of Louise Nevelson: Constructing a Legend* (New York: The Jewish Museum/New Haven: Yale University Press, 2007)

Harriet F. Senie

Nevins, Allan (*b* Camp Point, Ill., 20 May 1890; *d* Menlo Park, Calif., 5 March 1971). Historian. He wrote editorials for the *Evening Post* in 1913–23 and published a history of the newspaper in 1922; he became literary editor of the *Sun* in 1924 and a staff writer of the *New York World* in 1925. After teaching for a year at Cornell University he joined the faculty at Columbia University as an assistant professor of history in 1928 and became the DeWitt Clinton Professor of American History in 1931. At Columbia he formed the Society of American Historians (1939) and launched the country's first oral history program (1948). A leading authority on the Civil War, he led the Civil War Centennial Commission in 1961 and wrote more than 70 books, including biographies of John D. Rockefeller and Henry Ford; his *Grover Cleveland: A Study in Courage* (1932) and *Hamilton Fish: The Inner History of the Grant Administration* (1936) won Pulitzer Prizes. Nevins retired in 1958 and was honored by the Century Association and the New-York Historical Society for his contributions to the city.

Janet Frankston

New Alliance Party. Political party formed in 1979 by the social therapist Fred Newman to support such causes as feminism and gay rights. It challenged restrictive ballot access laws but used the same laws to challenge the ballot petitions of rival parties. With its antecedent, the International Workers Party, it formed alliances with the conspiracy theorist Lyndon LaRouche, the activist Al Sharpton, and the Brooklyn Democratic boss Vander Beatty (before his conviction for election fraud). Its first presidential candidate, Dennis Serrette, was on the ballot in 33 states in 1984 and received 35,000 votes; Lenora Fulani received 250,000 votes in 1988 and 100,000 in 1992. The New Alliance Party was accused of attempting to take over other progressive groups and grass-roots political organizations; it also attracted criticism for its social therapy practices, considered by some to be cult-like. In 1994 the New Alliance Party disbanded, and Fulani and Newman along with other members and supporters of the New Alliance Party joined the Independence Party of New York and the Patriot Party.

Jesse Drucker

New American Library. Firm of book publishers formed in 1947 by Kurt Enoch and Victor Weybright, who had been in charge of the U.S. office of Penguin Books. It was set up with two imprints: Signet for fiction of high quality and reference books, and Mentor for classics and serious nonfiction. Under the slogan "Good Reading for the Millions" the firm published paperbacks by such authors as William Faulkner, Thomas Mann, Eugene O'Neill, George Bernard Shaw, and Truman Capote. With "double volumes" selling for 50 cents a copy the firm broke the traditional 25-cent barrier for paperbacks. Sales reached 33 million copies in 1959, but in 1966 the original partnership disbanded in a dispute over a takeover by Times–Mirror. In the late 1960s New American Library published "broadsides" against the Vietnam War, as well as Ian Fleming's highly successful series of James Bond novels. In the early twenty-first century it continued to publish many successful editions, including several *New York Times* bestsellers. Its offices are located at 375 Hudson Street.

Victor Weybright, *The Making of a Publisher: A Life in the Twentieth Century Book Revolution* (New York: Reynal, 1967)

James E. Mooney

New Amsterdam. Capital of the Dutch colony of New Netherland. It was founded in the mid-1620s and was located at the southern tip of Manhattan, with a northern boundary at what later became Wall Street. On 2 February 1653 the settlement was granted a municipal charter by the Dutch Republic. In 1664, with the British takeover of the Dutch colony, its name was changed to New York City. In 1673 the Dutch regained possession of New Netherland during the third Anglo–Dutch War. At this time New York City's name was changed to New Orange; however, when the colony was negotiated back to England at the end of war, its English name was restored.

Russell Shorto

New Amsterdam Theatre. Theater built in 1903. On a narrow lot near Seventh Avenue and Broadway between 41st and 42nd Streets, architects Henry Herts and Hugh Tallant erected an office tower with a theater wing consisting of an ornate main stage and a rooftop theater. Beginning in 1913, the Ziegfeld Follies occupied the main stage; Florenz Ziegfeld, Jr., had an office in the tower and ran a nightclub on the roof until Prohibition. The 1927 Follies was the last of the series to occupy the main stage. Because of declining live theater attendance, in 1937 the New Amsterdam became a movie house. The Walt Disney Company bought the building and returned it to legitimate theater in 1997, after completing extensive repairs and restoring or reproducing many original details.

Mary C. Henderson, *The New Amsterdam: A Biography of a Broadway Theater* (New York: Hyperion Books, 1997)

Cathy Alexander

New Blazing Star. An early name for the ferry landing on the Arthur Kill near Long Neck in Staten Island (later called Linoleumville; now called Travis). The New Blazing Star Ferry to New Jersey was established in 1757 by Jacob Fitz Randolph and was operated for several decades by John Mersereau. From the ferry landing a road led to the Port Richmond Ferry, on which passengers could travel to Bergen Point, New Jersey, and Manhattan.

Barnett Shepherd

New Brighton. Residential neighborhood in northeastern Staten Island bounded on the north by the Kill van Kull, on the east by St. George, on the south by Castleton Avenue, and on the west by Sailors' Snug Harbor. The main streets are Richmond Terrace on the waterfront and Jersey Street running inland. Laid out in 1835 by entrepreneur Thomas E. Davis, it was one of the nation's earliest romantic suburbs, in which houses were laid out on wide streets with ample lawns and well shaded with ornamental trees. With views of New York Harbor and Manhattan, it was an elite suburban neighborhood of Manhattan-oriented businessmen. Large architecturally distinguished houses were built with extensive landscaped surroundings. One of these houses survives at 404 Richmond Terrace. St. George, named about 1886, comprises the eastern portion of early New Brighton.

The village of New Brighton was incorporated in 1866 and its village hall was erected in 1871 (demolished 2007). Almost entirely residential, the village did contain the U.S. Gypsum Company. Originally called the Windsor Plaster Mills, it was built on the shore in 1876. In 2010 the old gypsum building stands empty, with a salt depot using the grounds. Jersey Street, once the main shopping area, is now largely residential. The Richmond Terrace Houses, at the corner of Jersey Street, a New York City Housing Authority complex of 489 apartments, was built in 1963 with federal funds. The Cassidy–Lafayette Houses, a city housing authority apartment project on Cassidy Place, was built in 1970.

The oldest building in New Brighton is the Tysen–Neville House, 806 Richmond Terrace, a designated New York City landmark. It was built about 1780 when the area was farmland. Early nineteenth-century buildings include the Judge Jacob Tysen House, 355 Fillmore Street (circa 1835), and the Goodhue Mansion (circa 1845, now Goodhue Center, Children's Aid Society). The latter preserves the original 44-acre (17.8-hectare) estate. Hamilton Park, a small romantic suburban development, was created in New Brighton in the mid-1850s. Several original houses stand there. Designated New York City landmarks nearby are 22 Pendleton Place (circa 1855) and 1 Pendleton Place (1860). The original Christ Church New Brighton (Episcopal), on Franklin Avenue, was designed by James Renwick and built in 1850. That building was replaced by the present church in 1904. The original Unitarian church on Clinton Avenue was built in 1868; the present building, designed by Frank Quinby, replaced it in 1895. St. Stanislaus Kostka Roman Catholic church on York Avenue was constructed in 1923.

Kenneth T. Jackson, *Crabgrass Frontier: The Suburbanization of the United States* (New York: Oxford University Press, 1985); "St. George Historic District," New York City Landmarks Preservation Commission Designation Report, 1994

Barnett Shepherd

New Deal. President Franklin D. Roosevelt's New Deal programs focused on economic recovery from the Great Depression via work relief and business and financial reform. Although launched nationally from 1933 to 1936, social legislation had been tested in the previous decade in New York under Senator Robert Wagner, who ultimately wrote the National Industrial Recovery Act (1933), which created the Public Works Administration (PWA). Wagner also sponsored the National Labor Relations Act (1935). Under the Emergency Relief Appropriation Act of 1935, the Works Progress Administration (WPA) was established with approximately $5 billion in funding, providing public jobs for the unemployed—the largest jobs initiative in American history. Led by New York City social worker Harry Hopkins, the WPA paid for building or repairing schools, bridges, parks, hospitals, sewer lines, sports stadiums, streets, roads, and airfields. New York City had massive breadlines, unemployment, and makeshift "Hooverville" shacks in Central Park and on city streets. Hopkins established a separate WPA unit for the city that essentially treated it as the 49th state. Proposals from Fiorello H. La Guardia's Mayor's Committee on Federal Projects won prompt approval from Washington, partly because of the energy and efficiency of Robert Moses, the parks commissioner and head of the Triborough Bridge Authority.

Approximately two-thirds of city WPA employees built major public works projects including the Triborough Bridge, the Holland and Lincoln tunnels, the FDR Drive, the Henry Hudson and Belt parkways, and the New York Municipal (La Guardia) Airport, the most ambitious and costly WPA endeavor nationally. Workers also removed 33 miles of trolley tracks, and repaired, renovated, or built 50 bridges; 68 piers; 218 miles of water mains; 48 miles of sewers; sewage treatment plants; boardwalks in Coney Island and Staten Island; and 2000 miles of streets and highways, including Queens Boulevard, Jamaica Avenue, and the Grand Concourse. The WPA refurbished or expanded 287 parks, built 400 new ones, and constructed 17 municipal swimming pools, 255 playgrounds, Orchard Beach in the Bronx, Randall's Island stadium, and the new Central Park Zoo. In terms of health, education, and welfare, the WPA built Queens General Hospital, repaired Harlem Hospital, created a clinic for venereal disease, and started baby health stations; it renovated or built hundreds of schools, public libraries, courthouses, firehouses, police stations, enclosed municipal markets, homeless shelters, and armories; and with the Public Works Administration and the New York City Housing Authority cleared slums and erected housing projects like the Williamsburg and Harlem River Houses.

Unemployed white-collar professionals were engaged in new and innovative services like adult and preschool education, health care centers, dental clinics, elder care and public daycare, municipal record archiving, bookmobile libraries, and legal aid. The WPA also employed artists, musicians, actors, and writers by commissioning original artwork for municipal buildings, providing free concerts, funding new plays, and publishing the *WPA Guide to New York.*

Federal Writers' Project of the Works Progress Administration in New York City, *The WPA Guide to New York City: The Federal Writers' Project Guide to 1930s New York* (New York: Pantheon Books, 1982); Mike Wallace, *A New Deal for New York* (New York: Bell and Weiland, 2002)

Valerie Paley

New Dorp. Neighborhood in southeastern Staten Island, lying southeast of a portion of the hill that rises above Richmond Road. It was settled by the Dutch about 1671 as Niewe Dorp (new town), 10 years after the settlement of Oude Dorp (old town). The early settlers were Dutch, French, and English farmers and fishermen. In the early eighteenth century the junction of Richmond Road and Amboy Road became the site of several inns and taverns: the Vanderbilt family owned the Rose and Crown and the Black Horse, which were occupied by the British during the American Revolution. In the 1850s horse racing became popular because of the enthusiasm of William H. Vanderbilt, who lived on a large farm near the beach from about 1842 to 1863. The Seaview Association had a track near Richmond Road, races were held on

New Dorp Lighthouse, 2009

lower New Dorp Lane (now the main street), and hotels were built to accommodate spectators from New York City. The development of New Dorp was aided greatly by the construction in 1860 of a railroad line with a station at New Dorp Lane (Cornelius Vanderbilt assumed control of the line when it was declared bankrupt). The railroad also facilitated access to the beach. Among the structures designated landmarks by the city are the Gustav Mayer House, the *New Dorp Lighthouse,* and the art deco–style Lane Theater. Other notable sites include the Jacques Marchais Center of Tibetan Art (1947), built in the style of a Tibetan Buddhist monastery, and the New Dorp Moravian Church (whose founders included the Vanderbilts), its cemetery, and the adjoining Vanderbilt Mausoleum. The mausoleum was designed by Richard M. Hunt and the grounds landscaped by Frederick Law Olmsted. The Britton Cottage and the Guyon–Lake–Tysen House, which predate the American Revolution, were moved in the 1960s to Historic Richmond Town. In the early twenty-first century New Dorp residents are predominantly Italian.

Marjorie Johnson

New Dublin. Obsolete name of Egbertville.

Newfield, Jack (*b* Brooklyn, 18 Feb 1938; *d* New York City, 20 Dec 2004). Liberal muckraking journalist. A native of Brooklyn, and lifelong New Yorker, Newfield graduated from Hunter College in 1961, and was heavily involved with the Students for a Democratic Society (SDS) at its inception. He was a prominent antiwar activist, and published his first book in 1966, *A Prophetic Minority,* detailing the rise of the SDS, accounts of early sixties sit-ins and the desegregation movement, and the creation of the Student Nonviolent Coordinating Committee. After a short stint as assistant editor of the *Village Voice,* Newfield was hired at the *New York Post,* where he worked for most of his life. Although the *Post* changed ownership in 1977 and became more conservative, Newfield retained his liberal political position. He became well known for his many columns on the abuses of power by government officials and businesspeople. Among his many books are *The Full Rudy,* about former New York mayor Rudolph Giuliani, which won the American Book Award in 2003.

Benjamin Yakas

Newhouse [Neuhaus], **S(amuel) I(rving), Sr.** (*b* New York City, 24 May 1895; *d* New York City, 29 Aug 1979). Newspaper publisher. The son of Russian and Austrian Jewish immigrants, he grew up on the Lower East Side. When he was 20 years old he became the general manager of the *Bayonne Times* in New Jersey, and he soon had a share in its profits. In 1922 he gained a controlling interest in the *Staten Island Advance* and owned it outright from 1927; in 1932 he bought the *Long Island Press,* becoming unpopular with unions for reportedly having the police attack striking workers in 1937. With the help of his brothers Theodore, Louis, and Norman he began operations in Syracuse, New York, in 1939 and Oregon in 1950; expanded into broadcasting; and bought Condé Nast's magazines in 1959. By cutting costs and keeping profits in his family Newhouse built Advance Publications, one of the country's largest chains of newspapers, magazines, and broadcasters. He also donated more than $25 million to philanthropic causes and built the Mitzi E. Newhouse Theater (named for his wife) at Lincoln Center. In the early twenty-first century his conglomerate was run by his sons S. I. Newhouse, Jr., and Donald E. Newhouse.

Alana Erickson Coble

New Leader. Magazine. Founded in New York City in 1924, it began as a weekly newspaper of the American Socialist Party and evolved into an opponent of communism. It broke major stories and featured work by world-famous authors and intellectuals as well as its central preoccupation of opposing global communism. Its offices were first at 7 East 15th Street near Union Square; in 1966 it moved to 212 Fifth Avenue and in 1983 to 275 Seventh Avenue. The *New Leader* accepted contributions from everyone "except Trotskyists, Stalinists and Norman Thomas Socialists." It published early pieces by Martin Luther King, Jr., and Aleksandr Solzhenitsyn, and its editorial voice was shaped primarily by such New York City intellectuals as Sidney Hook, Irving Kristol, and Daniel Bell. During the 1950s it switched to a magazine format and was edited by Samuel "Sol" Levitas, who had fled revolutionary Russia disguised in the uniform of a Red Army colonel. During the cold war the State Department and Central Intelligence Agency supported the publication through various covert funding schemes. In the late 1960s it reached its peak circulation, at about 30,000. After the 1960s the magazine reinvented itself as a biweekly liberal–democratic journal of news and opinion and was edited by Myron Kolatch. In 2000 it became bimonthly. It stopped publishing a print version in 2006, but as of 2007 published a bimonthly online version.

See also Socialist Party of America.

Thai Jones

New Left. Term applied to the participants in a number of protest movements of the 1960s, especially the movements for civil rights in the South and against the Vietnam War. Although accounts of the activities of the New Left focus mainly on college campuses in places like Madison (Wisconsin), Berkeley (California), and Ann Arbor (Michigan), New York City was also an important center, and many members of the New Left in other parts of the nation were originally from there. Some of the first demonstrations in the North for civil rights took place in the city in 1960, when college students and other protesters picketed Woolworth's department stores to protest segregation at lunch counters in the South. In the early 1960s groups like Student SANE and the Student Peace Union protested the atmospheric testing of nuclear weapons, and pacifist groups gathered annually in City Hall Park to protest civil defense drills. Students for a Democratic Society (SDS), the main organizational body of the New Left, had its national office in the city from its formation in 1962 until 1965, when it moved to Chicago. During the spring of that year SDS sponsored a demonstration in front of the headquarters of Chase Manhattan Bank against its policies of investment in South Africa; 43 demonstrators were arrested in the protest, the first of any magnitude in the United States against apartheid.

When the war in Vietnam escalated in 1965, the New Left began to grow dramatically. In October 25,000 people marched down Fifth Avenue in the first major protest in the city against the war. A few days later David Miller burned his draft card in front of the Army Induction Center on Whitehall Street in lower Manhattan, an act for which he was later tried and imprisoned. In April 1967 about 250,000 people took part in the "spring mobilization" against the war by marching from Central Park to the United Nations. Students at Columbia University took over five buildings on campus in April 1968 to protest the cooperation of the university in research related to the war and the plans of the administration to build a gymnasium in Morningside Park; the occupation lasted for a week, until the police cleared the buildings of protesters, arresting 711 people and injuring more than 100.

The protest at Columbia became a model for others at dozens of campuses during the next few years and also led to the rise of the Weathermen, a militant faction that took control of SDS in 1969 and dissolved it within a few months. On 6 March 1970 an explosion destroyed a makeshift bomb factory in the basement of a town house on West 11th Street in Greenwich Village. Three members of the Weather Underground were killed, including Ted Gold, who had been an activist at Columbia. New York City was also the headquarters of groups like the Yippies, which were formed by Jerry Rubin and Abbie Hoffman; the Young Lords, a Puerto Rican radical group; and the local chapter of the Black Panther Party, of which 21 members were indicted for a bombing conspiracy and later acquitted. Radicalism in the 1960s culminated in the national student strike of May 1970, which followed the invasion of Cambodia by U.S. troops, and the killing of four students at Kent State University in Ohio by the National Guard. In New York City protests were largely peaceful until 8 May 1970, when students demonstrating in lower Manhattan against the war were attacked by a group of about 200 construction workers who injured 70 protesters and passersby. During the following autumn radicalism on college campuses began to subside, and by the mid-1970s there were few organizational traces of the New Left, but its effect on U.S. politics and culture was considerable.

Kirkpatrick Sale, *SDS* (New York: Random House, 1973); Nancy Zaroulis and Gerald Sullivan, *Who Spoke Up? American Protest against the War in Vietnam, 1963–1975* (Garden City, N.Y.: Doubleday, 1984)

Maurice Isserman

New Lots. Neighborhood in northeastern Brooklyn, bounded to the north by New Lots (Sutter) Avenue, to the east by Fountain Avenue, to the south by Linden Boulevard, and to the west by Pennsylvania Avenue; it is sometimes said to overlap East New York. A special patent for the area was granted by Governor Edmund Andros in 1677 to Dutch settlers from the town of Flatbush, who changed the name from Oostwoud to distinguish the land from that which they had left behind. A village was built that remained part of Flatbush until it was made a separate town in 1852; it eventually came to include parts of what are now Brownsville, East New York, and Cypress Hills. In 1886 the village was annexed to the City of Brooklyn. Much of the housing consists of two- and four-family attached houses. The main commercial thoroughfare, New Lots Avenue (especially between Pennsylvania and Van Siclen avenues), was once lined with family businesses. In the 1980s about half the immigrants settling in New Lots and its environs were from the Dominican Republic and Jamaica; many others were from Guyana, Haiti, and Honduras. By the twenty-first century New Lots had a reputation as one of New York City's most distressed neighborhoods. The Reformed Protestant Dutch Church (also called the New Lots Community Church) stands at 620 New Lots Avenue. In 2009 more than a quarter of New Lots residents had incomes below the poverty line.

Ellen Marie Snyder-Grenier

Newman, Arnold (Abner) (*b* New York City, 3 March 1918; *d* New York City, 6 June 2006). Portrait photographer. Unable to afford college, he learned photography at a portrait studio in Philadelphia. In the 1940s he began photographing artists like Marcel Duchamp, opening Arnold Newman Studios in New York City in 1946. His photographs appeared in *Harper's Bazaar, Life,* and *Look.* Newman's success stemmed from his practice of environmental portraiture; his portrait settings evoked and complemented the individual he was photographing. For example, his famous portrait of former Nazi Alfried Krupp was photographed in a sinister-looking factory. Newman made portraits of countless prominent individuals, including many U.S. presidents. He taught photography at Cooper Union and lived on the Upper West Side of Manhattan.

Kate Lauber

Newman, Barnett (*b* New York City, 29 Jan 1905; *d* New York City, 4 July 1970). Painter and sculptor. Born on the Lower East Side, Newman attended De Witt Clinton High School, took classes at the Art Students League in 1922, and received a BA in philosophy from City College (1923–27). He ran his father's garment business, the A. Newman Company, during the 1930s, and also worked as a substitute art teacher. During the 1940s Newman wrote for the art magazine *Tiger's Eye*. In 1948 he crystallized his style of "zip" paintings with *Onement I,* showing 20 such paintings in his first solo show at the Betty Parsons Gallery in 1950; later that year he completed his first sculpture, *Here I.* Newman's reputation increased through the 1960s. His series *Stations* *of the Cross: Lema Sabachthani* was exhibited at the Guggenheim Museum in 1966, and the M. Knoedler and Company gallery staged a well-received show of his late work in 1969. After his death Newman was recognized as a major figure in abstract expressionism. His wife, Annalee, founded the Barnett Newman Foundation in 1979.

Kate Lauber

Newman, Pauline M. (*b* Papilé, Lithuania, ?1889; *d* New York City, 8 April 1986). Labor leader. She immigrated to the United States in 1901 and settled in New York City, where she took up work in the factory that was later the site of the Triangle Shirtwaist fire in 1911. After eight years at the factory she was employed as an organizer by the International Ladies' Garment Workers' Union (ILGWU) and became active in the Women's Trade Union League and the Socialist Party. A lecturer on workers' rights and woman suffrage, she sought a seat in Congress in 1918 and became the education director of the new Union Health Center opened by the ILGWU. Newman provided workers with health education services for 65 years.

Robert D. Parmet

New Masses. Radical journal. The *New Masses* was founded by members of *The Liberator* and former contributors to *The Masses* after Communist Party ideologues took control of *The Liberator* and renamed it the *Worker's Monthly.* First published in 1926 in New York City, the *New Masses* advocated for a "Popular Front" to fight fascism. A leftward political shift during the Great Depression enhanced the stature of the *New Masses* in the United States, drawing writers such as Ernest Hemingway, Langston Hughes, and Thomas Wolfe as contributors to the periodical. Its stance against fascism, anti-Semitism, racism, and corporate abuse led to its being labeled as communist propaganda. The *New Masses* political cartoons famously lampooned Wall Street and the power elite, who in return attacked the magazine as unpatriotic and anti-American. The 1939 German–Soviet Non-aggression Pact was a blow to the credibility of the journal. After World War II the magazine declined; it ceased publication in 1948.

Nathan Morgante

New Museum of Contemporary Art. Founded in 1977 by Marcia Tucker and located at the New School for Social Research for the study and exhibition of multimedia art, it emphasizes controversial and provocative work by living artists using emerging technologies. In 1980 the museum established the High School Art Program, later renamed the Visible Knowledge Program, which eventually expanded into a national program dedicated to contemporary art education. In 2000 the museum founded the Zenith Media Lounge, which is the city's only museum space dedicated to new media exhibitions. Because of a series of location changes, the museum did not have a permanent exhibition space until it moved in 2007 to its current building at 235 Bowery, known for its unique "bento box" style of architecture.

Stephanie Miller

New Orange. Former Dutch name of New York City. It was given by the Dutch governor general Anthony Clove, who had commanded a fleet that took the city from the English on 8 August 1673. Under the Treaty of Westminster (19 February 1674) the province returned to English rule and the name New York was restored.

Robert Seder

New Republic. Weekly magazine launched in New York City in 1914 by Herbert Croly, Walter Weyl, and Walter Lippmann as a forum for progressive thought. It sought to influence young intellectuals and espoused the upper-middle-class liberal cosmopolitanism of the Northeast. The magazine supported the entry of the United States into World War I (although some of its writers such as Randolph Bourne opposed it) and embraced the status quo, which it hoped to improve through enlightened reform devised and implemented by an educated elite. Among its first writers were Felix Frankfurter and Raymond Moley. The magazine moved to Washington, D.C., in 1950–51.

David Seideman, *The New Republic: A Voice of Modern Liberalism* (New York: Praeger, 1986)

Lawson Bowling

newsboys. The emergence of PENNY PAPERS in the 1830s made newsboys essential to the distribution of newspapers in New York City. Often the orphaned and abandoned children of immigrants, newsboys (also called newsies) plied the streets of the city for the next century. The newsboys were loud, tough,

Newsboys

self-reliant entrepreneurs who spoke a distinct dialect, used colorful nicknames, and frequented the city's theaters; their subculture was often celebrated in novels, plays, and paintings. Homeless newsboys were subject to the malevolent influences of the saloon and the gambling den and soon drew the attention of reformers. In 1854 the Children's Aid Society opened the first of several Newsboys' Lodging Houses, which offered bed, board, and a minimum of night-schooling, and newsboys were sometimes sent west on orphan trains. The mass-circulation evening newspapers that catered to the commuters and theatergoers of the 1890s were especially dependent on newsboys. By then the typical newsboy was an Italian or Jewish immigrant boy 11 to 15 years old who lived at home and could hawk the evening papers after school. Girls also sold newspapers, but the practice was discouraged as unsafe. Boisterous newsboys were common in the heavily traveled areas near City Hall, Times Square, and the bridges across the East River. Attempts by reformers to license newsboys and reduce their late hours were only moderately successful; newsboys always preferred to police themselves and in 1899 organized a successful strike against the *Evening World* and the *New York Journal*. The newsboy eventually succumbed to adult competition, suburban home delivery, and the enclosed newsstand.

Charles Loring Brace, *Short Sermons to News Boys: With a History of the Formation of the News Boys' Lodging-house* (New York: Charles Scribner, 1866); David Nasaw, *Children of the City: At Work and at Play* (Garden City, N.Y.: Doubleday, 1985)

Mariam Touba

New School. Private university at 66 West 12th Street in Greenwich Village, formed in 1919 as an experimental institute to provide an alternative to the "academic authoritarianism" of Columbia University and other traditional schools. Originally called the New School for Social Research, from its earliest years the school prided itself on its unconventional character. Early faculty members included the economist Wesley Mitchell, the social theorist Thorstein Veblen, the philosopher Horace Kallen, and the historians Charles A. Beard and James Harvey Robinson. In 1922 it became clear that courses in the social sciences were not attracting enough students to meet expenses; Alvin Johnson, an economist trained at Columbia, took over the directorship and quickly transformed the school into a thriving institution by replacing the permanent faculty with visiting lecturers and allowing all to enroll in noncredit evening courses for a modest fee.

In the 1920s Johnson broadened the curriculum to include courses in literature, music, philosophy, psychology, and art. The interdisciplinary environment of the New School proved especially valuable to artists interested in collaborative efforts. In the interwar years the school attracted several important figures in the arts, including the composers Aaron Copland and Henry Cowell, the dancers Doris Humphrey and Charles Weidman, the art historian Leo Stein, the architectural historian Lewis Mumford, the painters Stuart Davis and Thomas Hart Benton, and the sculptor William Zorach. The school helped to popularize psychoanalysis, Marxism, expressionist drama, Keynesian economics, structuralism, Weberian sociology, and feminist theory.

After 1933 the New School became a sanctuary for Jewish and socialist scholars persecuted by Hitler. To provide an academic sponsor for displaced European scholars who would otherwise be denied entry into the United States, Johnson formed the University in Exile with the support of the Rockefeller Foundation; authorized by the state of New York in 1935 to grant graduate degrees, this later became the school's graduate faculty. The Dramatic Workshop was formed in 1940 to give the radical dramatist Erwin Piscator, a refugee from Berlin, a place to practice his craft. During its 11-year history the workshop provided a training ground for such actors and playwrights as Marlon Brando, Tennessee Williams, Rod Steiger, and Shelley Winters. In 1942 the École Libre des Hautes Études was formed as an autonomous division of the school by several leading intellectuals opposed to the Vichy government, among them the theologian Jacques Maritain, the philosopher Alexandre Koyré, the linguist Roman Jakobson, and the anthropologist Claude Lévi-Strauss, who developed his structuralist theory while teaching in New York City. A year later, the New School granted its first bachelor of arts degrees.

After World War II many of the academic innovations of the New School were adopted by conventional colleges and universities. Its adult education division attracted distinguished lecturers and permanent faculty such as the literary critic Alfred Kazin, the political theorist Hannah Arendt, the economist Robert Heilbroner, and the composer John Cage. As of 2008, the New School had eight schools and enrolled 13,000 continuing education students and 9400 undergraduate and graduate students.

Peter M. Rutkoff and William B. Scott, *New School: A History of the New School for Social Research* (New York: Free Press, 1986)

Peter M. Rutkoff, William B. Scott

Newspaper Row. Name applied from the 1840s to the early twentieth century to Park Row in lower Manhattan where the offices of many daily newspapers were situated, including the *Globe and Commercial Advertiser*, the *New York Times*, the *Recorder*, and more than a dozen others. The area was also occupied by paper manufacturers, advertising agencies, photographers, printers, and printmakers, including the renowned firm of Currier and Ives at 152 Nassau Street. Immediately south of the entrance to the Brooklyn Bridge stood the great golden dome of Joseph Pulitzer's World Building (1890, demolished). Nearby, extending above the skyline at Spruce and Nassau streets, was the redbrick clock tower of the Tribune Building (1870s, demolished). The demise of Newspaper Row began when the city's major daily newspapers moved uptown. The *New York Herald* was one of the first, moving in 1894 to 34th Street and Herald Square, and the *Times* followed in 1904, leaving Park Row for new quarters at Times Square. Some vestiges of Newspaper Row remain: the Associated Press was founded beneath the twin cupolas of the Park Row Building (1899), at 15 Park Row; 38 Park Row is the Potter Building (1883), where the *New York Press* and the *New York Observer* were published; 41 Park Row, the former New York Times Building (1889; later remodeled), is now part of Pace University.

Rebecca Read Shanor

newspapers. The first newspaper in Manhattan was the *New-York Gazette* (8 November 1725) of William Bradford, a member of a prominent family of newspaper publishers in Philadelphia who had moved to the city to become the government printer. New York was the third colony to have a newspaper, after Massachusetts and Pennsylvania. Displeased by the royalist leanings of the *Gazette*, a number of wealthy merchants and landowners supported the *New-York Weekly Journal*, which was printed from 5 November 1733 by John Peter Zenger, Bradford's former apprentice and partner. Zenger challenged the actions of the colonial government and was arrested on charges of seditious libel on 17 November 1734; his wife, Anna Catherine Zenger, continued the newspaper while he was in jail. His trial was the first of its kind in the colonies. Begun on 4 August 1735 and ending in his acquittal, it helped to win support for the concept of freedom of the press. From 1766 the *New-York Journal* was published by John Holt. In 1768–69 it was one of several colonial newspapers to print the "Journal of Occurrences," a series of anti-British articles written by Samuel Adams and the Sons of Liberty. During the years before the Revolution, Holt led efforts to distribute such tracts to printers from Boston to Charleston, South Carolina, and fled New York City as British troops moved in. The newspaper *Rivington's New-York Gazetteer; or, the Connecticut, New-Jersey, Hudson's River, and Quebec Weekly Advertiser* was first published in 1773 by James Rivington, a Tory who had opened the first chain of bookshops in the colonies; he renamed it the *Royal Gazette* after patriots refused his invitation to resolve

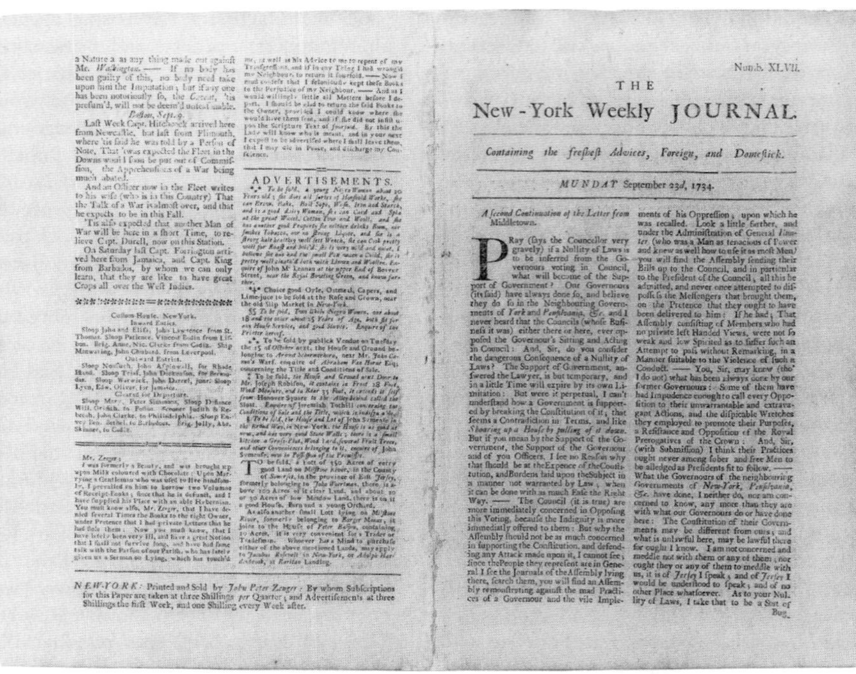
Numb. XLVII.

THE

New-York Weekly JOURNAL.

Containing the freshest Advices, Foreign, and Domestick.

MUNDAY September 23*d*, 1734.

The New-York Weekly Journal, *23 September 1734*

the colonial conflict through negotiation. The *New York Gazette and Mercury* was published by the Tory printer Hugh Gaine.

After the Revolution the number of newspapers in the city increased. Holt returned in 1783 and resumed publishing the *Journal,* which on his death in 1784 was run until the following year by his widow, Elizabeth Holt. The articles by Alexander Hamilton, John Jay, and James Madison that were later compiled as the *Federalist* were printed in the *New York Independent Journal* before being circulated throughout the new nation during 1787–88. The best-known Federalist newspaper was the *Gazette of the United States,* published in the city by John Fenno. The prominent Federalist Noah Webster was the editor of several newspapers, including the *Minerva* (daily, 1793). During the 1790s newspapers provided accounts of feuds between Federalists and the anti-Federalist supporters of Thomas Jefferson. After the Alien and Sedition Acts were passed in 1798, some anti-Federalist newspapers ceased publication, among them the *Time Piece* of John Burk; most of the city supported the Federalists. Hamilton began publishing the *New York Evening Post* in 1801 and in 1805 defended Harry Croswell (editor of the *Wasp,* a Federalist newspaper in Hudson, New York), who was accused of reprinting material from the *Evening Post* and committing libel against President Jefferson. Hamilton prevailed by maintaining that in libel cases the truthfulness of what a defendant had written or published was relevant and therefore admissible; this led to changes in New York State law in 1805 and later in federal law.

By 1800 there were five daily newspapers in New York City, which was already the nation's leading commercial center. One of the few that took up the cause of workers was the *Evening Post,* edited by the poet William Cullen Bryant from 1825; others included the *Working Man's Advocate* (1829) of George H. Evans and the *Free Enquirer* (1829) of Fanny Wright, which was supported by Walt Whitman. The country's first newspaper owned by blacks was *Freedom's Journal,* launched in the city on 16 March 1827 by John B. Russwurm,

Eighteenth-Century Newspapers in New York City, by Date of First Publication

(Frequencies of publication are given in chronological order.)

New-York Gazette (1725–44), weekly; pubd by William Bradford, later with H. DeForeest; continued by New-York Evening-Post

New-York Weekly Journal (1733–51), weekly; pubd by John Peter Zenger

New-York Weekly Post-Boy (1743–47), weekly; pubd by James Parker; continued by New-York Gazette, revived in the Weekly Post-Boy

New-York Evening-Post (1744–52), weekly; pubd by Henry DeForeest

New-York Gazette, revived in the Weekly Post-Boy (1747–52), weekly; pubd by James Parker; continued by New-York Gazette; or, the Weekly Post-Boy

Independent Reflector (1752–53), weekly; pubd by James Parker

New-York Mercury (1752–68), weekly;[1] pubd by Hugh Gaine; continued by New-York Gazette and the Weekly Mercury

Occasional Reverberator (1753), weekly; pubd by J(ames) Parker

New-York Gazette; or, the Weekly Post-Boy (1753–59), weekly; pubd by James Parker and William Weyman; continued by Parker's New-York Gazette; or, the Weekly Post-Boy

Instructor (1755), weekly; pubd by J(ames) Parker and W(illiam) Weyman

John Englishman. In Defence of the English Constitution (1755), weekly; pubd by J(ames) Parker and W(illiam) Weyman

Weyman's New York Gazette (1759), weekly; pubd by William Weyman; continued by New-York Gazette

Parker's New-York Gazette; or, the Weekly Post-Boy (1759–62), weekly; pubd by Samuel Parker; continued by New-York Gazette; or, the Weekly Post-Boy

New-York Gazette (1759–67), weekly; pubd by William Weyman

American Chronicle (1762), weekly; pubd by Samuel Farley

New-York Gazette; or, the Weekly Post-Boy (1762–66), weekly; pubd by John Holt; continued by New-York Journal; or, General Advertiser

New-York Pacquet (1763), weekly; pubd by John Mecom, printer

New-York Gazette; or, the Weekly Post-Boy (1766–73), weekly; pubd by James Parker

New-York Journal; or, General Advertiser (1766–82), weekly; pubd by John Holt; continued by Independent New-York Gazette

New-York Gazette and the Weekly Mercury (1768–83), weekly; pubd by Hugh Gaine

New-York Chronicle (1769–70), weekly; pubd by Alexander and James Robertson

Rivington's New-York Gazetteer; or, the Connecticut, New-Jersey, Hudson's River, and Quebec Weekly Advertiser (1773–75), weekly; pubd by James Rivington; continued by Rivington's New-York Gazette; or, the Connecticut, New-Jersey,

(*continued*)

Eighteenth-Century Newspapers in New York City, by Date of First Publication (*Continued*)

Hudson's River, and Quebec Weekly Advertiser

Constitutional Gazette (1775–76), semiweekly, pubd by John Anderson

New-York Packet, and the American Advertiser (1776–84), weekly, semiweekly; pubd by Samuel Loudon; continued by Loudon's New-York Packet

Rivington's New-York Loyal Gazette (1777), weekly; pubd by James Rivington; continued by Royal Gazette

Rivington's New-York Gazette; or, the Connecticut, New-Jersey, Hudson's River, and Quebec Weekly Advertiser (1777), weekly; pubd by James Rivington; continued by Rivington's New-York Loyal Gazette

Royal Gazette (1777–83), semiweekly, weekly; pubd by James Rivington; continued by Rivington's New-York Gazette, and Universal Advertiser

Royal American Gazette (1777–83), weekly, semiweekly; pubd by James Robertson

New-York Mercury; or, General Advertiser (1779–83), weekly; pubd by William Lewis

Brooklyne Hall Super-Extra Gazette (1782), irregular; pubd by Charles Loosely

New-York Evening Post (1782–83), thrice weekly; pubd by (Christopher) Sower (Jr.), (William) Morton, and (Samuel) Horner; continued by New-York Morning Post

Independent New-York Gazette (1783), weekly; pubd by John Holt; continued by Independent Gazette; or, the New-York Journal Revived

Rivington's New-York Gazette, and Universal Advertiser (1783), semiweekly; pubd by James Rivington

Town and Country Journal; or, the American Advertiser (1783), weekly; pubd by W(illiam) Ross

Independent Gazette; or, the New-York Journal Revived (1783–84), weekly, semiweekly; pubd by John Holt; continued by New-York Journal, and State Gazette

New-York Morning Post (1783–85), semiweekly; pubd by (William) Morton and (Samuel) Horner; continued by New-York Morning Post, and Daily Advertiser

New-York Gazetteer(, and Country Journal) (1783–86), weekly, semiweekly, thrice weekly;[2] pubd by Shepard Kollock; continued by New-York Gazetteer, or Daily Evening-Post

Independent Journal; or, the General Advertiser (1783–88), semiweekly, weekly; pubd by (Charles) Webster and (John) M'Lean; continued by New-York Daily Gazette

New-York Journal, and State Gazette (1784–85), weekly; pubd by Elizabeth Holt; continued by New-York Journal, and the General Advertiser

Loudon's New-York Packet (1784–85), semiweekly; pubd by Samuel Loudon; continued by New-York Packet

Daily Advertiser, Political, Commercial and Historical (1785), daily; pubd by F(rancis) Childs; continued by Daily Advertiser; Political, Historical and Commercial

New-York Journal, and the General Advertiser (1785), weekly; pubd by Elizabeth Holt; continued by New-York Journal; or, the Weekly Register

New-York Journal; or, the Weekly Register (1785–87), weekly; pubd by Eleazar Oswald; continued by New-York Journal, and Weekly Register

Daily Advertiser; Political, Historical and Commercial (1785–87), daily; pubd by F(rancis) Childs; continued by Daily Advertiser

New-York Morning Post, and Daily Advertiser (1785–88), daily; pubd by (William) Morton and (Samuel) Horner; continued by Morning Post, and Daily Advertiser

New-York Packet (1785–92), weekly, semiweekly, thrice weekly; pubd by Samuel Loudon; continued by Diary, or Loudon's Register

American Price-Current (1786), weekly; pubd by Francis Childs for Aeneas Lamont; continued by New-York Price-Current

New-York Gazetteer; or, Daily Evening-Post (1786), daily; pubd by (Shepard) Kollock, (George) Carroll, and (John) Patterson; continued by New-York Gazetteer; and, Public Advertiser

New-York Price-Current (1786), weekly; pubd by Francis Childs

New-York Gazetteer; and, Public Advertiser (1786–87), semiweekly; pubd by (George) Carroll and (John) Patterson

New-York Journal, and Weekly Register (1787), weekly, pubd by Thomas Greenleaf; continued by New-York Journal, and Daily Patriotic Register

New-York Journal, and Daily Patriotic Register (1787–88), daily; pubd by Thomas Greenleaf; continued by New-York Journal, and Weekly Register

Daily Advertiser (1787–1806), daily;[3] pubd by F(rancis) Childs; continued by People's Friend and Daily Advertiser

Impartial Gazetteer, and Saturday Evening Post (1788), weekly; pubd by (John) Harrisson and (Stephen) Purdy; continued by New-York Weekly Museum

New-York Museum (1788), semiweekly; pubd by John Russell

New-York Journal, and Weekly Register (1788–90), weekly; pubd by Thomas Greenleaf; continued by New-York Journal, and Patriotic Register

Morning Post, and Daily Advertiser (1788–92), daily; pubd by William Morton; continued by New-York Morning Post

New-York Daily Gazette (1788–95), daily; pubd by J(ohn) and A(rchibald) M'Lean; continued by New-York Gazette and General Advertiser

(New-York) Weekly Museum (1788–1817), weekly; pubd by John Harrisson and Stephen Purdy, Jr.,[4] continued by Ladies' Weekly Museum

Gazette of the United States (1789–93), semiweekly; pubd by John Fenno; continued by Gazette of the United States and Evening Advertiser[5]

New-York Journal, and Patriotic Register (1790–93), weekly; pubd by Thomas Greenleaf; continued by Greenleaf's New York Journal, and Patriotic Register

New-York Morning Post (1792), daily; pubd by William Morton

Diary, or Loudon's Register (1792–95), daily; pubd by Samuel Loudon, Jr.; continued by Diary, and Universal (Daily) Advertiser

Evening Mercury (1793), daily; pubd by John Buel

Journal des Révolutions de la Partie Française de Sainte-Domingue (1793), semiweekly; ed. Tanguy de la Boissiere; pubd by Thomas Greenleaf, printer

Columbian Gazetteer (1793–94), semiweekly; pubd by John Buel and Company; continued by New-York Evening Post

American Minerva (1793–96), daily;[6] pubd by George Bunce, and Company; continued by Minerva, and Mercantile Evening Advertiser

New-York Evening Post (1794–95), thrice weekly; pubd by L(evi) Wayland

Herald, a Gazette for the Country (1794–97), semiweekly;[7] pubd by George Bunce, and Company; continued by Spectator

Greenleaf's New York Journal, and Patriotic Register (1794–1800), weekly; pubd by Thomas Greenleaf; continued by Republican Watch-Tower

Argus and Greenleaf's New Daily Advertiser (1795), daily; pubd by Thomas Greenleaf; continued by Argus; or, Greenleaf's New Daily Advertiser

(*continued*)

Eighteenth-Century Newspapers in New York City, by Date of First Publication (*Continued*)

New-York Weekly Chronicle (1795), weekly; pubd by William Hurtin, Jr., and Andrew Commardinger
Mott and Hurtin's New-York Weekly Chronicle (1795), weekly; pubd by Jacob S. Mott and William Hurtin, Jr.; continued by New-York Weekly Chronicle
Gazette Française et Américaine (1795–96), thrice weekly; pubd by J(ohn) Delafond and by Labruère, Parisot and Company; continued by Gazette Française
Diary, and Universal (Daily) Advertiser (1795–96), daily; pubd by Samuel Loudon, Jr.; continued by Diary
Argus; or, Greenleaf's New Daily Advertiser (1795–96), daily; pubd by Thomas Greenleaf; continued by Greenleaf's New Daily Advertiser
New-York Gazette and General Advertiser (1795–1820), daily; pubd by A(rchibald) M'Lean; continued by New York Gazette and General Advertiser[8]
New-York Prices Current (1796–97), weekly; pubd by James Oram; continued by Oram's New-York Price-Current, and Marine Register
Diary (1796–97), daily; pubd by Cornelius C. Van Alen and Company; continued by Diary and Mercantile Advertiser
Minerva, and Mercantile Evening Advertiser (1796–97), daily; pubd by George Bunce and Company; continued by Commercial Advertiser
Register of the Times (1796–98), weekly;[9] pubd by Cornelius C. Van Alen and Company
Gazette Française (1796–99), thrice weekly; pubd by (Claude) Parisot and Company
Greenleaf's New Daily Advertiser (1796–1800), daily; pubd by Thomas Greenleaf; continued by American Citizen and General Advertiser
Youth's News Paper (1797), weekly; pubd by J(acob) S. Mott and C(harles) Smith
Diary and Mercantile Advertiser (1797–98), daily; pubd by (John) Crookes and (Robert) Saunders; continued by Mercantile Advertiser
Tablet; and Weekly Advertiser (1797–98), weekly; pubd by (John) Tiebout and (Thomas) Burling
Time Piece (1797–98), thrice weekly; pubd by Philip Freneau and Alexander Menut[10]
Oram's New-York Price-Current, and Marine Register (1797–99), weekly; pubd by James Oram; continued by New-York Price-Current
Spectator (1797–1804), semiweekly;[11] pubd by George F. Hopkins; continued by New-York Spectator
Commercial Advertiser (1797–1804), daily;[12] pubd by George F. Hopkins; continued by New-York Commercial Advertiser
Mercantile Advertiser (1798–1829), daily; pubd by John Crookes; continued by New-York Mercantile Advertiser[13]
Columbian Gazette (1799), weekly; pubd by (Robert M.) Hurtin and (Monteith) M'Farlane for J(ohn) M(ason) Williams
Courier, and Long Island Advertiser (1799), weekly; pubd by Thomas Kirk; continued by Courier, and New-York and Long Island Advertiser
Courier, and New-York and Long Island Advertiser (1799–1800), weekly; pubd by Thomas Kirk; continued by Long Island Courier
New-York Price-Current (1799–1802), weekly; pubd by James Oram; continued by Oram's New-York Price-Current[14]
Porcupine's Gazette (1800);[15] pubd by William Cobbett
Forlorn Hope (1800), weekly;[16] pubd by William Keteltas
Prisoner of Hope (1800), weekly, semiweekly; pubd by William Sing
American Citizen and General Advertiser (1800–1802), daily; pubd by D(avid) Denniston; continued by American Citizen (daily, 1802–10)
Temple of Reason (1800–1803), weekly; pubd by D(ennis) Driscol
Long Island Courier [Brooklyn] (1800–1803), weekly; pubd by Thomas Kirk
Republican Watch-Tower (1800–1810), semiweekly;[17] pubd by D(avid) Denniston; continued by Morning Star (semiweekly, 1810–13)

1. Other title was "No Stamped Paper to be Had."
2. Title varies.
3. Continued to 1809 under various titles.
4. Subsequently published by John Harrisson alone, by his wife Margaret Harrisson after his death, by his son C. Harrisson, and finally by James Oram (1814–17).
5. Published in Philadelphia.
6. Title varies. Companion to semiweekly Herald.
7. Companion to daily Minerva.
8. See list of daily newspapers.
9. Companion to the daily Diary.
10. Subsequent publishers were Philip Freneau and M. L. Davis and Company; M. L. Davis and Company; and R. Saunders for John D. Burk and James Smith.
11. Companion to daily Commercial Advertiser.
12. Companion to semiweekly Spectator.
13. See list of daily newspapers.
14. Continued under varying titles until 1817.
15. Published in Philadelphia; last issue published in New York City 13 Jan 1800.
16. Published in "the Prison, New York."
17. Companion to the daily American Citizen and General Advertiser. Published with James Cheetham from 1801 and by Cheetham alone from 1803.

Sources: Clarence S. Brigham, *History and Bibliography of American Newspapers, 1690–1820*, vol. 1 (Worcester, Mass.: American Antiquarian Society, 1947); Edward Connery Lathem, comp., *Chronological Tables of American Newspapers, 1690–1820* (Barre, Mass.: American Antiquarian Society/Barre Publishers, 1972); *Newspapers in Microform, United States, 1948–1983* (Washington, D.C.: Library of Congress, 1984); *United States Newspaper Program, National Union List*, 3rd edn, June 1989 (Dublin, Ohio: Online Computer Library Center); *United States Newspaper Program, New-York Historical Society Holdings*, April 1990 (Dublin, Ohio: Online Computer Library Center)

Compiled by Alana J. Erickson

who was the first black American to graduate from college (Bowdoin College, 1826), and the Presbyterian minister Samuel Cornish; it ceased publication in October 1829, and from 1837 Cornish was an editor of the *Weekly Advocate*, published by Philip A. Bell and renamed the *Colored American* before ceasing operations in 1842.

Gradually, presses were improved and printing became more efficient. Samuel Rust invented the Washington hand press (1827) in New York City, and steam-driven presses were introduced a few years later. By the late 1830s the presses manufactured by the New York City firm of Robert Hoe produced more than 4000 double impressions an hour. On 3 September 1833 Benjamin H. Day brought out the first issue of the *Sun*, which carried mostly human-interest stories and was aimed at a wide audience. Similar newspapers became popular in cities nationwide and were known as the penny press. Of the 35 PENNY PAPERS in New York City during the 1830s, the largest and most widely read was the *New York Herald* (1835). Under the direction of James Gordon Bennett, Sr., it aggressively gathered news and offered thorough coverage of sports, financial news, and foreign news. In 1841 it introduced regular Sunday editions. Soon there were 10 daily newspapers in the city. The main rival of the *Herald* was the *New York Tribune*, which began in 1841 under Horace Greeley and became known for its detailed reporting and its global perspective on farming, labor, and business. During the 1830s and 1840s aggressive coverage was also provided by the *Courier and Enquirer* of James Watson Webb and the *Journal of Commerce*, published by Arthur Tappan and later

Daily Newspapers Published within the Present Boundaries of New York City, by Date of First Publication (alphabetical index follows)

1780–1800

New-York Gazetteer[1] 1783–87
New-York Morning Post (, and Daily Advertiser)[2] 1783–92
New York Journal (i)[3] 1784–93
(New York) Daily Advertiser[4] 1785–1809
New-York Gazette (and General Advertiser) (i)[5] 1788–1840; continued by New York Journal of Commerce and Commercial
Diary[6] 1792–98; continued by (New-York) Commercial Advertiser
American Minerva 1793–96; continued by Commercial Advertiser
Evening Mercury 1793
Argus Greenleaf's New Daily Advertiser[7] 1795–1800; continued by American Citizen
(New-York) Commercial Advertiser 1797–1804
(New-York) Mercantile Advertiser 1798–1833; continued by Mercantile Advertiser and New-York Advocate
American Citizen (and General Advertiser) 1800–10; continued by New-York Morning Post

1801–1820

New York (Evening) Post (i) 1801–
Morning Chronicle (i) 1802–7
Public Advertiser[8] 1807–13
(New-York) Columbian[9] 1809–21; continued by New-York Statesman
New York (Morning) (Daily) Post (ii) 1810–12; continued by Statesman
Daily Telegraph (i) 1812–13
National Advocate 1812–29; continued by New York Morning Herald
Statesman 1812–13; continued by Daily Express
Daily Express 1813
Mid-day Courier 1814
Daily Items, for Merchants 1815–16
New York Commercial[10] 1815–1926; continued by New York Journal of Commerce and Commercial
New-York Courier 1815–17; continued by New-York Daily Advertiser
New-York Daily Advertiser 1817–36; continued by New York (Daily) Express
Republican Chronicle (and City Advertiser) 1817–19
New-York American, for the Country[11] 1819–45

1821–1840

New-York Statesman[12] 1822–29; continued by New-York Morning Herald
New York Gazette and General Advertiser 1822–40; continued by New York Journal of Commerce
New York Patriot (and Morning Advertiser) 1823–44
New York National Advocate 1824–26
New-York Enquirer 1826–29; continued by Morning Courier and New-York Enquirer Times
Brooklyn Evening Star 1827–63
(New York) Journal of Commerce (and Commercial) 1827–
New York Journal of Commerce 1827–93; continued by Journal of Commerce and Commercial Bulletin
Morning Chronicle (ii) 1827
Morning Courier 1827–29; continued by Morning Courier and New York Enquirer
(New-York) Standard 1827–34; continued by New York Times (i)
Merchants' Telegraph 1828
Morning Courier and New-York Enquirer 1829–61; continued by World
New-York Evening Journal 1829–32; continued by New-York Advocate and Journal
New-York Morning Herald 1829–30; continued by New York Standard (i)
New York Daily Sentinel[13] 1830–33
New-York American Advocate 1831–32; continued by New-York Advocate and Journal
New York Whig 1831–32
Democrat (i) [Brooklyn] 1832
Franklin Daily Advertiser 1832
New York Advocate and Journal 1832–33; continued by Mercantile Advertiser and New-York Advocate
New York Citizen 1832
New York Globe 1832
Evening Star (i) 1833–40; continued by New York Times and Evening Star
Mercantile Advertiser and New-York Advocate 1833–38
Morning Post and Family Gazette 1833
Sun[14] 1833–1950; continued by New York World–Telegram and the Sun
Adopted Citizen 1834
American Whig 1834
Brooklyn (Daily) (Morning) (Evening) Advertiser 1834–35; continued by American Citizen and Brooklyn Evening Advertiser
Constitution 1834
Democratic Chronicle 1834
Eagle 1834
Humorist; or, Real Life in New York 1834
Jeffersonian 1834–36
Major Downing's Advocate (and Mechanics' Journal) 1834
Man[15] 1834–?1835
New York Daily Bee 1834–?1836
New York Mechanic 1834
New York Times (i) 1834–39
New York Transcript[16] 1834–39
Penny Daily Gazette (i) 1834; continued by Constitution
Transcript and Wasp 1834–39
Truth (i) 1834
American Citizen and Brooklyn Evening Advertiser 1835; continued by Native American Citizen (and Brooklyn Evening Advertiser)
Business Reporter and Merchants' and Mechanics' Advertiser 1835
Mechanic 1835
Native American and Democratic Citizen 1835
Native American Citizen (and Brooklyn Evening Advertiser) 1835–[1837]
Native American Democrat 1835
New York General Advertiser and Daily Commercial Register 1835
New York (Morning) Herald[17] 1835–1924; continued by New York Herald Tribune
Williamsburg Gazette 1835–53
Age (i) 1836
American Banker[18] 1836–
Democrat (ii) 1836
(Ladies) Morning Star (i) 1836–37
New York (Daily) (Morning) Express 1836–64
Union (i) 1836
Daily News (i) 1837
Daily News (ii) 1837–38
Examiner 1837
New York Daily Whig 1837–40; continued by New York Gazette and General Advertiser
Omnium Advertiser 1837
Age (ii) 1838
Censor 1838
(New York) Times and Commercial Advertiser 1838–40; continued by New York Times and Evening Star
Evening Tattler (i) 1839–40; continued by Dispatch and Tattler
Morning Dispatch 1839–40; continued by Dispatch and Tattler
New York Evening Express ?1839–81; continued by Mail and Express
Penny Daily Gazette (ii) 1839
Ballot Box [campaign paper] 1840
Brooklyn Daily News (and Long Island Times) (i) 1840–43
Corsair 1840
Democratic Press 1840
Dispatch and Tattler 1840; continued by Evening Tattler (ii)
Evening Tattler (ii) 1840–?1842
Long Island Daily Times [Brooklyn] 1840–41
Morning Chronicle (and Tippecanoe Advertiser) (iii) 1840–?1841
New-York Planet 1840–41
New York Standard (i) 1840–44
New York Times and Evening Star [semiweekly] 1840–41; continued by Commercial Advertiser

(*continued*)

Daily Newspapers Published within the Present Boundaries of New York City, by Date of First Publication (*Continued*)

1841–1860

Brooklyn (Daily) Eagle[19] 1841–1955
Evening Mail (i) 1841
New York Advertiser ?1841–?1842
New York Democrat (i) 1841
New-York (Daily) Tribune 1841–1924; continued by New York Herald Tribune
New York Trumpet 1841
Penny Press 1841
Truth (ii) 1841
Daily Plebian 1842–45; continued by New York Morning News
Flushing (Evening) Journal 1842–1931; continued by North Shore Daily Journal
Morning Chronicle (and New York Penny-a-Line Advertiser) (iv) 1842–43
Morning Star (ii) 1842
New York Arena 1842–45; continued by Daily Plebian
New York Aurora 1842–44; continued by Daily Plebian
New York Commercial Transcript 1842
New-York Daily News 1842
Union (ii) 1842–43; continued by New York Aurora
Washingtonian Daily News 1842–43
American Patriot 1843–45; continued by Evening Gazette
(New-York) American Republican[20] 1843–45
Brooklyn Daily News (ii) 1843
Evening Tribune 1843–65
New-York Cynosure and Morning Chronicle 1843
True Sun[21] 1843–48
American Advocate for Equal Rights to Man 1844–?1845; continued by Daily Plebian
American Ensign 1844
Brooklyn Daily Advertiser (i) 1844–54; continued by United States Daily Freeman
Evening Mirror (i) 1844–59
(New York Daily) Evening Mirror (ii) 1844–45
New York Morning News 1844–46
Republic (i) 1844–45
(New-York) Daily Globe 1845–51
Daily Long Islander 1845
Evening Gazette 1845–46; continued by Gazette and Times
Evening Star (ii) 1845
Morning Telegraph (i) 1845–46; continued by Daily Telegraph (ii)
Daily Telegraph (ii) 1846
Daily Time 1846; continued by Gazette and Times
Gazette and Times 1846–47
New York Evening Ledger 1846
Daily American Artisan 1847
(New-York) (Evening) Day-Book 1848–61
Morning Star (iii) 1848–52
Williamsburgh Times[22] 1848–55; continued by Brooklyn Daily Times
Brooklyn Daily Freeman[23] 1849–50
Daily Dispatch 1849
Merchants' Day Book 1849
New-Yorker 1849–51
True National Democrat and Morning Star 1849–54
Daily Independent Press [Williamsburgh] 1850–55
New York Standard (ii) 1850
Brooklyn Morning Journal 1851–55
Journal of Commerce Jr. 1851–65
(Daily) National Democrat 1851–[1854]
New York Evening Times[24] 1851–57
New York Times (ii)[25] 1851–
Brooklyn Daily Journal 1852
Daily Half-Cent 1853
Woodhaven Advertiser and Literary Gazette 1853
United States Daily Freeman 1854
Brooklyn Daily Signal 1855–[1867]
Brooklyn Daily Times 1855–1932; continued by Brooklyn Times–Union
Dawn 1855
New York Daily News (ii) 1855–?1906
New York Daily Era (and Hotel Register) 1856–66
Daily Museum 1858–59
Gerrit Smith Banner [campaign banner] 1858
Brooklyn City News 1859–63; continued by Brooklyn Daily Union
New York Daily Transcript 1859–[1872]
World[26] 1860–1931; continued by New York World–Telegram

1861–1880

Brooklyn Daily Standard 1861
Brooklyn Daily Programme 1863–75
Brooklyn (Daily) Union (i) 1863–77; continued by Brooklyn Daily Union–Argus
Brooklyn Daily Advertiser (ii) 1864–72
Brooklyn Daily Whig 1864–65
Drum Beat 1864
(New York) Daily Commercial Bulletin and Auction Record[27] 1865–9; continued by New York Journal of Commerce and Commercial
Flushing Daily Times 1865–?1925
New York Evening Star and American Advertiser 1865
New York (Evening) Gazette (ii) 1866–67
Brooklyn Press 1867
Evening Telegram[28] 1867–1931; continued by New York World–Telegram
(New York) (Evening) Mail 1867–81; continued by Mail and Express
Evening Press 1868–70; continued by Globe and Evening Press
Every Afternoon 1868
New York Democrat (ii)[29] 1868–71
(New York) (Daily) Star 1868–91; continued by Daily Continent
Evening Republic 1869
Globe 1870–?1871
Globe and Evening Press 1870; continued by Globe
Journal of the Day 1870–71
New York Evening Free Press 1870–71
New-York Standard (iii) 1870–72
Evening Leader 1871
New York Daily Register 1871–89
New York Daily Witness 1871–79
Brooklyn Daily Argus 1873–77; continued by Brooklyn Daily Union–Argus
City Record 1873–
Daily Graphic 1873–89
Brooklyn Daily Post 1874
Republic (ii) 1874
(Long Island City) Daily Star 1876–1938; continued by Long Island Star–Journal
Brooklyn Daily Union–Argus 1877–83; continued by Brooklyn Union (ii)
Hotel Reporter 1877–[1925]
Truth (iii) 1879–84
Wall Street Daily News 1879–1907

1881–1900

Greenpoint Daily Star [1881]–?1900; continued by Daily Star
Mail and Express 1882–1904; continued by Evening Mail (ii)
New York (Morning) Journal (ii) 1882–97; continued by New York Journal and Advertiser
American Metal Market[30] 1883–2002
Brooklyn Union (ii) 1883–87; continued by Standard–Union
Dial 1884–?1885
Brooklyn Standard 1885–87; continued by Standard–Union
Daily Telegraph (iii) 1885
Up-Town News ?1885–?1889
Brooklyn Citizen[31] 1886–1947
Brooklyn Daily News (iii) 1886–1947
Daily Voice 1886
Staten Island Advance[32] 1886
Argus 1887
Evening Sun 1887–1920
Evening World 1887–1931; continued by New York World–Telegram
Investigator 1887–?1913
(New York) Press 1887–1916; continued by Sun
Standard-Union [Brooklyn] 1887–1932
New York Law Journal 1888–
Wall Street Journal 1889–
Journal of Finance (i) 1890–?1904
Bond Buyer 1891–
Daily Continent 1891; continued by Morning Advertiser
Journal of Finance (ii) 1891–1914
Morning Advertiser 1891–97; continued by New York Journal and Advertiser

(*continued*)

Daily Newspapers Published within the Present Boundaries of New York City, by Date of First Publication (*Continued*)

New York Advocate 1891–93
New York Recorder 1891–96
Daily Trade Record 1892–1916; continued by Daily News Record
Daily America 1893–94
Daily Mercury 1893–97
Wall Street Summary 1893–1910; continued by Financial America
Journal of Commerce and Commercial Bulletin, 1893–1926; continued by Journal of Commerce Commercial Bulletin and Commercial
Daily Racing Form 1894–
Daily Tattler 1896
New York (Evening) Journal (iii) 1896–1937; continued by New York Journal American
Morning Telegraph (ii) 1897–1972
New York Journal and Advertiser 1897–1901; continued by New York Journal and American
Wall Street Daily Investigator ?1898–1904
Daily People 1900–14

1901–1920

Daily Metal Reporter ?1901–61
Daily North Side News [Bronx] 1901–?1958
New York Journal and American 1901–2; continued by New York American and Journal
New York American and Journal 1902–3; continued by New York American
New York American 1903–37; continued by New York Journal–American
Evening Mail (ii) 1904–37; continued by Evening Telegram
Globe and Commercial Advertiser 1904–23
Wall Street Daily Investor 1905–?1914
(Bronx) Home News 1906–48; continued by New York Post Home News
Wall Street Daily Ticker 1906–?1907
Bromley Morning News 1908
New York (Evening) Call 1908–23; continued by New York Leader
Financial American 1910–24; continued by Wall Street News
Women's Wear Daily 1910–
Daily Long Island Democrat [Jamaica] 1911–12
Long Island Daily Advocate (i)[33] 1911–66
Film (and Television) Daily[34] 1915–72
Queens (County) (Evening) News 1915–39
Daily News Record 1916–
Daily Tank 1917
Evening Call[35] 1917–18
Daily News (iii)[36] 1919–
Market News ?1919–?1920

1921–40

Long Island Daily Press and Daily Long Island Farmer 1921–26; continued by Long Island (Daily) Press
Combined New York Morning Newspapers[37] 1923
New York Leader 1923
Daily Mirror 1924–57
New York Evening Bulletin 1924–[1925]
New York Evening Graphic 1924–32
New York Herald Tribune[38] 1924–66; continued by World Journal Tribune
Sunday Worker 1924–?1956
Wall Street News 1924–30; continued by Wall Street Journal
Long Island (Daily) Press [Jamaica] 1926–77
Daily Worker[39] 1927–58
Journal of Commerce Commercial Bulletin and Commercial 1927; continued by Journal of Commerce and Commercial
Journal of Commerce and Commercial 1927–96, daily 1948–96; continued by Journal of Commerce
New York Repository[40] 1931–33
New York World–Telegram[41] 1931–50; continued by New York World–Telegram and the Sun
North Shore Daily Journal 1931–38; continued by Long Island Star–Journal
Brooklyn Times–Union 1932–37
Brooklyn Daily 1933–63
Harlem Heights Daily Citizen ?1933–?1934
Westchester Globe (i) [campaign paper] 1933
Westchester Globe (ii) [campaign paper] 1935
New York Journal–American[42] 1937–66; continued by World–Journal Tribune
Long Island Star–Journal [Flushing][43] 1938–[1948]
PM 1940–48; continued by New York Star

1941–60

Long Island Daily Advocate (ii) [Ridgewood] 1948–66
New York Post Home News[44] 1948–49
New York Star[45] 1948–49; continued by Daily Compass
Retailing Daily 1948–57; continued Home Furnishings Daily
Daily Compass 1949–52
New York World-Telegram and the Sun 1950–66; continued by World Journal Tribune
Daily Bulletin 1955–
Home Furnishings Daily 1957–
New York Mirror 1957–63

1961–80

New York and Brooklyn Daily ?1963–[1971]
New York Standard (iv) 1963
World–Journal Tribune 1966–67
Daily World 1968–86; continued by People's Daily World
New York (Daily) Column (and the New York Knickerbocker) 1968–73
Daily Mirror 1971–73
Black American[46] 1972–90
Daily Challenge 1972–, daily 1984–
City News [1978]
New York Daily Press 1978
New York Graphic 1978
Trib 1978

1981–2003

New York City Tribune[47] 1983–92
Investor's Daily 1984–91; continued by Investor's Business Daily
New York Newsday ?1985–95
People's Daily World 1986–90
National 1989–91
Investor's Business Daily, 1991–
Brooklyn Daily Eagle and Daily Bulletin, 1996–
Journal of Commerce, 1996–2000
AM New York, 2003–

Note: Parts of names in parentheses were used during some part of a newspaper's run. Bracketed dates indicate first or last extant copy of a newspaper. List may not be comprehensive for business newspapers.

1. Daily in 1786; title varies.
2. Daily, 1785–92.
3. Daily, 1787–88; title varies.
4. Known as People's Friend 1806–7, L'Oracle and Daily Advertiser 1808.
5. Known as the New-York Daily Gazette 1788–95; title and publishers vary.
6. Title varies.
7. Title varies; see table of eighteenth-century newspapers.
8. Known as American Patriot and Public Advertiser 1811–12; frequency varies.
9. Known as the New York Evening Journal and Patron of Industry 1821.
10. Known as the Shipping and Commercial List and New York Price Current 1826–98.
11. Daily, 1820–45.
12. Known as the New York Statesman and Evening Advertiser 1822–23.
13. Daily edition of the weekly Working Man's Advocate (1830–36).
14. Merged in 1920 with Herald to form Sun and New York Herald (1920), which then divided again.
15. Daily edition of the weekly Working Man's Advocate (1830–36).
16. Known as the New York Transcript and Wasp 1839.
17. Founded as the weekly Thompson's Bank Note and Commercial Reporter (1836–87).
18. Merged in 1920 with the Sun to form Sun and New York Herald (1920), which then divided again.
19. Known as Brooklyn Eagle and King's County Democrat 1841–46.
20. Known as New York Citizen and American Republican 1844.
21. Published by striking compositors of the Sun.
22. Also known as East Brooklyn Daily Times.
23. Began as a weekly, became daily in 1849 or 1850.
24. Companion to the morning edition of the New York Daily Times.

(*continued*)

Daily Newspapers Published within the Present Boundaries of New York City, by Date of First Publication (alphabetical index) (*Continued*)

25. Known as the New York Daily Times 1851–57, companion of the New York Evening Times.
26. Known as the World, Morning Courier and New York Enquirer 1861–63.
27. Title varies.
28. Known as the New York Telegram (1925–31).
29. Title varies.
30. Weekly, 1883–1901. Also known as American Metal Market and (Daily) Iron and Steel Report 1902–26.
31. Daily to 1931.
32. Sometimes known as Richmond County Advance.
33. Also known as Knickerbocker News, Greater Ridgewood News.
34. Weekly to 1918.
35. The "night edition" of the New York Call.
36. Also known as the News, Illustrated Daily News.
37. Joint issue of morning newspapers during printers' strike (19–26 Sept).
38. Known as the New York Herald, New York Tribune 1924–26.
39. Published in Chicago 1924–26.
40. Published to retain franchise of Associated Press but never circulated.
41. Known as the Evening World, the World, the New York Telegram 1931.
42. Known as the New York Journal and American 1937–41.
43. Known as North Shore Daily Journal and Long Island Star 1938.
44. Name during this period of the New York (Evening) Post.
45. Known as New York Star, formerly PM 1948.
46. May not be daily throughout the run.
47. Also known as New York Tribune 1983.

Sources: Clarence S. Brigham, *History and Bibliography of American Newspapers, 1690–1820*, vol. 1 (Worcester, Mass.: American Antiquarian Society, 1947); Winifred George, ed., *American Newspapers, 1821–1936: A Union List of Files Available in the United States and Canada* (New York: H. W. Wilson, 1937; repr. Kraus, 1967); *Newspapers in Microform, United States, 1948–1983* (Washington, D.C.: Library of Congress, 1984); *United States Newspaper Project, National Union List*, 3rd edn, June 1989 (Dublin, Ohio: Online Computer Library Center); *United States Newspaper Project: New-York Historical Society Holding*, April 1990 (Dublin, Ohio: Online Computer Library Center)

INDEX

(*continued*)

Daily Newspapers Published within the Present Boundaries of New York City, by Date of First Publication (alphabetical index) (*Continued*)

Evening Tattler (i) 1839–40
Evening Tattler (ii) 1840–?1842
Evening Telegram 1867–1931
Evening Tribune 1843–65
Evening World 1887–1931
Every Afternoon 1868
Examiner 1837
Film (and Television) Daily 1915–72
Financial American 1910–24
Flushing Daily Times 1865–?1925
Flushing (Evening) Journal 1842–1931
Franklin Daily Advertiser 1832
Gazette and Times 1846–47
Gerrit Smith Banner [campaign banner] 1858
Globe 1870–?1871
Globe and Commercial Advertiser 1904–23
Globe and Evening Press 1870
Greenpoint Daily Star [1881]–?1900
Harlem Heights Daily Citizen ?1933–?1934
Home Furnishings Daily 1957–
(Bronx) Home News 1906–48
Hotel Reporter 1877–[1925]
Humorist; or, Real Life in New York 1834
Investigator 1887–?1913
Investor's Business Daily, 1991–
Investor's Daily 1984–91
Jeffersonian 1834–36
Journal of Commerce, 1996–2000
Journal of Commerce and Commercial, 1927–96, daily 1948–96
Journal of Commerce and Commercial Bulletin, 1893–1926
Journal of Commerce Commercial Bulletin and Commercial 1927
Journal of Commerce Jr. 1851–65
Journal of Finance (i) 1890–?1904
Journal of Finance (ii) 1891–1914
Journal of the Day 1870–71
Long Island Daily Advocate (i) 1911–66
Long Island Daily Advocate (ii) [Ridgewood] 1948–66
Long Island Daily Press and Daily Long Island Farmer 1921–26
Long Island Daily Times [Brooklyn] 1840–41
Long Island (Daily) Press [Jamaica] 1926–77
Long Island Star–Journal [Flushing] 1938–[1948]
(New York) (Evening) Mail 1867–81
Mail and Express 1882–1904
Major Downing's Advocate (and Mechanics' Journal) 1834
Man 1834–?1835
Market News ?1919–?1920
Mechanic 1835
(New-York) Mercantile Advertiser 1798–1833
Mercantile Advertiser and New-York Advocate 1833–38
Merchants' Day Book 1849
Merchants' Telegraph 1828
Mid-day Courier 1814
Morning Advertiser 1891–97
Morning Chronicle (i) 1802–7
Morning Chronicle (ii) 1827
Morning Chronicle (and New York Penny-a-Line Advertiser) (iv) 1842–43
Morning Chronicle (and Tippecanoe Advertiser) (iii) 1840–?1841
Morning Courier 1827–29
Morning Courier and New-York Enquirer 1829–61
Morning Dispatch 1839–40
Morning Post and Family Gazette 1833
Morning Star (ii) 1842
(Ladies) Morning Star (i) 1836–37
Morning Star (iii) 1848–52
Morning Telegraph (i) 1845–46
Morning Telegraph (ii) 1897–1972
National 1989–91
National Advocate 1812–29
(Daily) National Democrat 1851–[1854]
Native American and Democratic Citizen 1835
Native American Citizen (and Brooklyn Evening Advertiser) 1835–[1837]
Native American Democrat 1835
New York Advertiser ?1841–?1842
New York Advocate 1891–93
New York Advocate and Journal 1832–33
New York American 1903–37
New-York American Advocate 1831–32
New-York American, for the Country 1819–45
New York American and Journal 1902–3
New York and Brooklyn Daily ?1963–[1971]
New York Arena 1842–45
New York Aurora 1842–44
New York (Evening) Call 1908–23
New York Citizen 1832
New York City Tribune 1983–92
New York (Daily) Column (and the New York Knickerbocker) 1968–73
New York Commercial 1815–1926
New York Commercial Transcript 1842
New-York Courier 1815–17
New-York Cynosure and Morning Chronicle 1843
New-York Daily Advertiser 1817–36
New York Daily Bee 1834–?1836
New York Daily Era (and Hotel Register) 1856–66
New-York Daily News 1842
New York Daily News (ii) 1855–?1906
New York Daily Press 1978
New York Daily Register 1871–89
New York Daily Sentinel 1830–33
New York Daily Transcript 1859–[1872]
New York Daily Whig 1837–40
New York Daily Witness 1871–79
New York Democrat (i) 1841
New York Democrat (ii) 1868–71
New-York Enquirer 1826–29
New York Evening Bulletin 1924–[1925]
New York Evening Express ?1839–81
New York Evening Free Press 1870–71
New York Evening Graphic 1924–32
New-York Evening Journal 1829–32
New York Evening Ledger 1846
New York Evening Star and American Advertiser 1865
New York Evening Times 1851–57
New York (Daily) (Morning) Express 1836–64
New-York Gazette (and General Advertiser) (i) 1788–1840
New York (Evening) Gazette (ii) 1866–67
New York Gazette and General Advertiser 1822–40
New-York Gazetteer 1783–87
New York General Advertiser and Daily Commercial Register 1835
New York Globe 1832
New York Graphic 1978
New York (Morning) Herald 1835–1924
New York Herald Tribune 1924–66
New York Journal (i) 1784–93
New York (Morning) Journal (ii) 1882–97
New York (Evening) Journal (iii) 1896–1937
New York Journal–American 1937–66
New York Journal and Advertiser 1897–1901
New York Journal and American 1901–2
New York Journal of Commerce, 1827–1893
New York Law Journal 1888–
New York Leader 1923
New York Mechanic 1834
New York Mirror 1957–63
New-York Morning Herald 1829–30
New York Morning News 1844–46
New-York Morning Post (, and Daily Advertiser) 1783–92
New York National Advocate 1824–26
New York Newsday ?1985–95
New York Patriot (and Morning Advertiser) 1823–44
New-York Planet 1840–41
New York (Evening) Post (i) 1801–
New York (Morning) (Daily) Post (ii) 1810–12
New York Post Home News 1948–49
New York Recorder 1891–96
New York Repository 1931–33
New York Standard (i) 1840–44
New York Standard (ii) 1850
New-York Standard (iii) 1870–72
New York Standard (iv) 1963
New York Star 1948–49
New-York Statesman 1822–29
New York Times (i) 1834–39
New York Times (ii) 1851–
New York Times and Evening Star [semiweekly] 1840–41
New York Transcript 1834–39
New-York (Daily) Tribune 1841–1924
New York Trumpet 1841
New York Whig 1831–32
New York World–Telegram 1931–50

(*continued*)

Daily Newspapers Published within the Present Boundaries of New York City, by Date of First Publication (alphabetical index) (*Continued*)

New York World–Telegram and the Sun 1950–66
New-Yorker 1849–51
North Shore Daily Journal 1931–38
Omnium Advertiser 1837
Penny Daily Gazette (i) 1834
Penny Daily Gazette (ii) 1839
Penny Press 1841
People's Daily World 1986–90
PM 1940–48
(New York) Press 1887–1916
Public Advertiser 1807–13
Queens (County) (Evening) News 1915–39
Republic (i) 1844–45
Republic (ii) 1874
Republican Chronicle (and City Advertiser) 1817–19
Retailing Daily 1948–57
(New-York) Standard 1827–34
Standard–Union [Brooklyn] 1887–1932
(New York) (Daily) Star 1868–91
Staten Island Advance 1886
Statesman 1812–13
Sun 1833–1950
Sunday Worker 1924–?1956
(New York) Times and Commercial Advertiser 1838–40
Transcript and Wasp 1834–39
Trib 1978
True National Democrat and Morning Star 1849–54
True Sun 1843–48
Truth (i) 1834
Truth (ii) 1841
Truth (iii) 1879–84
Union (i) 1836
Union (ii) 1842–43
United States Daily Freeman 1854
Up-Town News ?1885–?1889
Wall Street Daily Investigator ?1898–1904
Wall Street Daily Investor 1905–?1914
Wall Street Daily News 1879–1907
Wall Street Daily Ticker 1906–?1907
Wall Street Journal 1889–
Wall Street News 1924–30
Wall Street Summary 1893–1910
Washingtonian Daily News 1842–43
Westchester Globe (i) [campaign paper] 1933
Westchester Globe (ii) [campaign paper] 1935
Williamsburg Gazette 1835–53
Williamsburgh Times 1848–55
Women's Wear Daily 1910–
Woodhaven Advertiser and Literary Gazette 1853
World 1860–1931
World–Journal Tribune 1966–67

Compiled by Alana J. Erickson

Foreign-Language Daily Newspapers in New York City, 1828–2009

ARABIC

Kawkab Amirka [Star of America], 1892–1909, daily 1897–1909
Al-Hoda [American Journal], 1898– , daily 1915
Mir'at al gharb [Mirror of the West; Daily Mirror], 1899–[1961], daily ?1913–32
Jurab-Ul Kurdy, 1907–?1913, daily 1912–?1913
As-Sayeh [The Traveler], 1912–58, daily 1928–30
Syrian Eagle [New York City Eagle], 1914–[1920]
As-Sameer [The Entertainer] [1945]
Al Ahrām [Ahrām al-dawlī], 1987–

CARPATHO–RUSYN

Den [The Day], 1922–26

CHINESE[1]

Mei hua shin pao [Mei hua ri bao; Chinese American], 1883
Chinese Daily News [Chinese Republic Daily], 1912
Chinese Nationalist, 1915–58
Mei-chou jih pao [Mei-zhou ri bao; Chinese Journal], 1926–[1976]
Min ch'i jih pao [Min qi ri bao; Chinese Nationalist Daily], 1927–58
Kung ho (jih) pao [Gong he (ri) bao, Kong wo (yat) bo; Justice (Daily) News], 1928–37, daily 1928–29
Mei-chou Hua chi'iao jih pao [Mei-zhou Hua qiao ri bao, Hua ch'iao jih pao; China Daily News], 1940–[1989]
Lian he ri bao [United Journal], 1940–
Hua mei ri bao [China Tribune], 1943–
Min chih jih pao [Min zhi ri bao; Min chih Journal], 1960–66
Sing Tao jih pao [Sing Tao Newspaper], published in New York City 1965–
Shi jie ri bao [World Journal], 1976–, daily 1991–
Pei Mei jih pao [Bei Mei ri bao; Peimei news], 1978–[1989]
Zhong guo ri bao [China Daily], 1981–
Qiao Bao [China Press], 1990–
Ming Pao [Daily News], 1997–2009

CROATIAN

Narodni List [National Gazette], 1898–1922
Jugoslovenski Svijet [Southern Slav World], 1908–23[2]; continued by Svijet Svijet [The World], 1924–38

CZECH

Delnik Americky [American Worker], 1882–85
Hlas Lidu [Voice of the People], 1886–?1921, daily 1905–?1921
New Yorkse Listy, 1886–1966, daily 1886–1923; continued by Americke Listy (weekly, 1962–89)

FRENCH

Le Courrier des États-Unis, 1828–?1937, daily 1851–32
Le Républicain, 1853–[1854]
Le Progrès, 1855–[1855]
Le Messager Franco Américain, 1860–83, daily 1860–83
Le Progrès [Le Journal Français aux États-Unis], 1909–[1910]

GERMAN

New Yorker Staats-Zeitung, 1834–1934; continued by New Yorker Staats-Zeitung und Herold
New-Yorker Staats-Demokrat, 1845–56, daily 1846–56; continued by New-Yorker Demokrat
Deutsche Schnellpost, 1848–51, daily 1850–51; continued by New-Yorker Deutsche Zeitung
New-Yorker Deutsche Zeitung, 1851–?1851
New-Yorker Demokrat 1856–1876; continued by New Yorker Allgemeine Zeitung
New Yorker Handels-Zeitung, 1857–58
New Yorker Journal, 1866–?1878
New-Yorker Tags-Nachrichten, ?1870–?1896
New-Yorker Presse, 1873–?1876
Brooklyner Freie Presse (und Long Island Anzeiger), 1873–?1918
Brooklyner Press, ?1875–?1876
New Yorker Allgemeine Zeitung, 1876–?1878; continued by New-Yorker Zeitung
New Yorker Volkszeitung, 1878–1932; continued by Neue Volks-Zeitung (weekly, 1932-49)
New-Yorker Zeitung, ?1879–1896; continued by Gross-New-Yorker Zeitung
New Yorker Herold Abend Zeitung, 1880–1934; continued by New Yorker Staats-Zeitung und Herold
Morgen Journal, 1890–1912; continued by Deutsches Morgen-Journal

(*continued*)

Foreign-Language Daily Newspapers in New York City, 1828–2009 (*Continued*)

Abendblatt der New Yorker Staats-Zeitung, 1892–1914; continued by New-Yorker Staats-Zeitung Abendblatt
Gross-New-Yorker Zeitung, 1896–1908; continued by New-Yorker Zeitung
New-Yorker Zeitung, 1908–?1913; continued by New Yorker Herold Morgenblatt
Deutsches Morgen Journal, 1912; continued by Deutsches Journal
Deutsches Journal, 1912–17; continued by New Yorker Deutsches Journal
New Yorker Herold Morgenblatt, ?1913–19; continued by New Yorker Staats-Zeitung und Herold Morgenblatt
New Yorker Deutsches Journal, 1917–18
New Yorker Staats-Zeitung und Herold Morgenblatt, 1919–?1921; continued by New Yorker Staats-Zeitung
New Yorker Staats-Zeitung, 1921–34; continued by New Yorker Staats-Zeitung und Herold
New Yorker Staats-Zeitung und Herold, 1934–, daily 1934–75

GREEK

Atlantis, 1894–1972, daily 1905–72
Thermopylae ?1900–?1907, daily ?1907
Ethnikos Kerux [National Herald], 1915–
Proini [Morning Paper], 1976–

HEBREW

Hadoar [The Post], 1921–, daily 1921–22

HUNGARIAN

Amerikai Magyar Nepszava [Hungarian American People's Voice], 1899–1969, daily 1904–69
Amerikai Magyar Vilag [Hungarian Daily World], 1901–[1938]
Elore [The Forward], 1904–21; continued by Uj elore
Egyetertes [The Concord], [1911]–1931; continued by A Kereszt-Egyetertes (weekly, 1932)
Uj elore [The New Forward], 1921–?1938
Magyar Ujsag [Hungarian News], 1932–[1933]
Magyar Jovo [Hungarian Daily Journal], [1945]–[1950]

ITALIAN

L'Eco d'Italia, 1849–?1896, daily 1881–?1896; continued by L'Eco D'Italia: Rivista Italo-Americana (weekly, ?1896–[1896])
Il Progresso Italo-Americano, 1880–1989
Cristoforo Colombo, 1887–97; continued by Il Progresso Italo-Americano
L'Araldo Italiano, 1889–1921
Bolletino Della Sera, 1898–1932
Il Movimento, ?1901–[1909]
Il Telegrafo, 1902–19
Corriere Della Sera, 1909–?1933
Il Giornale Italiano, 1909–22
Corriere d'America, 1922–[1937]
Il Nuovo Mondo, 1925–31; continued by La Stampa Libera
La Stampa Libera, 1931–38
Il Mondo, 1940–[1941]
America Oggi, 1988–[3]

JAPANESE

Yomiuri shinbun, 1985–2003, daily 1993–2003

KOREAN

Hangkook Ilbo New York Pan [Korea Times, New York Edition], 1967–
Korea Herald, U.S. Edition, 1975–
Sae gae Ilbo, 1982–, daily 1987–
Chungang Ilbo [The Korea Daily], 199?–

POLISH

Telegram Codzienny [Daily Telegram], 1913–25; continued by Nowy Swiat
Nowy Swiat [Polish Morning World], ?1919–71; continued by Nowy Dziennik
Nowy Dziennik [Polish Daily News], 1971–
Gazeta Polska, 199?–

RUSSIAN

Russkoe Slovo, 1910–20; continued by Novoye Russkoe Slovo
Novyi Mir, 1911–38, daily 1914–?1918; continued by Russkii Golos
Russkii Emigrant, 1911–15
Rodnaia Riech [Native Language], 1913–18
Russkaia Zemlia, 1915–[1916], daily 1916
Russkii Golos [Russian Voice], 1917–, daily 1917–?1963
Rassvet [The Dawn], 1918–26; continued by Russkii Vestnik I Rassvet
Novoye Russkoe Slovo, 1920–
Iskra [The Spark], 1921–[1921]
Utro [Morning], 1922
Russkaia Mysl [Russian Thought], 1923–[1924]
Rossiia, 1933–73, daily 1935–64
Novosti [1984]

SERBIAN

Srpski Dnevnik [Serbian Daily], 1911–[1932]

SLOVAK

(Dennik) Slovak v Amerike, 1899-[1989], daily 1913–1936, 1951
Slovenski Narod [Slovenic People], 1906–17, daily 1906–15
New Yorksky Dennik, 1913–62

SLOVENIAN

Glas Naroda [People's Voice], ?1893–?1963

SPANISH

Diario Cubano, 1870–[1870]
El Democrata (de Nueva York), 1870
Iberia, 1894–[1894]
(Diaro de) las Novedades, 1876–1918, daily 1909–?1910
La Prensa, 1913–1963, daily 1917-63; continued by El Diario de Nueva York, La Prensa
La Voz, 1937–39; continued by La Nueva Voz
La Nueva Voz, 1939–41
El Diario de Nueva York, 1948–63; continued by El Diario de Nueva York, La Prensa
El Diario de Nueva York, La Prensa, 1963; continued by El Diario–La Prensa
El Diario–La Prensa, 1963–
Noticias del Mundo, 1979–2004
El Daily News, 1995–
Hoy, 1999–2008; continued by El Diario–La Prensa

TURKISH

Hurriyet, 19??–

UKRAINIAN

Ukrain'ski Shchodenni Visti [Ukrainian Daily News], 1919-56; continued by Ukrain'ski Visti (weekly, 1957–)
Svoboda Ukrainian Daily, 1919–[4]

YIDDISH[5]

Yudishe gazeten, 1876–1927
Yiddisches Tageblatt [Yidishes tageblat], 1885–1928; continued by Der Morgen Zhurnal, Yidishes Tageblat
Der daily telegraf [Der Deyli telegraf], 1894–[1894]
Der Taglicher Herold [Der Taglikher herold], 1894–1905; continued by Der Tod, di Varhayt
Abend Blatt fur die Arbeiter Zeitung [Abend-blatt fun di Arbayter tsaytung], 1894–1902[6]
Forverts [Jewish Daily Forward], 1897–, daily 1897–1986
Tagliche Presse [Teglikhe prese], [1898]
Idische Welt [Idishe velt], 1899–1905; continued by New Yorker Morgenblatt un Idische Welt
New Yorker Abend Post, 1899–?1901
Morgen Zhurnal, 1901–28; continued by Der Morgen Zhurnal, Yidishes Tageblat
Di yidishe velt, 1902–5
New Yorker Morgenblatt un Idische Welt [Nyu-yorker morgenblat un Idishe velt], 1905
Di Varhayt [Jewish Daily Warheit], 1905–19; continued by Der Tog, di Varhayt
Morgen-zeitung [Morgen-tsaytung], 1906
Die Abend Zeitung [Di Abend tsaytung], 1906
Der Tog, 1914–19; continued by Der Tog, di Varhayt
Der Fihrer, 1915
Der Tog, di Varhayt, 1919–22; continued by Der Tog
Heint [Haynt], 1920
Die zeit [Di tsayt], 1920–22
Der Tog, 1922–53; continued by Der Tog, Morgen Zhurnal
Freiheit [Frayhayt], 1922–29; continued by Morgen Freiheit
Neue Warheit [Di Naye varhayt], 1925[7]

(*continued*)

Foreign-Language Daily Newspapers in New York City, 1828–2009 (*Continued*)

Der Morgen Zhurnal, 1938–53; continued by Der Tog, Morgen Zhurnal
Der Tog, Morgen Zhurnal, 1953–72; continued by Der Morgen Zhurnal, Yidisches Tageblat

1. Names are transliterations used by the newspaper; Pinyin transliteration, where different, follows in brackets.
2. Also contains articles in Slovenian.
3. Published in New Jersey.
4. Published in New Jersey.
5. Names are transliterations used by the newspaper; YIVO transliteration, where different, follows in brackets.
6. Also in German and English.
7. Also in Hebrew.

Note: Bracketed dates indicate first or last extant copy of a newspaper. Dates when a newspaper was daily are given only if the newspaper was not daily during its entire run.

Sources: Winifred Gregory, ed., *American Newspapers, 1821–1936: A Union List of Files Available in the United States and Canada* (New York: H. W. Wilson, 1937; repr. Kraus, 1967); *Newspapers in Microform, United States, 1948–1983* (Washington, D.C.: Library of Congress, 1984); *United States Newspaper Project, National Union List*, 3rd edn, June 1989 (Dublin, Ohio: Online Computer Library Center)

Compiled by Erica Judge, Meghan Lalonde, and Liza Weingarten

by David Hale and Gerard Hallock. The *New York Times* was launched in 1851 by Henry J. Raymond. Fierce competition led editors to use the Pony Express, pigeons, railroads, and steamboats in gathering news.

Of the penny newspapers introduced during the 1830s only the *Herald* and the *Sun* survived, but the development of the popular press changed journalism profoundly. Regular reports from Washington, D.C., were begun in 1822 by the *New-York Statesman* under the direction of Nathaniel Carter. Elias Kingman became the first permanent Washington correspondent (1830–61) and wrote for such publications as the *Journal of Commerce.* The Harbor News Association, the first cooperative organization for gathering news, was formed in 1849. A number of female journalists gained influence, including Margaret Fuller of the *Tribune.* Advertising became more sophisticated. By 1860 the *Herald* had a circulation of 77,000 and was the world's largest daily newspaper. The *Tribune,* particularly through its weekly edition, was popular outside the city.

Journalism played an important role before and during the Civil War. The weekly edition of the *Tribune* had a national circulation of more than 200,000 as early as 1852 and provided extensive coverage of the intense debates in the West before the war. By 1861 the *Herald* was printing 135,000 copies a day. Greeley inveighed against slavery, seeing its abolition as a moral issue that transcended the preservation of the Union, while Bennett supported President Abraham Lincoln's policies halfheartedly. Censorship was pervasive, and when the *New York World* and the *Journal of Commerce* in 1864 published a forged document concocted by a stock-market speculator, the government forced them to suspend publication for two days. Coverage of the draft riots of 1863 was sensational, and the presidential election year of 1864 saw angry debates over the policies of Lincoln, who was strongly endorsed by only five of the 17 daily newspapers in the city. New formats were introduced by *Frank Leslie's Illustrated Newspaper* (weekly, 1855) and *Harper's Weekly* (1857), which incorporated large illustrations printed from wood engravings. Greeley and Bennett both died in 1872; James Gordon

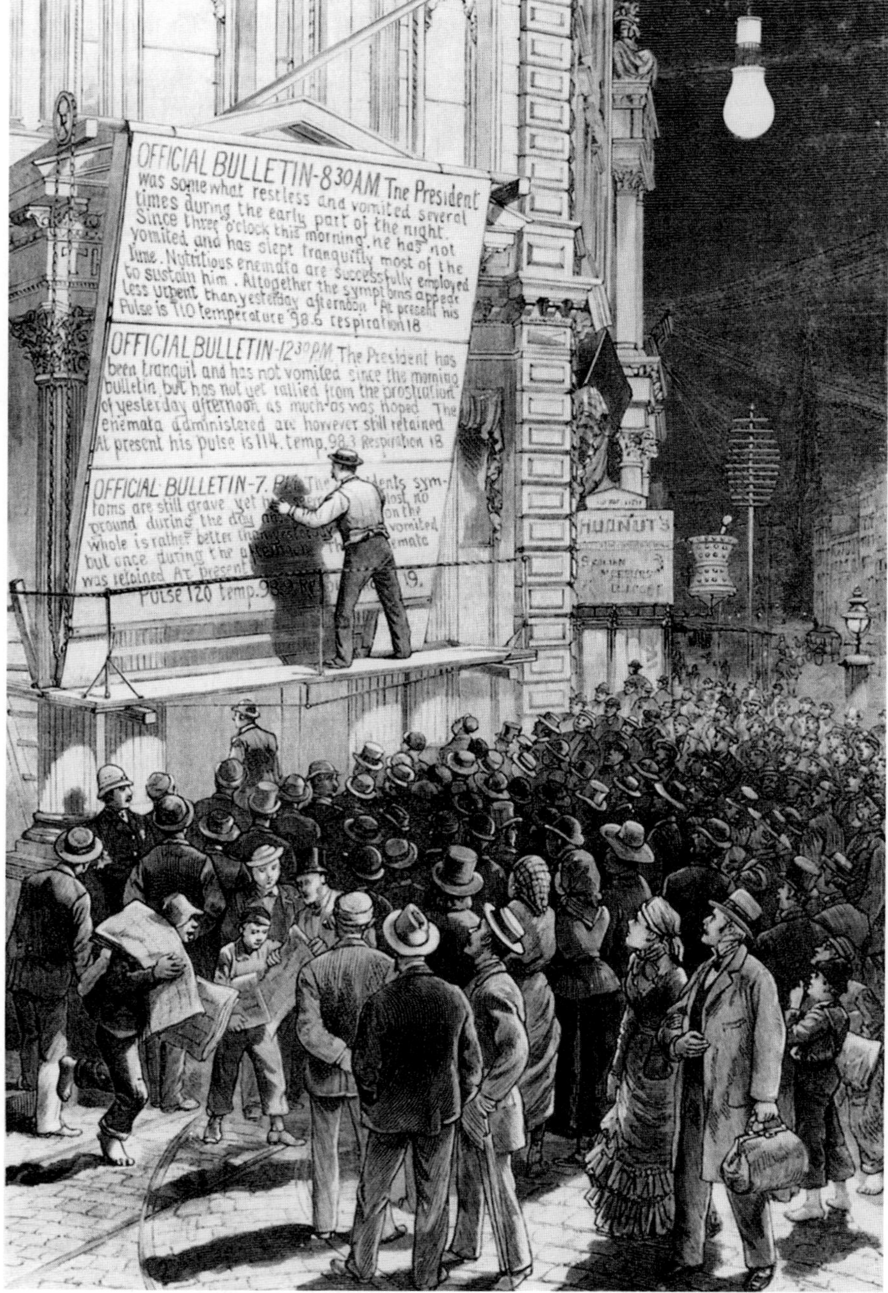

News bulletin outside the New York Herald *at Park Row and Ann Street, 3 September 1881. A reporter brings information from the telegraph in the office about President James A. Garfield's condition several weeks after he was shot by a disgruntled office seeker.*

Bennett, Jr., took over the *Herald* and remained in charge until his death in 1918. Newspaper staffs became larger, and the telephone was used more widely for gathering news. The city was the national center for writers, who were drawn by the quality of the morning daily newspapers (the *Post* under the direction of E. L. Godkin was the only evening newspaper of high quality at the time). The city's dailies provided extensive reports on local party politics. In 1871 the Tweed Ring was exposed by the *Times* and ridiculed by Thomas Nast in cartoons for *Harper's Weekly*.

Circulations continued to grow toward the end of the nineteenth century. The most important issue in the city was the large influx of immigrants; by 1890 about 80 percent of the population had a foreign-born parent, and the number of foreign-language newspapers increased accordingly. In 1880 the first halftone photograph of good quality appeared in the *New York Daily Graphic*. Joseph Pulitzer bought the *World* in 1883 and by 1887 had morning, evening, and Sunday newspapers that allowed him to dominate the newspaper business (the Sunday edition alone had a circulation of 250,000, the largest of any newspaper in the nation). In 1888 the *Sun* published photographs of life in the slums by Jacob A. Riis. The *Wall Street Journal* was begun in 1889 by the Dow Jones financial service. The *New York Age*, published by T. Thomas Fortune from 1890, became a leading newspaper of the black press.

By 1890 stereotyped plates invented during the Civil War were used in new kinds of presses, allowing 48,000 12-page newspapers to be produced in an hour. Color printing was first used by the *World* in 1893, and color comics became a feature of the Sunday edition. The best-known comic strip was *Hogan's Alley* by R. F. Outcault, which depicted life in a tenement. The central character, a toothless child wearing a nightshirt dotted with blobs of yellow ink, became known to readers as the Yellow Kid. In 1895 William Randolph Hearst moved to the city from San Francisco and purchased the *New York Journal*, which attracted reporters from Pulitzer, and published the Yellow Kid as well. The *Journal* and the *World* became sensational, cramming pages with enormous headlines and photographs. This style, called YELLOW JOURNALISM by critics, was adopted by daily newspapers nationwide during the Spanish–American War. Along with the *Sun* under Charles A. Dana and the *Herald* under Bennett, the *Journal* and the *World* nonetheless attracted some of the best writers of the day, who gathered in the newspaper offices on Park Row and at neighboring steakhouses. Well-known reporters included Nelly Bly, Lincoln Steffens, and Stephen Crane.

Competition among newspapers increased during the following decades. The *New York Times*, which had been strong under Raymond, lost considerable prestige during the 1880s and 1890s until it was taken over in 1896 by Adolph S. Ochs, who in 1904 appointed Carr Van Anda as his managing editor and moved operations to a new building on Broadway known as the Times Tower (1904). Of the $100 million that the *Times* earned between 1896 and 1921, Ochs reinvested $96 million in the newspaper, which was widely regarded as the city's finest and most dependable by the end of World War I. Hearst began newspapers in other cities, and Pulitzer devoted the last years of his life to relentless crusades in the MUCKRAKING spirit. The *Jewish Daily Forward* was launched in 1897, the *Amsterdam News* in 1909. The *Herald* continued to offer comprehensive coverage, but the quality of the *Tribune*, the *Sun*, and the *Post* deteriorated. A number of press associations were formed about this time. The ASSOCIATED PRESS, the successor to the Harbor News Association, was reorganized in 1900. It had cooperative agreements with foreign news agencies and controlled much of the flow of news until E. W. Scripps formed the United Press (1907) and Hearst the International News Service (1909). The socialist daily newspaper the *New York Call* began publication in 1908 and became popular, but it suffered after 1918 when the *Times* led the major daily newspapers in promoting a wave of anti-Bolshevik hysteria nationwide. The *Call* lost its mailing privileges under provisions of the Espionage Act of 1917; its offices were later ransacked by government agents and it was forced out of business in 1923. German-language newspapers were also attacked. Hearst's newspapers and the *World* were among the few publications that condemned these events. The communist newspaper the *Daily Worker* was formed in 1924 and later renamed the *Daily World*.

The 1920s saw the introduction of tabloid newspapers that incorporated large photographs and wild headlines. One of the first TABLOIDS was the *Illustrated Daily News* (26 June 1919), soon renamed the *Daily News*; its circulation reached 750,000 by 1924 and two million before World War II. In 1924 tabloid newspapers were introduced by Hearst (the *Mirror*) and Bernarr Macfadden (the *New York Evening Graphic*). Popular for their columnists and bold format, tabloids put tremendous pressure on other newspapers; the *Herald* and *Tribune* merged in 1924, and the *World* was sold to the Scripps–Howard chain in 1931, which promptly closed it down and merged the evening edition into the *World–Telegram*. The *Sun* was absorbed by the *World–Telegram* in 1950. After Ochs's death in 1935 the *Times* was taken over by his son-in-law Arthur Hays Sulzberger. It soon had more comprehensive coverage of major stories, foreign correspondents, and more Pulitzer Prizes than any competitor. The largest foreign-language newspaper was the *New York Staats-Zeitung*, which at one point had a circulation of 250,000. The *Village Voice* began in 1955 as a weekly alternative to the daily press. Radio and television increased the importance of the press associations, and in 1958 the United Press and the International News Service merged to form United Press International.

A series of strikes during the early 1960s hurt newspapers. The business retained an unusually complicated structure, with press operators, drivers, reporters, and typographers each represented by different unions. The number of daily newspapers decreased from eight to three; among those that closed were the *Herald Tribune* in 1966 and the *Journal–American* (owned by Hearst) and *World–Telegram and*

Stacks of the Sunday New York Times *near a newsstand in Greenwich Village on a Saturday night, 1991*

Sun (owned by Scripps–Howard) in 1967, which together were known briefly in 1966 as the *World Journal Tribune.* The *New York Times* won two important cases in the U.S. Supreme Court: one concerning libel (*New York Times v. Sullivan,* 1964) and the other concerning an attempt by the federal government to prevent the release of the Pentagon Papers (1971). In 1982 United Press International moved its offices to Washington, D.C.

During the 1990s there was intense competition for readers and advertisers, especially among the city's three tabloids: *New York Newsday,* the *New York Post,* and the *Daily News.* After a long strike the *Daily News* was bought first by Robert Maxwell and then by Mortimer B. Zuckerman, and the *Post* underwent several changes of management before being acquired in 1993 by Rupert Murdoch, who had owned the newspaper from 1976 to 1988. By the first decade of the twenty-first century, New York City had four major daily newspapers, more than any other U.S. city. In addition, it was home to more than 175 other newspapers that served various neighborhoods and ethnic communities. Many foreign-language papers, such as the *Jewish Daily Forward* and the *Ming Pao Daily News* (with a circulation of 108,000), thrived in the city. The decade also witnessed several significant changes in the newspaper field. In October 2003 the parent company of *Newsday,* the Tribune Company, began issuing a free morning paper, *AM New York,* which gained a circulation of more than 300,000 by 2005. A competitor, *Metro New York,* was launched in May 2005 and also distributed for free. These papers became a common sight in the morning subway commute. In 2007 Murdoch's News Corporation purchased the *Wall Street Journal.*

Frank Luther Mott, *American Journalism: A History of Newspapers in the United States through 250 Years, 1690 to 1940* (New York: Macmillan, 1941); Michael Emery, Edwin Emery, and Nancy L. Roberts, *The Press and America: An Interpretive History of the Mass Media* (Boston: Allyn and Bacon, 2000); Thorin Tritter, *Paper Profits in Public Service: Money Making in the New York City Newspaper Industry 1830–1930* (diss., Columbia University, 2000)

See also Photojournalism, Alternative press.

Michael Emery, Thorin Tritter

New Springville. Neighborhood in central Staten Island, adjoining the Greenbelt and bounded by Bull's Head, Travis, Willowbrook, Lighthouse Hill, and the Fresh Kills at Greenridge. It is part of Community District 2. The area was first settled in 1680 when it was called Carle's Neck, for the extension of land between Main Creek and Richmond Creek. By about 1840 it included a small hamlet, a dock, a Methodist church, and several freshwater springs, surrounded by a patchwork of modest farmsteads, and was known variously as Springville and New Springville. Extant structures from the nineteenth century include the former Asbury Methodist Church (1849, replacing an earlier building) and the Sylvanus Decker Farmhouse (circa 1810), both designated city landmarks, and the Basketmaker's House (circa 1810, now at Historic Richmond Town). New Springville remained an agricultural district and the center of truck farming in Staten Island until the end of the 1950s when subdivision for tract housing accelerated. From 1926 to 1964 two small airports were situated on Richmond Avenue, the main thoroughfare of the neighborhood and the focus of commercial development through the end of the twentieth century. The population grew rapidly after the opening of the Verrazano–Narrows Bridge in 1964 and became increasingly diverse after 1970, as many residents of Brooklyn moved to the area to occupy new townhouses, garden apartments, and condominiums built near the Staten Island Mall, which opened on Richmond Avenue in 1973. During the 1980s Korean and Chinese immigrants settled in New Springville. At the turn of the twenty-first century large numbers of Jewish and Korean families lived there; Indian and Filipino immigrants had also settled in the area.

Charles W. Leng and William T. Davis, *Staten Island and Its People: A History, 1609–1929* (New York: Lewis Historical Publishing, 1930)

Charles L. Sachs

Newsweek. Weekly international news magazine launched in Manhattan in 1933 by Thomas J. C. Martyn, formerly a foreign editor of *Time.* After the death in 1961 of its owner Vincent Astor it was sold to the Washington Post Company. The magazine made its reputation by incorporating objective reporting, signed commentaries, and (from 1967) advocacy issues. It publishes several editions overseas, including one in Japanese. Since 2000, the magazine has expanded to include Arabic, Polish, Russian, Spanish, and Chinese language editions. The circulation worldwide was more than four million and the readership more than 21 million as of 2010. The offices are at 251 West 57th Street.

Elliot S. Meadows

News World. Original name of the New York City Tribune.

Newtown. Name used in colonial times for Elmhurst and for one of the three towns that made up what is now the borough of Queens. The first European settlement in Queens was made at Maspeth in 1642, attacked by Indians in 1643, and abandoned in 1644. Another settlement was made in 1652 at what is now Queens Boulevard and Broadway, a site well inland and less vulnerable to raiding; it was at first named Middleburgh and in 1664 renamed Hastings. Settlers often referred to it as the "new town" to distinguish it from the first settlement, and when the English set up a system of towns and counties in 1683 the name Newtown was given to the village and the township. In 1895–96 an area north of Newtown was developed by Cord Meyer (ii), a real estate promoter who did not want his development to be associated with the pollution of Newtown Creek; in 1896 he prevailed on federal authorities to rename the area Elmhurst, although the name Newtown is retained by a high school and a subway station.

Vincent Seyfried

Newtown Creek. Tributary of the East River. It extends inland for a distance of 3.5 miles (5.6 kilometers), including a number of canals into Brooklyn, and is the boundary between Brooklyn and Queens. The creek was the route by which European colonists first reached Maspeth in 1642. During the American Revolution the British spent the winter near the creek, and the British military road that crossed Queens to what is now the Ma-

Newtown Creek, 2009

rine Air Terminal began at the town dock in Maspeth. Commercial vessels and small boats sailed the creek in the early nineteenth century. About 1860 the first oil and coal oil refineries opened along the banks and began dumping sludge and acids into the water; sewers were built to accommodate the growing neighborhoods of Williamsburg and Greenpoint and discharged their wastes directly into the creek, which by 1900 was known for pollution and foul odors. The water corroded the paint on the undersides of ships, and noxious deposits were left on the banks by the tides. High-level bridges over the creek were built from 1903 (some remain). State and city commissions sought unsuccessfully to improve the creek as it became one of the busiest commercial waterways in the country, second only to the Mississippi River in tonnage: 5,435,016 tons (4,929,560 metric tons) were transported in 1915 by 102,270 ships, which passed so frequently that traffic over the drawbridges was seriously disrupted. The channel was dredged constantly and widened by the federal government to accommodate marine traffic; the creek's natural depth was between 4 and 12 feet (1.2 and 3.7 meters). After World War II the creek's importance as a shipping route decreased, but it continued to be the site of many industrial plants. During the 1940s and 1950s, leaks at oil refineries including ExxonMobil and ChevronTexaco precipitated one of the largest underground oil spills in history. The spill was not discovered until 1978, and no action was taken until 1990 when ExxonMobil entered into consent decrees with the state to clean it up. The cleanup moved at a glacial pace through the early twenty-first century, when the 17-million-gallon oil spill covered more than 50 acres (20.2 hectares) underground. In 2004 residential property owners filed a lawsuit against the oil companies, and in 2008 efforts were under way to have the creek designated a federal Superfund site to speed the cleanup process. The Newtown Creek Alliance, Riverkeeper, and other organizations attempted to restore and protect the creek, and students reintroduced oysters, which act as natural filters, to its waters.

Vincent Seyfried

New Utrecht. Neighborhood in southwestern Brooklyn, lying within Bensonhurst. The land was inhabited by Nyack Indians in 1647 when the governor of New Netherland granted a deed to Anthony Jansen van Salee. It became one of the first six towns in Kings County and included what became Bensonhurst, Bath Beach, Dyker Heights, Mapleton, and Bay Ridge. The first European settlement was a house and a mill built in 1652 by Cornelius van Werckhoven (a schepen, or alderman, in Utrecht in the Netherlands), his two children, and their tutor, Jacques Cortelyou. After van Werckhoven's death in 1655 Cortelyou assumed leadership of the settlement, secured patents for land later occupied by Fort Hamilton, and divided the parcel into 20 plots of 50 acres (20 hectares) each, the last of which he reserved for the town's poor. In 1677 residents formed the Reformed Protestant Dutch Church: its building, erected in 1828, stands at 18th Avenue and 83rd Street.

By 1738 there were 282 inhabitants, of whom 119 were slaves. Farmers raised cattle and grew grains and tobacco. The population grew to 907 in 1810, 1009 in 1820, 2129 in 1850, and 4742 in 1880 as residents gradually sold land to developers who built suburban houses. The remaining truck farmers grew vegetables to sell to the growing population of Brooklyn. The opening of the Sea Beach, Coney Island, and West End steam railroads in the 1870s accelerated development of the area as a suburb. New Utrecht lost its identity when it was annexed by the City of Brooklyn in 1894 and is now considered a small neighborhood of Bensonhurst.

Mrs. Bleecker Bangs, *Reminiscences of Old New Utrecht and Gowanus* (New York: Brooklyn Daily Eagle Press, 1912)

Stephen Weinstein

Farm in New Utrecht

New Utrecht Reformed Church. Dutch Reformed church in southwestern Brooklyn, at 18th Avenue between 83rd and 84th streets. It opened in 1677 in the village of New Utrecht (1661) and was the fourth Dutch Reformed church in Kings County. The original building, erected in 1700, was repaired in 1774 and used as a hospital by the British during the American Revolution; it was demolished owing to structural weakness in 1827 and replaced in 1828 by a Georgian Gothic church built of granite with Victorian milk-glass windows in brick frames. A parsonage in the Dutch shingle style was added on 83rd Street in 1885 and a parish house in a Romanesque Revival style on 84th Street in 1892. It was declared a New York City landmark in 1966, and the church and the cemetery are both listed on the National Register of Historic Places. In 1998 the parish house was also landmarked.

Kevin Kenny

New Venice. Original name of EDGEMERE.

New Year's Eve. The first celebration of New Year's Eve in Times Square took place in 1906, sponsored by the *New York Times* to mark the completion of its new headquarters. The event was staged by the newspaper's publisher Adolph Ochs, who conceived of an elaborate "time ball" that would descend from atop a building precisely at midnight, intentionally recalling the globes used in most U.S. cities during the 1870s and 1880s to keep time and synchronize watches. The brightly lit ball of Times Square became an annual feature of the celebration, except for two years during World War II. Each New Year's Eve the spectacle drew hundreds of thousands of people to Times Square and millions of television viewers from across the nation. From the early 1990s onward, the Times Square Business Improvement District, now the Times Square Alliance, has hosted the New Year's Eve celebration. For the centennial of the New Year's Eve ball in 2008, the Times Square Alliance introduced a new LCD crystal ball that was twice as bright, had enhanced color capabilities, and was more environmentally friendly.

Michael O'Malley, *Keeping Watch: A History of American Time* (New York: Viking, 1990)

Michael O'Malley

New York, New Haven and Hartford Railroad. Railroad formed in 1872, the first to connect New York City with Boston. It superseded the New York and New Haven Railroad, which was chartered in 1844 to operate between Canal Street and New Haven, Connecticut; in New York City it used track owned by the New York and Harlem Railroad. Service to Boston and New England was taken over by Amtrak in 1971; the line between New York City and New Haven continued to serve commuters and became administered by the Connecticut Department of Transportation and the Metropolitan Transportation Authority of New York State.

John L. Weller, *The New Haven Railroad: Its Rise and Fall* (Mamaroneck, N.Y.: Hastings House, 1967)

See also RAILROADS.

John Fink

New York, Westchester and Boston Railroad. Railroad operating from 24 May 1912 as a modern, four-track subsidiary of the New York, New Haven and Hartford Railroad. It inherited the rights of the New York, Housatonic and Northern Railroad and the New York and Portchester Railroad, both defunct, and was built at a high price. The operators of the railroad believed that the commercial center of the city would continue to move north, but the zoning law of 1916 contained the central business district below 59th Street and the line ran no farther south than 133rd Street at the Harlem River in the Bronx. Hindered by their inability to transport passengers into Manhattan, the directors abandoned the line on 31 December 1937. The portion of the line in the Bronx reopened on 15 May 1941 as the Dyre Avenue shuttle of Interborough Rapid Transit. The New York, Westchester and Boston was the last important railroad built in New York City.

Roger Arcara, *Westchester's Forgotten Railway, 1912–1937* (New York: Quadrant, 1962)

John Fink

New York Academy of Arts. Original name of the AMERICAN ACADEMY OF THE FINE ARTS.

New York Academy of Medicine. Nonprofit corporation formed in 1847 to raise the standards of medical education and promote the health of the public. It originated at a time when physicians were struggling to establish themselves as members of an ethical and scientific profession. The academy's status rose with that of the profession, and by the time it moved into the building at 119 West 43rd Street in 1890, it was renowned for its expertise on issues of municipal health in New York City. The academy advocated improved public hygiene and sanitation as a means of staving off epidemics. It moved in 1926 into a building designed by the architects York and Sawyer at 2 East 103rd Street. Recommendations by special committees of the academy helped give rise to the Department of Hospitals (1928), to a review of maternal deaths in the 1930s, and to the New York City Health and Hospitals Corporation (1970). During the mid-1990s the academy was particularly well known in the field of medical education. Its health library, the second largest in the United States, contains more than 14 miles (23 kilometers) of shelves and nearly 700,000 catalogued works, including one of the world's finest collections of rare medical Americana and early European medical materials, and one of the world's largest collections of cookbooks (donated by a physician concerned with nutrition). Besides offering a wide range of information services to its fellows and to the general public, the institution serves as a regional library of medicine and coordinates cooperative services among health sciences libraries in 10 northeastern states and Puerto Rico. In 1991 the New York Academy of Medicine installed its first full-time president, Jeremiah A. Barondess, who at the request of Mayor David N. Dinkins launched a new study of the city's municipal hospital system. In the early twenty-first century the academy had more than 2100 fellows who worked in the fields of medicine, social work, nursing, law, education, and research.

Sandra Opdycke

New York Academy of Sciences. Organization formed as the Lyceum of Natural History by scientific polymath, educator, and politician Samuel Latham Mitchill (1754–1831), who convened the first meeting on 29 January 1817; most of the early members were students and faculty at the College of Physicians and Surgeons. Progress came haltingly, and it was not until 1823 that the Lyceum began regular publication of its journal *Annals of the New York Academy of Sciences,* which continues in the twenty-first century as one of the longest-published scientific journals in the United States. In 1836 the academy moved from rented rooms at the New York Dispensary to its own building on Broadway, but financial pressures forced the members to sell it in 1844. The following year, the Lyceum moved into the Medical School Building at New York University and shared quarters with the university for 32 years.

By 1860 the Lyceum maintained a library and a natural history museum, but eventually some functions of the Lyceum ceased: it no longer had any role as a natural history museum after its museum was destroyed by fire in 1866, and no scientific research was carried on within it after a professorate oriented toward research emerged at Columbia University. The Lyceum's role was also changed when its members helped to establish the American Museum of Natural History (1868), as science became increasingly specialized and emerged as a profession, and as societies devoted to individual disciplines grew. In 1876 the Lyceum reorganized as the New York Academy of Sciences. The new organization was controlled not by weekly membership meetings but by an elected council and was divided into four sections: biology; chemistry and technology; geology and mineralogy; and physics, astronomy, and mathematics. As a general scientific society the academy was responsible in 1887 for the organization of the first meeting of the American Association for the Advancement of Science, held in New York City. Under the leadership of Nathaniel Lord Britton the academy in 1891 organized the Scientific Alliance, a federation of scientific societies that published a monthly bulletin and from 1906 occupied quarters at the American Museum of Natural History. The early decades of the twentieth century were a time of prosperity for the academy; such scientists as Edmund Beecher Wilson, Thomas Hunt Morgan, Franz Boas, James McKeen Cattell, and Michael Pupin were active members. In 1912 the academy organized a survey of the geology, anthropology, and natural history of Puerto Rico and the Virgin Islands that continued for three decades. Under the auspices of the academy, scientists from many institutions in New York City conducted expeditions, the results of which the academy published.

From 1938 until the present day the New York Academy of Sciences has sponsored conferences on a wide range of scientific topics as a means of communicating research results to the scientific community. Among its notable "firsts" were conferences on antibiotics in 1946, on acquired immune deficiency syndrome (AIDS) in 1983, and on severe acute respiratory syndrome (SARS) in 2003. Since 2002 the academy has sponsored efforts to build scientific communities through programs such as the Frontiers of Science program and the Scientists Without Borders program, which is mobilizing and coordinating science-based efforts to address health, environmental, and other challenges in the developing world, and the creation of global science alliances with Mexico City, the United Kingdom, and China, among others. The academy's online offerings include eBriefings, its Science and the City Webzine, and access to its extensive library of *Annals* volumes. The organization also publishes a member magazine.

Throughout its history, the academy has counted among its membership leaders in the sciences, business, academia, and government, including U.S. presidents Thomas Jefferson and James Monroe, Thomas Edison, Louis Pasteur, Charles Darwin, Margaret Mead, and Albert Einstein. More recently, members include a number of Nobel laureates, such as Harold Varmus, Eric Kandel, Paul Greengard, and James Watson. The academy in the early twenty-first century had more than 25,000 members in 140 countries.

Herman Le Roy Fairchild, *A History of the New York Academy of Sciences* (New York: Herman Le Roy Fairchild, 1887); Simon Baatz, *Knowledge, Culture, and Science in the Metropolis: The New York Academy of Sciences, 1817–1970* (New York: New York Academy of Sciences, 1990)

Simon Baatz, Kenneth T. Jackson

New York African Society for Mutual Relief. Formed in New York City in 1808, it was incorporated in 1810 when Mayor DeWitt Clinton carried a special petition to the state legislature at Albany, making the organization the first to be incorporated by black Americans. Early members included the influential Episcopal minister Peter Williams, Jr.; the businessman William Hamilton, Sr.; John Teasman, an instructor at the New York African School; James McCune Smith, the nation's first black physician; Christopher Rush, one of the first African Methodist Episcopal bishops; Philip A. Bell, the antislavery journalist and editor of the *Colored American;* and Thomas Downing, proprietor of one of the most exclusive restaurants in Manhattan. All the members staunchly opposed slavery and promoted the black national convention movement and the independent black church movement. African Society Hall, a building constructed in the rear of the society's first property in lower Manhattan, was the meeting place of most of the African associations of antebellum New York City and contained a trap door so that it could fulfill its dual role as a stop on the Underground Railroad.

After the Civil War the society was struck by a number of internal scandals that shook its members' faith in mutual relief as a principle and collective action as a strategy. It came close to disbanding on more than one occasion but was saved by the inspired work of its oldest members: the printer John J. Zuille, one of the leading antislavery spokesmen in the city; E. V. C. Eato, grand master of the state's black Masons; William P. Powell, owner of a seaman's home and a nationally known abolitionist; and Peter Vogelsang, a veteran of the Union army. Together they brought a new unity to the society and a new commitment to its struggle for equality. By 1900 Booker T. Washington could refer to the New York African Society for Mutual Relief as the most influential and successful financial association among black Americans. During the decades that followed, the society became active in the politics of New York City and made public declarations on such national issues as the Scottsboro case in Alabama. Its membership included the city's foremost ministers, business leaders, politicians, and intellectuals. Among these were the real estate dealer John Nail and the dentist Walter N. Beekman.

From the 1880s to 1945 the already sizable holdings of the New York African Society increased by $1000 annually, and by 1910 each membership was worth several thousand dollars, although the initiation fee was far smaller. The members of the society therefore faced a dilemma: either the initiation fees and dues would need to rise to a prohibitive level, or each new membership would reduce the worth of all existing ones. The society struggled with declining membership for four decades until many of the society's benefits were duplicated by the New Deal. In 1945 the remaining members began the sad work of dismantling the society and liquidating its impressive holdings.

Craig Steven Wilder

New York Age. Weekly newspaper launched in 1887 as an organ of blacks who advocated equal rights. It was edited from 1889 to 1907 by the distinguished black journalist T. Thomas Fortune, who urged blacks to take part in the political process. In 1907 he sold his interests to Fred R. Moore, secretary and national organizer of the National Negro Business League, who continued to edit and publish the newspaper, with his son-in-law Lester A. Walton as its managing editor. In 1949 black ownership ended when the newspaper was purchased by Richard Bourne-Vanneck and his wife. It ceased publication in 1960.

Sandra Roff

New York and Harlem Railroad. First railroad in New York City, originating in 1832 with horses for motive power and connecting Union Square with 23rd Street and Fourth Avenue. Steam-powered operations began in 1835 when the railroad extended its line to 125th Street and Fourth Avenue in Harlem. It built the city's first major train station, at 27th Street and Fourth Avenue, and eventually built as far north as Chatham, New York, and as far east as Albany. In 1857 it merged with the New York and Hudson River Railroad to form the New York Central and Hudson River Railroad. The tracks of the railroad between New York City and Dover Plains through the Bronx River Valley form the backbone of the Metro-North Commuter Railroad in the twenty-first century.

See also Railroads, §1.

John Fink

New York and Mississippi Valley Printing Telegraph Company. Forerunner of Western Union Company.

New York and Sea Beach Railway. A railway that began operating on 18 July 1877 as a small steam line for transporting passengers from New Utrecht Avenue in Brooklyn to Coney Island over 4.5 miles (7 kilometers) of private track. It was the last line built specifically to profit from the enormous Coney Island summer traffic. The railroad's depot at Coney Island was the Sea Beach Palace, a building constructed for the Centennial International Exposition of 1876. The line was extended from New Utrecht Avenue to the ferry terminal at 65th Street in 1879 and was profitable to the end of the 1880s, but during the 1890s it was undermined by new trolley lines. The line was leased to the Brooklyn Rapid Transit (BRT) system in 1897, electrified, and linked to the elevated lines in Brooklyn. Its track was used by trolleys until 1907 and in 1915 was integrated into the Fourth Avenue subway line. Now known as the Sea Beach or "N" line, the line has four tracks, of which two furnish the normal

New York and Harlem Railroad, four-track viaduct over Harlem flats between 98th and 112th streets

service; there are nine stations and a terminus at Stillwell Avenue, Coney Island.

Vincent Seyfried

New York Aquarium. Aquarium opened by the City of New York at Castle Clinton in Battery Park in 1896. The New York Zoological Society took over the administration of the facility at the city's request in 1902; under the first director elected by the society, Charles H. Townsend, steps were taken to alleviate crowded conditions and maintenance problems. Charles M. Breder, Jr., succeeded Townsend in 1937 and helped to establish the aquarium's international reputation for scientific research. Aided by its location, the aquarium flourished for many years and drew 7000 visitors a day until the parks commissioner, Robert Moses, temporarily closed it in 1941 because of construction of the Brooklyn–Battery Tunnel; ensuing plans to demolish Castle Clinton and close the aquarium permanently aroused such strong protest that the castle was spared and the aquarium moved to the Bronx Zoo. Because of pressures to distribute funds for cultural attractions evenly among the boroughs, the Bronx was rejected as the site for a new aquarium in favor of Coney Island, where a new facility opened in 1957 near the boardwalk. An affiliated marine laboratory opened nearby in 1964 and was dedicated in 1967 as the Osborn Laboratories of Marine Sciences (named for Henry Fairfield Osborn), where research was conducted in fish genetics, fish pathology, aquaculture, and pharmacological applications of marine science. It was the first aquarium to breed and exhibit beluga whales, from 1961 through 2005, when the whales were transferred to a cooperative breeding program at the Georgia Aquarium. On 12 June 2007, Akituusaq, a 115-pound (52-kilogram) male Pacific walrus, was born, the first walrus born at the aquarium. In the early twenty-first century the aquarium's 14-acre (5.7-hectare) site is home to more than 8000 animals representing 350 species in outdoor and indoor habitats. The aquarium draws more than 750,000 visitors a year, mostly from Brooklyn, and is active in education, scientific research, and conservation.

Elliot S. Meadows

New York Association for New Americans [NYANA]. Resettlement agency. Formed in 1949, it became the largest agency of its kind in the United States by assisting more than a quarter of a million people referred by the Hebrew Immigrant Aid Society, including Jewish refugees from Europe (1949–53); Greece (1955–56); Hungary (1956–58); Egypt and Romania (1956–63); Cuba (1961–67); Czechoslovakia (1968–69); Poland (1968–69); the Soviet Union and Russia (from 1969), which eventually accounted for the largest number of refugees; Syria (1977); and Iran (from 1983). In 1975 the association began receiving federal funds to aid in the resettlement of non-Jewish refugees from Southeast Asia; it also received funds from the United Jewish Appeal, the United Way, private foundations, and government grants. From 1975 through 1990 the association assisted refugee "boat people" from Vietnam, Cambodia, and Haiti, as well as Ethiopian and Iranian Jews. In the mid-1990s the association resettled many Tibetans and Syrian Jews; it continues in the early twenty-first century to support services for refugees and immigrants.

Joseph S. Lieber

New York Association for the Blind. Name used from 1906 to 1990 by the Lighthouse.

New York Athletic Club. Private club at Central Park South and Sixth Avenue, formed in 1868 by William B. Curtis, Henry E. Buermeyer, and John C. Babcock in the backroom of the Knickerbocker Cottage on Sixth Avenue between 27th and 28th streets. On 11 November 1868 the club sponsored the New York Athletic Games, the first indoor amateur athletic meet in the United States, in the unfinished Empire Skating Rink on Third Avenue. The meet drew more than 1000 spectators, who saw six track and eight field events; among the innovations introduced at the meet were cleated athletic shoes and an early bicycle with a large front wheel called the velocipede. The club built a boathouse on the Harlem River in 1870, opened a clubhouse in Mott Haven in June 1874, and in 1880 purchased an island of 30 acres (12 hectares) in Long Island Sound as a training retreat for its elite competitors. Called Sheffields Island (later renamed Travers Island for the club's president William R. Travers), the island had two buildings in which as many as 70 athletes could live and train while carrying on business in New York City. By 1898 the club had many prominent businessmen in the city as members. In 1903 the club built the first squash courts in the United States. The club's building on 180 Central Park South opened with great fanfare on 22 January 1929 and now houses extensive athletic facilities, restaurants, and guest rooms. In the twenty-first century the club continues to offer its facilities to members at both its Manhattan and Travers Island locations.

Robert Hillenbrand

New York Bible Society. Organization formed on 4 December 1809 at the home of Theodorus Van Wyck to distribute English-language Bibles without note or comment in New York City. An auxiliary of the American Bible Society from 1829 to 1912, it had offices in the society's Bible House on Astor Place until 1919. After briefly occupying quarters on Madison Avenue, it moved in 1921 into a building at 5 East 48th Street donated by James Talcott and later named for him. Now known as the International Bible Society, it has moved to Colorado Springs.

David J. Fant, *The Bible in New York: The Romance of Scripture Distribution in a World Metropolis from 1807 to 1948* (New York: New York Bible Society, 1948)

Alana Erickson Coble

New York Botanical Garden. Public botanical garden in the Bronx. See Botanical gardens.

New York Cancer Hospital. See Memorial Sloan–Kettering Cancer Center.

New York Cares. Nonprofit organization that helps support 850 nonprofit agencies, public schools, and other social services in need of volunteers throughout the five boroughs. It is New York City's leading organization for unaffiliated volunteers and is the umbrella organization for 500 flexibly scheduled volunteer opportunities. It is known for organizing programs such as its annual coat drive, providing emergency response services, and restoring parks and cultural institutions throughout the city. Twice a year New York Cares sponsors New York Cares Day and Hands on New York Day, which deploys 12,000 volunteers into the city's parks and school systems. Because of the success of the program, the Hands On Network, a national volunteer and community service organization that works closely with New York Cares, was founded. In 2009 New York Cares garnered support from 48,000 volunteers, implementing programs at 1000 community organizations and assisting 400,000 New Yorkers.

Stephanie Miller

New York Central Lines LLC. Railroad company formed in 1998, named after the New York Central Railroad, which ran from 1832 to 1968. Owned and operated by CSX Transportation, since 2003 its trains continue to transport freight goods along lines in the Northeast, Midwest, and Canada.

Ben Silk

New York Central and Hudson River Railroad. Principal route for passengers and freight traveling west from New York City during the late nineteenth century. Its origins may be traced to the New York and Harlem Railroad (1832) and the Hudson River Railroad (1846); it was known as the New York Central Railroad until Cornelius Vanderbilt merged it in 1869 with the Hudson River Railroad. The railroad followed the course of the Hudson River and the Erie Canal and because of its easy grades gained a competitive advantage over other railroads and canals. In 1871 passenger train operations were consolidated at the new Grand Central Terminal on 42nd Street. Like its competitor the Pennsylvania Railroad, the New York Central and Hudson River cut the travel time between New York City and Chicago to 16 hours during the 1930s with its fastest train, the Twentieth Century Limited. In 1893 its Empire State Express set a speed record of 112 miles (180 kilometers) an hour. When the new Grand Central Terminal opened in 1913, the railroad's suburban electric trains, which carried commuters, used the lower level and its intercity trains the main level. In 1968 the railroad merged with the Pennsylvania Railroad to form the Penn Central, which declared bankruptcy in 1970. Its intercity routes were taken over in 1971 by the National Railroad Passenger Corporation (Amtrak), its commuter routes in 1972 by the Metropolitan Transportation Authority (MTA), and its freight operations in 1976 by the Consolidated Rail Corporation (Conrail).

Joseph R. Daughen and Peter Binzen, *The Wreck of the Penn Central* (Boston: Little, Brown, 1971); Carl W. Condit, *The Port of New York: A History of the Rail Terminal System* (Chicago: University of Chicago Press, 1980, 1981); Aaron E. Klein, *The History of the New York Central System* (New York: Bonanza, 1985)

See also Railroads.

Robert A. Olmsted

New York Chamber of Commerce. See Partnership for New York City (i).

New York City Ballet [NYCB]. Dance company, also known as City Ballet, formed in 1948 by Lincoln Kirstein and George Balanchine. In 1933 Kirstein invited Balanchine to the United States to establish a ballet school and company where American dancers could receive instruction from renowned ballet masters and perform new repertory for U.S. audiences. Balanchine agreed and the two first founded the School of American Ballet (SAB) in 1934, which served as an incubator for what would become New York City Ballet. To guarantee that the students would develop to fulfill the professional demands of the company, Balanchine supervised the training of his dancers, whom he taught to move with great precision, speed, and keen musicality. He served as SAB's artistic director and chairman of faculty and later as City Ballet's ballet master-in-chief. Balanchine created a unique American style that contrasted sharply with the previous classical aesthetic. In 1935 he and Kirstein founded their first professional company, the American Ballet. However, it ended soon after the collapse of both its exchequer and manager. During the following years several ballet companies were established and dissolved, and only the continued existence of SAB provided any indication that a permanent company in the future was possible. In 1946 Balanchine and Kirstein formed Ballet Society, which performed at New York's City Center of Music and Drama over the next two years. During that time Morton Baum, chairman of the City Center finance committee, began negotiations that led to Ballet Society joining City Center as a permanent ballet company called New York City Ballet. On 11 October 1948 NYCB opened its first season. Sixteen years later, City Ballet permanently moved to the David H. Koch Theater, named at the time New York State Theater, in Lincoln Center.

Balanchine worked with the music of Bach, Mozart, Tchaikovsky, Ravel, Ives, Gershwin, Sousa, Alexander Glazounov, and Mikhail Glinka, and music connoisseurs often attended NYCB performances to hear scores that were not played in concert halls. More than by any other composer, Balanchine was influenced by his friend and frequent collaborator Igor Stravinsky. For his eight-day Stravinsky festival (1972), Balanchine choreographed eight of the 20 new ballets presented. Balanchine also found inspiration with certain dancers he called his "muses," such as Suzanne Farrell. The Balanchine aesthetic predominated in the works of other company choreographers, including that of Frederick Ashton, Antony Tudor, John Taras, Todd Bolender, Peter Martins, and Jerome Robbins, an associate director of the company from 1949 to 1956 and again from 1969 to 1990. Robbins's work with the company was characterized by humor, introspection, and an impressive command of dance values. Among his most successful early ballets were *Cage, Concert,* and *Afternoon of a Faun,* an adaptation of the controversial work by Vaslav Nijinsky. His later ballets included *Dances at a Gathering, Goldberg Variations, Glass Pieces,* and *I'm Old Fashioned,* a tribute to Fred Astaire.

On Balanchine's death in 1983 Robbins and Martins, who joined the company in 1970 as a principal dancer, became the new ballet masters-in-chief. After several early pieces reflecting Balanchine's influence, Martins created a number of original ballets, including *Ecstatic Orange* (1987) and *Fearful Symmetries* (1990), both to minimalist scores, as well as his own renditions of *Swan Lake* (1999) and *Romeo+Juliet* (2005). Kirstein retired as the general director in 1989, and Robbins resigned in 1990; Peter Martins became the sole ballet master-in-chief after Robbins's resignation. During the early 1990s NYCB started the Diamond Project, an initiative to foster works by new choreographers and present them every two to four years. To honor its 50th anniversary, City Ballet received coverage and recognition from various outlets, including a major exhibition in the New-York Historical Society. In 2004 *Live from Lincoln Center* broadcast the NYCB celebration of the 100th birthday of George Balanchine in real time to fans on Lincoln Center Plaza and to television viewers at home. The company also received attention during the 2000s for its charitable works. After the terrorist attacks of 11 September 2001 the company performed a special show for the families of victims. Four years later NYCB ended the largest capital campaign ever conducted for a dance company, raising $58 million over five years. City Ballet and New York City Opera announced in 2009 that engineer and businessman David H. Koch had donated $100 million to modernize, enhance, and maintain New York State Theater, which was renamed the David H. Koch Theater. NYCB is considered one of the top ballet companies in the world. It employs about 100 dancers and offers more than 20 weeks of performances annually in the city.

Lincoln Kirstein, *The New York City Ballet* (New York: Alfred A. Knopf, 1973; rev. 1978 as *Thirty Years: Lincoln Kirstein's The New York City Ballet*); Nancy Reynolds, *Repertory in Review* (New York: Dial, 1977)

Nancy Reynolds, Frank Nestor

New York City Community College of Applied Arts and Sciences. Former name of New York City Technical College.

New York City Farm Colony–Seaview Hospital Historic District. First designated historic district on Staten Island, occupying an elevated site abutting and partly within the Greenbelt, bounded to the north by Walcott and Brielle avenues, to the east by Manor Road, to the south by Rockland Avenue, and to the west by Colonial Avenue and Forest Hill Road; it is bisected by Brielle Avenue. The Richmond County Poor Farm was founded in 1829 as a municipal poorhouse where residents farmed the land for their keep. After consolidation in 1898 it was renamed the New York City Farm Colony and in the early twentieth century supported more than 800 residents with fruit, vegetables, pigs, and chickens. New buildings were added west of Brielle Avenue by the Department of Public Charities from 1903 to 1914; the large, gambrel-roofed fieldstone dormitories and service buildings were designed by a number of firms including Renwick, Aspinwall and Owen to evoke colonial domestic architecture, contrasting with the severe institutional almshouses formerly used on Blackwell's Island. Four large neo-Georgian dormitories were added in 1934. In 1915 the Farm Colony merged with nearby Seaview Hospital; the farm became a geriatric facility from the 1950s until it closed in 1975. In 1982 the Department of General Services took possession and transferred 25 acres (10 hectares) to the Parks Department.

Seaview Hospital, built on the opposite side of Brielle Avenue, was the country's largest and most expensive municipal facility for treating tuberculosis. The original portion consisted of patients' pavilions, dining halls, nurses' and doctors' residences, and a surgical pavilion; it was carefully designed by Raymond F. Almiral for maximum efficiency and exposure to air, light, and pleasant vistas. The patient pavilions had capacious sleeping porches and solaria and were enlivened by distinctive tile roofs and mosaic friezes. The hospital was dedicated in 1913; later additions, including a number of open-air pavilions (1917), increased the capacity of the hospital to 2000 patients. In 1951 the first successful clinical trials of a nontoxic cure for tuberculosis were undertaken at Seaview, which was converted to other uses after 1961. In the early twenty-first century the hospital remains in operation, housing 300 beds in portions of the old complex and several modern buildings; it is known for its long-term-care brain injury unit. In 1985 the Landmarks Preservation Commission designated the area encompassing the Farm Colony and Seaview Hospital a historic district, including 120 acres (48.5 hectares) and 11 buildings.

Shirley Zavin, Kate Lauber

New York City Health and Hospitals Corporation [HHC]. Nonprofit corporation created by state law on 27 May 1969 to administer all municipal health facilities in New York City. It began operations on 1 July 1970 with a board of 15, of whom five members were municipal officials, five were appointed by the mayor alone, and five were appointed by the mayor with the approval of the City Council. Like its predecessor, the Department of Hospitals, HHC was required to focus on serving the city's poor. Its formation followed a decade of increasingly strident criticism of the municipal hospital system, and it was believed that a quasi-independent corporation would encounter fewer of the bureaucratic constraints that many investigative commissions had identified as a major difficulty in providing health care. HHC did have somewhat more autonomy than its predecessor, but not to the extent hoped for by its supporters. In addition to political obstacles it was impeded by the city's severe fiscal crisis. Caught between municipal deficits and rising medical costs, it was forced during the late 1970s and 1980s to close some hospitals and consolidate others. A series of untoward deaths in municipal emergency rooms in 1991 drew intense public scrutiny, as a result of which the director of HHC resigned and Mayor David N. Dinkins requested an investigation of the municipal system by the New York Academy of Medicine. At that time the system contained about 9000 beds, barely half the number managed by the Department of Hospitals in 1929, and its facilities cared for 30 percent of the city's newborn and pediatric patients, 40 percent of its substance abuse patients, and 50 percent of its psychiatric patients, as well as 10 percent of the patients hospitalized for AIDS in the entire United States. In the early twenty-first century HHC attempted a transformation in response to its critics, launching a $1.3 billion building and modernization plan; criticism was revived in 2008 when a patient died in the waiting room at Kings County Hospital Center. HHC remained the largest municipal hospital system in the country, with 11 acute-care hospitals, four skilled nursing facilities, six diagnostic and treatment centers, home health care, and more than 80 community clinics.

Health Care Needs and the New York City Health and Hospitals Corporation (New York: New York City Health and Hospitals Corporation, 1973)

See also Bellevue Hospital.

Sandra Opdycke

New York City Housing Authority. See Housing.

New York City Lunatic Asylum. Municipal residential facility located on the northern end of Roosevelt Island dedicated to the treatment and housing of the mentally ill during the mid- to late 1800s. By the early 1800s modern theories of mental illness emphasized the need for humane medical care in a peaceful, orderly environment. With these principles in mind, the Lunatic Asylum was designed by Alexander Jackson Davis and completed in 1839. Originally intended to be an expansive complex, the facility ultimately consisted of a central building, the Octagon, at the center of two long wings. The Octagon and its magnificent rotunda were built from gray stone in what Davis called the "Tuscan style," but the design also included strong Greek Revival influences.

Insufficient funding and a rapidly rising rate of mental illness led to overcrowding and substandard care (often provided by prisoners from the nearby penitentiary). Conditions at the asylum were exposed by the journalist Nelly Bly, who feigned mental illness in order to be committed. She reported on her experiences for the *New York World,* and later in a book, *Ten Days in a Mad-House.* By 1894 the task of managing the mentally ill would prove too great for the city, and the asylum's patients were transferred to state facilities. The Lunatic Asylum was renamed Metropolitan Hospital and became a general care facility.

Eric Hollingsworth

New York City Marathon. An annual footrace first staged in 1970. See Running.

New York City Mission Society. Missionary organization formed on 19 February 1827 to encourage religious conversions by distributing religious tracts. Originally known as the New York City Tract Society, it began operating mission stations in 1852. It was renamed the New York City Mission and Tract Society in 1866 and in 1870 shifted its efforts to opening churches in poor neighborhoods; the first, Mount Olivet, was at 63 East Second Street. With the Association for Improving the Condition of the Poor, the Charity Organization Society, and the Children's Aid Society, the New York City Mission and Tract Society received the United Charities Building at 105 East 22nd Street as a gift from John M. Kennedy in 1891. Given its current name in 1913, it advises churches and social service agencies into the twenty-first century.

Kenneth D. Miller and Ethel Prince Miller, *The People Are the City: 150 Years of Social and Religious Concern in New York City* (New York: Macmillan, 1962)

Alana Erickson Coble

New York City Opera. Formed in 1943 as the City Center Opera Company by Mayor Fiorello H. La Guardia and other prominent citizens, it was intended for lower- and middle-class New Yorkers who could not afford the Metropolitan Opera and to provide a forum for emerging American singers, conductors, and composers. In its early years and under the direction of Julius Rudel (1957–79) the company gave the premieres of works by Dominick Argento, Jack Beeson, Lee Hoiby, Leon Kirchner, Robert Kurka, Gian Carlo Menotti, Douglas Moore, Thomas Pasatieri, Ned Rorem, Robert Ward, and Hugo Weisgall and introduced many American singers, including soprano Beverly Sills and basses Norman Treigle and Samuel Ramey, as well as the Spanish tenors Plácido Domingo and José Carreras. The company performed at City Center on West 55th Street until 1966 when it moved to the New York State Theater at Lincoln Center. After retiring from the stage Sills managed the company from 1979 to 1989; she built a large audience by programming works from the operatic mainstream and musical comedies and by introducing supertitles (displaying below the proscenium arch an English translation of the text being sung), as a result of which a large deficit was eliminated and the company's operating budget was nearly tripled (to $28 million). Sills was succeeded in 1990 by the conductor Christopher Keene, who emphasized adventurous repertory of the sort that had characterized the company's early years. Under director Paul Kellogg (1996–2007) the company pursued unsuccessful attempts to build a new theater and sever its affiliation with Lincoln Center. The New York City Opera has proved resilient in the face of financial challenge, protracted union strikes, and the loss of its costumes in a warehouse fire in 1985. George Steel took the reins as general director in 2009 and oversaw the renovation of the David H. Koch Theater during the 2008–9 season.

Martin L. Sokol, *The New York City Opera: An American Adventure, with the Complete Annals* (New York: Macmillan, 1981)

James M. Keller

New York City Partnership. See PARTNERSHIP FOR NEW YORK CITY (ii).

New York City Technical College. College of the City University of New York at 300 Jay Street in Brooklyn, formed in 1946 by the state legislature as the New York State Institute of Applied Arts and Science, one of five experimental technical schools intended for returning veterans of World War II. In 1948 it became part of the State University of New York. The New York City Board of Estimate assumed responsibility for its administration in 1953 and changed the name to the New York City Community College of Applied Arts and Sciences, and the college joined the city university system in 1964. In 1971 it absorbed the Voorhees Technical Institute (originally the New York Trade School) and opened a branch campus at 450 West 41st Street in Manhattan (closed in 1987). Bachelor's degrees were first awarded in 1980 when the school took its current name. New York City Technical College is the only technical college in the city university system. It offers bachelor's degrees in hotel and restaurant management, legal assistant studies, telecommunications, and graphic arts, among other things. In 2002 it changed its name to New York City College of Technology. In 2009 about 15,400 students were enrolled in its degree programs.

Marc Ferris

New York City Transit Authority. Public authority created by the State of New York to operate and maintain the public transit system in New York City. It assumed responsibility for running the city's subways on 15 June 1953. In 1968 the authority became part of the Metropolitan Transportation Authority (MTA). New York City Transit Authority is the agency's legal name; in the mid-1990s MTA changed its common name to MTA New York City Transit. In addition to the city's subways it operates local buses, express bus routes, and the Staten Island Railway. From 1982 to the present the authority has implemented a massive capital renewal program, accompanied by management changes, that have revitalized the city's subway and bus systems. More than $45 billion was allocated to the capital program between 1982 and 2009. In 2007 the agency had an operating budget of $6.5 billion (58 percent of which was covered by fare revenues, the balance from subsidies), and 47,696 employees. On an average weekday in 2007, it had 7.5 million riders, including 5.1 million on the subway and 2.4 million on buses. Annual ridership in 2007 was more than 1.5 billion (the highest since 1952) for the subway, and 738 million for buses.

Peter Derrick

New York City triathlon. Annual endurance sporting event involving swimming, biking, and running. Begun in 2001 it quickly became one of the premier triathlons in the country, drawing Olympians from around the world as well as more than 3000 amateur athletes and fitness enthusiasts in 2008. The event is run on a course of the standard Olympic distance. The 1500-meter swim is held in the Hudson River, beginning at West 98th Street and finishing at the 79th Street boat basin. Competitors then transition to their bicycles for a 40-kilometer round-trip ride north on the Henry Hudson Parkway to the Mosholu Parkway and back again to 79th Street. Finally, they run south along Riverside Park and east across 72nd Street to Central Park where they complete their 10-kilometer run. The race has attracted more entrants each year at both the professional and novice levels.

David White

New York City Tribune. Daily newspaper founded in 1976 as the *News World* by the Korean spiritual leader and businessman Sun Myung Moon. It had its headquarters at 401 Fifth Avenue in Manhattan and was printed in Long Island City. The newspaper was promoted as an alternative to the other daily newspapers in New York City and became known for its conservative news coverage and editorials. The name was changed to the *New York Tribune* in 1983, prompting a copyright lawsuit from the *International Herald Tribune* that was settled in the following year when the name was changed again, to the *New York City Tribune.* Apart from a brief period during a newspaper strike in 1978, the *Tribune* failed to attract serious local interest, and after years of diminishing circulation and advertising revenues it ceased publication in January 1992.

James Bradley

New York Clearing House Association. Organization formed in 1853 by 52 commercial banks in New York City to make possible the daily settling of demand obligations among them, and the first organization of its kind in the United States. The plan for it was first advanced in 1831 by Albert Gallatin, former secretary of the treasury. The association was set up as a nonprofit, cost-recovering institution that derived its operating revenues from the bank owners belonging to it, who paid fees based on the volume of their clearings. Additional members were admitted on receiving approval from three-fourths of the existing membership. When the clearing house was in its heyday about 1908, each member bank had two representatives: a delivery clerk who presented currency or claims against other banks, and a settling clerk who received currency or checks from other banks. Each morning at 10 a.m. the delivery clerks formed a procession that paraded around the desks of the settling clerks, to whom they presented notices of accounts due. A third group of clerks, employed by the clearing house and known as proof clerks, then tallied the sums and calculated the amount due from or to each bank. As many as 2500 transactions were thus reduced to no more than 50 in a procedure that generally took only 35 to 40 minutes. Each member deposited gold or legal tender in its accounts at the clearing house, on which it could draw for debts owed to other member banks. The most common medium used in balancing accounts was the clearing house certificate, or CHC, which was issued to member banks in denominations of $5000, $10,000, $20,000, and $100,000, dollar for dollar, when member banks made their deposits of gold, silver, or other legal tender. CHCs were used exclusively as reserves and in clearing operations among members.

The New York Clearing House Association had virtually all the characteristics of a "bank of issue" or "central bank," except that it was privately owned and operated. It required weekly financial statements from its members and monitored their soundness and liquidity, and its members sometimes helped to set minimum reserve requirements that supplemented state and national banking laws. Eventually the association became a lender of last resort for members facing liquidity crises marked by high short-term interest rates, security liquidations, and bank closings. Its clearing house loan certificates (CHLCs), which were very similar to CHCs and had the same denominations, were issued to member banks as payment for secured loans that the clearing house made to them and were then used by the banks to settle their daily balances at the clearing house. These certificates prevented the hemorrhaging of specie and legal tender bank reserves and prevented sound but illiquid banks from failing. Over 50 years the New York Clearing House Association issued hundreds of millions of dollars in CHLCs with virtually no losses to banks or bank depositors. The role of the clearing house as a lender of last resort ended with the advent in 1914 of the Federal Reserve System, which duplicated most of its functions, but the association nevertheless continued to operate.

Restructed as the Clearing House Payments Company in 2004, the company's wire payment system (known as CHIPS) is responsible for 350,000 payments each day totaling $1.6 trillion. The association is the oldest bank association and forum in the United States. It publishes positions on issues of importance to its owner banks in the form of comment letters, amicus curiae filings, and other published materials.

Theodore Gilman, *A Graded Banking System* (Boston: Houghton Mifflin, 1898); James Graham Cannon, *Clearing Houses: Their History, Methods and Administration* (New York: D. Appleton, 1900); *New York Automated Clearing House* (New York: New York Clearing House Association, 1984); Richard H. Timberlake, Jr., "The Central Banking Role of Clearinghouse Associations," *Journal of Money, Credit and Banking* 16, no. 1 (1984), 1–15; *Clearing House Interbank Payments System* (New York: New York Clearing House Association, 1986)

Richard H. Timberlake

New York Clipper. Weekly newspaper. Founded in 1853 by Harrison Trent and Frank Queen (1823–82), its publisher and editor from 1857 until his death, it covered sport and the theater and catered to the tastes of lower- and middle-class Americans. It published detailed reports of blood sports, rowing, baseball, billiards, boxing, cricket, hunting, fishing, horse racing, winter pastimes, and other amusements, as well as news and circus reports, fiction and verse, and criticism of music and the theater. The newspaper reflected Queen's advocacy of athletics and physical training for both sexes and all classes and ages. It was bought by *Variety* in 1923.

George B. Kirsch

New York Coliseum. Former convention center at 10 Columbus Circle in Manhattan. Designed by Leon Levy and Lionel Levy and constructed in 1956 with federal urban renewal funds secured by Robert Moses on a site owned by the Triborough Bridge and Tunnel Authority, it was an architecturally undistinguished structure of gray brick that included an exhibition hall, a parking garage, and an office tower 25 stories tall. During the first 30 years of its existence, the Coliseum was the principal venue in New York City for large trade shows and for such public events as automobile and boat shows, but its small size and the many columns that obstructed its interior hindered exhibitors, from whom workers at the facility were also acknowledged to have extorted fees. In 1986, the opening of the Jacob K. Javits Convention Center rendered the Coliseum obsolete, and several plans were put forward to redevelop the site, most of them widely criticized because of the shadows the new structures would have cast over Central Park. A more modest plan designed by David Childs of Skidmore, Owings and Merrill was delayed in the early 1990s by the city's worsening economy; the Coliseum was demolished in 2000 and was replaced by the Time Warner Center.

John Voelcker

New York College for the Training of Teachers. Original name of Teachers College.

New York College of Podiatric Medicine. Private podiatric college opened in 1911 at 124th Street between Park and Madison avenues as the New York School of Chiropody. The oldest institution of its kind in the United States, the college also runs the seven Foot Clinics of New York.

Marc Ferris

New York Colored Mission. School and philanthropic association for blacks opened in 1865 on West 30th Street in the Tenderloin. Run by a group of Quaker educators and sponsored by the African Sabbath Association, it provided for the religious education of black children and evolved into one of the most active philanthropies in the city. The mission offered services by black and white ministers, a Sunday school, and Bible classes; maintained a physician and a nurse for medical care; and sent "friendly visitors" to black homes to distribute food, clothing, shoes, and coal to the poor and sick. It also sponsored socials on Friday evenings and athletic activities, served inexpensive meals, and had an employment office, rooms for young women, a night school, a nursery school, a sewing school, and a reading room. The mission remained in operation at least until 1938.

Seth M. Scheiner, *Negro Mecca: A History of the Negro in New York City, 1865–1920* (New York: New York University Press, 1965)

Mike Sappol

New York Commercial Association. Original name of the New York Produce Exchange.

New York Community Trust. One of the oldest and largest community foundations in the United States. Formed in 1924 by the United States Mortgage and Trust Company to manage permanent trusts for charitable purposes, it became more independent in 1926 when its first director, Ralph Hayes, arranged to work with several banks. The trust set itself apart from the community foundations in nearly all other large American cities by making grants not only in its home region but throughout the United States and abroad. Initially emphasizing its expert ability to invest money and execute donors' wishes, it grew slowly for three decades despite the establishment of such important entities as the Moritz and Charlotte Warburg Memorial Fund (to provide scholarships at the Hebrew University in Jerusalem) and a fund of $2.5 million from the Laura Spelman Rockefeller Memorial. By 1945 the trust held 77 funds with total assets of $17.6 million, making it one of the 50 largest U.S. foundations. It grew more quickly in the following decades, and by 1964 its 173 funds held nearly $40 million. Further growth was brought about by changes in the federal tax law in 1969, which tightened the regulation of private foundations and thus made community foundations more attractive. Herbert West, who succeeded Hayes in 1967, worked to form the New York Regional Association of Grantmakers (1975), the Tri-State United Way (1975), the Energy Conservation Fund (in the late 1970s), and the Citizens Committee on Substance Abuse (1989). It also provided technical services to other nonprofit organizations, and it undertook efforts directed at people with AIDS, the urban poor, undocumented immigrants, public schools, and the aged. During the 1970s and 1980s the trust became a national leader in serving suburban donors with regional affiliates. Four of these were set up, each with its own board: in Westchester (established 1975), Long Island (1977), Fairfield County, Connecticut (1982), and the Berkshire–Taconic region (1987). West led the trust until his death in 1989. In that year the trust held assets of more than $830 million, enabling it to make annual grants of $50 million. It continued to grow under his successor, Lorie A. Slutsky; by 2006 the Trust had assets of more than $2 billion.

The board of the New York Community Trust is selected in part by the participating banks and in part by public and private officials, including the chief judge of the U.S. Court of Appeals, the mayor, and the heads of the Association of the Bar of the City of New York, the New York Academy of Medicine, the New York Chamber of Commerce and Industry, and Lincoln Center for the Performing Arts.

David C. Hammack

New York Container Terminal. Commercial shipping port formerly known as Howland Hook Marine Terminal, located on the Arthur Kill north of Goethals Bridge in Staten Island. Built by the American Export Lines, the terminal was sold to New York City for $47.5 million in 1973. The city leased the 187-acre (76-hectare) facility to the Port Authority of New York and New Jersey in 1985; the facility largely shut down from 1986 to 1996. In 1995 the Port Authority leased the facility to Howland Hook Container Terminal Inc. The Port Authority acquired 124 adjacent acres (50 hectares) called Port Ivory in 2001 and as of 2007 was developing a 39-acre (16-hectare) rail terminal on the site. To accommodate larger ships at the Howland Hook and Bayonne docks, the Port Authority dredged the Arthur Kill channel to 41 feet (12 meters); the project was completed in 2006. In 2007 the Ontario Teachers' Pension Plan paid $2.4 billion to acquire the New York Container Terminal and three other shipyards from Hong Kong–based Orient Overseas International Ltd., which began running the facility in the 1990s. Along with the Brooklyn–

Port Authority terminal, the facility is one of the two major New York commercial shipping ports. It includes 412,000 square feet (38,000 square meters) of container cargo storage space; 82,000 feet (25,000 meters) of temperature-controlled storage; a 3,000-foot (900-meter)–long, 42-foot (13-meter)–deep ship berth; and onsite maintenance, trucking, and intermodal rail facilities. The International Longshoremen's Association Local 920 runs the facility, which employed roughly 420 longshoremen and 66 management employees in 2007.

Ben Silk

New York Cotton Exchange. Commodities market formed in 1870 at 142 Pearl Street by local merchants who dominated the cotton export business before the Civil War, as well as such notable merchants from the South as the Lehman brothers. It developed into the leading cotton futures market at a time when the nation imported more than 50 percent of the world's annual crop (compared with 90 percent in 1860). After World War II competition from other nations and growing domestic demand steadily reduced its share of trade. The exchange traded in wool futures in the 1950s but had little success because of trading irregularities and government scrutiny. In 1966 it successfully established futures contracts for frozen orange juice concentrate; its later trade in wool futures and tomato futures failed. Stricter requirements for self-regulation were established by the Commodity Futures Trading Commission in the 1970s and 1980s, with an especially great effect on trade in high-risk perishable items. The New York Cotton Exchange developed extensive trading in financial futures in the 1980s, including futures tied to two- and five-year notes of the U.S. Treasury, the U.S. dollar, and the European Currency Unit. In the early twenty-first century the exchange traded futures and options in cotton, frozen concentrated orange juice, and potatoes, as well as interest rates, currency, and index futures and options.

Jerry W. Markham, *The History of Commodity Futures Trading and Its Regulation* (New York: Praeger, 1987)

Morton Rothstein

New York County. One of the five counties of New York City, coextensive with the borough of MANHATTAN.

New York Curb Market (Agency) [New York Curb Exchange]. Stock exchange known from 1953 as the AMERICAN STOCK EXCHANGE.

New York Ecclesiological Society. Organization formed in 1848 to reintroduce to the Episcopal Church Catholic customs abandoned during the English Reformation; it was closely allied with the Oxford Movement. The society was influential in reviving Gothic architecture, especially the "middle pointed," or decorated, style popular in England during the fourteenth century, and it included the architect Richard Upjohn among its members. From 1848 to 1853 it issued the quarterly publication the *New-York Ecclesiologist,* which was devoted to ecclesiastical architecture, fixtures, furnishings, and ritual. It also published proceedings from British ecclesiological societies, to which the society deferred in virtually all matters. The ecclesiologists helped to eliminate Puritan influence from the Anglican liturgy and determine church architecture for many years. The society ceased operations in 1855, its objectives fulfilled with the success of the Gothic Revival.

Susanna A. Jones

New York Entomological Society. Organization formed on 29 June 1892 at the home of Charles Palm at 172 East 64th Street by a small group of insect collectors and naturalists that included the furrier Gustav Beyer. The society sponsored meetings, lectures, and from 1893 a yearly auction of beetles, moths, and butterflies. In March 1893 it launched the *Journal of the New York Entomological Society.* The Brooklyn Entomological Society (1872) was absorbed in 1968. In May 1992 the society organized a centenary dinner at the Explorers Club at which many of the dishes included insects as ingredients. The society has long been closely associated with the American Museum of Natural History, to which many members have donated important collections, scientific books, and periodicals.

Louis N. Sorkin

New Yorker. Weekly magazine launched in February 1925 by Harold Ross and Jane Grant with funds from the family that owned the Fleischmann Yeast Company. Aimed at an urbane, literate readership rather than at what Ross called "the old lady in Dubuque," it began as a sophisticated humor magazine and soon took on a more literary emphasis, affecting a breezy aloofness and a sardonic wit and combining characteristics of the *American Mercury, Vanity Fair,* the English magazine *Punch,* and the German magazine *Simplicissimus.* Regular features came to include a weekly miscellany of reportage and banter called "Talk of the Town," extended profiles of prominent figures, listings of cultural events, and "newsbreaks," which reprinted unintentionally amusing errors from other publications. Politically the magazine embraced a genteel liberalism. Members of the Algonquin Round Table figured prominently in the magazine during its early years, especially Alexander Woollcott, Robert Benchley, and Dorothy Parker. Apart from its illustrators all contributors initially used pseudonyms; no names appeared on the cover, the magazine did not print letters to the editor, and except in very early issues there was no masthead. Lionel Trilling remarked that the magazine's "corporate" existence fostered its polite, remote, and aseptic style. Others criticized the tone of the magazine, which Dwight Macdonald (later a contributor) likened to that of a cocktail party. Early on the magazine set itself apart from its competitors by maintaining a strict separation between its editorial and business offices, by insisting on scrupulous editing and fact checking, and by printing long, discursive pieces: an entire issue was devoted to John Hersey's "Hiroshima" in 1946. Ross's successor, William Shawn, published such influential pieces as James Baldwin's "The Fire Next Time" (1962), Hannah Arendt's "Eichmann in Jerusalem" (1963), Truman Capote's "In Cold Blood" (1965), and Charles Reich's "The Greening of America" (1970).

The *New Yorker* acquired a reputation as an institution, a reputation that it did everything to encourage. It adhered for decades to the graphic and typographic formulas established in its first issues, and on every anniversary it reprinted its first cover illustration—Rea Irvin's drawing of a dandy in a top hat named Eustace Tilley observing a butterfly through a monocle. But as the readership aged and advertising revenues declined, the *New Yorker* in the 1980s and early 1990s underwent changes in ownership and editorial practice. In 1985 the magazine was purchased by Advance Publications for $142 million and Shawn was replaced by Robert Gottlieb, who was in turn replaced by Tina Brown in 1992. The magazine departed from its traditional layout (by no longer insisting that advertisements conform to its three-column format), content (by devoting greater attention to popular culture and including letters to the editor), graphics (by printing photographs by staff photographer Richard Avedon and color illustrations), and tone (by eliminating features beginning with such phrases as "A friend in the country writes," a device widely parodied). At the same time as the magazine underwent editorial changes, for many years it was embroiled in a controversy over its publication in 1983 of a profile by Janet Malcolm of Jeffrey Masson, a former head of Freud's archives in London. A libel suit by Masson alleging that quotations attributed to him had been fabricated resulted in two trials, the second lasting until 1994, in which the author was faulted but the magazine was essentially exonerated.

Over the years contributors to the *New Yorker* have included the writers Katharine Sergeant Angell, Janet Flanner, Wolcott Gibbs, Lois Long, Ogden Nash, John O'Hara, S. J. Perelman, James Thurber, John Updike, E. B. White, and Edmund Wilson, and the cartoonists Charles Addams, Peter Arno,

Helen Hokinson, and Saul Steinberg. The magazine has also published theater criticism by Brendan Gill and film criticism by Pauline Kael, reviews of fiction and coverage of baseball by Roger Angell, and political coverage by Elizabeth Drew (from Washington) and Andy Logan (from City Hall).

Published from offices on West 43rd Street for more than 60 years, after the magazine was purchased by Condé Nast Publications its offices moved to 4 Times Square. David Remnick replaced Tina Brown as editor in 1998. As the magazine celebrated its 75th aniversary in 2000, it launched its first annual literary and arts festival. In 2004 the *New Yorker*'s circulation passed 1 million.

James Thurber, *The Years with Ross* (Boston: Little, Brown, 1957); Jane Grant, *Ross, the New Yorker, and Me* (New York: Reynal, 1968); Brendan Gill, *Here at the New Yorker* (New York: Random House, 1975)

Brenda Wineapple

New Yorkers for Parks. Nonprofit, independent watchdog for New York City's parks, beaches, and playgrounds, formed in 2001. The organization grew out of the Parks Council, organized in 1970 to preserve the city's open spaces and improve its recreational facilities. The Parks Council was established by a merger of the Park Association of New York City (formed in 1905 as the Parks and Playgrounds Association) and the Council for Parks and Playgrounds, a neighborhood organization dedicated to improving play facilities.

Ann L. Buttenwieser

New Yorker Staats-Zeitung. Weekly newspaper launched by G. A. Neumann in 1834 as an organ of the Democratic Party. It achieved a circulation of about 5000 by 1845 when Neumann sold it to Jakob Uhl, who began daily publication (1849) and increased circulation to more than 14,000. After Uhl's death in 1854 Oswald Ottendorfer became the editor and began directing the paper toward the German American business elite of the city. Circulation was nearly 50,000 by the early 1870s, and the newspaper's headquarters were moved to Printing House Square in 1873. Control of the newspaper passed successively to Hermann Ridder in 1890 and to his sons Bernard and Victor in 1915. When American participation in World War I undermined the position of their leading competitor the *Herold,* the Ridders absorbed it and renamed their newspaper the *Staats-Zeitung und Herold.* An attempt in 1933 by a Nazi agent authorized by Rudolf Hess to take over the newspaper was prevented by Victor Ridder. By 1938 the newspaper was the leading German American opponent of Nazi anti-Semitism, but it continued to advocate neutrality until Pearl Harbor. In the 1950s readership fell and the newspaper was forced to resume weekly publication. By 1991 its readership fell to 25,000 a week. It closed in 1993.

Stanley Nadel

New Yorker Volks-Zeitung. Newspaper launched in 1876 as the *Arbeiter-Stimme,* the official organ of the Workingmen's Party. It was transformed into a popular labor newspaper by Alexander Jonas and Adolf Douai, who took over as its editors in 1878, changed the name, and increased daily circulation to 10,000. By 1890 circulation exceeded 20,000 and the *Volks-Zeitung* was the leading socialist newspaper in the United States. It broke with the Socialist Labor Party in 1899 and helped to form the Socialist Party, which flourished until the anti-German and antisocialist campaigns of World War I. Under the editorship of Ludwig Lore after the war the newspaper was brought into the orbit of the Communist Party. After Lore was expelled from the party in 1925, he and the newspaper maintained an independent left-wing perspective. In 1932 the newspaper changed its name to *Neue Volks-Zeitung* and began publishing weekly; at the time it had 23,000 subscribers. It remained an important leftist and anti-Nazi force until it ceased publication in 1944.

Stanley Nadel

New York Evening Graphic. A tabloid newspaper launched in 1924 by Bernarr Macfadden. Edited for five years by Emile Gauvreau, it competed with the *Daily News* and the *Daily Mirror.* Beneath large headlines the newspaper propagated Macfadden's ideas on health and attacked organized medicine and censorship. Among its features were the first columns written by Walter Winchell and Ed Sullivan; contests; comic strips; advice and information columns; titillating photographs; stories emphasizing sex, sensation, and crime; and "Composographs," in which the faces of people in the news were superimposed on outlandishly inappropriate bodies. In libel suits totaling $7 million the *Graphic* lost only $5290. Although its circulation reached 600,000 the newspaper was eschewed by advertisers and it ceased publication in 1932.

Lester Cohen, *The New York Graphic: The World's Zaniest Newspaper* (Radnor, Pa.: Chilton, 1964)

Robert Ernst

New York Film Festival. Festival founded at Lincoln Center in 1963. The Film Society of Lincoln Center, established in 1969, hosts the festival, which features both American and foreign films and has introduced such directors as François Truffaut and Pedro Almodóvar to the United States. The festival is open to all genres and usually includes about 40 films. There are no categories and no prizes, although competition to be included is fierce.

Kate Lauber

New York Foundation. Charitable organization incorporated on 5 April 1909 by Alfred M. Heinsheimer. Initially, the foundation focused on medical care and research, social welfare, and education. In the 1950s programs in the arts and recreation were added, and the foundation began to contribute to regional and national organizations. Except during the period from 1950 to 1975, giving has been confined to New York City. In 1991 the New York Foundation had assets of $54.4 million and made grants totaling $2.7 million. In 2008 it gave $4.5 million in grants, half of which were geared toward youth or the elderly, and mostly poor communities. Its original headquarters were at 350 Fifth Avenue; in the twenty-first century the foundation relocated to 10 East 34th Street.

Kenneth W. Rose

New York Foundling Hospital. Institution formed on 11 October 1869 at 117 East 12th Street in Manhattan by Mary Irene Fitzgibbon (1823–96), a member of the New York Sisters of Charity who was inspired by the needs of abandoned infants in New York City and by similar institutions in Europe. The hospital moved to 3 South Washington Square in 1870, to Lexington Avenue at 68th Street in 1873, to Third Avenue at 68th Street in 1958, and finally to 590 Sixth Avenue in 1988, where it was still located in the early twenty-first century. It manages more than 40 programs for infants, youths, young parents, and families and emphasizes home care. The hospital opened the Mott Haven Academy Charter School in 2008, enrolling students in kindergarten through second grade, with plans to eventually serve about 300 students in grades K–8. The school is designed to meet the needs of children in the foster care and child welfare system, integrating social and educational goals.

Elsie Essmuller Vignec, *Children of Hope: Some Stories of the New York Foundling Hospital* (New York: Dodd, Mead, 1964)

Mary Elizabeth Brown

New-York Gallery of the Fine Arts. Art gallery opened in 1844 with the collection of Luman Reed by Jonathan Sturges and Reed's son-in-law Theodore Allen (1800–50). It was the first permanent art collection in the city and the nucleus of a national gallery. Additional paintings were donated by such artists as Thomas Cole, Asher B. Durand, and William Sidney Mount. The collection was exhibited at the National Academy of Design (1844, 1850–52) and the Rotunda in City Hall Park (1845–48) before being donated to the New-York Historical Society in 1858.

Timothy Anglin Burgard

New York Genealogical and Biographical Society. Formed in 1869, the organization is located at 122 East 58th

Street and is open to both members and nonmembers. The society hosts an extensive library with 75,000 volumes of published material and 30,000 manuscripts. Its collection is geared toward New York State (but also includes materials regarding other states and nations) and includes federal and state census records, burial and land records, New York City directories dating to 1786, and New Amsterdam court documents. The society also publishes the *New York Researcher,* formerly the *Bulletin* and the *Record* before 2004, which as of 2006 was the second-oldest journal of its kind in the nation.

Thomas E. Bird

New York Giants (i). Baseball team formed in 1883 as the New York Gothams when the National League expanded and awarded a franchise to John B. Day, already an owner of the Metropolitans of the American Association. The new team shared a field with the Metropolitans near the northern end of Central Park at Fifth Avenue and 110th Street, an area formerly used for polo matches. The manager, Jim Mutrie, called the players his "giants," a name that the team eventually adopted. Led by the pitchers Tim Keefe and Mickey Welch and the outstanding hitter Roger Connor, it won championships in 1888 and 1889, defeating St. Louis and Brooklyn. During the 1890s the team suffered financial difficulties and moved uptown to the new Polo Grounds, at Coogan's Bluff on 155th Street; there it remained for 67 years. In 1900 the pitcher Christy Mathewson joined the team, which in 1903 was purchased for $125,000 by John T. "Tooth" Brush. The catcher Roger Bresnahan and the pitcher Joe McGinnity were acquired from the Baltimore Orioles, and under its manager John J. McGraw the team had the second-best record in the league in 1903 and the best in 1904, although it refused to play the Boston Red Sox in the World Series (at the time an unformalized competition). In the first formal World Series (1905) the team defeated the Philadelphia Athletics, managed by Connie Mack, when Mathewson pitched three shutouts. McGraw's team dominated baseball for a generation, winning 10 pennants and three World Series between 1904 and 1924. Despite the addition of the pitcher Rube Marquard it lost the pennant to the Chicago Cubs in 1908 after Fred Merkle, playing in his first season, failed to touch second base on an apparent winning hit. The Giants lost a deciding playoff game amid rumors of bribery involving McGraw, who was later exonerated by a committee led by Brush.

When fire destroyed the original wooden grandstands of the Polo Grounds in 1911 the oddly proportioned stadium was rebuilt in concrete, a symbol of the importance of baseball in New York City. The Giants won four pennants there between 1911 and 1917, but no World Series. Two members of the team were banned from baseball for attempting to rig the outcome of games in 1919, as were a player and a coach in 1924 for arranging a bribe. The team was purchased in 1919 for $1 million by Charles A. Stoneham in a transaction arranged by McGraw, who received shares of the team, and the gambler Arnold Rothstein. The team proceeded to win four consecutive pennants (1921–24) and twice defeated the New York Yankees in the World Series. McGraw was succeeded in 1932 by Bill Terry, a player-manager who along with the power hitter Mel Ott and the pitcher Carl Hubbell led the team to three pennants: it defeated the Washington Senators in the World Series in 1933 but lost two series to the Yankees in 1936–37. The Giants are perhaps best known for their bitter rivalry with the Brooklyn Dodgers, and in particular for their defeat of the Dodgers for the National League pennant in 1951. Managed by Leo Durocher and including such players as the pitcher Sal Maglie and the center fielder Willie Mays (playing his first season), the team won the deciding game when Bobby Thomson hit a home run off Ralph Branca that became known as the "shot heard 'round the world." The team won another pennant in 1954, when Mays achieved a batting average of .341 and hit 41 home runs; it won its eighth World Series by winning four consecutive games against the Cleveland Indians, who had been heavily favored. After the end of the 1957 season Horace Stoneham moved the team to San Francisco, just as the Dodgers left Brooklyn for Los Angeles. See also SPORTS.

Jeffrey Scheuer

New York Giants (ii). Football team. Formed in 1925 by Tim Mara, a bookmaker (at the time a legal trade), whose son Wellington later became president of the team; it played its home games in the Polo Grounds until 1955, winning three National Football League (NFL) championships (1927, 1934, and 1938). Financial losses plagued the team during its early days and brought it to the verge of financial collapse toward the end of the first season; only when more than 70,000 spectators attended its last game, against Red Grange and the Chicago Bears, was a heavy debt turned into a modest profit. In 1930 the team easily won an exhibition game against former stars from the University of Notre Dame, thus demonstrating the appeal of professional football to a public that was still skeptical, while raising $115,153 for the New York Unemployment Fund.

The late 1950s and early 1960s was one of the finest periods in the history of the Giants, which had such outstanding players as Frank Gifford, Y. A. Tittle, Roosevelt Brown, Sam Huff, Andy Robustelli, and Emlen Tunnell and played for the NFL championship five times in seven years, winning the NFL title in 1956. The championship game of 1958, which the team lost in overtime to the Baltimore Colts by a score of 23–17 at Yankee Stadium, is often referred to as the greatest football game ever played. The team played its home games in Yankee Stadium from 1956 to 1973 and then at the Yale Bowl (1973–74) in New Haven, Connecticut, and Shea Stadium (1975), before moving to Giants Stadium in East Rutherford, New Jersey, in 1976.

The team struggled in the 1970s but after Bill Parcells became the head coach in 1983 its fortunes improved. In 1987, the Giants, led by quarterback Phil Simms and linebacker Lawrence Taylor, defeated the Denver Broncos in Super Bowl XXI by a score of 39–20. In 1991, the team won Super Bowl XXV against the Buffalo Bills, 20–19. From 1992 to 2006, the Giants made the playoffs five times, including a Super Bowl loss to the Baltimore Ravens in 2001. Coached by Tom Coughlin and led by veteran defensive end Michael Strahan and young quarterback Eli Manning, the Giants won Super Bowl XLII by a score of 17–14 in 2008, against the New England Patriots, who were trying to win their fourth Super Bowl of the decade and complete only the second undefeated season in NFL history.

Joseph A. Horrigan, David White

New York Golden Gloves. Amateur boxing tournament. *The Ring* magazine claims it was started first in Chicago in 1926, an idea promoted by Arch Ward, a sportswriter for the *Chicago Tribune.* But in 1927 Paul Gallico, sports editor of the New York *Daily News,* conducted an amateur boxing tournament and named it Golden Gloves. Ward suggested that the New York Golden Gloves champions come to Chicago to fight the Chicago champions in the Chicago Coliseum in 1928, thus beginning a rivalry that lasted until 1961. The Golden Gloves tournament spread to other cities, organized on a territorial basis to give all sections of the country representation, leading to a national Golden Gloves tournament. Some of the great champions to come out of the New York Golden Gloves are Sugar Ray Robinson, Floyd Patterson, Emile Griffith, and Mike Tyson.

Frank Dyer

New York Gold Exchange. Financial exchange that began in 1862 as Gilpin's Gold Room in a basement on New Street. At the time the Union was financing the Civil War by issuing paper money rather than raising taxes, and trading in gold was a popular means of speculating on the course of the war. Although such trading was banned by the New York Stock Exchange as unpatriotic and Gilpin's Gold Room itself was briefly banned in 1864, gold speculation continued in brokerage offices and shops along Broad and New streets and the room reopened as the New York Gold Exchange in October. Gold trading played an important role in the nation's foreign trade, but most trading was done for speculative purposes. In 1869 the gold market became unsettled when financier Jay Gould made an attempt to corner it by secretly buying up all available supplies and bribing members of President Ulysses S. Grant's inner circle to prevent sales of gold by the U.S. Treasury. Informed on 23 September by his contacts in the White House that the Treasury planned to sell gold nevertheless, Gould arranged for his associate Jim Fisk to execute numerous buy orders the next day to support the price while Gould sold his holdings. Gould and other members of his group made as much as $40 million in profits, but when it became widely known that gold was being sold by the Treasury, its price quickly fell: the ensuing panic ruined a number of brokers and many speculators (not including Fisk, who refused to honor his agreement to buy gold at a higher price), prompted an investigation by the U.S. Congress, and became known as "Black Friday." Gold trading slowed after 1870 as speculators turned their attention to Wall Street and as the price of gold stabilized, making speculation less profitable. From 1865 the New York Gold Exchange was part of the New York Stock Exchange. It ceased operations after specie resumption on 1 January 1879.

George Winslow

Pressroom of the New York Herald Tribune, *from* Frank Leslie's Illustrated Newspaper, *20 July 1861*

New York Guild for the Jewish Blind. Name used until 1960 by the JEWISH GUILD FOR THE BLIND.

New York Hall of Science. Originally built as a pavilion for the 1964–65 World's Fair, it was converted into a museum from 1966 to 1979. In 1986 the museum reopened with 25,000 square feet (2300 square meters) of space for more than 400 hands-on science exhibitions. The museum is dedicated to biology, chemistry, and physics education for children, families, and educators. It offers after-school programs, interactive workshops, and resources for educators. The museum is located at 47-01 111th Street in Queens.

Stephanie Miller

New York Harbor. See PORT OF NEW YORK.

New York Herald. Daily newspaper launched in 1835 by James Gordon Bennett, Sr. A pioneer in the use of railroads, steamships, and the telegraph to gather news, it became known for its thorough reportage on finance and society and its organized network of European correspondents. Its sensationalistic approach to scandal and crime, notably its coverage of the trial of Richard Robinson in 1836 for the murder of the prostitute Helen Jewett, led to widespread denunciation and a boycott against the newspaper in 1840. Despite these protests the newspaper had a circulation of 77,000 by 1860, the largest of any daily newspaper in the United States. It was usually Democratic in its politics and was considered more sympathetic toward the South than any other newspaper in the North, but it supported the Union during the Civil War, to which it assigned 63 correspondents in the field. The *Herald* was owned in turn by James Gordon Bennett, Jr. (1872–1918) and the publisher Frank A. Munsey before being purchased in 1924 by the Reid family and merged with the *New York Tribune* to form the *New York Herald Tribune.*

James L. Crouthamel, *Bennett's New York Herald and the Rise of the Popular Press* (Syracuse, N.Y.: Syracuse University Press, 1989)

Steven H. Jaffe

New York Herald Tribune. Daily newspaper formed in 1924 when the *New York Tribune,* under the direction of Ogden Reid, bought the *New York Herald,* owned by Frank Munsey. After Stanley Walker became its city editor in 1927, the newspaper gained a reputation for elegant writing and became one of the leading papers in the country. Among those who wrote for the newspaper were the war correspondents Marguerite Higgins and Homer Bigart; the columnists Joseph Alsop, Walter Lippmann, and Dorothy Thompson; and the sportswriter Red Smith. Under the direction of Helen Rogers Reid and her sons Whitelaw Reid and Ogden Reid, Jr., the *Herald Tribune* was rigorously anticommunist and supported such moderate Republican presidential candidates as Wendell Willkie (1940) and Dwight D. Eisenhower (1952). In 1958 it was purchased by the financier John Hay Whitney, who in 1963 introduced the magazine *New York* as a Sunday supplement to the newspaper. The writers Tom Wolfe and Jimmy Breslin began their careers at the *Herald Tribune* before it was merged in 1966 into the short-lived *New York World Journal Tribune* and ceased publication.

Richard Kluger, *The Paper: The Life and Death of the New York Herald Tribune* (New York: Alfred A. Knopf, 1986)

Steven H. Jaffe

New York Highlanders. Name used by the NEW YORK YANKEES from their inception in 1903 until 1913.

New York Hilton. Hotel at 1335 Sixth Avenue between 53rd and 54th streets, designed by William B. Tabler and opened in 1963 to accommodate business travelers and others. It has 2200 rooms, a conference center, and the Executive Tower, a separate building six stories tall. The New York Hilton owns an art collection that includes about 8500 paintings, sculptures, and lithographs. In the Mirage cocktail lounge stand two large marble sphinxes designed by V. Fontaine in Paris during the 1860s; they are adorned with bronze collars, ruffs, and saddles. A $148 million redesign was completed in 2006, with new features including an expanded lobby, a new full-service fitness club and spa, two new lounges, and two new restaurants.

Kevin Kenny

New-York Historical Society. Society formed in 1804 by business and government leaders, including Mayor DeWitt Clinton and John Pintard, the city inspector, to collect and preserve materials relating to the history of the United States and New York State; it is the oldest museum in continuous operation in the city, one of the most distinguished American independent research libraries, and the second-oldest historical society in the United States. Its first president was Egbert

Art gallery at the New-York Historical Society

New-York Historical Society, 2009

Benson, former chief justice of the Second U.S. Circuit Court, and its first quarters were rented rooms at the building on Wall Street formerly occupied by the federal government. Its first permanent building was erected in 1857 at Second Avenue and 11th Street, and the collection expanded in 1858 when the society received the holdings of the New York Gallery of the Fine Arts, which included works by nineteenth-century contemporary American artists such as Thomas Cole, Asher B. Durand, and William Sidney Mount. This was the city's only art museum until the Metropolitan Museum of Art was formed in 1872. Important acquisitions included 432 of the 435 watercolor illustrations used in John James Audubon's *Birds of America* (1827–38) in 1864 and the paintings by European masters collected by Thomas J. Bryan (1802–70) in 1867. In 1908 the society moved into its own building at 77th Street and Central Park West, where it still resides. From 1917 to 1980 it published the *New-York Historical Society Quarterly* (known as the *Quarterly Bulletin* until 1946).

In addition to its collections of fine art, the Historical Society's holdings include early American household utensils, needlework, shop signs, weathervanes, porcelain, and silver; a print collection that includes rare eighteenth-century engravings and nineteenth-century lithographs; political caricatures and posters; a large number of photographs; and documents and drawings from the city's architecture firms, including those of Cass Gilbert and McKim, Mead and White. Its library has one of the finest collections of eighteenth-century newspapers from the city; a complete file of city directories dating from the first one in 1768; seventeenth-century atlases of voyages and exploration; and slavery and antislavery pamphlets. Among its approximately two million manuscripts are letters from Charles II to Edmund Andros (1674) authorizing the takeover of New Netherland from the Dutch governor; the articles of General John Burgoyne's surrender; an orderly-book record of Nathan Hale's execution; letters of George Washington; orderly books and related papers from the French and Indian War through World War II; and papers of elite as well as ordinary New Yorkers.

In the late 1980s the New-York Historical Society experienced a financial crisis that forced it to close parts of its collections, and briefly in 1993, its entire collections. Potential mergers with the Museum of the City of New York or the New York Public Library ultimately failed. In 1994, Historical Society president Betsy Gotbaum oversaw a period of stabilization and revitalization that included deaccessioning the museum's European Old Masters, as well as the opening in 2000 of the Henry Luce III Center for the Study of American Culture, a permanent display of more than 40,000 treasures from the collections. During the presidency of Kenneth T. Jackson, the Historical Society collected artifacts and art associated with the terrorist attacks of 11 September 2001 and mounted 13 exhibitions on the World Trade Center. At this time the Historical Society began a $40 million renovation of the landmark building and signed a partnership agreement with the Gilder Lehrman Institute of American History, whose collection of more than 60,000 documents moved from the Morgan Library to the Historical Society. In 2004 Historical Society president Louise Mirrer led an institutional directive to focus its mission toward documenting the broader history of the United States as seen within the context of New York City and State. Once an exclusive institution that catered to New York City's white Protestant elite, the New-York Historical Society in the early twenty-first century is attracting a racially, religiously, and ethnically diverse constituency that is reflected in its board of trustees.

Ella M. Foshay, Valerie Paley

New York Hospital. Medical facility granted a charter by George III on 13 June 1771. It was located on Broadway between Anthony Street (now Duane Street) and Catharine Street (now Worth Street). Established as a voluntary general hospital, it treated mostly charity cases. The governors recognized that insanity was a treatable illness, and mental patients were among the first to be admitted. From 1776 to 1791 the hospital was used variously as a military barracks, a home for destitute immigrants, a hall for anatomical lectures, and a meeting place for the state legislature. Books were purchased for a medical library as early as 1796. The federal government entrusted the care of merchant and naval seamen to the hospital from 1799 to 1870. In 1821 the Bloomingdale Asylum, a psychiatric division of the hospital, opened in a rural area at what is now 116th Street and Broadway. A special marine department was set up in its own building in 1825.

By 1870 the original hospital had become too small and outmoded. While a new facility was being constructed the hospital maintained the Chambers Street House of Relief, which provided mostly emergency care. The new hospital, between Fifth and Sixth avenues at 15th and 16th streets, opened on 16 March 1877. In the same year the governors established a training school for nurses, thus guaranteeing a high quality of care for patients. The House of Relief moved in 1884 to Hudson Street, where it operated a clinic and provided emergency treatment to the community of lower Manhattan until 1917.

In 1912 New York Hospital became formally affiliated with Cornell University Medical College. The two institutions agreed on 14 June 1927 to build the New York Hospital–Cornell Medical Center on York Avenue between 67th and 68th streets, which began receiving patients on 1 September 1932. An ambulatory care facility was added in 1985. As of 2007 the hospital had 814 beds. Its better-known facilities include the Payne Whitney Clinic, a psychiatric division. New York Hospital is the oldest hospital in New York City and the second-oldest in the United States.

Milton L. Zisowitz, *One Patient at a Time: A Medical Center at Work* (New York: Random House, 1961); Eric Larrabee, *The Benevolent and Necessary Institution: The New York Hospital, 1771–1971* (Garden City, N.Y.: Doubleday, 1971)

Adele A. Lerner

New York Industrial Congress. Citywide assembly convened in June 1850 to work for labor reforms. It moved into a wing of City Hall in July 1850, where it coordinated efforts to reform the trades similar to those undertaken by the Luxembourg Commission under the direction of Louis Blanc in 1848: the proposals debated included those for land reform, municipal reform, banks run by the trades, and the replacement of the wage system with producers' cooperatives. The congress drew its energy from the revival of the trade-union movement in the summer of 1850 and especially from a militant tailors' strike. Irish and German craftspeople were prominent among the leaders, as were middle-class reformers like Horace Greeley and George Henry Evans. The congress evaded the turbulent national debate over expanding slavery and ignored the controversy over fugitive slaves' rights, focusing instead on city and state elections in the autumn of 1850. By forming nominating committees that were independent of Tammany Hall and by interrogating nominees, it helped a number of reform candidates to win. Its success as an independent organization was short-lived. Some delegates were loosely tied to the Democratic Party, which they hoped to reform from within, and during a meeting on 3 June 1851 the assembly was taken over and reorganized by politicians associated with Tammany Hall. The New York Industrial Congress briefly provided a vital forum for social, political, and labor reform; many of the ideas debated by its members were taken up in wider circles after the Civil War, including proposals for an independent labor party and a legislative campaign for an eight-hour workday.

Sean Wilentz, *Chants Democratic: New York City and the Rise of the American Working Class, 1788–1850* (New York: Oxford University Press, 1984); Iver Bernstein, *The New York City Draft Riots: Their Significance for American Society and Politics in the Age of the Civil War* (New York: Oxford University Press, 1990)

Iver Bernstein

New York Institute for Special Education. Private, nonprofit school for disabled children. It was formed in 1831 as the New York Institution for the Blind by the book publisher Samuel Wood, who on a visit to the city almshouse in the preceding year had been struck by the neglect of children left blind by a severe outbreak of conjunctivitis. With the help of Samuel Akerly, a Quaker physician who was the superintendent of the New York Institution for the Deaf, he sought to provide children with manual training and "moral education." From 1833 the institute occupied quarters at Ninth Avenue and 34th Street. It was the first institution in the United States to provide formal education for blind children and the only school of its kind in New York State until 1865; it remained the most prominent and innovative even as other schools opened around the country later in the century. In 1866 William Wait, long the director of the institute, developed a method of reading for the blind called the New York point system that became increasingly popular until it was supplanted in 1890 by Braille, a system more adaptable to the new process of machine embossing. Among the instructors at the school were Grover Cleveland (for two years) and Fanny Crosby, a writer of Methodist hymns who had earlier been a student there.

In 1912 the school changed its name to the New York Institute for the Education of the Blind and replaced its curriculum, which had been principally vocational, with the fuller one of the state, including preparation for the examinations of the New York State Board of Regents. After the school was enabled by a bequest from F. Augustus Schermerhorn to move in 1924 to 999 Pelham Parkway in the Bronx, it gradually expanded its programs to help children with a wider range of disabilities, beginning with a program in 1940 for the deaf blind. By the 1980s it taught children who were blind, as well as those with emotional and learning disabilities, infants and preschoolers who were developmentally delayed, and children with multiple disabilities. To reflect its expanded programs the school adopted its current name in 1986.

Sandra Opdycke

New York Institute of Technology. Private college opened in 1955 in Brooklyn; it at first offered a two-year course of study and granted associate degrees in applied science. In 1958 the college moved to 61st Street and Broadway in Manhattan, a site now known as the Metropolitan Center. It became a four-year college in 1960 and went on to open two campuses on Long Island. In the early twenty-first century the New York Institute of Technology had 11,000 students on its three campuses and offered associate, bachelor's, and master's degrees and a doctorate in osteopathy.

Erica Judge

New York Jets. Football team. Formed in 1960 as the New York Titans by Harry Wismer, it was an original member of the American Football League (AFL). The team played its home games at the Polo Grounds from 1960 to 1963 before moving to Shea Stadium in 1964 and then to Giants Stadium in East Rutherford, New Jersey, in 1984. The AFL took over its operations in November 1962 after Wismer was unable to meet his payroll. In 1963 the team was bought by a syndicate led by MCA-TV president David A. "Sonny" Werblin, who renamed the team the Jets and hired Weeb Ewbank as the head coach and general manager. The team's 1965 draft of University of Alabama quarterback Joe Namath resulted in a contract reportedly worth more than $427,000 over three years. Namath brought instant credibility to both the Jets and the AFL. He was named AFL Rookie of the Year in 1965 and in 1967 became the first professional player to pass for more than 4000 yards in a season.

In 1969 the Jets recorded one of the most famous upsets in the history of professional football when it became the first AFL team to win a Super Bowl (Super Bowl III), defeating the Baltimore Colts by a score of 16 to 7. The Colts had been heavily favored to win by as many as 21 points. The following year the Jets lost to Kansas City in the first round of the playoffs. Namath, Don Maynard, and Ewbank, all part of the 1969 Super Bowl team, were elected to the Pro Football Hall of Fame.

The Jets qualified for the playoffs four times during the 1980s and twice during the 1990s. In 1982 and 1998 they reached the American Football Conference championship game but each time fell a win short of making it back to the Super Bowl. The team reached the playoffs multiple times during the first decade of the twenty-first century under head coaches Herman Edwards and Eric Mangini.

Joseph A. Horrigan

New York Journal–American. Daily newspaper launched in 1937 by Clarence J. Shearn, who sought to rescue William Randolph Hearst's empire from bankruptcy by combining his three newspapers in New York City: the *American* (acquired in 1895 as the *New York Journal*), the *Evening Journal* (launched in 1896), and the *Mirror* (a tabloid launched in 1924). Although Hearst himself had nominally retired by this time, the newspaper reflected his isolationist views on foreign policy and stressed sensational news and entertainment features, much like his earlier newspapers. Under the city editor Paul Schoenstein the staff won a Pulitzer Prize in 1944 after the newspaper had wielded its influence to obtain the rare drug penicillin for a small child. William Randolph Hearst, Jr., won a second Pulitzer Prize in 1955 after leading a team of editors for the *New York Journal–American* to Moscow, where they were permitted to report on events in the Soviet Union without hindrance. The newspaper was best known for its columns, most of long standing, including "Cholly Knickerbocker" by Maury Paul, "New York Day by Day" by O. O. McIntyre, and "Hollywood News" by Louella Parsons. Despite the newspaper's popularity, circulation and advertising declined during the early 1960s because of shifts in population. To stave off bankruptcy the newspaper merged with the *New York Herald Tribune* and the *New York World–Telegram* in 1966 to form the *World–Journal Tribune,* which lasted less than a year. For many years the newspaper was published at 220 South Street.

W. A. Swanberg, *Citizen Hearst: A Biography of William Randolph Hearst* (New York: Charles Scribner's Sons, 1961); Joseph Sage, *Three to Zero: The Story of the Birth and Death of the World Journal Tribune* (New York: American Publishers Association, 1967); John Hohenberg, *The Pulitzer Prizes: A History of the Awards* (New York: Columbia University Press, 1974)

Julian S. Rammelkamp

New York Journalistic Fraternity. Original name of the New York Press Club.

New York Kehillah. Community organization formed in 1908 by Jews in New York City to handle religious, educational, and social problems. Its formation marked the first attempt by the Jewish community to govern itself along the lines of a traditional Jewish polity since colonial times. The group was begun in response to a statement by Theodore Bingham, the police commissioner, that Jews were responsible for 50 percent of the city's crime. The charge aroused calls for his resignation and also rekindled concern about Jewish prostitution and gambling. The Kehillah was nurtured by Judah Magnes, a Reform rabbi, and consisted of bureaus for education, social morals, labor relations, and the supervision of dietary laws. Its most successful efforts were training a core of teachers and providing Jewish education. Undercover agents of its Bureau of Social Morals provided the police with information about criminal activity. The Kehillah met with opposition from some quarters, especially Orthodox Jews and socialists, who never offered their full cooperation in its efforts. Paralyzed by forces within the community by 1917, the organization suffered from a lack of legal enforcement for its sanctions and ceased operations in 1922.

Arthur A. Goren, *New York Jews and the Quest for Community: The Kehillah Experiment, 1908–1922* (New York: Columbia University Press, 1970)

Henry Feingold

New York Knicks. Professional basketball team. An original member of the Basketball Association of America, a forerunner of the National Basketball Association (NBA), the team played its first game on 1 November 1946, defeating the Toronto Huskies by a score of 68 to 66. Coached by Joe Lapchick, the Knicks made the playoffs in each of their first 10 seasons, including three appearances in the championship series, which they lost in 1951 to Rochester and in 1952 and 1953 to Minneapolis. The team was led in its early years by Carl Braun, Harry Gallatin, Dick McGuire, and Nat "Sweetwater" Clifton, one of the first black players in the NBA. The team had mixed success from the late 1950s into the 1960s.

The Knicks enjoyed their greatest success after Red Holtzman took over as head coach in 1968; in 1969–70 they won their first league title. Led by Willis Reed, the team also included Walt Frazier, Bill Bradley, and Dave DeBusschere (all four were later elected to the Basketball Hall of Fame) and Dick Barnett. One of the most memorable moments in NBA and Madison Square Garden history occurred in the decisive game seven of the 1970 championship series, when an injured Willis Reed, who was not expected to play, emerged from the locker room for the game's opening tip-off to raucous cheers from the Garden crowd. While ineffective for most of the night, Reed scored the team's first two baskets of the game and was widely credited as having inspired the Knicks to their 113–99 victory. Reed's example has been referenced by the media ever since when an injured athlete takes part in a crucial competition. Earl "the Pearl" Monroe joined the Knicks in 1971–72 to form an outstanding backcourt with Frazier, and in the following year the team won its second league title.

After reaching the playoffs for nine consecutive seasons the Knicks played unremarkably from the mid-1970s until 1984, when they forced a seventh game in the semifinals of the Eastern Conference of the NBA against the Boston Celtics (who eventually won the championship). They reached the playoffs in 1987–88 for the first time in four years and in 1988–89 won the Atlantic Division for the first time in nearly two decades. Coach Pat Riley then built the foundation for a team that made the playoffs every year in the 1990s. The early part of the decade was marked by a resurgent fan base, memorable playoff games, and heated rivalries with the Chicago Bulls, who won six championships in the 1990s, and with the Indiana Pacers. The team reached its pinnacle in 1994, returning to the NBA finals for the first time in 21 years, but squandered a three games to two lead and lost the championship to the Houston Rockets in seven games. After Riley left the Knicks in 1995 to coach the Miami Heat, his new team became one of the Knicks' biggest rivals for the latter half of the decade, during which the Knicks reached the NBA finals in 1999.

The trade of Patrick Ewing at the twilight of his career in September 2000 marked the end of one of the most successful eras in the franchise's existence and ushered in one of the worst periods in its history. The Knicks made the playoffs in 2001 but failed to do so for the next eight seasons. In December 2003 the Knicks' management was overhauled when former Detroit Pistons Hall of Famer Isiah Thomas was made general manager. From 2004 to 2010 the Knicks continued to lose, and the team management was ridiculed extensively in the New York City and national media for having the highest payroll, yet one of the worst records in the league.

Albert Figone, David White

New York Landmarks Conservancy. Private, non-for-profit organization founded in 1973 dedicated to preserving, revitalizing, and reusing architecturally significant buildings. Early in its history, it fought to save the Custom House and the Fraunces Tavern Block, both in lower Manhattan, and St. Ann and the Holy Trinity Church in Brooklyn Heights. The conservancy's work has expanded into providing technical assistance to owners of historic buildings; providing loans, through a revolving fund created as part of the conversion of the Federal Archive Building in Greenwich Village into apartments; and assisting historic religious properties with grants and loans through its Sacred Sites program.

Andrew S. Dolkart

New York Law Institute. Private subscription library opened in 1828 to make legal materials available to judges and lawyers practicing in New York City. The institute moved frequently during the nineteenth century to remain close to the federal courts; in 1915 it settled in the Equitable Building at 120 Broadway, where it housed a collection of more than 300,000 law reports, legal treatises, and scholarly journals. In the early twenty-first century it remained the oldest—and the only circulating—law library in the city.

Elliott B. Nixon

New York Law School. Private law school. It was founded in 1891 by George Chase, who resigned from Columbia Law School after a dispute with the president of the university, Seth Low, an opponent of the practical approach to legal education practiced by Theodore Dwight; several professors and students also left Columbia for the new institution. The school rented space in the Equitable Life Assurance Building and by 1906 had 1000 students, at the time the highest enrollment of any law school in the United States. It moved to the McBurney Young Men's Christian Association on West 23rd Street in 1919. Hurt by the Depression and war, the school closed in 1941; it was able to reopen in 1947 at 244 William Street, in part because of the G.I. Bill. The school moved to its current address at 57 Worth Street in Manhattan in 1962 and later expanded to three adjacent buildings. In the early twenty-first century the school had more than 80 full-time faculty members, who taught more than 1500 students. Among those who have taught at New York Law School are Charles Evans Hughes (1893–1900), Woodrow Wilson (1891–98), Roy Cohn (1950–60), William Kunstler (1952–60), and Nadine Strossen (from 1988), president of the American Civil Liberties Union. Alumni include Senator Robert F. Wagner (i; 1900), the poet Wallace Stevens (1903), the Supreme Court justice John Marshall Harlan (1924), and Chester F. Carlson (1939), who invented xerography.

Marc Ferris

New York Ledger. Literary magazine. It began as the weekly trade publication the *New York Merchant's Ledger,* which was bought by the publisher Robert Bonner in 1851; he transformed it into what he called a "family weekly," a story newspaper containing short novels, poems, and sketches; editorials on topics ranging from New York City to faithless husbands; a section of "wit and humor"; and an advice column. The newspaper enjoyed enormous success and was widely imitated, marking the beginning of an ebullient phase in the city's popular literary culture. From 1850 to 1870 it attracted many popular writers, including E. D. E. N. Southworth, Fanny Fern (Sara Parton), Lydia Sigourney, and Sylvanus Cobb, Jr., as well as Henry Ward Beecher, Horace Greeley, Edward Everett, George Bancroft, Charles Dickens, and Edgar Allan Poe. Bonner was perhaps best known for his sensationalist advertisements in other newspapers (he allowed no advertising in his own); he bought full pages in the *New York Tribune* and the *New York Herald* to announce the latest "thrilling story" in the *Ledger* and sometimes to settle feuds with other publishers. He also caused a sensation with other promotional tactics, among them the firing of 100 cannons in City Hall Park to advertise Cobb's story "The Gun-maker of Moscow." The *Ledger* was overshadowed in the 1870s by other newspapers, including the *Family Story Paper* and the *New York Weekly.* After Bonner's retirement in 1887 it was left to his sons and ceased publication in 1903.

Alice Fahs

New York Liberty. Women's professional basketball team. One of the eight original members of the Women's National Basketball Association (WNBA), the Liberty has played its home games every summer at Madison Square Garden since the franchise's inception in 1997. The team reached the playoffs in all but three of its first 12 seasons, but failed to win a championship, losing in the finals four times. Teresa Weatherspoon was the team's star player from 1997 until 2003 and made one of the most memorable shots in league history when she scored from halfcourt as time expired to force a decisive final game against the Houston Comets in the 1999 finals. The Liberty played six games at Radio City Music Hall in 2004 as Madison Square Garden was prepared for the Republican National Convention. In July 2008 it played in the first outdoor regular season game in league history.

David White

New York Life Insurance Company. Firm of life insurers formed as the Nautilus Insurance Company in 1845 by Pliny Freeman. A mutual firm, it had its first headquarters at 44 Wall Street and adopted its current name in 1849. The first board of directors included such distinguished New Yorkers as Albert Woodhull, Caleb Woodhull, Henry W. Hicks, and Loring Andrews; the first president was James De Peyster Ogden, a businessman and former president of the New York State Chamber of Commerce. The firm was one of the first to introduce soliciting and soon devised the general agency system, under which an agent controlled a territory, recruited and trained a sales force at his or her own expense, and received a percentage of sales from the home office. Branches were opened nationwide, and a 12-story headquarters of white marble was built at 346 Broadway in 1870 and redesigned between 1894 and 1898 by the firm of McKim, Mead and White (designated a landmark in 1987). Annual sales rose from $22 million in 1880 to $159 million in 1890; during the same decade several men who later became influential joined the firm, including John A. McCall, George W. Perkins, Darwin P. Kingsley (1862–1932), and Thomas A. Buckner. At the turn of the twentieth century the firm became the first in the world to have more than $1 billion of policies in force.

New York Life Insurance Building (designed by Cass Gilbert) between 26th and 27th streets along Madison Avenue, ca 1935–40

Kingsley, president from 1907 to 1931, sought to expand the firm's operations abroad and develop new policies. Under one program, "Nylic for Agents," agents earned a monthly income for life after 20 years of service. The firm remained successful during the first decades of the twentieth century despite World War I and the influenza epidemic of 1918–19, which doubled the company's payments of death benefits. Headquarters designed by Cass Gilbert were built in 1928 at Madison Avenue between 26th and 27th streets, the former site of Madison Square

Garden. In 1929 Calvin Coolidge, the former president, joined the board of directors. After World War II the firm enjoyed continuous prosperity and funded several housing developments in the city; the best known were the Fresh Meadows Housing Development (1949), a project built on 166 acres (67 hectares) in Fresh Meadows, and Manhattan House (1951), a 19-story building covering the block bounded by 66th Street, Second Avenue, 65th Street, and Third Avenue. By the twenty-first century New York Life was one of the oldest life insurers in the United States.

James Bradley

New York Lung Association. Organization formed in 1902 as the New York Society for the Prevention of Tuberculosis. Its first headquarters were on West 43rd Street. The association focuses its efforts on the local population; it sponsors research fellowships and educational programs about smoking, asthma, and tuberculosis.

A Half Century's Progress against Tuberculosis in New York City, 1900 to 1950 (New York: New York Tuberculosis and Health Association, 1952)

Andrea Balis

New York magazine. Weekly magazine that originated in 1963 as a supplement to the Sunday edition of the *New York Herald Tribune.* In 1964 Clay S. Felker became the editor, and in 1967 he bought the rights to the name. With his partner, the graphic designer Milton Glaser, he launched *New York* as an independent magazine in the following year: they mixed humor and seriousness in a format that emphasized graphics and typography and made the magazine one of the most widely imitated publications of its time. In the first issues it printed stories on subjects as diverse as celebrity watching in the Hamptons (by Jimmy Breslin) and the conditions of skid row (by Tom Wolfe). Felker supported efforts by Wolfe and others to propound a style of writing known as "new journalism," which employed the tone and descriptive techniques of fiction writing. Nicholas Pileggi, who became a contributing editor in 1968, wrote investigative pieces on corruption in city government and organized crime. The magazine became known for its opinionated and at times sardonic tone. Among its more popular writers were Breslin; Gloria Steinem; Pete Hamill; Gael Greene, who used sensual images in her restaurant reviews; and the theater critic John Simon. In January 1977 the magazine was bought by the Australian newspaper magnate Rupert Murdoch, who merged it in 1980 with *Cue,* a weekly guide to cultural events and entertainment. In 1991 Murdoch sold it to K-III Communications, a group headed by Henry Kravis, and in 2003 Bruce Wasserstein bought it for $55 million. The magazine has won numerous awards and has a popular Web site.

Rachel Sawyer

New York Manumission Society. Organization established in 1785 to promote the abolition of slavery in New York State. The group was founded as the New-York Society for Promoting the Manumission of Slaves, and Protecting Such of Them as Have Been, or May Be Liberated. It was composed of prominent white men such as John Jay, Alexander Hamilton, and James Duane. Some were members of the Religious Society of Friends, or Quakers, which opposed slavery, while other members were slaveowners themselves, including the organization's first president, John Jay. Perhaps influenced by this, the organization advocated gradual rather than immediate abolition. The society was successful in pressing the New York State legislature for the passage of the 1799 Gradual Emancipation Law. It also encouraged individual slaveowners to manumit their slaves voluntarily, provided legal representation to slaves seeking manumission, and protected blacks from kidnappers wanting to sell them elsewhere. In 1787 the society opened the first of seven AFRICAN FREE SCHOOLS for free and slave black children in New York City. It wanted to provide education for black children as well as prepare them for what it viewed as the responsibilities of freedom. The schools educated thousands of children until 1834, when they became part of the New York City public school system. The Manumission Society continued its work even after slavery in New York had been abolished. As the society's importance diminished, it dissolved in 1849 and had its assets transferred to the Association for the Benefit of Colored Orphans.

David N. Gellman, *Emancipating New York: The Politics of Slavery and Freedom, 1777–1827* (Baton Rouge: Louisiana State University Press, 2006)

Maurita Baldock

New York Medical College. Medical school formed in 1860 as the New York Homoeopathic Medical College at Third Avenue and 20th Street. The first president of its board of trustees was the poet William Cullen Bryant, a long-time advocate of homoeopathy. Although the college was the first in the city with a homoeopathic orientation, it was receptive from the outset to traditional (allopathic) medical practice. Early in its history the college had its own teaching hospital (Metropolitan Hospital), and it also maintained clinical facilities at Hahnemann Hospital (later reorganized as Fifth Avenue Hospital), Flower Hospital, and Ward's Island Hospital. A pioneer in women's medical education, in 1918 the college absorbed the New York Medical College for Women (founded in 1863). By the 1920s the college no longer offered instruction in homoeopathy, and in 1936 it assumed its current name. In 1938 it became part of an institution known as New York Medical College, Flower and Fifth Avenue Hospitals. The college moved in 1972 to suburban Westchester County, while maintaining its affiliations with clinical teaching hospitals in the city.

Leonard P. Wershub, *One Hundred Years of Medical Progress: A History of New York Medical College, Flower and Fifth Avenue Hospitals* (Springfield, Ill.: Charles C. Thomas, 1967)

Francesco Cordasco

New York Medical Repository. Medical and scientific journal, the first in the United States, launched in 1797 by Samuel Latham Mitchill and Elihu Smith, both physicians of New York City, and published quarterly. The contents were edited primarily by Mitchill and reflected his wide-ranging interests in medicine, chemistry, biology, botany, zoology, mineralogy, agriculture, geography, and meteorology. Each issue included original scientific essays, weather observations, news of scholarly work in Europe, and book reviews. Mitchill was particularly interested in the prevention of epidemics; Smith, a physician at New York Hospital, died in an epidemic during the journal's first year, and another collaborator, Edward Miller, who was a resident physician for the city, died in an epidemic in 1812. Mitchill retired in 1821 and the journal ended publication in 1824.

Sandra Opdycke

New York Mercantile Exchange [NYMEX]. Commodities and futures exchange formed in 1872 as the Butter and Cheese Exchange by a group of wholesale grocery merchants on the West Side of Manhattan, and given its current name in 1882. It moved in 1886 to the corner of Hudson and Harrison streets. In the early years, trading in eggs, butter, and other foodstuffs was mostly in cash; futures in butter and eggs were traded as early as 1903. Potato futures were introduced in 1941 and soon dominated trading. During the 1960s and 1970s NYMEX sought to increase its volume by offering trading in more futures and in new commodities such as platinum. It introduced a highly successful contract in heating-oil futures in 1978, and eventually it came to play an important role in setting oil prices around the world. In 1977 NYMEX moved to 4 World Trade Center. In 1994 it merged with the New York Commodities Exchange (COMEX) and in 1997 moved to its current

New York Mercantile Exchange, 1850

World Financial Center location at 1 North End Avenue. On 17 November 2006 the parent company NYMEX Holdings began trading publicly on the New York Stock Exchange.

George Winslow

New York Metropolitans. Baseball team. Formed in September 1880, the team competed in the American Association from 1883 to 1887 and played its home games at the Polo Grounds. After winning the championship of their league in 1884, the Metropolitans lost three consecutive games to the Providence Grays of the National League in a playoff that some baseball historians describe as the first World Series. The Metropolitans were owned by John B. Day, a businessman who also controlled the New York Giants of the National League. Day's sale of the Metropolitans to Erastus Wiman in 1885 was unsuccessfully challenged by the American Association, which sought to expel the club. After a court blocked the expulsion Wiman sold the team to the Brooklyn Trolley-Dodgers of the American Association in 1887. Although this sale marked the end of the Metropolitans, their name was revived in 1962 when the New York Mets joined the National League.

George B. Kirsch

New York Metropolitan Transportation Council [NYMTC]. Metropolitan planning organization responsible for coordinating and allocating federal transportation funds in the tri-state region. It was created in 1982 after the Tri-State Regional Planning Commission was dissolved. NYMTC absorbed the remaining staff and files of Tri-State, focusing on the downstate New York area including New York City and five of its 26 suburban counties—Nassau, Suffolk, Westchester, Putnam, and Rockland. Each suburban county, New York State (Department of Transportation), New York City (Department of Transportation and City Planning Commission), and the Metropolitan Transportation Authority have representatives on the council, and current rules call for voting by consensus. Nonvoting members include the Port Authority of New York and New Jersey, New Jersey Transit, the North Jersey Transportation Planning Authority, the New York State Department of Environmental Conservation, the Federal Highway Administration, the Federal Transit Administration, and the U.S. Environmental Protection Agency. NYMTC has continued many of the transportation planning programs begun by Tri-State, although at a less ambitious level of detail. The terrorist attacks of 11 September 2001 destroyed NYMTC's offices and files, and three staff members died. The agency has since operated out of new headquarters in lower Manhattan.

George Haikalis

New York Mets. Professional baseball team, formed as one of two new teams in the National League in 1962. New York City received the franchise largely through the efforts of William A. Shea, who was charged by Mayor Robert F. Wagner with bringing a team to the city after the Brooklyn Dodgers and the New York Giants left for California in 1957. Joan Whitney Payson was the principal owner of the new team, which played its first two seasons at the Polo Grounds in upper Manhattan (former home of the Giants). It chose as its colors blue (to represent the Dodgers) and orange (to represent the Giants) and as its logotype a stylized rendering of the city's skyline. During its first season the team compiled a record of 40 wins and 120 losses, second worst in the history of the major leagues, and it fared little better during the years immediately following. It saw itself through this trying period by cultivating an image of likable ineptness and relying on the showmanship of its manager, Casey Stengel. In 1964 the team moved to Shea Stadium in Queens, a venue more accessible to residents of the suburbs, and in 1965 Wes Westrum replaced Stengel as the manager. By this time a number of fine players were emerging from the team's farm system, including outfielders Cleon Jones and Ron Swoboda, shortstop Bud Harrelson, and pitchers Tom Seaver, Jerry Koosman, Jim McAndrew, Nolan Ryan, and Gary Gentry. The team also acquired outfielder Tommy Agee and the first baseman Donn Clendenon through trades. Gil Hodges, who had played first base for the team early in its history, managed the team from 1968 to 1972.

The Mets in 1969 accomplished a feat with few parallels in professional sports. Having failed in each of its first seven seasons to win as many games as it lost or to finish higher than ninth among 10 teams, the team overtook the Chicago Cubs late in the season to win the championship of the Eastern Division, winning 100 games and losing 62. The team then defeated the Atlanta Braves for the National League pennant in three games and won the World Series in five games against the heavily favored Baltimore Orioles. The feeling of optimism and confidence generated in New York City by the Mets' victory is widely regarded as having helped to reelect Mayor John V. Lindsay. The Mets remained competitive for the next five years, winning the National League pennant in 1973 under manager Yogi Berra before losing the World Series to the Oakland Athletics in seven games.

The Mets foundered under lackluster ownership after Payson's death in 1975. The decision to trade Seaver to the Cincinnati Reds in 1977 is considered the low point in the team's history. Managed by Berra, Joe Frazier (1976–77), Joe Torre (1977–81), George Bamberger (1982–83), and Frank Howard (1983), the Mets between 1974 and 1983 finished last five times and next to last three times. Rebuilding began in 1980, when publisher Nelson Doubleday and real estate executive Fred Wilpon bought the team. Wilpon became the team's sole owner in 2002. A new general manager, Frank Cashen, assembled a powerful team by combining players developed through the farm system, notably Dwight Gooden, Darryl Strawberry, and Wally Backman, with others, such as Keith Hernandez, Gary Carter, and Howard Johnson, acquired through trades. The team was competitive between 1984 and 1990 under manager Davey Johnson, winning 108 games and the World Series in 1986 and the Eastern Division of the National League in 1988. The Mets rallied on their last strike in the sixth game of the 1986 World Series to overcome a two-run lead by the Boston Red Sox.

The Mets underwent a sharp decline during the early 1990s, finishing last in the Eastern Division in 1993 (59 wins, 103 losses). Bud Harrelson replaced Johnson as the manager in 1990. Jeff Torborg (1991–93), Dallas Green

(1993–96), Bobby Valentine (1996–2002), Art Howe (2003–4), and Willie Randolph (2005–) subsequently managed the team. Under Valentine, the Mets won two consecutive Wild Cards in 1999 and 2000. Led by pitcher Al Leiter and catcher Mike Piazza, the team defeated the Arizona Diamondbacks, three games to one, in the 1999 National League Divisional Series before losing to the Atlanta Braves in the League Championship Series, four games to two. After winning the National League pennant in 2000, the Mets lost the 2000 World Series, the first Subway Series since 1956, to the crosstown Yankees. A Mets 3–2 victory over the Atlanta Braves 10 days after the terrorist attacks of 11 September 2001, highlighted by Mike Piazza's eighth-inning home run, is seen as beginning the city's comeback after the tragedy.

In the mid-2000s general manager Omar Minaya built the Mets around Latino players Carlos Beltran, Pedro Martinez, and Jose Reyes, who along with Tom Glavine, Billy Wagner, and David Wright signed long-term contracts. Shea Stadium, the site of seven Mets postseason appearances and a staging area for relief efforts after 9/11, was replaced on the same site in 2009 by Citi Field, designed to resemble Ebbets Field, home of the Brooklyn Dodgers until 1957.

Leonard Koppett, *The New York Mets: The Whole Story,* 2nd edn (New York: Collier Books, 1974); Peter Simon and Jack Lang, *The New York Mets: Twenty-Five Years of Baseball Magic* (New York: Henry Holt, 1986); Jimmy Breslin, *Can't Anybody Here Play This Game?* (New York: Penguin, 1963; repr. 2003); Bruce Markusen, *Tales from the Mets Dugout* (Champaign, Ill.: Sports Publishing, 2007).

Harold S. Wechsler

New York Mothers' Home of the Sisters of Misericordia. Original name of Our Lady of Mercy Medical Center.

New York Nautical Training School. Original name of the Maritime College.

New York Naval Shipyard. Official name of the Brooklyn Navy Yard.

New York/New Jersey Metrostars. Major League Soccer team in New York City, renamed the New York Red Bulls in 2005.

New York Newsday. Daily newspaper launched in 1985. Its parent newspaper, *Newsday,* was founded in 1940 in Hempstead, Long Island, by Alicia Petterson, who as the editor and publisher shaped it into a tabloid best known for its local investigative reporting. The newspaper began expanding its circulation into New York City after being purchased by the Times–Mirror Company in 1970. *New York Newsday* maintains its own headquarters in Manhattan and a separate editorial staff. In 2004 it was revealed that beginning in 2000 the newspaper had inflated its circulation numbers by more than 100,000 copies. In 2006 its daily circulation was more than 400,000, and it was home to several widely read columnists, including Sydney Schanberg, Murray Kempton, Jimmy Breslin, and Liz Smith.

Robert F. Keeler, *Newsday: A Candid History of the Respectable Tabloid* (New York: William Morrow, 1990)

Madeline Rogers

New York Newspaper Guild. Labor organization formed in New York City in November 1933; its members elected Allen Raymond of the *New York Herald Tribune* their first president and Heywood Broun of the *New York World–Telegram* their vice president. The organization was instrumental in forming the American Newspaper Guild.

Michael Green

New York Observer (i). Weekly newspaper launched on 17 May 1823 by Sidney E. Morse and Richard C. Morse and published until 30 May 1912. It reflected Presbyterian orthodoxy and was the first religious newspaper published in New York City. Soon after it began publication the newspaper began a fervent campaign against the city's theaters. For many years it was edited by Samuel Irenaeus Prime, who published a popular series of letters under the pseudonym "Irenaeus" and exploited anti-Catholic sentiment among evangelical Protestants. By mid-century he broadened the scope of the newspaper beyond a denominational readership. The founders of the newspaper, sons of the geographer Jedidiah Morse, introduced in 1839 a wax-engraving technique suitable for printing maps. Their brother, the artist and inventor Samuel F. B. Morse, was a contributor to the *Observer;* his letter from Paris published on 20 April 1839 was the first American report of the daguerreotype.

Mariam Touba

New York Observer (ii). Weekly newspaper launched in 1987 by investment banker Arthur L. Carter. Printed on peach-colored paper in a broadsheet format, it aimed to offer bold, irreverent coverage of cultural, social, political, and business life in New York City. The newspaper catered unabashedly to the wealthy and powerful elite of Manhattan. It became well-known for its regular columns on politics by Joe Conason and Terry Golway, on the arts by Hilton Kramer, on nightlife by Rex Reed, and on film by Andrew Sarris; it also published Candace Bushnell's column "Sex and the City," on which a popular television series of the same name was based. In 2006 Carter sold the *Observer* to Jared Kushner, a graduate student in business and law at New York University. In 2007 Kushner transformed the newspaper from a broadsheet to a tabloid. In 2010 the *Observer* had a paid circulation of 52,000.

James Bradley

New York One [NY1]. Twenty-four-hour local news channel owned by Time Warner. Richard Aurelio of Time Warner founded the channel in 1991 and became its first president; it began broadcasting in 1992 in a studio at 460 West 42nd Street. In 2002 NY1 moved to new studios in the Chelsea Market Building at 75 Ninth Avenue.

Kate Lauber

New York Palace. Luxury hotel on Madison Avenue between 50th and 51st streets, designed by the firm of Emery Roth and Sons

Interior of the New York Palace Hotel, 1980

and completed in 1986; it is built over the Villard Houses, a palazzo designed by the firm of McKim, Mead and White in 1882. Known as the Helmsley Palace from 1981 to 1992, the hotel has 55 stories, 962 rooms, a courtyard facing Madison Avenue, and a facade of dark bronzed glass and anodized aluminum; its two-story marble lobby was designed by Tom Lee. Four antique Florentine lanterns adorn the main entrance, and two tiers of nineteenth-century bronze and glass marquees overhang the other two. The great hall of the palazzo is known for its spectacular features, including a red Verona marble fireplace in the grand foyer of the upper lobby (designed by Augustus Saint-Gaudens) and a clock decorated with the signs of the zodiac (Saint-Gaudens and Stanford White). Some of the most elegant rooms are the Drawing Room and the Madison Room, designed by White for the newspaper publisher Whitelaw Reid. In 2007 renovation was completed, transforming the fourth and fifth floors of the Villard Houses into a luxurious 13,000-square-foot (1200-square-meter) venue dubbed the Mansion Rooms.

Janet Frankston

New York Peace Society. Forerunner of the AMERICAN PEACE SOCIETY.

New York Philharmonic. Oldest orchestra in the United States. Officially the Philharmonic-Symphony Society of New York, it was formed in 1842 as the Philharmonic Society, a cooperative organization of musicians led by conductor Ureli Corelli Hill. The first concert took place on 7 December in the Apollo Rooms on lower Broadway, with 63 musicians performing before an audience of 600; the concert began with Hill conducting Beethoven's Symphony no. 5. German music and musicians dominated the orchestra in its early years, during which the conductor's post was shared by several men, chiefly Theodore Eisfeld and Carl Bergmann. During 1877–78 and 1879–91 performances were brought to a virtuoso level by the German-born Theodore Thomas. His successor Anton Seidl (1891–98) was a conductor of Wagner whose Romantic interpretations inspired both adulation and controversy.

After a group of wealthy patrons formed the Guarantors' Committee in 1909, the orchestra enjoyed financial stability. The guarantors were responsible for engaging Gustav Mahler as the principal conductor of the orchestra and for expanding the performance season. Under the leadership of Josef Stransky (1911–23) the orchestra broadened its repertory to include works by American composers as well as new Europeans such as Debussy, Schoenberg, and Stravinsky and made its first commercial recording in January 1917. Willem Mengelberg first conducted the orchestra in 1921; during his tenure concerts were also conducted by Stravinsky, Wilhelm Furtwängler, and ARTURO TOSCANINI. The orchestra absorbed several others: in 1921 the National Symphony Orchestra (formed as the New Symphony in 1919), in 1923 the City Symphony Orchestra (formed in 1922), and in 1928 the Symphony Society of New York (formed in 1878 by Leopold Damrosch). This period marked the beginning of an expanded educational program, radio broadcasts (1922), summer concerts at Lewisohn Stadium (1922), and children's concerts under the direction of Ernest Schelling (1924).

Toscanini became the conductor of the newly combined orchestra in 1929. Nationwide radio broadcasts began in 1930 and continued until 1967. From 1936 the orchestra was led principally by John Barbirolli and Artur Rodzinski (to 1947), whose assistant conductor LEONARD BERNSTEIN made a spectacular debut leading the orchestra as a substitute for Bruno Walter. The years following Rodzinski's resignation were dominated by Walter, Leopold Stokowski, Dimitri Mitropoulos, and Bernstein (from 1957), whose tenure was a period of great change and growth. Two television series were begun in 1958, and in 1962 the orchestra left Carnegie Hall after 69 years and moved to Philharmonic Hall (now Avery Fisher Hall) at Lincoln Center. In 1964 it became the first American orchestra to offer a year-round contract to its members, leading to expanded programming. In the autumn of 1969 Bernstein was given the orchestra's first lifetime position of laureate conductor. Pierre Boulez, the music director from 1971, became known for his emphasis on twentieth-century music and his innovative programming. Zubin Mehta, music director from 1978 to 1991, specialized in late Romantic composers. Kurt Masur became the music director in September 1991; he was succeeded by Lorin Maazel in 2002, who was himself succeeded in 2009 by Alan Gilbert. In the early twenty-first century the orchestra continued to support contemporary composers, commissioning and performing John Adams's Pulitzer Prize–winning *On the Transmigration of Souls,* a piece inspired by the terrorist attacks of 11 September 2001. In 2006 it led other major orchestras in the digital age as the first to produce downloadable concerts. The New York Philharmonic has 106 permanent musicians and performs about 180 concerts a season; it has performed more than 14,000 concerts since its founding.

Walter Damrosch, *My Musical Life* (New York: Charles Scribner's Sons, 1923); Howard Shanet, *Philharmonic: A History of New York's Orchestra* (Garden City, N.Y.: Doubleday, 1975); Vera Brodsky Lawrence, *Strong on Music: The New York Music Scene in the Days of George Templeton Strong, 1836–1875,* vol. 1, *Resonances, 1836–1850* (New York: Oxford University Press, 1988); Vera Brodsky Lawrence, *Strong on Music: The New York Music Scene in the Days of George Templeton Strong, 1836–1875,* vol. 2, *Reverberations, 1850–1856* (Chicago: University of Chicago Press, 1995)

Barbara Haws

Music Directors, Music Advisers, and Principal Conductors of the New York Philharmonic

Term	Name
1842–49	Ureli Corelli Hill, Henry Timm, Alfred Boucher, Louis Wiegers, Denis Etienne, William Alpers, George Loder
1849–54	Theodore Eisfeld
1854–55	Theodore Eisfeld and Henry Timm
1855–56	Carl Bergmann
1856–58	Theodore Eisfeld
1858–59	Carl Bergmann
1859–65	Theodore Eisfeld and Carl Bergmann
1965–76	Carl Bergmann
1876–77	Leopold Damrosch
1877–78	Theodore Thomas
1878–79	Adolph Neuendorff
1879–91	Theodore Thomas
1891–98	Anton Seidl
1898–1902	Emil Paur
1902–3	Walter Damrosch
1906–9	Wassily Safanoff [Vasily Safonov]
1909–11	Gustav Mahler
1911–23	Josef Stransky
1922–28	Willem Mengelberg
1928–36	Arturo Toscanini
1936–42	John Barbirolli (began as a guest conductor)
1943–47	Artur Rodzinski
1947–49	Bruno Walter (adviser)
1949–50	Leopold Stokowski (co-principal conductor)
1949–58	Dimitri Mitropoulos
1958–69	Leonard Bernstein
1969–70	George Szell (adviser)
1971–77	Pierre Boulez
1978–91	Zubin Mehta
1991–2002	Kurt Masur
2002–9	Lorin Maazel
2009–	Alan Gilbert

New York Pops. Largest independent symphonic orchestra in the country. Founded in 1983 by SKITCH HENDERSON, the Pops employs 77 musicians and performs popular American music, including works by Leonard Bernstein, Irving Berlin, Aaron Copland, Duke Ellington, George Gershwin, and Cole Porter. In 1990 the orchestra began free education programs in New York City public schools. Its annual series is held at Carnegie

Hall, and its Summermusic concerts are performed throughout the city.

Kate Lauber

New York Port of Embarkation. Military command during World War II. Between 1942 and 1945 it organized the shipping overseas of three million U.S. soldiers and their equipment and more than 63 million tons of additional war supplies. Its facilities included a complex network of railroad lines, highways, waterways, wharves, and warehouses. At its peak in 1944 the port comprised 10 terminals and three areas for staging troops and employed more than 55,000 men and women. Its three principal facilities were the Brooklyn Army Terminal, where the commander of the port, Major General Homer M. Groninger, had his headquarters; Bush Terminal, which extended from 28th to 50th streets along First and Second avenues in Brooklyn and comprised 26 eight-story warehouses built between 1895 and 1926; and Staten Island Terminal. Together these terminals handled about half the wartime shipments from the port. Other facilities on Staten Island included Fox Hills Terminal and Howland Hook Terminal, the principal point from which petroleum, oil, and lubricants were shipped. In Manhattan the North River Terminal, at 12th Avenue and 46th Street, was an important point of embarkation for troops. Seven piers on the Hudson River permitted the loading of troop ships and ocean liners. The Army Postal Terminal, at 464 Lexington Avenue in Manhattan, handled more than three billion pieces of mail during the war. Across the harbor in New Jersey were the terminals of Port Johnson and Claremont. The Special Service Supply Terminal had offices in Manhattan and Brooklyn. Troops bound overseas were routed into the port from three staging areas: Camp Kilmer (New Brunswick, New Jersey), Camp Shanks (Orangeburg, New York), and Fort Hamilton (Brooklyn).

Joseph F. Meany, Jr.

New York Post. Daily newspaper. Launched in 1801 by Alexander Hamilton as the *Evening Post* with William Coleman as its first editor, it was produced in offices on Pine Street and published shipping notices and anti-Jeffersonian invective. Coleman was succeeded on his death in 1829 by William Cullen Bryant, under whose guidance the newspaper abandoned its conservative politics and broadened its appeal. During the party realignments of the 1820s and 1830s it supported Andrew Jackson and the Democratic Party, and opposed high tariffs, the Bank of the United States, and the nullification acts of South Carolina. Bryant tempered the blustery, radical brand of Jacksonianism embraced by his associate William Leggett (to 1836), and avoided the sensationalism of the penny press, notably the *Herald* of James Gordon Bennett, Sr. With his later associate John Bigelow (from 1848) he opposed slavery and expressed frustration with the Democrats for equivocating on the issue. In 1850 the offices of the newspaper were moved to the corner of Liberty and Nassau streets. Bigelow introduced a broad range of new issues through a weekly column of fictional interviews with a "Jersey ferryman" that related political gossip, and in 1851 he published an exposé of Jared Sparks's sanitized edition of George Washington's correspondence.

In 1855 the *Post* became a supporter of the Republican Party. Bigelow left the newspaper in 1860 and was replaced by Charles Nordhoff, who supported Abraham Lincoln and advocated the vigorous prosecution of the Civil War. During the draft riots (1863) he wrote an account of 8000 words suggesting that the riots had been instigated by Copperhead Democrats, and after attaching a hose to the steam boiler of the newspaper's offices he threatened to repel attackers with blasts of scalding water. After the war Bryant and Nordhoff backed President Andrew Johnson's mild Reconstruction program and the 14th Amendment, and opposed Johnson's impeachment and a silver-based monetary system. The offices of the *Post* were moved to Broadway and Fulton Street in 1875, at a time when the newspaper was faring well commercially. Bryant died in 1878 and was succeeded as the chief editor of the newspaper by his son-in-law Parke Godwin. In 1881 the newspaper was purchased by Henry Villard, who installed the editorial triumvirate of Horace White, E. L. Godkin, and Carl Schurz. Under their leadership the newspaper continued to oppose free silver and supported lower tariffs and civil service reform. As the sole editor from 1883 Godkin waged a relentless attack against Tammany Hall: in 1890 he published a series of scathing biographical sketches of its leaders, whom he described as "liquor-dealers," "pugilists," "dive-keepers," and "convicted murderers."

The Villard family relinquished control of the *Post* in 1917, which under the ownership of Thomas Lamont (1917–22) and Cyrus Curtis (from 1924) became a forum for more conservative views. The political perspective changed again in 1936 when the newspaper was bought by J. David Stern, a supporter of the New Deal. By this time the newspaper was declining in profitability, and when Dorothy Schiff assumed control in 1939 it ranked third in circulation among afternoon newspapers in the city. In an effort to attract readers Schiff and her third husband, Theodore O. Thackrey, emphasized scandal and human-interest stories, and in 1942 the format was changed from broadsheet to tabloid. James A. Wechsler, the chief editor from 1949, crusaded for civil liberties, attacked Senator Joseph R. McCarthy, and was himself attacked for his early association with the Young Communist League; in 1954 vandals splashed red paint on the newspaper's building on West Street. Paul Sann assumed the editorship in 1961 and increased coverage of crime and sports.

By 1967 the *New York Post* was the only afternoon newspaper left in the city. It benefited little from the demise of its competitors, because the same demographic and cultural changes that had driven them out of business were hurting the *Post* as well. Financial losses led Schiff to sell the newspaper in 1976 to the Australian press magnate Rupert Murdoch, who sought to replace the newspaper's traditional readership, which was largely white, middle class, and aging, with a newer one that was racially diverse, working class, and young. Murdoch introduced marked changes: a stridently conservative editorial stance, frequent blurring of the distinction between reporting and opinion, sensationalistic and at times smirking coverage of crime, sex, accidents, scandal, and celebrities, and deliberately outrageous headlines, of which perhaps the most memorable was "Headless Body in Topless Bar." The newspaper also ran sweepstakes that it promoted aggressively, and within a few years circulation increased sharply. The *Post* nevertheless remained unprofitable, largely because of its inability to sell display advertising to large retailers (who recognized that most readers of the *Post* also read other newspapers, and therefore believed that advertising in the *Post* was redundant). Murdoch lost about $150 million by 1988, when he was forced to sell the newspaper because of a federal regulation barring common ownership of television stations and newspapers in the same market. The *Post* was purchased by the real estate investor Peter Kalikow, who won $22 million in concessions from the newspaper's labor unions. Kalikow in turn sold the newspaper in 1993 when he became bankrupt. Granted a waiver of the regulation that had forced him to sell the newspaper years before, Murdoch again became the owner in 1993. In 2000 it cut its price from 50 cents to 25 cents. As of 2009 it had 508,000 weekday readers and 343,000 Sunday readers. It is the only paper in the United States to have published daily for 200 years continuously.

Allan Nevins, *The Evening Post: A Century of Journalism* (New York: Boni and Liveright, 1922); James A. Wechsler, *The Age of Suspicion* (New York: Random House, 1953); Charles H. Brown, *William Cullen Bryant* (New York: Charles Scribner's Sons, 1971); Jeffrey Potter, *Men, Money, and Magic: The Story of Dorothy Schiff* (New York: Coward, McCann and Geoghegan, 1976)

Robert Stinson

New York Presbyterian Hospital. First academic medical center in the world to combine a major hospital with a medical school. It resulted from an affiliation spearheaded by

Edward S. Harkness between Presbyterian Hospital and Columbia University's College of Physicians and Surgeons in 1911 to advance medical care, education, and research. However, intensive planning did not begin on the center until after the hospital and university signed a second affiliation agreement in 1922. The center opened in 1928 in Washington Heights between 165th and 168th streets and between Broadway and Fort Washington Avenue on 22 acres (9 hectares) donated by Harkness and his mother, Mrs. Stephen Harkness, along with construction funds. Presbyterian Hospital moved into a facility with 694 beds that included the Harkness Pavilion (150 private-room beds) and the Squier Urological Clinic. Its affiliates—the New York State Psychiatric Institute and Hospital, Sloane Hospital for Women, Vanderbilt Clinic, Babies Hospital, and the Neurological Institute—also moved into new facilities in Washington Heights. In 1933 the center opened the Institute of Ophthalmology with 100 beds; this was integrated with the Herman Knapp Memorial Eye Hospital in 1939. The Mary Harkness Convalescent Home was opened in Port Chester in 1937 on land donated to the center. In 1938 the center added an additional 7.5 acres (3 hectares) to its property holdings between 163rd and 165th streets between Fort Washington Avenue and Riverside Drive. To meet the demand for semiprivate beds, the Harkness Pavilion was enlarged to accommodate an additional 500 beds. As a result of negotiations begun in 1940 with the city for a cancer hospital, the Francis Delafield Hospital, a 300-bed facility funded by the city, opened in 1950 at the center. The New York Orthopaedic Dispensary and Hospital, affiliated with Presbyterian Hospital from 1945, moved to the center in 1950. Expansion continued with the opening of the Millstein Pavilion (1988) and the Allen Pavilion (1989). Along with the College of Physicians and Surgeons, the center is home to Columbia University's Mailman School of Public Health, College of Dental and Oral Surgery, and School of Nursing. By the 1980s the center was the leading organ transplant center in the Northeast, a federally designated comprehensive cancer center, and renowned for its neonatal care and work with patients suffering from Parkinson disease. By the mid-1990s, Columbia–Presbyterian Medical Center was the largest hospital in New York City, with 1548 beds, and as many as 35 percent of its patients were from outside the city. Clinical advances made by Columbia faculty include the blood test for cancer, medical use of the laser, and successful transfer of genes from one cell to another. To fulfill the center's research mission, affiliated research centers are located on the campus that also receive funding from government agencies, corporations, and private benefactors. They focus on research in molecular neurobiology; cancer; diabetes; nutrition; sickle cell anemia; biotechnology; aging brain, Alzheimer disease, and other degenerative neurological conditions; immunology; and rheumatology. In 1997 the New York–Presbyterian Healthcare System was formed with the merger of the Cornell and Columbia medical centers and New York and Presbyterian Hospitals and the network of all their affiliated hospitals in the tri-state region to create one of the most comprehensive hospitals in the world. A merger between the two hospitals and medical centers had been explored approximately 70 years earlier (1916) and rejected. In 2003 the center was renamed Columbia University Medical Center. In its 2009–10 Honor Roll, *U.S. News and World Report* ranked New York–Presbyterian University Hospitals of Columbia and Cornell as sixth best in the nation, with top rankings in the country for kidney disease, neurology and neurosurgery, psychiatry, gynecology, endocrinology, urology, cardiology, orthopedics, and pediatrics.

Jane E. Mottus

New York Press Club. Professional organization of members and former members of the news media. Originally formed in 1872 as the New York Journalistic Fraternity, it was incorporated in 1874 under its current name. Its activities included charity work as well as banquets and shows at which such speakers as Governor Alfred E. Smith and Mayor James J. Walker appeared. The club disbanded in 1933 after going into receivership but was revived in 1948. In the twenty-first century it sponsors debates and speeches, aids reporters charged with libel or contempt, and works to protect the freedom of the press, publicize election debates, and recognize excellence in journalism. It hosts an annual award ceremony to recognize all branches of media and publishes *Byline Magazine* annually. Its headquarters are at 1636 Third Avenue.

Michael Green

New York Printers' Union. Original name of New York Typographical Union no. 6.

New York Produce Exchange. Commodities market formed in 1861 as the New York Commercial Association by merchants and ship brokers who gathered outside the Merchants' Exchange; it was renamed in 1868. It was at first a cash spot market: merchants based their transactions on samples from individual lots of grain rather than on inspection, grades, and negotiable warehouse receipts (the system used in Chicago). Members included agents of European firms buying for shipment abroad, often through other ports. The leaders of the exchange overcame the resistance of exporters and in 1874 established trading "pits" for transactions in inspected and graded grains. From 1885 the exchange was housed in a building at 2 Broadway. As the nation's leading export market for wheat, flour, lard, and cottonseed oil, the exchange attracted many respected merchants. In the 1870s Franklin Edson, later mayor of New York City, was its president for three terms. Shrinking foreign trade after 1920 forced the exchange to broaden its scope and offer both spot and futures trading in such commodities as hay, hops, butter, and cheese. Later retrenchment confined its operations by the

New York Produce Exchange, 1890

1950s to trading in cottonseed oil, tallow, fishmeal, and pepper. After several years of heavy losses, the New York Produce Exchange was reorganized in 1973 into a real estate investment trust, and its commodities business was taken over by other exchanges.

Morton Rothstein

New York Public Library at Seventh Avenue, ca *1910*

New York Public Library [NYPL]. Library formed in 1895 by the consolidation of the Astor and Lenox libraries and the Tilden Trust. New York City had no major library when John Jacob Astor provided a bequest of $400,000 for a library in the 1830s. In 1854 the Astor Library was erected on Astor Place on a noncirculating basis open to the public free of charge. Although members of the Astor family continued to make contributions, the library often suffered financial difficulties. James Lenox (1800–80) transferred land and his collection of books and art to the Lenox Library, incorporated in 1870. Opened in 1877 in a building designed by Richard Morris Hunt, the library was used primarily for art exhibitions, and its books were so poorly cataloged that they could not easily be consulted. Under public pressure the library gradually extended its hours and eased its admission policies even as it faced recurrent financial problems. In 1886 Samuel J. Tilden, the former Democratic governor and presidential candidate, left the city a trust to set up a free library. Family members contested the will and were awarded the entire estate by a court decision in 1891, but one heir donated Tilden's personal library and more than $2 million to the trust. Negotiations to merge the trust and the Astor Library were eventually extended to include the Lenox Library; they ended on 23 May 1895 with the formation of the New York Public Library, Astor, Lenox and Tilden Foundations, a private institution open to the public.

Confronted with the task of building a strong institution from two weak ones, the board of trustees appointed as their first director John S. Billings, a former army surgeon who had built the country's foremost medical library. He combined the often inaccessible Astor and Lenox collections into the reference department, a major noncirculating research library intended as a library of record. Maintained by the Astor, Lenox, and Tilden endowments, it was especially strong in Americana, English and American literature, music, dance, theater, foreign languages, and genealogy and had comprehensive collections of illustrated books, periodicals, government publications, maps, and newspapers. Billings reorganized the staffs of the former libraries, built new collections, devised a unique classification scheme, and drew a sketch that became the basis for the main building at Fifth Avenue and 42nd Street, which was designed by John M. Carrère and Thomas Hastings and opened to the public on 23 May 1911. The trustees left open the possibility of adding neighborhood branches. The city's existing free libraries were small, independent institutions sponsored primarily by charitable and religious organizations to promote the moral, civic, and intellectual growth of immigrants and workers; they were popular but lacked coordination and financial support. The branches of the New York Free Circulating Library (formed 1878), the largest of the city's free libraries with 11 branches by 1899, were absorbed by NYPL in 1901 and converted into a circulation department.

A month after the circulation department was formed, Andrew Carnegie offered $5.2 million to erect 65 branches if the city would provide the sites and maintenance. The city agreed, and between 1902 and 1914, 37 branches operated by NYPL under contract with the city were built in Manhattan, the Bronx, and Staten Island. In 1906 the superintendent of work with children (now the office of children's services) was established, one of the first libraries to welcome children regardless of age. During the same year the superintendent of work with schools (now the office of young adult services) was also established, the first office of its kind in the United States. By 1921 there were 43 branches. Shifts in population placed new demands on the library: in such areas as the Lower East Side, where there were several branches, the population was decreasing, while in others such as the Bronx there were few libraries for a population that was rapidly expanding. Seven branches opened between the world wars, but inflation and a lack of municipal funds left some needs unmet. The library responded by opening 14 subbranches with abbreviated hours and deposit stations in community institutions and by providing "bookmobiles" to unserved areas of the Bronx and Staten Island. Severe strains developed during the Depression. Staff was furloughed, hours were shortened,

New York Public Library, 40th Street and Fifth Avenue, 1911

New York Public Library (designed by Carrère and Hastings), 42nd Street and 5th Avenue, ca *1945*

and book purchases declined. At the same time the reference department experienced such an increase in use that it became known as the "people's university." Some library operations were maintained in part by workers in federal relief programs.

After World War II the branch system demanded renovations and additions, forcing the library to seek new sources of income. During the 1940s it shifted its goals from large gifts to a greater number of small gifts in annual campaigns. It also revamped its administration, adding an office of adult services (1946) and departments of public relations and personnel. After 1950 state and city funding for the circulating department rose sharply. Between 1945 and 1956 the number of branches grew from 50 to 80, and they gave attention to such materials as films, discs, and tapes; developed radio and television programs for audiences of all ages; and expanded their range of free programs to include film screenings, concerts, dramatic readings, art exhibitions, and lectures. The branch libraries during the 1960s intensified their efforts in neighborhoods dominated by ethnic minorities. NYPL in 1965 established a Library for the Performing Arts at Lincoln Center (now the New York Public Library for the Performing Arts, Dorothy and Lewis B. Cullman Center). The reference department developed programs in book preservation, microfilming, exhibits, and bibliographic publications and was renamed the research libraries in 1966. In 1974 the library helped to form the Research Libraries Group, a cooperative for sharing resources.

In 1970 the first large circulation building opened in midtown Manhattan. The branch staffs were reduced by 20 percent in the early 1970s because of budget cuts, and the situation was exacerbated by high inflation and the city's fiscal crisis of the mid-1970s. From 1975 branch programs and hours were curtailed, deficits grew, and hours for the central building, until then open 84 hours a week, were reduced by nearly half. Finances improved in the late 1970s with an influx of funds from New York State, the federal government, and private contributors. Circulation and hours did not increase again until the early 1980s, and the system did not fully regain its earlier service levels. The appointment of Vartan Gregorian as president in 1981 was an important step toward revitalization. During his tenure the library renovated the central building and many branches, introduced new programs, reduced cataloging backlogs, increased hours, and successfully completed a campaign to raise $300 million. The research libraries continued to be supported primarily by private endowment, the branch libraries by the city.

Lack of space became a problem in the late twentieth and early twenty-first century. During the Bryant Park restoration of the late 1980s, a plan was formulated to expand stack space underneath the park, which is adjacent to the main library at 42nd Street and Fifth Avenue. Excavations began in 1988 and in 1991; 40 miles (64.3 kilometers) of subterranean shelf space were completed. Under Paul LeClerc, who became president of NYPL in 1993, the main library's space was further increased: its open-air courtyard was enclosed, and a six-story glass structure designed by Davis Brody Bond opened in its place in 2002. The addition, called South Court, added 40,000 square feet (3716 square meters) of classrooms, the 178-seat South Court Auditorium, and office space. In 2006, after renovations, the Bronx Library Center (formerly the Fordham Library Center) opened with greatly expanded facilities, including a 150-seat auditorium. In 2008 NYPL announced a $1 billion plan to transform the entire library system. Stephen A. Schwarzman, chairman of the Blackstone Group,

South Reading Room at the New York Public Library, 42nd Street and Fifth Avenue

donated $100 million toward the plan, the largest gift in the library's history. In recognition, the trustees renamed the main facility, the Humanities and Social Sciences Library at 42nd Street and Fifth Avenue, the Stephen A. Schwarzman Building. As part of the planned transformation, the Schwarzman Building will be renovated to include both circulating and reference collections; large hub libraries will be built in Manhattan, the Bronx, and Staten Island; and the library's online catalog and digital collections will be revamped.

The New York Public Library holds about 50 million items in its research and circulating collections. The Schwarzman Building houses research divisions and sections devoted to economics and public affairs; the history of the United States, local history, and genealogy; the humanities and social sciences; Judaica; the Far East; the Slavic and Baltic regions; periodicals; maps; and science and technology. Nearly one million rare items are held in the library's special collections, including the Miriam and Ira D. Wallach Division of Art, Prints, and Photographs; the Rare Books and Manuscripts Division; the Carl H. Pforzheimer Collection of Shelley and His Circle; the George Arents Collection on the History of Tobacco and Tobacco-Related Literature; the Spencer Collection of Illustrated Books, Illuminated Manuscripts, and Fine Bindings; and the Berg Collection of English and American Literature. In addition to the Schwarzman Building's main research collections and the Library for the Performing Arts, NYPL operates two other special research libraries: the Schomburg Center for Research in Black Culture, in Harlem, and the Science, Industry, and Business Library, on Madison Avenue and 34th Street. The library issues borrowers' cards to anyone who lives, works, or attends school in New York State. In the early twenty-first century there were 87 branch libraries containing seven million circulating items; 15 million people visited the library annually, and there were 1.86 million cardholders.

Harry Miller Lydenberg, *History of the New York Public Library* (New York: New York Public Library, 1923); Phyllis Dain, *The New York Public Library: History of Its Founding and Early Years* (New York: New York Public Library, 1972); Henry Hope Reed, *The New York Public Library: Its Architecture and Decoration* (New York: W. W. Norton, 1986)

Robert Sink

New York Public Library for the Performing Arts. Research center of the New York Public Library, opened at Lincoln Center in 1965. The Lincoln Center facility, now named the New York Public Library for the Performing Arts, Dorothy and Lewis B. Cullman Center, allowed the library to unite all its performing arts collections, which had previously functioned as separate units. It houses some nine million items and offers exhibitions and live events, including dance and music performances, panel discussions and lectures, films, and play readings. The research collections are devoted to dance, music, recorded sound, and theater. Among the holdings of the Jerome Robbins Dance Division are choreographic records, costume and set designs, photographs and moving images, and recorded interviews. It houses archives related to many eminent dance figures, including Vaslav Nijinsky, Agnes de Mille, and Merce Cunningham. The music division's resources range from classical music and opera to spirituals, jazz, and musical comedy, to rock and contemporary music. The division contains manuscripts of works by Bach, Mozart, and Beethoven, as well as more recent materials, such the extensive American Music Collection. The Rodgers and Hammerstein Archives of Recorded Sound include wax roll recordings of early twentieth-century Metropolitan Opera performances and Fiorello H. La Guardia's radio broadcasts. Staff undertake special recording projects to augment the collection. The Billy Rose Theatre Collection comprises approximately five million items related to the theatrical arts, including scripts, production designs, and more than 4500 video recordings of performances, documentaries, and interviews.

Helen Graves

New York Rangers. Ice hockey team formed on 15 May 1926, sometimes called the Broadway Blues. The team played its first game on 16 November 1926 in Madison Square Garden under the direction of Lester Patrick, the coach and manager. In 1928 it won the Stanley Cup after defeating the Montreal Maroons in five games; it also reached the Stanley Cup finals in 1929 and 1932 largely because of the efforts of Frank Boucher, Ivan "Ching" Johnson, and brothers Bill and Bun Cook. The team won the Stanley Cup in 1933 and again in 1940 when it defeated the Toronto Maple Leafs in six games: members of the team included Babe Pratt, Lynn Patrick, Art Coulter, Neil Colville, and Bryan Hextall. The Rangers finished first in the National Hockey League in 1941–42 and reached the finals in 1949–50, but they failed to win consistently again until 1965–66, when Emile Francis became the coach. During the 1960s and 1970s the team had such well-known players as Rod Gilbert, Jean Ratelle, Brad Park, Ed Giacomin, and Phil Esposito. The Rangers made the Stanley Cup finals in 1972 and 1979 and finished first in the Patrick Division in 1989–90 and 1991–92 but failed to win the league championship.

In 1994 players such as Brian Leetch, Adam Graves, Mark Messier, and Mike Richter led the team to its first Stanley Cup championship in 54 years after successively defeating the New York Islanders, the Washington Capitals, the New Jersey Devils, and the Vancouver Canucks. In 1996 the team signed hockey legend Wayne Gretzky for the final three years of his career. Beginning in 1998–99, the Rangers failed to make the playoffs for seven consecutive seasons until team captain Jarmoir Jagr and goalie Henrik Lundqvist led them back in 2005–6.

Stan Fischler, *New York Rangers: The Iceman Cometh* (Englewood Cliffs, N.J.: Prentice Hall, 1974)

James Duplacey

New York Red Bulls. Major League Soccer (MLS) team known as the New York/New Jersey MetroStars until it was bought and rebranded in March 2006 by Red Bull Company GmbH. The MetroStars played its first game as one of the league's original 10 teams on 13 April 1996 against the Los Angeles Galaxy at the Rose Bowl. The club had 10 managers during its first 11 years and compiled a 146–168–54 record. The team reached the MLS Cup semifinals in 2000 and was a runner-up in the 2003 U.S. Open Cup. The Red Bulls currently play home games in Red Bull Park, a 25,000-seat soccer-specific stadium in Harrison, New Jersey.

Joshua Robinson

New York Review of Books. Literary magazine, published every two weeks, launched as a book review by Robert Benjamin Silvers and Barbara Epstein during a newspaper strike in February 1963. Once jokingly called the "New York review of each other's books" by the historian Richard Hofstadter, it took up the cause of the New Left and was soon one of the most influential publications of its kind in academe. Its rise coincided with the decline of intellectuals of New York City as a cohesive group. The *Review* became known for publishing long, wide-ranging essays about several books. In the 1960s the magazine *Commentary* criticized it for publishing leftist material, particularly a detailed cover illustration of a "Molotov cocktail." Among frequent contributors were Noam Chomsky, Joan Didion, Theodore Draper, Stephen Jay Gould, Andrew Kopkind, Felix G. Rohatyn, and I. F. Stone, and the cartoonist David Levine. Over the years the *Review* evolved into a sober journal of ideas open to different political points of view and not strongly oriented toward writers from New York City. In the early twenty-first century its circulation was about 140,000.

Philip Nobile, *Intellectual Skywriting: Literary Politics and the New York Review of Books* (New York: Charterhouse, 1974)

Thomas E. Bird

New York Road Runners. Running organization founded on 4 June 1958 by some 40 dedicated long-distance runners who met at Macombs Dam Park in the Bronx. Its first president was Ted Corbitt. Over the course of the twentieth century New York Road Runners expanded to more than 50,000 members, the largest organization in the world of its kind, and became a leading presence in the local, national, and international running communities. Under the leadership of president FRED LEBOW, the club organized the first New York City Marathon in Central Park in 1970, growing it into an internationally renowned event that by 2009 took nearly 50,000 runners on a trip through all five boroughs. In the early twenty-first century the club was led by president Mary Wittenberg and continued to serve as the organizer of the New York City Marathon as well as more than 50 additional road races held throughout the year. New York Road Runners also became a pivotal force in helping to develop New York City's parks, world-class distance running in the United States, and the World Marathon Majors series. In addition, through the NYRR Foundation, the club establishes community running programs throughout the city to serve children who have little access to athletic programming. Its headquarters are located at 9 East 89th Street in Manhattan.

David White

New York School. Name given to a group of abstract expressionist artists in New York City who became well known after World War II and were active throughout the 1950s. The painters included William Baziotes, Elaine de Kooning, Willem de Kooning, Helen Frankenthaler, Arshile Gorky, Adolph Gottlieb, Philip Guston, Grace Hartigan, Hans Hofmann, Franz Kline, Lee Krasner, Norman Lewis, Robert Motherwell, Barnett Newman, Jackson Pollock, Ad Reinhardt, Mark Rothko, Hedda Sterne, Theodore Stamos, Clyfford Still, Bradley Walker Tomlin, and Jack Tworkov. Sculptors included David Hare, Herbert Ferber, Isamu Noguchi, Ibram Lassaw, Seymour Lipton, Theodore Roszak, and David Smith. This diverse group drew inspiration from many sources: European abstract and surrealist artists living in New York City during the 1940s, including John Graham, Max Ernst, Marcel Duchamp, André Masson, Piet Mondrian, Yves Tanguy, and the Chilean Roberto Matta Echaurren; exhibitions on cubism and surrealism held in New York City; the psychoanalytic theories of Carl Jung; Greek myth; existentialism; and American Indian art. Rejecting social realism and American scene painting, many sought through form to express inner states of feeling. The work of these artists was shown at the galleries of Peggy Guggenheim, Betty Parsons, Charles Egan, Sam Kootz, and Sidney Janis and championed by the art critics Clement Greenberg, Harold Rosenberg, Tom Hess, and Meyer Schapiro.

Dore Ashton, *The New York School: A Cultural Reckoning* (New York: Penguin, 1979); Lisa Phillips, *The Third Dimension: Sculpture of the New York School* (New York: Whitney Museum of American Art, 1984)

Patricia Hills

New York School for Fine and Applied Art. Former name of the PARSONS THE NEW SCHOOL FOR DESIGN.

New York School of Chiropody. Original name of the NEW YORK COLLEGE OF PODIATRIC MEDICINE.

New York School of Interior Design. Private college at 170 East 70th Street. It was founded in 1916 as the School of Interior Decoration by the architect Augustus Sherrill Whiton (1887–1961) and several other designers, artists, and decorators. It offers certificates, associate degrees, and bachelor's degrees. In the early twenty-first century the school had some 750 students and 70 faculty members.

Marc Ferris

New York School of Social Work. Institution that later became the School of Social Work at COLUMBIA UNIVERSITY.

New York's Hotel Pennsylvania. Twenty-two-story hotel at 401 Seventh Avenue. Designed by the firm of McKim, Mead and White for the Pennsylvania Railroad, it opened in 1919 as the Hotel Pennsylvania under the management of Ellsworth Statler, a prominent hotel owner. Catering primarily to travelers who used the original Pennsylvania Station (the hotel had underground passages that connected to the station), it had 2200 rooms and the world's first high-rise elevator system. During the 1930s and 1940s it was famous for its Cafe Rouge Ballroom, a popular nightclub that featured Big Band musicians such as Benny Goodman, Count Basie, and Duke Ellington. The Glenn Miller Orchestra broadcast a "Live from the Cafe Rouge" segment, and in 1938 Miller immortalized the hotel's telephone number with his song "Pennsylvania 6-5000." The exterior of the building remains virtually unaltered. The hotel was successively renamed the Hotel Statler (1948), the Statler–Hilton Hotel (1954), the New York Statler Hotel (1979), and the New York Penta Hotel (1983); it took its current name in 1992.

Jessica Montesano, May N. Stone

New York Society Library. Public library opened by subscription in 1754 in City Hall to members who paid an annual fee. Most of its holdings were destroyed or lost during the American Revolution, after which it experienced financial problems and faced competition from the increasingly popular free public libraries. The library moved to Nassau Street in 1795 and in 1839 absorbed its rival, the New York Athenaeum. The city's upper classes accounted for most of its members, and as they moved uptown the library followed, to Broadway and Leonard Street in 1840 and then to University Place in 1856. From 1850 the library received several generous bequests that ensured its long-term prosperity, and from 1882 it offered delivery service to its patrons. The trustees considered leaving University Place as early as 1900 but delayed moving until 1937 when they renovated and expanded a five-story townhouse at 53 East 79th Street. By the time of its bicentenary the New York Society Library owned roughly 300,000 items, including many rare books and manuscripts. It is the oldest library in New York City and the fourth-oldest in the United States.

Austin Baxter Keep, *History of the New York Society Library* (New York: De Vinne, 1908); Marion King, *Books and People: Five Decades of New York's Oldest Library* (New York: Macmillan, 1954)

Cynthia A. Kierner

New York State Institute of Applied Arts and Science. Original name of NEW YORK CITY TECHNICAL COLLEGE.

New York State Psychiatric Institute. Psychiatric research institute, now a teaching and research hospital that is part of the Columbia University Medical Center. Founded in 1895 as the Pathological Institute, it was the product of increasing interest in the scientific study of biological causes underlying mental illness. It was the first psychiatric facility in the country with a research and teaching mandate. The institute was originally located at Madison Avenue and 23rd Street before relocating to WARDS ISLAND for proximity to the clinical activities of the Manhattan State Hospital. It moved again to Washington Heights before becoming affiliated with Presbyterian Hospital in 1925.

Eric Hollingsworth

New York Stock Exchange [NYSE]. The principal securities market in the United States and the world's largest cash equities market. New York City had an active securities market by 1790, stimulated by the issuance in that year of bonds by Alexander Hamilton, the first secretary of the treasury, to consolidate and refund debts incurred during the American Revolution. There is, however, little evidence to support the claim that the "Buttonwood Agreement" of 1792 (signed by 22 stockbrokers and merchants on 17 May and by two more later in the year) marks the beginning of the NYSE itself. Within a few months of the bankruptcy of

William Duer in the spring of 1792 the city's securities market was largely inactive, not to be revived until after the War of 1812.

The NYSE was organized on 8 March 1817, when a group of 28 brokers adopted a constitution and set up formal membership rules. The initial name was the New York Stock and Exchange Board; the name New York Stock Exchange dates to 1863, and the exchange is popularly referred to as the Big Board. In its early years the exchange functioned as a call market, in which the name of each stock was called out in turn as brokers bid on only one security at a time. Its business at first consisted almost entirely of bank and insurance stock. Railroad securities began to dominate by the 1830s and 1840s and continued to do so until the end of the century. The early exchange was a small operation: only a few dozen brokers regularly attended the twice-daily calls, and daily volume was only a few thousand shares. Between 1817 and 1865, when the exchange opened its first permanent headquarters on its current site at Broad and Wall streets, it moved its base of operations 10 times.

The 1860s were a decade of major change at the NYSE. Fueled by wartime speculation, trading flourished at the exchange and at other sites in lower Manhattan. A number of rival exchanges opened, among them the Open Board of Stock Brokers, which from 1863 to 1869 often matched the NYSE in trading volume. When the NYSE absorbed its rival in 1869 it became a body of 1060 members, more than 10 times the number of a decade earlier. Membership on the exchange became a salable property right in 1868, with seats selling for $4000 in the 1870s. (The price remained relatively stable over the years, although it did surpass $1.1 million in 1987.) The number of seats increased to 1100 in 1880, and in another sign of growth the call market was replaced in 1871 by a continuous-auction market, which remains the principal means of trading.

Growth continued in the late nineteenth century, with occasional reverses. In 1873 the exchange closed for 10 days after the failure of Jay Cooke and Company. On 15 December 1886 the volume of shares traded first exceeded one million, and by the turn of the century industrial securities were traded for the first time. The coming of age of industrial listings was confirmed in 1901, when the newly formed U.S. Steel Corporation became the first company capitalized at more than $1 billion. In the same year the exchange witnessed perhaps the most remarkable of several attempted "corners," when Edward H. Harriman and Jacob Schiff battled James Hill and J. P. Morgan for control of the North Pacific Railroad: in the course of a single trading session the price of a share quintupled, to more than $1000. The struggle took place in borrowed quarters, the exchange having moved out of its former building while a new one was being erected on the same site. The new building, the current home of the NYSE, was designed by George B. Post and completed in 1903 at a cost of $2 million and features a magnificent Renaissance facade on Broad Street and a trading floor 100 feet (30 meters) wide, 183 feet (56 meters) long, and 79 feet (24 meters) high.

The NYSE was closed for six months in 1914 because of war, but it emerged from the war much stronger, as did the economy of the United States, which for the first time became a creditor nation. The exchange was in the forefront of the great securities boom of the 1920s, and 275 new seats were created in 1929. The boom ended abruptly with the stock market crash of the same year. On "Black Tuesday," 29 October, more than 16 million shares were traded (a record that stood for nearly 40 years), and by the end of the trading session the Dow Jones Industrial Average had declined more than 23 percent from its closing level of the preceding week. This marked only the beginning of the Depression: by the time the Dow Jones average reached its lowest level in the summer of 1932, it had only about one-tenth its value of three years earlier. Public confidence in the exchange was shaken, and after extensive congressional hearings the Securities and Exchange Commission (SEC) was formed in 1934. The commission tightened reporting and listing requirements and

Trading floor at the New York Stock Exchange, from Harper's Weekly, *10 September 1881*

implemented other reforms, arousing considerable opposition from an exchange that for decades had operated with little or no governmental oversight. The leader of the opposition was Richard Whitney, president of the exchange from 1930 to 1935, who in the view of his many enemies received his just reward in 1938 when he was convicted of swindling his customers. After his downfall the exchange accepted the reforms of the SEC, and in 1938 it initiated random supervisory audits of member firms to protect customers' assets in brokerage accounts.

After World War II the exchange mounted extensive advertising and promotional campaigns in an effort to attract small investors. But by the 1960s the dominant force was the institutional market, comprising private pension funds, trust funds, insurance companies, and open-end investment companies, or mutual funds. The reputation of the exchange as dependable and secure was reinforced by the successful resolution of the so-called salad-oil scandal in 1963. The crisis was brought on when the failure of a member firm, Ira Haupt and Company, endangered $450 million worth of its customers' cash and stock, which were pledged to banks as security for loans. Although under no legal obligation to do so, the NYSE set up a special trust fund to protect the firm's customers. When four member firms were liquidated in 1969 and 10 more followed in 1970, customers were protected against losses by the trust fund and by the Securities Investors Protection Corporation. In 1971 the NYSE was incorporated for the first time, as a nonprofit corporation. A long-standing rule mandating fixed commissions for stock transactions was repealed in 1975, leading to the rapid growth of discount brokers and to negotiable commissions from full-service brokers.

Further changes were brought about by the stock market crash of 1987, which followed an extended "bull market" during which prices and trading volume rose sharply. On 20 October 608 million shares were traded, with a value of about $21 billion, and the Dow Jones average declined by more than 500 points. Because much of the sudden decline in the market had been caused by "program trading," under which transactions are executed by computer when prices reach a certain level, the exchange implemented "trading collars" to make the market less volatile. Among these were special controls that take effect when the Dow Jones declines by 50 points from the closing level of the preceding day. By the early 1990s program trading still accounted for 12 percent of all trading volume on the exchange, but its tendency to exaggerate swings in the market had apparently been neutralized.

In a 12-year period beginning in the early 1980s the NYSE spent more than $1 billion on technology, to increase the volume of trading that could be handled to more than one

New York Stock Exchange, 2009

billion shares each day, about four times the average daily volume in 1993. In the mid-1990s about 90 percent of all customers' orders were processed electronically, with the trade confirmed in seconds and a record of the transaction instantaneously made available to investors worldwide. As of January 2007 all stocks could be traded electronically except for a few very high priced ones. In 2005 the NYSE reorganized as a for-profit publicly traded company after it acquired the securities exchange Archipelago; it adopted the name NYSE Group in 2006. Then in 2007 the NYSE Group merged with the European electronic stock exchange Euronext to form the transatlantic holding company NYSE Euronext. NYSE Euronext exchanges are located in six countries and in the early twenty-first century had nearly 4000 listed companies with a market capitalization of $28.5 trillion.

The NYSE has 1366 members, a number fixed in 1953. A firm seeking to have its shares traded on the exchange must satisfy very strict requirements with respect to financial condition, reporting, and registration with the SEC. Membership on the NYSE is generally considered an endorsement of a firm's status and is eagerly sought after. NYSE Euronext is governed by an annually elected board of directors, the majority of whom are not affiliated with any other NYSE exchange board; it also includes an independent, nonexecutive chair and deputy chair and a chief executive officer and deputy chief executive officer.

Robert Sobel, *NYSE: A History of the New York Stock Exchange, 1935–1975* (New York: Weybright and Talley, 1975); Walter Werner and Steven T. Smith, *Wall Street* (New York: Columbia University Press, 1991); Peter Eisenstadt, "Forgetting the Origins of the New York Stock Exchange: How the Buttonwood Tree Grows," *Prospects* 19 (1994)

New York Sun (i). Newspaper launched in 1833 by Benjamin Day. Its humorous crime reports, its coverage of murder trials, and its exploitation of sensational hoaxes soon gave it the highest daily circulation of any newspaper in the United States. In 1852 Moses Sperry Beach became the editor and sole proprietor of the *Sun*, which he sold in 1868 to a syndicate led by Charles A. Dana. Under Dana the newspaper emphasized human interest reporting and independent but largely Republican conservatism. It was celebrated as a school for journalists, including Julian Ralph, Arthur Brisbane, Jacob A. Riis, and Will Irwin. In 1897 Francis P. Church wrote the most famous editorial in American journalism, "Yes, Virginia, there is a Santa Claus," in response to a letter from an eight-year-old girl. The newspaper was purchased in 1916 by Frank Munsey. In 1950 the *Sun* was absorbed by the *New York World-Telegram*.

Steven H. Jaffe

New York Sun (ii). Newspaper. First published in 2002, it saw itself as a right-of-center alternative to the *New York Times*. The *Sun* was known for its broad coverage of Manhattan and New York State, its arts section, and its focus on Jewish-related issues. A conservative newspaper that nonetheless had the respect of the political left, the *Sun* was published five days per week until it ceased publication in September 2008 because of financial difficulties.

Elaine S. Abelson

New York Theological Seminary (i). Original name of Union Theological Seminary.

New York Theological Seminary (ii). Nondenominational Protestant seminary formed in 1900 as the Bible Teachers College in suburban Montclair, New Jersey, by Wilbert Webster White (1863–1944), a minister of the United Presbyterian Church. It moved in 1902 to New York City, where its classes were held first at the Broadway Tabernacle on Sixth Avenue and 34th Street (built 1859), then at an optician's office nearby, at a building on 49th Street between Lexington and Third avenues (from 1918), and at the Marble Collegiate Church on Fifth Avenue and West 29th Street (from 1976). The seminary was renamed successively the Bible Teachers Training School (to bring it into compliance with regulations of the New York Board of Regents) and the Biblical Seminary in New York (1921) before adopting its current name in 1965. The course of instruction reflected White's belief that scriptural study belonged at the center of the theological curriculum. As president of the seminary until 1940 White oversaw the training of scores of pastors, directors of Christian education, teachers, and missionaries. Although enrollment declined in the 1950s and 1960s the fortunes of the seminary revived after it radically restructured its programs in 1970 to provide an affordable theological education for the growing black, Spanish-speaking, and Asian population in the metropolitan area. In 2002 it moved to Morningside Heights in Manhattan and began operating out of the Union Theological Seminary, Riverside Church, and the Interchurch Center. Although Bible study remained central to the curriculum, various experimental offerings sought to equip members of the clergy and lay leaders for diverse urban ministries; one innovative program known as the seminary behind bars was established to train prison ministers.

Peter J. Wosh

New York Times. Daily newspaper launched on 18 September 1851 by bankers from Albany, New York, led by Henry J. Raymond, who had worked for Horace Greeley's newspaper the *New York Tribune* and James Watson Webb's *Courier and Enquirer.* Although less influential and widely read at the time than the *New York Tribune* and the *New York Herald* of James Gordon Bennett, Sr., it became successful by offering comprehensive reporting while at the same time reflecting Raymond's sympathy toward the Whig and Republican leaders William H. Seward and Thurlow Weed. Its coverage during the Civil War lent the newspaper respect and helped Raymond not only to win a seat in the U.S. Congress but also to become the Republican national chairman. After the war Raymond's hesitancy to break with the conservative Reconstruction policies of President Andrew Johnson alienated him from the mainstream of the party and diminished the newspaper's circulation and power, though he reconciled with the Republican Party when he supported Ulysses S. Grant for the presidency in 1868. After Raymond's death in 1869 control of the newspaper passed to George Jones, who with Louis Jennings as his editor aggressively pursued and exposed William M. "Boss" Tweed in the early 1870s (this despite Tweed's demands that they desist and notwithstanding the risk of financial ruin). In 1884 the newspaper sided with liberal Republicans who endorsed the Democratic presidential candidate Grover Cleveland over his Republican opponent James G. Blaine, as a result of which the newspaper lost its old Republican support. Jones died in 1891; by 1896, in the unbusinesslike hands of its editor Charles R. Miller and several other staff members, as well as after the financial panic of 1893, daily circulation was down and the newspaper was nearly bankrupt.

Fortunes changed when Adolph S. Ochs became the principal owner of the *New York Times* in the hopes of earning revenue for his struggling newspaper the *Chattanooga Times.*

New York Times Building (designed by Eidlitz and MacKenzie), 1905

This was done with the proviso that he could become the sole owner if he were able to retire all the newspaper's debt. Having satisfied this condition he assumed control on 19 August 1896. Ochs improved the layout, increased the amount of financial news, and used the editorial page to print letters to the editor and articulate his own conservative Democratic positions. He also sponsored a contest for a slogan but eventually chose his own, "All the News That's Fit to Print," which first appeared on the front page on 10 February 1897. By late 1898 the sensational coverage of the Spanish–American War in the newspapers of William Randolph Hearst and Joseph Pulitzer cut into the circulation of the *Times.* In response Ochs reduced its price from three cents to one cent, and readership tripled within a year. Shortly after the turn of the century the newspaper moved from 41 Park Row in lower Manhattan to Long Acre Square, which soon became known as Times Square. In 1913 it moved again, to 43rd Street between Seventh and Eighth avenues.

Carr Van Anda became the managing editor in 1904 and during the next 20 years strove to make the *Times* the "paper of record," in part by emphasizing such scientific events as Robert Peary's exploration of the North Pole and Albert Einstein's discoveries. After Miller's death in 1922 his position as editorial page editor was filled successively by Rollo Ogden, John Finley, and Charles Merz. In 1923 Lester Markel began a 40-year tenure as editor of the Sunday newspaper; he introduced the "News of the Week in Review" among other sections. After Van Anda retired in 1925 his assistant Frederick Birchall discharged the duties of managing editor while formally remaining acting managing editor, owing to his British citizenship. At the end of 1932 the position of managing editor was assumed by Edwin L. James, a foreign correspondent distinguished for his coverage of World War I and the "lead" of his story about the first solo flight across the Atlantic: "Lindbergh did it." In the same year Arthur Krock became the chief of the Washington bureau; later a columnist, he enjoyed a career at the newspaper that lasted until 1966, during which he won four Pulitzer Prizes.

The new publisher of the *Times* after Ochs's death in 1935 was Arthur Hays Sulzberger, who had married Ochs's only child, Iphigene, and served a long apprenticeship as his assistant. He modernized the printing plants, named Anne O'Hare McCormick foreign affairs columnist, and added a crossword puzzle and sections on fashion and food. He made a large commitment of money and staff to covering World War II at a time when other newspapers were cutting back on the space devoted to news. Turner Catledge became the managing editor after James's death in 1951 and later served as editor in chief until 1968. In the following years Catledge added a feature called "Man in the News," demanded sharper writing, and gave charge of design and copyediting to Theodore Bernstein, a crusader for grammatical rectitude. He also chose the next generation of editors, mostly foreign correspondents: Clifton Daniel, his successor as managing editor; Harrison Salisbury, the first editor of the "op-ed" page when it began in 1970; and A. M. Rosenthal, who became city editor in 1963 and dominated news coverage at the newspaper until the mid-1980s. James Reston succeeded Krock as head of the Washington bureau in 1953, became one of the nation's most influential and popular columnists, and engaged the reporters and columnists Russell Baker, Tom Wicker, and Anthony Lewis. In 1954 C. L. Sulzberger, a nephew of the publisher, became the foreign affairs columnist. After Merz retired in 1961 Ochs's nephew John B. Oakes took charge of the editorial page.

During the early 1960s the newspaper changed publishers twice in two years: first in 1961 when Sulzberger was succeeded by his son-in-law Orvil Dryfoos, then in 1963 when Dryfoos died, just after the settlement of a printers' strike that lasted 114 days. About the same time an advertisement placed in the *Times* concerning civil rights in Montgomery, Alabama, led to a lawsuit against the newspaper for libel. The case resulted in a ruling in favor of the newspaper by the U.S. Supreme Court, which in *New York Times Company v. Sullivan* (1964) narrowed the definition of libel in cases concerning public figures and reaffirmed the principle of freedom of the press. Sulzberger's son Arthur Ochs Sulzberger, who became the publisher in 1963, introduced changes in the newspaper's format and helped the owners to expand into magazine publishing and broadcasting.

Rosenthal became managing editor of the *Times* in 1969 and was executive editor from 1976 until he retired in 1986. With his longtime aide Arthur Gelb he oversaw the restructuring of the newspaper's format: after several years of being printed in only two sections, local editions were now being printed in four, which allowed more space for full-page advertising and increased revenues that underwrote the paper's commitment to worldwide reporting. Rosenthal directed major investigative stories about the Central Intelligence Agency and about the "Pentagon papers" in 1971, a government record of the Vietnam War that the federal government tried to prevent the *Times* and the *Washington Post* from publishing. By a decision of the U.S. Supreme Court, publication was allowed to proceed on the grounds that efforts to suppress the papers constituted "prior restraint" of free speech.

Restructuring continued under the executive editor Max Frankel, who during a decade in charge of the editorial page had made it more politically moderate and more literary, and the managing editor Joseph Lelyveld. Through the 1980s the *Times* maintained the traditional appearance that earned it the nickname the "great gray lady." In the 1990s the *Times* began color printing in most of its Sunday sections and expanded coverage of local news and sports. The *Times* also continued to dominate the Pulitzer Prizes: in 2008 it won its 97th, meaning it had won nearly 10 percent of all the prizes awarded since they began in 1917.

By the terms of a trust set up by Iphigene Ochs Sulzberger, on her death in 1991 at the age of 97 control of the newspaper passed to her four children, Arthur Sulzberger, Judith Sulzberger, Marian Heiskell, and Ruth Holmberg; on their death control would pass to their 13 children, including Arthur Ochs Sulzberger, Jr., who succeeded his father as publisher in 1992. In 2007 the *New York Times* moved into a new building on Eighth Avenue between 40th and 41st streets designed by Renzo Piano. Erected on property cleared by New York State through the use of eminent domain, the new *Times* building is the result of a joint venture between the newspaper and developer Forest City Ratner Companies. Standing 52 stories tall, the lower portion is used by the newspaper, and the upper tower remains in the hands of Forest City Ratner. The new building includes no printing facilities. Although the presses in the 43rd Street building were used until June 1997, in 2008 the *Times* relied on the printing plants it had opened in Edison, New Jersey, in 1993 and in College Point, Queens, in 1997.

In 2008 the *New York Times* had a daily circulation of 1.07 million and a Sunday circulation of 1.5 million. The *Times* published a national edition in half a dozen satellite plants around the country and shared ownership with the *Washington Post* of the *International Herald Tribune*. It also owned television and radio stations, magazines, and other newspapers, mostly in the South and Southwest.

Gay Talese, *The Kingdom and the Power* (New York: World, 1969); Harrison E. Salisbury, *Without Fear or Favor: The New York Times and Its Times* (New York: Times Books, 1980); James Reston, *Deadline: A Memoir* (New York: Random House, 1991); Nan Robertson, *The Girls in the Balcony: Women, Men, and the New York Times* (New York: Random House, 1992)

Harrison Salisbury, Thorin Tritter

New York Times Building, 2009

New York Titans. Name by which the New York Jets were known from 1960 to 1963.

New York Trade School. Original name of Voorhees Technical Institute.

New York Transit Museum. Museum in Brooklyn, operated under the auspices of the New York City Transit division of the Metropolitan Transportation Authority (MTA) and displaying the history of mass transit in New York City. It is situated underground in the former Court Street station of the Independent Subway System (IND), at the corner of Schermerhorn Street and Boerum Place in Brooklyn Heights. Exhibits at the museum include antique signals, fareboxes, turnstiles, and rapid transit maps dating from as early as 1892 (before the opening of the subway system). The museum holds an extensive collection of mosaics, friezes, terra-cotta plaques inspired by the "city beautiful" movement of the early twentieth century, and architectural drawings of ticket booths and stations that reveal a uniformly high quality of design. The lower level of the station, formerly the station's platform, houses many subway and elevated railway cars dating to 1903. These cars are occasionally employed as a "Nostalgia Train" by the MTA: for example, on 10 September 2007, a train composed of six pre–World War II cars was run on the Eighth Avenue A express line to celebrate the 75th birthday of the IND.

Barbara Grcevic

New York Tribune. Daily newspaper launched by Horace Greeley in 1841. It supported Whig politics and reformist causes favored by its publisher, including temperance, the labor movement, utopian socialism, and opposition to the expansion of slavery. The staff during the 1840s included Solon Robinson and George "Gaslight" Foster, who together wrote about the plight of the city's slum dwellers and sweatshop workers, and the feminist Margaret Fuller. It also published a weekly edition that was the most influential Republican newspaper in the nation and by the 1850s had a circulation of more than 200,000. The newspaper was instrumental in persuading Abraham Lincoln to enact the Emancipation Proclamation in 1863. It was purchased in 1872 by the editor Whitelaw Reid, under whose direction it took a more conservative turn and engaged in an eight-year battle (1884–92) with striking printers. In 1886 the *Tribune* was the first newspaper to install Ottmar Mergenthaler's slug-casting linotype machine, which revolutionized typesetting. Reid's son Ogden Reid, Sr., became the president and managing editor in 1912; with his wife Helen (Miles) Rogers Reid he revamped the newspaper's news coverage and layout. In 1924 the Reid family bought the *New York Herald* and merged it with the *Tribune* to form the NEW YORK HERALD TRIBUNE.

Steven H. Jaffe

New York Typographical Union no. 6. Trade union representing typographers, organized as the New York Printers' Union in Manhattan in 1850 by Horace Greeley, its first president. In 1852 it formed an affiliation with the National Typographical Union (renamed the International Typographical Union in 1869). Known as the "Big Six," the union at first included all craft workers in the trade; eventually it included only compositors and book and job printers when press operators, bookbinders, stereotypers and electrotypers, and photoengravers formed their own unions. Separate unions formed by female typesetters in 1868 and by German American printers in the following year were later reincorporated into the Big Six. The union represented most newspaper compositors and many workers in the larger commercial shops in the city. Known for aggressiveness, it engaged in prolonged strikes against newspapers in 1934 and 1962–63. The International Typographical Union (ITU) merged with the Communications Workers of America (CWA) in 1987 and the local became known as ITU Local 6/CWA Local 14156.

George A. Stevens, *History of New York Typographical Union No. 6* (Albany, N.Y.: J. B. Lyons, 1914); Harry Kelber and Carl Schlesinger, *Union Printers and Controlled Automation* (New York: Free Press, 1967)

William S. Pretzer

New York University. Private university formed in 1831 in Washington Square as the University of the City of New York by a committee led by Albert Gallatin, secretary of the treasury under Presidents Thomas Jefferson and James Madison. From the beginning it was the subject of debate over the purpose of education. The banker John Delafield and Dutch merchants such as Myndert Van Schaick argued that the university should provide practical instruction for those who could not afford to attend an expensive college; an influential group of Presbyterian and Dutch Reformed ministers advocated a religious approach to education and resisted any separation of science and morality. The first chancellor was James M. Mathews (1785–1870), a minister whose adoption of a traditional religious orientation for the university prompted Gallatin to resign as a trustee. He was followed by a succession of Dutch Reformed and Presbyterian ministers who tried to sustain the evangelical character of the institution and who were opposed by such prominent faculty members as Samuel F. B. Morse, professor of fine arts and inventor of the telegraph, and John Draper, chemist, historian, and an early developer of photography. In spite of the religious commitments of its leaders, the university's curriculum was nondenominational: religion was a central feature, but so were classics, natural history, and mathematics.

The first students reflected the evangelical inclinations of the first chancellors. During the 1830s and 1840s Presbyterian students were twice as numerous as those of any other denomination, and nearly all were from outside the city until the 1850s, when the proportion decreased to one half. By the 1890s the university drew 65 percent of its students from New York City and began to reflect the heterogeneity of the city. Virtually every Protestant denomination including Quakers was represented, as were Catholics and Jews. Henry Mitchell MacCracken (1840–1918), a professor

New York University, Kimmell Center, 2009

of philosophy from 1884, became a vice chancellor in 1885 and chancellor in 1891: he transformed the university into a modern institution by moving the undergraduate college to a campus in the Bronx designed by Stanford White, and developing a graduate school of arts and sciences, a law school, and a medical school (which forged an affiliation with Bellevue Hospital). In addition he founded the university's graduate school of education (the first in the United States) and a school of commerce, accounts, and finance. These changes were effected without benefit of endowment, in part because enrollment increased from less than 100 to nearly 4000, and in part because a change in the by-laws authorized the university to acquire investment property. This rapid growth made for overcrowded classrooms, transient faculty, and fluctuating standards, and yet opened the university to students who had neither the means nor the preparation to study at more selective institutions. In 1896 the university took its current name.

Elmer Ellsworth Brown resigned from his position as commissioner of education under President William Howard Taft to succeed MacCracken in 1911. During his long tenure (to 1933) the university became one of the largest in the United States: between 1912 and 1917 alone enrollment increased from 4300 to 9300. Brown continued the emphasis on professional training by moving the school of business to Wall Street (1920), opening a school of dentistry (1925) and a school of fine arts (1928), and imposing more stringent requirements for admission to the schools of law (two years of college) and medicine (a college degree as of 1930). He also established New York University Press (1916) and strengthened the libraries. By the university's centenary in 1931 enrollment reached a peak of 40,000. After the Depression the chancellors Harry W. Chase (1883–1955) and Henry T. Heald (1904–75) reduced building and curtailed enrollment in an effort to raise academic standards. The School of Continuing Education (1934) and the School of Public Administration (1938, now the Robert F. Wagner Graduate School of Public Service) were the only new structures erected during their tenures. The GI Bill brought an influx of older students after World War II who tended to raise the academic quality of the university. During the McCarthy period two popular professors were dismissed for their political views, bringing about a censure by the American Association of University Professors that was not lifted until the 1960s. Carroll V. Newsom (1905–90), an outspoken critic of McCarthyism, was inaugurated the university's 10th chancellor in 1956.

Efforts to improve academic standards and make the university a leading research institution were undertaken in the following decades by the chancellors James Hester, John Sawhill, and John Brademas. Visible symbols of these efforts were the construction of Warren Weaver Hall for the Courant Institute of Mathematical Sciences and of the Elmer Holmes Bobst Library on Washington Square (1967–72), a 12-story structure of red sandstone designed by Philip Johnson and Richard Foster. Sawhill and Brademas also mounted a successful campaign to increase the university's endowment. The campus in the Bronx was sold to the city in 1973 and eventually housed Bronx Community College. Several additional developments further concentrated the university's presence near Washington Square, notably the reorganization of the Tisch School of the Arts nearby and of the Robert F. Wagner Graduate School of Public Service, and the removal of the Leonard N. Stern School of Business to a modern facility designed by Robert Geddes. The construction of dormitories and the acquisition of apartments to enable students and faculty to reside on campus aroused protests from community groups, as well as from alumni who feared that the university's commitment to the commuting student would be undermined. Another sign of academic self-confidence was the appointment in 1991 of the historian L. Jay Oliva, the first president ever chosen from the ranks of the academic faculty.

In the early twenty-first century the university's growth was a central priority under the helm of John Sexton, a former dean of the law school who was appointed president in 2001. As of 2008 Sexton had raised $2.5 billion and aggressively expanded the university's physical presence both in New York and abroad. Greenwich Village residents, wary of the university's presence for decades, had a mixed response to Sexton's work. In the 1960s some residents opposed the construction of I. M. Pei's University Village: also known as the Silver Towers, the complex included two 32-story buildings housing faculty and one that was leased to a Mitchell–Lama cooperative for middle-income families. The buildings were constructed on land Robert Moses obtained during his controversial slum clearance program; residents feared the super block development would damage the character of the neighborhood and accused the university of working without community cooperation. Half a century later the 10-story Kimmel Center for Student Life, designed by Kevin Roche John Dinkeloo and Associates, replaced the old student center on Washington Square Park South; residents voiced concerns that it would overshadow the park, as they had when the nearby Bobst Library was built in 1967. NYU Plans 2031, the university's 25-year development plan, aimed to increase the university's footprint by 6 million square feet (557,418 square meters) (from almost 15 million square feet [1.4 million square meters] in Greenwich Village, the East Village, and Union Square). To facilitate a better relationship with neighborhood residents, the university began holding community open houses in 2007 and displayed plans for perusal. It expanded to the outer boroughs upon acquisition of the 150-year-old Polytechnic University, an engineering school in downtown Brooklyn, in 2008. Sexton also strove to establish the university globally, planning a campus in the United Arab Emirates, NYU Abu Dhabi, which opened the doors to its downtown campus in December 2009, with an inaugural class of 100 students entering in August 2010; its residential campus is expected to open in 2014. More than 40,000 students were enrolled in the university's 14 schools in the early twenty-first century, taught by 3100 full-time faculty; with more than 16,000 employees, it was one of the largest employers in the city.

Theodore Francis Jones, *New York University, 1832–1932* (New York: New York University Press, 1933); Thomas J. Frusciano, *New York University and the City: An Illustrated History* (New Brunswick, N.J.: Rutgers University Press, 1997)

Kate Lauber, Paul H. Mattingly

New York University Medical Center. Teaching hospital, established in 1947 in Manhattan between 30th and 34th streets and First Avenue and FDR Drive. In 1948 the New York Post-Graduate Medical School and Hospital (renamed University Hospital) joined the center and the Howard A. Rusk Institute of Rehabilitation Medicine opened. Tisch Hospital (1963) is an acute-care general hospital. The center is now composed of Tisch Hospital, Rusk Institute of Rehabilitation Medicine, New York University Hospital for Joint Diseases, and New York University School of Medicine (1841) and its affiliated hospitals, which include Bellevue, Veterans Affairs, Lenox Hill, and North Shore University Hospitals and Gouverneur Healthcare Services. Its more than 50 centers and institutes focus on AIDS, biomolecular medicine, cancer, translational (patient-oriented) medicine, aging, dementia and Alzheimer's disease, brain health, epilepsy, heart and vascular disease, environmental medicine, mental health issues, spinal cord injury, and immunology and infectious diseases.

Jane E. Mottus

New York Water Taxi. Transportation company operating in the New York Harbor. Frequented by both local commuters and tourists, New York water taxis run on fixed schedules and carry up to 149 passengers. As of 2007 the company operated year-round commuter routes between lower Manhattan and downtown Brooklyn and Queens, South Brooklyn, and Yonkers during rush hour. During the warmer months the company offers shuttles to Mets games, assorted harbor tours and local cruises, and "hop-on, hop-off" routes for sightseers that travel between Long Island City in Queens, Fulton Ferry in Brooklyn, and many different stops in Manhattan; passengers can pay per ride or purchase one- and two-day unlimited use passes, allowing them to get on and off frequently and visit many parts of New York City for one price on their own schedule.

Ben Silk

New York Women's Trade Union League. Labor organization formed in 1903 by Jane Addams and other social reformers to help working women organize unions. During its early years the league was mistrusted by union leaders and working-class women because its executive board was dominated by reformers from the middle class. Leonora O'Reilly, an Irish shirtmaker and union organizer and the league's most influential working-class member, set out to remedy this by attracting talented trade-union women to the league. In 1905 she recruited as a member Rose Schneiderman, a Jewish immigrant cap maker who brought solid credentials as an organizer and as the first woman elected to the executive board of a national union (the United Cap and Hat Makers). Elected vice president of the league in the following year, Schneiderman brought a new perspective to the league's organizing work. She suggested that the league extend aid only to those working women who asked for it, asserted that previously they had acted more like social reformers than union organizers, and studied industries that had the worst conditions so they could organize their workers. Despite a severe depression in 1907–8, Schneiderman made progress among Jewish immigrant garment workers, laying the groundwork for a strike led by shirtwaist makers in 1909–10 called the "uprising of the

New York Water Taxi, 2009

thirty thousand." This was the largest strike by American women up to that time.

The uprising brought a dynamic group of women workers into the league, among them the Lithuanian-born shirtwaist maker Pauline M. Newman, and Clara Lemlich, a Ukrainian immigrant whose fiery speech moved the workers to strike over the objections of both male union leaders and the middle-class leadership of the league. But the emergence of a strong working-class core led to conflict. Some middle-class members, particularly the league's secretary, Helen Marot, argued that too much energy was being devoted to Russian Jewish immigrant women at the expense of American-born workers. This conflict highlighted the tensions of class and ethnicity that plagued the league in its early years. Schneiderman and Newman, supported by O'Reilly, complained that middle-class "allies" were too domineering and that the league should be run by working women. They contemplated resigning when Marot accused Russian Jews of being too emotional and unused to constructive work. Before World War I working-class members were unable to successfully challenge the middle-class officers, because the league drew its financial support not from unions but from wealthy women.

After 1917 the working-class leaders attracted a new group of wealthy supporters to the league who shared their belief that the organization should be run by working women themselves. In 1917 Schneiderman was elected president and Newman vice president. The two gathered around them an executive board made up almost entirely of working women, which shaped the policies of the league for the rest of its existence. From the 1920s until the 1940s the league adopted a strategy for improving the lives of working women that was based on education, organization, and legislation. It ran a school for working women from 1923 to 1955 that offered courses in history, literature, current events, and economics, as well as labor relations, labor history, and lobbying, and the school became a model for adult education in the United States. The league sought both to train women academically and to encourage the growth of a professional network that would extend beyond the classroom. In its organizing drives it took a special interest in unskilled workers overlooked by the American Federation of Labor and the Congress of Industrial Organizations. League organizers helped build the garment unions and supported them during the 1920s and 1930s; they embarked on a decades-long campaign to unionize the city's largely black and Puerto Rican laundry workers and hotel maids, and during the 1940s they were advocates for women in the defense industries.

Finally the league was instrumental in making New York State a testing ground for labor legislation. During the second decade of the twentieth century it successfully lobbied for maximum hours and occupational safety legislation for women workers. Over the next 30 years it fought for minimum wage, fire safety, equal pay, maternity insurance, and the extension of social security to domestic workers. It also fought for publicly funded child care and comparable worth (the principle that jobs of equal worth to an employer should be equally paid). Franklin D. Roosevelt and Eleanor Roosevelt gave it influence on a national level. It also enjoyed close relations with municipal and state officials, and during the late 1930s and early 1940s the state Department of Labor was dominated by league members. Dwindling financial support and the postwar "red scare" combined to cripple the league by the 1950s, and it disbanded in 1955.

Nancy Schrom Dye, *As Equals and as Sisters: Feminism, Unionism and the Women's Trade Union League of New York* (Columbia: University of Missouri Press, 1980); Annelise Orleck, *Common Sense and a Little Fire: Working Class Women's Activism in the 20th Century United States* (Chapel Hill: University of North Carolina Press, 1995)

Annelise Orleck

New York Workers School. First communist adult school in the United States, opened on New York City's Lower East Side in October 1923 to train militants for the class struggle. In a typical term the school offered more than 100 courses, the basic ones being principles of communism, political economy, and Marxism–Leninism. Trade union issues were also taught, along with U.S. history, literature, elementary and intermediate Russian, and English. After two years of internal party disorganization Bertram R. Wolfe put the school on a firm basis. Teachers received $12 a week to instruct the students, men and women, communists as well as noncommunists, who attended the evening classes after day jobs in offices and light industries—and often marched with them in demonstrations and rallies. The school and its several annexes in the five boroughs flourished until a major split in the Communist Party developed in 1929. Wolfe was ousted and a long-time teacher at the Workers School, Abraham Markoff, became director in 1930 and guided the school through the Depression and into the Popular Front period. He died in 1938, and William Weinstone, a party leader, took over the Workers School, which was superseded in 1944 by the Communist Party's Jefferson School of Social Science.

Marvin E. Gettleman, "The New York Workers School, 1923–1943: Communist Education in American Society," in Michael E. Brown et al., *New Studies in the Politics and Culture of U.S. Communism* (New York: Monthly Review Press, 1993), 261–80

Marvin E. Gettleman

New York World–Telegram. Daily newspaper launched in 1931 by Roy W. Howard, director of the Scripps–Howard chain, through a merger of the *New York Telegram,* which he acquired in 1925, with the *New York World,* formerly owned by Joseph Pulitzer. In the tradition of its politically liberal founder, Edward W. Scripps, the chain gave the newspaper autonomy in local news but maintained strict control over national coverage and the editorial page. The staff of the *World–Telegram* also adhered to the crusading tradition of Scripps even though Howard made the newspaper more conservative and was critical of the New Deal. The Pulitzer Prize was awarded to the newspaper in 1933 for its campaign against local misgovernment; in 1940 and 1941 to a group of its writers, including Westbrook Pegler, for helping to convict dishonest public officials; and in 1947 to Frederick Woltmann for exposing communist activity in the United States. In 1950 the newspaper absorbed Charles A. Dana's *Sun,* becoming the *World–Telegram and Sun.* Although its reporters won another Pulitzer Prize in 1963 for their coverage of an airplane disaster, the newspaper lost much of its circulation and advertising revenue by 1966 because of shifts in population. In 1966 the *World–Telegram* combined with the *New York Herald Tribune* and the *New York Journal–American* to form the *World–Journal Tribune,* which lasted less than a year. For many years the newspaper was published at 125 Barclay Street in lower Manhattan.

Joseph Sage, *Three to Zero: The Story of the Birth and Death of the World Journal Tribune* (New York: American Publishers Association, 1967); John Hohenberg, *The Pulitzer Prizes* (New York: Columbia University Press, 1974)

Julian S. Rammelkamp

New York Yacht Club. Oldest yacht club in the United States, and one of the world's most influential and prestigious boating organizations. It was founded in 1844 by John Cox Stevens and eight other pleasure-boat sailors on Stevens's schooner *Gimcrack,* anchored off the Battery. The next year a simple one-room clubhouse was built at Elysian Fields, the commercial park owned by the Stevens family at Hoboken, New Jersey. Many early races started on the Hudson River, went out through the Narrows to the Lower Bay or into the Atlantic, and returned to finish off Elysian Fields. As the harbor became crowded during the 1850s the start and finish were moved to near Bay Ridge, Brooklyn. By 1900 the club was running most of its races on Long Island Sound or in New England waters.

After leaving Hoboken in 1869 the club had clubhouses on Staten Island and in 11 small buildings called "stations" between New York and Maine, while renting rooms in Manhattan for winter gatherings. Since 1901 (when the membership was nearly 2000) the club has occupied a beaux-arts clubhouse (designated a U.S. National Historic Landmark in 1987) at 37 West 44th Street that was designed by Whitney Warren; it has so many maritime motifs that a visitor commented, "Except for the absence of motion, one might fancy oneself at sea." Since 1987 there has been a second clubhouse, Harbour Court, in Newport, Rhode Island.

The club has been a leader in writing racing rules and organizing races, including the first long-distance ocean race, from New York to England (1866), and the AMERICA'S CUP, which the club held from 1851 until 1983. Although five Morgans, two Vanderbilts, and many other men of wealth have been the club's commodore (the equivalent of president), membership has been varied, and its squadron has consisted of boats of all sizes. The chief qualification for membership is a serious interest in sailing or powerboating. Women were first admitted as full members in 1984. In the early twenty-first century the club had more than 3000 members, with representation from across North America, the United Kingdom, Europe, Latin America, and the Pacific Rim.

John Parkinson, Jr., *The History of the New York Yacht Club* (New York: New York Yacht Club, 1975); John Rousmaniere, *History of the New York Yacht Club* (New York: New York Yacht Club, 2008)

John Rousmaniere

New York Yankees. Baseball team. It began in 1903 as the New York Highlanders when Frank Farrell and Bill Devery acquired the Baltimore Orioles for $18,000 and moved them to New York City. The team played its home games at Hilltop Park, on the west side of Broadway between 165th and 168th streets. One of its first outstanding players was the pitcher Jack Chesbro, who won 41 games in 1904, a major league record. The Highlanders played well for a few years but gradually weakened and ended last in their league in 1912. In the following year they were renamed the Yankees and abandoned Hilltop Park for the Polo Grounds. Farrell and Devery sold the club in 1915 for $460,000 to Colonel Tillinghast L'Hommedieu Huston, a wealthy engineer, and Colonel Jacob Ruppert, a millionaire who owned a brewery and had served four consecutive terms as a Democratic congressman from New York City (1899–1907). In 1920 Ruppert and Huston bought from the Boston Red Sox the contract of BABE RUTH, with whom the Yankees, managed by Miller Huggins, won their first American League pennant in 1921 and their first World Series in 1923. Ruth and his teammates, including first baseman LOU GEHRIG who started in 2130 consecutive games but whose brilliant career and life were cut short by illness in 1941, became known as "murderer's row" because of the difficult task opposing pitchers faced against the Yankee lineup. The team won six American League pennants and three World Series titles in the 1920s. Ruth electrified the world of baseball with his unprecedented skill at hitting home runs. His popularity led the Yankees to build their own ballpark, YANKEE STADIUM, at River Avenue between 157th and 161st streets in the Bronx, across the Harlem River from the Polo Grounds. More than 74,000 fans attended its dedication on 18 April 1923; nearly 25,000 others were turned away. The sportswriter Fred Lieb of the *New York Evening Telegram* referred to the magnificent new stadium as "the house that Ruth built," a name that continued to be used until it was closed in 2008. Ruppert bought Huston's share in the team in 1923 and remained the sole owner until his death in 1939.

In 1927 the Yankees won 110 games and lost only 44, one of the best records in the history of baseball, but in 1929 Huggins died and the early 1930s saw the retirement of many players, including Ruth. By the late 1930s another strong team had been assembled: led by JOE DIMAGGIO, Tommy Henrich, Charlie Keller, and Bill Dickey and managed by Joe McCarthy, it was acquired in 1945 for $2.8 million by Dan Topping, Larry MacPhail, and Del Webb. This team won seven pennants and six World Series between 1936 and 1943. The team that emerged in the 1950s was managed first by Casey Stengel and later by Ralph Houk, and included PHIL RIZZUTO, MICKEY MANTLE, Roger Maris, WHITEY FORD, and YOGI BERRA. The team won the World Series every year from 1949 to 1953, and between 1954 and 1964 won four World Series and nine pennants. Elston Howard became the first black member of the Yankees in 1955. Topping and Webb sold the team to the Columbia Broadcasting System (CBS) for $14 million in 1964.

The Yankees were mediocre in the late 1960s and early 1970s but improved when a syndicate controlled by GEORGE STEINBRENNER, a shipbuilder from Cleveland, bought them from CBS in 1973, reportedly for $10 million. In 1974 and 1975 the team played at Shea Stadium while Yankee Stadium was being renovated. When the cost of the project reached $100 million, well over its budget, the City of New York agreed to assume ownership of Yankee Stadium and pay for its renovation; the Yankees signed a lease to remain there for a quarter century, until 2002. Under Steinbrenner's ownership the Yankees aggressively sought free agents, and with Catfish Hunter, Reggie Jackson, Thurman Munson, Sparky Lyle, and Ron Guidry the team won the World Series in 1977 and 1978 and pennants in 1976 and 1981. The Yankees played poorly in the 1980s, a period marked by Steinbrenner's summary dismissal of several managers: Billy Martin (1928–89) alone was dismissed five times.

Beginning in 1995, the team made the playoffs for 13 consecutive seasons, winning the World Series in 1996, 1998, 1999, and 2000. Joe Torre was the team's manager for all four championships and its star players included Derek Jeter, Mariano Rivera, Bernie Williams, Paul O'Neill, Andy Pettite, and Tino Martinez. The Yankees lost the World Series in 2001 four games to three to the Arizona Diamondbacks, but won two memorable extra inning games at Yankee Stadium, and the team was widely credited for providing the city with an emotional lift in the aftermath of the 11 September 2001 terrorist attacks. The team reached the World Series again in 2003 but lost to the Florida Marlins and a year later fell one game short of making it to the series when they squandered a three games to zero lead in the American League Championship Series to the archrival Boston Red Sox. In 2008 George Steinbrenner turned over control of the team to his sons Hal and Hank. In 2009 the Yankees played their first game in the new Yankee Stadium, located across East 161st Street from the old stadium, which was to be taken down and replaced by park land. The New York Yankees, often known as the "Bronx Bombers," dominated baseball from the early 1920s and are perhaps the most famous team in the history of sport. By 2009 they had won 27 World Series and 40 American League pennants.

Frank Graham, *The New York Yankees: An Informal History* (New York: G. P. Putnam's Sons, 1948); Donald Honig, *The New York Yankees* (New York: Crown, 1981); Mark Gallagher, *Day by Day in New York Yankees History* (Champaign, Ill.: Leisure Press, 1983)

See also SPORTS and BASEBALL.

Lawrence S. Ritter, David White

Niblo's Garden. Entertainment center at Broadway and Prince Street. When purchased in 1823 by the Irish impresario William Niblo, the site was known as the Columbian Gardens and frequented for open-air events. Niblo added the Sans Souci Theatre to the landscaped grounds in 1827; with the further addition of a saloon and hotel the complex was renamed Niblo's Garden and opened on 18 May 1829. The facility could seat 3000 and soon became famous for fashionable entertainment. It was the site of first performances by Joseph Jefferson, Charles Kean, Edwin Forrest, James and Lester Wallack, Charlotte Cushman, Dion Boucicault, and Adelina Patti and of early performances by the Philharmonic Society; also, the polka was reportedly introduced there in 1844. Destroyed by fire in 1846, the facility reopened in 1849. On 27 September 1855 George F(rederick) Bris-

Niblo's Garden

tow's *Rip van Winkle,* the first American opera on an American subject, premiered there. Niblo retired in 1858, and Niblo's Garden was soon acquired by A. T. Stewart. The last performance in the theater was given on 23 March 1895.

Marion R. Casey

Nicholas Brothers. Team of tap dancers, consisting of the brothers Fayard (Antonio) Nicholas (*b* Mobile, Ala., 20 Oct 1914; *d* Toluca Lake, Calif., 24 Jan 2006) and Harold Nicholas (*b* Winston–Salem, N.C., 17 March 1921; *d* New York City, 3 July 2000). Their parents were musicians in a vaudeville pit band, and the boys learned to dance by watching other performers. The family moved from Philadelphia to Harlem in 1932, and the brothers were soon the regular final act at the Cotton Club, where they worked alongside performers Duke Ellington, Cab Calla-way, and Ethel Waters. They combined classical tap dancing with ballet and rigorous acrobatics, using their entire bodies with the grace and agility of the most skilled adult tap dancers. In 1930 they made their debut on Broadway in the first production of *Babes in Arms* (choreography by George Balanchine). They performed at the Cotton Club throughout the 1930s even while they made their first motion pictures; they also appeared in many musicals in Hollywood, among them *Stormy Weather* (1943) with Lena Horne and *The Pirate* (1948) with Gene Kelly. In 2003 the Nicholas Brothers were inducted into the National Museum of Dance and Hall of Fame in Saratoga Springs, New York.

Rusty E. Frank, *Tap!: The Greatest Tap Dance Stars and Their Stories, 1900–1955* (New York: William Morrow, 1990)

Amanda Aaron

nickel fare. By the late nineteenth century most urban railways in the United States charged passengers a standard fare of five cents for a single ride of unlimited distance. This uniform nickel fare was adopted in 1900 in the original contract between the City of New York and the Interborough Rapid Transit Company (IRT) and retained in 1913 when the IRT and its competitor, the Brooklyn Rapid Transit Company, signed contracts for additional lines. Inflation before and during World War I lowered the real value of the nickel of 1904 to 2.25 cents by 1920, so that in the 1920s and 1930s even the poor could ride the subway frequently. But the low fare also deprived the transit companies of the income they needed to maintain service: between 1916 and 1919 the cost of steel increased from $30 to $90 a ton and that of coal from $3.23 to $6.07 a ton, and the cost of brake shoes increased by 150 percent. The companies kept wages low, introduced labor-saving machinery such as turnstiles and automatic door openers, and deferred maintenance. The result was that the subways physically declined. Company demands for an increase in the fare were extremely unpopular. In his reelection campaign in 1921 Mayor John F. Hylan called the nickel fare a "property right" for middle- and working-class citizens; his landslide victory was widely attributed to his strong position on the issue. As a result the five-cent fare became an article of faith honored by every mayor until 1948, when Mayor William O'Dwyer reluctantly doubled it.

Clifton Hood

Niebuhr, Reinhold (*b* Wright City, Mo., 21 July 1892; *d* Stockbridge, Mass., 1 June 1971). Prominent theologian and social theorist. The son of a midwestern German pastor, he graduated from Elmhurst College (1910) and Eden Theological Seminary (1913) and earned a bachelor's degree in divinity (1914) and a master of arts (1915) at Yale University. From 1915 to 1928 he was the pastor of Bethel Evangelical Church in Detroit. He moved to New York City in 1928 to teach "applied Christianity" at Union Theological Seminary, remaining there until 1960. While in the city he wrote more than a dozen books and hundreds of articles and was a speaker and consultant for many groups. From its formation in 1941 he edited *Christianity and Crisis,* a religious journal of social and political commentary. He sought election to Congress as a Socialist in 1930, but by 1936 gravitated to the Democratic Party; he later became a consultant to the State Department and after World War II helped to form the Americans for Democratic Action. Considered "neo-orthodox" by many, he renounced the ideals of human goodness, inevitable progress, and adaptive personality that were central to liberal Protestantism and urged his followers to embrace a brand of realism in which they recognize and repent for the evils they necessarily commit. He considered life fraught with paradox and tension and explicable only by dialectical analysis, believing that God demands mankind's intense engagement in history, which nonetheless acquires meaning only through his transcendent purposes. Liberal in his theological method, to which he gave broad secular applications, Niebuhr was instrumental in reshaping Protestantism to protest an age of totalitarianism, economic depression, and impersonality. A part of West 120th Street between Broadway and Riverside Drive is named in his honor.

Charles W. Kegley, ed., *Reinhold Niebuhr: His Religious, Social, and Political Thought* (New York: Macmillan, 1956); Richard W. Fox, *Reinhold Niebuhr: A Biography* (New York: Pantheon, 1985)

James D. Bratt

Nielsen, A. C. See ACNielsen.

Nightingale–Bamford School. Private girls' elementary and secondary school opened in 1920 in Manhattan as Miss Nightingale's School by Frances N. Nightingale, a teacher since 1906, and Maya Stevens Bamford. It took its current name in 1929, when it moved to 20 East 92nd Street. In 1989 the original schoolhouse was renovated and an adjacent brownstone was added. In the twenty-first century the school offers a classical, 13-year college preparatory program for 560 students; it had only five headmistresses in its first 70 years.

Richard Schwartz

Nine Eleven (9/11). See September 11.

92nd Street Y(M-YWHA). Jewish community center at 1395 Lexington Avenue in Manhattan, formed in 1874 as the Young Men's Hebrew Association (YMHA) by German Jews as a social and literary society for Jewish young adults. In 1882 a branch for Russian Jewish immigrants opened on the Lower East Side, which evolved into the Educational Alliance (1889). A broad range of social, religious, educational, and recreational activities was developed in the late 1890s to appeal to young people who were not reached by synagogues and to encourage support from the Jewish community. Jacob H. Schiff purchased the 92nd Street property and paid for construction of a building, occupied from 1900 to 1928. This facility was replaced in 1930 by the present structure, to which an addition was made in 1968. In 1942 the 92nd Street Y absorbed the Young Women's Hebrew Association (YWHA, founded in 1902), which moved its programs to 92nd Street from Harlem and at the same time opened Jewish neighborhood centers in other areas of the city. Reincorporated in 1945 as the YM-YWHA, the 92nd Street Y merged in 1962 with the Clara de Hirsch Home for Working Girls (1897), which had begun as a trade school and residence for immigrants and had become solely a residence during the 1920s.

In the twenty-first century the 92nd Street Y remains a nonsectarian agency offering diverse cultural, educational, and recreational activities, including concerts, lectures, and films, as well as classes in Jewish education, the humanities, dance, fine arts, and music. It also operates a nursery school and kindergarten, after-school programs, summer day camps, adult travel programs, a health and fitness center, a senior adult center, a residence for young adults, and a library and archives.

Alfred Stern, ed., *Building Character for Seventy-Five Years* (New York: YM-YWHA, 1949)

Steven W. Siegel

Nixon, Richard M(ilhous) (*b* Yorba Linda, Calif., 9 Jan 1913; *d* New York City, 22 April 1994). Thirty-seventh president of the United States. After graduating from law school in 1937 he failed to secure a position on Wall Street and returned to California to work for a law firm in Whittier and enter politics. He served in the U.S. Congress from 1947 to 1953 and as vice president of the United States under Dwight D. Eisenhower from 1953 to 1961. After running unsuccessfully for the presidency in 1960 and for the governorship of California in 1962 he moved with his family to New York City, where he lived at 810 Fifth Avenue and worked for the law firm of Mudge, Rose, Guthrie and Alexander. He soon became a partner in the firm and began to rebuild his political career with the help of his colleague John N. Mitchell. After being elected president of the United States in 1968 he left the city for Washington, D.C. (Mitchell served as his attorney general). Reelected in 1972, he resigned in 1974 during the Watergate scandal and moved to San Clemente, California. In 1980 he returned with his wife to New York City, where he took up residence in a cooperative apartment at 142 East 65th Street and rented an office suite at 26 Federal Plaza. He sold the apartment in 1981 and moved to suburban New Jersey. In 1984 he tried to buy a cooperative apartment at 760 Park Avenue but withdrew his offer in the face of objections from other residents. He moved his office in 1988 to Short Hills, New Jersey.

Stephen E. Ambrose, *Nixon* (New York: Simon and Schuster, 1987–89)

Edward T. O'Donnell

Nizer, Louis (*b* London, 6 Feb 1902; *d* New York City, 10 Nov 1994). Lawyer. After moving to New York City, he lived in Brooklyn where his father had a cleaning and dyeing shop. After graduating from Columbia College (where he won two oratory prizes) and Columbia Law School (1924) he studied copyright law and started the law firm of Phillips, Nizer, Benjamin, Krim and Ballon. He worked for such celebrities as Johnny Carson, Salvador Dali, Julius Erving, Charlie Chaplin, and Mae West. In 1954 he won a libel suit on behalf of Quentin Reynolds against the columnist Westbrook Pegler and the Hearst Corporation, inspiring a play on Broadway, *A Case of Libel* (1963). In 1962 he represented Henry Faulk, a CBS radio personality, who was accused of being a communist. His success in this case led to the end of blacklisting in broadcasting. The Motion Picture Association of America became his client in 1966. Nizer's published writings include *My Life in Court* (1961), *Implosion Conspiracy* (1972), and *Catspaw* (1992). He was also a prominent Jewish philanthropist, and Yeshiva University honored him in 1957 with an award for "honoring the spiritual and cultural heritage of Judaism in America."

George J. Lankevich

NL Industries [National Lead Industries]. Firm of lead and titanium producers. Incorporated in New Jersey on 7 December 1891 as the National Lead Company, by 1920 it operated plants in Brooklyn, Long Island City, Staten Island, and four other places around the United States. It became one of four firms that produced 90 percent of all American-made white lead used in the manufacture of paint. After heavy investment in titanium pigments the firm acquired the Titanium Pigments Company (1932), which soon became a major division. In 1935 the largest titanium pigment plant in the United States opened at Sayreville, New Jersey. Additional foreign and domestic acquisitions further diversified the firm, and on 16 April 1971 it took its present name. The firm long maintained its headquarters at 445 Park Avenue in Manhattan but by the early twenty-first century operations had moved to Texas.

David B. Sicilia

Noah, Mordecai M(anuel) (*b* Philadelphia, 19 July 1785; *d* New York City, 22 March 1851). Journalist, public official, and playwright. He edited six newspapers in New York City, including the lively and influential *National Advocate* (1817–24), the *New-York Enquirer* (1826–29), and the *Evening Star* (1833–40). His variable political loyalties ranged across the spectrum from Tammany Democrat to Jacksonian to Whig, and he served the city in various patronage positions: sheriff, judge, and surveyor of the Port of New York. His promotion of Jewish causes and his successful presidency of the Hebrew Benevolent Society (1842–51) made him the most visible spokesman of American Jewry. Among his plays are *She Would Be a Soldier* (1819) and *Marion; or, the Hero of Lake George* (1821). Noah was a spirited nationalist with an interest in many social and municipal reforms.

Mariam Touba

Nobel Prize. Named for the scientist and inventor Alfred Nobel, the Nobel Prizes have been awarded every year since 1901. As of 2009, about 150 people born in New York City or who have affiliations with city institutions have been honored with the Nobel Prize.

Nobel Laureates Associated with New York City Institutions at Time of Award

Name	Nobel Prize	Institution
Richard Axel	Physiology or Medicine (2004)	Columbia University
Nicholas Murray Butler	Peace (1931)	Columbia University
Martin Chalfie	Chemistry (2008)	Columbia University
André F. Cournand	Physiology or Medicine (1956)	Bellevue Hospital
Clinton Davisson	Physics (1937)	Bell Telephone Laboratories
Robert F. Engle III	Economic Sciences (2003)	New York University
Robert F. Furchgott	Physiology or Medicine (1998)	SUNY Health Science Center
Eric R. Kandel	Physiology or Medicine (2000)	Columbia University
Tsung-Dao Lee	Physics (1957)	Columbia University
Robert A. Mundell	Economic Sciences (1999)	Columbia University
Edmund S. Phelps	Economic Sciences (2006)	Columbia University
Isidor Isaac Rabi	Physics (1944)	Columbia University
James Rainwater	Physics (1975)	Columbia University
Dickinson W. Richards	Physiology or Medicine (1956)	Columbia University
Joseph E. Stiglitz	Economic Sciences (2001)	Columbia University
Horst L. Störmer	Physics (1998)	Columbia University
Max Theiler	Physiology or Medicine (1951)	Rockefeller Foundation
Harold C. Urey	Chemistry (1934)	Columbia University
William Vickrey	Economic Sciences (1996)	Columbia University
Rosalyn Yalow	Physiology or Medicine (1977)	Veterans Administration Hospital
Hideki Yukawa	Physics (1949)	Columbia University

Source: Nobelprize.org

In addition to recognizing achievements in the fields of physics, chemistry, economics, literature, and physiology or medicine, the Nobel Peace Prize is given for excellence in humanitarian efforts. The first Nobel Peace Prize was awarded to native New Yorker Theodore Roosevelt in 1906. A small sampling of the New York laureates includes Kenneth Arrow (Economics, 1972), Nicholas Murray Butler (Peace, 1931), Richard Feynman (Physics, 1965), and Steven Weinberg (Physics, 1979).

Noble, John A(lexander) (*b* Paris, 17 March 1913; *d* New York City, 15 May 1983). Maritime artist. Noble moved to the United States in 1919 with his parents, American impressionist painter John "Wichita Bill" Noble and Amelia Peische Noble. He attended Friends Seminary and the National Academy of Design in the city and began working as a seaman when he was 15, settling in Staten Island in his late 20s. In the 1940s he devoted himself fully to his art, building a floating studio across the Kill van Kull in suburban Bayonne, New Jersey. Noble named his studio Graveyard; there he depicted the New York harbor in oil paintings, charcoal drawings, and stone lithographs. The Noble Maritime Collection opened at the Snug Harbor Cultural Center in 2000.

Kate Lauber

No Deal Party. Political party formed in 1945 by Mayor Fiorello H. La Guardia to provide a position on the ballot for Newbold Morris, president of the City Council and a candidate to succeed La Guardia as mayor. Morris's candidacy was a deliberate effort to draw votes away from the Republican Party, with which La Guardia was engaged in a dispute. The party drew 21 percent of the vote and disbanded soon after the election.

Chris McNickle

Noguchi, Hideyo [Seisaku] (*b* Inawashiro, Japan, 24 Nov 1876; *d* Accra [now in Ghana], 21 May 1928). Bacteriologist, parasitologist, and immunologist. He moved to the United States in 1899 after meeting the American microbiologist Simon Flexner, with whom he joined the Rockefeller Institute at its inception in 1904; he remained there for the rest of his career and conducted innovative studies of syphilis, rabies, polio, and yellow fever. On a trip to Africa to study the relationship between the South American and African strains of the virus that causes yellow fever he contracted the disease and died.

Joseph S. Lieber

Noguchi, Isamu (*b* Los Angeles, 17 Nov 1904; *d* New York City, 30 Dec 1988). Sculptor. In 1923 he moved to New York City to study medicine at Columbia University. He turned to sculpture in 1924 after taking classes at Leonardo da Vinci Art School and set up his first studio at 127 University Place. From 1935 to 1966 he created set designs for the choreographer Martha Graham. In 1938 he designed his first fountain, Ford Fountain (destroyed), for the 1939 New York World's Fair. In 1940 his stainless-steel relief *News* was installed over the entrance of the Associated Press Building at 50 Rockefeller Plaza. In sculptures that took the form of a waterfall wall and undulating ceiling (1956–58, aluminum and steel), he incorporated sound and light into the design of a lobby installation at 666 Fifth Avenue. His first sculpture garden in the city, at Chase Manhattan Bank Plaza (1961–64), used granite and basalt rocks imported from Kyoto. Placed in a glass enclosure below ground, it is open to the sky and visible from above. In 1968 a major retrospective of his work was held at the Whitney Museum of American Art, his sculpture *Red Cube* was permanently installed at 140 Broadway, and his autobiography *A Sculptor's World* was published. His many unrealized designs for the city included playgrounds at the United Nations and in Riverside Park and a sculpture garden for the courtyard of Lever House. From the early 1950s until the end of his life he divided his time between studios in New York City and Japan. In 1985 the Isamu Noguchi Garden Museum, designed and built by the artist to display his works, opened across the street from his studio in Long Island City in Queens.

Harriet F. Senie

NoHo. Neighborhood and historic landmark district in lower Manhattan (2010 pop. *ca* 5000), bounded to the north by Ninth Street, to the east by Third Avenue and the Bowery, to the south by Houston Street, and to the west by Mercer Street; its name is an acronym for the phrase "north of Houston." The land was once the site of Jacob Sperry's Botanic Gardens, which were purchased in 1803 by John Jacob Astor for development. In the 1830s the area attracted fashionable residents such as Warren Delano, Philip Hone, Julia Ward Howe, and James Roosevelt and became known as Astor Place. Commercial ventures such as publishing moved in after the Civil War. Later the area was variously considered part of the Lower East Side, part of the East Village, and part of the warehouse district (which also included SoHo and Tribeca). In the 1970s NoHo became trendy after artists, such as Chuck Close, Robert Mapplethorpe, Robert Rauschenberg, and Frank Stella, moved into century-old loft buildings. The population is generally economically middle class and includes many artists and professionals, as well as celebrities such as Cher, Lauren Hutton, Keith Richards, Russell Simmons, and Britney Spears.

Val Ginter

noise. From its founding New York City was filled with noise, such as the sounds of commerce, drinking songs, and animals freely roaming the streets. During the nineteenth century the din of horse-drawn carriages clattering over cobblestones was deafening, and in the 1870s and 1880s several city ordinances attempted to control noise. As horses disappeared, they were replaced with screeching elevated railways and honking automobiles. Antinoise campaigns ensued. In 1906 Julia Barnett Rice formed the Society for the Suppression of Unnecessary Noise, recruiting Mark Twain as president of a committee that persuaded children to be quiet near hospitals. The city passed its first comprehensive noise code in 1972 despite significant opposition by the construction industry; the code, which is overseen by the Department of Environmental Protection, was overhauled in 2005. The code placed restrictions on construction work, one of the biggest auditory culprits, by limiting most work to weekdays from 7 a.m. to 6 p.m. Even ice cream trucks were barred from playing their jingles while stationary. The new code expanded restrictions on music from bars and restaurants by taking into account bass sounds as well as decibel level. Barking dogs, air conditioners, garbage trucks, cars, and motorcycles were addressed in the code, which made honking illegal except in an emergency. In the early twenty-first century complaints about noise topped the list at 311, the city's government hotline.

Kate Lauber

Nooten Eylandt. Former name of GOVERNORS ISLAND.

Norddeutscher Lloyd. See NORTH GERMAN LLOYD STEAMSHIP LINES.

Normal College High School. Former name of HUNTER COLLEGE HIGH SCHOOL.

Normal College of the City of New York. Name used from 1870 to 1914 by HUNTER COLLEGE.

Normandie. Ocean liner built in France during 1931–32. At more than 1000 feet (300 meters) long and 83,000 tons, it was the largest and heaviest vessel at that time. The ship crossed the Atlantic regularly until 1939 when the outbreak of World War II prevented its return to Europe. Moored at Pier 88, the Coast Guard boarded the ship toward the end of 1941 and claimed it for the federal government. While being converted into a troopship in 1942, the SS *Normandie* caught fire and rolled onto one side, remaining thus until the superstructure was stripped and the hull raised and taken to Columbia Pier in Brooklyn. Two portals salvaged from the ship are now part Our Lady of Lebanon Maronite Cathedral.

Harvey Ardman, *Normandie: Her Life and Times* (New York: Watts, 1985)

James E. Mooney

North Beach. A former resort in northwestern Queens, lying along the shoreline of Bowery Bay and the East River from 80th Street to the shore of Flushing Bay. It was opened on 19 June 1886 as Bowery Bay Beach by the piano maker William Steinway, who wished to provide a local beach resort for workers, with financial support from the brewer George Ehret. The resort was renamed North Beach in February 1891. Between 1895 and 1915 it reached its peak: there were hotels, carousels, scenic railways, restaurants, shooting galleries, dance halls, beer gardens, Ferris wheels, swimming pools, theaters, bowling alleys, picnic grounds, weekly fireworks displays, and boat rides known as chutes. Steamboats carried large crowds from Manhattan and the Bronx, and trolleys ran from Long Island City and Brooklyn. During World War I attendance began to decrease, and it ceased altogether during Prohibition. In the 1920s some of the land was used for Glenn L. Curtiss Airport, which opened in 1939 and was later renamed La Guardia Airport. The runways entirely cover the old pleasure grounds and beach.

Vincent Seyfried

North Brother Island. Island in the western arm of the East River, at the entrance to Long Island Sound. It has an area of 20.5 acres (8.3 hectares) and is part of the Bronx. The Dutch called the island and its neighbor South Brother Island (about a third of a mile, or half a kilometer, to the west) the Gezellen (Companions). For many years North Brother Island was in private hands, until it was purchased in 1871 by the Town of Morrisania. A tuberculosis hospital built there by the Sisters of Charity closed in 1885 when the city took possession of the island and built Riverside Hospital for the treatment of infectious diseases, mostly victims of smallpox. The best-known patient was Typhoid Mary (Mary Mallon). That year the hospital was moved to Welfare (now Roosevelt) Island. On 15 June 1904 the steamboat GENERAL SLOCUM, with passengers on a church-sponsored excursion, caught fire in the East River and was beached on the shore off the island; about 1200 people, mostly women and children, died. With the severe housing shortage after World War II, the city rented out the disused hospital and some Quonset huts to returning veterans studying under the GI Bill. The hospital was later used as a drug rehabilitation center before closing in 1964. In the early twenty-first century the island was off-limits to the public, with its deteriorating buildings obscured by dense vegetation.

Gerard R. Wolfe

Northern Dispensary. Privately funded clinic opened in 1827 to provide health care for the residents of Greenwich Village at little or no cost. The clinic moved in 1831 to a triangular building at the intersection of Waverly Place, Grove Street, and Christopher Street. It became a dental clinic after World War II and remained so until 1989, when a shortage of funds compelled it to cease operations and transfer its land and building to the Roman Catholic Archdiocese of New York.

Northern Dispensary: By-Laws for the Government of the Board of Trustees (New York: William Van Norden, 1829)

Elliott B. Nixon

Northfield. Former administrative district in northwestern Staten Island, bounded to the north by the Kill van Kull, to the east by Rockland and Brielle avenues, to the south by Richmond Road, Richmond Creek, and Fresh Kills Creek, and to the west by the Arthur Kill. The area was known variously as the North Side, the North Division, and the North Quarter until after the American Revolution, when it became one of four administrative districts on the island. Towns within its boundaries included Port Richmond, Mariners Harbor, Old Place, Graniteville, Bulls Head, Travis, Chelsea, and New Springville. The district became obsolete when the city was consolidated in 1898; the last seat was Port Richmond.

Marjorie Johnson

North German Lloyd Steamship Lines [Norddeutscher Lloyd]. A German shipping firm formed in 1858 to connect its home port of Bremen with New York City. Service began in June with crossings by the *Bremen,* the first of three steamships, and in 1863 the firm acquired extensive dock facilities in Hoboken, New Jersey. From the 1860s emigrants from Germany and eastern Europe accounted for much of the westbound traffic. When the United States was still neutral during the early years of World War I, several of the firm's ships sought refuge in New York City, only to be seized by the U.S. Navy when the United States entered the war in 1917. Service to New York City resumed in 1920 but was later interrupted by World War II when several ships again sought refuge in the city; one that did not was the *Bremen,* which raced across the North Atlantic to Murmansk in the Russian Soviet Federative Socialist Republic before safely reaching Bremen several months later. After service resumed in 1951 Lloyd ran the *Bremen* (reconditioned), the *Europa,* and the *Berlin* from New York City to Bremerhaven until 1971. In 1970 it merged with its longtime competitor Hamburg–America Lines. The new firm, Hapag–Lloyd, continued into the 1990s to offer container service to New York City and to operate the *Europa* as a cruise ship. The fleet of North German Lloyd included some ships that held speed records: in 1881 the steamer *Elbe* sailed from Southampton to New York City in eight days, a record that held until 1900, and in 1929 the new *Bremen* set a record for the fastest transatlantic crossing.

Otto J. Seiler, *Bridge across the Atlantic: The Story of Hapag–Lloyd's North American Liner Services* (Herford, Germany: Mittler and Sohn, n.d.)

Rohit T. Aggarwala

North New York. Disused name for a part of the southwestern Bronx lying within the present Mott Haven and bounded to the north by 147th Street, to the east by the neighborhood of Port Morris, to the south by 134th Street, and to the west by Third Avenue. Irish factory workers settled the area during the 1840s, the name North New York first being used as a postal address in 1862. After World War II the neighborhood became the site of two low-income, high-rise housing projects, John Purroy Mitchel Houses and Mott Haven Houses. Some brick apartment buildings from the turn of the century survive; the northern section is more commercial. The population in 2010 is mostly black and Latin American.

Lloyd Ultan

North River. Name by which the Hudson River is known at its southern end.

North River Steamboat. See Clermont.

North Side [Great North Side]. Name applied between 1874 and 1898 to the land north of the East River in what is now the Bronx. Its use was promoted by the North Side Board of Trade (organized on 6 March 1894) as an alternative to the name Annexed District, which many residents disliked. Among the organizations and businesses that used the name were the North Side Savings Bank, the North Side Brewing Company, the North Side Hotel, and the *North Side News,* a Democratic newspaper launched in April 1897. The name fell into disuse after the Bronx became a borough in 1898.

The Great North Side (Bronx: North Side Board of Trade, 1897)

Gary D. Hermalyn

Northside Center for Child Development. Social service organization founded in 1946 by Kenneth B. Clark and Mamie Phipps Clark to provide psychological counseling for troubled youth in Harlem. It was originally called the Northside Testing and Consultation Center and started in a basement apartment of the Dunbar housing project on 135th Street. In 1974 it moved to its present location in the Schomburg Houses on Fifth Avenue and 110th Street. In the twenty-first century the organization offers mental health and educational services to children and families.

David Rosner

North Side News. Democratic newspaper launched on 4 April 1897 and published weekly; it was the first important newspaper in the North Side, the familiar name for the Annexed District, which later became part of the Bronx. The newspaper appeared daily from October 1901 until it ceased publication in the mid-1950s.

Stephen Jenkins, *The Story of the Bronx* (New York: G. P. Putnam's Sons, 1912)

Gary D. Hermalyn

North Side Savings Bank. Savings bank founded in 1905 in the Bronx where there were few similar institutions at the time. The first president was John J. Barry, a wealthy builder born in Ireland, and the first office was at 3196 Third Avenue (near 161st Street); it moved in 1910 to 3230 Third Avenue (near 163rd Street). The bank grew along with the Bronx, and in 1951 the main office was moved to 185 West 231st Street, adjacent to the Major Deegan Expressway. In 1986 the bank was converted from mutual to stock ownership, and in 1997 it was acquired by North Fork Bancorporation.

Chad Ludington

Norton, C(harles) McKim (*b* Lake Forest, Ill., 6 Jan 1907; *d* Lexington, Mass., 10 May 1991). Planner. After graduating from Harvard College in 1929 and Harvard Law School in 1932, he worked as a lawyer in New York City. Norton was elected in 1937 to the board of directors of the Regional Plan Association (RPA), of which his father, Charles Dyer Norton, had been the founding chairman. At RPA, he was responsible for developing a second regional plan for greater New York in the late 1950s. The plan was notable for its public involvement and for its acknowledgment of the dangers of urban sprawl. Norton advocated clustered urban development, strong downtowns, and public parks. He was instrumental in creating the 26,000-acre (10,522-hectare) Gateway National Recreation Area, the country's first urban national park. A supporter of public transit, he also helped to form the Metropolitan Transportation Authority (MTA) in 1968. Norton retired as president of RPA in 1969.

Shan Jayakumar

Norwegian Lutheran Deaconesses' Home and Hospital. Forerunner of the Lutheran Medical Center.

Norwegians. Norwegians emigrated in the seventeenth century to New Amsterdam, where they became shopkeepers, innkeepers, carpenters, traders, and shipbuilders, and introduced a style of clapboard house that became common in the colony. One immigrant was Anneken Henriksen from Bergen, who in 1650 married Jan Arentzen van der Bilt, forebear of the Vanderbilt family. The bustling port of New York attracted Norwegian sailors, carpenters, and those skilled in other aspects of maritime industry.

More Norwegians settled in the city and its environs after 1825. About 6000 lived there in 1869, and by the end of the century many were concentrated in Brooklyn. The largest neighborhood was around the docks, piers, and shipyards along Hamilton Avenue near what is now Red Hook. Several humanitarian organizations were formed, including the Independent Order of Good Templars (1879), a secret temperance society in Brooklyn. The Voluntary Relief Society for the Sick and Poor among Norwegians in New York and Brooklyn, organized in 1883 by the Lutheran deaconess Sister Elizabeth Fedde (1850–1921) and eight clergymen, was incorporated in 1892 as the Norwegian Lutheran Deaconesses' Home and Hospital and situated at Fourth Avenue and 46th Street in Brooklyn. Important churches in Brooklyn included the Trinity Lutheran Church (411 46th Street), established in 1890, and Our Saviour's Lutheran Church (414 80th Street). For many years the Norwegian Seamen's Church owned an impressive edifice at 33 First Place in Carroll Gardens before moving to smaller quarters in Manhattan. The weekly newspaper *Norway Times/Nordisk Tidende,* one of the major Norwegian newspapers in the country, began publication in 1891; among its influential editors was Andreas Nilsson Rygg (1912–29). Many Norwegians settled about the turn of the century in Bay Ridge, a Brooklyn neighborhood that supported a wide range of Norwegian cultural institutions and businesses. The year 1895 saw the formation of the national fraternal order the Sons of Norway and of the American-Scandinavian Foundation, with headquarters in Manhattan; the foundation in 1913 began publishing the quarterly journal *Scandinavian-American Review* (now known as *Scandinavian Review*) and also distributed books, translations, and scholarly works about the five Scandinavian countries. Social clubs and athletic clubs became an essential part of Norwegian culture in the city.

The Norwegian National Federation, formed in 1905, had 40 societies affiliated with it by 1914.

As many as 55,000 first- and second-generation Norwegians lived in New York City in 1940, most of them in Bay Ridge. From 1940 to 1963 Carl Soyland was the editor of the *Norway Times* and was instrumental in promoting Norwegian cultural affairs, especially plays produced with the help of the actress Borgny Hammer. During World War II tons of food and clothing were sent to Norway by American Relief for Norway. The Norwegian Lutheran Deaconesses' Home and Hospital merged in 1956 with the Lutheran Hospital of Manhattan, was renamed the Lutheran Medical Center, and later became a city hospital at Second Avenue in the 50s in Brooklyn. Other health facilities included the Norwegian Children's Home on 84th Street in Dyker Heights, the Norwegian Christian Home and Health Center for the elderly on 67th Street in Brooklyn, and the Eger Home on Staten Island. Bay Ridge lost some of its Scandinavian character during the later decades of the twentieth century as second- and third-generation Norwegians moved to the suburbs. In the mid-1980s the *Norway Times* began to print most of its contents in English, and by 1990 the Norwegian population in the city had fallen to about 10,000. The Sons of Norway continued to operate six lodges in the metropolitan area. More than 20,000 people reported Norwegian ancestry in 2007. Prominent Norwegian immigrants to the city and its environs have included Ole Singstad, who built the Holland Tunnel, and Thor Solberg, a pioneer aviator who in 1935 was the first person to fly solo from the United States to Norway.

A. N. Rygg, *Norwegians in New York, 1825–1925* (New York: Norwegian News, 1942); Erik J. Friis, ed., *They Came from Norway* (New York: Norwegian Immigration Sesquicentennial Commission, 1975)

Erik J. Friis

Norwood. Neighborhood in the northwestern Bronx, bounded to the north by Van Cortlandt Park and Woodlawn Cemetery, to the east by Bronx Park, and to the southwest by Mosholu Parkway. The name is probably a contraction of "north wood." During the American Revolution the area was the site of several skirmishes around the Valentine-Varian House. Although the Williamsbridge Reservoir was built in the area by the city in 1888, most of the land until 1905 was part of a dairy farm belonging to the Varian family. Development began in the early twentieth century after the extension of the Third Avenue elevated line and the subway system created shopping streets along 204th Street and Jerome Avenue. Montefiore Hospital was built in the neighborhood in 1912. Starting in the 1980s and continuing into the early twenty-first century, Norwood attracted a diverse population of new residents, including many from Puerto Rico, the Dominican Republic, India, Cambodia, Vietnam, Korea, the Philippines, and Ireland. There is also a sizable Jewish population. The housing stock consists of apartment buildings and one- and two-family houses.

Lloyd Ultan

Noticias del Mundo. Daily Spanish-language newspaper, launched in 1980 by the Korean spiritual leader and businessman Sun Myung Moon. It covered local, national, and international news from a politically conservative point of view. The newspaper ceased operations in April 2004.

James Bradley

Novelty Ironworks. Firm of iron founders between 12th and 14th streets on the East River in Manhattan, just north of where the Jacob Riis Houses now stand. It was formed in the mid-1830s by the president of Union College, Eliphalet Nott, to build an engine for his anthracite-burning steamboat the *Novelty* (1836), and under the leadership of Thomas B. Stillman and Horatio Allen from 1842 it became the city's largest foundry. The firm made castings for a variety of machinery, and, because it specialized in steam engines, for oceangoing ships during the shipbuilding boom of the early 1850s. Eighteen departments occupied two city blocks and two slips along the river and employed more than 1000 men, most of whom were skilled machinists earning some of the highest wages in the city. Operations were carried out on a vast scale: the bedplate alone for the engine of the steamboat *Arctic* weighed 60 tons (54 metric tons). The immensity of operations at the works and the consequent need for thorough organization and supervision made it the best-known industrial workplace in New York City and a symbol of industrial progress. From the late 1850s engine-building businesses moved their operations to Philadelphia, and although the iron industry prospered during the Civil War most of the large works in the city were in financial straits by the late 1860s. The Novelty Ironworks closed in 1870.

Richard Stott

Novoye Russkoye Slovo [New Russian Word]. Independent, illustrated Russian-language daily newspaper, launched in 1910 as *Russkoye Slovo;* it describes itself as the oldest continuously published newspaper of its kind in the world. Renamed in 1920, it was edited for 50 years by Mark Weinbaum and after 1973 by Andrei Sedych. Until the last years of the Soviet Union the newspaper published material that could not be published there. As of 2007 the circulation was about 45,500. Local news is emphasized, but it also includes reports on international and national events as well as pieces on literary and historical topics.

Robert A. Karlowich, *We Fall and Rise, 1889–1914: Russian-Language Newspapers in New York City* (Metuchen, N.J.: Scarecrow, 1991)

Thomas E. Bird

Novy Zhurnal. Russian-language quarterly journal launched in June 1942 in New York City by Mark Aldanov and Mark Zetlin. Initially known for publishing a wide range of items, it later espoused values of traditional Russian culture and advocated the defense of individual freedoms, publishing material censored in the Soviet Union. It was edited for about 25 years by the influential scholar Ro-

Novelty Ironworks, at the foot of 12th Street

man Gul and, since 1994, by Vladimir Kreid. The journal is especially important to Russians living in the city, who contribute memoirs, correspondence, and bibliographies.

Thomas E. Bird

Nowy Dziennik [Daily News]. Polish-language newspaper, launched in 1971 and published six days a week in New York City. It focuses on Polish and Polish American affairs. In the twenty-first century, it remained one of the major Polish-language daily newspapers in the United States and was headquartered at 333 West 38th Street.

James S. Pula

Nowy Swiat [New World]. Polish-language newspaper published in New York City from 1919 to about 1971. It provided detailed coverage of Polish politics and during the interwar period was a leading supporter of Joseph Pilsudski's regime.

James S. Pula

NRA. See NATIONAL RIFLE ASSOCIATION.

numbers. Term used for illegal gambling operations that usually involve wagers on three-digit numbers from 000 to 999. The winning number, or "hit," is a well-publicized number agreed on by custom: sometimes it is taken from the financial or sports pages (for example, the last three digits of the daily handle, or total amount wagered, at a racetrack). The bettor chooses a number and places a "policy" (a nickname derived from the penny insurance once popular in poor neighborhoods); a "runner" or "writer" usually records bets on slips of paper and takes them to a "spot" (where bets are also accepted) or "store." Betting slips are then collected by "pick-up men" and taken to a "controller" who takes them to the "policy bank," a central facility where the day's hits are tallied and the split of the profits among the spots and runners is figured. Because the payoff on a winning number is usually 600 to 1 and the odds of winning are 999 to 1, about 40 percent of the total amount wagered accrues to the operators, a higher return than in other forms of gambling.

One of the first well-known numbers operators in New York City was Al Adams, who dealt in favors for Tammany Hall and William M. "Boss" Tweed. He had about 1000 policy shops in the 1880s and was known as the meanest gambler in the city because by rigging the numbers he drove other operators out of business. The 1910s and 1920s saw the development of penny ante numbers, a game intended for residents of the poorest neighborhoods. It became popular and was soon the most lucrative kind of numbers game for its operators. Influential operators like Madame St. Clair and Casper Holstein, both of Harlem, made fortunes by running numbers banks. Numbers operators often became influential figures, giving charity as well as investing numbers money in legitimate businesses and other rackets in their neighborhoods. St. Clair's racket, as well as many others in Harlem, was taken over by Dutch Schultz, who terrorized "bankers" into buying his protection and then took control of their businesses. Schultz's underling, Otto "Abbadabba" Berman, later developed a rigging system that prevented numbers heavily bet on from winning. After Schultz's murder in 1935 the racket in Harlem was taken over by white mobsters Lucky Luciano, Meyer Lansky, and Vito Genovese.

The numbers game remained widely played through the 1970s, often operated by organized crime with the complicity of bribed police officers. In 1966 New York State instituted its first lottery, which initially didn't do as well as expected because of the relative simplicity of the numbers, popular trust in the numbers banks, and the numbers' tax-free payoffs. In recent years law enforcement and growing public use of official lotteries have significantly cut into the business of the numbers rackets still in operation in the twenty-first century.

Jesse Drucker, Ben Silk

numismatics. Numismatics, or coin collecting, became popular in the United States in 1857 when the replacement of the large cent by the flying-eagle cent led many enthusiasts to collect a cent from each year since 1793. The American Numismatic Society, formed in New York City on 6 April 1858 as the second such society in North America (after the Numismatic and Antiquarian Society of Philadelphia), was for many years a collectors' club. In 1908 it moved to its own building on 155th Street and focused on scholarship. This shift in emphasis led to the formation of the New York Numismatic Club in the same year, which included among its members Victor D. Brenner, the designer of the Lincoln cent. The Brooklyn Coin Club was organized on 12 November 1932, followed by the Bronx Coin Club on 10 October 1933. Other coin clubs in the city have included those operated in association with the Chase Manhattan Money Museum, the Numismatic Forum of New York, and the Flushing Coin Club. Since 1952 the American Numismatic Society has conducted a summer seminar, which trains graduate students in history, art history, and the classics in numismatics. In 2003 the American Numismatic Society moved from 155th Street to Fulton and William streets in downtown Manhattan.

Howard L. Adelson, *The American Numismatic Society, 1858–1958* (New York: American Numismatic Society, 1958)

See also STAMP AND COIN DEALERS.

John M. Kleeberg

Nurses' Settlement. Name by which the HENRY STREET SETTLEMENT was known from 1898 to 1913.

nursing. Until the early twentieth century medical and nursing care was usually administered at home. At the first hospitals in New York City, opened during colonial times primarily to quarantine infected sailors and immigrants, nursing care was provided by untrained attendants and recovering patients. The first recorded effort to train nurses in the United States was made at New York Hospital in 1798 by Valentine Seaman, a doctor who taught a course in maternity and child care. Nursing of a more professional sort was provided in 1817 by the Sisters of Charity, who were sent to Manhattan from their motherhouse in Maryland by Mother Elizabeth Bayley Seton. After serving in schools, hospitals, and orphanages they founded St. Vincent's Hospital (1849), the Half Orphan Asylum (1856), and New York Foundling Hospital (1869); they also worked at the contagion hospitals on Wards Island, Blackwell's Island, and Randalls Island during outbreaks of smallpox, cholera, and yellow fever.

Racial segregation led to the founding in 1839 of Lincoln Hospital by the Society for the Relief of Worthy, Aged, Indigent Colored Persons. Only African American women were admitted to the training program for nurses offered there from 1898. A training program for nurses was established at the New York Infirmary for Women and Children (1857) by three doctors: Elizabeth Blackwell, the first woman in the United States to earn a medical degree, her sister Emily Blackwell, and their colleague Marie E. Zakrzewska. Elizabeth Blackwell also trained nurses at Bellevue Hospital in 1861 for service in military hospitals during the Civil War. The brutality of war demonstrated the need for better nursing care. The State Charities Aid Association, formed after the war by the philanthropist Louisa Lee Schuyler, sponsored visiting committees to investigate conditions in schools, asylums, and hospitals in the city. After finding filth and depravity at Bellevue Hospital the association in 1873 opened there the first Nightingale school for nurses' training in the United States. Student nurses cared for patients under the supervision of only a superintendent and one or two head nurses, who taught them procedures. Their formal education consisted of lectures delivered sporadically by hospital physicians at night. Admitting women students of good character and holding them to a strict regime of discipline was considered critical to the success of the school's reform mission.

Nightingale schools opened at many other hospitals in the city, where by the 1920s most nursing was provided by students. Graduates of the nursing programs found work mainly in private households but also joined the public health sector and filled the few positions available on hospital staffs. The women's branch of the New York City Mission and Tract Society established Visiting Nursing in 1877, the first organization in the United States to send trained nurses into the homes of indigent patients. The American School for Male Nurses opened in 1886 in connection with the City Training School on Blackwell's Island, followed by the Mills Training School for Male Nurses in 1888 at Bellevue. In 1893 the National League for Nursing was formed and Lillian Wald, a graduate of the nursing school at New York Hospital, organized a settlement later known as the Henry Street Settlement, which became the model for visiting nursing programs in the United States. The American Nurses Association was formed in the city in 1896. The *American Journal of Nursing* was first published there in 1899, and during the same year a course on hospital economics was given at Teachers College, from which a program in higher education for nurses evolved. The Division of Nursing Education at Teachers College later granted advanced degrees and led the effort to professionalize nursing during the first half of the twentieth century. Legislation was passed to set standards (in 1903 for New York State), control practice, and register nurses. M. Adelaide Nutting became the first professor of nursing in the world at Teachers College in 1906. The first meeting of the National Association of Colored Graduate Nurses (NACGN) was held in New York City in 1908. Fifty-eight organizations employed 372 visiting nurses by 1909 to serve the city's neighborhoods. From 1912 to 1950 the National Organization of Public Health Nurses had its headquarters in the city.

Following the influential efforts of female nurses during World War I, education in the field began to grow in popularity particularly for women. In 1932, a College of Nursing was added to New York University while medical education became more accessible and popular within the city and the United States. In 1980, New York City College of Technology began to offer two professional nursing programs as part of the School of Professional Studies in which students can receive an associate's degree in applied science and a bachelor of science required by the New York State Education Department for all registered nurses (RNs). Pace University also added the Leinhard School of Nursing in 1966.

Pregnant women were cared for principally by midwives and nurse-midwives, some of whom were immigrants trained at Bellevue Hospital, which had a program in midwifery from 1911 to 1935. Despite opposition, community-based maternity centers were organized, such as the Maternity Center Association in 1915. The first birth control clinic in the nation was opened in Brooklyn on 16 October 1916 by Margaret Sanger, a nurse who led the struggle to provide birth control to women. Nurses in the city's health department initiated preventive care in school health and child hygiene programs and home visits to postpartum women and their infants.

By the 1920s Lincoln Hospital had the largest nursing school for African Americans in the United States. Before closing in 1961 it granted diplomas to 1864 nurses. Another nursing school for black women opened in 1923 at Harlem Hospital. Through the efforts of the NACGN under the leadership of Adah Belle Thoms, Geneva Estelle Massey Riddle, and Mabel Keaton Staupers discrimination against black nurses was contested and racial quotas in the armed services were eliminated during World War II.

After the war nursing care became increasingly complex. Several levels of certification developed, including those of licensed practical nurse and research nurse (which requires a doctorate). The GI Bill and federal grants financed college education for nurses, and university and college programs gradually replaced the hospital schools: only two of the 26 programs that trained registered nurses in the city in 1989 were offered by hospitals; of the rest nine were senior (baccalaureate) programs and 15 were associate degree programs in community colleges. In 1989 a survey of registered nurses in New York State showed that of those in the five boroughs 49 percent were white, 29 percent African American, 18 percent Asian, 5 percent Puerto Rican and Latin American, and fewer than 1 percent American Indian.

In the mid-1990s nurses in New York City began to earn doctorates and conduct research, and manage large hospital budgets, in addition to providing bedside care in hospitals, visiting the sick in their homes, and ministering to the needy in the community. In 2009 New York State registered 252,662 individuals licensed and registered as professional nurses. According to the New York State Nurses Association, New York City employed over 6400 registered professional nurses in city health care facilities as of 2007.

Jane Mottus, *New York Nightingales: The Emergence of the Nursing Profession at Bellevue and New York Hospital, 1850–1920* (Ann Arbor, Mich.: UMI Research Press, 1981); Darlene Clark Hine, *Black Women in White* (Bloomington: Indiana University Press, 1989)

Meghan Lalonde

nursing-home scandals. Nursing homes in New York City have been the subject of several major scandals. In the late 1950s night raids by the city's department of investigations revealed poor living conditions and lax management at several nursing homes, and other investigations by the welfare department uncovered extensive overcharging by the homes. Several nursing homes were closed as a result, including 10 owned by Bernard Bergman (1911–84). In 1960 a report by the city's investigations commissioner, Louis I. Kaplan, depicted widespread abuse and neglect at the city's nursing homes. None of these investigations attracted much publicity or led to major reforms. The government's initial failure to crack down on rogue nursing-home operations had serious repercussions, because illegal activities worsened after the advent of Medicaid and its system of reimbursements in 1967.

In October 1974 a four-part series in the *New York Times* by John L. Hess broke open the nursing-home scandals. Other journalists also exposed nursing-home fraud, including Jack Newfield of the *Village Voice* and Steve Bauman of the television station WNEW. Governor Hugh L. Carey then appointed a special prosecutor, Charles J. Hynes, to investigate nursing homes throughout New York State, and Assemblyman Andrew Stein of Manhattan held dramatic hearings that brought widespread corruption to light. The most notorious figure to emerge from the scandals was Bergman, who controlled 37 nursing homes in the city, notably the Park Crescent and the Towers Nursing Home on the Upper West Side. Convicted of Medicaid fraud and bribery, he served a year in prison and paid nearly $2 million in fines. Eugene Hollander, who owned four nursing homes in the city, achieved particular notoriety for having purchased valuable paintings with Medicaid payments. He avoided prison by agreeing to divest himself of all his nursing-home interests.

In the end the city's worst nursing homes, including Bergman's, were closed, and a permanent office of special prosecutor was established to oversee the business. The nursing-home scandals also played a role in bringing down two leaders of the state assembly: Stanley Steingut of Queens and Albert H. Blumenthal of Manhattan. The scandals launched the political careers of Stein, who became borough president of Manhattan and president of the City Council, and Hynes, who became district attorney of Brooklyn.

James Bradley

Nutten Island. Former name of Governors Island.

Nutting, M(ary) Adelaide (*b* Frost Village, Quebec, 1 Nov 1858; *d* New York City, 3 Oct 1948). Nursing educator. She moved to New York City in 1899 after becoming known at Johns Hopkins University as a champion of improved nursing education and better working conditions for nurses. She taught in various departments at Teachers College, Columbia University (1899–1925) and in 1906 became the first professor of nursing in the world. One of the most prominent figures in modern nursing, she was instrumental in establishing the Department of Nursing and Health at Teachers College and was the first person to lead it (1910–25).

Joseph S. Lieber

Nuyorican Poets Cafe. A meeting and performance space opened in October 1975 at 505 East Sixth Street in Manhattan. It was established by members of the Nuyorican movement, an informal association of Puerto Rican artists, musicians, and writers living in New York City (the term *Nuyorican* is a blending of "New York" and "Puerto Rican"), whose art focused on their experiences as members of the Puerto Rican diaspora in the city. The cafe was an outgrowth of a salon held from 1973 by Miguel Algarín and Richard August at their apartment in the East Village, which attracted such writers as Lucky Cienfuegos, Miguel Piñero, Pedro Pietri, Tato Laviera, Bittman "Bimbo" Rivas, and Sandra Esteves and where works such as Piñero's *Short Eyes* (1974) and Pietri's *Puerto Rican Obituary* (1974) were written and revised. Although many of the writers associated with the cafe were Spanish-speaking, it also drew such figures as Allen Ginsberg, Gregory Corso, Amiri Baraka, and Ntoszake Shange. The cafe moved in 1980 to an abandoned tenement building at 236 East Third Street. Closed in 1983, it reopened in 1989. In addition to sponsoring readings of poems and screenplays, the Nuyorican Poets Cafe produced more than two dozen plays and published poetry anthologies such as *Aloud: Voices from the Nuyorican Poets Cafe* (1994).

Roland Legiardi-Laura

N. W. Ayer and Partners. Advertising agency formed in 1869 in Philadelphia as N. W. Ayer and Son. The firm opened an office in the Flatiron Building in New York City in 1903, and the city gradually became its unofficial headquarters; the headquarters were formally moved to New York City in 1973. Over the years the firm became known for several innovations in advertising, including the first color print advertisement (1893) and the first radio advertisement (1922); for long-running campaigns on behalf of such clients as the National Biscuit Company, Steinway and Sons, and American Telephone and Telegraph (an association that began in 1908 and continued into the early twenty-first century); and for several memorable advertising slogans, including "A Diamond Is Forever" (for DeBeers Consolidated Mines), "Reach Out and Touch Someone" (for American Telephone and Telegraph), and "Be All That You Can Be" (for the U.S. Army). In 2002 N. W. Ayer and Partners merged with the Kaplan Thaler Group, another advertising agency, and began operating under the Kaplan Thaler name. Up until this merger, it was the oldest agency in continuous operation in the United States.

Nyad, Diana (*b* New York City, 22 Aug 1949). Long-distance swimmer and radio commentator. On 6 October 1975 she swam around Manhattan Island in record time—seven hours, 57 minutes—and in 1979 she set the world distance record, 102.5 miles (165 kilometers). Since 1980 she has been a commentator for CNBC, National Public Radio, Fox, and ABC Sports.

Diana Nyad, *Other Shores* (New York: Random House, 1978); Valjean McLenighan, *Diana: Alone against the Sea* (New York, Heinemann, 1980)

Jameson W. Doig

NYANA. See New York Association for New Americans.

NYC Condom. The nation's first official city-branded condom, unveiled by the New York City Department of Health and Mental Hygiene on 14 February 2007. Health department clinics have distributed condoms for free since 1971. The program expanded to include community-based organizations during the 1980s after the AIDS epidemic was recognized as a public health crisis. In 2005 the health department launched an Internet-based system for bulk ordering, a move that increased distribution to more than 1.5 million condoms per month through clinics, community centers, bars, clubs, and retail and commercial centers. On Valentine's Day 2007 more than 150,000 newly designed NYC Condoms were distributed throughout the city in an initiative that directed attention toward New York City's awareness of the importance of sexual health and free condom distribution. That year, the health department handed out 39 million free condoms in more than 900 locations, a distribution growth of 120 percent. In February 2008 industrial designer Yves Béhar redesigned NYC Condom packages and dispensers. For this, he won an International Design Excellence Award in the Design Strategy category.

Anne Epstein

NYPL. See New York Public Library.

Oakland Gardens. Neighborhood in northeastern Queens, bounded to the north by Oakland Lake and 48th Avenue, to the east by Alley Pond Park, to the south by Union Turnpike, and to the west by Cunningham Park. A housing development of the same name is bounded by the Long Island Expressway, Cloverdale Boulevard, 69th Avenue, and Springfield Boulevard. The area was settled in 1645 by John Hicks, one of the original patentees of Flushing. In the early nineteenth century his property passed into the Lawrence family, and about 1847 Frederick Newbold Lawrence built a mansion named the Oaks, which lent its name to the nearby lake. Manhattan restaurateur John Taylor bought the estate in 1859 and with John Henderson transformed it into a horticultural establishment of more than 30 greenhouses specializing in roses and orchids. In 1886 Taylor's son, John H. Taylor, inherited the property; he organized the Oakland Golf Club in 1896 and became its first president. Among the members were Alfred E. Smith, Robert F. Wagner (1), and Bernard Baruch. After 1911 the club bought the golf course; the Draper Realty Company of Manhattan bought the rest of the land and divided it into building lots. Morton Pickman of Forest Hills bought the club in 1952. His plan to erect high-rise apartment buildings was blocked, and he sold the property to Marvin Kratter in 1958. The City of New York bought the golf club in the early 1960s and built Public School 203, Benjamin Cardozo High School, and a new 34-acre campus for Queensborough Community College (1978). In 1963 Alexander Muss and Sons bought the remaining 65 acres of the golf course and built about 700 one- and two-family houses (initially selling for $33,745 to $45,240). William K. Vanderbilt's Long Island Motor Parkway (1908) cuts through Oakland Gardens east from Cunningham Park. In the early 1960s many homes were demolished and others moved for the Clearview Expressway. Oakland Lake, a glacial kettle pond, was part of Flushing's water system; it was degraded by development and drainage of the wetlands in the twentieth century, but in 1988 the New York State Department of Environmental Conservation designated the lake area as a protected wetland. In the twenty-first century, the lake has been rehabilitated and is home to many species of fish and birds.

Jeffrey A. Kroessler

Oakwood. Neighborhood in east central Staten Island, lying near the southern shore and bounded to the north by Ebbitts Street, to the east by the Atlantic Ocean, to the south by Great Kills Park, and to the west by the tracks of the Staten Island Railway (SIR); it stretches along a flat corridor between the Atlantic Ocean and the hilly interior of the island. During the nineteenth century the area was an ocean resort. Development increased for a time after a subway tunnel under the Narrows was proposed in the 1920s that would have linked the SIR and the Fourth Avenue subway (now the R line to Bay Ridge). The commercial thoroughfare Hylan Boulevard splits the neighborhood between the beach to the southeast and Oakwood Heights to the northwest. In the early twenty-first century Oakwood was a middle-class neighborhood of one- and two-family homes and garden apartments; overdevelopment had become a neighborhood concern.

Andrew Sparberg

Obama, Barack (Hussein) (*b* Honolulu, 4 Aug 1961). The 44th president of the United States of America. Barack Obama was born in Hawaii. After his parents divorced, Obama moved with his mother and stepfather to Jakarta, Indonesia, in 1967, but returned to live with his grandparents in Hawaii in 1971. In 1979 Obama moved to Los Angeles to attend Occidental College but transferred two years later to Columbia University. In his memoir, *Dreams from My Father,* he tells the story of being locked out of his apartment at 142 West 109th Street and sleeping in an alleyway between 108th and 109th streets near Amsterdam Avenue. In his senior year Obama moved to 339 East 94th Street. Following his graduation from Columbia in 1983 with a degree in political science, Obama worked for a few months at the Business International Corporation to pay off his student loans, then as a community organizer for the New York Public Interest Research Group located at the City College of New York.

Obama moved to Chicago in 1985 and worked as a community organizer before entering Harvard Law School in 1988. After graduation Obama returned to Chicago, where he served as a lecturer at the University of Chicago Law School for 12 years. In 2004 he won election to the U.S. Senate, and on 4 November 2008 he became the first African American president.

Anne Epstein

Obelisk. See Cleopatra's Needle.

Obie Award. Award instituted in 1955 by the *Village Voice* to acknowledge the achievements of Off-Broadway theater (and later Off-Off-Broadway theater). Citations are given for acting, directing, playwriting, and design, with special awards for distinguished or sustained achievement.

Ross Wetzsteon, ed., *The Obie Winners: The Best of Off-Broadway* (New York: Doubleday, 1980)

D. S. Moynihan

O'Brien, John P(atrick) (*b* Worcester, Mass., 1 Feb 1873; *d* New York City, 22 Sept 1951). Mayor. After a successful career as the corporation counsel of New York City and surrogate, he won a special election in 1932 to finish James J. Walker's unexpired term as mayor. His ineptitude in public relations turned voters against him, and he finished third in the election of 1933, which was won by Fiorello H. La Guardia.

Frank Vos

Observatory Place. One of the five open spaces provided for in the pivotal 1811 Commissioners' Plan. Consisting of 26 acres, it ran from 89th to 94th streets between Fourth Avenue (Park) and Fifth Avenue. The land was private. Starting in the 1830s, portions were sold off for building lots. It was abolished in 1865 in order to extend local streets.

Lisa Keller

occupational health. In the late nineteenth and early twentieth centuries, reformers working with the urban poor focused on improving health and safety in the workplace. Such crusaders as Alice Hamilton and Florence Kelley, who were associated with the settlement movement, paid particular attention to the link between illness and working conditions. In 1890 workers for charities and settlement houses in New York City found that nearly one person in every four families died of tuberculosis (then called consumption); in poorer neighborhoods the toll was higher and entire communities were devastated. The Triangle Shirtwaist fire, which killed 146 workers, shocked the public and persuaded the state legislature to organize a factory inspection commission. The commission held hearings on the dangers of several occupations and issued a report that marked a turning point in efforts to prevent occupational disease and accidents. The publicity surrounding these hearings spurred the passage of workers' compensation laws in New York City, and several members of the commission later played an important role in the administration of Franklin D. Roosevelt, including Kelley, Frances Perkins, and Robert F. Wagner.

During the second decade of the twentieth century the Consumers' League joined forces with the International Ladies' Garment Workers' Union to seek better working conditions and control the spread of communicable diseases in the workplace; the "union label" attached to garments came to symbolize clean working conditions. Activist organizations like the Workers' Health Bureau of America continued to aid labor groups such as the

Bakers' and Confectioners' Union and the Amalgamated Clothing Workers in investigating hazards in the workplace. At the same time the widespread introduction of lead into paint and gasoline and the increased smelting of ores heightened awareness of dangers to workers and the public. John B. Andrews and the American Association for Labor Legislation, which had its headquarters in New York City, led the campaigns against "phossy jaw" and lead poisoning, and industrial hygienists and occupational physicians tested the exposure to lead of painters and battery workers.

As the political power of progressive reformers waned in the 1920s, professional industrial hygienists replaced labor advocates as custodians of health and safety in the workplace. Such organizations as the National Safety Council and the Industrial Hygiene Association encouraged workers and management to assume greater responsibility in reducing injuries and disease. The Workers' Health Bureau, based in New York City and led by progressive women, was one of the few organizations that maintained the traditional alliance with labor; it helped in particular to focus public attention on the plight of watchmakers who were suffering from chronic diseases because of their ingestion of radium. During the Depression labor unions regained their earlier power, and the number of liability suits increased. Among occupational diseases silicosis was of particular concern because it affected workers who inhaled silica dust in the rapidly growing construction industry. The Congress of Industrial Organizations used the deplorable health and safety conditions of these heavy industries as a vehicle for organizing unions.

The decline of heavy industry after World War II and the rise of white-collar and service industries led to a general belief that occupational diseases would be virtually eliminated. Instead, however, occupational health problems took on new forms. Dangers associated with the telecommunications and electrical industries received much attention, as did the proliferation of video display terminals: in the 1980s some studies suggested a link between exposure to low-level radiation from the terminals and miscarriages. Many office workers using computer keyboards also became afflicted with repetitive strain injuries such as carpal tunnel syndrome. The New York Committee on Occupational Safety and Health, an organization of industrial hygienists, union activists, and officials, has been in the forefront of efforts to protect the workforce since the early 1970s.

David Rosner and Gerald Markowitz, eds., *Dying for Work: Workers' Safety and Health in Twentieth-Century America* (Bloomington: Indiana University Press, 1987)

See also PHYSICAL DISABILITIES.

David Rosner

Ocean Breeze. Neighborhood in east central Staten Island, lying southeast of Hylan Boulevard. Often considered the southern section of SOUTH BEACH, it was originally a summer beach colony of bungalows and tents; the beach is now part of the city parks system. Part of an effort to revitalize Staten Island beaches, the 835-foot Ocean Breeze Fishing Pier opened in 2003. Seaview Avenue is the main thoroughfare. Near Hylan Boulevard is a residential area of small one-family houses.

Marjorie Johnson

Ocean Hill. Neighborhood in east central Brooklyn, bounded to the north by Broadway, to the east by Van Sinderen Avenue, to the south by East New York Avenue, and to the west by Ralph, Atlantic, and Saratoga avenues. It was developed as an exclusive neighborhood in the 1890s. By the early twentieth century there were department stores, theaters, and some industrial facilities, and Broadway and Rockaway Avenue were the main thoroughfares. With neighboring Brownsville the neighborhood formed one of three districts designated in the 1960s to test community control over local schools, with support from the Ford Foundation. Conflict ensued between school leaders, members of the community, and the United Federation of Teachers, sparking a bitter teacher strike. After 1970 houses were abandoned, and many stores along Broadway were destroyed by fire during a blackout in 1977. In the twentieth and twenty-first centuries two- to four-family houses predominated; the city planned to rebuild one- and two-family houses on vacant lots and to renovate vacant apartment buildings along Eastern Parkway and multifamily houses. The East Broadway Merchants' Association and the Ocean Hill Bushwick Bedford–Stuyvesant Development Corporation undertook the improvement of Broadway, which remained an important thoroughfare. In the early twenty-first century the population was largely African American; a small Latino community lived in the northern section near Broadway. In 2009 a new, green, 41-unit condominium opened for area residents, built by Habitat for Humanity.

Ellen Marie Snyder-Grenier

Ocean Parkway. Divided thoroughfare running about 6 miles (10 kilometers) north to south from Prospect Park to the southeastern edge of Coney Island. The parkway was suggested in the 1860s in reports to the park commissioners of Brooklyn by Frederick Law Olmsted and Calvert Vaux, who together drew up a plan influenced by boulevards in Paris and Berlin. The city of Brooklyn acquired the land for Ocean Parkway in 1868 and began construction in 1874. It was completed six years later and resembled the Eastern Parkway: it had a width of 210 feet (64 meters), a central roadway, two malls, two side roads, and two sidewalks and was lined with trees, benches, and playing tables. The country's first bicycle path runs the length of the parkway. The central drive was used for horse and carriage races, hence its nickname, the Ocean Parkway Speedway. It ran through several neighborhoods, including Parkville and Windsor Terrace; later, other neighborhoods such as Kensington were built along the parkway. About the turn of the twentieth century, houses were constructed along the edges, attracting buyers from Bushwick, Bedford–Stuyvesant, and Brooklyn Heights. Many grand houses were built about the time of World War I, which marked the end of a period of suburban affluence in the neighborhood. In the 1920s rows of one- and two-family houses and small apartment buildings were erected, and the upper reaches of the parkway became the site of luxury apartment buildings with elevators; after World War II apartment buildings replaced older houses on streets near the parkway. Parallel to Ocean Parkway and several blocks to the east is Coney Island Avenue, an important commercial street. In 1975 the city designated Ocean Parkway as a scenic landmark.

Ellen Marie Snyder-Grenier

Ochs, Adolph S(imon) (*b* Cincinnati, 12 March 1858; *d* Chattanooga, Tenn., 8 April 1935). Newspaper publisher. He began his career in journalism in 1872 as an apprentice at the *Knoxville Chronicle* in Tennessee and worked as a printer in Knoxville and Chattanooga until 1878 when he borrowed money and bought the struggling daily *Chattanooga Times.* The newspaper thrived under his stewardship, but after the financial panic of 1893 he was forced to seek new sources of capital. In 1896 he rescued the *New York Times* from receivership, quickly making the newspaper profitable and respectable by emphasizing objective news rather than opinion and sensationalism. He coined the slogan "All the News That's Fit to Print" and resolved to keep the newspaper in his family. For many years he lived at 308 West 75th Street (later the site of the Manhattan Day School); he was active as the publisher of the *Times* to the end of his life.

Gerald W. Johnson, *An Honorable Titan: A Biographical Study of Adolph S. Ochs* (New York: Harper and Brothers, 1946)

See also NEW YEAR'S EVE.

Harrison Salisbury

O'Connor, John Joseph Cardinal (*b* Philadelphia, 15 Jan 1920; *d* New York City, 3 May 2000). Roman Catholic cardinal. He moved from being a Philadelphia priest (1945–52), to naval chaplain (1952–79), to bishop of Scranton, Pennsylvania (1983). In 1984 he became archbishop of New York and cardinal in 1985. Upon arrival in New York, he joined a coalition that successfully challenged in the courts a directive prohibiting employment discrimination on the basis of sexual orientation. In 1984 he clashed with vice presidential candidate Geraldine Ferraro over abortion; in 1990 he warned that Catholic politicians who deviated from church teaching risked excommunication. His condemnation of homosexuality and birth control led protesters in 1989 to disrupt his Mass at St. Patrick's Cathedral. Other of his decisions proved more popular. O'Connor defended labor and kept parishes open that had lost most of their communicants. He advocated new charities, opening a hospice for people with AIDS (1985), and forming a religious order, the Sisters of Life (1991). He tendered his resignation at the age of 75 as canon law required, but Pope John Paul II kept him in his position until his death from brain cancer. He is buried beneath St. Patrick's Cathedral, and his papers are in the archdiocesan archive.

Nat Hentoff, *John Cardinal O'Connor: At the Storm Center of a Changing American Catholic Church* (New York: Charles Scribner's Sons, 1988); John Cardinal O'Connor and Edward I. Koch, *His Eminence and Hizzoner: A Candid Exchange* (New York: William Morrow, 1989); Terry Golway, *Full of Grace: An Oral Biography of John Cardinal O'Connor* (New York: Atria/Simon and Schuster, 2001)

Mary Elizabeth Brown

John Garfield, Morris Carnovsky, J. E. Bromberg, Stella Adler, Luther Adler, Sanford Meisner, and Art Smith in Clifford Odets's Awake and Sing! *at the Belasco Theatre, 1935*

Octagon Tower. Restored former ruin on Roosevelt Island, built in 1839 as the New York City Lunatic Asylum. It consists of a rotunda 62 feet (19 meters) tall surrounded by a spectacular flying staircase. The structure once served as the hub between the southern and western wings of a much larger building. The wings were demolished in 1970, and the dome was destroyed by fire in 1982. In 1994 the Roosevelt Island Operating Corporation asked for permission to stabilize the building and open part of it to the public, and Octagon Park was created in 1995. In 2004 the corporation gave approval to the firm of Becker and Becker to build the Octagon, a 500-unit residential development in Octagon Park. In 2006 they restored the tower, which became the main lobby of the building and houses the exercise room, community room, lounge, and offices. It is flanked on both sides by luxury apartments built on the site of the razed wings of the asylum.

Kenneth T. Jackson

Odets, Clifford (*b* Philadelphia, 18 July 1906; *d* Los Angeles, 14 Aug 1963). Theater director, playwright, and actor. He began his career as an apprentice actor in New York City with the Group Theatre, an experimental troupe led by Harold Clurman, Lee Strasberg, and Cheryl Crawford. In 1933 he rented an apartment at 82 Horatio Street, where he lived until moving to 1 University Place. He gained national prominence in 1935 for his militant one-act play *Waiting for Lefty;* several weeks later the Group Theatre mounted his second play, *Awake and Sing!* with the actors Stella Adler, Morris Carnovsky, and John Garfield. During an association with the company that lasted seven years he wrote *Golden Boy* (1937) and several other plays. He then moved to Hollywood, where he struggled as a screenwriter. His success as a playwright nevertheless continued, and his play *The Country Girl* (1950) was staged on Broadway. In 1952 Odets testified before the House Un-American Activities Committee about his political activities in the 1930s.

Margaret Brenman-Gibson, *Clifford Odets, American Playwright: The Years from 1906 to 1940* (New York: Atheneum, 1981)

Peter M. Rutkoff, William B. Scott

Paul O'Dwyer, 1968

O'Dwyer, (Peter) Paul (*b* Bohola, County Mayo, Ireland, 29 June 1907; *d* Goshen, N.Y., 24 June 1998). Lawyer and reformer, brother of William O'Dwyer. He grew up in Brooklyn, attended law school at St. John's University, and worked as a lawyer on behalf of miners in Kentucky and blacks in Mississippi and Alabama. In 1958 he joined with Eleanor Roosevelt, Herbert H. Lehman, and others in establishing the Committee for Democratic Voters, which marked the beginning of the Democratic reform movement in New York State. As the Democratic nominee for the U.S. Senate in 1968 he was defeated by Senator Jacob K. Javits. He was president of the City Council of New York from 1974 to 1977. He wrote *Counsel for the Defense: An Autobiography* (1979).

B. Kimberly Taylor

O'Dwyer, William (*b* Bohola, County Mayo, Ireland, 7 July 1890; *d* New York City, 24 Nov 1964). Mayor, brother of Paul O'Dwyer. As the district attorney of Brooklyn during 1940–41 he successfully prosecuted members of the criminal organization Murder Incorporated. He won the Democratic mayoral nomination in 1941 but was defeated in the general election by Fiorello H. La Guardia. In 1945 he was elected mayor as the candidate of the Democratic and American labor parties. He had a reputation as a capable administrator responding ably to a postwar surge in labor unrest and to the need for affordable housing for returning veterans, and for investments in infrastructure deferred since the Depression. He also helped bring the United Nations headquarters to New York City. His career was marked by accusations

William O'Dwyer, 1949

of an unpredictable personality and allegations of complicity with organized crime. Reelected in 1949, he resigned in 1950 and became U.S. ambassador to Mexico.

George Walsh, *Public Enemies: The Mayor, the Mob and the Crime That Was* (New York: W. W. Norton, 1980)

Chris McNickle

Off Broadway. Medium-sized commercial theaters in New York, having more than 100 but fewer than 499 seats. Unlike Broadway theaters, which primarily offer productions that run as long as they can be sustained, many Off-Broadway theaters offer three or four play seasons with limited runs and rely heavily upon a subscription base. This means that many of them seek to establish a reputation for a certain kind of work, such as classic revivals (Classic Stage Company), drama of certain nations (Irish Repertory), new plays and musicals (Manhattan Theatre Club), revivals (Second Stage), or particularly innovative new work (New York Theatre Workshop). There were about 200 Off-Broadway theaters in the five boroughs in the early twenty-first century.

Marvin Carlson

Off Off Broadway. Performing groups and theaters in New York with audiences of fewer than 100 people. Off Off Broadway began in the late 1950s in Greenwich Village as a reaction to Off Broadway, which was seen as becoming too commercial and conservative. Off Off Broadway is found throughout New York City and is extremely varied in its offerings. Some companies have their own home, such as the Ontological-Hysteric Theater of Richard Foreman or the Performing Garage of the Wooster Group, but most use found spaces or ongoing Off-Off-Broadway venues like the Café La Mama, HERE, or St. Ann's Warehouse in DUMBO.

Marvin Carlson

Off-Track Betting (Corporation, New York City) [OTB]. Public-benefit corporation formed in April 1971 by the state legislature of New York to allow wagering at locations away from the racetrack on thoroughbred and harness races. Although objections were raised by opponents of gambling and by the New York Racing Authority, which represented racetracks throughout the state, the supporters of off-track betting promoted it as a means of producing revenue for the city and state, weakening the illegal gambling operations of organized crime, and reviving horse racing. The corporation was overseen by a board of directors appointed by the mayor. The first head of OTB was Howard Samuels, a successful businessman active in Democratic politics. Patrons could bet on local races and on events outside the state, including the Kentucky Derby and the Preakness; they placed their bets at small outlets, modeled after betting parlors in Britain, that were the first of their kind in the United States, as well as by telephone. Although the betting outlets were not initially intended as gathering places, they eventually included restrooms, snack bars, and television monitors on which races were broadcast. By 1978 157 branches were scattered throughout the city. From that time the volume of wagers declined because of competition from the state lottery and other forms of gambling, the general decline in the popularity of horse racing, and the imposition by OTB of an unpopular surtax on winnings. In 1990 OTB had 100 branches in the city, employed 1700 workers full time and 600 part time, and raised $40 million for the city, $17 million for the state, and $8 million for other local governments. In the early 1990s OTB became unprofitable and remained that way as of 2010, despite the state taking over control in 2008. There were 65 branches in 2010, but the future remained uncertain as an interim agreement was to be put in place to prevent the closure of all facilities because of bankruptcy.

Edward T. O'Donnell

Ogilvy, David (Mackenzie) (*b* West Horsley, near Guildford, England, 23 June 1911; *d* Touffou, France, 21 July 1999). Advertising executive. After attending Oxford University he worked in Paris as a chef and in Scotland as a door-to-door stove salesman until his brother Francis helped him secure a position with the advertising firm Mather and Crowther in London in 1935. He went to the United States in 1938 to learn about American advertising and decided to stay; from the following year he conducted 439 nationwide surveys for George Gallup. He served during World War II with the British embassy in Washington. In 1948 he formed the advertising agency Hewitt Ogilvy Benson and Mather with Anderson Hewitt in New York City: he became well known for distinctive campaigns such as one for Hathaway shirts featuring a man with an eye patch, and for placing advertisements in respected publications such as the *New Yorker.* In 1975 he retired as the chairman of Ogilvy and Mather International and became its worldwide creative head, a position from which he retired in 1983. He wrote *Confessions of an Advertising Man* (1963), *Ogilvy on Advertising* (1983), and an autobiography, *Blood, Brains, and Beer* (1978).

Marjorie Harrison

O'Hara, Frank [Francis Russell] (*b* Baltimore, 27 March 1926; *d* Mastic Beach, N.Y., 25 July 1966). Poet. He studied at Harvard University (AB 1950) and served in the navy during World War II. He moved to New York City in 1951 and worked at the Museum of Modern Art, becoming assistant curator of the Department of Painting and Sculpture Exhibitions in 1960. Influenced by abstract expressionist painting, he cultivated friendships with Jackson Pollock and Franz Kline and became associated with the New York School of poetry. He developed an unconstrained poetic style characterized by spontaneous observations of everyday life; the collection *Lunch Poems* (1964) provides a quasi-photographic view of New York City at midday. Many of his other works, such as *Love Poems* (1965), celebrate his homosexuality. After O'Hara's death in an automobile accident his friend Allen Ginsberg paid tribute to him in the poem "City Midnight Junk Strains" (1966).

Brad Gooch, *City Poet: The Life and Times of Frank O'Hara* (New York: Alfred A. Knopf, 1993)

Shan Jayakumar

O. Henry [Porter, William Sydney] (*b* Greensboro, N.C., 11 Sept 1862; *d* New York City, 5 June 1910). Short-story writer known for surprise endings. After leaving school at age 15 he lived in Texas and Honduras and spent three years at the Ohio State Penitentiary for embezzlement, though it is not certain whether the charge was accurate. He wrote his first short stories in prison and coined the pen name O. Henry upon release. He lived briefly in Pittsburgh before settling in New York City in 1902. He lived at 55 Irving Place from 1903 and in 1906 moved to the Caledonia Hotel at 28 West 26th Street; he kept a room there for writing after moving to the Chelsea Hotel at 222 West 23rd Street. O. Henry wrote dozens of stories a year, many of them inspired by life in the city, and published them in such collections as *The Four Million* (1906) and *The Voice of the City* (1908).

Richard O'Connor, *O. Henry: The Legendary Life of William S. Porter* (New York: Doubleday, 1970)

James E. Mooney

Ohrbach's. Firm of clothing retailers. It began as a store opened in 1923 in Union Square by Nathan M. Ohrbach (*b* Vienna, 31 Aug 1885; *d* New York City, 19 Nov 1972), who sold ready-to-wear clothing at low prices. He profited by selling in bulk for cash, offering minimal sales service, and forgoing delivery, decorative wrappings, and alterations. His slogan was "More for less, or your money back"; customers who could prove that another store had undersold his were refunded their money and also received 10 percent of the competitor's selling price. After the store moved to 5 West 34th Street, its annual sales exceeded $30 million. Ohrbach later specialized in inexpensive copies of European designer clothes and fulfilled his aspiration of becoming to discount retailing what Bergdorf Goodman was to high-priced retailing. The firm was later sold to the Brenninkmeyer family of the Netherlands, then ceased operations in February 1987.

Nathan Ohrbach, *Getting Ahead in Retailing* (New York: McGraw-Hill, 1935)

Leslie Gourse

O'Keeffe, Georgia (*b* Sun Prairie, Wis., 15 Nov 1887; *d* Santa Fe, N.Mex., 6 March 1986). Painter. She moved to New York City in 1907 to study at the Art Students League with William Merritt Chase and first encountered modern art in the following year at Alfred Stieglitz's gallery "291." After working as an illustrator in Chicago (1909–10) and studying at the University of Virginia (1912), she returned to the city in 1914 to study with Arthur Wesley Dow (1857–1922) at Teachers College, Columbia University. In South Carolina she completed abstract drawings that in 1916 gained the attention of Stieglitz, who included her work in two group exhibitions, presented the first solo exhibition of her drawings and watercolors in 1917, and invited her to leave a teaching post in Texas and return in 1918 to New York City, where from July to the end of 1920 she lived and worked at 114 East 59th Street. After the two were married in 1924 she moved into the Hotel Shelton at 525 Lexington Avenue, which became her residence in the city for the next 10 years. During this period she also spent time in Lake George (New York) and New Mexico. Her work from these years ranges from organic abstractions to floral still lifes, stark landscapes, and "precisionist" paintings and drawings inspired by the dramatic architecture of the city (1924–29). She lived from the autumn of 1936 at 405 East 54th Street and from October 1942 at 59 East 54th Street. On Stieglitz's death in 1946 she organized and dispersed his art collection and operated An American Place gallery, which lasted until 1950. The Metropolitan Museum of Art and the Whitney Museum of American Art own important examples of O'Keeffe's work.

Lloyd Goodrich and Doris Bry, *Georgia O'Keeffe Retrospective Exhibition* (New York: Whitney Museum of American Art, 1970); Laurie Lisle, *Portrait of an Artist: A Biography of Georgia O'Keeffe* (New York: Seaview, 1980); Patterson Sims, *Georgia O'Keeffe: A Concentration of Works from the Permanent Collection* (New York: Whitney Museum of American Art, 1981); Charles C. Eldredge, *Georgia O'Keeffe* (New York: Harry N. Abrams, 1991)

Judith Zilczer

Olatunji, Babatunde Michael (*b* Ajido, Nigeria, 7 April 1927; *d* Salinas, Calif., 6 April 2003). Drummer. After attending Baptiste Academy in Lagos he earned his BA from Morehouse College in 1954 and in 1958 opened the Center for African Culture at 43 East 125th Street, which became a national center for African drumming and culture; for more than 25 years he taught students from all over the world and introduced to new audiences such performers as John Coltrane, Ladji Camara, and Yusef Lateef. His first album, *Drums of Passion* (1959), brought traditional African music into the commercial mainstream, and his song "Jingo-lo-ba" became well known through a version done by Carlos Santana in 1968. He and Bill Lee wrote the score for the Spike Lee film *She's Gotta Have It* (1986). Olatunji's students and associates included the percussionists Chief James Hawthorne Bey, Taiwo Duvall, Moses Miann, Ladji Camara, Kehinde Stewart O'Uhuru, Montego Joe, Sonny Morgan, Sule Greg C. Wilson, and Mickey Hart of the Grateful Dead. Olatunji moved to California and taught at the Esalen Institute before his death.

Babatunde Olatunji, and Robert Atkinson, *The Beat of My Drum: An Autobiography* (Philadelphia: Temple University Press, 2005)

Sule Greg C. Wilson

Old Blazing Star. An early name for the area on the shore of the Arthur Kill near Rossville in Staten Island. The name refers to a comet, but its origin is unknown. The *Blazing Star* ferry to New Jersey docked there from 1722, and later there was also a Blazing Star Tavern. When a new ferry service was begun at Long Neck north of Blazing Star, the "old" was added, and after 1837 the name was changed to Rossville.

Barnett Shepherd

Oldenburg, Claes (Thure) (*b* Stockholm, 28 Jan 1929). Sculptor. He studied at Yale University (BA 1951) and the Art Institute of Chicago (1952–54). He moved to New York City in 1956. His early works include *The Street* (1960), constructed of debris from the streets of New York City. In the 1960s he became widely known for his outdoor public works—oversized soft sculptures of everyday objects, often made of vinyl, papier-mâché, or canvas and stuffed with kapok or a similar material. Typical examples include *Soft Typewriter* (1963) and *Bacon, Lettuce and Tomato* (1963). Exploring the relationship between architecture and sculptor, he has collaborated with architects such as Frank Gehry.

Shan Jayakumar

Old Place. Neighborhood in northwestern Staten Island, near the approach to the Goethals Bridge. The original settlement grew up around a tide mill built by the 1750s on Old Place Creek, which empties into the Kill van Kull. The eastern portion of the settlement, along Forest Avenue, was called Summerville. Old Place remained largely uninhabited because of its marshes, swamps, and creeks, and the mosquitoes with which they were infested. Much of the marsh was filled in and the land zoned for industrial use. Procter and Gamble had a factory on Western Avenue from 1907 to 1991; known as Port Ivory, in the 1920s it employed 1500 workers. The remaining marshland has been designated as Wetlands; the nearly 70-acre Old Place Creek Wetland is part of the larger Harbor Herons Wildlife Complex.

Marjorie Johnson

Old Town. Former neighborhood in northeastern Staten Island, lying east of Richmond Road. The first permanent European settlement on the island was made near the beach adjoining Fort Wadsworth in 1661 by Dutch, French, and English farmers and fishermen. The town was called Dover by the English but became known as Old Town when a new town was formed at New Dorp. In the late nineteenth century the beach area became a summer resort and amusement park known as South Beach, and a spur line of the railroad was built to accommodate tourists. After the turn of the century many western, war, and adventure films were shot at the farm of Fred Scott just inland from the beach. Hylan Boulevard, which runs the length of Staten Island, bisects the area and is its principal commercial thoroughfare. Below Hylan Boulevard is a large marshy area that has been designated a protected Wetlands. Staten Island Railway crosses the northern section of the area; in the early twenty-first century Old Town was less a neighborhood than a train stop.

Marjorie Johnson

Olinville. Neighborhood in the north central Bronx, bounded to the north by 215th Street, to the east by White Plains Road, to the south by Burke Avenue, and to the west by the Bronx River. It began as Olinville no.1 and Olinville no. 2, two villages named for Stephen Olin, a bishop in the Methodist Church, that were formed in the 1840s after a railroad station of the New York and Harlem River Railroad opened nearby in Williamsbridge. The villages were separated by Olin Avenue (formerly Gun Hill Road between the Bronx River and White Plains Road) and incorporated between 1852 and 1854. The population grew after the Third Avenue elevated line was extended to meet the recently completed branch of the subway to White Plains Road. In 2005 the neighborhood was rezoned to preserve its low-density character. In 2010 most of the population was African American. Many who live in the neighborhood consider themselves residents of Williamsbridge.

John McNamara, *History in Asphalt: The Origin of Bronx Street and Place Names* (New York: Bronx County Historical Society, 1984)

Gary D. Hermalyn

Olitski, Jules [Demikovsky, Jerd] (*b* Snovsk, Russian SFSR [now Shchors, Ukraine], 27 March 1922; *d* New York City, 4 Feb 2007). Painter and sculptor. He was taken as a baby to New York City after his father had been executed by the Bolsheviks on political charges. He demonstrated artistic talent at an early age and trained in Manhattan at the National Academy of Design and at the Beaux-Arts Institute of Design. He won critical attention with a solo show at the Alexander Iolas Gallery in New York City in 1958. In the 1960s Olitski became a leading exponent of color field painting, an outgrowth of American abstract expressionism, and in 1969 he became only the third living artist to have a one-man show at the Metropolitan Museum of Art. Ultimately, he had more than 150 exhibitions around the world.

Kenneth T. Jackson

Olmsted, Frederick Law (*b* Hartford, Conn., 26 April 1822; *d* Belmont, Mass., 28 Aug 1903). Landscape architect. After moving to New York City in 1840 he worked as a clerk in a mercantile house and lived from 1848 to 1854 in Staten Island at what is now Woods of Arden Road (his farmhouse stands at 4515 Hylan Boulevard). Several accounts of his travels in the southern United States were published during the 1850s and 1860s. He became best known for his work as a landscape architect from 1858 with Calvert Vaux; together they designed Central Park (the construction and use of which Olmsted oversaw as its architect-in-chief and superintendent), Riverside Park, and smaller recreational areas in Manhattan; proposed a street plan for Washington Heights; and were the landscape architects of Prospect Park, Fort Greene Park, Ocean Parkway, Eastern Parkway, and several smaller parks in Brooklyn. Olmsted also prepared comprehensive plans for the Bronx (with the engineer J. J. R. Croes) and Staten Island and for a resort at Rockaway Point. In addition to working as a landscape architect he was an experimental farmer on Staten Island and a founder of the Union League Club and the Metropolitan Museum of Art.

Olmsted's career in the city was hindered and eventually cut short by politics. He fought bitterly against Tammany Hall, reform Democrats (notably Andrew Haswell Green), and Republicans, whom he accused of interfering with his designs and according more importance to patronage than to the proper administration of the parks. After his dismissal by the Department of Public Parks in 1878 he moved in 1882 to Brookline, Massachusetts, but continued to concern himself with the fate of the public parks in New York City. During his last years he opposed the addition to the parks of neoclassical structures designed by McKim, Mead and White and other architects and oversaw the construction of parks that he had designed in southern Brooklyn. Ill health forced his retirement in 1895.

In his designs Olmsted sought to provide relief from the density, congestion, and incessant pace of New York City. He considered his landscapes both works of art and social experiments that would have a civilizing influence. He denounced the gridiron system of streets as a relic of an earlier stage of urbanization and envisioned instead a compact business district surrounded by more open residential neighborhoods and spacious, naturalistic parks; this vision is most clearly set forth in his proposals for the Bronx and for the parkways in Brooklyn. Although often frustrated by political maneuvering and competing ideas of what a park should be, Olmsted and his collaborators had a profound influence on New York City.

Laura Wood Roper, *FLO: A Biography of Frederick Law Olmsted* (Baltimore: Johns Hopkins University Press, 1973); Charles C. McLaughlin et al., eds., *The Papers of Frederick Law Olmsted* (Baltimore: Johns Hopkins University Press, 1979–)

See also U.S. Sanitary Commission.

David Schuyler

Eastern Parkway (designed by Frederick Law Olmsted), ca 1895

Olvany, George W(ashington) (*b* New York City, 20 June 1873; *d* New York City, 15 Oct 1952). Lawyer and politician. After Charles F. Murphy's death in 1924 Olvany was named head of Tammany Hall. Citing poor health, he resigned in March 1929 after his close political ally Governor Alfred E. Smith had failed to win the presidential election of 1928. An investigation of government corruption by Samuel Seabury in 1931 revealed that during Olvany's tenure as the boss of Tammany Hall his law firm, Olvany, Eisner and Donnelly, had taken bribes from real estate interests and fixed licenses.

Frank Vos, Max Seppo

Olympia and York. See Brookfield Properties.

omnibuses. See Buses.

Omnicom Group. Advertising holding group formed in 1986 by the merger of Batten, Barton, Durstine, and Osborn; Doyle Dane Bernbach; and Needham Harper. It operates three independent agency networks: BBDO Worldwide Network, DDB Needham Worldwide Network, and TBWA International (acquired in 1993). It also manages specialty advertising companies through Diversified Agency Services (DAS) and Omnicom UK. It has offices at 437 Madison Avenue in Manhattan.

Janet Frankston

Onassis [Kennedy; née Bouvier], **Jacqueline (Lee)** (*b* East Hampton, N.Y., 28 July 1929; *d* New York City, 19 May 1994). Editor. As a young woman she lived in her family's apartment on Park Avenue. She married John F. Kennedy in 1953 and moved to the White House in 1961 when he was elected president. After his 1963 assassination, she chose to live permanently in New York City and purchased a cooperative apartment on Fifth Avenue in 1964. She married Aristotle Onassis in 1968 and often lived abroad until his death in 1975. She was a consulting editor at Viking Press until she moved to Doubleday in 1978 where she became a senior editor. A leader in the city's landmarks preservation movement, she was instrumental in protecting Grand Central Terminal from destruction. She also helped to form the 42nd Street Development Corporation and was a member of the Municipal Art Society, the International Center of Photography, and the Century Association. After her death the reservoir in Central Park was renamed in her honor.

Patricia U. Bonomi

Onderdonk House. Historic house at 1820 Flushing Avenue in Queens, also known as the Vander Ende–Onderdonk House. It was built in 1709 by Paulus Vander Ende in a blend of English, Georgian, and Dutch styles found only in the metropolitan area and along the Hudson River. It was bought in the 1820s by Adrian Onderdonck, a farmer who had married a member of the Wyckoff family, and was occupied by his descendants until 1905. After a devastating fire in the mid-1970s the house was restored by the Greater Ridgewood Historical Society between 1975 and 1981. In 1977 it was listed on the National Register of Historic Places, and in 1978 was added to the New York State Register of Historic Places. In 1996 it received New York City Landmark status. The Onderdonk House was the oldest surviving farmhouse in the area in the early twenty-first century.

Eric Wm. Allison

O'Neill, Eugene (Gladstone) (*b* New York City, 16 Oct 1888; *d* Boston, 27 Nov 1953). Playwright. Born in room 236 of Barrett House, on 43rd Street off Broadway, he spent much of his life in New York City. As a child he toured with his father, the romantic actor James O'Neill (1847–1920), and after a year at Princeton University he worked in a variety of jobs and as a seaman. He contracted tuberculosis and while recovering in a sanitarium decided to become a playwright. In 1916 he became the leading writer for a theater group on Cape Cod that moved to Greenwich Village as the Provincetown Players. He joined the troupe in New York City, living at 38 and 42 Washington Square South and spending time at Jimmy the Priest's, a boardinghouse at 252 Fulton Street that is the setting of his play *Anna Christie,* and at the Hell Hole (on Fourth Street and Sixth Avenue), an Irish saloon where he often slept. The Provincetown Players gave the premieres in Off-Broadway theaters at 133 and 139 MacDougal Street (1916–19) of 10 of his one-act plays, and on Broadway of his first full-length play, *Beyond the Horizon* (1920), for which he won a Pulitzer Prize; he also won the prize for *Anna Christie* (1921), *Strange Interlude* (1928), produced by the Theatre Guild, and *Long Day's Journey into Night,* his best-known work, completed in 1941 and produced posthumously in 1956. Other major works include *The Emperor Jones* (1920), *Desire under the Elms* (1924), *Mourning Becomes Electra* (1931), and *The Iceman Cometh,* first produced in 1946 but not recognized as a work of genius until its revival in 1956 at the Circle in the Square, staged by José Quintero and featuring Jason Robards.

Although he experimented in a wide range of theatrical genres and production styles, O'Neill is best known for his stark, realistic drama. His plays offer intense psychological treatments of alcoholism, insanity, suicide, and sexual passion. Most of his works are autobiographical and draw on his experiences in waterfront hovels and in Greenwich Village. He received the Nobel Prize for literature in 1936.

Arthur Gelb and Barbara Gelb, *O'Neill* (New York: Harper and Brothers, 1960)

Martha S. LoMonaco

Onion. Fake news organization with headquarters in New York City that publishes satirical content via a weekly free newspaper, a Web site, and video and radio/podcast segments on the Web. It was founded in Madison, Wisconsin, in 1988; it moved to New York City in 2001. The newspaper satirizes all of the major components of a real paper, including national and international news, human interest stories, op-eds, on-the-street polls, news graphics, and weather, wedding, funeral, real estate, stock, and television listings. The "AV Club" section contains nonsatirical pop-culture interviews and reviews. The paper has local editions in New York City and nine other cities that include local advertising and entertainment coverage. The paper claims a national print circulation of 690,000. In 1999 the organization started its book series by publishing *Our Dumb Century: The Onion Presents 100 Years of Headlines.* Its Web site, launched in 1996, was redesigned and fully developed in 2005 when the Onion Radio News was added. In 2007 television-style news broadcasts were added to the Web site under the name Onion News Network. *The Onion Movie,* a direct-to-DVD film, was released in 2008. The *Onion* has its own fictional history, according to which the paper was founded in the mid-1700s by Herman Ulysses Zweibel. Its motto is *Tu Stultus Es* ("You Are Stupid," in Latin).

Jacqueline Lalley

Opdyke, George (*b* Kingwood Township, near Frenchtown, N.J., 7 Dec 1805; *d* New York City, 12 June 1880). Merchant and mayor. He became a prosperous clothing manufacturer and moved to New York City in 1832 to open the first large clothing factory there. In 1846 he turned the business over to his brother-in-law and became an importer of wholesale dry goods. A millionaire by 1853, he later organized a bank and was elected to the state assembly, where he advocated various reforms. As mayor during the draft riots of 1863 he refused to compromise with rioters and abandoned City Hall for the shelter of St. Nicholas Hotel.

James E. Mooney

Open Theater. Avant-garde theater company founded in New York City in 1963 by Joseph Chaikin (1935–2003), a former member of Living Theatre, and Peter Feldman (*b* 1936). The group created collaborative productions in workshops, often using the concept of "transformations," where actors transformed from one character or object into another. Its most significant works included *American Hurrah* (1965) and *Viet Rock* (1966), which were created with playwrights Jean-Claude van Itallie and Megan Terry and staged at La Mama Experimental Theatre Club. Its later works included *The Serpent* (1968), *Terminal* (1969), *Mutation Show* (1969), and *Nightwalk* (1973). Open Theater dissolved in 1973.

Kate Lauber

opera. Although rooted in a repertory and a tradition dating largely from the nineteenth century, opera in New York City is as cosmopolitan and varied as its audience. The earliest opera performances in the city took place in 1750, when the Nassau Street Theatre presented ballad operas such as John Gay's *The Beggar's Opera,* musical plays, and pastiches (selections by different composers). Carl Maria von Weber's *Der Freischütz* was performed in English at the Park Theatre in 1825 by a troupe including the celebrated tenor Manuel García and four members of his family; the youngest, Maria Felicia, achieved early success in the city before building an important career in Europe as Maria Malibran. That year the troupe staged the first foreign-language operas in the city, a series of 80 performances sponsored by the wine importer Dominick Lynch with encouragement from Lorenzo da Ponte, who taught in New York City after writing librettos for Mozart; the series included operas by Rossini and Mozart, all sung in Italian. Signora Bartolini sang "operatic airs between the plays" at Chatham Garden, near City Hall; in 1832 the French tenor Jacques Montresor presented an Italian series at Richmond Hill, Aaron Burr's former mansion at Varick and Charlton streets.

The Austin-Wood and Inverarity companies, run by English and Scottish singers, performed at the Park Theatre in the 1830s, while the Shireff-Seguin-Wilson troupe (also English) followed at the National and at Niblo's Garden (at Broadway and Prince Street), where admission cost only 50 cents. Da Ponte helped to form the Rivafinoli troupe and in 1833 raised money to build the Italian Opera House, the first in the city. The venture had a single season of 60 performances before the theater burned in 1839; Palmo's Opera House on Chambers Street came to a similarly abrupt end in 1844. In late 1847 the Astor Place at Broadway and Eighth Street also opened for a single brief season. Although its boxes were likened to "pens for wild beasts," the Park Theatre remained the principal venue for opera in the city until 1848, when it also burned. Jenny Lind made her American debut in 1850 at Castle Garden, a venue that appealed to the masses much as the Park Theatre had appealed to the elite. Among the few American operas to be performed were George Frederick Bristow's *Rip van Winkle* (1855) and William Henry Fry's *Leonora* (1858).

As the city grew northward its first major opera house, the Academy of Music (seating 4600), was built on Irving Place at 14th Street. The inaugural season began in October 1854 with Vincenzo Bellini's *Norma* sung by Giulia Grisi and her husband, the tenor Mario Grisi. In the same year 16-year-old Adelina Patti made her opera debut in Gaetano Donizetti's *Lucia di Lammermoor*; she was a mainstay of the Academy of Music during the management of Max Maretzek and later of the English impresario James H. Mapleson. Destroyed by fire in 1866, the house was rebuilt but eventually overshadowed by the new Metropolitan Opera House, built in 1883. As the nineteenth century progressed, the dominance of European singers was challenged by American performers, including Clara Louise Kellogg, Minnie Hauk, and Annie Louise Cary. At the same time the Metropolitan Opera consolidated its position as the leading company in the city. Its only serious competitor was the Manhattan Opera House, opened on 34th Street by Oscar Hammerstein in 1906, where the performers included Mary Garden, Emma Calvé, Luisa Tetrazzini, and John McCormack and much of the repertory was French; backers of the Metropolitan Opera bought out Hammerstein in 1910. The City Center Opera, formed in 1943 at the former Mecca Temple on 54th Street, established itself as the second-most important company in the city when it moved to Lincoln Center in 1966 and became the New York City Opera.

Dozens of local opera companies have come and gone in New York City, including the Amato Opera Theater (founded in 1948), the Queens Opera (1961), the Bronx Opera Company (1967), the New York Grand Opera (1973), Dicapo Opera Theatre (1981), and the Opera Company of Brooklyn (2000). The Opera Orchestra of New York, formed in 1968 by Eve Queler, specialized in concert readings of rarely heard works. The Brooklyn Academy of Music became an active presenter of operas in the late 1980s. In the early twenty-first century operas were also performed by students at the Juilliard School, the Manhattan School of Music, and Mannes College the New School for Music.

John Dizikes, *Opera in America: A Cultural History* (New Haven: Yale University Press, 1993)

John W. Freeman

Opportunity: A Journal of Negro Life. The journal of the National Urban League, launched in 1923 and issued monthly for most of its duration. Associated with the Harlem Renaissance, the journal published news of the National Urban League and its local affiliates, including the work of black artists and writers, and discussed issues of interest to blacks. Its first editor, Charles Johnson, was succeeded in 1928 by Elmer Carter. In 1943 the journal became a quarterly. Editorial direction was assumed in 1945 by Madeline Aldridge and in 1947 by Dutton Ferguson. In 1949 *Opportunity* ceased publication.

Cheryl Greenberg

Opus Dei. Catholic organization with U.S. headquarters in New York City founded in 1928 by the Spanish priest Josemaría Escrivá. It first came to the United States in 1949. The organization was made a personal prelature of the pope in 1982. It has been criticized by some who say that it is secretive and a radical form of Catholicism. The U.S. headquarters are located on East 34th Street, and there is also a dormitory for men, called the Riverside Study Center, located on the Upper West Side. Opus Dei, which means "the work of God," is involved in many social programs, including a supplementary education program in the South Bronx.

Nathan Morgante

Orange Order. Fraternal organization formed in Ireland in 1795 "to maintain and uphold the Protestant faith." Named for William III, prince of Orange, who defeated James II at the Battle of the Boyne in Ireland (1690), it advocates the continued membership of Northern Ireland in the United Kingdom. During its early years in New York City the order organized an annual parade on 12 July: in 1824 Thomas Addis Emmet, an exiled member of the United Irishmen, recorded that the marchers received a "humiliating thrashing" from the "green" Irish. More violent disruptions in 1870 and 1871 became known as the Orange riots. A sharp decline in Irish Protestant immigration during the late nineteenth century weakened the order in the city, and the parades were eventually discontinued.

Tony Gray, *The Orange Order* (London: Bodley Head, 1972); Michael A. Gordon, *The Orange Riots: Irish Political Violence in New York City, 1870 and 1871* (Ithaca, N.Y.: Cornell University Press, 1993)

William McGimpsey

Orange riots. Violence that occurred during parades in 1870 and 1871 held to commemorate the anniversary of a major victory of the Protestants over the Catholics in Ireland, that of William III, king of England and prince of Orange, over King James II at the Battle of the Boyne. On 12 July 1870 a group of Irish Protestants (Orangemen) held a parade up Eighth Avenue to Elm Park at 19th Street; they were followed and harassed by 200 Catholic Irish, who with 300 Irish laborers working near the park attacked the Orangemen. The police intervened, but eight persons were killed in several skirmishes nearby. The following year the police commissioner, James J. Kelso, banned the parade, fearing another outbreak of violence. He was quickly overruled by Governor John T. Hoffman, who ordered that the marchers be protected by the police and the militia: Tammany Hall was then under attack from reformers and felt obliged to prove that it could maintain order among the people who were the source of its power. The parade went forward with an escort of several hundred police officers and five regiments of the National Guard. With provocation but without orders, many of the guardsmen fired into the crowd. Sixty-seven persons (including militiamen and police officers) were killed and more than 150 were injured. The incident further compromised Tammany Hall and led to efforts to improve the National Guard.

Stephen J. Sullivan, "The Orange and Green Riots (New York City: July 12, 1870 and 1871)," *New York Irish History* 6 (1991–92), 3–12, 46–59

Russell S. Gilmore

Oratorio Society of New York. The oldest amateur chorus in New York City, founded in 1873 by Leopold Damrosch. In 1873 it started the tradition of performing Handel's *Messiah* each Christmas. It gave the American premieres of Berlioz's *Romeo and Juliet* (1882) and Wagner's *Parsifal* (1886). Early performances were given at the Metropolitan Opera House and Steinway Hall. In 1888 Andrew Carnegie became president of the society, a position he retained for 30 years, and in 1891 he built it a new home, Carnegie Hall. In 1973 it was given the Handel Medallion, the city's highest cultural award. In 1977 it started what is now known as the Lyndon Woodside Oratorio Solo Competition. It was honored again in 1998 by Mayor Rudolph Giuliani in its 125th year. Many famous conductors have led the Oratorio Society, including Tchaikovsky, Leonard Bernstein, and Aaron Copland.

James Bradley

Orbach, Jerry [Jerome Bernard] (*b* Bronx, 20 Oct 1935; *d* New York City, 28 Dec 2004). Actor. Though born in New York City, Orbach lived in numerous places before returning to New York in 1955 to study at the Actor's Studio in Manhattan. After starring in an Off-Broadway production of *The Threepenny Opera,* Orbach achieved acclaim for his performance in *The Fantasticks.* In 1992 he joined the cast of *Law and Order* as Detective Lennie Briscoe, a role he played until his death. In 2002 Orbach and *Law and Order* cast mate Sam Waterston were named "Living Landmarks" by the New York City Landmarks Conservancy. In 2007 a stretch of 53rd Street near Eighth Avenue, in the Manhattan neighborhood where Orbach lived for many years, was renamed Jerry Orbach Way.

Anne Epstein

Orchard Beach. The only beach in the Bronx, located on Pelham Bay in Pelham Bay Park. It is 1.1 miles (1.77 km) long and 115 acres

(46.54 hectares) with a promenade of shops, playgrounds, picnic areas, and more than two dozen sports courts. The beach was the vision of Parks Commissioner Robert Moses, who designed it to be the "Riviera of New York." Originally a well-established campsite in the 1930s, the beach was named for the orchards that used to grow on private estates in the area. Moses devised a plan to renovate the area and create a place the entire city could enjoy. The renovation was completed in 1938, but heavy demand led to an early opening in 1936 while sand and facilities were still being put in place. Following budgetary cutbacks in the 1970s, the beach was neglected, but in the early twenty-first century it was being restored.

Meryl Cates

O'Reilly, Leonora (*b* New York City, 16 Feb 1870; *d* Brooklyn, 3 April 1927). Labor activist. The child of Irish immigrants who appreciated activism and were involved with labor unions, she was three when her father died, and her mother, a garment worker, raised her in Brooklyn and introduced her to radical politics. At age 11 O'Reilly began work in a shirt collar factory, and a few years later, in 1886, she helped to organize the Working Women's Society, both a trade union and a mutual aid society. The organization impressed the philanthropist Josephine Shaw Lowell, who drew O'Reilly into social reform circles, where she won the admiration of influential reformers like Lillian Wald of the Henry Street Settlement and Felix Adler of the Ethical Culture Society. In 1897 O'Reilly organized the first women's local of the United Garment Workers of America and a garment workers' cooperative. She helped to form the New York Women's Trade Union League in 1903 and remained an active member until 1915, attracting thousands to unionism with her moving speeches. A believer in the importance of education, she attended the Brooklyn Pratt Institute and went on to teach at the Manhattan Trade School for Girls from 1902 to 1909. She was also an impassioned antiwar activist, helped found the National Association for the Advancement of Colored People (NAACP), and in 1909 was active in the labor division of the state's Woman Suffrage Party. She also worked to the end of her life for the independence of Ireland.

Annelise Orleck

organized crime. The business of crime in New York City is defined by three eras. From the mid-nineteenth century to the early twentieth, its rackets were locally oriented and conducted with the approval of political organizations. With the onset of Prohibition in the 1920s, organized-crime figures in the city became pivotal in national organizations and so powerful that they influenced city government. After the 1960s a combination of law enforcement initiatives, the aging and weakening of old crime families, and the emergence of new criminal combinations forced a restructuring of organized crime in the city.

During the first of these three stages the distinction between ward leader and gang leader sometimes blurred. Street gangs controlled the ballot box on behalf of politicians who in return gave protection to saloons, brothels, and gambling houses. Gambling was the major source of revenue for these combines, which provided a base for a generation of politicians. Among the best known was John Morrissey, a prizefighter and Democratic politician who opposed efforts by the Anti-Gambling Society to raid gambling houses in 1867. Leaders of Tammany Hall, police officers, and gamblers cooperated, and the chain of influence reached from the neighborhoods, where gamblers made deals with leaders of assembly districts, to the county party organizations to the highest levels of municipal government. Morrissey amassed wealth and power through his scheming, as did others later, such as Big Tim Sullivan, a ward boss from the Bowery. But their machinations were local, rooted in backroom politics and the give and take of the city streets, and had little effect beyond New York City and its environs.

The first generation of Jewish and Italian criminals around the turn of the century did little to alter the localism of organized crime. Like their predecessors they formed gangs: the mostly Italian Five Points Gang of Paul Kelly, included such criminals as Al Capone, Lucky Luciano, Frankie Yale, and Johnny Torrio; it enjoyed connections to Democratic organizations. Shadowy "black hand" gangs run by Italians conducted extortion rackets, but they confined their activities to Italian neighborhoods and in retrospect it seems that their power and cohesion were exaggerated. In the early twentieth century a number of widely publicized murders linked to organized crime helped to give the city a reputation for corruption and intrigue. The murder in 1909 of police lieutenant Joseph Petrosino while he was pursuing an investigation in Palermo, Sicily, was suspected by some of being part of an international conspiracy. In a case of official corruption a few years later police lieutenant Charles Becker and four accomplices were executed for the killing in 1912 of the gambler Herman Rosenthal. Becker's guilt was later called into question but not before his case had advanced the career of Charles Whitman, the Republican district attorney who prosecuted Becker and was later elected governor.

Italian gangs in the early 1920s were parochial and somewhat inflexible. Old gang leaders such as Giuseppe "Joe the Boss" Masseria recruited members according to their place of origin in Sicily or Italy. They disdained cooperation with those who were not Italian but were willing to wage gang wars against those who were. In the late 1920s, for example, Masseria fought for control of the rackets against Salvatore Maranzano in what was known as the Castellammarese War.

With the onset of Prohibition in the 1920s organized crime became more sophisticated. Those who controlled the rackets in the city were now in charge of a national operation. Neighborhood hoodlums put aside their ethnic and regional differences and agreed to divide responsibilities and territories rather than battle with each other. Within the Mafia there developed a peculiarly American institution known as the "family." In most American cities one Mafia family was in control; in New York City there were five families, known by the surnames of their leaders: Genovese, Bonanno, Gambino, Profaci, and Lucchese. The new generation of organized-crime leaders included Lucky Luciano, Meyer Lansky, Frank Costello, and Joe Adonis and followed the businesslike example set by the gambler Arnold Rothstein. Luciano took charge of efforts to eliminate the influence of the older generation by ingratiating himself with Masseria and then engineering in 1931 the killing of both Masseria (at a restaurant in Coney Island) and Maranzano. He also cultivated his power in city government, as in 1931 when his gunmen threatened Harry Perry, a district leader from the Lower East Side who subsequently chose not to seek reelection and was replaced by Luciano's preferred candidate, Albert Marinelli.

The actions of Luciano and his organization of enforcers, known in the tabloid newspapers as Murder Incorporated, became a source of fascination among the press, in works of fiction and films, on radio, and later on television. Perhaps for this reason they have sometimes been exaggerated: the killing of older organized-crime leaders was not indiscriminate, and the new national crime syndicate did not run as smoothly as a legitimate business. Nevertheless, Luciano and his accomplices gave organized crime in New York City a stability and structure that it had lacked and helped to make it a formidable force in American life.

Mayor Fiorello H. La Guardia inveighed against organized crime during the 1930s and campaigned successfully to ban Costello's slot machines. At the same time Thomas E. Dewey launched his own political career by winning convictions of Luciano on charges of prostitution in 1936 and of the Democratic district leader James J. Hines on charges of protecting the numbers racket of Dutch Schultz. Although Luciano managed to retain some of his power when he went to prison in 1936, his enforced absence made possible a grander role for Costello, who like others was compelled by the repeal of Prohibition in 1933 and the consequent end of the vast bootlegging business to seek different sources of profit. Gambling, loan-sharking, labor racketeering, and prostitution were reinvigorated; most organized-crime leaders were involved in the sale of illegal drugs (contrary to widespread belief); and Lansky used his financial and organizational abilities to channel illegitimate gains into legitimate businesses such as casinos and resorts. Criminals infiltrated the garment industry, vegetable markets, and other businesses that were disorganized and decentralized. Often they entered a business by force; at other times labor or management invited them.

During the 1940s organized-crime leaders used their newly gained wealth to colonize Tammany Hall. Whereas earlier the racketeers had flourished with the sufferance of political leaders, they were now political leaders themselves. Adonis wielded political influence in Brooklyn while controlling the drug trade and the docks. Costello established even more extensive connections in government and used the money he made in gambling and from a slot machine network in Louisiana to function as a kind of political patron. He gained a large measure of control over a Tammany Hall weakened by La Guardia's reform mayoralty and appears to have rigged some judicial appointments. During the 1950s Costello lost power in the rackets to Vito Genovese, who had fled the United States for Italy to avoid a murder charge but returned after World War II. Genovese failed in an attempt on Costello's life but succeeded in one against Costello's ally Albert Anastasia in the Park Sheraton Hotel. Costello was eventually persuaded to retire. Genovese was soon undone by internal struggles with rivals: Costello, Lansky, and Luciano are widely believed to have arranged the arrest on a federal drug charge that led to his imprisonment in 1959.

The 1950s and early 1960s saw repeated challenges to organized crime in New York City. Mayor William O'Dwyer, who became well known for prosecuting the members of Murder Incorporated, was forced to resign from office in 1950 because of allegations that he himself had links to organized crime and gamblers. In that year an investigatory committee in Washington, D.C., led by Senator Estes Kefauver began hearings on organized crime. Costello's testimony before the committee revealed his connections to Tammany Hall and also gave credence to the allegations surrounding O'Dwyer. In the city, political reforms weakened the bonds between organized crime and politics. From 1952 district leaders were chosen by direct election, which lessened the chances that the process could be manipulated and freed the office of district leader from its disreputable past. Mayor Robert F. Wagner, who rose in politics with Tammany support, eventually repudiated his sponsors. By the end of the decade the longstanding ties between organized crime and the Manhattan Democratic machine had been broken.

Organized crime in New York City was further weakened in the 1960s by the enforcement efforts of Robert F. Kennedy during his tenure as attorney general of the United States, the extent of information about criminal activities revealed by Joseph Valachi to the U.S. Department of Justice and in testimony before an investigatory committee of the U.S. Senate, and the aging of the organized-crime families, which often fought brutally for control of the rackets. Early in the decade the Profacis prevailed against the Gallos in a violent dispute over the rackets in Brooklyn; later in the decade the Bonannos unsuccessfully waged the so-called banana war in an effort to expand their power.

By the late 1960s Carlo Gambino emerged as the dominant organized-crime leader in the city (he died of natural causes in 1976). Joey Gallo, imprisoned during the struggle with the Profacis, was freed in 1971 and soon became something of a celebrity. He advocated bringing blacks into organized crime to broaden the base and effectiveness of criminal combinations, much as Luciano had once advocated an alliance between Italians and Jews. About the same time Joe Colombo, who had emerged as the head of the Profaci family, organized the Italian-American Civil Rights League to bring pressure to bear against stereotypes of Italians as organized-crime figures. Carmine Galante, who had taken charge of the Bonanno family in the mid-1970s, moved to expand his power at the end of the decade. Colombo was shot and paralyzed at a rally in 1971; Gallo was fatally shot in Little Italy in 1972; and Galante was fatally shot at a restaurant in Brooklyn in 1979.

The means of prosecuting organized crime changed radically after Congress passed the Racketeer Influenced and Corrupt Organizations (RICO) laws as part of the Organized Crime Control Act of 1970. The laws made it easier for the government to prove criminal conspiracies and to prosecute criminal organizations instead of only individuals; they also imposed heavy penalties on those convicted and enabled prosecutors to seize the assets of criminal enterprises. After the death in 1972 of J. Edgar Hoover, director of the Federal Bureau of Investigation, the bureau no longer focused its energies on the fight against communism and began to work more closely with the Drug Enforcement Agency. Local police also devoted more of their resources to fighting organized crime. In New York City federal prosecutor Rudolph W. Giuliani gained renown and political power from a series of highly publicized cases. Organized crime also became less glamorous in the city owing to its heavy involvement in the heroin trade, which by the early 1970s had caused a drug-abuse problem of dangerous proportions. Some of the glamour attached to organized crime was restored by Mario Puzo's novel *The Godfather* (1969) and the motion pictures that it inspired: organized-crime leaders were no longer depicted only as parasites who preyed on the city but also as exemplars of ethnic pride, old-fashioned men of honor, and businessmen who supplied needed if morally questionable services.

As organized-crime families continued to weaken, they were governed increasingly by younger and inexperienced criminals. At the same time new rackets and new gangs appeared. Asian gangs based in Chinatown thrived on extortion, racketeering, gambling, and drug dealing. Black and Latin American gangs gained enough power to control drug operations once dominated by the Mafia, which was weakened by the breaking in 1987 of a heroin-smuggling ring known as the "pizza connection" that operated under the cover of pizza parlors. Criminal immigrants from Russia and Cuba transferred their illicit operations to the United States. The five original organized-crime families, however, continued to pursue illegal activities ranging from waterfront rackets to the theft of stock certificates and to infiltrate legitimate businesses in the meatpacking, garbage disposal, construction, and garment industries. During the 1990s state and federal efforts, complemented by municipal action under Mayor Giuliani, further diminished the strength of organized crime in New York City, and the five families were gravely damaged. The Bonanno organization revived briefly under the leadership of Joseph Massino, but his 2004 conviction for racketeering undid his efforts.

With the leadership of organized crime disrupted and organizational discipline weakened, the image of the mob in the media changed. Up until 1992, when he was convicted on felony charges and imprisoned, the best-known racketeer in New York City was the flashy John Gotti. When Gotti died behind bars in 2002, the city's best-known racketeer was the beleaguered Tony Soprano, a fictional character in a television series who lived and worked in New Jersey but occasionally conducted business in New York. The business of crime persists in New York City, particularly in drug dealing with ties to Latin America and in gangs with Asian and Russian roots. But the traditional five families, while still active in rackets such as credit card fraud and CD bootlegging, entered the twenty-first century in a weakened state.

Humbert S. Nelli, *The Business of Crime: Italians and Syndicate Crime in the United States* (New York: Oxford University Press, 1976); Alan A. Block, *East Side, West Side: Organizing Crime in New York, 1930–1950* (New Brunswick, N.J.: Transaction, 1983); James B. Jacobs with Coleen Friel and Robert Radick, *Gotham Unbound: How New York Was Liberated from the Grip of Organized Crime* (New York: New York University Press, 1999)

Robert W. Snyder

Original Celtics. Professional basketball team. Frank McCormack founded the New York Celtics in 1915 with a group of teenage basketball players from Manhattan's West Side. Unable to use the old name, James Furey reorganized the team in 1918 as the Original Celtics after it had disbanded during World War I. The Original Celtics had older players, traveled frequently, and were managed and promoted professionally. The Celtics dominated most of their opponents in the 1920s, compiling 700 victories and only 60 losses during the decade. Whirlwind national tours took the team more than 150,000 miles per year to play 140 games. With its unparalleled success and travel schedule, the team popularized professional basketball in the United States. On 16 April 1921, at the 71st Regiment Armory, the Celtics played in front of 11,000 fans, the largest crowd to ever watch a basketball game at the time. The team gradually lost popularity from the 1930s to 1950s as it faced greater competition from other professional leagues and teams, including the Harlem Globetrotters, which purchased the Celtics as a minor league team in 1949. The team played its final game in 1953. Throughout their history the Celtics frequently hosted games at the Amsterdam Opera House on West 44th Street, the Central Opera House at 205 East 67th Street, the second Madison Square Garden at Madison Avenue and 23rd Street, and the Hippodrome on Sixth Avenue between 43rd and 44th streets.

David White

orphanages. For information on orphanages see Child welfare.

Orphan Asylum Society. Charitable organization formed in 1806 by a group that included Isabella Graham, her daughter Johanna Bethune, Sarah Hoffman, and Elizabeth Hamilton (widow of Alexander Hamilton). It occupied a small rented house on Raisin Street where six recently orphaned children received care. Rapid growth prompted the society to purchase land for a new building on Bank Street in 1807; in the following year the state legislature raised $5000 for the orphanage by lottery. The orphanage moved in 1836 to Riverside Drive and 73rd Street, where there was room for about 200 children. In 1899 the society named its first professional superintendent as part of a plan to emphasize higher education. Scholarship support was soon provided by a legacy from Mrs. R. G. Dun, wife of the founder of Dun and Bradstreet. In 1902 the society decided to sell its property in Manhattan to Charles Schwab and buy a site in suburban Hastings-on-Hudson in Westchester County.

The Orphan Asylum Society was an innovative institution that was among the first to employ the "cottage system," under which about 20 children of various ages, separated by gender, lived in a cottage under the supervision of house parents. At the age of 11 or 12 each child was indentured to a family, which paid $25 at the outset and an additional $25 to the child when he or she turned 18. The program required that each family taking part belong to a Protestant church and that the father be employed. In 1929 the society was renamed the Graham School in honor of its founder; in 1989 the name became Graham Windham.

The society celebrated its bicentennial in 2006 and continues to provide vital preventive services, education, protection, and assistance to the most disadvantaged and vulnerable children of New York City.

Joanna H. Mathews, *A Short History of the Orphan Asylum Society in the City of New York, Founded 1806* (New York: A. D. F. Randolph, 1893)

Phyllis Barr, Page Putnam Miller, Stephen Weinstein

Orphan Train Movement. Program of resettlement for urban poor children and a small number of adults from the east westward. Named after the new railroads that carried them, the orphan trains ran roughly from 1850 to 1930 and traveled mostly to midwestern and western states. The program was the idea of Charles Loring Brace of the Children's Aid Society, which was based in New York City, but was soon imitated by other organizations, including the New York Foundling Hospital. Because of variances in record keeping between organizations, the exact number of children "placed out" is uncertain but estimated to be around 250,000. Brace viewed rural America as expanding and in need of labor. Some of the children sent west were orphans but many had living parents who were simply unable to take care of them. Taken from city streets or from orphanages, the children generally went out in groups of five to 30 with an adult agent. Some children were placed with prearranged families whereas others were selected by families at stops along the route. The children not chosen would continue on the train line until they had all been placed. There was generally no screening of foster parents and little follow up. Some children were mistreated or ran away. The Children's Aid Society trains were also criticized for placing non-Protestant children with Protestant families. The orphan trains ended in the late 1920s with the development of foster care, legal adoption, and the notion that having children stay with their original families was a better option.

Marilyn Irvin Holt, *The Orphan Trains: Placing Out in America* (Lincoln: University of Nebraska Press, 1992); Stephen O'Connor, *Orphan Trains: The Story of Charles Loring Brace and the Children He Saved and Failed* (Boston: Houghton Mifflin, 2001); Linda Gordon, *The Great Arizona Orphan Abduction* (Cambridge, Mass.: Harvard University Press, 2001)

Maurita Baldock

Osborn, Henry Fairfield (*b* Fairfield, Conn., 8 Aug 1857; *d* Garrison, N.Y., 6 Nov 1935). Biologist. He was appointed in 1891 to a dual position at Columbia University and the American Museum of Natural History, where he established programs in biology and vertebrate paleontology. As president of the museum during 1908–33 he promoted worldwide expeditions and oversaw the construction of massive exhibition halls. Osborn was also president of the New York Zoological Society and took part in opening and administering the Bronx Zoo.

Ronald Rainger

Oscar of the Waldorf. Nickname of the headwaiter Oscar (Michel) Tschirky (*b* Switzerland, 28 Sept 1866; *d* New York City, 6 Nov 1950) at the Waldorf Hotel in New York City. He arrived in the city with his mother on 14 May 1883 and the next day began working as a busboy at the Hoffman House. Over the next four years he advanced to the rank of waiter in its private dining room, and he then worked as a waiter at Delmonico's. In 1893 he became the headwaiter at the Waldorf Hotel (which had recently opened) and eventually he was the most famous one in New York City. He originated the Waldorf salad and many other recipes, which he published in a collection of nearly 1000 pages called *The Cook Book, by "Oscar" of the Waldorf* (1896). In 1943 he took an advisory position with the hotel.

Karl Schriftgiesser, *Oscar of the Waldorf* (New York: E. P. Dutton, 1943)

Allen J. Share

Oscar Wilde Bookshop. Opened in 1967 by gay activist Craig L. Rodwell, the store on Mercer Street was one of the world's first gay bookstores that refused to stock pornography. In 1973 the store moved to 15 Christopher Street, one block from Stonewall. More than a bookstore, it served as a meeting place and discussion site for the gay and lesbian community. After financial troubles in the first decade of the twenty-first century, the store closed in 2009.

Jessica Montesano

O'Sullivan, John Louis (*b* Harbor of Gibraltar, 15 Nov 1813; *d* New York City, 24 Mar 1895). Writer and diplomat. He earned degrees from Columbia College in 1831 and 1834, practiced law, and in 1837 launched the *Democratic Review,* a literary journal in which he coined the term *manifest destiny* to refer to the westward expansion of the United States. He was elected to the state legislature and with Samuel J. Tilden launched the *New York Morning News,* which he edited from 1844 to 1846, and was a regent of New York State University until 1854. O'Sullivan was a diplomat in Portugal until 1879 when he returned to the city.

James E. Mooney

Oswald, Lee Harvey (*b* New Orleans, La., 18 Oct 1939; *d* Dallas, Tex., 24 Nov 1963). Assassin of John F. Kennedy. He lived in New York City for 17 months about a decade before his role in the assassination of President John F. Kennedy. In August 1952 he moved to the city with his mother, the two living successively with his half-brother at 325 East 92nd Street in Manhattan, in a basement apartment at 1455 Sheridan Avenue in the Bronx, and at 825 East 179th Street in the Bronx (from

January 1953). During this period he attended Trinity Evangelical Lutheran School (to 26 September 1952), Public School 117 (from 30 September 1952 to 16 January 1953), and Public School 44 (from 23 March 1953), but because of his perpetual truancy he was remanded to Youth House for psychiatric evaluation on 16 April 1953. His problems at school continued after he re-enrolled at Public School 44 on 24 September. Oswald and his mother left New York City for New Orleans in early January 1954. Oswald was killed while in police custody in Dallas shortly after the assassination of President Kennedy.

OTB. See Off-Track Betting.

Ott, Mel(vin Thomas) (*b* Gretna, La., 2 March 1909; *d* New Orleans, La., 21 Nov 1958). Baseball player. A popular outfielder for the New York Giants from 1926 to 1947, he was one of the leading power hitters in the National League, leading the league in home runs six times and compiling a lifetime batting average of .304. He became known for a distinctive batting style that involved raising the front leg before swinging. Ott retired with 511 career home runs, a league record at the time. From 1942 to 1948 he managed the Giants. He was inducted into the Baseball Hall of Fame in 1951.

Milton J. Shapiro, *The Mel Ott Story* (New York: Messner, 1959)

Jeffrey Scheuer

Ottley, Roi (*b* New York City, 2 Aug 1906; *d* New York City, 1 Oct 1960). Writer and broadcaster. Born to Grenadian parents Jerome P. and Beatrice (Brisbane) Ottley, he excelled at track and earned a scholarship to St. Bonaventure University in upstate New York. Ottley contributed articles to the university's literary magazine and newspaper. He then worked as a reporter, columnist, and editor for the *Amsterdam News* until 1935 when he became an editor for the Federal Writers' Project. His first book, *New World A-Coming,* which called for full racial equality, was published in 1943. Ottley became a commissioned officer in the U.S. Army in 1948 and covered the Korean War as the first African American war correspondent. He wrote for the *Chicago Tribune* and hosted his own radio program in Chicago. Ottley's published writings include *Black Odyssey* (1948), *No Green Pastures* (1951), *The Lonely Warrior* (1955), and (with William J. Weatherby) *The Negro in New York: An Informal Social History* (1967).

Our Lady of Lebanon Maronite Cathedral. Cathedral at the intersection of Remsen and Henry streets in Brooklyn Heights housing an Eastern Catholic, or Maronite, congregation. Designed in the Romanesque Revival style by Richard Upjohn, the cathedral was built between 1844 and 1846 and opened as the Church of the Pilgrims (Congregational). When the congregation merged with nearby Plymouth Church in 1934, the cathedral's Tiffany windows were moved to Hillis Hall behind Plymouth Church, which was renamed Plymouth Church of the Pilgrims. The doors at the western and southern portals of the cathedral depict Norman churches and were salvaged from the ocean liner *Normandie,* which caught fire in 1942. The Maronites purchased the cathedral in 1944, and it took its current name in June 1977 when the Eparchy of St. Maron was transferred to Brooklyn. In 2010 the congregation consisted of about 600 Lebanese families and a handful of Syrians, and services were offered in English, Aramaic, and Arabic.

Thomas E. Bird

Our Lady of Mercy Medical Center. General-care hospital started by the Misericordia Sisters of Montreal. Opened on Staten Island in 1887 as a home for unwed mothers, it was originally called the New York Mothers' Home of the Sisters of Misericordia. The facility moved in 1888 to 106 West 123rd Street in Manhattan and in 1889 to East 86th Street. It expanded to a general-care hospital known as Misericordia Hospital by 1905. The affiliated Misericordia School of Nursing began graduating nurses in 1913. In 1958 the hospital moved to East 233rd Street in the Bronx; in 1976 the Archdiocese of New York assumed control of the hospital, which took its current name in 1984. The center, a university affiliate of New York Medical College, became a member of the Montefiore Health System in 2007. The Misericordia Sisters continue to sponsor Rosalie Hall, a residential program for unwed mothers.

Matthew J. Brennan

Outcault, R(ichard) F(elton) (*b* Flushing [now in Queens], 14 Jan 1863; *d* Lancaster,

Richard Felton Outcault, The Yellow Kid

Ohio, 5 Sept 1928). Cartoonist. He is regarded as having created the first comic strip: a series of cartoons about immigrants in New York City that appeared in the *New York World* as "Hogan's Alley" from the mid-1880s to 1896. Retitled "The Yellow Kid" after its central character, the strip was published from 1896 to 1898 in a color supplement to the *New York Journal* called *American Humorist*. He also drew the comic strip "Buster Brown" (*New York Herald* 1902–5, *New York Journal* 1906–20); Buster Brown, his friend Mary Jane, and his bulldog Tige were among the first comic strip characters used to merchandise products. Outcault lived in Flushing.

See also CARTOONING.

Patricia A. Perito

outdoor advertising. Billboards promoted circuses and theaters as early as the 1840s, when P. T. Barnum used huge banners and woodcuts to advertise his American Museum at Broadway and Ann Street. In the antebellum period the first sandwichmen, or "walking billboards," paraded on busy thoroughfares such as Broadway, often advertising entertainments or patent medicines. Gaslight signs, favored especially by entertainment halls, taverns, and tobacco shops, became widely used by the end of the Civil War. The development of roads, streetcars, and elevated lines spurred larger and more numerous billboards, often in color. Posters covered the pillars of the elevated trains, and fences lining streetcar routes were covered with bills promoting such products as Hood's sasparilla, Quaker oats, Dutch cleanser, Sapolio soap, St. Jacob's oil, Bull Durham tobacco, and five-cent cigars. The largest early outdoor advertising firms in New York City were those of Kissam and Allen (1872–78), Bradbury and Houghtaling (1870–83), and O. J. Gude of Brooklyn. Until the business began to regulate itself in the late nineteenth century, bill stickers would post their advertisements atop those of competitors.

When chromolithography was developed in the 1880s, advertisements grew larger and more colorful. The first lithograph for a billboard was an illustration for a theatrical production of *Uncle Tom's Cabin*, depicting Eliza fleeing the bloodhounds across the ice floes. O. J. Gude put up the first electric sign in 1891 on a rooftop in Madison Square, composed of 1457 lamps that spelled out "Manhattan Beach Swept by Breezes" to advertise Manhattan Beach. By 1910 posters covering more than 200 square feet (19 square meters) were common, and often posted in multiple copies. Riverside Drive and Central Park, where carriages paraded on Sundays, were bordered with huge signs, and posters were affixed to fences surrounding construction sites. Reformers criticized these large displays as an eyesore and complained that they provided a hiding place for "immoral acts." In response, outdoor advertisers erected neater, permanent signboard stands of metal and often landscaped the area around them.

During the Progressive era the Municipal Art Society and adherents of the "city beautiful" movement raised a great outcry against outdoor advertising. Raymond Fosdick, the commissioner of accounts for New York City, led a commission that investigated the "billboard nuisance" in 1912. By 1918 the city had passed an ordinance regulating billboards, allowing them only outside residential and scenic areas and prohibiting the posting of small bills by individuals; far from ruining the billboard business, this helped it by eliminating a source of informal competition. Neon signs were popular by the 1920s, and Times Square became well known as a center of outdoor advertising: an advertisement for Wrigley's Spearmint chewing gum that depicted a "spearman" launching his weapon took up more than two blocks along Broadway. In the 1930s movie theaters in midtown erected enormous lighted signs to promote their attractions. The spot beneath the Budweiser sign, which showed a team of Clydesdale horses hauling a great wagon of barrels, was a favorite meeting place in Times Square, as was that beneath the Pepsi-Cola waterfall atop the Bond Building. During both world wars giant outdoor displays urged the public to buy war bonds.

Theaters and movie houses in the 1950s continued to commission both lighted displays and giant billboards, which often depicted shapely, reclining actresses and provoked some public indignation. Outdoor advertising became the subject of several films: *It Should Happen to You* (1953), directed by George Cukor, tells the story of an actress who rents a billboard on Columbus Circle to promote herself, and the signs of Times Square are featured in William Klein's *Broadway by Light* (1958). Audacious cutout figures and moving designs appeared on billboards during the 1960s, and in 1966 the Sunkist "smellacular" sign emitted a citrus aroma over the West Side Highway. In the following decades Times Square increasingly became the site of advertisements for the products of Japanese electronics firms.

A major concern of many environmentalists in the city was the amount of energy consumption required for the advertisements in and around both Times Square and Broadway. Above the Chase sign at 42nd Street and Seventh Avenue, Ricoh Americas Corporation developed a billboard entirely powered by wind and sunlight in 2008. When no wind or sun is usable, the billboard goes dark and has no alternative source of energy.

While billboards line the highways throughout the five boroughs, they also line the subway platforms in the form of large-scale posters and on the trains themselves and inside the tunnels. In 1998 CBS Outdoor, a division of the CBS conglomerate, gained limited rights to handle advertising space within subway stations and began selling wall space and floor space to advertisers, while the Metropolitan Transit Authority (MTA) handles advertising space on the station walls. In 2009 the *New York Times* and MTA placed ads on the walls of subway tunnels for the 1, 2, 3, 4, 5, 6, 7, and shuttle trains. The History Channel became the first company to develop a marketing campaign specifically designed for display on the exterior of the shuttle between Times Square and Grand Central Terminal in 2008 for the show "Cities of the Underworld." The advertisements were a version of those that appeared on the sides of MTA buses. These campaigns were often placed in a string of transit locations, including the station walls, interior of subway cars, buses, and bus stops. In addition to advertisements within the tunnels and on the exterior car panels, the MTA organized the sale of advertising space on turnstiles, digital screens inside stations and above station entrances, and projections against subway station walls as a means of aiding the MTA's financial struggles. See also ADVERTISING.

Kathleen Hulser, Meghan Lalonde

Outerbridge Crossing. Steel cantilevered bridge spanning the Arthur Kill between southwestern Staten Island and Perth Amboy, New Jersey. It was designed by Alexander Waddell and opened to traffic on 29 June 1928 at the same time as the smaller Goethals Bridge (built upstream and also designed by Waddell). The two bridges were the first crossings for motor vehicles between Staten Island and the mainland. The bridge has a span of 750 feet (229 meters), clears Arthur Kill by 135 feet (41 meters) and has a long-graded approach viaduct, making the total length 10,140 feet (3093 meters). Outerbridge Crossing is named for Eugenius Outerbridge, the first chairman of the Port of New York Authority and a resident of Staten Island.

Rebecca Read Shanor

Overseas Press Club of America. Club based in New York City for both foreign correspondents and American reporters. Its formation was first suggested by Charles Ferlin, a longtime reporter for the Associated Press and the United Press, at a meeting on 2 April 1939 at the Algonquin Hotel, where the club first set up offices. The club holds banquets and meetings, and gives annual awards for outstanding reporting; it has also published several volumes of reporting and recollections by its members, including *The Inside Story* (1940). It came under fire for commending NPR's controversial coverage of the Israeli–Palestinian conflict in 2006. It also awards 12 scholarships annually to students aspiring to careers as foreign correspondents. The offices are at 40 West 45th Street.

Michael Green

Ovington, Mary White (*b* Brooklyn, 11 April 1865; *d* Newton Highlands, Mass., 15 July 1951). Writer, social worker, and civil rights activist. After becoming the registrar at the Pratt Institute in 1893 and the head social worker at the Greenpoint Settlement in 1895, she helped to form the National Association for the Advancement of Colored People (NAACP) in 1909, of which she was later executive secretary, treasurer, and chairwoman of the board. Her book *Half a Man: The Status of the Negro in New York* (1911) examined racial discrimination encountered by blacks seeking employment or housing. She also wrote a novel, children's books, and *The Walls Came Tumbling Down* (1947), both a memoir and a history of the NAACP.

R. L. Harris, Jr.

Oxford University Press. University press in England, the American branch of which was formed in 1896 at 91 Fifth Avenue to facilitate the marketing and sale of Oxford Bibles in the United States. In the following year the branch took over from Macmillan the American marketing of all books published by its parent. The American office underwent rapid growth between 1928 and 1936, eventually becoming one of the leading university presses in the United States. Its primary emphasis is on scholarly and reference books, Bibles, and college and medical textbooks. In 1995 it moved its offices to the former B. Altman building at 198 Madison Avenue.

Eileen K. Cheng

Oyster Bar at Grand Central. Old-style seafood restaurant, located on Grand Central Terminal's lower level since 1913. When the Oyster Bar opened in the new Grand Central, it was distinguished by the vast herringbone-patterned, tile-vaulted ceiling fabricated by the Guastavino Fireproof Construction Company. After a devastating fire in 1997, the restaurant was quickly rebuilt. With a substantial raw bar and an extensive menu, it boasts 28 different kinds of oysters on the half shell.

Margaret Latimer

Oyster Island. Island that no longer appears on charts of Upper New York Bay, surviving only as a patch of shoal water to the south of Liberty Island. Well into the nineteenth century three islands were shown on charts roughly equidistant in a line from north to south: Ellis Island, Bedloes (later Liberty) Island, and Oyster Island. The name came from the oystering industry important in the area until it succumbed to overharvesting and pollution.

Norman J. Brouwer

oysters. Up until the late 1920s oysters were important in New York City life. The *Crassostrea virginica,* the dominant oyster on the eastern seaboard from Labrador to the Gulf of Mexico, flourishes in brackish water, particularly where freshwater runs into seawater, such as the estuary of the Hudson River. Oysters grew in the Hudson River as far up as Ossining, in the East River, in Jamaica Bay and around Rockaway, on the coast of Brooklyn, all around Staten Island and City Island, along the New Jersey coast to Keyport, and along the Keyport, Hackensack, and Raritan rivers. They surrounded Ellis Island and Liberty Island, which was why the Dutch named them Little Oyster Island and Great Oyster Island. Some historians estimate that at the time of Dutch New Amsterdam, New York Harbor contained half of the world's oysters.

Oyster vendor, ca *1890*

Before the arrival of Europeans, the Lenape and the native peoples before them ate copious quantities of oysters, leaving tremendous piles of shells, called shell middens, which have been found throughout the New York City area. Some of these middens are as deep as 4 feet (1.2 meters) and are the most common marker of pre-European settlement around the mouth of the Hudson. One such midden gave Pearl Street its name. As recently as the end of the nineteenth century huge shell middens were seen on the Rockaway peninsula, especially the Bayswater section of Far Rockaway. Many middens in Manhattan and Westchester were lost in the nineteenth century when the Hudson rail line was built; however, middens still sometimes turn up when construction workers start digging. The oldest dated shell midden was in Dobbs Ferry and was carbon dated to about 6950 BCE.

Most of the early Europeans who traveled to New Amsterdam commented on the great size and fine flavor of the oysters, though some chroniclers were more pragmatic, such as Rev. Jonas Michaëlius, who arrived in New Amsterdam in 1628 and wrote of the "large quantity of oyster shells to burn for lime." Burned oyster shells were the standard material for mortar in early New York City buildings, including Trinity Church, until a 1703 ordinance banned the practice because of complaints about the noxious smoke. In Dutch times settlers simply walked to the water's edge and picked up their dinner. But eventually, boats traveled around the waters of the city, gathering oysters to sell from stalls on every street corner. They were featured in sleazy basement bars known as oyster cellars, always marked from the sidewalk stairway with a red balloon and known as places to meet prostitutes. Until the late nineteenth century oysters were sold grilled, fried, stewed, or raw at large outdoor food markets. People who worked in Manhattan and lived in Brooklyn would stop for oysters before taking a ferry home. The markets bought the oysters from barges that tied up along the Hudson or East rivers and maintained an office for running a wholesale trade and a deck on which shuckers worked.

Oysters were cheap, and it was said that the poor of New York City had nothing to eat but bread and oysters. In the nineteenth century restaurants offered what was known as the "Canal Street plan," named after the popularity of oyster cellars along Canal Street, which meant all the oysters one could eat for six cents. Nevertheless, oysters were also popular with the wealthy and were often featured at extravagant New York City banquets and in grand restaurants. The city was so associated with the consumption of oysters, millions of them a year by the nineteenth century, that when someone traveled to New York City it was common to say to them, "Enjoy the oysters." With the building of the Erie Canal, the western railroads, and faster transatlantic crossings, oysters became an export product to markets in San Francisco, London, and elsewhere.

As early as the eighteenth century New York oyster beds started showing signs of exhaustion and would have been completely stripped by the nineteenth century if oystermen had not learned how to plant seed oysters, or fingernail-sized young oysters, from other areas. Tremendous quantities of seed oysters were brought up from the Chesapeake Bay and planted in the famous New York beds from Stratford to Bridgeport. The planting process brought many free blacks from Virginia and Maryland to pre–Civil War New York City where they enjoyed greater freedom. One important free black oystering community was called Sandy Ground in southern Staten Island. African Americans became involved in the New York oyster trade, particularly as street vendors and oyster cellar operatives. Thomas Downing, who ran the most famous oyster cellar in the city before the Civil War, was one of the city's first prominent African Americans.

Eventually, centuries of dumping untreated sewage in water around the city forced oyster beds to close down because of health risks. In 1927 the last New York City oyster bed, in Raritan Bay off Staten Island, was closed. In the twenty-first century city water is once again clean enough for oysters to grow, and environmentalists have been replanting some beds, but the presence of polychlorinated biphenyls (PCBs) and heavy metals in the water continues to make New York City oysters unsafe to eat.

Mark Kurlansky, *The Big Oyster: History on the Half Shell* (New York: Ballantine Books, 2006)

Mark Kurlansky

Ozone Park. Neighborhood in southwestern Queens, bounded to the north by Atlantic Avenue, to the east by 104th Street, to the south by Liberty Avenue, and to the west by 96th Street. It was developed by the music publisher Benjamin W. Hitchcock and Charles C. Dunton after railroad service was extended to the area in 1880 by the New York, Woodhaven, and Rockaway Railroad, which provided a direct route to Brooklyn and Rockaway Beach. Hitchcock and Dunton filed a survey map in July 1882, and their land was divided into 25-by-100-foot lots. In 1883–84 they bought more land, enlarging Ozone Park from 316 to 630 lots that were sold at auction; streets and sidewalks were laid out and shade trees planted. A post office opened in 1889 when the number of residents reached the required level of 600. The population reached 1100 by 1900 and 3000 by 1910, and consisted mostly of young families from Brooklyn. Development was spurred by the need to house workers at the tinware plant of Lalance and Grosjean in Woodhaven.

The success of Ozone Park led to the development in 1896 of Ozone Park Heights, which extended as far south as Rockaway Boulevard, and the formation of the Ozone Park Home Company. The area's popularity increased after the Brooklyn Rapid Transit extended the Fulton Street elevated line along Liberty Avenue to Lefferts Boulevard (119th Street) in September 1915, enabling residents to commute to Manhattan for only 5 cents. The neighborhood became entirely built up as the demand for housing increased during the 1920s; the last open spaces were used for blocks of row houses and attached houses. In April 1956 the Independent subway was connected at Grant Avenue to the Fulton Street elevated line, which became obsolete. The neighborhood is home to Aqueduct Racetrack at Rockaway Boulevard and Southern Parkway, opened in 1894, and John Gotti kept his headquarters at the Bergin Hunt and Fish Club at 98–04 101st Avenue. During the late twentieth century most inhabitants were of German, Irish, Italian, and eastern European ancestry; by the early twenty-first century the number of residents from the Caribbean, Latin America, and Asia had increased.

Vincent Seyfried

P

Pace University. University incorporated as Pace College in 1947. Its forerunner was a course developed by Homer St. Clair Pace to tutor candidates for state certifying examinations for public accountants. With his brother Charles Ashford Pace he opened a school of accountancy in 1906 at the New York Tribune Building in lower Manhattan. The two also offered the Pace Standardized Course in Accounting at Young Men's Christian Associations in Brooklyn, Manhattan, and New Jersey. Enrollment in the metropolitan area exceeded 300 by 1909 and 4000 by 1919; in 1927 the school moved from the Hudson Terminal Building on Church Street to the new Transportation Building on Broadway. Pace Institute was incorporated in 1935 as a nonprofit institution of higher education. In 1942 it received its permanent charter and the administration was taken over by Homer Pace's sons Robert Scott Pace, who became president, and C. Richard Pace, who became secretary. When the institute became Pace College, Edward J. Mortola was appointed an assistant dean. The college bought the New York Times Building on Park Row in 1951; in 1953 it moved into its new quarters and was authorized to grant bachelor's degrees. It offered the master of business administration from 1958 and in 1961 inaugurated Mortola as its third president. During his administration the school opened a campus in suburban Pleasantville, New York (1962), and schools of arts and sciences, education, and nursing (1966); introduced graduate programs in education (1969); completed the Pace Plaza Building in lower Manhattan (1970); attained university status (1973); effected a merger with the Colleges of White Plains (1975); opened a law school and a midtown campus (1976); acquired the former campus of Briarcliff College (1977); and began a doctoral program in school and community psychology (1979) and a school of computer science and information systems (1983). On being named chancellor in 1984 Mortola was succeeded by William B. Sharwell, who oversaw the introduction of a master's program in publishing (1985) and new programs in information systems (1986), as well as the opening of the Lubin Graduate Center in White Plains, New York (1987). In 1990 Patricia O'Donnell Ewers was named president of the university. During the Ewers administration undergraduate programs in Westchester were consolidated on the Pleasantville campus (1995) and the Ann and Alfred Goldstein Academic Center opened in Pleasantville (1995). In 1996 the Lubin School of Business became accredited and the university acquired both a midtown center and the World Trade Institute. At the end of the decade a new law school academic building was dedicated on the White Plains campus (1999). In 2000 David A. Caputo became Pace's sixth president. A year later the university lost staff members, alumni, and its World Trade Institute facilities in the terrorist attacks on the World Trade Center. In 2007 Caputo was succeeded by Stephen J. Friedman as president.

Marilyn E. Weigold

Packer Collegiate Institute. Private coeducational elementary and secondary school opened in 1854 as the Brooklyn Female Academy. It is the oldest independent school in Brooklyn and the fifth-oldest in New York City. The college division of the school in 1919 became the first junior college to be approved by the Regents of the State of New York. In 1972 the school became coeducational and the junior college was discontinued. Packer is known for its magnificent neo-Gothic chapel, designed by Minard Lafever, and for its alumni garden, awarded the National Nurserymen's Prize for best urban school garden in 1980.

Richard Schwartz

Paderewski, Jan Ignace (*b* Kuryłnowka, Podolia, 12 Nov 1860; *d* New York City, 29 June 1941). Pianist, composer, and statesman. The most popular pianist in the world during his lifetime, he made many concert tours to New York City and lived there on several occasions. He died in the city shortly after returning to the United States to plead the case for Poland when the nation was overrun by the German army in the early days of World War II.

Kenneth T. Jackson

Paerdegat Basin. A channel in Brooklyn 1¼ miles (2 kilometers) long that empties into Jamaica Bay, and by extension the surrounding neighborhood, which is bordered by Canarsie, Flatlands, and Bergen Beach. After the city failed to transform Jamaica Bay into a major port in the 1920s, the area remained undeveloped until the 1960s. In 1972 local residents defeated a proposal to construct a city-sponsored complex of garden apartments for nearly 4000 residents. Paerdegat Basin now consists of one- and two-family suburban houses.

Stephen Weinstein

Page, Geraldine (*b* Kirksville, Mo., 22 Nov 1924; *d* New York City, 13 June 1987). Actress. In 1945 she moved to New York City and made her debut in a production of *Seven Mirrors* by the Blackfriars Guild. She studied voice with Alice Hermes and acting with Uta Hagen at the Berghof Studios and the Theater Wing School. In 1952 she became well known for her performance in Tennessee Williams's *Summer and Smoke* at the Sheridan Square Theater in Greenwich Village. In the following year she played the role of Lily Barton in Vina Delmar's *Midsummer* at the Vanderbilt Theater, for which she won the Theater World Award, the Donaldson Award, and the Drama Critics Award; after this she seldom left the city or the public eye. She made her first motion picture, *Hondo* (with John Wayne), in 1954. During the 1960s she worked with the Actors Studio in the city and played many roles on Broadway in productions directed by Lee Strasberg. With her second husband, the actor Rip Torn, she formed the Sanctuary Theater Company. Known for the enthusiasm she brought to her roles, she performed in dozens of plays, films, and television productions and won two Emmys, as well as an Academy Award for her performance in *A Trip to Bountiful* in 1985. At the end of her life she lived at 435 West 22nd Street and appeared on Broadway as Madame Arcate in Noël Coward's *Blithe Spirit.*

Chad Ludington

Paine, Thomas (*b* Thetford, England, 29 Jan 1737; *d* New York City, 8 June 1809). Political theorist and writer. After a series of false starts as a corset maker, excise official, and pamphleteer, he left England in 1774 and settled in Philadelphia. He was drawn into political controversy and became a brilliant proponent of American independence. His popular pamphlet *Common Sense* (1776) laid out the patriot case and galvanized public opinion. Regarded as a leading spokesman for democracy well into the 1790s, he ran afoul of respectable opinion for his activities in connection with the French Revolution and especially after publishing *The Age of Reason* (1795), a deist critique of Christianity. This and other writings were condemned in the United States as irrelevant to American political concerns

Thomas Paine, 1827

by some, and as blasphemy by others. After returning to the United States in 1803 he settled at his farm in New Rochelle, New York, a gift from the state assembly after the American Revolution. He was drawn back to New York City repeatedly to spend time with sympathetic freethinkers and Republicans, and also to escape his pious, unfriendly neighbors. In 1804 he lived at 16 Gold Street before moving to 36 Cedar Street. He settled permanently in the city in 1806, moving successively from 85 Church Street to 63 Partition Street (now West Fulton Street) in 1807 and to 309 Bleecker Street in 1808. During the following year he lost many friends in quarrels and suffered bouts of apoplexy that left him an invalid; he also wrote prolifically, replying to personal attacks, lambasting the Federalists, and encouraging his friends and supporters. (His fiery example inspired several young admirers who became leading radical spokesmen during the 1820s and 1830s.) Lonely and ill, in May 1809 he begged a longtime friend from his days in France, Marguerite Bonneville, to take him into her household. She grudgingly agreed and rented a house for him at 59 Grove Street adjoining her own.

Sean Wilentz

Paine Webber. Firm of securities brokers, formed in 1942 as Paine, Webber, Jackson and Curtis by the merger of Jackson and Curtis (1879) and Paine, Webber and Company (1880). Originally based in Boston, the firm moved its headquarters to New York City in 1963. It became a publicly owned corporation in 1972 and took its current name in 1974. Although best known for its nationwide network of retail brokerage offices, the firm also provides institutional investment banking services. Shares in Paine Webber are traded on the New York Stock Exchange. The headquarters were at 1285 Sixth Avenue in Manhattan. In 2000 it merged with UBS AG of Switzerland, and in 2003 "Paine Webber" disappeared from the company name.

Paine, Webber and Company, 1880–1930: A National Institution (Boston: Paine, Webber, 1930)

Owen D. Gutfreund

painting. During the eighteenth century in New York City several artists made their living painting portraits of wealthy residents. The most successful painters were the members of the Duyckinck family, especially Gerardus Duyckinck II (1723–97), who had skills in varnishing, Japanning, gilding, silvering, and glazing. Several painters trained in Europe visited the city, including John Smibert, who had settled in Boston, and John Watson, from Perth Amboy, New Jersey. The most cosmopolitan artist of the period was London-born John Wollaston, who worked in New York City from 1749 to about 1752, when he moved to Maryland. Other portrait painters working in the late eighteenth century included Lawrence Kilburn, Thomas McIlworth, John Mare (*b* circa 1737; *d* 1795), and Abraham Delanoy. John Durand (*fl* 1766–82), Matthew Pratt, Gilbert Stuart, and John Singleton Copley worked only briefly in the city.

In the early years of the republic, portraiture continued to employ painters such as Samuel Lovett Waldo and his student William Jewett, who together formed a portraiture business. By the 1820s many painters also pursued other interests, such as Robert Fulton (1765–1815) and Samuel F. B. Morse. John Trumbull, a history painter, was president of the American Academy of Fine Arts. William Dunlap, a painter and playwright, helped to found the National Academy of Design; his *History of the Rise and Progress of the Arts of Design in the United States* (1834) set the standard for art criticism. After years of living in France, portraitist John Vanderlyn settled in New York City in 1815 and exhibited his panorama *Palace and Gardens of Versailles* (Metropolitan Museum of Art) in a specially built rotunda in City Hall Park. Charles Loring Elliott and Daniel Huntington continued to fill major portrait commissions during the antebellum years. Publishers often commissioned views of the city, which were popular among both residents and tourists. William Guy Wall (*b* Ireland, 1772; *d* circa 1864), Nicolino Calyo, and Francis Guy (*b* Burton-in-Kendal, England, 1760; *d* Brooklyn, 1820) were artists painting city scenes.

A rising elite of merchants, bankers, and railroad directors such as Luman Reed, Jonathan Sturges, Philip Hone, and Marshall O. Roberts bought the work of the artists of the Hudson River School, including Thomas Cole, Asher B. Durand, John Frederick Kensett, and later Jasper F. Cropsey (1823–1900), Sanford Robinson Gifford (1823–80), Albert Bierstadt (1830–1902), Thomas Worthington Whittredge (1820–1910), and Frederic E. Church. The collections of Reed and Sturges eventually were left to the New-York Historical Society. Popular historical painters included Henry Peters Gray (1819–77), Daniel Huntington, Thomas P. Rossiter (1818–71), and Emanuel Leutze (1816–68). At the several private clubs of the city, notably the Century Association, patrons socialized with artists, and with literary figures such as the poet and journalist William Cullen Bryant, they promoted American art through the American Art-Union (1839–52).

Although landscape painting dominated in terms of numbers at the annual exhibitions of the National Academy of Design, genre paintings appealed to art writers and journalists at mid-century and during the two decades after the Civil War. The first generation of genre painters included the banker Francis Edmonds (1806–63); William Sidney Mount; Henry Inman; James H. Cafferty (1819–96); Arthur Fitzwilliam Tait (1819–1905), who often drew for Currier and Ives; and the eccentric John Quidor (1801–81), who painted scenes from the stories of Washington Irving. Two Ohio artists became successful in New York City: William Holbrook Beard (1824–1900) specialized in humorous depictions of anthropomorphized animals such as *Bulls and Bears of Wall Street* (New-York Historical Society), and Lilly Martin Spencer (1822–1902) painted sentimental pictures of domestic subjects. Many of the genre artists achieving prominence during the 1840s and 1850s, including John George Brown (1831–1913), Thomas Hicks (1823–90), John Whetten Ehninger (1827–89), and Eastman Johnson, studied in the European centers of art—London, Düsseldorf, and Paris.

At the onset of the Civil War the artists Sanford Gifford and Jervis McEntee enlisted in the Union army. Johnson, Edwin Forbes, and Winslow Homer followed the troops—Johnson to find subjects for his genre scenes, Forbes as a staff artist for *Frank Leslie's Illustrated Newspaper,* and Homer as an artist for *Harper's Weekly.* Artists and patrons together organized the art exhibition of the Metropolitan Fair (1864) to raise funds for the U.S. Sanitary Commission.

The moralizing genre painting and the detailed landscape painting of the Hudson River School declined after the Civil War. At that time younger American painters, including William Merritt Chase and Julian Alden Weir, flocked to Paris and Munich to learn cosmopolitan European styles and new attitudes about art. In 1877 Augustus Saint-Gaudens, Walter Shirlaw (1838–1909), Wyatt Eaton (1849–96), and Helena de Kay Gilder (1848–1916) formed the Society of American Artists to promote the new trends in art. From 1878 the society held annual exhibitions that displayed the work of Chase, Weir, Will Hicok Low (1853–1932), Maria Richards Oakey (1845–1927), George Inness (1825–94), Albert Pinkham Ryder (1847–1917), John La Farge, Homer Dodge Martin (1836–97), Thomas Dewing (1851–1938), and John Singer Sargent (1856–1924). The Society of American Artists merged with the National Academy of Design in 1906.

The major tendencies in painting at the end of the nineteenth century included the poetical landscapes of Ryder and Ralph Blakelock and the impressionism of Chase and Childe Hassam, a founding member of the group Ten American Painters (1898). Academic, neoclassical styles of painting still flourished: their exponents included Edwin Howland Blashfield (1848–1936) and Kenyon Cox (1856–1919), both of whom painted murals for the numerous private mansions and public buildings then being constructed.

Early in the twentieth century Robert Henri led a group of artists who rejected impressionism and insisted on a realism that represented the "spirit" of the people and the new age of urbanization. Influenced by Walt Whitman, the European tradition of graphic realism, and the realist novelists, the painters George Luks, William James Glackens, John Sloan, and Everett Shinn depicted the leisure life of the working classes. To counter the conservatism of the National Academy, Sloan and Henri organized an exhibition at the Macbeth Gallery (1908) that included their own work as well as that of Luks, Glackens, Shinn, Arthur B. Davies (1862–1928), Ernest Lawson (1873–1939), and Maurice Prendergast (1859–1924); the participants in this show became known as "The Eight," and later "the Ashcan School." In 1912 Sloan became the unpaid art director of the radical socialist publication *The Masses,* edited by Max Eastman, which also featured the drawings of George Bellows and Stuart Davis.

The early twentieth century saw the development of a semiabstract style that expressed the responses of artists to the increasing mechanization of the modern era. The photographer and gallerist Alfred Stieglitz brought European cubism and African art to New York City through exhibitions at his Little Galleries of the Photo Secession (also known as "291") at 291 Fifth Avenue. He showed the work of avant-garde photographers and the paintings of John Marin (1870–1953), Abraham Walkowitz (1878–1965), Max Weber, and Georgia O'Keeffe, which conveyed the vitality of the city. Other early modern artists included Alfred H. Maurer (1868–1932) and Joseph Stella, who painted Coney Island and the Brooklyn Bridge using an abstract style.

The realists and semiabstractionists together organized the International Exhibition of Modern Art, known as the Armory Show, which opened at the 69th Regiment Armory in New York City in 1913 with more than 1600 European and American works. The critical reception of the show was largely negative and focused on the controversial work of the French artist Marcel Duchamp, whose *Nude Descending a Staircase* (1912, Philadelphia Museum) was humorously called "Explosion in a Shingle Factory." Duchamp and the American artist Man Ray were part of the dadaist movement, which grew out of a wartime cultural malaise, emphasized the mental conception of an artwork rather than its craftsmanship, and was often highly irreverent. Many of the avant-garde artists frequented the weekly salons of Louise and Walter Arensberg, Mabel Dodge, and the Stettheimer sisters Ettie, Carrie, and Florine.

During the 1920s and 1930s Charles Sheeler, Charles Demuth (1883–1935), and Niles Spencer (1893–1953) depicted industrial America in a modernist style often called precisionism or cubist realism and characterized by precise lines and reductive forms. O'Keeffe, Marsden Hartley, and Arthur B. Dove (1880–1946) developed a style based on natural forms. The society figure and sculptor Gertrude Vanderbilt Whitney created many important exhibition spaces, including the Whitney Studio (1914–17), the Whitney Studio Club (1918–28), and the Whitney Studio Galleries (1928–30), which regularly showed the paintings of Sloan, Alexander Brook (1898–1980), and Guy Pène du Bois (1884–1958). In 1930 she founded the Whitney Museum of American Art. Sloan, du Bois, and Kenneth Hayes Miller taught at the Art Students League.

When the Depression began many artists in New York City joined the John Reed Club, which served as a social club for artists who advocated an art by and for the working classes. Among those active as organizers or as cartoonists and writers for leftist political journals were the artists Rockwell Kent, Hugo Gellert (1892–1985), William Gropper (1897–1977), Louis Lozowick (1892–1973), Ben Shahn, Bernarda Bryson Shahn, and Philip Evergood; the most prominent journal was *Art Front,* the monthly magazine of the Artists' Union, edited successively by Davis, Joe Solman, and Clarence Weinstock (1910–64). Lozowick, Raphael Soyer, and Philip Reisman (1904–92) were among the teachers at the John Reed Club School of Art. Politically oriented artists organized protests when the mural *Man at the Crossroads* painted by the Mexican painter Diego Rivera for Rockefeller Center was covered over and then destroyed in 1933–34.

In the mid-1930s, with the rise of fascism in Europe, leftist groups of artists, including those friendly with the Communist Party, formed alliances with liberal groups. Together they organized the American Artists' Congress, which held a conference in February 1936 attended by artists, musicians, and such writers as Lewis Mumford and Meyer Schapiro. Not all figurative artists at the time were overtly political in their painting: Isabel Bishop (1902–88) was more inclined to paint the shop girls of Union Square; Reginald Marsh depicted bathers at Coney Island and derelicts of the Bowery; Thomas Hart Benton, living in the city for the first half of the 1930s and influencing artists through his teaching at the Art Students League, painted murals for the New School for Social Research that celebrated the various regions of the United States. Edward Hopper, who did not join groups, avoided politics altogether.

Harlem during the late 1920s and 1930s was another lively artistic center. Aaron Douglas and Charles Alston (1907–77) painted murals that incorporated African and black American imagery with modernist techniques. Romare Bearden and Jacob Lawrence (1917–2000) were heirs to the ideals and institutions of the Harlem Renaissance and learned from such dynamic figures as the sculptor Augusta Savage. Other painters associated with Harlem were William H. Johnson, Palmer Hayden, Malvin Gray Johnson, and Norman Lewis (1909–79).

The major patron for artists in the late 1930s was the federal government. In December 1933 the Public Works of Art Project was formed to provide relief for unemployed artists; in New York City the project was directed by Juliana Force (then head of the Whitney Museum) and lasted about five months. A more ambitious program, the Federal Art Project of the Works Progress Administration (1935–43), hired artists to supply paintings to government offices or execute murals for public schools, housing projects, and radio stations. The Section, a program operated by the Department of the Treasury, commissioned murals for post offices, other federal buildings, and airports. These government programs for the most part supported figurative painting, but they also employed such abstract artists as Stuart Davis, Arshile Gorky, Burgoyne Diller (1906–65), and Ilya Bolotowsky (1907–81).

During the late 1930s and the 1940s the Museum of Modern Art presented exhibitions of modern European abstract, cubist, and surrealist paintings, yet its curators tended to ignore American abstraction. Thus, the American Abstract Artists was formed in 1936; its members, including George L. K. Morris, worked in a hard-edged abstract style. A more expressive form of abstraction began to develop because of the influence of émigré abstract and surrealist artists, including Duchamp, John Graham (1881–1961), Max Ernst, Yves Tanguy, Hans Hoffman (1880–1966), and the Chilean artist Roberto Matta Echaurren. Its adherents, who became known as the New York School, drew on mythology, American Indian art, and their experiences with psychoanalysis to create paintings that focused on self-examination and the work of art itself. Jackson Pollock and Willem de Kooning emerged as the leading exponents of this new style, variously called abstract expressionism and "action painting" (a term coined by the critic Harold Rosenberg).

Painting after World War II represented a diversity of styles, and art galleries flourished. Artists such as Yasuo Kuniyoshi, Stephen Greene, Rico LeBrun (1900–64), Alice Neel, Fairfield Porter (1907–75), and Raphael Soyer practiced a figurative art ranging from naturalist to expressionist. By the mid-1950s Robert Rauschenberg and Jasper Johns were drawing on images from popular culture, foreshadowing the movement later known as pop art.

A number of new painting styles took hold during the 1960s. Pop art by Andy Warhol, Roy Lichtenstein, and James Rosenquist celebrated the banality of everyday objects; the hard-edged painting of Ellsworth Kelly, Jack Youngerman, and Jules Olitski was based on simple shapes; minimalist works by Frank Stella, Agnes Martin, and Robert Ryman used stripes, grids, and patterns; and the lyrical abstraction of Helen Frankenthaler was characterized by broad areas of thin paint that penetrated the surface of the canvas. New realists in the 1960s and 1970s included Larry Rivers, Philip Pearlstein, Alex Katz, and Janet Fish; photorealists included Richard Estes and Audrey Flack. Political art by Rudolf Baranik, Leon Golub, Nancy Spero, and May Stevens criticized imperialism, sexism, and racism during the 1970s and 1980s. At the end of the twentieth century a number of women, blacks, Asian Americans, American Indians, and Latin Americans came to the forefront of painting, notably Emma Amos, Ida Applebroog, Luis Cruz Azaceta, Jean-Michel Basquiat, Howardena Pindell, Katherine Porter, Faith Ringgold, Juan Sanchez, Miriam Schapiro, Joan Semmel, Sylvia Sleigh, Joan Snyder, and Joyce Kozloff. However, by the beginning of the twenty-first century many artists were working as video, installation, performance, and new media artists.

Doreen Bolger Burke, *American Paintings in the Metropolitan Museum of Art,* vol. 3, *A Catalogue of Works by Artists Born between 1846 and 1864* (New York: Metropolitan Museum of Art, 1980); Natalie Spassky, *American Paintings in the Metropolitan Museum of Art,* vol. 2, *A Catalogue of Works by Artists Born between 1816 and 1845* (New York: Metropolitan Museum of Art, 1985); John Caldwell and Oswaldo Rodriguez Roque, *American Paintings in the Metropolitan Museum of Art,* vol. 1, *A Catalogue of Works by Artists Born by 1815* (New York: Metropolitan Museum of Art, 1994)

Patricia Hills

paints, dyes, and varnishes. There was little demand for paints, dyes, and varnishes in New York City during the colonial period: for cultural reasons early settlers refrained from painting buildings, and as of 1712 lampblack was the only pigment legally produced in the colony of New York. In 1754 William Post began mixing, grinding, and importing pigments at a shop on Fletcher Street that was the forerunner of the Devoe and Raynolds Company. New Yorkers in the 1770s made dyes from dogwood, redwood, and indigo and had halted much of the importation of dyed goods, linseed oil, and related products. William Partridge began grinding dyestuffs at a horse-propelled capstan mill in Greenwich Village in 1798 and introduced into the United States argols, lac dye from India, Nicaragua wood, and potassium dichromate for use as a mordant; his enterprise was the precursor of the American Dyewood Company (1904), the first giant in the field. Several patents were issued for dyes and leads during the early nineteenth century. In 1819 Mordecai Lewis began making lead pigments, and Joel West opened a turpentine distillery. The New York Chemical Manufacturing Company (1823) made paints and dyes, and by 1825 several small plants ground imported white lead and colored paints. Pascal B. Smith developed a spar varnish at his shop on East Sixth Street in 1827 and built a large business. In the same year the merchant David Leavitt, the distillers Augustus and John Bell Graham, and others formed the Brooklyn White Lead Works, and in 1827 the brothers Whitehead, Peter, and George Cornell formed the Union White Lead Company of Brooklyn (incorporated in 1841).

Several large lead factories opened between 1840 and 1850: Robert Colgate formed the Atlantic White Lead Company of New York (which became the nucleus of the National Lead Company), and John Jewett and Sons opened a plant in Staten Island. After the Civil War Hall, Bradley and Company built a large plant in Brooklyn, the Bradley White Lead Company. In 1865 the production of aniline dyes began in Brooklyn at the plant of Thomas and Charles Holliday, and by 1880 factories in New York State accounted for all of the 80,000 pounds (36,000 kilograms) of aniline dyes produced in the United States. But manufacturers of dyes could not compete with the flood of German imports, which eliminated most domestic producers by 1900; one of few that remained was the American Dyewood Company, which in 1904 had sales of $3 million. From about the turn of the century factories moved from Manhattan to Brooklyn and other surrounding communities where tall stacks carried off the noxious fumes. Paint and varnish manufacturers in New York City continued to prosper: between 1890 and 1919 they increased in number from 27 to 113, in employment from 783 to 5243, and in the total value of their products from $3.8 million to $31.2 million (an increase only partly explained by the consolidation of the city in 1898), and in 1919 the metropolitan area accounted for half of all the varnish made in the United States. In 1929 the value added for the 206 paint and varnish makers in the region was $58.6 million. Production levels in New York City were uneven in the 1970s and 1980s, but there was a clear trend toward the consolidation of firms. In the late 1970s only 115 producers of paint and allied products remained in the metropolitan area, with a total value added of $78.4 million.

Notes for a History of Lead (New York: D. Van Nostrand, 1888); Williams Haynes, *American Chemical Industry,* vol. 1, *Background and Beginnings, 1609–1911* (New York: D. Van Nostrand, 1954)

David B. Sicilia

Pakistanis. Muslims from India arrived in the United States in the early 1900s. Pakistan achieved independence from India in 1947, but it was not until 1965 that immigration restrictions were lifted and allowed Pakistanis to immigrate to New York City in larger numbers. Between 1990 and 2000 the city's Pakistani population more than doubled in size. According to the Asian American Federation of New York, in 2000, 47 percent of Pakistani immigrants lived in Queens, 33 percent in Brooklyn, 10 percent in the Bronx, 8 percent in Manhattan, and 2 percent in Staten Island. Neighborhoods with large Pakistani populations include Bensonhurst, Kensington, Midwood, Astoria, and Flushing. An annual parade to commemorate Pakistani independence is held annually in Manhattan in late August. Pakistanis ranked 18 in the top 20 foreign-born groups in New York City in 2000.

Penelope Gelwicks

PAL. See Police Athletic League.

Palace Theatre. Theater at Seventh Avenue and 47th Street, built by the impresario Martin Beck. It opened in 1913 and through several questionable transactions was taken over by E. F. Albee, head of the Keith vaudeville circuit, under whose management it became the pinnacle of vaudeville. Performers there could win a national audience, and the sidewalks outside were often crowded with those seeking bookings. The top floor was used for offices by agents preparing cross-country tours for performers. During the Depression vaudeville was largely replaced by sound motion pictures, and in 1932 the Palace became a movie house. The management then introduced a combination of films and live acts before offering films alone from 1935 to 1949. After a performance in the 1950s by Judy Garland the theater became a national stage for Danny Kaye, Jerry Lewis, Harry Belafonte, and others. From 1960 to 1965 it reverted to showing motion pictures. It was bought by the Nederlander family and reopened as a theater for live performance in 1966. During a complicated review of its historic status the interior was named a landmark, but the building surrounding the auditorium was destroyed and replaced by a hotel. The auditorium reopened in 1991 for a performance of the musical *The Will Rogers Follies,* and in 1994 *The Beauty and the Beast* had a five-year run there. In the early twenty-first century the theater continued to host main stage productions.

Marian Spitzer, *The Palace* (New York: Atheneum, 1969); Robert W. Snyder, *The Voice of the City: Vaudeville and Popular Culture in New York* (New York: Oxford University Press, 1989)

Robert W. Snyder

Pale Male. Red-tailed Hawk who lives in a nest at 927 Fifth Avenue. A group of Central Park birdwatchers first spotted Pale Male in 1991 and named him for his light color; he and his mate First Love built the first known hawk nest in the park's history on the southwest corner of the Great Lawn. In 1993 Pale Male and his new mate Chocolate built their nest on the 12th-floor ledge of an apartment building at 927 Fifth Avenue, near 74th Street. Pale Male has returned to the nest yearly, siring more than 20 baby hawks whose descendents have been spotted breeding in nests all over the city. Since 2004 Pale Male and his mate Lola have been unable to successfully reproduce although they have built a new nest on the building each year.

Marie Winn, *Red Tails in Love* (New York: Pantheon Books, 1998)

Kate Lauber

Palestinians. After the formation of Israel in 1948 many Palestinians moved to the United States, and large numbers came to New York City starting in the late 1960s. More immigrants came after the Lebanese civil war in the 1980s and the Gulf War in the early 1990s. Palestinians initially lived near Syrian and Lebanese enclaves in lower Manhattan but later settled primarily in Brooklyn. Organizations such as the Union of Palestinian Women's Associations (1986), the Palestinian American Youth Club, the Palestinian–American Community Center, and various student groups encouraged their members to be politically active, especially in working toward an independent Palestinian state. In the mid-1990s the largest Palestinian community in the city was in Sunset Park. Many Palestinians belong to village clubs like the Al-Bireh and Beit Hanina clubs and the Ramallah Federation. Religious institutions include the Al-Faruq Mosque and St. Nicholas Cathedral, both in Boerum Hill. Because a Palestinian may carry a passport from one of several nations, estimates of the Palestinian population in the city are rough, ranging from 10,000 to 40,000 in the early twenty-first century. A well-known Palestinian was Edward Said (1935–2003), an influential literary theorist and professor of English and comparative literature at Columbia University from 1963 until his death.

Inea Bushnaq

Paley, William S. (*b* Chicago, 28 Sept 1901; *d* New York City, 26 Oct 1990). Entrepreneur. He moved to New York City in 1928 and consolidated a loosely connected group of radio stations to form the Columbia Broadcasting System (CBS). Under his direction the firm invested in Broadway musicals and made acquisitions ranging from the New York Yankees to the piano makers Steinway and Sons. Paley was also an art collector and the long-time president and trustee of the Museum of Modern Art. From the mid-1960s until his death he lived at 820 Fifth Avenue in Manhattan. Paley Park is on 53rd Street.

David Halberstam, *The Powers That Be* (New York: Alfred A. Knopf, 1979); Sally Bedell Smith, *In All His Glory: The Life of William S. Paley* (New York: Simon and Schuster, 1990)

JillEllyn Riley

Paley Center for Media. Museum opened in 1975 as the Museum of Broadcasting by William S. Paley, founder and chairman of the Columbia Broadcasting System, to collect and preserve radio and television programs and make them available to the public. Its collection covers more than 70 years of broadcast history and has more than 40,000 programs, including news, public affairs, documentary, performing arts, children's, sports, comedy, and dramatic programming, as well as advertising. Exhibitions and seminars highlighting the museum's extensive collection are presented annually. In 1991 the museum was renamed the Museum of Television and Radio and moved into a new building at 23 West 52nd Street. On 5 June 2007 it was renamed the Paley Center for Media, reflecting emerging broadcasting technologies such as the Internet and mobile video.

Laura Gwinn

Palm. Steakhouse, opened by Pio Bozzi and John Ganzi in 1926 at 837 Second Avenue. For decades it was a popular meeting place for writers and members of the media. The Palm is also known for its caricatures of celebrities on the walls.

Jessica Montesano

Palmer [née Worrall], **Phoebe** (*b* New York City, 18 Dec 1807; *d* New York City, 2 Nov 1874). Evangelist and writer. Born to a devout Methodist family, she married Warren C. Palmer, a Methodist physician, and with him underwent a religious renewal from 1832 to 1837 that led her to believe in "entire sanctification," an ideal of total personal consecration achieved in a distinct experience. Her idea adapted Wesleyan perfectionism to Victorian standards of urban domesticity and moderate social reform and was crucial in shaping the American holiness tradition. She spread her ideas in books, in her magazine *Guide to Holiness* (1864–74), and in weekly meetings at her home. She held revival meetings across the eastern United States and Canada during the 1850s and in the British Isles during the Civil War but otherwise lived in New York City for her entire life.

Charles Edward White, *The Beauty of Holiness: Phoebe Palmer as Theologian, Revivalist, Feminist, and Humanitarian* (Wilmore, Ky.: Francis Asbury, 1986)

James D. Bratt

Palmer Raids. A series of nationwide roundups of radicals launched by the federal government on 7 November 1919 and 2 January 1920. The raids were organized by the Department of Justice under the leadership of Attorney General A. Mitchell Palmer in response to public concern over the threat of radicalism during the year following the end of World War I. Thousands of strikes and the formation in the United States of organizations inspired by the Bolshevik Revolution of 1917 convinced many Americans that there was an organized effort to overthrow the U.S. government. The threat appeared to be confirmed on 2 June when eight bombs exploded in eight different cities, including New York City where the home of a federal judge was damaged and a watchman killed. The Palmer Raids were intended to eliminate the revolutionary threat by expelling foreign-born radicals under a law that made it a deportable offense for an alien to advocate the overthrow of the government.

The November raids targeted the Union of Russian Workers (URW), an organization that had been formed in 1907. Simultaneous raids in 12 cities seized 300 URW officers and members. In New York City federal agents supported by local police entered the Russian People's House at 133 East 15th Street shortly after 9 p.m., searching for members of the URW, which had an office there. Most of the people in the building were Russian immigrants attending night classes. More than 200 people were arrested, and many were beaten and seriously injured. Most were later released; only 39 were held for deportation. The next day 500 more suspected radicals were picked up at 70 locations in all five boroughs. These raids were conducted by local officials at the urging of a state legislative committee headed by state senator Clayton R. Lusk. The Lusk Committee had been investigating radical activity since the summer and had already conducted several smaller raids. Nearly 250 of the aliens seized during the two days of raids were declared to be deportable radicals and were held on Ellis Island. On 21 December, most of them sailed out of New York City under heavy guard aboard an old government ship, the *Buford.* Thirty-five men arrested in the raids were prosecuted under the New York criminal anarchy law, including Benjamin Gitlow, a former socialist assemblyman from the Bronx, and James Larkin, an Irish labor leader. Both were convicted and sentenced to five to 10 years in Sing Sing Prison.

An even larger series of raids was launched on 2 January 1920 and captured 3000 people across the country. In New York City agents held deportation warrants for 800 members of the Communist Party and the Communist Labor Party and immediately seized several hundred. However, the raids failed to achieve their goal of deporting all foreign-born radicals after Louis F. Post, an official of the Department of Labor, declared that most of the people caught in the raids were not a threat and canceled more than 2000 deportation orders. In the end, the government deported more than 800 communists.

The war against radicalism continued in the city for several more months. The New York Assembly declared that members of the Socialist Party could not be loyal Americans and expelled four socialist representatives from the city. The Lusk Committee also persuaded the legislature to pass several laws aimed at suppressing radicalism. By then, however, the Red Scare had begun to wane. Governor Alfred E. Smith opposed the expulsion of the socialists and vetoed the Lusk laws as violations of the First Amendment.

Robert K. Murray, *Red Scare: A Study of National Hysteria, 1919–1920* (Minneapolis: University of Minnesota Press, 1955); Kenneth D. Ackerman, *Young J. Edgar: Hoover, the Red Scare, and the Assault on Civil Liberties* (New York: Carroll and Graf, 2007); Christopher M. Finan, *From the Palmer Raids to the Patriot Act: A History of the Fight for Free Speech in America* (Boston: Beacon, 2007)

Christopher M. Finan

Palmo's New York Opera House. Opera house opened in February 1844 at 67 Chambers Street by Ferdinand Palmo (1785–1869), an Italian immigrant. It initially attracted a genteel clientele and was the focus of a brief vogue for Italian opera during the mid-nineteenth century. The house was the site in 1845 of the local debut of the German Opera Company (in productions that were a critical success and a popular failure) and in 1847 of the first performance in New York City of an opera by Giuseppe Verdi (*I Lombardi*). In the end Palmo's was hurt by its location too far downtown, and in 1848 it was sold to William Burton, who abandoned opera in favor of dramatic performances.

Marc Ferris

Panamanians. Panamanians of West Indian origin settled in New York City before 1950 to work in conjunction with the shipping and air routes from Panama. Panama was exempt from the immigration quotas imposed in 1924 and 1952. During the 1950s a sizable number of Panamanians immigrated to the United States because of changes in employment in the Canal Zone, a large-scale retirement of older workers, and the voluntary entry of young men looking to serve in the U.S. armed forces during the Korean War. The U.S. Bureau of the Census first recorded the country of origin of immigrants from Central and South America after 1960, when the largest number of Panamanian immigrants settled in the city.

Panamanians who arrived before 1970 were of different backgrounds. They were West Indian, of black and mixed race, and originated from the Canal Zone and the cities of Panamá and Colón. They settled in the Haitian and Caribbean enclaves and African American neighborhoods of Brooklyn and in Spanish-speaking enclaves in Queens, Manhattan, and the Bronx. A military coup in 1968 spurred an influx of Panamanians of European ancestry who settled mostly in Miami and in wealthy neighborhoods in Manhattan and Queens. During the 1970s and 1980s the number of poor Panamanian immigrants increased, accounting for part of the purportedly large undocumented population in the city before the passage of the Immigration Reform and Control Act of 1986. Legal status was granted to canal workers (many of West Indian origin) who were displaced by the terms of a treaty signed by General Omar Torrijos and President Jimmy Carter in 1979. One of the few organizations in New York City intended strictly for Panamanians was Las Servidoras, formed by Sarah Anesta Samuel in Brooklyn in 1953; later renamed the Dedicators, by the mid-1990s it had provided hundreds of thousands of dollars in college scholarships for Panamanian immigrants and other minority students. Panamanians in the city also joined alumni associations affiliated with secondary schools in the Canal Zone and organized large groups that traveled to Panama for an annual festival. The *Panama Chronicle,* a bilingual quarterly newspaper published from 1977 to 1992, was distributed free of charge and provided news about events in Panama. Prominent Panamanians include the state assemblyman Ed Griffith, the former state senator Waldaba Stewart, the composer Roque Cordero, the singer and actor Rubén Blades, the playwright Carlos Quintero, the classical pianist Jaime Ingram, the baseball players Hector Lopez and Rod Carew, the bantamweight boxing champion "Panama Al" Brown, and the basketball player Rolando Blackman. According to the federal census more than 23,000 Panamanians lived in New York City in 2000, most of them in Brooklyn and Queens.

Marcia Bayne-Smith, Roy S. Bryce-Laporte

Pan American Airways. International airline formed in 1927 by Henry "Hap" Arnold and taken over in the same year by Juan Trippe, a World War I naval pilot. Headquartered on East 42nd Street, the airline was so successful in cultivating the favor of regulators in the United States and Latin America that by 1931 its routes covered 20,308 miles (32,676 kilometers) in 20 countries. As the only international carrier in the United States from 1931 to 1942, it helped to establish New York City as a center of international aviation and was responsible for a number of innovations in air travel. Scheduled transatlantic service from the city began on 20 May 1939 from the Marine Air Terminal at La Guardia Airfield (at the time unfinished) and was provided by Boeing 314 seaplanes that traveled at 193 miles (311 kilometers) an hour and could carry 74 passengers or provide berths for 40. Between 1942 and 1945 the airline was active in the planning of what later became John F. Kennedy International Airport. Service around the world was inaugurated in 1947; the airline also introduced jet service from New York City to London with the Boeing 707 (26 October 1958) and the first "jumbo" jet, the Boeing 747 (from Kennedy Airport in 1969). In 1964 it opened new headquarters at 200 Park Avenue, at the time the largest office building in the world. Pan American was the dominant international airline in the United States until the early 1980s but toward the end of the decade encountered financial difficulties. The airline's headquarters building was acquired by the Metropolitan Life Insurance Company; in 1991 it sold its European routes to Delta Airlines and was forced to cease operations in 1992. The Pan American name was bought in bankruptcy proceedings, and the new company offered limited service until the early twenty-first century.

Marilyn Bender and Selig Altschul, *The Chosen Instrument: Pan Am, Juan Trippe, the Rise and Fall of an American Entrepreneur* (New York: Simon and Schuster, 1982); R. E. G. Davies, *Pan Am: An Airline and Its Aircraft* (New York: Orion, 1987)

See also W. R. Grace and Co.

Paul Barrett

Panorama of New York City. A huge, three-dimensional reproduction of New York City at the Queens Museum in Flushing Meadows–Corona Park. Constructed as the New York City exhibit for the World's Fair of 1964–65, it is the world's largest scale model, occupying 9335 square feet (867 square meters). At a scale of 1200:1 it reproduces the city's 860,000 buildings, thousands of streets and parks, and dozens of major bridges. The project was conceived by Robert Moses, the long-time municipal builder and president of the World's Fair Corporation, and fabricated by the model-making firm of Lester Associates. The task took more than three years and required the full-time labor of hundreds of workers. Visitors to the museum observe the model from overhead. Completely renovated between 1992 and 1994, with lighting and other updates performed from 2004 to 2005, the Panorama of New York remains the best way to understand the geography and infrastructure of the metropolis.

Kenneth T. Jackson

Pantoja, Antonia (*b* San Juan, Puerto Rico, 13 Sept 1922; *d* New York City, 24 May 2002). Educator and community activist. She was born into a poor, working-class family, became a teacher, and moved to New York City in 1944. She formed a network of community institutions, including the Puerto Rican Association for Community Affairs (1953), the Puerto Rican Forum (1957), and Aspira (1961), that she viewed as tools for progressive struggle. Pantoja established Universidad Boricua in New York City, which became Boricua College in 1970. Later she returned to Puerto Rico and formed an economic development corporation called Producir with Wilhelmina Perry. She received the Presidential Medal of Freedom in 1996. Pantoja's autobiography,

Memoir of a Visionary: Antonia Pantoja, was published in 2002.

Virginia Sánchez Korrol

Papanicolaou, George N(icholas) (*b* Kimi, Greece, 13 May 1883; *d* Miami, Fla., 18 Feb 1962). Inventor of the Papanicolaou test, or Pap test. After earning his MD from the University of Athens (1904) and doctorate from the University of Munich (1910), he moved to New York City and became a professor in the department of anatomy at Cornell University Medical College. During an association with the college lasting 47 years, he invented the gynecological procedure named after him (also called the Pap smear) that allows for the early detection of cervical cancer. He also perfected the diagnostic techniques of exfoliative cytology, which are used to find malignant cells in many other areas of the body, and wrote the *Atlas of Exfoliative Cytology* (1954). His work is considered an important contribution to modern cancer research.

Daniel Erskine Carmichael, *The Pap Smear: Life of George N. Papanicolaou* (Springfield, Ill.: Thomas, 1973)

Adele A. Lerner

paper. For American colonists, paper was not a vital necessity and the little they did need was imported from Europe. The first paper mill in America began production in 1690 in Philadelphia using rags as its raw material. It was owned and operated by William Bradford who moved to New York City in 1693 and became well known as a printer and publisher. He may have printed the first book in New York City, a testimonial to the martial exploits of Colonel Benjamin Fletcher, who served as governor of New York beginning in 1692. In 1725 Bradford established *The New York Gazette,* the city's first newspaper. In 1775 Robert Bowne opened Bowne and Company at 39 Queen Street (now Pearl Street) in Manhattan, selling writing papers, account books, quills and pens, binding and printing materials, and other dry goods. Within a few years he added printing to his business services. (In 2010 it was the oldest company listed on the New York Stock Exchange and still maintained offices in New York City.) During the American Revolution paper supplies were tight because of the British blockade but eased after the war. During the mid-1800s, as New York City became the commercial center of the country, it also became the information capital and home to many book, magazine, and newspaper publishers. By the late 1850s printing was the city's fastest growing industry, and demand for paper was strong. Its paper trade became centered in the area east of Printing House Square (now Park Row), also known as Newspaper Row. Up until the second half of the 1800s paper was generally made of recycled materials such as rags or linen, but after that time wood pulp became the primary raw material.

Over the past century the role of paper in the economic life of New York City has diminished. In 1987 International Paper Company, which had been based in New York City since its formation in 1898, moved its operational headquarters to Memphis, Tennessee. In the early 1990s there were 245 firms in the city employing more than 10,000 people making paper products worth $888.1 million. A decade later the paper industry in New York City produced shipments valued at $549.3 million. During the first half of 2007 there were 83 establishments and an average of 2545 people employed in the city's paper industry. More telling, in 1962, when New York City honored astronaut John Glenn, the first American to orbit the earth, with a ticker-tape parade, 3474 tons of paper fell to the streets. Forty-six years later, in February 2008, when the New York Giants marched up Broadway after their victory over the New England Patriots in the Super Bowl, only 36.5 tons were tossed in celebration.

Lyman Horace, *A History of Paper-Manufacturing in the United States 1690–1916* (New York: Lockwood Trade Journal Company, 1916)

Catherine Mathis

Papp, Joseph [Papirofsky, Yosl] (*b* Brooklyn, 22 June 1921; *d* New York City, 31 Oct 1991). Theater director and producer. Born to Jewish immigrants from Poland, he started the New York Shakespeare Festival in 1954. In 1957 the company was granted the use of Central Park for summer productions, with the Delacorte Theater being built in 1962 for use by the festival. Papp oversaw the conversion of the Astor Library on Lafayette Street into a multistage theater complex opened in 1967 as the Public Theater. There he staged both new works by young playwrights such as Caryl Churchill, Miguel Piñero, David Mamet, and Sam Shepard and innovative interpretations of standard works by Shakespeare, Bertolt Brecht, and Anton Chekhov. A number of productions first staged at the Public Theater transferred to Broadway, achieving great success and allowing Papp to use the profits they generated to support his less commercially successful artistic ventures. These include the musical *Hair,* which premiered at the Public Theater in 1967; *A Chorus Line* (1975) (which ran for a record 6137 performances on Broadway from 1975 to 1990); and a musical adaptation of Shakespeare's *Two Gentlemen of Verona,* which hit Broadway in December 1971. A strong supporter of experimental and noncommercial theater, Papp also worked to bring to light the work of minority playwrights and was among the first to cast minority actors in Shakespearean and other classical roles. He remained the artistic director of the Public Theater until his death in 1991. In 1992 the Public Theater was renamed the Joseph Papp Public Theater in his honor.

Patrick Barrett

parades. Among the first parades in New York City were military reviews and musters, which were common during the seventeenth century. The first St. Patrick's Day Parade was held in 1766 by Irish soldiers in the British army. Large annual parades during the late eighteenth century commemorated events of national importance: American independence, Evacuation Day (marking the evacuation of the British from the city in 1783), and the ratification of the Constitution in 1788. Civic and ethnic parades were sponsored by political parties, immigrant groups, and city government. In the first half of the nineteenth

Hudson–Fulton Parade, 1909

century New York City sponsored parades and festivities for prominent visiting foreigners. A large parade was given in 1824 to welcome the Marquis de Lafayette to the city, and another in 1851 for the Hungarian revolutionary Louis Kossuth. Important public works projects were also celebrated with parades, including the opening of the Erie Canal in 1825 and of the Croton Water Works in 1842. A spectacular parade in 1860 welcomed the Prince of Wales (later Edward VII), and the end of the Civil War was celebrated with a large parade in 1865. The Easter Parade, first held in the 1870s, became an annual event in which marchers (or more accurately strollers) gathered along Fifth Avenue on Easter Sunday to display new spring outfits and hats.

Ticker-tape parades were first organized by the city in the mid-1880s around Wall Street. Union Square was the site of many rallies and parades on May Day sponsored by radical groups and labor organizations; the first Labor Day Parade was held there in 1882. The frequency of these gatherings diminished after World War II as the American left declined, but an annual Labor Day Parade lasted until 1986, when it was canceled because of decreased popularity among union members. More than 110,000 marchers took part in the Business Men's Republican and Sound Money Parade of 1896 in support of William McKinley's presidential candidacy. In 1899 the Dewey Arch, an elaborate triumphal arch, was erected across Fifth Avenue at 23rd Street for a celebration of Admiral George Dewey's victorious return from the Philippines. Henry Hudson's explorations and Robert Fulton's invention of the steamboat were celebrated in 1909 with parades and performances in city parks.

Parades sponsored by commercial firms began in the twentieth century, including Macy's Thanksgiving Day Parade (annual from 1924), one of the most popular in the city. The Columbus Day Parade on Fifth Avenue began in 1929, and the Puerto Rican Day Parade began in 1958 in El Barrio, drawing about two million people annually in the early twenty-first century. Steuben Day, celebrated by German Americans, started in the 1950s and was typical of ethnic parades. The Halloween Parade in Greenwich Village was organized by the performance artist Ralph Lee in 1973 and became an annual event; its irreverence and wide participation caused it to outgrow the sidestreets of Greenwich Village, and it moved to Sixth Avenue. The American bicentennial (1976), the 100th anniversary of the Brooklyn Bridge (1986), and the reopening of the Statue of Liberty (1986) were celebrated with parades on land and water. The first Gay Pride Parade was organized in 1970. The nation's largest art parade, the annual Mermaid Parade in Coney Island, was founded in 1983 and celebrates the beginning of summer; it features paraders dressed

Gay and Lesbian Pride Parade, June 2009

Major Parades in New York City

African–American Day Parade (1969), Adam Clayton Powell Boulevard, 111st to 142nd streets, Manhattan, September
American Ethnic Parade, Columbus Circle, along Central Park South to Sixth Avenue to 43rd Street, Manhattan
Armenian Martyr's Day Parade [Armenian Genocide Remembrance Day Parade] (1961), Times Square, Manhattan, April
Brazilian Summer Carnival Parade (1986), Lower East Side, Manhattan
Bronx Week Parade (1971), Grand Concourse, 198th to 153rd streets, Bronx, May–June
Captive Nations Week Parade (1959), Fifth Avenue, Manhattan, July
Children's Parade for Peace, Manhattan, October
Chinese New Year Parade, Chinatown, Manhattan, February
Columbus Day Parade (1909), Fifth Avenue, 44th to 86th streets, Manhattan, 12 October
Cuban Day Parade (1904), Madison Avenue, 56th to 37th streets, Manhattan, May
Dance Parade (2007), Sixth Avenue, 28th Street to Tompkins Square Park, Manhattan, May
Dominican Day Parade (1981), Madison Avenue, 57th to 37th streets, Manhattan, August
Easter Parade (*ca* 1870), Fifth Avenue near St. Patrick's Cathedral and 50th Street, Manhattan, April
Ecuador Day Parade (1984), 35th Avenue, 70th to 89th streets, Queens, August
Flag Day Parade, Fulton and Water streets to Fraunces Tavern Museum, Manhattan, June
Greek Independence Day Parade (1893), Fifth Avenue, 62nd to 79th streets, Manhattan, March–April
Greenwich Village Halloween Parade (1974), Houston Street from West Street to Sixth Avenue, north to 14th Street, east to Union Square, Manhattan, 31 October
Hispanic Day Parade (1965), Fifth Avenue from 44th to 86th streets, Manhattan, October
Hispanic Parade of Queens (1976), 37th Avenue between 69th and 89th streets, Queens, September
India Day Parade, Madison Avenue, 54th to 26th streets, Manhattan, August
India Independence Day Parade, Madison Avenue, 41st to 23rd streets, Manhattan, August
International Cultures Day Parade, Sixth Avenue, 35th to 56th streets, Manhattan, June
International Immigrants Parade (1986), Madison Avenue, 37th to 57th streets, Manhattan, October

(continued)

Major Parades in New York City (*Continued*)

Korean American Day Parade (1980), Broadway, 40th and 24th streets, Manhattan, September
Krishna Procession, Fifth Avenue and 59th Street to Washington Square Park, Manhattan
Labor Day Parade (1882), Fifth Avenue, 44th to 79th streets, Manhattan, September
Lesbian and Gay Pride Day Parade (1970), Fifth Avenue, Columbus Circle, and Christopher Street, Manhattan, June
Loisaida Fair (1986), Avenue C, Third to 10th streets, Manhattan, May
Macy's Thanksgiving Day Parade (1924), Central Park West, 77th to 59th streets, down Broadway to 34th Street, Manhattan, November
Martin Luther King, Jr., Day Parade (1968), Fifth Avenue, 61st to 86th streets, Manhattan, January
Memorial Day Parade (1896), 72nd Street and Broadway, west on 86th Street to Soldiers' and Sailors' Monument, Manhattan, May
Mermaid Parade (1983), Steeplechase Park to West Fifth Street, Brooklyn, June
Norwegian Constitution Day Parade (1951), Fifth Avenue, 95th to 67th streets, Brooklyn, May
Pakistan Independence Day Parade, Madison Avenue, 41st to 26th streets, Manhattan, August
Parade of Liberty, 4 July
Presidents Day Parade, Fifth Avenue, 35th to 50th streets, Manhattan, February
Puerto Rican Day Parade (1956), Fifth Avenue, 44th to 86th streets, Manhattan, June
Puerto Rican Day Parade [Bronx] (1987), Grand Concourse, Bronx, May
Pulaski Day Parade (1937), Fifth Avenue, 26th to 52nd streets, Manhattan, October
Queens Purim Parade (1980), Main Street, 68th Drive to 73rd Avenue, Kew Gardens, Queens, March
Ragamuffin Day Parade, Brooklyn, October
St. Patrick's Day Parade (1853), Fifth Avenue, 44th to 86th streets, Manhattan, 17 March
Salute to Israel Parade (1964), Fifth Avenue, 57th to 86th streets, Manhattan, May–June
Solidarity Day Parade, Fifth Avenue, Manhattan, May
Steuben Day Parade (1957), Fifth Avenue, 67th to 86th streets, Manhattan, September
Three Kings Parade (1977), Third Avenue, 106th to 116th streets, Manhattan, January
Turkish-American Day Parade (1982), Madison Avenue, 56th to 47th streets, May
United Hispanic American Day Parade (1965), Fifth Avenue, 44th to 72nd streets, Manhattan, October
Veterans Day Parade (1918), Fifth Avenue, 39th to 23rd streets, Manhattan, November
Washington's Birthday Parade, Manhattan, February
West Indian–American Day Carnival and Parade (1967), Eastern Parkway, Utica Avenue to Washington Avenue, Brooklyn, September

as mermaids and other sea creatures, led by Queen Mermaid and King Neptune.

In the twenty-first century religious processions on Roman Catholic saints' days and holy days such as Good Friday continued in Latino neighborhoods on the Lower East Side and in Harlem, and in Italian neighborhoods in Greenwich Village and Brooklyn. In Greenpoint the *giglio* procession celebrated the festival of Our Lady of Mount Carmel and St. Paulinus, in which a tower 60 feet (18 meters) high is "danced" through the streets by young men from the parish. For the San Gennaro Festival in Little Italy in Manhattan a statue of the saint is carried in a procession. The West Indian Day Parade on Labor Day weekend in Crown Heights is one of the largest in the city. In 2001 new parades were banned from Fifth Avenue, the most famous parade route in the city, although any founded before July of that year could continue to use the route.

Gary Jennings, *Parades!: Celebrations and Circuses on the March* (Philadelphia: J. B. Lippincott, 1966)

Brooks McNamara

Paramount Communications. International conglomerate of entertainment and publishing firms. It began as a maker of automobile parts incorporated as Michigan Bumper in 1934; the business was renamed the Michigan Plating and Stamping Company in 1955, the Gulf and Western Corporation in 1958, and Gulf and Western Industries in 1960. It was headquartered in New York City from 1969 until 1994. During the 1960s the firm acquired many manufacturers of automobile parts, electronics, metals, plastics, and tools. It entered the field of communications in 1966 by acquiring a majority interest in the Paramount Pictures Corporation. In the 1970s and 1980s it increased its holdings in the entertainment and publishing industries, acquiring Madison Square Garden, the basketball team the New York Knicks, the hockey team the New York Rangers, cable television networks, chains of movie theaters, film production and distribution companies, the publishing house Simon and Schuster, several educational and trade publishers including Prentice Hall, and a number of companies providing computer software and electronic information services to business. In 1983 the firm was restructured, resulting in the divestiture of $1 billion of its securities portfolio and the sale of its consumer and industrial products group. It sold its consumer and commercial finance business, the Associates First Capital Corporation, to the Ford Motor Company for $3.4 billion in 1989 and changed its name to Paramount Communications. In 1990 the conglomerate had 117.6 million common shares outstanding, 30,000 stockholders, 12,400 employees, and gross revenues of $3.87 billion. In 1994 it was acquired for $10 billion by Viacom, which later that year agreed to sell its sports assets, including the Knicks and Rangers, for $1.1 billion. It sold its headquarters in Manhattan at 15 Columbus Circle to the Trump Corporation in 1997. In 2006 Viacom split in two, dividing the assets of the former Paramount Communications.

Edward T. O'Donnell

paratransit. Demand-responsive, point-to-point transit provided for disabled people. U.S. government regulations, first enacted in 1973 and later amended, mandate that mass transit agencies provide service to disabled individuals unable to use conventional public transportation. In New York City the city's Department of Transportation initially operated the paratransit service, Access-A-Ride (AAR); in 1993 the Metropolitan Transportation Authority assumed responsibility for AAR and contracted with private transportation companies to deliver the service. Small buses and vans with wheelchair accessibility are used for the prearranged trips. Paratransit customers are prescreened to ensure that their disabilities meet the legal requirements for such service and are issued identification cards documenting their eligibility. The fare is the same as a full-fare bus or subway trip. In 2000 AAR provided approximately 2.3 million trips; in 2005, 4.7 million trips.

Andrew Sparberg

Parish, Sister [Kinicutt, Dorothy May] (*b* Morristown, N.J., 15 July 1910; *d* Dark Harbor, Maine, 8 Sept 1994). Interior designer. Born to a wealthy family, she founded a one-room business in Far Hills, New Jersey, in 1933 that evolved into the noted decorating firm of Parish–Hadley Associates, based in New York City. She became the best-known woman in interior design and is credited with having originated the American country style during the 1960s. Her work was expensive, and she went to great lengths to please her clients: in a single bedroom for William S. Paley, chairman of the Columbia Broadcasting System (CBS), she had a painter work for five months applying 18 coats of paint, including six shadings for the base alone. Parish lived on East End Avenue in Manhattan.

Kenneth T. Jackson

Park Avenue. Avenue in Manhattan and the Bronx between 32nd Street and Fordham Road. Originally known as Fourth Avenue within Manhattan, the stretch between 32nd and 133rd streets was renamed between 1860 and 1900. Metro-North (originally New York Central) Railroad tracks follow Park Avenue continuously from 42nd Street northward using tunnels, viaducts, and open cuts. Grand Central Terminal's construction between 1906 and 1913 created Park Avenue's upscale business and residential districts between 46th and 96th streets.

Andrew Sparberg

Park Avenue Hotel. Building opened in April 1878 on the west side of Park Avenue between 32nd and 33rd streets. A seven-story building of cast iron with a mansard roof, it was built for the merchant and philanthropist A. T. Stewart by his favorite architect, John Kellum. It began as a working women's hotel, but strict residence rules for the women soon caused its failure. Reopened after two months as a stylish public hostelry popular for its palm court and band music, it was demolished in 1927.

"The Women's Hotel," *Harper's Weekly*, 3 April 1889, pp. 294–97

Margot Gayle

Parkchester Oval, 2009

Parkchester. Housing development and neighborhood in the eastern Bronx, bounded to the north by East Tremont Avenue; to the east by Purdy Street, St. Raymond Avenue, and Olmstead Avenue; to the south by McGraw Avenue; and to the west by White Plains Road. It was once the site of the New York Catholic Protectory, a self-sufficient farm and trade school for wayward boys opened by the Christian Brothers after the Civil War. It had a bakery and printing, carpentry, shoemaking, and tailor shops. The playing fields were also used by semiprofessional baseball teams for many years. Between 1938 and 1942 a complex designed and owned by the Metropolitan Life Insurance Company was built on a site of 129 acres (52 hectares) as the largest housing development in the United States that was not itself a city. There were 12,273 units divided among buildings of seven to 13 stories each, standing in four quadrants around landscaped grounds; amenities included a large shopping area with more than 100 stores (among them the first branch outside Manhattan of Macy's), a movie theater, and a bowling alley. The design of the residential buildings was based on three core plans and five wing plans (and their variants). A wing consisted of two dwelling units, each having two to five rooms. The facades were of sheer brick, patterned at the tops of buildings and around entrances, and there were also small decorative sculptures. Parking could accommodate 3000 automobiles. Storefronts had curving facades, art deco detailing, and stylized signage. The development was named for two adjoining neighborhoods, Park Versailles (a name that went out of fashion) and Westchester. In the mid-1960s the Metropolitan Life Insurance Company was accused by the city's commission on civil rights of limiting tenancy to whites. The neighborhood became more diverse racially as a result, and in 1968 Metropolitan Life sold Parkchester to the large real estate firm Helmsley–Spear, which converted the north quadrant of the project into a condominium. Helmsley–Spear was dogged by allegations of neglect, and the development declined until the late 1990s. In 1998 the Helmsleys sold Parkchester to the Community Preservation Corporation. Meanwhile, many new immigrants settled there, mostly from Jamaica, the Dominican Republic, Guyana, the Soviet Union, India, China, and the Philippines.

John McNamara, *McNamara's Old Bronx* (New York: Bronx County Historical Society, 1989); Gary D. Hermalyn and Robert Kornfeld, *Landmarks of the Bronx* (New York: Bronx County Historical Society, 1990)

Gary D. Hermalyn

Park East Synagogue. Orthodox synagogue at 163 East 67th Street. It was originally called the Congregation Zichron Ephraim after Ephraim Weil, whose sons Jonas and Samuel provided the land and funds for the building in 1888. Schneider and Herter designed the elaborate Byzantine temple, which was completed in 1890. In 2008 Pope Benedict XVI made history by attending a service at Park East and becoming the first pope to visit an American synagogue.

Kate Lauber

Parker, Charlie [Charles, Jr.] (*b* Kansas City, Kans., 29 Aug 1920; *d* New York City, 12 March 1955). Saxophonist and composer. He worked with a number of big bands in Kansas City and moved in 1939 to New York City, where he worked as a dishwasher at Jimmy's Chicken Shack in Harlem and lived

Charlie Parker, ca 1940–45

from the early 1940s at 411 Manhattan Avenue. He performed in 1942 as a featured soloist with Jay McShann's big band at the Savoy Ballroom, and during jam sessions held after hours at nightclubs in Harlem such as Minton's Playhouse and Monroe's Uptown House, he experimented with new sounds that laid the groundwork for bop in the early 1940s. When the focus of bop shifted to 52nd Street in the mid-1940s, he played there regularly at several clubs. His first recordings as a leader were made in November 1945 and include *Now's the Time* and *Ko-Ko*; his sidemen were trumpeters Dizzy Gillespie and Miles Davis, double bass player Curly Russell, pianist Sadik Hakim, and drummer Max Roach. Parker left for Los Angeles in December 1945, returned to New York City in April 1947, and formed a quintet with Davis and Roach. About this time he lived in a series of hotels, among them the Dewey Square Hotel on West 117th Street, which inspired his composition *Dewey Square* (1947). From 1946 he worked with the record producer Norman Granz, under whose direction he performed at a famous concert at Carnegie Hall in September 1949 and took part in several recording sessions in which he was backed by a string section. During this period he lived with his companion, Chan Richardson, at 151 Avenue B in the East Village. He made his last public appearance on 5 March 1955 at the club Birdland (so called after his nickname "Bird"); he died in a friend's suite at the Hotel Stanhope at 995 Fifth Avenue. His death received little notice in the newspapers, but his fans paid him tribute by scrawling the words "Bird Lives!" on walls throughout the city. Among his compositions inspired by New York City is *Scrapple from the Apple* (1947); *52nd Street Theme,* though composed by Thelonious Monk, was closely associated with Parker, and he used it to open and close many of his sets. A virtuoso alto saxophonist, Parker was the most important figure in the evolution of bop.

Lawrence O. Koch, *Yardbird Suite: A Compendium of the Music and Life of Charlie Parker* (Bowling Green, Ohio: Bowling Green University Press, 1988)

Peter Keepnews

Parker [née Rothschild]**, Dorothy** (*b* West End [now in Long Branch], N.J., 22 Aug 1893; *d* New York City, 7 June 1967). Writer. She grew up at 57 West 57th Street and worked as a staff writer for *Vanity Fair* (1917–20), from which she was discharged for writing unflattering reviews of three major plays. Her epigrammatic, satiric verses won her a devoted readership, as did her trenchant book reviews in the *New Yorker* (1927–33), signed "Constant Reader." As one of the first members of the Algonquin Round Table and one of its few female members, she became well known for her mordant wit. She was also a critically successful but not prolific writer of short stories, in which she exposed the urbane world of sophisticates with wry, Swiftian clarity. She was arrested in 1927 for demonstrating against the execution of Sacco and Vanzetti. Parker lived from 1953 to the end of her life at the Volney Hotel, 23 East 74th Street; she left her estate to Martin Luther King, Jr., and asked that it eventually be ceded to the National Association for the Advancement of Colored People.

Marion Meade, *Dorothy Parker: What Fresh Hell Is This?* (New York: Villard, 1988)

Brenda Wineapple

Parker, James (*b* Woodbridge, N.J., *ca* 1714; *d* Burlington, N.J., 2 Jul 1770). Colonial printer and newspaper editor. Apprenticed to William Bradford and financially supported by Benjamin Franklin, he began publishing the city's third newspaper, the *New-York Weekly Post-Boy* in 1743, building up a successful printing business through occasional, acrimonious partnerships with William Weyman and John Holt. While holding various administrative positions in the postal system, serving as keeper of the city's lending library, and maintaining presses in Woodbridge and Burlington, New Jersey, and New Haven, Connecticut, Parker acted for 16 years as public printer for the province of New York. A technically able printer, he issued four short-lived periodicals, and his volume of psalms was the first book of music set from type in America. Parker published two of the colonial city's defining documents: Daniel Horsmanden's justification of the prosecution of the 1741 "Negro plot," *A Journal of the Proceedings in the Detection of the Conspiracy* (1744), and Alexander McDougall's 1769 incendiary anonymous broadside *To the Betrayed Inhabitants of the City and Colony of New York.* Parker's reluctant testimony, just before his death, identifying McDougall as the author led to the latter's imprisonment and the launch of New York's revolutionary movement of the 1770s.

Mariam Touba

Parkhurst, Charles H(enry) (*b* Framingham, Mass., 17 April 1842; *d* New York City, 8 Sept 1933). Minister. After graduating from Amherst College and serving as a minister in Lenox, Massachusetts, he served at Madison Square Presbyterian Church on 24th Street and Madison Avenue from 1880 to 1918, when it merged with First Presbyterian Church. A leader in the Social Gospel movement, he became president of the Society for the Prevention of Crime in 1891. During a rousing sermon on 14 February 1892 he inaugurated a campaign to root out "the polluted harpies that under the pretense of governing this city, are feeding day and night on its quivering vitals." He visited saloons, brothels, and gambling dens in disguise and revealed the names of dishonest politicians in sermons and in court testimony. His exposés contributed to the establishment of the Lexow Commission, the election of William L. Strong as a reform mayor (1894), the appointment of Theodore Roosevelt as chairman of the Police Board (1895), and the consolidation of New York City in 1898. He resigned from the Society for the Prevention of Crime in 1908. Parkhurst wrote *Our Fight with Tammany* (1895) and *My Forty Years in New York* (1923). He lived at 133 East 35th Street.

Charles Parkhurst

David Meerse

parking. Parking became a concern in New York City in the late 1920s but only at special times and at special events. Simple on-street parking rules were instituted in business districts in the 1930s. After World War II, when New Yorkers started to acquire motor vehicles for routine personal use, the problems of storing them for shorter or longer periods intensified. To date, the city has not been able to develop a simple and effective parking policy. Automobile owners tend to believe that they have a right to use street space as they see fit; retailers and restaurateurs insist that they will lose business if their customers cannot park conveniently; and traffic managers have concluded that the best ways of controlling the volume of street traffic and level of air pollution is to ban or restrict parking. Another reason why parking policies and programs are confusing is the presence in New York City of widely different districts, each with their own parking needs and possibilities.

Per capita automobile ownership in New York City is only half as large as in other U.S. communities (205 registered cars per 1000 population, compared with the national average of 465), but the concentration of business districts, hospitals, and sports venues; the trend toward large retail stores; the heightened priority placed on personal comfort and

Muni-Meter, 2009

convenience (use of the car rather than public transportation); and expected future population growth all mean that the parking demand will become much larger. Contrary to popular belief, most of the motorists who drive to work in New York City are local residents, not suburbanites.

In midtown and lower Manhattan business districts, off-street parking spaces in commercial garages can almost always be found, but they are expensive, and the locations are not always convenient. Legal curbside parking for ordinary users, however, simply does not exist during the workday as such space is reserved for loading, commercial and diplomatic vehicles, taxis, bus lanes, and other priority functions. A special problem in high-intensity districts in New York City is the presence of large numbers of vehicles with privileged plates (such as medical doctors, members of the press, judges, clergy, federal agents, police), which are not always engaged in official duties. Diplomats have immunity from local regulations, and the city on a few occasions has been on the verge of starting an international incident by battling flagrant abuses—until a protocol of agreement was signed with the diplomatic corps in 2002.

The first parking meter was introduced in New York City in 1951, and the city's 63,000 meters are a common presence in all business districts and along major arteries. Muni Meters (machines that dispense a receipt that is left on the vehicle dashboard) were introduced in 1999, and their numbers are growing. Parking in high-intensity districts largely has been supervised by uniformed parking enforcement officers since 1960. Originally, these were the "meter maids" (under the Department of Traffic), later expanded to a force of "brownies" (under the New York City Department of Transportation), whose traffic responsibilities were progressively broadened but who also encountered jurisdictional disputes with the New York Police Department (NYPD). In 1996 all these functions were assumed by the NYPD Traffic Control Division, which has their own traffic enforcement agents. Classified as civilian employees, they wear a uniform closely resembling that of regular police, generating more respect and fewer personal attacks by irate motorists. The 800 agents assigned to parking control issue some 25,000 tickets each average weekday; others are written by regular police officers and fire and sanitation inspectors.

A Parking Violations Bureau was established under Mayor John V. Lindsay (1966–73) to "decriminalize" parking violations and streamline the collection of fines. These goals were achieved, but the bureau experienced several scandals in the handling of funds and contracts. Parking fines are now collected by the city's Department of Finance. Before collection procedures were improved, some scofflaws managed to accumulate more than $10,000 in fines; the worst offenders were diplomats and federal agents.

The parking regulations in New York City central business districts are elaborate and complex—not to deliberately discourage motorists but to squeeze the last drop of utility from scarce space. A distinction is made among *parking* (the driver leaves the vehicle), *standing* (the driver remains in the vehicle), and *stopping* (the vehicle halts for less than a minute), which is banned in many areas. The common signs "Do not even THINK about parking here!" and "No Parking, No Standing, No Stopping, NO KIDDING!" became internationally famous. In the core of lower Manhattan a Blue Zone has been established in which all parking and standing is banned from 7 a.m. to 7 p.m. on weekdays. Such constraints challenge the ingenuity of New Yorkers, and a common strategy is the "car sitter"—a second person who remains in the vehicle while the driver runs errands—and drivers take chances with double and triple standing. Despite restrictions, regulations, and improved enforcement practices, traffic loads have continued to grow, except where they have reached capacity ceilings. The peak period for parking demand in midtown is 4 to 6 p.m., when entertainment traffic overlaps with normal business traffic.

Given that traffic volumes have reached a saturation point for most of the working day, the city has established a policy of not issuing any new licenses for commercial parking garages in the core of the central business districts. An unusual zoning clause for U.S. cities forbids the incorporation of parking spaces, beyond a few, in any new nonresidential buildings in Manhattan below 110th Street and downtown Brooklyn. On the other hand, government agencies at the federal, state, and municipal levels try to assure free parking for their employees.

Deliveries of supplies and removal of products by truck (*loading*) is a special problem. All new commercial, manufacturing, and storage buildings (as well as hospitals, prisons, and funeral parlors) are now required to provide adequate off-street docks. The number depends on the type of building, its size, and the characteristics of the district around it. All this, however, does not help to accommodate the service demands of older establishments. Loading trucks usually have to double park, and during parts of the day they form solid lines along major commercial arteries, limiting street carrying capacity, encroaching on sidewalks, and blocking movement. Solutions, such as cooperative ventures and jointly used loading spaces, have not worked because drivers refuse to leave their vehicles out of sight for fear of pilferage and owners of commercial establishments are unwilling to depend on any but their own vans and trucks to support their activities.

For new commercial and community facility buildings not in the central business districts the provision of off-street parking is usually required, depending on the type (in terms of traffic-generating characteristics) and size of activities supported, the type and density of the district in which they are located, and the availability of public transport services. Thus, a store located in a suburban district would have to create a large parking facility, and one in a dense area would not be allowed to provide any parking at all.

The parking requirements for residential uses reflect the same philosophy of setting norms in response to the characteristics of an area. Therefore, a single-family residence in a low-density district with no subway access has to be provided with at least one off-street parking space. As the density increases, however, the norms are changed such that in some districts only 40 percent of the dwelling units must have a parking space. Many New Yorkers, however, particularly those living in high-density areas with high garage fees, keep their cars in remote garages for weekend use only. In some instances owners of apartment buildings with the required parking spaces have not been able to rent them and therefore have received licenses to open their garages to commercial use.

Parking in residential districts of New York City has been governed since 1950 by alternate-side-of-the-street rules, which prohibit parking during several hours on one or two weekdays on one side of the street so that street sweepers can move along the curb. Since double parking during those hours is usually tolerated on the other side, New Yorkers have to know exactly when to move their car back and forth and not get blocked in if they need the vehicle during the double park hours. Some years ago paying for an occasional parking ticket was considered an acceptable price for living in New York City, but by the twenty-first century the charge has reached a painful $65 to $115. In some neighborhoods the total length of curbs is sufficient for all the cars owned by the local residents, but this is rarely the case in zones with apartment buildings. A new problem has emerged in some districts with originally one-family homes on tight lots. If these buildings become occupied by households with several cars, people use the front and back yards for parking, thereby violating zoning ordinances and changing the appearance of the neighborhood.

Parking garages and lots are scattered throughout the boroughs. In Manhattan alone there are about 100,000 off-street parking spaces in some 1600 facilities. These may be public and purely commercial (open to anybody for a charge, licensed by the Department of Consumer Affairs), partially supported by local merchants (validated sales slips), open to customers of specific establishments (usually without charge), municipal (owned and operated by the Department of Transportation), owned and operated by institutions and firms for their own employees and visitors, and exclusive accessory facilities for residences.

See also Traffic and Streets and highways.

Sigurd Grava

Park Row. Street in lower Manhattan, location of City Hall and the Municipal Building, running diagonally between Broadway and Chatham Square. During the nineteenth century it was called Newspaper Row because most of the city's dailies were published there, taking advantage of City Hall's proximity. Trolley and elevated train routes crossing the Brooklyn Bridge used a large terminal on Park Row that was demolished in 1944. In the early twenty-first century Police Department headquarters and Pace University were both on Park Row.

Andrew Sparberg

parks. New York City has the largest urban parks system in the United States, occupying some 28,000 acres (11,331 hectares) exclusive of state and federal lands and comprising more than 1700 parks and playgrounds, as well as recreation centers, golf courses, ballfields, zoological and botanical gardens, monuments, historic houses, beaches, forests, meadows, and wetlands. These are administered by the New York City Department of Parks and Recreation. The city's few early parks included Bowling Green (1733, the city's oldest park), Battery Park, and City Hall Park. The first street plan, the 1811 Commissioner's Plan, provided for a "grid" with no public parks. It did leave open several spaces, designated as squares, and some of these—such as Tompkins Square, Union Square, Madison Square, and Mount Morris (now Marcus Garvey Park)—later became parks. In Brooklyn, an independent city for most of the nineteenth century, the first major park was Fort Greene Park (1847); the effort to acquire this hilly site well-known for its role during the American Revolution had been championed by Walt Whitman, then the editor of the *Brooklyn Daily Eagle.* Nineteenth-century cemeteries were often parklike, and Green-Wood Cemetery opened in 1838 and became a popular site for strolling and picnics; the following year 11 park sites were proposed in Brooklyn by a three-member commission.

By the mid-nineteenth century, as the city's population spread northward, demand increased for more open, green spaces, resulting in the creation of Central Park (opened 1859). Acquisition by the state of the 843 acres (340 hectares) of swampy land with rocky outcroppings started in 1853. The park was designed by Frederick Law Olmsted and Calvert Vaux and was based on the English pastoral style. Olmsted and Vaux also designed Riverside Park in Manhattan and Prospect Park in Brooklyn (often considered their masterpiece) and planned a system of parkways, or landscaped routes, intended to link parks within a system: Eastern Parkway (1868–74) and Ocean Parkway (1869–76) in Brooklyn were early examples. In mid-century Madison Square Park and Reservoir Square (later Bryant Park) were added in Manhattan.

The Department of Public Parks was formed in 1870 to oversee these new green spaces in Manhattan. Brooklyn had its own department, which also administered Forest Park in Queens and other lands. Lower Westchester (later the Bronx) was largely undeveloped and became the focus of parks advocates in the 1880s. As population surged, citizen groups lobbied for more park space to provide "lungs" for the city. In 1881 the New York Park Association argued that open spaces not only improved the quality of life, but also raised the value of adjacent property. Their efforts resulted in two major additions of parks spaces. The 1887 Small Parks Act led to the creation of parks in severely overcrowded areas, including Mulberry Bend (now Columbus Park) and DeWitt Clinton Park. In 1888 a New Park Commission set up by the state legislature led to the adoption of St. Mary's, Claremont, Crotona, Bronx, Van Cortlandt, and Pelham Bay Parks, totaling an additional 3495 acres (1414 hectares) of new Bronx parks; the cost, assessed on the city at large, was $9.5 million. This resulted in the quintupling of the parkland in the city. Other new parks in New York City during the late nineteenth century included Brooklyn Forest Park (Forest Park, Queens), Lincoln Terrace, Bensonhurst Beach Park, Canarsie Beach Park, and Dyker Beach Park. At the same time the parks department created the Prospect Park–Coney Island Bicycle Pathway on Ocean Avenue (1894) and the Van Cortlandt Park Golf Course (1895), the first municipal course in the United States.

Following the 1898 consolidation of the boroughs, Manhattan had approximately 1300 park acres (526 hectares), Brooklyn and Queens had 1574 acres (637 hectares), the Bronx 4058 acres (1642 hectares), and Staten Island 3 acres (1.2 hectares). In addition to the continuous addition of small parks, recreation facilities expanded considerably during the twentieth century. A kindergarten and gymnasium were opened in Hamilton Fish Park, and the first children's farm garden (which introduced children to country living) was established in DeWitt Clinton Park in 1902.

Robert F. Wagner Park, 2009

In October 1903 Seward Park on the Lower East Side became the first municipal park in the country to be equipped with a permanent playground; the Bureau of Recreation in the parks department began in 1911, and by 1915, 70 PLAYGROUNDS existed.

During the second and third decades of the twentieth century interborough athletic championships drew as many as 10,000 spectators to city parks, which also became the sites of outdoor concerts, historical pageants, and film showings. The Park Association of New York City, a privately sponsored advocacy group, began in 1926; it later evolved into the Parks Council (incorporated in 1970). Efforts continued to add park space during the 1920s, particularly in the growing areas of the outer boroughs; new parks in Queens included Cunningham Park (350 acres [142 hectares]) and Alley Pond Park (654 acres [265 hectares]), and in Staten Island, Clove Lakes (195 acres [79 hectares]), Wolfe's Pond (317 acres [128 hectares]), and La Tourette (550 acres [223 hectares]) Parks.

Robert Moses became parks commissioner in 1934 and consolidated the separate borough departments. He formed a large professional staff and with federal relief work funds employed tens of thousands of laborers. Over the ensuing decade he oversaw the building and opening of hundreds of new playgrounds and 11 large outdoor pools, the improvement of miles of beachfront, and the rising of Flushing Meadows Park (now FLUSHING MEADOWS–CORONA PARK) on what had once been industrial ash heaps. Outlying areas such as Jamaica Bay and Marine Park were rescued from development and kept in a largely natural state. Construction slowed during World War II, but in the 1950s new indoor recreation centers in Brownsville, Bedford–Stuyvesant, and Mott Haven addressed the need for year-round places of play in poor, underserved neighborhoods. By the time Moses retired from his position in 1960 the parks system had nearly tripled in size.

Many experiments were introduced in the late 1960s as land grew more scarce. Under Park Commissioner August Heckscher, ten vest pocket parks opened in 1967 in vacant city lots of one-quarter acre or less. The Thomas Pell Wildlife Refuge in Pelham Bay Park, the second such refuge in the city, was created in 1967; and new types of equipment were tried in "adventure" playgrounds. Central Park and the other large parks hosted concerts and other events. Growing concern for the environment and a desire to preserve forests and wetlands led to the securing of the Greenbelt in Staten Island and Udalls Cove in Queens. The decline in port traffic inspired proposals to build waterfront parks, while a greater concern for existing parks gave rise to private groups such as the Central Park Conservancy. In the 1980s citizen advocacy groups came into being to help support parks. In the early 1990s three urban parks opened with the sponsorship of the state and public authorities: Riverbank State Park (May 1993), occupying 28 acres (11.3 hectares) atop a waste treatment plant in Harlem; Octagon Park (October 1992), a sports complex and community garden of fifteen acres at the northern end of Roosevelt Island; and Hudson River Park (June 1992), an 8-acre (3.2-hectare) park in lower Manhattan with a fine view of New York Harbor.

Hudson River Park, 2009

At the start of the twenty-first century, New York City had more than 1700 parks, playgrounds, and recreation facilities across the five boroughs. The largest parks are Pelham Bay Park, Bronx (2765 acres/1119 hectares); Greenbelt, Staten Island (1778 acres/720 hectares); Flushing Meadows–Corona Park, Queens (1255 acres/508 hectares); Van Cortlandt Park, Bronx (1446 acres/585 hectares); Central Park, Manhattan (844 acres/342 hectares); Marine Park, Brooklyn (798 acres/323 hectares); Bronx Park, Bronx (718 acres/291 hectares); Alley Pond Park, Queens (655 acres/265 hectares); Franklin D. Roosevelt Boardwalk, South and Midland Beaches, Staten Island (638 acres/258 hectares); and Forest Park, Queens (544 acres/220 hectares). The parks system also supports 34 outdoor pools, 19 outdoor mini-pools, and 12 indoor pools. These evolved from the public baths created at the end of the nineteenth century, which were used mostly for bathing but also swimming; by 1911 Manhattan had 12 bathhouses. In 2010 city parks supported six zoos; 14 miles of public beaches; 14 floating baths; ice skating facilities; lawn bowling, boules, and bocce (the most popular, located in 39 parks); running marathons; and numerous recreational activities ranging from chess to exercise.

Elizabeth Barlow Rogers, *Frederick Law Olmsted's New York* (New York: Praeger, 1972); New York City Department of Parks and Recreation, http://www.nycgovparks.org

Lisa Keller, Jonathan Kuhn

Parks, Sam(uel J.) (*b* County Down, Ireland, 1864; *d* Ossining, N.Y., 4 May 1904). Labor leader. He moved to Chicago in 1892 and to New York City in 1896, where he learned the housesmith's trade. Known for his enormous size and strength, he helped to win for the Housesmiths and Bridgemen's Union an increase in the daily wage advance from $2.50 to $4.50 as he worked his way through the building trades. Later he was the president of the union and of the New York City Board of Building Trades and became a well-known racketeer, often sending workers out on strike to help a contractor destroy its competitors. He remained popular among union members because of his success at enforcing union rules, maintaining job security, and helping ironworkers to win wage advances and increases; through his efforts daily wages rose from $1.50 to $5. Parks was indicted for blackmail in 1903 and sentenced to two and a half years in prison, where he died.

Ray Stannard Baker, "Trusts and Labour in America: The Amazing Story of Sam Parks," *World's Work* 3 (1903), 40–52

Kerry Candaele

Park Slope. Neighborhood in northeastern Brooklyn (2000 pop. *ca* 62,200), bounded to the north by Fourth and Flatbush avenues, to the east by Flatbush Avenue and Prospect Park West, to the south by Prospect Park West and 15th Street, and to the west by Fourth Avenue. It was developed after Prospect Park was completed and street railways were extended to the area in the 1870s. Mansions and four-story row houses were built north of Ninth Street near Grand Army Plaza for professionals and entrepreneurs, many of whom used new streetcar lines that extended over the Brooklyn Bridge (1883) to travel to work in downtown Brooklyn and Manhattan. From about this time Prospect Park West from the plaza to First Street was known as the "gold coast." Modest row houses and apartment buildings were built west of Seventh Avenue and south of Ninth Street to house workers in local factories like that of Ansonia Clock at 12th Street and Seventh Avenue, which was the largest clock factory in the world. Development slowed about the time of World War I, when real estate firms took interest in open land south of Prospect Park that had become accessible by subway and automobile. The lower, less elegant working-class sections of Park Slope were largely Irish. The neighborhood became less fashionable after World War II with the increase of suburban settlement on Long Island. Working-class families moved into the residences in the northern

Brownstones on Carroll Street in Park Slope, 1991

sections, many of which were used as rooming houses.

In the 1960s Eighth Avenue between the plaza and First Street became known as "doctor's row," and in the following years row houses were bought cheaply and restored. A landmark district (the largest in Brooklyn) was formed in 1974 in an area containing about 1600 historic buildings and bounded by Flatbush Avenue, Prospect Park West, 14th Street, and Eighth Avenue. The Ansonia Clock factory was converted into a housing cooperative in 1982. The 14th Regiment Armory on Eighth Avenue became a women's shelter; its exterior was landmarked in 1998.

The commercial districts lie along Seventh Avenue and on Fifth Avenue, especially south of Ninth Street. Many noteworthy buildings are in the landmark district near Grand Army Plaza, including the Montauk Club (designed after the Ca' d'Oro in Venice) and Romanesque Revival and neoclassical row houses (many built before 1916) along side streets. The area attracted a small number of new immigrants in the 1980s, principally from the Dominican Republic and Jamaica. In the late twentieth century the population consisted of young professionals near Prospect Park, attracted by the proximity of the neighborhood to Manhattan and the low cost of housing; Latin Americans west of Seventh Avenue; and many Irish Americans in an enclave south of Ninth Street. By 2008 Park Slope had become the poster neighborhood for the revival and gentrification of Brooklyn as young families flocked to the neighborhood for its proximity to Prospect Park and its beautiful, increasingly expensive housing.

John J. Gallagher

Park Theatre. Theater on Park Row facing City Hall Park, designed by Joseph François Mangin and built in 1798. It became one of the city's most important entertainment venues, where English stock companies produced farces, musical plays, and melodramas and helped introduce the "star system" in the entertainment business. From 1825 the theater's custodian Edward Simpson staged operas and classical music performances, including the local premiere in 1839 of Beethoven's *Fidelio* and the debut in 1843 of the Norwegian violinist Ole Bull. The theater was destroyed by fire on 16 December 1848 and rebuilt as a row of retail shops.

See also Theater, §2.

Marc Ferris

Park Versailles. Disused name for a part of the eastern Bronx bounded to the north by East Tremont Avenue, to the east by White Plains Road, to the south by Westchester Avenue, and to the west by Croes Avenue. The area was once occupied by the Archer–Mapes farm, which was auctioned off in the 1860s, and was named by developers who believed that its wide, tree-lined avenues recalled the grounds of Versailles. In the early twenty-first century this neighborhood is often considered part of Parkchester.

John McNamara, *History in Asphalt: The Origin of Bronx Street and Place Names* (New York: Bronx County Historical Society, 1984)

Gary D. Hermalyn

Parkville. Neighborhood in central Brooklyn, bounded to the north by Ditmas Avenue, to the east by Coney Island Avenue, to the south by Avenue H and Walsh Court, and to the west by McDonald Avenue; it is considered part of Flatbush. Known as Greenfield until 1870, the United Freeman's Association laid out the neighborhood on land purchased in 1851 and 1852 from the Tredwell and Ditmas families. With Windsor Terrace it lay on both sides of what is now Ocean Parkway. After streets were plotted in 1853, the area became a comfortable, middle-class suburb of Brooklyn, largely Jewish and Italian. In the 1980s many immigrants from China moved to the neighborhood and its environs, as did smaller numbers of newcomers from the former Soviet Union, Italy, Israel, and Poland. In 2000 the population exceeded 45,000.

Ellen Marie Snyder-Grenier

parkways. Limited-access highways that are common in the New York metropolitan area and uncommon elsewhere in the United States, bordered and often divided by ribbons of land that are carefully landscaped with trees, grass, and other plantings. They are generally closed to trucks and commercial traffic and free of advertising billboards. The term was originally applied to the roads built for pedestrians and carriages in public parks at the end of the nineteenth century. The first modern parkway built for automobiles was the Bronx River Parkway (proposed in 1906, opened in 1923). By mid-century an innovative network of landscaped parkways spread throughout the New York City area, providing easy access within the city and to the farthest reaches of Westchester and Long Island. Many of these roads were built under the supervision of Robert Moses. Besides the Bronx River Parkway, other well-known examples in New York City are the Henry Hudson Parkway (1936), the Grand Central Parkway (1936), and the Belt Parkway (1940).

Owen D. Gutfreund

Parrish, (Frederick) Maxfield (*b* Philadelphia, 25 July 1870; *d* Plainfield, N.H., 30 March 1966). Painter and illustrator. Educated abroad and at Haverford College and the Pennsylvania Academy, he achieved his first commercial success with a cover for *Harper's Weekly* and was soon engaged by the magazines *Collier's, Scribner's,* and *Ladies' Home Journal;* he later illustrated such books as Edith Wharton's *Italian Villas* and Francis Turner Palgrave's *Golden Treasury* (1911). During the winter of 1918–19 he painted at 49 East 63rd Street. He became known for advertisements for tires, light bulbs, and Jell-O desserts and for a mural 28 feet (8.5 meters) long at the Hotel Knickerbocker, *Old King Cole,* depicting the legendary king of the nursery tale surrounded by his court; this was moved to the St. Regis Hotel in 1933 and became a favorite of New Yorkers for decades. An exhibition of his work was held at the Gallery of Modern Art in 1964. Parrish received the gold medal of the Architectural League.

Coy L. Ludwig, *Maxfield Parrish* (New York: Watson–Guptill, 1973)

James E. Mooney

parrots, wild. Bands of wild parrots have inhabited Brooklyn since the late 1960s. Of the species *Myiopsitta monachus,* also known as monk parakeets or Quaker parrots, they are thought to have escaped from John F. Kennedy Airport in the late 1960s en route from Argentina; other theories suggest that the birds escaped from pet stores or were released from the Brooklyn Botanic Gardens. The parrots were first sighted in the early 1970s and since then have lived in colonies at Brooklyn College and Green-Wood Cemetery; some parrots call Coney Island, Bay Ridge, and other Brooklyn neighborhoods home, and a few have ventured outside the borough to Pelham Bay Park in the Bronx. The birds were initially classified as an invasive species, and federal eradication teams were sent in 1973 to wipe them out, although one band living at Rikers Island mysteriously escaped its hunters. In 2006 Brooklyn parrot advocate Steve Baldwin created the Brooklyn Parrot Society, a nonprofit organization to educate the public about the birds. The parrots, which eat plants, berries, and pizza, continue to build their 400-pound (181-kilogram) nests atop the light poles of the Brooklyn College athletic field and the front gate of Green-Wood Cemetery.

Kate Lauber

Parsons [née Clews]**, Elsie (Worthington)** (*b* New York City, 27 Nov 1874; *d* New York City, 19 Dec 1941). Sociologist, anthropologist, and folklorist. Born to a wealthy and socially prominent family, she graduated from Barnard College in 1896 and earned a doctorate in sociology from Columbia University in 1899. Under the influence of Franz Boas she began to concentrate on anthropology about 1915, becoming known for her studies of the Indian tribes of the southwestern United States. She helped to found the New School for Social Research and the magazine the *New Republic* and was active in the salon of Mabel Dodge and other artistic and intellectual circles. Parsons was also a noted feminist, pacifist, and social critic. Her published writings include *The Family: An Ethnographical and Historical Outline with Descriptive Notes* (1906), *Mitla, Town of the Souls, and Other Zapoteco-Speaking Pueblos at Oaxaca, Mexico* (1936), and *Pueblo Indian Religion* (1939).

Desley Deacon, *Elsie Clews Parsons: Inventing Modern Life* (Chicago: University of Chicago Press, 1997)

Ira Jacknis

Parsons, William Barclay (*b* New York City, 15 April 1859; *d* New York City, 9 May 1932). Civil engineer. He graduated from Columbia University (AB 1879, civil engineering degree 1882). As the chief engineer for the Rapid Transit Commission of New York (1894–1905) he supervised the planning and construction of the city's first subway line, the Interborough Rapid Transit. A trustee of Columbia (from 1897) and later the chairman of the board of the Columbia Medical Hospital, he took an active role in establishing the university's campus in Morningside Heights at the turn of the century and in the building of Presbyterian Hospital. He was also a surveyor for the Chinese railway system (1898–99), the chief engineer for the Cape Cod Canal (1905–14), a consulting engineer for the Panama Canal (1905), and chairman of the Chicago Transit Commission. Parsons's practice was a forerunner of the firm of consulting engineers Parsons–Brinkerhoff. His published writings include *Track* (1885), *Turnouts* (1885), and *Robert Fulton and the Submarine* (1923). A vestryman at Trinity Church, he lived for many years at 35 East 50th Street.

Shan Jayakumar

Parsons School of Design. See Parsons The New School for Design.

Parsons The New School for Design. Private art school at Fifth Avenue and 13th Street in Manhattan, opened in 1896 as the Chase School of Art by the painter and art teacher William Merritt Chase. The school was known as the New York School for Fine and Applied Art when it was led from 1905 to 1930 by Frank Alvah Parsons (1866–1930), who shifted the emphasis away from painting and sculpture and toward design and the applied arts and introduced a unique curriculum that included courses in interior decoration, costume design, teacher training, and advertising design. By 1922 the school had established a full-time program in Paris that was the first program for study abroad supported by an American art institution. It was renamed Parsons School of Design in 1940. As of 2007 about 4000 students were enrolled at the school, which offers undergraduate and graduate degrees in design, the visual arts, and the fine arts. The work of students and of artists and designers from the United States and abroad is shown at the Parsons Exhibition Center, one of the largest public galleries in lower Manhattan. Parsons became an affiliate of the New School for Social Research in 1970 and was renamed Parsons The New School for Design in 2005.

David C. Levy, *An Historical Study of Parsons School of Design and Its Merger/Affiliation with the New School for Social Research* (New York: New York University Press, 1979)

Linda Elsroad

partisan press. An openly partisan form of journalism developed during the nineteenth century as political parties began to subsidize and control newspapers across the country and particularly in New York City. The *Evening Post,* a Federalist newspaper, was launched in the city in 1801 by Alexander Hamilton to counteract Republican opposition. John D. Burk, anti-Federalist editor of the *Time Piece,* feared prosecution for his political outspokenness under the Alien and Sedition Acts and went underground for two years. Both newspapers blurred the distinction between news and opinion and commonly printed party slogans on their mastheads. During the 1830s the *Evening Post* shifted its allegiance from the Federalists to the Democrats and lent critical political support to Andrew Jackson. Partisan journalism took its extreme form in short-lived campaign newspapers that existed solely to promote candidates, among them the Whig newspaper the *Log Cabin.* To counteract the domination of Democratic newspapers in New York City the Whigs founded the *New York Tribune* (1841), which by the 1870s turned Republican and engaged its opponent, the Democratic *World,* in heated partisan headline warfare. Journalists who displayed loyalty toward a party were often rewarded with lucrative state printing contracts and appointments to political office. The economic ties between the press and political parties weakened as newspapers increasingly relied on advertising for revenues, a trend that began in New York City in the middle of the nineteenth century. Although partisan journalism continued, editors such as Horace Greeley of the *New York Tribune* seized control of the political content of their newspapers from the parties. During the 1930s the labor press in New York City began promoting objective journalism, which it maintained would enable citizens to make independent political judgments. During the 1840s the use of wire services in New York City made news more homogeneous than before and partisan distortions more obvious. The *New York Times* led efforts to professionalize journalism in the 1870s by making objective, independent reporting its highest goal. It led a crusade against the Tweed Ring during 1870–71 and later against political parties themselves. Partisanship in journalism was further disclaimed by editors such as E. L. Godkin, who led a movement for liberal reform in the late nineteenth century. By the 1880s New York City emerged as a center of independent journalism, as large daily newspapers embraced objectivity and symbolically replaced partisan mastheads with ones extolling factuality.

Edwin Emery and Michael Emery, *The Press and America: An Interpretive History of the Mass Media* (Englewood Cliffs, N.J.: Prentice Hall, 1978); Michael Schudson, *Discovering the News: A Social History of American Newspapers* (New York: Basic Books, 1978)

Becky M. Nicolaides

Partisan Review. Quarterly magazine launched by the John Reed Club in 1935. It was reshaped in 1937 as an independent radical publication by Philip Rahv and William Phillips. The magazine challenged communist domination of leftist thought, quickly becoming the most important forum for anti-Stalinism and the most influential publication of its kind in the nation. In May–June 1954 it sponsored an influential symposium, "Our Country and Our Culture," that included such participants as Norman Mailer, Reinhold Niebuhr, David Riesman, and Lionel Trilling. Its influence declined after 1960. Phillips remained the principal editor until just before his death in 2002; the magazine ceased publication the following year.

James Burkhart Gilbert, *Writers and Partisans: A History of Literary Radicalism in America* (New York: John Wiley and Sons, 1968); *Partisan Review: The Fiftieth Anniversary Edition* (New York: Stein and Day, 1984)

Lawson Bowling

Partnership for New York City (i). Association for the development of New York City's economy. Formed on 5 April 1768 as the New York Chamber of Commerce by 20 merchants at Fraunces Tavern, it was granted a royal charter on 13 March 1770 by George III. It was the first business association in the city to be unaffiliated with any government body. From its earliest days the chamber mediated business disputes and supported public works and legislation that promoted business. Meetings were held at the Royal Exchange, the Merchants' Coffee House, the Tontine Coffee House, and the Merchants' Exchange; the first president was the Loyalist former mayor John Cruger. The chamber was an administrative base for the Loyalists until their defeat, and it subsequently lost power at the end of the war. It was reorganized on 13 April 1784 as the Chamber of Commerce of the State of New York. On 3 January 1786 it issued the first proposal for the Erie Canal.

Membership increased through the mid-nineteenth century, and the chamber was deeply engaged in the affairs of the city after the Civil War. It funded the Committee of Seventy, investigated the political corruption of the Tweed Ring, proposed the consolidation of New York City, and supported the establishment of a rapid transit system. It encouraged the development of the Catskill Aqueduct in 1912 and in 1916 proposed the formation of the Port of New York Authority. In November 1902 the chamber constructed its first building, a four-story structure of Vermont marble at 65 Liberty Street; after World War II, permanent staff members replaced volunteers.

In 1973 the chamber merged with the Commerce and Industry Association (formerly the Merchants' Association) and became the New York Chamber of Commerce and Industry. In 1979 David Rockefeller founded the New York Partnership; in 2002 the partnership and the chamber combined to form the Partnership for New York City, expanding the chamber's mission from business advocacy to a broader economic vision of the city. In 2010 the partnership was headquartered at One Battery Park Plaza; the chamber's archival records (1768–1973) are held at the Columbia University Rare Book and Manuscript Library.

Joseph Bucklin Bishop, *A Chronicle of One Hundred and Fifty Years: The Chamber of Commerce of the State of New York, 1768–1918* (New York: Charles Scribner's Sons, 1918)

Donald R. Stabile

Partnership for New York City (ii). Coalition of leaders in business, nonprofit organizations, and education formed in 1979 by David Rockefeller as the New York City Partnership to work with government agencies on economic development, education, and housing. It introduced a summer employment program for low-income youth and developed housing for middle-income families through the New York City Housing Partnership, formed in 1982. The organization has studied obstacles to development in the five boroughs, especially those posed by the environmental review process and those that discourage technologically advanced industries. In 2002 the New York City Partnership merged with the New York City Chamber of Commerce to form the Partnership for New York City.

Rosalie Genevro

Pastor, Tony [Antonio] (*b* New York City, 28 May 1837; *d* Queens, 26 Aug 1908). Theater manager and variety performer. He began singing at age six and started his stage career in 1846 at P. T. Barnum's American Museum. Pastor performed as a clown, minstrel, and comic singer before opening Tony Pastor's Opera House in 1865 at 201 Bowery. He opened Tony Pastor's New Fourteenth Street Theatre in 1881, where he promoted tamer vaudeville shows to appeal to women and families instead of the traditional male audiences. Pastor's innovations were widely imitated and he became called the "father of vaudeville" for his role in making it popular among mainstream audiences.

See also Vaudeville.

Ben Silk

Paterson, David A(lexander) (*b* Brooklyn, 20 May 1954). New York State governor. The son of politician Basil Patterson, he graduated from Columbia University in 1977 and Hofstra Law School in 1983. During 1983–85 he worked as an assistant district attorney in Queens County, in the Manhattan Borough President's Office, and in the administration of Mayor David Dinkins. In 1985 he was appointed to the New York State Assembly to serve out the remainder of a deceased senator's term and was later elected to the position, filling the seat once occupied by his father. In 2002 he became the minority leader of the state senate and was known as a consensus builder. In 2007 Patterson, who is legally blind, became the first African American lieutenant governor of New York under Governor Eliot Spitzer. Upon Spitzer's abrupt resignation from office in March 2008, Patterson succeeded as governor. He has long supported controversial issues such as stem cell research, voting rights to noncitizens, and the legal recognition of same-sex marriage.

Sherrill Wilson

PATH [Port Authority Trans-Hudson Corporation] **and PATH Station.** Fourteen-mile interstate rapid transit system that connects Manhattan with Hoboken, Jersey City, and Newark, New Jersey. Originally constructed between 1874 and 1909, under a progression of ownerships that overcame formidable engineering obstacles, it opened as the Hudson and Manhattan Railroad, more popularly known as the Hudson Tubes or H & M. Its two pairs of trans-Hudson tunnels were recognized as a pioneering engineering achievement. PATH uses subway-type third

PATH station, 2009

rail electric trains; its two Manhattan branches are a midtown route terminating at 33rd Street and Sixth Avenue (opened in 1908, including four additional stations between 23rd and Christopher streets) and a downtown route terminating at Hudson Terminal, the World Trade Center site (opened in 1909). The Holland and Lincoln tunnels, opened in 1927 and 1937, respectively, siphoned customers from the H & M, which experienced many years of financial difficulties culminating in its 1954 bankruptcy. In 1962 the Port Authority of New York and New Jersey bought the H & M, took over its operations, spent millions of dollars to repair and replace old infrastructure, purchased a new car fleet, and renamed the system PATH.

As part of the bistate compact that allowed the Port Authority to create PATH, it also built the World Trade Center complex in lower Manhattan atop the Hudson Terminal station. A brand new PATH station under the trade center complex opened in 1971. The terrorist attacks of 11 September 2001 destroyed the station and flooded the tunnels halfway to Exchange Place in Jersey City. Thanks to quick action by PATH employees, train service was immediately stopped at the onset of the attacks and all passengers in the station or en route to Manhattan were taken to New Jersey, so no PATH customers or employees were trapped on trains when the towers collapsed. For the next 26 months no service operated to the World Trade Center site; on 23 November 2003 a temporary station was opened. A permanent station will ultimately replace the 2003 facility when the entire site is rebuilt.

After celebrating its 100th anniversary in February 2008, PATH continues to be a vital transit link between Manhattan's business core and nearby New Jersey communities. Many PATH patrons transfer to commuter trains and buses at three major New Jersey hubs (Newark, Journal Square, and Hoboken). Approximately 227,000 weekday fares are collected; annual passenger trips in 2006 totaled nearly 67 million; the fare was $1.50 in 2007 and rose to $1.75 in March 2008, with discounted rates for regular riders. A new 340-car fleet is currently under construction and will replace all current (1965–1986) rolling stock.

Andrew Sparberg

Pathmark. Chain of supermarkets operated by the Great Atlantic and Pacific Tea Company and one of the 10 largest grocery chains in the United States. It was formed in 1968 under the direction of Milton Perlmutter by several members of the Wakefern Cooperative, which operated supermarkets in New York City and its environs under the name Shop Rite. The firm encouraged the operators of its stores to heed local preferences and also followed a policy of community involvement. In 1977 it entered into an agreement with the Bedford Stuyvesant Restoration Corporation to build a supermarket in one of the most severely depressed parts of Brooklyn. Pathmark opened a supermarket at Pike Slip in Manhattan in the mid-1980s after persuading local merchants that the store would help the local economy rather than drive competitors out of business. As of 2010 there were four Pathmark supermarkets in Manhattan, five in Brooklyn, three in the Bronx, two in Queens, and one in Staten Island.

Chad Ludington

Patrolmen's Benevolent Association of the City of New York [PBA]. Labor organization formed as a protective society in 1894 to assure proper burials for police officers who died during an influenza epidemic. In 1911 it won its first important legislative victory when it secured passage of a "three platoon" law, which replaced the system of two 12-hour work shifts with three eight-hour shifts; the law was amended in 1969 in order to allow for greater managerial flexibility in duty assignments. From 1914 to 1935 the president of the PBA was Joseph P. Moran; his retirement was followed by a period of instability that lasted until John E. Carton was elected president in 1947 by defeating Raymond Donovan, who advocated that the PBA break with tradition by declaring itself a union. In 1951 Donovan led a small faction of officers who joined the United Patrolmen's Association, an affiliate of the Transit Workers Union; their insurgency ended when the police commissioner, George P. Monaghan, threatened to take disciplinary action. Carton remained president until 1958 and won large pay increases for his men. His successor, John J. Cassese, soon revived the controversy over the formal status of the organization: he threatened to form an affiliation with the International Brotherhood of Teamsters, owing to the city's refusal in 1958 to have the PBA collect membership dues through payroll deductions, a source of operating income that most other municipal unions had been granted. In 1963 Mayor Robert F. Wagner extended this right to the PBA and recognized it as the exclusive collective bargaining unit for police officers. The years 1966 to 1973 were tumultuous, when the PBA became embroiled in a controversy over the creation of a civilian review board and firefighters and sanitation workers demanded pay parity with police officers. After Cassese retired in 1969 the PBA experienced another period of instability until Philip R. Caruso's election as president in 1980, which lasted until 1995. Since 2001 the union has been active in the passage of legislation that would provide benefits for deaths or injuries to officers that resulted from the terrorist attacks on the World Trade Center of 11 September 2001.

Emma Schweppe, *The Firemen's and Patrolmen's Unions in the City of New York* (New York: King's Crown, 1948); Joseph P. Viteritti, *Police, Politics and Pluralism in New York City* (Beverly Hills, Calif.: Sage, 1973)

Joseph P. Viteritti

patronage. See Civil service.

pattern making. The first unsized clothing patterns appeared in fashion magazines in the early 1850s; sized patterns were introduced in 1864 and made it possible for amateur seamstresses and women working at home to produce fashionable clothes tailored to the wearer. During the second half of the nineteenth century the focus of the pattern business shifted to New York City when the three largest companies moved there (E. Butterick and Company, Madame Demorest, and McCall), as did several smaller ones. Patterns were a practical and economical alternative to drafting systems and dressmakers and became popular throughout the United States and Europe, especially among women who lived far from cities; Butterick's patterns sold for 10 to 75 cents each in 1867; Demorest's skirt and bodice patterns were as little as 30 cents each in 1877. At its height in the 1870s Demorest purchased 5000 reams of tissue paper and two million envelopes at a time and reportedly sold 50,000 copies of its most popular styles. Butterick sold between four and six million patterns annually. The pattern business helped to make New York City the fashion capital of the United States and to set national standards of style and taste by reinterpreting Parisian vogues for American consumers. Pattern manufacturers sometimes published fashion magazines: *Mme. Demorest's What to Wear, Demorest's Monthly Magazine,* and *The Quarterly Mirror of Fashion* by Demorest; *The Ladies' Quarterly Report of Fashions, The Metropolitan,* and *The Delineator* by Butterick; and *The Queen* and *The Bazar Dressmaker* by McCall. These reached a combined readership of nearly 400,000 by the 1880s. In the early twentieth century women's ready-made apparel replaced pattern making as the primary fashion enterprise in New York City, although home sewing remains a popular hobby. A few of the large pattern manufacturers are still in existence. McCall acquired Butterick and Vogue Patterns in 2001, and the company continues to provide high-quality patterns to home sewing enthusiasts. McCall Pattern Company maintains headquarters at 120 Broadway.

Claudia B. Kidwell, *Cutting a Fashionable Fit: Dressmakers' Drafting Systems in the United States* (Washington: Smithsonian Institution Press, 1979); Margaret Walsh, "The Democratization of Fashion: The Emergence of the Women's Dress Pattern Industry," *Journal of American History* 66 (1979), 299–313; Nancy Page Fernandez, "'If a Woman Had Taste . . .': Home Sewing and the Making of Fashion, 1850–1910" (diss., University of California, Irvine, 1987)

Wendy Gamber

Patterson, Alicia (*b* Chicago, 15 Oct 1906; *d* New York City, 2 July 1963). Newspaper editor and publisher. She learned the newspaper business from her father, Joseph Medill Patterson, founder of the *Daily News.* In a financial partnership with her husband, Harry Guggenheim, in 1940 she launched *Newsday,* a tabloid newspaper that she made into a powerful force on Long Island by means of local reporting, aggressive efforts to increase regular readership through home delivery, and coverage that treated the island as a unified political and economic region. In her later years she opposed the isolationist views of her father, who responded by reneging on plans to give her control of the *Daily News.*

Robert F. Keeler, *Newsday: A Candid History of the Respectable Tabloid* (New York: William Morrow, 1990)

Madeline Rogers

Patterson, Joseph Medill (*b* Chicago, 6 Jan 1879; *d* New York City, 26 May 1946). Newspaper publisher and father of Alicia Patterson, founder and editor of *Newsday.* A grandson of Joseph Medill, founder of the *Chicago Tribune,* and son of Robert Wilson Patterson, its editor in chief, he went to work as a reporter for the *Tribune* after graduating from Yale. Patterson was elected to the state legislature of Illinois in 1903, managed Eugene V. Debs's presidential campaign in 1908, wrote two novels, and had three of his plays produced on Broadway before returning to the *Tribune* as a coeditor in 1912. From 1914 he worked as a war correspondent in Mexico, Belgium, Germany, and China. In 1919 he launched the *Illustrated Daily News,* published in New York City while he remained in Chicago. Renamed the *Daily News,* the newspaper became the first successful American tabloid and by 1924 was the most popular newspaper in the United States, reaching 750,000 readers daily. In 1925 he moved to New York City to manage the newspaper full time. Circulation exceeded one million by 1926 and two million by 1940. As an editor Patterson was famous for paying his trusted employees high salaries and staying in touch with everyday New Yorkers, frequenting nightclubs in Coney Island, Times Square, and the Bowery. He served as a close adviser to President Franklin D. Roosevelt and defended Roosevelt's candidacy for a third term in 1940, winning him a Pulitzer Prize. The relationship between the two men deteriorated when Patterson espoused isolationism during World War II. He ran the *Daily News* until his death.

John Tebbel, *An American Dynasty* (New York: Greenwood, 1968); Leo E. McGivena et al., *The News: The First Fifty Years of New York's Picture Newspaper* (New York: News Syndicate, 1969)

Steve Rivo

Patz, Etan (Kalil) (*b* Manhattan, 9 Oct 1972, *d* unknown). Six-year-old boy who disappeared on 25 May 1979 while walking from Prince Street in SoHo to the West Broadway school bus stop. His disappearance galvanized awareness of and gave rise to new legislation and new methods for tracking down missing children, most famously the milk cartons of the 1980s, which showed names and photos of lost children above law enforcement contact information. In 1983 President Ronald Reagan declared the day of Etan's disappearance, May 25, as National Missing Children's Day. The Patz family continued to live in the city after Etan's disappearance. His body was never discovered. He was declared legally dead in 2001, and in 2004 a Manhattan judge ruled that José Ramos, a convicted pedophile acquainted with a former babysitter for the Patz family, was responsible for Etan's death.

Kenneth T. Jackson

Paulding, James Kirke (*b* Great Nine Partners, Putnam County, N.Y., 22 Aug 1778; *d* New York City, 6 April 1860). Writer and naval officer, brother of William Paulding, Jr. He grew up in Tarrytown, New York, where he became a friend of Washington Irving; together they published the whimsical journal *Salmagundi* during 1807–8. Paulding soon wrote *The Diverting History of John Bull and Brother Jonathan* and poetry that he defended in *The United States and England* (1815). He was later appointed secretary of the navy commissioners (1815–23), naval agent for New York State (1824–38), and secretary of the navy (1838–41). His works include a life of George Washington, studies of the South, dozens of tales, and novels about New York City such as *The Dutchman's Fireside* and *The Old Continental.* He is buried in Green-Wood Cemetery in Brooklyn.

Larry J. Reynolds, *James Kirke Paulding* (Boston: Twayne, 1984)

James E. Mooney

Paulding, William, Jr. (*b* Tarrytown, N.Y., 7 March 1770; *d* Tarrytown, 11 Feb 1854). Congressman and mayor, brother of James Kirke Paulding. He practiced law in New York City for several years before his election to the U.S. House of Representatives as a Democrat from the twelfth district (1811–13). During the War of 1812 he was a brigadier general in the state militia. A delegate to the state constitutional convention of 1821, he was the state's adjutant general before his election as mayor in 1824; he remained in office until 1825, when he was replaced by Philip Hone, but won reelection and held office again from 1826 to 1829.

James E. Mooney

paving. The first recorded paving of a street in New Amsterdam took place in 1658, when at the request of nearby residents cobblestones were laid along what later became Stone Street between Whitehall and Broad streets. In May 1684 the Common Council ordered that principal streets be paved, the expense to be borne by the owners of adjacent property. Legislation passed on 20 May 1708 mandated stricter enforcement of paving regulations and noted that earlier measures had gone unheeded. In 1748 the streets of New York City were said by visitors to be spacious and well paved, but they were reported to be filthy and often impassable on 6 April 1787 when the state legislature granted the power to pave the streets to the

Paving blocks on 28th Street between Broadway and Sixth Avenue, 2 October 1930

Common Council. Legislation passed by the council in April 1789 imposed severe penalties for the breach of paving regulations. From the 1830s experiments were undertaken with different paving materials, including macadam, woodblocks, and cut stone block. Rectangular, granite paving stones called Belgian blocks and rectangular blocks made of trap stone became widespread in 1852, replacing the common round cobblestones. In 1876 there were 299 miles (481 kilometers) of paved streets in New York City, of which Belgian and trap blocks accounted for 146 miles (235 kilometers), cobblestones for 86 miles (138 kilometers), and other materials including concrete, wood, macadam, and gravel for 67 miles (108 kilometers). Asphalt pavement was introduced in the city in 1884 and represented a marked improvement over stone block, which was bumpy and noisy; it was officially adopted on 6 January 1890 for streets not extensively used for business purposes and remained in use more than a century later to pave the more than 6300 miles (10,100 kilometers) of streets and highways in the five boroughs.

James Ford, *Slums and Housing, with Special Reference to New York City: History, Conditions, Policy* (Westport, Conn.: Negro Universities Press, 1971)

Craig D. Bida

Pavlova, Anna (Pavlovna) (*b* St. Petersburg, 12 Feb 1881; *d* The Hague, 23 Jan 1931). Dancer. She was trained at the Imperial School of Ballet in St. Petersburg. In 1909 her performance with Sergei Diaghilev's Ballets Russes was seen by Otto H. Kahn, director of the Metropolitan Opera, who signed her and her partner Mikhail Mordkin to a one-month contract; the two opened on 28 February 1910 in *Coppélia* to great success. Although Pavlova occasionally returned to Russia before World War I, she spent much of her career in New York City.

Keith Money, *Anna Pavlova: Her Life and Art* (New York: Alfred A. Knopf, 1982)

Barbara Barker

pawnshops. The first pawnshop in New York City was opened in 1822 at 25 Chatham Street by an Englishman named William Simpson. The many secondhand shops operated by usurers at the time also lent money on personal property, but unlike pawnshops they required customers to sign conditional bills of sale. Typically customers exchanged items such as jewelry or clothing for money and agreed to repay the amount borrowed plus interest to redeem their property, which those who could not pay would forfeit. Pawnbrokers appraised merchandise and gave their customers pawn tickets, which were either used to redeem pledges or sold to hock-ticket peddlers (pawnshops were also known as hockshops). In 1838 Simpson paid $5 for coats, $1 for watches, and 50 cents for pants. A typical business day in 1841 brought in 153 items valued at $655.71, and in 1842 his vault held jewelry on which $34,504.31 was lent. Other pawnshops soon opened and in time enjoyed a virtual monopoly of the lending field, in part by remaining open 24 hours a day. They ran the risk that the property they accepted would later be found to have been stolen, and they were sometimes embroiled in disputes over the ownership of valuables in businesses that were jointly owned. From 1891 to 1916 Simpson made $100,000 to $200,000 a year.

In the late 1980s pawnshops experienced a resurgence, as members of the middle class and the affluent turned to them during a period of layoffs, bankruptcies, foreclosures, tight credit, high medical bills, and costly divorce settlements. Nationwide the number of pawnshops increased by more than half from 1986 to 1991. At the same time there was a trend toward publicly owned operators of pawnshops, such as Cash American Investments and Ezcorp. Edward Lewis Wallant's novel *The Pawnbroker* (1961), which was made into a popular film, is set in New York City.

William R. Simpson, Florence K. Simpson, and Charles Samuels, *Hockshop* (New York: Random House, 1954)

Mary Ann Romano

Payton, Philip A. (Jr.) (*b* Westfield, Mass., 1876; *d* Allenhurst, N.J., 29 Aug 1917). Businessman. A graduate of Livingston College (1898), he moved in 1899 to New York City, where as the president of the Afro-American Realty Company (incorporated 1904) he was the first real estate agent to rent apartments in Harlem to blacks. His success inspired other blacks to become real estate agents, including John E. Nail and Henry C. Parker. Afro-American Realty declared bankruptcy in 1908, after which Payton bought and managed buildings from an office at 67 West 134th Street.

Alana Erickson Coble

peace movements. Organized opposition to war began in New York City during the colonial period when Dutch Mennonites, Quakers, and Moravians from central Europe refused to take up arms or pay taxes specifically intended for war. On 14 August 1815 the Christian pacifist and wealthy merchant David Low Dodge formed the New York Peace Society, one of the first organizations in the world to hold the abolition of war as its single goal. The society condemned all warfare as opposed to the example of Jesus and insisted that all its members be affiliated with an evangelical church. A kindred organization, the American Peace Society (1828), had its headquarters for a time in New York City. The peace movement declined at the onset of the Civil War, as most of its adherents had an equally strong commitment to the crusade against slavery.

When the peace movement was revived in the late nineteenth century, its earlier religious basis was replaced by a secular internationalism. The emergence of New York City as a center of international finance and trade made many local businesspeople become more concerned with foreign affairs, and the New York Peace Society was revived; under Andrew Carnegie's leadership it soon became the largest branch of the American Peace Society. The society campaigned for the international arbitration treaties negotiated during the presidency of William Howard Taft and organized the highly successful National Arbitration and Peace Congress held in New York City on the eve of the conference at The Hague in 1907. The peace movement before World War I was mostly sustained by elites who sought to avoid a war among the great powers: they equated peace with the preservation of a stable international order and were generally accepting of the existing imperial system.

The outbreak of war produced an extraordinary transformation of the pacifist movement, as women emerged in leadership roles. On 29 August 1914 1500 women in mourning dress marched in silence down Fifth Avenue behind a large white banner depicting a dove holding an olive branch. A coalition of women's groups in 1915 formed the Woman's Peace Party under the leadership of Jane Addams and Carrie Chapman Catt; the group was founded in Washington, D.C., but had a very active branch in New York City. Many members were suffragists, and most believed that the nurturing role of women led them naturally to oppose violence and war. Ignoring the wrath of critics, they organized a conference at The Hague that brought together women from the warring nations. Leaders of the conference met with heads of state in an unsuccessful effort to mediate the conflict. In later years participants in the conference formed the Women's International League for Peace and Freedom, which had an active, sometimes faction-ridden chapter in New York City that remains active into the twenty-first century. Another activist organization, the American Union against Militarism (1916), grew out of a meeting of reformers at the Henry Street Settlement. Led by Lillian Wald and Paul Kellogg, editor of the magazine the *Survey,* the group argued that war would prevent the implementation of domestic reforms and sought to mobilize public pressure on President Woodrow Wilson to mediate among warring nations to end the conflict. A group of well-known internationalists led by Taft and A. Lawrence Lowell, the president of Harvard University, formed the League to Enforce Peace in 1915 during a series of meetings at the Century Club in New York City. The league urged that after the war nations should settle their disputes through an international tribunal, failing which it favored collective retaliation against offenders. The carnage in Europe lent weight to this message, and the league became the catalyst for the formation of a postwar league of nations.

U.S. entry into the war dealt a series of blows to organizations that had opposed it; many suffragists in the pacifist movement aided the war effort as a means of winning public support and gaining the vote, and the city's trade unions were faced with the choice between making gains by cooperating with the war effort and being persecuted for opposing it. After the war, internationalists in 1919 organized the League of Free Nations Association (which became the Foreign Policy Association in 1921); its program favored planned reconstruction, liberalized trade, and social democracy. Although some pacifists continued to press for U.S. membership in the League of Nations after the Senate blocked it, many others were discouraged by the punitive Treaty of Versailles and by postwar xenophobia.

During the 1920s and 1930s the Women's Peace Union, based primarily in New York City and led by Elinor Byrns, campaigned for a constitutional amendment that would limit U.S. participation in future wars. The Fellowship of Reconciliation, formed in 1915 in suburban Garden City, New York, advocated absolute pacifism; its leaders, including A. J. Muste and John Haynes Holmes, successfully appealed to many Protestant members of the clergy who had come to regret their enthusiasm for the war. Pacifist groups had substantial appeal during the 1930s until Hitler's stunning conquest of France and the Battle of Britain in 1940, and above all the Japanese attack on Pearl Harbor. Pacifists were now a tiny, embattled minority, their efforts reduced to protecting the rights of conscientious objectors.

With the end of World War II and the beginning of the atomic age many internationalists believed that U.S. membership in the United Nations was insufficient to achieve world peace. The United World Federalists, formed in 1947 at a convention in Asheville, North Carolina, by the end of the following year claimed 659 chapters and 40,000 members, many of whom were in New York City. The group advocated a world government with the authority to create an international police force, and it grew rapidly when it enlisted a number of scientists fearful of an atomic arms race. In 1957 Norman Cousins, editor of the *Saturday Review,* brought together at the Overseas Press Club in New York City a coalition of pacifists, liberals, and scientists disturbed by the dangers of radiation from atmospheric nuclear testing; the psychologist Erich Fromm named the group the Committee for a Sane Nuclear Policy (SANE). Peace activism was unpopular during the cold war. Critics demanded that SANE purge its ranks of communists, and when Cousins acquiesced some leaders like Linus Pauling resigned and several chapters in New York City refused to investigate their own members. SANE survived the purge but was weakened in the process.

President Lyndon B. Johnson's escalation of the Vietnam War led to protests from peace organizations, and opposition broadened when the demands imposed by the war led to the sacrifice of domestic programs. Residents of New York City organized candlelight vigils, public readings, "teach-ins" on college campuses, petition campaigns, and marches on Washington, D.C. Columbia University was the scene of a violent confrontation between students and police in 1968. Leading antiwar organizations active in the city included Women Strike for Peace, the Fifth Avenue Peace Parade Committee, Vietnam Veterans against the War, and Clergy and Laymen Concerned about Vietnam. President Richard M. Nixon's continuation of the war led to mass protests known as moratoriums in October and November 1969. The protests diminished only when Nixon began to withdraw forces from Vietnam and discontinued the military draft.

A widespread reluctance among Americans to become embroiled in military conflicts after the Vietnam War took some of the urgency from the peace movement, which in the 1980s focused its efforts on slowing the buildup in nuclear arms by the United States and the Soviet Union. One of the stronger organizations in New York City was Physicians for Social Responsibility, formed in 1982 in Boston. On 12 June 1982 peace advocates from every region of the country gathered in New York City for the United Nations Special Session on Disarmament, and nearly one million people marched from the United Nations to Central Park to call for a nuclear freeze.

During the crisis in the Persian Gulf in 1990 New York City was the focus of considerable dissent against President George H. W. Bush's decision to deploy troops. The calls for sanctions rather than war mirrored the debate taking place in the U.S. Congress. The reluctance among New Yorkers to support military conflict displayed its full form during the war in Iraq beginning in 2003; massive rallies and protests, some of the largest in recent history, took place in New York City, particularly after it was discovered that Iraq had no weapons of mass destruction and therefore the main reason the United States had entered into the war was based on false information. Despite lawsuits, protests, and starkly decreased numbers of supporters of the war, peace efforts had little effect on President George W. Bush's policy in Iraq.

Peter Brock, *Pacifism in the United States, from the Colonial Era to the First World War* (Princeton, N.J.: Princeton University Press, 1968); Charles DeBenedetti, *The Peace Reform in American History* (Bloomington: Indiana University Press, 1980); Charles DeBenedetti and Charles Chatfield, *An American Ordeal: The Antiwar Movement of the Vietnam Era* (Syracuse, N.Y.: Syracuse University Press, 1990)

Michael A. Lutzker

Peale, Norman Vincent (*b* Bowersville, Ohio, 31 May 1898; *d* Pawling, N.Y., 24 Dec 1993). Preacher, writer, and religious counselor. The son of a Methodist physician who became a minister, he lived in several small towns in Ohio during his childhood and attended Ohio Wesleyan University (BA 1920) and Boston University (MA, STM 1924); he was ordained a Methodist minister in 1922. After leading parishes in Rhode Island, Brooklyn, and Syracuse, New York, he became the pastor of Marble Collegiate Church on Fifth Avenue in 1932, where he developed "positive thinking," a program that blended popular psychology and Christian idiom into a practical philosophy that found many adherents, especially among professionals in Manhattan. Peale proposed that a willful and practiced change in attitude can bring about prosperity, inner peace, and health, views that he articulated in his book *The Power of Positive Thinking* (1952). As a member of various local organizations he opposed the New Deal in the 1930s, communism in the 1950s, and the presidential candidacy of John F. Kennedy in 1960. Despite such controversies he concentrated on spreading his message: he launched a radio program (which became nationally syndicated) and the monthly magazine *Guideposts* and also had a newspaper column, wrote more than 20 books, and gave many speeches. He was president of the Protestant Council of the City of New York from 1965 to 1969. Toward the end of his life Peale had the largest outpatient psychiatric clinic in the country and remained one of the country's best-known religious figures. In 1984 he received the Presidential Medal of Freedom.

Donald B. Meyer, *The Positive Thinkers: A Study of the American Quest for Health, Wealth and Personal Power from Mary Baker Eddy to Norman Vincent Peale* (Garden City, N.Y.: Doubleday, 1965; rev. Middletown, Conn.: Wesleyan University Press, 1988)

James D. Bratt

Pecora, Ferdinand (*b* Nicosia, Italy, 6 Jan 1882; *d* New York City, 7 Dec 1971). Judge. He moved to New York City with his family in 1887 and later earned a degree from New York Law School. After working in the district attorney's office for 12 years he was appointed counsel to the committee on banking of the U.S. Senate in 1933–34; his investigations uncovered questionable practices on Wall Street and led to the passage of the securities acts of 1933 and 1934. He was the first director of the Securities and Exchange Commission, resigning to become a justice of the Supreme Court of New York. In 1950 he sought election as mayor. He was also counsel to the law firm of Schwartz and Frolich and a director of Freedom House. Pecora's writings include *Wall Street under Oath* (1939).

See also Civil Service Unions.

James E. Mooney

Peerce, Jan [Perelmuth, Jacob Pincus] (*b* New York City, 3 June 1904; *d* New York City,

15 Dec 1984). Tenor. After attending DeWitt Clinton High School and Columbia University, Peerce made his operatic debut in 1939 and first sang at the Metropolitan Opera in 1941 as Alfredo in *La Traviata.* His career encompassed 324 performances in 11 operas, including *La Bohème, Carmen,* and *Rigoletto.* A favorite of the conductor Arturo Toscanini, Peerce was known for his refinement and rich tone. He appeared in several movies and gave concerts into the 1970s. He was related by marriage to the tenor Richard Tucker.

David J. Weiner

Pei, I(eoh) M(ing) (*b* Canton, China, 26 April 1917). Architect. After graduating from the Massachusetts Institute of Technology he began practicing architecture in New York City in 1939. In 1955 he formed I. M. Pei and Associates (now Pei Cobb Freed and Partners), one of the best-known architectural firms in the city. His projects in the city include the Jacob K. Javits Convention Center, the National Airlines Terminal at John F. Kennedy International Airport, New York University Plaza, and Kips Bay Plaza. His offices are at 600 Madison Avenue.

Carter Wiseman, *I. M. Pei: A Profile in American Architecture* (New York: Harry N. Abrams, 1990)

Elliot S. Meadows

Pelham Bay. Neighborhood in the northeastern Bronx, south of Pelham Parkway and east of Pelham Bay Park. It took shape about 1920 around a recently completed terminal station of Interborough Rapid Transit. The housing stock consists of brick apartment buildings dating from the 1920s and the years after World War II, along with some one-family houses. The population is mostly Italian and Irish. Westchester Avenue is the principal commercial thoroughfare. One well-known resident of Pelham Bay was George Meany, first president of the American Federation of Labor and Congress of Industrial Organizations (AFL–CIO); another was the author Cynthia Ozick.

Lloyd Ultan

Pelham Bay Park. Public park in the northeastern Bronx, bounded to the north by Westchester County, to the east by City Island and Long Island Sound, to the south by Watt Avenue and Bruckner Boulevard, and to the west by the Hutchinson River Parkway. Including Orchard Beach it comprises 2764 acres (1120 hectares), making it three times the size of Central Park in Manhattan and among parks in New York City second in area only to the Gateway National Recreation Area. The land was the site in 1776 of the Battle of Bell's Point, in which Colonel John Glover and his militia held off the Hessian army of Sir William Howe, allowing General George Washington and his army to escape to White Plains. It was acquired by the state legislature at the urging of the New York Park Association in 1888, when the surrounding area was largely undeveloped. Within the park are the Bartow–Pell Mansion (1836–42), the only surviving estate from among more than two dozen that once overlooked Pelham Bay; the Pelham Bay Golf Course (1914); and the Split Rock golf course (1936), which is named for a nearby boulder and Indian trail and has a clubhouse reminiscent of a mansion on a southern plantation. Orchard Beach, a large public bathing facility on Long Island Sound that opened in the mid-1930s by dredging of the nearby waters, links the mainland to Hunter's Island, now a wooded nature sanctuary. The inlet formerly connected to the sound became a lagoon where the trials for the U.S. Olympic rowing team were held in 1964. Pelham Bay Park has more than 9 miles (14 kilometers) of shoreline, two public golf courses, ballfields, bridle paths, tennis courts, nature preserves, and a firing range of the New York Police Department at Rodman's Neck; two important highways and the main line of Amtrak run through it.

Gary D. Hermalyn, Jonathan Kuhn

Aerial view of Pelham Bay Park and Orchard Beach

PEN [Poets, Playwrights, Editors and Novelists]. International literary and human rights organization formed in 1921 by the English writer Catherine Amy Dawson as a dining club in London and later including 144 centers in 101 countries. Its activities in the United States are centered in New York City at the PEN American headquarters at 588 Broadway. The group often meets at the Salmagundi Club at 47 Fifth Avenue and produces the PEN World Voices Literary Festival each spring at such venues as the New York Public Library and the 92nd Street Y.

Anthony Gronowicz

Penfield, Edward (*b* Brooklyn, 2 June 1866; *d* Beacon, N.Y., 8 Feb 1925). Painter and illustrator. He studied at the Art Students League before working as the art editor of *Harper's New Monthly Magazine* in 1890, where he became famous for his placard illustrations. In his murals and posters he used designs based on Japanese principles of simplicity. He resigned in 1901 to devote himself to his own work, which included illustrating John Kendrick Bangs's book *Dreamers* (1899) and the books *Holland Sketches* (1907) and *Spanish Sketches* (1911). Penfield lived at 163 West 23rd Street and then in suburban Pelham Manor.

James E. Mooney

Penn Central Transportation Co. v. City of New York. Case decided in 1978 (438 U.S. 104) by the U.S. Supreme Court that upheld the application of the Landmarks Preservation Law of New York City to a proposed development involving Grand Central Terminal. The law prevented Penn Central, which owned the building, from constructing a 55-story office tower over the terminal and stripping off part of its facade. The court held that the restriction on the development, which did not interfere with the use of the terminal and permitted the owner to transfer the air rights over the terminal to other parcels of land in the vicinity, was "substantially related to the promotion of the general welfare" and did not constitute a "taking" of property without just compensation.

Richard Briffault

Pennington, J(ames) W(illiam) C(harles) (*b* Maryland, 1807; *d* Jacksonville, Fla., 20/22 Oct 1870). Minister and writer.

After escaping from slavery in Maryland about 1828 he was educated by Quakers, worked as a blacksmith, and was a pastor on Long Island, in Connecticut, and then at the First (Shiloh) Presbyterian Church on Prince Street in New York City (1847–55). A strong supporter of John Brown, he was among the most radical black ministers in antebellum New York City. He received the doctorate of divinity from the University of Heidelberg in 1851 and later wrote an important narrative of his years as a slave and a history of blacks in colonial America. In 1855 he helped to form the New York Legal Rights Association, which sued the city to secure the right for blacks to use public transit facilities.

Graham Hodges

Pennsylvania Hotel. See NEW YORK'S HOTEL PENNSYLVANIA.

Pennsylvania Railroad. Railroad company, originally chartered in 1846 by the Commonwealth of Pennsylvania to build a rail line in that state. Through mergers and acquisitions the Pennsylvania Railroad (PRR) became the principal rail route between New York City and Philadelphia, Baltimore, and Washington, D.C. In 1871 PRR acquired control of railroads between Philadelphia and Jersey City, its original New York access, where barges and ferries transported freight and passengers to Manhattan and Brooklyn. In 1900 PRR purchased the Long Island Rail Road (LIRR), which facilitated construction of its New York Tunnel Extension Project, encompassing two tunnels between New Jersey and Manhattan, Pennsylvania Station, four tunnels under the East River, Sunnyside Yards in Long Island City, and use of electric power in this area. This massive civil engineering feat allowed PRR and LIRR trains direct access to Manhattan; it also grew to encompass the joint PRR/New Haven Railroad Hell Gate Bridge project (1917) between Queens and the Bronx, permitting direct rail service between Washington, D.C., and Boston.

Electric train power expanded between 1933 and 1938 to include the entire PRR New York/Philadelphia/Washington, D.C., route, solidifying PRR's dominance in this market. In 1966 PRR sold LIRR to New York State. Growing competition from air and highway travel caused PRR and the New York Central Railroad to merge in 1968 and form the Penn Central Railroad, which in turn declared bankruptcy in 1970; its long-distance passenger routes became part of the National Railroad Passenger Corporation (Amtrak) in 1971. In 1976 the U.S. government created the Consolidated Rail Corporation (Conrail) by merging Penn Central with five other northeastern railroads. Conrail operated former PRR commuter services between New York City and New Jersey until 1983; since then New Jersey Transit Corporation has controlled that service. Conrail's freight operation, in turn, was split in 1997 between the CSX and Norfolk Southern railroads.

George H. Burgess and Miles C. Kennedy, *Centennial History of the Pennsylvania Railroad Company* (Philadelphia: Pennsylvania Railroad Company, 1949); Carl W. Condit, *The Port of New York: A History of the Rail Terminal System from the Beginnings to Pennsylvania Station* (Chicago: University of Chicago Press, 1980)

Robert A. Olmsted, Andrew Sparberg

Pennsylvania Station [Penn Station]. Name used by a station of the Pennsylvania Railroad and later by a station of the National Railroad Passenger Corporation (Amtrak). The first of the two was designed by the firm of McKim, Mead and White and covered two blocks bounded by 31st and 33rd streets and Seventh and Eighth avenues. The Pennsylvania Railroad long wished to build a station in New York City to compete with Grand Central Terminal of the New York Central Railroad but could not build a bridge or tunnel across the Hudson River from its terminal in Hoboken, New Jersey. In the 1890s the use of electric tracks and advances in civil engineering permitted a tunnel to be dug to Manhattan. By 1895 Alexander Cassatt, president of the railroad, made plans for a station that would be the first in the United States to accommodate large-scale use of electric traction. McKim, Mead and White designed a monumental gateway to the city modeled after the Baths of Caracalla in ancient Rome and consistent with principles of the "city beautiful" movement: they provided for a rational distribution of space and traffic, took into account the civic function of the building, and incorporated references to classical precedents. Construction began in 1902 and was hastened by legislation in 1908 banning steam locomotion on passenger trains.

At its completion in 1911 the station facilitated the orderly movement of both commuters using the Long Island Rail Road and passengers traveling to New England and southern cities along the East Coast. Access streets running through the building enabled passengers and baggage to be let off and picked up with minimal disruption of city traffic. The tracks were laid below grade about 18 feet (6 meters) under a concourse for the Long Island Rail Road. Above this was the austere, monumental waiting room of the Pennsylvania Railroad, adjacent to a concourse of glass and wrought iron. Flights of stairs connected the various levels. A row of colossal Tuscan columns extended across the eastern frontage, behind which a shopping arcade led to the waiting room. The railroad decided in 1962 to replace the station with a new one, and despite heated objections from preservationists, Pennsylvania Station was demolished in 1965. This, together with threats to properties in Greenwich Village, resulted in the city forming the Landmarks Preservation Commission in 1965 and helped to spur a national interest in preserving historic buildings. Photographs of Pennsylvania Station survive in the work of Berenice Abbott and many others.

The second Pennsylvania Station was completed in 1968 in the same location as part of a complex that also houses Madison Square Garden and offices. The railroad functions are confined to the cramped basement levels. From 1992 through 2007 several schemes to redevelop the station were proposed. A proposal of October 2007 called for demolishing the existing Madison Square Garden and station and building in its place a new station with retail space; turning the post office into an adjunct station, post office, and new sports

Facade of Pennsylvania Station on Seventh Avenue, 1915

Interior of Pennsylvania Station, 1911

arena; and constructing new office towers on adjacent properties. Pennsylvania Station is the busiest train station in North America. Its 21 tracks handle more than 7.5 million passengers a year, sometimes at the rate of 1000 patrons every 90 seconds.

Leland M. Roth, *McKim, Mead and White, Architects* (New York: Harper and Row, 1983); Hilary Ballon, *New York's Pennsylvania Stations* (New York: W. W. Norton, 2002)

Mary Beth Betts

penny arcades. Enclosed areas in amusement parks and other bustling places filled with machines offering entertainment bought by dropping a coin (usually a penny) into a slot. They were well known at Coney Island as early as the 1880s. Some machines played a tune while model locomotives and steamboats ran in place; others depicted such sights as "Munich's Beer Drinking Festival," "The Island of Pango-Pango," "Mountain Climbing in Switzerland," and "Life among the Head Hunters in Borneo." Other machines allowed customers to measure the strength of their grip, the size of their chest, or the force of their punch; they could also view pictures of the golfer Bobby Jones demonstrating good form and scenes from fights between such well-known boxers as Jack Dempsey and Gene Tunney. For a dime the "photomat" produced framed portraits. The "love teller" rated a customer's capacity as a lover on a scale from hot to cold, and in other machines risqué scenes were shown under such titles as "Artists and Models," "Red Hot Momma," "Jazz Baby," "They Forgot to Lower the Curtain," "The Girls and the Burglar," "Cleo, Queen of the Harem," "The Chemise Girl," "The Queen of Sin," and "Bare in the Bear Skin." Machines also told fortunes and provided horoscopes. To the dismay of some, penny arcades and burlesque theaters moved to the formerly elegant area around Times Square during the Depression. The arcades survived in slightly altered form into the 1960s until they finally disappeared with the advent of more sophisticated electronic machines.

Sodom by the Sea: An Affectionate History of Coney Island (Garden City, N.Y.: Doubleday, Doran, 1941); Jill Stone, *Times Square: A Pictorial History* (New York: Macmillan, 1982)

James O. Drummond

penny papers. Term used to describe the mass circulation daily newspapers that revolutionized American journalism during the 1830s; New York City played a dominant role in their development. The penny papers were intended to have broader popular appeal than the conventional political and mercantile daily newspapers that sold expensive annual subscriptions and catered to an elite readership. Horace Greeley's experimental newspaper the *Morning Post,* launched in January 1833 and sold at two cents a copy, was unsuccessful; but the *Sun,* begun in September of that year by Benjamin Day and priced at one cent, achieved an unparalleled circulation of 20,000 by 1835. Day's innovations included an avowedly nonpolitical editorial stance, a heavy emphasis on local crime and sports, and the use of NEWSBOYS to sell the *Sun* in the city's streets. The *Sun* inspired numerous imitators, the most successful of which were the *Transcript* (1834–39) and the *New York Herald* of James Gordon Bennett, Sr. Rising circulation led these newspapers to experiment with new forms of printing technology, such as steam power and presses with several cylinders. The most politically radical of the penny papers was George Henry Evans's *Man* (1834–35). Although often sympathetic to the city's working class, the *Sun,* the *Transcript,* and the *New York Herald* were racist and sometimes nativist. Their sensationalistic exploitation of murder trials led to boycotts and denunciations of the "gutter press," and their editorial attacks prompted numerous libel suits. At the same time they competed to obtain the latest and most accurate national and international news by means of horse expresses, trains, and newsboats. The *New York Tribune* (1841) and the *New York Times* (1851) inaugurated an era of more restrained penny papers. Most of these newspapers eventually raised their daily price to two or three cents. The penny papers invigorated competitive news gathering in New York City, freed the press from the necessity of political partisanship, and created a new mass readership that included workers and artisans. Many of their innovations prefigured the methods of yellow journalism and the tabloids.

Dan Schiller, *Objectivity and the News: The Public and the Rise of Commercial Journalism* (Philadelphia: University of Pennsylvania Press, 1981); Alexander Saxton, *The Rise and Fall of the White Republic: Class Politics and Mass Culture in Nineteenth-Century America* (London: Verso, 1990); Frank Luther Mott, *American Journalism: A History of Newspapers in the United States through 250 Years, 1690 to 1940* (New York: Macmillan, 1941; repr. New York: Routledge, 2000)

Steven H. Jaffe

Penthouse. Men's magazine launched in 1965 by Bob Guccione, a native of Brooklyn. It was originally introduced in England, and Guccione opened an office in New York City in 1969. The magazine's combination of nude photography and investigative journalism attracted a devoted following. Facing competition from Web sites during the 1990s, the magazine's circulation declined by nearly 50 percent, leading to bankruptcy and financial restructuring. New owners increased readership with greater emphasis on mainstream popular culture and greater Internet presence. It has offices at 2 Penn Plaza.

Robert Sanger Steel

People's Institute. Institute formed in New York City in 1897 by Charles Sprague Smith, a professor at Columbia University. It played a role in efforts by the state legislature to improve the conditions of workers. Soon it focused on leisure as an important element of social progress and the elimination of crime. With the Women's Municipal League it investigated the spread of "cheap amusements" in the city, leading to the formation of the National Board of Review of Motion Pictures in 1908. It sponsored the Cooper Union Forum and the People's Symphony concerts, designated "play streets," offered discounted theater tickets, and set up community centers in public schools. The People's Institute closed in 1934.

Robert B. Fisher, "The People's Institute of New York City, 1897–1934: Culture, Progressive Democracy, and the People" (diss., New York University, 1974)

Peter G. Buckley

people's token. Counterfeit of the bull's-eye subway token that circulated during 1986–95. Alan Campbell had made brass slugs since 1970, and he joined forces with Kim Gibbs, who owned a bicycle messenger business. Campbell produced the slugs in Paterson, New Jersey, and dropped them off at self-storage sites in Brooklyn; Gibbs's messenger business doubled as a distribution network known as the Ministry. The tokens were sold at prices ranging from 20 to 55 cents; a legitimate token was then $1.15. In 1991 the Ministry was selling 10,000 tokens a week. Campbell and Gibbs were arrested in June 1991. Campbell was convicted of two felonies and served 19 months; Gibbs was convicted of four felonies and served nearly six years. Despite the arrests, the people's token operation was continued by others; the fakes were still seen in circulation through 1995 when another design change ended their career.

See also Tokens.

John M. Kleeberg

People's Weekly World. Newspaper of the American Communist Party and historically the most influential newspaper of the American left. Known during its heyday as the *Daily Worker,* it was launched in Chicago in 1924 and moved to New York City in 1927. The newspaper wielded its greatest influence during the 1930s, when it had a circulation of more than 100,000 and defended the "Scottsboro boys." After the war many members of its staff were harassed and jailed by federal authorities. Absorbed in 1958 by the *Worker,* it resumed publication in 1968 as the *Daily World,* became the *People's Daily World* in 1986, and took its current name in 1990.

Anthony Gronowicz

Peppermint Lounge. Popular nightclub and celebrity haunt at 128 West 45th Street (1961–65), allegedly controlled by Matthew Ianniello, head of the Genovese crime family. The house band, Joey Dee and the Starliters, had a number-one hit in 1961 with the song "Peppermint Twist," and the club became closely associated with the Twist dance craze.

Caleb Smith

Pepsico. Conglomerate of snack-food and soft-drink makers and restaurateurs formed by the merger of the Pepsi-Cola Company and Frito-Lay in 1965. A forerunner was the Pepsi-Cola Company, which formulated the soft drink Pepsi-Cola in 1893. Under the direction of Alfred Steele and his wife, Joan Crawford, corporate headquarters were moved in 1948 from Long Island City in Queens to Manhattan. In 1998 the company merged with Tropicana. Another merger followed three years later when Pepsico acquired the Quaker Oats Company. As of 2008 the firm had annual sales of more than $35 billion and more than 185,000 employees. Pepsico has its headquarters in suburban Purchase, New York.

James O. Drummond

Perelman, S(idney) J(oseph) (*b* New York City, 1 Feb 1904; *d* New York City, 17 Oct 1979). Essayist and playwright. He grew up in Providence, Rhode Island, and after graduating from Brown University worked as a cartoonist for the weekly magazine *Judge* in New York City before devoting himself to writing. A master of language and wordplay, he contributed comic essays to the *New Yorker* from the 1930s to the 1970s, and with his wife, Laura West, he wrote the play *All Good Americans* (1933). He also wrote the musical *One Touch of Venus* (1943) and the play *The Beauty Part* (1962), as well as screenplays for the Marx Brothers' *Monkey Business* (1931) and *Horse Feathers* (1932); he won an Academy Award for his screenplay of *Around the World in Eighty Days* (1956). His published writings also include *Westward Ha!* (1948) and *Baby It's Cold Inside* (1970), in which he introduced the Irish poet Shameless McGonigle. Perelman lived at 134 West 11th Street from 1955 until 1966 and at the Gramercy Park Hotel (52 Gramercy Park North) from 1972.

Walter Friedman

performance art. Art form developed in the 1970s that combined elements from diverse media such as music, dance, sculpture, film, and videotape. It challenged the conception of art as a commodity and often blurred the boundary between performer and audience. A performance art event could be as short as several minutes (often dozens of short pieces were presented in an evening) or as long as several days. The roots of performance art may be traced to such art movements of the early twentieth century as constructivism, Futurism, Dada, and surrealism and more immediately to conceptual art, Happenings, and the Fluxus movement, in which Dick Higgins, Alison Knowles, and Nam June Paik were leading figures in New York City from the 1950s to the 1970s. Performance art events took place in private, public, official, and unofficial spaces: the artist Jean Dupuy presided over many events at his loft at 405 East 13th Street and later at 537 Broadway; performers from many nations appeared in festivals and performance events at the Judson Memorial Baptist Church on Washington Square; the composer Charlie Morrow once led a band of players blowing conch shells through the Port Authority Bus Terminal; and one summer afternoon the "sanitation artist" Mierle Laderman Ukeles staged a "wedding" of two barges at a refuse transfer station on the Hudson River. Dancers such as Yvonne Rainer, Trisha Brown, Simone Forti, and Steve Paxton became known for a style of movement that drew on everyday gestures, and Vito Acconci staged "self-dramatizations": these included "Following Piece," in which he followed a person on the street chosen at random, and "Conversions," in which he burned off his chest hairs and hid his penis so that he could experience the sense of not being a man.

By the mid-1970s a second generation of performance artists appeared at small performance spaces and clubs in SoHo and Tribeca such as the Kitchen on Broome Street, Artist's Space, Franklin Furnace, the Mudd Club, TR 3, and Roulette. Feminist ideas influenced the performance art of Martha Wilson, Linda Montano, and Adrian Piper, who experimented with disguises and perceptions of women's appearance, and Vanalyne Green and Joan Jonas, who combined live and videotaped performances to examine the intersection of the personal and the political. A number of performance artists began their careers in obscurity in New York City and later became nationally known, among them Wilson, Piper, Laurie Anderson, and Michael Smith. Considered the most important historian and writer on the performance arts movement, RoseLee Goldberg founded PERFORMA, a nonprofit organization dedicated to the advancement of performance art, in 2004. The following year New York City hosted the first in what would become a biennial series, PERFORMA 2005. The festival lasted three weeks and included live performances, exhibitions, installations, film screenings, and symposia that were hosted throughout the city at prominent cultural venues. PERFORMA 07 also met critical success, as did PERFORMA 09, which featured more than 150 performances from artists around the world. One performance art group, the Upright Citizens Brigade Theatre, specialized in improvisational comedy. Housed at West 26th street, it spawned numerous projects, including Improv Everywhere. Founded in 2001 this group mobilized members on the Internet to engage in large-scale, preplanned pranks. The most notorious was the annual No Pants! Subway Rides, an activity involving subway riders casually "depantsing" en masse during a rush hour subway commute. In 2009, 1200 New Yorkers participated, and several were arrested for disorderly conduct. New York City has also witnessed a resurgence in burlesque, an exotic dance that couples vaudeville entertainment and strip teasing that was prominent in the late nineteenth and early twentieth centuries. Prominent New York City performers included Julie Atlas Muz, Tigger!, the World Famous *BOB*, Dirty Martini, and newcomer Suspicious Package. Burlesque performances generally took place in East Village and Williamsburg venues such as Fez, RiFiFi, and Galapagos Art Space.

An important performance art venue was PS 122, a converted former schoolhouse in the East Village that hosted experimental art after 1980, particularly performance art that blurred the line between dance, theater, music, and performance. Other examples of theater-based performance art included Under the Radar, an annual festival hosting experimental theater from around the world, and Elevator Repair Service, a New York City–based experimental theater group. The major political performance art to emerge early in the twenty-first century was spearheaded by Reverend Billy (Bill Talen), a flamboyant faux preacher denouncing real estate overdevelopment in the city, including what he called the "Disneyfication" of Times Square. Reverend Billy founded the Church of Life after Shopping to denounce consumerism and materialism, and he ran for New York City mayor on the Green Party ticket in 2009. Although performance art flourished in its traditional bases, such as the West Village and East Village in Manhattan and Williamsburg in Brooklyn, there were many venues throughout the city.

Gregory Battcock and Robert Nickas, eds., *The Art of Performance: A Critical Anthology* (New York: E. P. Dutton, 1984)

Janos Marton, Kathleen Hulser

Performance Group. Theater troupe. It was started by director Richard Schechner in 1967 and originally based in The Performing Garage in the SoHo district at 33 Wooster Street. Drawing on the principles of the French Theatre of the Absurd, the Fluxus movement, and the happenings that in the preceding decade had explored new and innovative forms of theatrical expression, the Performance Group emphasized the organic creation of work that was both intellectually and socially challenging. Focusing on renegotiating the relationship between the audience and the performers through unconventional use of space and on the use of many forms of media in performance (the group's work was often referred to as "intermedia"), Schechner and his associates sought to break down the barriers between different artistic disciplines and combine them into a single theatrical experience. Productions ranged from presentation of new work to radical deconstructions of classical texts and were largely directed by Schechner, though others such as Joan MacIntosh, Elizabeth LeCompte, and Spalding Gray also directed and wrote for the group, often working off of cast improvisations to create their material. Among the works presented by the group were Schechner's *Dionysus in 69* (an adaptation of Euripides' *The Bacchae*) and Bertolt Brecht's *Mother Courage and Her Children* (1975). The group later dissolved, with many of its members going on to form the Wooster Group.

Patrick Barrett

Perkins, Frances (*b* Boston, 10 April 1880; *d* New York City, 14 May 1965). Reformer and public official. Brought up in Worcester, Massachusetts, and educated at Mount Holyoke College, she worked for the New York City Consumers League from 1910 and in 1912 prevailed on the state legislature to pass an important bill limiting the work week for women and children to 54 hours. Under the league's director Florence Kelley she investigated sanitary conditions in the city's bakeries and fire hazards in factories. After the Triangle Shirtwaist fire in 1911 she was an expert witness and later an inspector for the Factory Investigating Commission of the state legislature, which included Robert F. Wagner and Alfred E. Smith. In 1918 her concern over inadequate care for poor pregnant women and infants led her to help form the Maternity Center Association in New York City, for which she worked as an unpaid executive secretary. She became the first woman to hold high state office in New York in 1919 when Smith, now governor, appointed her to the Industrial Board (forerunner of the Department of Labor), citing her command of facts and figures. As Governor Franklin D. Roosevelt's industrial commissioner from 1928, her priorities included occupational health and safety, enforcement of workers' compensation, and an end to child labor. After Roosevelt became president in 1933 he named her secretary of labor, then the highest public office ever held by a woman in the nation. Perkins served until 1945, and as the head of the Committee on Economic Security she was a leading force behind the drafting of the Social Security Act. In Washington, D.C., the main building of the U.S. Department of Labor is named for her.

George Whitney Martin, *Madam Secretary: Frances Perkins* (Boston: Houghton Mifflin, 1976)

Marjory Potts

Perkins, (William) Maxwell (Everts) (*b* New York City, 20 Sept 1884; *d* Stamford, Conn., 17 June 1947). Editor. He attended Harvard University and in 1910 joined the advertising department at Charles Scribner's Sons in New York City, where he became an editor in 1914 and worked for the remainder of his career. After persuading the firm in 1919 to publish F. Scott Fitzgerald's *This Side of Paradise* he became the editor for such writers as Erskine Caldwell, Ernest Hemingway, James Jones, Ring Lardner, Marjorie Kinnan Rawlings, and Alan Paton. He is perhaps best known as the editor for Thomas Wolfe, whose manuscripts for *Look Homeward, Angel* (1929) and *Of Time and the River* (1935) he subjected to aggressive editing. Perkins's dedication to his authors and his insightful criticism set a standard for modern editors. From 1932 to 1938 Perkins lived at 246 East 49th Street in Manhattan.

A. Scott Berg, *Max Perkins, Editor of Genius* (New York: E. P. Dutton, 1978)

Marc H. Aronson

Perlea, Ionel (*b* Ograda, Romania, 13 Dec 1900; *d* New York City, 29 July 1970). Conductor. He completed his studies in music in Germany and before World War II directed the Bucharest Opera. He moved to the United States in 1949 and soon made his American debut conducting *Tristan and Isolde* at the Metropolitan Opera in New York City. In 1952 he joined the faculty of the Manhattan School of Music where he taught until the end of his life. After a heart attack and a stroke paralyzed his right hand, he continued conducting using his left hand. Perlea made more than 50 recordings of orchestral works for Vox and RCA.

Vladimir Wertsman

permits. See Public order.

Peruvians. The recorded settlement of Peruvian immigrants in New York City began in the early 1970s; there were about 40,000 in the city by the late 1980s, when many others arrived, fleeing terrorism and economic crisis in Peru. According to the Peruvian consulate about 100,000 Peruvians were living in the metropolitan area by the early 1990s. More than half of those lived in Queens, especially Sunnyside and Elmhurst. More than 27,000 more immigrants arrived in 2000. Many are professionals, especially physicians, and others work service industries, in manufacturing, and as domestic servants. Several weekly and monthly newspapers cater to Peruvians, among them *Nueva Imagen, Imagen del Sur,* and the *Prensa Peruana*. The feast of El Señor de los Milagros is celebrated with a street fair on West 53rd

Street in Manhattan during the last week of October.

Graciela M. Castex

Peter Cooper Village. Housing development in Manhattan (2000 pop. *ca* 5000), adjacent to Stuyvesant Town and bounded to the north by 23rd Street, to the east by Franklin D. Roosevelt Drive, to the south by 20th Street, and to the west by First Avenue. Planned in 1943 as part of a project to redevelop the Gashouse District, it was built by the Metropolitan Life Insurance Company to serve a middle-class constituency and was one of four such complexes they built; the others are Stuyvesant Town, Parkchester, and Riverton, and in total they provided 25,000 apartments. After more than 500 existing buildings in the area were demolished in the autumn of 1945, construction began on 21 apartment buildings ranging in height from 12 to 15 stories and containing 2495 apartments, many with a view of the East River. The development was landscaped with lawns, paths, and play areas adorned with trees and shrubs and offered 15 recreational facilities. The apartments were spacious, and rents were higher than Stuyvesant Town, attracting more prosperous tenants. The first tenants moved in on 1 August 1947, and by 1 June 1949 all the apartments had been leased. In 2008 Peter Cooper Village remained desirable because of its location, apartment size, and affordability. In October 2006 Metropolitan Life sold Stuyvesant Town and Peter Cooper Village to the real estate firm Tishman Speyer Properties for $5.4 billion, a record-high price for such a transaction. In 2010 the firm defaulted on its payments and creditors took over the property.

James O. Drummond

Peter Luger Steak House. Restaurant at 178 Broadway in Williamsburg, opened in 1887 as Charles Luger's Cafe, Billiards, and Bowling Alley. It is known for its white oak tables, wood-paneled walls, ornate pressed-tin ceilings, and what Alfred Hitchcock once called "the best steak in the world." For at least its first 120 years, it also had a reputation for not advertising and not accepting credit cards.

Kenneth T. Jackson

Peter Luger Steak House, 2009

Pete's Tavern, 2009

Pete's Tavern. Oldest continually operating drinking establishment in New York City, opened in 1864 on the corner of 18th Street and Irving Place, near Gramercy Park. The tavern once offered nightly lodging and stables for horses in addition to food and drink. It was a favorite meeting place of politicians connected with Tammany Hall, which was situated a few blocks south. At the turn of the century O. Henry lived in a nearby boarding house and spent many hours at the tavern, where he wrote *The Gift of the Magi* (1905). During Prohibition (1920–33) the front of the tavern was converted into a sham florist shop while in the back rooms, entered through a dummy refrigerator door, a speakeasy catered to local politicians. Pete's Tavern has been used in many television commercials and films, including parts of Milos Forman's *Ragtime* (1981).

Chad Ludington

Petit, Philippe (*b* Nemours, France, 13 August 1949). High-wire artist known for his 1974 walk across the twin towers in the World Trade Center. With a cable strung a quarter-mile above the street, 24-year-old Petit crossed seven times in 45 minutes before he surrendered to waiting police. Petit had been planning the crossing even before the towers were built. He said he had hatched the idea in 1968, when he was saw an article about the plans for the towers. Petit's adventure was made into a documentary film, *Man on Wire* (2008), which won an Oscar in 2009 in that category.

Meryl Cates

petroleum. The petroleum industry in New York City dates to 1859, when John D. Rockefeller, a partner in a small refinery, opened a sales office in the city after oil was discovered near Titusville, Pennsylvania. His brother William joined the firm and in 1867 moved to the city to handle domestic sales, develop foreign markets, and aggressively buy up shares in oil concerns. The firm eventually became the banker for the Standard Oil Alliance, which disbanded in 1882 to form several companies, including the Standard Oil Company of New York (Socony). William Rockefeller was named president of Socony and soon merged with the firm of Charles Pratt. By 1899 Socony was the most important company in the Standard Oil network. In later years the growth of the oil industry in New York City was hindered by adverse state laws governing joint stock companies and partnerships. Despite these obstacles the city's oil businesses flourished. Many oil corporations availed themselves of more lenient corporate laws in New Jersey and Delaware while transacting most of their business in New York City. Among these were two of the giants in the industry, Mobil Oil and the Exxon Corporation, descendents of Socony, although both these firms moved away in 1990, later merging to form ExxonMobil. Oil refineries operated in the city from the 1860s, and in the early twenty-first century several remained on Newtown Creek, where ExxonMobil was involved with one of the largest underground oil spills in history.

Oil's First Century (Cambridge, Mass.: Harvard Graduate School of Business Administration, 1960)

Bennett H. Wall

Petrosino, Joseph (*b* Padula [now in Italy], 30 April 1860; *d* Palermo, Sicily, 12 March 1909). Detective. He immigrated to the

United States in 1873, settling in New York City, and became a police officer on 19 October 1883 and a detective on 20 July 1895. In December 1908 he was appointed to lead a secret service charged with eliminating the criminal organization known as the Black Hand. His work disproved the widespread notion that there was an international criminal syndicate based in Sicily that had a branch in the city. Petrosino was murdered while checking criminal records in Palermo during a deportation inquiry. The case remained unsolved; the most likely suspect, Don Vito Cascio Ferro, died in 1943. A small plaza just north of the old police headquarters at 240 Centre Street is dedicated to Petrosino's memory.

Arrigo Petacco, *Joe Petrosino,* trans. Charles Lam Markmann (New York: Macmillan, 1974)

Mary Elizabeth Brown

Pfaff's Cellar. Basement restaurant and beer hall opened in 1856 by German restaurateur Charley Pfaff at 647 Broadway, then within the entertainment district. It became the meeting place of a famous roundtable led by Henry Clapp, editor and founder of the countercultural newspaper the *Saturday Press.* The members (as many as 30) called themselves bohemians, perhaps the first in the United States, and included actresses Ada Clare and Adah Isaacs Menken, journalist Horace Greeley, novelist William Dean Howells, political cartoonist Thomas Nast, and poet Walt Whitman. Pfaff's closed after the Civil War with northward expansion of the city. The building is extant and renovated.

Val Ginter

Pfizer. Firm of pharmaceutical manufacturers formed in Brooklyn in 1849 by Charles Pfizer and Charles Erhart, chemists trained in Germany. During the nineteenth century its main factory was at Bartlett Street and Harrison Avenue in Williamsburg, then a mostly German area; its administrative office was at 81 Maiden Lane in Manhattan. The firm was known for the fine quality of its chemicals, especially its santonin, tartaric acid, and citric acid, which it sold in bulk to pharmaceutical wholesalers. It was incorporated in 1900 but remained essentially a family business until 1942. During World War I the firm developed a method of producing citric acid with sugar (later molasses) rather than imported limes, and in the 1930s and 1940s its research led to the production of vitamins. During World War II the firm was part of a consortium led by the government to produce penicillin, which was scarce. The president of the company, John L. Smith, risked government sanctions by supplying penicillin to the physician Leo Lowe at Brooklyn Jewish Hospital. After the war the major products of the firm were vitamins and antibiotics (including Terramycin) rather than iodides, mercurials, and citric acid. The marketing of pharmaceuticals abroad began in 1946. Under its president John McKeen the firm during the 1950s and 1960s acquired manufacturers of petroleum, paints, rubber, composite metals, plastics, cosmetics, toiletries, and baby care products. International headquarters opened in 1961 on Second Avenue and 42nd Street. During the 1970s and 1980s John Powers and Ed Pratt oversaw the sale of divisions unrelated to the production of pharmaceutical, agricultural, consumer, and chemical products. The firm made 46 percent of its sales abroad in 1989, by which time it was the only pharmaceutical firm that continued to manufacture its products in New York City. Pfizer maintained an active relationship with New York City during the late twentieth century; it created affordable housing at the company's original facility in Williamsburg, and in 1989 donated and renovated an adjacent building to be used for the Beginning with Children Charter School. In return for maintaining and expanding its operations in New York City, in 2003 the administration of Mayor Michael Bloomberg granted Pfizer $46 million in tax cuts, but four years later Pfizer announced that it would close its Williamsburg facility, eliminating 600 jobs. In January 2008 Pfizer began to solicit proposals from private developers for the redevelopment of the Williamsburg site, with an emphasis on affordable housing and job creation. In response, Assemblyman Vito Lopez began calling for the city to acquire the site by eminent domain. The site's future in the early twenty-first century remained uncertain. Pfizer itself accrued $48.6 billion in revenues in 2007, with $7.5 billion spent on research and development.

Pfizer Quality: 100th Anniversary, 1849–1949 (New York: Pfizer, 1949); Samuel Mines, *Pfizer: An Informal History* (New York: Pfizer, 1978)

David J. S. King

pharmaceuticals. The first pharmaceutical firm in New York City was formed in 1781 by Effingham Lawrence and survived well into the twentieth century as Schieffelin and Company. Five druggists were listed in the city directory of 1786: Lawrence and the firm of Besley and Goodwin on Pearl (Queen) Street, and Francis Wainwright, Timothy Hurse, and Oliver Hull in Hanover Square. By the early nineteenth century druggists stocked not only chemicals used to prepare medicines but such goods as glassware, oils, and paints. The most important of these early firms included Lawrence and Keese, J. A. and W. B. Post, Thomas S. Clark, John and William Penfold, John M. Bradhurst, R. and S. Murray, Silas Carle, and John C. Morrison. Medicines were produced in small laboratories attached to druggists' shops, and some firms eventually specialized in making common preparations on a large scale. Most pharmacies derived their preparations from plants and found a market for herbal remedies such as jalap, ipecac, sarsaparilla, and balsam. Firms kept pace with their European counterparts, introducing European drugs in the city soon after they were developed. In 1825, only five years after Pierre Joseph Pelletier and Joseph B. Caventou published their methods for isolating quinine from cinchona bark to treat malaria, John Currie set up a factory to produce quinine sulfate in New York City. Quinine extracted from cinchona bark remained an important product until synthetic antimalarial drugs were developed in the 1940s.

In the mid-nineteenth century the city became the national center of the pharmaceutical industry. Patent medicines such as William Brandeth's Life-Extension pills were manufactured and advertised there. The New York College of Pharmacy opened in 1829, and the firm of Olcott and McKesson (later McKesson and Robbins) was formed in 1833 to produce gelatin-coated pills. From 1846 a naval hospital in Brooklyn operated a laboratory to assure the purity of its medicines; production there increased between 1852 and 1856 during the tenure of E. R. Squibb, who formed a company in Brooklyn to continue his work after the naval laboratory ceased to be funded. In 1849 the firm of Pfizer and Company was formed in Brooklyn by Charles Pfizer and Charles F. Erhart, chemists trained in Germany. A shop for laboratory supplies was opened in 1851 at Third Avenue and 18th Street by Bernard G. Amend, once an assistant to the influential German chemist Justus Liebig; it was expanded by Amend and Carl Eimer in 1856 into one of the first prescription laboratories in the area. In 1885 Charles Robbins formed the New York Quinine and Chemical Works, which became a leading manufacturer of quinine. Foreign companies were attracted to the city by its port; among them was E. Merck, a German firm that established an agency in the city in 1890. The large local market prompted the William R. Warner Company and many other American firms to open sales offices, and the city became the largest center for distribution in the country.

During World War I American firms were spurred to develop synthetic substitutes for raw materials that had become difficult to import, such as limes for the manufacture of citric acid. After German companies (which had dominated the industry) and their patents ceased to be protected by law, the American branch of the Bayer Company was acquired by Sterling Products, incorporated in the city in 1901. American firms grew rapidly after the war and established active research laboratories. In the early twenty-first century several firms headquartered in the city, including Pfizer (which acquired Warner–Lambert in 2000) and Bristol–Myers Squibb (formed by a 1989 merger) remained national leaders, although commercial manufacturing, research, and development gradually moved elsewhere. The city continued to be a center for pharmaceuticals administration, marketing, and finance, and educational institutions such as Rockefeller University and Columbia University remained top biological research and development centers.

William Haynes, *American Chemical Industry* (New York: D. Van Nostrand, 1945–54); Tom Mahoney, *The Merchants of Life: An Account of the American Pharmaceutical Industry* (New York: Harper and Brothers, 1959)

David J. S. King

Phelps Stokes Fund. Foundation organized in 1911 with a bequest from Caroline Phelps Stokes (1854–1909) to improve low-income housing in New York City and expand educational opportunities for American Indians, black Americans, Africans, and poor whites; it is one of the oldest foundations in the city. Members of the Phelps Stokes family served on the board of directors and played a major role in shaping the agenda of the fund, especially I. N. Phelps Stokes (member of the board from 1911 to 1938) and his brother Anson Phelps Stokes, Jr. (member from 1911 to 1946). Some of the first initiatives were studies of educational policy, aid to southern black colleges, and competitions for better housing design in New York City. The fund also subsidized James Ford's research for *Slums and Housing* (1936). After World War II it concentrated on social policy, seeking to better race relations and to encourage racially integrated housing in New York City. During the 1970s and 1980s it shifted its focus to broadening educational opportunities for American Indians and black South Africans. As of 2008 it ran the Smart Teachers as Role Models (STAR) program, which with the cooperation of the University of Michigan aims to diversify the population of future teachers.

Deborah S. Gardner

philanthropy. Philanthropy during the colonial period generally supplemented government funding and emphasized religion; notable gifts, often from Britain, to Trinity Church, King's College (later Columbia University), and New York Hospital were designed to advance the Church of England in America and met with criticism from New Yorkers who adhered to other religious traditions. Although the American Revolution created conditions that encouraged an expansion of private philanthropy, most early social welfare institutions received more government than philanthropic funds. These included the Humane Society (1787), which helped debtors and the poor; the African Free School (1787); New York Hospital (from 1791) and its Bloomingdale Asylum for the Insane (1821); the Free School Society (1805); the New York Orphan Society (1807); and the Society for the Prevention of Pauperism (1818). New York governments also subsidized colleges, and after 1815 the city provided space to learned societies and museums. Jacksonians, however, condemned such public subsidies as wasteful indulgence of dilettantes and evicted the societies in 1831, just as they cut municipal subsidies to nonprofit charities and sought to shift responsibility for social welfare from the city to private organizations, including workers' mutual benefit organizations.

Protestant revivals after 1816 made New York City the national center of a "benevolent empire" of new philanthropies such as the American Bible Society (1816), the American Tract Society (1825), and the New York Sunday School Union. Arthur and Lewis Tappan and other evangelicals financed abolitionists and many western colleges. Within the city, evangelicals (often women) created the Association for Improving the Condition of the Poor (1843) and the Five Points House of Industry (1854) as well as several Protestant schools and homes for orphans, widows, unwed mothers, the handicapped, and the unemployed. Nonevangelicals objected that these were sectarian, so Catholics (especially orders of nuns) and Jews accordingly created their own institutions (orphanages, schools, hospitals, and community centers), which evangelicals criticized in their turn. In 1875 the state sought to resolve religious conflicts by legislating that orphans go to institutions "of the same religious faith as the parents." Episcopalians generously supported many institutions within the mainstream; Quakers developed notable institutions for blacks and others excluded from the mainstream. From the 1870s William E. Dodge joined with other Protestant philanthropists in the national anti-"obscenity" and anti–birth control campaigns of Anthony Comstock's New York Society for the Suppression of Vice; Margaret Sanger and advocates of birth control eventually responded with the country's first family planning clinic in 1916.

Large fortunes enabled individual philanthropists to take striking initiatives. Robert Richard Randall's 1801 bequest enabled religious leaders to open Sailors' Snug Harbor, a home for elderly and disabled sailors on Staten Island. John Jacob Astor's 1849 will provided $400,000 for a library; Peter Cooper endowed the Cooper Union for the Advancement of Science and Art (1859) with wealth from his glue business. Individual gifts also created the Lenox Library (1870); the Pratt Institute (1886); limited-rent houses (1878–90) (predecessors of those funded by Alfred T. White of Brooklyn); Carnegie Hall (1891), which combined a gift with income-earning provision of service; and Rockefeller University (1901). From the 1880s several philanthropists made possible the expansion of Columbia University.

From the 1860s Democrats and Republicans alike restored the city's earlier pattern of government subsidies. The Central Park Commission provided city-owned land and subsidies to such private cultural institutions as the Metropolitan Museum of Art and the American Museum of Natural History; similar aid went later to the New York Zoological Society, the New York Botanical Garden, the Brooklyn Museum, and the Brooklyn Botanical Garden. Under William M. "Boss" Tweed's "welfare program" of the late 1860s, private welfare organizations received subsidies from the city.

Women played key roles in nineteenth-century philanthropy and led the two most important efforts to reorganize it at the century's end. The State Charities Aid Association, under Louisa Lee Schuyler, monitored both government agencies and private charities. In 1899 it argued that appropriations to private charities discouraged them from gaining private support and deprived public hospitals of needed funds. The Charity Organization Society of the City of New York (1882), founded by Josephine Shaw Lowell, coordinated Protestant charities (and to some extent Jewish and Catholic ones) through the annual *Charities Directory* and a clearinghouse for aid applications at the central United Charities Building (donated by John S. Kennedy). Its New York School of Social Work worked closely with the Russell Sage Foundation. Parallel and separate Jewish organizations included the United Hebrew Charities, which had its own building not far from the United Charities Building. The Catholic Charities of the Archdiocese of New York (1920) and a similar organization in the Diocese of Brooklyn appeared at the same time. Organization along religious lines, especially those providing services for children and families, characterized New York City philanthropy, as did the presence of strong mutual benefit organizations ranging from the Workmen's Circle, which served Yiddish-speaking residents, to black churches.

Throughout much of the nineteenth century the law and the courts of New York State discouraged endowments, forcing nonprofit organizations to rely on annual contributions. "Charity balls" grew so prominent by the 1880s that they were less important in fund raising than in establishing membership in "society." New legislation passed after the disputed probate of the estate of Samuel J. Tilden made it easier to create endowments and for the first time legalized general-purpose foundations. During the first half of the twentieth century the several Rockefeller and Carnegie foundations led others in making New York City the national center for foundation activity and connecting philanthropic work in medicine, science, higher education, and the arts in the United States with that in the rest of the world.

Some philanthropic efforts aimed at specific religious communities: Beth Israel Hospital and Yeshiva University were identified with Jews from eastern Europe; Catholics built Fordham and St. John's universities and an extensive system of parochial schools; and each religious community developed its own seminaries. Yet on the whole large-scale philanthropy did not become organized along ethnic lines, even as black, Latin American, and Asian New Yorkers became increasingly prominent. Some Catholics and Jews, like many Protestants, shifted their focus from religion to the more secular fields of education, medicine, science, and the arts. The highly publicized philanthropy of J. P. Morgan, Henry Clay Frick, and others benefited art museums; the Museum of Modern Art, the Solomon R. Guggenheim Museum, and the Whitney Museum of American Art celebrated art that appealed to their donors; Rockefeller family philanthropy created the Cloisters and the Asia Society and contributed to Lincoln Center; and banker Robert Lehman put a personal stamp on the Metropolitan Museum of Art by donating thousands of works of art to its collection. Another group of major donors supported the renewal of old institutions, notably Elmer Holmes Bobst and Laurence Tisch (New York University) and Lila Acheson Wallace and Brooke Astor (the New York Public Library).

After World War II New York City's position as the country's philanthropic center grew stronger when the library of the Russell Sage Foundation evolved into the Foundation Center in 1947, the Ford Foundation (in 1953) and others moved to the city, and big business developed corporate foundations. At the same time national policy reinforced the city's strong traditions of government and private philanthropy. Antipoverty programs begun in the 1960s (including Harlem Youth Opportunities Limited, Mobilization for Youth, and the Bedford Stuyvesant Restoration Corporation) received support from the Ford Foundation and private donors. By the 1960s social service organizations became more dependent on federal than on municipal or private funds. In the 1980s and later, "Friends" groups, supported by both philanthropy and business, formed for many city parks, but 31 of the city's museums and performing arts organizations continued to rely somewhat on municipal subsidies.

Together, government and private philanthropy created in New York City the nation's largest nonprofit sector of privately managed educational, cultural, medical, and social service organizations. By the early twenty-first century the 9000 largest New York City nonprofits spent a total of $43 billion and provided one job in every seven, more than 525,000, and were growing quickly. They continued to receive a third or more of their income from current philanthropy and endowments and to benefit from the work of thousands of volunteers. The metropolitan region accounted for 17 percent of the nation's nonprofit activity, twice its share of population. New York philanthropy continued to be diverse and decentralized, although the rise of wealthy philanthropists on the West Coast to some extent balanced New York's position by the early twenty-first century.

See also Foundations.

David C. Hammack

Philip Morris. Firm of tobacco and food processors. Initially a British firm, it opened its first branch in the United States on Broad Street in New York City in 1902 and became a publicly traded U.S. company in 1919. After moving several times during the next few years it set up headquarters in 1929 at Fifth Avenue near 21st Street. The firm and its products soon became widely known through a number of clever advertising themes, including the "call for Philip Morris" by Johnny the bellhop (first given in the lobby of the Hotel New Yorker in 1933) and the "Marlboro man" (begun in 1955 and lasting into the 1990s). Marlboro became the most popular brand of cigarette in the world, and during the 1960s the firm expanded, buying several tobacco companies in Britain and the United States. By the 1970s the company entered other industries, including brewing and soft-drink and paper manufacturing. The firm erected a 26-story building at Park Avenue and 41st Street for its headquarters in 1980. During the next decade it made several leveraged buyouts that permitted it to acquire such firms as General Foods and Kraft. To combat antismoking legislation it made a determined and highly controversial defense of the "right to smoke." Throughout the last decade of the twentieth century Philip Morris faced various lawsuits brought by current and former smokers. Because of the pressure of a federal investigation the company admitted in 1999 that smoking increases the risk of cancer and other serious illnesses. It later launched a corporate responsibility initiative that assists smokers wanting to quit and encourages parents to talk to their children about the dangers of smoking. In 2003 Philip Morris changed its name to the Altria Group in an effort to distance itself from tobacco litigation. In 2008 the Altria Group moved its headquarters to Virginia.

Peter Taylor, *The Smoke Ring: Tobacco, Money, and Multinational Politics* (New York: Pantheon, 1984); Richard Kluger, *Ashes to Ashes: America's Hundred-Year Cigarette War, the Public Health, and the Unabashed Triumph of Philip Morris* (New York: Vintage Books USA, 1997)

James Bradley

Philipse, Frederick [Flypsen, Vredrych] (*b* Bolswaert [now Bolsward], Netherlands, 1626; *d* New York City, 6 Nov 1702). Political and mercantile leader. He settled in New Amsterdam in the 1640s as a carpenter, or master builder, rose rapidly within the community, and by 1658 began purchasing land in Manhattan. His marriage about late 1662 to Margaret Hardenbroeck De Vries, a wealthy widow from a family engaged in international shipping, increased his wealth, his fleet, and his contacts, and he became a prosperous merchant with a residence on De Brower Straat (Stone Street). When the English came to power, he swore allegiance to the Crown and anglicized the spelling of his name. His loyalty and wealth brought appointment to many local offices, including a seat on the governor's council from 1675 to 1699. During Leisler's Rebellion he withdrew from politics. His overseas activities included the importation of slaves and trade with pirates from Madagascar. With the profits he expanded his land holdings in Manhattan along with property to the north, and he obtained a patent for the Manor of Philipsburgh that recognized his control over lands from the northern tip of Manhattan to the Croton River. He adopted his first wife's daughter, Maria, renamed Eva, who later married Jacobus Van Cortlandt, the brother of his second wife, Catherine (1652–1730). He gave the couple a farm on land that now makes up a large part of Van Cortlandt Park.

"Frederick Philipse and the Madagascar Trade," *New-York Historical Society Quarterly* 50 (1971), 354–74; Patricia U. Bonomi, *A Factious People: Politics and Society in Colonial New York* (New York: Columbia University Press, 1971)

Jacob Judd

Phipps Houses. Nonprofit foundation formed about 1905 by the philanthropist Henry Phipps to build model tenements. Its first undertaking was a tenement designed by Grosvenor Atterbury on East 31st Street in Manhattan. In 1911 it built a similar complex between West 63rd and 64th streets in Manhattan (Whitfield and King, architects); the interior design influenced plans for other low-income apartments. In 1928 the foundation built the Phipps Garden Apartments in Sunnyside Gardens, a complex of four- to six-story buildings surrounding a courtyard, designed by Isador Rosenfeld. Phipps Houses was one of few associations of its kind to survive the Depression and changing real estate markets after World War II. In 1973 it built the Lambert Houses, a six-story apartment complex in the Bronx with a shopping plaza and parking garage, designed by the firm of Davis, Brody and situated on Boston Road between Bronx Park South and East Tremont Avenue. Phipps Houses continue to sponsor and develop housing for low- and moderate-income families in the early twenty-first century.

Richard Plunz, *A History of Housing in New York City* (New York: Columbia University Press, 1990)

Eric Wm. Allison

Phoenix House Foundation. Nonprofit agency formed in New York City in 1967 that treats teenagers and adults for drug and alcohol abuse. It was one of the first agencies to give treatment designed to address the underlying causes of addiction and to use only medical supervision and psychological, vocational, and educational counseling. The foundation offers drug education and after-school drug intervention programs in schools as well as special programs for working adults, prisoners, and the homeless. In the early twenty-first century it had more than 30 residential and outpatient programs in the New York City area and treated about 2500 people a day. Its main office is at 164 West 74th Street in Manhattan.

Gilbert Tauber

Phoenixville. Name applied to BULLS HEAD when it was rebuilt after a fire at a seventeenth-century tavern.

photographic agencies. Firms supplying photographs to publishers and individuals appeared in New York City soon after photography was introduced. From the 1850s customers at the portrait gallery of MATHEW B. BRADY on Broadway were able to purchase photographs of well-known individuals that they selected from albums; Brady was unable to keep up with demand and had his most popular photographs printed by the firm of E. and H. T. Anthony. Edward Anthony (1818–88) and his brother Henry (1814–84) later distributed Brady's photographs, including many from his series documenting the Civil War. After 1888 the Anthonys' firm merged with the Scovill Manufacturing Company, a maker of photographic supplies, to form Ansco. Many commercial photographers earned a steady income documenting the architecture of the city. Some of the most prominent firms that provided architectural photographs were those of Underwood and Underwood, Joseph and Percy Byron, George P. Hall and Sons, Wurts Brothers, Gottscho–Schleisner, and F. S. Lincoln. Thomas Airviews, formed in 1936, was for more than five decades the best-known firm engaged in aerial photography: a collection of its prints and negatives at the New-York Historical Society includes some documenting the construction of Stuyvesant Town, Rockefeller Center, and the World Trade Center.

The popularity of photographic essays in magazines such as *Life* and *Look* led to the formation of several photographic agencies, including MAGNUM PHOTOS and Black Star. Magnum, formed in 1947 by the freelance photographers Robert Capa, Henri Cartier–Bresson, George Rodger, David (Chim) Seymour, and William Vandivert, became instrumental in protecting photographers' rights. Members retained control over the use of their photographs and ownership of their negatives; the high quality of their work attracted publishers. Stock photographic agencies were formed during the 1930s to supply photographs to publications. The BETTMANN ARCHIVE (1935) grew by purchasing collections from photographers and from newspapers that had ceased publication. In 1954 Helen Gee opened the Limelight Gallery/Cafe, the first gallery in the city devoted to photography, which became a popular meeting place for photographers before closing in 1961. The success of this space along with the Witkin Gallery (1969), run by Lee D. Witkin, led to the opening of other galleries. At the beginning of the twenty-first century more than 50 photographic agencies operated in New York City. Though they varied in size and focus, most agencies continued to concentrate on PHOTOJOURNALISM while relying on providing photographs for annual reports and other projects with large budgets. Stock photographic agencies continued to be an important source of historic photographs.

William Welling, *Photography in America: The Formative Years, 1839–1900* (New York: Thomas Y. Crowell, 1978); Peter Bacon Hales, *Silver Cities: The Photography of American Urbanization, 1839–1915* (Philadelphia: Temple University Press, 1984)

Dale L. Neighbors

photography. Always a world leader in photography, New York City was the site of experiments in late 1839 in daguerreotyping, a process for making a unique but reversed image on a plate coated with silver. Some of the first daguerreotypes of city scenes were made by Samuel F. B. Morse. John W. Draper (1811–82), a professor of chemistry at the University of the City of New York (now New York University), also claimed to be successful with the process (no examples by either survive). A negative-positive process on paper devised in 1839 attracted little interest in the city but was used by the French photographer Victor Prévost (active 1820–81) to photograph architecture in the city. In the following decades making daguerreotype portraits, sometimes by students of Morse, became a flourishing business. Concentrated along Broadway between Fulton and Canal streets, salons were opened by highly regarded portraitists, among them MATHEW B. BRADY and in the 1860s Jeremiah Gurney and the brothers Henry and Charles Meade. Eventually more than 70 firms offered a range of facilities and prices, and in 1856 the *Cosmopolitan Art Journal* reported that even "the humblest cottage" had "some beautiful image of friend and relative." During the 1840s ancillary businesses in the city made and distributed equipment and chemicals, besides photographs. The city also became a center for publishing photographs and works on photography: the first portfolio of portraits of national figures (1847), based on photographs by John Plumbe, Jr. (1809–57); *The History and Practice of the Art of Photography* (1849), by Henry Hunt Snelling (1817–97); the *Daguerreian Journal* (1850; later *Humphrey's Journal*); Brady's *Gallery of Illustrious Americans* (1851); and the *Photographic Art Journal* (1851), edited by Snelling.

About 1851 a process was introduced by which albumen paper prints were made from a negative of collodion and silver salts on glass. This supplanted the earlier processes and remained the most commonly used one in the city until the late 1880s. Portraitists in New York City were the first in the nation to use the new technology for commercial purposes. They responded to sharp competition and periods of economic depression between 1860 and 1890 by offering a choice of processes and a range of sizes and formats: ambrotypes, tintypes, cartes-de-visite, and cabinet- and imperial-sized portraits. Some photographers, including Brady and Napoleon Sarony, sold small and large prints of well-known people (President Abraham Lincoln maintained that a carte-de-visite portrait made during his visit to the city on 27 February 1860 by Brady helped him to win the presidential election). Sarony and one of his competitors, Jose Mora (active in the 1880s), paid well-known figures in the theater for the right to make and sell their portraits. After the Civil War periodicals published in the city relied increasingly on photographs, first as models for drawn illustrations and later in direct reproduction. The first lithographic transcription of a photograph for a newspaper appeared in the *Daily Graphic* in 1873. The halftone process plate was introduced in the late 1880s, and publishers soon became interested in recording with camera images what the *Illustrated American* called "contemporaneous history." Such images were eventually the most widely used kind of illustration, especially valued in the growing field of advertising. The development of new technology for printing coincided with the advent of social documentation in the slums of New York City. Among the first books to contain reproductions from halftone process plates was Jacob A. Riis's *How the Other Half Lives* (1890).

Scenes of the city were often photographed, especially views of midtown Manhattan, the Bowery and Broadway, and the waterfront along the East River. Photographs of the city were frequently used by real estate developers and illustrators and were also sold for use in stereoscopes. Well-known landscape photographers included Edward T. Anthony (1818–88) and John S. Johnston (active in the 1870s). After simplified equipment and procedures were introduced in the late 1880s views of the city were photographed by amateurs, who organized such groups as the Society of Amateur Photographers (later the Camera Club of New York) to promote pictorialism, or the practice of photography as an art form. Among those who photographed buildings and street life in the late nineteenth century were Alice Austen, Robert Bracklow (1849–1920), and ALFRED STIEGLITZ; they favored picturesque scenes reproduced in a "straight" style, with relatively little manual or chemical manipulation. As pictorialism evolved under Stieglitz's auspices within the group known as the Photo-Secession, some artistic photographers did use soft focus and hand retouching in their city views. Alvin Langdon Coburn (1882–1956) and Karl Struss (1886–1980) were members of the Photo-Secession who sought to symbolize rather than depict the unique vitality of the city. Commercial photographs of the city continued to be produced by firms such as that of the Byron family (Joseph, 1844–1923, and Percy, 1878–1959), which supplied private patrons and publishers with photographs of many aspects of urban life, including the homes of the wealthy. Just before the turn of the twentieth century commercial portraiture suffered from a depressed economy and from the popularity of snapshots. It was revitalized by Gertrude Käsebier and Zaida Ben-Yusuf (active between 1896 and 1915), whose studios on Fifth Avenue catered to the wealthy and set an elegant style imitated into the 1920s by Arnold Genthe (1868–1942) and others. Documentary photographs by LEWIS HINE and by JESSIE TARBOX BEALS were made in the early twentieth century to promote the social policies of the Progressive era.

After 1912 the pictorialist movement gave way to a modernist aesthetic that relied on abstraction and geometric form to portray the city as a vital center. Some of the best-known examples of the clean, precise modernist style occur in the early work of Charles Sheeler and Paul Strand (1890–1976), who photographed streets and buildings in the years surrounding 1920; together they made the first short art film about the city, *New York the Magnificent* (1921; later known as *Manhatta*). During the 1920s notable works by amateur photographers included portraits by Doris Ulmann (1882–1934) of Sinclair Lewis and other literary figures and by Carl Van Vechten of prominent black New Yorkers. Celebrity portraiture was later taken over by photographers working for magazines like *Vogue* and *Vanity Fair* and became linked with fashion photography. The sleekness of photographs by Edward Steichen and the surreal mystique of those by George Platt Lynes (1907–55) inspired such later photographers as RICHARD AVEDON (1923–2004), Arnold Newman (*b* 1918), and Irving Penn (*b* 1917) to develop unique styles in their work with celebrities. Hine was one of few in the 1920s who considered working people suitable subjects for art photography. Neighborhood life was documented by such portraitists as JAMES VAN DER ZEE (1886–1983), who photographed blacks in business and the professions in Harlem.

The establishment in Manhattan of major news bureaus, advertising agencies, and fashion and entertainment firms between 1925 and 1950 led to a greater role for photography in publishing. The color process Kodachrome was invented in 1935 by the musicians and amateur chemists Leopold Godowsky and Leopold Mannes, and after World War II color processes expanded and became increasingly popular. PHOTOGRAPHIC AGENCIES were formed, and Black Star, Underwood and Underwood, and MAGNUM PHOTOS expanded the business and supplied specialized products.

Interest in social documentation revived during the 1930s. Late in the decade photographers abandoned pictorialist conventions to record the street life of working-class neighborhoods in projects under the aegis of the PHOTO LEAGUE and the Works Progress Administration. Hine, BERENICE ABBOTT (1898–1991), and Margaret Bourke-White (1904–71) were commissioned in the 1930s to photograph new skyscrapers, notably the Empire State, RCA, and Chrysler buildings; Abbott used her photographs to examine architectural connections and transformations in *Changing New York* (1939), for which text was provided by the art historian Elizabeth McCausland. In some of his last photographs of buildings in midtown Manhattan, Stieglitz expressed his deepest feelings about the city. At this time Walker Evans began photographing urban street scenes and street signs. Picture books about the city by such photographers as Alexander Alland (1902–89) and Andreas Feininger (*b* 1906) were also popular.

The launching of the magazines *Fortune, Life,* and *Look* in the late 1920s and 1930s helped to make New York City the center of PHOTOJOURNALISM, which attracted among others Bourke-White, Feininger, and W. Eugene Smith (1918–78). The demand for photographs was great, and several photographers escaping upheaval in Europe found work in New York City–based publications as photojournalists, including ALFRED EISENSTAEDT, Philippe Halsman (1906–79), and André Kertész (1894–1985). City life also attracted unaffiliated photographers who supported their projects with exhibitions, publications, teaching, and grants. Helen Levitt (*b* 1918), Lisette Model (1906–83), and Walter Rosenblum (1919–2006) photographed street life almost exclusively; DIANE ARBUS (1923–71) and Bruce Davidson (*b* 1933) explored both public and more intimate happenings. A department of photography was set up in 1939 at the Museum of Modern Art, and photographs became widely considered worthy of collection and exhibition by other museums, galleries, dealers, and auction houses, some of which specialized in photographs. Encouraged by the respect accorded to photography, many photographers experimented with color, multiple exposure, and unusual scale; artists began to combine photographs with paint and other graphic media. Courses in photography and the history of photography were introduced into the curricula of major universities and art schools in the city, and publishers offered a greater number of books on photography. Centers for teaching, publication, and exhibition were established, among them the International Center for Photography, and the Aperture Foundation moved to the city in 1980. As new electronic imaging techniques were developed in the mid-1990s older methods of producing images by silver-based techniques were supplanted by digital methods. Black and white images became less common, as both amateur snapshot and professional photographers turned to color, which began to enliven newspaper reportage. In the early twenty-first century, with more than 100 galleries devoted to showing photographs, New York City continued to attract photographers and to be a center for producing, publishing, and distributing photographic art.

Andreas Feininger and Susan E. Lyman, *The Face of New York* (New York: Crown, 1954); Berenice Abbott, *Changing New York,* with text by Elizabeth McCausland (New York: E. P. Dutton, 1939; repr. New York: Dover, 1973, as *New York in the Thirties, as Photographed by Berenice Abbott*); Roy Meredith, *Mathew Brady's Portrait of an Era* (New York: W. W. Norton, 1982); Alan Trachtenberg, *Reading American Photographs: Images as History, Mathew Brady to Walker Evans* (New York: Hill and Wang, 1989); Raymond Jacobs, *My New York* (New York: Pointed Leaf Press, 2006)

Naomi Rosenblum

photojournalism. The use of photographs to convey news became important in New York City during the 1860s. *Frank Leslie's Illustrated News* and *Harper's Weekly* regularly illustrated articles with wood engravings adapted from daguerreotype portraits and other photographs. Photomechanical methods, in which photographic images are used directly in the preparation of ink printing plates, were employed as early as 1873 by experimental processes in the *Daily Graphic,* but photographs were not widely used in newspapers until a patent was granted in 1878 for the halftone process, which reduced continuous tones into patterns of dots and produced images of a quality similar to that of original photographs. By the turn of the twentieth century photojournalism was well established. Among early professionals were several women, including JESSIE TARBOX BEALS, the first female press photographer, who opened a studio in the city in 1905 and contributed often to the *New York Herald* and the *New York Tribune,* and Francis Benjamin Johnston (1864–1952), who was well known for her work before World War I and worked on many freelance assignments, including a documentation of the building of the New Theatre in 1909.

Photojournalism changed after small, handheld cameras with fast lenses were introduced in the 1920s, permitting photographers to take candid photographs and to cover news events as they happened. The new style of photojournalism led to the success of picture magazines, most of which had headquarters in the city and began publication during the 1930s and 1940s. One of the first was *Fortune* (1929), which engaged as its first staff photographer Margaret Bourke-White (1904–71), a former pupil at the Clarence White School of Photography who was admired for her simple, bold compositions. She executed many photographic essays on industrial and social subjects and was one of the first four staff photographers for *Life,* which used her photograph of Fort Peck Dam as the cover illustration for its first issue (23 November 1936). At its peak

Life had more than 40 staff photographers, including ALFRED EISENSTAEDT, Andreas Feininger (*b* 1906), and W. Eugene Smith (1918–78). Other magazines influential in the development of photojournalism were *Look, Focus,* and *Holiday.* The format of picture magazines led to the development of fashion photography and photography for advertising. In 1932 Anton Bruehl (1900–83) made some of the first color photographs for editorial work and advertisements under contract with Condé Nast. The work of Richard Avedon, Louise Dahl-Wolfe, and Paul Outerbridge was reproduced in *Vogue* and *Harper's Bazaar.*

By the middle of the twentieth century some of the most distinctive photojournalism in the city was the work of WEEGEE, whose gritty images were featured in the *Daily News.* By using a police radio he often reached crime scenes before the police and became renowned for his stark images of murders, fires, and the chaos of urban life. In 1945 he published *Naked City,* a collection of photographs of crime. Picture magazines declined during the 1960s after television began to provide immediate coverage of news. *Look* ceased publication in 1971, and *Life* in 1972. In the mid-1990s interest in photojournalism revived owing to the demand for images more vivid than those of television, and often photojournalists concentrated on issues of social reform. PHOTOGRAPHIC AGENCIES became important to photojournalism for directing photojournalists to parts of the world discussed in the news and matching photographers with buyers for their images. MAGNUM PHOTOS (formed in the city in 1947) and other leading agencies helped to shape the future of photojournalism.

In the early twenty-first century, the increasing consumption of online news over print journalism, as well as the advent of inexpensive digital technology, transformed photojournalism, including in New York City. Amateur photojournalists, or "citizen photojournalists," abounded: for instance, on 11 September 2001 people watching the terrorist attacks on the World Trade Center took photographs with digital cameras and cell phones that were published in print and online and shown in television news broadcasts.

Tim N. Gidal, *Modern Photojournalism: Origin and Evolution, 1910–1933* (New York: Collier, 1973); Lee D. Witkin and Barbara London, *The Photograph Collector's Guide* (Boston: New York Graphic Society, 1979)

See also DOCUMENTARY PHOTOGRAPHY; PHOTOGRAPHY.

Dale L. Neighbors

Photo League. Group formed by photographers in 1936 to document working-class life in New York City and to photograph social and political events from a radical ideological perspective. Eventually it attracted photographers with a more diverse political perspective, including Berenice Abbott, Dorothea Lange, Beaumont Newhall, Nancy Newhall, W. Eugene Smith, Paul Strand, and Edward Weston, who considered the Photo League a lively alternative to the conservatism of the Camera Club of New York and the Pictorial Society of America. It sponsored projects concerned with city life; it also had a gallery and publication. In a school directed by Sid Grossman amateurs learned about basic problems in documentation by involving themselves in executing structured projects such as "Men at Work," supervised by Lewis Hine, and the Harlem Document, supervised by Aaron Siskind; pupils included Morris Engel, Arthur Leipzig, Walter Rosenblum, and Dan Weiner. The avant-garde photographers John Heartfield and Barbara Morgan and the photojournalist Weegee were among those whose work was exhibited at the gallery. The publication *Photo Notes* informed members of activities and published criticism by Elizabeth McCausland, the Newhalls, and Strand, among others. At its peak in 1948 the Photo League found itself listed as a "subversive" organization and in 1952 was forced to close.

Naomi Rosenblum

phrenology. Pseudoscience that purports to analyze character by studying the shape of the skull. It was introduced to New York City in 1835 by the brothers Lorenzo and Orson Squire Fowler, who opened an office, museum, lecture hall, and examination room at 135 Nassau Street, a brick building called

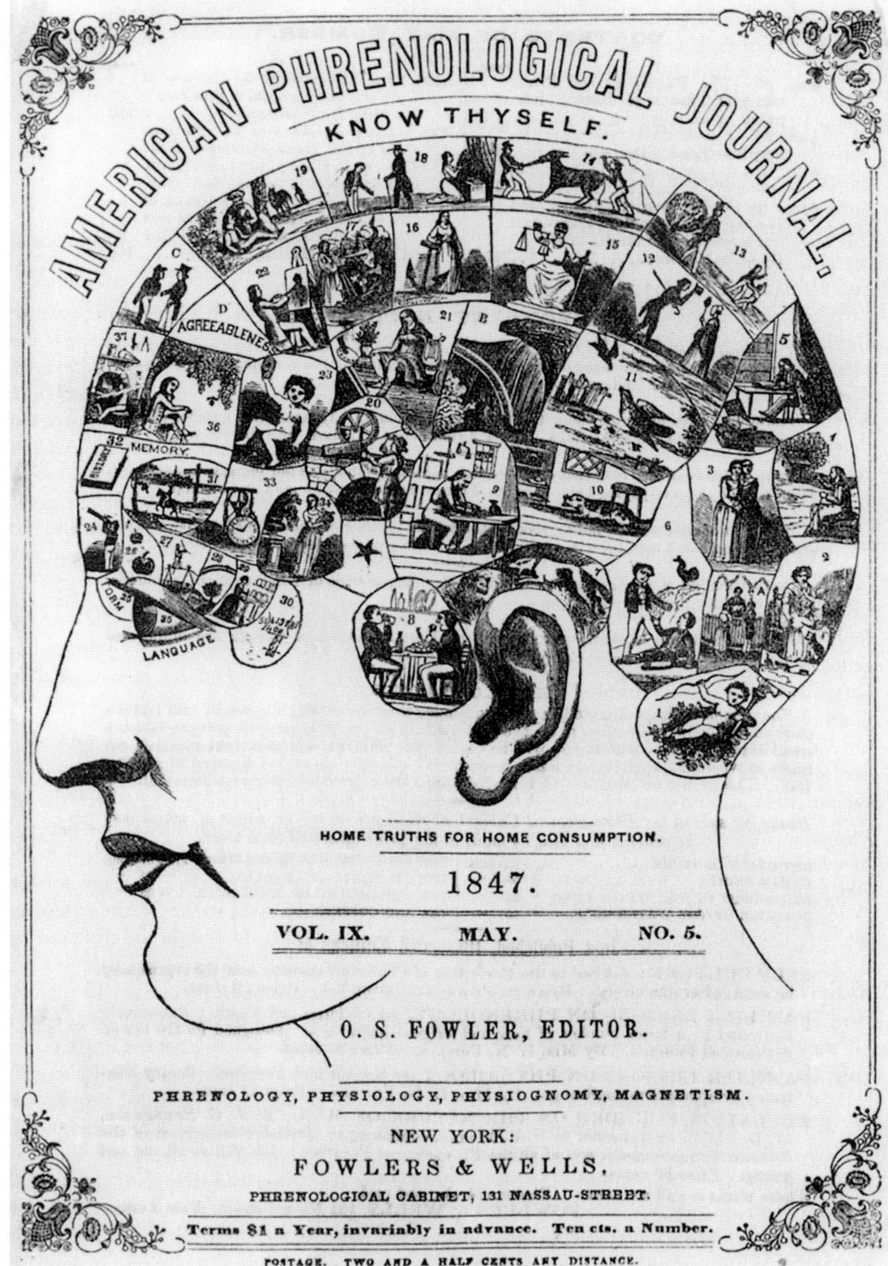

American Phrenological Journal, *May 1847*

Clinton Hall. In the same year Orson Fowler published the book *Phrenology Proved, Illustrated and Applied,* which sold tens of thousands of copies and went through 62 editions during the next two decades. The business of "practical phrenology" proved lucrative, and the two brothers called on their sister Charlotte to join them. She helped Lorenzo on the lecture circuit and with head-reading while Orson dashed off more books, among them *Matrimony; or, Phrenology and Physiology Applied to the Selection of Congenial Companions for Life, including Directions to the Married for Living Together Affectionately and Happily* (1843). The Fowlers' enterprise attracted widespread interest (one of their customers was Walt Whitman, whom they described as having "friendship and sympathy," as well as "indolence and a tendency to the pleasures of voluptuousness"), and they moved to larger quarters at 308 Broadway. Others were more skeptical: as early as 1838 David Meredith Reese denounced phrenology in his book *Humbugs of New-York.* Lorenzo's wife, Lydia, joined the business in 1844, and during the same year the Fowler brothers formed a partnership with Samuel Roberts Wells, who married Charlotte, and with him set up the publishing house of Fowler and Wells. All five gave lectures and wrote books. In 1855 Orson and Lorenzo Fowler sold their interests in the publishing house to the Wellses. Fowler and Wells's Phrenological Museum moved to successively larger quarters at 389, 737, 753, and 775 Broadway; the Lorenzo Fowlers and the Wellses eventually shared an elegant residence at 233 East Broadway. In 1860 Lorenzo and Lydia Fowler moved to London. On Lydia's death in 1879 their daughter Jessie helped her father in phrenological undertakings. Fowler and Wells continued to publish phrenological tracts into the first decade of the twentieth century. Jessie Fowler, a resident of New York City from 1896, wrote a number of books on phrenology, and as late as 1928 was listed as a phrenologist in local directories. She died at her home at 843 West 179th Street, the last of the phrenological Fowlers.

Madeleine B. Stern, *Heads and Headlines: The Phrenological Fowlers* (Norman: University of Oklahoma Press, 1971)

Allen J. Share

Phyfe [Fife], **Duncan** (*b* Scotland, 1768; *d* New York City, 16 Aug 1854). Cabinetmaker. He moved from Albany, New York, to New York City by 1792, when he joined the General Society of Mechanics and Tradesmen. He was first listed in city directories in 1793 and by 1795 moved his shop to 35 Partition (now Fulton) Street. He employed many apprentices and journeymen, who struck when he reduced wages during the panic of 1819. He marketed his work in the city and in ports of the South and the West Indies. Between 1817 and 1822 he had customers in Savannah, Georgia, and briefly stationed an agent there to take orders and sell furniture. Phyfe was well-known in his day for his elegant designs; his name now identifies American neoclassical furniture generally. In *Wealth and Biography of the Wealthy Citizens of New York City* (1845) his estate was valued at $300,000 and his firm was described as the largest and most fashionable in the country. He retired from the trade in 1847.

Duncan Phyfe, sideboard and cellarette, ca *1825*

Nancy McClelland, *Duncan Phyfe and the English Regency, 1795–1830* (New York: W. R. Scott, 1939)

Deborah Dependahl Waters

physical disabilities. Before the mid-nineteenth century there were few services in New York City to assist the physically disabled. The number of handicapped people in the city became particularly evident during the winter of 1842, when city inspector John Griscom submitted to the Common Council a long and critical report of the city's sanitary conditions, and clinics for the disabled were set up at local medical colleges. In the 1850s James Knight, a physician who made home visits for the Association for the Improvement of the Condition of the Poor (AICP), reported that a large number of crippled people could not leave their homes. In response the AICP formed the New York Society for the Relief of the Ruptured and Crippled (1862), which opened an asylum for 25 crippled children and supplied trusses and bandages for the disabled in a small building at 97 Second Avenue. The society eventually moved to new quarters at Lexington Avenue and 42nd Street, where it established an asylum and hospital that housed 200 children. The financial support provided by the city and by private sources such as the Hospital Sunday Fund allowed the society to offer most of its services free of charge. The society later evolved into the Hospital for Special Surgery.

In 1868 the New York Orthopedic Dispensary opened at 126 East 59th Street to provide free mechanical and surgical treatment of diseases and deformities of the spine and joints, infantile paralysis, bow-legs, club-feet, and other physical handicaps. In 1875 the dispensary opened a hospital with 50 beds that offered most of its services to children aged four to 14 suffering from curable handicaps; Theodore Roosevelt was the organization's treasurer for several years in the 1870s. During this same period the city's Charity Hospital on Blackwell's Island set up a paralytic hospital to provide chronic care for those afflicted by paralysis or epilepsy. The Hospital for Deformities and Joint Diseases opened in 1905 at Madison Avenue and 123rd Street (it now operates as the Hospital for Joint Diseases Orthopaedic Institute at 301 East 17th Street). Among the many residential programs established for crippled children about the turn of the twentieth century were the House of St. Giles the Cripple at 417 Clinton Street in Brooklyn (by Episcopalians in 1891), the House of the Annunciation for Crippled and Incurable Children on the Upper West Side (by the Sisters of the Annunciation of the Blessed Virgin Mary in 1893), the Darrach Home for Crippled Children (1903), and the

New York Home for Destitute Crippled Children (1904). The Association for the Aid of Crippled Children (1899) at Stuyvesant Square provided home nursing and transportation assistance and helped handicapped children, especially the blind, to obtain care elsewhere.

By the late 1890s there was a growing emphasis on helping physically handicapped children become self-sufficient. The Children's Aid Society organized the Guild for Crippled Children of the Poor of New York City (1896) at 224 West 63rd Street; renamed Classes for Crippled Children, this organization had a kindergarten and offered vocational training for older children. Vocational training was also provided by the William H. Davis Free Industrial School for Crippled Children at 471 West 57th Street, the Crippled Children's East Side Free School at 157 Henry Street (1902, later known as the New York Service for the Orthopedically Handicapped), and the Brearley League Industrial School for Cripples at 350 East 88th Street (1908, later known as the Rhinelander School). In 1903 the city's health department began routine screening of schoolchildren for orthopedic and visual problems. The city's first public school classes for crippled children opened in 1905, and in the following year Henry Goldman, head of the East Side Free School, persuaded the Board of Education to establish a special public school for children with physical disabilities.

Services for handicapped adults were much slower to develop than those available for children: a state commission revealed that only 12 percent of the 414,000 workers injured in industrial accidents from 1906 to 1908 received compensation. Reform legislation established local industrial commissions to adjudicate compensation cases impartially, but in the 1930s an exposé of these agencies in New York City and Chicago by the legal scholar Walter Dodd revealed exploitation of the immigrants who filed most of the claims and a marked tendency to favor the interests of insurance companies rather than those of the injured workers. Righting these wrongs became a new priority of reformers.

Medical advances helped to reduce the number of seriously handicapped children, but even as late as 1912 nearly one-third of schoolchildren in New York City had physical disabilities. Special classes for children with cardiac problems were begun in 1917 (discontinued in 1941 by recommendation of a mayoral commission). State support became available to assist the city's school programs in the same year, when New York became one of only two states in the country to pass laws aiding handicapped children not confined to institutions. In 1925 the New York Academy of Medicine reported that the efforts of private agencies such as the Association to Aid Crippled Children were reaching only about one-sixth of the estimated 18,000 disabled children in the city, a gap in services that was confirmed in 1938 by the Commission for the Study of Crippled Children appointed by Mayor Fiorello H. La Guardia. At the recommendation of the new commission the mayor formed the Division of Physically Handicapped Children in the health department, which was made responsible for maintaining a central registry of physically handicapped children in the city set up by the commission. As death rates from infectious diseases diminished, public health officials gave greater attention to broader issues of health and welfare in the city. This change of emphasis was highlighted in 1945 when the responsibility for administering state aid to the handicapped was moved from the city's Domestic Relations Court to its health department.

Although New York State provided more financial assistance than most other states for disabled adults, it did not significantly improve its vocational training programs for the disabled until after World War I, when the needs of wounded veterans sparked public interest and generated federal grants for state training programs. This support led to the formation of the city's Rehabilitation Center for the Disabled in 1924 and of the Rehabilitation Bureau in the state education department, both of which received vocational rehabilitation funds granted under the Social Security Act of 1935. The training programs developed during these years focused on workers who could be restored to ordinary functioning. Several important steps were taken in the 1950s to improve health care for disabled children. The Division for Physically Handicapped Children in the health department was given the status of a bureau in 1951, and city and state funds were set aside to cover medical and rehabilitation costs for children with severe orthopedic problems, congenital heart disease, cleft palates, harelips, and conditions requiring plastic surgery; state funds supported the opening in 1953 of a cleft-palate rehabilitation center at Mount Sinai Hospital. Classes were offered in the public schools for brain-injured children, amputees, and children with cerebral palsy, and programs for the handicapped were extended into high school. The development of Medicare and Medicaid in 1965 expanded the health care available to disabled adults. Additional benefits were provided by amendments to the Vocational Rehabilitation Act (1965), which provided the federal support to cover 90 percent of the cost of programs that trained the physically handicapped.

A new emphasis was placed on social equality for the disabled during the civil rights movement of the 1960s. The claim by advocacy groups in New York City that the disabled had a right to full participation in the life of the city met with growing acceptance from the federal government and the public. The Housing Act of 1972 extended subsidies to make new housing accessible to the handicapped; the Vocational Rehabilitation Act of 1973 increased funding for vocational programs and in Section 504 mandated an end to all discriminatory exclusion of the disabled from community services. How and where to apply Section 504 became a matter of bitter controversy in the city. The disclosure that fewer than one-third of the city's 3600 buses had wheelchair lifts led to a lawsuit by advocacy groups in 1982, as a result of which lifts were installed on 80 percent of the city's buses by 1991. The Americans with Disabilities Act (ADA), passed by Congress in 1990, required that all new mass transit vehicles be accessible to the disabled, and in the following year the city installed elevators or ramps in 10 of its 54 major subway stations (it was required to do the same in the remaining stations by 1995, a project that remains incomplete in the early twenty-first century). The Education for Handicapped Children Act of 1978 (Public Law 94-142) affirmed the equal right of all disabled children to publicly funded education. By 1991 special education classes were offered in nearly every public elementary school in New York City, and the city was moving toward expanding its preschool programs for the disabled.

In the twenty-first century the Mayor's Office for People with Disabilities has made these and many other programs come to fruition, including further housing, building codes that allow accessibility, employment opportunities, and tax breaks for those with disabilities. The department partners with private organizations to meet these goals. Another program in compliance with the ADA's paratransit requirements is Access-A-Ride, a bus service established in 1990 that costs no more than a ride on the subway. Those with disabilities can call a hotline to arrange individual trips or daily trips. A care assistant may accompany the rider at no charge. MetroCards are available at a reduced fare for the disabled, and more subway stations throughout the city have installed elevators. In 2008 the mayor's office hosted Disability Mentoring Day, a day dedicated to putting more physically disabled people into the workforce. Through the Access New York initiative, the mayor's office also compiled information about transportation and city services for the disabled. Many of these programs extend to the elderly population of the city as well.

The New York City Department of Parks and Recreation has also tried to accommodate ADA requirements for park users. City parks partnered with U.S. Paralympics for programming initiatives, offering wheelchair tennis, football, basketball, softball, and soccer. In addition some parks offered free aquatics programs and accessible camping activities. In 2007 the parks department made beaches more accessible for the disabled and elderly by laying mats on the sand for wheelchair use. Other innovations made a public pool accessible in Flushing Meadows–Corona Park. In addition, the Owen Dolen Center in Westchester Square in the Bronx was a facility especially designed for children with disabilities; it provided field trips and day camps. The city's ADA compliance has enabled many families to more easily care for elderly relatives or those with physical disabilities.

David M. Schneider and Albert Deutsch, *The History of Public Welfare in New York State, 1867–1940* (Chicago: University of Chicago Press, 1941); John Duffy, *A History of Public Health in New York City* (New York: Russell Sage Foundation, 1968, 1974)

See also Blindness.

Sandra Opdycke, Penelope Gelwicks

physics. Creative genius in the physical sciences in the eighteenth- and nineteenth-century United States was isolated rather than sustained, as exemplified by the work of Benjamin Franklin, Benjamin Thompson ("Count Rumford"), Joseph Henry, Josiah Willard Gibbs, and A. A. Michelson. There was nothing yet comparable with either the established tradition of Europe or its recent growth and scientific professionalization. The situation was such that at a meeting in New York City in 1880 of the American Association for the Advancement of Science, Henry Rowland, the first American professor of physics (at Johns Hopkins University), described American science as "a thing of the future and not of the present or the past." But soon the scene quickly began to change, and many of the changes radiated from New York City and its environs.

The rapid transformation of physics was fueled by a series of sensational discoveries in the burgeoning field of electrical science and applied electricity (x-rays in 1895, radioactivity in 1896, the electron in 1897, quantum phenomena from 1900), by the inexorable transformation of the United States from an agricultural to a manufacturing society, and by the steady growth of population in the metropolitan area, adding to its wealth and reinforcing its ambitions. Early work in industrial physics was conducted in the city by Thomas Edison, Alexander Graham Bell, Nikola Tesla, and others. Columbia University contributed ideas, students, and teachers to academia and industry: the American Physical Society was founded at the university in 1899 and held many of its meetings there for several decades; George Pegram of Columbia in 1927 became the treasurer of the society; the university for many years housed the editorial offices of the *Physical Review*, the leading professional journal; and in 1905 the university awarded its first PhD in physics to R. A. Millikan, later much celebrated. At Columbia Michael Pupin, although himself essentially an engineer, vigorously defended basic scientific research. In 1927 Columbia opened new physics laboratories named in honor of Pupin after his death in 1934. Many of the accomplishments of the 1930s and after in the new laboratories were overseen by Pegram and inspired by I. I. Rabi. One landmark was the discovery by Harold C. Urey in 1932 of heavy hydrogen. This was closely followed by developments in the field of molecular-beam physics by Rabi and his colleagues, who brought the field to a new level of precision and sophistication. Their work earned the Nobel Prize in 1944.

World War II diverted scientific energies. The Pupin laboratories became the site in 1940 of the Manhattan Project, in which Pegram, Urey, and Enrico Fermi played leading roles. After the war the new molecular-beam techniques were applied to the investigation of the refined properties of atoms, molecules, nuclei, and electrons (by Polykarp Kusch and Willis Lamb) and to new precision methods of measuring time (by Norman Ramsay). And the study of the subtleties of electromagnetic interactions launched the era of masers and lasers. During this same period new and increasingly powerful techniques were used to explore the new field of "elementary particle" physics and especially to examine the basic symmetries of these particles and their interactions. Physicists at Columbia, notably T. D. Lee, Chien-shiung Wu, Melvin Schwartz, Leon Lederman, and Jack Steinberger, figured prominently in this work. By this time physics had become part of a huge international enterprise. Columbia maintained some close links with the giants of industrial physics, especially Bell Telephone Laboratories (now greatly expanded in New Jersey) and International Business Machines (through its on-campus research institute, the Watson Laboratory).

By the late twentieth century several trends had combined to diminish the former significance of New York City as a center of physics: the growth and globalization of physical research; the more elaborate and extensive involvement of the physical sciences in industry and government; and social, economic, and demographic changes in the metropolitan region. The gargantuan machines used for "elementary particle" research had outgrown the confines of a university campus or city, perhaps even of a single country. Much of the nuclear science and technology that emerged from the Manhattan Project had become environmentally inappropriate to an urban setting. The headquarters of the American Physical Society and later of the Institute of Physics left New York City for enlarged premises strategically closer to Washington, D.C. In the twenty-first century New York City remains an integral part of scientific studies and research in the state and the United States as a whole. Nobel Prizes for physics were awarded to New Yorkers Arno Penzias (1978), Leon Lederman (1988), and Robert Hofstadter (1961).

Celebration of the Fiftieth Anniversary of the Pupin Laboratories (New York: Columbia University, 1978); Melba Phillips: "The American Physical Society: A Survey of Its First 50 Years," *American Journal of Physics* 58, no. 3 (1990)

Samuel Devons, Danielle Molinski

Pierpont Morgan Library. Original name of the Morgan Library and Museum.

Pierre Hotel. Hotel at Fifth Avenue and 61st Street in Manhattan. Opened in October 1930, it joined a group of luxury hotels near the southeastern corner of Central Park, including the Sherry–Netherland, the Plaza, and the Savoy–Plaza (now demolished). The architects, Schultze and Weaver, designed a conservative 44-story tower to replace the château-like mansion of Commodore Elbridge T. Gerry. The design facilitated the creation of more than 700 rooms, most of which were leased annually by the hotel's wealthy clientele. Named for the hotel's first manager, Charles Pierre Casalasco, financing was provided by a group of investors including Walter Chrysler and Edward F. Hutton. Despite the hotel's upscale reputation, the Pierre fell into bankruptcy during the Great Depression only to be pulled out in 1938 when J. Paul Getty bought the building for $2.5 million and converted many of the original 712 rooms into cooperative apartments. Through the changes the hotel continued to foster loyalty among such bold-faced names as Audrey Hepburn, Cary Grant, Elizabeth Taylor, and President Richard Nixon. By 1960 most of the suites had been sold as cooperatives, and in 1981 the hotel came under the control of Four Seasons. On 2 January 1972, the Pierre was the site of what at the time was the largest and most successful hotel robbery in history. Four men, most associated with the Lucchese crime family, successfully pried open lock boxes maintained for guests in an open vault. The four perpetrators, working in the early morning darkness, handcuffed 19 hostages for as much as two and a half hours before escaping with millions of dollars in valuables. In 2005 the cooperative board that controlled the Pierre signed a 30-year management contract with Taj Hotels. From 2007 to 2009, the Pierre underwent an extensive $100 million renovation of its hotel lobby and its remaining 200 rooms.

Carol Willis, Kenneth T. Jackson

Pierrepont, Henry E(velyn) (*b* Brooklyn, 8 Aug 1808; *d* Brooklyn, 28 March 1888). City planner and businessman, second son of Hezekiah B. Pierrepont. In addition to managing his family's properties he worked to establish ferry connections across and up the East River and was a founder and later a trustee of Green-Wood Cemetery in Brooklyn. He is regarded as one of the first city planners in the United States: active in planning the expansion of Brooklyn and known as its "first citizen," he also studied many European cities firsthand. His elder brother, William Constable Pierrepont, dedicated himself to managing the family properties in upstate New York.

John J. Gallagher

Pierrepont [Pierpont], **Hezekiah B(eers)** (*b* New Haven, Conn., 1768; *d* Brooklyn, 1838). Merchant, early suburban developer, father of Henry E. Pierrepont. Born to a family long established in New England, he settled in Brooklyn in 1802 and restored the spelling of his surname to its original French form. He amassed a small fortune as a merchant adventurer and was once captured by French privateers in the China Sea. Through his marriage to Anna Maria Constable, the daughter of a prominent merchant in Manhattan, he inherited considerable properties in upstate New York. In Brooklyn Ferry (now Brooklyn Heights) he bought 60 acres (24 hectares) of the Benson farm and built a mansion on the heights above the East River. He was a prominent investor in Robert Fulton's steam ferry connecting Brooklyn to Manhattan, as well as in the local development that ensued. Pierrepont was the first important suburban real estate developer in U.S. history and was advertising and selling lots in Brooklyn Heights to prominent business leaders from Manhattan by 1823. Among the proposals that he made but did not see realized was one for a promenade along Brooklyn Heights.

Kenneth T. Jackson, *Crabgrass Frontier: The Suburbanization of the United States* (New York: Oxford University Press, 1985)

John J. Gallagher

piers. See Recreation piers.

pigeons. See Rock Pigeon.

Pigtowns. Name applied during the nineteenth and early twentieth centuries to two neighborhoods in Flatbush, one near Bedford Avenue and Montgomery Street and the other about half a mile (1 kilometer) to the east near Lincoln Terrace Park. The neighborhoods were far from urban development and had many wooden shacks, pigpens, and chicken coops. In 1908 Charles Ebbets, owner of the Brooklyn Dodgers, began buying lots in anticipation that the Interborough Rapid Transit company would extend its subway along Eastern Parkway and by 1913 completed Ebbets Field. After the subway was extended into East Flatbush in 1914, both Pigtowns disappeared.

Stephen Weinstein

Piñero, Miguel [Gomez, Antonio, Jr.] (*b* Puerto Rico, 19 Dec 1946; *d* New York City, 17 June 1988). Playwright. He moved with his family from Puerto Rico to the Lower East Side in 1950. His arrest and imprisonment for burglary in 1964 began a 10-year series of convictions for petty crimes related to his drug addiction. He was eventually sent to the Otisville State Training School for Boys and earned his high school equivalency diploma while an inmate at Manhattan State Hospital. In 1971 he took part in Clay Stevenson's acting workshop at Ossining Correctional Facility and began writing plays. Prison life became the basis of his best-known work, *Short Eyes* (1974), which was presented Off-Broadway and made into a motion picture; brutally realistic portrayals of life in prison and on the city streets characterize 12 other plays, including *Eulogy for a Small-Time Thief* (1977), two screenplays, and two books of poetry. Piñero helped to form the Nuyoricans, a group of Puerto Rican poets based in the city. In 1974 he won an Obie Award, the New York Drama Critics' Circle Award, and the Drama Desk Award.

James Pelton

Pintard, John (*b* New York City, 18 May 1759; *d* New York City, 21 June 1844). Businessman. After graduating from Princeton College in 1776 he entered business, focusing his efforts in the China and East India trade; by 1792 he was one of the most successful merchants in New York City. He later declared bankruptcy, however, and was imprisoned for debt before finding work as an auctioneer of books and editor of the *Daily Advertiser*; he was eventually engaged as the secretary of the city's first fire insurance company. As clerk of the corporation and inspector for the city he developed a system for keeping vital statistics. Under the auspices of the Tammany Society, in which he was a sagamore and grand sachem, he organized a historical museum; he also helped to organize the New-York Historical Society in 1804 and the General Theological Seminary, served for many years as the secretary of the American Bible Society, and was influential in strengthening the New York Chamber of Commerce. An alderman and a member of the state legislature, Pintard promoted the Erie Canal and organized the city's first savings bank, of which he was president.

James E. Mooney

Miniature of John Pintard by John Ramage, 1787

Piscator, Erwin (*b* Ulm, Germany, 17 Dec 1893; *d* Starnberg, West Germany, 30 March 1966). Theatrical producer and director. He owned his own theater in Germany, and in 1936 his collaboration on the stage adaptation of Theodore Dreiser's *An American Tragedy* ran on Broadway for 19 performances. Three years later he immigrated to the United States with his wife. In 1940 he became the director of the New School's Dramatic Workshop. His students included Marlon Brando, Tony Curtis, and Tennessee Williams. He returned to Germany in 1951 and until his death remained a major exemplar of expressionist staging and contemporary, epic style theater. His wife, Maria Ley-Piscator, died in New York City in 1999.

Jessica Montesano

pizza. New York City's first pizzeria was opened in 1905 as an outgrowth of Gennaro Lombardi's grocery store in the heart of Little Italy at 53½ Spring Street. Fired in a coal-burning oven, the five-cent pizzas conformed to the style of their Neapolitan ancestors, with only a few adaptations, borne of necessity. Because Lombardi could not find the buffalo mozzarella cheese or the San Marzano tomatoes used in his native Naples, he used local tomatoes and mozzarella made from cow's milk. The poverty of his clientele, almost exclusively Italian immigrants, was the source of another New York innovation: the slice. Whereas pizzas in Italy were sold whole, some of Lombardi's customers could not afford to spend a nickel, and so they were given triangular slices of the pie corresponding to their payments of one or two cents. Some of the most famous New York pizza dynasties have roots at Lombardi's, which closed in 1984 only to be reopened by the founder's grandson one block away 10 years later. Antonio Totonno Pero, founder in 1924 of Totonno's in Coney Island, learned the trade as one of Lombardi's first pizzaiolos. John Sasso left the same job at Lombardi's to open John's on Bleecker Street in 1929. Patsy Lancieri, whose name now decorates four New York pizzerias and whose nephew founded Grimaldi's, another New York pizza institution, also worked briefly at Lombardi's. Until World

Grimaldi's Pizzeria, 2009

War II the few pizzerias in New York City catered primarily to the city's Italian American communities. But during the decade after the war American soldiers who had been stationed in Italy popularized this "ethnic" food, spurring a nationwide pizza boom. In 2010 more than 400 pizzerias were listed in New York City, along with innumerable Italian restaurants that served pizza as a secondary matter.

Nationally, New York City is known for a pizza style that resembles an oversized version of Neapolitan pizza: thin, flexible slices—often folded in half while eaten—that are light on cheese and other toppings. Pizzerias around the country sell slices under the banner of "authentic New York pizza." A theory that attributed the flavor of New York's pizza crusts to the mineral content of the city's tap water gave rise to the urban legend that purist purveyors in other cities imported their water from New York City. In recent years pizza aficionados have decried the decline of New York–style pizza in the city and the ascendance of a thicker, cheesier variety, proffered most notably by a chain of unaffiliated pizzerias sharing the name Ray's. Another departure from classic New York style is the world's most expensive pizza, served at Nino's Bellissima with a price tag of $1000, and featuring crème fraîche, lobster, and four varieties of caviar.

Rowan Moore Gerety

planetarium. See Hayden Planetarium.

Planned Parenthood Federation of America, Inc. Nonprofit organization devoted to reproductive health care, the oldest and largest of its kind in the United States. Among its forerunners was the country's first birth control clinic, opened in Brooklyn in 1916 by Margaret Sanger. After her arrest and indictment for distributing contraceptive devices, the organization continued in various forms until 1939 when the Birth Control Clinical Research Bureau of America merged with the American Birth Control League to form the Birth Control Federation of America. Headquarters were established in the city and the current name was adopted in 1942. Planned Parenthood has its offices at 810 Seventh Avenue; in the early twenty-first century its 97 affiliates operated 880 centers nationwide.

See also Family Planning.

Chad Ludington

Platt, Thomas C(ollier) (*b* Oswego, N.Y., 15 July 1833; *d* New York City, 6 March 1910). Political leader. He was well-known in business and politics when he moved to New York City in 1880. Soon elected to the U.S. Senate, he led the New York State delegation to the Republican National Convention in 1888. Through political maneuvering he unsuccessfully sought an appointment as secretary of the treasury. As a leading figure in city politics he gained power in state government and became the leader of the Republican Party in New York State. After Platt's reelection to the Senate in 1904 his influence declined and he left politics. He lived at 2 Rector Street in lower Manhattan.

James E. Mooney

Players. Club incorporated in 1888 for men active in the theater, music, literature, and the arts. One of its founders, the actor Edwin Booth, purchased a building for the club on Gramercy Park South. Erected in 1845 in the Gothic Revival style as one of the first brownstones in New York City, the building was remodeled by Stanford White to resemble an Italian Renaissance palace, leaving the proper residents of the neighborhood aghast. Inside the building are comfortable quarters and a working library of theater history that is based on the collection of Booth, much augmented. Quotations from Shakespeare adorn the walls of every room.

James E. Mooney

playgrounds. The movement to build playgrounds in New York City began in the 1880s, as street play became dangerous with the city's increasing traffic. The first playgrounds were sponsored by settlement houses and consisted of backyard spaces with sandboxes and other simple equipment. In 1891 Charles Stover formed the New York Society for Parks and Playgrounds, which demonstrated play equipment and pressured the city to build playgrounds. More support was given in 1897 by the Small Park Advisory Committee, led by journalist Jacob A. Riis. In 1898 Stover and Lillian Wald, the Henry Street Settlement director, formed the Outdoor Recreation League, which built nine privately sponsored playgrounds taken over by the Parks Department in 1902. They supplied slides and seesaws, the mainstays of playgrounds. In the following year the first permanent playground built by the city opened in Seward Park at Essex Street and East Broadway on the Lower East Side. Others were also located in slum districts, such as Seward and DeWitt Clinton Parks.

Parks commissioner Stover formed the Bureau of Recreation in 1911 to accommodate the growing role of athletics in park design and operation. About the same time the city opened playgrounds atop active commercial waterfront piers. Between 1910 and 1920 thousands of children took part in interborough sports tournaments at playgrounds that drew large crowds of spectators. The first playgrounds in Central Park were built in the

Playground at 10 West 28th Street, ca *1890*

1920s. During the tenure of Robert Moses as the parks commissioner (1934–60) the number of playgrounds in the city rose from 119 to 777. Many were built by federal relief workers during the 1930s; the standard designs of mass-produced sandboxes, wading pools, swings, and benches gave them a uniform look throughout the five boroughs. Employees of the city known as "parkies" led children's activities and conducted preschool classes. In 1938 the Parks Department worked with the Board of Education to develop additional playgrounds on sites adjacent to schools.

From the 1960s designers experimented with new equipment and materials. The city's first "adventure playground," designed to foster free-form, unprogrammed play in children, opened in 1967 on the west side of Central Park; like its European forerunners, it was built after a planning stage during which the opinions of children were solicited. Temporary playgrounds were set up on vacant lots. The Playground for All Children at Flushing Meadows–Corona Park (1984) was the first playground in the nation designed specifically for physically disabled children; another was added at Asser Levy Recreation Center in 1993. Efforts increased to involve communities in the design, construction, and maintenance of playgrounds. In addition to the many outdoor playgrounds, others are indoors, including one at the Pelham Fritz Recreation Center in Marcus Garvey Park. In 2009, according to the Parks Department there were 188 parks in the Bronx, 290 in Brooklyn, 259 in Queens, 208 in Manhattan, and 56 in Staten Island.

A Playground for All Children: City of New York (Washington, D.C.: U.S. Department of Housing and Urban Development, 1976–78); New York City Department of Parks and Recreation, http://www.nycgovparks.org

Jonathan Kuhn, Lisa Keller

Playwrights Horizons. Off-Broadway theater. Founded in 1971 by Robert Moss at the Clark Center for the Performing Arts at the Westside Young Men's Christian Association, it moved to 416 West 42nd Street in 1974 in a space that formerly housed a burlesque (razed and rebuilt; reopened in 2003), after a brief stay in a nearby pornography theater. Dedicated to the production of works by new American writers, composers, and lyricists, Playwrights Horizons was instrumental in the revitalization of West 42nd Street during the late 1970s as one of the first theaters to open on what is now known as Theater Row. The theater also operates, in conjunction with New York University's Tisch School of the Arts, the Playwrights Horizons Theater School at 440 Lafayette Street in Manhattan. Artists whose work has been presented at the theater include Kenneth Lonergan, Christopher Durang, A. R. Gurney, and Pulitzer Prize winners Doug Wright (*I Am My Own Wife*), Stephen Sondheim and James Lapine (*Sunday in the Park with George*), Alfred Uhry (*Driving Miss Daisy*), and Wendy Wasserstein (*The Heidi Chronicles*).

Patrick Barrett

Plaza Hotel. Hotel at 59th Street and Fifth Avenue, overlooking Grand Army Plaza. The site was once occupied by a shallow pond that the wealthy used for ice skating. In 1890 the first Plaza Hotel opened on the site, but it was unprofitable. The George A. Fuller Company bought the building in 1902, and demolished it in 1905. Henry J. Hardenbergh then designed a new 19-story hotel with 800 rooms and several grand entertaining areas. It opened on 1 October 1907 when the first guest, Alfred Gwynne Vanderbilt, was greeted by a grand welcoming committee. Single rooms initially cost $2.50 a night. The new Plaza became the best-known hotel in the city, featuring the Oak Room Bar and Palm Court restaurants. Among its famous guests were the Duke and Duchess of Windsor, F. Scott Fitzgerald, Frank Lloyd Wright (who lived there while he was working on the Guggenheim Museum), and the Beatles, who stayed there during their first trip to the United States in 1964. Truman Capote hosted the famous Black and White Ball in the Plaza's Grand Ballroom in 1966. In the Eloise books by Kay Thompson, the main character, a six-year-old girl, lives in a room on the "tippy-top floor" of the hotel. The Plaza has also been the setting for scenes in several movies including *North by Northwest* (1959), *Plaza Suite* (1971), *Barefoot in the Park* (1967), *The Way We Were* (1973), and *Funny Girl* (1968). In 2005 the new owners, El-Ad Properties, closed the Plaza for a two-year-long renovation that included turning many of the rooms into

Plaza Hotel

private residences. The hotel reopened on 1 March 2008.

Anne Epstein

Pleasant Plains. Neighborhood in southern Staten Island, northeast of Tottenville. Throughout the nineteenth century many oystermen lived there. The area was named after the Staten Island Railroad built a station in the 1860s at a bend in the Amboy Road; the business and entertainment district took shape nearby. Many of its one-family houses remain from the late nineteenth century, when John C. Drumgoole formed Mount Loretto, a home for destitute orphaned boys from Manhattan that covered 600 acres (240 hectares). Part of the property became the Cemetery of the Resurrection in 1988. Pleasant Plains retains a bit of its rural character. Well-known residents have included the harpist Maud Morgan and the opera manager Max Maretzek.

Marjorie Johnson

P. Lorillard and Company. Firm of tobacco products manufacturers. It began as a snuff factory opened in 1760 by Pierre Lorillard (1742–*ca* 1778) in a rented house on Chatham Street in Manhattan. After Lorillard was killed by British troops seeking refuge in the house, his sons Peter and George took over the firm in 1792; they maintained the building in Manhattan as their headquarters and moved the factory to a wooden grist mill in Westchester County along the Bronx River (now in the Bronx), where they experimented with using water power in production. The mill produced more tobacco than any other facility in the country by the end of the eighteenth century and was later replaced with a larger granite building, which was sold in 1870. The firm left the city in 1891 and became part of a trust formed by the American Tobacco Company; when the trust was declared illegal in 1911 by the U.S. Supreme Court, Lorillard again became independent. The mill was acquired by the New York Botanical Garden in 1937 and converted into a restaurant. In 1959 the firm's headquarters were moved to Manhattan. Lorillard was bought by the Loews Corporation in 1969.

Lorillard and Tobacco, 200th Anniversary, P. Lorillard and Company, 1760–1960 (New York: P. Lorillard, 1960)

James Bradley

Plum(b) Beach. Former neighborhood in southeastern Brooklyn, connected to Sheepshead Bay by a neck of land extending east from the foot of Emmons Avenue. Named for the beach plums growing in the area, the site was known variously as Plum Island and Plumb Island until it was joined to the mainland with dredgings from the construction of the Belt Parkway. In the late 1890s it was bought by the federal government as a site for a military fortification, but this project was abandoned and the land was then leased with the stipulation that it be used as a summer resort. It became a bungalow colony that in 1934 still had no electricity, gas, or telephone service. In the 1950s the U.S. Department of Agriculture opened a laboratory there to study animal diseases. No longer inhabited, the area lies within the Gateway National Recreation Area and is partly owned by the city.

Ellen Marie Snyder-Grenier

Plunders Neck. Former neighborhood in southeastern Brooklyn, lying within New Lots and bordered to the north by East New York and the Queens County line, to the east by Spring Creek, to the south by Jamaica Bay, and to the west by Betts Creek (Fountain Avenue). The area was the site of farming and fishing, and during the late nineteenth century about 50 families lived in wooden houses isolated from the rest of Kings County. A small hotel stood at Forbell's Landing adjacent to Mill Pond. The land later became the site of the Louis H. Pink housing project and the Pitkin Avenue subway yards.

Stephen Weinstein

Plunkitt, George Washington (*b* New York City, 1842; *d* New York City, 19 Nov 1924). Political leader. Known as "the sage of Tammany Hall," he held office as an alderman and state senator; for many years he was a Democratic district leader on the West Side and a sachem of the Tammany Society, of which he became Father of the Council. Plunkitt is remembered for his frank statements about "honest graft" and why reform movements are doomed in New York City. Many of his views are recorded in William Riordan's book *Plunkitt of Tammany Hall* (1905). Plunkitt lived at 323 West 51st Street.

Frank Vos

Plymouth Church of the Pilgrims. Congregational church organized on 13 June 1847 by a group of merchants, most of them abolitionists from New England. It opened in a building at the corner of Orange and Hicks streets in Brooklyn Heights, with Henry Ward Beecher as its minister. After being destroyed by fire on 13 January 1849 the building was replaced in 1850 by a much larger one, which had ample standing room and a large semicircle of pews around a platform that served as a pulpit. The number of full members rose from 21 in 1847 to 1460 in 1859, when the congregation on Sundays reached nearly 3000 (many Congregational churches had fewer than 100 communicants at the time). The congregation took keen interest in temperance and abolition and opened the church as a station on the Underground Railroad to offer asylum to runaway slaves. During the Kansas–Nebraska crisis of the mid-1850s it dispatched rifles to the antislavery settlers; the rifles quickly became known as "Beecher's bibles" and the church as the "church of the holy rifles." Most members supported Beecher when accusations of adultery were brought against him in the 1870s, and when he died in 1887 50,000 mourners passed through the church. The church continued to thrive under his successor, Lyman Abbott. A parish house enclosing a garden court was added in 1914. After merging with the Congregational Church of the Pilgrims in 1934 the church was renamed Plymouth Church of the Pilgrims; it remained in its building on Orange Street, where in Hillis Hall the Tiffany windows from the former Congregational Church of the Pilgrims (113 Remsen Street) were installed. In 2010 Plymouth Church continued to serve the community with regular worship services.

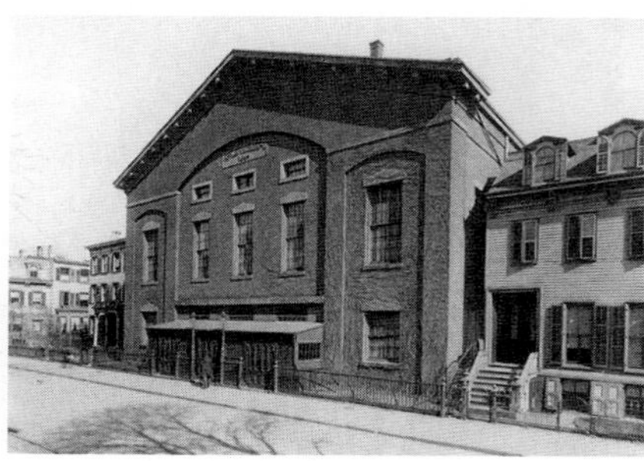

Plymouth Church of the Pilgrims (designed by Joseph C. Wells), Brooklyn Heights, ca *1900*

Stephen Morrell Griswold, *Sixty Years with Plymouth Church* (New York: Revell, 1907)

Kevin Kenny

PM. Daily newspaper launched in New York City in 1940 and shaped by the idealism of its editor and publisher, Ralph Ingersoll, who had worked for the publishers of *Time* as an editor of *Fortune* and a founder of *Life.* It had a magazine format, carried no advertising, and became known for its crusading journalism. Among the newspaper's innovations were its coverage of the labor movement and its features of interest to consumers. Its prominent writers and photographers included Ben Hecht, Ernest Hemingway, Max Lerner, I. F. Stone, James A. Wechsler, Margaret Bourke-White, and Weegee. Despite these strengths the newspaper was not profitable, owing largely to Ingersoll's inability to manage the company. When it began accepting advertising in 1946 at the insistence of the investor Marshall Field III, Ingersoll resigned in protest. The newspaper became the *Star* in 1948 and ceased publication later that year.

Roy Hoopes, *Ralph Ingersoll: A Biography* (New York: Atheneum, 1985)

Madeline Rogers

pneumatic subway [Beach Pneumatic Transit]. New York City's first passenger subway, built in 1870. At the American Institute Fair in 1867, Alfred Ely Beach, the editor of *Scientific American,* showcased the air-powered tubes that would later serve as the prototype for his subway. Though these tubes were first used in England for both package dispatch services and passenger railroads, Beach was the only person to successfully adapt the system as a subterranean railroad in the United States. In 1870 Beach completed the 312-foot (95-meter) tunnel from Warren Street to Murray Street under Broadway in 58 days; his urban novelty operated with one train and one station until 1873. While serving no functional purpose, the railroad operated to convince the public and possible investors of its potential; a fountain and grand piano were placed in the waiting area to impress passengers. It is nonetheless unlikely that pneumatic power could have been adapted to suit the needs of New York City on the scale of the modern subway. In 1912 the tunnel was destroyed during the construction of the new subway line under Broadway by the Brooklyn Rapid Transit Company.

Michael C. Repka

Podhoretz, Norman (*b* Brooklyn, 16 Jan 1930). Editor and writer. A son of immigrants, he earned a BA in English from Columbia University and later studied for two years at Cambridge University. In New York City he joined the staff of *Commentary,* a monthly magazine edited by Elliot Cohen. In 1956 he married Midge Decter, Cohen's secretary and later an editor and political analyst. In 1960 Podhoretz became the magazine's editor; in 1995 he became the editor-at-large. For a short time he was allied with the New Left, publishing critical essays on the cold war, the Vietnam War, and American life. His memoir *Making It* was published in 1968. He moved to the right during the mid-1960s; by the early 1970s he abandoned literary interests for political ones and became a leading spokesman for neoconservatism.

Alexander Bloom

Poe, Edgar Allan (*b* Boston, 19 Jan 1809; *d* Baltimore, 7 Oct 1849). Short-story writer, poet, and critic. Orphaned in 1811, he grew up in Virginia and England. His early career was marked by frequent changes of residence and a conspicuous lack of success as a writer. He lived in New York City during 1837–38 and spent the summers of 1843 and 1844 in a farmhouse on West 84th Street, just west of Broadway. He again took up permanent residence in the city in 1844. While living at 85 Amity Street (now West Third Street) he wrote the poem "The Raven," which he published anonymously in February 1845 in the *American Review* to critical success. During the same year he became the editor of the *Broadway Journal,* a weekly publication through which he sought to challenge the city's best-known literary journals, especially the *Knickerbocker Magazine,* leading him into several damaging controversies. His charge that Henry Wadsworth Longfellow's poetry was plagiarized contributed to the demise of the journal in December. In 1846 he moved to Fordham Cottage at 2640 Grand Concourse near East Kingsbridge Road; the building is now known as Poe Cottage. Critical intrigue continued to influence his work. For the popular magazine *Godey's Lady's Book* he wrote the series "The Literati of New York," which resulted in a libel suit against him by Thomas Dunn English, one of his subjects. *Godey's* dropped the series but published his short story "The Cask of Amontillado," a veiled parody of his literary troubles. After the death of his wife Poe left the city in 1849.

Kenneth Silverman, *Edgar A. Poe: A Mournful and Never Ending Remembrance* (New York: Harper Collins, 1991)

See also Literature, §1.

Jeff Finlay

Poe Cottage. Last home of Edgar Allan Poe (from 1846 to 1849), built about 1812 on the Grand Concourse and East Kingsbridge Road in the Bronx. Poe moved to the site in the hope that its setting would prove salutary to his wife, who was gravely ill, and because of its access to Manhattan by the New York and Harlem River Railroad. While living in the cottage Poe wrote such well-known poems as "Annabel Lee," "Ulalume," "The Bells," and "Eureka." Poe's wife died of tuberculosis at the cottage in 1847. In 1913 it was moved to Poe Park across the street to avoid demolition, and in 1917 it opened as a historic house museum. Now a national and city landmark, it is administered by the Bronx County Historical Society.

Gary D. Hermalyn

poetry slam. Competition in which poets perform their work for an audience. In their current form, poetry slams began in Chicago in the mid-1980s; the first poetry slam in New York City took place at the Nuyorican Poets Cafe in 1988. Initially hosted by poet Bob Holman, these events have been a feature of the cafe's programming ever since, and poetry slams have remained popular in the city. In 2008 weekly slams were sponsored by the Nuyorican, the LouderARTS Project, and NYC–Urbana at the Bowery Poetry Club, a venue founded by Holman in 2002. Youth programs have been established. Teams from New York City regularly participate in the annual National Poetry Slam. At "open" slams all audience members may have the opportunity to participate. At invitational slams the poets competing have been selected in advance. Judges—audience members who have been selected by the host—rate each three-minute performance on a scale of one to 10. Slams frequently last multiple rounds, with the lowest-scoring poets gradually being eliminated. The styles participants use may vary from hip-hop music to traditional poetry recitation, and subject matter is also diverse. Quality of performance, as well as content, is a factor in scoring. Criticism of poetry slams has focused on the uneven quality of the poetry performed; however, advocates point to the value of the strong connection formed between poet and audience.

Cristin O'Keefe Aptowicz, *Words in Your Face: A Guided Tour through Twenty Years of the New York City Poetry Slam* (New York: Soft Skull Press, 2008)

Helen Graves

Poe Cottage, ca 1915

Poets, Playwrights, Editors and Novelists. See PEN.

Poets House. Founded in 1985 by the late poet Stanley Kunitz and arts administrator Elizabeth Kray, this 45,000-volume poetry library is located on the second floor of 72 Spring Street. Its collection of books, journals, chapbooks, audiotapes, videos, and electronic media is free and open to the public. It has a sunny reading room, and a children's room is decorated with colorful paper cranes. Each year Poets House holds more than 50 panel discussions, lectures, seminars, and workshops, both onsite and in city libraries. The annual Poets House Showcase is an exhibit of all the poetry books published nationwide that year. In the late 2000s Poets House planned to double its space and expand its services by moving to a new building in Battery Park City where it will be exempt from rent through 2069.

Katarzyna Nikhamina

Poets' Walk. Informal name for the sculpture-lined southern end of the Central Park Mall near 69th Street. Also known as Literary Walk, the promenade is distinguished by quadruple rows of American elms that flank the 40-foot-wide (12-meter-wide) walkway, creating a canopy. In 1873 park commissioners designated the mall for the installation of sculptures in order to preserve the naturalistic feel that Frederick Law Olmstead and Calvert Vaux had created in the rest of the park. As a result, the walkway became lined with sculptures of the literary figures William Shakespeare, Robert Burns, Fitz-Greene Halleck, and Sir Walter Scott. Nonliterary sculptures in the vicinity include those of Ludwig van Beethoven and Christopher Columbus. The path inspires photographers in all seasons and has been featured in numerous films shot in New York City.

Talia Falk

Poles. The Polish presence in New York City dates to the early seventeenth century, when a number of merchants, soldiers, and teachers from Poland settled in New Amsterdam. Among them were Alexander Curtius, founder of the first school in Manhattan; Daniel Litscho, a leading supporter of Peter Stuyvesant on the council of burgomasters and schepens; Olbracht Zaborowski, a landowner who held title to much of New Jersey; and Marcin Krygier, who was elected burgomaster at least three times. In 1834 two Austrian warships arrived in New York Harbor carrying 234 Polish exiles from the failed uprising of November 1830. Some settled in the city, where they worked to free Poland from foreign domination. Gaspard Tochman founded the Polish–Slavonian Literary Association (1846), and several others published literary and historical works. More groups of Polish immigrants settled in New York City after the unsuccessful Polish revolts of 1846 and 1848 and the January Revolt of 1863. Many of the immigrants were highly educated, eventually entered the professions, and often took part in reform movements such as that against slavery. During the Civil War Colonel Wladimir Krzyzanowski raised the 58th New York Infantry, known as the Polish Legion, and Major Alexander Raszewski led a Polish unit, Company C, of the 31st New York Infantry.

Most of the Poles settling in New York City between 1870 and 1920 were rural laborers seeking economic opportunity who were originally from parts of Poland occupied by Austria and Russia. Called the *za chlebem* ("for bread") immigrants, they generally found employment in construction and manufacturing, especially textiles. Once established they proved to be enthusiastic supporters of the labor movement, many becoming leaders in union locals. The first neighborhood of the za chlebem took form on the Lower East Side, where St. Stanislaus Bishop and Martyr Church was erected in 1872. Gradually these immigrants expanded into the southern and northeastern Bronx, Fort Greene, South Brooklyn, Elmhurst, and in 1890 Greenpoint, where they established St. Stanislaus Kostka Church in 1896. The Catholic Church proved important in the daily lives of Polish immigrants, providing a social focus as well as a religious one. Two parishes of the Polish National Catholic Church were eventually formed in the city: Holy Cross Parish in South Brooklyn and the Church of the Resurrection in Greenpoint. The Polish population of New York City was swelled by refugees from Nazi atrocities during World War II, displaced persons after the war, refugees from communist persecution during the cold war, and the rise of the labor movement Solidarity. These new immigrants tended to be educated and highly skilled, and many settled in traditional Polish neighborhoods. In the 1970s, when the Polish population of the city was at its height, about 292,000 residents were of Polish birth and about 500,000 others were of Polish heritage. Among those of Polish birth 38 percent lived in Brooklyn, 33 percent in Queens, 14 percent in Manhattan, 11 percent in the Bronx, and 4 percent in Staten Island. The largest Polish neighborhood was Greenpoint, where Manhattan Avenue was lined with Polish bookstores, butcher shops, restaurants, and travel agencies. One of the most influential Polish-language newspapers, *Nowy Dziennik,* was launched in the city in 1971. The number of Polish-born residents in New York City fell in the quarter century after 1985, partly because of tighter immigration enforcement, partly because of the aging of the population, and partly because of Poland's admission to the European Union in 2004, which spurred a return migration. According to the Department of City Planning, the Polish-born population in the five boroughs in 2006 was 60,153.

In the early twenty-first century Polish fraternal, cultural, and educational organizations in New York City included the Kosciuszko Foundation, the Polish Institute of Arts and Sciences of America, the Polish National Alliance of Brooklyn, the Roman Dmowski Institute, and the Joseph Pilsudski Institute of America for Research in the Modern History of Poland. There were also 24 Roman Catholic parishes recognized as Polish, eight major Polish veterans' organizations, 10 Polish political organizations, nine professional associations, six artistic and theatrical societies, and 12 periodicals. The most important Polish social and cultural celebration of the year is the annual Pulaski Day Parade in October.

James S. Pula

police. For the first 200 years of its existence New York City maintained public order much like that of other colonial cities. In New Amsterdam a *schout fiscal* (sheriff attorney) administered the rules established by the Dutch West India Company, and a burgher guard looked out for Indians at times of expected raids. When fears of Indians became widespread, Governor Peter Stuyvesant initiated a paid nighttime foot patrol consisting of a captain and eight men armed with rattles. The patrol was intended to alert residents of impending raids; to control rowdy sailors, drunkards, and prostitutes; and to watch for fires. Under British control in the late seventeenth century New York City was subject to military rule. A notable exception to the pattern was a night watch, 45 strong, that patrolled from 1684 to 1689 and briefly made the city perhaps the best-protected in the colonies, a distinction of which the city was soon deprived by political unrest and war. From the end of the seventeenth century until well into the nineteenth New Yorkers falteringly sought to navigate between competing approaches to policing. Under the charter promulgated by John Montgomerie in 1731 all citizens living south of the Collect Pond could be called on for night-watch duty. A constable in each ward took eight men with him every night to serve watch (although women were eligible, there is no record of any having served). The reluctance of local residents to be pressed into service, even for a night, abruptly ended the citizens' watch in 1734, when it was replaced by a paid force of three to a dozen men standing guard over a city of 10,000.

Policeman of 1693, from Harper's New Monthly Magazine

Number of Police Officers in New York City, 1826–2008

Year	Officers
1826	200
1840	948
1844	1,132
1850	901
1855	1,116
1860	1,473
1865	2,474
1870	2,325
1875	2,544
1880	2,159
1885	2,898
1890	3,525
1895	3,825
1900	7,426
1905	8,766
1910	10,173
1915	10,664
1920	10,905
1925	14,216
1930	18,595
1935	17,842
1940	19,747
1945	15,579
1950	19,789
1955	22,024
1960	26,993
1965	29,407
1970	38,927
1975	42,165
1980	28,691
1985	30,705
1990	26,911
1993	36,340
2000	40,800
2005	36,149
2006	35,690
2008	37,838

Note: There was no official police department before 1844.

From the 1740s residents believed their city to be besieged by crime and disorder and were unsure of the remedy. The "Negro plot" in 1741 frightened the city into organizing a temporary militia, which was immediately succeeded by another paid force, this time of 36 men, a dozen of whom were on duty on any given night. Within a year the paid force was replaced by another citizens' watch; like its predecessors this proved both inadequate to the task and burdensome to the citizenry, particularly the poor, who could ill afford the time needed to serve or the money to secure a substitute. As a result impoverished residents found themselves guarding their more affluent neighbors, an arrangement that continued when the state government in 1747 set up a force with characteristics of both a militia and a citizens' watch, prompting the city to organize yet another paid police force in 1762. In 1774 there was a force with the equivalent of 20 full-time positions: 16 regular watchmen served nightly for £32 a year, and eight served on alternate nights for £16 a year. The force looked out for fires but was scarcely able to control the city's burgeoning, boisterous populace. When the British army occupied New York City in 1776, it assumed primary responsibility for policing, but many residents maintained a voluntary watch throughout the war. A formal constabulary system and night watch were reintroduced after the British evacuated in 1783. To provide incentives for enforcing the law, the state legislature soon established a fee schedule by which constables were paid according to each task: fees were set for serving a warrant, issuing fines, making arrests, detaining prisoners, serving summonses, and performing similar duties.

In 1800, 16 constables patrolled the city by day along with about 40 marshals appointed by the mayor. Together they were responsible for suppressing riots, maintaining order in the streets, acting as court officers, and arresting offenders. Much of the work of law enforcement in the early nineteenth century was done by one man, Jacob Hays, who governed the small constabulary force for nearly 50 years after Mayor Edward Livingston appointed him high constable in 1802. At night a ragtag force of 72 men served in the watch in 1800 under two captains and two deputies and was entrusted with lighting the street lamps, subduing wrongdoers, looking out for fires, and guarding the Potter's Field from grave-robbing medical students. Paid too little to support themselves on watch work alone, the watchmen labored during the day as mechanics, teamsters, stevedores and the like, then often dozed their way through guard

Police Commissioners of New York City after Consolidation

Bernard J. York	1898–1901*
John B. Sexton	1898–1901
Theodore L. Hamilton	1898
William E. Phillips	1898
Jacob Hess	1898–1901
Henry E. Abell	1899–1901
Michael C. Murphy	1901–2
John N. Partridge	1902–3
Francis V. Greene	1903–4
William McAdoo	1904–5
Theodore A. Bingham	1906–9
William F. Baker	1909–10
James C. Cropsey	1910–11
Rhinelander Waldo	1911–13
Douglas I. McKay	1913–14
Arthur Woods	1914–17
Frederick H. Bugler	1918
Richard E. Enright	1918–25
George V. McLaughlin	1926–27
Joseph A. Warren	1927–28
Grover A. Whalen	1928–30
Edward P. Mulrooney	1930–33
James S. Bolan	1933
John F. O'Ryan	1934
Lewis J. Valentine	1934–45
Arthur W. Wallander	1945–49
William P. O'Brien	1949–50
Thomas Francis Murphy	1950–51
George P. Monaghan	1951–53
Francis W. H. Adams	1954–55
Stephen P. Kennedy	1955–61
Michael J. Murphy	1961–65
Vincent L. Broderick	1965–66
Howard R. Leary	1966–70
Patrick V. Murphy	1970–73
Donald F. Cawley	1973–74
Michael J. Codd	1974–77
Robert J. McGuire	1978–83
Benjamin Ward	1984–89
Richard J. Condon	1989–90
Lee P. Brown	1990–92
Raymond W. Kelly	1992–94
William J. Bratton	1994–96
Howard Safir	1996–2000
Bernard Kerik	2000–1
Raymond W. Kelly	2002–

*Before 1901, the city had concurrent commissioners.

duty. Like the constables and marshals the watchmen wore no uniform apart from leather helmets, for which they became known as leatherheads.

During the first half-century after independence New Yorkers tolerated their meek and modest police system and accepted a remarkable degree of unchallenged lawlessness in the streets, largely because their fears of a standing army made them wary of delegating greater coercive power to local government. But by 1830 many came to see their fractured police force as incompetent and ineffective. As immigrants, tenements, and factories became more numerous, tensions relating to class, race, and ethnicity heightened and crime increased accordingly. There were frequent riots, robberies around the wharves and businesses of the first ward, violence and vice in the slums of the Five Points, and prostitution and gambling throughout the city, all signaling the breakdown of communal order. At the same time the constables and night watch were increasingly criticized for paying less attention to public safety than to the fees they could earn and the political favors they owed to the politicians who had appointed them. Inspired by the example set in London, officials in the early 1840s resolved to make New York City the first American city to adopt a full-time, professional police force that could prevent crime as well as respond to it. A measure to reorganize the force introduced by Mayor Robert H. Morris and signed into law in 1845 by Mayor William F. Havemeyer established a "Day and Night Police" of as many as 800 men, identified by a star-shaped badge that gave the new force the nickname "star police."

Reformers were still fearful that the power vested in a strong, independent police department could be abused, and they sought to make the police strictly accountable to the public by subjecting them to the control of elected officials. In solving one problem they nevertheless created others. By commingling control of the police and partisan politics they made the mayor's authority to appoint police officers dependent on the recommendations of aldermen; patrol districts coincided with ward boundaries, local politicians used the police for their own venal purposes, party officials controlled the appointment of magistrates to the police courts, and aldermen enjoyed the right to have criminal charges dismissed. Because the fee schedule was replaced by a system of fixed salaries, the most lucrative part of police work became the taking of bribes from those engaged in gambling, prostitution, and other illicit businesses. The same reformers who were eager to organize a police force were reluctant to pay for it, and the force remained small in relation to the city's population, numbering only 1200 in 1855 (when the city's population exceeded 600,000). Furthermore, the absence of a modern system of social services forced the police to shoulder many duties having little relation to crime fighting: police directed traffic, found shelter for the homeless, searched for lost children, settled domestic disputes, and escorted drunkards home or to the precinct house. In 1850 the police were outfitted with uniforms.

The police in 1853 were placed under the control of a board of commissioners composed of the mayor, the recorder, and the city judge. In the same year some formal training began, and officers were armed with nightsticks. It was hoped that the new board would wrest control over law enforcement from the corrupt council, but soon Mayor Fernando Wood demonstrated his capacity to use the police for his own purposes. In 1857 a state legislature dominated by Republicans decided to take power away from the city's Democrats and into its own hands when it established the Metropolitan Police District. Composed of New York, Kings, Westchester, and Richmond Counties, the new district was governed by a board of five gubernatorial appointees and the mayors of New York City and Brooklyn. Wood, a Democrat, resisted the establishment of a state force within the city and vowed to maintain a municipal counterpart. The two forces coexisted for several months until the Metropolitans in June sought to arrest the recalcitrant mayor for inciting a riot, and a bloody battle ensued on Broadway. The confrontation ended when the state militia intervened, and the crisis was resolved a month later when the New York State Court of Appeals upheld the constitutionality of the state force. In the same year officers were authorized to carry a service revolver. The seats on the board reserved for the mayors of New York City and Brooklyn were eliminated in 1860, and the total number of members was reduced to three (all appointed by the governor), thus guaranteeing that Republicans would have unlimited access to the patronage afforded by the police department. The Metropolitan Police District was abolished in 1870 by the state legislature, now controlled by the Democrats, and the governance of the department was returned to a local board composed of Democrats loyal to Tammany Hall and a few Republican allies, giving impetus to a reform movement already under way. All precinct detectives in 1883 were placed under the jurisdiction of the Central Detective Bureau at the request of its commanding officer Thomas Byrnes, ostensibly to fight corruption, and in the following year the police came under the jurisdiction of civil service regulations already applicable to other municipal agencies. Service revolvers were officially issued to officers in 1887. After a long campaign by the Women's Temperance Union, New York City in 1891 became one of the last large American cities to employ police matrons.

The police department was a symbol of corruption in the late nineteenth century and for much of the twentieth, owing largely to the close connections between policing and politics. An investigative commission led by State Senator Clarence Lexow in 1894–95 disclosed involvement by the police in vice operations and found officers responsible for rigging elections and for physical brutality. In 1930 an investigation led by Samuel Seabury uncovered widespread corruption, as well as the harassment of innocent women by police vice squads. Periodic scandals inspired attempts to reform the police force and make it more professional, but these proved slow and difficult to bring about.

One effort to instill professionalism was the formation of specialized, technically trained units with specific functions. In response to a spate of anarchist terrorism, a bomb squad was created in 1903. Traffic control was adopted as an official activity in 1908. Radio motor patrol cars (RMPs) were introduced in 1923, and the Emergency Services Division was created in 1930. Two-way communication between patrol cars and precincts began in 1937; a fully automated communications system known as the Special Police Inquiry Network (SPRINT) became operational in 1969. In 1959 the department organized the Tactical Patrol Force (TPF), a specially trained corps of physically imposing, college-educated police officers intended to deal with gang violence. By the mid-1960s the TPF became an important instrument for the suppression of civil unrest. The force, later disbanded, was admired by some for its proficiency and resented by others, especially among racial minorities, as an army of occupation. Skepticism toward the department among minority groups stemmed from its long history as an all-white organization: it did not appoint its first black officer, Samuel Battle, until 1911, and its first black precinct commander, Lloyd Sealy, until 1964.

Efforts at reform took on a new urgency during the 1960s with the onset of the civil rights movement, racial unrest, and charges of police brutality. Demands that the police be sensitive to the concerns of racial and ethnic minorities became widespread. In 1966 the Patrolman's Benevolent Association became embroiled in a heated political battle over a referendum to form a civilian review board. By the end of the decade two national commissions had stressed the need for urban police departments to recruit more officers from racial minority groups. A commission led by Whitman Knapp in 1972 confirmed allegations that the leadership of the police department had tolerated systemic corruption and that many officers routinely collected payoffs from owners of small businesses. In 1972 the Civil Rights Act was amended to bring state and local governments under federal guidelines for employment, and between 1974 and 1983 the Guardians, an association of black officers, filed four successful lawsuits against the city because of racial bias in entry-level and promotional examinations. The city's first black police commissioners were named in the following years: Benjamin Ward in 1984 and Lee P. Brown in 1990. In 1985 Mayor Edward I. Koch appointed a committee led by John E. Zuccotti to investigate management and personnel practices in the department. The committee

New York City Police Department Precincts

MANHATTAN

Precinct	Address
1st	16 Ericsson Place
5th	19 Elizabeth St.
6th	233 West 10th St.
7th	19½ Pitt St.
9th	130 Ave. C
10th	230 West 20th St.
13th	230 East 21st St.
14th (Midtown South)	357 West 35th St.
17th	167 East 51st St.
18th (Midtown North)	306 West 54th St.
19th	153 East 67th St.
20th	120 West 82nd St.
22nd (Central Park)	86th St. and Transverse Rd.
23rd	162 East 102nd St.
24th	151 West 100th St.
25th	120 East 119th St.
26th	520 West 126th St.
28th	2271–89 Eighth Ave.
30th	451 West 51st St.
32nd	250 West 135th St.
33rd	2207 Amsterdam Ave.
34th	4295 Broadway

BRONX

Precinct	Address
40th	257 Alexander Ave.
41st	1035 Longwood Ave.
42nd	830 Washington Ave.
43rd	900 Fteley Ave.
44th	2 East 169th St.
45th	2877 Barkley Ave.
46th	2120 Ryer Ave.
47th	411 Laconia Ave.
48th	450 Cross Bronx Expressway
49th	2121 East Chester Rd.
50th	3450 Kings Borough Ave.
52nd	3016 Webster Ave.

BROOKLYN

Precinct	Address
60th	2951 West Eighth St.
61st	2575 West Coney Island
62nd	1925 Bath Ave.
63rd	1844 Brooklyn Ave.
66th	5822 16th Ave.
67th	2820 Snyder Ave.
68th	333 65th St.
69th	9720 Foster Ave.
70th	154 Lawrence Ave.
71st	421 Empire Blvd.
72nd	830 Fourth Ave.
73rd	1470 East New York Ave.
75th	1000 Sutter Ave.
76th	191 Union St.
77th	127 Utica Ave.
78th	65 Sixth Ave.
79th	263 Tompkins Ave.
81st	30 Ralph Ave.
83rd	480 Knickerbocker Ave.
84th	381 Gold St.
88th	298 Classon Ave.
90th	211 Union Ave.
94th	100 Meserole Ave.

(*continued*)

QUEENS

Precinct	Address
100th	92–24 Rockaway Beach Blvd.
101st	16–12 Mott Ave.
102nd	87–34 118th St.
103rd	168–02 P.O. Edward Byrne Ave.
104th	64–2 Catalpa Ave.
105th	92–08 222nd St.
106th	103–53 101st St.
107th	71–01 Parsons Blvd.
108th	5–47 50th Ave.
109th	3705 Union St.
110th	94–41 43rd Ave.
111th	42–06 215th St.
112th	68–40 Austin St.
113th	167–02 Baisley Blvd.
115th	92–15 Northern Blvd.

STATEN ISLAND

Precinct	Address
120th	78 Richmond Terrace
122nd	23–20 Highland Blvd.
123rd	116 Main St.

Source: New York Police Department Web site, http://www.nyc.gov/html/nypd/html/home/home.shtml

Compiled by Jessica Montesano and Frank Nestor

found that the major obstacle to achieving a racially balanced police force was an overreliance on written civil service examinations for selection and promotion. It also found that systematic corruption in the department had been essentially eliminated. Other problems facing the department included charges by female officers of sex discrimination and renewed concerns about police brutality. In response to the large number of officers shot in the line of duty, bullet-proof vests were introduced in the early 1980s and made compulsory in 1991.

A surge in violent crime that began in the 1970s and culminated in increased drug-related shootings in the 1990s earned New York City a reputation as a dangerous place. Brown and Mayor David N. Dinkins responded by reintroducing foot patrols in many neighborhoods and developing a plan called "Safe Streets, Safe City," which called for the addition of many hundreds of police officers between 1991 and 1996. The new emphasis on community policing was consistent with a national trend, but it also increased the risk of corruption. In a direct contradiction of the recommendations made by the Knapp Commission, it placed more officers on foot patrol and closer to the people at a time when the drug trade put an unprecedented volume of tainted money on the street. When drug-related corruption in several precincts was uncovered in 1992, Mayor Dinkins appointed an investigatory panel led by Judge Milton Mollen of the New York State Supreme Court. Although the panel did not find the widespread, systemic corruption of the sort unearthed by the Knapp Commission 20 years earlier, it warned that the department had failed to uproot corruption and had tolerated a culture that fostered misconduct and concealed lawlessness.

Police boat, 2009

When former federal prosecutor Rudolph W. Giuliani became mayor in 1994, he pledged to make crime reduction his number one priority. His first police commissioner, William J. Bratton, instituted the "broken windows" approach to policing, which treated quality-of-life issues as precursors to more serious crimes. Bratton also established COMPSTAT (Computer Generated Comparative Statistics), a management reporting system that held precinct commanders personally responsible for crimes committed in their jurisdictions. In 1995 the Housing Authority Police Department and Transit Authority Police Department, which once operated as separate units, were merged into the New York Police Department. In 1998 the Division of School Safety, an unarmed security force within the school system, was also put under the jurisdiction of the department.

Beginning in 1993 New York City experienced significant drops in crime that continued into the administration of Mayor Michael R. Bloomberg, and his police commissioner Raymond W. Kelly, who had also served under Mayor Dinkins. From 1997 to 2006 index crime (the eight crimes used by the Federal Bureau of Investigation [FBI] to compile its annual crime index: willful homicide, forcible rape, robbery, burglary, aggravated assault, larceny over $50, motor vehicle theft, and arson) dropped 42.4 percent, and as of 2006 New York City had the lowest index crime rate among the nation's 25 largest cities. The terrorist attack on the World Trade Center in 2001 had a serious effect on the Police Department, which lost 23 officers and left many others with physical and psychological injuries. In 2002 the department established deputy commissioners for intelligence and counterterrorism, the latter heading a counterterrorism unit that coordinates efforts with the Joint Terrorism Task Force of the FBI. In 2006 a new Office of Emergency Management headquarters was opened to coordinate the response of police, fire, and medical units to emergency situations.

Police memorial, 2009

In 2005 the New York City Police Academy had its first graduating class in which a majority of its officers were nonwhite (45.2 percent non-Latino white, 18.3 percent black, 28.2 percent Latino, and 8 percent Asian). In 2006 there were 35,645 sworn officers in the department: 55.8 percent white, 24 percent Latino, 16.2 percent black, 4 percent other, and 17.3 percent female; the department also included 17,683 civilian personnel. As of 2006 Police Academy cadets received an annual salary of $25,100 plus benefits, which would increase in six months to $32,700. While competitive on a national level, the salary lagged behind salaries earned by police officers in adjoining suburban counties, making it difficult for the department to recruit personnel.

The basic unit of command from which officers are deployed for patrol duty is the precinct, of which there are 76, organized within eight borough commands. There are four civil service ranks in the department that are granted on the basis of a written examination: police officer, sergeant, lieutenant, and captain. A member of the force is awarded a gold shield of the detective rank for meritorious service at the discretion of the police commissioner. All promotions to executive ranks above captain are also at the discretion of the commissioner: these ranks include deputy inspector, inspector, deputy chief, assistant chief, and chief. In 2006 Mayor Bloomberg announced long-awaited plans to move the Police Academy from its Gramercy Park location on East 20th Street, where it had been since 1964, to a new 33-acre (13-hectare) facility in College Point, Queens. Ground was broken for the new facility in December 2009.

James F. Richardson, *The New York Police: Colonial Times to 1901* (New York: Oxford University Press, 1970); Robert M. Fogelson, *Big City Police* (Cambridge, Mass.: Harvard University Press, 1977); Joseph P. Viteritti, *Police Professionalism in New York City: The Zuccotti Committee in Historical Context* (New York: Center for Research in Crime and Justice, New York University School of Law, 1987); James Lardner and Thomas A. Reppetto, *NYPD: A City and Its Police* (New York: Henry Holt, 2000)

Joseph P. Viteritti

Police Athletic League [PAL]. Nonprofit organization run by volunteer police officers and dedicated to the educational, cultural, and recreational enrichment of disadvantaged children in New York City, formed in 1914 as the Junior Police by Captain John Sweeney of the New York Police Department. It became well known for its programs in athletics, notably boxing, and later added employment training, courses in remedial reading, drug-abuse counseling, creative writing contests, day-care centers, after-school clubs, and educational summer day camps. By the early twenty-first century a $40 million capital campaign had funded new PAL community centers in Harlem, the South Bronx, and South Jamaica. More than 70,000 youths a year take part in activities sponsored by the league.

Stephen Weinstein

polio (poliomyelitis). Viral infection that attacks nerves and can cause paralysis, brain damage, and death. Although cases of polio were commonly observed and treated by physicians in New York City during the eighteenth and nineteenth centuries, the first recorded epidemic of polio in the city did not occur until 1907. In 1910 the New York City Board of Health classified polio as a communicable disease requiring immediate reporting and isolation of the patient. The city suffered its worst polio epidemic during the summer of 1916. Before its end in late October the epidemic claimed 8991 victims, with 2449 deaths. About 95 percent of all the polio cases in the city that summer were children younger than 10. By declaring that the city was in a "state of great and imminent peril," Mayor John Purroy Mitchel justified closing theaters and parks, postponing the opening of the city's public schools, forcibly removing victims from their homes, and other harsh measures. Less severe epidemics of polio occurred in New York City during the summers of 1931, 1935, and 1936, with sporadic outbreaks during the 1940s and 1950s. Although polio was already waning before the advent of the Salk and later the Sabin polio vaccines, their implementation between 1955 and 1965 led to its end as a major killer of children.

John R. Paul, *A History of Poliomyelitis* (New Haven: Yale University Press, 1971); John Duffy, *A History of Public Health in New York City* (New York: Russell Sage Foundation, 1968, 1974); David Oshinsky, *Polio: An American Story* (New York: Oxford University Press, 2005)

Howard Markel

Polish Institute of Arts and Sciences of America. Research institution formed in 1942 by Polish scholars exiled by the Nazi invasion of their homeland. It severed ties with the communist government of Poland, and only reassociated with Poland in 1989. The institute sponsors an annual scholarly meeting, maintains a library and archives for research on Polish history and culture, publishes books, supports lectures and art exhibitions, and has published, since 1956, the internationally recognized journal *Polish Review.* In the early twenty-first century it had roughly 1500 members including the former national security adviser Zbigniew Brzezinski, the poet Czeslaw Milosz, and the ambassador John Gronouski. Its offices were at 208 East 30th Street in Manhattan.

James S. Pula

Polish Legion. Popular name for the 58th New York Volunteer Infantry, recruited in 1861 from among Polish, German, and other immigrants in New York City and organized by Colonel Wladimir Krzyzanowski. It fought during the Civil War at Cross Keys, Groveton, Second Bull Run, Chancellorsville, Gettysburg, Lookout Mountain, and Wauhatchie.

James S. Pula

Polish National Alliance of Brooklyn. Fraternal organization formed in 1905 to provide immigration services and cultural activities for Poles. From the outset it offered insurance, provided scholarships for college students, and promoted Polish heritage. In the late twentieth century it was the largest Polish fraternal organization in New York City, with members throughout New England and the eastern states. Its headquarters are at 155 Noble Street in Brooklyn.

James S. Pula

political clubs. The first political clubs in New York City were caucuses formed during the American Revolution to support the Livingstons (patriots) and the De Lanceys (Loyalists). After the first formal party system took shape in the early 1790s clubs supported the Democratic Republicans (led by Thomas Jefferson) and the Federalists (led by Alexander Hamilton). The Democratic Republicans dominated the city's civic activities, and their influence increased after the War of 1812. Their success was due to the ward system, which enabled a quasi-democratic political system to develop. Political clubs ranged in size from those covering one ward (such as the Young Hickory Association in the eighth ward) to citywide organizations like the Democratic Empire Club; the more powerful ones conducted meetings in their own halls or saloons. By the 1840s even the Catholic Church had its own political club, Carroll Hall, run by Bishop John Hughes. Other clubs in the city included the Empire Club, led by Captain Isaiah Rynders, and Mike Walsh's Spartan Club, which drew its membership from newly arrived, exploited Irish immigrants.

Political clubs grew in importance during the nineteenth century, reaching a peak when the Democratic Party became institutionalized and the city in the early 1840s underwent unprecedented population growth. In 1849 the refusal of the Spartan Club to support the mayoral candidate of Tammany Hall led to the victory of Fernando Wood, a Whig sponsored by Mozart Hall. A resumption of growth after the Civil War resulted in more centralized and less democratic politics, in part a reaction to the scandals of the Tweed Ring, and political clubs diminished in importance. In the late nineteenth century political clubs remained active in Brooklyn; in addition to those allied to the Democratic and Republican Parties, Brooklyn had clubs organized around specific issues such as Prohibition (the Anti-Saloon Republican League, 1888) and women's rights (the Equal Rights Club, 1890). During the first half of the twentieth century some socialist and communist clubs were formed.

After World War II the influence of political clubs declined precipitously. Their number fell from 2819 in 1933 to just 268 in 1972, with the largest number in Queens. Much of the clubs' residual power, especially within the Democratic Party, accrued because organized crime had filled a patronage vacuum left by the federal government, which saw its role formally eliminated when the Hatch Act (1940) forbade federal employees to contribute money to political organizations. Frank Costello (1891–1973) became the covert head of Tammany Hall, and organized-crime figures were dominant in Democratic clubs in Brooklyn and Manhattan.

Although the number of political clubs had decreased to about 100 by the 1990s, their influence lingered: Mayor Ed Koch began his political career with the Village Independent Democrats; Mayor David Dinkins was supported by the George Washington Carver Democratic Club of Harlem; and U.S. Representative Charles B. Rangel maintained power through the Martin Luther King Democratic Club of Harlem. In the early twenty-first century many political clubs drew their support from new immigrants and ethnic groups such as Dominicans in Washington Heights, who were active participants in the Northern Manhattan Democrats for Change and the Concerned Democratic Coalition of Northern Manhattan. The Thomas Jefferson Democratic Club in Canarsie, home to former Brooklyn Democratic chief Meade H. Espisto, was transformed by new Caribbean and Latino members. Clubs also remained powerful in the judicial selection process. Other significant political clubs included the North End Democratic Club in the Bronx, home to former borough president Fernando Ferrer, state assemblyman Jose Rivera, and borough president Adolfo Carrion, Jr.; the Community Free Democrats in Manhattan, home to U.S. Representative Jerrold L. Nadler; and the Robert F. Kennedy Democratic Club and Guy R. Brewer Democratic Club in Queens.

Roy V. Peel, *The Political Clubs of New York City* (New York: G. P. Putnam's Sons, 1935); Norman Adler, *Political Clubs in New York City* (New York: Praeger, 1975)

Anthony Gronowicz

politics. See Government and Politics.

Pollock, (Paul) Jackson (*b* Cody, Wyo., 28 Jan 1912; *d* East Hampton, N.Y., 11 Aug 1956). Painter. After following two of his brothers to New York City in 1930 he studied at the Art Students League with Thomas Hart Benton, whose figurative painting influenced his early style. In 1935 he worked on the Federal Art Project of the Works Progress Administration, and in the following year he joined an experimental workshop run by David Alfaro Siqueiros. Shortly after leaving the Federal Art Project Pollock met his future patron, Peggy Guggenheim, who had recently opened her gallery Art of This Century at 30 West 56th Street. In 1943 the Museum of Modern Art purchased his painting *The She-Wolf.* He married the artist Lee Krasner in 1945, with whom he moved to Springs, Long Island; there he set up a studio in a barn, where he developed a technique of pouring paint directly on the canvas that became typical of his mature works and proved highly influential. He died in an automobile accident. Although controversial during his life, Pollock achieved great recognition after his death as a key figure in the American abstract expressionist movement. His residences in New York City included 46 Carmine Street (1932–33), his brother's apartment at 46 East Eighth Street (1935–45), and a carriage house at 9 MacDougal Alley (1949 and 1950).

Francis Valentine O'Connor and Eugene Victor Thaw, *Jackson Pollock: A Catalogue Raisonné of Paintings, Drawings, and Other Works* (New Haven: Yale University Press, 1978); Ellen G. Landau, *Jackson Pollock* (New York: Harry N. Abrams, 1989)

Mona Hadler

pollution. Contamination of New York City's water, air, and land is one the most complex problems facing the city, where the effects of pollution are magnified by the density of population.

The purity of drinking water was an early environmental concern. Although clear ponds, streams, and freshwater wells provided an adequate supply for American Indians and Dutch and English colonists, by the mid-eighteenth century surface waters and some public and private wells were becoming fouled by seepage from cesspools and street runoff. A shortage of potable water in 1832 contributed to a cholera epidemic that killed 3513 city residents. Most of the populace still depended on well water when New York City voters approved plans in 1835 to dam the Croton River in Westchester County and construct an aqueduct to transport clean water to the city (completed 1842). During the twentieth century the city markedly expanded its upstate supply of pristine water, building six large reservoirs in the Catskill and Delaware watersheds from 1907 to 1964. Over the following decades these supplies provided the city with high-quality water that exceeded state and federal standards. But by the late twentieth century rapid residential and commercial development and sewage discharges, especially in the suburbanized Croton watershed, contributed to some declines in the quality of reservoir water and occasional discoloration of Croton tap water, which federal and state officials directed to be filtered to safeguard its quality. Construction began in 2004 on a 300-million-gallons-per-day (1.14-billion-liters-per-day) underground filtration plant at Van Cortlandt Park in the Bronx. Additionally, to protect the city's water supply at its source, government officials began in the early 1990s to accelerate pollution-prevention efforts throughout the upstate watershed region. By 2008 the city had acquired or preserved nearly 90,000 acres (36,400 hectares) of ecologically important lands, mostly in the unfiltered Catskill and Delaware watersheds, and had funded upgrades to more than 100 sewage treatment plants located in all three watersheds. Nevertheless, intense rainstorms, large-scale development projects near the reservoirs, and the possibility of natural gas drilling on watershed lands remained long-term threats to the drinking water supply.

The rivers and bays of New York City have been polluted, mostly by sewage and to a lesser extent by toxins and garbage, since the industrialization and population growth of the late nineteenth century. The city's first, primitive sewer was constructed along Broad Street in lower Manhattan in the late seventeenth century, but a comprehensive network of underground sewers was not laid until the mid-nineteenth century. Although in the following decades rudimentary devices were installed at outflow pipes to filter solid biological wastes, virtually all the city's raw sewage was dumped directly into local waterways until the early twentieth century, by which time it had largely destroyed a prosperous shellfish industry and was endangering the health of bathers. In 1935 the city opened its first modern sewage treatment plant on the shores of Coney Island. By the time the North River plant in West Harlem began operating in 1986, 14 sewage plants were treating nearly all the raw waste generated in the city during dry weather, or approximately 1.7 billion gallons (6.4 billion liters) a day. Despite such progress, in the early twenty-first century 27 billion gallons (102 billion liters) of combined raw sewage waste and polluted rainwater were still being flushed directly into the city's waterways every year: because of the city's nineteenth-century unified sewer system, in which wastewater and storm runoff are collected in common pipes, treatment facilities are overloaded during even moderate rainfall. Although unhealthy bacteria levels continued to contaminate shellfish beds and limit swimming along sections of the waterfront, overall pollution related to sewage began a steady decline in the 1970s and continued into the twenty-first century. Sewage sludge, the end product of sewage treatment, was for many years dumped 12 nautical miles (22.2 kilometers) offshore and later 106 miles (170.6 kilometers) offshore. Because of its harm to the marine ecology, ocean dumping of sewage sludge was prohibited by federal law as of 1992. In the early twenty-first century the city's roughly 1200 tons (1090 metric tons) per day of sewage sludge has first been "dewatered" at city treatment plants and ultimately used as fertilizer or for other land applications around the country. The waters surrounding New York City have also been subject to toxic pollution. From the late 1940s to the mid-1970s two manufacturing plants operated by General Electric north of Albany, New York, sent more than 500,000 pounds (227,000 kilograms) of polychlorinated biphenyls (PCBs) directly into the Hudson River. These toxic PCBs were detected in more than 20 species of fish taken from the river, of which more than half a dozen were declared off-limits to commercial fishing in New York State. After World War II and continuing for several decades, hundreds of businesses drained chemical wastes into the city's sewers: every day thousands of pounds of heavy metals such as zinc, copper, lead, chromium, and nickel entered sewage plants, which funneled much of the chemical loadings into surrounding waters; however, these discharges have declined sharply in the twenty-first century. Another problem of continuing concern has been ubiquitous urban runoff, such as automotive fluids. These pollutants, as well as occasional oil spills in the Arthur Kill along Staten Island, were still adding to the toxic flow dumped into New York Harbor in the first decade of the twenty-first century.

Garbage is another source of water pollution. In the 1850s the city began loading trash on barges to be jettisoned offshore, a practice that was halted in 1934 by order of the U.S. Supreme Court after garbage repeatedly washed onto the New Jersey coast. For decades the city relied on landfills as the primary means of trash disposal, ultimately destroying tens of thousands of acres of saltwater wetlands. Ecologically sensitive marshes in all five boroughs vanished, and pollution seepage from uncontrolled dumps contributed to the contamination of waterways. The number of landfills in the city peaked at 89 in 1934, after which they began closing as they reached capacity and their damaging effects were recognized. In 2001 the city's last landfill, the 2200-acre (890-hectare) Fresh Kills Landfill on Staten Island, stopped receiving trash. In addition to polluting water, the city's trash landfills left a legacy of contaminated land throughout all five boroughs. Indeed, five former city landfills are included on New York State's 2008 listing of hazardous waste sites; four are still classified as posing a "significant threat to the public health or environment." Counting properties contaminated by pollution from all sources, there were 42 hazardous waste sites in New York City, according to the state's 2008 listing. City officials also identified as many as 7600 acres (3075 hectares) of less polluted dump sites, vacant lots, and abandoned commercial properties scattered across the boroughs. A sweeping 2003 state law sought to encourage the cleanup and redevelopment of such sites. In 2008 the city generated about 24,000 tons (21,800 metric tons) of residential, institutional, and commercial trash a day; another roughly 27,000 tons (24,500 metric tons) per day of construction rubble and dirt was also generated. As of 2008 close to one-fifth of the city's residential and institutional waste was being recycled (see Recycling) under a curbside collection program begun in 1989. The remainder of such city-collected waste was being exported, at increasing cost, to out-of-state landfills and regional incinerators.

The air in New York City after the American Revolution was often foul: pungent odors were emitted by overflowing outhouses, open sewers, manure and refuse in the streets, as well as fat, bones, and other wastes discarded by butchers, fishmongers, and tradespeople. The unpleasant smells caused by the rending of tallow and other aspects of soap making were one reason why the city in 1796 restricted the manufacture of soap and candles to the suburbs. Until the mid-nineteenth century garbage was often left for pigs and other scavengers in streets and alleys, dumped in low-lying lands, or discarded at the water's edge. The nation's first refuse incinerator was built on Governors Island in 1885, and the use of incinerators increased after the U.S. Supreme Court banned ocean dumping of garbage. By the early twentieth century the burning of coal to power utility plants and to heat residences often filled the city's skies with plumes of dark smoke. A boom in automobile travel after World War II compounded the problem. In November 1953 a temperature inversion trapped sulfur dioxides, particulates, and other contaminants over the city, resulting in the deaths of perhaps 200 people and the hospitalization of many more. During the 1960s more than 17,000 incinerators in apartment buildings and 11 municipal garbage-burning plants added soot and toxins to the atmosphere. A mayoral task force warned in 1966 that in proportion to its area New York City was pumping more poisons into its air than any other major city in the country. The city then took important steps to reduce such pollution. The City Council lowered the sulfur content allowed in coal and heating oil in 1966 and 1971, yielding significant reductions in sulfur dioxide and soot. Lead in gasoline was reduced by the U.S. Environmental Protection Agency starting in 1973, and as a result airborne lead concentrations in the metropolitan region had fallen by 95 percent by the mid-1990s. The City Council prohibited new incinerators in apartment buildings as of 1970; those that remained were phased out by 1993. And by the mid-1990s, federally required pollution controls on automobiles and annual automobile emissions inspections had helped to lower official carbon monoxide readings from the harmful levels of the preceding decades. In 1988 and 1995 the council restricted tobacco smoking, a primary source of indoor pollution, in nearly all enclosed public spaces in the city, leading to the city's 2002 Smoke-Free Air Act, which made virtually all workplaces smoke free. Air quality in the city has markedly improved since the 1960s but continued in the early twenty-first century to violate national standards for particulates and ozone smog. Among the major contributors to the problem were diesel-powered vehicles and construction equipment, as well as a growth in regional motor vehicle travel. A "congestion pricing" plan to reduce traffic in Manhattan and to raise funds for public transportation was widely discussed in 2007 but was not approved by the state legislature.

Noise pollution became a problem in New York City with the introduction of elevated railways in the 1870s and worsened with increased traffic, especially after World War II. Some improvements resulted when the city adopted one of the nation's first noise-control codes in 1972. The code was revised in 2005, by which time the city was issuing 2000 to 3000 summonses a year for noise violations. However, excessive noise from construction activities, loud air conditioners, honking horns, barking dogs, roaring subways, piercing sirens, and jet takeoffs from area airports remained an annoyance in many neighborhoods, sometimes interfering with hearing and sleep.

As pollution problems attracted greater public attention during the 1960s and 1970s, tens of thousands of New York City residents joined environmental groups; Mayor John V. Lindsay in 1968 formed what later became the Department of Environmental Protection. On 22 April 1970 more than 100,000 New Yorkers joined with Americans across the country to celebrate the first Earth Day; they gathered in Union Square to learn about environmental issues or strolled down Fifth Avenue, which was closed to traffic between 14th and 59th streets. During the 1970s and 1980s there was a growing recognition that some of the more troubling environmental problems (such as lead poisoning from paints and the siting of garbage transfer stations) were having a disproportionate effect on the poor and minorities. This led to the formation of grassroots organizations dedicated to securing "environmental justice."

During the first decade of the twenty-first century scientists and public officials warned that global warming from the burning of fossil fuels could lead in future decades to increased inland and coastal flooding and stresses to the city's water supply and sewage infrastructure. In part to advance local solutions to the emerging climate crisis, Mayor Michael Bloomberg in 2007 unveiled PlaNYC 2030, a 127-point initiative to sustainably enhance the city's urban environment and refurbish its infrastructure, and created a new Office of Long-Term Planning and Sustainability. The City Council also took action to cut carbon dioxide emissions, including the passage of laws that require new government buildings to meet standards for Green Buildings and call for a 30 percent reduction in such emissions from all government operations by 2017. Ironically, New York

City residents generate less air pollution, use less energy, and consume less water per capita than do their rural and suburban counterparts largely because of the city's compact living patterns and high public transit usage. And in the early twenty-first century New York City's immediate pollution dangers were less acute than those in many other cities of comparable size. But long-term assaults on its water, air, and land continued.

Freedom to Breathe: Report of the Mayor's Task Force on Air Pollution in the City of New York (New York: City of New York, 1966); John Duffy, *A History of Public Health in New York City* (New York: Russell Sage Foundation, 1968, 1974); Charles H. Weidner, *Water for a City: A History of New York City's Problem from the Beginning to the Delaware River System* (New Brunswick, N.J.: Rutgers University Press, 1974); Eric A. Goldstein and Mark A. Izeman, *The New York Environment Book* (Washington, D.C.: Island, 1990)

See also Sanitation.

Eric A. Goldstein, Mark A. Izeman

Polo Grounds. Name of several sporting facilities in New York City. The first opened in 1876 between 110th and 112th streets between Fifth and Sixth avenues in Manhattan for polo and became the home of the baseball Giants and Metropolitans in 1883. It was abandoned when streets were cut through in 1889. The name was revived in 1891 when the Giants took over Brotherhood Park, then a year old, overlooking the Harlem River at 157th Street. Destroyed by fire on 13 April 1911, it was replaced the same year by a structure of concrete and steel seating 38,000 (eventually 55,987) and notable for its unusual dimensions (279 feet [85 meters] to left field; 483 feet [147.2 meters] to center field; and 258 feet [78.6 meters] to right field). This facility was the home of the baseball Giants (to 1957), the football Giants (1925–55), and the New York Mets (1962–63) before being demolished in 1964 to make way for a public housing project.

Steven A. Riess

Polytechnic Preparatory Country Day School. Private coeducational secondary school opened in 1854 on 25 acres (10 hectares) in Bay Ridge, Brooklyn. It was one of the first private schools in the United States to adopt the model of the country day school: a full day's program of academics, arts, athletics, and college preparation, and shared responsibility with the family in providing guidance to students.

Richard Schwartz

Polytechnic University. Private educational institution opened in 1854 as the Brooklyn Collegiate and Polytechnic Institute, a college preparatory school for boys at the edge of Brooklyn Heights. The school was led in its first decade by John H. Raymond, later the first president of Vassar College. It gradually focused on scientific and technical education under its second president, David H. Cochran, and as the industrial economy of Brooklyn expanded during the 1880s, it implemented a four-year scientific curriculum emphasizing engineering. In 1890 the name was changed by state charter to the Polytechnic Institute of Brooklyn. Graduates of the school readily found employment in the growing metropolitan area, especially after Brooklyn became a part of New York City in 1898. At the same time inadequate physical resources kept the school crowded into downtown Brooklyn. During the early decades of the twentieth century the school had a distinguished scientific and technical faculty that included an extraordinary group of Viennese refugees from fascism, under whose leadership the doctorate was first offered in several fields during the 1930s and important research was carried on during the 1940s. Advances were made in the field of polymers by the chemist Herman F. Mark. Developments in microwave research by the electrical engineer Ernst Weber were crucial to the development of U.S. radar during World War II. The school's achievements during these years helped its reputation extend as far as India, Taiwan, and Iran.

Women were admitted as students in the 1940s. During the administration of its fifth president, Harry Rodgers, the school acquired nearby facilities that had been vacated in the late 1950s by the American Safety Razor Company. Baccalaureate degrees in the humanities and social sciences were added in the late 1960s. Financial problems during the following years limited the school's ability to attract students and retain faculty, even after a merger in 1973 with the engineering school of New York University strengthened the faculty and increased the amount of state aid. In 2008 the trustees accepted a merger with New York University.

John J. O'Connor, *Polytechnic Institute of Brooklyn: An Account of the Educational Purposes and Development of the Institute during Its First Century* (New York: Polytechnic Institute, 1955)

Marvin E. Gettleman

The Harlem River Speedway (center) and the Polo Grounds (right), 1914

Pomander Walk. Private row of facing two-story cottages in a Tudor style from 94th to 95th streets between Broadway and West End Avenue, built in 1921 by the developer Thomas Healy. Healy acquired the land and engaged the firm of King and Campbell to design a development based on the quaint English village depicted in Louis N. Parker's popular play *Pomander Walk* (opened in New York City in 1911). Along Broadway Healy built one of the first indoor skating rinks in Manhattan and the restaurant Sunken Gardens. Pomander Walk stands out from its surroundings for its style and ambience: it is ornamented with colorful trim (including shutters of aqua, blue, red, and green), old-fashioned lampposts, a small wooden sentry box, and hedges and flower boxes lining the walk. Its residents have included such actors as Dorothy and Lillian Gish, Mary Martin, Humphrey Bogart, and Rosalind Russell. Pomander Walk

Pomander Walk, 2009

was designated a New York City landmark in 1982 and included on the National Register of Historic Places in 1983.

See also TAXPAYERS.

Amanda Aaron

Pomonok. Neighborhood in central Queens centered at Kissena Boulevard and Jewel Avenue, bounded on the north by the Long Island Expressway; originally part of the Town of Flushing. The name derives from an Indian word applied to an area of eastern Long Island and probably means "land of tribute" or "land where there is traveling by water." In early deeds it is spelled Pommanocc (1639), Paumanacke (1659), and Pommanock (1665). The Pomonok Country Club opened around 1920 and hosted the Professional Golfers Association tournament in 1939. In 1949 the members voted to sell the land to Local 3 of the International Brotherhood of Electrical Workers, which built Electchester, a cooperative apartment development with 2500 units in 38 buildings, and the New York City Housing Authority, which built the Pomonok Houses, a 35-building complex with 2070 units completed in 1952; the Queens Borough Public Library opened a branch in the Pomonok Houses in 1951. Queens College opened on the site of the Parental School (1908) on Kissena Boulevard in 1937.

Patricia A. Doyal, Jeffrey A. Kroessler

Pondiac Democratic Club. Political club formed in the Bronx in 1921 by Albert Cohn at the behest of Edward J. Flynn, the Democratic leader of Bronx County (1922–53). It was intended to erode the political base of the rival Democratic district leader Patrick Kane, who unsuccessfully challenged Flynn for the office of sheriff of the Bronx in 1921. The club met on the second floor of 809 Westchester Avenue and was originally called the Pontiac Club after an American Indian chief of the Ottawa tribe (the name was misspelled when the club was registered). At first the 200 dues-paying members of the club were predominantly Jewish and Irish. The club gained influence because of its ability to guarantee an extraordinarily high turnout among voters and was the first Democratic club to draw members from the growing Latin American community in the Bronx. In 1953 its member Felipe Torres became the first Latin American elected to the state assembly, and in 1967 its leader Eugene Rodriquez, also an assemblyman, became the first one elected to the state senate. Rodriquez's conviction of attempted extortion in 1967 led to the collapse of the club, and it disbanded when his rival Louis Gigante was elected a Democratic district leader in 1972 with the backing of a neighboring club. Other members of the Pondiac Club included James J. Lyons, Stanley Friedman, Clara Gompers, Ed Gilhooley, Robert Garcia, Salvador Almeida, and David Ross.

Neal C. Garelik

Poole, Butcher Bill [William] (*b* New Jersey, July 1821; *d* New York City, 8 March 1855). Nativist. A butcher, a notoriously ferocious street fighter, and a gang leader, he was involved in gambling and liquor sales but was best known for his association with various anti-immigrant groups, including the Bowery Boys. He was also a "shoulder hitter" (strong-arm man) for nativist political causes. His dispute with the Irish-born heavyweight boxer John Morrissey led to his fatal shooting by Lewis Baker, a Welshman; his last words were reportedly "Good-bye boys, I die a true American." Nativist newspapers exploited the incident by glorifying Poole and portraying him as the innocent victim of an Irish conspiracy. As many as 250,000 people attended his funeral, and the trial that followed his death led to increased tension between Irish immigrants and native-born Americans. In the 2002 film *Gangs of New York* a character based on Poole was portrayed by Daniel Day-Lewis, who was nominated for an Academy Award for the performance.

Elliott J. Gorn, "'Good-bye Boys, I Die a True American': Homicide, Nativism, and Working-Class Culture in Antebellum New York City," *Journal of American History* 74 (1987), 388–410

Elliott J. Gorn

Poole, Ernest (*b* Chicago, 23 Jan 1880; *d* Franconia, N.H., 10 Jan 1950). Journalist and novelist. He graduated from Princeton University in 1902. A reformer, his magazine reporting in *McClure's* led to changes in child labor laws and tenement reform as well as helped to fuel an antituberculosis campaign. His first novel, *The Voice of the Street* (1906), a story of New York tenement life, also had a social message. Poole wrote *The Harbor* (1915) against the backdrop of the changing Brooklyn docks during the transition of marine transport from sail to steam power. His novels portrayed labor unions in a sympathetic light. As a correspondent for the *Saturday Evening Post* during World War I he reported on Europe, and in 1917 he traveled to Russia and reported on the effects of the Russian Revolution on the population. In 1918 he won the Pulitzer Prize for *His Family,* a novel detailing the rise in social mobility after the war. Throughout the 1920s and 1930s Poole's work was published in *Harper's Magazine.* He famously chronicled the urban squalor of "The Lung Block," a section of New York City's Lower East Side notorious for its high incidence of tuberculosis; decades later his reporting led to the demolishing of the infamous tenements and the construction of Knickerbocker Village. His autobiography *The Bridge* was published in 1940.

Nathan Morgante

pooper-scooper law [Canine Waste Law]. Law passed in 1978, with a major push by activist group Children before Dogs, that requires dog owners to remove their dog's waste from the sidewalk. Since the 1930s "Curb Your Dog" signs have been visible in the city. New York City's Departments of Health, Sanitation, and Parks and Recreation can issue tickets for any violations of the law. By the early twenty-first century the sidewalks of the city were almost entirely clear of animal waste, a dramatic improvement over the decades before World War II.

Michael Brandow, *New York's Poop Scoop Law: Dogs, the Dirt, and Due Process* (West Lafayette, Ind.: Purdue University Press, 2008)

Jessica Montesano

poorhouses. See ALMSHOUSES.

Pope, Generoso (*b* near Naples, 1 April 1891; *d* New York City, 28 April 1950). Businessman and community leader. He moved to New York City in 1906 and first worked as a waterboy for the Colonial Sand and Gravel Company, a tunnel excavation company that he owned by 1920; he had enterprises in real estate, banking, and communications. He bought the leading Italian American daily newspaper *Il Progresso Italo-Americano* in 1928 and the weekly newspaper *Il Corriere d'America* in 1929. A supporter of Mussolini, he received medals from the Italian fascists in 1926, 1928, and 1930; in 1931 leftists tried to assassinate him with a letter bomb. In 1936 he voiced his support for neutrality, thus aiding the fascists in the Second Italo-Ethiopian War. He was a powerful figure in Tammany Hall politics, and his friendship with Mayor James J. Walker prompted his investigation by the Seabury Commission (he was eventually cleared). Initially opposed to Fiorello H. La Guardia's mayoral candidacy, he later supported it; in later years he returned to endorsing Democratic candidates. He repudiated fascism in an editorial in *Il Progresso* in 1941. During the late 1940s he organized Italian relief efforts and established a college scholarship fund for graduates of the city's Catholic schools. In 1949 he bought the radio station WINS. Pope left the bulk of his estate to charity.

Mary Elizabeth Brown

Poppenhusen, Conrad (*b* Hamburg, 1 April 1818; *d* College Point [now in Queens], 12 Dec 1883). Businessman. The son of a prosperous textile trader, he moved to New York City in 1843 to run the offices of the whalebone merchant H. C. Meyer and in 1844 became a partner in the firm of Meyer and Poppenhusen. At its plant in Brooklyn the firm processed whalebone into buttons, corset stays, combs, spoons, medical products, and various other articles, and in 1852 it secured a license for the manufacture and sale of hard rubber (developed by Charles Goodyear). With the assistance of a new partner, Frederick Koenig, the plant was converted to the manufacture of hard-rubber household goods, but it soon proved too small for the rapidly expanding business; in 1854 the firm was reestablished in Queens as the India Rubber Comb Company, later the Enterprise Works. The new location easily accommodated the factory workers, and in the following years Poppenhusen built streets, houses, businesses, and schools (including the Poppenhusen Institute, 1868, which remains open as of 2007). In 1870 the community became the village of College Point, incorporating the neighborhoods of Flammersburg and Strattonport. Poppenhusen built the Flushing and North Side Railroad and entrusted it to his sons, but their inexperience in management and fierce competition led to ruin. Although he tried to remedy the damage, in 1877 he was forced to declare bankruptcy; in his final years he made a limited financial recovery.

Vincent Seyfried

popular entertainment. Parades, festivals, and informal recreations in streets and taverns were some of the popular entertainments available in New York City during the colonial period. Most participants were men. The growth of the city in the first half of the nineteenth century encouraged some entrepreneurs to open theaters, and soon melodramatic plays and minstrel shows were introduced. Both genres relied on a range of ethnic, racial, and regional stereotypes (the worst of which were reserved for blacks), and by the early 1830s they were well established. To accommodate the wide audience that the performances attracted, theaters were divided into an upper tier, or gallery, for rowdies and prostitutes and a mezzanine for families. By the middle of the century there were many theaters and different kinds of entertainment for each social class: the Bowery became the entertainment district for immigrants and the working class and Broadway for the middle and upper classes. During the 1880s entrepreneurs hoping to appeal to all segments of the population developed vaudeville theater, in which old-fashioned variety shows were presented in new settings; there was enough propriety and enough raciness to suit most tastes and offend few, and drunkenness was not tolerated. Manhattan soon became a national center for vaudeville, which along with amusement parks, cafés, dance halls, and nickelodeons helped to subvert Victorian ideas of propriety and sexuality by permitting working women to mingle unsupervised with men. After the introduction of sound motion pictures in the late 1920s vaudeville theater declined and could not survive the Depression. By the 1930s motion pictures became the most popular form of entertainment. Virtually every commercial district had its own movie house, usually a renovated vaudeville theater or an enormous new motion picture "palace" with extravagant decor. Many New Yorkers went to the movies weekly. After World War II popular culture in the city changed immensely. Racial and ethnic minorities demanded an end to offensive stereotypes in theatrical productions and broadcasts. After television was introduced, popular forms of entertainment were usually broadcast rather than performed in public for audiences. Fear of crime and racial conflict also decreased the public nature of popular entertainment. Still, New York City remained a center for live performance. Rap music was developed on the streets and spread worldwide. Movie theaters showed first-run films from Hollywood and classic and foreign films, and public celebrations for the Fourth of July and other occasions were well attended. The decline of crime during the 1990s brought a greater sense of ease to going out. The popularity of nightclubs and comedy clubs grew, and bars offered televised sports, billiards, and other diversions. Rising property values, however, brought down some old clubs, such as CBGB on the Bowery. In the early twenty-first century the immigrant presence in the city fostered new venues for entertainment. International forms of music, particularly Latin music, grew more prominent in the city's nightlife.

Robert W. Snyder, *The Voice of the City: Vaudeville and Popular Culture in New York* (Chicago: Ivan R. Dee, Publisher, 2000)

Robert W. Snyder

popular fiction. In the mid-nineteenth century about half the popular fiction books written on urban subjects were set in New York City, which was presented with all its promises and threats as the archetypal American city. During this period of widespread moral evangelism from about 1820 to 1870, the city was seen by some as harboring all the temptations of sin: greed on Wall Street, licentiousness on the Bowery, and artifice on Broadway. It was the ultimate proving ground for personal character, a challenge to the innocent and a lure to the weak. Many early authors of popular fiction contrasted images of the smoke-shrouded city with sentimental notions of the idyllic countryside and used this contrast to promote the supposed rural virtues of simplicity, chastity, honesty, industry, and frugality. Frequently a country-born protagonist approached the city with a mixture of awe and dread: in Cornelius Mathews's *Moneypenny* (1849) the title character regarded the city "with fear and trembling, as though it were some beast of prey crouching on the river-bank in the dark." Another common device was to relate a tale of heroism from the perspective of an innocent, virtuous child, as in *The Newsboy* (1854) and other works by Elizabeth Oakes Smith, or of a sober, religious wife, as in the works of Ann Sophia Stephens and Maria Susanna Cummins, in which the heroine provides shelter from the immorality of the streets. A harsher genre of popular fiction known as "rogue fiction" featured the outlaw or cowboy as its protagonist.

Across the United States readers of popular fiction became familiar with such stock details of New York City as the Five Points, the Tombs, gambling houses, concert saloons, dancehalls, oyster cellars, prostitutes, newsboys, and firefighters, and the prevalent style in popular fiction shifted from sentimentalism to realism. The standards of the period were set in such best sellers as *Letters from New-York* (1843) by Lydia Maria Child and *The Mysteries and Miseries of New York* (1848) by Ned Buntline (a pseudonym of Edward Zane Carroll Judson), which combined elements of fiction, journalism, realism, and sensationalism. George G. Foster employed a symbolism of sunlight and shadows to denounce the filth and misery of the city in the novel *Celio; or, New York Above-ground and Under-ground* (1850), and the city was portrayed as "part Paradise, part Pandemonium" in works such as John D. Vose's *Seven Nights in Gotham* (1852), a luridly detailed chronicle of the nightlife and sexual adventures of the wealthy and sophisticated. The less decadent lives of the working class were explored in novels that romanticized the hardy workman and his virtuous wife. Although many writers deplored the exploitation of the working class and sympathized with the downtrodden, they did not champion radical social reform. Working-class readers were assured that they would eventually be rewarded and that the idle rich would be punished. In works like *Celio* and George Lippard's *New York: Its Upper Ten and Lower Million* (1853) the salvation of the working-class hero comes from above, perhaps in the form of an inherited fortune, rather than from such active remedies as politics, strikes, riots, or crime.

One of the most sensational portrayals of the suffering of the poor in the shadow of splendor was Solon Robinson's *Hot Corn: Life Scenes in New York Illustrated* (1854), which sold 50,000 copies in six months. William Wirt Howe wrote in his popular novel *The Pasha Papers* (1859) that the city had "more trade, more wealth, more houses, more dirt, more misery, more political corruption than any other great city in the country," that it was "a place of very great importance particularly self-importance." By 1865 the publishing house of Beadle and Adams had produced four million copies of "dime novels." Writers of popular fiction in the 1860s and 1870s began to share the concerns of civic reformers and denounced incompetent civil servants, corrupt police officers, and self-serving politicians. Howe's *The Pasha Papers* and Henry L. Williams's *Gay Life in New York; or, Fast Men and War Widows* (1866) blasted Tammany Hall and wistfully recalled a supposed golden era of enlightened rule. In the last third of the nineteenth century popular fiction contributed to the emerging image of New York City as a place of civilization and progress. The urban mysteries that had entranced and bewildered earlier generations of readers were now explained in fictional works that doubled as success manuals. Foremost among these were the novels of Horatio Alger, which were so popular that after his death his name was attached to the works of other writers. In *Ragged Dick; or, Street Life in New York* (1867) and about 120 subsequent novels, Alger provided a mostly rural audience with detailed descriptions of the city and practical information on employment, transportation, and lodging. He reassured his readers that anyone could get along in the city with enough "street smarts," charm, aggressiveness, and good fortune.

After the Civil War improvements in law enforcement in the city led to a more favorable view of fictional police officers and detectives, who were no longer seen as unsavory types consorting with criminals and meddling in marital affairs and labor disputes. The detective story, a genre developed earlier in the century by Edgar Allan Poe, became an important form of popular fiction in the late 1880s. Individual wit and will triumphed in a dangerous and deceitful world in such stories as Harlan Halsey's *Lady Kate, the Dashing Female Detective* (1886), in which a female protagonist in New York City alternates between explicitly male and female roles and flirts with the objects of her professional and romantic attention. The celebrated head of the detective bureau of the city police, Thomas Byrnes (1880–92), was instrumental to boosting the reputation of real and fictional detectives through his collaboration with Julian Hawthorne (son of Nathaniel Hawthorne) on five novels loosely based on his own casework and published in 1887–88. Over time the detective genre evolved to reflect changing attitudes toward law and order in the city, and detectives were variously incarnated in stock roles such as spy, scientist, vigilante, and police officer, all adept at disguising themselves and infiltrating milieus ranging from fashionable society to the underworld. In Norman Munro's *Black Tom, the Negro Detective; or, Solving a Thompson Street Mystery* (1893) the hero is "a mysterious individual who came and went into and out of the negro quarters of the city" who unravels the mystery of a white woman found dead in the black part of town, only to be revealed himself as a white detective in disguise.

Government regulation and a changed marketplace brought a rapid end to the dime novel in the 1890s and led to the development of the pulp magazine. One of few fictional detectives to enjoy popularity in both the old and new types of publication was Nick Carter, a hardy, all-American Protestant youth from New York City who appeared in more than 1000 stories from the 1890s to the 1920s. The character was created in "The Old Detective's Pupil; or, the Mysterious Crime of Madison Square," published in the *New York Weekly* in September 1886, and remained a constant for 17 years under the byline of Frederick Marmaduke Van Rensselaer Dey. Carter was pictured in various disguises, including those of a farmer, an Irish political boss, a Chinese boy, and a woman. During a time of imperialism, nativism, and moralism, he embodied traditional middle-class values, eschewing alcohol, tobacco, and profanity: Dey boasted that he "never wrote a Nick Carter story that he wouldn't read to a Bible class." After the turn of the twentieth century the widely held opinion that science was a remedy for urban ills helped to transform the detective from a disguise artist into a scientist. Arthur B. Reeve began a successful series of novels with *The Silent Bullet* (1912), about a professor of "criminal science" at Columbia University who solves crimes with such advanced techniques as "soul analysis." The detective as a force for Progressivism was exemplified by Average Jones, created by the prominent muckraking journalist Samuel Hopkins Adams. After inheriting a fortune on the condition that he live in New York City for 10 years, Jones became an "Ad-Visor," using his powers of detection to ferret out fraud in newspaper advertising; much as earlier detectives had protected New Yorkers from the hidden menaces of the industrial metropolis, Jones protected them from quack doctors, greedy trusts, and corrupt politicians.

As the city grew more complex the craft of the fictional detective grew more esoteric: having at first consisted of knowledge of the street and disguises and then of scientific techniques, it now further evolved into an ability to solve crimes through pure analytical reasoning. The detective as a gentleman of leisure who lent his intellectual powers to solving bizarre and sophisticated crimes was exemplified in Willard Huntington Wright's *The Benson Murder Case* (1926), the first novel featuring his highly popular detective Philo Vance, the scion of an aristocratic New York City family who recalled such characters from British detective fiction as Agatha Christie's Hercule Poirot and Dorothy Sayers's Lord Peter Wimsey. Vance solved crimes nonchalantly with the aid of psychology, criminal anthropology, and a sound knowledge of art; his popularity continued through several sequels until Wright's death in 1933. Frederic Dannay and Manfred B. Lee wrote a long series of novels beginning with *The Roman Hat Mystery* (1929) in which both the pseudonymous author and the detective were Ellery Queen, who lived with his father on West 87th Street and regarded the city with scientific detachment through rimless pince-nez. Rex Stout introduced Nero Wolfe in *Fer-de-lance* (1934), and by 1975 there were more than 60 sequels. Unsoiled by the street life of the city, Wolfe was an obese, cerebral detective who remained ensconced in his apartment on West 35th Street while his energetic assistant Archie Goodwin did the legwork. In an increasingly confounding and hazardous world of crime, Wolfe's renowned brownstone was a fortress from which reason ruled. The detective became an antihero in the work of Dashiell Hammett, who made New York City the setting for parts of *The Glass Key* (1931) and for his last novel, *The Thin Man* (1934), which inspired a series of motion pictures. Its central character is a retired detective named Nick Charles, who while on vacation amid the decadent leisure class of New York City is thrust into the investigation of a murder. Clearly more enthusiastic about drinking and cavorting than about pursuing the case, Charles nevertheless solves it while doing hardly any investigative work of his own. Several other fictional detectives became popular during the 1930s and 1940s: Hildegarde Withers, a spinster schoolteacher and police buff introduced in Stuart Palmer's *The Penguin Pool Murder* (1931) who later appeared in a series of books and films; Bill Crane, a private detective created by John Latimer in *Murder in the Madhouse* (1935); and Scott Jordan, a lawyer and classical music aficionado in New York City created by Harold Q. Masur in *Bury Me Deep* (1947).

At the same time as Vance and Wolfe relied on their deductive powers, the brawling, "hard-boiled" private investigator of pulp fiction pulled the genre of detective fiction in the opposite direction. The most extreme example of the detective as a vengeful urban vigilante is Mike Hammer in more than 20 novels by Mickey Spillane beginning with *I, the Jury* (1947); the character helped to make Spillane the best-selling mystery writer in the world. The ingredients of these stories are deserted, rainy New York City streets; a few luxury penthouses; and an endless maze of tenements, bars, and alleyways, as well as a distrust of lawful authority and a rejection of liberal idealism. The leading postwar writer of the "police story" was Ed McBain (pseudonym of Evan Hunter), who in *Cop Hater* (1956) and later novels drew a similarly bleak portrait of the city. The citizens of "Isola," McBain's version of New York City, are vulnerable "cave-dwellers" who cower in their apartments while the city crumbles around them. Unlike Spillane, whose despair over the individual's loss of power led him to create an armed and dangerous outlaw in Hammer, McBain abandoned individual heroics altogether in favor of the collective authority of the police. His fictional 87th Precinct replaced the lone detective, and teamwork and the power of law replaced individual will.

During the 1950s the detective story began to depict Harlem. Chester Himes created the police detectives Grave Digger Jones and Coffin Ed Johnson and broached the subject of racism. In *Blind Man with a Pistol* (1969) and *The Real Cool Killers* (1985) the possibilities for heroism are tightly circumscribed by the drugs, prostitution, filth, and despondence of Harlem, but Jones and Johnson are nevertheless able to fight crime by relying on the law and their partnership. Ernest Tidyman introduced the first fictional black private detective in *Shaft* (1971), the original cover of which announced: "Shaft has no prejudices . . . He'll kill anyone black or white." Against a backdrop of racial unrest, Shaft and a team of black revolutionaries confront a band of kidnappers seeking to take over the heroin trade in Harlem. Like many other detective stories *Shaft* is infused with sardonic humor: at one point the main character ignites a riot by running through the streets crying "The niggers are coming!" Other detectives specialized in the sort of crime found only in the international capital of finance: under the pseudonym Emma Lathen, Mary J. Latis and Martha Hennisart wrote a series of books including *Banking in Death* (1961) in which the expertise of John Putnam Thatcher, an executive at a bank on Wall Street, allows him to uncover elaborate financial chicanery. Arthur Maling wrote several novels, including *Ripoff* (1976), in which the hero is Brock Potter, a partner in the fictional brokerage house of Price, Potter, and Petacque.

In the early twenty-first century many works of popular fiction focused on women in the city: *The Nanny Diaries* (2002), by former nannies Emma McLaughlin and Nicola Kraus, portrays an Upper East Side mother from the perspective of her overworked nanny; *The Devil Wears Prada* (2003) is a fictionalized account of author Lauren Weisberger's job as an assistant to Anna Wintour at *Vogue*; and "Sex and the City" columnist Candace Bushnell's *Lipstick Jungle* (2005) follows the lives of four powerful New York City women. Urban fiction by black authors, also known as hip-hop or street lit, also flourished, sold by sidewalk book vendors as well as mainstream and independent publishers. Authors included activist Sister Souljah, author of *The Coldest Winter Ever* (1999), about Winter Santiaga, the teenage daughter of a Brooklyn drug dealer; and Omar Tyree, whose novel *The Last Street Novel* (2007) chronicled the adventures of a crime writer in Harlem.

Adrienne Siegel, *The Image of the American City in Popular Literature, 1820–1870* (Port Washington, N.Y.: Kennikat, 1981); T. J. Binyon, *"Murder Will Out": The Detective in Fiction* (Oxford: Oxford University Press, 1989)

Jeff Sklansky

Popular Library. Firm of book publishers, formed in 1942 by Ned Price and specializing in paperbound editions. In the mid-1950s it created a stir in the book trade by purporting to have the "fastest selling pocket-size book line in the nation." The firm sold as many as 85 million books a year by publishing the work of such varied authors as Fulton Sheen and Polly Adler. It later became a profitable imprint of Fawcett and the Columbia Broadcasting System (CBS) before being acquired by Warner Communications in 1982.

James E. Mooney

population. According to the first known colonial census, the area comprising what is now New York City probably had about 10,000 inhabitants in 1698, including 4937 in New York County (Manhattan, settled mostly at the southern tip), 2017 in Kings County (Brooklyn), 727 in Richmond County (Staten Island), and a few others in Queens County (which extended into what is now Nassau County) and the part of southern Westchester County that later became the Bronx. Although the area in the seventeenth century was populated mostly by Dutch and English, many other ethnicities were represented. The city's status as a commercial center and the Dutch reputation for tolerance attracted myriad ethno-religious groups that were seeking refuge from oppression or looking for economic opportunities; these included French-speaking Walloons; Calvinists; Quakers; Puritans; Lutherans; Mennonites; Huguenots; and Jews with diverse origins, such as Brazil, Spain, and Portugal. A substantial flow of African slaves also characterized early settlement in the colony. In fact, by the late 1700s blacks likely comprised close to one-fifth of the city's population. The first federal decennial census, conducted in 1790, showed the city with a population of 33,131 (an additional 16,000 lived in the outlying settlements and farms that later became part of the city). The next-largest cities were Philadelphia (28,522), Boston (18,320), Charleston (16,359), and Baltimore (13,503).

New York City's population was transformed starting in the 1830s with the onset of immigration from northern and western Europe, primarily from Ireland and Germany. These flows marked the onset of mass immigration that would last 100 years, culminating in New York City's permanent status as the nation's largest city. The city increased from 203,000 people in 1830 to 814,000 by 1860, largely on the heels of Irish emigration spurred by the Potato Famine of the 1840s. In 1860 close to one-half of the city's population was foreign-born, with the largest contingent from Ireland. Even in the face of westward migration and the Civil War, immigration continued to propel the city's population upward during the 1860s and 1870s. The city, which now included a portion

Population of Selected Counties of the Colony of New York, 1698–1786

	New York	Kings	Queens	Richmond	Westchester
1698	4,937	2,017	3,565	727	1,063
1703	4,375	1,912	4,392	504	1,946
1712	5,841	1,925	N/A	1,279	2,818
1723	7,248	2,218	7,191	1,506	4,409
1731	8,622	2,150	7,995	1,817	6,033
1737	10,664	2,348	9,059	1,889	6,745
1746	11,717	2,331	9,640	2,073	9,235
1749	13,294	2,283	7,940	2,154	10,703
1756	13,046	2,707	10,786	2,132	13,257
1771	21,863	3,623	10,980	2,847	21,755
1786	23,614	3,986	13,084	3,152	20,554

N/A=Not Available.

Source: U.S. Bureau of the Census, *A Century of Population Growth* (1909)

of present-day Bronx County, officially exceeded a population of one million in 1880. Although immigration continued unabated, the origin countries began to change during the 1880s, with immigration from northern and western Europe giving way to flows from southern and eastern Europe, most notably from Italy, Russia, and Poland. The five boroughs were consolidated into New York City in 1898, with a population of 3.4 million people. It was by far the largest city in the country, well above Chicago (1.7 million), Philadelphia (1.3 million), St. Louis (575,000), and Boston (561,000).

The physical city started to expand after the first subway line was opened in 1904 and subsequent large-scale housing development outside Manhattan began. During the first decade of the twentieth century alone, the city added 1.3 million residents, reaching 4.8 million in 1910, with 41 percent of the population foreign-born. The year 1910 also saw Manhattan reach a peak of 2.3 million residents, but it no longer accounted for a majority of the city's population, as the subways increased settlement in the other boroughs. Still, population was highly concentrated in lower Manhattan, with densities in tenement neighborhoods sometimes exceeding 600 people per acre (compared with today's densities of less than half that number for most Manhattan high-rise neighborhoods). With continued growth, New York City's 6.9 million residents in 1930 were at the hub of a metropolis of more than 12.6 million. Fear regarding the ability of new immigrants to assimilate spurred the passage of restrictionist immigration legislation during the 1920s. Various country quotas were established at the national level with the goal of limiting immigration from southern and eastern Europe. When combined with the effects of the Great Depression, these quotas led to sharp declines in immigration to New York City; however, it continued to grow because of a surge in domestic migration from the southern states and from the island of Puerto Rico, propelling the population to 7.9 million in 1950.

The Immigration and Nationality Act of 1965 led to a resurgence of immigration in many cities, including New York City, which saw an increase in immigrants from Latin America, Asia, and the Caribbean. This increase came amidst large-scale suburbanization and a loss of central-city manufacturing employment, a common experience in most cities of the Northeast and Midwest during the decades after World War II. In New York City, net migration turned negative, meaning that the city became a net exporter of people. This trend was most pronounced during the 1970s, with the city registering a loss through net domestic migration of nearly two million people. However, this large population loss was followed by population growth during the 1980s and 1990s that was fueled by continued immigration and the fertility of new immigrant populations. By 2000 New York City's population reached a new peak, crossing the eight million mark for the first time. The share of foreign-born population rose from just 18 percent in 1970 to 36 percent in 2000. The population dynamic that took root in the 1960s continues today: net export of population to other states, offset by immigration and positive natural increase (more births than deaths). New York City's population stood at 8.25 million in 2006, with the foreign-born population numbering 3.04 million or 37 percent of all people. The city's population continues to be defined by immigrants, with challenges that rival those of a century ago. For instance, some 1.8 million city residents, about one-quarter of the population aged five years and older, are not proficient in English.

Around the time of incorporation, New York City's population was young, with close

Population of New York City Boroughs (as Defined by Consolidation of 1898), 1790–2000

	Bronx	Brooklyn	Manhattan	Queens	Staten Island	Total
1790	1,781	4,495	33,131	6,159	3,835	49,401
1800	1,755	5,740	60,515	6,642	4,563	79,216
1810	2,267	8,303	96,373	7,444	5,347	111,734
1820	2,782	11,187	123,706	8,246	6,135	152,056
1830	3,023	20,535	202,859	9,049	7,082	242,278
1840	5,346	47,613	312,710	12,480	10,965	391,114
1850	8,032	138,882	515,547	18,593	15,061	696,115
1860	23,593	279,122	813,669	32,903	25,492	1,174,779
1870	37,393	419,921	942,292	45,468	33,029	1,478,103
1880	51,890	599,495	1,164,673	56,559	39,991	1,911,698
1890	88,908	838,547	1,441,216	87,050	51,693	2,507,414
1900	200,507	1,166,582	1,850,093	153,999	67,021	3,437,202
1910	430,890	1,634,351	2,331,542	284,041	85,969	4,766,883
1920	732,016	2,018,356	2,284,103	469,042	116,531	5,620,048
1930	1,265,258	2,560,401	1,867,312	1,079,129	158,346	6,930,446
1940	1,394,711	2,269,285	1,889,924	1,297,634	174,441	7,454,995
1950	1,451,277	2,738,175	1,960,101	1,550,849	191,555	7,891,957
1960	1,424,815	2,627,319	1,698,281	1,809,578	221,991	7,781,984
1970	1,471,701	2,602,012	1,539,233	1,986,473	295,443	7,894,862
1980	1,168,972	2,230,936	1,428,285	1,891,325	352,121	7,071,639
1990	1,203,789	2,300,664	1,487,536	1,951,598	378,977	7,322,564
2000	1,332,650	2,465,326	1,537,195	2,229,379	443,728	8,008,278

Note: From 1874 to 1895 New York City consisted of Manhattan and part of the Bronx. The total population of the city was 1,206,299 in 1880 and 1,515,301 in 1890.

Sources: U.S. Bureau of the Census, *Census of Population*, 1960 (vol. 1, part A, table 29), 1970, 1980, 1990; "State and County Quick Facts," http://quickfacts.census.gov/qfd/states/36/3651000.html

Population of New York City by Race and Hispanic Origin, 1950–2006 (in Thousands)

Year	Total Population	Black Non-Hispanic	Hispanic	Asian and Other Non-Hispanic
1950	7,892	728	246	28
1960	7,782	1,063	613	53
1970	7,895	1,526	1,279	118
1980	7,072	1,695	1,406	268
1990	7,323	1,847	1,784	529
2000	8,008	1,962	2,161	1,084
2006	8,214	1,947	2,268	1,145

Sources: U.S. Bureau of the Census, *Census of Population, 1950–2000*; *American Community Survey*, 2006

Compiled by Frank Nestor

to one-third of residents younger than 15. Overcrowded conditions were fairly common in most parts of the city, a function of large families living in tenement buildings. Over the past 50 years, the household and living arrangements of city residents have shifted. Starting in the 1960s, the number of single-parent families has risen because of myriad social, economic, and cultural factors, including the increased number of women participating in the labor force, delayed marriage and childbearing, and increases in divorce. More than one-third of all children live in single-parent households. The number of nonfamily households (mostly consisting of one person living alone) has also risen, primarily in Manhattan. At the same time, households in parts of New York City have grown more complex as a result of larger, extended immigrant families. Overall, approximately 20 percent of city residents live in poverty, a rate that has been relatively unchanged for more than three decades.

The city has continued to grow in racial and ethnic diversity. One hundred years ago, European ethnic groups dominated, but by the middle of the twentieth century large increases in black and Puerto Rican migration to the city began to change its racial and ethnic composition. By 1960 more than 600,000 Puerto Ricans lived in the city, and by 1970 the overall number of Hispanics exceeded 1.25 million. These increases were accompanied by the outmigration of European whites, who last comprised a majority of the city's population in 1980 and whose outward movement has transformed the city from a largely white European city to one with no dominant racial group. In 2006 the city was 35 percent white non-Hispanic, 24 percent black non-Hispanic, 28 percent Hispanic, and 14 percent Asian non-Hispanic, numbers that fail to do justice to the substantial mix of ethnic subgroups within each of these categories.

New York City's 2006 population of 8.25 million still makes it by far the largest city in the United States, easily exceeding the population of Los Angeles (3.83 million) and Chicago (2.84 million). Four of five New York City boroughs would qualify as top 10 U.S. cities as ranked by population.

Joseph J. Salvo, Arun Peter Lobo

Population Council. Nonprofit organization formed in 1951 by John D. Rockefeller III to study and control population. Initially its goal was to expedite population policies in the third world, but it eventually sought also to control fertility in the United States in the interest of preserving advances in education, culture, and development. The first benefactors were Rockefeller (who gave $1,893,000), chairman for the first 25 years; the Ford Foundation ($600,000); the Rockefeller Brothers Fund ($120,000 a year for three years); and several large corporations. By 1985 the council had received $63 million from the Ford Foundation and $50 million from various funds controlled by Rockefeller. Special projects were financed by the U.S. Agency for International Development and the National Institutes of Health. In 2007 the council had a staff of more than 500, projects in more than 60 countries, and a budget of $71.6 million supported by contributions from foundations, governments, individuals, and international organizations. The council directs social programs (including many related to health), conducts research on issues pertinent to developing countries, seeks to improve contraceptive technology, and provides advice and technical assistance to governments, international agencies, and private organizations; it also issues publications and sponsors conferences, seminars, and workshops. Its main areas of focus center on the human immunodeficiency virus (HIV) and AIDS; poverty, gender, and youth; and reproductive health. The Population Council is credited with having defined the importance of population growth and made the study of population a scientific endeavor.

Thomas M. Shapiro, *Population Control Politics: Women, Sterilization, and Reproductive Choice* (Philadelphia: Temple University Press, 1985)

Jane Allen

pornography. New York City became a central market for erotic materials as early as the 1840s, when the first examples of published pornography were probably imported from England and France. In 1846 William Haynes, a surgeon in New York City, published John Cleland's *Fanny Hill: Memoirs of a Woman of Pleasure,* the first known pornographic work produced in the United States. He reinvested the profits to publish racy novels, which by the 1860s were so widely available that they attracted the notice of Anthony Comstock, later the city's leading figure in a lengthy campaign against vice. Pornographic items were sold by some pushcart vendors and stationery stores, and at the end of the nineteenth century even reputable vendors sold postcards with graphic images, drawings with suggestive captions, and photographs of scantily clad women. Occasionally between 1900 and 1920 brazen individuals hawked sexually explicit cards openly on market streets, usually attracting crowds of young men and risking arrest. In some neighborhoods saloon owners and shopkeepers used pornographic paintings, photographs, and figurines to attract customers. Several bars in lower Manhattan and Brooklyn offered slot machines that showed 12 to 15 provocative pictures for a nickel or a dime. Such neighborhoods as Greenwich Village and the East Village were known for tolerating expressions of sexuality that were persecuted elsewhere. During the 1920s and 1930s an underground homosexual culture developed in Times Square. Known as the "Crossroads," the neighborhood attracted both homosexual and heterosexual patrons to entertainments that became increasingly explicit.

The port also served as the illegal point of entry for such literary works as Boccaccio's *The Decameron* and James Joyce's *Ulysses.* Restrictions on printing erotica were loosened after the U.S. Supreme Court allowed the importation of *Ulysses* in 1933, and New York City became the first market for such works as William Faulkner's *Sanctuary* and James Farrell's Studs Lonigan trilogy. Virtually all sexual images and explicit works were deemed obscene until a series of rulings by the U.S. Supreme Court beginning in 1957 narrowed the definition to allow the open sale of pornographic materials. The editor Ralph Ginzburg tested obscenity laws in 1963 by launching *Eros,* a quarterly hardbound magazine devoted to sexuality; for 10 years he unsuccessfully fought a three-year prison sentence while a growing number of businesses, particularly on 42nd Street, offered a vast array of far more explicit magazines, books, movies, "peep shows," and live performances. In a landmark decision, *Memoirs v. Massachusetts* (1966), the Supreme Court ruled that materials needed to be "utterly without redeeming social value" to be found obscene, and observers soon noted that pornography was the fastest-growing segment of the economy on the West Side. Publishers churned out more and varied erotica, including magazines ranging from *Screw,* edited by Al Goldstein, to *Lesbian Lust.*

By 1969 the city's pornography trade became a prominent issue in local politics. The evangelist Billy Graham condemned Times Square as an "open sewer running through the heart of the city" and called on the three mayoral candidates to oppose pornography in their election campaigns. Mayor John V. Lindsay did make pornography a priority, establishing a task force to combat it and enforcing new laws against unlicensed peep shows and the display of sexually oriented magazines. In 1973 a vigorous campaign against obscenity yielded 529 arrests and a conviction rate of 85 percent. Municipal and federal authorities began to look at pornography as an aspect of organized crime, as three crime families were linked to adult bookstores and movie theaters. The resulting crackdown was challenged by some on the grounds of free speech. Goldstein tested the limits of sexual speech by depicting a wide range of sexual acts and lampooning national leaders in *Screw*; he and the publisher were fined on more than one occasion. The magazine maintained a circulation of well over 100,000 and was identified as the leading publication of its kind in an early 1980s survey. Feminists refocused opposition to pornography by arguing that it oppressed women: Women against Pornography, formed in 1979, gave tours of 42nd Street. They found allies in the U.S. Attorney General's Commission on Pornography (1984–86), whose Meese Report condemned a range of materials including sadomasochistic and homosexual literature.

In the following years the pornography trade in the city, as both an economic activity and a political issue, faded somewhat. Efforts to redevelop 42nd Street restricted the number of storefronts and theaters devoted to pornography, and the introduction of adult telephone services and video recordings diminished the industry's association with the city. Concentrations of adult video stores in Chelsea and Flushing drew protests and calls for new zoning laws; at the same time, campaigns against sexual expression were contested by feminists opposed to censorship and by AIDS activists.

In the twenty-first century access to pornography has become easier with Internet sites and chat rooms, and cable television brings X-rated programs into living rooms at modest charges. Sex stores serving both high- and low-end customers are common throughout the city and cater to the "adult entertainment" industry. A number of groups have lobbied to prevent stores from selling pornography near schools and areas where children congregate. Police crackdowns on places selling pornography have elicited complaints from free speech advocates and gay rights groups who say that they have been targeted unfairly. In 2002 the city's first Museum of Sex opened at 233 Fifth Avenue, with a permanent collection of 15,000 objects. New York City became the location of the television show *Sex and the City,* broadcast on HBO from 1998 to 2004 and focusing on the social, and sexual, lives of single women in the city.

John D'Emilio and Estelle B. Freedman, *Intimate Matters: A History of Sexuality in America* (New York: Harper and Row, 1988)

Elizabeth Hovey

Port Authority Bus Terminal. Huge bus depot on the west side of Eighth Avenue between 40th and 42nd streets, designed, financed, and erected during 1947–50 by the Port of New York Authority at a cost of $24 million and opened to the public on 15 December 1950. All commuter and interstate bus companies moved into the new terminal except for the Greyhound Corporation, which did so in 1963. The facility was enlarged in 1963 at a cost of $30 million and again during 1979–80 at a cost of $226 million, mostly to accommodate heavier bus traffic to the New Jersey suburbs across the Hudson River. It is the largest bus terminal in the United States and one of the world's busiest mass transit facilities, accommodating more than 200,000 passengers and 7000 buses on a typical weekday. The 1979–80 expansion included 52 new bus-loading platforms and an indoor mall with 70 shops. In the 1990s, as the nearby Times Square area underwent a significant revitalization, the bus terminal management expanded efforts to provide first-class security and services to terminal customers. In late 2007 plans were announced to construct a large office atop the terminal. Construction was expected to begin in 2010 and take four years to complete.

Andrew Sparberg

Port Authority of New York and New Jersey. Government agency created in 1921 by the states of New York and New Jersey as the Port of New York Authority and charged with improving transportation and terminal facilities in the port and the surrounding bi-state region. Given no taxing power, it was authorized to issue bonds and charge fees for use of its facilities. Appointments to the board of commissioners were divided equally between the state governors and set for fixed, overlapping terms; in 1927 the governors were granted veto power over commissioners' actions. When the agency sought to improve rail-freight transportation in the 1920s, its proposals were blocked by the railroads, which argued that the proposed unified network would weaken their ability to compete for business and that the capital costs to be borne by those carriers under the plan (for new tunnels under the Hudson River and New York Bay) would exceed any benefits they would reap. Local pressures and a campaign by engineer O. H. Ammann led the authority to construct vehicular bridges between New Jersey and Staten Island and the George Washington Bridge; they were completed between 1928 and 1931, ahead of schedule and within budget, giving the agency a reputation for efficiency and political independence. The Port Authority was then awarded control over the Holland Tunnel (opened in 1927) in 1930–31 and began work on the Lincoln Tunnel.

As toll revenue declined during the Depression, the agency drifted, but beginning in the 1940s it became a major regional power under the leadership of executive director Austin J. Tobin, who gathered political support that permitted the Port Authority to take over La Guardia and Idlewild (now John F. Kennedy) airports in New York City as well as Newark Airport in 1947, build the Port Authority Bus Terminal (1947–50), and expand the Lincoln Tunnel. With Robert Moses it devised plans in 1954–55 that led to the construction of the Verrazano–Narrows Bridge, the Throgs Neck Bridge, and the lower deck of the George Washington Bridge. In 1947 the authority took over the marine terminal at Newark, but New York City rejected the agency's offer to take control of and modernize the city's piers. During the 1950s the authority built a major container port at Newark/Elizabeth.

While Tobin was executive director, the Port Authority was often criticized for neglecting the region's rail facilities. In 1961, with most railroads in bankruptcy, Tobin reluctantly agreed to take over the Hudson and Manhattan Railroad, and the railroad (now the Port Authority Trans-Hudson Corporation, or PATH) remains a crucial commuter line despite a large deficit. Tobin's plans to build the World Trade Center were approved in the 1960s, and it was finished in the 1970s. Beset by conflicts over rail-commuter and other issues, he retired in 1972. On 1 July 1972 the authority took its current name.

After several years adrift, in 1977 the agency named Peter C. Goldmark, Jr., executive director. It then developed an industrial park in South Bronx and built a satellite communications center, Teleport, on Staten Island. It also expanded the bus terminal in Manhattan and proposed other projects that encountered criticism, partly because they were outside the agency's transportation mandate. Goldmark's successor, Stephen Berger (1985–90), concentrated on refurbishing aging facilities. Under Stanley Brezenoff (1990–95) and his successors, the authority faced recurrent demands to improve transportation facilities, and monorails from Newark and John F. Kennedy airports to Manhattan were completed. In recent years the agency has experienced continuing growth in passengers and income; its gross operating revenues reached $3 billion in 2006. That year the Port Authority began a 10-year capital plan that includes building a new commuter tunnel under the Hudson River, modernizing the three airports and adding Stewart Airport as a fourth major jetport, and reconstructing the World Trade Center site.

Jameson W. Doig, *Empire on the Hudson* (New York: Columbia University Press, 2001); James Glanz and Eric Lipton, *City in the Sky* (New York: Times Books, 2003)

Jameson W. Doig

Port Authority Trans-Hudson Corporation. See PATH and PATH Station.

Porter, Cole (Albert) (*b* Peru, Ind., 9 June 1891; *d* Santa Monica, Calif., 15 Oct 1964). Composer. The son of prosperous parents, he attended Yale University (BA 1913), where he wrote the "Yale Bull Dog Song" and "Bingo Eli Yale." Later he studied music at Harvard University and with Vincent d'Indy in France. His family opposed his decision to pursue a career as a songwriter until he was freed from financial worry by his marriage to Linda Lee Thomas (?1883–1954), a woman from a wealthy family. His first production on Broadway was *See America First* (1916). He became well known for Broadway musicals and film scores that included many memorable songs, such as "What Is This Thing Called Love?" (1930), "You Do Something to Me" (1929), "Love for Sale" (1930), "Night and Day" (1932), "Anything Goes" (1934), "Begin the Beguine" (1935), "I've Got You under My Skin" (1936), and "In the Still of the Night" (1937). Several of his songs were inspired by New York City, including "Washington Square" (1920), "Happy Heaven of Harlem" (1929), "I Happen to Like New York" (1930), "Take Me Back to Manhattan" (1930), and "Down in the Depths on the 90th Floor" (1936). He maintained an elegant residence at the Waldorf Towers at 100 East 50th Street. Three of his finest works for the theater are *Kiss Me Kate* (1948, book by Bella and Samuel Spewack), *Can-Can* (1953, book by Abe Burrows), and *Silk Stockings* (1955, book by Burrows, George S. Kaufman, and Leueen MacGrath). Porter wrote his own lyrics, which are characterized by elegant turns of phrase, urbane wit, emotional restraint, and sexual innuendo.

Robert Kimball and Brendan Gill, *Cole* (New York: Holt, Rinehart and Winston, 1971); Charles Schwartz, *Cole Porter: A Biography* (New York: Dial, 1977)

Nicholas E. Tawa

Porter, Edwin S(tanton) (*b* Connellsville, Penn., 21 April 1870; *d* New York City, 30 April 1941). Filmmaker. He moved to New York City in the mid-1890s and began building motion picture equipment and working as a film exhibitor; he showed outdoor advertising films at Herald Square and more sophisticated programs at the Eden Musée on 23rd Street. In 1901 he became a camera operator and studio manager for the Edison Manufacturing Company, for which he produced a range of comedies and dramas, including *The Great Train Robbery* (1903), *East Side Urchins Bathing in a Fountain* (1903), and *Dream of Rarebit Fiend* (1906). He later designed Edison's much larger studio in the Bronx, which went into operation in 1907. After leaving Edison in 1909 he formed the Rex Motion Picture Manufacturing Company at 573 11th Avenue, which soon became part of Carl Laemmle's Universal Film Manufacturing Company. In 1912 he sold his stake in Universal and formed the Famous Players Film Company with Adolph Zukor; from their studio at 213 West 26th Street he directed James Hackett in the first film version of *The Prisoner of Zenda* (1913) and Mary Pickford in *Caprice* (1913). He sold his one-quarter interest in the company to Zukor for $800,000 in 1915 and began manufacturing the simplex projector, which became the foremost motion picture projector of the time. Porter eased into retirement, became a recluse during the 1930s, and died at the Taft Hotel in 1941.

Charles Musser, *Before the Nickelodeon: Edwin S. Porter and the Edison Manufacturing Company* (Berkeley: University of California Press, 1991)

Charles Musser

Porter, William Sydney. See O. Henry.

Porter, William T(rotter) (*b* Newbury, Vt., 24 Dec 1809; *d* New York City, 19 July 1858). Editor and publisher. He began his career working for two small newspapers in New England before moving to New York City, where in 1831 he founded the *Spirit of the Times*. In 1839 he purchased the *American Turf Register* and *Sporting Magazine*. A pioneer of sporting journalism in the United States, Porter was also an enthusiastic sportsman, a founder of the New York Cricket Club, and an avid supporter of horse racing, field sports, and recreational athletics.

Norris Wilson Yates, *William T. Porter and the* Spirit of the Times (Baton Rouge: Louisiana State University Press, 1957)

George B. Kirsch

Port Ivory. Industrial area in the northwestern corner of Staten Island, named after the former factory complex operated by Procter and Gamble on the site. It opened in 1907 to manufacture Ivory and other brand-name soap bars, flakes, and granules, as well as other household products intended for the northeastern United States, including shortening (Crisco), and from about 1930 to about 1980 synthetic detergents and cleansers, cooking oils, baking goods (Duncan Hines), and orange juice (Citrus Hill). At its height in the 1920s the complex occupied 129 acres (52 hectares) and employed 1500 workers. Because of mounting costs Procter and Gamble closed Port Ivory in 1991. The site was purchased by the Port Authority of New York and New Jersey in 2001 for expansion of the adjoining Howland Hook Marine Terminal (reactivated in 1996). In 2008 the Port Authority was completing construction of a new 39-acre (16-hectare) intermodal container transfer rail facility on the site, to link with the reactivated freight rail line over the Arthur Kill lift bridge that reopened in April 2007, as well as leasing some of the property for warehousing.

Robert Davidson, *"Alive at 75": A Short History of the Port Ivory Plant of Procter & Gamble* (New York: Procter and Gamble, 1973); Charles L. Sachs, *Made on Staten Island: Agriculture, Industry, and Suburban Living in the City* (New York: Staten Island Historical Society, 1988)

Charles L. Sachs

Port Mobil. Section of southwestern Staten Island on the shore of the Arthur Kill just north of Charleston. It is named for a plant of the Mobil Oil Terminal Company built in 1936 on 200 acres (81 hectares) of marshland. There is an oil storage and distribution center with a steel bulkhead 2000 feet (600 meters) long for loading and unloading oceangoing tankers, and a pipeline under the Arthur Kill that delivers petroleum from Linden, New Jersey. The nearest main road is Arthur Kill Road; there are few houses.

Marjorie Johnson

Port Morris. Neighborhood in the extreme southeastern corner of the Bronx, bounded to the north by the Bruckner Expressway, to the east and south by the East River, and to the west by the Bronx Kill. The land was once part of Morrisania and was developed as a seaport by Gouverneur Morris II. The first factories opened in the 1850s, and the area was annexed to New York City in 1874. Morris's home in the southern end was demolished and replaced by the yards of the New York, New Haven and Hartford Railroad, which were built in 1906. In the mid-1990s the port was used mostly for unloading oil and coal for storage nearby, and manufacturing remained a dominant enterprise in the neighborhood. In 1997 the area was rezoned for residential use, and in the early twenty-first century the area began to attract artists and young professionals.

Gary D. Hermalyn

Port of New York. Upper New York Bay was quickly developed as a port by colonists because it was large and close to the open sea, with deep channels, deep water next to the

Plan of the City of New York in North America, surveyed in 1766–67 by Bernard Ratzer

Berenice Abbott, Watuppa *(1936)*

shore in many places, sufficient anchorage, shelter from the prevailing winds, and little ice in winter; it was also easy to defend because its entrances were narrow and there were enough of them to make blockade difficult. Its location at the mouth of the Hudson River made the port a terminus of trade routes extending into Canada north from Lake Champlain and northwest from the Mohawk River and Lake Ontario. From the seventeenth century furs and other goods traded with the Iroquois were sent to the port from a Dutch outpost upstate at Fort Orange (later Albany). The first wharf at the lower end of Manhattan, built in 1648 by Governor Peter Stuyvesant, was situated on the western bank of the East River in an area sheltered from the prevailing westerly winds and from ice that strayed from the Hudson, and it remained the center of the port throughout the colonial period. Flour produced by German farms west of the Hudson and in the valleys of the Mohawk River and Schoharie Creek was shipped through the port to the West Indies, where it was traded for sugar that was sold in Europe to buy manufactured goods later sold in the city. During the early eighteenth century the city's shipbuilding district was north of the port, near what is now South Street Seaport. Trade and agriculture along the Hudson were secured after the British captured Canada from the French in the Seven Years' War (1756–63).

The port was the third- or fourth-largest in the colonies about the time of the American Revolution and grew rapidly afterward. American firms were no longer restricted to trading only with the colonies and European trade partners of Britain, and they soon sent vessels all over the world. The first to leave the port for China was the *Empress of China,* which set sail in February 1784. Weakened by its alliance with Britain, the Iroquois Confederation ceased to control upstate New York, and settlement along the waterways there increased rapidly. Travel westward improved during the 1790s, when locks were built around the falls and rapids of the Mohawk and wagon roads were extended from the Hudson to Buffalo, New York. By the early nineteenth century shipbuilding facilities moved north to Corlear's Hook. There in 1807 the shipyard of Charles Brown(e) launched the *North River Steamboat*, which was designed by Robert Fulton and became the first successful steam-powered vessel in the world; in August it began operating between the city and Albany, and Fulton was granted a monopoly on the operation of steam-powered vessels in New York State and to points in adjoining states. He designed ferries for use on routes from New York to Jersey City, New Jersey, and to Brooklyn, and in 1813 he launched the *Fulton,* a steamboat intended to run on Long Island Sound between the city and southern New England. It ran on the Hudson during the War of 1812 and with the steamship *Connecticut* was later used on the route between the city and New Haven, Connecticut.

The growth of the port accelerated after the war. The world's first steam-powered warship, designed by Fulton, was under construction in New York City by 1815. A steam towing service for becalmed sailing ships was introduced in 1818 by the *Nautilus,* a ferry to Staten Island that towed ships into Upper New York Bay. During the same year the first packet service began between the city and Europe: a fleet of four ships was assembled by the Black Ball Line, allowing it to schedule regular sailings in each direction between New York City and Liverpool (previous sailings were unpredictable because they were undertaken whenever the loading of cargo was completed). Although it was more expensive than others the service was soon in demand, and a number of new firms provided service to Liverpool, London, and ports in continental Europe, where grain and cotton were delivered, emigrants embarked, and manufactured goods bound for the city were loaded. Regular steam service was initiated in 1819 between the city and Charleston, South Carolina, by the *Robert Fulton,* a sidewheel steamer fitted with sails; the service was abandoned after five years. The first transatlantic crossing by a ship with steam capability was made in 1819 by the *Savannah,* a packet ship built in the city; the ship's engine was used little and regular service was not established, largely because the amount of fuel required for steam power left insufficient space for cargo. The steamboat route from the city to New England was extended to Providence, Rhode Island, in 1822. The development of steamboat travel was hindered by Fulton's monopoly, which was declared unconstitutional by the U.S. Supreme Court in *Gibbons v. Ogden* (1824).

The port expanded at an unprecedented rate after the Erie Canal was completed from Albany to Buffalo in 1825. Goods could be shipped from Buffalo to the city in eight days rather than 20, and the cost was reduced from $100 to $15 per ton ($90 to $13.50 per metric ton); the most important commodity was grain from the Western Reserve of Ohio. A second canal was built from the Hudson River to Lake Champlain, and several other states built canals that also served the Port of New York: the Delaware and Hudson Canal was built with money from investors in New York City to carry coal to the port from northeastern Pennsylvania, as was the Morris Canal, which ran across northern New Jersey; the Delaware and Raritan Canal connected the Delaware and Raritan Rivers in New Jersey, permitting cargo to be shipped into Lower New York Bay. Most boats used on the canals were pulled by horses or mules and required steam tugs to tow them to the port. The first vessel designed as a towboat was the *Rufus King,* a sidewheel steamboat built in the city in 1825. Larger sidewheelers were later developed to tow canal boats to the port in rafts of 40 or more moored together. Steam travel was introduced on most waterways and there was keen competition among shippers, particularly on the Hudson.

By the mid-nineteenth century the port handled more goods and passengers than all the other ports in the country combined and was one of the most important in the world. Transatlantic steamship service began in 1838, when vessels of two rival British companies arrived at the port within hours of each other. For a brief period in the early 1850s the steamers of the New York City–based Collins Line were the fastest and most luxurious vessels on the North Atlantic. In 1847 the Fall River Line was introduced to provide overnight steamboat service from lower Manhattan to Fall River, Massachusetts, where passengers boarded an express train to Boston; this became the most successful ferry company operating in the sound. Sailing ships continued to dominate long trade routes, and in 1845 one of the world's first clipper ships, the *Rainbow,* was launched from the city to engage in trade in China. Many clippers were built after gold was discovered in California, but construction ceased during a depression in shipping in 1857. A railroad line that later became the New York Central Railroad was completed in 1851 from Albany to New York City. Shipbuilding facilities opened on East 14th Street and in Williamsburg and Greenpoint, and before the Civil War the city was the leading center of wooden shipbuilding in the nation. Atlantic Basin and Erie Basin, the first large-scale cargo terminals, were built in Red Hook during the 1850s and 1860s.

Port of New York and New Jersey Container Traffic and Total Foreign Trade (metric tons), 1990–2008

Year	TEUs	Total Foreign Trade (Imports and Exports)	Total Imports	Total Exports
1990	1,898,426	N/A	N/A	N/A
1991	1,865,471	42,785,520	35,421,534	7,363,986
1992	2,014,052	38,702,896	31,930,247	6,772,649
1993	1,972,692	41,418,668	34,675,440	6,743,228
1994	2,033,879	47,296,793	40,360,139	6,936,654
1995	2,262,792	45,024,214	36,771,942	8,252,272
1996	2,269,500	53,181,462	46,512,115	6,669,347
1997	2,456,886	51,903,582	45,154,737	6,748,845
1998	2,466,013	56,918,581	50,921,670	5,996,911
1999	2,828,878	62,774,380	53,014,948	6,044,894
2000	3,050,006	64,817,274	58,310,713	6,506,561
2001	3,316,275	73,549,829	65,276,313	8,273,516
2002	3,749,014	70,113,123	59,933,907	10,179,216
2003	4,067,812	78,465,541	68,879,750	9,585,791
2004	4,478,480	80,643,991	70,340,708	10,303,283
2005	4,785,318	84,754,023	73,686,157	11,067,866
2006	5,092,806	86,162,562	71,294,314	14,868,248
2007	5,299,105	87,231,330	69,161,316	18,070,014
2008	5,265,053	88,906,267	67,386,591	21,519,676

Note: TEU=Twenty-foot equivalent unit, a standard linear measurement used in quantifying container traffic flows. As examples, one 20-foot-long container equals 1 TEU, and one 40-foot container equals 2 TEUs (that is, 40/20=2). N/A=Not Available.

Source: American Association of Port Authorities and Port of New York and New Jersey Trade Statistics, 1991–2007

Compiled by Frank Nestor

Industrial activity increased during and after the Civil War. Wooden shipbuilding declined, and the centers of iron and steel shipbuilding gradually moved elsewhere, although a few shipbuilders remained in the city as late as the 1970s. The harbor was altered to accommodate ever larger steamships; dangerous reefs were blasted out of Hell Gate in 1876 and 1885, and work on the Harlem River Ship Canal was conducted between 1826 and 1938. By the early 1870s the shoreline of Brooklyn from the navy yard to Red Hook was lined with multistory brick warehouses. Three companies garnered most of the shipping on the Hudson: overnight steamboats were operated between the city and Albany by the Peoples' Line and between the city and Troy, New York, by the Citizens' Line, and day steamboats were operated by the Hudson River Day Line between New York and Albany. By the 1880s, 11 major railroads built terminals in the city. Those of the New York Central and the New Haven railroads were in Manhattan, and that of the Long Island Railroad in Brooklyn at the foot of Atlantic Avenue and later in Long Island City; the Baltimore and Ohio railroad had a freight terminal in Staten Island; and the other lines had terminals on the shore of the harbor in New Jersey. Until tunnels were built under the Hudson after the turn of the twentieth century, railroads in New Jersey operated thousands of ferries and lighterage vessels that ran from freight and passenger terminals in New Jersey (many built on landfill) to terminals in Manhattan and Brooklyn. Entire trains were moved on the East River from Jersey City to the Bronx, and strings of freight cars were carried on barges called car floats and moved by tugboats. Cargo also traveled in open scows, covered barges, hold barges, derrick lighters, and steam lighters and was transferred to ships by crane barges and floating elevators.

The Port of New York became the busiest port in the world around 1912 and remained so for more than 50 years. Steamboat companies on the Hudson and the sound operated some of the largest and most elegant sidewheel steamboats ever built. Many had a length of about 300 feet (91 meters) (the *Commonwealth,* built in 1908 and operated by the Fall River Line, was 456 feet [139 meters] long), and they were furnished and decorated so splendidly that they became known as floating palaces. To accommodate such large vessels piers were built on the Hudson in Manhattan, along the shore of Brooklyn beneath Brooklyn Heights, and in Jersey City and Hoboken, New Jersey, many of them covered with sheds to protect cargo from the weather and theft. The Ambrose Channel, completed in 1912 to provide a deeper and more direct entrance to the port, was later used by enormous passenger liners. Sailing ships continued to use berths off the East River in Manhattan into the early twentieth century. The year 1921 marked the formation of the Port of New York Authority (later renamed the Port Authority of New York and New Jersey), which was intended to improve terminals in the port and related transportation facilities. The port operated to full capacity during World War II, handling half the troops and one-third of the supplies sent overseas. The handling of goods and passengers remained largely unchanged into the 1950s, and the port gradually lost business to truck transport after the George Washington Bridge, the Lincoln and Holland tunnels, and various roads were built in the 1930s. The Fall River Line ceased operations in 1937 and overnight services on the Hudson were discontinued in 1939; the Hudson River Day Line retired its last sidewheel steamer, the *Alexander Hamilton,* in 1971.

The world's first ship adapted to carry standardized steel freight containers sailed from Port Newark in New Jersey for Houston, Texas, in 1956. Containerization was introduced to speed the handling of freight and reduce ships' stays in port from weeks to days, allowing ships to make more voyages and carry more cargo. It also was adaptable to road, rail, and air transportation, and containers protected goods from damage and pilferage. In the twenty-first century ships more than 900 feet (274 meters) in length with a container capacity in the thousands call at the Port of New York. Special terminals were built in Brooklyn, Staten Island, and New Jersey for the transfer of containers using large mobile cranes. This efficient handling system greatly reduced the number of workers employed in the port. By 2008 the port's active container handling facilities were American Stevedoring in Red Hook, Brooklyn; Howland Hook Terminal on the west shore of Staten Island; Global Terminal on the west side of the Upper Bay in south Jersey City; Universal Maritime in Port Newark; and the Maher Terminal in Port Elizabeth, New Jersey. The latter, covering an area of more 600 acres (243 hectares), is the largest container terminal in the country.

The change in cargo handling methods rendered hundreds of covered piers and warehouses along the shores of Manhattan, Brooklyn, Staten Island, and Hoboken, New Jersey obsolete. Most were eventually demolished and replaced by office and residential developments or public spaces, including South Street Seaport and Battery Park City in lower Manhattan, Hudson River Park on the West Side of Manhattan, and Brooklyn Bridge Park on the Brooklyn shoreline between the Manhattan Bridge and Atlantic Avenue. The large piers built between West 48th and West 52nd streets in Manhattan for ships like the *Normandie* were rebuilt in the 1970s to create a modern passenger ship terminal. With the continued popularity of cruise ships, additional terminals for these vessels have been created on the west side of the Upper Bay at the former Military Ocean Terminal in Bayonne, New Jersey, and on the south Brooklyn waterfront opposite Governors Island. Most federal facilities in the port have also been closed and offered to local communities for development. The New York Naval Shipyard in Brooklyn is now managed by the Brooklyn Navy Yard Development Corporation, which has leased out most of the space for a wide variety of businesses. The navy yard dry docks continue to be used for ship repairs and alterations. The piers at the former Brooklyn Army Terminal at 59th Street in South Brooklyn have been removed, and the large Cass Gilbert–designed concrete warehouses have been refurbished and leased out as office space. Governors Island, last occupied by the Coast Guard, is being redeveloped as new park land. The old Lighthouse Service Depot in St. George, Staten Island, has been partially converted to a repair facility for Staten Island ferries. The remaining historic buildings were to house the National Lighthouse Museum, although in 2008 the project was on hold because of lack of funding. The immigrant processing station on Ellis Island was opened in 1990 as a museum of immigration. As the central harbor ceased to be used by commercial traffic, it increasingly attracted sailboats, motor boating, and excursion vessels in the twenty-first century. High-speed ferries carry passengers between Manhattan and points as far away as Sandy Hook (New Jersey), Jamaica Bay, and the north shore of Long Island. Commercial traffic continued to flow through the Narrows, most of it approaching or leaving the container terminals, oil depots, and refineries of New Jersey; and tugs are constantly passing through the harbor moving barges loaded with fuel, cement, and crushed stone.

A Maritime History of New York (Garden City, N.Y.: Doubleday, Doran, 1941)

Norman J. Brouwer

Port Richmond. Neighborhood in northwestern Staten Island, lying south of the Kill van Kull. The area was known in 1700 as the Burial Place, after a cemetery of the Dutch Reformed church near the shore on Richmond Avenue. It was a transfer point for freight and passengers traveling by boat between New York City and New Brunswick, New Jersey, and a ferry landing known variously as Ryer's Landing, Mersereau's Landing, and Decker's Landing was built as a terminus for a route to Bergen Point (now in Bayonne), New Jersey; ferries ran continually until shortly after the Bayonne Bridge was built in 1931. The area also became the site of an important stop on a coach route between the city and Philadelphia. A public park was built in 1836. Irish and Germans settled in the neighborhood in the mid-nineteenth century. Some small industries were established, including the only whaling company on the island in 1838. Its whale-oil processing plant was destroyed by fire in 1842 and replaced by a factory of the Jewett White Lead and Linseed Oil Company, which operated into the twentieth century. Lumber and coal yards moved near the waterfront during the nineteenth century. A large cloth-dyeing plant was built inland in 1851 by the Barrett Nephews Company, an offshoot of the New York Printing and Dyeing Company in West New Brighton that flourished until the early twentieth century (a shopping mall now stands on the site).

The neighborhood was incorporated as Port Richmond in 1866 and in 1883 was described as a model village. During the 1880s the Staten Island Railroad built a northern line with a station at Richmond Avenue, the main shopping area. By the 1890s there was an African American church in the neighborhood. Port Richmond Square eventually became a transfer point for streetcars and later for bus lines, encouraging the growth of a prosperous commercial center and a large population. Italians, Poles, Norwegians, and Swedes moved into the neighborhood early in the twentieth century. Several buildings soon lined three sides of the park: Public School 20 (now a city landmark), a public library provided by Andrew Carnegie in 1902, and three churches. A synagogue was built in 1907. Faber Park and Pool opened in 1932; sporting events were held during the 1940s and 1950s at privately owned Weinglass Stadium.

The housing consists of modest one-family houses on small lots, especially in the downtown. Larger Victorian houses line Herberton Avenue, and attractive one-family houses built in the 1920s are just north of Forest Avenue (Port Richmond Center). Two lumberyards and 10 churches are features of the area.

Marjorie Johnson

Post [née Price]**, Emily** (*b* Baltimore, 27 Oct 1872; *d* New York City, 25 Sept 1960). Writer. She grew up in New York City, where she attended Miss Graham's Finishing School for Young Ladies and from the age of 12 lived at 12 West 10th Street. After her marriage ended in divorce, she devoted herself to writing. By 1921 she was commissioned to write a book on etiquette; more than 666,000 copies were sold, and she later wrote columns for *McCall's* and 150 newspapers and had a weekly radio program on which she answered questions about etiquette. One of her most famous quotes was "manners are a sensitive awareness of the feelings of others. If you have that awareness you have good manners, no matter what fork you use." By 1946 she opened the Emily Post Institute. She lived at 39 East 79th Street from about 1925 until the end of her life.

James E. Mooney

Post, George B(rowne) (*b* New York City, 15 Dec 1837; *d* Bernardsville, N.J., 28 Nov 1913). Architect. He graduated from New York

The World Building, designed by George B. Post, at Park Row and Frankfort Street, ca 1900 (demolished)

University in 1858 and was engaged as the consulting architect in charge of elevators and ironwork for the Equitable Building (1868–70, demolished), considered the first skyscraper in New York City; he later designed the Western Union building (1872–75, demolished) and used metal-framed interior walls in his New York Produce Exchange (1881–84, demolished) that anticipated the skeleton framing later adopted for skyscraper construction. Post is also known for such works as the Williamsburgh Savings Bank in Brooklyn (1869–75), the World (Pulitzer) Building (1889–90, demolished), the New York Stock Exchange (1901–4), and the campus of City College (1897–1907).

Sarah Bradford Landau, *George B. Post, Architect: Picturesque Designer and Determined Realist* (New York: Monacelli Press, 1998)

Sarah Bradford Landau

post offices. Postal service was first offered in New Amsterdam in 1660. The rotunda on Chambers Street housed the city's only post office until 1835 when a branch opened near Wall Street. In 1845 the main post office moved to the former Middle Dutch Church on Nassau Street and the branch office to Chatham Square. Post offices were first erected by the federal government during the mid-nineteenth century, and after the Civil War the Office of the Supervising Architect of the Treasury designed and built a number of large post offices, many of them also containing courthouses. In 1875 the main post office on Nassau Street was replaced by an enormous facility in City Hall Park designed in the Second Empire style by Alfred Mullet (demolished). In 1885, during Mifflin Bell's tenure as supervising architect, work began on the Brooklyn Post Office and Courthouse, built in the Romanesque Revival style (restored 2004; this remains the city's oldest post office in use). The Tarnsey Act of 1893 authorized the federal government to award commissions to private architects, and before its repeal in 1912 two of the city's largest post offices were erected: Grand Central Station (1909), designed by Warren and Wetmore, architects of the adjoining railroad terminal; and the General Post Office (1913), designed in a Classical Revival style by McKim, Mead and White (William Kendall, partner in charge) to complement Pennsylvania Station. During the late 1920s and early 1930s Congress authorized the construction of a large number of branch offices, including those in Long Island City (1929) and Staten Island (1932).

Old Post Office (designed by Alfred Mullett; demolished), ca *1910*

Post office construction expanded rapidly during the Depression. Between 1932 and 1941, 29 post offices were erected in the city with New Deal funds, four designed by Louis Simon, the supervising architect of the Treasury, and the rest by local architects employed by work relief programs. The number of commissions for federal buildings increased so rapidly that Simon's office became unable to handle them, and in 1930 Congress again permitted commissions to be awarded to private architects. Dwight James Baum designed the Flushing post office (1934); Cross and Cross designed the Jamaica post office (1934) and collaborated with Pennington, Lewis and Mills on Church Street Station, both a post office and an office building (1938). By 1934 funds for so many new post offices had been allocated that the government undertook a novel plan to acquire designs: important commissions were given to a group of unemployed architects who were moved temporarily to Washington, D.C.; architects from New York City, including Thomas Harlan Ellett, William Dewey Foster, Eric Kebbon, Alan Balch Mills, Carroll Pratt, and Lorimer Rich, were responsible for at least 20 buildings.

Most of the new post offices were designed in the Colonial Revival style popular in Federal architecture. Rich designed branches in Flatbush (1936) and West Farms (1936) to resemble farmhouses from the eighteenth and early nineteenth centuries; Kebbon designed Lenox Hill (1935) and Planetarium (1936) stations to resemble townhouses and was also responsible for the branch in Far Rockaway (1936), an adaptation of Monticello. A few post offices in the city were designed in the austere Modern Classical style that became popular for public buildings during the 1930s,

Branch U.S. Post Office Station "S" in the Bronx, ca *1880*

including Madison Square Station (1937, Rich) and the main post office in the Bronx (1937, Ellett), and a few were examples of modernism, notably Forest Hills Station (1938, Rich). The Treasury also commissioned works of art for 10 of the new buildings, including the painting *First Amendment* (Woodhaven Station) and the fresco cycle *Americans at Work* (Bronx post office), both by Ben Shahn; two murals with scenes of the city by Louis Lozowick (General Post Office); and eight murals with urban street scenes by Kindred McLeary (Madison Square Station). Fewer post offices were built after the relief projects were discontinued in 1941, and in later years the U.S. Postal Service erected few notable buildings, preferring instead to lease space in existing buildings. Most of the city's older post offices are still in use, having undergone modest modernization projects during the late twentieth century. By 2008 the future of the General Post Office was in flux, with plans to convert it into a train station and into the site for a new Madison Square Garden.

Andrew S. Dolkart

Potter, Edward T(uckerman) (*b* Schenectady, N.Y., 25 Sept 1831; *d* New York City, 21 Dec 1904). Architect, brother of Henry Codman Potter and half-brother of William A. Potter. He was known for designing churches and college buildings, many in the High Victorian Gothic style. In New York City his buildings include the Church of the Heavenly Rest (1868–71, demolished), St. Paul's Memorial Church and rectory in Staten Island (1866–70), and the original Brown Brothers Building (1864–65, demolished), a marble palazzo on Wall Street.

Sarah Bradford Landau, *Edward T. and William A. Potter* (New York: Garland, 1979)

Sarah Bradford Landau

Potter, Henry Codman (*b* Schenectady, N.Y., 25 May 1834; *d* Cooperstown, N.Y., 21 July 1908). Bishop, brother of Edward T. Potter and half-brother of William A. Potter. He graduated from Virginia Theological Seminary in 1857. He was the rector of small parishes in Pennsylvania and New York State before becoming successively the assistant rector of Trinity Church in Boston (1866); the rector of Grace Church in New York City (1868), the largest and wealthiest Episcopal parish in the nation; an assistant bishop (1883); and the bishop of the Diocese of New York (1888), a position he held to the end of his life. During his career in the city he became known for his conviction that urban churches must concern themselves not only with wealthy, educated parishioners but also with the working class, prisoners, the poor, and the uneducated. Although his church was supported by the wealthy, he became identified with the cause of labor and joined forces with religious and civic leaders who were trying to improve the conditions of the poor. Among the organizations for social betterment that he supported or helped to form were the Church Association for the Advancement of the Interests of Labor, the Seamen's Church Institute, and the Actors' Church Alliance; he was also an important figure in the settlement and institutional church movements and came to be known by some as the "people's bishop" and "citizen bishop." Potter tended toward the Low Church and was theologically liberal, but through his tolerance, skill, diplomacy, and strong personality he was able to secure the cooperation of diverse elements in the diocese. He eagerly pursued the construction of the Cathedral of St. John the Divine, hoping that a great metropolitan cathedral would join with other educational, religious, cultural, and philanthropic institutions to make the city a leader in moral ideas, letters, sciences, and the arts; he secured a site, raised the initial funds, and in 1892 laid the cornerstone. Some consider his episcopate to be the height of the Episcopal Church in the city. He published *Brilliants: Selected from the Writings of Henry Codman Potter* in 1893.

George Hodges, *Henry Codman Potter, Seventh Bishop of New York* (New York: Macmillan, 1915); James Sheerin, *Henry Codman Potter, an American Metropolitan* (New York: Fleming H. Revell, 1933)

Jane Allen

Potter, William A(ppleton) (*b* Schenectady, N.Y., 10 Dec 1842; *d* Rome, 19 Feb 1909). Architect, half-brother of Henry Codman Potter and Edward T. Potter. He was known for designing church and college buildings, including the Holy Trinity Church complex (1887–89; now St. Martin's Church) on Lenox Avenue and 122nd Street, the campus of Teachers College (1892–97), and the Universalist Church of the Divine Paternity and parish house (1897–98; now Universalist Church of New York City) at Central Park West and 76th Street.

Sarah Bradford Landau, *Edward T. and William A. Potter* (New York: Garland, 1979)

Sarah Bradford Landau

potter's fields. Burial places for indigents. New York City's first known potter's field was at Washington Square; it was replaced successively by one at Madison Square and another at Bryant Park. A small field was shared during the nineteenth century by Jamaica, Flushing, Newtown, Hempstead, North Hempstead, and Oyster Bay (it is now a schoolyard in Queens Village). HART ISLAND in the Bronx became the city's potter's field in 1869 and has

Jacob A. Riis, The Potter's Field; The Common Trench *(ca 1890). Convicts lower wooden coffins into a common grave on Hart Island.*

remained the world's largest burial place for the poor ever since.

Edward F. Bergman

Pottier and Stymus. Firm of furniture manufacturers and decorators, formed in 1859 as the partnership of the upholsterer William Pierre Stymus and Auguste Pottier (1823–96), a wood sculptor trained in France who settled in New York City in 1850. By 1871 it operated an integrated factory on Lexington Avenue between 41st and 42nd streets to handle large contracts for complete interiors in diverse styles. In 1876 it showed neo-Grec and Henry II wares at the Centennial Exhibition in Philadelphia, including two black walnut chairs (circa 1875, now at the Metropolitan Museum of Art). Its customers included President Ulysses S. Grant and the financier Henry Morrison Flagler. After a fire in 1888 Pottier left the firm, which reorganized, rebuilt its factory, and remained in operation until 1918–19.

Deborah Dependahl Waters

Pouch Terminal. Former Staten Island marine terminal and cargo warehouse along the island's eastern shoreline in Clifton (between St. George Ferry Terminal and the Verrazano Bridge). Constructed in 1917 by Alonzo Pouch, a descendant of the family that founded the American Dock Company (in nearby Tompkinsville, Staten Island) in 1872, Pouch Terminal consisted of three piers and adjacent warehouses. From 1977 to 1983 two of the piers were used for storing part of Staten Island's bus fleet. Part of the old warehouse buildings were renovated and became office space; in the twenty-first century the piers no longer exist.

Andrew Sparberg

poverty. In the early seventeenth century the Dutch Reformed Church established a poor-relief system to alleviate poverty in New Amsterdam. Under this system, church officials apprenticed orphans, provided medical services, and built a small almshouse for the aged poor. Laws enacted by the colony in 1661 required that each community collect donations to maintain a poor fund, a system replaced in 1683 by British colonial poor-law legislation that shifted responsibility for caring for the poor to counties. The wardens of the Anglican Church who administered the new system listed only 35 permanent paupers in 1700, a number that increased to about 100 during the 1730s. City relief at that time cost an average of £500 a year and commonly took the form of food, firewood, shoes, clothing, medical care, funeral expenses, and small cash payments for those who met the residency requirements.

Poverty became more serious in New York City during the eighteenth century. Rising immigration brought indentured servants and other dependent people to the city, while colonial wars and economic depressions periodically created hardships. In 1734 the Common Council authorized construction of a large municipal almshouse that by 1772 sheltered 425 paupers. Large numbers of "outdoor" poor were also supported, making the poor-relief effort one of the city's largest annual expenditures. Economic dependence intensified during the Revolution, as private charity emerged to supplement public action. Founded by civic leaders in 1787, the Humane Society initially aided imprisoned debtors but expanded activities after 1800 to include medical care for the poor, child labor reform, and support of a soup house.

During the first half of the nineteenth century, rising immigration and periodic epidemics significantly increased New York City's welfare burden. Severe winters caused annual emergencies in the city as construction workers and other outdoor laborers became unemployed and appealed to relief officials for food and fuel. A three-story poorhouse completed in 1797 was replaced in 1816 by a much larger structure called the Bellevue Establishment, which by the 1820s housed about 1700 people. Hundreds of other dependents were confined in a public hospital, an orphanage, an insane asylum, and a juvenile reformatory. Throughout this period public welfare accounted for about one-fourth of the city's annual budget, more than any other item. By 1825 several dozen specialized societies had formed, including religious and medical philanthropies, societies to provide for widows and orphans, and mutual benefit associations.

The growing belief that poverty was the result of individual moral failure was reflected in these groups' efforts to reform paupers. Adherents of a vigorous urban missionary movement of Bible and tract societies, Sunday schools, and temperance crusades dedicated themselves to providing moral education for the poor. Groups such as the New York Society for the Prevention of Pauperism, established in 1817, discouraged material assistance by emphasizing the social dangers of dependence. New attitudes toward social welfare led to the enactment of state legislation in 1824 that abolished "outdoor" relief and required institutionalization of the truly needy. Work was viewed as a means of combating public dependence and cutting municipal welfare costs, and the Common Council after 1830 required even the most feeble paupers in the almshouse to perform some kind of work. Changing public attitudes toward benevolence also underlay the formation of the New York Association for Improving the Condition of the Poor, founded by religious leaders in 1843. Under the direction of Robert M. Hartley, it introduced the district visitor system to provide moral and spiritual advice and to distinguish between the worthy and unworthy poor. The moralistic approach to poverty also guided the Children's Aid Society (1853), which by 1890 placed some 90,000 homeless and delinquent children in rural homes in the Midwest, away from the presumed temptations of the big city.

Poverty intensified during the 1870s and 1880s. Economic depressions brought massive unemployment. Labor's demand for municipally sponsored work relief failed. During the winter of 1893–94 police stations in the city provided temporary shelter for more than 20,000 homeless people. A Catholic periodical estimated that 40,000 children lived as vagrants in New York City during the late

"Stepping mill" for grinding grain, operated by convicts, 1823

James Henry Cafferty, The Sidewalks of New York *(1859; also known as* The Encounter*)*

nineteenth century, a deplorable condition captured by Jacob A. Riis's photographs of street children in the city in the 1890s. Robert Hunter argued in *Poverty* (1904), a classic study of the urban poor, that economic forces such as low wages kept most working-class families on the edge of subsistence. By 1907 New York City had four ALMSHOUSES that sheltered almost 5000 people, as well as a number of specialized institutions that provided care for the blind or physically handicapped or housed juvenile delinquents. Moralistic views about poverty nevertheless continued to shape welfare programs. Those temporarily unemployed were often unable to find public assistance; the city suspended outdoor relief during a depression in 1874 (as did Brooklyn in 1878); and the new charter that took effect on consolidation in 1898 prohibited home relief.

Private philanthropy was transformed when the Charity Organization Society introduced "scientific charity" to the city during the late nineteenth century. Initiated in Buffalo, New York, in 1877, the charity organization movement sought to systematize private relief by investigating each applicant's case and weeding out the unworthy. Its "friendly visitors" provided counseling for poor families because they viewed poverty as a moral rather than an economic problem. The local director, Josephine Shaw Lowell, became a national spokeswoman for reform. Officials of the organization formed the nucleus of the National Conference on Charities and Correction in 1874 (renamed the National Conference of Social Work in 1917). Toward the end of the century the settlement house movement, begun in London in 1884, increasingly saw poverty as the product of structural problems in the urban economy. The movement found support in New York City among members of churches involved in the Social Gospel movement such as Stanton Coit, who opened the Neighborhood Guild in 1886. Other SETTLEMENT HOUSES soon followed, including the College Settlement (1889), East Side House (1891), the Henry Street Settlement (1893), the Lenox Hill Settlement (1894), the Union Settlement (1895), and Greenwich House (1902). In addition to promoting child labor reform, tenement house legislation, and the building of parks and playgrounds, the settlement houses worked to improve education and public health. Tensions between the Charity Organization Society and the settlement houses grew during the 1920s when the state legislature enacted a "mother's pension" law providing cash assistance for dependent mothers. The Charity Organization Society denounced the law, which it viewed as an infringement on private philanthropy.

During the Depression of the 1930s the notion grew that relief was not a charity but a right, and that caring for the poor was not the responsibility of the state. In his book *The American Poorfarm and Its Inmates* (1926) Harry C. Evans shocked New Yorkers with his descriptions of children living among the insane in poorhouses. The state legislature ordered an inquiry in response to the report and to a study which showed 50 to 75 percent of the almshouse population to be chronically ill. By 1929 the legislature passed the New York State Public Welfare Act, which restored home relief for the poor. Similarly, the 1930 Old Age Security Act made New York the first state to provide benefits for the elderly. Between 1930 and 1933 the number of unemployed workers in New York City tripled. With a population of almost seven million in 1930, the city faced especially severe problems with welfare, unemployment, and housing. A shantytown called Hoover Valley was built on the Great Lawn of Central Park. Groucho Marx quipped that he knew things were bad when he saw pigeons in the park feeding people.

Mayor James J. Walker in 1930 formed a committee to raise cash for the needy. In 1931 the Board of Aldermen appropriated $80 million for work relief programs on roads and parks, but by summer the money was exhausted; to avoid bankruptcy the city appealed to the state, which was sympathetic because a number of its officials were reformers who had spent much of their life in the city. Shortly after Governor Franklin D. Roosevelt asked the state legislature for emergency action in 1931, the Temporary Emergency Relief Administration was formed and New York became the first state to provide unemployment relief. But state funds too were exhausted in 1932, leaving 88,000 approved applicants waiting for work relief, so Congressman Fiorello H. La Guardia and Senator Robert F. Wagner secured a relief appropriation of $2 billion from the U.S. Congress. The city obtained additional sums of federal money for public works after the election of La Guardia as mayor and Roosevelt as president, and eventually New York became known as the unofficial capital of the New Deal. The Works Progress Administration in 1935, Aid to Families with Dependent Children, and the Social Security Act temporarily revived the social welfare system in New York City.

In the 1940s and 1950s poverty steadily decreased in New York City despite demographic and manufacturing changes that weakened the economy. Large numbers of southern African Americans moved to the city because of the promise of better economic conditions, but many were disappointed by the scarcity of unskilled work. While total employment in the city increased, the manufacturing sector began to decline after 1954. As part of his war on poverty, President Lyndon B. Johnson expanded welfare benefits with programs such as Head Start. Mayor John V. Lindsay raised welfare benefits to the highest level in the nation and relaxed requirements for eligibility, in part to ease racial tension. The number of people receiving public assistance in New York City increased from 328,000 in 1960 to 1.1 million in 1972. Public resentment grew as reports showed that the welfare system created a disincentive to work and encouraged women to give birth out of wedlock.

In 1978 the administration of Mayor Edward I. Koch began cutting the welfare rolls and limiting payments to recipients. These measures contributed to widespread homelessness, as did the continued erosion of manufacturing employment. Tax concessions granted to developers by Koch, an incentive to encourage new commercial and residential development and to improve the city's tax base after the fiscal crisis, led to the destruction of as many as 100,000 single-room occupancy units (SROs) that had served as cheap housing for the mentally ill and the elderly. During the 1980s the federal government also reduced its housing programs, and families were increasingly forced to double up in cramped apartments. The Coalition for the Homeless and the Legal Aid Society successfully sued the city to establish a legal right to housing for the poor and forced the city to open and maintain shelters for the homeless. Soup kitchens opened in hundreds of churches for the first time since the Depression; abandoned psychiatric institutions were reclaimed to house the mentally ill; and orphanages, called "congregate care facilities," were built to house homeless and abandoned children.

Under the administration of President Ronald Reagan the federal government restricted welfare, disability payments, school hot-lunch programs, and food stamps. David N. Dinkins was elected mayor in 1989 after pledging to improve the lot of the poor, but his promise to finish a massive public housing program begun by Koch was forestalled by another fiscal crisis. Public sentiment toward the poor, initially sympathetic when the homeless first became visible in the early 1980s, turned as beggars seemed more threatening and demanding. There was little opposition when Dinkins closed several public shelters and removed encampments of homeless people from Tompkins Square Park and Columbus Circle. In the 1990s New York City sought to reduce welfare rolls by cutting relief programs and medical care for the poor. By the twenty-first century the number of people on welfare had not diminished substantially, despite efforts to cut down on applicants for welfare by applying new work rules and time limits, reforms started in the late 1990s to stem the increasing number of applicants. From 1975 through 2005 the poverty rate in New York City ranged from 15 to 26 percent, placing the city ninth in the rankings of poverty rates in U.S. cities.

Raymond A. Mohl, *Poverty in New York, 1783–1825* (New York: Oxford University Press, 1971); Paul T. Ringenbach, *Tramps and Reformers, 1873–1916: The Discovery of Unemployment in New York* (Westport, Conn.: Greenwood Press, 1973); Philip Hosay, *The Challenge of Urban Poverty: Charity Reformers in New York City, 1835–1890* (Manchester, N.H.: Ayer, 1980); New York City Commission for Economic Opportunity, Report to Mayor Michael R. Bloomberg, "Increasing Opportunity and Reducing Poverty in New York City," September 2006, http://www.nyc.gov/html/om/pdf/ceo_report2006.pdf

Clara J. Hemphill, Raymond A. Mohl

Powell, Adam Clayton, Jr. (*b* New Haven, Conn., 29 Nov 1908; *d* Miami, Fla., 4 April 1972). Congressman, minister, and civil rights leader, son of Adam Clayton Powell, Sr. He

Adam Clayton Powell, Jr., with Haile Salassie

grew up in New York City and attended Colgate University. His complexion was light, and at college he allegedly tried for a time to pass as white. He graduated in 1930, became an assistant pastor at the Abyssinian Baptist Church in New York City (where his father was the pastor), and received a master's degree in religious education from Columbia's Teachers College in 1932 and a doctor of divinity degree from Shaw University in 1938. After leading a night school, an employment bureau, and a soup kitchen at his church he took over the pastorate in 1938. He helped to organize the Equal Employment Coordinating Committee and led boycotts of companies in Harlem and elsewhere that refused to employ black workers. An adroit politician, he secured backing for his movement from opposing groups of communists and black nationalists. In 1941 he became the first black member of the City Council, and after a congressional district with a black majority was drawn in Harlem, he was elected to represent it in 1945. During more than two decades in Congress he unsuccessfully introduced many amendments intended to ensure nondiscrimination in federally funded programs. In 1960 he became the first black chairman of a major committee, that on education and labor; he used this position to further the domestic programs of President Lyndon Johnson's Great Society by helping to design and pass legislation in support of education, housing, and civil rights.

Powell alienated many of his white colleagues, who considered his brash, assertive style arrogant and disapproved of his reputation as a libertine, which was furthered by his marriage to the entertainer Hazel Scott. He retained his post as the pastor of the Abyssinian Baptist Church, and his weekly trips to New York City and frequent vacations on the Caribbean island of Bimini left him little time for legislative and committee work. His amendments sometimes killed progressive legislation by costing it the votes of southerners and conservatives. In 1960 he was sued for slander by a woman in Harlem whom he had accused of collecting racketeering payoffs for the police; he ignored the suit and claimed congressional immunity. Convicted in 1966 of contempt of court for refusing to answer a subpoena, he responded by remaining outside of New York City except on Sundays, when legal papers could not be served. In the following year Congress voted to deny him his seat on the grounds that he had misused campaign funds. Asserting that he was the victim of a "Northern-style lynching," he sought reelection to his seat in the special election that followed, won by a huge margin, but declined to take his seat. In 1968 he won the seat again in a regular election, but Congress denied him seniority and committee assignments. The U.S. Supreme Court ruled in 1969 that Powell's exclusion in 1967 had been unconstitutional. In the following year Powell was defeated in the Democratic primary by Charles B. Rangel, and he retired to Bimini. After his death, Seventh Avenue in Harlem was renamed Adam Clayton Powell Jr. Boulevard in his honor.

Charles V. Hamilton, *Adam Clayton Powell: The Political Biography of an American Dilemma* (New York: Atheneum, 1992); Wil Haywood, *King of Cats: The Life and Times of Adam Clayton Powell, Jr.* (Boston: Houghton Mifflin, 1993)

Greg Robinson

Powell, Adam Clayton, Sr. (*b* Franklin County, Va., 5 May 1865; *d* New York City, 12 June 1953). Minister, father of Adam Clayton Powell, Jr. He graduated from Wayland Seminary in 1892 and briefly assumed the pastorate at Ebenezer Baptist Church in Philadelphia in 1893. That same year he was named a minister by the Immanuel Baptist Church in New Haven, Connecticut, and in 1895–96 he attended Yale Divinity School as a special student. He moved in 1908 to the Abyssinian Baptist Church in New York City, then on West 40th Street. A dynamic, powerful figure, he tried repeatedly to persuade the congregation to move to the developing black neighborhood of Harlem. For this purpose he raised a large sum of money, and in 1920 the congregation bought land on West 138th Street; construction of the new church was completed in June 1923 at a cost of some $350,000. He also built an old-age home on St. Nicholas Avenue, which was named in his honor. During the 1930s Abyssinian Baptist Church became the largest Baptist church in the United States, and he became widely known and much sought after as a speaker. A political moderate, he was influential in the Republican Party. After retiring as a pastor in 1938 in favor of his son he wrote several books, including an autobiography, *Against the Tide* (1938); *Riots and Ruins* (1945), a discussion of race riots; and *Upon This Rock* (1949), a history of the Abyssinian Church.

Greg Robinson

Powell, Bud [Earl] (*b* New York City, 27 Sept 1924; *d* New York City, 1 Aug 1966). Pianist. After leaving high school to work as a pianist in Coney Island, Greenwich Village, and Harlem, Powell lived on St. Nicholas Avenue between 140th and 141st streets and soon was taking part in jam sessions at Minton's Playhouse (West 118th Street). He toured and recorded in the big band of the trumpeter Cootie Williams (1942–44) and then worked with swing and bop musicians on 52nd Street. Continuing psychological troubles were worsened by a head injury in 1945, and he spent extended periods in mental institutions. Nonetheless, he played regularly into the 1950s and became the foremost piano soloist in bop owing to an unparalleled ability to transfer to the keyboard the improvisational style of the alto saxophonist Charlie Parker. Powell lived in Paris from 1959 to 1964 and then spent the rest of his life in New York City.

Marc Ferris, Barry Kernfeld

Powell, Charles Underhill (*b* Glen Head, Long Island, 16 Jul 1876; *d* Flushing, Queens, 26 Mar 1956). Urban planner and civil engineer. A descendant of two notable Queens families, he was chief engineer for the Queens Topographical Bureau from 1915 to 1942 and took the lead role in transforming the city's largest borough from a loose collection of 60 rural villages with a population of 250,000 into a unified, metropolitan suburb of 1.3 million. His office planned 75,000 acres (30,351 hectares) of property and 2500 miles (4023 kilometers) of streets and parkways and laid out 1100 acres (445 hectares) of public parks and the beaches of the Rockaways. He imposed a new street grid of west-to-east–running avenues and north-to-south–running streets, changing almost all street names to numbers (32 thoroughfares named for George Washington were reduced to only four). Each house was given a hyphenated three-number address that identifies the nearest cross thoroughfare, the house's number, and the thoroughfare the house is on. As he reconfigured Queens, Powell became an active historian, writing and lecturing about the histories of its streets, Flushing's community of Friends (of which he was a member), and other aspects of the area's past. When his road-building project uncovered old burial grounds, he surveyed them, transcribed headstone inscriptions, and wrote a book that is still used by genealogists and New York historians.

Charles U. Powell, *Description of Private and Family Cemeteries in the Borough of Queens,* ed. Alice H. Meigs (Jamaica, N.Y.: Long Island Collection, Queens Borough Public Library, 1932); Vincent F. Seyfried, *The Story of Woodhaven and Ozone Park* (1985; repr. Woodhaven, N.Y.: Woodhaven Cultural and Historical Society, 1994)

John Rousmaniere

Powell, Colin L(uther) (*b* New York City, 5 April 1937). Statesman and military leader. The son of Jamaican immigrants, he grew up on Kelly Street in the South Bronx and in 1954 graduated from Morris High School. In 1958 he earned a BS from City College of New York and enlisted in the army at the rank of second lieutenant. He fought two tours of duty in Vietnam, where he won many medals, including the Purple Heart. He later commanded the elite 101st Airborne Division. A White House Fellow in the early 1970s, he worked in the Pentagon by the late 1970s and quickly became the highest-ranking African American member of the military. He was named national security adviser in 1987 by President

Ronald Reagan; in 1989 he became a four-star general and the first African American chairman of the Joint Chiefs of Staff for Presidents Reagan, George H. W. Bush, and Bill Clinton. Powell was instrumental in leading U.S. forces in the Gulf War in 1991. He retired from the army in 1993. In January 2001 he was selected as the first African American secretary of state under George W. Bush. His autobiography, *My American Journey,* was published in 1995.

James Bradley, Meghan Lalonde

Powell, Samuel S. (*b* New York City, 16 Feb 1815; *d* 6 Feb 1879). Mayor of Brooklyn. Born to a family from Long Island, he moved to Brooklyn at age 13 and enjoyed a successful career in business; he was a director of insurance companies, of a utility, and of a bank. He was elected mayor as a Democrat and served from 1857 to 1861 and from 1872 to 1873; the total length of his tenure, six years and four months, was one of the longest of any mayor of Brooklyn.

Ellen Fletcher

Power Memorial Academy. Catholic high school for boys, opened in 1931 and run by the Congregation of Christian Brothers. It was named for James Power, the pastor of All Saints Church in Harlem, who introduced the order to the United States in 1906. Originally at 15–19 West 124th Street, the school moved in 1938 to a former hospital building 10 stories tall at Amsterdam Avenue and West 61st Street. The school was known for its consistently strong athletic teams until it ceased operations in 1984. One of its best-known alumni was the basketball player Lew Alcindor (class of 1965), who later took the name Kareem Abdul-Jabbar.

Gilbert Tauber

Powers, Bertram A. (*b* Cambridge, Mass., 8 March 1922; *d* Washington, D.C., 23 Dec 2006). Labor leader. After getting his start as a printer in Fitchburg, Massachusetts, he moved to New York City in 1946 and joined Local 6 of the International Typographical Union. As president of the printer's union from 1961 until 1990, Powers was a no-nonsense bargainer who led one of America's longest and most debilitating work stoppages, a 114-day strike in 1962 and 1963 that was blamed for the collapse of four large daily newspapers during the next five years. Eventually, Powers negotiated settlements that guaranteed his members jobs for life in return for allowing for the automation of the industry. Although Powers was reviled by much of the public and was even rebuked by President John F. Kennedy, he was popular with the 20,000 members of his union and was almost comparable in power and influence with George F. Meany and Jimmy Hoffa.

Kenneth T. Jackson

Prall's Island. Uninhabited island in the Arthur Kill off the western shore of Staten Island. Originally known as Dongan's Island after New York Governor Thomas Dongan (1634–1715), Prall's Island is believed to be named after either a prominent farming family or the man who purchased the island; the current name took hold in the late nineteenth century. Once a major farming center of the cash crop salt hay, it currently serves as a bird sanctuary. The New York City Department of Parks and Recreation was assigned the island in 1984, and since then the Audubon Society has documented 400 pairs of nesting birds on the 80.3-acre (32.5-hectare) island.

Jessica Montesano

Pratt, Charles (*b* Watertown, Mass., 2 Oct 1830; *d* New York City, 4 May 1891). Businessman and philanthropist. As a young man he worked as a salesman in a number of mercantile establishments in Watertown and New York City, to which he moved in 1851. He formed a partnership with Henry Huttleston Rogers, and the two entered the oil business in 1867 as the firm of Charles Pratt and Company. Their refinery at Green Point, in what is now Brooklyn, produced 1500 barrels a day and quickly established its product, Pratt's Astral Oil, as among the best on the market. In 1874 John D. Rockefeller bought the company, not only because of the good reputation of its product but to obtain the talents of the two owners, who proved to be outstanding executives with Standard Oil. Pratt's concern with engineering training often took him to western European nations to study their secondary technical training systems. After several years of such study he founded the Pratt Institute, which opened on 12 October 1887 and of which he served as president until his death. He also founded the Pratt Institute Free Public Library at a time when no such institution existed in Brooklyn or Manhattan, and in 1888 he organized the Thrift, one of the first savings and loan institutions. As a leader of Standard Oil, Pratt promoted increased efficiency and product marketing throughout the corporation, and he was known for his attention to detail.

Paul H. Giddens, *The Birth of the Oil Industry* (New York: Macmillan, 1938); Ralph W. Hidy and Muriel E. Hidy, *History of Standard Oil Company (New Jersey),* vol. 1, *Pioneering in Big Business, 1882–1911* (New York: McGraw–Hill, 1955)

Bennett H. Wall

Pratt Institute. Private art and design college in Brooklyn, opened in 1887 by the oil baron Charles Pratt to provide training in practical subjects. Raised in modest circumstances, Pratt wrote in his journal at age 17 that he was determined "to improve my mind in every way possible." After becoming a trustee of John D. Rockefeller's Standard Oil trust and accumulating considerable wealth, he turned to philanthropic pursuits. Concluding that useful education was not available at either public or private schools, Pratt decided to establish a school for "rich and poor alike" that would "embrace all branches of education," one that "combines headwork with handwork." The institute began with 12 students and one drawing class and soon had several thousand students; it offered courses in mechanical and applied arts, domestic arts and sciences, library training, and kindergarten training. From the outset it was coeducational and admitted students of all backgrounds. The institute pioneered particularly in recognizing the critical need for teacher training. Many of its programs were among the first of their kind in the United States; it had the first public library in Brooklyn and the first manual training high school (similar to today's vocational schools) in New York City. Institute-related activities included a neighborhood association, workers' housing, and a savings bank, as well as involvement in the new kindergarten movement. Charles Pratt wrote in 1888 that he wanted the institute "to be a model, and to do the experimental work of this kind of education for the people of this country." His work helped inspire the founding of such schools as Drexel University, Carnegie Mellon University, the California Institute of Technology, and the California Institute of the Arts. Its innovative programs continued in the areas of advertising and interior, fashion, industrial, and graphic design. In the twenty-first century Pratt Institute's community involvement has continued with such initiatives as the Pratt Center, which has been an effective advocacy organization since 1963. It has more than 4500 students and grants associate, undergraduate, and graduate degrees at its schools of art and design, architecture, information and library science, liberal arts and sciences, and continuing education and professional studies. In addition to its 25-acre (10-hectare) Brooklyn campus, the institute has a facility on West 14th Street in Manhattan and operates a joint program with Munson–Williams–Procter Art Institute in Utica, New York.

Margaret Latimer

Prep for Prep. Pioneering teaching program for placing minority students in highly competitive independent New York City schools. Founded in 1978 by public school teacher Gary Simons, it identifies promising fifth and seventh graders, offering them a rigorous preparatory curriculum, character development, and ongoing counseling. Prep classes meet Saturdays, a weekday afternoon, and all week during summers.

Peter L. Donhauser

"preppy murder." Notorious crime that occurred on the morning of 26 August 1986 when Jennifer Dawn Levin, the 18-year-old daughter of a wealthy family, was strangled to death during a sexual encounter in Central Park near the Metropolitan Museum of Art. The assailant was Robert E. Chambers, a 19-year-old man she had met several hours earlier at Dorian's Red Hand, a bar on East 84th Street. The case attracted widespread notice because of the youth and privileged background of both Chambers and Levin. Chambers pleaded guilty to manslaughter and served 15 years in prison for two counts of second-degree murder. In 2003 he was released but has since been indicted for various other charges, including drug sale and use.

Melissa M. Merritt

Presbyterian Hospital. Charitable hospital incorporated in 1868 opened in 1872 by James Lenox (1800–80) and other philanthropists. Situated between 70th and 71st streets and Madison and Fourth (Park) avenues on land donated by Lenox, it opened with 32 ward beds and private rooms. Expansion began with an outpatient dispensary (1888); two ward buildings, increasing capacity to 200 beds (1892); a school of nursing (1892); a surgical pavilion (1893); social services (1904); and a surgical pathology lab (1912). Presbyterian's wartime service included a 40-bed military ward during the Spanish–American War and overseas base hospital units for World Wars I and II. By 1908 the medical board recommended a new hospital be constructed; in 1910 Edward S. Harkness (1874–1940), a board member, proposed an affiliation with the College of Physicians and Surgeons of Columbia University. Other affiliations followed: a new state psychiatric institute and hospital (1924), Sloane Hospital for Women, the Vanderbilt Clinic, Babies Hospital, and the Neurological Institute (1925). Columbia–Presbyterian Medical Center opened in 1928 and Presbyterian moved to a 694-bed facility that included Harkness Pavilion (150 private rooms) and the Squier Urological Clinic located in Washington Heights between 165th and 168th streets and between Broadway and Fort Washington Avenue on land donated by the Harkness family. In 1997 New York Hospital and Presbyterian Hospital merged to form New York–Presbyterian Hospital System, which includes the two medical centers and their networks of affiliated hospitals throughout the tri-state region, forming one of the most comprehensive and prestigious university hospitals in the world.

See also Hospitals.

Jane E. Mottus

Presbyterians. Organized Presbyterianism in New York City began with the founding in Queens of First Presbyterian Church, Newtown (1652), and of First Presbyterian Church, Jamaica (1662). During the early eighteenth century the Anglican colonial governors Benjamin Fletcher and Lord Cornbury sought to suppress Presbyterians, who were classed as "dissenters," by forcing Newtown and other Presbyterian congregations to accept Anglican ministers. When services were led in a private home on 20 January 1707 by Francis Makemie, the father of American Presbyterianism and moderator of the first American presbytery (at Philadelphia in 1706), Cornbury arrested him for preaching without a license. Jailed for three months before trial, Makemie defended himself under the English Toleration Act (1689) and was acquitted, although forced to pay all costs of the trial, the unpopularity of which contributed to Cornbury's removal (1708). The First Presbyterian Church, Manhattan, formed in 1716, began holding services at its site on Wall Street in 1719; a Presbyterian church in Staten Island was formed in 1717 (destroyed during the American Revolution and rebuilt in 1856).

Presbyterian lay leaders were active in the political, economic, and intellectual life of the city during the Revolutionary period. Leaders in the war such as William and Philip Livingston, William Smith, Jr., John Morin Scott, and Alexander McDougall were members of First Presbyterian in Manhattan, which became known as the "church of the patriots." The revolutionary activities of John Rodgers, pastor of First Presbyterian from 1765 to 1811, caused him to flee the city during the British occupation. Rodgers was later a vice chancellor of the New York Board of Regents (1784), president of the Society for the Relief of Distressed Debtors (1787), and moderator of the first Presbyterian General Assembly (1789). He and others in the General Assembly took steps to educate the clergy and laity during the late eighteenth century. To make a "priesthood of all believers" the church leadership opened the James Robertson School (1788), the first school for blacks (1787), the first Sunday schools in Manhattan (1793, run by a black woman at Scotch Presbyterian Church) and in Brooklyn (1824), the Free School Society (1805), the New York Sunday School Union (1816), and the first free school for infants (1827, at the Canal Street Presbyterian Church).

In 1836 Samuel Miller's report to the General Assembly on slavery and the church contributed to a denominational schism. On one side was the New School, which dominated Union Theological Seminary; it opposed slavery, was receptive to revivalism, advocated a union with Congregationalism under a plan put forth in 1801, and supported such ecumenical organizations as the American Board of Commissioners for Foreign Missions, the American Tract Society, and the American Sabbath School Union. The Old School disapproved of revivalism, supported missionary work and the expansion of frontier churches, and was not openly opposed to slavery; it was centered at Princeton Theological Seminary, and a number of congregations in New York City were aligned with it, among them Brick Presbyterian Church, Fifth Avenue Presbyterian Church, and First Presbyterian Church, Manhattan. New School churches such as Spring Street Presbyterian Church (Manhattan), Laight Street Presbyterian Church (Manhattan), and First Presbyterian Church, Brooklyn, were threatened by mob violence because of their opposition to slavery. Unity within the Old School was maintained until 1861, when a resolution in support of the Union by Gardner Spring, the pastor of Brick Presbyterian, split the Old School General Assembly and created the Southern Presbyterian Church. In 1869 the faction that supported the Union

Madison Avenue Presbyterian Church (designed by James E. Ware), ca 1904

sought reconciliation with the New School during a joint communion service of the General Assemblies led by Spring at the Brick and Covenant churches.

The period after the Civil War saw renewed Presbyterian leadership in social, missionary, and political causes. Among the institutions formed were Presbyterian Hospital (1868, now Columbia–Presbyterian Medical Center), by James Lenox, elder of First Presbyterian Church, Manhattan; the Presbyterian Home for Aged Women (1866), forerunner of the James Lenox House (49 East 73rd Street), by the Lenox family; and the Riverdale Neighborhood House (1872), by the Dodge family. In 1884 Horace Underwood was commissioned as the first Presbyterian missionary to Korea by the Lafayette Avenue Presbyterian Church, and in the 1890s Charles H. Parkhurst of the Madison Square Presbyterian Church became a champion of municipal reform. The Presbyterian national headquarters opened at 156 Fifth Avenue in Manhattan on 1 May 1895. The Social Gospel movement, enunciated by Henry Sloane Coffin and others, took root in the Labor Temple, led by Charles Stelzle and formally organized as the American International Church in 1915. Presbyterians were also embroiled in two major controversies over theology when Charles A. Briggs of Union Theological Seminary (1893) and Harry Emerson Fosdick, pastor at First Presbyterian Church, Manhattan (1923), were brought to trial before the General Assembly. The church saw remarkable growth during these years despite increasing divisions: the Church Extension Committee of the Presbytery and the Presbyterian Progress Foundation provided buildings for Featherbed Lane Presbyterian Church (1919), Eastchester Presbyterian Church (1930) in the Bronx, Fort George Presbyterian Church (1918), and Rendall Memorial Presbyterian Church (1927) and transferred declining congregations to congregations in other neighborhoods. The activity of William Adams of the national Board of Home Missions drew many other Presbyterian agencies to the city in the mid-1950s.

More than 30 moderators of the General Assembly have been residents of New York City, including Rodgers (1789), Miller (1806), Coffin (1943), Edler Hawkins (1964, the first black moderator), Thelma Adair (1976, the first black female moderator), and Robert Davidson (1981). Among those who have contributed to the rich musical heritage of the church are Clarence Dickinson of Brick Church, founder of the American Guild of Organists and editor of the *Presbyterian Hymnal* published in 1933, and John Weaver, organist at Madison Avenue Presbyterian Church and a major contributor to the *Hymnal* published in 1990. In 1983 the Presbyterian Church (U.S.) reunited with the United Presbyterian Church (United States of America) to end the division that began during the Civil War, and the reunited Presbyterian Church (United States of America) moved the denominational headquarters to Louisville, Kentucky. During this period the church reaffirmed its commitment to including members of minority groups in its congregations.

Even during this period of reconciliation, however, the church was dividing over the recognition of homosexual clergy members. In 1978, after the General Assembly prohibited the ordination of openly homosexual people, the West Park Presbyterian Church, located on Manhattan's Upper West Side, declared itself a conscientious objector to the policy, welcoming gays into its congregation. In 1992 the More Light Churches Network was founded to organize gay-welcoming Presbyterian churches, merging in 1998 with former Presbyterians for Gay and Lesbian Concerns to form More Light Presbyterians. New York City churches have played a prominent role in the More Light movement; in the twenty-first century 13 of them were signatories.

Robert Hastings Nichols, *Presbyterianism in New York State: A History of the Synod and Its Predecessors* (Philadelphia: Westminster, 1963); Dorothy Ganfield Fowler, *A City Church: The First Presbyterian Church in the City of New York, 1716–1976* (New York: First Presbyterian Church in the City of New York, 1981)

David Meerse, Janos Marton

presidents. Many American presidents have had associations with New York City. The first Executive Mansion, at 3 Cherry Street in Manhattan, was the home of President George Washington from April 1789 to February 1790. Vice President John Adams lived in the Mortier House (also known as Richmond Hill) at what is now Charlton Street in Greenwich Village. When he became president himself he moved to the Vincent–Halsey House in Eastchester (now in the Bronx) for two months in 1797 to avoid a yellow fever epidemic in Philadelphia. As Washington's secretary of state, Thomas Jefferson lived briefly at 57 Maiden Lane in 1790. James Monroe retired to his son-in-law Samuel Gouverneur's home, a small, Dutch-roofed house at Lafayette and Prince streets where he remained for the rest of his life. While campaigning for the presidency in 1860 Abraham Lincoln delivered one of the most important speeches of his career at the Great Hall of Cooper Union; after his assassination his funeral cortège passed through the city, and his body lay in state at City Hall. From 1881 to 1885 Ulysses S. Grant lived in a brownstone at East 66th Street where he wrote his memoirs and made several disastrous investments; he is the only president buried in the city (see Grant's Tomb). Chester A. Arthur built his career in Manhattan, where he first worked as a civil rights lawyer and eventually oversaw the New York Customs House; after his term in the White House he lived out his life in the city. Between his two presidential terms Grover Cleveland lived on Madison Avenue and 68th Street and worked for a prominent law firm on Wall Street. Born on East 20th Street near Gramercy Park, Theodore Roosevelt spent his childhood in Manhattan and was active in city politics as a state assemblyman, police commissioner, and mayoral candidate. After Calvin Coolidge was president he became a director of the New York Life Insurance Company and often stayed in a reserved suite in the Vanderbilt Hotel. Similarly, Herbert Hoover lived in a suite in the Waldorf Towers on East 50th Street from 1934 until his death. Franklin D. Roosevelt lived in the city between 1905 and 1933. As president of Columbia University, Dwight D. Eisenhower lived at 60 Morningside Drive from 1948 until he became a presidential candidate in 1952. John F. Kennedy lived in the Bronx as a boy, from 1926 to 1929. During his brief retirement from politics Richard M. Nixon moved to the city in 1963 to join the law firm of Mudge, Rose, Guthrie and Alexander, and he lived in the city again from 1980 to 1981. George H. W. Bush lived in the Waldorf Towers from 1970 to 1972 while he was the U.S. ambassador to the United Nations. After the White House, Bill Clinton moved to suburban Chappaqua, New York, and set up an office in Harlem. President Barack Obama graduated from Columbia University (BA 1983) after living for two years on the Upper West Side.

James Bradley

Presidential Nominating Conventions in New York City, and Nominees

1868, Horatio Seymour (Democrat)
1916, Charles Evans Hughes (Republican)
1924, John W. Davis (Democrat)
1976, Jimmy Carter (Democrat)
1980, Jimmy Carter (Democrat)
1992, Bill Clinton (Democrat)
2004, George W. Bush (Republican)

Press Club. See New York Press Club.

Prial, Frank J. (*b* 11 Aug 1875; *d* Brooklyn, 24 Feb 1948). Labor leader. A deputy city comptroller from 1918 to 1933, he formed and led the Civil Service Forum and also published and edited the *Chief,* a civil service newspaper. He was the most influential spokesman for city workers in the years before municipal unionism. He opposed collective bargaining, preferring instead to achieve his goals through personal connections. A well-known figure in the Democratic Party, he ran unsuccessfully in several elections. Prial's influence diminished after Fiorello H. La Guardia became mayor and as civil service unions grew in the late 1930s.

Joshua B. Freeman

Price, Bruce (*b* Cumberland, Md., 12 Dec 1845; *d* Paris, 29 May 1903). Architect. He studied architecture with the firm of Niernsee and Neilson in Baltimore, where he began his career before moving to New York City in 1877. His major contribution in the city was his exploration of the design of "tower" skyscrapers, set forth in a series of projects that treated the building as a tripartite column. These included the Sun Building (1890, unexecuted), the American Surety Building at 100 Broadway (1894–96), the St. James Building at 1133 Broadway (1896), the International Bank Building at Broadway and Cedar (1899, demolished), and the Bank of the Metropolis at Union Square West (1902–3). Price's skill in designing urban residences is displayed in the King Model Houses, built in Harlem in two rows on West 138th and 139th streets (1891, with Clarence S. Luce) and now known as Strivers' Row.

Lamia Doumato, *Bruce Price, 1845–1903* (Monticello, Ill.: Vance, 1984)

Marjorie Pearson

Price, (Mary) Leontyne (*b* Laurel, Miss., 10 Feb 1927). Singer. The daughter of a sawmill worker and a midwife, she graduated from Central State College in Wilberforce, Ohio, and embarked on a career as a classical soprano. She studied for four years at the Juilliard School of Music in New York City, where she was coached by Florence Page Kimball, and sang the part of Alice in Verdi's *Falstaff.* Her debut in the city in Virgil Thomson's *Four Saints in Three Acts* (April 1952) attracted the attention of Ira Gershwin; he chose her to sing the role of Bess in his revival of his brother's opera *Porgy and Bess,* which played in the city from 1952 to 1954 before touring the rest of the country and western Europe. Known for her soaring phrasing and subtle inflections, she was chosen for the title role in a production of Puccini's *Tosca* broadcast on television in 1955. Although some American opera houses were hesitant to engage her because she was black, in Europe she was welcomed and cast in the lead role of Verdi's *Aïda,* to which her vocal sheen, stamina, and phrasing were well suited. She later earned acclaim singing the role in Vienna (1959), at Covent Garden (1959), and at La Scala (1960). In January 1961 she was given a 45-minute ovation after her debut at the Metropolitan Opera as Leonora in Verdi's *Il Trovatore* opposite the tenor Franco Corelli. During the following decades she spent most of her career at the Metropolitan Opera and lived in New York City. She sang leading roles in operas by Mozart, Puccini, Massenet, and Tchaikovsky but was most admired for her performances of Verdi's music. She made successful recordings as Aïda, Tosca, Carmen, and Verdi's Leonoras. She retired in 1997, taught at Juilliard, and wrote a children's version of *Aïda.* She has won the Presidential Medal of Freedom, 19 Grammy awards, the National Medal of Arts, and the Kennedy Center Honors. She lives in Greenwich Village.

S. D. R. Cashman

Leontyne Price in Verdi's La forza del destino

PricewaterhouseCoopers. Accounting firm, begun as a British entity that opened a branch office in New York City in 1890 to investigate and audit American companies for British investors. The firm, originally called Price Waterhouse, became an independent American partnership by the turn of the twentieth century and began working for several of the nation's largest corporations, including U.S. Steel in 1902. During the 1920s the firm evolved into a distinctly American entity. By the following decade it had become the most highly respected accounting firm in the United States because of its many successful clients and the reputation of its senior partner, George O. May, the foremost accounting theorist of his time. In 1997 Price Waterhouse merged with Coopers and Lybrand to create the biggest accounting firm in the world, taking its current name in 1998. In 2008 PricewaterhouseCoopers was one of the four biggest accounting firms; its revenues for the 2007–8 fiscal year were $28.2 billion, and it employed more than 150,000 people in more than 150 countries, maintaining its global headquarters at 300 Madison Avenue.

David Grayson Allen and Kathleen McDermott, *Accounting for Success: A History of Price Waterhouse in America, 1890–1990* (Boston: Harvard Business School Press, 1990)

Kathleen McDermott

Primerica Corporation. Name used from 1987 by the financial services firm that had originated as the packing company American Can. The firm used the name until 1993, when it became the Travelers.

Janet Frankston

Prince, Hal [Harold Smith] (*b* New York City, 30 Jan 1928). Broadway producer and director. After attending the University of Pennsylvania (AB 1948) he first worked as an assistant under producer and director George Abbott. In 1950 he was drafted into the army and served in Germany. At age 26 he emerged as a producer on the original production of *The Pajama Game* (1954), which won the Tony Award for Best New Musical in 1955. He collaborated with Frederick Brisson and Robert E. Griffith on this production as well as Tony Award–winning productions of *Damn Yankees* (1955) and *West Side Story* (1957). He also produced works by Jerry Bock and Sheldon Harnick (*Fiorello!,* 1959, with Griffith; and *Fiddler on the Roof,* 1964) and became a frequent collaborator of Stephen Sondheim (*A Funny Thing Happened on the Way to the Forum,* 1962; *Company,* 1970; *Sweeney Todd,* 1979). In the late 1970s Prince found inspiration in the young talent of Andrew Lloyd Webber, with whom he worked on *Evita* (1979) and *The Phantom of the Opera* (1987), among others of Webber's works. As of 2007 Prince had won 21 Tony Awards, including one for Lifetime Achievement in the Theater, which he received in 2006. In 2007 he produced *LoveMusik,* and he remained an active director in 2010.

Prince's Bay. Neighborhood in southwestern Staten Island, bounded to the north by Amboy Road and to the south by Raritan Bay. The area is possibly named for an unknown English prince who anchored his ship there during the American Revolution, although a conflicting tradition holds that the area was named for a family called Prince. From the earliest times fishing was an important activity, particularly the harvest of clams and oysters that were considered the best in the metropolitan area. A plant for processing palm oil and making candles was built at Seguine Point in 1846. The Johnson Brothers Supply Company was formed after the Civil War and in 1888 was taken over by S. S. White Dental Works, which became the world's largest manufacturer of dental equipment. In the 1860s the Staten Island Railroad built a line through the area with a station on Seguine Avenue near Amboy Road. A small business district took form around the station. After

1900 state officials banned all fishing in the bay because of pollution. The buildings of the dental works were demolished in the 1970s after the firm moved to New Jersey, and a townhouse complex was built on the site. Elegant houses are located inland and on the waterfront. Richmond Memorial Hospital (1919) became part of Staten Island Hospital in 1988 (later Staten Island University Hospital). Many older one-family houses remain near the railroad station. The neighborhood has several recreational facilities: Wolfe's Pond Park, extending from the shore to Hylan Boulevard; Lemon Creek, which has berths for 400 pleasure boats; and the Seguine Mansion at Lemon Creek, built in the Greek Revival style and designated a landmark by the city. Nearby stands the Manee–Purdy House, built in the eighteenth century and also a landmark.

Marjorie Johnson

Princeton Club. Club incorporated in 1899 as an outgrowth of a local alumni association. It first occupied a clubhouse on the corner of 34th Street and Park Avenue, before moving into the former home of Stanford White on Gramercy Park North and Lexington Avenue, where it remained for 10 years. During World War I, when many members were serving overseas, the club shared facilities and membership with the Yale Club at 44th Street and Vanderbilt Avenue. In 1922 the club purchased a mansion on the corner of Park Avenue and 39th Street, to which it added a 10-story annex. It remained there for 40 years. By 1955 there were about 4000 members, and the old facilities were both aging and growing crowded. A new building at 15 West 43rd Street opened in 1963; its facilities include dining rooms, library and reading rooms, squash courts and other sporting facilities, and sleeping accommodations. The club has associate members who belonged to defunct sister clubs, such as that of Columbia University.

James E. Mooney

printing. The first printing press on Manhattan Island was set up in 1693 by William Bradford (1663–1752), who had earlier trained in London and introduced printing in Pennsylvania. He began his operation in a shop near what is now 81 Pearl Street and soon printed pamphlets concerning a trial that he faced in Philadelphia (for printing material critical of the Quaker faith). Bradford held the position of royal printer until 1742 and in the course of nearly 50 years was responsible for printing the first legislative proceedings in America (1694), the first paper money in New York City (1709), the first American edition of the *Book of Common Prayer* (1710), the first edition of an American play (Governor Robert Hunter's *Androboros,* 1714), the first newspaper in New York City (the *Gazette,* 1725–44), and the first map of the city (by James Lyne, 1731). Bradford's former apprentice John Peter Zenger, who served for a short period as the public printer in Maryland, returned to New York City in 1725 and opened a printing shop. Opponents of Governor William Cosby, who despised Bradford's newspaper for representing the government, asked Zenger to launch another paper in 1733. Zenger's *Weekly Journal* appeared on 5 November 1733, edited by James Alexander, a leader of the opposition. Its insistent attacks on Cosby's administration led after a year to Zenger's imprisonment for seditious libel and to a trial (4 August 1735) at which the renowned Andrew Hamilton of Philadelphia secured Zenger's acquittal. News of the trial spread quickly; Alexander's *A Brief Narrative* (1736), in which it was described, was widely reprinted in America and abroad and required some 20 editions before 1800. Although Zenger's trial had no force as legal precedent, it became a popular symbol of the struggle for free speech in America.

Another former apprentice of Bradford, James Parker (1714–70), established the third printing office in New York City in 1742 and the third newspaper, the *Weekly Post-Boy,* in 1743. After Bradford's retirement in 1744 and Zenger's death in 1746, a new generation took over the printing trade in New York City. Under Bradford's successor Henry DeForeest (*b* 1712; *d ca* 1766), the first American-born printer in the city, the *Gazette* became the *Evening Post* (1744–53). Parker printed a number of substantial books during the 1740s, including Samuel Richardson's *Pamela* (the earliest "best seller" in New York City); entered into a partnership with William Weyman (1753); and opened printing offices in New Jersey and Connecticut. His firm produced the earliest magazine in New York City, the *Independent Reflector* (1752–53), noted for publishing the essays of William Livingston. In 1760 Weyman left Parker's firm, and John Holt (1721–84), who worked for the firm in New Haven, Connecticut, moved to New York City to edit Parker's newspaper (now called *New-York Gazette and Weekly Post-Boy*). Holt became one of the most active supporters among printers of the revolutionary cause, serving as a printer to the province and continuing his own newspaper (the *New-York Journal,* launched 1766) outside the city during British occupation.

In 1776 the prolific printer Hugh Gaine left the city (as did many other printers); he supported the Revolution from Newark, New Jersey, where he published his own newspaper, begun as the *Mercury* in 1752. To the shock of many patriots he returned to New York City seven weeks later and transformed his newspaper into an outlet for Loyalist sentiment. His equivocation prevented him from being named the royal printer during the war; in 1777 the position went instead to James Rivington (1724–1802), a bookseller specializing in books from England who also published the *Gazetteer* (from 1773), a widely circulated newspaper that he later renamed the *Loyal Gazette* and then the *Royal Gazette.* The most prominent Loyalist printers in New York City during the war were the brothers James Robertson (*b* 1740; *d ca* 1810) and Alexander Robertson (1742–84), who opened a shop and published two newspapers, the *Chronicle* (1769) and the *Royal American Gazette;* leading patriots included John Anderson (*d* 1798), who printed an edition of Thomas Paine's *Common Sense* (1776), and Samuel Loudon (*b ca* 1727; *d ca* 1813), who created a furor by printing a reply to Paine, both of whom were forced to leave the city in 1776.

The typical printing shop of the colonial and revolutionary periods had one or two presses, four or five fonts of type, and employed two journeymen besides family members and apprentices. It printed forms, almanacs, primers, literary and political writings, and (if it was an official printer) government documents. From 1693 to 1783 there were about 2500 known items printed in New York City (excluding forms and newspapers); about two dozen printers' names appear on these items, but nearly half the total was produced by the two largest printers and 90 percent by the seven largest (in decreasing order of output: Bradford, Gaine, Parker, Holt, Weyman, Rivington, Zenger). Most materials produced during the period were typographically undistinguished, but the number of significant books produced was impressive.

The printing trade was profoundly transformed by technological innovations made in New York City after the Revolution. In 1790 Adam Mappa introduced typefounding and in 1795 Alexander Anderson popularized boxwood engraving, a process used to produce woodcut illustrations. By 1800 there were about 15 printing offices in the city, together employing 70 or 80 journeymen printers. Knowledge of the art of stereotyping was imported in 1813 from England by the printer David Bruce, who made molds of composed type and engravings for cast printing plates. By 1820 there were nine stereotype foundries in the city. Although New York City had 20 printers in 1820, its trade was subordinate in output and reputation to that of Boston and Philadelphia. R. Hoe and Company introduced an iron toggle-jointed hand press in 1822 and by the mid-1830s produced the Washington press, which became the standard iron hand press for the rest of the century; the company also made flatbed cylinder presses for newspaper work.

During 1820–40 the printing trade diversified into a number of branches, including newspaper, book, and commercial printing; at the same time bookbinding, typefounding, equipment manufacturing, and other auxiliary trades expanded. The city's reputation as a center of book and periodical printing was enhanced by the formation of several influential firms with national distribution: the Methodist Book Concern, the Tract Society, and Harper and Brothers. Faster production methods gave rise in the 1830s to the penny press, a term used to describe inexpensive daily newspapers that focused on commercial information and gossip. James Gordon Bennett, Sr., and Horace Greeley were two of the city's most successful newspaper editors at the time. George Bruce, Jr., in 1838 introduced his pivotal typecasting machine, a device that mechanized typefoundries and increased productivity by 600 percent. In 1847 Richard M. Hoe developed a large rotary, type-revolving press for metropolitan newspapers. A successful treadle-driven press invented by George P. Gordon in 1851 encouraged the production of job work and the proliferation of small shops. The presence of these aggressive entrepreneurs, industrial growth, and the commercial and financial influence of New York City made the city the printing capital of the United States by the 1850s, when more than 1000 printers worked in the city.

By the mid-nineteenth century newspaper companies clustered around Printing House Square at the intersection of Park Row and Nassau Street, and job shops spread from Park Row to the East River along John, Fulton, Ann, Beekman, and Spruce streets; their proximity reinforced competition and promoted the growth of trade associations and labor unions. In 1852 journeymen printers formed New York Typographical Union no. 6, which became the longest-lasting printers' organization in the city. Master printers organized a short-lived employers' association, the Typothetae of the City of New York, in 1865. Dominated by entrepreneurial book and job printers such as Theodore Low De Vinne, the Typothetae opposed the growth of trade unionism. By the 1860s the city had 51 newspaper offices (employing about 2400), 17 book publishers (employing more than 2100 production workers), and 81 job offices (employing 870). Twenty years later, New York City also had become the center of periodical publishing and printing.

Four independent type foundries were consolidated in 1893: American Type Founders Company, J. Conners, D. and G. Bruce, and A. D. Farmer and Son. By the mid-1890s press workers, electrotypers and stereotypers, and bookbinders who were members of New York Typographical Union no. 6 organized their own unions and then formed the Allied Printing Trades Council. After an acrimonious strike in 1906 a group of master printers led by Charles Francis formed the Printers' League. It joined forces with the Typothetae in 1916 to form the New York Employing Printers' Association, forerunner of the New York Employing Printers Association and the Association of the Graphic Arts (formerly the Printing Industries of Metropolitan New York). During the first half of the twentieth century nearly 20 percent of all workers in printing and publishing in the United States were employed in New York City. Increasingly, publishers of magazines and books moved into offices in Manhattan but commissioned their printing to businesses in the surrounding counties, whereas newspaper and commercial printing remained centrally situated. In 1940 the federal census of manufactures found that New York City had more than 18,400 compositors and typesetters, 7700 other printing workers, 700 electrotypers and stereotypers, 3600 photoengravers and lithographers, and 3400 press workers and plate printers.

The number of daily newspapers decreased from 43 in 1892 (when there were also 294 weekly newspapers) to seven in the 1950s. There were just four dailies published in 1990 as digital technology and economic conditions forced industrial restructuring between 1980 and 2000. Firms offering computerized desktop publishing displaced most compositors and printing press plate makers. In 2008 newspaper and book printing were virtually nonexistent in the city as land prices were prohibitive and changes in transportation and computerized printing allowed large production facilities to move to the suburbs, or out of the country. Approximately 1000 firms employed 15,000 production workers in the five boroughs. Two-thirds of these firms, employing about 75 percent of the labor force, were commercial printers, many serving legal and financial clients near City Hall, retail stores near Eighth Avenue and 34th Street, and advertising firms east of Madison Avenue above 42nd Street (see Financial Printing).

Charles R. Hildeburn, *Sketches of Printers and Printing in Colonial New York* (New York: Dodd, Mead, 1895); Douglas C. McMurtrie, *A History of Printing in the United States* (New York: R. R. Bowker, 1936); Lawrence C. Wroth, *The Colonial Printer* (New York: Grolier Club, 1931; rev. Portland, Maine: Southworth–Anthoensen, 1937); G. Thomas Tanselle, *Guide to the Study of United States Imprints* (Cambridge, Mass.: Harvard University Press, 1971); New York Industrial Retention Network, *Printed in New York: The Transformation of New York City's Printing Industry* (Brooklyn, N.Y.: New York Industrial Retention Network, 2002)

William S. Pretzer, G. Thomas Tanselle

Printing House Square. Nickname given to the area near City Hall where the major New York City newspapers had offices during the mid-nineteenth century. Considered the most important press center in the United States at the time, these papers had a daily circulation of more than a quarter of a million. The square was located at the north end of Nassau Street, at Park Row and Spruce Street. The *Tribune, Times, Herald, Sun, Express, Daily News, Mercury,* and *Ledger* were among the publications that had offices there. Statues of Benjamin Franklin and Horace Greeley were on the square. These newspapers began to move uptown in the early twentieth century, and most of them no longer exist.

Lisa Keller

printmaking. Printmaking was the first of the visual arts to herald the birth of New York City. The earliest images of the nascent city were prepared by Dutch artists, followed by the work of British printmakers when England laid claim to the Dutch colony. The few prints that circulated in the seventeenth century were all issued by European presses. A stunning copper engraving of 1717 conceived by the Englishman William Burgis is titled "A South Prospect of the Flourishing City of New York" and depicts the port in four combined images printed from four plates. A few caricatures of political figures were also produced in the eighteenth century. During the first decades of the nineteenth century a group of artists from abroad made topographic albums of the city that were published as collections of aquatints, *Picturesque Views of American Scenery* (1819–21) and *The Hudson River Portfolio* (1821–25), and as a collection of lithographs, *Itinéraire pittoresque du fleuve Hudson* (1828–29).

The quality of topographic views made in the city improved through the work of several artists trained in England, including William James Bennett, Francis Guy, John Hill, William Guy Wall, and William Winstanley; their prints later inspired the artists of the Hudson River School. Alexander Anderson and Cornelius Tiebout were among the first engravers who lived in the city. Formal training in printmaking was first offered by the National Academy of Design (1826), which was modeled on the Royal Academy of Art in London and had a gallery devoted to exhibitions of prints. Members included such printmakers as Bennett, F. O. C. Darley, Alfred Jones, J. F. E. Prud'homme, and James Smillie. Etchings and lithographs lampooning President Andrew Jackson increased the popularity of political caricatures. The Apollo Association, formed in 1839 and later renamed the American Art-Union, awarded many commissions to engravers for reproductions of American paintings; print exhibitions held in its galleries became fashionable.

As the market for prints expanded during the nineteenth century, the number of printmakers increased and thousands of prints were issued by the firms of John Bachman, Lewis P. Clover, Charles Magnus, Ferdinand Mayer and Sons, H. R. Robinson, and Endicott. The most successful firm was that of Currier and Ives, which had its plant at Spruce and Nassau streets and remained in operation from 1857 to 1907. The firm was best known for more than 7000 lithographs depicting scenes of daily life, many of them executed by such well-known artists as George Catlin, George Inness, Eastman Johnson, Louis Maurer, Fanny Palmer, Charles Parsons, and Arthur F. Tait. It was also the best-known publisher of political caricatures, a good number of which were issued around the time of the Civil War by popular artists such as Thomas Worth. The introduction of wood engraving, a process using the grain side of boxwood blocks, allowed illustrations to be printed on the steam-powered presses used to print periodicals and books. Scenes of city life appeared in such periodicals as the *Mirror, Family Magazine,* the *Picture Gallery, Godey's Lady's Book, International Monthly, National Magazine, United States Magazine, Frank Leslie's Illustrated Newspaper, Harper's Weekly,* and the *Illustrated News.* The largest illustrations required several blocks prepared by different engravers and screwed together for printing; among the illustrators who became widely known was Winslow Homer. In addition to wood engraving, intaglio and planographic techniques were used to make illustrations for books. During the 1850s Darley became extremely popular for his illustrations of works by William Shakespeare, Charles Dickens, Edgar Allan Poe, Henry Wadsworth Longfellow, Washington Irving, James Fenimore Cooper, and Joseph C. Neal. A growing number of illustrators were women, who were able to learn printmaking techniques in workshops and classes offered by large cultural institutions such as the National Academy of Design.

Etching became a popular technique in the city after mid-century when artists in France and England demonstrated its expressive possibilities in rendering landscapes. It was embraced by Thomas Moran, Mary Nimmo Moran, Robert Swain Gifford, Samuel Colman, and Stephen Parrish. Their prints were made on fine paper in small runs in print dealers' shops and soon became much sought after, leading in 1877 to the formation of the New York Etching Club, an exclusive organization that sponsored exhibitions until 1893. Many painters were influenced by the work of James McNeill Whistler, whose first exhibition of prints in the United States was held at the Wunderlich Gallery in the city in 1883. About this time political cartoons became popular nationwide in a number of periodicals issued in the city, among them *Yankee Doodle, Phunny Phellow, Vanity Fair,* the *Daily Graphic, Frank Leslie's Illustrated Newspaper,* the *New York Herald, Scribner's,* and especially *Puck,* which developed a format that later became the basis for the editorial page of the *New York Times.* The best-known cartoonist was Thomas Nast, who produced a biting series of cartoons about the Tweed Ring and the first cartoon of a fat, jovial, bearded Santa Claus.

During the 1890s posters became the most popular form of graphic art. Posters by French artists were exhibited in 1890 and 1893 at the Grolier Club. A poster by Edward Penfield advertising the April issue of *Harper's Monthly Magazine* in 1893 set a standard for a bold, simple style that was soon adopted by other American artists. Will H. Bradley, Elisha Brown Bird, Howard Chandler Christy, Arthur Wesley Dow, Joseph Christian Leyendecker, Florence Lundborg, Maxfield Parrish, and Louis John Rhead became well known for their posters, many of which were commissioned by publishers in the city. Posters reached the height of their popularity about 1895: nearly 1500 were shown in an exhibition at the Fidelis Club in Manhattan in 1899. Several members of the exclusive Society of Illustrators including Christy, Leyendecker, Charles Dana Gibson, James Montgomery Flagg, and Jessie Willcox Smith used the grand style popular at the turn of the twentieth century for posters designed to encourage support for the entry of the United States into World War I. By this time prints had been supplanted by photographs as a medium for illustrating newspapers and periodicals. Some artists such as Joseph Pennell expanded the scope of printmaking as an art form; other printmakers and art studios accepted commissions for advertising.

Many innovations in printmaking date from the Depression. Under the auspices of the Works Progress Administration workshops were organized between 1935 and 1941 to encourage experimentation with different techniques. More than 300,000 prints were made nationwide during these years, many of them by a workshop in the city that was the country's largest. American prints became noted for their original compositions, lush colors, and technical innovation, and New York City, known as a center for printmaking, attracted such prominent artists as John Sloan, Edward Hopper, John Marin, George Bellows, Martin Lewis, Louis Lozowick, and Reginald Marsh, and later Andy Warhol, Helen Frankenthaler, Robert Indiana, and Ellsworth Kelly. More workshops were formed; one of the most important was Atelier 17, opened in 1940 by the English printmaker Stanley William Hayter, which promoted new approaches to printmaking until it closed in 1955. A workshop called Universal Limited Art Editions, opened in 1957 by Tatyana Grosman, attracted major painters to printmaking, among them Larry Rivers, Robert Rauschenberg, and Jasper Johns, and became a model for later works.

Prominent early views of the city are held in the print collections of the Museum of the City of New York, the New-York Historical Society, the New York Public Library, and the Metropolitan Museum of Art. Several Manhattan galleries specialize in prints, among them the Hirschl and Adler Galleries, the Susan Sheehan Gallery, and The Old Print Shop.

I. N. Phelps Stokes, *The Iconography of Manhattan Island, 1498–1909, Compiled from Original Sources and Illustrated by Photo Intaglio Reproductions of Important Maps, Plans, Views and Documents in Public and Private Collections* (New York: Robert H. Dodd, 1915–28; repr. Arno, 1967); James Watrous, *American Printmaking: A Century of American Printmaking, 1880–1980* (Madison: University of Wisconsin Press, 1984); Gloria Gilda Deák, *Picturing America, 1497–1899: Prints, Maps and Drawings Bearing on the New World Discoveries and on the Development of the Territory That Is Now the United States* (Princeton, N.J.: Princeton University Press, 1988); *Picturing New York: The City from Its Beginnings to the Present* (New York: Columbia University Press, 2000)

Gloria Deák

Priscilla. Steamboat designed by George Peirce and built in 1893. It measured 440 feet (134 meters) by 52 feet (16 meters), and its sidewheels were 35 feet (11 meters) by 14 feet (4 meters). The ship had five boilers, a four-cylinder double-inclined compound engine, and 8500 horsepower. There were 1500 passenger berths, and the ship could carry 800 tons of freight. Frank Hill Smith designed the interior in a Renaissance style. The *Priscilla* was operated by the Fall River Line from 1894 until 1937 and ran between Manhattan and Fall River, Massachusetts.

Arthur G. Adams

prisons. See Jails.

prison ships. Between 1776 and 1783 thousands of American soldiers, sailors, and civilians perished aboard British prison ships anchored off Manhattan. This little-known story began on 15 September 1776, the day that British forces again routed Washington's army and seized New York City, bringing with them more than 1000 Americans captured in the fighting on Long Island (26–31 August). To hold them all, public buildings, sugar houses, churches, and even private residences were commandeered for use as stockades. But space in the occupied city was at a premium, especially after a third of it burned in a disastrous fire on 21 September. When several thousand more prisoners were brought in after the capitulation of Fort Washington on 16 November, conditions in the vastly overcrowded, pestiferous prisons went from bad to appalling. In December 1776 the British began shifting some captured Americans to broken-down transports and warships that had been stripped of ordnance, spars, rigging, canvas, rudders, and other reusable equipment. The first of these floating prisons were the *Whitby* and *Grosvenor.* Their appearance did not improve conditions in the city's stockades, however, because British naval operations as well as military forays into the countryside around New York City ensured the arrival of hundreds of new captives every year. Down to the final year of the war, as a result, additional prison ships would be pressed into service as needed: *John, Glasgow, Preston, Good Intent, Good Hope, Prince of Wales, Falmouth, Stromboli, Lord Dunlace, Scorpion, Judith, Myrtle, Felicity, Chatham, Kitty, Frederick, Woodlands, Scheldt, Clyde, Hunter, Perseverance,* and *Bristol Packet.* The great majority were used only temporarily, and there were never more than five or six in use at a time—usually (but not always) anchored in Wallabout Bay, a shallow cove on the Brooklyn side of the East River, directly across from Corelear's Hook on Manhattan.

Most notorious of the Wallabout prison ships was the *Jersey,* originally a 64-gun frigate that saw decades of service in the Mediterranean before the Royal Navy converted it (circa 1771) to a hospital ship. Sent to America in 1776, the ship spent four years anchored off the East River waterfront where its great black hull—41 feet (12.5 meters) at the beam and 144 feet (44 meters) from stem to stern—became a landmark of sorts among residents of the occupied city. Sometime over the summer of 1780 the *Jersey* was converted to a prison ship and towed up to Wallabout Bay. It remained there for the remainder of the war, packed with as many as 1100 captured Americans at a time, triple its normal complement of crew.

The nightmarish conditions aboard the *Jersey* made it an enduring symbol of British inhumanity during the Revolutionary War. In letters, diaries, and memoirs, prisoners confined in its dim, steaming hold gave graphic descriptions of sadistic guards, scanty and barely edible provisions, stinking water, overflowing waste tubs, and rampant disease (scurvy, yellow fever, typhus, dysentery, and smallpox). From six to 10 men were said to have died between its decks every night, and every morning a gang of prisoners known as the "working party" gathered up the corpses and hastily interred them, along with those from other ships, in graves on nearby beaches. The actual death toll cannot be reconstructed from the surviving records, but it is probable that as many as 12,000 Americans perished aboard the *Jersey* and other British prison ships in New York City—almost twice the 6824 believed to have been killed in action during the war.

The deaths of these and other prisoners in New York hardened anti-British opinion in the former colonies and figured importantly in the negotiations that led to American independence in 1783. Once the war ended, it was a different story. For decades, rotting timbers of the *Jersey* were still visible at low tide in the mud flats of Wallabout Bay, and its beaches remained littered with human remains washed out of shallow gravesites. But despite repeated calls for a permanent marker to honor the dead, nothing materialized until 1873, when a mausoleum for their bones was incorporated by Frederick Law Olmsted and Calvert Vaux into the design of Brooklyn's Washington (now Fort Greene) Park. In 1908, after a national campaign orchestrated by the Daughters of the American Revolution, a proper memorial—the Prison Ship Martyrs' Monument—was belatedly erected over the mausoleum, facing Wallabout Bay.

Edwin G. Burrows, *Forgotten Patriots: The Untold Story of American Prisoners during the Revolutionary War* (New York: Perseus Book Group, 2008)

Edwin G. Burrows

private schools. See Independent Schools.

Procter and Gamble. Firm of household products manufacturers. Formed in Cincinnati in 1837, it opened an industrial plant at Port Ivory, Staten Island, in 1907, which manufactured soaps, detergents, toilet goods, vegetable oil, and food and paper products. At its height during the 1920s the plant occupied 129 acres (52 hectares) and employed 1500 workers to manufacture soap bars, flakes, and granules (most under the brand name Ivory), vegetable shortening (Crisco), and related products for the northeastern United States. As the firm diversified during the following decades, the factory also made synthetic detergents and cleansers (such as Tide), cooking oils, baking goods under the name Duncan Hines, and orange juice (Citrus Hill). Because of mounting costs the firm began phasing out selected operations in the mid-1980s, and it closed all of Port Ivory in 1991. Procter and Gamble was an innovator in developing close relations with advertising and communications firms in Manhattan; it was the first firm to use direct radio promotion (1923) and produce daytime serial "soap operas" on radio (1933) and television (1950). In the early twenty-first century, the firm owned and produced, through its affiliate Procter and Gamble Productions, the television soap operas *As the World Turns* and *Guiding Light* in Manhattan, where it maintained its production, casting, publicity, and writers' offices.

Robert Davidson, *"Alive at 75": A Short History of the Port Ivory Plant of Procter & Gamble* (New York: Procter and Gamble, 1973); Charles L. Sachs, *Made on Staten Island: Agriculture, Industry, and Suburban Living in the City* (New York: Staten Island Historical Society, 1988)

Charles L. Sachs

Produce Exchange. See New York Produce Exchange.

progressive education. The progressive education movement began in the decades after the Civil War as a reaction to the corrupt political control and rote instruction that characterized most public schools in the United States. Many of the goals and tenets of progressive education were conceived and implemented in New York City. The early focus of the movement on hands-on experience was inspired by a display of the Moscow Imperial Technical School at the Philadelphia Centennial Exposition of 1876, where Victor Della Vos exhibited tools, models, and drawings to stress the importance of manual training in instruction shops. Interest in manual training led to the opening of the New York Trades Schools by Richard T. Auchmuty in 1881 and of the Pratt Institute in Brooklyn and the Baron de Hirsch School in the 1890s. The drive to open new schools gained further momentum in 1892 when Joseph Mayer Rice of New York City wrote a series of muckraking articles about the conditions of public schools in the monthly publication the *Forum.*

During the 1880s progressive educators focused on improving the lives of immigrants pouring into New York City. They formed settlements modeled on those of England where university students in the 1880s assisted and lived with the poor. In 1886 the Lily Pleasure Club (later renamed the University Settlement) was opened at 146 Forsyth Street in Manhattan by Stanton Coit (1857–1944), followed by the New York College Settlement (1889), Everett Wheeler's East Side House (1891), Lillian Wald's Nurses' Settlement (1895, later renamed the Henry Street Settlement), the Hudson Guild (1895), and Greenwich House (1902). The settlements' kindergarten programs, health and nutrition classes, cultural activities, manual training, and courses led to reforms in schools throughout the city.

The growth of progressive education, the development of psychology, and the influence of John Dewey gave rise to professional schools of education, notably Teachers College of Columbia University (1887) and the Bank Street College of Education, formed by Lucy Sprague Mitchell in 1916 as the Bureau of Educational Experiments. The graduates of these colleges founded and taught at such experimental schools in New York City as the Play School (1914), the Walden School (1915), the Lincoln School of Teachers College (1917), the Dalton School (1919), and the Little Red School House (1921). At these schools traditional, formalist methods were rejected in favor of programs stressing self-expression and learning by doing. The progressive movement waned during the 1950s, but many progressive schools continued to operate according to the principles on which they were founded.

Lawrence A. Cremin, *The Transformation of the School* (New York: Alfred A. Knopf, 1961)

Alfonso J. Orsini

Progressive Party. Political party formed in 1912 and best known for its role in the presidential election of the same year; it is often referred to as the Bull Moose Party. It advocated far-reaching regulatory and social reforms, including the abolition of sweatshops; laws regulating employer liability, child labor, and wages and hours; public ownership of natural resources; a graduated income tax; the direct election of U.S. senators; woman suffrage; and old-age, health, and unemployment insurance. New York City played an important role in the history of the party. The national headquarters was on 42nd Street, and the party's presidential nominee, Theodore Roosevelt, often consulted with party leaders in Manhattan from his residence at Oyster Bay on Long Island. Leading social scientists and social reformers from the city were instrumental in writing the party's political platform. Frances Kellor, executive director of the party's Progressive Service (based in Manhattan), directed research, education, and legislative efforts. Samuel McCune Lindsay, professor of social legislation at Columbia University, and John B. Andrews, secretary of the American Association for Labor Legislation (also based in Manhattan), addressed delegates at the national convention and were notable contributors to the party's agenda. Other New Yorkers prominent in the party included Edward T. Devine, George W. Kirchwey, and E. R. A. Seligman, all professors at Columbia, and the social reformers Florence Kelley, Pauline Goldmark, Henry Moskowitz, and Homer Folks. The philosopher John Dewey was briefly a codirector of the party's Committee on Education. In addition, Herbert Croly had a formative influence on Roosevelt through his book *The Promise of American Life* (1909).

The Progressive Party engaged in internecine battles with the Republican Party, from which it had broken, and had only slight support from organized labor (Samuel Gompers and the American Federation of Labor endorsed Democratic candidate Woodrow Wilson). As a result the Progressives fared poorly in New York State and elsewhere, electing only one governor, two senators, 16 representatives, and a few hundred local officials nationwide. Nevertheless, the Progressive Party retains a central role in the rise of the modern welfare state and the history of party politics in the twentieth century.

John Recchiuti

Prohibition. The 18th Amendment to the Constitution of the United States went into effect in 1920, making illegal the manufacture, sale, and transport of all alcoholic beverages. The sympathy toward the temperance movement of the national majority thus overrode an antipathy toward it in New York City that was personified by Fiorello H. La Guardia, who as a congressman excoriated the "noble experiment" of Prohibition as unenforceable, discriminatory toward immigrants and workers, and likely to breed contempt for the law. Prohibition did create new opportunities in the city for leaders of organized crime, who recognized the advantages of the harbor for the illegal importation of alcohol, known as rumrunning: their fleets ran liquor past the coast guard, their trucks transported it nationwide, and bootlegging replaced gambling as their main source of revenue. The city provided the country not only with much of its liquor, but also with many of its organized-crime leaders, among them Johnny Torrio and Al Capone, who had criminal careers in Brooklyn before moving to Chicago; Charles "King" Solomon, who used his connections in the city to dominate the rackets in New England from his base in Boston; and the members of the Purple Gang of Detroit.

New York City was also a leading source of demand for illegal alcohol, and with the onset of Prohibition speakeasies, ranging from squalid to elegant, opened throughout the city. Police Commissioner Grover Whalen estimated that the city had 32,000 speakeasies, twice the number of the legal saloons in the city before Prohibition. Some speakeasies restricted their clientele to males, others encouraged the mingling of the sexes, and still others aimed at college students. The part of 52nd Street between Fifth and Sixth avenues was reputed to have the city's greatest concentration of speakeasies, which to the chagrin of the proper old families in the neighborhood took over many of the fine brownstone town houses. The best-known speakeasy on the block and indeed in the city was Jack and Charlie's 21, favored by such literary figures as Robert Benchley, Dorothy Parker, and Alexander Woollcott: it was equipped with a chute so evidence could be quickly disposed of during a raid. The owners of speakeasies had to pay off not only the precinct police captains but the leaders of organized crime, some of whom like Jack "Legs" Diamond made extortion a specialty. They also had to look out for operatives of the Prohibition Bureau, a federal strike force with 1500 agents, of whom the best-known were two partners from the Lower East Side, Izzy Einstein and Moe Smith. They slipped into speakeasies by disguising themselves as milk-wagon drivers, streetcar conductors, visiting musicians, icemen, and once as gravediggers to raid a speakeasy across from Woodlawn Cemetery. Newspapers given to sensational coverage of crime found them colorful, and in time they staged their raids to accommodate newspaper deadlines. In 1925 the Prohibition Bureau was sufficiently embarrassed by their celebrity to discharge them "for the good of the service." By this time the local police had largely relinquished its role in enforcing Prohibition and left it to an increasingly ineffectual federal force.

It is unsurprising that the first presidential candidate to call for the repeal of Prohibition was Alfred E. Smith, a product of the immigrant Lower East Side and Tammany Hall.

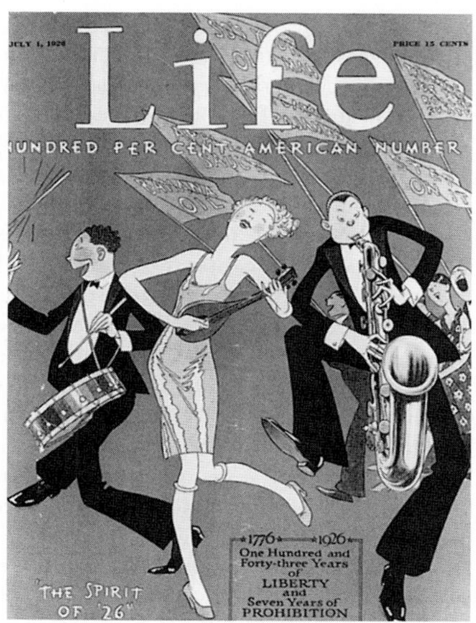

"One Hundred and Forty-three Years of Liberty and Seven Years of Prohibition," cover for Life, *1 July 1926*

Although he lost the election of 1928, Prohibition had by then nearly run its course and was repealed in 1933. It left no discernible effect on the drinking habits of New Yorkers but unquestionably invigorated organized crime in the city, and gangs that profited on bootlegging during Prohibition were later able to diversify their operations.

Herbert Asbury, "The Noble Experiment of Izzy and Moe," *The Aspirin Age, 1919–1941,* ed. Isabel Leighton (New York: Simon and Schuster, 1949); John Kobler, *Ardent Spirits: The Rise and Fall of Prohibition* (New York: G. P. Putnam's Sons, 1973)

Warren Sloat

property and liability insurance. The insurance business was established in New York City in the early eighteenth century as maritime insurance became a routine element of commerce. Colonial merchants usually bought their insurance from underwriters in Amsterdam and London, which perfected marine insurance practices; often the distance imposed a long delay, and gradually agents in the ports of Boston, New York City, Philadelphia, Baltimore, and Charleston, South Carolina, accepted applications for marine insurance and offered them to local underwriters in a manner similar to that of Lloyd's of London, where individual insurers wrote their names under descriptions of the voyages they were willing to guarantee. In 1719 Parliament prohibited the formation of stock insurance companies in the colonies, and underwriters in the colonial ports had insufficient capital of their own to meet the demand for insurance.

After the American Revolution joint stock companies that were organized with limited liability raised more capital for insurance operations. The formation of the Insurance Company of North America in Philadelphia in 1792 freed American shipowners from relying on insurers in London, and the success of the firm inspired entrepreneurs to provide marine insurance in other port cities. Within two years the United States Insurance Company and the Pacific Insurance Company began marine insurance operations in New York City. The city's expansion also led to the formation of several fire insurers: the United Insurance Company (1787), the New York Insurance Company (1798), the Columbian Insurance Company (1801), and the Eagle Fire Insurance Company (1806). By the end of the eighteenth century marine insurance, fire insurance, and life insurance were established lines of business in the United States.

Fire insurers were crippled by the Great Fire of 1835 in the city. Nearly 600 buildings were destroyed, generating losses of about $15 million. Of the 26 fire insurers in business at the time, 23 exhausted their reserves by paying claims and declared bankruptcy. Another severe fire in 1845 destroyed 450 buildings and caused the failure of more insurers, most of which were joint stock companies. The mutual form of organization later came to dominate but proved no more stable. A general insurance law passed by New York State in 1849 placed the licensing and supervision of companies under the authority of the state comptroller and abolished chartering by the legislature. In the following years a number of companies were organized imprudently: 47 of 54 formed after 1849 failed by 1860 and together left unpaid losses of more than $2 million. To protect policyholders the state moved to regulate companies. In 1859 the office of the superintendent of insurance was established, and companies were required to submit financial reports and meet minimum standards.

The New York Board of Fire Underwriters was chartered on 9 May 1867 by the state legislature to "inculcate just and equitable principles in the business of insurance, operate the Fire Patrol and assess all companies writing fire insurance in the City for maintenance of the Patrol." For a short time the board attempted to control rates but ceased to do so in 1877 because members frequently deviated from established rates. The board did succeed in reducing fire hazards by inspecting buildings, investigating arson, and researching technology for firefighting. A standard fire policy was drafted by a committee of the board and in 1888 made mandatory by the state legislature for all fire insurers.

Marine insurers benefited from the great success of American clipper ships but suffered during the era of free trade after the Civil War, when British steam-propelled metal ships carried an increasing share of American exports and British insurers captured most of the market for American marine insurance. Of the 13 domestic marine insurers listed in the first report of the state insurance department in 1864, only Atlantic Mutual survived to the end of the century. British insurers held almost all policies for hull insurance, since most ships were British; American insurers continued to provide large amounts of insurance for cargo.

The city's property and liability insurers did not achieve the same degree of national prominence during the second half of the nineteenth century as its life insurers did. Resentment in the Midwest of eastern financiers led to the establishment there of local and regional insurance companies that competed vigorously with companies in New York City; many states taxed insurers from out of state. Regional distrust was exacerbated by the findings of the Armstrong Commission (1905) of abuses by major life insurers, and those of the Merritt Committee (1910), which examined the sharp increases in fire insurance rates in the city during the 1890s and the early twentieth century.

The revival of the American merchant marine early in the twentieth century improved conditions for American marine insurers. The American Institute of Marine Underwriters, formed in 1920, helped American companies to regain some hull insurance business through syndication. New kinds of insurance were developed about this time, against automobile accidents and theft, burglary, public liability, and inland marine losses; insurers in the city also provided fidelity and surety bonds. Workers' compensation resulted from the efforts of reformers and from the mistrust of business spurred by the investigations by the Armstrong Committee in 1906, which examined the business practices of the insurance industry in the state; the first law in the United States establishing workers' compensation was enacted in New York State in 1910. Several new private insurers and a state fund were formed to provide coverage, in part because many traditional insurers supported employers' resistance to the principle that compensation for work-related injuries should be provided regardless of fault. Eventually many of the traditional insurers did provide workers' compensation insurance.

Insurers became limited to underwriting either fire and marine insurance or casualty and surety by the Appleton rule, first promulgated in 1901 by the deputy superintendent of insurance for New York State, H. D. Appleton, and incorporated into the insurance law of 1939. This rule led to the adoption nationwide of the insurance practices of New York State, although other states were less stringent. The first law in the nation for insurance guaranty was passed in 1947 and assessed all insurers a percentage of their premiums for a guaranty fund to pay the unsatisfied claims against insolvent insurers; it became an important consumer protection measure and was later adopted by all the other states. In 1949 a new law granted full underwriting powers to both fire and marine insurers and casualty and surety insurers, enabling firms to combine different types of coverage in a single policy.

Those Who Underwrite Metropolitan New York (New York: Roberts, 1943)

Robert J. Gibbons

Prospect Heights. Neighborhood in northwestern Brooklyn, lying along the northern edge of Prospect Park and bounded to the north by Atlantic Avenue, to the east by Washington Avenue, to the south by Eastern Parkway (which begins in the neighborhood at Grand Army Plaza), and to the west by Flatbush Avenue. It was developed after Prospect Park was completed in the 1870s. The population consisted mostly of middle-class Italians, Irish, and Jews until after World War II, when it became predominantly African American. Eventually many buildings were abandoned and the neighborhood declined, and during the 1960s Washington Avenue was the site of race riots and arson that destroyed many buildings. In the mid-1980s the city sold off clusters of abandoned buildings to encourage the development of middle-income housing. A wave of speculation resulted, and during the next eight years almost one-third of the neighborhood's housing was renovated. Middle-class residents were attracted by relatively inexpensive condominiums and cooperatives and by the proximity of the neighborhood to Park Slope, Prospect Park, and Manhattan. Most of the immigrants who settled in Prospect Heights during the 1980s were from the Caribbean, especially from Jamaica, Haiti, and Guyana and to a lesser extent from Trinidad and Tobago, the Dominican Republic, Barbados, and Panama. The population in the early twenty-first century included working-class and middle-class homeowners and low-income renters and was largely African American, with some whites, West Indians, and Latin Americans. Along Eastern Parkway stand the Brooklyn Museum, the Brooklyn Botanic Garden, and the Brooklyn Public Library; the side streets are lined with brownstones and town houses built at the beginning of the twentieth century, along with small apartment buildings.

Judith Berck

Prospect–Lefferts Gardens. Neighborhood in northwestern Brooklyn, lying within northern Flatbush and bounded to the north by Empire Boulevard, to the east by New York Avenue, to the south by Clarkson Avenue, and to the west by Ocean Avenue. Founded in 1660 by Leffert Pietersen van Haughwout, the area was farmland until 1893 when James Lefferts divided it into building lots. Rowhouse development began almost immediately. The most active period for construction was between 1905 and 1911, when more than 500 limestone houses were built. By 1919 the Lefferts Manor Association was formed. The core of this area was called Lefferts Manor, an eight-block restricted zone with building covenants designed by Brooklyn architect Axel Hedman. Maple Street, the heart of Lefferts Manor, has long been known as "Doctors' Row." The Lefferts Homestead (on which the neighborhood was built) and the nearby Brooklyn Botanic Garden offer visual variety. The Peter Lefferts House (built between 1777 and 1783) was moved to Prospect Park in 1918. Residents of Prospect–Lefferts Gardens are racially integrated, professional, and middle class; it was designated a historic district in 1979. In the early twenty-first century residents were from Jamaica, Haiti, the Dominican Republic, and Puerto Rico as well as from white ethnic groups. Housing consists of row houses and some semidetached and detached houses, as well as apartment buildings with storefronts along Rogers and Flatbush avenues, mostly built between the 1890s and the 1920s. Flatbush Avenue is the main thoroughfare, and there is additional shopping along Nostrand Avenue. The annual Prospect–Lefferts Gardens House Tour attracts many visitors.

Andrew S. Dolkart, *This Is Brooklyn: A Guide to the Borough's Historic Districts and Landmarks* (New York: Fund for the Borough of Brooklyn, 1990); Andrea Reynolds, ed., *Historic Houses in New York City* (New York: Historic House Trust of New York City and City of New York Parks and Recreation, 2nd edn 1992); Kenneth Jackson and John Manbeck, eds., *The Neighborhoods of Brooklyn* (New Haven: Yale University Press, 2nd edn 2004)

John Manbeck, Elizabeth Reich Rawson

Prospect Park. Public park in west central Brooklyn, bounded to the north by Eastern Parkway, to the east by Flatbush Avenue, to the south by Parkside Avenue, and to the west by Prospect Park Southwest and Prospect Park West. It occupies 526 acres (213 hectares). Part of the site was acquired by the City of Brooklyn in 1860; the present configuration of the park was first sketched by Calvert Vaux in February 1865 at the behest of James S. T. Stranahan, president of the Prospect Park Commission. A comprehensive plan for development was submitted in the following year by Vaux and Frederick Law Olmsted. The principal features of their design were the Green, or Long Meadow, a rolling expanse of lawn and trees; a rocky, heavily wooded area called the Ravine; and Prospect Lake. Meadowport Arch, Endale Arch, East Wood Arch, and other arches throughout the park separated pedestrian from equestrian and vehicular traffic. The Parade, across Franklin Avenue from the park, provided additional facilities for recreation, and the Plaza (now Grand Army Plaza) routed traffic into and around the park and served as a grand ceremonial space. From 1866 Olmsted supervised construction, a massive undertaking that employed as many as 1800 men to move earth; lay an underground drainage system; create miles of roads and paths; plant grass, trees, and shrubs; and erect bridges. Vaux and a number of associates designed the Thatched Shelter, the Dairy, the Concert Grove and its pavilions, and numerous rustic arbors. Shortly after its opening Prospect Park became a favorite place of resort. In 1868 about two million people visited it to enjoy the scenery or a family picnic, row or skate on the lake, listen to weekly concerts, and take part in athletic contests on the Parade. By the end of the nineteenth century there were perhaps as many as 15 million visitors each year.

Olmsted and Vaux considered Prospect Park integral to the future of Brooklyn and the metropolitan area. As early as 1866 they urged that it be connected to Central Park in Manhattan by a series of wide boulevards, and although this plan was never realized they were able to forge a comprehensive park and avenue system by rearranging the streets approaching Prospect Park, constructing Ocean Parkway and Eastern Parkway, and designing other public spaces. In later years Olmsted was distressed by changes made to the park, particularly the addition of gateways and structures designed by McKim, Mead and White and other architects and the more formal treatment of parts of the landscape. In the twentieth century the advent of the automobile made it necessary to widen and straighten the drives, and playgrounds and other recreational facilities were added. During the Depression the city's parks commissioner, Robert Moses, rehabilitated the landscape and restored many buildings; he also added such new structures as the Wollman Skating Rink (on part of the Concert Grove) and the zoo. Despite these major changes to the original landscape Prospect Park remains the centerpiece of the park system in Brooklyn and one of the greatest of the urban parks designed by Olmsted and Vaux.

Clay Lancaster, *Prospect Park Handbook* (New York: W. H. Rawls, 1967); David Schuyler et al., eds., *The Papers of Frederick Law Olmsted,* vol. 6, *The Years of Olmsted, Vaux and Company, 1865–1874* (Baltimore: Johns Hopkins University Press, 1992)

David Schuyler

Prospect Park and Coney Island Rail Road [Culver Line]. Railroad formed by Andrew Culver in 1874 after consolidating the Park Avenue Horsecar Line in Brooklyn and the steam-operated Greenwood and Coney Island Rail Road, which joined at 20th Street and Ninth Avenue in Brooklyn. Horsecar routes served ferry ships at Catherine Street and Hamilton Avenue. In 1879 Culver leased the New York and Coney Island Rail Road, which ran between Coney Island and Norton's Point near Sea Gate. It was bought by Brooklyn Rapid Transit in 1893 and electrified in 1899. The completion of an elevated line on McDonald Avenue in 1919 provided faster service to Manhattan. During the early 1930s the railroad tested a new trolley car known as the PCC car (for Presidents Conference Committee, an organization of electric railway presidents that redesigned trolleys so that they could compete with automobiles and buses). Trolley service was offered on McDonald Avenue until 1956.

James C. Greller and Edward B. Watson, *The Brooklyn Elevated* (Hicksville, N.Y.: N.J. International, 1986); James C. Greller and Edward B. Watson, *Brooklyn Trolleys* (Hicksville, N.Y.: N.J. International, 1986)

John Fink

Prospect Park South. Neighborhood in northwestern Brooklyn covering 60 acres (24 hectares) and bounded to the north by Church Avenue, to the east by the tracks of the B and Q subway lines, to the south by Beverley Road, and to the west by Coney Island Avenue. Located in the heart of the original Town of Flatbush and once owned by the Dutch Reformed Church (1795) of Flatbush, the area was developed in 1899 by Dean Alvord after the extension of rail service reached Prospect Park South from Manhattan and downtown Brooklyn. Alvord planned the neighborhood to resemble a spacious suburb, a "country in the city," and he engaged John J. Petit as architect and John Aitkin as landscape architect to establish stringent standards. With buried utility lines, the freestanding houses were set back 30 feet (9 meters) from the sidewalk and were built in a variety of styles, including Georgian, Prairie, Queen Anne, Elizabethan, neo-Tudor, Pediment, Japanese, Colonial Revival, French Revival, and Mission. A strip of land 8 feet (2.4 meters) wide between the street and the sidewalk allowed for trees set on the property line to give an illusion of wider streets. Buckingham and Albermarle roads have central planting malls. A neighborhood association dates from 1905. The neighborhood in the early twenty-first century remained mostly upper middle class; the main commercial thoroughfares are Cortelyou Road with its Flatbush Food Co-op, a popular bookstore/café, and multiethnic restaurants along Church and Coney Island avenues. Nearby on East 18th Street is the privately owned Knickerbocker Tennis Club (1889) that burned in 1988 but was later restored. Among the outstanding homes are the former Alvord Mansion at 1522 Albemarle Road and the Japanese house (1902) at 131 Buckingham Road. The journalist Nellie Bly (Elizabeth Cochran) lived on Marlborough Road. The official residence of the president of Brooklyn College is at 15 Westminster Road. Prospect Park South was named a historic district in 1979. Each spring the neighborhood participates in the Flatbush Victorian House Tour.

Herbert F. Gunnison, ed., *Flatbush of To-day* (New York: Privately printed, 1908); Kenneth Jackson and John Manbeck, eds., *The Neighborhoods of Brooklyn* (New Haven: Yale University Press, 2nd edn 2004)

John J. Gallagher, John Manbeck

Prospect Park Zoo. Zoo on Flatbush Avenue, near Prospect Park's Ocean Avenue entrance. It originated as a menagerie in the late nineteenth century, and the Central Park and Bronx zoos sent animals, including zebras, sheep, and baboons, to supplement it in 1902. A 1906 inventory listed a coyote, two timber wolves, and an angora goat for sale to the public, along with a broken-down automobile and a steam roller. In 1914 the menagerie began its transformation to a proper zoo with the purchase of the Bostock collection of animals from the Anglo-American Exposition grounds in London, which was had cheaply — for $12,000 — because of World War I. The new Prospect Park Zoo opened in April 1916, consisting of a $20,000 one-story brick and stone building. By 1923 the zoo had obtained its own elephant. In 1934 Parks Commissioner Robert Moses obtained Works Progress Administration funds to build a new zoo in the park, which opened in 1935 with three new animal houses, a seal pool, and a restaurant. Through the late twentieth century the zoo fell into obsolescence. During the 1980s the Wildlife Conservation Society entered into a partnership with the city to renovate and manage a new facility, and a $37 million renovation began in August 1989, replacing the zoo's old cages and pits with natural habitats. The new zoo opened in 1993. Although much smaller than the Bronx Zoo, in 2008 the Prospect Park Zoo was home to almost 400 animals representing more than 100 species and received almost 240,000 visitors annually.

Kate Lauber

prostitution. The earliest evidence of prostitution in New York City was reported by late-seventeenth-century visitors who noticed Dutch and English "lasses" soliciting along the Battery. Throughout the colonial period "disorderly houses" along the waterfront catered to sailors who frequented nearby taverns. During the American Revolution prostitutes did most of their business with British soldiers. Commercial sex in the eighteenth and early nineteenth centuries was concentrated in three areas: the "holy ground" adjacent to St. Paul's Chapel and a block east of the Hudson River on land owned by Trinity Church; George Street (later Spruce Street) on the northern edge of the city near the Park Theatre and the "Common" (later City Hall Park); and East George Street (later Market Street) along the East River. Prostitution flourished after 1810. Property owners willingly rented space to prostitutes because they had more money and proved more stable than working-class tenants. Under common law, landlords who owned houses of prostitution were not considered accessories. Prostitution was treated as vagrancy or disorderly conduct, both misdemeanors for which most participants went unpunished. A Victorian double standard sanctioned male sexual activity outside marriage and divided women into two groups: the respectable, who were considered "passion-less," and the unrespectable, who were irredeemable and available for purchase.

Nineteenth-century urban prostitution thrived for several reasons. The number of single, underemployed young women who moved to New York City from rural areas and abroad grew dramatically after 1820. They earned such low wages for what was considered legitimate work that many were forced to seek additional income. Probably 5 to 10 percent became prostitutes because they could earn more in an evening than other employment might bring in a week. Most were prostitutes for only a short time, eventually securing more socially acceptable employment or getting married. Some women attained a social or economic status that transcended their identity as prostitutes. Elizabeth "Eliza" Bowen abandoned prostitution to marry the wealthy French wine merchant Stephen Jumel in 1804 and was reportedly the wealthiest woman in the United States on his death in 1832 (she married Aaron Burr in 1833). Before the Civil War the madams Julia Brown, Adeline Miller, and Rosina Townsend were celebrated figures. The murder of the courtesan Helen Jewett in 1836 and the ensuing trial of her lover and alleged killer Richard Robinson attracted national interest, exposing the popularity of prostitution among men from all ranks of life. By the end of the century Rosie Hertz, the reputed "godmother" for prostitutes in the city, ran several brothels on the Lower East Side while living in an affluent neighborhood of Brooklyn.

Increasingly commercialized leisure activities appealed to a young, transient male population. After the Civil War leading concert saloons like Harry Hill's used "waiter girl" prostitutes to attract these "Bowery B'hoys" as well as prominent businessmen and politicians. From the 1830s procurers, or "pimps," managed prostitutes and lived off their earnings. Nicknamed "Broadway statues," "bullies," and the "fancy men" of prostitutes, they were fixtures in the sexual underworld by mid-century. Prostitution was preeminent in the city's underground economy. Brothels, unlicensed saloons, and illegal gambling dens corrupted neighborhood politicians and police, and antebellum theater proprietors routinely allowed prostitutes to conduct business in the "third tier" of their establishments. The leading "parlor houses" employed 15 to 20 women on weekends, the smaller establishments four or six. Many even advertised their services in local newspapers and guidebooks. From 1820 to 1850 the largest concentrations of prostitutes were found in the Five Points and at Corlear's Hook, Water Street, Church Street, and Chapel Street. By 1860 New York City reportedly had 500 brothels.

8

Her furniture is of the most costly, and the decorations and upholstering will vie with any we have seen. Her lady boarders are courteous, pretty and accommodating. The hostess is a lady of pleasing manners, sociable, and well understand the art of entertaining visitors. The wines are the best the market affords, selected from the best brands, and cannot be surpassed. In fact, she seeks nothing but the pleasure of her visitors. We know of no better house to recommend strangers and others to, than this.

MRS. EVERETT,

No. 158 Laurens St.

This is a quiet, safe and respectable house, and altogether on the assignation order, and conducted on true Southern principles. She accommodates a few charming and beautiful lady boarders, who are from the sunny South, and equal to any of its class in the city. The proprietress strictly superintends the operations of her household, which is always in perfect order. The beautiful senoritas are quite accomplished, sociable and agreeable, and pattern after the much admired landlady. Gentlemen visitors from the South and West, are confidently recommended to this pleasant, quiet and safe abode. The landlady possesses all the charming mannerisms which so highly characterize that soothing clime. The very best wines constantly kept on hand, and selected from the best brands the market affords.

9

MISS. CLARA GORDON,

No. 119 Mercer St.

We cannot too highly recommend this house, the lady herself is a perfect venus: beautiful, entertaining and supremely seductive. Her aids-de-camp are really charming and irresistible, and altogether honest and honorable. Miss G. is a great belle, and her mansion is patronized by Southern merchants and planters principally. She is highly accomplished, skilful and prudent, and sees her visitors are well entertained. Good Wines of the most elaborate brands, constantly on hand: and in all, a finer resort cannot be found in the city.

MISS THOMPSON.

No. 75 Mercer st.

This lady keeps one of the largest and most magnificiently furnished mansions in the central part of the city. She has spared no expense in fitting up this establishment—which is furnished and decorated in the most suberb style. The hostess is a great favorite, and always happy to see her friends and visitors. She accommodates a number of handsome lady boarders, who are agreeable and accomplished. We recommend visitors and others to give them a call, and partake of the good things of this life.

MISS MARY TEMPLE,

No. 122 Green st.

This is an elegantly fitted up mansion, conveni-

Nineteenth-century advertisements for prostitutes from the Directory to the Seraglios

After 1850 the city's first exclusive sex and entertainment district took shape in the streets north of Canal Street and parallel to Broadway (the area now known as SoHo). It was eclipsed in importance shortly after the Civil War by the Tenderloin, an area in the heart of Manhattan between Fifth and Eighth avenues, extending as far south as 23rd Street and as far north as 34th Street by 1870, 42nd Street by 1880, and 50th Street by 1900. Allen Street on the Lower East Side and Union Square were also centers of prostitution. Despite controversy, prostitution was never segregated: concert halls, saloons, cigar stores, restaurants, masquerade balls, and later cabarets resorted to commercial sex to attract patrons, and elegant bordellos could be found in elite areas like Gramercy Park. In 1896 the assemblyman and district leader Martin Engel of Tammany Hall and his ally Max Hochstim formed the Independent Benevolent Association. The first "syndicate," it had a membership of several hundred madams, landlords, doctors, and municipal officials and collected dues to pay for "protection" and legal expenses, settled disputes, and organized prostitution on the Lower East Side.

Antiprostitution movements took different forms. In 1831 the young Presbyterian minister John R. McDowall formed a magdalen society to reform prostitutes, followed within a decade by the New York Female Benevolent Society, the New-York Society of Public Morals, and the New-York Female Moral Reform Society (see MAGDALEN SOCIETIES). In 1843 the Roman Catholic Sisters of Mercy and the Sisters of the Good Shepherd began efforts to reform and assist prostitutes. In 1852 evangelical Methodists tore down the notorious Old Brewery and built the Five Points Mission on the same site a year later. Other antiprostitution movements were linked to temperance and emphasized conversion to a morally pure way of life. These purity crusades, however, were sporadic and ineffective in diminishing prostitution. To Judge Charles Daley in 1849 and the newspaper editor Walt Whitman in the 1850s legalizing the trade was the only way to control it. Physicians like William Sanger supported regulation to protect public health and prevent venereal disease. Measures to legalize prostitution were debated by the state legislature in 1871 and 1875 but defeated by a coalition led by the women's rights advocate Susan B. Anthony.

At century's end vice crusades grew in number and significance. The Presbyterian pastor Charles H. Parkhurst instigated an antiprostitution campaign that contributed to an electoral defeat for Tammany Hall in 1892, and within a decade committees led by Senator Clarence Lexow and Assemblyman Robert Mazet further exposed links between the city's sex entrepreneurs and law enforcement officials. Wealthy businessmen, university professors, and other progressive reformers organized the Committee of Fifteen (1900–2) and the Committee of Fourteen (1905–32), which helped pass the Tenement House Law (1901), establish a women's night court (1907), eliminate "Raines Law" hotels (1905), and pass an injunction and abatement law penalizing landlords involved in commercial sex (1914).

Federal intervention also affected prostitution in New York City. Congressional legislation in 1903 and 1907 outlawed the importation of prostitutes and authorized the deportation of immigrants convicted of prostitution. The Mann Act (1910) made it illegal to transport women across state lines for "immoral purposes." Above all the Commission on Training Camp Activities during World War I suppressed open prostitution in the Tenderloin. Municipal officials similarly grew less tolerant of commercial sex and increasingly worked to repress or isolate it. During the 1930s a commission led by Samuel Seabury, the Committee of 100, and Mayor Fiorello H. La Guardia exposed police ties to various sex entrepreneurs. As the brothel and open prostitution became obsolete, prostitutes worked more clandestinely in tenements, dance halls, massage parlors, and "call houses"; they could no longer advertise and had to move their places of business frequently. During Prohibition prostitution developed close ties with the illegal alcohol trade and organized-crime figures such as Lucky Luciano, who by 1935 reportedly dominated prostitution in the city. The best-known madam, Polly Adler, was professionally connected with Al Capone, Dutch Schultz, Frank Costello, Arnold Rothstein, and Vincent Coll.

After 1965 prostitution became more public. Massage parlors proliferated when the City Council ended licensing requirements in 1967, with almost 100 around Times Square by 1976. In midtown and on the East Side many landlords leased their property to prostitutes in the face of rising vacancy rates and foreclosure in a weak economy. Local and federal law enforcement agencies, as well as the general public, increasingly treated prostitution as a "victimless" crime. During the 1970s and 1980s police officials estimated that 25,000 prostitutes worked in New York City. Although most of them lived at the poverty line, exclusive escort services charged $175 an hour to $1000 an evening for their "call girls." These lucrative ventures came to public attention with the arrest in 1984 of Sydney Biddle Barrows, the proprietor of a successful escort business who was known as the "Mayflower Madam" because of her socially prominent ancestry. Prostitutes themselves grew more assertive. During the 1970s the first known labor organization for prostitutes, COYOTE (Call Off Your Old Tired Ethics), defended prostitution as legitimate women's work and attacked laws against it as an invasion of privacy. The high cost of prosecution ($2000 a case) also increased support for legalization.

After 1980 prostitution came under renewed attack, with the feminist group WHISPER (Women Hurt in Systems of Prostitution Engaged in Revolt) condemning prostitution as a form of male domination. Kathleen Barry exposed the pernicious effects of the international traffic in prostitutes. During the 1990s Mayor Rudolph Giuliani led a movement to revise city zoning laws for the purpose of suppressing visible prostitution and other forms of commercial and public sex. Child and male prostitution drew increasing attention because of the efforts of Covenant House, which operates shelters for homeless and runaway youth; growing concerns about child abuse; and the 1986 report of the Attorney General's Commission on Pornography (the Meese Report). In 2002 the New York City Council investigated the alleged rise in teenage prostitution. Finally, fears of venereal infection revived when medical surveys found that 10 to 15 percent of "streetwalkers" were infected with the virus that causes AIDS.

William W. Sanger, *The History of Prostitution: Its Extent, Causes, and Effects throughout the World* (New York: Harper and Brothers, 1858; repr. Arno, 1972); Christine Stansell, *City of Women: Sex and Class in New York, 1789–1860* (New York: Knopf, 1986); Timothy J. Gilfoyle, *City of Eros: New York City, Prostitution and the Commercialization of Sex, 1790–1920* (New York: W. W. Norton, 1992); Patricia Cline Cohen, *The Murder of Helen Jewett: The Life and Death of a Prostitute in Nineteenth-Century New York* (New York: Knopf, 1998); Elizabeth Alice Clement, *Love For Sale: Courting, Treating, and Prostitution in New York City, 1900–1945* (Chapel Hill: University of North Carolina Press, 2006)

Timothy J. Gilfoyle

Provident Loan Society of New York. Nonprofit lending organization formed by the Charity Organization Society in 1894. Initially it was a pawn brokerage that also made loans to hospitals and charitable, religious, and educational institutions. Its original headquarters were in the United Charities Building on 22nd Street and Fourth Avenue. The society declined in importance during the 1980s. In 2007 it had five branches in the city in addition to its headquarters (1909) at Park Avenue South and 25th Street.

The Provident Loan Society of New York, 1894–1944: Fifty Years of Remedial Lending (New York: Provident Loan Society of New York, 1944); Peter Schwed, *God Bless Pawnbrokers* (New York: Dodd, Mead, 1975)

James Bradley

Provincetown Players. Theater company formed in 1915 by a group of summer residents of Provincetown, Massachusetts; in 1916 they produced Eugene O'Neill's *Bound East for Cardiff* and were encouraged by their success to move their operation to New York City. Led by the writers George Cram "Jig" Cook and his wife Susan Glaspell, both committed socialists, the group also included the painter Ida Rauh, the arts patron Mabel Dodge, and the political agitator John Reed. The members of the company wrote their own productions and staged them in living rooms and on porches in Provincetown until moving into a makeshift theater on a wharf. In New York City they rented a theater in Greenwich Village and staged one-act plays, including most of O'Neill's early dramas. Their greatest success, a production of O'Neill's *The Emperor Jones* in 1920, also led to their undoing when the play moved to Broadway, bringing renown to the company but also effectively destroying its amateur nature. In 1922 Cook and Glaspell left for Greece and the original Provincetown Players dissolved. The name of the company (although not the spirit of volunteerism) was resurrected in 1923 when O'Neill, the designer Robert Edmond Jones, and the writer Kenneth MacGowan presented a mixture of new plays and classics under the banner of the Experimental Theatre at the Provincetown Playhouse, an effort that ended after four seasons.

Helen Deutsch and Stella Hanau, *The Provincetown: A Story of the Theatre* (New York: Farrow and Rinehart, 1972); Robert K. Sarlos, *Jig Cook and the Provincetown Players: Theatre in Ferment* (Amherst: University of Massachusetts Press, 1982)

See also Theater.

D. S. Moynihan

Provoost, Samuel (*b* New York City, 26 Feb 1742; *d* New York City, 6 Sept 1815). Episcopalian bishop. The son of Dutch Calvinists, he graduated from King's College and later attended St. Peter's College, Cambridge University, where he studied to become an Anglican priest. He was ordained a priest on 23 March 1766 by the bishop of Chester. Later in 1766 he became an assistant minister of Trinity Parish in New York City. A strong advocate of the patriot cause, he disagreed with the vestry on theological and political issues and resigned after several years. He moved to Dutchess County, where he remained for 14 years, returning to the city after the British evacuated. He and Benjamin Moore, a Loyalist, were chosen by different factions to become the rector of Trinity Parish; after Moore stepped aside, Provoost took the office in 1784 and retained it until 1800. He was appointed the first chaplain to the U.S. Senate and conducted a service of thanksgiving for President George Washington after his inauguration. He also oversaw the construction of a new building for Trinity Church that was consecrated on 25 March 1790. A founder of the Protestant Episcopal Church of the United States of America, he was the first bishop of the diocese in New York City (1787–1801) and represented New York State in the general convention of the church. His insistence that the laity should have representation there brought him into conflict with Samuel Seabury, whose consecration as the first bishop of Connecticut he opposed (the two were later reconciled). Provoost was buried in Trinity Church Yard and reinterred in Trinity Cemetery at 155th Street.

Morgan Dix, *A History of the Parish of Trinity Church in the City of New York* (New York: G. P. Putnam's Sons, 1901)

Phyllis Barr

Prudden, T(heophil) Mitchell (*b* Middlebury, Conn., 1849; *d* New York City, 10 April 1924). Pathologist and bacteriologist. He was educated at the Sheffield Scientific School of Yale University (BS 1872), and Yale Medical School (MD 1875). He studied for several years in Heidelberg, Vienna, and Berlin, where he became influenced by many of the major bacteriologists of the late nineteenth century, including Robert Koch. On returning to the United States he took an academic post as a professor of histology, pathology, and bacteriology at Columbia University's College of Physicians and Surgeons in New York City, where he was noted as an inspiring teacher, speaker, author, and bacteriological investigator. He was also involved as a consultant and ex officio member with such organizations as the New York City Board of Health, the Rockefeller Institute of Medical Research, the Rockefeller Foundation, the New York State Public Health Department, the New York Academy of Medicine, and the National Academy of Sciences. Prudden is often credited with having brought the techniques of germ theory from the European laboratories to American shores in 1885. He lived at 437 West 59th Street.

Lillian E. Prudden, ed., *Biographical Sketches and Letters of T. Mitchell Prudden, M.D.* (New Haven: Yale University Press, 1927)

Howard Markel

Prudential Securities. Firm of investment bankers. It was formed as Cahn and Company in 1879 by Leopold Cahn (1836–1904), a member of the New York Stock Exchange and a banker. After the headquarters were moved to 42 Broadway the firm was renamed J. S. Bache and Company when Cahn's nephew Jules S. Bache (1861–1944) became its chairman in 1892. A retail brokerage, it was dedicated to small investors, especially eastern European Jews who set up garment businesses. In 1945 the firm was renamed Bache and Company, and its offices were moved to 36 Wall Street when Harold Bache (1894–1968) became the chairman. During his tenure the firm expanded rapidly, opening branches throughout the country and introducing commodity trading and mutual funds: it was soon the second-largest brokerage house in the United States. Headquarters designed by the firm of Guzen and Partners were built in 1969 at 100 Gold Street and became known as Bache Plaza. The ill-fated attempt by the brothers Nelson Bunker Hunt and W. Herbert Hunt to corner the silver market in 1980 left the firm nearly insolvent, and in 1981 it was sold for $385 million to the Prudential Insurance Company (based in Newark, New Jersey). Under the name of Prudential–Bache Securities the firm became the first broker on Wall Street to offer services in nearly every area of the financial industry. It moved its headquarters to 1 Seaport Plaza in 1986 and took its current name in 1991. In 2001 it started trading on the New York Stock Exchange under the name PRU. As of 2007 its assets were $630 billion.

James Bradley

P.S.1 Contemporary Art Center. Founded in 1971 by Alanna Heiss as the Institute for Art and Urban Resources, the institute began to operate P.S.1, a former 100-room Romanesque Revival schoolhouse in the Long Island City section of Queens in 1976 and transformed it into an exhibition, performance, and studio space for artists. It gained renown as a center for contemporary, often avant-garde, art. In order to highlight the constantly changing exhibits, P.S.1 never established a permanent collection of its own. In 1994 it closed for major renovations and expansions. At 125,000 square feet (11,613 square meters), P.S.1 reopened as one of the largest centers for contemporary art in the world. In 1999 it merged with the Museum of Modern Art (MoMA), which increased P.S.1's visibility and gave MoMA a foray into a younger and more cutting-edge art movement. The first major collaboration between the two institutions took place in the 2000 exhibit *Greater New York,* which showcased emerging New York City artists. Over the years, P.S.1 has hosted such artists as Richard Serra, Christopher Wool, Robert Rauschenberg, Rachel Whiteread, Keith Sonnier, and Pipilotti Rist. In 1999 P.S.1 and MoMA started an annual competition called the Young Architects Program, in which young architects submit design proposals for P.S.1's courtyard. The winning design is implemented to transform the courtyard into a musical performance and party space for the weekly Warm Up music series P.S.1 hosts in the summer. In addition to its exhibit space in Queens, P.S.1 also runs WPS1, an Internet art radio station, from the Clocktower Gallery at 108 Leonard Street in downtown Manhattan.

Breanne Scanlon

Performance Space 122 [P.S. 122]. Theater and performance art venue in a former public school on First Avenue and East Ninth Street. In 1979 a group of choreographers and performance artists created rehearsal and performance space out of the abandoned Public School 122. Since then, the structure has evolved into a center for avant-garde and experimental theater and performance art. John Leguizamo, Eric Bogosian, and Spalding Gray, among others, have debuted work at P.S. 122.

Melissa Baldock

psychoanalysis. Theory of human behavior developed by Sigmund Freud (1856–1939) and his "Vienna Circle," starting in 1900; it emphasizes unconscious motivation, sexuality, dreams, and childhood experiences. It was introduced to the United States by Freud's disciple, Abraham A. Brill (1874–1948), who formed the New York Psychoanalytic Society in 1911. In 1913 Fordham Medical School professor Smith Ely Jelliffe and William Alanson White cofounded in the city the field's premier journal, *Psychoanalytic Review.* New York City soon became the world center for psychoanalysis. For more than 40 years, following the influx of European émigrés such as Karen Horney, Franz Alexander, and Otto Rank in the 1940s, the number of psychoanalysts concentrated on the Upper East Side of Manhattan (Park and Madison Avenues) exceeded that of all other U.S. cities combined. As of 2009 the city was the home of more than 50 psychoanalytic training institutes. In 2006, despite controversy, New York State became the first state to offer a governmental license for the practice of psychoanalysis.

Henryk Misiak and Virginia S. Sexton, *History of Psychology: An Overview* (New York: Grune and Stratton, 1966)

Harold Takooshian

psychology. The science of behavior. It is typically dated from 1879 when Wilhelm Wundt formed the first psychology laboratory in Leipzig, Germany. In the twentieth century New York City has been instrumental in the developing science and practice of psychology. Besides premier institutions such as Bellevue Psychiatric Clinic, Northside Center, and the Psychological Corporation, New York City has been a base for hundreds of pioneering individuals in the field, such as Anne Anastasi (Fordham University), Neal Miller (Rockefeller University), Kenneth B. Clark and Stanley Milgram (City University of New York), Otto Klineberg and Stanley Schacter (Columbia University), Max Wertheimer and Leon Festinger (The New School), Jerome Bruner and Philip Zimbardo (New York University), Florence L. Denmark (Pace University), and Benjamin B. Wolman (Long Island University).

In 1891, Columbia University formed a psychology department chaired by Wundt's student James McKeen Cattell. Much important early work was done there in experimental psychology, and during the early twentieth century Columbia awarded more doctorates in psychology than any other school in the United States. By the 1920s Cattell, Edward L. Thorndike, and other quantitative psychologists at Columbia had laid the groundwork for the behaviorist school. In the 1930s a rift emerged between academic and practicing psychologists. A group of clinical psychologists in New York City withdrew from the American Psychological Association (APA) to form the Association of Consulting Psychologists, and in 1937 the entire clinical division of the APA seceded and formed the American Association of Applied Psychology. The two opposing groups were reconciled after World War II, when psychologists in general began to expand their roles. Psychological testing was used increasingly to assess schoolchildren, college and job applicants, prisoners eligible for parole, the mentally ill, and a host of others. In 1954 Mamie P. Clark and Kenneth B. Clark of the City University of New York made a historic contribution in the field of social psychology when their research into the effects of racial prejudice on children was cited in the U.S. Supreme Court school desegregation case *Brown v. Board of Education.* With the growth of community mental health services during the 1960s and 1970s, psychologists became more active in providing psychological therapy. In the early twenty-first century more than 3000 psychologists were licensed in New York City, of whom more than two-thirds were in Manhattan.

Ernest R. Hilgard, *Psychology in America: A Historical Survey* (San Diego: Harcourt Brace Jovanovich, 1987); S. Baatz, "Knowledge, Culture, and Science in the Metropolis: The New York Academy of Sciences, 1817–1970," *Annals of the New York Academy of Sciences* 584 (1990), 1–269; Donald A. Dewsbury, ed., *Unification through Division: Histories of the Divisions of the American Psychological Association* (Washington, D.C.: American Psychological Association, 1996)

Sandra Opdycke, Harold Takooshian

public advocate. Municipal office created in 1993–94 to replace that of president of the City Council, which had its powers redefined and curtailed by the charter revisions of 1989. The public advocate presides at meetings of the City Council and is an ex officio member of all its committees but votes only in the event of a tie; she or he can introduce legislation and is first in the line of succession to the mayor's office. The public advocate answers complaints about municipal government and investigates agencies and programs. Democrat Mark Green was elected the city's first public advocate in 1993 and served two terms; Democrat Betsy Gotbaum replaced him in 2002 and also served two terms; in January 2010 she was succeeded by Democrat Bill de Blasio.

public authorities. Semiautonomous government agencies, legally known as public-benefit corporations. They have been used for many different purposes, but their main advantage to policy makers has been their ability to raise money for public improvements by issuing tax-exempt bonds without the need for voter approval and unconstrained by constitutional or statutory debt limits. Also, public authorities have often been used to build and manage public facilities such as transit systems, toll roads, airports, convention centers, and stadiums. They have eased access to the capital markets for nonprofit institutions like hospitals, museums, and universities, providing for long-term loans at relatively low borrowing costs; bonds have also been issued to make low-interest loans to developers of affordable housing and to make funds available for mortgage loans to low-income borrowers. In some cases, the charters for public authorities authorize them to take property using the power of eminent domain. In this process, the authority "condemns" the property and pays the owner a price determined by the courts. Public authorities are typically governed by an appointed board of directors and often operate without any direct control by voters or elected officials.

The Port of New York Authority, formed in 1921, was the first modern public authority in the United States. Under the leadership of Julius Cohen and Austin Tobin, it established many precedents that would be followed by other public authorities, in the New York City area and nationwide. The agency, which later became a bi-state public benefit corporation and was renamed the Port Authority of New York and New Jersey, is responsible for financing, constructing, and operating all of the shipping facilities and airports in the metropolitan area, as well as of the trans-Hudson transportation links, including the George Washington Bridge, Lincoln Tunnel, Holland Tunnel, and the Port Authority Trans-Hudson Corporation (PATH) train system. Another important New York public authority, one of the many that was formed by state and local governments during the New Deal as conduits for loans from federal agencies, was the Triborough Bridge Authority (later renamed the Triborough Bridge and Tunnel Authority), which under the leadership of Robert Moses was used to rebuild and overhaul New York City's transportation infrastructure from the 1930s through the 1960s. In 1968 it was merged into a newly formed public authority, the Metropolitan Transportation Authority, which also took over six other public authorities involved in transportation throughout the metropolitan area.

Two other noteworthy public authorities that operate in New York City are the Urban Development Corporation (later renamed the Empire State Development Corporation) and the Municipal Assistance Corporation. The Urban Development Corporation was responsible for extensive real estate development initiatives, including Roosevelt Island,

Battery Park City, and the redevelopment of Times Square. The Municipal Assistance Corporation was created as a solution to New York City's crippling debt crisis in the early 1970s. Dozens of other less well-known public authorities have operated in New York City, building schools, public hospitals, museums, college dormitories, and public housing projects. Collectively, public authorities in New York City have issued billions of dollars in public debt, several times that of the state and city.

Owen D. Gutfreund

public baths. See BATHHOUSES.

public executions. Public executions were common in the early history of New York City. The first civilian execution was in 1646 when Jan Creoli was strangled for pederasty. By 1700 there had been nine executions, 93 by 1750, and 219 by 1824. The gallows were initially on Park Row, then at the intersection of Bleecker and Mercer Streets near Washington Square Park, and finally at the south end of Union Square. Hanging was the preferred method for executions, although some early convicts were burned at the stake, slowly roasted, suspended in chains until dead from exposure, forced into a barbed cage, or gibbeted. Executions in the early 1800s were spectacles. Cavalry and a band escorted a procession from the jail to the scaffold, with the condemned wearing a white costume and hat with black trim. A noose was draped around the condemned's neck, and a coffin preceded him or her on a wagon. Officials and the criminal gave short speeches. In 1824 the execution of John Johnson drew 50,000 people—one-third of the city—along a mile-long route from the Bridewell prison near City Hall to 13th Street and Second Avenue. The popularity of executions made them increasingly difficult to administer as the city grew. In 1825 authorities switched from conducting executions on traditional Fridays to nonworking Saturdays to reduce disruption. In 1829 they moved the gallows to Roosevelt Island, but the public was undeterred: chartered steamboats packed with spectators and hundreds of small sailboats assembled to watch a double hanging. Several capsized and drownings were rumored. To ensure executions without disruption, the Common Council decreed that they should take place in prison yards. This regulation was the first of its kind in the world; New York State adopted a similar rule in 1835. Such executions could initially be seen by ticket holders and from rooftops. A scalping market developed for the former, and landlords rented viewing places for the latter. In 1860 the last truly public execution in New York City was conducted by military officials at the federal base on Liberty Island, outside local and state jurisdiction. The gallows was built on a high terrace now occupied by the Statue of Liberty. Thousands watched from boats. In 1867 authorities, again concerned with order and efficiency, erected awnings around the gallows and deployed police to clear nearby roofs, but thousands still gathered. Finally in 1888 the New York State legislature passed the Electrical Execution Act, which mandated the exclusive use of electrocution for state killings. The electric chair, deep inside a prison, was first used in New York City on 7 July 1890 and ended public executions.

Robert M. Neer

People from New York City Executed 1639–1963

Century	Number
1600s (earliest: 1639, mutiny)	16
1700s	185
1800s	109
1900s (latest: 1963, robbery/murder)	384
Total	694
Gender	
Female	21
Male	673
Race	
Asian	10
African American	207
Latino	11
Native American	2
Unknown	36
White	428
Crimes committed	
Armed robbery	4
Arson	15
Attempted rape	4
Burglary	28
Coining	2
Conspiracy to murder	14
Conspiracy and sedition	21
Counterfeiting	2
Cowardice	1
Dereliction of duty	1
Desertion	9
Espionage	3
Forgery	15
Grand larceny	5
Highway robbery	8
Horse stealing	2
Murder	489
Accessory to murder	16
Mutiny	4
Parole violation	1
Pederasty	2
Pickpocketing	2
Piracy	15
Poisoning	1
Private stealing	1
Rape	1
Robbery	17
Robbery and assault	2
Slave revolt	1
Sodomy	1
Theft	1
Treason	2
Unknown	4
Total	694

Sources: M. Watt Espy and John Ortiz Smykla, *Executions in the United States, 1608–2002: The Espy File* [online], 4th ICPSR ed., Inter-University Consortium for Political and Social Research, 2004, http://www.ICPSR.UMich.edu; Daniel A. Hearn, *Legal Executions in New York State: A Comprehensive Reference, 1639–1963* (Jefferson, N.C.: McFarland, 1997); Death Penalty Information Center, www.DeathPenaltyInfo.org/executions

Compiled by Bob Neer

public health. Marshes and an inadequate water supply were among the health risks in New Amsterdam during the early seventeenth century. Outbreaks of disease were nonetheless manageable as long as the population remained sparse. Governor Peter Stuyvesant enacted a number of ordinances designed to improve sanitary conditions, including one in 1648 prohibiting goats and hogs from roaming the streets and another in 1657 forbidding the disposal of refuse in the streets. Strict quarantine laws were also introduced under Dutch rule. After the British took control in 1664 new laws sought stricter management of farm animals, waste disposal, street cleaning, and food distribution. Religious organizations also played a role in making decisions that affected public health.

Until the mid-nineteenth century there was broad disagreement regarding the origin and spread of infectious disease. *Sanitarians* believed that disease was transmitted by "miasmas"—vapors from fetid water, open sewage, animal carcasses, and rotting food—and sought to improve sanitary conditions. *Contagionists* believed that it was transmitted from person to person and could best be controlled by quarantines. *Anticontagionists* saw disease as arising from the peculiar social or moral conditions of the victim. Most settlers saw epidemics as manifestations of divine judgment or a statement about the individual morality of the victim or the community from which the victim came. Being Irish, African American, or German was important in understanding both the cause of illness and the means of treatment. Hence, American public health practice often contained a strain of victim-blaming, in which ethnicity, economic status, personal habits, and stereotypes were seen as factors that led to differential susceptibility. Health officials therefore tended to engage in programs aimed at modifying individual behavior rather than social programs aimed at improving access to better food, housing, or health care.

During the seventeenth and eighteenth centuries epidemics of SMALLPOX or YELLOW FEVER did not spread far beyond the borders of the town in which they broke out. But in the nineteenth century CHOLERA, yellow fever, typhoid, and typhus began to affect entire regions of the country as new commercial trade routes tied the nation together. Furthermore, as poverty, crowding, and a lack of proper sanitation and pure water characterized growing cities, tuberculosis, diarrheal, and intestinal diseases became endemic. Moralists blamed the poor for bringing disease on themselves and accused them of living in filth and depravity by their own choice. Smallpox struck the city in 1679–80, 1690, 1731 (when as much as 8 percent of the population died), and 1752–66; measles in 1729; and yellow fever in 1702 (when a tenth of the population died) and 1743. Malaria became less frequent as swampy areas were filled in for development.

Public health problems increased after the Revolution. Yellow fever epidemics, which devastated the city frequently between 1791 and 1822, deepened the rift between sanitationists and contagionists and also led to the enactment of stricter laws governing burial and waste disposal. In 1796 the state legislature gave the city the power to make its own sanitation laws. Yellow fever in 1798 killed more than 2000 residents, or about 3 percent of the population; death tolls were highest in poor neighborhoods, which were often in swampy areas where mosquitoes bred. In the same year a municipal pesthouse was opened as a quarantine station (it later became the site of Bellevue Hospital). Mortality statistics were first compiled in the early nineteenth century under the direction of the city inspector John Pintard and were important in the development of epidemiology. In 1805 the state authorized the Common Council to appoint a standing board of health. When a smallpox vaccine became available shortly after 1800, many physicians and public health officials argued forcefully for compulsory vaccination; their efforts failed because of suspicion and apathy among the population, but they worked to provide free vaccinations to all who wanted them. The well-known physicians David Hosack and John Griscom were influential in the construction of the city's first working sewage system during the 1820s. Concerns over public health often inspired social legislation: conditions in the debtors' prison were improved in 1811 after an outbreak of disease, and the country's first school for blind children (now the New York Institute for Special Education) opened in 1832 after many children in the almshouse were left blind by an outbreak of conjunctivitis.

Cholera epidemics in 1832 and 1849 spread beyond poor neighborhoods and threatened the entire population of the city, providing motivation for reform during the mid-nineteenth century. Attention focused on overcrowding, but the sanitation movement was nonetheless tinged by a pervasive moralism: many reformers believed that better conditions would uplift the poor spiritually and thus improve the health of society. A campaign to form a powerful municipal health agency was waged by the surgeon Stephen Smith, the epidemiologist Elisha Harris, the reformer Robert M. Hartley, such civic leaders as Dorman B. Eaton and Peter Cooper, and the writer William Cullen Bryant. Public acceptance of immunization grew after a law was passed in 1860 allowing communities to require vaccinations for schoolchildren. In 1866 the Metropolitan Board of Health was established and given enormous powers; Harris was appointed the first registrar. The first agency of its kind in the country, it became a model for cities nationwide after it helped prevent a cholera epidemic in 1866 by removing thousands of tons of manure from the city.

After 1866 physicians gradually replaced businessmen and social reformers as makers of public health policy. Most physicians supported the public health movement, but some protested requirements that they report cases of infectious diseases. At this time political machines supported public health programs because health agencies provided many positions that could be given to loyal followers. By the 1890s leaders such as Charles Francis Murphy of Tammany Hall agreed that scientific advances in public health made it necessary for appointees to have an adequate knowledge of medicine. The health department assumed a central role in regulating sewage facilities, refuse collection, the water supply, and food inspection. Health authorities also had a say in making policies governing public baths and toilets, schools, clinics, hospitals, subsidized housing, and programs to promote kitchen gardening and outdoor recreation.

Toward the end of the nineteenth century new programs emerged aimed at managing health care for the poor. Public health physicians from the U.S. Maritime Hospital Service (soon to be renamed the U.S. Public Health Service) set up extensive screening procedures at Ellis Island and collaborated with city officials in establishing a quarantine hospital on the island for immigrants suspected of carrying disease. William H. Welch, Edward Delafield, and T. Mitchell Prudden were influential in gaining public acceptance of bacteriology as the basis of modern medicine, and in 1892 the world's first municipal bacteriological laboratory for routine diagnosis opened in New York City under the direction of William Park and Hermann M. Biggs. These years also saw the rise of nursing as an important field. Nurses organized treatment during epidemics and provided education and case-finding services in homes, schools, courts, and clinics. The Henry Street Settlement, opened by Lillian Wald in 1893, became a model for visiting nursing services throughout the country. The first public health nurse, Lina Rogers, was employed by the health department in 1902 and sent visiting nurses to homes and public schools to encourage preventive medicine. Physicians often resented the increasing number of clinics that provided free or inexpensive medical care for the poor. Against physicians' staunch opposition Biggs gained Murphy's support for his campaign to improve care for TUBERCULOSIS patients and to require physicians to report cases of the disease. One of Biggs's colleagues in fighting the disease was Homer Folks, executive secretary of the New York State Charities Aid Association. Labor leaders pressed industry and government to provide income and health services to those disabled at work (see OCCUPATIONAL HEALTH).

The advent of bacteriology led health agencies to focus on killing germs and improving the environment. Many infectious diseases were soon eradicated, and by the early twentieth century New York City's sewer system was extended into poor neighborhoods. Pollution of the city's waterways by raw sewage also attracted public attention. Public baths were built after 1901, often by philanthropists. The Milbank Memorial Baths were sponsored by the Milbank family and built by the Association for Improving the Condition of the Poor (AICP) on East 38th Street in 1904. A campaign to improve children's health was begun, inspired in part by an epidemic of POLIO during the early years of the twentieth century. The Rockefeller Institute (formed in 1904) conducted research on the disease. Such private charities as AICP led the school lunch movement after the turn of the twentieth century, and in 1908 the pediatrician S. Josephine Baker formed a division of child hygiene in the health department that became a model for other U.S. cities. The city's water supply was chlorinated in 1911, and a program for pasteurizing milk was introduced in 1912. Nathan Straus and other philanthropists set up stations to provide pasteurized milk free of charge.

Advances in public health continued to be made into the early years of World War I. The Rockefeller Foundation (1913) funded many health projects, and the health commissioner S. S. Goldwater (1914–15) devised an innovative system of district health centers in Manhattan; he also set up health education programs, encouraged women to enroll their infants in milk stations, expanded medical record keeping, and formed close ties with private agencies, community groups, and private physicians. His successor, Haven Emerson (1915–17), extended the health district plan to Queens and waged a public campaign

Average Annual Number of Deaths from Leading Causes in New York City, 1804–2007

	1804–9	1810–14	1815–19	1820–24	1825–29	1830–34	1835–39	1840–44	1845–49	1850–54	1855–59	1860–65
Bronchitis	N/A	N/A	N/A	N/A	N/A	N/A	N/A	77	134	238	335	408
Cholera infantum	102	146	48	130	179	279	396	549	753	1,140	1,107	1,484
Convulsions	184	149	180	197	323	538	690	577	1,065	1,728	1,714	1,648
Diarrhea	11	17	40	54	86	88	112	107	424	716	585	591
Dysentery	39	59	117	142	162	115	137	158	627	876	384	310
Measles	12	13	17	80	75	120	195	105	126	277	338	221
Pneumonia	102	146	176	176	279	396	549	592	753	1,140	1,107	1,484
Scarlet fever	6	1	2	3	47	264	274	324	136	505	1,034	1,082
Smallpox and varioloid	73	131	162	108	130	72	141	130	504	566	226	368
Tuberculosis	437	593	608	677	856	1,229	1,390	1,407	1,848	2,511	2,842	3,313
Typhoid and paratyphoid fever	N/A	N/A	N/A	N/A	N/A	N/A	3	19	172	114	159	436
Typhus fever	73	131	162	108	130	72	141	130	504	566	226	368
Whooping cough	38	62	66	59	93	117	144	111	143	196	299	195

	1866–70	1871–75	1876–80	1881–85	1886–90	1891–95	1896–97	1898–1900
Bronchitis	828	1,052	1,214	1,524	1,907	1,979	1,393	2,375
Cancer	1,472	1,824	2,525	2,112	2,425	1,747	1,206	2,144
Cerebral hemorrhage	808	606	589	821	943	1,227	1,249	1,231
Cholera	142	83	70	100	68	65	36	65
Convulsions	1,530	737	679	615	574	513	508	675
Diarrhea and extremis	4,291	4,083	3,517	4,015	4,153	4,355	3,948	6,595
Diphtheria	862	1,811	1,740	2,242	2,496	2,297	1,677	1,993
Dysentery	574	207	199	310	239	145	131	304
Heart disease	714	781	962	1,421	1,802	2,158	2,248	3,819
Liver disease and cirrhosis	348	396	299	373	365	502	572	1,012
Measles	425	333	302	711	645	659	N/A	N/A
Meningitis	800	685	591	727	887	982	770	1,231
Nephritis	928	1,073	1,262	1,901	2,390	2,589	2,669	5,215
Pneumonia	1,928	2,302	2,471	3,391	4,143	5,732	5,002	9,036
Scarlet fever	1,094	844	1,014	1,188	794	753	N/A	N/A
Smallpox and varioloid	117	723	77	150	43	70	N/A	N/A
Respiratory tuberculosis	4,115	4,160	4,351	5,257	5,334	5,236	4,919	7,964
Typhoid and paratyphoid fever	473	332	334	533	396	363	N/A	N/A
Typhus fever	200	46	10	56	4	49	—	N/A
Whooping cough	303	439	408	451	494	407	372	605

(*continued*)

against alcoholism. Under Charles Bolduan a bureau of public health education was formed in 1914 as the world's first such agency affiliated with a municipal health department. In October 1916 Margaret Sanger and her sister Ethel Byrne challenged state law by opening a birth control clinic in Brooklyn, the nation's first, which police soon closed; Sanger continued to fight for birth control in the city and in the 1920s formed organizations that eventually merged to become the Planned Parenthood Federation of America.

The influenza pandemic that battered the country during 1918–19 killed more than 12,000 people in the city. The incidence of DIPHTHERIA declined sharply after Béla Schick developed a means of testing immunity to the disease (1921), allowing the health department to broaden its vaccination program with the help of the financier Thomas W. Lamont. Under John A. Kingsbury (1922–35) the Milbank Memorial Fund sponsored programs for child welfare and presented health demonstrations from 1924 in Yorkville. The Department of Hospitals was formed in 1928 and became the sole administrator of 26 municipal facilities, ending a system of divided jurisdiction under which some hospitals had been run by the Department of Health, others by the Bellevue Board of Directors, and still others by the Department of Public Charities. The department was the largest of its kind in the country and also had under its auspices an independent bureau of nursing (1928), which oversaw work in public school health programs, visits to tuberculosis patients, and the staffing of infant health stations.

During the 1930s the health care system improved owing to the efforts of Mayor Fiorello H. La Guardia and the health commissioner John L. Rice. The health department

Average Annual Number of Deaths from Leading Causes in New York City, 1804–2007

	1901–5	1906–10	1911–15	1916–20	1921–25	1926–30	1931–35	1936–40	1941–45	1946–48
Cancer	2,621	3,334	4,256	4,993	6,229	7,637	9,062	11,257	13,169	14,627
Circulatory system	5,954	9,148	12,669	14,792	18,114	21,815	23,706	25,711	30,886	32,539
Homicide	143	247	293	271	334	405	522	351	265	362
Diabetes	520	690	916	1,063	1,284	1,624	2,140	2,787	3,131	3,423
Infant deaths (<1 year)	15,611	16,609	14,060	12,004	8,895	7,662	5,521	4,079	3,828	4,298
Influenza	449	412	393	4,480	725	874	625	250	108	48
Liver disease, cirrhosis	814	1,076	900	500	338	413	584	922	1,052	1,500
Measles	616	925	630	559	405	255	107	31	14	16
Nephritis, nephrosis, etc.	5,752	5,600	5,499	5,676	4,108	3,411	3,608	3,675	3,081	2,574
Pneumonia	9,976	10,573	10,135	12,656	8,210	9,115	7,580	5,087	3,345	2,966
Respiratory tuberculosis	8,154	8,832	8,745	7,915	4,937	4,574	4,068	3,680	3,281	2,932
Suicide	761	825	686	742	842	1,163	1,369	1,191	907	930

	1949–51	1952–55	1956–60	1961–65	1966–70	1971–75	1976–80	1981–85
Cancer	15,556	16,553	16,869	17,398	17,814	17,315	16,549	15,889
Cardiovascular diseases	36,206	37,724	38,988	39,943	41,981	40,639	37,978	37,818
Diabetes	1,583	1,644	1,581	1,789	1,867	2,064	1,547	1,436
Drug abuse	N/A	81	96	263	551	677	414	573
Homicide	318	340	366	592	992	1,663	1,700	1,763
Infant deaths (<1 year)	3,882	4,021	4,290	4,333	3,477	2,312	1,875	1,624
Influenza	57	51	68	32	63	27	35	7
Liver disease, cirrhosis	1,440	1,858	1,858	2,386	2,936	2,440	2,185	1,789
HIV/AIDS	—	—	—	—	—	—	—	768
Nephritis, nephrosis, etc.	570	556	573	509	447	372	381	383
Pneumonia	2,412	2,613	3,391	3,362	3,499	3,137	2,965	2,733
Respiratory tuberculosis	2,173	1,178	824	624	432	235	141	125
Suicide	863	649	711	908	680	641	711	603

	1986–90	1991–95	1996–2000	2001–5	2006	2007
Cancer	11,623	15,191	14,335	13,717	13,116	13,251
Cardiovascular diseases	33,527	32,074	29,330	26,663	24,760	24,300
Diabetes	1,198	1,348	1,659	1,770	1,708	1,560
Drug abuse	787	947	875	866	903	N/A
Homicide	1,902	1,815	778	624	624	517
Infant deaths (<1 year)	1,549	1,339	881	760	740	697
Liver disease, cirrhosis	1,289	946	697	521	454	453
HIV/AIDS	3,644	6,257	2,716	1,603	1,209	1,115
Nephritis, nephrosis, etc.	816	311	564	654	468	435
Pneumonia, influenza	3,351	2,810	2,548	2,726	2,578	2,247
Respiratory tuberculosis	174	135	39	25	15	14
Suicide	600	599	514	483	459	477

Dash denotes zero; N/A=Not Available.

Source: New York City Department of Health and Mental Hygiene, Bureau of Vital Statistics, Summary of Vital Statistics

Compiled by James Bradley and Andrew A. Kryzak

opened a bureau of district health and expanded the health center system. Other federal projects supported the building of hospitals and clinics and the introduction of programs to promote the health of mothers and children and to fight cancer and chronic diseases. The first major citywide study of the demand for services related to chronic diseases was conducted in 1932, and in 1939 Welfare Island Hospital opened as a clinical research center devoted to chronic disease (renamed Goldwater Hospital in 1941).

From the 1930s labor and business leaders bargained collectively for insurance coverage, which reduced the pressure on public funds to finance the catastrophic cost of illness and injury for workers. The state played an important role in determining the availability of private health insurance in the city, the number and location of hospitals, the purchase of medical technology, and the amount of reimbursements to hospitals by public and private customers. The Bureau of Social Hygiene (1935) overcame a long-standing social taboo when it launched a campaign against venereal disease, which was later brought under control after penicillin was introduced during the 1940s. The city's first facility for detecting and preventing cancer, the Strange Cancer Prevention Clinic at the New York Infirmary, was opened in 1937 by Élise L'Espérance.

Programs dealing with chronic and degenerative ailments such as cancer, heart disease, diabetes, and glaucoma increasingly emphasized early diagnosis and treatment. Improved medical care and education became available to children and pregnant women, and programs were introduced to discourage smoking, drinking, and drug abuse. The health department sponsored on-site screenings for residents unlikely to seek treatment otherwise, using new technology such as the Pap test for cervical cancer developed by George Papanicolaou at New York Hospital in 1943. Under the direction of Thomas M. Rivers, the Public Health Research Institute of the City of New York (1941) worked on such varied topics as communicable disease and nutrition. From 1943 to 1949 the federal government provided prenatal and postnatal services to the families of military personnel under the Emergency Maternity and Infant Care Program. The city's infant mortality rate was halved during the 1940s, and local facilities became national leaders in the care of premature infants. The incidence of chronic disease soon declined, and the city focused on the elderly and on substance abuse, which was soon classified as a chronic disease and recognized as a public health threat. In 1952 the Department of Hospitals remodeled Riverside Hospital, a former tuberculosis hospital on North Brother Island, as a center for the study and treatment of addiction among young people.

Gains made during the New Deal and the postwar years were consolidated through the efforts of Leona Baumgartner, the first woman appointed health commissioner. During her tenure (1954–62) the health department in 1955 began administering the Salk vaccine against polio; 94 percent of all schoolchildren had received the vaccine by 1962, effectively eliminating polio in the city. She also oversaw the formation of the Poison Control Center (1955) and argued forcefully for fluoridating the city's water supply, which was done in 1965–66 after years of angry debate. In 1959 the use of leaded paint was restricted in the city after researchers found that children who ingested it suffered neural damage; the paint was later banned nationwide and efforts were made to remove it from public buildings. Sunset Park Alcoholic Clinic opened in 1962 and received funds from the city, the Health Research Council of Greater New York, and Downstate Medical School. Methadone was first used as a substitute for heroin in 1964 at Beth Israel Hospital, and in the following year methadone clinics were opened at municipal hospitals. The 1960s saw the federal government increase support for urban health projects. Among the new programs were Medicaid and Medicare, which were established in 1966 and soon paid a large portion of the medical expenses of the city's elderly and poor. Widespread immunizations virtually eradicated measles. During the late 1960s there was a sharp increase in the incidence of sexually transmitted diseases, partly due to changing sexual mores.

A number of public health crises occurred during the 1970s and 1980s. Many shipbuilders who had been exposed to asbestos in the Brooklyn Navy Yard in the 1930s were diagnosed with lung cancer as well as the debilitating lung disease asbestosis; applications of asbestos declined after the early 1970s and were largely banned by the 1990s, and asbestos was removed from most public buildings (a decision to remove asbestos from all 1069 of the city's public schools caused delays in schools opening in 1993). Federal health services were severely reduced during the 1980s, making basic health care unavailable to many poor people. Modern sanitation facilities reduced threats posed by waste, but tuberculosis, hepatitis, and measles reappeared as drug abuse intensified. Sharp disparities in life expectancy and infant mortality persisted along racial lines: in Harlem during the early 1990s only about 40 percent of all men lived to the age of 65, a figure lower than in many developing nations. Nearly half the reported cases of lead poisoning between the 1970s and the 1990s occurred in low-income neighborhoods in central Brooklyn and the southern Bronx. Although city screening programs identified between 600 and 900 annual cases of undue lead exposure, officials believed that the number of children at risk exceeded 200,000.

The AIDS epidemic profoundly affected the Department of Health during the 1980s and 1990s. The causes and treatment of the disease were little understood during the early years of the epidemic, and controversies about the balance between personal rights and confidentiality versus the need to document and track illness led to serious ethical and political dilemmas for the department. Needle exchange policies, educational campaigns, and other traditional public health methodologies also came under attack from a variety of sources. But the development of antiretroviral therapy during the 1990s gave a powerful new tool to the department in its attempt to regain its authority.

In the early twenty-first century the Department of Health has been particularly affected by the increased attention to potential terrorist attacks and appropriate public health responses. The department was scrutinized, for instance, for its ambiguous role in allowing children to return to school in lower Manhattan and residents to return to their apartments after the destruction of the World Trade Center towers on 11 September 2001 despite the potential negative health effects of the toxic dust that lingered in the area for months. Thousands of people suffer from 9/11-related illnesses, and in 2007 Mayor Michael Bloomberg established the World Trade Center Medical Working Group to review research and the adequacy of health and mental health services for those affected by the attacks. The New York City Department of Health and Mental Hygiene helps to cover the costs of treatment and maintains "9/11 Health," a Web site that keeps the public informed about ongoing research and services. In other areas the department remains noted for innovations in chronic disease surveillance, diabetes control, and the regulation of tobacco smoking in public.

Leona Baumgartner, "One Hundred Years of Health: New York City, 1866–1966," *Bulletin of the New York Academy of Medicine* 45 (1969), 555–86; John Duffy, *A History of Public Health in New York City* (New York: Russell Sage Foundation, 1968, 1974); David Rosner, ed., *Hives of Sickness: Epidemics and Public Health* (New York: Museum of the City of New York, 1994); Sandra Opdycke, *No One Was Turned Away: The Role of Public Hospitals in New York City since 1900* (New York: Oxford University Press, 1999); David Rosner and Gerald Markowitz, *Are We Ready? Public Health and 9/11* (Berkeley: University of California Press/Milbank Fund, 2006)

Joseph S. Lieber, Sandra Opdycke, David Rosner

public housing. Public housing, as initially conceived in the early twentieth century, was intended to eradicate dilapidated structures to provide better dwellings for lower income families and to serve as a unifying element in urban redevelopment projects in New York City and across the nation. Because of an especially enduring coalition of labor unions, housing reformers, and commercial interests, New York City's public housing program retained broad public support and critical levels of funding even as disillusionment undercut similar programs in other U.S. cities.

Formed in 1934 the New York City Housing Authority (NYCHA), the first such local authority in the United States, became the central agency assigned to administer a broad mixture of state, city, and federally funded projects. In 1935 NYCHA completed the First Houses (Frederick Ackerman, architect) with 123 apartments on Third Street west of Avenue A on the Lower East Side. The U.S. Housing Act of 1937 set aside $100 million for housing construction, and in the same year the Housing Division of the Public Works Administration opened the first federally subsidized housing in the country, the Harlem River Houses (Archibald Manning Brown, Horace Ginsbern, and John Louis Wilson), with 576 units at 153rd Street and the Harlem River.

The First Houses and Harlem River Houses were based on "model" tenement plans that originated in the nineteenth century; both were low-rise, walk-up projects with well-designed apartments, playgrounds, shops, and areas for community meetings. Each apartment had a full bathroom, a kitchen with windows, and access to outdoor light and air on two sides. These features made the dwellings desirable at a time when most of the old tenements offered only windowless rooms and communal water closets. Low-rise designs were also used in the Williamsburg Houses in Brooklyn (1938; Shreve, Lamb and Harmon in association with William Lescaze) and the Vladeck Houses (1940; Richmond Shreve, William Ballard, and Sylvan Bien), which were built on the Lower East Side by the U.S. Housing Authority (which suc-

Williamsburg Houses, 1938. Built by the Public Works Administration in brick and concrete, the project followed the "superblock" principle, replacing 12 regular city blocks. Its low-rise units, compatible with the existing scale of the neighborhood, housed more than 1600 families.

ceeded the Housing Division of the Public Works Authority with the passage of the Wagner–Steagall Act of 1937).

From the inception of public housing, NYCHA officials struggled to balance social and economic realities with the program's original goals and vision. From the start, demand far outstripped supply; in 1938 NYCHA, which controlled 13,000 apartments in both municipal and federal projects and had few vacancies, received 36,000 applications. A family applying for public housing faced stringent requirements: at least one member had to be a U.S. citizen (a major obstacle in a city dominated by immigrants), the family had to have bank accounts and insurance (even during the Depression), and family income had to be at least a certain multiple of the annual rent (which, for a time, effectively excluded the poor).

Racial steering was another key element of the tenant selection process. This policy was based on the belief that public housing had to reflect the racial character of the adjacent community. The segregated neighborhoods of the period caused projects to have almost exclusively white or black tenants. These and other policies reinforced a tendency to relegate the poor to other areas, especially industrial and waterfront sites. Properties intended for redevelopment were often divided among many property owners, and as a result the high cost of the real estate precluded anything but a middle-income project.

In the late 1930s the designs used during the nineteenth and early twentieth centuries were abandoned in favor of high-rise designs based loosely on the concept of the "tower in the park." The first projects to use these were the Red Hook Houses in Brooklyn (1939; Alfred Easton Poor) and the East River Houses in Manhattan (1941; Voorhees, Walker, Foley and Smith). Groups of tall buildings with elevators housed more people and were cheaper to construct, and they became the norm when building costs rose sharply after World War II (doubling in a single 14-month period during 1946–47). NYCHA achieved additional economies by reducing room dimensions, omitting closet doors, and painting rather than plastering concrete-slab ceilings.

During the 1950s construction of public housing peaked at a yearly average of 7500 units, and large high-rise projects were erected in deteriorating neighborhoods in East Harlem, the southern Bronx, and central Brooklyn. These and other projects caused population displacement that worked particular hardship on the poor, the elderly, and long-term residents. The Housing Act of 1954 tried to address the needs of those displaced by urban renewal by giving them priority for apartments and promoting new housing development. The Limited-Profit Housing Companies Law of 1955 (known as the Mitchell–Lama program) provided low-cost mortgages to the builders of middle-income housing, and in 1960 the housing laws of New York State were amended to allow the construction of buildings that could be sold to nonprofit cooperatives. As construction waned, different forms of housing followed the principle of "scatter-site" planning, which provided for small high-rise and low-rise projects, compatible with local neighborhood conditions that were fit into existing residential blocks to minimize the displacement of population. Such projects were built on the Upper West Side, at Twin Parks in the Bronx, and in East New York. In 1967 NYCHA transferred its responsibility for construction to the Housing and Development Administration, while retaining the responsibility for managing its huge inventory of apartments. To further expand housing options, the federal government began in 1976 the Section 8 Housing Assistance Program to encourage the lease of privately owned apartments rather than the construction of new buildings.

As the social and economic profile of some housing projects improved, those of others declined. During the 1960s the city's welfare department successfully pressured NYCHA to change its tenant selection standards to allow in more recipients of public assistance, such that by the 1970s their numbers among the public housing population had skyrocketed. African and Latino Americans became the majority of the tenants during the 1960s (though a portion of housing projects remained predominantly white). By the 1970s NYCHA was forced to take in the homeless in large numbers (in 2001 about 29,115 formerly homeless families were in residence, 77,229 people, or about 18 percent of NYCHA residents).

As the welfare caseload and homeless numbers grew and surrounding communities deteriorated, social disorder mounted. By the 1960s about 60 percent of projects suffered from problems with vandalism. By the 1980s person-on-person crime in public housing was nearly equal in severity to that of the city as a whole. A new shift in policy during the late 1980s tried to grapple with rising levels of crime and the crack epidemic. In 1989 the federal government permitted a speed-up in evictions for families with misbehaving children; by 1999 evictions numbered about 1200 a year.

Despite these setbacks and even as public housing across the country tended to deteriorate and lose public support, NYCHA officials continued to put huge resources into the maintenance and upkeep of the city's vast public housing stock. New York City lost none of its public housing during the 1970s, in contrast to cities like Newark, New Jersey, and St. Louis, which saw many cases of forced closure or demolition. In areas such as the South Bronx and East New York, where property abandonment during the 1970s was widespread, high-rise projects remained as residential islands on empty landscapes. NYCHA made unprecedented investments in tenant patrols, security devices, and the development and expansion of the housing authority police. By the late 1970s NYCHA spent a greater proportion of its budget on security than any other authority in the country. At the same time, NYCHA also made large investments in grounds keeping, maintenance, the development of community centers and health facilities, and a wide range of other social services.

Over the decades, despite national disillusionment with public housing, New York City remained committed to NYCHA and its public housing stock. City officials effectively resisted large-scale demolition or, worse, prolonged underfunding. In the early twenty-first century the city maintains the largest inventory of public housing in the nation.

Richard Plunz, *A History of Housing in New York City* (New York: Columbia University Press, 1990); Nicholas Dagen Bloom, *Public Housing That Worked: New York in the Twentieth Century* (Philadelphia: University of Pennsylvania Press, 2008)

Roy Strickland, Jared Day

public order. New York City's ascendancy to a world capital was facilitated by a drive to establish an orderly city that promoted growth and prosperity. Over the course of two centuries, officials and residents sought to banish chaos and to create an environment in which it was safe to work, live, and play. Starting in the nineteenth century New York City created agencies, policies, and laws that provided for a stable urban foundation. The city's phenomenal growth (from 60,000 inhabitants in 1800 to more than eight million in 2000) required the establishment of public behavior standards and the creation of a police force, specialized regulations, and municipal agencies to enforce them. Public officials became responsible for preventing crime; arresting law-breakers; ensuring access to public spaces, light, water, and sewage services; and preventing disturbances of the public peace. Local residents embraced this structure as a means to improve their lives, thereby agreeing to the new rules.

The period between 1625 and 1850 was marked by significant disorder. Raucous meetings, riots, and unpaved and dirty streets made for a difficult environment. But by the mid-nineteenth century the city began to establish a new platform of order and basic services. In 1842 it opened the country's first public water system. In 1845 a paid, professional police force replaced the volunteer civilian militia and became the first secular local authority to enforce a wide variety of new regulations. The violence of the draft riots of 1863 marked a turning point for the city; it was one of the only times the city virtually shut down. Afterward, the drive for order accelerated. The local police force, reestablished in 1870 after a 13-year takeover by the state government, became aggressive in the creation a "safe" city. Its mandate included the prevention of crime, as opposed to just arresting those who had committed crimes. At the same time the police became the enforcers of hundreds of new regulations controlling traffic, animals, signage, vagrants, pollution, peddlers, and public behavior. Municipal authorities built paved roads and expanded public transit, lighting, and gas and electric infrastructure. Commerce and traffic regulation increased dramatically, as did the number of permits for various commercial activities. Concerns over public health and safety led to the creation of housing and health regulations, a sewage system, fire hydrants, pollution controls, and food safety measures. New regulations controlled drinking, prostitution, gambling, and any activity that caused disruption on the streets. From spitting to begging, personal activity in public became the subject of control, redefining unacceptable public behavior to include drunkenness, urination, and sexual activity. A major step toward controlling public spaces occurred in the 1870s when new laws required permits for preaching, demonstrating, or marching on public streets, making New York City the first major U.S. city to control such activities.

By the twentieth century the foundation for the ordered city was well-established in the country's largest urban center. Authorities enacted policies to ensure that the millions living in Greater New York (formed 1898), including record numbers of immigrants, could live in relative peace and increasing prosperity. Overcrowded tenements, a booming pushcart trade, and burgeoning commerce led to even more regulations to ensure safety and security. Mass transit, including the new subway and expanded bus service, made possible an orderly commute to and from work; new traffic regulations helped ease street congestion. A reorganized Sanitation Department ensured that garbage was picked up and roads cleaned. The Fire Department expanded to help eliminate major fires. Police fulfilled their mandate for order by pursuing both criminal activity and quality-of-life issues, increasingly challenged by the difficulties in dealing with Prohibition, organized crime, street gangs, and a proliferation of guns. Maintaining public order also involved preventing processions and demonstrations, especially when left-wing groups were involved. At the start of the twentieth century the Industrial Workers of the World, or Wobblies, engaged in raucous protests, often ending in arrests. Communists, socialists, suffragettes, antiwar activists, and others used Union Square as their main gathering ground up to World War II. Such demonstrations were quiescent during the 1940s and 1950s, but in the 1960s and 1970s Union Square once again became the setting for public protest, particularly in connection with the Vietnam War. Under liberal city administrations New York City became the setting for numerous feminist and gay rights protests and marches. By the 1970s, coinciding with an increase in crime, the perception of street disorder led to the diminution of these political streets activities. Ethnic and racial unrest resulted in numerous minor riots in the twentieth century, such as those in 1900, 1935, and 1943 involving African Americans. The solid foundation of public order was a major factor in sparing the city from the major violence that engulfed many U.S. cities during the mid-1960s. Throughout varied disruptions, such as blackouts, mass transit strikes (1969, 1980, and 2005), political protests, and labor demonstrations, stability was maintained and daily life functioned efficiently.

The demand for public order gained new urgency in the twenty-first century after the terrorist attacks of 11 September 2001. This marked the beginning of new national and local actions to increase security and maintain public order. City officials enacted measures to keep a watchful eye over potential terrorist threats, and these parameters expanded to include increased requirements for identification, more public and private surveillance, and more limitations on the use of streets, parks, and other spaces for public assembly. In lower Manhattan, a "ring of steel" was constructed in the financial district to thwart terrorists by blocking vehicles through the raising and lowering of steel plates in the streets. New York City police strictly enforced public meeting permit rules, discouraging or disallowing noncelebratory and noncommercial use of public streets and squares. Barriers, usually concrete, were placed in many locations throughout the city to prevent vehicles from accessing sidewalks and buildings. This period also witnessed a significant decline in the city's crime rate.

Lisa Keller, *Triumph of Order: Public Space and Democracy in New York and London* (New York: Columbia University Press, 2008)

Lisa Keller

public relations. In the nineteenth century press agents working on commission in New York City promoted entertainers by means of stunts, hoaxes, and cleverly written press releases. At the start of the twentieth century railroads, utilities, and manufacturers sought the aid of press agents to improve their images and ward off angry customers and stockholders. Some firms engaged independent press agents, while others opened or expanded public relations departments. Ivy L. Lee formed a publicity agency in 1904 and counted the Rockefeller family among his clients. He attracted many advertisers and journalists to the field, including his friend Pendleton Dudley, who left the *Wall Street Journal* in 1909 to open his own publicity agency. In 1919 public relations agencies were formed by Edward L. Bernays, a Broadway press agent who had engaged in wartime government propaganda, and John Price Jones, a newspaper reporter and advertising man who concentrated on fund raising for nonprofit organizations. Richard Maney (1891–1968) began working on Broadway in 1920 and, widely respected for his witty prose, became its most celebrated press agent. In 1923 Bernays taught the first course on public relations at New York University.

The late 1920s and the 1930s saw the formation of many new public relations agencies and corporate public relations departments in New York City. Among those who had successful firms were Harry Bruno, William H. Baldwin, Carl Byoir, Benjamin Sonnenberg, Stephen Hannagan, Glenn and Denny Griswold, and Earl Newsom. Arthur Page became the head of public relations at American Telephone and Telegraph in 1927, and Paul Garrett led the public relations department at General Motors from 1931. The first public relations trade organization was formed in the 1930s, and by 1948 two such organizations merged to establish the Public Relations Society of America. Hill and Knowlton (formed in Cleveland) opened a branch in the city in 1938 and after moving its headquarters there in the mid-1940s became the largest public relations firm in the United States.

The public relations business enjoyed tremendous growth in New York City after World War II. Companies increasingly turned to public relations for protection against the undesirable consequences of government regulation, scandal, and hostile takeovers. Founded in 1954, Howard J. Rubenstein Associates remained one of the city's foremost public relations agencies more than 50 years later. In the early twenty-first century public relations firms in the city remained essential to managing the images of the city's museums and cultural institutions, sports teams, schools, hospitals, nonprofit organization, and financial, media, and real estate companies, as well as actors, musicians, fashion designers, and chefs.

Irwin Ross, *The Image Merchants: The Fabulous World for Favorable Opinion* (Garden City, N.Y.: Doubleday, 1959); L. L. L. Golden, *Only by Public Consent: American Corporations Search for Favorable Opinion* (New York: Hawthorne, 1968); Richard S. Tedlow, *Keeping the Corporate Image: Public Relations and Business, 1900–1950* (Greenwich, Conn.: JAI, 1979)

Alan R. Raucher

public schools. During much of New York City's history public education was not perceived as the function of a government agency. Throughout the colonial period and well into the nineteenth century, education was provided primarily through private efforts and voluntary organizations. Independent schoolmasters took in students for a fee, teaching everything from basic literacy to such practical subjects as surveying, French, and bookkeeping; the Dutch Reformed and Anglican Churches opened schools for the poor where the rudiments were taught without charge; and King's College offered a full academic, college preparatory course. The frequency with which people signed their names and the extent of newspaper circulation in 1775 indicate that literacy was widespread at the end of the colonial period.

After the American Revolution a new commitment to public education was made. George Clinton, the first governor of New York, in 1792 articulated the belief that education was the basis of republicanism when he declared that the "diffusion of knowledge is essential to the promotion of virtue and the preservation of liberty." In 1784 the regents of the University of the State of New York were created to oversee academies providing secondary education, as well as Columbia College. The regents granted one of their first charters to Erasmus Hall Academy in Flatbush (1787); with land from the Dutch Reformed Church and funds from its trustees and from tuition, the academy operated both a day school and a boarding school. The State of New York began to fund public education in 1795: in New York City these funds were distributed to the charity schools.

Many peer and immigrant children did not go to school in New York City in the early nineteenth century, in contrast to rural towns and villages of New York State. To make attendance more universal, the city's leaders formed the Free School Society (later renamed the Public School Society), a voluntary agency that channeled private and public funds into schools for poor and working-class youth. At a school dedication in 1809 Mayor DeWitt Clinton described what motivated the society: "A number of benevolent persons had seen, with concern, the increasing vices of the city, arising, in a great degree, from the neglected education of the poor." The schools opened by the society were modeled after the economically operated monitorial schools developed by Joseph Lancaster in London, in which a teacher trained a group of student monitors who in turn instructed a group of pupils; in theory this system enabled one teacher to educate hundreds of children. To encourage attendance the society explicitly defined its schools as nondenominational. The schools multiplied and in effect became the city's public school system, serving a majority of the city's children and receiving a large share of its funds, while more prosperous families continued to patronize private and denominational schools.

By the mid-1820s members of the Baptist and Catholic Churches increasingly asked why schools that they sponsored did not receive public funds. Objections from the Catholic Church held special weight because of the large number of Catholic immigrants from Ireland and Germany, who perceived the Public School Society as essentially Protestant. After years of controversy the state legislature established a new public school system in 1842, governed by elected ward trustees and a central board of education. The new system of "ward schools" grew at the expense of the Public School Society and by 1853 absorbed its remnants.

The school system in Brooklyn evolved much like those of the rural areas of New York State, which were organized within districts supported by state aid, tuition fees, and local taxes. Like many other cities Brooklyn combined these districts under a municipal board of education in 1843. With the absorption of Williamsburgh by Brooklyn in 1855 a unified board assumed responsibility for the schools of the greater city, with small committees assigned to oversee each school.

The curriculum used in the public elementary schools in New York City during the nineteenth century combined basic instruction in language, arithmetic, singing, draw-

Public school in Fort Greene, ca 1900

ing, and calisthenics with moral and social training; in the higher grades science, history, and civics were taught as well. Early in the century children entered school as young as five, but by mid-century the age of six or seven was more common. Six terms (three years) of primary school followed by eight terms (four years) of grammar school constituted a full course, usually completed by about the age of 14. Secondary education was limited because unlike most northeastern cities, New York City lacked a public high school system. Students who wished to continue their education attended supplementary classes given by grammar school principals, introductory courses at the College of the City of New York (opened as the Free Academy in 1847), and courses at the Evening High School (for men, opened in 1866), the Normal College (opened in 1870), and private preparatory schools. Black children in both Manhattan and Brooklyn were required to attend separate "colored schools" until the 1880s, when both districts opened the regular schools to children of all races; in 1900 the last school to be explicitly separate racially was closed.

Immigration challenged the public education system in New York City during the late nineteenth century. Building enough schools to house a population of students that reached half a million in 1898 was a goal beyond reach. Thousands of children were turned away from school because of a lack of seats, making ineffective the compulsory school law adopted in New York State in 1874. Many schools resorted to half-day sessions so that each classroom could be used twice. After consolidation the city drew on the new capital resources made available, and under C. B. J. Snyder, superintendent of school buildings, it directed these resources toward the building of imposing new schoolhouses throughout the city.

The new schools tried to fulfill their social mission by extending their reach in many directions: they offered expanded kindergartens to accommodate the children of poor families at an earlier age; special education programs for students with physical or mental disabilities; fresh-air classes, usually held in rooms with wide-open windows, for students with health problems such as "pretuberculosis" and anemia; special classes at Bellevue Hospital for the hospital-bound; and schools for truants such as the Parental School in Flushing, in a campus setting far from the centers of population. Day high schools were finally opened throughout the city, with DeWitt Clinton High School and Wadleigh High School in Manhattan, Morris High School in the Bronx, and Curtis High School in Staten Island joining Girls High School, Boys High School, and Erasmus High School in Brooklyn and Bryant High School in Queens. Although New York City was the last major city in the United States to open high schools, it emerged as an innovator by creating schools that specialized in fields such as navigation and the printing trades, a trend that continued as a high school education came to be considered a requirement for entry into many businesses.

The schools also offered programs to help immigrants assimilate: intensive language courses for children who did not speak English, and evening classes in English and civics for adults at several elementary schools. To meet the demand for self-improvement, the schools offered a range of adult vocational classes at night, teaching clerical and business subjects, dressmaking, millinery, and industrial arts. A people's university emerged in the form of a program of Public Evening Lectures conducted from 1888 to 1917, offering hundreds of evening courses throughout the city in science, literature, art, music, and history taught in English, Yiddish, and Italian.

In the mid-nineteenth century school trustees filled most teaching positions with young women who had limited training; but as schools became more elaborate, the standards of training, evaluation, and appointment of teachers were raised. Licensing examinations and a merit-based employment system were established, and increasingly teachers claimed a degree of professional standing. Reflecting an emerging sense of assertiveness as well as the currents of the labor movement, teachers formed the New York City Teachers Union in 1916, affiliated with the American Federation of Teachers. Although it lacked recognition as an official bargaining agent, the union gave teachers a voice in setting salaries, budgets, and employment and educational policies. The union argued that the needs of teachers and students went hand in hand and demanded expanded resources for the city's schools and progressive educational reforms. Parents sought to exert their influence on the schools by forming the citywide United Parents Associations in 1921, the members of which became active in shaping educational policies. During the Depression membership in the teachers' union increased; however, its effectiveness was undermined when an anticommunist faction in 1935 accused the leadership of having communist sympathies and when the union was expelled from the American Federation of Labor in 1941. The expulsion was followed in the 1950s by an anticommunist purge aimed at union members.

During the 1950s the public school system in New York City enrolled more than a million students. At its best the system was a model known for its innovations in teaching and for graduating many students who went on to college and successful careers; Stuyvesant High School (1904) and the Bronx High School of Science (1938) became widely known for academic excellence. Yet at the same time the system contained the worst problems associated with urban education. The proportion of dropouts was high, especially in schools serving poorer neighborhoods and ethnic minorities. Residential segregation in the city led to racial segregation in elementary schools and racially identifiable "tracking" in high schools (the practice of assigning students to separate courses of study). Voluntary transfers and redistricting were implemented during the 1950s and 1960s, but the schools remained virtually segregated and the proportion of white students declined. As the schools came to be perceived as inadequate in the 1960s, parents' and citizens' groups began demanding "community control." Various experts also proposed decentralization of authority, and the Ford Foundation in 1967 funded three "demonstration districts" governed by community boards. The efforts led to years of community demonstrations and teachers' strikes; an especially acrimonious conflict was centered in the Ocean Hill–Brownsville district in 1968, and the United Federation of Teachers, led by Albert Shanker, became increasingly assertive. Tensions were relieved when the state legislature passed the school decentralization law of 1970, which assigned the governance of elementary and junior high schools to 32 elected community school boards while retaining control of high schools by the Board of Education. The community school boards partially transformed the educational system by exercising their power to define the educational goals of their districts and to select principals and community superintendents. But the central administration, led by the chancellor (the new name for the central superintendent of schools), retained significant power over allocation of resources, effectively limiting the ability of community school boards to innovate, especially during periods of fiscal constraint.

The schools during the 1970s and 1980s were affected both by changes in leadership and by broad national movements aimed at meeting the needs of all children. Bilingual education, introduced in Florida and advanced by rulings of the U.S. Supreme Court, was accepted by New York City in 1974 through a consent agreement settling a suit brought against the Board of Education by Aspira, a Puerto Rican community organization. Special-education classes were given more attention after the passage of the Education of All Handicapped Children Act in 1975. The national movement for options in education quickly took root because of the diversity of the city, and an array of experimental, alternative, and magnet schools were opened. At the same time schools were faced with an increasing fear of violence, often related to illegal drugs; in some schools metal detectors were installed.

By the 1990s, two decades of community participation notwithstanding, the public

Fort Hamilton High School, 2009

schools in New York City still faced serious problems. Insufficient academic achievement, unacceptably high dropout rates, and the abandonment of the public schools by much of the middle class were obvious threats. Inadequate financing in comparison with wealthy suburbs, and cuts in municipal and state budgets, seemed to frustrate efforts at improvement. Moreover, the leaders of the school system seemed to get bogged down in conflicts. A chief area of controversy was curriculum reform. A proposed curriculum on sex education, keyed to the prevention of AIDS, generated opposition from some central board members. A draft "rainbow" curriculum for multicultural studies similarly split the board into factions. With the board divided, Mayor Rudolph Giuliani was able to force the resignation of Chancellor Ramon Cortines to influence the selection of his replacement, Rudy Crew, and then to push out Chancellor Crew once he had lost the mayor's favor. In 2002, arguing that the governance structure had contributed to a general failure to meet the educational needs of the city's youth, Mayor Michael Bloomberg succeeded in persuading the state legislature and governor to abolish the Board of Education, to abolish the elected community school boards, and to give full control of the school system to the mayor. This change was in part a response to the national movement for accountability in schooling. In that spirit, Bloomberg and Chancellor Joel Klein set about making a series of administrative changes, including breaking up large high schools and devolving greater administrative responsibility upon principals, who would then be held accountable for results.

The public schools of New York City brought with them into the twenty-first century most of the problems and strengths that had defined them in previous decades. The challenge to provide a full democratic education to the children of a city with manifest economic disparities and uniquely diverse racial and ethnic groups had never completely been met. But the city's leaders had placed a commitment to that ideal high among their expressed goals.

Sol Cohen, *Progressives and Urban School Reform: The Public Education Association of New York City, 1895–1954* (New York: Teachers College Press, 1964); Carl Kaestle, *The Evolution of an Urban School System: New York City, 1750–1850* (Cambridge, Mass.: Harvard University Press, 1973); Diane Ravitch, *The Great School Wars: New York City, 1805–1973: A History of the Public Schools as Battlefield of Social Change* (New York: Basic Books, 1974); Diane Ravitch and Ronald K. Goodenow, eds., *Educating an Urban People: The New York City Experience* (New York: Teachers College Press, 1981); Kate Rousmaniere, *City Teachers: Teaching and School Reform in Historical Perspective* (New York: Teachers College Press, 1997)

David Ment

Public Theater [Joseph Papp Public Theater]. Theater founded by Joseph Papp (1921–91) and housed at 425 Lafayette Street in the original Astor Library (built in 1854). After the Hebrew Immigrant Aid Society sold the building to a developer in 1965, Papp worked with the Landmarks Preservation Commission to prevent its demolition. In its first big victory, the commission arranged for Papp, producer of the Shakespeare in the Park festival, to buy the building as an indoor venue for $560,000. Architectural preservationist Giorgio Cavaglieri converted the space into a theater. The Public, which produced new plays as well as Shakespeare and other classical theater, opened on 29 October 1967 with the controversial musical *Hair.* This production, along with other commercially successful work including *A Chorus Line* (1975), which later had a 15-year run on Broadway, allowed Papp to produce the Shakespeare festival at the Delacorte Theater in Central Park and to nurture emerging playwrights like David Rabe, John Guare, James Lapine, David Henry Hwang, and Suzan-Lori Parks. Notable Public Theater productions include *The Basic Training of Pavlo Hummel* (1971), *That Championship Season* (1972), *Bring in 'da Noise, Bring in 'da Funk* (1995), *Topdog/Underdog* (2001), and *Passing Strange* (2007). Papp died in 1991, and in 1992 the theater was named the Joseph Papp Public Theater in his honor. Shortly before his death Papp resigned from the theater and named as his successor JoAnne Akalaitis, former member of the theater company Mabou Mines. She was soon replaced by George C. Wolfe as artistic director in March 1993; Oskar Eustis took over in 2004. Mara Manus became executive director in 2002, and until her resignation in 2008 she stabilized the theater's finances, increasing its operating budget, subscriber base, and corporate support. Manus was succeeded by Andrew Hamingson, former managing director of the Atlantic Theater Company. The theater, which is owned by the city, contains six performance spaces, including the cabaret-style Joe's Pub, which opened in 1998; the Public also operates the Delacorte Theater and offers theater education and outreach services to students in the five boroughs. In the early twenty-first century the city had contributed $19 million and the Public raised $6 million toward a renovation plan for the Lafayette Street Theater. As of 2008 the Public's productions had won 40 Tony Awards, 141 Obies, 39 Drama Desk Awards, 23 Lucille Lortel Awards, and four Pulitzer Prizes.

Kate Lauber

public transportation. The New York metropolitan region has the most extensive public transportation system in the United States, and along with Tokyo, the most heavily used and complex network in the world. In the early twenty-first century the system included subways, regular buses, express buses, taxis, commuter trains, ferries, water taxis, and trams stretching across the five boroughs. The city has been a public transit mecca since the early nineteenth century, when horse-drawn streetcars and omnibuses carted residents about Manhattan. Metropolitan New York boasts the highest rate of public transit use in the United States, with more than seven million public transit riders per day in 2008, or 40 percent of the national total. More than half of the city's workers use public transportation in their commute—which is also the longest, on average, of any major U.S. city.

See also Buses; Cable Cars; Elevated Railways; Ferries; Horses; Metropolitan Transportation Authority; New York City Transit Authority; New York Water Taxi; Parsons; William Barclay; Paratransit; Railroads; Streetcars; Subways; Taxicabs; Transport Workers Union of America.

Kenneth T. Jackson

Publishers Weekly. Periodical launched in 1872 by Frederick Leypoldt as the *Publishers' and Stationers' Weekly Trade Circular;* it took its current name in the following year. Originally intended for both the book and stationery trades, it soon focused exclusively on book publishing. *Publishers Weekly* is owned by Reed Elsevier Inc. and has offices at 360 Park Ave South. It was published 51 times a year with a circulation of 25,000 in 2007.

Eileen K. Cheng

publishing. See Book Publishing, Children's Book Publishing, Magazines, and Newspapers.

Puck. Humor magazine that began as a German-language publication of the same name, launched in September 1876 by the cartoonist Joseph Keppler and the publisher Adolph Schwarmann. It was named for the character in Shakespeare's *A Midsummer Night's Dream.* In March 1877 an English-language version with the subtitle "Oh What Fools These Mortals Be!" was introduced under the direction of Henry Cuyler Bunner. Printed in a large format, this attracted some of the best-known cartoonists of the day, among them Frederick Burr Opper, F. Graetz, and Grant Hamilton. It soon surpassed the German edition, becoming the first successful humor magazine in the country. Closely allied with Democratic causes, it opposed free silver, supported the civil service, favored lower tariffs, and often lashed out against big business and monopolies. Circulation exceeded 90,000 by the 1880s when the magazine enjoyed wide influence: Grover Cleveland attributed his victory in the presidential election of 1884 to the magazine's attacks on his Republican opponent, James G. Blaine. The magazine inspired several other publications, including *Puck's Monthly Magazine and Almanac, Puck's Quarterly,* and *Puck's Annual.* Gradually overshadowed in political importance by daily newspapers, it took a more general approach during Harry Wilson's tenure as editor from 1896. Under the editorship of Arthur Hamilton Folwell (from 1905) and his successors circulation declined, and the magazine was eventually taken over by Nathan Straus, who reorganized it and added such regular columns as "The Seven Arts," "Puppet Show," and "Puck's Golf Idiot." The format was reduced in size in 1915 and again in 1917, color illustrations were eliminated under Karl Schmidt, and the magazine was published fortnightly and then monthly under William Randolph Hearst. Puck ceased operations in September 1918. For many years the magazine occupied a building at 295–307 Lafayette Street in Manhattan, designed by the architect Albert Wagner and erected in 1886 as a printing plant. The building is a handsome structure of red brick. Above the entrance is a gold-leaf statue of Puck; a larger one adorns the northeast corner of the building. Wagner extended the building to the south in 1893 and supervised the moving of the west facade to accommodate the widening in 1899 of Elm Place (now Lafayette Street).

Walter Friedman, Sandra Opdycke

Puerto Rican Forum. Original name of the National Puerto Rican Forum.

Puerto Rican Legal Defense and Education Fund. See LatinoJustice PRLDEF.

Puerto Ricans. During the seventeenth and eighteenth centuries a few entrepreneurs and their families were among the first to move to New York City from Puerto Rico; they traded sugar, rum, tobacco, and molasses grown in Puerto Rico for food staples from the Northeast. Later the city attracted merchants, workers, and students, but from the 1860s to the 1890s most immigrants were political exiles, followed by a growing number of contract and noncontract laborers. During the late 1860s the city became a haven for supporters of El Grito de Lares, a failed attempt in 1868 to make Puerto Rico independent of Spain: Ramón Emeterio Betances, Eugenio María de Hostos, Segundo Ruiz Belvis, and Lola Rodríguez de Tío were among those who joined with Cubans and other Latin Americans in the city to promote Antillean liberation using traditional methods of organizing, meeting, and disseminating propaganda. La Sociedad Republicana de Cuba y Puerto Rico (1865) was the earliest association of Cuban and Puerto Rican exiles formed to promote independence. Several Spanish-language newspapers began publication, including *El Buscapié* (1877), *América* (1883), *El Latino-Americano* (1885), *Las Novedades* (1887), *Revista de Literatura, Ciencias y Artes* (1887), *El Avisador Cubano* (1888), *El Economista Americano* (1887), and *La Juventud* (1889). By 1892 a renewed commitment to independence increased membership in the liberation movement. José Martí formed the Cuban Revolutionary Party, and Sotero Figueroa edited and published the first issue of *Patria,* the official organ of the movement. Independence clubs formed the bases of the movement, including Figueroa's Club Borinquen and Inocencia Martínez Santaella's Club Mercedes Varona. Clubs supported liberation through fund-raising activities advocating emancipation through various means, including swaying public opinion in newspapers such as *Patria, El Porvenir* and *La Revolución.* The Puerto Rican branch of the Cuban Revolutionary Party formed in the city after Martí's death in 1895 and flourished under the leadership of activists like Figueroa, Martínez Santaella, Julio J. Henna, Roberto Todd, Gerardo Forest, Juan de Mata Terreforte, Francisco Gonzálo Marín, and Antonio Vélez Alvarado. Many groups actively supported liberation: Hijas de Libertad, Los Independientes, Rifleros de la Habana, and Dos Antillas. The work of Jesús Colón confirms the observations of writer Bernardo Vega that membership was not determined by race: groups like La Liga Antillana, an association of working-class women devoted to raising funds and establishing international networks, could meet only in centers that admitted people of different races, cultures, or religions, such as the headquarters of the Socialist Party and of the Cigar Makers' International Union.

Black Puerto Ricans like physician José N. Cesteros lived in segregated neighborhoods but took part in social and political activities with other Puerto Ricans. The leadership of Dos Antillas was shared by two black Puerto Ricans: Rosendo Rodríguez and the Africanist historian and bibliophile Arthur Schomburg, a former student of island abolitionist José Julián Acosta. After his arrival in 1891, Schomburg committed to the Antillean liberation movement but is best remembered in subsequent decades for his involvement with the African American community during the Harlem Renaissance. Most Puerto Rican organizations formed in the city during the nineteenth century disbanded in 1898 after Puerto Rico was surrendered to the United States following the Spanish–American War. Former members used their networks and experience as leaders to direct civic, cultural, and political affairs in the barrios. Henna, a well-known physician, helped to establish the

French Hospital. Toward the end of the nineteenth century cigar makers built settlements in Chelsea and on the Lower East Side near Spanish-owned tobacco factories. Practices like *la lectura* strengthened cultural and political awareness: employees in tobacco factories engaged readers to read aloud twice during the workday (once for news, once for literature and political writing), and discussions followed each session. The first female reader in the tobacco factories was the feminist and labor activist Luisa Capetillo, who lived in New York City in 1912 and ran a boarding house on 22nd Street and Eighth Avenue.

More working-class Puerto Ricans moved to the city during the first decades of the twentieth century to escape from economic hardship in Puerto Rico brought on by a series of natural disasters that crippled the sugar and coffee industries, as well as by tumultuous strikes and chronic unemployment. Between 1909 and 1916 a total of 7394 Puerto Ricans moved to the United States, where some were contract laborers on farms in the East; others worked in urban factories. During the next few decades immigration fluctuated according to the availability of work. Fewer than 2000 Puerto Ricans lived in the city by 1910; but during World War I 13,000 Puerto Ricans moved to the United States to work in war industries. After receiving U.S. citizenship under the Jones–Shafroth Act, 10,812 Puerto Ricans moved to the city in 1917, and they were soon followed by a large number of military conscripts.

During these years there were slightly fewer Puerto Rican women than men, and more whites than blacks; most were young, skilled, or semiskilled workers from cities. Many disembarked and settled in Brooklyn, finding work in the Brooklyn Navy Yard and in factories along the waterfront. They created *colonias* around the navy yard and in Greenpoint, Williamsburg, and Red Hook. Others moved across the East River to Chelsea and East Harlem where they formed the large community known as El Barrio. By 1926 most lived in two areas of Manhattan: from 90th Street to 116th Street between First and Fifth avenues, and from 110th Street to 125th Street between Fifth Avenue and Manhattan Avenue. They were attracted to colonias and barrios where other Puerto Ricans lived and Puerto Rican ways of life were preserved. The difficulties of adapting to North American culture were mitigated by forming home town clubs, mutual aid and self-help associations; cultural, social, and political groups also helped Puerto Ricans to adjust to their new surroundings. Books, magazines, newspapers, and Spanish-language radio stations were widely available and enabled Puerto Ricans to network with other Spanish speakers. By the first decades of the twentieth century the newspapers *Cultura Proletaria, El Heraldo, La Prensa, Gráfico,* and *Artes y Letras* were published, in addition to several that had begun publication in the late nineteenth century; many organizations also issued reports and newsletters. More than 40 organizations looked to the interests and needs of Puerto Ricans, including Alianza Obrera, Porto Rican Brotherhood of America, Liga Puertorriqueña e Hispana, and Asociación de Escritores y Periodistas Puertorriqueños.

Most Puerto Ricans worked for low wages in light and heavy industry, domestic service, cigar factories, hotels, restaurants, and laundries. During the 1920s about 60 percent of working Puerto Ricans in New York City were employed in the tobacco industry. Seasonal workers continued to be recruited for farm labor. By 1930 the number of Puerto Ricans in the city was estimated at 53,000 by the U.S. Bureau of the Census, at 100,000 by the New York Mission Society and the *New York Times,* and at 100,000 to 150,000 by the Porto Rican Brotherhood of America. During the Depression more Puerto Ricans left the United States than moved there. By the 1930s many worked in the merchant marine, the postal service, and small businesses. Most struggled with inadequate housing, wages, health care, and sanitation. Their race and ethnicity, as well as their limited skills, barred them from many kinds of work, and they fought to maintain dignity and family values. Women were expected to fulfill traditional family roles even as they entered the workforce in increasing numbers; often they provided the primary income for their families as domestic workers or as workers in restaurants, laundries, the garment trades, and cigar factories. In their own homes they earned a living doing piecework or caring for the children of others. Leaders included members of the small professional class, merchants, owners of bodegas and botánicas, nuns, priests, ministers, missionaries, *santeros* (priests and priestesses of Santería), and spiritualists. Inured in a tradition of activist politics, in 1937 the East Harlem community elected the first Puerto Rican to serve in the New York State Legislature—Oscar García Rivera.

By the mid-twentieth century rapid population growth and unemployment in Puerto Rico spurred massive emigration. Between 1940 and 1970 the Puerto Rican population of the city rose from 61,000, less than 1 percent of the total for the city, to 817,712, more than 10 percent of the total. There were more women, unskilled laborers, and people from rural areas than before. Many Puerto Ricans served in World War II, bringing the total for both world wars to 83,000. As early as 1948 a branch in New York City of the Migration Division of the Department of Labor of Puerto Rico offered assistance in finding work and services, monitored the movements of seasonal contract laborers, and offered protection, legal advice, and links with Puerto Rico; later renamed the Office of the Commonwealth, the department provided citywide leadership that was sometimes compromised by the perception that it was a political intermediary between Puerto Rico and Puerto Rican communities in the United States. Several community organizations were formed before the end of the 1950s, including a coordinating committee for the Puerto Rican Day Parade and the Council on Hometown Clubs. A cadre of young professionals including Antonia Pantoja, Josephine Nieves, Luis Nunez, Yolanda Sánchez, and Eddie González, among others, emerged to help advance the community. They were instrumental in creating the Young Hispanic Adult Association, which became the Puerto Rican Association for Community Affairs (1953). The Puerto Rican Forum (1957) and the Puerto Rican Family Institute (1960) also promoted cultural heritage and education. The Puerto Rican Forum developed a plan for advancing the community that prioritized the formation of local groups. One of its most successful projects was the creation of the education and leadership association Aspira (1961). The forum represented the interests of Puerto Ricans in city and state governments.

The war on poverty in the 1960s did little to improve economic conditions for Puerto Ricans. Militant leaders focused on the status of Puerto Rico as a commonwealth, which they likened to that of a colony. Many community organizations became so dependent on federal funds as to become virtual extensions of the government. New groups such as the Young Lords, the Puerto Rican Socialist Party, El Comité, and the Puerto Rican Students' Union drew their membership mostly from second-generation Puerto Rican New Yorkers and sought to remedy social problems through radical politics; they protested poor sanitation and living conditions and fought for breakfast programs, clothing, day care, and health clinics. These groups took to the streets to advocate open enrollment and Puerto Rican studies programs in the city university system as well as bilingual education in the public schools. Criticizing the established Puerto Rican leadership for being conservative and unresponsive, they challenged the effectiveness of the bureaucracy through which many Puerto Rican leaders had risen to prominence, including Ramón Vélez and Gilberto Gerena Valentín (others such as Herman Badillo made their careers in the reform wing of the Democratic Party).

Most Puerto Ricans were hurt by the decline of manufacturing in the local economy during the 1970s, as factories moved to outlying areas, the South, and countries where labor was cheaper. Discrimination further limited the opportunities available to Puerto Ricans. Urban renewal programs disrupted working-class communities where crumbling tenements were replaced by highways and low- and middle-income housing. Businesses moved and barrios disappeared. Writers called attention to racial and ethnic discrimination encountered by Puerto Ricans and Nuyoricans (those born to Puerto Ricans in the city); Piri Thomas, Pedro Prieti, Tato Laviera, Nicholasa Mohr, Edward Rivera, and Sandra Maria Esteves were among those who criticized the institutional neglect of the community and the failure of democratic principles in the city. By 1969 educators and professionals established El Museo del Barrio, and during the 1970s many Puerto Rican organizations focused on addressing the issues raised by radical groups. Clubs, social and religious groups, athletic teams, and cultural pageants were organized, as well as political institutions that sought to improve relations with other segments of American society. Some who arrived in the city at mid-century proposed methods for teaching English to Spanish-speaking students that later became the foundation of bilingual education programs across the city. Substitute auxiliary teachers linked the schools with the community and formed the Society of Puerto Rican Auxiliary Teachers and later the Puerto Rican Educators' Association. These groups advocated professional recognition and licensing of bilingual teachers. By 1972 the Puerto Rican Legal Defense and Education Fund had established preprofessional programs and offered educational guidance and counseling for urban youth. It became well known for representing Aspira in a suit against the Board of Education, which was charged with not providing educational opportunities to Spanish-speaking children. The resulting consent decree mandated a transitional bilingual program for all students of limited proficiency in English. In 1973 the Centro de Estudios Puertorriqueños was established at the City University of New York led by Frank Bonilla to promote scholarly research, archive historical documents, and maintain secondary and primary resources on the Puerto Rican experience. The following year Boricua College, designed to cater to the bilingual needs of Puerto Ricans and other Latinos, opened its doors in Washington Heights, followed by campuses in Brooklyn and the Bronx. By the mid-1990s Puerto Ricans were no longer the only visible Latino group in the city. In 2000 the Puerto Rican population had increased to more than four million in the United States but had declined in New York City. However, at 800,000 individuals, it remained the largest Puerto Rican community of any U.S. city and numbered twice the population of San Juan. Despite continuing hardships since the nineteenth century Puerto Ricans have shaped the city's multicultural dimensions; contributed to music, literature, and the arts; crafted influential organizations; and advanced politics and education. The educational and economic attainment of each generation has improved. Most Puerto Ricans continue to identify themselves as Puerto Rican and retain ties with the island.

César Andreu Iglesias, ed., and Juan Flores, trans., *Memoirs of Bernardo Vega* (New York: Monthly Review Press, 1984); Edna Acosta-Belén and Virginia Sánchez Korrol, eds., *Jesús Colón: The Way It Was and Other Writings* (Houston, Tex.: Arte Público Press, 1993); Virginia Sánchez Korrol, *From Colonia to Community: The History of Puerto Ricans in New York City* (Berkeley: University of California Press, 2nd edn 1994); Gabriel Haslip-Viera et al., eds., *Boricuas in Gotham: Puerto Ricans in the Making of Modern New York City.* (Princeton, N.J.: Marcus Weiner, 2004)

Virginia Sánchez Korrol

Puerto Rican Traveling Theater. Formed by Miriam Colón in 1967, it performed initially in warehouses and storefronts. In 1974 it began renting from the city the former firehouse of Engine Company no. 54 at 304 West 47th Street, which at a cost of $1.6 million it converted into an auditorium with 196 seats; the first production there opened in 1981. The company performs each of its plays in two languages, with the same cast: on Wednesday, Thursday, and Friday in English, and on Saturday and Sunday in Spanish. It also presents its productions on a portable stage in the streets of poorer neighborhoods. It operates a free program to train aspiring young performers, offers a play-writing curriculum, and tours the five boroughs and New Jersey during the summer months. It has won the New York State Governor's Arts Award, the National Association of Latino Arts and Culture (NALAC) Lifetime Achievement Award, and the U.S. President's Lifetime Achievement Award. In 2008 it premiered the play *Three Calla Lilies* by Abniel Marat.

Melissa M. Merritt

Pulitzer, Joseph (*b* Makó, Hungary, 10 April 1847; *d* harbor of Charleston, S.C., 29 Oct 1911). Newspaper publisher. He immigrated to the United States and soon after his arrival joined the Union army in the Civil War. After his discharge in 1865 he moved to St. Louis; there he worked for Carl Schurz's *Westliche Post* and in 1878 acquired the *Dispatch,* which he merged with another newspaper to form the *Post–Dispatch.* The sensational style of journalism that he developed at this time was perfected in 1883 when he moved to New York City and purchased the *New York World.* Known for its profuse illustrations, entertainment features, and popular "crusades," the newspaper was often criticized for its loose mixture of fact and gossip. Its circulation war with the *New York Journal* (operated by William Randolph Hearst) marked the beginning of yellow journalism. Pulitzer defended his techniques as an effective means of increasing circulation and advertising. His newspapers achieved a combined circulation of 750,000 and quickly made him a millionaire. He provided $16,500 in 1904 to Columbia University for the establishment of the Pulitzer Prize. He lived from 1883 to 1885 at 17 Gramercy Park South; from 1887 to 1900 at 10 East 55th Street (now the St. Regis Hotel Pharmacy); from 1900 to 1904 in the Sloane Mansion, 9 East 72nd Street (now the Lycée Français de New York); and from 1904 at 9 East 73rd Street.

George Juergens, *Joseph Pulitzer and the New York World* (Princeton, N.J.: Princeton University Press, 1966); W. A. Swanberg, *Pulitzer* (New York: Charles Scribner's Sons, 1967)

Julian S. Rammelkamp

Pulitzer Prize. Award conceived by Joseph Pulitzer in his 1904 will granting Columbia University $16,500 to establish four prizes in journalism, four prizes in letters and drama, one prize in education, and four traveling scholarships (Pulitzer also bestowed $2 million to establish the School of Journalism at Columbia). The Pulitzer Prizes began in 1917, when panels of specialists recommended awards to an advisory board of journalists, and prizes were granted by the university's board of trustees. Pulitzer's will gave the advisory board the power to change or expand the award system and to withhold any award if they deemed all entries substandard. Thus, new award categories were added for cartoons (1922), photography (1942), and musical composition (1943), and over the years the number of categories increased to 21. Beginning in 1999 online components were permitted in the public service journalism category, and in 2006 online content was allowed in all journalism categories. More than 2400 entries are submitted annually and judged by 102 individuals serving on 20 different juries. The public service winner receives a gold medal designed in 1918 by sculptor Daniel Chester French, and winners in the other categories receive an award of $10,000. The Pulitzer endowment was depleted in the 1970s and a second endowment was created in 1978; the two endowments are managed by Columbia and fund the cash prizes and stipends for the jurors in letters, music, and drama. Journalism jurors receive no compensation. Although the prize money and the award ceremony at Columbia's Low Library are modest, the Pulitzer awards carry great prestige.

John Hohenberg, *The Pulitzer Prizes* (New York: Columbia University Press, 1974)

Kate Lauber

Punkiesberg. Dutch name for Cobble Hill.

Pupin, Michael [Mihajlo] **(Idvorsky)** (*b* Idvor, near Pancevoy, Serbia, 4 Oct 1858; *d* New York City, 12 March 1935). Nobel laureate, physicist, and inventor. He immigrated to the United States in 1874 and in 1879 enrolled at Columbia College, graduating with honors. In 1889 he received a doctorate from the University of Berlin and began teaching mathematical physics at Columbia, where he later became a professor of electromechanics (1901–31). His inventions in carrier-wave rectification had important applications in radio broadcasting, and his "Pupin coil" extended the range of long-distance telephony. Through his discovery of secondary radiation, he reduced patients' exposure to X-rays. Busts of Pupin by Ivan Mestrovic stand beside the Serbian Orthodox Cathedral of St. Sava (15 West 25th Street) and inside Columbia University's Pupin Hall. His autobiography *From Immigrant to Inventor* (reprint 2005) won the 1924 Pulitzer Prize. In addition to having a Connecticut estate, Pupin lived at the Dakota in New York City. He is buried in Woodlawn Cemetery in the Bronx.

Val Ginter

pushcart vendors. See Street Vendors.

Putnam. See G. P. Putnam's Sons.

Putnam's Monthly Magazine. Literary magazine launched in 1853. Briefly the foremost magazine of its kind, it was edited by Charles F. Briggs with George William Curtis, Charles A. Dana, Frederick Law Olmsted, and Parke Godwin and was unique in its outspoken commitment to American literature at a time when English serials predominated in such magazines as *Harper's.* It published many stories and articles about life in New York City, among them Herman Melville's short story "Bartleby the Scrivener" (1853). Other contributions were made by Henry Wadsworth Longfellow, James Russell Lowell, Henry David Thoreau, Horace Greeley, William Cullen Bryant, and Henry James. The magazine ceased publication in 1857 and was revived in 1868 without much success.

Alice Fahs

Q

Quakers. Members of the Religious Society of Friends; for practicing members of the religion, the terms *Quakers* and *Friends* mean the same thing. The first English Quakers were missionaries who arrived in New Netherland in 1657. They were unwelcome among the Dutch but found acceptance in some English towns on Long Island under Dutch jurisdiction, including Gravesend, Jamaica, Hempstead, and especially Flushing, a village formed by New Englanders who found the Quaker unpaid ministry to their liking. Soon many were holding Quaker meetings in their homes, attracting the attention of the Dutch civil authorities. New Netherland passed a law against visiting Quakers and those residents who might entertain them, and in 1657 Henry Townshend of Flushing became the first person convicted under it. He was fined, and other residents of Flushing quickly came to his support. Thirty-one signed a petition, later known as the Flushing Remonstrance, articulating their view that residents of Flushing were free to worship as they pleased. Colonial officials soon made clear that such action was unacceptable, and most signers of the original statement withdrew their support for it. Coercion was only briefly successful, for Friends continued to hold meetings. In 1662 John Bowne, another Quaker from Flushing, was arrested, imprisoned, and fined for allowing Quakers to meet in his house; he appealed to the Dutch West India Company, which subsequently instructed Governor Peter Stuyvesant not to persecute dissenters as long as they did not disrupt the workings of the colony. This was a powerful early statement of freedom of religion.

After the English conquest in 1664 Quakers ceased to be targets of persecution, except in wartime when authorities were sometimes reluctant to recognize the validity of the Quakers' support of pacifism. For the next century most Quakers remained in the countryside of western Long Island, especially in Flushing, Hempstead, and Oyster Bay, and for the most part Quakerism expanded north up the Hudson River and later to the west before the twentieth century. Some were attracted by the mercantile opportunities in Manhattan, where a meetinghouse was built in 1696 on Green Street (now Liberty Place).

By the early nineteenth century Friends in New York City were a powerful minority among those of New York State. They were usually wealthier than their counterparts in the country, and their contact with the wider world through commerce introduced them to evangelical groups in England; they stressed such doctrinal issues as atonement and the Trinity and placed greater emphasis on the Bible, putting them at odds with many rural Quakers who continued to emphasize the "inner light" of God in all. After a struggle to control Quakerism in New York State, the two groups formally divided into two factions in 1828. Elias Hicks symbolized the traditionalists of Long Island and elsewhere, who became known as Hicksites. Their beliefs were considered well beyond the bounds of Christian respectability by Friends in the city, who adopted the major tenets of evangelical Christianity and became known as Orthodox Quakers. Both factions opposed slavery and after the Civil War helped freed blacks through such organizations as the New York Colored Mission (1871). The Friends' Employment Society (1862) trained young women for work, especially in hospitals. Among the Quaker agencies for children were the Young Friends' Aid Association (1873) and the Society for the Prevention of Cruelty to Children (1875). Quakers also continued to pursue peace efforts and actively assist noncombatants during the world wars. In the following years they shifted their focus toward social action, and in 1955 the Hicksite and Orthodox factions reunited to strengthen their assault on contemporary problems.

George L. Smith, *Religion and Trade in New Netherland: Dutch Origins and American Development* (Ithaca, N.Y.: Cornell University Press, 1973); Arthur J. Worrall, *Quakers in the Colonial Northeast* (Hanover, N.H.: University Press of New England, 1980)

Arthur J. Worrall

Friends Meeting House on Northern Boulevard, Flushing, 1927

Quantum Chemical Corporation. Firm of distillers and chemical manufacturers. It was formed in 1924 as the National Distillers Products Corporation in a bankrupt distillery by Seton Porter (1882–1953), who made spirits for medicinal and religious purposes and after the repeal of Prohibition in 1933 was able to sell alcoholic spirits. The headquarters were at 52 Williams Street until being moved to 99 Park Avenue in the mid-1950s. After buying U.S. Industrial Chemicals, the firm was renamed the National Distillers and Chemical Corporation. It concentrated entirely on chemicals from the 1970s and in 1988 took its current name. In 2007 Quantum Chemical had sales of $2.3 billion and 8850 employees.

James Bradley

Quarantine Riots. The name of two violent incidents in Staten Island in the late 1850s, resulting from lax enforcement of quarantine laws at the quarantine station on Seguine's Point. Before the riots nearby residents of Tompkinsville and Castleton had set up vigilance committees to keep the arriving sailors and immigrants inside the station until they were cleared of disease. In July 1857 protesters attacked the station but were beaten back by the police. On 2 September of the following year, when several victims of yellow fever arrived at the quarantine hospital, a much larger mob attacked the station and burned all its buildings to the ground. One hospital employee was shot, and many patients were dragged out of the building and beaten.

A large force of Marines and policemen from Manhattan were called to Staten Island to quell the violence, and many of the rioters were arrested. In the next few years local public health officials decided to move the quarantine station to various floating hospitals and uninhabited islands in Lower New York Bay.

Chad Ludington

Queen Elizabeth. Ship. Built in the 1930s, it made its maiden voyage from Clydebank, Scotland, on 3 March 1940, arriving in New York six days later. Used as a troopship during World War II, it carried more than 750,000 soldiers and sailed some 500,000 miles. After the war the ship again became a passenger liner, mainly on the transatlantic route. In 1968 it was retired and was replaced by the *Queen Elizabeth 2.*

Jessica Montesano

Queen Elizabeth 2. Ship. Launched in 1967, the *QE2* was the longest-serving ship in the Cunard Line's history and the fastest passenger ocean liner then in service. The vessel crossed the Atlantic more than 800 times and carried more than 2.5 million passengers before its 806th and last voyage in 2008 out of New York Harbor.

Jessica Montesano

Queen Mary. Transatlantic passenger liner that sailed between England, France, and New York City. It was owned by Cunard–White Star Limited, which, legend has it, wanted to name it the *Victoria*. However, when Sir Percy Bates and Sir Ashley Sparks, leading officials of the firm, told King George V that they planned to name the ship after the greatest queen of England, the king replied that his wife, Queen Mary, "would be delighted." After its maiden voyage to New York City in 1936, the ship held the transatlantic speed record for many years. During World War II it ferried entire army divisions (14,000 men) to Britain and sailed alone because its speed allowed it easily to outrun German U-boats. The ship retired in 1967, and as of 2010 it was a museum and hotel docked at Long Beach, California.

Frank O. Braynard

Queen Mary 2. Ocean liner. Cunard ocean liners had been arriving in New York since 1847 when the line's new flagship, the new Royal Mail Ship *Queen Mary 2,* went into service in 2004. The longest ocean liner ever built at 1132 feet (345 meters), it succeeded the *Queen Elizabeth 2* and the first *Queen Mary* (later a floating hotel in Long Beach, California) as the queen of the transatlantic route. The *Queen Mary 2* is about three times as long as the *Titanic* and twice as long as the *Queen Elizabeth 2.* The ship's name refers to the consort of British king George V, grandfather of Queen Elizabeth II. Built in France by Chantiers de l'Atlantique, and capable of carrying 2620 passengers and making an open ocean speed of 30 knots (34.5 m.p.h.), the *QM2* docked either at the Manhattan Cruise Terminal near 55th Street on the Hudson or at the new Brooklyn Cruise Terminal at Pier 12 at Red Hook, formerly a commercial wharf. On 13 January 2008 the ship participated in one of the most spectacular displays in New York Harbor history when it, the new *Queen Victoria,* and the 39-year-old *Queen Elizabeth 2* rendezvoused near the Statue of Liberty. This reportedly was the first time three Cunard *Queens* were present in the same location.

John Rousmaniere

Queens. The largest borough in land area, comprising 37 percent of the city. At 13.75 miles (22 kilometers) from east to west and 15 miles (24 kilometers) north to south, Queens covers about 120 square miles (311 square kilometers) and is almost as large as Manhattan, the Bronx, and Staten Island combined. It is bounded to the north by the East River and Long Island Sound, to the east by Nassau County, to the south by the Atlantic Ocean, to the southwest by Brooklyn, and to the west by the East River.

1. To the Mid-Nineteenth Century

American Indians lived near bays and inlets along the coast, including Flushing Bay, Little Neck Bay and Oakland Lake, Jamaica Bay, the Rockaway Peninsula, and the headwaters of Newtown Creek. Beginning in 1609 the Dutch explored the region and established the colony of New Netherland; by 1638 some farming began in Queens along the East River in what became Hallett's Point in Astoria. None of these pioneer settlements in Queens endured, but the loamy soils, oak forests, and salt marshes of Long Island soon lured others seeking to raise hay, grain, and livestock and extract timber and firewood. Dutch authorities granted English settlers from New England permission to settle western Long Island. In 1642 Governor Willem Kieft gave Rev. Francis Doughty a patent to settle Mespat at the head of Newtown Creek (Maspeth). That settlement was destroyed in the Indian war the next year, but within a decade English and Dutch settlers built permanent settlements. The Indians left little behind but place-names and trails that became roads, though wampum continued as local currency into the eighteenth century.

While governed from New Amsterdam under Dutch laws and institutions, many of the early residents were English Protestants. They founded Vlissingen (Flushing) in 1645, Middleburgh (Newtown, and later Elmhurst) in 1652, and Rustdorp (Jamaica) in 1656. The Dutch gave each village a Dutch name and installed the Dutch form of government. By the late seventeenth century many families that later became prominent were established, including the Halletts of Newtown, the Lawrences of Flushing, and the Van Siclens of Jamaica. English settlers disliked Dutch rule, particularly in matters of religion and local administration. Only adherents of the Dutch Reformed Church could worship openly. In the most important event in the county's colonial history, Flushing residents signed the Flushing Remonstrance on 27 December 1657, formally protesting the denial to Quakers of freedom of worship guaranteed by the town charter. Governor Peter Stuyvesant immediately arrested and fined several petitioners. In 1662 Stuyvesant imprisoned John Bowne for allowing Quaker meetings in his Flushing home, then banished him from the colony. Bowne traveled to the Netherlands and appealed his banishment to the Dutch West India Company, which upheld him and guaranteed religious freedom for all Protestant sects in the colony. Vindicated, Bowne returned to Flushing. His house, a "Shrine to Religious Freedom," is a city landmark, as is the nearby 1694 Quaker Meeting House.

The English took over New Amsterdam in 1664 and in 1683 divided their new province of New York into 10 counties, including Queens, originally extending east to Suffolk. The new county was divided into five townships: Newtown, Flushing, Jamaica, Hempstead (out of which North Hempstead was formed after the Revolution), and Oyster Bay. The western towns, plus the Rockaway Peninsula, correspond to present-day Queens; the boundaries reflected natural features of the terrain, which influenced the social divisions and the movement of goods and people well into the twentieth century. The terminal moraine, the southern limit of the last ice age, runs through the middle of the borough (roughly the route of the Interborough Parkway and the Grand Central Parkway east of Kew Gardens). Newtown and Flushing are north of the moraine, separated by Flushing Bay and Flushing Creek, meandering south through 3 miles (5 kilometers) of salt marsh (now Flushing Meadows–Corona Park) to the moraine. Flushing Meadows prevented continuous travel by land through northern Queens; the first bridge was built in 1800 at what became Northern Boulevard. Jamaica occupies the sandy outwash plain, the flat expanse created when the glacier melted, to Jamaica Bay, a saltwater lagoon shielded from the ocean by Rockaway Peninsula and noted for its fish, shellfish, water fowl, and salt-marsh meadows.

Jamaica Village was the first county seat, 12 miles (19 kilometers) from the Brooklyn ferry on the East River along an Indian trail to Jamaica. In 1703 the colonial legislature designated this road the King's Highway and authorized its continuation to East Hampton on the east end of Long Island; in Queens it became Jamaica Avenue. The population was largely engaged in agriculture, with a small

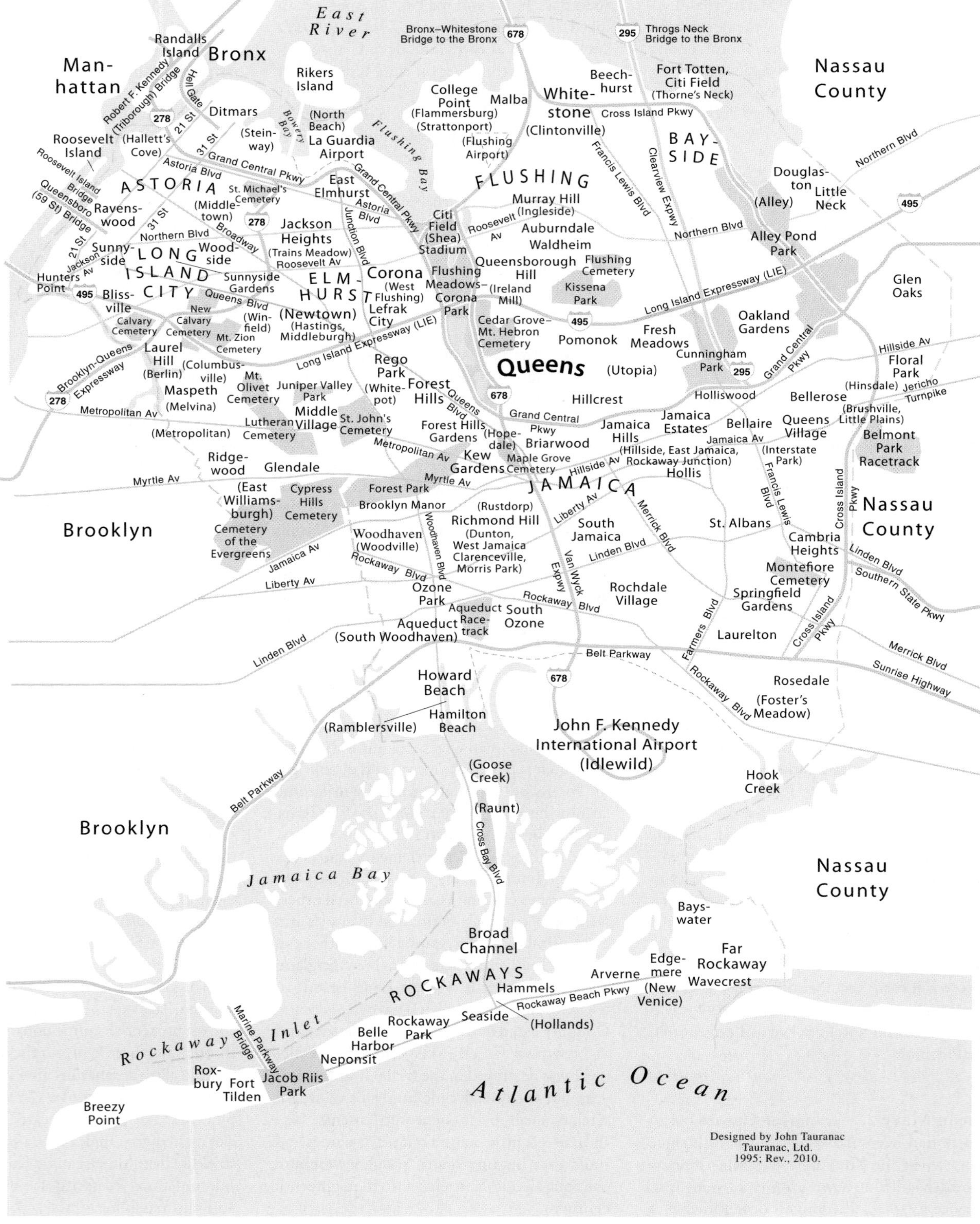
East River
Bronx–Whitestone Bridge to the Bronx
678
295
Throgs Neck Bridge to the Bronx
Randalls Island
Bronx
Man-hattan
Robert F. Kennedy (Triborough) Bridge
Hell Gate
278
21 St
Rikers Island
Ditmars
Nassau County
Beech-hurst
Fort Totten, Citi Field (Thorne's Neck)
College Point (Flammersburg) (Strattonport)
Malba
White-stone (Clintonville)
Cross Island Pkwy
Roosevelt Island
(Hallett's Cove)
31 St
(Stein-way)
Bowery Bay
(North Beach) La Guardia Airport
Flushing Bay
(Flushing Airport)
BAY-SIDE
Northern Blvd
Roosevelt Island Bridge
Queensboro (59 St) Bridge
Astoria Blvd
Grand Central Pkwy
ASTORIA
St. Michael's Cemetery
East Elmhurst
Grand Central Pkwy
FLUSHING
Francis Lewis Blvd
Clearview Expwy
Douglas-ton
Little Neck
(Alley)
495
Ravens-wood
(Middle-town)
31 St
278
Jackson Heights (Trains Meadow)
Astoria Blvd
Citi Field (Shea) Stadium
Murray Hill (Ingleside)
Roosevelt Av
Auburndale
Waldheim
Northern Blvd
Alley Pond Park
Northern Blvd
Broadway
Junction Blvd
21 St
Jackson Av
Sunny-side
LONG ISLAND CITY
Wood-side
Roosevelt Av
Flushing Meadows–Corona Park
Queensborough Hill
Flushing Cemetery
Kissena Park
Glen Oaks
Hunters Point
495
Bliss-ville
Sunnyside Gardens
Queens Blvd
ELM-HURST
Corona (West Flushing)
Lefrak City
(Ireland Mill)
Long Island Expressway (LIE)
Oakland Gardens
Calvary Cemetery
New Calvary Cemetery
Mt. Zion Cemetery
(Win-field)
(Newtown) (Hastings, Middleburgh)
Long Island Expressway (LIE)
Cedar Grove–Mt. Hebron Cemetery
495
Pomonok
Fresh Meadows
Cunningham Park
295
Grand Central Pkwy
Hillside Av
Brooklyn-Queens Expressway
Laurel Hill (Berlin)
(Columbus-ville)
Mt. Olivet Cemetery
Juniper Valley Park
Rego Park (White-pot)
Forest Hills
Queens Blvd
Queens
(Utopia)
Floral Park
(Hinsdale)
Jericho Turnpike
278
Maspeth (Melvina)
Metropolitan Av
Middle Village
678
Hillcrest
Holliswood
Bellerose
(Brushville, Little Plains)
(Metropolitan)
Lutheran Cemetery
St. John's Cemetery
Grand Central Pkwy
Forest Hills Gardens
(Hope-dale)
Briarwood
Jamaica Hills
Jamaica Estates
Bellaire
Queens Village
Belmont Park Racetrack
Metropolitan Av
Kew Gardens
Maple Grove Cemetery
(Hillside, East Jamaica, Rockaway Junction)
Jamaica Av
(Interstate Park)
Ridge-wood
Glendale
Myrtle Av
Myrtle Av
Hillside Av
Hollis
Myrtle Av
(East Williams-burgh)
Cypress Hills Cemetery
Forest Park
JAMAICA
Brooklyn Manor
(Rustdorp)
Liberty Av
Merrick Blvd
Cross Island Pkwy
Nassau County
Brooklyn
Woodhaven Blvd
Richmond Hill (Dunton, West Jamaica Clarenceville, Morris Park)
South Jamaica
St. Albans
Francis Lewis Blvd
Cambria Heights
Cemetery of the Evergreens
Woodhaven (Woodville)
Van Wyck Expwy
Linden Blvd
Linden Blvd
Jamaica Av
Rockaway Blvd
Montefiore Cemetery
Southern State Pkwy
Liberty Av
Ozone Park
Rochdale Village
Springfield Gardens
Rockaway Blvd
Aqueduct Race-track
South Ozone
Aqueduct (South Woodhaven)
Farmers Blvd
Laurelton
Cross Island Pkwy
Linden Blvd
Belt Parkway
Merrick Blvd
Howard Beach
678
Rosedale
Sunrise Highway
Rockaway Blvd
(Foster's Meadow)
(Ramblersville)
Hamilton Beach
John F. Kennedy International Airport (Idlewild)
(Goose Creek)
Hook Creek
Belt Parkway
(Raunt)
Brooklyn
Cross Bay Blvd
Jamaica Bay
Nassau County
Bays-water
Broad Channel
Far Rockaway
Wavecrest
Edge-mere
Arverne
ROCKAWAYS
Hammels
(New Venice)
Rockaway Beach Pkwy
Seaside
(Hollands)
Rockaway Park
Belle Harbor
Marine Parkway Bridge
Rockaway Inlet
Neponsit
Rox-bury
Fort Tilden
Jacob Riis Park
Atlantic Ocean
Breezy Point
Designed by John Tauranac
Tauranac, Ltd.
1995; Rev., 2010.

Population of Selected Towns in Queens, 1790–1890

	Flushing	Jamaica	Long Island City	Newtown
1790	1,607	1,675	N/A	2,111
1800	1,818	1,661	N/A	2,282
1830	2,822	2,376	N/A	2,610
1840	4,124	3,781	N/A	5,054
1850	5,376	4,247	N/A	7,208
1860	10,188	6,515	N/A	13,725
1870	14,650	7,745	3,867	20,274
1880	15,960	10,088	17,129	N/A
1890	19,803	14,441	30,506	17,549

N/A=Not Available.

Note: Population figures for towns were not included in the censuses of 1810 and 1820.

Compiled by James Bradley

number living in the three village centers. By the early eighteenth century land prices rose steadily and the size of farms decreased; most land was still held by established families. Many families owned slaves, although few owned more than two. The first census (1790) recorded 5393 inhabitants, including 1095 slaves.

In the eighteenth century Queens supplied Manhattan with produce, exporting it also to the Caribbean and England. Around 1730 farmers developed a new variety of apple, the Newtown pippin, which soon spread throughout Long Island and was the first American-grown apple exported to England, where it was considered a luxury and commanded a high price. As early as 1737 William Prince opened the first commercial nursery for trees and plants in America in Flushing, and in the nineteenth century the Prince and Parsons nurseries were cultivating and selling fruit trees and ornamentals from Europe and Asia, making Queens the horticultural center of the nation (the remains of the Parsons nursery can be seen in Kissena Park).

The American Revolution divided Queens. Except in Newtown most residents strongly favored the British. George Washington's defeat in the Battle of Long Island on 27 August 1776 gave the British control of western Long Island, and thousands of troops were quartered in Queens, which became a major staging area for military operations. The British enjoyed nearly total security, disturbed only by the inconsequential raids of rebels from Connecticut in whaleboats. The seven-year occupation left a ravaged countryside and lasting memories of hardship. Officers billeted themselves in homes, the army requisitioned crops and livestock, and soldiers acting on their own stole produce, stripping the land of timber and even fenceposts for firewood. After the peace treaty was signed, Queens became a staging ground for the evacuation of thousands of Loyalists from all over America. The last British troops in New York marched out of Jamaica on 8 December 1783.

In 1788 the county seat was transferred from Jamaica to Mineola in North Hempstead (in 1872 it was moved to Long Island City, reflecting the shift in population and economic growth). Six turnpikes built between 1801 and 1816, two running between Flushing and Brooklyn through Newtown and two separately linking Jamaica and Brooklyn, improved access to urban markets. Between 1800 and 1830 the population rose from 5791 to 7806. The opening of the Erie Canal in 1825 had a dramatic impact on Queens, as farmers shifted from grain to truck gardens supplying the growing city with fruits, vegetables, and flowers. During the 1830s the population grew by 5153.

The greatest agent for change in the nineteenth century was the Long Island Rail Road (LIRR), which began running between Brooklyn and Jamaica in 1836. By the 1860s there were three rival railroads: the Long Island, the Flushing and North Side, and the South Side (both became part of the LIRR in 1889). The railroads not only served the agricultural sector, but also opened up the county to suburban development. In 1839 Astoria became the first village to be incorporated in Queens since the seventeenth century. Ravenswood began as a fashionable suburb along the East River in 1848 and became the first iteration of the "gold coast," which eventually expanded to the east along the northern shore of Long Island through Flushing, Malba, Bayside, and Douglaston and into Nassau County. After the state passed the Rural Cemeteries Act in 1847, banning burials in Manhattan for sanitary reasons, cemeteries were opened in Newtown, including Cavalry (1848) and Lutheran (1852). In the early years cemeteries served as popular picnic sites. Manufacturers scattered widely, building factories in Whitestone, Woodhaven, and College Point.

By the 1850s residential development extended into new sections. Speculators bought up farms between 1852 and 1854 for resale as village lots in Hunters Point, Maspeth, Winfield, and West Flushing (Corona) along the proposed route of the Flushing Railroad. The railroad, financed by wealthy residents of Flushing, began running in 1854 to Hunters Point, and in the late nineteenth century Flushing became preeminent as a commuter suburb and genteel summer colony. Large numbers of Irish and German immigrants moved into Queens about this time. Those displaced by the potato famine in Ireland in the late 1840s settled mostly in Astoria but also in Jamaica and Flushing. Many Germans moved to Queens from Brooklyn, settling along Metropolitan and Myrtle avenues. Middle Village, which had been English in the 1840s, became almost entirely German by 1860.

2. From Mid-century to Consolidation

Industrialists discovered Queens in the 1850s, accelerating the growth of western Queens. Conrad Poppenhusen moved his hard rubber factory from Williamsburg to College Point in 1854 and became a benefactor of the community, even paying the salaries of his workers serving in the Civil War. His 1868 Poppenhusen Institute is a designated landmark. From 1865 to 1898 western Queens grew much faster than the eastern sections. Distilleries, varnish factories, chemical works, and oil refineries opened in Long Island City along Newtown Creek and the East River, facilitated by the relocation of the LIRR terminus from Brooklyn to Hunters Point in 1861. Lalance and Grosjean opened its tinware factory in Woodhaven in 1863; William Steinway moved his piano factory from Manhattan to Astoria in 1871. Sohmer Piano opened along the East River in 1886. Breweries were established in Ridgewood near the Brooklyn line. By 1920 Queens ranked 15th in the nation in industrial output, and though declining, industry persisted into the early twenty-first century in Long Island City, College Point, and Maspeth.

Transformation of the rural landscape into suburban communities accelerated in the second half of the nineteenth century. In fact, suburbanization characterized the development of Queens until the late twentieth century. The first houses in Glendale went up in 1868–69, and Queens Village developed in 1871. Richmond Hill, the first planned suburb in Queens, was begun in 1869 by Albon Platt Man; it was later home to Jacob Riis. Some large farms in Bayside were converted into building lots in 1872, and South Flushing between the old village and what is now Kissena Park was subdivided in the following year. New, privately owned excursion parks catered to working-class German families, and on weekends thousands of visitors went to College Point and Ridgewood, both heavily German, to enjoy the waterfront, the picnic groves, the dance pavilions, and the beer. After the Brooklyn City Railroad built its car barns just across the line in Ridgewood in 1881, that area grew into a prosperous working-class, primarily

German community, and the opening of the Myrtle Avenue elevated railroad in 1888 spurred further growth. Development of Ozone Park (named for the breezes off Jamaica Bay) began in 1882, Morris Park in 1884, and, along the Long Island Rail Road, Hollis in 1885. From 45,468 in 1870, the population nearly doubled to 87,050 in 1890.

By 1890 Queens was a mix of suburban wood-frame homes, noxious industrial facilities along Newtown Creek and other areas, and farms. A handful of Chinese-run vegetable farms in Astoria grew bitter melon, bottle squash, bok choy, and other produce for homes and restaurants in Chinatown in Manhattan. Large greenhouses in Flushing and Bayside provided cut flowers to wholesalers in the city. Floral Park, in far-eastern Queens, supplied tulips and carnations from vast fields to hotels and restaurants in Manhattan. In 1886 William Steinway and brewer George Ehret built Bowery Bay Beach (now the site of La Guardia Airport); renamed North Beach in 1891, it featured picnic grounds, swimming, dance halls, and amusement rides. It closed during Prohibition. The Rockaways also became a leisure destination. The first hotel opened in 1833, and railroad service began in 1869. The area featured large summer cottages in Far Rockaway and Arverne, and smaller bungalow communites and tent colonies, as well as amusement areas, by 1900.

In the 1894 nonbinding referendum on consolidation, Queens voted to join the proposed Greater New York, with Jamaica, Newtown, and Long Island City voting in favor, while Flushing and other parts of eastern Queens were opposed. On 1 January 1898 the municipal borough of Queens was created, consisting of Long Island City, Newtown, Flushing, and Jamaica. In addition, the Rockaway Peninsula, part of the town of Hempstead, was also included to give the new city total control over Jamaica Bay. Consolidation created the untenable condition that part of Queens County was in the city, while the towns of Hempstead, North Hempstead, and Oyster Bay were in Queens County but not in the city, so on 1 January 1899 they formed Nassau County.

3. The Twentieth Century and After

In the first three decades of the twentieth century Queens grew by 750 percent, from 152,999 in 1900 to 1,079,129 in 1930, with nearly half a million arriving during the 1920s. New transportation systems stimulated this growth. The Pennsylvania Railroad bought the Long Island Rail Road in 1900, electrified its route through Queens (1905–8), and opened tunnels under the East River in 1910 to the new Pennsylvania Station, bringing most of Queens within commuting distance of Manhattan. This precipitated the decline of Hunters Point, where passengers had transferred from the LIRR to ferries. The opening of the Williamsburg Bridge in 1903 made possible new elevated lines along Liberty Avenue to Richmond Hill (1915), to Metropolitan Avenue in Middle Village (1915), and along Jamaica Avenue to Jamaica (1918), as well as direct trolley service into Manhattan. The Queensboro (originally Blackwell's Island) Bridge opened in 1909 and had a dramatic impact on the borough, increasing land values and facilitating a building boom along the routes of the new dual subway lines to Astoria (1917) and Corona (1917, extended to Flushing in 1928). In the first decade after consolidation the Topographical Bureau laid out the borough's street network in 1908, including Queens Boulevard, and a new street- and house-numbering system unique to the borough was imposed (the first number in the hyphenated address refers to the cross street).

In addition to the thousands of one- and two-family brick and wood-frame houses (such as those built by the Real Good Construction Company in Rego Park), many distinctive model-housing communities, variations of the garden-apartment idea, were built in the first half of the twentieth century. The Russell Sage Corporation began building Forest Hills Gardens in 1912; the Queensboro Corporation built the first garden apartments in Jackson Heights in 1914; the City Housing Corporation built Sunnyside Gardens between 1924 and 1928 (home to Lewis Mumford); and the Metropolitan Life Insurance Company erected model tenements in Sunnyside, Woodside, and Astoria in the early 1920s. The G. X. Mathews Company built block after block of three-story model tenements, all in distinctive yellow and orange Kreischer brick, across western Queens from Ridgewood to Astoria. After the war the New York Life Insurance Company built Fresh Meadows, a complex housing 14,000 much praised by Lewis Mumford (1947). Parkway Village was built for employees of the United Nations (1946); and Glen Oaks, garden apartments with garages, quickly filled with returning veterans (1946).

As thousands of immigrant families moved from Manhattan and Brooklyn, new ethnic neighborhoods grew in Queens. Italians settled in Astoria and Corona, Germans in Astoria, College Point, Ridgewood, and Middle Village, and Irish in Woodside and Sunnyside. The borough's varied and picturesque settings attracted at least 20 film companies, making Queens the national center of the silent-film industry. This continued until World War II, as many Broadway stars shot films during the day before appearing onstage at night.

The Great Depression stopped virtually all private-sector construction in Queens, but few places benefited more from President Roosevelt's New Deal. An extraordinary collection of public works was built between 1933 and 1941. The Triborough Bridge, begun by the city in 1929, was completed with funding from Washington in 1936; the Grand Central Parkway opened the same year from the bridge to Kew Gardens. The Cross Island, Interborough, Whitestone, and Belt parkways were built, as were the Bronx-Whitestone, Cross Bay, and Marine Park bridges and the Queens Midtown Tunnel. Other projects included La Guardia Airport, the Independent Subway System (IND) Queens Boulevard Line, Boulevard Gardens apartments in Woodside and the Queensbridge and South Jamaica housing projects, Astoria Pool, and the 1939 World's Fair in Flushing Meadow.

The borough experienced a second growth spurt after World War II, facilitated by the transportation infrastructure built during the New Deal. Most of the remaining farms and many private golf courses succumbed to development. The Klein farm in Fresh Meadows, the borough's last working private farm, was sold in 2002 (in 2008 the Queens County Farm Museum in Floral Park occupied a site that has been under cultivation since 1697, the oldest continuously farmed site in the state). Much of the new housing consisted of large apartments, particularly along the subway lines. In those neighborhoods the suburban scale was compromised or lost entirely. Public housing projects were erected in Astoria, Woodside, Flushing, and especially the Rockaways. Transportation infrastructure built after the war included the Throgs Neck Bridge, the Long Island, Van Wyck, and Clearview expressways, and Idlewild Airport (1948), renamed John F. Kennedy Airport in 1963. Postwar growth culminated in the World's Fair of 1964–65 in Flushing Meadow Park (renamed Flushing Meadows–Corona Park in 1967), but already the city was beginning a period of slower growth and declining economic vitality that hit a low point with the fiscal crisis of 1975. The borough lost nearly 100,000 residents in the 1970s, the only time the population fell. That was also when Archie Bunker came to personify blue-collar Queens in the popular television show *All in the Family*.

Following the Immigration and Nationality Act of 1965, many immigrants settled in Queens, especially Asians and Latin Americans, making it the most diverse place in the nation. The population rebounded by a modest 60,273 during the 1980s, and by an impressive 277,781 in the 1990s. In 1980 about 56 percent of the foreign-born residents of Queens had arrived in the preceding 15 years. By 2000 almost half the borough's inhabitants were foreign born, up from about 36 percent in 1990, the most in the city. Less than half the population was white, and African Americans accounted for 20 percent, while Hispanics accounted for 25 percent. By the 2010 census, the Asian population is projected to surpass the number of African Americans. Chinese and Koreans, and immigrants from South and Southeast Asia, transformed Flushing, Jackson Heights, Elmhurst, and Corona, but with upward mobility many families moved into the suburban neighborhoods of eastern Queens. Jews from the former Soviet Union moved into Forest Hills and Rego Park. Astoria, which grew a sizable Greek population in mid-century, began attracting Muslim immigrants, while Guyanese moved into Richmond Hill, South Ozone Park, and Jamaica. Some schools enrolled a student body speaking over 30 different languages. Jamaica and the communities of southeast Queens, including Cambria Heights, Springfield Gardens, Laurelton, St. Albans, and Hollis, remained the core of black residence. Recent immigrants from the West Indies, primarily Jamaica and Haiti, also moved to those neighborhoods, which were home to many prominent African American jazz musicians and entertainers, including Lena Horne, Ella Fitzgerald, and Count Basie. Louis Armstrong lived in Corona, and his home is now a museum.

Queens has long had a reputation for a tainted political system. In the early 1900s three successive borough presidents had legal problems: Joseph Cassidy went to Sing Sing for corruption, Joseph Bermel resigned and fled to Europe, and Lawrence Gresser was removed by the governor. For much of the twentieth century Queens regularly elected Republicans, but by 2000 the Democrats controlled almost every state, local, and national office. Under first Matthew Troy and then Donald Manes, the Queens Democratic organization was the second largest in the state in the 1970s and 1980s (Troy was convicted of corruption, and Manes committed suicide over the Parking Violations Bureau scandal). Mario Cuomo grew up in Jamaica and rose to prominence brokering a compromise between middle-class homeowners and advocates of low-income housing over new public housing projects in Forest Hills in the early 1970s; he served three terms as governor (1983–1994).

Queens has a long sporting tradition. The first recorded horse races in the colonies were staged on the Hempstead Plains in 1665, and by 1700 there was a course around Beaver Pond in Jamaica. New York State banned horseracing from 1802 to 1821, although "trials of speed" were permitted in Queens. At Union Course in Woodhaven in 1823 a crowd of 60,000 saw Eclipse, the champion New York horse, beat southern champion Sir Henry in three heats. The track saw many such match races, including the Fashion-Peytona contest in 1845. Aqueduct Racetrack opened in 1894 and Jamaica in 1903 (it closed in 1959 and Rochdale Village rose on the site); Belmont Park opened just across the line in Nassau in 1905. By 1930 there were 18 golf courses in Queens, all private but the 1901 Forest Park course, more than any other borough. Fresh Meadows Country Club hosted the PGA Tournament in 1930 and the U.S. Open in 1932, and Pomonok hosted the PGA in 1939 (both were sold for housing after the war). In 1925 Germans and Hungarians opened Metropolitan Oval in Maspeth, today the oldest soccer field in continuous use in the nation. Championship tennis was practically synonymous with the West Side Tennis Club in Forest Hills, which hosted the national championships from 1914 until 1977, when the U.S. Open moved to Flushing Meadows–Corona Park; Arthur Ashe Stadium opened there in 1997. During the 1930s many title fights were staged at Madison Square Garden Bowl on Northern Boulevard in Long Island City; other boxing venues included Sunnyside Garden and Ridgewood Grove. The New York Mets moved into Shea Stadium in 1964, and in 2009 moved into Citifield, built adjacent. Until the 1950s Queens also had many semi-pro teams, most notably the Bushwicks, who played baseball in Dexter Park in Woodhaven (site of the first night game in the city).

There are five institutions of higher education in Queens. St. John's University moved from Brooklyn to a new campus on the site of Hillcrest Golf Club in 1956, and there are four branches of the City University of New York: Queens College (1937), Queensborough Community College (1958), York College (1966), and La Guardia Community College (1971). The Queens Borough Public Library (founded in 1896 as the Long Island City Public Library) has had the nation's highest circulation since the 1980s, while serving the most diverse population on the planet.

William Munsell, ed., *A History of Queens County, New York* (New York: W. W. Munsell, 1882); Vincent F. Seyfried, *Queens: A Pictorial History* (Norfolk, Va.: Donning, 1983); Jon A. Peterson, ed., and Vincent F. Seyfried, consultant, *A Research Guide to the History of the Borough of Queens, New York City* (New York: Department of History, Queens College, City University of New York, 1987); Vincent F. Seyfried and William Asadorian, *Old Queens, N.Y. in Early Photographs* (New York: Dover, 1991)

Jeffrey A. Kroessler, Jon A. Peterson, Vincent Seyfried

Queensboro Bridge. Steel, two-leveled bridge with two cantilevered lengths spanning the East River between 59th Street in Manhattan and Long Island City in Queens, by way of an intermediate link on Roosevelt Island. Completed in 1909, it was designed by Gustav Lindenthal and decorated with ornate ironwork and finials by the architect Henry Hornbostel. The bridge was the first

Queensboro Bridge, 2009

major span in New York City to depart from the suspension form and the third of eight bridges built across the East River. It measures, including approaches, 7450 feet (2272 meters) long and 135 feet (41.1 meters) tall. Often referred to as the 59th Street Bridge, it is a city landmark.

Rebecca Read Shanor

Queensborough Community College. Junior college of the City University of New York, opened in 1958 on the grounds of the Oakland Golf Course. Students attended classes at several locations nearby until a new campus of 34 acres (14 hectares) was completed in 1978 at 56th Avenue and Springfield Boulevard in Bayside. The college offers the only program in the state in laser and fiber optics and is highly regarded for its program for the homebound. In 2006 the college enrolled more than 12,000 students in one of its associate degree or certificate programs and about 10,000 students in its continuing education program.

Marc Ferris

Queensborough Hill. Neighborhood in north central Queens, lying within Flushing and bounded to the north by Booth Memorial Drive, to the east by Main Street, to the south by Mount Hebron Cemetery and Cedar Grove Cemetery, and to the west by College Point Boulevard. The land rises steeply from Flushing Creek to a height of 81 feet (25 meters) above sea level. In the nineteenth century the area was called Ireland Mill after a gristmill on the creek at what is now College Point Boulevard. Residential development began in the 1930s, but most of the homes and businesses were built in the 1940s and 1950s. The population in 2008 was about 15,400: 49 percent Asian, 33 percent white, and 14 percent Hispanic.

Vincent Seyfried

Queens Borough Public Library. See Queens Library.

Queens College. College of the City University of New York (CUNY). It began as a group of extension centers formed by Hunter College and City College in the 1920s and became autonomous in 1937, when it first occupied a campus off Kissena Boulevard in Flushing on grounds used initially as a school for juvenile delinquents. The college became part of CUNY in 1961. The original complex of cottages in the Spanish style was supplemented during the next half-century by a modern campus that in the early twenty-first century spanned 77 acres and included the Kupferberg Center for the Visual and Performing Arts, Townsend Harris High School (part of City College until 1942), and the CUNY School of Law. The college emphasizes the liberal arts and offers undergraduate and graduate degrees. Its 582 full-time faculty has included such distinguished figures as writer Michael Harrington (from 1972 until his death), geologist Barry Commoner, composer Thea Musgrave, and mathematician Dennis Sullivan. In 2008 the college enrolled 18,494 students, including 14,384 undergraduates and 4110 graduate students. Notable alumni include Jerry Seinfeld, Ray Romano, and Carole King.

Selma Berrol

Queens County Farm Museum. New York City's largest piece of continuously farmed land and the oldest such farm in the state, located at 73-50 Little Neck Parkway in Floral Park. The Adriance family, Dutch subsistence farmers, started the farm in 1697. John Bennum, Sr., bought it in 1808, farming for nearly 25 years before selling to Daniel Lent. Peter Cox bought the land in 1833 during a period of exponential agricultural growth in the United States and expanded the original Adriance farmhouse. His son, Henry, joined the Queens Agricultural Society and transformed the farm into a commercial operation, becoming the largest market crop producer in the county by 1879 and increasing the farm's worth almost four times before selling to Daniel Stattel in 1892. Stattel modernized the farm and further increased its value during the age of truck farming, sending his crops to market on wagons. Real estate investor Pauline Reisman bought the farm in 1926 and then quickly sold the land to the state for expansion of the Creedmoor Psychiatric Center. The hospital demolished all the buildings on the farm except the original farmhouse, building new facilities so that its psychiatric patients could help grow produce for the kitchens. Creedmoor moved in 1973; two years later the Colonial Farmhouse Restoration Society of Bellerose founded the Queens County Farm Museum. Seven acres (2.8 hectares) of the farm, including the farmhouse and outbuildings, won landmark designation in 1976, and the state transferred ownership to the Department of Parks and Recreation in 1981. In the early twenty-first century the 47-acre (19-hectare) farm was a historical and educational facility as well as a working farm: it produced fruits and vegetables and raised livestock and honeybees, working toward sustainable production and selling to city restaurants and markets.

See also Adriance Farmhouse.

Kate Lauber

Queens Library. The origins of the public library system in Queens date to the mid-nineteenth century. Three libraries joined to form the Long Island City Public Library, chartered in 1896. About the turn of the century four other libraries joined the system, now called the Queens Borough Library. Andrew Carnegie donated $240,000 in 1901 to build eight additional branches, and New York City was authorized to provide operating funds. The Flushing Library, organized in 1858, joined the system in 1902. In 1907 the enlarged system was incorporated under its present name. The library had administrative offices in Long Island City until 1908 when they were moved to Jamaica. The Central Library, built in 1966 at 89-11 Merrick Boulevard in Jamaica, acquired collections in art, music, history, language, literature, the social sciences, science, and technology. In 1978 the Queens Borough Public Library became the first automated library system in the city, and from 1986 into the 1990s it had the highest circulation of any municipal library in the United States (13.2 million items circulated in 1993). By 1994 it was also the fifth-largest public library system in the country, with 62 branches, about one million registered patrons, and a collection of nearly 9.5 million items. Its adult literacy program was the first to use computers and offer driver's education and classes for the deaf. Through its New Americans Project the library also offered cultural programs and classes in English for immigrants, who by the mid-1990s accounted

Bus to the Queens Borough Public Library, ca *1937*

for one-third of the population of the borough. The Chinese-language "Ni Hao" collections were available in 24 branches, the Spanish-language "Say Sí" collections in 16.

In addition to books the Central Library circulates films, videocassettes, compact discs, and magazines and has divisions for teenagers and children; in the Toddler Learning Center children aged one to three years can play with educational toys while their parents meet with child-care professionals. A special collection called the Long Island Division focuses on the history of the four counties of Long Island (Brooklyn, Queens, Nassau, and Suffolk) and contains photographs, slides, manuscripts, maps, postcards, reference books, newspapers, and genealogies. The Langston Hughes Community Library and Cultural Center houses the Black Heritage Reference Collection. The library mails books to the homebound and maintains Kurzweil readers, which convert printed text into synthesized speech, and telecommunications devices for the deaf. In 1993 an online public access catalogue was introduced at the Central Library, providing access to databases, listings of library programs, community information, and library catalogues worldwide. Each branch has Quick Cat, a CD-ROM catalogue that provides access to all catalogued materials in the collections of the Central Library and the branches; online databases may be used free of charge. In 2008 14 million people visited the library, and the system was still number one in the nation for circulation, with more than 21 million loans as of 2007.

How Far That Little Candle . . . : The Queens Borough Public Library: Fifty-Five Years, 1896–1951 (New York: Queens Borough Public Library, 1951)

GraceAnne A. DeCandido

Queens–Midtown Tunnel. Double tunnel under the East River between 36th Street in Manhattan and Long Island City in Queens. Designed by Ole Singstad and opened to traffic in 1940, it is the third of four tunnels built to provide access to Manhattan for motor vehicles. The tunnel has a length of 6300 feet (1921 meters); ventilation towers with large, computer-controlled fans at either end of the tunnel provide a complete change of air every minute and a half. Advanced construction techniques made it possible for the Queens–Midtown Tunnel to be completed in four years. The first renovations for the tunnel began in 1998 by the Metropolitan Transit Authority; the approximately $132 million project, which included strengthening the ceiling, improving lighting, and upgrading fire protection, was completed in 2004. The tunnel is closed for one night each spring before the circus opens at Madison Square Garden to allow for the Ringling Brothers and Barnum & Bailey Circus Animal Walk.

Rebecca Read Shanor

Queens Museum of Art. Center for the visual arts in Flushing Meadows–Corona Park. Dedicated in 1972, it occupies the New York City Building constructed for the World's Fair of 1939–40. Best known for its extraordinary panorama of New York City, the largest three-dimensional model of an urban area in the United States, the museum offers a wide array of exhibitions, from classical sculpture to the avant-garde. It also maintains a permanent collection, operates an extensive school-tour and workshop program, and offers gallery talks, performances, and films. In 1994 it underwent major renovations, and in 2010 another renovation project that would double its space was under way.

Kenneth T. Jackson

Queens Village. Neighborhood in east central Queens, bounded to the north by Union Turnpike, to the east by the Cross Island Parkway, to the south by Murdock Avenue, and to the west by Francis Lewis Boulevard. The area was known during colonial times as the Little Plains because it marked the western edge of the treeless plain that extended to Wantagh. Thomas Brush opened a wheelwright and blacksmith shop in 1824 and later built a tavern, a country store, and a shed for curing tobacco. These enterprises became the center of a hamlet on Springfield Boulevard that came to be called Brushville. In April 1854 residents voted to change the name to Queens; Callister's Wagon Works opened in the same year. Extensive development began in 1870 when Scott R. Sherwood subdivided a parcel south of the tracks of the Long Island Rail Road into 700 building lots, and Colonel Alfred Wood persuaded the railroad to build a station. A map of 1873 shows 50 houses; the population increased from 675 in 1891 to 900 in 1898. Growth accelerated after the construction of Interstate Park, a venue for pigeon- and trapshooting (1900) and the opening of Belmont Park (1905). Many streets and houses were added during the 1920s. To obviate confusion with the name of the county, the Long Island Rail Road added "village" to the name of its local station, a change that was soon made to the name of the neighborhood as well. After World War II African Americans from Hollis and St. Albans moved in, along with Latin Americans. In the 1980s many new immigrants settled in Queens Village, especially from Guyana, Haiti, India, and Jamaica, and to a lesser extent the Philippines and Colombia. The population in 2005 was 57,000, about 44 percent African American. Queens Village remained suburban and residential into the twenty-first century.

Vincent Seyfried

Queens West. A redevelopment project along the Queens side of the East River in Hunters Point, authorized by the state legislature in 1984. The site occupies 74 acres (30 hectares), including more than 1 mile (1.6 kilometers) of shoreline between 47th Road and 54th Avenue. The proposal called for apartment towers of as much as 42 stories, as well as a four-block hotel and office complex intended to house agencies of the United Nations in New York City. Ground was not broken until September 1994, and then only for a sliver of park two blocks from the river. In 1997 the 42-story City Lights residential tower opened (Cesar Pelli and Associates, architects), and in 1998 the two-and-a-half-acre Gantry Park was completed, featuring two Long Island Rail Road gantries on the river. The 32-story Avalon Riverview opened in 2002. The site of the Pepsi-Cola bottling plant was slated for additional housing; the plant's large neon sign, a designated landmark, was moved to an adjacent location. Queens West was to have been the site of the Olympic Village had the city bid successfully for the 2012 games.

Kenneth T. Jackson

Queens Zoo. Small zoo formerly known as Flushing Meadows Zoo. Opened in 1968 on the grounds of the 1964 World's Fair, the zoo was built by Robert Moses's Triborough Bridge and Tunnel Authority and by the Metropolitan Transit Authority after Moses resigned. The zoo, which had free admission, collected American animals and had no cages. The aviary was housed in the former Winston Churchill Pavilion, a geodesic dome designed by Buckminster Fuller for the World's Fair, although it was closed for many years: the lack of any boundary between visitors and birds proved problematic. Several years after its opening, the $3.5 million zoo was still a little-known facility at 111th Street and 52nd Avenue. In 1975 several animal-rights groups advocated for closing the zoo, along with the Prospect Park and Central Park zoos, and moving the animals to the Bronx; in the late 1970s the city began negotiations with the Wildlife Conservation Society to take over management of the zoo. After an extensive $16-million renovation, it reopened in June 1992. Otis, a coyote caught in Central Park in 1999, is a resident of the zoo, which continues to focus on North and South American species, including the endangered spectacled bear of the Andes. About 250 animals and 40 different species lived at the zoo in the early twenty-first century.

Kate Lauber

Quill, Michael J(oseph) (*b* Ireland, 18 Sept 1905; *d* New York City, 28 Jan 1966). Labor leader. As a young man he fought in the Irish Republican Army before moving in 1926 to New York City, where he worked in the subway system. He helped to form the Transport Workers Union (TWU) in 1934 and the next year was elected its president. He won a seat on the City Council as a candidate of the

American Labor Party in 1937. Defeated in 1939, he was returned to office in 1943, remaining until 1949. He worked closely with the Communist Party, an influential force in the TWU, until renouncing it in 1948. As a vice president of the Congress of Industrial Organizations and the head of its council in the city, he was a leading labor spokesman and liaison between unions and city government during the 1950s. Quill's ties to communists, outspoken Irish nationalism, strong support for civil rights and other liberal causes, and repeated threats to call subway strikes made him a controversial figure throughout his career. Sharp-tongued and humorous, he was constantly an object of attention from the press and appeared often on radio and television. He died shortly after leading a 12-day strike of bus and subway workers during which he was imprisoned for contempt of court.

Joshua B. Freeman, *In Transit: The Transport Workers Union in New York City, 1933–1966* (Philadelphia: Temple University Press, 2001)

Joshua B. Freeman

Quinn, Anthony (Rudolph Oaxaca) (*b* Chihuahua, Mexico, 21 April 1915; *d* Boston, 3 June 2001). Actor. He made his debut on Broadway in 1947. Although best known for his work in films like *Lawrence of Arabia* (1962) and *The Guns of Navarone* (1961), he appeared in Broadway and touring productions of several plays, including Tennessee Williams's *A Streetcar Named Desire* (1961) and *Zorba* (1983–84). He maintained his principal residence in New York City into the 1990s.

Quinn, Christine (*b* Glen Cove, N.Y., 25 July 1966). Speaker of the City Council. In 1999 she ran for City Council in the third district and in 2007 became City Council speaker. A Democrat, she was the first openly gay woman on the City Council.

Jessica Montesano

Quinn, John (*b* Tiffin, Ohio, 24 April 1870; *d* New York City, 28 July 1924). Lawyer and art collector. He became a legal adviser to such clients as Thomas Fortune Ryan and was a strong advocate of the Alien Property Act (October 1917), the constitutionality of which he successfully defended in April 1920. He amassed the largest private collection of modern art and literature of his day. A patron of John Butler Yeats, Gwen John, James Joyce, Joseph Conrad, and Ezra Pound, he was also the contact in New York City for Irish artists and politicians. He incorporated the Association of American Painters and Sculptors, of which he was made an honorary member; in 1912 he arranged for the rental of the 69th Regiment Armory for its important 1913 exhibition of modern art known as the Armory Show. In addition to lending 77 items from his collection to the show, he made the largest purchase from it by a private collector. The library in his apartment at 58 Central Park West contained 18,000 items, including the complete manuscript of Joyce's *Ulysses,* a work that he defended (and lost) against obscenity charges in 1921.

B. L. Reid, *The Man from New York: John Quinn and His Friends* (New York: Oxford University Press, 1968)

Marion R. Casey

Quintero, José Benjamin (*b* Panama City, Panama, 15 Oct 1924; *d* New York City, 26 Feb 1999). Director and pioneer of Off-Broadway theater. He came to the United States to study medicine at the University of Southern California before becoming involved in the theater. He was instrumental in the rebirth of Off-Broadway theater as a viable alternative to large Broadway productions and was a founding member of the original Circle in the Square Theatre in Greenwich Village. His work helped to establish Off-Broadway theaters as venues worthy of critical and audience attention. Quintero revived interest in Eugene O'Neill and became known as the premier director of the playwright's work, staging *The Iceman Cometh* (1956), which launched the career of Jason Robards, Jr.; the Broadway debut of *Long Day's Journey into Night* (1956), in which Robards starred alongside Fredric March; *Moon for the Misbegotten* (1973); and a 1988 revival of *Long Day's Journey into Night* that included actress Colleen Dewhurst. He also directed Tennessee Williams's works, including *Summer and Smoke* in 1952 (a production that brought actress Geraldine Page to stardom) and *The Seven Descents of Myrtle* in 1968. Quintero struggled with bouts of depression and alcoholism throughout his life, and his larynx was removed in 1987 because of throat cancer. He continued to direct plays, however, with the use of a mechanical voice box until his death. The Jose Quintero Theatre at 534 West 42nd Street is named after him.

Patrick Barrett

Quintero, Luisa (*b* Toa Baja, Puerto Rico, 1903; *d* New York City, August 1987). Journalist. She began her career in New York City in 1928 writing and editing for the Spanish-language newspaper *La Prensa.* During her early years in the city, Quintero wrote or edited for other publications, including the United Nations Spanish Bulletin, and was a founder of the Puerto Rican Day Parade. She was best known for "Marginalia," the daily column she wrote for *El Diario–La Prensa* on religion, culture, education, history, current events, and politics.

Virginia Sánchez Korrol

R

Rabbinical Seminary of America. Orthodox rabbinical college opened in 1933 at 135 South Ninth Street in Williamsburg in Brooklyn and moved in 1955 to larger quarters at 92-15 69th Avenue in Forest Hills, Queens. It is alternately known as Yeshivas Chofetz Chaim. It has three elementary schools and three high schools in Queens and Brooklyn, as well as eight other schools across the United States and Canada, synagogue centers in California, Arizona, Texas, and Buffalo, and an extension program in Jerusalem. In New York City the seminary also administers Congregation Chofetz Chaim, a Hatzolah volunteer ambulance unit, and Yeshiva Rabenu Yisroel Meir Hakohen, which trains Orthodox rabbis.

Marc Ferris

Rabi, I(sidor) I(saac) (*b* Rymanów [now in Poland], 29 July 1898; *d* New York City, 11 Jan 1988). Physicist and Nobel laureate. As an infant he moved to the United States with his family. After graduating from Cornell University he earned his doctorate in 1927 at Columbia University where he established the physics research center and taught for 60 years. In 1944 he won the Nobel Prize in physics for devising a method of measuring magnetic properties of atoms, molecules, and nuclei. A consultant to the federal government, he was influential in building Brookhaven National Laboratory and advocated controlling atomic energy. Rabi wrote an autobiography, *My Life and Times as a Physicist* (1960).

John S. Rigden, *Rabi, Scientist and Citizen* (New York: Basic Books, 1987)

James E. Mooney

radio. The technological forerunner of radio was wireless telegraphy, introduced in the United States by its inventor Guglielmo Marconi in October 1899. With the sponsorship of James Gordon Bennett, Jr., owner of the *New York Herald,* he broadcast from New York Harbor coverage of the immensely popular race for the America's Cup by following its progress from a steamship and sending frequent reports to a station at 34th Street; these were posted at the Herald Building, where crowds blocked traffic, and at bulletin boards throughout the city. The telegraph was used into the 1920s by a growing number of amateur operators ("hams") to send messages across the metropolitan area. Lee De Forest invented the audion vacuum tube in 1906 and demonstrated it in the city; in 1910 he broadcast a performance by Enrico Caruso from the Metropolitan Opera and by 1916 made regular broadcasts of music and news, including election results. Operators in the city reported on the sinking of the *Titanic,* for which the wireless was the primary source of information. The invention of the regenerative circuit in 1913 by Edwin H. Armstrong, a student at Columbia University, made earphones unnecessary for reception. By the early 1920s a growing audience in the city appreciated the potential of the telegraph. Armstrong invented frequency modulation (FM) between 1925 and 1933.

After the first radio station sponsored by a corporation began broadcasting as KDKA in Pittsburgh, the Radio Corporation of America (RCA), American Telephone and Telegraph (AT&T), and other firms established stations in New York City and the surrounding region: WJZ (1921), WEAF (1922), and WJY (1923). From late 1921 performances by Vincent Lopez and his orchestra were broadcast from the Hotel Pennsylvania, and WHN gave early exposure to such jazz musicians as Fletcher Henderson with its broadcasts from the Club Alabam on West 43rd Street. Some stations in the metropolitan area were operated by colleges, newspapers, churches, hotels, and other enterprises: WOR by Bamberger's department stores, WEVD by the Socialist Party, and WNYC by the city. In 1922 AT&T proposed a "phone booth of the air" for the city: anyone could address the public for 10 minutes in the afternoon for $50 or in the evening for $100, and eventually there would be a chain of stations. The first station to be licensed under the plan was WEAF (based during its first year on lower Broadway and then at 711 Fifth Avenue), which on 28 August 1922 broadcast the first paid advertisement (sold for $50), for a cooperative housing complex in Jackson Heights, and which aggressively exploited the commercial potential of radio. Marion Davies gave a talk called "How I Make Up for the Movies" for the beauty product Mineralava and offered autographed pictures that drew hundreds of requests, and Will Rogers was reportedly paid $1000 to speak during the *Eveready Hour.*

Initially advertising over the radio was controversial, but by the late 1920s it was the primary financial support for broadcasting. The city became the center of commercial radio after the first networks were formed there: the National Broadcasting Company (NBC; November 1926), led by David Sarnoff and comprising WEAF as its "flagship" and 25 affiliates nationwide, and the Columbia Broadcasting System (CBS; 1927), which had WOR as its flagship. In 1927 NBC was divided into the Red Network (with 19 affiliates) and the Blue Network (which offered cultural and public service programs; it was sold by NBC in 1942 and later evolved into the American Broadcasting Company). From 1927 CBS and then NBC broadcast performances at the Cotton Club by Duke Ellington and later Cab Calloway. As governor of New York in the 1920s, Franklin D. Roosevelt made broadcasting an important force in politics by discussing his decisions over the radio.

Programming for radio was influenced by cultural activities in the city. After 1929 many unemployed performers and musicians were engaged for radio programs. A brand of urban, ethnic humor made popular on the vaudeville stage in New York City by Al Jolson, George Burns and Gracie Allen, Ed Wynn, Jack Benny, Fred Allen, and Jack Pearl (as Baron Munchausen) was introduced on the radio to a national audience. Music programs were a staple for most stations: the performances of Bing Crosby, Rudy Vallee, and Arturo

Broadcast of the "March of Time" over the Columbia Broadcasting System, ca *1937*

FOURTH SECTION. **THE NEW YORK HERALD.** PAGES 1 TO 14.

NEW YORK, SUNDAY, OCTOBER 1, 1899.—[COPYRIGHT, 1899, BY JAMES GORDON BENNETT.] PRICE FIVE CENTS.

THE PONCE FROM WHICH DESPATCHES WILL BE SENT

MARCONI WILL REPORT THE YACHT RACES FOR THE HERALD BY HIS WIRELESS SYSTEM.

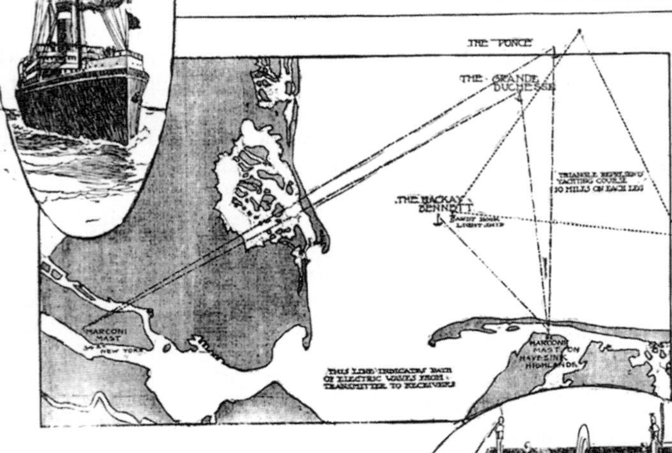

THE TRANSMITTER

THE GRANDE DUCHESSE

COMPLETE DETAILS OF THE MARVELLOUS INVENTION BY WHICH NEWS IS REPORTED FORTY MILES AWAY WITHOUT THE USE OF WIRES.

Absolute demonstration of the value of the Marconi system of wireless telegraphy will be furnished the Western world for the first time during the yacht races this week by Signor Marconi and a corps of assistants, who will report every movement of the contending yachts to the HERALD.

This will be a feat unparalleled in the history of journalism. During the last international contest for the America's Cup the cable laying steamer Mackay-Bennett flashed the news by submarine cable to the HERALD, and thence to an eagerly awaiting world. This year there will be no cable, no wires—only the thin air and the Marconi instruments to flash the news instantaneously from the decks of the steamers Ponce and Grande Duchesse, which will follow the yachts, direct to New York.

Elaborate preparations have been made to make the service instantaneous, accurate, complete. In the following article the principle and workings of the Marconi system are described. Sufficeth it here to say that wireless telegraphy is exactly what the term implies. From a mast by means of a transmitter waves are sent to other masts, where receivers collect the waves and reduce them to the ordinary Morse alphabet, so well known to telegraphers. That is all. Electric waves pass from transmitter through the air to receiver without a wire to guide them. And this is not so remarkable when one considers that the earth is a return wire for every ordinary telegraph current. Originally Professor Morse had two wires on every line to complete the electrical circuit. It was soon found that the earth would do half the work. Every telegraph wire in the world depends on the earth to complete the electric circuit. Marconi simply dispensed with the other wire, and the air takes the place of the remaining wire, which had endured for fifty years.

This sounds complex, incomprehensible, impossible. Really it is simple. From the masts of the Ponce and Grande Duchesse waves corresponding in duration to the currents of an ordinary battery will be by a Marconi transmitter sent forth in the air. They will be received by properly adjusted receivers, connected with wires for the purpose, on the Mackay-Bennett, anchored near the Sandy Hook Lightship, where the races begin; a mast specially erected on the Navesink Highlands and a mast on top of a high building in Thirty-fourth street. From each of these three stations every movement of the Columbia and the Shamrock will be sent all over the world.

The HERALD will thus prove a boon not only to science, but to millions of persons who await with eagerness the result of a contest that has excited more interest than any in the history of the America's Cup.

That Marconi and his instruments will do all that is expected from them seems certain. During the recent British naval manoeuvres this system of wireless telegraphy was thoroughly tested, and was found to yield excellent results. Messages were received and transmitted on this occasion over a distance of more than forty miles. This in its way was even a more remarkable success than the transmission of messages between Newhaven and Dieppe, for the reason that during the manoeuvres both the receiver and the transmitter were on swift moving ships during the time that the messages were being sent.

Scientists everywhere have watched Signor Marconi's successive experiments with deep attention, and it is needless to say that they will be much interested in those which will take place during the yacht races. To the unscientific reader the term experiment may appear to be erroneous in this connection, for it may be claimed, and with much justice, that this work is no longer experimental, but as accurate and sure as any work of the kind can be. That the truth of this claim will be further manifested when the story of the yacht race is flashed from the water into the HERALD office is the firm belief of all those who know what Marconi has done hitherto.

By W. B. Bradfield.

Assistant to Signor Marconi.

FEW words about the apparatus used and the actual working of a wireless telegraph station may not prove altogether uninteresting, and in view of the many erroneous descriptions that have already been published are perhaps necessary.

As is, of course, well known, the Marconi system is worked by means of Hertzian waves, so called after the late eminent German professor, Heinrich Hertz, who first experimentally proved their existence thirty years or so after Clerk Maxwell had mathematically predicted them.

At his New Jersey station Mr. Marconi employs the following apparatus to generate and collect these waves:—The first thing that is apparent to the observer is a tall mast, 150 feet high, from the top of which is suspended a wire—it is actually an ordinary insulated copper wire, such as is used for electric lighting purposes—which passes through a window of the operating room and is joined up inside with the apparatus. There is nothing strange in the appearance of the mast itself, and no effort is made to clothe this part of the apparatus with mystery. With regard to apparatus within the room, simplicity is the most amazing part of it. The whole apparatus is fixed on a small table about four feet long and two feet wide, and the battery for supplying the power is packed underneath it.

This battery consists of ninety-eight dry cells, which are connected up fourteen in series and seven in derivation, and is joined up in parallel with eight accumulator cells to give a steady current of six amperes. The actual generator of the waves is an ordinary inductor or Ruhmkorff coil, such as is used for the production of X rays, and is capable of giving a ten inch spark. Each end of the secondary winding of this coil is fitted with a sparking rod, to which is attached a brass ball one and a half inches in diameter.

To one of these balls is connected the vertical wire; the other is joined to earth. With the single addition of a Morse key in the primary circuit the transmitting apparatus is complete.

What Happens.

Consider for a moment what happens when this key is depressed. The immediate and apparent result is a loud, crackling spark discharge between the two brass balls, which are adjusted to be about two centimetres apart. The more important result is that the vertical wire at the moment the spark passes emits waves which go out into space in all directions, and continue to do so as long as the key is depressed. It is quite easy to understand, therefore, that by depressing the key for a short or a long period short and long series of waves or oscillations are emitted, and the Morse alphabet, which is used in ordinary telegraphy, may be employed.

The only thing that remains is to get something that will pick up and indicate the presence of these oscillations.

The apparatus which Marconi employs to do this is what is commonly known as a "coherer," a name which is due to Professor Oliver Lodge, of Liverpool. An Italian named Calzecchi was the first to discover the sensibility of coherers and filings tubes to Hertz waves. He found that metallic filings in a loose state of contact offered an appreciable resistance to the passage of a current. He found also, however, that on exposing these filings to the action of Hertzian waves the resistance fell enormously, but that on shaking them up the resistance was increased again to its original value. Marconi's coherer works on the same principle, but is vastly more sensitive and reliable than those used by Calzecchi, Branly and others.

It consists of a small glass tube about two inches long, in which two small silver plugs a quarter of an inch long are tightly fitted and separated from each other by about one-thirtieth of an inch, the gap between them being partially filled with a mixture of nickel and silver filings, these metals having been found to be the most sensitive and reliable after a long series of experiments. The coherer exhausted to a vacuum of four millimètres.

So much for the coherer. The rest of the receiving apparatus is perfectly easy to understand. In circuit with the coherer is a single dry cell and a telegraphic relay of the ordinary type. This relay is used to close the circuit of a local battery, which works a Morse writing instrument and also an electric bell hammer, which strikes the coherer a smart tap to restore it to its normal high resistance after it has received an impulse from the distant transmitter.

To protect the coherer from the too powerful effects of the local transmitter the whole receiver is enclosed in a metallic box.

Receiving a Message.

To receive a message all that is now necessary is to connect the vertical line either directly or through a small induction coil to one end of the coherer, the other end of it being connected to earth.

Such is the Marconi apparatus in use at the HERALD's New Jersey land station, and it is in exact duplicate aboard the steamer Ponce, which is to report the progress of the yacht racing this week. She has been specially rigged with a new topmast to give the same height of wire as that at the land station, and the instruments are installed in the chart house.

The distance that will have to be bridged will probably not exceed thirty-five miles; the apparatus employed would, however, be capable of sending and receiving messages at a distance of nearly eighty miles.

The chief factor in determining the distance possible is the height of the vertical wire. Mr. Marconi finds that by doubling the height the distance becomes quadrupled. That is, assuming twenty feet will give one mile, forty feet will give four miles, eighty feet sixteen miles, and so on. There are, of course, other factors, such as the sensitiveness of the coherer and the adjustment of the apparatus generally, but apparently they are not so marked in their effects.

Why this vertical wire is necessary for long distances is not very certain. It has been suggested that the earth's curvature may have something to do with it. Compare this, however, with Mr. Marconi's results in the English naval manoeuvres this summer, when with one hundred and fifty feet of wire at each end he succeeded in telegraphing seventy-five miles. To do this the waves must have passed through a "hill" of water thirty-five miles long and seven hundred feet high. More probably the vertical wire is necessary because its use lengthens the waves and propagates them in a plane vertical to the surface of the earth, and they are, therefore, less likely to be absorbed by it. The fact that the waves are lengthened of course causes them to be more penetrative and capable of affecting a receiver at a greater distance.

Of the working of a wireless telegraph station there is not much to say, as it is essentially the same as that of any other telegraph office. At present the speed of transmission is rather less; it does not ordinarily exceed about fifteen words a minute, but this will of course increase with time. A call is indicated by a bell which is switched off during the reception of a message. As before stated, the telegrams are printed in dots and dashes on an ordinary Morse inker, the operator having merely to read them from the tape.

The key used is of a slightly different form from the usual Morse key, the back contact being used to connect the vertical wire to the receiver, so that no changing over from the transmitter to the receiver is necessary after sending a message.

POPULAR EXPLANATION OF MARCONI'S METHOD

From Pearson's Magazine for July.

[Copyright, 1899, by Pearson Publishing Co.]

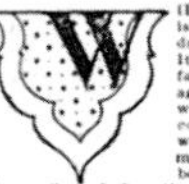

IRELESS telegraphy is now no longer the dream of the scientist. It is an accomplished fact. A year or two ago it was thought wonderful that you could signal without wires across half a mile. Now signals have been sent over thirty-four miles. Before the century is out wireless telegraphy between America and England will probably have been accomplished, and the great ocean liners on the high seas will be able to keep up constant communication with the land on either side.

Some few months since, Mr. Marconi, whose name will be familiar to most readers of this magazine, succeeded in sending messages between the two English towns Salisbury and Bath, a distance of thirty-four miles, although there was no connection in the shape of a cable between them.

This remarkable feat did not arouse the public interest that it deserved, and has been put into the shade by Mr. Marconi's most recent achievement in telegraphing without wires between England and France.

It was on March 28 that the very first wireless message was sent across the Channel. The instruments had been taken over to France a week before in charge of two assistants, and a house, the Châlet l'Artois, at Wimereux village, two miles west of Boulogne, was hired to serve as a station.

A suitable pole one hundred and fifty feet high was then erected, and within a week from the start telegraphic communication was established between the coasts of England and France. The station on the English side is at the South Foreland lighthouse, near Dover. In the presence of the committee appointed by the French government, consisting of Colonel le Comte du Pontavice de Heussey, Captain Ferrié and M. Voisenet, the first message was sent from France to England, across thirty two miles of sea, by Mr. Marconi, and the reply was promptly returned by his assistant at Dover.

It was only natural that these experiments across the English Channel should arouse more general interest than those before mentioned between Salisbury and Bath, because it is always more difficult to establish telegraphic communication between two points separated by water than two places with no water barrier between them.

Wonderful, however, as is wireless telegraphy between two fixed points, it is even more wonderful that you should be able to signal across space from a moving boat to any selected point.

During the summer of 1898 His Royal Highness the Prince of Wales spent some weeks on board the royal yacht Osborne, while slowly recovering from the effects of the serious accident to his knee which he sustained at Waddesdon Manor, while on a visit to the late Baron Ferdinand Rothschild.

The Prince had read with interest the account that had been published concerning the experiments made by a young Italian in signalling across space without the employment of connecting wires, and it occurred to him that his period of enforced rest, until the fractured knee should have quite recovered, might be considerably enlivened were the system put to a practical test under his special notice.

An invitation was accordingly sent to Mr. Guglielmo Marconi, asking him to establish wireless telegraphic communication between the royal yacht Osborne and Osborne House, Isle of Wight, in order that Her Majesty might communicate with H. R. H. the Prince of Wales from Osborne House

(CONTINUED ON SECOND PAGE.)

Article in the New York Herald *about Guglielmo Marconi's plans to report the America's Cup using "wireless telegraphy," 1 October 1899*

Toscanini with the New York Philharmonic were heard throughout the country, and from 1935 Martin Block, one of the first disc jockeys, broadcast his *Make Believe Ballroom* on WNEW, on which he played selections by several bands rather than only one (the program became one of the most popular of the following decade). Probably the most notorious program of the time was *War of the Worlds,* Orson Welles's highly realistic radio play about an invasion of New Jersey by Martians, broadcast on the eve of Halloween in 1938. Public reaction to the play demonstrated how much New Yorkers relied on radio for news bulletins and live reports; residents created havoc as they fled their homes in panic. After the outbreak of World War II radio became a vital source of information about world events. It was still being broadcast by amplitude modulation (AM), as the commercial development of FM was thwarted by RCA until the 1950s and 1960s, when it became used mostly to broadcast classical music.

After the introduction of television the popularity of radio comedies, dramas, and variety programs broadcast by the networks declined while that of local programs featuring the music of Tin Pan Alley increased. Recorded music gained in importance and by the early 1960s accounted for some of the most popular programming in the city. Disc jockeys such as Alan Freed, Murray the K, Cousin Brucie, and Scott Muni played rock-and-roll and popular music on powerful stations like WINS, WABC, and WMCA, which adopted a format known as "Top 40" (their playlists always consisted of the 40 best-selling records). Many considered the new programs emblematic of the frenzied pace of life in the city and its growing youth culture. As AM radio was increasingly given over to top forty, FM stations like WNEW and WOR developed a new format known as "underground," or "progressive rock," in which advertisements, the banter of disc jockeys, and station identification were kept to a minimum. By the mid-1970s AM had declined in popularity. In the following decades FM stations directed their programming at narrow segments of the audience and specialized increasingly in one type of programming: Top 40 (which remained the dominant format), oldies, easy listening, country, rhythm and blues, rap, jazz, classical music, foreign-language programming, news, and talk. Controversial disc jockeys like Howard Stern also became popular for developing a genre known as "shock," or "raunch," radio, characterized by savage humor and sexual innuendo. Broadcasters in the 1990s sought to cater to the diverse population of the city, which remained a national center for radio broadcasting.

In the early twenty-first century subscription satellite radio transformed the airwaves. XM Satellite Radio and Sirius Satellite Radio began broadcasting in 2001 and 2002, respectively, and the two merged in 2008; Sirius XM is headquartered at Rockefeller Center and broadcasts 130 channels. Subscription satellite radio attracted Stern and other New York shock jocks like Opie and Anthony because it provided freedom from Federal Communications Commission regulations. Internet radio stations also abounded, and stations like WNYC allowed audiences to listen to live radio broadcasts online or as downloadable podcasts.

Erik Barnouw, *A History of Broadcasting in the United States* (New York: Oxford University Press, 1966–70); Christopher H. Sterling and John M. Kittross, *Stay Tuned: A Concise History of American Broadcasting* (Belmont, Calif.: Wadsworth, 1978)

Susan J. Douglas

Radio City Music Hall. Large indoor theater situated at Rockefeller Center. Conceived by Samuel Rothafel as a palatial entertainment center affordable to the general public, it was designed by Donald Deskey in the art deco style with an opulent interior and 5874 seats and opened on 27 December 1932 with a performance by Martha Graham, Ray Bolger, and Gertrude Niesen. The ceiling gives the illusion of a giant sunset; three large elevators on an enormous stage make possible fast and extensive scene changes and such effects as whole choruses rising up through the floor. The opulent foyer has a ceiling 60 feet (18 meters) high and drapes extending from the ceiling to the floor, ornate mirrors, and long, slender chandeliers. Soon after its opening the theater offered programs combining feature films with stage shows, a format that remained popular for almost 50 years. In 1979 the interior was declared a landmark and restored. Under Robert Jani's direction the theater became principally a venue for live spectacles and television events. Among the events staged there in the 1980s and early 1990s were the Grammy Awards, performances by the Moscow Circus, the annual Radio City Christmas Spectacular, and concerts by Michael Jackson, Frank Sinatra, Liza Minnelli, and Shirley MacLaine. In the early twenty-first century the hall continues to draw international music stars and is frequent host to the Grammys, the Tony Awards, the MTV Music Awards, and the Daytime Emmy Awards; the Christmas Spectacular is seen by more than a million people each year. The best-known act to perform at Radio City Music Hall is the Rockettes, a company of 36 long-legged, bejeweled dancers who first appeared in 1933 and soon became emblems of the entertainment business and the city.

Mary C. Henderson, *The City and the Theater: New York Playhouses from Bowling Green to Times Square* (Clifton, N.J.: James White, 1973)

Robert Seder

Radio Corporation of America. Former name of the RCA Corporation.

Raffeiner, John Stephen (*b* Mals [now in Austria], 26 Dec 1785; *d* Brooklyn, 16 July 1861). Missionary. After training as a physician and priest he volunteered for missionary work in the United States and moved to New York City in 1833. He organized the first German Catholic congregation there in 1834; under his direction it built St. Nicholas's

Radio City Music Hall, ca 1937

Church (1836) on East Second Street where he was a pastor until 1840. He was instrumental in organizing many churches in New York City, including St. John the Baptist (1840) on West 30th Street in Manhattan and the Church of the Holy Trinity (1841) in Williamsburgh, Brooklyn, where he was pastor from 1841 to 1861. Raffeiner was also vicar general of the dioceses of New York (1843–61) and Brooklyn (1853–61).

Thomas F. Meeham, "Very Rev. Johann Stephan Raffeiner," *[U.S. Catholic Historical Society] Historical Records and Studies* 9 (1916), 161–75

Kevin Kenny

ragtime. The term *ragtime* is probably derived from "ragged time," a phrase that evokes the syncopated rhythms of the music. Its beginnings in New York City may be traced to the minstrel shows of the 1880s, but ragtime did not become popular until 1896 when singer and pianist Ben Harney introduced it to the city's vaudeville stages. Piano ragtime quickly developed into an improvised idiom that prefigured jazz and lent itself to performance competitions, such as one held at Tony Pastor's vaudeville house in 1900, in which Mike Bernard was declared the reigning champion of ragtime. Although it is frequently thought of exclusively as piano music, ragtime was also played by instrumental ensembles and was even more popular as a song style marked by lively rhythms and often by lyrics in African American dialect. Ragtime of all types was heard often in African American cabarets. During the first decade of the twentieth century the outstanding cabarets were in the Tenderloin and Black Bohemia districts (on the West Side from the 20s to the 50s) and in the "Jungles" (the West 60s). These clubs included Ike Hines's (West 27th Street), the Douglass Club (West 31st Street), Barron Wilkins's Savoy Club (West 35th Street), the club at the Marshall Hotel (West 53rd Street), and Jim Allen's (West 61st Street). In the second decade of the twentieth century the leading cabarets were in the West 130s in Harlem and included Leroy's, Barron's Astoria Cafe, and Connor's Royal Cafe. Well-known pianists heard at these clubs included Eubie Blake, James P. Johnson, Willie "the Lion" Smith, Luckey Roberts, and Jelly Roll Morton, all of whom were published composers as well. Scott Joplin and his protégé Joseph F. Lamb, both living in New York City at the time, were atypical in that they were major composers of piano ragtime who were not also active as performers. The most important composer of vocal ragtime was Irving Berlin, who composed the song "Alexander's Ragtime Band" (1911).

Ragtime was disseminated nationwide principally through sheet music, and most of the largest publishers were in New York City. At the turn of the twentieth century many of these publishers were on a single block—West 28th Street between Broadway and Sixth Avenue—which became known as Tin Pan Alley because of the clamor of piano playing and singing emanating from the offices there. As publishers moved elsewhere in the city, Tin Pan Alley came to refer to the entire music publishing business. Most purchasers of ragtime sheet music were young. Older generations usually disapproved of the music: whites did so because they feared the effects of African American music on impressionable white youth, and many African Americans did so because they feared that their own youth would be corrupted by a music associated with brothels and cabarets and because they found the texts of ragtime songs racially demeaning. In New York City this disapproval was manifested officially as ragtime was banned from the free pier concerts in the summer of 1902 and from school music programs in 1914.

Ragtime was always associated with dances. In the early days these included the cakewalk, the two-step, the slow drag, and the syncopated waltz. During the second decade of the twentieth century new dances associated with ragtime proliferated: the grizzly bear, the turkey trot, the fox trot, the one-step, the hesitation waltz, and two Latin American dances that shared some of the rhythmic traits of ragtime, the tango and the maxixe. These new dances were eagerly learned by the middle and upper classes, prompting the installation of dance floors at elegant restaurants in midtown (known as "lobster palaces"), including Murray's Roman Gardens, Bustanoby's, Rector's, and Martin's Café de l'Opéra. The leading musician associated with these new dances was James Reese Europe, whose work with the dance team of Vernon and Irene Castle helped to make his recordings well known throughout the country.

About 1917 the popularity of ragtime declined, but many of its elements were retained in jazz and in such idioms as novelty piano and Harlem stride. During the 1940s ragtime was rediscovered by bands seeking to reclaim the roots of jazz: although their popularity was short-lived they inspired an interest in ragtime that led to the formation of fan clubs and to research by collectors of sheet music, recordings, and piano rolls. These activities had only a limited influence until the 1970s, when Scott Joplin's music, fashioned into a film score for the movie *The Sting,* won an Academy Award and launched a nationwide ragtime revival.

Edward A. Berlin, *Ragtime: A Musical and Cultural History* (Berkeley: University of California Press, 1980); Edward A. Berlin, *Reflections and Research on Ragtime* (New York: Institute for Studies in American Music, 1987); Terry Waldo, *This Is Ragtime* (New York: Da Capo Press, 1991)

Edward A. Berlin

Rahv, Philip [Greenberg, Ivan] (*b* Ukraine, 10 March 1908; *d* Cambridge, Mass., 23 Dec 1973). Editor. As an editor of the *Partisan Review* from 1934 to 1969 he helped to shape intellectual life in New York City. A communist early in his career, he became a leading anti-Stalinist after 1937, supported World War II, opposed McCarthyism, and was skeptical of the intellectual fashions of the 1960s. Rahv took pride in promoting new writers, including Delmore Schwartz and Saul Bellow. In such works of literary criticism as *Image and Idea* (1949) and *The Myth and the Powerhouse* (1965) he rejected the methods of "New Criticism" and emphasized the need to interpret literature within its cultural context.

Terry A. Cooney

railroad apartments. Apartments with narrow, oblong layouts recalling those of railroad cars. They had no hallway, and each room opened directly onto the next. The railroad apartment became prevalent in multistory tenement buildings in New York City after 1850 when available land was becoming scarce and the demand for housing was increasing. The buildings usually stood on lots with 25 feet (8 meters) of frontage and a depth of 100 feet (30 meters), contained an average of four railroad apartments on each floor, often occupied more than 90 percent of their lots, and had windows only at the front and rear, causing interior rooms of the apartments to be narrow, dark, and poorly ventilated.

James Ford, *Slums and Housing, with Special Reference to New York City: History, Conditions, Policy* (Westport, Conn.: Negro Universities Press, 1971)

Craig D. Bida

railroads. Freight and passenger rail have played an important role in the development of New York City. Although freight trains have been surpassed by airplanes and trucks, New York City remains much more dependent on passenger rail service than other cities in the United States.

1. To 1900

The age of the railroad in New York City began on 24 November 1832 when the New York and Harlem Railroad began service connecting Union Square with 23rd Street and Fourth Avenue. Service in Brooklyn began on 1 April 1836 when the Brooklyn and Jamaica Railroad began running along Atlantic Avenue. The Brooklyn and Jamaica also built a tunnel 3000 feet (900 meters) long under Atlantic Avenue between Boerum Place and Willow Street to serve a shoreline freight terminal; in 1861 the city banned steam service in the tunnel, which was then sealed. The Long Island Rail Road (LIRR) was chartered on 24 April 1834 to construct a line between Brooklyn and Greenport, with the purpose

View of Grand Central Station from Fourth Avenue, ca *1896*

of improving connections between New York City and Boston. Lease of the Brooklyn and Jamaica provided direct service between the East River and eastern Long Island. Steam service was introduced in the city in 1837 by the New York and Harlem Railroad, which built a freight depot two blocks south of Canal Street between Franklin and White streets, and a line along Fourth (now Park) Avenue between 125th Street and a terminal between 26th and 27th streets; until 1876 the city required that the trains be powered by horses south of 32nd Street. The New Jersey Rail Road was the first rail company to establish regular ferry service between New Jersey and Manhattan (1838). The New York and Harlem Railroad built a bridge over the Harlem River in 1840 and completed the Williams Bridge over the Bronx River in 1842. In 1844 the LIRR reached Greenport, and the New York and New Haven Railroad was incorporated; it connected with the Harlem line just northeast of Woodlawn Cemetery and began service from New Haven, Connecticut, to Manhattan in 1848, sharing track and renting terminals in Manhattan and the Bronx that belonged to the Harlem line. The completion of the New York and New Haven Railroad hastened the suburban development of the coastal regions of eastern Westchester County and southern Connecticut. It also took the business of the LIRR, which was forced into receivership in 1850.

Steam rail service linking Manhattan with the Bronx and the rest of the mainland was begun in October 1851 by the New York and Hudson River Railroad, which had been chartered in 1846 and had track running along the eastern bank of the Hudson River to Rensselaer. This was the first line to carry freight directly into Manhattan, and it played a role in developing the Upper West Side. Later the railroad was enjoined from using steam engines south of its terminal at 30th Street and 11th Avenue and so carried cargo by horse to its warehouse and handling center on Chambers Street. The first railroad to provide service between the Midwest and the Great Lakes and the western shore of the Hudson River was the New York and Erie Railroad, which in October 1852 leased three small rail systems in northern New Jersey. In 1853 the Harlem line acquired a local track between Melrose and Port Morris in the southeastern section of the Bronx. Settlement on the Upper East Side and in parts of the Bronx and lower Westchester County was aided by the Harlem line, which ran as far upstate as Chatham by 1857. In 1861 the New York and Erie Railroad built elaborate terminal facilities at Jersey City. These and similar facilities of the Delaware, Lackawanna and Western Railroad in Hoboken, New Jersey, and the New Jersey Central Railroad in Jersey City placed New York City, its market, and its port within reach of the coalfields of Pennsylvania. By 1863 two rail routes joined New York City and Philadelphia: that of the Pennsylvania Railroad; and one formed by the New Jersey Central Railroad and the Philadelphia and Reading Railroad (which had a junction in Trenton, New Jersey). More than 50 railroads were built in Brooklyn during the nineteenth century; many were horsecar lines that were electrified and converted into trolley lines during the 1890s. The first, opened on 3 July 1854 by the Brooklyn City Railroad, ran from Fulton Ferry to Marcy and Myrtle avenues.

The rest of the track on Long Island was laid by five small commuter railroads that were eventually absorbed by a renascent LIRR. By 1860 the LIRR was a fully developed commuter railroad that helped to settle outposts formerly considered remote, such as Flushing and Maspeth. All tracks fed into a terminal in Flatbush owned by the company and into a large facility at Hunter's Point in Long Island City on the East River, which was connected with Jamaica in 1861; until 1910 Hunter's Point was the interchange point for all traffic bound to the LIRR in Manhattan and included a freight station, passenger areas, ferries, docks, a coach yard, an engine house, and a machine shop. The first railroad in Staten Island was the Staten Island Railway (SIR), completed in 1860, which ran between Clifton and Tottenville. Renamed the Staten Island Rapid Transit Railroad (SIRTRR), it built a line along the northern shore and connected at Cranford Station, New Jersey, with the Lehigh Valley Railroad and the New Jersey Central (later renamed the Central Railroad of New Jersey). In the 1880s the Baltimore and Ohio Railroad, the first railroad company established in the western hemisphere, began providing financial backing for the SIRTRR and acquired full control in 1899, including the connecting ferries to Manhattan (in 1905 the ferries were transferred to New York City's government, in response to a 1901 accident).

Cornelius Vanderbilt became a lessee of the highly successful Harlem line, acquired a majority of its stock in 1864, and built a large freight and passenger terminal at St. John's Park, bordered by Varick, Hudson, Beach, and Laight streets just south of Canal Street. In 1867 he became the president of the New York Central Railroad, a trunk line from Albany to Buffalo with connections to the Midwest. He soon recognized that separate terminals in Manhattan were an inconvenience to passengers and reduced profits, so in 1869 he consolidated the New York and Harlem Railroad and the New York and Hudson River Railroad to form the New York Central and Hudson River Railroad, connecting the lines with a track between Spuyten Duyvil and Morrisania in the Bronx. He then excavated a site between 42nd and 57th streets and Lexington and Madison avenues for the Grand Central Depot, which was completed in 1871. Trains were run in an open cut to obviate dangerous grade crossings on Fourth Avenue.

Between 1865 and 1900 terminals were built along the shore of New Jersey by several railroads, including the New York, Ontario and Western Railroad and the New York, West Shore and Buffalo Railroad, both of which established terminals in Weehawken. Several trunk lines provided rail service from the

New York Railways System ("Green Lines")

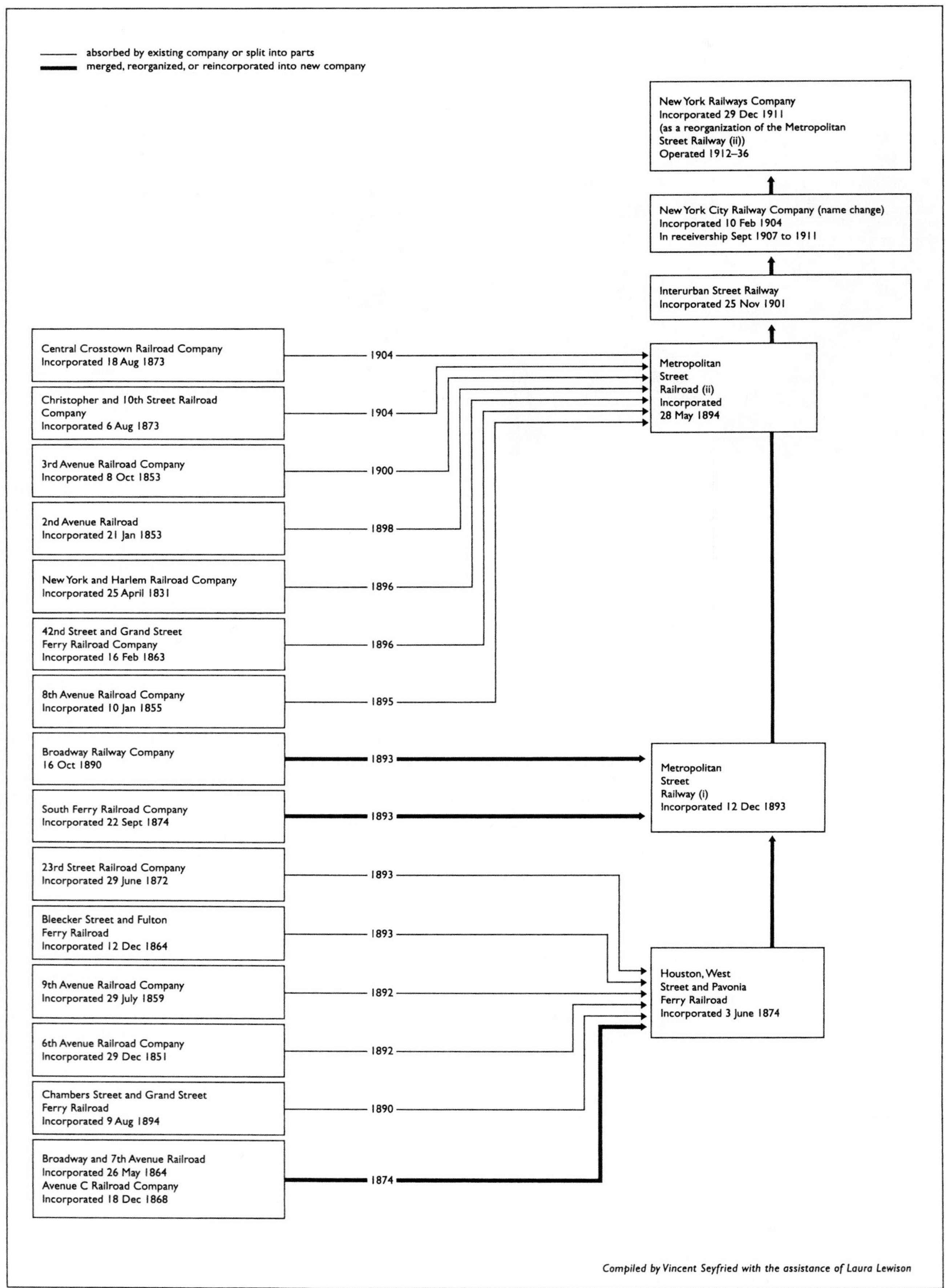

Compiled by Vincent Seyfried with the assistance of Laura Lewison

Third Avenue Railway System

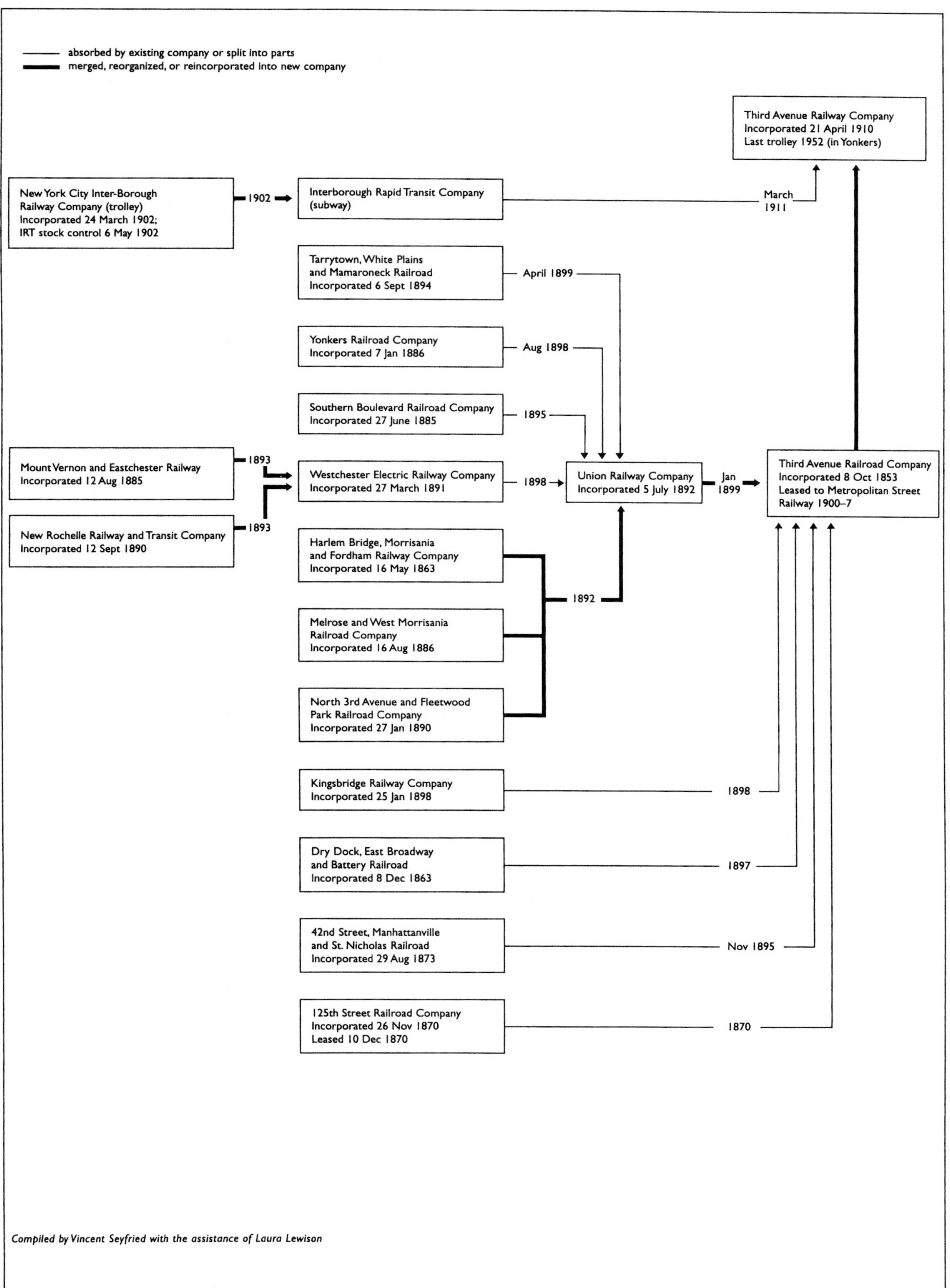

Compiled by Vincent Seyfried with the assistance of Laura Lewison

Railway Companies in Queens

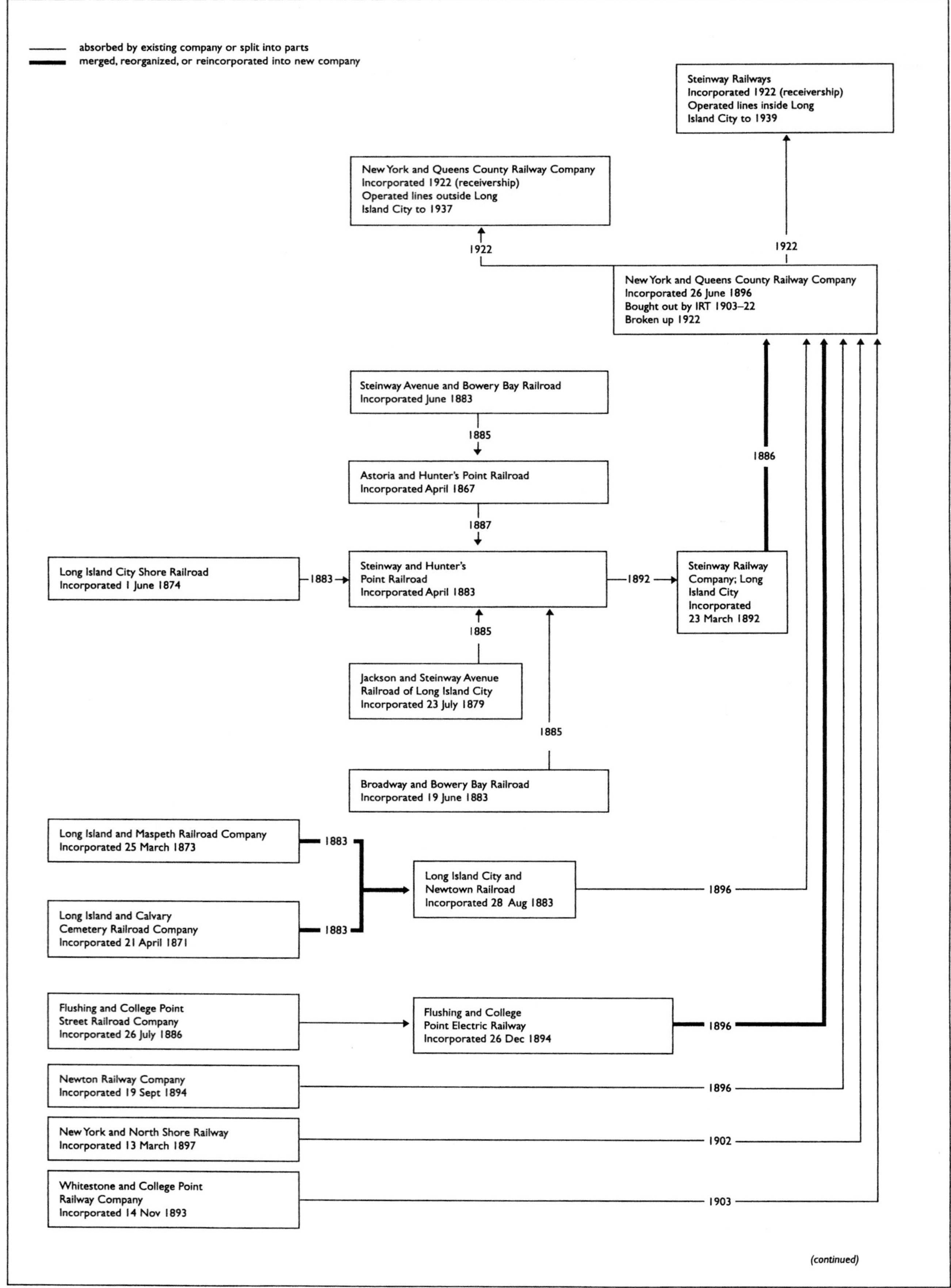

(continued)

Railway Companies in Queens (Continued)

Rockaway Village Railroad
(horse cars in Far Rockaway)
Incorporated 6 March 1886
1898
Ocean Electric Railway
subsidiary of LIRR
(trolleys from Neponsit to
Far Rockaway; to 1928)
Incorporated 27 Feb 1899
Mineola, Hempstead and Freeport
Traction Company
Incorporated 27 Feb 1899
1902
New York and Long Island Traction Company
Incorporated 22 Sept 1902
Bought out by LIRR and IRT 1905–6
(Trolleys in Woodhaven, Ozone Park,
Springfield, Rosedale, Jamaica,
Hollis, Queens Village, to 1926)
Long Island Electric Railway
Incorporated 5 March 1894; foreclosed 1926
1926
Jamaica Central Railways
(reorganization 1926–33)
Bought out by LIRR and IRT 1905–6
(trolleys in Richmond Hill, Jamaica,
Hollis, Queens Village, Springfield,
Hook Creek, Inwood, Far Rockaway)
Mineola, Roslyn and Port
Washington Traction Company
Incorporated 6 Aug 1902
1907
New York and North Shore Traction Company
Incorporated 26 Aug 1907; abandoned 1920
(trolleys in Flushing, Bayside,
Little Neck, Whitestone, to 1920)
South Shore Traction Company
Incorporated 2 March 1903
1912
Manhattan and Queens Traction Company
Incorporated 2 Nov 1912
(trolleys on Queens Boulevard and Sutphin Boulevard
in Long Island City, Woodside, Elmhurst, Forest
Hills, Kew Gardens, Jamaica, South Jamaica, to 1937)
Compiled by Vincent Seyfried

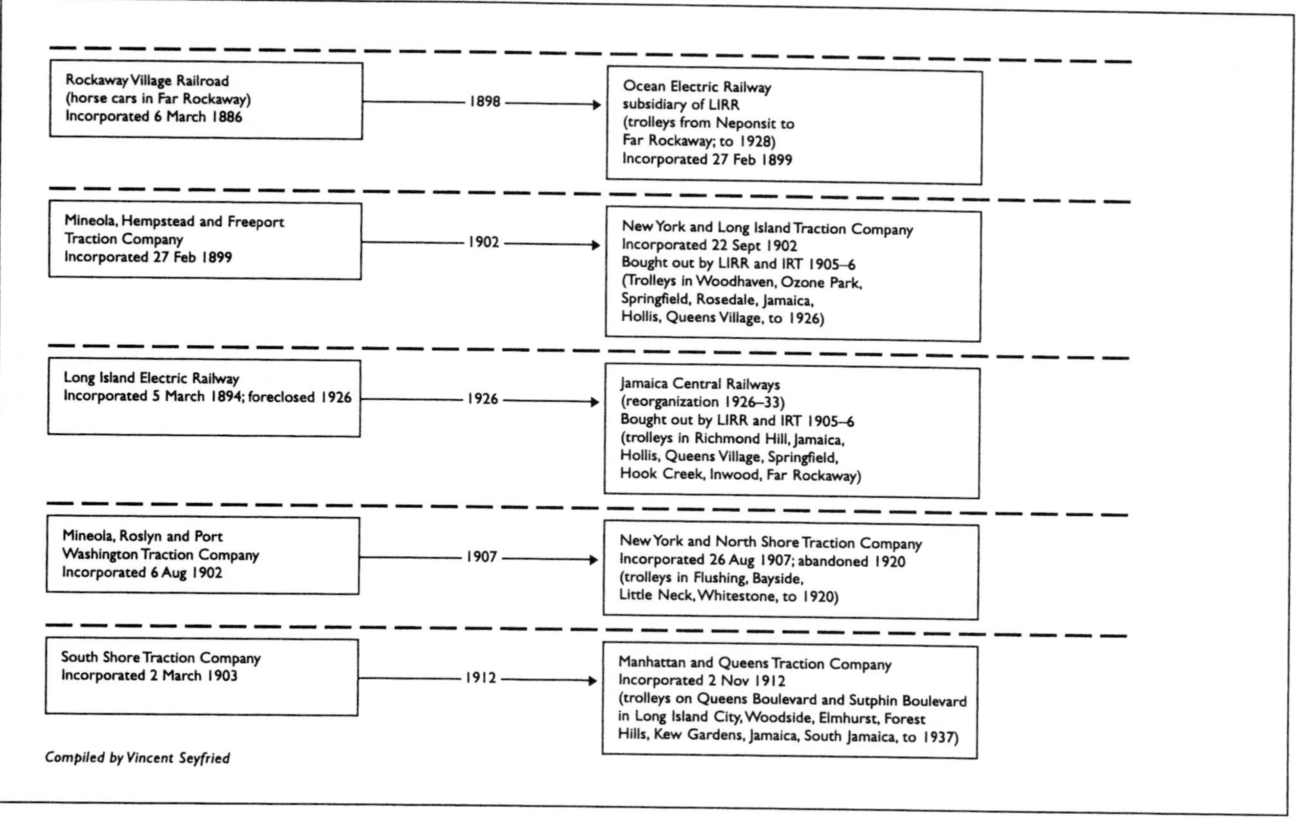

Railways of Staten Island

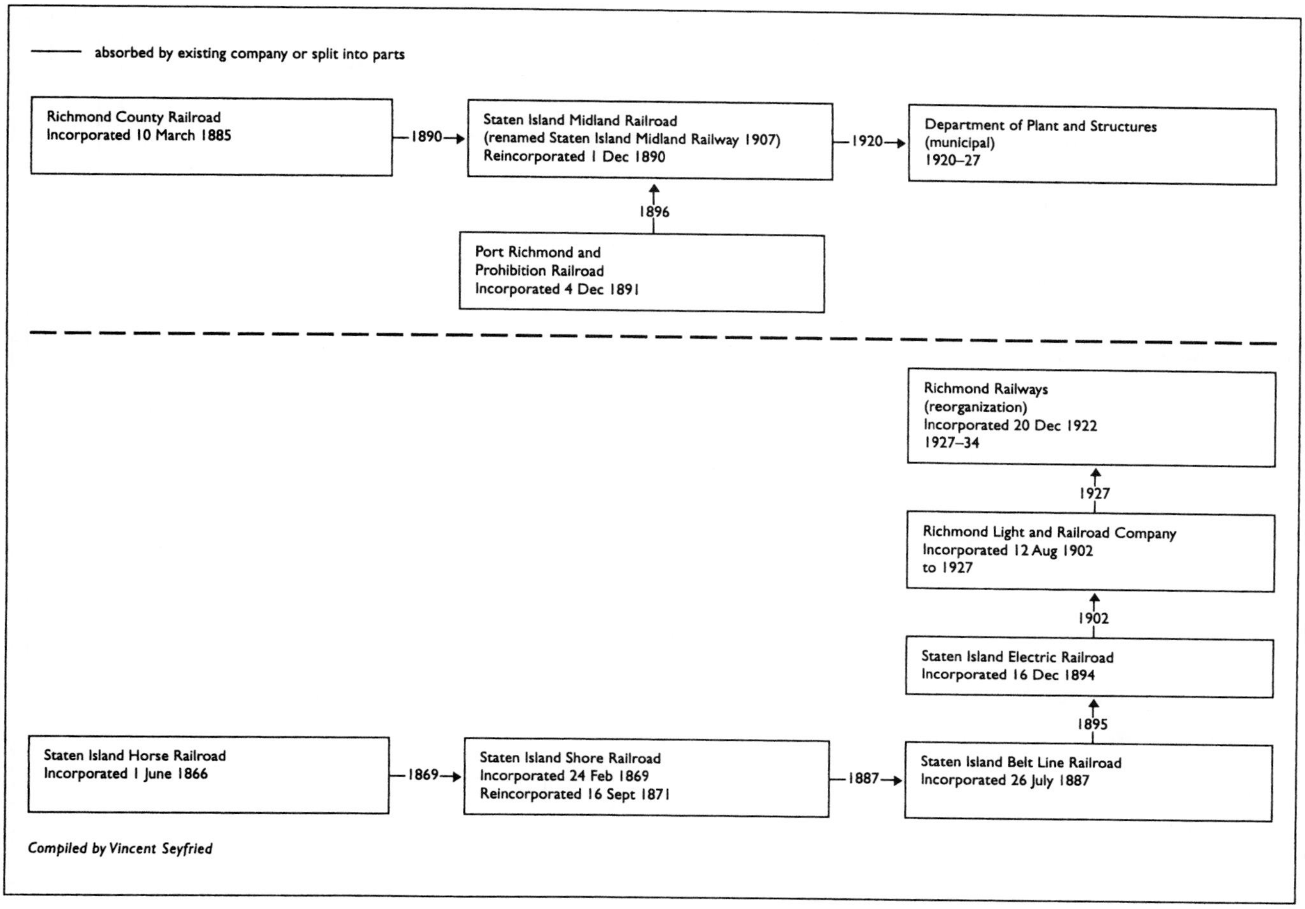

absorbed by existing company or split into parts
Richmond County Railroad
Incorporated 10 March 1885
1890
Staten Island Midland Railroad
(renamed Staten Island Midland Railway 1907)
Reincorporated 1 Dec 1890
1920
Department of Plant and Structures
(municipal)
1920–27
1896
Port Richmond and
Prohibition Railroad
Incorporated 4 Dec 1891
Richmond Railways
(reorganization)
Incorporated 20 Dec 1922
1927–34
1927
Richmond Light and Railroad Company
Incorporated 12 Aug 1902
to 1927
1902
Staten Island Electric Railroad
Incorporated 16 Dec 1894
1895
Staten Island Horse Railroad
Incorporated 1 June 1866
1869
Staten Island Shore Railroad
Incorporated 24 Feb 1869
Reincorporated 16 Sept 1871
1887
Staten Island Belt Line Railroad
Incorporated 26 July 1887
Compiled by Vincent Seyfried

Trolley and Elevated Lines in Brooklyn (slightly simplified)

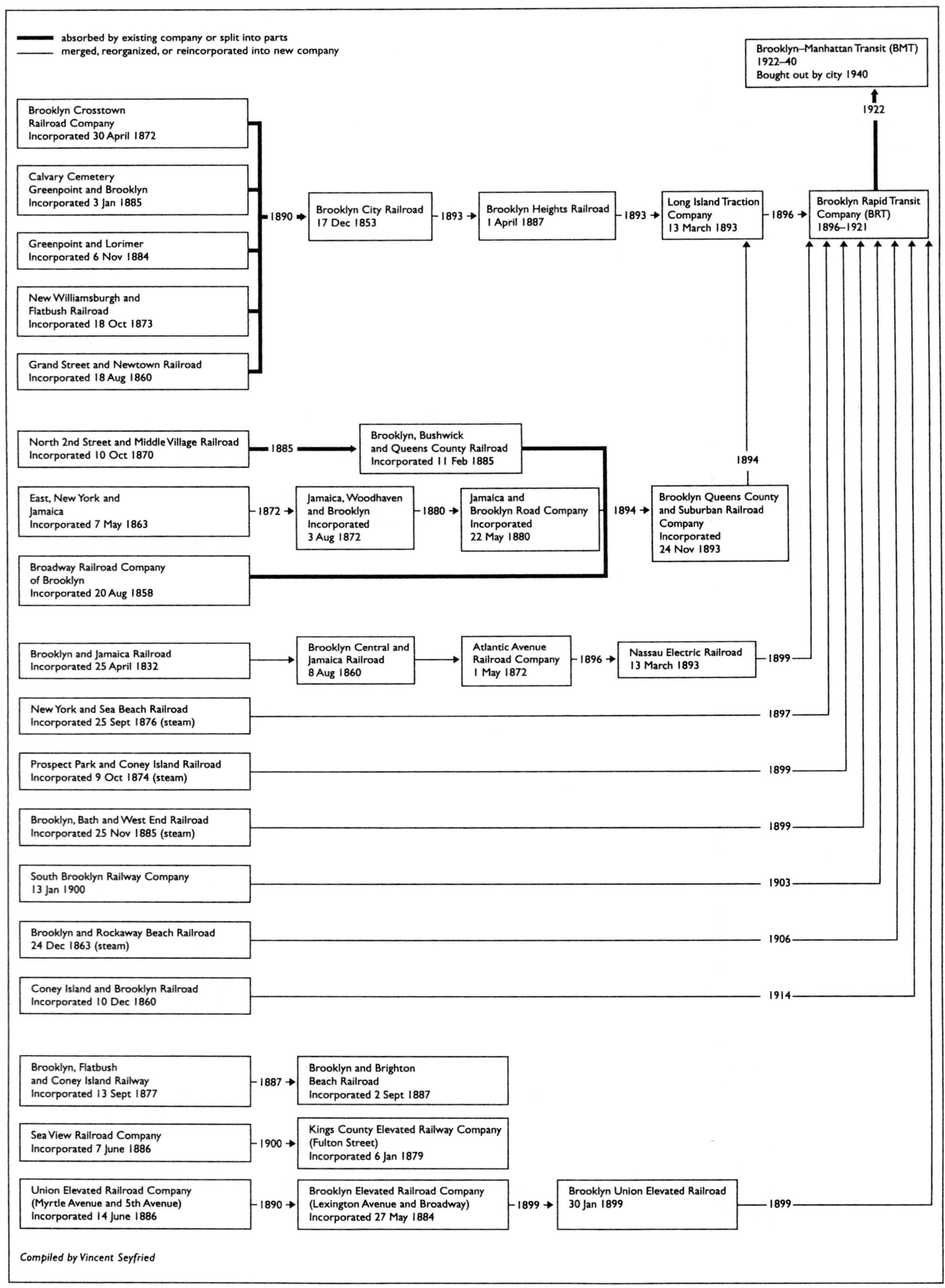

Midwest and the Great Lakes to the western shore of the Hudson River. In 1868 the New Haven line added a short spur from New Rochelle in lower Westchester County to Port Morris in the Bronx to increase its freight capabilities and provide ferry service between connecting lines at Jersey City. Freight service to New Jersey allowed the shipping of goods to the metropolitan region from the South and the West, particularly coal and food. New York City was then the busiest port in the world and the hub of a vast shipping network.

The New York and New Haven Railroad built rail yards in the Bronx at East 132nd Street (Harlem River) and East 149th Street (Oak Point). It had almost a monopoly in New England and changed its name to the New York, New Haven and Hartford Railroad in 1872. The Pennsylvania Railroad built extensive facilities on the Hudson riverfront (Jersey City) in 1876 that included a new station, repair and maintenance shops, freight-handling terminals, and ferry and lighterage docks for conveying passengers and cargo across New York Harbor. The LIRR passed into a second receivership in 1877 and was restored to solvency only after Austin Corbin bought a majority of its stock in 1880. To gain access to the markets of the city, the Philadelphia and Reading Railroad obtained control of the system operated by the Central Railroad of New Jersey in 1883.

During the same era steam-powered elevated railroads appeared in Manhattan and Brooklyn. Between 1867 and 1881 four north-south routes were built in Manhattan along Second, Third, Sixth, and Ninth avenues; beginning in 1887 an extension of the Second and Third avenue routes was built farther northward into the Annexed District (the Bronx). This entire system ultimately became the Manhattan Railway Company. In Brooklyn the first elevated was the Lexington Avenue line, opened on 13 May 1885 by the Brooklyn Elevated Railroad. Several lines ran directly to Coney Island, where many workers spent their leisure time: the Prospect Park and Coney Island Rail Road; the New York and Sea Beach Railway; the Brooklyn Bath and West End Rail Road; the Brooklyn, Flatbush and Coney Island Railway; and the Brooklyn, Canarsie and Rockaway Beach Rail Road were in service by 1890 (these lines later became part of the city's subway system). Most elevated lines and trolley lines in Brooklyn came under the control of the Brooklyn Rapid Transit Company. Trolley traffic in Brooklyn was so busy that the baseball team there, the Dodgers, was named for a local practice known as trolley dodging. The Lehigh Valley Railroad in 1891 reached Jersey City, to which it provided service from the Midwest via Buffalo. In 1897 the New York Central and Hudson River Railroad improved service to Manhattan with a four-track bridge over the Harlem River. The railroads around the city hastened the industrialization of southern Bronx, Long Island City, and New Jersey between the ports of Weehawken and Elizabeth, and along the waterfront in Brooklyn and the western shore of the East River in Manhattan. Residential settlements developed along commuter routes and increased land values in Queens, the Bronx, and Brooklyn.

2. After 1900

The Pennsylvania Railroad increased its share in the railroads of the city by buying a majority of the stock of the LIRR in 1900. Takeovers and consolidations became commonplace as financiers like Vanderbilt, Jay Gould, Daniel Drew, and J. P. Morgan engaged in railroad speculation. Overlapping corporate directorships, competition in a constricted market, and superfluous and unconnected rail networks embroiled the rail companies as well as the municipal, state, and federal governments in scandal and confusion.

By the turn of the century the network of rails in the area was complete but lacked facilities for direct shipment of goods from rails to ships (except in New Jersey); therefore, other forms of transport were also used. Almost every line that served the Port of New York built elaborate facilities for equipment maintenance and freight handling, including those along the Hudson River from Christopher Street to 23rd Street, the rail compound between 60th and 72nd streets operated by the New York Central and Hudson River Railroad, the large yard at Mott Haven, and extensive facilities along the waterfront in Brooklyn. Upper New York Bay and the rivers around the city were crowded with ferries shuttling passengers from New Jersey and Long Island City to Manhattan. Loaded railroad cars were carried by floats, and goods were transferred from rail to ship by lighters (specially designed freight ferries).

Several carriers with terminals in New Jersey extended rails into the heart of the city. The Hudson and Manhattan Railroad, a subway system, built the first tunnel under the Hudson River to the city, offering service between Newark, Jersey City; Hoboken; and Manhattan from 1908. The Pennsylvania Railroad (PRR) had a tunnel dug under the Hudson and East rivers, principally by Irish and Italian laborers. With the permission of a charter granted by the Common Council in 1902, the company built Pennsylvania Station between 31st and 33rd streets and Seventh and Eighth avenues to rival Grand Central Depot and serve passengers on the Pennsylvania and Long Island railroads. The well-known architectural firm of McKim, Mead and White designed the station, which opened for the LIRR on 8 September 1910 and for the PRR on 27 November 1910. To the east the Pennsylvania electrified its lines initially to Sunnyside where it built what was then the largest coach yard in the world. With the New York, New Haven and Hartford Railroad, the Pennsylvania improved the circulation of through-traffic by building the New York Connecting Railroad, which linked the PRR and LIRR with the New Haven line at Port Morris over the elaborate Hell Gate Bridge. About this time the New York Central and Hudson River Railroad rebuilt Grand Central Depot according to the ambitious plans of the engineer William J. Wilgus. He envisioned a terminal with 67 tracks along double levels and a highly sophisticated signaling and interlocking system that could efficiently serve 70,000 passengers an hour while concealing the train traffic. Completed in 1913 and renamed Grand Central Terminal, the facility was the largest railroad complex in the world.

Concurrent with main line railroad developments, New York City provided capital funds for new underground rapid transit routes (subways) and gave two private companies franchises to operate these routes, which encompassed all boroughs excepting Staten Island. The Interborough Rapid Transit (IRT) began operations in 1904; a year earlier it leased for 999 years the Manhattan Railway network (in Manhattan and the Bronx) in order to coordinate operations with the new subways. The Brooklyn Rapid Transit Company (BRT) had acquired control of all Brooklyn elevated routes by 1900. In 1913 the so-called dual contracts allowed the IRT and BRT operating rights over a large network of new subways in all boroughs except Staten Island.

The pollution from steam-powered trains operating in closed tunnels drew criticism from urban reformers and lowered property values along routes where trains ran above ground or in open cuts. Public complaints prompted several companies to undertake the demanding project of electrifying their lines. The LIRR's Atlantic Avenue (Brooklyn) route and connecting lines through Queens to Far Rockaway and Rockaway Park were electrified using a third-rail system in 1905, which represented the first large-scale railroad electrification in North America; the remaining LIRR routes in Queens were electrified between 1908 and 1917 as part of the overall Penn Station project. The PRR's main line west from Penn Station into New Jersey was initially electrified using the same third-rail system that extended to a junction just east of Newark known as Manhattan Transfer, where steam power took over. In 1935 an overhead catenary system replaced the third rail and ultimately was used on the entire route to Philadelphia and Washington, D.C. Lines were electrified by the New York Central and Hudson River Railroad between Grand Central Terminal and Harmon, New York (Hudson Line), and White Plains, New York (Harlem Line) in 1906, using an unusual under-running third-rail system, and by the New York, New Haven and Hartford Railroad between Woodlawn Junction (Bronx) and

New Haven by 1914 using an overhead catenary. Electrification altered the landscape of Park Avenue. Between 1921 and 1924 the New York Central and Hudson River Railroad covered the train yards that stretched to 57th Street and the open cut that ran up the middle of Fourth Avenue; it then rented the air rights above its property, and a new complex of hotels and office buildings known as Terminal City changed the character of midtown Manhattan. Park Avenue then became one of the most fashionable residential streets in the world.

Despite these improvements the railroads remained inadequate and congestion increased during World War I. When bottlenecks on the rails threatened the war effort, the federal government formed the U.S. Railroad Administration in December 1917 to operate the rails. Locally the BRT declared bankruptcy and was succeeded by the Brooklyn Manhattan Transit Company after a severe accident on 1 November 1918 at the Malbone Street (now Empire Boulevard) underpass. The Port of New York Authority was formed in April 1921 to increase freight-handling capabilities in the region. The authority was caught between public and private interests and hindered by jurisdictional conflicts (between state and city and between New York and New Jersey), and it eventually abandoned the rails to promote highways and airports. Also in 1921 the Erie Railroad began using trucks to transport freight, and traffic on the waterways around the city declined as other railways followed. A decade later the Port of New York Authority opened the first rail and truck terminal, the Union Inland Freight Station, between Eighth and Ninth avenues and 15th and 16th streets. In 1925 the Baltimore and Ohio's (B&O) Staten Island Railway was electrified using a subway-type third rail and cars.

By the 1930s changes to the rail system were hastened by corporate debt, mismanagement, and competition from trucks, buses, and airplanes. The Depression forced the New York, New Haven and Hartford Railroad to file for bankruptcy in 1935, marking the ascendancy of the automobile; this bankruptcy lasted until 1947. In the mid-1930s the New York Central relocated its West Side freight tracks from 11th Avenue into a depressed cut south of 59th Street, and north of 72nd Street it relocated its riverside tracks into a new tunnel constructed as part of Robert Moses's Henry Hudson Parkway project. In June 1940 New York City purchased the Brooklyn–Manhattan Transit and IRT companies and merged both into the Board of Transportation (which already operated the Independent Subway System) to form the New York City Transit System (today, the New York City Transit Authority).

Although the number of rail passengers peaked during World War II and the Port of New York remained the busiest in the nation until 1960, the railways in the region lost about two-thirds of their passenger traffic and half their freight tonnage between 1945 and 1970. Companies abandoned their facilities along the waterfront in New Jersey and their yards in Mott Haven, as well as rights of way throughout the region; the New York Central and Hudson River Railroad abandoned its yard on the Hudson River between 60th and 72nd streets. Several bankruptcies, mergers, and takeovers also occurred. In 1957 the state legislatures of New York and New Jersey established the Metropolitan Rapid Transit Commission, which recommended a rapid transit loop system connecting Manhattan with various commuter railroad terminals in Hudson County, New Jersey. Nothing ever came of this recommendation, but in 1962 the Port of New York Authority purchased the bankrupt Hudson and Manhattan Railroad, which became the PATH (Port Authority Trans-Hudson) system.

Railroads in the metropolitan region continued to decline during the 1960s. The New York, New Haven, and Hartford Railroad entered a second and final bankruptcy in 1961. The landmark Pennsylvania Station was demolished in 1964 and replaced by a smaller underground station and a new Madison Square Garden above street level. In the following year the State of New York, as directed by Governor Nelson A. Rockefeller, purchased the troubled LIRR and took over its operation; in March 1968 it became part of the much larger Metropolitan Transit Authority (MTA). Later that year the Interstate Commerce Commission effected what was then the largest corporate merger in history by joining the three largest metropolitan rail companies—the New York Central, the Pennsylvania, and the New Haven railroads—to form the Penn Central Corporation, which ultimately failed in 1970; in 1971 the administration of its long-distance passenger lines was assumed by the National Rail Passenger Corporation (Amtrak), an agency newly established by the federal government. Despite this assistance, several railroads in the area remained bankrupt, particularly in New Jersey. Besides the Penn Central, this group included the Erie–Lackawanna, the Central of New Jersey, the Reading, the Lehigh Valley, and the Lehigh and Hudson River. The United States Railway Association formed the Consolidated Rail Corporation (Conrail) to take over commuter and freight operations of these six railroads in April 1976.

The MTA continued to manage service on the LIRR and after 1971 leased commuter operations on the Hudson, Harlem, and New Haven lines to the Penn Central Conrail, and in conjunction with the New Jersey Department of Transportation leased services between Hoboken, N.J., and Manhattan, and to Rockland and Orange counties in New York. The passenger service of B&O's Staten Island Railway came under MTA operation in 1971. To prevent Conrail from becoming a permanent government agency, the federal government during President Ronald Reagan's administration sought to make it attractive to private buyers. Conrail was divested of its commuter operations, which required large investments of labor and capital, on 1 January 1983. The MTA created a new subsidiary, Metro-North Commuter Railroad, to operate the Hudson and Harlem lines, as well as the New Haven line, for which it shared jurisdiction with the Connecticut Department of Transportation. New Jersey Transit, an agency established by the State of New Jersey in 1979, in 1983 assumed responsibility for managing the complex commuter rail systems in the Garden State, which fed into Newark, Manhattan's Pennsylvania Station, and the former terminal of the Erie–Lackawanna at Hoboken. After 1983 the federal government dismantled the U.S. Railroad Administration and in 1987 sold to private buyers its share of 85 percent in Conrail, which by 1991 was a prosperous freight carrier. In 1999 Conrail in turn was split and roughly equal portions were sold to CSX Transportation and Norfolk Southern, the two largest freight railroads in the United States east of the Mississippi River. In 2000 the CSX route along the Hudson's east bank between Albany and the Bronx was significantly improved when the New York State Department of Transportation opened its 1.9-mile (3-kilometer) Oak Point Link, which connects High Bridge (just north of Yankee Stadium) to the Harlem River and Oak Point yards in South Bronx. The link eliminated a complicated interface with MTA Metro North Railroad and permitted CSX to use the Hell Gate Bridge for access to Queens, Brooklyn, and Long Island. Both CSX and Norfolk Southern railroads continued to provide freight service into New York City in 2008.

In the early twenty-first century New York City's metropolitan population depended more heavily on commuter rail than did the residents of any other area in the United States. To meet this demand, beginning in the late 1980s, the commuter and intercity rail operators undertook major capital projects that altered the city's railroad landscape. In 1987 the LIRR constructed a new passenger train yard west of Penn Station, on the site of the New York Central's old freight facility, between 30th and 33rd streets and 10th and 12th avenues; in 2008 the MTA was reviewing proposals to lease the air rights over this facility. Amtrak in 1990 rerouted its New York–Albany–Buffalo traffic from Grand Central Terminal to Pennsylvania Station, thus consolidating all New York intercity trains there, by restoring the Spuyten Duyvil Bridge and using the old New York Central freight tracks on Manhattan's West Side. The LIRR replaced its electric car repair shops in Morris

Park, Queens, with the Hillside Maintenance Complex, a modern facility in Hollis, Queens, covering 26 acres (11 hectares).

New Jersey Transit completed three important projects that vastly improved Manhattan access for Erie–Lackawanna lines formerly terminating only at Hoboken. The Kearny Connection (1996) allowed Morristown and Gladstone Line trains a direct entrance into Penn Station; the Montclair Connection (2002) did the same for the combined Boonton and Montclair branches. In 2003 a huge new station in Secaucus, New Jersey, permitted passengers to transfer between diesel-powered train services based at Hoboken and electric trains operating to and from Penn Station. Thus, rail customers originating in Bergen, Rockland, and Orange counties received Penn Station access. In 2008 New Jersey Transit was designing a new trans-Hudson tunnel to double its capacity into the Penn Station vicinity.

Also in 2008 the LIRR East Side Access project was constructing new tunnels in Queens and Manhattan, enabling trains to use the previously unused lower level of the 63rd Street tunnel originally built in the 1970s. In Queens a connection to existing LIRR lines in the Sunnyside area is under construction. On the Manhattan side, new tunnels will lead to a new terminal directly below Metro-North's existing Grand Central; the entire project is scheduled for completion in 2013.

The LIRR, the largest commuter line in North America, carried 282,000 passengers on an average weekday in 2006; Metro-North carried about 260,000. New Jersey Transit carried about 250,000 weekday riders, which included trips on lines operating from Hoboken through Bergen County (New Jersey) terminating in Rockland and Orange counties (New York) operated jointly with Metro-North. The vast majority of these riders traveled to or from Manhattan's two rail terminals or accessed Manhattan via rapid transit connections at Brooklyn (Atlantic Terminal), Queens (Long Island City), Hoboken, and Newark.

Carl W. Condit, *The Port of New York: A History of the Rail Terminal System* (Chicago: University of Chicago Press, 1980, 1981)

See also Elevated railways and Subways.

John Fink, Andrew Sparberg

Rainbow Room. Restaurant and nightclub opened in the new RCA Building (later the GE Building) in Rockefeller Center in October 1934. It was the first large dining and dancing club atop a modern skyscraper. The name was inspired by an organ on the premises that translated music into shifting color patterns. For many decades the restaurant was considered one of the most elegant in New York City. It offered stunning views of the skyline and a revolving dance floor and over the years featured the music of Duke Ellington, Noël Coward, and other leading performers. A renovation in 1974 at a cost of $25 million restored the restaurant's grandeur. In 1998 the Cipriani family, known for its Italian restaurants across New York and the world, took over the operation of the Rainbow Room. Restaurant operations ceased in the summer of 2009, when the Ciprianis surrendered possession of the restaurant. As of 2010 a new operator had not been named, and the bar, restaurant, and banqueting facilities remained closed.

James Bradley

Raines Law. Law passed by the New York State Legislature in 1896 to discourage the consumption of alcohol and increase state revenue. Introduced by Senator John Raines and passed at the urging of the state Republican leader Thomas C. Platt, it replaced local (often Democratic) excise boards with a state (often Republican) excise commission, raised liquor license fees, and limited the sale of liquor on Sundays to hotels. When the excise commission defined a "hotel" as an establishment that served meals and had at least 10 furnished rooms to let, many taverns in the city qualified by renting tenements in the buildings that they occupied. Reformers including Charles H. Parkhurst and William Travers Jerome denounced these "Raines Law hotels" for prostitution and gambling; journalist Lincoln Steffens emphasized their corruption of police officers. Efforts to shut down the hotels were opposed by those who argued that workers had a right to drink on their only day off, including many Germans, Czechs, and others whose votes could swing mayoral elections in New York City. Battles over the enforcement of the Raines Law bedeviled police commissioners from Theodore Roosevelt to Francis V. Greene and gave Mayors William L. Strong and Seth Low reputations for puritanism that may have contributed to their failure to serve more than a single term.

David C. Hammack

Ramaz School. Coeducational Jewish day school opened in 1937 by Joseph H. Lookstein. Its name is derived from letters contained in the name of the rabbi Moses Z. Margolis. The school was among the first Orthodox Jewish day schools to have a curriculum comparable to that of secular high schools. Ramaz offers both a traditional general curriculum and a comprehensive Judaic studies program. In 2006 it had a combined enrollment of about 1100 in the lower school (nursery to the eighth grade) at 125 East 85th Street and the upper school (ninth to 12th grades) at 60 East 78th Street.

Erica Judge

Ramblersville. Name applied until 1916 to Howard Beach.

Rand, Ayn [Rosenbaum, Alissa] (*b* St. Petersburg, 2 Feb 1905; *d* New York City, 6 March 1982). Philosopher and novelist. She moved to the United States in 1926 and to New York City in 1951 and formulated a philosophy of radical individualism "upholding capitalism in politics, egoism in ethics, and reason in epistemology." In reclusion she wrote essays and books that became available at the Objectivist Book Service on East 34th Street. The Nathaniel Branden Institute offered information and courses about objectivism from 1958 to 1968. During the 1960s Rand acquired a following on college campuses; her program "Commentary" was broadcast by the radio station WBAI, and "Ayn Rand on Campus" was broadcast by WKCR, the radio station of Columbia University. Rand's best-known works are novels such as *The Fountainhead* (1943) and *Atlas Shrugged* (1957) that exemplify her philosophy; she also wrote *We the Living* (1959) and *The Virtue of Selfishness* (1964). She is buried in Kensico Cemetery in Westchester County.

David A. Balcom

Randall, Tony [Rosenberg, Leonard] (*b* Tulsa, Okla., 26 Feb 1920; *d* New York City, 17 May 2004). Actor. He attended Northwestern University and Columbia University, and studied at the Neighborhood Playhouse with Sanford Meisner. He made his debut on Broadway in 1941, later appearing in Rudolf Besier's *The Barretts of Wimpole Street* (1947), *Antony and Cleopatra* (1948), George Bernard Shaw's *Caesar and Cleopatra* (1950), and Jerome Lawrence and Robert E. Lee's *Inherit the Wind* (1955–56). He became best known for his performance as the fastidious Felix in the television series *The Odd Couple* (1970–74), based on the play by Neil Simon. For many years Randall lived in a 10-room apartment in the Beresford at 81st Street and Central Park West. In 1991 he founded a nonprofit subscription company called the National Actors Theatre to stage works by Gogol, Ibsen, Shaw, and others at popular prices, and in its first two seasons he directed and acted in some of its productions. Through this theater company Randall met his second wife, Heather Hanlan. They married in 1995, three years after the death of Florence Gibbs, his wife of 53 years. Tony and Heather Randall had two children before he died from pneumonia following heart surgery in 2004.

Randall Manor. Neighborhood on the northern shore of Staten Island. It was formed in the 1930s on 50 acres (20 hectares) of woodland in the southern section of Sailors' Snug Harbor (now the Snug Harbor Cultural Center) and is named for Captain Robert R. Randall, who bequeathed his fortune to build Sailors' Snug Harbor, a home for retired sailors. The original homes are in the Tudor, Colonial, or Federal Revival styles and are well maintained. At the center of the neighborhood is Allison Pond and Park, a picturesque public recreation area. Henderson Avenue, the main thoroughfare, is residential; most shops lie along Castleton Avenue nearby.

Marjorie Johnson

Randalls Island. An island of 273 acres (111 hectares) at the confluence of the East River and the Harlem River, legally part of Manhattan. It was called Minnehanonck by the Indians; Barent Eylandt by Wouter van Twiller, who purchased it in 1637; and Montresor Island by the British army before it was renamed Randalls in 1784 by its new owner, Jonathan Randal (or Randell). Five years after his death in 1830, his heirs sold it to the city for $60,000. It was then used successively for a potter's field, an almshouse, a smallpox quarantine station, a reformatory called the House of Refuge, the Idiots' and Children's Hospital, and the Inebriate Asylum. These institutions were later moved to Welfare Island (now Roosevelt Island), and the island was cleared to make way for construction of the Triborough Bridge. In the 1930s the Triborough Bridge and Tunnel Authority set up its headquarters on the island. Randalls Island is connected to Wards Island by landfill.

The flat terrain of Randalls Island makes it ideally suited for athletic facilities. Municipal Stadium, built in 1936 (also called Triborough Stadium and Randall's Island Stadium), was renamed Downing Stadium in 1955 to honor the former director of recreation John J. Downing. Among its notable sporting events was Jesse Owens's victory in the 100-yard dash conducted at the 1936 Olympic trials. After the stadium stopped being a major sporting facility, it hosted concerts and music festivals, including the three-day New York Pop Festival in 1970. In 2005 the new Icahn Stadium, built on the site of the old stadium, was opened. It is maintained by the Randall's Island Sports Foundation (RISF), founded in 1992, together with the New York City Department of Parks and Recreation. Other facilities on the island include soccer and baseball fields, a tennis center, a golf center, a ferry dock, picnic areas, and playgrounds. RISF also organizes the free Randall's Island Kids (RIK) program, outdoor and sporting events and camps that bring as many as 14,000 children from Harlem and the South Bronx to the island year round. Furthermore, RISF has worked with the city and parks department to restore freshwater wetlands and a saltwater marsh on the island. The familiar *Discus Thrower* statue by Greek sculptor Kostas Dimitriadis (1926) once stood on Downing Stadium's plaza. Over the years it was vandalized and was removed in 1970, but in 1999 it was restored and placed at the entrance to the island.

Gerard R. Wolfe

Randel, John, Jr. (*b* Albany, 1787; *d* Brooklyn, 1865). Surveyor and civil engineer. After conducting early survey work for the state in the Albany area, Randel was hired in 1807 by the state commission charged with planning the future streets of Manhattan. After completing an initial survey, he produced a map for the Commissioners Plan of 1811, which featured a rigid grid of streets and avenues stretching from North (now Houston) Street to 155th Street. Over the next decade Randel and his survey crews ranged over Manhattan's rural landscape, enduring arrests, lawsuits, and verbal and physical abuse (including, allegedly, unleashed dogs and hurled cabbages and artichokes) precipitated by landowners who preferred that their farms, homesteads, and country estates not be divided by the grid. Randel's men marked every future intersection with over 1500 white marble monuments, each engraved with its prospective street, avenue, and elevation; where the landscape was rocky they used iron bolts as markers. Randel also produced dozens of large-scale topographical maps covering the survey area; these highly detailed folio sheets form the most accurate document of Manhattan's pre-grid landscape. Randel laid out numerous other streets in New York State, including Syracuse and the Brooklyn Navy Yard. He was also an engineer for the Erie Canal and other significant canal and railroad projects outside of New York. In 1848 he proposed the first elevated railroad for Manhattan and displayed a working model at the New York Crystal Palace; it featured such innovations as express/local service and passenger elevators. He founded the community of Randalia, Maryland, in the 1840s, but soon returned to New York City and lived the remainder of his life in Brooklyn.

Gerard Koeppel, Caleb Smith

Random House. Firm of book publishers formed in 1927 at 73 West 45th Street by Bennett Cerf and Donald S. Klopfer, also the owners (since 1925) of the Modern Library. It was so named because Cerf thought they might "publish a few books on the side at random." The firm began as a publisher of costly, elegant limited editions but developed into a trade publisher by the early 1930s. The firm made bold choices: working against censorship laws, it was the first to publish James Joyce's *Ulysses* in the United States, in 1934. The acquisition of Alfred A. Knopf and Vintage Books in 1960 made Random House one of the nation's largest publishers of high-quality books. It became known as well for its substantial and profitable children's department and for its commitment to publishing dramatic works. The firm was acquired in 1966 by the Radio Corporation of America, which sold it in 1980 to Newhouse Publications; in 1998 it was acquired by German media conglomerate Bertelsmann. Among the well-known books published by the firm are Whittaker Chambers's *Witness* (1952), Ayn Rand's *Atlas Shrugged* (1957), Truman Capote's *In Cold Blood* (1965), William Styron's *The Confessions of Nat Turner* (1967), Philip Roth's *Portnoy's Complaint* (1969), and the works of such diverse authors as William Faulkner, Robert Penn Warren, Eugene O'Neill, Lillian Hellman, Gertrude Stein, and Theodor Geisel, aka Dr. Seuss. Bertelsmann appointed Markus Dohle chief executive in May 2008; with headquarters at 1745 Broadway, Random House was the largest English-language trade-book publisher in the world in the early twenty-first century.

See also Book publishing.

Eileen K. Cheng

Ranelagh Gardens. Tavern and pleasure garden at Broadway and Thomas Street, opened by John Jones in 1765 and named after a similar establishment in London. Once the homestead of Anthony Rutgers (*d* 1746), it had a house, garden, and orchard. At night the grounds were illuminated and used for concerts, fireworks, and other entertainments. Samuel Fraunces, owner of Fraunces Tavern in New York City, was the lessee in 1769, apparently its last year in operation. The house, which stood at what is now 232–36 Church Street, was demolished in 1796.

Gilbert Tauber

Rangel, Charles B(ernard) (*b* New York City, 11 June 1930). Congressman. He served in the U.S. Army from 1948 to 1952 and received the Bronze Star for Valor and the Purple Heart during the Korean War. After graduating from New York University (1957) and St. John's University School of Law (1960), he was an assistant U.S. attorney for the Southern District of New York (1961–62). He was elected as a Democrat to the New York State Assembly in 1966 from Harlem and to the U.S. Congress in 1970 from the fifteenth congressional district after defeating Adam Clayton Powell, Jr., in the Democratic primary. He was a member in 1974 of the House Judiciary Committee, which voted articles of impeachment against President Richard M. Nixon. In 1983 he was appointed deputy whip of the Democratic Party in the House of Representatives and in July 1984 he was named a chairman of the Democratic presidential campaign of Walter F. Mondale. In 2006 he was elected to a 19th term in Congress and in 2007 became the chair of the House Ways and Means Committee. In 2008 Rangel was confronted with a series of accusations concerning tax evasion, which prompted an investigation by the House Ethics Committee into his personal and campaign finances. In 2010 he took a leave of absence from his position as chair of the House Ways and Means Committee.

Charles Rangel and Leon Wynter, *And I Haven't Had a Bad Day Since: From the Streets of Harlem to the Halls of Congress* (New York: St. Martin's, 2007)

Larry A. Greene

rap. See Hip-Hop and rap.

Rapelye, George Bernard (*b* New York City, 1784; *d* New York City, 27 March 1863). Antiquarian and real estate magnate. He worked as a merchant's clerk from 1802 to 1806 before setting up a real estate business in 1807. He owned nearly all the houses in the area bounded by 40th Street, Eighth Avenue, 13th Street, and 11th Avenue but lived in miserly circumstances in a one-room apartment on Broadway. He also bought stocks and collected materials associated with the history of the city, including autographs, maps, and directories. Rapelye was a friend of John Pintard, an organizer of the New-York Historical Society, and a vestryman of St. Thomas's Church on Broadway.

James E. Mooney

Rapp–Coudert Committee. Committee of the state legislature active during 1940–41. It was led by George Rapp of upstate New York and the very active co-chairman Frederic R. Coudert of the law firm Coudert Brothers. The committee originally was charged with investigating allegations of excessive spending in schools but soon shifted its focus toward purging communists from the municipal colleges and particularly from City College of New York and Brooklyn College. In addition to being centers of student radicalism, these colleges had large communist units among faculty and staff that published lively shop papers, demanded improved working conditions, led local chapters of the College Teachers Union (affiliated with the American Federation of Labor), and supported the Soviet Union on major issues. The committee induced informers to testify about communists on the campuses and then called those who were implicated to testify themselves; uncooperative faculty members were dismissed by the New York City Board of Higher Education. The committee abruptly halted its investigations when the Nazis invaded the Soviet Union, but after the war its work was continued by such arms of the U.S. Congress as the Internal Security Subcommittee of the Senate Judiciary Committee, which also adopted many of its techniques and employed some of its staff members. With the cooperation of the Board of Higher Education several professors at Brooklyn College who had been overlooked earlier were dismissed during the 1950s, as were scores of teachers in the city's elementary and secondary schools.

Ellen W. Schrecker, *No Ivory Tower: McCarthyism and the Universities* (New York: Oxford University Press, 1986)

Marvin E. Gettleman

Raritan Bay. Body of water at the southernmost point in New York City and State, at the confluence of the Raritan River, Arthur Kill, and Atlantic Ocean. Raritan Bay separates Middlesex and Monmouth counties (New Jersey) from the southern end of Staten Island, touching the neighborhoods of Tottenville and Pleasant Plains. The name *Raritan* derives from an Algonquin word meaning "stream overflows"; it was also an Indian tribe on Staten Island that existed before European settlement.

Clyde L. Mackenzie, Jr., *The Fisheries of Raritan Bay* (New Brunswick, N.J.: Rutgers University Press, 1992)

Andrew Sparberg

Raunt. Former neighborhood in south central Queens, lying on several marshy islands along a wide channel of the same name in Jamaica Bay; the name is of unknown origin. A fishing platform once stood on the southern shore of a marshy island facing the channel, and from July 1888 it was a station on the Cross Jamaica Bay line of the Long Island Rail Road. Small hotels on piles accommodated weekend fishing parties, and the area was soon favored by rod and gun clubs, but it was abandoned after the Board of Health declared Jamaica Bay too polluted for fishing in 1916. Railroad service was suspended after the railroad trestle was destroyed by fire on 7 May 1950. When the city rebuilt the line in 1956 as part of the rapid transit system, the channel was filled in.

Vincent Seyfried

Rauschenberg, Robert (*b* Port Arthur, Tex., 22 Oct 1925; *d* Captiva, Fla., 12 May 2008). Painter. Drafted into the Marines during World War II, he saw his first paintings while traveling in the service, in California at the Huntington Art Gallery. He first saw European paintings in 1943. After moving to New York City in 1949 he became acquainted with the composer John Cage and the choreographer Merce Cunningham (with whom he later collaborated) and began to experiment with the economical medium of blueprint paper. His display windows for the clothing store Bonwit Teller brought him to the attention of *Life* in 1951; critics disdained his exhibition of white oil paintings in the same year and his all-black paintings soon after. He then executed a series of "combine-paintings," in which he sought to communicate a coherent message through disparate images. These wildly imaginative, bizarre collages juxtaposed diverse everyday objects (one consisted of a paint-splattered bed and pillow). He won prizes at the Venice Biennale (1954) and the Corcoran Gallery (1955) and in 1958 was given a one-man show by Leo Castelli. Rauschenberg was a leading figure in the avant-garde movement and one of the founders of pop art. After suffering a stroke in 2002, he learned to paint with his left hand. His work was shown at major exhibitions in Paris (1981), at the Guggenheim (1997), and in Los Angeles (2005); these works are now in the Metropolitan Museum. He also photographed, choreographed, and took part in performance art.

Leslie Gourse

Rauschenbusch, Walter (*b* Rochester, N.Y., 4 Oct 1861; *d* Rochester, N.Y., 25 July 1918). Theologian. Educated as a minister in Rochester and abroad, he moved to New York City in 1886 as a pastor of the Second German Baptist Church. While ministering to his congregation during the blizzard of 1888 he contracted influenza that left him deaf. He had a strong social conscience, and after becoming acquainted with Henry George and studying economics and theology he helped to formulate the Social Gospel, a theology based on social reform. He became known nationally for his book *Christianity and the Social Order* (1907). Toward the end of his life Rauschenbusch was disillusioned by the social breakdown that he believed had contributed to World War I.

Paul M. Minus, *Walter Rauschenbusch: American Reformer* (New York: Macmillan, 1988)

James E. Mooney

Ravenswood. Former name for the shore of Long Island City in Queens along the East River. The land was acquired in 1814 and developed by Colonel George Gibbs, a businessman from Manhattan. After his death in 1833 his land was divided by three developers into nine estates, and from 1848 there were several fine mansions lining the shore. In 1875 the first commercial buildings were erected, and the mansions eventually became offices and boardinghouses. The area was heavily commercial by 1900. The name Ravenswood survives in that of the large housing project

Proposed development along the East River in Ravenswood, Long Island, near Hallett's Point, ca 1836

bounded by 34th Avenue, 24th Street, 36th Avenue, and 12th Street.

Vincent Seyfried

Ravitch, Richard (*b* New York City, 7 July 1933). Public official, lawyer, and businessman. After graduating from Columbia and receiving his law degree from Yale, he worked in Washington, D.C., in 1959–60. He then became a principal of the HRH Construction Corporation, where he was responsible for the development, financing, and construction of 45,000 units of affordable housing in New York City and other locations. In 1975 he was appointed by Governor Hugh Carey to serve as chairman of the New York State Urban Development Corporation (UDC), an agency with 30,000 dwelling units then under construction, which had become insolvent and faced bankruptcy. He designed a bailout plan for UDC, part of which involved the creation of the New York State Project Finance Agency to issue credit-worthy revenue bonds secured by UDC's federal subsidy payments. This, together with other actions, helped to restore New York State's fiscal credibility. Later in 1975 and in 1976 Ravitch assisted New York City and New York State officials in resolving the city's defaults.

In November 1979 Ravitch was appointed by Governor Carey chairman and CEO of the Metropolitan Transportation Authority (MTA). At the time the subway and bus systems, the Long Island Rail Road, and the commuter rail services that were to become Metro-North Railroad in 1983 were not in a state of good repair because of long-term disinvestment in the capital plant and equipment, poor maintenance, and inadequate management. Ravitch worked with the New York State legislature to increase capital funding, including selling bonds backed by future operating revenues; he also implemented the first MTA five-year capital programs (one for the commuter railoads, the other for the city's subway and bus systems), for 1982–86, which committed $8.5 billion in total to begin rebuilding the MTA transit network and to purchase new buses and subway and commuter rail cars. Ravitch was also able to convince the state to approve a set of regional taxes to provide increased operating subsidies for MTA services, while also asking the MTA Board to approve fare increases; he also argued for the need for a stable source of revenue for capital expenditures. Although he resigned as MTA chairman in August 1983, MTA's rebuilding efforts continued over the next 25 years at these increased levels, and transit services improved substantially. In addition, his effort to introduce a fare card in New York finally came to fruition with the introduction of Metrocard in the late 1990s. In part as a result of improved service, as well as the introduction of free bus to subway transfers, ridership on MTA services boomed.

Following his MTA service, he led an effort to recapitalize the Bowery Savings Bank. In 1989 he ran unsuccessfully for mayor. In 2008 Ravitch's attention returned to MTA issues, when he was asked by Governor David A. Patterson to head a commission charged with recommending long-term solutions to the authority's capital and operating funding problems. Paterson, who had assumed the position of governor in March 2008 when the elected governor, Eliot Spitzer, resigned, subsequently appointed Ravitch as lieutenant governor in July 2009.

Peter Derrick

Raymond, Henry (Jarvis) (*b* Lima, N.Y., 24 Jan 1820; *d* New York City, 18 June 1869). Newspaper editor and congressman. He began his career in journalism as an assistant to Horace Greeley at the weekly journal the *New Yorker* and in 1841 helped Greeley to publish the first *New York Tribune;* in 1843 he joined the *Courier and Enquirer,* published by James Watson Webb. With George Jones and several other bankers from Albany, New York, he launched the *New York Times* on 18 September 1851. The success of the newspaper helped Raymond's political career: he replaced Greeley as the principal advocate for such prominent Republicans as William H. Seward and Thurlow Weed, and he became a state assemblyman and lieutenant governor. In 1864 he led President Abraham Lincoln's reelection campaign and was elected to the U.S. Congress, but after Lincoln's death he espoused President Andrew Johnson's Reconstruction policy at a time when most Republicans had abandoned its racist principles; as a result his influence and that of the newspaper declined. Raymond eventually returned to the mainstream of the Republican Party and worked on rebuilding the *Times* until the end of his life.

Francis Brown, *Raymond of the Times* (New York: W. W. Norton, 1951)

Harrison Salisbury

Razaf, Andy (*b* Washington, D.C., 16 Dec 1895; *d* New York City, 3 Feb 1973). Lyricist. The son of a Malagasy nobleman and an African American woman, he moved to Manhattan in 1905 where for more than 50 years he was a songwriter in Harlem and Tin Pan Alley and on Broadway. Over the years he collaborated with many musicians, including his principal songwriting partners Fats Waller and Eubie Blake. Some of Razaf's most popular lyrics are those to the songs "Ain't Misbehavin'," "Honeysuckle Rose," and "Memories of You."

Barry Singer

RCA Corporation. Firm of radio and television equipment manufacturers, formed in 1919 as the Radio Corporation of America (RCA) at the urging of the U.S. Navy, which was convinced by wartime experience of the need for a communications system under U.S. ownership. The corporation was a monopoly that held all the patents in the new field of wireless communication. Its stock was controlled by such companies as General Electric and American Telephone and Telegraph under the leadership of Owen D. Young, later joined by Westinghouse. In broadcasting it also competed with Westinghouse, on the whole unsuccessfully until 1921, when David Sarnoff, then 30 years old, was brought in as the general manager and promptly broadcast the heavyweight boxing match between Jack Dempsey and Georges Carpentier to an audience of three million. Sarnoff then carried out his intention to manufacture radio receiver sets for less than $100 each and had sales in the hundreds of thousands each year. In 1926, with one station in Providence, Rhode Island,

"His Master's Voice," advertisement for RCA's Victor Phonograph

RCA went on the air as the newly incorporated National Broadcasting Company (NBC), which within a few months was operating on two networks. The federal government broke up the firm in the 1930s, and RCA became an independent corporation with NBC as its sole property. Among its many successes was the *Amos 'n' Andy Show,* to which half the receivers in the United States were tuned for each program. RCA helped to fund the construction of and operated out of 30 Rockefeller Plaza, known as the RCA Building upon its completion in 1933.

While having great success in broadcasting and the manufacture of radios, RCA allocated $1 million in 1935 for testing television, largely in an important research laboratory founded by Sarnoff. The firm launched commercial television in July 1941, but only a few hundred sets were able to receive the signals, and when war broke out the full production effort of RCA was given over to military purposes: its research staff had experience in developing radar and such other electronic systems as loran, sonar, and walkie-talkies, and many of the tubes designed for television sets were used in radar rooms. Sarnoff also went off to war, using as his entry a commission as a lieutenant colonel in the reserve of the Signal Corps that he had received in 1924 and his promotion to colonel in 1930. He served with General Dwight D. Eisenhower as a communications expert for the invasion of northern Europe and went with the troops to France, where he restored communications. Promoted to the rank of brigadier general, he returned to RCA by the end of 1944, where he resumed full control.

Postwar life for RCA and Sarnoff meant television, and the first sets began to reach the public in late 1946. During the next year a quarter of a million sets were sold, four-fifths of them made by RCA and all of them black and white. The Columbia Broadcasting System (CBS) was working on a color television but could not get its mechanical system approved by the Federal Communication Commission. Benefiting from this delay and from the resources of its electronics laboratory in suburban Princeton, New Jersey, RCA prevailed in the race to develop color television by successfully arguing to regulators that the approach to color television taken by CBS would be incompatible with the millions of monochrome sets in U.S. homes. As a result of this victory RCA had annual sales in the range of $100 million in the late 1950s and twice that in 1965 (by which time color sets accounted for half of total sales). In that year Sarnoff resigned as chief executive of the firm and became chairman. His son took over as president and introduced a number of changes, two of which were scorned by his father: the adoption by the firm of its acronym as its official name, and its expansion into such disparate businesses as automobile rentals, frozen foods, greeting cards, and office buildings. Sarnoff died in 1971; his son's contract was not renewed by the board in 1975.

Anthony Conrad's resignation from the board in 1976 and the failure of several commercial ventures left the firm with a debt of $1 billion by 1981. After a series of changes in management the firm reverted to its original businesses: electronics, communications, and entertainment. Sales and profits increased by the mid-1980s, but soon afterward a plan to acquire RCA was put forth by General Electric, and despite protests by some staff and stockholders, the acquisition was realized in 1986.

Kenneth Bilby, *The General: David Sarnoff and the Rise of the Communications Industry* (New York: Harper and Row, 1986)

James E. Mooney

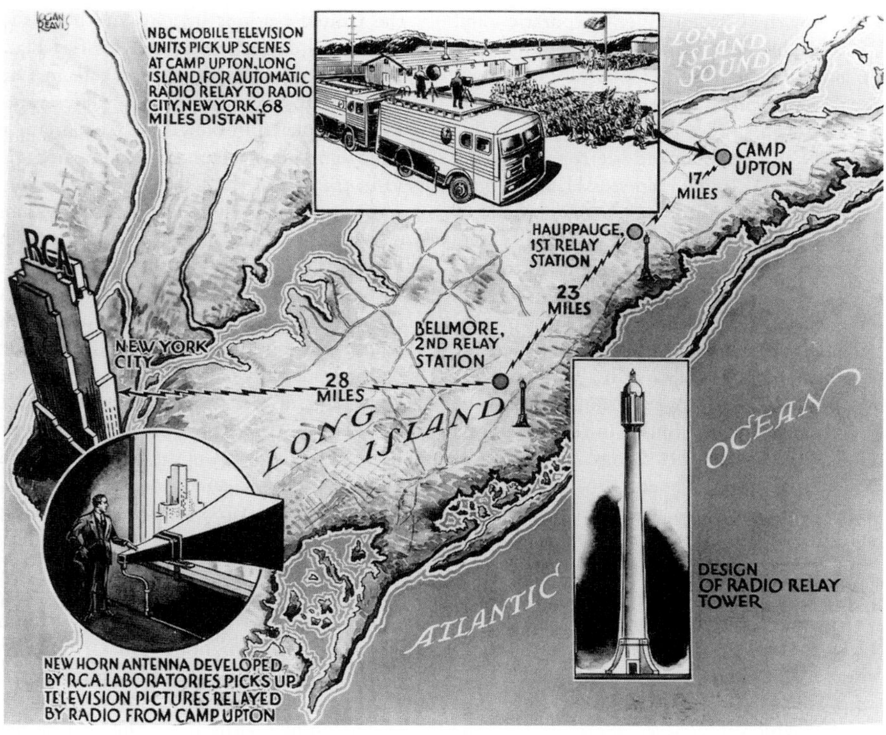

Illustration of RCA television relay

Reader's Digest. Monthly magazine, launched in 1922 from a basement office on Minetta Lane in Greenwich Village by DeWitt Wallace (1889–1981) and Lila Acheson Wallace (1889–1984). Only a few issues were published in New York City. In 1922 the office was moved to Pleasantville and then to Chappaqua, both in Westchester County. The company retained its Pleasantville mailing address in the early twenty-first century.

real estate. From colonial times the development of New York City was heavily influenced by shortages of land and housing that led city and state government aggressively to encourage investment and private development through urban planning, the provision of infrastructure, tax abatement, and other incentives. One of the city's first efforts toward this end was the implementation of a street plan in 1811 (see GRID PLAN). As the population increased and the developed city expanded northward, land in Manhattan gradually became scarce and valuable. During the first half of the nineteenth century John Jacob Astor became the wealthiest man in the United States largely by buying up land in the city; he built his empire in part by foreclosing on mortgages and buying land during the panic of 1837, when others could not afford to keep distressed property, and holding it until it regained value. During the second half of the century real estate developers gained readier access to debt and equity capital, as the city became the most important financial center in North America. The intense demand for increasingly limited space led developers to erect ever-taller buildings, and during the 1860s multistory office buildings, apartment buildings, and TENEMENTS were introduced. Apartments were generally designed for middle- and upper-class tenants; many began as luxury units for rent and were later owned cooperatively. Tenements covered virtually the entire lot on which they were built and could accommodate many tenants, allowing landlords to collect a large rental income; the high value of such properties deterred architects from incorporating open spaces and recreational facilities into their design. Overcrowding became so severe that the city enacted tenement regulations in 1867, the first in the United States. Efforts to relieve the housing crisis were made by a number of private concerns, among them the City and Suburban Homes Company of Alfred T. White, which during the late nineteenth century built model housing projects for workers. At the same time the number of skyscrapers increased, as did the number of loft buildings, which had rooms with open floors and high ceilings for use as workshops and showrooms.

As the rate of development increased, real estate interests became more highly organized, and public concern grew for controlling building standards more closely. One of the first trade publications, the weekly *Real Estate Record and Builders' Guide,* was launched in 1868 by the Real Estate Record Association, which later published the influential books *A History of Real Estate, Building, and Architecture in New York City* (1898) and Richard M. Hurd's *Principles of City Land Values* (1903), the first systematic attempt to analyze patterns of urban development in the United States. Hurd, president of the Lawyers Mortgage Company and vice president of the Mortgage Bond Company, was a leading lender for office and apartment buildings at the turn of the century. The Real Estate Board of New York (1896) was one of the first organizations of its kind in the country. From the 1890s private developers in the city vied with each other to build the world's tallest buildings, and successively taller skyscrapers were built: the Pulitzer and Flatiron buildings, the Times Tower, the Singer Building, the Metropolitan Life Tower, and the Woolworth Building (1913), which at nearly 800 feet (243 meters) held the record for almost two decades. Large-scale projects such as the Equitable Building, built by the Du Pont family in 1915, received a great deal of publicity and aroused much public concern, leading to demands for public control. About this time reformers sought to regulate development more tightly. Efforts to improve building standards, eliminate unsanitary conditions, and relieve overcrowding in tenements culminated in the Tenement House Law of 1901, which prescribed minimum standards for light, air, indoor plumbing, and other housing improvements. During the first decade of the twentieth century owners and tenants of office buildings, hotels, department stores, and boutiques fought to prevent the garment industry from building lofts in commercial districts; they eventually won such protection through ZONING. In 1916 the city implemented the country's first comprehensive zoning regulations controlling the height, bulk, and use of all private structures. The new zoning law required skyscrapers to be built with setbacks above a certain height, thus allowing more light, air, and open space between buildings and also leading to fundamental changes in the design of skyscrapers.

The 1920s saw a tremendous increase in the construction of residential housing and commercial buildings. Large-scale projects were undertaken by such developers as Fred F. French, Harry Black, Henry Mandel, Abraham E. Lefcourt, Irwin Chanin, Leo Bing, and Alexander Bing, financed by such lenders as Chase Manhattan Bank, Bowery Savings Bank, and Dime Savings Bank. Skyscrapers were concentrated near Wall Street and on lower Broadway until the 1920s, when the first ones were built around Grand Central Terminal. Midtown Manhattan soon flourished and became the site of the garment district after a number of developers led by Lefcourt built lofts along Seventh Avenue. By this time the city had more buildings of at least 20 stories than all other U.S. cities combined. Competition to build the world's tallest building escalated, and the Woolworth Building was surpassed by the Bank of Manhattan (1929), followed by the Chrysler Building (1930).

An acute housing shortage led the city to introduce property tax benefits and bold policies for encouraging the construction of more housing. Various philanthropic organizations and limited-dividend ventures also sought to promote innovative residential planning and to reduce rents and the cost of housing. They built such developments as Forest Hills Gardens, a middle-income community in Queens financed by the Russell Sage Foundation and designed by Frederick Law Olmsted, Jr., and Grosvenor Atterbury; the Paul Lawrence Dunbar apartment buildings in Harlem, built by the Rockefeller family; and Sunnyside Gardens in Queens, sponsored by the City Housing Corporation and planned by Alexander Bing and the architects Clarence S. Stein and Henry Wright. Large-scale developments were also undertaken by such life insurance companies as Equitable Life, New York Life, and Metropolitan Life, which in 1924 under Frederick H. Ecker built Sunnyside, a 2125-unit apartment complex in Queens. The greatest number of units were built by limited-dividend cooperative housing organizations, often formed by labor unions; the largest was the United Housing Foundation of the Amalgamated Clothing Workers, directed for six decades by Abraham E. Kazan. Its first projects, completed in the 1920s, were the Amalgamated Houses in the Bronx and the Amalgamated Dwellings on the Lower East Side. Building codes for apartment buildings improved, especially under the Multiple Dwellings Law of 1929, which strengthened minimum housing quality and development standards.

Real estate developments grew in scale and increasingly attracted the public's attention. Publicity focused on such projects as the Empire State Building, financed by the Du Pont family, which at 1250 feet (381 meters) was the world's tallest building from its completion in 1931 until the World Trade Center surpassed it in the mid-1970s. Rockefeller Center, built by the Rockefeller family in the 1930s, was even more ambitious and costly and became a model for mixed-use projects with buildings containing offices and retail space. In addition to these spectacular successes, the high cost of property and the importance of the real estate market in the local economy also caused devastating failures, such as that of French in the Depression. During these years the New York City Housing Authority began erecting PUBLIC HOUSING; the number of units reached 175,000 by the mid-1990s. City government also encouraged private development by expanding public infrastructure, a practice engaged in to an unprecedented degree by Robert Moses, who oversaw the construction and maintenance of bridges, highways, parks, and such public projects as the world's fairs of 1939–40 and 1964–65 in Flushing Meadow. Government agencies and special public authorities also built tunnels, airports, and convention centers. The Metropolitan Life Insurance Company sponsored Parkchester, a complex of more than 12,000 apartments in the Bronx opened in 1941, as well as Stuyvesant Town and Peter Cooper Village on the East Side and Riverton in Harlem, which became prototypes for national redevelopment programs. In the 1950s the state and city introduced the MITCHELL–LAMA program of subsidized mortgages and property tax abatements for the construction of middle-income rental housing. Urban renewal projects were undertaken by the private developer William Zeckendorf, who assembled the land for the site of the United Nations in 1946 and built such residential developments as Kips Bay Plaza, Lincoln Towers, and Park West Village. During the 1940s and 1950s, 30 major skyscrapers were completed in New York City (many of them in midtown Manhattan), compared with 10 in the rest of the United States. By mid-century multifamily housing occupied most of Manhattan and much of Brooklyn, the Bronx, and Queens.

The pace of development accelerated and the price of property in the city rose. By the 1960s office towers dominated midtown Manhattan, especially Park Avenue, and the redevelopment of lower Manhattan resulted in the construction of the Chase Manhattan Bank and the planning of the World Trade Center. The city cleared a number of sites for urban renewal projects, among them the site of Lincoln Center for the Performing Arts. Many developers prospered, including HRH–Starrett, Tishman Speyer, Rose Associates, the Trump Organization, Levitt and Sons, the Durst Organization, and Helmsley–Spear; a decline in the market forced Zeckendorf into bankruptcy in 1965. Under the leadership of Austin Tobin the Port of New York Authority built much of the region's infrastructure as well as the World Trade Center, an office complex dominated by twin towers 1350 feet (411 meters) tall. Programs to build and rehabilitate rental housing, condominiums, and cooperatives were begun by nonprofit community development corporations, sometimes using "sweat equity," under which prospective owners and tenants rehabilitated buildings with their own labor. During the 1960s and 1970s the city led the nation in generating capital for real estate investment trusts (REITs). Under Kazan the United Housing Foundation in the late 1960s and early 1970s built Co-op City in the Bronx, one of the largest residential complexes in the world (15,372 units). During a slump in the city's real estate market in 1977 the Canadian firm of Olympia and York attracted international attention by buying eight office buildings at "distress" prices: when the market later improved, the value of the buildings quadrupled. In the 1980s public authorities built the new communities of Roosevelt Island and Battery Park City, both highly successful; Battery Park City in the mid-1980s became the site of the World Financial Center, a flourishing development by Olympia and York. Homeownership programs for low- and middle-income families in the outer boroughs were sponsored by the East Brooklyn Congregations and churches in the southern Bronx, and by the New Homes Program of the New York City Housing Partnership, inspiring similar efforts by other community builders. The developer Donald Trump amassed real estate holdings worth billions of dollars; he experienced severe financial difficulties, as did Olympia and York, after a decline in the real estate market brought on by the stock market crash of 1987 and the loss of jobs in financial services. The downturn in prices continued well into the next decade. By 1993 the crime rate in the city began to fall, and financial services employment began to rise. The recovery of the real estate market followed, and by the turn of the twenty-first century, New York City was booming once again and the suburbs began to lose relative to Manhattan.

The terrorist attacks on the World Trade Center on 11 September 2001 persuaded many observers that high-rise development would be less attractive and that both employers and citizens would flee from the dense environment of Manhattan. Such predictions proved to be wrong, as new towers for corporate headquarters began to soar in midtown, such as the Bloomberg, New York Times, Hearst, and Time Warner buildings. High-end residential buildings of considerable height also began to answer a strong demand for luxury units in Manhattan. Neighborhoods became more desirable in all five boroughs. Particularly significant was the transformation of older industrial sections, such as DUMBO and Williamsburgh in Brooklyn and the meatpacking district and the Bowery in Manhattan. Hotels, bars, and boutiques soon followed.

Eugene Rachlis and John E. Marquesee, *The Land Lords* (New York: Random House, 1963); Tom Shachtman, *Skyscraper Dreams: The Great Real Estate Dynasties of New York* (Boston: Little, Brown, 1991)

See also HOUSING.

Marc A. Weiss

Real Estate Board of New York [REBNY]. Trade association of real estate brokers formed in 1896 as the Real Estate Board of Brokers. Among its forerunners were the New York Real Estate Exchange (1847), the first real estate trade organization in the United States (which lasted only a year), and the Real Estate Exchange of the City of New York, formed in 1885 by property owners and brokers to standardize practices and win public confidence in real estate transactions; the latter worked closely with trade magazine REAL ESTATE RECORD AND BUILDERS' GUIDE (1868). In 1904 REBNY introduced an education program at the West Side YMCA that was one of the first of its kind; it supported the city's 1916 ZONING law and took part in national efforts to introduce licensing for real estate agents. In 2008 it had about 12,000 members, including developers, brokers, property owners, managers, and lenders. REBNY works as an advocate for tax policies and other public programs to encourage real estate development in the city, and supports education and research programs.

Pearl Janet Davies, *Real Estate in American History* (Washington, D.C.: Public Affairs Press, 1958); Tom Shachtman, *Skyscraper Dreams: The Great Real Estate Dynasties of New York* (Boston: Little, Brown, 1991)

Marc A. Weiss

Real Estate Record and Builders' Guide. Weekly trade publication for the real estate and building industries of Greater New York. It was launched in 1868 by Clinton W. Sweet, the publisher for four decades. The journal was at its peak during the late nineteenth century when Manhattan developed into the hub of the integrated metropolitan area. It made itself indispensable to large development interests in the city by publishing regular, accurate, and geographically comprehensive reports of lot transactions, mortgage rates, and failures; copies of building plans and tabulations of building costs that helped to rationalize the metropolitan markets in real estate, credit, and building supplies; and "insider" columns and editorials. With the West Side Association, the powerful defender of property owners' interests, it advocated a visionary program of planned growth through comprehensive park, street, transit, and other public improvements, and it was an early supporter of using planning and landscape design to coordinate private development. Although its influence over development policies and planning debates declined early in the twentieth century, the *Record and Guide* continued to be published into the twenty-first century.

David Scobey

Recovery Party. Party label used during the three-way mayoral election of 1933 by Joseph V. McKee, who was running against John P. O'Brien and Fiorello H. La Guardia. McKee, who had served briefly as acting mayor of New York City after James J. Walker resigned in September 1932, had counted on support from Franklin D. Roosevelt that never materialized. McKee outpolled the incumbent mayor, O'Brien, but the winner was the fusion candidate, La Guardia.

Frank Vos

recreation piers. According to its charters, New York City initially had use of its waterfront only for shipping and commerce, but in 1892 these restrictions were eased by the state legislature, which permitted the upper stories of certain piers to be set aside for public use. In 1897 the Third Street Recreation Pier at Corlear's Hook was built by the Dock Department; measuring 350 by 60 feet (107 by 18 meters), it had space on the first story for landing produce and a pavilion in a French Renaissance style with seating for 500 on the second story. Similar facilities were soon opened on the East River at 112th Street and on the Hudson River at Christopher and at 50th streets. Attendants were present and offerings included music on weekday evenings, inexpensive food concessions, and free milk. By the time of World War II the oldest recreation piers were closed. During the 1980s the city and state opened unused piers in Manhattan, Brooklyn, and Queens for fishing, sunning, and jogging. Food concessions, shopping, and cultural programs were introduced at the foot of Wall Street (at Piers 15–17 in South Street Seaport); a pavilion built by Robert Moses at 107th Street was refurbished for fishing and community events; and indoor sports were offered in the Cromwell Recreation Center, a renovated commercial pier shed built in 1936 in an art deco style at the foot of Victory Boulevard in Tompkinsville. Pier 84 on the Hudson became the site of rock concerts during the summer. In the early 1990s the city and state began renovating piers on the Hudson between Battery Park City and West 72nd Street for recreational use. By 2008 plans were complete for the transformation of Pier 15 on the East River in Manhattan and former Port Authority piers below Brooklyn Heights in Brooklyn.

Ann L. Buttenwieser

recycling. New York City generates more refuse than any other city in the United States:

Recycling signs, 2009

nearly 41,000 tons (37,195 metric tons) each day. The need to recycle became especially pressing during the 1980s as the environmental hazards of burning garbage became more apparent and landfills rapidly neared capacity (the city's only operating landfill, at Fresh Kills on Staten Island, was closed in March 2001; it was temporarily reopened to accept waste after the terrorist attacks of 11 September 2001). A state law requiring a deposit on most glass bottles and aluminum cans in which beverages are sold was enacted in 1982 and took effect in the following year. The city's recycling program began in earnest with the passage in 1989 of Local Law 19, a measure intended to combat the air pollution caused by large-scale incineration of garbage. In 1992 the city began phasing in mandatory recycling, and by 1997 residents of all five boroughs were required to place newspapers, magazines, corrugated cardboard, glass, metal, plastic containers, and aluminum foil in special containers or clear plastic bags. The materials are collected by sanitation workers and then stored until they can be processed for resale to manufacturers. Superintendents in apartment buildings must provide space and bins for their residents, and sanitation enforcement officers are authorized to ensure that recyclable materials are not discarded along with garbage; fines for violations range from $25 to $500. In 2002 Mayor Michael Bloomberg announced plans to eliminate glass, plastic, paper, and metal recycling because of a budget deficit. Public opposition led metal and paper recycling to be retained, and collection of glass and plastic recyclables returned in 2004 when the city signed a 20-year contract with the Hugo Neu Corporation to recycle glass, metal, plastic, and eventually paper.

Materials collected through municipal recycling increased 54 percent from 1991 to 1992. In 1993 13 percent of the city's residential refuse was being diverted from landfills and incinerators to recycling plants. The figure rose to 20 percent by 2001 but had dropped to 13 percent in 2006.

Jacqueline Lalley

Red Hook. Neighborhood in southwestern Brooklyn (2000 pop. *ca* 10,200), occupying a peninsula of 680 acres (275 hectares) that is bounded to the northeast by the Gowanus Expressway and the entrance to the Brooklyn–Battery Tunnel, to the south by Gowanus Bay, to the west by Upper New York Bay, and to the northwest by Buttermilk Channel. Settled by the Dutch in 1636, initially for farms and mills in the wetlands, the area was called Roode Hoek for the color of its soil and its shape, and for 200 years it remained a marshy, rural enclave. The opening of Atlantic Basin in the 1840s, with its influx of Scandinavian, German, and Irish workers, brought about rapid maritime, industrial, and residential development in the 1850s, and the area became one of the busiest shipping centers in the nation; it was the second row-house district to be extensively developed in Brooklyn (after Brooklyn Heights). By the time of the Civil War ships from all over the world docked at Red Hook to receive and unload cargo and for repair where William Beard's wharves and warehouses serviced Union forces. Hundreds of grain barges from the Erie Canal clustered at the mouth of the Gowanus Canal; there were also a few shipyards such as Todd Shipyards from the 1860s until 1985. The neighborhood at the turn of the century, known generally as South Brooklyn because it was south of the original city of Brooklyn, was a tough, lively, bustling place where Al Capone worked as a petty criminal before moving to Chicago. Although dominated by Italian dockworkers, it also had a small but thriving colony of immigrants from Puerto Rico and from the Middle East centered along Atlantic Avenue. In 1936 the Red Hook Houses and the Red Hook Recreation Center were built for the families of the dockworkers. This was one of the first housing projects in the city and also one of the largest, and continued into the 1990s to house most of the local residents. The ambience of the neighborhood in the 1930s and 1940s is conveyed in Arthur Miller's play *The View from the Bridge,* Elia Kazan's film *On the Waterfront,* Hubert Selby's novel *Last Exit to Brooklyn.* and H. P. Lovecraft's short story "The Horror at Red Hook."

The deterioration of Red Hook was brought on by the construction of the Gowanus Expressway (1964), the Brooklyn–Queens Expressway (1957), and the Brooklyn–Battery Tunnel (1950), which cleaved the waterfront from Columbia Street (which eventually reemerged as the Columbia Street Waterfront District) and the rest of the neighborhood, and the neighborhood from the rest of the city. After reaching 25,000 in 1960 the population declined sharply. The chief means of employment, break-bulk shipping, was displaced in the 1960s by container shipping. In 1964 the city decided to replace much of the neighborhood with a container port that opened in 1981, but although this consumed much land it provided little employment, as most shipping activity had already shifted to New Jersey. The neighborhood became desolate and poor with high crime statistics; eventually some 90 percent of the population was African American or Latin American. They organized into two sections: "The Front" or "The Houses" and "The Back" or "The Point."

Red Hook, 2009

The Fishport at Erie Basin, operating briefly in 1987–88, did little to help, but the late 1980s saw a slow, hopeful renaissance along Columbia Street. With notoriously poor public transportation, the principal commercial thoroughfares remain Atlantic Avenue and Court and Smith streets.

In recent years, Red Hook has developed as an attractive neighborhood with townhouses, warehouse condos, and rental apartments. Artists have acquired subsidized housing and have created the Brooklyn Waterfront Artists' Coalition; the Hudson Waterfront Museum, a former railway barge, is docked at Conover Street; and the Pier 41 Association, another artists' group, has been formed. The Red Hook Waterfront Arts Festival includes opera performances on decommissioned ships. Controversy over land use and gentrification have attended the neighborhood's transformation. In 1996 Home Depot, the first "big box store," appeared in the area. Restoration of the Beard Street piers by developer Greg O'Connell included the arrival of Fairway Foods. In 2006 Carnival Cruise Lines took over Pier 12 to dock their "Princess" ships and their Cunard Lines, the QM2, or Queen Mary 2. In 2006 the Swedish furniture store IKEA opened and began providing free transportation out of Red Hook by bus or water taxi. The same year the abandoned Revere Sugar Works factory was demolished, and Thor Equities planned to build on the cleared space. Meanwhile, the Visitation Roman Catholic Church (1897) continued as a bulwark, and from the row houses on Visitation Place, people could reconnect to the waterfront when visiting several new restaurants and microbreweries such as the Liberty Heights Taproom.

Toby Sanchez, *Red Hook Neighborhood Profile* (New York: Brooklyn in Touch Information Center, 1986); Kenneth Jackson and John Manbeck, eds., *The Neighborhoods of Brooklyn,* 2nd edn (New Haven: Yale University Press, 2004)

Ellen Fletcher, John J. Gallagher

Reed, John (Silas) (*b* Portland, Ore., 22 Oct 1887; *d* Moscow, 19 Oct 1920). Journalist and revolutionist. Educated at Harvard University, he moved to New York City to work for the *American Magazine,* where he became acquainted with Lincoln Steffens and Ida M. Tarbell; he then went to work for *The Masses,* was imprisoned for supporting strikers, and worked as a war correspondent in Mexico and Europe for *Metropolitan Magazine.* He lived at 42 Washington Square South (1911–12) until moving to the mansion of Mabel Dodge at 23 Fifth Avenue (1913–14). In January 1916 he began living with Louise Bryant at 43 Washington Square South. Declared ineligible for military service for reasons of health, he traveled to Russia, witnessed the October Revolution, and wrote articles for *The Masses* that led to charges of sedition. On his return to the city he lived briefly at 1 Patchin Place before settling in the autumn of 1918 at 147 West Fourth Street where he wrote his best-known work, *Ten Days That Shook the World* (1919). After a number of problems with the law he escaped to Russia using a forged passport but soon died of typhus. He is buried with Lenin and several other Soviet leaders in Red Square in Moscow.

David C. Duke, *John Reed* (Boston: Twayne, 1987)

James E. Mooney

Reed, Lou(is Alan) (*b* Brooklyn, 2 March 1942). Singer and songwriter. He grew up on Long Island, learned to play the guitar, and earned his BA at Syracuse University, where he studied with the poet Delmore Schwartz. In 1963 Reed moved to New York City, accepting a job as a staff songwriter at Pickwick Records. With John Cale (with whom he lived on the Lower East Side) he led the Velvet Underground from 1965 to 1970, a rock group inspired by the work and ideas of the artist Andy Warhol. The poignant and often lurid imagery of its music violated taboos by evoking such themes as sadomasochism and heroin addiction, and stood in sharp contrast to the innocence and optimism of much popular music of the late 1960s. The group was regularly seen at the Manhattan nightclub Max's Kansas City. After the group disbanded, Reed's work was extremely erratic; his most accomplished record albums include *The Blue Mask* (1982, with the guitarist Robert Quine), and *Songs for Drella* (1990, with Cale), a tribute to Warhol. Much of Reed's work has incorporated his New York roots, including the albums *Coney Island Baby* (1976) and *New York* (1989) and a book of photographs, *Lou Reed's New York* (2006). He has performed with avant-garde performance artist Laurie Anderson, whom he married in 2008. Although best known for his low monotone voice and abrasive guitar style, Reed is more highly regarded by critics for his lyrics and his poetry.

Gene Santoro

Reed, Luman (*b* Green River, N.Y., 4 Jan 1785; *d* New York City, 7 June 1836). Merchant and art patron. Brought up in Coxsackie, New York, on the Hudson River, in 1815 he moved to New York City and opened a produce shop at 13 Coenties Slip; in 1821 he established the mercantile firm of Reed and Lee at 125–27 Front Street. His neoclassical mansion at 13 Greenwich Street was designed by Isaac Green Pearson and completed in 1832; he converted the third story into a private art gallery. Initially a collector of works by Flemish, Dutch, German, and Italian masters, he was inspired by patriotism to buy paintings by American artists. From Thomas Cole he commissioned "The Course of Empire," a series of five paintings, and he gathered portraits and historical and genre paintings by Asher B. Durand, William Sidney Mount, and George W. Flagg (1816–97) to fill his gallery, which opened to the public once a week (it was one of a few institutions with public viewing hours). He was a member of the Sketch Club (circa 1834) and a patron and honorary member of the National Academy of Design (1834). In 1844 Reed's collection was bought by his son-in-law Theodore Allen (1800–50) and his business partner Jonathan Sturges to form the New-York Gallery of the Fine Arts (1844–58); the collection was given to the New-York Historical Society in 1858.

Wayne Craven, "Luman Reed, Patron: His Collection and Gallery," *American Art Journal* 12 (Spring 1980), 40–59; Ella M. Foshay, *Mr. Luman Reed's Picture Gallery: A Pioneer Collection of American Art* (New York: Harry N. Abrams/New-York Historical Society, 1990)

Timothy Anglin Burgard, Ella M. Foshay

Reed, Willis, Jr. (*b* Hico, La., 25 Jul 1942). Basketball player. He played for the New York Knickerbockers from 1964 to 1974, leading the team to its only two National Basketball Association (NBA) championships in 1970 and 1973. Reed is best remembered for his performance in the 1970 NBA finals when after missing game six of the series with a torn thigh muscle he limped onto the Madison Square Garden court and scored the Knicks' first four points of the decisive game seven, igniting the crowd and inspiring the team to victory over the Los Angeles Lakers. Reed retired in 1974 with a career average of 18.7 points and 12.9 rebounds per game. He later coached the Knicks (1977–78), worked in the front office of multiple NBA teams, was enshrined in the Basketball Hall of Fame (1982), and was named one of the 50 greatest players in NBA history (1996).

Ben Silk

Reformed Church in America. Protestant denomination originally known as the Dutch Reformed Church. Its first congregation in New Amsterdam was formed in 1628 and administered by Jonas Michaëlius, who reported 50 communicants at the first communion that he celebrated there. This was the official church of the colony, and through its influence Dutch Calvinism expanded steadily under the supervision of the classis of Amsterdam. After the English assumed control in 1664, they aggressively replaced Dutch customs and institutions with English ones. Little resistance was offered by Dutch merchants and traders or by Dutch ministers, or dominies, who felt compelled to cooperate in the interest of preserving their freedom to worship: they generally won a measure of autonomy from English magistrates, despite Governor Edmund Andros's efforts to install a dominie with Anglican orders in the Dutch Reformed Church in Albany, New York. Irked by the economic hardship incurred during the English conquest, many congregations disputed the salaries of dominies willing to assimilate. In 1689 Jacob Leisler led an uprising of lower-class Dutch settlers against Andros, English rule, and a perceived threat of papism, and soon the rebels also found themselves pitted against the dominies and the Dutch mercantile elite (see LEISLER'S REBELLION). When the rebellion was put down in 1691, Henricus Selyns, minister of the Dutch Reformed Church in New York City, lambasted Leisler and praised the restoration of political order. He later persuaded Governor Henry Sloughter to sign the warrant for Leisler's execution. During the following decade the Dutch Reformed Church was torn by feuding between supporters and opponents of Leisler, whose rebellion came to be viewed as a protest against assimilation to English ways; control of church offices was sought by both factions. In 1698 supporters were permitted by the governor to exhume the bodies of Leisler and Jacob Milborne, his lieutenant, which were reinterred in the city's Dutch church after a cavalcade through the streets. Tensions within the Reformed Church eased somewhat as many of Leisler's supporters moved to New Jersey to escape political and ecclesiastical factionalism. A greater degree of harmony was restored after Selyns's death in 1701.

For the first half of the eighteenth century Gualtherus Du Bois led the city's Dutch Reformed churches, which faced steady attrition owing in part to the success of the Society for the Propagation of the Gospel (1701), an organization of Anglican missionaries who distributed the Book of Common Prayer in Dutch and also opened schools that taught Anglican theology and English. The society's efforts were reinforced by several governors who sought to advance Anglicanism, which they considered the official religion of the colony according to the Ministry Act of 1693. Education was left increasingly to Anglicans as the Dutch churches allowed their own schools to decline. Recognizing that the future of the colony lay with the English, many young people became Anglicans and Presbyterians, and to encourage their return to the Dutch church, congregants at mid-century called on Du Bois to appoint an English-speaking minister. William Livingston, publisher of the *Independent Reflector,* lamented the "melancholy declension" of the Dutch churches because the young, "forgetting the religion of their ancestors, wandered in search of new persuasions"; he himself had left the Dutch Reformed Church because he could not understand the Dutch language. In 1763 the Dutch church in the city engaged Archibald Laidlie, an English-speaking minister who had graduated from the University of Edinburgh. His sermons soon drew three times as many congregants as those of Dutch dominies. By the time of the American Revolution the Dutch Reformed Church was one denomination among many in the city. The denomination took its present name in 1867 and remained active in the early twenty-first century. One of its better-known congregations was the MARBLE COLLEGIATE CHURCH in Manhattan.

John M. Murrin, "English Rights as Ethnic Aggression: The English Conquest, the Charter of Liberties of 1683, and Leisler's Rebellion in New York," *Authority and Resistance in Early New York,* ed. William Pencak and Conrad Edick Wright (New York: New-York Historical Society, 1988), 56–94; Richard W. Pointer, *Protestant Pluralism and the New York Experience: A Study of Eighteenth-Century Religious Diversity* (Bloomington: Indiana University Press, 1988); Randall Balmer, *A Perfect Babel of Confusion: Dutch Religion and English Culture in the Middle Colonies* (New York: Oxford University Press, 1989)

Randall Balmer

Reformed Church of South Bushwick. Church at 15 Himrod Street in Brooklyn, organized in 1851. Known as the White Church, it is a white-frame structure with Greek Revival elements, a central tower, and a steeple.

Kenneth T. Jackson

Reformed Dutch Church of Newtown. One-story church at 85-15 Broadway in Elmhurst. Erected in 1831 in Greek Revival style, it is one of the city's few remaining churches built entirely of wood. The building replaced a small octagonal church built in 1735 in the colonial settlement of Newtown that the British used as a powder magazine in 1780. The 1970s saw many Asian immigrants move into the neighborhood, and a Taiwanese ministry was initiated in August 1980. This influx of immigrants led to the creation of a second head pastor position to minister in Taiwanese and Tamil. In 1995 the church began offering services in Mandarin. It is part of the Reformed Church in America.

Amanda Aaron

Reformed Episcopal Church. Religious movement launched at a meeting in the Young Men's Christian Association Hall (Fourth Avenue and 23rd Street) on 2 December 1873 by George David Cummins. Its formation was the result of a breach opened in the 1840s between the evangelical wing of the Protestant Episcopal Church (of which Cummins, the assistant bishop of Kentucky, was a member) and the Anglo-Catholic movement (which entered the church through the General Theological Seminary of New York City), and more immediately of Cummins's participation in the closing communion service of the Evangelical Alliance in New York City (2–12 October 1873), for which he received a severe censure from Bishop Horatio Potter that led him to resign from the church on 10 November. The new movement advocated a moderate episcopacy but failed to attract many evangelicals and suffered a serious setback when Cummins died in 1876; its national membership never grew beyond 12,000 (in the 1920s). The Reformed Episcopalians at one time had 12 parishes in New York City, but in 2008 only the First Reformed Episcopal Church on East 50th Street remained.

Allen C. Guelzo, *For the Union of Evangelical Christendom: The Irony of the Reformed Episcopalians, 1873–1930* (University Park: Pennsylvania State University Press, 1994)

Allen C. Guelzo

Reformed Protestant Dutch Church. Church at 630 New Lots Avenue in Brooklyn, also known as the New Lots Community Church and the New Lots Reformed Dutch Church. The building was erected in 1823 by local Dutch farmers who had grown weary of the weekly trek to the Flatbush Reformed Church. A registered landmark, it is a simple wood clapboard church with a pitched roof, an impressive steeple, and Gothic Revival stained-glass windows.

Kenneth T. Jackson

Regional Plan Association of New York [RPA]. Private organization formed in 1929 to implement the *Regional Plan of New York and Its Environs,* a study comprising 10 preliminary and two final volumes proposed by the Committee on the Regional Plan of New York and Its Environs, which was founded in 1922. RPA superseded the committee, which continued to function until the two organizations completed their merger in 1931. Among the many experts in urban development who contributed to the plan were Edward Bassett, the attorney who wrote the zoning law of 1916; Clarence Arthur Perry, who developed the concept of the "neighborhood unit"; Raymond Unwin, founder of the urban planning program at Columbia University; and other well-known planners such as Harland Bartholomew, Edward Bennett, and George Ford. The authors of the plan proposed a detailed system of land use and transportation improvements for Manhattan, the outer boroughs, and surrounding areas in New York State, New Jersey, and Connecticut. They intended to maintain the New York metropolitan region as the economic center of the United States by strengthening the financial and commercial centers, improving the upper-income residential areas of Manhattan, and dispersing manufacturing throughout the region. Special attention was given to highway and bridge construction and to the preservation of open space. Upon the plan's release funds for monitoring its success were granted by the Russell Sage Foundation.

With the support of the Ford Foundation and the Rockefeller Brothers Fund the association sponsored further planning studies during the 1950s and early 1960s, including the New York Metropolitan Region Study, directed by the economist Raymond Vernon, and *Spread City,* an influential forecast of suburban sprawl published in 1962.

C. McKim Norton, son of Charles Dyer Norton and president of the RPA, guided the preparation of the *Second Regional Plan* in 1968. The plan proposed to control suburbanization in the region and revitalize its core by coordinating the construction of office buildings and the planning of public transit; building the Citicorp Center, the World Trade Center, and new plazas and arcades in Manhattan; reviving downtown Brooklyn; and redeveloping the region's waterfronts. In 1996 the RPA released *A Region at Risk: The Third Regional Plan for the New York–New Jersey–Connecticut Metropolitan Region,* which urged cooperation between the public and private sector in improving the metropolitan region and was organized into five areas: greensward, mobility, centers, workforce, and governance. In the early twenty-first century the RPA remained actively involved in the future of the metropolitan region, including the redevelopment of lower Manhattan after the terrorist attacks of 11 September 2001, the transfer of Governors Island to the people of New York in 2003, and improving the region's rapid transit system.

Forbes B. Hays, *Community Leadership: The Regional Plan Association of New York* (New York: Columbia University Press, 1965)

John T. Metzger, Marc A. Weiss

Regis High School. Jesuit day school for boys at 55 East 84th Street, opened in 1914. Its building, designed by the firm of Maginnis and Walsh, was completed in 1917 and later designated a city landmark. The school is known for its competitive admissions and rigorous academic program, and all its students receive scholarships covering all expenses except laboratory and activity fees. In 2005 it enrolled 530 students drawn from the entire metropolitan area, including New Jersey and Connecticut.

Gilbert Tauber

Rego Park. Neighborhood in east central Queens, bounded to the north by Queens Boulevard, to the east by Yellowstone Boulevard, to the south by the intersection of Yellowstone and Woodhaven boulevards, and to the west by Woodhaven Boulevard. The name is derived from that of the Real Good Construction Company, which developed the neighborhood in the 1920s. Until 1920 the area was covered by farms and had one road, Remsen's Lane (now 63rd Drive, Fleet Court, and 64th Road), which abutted the Zeiler farm; for several years Chinese farmers who kept strictly to themselves grew vegetables there for sale in Chinatown. The Rego Construction Company bought out the farms during the 1920s and built one-family row houses, multi-family houses, and apartment buildings, and in 1923 the area was named by the developers Henry Schloh and Charles I. Hausmann. The core of the development was 525 eight-room houses costing $8000 each; the first stores were built in 1926 on Queens Boulevard and 63rd Drive. Apartment buildings were erected in 1927–28, among them Jupiter Court, Remo Hall, and Marion Court. A railroad station was open from 1928 to 1967. The IND subway line to Union Turnpike began service on 31 December 1936. In 1939–40 the World's Fair spurred development. The city's first Howard Johnson restaurant was built on Queens Boulevard for the fair (demolished 1969). The Rego Park Jewish Center was dedicated in 1948. In 1945 construction began on the Long Island Expressway from the Brooklyn Queens Expressway through Rego Park. Part of the neighborhood south of the boulevard with handsome single-family homes is known as the Crescents for the concentric curving streets. Lefrak City (1962–67), a huge housing complex adjacent to the Long Island Expressway, at first was predominantly Irish, German, and Italian, but in the 1970s it attracted many immigrants from the Soviet Union and Asia. About 15 percent of the immigrants settling in Rego Park in the 1980s were Chinese, but many more were Jews from the Soviet Union, Iran, and Israel; there were also enclaves of Indians, Colombians, Koreans, and Romanians. The population in 2008 was about 25,000: half white, 27 percent Asian, 16 percent Hispanic. Queens Boulevard remains a lively retail center, with several national chains as well as local businesses.

Vincent Seyfried

Reid, Whitelaw (*b* near Xenia, Ohio, 27 Oct 1837; *d* London, 15 Dec 1912). Journalist and diplomat. After covering the Civil War for the *Cincinnati Gazette* he joined the staff of the *New York Tribune* in 1868. On Horace Greeley's death in 1872 he became the principal owner and editor in chief of the newspaper and was considered by many to be the nation's most influential Republican editor. He relinquished active editorship of the *Tribune* in 1889 but retained financial control. In the same year he was appointed minister to France by President Benjamin Harrison, and in 1892 he returned to the United States and was the unsuccessful Republican candidate for vice president. He became President Theodore Roosevelt's ambassador to Great Britain in 1905, a position he held until his death.

Bingham Duncan, *Whitelaw Reid: Journalist, Politician, Diplomat* (Athens: University of Georgia Press, 1975)

Steven H. Jaffe

Reinhardt, Ad(olf D. Frederick) (*b* Buffalo, N.Y., 24 Dec 1913; *d* New York City, 30 Aug 1967). Painter. He grew up in Brooklyn and Queens and studied at Columbia University from 1931 to 1935. While working in a studio next to Stuart Davis's in 1938 he began a series of brightly colored abstract paintings inspired partly by what he called Davis's "loud ragtime jazz records" and "loud colored shirts on the clothes-line." Reinhardt had his first major exhibition in 1946 at the Betty Parsons Gallery. Unlike most other painters of the New York School, he opposed painterly expressionism and decried what he considered the corrupt relationship of artists, dealers, and critics (especially Clement Greenberg). During the 1940s he drew cartoons for the newspaper *PM* that satirized the art world and was himself the subject of "Pure Paints a Picture" (1957), a spoof written by Elaine de Kooning. He also took part in a protest in November 1940 against the Museum of Modern Art because of its reluctance to exhibit contemporary abstract painting. From 1947 to 1967 he taught at Brooklyn College. Reinhardt's paintings were eventually acknowledged as some of the most theoretically rich work produced by the New York School. Though he took Greenberg's formalism to an extreme, his work also directly influenced the antiformalist minimal and conceptual movements that took shape during the decade after his death. In 1991 he was given a posthumous retrospective exhibition at the Museum of Modern Art. Reinhardt is best known for a series of black monochrome paintings exhibited at a retrospective exhibition at the Jewish Museum in Manhattan in 1966 and for his writings on art, which address notions of autonomy and purity in painting and set forth a dogma of radical formalism.

Lucy R. Lippard, *Ad Reinhardt* (New York: Harry N. Abrams, 1981)

Melissa M. Merritt

reinsurance. Insurance by firms that spread their risks by transferring some of them to other insurers. The validity of reinsurance contracts was recognized by the supreme court of New York State in *New York Bowery Insurance Company v. New York Fire Insurance Company* (1837). One of the first companies to offer reinsurance was founded in New York City: Atlantic Mutual, which had a reinsurance agreement with the Insurance Company of North America that enabled both companies to provide larger amounts of insurance for single ships. Reinsurance became vital for fire insurers after the Great Fire of 1835 and the fire of 1846 in New York City, and the fire of 1871 in Chicago, when companies that wrote most of their policies in a single geographic area found that they had to pay losses on many of the policies simultaneously. Lower Manhattan was found to be a convenient location for firms offering primary insurance and reinsurance. The opportunities there about the turn of the twentieth century also attracted many foreign firms, such as Cologne Re and Munich Re in 1898, Skandia in 1900, and North American Re, a branch of Swiss Re that in 1910 opened offices in the city to transact business throughout the nation; the city soon emerged as one of the leading reinsurance centers in the world. After the terrorist attacks of 11 September 2001 on the World Trade Center, the insurance and reinsurance industries were hit with huge losses; Swiss Re and six other companies were involved in a nearly six-year legal battle over claims by Larry Silverstein, the developer who leased the World Trade Center shortly before the attacks. Under a 2007 settlement the seven companies agreed to pay Silverstein $2 billion, on top of $2.55 billion previously paid by other insurers; the $4.55 billion—the largest single insurance settlement in history—went toward rebuilding the World Trade Center site.

Bernard L. Webb et al., *Principles of Reinsurance* (Malvern, Pa.: Insurance Institute of America, 1990)

Robert J. Gibbons

Reisman, Philip (*b* Warsaw, 1904; *d* New York City, 17 June 1992). Painter and printmaker. After arriving in New York City in 1908 he studied at the Art Students League during the 1920s and had his first solo show at the Painters and Sculptors Gallery in 1931. He worked in the tradition of the Ashcan School and was especially known for his views of the teeming streets, tenements, parks, and bars of the city. In 1979 the Museum of the City of New York presented an exhibition of Reisman's work.

Kenneth T. Jackson

Rejection Show. Live show in New York City in which writers, comedians, artists, and others read or perform pieces on the theme of rejection. The show was created in 2003 by writer and comedian Jon Friedman. In 2006 it began being performed monthly at the Upright Citizens Brigade Theatre in Manhattan. Past venues included The Tank and Performance Space 122, as well as Mo Pitkin's, where it ran weekly in summer 2006. While much of the material is presented by professionals in the entertainment and publishing industries whose work has been rejected, laypeople are also invited to tell stories involving rejection of a personal, romantic, professional, or other sort. Regular guests include writers for *Saturday Night Live* and the *Onion* as well as cartoonists from the *New Yorker*. Often the presenters' comments and stories of the rejection process are emphasized as much as the work itself. Friedman edited the anthology *Rejected: Tales of the Failed, Dumped and Canceled* (2009). Recordings and written material from the show are also available on a broadband channel.

Jacqueline Lalley

Reles, Abe (*b* Brooklyn, 1907; *d* Brooklyn, 12 Nov 1941). Gangster. Born in the Brownsville neighborhood of Brooklyn, he began his criminal career as an adolescent. Also known as "Kid Twist," Reles worked for the Shapiro brothers before being caught and sent to juvenile detention for two years. Upon his return, Reles and childhood friend Buggsy Goldstein killed the Shapiros and took control of the Ocean Hill and Brownsville rackets. Reles's growing stature in organized crime led him to work with Louis "Lepke" Buchalter, a leader in the gang of contract killers known as Murder Incorporated that performed many mob executions during the 1930s. Linked to well over a dozen killings, Reles once told an attorney he got used to killing men the same way the attorney grew accustomed to trying cases. After being picked up on murder charges, Reles turned informant in 1940, implicating Goldstein and Buchalter as well as other members of Murder Incorporated. Held at the Half Moon Hotel on Coney Island under police surveillance, Reles fell to his death from a sixth-story window before he could testify against Albert Anastasia and other high-ranking crime figures. Although many believed the police allowed Reles to be pushed from the window or did it themselves, Reles's death was officially ruled an accident sustained during an escape attempt. The fall earned Reles the nickname, "the Canary who sang but could not fly."

Ben Silk

religion. A tradition of religious diversity was established in New York City by Dutch colonists and strengthened by the position of the city as a trading post. The colonists espoused toleration, and the Dutch West India Company did not want the enforcement of the Dutch Reformed faith to interfere with trade. The difficulty of attracting settlers led the company to accept a religiously diverse population that included Italians, Danes, Dutch from the lower classes, and refugees of religious persecution, including 30 Protestant Walloon families in 1624. The practice of Dutch Pietism, as represented by the Reformed Church, was not enforced by the first governor, Peter Minuit, a nominal Huguenot. For this he drew criticism from Jonas Michaëlius of the Dutch Reformed Church, with whom he often disagreed. After becoming governor in 1647 Peter Stuyvesant tried unsuccessfully to establish the exclusive rights of the Dutch church, which was poorly staffed and attended. Most able *predikanten* (pastors) were unwilling to cross the Atlantic for a frontier ministry, and less able ones in the colony attracted few congregants. At this time the city was rapidly evolving from a trading post into a diverse, international community. In 1654 Stuyvesant protested the emigration to the city of Jews from Recife, Brazil, for fear of encouraging other immigrants who did not belong to the Dutch Reformed Church, but the Dutch West India Company welcomed Brazilian Jews for their knowledge of international affairs; that the company had Jews among its prime stockholders in Amsterdam may also have played a part. One of Stuyvesant's supporters was Dominie Johannes Megapolensis, who in 1655 complained to officials in Amsterdam: "We have here Papists, Mennonites and Lutherans among the Dutch [and] also many Puritans or Independents and many atheists and various other servants of Baal."

When the English took control of the city in 1664 they made efforts to establish the Church of England, which had a growing number of adherents in the colony. In the 1680s the Dutch Reformed Church in New York City was led by Dominie Hendrik Selijns, who had integrity and was popular among merchants. At times fierce disputes arose between members of the Anglican, Dutch Reformed, and Presbyterian faiths, but in general there was widespread tolerance of religious difference. The African Methodist Episcopal Zion Church, formed in 1821, was the first African American church in the city. The New York City Mission Society was formed as an interdenominational organization in 1812 by clergy and laymen to help the poor. Members raised funds for charitable causes and worked in slums to promote good health and education; they also used religious motivations grounded in congregants' understanding of benevolence and formed religious organizations to combat urban problems. Several other charitable organizations were formed during these years, among them the New York City Mission and Tract Society, the New York Female Moral Reform Society, and the New York Society for the Relief of Widows and Orphans of Medical Men. The American Bible Society was formed in 1816. After the founding of Union Theological Seminary by Presbyterians in 1836 Protestantism developed a new intellectual focus. Scholars at the seminary were pioneers in ecumenism who experimented with liberal theology. Among the faculty members was the religious historian Philip Schaff, who urged American Protestant churches to join in a federation.

Like most other parts of the United States, New York City remained heavily Protestant until emigration of Catholics from Ireland and continental Europe began in the 1830s. The leaders of the city were reluctant to welcome immigrants whom they feared would be resistant to evangelistic appeals and unwilling to adopt such Protestant customs as observing a quiet Sabbath and abstaining from alcohol. In 1833 there were five Catholic churches in New York City. Tension between

Hindu Temple Society in Flushing, 1992

Catholics and Protestants in the city peaked after controversies over religion in public schools and an attack on Catholics in Philadelphia in the early 1840s. Bishop John Hughes staved off attacks in New York City by threatening to arm his churches. By 1863 the city was the Catholic center of the country and had 32 Catholic churches, many of which drew large congregations. Some Protestant evangelists tried to convert Catholics in the city, as they had done in small towns upstate and in other parts of the nation. The best-known evangelist of the day, Charles G. Finney, worked closely with wealthy merchants, including Arthur and Lewis Tappan, who built for him on Broadway a tabernacle that resembled a theater and attracted large crowds. Nevertheless, few Catholics attended his sermons: most of his adherents were Protestants displaced from small towns.

At the end of the nineteenth century hundreds of thousands of Jews fleeing pogroms in eastern Europe immigrated to the United States and settled in New York City. German Jews were at the time forming Conservative and Reform congregations in the city and often conflicted with the Jewish immigrants from eastern Europe, who either remained Orthodox and organized small shuls or ceased to practice their religion altogether. Reform and Conservative Judaism later became influential: about the turn of the twentieth century the founding of the Jewish Theological Seminary established an intellectual focus for Conservatism; Reform temples were presided over by rabbis who became known throughout the nation.

In 1892 Episcopalians laid the foundation in Morningside Heights for the Cathedral of St. John the Divine. Designed to overshadow St. Patrick's Cathedral, it became the largest church in the United States and the largest Gothic cathedral in the world. Churches well known for their fine music and splendid architecture drew many tourists. Protestant ministers who hoped to influence elite New Yorkers and become known through religious publications aspired to a fashionable pulpit in the city. There were also a number of well-known ministers in Brooklyn, the "city of churches," among them Henry Ward Beecher. Some ministers, including William S. Rainsford (1850–1933) of St. George's Episcopal Church, became known as reformers. They attacked Tammany Hall and other corrupt political organizations and fought against social vices such as prostitution and liquor trafficking. Rainsford and others solicited funds from philanthropists like J. P. Morgan to found "institutional churches" that offered gymnasiums, health centers, game rooms, and educational facilities for the poor. Charles A. Briggs of Union Theological Seminary was tried in 1892–93 for heresy by his fellow Presbyterians for offering new, critical views of the Bible. After his acquittal the seminary became interdenominational and eventually led the mainstream of the Protestant ministry in the city; in 1910 it moved to Morningside Heights next to Columbia University.

The city was a major center after the 1890s for the Social Gospel, a movement begun by liberal Protestants. Its best-known leader, Walter Rauschenbusch, was a Baptist who worked in Hell's Kitchen, where he could occasionally be seen leading his fellow Baptist John D. Rockefeller through the streets to gain his support for ministries to immigrants. For members of many ethnic groups that settled in the city, religion became a way of preserving ethnicity and finding community. They continued to practice the religions of their native countries and also used their houses of worship for social gatherings. Christians from Russia, Greece, eastern Europe, and the Middle East erected Orthodox and national Catholic churches (independent of papal authority) that were influential in their neighborhoods, although less so in the nation. Chinese houses of worship were first recorded in the census of 1890.

About the time of World War I large numbers of blacks moved from the South to New York City. Most settled in Harlem, displacing Jews. Black Protestant congregations often met in disused churches and synagogues that became rallying points for the concerns of the community. Some ministers, including Adam Clayton Powell, Sr., and Adam Clayton Powell, Jr., of the Abyssinian Baptist Church, inspired their large followings to take up political causes. In the 1920s Marcus Garvey formed a "back to Africa" movement that incorporated religious imagery, attracted the support of some ministers, and led to the rise of the African Orthodox Church, which remained a small denomination. Many black radicals active in the Harlem Renaissance found religion confining and became averse to it, but African American spiritual lore did find its way into the work of some poets, soul and gospel musicians, and playwrights. After 1920 many Puerto Ricans moved into an area of New York City that became known as Spanish Harlem. Most remained Catholic but did not practice Catholicism the way Europeans did: one estimate suggested that only 4 percent of Puerto Rican Catholics attended church regularly, less than one-tenth the proportion for all Catholics in the nation.

Religious and social conscience took new forms in New York City in the mid-twentieth century. George Baker assumed the name Father Divine and in the 1930s formed the Father Divine Mission, which attracted a largely black congregation and became known nationally. Dorothy Day, a convert to Catholicism, began publishing the *Catholic Worker* in 1933 and with her colleagues ministered to the poor and promoted social justice. The best-known liberal Protestant minister of the century, Harry Emerson Fosdick, was helped by John D. Rockefeller, Jr., to build Riverside Church at 120th Street and Riverside Drive in Morningside Heights. This interdenominational church helped to shape American theology for decades. At mid-century the faculty of Union Theological Seminary included the preeminent religious thinkers Reinhold Niebuhr and Paul Tillich; Francis Cardinal Spellman was the head of the Archdiocese of New York and often regarded as the leader of American Catholicism; and Rabbi Abraham J. Heschel dominated Jewish theology. With funds from John D. Rockefeller, Jr., Protestants opened the Interchurch Center in 1958 in Morningside Heights at 475 Riverside Drive, nicknamed the God Box for its architecture and function.

In 1957 the evangelist Billy Graham began a crusade in Madison Square Garden, where he held nightly gatherings that were broadcast on national television. His large audiences were drawn from churches in the city and even from congregations hundreds of miles away. He made thousands of conversions and gained the approval of the Protestant Council of New York, which was often skeptical of conservative evangelists. He also won many friends, some of them celebrities, and fended off criticism from theologians like Niebuhr who found his evangelism lacking in social justice and relevance to the modern world. By the 1960s other Protestant evangelists, many of them Pentecostalists, came into conflict with the Catholic Church by attracting Puerto Ricans and other Latin Americans. As elsewhere in the United States, Pentecostal congregations prospered notably in the quarter century after 1985, becoming commonplace in all the boroughs with substantial Latino populations, with a special appeal to recently arrived immigrants from Mexico and Latin America. The ministry of the Nation of Islam (the members of which were known as the Black Muslims) formed in the city and led by Malcolm X during the 1960s suffered losses after his assassination in 1965 but also presaged the rise of a modest Islamic presence generally within the city's African American communities.

Pluralism continued to flourish in the city in the early twenty-first century, creating community amid urban anonymity. Perhaps ironically, given its secular reputation, New York City remained an important center of national denominational enterprise. Some denominations and many interdenominational agencies continued to make their headquarters there, including the National Council of Churches and Church Women United USA (both at the Interchurch Center on Riverside Drive). Other less ecumenical Christian organizations also were well established in the city. The Watchtower in Brooklyn Heights became the international headquarters of the Jehovah's Witnesses, and many evangelical denominations were strongly represented in the mid-1990s, including the American Bible Society (at 1865 Broadway). The Young Women's Christian Association (YWCA), not as explicitly religious as it had been in its early years, established its national headquarters on Broadway. The major interfaith organization in the United States, the National Conference of Christians and Jews, maintained offices on Fifth Avenue, and Religion in American Life, also a national organization, had offices on Second Avenue.

Many of the world's religions continued to be practiced in the city, including Islam, Buddhism, and Hinduism. The largest denomination was Catholicism, with 2.35 million adher-

Estimated Number of Houses of Worship for Principal Faiths in New York City

	1855	1901	1926	1960	1986	1990	2009
PROTESTANT CHURCHES							
African Methodist Episcopal	11	15	22	36	37	5	40
African Methodist Episcopal Zion			13	16	25	4	18
Apostolic				9	35	72	77
Assembly of God			6	67	131	47	169
Baptist	46	118	88	250	606	471	460
Bible					10	10	11
Christian and Missionary Alliance			3	10	24	14	18
Christian Church (Disciples of Christ)	1	5	15	26	41	28	45
Christian Church of North America					11	63	84
Christian Scientist		7	33	35	27	47	13
Church of Christ					23	50	46
Church of God				28	115	37	59
Church of God (Anderson)				4	14		17
Church of God in Christ				17	52	29	24
Church of Jesus Christ of Latter-day Saints		1	3	3	6	27	32
Church of the Nazarene			8	6	15	16	43
Congregationalist / United Church of Christ	22	54	52	42	64	26	53
Divine Science			2	2	2		1
Episcopal	88	180	194	169	149	163	140
Evangelical	4	9	14	22	15	36	75
Friends	9	4	5	4	5	3	9
Jehovah's Witnesses				16	57	54	60
Lutheran	7	114	192	199	175	161	105
Mennonite				4	11	10	16
Methodist	93	149	145	127	136	123	120
Moravian	3	8	12	12	9	9	10
Pentecostal		4	3	36	324	391	450
Plymouth Brethren		1	19	15	19	12	9
Presbyterian	69	132	138	103	113	159	104
Reformed	52	87	85	70	69	37	58
Seventh-Day Adventist			17	38	70	116	175
Spiritualist			61		11	12	17
Unification					6	3	1
Unitarian	5	7	10	8			
Unitarian Universalist					9	12	7
Universalist	5	8	5	2			
ORTHODOX CHURCHES							
African Orthodox			6	9			
Greek Orthodox			6	30	27	40	42
Russian Orthodox			11	18	11	69	56
Other Orthodox		4	16	19	37	1	24
CATHOLIC CHURCHES							
American Catholic Church			2				
Liberal Catholic			2	2	3	3	1
Roman Catholic	53	224	430	442	430	403	396
Other Catholic		4	16	19	37	1	12
JEWISH SYNAGOGUES	11	104	1044	1240	410	437	466
BAHA'I TEMPLES			1		2	1	1
HINDU TEMPLES				7	9		27
BUDDHIST TEMPLES				4	30	16	20
MUSLIM MOSQUES			1	5	50	60	150

Compiled by Andrew A. Kryzak

ents in the early twenty-first century. The city continued to have the largest Jewish community in the nation, invigorated by plural communities of Reform, Conservative, Orthodox, and sectarian Hasidic Jews. By 2000 the city was home to more than 700,000 Muslims worshipping in more than 80 mosques. The city's well-known black Protestant congregations continued as principal institutions within New York's African American communities, and the city's prominent white Protestant congregations retained an influence beyond their numbers. "Megachurches," such as the 10,000-member Brooklyn Tabernacle, aligned "born-again" New Yorkers with the national evangelical Protestant movement. New York City's several thousand churches, synagogues, and mosques testified to a 300-year engagement with religion that belied its reputation as the epitome of American secularism.

George L. Smith, *Religion and Trade in New Netherland: Dutch Origins and American Development* (Ithaca, N.Y.: Cornell University Press, 1973); David W. Dunlap, *From Abyssinian to Zion: A Guide to Manhattan's Houses of Worship* (New York: Columbia University Press, 2004)

Martin E. Marty, Jon Butler

remittances. Payments made by immigrants back to their home countries. As New York City has always had the nation's largest immigrant community, it has become a center for remittances. In 2006 the Inter-American Development Bank estimated that people living in New York State sent more than $3.7 billion in remittance payments to Latin America alone. Much of the money is sent through informal channels that are untraceable, thus there are few estimates on payments to other regions because informal channels make up the bulk of monetary transfers from the United States to these regions.

Nathan Morgante

Remsen Village. East Flatbush neighborhood in northeastern Brooklyn, bounded to the north by Linden Boulevard, to the east by Rockaway Parkway, to the south by Ditmas Avenue, and to the west by Ralph Avenue; it is named for Remsen Avenue, which bisects it. In the late 1930s real estate developer Fred Trump built blocks of attached and semiattached brick houses that he called bungalows on Remsen Avenue, a site that formerly housed quarters for the Barnum & Bailey Circus. Remsen Village's modest homes attracted a growing Jewish population that formed an active community council. By the 1970s many had moved to the outer suburbs and were replaced by immigrants from the Caribbean, chiefly Jamaica, Haiti, and Guyana. The main commercial district lies along Remsen Avenue; small industries and shopping pockets line Linden Boulevard, while the Brooklyn Terminal Market, which replaced Fort Greene's Wallabout Market, sits off Ditmas Avenue.

Kenneth Jackson and John Manbeck, eds., *The Neighborhoods of Brooklyn,* 2nd edn (New Haven: Yale University Press, 2004)

Elizabeth Reich Rawson, John Manbeck

rent regulation. Government regulation of the amount of rent charged for housing. Its goal is to protect tenants from steep rent increases and unfair eviction, and ensure that landlords keep buildings in good order; at the same time it aims at allowing landlords reasonable increases in rents with adjustments for cost of living. In New York City rent stabilization/control means that the landlord/owner can only charge rents determined by government agencies. Rent control covers tenants who have lived continuously in the same apartment from before 1971, or family members who succeeded to those tenancies before 1947. Rent stabilization covers buildings built before 1974 with six units or more. Rent levels are based on criteria including length of residency, size of building, and economic factors. To qualify, the tenant must have been living in the apartment continuously for an extensive period of time. The rent formula (maximum base rent, or MBR) takes into consideration the costs for the owner, including taxes, water and sewer costs, and other carrying costs. The formula is changed every two years, subject to public hearings that are usually contentious. Rent laws in New York City are subject to approval by the state legislature in Albany. The New York City rent control program, formally started in 1943, is the oldest in the United States.

In New York City a housing shortage and high rents after World War I prompted the state legislature to pass emergency laws enabling tenants to challenge "unjust, unreasonable and oppressive" rent increases in magistrates' courts. These laws were annually renewed until 1928; residents of " old-law" tenements that were in violation of these rent regulations gained further protection under the Minkoff Law (1939), which prohibited rent increases in old-law housing that did not fully comply with the Multiple Dwellings Law of 1929 (which regulated structural, maintenance, and hygienic standards in apartment housing).

During World War II the U.S. Office of Price Administration (OPA) declared the city a "defense rental area" to encourage landlords to maintain fair rents voluntarily. In 1942 the Metropolitan Fair Rent Committee, an influential group of large-apartment owners, promised that the landlords whom it represented would comply, but there were still reports of exorbitant rents. They precipitated a riot in Harlem in August 1943. On 1 November the OPA froze the rents of 1.4 million dwellings at the level of 1 March, with some exceptions: landlords were permitted to increase rents by 15 percent in cases of hardship and to evict tenants to provide housing for their immediate families. Despite charges that rent controls were creating a black market, they were maintained by the OPA until 1947, whereupon tenant groups persuaded Governor Thomas E. Dewey and Mayor William O'Dwyer to impose a state-run system that placed controls on apartments built before 1947 (landlords were allowed a "catch-up" rent increase of 15 percent); it was at this point that the year when a building was constructed became a factor in determining how much rent could be charged. Under the new system the vacancy rate was measured at three-year intervals: a rate below 5 percent constituted a housing emergency that could justify a renewal of rent controls by the state legislature. Landlords were granted occasional rent increases of as much as 15 percent.

New York City and New York State began shared administration of rent regulation in 1962. By 1968, 75,000 high-rent apartments were gradually deregulated. Rents kept increasing, and in 1969 the Rent Stabilization Law affected units built after the 1947 cutoff for buildings to be eligible for rent control, covering approximately 325,000 units in New York City. Rent increases were subject to self-enforcement by landlords belonging to the Rent Stabilization Association. The method of setting rent control prices changed with the Local Law 30 of 1970, which, using the maximum base rate, adapted prices to the changing costs faced by landlords, allowing them to pass those costs on to renters. Fears that housing abandonment would become chronic moved the legislature to weaken rent controls in 1971; it allowed a rent increase of 15 percent and an inflation adjustment of 7 percent, and linked stabilized rents to a "maximum base" calculated according to a reasonable return on investment. In 1972 it adopted "vacancy decontrol," under which apartments were removed from rent control altogether when they became vacant, but owing to pressure from tenant groups it reimposed rent stabilization on decontrolled apartments in 1974. Landlords in the 1980s increasingly perceived rent control as permanent, and as a result many converted rental apartments to cooperatives and condominium units. In 1997 the Rent Regulation Reform Act provided that stabilization be applied only to apartments with rents under $2,000 per month. Such apartments would be deregulated after that amount if vacated or if renters' household gross income surpassed $175,000 for two years. The house must be a primary residence. There are also programs for renovated or new buildings, and provisions for temporary stabilization.

In the first decade of the twenty-first century there were 2.5 million tenants living in one million apartments subject to rent control. Rent regulation continued to be fiercely debated. Opponents of the system contend that it contributes to abandonment and reduced revenues from property taxes. They also argue that rent regulation benefits the middle class rather than the poor: regulated rents do not take into account a tenant's income (except in the highest-priced rent-stabilized apartments, because of a limited provision passed in 1993), and the higher turnover of apartments in poor neighborhoods allows for more frequent rent increases. Defenders of the system maintain that the inadequate supply of affordable housing stems not from regulation but from more fundamental problems, and that in any case rent regulation does not apply to new construction. They also doubt whether a repeal of regulation would achieve its purported benefits, arguing that rents in poor neighborhoods would still be higher than what local residents could afford to pay, and that a repeal would lead to widespread price gouging. Rent-regulated apartments in the city are highly sought after and are often the subject of legal disputes, especially concerning tenants' principal domicile, subletting, and rights of succession.

George Sternlieb and James W. Hughes, *Housing and Economic Reality: New York City, 1976* (New Brunswick, N.J.: Rutgers University Center for Urban Policy Research, 1976); Ronald Lawson, ed., *The Tenant Movement in New York City, 1904–1984* (New Brunswick, N.J.: Rutgers University Press, 1986)

Joel Schwartz, Lisa Keller

Renwick, James (*b* New York City, 1 Nov 1818; *d* New York City, 23 June 1895). Architect. Trained as an engineer, he oversaw the construction of a reservoir on the site at 42nd Street now occupied by the New York Public Library. He soon won a competition to design Grace Church, a success that led to commissions for St. Bartholomew's Church and St. Patrick's Cathedral; he also designed the fountain at Bowling Green, the Free Academy, hotels including the St. Denis, banks, palatial residences such as that of Charles Morgan, and buildings on Blackwell's, Wards, and Randalls islands for the Department of Charities and Correction. Toward the end of his life he was a senior warden of Grace Church.

See also Terra-cotta.

James E. Mooney

Republican Party. From its creation in 1854, the Republican Party has always been a minority party in New York City, but with a disproportionately large effect on local, state, and national politics. Its origins were among free-soil, antislavery advocates. Although some of the city's most prominent newspapers, including the *Tribune,* the *Evening Post,* and the *New York Times* supported Republicans, the party had limited political appeal. Most Republicans tended to be affluent Protestants of English descent. Irish Catholics and other poor and working-class immigrants were put off by Republican support for moral reforms such as abolition and temperance and had little in common culturally with Republicans, some of whom had been members of the anti-immigrant and anti-Catholic Know-Nothings.

By the late 1850s Republicans dominated New York State government and often clashed with Democratic city officials, going so far as to revise the city's charter in 1857 to weaken Democratic control. Before the Civil War, New York City was the center of the cotton trade, which led many Manhattan business leaders to become advocates for the South and oppose the abolition of slavery. Though Abraham Lincoln's path to the presidency began with a famous speech at Cooper Union in 1860, he found little political support in the city during the Civil War, which became a hotbed of anti-Lincoln Copperhead Democrats. The draft riots of 1863 showed how deep the resentment of Republican war policies was among working-class New Yorkers.

In the second half of the nineteenth century, Republicans were often at the forefront of attacks against the corruption of Tammany Hall, the city's Democratic political machine. Republicans were also supporters of a wide range of municipal reforms. In 1882 a young Manhattan-born patrician named Theodore Roosevelt was elected to the state assembly as a Republican. He ran unsuccessfully for mayor as a Republican in 1886 and was appointed head of the city's Police Commission by Republican mayor William Strong in 1895. By 1901 Roosevelt would be living in the White House. Like many Republicans in twentieth-century New York City, Roosevelt often clashed with party leaders at home and in Washington, D.C.

In the same year that Roosevelt ascended to the presidency, his friend Seth Low was elected mayor as a reformer. Realizing that Republican support was not enough for victory, Low ran as a "fusion" candidate with the support of the Citizens Union. Throughout the twentieth century, Republican mayoral candidates followed Low's example and created their own anti-Tammany fusion tickets. One of the city's most famous Republican politicians was Fiorello H. La Guardia, although he wore his Republican identity loosely. First elected mayor in 1933 La Guardia was a strong supporter of the New Deal and organized labor. In each of his three mayoral victories, he ran as a fusion candidate.

New Yorkers played an important role in the national Republican Party in the mid-twentieth century. Thomas E. Dewey and Wendell Wilkie headed the national Republican tickets in 1940, 1944, and 1948. Jacob K. Javits began a decades-long career as a leading liberal Republican in Congress. Nelson A. Rockefeller was governor from 1959 to 1973 and was appointed vice president by Gerald Ford in 1974. Rockefeller was a national leader of the liberal wing of the Republican Party, which soon drew opposition from conservative Republicans such as Barry Goldwater and Ronald Reagan.

John V. Lindsay was the embodiment of postwar liberal New York Republicans. He had represented the affluent "silk stocking district" of Manhattan's East Side in Congress and was elected mayor in 1965 running on both the Republican and Liberal party lines. During his first term, Lindsay became a polarizing figure and was defeated in the Republican primary in 1969 by Staten Island's John Marchi, but he won reelection by running on the Liberal and Independent lines. As his politics drifted leftward, Lindsay grew uncomfortable in an increasingly conservative Republican Party. In 1971 he formally switched parties before making an unsuccessful run for the Democratic presidential nomination.

During this time the base of the city's Republican Party shifted away from liberal and wealthy silk stocking district voters and became increasingly located among middle-class Irish and Italian Americans living in Staten Island, southern Brooklyn, and central and eastern Queens. These voters were represented by politicians such as Marchi, Vito Battista, and Guy Molinari. A dwindling number of liberal Republicans remained on Manhattan's Upper East Side, represented by politicians such as Roy Goodman, Bill Green, and John Ravitz, but by 2002 no silk stocking Republican remained in elected office.

While the Republican Party flourished nationally during the 1980s, it stagnated in the city. In 1989 a former prosecutor named Rudolph Giuliani ran for mayor on both the Republican and Liberal party lines. Though Giuliani lost to Democrat David Dinkins, he won in a rematch four years later, again running as a fusion candidate. Though Giuliani was liberal on abortion and gay rights, he was pro-business and took conservative positions on taxes, welfare, and crime. He crossed party lines in 1994 to support Mario Cuomo for governor but would become popular among national Republicans because of his actions in response to the terrorist attacks of 11 September 2001. Giuliani's successes as mayor did little to strengthen the city's Republican Party; many conservative and moderate Democrats happily voted for Giuliani while retaining their party membership and voting for Democrats for other offices. Despite this, the Republican line for mayor was still a highly prized commodity. Billionaire Michael Bloomberg, a lifelong Democrat, switched parties in 2001 and successfully ran for mayor. He was reelected in 2005 as a Republican, but it proved to be a marriage of convenience. In 2007 Bloomberg left the party and became an independent; he was elected again in 2009, this time on the Republican and Independent party lines. In 2008 Rudolph Giuliani unsuccessfully sought the Republican nomination for president.

Throughout the 1990s and the first decade of the twenty-first century the Republican

Party became weaker throughout the Northeast. In New York City the party's already small numbers grew even smaller. In 1996 Republicans made up 13.8 percent of registered voters in the city; by 2008 that figure was down to 11.6 percent. At that time Republicans accounted for only three of the 51 seats in the City Council; three of the 27 seats in the city's delegation to the state senate; and only one of the 65 seats in the city's delegation to the state assembly.

Vincent J. Cannato

Republic New York Corporation. Commercial bank, formed in 1966 as the Republic National Bank of New York by Edmond J. Safra (1932–99) with headquarters at the Knox Hat Building on Fifth Avenue and 42nd Street (declared a landmark in 1980 and incorporated in 1986 as the National Bank Tower). The bank undertook a series of mergers and acquisitions beginning in 1974, when it bought the Kings Lafayette Bank, based in Brooklyn. Later acquisitions included 12 branches from Bankers Trust Company (1980), the Williamsburgh Savings Bank (1987), and the Manhattan Savings Bank (1990). In 1990 the bank adopted its current name. By 2007 Republic was one of the 15 largest commercial banks in the city, with nearly $40 billion in assets.

James Bradley

rescue dogs. Trained dogs that helped search for survivors and human remains after the terrorist attacks of 11 September 2001 on the World Trade Center. More than 300 dog and handler teams from across the country assisted the New York City Police Department's K-9 Unit with the search effort. Despite some handlers' concerns, a study undertaken between 2001 and 2004 found that the dogs' health did not suffer as a result of their exposure to toxic air at Ground Zero. DOGNY, a 2002 sculpture project sponsored by the city and the American Kennel Club, placed 300 life-sized sculptures of rescue dogs throughout the city to commemorate their work.

Kate Lauber

restaurants. The restaurant as Americans know it began in New York City in 1827 when the Swiss brothers Giovanni and Pietro Delmonico opened a small establishment on William Street where businesspeople could order a variety of hot meals. Taverns, coffeehouses, and eating houses existed in most American cities at the time, but restaurants that offered fine dining did not. Based on the Parisian model, Delmonico's established the pattern for all restaurants in the United States. It became a favorite place for eating and socializing and eventually expanded to four restaurants; one of these, at Fifth Avenue and 14th Street, was the place from which Samuel F. B. Morse sent the first cablegram across the Atlantic Ocean. After the Civil War Delmonico's competed with opulent establishments decorated with Italian marble, fine oak, and velvet draperies, such as Louis Sherry's, Rector's (at Broadway and 54th Street), the Maison D'Orée, and the restaurant at the Waldorf Hotel (opened in 1893 at Fifth Avenue and 34th Street), where the maître d', Oscar Tschirky, installed a velvet rope at the door to keep out those deemed unworthy of a table. In 1899 the Café Martin on Fifth Avenue and 26th Street introduced banquette seating, and Rector's introduced dancing. Along Broadway extravagant new restaurants like Churchill's, Murray's Roman Gardens, Shanley's, the Knickerbocker Grill, and Maxim's appealed to theatergoers; large oyster bars identified by red and white signs in the shape of a balloon appealed to everyone, offering an unlimited number of servings under the "Canal Street plan" (see OYSTERS). The best-known of the oyster palaces was the Grand Central Oyster Bar and Restaurant, opened on the lower level of the Grand Central Terminal and still in operation in the early twenty-first century.

The city's selection of restaurants was enriched by the arrival of immigrants during the late nineteenth century. The food served in the first Italian restaurants in the city was adapted from recipes of Naples and Sicily. Pizza was a Neapolitan food uncommon in most of Italy but popular in New York City after Gennaro Lombardi opened a pizzeria on Spring Street in 1905. Barbetta, opened in 1906 by Sebastiano Maioglio on West 39th Street (moved in 1925 to West 46th Street), served Piedmontese cuisine to the musicians who played at the Metropolitan Opera House nearby, and Sardi's (1927) became a favorite of theatergoers. The most popular Italian restaurant of the time was Mamma Leone's, which began in 1906 over a wine cellar near the back of the original Metropolitan Opera House and then moved to West 48th Street after World War I. Of the many German restaurants that opened at the turn of the twentieth century, the most famous was Lüchow's on East 14th Street, run by August Guido Lüchow. Jewish immigrants had grocery-restaurants called DELICATESSENS, some strictly kosher, which offered an array of breads, smoked salmon, dried fish, noodle pudding, frankfurters, pastrami, pickles, and cream soda. In Chinese restaurants New Yorkers were introduced to dishes developed for American tastes such as chop suey, egg foo young, and chow mein. Russian restaurants of the early twentieth century, such as the Russian Tea Room on West 57th Street next to Carnegie Hall, were often run by émigrés and patronized by artists and writers. Later Russian immigrants in Brooklyn opened large, colorful family restaurants like the National and the Zodiac. At the same time soul food such as fried chicken, biscuits and ham, and fried pies was served at restaurants in black neighborhoods and during the 1930s and 1940s at nightclubs in Harlem like Connie's Inn, the Cotton Club, and Smalls' Paradise, where the clientele was largely white (sometimes exclusively so).

The onset of Prohibition in 1920 crippled fine dining in New York City, and Delmonico's, Louis Sherry's, Rector's, and other such places closed by the early 1920s. In their place rose the speakeasies, which at first were nothing more than illicit saloons but later developed into private eating houses for what the *New York Journal American* columnist "Cholly Knickerbocker" (Maury Paul) called café society. The best-known speakeasy, the "21" Club (1922) at 21 West 52nd Street, the last of many such establishments opened by Jack Kriendler and Charlie Berns, was a multistoried restaurant and bar where good food was served at exorbitant prices to the important and glamorous; a system of trapdoors ensured that no liquor would be found during police raids. After the end of Prohibition, "21" continued to dominate the social scene in New York City, rivaled only by the Colony Club, which itself began as a speakeasy and later developed into a fine restaurant. In the outer boroughs notable restaurants included Gage and Tollner and the steakhouse Peter Luger in Brooklyn.

Americans were introduced to authentic French cuisine at the World's Fair of 1939–40, after which Henri Soulé, maître d' at the restaurant of the French pavilion, opened a deluxe French restaurant called Le Pavillon on East 55th Street. It set the standard for fine French restaurants in the United States and became a training ground for chefs and restaurateurs. Other important French restaurants in the city included Lutèce and later Le Cirque. Japanese restaurants opened in New York City during the 1950s and 1960s: Toyo-Kwan, Daruma, and Miyako served sukiyaki, teriyaki, and tempura; Saito on West 52nd Street, run by Moto Saito, had the first sushi bar (1957); and Benihana of Tokyo, opened in 1964 by Rocky Aoki, was the first Japanese steakhouse (the formula was later copied in Japan, where the restaurant was called Benihana of New York). During the late 1950s and 1960s the firm Restaurant Associates developed Zum Zum (a German sausage restaurant), Trattoria (an Italian restaurant in the Pan Am Building), the Forum of the Twelve Caesars (an extravagant rendering on West 48th Street of an imperial Roman dining room), La Fonda del Sol (a Latin American restaurant in the Time-Life Building), and the Four Seasons Restaurant (opened in 1959 in the Seagram Building). T.G.I. Friday's, founded in New York City in 1965, is often considered to have been the first "singles bar."

Partly as a result of growing immigration, the 1970s saw a proliferation of ethnic restaurants in the city, which in addition to the now well-known cuisines of Italy, China, and Japan introduced New Yorkers to those of India, Thailand, and Ethiopia. At the same time French restaurants expanded their offerings to include "nouvelle cuisine" as well as more traditional dishes. The trend toward increasingly lavish restaurants was exemplified by Windows on the World, built at a cost of $6 million on the 107th floor of the World Trade Center in 1976. Restaurants became still more extravagant during the 1980s, and prices reached unprecedented levels. Several developments were in evidence at the end of the decade: young chefs like Larry Forgione of An American Place on Park Avenue and 32nd Street sought to fashion inventive menus and promoted what was called "new American cuisine," a rendering of traditional American dishes with modern refinements; innovations in seafood dishes were made by such chefs as Gilbert LeCoze of Le Bernardin, which opened on West 51st Street in 1988; and casual Italian trattorias and French bistros appealed to a clientele increasingly concerned with saving money.

Owing to high real estate prices in midtown, more and more of New York City's finest, well-trained chefs and restaurateurs moved or opened casual, innovative places downtown, in the Flatiron District, Tribeca, the Lower East Side, the West Village, the meatpacking district, and Nolita (North of Little Italy). Steakhouses, bistros, and huge Asian restaurants opened along with casual corner eateries such as The Spotted Pig in the West Village, which became as well known for its cuisine as for its bar scene, while at wd~50 on the Lower East Side chef Wylie Dufresne became the first chef in the city to emulate the experimental "molecular cuisine" of Spain's eminent chef Ferran Adrià. Across the Brooklyn Bridge in newly gentrified neighborhoods like Park Slope, Carroll Gardens, and DUMBO, similar casual restaurants with serious French, American, and Mediterranean menus flourished, while in other sections of the borough immigrants from Central and South America, the Caribbean, Russia, Croatia, and Albania took up residence in neighborhoods that were revitalized by cafés, luncheonettes, take-out establishments, and restaurants featuring those ethnic food cultures. In the early twenty-first century there are approximately 26,000 food-service establishments throughout New York City, including about 18,700 restaurants, with total sales of $15 billion annually.

See also Food.

John F. Mariani

New York City's Largest Retailers by Number of Outlets, July 2008

Retailer	Total	Manhattan	Brooklyn	Queens	Bronx	Staten Island
Dunkin' Donuts	341	78	89	96	49	29
Subway	335	136	57	77	44	21
McDonald's	248	72	57	67	41	11
Starbucks	235	186	18	21	4	6
Duane Reade	216	139	31	27	11	8
Baskin-Robbins	215	46	58	70	26	15
Rite Aid	209	37	57	68	42	5
Radio Shack	116	40	27	25	18	6
GNC	115	41	29	28	14	3
Payless	109	21	36	27	20	5
CVS	108	27	22	34	11	14
Sleepy's	105	34	26	24	12	9
Burger King	92	21	24	24	15	8
AT&T Wireless	85	40	21	15	7	2
Jackson Hewitt Tax Service	83	16	19	22	19	7
T-Mobile	82	31	26	14	10	1
Domino's Pizza	74	21	20	15	14	4
Golden Krust	72	13	28	14	17	0
KFC	70	11	24	20	11	4
GameStop	69	17	16	16	14	6
Carvel	62	5	13	25	11	8

Source: Center for an Urban Future

Compiled by Frank Nestor

Restell, Madame. Pseudonym of Ann Trow Lohman.

Retail, Wholesale and Department Store Union [RWDSU]. Labor union formed in New York in 1937 as the United Retail Employees of America; it took its current name in 1940. In 1941 RWDSU struck against Gimbel's department store and won a 40-hour workweek. The number of members increased dramatically during the late 1930s and early 1940s, but the union was divided up by the international leadership in the 1940s and 1950s. RWDSU was resurrected in 1954 when it merged with the Distributive Processing and Office Workers of America and the Playthings, Jewelry, and Novelty Workers International Union. In 1993 RWDSU affiliated with United Food and Commercial Workers.

Kerry Candaele

Reuben's. Delicatessen opened in 1908 by Arnold Reuben (1883–1970), a German immigrant, at 802 Park Avenue near 75th Street. It moved successively to Broadway and 82nd Street, Broadway and 73rd Street (1916), 622 Madison Avenue at 59th Street (1918), and 6 East 58th Street (1935), where it became well known among entertainment figures and tourists. The restaurant popularized but did not originate the Reuben sandwich (corned beef, Swiss cheese, sauerkraut, and Russian dressing on rye bread). Reuben retired in 1964 and although the restaurant closed in 1966, the brand name continued in different locations into the 1990s under various owners.

Val Ginter

Reverend Ike [Eikerenkoetter, Frederick J.] (*b* Ridgeland, S.C., 1 June 1935). Evangelist. The son of a Baptist minister and a teacher, he served as a chaplain in the U.S. Air Force before becoming an assistant pastor at the Bible Way Church in Ridgeland, South Carolina, in 1958. In 1962 he formed the United Church of Jesus Christ for All People and the United Christian Evangelistic Association. He moved to Boston in 1964, where he opened the Miracle Temple, and to New York City in 1966, where in the former Sunset movie theater on 125th Street he gave sermons based on the principle that "no one has to be poor, and no one has to be a failure." He soon made radio broadcasts and undertook national tours. During the following years Reverend Ike developed the Science of Living, a program of self-awareness and motivation, and in 1969 he bought the huge Loews theater at 175th Street and Broadway, which became the site of the United Church, Science of the Living Institute. The church flourished during the 1970s and was known for such catchphrases as "Welfare has its place but don't make it a resting place"; "I believe in God, therefore I believe in myself"; and "The best thing you can do for the poor is to not be one of them." A semimonthly magazine, *Action,* reached a circulation of 1.5 million, and Reverend Ike's broadcasts were eventually heard on more than 1500 radio stations. Known for his flamboyant demeanor and clothes as well as extensive real estate holdings and Rolls Royces, Reverend Ike continued to give sermons at the United Church in the early twenty-first century but keeps somewhat of a lower profile.

Eric Wm. Allison

revivalism. A movement in Protestant churches to renew, or revive, religious ardor and spirituality of adherents and to convert others. It was introduced to New York City by the English missionary George Whitefield, who on 14 November 1739 preached to an audience of 2000 outside the Wall Street Presbyterian Church. Whitefield's style was adopted by other revivalists who, like him, were attracted to the city because of its size and prominence, held mass meetings at unconventional times and places, and relied on charisma, sensational publicity, and fervent preaching. By 1829 the Methodists' success led Presbyterians in the city to engage Charles G. Finney, the best-known revivalist of his time. During the next six years he organized seven free churches, which did not charge rent for pews, to attract the poor. Finney also organized the first city mission, which visited the poor and campaigned against vice in nearby Five Points. During a financial panic in 1857, prayer meetings attracted thousands in lower Manhattan and inspired the only national revival that began in the city. In October 1872 Jerry McAuley, a former alcoholic, formed the Water Street Mission and emphasized the spiritual power to overcome addiction; the mission opened branches throughout the city and established the Crittenden (1883) and the Door of Hope (1890), homes for "fallen women," which grew into national organizations linked by the *Christian Herald,* a magazine published in the city from 1878. Several missions gave rise to denominations, including the Christian and Missionary Alliance, which was led in the 1880s by Presbyterian minister Albert B. Simpson and eventually became one of the largest evangelical denominations in the country.

In his campaign from 7 February to 19 April 1876 Dwight L. Moody adapted music hall entertainment to a brand of revivalism carefully fashioned for the middle class. Moody spoke to audiences of 10,000 a day in P. T. Barnum's Hippodrome at Madison Avenue and 27th Street and claimed to inspire 5000 conversions. With the help of meticulous planning by a professional staff, Billy Sunday became the best-known revivalist in the city from 1896 to 1935: his comic rhetoric, frenzied stagecraft, and adaptation of vaudeville entertainment attracted audiences of 1.4 million to his meetings, where there were 65,000 conversions. He reached the height of his career during a rally that lasted from April to June 1917. Billy Graham came to prominence in the city during his 1957 revival in Madison Square Garden that lasted from 15 May to Labor Day; he addressed two million people, among whom he claimed 55,000 as converts. He made his national debut on television in the city on 1 June 1957, launching the "electronic church," which soon became the largest outlet for revivalism. Graham's return visits in 1960 and 1969 were not as successful. More notable was a mission to drug addicts begun in the city in 1958 by the Pentecostal pastor David Wilkerson and expanded into the nationwide ministry Teen Challenge.

William G. McLoughlin, *Modern Revivalism: From Charles Grandison Finney to Billy Graham* (New York: Ronald, 1959); Carroll Smith Rosenberg, *Religion and the Rise of the American City: The New York City Mission Movement, 1812–1870* (Ithaca, N.Y.: Cornell University Press, 1971); Norris A. Magnuson, *Salvation in the Slums: Evangelical Social Work, 1865–1920* (Metuchen, N.J.: Scarecrow, 1977)

James D. Bratt

Jerry McAuley Bowery Mission, 1897

Revlon. Cosmetics firm formed in 1932. The company achieved success with a nail polish developed by its founders, Charles Revson (1906–75), his brother Joseph, and a chemist, Charles Lachman, for whom the "L" was included in the company name Revlon. Revson introduced in 1940 the first color-coordinated nail polish and lipstick ("matching lips and fingertips") and the first pink nail polish, and by 1941 he achieved a near monopoly for his products in beauty salons. He introduced new color lines each spring and autumn and devised advertisements that associated his products with heightened sexuality (an advertising campaign in 1952 based on the slogan "fire and ice" caused a sensation). His firm also sponsored a television program (*The $64,000 Question*) and made vitamins, toilet bowl cleaners, and shoe polishes. For many years Revlon enjoyed a rivalry with Estée Lauder; at one point both firms had their headquarters in the General Motors Building at 767 Fifth Avenue. At the time of Revson's death in 1975, Revlon was the second-largest cosmetics firm in the world. In 1985 the company was sold to a subsidiary of MacAndrews and Forbes Holdings, and in 1996 it became a public company. In the early twenty-first century its headquarters are located at 237 Park Avenue.

Andrew P. Tobias, *Fire and Ice: The Story of Charles Revson, the Man Who Built the Revlon Empire* (New York: William Morrow, 1976)

Marc Ferris

Revolution. Weekly periodical launched in 1868 in New York City by Susan B. Anthony. It emphasized news of the reform movement and favored an informed electorate and the abolition of standing armies. The publication was edited by Elizabeth Cady Stanton and Parker Pillsbury until Laura J. Curtis Bullard took charge in 1870; under her direction the focus was more on the well-being of women than on their equality. In 1871 *Revolution* was bought by W. T. Clarke, who tried unsuccessfully to transform it into a literary journal. It merged in February 1872 with the *Liberal Christian.*

Sandra Roff

Rheingold Breweries. Firm of brewers formed in Brooklyn in 1855 by Samuel Liebmann, a German immigrant. After his death in 1872 the firm of Liebmann Breweries was taken over by his sons, who expanded it by buying smaller local breweries, and during the 1880s Rheingold became its principal marque. From 1940 to 1965 the firm achieved wide publicity by running a promotional beauty contest in which customers cast ballots to choose Miss Rheingold. Like other smaller

Macy's food counter, 1902

brewers it could not survive the competition from large firms with modern facilities, national distribution, and enormous advertising budgets. In 1964 it took its current name after being sold by the family to Pepsi-Cola United Bottlers. Sales declined, the firm was put up for sale in 1974, and a purchase by Chock Full O'Nuts was arranged by the city. Under the new ownership sales continued to decline, and the factory in Brooklyn closed in 1976 when operations were moved to Orange, New Jersey. The beer returned to New York City bars and grocery shelves in 1998, however, when Walter Liebman and Michael Mitaro restarted the company. They also launched a new Miss Rheingold campaign. In 2005 the company was purchased by Drinks America.

K. Austin Kerr

R. H. Macy. Department store founded in 1858 by Rowland H. Macy. It began as a small shop on Sixth Avenue between 13th and 14th streets, far north of the existing dry-goods district bounded by Broome Street, the Bowery, Grand Street, and Broadway. The early Macy's was an innovative operation. Specializing in "fancy" and imported dry goods for women, the store was known for odd pricing (setting prices only one cent or a few cents below a full-dollar amount), a "cash-only" policy (which lasted until the 1950s), good value, and a money-back guarantee. Throughout the nineteenth century there was a factory on the premises; and before ready-to-wear women's clothing was introduced, more than 200 employees, mostly women, sewed made-to-measure suits, coats, jackets, and undergarments for women and shirts for men. The store grew rapidly and by the 1870s had an unprecedented number of departments, among them a large and profitable one devoted to home furnishings, and a range of merchandise that included toys, china, glassware, men's furnishings, jewelry, candy, and books. Macy's helped to secularize the American Christmas. Illuminated window displays, introduced in 1874, became a tradition that signaled the beginning of the Christmas shopping season; a Santa Claus first appeared in the store during the 1870s and afterward remained a fixture of the modern Macy's Thanksgiving Day Parade.

The firm was taken over in 1888 by Isidor and Nathan Straus, who moved the store from the declining shopping district on 14th Street to a building that they erected in 1902 at 34th Street and Broadway. A National Historic Landmark and the largest department store in the world, Macy's flagship store at Herald Square was the first large store above 23rd Street; despite the proximity of the Sixth Avenue elevated line, Macy's initially had to run a steam wagonette between 14th and 34th streets for customers reluctant to make the trip so far north.

For many years Macy's was characterized by a remarkable profitability and continuity of ownership. The Straus brothers' partnership became a family partnership in 1919 and a public corporation in 1922. The Straus family remained at the helm until the firm became privately held once again in 1986 after a leveraged buyout led by senior management. The buyout, coupled with the economic recession of the late 1980s, put such a strain on the operations of the firm that in January 1992 Macy's filed for bankruptcy. Not until it merged with Federated Department Stores in 1994 did the corporation emerge from bankruptcy protection. The merger created a true retail giant that has grown even larger in recent years with the "rebranding" of local, nameplate stores in major cities across the country. Chicago's legendary State Street store Marshall Field and Company is now a Macy's, as are stores in 45 states. Featured in movies (*Miracle on 34th Street*) and television (*Desperate Housewives*); sponsoring a spectacular fireworks display on the East River on the Fourth of July, a tap dance extravaganza in Herald Square, and the traditional Thanksgiving Day Parade; Macy's has become a New York institution and is often a stop on the itinerary of foreign visitors.

Ralph M. Hower, *History of Macy's of New York, 1858–1919: Chapters in the Evolution of the Department Store* (Cambridge, Mass.: Harvard University Press, 1943)

Elaine S. Abelson

R. Hoe and Company. Firm of printing-equipment manufacturers formed in New York City in 1822. It was famous for innovative printing presses, including the Washington press, a toggle-jointed iron hand press; a flatbed cylinder newspaper press; and a type-revolving, rotary press invented in 1847 by Richard M. Hoe (1812–86). The firm occupied buildings on the Lower East Side until 1930 when it moved to the Bronx; it was dissolved by bankruptcy in 1977.

Frank E. Comparato, *Chronicles of Genius and Folly: R. Hoe and Company and the Printing Press as a Service to Democracy* (Culver City, Calif.: Labyrinthos, 1979)

William S. Pretzer

Rice, (Henry) Grantland (*b* Murfreesboro, Tenn., 1 Nov 1880; *d* New York City, 13 July 1954). Sportswriter. He studied classics at Vanderbilt University (BA 1901) and worked for newspapers in Nashville; Washington, D.C.; Atlanta; and Cleveland before moving to New York City in 1911 to write for the *New York Evening Mail.* In 1914 he joined the *New York Tribune,* with which he remained associated until 1930. Rice's effusive, hyperbolic writing style, often painting the athlete in heroic terms, was immensely popular and influenced a generation of sportswriters. He wrote three volumes of verse and an autobiography, *The Tumult and the Shouting: My Life in Sport* (1954). In New York City he lived at 450 Riverside Drive (1911–30) and 1158 Fifth Avenue (from 1930).

Charles Fountain, *Sportswriter: The Life and Times of Grantland Rice* (New York: Oxford University Press, 1993); Mark Inabinett, *Grantland Rice and His Heroes: The Sportswriter as Myth-maker in the 1920s* (Knoxville: University of Tennessee Press, 1994)

Rice, William Marsh (*b* Springfield, Mass., 14 March 1816; *d* New York City, 23 Sept 1900). Businessman and philanthropist. He moved to Houston, Texas, in 1838 and became a partner in the mercantile firm of Nichols (renamed Rice and Nichols) and then moved to Mexico at the beginning of the Civil War and to New York City in 1865, where he oversaw finances and purchases for the Houston and Texas Central Railroad. For many years he lived in hotels, but by 1883 he had an apartment in the Grenoble on 57th Street. After his wife's death in 1896 he moved to an apartment at 500 Madison Avenue. He was murdered by his valet, Charles F. Jones, at the instigation of a lawyer, Albert T. Patrick, who hoped to gain some of Rice's wealth through a forged will. Most of Rice's estate went to form the William Marsh Rice Institute in Houston, which opened in 1912 and is now Rice University.

Sylvia Stallings Morris, ed., *William Marsh Rice and His Institute: A Biographical Study* (Houston: William Marsh Rice University, 1972)

Eileen K. Cheng

Rice High School. Catholic high school for boys in Harlem, opened in 1938 and run by the Congregation of Christian Brothers. Named for the founder of the Christian Brothers, Edmund Ignatius Rice (1762–1844), it once occupied three buildings that had previously been the campus of Power Memorial Academy. In 1940 it moved to its current facility, which the Young Women's Christian Association (YWCA) formerly occupied. It is well known for high academic standards and a consistently superior basketball team.

Gilbert Tauber

Richmond, Mary E(llen) (*b* Belleville, Ill., 5 Aug 1861; *d* New York City, 1928). Social worker. She moved to New York City in 1909 as the first director of the charity organization department of the Russell Sage Foundation. Richmond believed that the complex problems of impoverished people could be solved only by trained caseworkers in privately funded social service agencies and not by public welfare programs. A pioneer in the professionalization of social work, she developed casework techniques while opposing popular measures for public assistance, such as widows' pensions. Her books *Social Diagnosis* (1917) and *What Is Social Case Work?* (1922) greatly influenced the first generation of academically trained social workers. Richmond lived in an apartment on West 120th Street near Columbia University.

Sarah Henry Lederman

Richmond County. One of the five counties of New York City, coextensive with the borough of Staten Island.

Richmond Hill. Neighborhood in east central Queens, lying adjacent to Jamaica and bounded to the north by Myrtle and Hillside avenues, to the east by the Van Wyck Expressway, to the south by Linden Boulevard, and to the west by 100th Street. The 2000 population was about 46,000: 35 percent Hispanic, 29 percent white, 16 percent Asian, 8 percent African American. The area was mostly farmland until it was developed by Albon P. Man, a wealthy lawyer of the firm of Man and Parsons in New York City who in 1867 engaged the landscape architect Edward Richmond to buy land and lay out a community. Between 1868 and 1874 streets were laid out, a school was built, trees were planted, and a railroad station began service. Together with Morris Park and Clarenceville, Richmond Hill was incorporated as an independent village in 1894. Most residents were businessmen from Manhattan who erected large houses in the Queen Anne style costing from $2500 to $5000 each on generous plots. Jacob Riis moved there in 1886 (his home on 120th Street was demolished). By 1900 the high school had opened and a hilly section toward Kew Gardens was covered by luxurious houses costing $8000 each. The City of Brooklyn began creating Forest Park abutting Richmond Hill in 1895. The Episcopal Church of the Resurrection began in 1874, followed by Union Congregational Church (1902), St. John's Lutheran Church (1903), and Holy Child Jesus Christ Catholic Church (1910). The Richmond Hill library opened in 1899, and in 1905 a Carnegie library opened (one of only seven in the borough); the Works Progress Administration (WPA) mural *The Story of Richmond Hill* by Philip Evergood was finished in 1938. The Republican Club building opened in 1908, and like the library is a city landmark. Real estate development intensified and Jamaica Avenue became commercialized after the Jamaica Avenue elevated line reached the area in 1918. By 1920 there was no open land and the only sort of development possible was infilling (building new houses in between older ones, often on substandard lots, or demolishing large houses and putting up smaller ones in their place). The population was mostly German and Irish until an influx of Latin Americans began after 1975. In the 1980s almost 40 percent of the immigrants who settled in Richmond Hill were from Guyana; others were from the Dominican Republic, Colombia, Ecuador, India, and Jamaica. Early in the twenty-first century, Richmond Hill was a well-maintained residential neighborhood retaining many elegant structures from the turn of the twentieth century. The center of the neighborhood is the Triangle, formed by the intersection of Lefferts Boulevard with Myrtle and Jamaica avenues. Nearby, the Triangle Hofbrau was an inn and restaurant from 1864 to 1999. The Richmond Hill Historical Society began lobbying for historic district status in the 1990s, but the Landmarks Preservation Commission resisted, claiming that too many houses had been altered.

Vincent Seyfried, Jeffrey A. Kroessler

Richmondtown. Neighborhood in Staten Island near the geographic center of the borough. Its main streets are Richmond Road and Clarke Avenue. In the 1690s the area was the site of a crossroads settlement known as Cocclestown because of its abundance of oyster shells. It later became Richmond Town, the county seat and the site of the county jail (1710) and courthouse (1728). The first building of the Church of St. Andrew (Episcopal) was constructed from 1711 to 1713. In 1837 a local entrepreneur named Henry Seaman bought the Swaim farm, divided it into lots, and constructed five houses (three of which

Richmondtown Courthouse, 2009

remain standing in the early twenty-first century). In the same year a new Greek Revival courthouse was built, followed by a new jail in 1860 (later demolished). The Church of St. Patrick (Roman Catholic) was erected in 1868. Consolidation in 1898 led to the gradual removal of county government operations to St. George, but the neighborhood continued to grow after Staten Island Rapid Transit was built to its south. In the early twenty-first century Richmondtown is a middle-class residential neighborhood. The firehouse at 3664 Richmond Road is the home of one of the two remaining volunteer fire companies in New York City.

Barnett Shepherd

Richmondtown Restoration. Former name of Historic Richmond Town.

Richmond Valley. Neighborhood in southwestern Staten Island, bounded to the north by Outerbridge Crossing Plaza and the exchanges of the Richmond Parkway and West Shore Expressway, to the south by Mill Creek and Amboy Road, and to the west by the Arthur Kill. A mill that stood on the creek for centuries was run by the Dissosway, Weir, and Cole families. The area was named by the Staten Island Railroad, which opened a station there in the 1860s. Luxury houses and warehouses were built in the 1980s. Since 2000 several "big box" shopping centers, commercial building, and office buildings have been constructed.

Marjorie Johnson

Rickard, Tex [George Lewis] (*b* Leavenworth, Kans., 2 Jan 1871; *d* Miami, 6 Jan 1929). Boxing promoter. The first boxing match that he promoted in New York City was the heavyweight championship between Jess Willard and Frank Moran on 25 March 1916 at Madison Square Garden, the first heavyweight title fight in the city since 1900. In the following years Rickard made Madison Square Garden into the best-known boxing venue in the nation, especially when he made it the site of Jack Dempsey's defense of the heavyweight title against Georges Carpentier on 2 July 1921, the first fight to draw $1 million in gate receipts. This figure was exceeded by a fight that Rickard promoted between Dempsey and Luis Firpo on 14 September 1923 at the Polo Grounds before 75,000 fans. In 1925 Rickard's syndicate built a new Madison Square Garden that featured boxing, ice hockey, and six-day bicycle races.

Steven A. Riess

Rickey, (Wesley) Branch (*b* Little California [now in Stockdale], Ohio, 20 Dec 1881; *d* Columbia, Mo., 9 Dec 1965). Baseball executive. After a career as a player and manager he spent 26 years as an executive with the St. Louis Cardinals. As president and general manager from 1942 of the Brooklyn Dodgers he was influential in having Jackie Robinson enter the major leagues in 1947. Forced from the Dodgers in 1950 by the team's owner Walter O'Malley, he tried with the lawyer William A. Shea to form a new baseball league in the late 1950s; their efforts led indirectly to the admission of the New York Mets into the major leagues in 1962. From 1943 to 1950 Rickey lived at 215 Montague Street in Brooklyn Heights.

Murray Polner, *Branch Rickey: A Biography* (New York: Atheneum, 1982)

Joseph S. Lieber

Ridgewood. Neighborhood in Brooklyn and Queens bounded to the north by Metropolitan Avenue, to the east by the tracks of the Long Island Rail Road and Conrail, to the south by Central Avenue, and to the west by Flushing Avenue. The area was inhabited by Mespachtes Indians and during the seventeenth and eighteenth centuries was tilled by Dutch farmers. The only surviving Dutch farmhouse is the Adrien Onderdonck House (1731); it burned in the 1970s but was restored by the Greater Ridgewood Historical Society and became a city landmark in 1996. Arbitration Rock was set at Onderdonk and Montrose avenues to end a dispute over the boundary between the towns of Bushwick and Newtown that lasted from 1660 to 1769; the rock was unearthed and moved to the Onderdonk House in 2001. English settlers in the early eighteenth century named the area for its high wooded terrain. Transportation links to Brooklyn facilitated development in the mid-nineteenth century. The horsecar line along Myrtle Avenue was extended to Broadway in 1855, as was the elevated rapid transit line in 1879; the Brooklyn City and Bushwick trolley lines built large depots at Myrtle and Wyckoff avenues in 1881; and the Myrtle Avenue elevated line was extended to Wyckoff Avenue in 1888. Brooklyn built the Ridgewood Reservoir for its water system in 1858, and it remained in service until 1959. From the late 1880s until the end of World War I the area was sometimes known as Evergreen, in deference to a community on Long Island that claimed priority in using the name Ridgewood. The population was largely middle class and German and supported many local businesses, including several breweries and knitting mills. At first small frame houses were erected, and from 1906 Gustav Mathews acquired the remaining farmlands and built the Mathews Flats, more than 800 six-family row houses of three stories each in distinctive yellow and orange brick from the Kreischer brick works on Staten Island (a few blocks were designated as city landmarks). The houses sold for more than $11,000 or rented for $15 a month. Paul Stier built a similar development from 1908 to 1914 between 67th and 70th avenues, using tan brick and lumber of the highest quality (much of the housing in the neighborhood consists of his row houses, about half of which are occupied by their owners). The homes on Stockholm Street, and the brick street itself, comprise another historic district. In the 1920s the boundary between Brooklyn and Queens was redrawn, changing the historic straight line to a line following the street grid, eliminating the situation where the border cut through houses.

After World War II a large number of Romanians, Italians, and Slovenes settled in the neighborhood. In an effort to disassociate themselves from Bushwick, a largely African American area to the south with high rates of crime and arson, the local residents in 1979 voted to change from a postal zone in Brooklyn to one in Queens. In September 1983 an area comprising 2980 buildings was listed on the National Register of Historic Places, the largest such historic district in the nation. Some six-family apartment buildings were converted into cooperatives in the late 1980s to attract young working-class families. In addition to its large German community Ridgewood during the 1980s attracted many immigrants from eastern Europe, especially Romania (accounting for more than a quarter of all immigrants settling there), the former republics of Yugoslavia, and Poland. The neighborhood also drew large numbers of Chinese, Dominicans, Italians, Koreans, and Ecuadorians. In 2000 the population was about 88,000: 46 percent white, 43 percent Hispanic, 7 percent Asian.

Vincent Seyfried, Stephen Weinstein

Ridiculous Theatrical Company. Theater company formed in 1967 by Charles Ludlam as an offshoot of John Vaccaro's Play-House of the Ridiculous. As the company's producer, director, playwright, and leading actor, Ludlam took much of his material from popular culture and used exaggerated characterizations and sexual ambiguity in his performances. After Ludlam's death in 1987, his duties were assumed by his companion Everett Quinton. The company shut down two years later.

D. S. Moynihan

Rihani, Ameen [Amin] **(Fares)** (*b* Freika, near Bikfaya, Lebanon, 24 Nov 1876; *d* Freika, 14 Sept 1940). Writer. After moving to New York City in 1888 he worked in his father's dry-goods shop on Washington Street. He became a member of al-Rabitah al-Qalamiyya (the Pen League), an influential literary circle of Syrian émigré writers, and wrote *The Book of Khaled* (1911), believed to be the first novel about the earliest Syrian immigrants in America. As a writer he sought to bridge two cultures and therefore returned often to the Middle East. Rihani was one of the first Syrians in New York City to speak out against militant Zionism. His writings on the Arab world include the book *Maker of Modern Arabia* (1928) and articles in the *New York Times, Harper's Weekly,* and the *Nation.*

Paula Hajar

Riis, Jacob A(ugustus) (*b* Ribe, Denmark, 3 May 1849; *d* Barre, Mass., 26 May 1914). Social reformer, photographer, and writer. After immigrating to the United States from Denmark in 1870 he worked as a police reporter for the *New York Tribune* from 1877 to 1888 and became known for his vivid descriptions of crime along Mulberry Bend in the Five Points neighborhood. The extreme poverty and overcrowding that he witnessed there led him to become an advocate for immigrants. Riis' lurid and sensationalist photographs that accompanied his stories forced his middle-class readers to confront the filth and degradation of the slums. His article "Flashes from the Slums" (1888) in the *Sun* was highly successful, and in 1890 he became nationally known for his book *How the Other Half Lives,* an account of the squalid conditions on the Lower East Side. A showman, he also gave lantern slide lectures to religious and charitable organizations, seeking to close police lodging houses and promoting tenement regulation, care for homeless children, and the construction of playgrounds. He eventually left newspaper work to write and give lectures full time. Among his supporters was Theodore Roosevelt, who as the city's police commissioner closed the police lodging houses. In 1887 Riis built a house at 84-41 120th Street in Richmond Hill, his home until 1911. Later he lived at 524 North Beech Street in Richmond Hill.

Alexander Alland, *Jacob A. Riis, Photographer and Citizen* (Millerton, N.Y.: Aperture, 1974); Bonnie Yochelson and Daniel Czitrom, *Rediscovering Jacob Riis* (New York: The New Press, 2008)

Bonnie Yochelson

Jacob A. Riis

Rikers Island. Located in the East River off the southeastern edge of the Bronx, it originally covered 87 acres (35 hectares) of land and belonged to descendants of Abraham Rycken, a settler who moved to Long Island in 1638. The city bought the island from the family in 1884 and used it as a prison farm. In 1931 it opened a prison for men there to replace its crumbling one on Blackwell's Island. After 1954 landfill was added to enlarge the area of the island to 415 acres (168 hectares), enabling the prison facilities to expand. The only transport was a ferry to the Bronx until 1966, when a three-lane bridge 4200 feet (1280 meters) long was extended to Queens. In 1985 the Rose M. Singer Center for women opened the nation's first jail-based nursery. The facility also included a bakery, laundry, tailor shop, print shop, power plants, and infirmary. By most measures Rikers Island, with a capacity for 17,000 inmates, is the largest jail facility in the United States.

Jennifer Wynn, *Inside Rikers: Stories from the World's Largest Penal Colony* (New York: St. Martin's Press, 2001)

Joseph P. Viteritti

Rio de San Antonio. Former name of the Hudson River, given by Estevan Gomez (*ca* 1483–1538), a Portugese explorer who arrived at the river's mouth in 1524.

riots. Although New York City was considered a center of Loyalist sentiment during the American Revolution, British imperial policy frequently drove the local populace into the streets in the years before armed revolt. The English traditions that shaped colonial New York sanctioned rioting, and in the eighteenth and early nineteenth centuries it was an established part of the city's political culture. On 1 November 1765 mobs demonstrated against the Stamp Act by parading with effigies of Cadwallader Colden, the lieutenant governor of New York; they controlled the streets until the act was repealed the next spring. Other effigy processions took place in opposition to the Townshend Duties on 14 November 1768, 10 May 1770, and 5 November 1770. On 15 June 1774 a crowd paraded with effigies of British officials to protest the Boston Port Bill. British soldiers and residents of New York City defending the Liberty Pole clashed several times from 10 August 1766 to 18 January 1770 (the Golden Hill Riot). Crowds harassed royal officials, whom they threatened with bodily harm and sometimes tarred and feathered.

The end of hostilities with Britain and the departure of the redcoats did not bring peace to the streets. On 26 July 1788 enraged supporters of the proposed Constitution gutted the printing office of the anti-Federalist Thomas Greenleaf. Political differences led to several disturbances in the 1790s, including a demonstration against the Jay Treaty at which Alexander Hamilton maintained that the crowd pelted him with stones. The Doctors' Riot of 1788 began on 13 April when 5000 people marched on New York Hospital to protest the purported theft of cadavers for dissection. Searching for evidence of illegal behavior, the rioters destroyed laboratories, ransacked offices, and buried (or reburied) every cadaver they found. They took into custody a group of medical students (whom they later surrendered to the authorities for "safekeeping"). The rioters returned the next day to search the homes of physicians and other facilities and then disarmed a small militia detachment and threatened to storm the jail where the students were being held. The authorities reacted by firing on the crowd and killing three people. Concerns about immoral behavior inspired two riots aimed at bawdy houses (14–15 October 1793 and 17–20 July 1799).

During the nineteenth century ethnic and religious differences, politics, and racial prejudice led to the most violent rioting in the city's history, typified by a battle on Christmas Day 1806 in the sixth ward between Catholics (mostly Irish) and Protestants (mostly native born). There were also violent strikes by stevedores (1825 and 1828), weavers (1828), and stonecutters (1829). Many regard 1834 as the city's worst year for riots because of election rioting between Whigs and Democrats (9–10 April) and mob attacks on abolitionists and blacks (7–11 July). Both these disturbances and several others in the 1830s were marked by intense physical violence. The Flour Riot (12 February 1837) was different: after a political meeting decrying the plight of the poor, a large crowd attacked Eli Hart's warehouse and gave away flour; two other warehouses also were attacked. The police were powerless to stop fights on 4–5 July 1857 between the Protestant street gang the Bowery Boys and the Catholic gang the Dead Rabbits, and 12 lives were lost as a result.

By this time widespread crowd violence had become commonplace, setting the stage for the second-most serious riot in the city's history. The Astor Place Riot (10–11 May 1849) began when supporters of the American actor Edwin Forrest interrupted a performance by his English rival, William C. Macready. Protests both in and outside the Astor Place Opera House brought forth the militia and the police, who killed 22 people (nine more may have died later of their injuries) and wounded 48 when they fired into a crowd that refused to disperse, and 50 to 70 policemen were injured when the crowd retaliated. The riot reflected deep ethnic and class resentments within the city. In the Kleindeutschland Riot (12–13 July 1857) the police killed one man and wounded several others in a

Lithograph of the Astor Place Riot, 1849

disturbance in a German neighborhood that began when police officers attempted to break up a street brawl.

The DRAFT RIOTS of 13–16 July 1863, the bloodiest riots in U.S. history, began in front of a conscription office on Third Avenue and 47th Street when the city's Irish poor arose against a new law exempting from conscription anyone who paid a fee of $300. The riot assumed a racial dimension: some blacks were hanged, many were assaulted, and African American institutions and homes were destroyed. Contemporary estimates reported from 105 to 1000 deaths, though the most widely accepted figure is around 100. Eight people were killed and 15 were injured in the Orange riot of 12 July 1870, in which Irish Catholics attacked Irish Protestants commemorating the victory of William of Orange over French and Irish forces in 1690 (see ORANGE RIOTS). In the following year Catholics assaulted a truncated Protestant parade on the same anniversary despite the presence of a large police and militia guard.

Hard times after the Civil War prompted a resurgence of labor strife, which became the principal source of rioting in the late nineteenth century. The Tompkins Square Riot (13 January 1874) was the result of a demonstration planned by the Committee of Safety, a political group with many members in the communist organization the International Workingmen's Association, or First International. The police board and the parks commissioner at first seemed cooperative but at the last moment denied the necessary permits. Although the organizers revised their plans and canceled part of the proceedings, most of the participants were left uninformed of any changes, and in the ensuing confusion about 7000 men and women gathered in Tompkins Square. The demonstrators were ordered to disperse by the police commissioner and soon after were charged by a force of 1600 police officers, who indiscriminately beat and arrested demonstrators and bystanders. News of the riot spread, and hundreds of demonstrators converged on police headquarters to demand the release of those arrested, but city officials were aware that the behavior of the police was largely sanctioned by middle-class New Yorkers and ignored the demands for an inquiry. On 22 April 1886 eastern European sugar refinery workers attacked delivery wagons and fought with police in Williamsburg.

The employees of the city's many privately owned streetcar and elevated railroad companies were particularly noted for aggressive behavior, especially during strikes over wages and working conditions. Although riots took place on several occasions (notably in Manhattan in 1886), the most serious were the Brooklyn Surface Railroad Riots (14 January to 2 February 1895), in which strikers tore down electrical wires, damaged tracks, beat nonunion workers, and confronted the police and militia. Shots fired by rioters on 21 January wounded two police officers, and in partial retaliation soldiers charged into the crowd with bayonets and injured many people. Almost 7000 militia members were deployed along the rail lines to guard the streetcar tracks against sabotage, and on 23 January the militia shot and killed one man. Race relations remained a persistent problem. Whites attacked African Americans in 1889 and in response to an arrest did so again in 1900 in San Juan Hill.

In the early and mid-twentieth century riots in New York City resulted less from conflict between whites and African Americans than from attacks on property that pitted blacks against the city's police force. On the whole riots caused fewer deaths than they had previously. There were riots in Harlem in 1935 (killing three people), 1943 (killing six), 1964, and 1965 and during the citywide power blackout of 1977. Protests of the antiwar movement and the student Left in the 1960s

Newspaper illustration of the Whisky War in the City of Brooklyn

and early 1970s sometimes resulted in politically motivated riots. The best-known incident of the period took place between 23 April and 1 May 1968 at Columbia University, where students protested the university's cooperation with the Institute for Defense Analysis and its decision to build a gymnasium in Morningside Park, the dividing line between the university and poor residents of Harlem. The students staged large rallies, destroyed fences at the construction site, occupied campus buildings, held three university officials hostage for more than 24 hours, and ransacked several offices, including that of President Grayson Kirk in Low Library. With classes mostly suspended and the university in turmoil, police removed the protestors forcibly on 30 April. Four faculty members, 132 students, and 12 police officers were injured in clashes on the first day, as were five more police officers and six students the next day. The confrontation did not subside until the end of the spring semester, and the bitterness on both sides remained for many years. The Stonewall Riots of 28 June 1969, precipitated by a police raid at the Stonewall Inn, a gay bar at 53 Christopher Street, marked the beginning of the gay-rights movement. Another violent incident connected with the Vietnam War occurred in 1970, when construction workers attacked antiwar demonstrators on Wall Street.

Disagreement about a park curfew and its effect on the homeless led to a confrontation between the community and the police in the Tompkins Square Riot of 6 August 1988, characterized as a "police riot" because of the manner in which the police dealt with the protestors. During the summer of 1991 an automobile in the motorcade of Menachem Mendel Schneerson, the spiritual leader of the Lubavitcher sect of Hasidim in Crown Heights, struck and killed a Guyanese boy named Gavin Cato who was playing on the sidewalk. A group of black men killed a visiting Hasid, Yankel Rosenbaum, in retaliation. Existing tensions between Lubavitchers and West Indian residents of the neighborhood boiled over and several days of rioting ensued; about 200 people were injured. Accusations that Mayor David Dinkins did not act quickly enough to quell the riots became a major issue in his reelection campaign against Rudolph Giuliani. As of the early twenty-first century the incidents in Crown Heights were the last violent riots in the city. Although demonstrations were staged in response to allegations of police brutality in such cases as the shooting of Amadou Diallo in the Bronx (1999) and Sean Bell in Queens (2006), the protests did not escalate to violent rioting as many had in the past.

Adrian Cook, *The Armies of the Streets: The New York City Draft Riots of 1863* (Lexington: University Press of Kentucky, 1974); Paul O. Weinbaum, *Mobs and Demagogues: The New York Response to Collective Violence in the Early Nineteenth Century* (Ann Arbor, Mich.: UMI Research Press, 1979); Paul A. Gilje, *The Road to Mobocracy: Popular Disorder in New York City, 1763–1834* (Chapel Hill: University of North Carolina Press, 1987)

Paul A. Gilje

Ripley, Robert [LeRoy] (*b* Santa Rosa, Calif., 25 Dec 1890; *d* New York City, 27 May 1949). Originator of Ripley's "Believe It or Not!" In 1913 he moved to New York to try out for the New York Giants baseball team and was accepted. However, an injury in his first game ended his baseball career before it started. That same year, the *New York Globe* hired him to draw sports cartoons. He titled one cartoon about unusual sports events "Believe It or Not!" which formed the basis for a weekly column about odd achievements. He traveled around the world to collect inspiration for the cartoons. When, in 1923, the *New York Globe* shut down operations, the *New York Post* hired Ripley to continue to publish his popular cartoons. Ripley continued to have a presence in sports and in 1926 won the title of New York City handball champion. In 1929 "Believe It or Not!" was syndicated and began to be published around the world. The year 1930 marked the beginning of a 14-year career in radio, which centered on live radio broadcasts from places underwater, in the sky, in snake pits, and in other unusual places. Through the 1930s Ripley opened Ripley's "Believe It or Not!" Odditoriums in Illinois, California, Texas, and New York City. His popularity reached such a height that in 1936 members of the Boys Club of New York voted his job as the most desirable and popular in America, with the presidency of the United States coming in second place. In 1949 during the taping of the 13th weekly installment of his television show, which that week was dealing with death and death rituals, Ripley died from heart failure.

Breanne Scanlon

Ritz Tower. Luxury hotel and apartment building. When it opened in 1926 on the corner of 57th Street and Park Avenue, it was the world's tallest residential building. At 540 feet (165 meters) and 41 stories the building signaled the increasing height and luxury of Park Avenue apartment buildings. Developer Arthur Brisbane, a popular columnist for the *Evening Journal,* developed the hotel as an apartment hotel, which provided furnished public rooms and restaurants on the building's lower floors and suites of private rooms above. Such buildings were not subject to the height restrictions of other residential buildings, and they also addressed the growing realization that multifamily housing was the only way to accommodate Manhattan's many residents. As such, the Ritz Tower served a significant residential population but also had facilities for transient guests. The building created by primary architect Emery Roth and contributing architect Thomas Hastings is a testament to the belief that classical design is applicable in modern architecture. Its steel frame is clad in limestone, brick, and terracotta and adorned with decorative details of the Italian Renaissance. The building's setback structure created terraces meant to enhance the living quarters of residents and to draw the eye upward from street level. The Ritz-Carlton Company was hired by Brisbane to provide services to the building's residents and manage the building and its restaurants.

In return the company lent the building the use of the company's famous name to increase the building's appeal. When Brisbane later realized he could not handle the heavy debt of the $4 million mortgage he had taken out for the project, he offered the property to his friend and employer William Randolph Hearst and moved to less spectacular quarters in the building. In 1955 the building was purchased by the Sonnabend hotel chain, and the interior was redecorated by designer Dorothy Draper. After the renovation, the building was converted to cooperative apartments while it continued to provide luxury hotel services. In 1987 the Ritz Tower discontinued transient rentals. In the early twenty-first century it is still considered one of the city's most desirable addresses.

Carol Willis, Joe Piscina

Riverbank Park, 2009

Rivera, Diego (*b* Guanajuato City, Mexico, 8 Dec 1886; *d* Mexico City, 24 Nov 1957). Painter and muralist. After gaining fame in Mexico and Europe, Rivera's first American one-man exhibition, Frozen Assets, was shown at the Museum of Modern Art (MoMA) in December 1931. The following year he was commissioned to paint a mural for the west wall of the Grand Lobby of 30 Rockefeller Plaza, which was then under construction. The work was titled *Man at the Crossroads Looks Uncertainly but Hopefully towards the Future,* and was intended to depict the themes of "human intelligence controlling the powers of nature" and "the era of science." Rivera began the fresco in April 1933 but controversy soon arose when he included a portrait of Vladimir Lenin leading a May Day parade. The Rockefeller family considered the portrait inappropriate and asked Rivera to remove it, but he refused. In spite of his offer to add a portrait of Abraham Lincoln on the opposite side of the mural, Rivera was removed from the commission. After being paid his full fee, he was barred from the site, and the mural was covered up by a large curtain. The Museum of Modern Art unsuccessfully petitioned to have the mural removed and added to their collection, but despite demonstrations by supporters, ax-wielding workmen destroyed the work on 10 February 1934. The mural was soon replaced by José María Sert's painting *American Progress,* and Rivera never worked in the United States again. However, in 1935 he re-created the frescoes in the Palace of Fine Arts in Mexico City, with the addition of an unflattering portrait of John D. Rockefeller, Jr. in a nightclub.

Caleb Smith

Riverbank State Park. State park running from 137th Street to 145th Street between Riverside Drive and the Hudson River in Manhattan. The Board of Estimate approved the site in 1985; construction began in 1992, and the park opened a year later. Sitting 69 feet (21 meters) above the Hudson River over a wastewater treatment facility and modeled after Japanese urban rooftop designs, Riverbank offers panoramic views of lower Manhattan, the Hudson River, the Palisade Mountains, and the George Washington Bridge. The park's outdoor facilities include playgrounds, lawns, and picnic areas; a carousel; community gardens; basketball, tennis, and handball courts; a running track; a swimming pool; and a football field. The park also has a 900-seat indoor amphitheater at water level, a 2500-seat athletic complex with a fitness room, an Olympic-sized swimming pool, a covered rink for ice skating and roller skating, a greenhouse, and a restaurant. During the summer the park holds free concerts and plays as well as special events for children and senior citizens. Riverbank is the only state park in Manhattan and receives more than two million visitors annually.

Ben Silk

River Café. Restaurant moored on the East River at 1 Water Street in Brooklyn Heights. It took many years for restaurateur Michael "Buzzy" O'Keeffe to gain city approval for a barge café in this once seamy waterfront area known as DUMBO. The 130-seat River Café, which opened in May 1977 and faces the Manhattan skyline, was called by the *New York Times* "the restaurant that launched a thousand chefs," including Larry Forgione and Rick Laakkonen. The French restaurant guide Gault Millau rated the River Café one of the five best restaurants in New York City.

Harold Takooshian

Riverdale. Neighborhood in the northwestern Bronx, lying on the ridge east of the Hudson River south of Westchester County. Its eastern and southern boundaries are constantly in dispute. It began as a railroad station of the Hudson division of the New York Central Railroad called Riverdale-on-Hudson. In the 1860s the high ground overlooking the Hudson was an ideal site for the summer mansions of the city's industrial and mercantile elite, who could travel easily by rail to and from their offices in Manhattan. Before World War II a number of luxurious one-family houses were built on landscaped grounds near the mansions. The construction in the 1930s of the Henry Hudson Parkway spurred development, as did the addition of a bus line connecting the neighborhood to the Seventh Avenue line of Interborough Rapid Transit at 231st Street and to the Eighth Avenue line of the Independent Subway System in northern Manhattan. During the years after the war most of the estates were sold to institutions and developers. Fewer high-rise apartment buildings were erected than in nearby Spuyten Duyvil.

Many structures dating from the nineteenth century are local landmarks: Fieldston Hill (circa 1865) at the western end of 246th Street, Greyston (1864) at 247th Street and Independence Avenue, Wave Hill (1844) at 249th Street and Independence Avenue, and Stonehurst (1861). From the same period are Christ Church (1866) and the Riverdale Presbyterian Church (1863), which stand on either side of the Henry Hudson Parkway. The College of Mount St. Vincent, operated by the Sisters of Charity, has a castle originally built in 1852 for the well-known Shakespearean actor Edwin Forrest, as well as his cottage and stable. The college's administration building was built in stages from 1857 to 1908. Along Sycamore Avenue between 252nd and 254th streets is the Riverdale Historic District, the residences of which were originally the barns and carriage houses of the nearby estates. North of Manhattan College Parkway is the Fieldston Historic District with beautiful landscaped grounds and sumptuous homes. Major institutions in Riverdale include the Riverdale Country School, the Wave Hill Center, the Henry Ittleson Center for Child Research, the Cardinal Spellman Retreat House, and the Hebrew Home for the Aged. Riverdale is geographically separated from the rest of the city because of its ridge. It has few major commercial thoroughfares, giving the neighborhood a distinctive suburban character.

William A. Tieck, *Riverdale, Kingsbridge, Spuyten Duyvil: New York City* (Old Tappan, N.J.: Fleming H. Revell, 1968); Gary Hermalyn and Robert Kornfeld, *Landmarks of the Bronx* (New York: Bronx County Historical Society, 1989)

Lloyd Ultan

Riverdale Country School. Coeducational elementary and secondary school opened in 1907 by Frank Sutcliff Hackett and his wife, Frances Hackett, on a country estate high above Van Cortlandt Park. In 1935 the Riverdale Country School for Girls opened on a nearby estate west of the original campus. Riverdale Country School became fully coeducational in 1972; the original campus became the site of its secondary school, and the former girls' school the site of its elementary school. The enrollment stood at 1060 students in 2006.

Richard Schwartz

Riverdale Presbyterian Church. Church formed in 1863 at 4765 Henry Hudson Parkway West by J. Joseph Eagleton, Samuel W. Dodge, William Earl Dodge, Jr., Robert Colgate, and John Mott. The building was designed by James Renwick on land donated by Joseph Delafield. With the active support of the philanthropist Grace Hoadley Dodge, church members established Riverdale Neighborhood House (1872) and the Riverdale Neighborhood and Library Association. Notable members of the congregation included Cleveland H. Dodge and George W. Perkins. In 1965 the city designated the church building and the attached Grace H. Dodge Church House as landmarks.

David Meerse

Riverside Church. An interdenominational church on the east side of Riverside Drive between 120th and 122nd streets. It occupies a huge, steel-framed Gothic Revival building, financed by John D. Rockefeller, Jr., and completed in 1930. The congregation began as a Baptist church in 1841 in lower Manhattan and soon became known for its interracial and international character. The first minister at the new site uptown was the controversial and influential Harry Emerson Fosdick. The church seats 2500 people and is notable for the excellence of its stone carving and stained glass. The Laura Spelman Rockefeller Memorial Carillon, the largest in the world, contains 74 bells and occupies a space extending from the 23rd story to what would be the 28th; it was the first carillon in history to achieve a compass of five octaves, and its Bourdon, or hour-bell, is the largest and heaviest carillon bell ever cast. An observation platform 355 feet (108 meters) above the ground is served by the tallest elevators in any church in the world. Riverside Church is affiliated with both the American Baptist churches in the United States and the United Church of Christ.

Kenneth T. Jackson

Riverside Park. Public park in Manhattan, situated on a 4-mile (6.4-kilometer) strip of land along the Hudson River from 72nd Street to 125th Street and from 135th Street to 158th Street, and occupying more than 323 acres (131 hectares). Prehistoric glaciers left rocky outcroppings and steep bluffs on the site, and before European settlement the rough terrain was only sparsely populated by American Indians. In 1846 the Hudson River Railroad was built along the shoreline. A proposal for a scenic drive and park was advanced in 1865 by William R. Martin, a commissioner on the Board of Central Park. During the next two years the city acquired land between the railroad and the bluffs, for which a park was commissioned in 1873 by the park board from the chief designer of Central Park, Frederick Law Olmsted. His proposal, calling for a parkway that would adapt to the rolling contours of the land, was accepted in 1875; the final plans were drawn up by others, including Samuel Parsons, Julius Munkwitz, and Calvert Vaux, and implemented during the next 25 years. The park was built in English pastoral style, with a rustic retaining wall, informally arranged plantings, and meandering paths. Dockside industries and noisy railroads along the riverfront, however, threatened the park. A plan made as early as 1891 to build a bridge over the tracks was neglected for more than 40 years. Proponents of the "city beautiful" movement at the turn of the twentieth century introduced formal elements into the park, including the Soldiers' and Sailors' Monument and its plaza at 89th Street, Grant's Tomb at 121st Street, and the Firemen's Memorial at 100th Street. Between 1934 and 1937 a plan known as West Side Improvement was executed along the riverfront under the guidance of Robert Moses, who expanded earlier proposals, including one by McKim, Mead and White from the 1920s, to build a rotunda and a marina at 79th Street and to double the size of the park by adding to it the West Side Highway and Henry Hudson Parkway. The architect and engineer Clinton Lloyd replaced rustic stone with granite, bluestone, and concrete to give the park a more orderly appearance; the landscape architect Gilmore Clarke contributed a complementary planting scheme. Most of the labor was provided by relief workers, who enclosed the railroad tracks and built a promenade over them and added a lower level on landfill for athletic fields and tennis courts. When their work was completed, the park incorporated

Riverside Park, 2009

Soldiers' and Sailors' Monument (designed by Stoughton and Stoughton with Paul E. M. Duboy) on Riverside Drive, ca *1900*

elements of several styles of landscape design. In 2000, 7 acres (2.8 hectares) of land stretching between 68th and 72nd streets were developed into Riverside Park South, which included a soccer field, three basketball courts, and a public pier extending 750 feet (289 meters) into the Hudson River.

Jonathan Kuhn

Rizzuto, Phil(ip Francis) [The Scooter] (*b* Brooklyn, 25 Sept 1917; *d* West Orange, N.J., 10 Aug 2007). Baseball player and broadcaster. A Brooklyn-born graduate of Richmond Hill High School in Queens, he played shortstop for the New York Yankees (1941–42, 1946–56), was the American League's Most Valuable Player (1950), and became a member of the Baseball Hall of Fame in 1994. Rizzuto was well known as an elite defensive infielder and was also regarded as one of the best bunters in the major leagues. When he retired, his 1217 career double plays ranked second in major league history. Beginning in 1957 he broadcast Yankee games on radio and television for nearly 40 years; his signature phrase "Holy cow!" and birthday wishes to fans made him a New York City institution.

Andrew Sparberg

RJR Nabisco. Firm of food processors formed in 1890 as the New York Biscuit Company by the lawyer William Henry Moore. In 1898 it acquired the brands Fig Newtons and Premium Saltines when it merged with the American Biscuit Company to form the National Biscuit Company, a group of 114 bakeries with total capitalization of $55 million. Under the direction of Adolphus Greene, during the following decade it introduced small, sealed cardboard boxes of soda crackers known as Uneeda Biscuits, which were tremendously successful owing largely to an advertising campaign handled by the firm of N. W. Ayer and Son; it also developed uniform production standards, innovative packaging, and trademarks. The firm moved its headquarters from Chicago to New York City in 1906 and introduced several brands, among them Oreo cookies and Barnum's Animal Crackers, and was soon the leading manufacturer of cookies and crackers in the United States. It also operated a bakery at 10th Avenue and 14th Street in Manhattan that was the largest in the world; the name Nabisco became a trademark in 1941. After a period of losses during the 1930s and World War II, the firm recovered by expanding its line of products and marketing them aggressively. By the 1970s it was again the country's leading cookie and cracker manufacturer; the headquarters were moved to suburban East Hanover, New Jersey, in 1975. The firm merged in 1981 with Standard Brands, a food and beverage manufacturer, to form Nabisco Brands. After being acquired by R. J. Reynolds Industries in 1985, Nabisco Brands became part of RJR Nabisco, a firm with annual sales of more than $19 billion that was the largest consumer-products company in the United States. An attempt in 1988 by F. Ross Johnson, president of the firm, to take it private led to one of the costliest corporate bidding wars in history; Johnson's group eventually lost out to another led by the brokerage firm Kohlberg Kravis Roberts, which prevailed by bidding nearly $25 billion in cash, notes, and securities. Despite the debt incurred by its new owners, RJR Nabisco remained successful. In 1999 RJR Nabisco became the Nabisco Group to distance itself from tobacco litigation. The following year Philip Morris Companies (now known as Altria Group) acquired Nabisco and merged it with Kraft. Nabisco, along with the other Kraft Foods brands, was spun off as an independent entity in 2007.

Peter A. Coclanis

Robards, Jason (Nelson, Jr.) (*b* Chicago, 26 July 1922; *d* Bridgeport, Conn., 26 Dec 2000). Actor. Robards's family moved to Manhattan when he was six years old, but lived there only a year before relocating to Los Angeles (his father, Jason Robards, Sr., was an actor). Robards attended Hollywood High School. He served in the navy during World War II, receiving multiple citations for valor, including the Navy Cross. After the war Robards moved to New York to pursue an acting career and found small roles on stage and in radio. He attended the American Academy of Dramatic Arts (1946) and performed at the Circle in the Square in 1953 under the direction of José Quintero. On Broadway he appeared in *The Iceman Cometh* (1956) and *Long Day's Journey into Night* (1956–58) by Eugene O'Neill, the playwright with whom he became most strongly associated. He also won a Tony Award for his performance in Budd Schulberg's *The Disenchanted* (1958–59) and was nominated for eight others. In later years Robards appeared in Arthur Miller's *After the Fall* (1964) and revivals of *Long Day's Journey* (1976, 1988), as well as in many television shows and films, while maintaining a residence in the Southport section of suburban Fairfield, Connecticut. Robards died of lung cancer in 2000.

Jessica Montesano, Meghan Lalonde

Robbins [Rabinowitz], **Jerome (Wilson)** (*b* New York City, 11 Oct 1918; *d* New York City, 29 July 1998). Dancer, choreographer, and director. He joined Ballet Theatre in 1940 and became a soloist in 1941. Robbins danced and choreographed for, and subsequently became artistic associate director of, George Balanchine's New York City Ballet from 1949 to 1956. From the 1940s to the 1960s he choreographed and directed numerous Broadway shows. Under Robbins, dance advanced the plot, and dialogue and music grew out of the physical action onstage. Among his Broadway musicals are *On the Town* (1944; based on his 1944 ballet *Fancy Free*), *High Button Shoes* (1947), *Call Me Madam* (1950), *The King and I* (1951), *Peter Pan* (1954), *West Side Story* (1957, film version 1961), *Gypsy* (1959), and *Fiddler on the Roof* (1964). *Jerome Robbins' Broadway* (1989) was a retrospective of his choreography from nearly a dozen musicals. In 1958 he formed the Lena Robbins Foundation to increase public awareness of new choreographers and to develop a film library dedicated to the preservation of dance. For the Spoleto Festival of 1958 he formed his own company, Ballets U.S.A., which he reconvened on and off for four years. Robbins left Broadway and returned to New York City Ballet in the 1960s, becoming its ballet master in 1969. With Peter Martins he became ballet master-in-chief on Balanchine's death in 1983, a position he retained until 1990. Robbins's work includes more than 60 ballets, among them *The Cage* (1951), *Interplay* (1952), *Afternoon of a Faun* (1953), *New York Export: Opus Jazz* (1958), *Moves* (1961), *Dances at a Gathering* (1969), *In the Night* (1970), *The Goldberg Variations* (1971), *Watermill* (1972), *In G Major* (1975), *The Four Seasons* (1979), *Glass Pieces* (1983), *I'm Old Fashioned* (1983), *In Memory Of...* (1985), and *Ives, Songs* (1988). Robbins received numerous awards, including five Tony Awards, five Donaldson Awards, two Academy Awards, an Emmy Award, the Screen Directors' Guild Award, the New York Drama Critics' Circle Award, a Kennedy Center Honor, the French Legion of Honor, a Capezio Dance Award, and the National Medal of Arts.

Norma Adler

Robert F. Kennedy Memorial Bridge [Triborough Bridge]. Viaduct structure containing three steel bridges and spanning the waters among Manhattan, the Bronx, and Queens, designed by Othmar H. Ammann and the architect Aymar Embury II. Construction began on 25 October 1929; on the same day the stock market crashed, and construction soon halted when investors were unwilling to purchase municipal bonds. The Triborough Bridge Authority was formed as an alternative source of funds in 1933, and the bridge opened to traffic on 11 July 1936 as the first of several structures built by the authority in New York City. During its first year it carried 9.65 million vehicles and generated $2.72 million in tolls. The most prominent feature is a suspension bridge spanning the East River between Queens and Wards Island that is 2780 feet (848 meters) long, with a height above water of 143 feet (43.6 meters). A lift bridge of 770 feet (235 meters) spans the Harlem River between 125th Street in Manhattan and Randalls Island, and a truss bridge of 1217 feet (371 meters) links Randalls Island to the Bronx. The bridge was renamed in 2008 to commemorate New York senator Robert F. Kennedy, who had been assassinated in Los Angeles 40 years earlier.

Rebecca Read Shanor

Roberto Clemente State Park. First state park in New York City. Opened in August 1973 as Harlem River–Bronx State Park, it spanned 25 acres (10 hectares) of land along the Harlem River north of the Washington Bridge in the Bronx. The site was occupied by boating clubhouses and shipyards in the nineteenth century. It was given its current name in September 1974 in memory of the Pittsburgh Pirates baseball player killed in a plane crash while on a relief mission to earthquake victims in Nicaragua. The park has a large outdoor pool, a gymnasium, and ballfields and abuts the River Park Towers.

Gary D. Hermalyn

Robertson, R(obert) H(enderson) (*b* Philadelphia, 29 April 1849; *d* New York City, 4 June 1919). Architect. An early association with the architect William A. Potter helped him to achieve a reputation as a skilled designer of religious and commercial buildings. His most important projects included St. Luke's Church, a Romanesque Revival structure at 285 Convent Avenue (1892–95), and the classically inspired St. Paul's Methodist Church (now the Church of St. Paul and St. Andrew) at West End Avenue and 86th Street (1896). Robertson explored diverse solutions to the problems encountered in designing tall office buildings while working on the Lincoln Building (1889–90, Union Square West), the McIntyre Building (1890–92, 874 Broadway), the Corn Exchange Bank (1892–94, Beaver and William streets, demolished), the American Tract Society Building (1894–95, Nassau Street), and the Park Row Building (1896–99, 15 Park Row), on its completion the world's tallest building.

Marjorie Pearson

Robeson, Paul (Leroy) (*b* Princeton, N.J., 9 April 1898; *d* Philadelphia, 23 Jan 1976). Actor, singer, athlete, and civil rights activist. Born to Maria Louisa Bustill and William Drew Robeson, a runaway slave and Methodist minister, he attended Rutgers University on an academic scholarship. The only African American student then at Rutgers, he was the valedictorian and a star football player. Robeson pursued professional football and boxing while attending law school at Columbia University in the early 1920s. During a performance in an amateur play at the YMCA, he captured the attention of playwright Eugene O'Neill, who cast Robeson in *Taboo, The Emperor Jones,* and *All God's Chillun Got Wings;* he later became known as one of the first actors to portray realistic, nuanced black characters in motion pictures. One of the most popular baritone singers of his time, he mastered many languages and performed classical repertory, spirituals, and folk songs from around the world in concert. "Old Man River," which he sang in both the film and stage versions of *Showboat,* was his signature song. From 1939 to 1941 he lived at 555 Edgecomb Avenue in Harlem (the house was later designated a National Historic Landmark). During World War II he was one of the first to sing on behalf of the war effort. Inspired by his experience of discrimination in law and by the perspectives he gained while touring abroad, he later joined several causes devoted to labor and antifascism and also spoke out for civil rights; the government subsequently suspended his passport from 1950 to 1958, cutting short his career. He was banned from appearing on television during the 1950s and many of his films were deemed illegal. In protest Robeson spent many of his latter years in England and the Soviet Union. His last home in the city was at 16 Jumel Terrace in Manhattan, where he lived from 1963 to 1966.

Martin Bauml Duberman, *Paul Robeson* (New York: Alfred A. Knopf, 1988)

Amanda Aaron

Robinson, Bill (Luther) "Bojangles" (*b* Richmond, Va., 25 May 1878; *d* New York City, 25 Nov 1949). Tap dancer, actor, humanitarian. Robinson performed from a young age in the taverns of Richmond, Virginia, and later Washington, D.C. He was already a veteran performer when he developed his own vaudeville show with comedian George Cooper in 1905, around the same time he got the nickname Bojangles. Robinson spent the next two decades touring as one of the biggest performers during vaudeville's twilight years, sometimes earning more than $3000 as a solo performer beginning in 1914. He moved to New York City in 1928 where he found Broadway fame in the revue *Blackbirds of 1928.* He appeared in more than a dozen major films over the next 15 years, notably opposite Shirley Temple in *Rebecca of Sunnybrook Farm* (1938) and *The Little Colonel* (1935), and with Lena Horne and Fats Waller in *Stormy Weather* (1943). Robinson is reported to have contributed nearly $1 million to charitable causes, from black hospitals and schools to orphanages and cancer research. Robinson performed at as many as 400 benefits a year, including an annual concert for the blind on his birthday.

Robinson's most famous stage performance was in *The Hot Mikado* (1939), a jazz adaptation of Gilbert and Sullivan's operetta that was popular among both critics and Broadway audiences. Robinson was a cofounder of the Negro Baseball League's New York Black Yankees and mascot for the New York Giants. He never left home without a gold-plated, pearl-handled .32 revolver that was the gift of retired officers of the New York Police Department, and he was the only nonofficer in New York City with a permit to carry such a gun. He lived on 149th Street and Seventh Avenue for 20 years, and was appointed unofficial mayor of Harlem in 1934. When he died, Harlem schools closed while his body lay in state at the 142nd Street Armory, and police estimated that half a million people lined 8 miles (13 kilometers) of streets to watch his funeral procession from Abyssinian Baptist Church, where he was eulogized by Adam Clayton Powell, Sr., to his burial in Brooklyn's Evergreens Cemetery.

Rowan Moore Gerety

Bill "Bojangles" Robinson, with a pearl-handled gold revolver given to him by the 32nd police precinct of New York City, a platinum key to the city of Richmond, Virginia, two gold deputy sheriff's badges from New York City and Brooklyn, and a gold badge for the honorary mayoralty of Harlem, all awarded to him for charitable work.

Robinson, Boardman (*b* Somerset, Nova Scotia, 6 Sept 1876; *d* Stamford, Conn., 5 Sept 1952). Canadian American illustrator, cartoonist, and socialist. Boardman began his career drawing distinctive ink wash and black crayon cartoons for the *New York Times* and the *New York Tribune.* In 1917, as an illustrator for the socialist journal *The Masses,* he was accused of violating the Espionage Act of 1917 for his controversial political cartoon titled "Making the World Safe for Democracy." He was later acquitted, but *The Masses* was forced to cease publication as a result of the litigation. Robinson later worked as an illustrator and contributing editor for other left-wing magazines such as *The Liberator* and *The New Masses.* He illustrated several books, including John Reed's *The War in Eastern Europe* (1916), which depicted his travels with Reed through Russia and the Balkans. He taught at the Art Students League in New York City from 1919 to 1930, and in 1932 was commissioned to paint a mural in the RKO Building in Rockefeller Center, which he described as the "supremacy of man's spiritual nature over industrialization." Robinson left New York in 1936 to become director of the Colorado Springs Fine Arts Center.

Caleb Smith

Robinson, Jackie [John Roosevelt] (*b* Cairo, Ga., 31 Jan 1919; *d* Stamford, Conn., 24 Oct 1972). Baseball player. He became the first student at the University of California–Los Angeles to earn four letters (one each in football, baseball, basketball, and track). During World War II he was nearly court-martialed when he refused to play on the football team at Fort Hood in Texas, an act of protest prompted by having been forced to move to the back of an army bus. After the war he played baseball in the Negro Leagues for the Kansas City Monarchs; soon many believed that he would become the first black player in the major leagues. At the East–West Game of the Negro Leagues in 1945 he was approached by a scout for Branch Rickey, president of the Brooklyn Dodgers. After secret negotiations Rickey announced on 23 October 1945 in Montreal that he had signed Robinson, who soon joined the Dodgers' farm team the Montreal Royals. He was promoted to the major leagues on 9 April 1947. In 10 years as a second baseman for the Dodgers he batted .311, stole 197 bases, had 1518 hits in 1382 games, and played in six World Series. His performance on the field and his ability to handle the pressures of his role became an inspiration to all who fought bigotry. He was elected to the Baseball Hall of Fame in 1962, the first year he was eligible. From 1947 to 1949 he lived at 5224 Tilden Street in Flatbush; for most of his years as a player he lived in St. Albans in Queens. After his retirement from baseball he was a business executive, a founder of Freedom National Bank in Harlem (1964), a civil rights activist, and a prominent Republican. In 1990 *Life* named him one of the 100 most influential Americans of the twentieth century. Robinson wrote an autobiography, *I Never Had It Made* (1972).

Arthur Ashe, *A Hard Road to Glory* (New York: Amistad/Warner, 1988)

Arthur Ashe

Robinson, Sugar Ray [Smith, Walker, Jr.] (*b* Detroit, 3 May 1921; *d* Culver City, Iowa, 12 April 1989). Boxer. At the age of 12 he moved with his mother to New York City where he attended DeWitt Clinton High School for three years. After a successful career as an amateur boxer he turned professional in 1940 and won the world welterweight title in 1946 in a 15-round decision over Tommy Bell. In 1951 he defeated Jake La Motta in a contest for the world middleweight title, a championship he held five times during his long career. Although he retired several times, financial problems forced him back into the ring. At the time of his final retirement in 1965 after a loss to Joey Archer, his record stood at 174 wins, 19 losses, six draws, one no-decision, and one no-contest. He was elected to the Boxing Hall of Fame in 1967. With Dave Anderson he wrote *Sugar Ray* (1970).

Randy Roberts

Rochdale Village. Limited-equity cooperative in southeastern Queens (2007 pop. *ca* 25,000), lying within South Jamaica and bounded to the north by Baisley Boulevard and Bedell Street, to the east by Bedell Street, to the south by 137th Avenue, and to the west by Guy R. Brewer Boulevard. Built on the site of the former Jamaica Racetrack, it was a favorite project of Robert Moses and was built for $86 million as a middle-income cooperative by the United Housing Foundation. Its 20 cruciform redbrick buildings of 14 stories each contained 5860 apartment units in all. Laid out on 170 acres (69 hectares), the cooperative also contains two shopping malls, three schools, a community center, and recreational facilities. When Rochdale opened in 1963 it was the largest cooperative housing complex in the world and was the largest experiment in integrated housing in New York City. At first its population was 80 percent white and 20 percent African American. Integration did not last, and white families started leaving in the late 1960s. In 2008 its population was predominantly African American.

James Bradley, Peter Eisenstadt

rock. New York City played an important role in the development of rock and of its precursors rock and roll and rhythm and blues. In the 1940s and 1950s rhythm and blues recorded in Kansas City, East St. Louis (Illinois), Chicago, Cincinnati, New Orleans, Texas, and California was transferred to disc at Bell Studios. Atlantic Records began in the city as a small independent record label led by Ahmet Ertegun, Nesuhi Ertegun, Herb Abramson, and (later) Jerry Wexler; it recorded such rhythm-and-blues musicians as Big Joe Turner. Record companies in the city helped to develop a style of rhythm and blues that was more polished and jazz-oriented than its counterpart elsewhere by engaging as studio musicians a number of sidemen from big bands, including those of Duke Ellington and Count Basie: among the best-known studio players were the guitarist Mickey Baker and the saxophonist King Curtis (both of whom recorded for Atlantic), the guitarist Cornell Dupree and the drummer Bernard Purdie (both members of Curtis's band), and the guitarist Jimmy Spruill (who recorded for the labels Fire, Joy, and Fury, all owned by Bobby Robinson). Early rhythm-and-blues recordings by Fats Domino and Little Richard were broadcast on the radio station WINS in New York City from 1954 by the disc jockey Alan Freed (who is believed to have originated the term *rock and roll*); he later organized concerts at the Paramount Theater in Brooklyn. Other disc jockeys in the city included Murray the K (Murray Kaufman), Cousin Brucie (Bruce Morrow), and B. Mitchell Reid.

The line between rhythm and blues and rock and roll became increasingly blurred by white performers like Elvis Presley, Buddy Holly, and Bill Haley, who found a wide audience by combining elements of rhythm and blues and country music. Berry and Holly were among the few rock-and-roll performers who wrote their own songs: most relied on material written by other songwriters that adhered closely to the popular-song formulas of Tin Pan Alley. Many of these songwriters worked in the Brill Building at 1619 Broadway, including Jerry Lieber and Mike Stoller, Gerry Goffin and Carole King, Neil Sedaka, Bert Berns, Ellie Greenwich, Barry Mann, Bobby Darin, and Neil Diamond (all employed by Don Kirshner's firm Aldon Music), Doc Pomus and Mort Shuman, and Burt Bacharach and Hal David. By the early 1960s songwriters were powerful figures in the music business, and many began performing themselves: among those who did was Paul Simon. Doo-wop emerged as a genre of rock and roll that combined the smooth, intricate harmonies of the barbershop quartet, the rhythmic drive of black gospel music, and often ludicrous lyrics. Early doo-wop groups included the Mills Brothers and the Ink Spots; the gospel element predominated in the work of later groups like the Ravens, the Orioles, the Dominos, the Clovers, the Drifters, the Platters, and the Coasters. Popularized by Freed and often performed on street corners, doo-wop had an enormous impact on white, black, and Latin American teenagers in New York City in the late 1950s and early 1960s. Italian groups were especially numerous, among them Johnny Maestro and the Crests (1958–60, best known for their recording "16 Candles"), the Brooklyn Bridge (also formed by Maestro), Dion DiMucci and the Belmonts (named for the predominantly Italian neighborhood in the Bronx), Frankie Valli and the Four Seasons, Joey Dee and the Starlighters (whose recording "Peppermint Twist" was named for the Peppermint Lounge, a discotheque in the city), and Danny and the Juniors (well known for their recording "At the Hop"). In the early 1960s doo-wop was largely eclipsed by the music of the Beatles and other groups from Britain.

At the same time small clubs like Gerde's Folk City, the Bitter End, the Cafe Wha?, and the Gaslight achieved success as venues for folk music and blues, both associated in the popular mind with the bohemianism then fashionable and the brand of leftist populism embodied by such folk musicians as Woody Guthrie and Pete Seeger. The clubs drew college-educated listeners familiar with the music of Doc Watson, Bill Monroe, Sonny Terry and Brownie McGhee, Elizabeth Cotten, Mississippi John Hurt, Skip James, Muddy Waters, and the Reverend Gary Davis. Among the more distinctive performers were Phil Ochs and Dave Van Ronk; others were dutiful imitators of genres ranging from Scottish ballads to Mississippi Delta blues. Bob Dylan, who began his career by performing folk music on the acoustic guitar, took up the electric guitar at the Newport Folk Festival in

1965 and soon gained a large following. His album *Highway 61 Revisited* and such songs as "Like a Rolling Stone" had a profound influence on the Beatles, the Rolling Stones, and other groups, who in their music and especially their lyrics now gave greater attention to irony and political topicality. Rock was first played on FM radio in New York City in 1966 on the classical-music station WOR by the disc jockey Scott Muni; he later moved to WNEW-FM, where he became known for innovative programming that demanded rather more from his listeners than the steady regimen of pop singles to which they were accustomed. Rock was also broadcast by WBAI, which combined highly eclectic music programming with counterculture politics.

The musical explorations of the Beatles in their albums *Revolver, Rubber Soul,* and *Sgt. Pepper's Lonely Hearts Club Band* contributed further to the growing self-consciousness and diversity of rock. Musicians largely abandoned the conventions of Tin Pan Alley in favor of adventurous material of their own composition. Their lyrics became more sophisticated and ambitious, and they freely drew on inspirations as diverse as the music of Erik Satie and the cacophony of the city. On disc and at clubs like the Electric Circus, Lou Reed and his influential band the Velvet Underground sang about sadomasochism and drugs to the accompaniment of shrieking, microtonal viola lines, guitar feedback, and a thundering rhythm section. The Fugs and the Mothers of Invention engaged in anarchic musical satire; blues and soul were performed by the Blues Project, by Aretha Franklin and B. B. King (both of whom recorded with Curtis), and by a number of "garage" bands, including the Young Rascals, Vanilla Fudge, and Mountain. The recording studio took on a more prominent role as overdubbing and editing were used to create increasingly dense sounds. From the late 1960s the producer Bill Graham presented concerts featuring three or four widely disparate groups at the Fillmore East, a converted vaudeville house on lower Second Avenue, and a club called the Scene in a basement in the West 40s offered performances by Buddy Guy, Johnny Winter, Jerry Garcia, and Jimi Hendrix, who regularly played at the Cafe Wha? and had a recording studio at 55 West Eighth Street called the Electric Lady Studio. Inspired by the innovative guitar playing of Hendrix, the jazz trumpeter Miles Davis added electric instruments to his band and helped to launch a genre known as jazz-rock, which was heard at venues like the Fillmore East and appealed to a broader audience than jazz had reached for some time.

By the mid-1970s, a new genre called punk rock emerged, centered on the Lower East Side and played at places such as CBGB-OMFUG (Country, Bluegrass, and Blues, and Other Music for Uplifting Gourmandizers) on the Bowery. Inspired by the garage bands of the 1960s, the Velvet Underground and the New York Dolls, and often the jazz musicians John Coltrane, Ornette Coleman, and Albert Ayler, punk musicians created a raw, stripped-down sound; among the better known were Television (which included the guitarists Tom Verlaine and Richard Lloyd), Richard Hell and the Voidoids (including the guitarist Robert Quine), Patti Smith, the Ramones, Talking Heads, and Blondie. The music influenced English bands like the Clash and the Sex Pistols (overtly modeled after the Voidoids by Malcolm McLaren, a former manager of the New York Dolls), some of which performed in New York City in the late 1970s, achieving success that in turn helped some bands from the city to sign record contracts with Sire (Talking Heads and the Dead Boys), Chrysalis (Blondie), Elektra (Television), Arista (Smith), and Capitol (Mink DeVille). A few bands were heard on commercial radio (Blondie and Talking Heads made hit recordings), but locally most were broadcast on college stations and briefly in 1978 on WPIX-FM. At the end of the decade punk rock thrived at such clubs as Max's Kansas City, Hurrah, the Mudd Club, Danceteria, and the Ritz (on East 11th Street), though by this time the musical differences among the bands had become accentuated and punk rock soon fragmented into such genres as new wave, noise rock, hardcore, and thrash. Although punk rock was a spent force by 1981, it achieved a lasting impact by bringing more women into rock and animating nightlife in lower Manhattan.

Other rock musicians were more difficult to categorize. Elements from such disparate sources as avant-garde jazz, the music of John Cage, and conceptual art were incorporated into the work of Eugene Chadbourne, Glenn Branca, Laurie Anderson, and the groups Curlew, DNA, the Lounge Lizards, and Naked City (consisting of the saxophonist John Zorn and the guitarists Fred Frith and Bill Frisell). An amalgam of punk rock and funk was forged by Material (the electric bass guitarist Bill Laswell and the electric guitarist Ronnie Drayton) and the Music Revelation Ensemble (the saxophonist David Murray and the electric guitarist James Blood Ulmer). James Chance, a white saxophonist, led a largely black band at the Squat Theater called James White and the Blacks that evolved into Defunkt, led by the trombonist Joseph Bowie. In the early 1990s New York City had become more inhospitable to rock musicians, with much of the prominent rock music coming out of other major cities such as Seattle (grunge). A prominent exception was Living Colour: led by the virtuoso electric guitarist Vernon Reid, it developed a distinctive style by drawing on jazz, calypso, and heavy metal. The band was active in the Black Rock Coalition, a group formed in the city to combat racism in the record business.

In the twenty-first century rock music went through a renaissance with the Garage Rock Revival, led by New York City groups such as the Strokes, Interpol, and the Walkmen, who combined the spirit of 1960s garage rock with post-punk and 1990s melodic indie rock. This reinvigorated New York as the cutting edge of new rock music. Many of these bands had commercially successful albums initially, but their careers proved short-lived. At the same time increasing rent prices pushed many artists out of Manhattan and into Brooklyn, particularly into the Williamsburg neighborhood, where a tight-knit indie rock scene took root and thrived. Many of these bands combine art rock, electronics, funk, and more experimental forms of rock music to create ebullient, challenging work with little regard for mainstream success. The scene also took a lot of inspiration from the DIY (do-it-yourself) spirit of punk, and over the decade featured a flourishing live scene, much of which revolved around organizer and promoter Todd P. Despite the insular nature of the scene, it has produced several breakout artists, including the Yeah Yeah Yeahs, TV on the Radio, MGMT, Liars, Grizzly Bear, and Animal Collective, who have all jumped into the national landscape, playing to sold-out crowds across the country, and scoring top-20 albums on the Billboard charts as well as appearances on late-night shows.

Gene Santoro, George Winslow, Benjamin Yakas

Rockaway Junction. Former name of HILLSIDE.

Rockaway Park. Neighborhood in southern Queens, lying on the Rockaway Peninsula and bounded to the north by Rockaway Inlet, to the east by Beach 110th Street, to the south by the Atlantic Ocean, and to the west by Beach 126th Street. There was rapid development after the New York, Woodhaven and Rockaway Railroad was extended to the area in 1880. On 25 July 1889 Austin Corbin, president of the Long Island Rail Road, set aside 300 acres (120 hectares) with one-half mile (1 kilometer) of beachfront for an exclusive residential neighborhood. The failure of the Hotel Imperial, built for $1 million, slowed development. In 1900 the owners of the beach resumed promotional efforts and invested $500,000 to fill in 23 acres (9 hectares) of the bay and build a boulevard along the ocean and a boardwalk 12 blocks long; 14 streets were laid out, utilities were installed, and Rockaway Beach Amusement Park in Rockaway Beach nearby opened in 1901. Soon there were large crowds of summer visitors and hundreds of houses by the time of World War I. A smaller amusement park called Rockaway Playland, also in Rockaway Beach, lasted until 1987. Rockaway Park, an attractive residential neighborhood, now draws few vacationers but has a larger permanent population.

Vincent Seyfried

Rockaway Peninsula [Rockaway]. Narrow peninsula consisting of a barrier beach 4 miles (6 kilometers) long and less than 1 mile wide in southern Queens, bounded to the north by Rockaway Inlet, to the east by Nassau County, and to the south and west by the Atlantic Ocean; it includes Fort Tilden and Jacob Riis Park as well as the neighborhoods (west to east) of Breezy Point, Roxbury, Neponsit, Belle Harbor, Rockaway Park, Rockaway Beach, Holland, Hammels, Arverne, Edgemere, and Far Rockaway. The area was uninhabited until a fishing shack was built in 1856. Transportation for the first summer visitors was provided by a ferry from Canarsie in 1864. In 1869 the South Side Railroad was constructed from the Queens mainland through Valley Stream to Far Rockaway, and hotels were soon built, leading to the peninsula's development as a summer resort. The Long Island Rail Road (LIRR) absorbed the Rockaway service in 1876; in 1880 LIRR built a timber trestle across Jamaica Bay to provide direct service between the Queens mainland and all communities between Rockaway Park and Far Rockaway; LIRR electrified the trestle route in 1905. Summer-only residents, who often rented small bungalows for the season, could now easily commute to jobs in Manhattan and Brooklyn. At the same time electric train service began Rockaway's slow transformation from a summer resort into a year-round urban neighborhood. The trestle was subject to fires; after a particularly serious one in May 1950 New York City bought the LIRR route (September 1952), rebuilt the trestle using concrete, and connected it to Brooklyn's Fulton Street subway in 1956. In the 1960s many of the old summer bungalows in Arverne and Hammels were removed as part of a redevelopment effort that never became reality, leaving large areas of vacant beachfront land. By the late 2000s the Rockaway Peninsula was a beachfront residential community with a mixture of private homes, large apartment complexes, and a sprinkling of summer-only residential units. Some long-vacant land in Arverne was being redeveloped with new, low-rise housing.

Lawrence and Carol P. Kaplan, *Between Ocean and City: The Transformation of Rockaway, New York* (New York: Columbia University Press, 2003)

Vincent Seyfried, Andrew Sparberg

Rockefeller, David, Sr. (*b* New York City, 12 June 1915). Banker and businessman. The youngest of six children of John D. Rockefeller, Jr., and Abigail "Abby" Aldrich Rockefeller, he graduated from Harvard College and studied for a year at the London School of Economics before taking his doctorate in economics at the University of Chicago in 1940. He served as an intelligence officer in North Africa and southern France during World War II and then as an assistant military attaché at the American embassy in Paris until late 1945. In the following year he returned to New York City to work for Chase National Bank. He was the chairman during the late 1940s and 1950s of a coalition of educational and religious groups that sought to improve conditions in Morningside Heights by building low-cost cooperative apartments with federal funds. In the early 1950s he was instrumental in the Chase Bank decision to remain in lower Manhattan and build a new headquarters there rather than in midtown or outside the city, a decision that led most of the large banks and brokerage houses in the city to remain near Wall Street. In 1956 he led the merger of Chase with the Bank of Manhattan. He became president and vice chairman of Chase in 1959 and chairman of the board and chief executive officer in 1969. Under his direction the bank expanded overseas, increased its capitalization and asset base, and began lending to the third world after the first Arab oil embargo in 1973. During the city's fiscal crisis of the mid-1970s he joined with Walter Wriston of Citicorp, Felix G. Rohatyn of Lazard Frères, and many others to form the Municipal Assistance Corporation, which stabilized the city's finances. After retiring from Chase in 1981 he continued to serve as the chairman of its international advisory committee; he was also chairman of the Downtown–Lower Manhattan Association, which helped to plan the South Street Seaport, the World Trade Center, and Battery Park City, and of the New York City Partnership, an organization of major corporations that constructs low-cost housing and works with city agencies to improve the delivery of services. An important collector of modern art, Rockefeller was a patron for 60 years of the Museum of Modern Art, to which he gave $100 million in 2008.

Alvin Moscow, *The Rockefeller Inheritance* (New York: Doubleday, 1977); John Willson, *The Chase* (Boston: Harvard Business School Press, 1986)

Peter J. Johnson

Rockefeller, John D(avison) (*b* near Richford, N.Y., 8 July 1837; *d* Ormond Beach, Fla., 23 May 1937). Businessman and philanthropist. In 1859 he opened a sales office in New York City that was the forerunner of the Standard Oil Company of New York, of which he became the principal shareholder. He organized the firm as a holding company, or trust, with national and international networks of production, refining, transportation, and distribution. Under his guidance Standard Oil reached a position of near-monopoly in an industry that had previously been characterized by ruinous competition. He moved with his family to New York City in 1884, taking up residence at 4 West 54th Street (now the site of the garden of the Museum of Modern Art). He also purchased an estate of 5000 acres (2000 hectares) in Westchester County. In the late 1880s he made large charitable donations to the Northern Baptist Convention and the educational and welfare agencies affiliated with it. On the advice of his associate Frederick T. Gates he shifted his support in the late 1890s to such causes as the settlement house movement, public health, education, housing, and municipal reform. For many years he was the principal supporter of the Bureau of Municipal Research, which had a profound influence on the structure of the city's government and led to reform of the police force, schools, and public health system. He remained active in the daily management of Standard Oil until 1897 and retained the title of president until 1912, the year following the dissolution of the firm by the U.S. Supreme Court. Considered the richest person in the world, Rockefeller later formed several major philanthropic foundations: the Rockefeller Institute for Medical Research (1901; now Rockefeller University), the General Education Board (1903), and the Rockefeller Foundation (1913). He also played a major role in the establishment of the Riverside Church and the University of Chicago.

John Ensor Harr and Peter J. Johnson, *The Rockefeller Century* (New York: Charles Scribner's Sons, 1988); John Ensor Harr and Peter J. Johnson, *The Rockefeller Conscience: An American Family in Public and in Private* (New York: Macmillan, 1991); Ron Chernow, *Titan: The Life of John D. Rockefeller, Sr.* (New York: Random House, 1998)

Peter J. Johnson

Rockefeller, John D(avison), Jr. (*b* Cleveland, Ohio, 28 Jan 1874; *d* Tucson, Ariz., 12 May 1960). Businessman and philanthropist, father of John D. Rockefeller, III; Nelson A. Rockefeller; and David Rockefeller. He was the only son and principal heir to the fortune of John D. Rockefeller. In his early thirties he married Abigail "Abby" Greene Aldrich, the daughter of Senator Nelson W. Aldrich of Rhode Island, and devoted himself to managing his father's business and philanthropic affairs. He was deeply influenced by his friend Harry Emerson Fosdick, who advocated Christian involvement in social problems, and by Frederick W. Taylor's writings on scientific management. His family's involvement with the mining strikes surrounding the 1914 Ludlow Massacre in Colorado turned him toward a greater involvement with issues of reform. His personal fortune, which reached $1 billion by 1929, enabled him to help finance the Paul Lawrence Dunbar Apartments in Harlem, the Thomas Garden Apartments in the Bronx, and Sunnyside Gardens in Queens. He was also active in creating public parks and open spaces: Fort Tryon Park, site of the Cloisters, was developed with his personal funds and then contributed to the city in the 1930s, and in 1946 he donated to the United Nations a parcel of land in Turtle Bay that he had purchased for $8.5 million, which became its permanent site. He also supported the early efforts of Margaret

Sanger and her colleagues to promote contraception. Rockefeller Center, built almost entirely with his own money during the Depression, became a focus of the city's life and had an enduring effect on urban design. Rockefeller's residences in New York City included 13 West 54th Street (1901–8), 10 West 54th Street (1908–36), and 740 Park Avenue (from 1936). He also lived at the huge Rockefeller estate at Pocantico Hills in Westchester County.

Raymond B. Fosdick, *John D. Rockefeller, Jr.: A Portrait* (New York: Harper and Brothers, 1956); John Ensor Harr and Peter J. Johnson, *The Rockefeller Conscience: An American Family in Public and in Private* (New York: Macmillan, 1991)

Peter J. Johnson

Rockefeller, John D(avison), III (*b* New York City, 21 March 1906; *d* Tarrytown, N.Y., 10 July 1978). Philanthropist. The eldest son of John D. Rockefeller, Jr., and Abigail "Abby" Aldrich Rockefeller, he graduated from Princeton University in 1929 and embarked on a world tour. He returned to the United States just after the stock market crash and went to work for his father, serving on the boards of more than 30 foundations and nonprofit organizations. He also took part in the development of Radio City Music Hall and the other theaters in Rockefeller Center. After World War II he prevailed on the Rockefeller Foundation to conduct research on world population growth, agriculture, and agricultural economics. Frustrated by the resistance of the foundation's trustees and officers, he used his own funds to form the Population Council and the Agricultural Development Council in the early 1950s. Both organizations made enormous contributions to the development of safe and effective contraceptives and to a better understanding of economic development. During the 1950s and 1960s he formed the Asia Society, revived the Japan Society, and was a leader of the group that planned and built Lincoln Center for the Performing Arts (of which he served as chairman for 15 years). He lived at 1 Beekman Place from 1934 to 1978, as well as at the huge family estate in Westchester County.

Alvin Moscow, *The Rockefeller Inheritance* (New York: Doubleday, 1977); John E. Harr and Peter J. Johnson, *The Rockefeller Century* (New York: Charles Scribner's Sons, 1988); John Ensor Harr and Peter J. Johnson, *The Rockefeller Conscience: An American Family in Public and in Private* (New York: Macmillan, 1991)

Peter J. Johnson

Rockefeller, Nelson A(ldrich) (*b* Bar Harbor, Maine, 8 July 1908; *d* New York City, 26 Jan 1979). Governor and vice president of the United States. A grandson of John D. Rockefeller, he attended the Lincoln School, a private school in Manhattan. One of the family's three homes was at 10 West 54th Street. After graduating from Dartmouth College in 1930 he returned to the city in the following year, settling into an apartment on East 67th Street; he later moved to Fifth Avenue and 63rd Street. In 1932 he became a trustee of the Museum of Modern Art, marking the beginning of an increasingly active career as an art collector and patron. Under his presidency in 1939 and 1959 the museum developed into a prominent and popular cultural institution. He also assembled an exceptional private collection of modern and primitive art, and used his own collection of primitive sculpture to found the Museum of Primitive Art in 1954. From 1931 he worked at various branches of the family's business. He became president of Rockefeller Center in 1938. His political career grew out of his 1935 investment in Creole Petroleum, the Venezuelan subsidiary of Standard Oil. His involvement in Latin American affairs led to his appointment as coordinator of Inter-American Affairs in the U.S. Department of State in 1940, and assistant secretary of state for the American Republics in 1944.

After serving in appointed posts under Presidents Harry S. Truman and Dwight D. Eisenhower, Rockefeller turned his attention to elective office. Nominated by the Republicans for the governorship of New York in 1958, he defeated the incumbent, W. Averell Harriman. He became a leader of the moderate wing of the Republican Party, and mounted unsuccessful campaigns for the Republican presidential nomination in 1960, 1964, and 1968. Despite these setbacks he was reelected governor in 1962, 1966, and 1970. Rockefeller was the first governor to establish a permanent office in New York City, and he governed the state largely from headquarters at 22 West 55th Street, staying in Albany for legislative sessions. For many years he feuded with Mayor John V. Lindsay (initially an ally) and with Robert Moses, who lost his commanding influence over the city's politics in 1968 when Rockefeller established the Metropolitan Transit Authority, which absorbed Moses's last base of power, the Triborough Bridge and Tunnel Authority. As governor, Rockefeller's tough stances left a mixed legacy: when inmates at the Attica State Penitentiary rioted in 1971, he ordered state troopers and National Guardsmen to retake the prison by force, resulting in the deaths of 29 prisoners and 10 hostages. Two years later he pushed the severe "Rockefeller drug laws" through the state legislature, establishing mandatory prison sentences for the possession and sale of drugs; opponents noted the laws' unfairness toward first-time and nonviolent offenders, as well as African Americans and Latinos. He also pushed for increased access to higher education and a major expansion of the State University of New York. In 1973 Rockefeller resigned as governor to lead the National Commission on Critical Choices for Americans. He returned to public office the following year when Richard Nixon resigned the presidency and was succeeded by Gerald Ford, who nominated Rockefeller as his vice president. Rockefeller withdrew from consideration as Ford's running mate in 1976, and when Ford's term ended in 1977 he retired from politics.

Eileen K. Cheng

Rockefeller Center. Complex of 19 commercial buildings in Manhattan, bounded by 52nd and 49th streets, and Fifth and Seventh avenues. It has inspired developers elsewhere, including those for Battery Park City. The land, earlier occupied by tenements, was leased by Columbia University to John D. Rockefeller, Jr., who in early 1929 planned to increase the area's value by erecting three tall office buildings and a new Metropolitan Opera House around a plaza. After the stock market crashed in October, the opera could not afford to move, so Rockefeller reconceived the development as entirely commercial. He engaged development consultants Todd, Robertson and Todd, along with three architecture firms: Reinhard and Hofmeister (expert in dividing office spaces); Corbett, Harrison and MacMurray (known for civic concern and sober design); and Hood, Godley and Fouilhoux (known for innovative design). The first group of office towers and theaters surrounding a sunken plaza was completed in 1929, bounded by 51st and 49th streets, and Fifth and Sixth avenues. Four low buildings on Fifth Avenue provide an entrance of inviting scale to the two northern blocks. A downward slope in the central block between the low buildings leads pedestrians past shop windows toward the sunken plaza where plants, flags, sculptures, and fountains were installed. An outdoor restaurant operates in summer and an ice-skating rink in winter. West of the plaza, on a street added to relieve traffic, the architects placed the tallest tower, the RCA (now GE) Building. Two theaters on Sixth Avenue occupied less desirable lots but were visible from the theater district. The Center Theater was demolished in 1954, but Radio City Music Hall survives, used now for popular music shows rather than the original vaudeville acts and films. Some of the elegant shops that lined Fifth Avenue and the plaza have been replaced by chain stores. Rooftop gardens and an observation deck produced income, as did the Rainbow Room restaurant (opened 1934), which is still among the city's most glamorous. The owner commissioned many murals and works of sculpture, including the massive *Atlas* by Lee Lawrie with René Chambellan (1937) at the entrance to 630 Fifth Avenue, and *Prometheus* in the sunken plaza by Paul Manship (1934).

Todd, Robertson and Todd planned an underground corridor leading to a subway station at 47th–50th streets along a new Sixth Avenue line that opened in 1940. Shops and

Rockefeller Center Plaza, 2009

services flank the corridors. A second underground system clears traffic from the area by providing off-street truck loading and delivery. The imaginative design and high standards for construction and maintenance continue to attract tenants and tourists.

The center's increasing profitability during and after World War II inspired the owners to add buildings on the northern and western sides after 1947, including four coordinated office towers designed by Harrison and Abramovitz on Sixth Avenue between 48th and 57th streets. The first, the Time–Life Building, was erected in 1960, the three south of it in 1973. These tall prismatic towers surrounded by open space reflected the new standards introduced by the zoning changes of 1961, but they drew less admiration than the earlier buildings had. Gensler Associates created a sensitively inserted addition for Christie's auction house on 49th Street in 1999. The Rockefeller Group bought the land in 1985, sold a part interest to Japanese investors, and in 2000 sold the center to Tishman–Speyer, a real estate company. The new owners altered the center's Fifth Avenue facades and remodeled the underground shopping street in white marble. Other architectural changes have been made to the buildings that are not landmarks.

Daniel Okrent, *Great Fortune: The Epic of Rockefeller Center* (New York: Viking, 2003)

Carol Krinsky

Rockefeller Foundation. Charitable foundation, one of the oldest and largest in the United States. It was formed in 1913 "to promote the well-being of man-kind through out the world" by John D. Rockefeller and his advisers Frederick T. Gates (1853–1929) and John D. Rockefeller, Jr., who had also formed the Rockefeller Institute for Medical Research (1901; later Rockefeller University), the General Education Board (1903), and the Rockefeller Sanitary Commission for the Eradication of Hookworm Disease (1909). The work of these institutions influenced the direction of the fund: its trustees set up the International Health Division (1913–51) to enable the sanitary commission to combat malaria, tuberculosis, and yellow fever in addition to hookworm, and the China Medical Board (1914–28) to promote modern Western medicine in China; the fund also financed the construction of the Peking Union Medical College. Under the leadership from 1917 to 1929 of George E. Vincent (1864–1941), the fund was active principally in public health and medical education. A reorganization of the Rockefellers' various philanthropies in 1928 left the fund with five divisions devoted to international health, the medical sciences, the natural sciences, the social sciences, and the humanities. It merged with the Laura Spelman Rockefeller Memorial, a foundation formed in 1918 by John D. Rockefeller in honor of his late wife, and also continued the work of the International Education Board, formed by John D. Rockefeller, Jr., in 1923. The China Medical Board became an independent foundation charged with operating the Peking Union Medical College; by 2008 its endowment was $270 million, and it had granted nearly $1 billion since its inception.

The efforts of the Rockefeller Foundation in the natural and medical sciences were strengthened during the presidencies of Max Mason (1877–1961) from 1929 to 1936 and of Raymond B. Fosdick (1883–1972) from 1936 to 1948. Under the direction of Dean Rusk from 1952 to 1961 and J. George Harrar (1906–82) from 1961 to 1972, attention shifted to agricultural development, equal opportunity, and population concerns. Led from 1972 to 1979 by John H. Knowles (1926–79), the foundation began to fund social history projects, established a fellowship program in the humanities, and expanded its work in agricultural and medical science in the third world. Under the presidency of Richard Lyman (*b* 1923) from 1980 to 1988, the foundation continued its work in developing countries with scientifically based development programs and also undertook new initiatives in secondary education and the fight against persistent urban poverty. Peter C. Goldmark, Jr., served as president from 1988 to 1997 and brought about a clearer focus on housing, education, and the environment. Goldmark was succeeded by Gordon Conway, who served from 1998 to 2004 and Judith Rodin (*b* 1944) in 2005. In the early twenty-first century the foundation's New York City–focused initiatives included Opportunity NYC, aimed at lifting up poor families, the NYC Cultural Innovation Fund, and the Jane Jacobs Medal, which is awarded annually to two individuals whose work embodies Jacobs's urbanist ideals. Many universities, health-care facilities, and cultural institutions in the city have received support from the foundation for experimental and model programs: by 2008 the Rockefeller Foundation had granted about $14 billion since its founding and maintained more than $4 billion in assets.

The Rockefeller Foundation is one of several independent foundations based in New York City that carry the Rockefeller name. The Rockefeller Brothers Fund, formed in 1940 by John D. Rockefeller's grandchildren, had assets in 2008 of $923.5 million and granted more than $30 million in 2007; one component of its programs focuses on New York City. Rockefeller's great-grandchildren in 1967 formed the Rockefeller Family Fund, which in 2006 held assets of nearly $90 million and granted more than $6 million.

Kenneth W. Rose

Rockefeller University. Research institute offering graduate training in the physical and medical sciences. Founded in 1901 by John D. Rockefeller as the Rockefeller Institute for Medical Research, it first occupied quarters on Lexington Avenue and 50th Street. In 1906 the institute moved to its present site at 1230 York Avenue, between 63rd and 68th streets, where it opened Central Laboratory (now Founder's Hall). The hospital built for the institute in 1910 combined the study and treatment of human disease. Rockefeller's two chief philanthropic advisers, John D. Rockefeller, Jr., and Frederick T. Gates, were determined to create a world-class research institute on American soil. Rockefeller gave $2.6 million to the institute in 1907 and $3.8 million in 1910.

At its inception the institute functioned as a grant-giving body that supported private and public scientific research. In cooperation with the city's health department, one of its first grants supported a study of the city's milk supply. The institute's early research emphasis on the biology of infectious disease broadened by 1935 to keep pace with new developments in biological research. The first director, Simon Flexner (1901–35), developed the institute's administrative organization. By the 1950s the institute was one of the leading research facilities in the nation; it became a degree-granting institution in 1954 and first awarded the PhD in 1959. The current name was adopted in 1965, reflecting a commitment to the academic exploration of science. Twenty-three Nobel laureates have been associated with the institution, among them Alexis Carrel, Karl Landsteiner, Peyton Rous, Fritz Lipmann, Joshua Lederberg, David Baltimore, and Paul Greengard. Other prominent scientists who have worked there include Rebecca Lancefield, Hideyo Noguchi, Louise Pierce, Oswald Avery, and René Dubos. The university and its hospital have been the site of important developments and research in diverse areas, including human blood groups, antibiotics, viral cancers, DNA, vision, taste, and smell, methadone-based drug rehabilitation, aging, tuberculosis, neurobiological disorders, obesity, schizophrenia, hepatitis C, poliomyelitis, yellow fever, heart disease, diabetes, leukemia, arthritis, AIDS, alcoholism, parasitic diseases, and genetic disorders. The first effective treatment for African sleeping sickness was also developed there. The laboratory led by a senior professor is the basic unit of organization; there are no academic departments. Graduate courses, discussion groups, tutorials, and research apprenticeships all revolve around the laboratory. Students attend tuition-free and receive a yearly stipend. Unlike most universities it is dedicated exclusively to graduate study, conferring only earned doctorates and honorary degrees.

George W. Corner, *A History of the Rockefeller Institute: 1901–1953, Origins and Growth* (New York: Rockefeller Institute Press, 1964)

See also Science.

Lee R. Hiltzik, Renee D. Mastrocco

Rockettes. Precision dance team. Modeled on the 16 Missouri Rockettes, the group was formed by Russell Markert for the opening of Radio City Music Hall at Rockefeller Center on 27 December 1932. As they first performed at the Roxy Theater, the dancers were called the Roxyettes until 1934. When motion pictures were shown in the theater, they performed at least three times a day and learned new routines every week. The ensemble participated in United Service Organizations (USO) tours during World War II and began appearing in the Macy's Thanksgiving Day Parade in 1957. Decades of controversy over the all-white membership of the troupe ended when Jennifer Jones became the first black member in December 1987. Known for their high kick line and lavish costumes (the toy soldier uniform takes 12 hours to make), the ensemble maintains the illusion of uniform height by lining the tall dancers in the middle and arranging the shorter dancers at the ends, and then adjusting the size of their hats. As of 2007 the group had 36 members.

Charles Francisco, *The Radio City Music Hall: An Affectionate History of the World's Greatest Theater* (New York: E. P. Dutton, 1979)

Barbara Cohen-Stratyner

Rock Pigeon [domestic pigeon]. Plump bird about 13 inches (33 centimeters) long with a short, fan-shaped tail, a white rump, two black wing bars, and an iridescent green neck patch; it is usually blue gray but the color varies from black to white. Originally a cliff dweller, it was introduced to New York City from Europe at an unknown time and soon proliferated; pigeons are especially common in Central and Prospect parks. The birds build nests in trees, and more often on windowsills and cornices, usually producing clutches of two eggs three times a year. Pigeons are ubiquitous in New York City and referred to as "rats with wings"; their droppings have often angered city residents.

Racing or homing pigeons, also part of the Rock Pigeon family, have a long history in New York City; European immigrants brought the tradition with them in the nineteenth century, and residents have kept pigeons in rooftop coops since then. In 1880 a homing pigeon sold to someone in Waltham, Massachusetts, found its way back to the city, 185 miles (298 kilometers) away, a year later. Hoboken, New Jersey, just across the Hudson River, was the center of rooftop pigeon culture, as seen in Elia Kazan's 1954 film *On the Waterfront.* In the early twenty-first century, although pigeon keepers had greatly diminished in number, some continued to race their birds, especially in Brooklyn. Organizations like the Frank Viola Homing Pigeon Club in Coney Island organized competitions, driving hundreds of birds between 100 and 500 miles (161 to 805 kilometers) from the city and releasing them; pigeon keepers wait by their coops for the birds—equipped with electronic bracelets to clock their time—to return.

John Bull, Kate Lauber

Rockwell, Norman (*b* New York City, 3 Feb 1894; *d* Stockbridge, Mass., 9 Nov 1978). Painter and illustrator. He was born at Amsterdam Avenue and 103rd Street; his family later lived in apartments in Harlem, including one at St. Nicholas Avenue and 147th Street from 1896 to 1900. In 1908 he enrolled in art classes at the New York School of Art (formerly the Chase School of Art, 57 West 57th Street) and two years later transferred to the National Academy; he finally completed his formal art education at the Art Students League (215 West 57th Street). Rockwell won the affection of the public for his nostalgic portrayals of life in small towns and sought above all to provoke an emotional response in his audience, leading some to criticize him for avoiding the stark realities of his time. He is best known for 317 cover illustrations executed for the *Saturday Evening Post* between 1916 and 1963.

Donald Walton, *A Rockwell Portrait: An Intimate Biography* (Kansas City, Kans.: Sheed Andrews and McMeel, 1978)

Andrew Wiese

Rodgers, Richard (*b* Queens, 28 June 1902; *d* New York City, 30 Dec 1979). Composer. He attended Columbia College and the Institute of Musical Art in New York City but learned music largely through his own study of the operettas of Victor Herbert and the musicals of Jerome Kern. He wrote the music for several successful Broadway shows to which Lorenz Hart contributed the lyrics: *Garrick Gaieties* (1925); *On Your Toes* (1936), well known for the dance sequence "Slaughter on Tenth Avenue" and the song "There's a Small Hotel"; and *Babes in Arms* (1937), which included the songs "The Lady Is a Tramp," "My Funny Valentine," and "Where or When." Their show *Pal Joey* (1940, book by John O'Hara) was considered bold for its time: it tells the story of an unprincipled protagonist in a trashy environment and features a ballad of troubled love, "Bewitched, Bothered and Bewildered." Many of the works of Rodgers and Hart celebrate life in New York City, among them their first hit song, "We'll Have Manhattan" (1925); the show *Fifth Avenue Follies* (1926); and the songs "Coney Island" (1930), "Harlemania" (1930), "I Gotta Get Back to New York" (1933), "Manhattan Melodrama" (1934), "The Circus Is on Parade" (1935), "Memories of Madison Square Garden" (1935), "There's a Boy in Harlem" (1938), "At the Roxy Music Hall" (1938), and "Give It Back to the Indians" (1939). After Hart's death Rodgers wrote a number of successful musicals with Oscar Hammerstein II, including *Oklahoma!* (1943), *Carousel* (1945), *South Pacific* (1949), *The King and I* (1951), and *The Sound of Music* (1959).

David Ewen, *Richard Rodgers* (New York: Holt, Rinehart and Winston, 1957)

See also Hart, Lorenz.

Nicholas E. Tawa

Rodman, Henrietta (*b* Astoria [now in Queens], 1878; *d* New York City, 23 March 1923). Schoolteacher and activist. She was instrumental in forming both the Feminist Alliance, a group based in Greenwich Village dedicated to abolishing sex discrimination, and the Liberal Club (1913), in which she caused a split by insisting on the admission of blacks. A socialist, suffragist, member of the Women's Trade Union League, and advocate of dress reform, she prevailed on the Board of Education to allow female teachers to marry, bear children, and retain their positions. She also fought to secure cooperative housing and child care for professional women. Rodman's apartment on Bank Street was a popular gathering place for bohemians and social reformers before World War I.

Jan Seidler Ramirez

Rodman's Neck. Section of Pelham Bay Park in the Bronx, jutting prominently into Eastchester Bay. After the late seventeenth century it was given several names, including Ann Hoeck and Ann's Neck (after ANNE HUTCHINSON, who settled nearby in 1643). The land was acquired in 1888 with the intention of making it a park, but it was used for various purposes in the following century: as a naval training station between 1917 and 1919; as a park in the 1920s; as the site, between 1930 and 1936, of Camp Mulrooney, the summer home of the New York City Police Academy; and as a firing range for the police department between 1959 and 1989. In the early twenty-first century the area continues to be used as a firing range for the police department and a site for detonating unexploded bombs and seized illegal fireworks. In 2007 plans were announced to relocate the firing range to College Point in the borough of Queens over a multiyear period; it was unclear whether Rodman's Neck would remain the chief site for bomb destruction or whether it would pass necessary environmental tests for lead contamination so that it might again be used as a park.

Kenneth T. Jackson

Rodrigues, Jan [Juan]. Fur trader. In 1613, as a free black sailor from Santo Domingo (in what is now the Dominican Republic), he started a fur-trading business with Native Americans. He was left on Manhattan Island by his former Dutch employer, ADRIAEN BLOCK (also a fur trader). Rodrigues was perhaps the first non–Native American inhabitant of Manhattan and is said to have played a role in the Dutch–Native American deal to execute the purchase of Manhattan.

Celedonia Jones

Roebling, Emily Warren (*b* Cold Spring, N.Y., 23 Sept 1843, *d* 28 Feb 1903). Engineer. The daughter of a building contractor, Emily excelled at math and science from an early age. She married Washington Roebling, son of John Roebling, the primary engineer of the Brooklyn Bridge. Washington took over the project after his father's death, but in 1872 he became immobilized by decompression sickness, so Emily directed the project until its completion in 1883. To accomplish this, she studied engineering. Although she kept her husband as the project's official chief engineer, she oversaw the day-to-day construction and managed the relationships with the bridge's trustees and other engineers, politicians, and the press. After the bridge's completion, she received a legal education from New York University and worked for women's rights. She is memorialized by plaques on both the Brooklyn and Manhattan towers of the bridge.

Marilyn E Weigold, *Silent Builder: Emily Warren Roebling and the Brooklyn Bridge* (New York: National University Publications, 1984)

Ben Silk

Roebling, John Augustus (*b* Mühlhausen in Thüringen, Germany, 12 June 1806; *d* Brooklyn, 22 July 1869). Engineer, inventor, and designer of the Brooklyn Bridge. The son of a poor tobacconist, he studied in Berlin and immigrated to the United States in 1831, where he settled with other Thuringians in a farming colony near Pittsburgh. While working as an engineer in the canals of Pennsylvania, he developed wire cable as a sturdier substitute for rope made of hemp, which often caused accidents when boats were pulled uphill. He tested his invention on a series of suspended aqueducts over the Allegheny River and then formed a wire-cable works in Trenton, New Jersey (the firm remained in business until the 1980s). Roebling built iron suspension bridges in Ohio and upstate New York before designing the Brooklyn Bridge in 1867. He oversaw the beginning of its construction before dying of tetanus contracted during a building accident.

Hamilton Schuyler, *The Roeblings: A Century of Engineers, Bridge-Builders and Industrialists* (Princeton, N.J.: Princeton University Press, 1931); David B. Steinman, *The Builders of the Bridge: The Story of John Roebling and His Son* (New York: Harcourt, Brace, 1945)

Ellen Fletcher

Roebling, Washington (Augustus) (*b* Saxonburg, Pa., 26 May 1837; *d* Trenton, N.J., 21 July 1926). Civil engineer, son of John Augustus Roebling. After studying engineering at Rensselaer Polytechnic Institute, he joined his father in the work of designing suspension bridges. He served as a bridge builder and soldier for the Union army during the Civil War and then moved to Brooklyn Heights (137 Hicks St.) to assist his father in building the Brooklyn Bridge. With the death of his father in 1869, Washington Roebling took charge of the bridge's construction; however, in the summer of 1872 he became ill with decompression sickness and thereafter depended on his wife, Emily Warren Roebling, who was also an engineer. She heavily aided her husband and oversaw the construction until the bridge's completion in 1883.

Hamilton Schuyler, *The Roeblings: A Century of Engineers, Bridge-Builders and Industrialists* (Princeton, N.J.: Princeton University Press, 1931); David Steinman, *The Builders of the Bridge: The Story of John Roebling and His Son* (New York: Harcourt, Brace, 1945)

Ellen Fletcher

Rohatyn, Felix G(eorge) (*b* Vienna, 29 May 1928). Investment banker. After graduating from Middlebury College in 1948, he went to work for Lazard Frères, where he became a partner in 1960. During the 1970s he was a member of the board of governors of the New York Stock Exchange. In 1975 he was appointed chairman of the Municipal Assistance Corporation (MAC) by Governor Hugh L. Carey, and during the fiscal crisis of the following years he played a critical role in returning the city to solvency. He left the MAC in May 1993. In 2006 he was appointed as a chairman of the International Advisory Committee and as a senior adviser by Lehman Brothers.

Janet Frankston

Rolling Stone. Monthly magazine launched in 1967 in San Francisco by Jann Wenner, a 20-year-old former student at the University of California, Berkeley. It moved to New York City in 1977. Begun as a small alternative newsletter, it featured John Lennon on the cover of its first issue and sold 6000 copies. The magazine soon became a voice for the counterculture in the Haight–Ashbury district of San Francisco. In the early 1970s it turned to more serious topics such as the Vietnam War and corruption in U.S. politics. It also boosted the career of several journalists, including Greil Marcus, Tim Cahill, Joe Eszterhas, Hunter S. Thompson, and P. J. O'Rourke, as well as the photographer Annie Liebovitz. Articles on Charles Manson, the presidential campaign of 1972, and the abduction of Patricia Hearst attracted critical accolades and a broader audience. After Wenner moved the magazine to New York City, it developed a slicker, more commercial style and cultivated major advertisers. In the 1990s the magazine faced competition from the Internet and criticism that it favored the interests of the aging baby boomer generation over new genres of popular music. However, it maintained high circulation numbers by introducing several international editions and expanding onto the Internet with a popular site that has interactive message boards and streaming videos. In 2007 when *Rolling Stone* celebrated its 40th anniversary, it had received a total of 13 national magazine awards. Its offices are at 1290 Sixth Avenue.

Robert Sanger Steel

Rollins, Sonny [Theodore Walter] (b New York City, 7 Sept 1930). Saxophonist. He grew up in Harlem and attended public schools in New York City. Rollins's early recordings "Saxophone Colossus" (1956) and "Freedom Suite" (1958) made him known for his rich tone on the tenor saxophone and his ability to transcend the harmonic limitations of "hard bop." He took several leaves from his career as a performer. During one of these breaks in the early 1960s, Rollins and his wife, Lucille, were living on Grand Street in the Lower East Side of Manhattan near the Williamsburg Bridge. He discovered that practicing on the bridge meant that he could play as loudly as he wanted to without disturbing anyone. At times Rollins was spending 15 hours a day playing on Williamsburg, a period commemorated by his album *The Bridge* (1962). In 2004 he was presented with a Lifetime Achievement Grammy Award. On 18 September 2007 Rollins performed a special concert at Carnegie Hall commemorating the 50th anniversary of his first appearance on that stage.

Charles Blancq, *Sonny Rollins: The Journey of a Jazzman* (Boston: Twayne, 1983); Eric Nisenson, *Open Sky: Sonny Rollins and His World of Improvisation* (New York: St. Martin's, 2000)

Marc Ferris

Roma. See Gypsies.

Romanians. A Romanian community formed in New York City between 1900 and World War I. Most immigrated from Transylvania and Banat, regions under Austro-Hungarian rule, and a few were Macedo-Romanians from Greece and Albania. Most were factory workers, craftsmen, or innkeepers. The community was served by several general-interest publications: *Curierul Romano-American* (Romanian-American Courier, 1900), *Vremea Noua* (New Time, 1900), and *Ecoul Americei* (America's Echo, 1904), which provided cultural and political news. Some of the first organizations were cultural and mutual-aid societies, among them Dorul (1903–), Farsarotul (1903– ; Macedo-Romanian), Unirea (1909–), Perivolea (1909; Macedo-Romanian), and Avram Iancu (1909–). Specialized publications covered diverse topics: religious news was given in *The Romanul American* (1910–12), edited by a Roman Catholic (Eastern Rite) priest; *Desteapta-te Romane* (Awake Thee, Romanian, 1911–16) took a pro-Hungarian stand on the issue of Transylvania; *Steaua Noastra* (Our Star, 1911–24) promoted Romanian books sold in the bookstore of the editor, P. Axelrad, the compiler of a Romanian-English dictionary; and *Curierul Roman* (1923–24) provided news of the city's Macedo-Romanians. From the time of World War I Romanians in the city strongly supported Romanian sovereignty over Transylvania. Improving relations with Romania was the goal of the Society of Friends of Romania (1928–32), which published the periodical *Romania,* and of the Sons of Romania (1932–34), which issued a bulletin. The publications *Porunca Vremii* (Imperative of the Time, 1937–), *Fii Daciei* (Sons of Dacia, 1938–), and later the *Romanian Boian News* (1968–) opposed communism and sought to promote chauvinism; they had limited circulation.

Romanians in the city protested the fascist regime in Romania of Ion Antonescu (1940–44) and the communist regimes of Gheorghe Gheorghiu-Dej and Nicolae Ceausescu. The Free Romania Committee (1941–44) and the Democratic Union of Free Romania (1948–56) sought to revive the Romanian monarchy; the Romanian National Committee (1951–67) attacked the communist government; and the Romanian Welfare Organization (1948–74) helped refugees to settle in the United States. Formed to preserve Romanian heritage, the Iuliu Maniu Romanian American Foundation (1952–) amassed a library and a collection of Romanian costumes and set up a scholarship program. Refugees and political exiles moved to the city in the 1950s and late 1980s. In 1970 an association called Truth about Romania was formed to monitor violations of human rights and international treaties by the government of Romania. Devoted to local, national, and international news, the periodicals *Micro-Magazin* (1972–), *Lumea Libera* (Free World, 1987–), and *Epoca* (1987–) became popular; the political journals *Dreptatea* (Justice, 1973–) and *Spectatorul* (1975–) found smaller audiences. Through its newspaper *Actiunea Romaneasca* the Romanian National Council (1974–) sought to publicize Romanian achievements and help immigrants adjust to the United States. The Romanian Cultural Center (1980–) organized celebrations of Romanian national holidays and other cultural events. In December 1989 Romanians in the city celebrated the fall of the Romanian communist government.

In 2000 more than 19,000 people in New York City were of Romanian ancestry, and the majority lived in Queens. They were professionals, engineers, musicians, writers, teachers, office workers, small businesspeople, taxi drivers, and maintenance workers. About 80 percent of Romanian churchgoers were Eastern Orthodox and belonged to six churches: St. Dumitru in Manhattan; and St. Maria, Holy Trinity, Descending of the Holy Ghost, St. Nicholae, and Three Hierarchs in Queens. Other churches in Queens were the St. Mary Roman Catholic Church, two Baptist churches, a Pentecostal church, and a Seventh-Day Adventist church. Well-known Romanians in the city have included the soprano Stella Roman, the broadcaster Liviu Floda, the stage director Andrei Serban, and the graphic artist Eugen Mihaesco.

Vladimir Wertsman, *The Romanians in America, 1748–1974: A Chronology and Fact Book* (Dobbs Ferry, N.Y.: Oceana, 1975)

Vladimir Wertsman

Ronan, William J. (*b* Buffalo, N.Y., 8 Nov 1912). Public official. He attended public schools in Buffalo and graduated from Syracuse University in 1934; he earned his PhD from New York University (NYU) in 1940. He established the Graduate School of Public Administration at NYU (now the Wagner Graduate School of Public Service) as well as NYU'S School of Social Work. While at NYU, as executive director of New York State's Commission on Coordination, he produced a report on public authorities in the state. After working as a deputy city administrator for Mayor Robert F. Wagner, he became the chief strategist for Nelson A. Rockefeller in his successful gubernatorial campaigns from 1958 on. As secretary to Governor Rockefeller, Ronan helped set up the Tri-State Regional Transportation Commission and was a leader in dealing with the problems of the commuter railroads. A strong advocate for public transit, he helped set up the Metropolitan Commuter Transportation Authority (MCTA) in 1965, which purchased the Long Island Rail Road (LIRR) from the Pennsylvania Railroad. Under state legislation, in 1968 the MCTA was transformed into the Metropolitan Transportation Authority (MTA), which became responsible for the LIRR, the New York City Transit Authority, and the Triborough Bridge and Tunnel Authority. The MTA also became responsible for improving service on the New York Central and New Haven commuter rail systems serving areas north of Manhattan (which later became Metro-North Railroad) and for the bus system in Nassau County, as well as for Stewart and Republic airports. As chairman of the MTA from 1 March 1968, Ronan led the effort to upgrade and improve public transportation services in the region, which included new commuter rail cars serving new high-level platforms, and further electrification of commuter rail lines, as well as the rehabilitation of the existing transit network. He resigned as MTA chairman on 26 April 1974.

Michael N. Danielson and Jameson W. Doig, *New York: The Poliitics of Urban Regional Development* (Berkeley: University of California Press, 1982)

Peter Derrick

Ronson Ship. Vessel used in the trade between New York City and the Caribbean, sunk in the 1740s for use as landfill. It was recovered in 1982 during the archaeological excavation of 175 Water Street.

Nan A. Rothschild

Roosevelt, (Anna) Eleanor (*b* New York City, 11 Oct 1884; *d* New York City, 7 Nov 1962). First Lady. She was brought up at 11 West 37th Street by her maternal grandmother, who sent her to boarding school in England. A débutante in 1901, she married her cousin Franklin D. Roosevelt in 1905 and lived successively at 125 East 36th Street (1905–8) and in a townhouse at 47–49 East 65th Street. The family moved to Albany, New York, in 1910, to Washington, D.C., in 1913, and back to New York City in 1920 when she became involved with the League of Women Voters. In 1924 she was the head of the women's platform committee at the Democratic National Convention in Madison Square Garden. After her husband's death in 1945 she divided her time between Hyde Park (New York) and several addresses in the city, including 29 Washington Square West (from 1945), the Park Sheraton at 870 Seventh Avenue (1949–53, 1958), and 211 East 62nd Street (1953–59). In 1946–52 she was a delegate to the United Nations and a regular presence at its headquarters. In addition to her official duties she was embroiled in notable disputes with such figures as Francis Cardinal Spellman and Carmine DeSapio. In 1959 she moved to a townhouse at 55 East 74th Street, where she spent the rest of her life.

Eleanor Roosevelt reviews the Waves at the Naval Training School for Women's Reserves in the Bronx, 2 August 1943

J. William T. Youngs, *Eleanor Roosevelt: A Personal and Public Life* (New York: Longman, 2005)

Lois Scharf

Roosevelt, Franklin D(elano) (*b* Hyde Park, N.Y., 30 Jan 1882; *d* Warm Springs, Ga., 12 April 1945). Thirty-second president of the United States. Born in Dutchess County, he was educated at Groton Preparatory School and Harvard University. He moved to New York City and studied law at Columbia University. He married his cousin Eleanor in 1905 and lived with her at 125 East 36th Street (1905–8) before moving to a townhouse at 47–49 East 65th Street. As a state senator in Albany from 1910 he enraged Tammany Hall by leading party insurgents in blocking the legislative election of its candidate William P. Sheehan. The insurgents refused to attend the binding party caucus, which Tammany Hall dominated, and voted for the opposition, reform candidate; a stalemated state senate chose a third candidate in a compromise. Roosevelt served as an assistant secretary of the navy from 1913 and returned to New York City in 1920. Stricken with polio in 1921, he resumed his political career. He supported Alfred E. Smith's candidacy for the governorship in 1924 and for the presidency in 1929 but pointedly ignored him after becoming governor himself (elected 1928, reelected 1930). Nominated by the Democrats for the presidency in 1932, he defeated President Herbert Hoover by a wide margin. During the Depression he assisted the city through the Works Progress Administration and the Public Works Administration, which helped finance the construction of the Triborough Bridge in 1936, and built housing projects and schools. He also established the Securities and Exchange Commission.

Lois Scharf

Roosevelt, Isaac (*b* New York City, 8 Dec 1726; *d* New York City, 13 Oct 1794). Political and mercantile leader, great-great-grandfather of Franklin D. Roosevelt. He opened a wholesale sugar refinery on Wall Street in 1745, soon became one of the most successful businessmen in New York City, and helped to form the New York Chamber of Commerce and the Society of the New York Hospital (the first hospital in the city). A patriot during the American Revolution, he represented the city during the state constitutional convention of 1776. In his later years he was a close ally of Alexander Hamilton; he helped to form the Bank of New York in 1784 and was a strong supporter of Federalist causes.

Allen Churchill, *The Roosevelts: American Aristocrats* (New York: Harper and Row, 1965)

James Bradley

Roosevelt, Theodore(, Jr.) (*b* New York City, 27 Oct 1858; *d* Oyster Bay, N.Y., 6 Jan 1919). Twenty-sixth president of the United States. He was born at 28 East 20th Street. His grandfather Cornelius Van Schaanck Roosevelt (1794–1871) was a real estate investor, a founder of Chemical Bank, and one of the city's wealthiest citizens. His father, Theodore Roosevelt, Sr. (1831–78), was a leading philanthropist who supported many charitable and cultural institutions, notably the Metropolitan Museum of Art and the American Museum of Natural History. In his youth Roosevelt suffered from asthma, and in 1873 his family moved to a larger home at 6 West 57th Street so that he could practice his physical conditioning. His health gradually improved, and in 1876 he entered Harvard College. After he married Alice Lee, the couple moved to New York City to live with his widowed mother. Roosevelt enrolled at Columbia Law School, became involved in local politics, and joined the district Republican club; he won a seat in the state assembly in 1882, where he represented the relatively wealthy twenty-first district of midtown Manhattan. He became a member of the city affairs committee and received extensive publicity when he accused the financier Jay Gould of corrupting a state supreme court judge in an attempt to control the Manhattan Elevated Railroad; he persuaded the assembly's judiciary committee to hold investigative hearings, and although Gould was exonerated Roosevelt secured a reputation as a reformer and fighter of corruption. In February 1884 his political career was interrupted by the death of his mother and wife on the same day, and later that year he chose not to seek reelection.

Roosevelt returned to politics in 1886 as a candidate for the mayoralty against the Democrat Abram S. Hewitt and the Union Labor candidate Henry George, an economist who advocated a "single tax" on land, but Hewitt won the election and Roosevelt finished third. He was the city's civil service commissioner in 1889–95, and in 1895 he was appointed president of the police board in the reform administration of Mayor William L. Strong. Roosevelt's boundless energy and

Theodore Roosevelt statue, 2009

impromptu social visits to policemen made him popular with the press, but he faced clamorous opposition when he decided to enforce the Sunday closing law on saloons, and his imperious, determined nature made for troubled relationships with the mayor and other members of the police board. In 1897 he resigned his office to accept an appointment as the assistant secretary of the navy under President William McKinley. During the Spanish-American War he was one of the organizers of the Rough Riders and earned fame for his efforts in the Battle of San Juan Hill. In 1898 he was elected governor of New York, and in 1900 he was selected as McKinley's vice presidential candidate; he became president after McKinley was assassinated in 1901, serving for seven and a half controversial years. His mediation of the Russo–Japanese War in 1905 earned him the Nobel Peace Prize. In 1909 he left office and traveled extensively abroad. On his return to the United States in June 1910 his ship docked at New York City, and he was greeted with a thunderous reception and a ticker-tape parade of unprecedented size. Roosevelt became an editor at *Outlook,* with an office on Fourth (now Park) Avenue, and a contributor to *Metropolitan Magazine.* His remaining years were marked by an unsuccessful campaign as the presidential candidate of the Progressive Party in 1912 and his open criticism of President Woodrow Wilson. Roosevelt's birthplace was demolished in 1916 but replicated by Theodate Pope Riddle in 1923, and in 1962 it was named a National Historic Site and opened to the public. A memorial statue of Roosevelt designed by John Russell Pope and erected in 1940 stands 15 feet (4.5 meters) tall in front of the American Museum of Natural History. Roosevelt is the only native of New York City to have achieved the nation's highest office.

Nathan Miller, *Theodore Roosevelt: A Life* (New York: William Morrow, 1992); David McCullough, *Mornings on Horseback: The Story of an Extraordinary Family, a Vanished Way of Life and the Unique Child Who Became Theodore Roosevelt* (New York: Simon and Schuster, 2001); Edmund Morris, *The Rise of Theodore Roosevelt* (New York: Modern Library, 2001)

Richard Skolnick

Roosevelt Hospital. Private hospital incorporated in 1864 and funded by a bequest from James H. Roosevelt, an uncle of Theodore Roosevelt. It opened in 1871 at 58th Street and 10th Avenue, where it remains in the early twenty-first century, and became the site of many medical innovations: William Halstead in the 1880s was the first surgeon in the United States to use rubber gloves during surgery; the Syms Operating Pavilion, opened in 1891, was the first modern operating theater in New York City and is now a landmark; William McBurney developed the technique for performing an appendectomy during the 1890s (an operation performed on the Duchess of Windsor at the hospital in 1944); and Karl Connell developed the gas mask used by U.S. troops during World War I. The Smithers Alcoholism Treatment and Training Center opened in 1968; it is named for R. Brinkley Smithers, who donated more than $10 million to the center. The inpatient unit of Roosevelt Hospital is housed in a mansion in the East 90s formerly owned by the showman Billy Rose. The hospital merged with St. Luke's Hospital in 1979 to form St. Luke's–Roosevelt Hospital Center.

Andrea Balis

Roosevelt Island. Island in the East River (2000 pop. 9,250), equidistant between the Upper East Side of Manhattan (51st Street to 86th Street) and Long Island City in Queens. It is about 800 feet (240 meters) wide and 1.75 miles (2.8 kilometers) long. The Queensboro Bridge crosses overhead, carrying an aerial tramway that connects the island to Manhattan. The island was called Minnehanonck by the Indians and Varcken Eylandt by the Dutch. Its first European owner was Wouter van Twiller, who bought it from the Indians, as he had done with what are now known as Wards, Randalls, and Governors islands. In 1668 the island was bought by Captain John Manning, who retired to it in disgrace after having surrendered the colony of New York to the Dutch in 1673. By the early eighteenth century title to the property was taken by Robert Blackwell, who had married Manning's daughter Mary. He lived and farmed on the island, which came to bear his name; a farmhouse believed to have belonged to his descendants still stands just south of the Queensboro Bridge. Blackwell's Island, as it

Roosevelt Island, 2009

was known then, was acquired in 1828 by the city, which by 1860 built on it a prison, an almshouse, a workhouse, and three hospitals: Metropolitan Hospital (A. J. Davis, 1839), designed as a lunatic asylum with an octagonal tower (the Octagon) that survived into the twenty-first century (without its original wings); City Hospital (James Renwick, Jr., 1859), a charity hospital built of stone quarried on the island by convicts imprisoned there; and Smallpox Hospital (James Renwick, Jr., 1856), a small Gothic Revival structure that is now a gray, crenellated ruin. Later structures include the Chapel of the Good Shepherd (Frederick Clarke Withers, 1889), which served patients and staff, and the Blackwell Lighthouse (James Renwick, Jr., 1872) at the northern tip of the island. By 1921 the prison and the workhouse had achieved such a reputation for overcrowding, violence, and drug trafficking that the city renamed the island Welfare Island. A series of new hospitals was begun in the 1920s, of which the most important is Goldwater Memorial for the chronically ill (Isadore Rosenfield; Butler and Kohn; York and Sawyer, 1939). The prison was moved to Rikers Island in 1935, leaving Welfare Island to the aged and the sick.

The Urban Development Corporation (UDC) of New York State in 1971 undertook to transform Welfare Island into a densely developed residential community to be called Roosevelt Island, named for Franklin D. Roosevelt. A master plan by Philip Johnson and John Burgee called for a neighborhood free of automobiles, with apartment buildings and stores connected by a central street, restored historic buildings, river views, and a park at each end of the island. Because of changes to the plan, inflation, and the fiscal collapse of the UDC, only part of the plan was realized in the mid-1970s. Southtown (Sert, Jackson, and Associates; Johansen and Bhavnani, 1975–76), a complex of four large apartment buildings with both subsidized and market-rate apartments, was built around a quiet street paved with brick. Higher-priced apartments face the Upper East Side, lower-priced ones Long Island City. Roosevelt Island was slow to achieve popularity but by the 1980s had become sought after as a quiet neighborhood offering fine views of Manhattan. Automobiles can reach the island only from Queens and are allowed to go no farther than the Motorgate garage and entry complex; the tramway was the only means of access from Manhattan until a subway station opened on the island in 1989. Throughout the first decade of the twenty-first century, Southtown underwent much development, and the ruins of the former Smallpox Hospital, which lies on the southern tip of the island and is visible from FDR Drive, have been the center of much dispute among New York City preservationists. The Octagon was restored in 2006 and transformed into a high-end apartment community.

Roosevelt Island Tramway System Assessment (Washington, D.C.: U.S. Department of Transportation, 1979)

See also Roosevelt Island Tramway.

Ellen Fletcher

Institutions on Blackwell's Island

Roosevelt Island Tramway. First commuter aerial tramway in the United States. Spanning the East River, the tram connects Roosevelt Island with Manhattan, landing at 59th Street and Second Avenue. Built in 1976, it was meant as a temporary solution while a subway station for the F line was constructed, which opened in 1989. It was designed by Prentice and Chan, Ohlhausen and built by Vonroll at a cost of $5 million. Each tram holds 125 people (10 seats and 115 standing) and travels for 3100 feet (945 meters) alongside the Queensboro Bridge at an average speed of 16 miles (25.7 km) per hour, rising to a height of 250 feet (76.2 meters). The trip takes about four and a half minutes, and the trams run every seven and a half minutes during rush hour and every 15 minutes at other times, from 6:00 a.m. to 2:00 a.m. (3:30 a.m. on weekends). Before the tram was built, a trolley on the Queensboro Bridge stopped halfway across and let passengers off to catch an elevator to the ground on Roosevelt Island. On 18 April 2006 both trams lost power and remained suspended midair for over seven hours, stranding 68 passengers. The trams—which are managed by the Roosevelt Island Operating Corporation—were taken out of service and overhauled, reopening in September 2006. In the early twenty-first century Roosevelt Island residents continued to use the tram, many preferring it to the overcrowded F train station.

Kate Lauber

Roosevelt Island Tramway, 2009

Root, Elihu (*b* Clinton, N.Y., 15 Feb 1845; *d* New York City, 7 Feb 1937). Statesman. After graduating from Hamilton College he attended New York University Law School and became successful on Wall Street. From 1871 to 1878 he lived at 20 Irving Place. Theodore Roosevelt sought his legal advice while serving as the city's police commissioner and later as governor of New York. Under President William McKinley he was appointed secretary of war in 1899, a position he retained until Roosevelt, now president, made him secretary of state in 1905. Root was elected to the U.S. Senate from New York State in 1909 and won the Nobel Peace Prize in 1912. Root worked for the Allies during World War I and was active in the Carnegie benefactions; he returned to private life in 1915. His homes in New York City included a house that he built at 733 Park Avenue in 1903 and another at 998 Fifth Avenue, where he lived from about 1912 until the end of his life.

Richard W. Leopold, *Elihu Root and the Conservative Tradition* (Boston: Little, Brown, 1954)

James E. Mooney

rope and cordage. The manufacture of rope and cordage is closely linked to the port economy and requires large amounts of land. In colonial Manhattan rope yards lined the northern fringes of Broadway and the banks of the Collect Pond. By 1824 eight rope factories in Brooklyn operated within 1 mile (1.5 kilometers) of the East River, employed 200 workers, and each year produced about 1130 tons (1025 metric tons) of cordage. John Good, a rope maker in Brooklyn, received the first American patent for spreaders and breakers in 1869, and within 10 years his inventions had revolutionized the manufacture of cordage. Large rope makers included Tucker, Carter, and Company, Elizabethport Steam Cordage, and William Wall and Sons in Brooklyn (1830). Increased output and fierce competition prompted four firms in Manhattan to organize a cartel in 1887 called the National Cordage Company, which lasted until 1893; a similar effort led to the formation of the United States Cordage Company, which passed into receivership in 1895. The shift from sailpower to steam, spiraling land costs in the city, and the nationwide railroad network drove rope factories from New York City, and few mechanized plants remained by the turn of the century. The largest was the Waterbury Rope Company, which operated a fortress-like factory in Brooklyn where it made several grades of cordage from Philippine manila and Yucatan sisal. The industry benefited from the building boom of the 1920s, but many firms, such as the American Manufacturing Company and the Chelsea Fibre Mills, nevertheless diversified into related products like twine, shoelaces, and wire rope. The Depression essentially ended rope making in the city.

Solveig Paulson Russell, *Twist and Twine: The Story of Cordage* (New York: Parents' Magazine, 1969)

Marc Ferris

Rorem, Ned (*b* Richmond, Ind., 23 Oct 1923). Composer and writer. He grew up in Chicago and studied music in New York City at the Juilliard School and with Virgil Thomson, who exerted a strong influence on his style. After living in Paris and Morocco he returned to the city in 1958. During the following decades he became known as a composer of emphatically tonal works, particularly art songs, and as an essayist who wrote provocatively about music and other topics in such collections as *New York Diary* (1966) and *Paris Diary* (1967). In 1976 he won a Pulitzer Prize for his orchestral composition *Air Music.* During the 1990s Rorem composed new works for Carnegie Hall and the New York Philharmonic. Rorem lived for almost 30 years at West 70th Street.

Janet Frankston

Rose, Alex [Royz, Olesh] (*b* Warsaw, 15 Oct 1898; *d* New York City, 28 Dec 1976). Labor leader. He arrived in New York City in 1913, became a millinery worker, and in 1914 joined the Millinery Workers' Union. A leading organizer in 1936 of the American Labor Party, he became increasingly concerned that the party was being infiltrated by communists, and after a leftist faction gained control in 1944 he left with David Dubinsky to form the Liberal Party. Despite a lack of mass support and funds, Rose used his political skills to make the party a powerful force in politics at both the city and state levels. In addition to leading the party he was president of the United Hatters, Cap and Millinery Workers' International Union from 1950 until his death.

Eileen K. Cheng

Rose, Billy [Rosenberg, Samuel Wolf] (*b* New York City, 6 Sept 1899; *d* New York City, 10 Feb 1966). Songwriter, theater and nightclub owner, and producer. He first worked in

Washington, D.C., as the head of the Reports Division of the War Industries Board, then led by Bernard Baruch. After World War I, he returned to New York City, where he lived at a church mission on 46th Street and studied popular songs at the New York Public Library. He published his first song in 1921 and over the years he took credit for nearly 400 more, although in many cases he was probably no more than a coauthor of the lyrics. In February 1929 he married the entertainer Fanny Brice, with whom he moved to an apartment at 15 East 69th Street (now the Westbury Hotel). During the same period he helped to form the Songwriter's Protective Agency (serving as its first president) and used his money from songwriting to purchase the Back Stage Club.

Rose's club was supported by organized crime and highly profitable. He had similar support at the Casino de Paree and the Billy Rose Music Hall, and when he eventually tried to break free from criminal influence he was forced to seek protection from the Federal Bureau of Investigation. In 1931 he had his first success as a producer with the show *Crazy Quilt,* a touring production that was able to make money during the Depression. He next joined with Jimmy Durante and an elephant in the Broadway spectacular *Jumbo* (1935) and produced shows in Cleveland and in Fort Worth, Texas, where he met Eleanor Holm, the star of an aquatic musical revue; she became his second wife in 1939 and was featured in New York City in his next "aquacade," at the World's Fair of 1939–40. From 1939 to 1952 he lived at 33 Beekman Place and managed the popular nightclub the Diamond Horseshoe. His Broadway productions during these years included *Carmen Jones* (1943), an all African American version of Bizet's opera set in a parachute factory during World War II, and *The Seven Lively Arts* (1944), produced in collaboration with Igor Stravinsky, Cole Porter, Benny Goodman, Bert Lahr, and Beatrice Lillie. Between 1947 and 1959 he wrote a newspaper column focusing on show business. From 1956 until his death Rose lived at 56 East 93rd Street. He bequeathed almost his entire estate of $54 million to the Billy Rose Foundation, which gave major support to the Billy Rose Theatre Collection at the New York Public Library for the Performing Arts, and to other causes in the arts and medicine.

Earl Conrad, *Billy Rose, Manhattan Primitive* (Cleveland: World, 1968); Polly Rose Gottlieb, *The Nine Lives of Billy Rose* (New York: Crown, 1968)

Chad Ludington

Rosebank. Neighborhood in northeastern Staten Island, bounded to the east by Upper New York Bay, to the southwest by the Staten Island Expressway, and to the northwest by Clifton. Until 1880 the area was part of Peterstown, so named by the German settlers who lived in the northern part. In 1873 New York State purchased eight and a half acres (three and a half hectares) of waterfront for a maritime quarantine facility, which was the principal facility of its kind in the United States from the late 1930s until quarantine functions were transferred to Governors Island in 1971. The neighborhood is the site of Alice Austen's home, portions of which date to the eighteenth century; the house was extensively renovated in 1846 and opened to the public in 1985 as a place of exhibit for some of Austen's finest photographs. The Italian revolutionary Giuseppe Garibaldi lived in the area for several years during his exile from Italy, and a later resident, Antonio Meucci, is credited by some as the rightful inventor of the telephone; both are commemorated in the Garibaldi-Meucci Museum. In the late 1880s families that had lived in the area for many years were displaced from parts of Rosebank by immigrants from southern Italy who intended to farm the land but found that the small plots made even truck farming difficult; many soon sought other work. Rosebank retains a strong Italian American identity and has well-maintained small houses, gardens, grape arbors, and fig trees. Catholic and Italian festivals are important events in the neighborhood; St. Mary's School is a stable institution. The shrine of Our Lady of Carmel near St. Joseph's Roman Catholic Church reflects Italian vernacular architecture and was added to the National Register of Historic Places in 2002. The neighborhood is working class and has experienced some tensions as new Polish, African, Asian, and Mexican families have created a more diverse community. The shutdown of the 100-year-old Sun Chemical Factory may affect any redevelopment.

Howard R. Weiner

Rose Center for Earth and Space. Astrophysics center named for Frederick and Sandra Rose, located at West 81st Street between Columbus Avenue and Central Park West at the American Museum of Natural History. Opened in 2000, the center houses the new Hayden Planetarium, Cullman Hall of the Universe, Gottesman Hall of Planet Earth, and Space Theater. Rose exhibitions focus on the history and evolution of the phenomena of the universe, galaxies, stars, and planets through the innovations of modern astrophysics. Notable features include the customized Zeiss Mark IX Star Projector, an ecosphere, sulfide chimneys, and the Willamette Meteorite.

Dianna Ng

Rosedale. Neighborhood in southeastern Queens, bounded to the north by Merrick Boulevard, to the east and south by Hook Creek, and to the west by Brookfield Park; beyond the park is JFK Airport. The area was settled in 1647 by Thomas and Christopher Foster and became known as Foster's Meadow. A hamlet was built after a railroad station opened in 1870; developers changed the name to Rosedale in 1892. Most of the housing was erected in the 1920s, and until the 1930s the population was Irish and German. After World War II the neighborhood attracted a more diverse population, including Italians, Jews, and African Americans. Racial tension simmered in the 1970s, as Rosedale remained a white enclave pressed by adjacent black communities. In the 1980s a number of immigrants from the Caribbean moved to Rosedale and its environs, almost half from Jamaica and many others from Haiti and Guyana. Regardless of the demographic changes, Rosedale maintained a suburban character into the twenty-first century.

Vincent Seyfried

Rose Hill. Park located in the Bronx at the intersection of East Fordham Road and Webster Avenue. The name comes from the estate of Robert Watt, who owned the land that is now occupied by Fordham University. In 1787 John Watt purchased the land and gave it to his brother, Robert, who named it after the family seat in Scotland. In 1839 the land was sold to the Catholic Church for the construction of St. John's College, which eventually became Fordham University. The park underwent renovations in the 1960s, and in 1991 the cobblestone walkways and comfort station were rebuilt.

Nathan Morgante

Roseland Ballroom. Dance hall that opened on 1 January 1919 at 1658 Broadway, near 51st Street. It became a notable venue for jazz bands, including McKinney's Cotton Pickers and the bands of Sam Lanin, Fletcher Henderson, A. J. Piron, Claude Hopkins, Earl Hines, and Ella Fitzgerald. The hall was considered safer and more elegant than the taxi dance halls where patrons paid 10 cents for each dance; its location in the theater district, lavish decor, and national radio broadcasts made it especially prominent. The building that housed the ballroom was demolished in December 1956 and superseded by Roseland Dance City in 1957 on West 52nd Street. Disco nights were shut down in 1990 because of safety concerns. In the early twenty-first century this dance hall remained popular, entertaining a diverse clientele, presenting ballroom dancing on weeknights, occasional rock shows, and Latin dancing on weekends. After a multimillion-dollar renovation it became a concert and event space, showcasing major acts such as the Rolling Stones and Madonna (2008).

Kathy J. Ogren

Rosenberg case. The most celebrated court case of the cold war, in which a husband and

Rosenberg Complex, 2009

wife were convicted of spying for the Soviet Union and executed at Sing Sing Prison (Ossining, New York) on 19 June 1953. In 1950 the Federal Bureau of Investigation arrested Julius Rosenberg (1918–53), his wife, Ethel (1915–53), and his brother-in-law David Greenglass after revelations about a spy ring in New York City that included the atomic scientist Klaus Fuchs. The Rosenbergs, who lived at 10 Monroe Street on the Lower East Side, were accused of conveying atomic secrets to the Soviet Union while Julius Rosenberg, a devoted communist, was a civilian employee of the U.S. Signal Corps from 1940 to 1945; Greenglass had had access to classified information while working at atomic facilities in Los Alamos, New Mexico, in 1944. Greenglass became a federal witness, testified against the Rosenbergs, and received a prison sentence. The death sentence imposed on the Rosenbergs was widely regarded as severe.

Ronald Radosh and Joyce Milton, *The Rosenberg File: A Search for the Truth* (New York: Holt, Rinehart, 1983); Joseph H. Sharlitt, *Fatal Error: The Miscarriage of Justice That Sealed the Rosenbergs' Fate* (New York: Charles Scribner's Sons, 1989)

Martin Ebon

Rosenfeld, Morris (*b* Boksze, near Suwalki, Poland, 28 Dec 1862; *d* New York City, 22 June 1923). Poet. After living in Warsaw he immigrated to the United States in 1886 and worked for a time in the garment industry in New York City. He wrote verses about the travails of the sweatshop, immigrant longings, and socialist ideals that were often published in the Yiddish press and sung at workers' meetings and rallies. He was regarded as the bard of the Jewish labor movement. Several collections of his work were issued. In 1898 Rosenfeld became the first American Yiddish writer to achieve fame beyond the immigrant community when Leo Weiner translated his verses in *Songs from the Ghetto.*

Hutchins Hapgood, *Four Poets of the Ghetto* (Berkeley Heights, N.J.: Oriole, 1963)

Jeffrey Shandler

Ross, Charles. Alias of Lucky Luciano when he lived in the Waldorf Towers.

Ross, Harold (Wallace) (*b* Aspen, Colo., 6 Nov 1892; *d* Boston, 6 Dec 1951). Legendary magazine editor. During World War I he worked in Paris with Alexander Woollcott as a member of the editorial board of the military newspaper *Stars and Stripes.* After settling in New York City he launched the *New Yorker* with his wife, Jane Grant, who had written for the *New York Times;* in this endeavor he drew on the literary talents of the members of the Algonquin Round Table and the financial resources of Raoul Fleischmann, who had earned his fortune in the baking business. As the editor of the magazine for the next 26 years, he acquired a reputation for intelligence, brusqueness, and fanatical dedication to good writing. Although he seldom was publicly outspoken, just before his death he successfully protested the broadcasting of advertisements over loudspeakers in Grand Central Terminal. Ross lived from 1919 to 1920 at 56 West 11th Street in Manhattan, from August 1920 to August 1922 at 231 West 58th Street (at the same time also living for about a year at 333 West 85th Street), from 1922 to 1928 at 412 West 47th Street, and in the early 1930s at the Ritz-Carlton Hotel, 374 Madison Avenue.

James Thurber, *The Years with Ross* (Boston: Little, Brown, 1957); Jane Grant, *Ross, the New Yorker, and Me* (New York: Reynal, 1968); Thomas Kunkel, *Genius in Disguise: Harold Ross of the New Yorker* (New York: Random House, 1995)

Brenda Wineapple

Rossville. Neighborhood in southwestern Staten Island (2009 pop. *ca* 5500), bounded on the north by the Arthur Kill, on the east by the South Shore Golf Course, on the south by Woodrow Road, and on the west by Bloomingdale Road. The main streets are Arthur Kill Road and Rossville Avenue. The West Shore Expressway, built in 1976, cuts through historic Rossville. The area was settled during the seventeenth century and was known before the American Revolution as Blazing Star (see Old Blazing Star) after a comet and the local tavern. It was linked to the region by the Blazing Star Ferry and later by coastal steamships. During the nineteenth century it became a prosperous farming community and the post office location for southwestern Staten Island. In 1836 it was renamed for Colonel William E. Ross, a wealthy gentleman who lived there in "Ross Castle" on the shore. Passed over by rapid transit in the early twentieth century, Rossville declined until the mid-1970s when the opening of the expressway stimulated development. Two enormous liquefied natural gas tanks were built on the shore around 1971. After lengthy community opposition they were never used for that purpose, and at the end of the first decade of the twenty-first century they still stood empty. The population is Italian, Jewish, Indian, Pakistani, Filipino, and Korean. On Arthur Kill Road are many nineteenth-century houses, two historic cemeteries, a large catering hall, several automobile repair shops, a power transformer, and a marine junkyard. The Arthur Kill Correctional Facility, operated by the New York State Department of Corrections, opened in 1976. Condominiums and large, one-family houses stand along Rossville Avenue and Bloomingdale Road.

Charles W. Leng and William T. Davis, *Staten Island and Its People: a History, 1609–1929* (New York: Lewis Historical, 1930); John B. Woodall, "St. Luke's, Rossville: Life and Death of a Parish and Community," *Staten Island Historian* (Winter 1989), 24–30

Carol V. Wright, Barnett Shepherd

Roth, Henry (*b* Tysmenia, Galicia (now in Ukraine), 8 Feb 1906; *d* Albuquerque, N.M., 13 Oct 1995). Novelist and short-story writer. Roth immigrated to New York City in 1907 and grew up in Brownsville, the Lower East Side, and Harlem; he graduated from DeWitt Clinton High School in 1924 and from City College in 1928. In 1934 he published *Call It Sleep,* a novel in a documentary realist style set on the Lower East Side in the first decades of the twentieth century. After its publication Roth worked as a substitute teacher, laborer, and precision tool grinder in the city before moving to Maine with his wife, Muriel Parker. Decades of writer's block followed *Call It Sleep,* which was rediscovered and reissued in 1960 and 1964, and is considered by critics a literary masterpiece. His second book, *Shifting Landscape: A Composite (1925–1987)* (1987), was a collection of his short stories. In the 1970s he began a six-volume quasi-autobiographical work called *Mercy of a Rude Stream.* Only four volumes were completed before Roth's death: *A Star Shines over Mt. Morris Park* (1994), *A Diving Rock on the Hudson* (1995), *From Bondage* (1996), and *Requiem for Harlem* (1998).

Bonnie Lyons, *Henry Roth: The Man and His Work* (New York: Cooper Square, 1976); Steven G. Kellman, *Redemption: The Life of Henry Roth* (New York: W. W. Norton, 2005)

B. Kimberly Taylor, Kate Lauber

Roth, Philip (Milton) (*b* Newark, N.J., 19 May 1933). Novelist and short-story writer. He attended Weequahic High School in Newark and studied at the University of Chicago (MA, 1955), gaining renown after the publication of

Goodbye, Columbus (1959) and the comic novel *Portnoy's Complaint* (1969), which portrays Alexander Portnoy, "Assistant Commissioner of Human Opportunity for the City of New York." After the runaway success of *Portnoy's Complaint,* Roth escaped celebrity by immersing himself in the Czech community of New York, attending classes with writer Antonin Liehm on Staten Island and eating in Czech restaurants in Yorkville. He taught at Hunter College from 1989 to 1992, returning to Weequahic in the Pulitzer Prize–winning *American Pastoral* (1997) and *The Plot against America* (2004). In *Exit Ghost* (2007) Roth's alter ego Nathan Zuckerman returns to post-9/11 New York. In the early twenty-first century Roth maintained a studio on the Upper West Side of Manhattan and lived in Connecticut.

Shan Jayakumar, Kate Lauber

Roth, Samuel (*b* Nustscha, Galicia, 17 Nov 1894; *d* New York City, 3 July 1974). Prolific New York publisher of racy literature; imprisoned four times for obscenity; best known as defendant in the first major obscenity case to reach the Supreme Court (in 1957). Roth published under numerous imprints, both his own work and the (often pirated) works of European authors including D. H. Lawrence and James Joyce.

Roth arrived on Manhattan's Lower East Side with his family at age four. As a child, he worked as an egg candler, a newsboy, and a baker; at age 16 he was a reporter for the *New York Globe.* He published poetry in little magazines; attended Columbia University for a year; started his first magazine, *The Lyric;* then opened a poetry bookstore in Greenwich Village with his wife Pauline. In 1925, he published portions of Joyce's work in progress, *Finnegans Wake,* in his magazine, *Two Worlds;* the next year, he began to serialize Joyce's *Ulysses,* a risky venture both because Joyce said he did not have permission (Roth contested the point), and because a Manhattan court five years before had ruled portions of the book obscene. Although attacked by prosecutors and many in the literary establishment as a pornographer and copyright pirate, Roth was a pioneer in publishing sexual classics, such as *Fanny Hill,* and a determined defender of free expression. Roth conducted his publishing enterprises at 110 Lafayette Street in Manhattan; during his jail terms, Pauline carried on the business. In 1932, Roth published a bizarre anti-Semitic tract, *Jews Must Live.*

In 1955, Roth was indicted on 26 counts of obscenity; he was convicted on four, one of which involved a glossy quarterly, *American Aphrodite,* which he had published since 1951. The issue in question contained the story of Venus and Tannhauser, as told in prose and illustrations by the artist Aubrey Beardsley. The Supreme Court affirmed Roth's conviction, but ruled that not all sexual material is obscene; works with even "slightest redeeming social importance" are protected by the First Amendment.

Roth served time at Lewisburg federal prison after this conviction, but soon returned to publishing. He retired to an apartment on Central Park West.

Leo Hamalian, "Nobody Knows My Names: Samuel Roth and the Underside of Modern Letters," *Journal of Modern Literature* 3, no. 4 (April 1974), 889; *Roth v. United States,* 354 U.S. 476 (1957).

Marjorie Heins

Rothko, Mark [Rothkowitz, Marcus] (*b* Dvinsk [now Daugavpils, Latvia], 25 Sept 1903; *d* New York City, 25 Feb 1970). Painter. After immigrating to Portland, Oregon, as a child, he moved permanently in 1925 to New York City, where he became a pupil of Max Weber at the Art Students League. He frequented Milton Avery's studio and in 1935 joined Adolph Gottlieb and other artists in a group called The Ten. With Gottlieb and Barnett Newman he wrote a letter on 7 June 1943 to Edward Alden Jewell, the art critic for the *New York Times,* that described their art as "the simple expression of the complex thought." His first solo exhibition was held in 1945 at Art of This Century, a gallery owned by Peggy Guggenheim. After the gallery closed, he was represented by the Betty Parsons Gallery, which from 1947 mounted five solo exhibitions of his works. By 1950 he had eliminated all vestiges of representational imagery from his art and developed the style, characterized by large rectangles of color hovering in the canvas field, for which he became known. Toward the end of the decade his work became progressively more somber, as evidenced by a series of large-scale canvases that he painted during 1958–59 for the restaurant the Four Seasons in the Seagram Building. Soon after completing his last series of paintings, which were limited in color to black, gray, and brown, he took his own life. Rothko's residences in New York City included 19 West 102nd Street (1924–29), 137 West 72nd Street (1932–36), 313 East Sixth Street (1936–40), 29 East 28th Street (1940–43), 22 West 52nd Street (from 1945), 1288 Sixth Avenue (from late 1946 to 1954), 102 West 54th Street (from 1954), 118 East 95th Street (1960–64), and his studio at 157 East 69th Street (where he worked from 1964 and lived from January 1969 until his death).

Anna G. Chave, *Mark Rothko: Subjects in Abstraction* (New Haven, Conn.: Yale University Press, 1989); James E. B. Breslin, *Mark Rothko: A Biography* (Chicago: University of Chicago Press, 1993)

Mona Hadler

Rothstein, Arnold (*b* New York City, 1882; *d* New York City, 6 Nov 1928). Gambler and organized-crime figure. Born into a wealthy family, he hung out as a young man in the poolrooms and gambling parlors of the Lower East Side, where he met the gang leader Monk Eastman and Tammany Hall ward boss Big Tim Sullivan. Rothstein used his connections to Eastman, Sullivan, and others to become a leading gambler, bootlegger, drug dealer, and labor racketeer. Called the Big Bankroll, the Great Brain, and the Man Uptown, Rothstein was dapper and refined. He applied techniques of business to crime that were later perfected by Meyer Lansky, Lucky Luciano, and others. Rothstein did most of his work at Lindy's Restaurant in Times Square. He was accused of having engineered the outcome of the World Series of 1919, although he denied having done so. He almost certainly supplied strong-arm helpers and finances for communist unionists in the garment industry, in which he apparently mediated labor disputes. Rothstein was shot and mortally wounded in room 349 of the Park Central Hotel (Seventh Avenue and 56th Street), perhaps for refusing to pay a gambling debt. Although Mayor James J. Walker supervised the investigation, the assailant was never found, leading some to conclude that Tammany Hall had sabotaged the investigation to hide Rothstein's links to city government. He lived in the 1920s at 355 West 84th Street and at the Ritz-Carlton Hotel, 374 Madison Avenue, and in his final years at 912 Fifth Avenue. He served as the inspiration for Meyer Wolfsheim in F. Scott Fitzgerald's *The Great Gatsby* and Nathan Detroit in *Guys and Dolls.* Rothstein's life has been the subject of many books and movies, including *King of the Roaring 20s: The Story of Arnold Rothstein* (1961) starring David Janssen, which was rereleased in 2006.

David Pietrusza, *Rothstein: The Life, Times, and Murder of the Criminal Genius Who Fixed the 1919 World Series* (New York: Carroll and Graf, 2003)

Robert W. Snyder, Meryl Cates

rotisserie baseball. Game played by baseball enthusiasts, often called fantasy baseball. It was invented in 1979 by a group including the writer Daniel Okrent, the editor Cork Smith, and Robert Sklar, a professor of film at New York University, at La Rotisserie Française, a restaurant on 52nd Street between Third Avenue and Lexington Avenue. Participants in the game form fictitious teams that include real baseball players; by means of statistical formulas the performance of the teams is determined according to that of the players in the major leagues. The Fantasy Sports Trade Association estimated that 18 million adult Americans played fantasy-based games in 2008.

Joseph S. Lieber, Caleb Smith

row houses. Introduced in New Amsterdam by the Dutch in the mid-seventeenth century, the earliest row houses were simpler than those in the Netherlands: they were 20 feet (6 meters) wide, built of brick in Flemish bond with their gable end on the street (often pictured showing their distinctive Dutch stepped rooflines), and had a kitchen in the basement (the top of which extended above ground level), a parlor on the first story, and sleeping quarters on the upper story. Flush with either the left or right side of the building was a grand exterior staircase called the stoop (from a Dutch word for step or platform) that led from the street to the first story, with benches on either side of the landing; the family entered and left the building through a passage under the stoop and spent most of its time in the basement. Two-part Dutch doors allowed for ventilation while keeping children in and animals out; initially chimneys were made of wood with a clay lining and required frequent cleaning. Stepped gables were a convenience for chimney sweeps and for the fire brigade and were important for householders before fire-resistant brick and tile became readily available.

The Dutch row house offered a practical means of housing large families in a small space: it was sturdily built, cost little to maintain and heat, had separate family and reception areas, and was more comfortable than the English row house that was common in Boston and Philadelphia. In addition the design of the row house was adaptable: the building could be appointed lavishly for a wealthy family or sparely for a worker's family with as many as eight members; it could also be subdivided into several rental units and then converted back again into a one-family house, and the lower stories could be rented out to shops or restaurants. The parlor on the first story was used only for important occasions such as St. Nicholas Day, weddings, and funerals; Washington Irving wrote in *A History of New York* that the parlor was so inviolable that it was to be entered only for its weekly cleaning and that the brass lion's-head knocker on the front door was worn out from polishing more often than from use.

After the British took the city from the Dutch in 1664 the row house evolved into a simplified Georgian style characterized by brickwork in English bond, dormer windows, eaves parallel to the street, a low stoop of three or four steps, and railings and gates in wrought iron. The Federal style that took hold after independence was similar to the Georgian, except that the brickwork was now done in American running bond, and applied decoration often included an eagle.

The appearance of the row house changed again with the onset of the Greek Revival. Used first in churches, courthouses, and other public buildings, the new style became popular in private houses during the 1820s when the rising up of the Greek people against the Ottoman Empire in 1821–28 rekindled an interest in ancient Greece (during the same period a number of American cities were given Greek names). During the Greek Revival the row house acquired such classical features as egg-and-dart moldings, eaves featuring the beamlike triglyph and metope of the Greek pediment, lights atop and beside the main entrance, and balanced colonettes with capitals on either side. Pineapples, symbols of hospitality, were commonly used as finials on the newel posts. The windows had flat lintels, sometimes with a Greek key or other geometric fretwork, and the basement was visually separated from the rest of the house by a distinctive string course. The brickwork was frequently in American running bond. As in the Federal style the stoop was low, the railings were of wrought iron, and there was a high proportion of window space to wall.

The Gothic Revival enjoyed a brief popularity partly due to the writings of John Ruskin (1785–1864), who believed that people's actions were in part determined by their surroundings and that human simplicity and goodness were at their peak during the high Middle Ages. Although the Gothic Revival in the United States is associated principally with rectories and manses, a small number of private row houses were built in this highly decorative style, which is characterized by broken arches, trefoils and quatrefoils in railings and ballisters, crockets on finials, and the triescalon motif in frets. In New York City the windows of Gothic Revival buildings were surmounted by balanced, L-shaped drip moldings designed to keep rainwater away from the opening.

By the 1840s the first story was divided by sliding doors, which separated the parlor (often called the salon in wealthy families and the front room in working-class families) from the rooms to the rear. Behind the parlor and in front of the dining room was a music room, a space about 6 or 8 feet (2 to 2.5 meters) deep marked off by columns, demi-walls, or a scrollwork lattice. The room usually contained a piano and was the center of family entertainment. During this period architects exploited the easy reversibility of the floor plan of the row house: the stoops in a row would be on the right side between the left-hand cap house (a more substantial building at the end of the row) and the middle of the row, those in the other half of the row would be on the left, and a combined stoop would be formed in the middle.

The row houses built of soft, brownish sandstone and known as brownstones became popular during the Anglo-Italianate period that began in the late 1860s. The style was derived from that of English rows and crescents, which was in turn influenced by the style of Italian palazzi visited by young Britons during the eighteenth century. In New York City the Italianate buildings were distinguished by deep cornices over the windows; an impressive cornice over the main door (often supported by S-shaped console brackets); a heavy, imposing stoop with cast-iron baluster and newel posts; floor-to-ceiling windows on the parlor story; and arched windows in an elevated basement. Two new styles called Romanesque Revival and Queen Anne vied for popularity from the mid-1870s, at a time when architecture became established as a profession. Romanesque Revival was also known as Richardson Romanesque, after H. H. Richardson, one of the first Americans to study at the École des Beaux-Arts in Paris (with Eugène Viollet-le-Duc). The style was a late Victorian interpretation of the buildings of the later Roman Empire, particularly the fortified buildings. Its features included bases of heavy, rusticated stone; masonry arches (usually for the entrance); towerlike elements; engaged colonettes; elaborate floral panels of curved stone (called Byzantine scrollwork); and sometimes gargoyles. Buildings were generally constructed of Roman bricks (which were longer and slimmer than common bricks). The Queen Anne was an eclectic, Anglophile style that strove to use all the motifs associated in the popular imagination with historical England. Its buildings were constructed of such diverse materials as cast iron, terra-cotta, carved stone, force-molded concrete, and decorative burnt brick. Many were asymmetrical and combined antithetical elements; they could include Flemish gables and bulbous, Victorian towers. Both the Romanesque Revival and Queen Anne styles emphasized texture and the voluptuous use of materials (especially brick), as well as large buildings or at least the appearance of large buildings: a row of houses would often be designed with a unified front to make the final product resemble a palace. During these years the interior design of the row house underwent one of its few changes, as the affordability of furnaces and central heating from the 1870s made it practical to dig cellars.

Innovative builders in the late 1880s added to the grandeur of the row house by introducing the box stoop, which at first had two levels and eventually as many as three or (rarely) four. At the same time a new style of row house was imported from England, called variously the London Basement Plan and the American Basement Plan. Its main departure from earlier designs was the location of the grand ceremonial staircase inside the house, and of the entrance at ground level or at most two or three steps above it. Some of the row houses built according to the new plan were Georgian (a classic style filtered through English sensibilities of the eighteenth century); others were neo-Classic (based on Greek and Roman styles as viewed by the École des Beaux-Arts).

The row house housed many Irish and Italian immigrants in Brooklyn and the Bronx in the early twentieth century. It continued to be used much as it had been by the Dutch: the family spent most of its waking hours near the kitchen in the basement, reserved the front room for Sunday dinner and other important events, and used the stoop as a meeting place. The parents usually slept in the quieter bedroom, at the rear of the second story; the front bedroom was used by children and other relatives. Over the years stories could be added and interior modifications made, but the floor plan and the use of the rooms remained essentially the same. Grander row houses often had two stories for receiving guests, the parlor story and the one above. On the parlor story the salon was in the front and the library in the rear. In imitation of the customs of grand English houses, the family ate its daytime meals in the library, served by a dumbwaiter from the basement kitchen. On the story above the front room might be a drawing room to which the women could withdraw after supper, or a billiard room for the men (in which case the women used the library). At the back of this story was the formal dining room, also served by dumbwaiter, with a butler's pantry next to it used for the final preparation and reheating of food. The latter Georgian and neo-Classic row houses were the grandest ever built in New York City: fine examples are on West 74th Street off Central Park West (1904).

The row house began its decline about 1916. Then the subways were reaching into the unsettled parts of Brooklyn and the Bronx, where there was sufficient space to build semidetached and free-standing houses with larger lawns and backyards. At the same time the automobile was becoming affordable to an upwardly mobile middle class, which was increasingly likely to buy a house with a driveway and a garage. To accommodate this new development the design of row houses sacrificed living space. The garden cottage, developed during the 1940s, had a garage built below ground level that was reached by an inclined driveway; the automobile occupied the basement, the family was forced upstairs, and the upper stories and separate reception area disappeared. By the 1950s the family automobile was so large and important that the garage was moved to street level and seemed to be the most important design element of the building.

See also Bricks and Brownstones.

John J. Gallagher

rowing. Before steam ferries and bridges, one of the few ways to cross the city's many waterways was by rowing gigs and larger pulling boats. When rowers were not making a living, they raced each other for wagers before crowds of spectators. In 1825 New York City was the site of the first known international rowing contest when a visiting British ship challenged the Whitehall Landing crew to a race from Bedloe's Island to Hoboken, New Jersey, and then to the finish at the Battery.

Rowing bloomed in the 1830s with the formation of new clubs, some for middle- or upper-class amateur rowers and others for professionals. In races run by the Castle Garden Amateur Boat Club Association and other organizations, one of the most successful crews was the Wave Club, which rowed boats built by Clarkson Crolius. The first recorded individual race by solo rowers occurred in 1837, and professional racing in single sculls was a popular spectator sport until it gained a seamy reputation for fixed races and ceased to exist by the early twentieth century. Amateur rowing thrived in New York City. The city's first collegiate crew was formed by Columbia College in 1859, and the National Association of Amateur Oarsmen was organized in the city in 1872, when it defined amateurism. In 1905 there were 31 boathouses for rowing clubs and college crews, many on "the Speedway" on the Harlem River's western bank or "Scullers' Row" on the Hudson between 125th and 135th streets. When most of Scullers' Row was demolished in 1928, some clubs moved uptown to near Dyckman Street. Races between ethnic rowing clubs continued into the 1950s in the five boroughs. The last wooden Victorian boathouse, owned by the Fordham Rowing Association, was lost to arson in 1978.

Bolstered by the revival of interest in club sports and community waterfront facilities, rowing revived in New York City during the 1990s and early 2000s. Among the active organizations were the New York Athletic Club (rowing on Orchard Beach Lagoon), the New York Rowing Association (NYRA, at the Peter Jay Sharp Boathouse on the Harlem River), the Power Ten crew (based at the fire department boathouse near Gracie Mansion on the East River), and the Empire State Rowing Association (based at Roberto Clemente State Park in the Bronx). Community rowing programs were organized in conjunction with the Police Athletic League. Local colleges with rowing programs included Columbia, Manhattan College, Fordham University, St. John's University, and the State University of New York Maritime College. Still, most New Yorkers were unaware that the city's waters were used by rowers until a fatal collision between a powerboat and a scull making a predawn training run on the Harlem River in 2005.

According to the NYRA, more than 1000 teenagers were active in youth rowing programs between 2004 and 2007. A "Head of the Harlem" regatta was held every September. Several New York City public high schools had rowing clubs, and two, the Bronx High School of Science and Beach Channel High School, had crews in competition. In 2005 Beach Channel (Rockaway Beach, Queens) won five medals at the Eastern States Interscholastic Championships.

Arthur Ruhl and Samuel Crowther, *Rowing and Track Athletics* (New York: Macmillan, 1905); Melvin L. Adelman, *A Sporting Time: New York City and the Rise of Modern Athletics, 1820–1870* (Urbana: University of Illinois Press, 1986)

Joseph S. Lieber, John Rousmaniere

Roxbury. Neighborhood in southwestern Queens, lying near the western end of Rockaway Peninsula and bounded to the north by Rockaway Inlet, to the east by a station of the U.S. Coast Guard, to the south by State Road, and to the west by a section of the Gateway National Recreation Area. A summer colony grew in the early 1900s; in 1960 the Atlantic Improvement Company purchased the last vacant land and built homes and stores. Early in the twenty-first century most of the housing consisted of small bungalows, many of them winterized; the population remained largely Irish and middle class, and almost entirely white. With Breezy Point, Roxbury is part of the Breezy Point Cooperative, and the association approves all sales, rentals, and construction.

James Bradley

Roxy Theater. Movie theater opened in 1927 on 50th Street and Seventh Avenue at a cost of about $12 million. It was designed by the architect W. W. Ahlschlager and promoted and managed by Samuel Rothafel. Called the "cathedral of the motion picture," the theater seated more than 6000 and had the largest music library found in any theater, an advanced refrigeration and ventilation system, its own infirmary, and a power plant large enough to light a city of 250,000. The Roxy Theater was razed in 1961.

Roxy: A History (New York: Film Daily, 1927)

David Nasaw

RPA. See Regional Plan Association of New York.

Rubenstein Associates. Public relations firm established in Brooklyn in 1954 by Howard Rubenstein. After Rubenstein managed the successful mayoral campaign of Abraham D. Beame in 1973, the firm gained several major clients in municipal government and business. In 1984 it moved to Manhattan, where it served about 200 clients, including many of the city's most powerful builders, trade associations, and labor unions. For 34

Interior of Roxy Theater

of these clients it worked as a registered lobbyist. By this time Rubenstein Associates was one of the largest and most influential public relations firms in the city. In the early twenty-first century it had more than 200 employees and approximately 450 clients. Its headquarters were at 1345 Sixth Avenue.

Alan R. Raucher

Rubin, I(sidor) C(linton) (*b* Vienna, 8 Jan 1883; *d* London, 10 July 1958). Gynecologist. He settled in New York City as a child. In 1919 he developed a test for sterility in women for which he became internationally known; he also conducted important research in cervical cancer. Rubin taught at the College of Physicians and Surgeons (1937–47), was chief of gynecology at Mount Sinai Hospital (1937–46), and was also associated with Beth Israel Hospital, Montefiore Hospital, and Harlem Hospital.

Joseph S. Lieber

Rubinstein, Helena (*b* Kraków, Poland, *ca* 1871; *d* New York City, 1 April 1965). Leading cosmetics businesswoman. She moved to New York City in 1914 by way of London and in the following year opened the Maison de Beauté de Valaze at 14 East 49th Street, which featured her immediately popular Crème Valaze. Her factory-made but narrowly marketed products soon became successful, and she expanded her salons and product line to several American and European cities. Some of her products became the target of federal regulators after the passage of the Pure Food and Drug Act of 1936, but in the long run her profits were scarcely affected. Advertisements that showed her wearing a white laboratory coat and inspecting her products extolled a scientifically designed beauty program, a marketing strategy that became widely imitated. She also offered the first line of cosmetics for oily, dry, and normal skin, and introduced a mascara applicator that remained in use into the 1990s. Rubinstein was well known for her idiosyncrasies and for most of her career had a highly publicized rivalry with Elizabeth Arden. From her headquarters at 655 Fifth Avenue she oversaw a cosmetics empire that by the time of her death in 1965 included more than 500 products and employed about 26,000 persons in salons, factories, and laboratories in 14 countries. She also owned the apartment building at 625 Park Avenue, which was one of her many residences throughout the world.

Marc Ferris

Rucker Tournament. Playground basketball league. Founded by Holcombe Rucker, a Harlem English teacher and parks department recreation director credited with helping hundreds of youngsters go to college, the tournament began in the late 1940s. It was held in a number of parks before moving to its current location at 155th Street and Frederick Douglass Boulevard in 1965, named Rucker Park in 1969. At its peak from the 1950s to 1970s, Rucker Pro League teams featured National Basketball Association (NBA) legends like Wilt Chamberlain, Julius Erving, and Nate "Tiny" Archibald competing with talented playground legends like Earl "The Goat" Manigault, Joe Hammond, and Pee Wee Kirkland. The original Rucker Tournament collapsed in the early 1980s; since 1982 the Entertainers Basketball Classic (EBC) has run a tournament at Rucker Park that combines basketball with a sideline disc jockey and wisecracking announcer on the court calling the play-by-play. NBA stars Stephon Marbury and Ron Artest played on EBC teams owned by New York City rappers such as Sean Combs, Fat Joe, and Ja Rule. Rucker Park has appeared in Nike commercials, video games, and NBA television broadcasts. The Rucker Tournament was portrayed in the documentary film *Gunnin' for That #1 Spot* (2008).

Ben Silk

Ruder Finn. Public relations firm, formed in 1948 by Bill Ruder (*b* 1921) and David Finn (*b* 1921). Based in a small room at the Lombardy Hotel on East 56th Street, it began as an organization called Art in Industry that was intended to promote business sponsorship of the arts. The firm soon took its current name and became successful as a public relations firm for entertainers such as Perry Como, Dinah Shore, the Mills Brothers, and Jack Lemmon. It later acquired a more diverse list of clients, including large corporations, colleges and universities, and foreign governments. Ruder served as an assistant secretary of commerce under President John F. Kennedy. In 2010 Ruder Finn had headquarters at 301 East 57th Street in Manhattan and more than 100 offices worldwide.

James Bradley

Rudin, Lewis [Lew] (*b* Bronx, 4 April 1927; *d* New York City, 20 Sept 2001). Real estate mogul. He graduated from De Witt Clinton High School in the Bronx and the New York University School of Commerce. His father founded Rudin Management in 1924, when he built his first apartment house, a six-story tenement in the Bronx that still stands. Along with his brother Jack, Lewis Rudin became cochairman of a company that in 2001 included 40 buildings in the New York metropolitan area, including 16 office towers, valued at more than $2 billion (in 2001). In 1955 the Rudins built their first office building at 415 Madison Avenue. In the 1980s and 1990s the family continued building office towers. In 1993 Rudin's son, William, became president of Rudin Management Company and spearheaded the Reuters Tower in Times Square.

Committed to the health and vitality of New York City, Rudin rallied the real estate and business communities during the city's 1970s fiscal crisis to prepay their real estate taxes in a successful effort to help the city avoid bankruptcy. In the 1980s he lobbied Congress to protect the deductibility of state and local taxes. He was a recipient of the Bronze Medallion, New York City's highest civic award, and was named a "Living Landmark" by the New York Landmarks Conservancy. He also held the title of honorary police commissioner of New York City. Rudin was known for his philanthropic pursuits, especially his cofounding of the Association for a Better New York in 1971. He popularized the New York Marathon and played a key role in moving it out of Central Park and onto the streets of the city's five boroughs. Rudin and his brother sponsored the Samuel Rudin Trophy in honor of their father, a marathon runner.

Jessica Montesano

Rudin, Samuel (*b* 1896; *d* New York City, 22 Dec 1975). Real estate developer. He erected apartment buildings in New York City before World War II and then became known for modern apartment towers on the Upper East Side furnished with such conveniences as insulated plumbing, air-conditioned hallways, and street-level stores; he promoted the apartments as "walk-to-work" residences for executives. He also erected such office buildings as 1 Battery Park Plaza, the New York Merchandise Mart, and 345 Park Avenue, chosen by the firm of Bristol–Myers as its headquarters over properties outside the city. An active philanthropist, Rudin helped to form the Association for a Better New York and sponsored the New York City Marathon. His sons Lewis Rudin and Jack Rudin also became prominent developers.

Marc A. Weiss

Rugby. Neighborhood in central Brooklyn, encompassing the land north of Holy Cross Cemetery and that surrounding Kings County Hospital and bounded to the north by Church Avenue, to the east by 57th Street, to the south by Clarendon Road, and to the west by Albany Avenue; it is considered one of the four sections of East Flatbush. The area was once covered by potato farms and was renamed in the late 1890s by developers who thought Flatlands an unattractive name. In 1900 the real estate firm of Wood, Harmon bought many acres of farmland for development as suburban lots and contracted with Brooklyn Rapid Transit to build 50 houses within a year in return for the extension to the area of a trolley line along Reid Avenue. Growth increased after Interborough Rapid Transit extended the subway to Nostrand Avenue in 1912. The housing stock consists of one- and two-family detached and semidetached houses built mostly in the 1920s and 1930s and a few apartment buildings dating from after World War II. The main retail shopping area developed along Utica Avenue and Church Avenue. From the 1920s to the 1960s many Italians and American-born Jews moved to the neighborhood, and the population became increasingly diverse after 1965, with a large number of blacks and immigrants from the Caribbean (especially Jamaica, Haiti, and Guyana). In the early twenty-first century the neighborhood was known as East Flatbush.

Ellen Marie Snyder-Grenier

Ruggles, David (*b* Norwich, Conn., 15 March 1810; *d* Florence, Mass., 26 Dec 1849). Writer, publisher, and abolitionist. He grew up in Norwich and in 1827 moved to New York City, where he operated a grocery. In 1834 he opened a bookshop at 67 Lispenard Street that served blacks and abolitionists until it was destroyed by a mob in the following year. He launched the first black magazine in the United States, the *Mirror of Liberty,* in 1838, and wrote numerous pamphlets satirizing American colonialism. In 1835 he became the leader of the New York Vigilance Committee, which helped fugitives from slavery such as Frederick Douglass to evade capture.

Graham Hodges

Ruggles, Samuel B(ulkley) (*b* New Milford, Conn., 11 April 1800; *d* Fire Island, N.Y., 28 Aug 1881). Real estate developer. He moved to New York City in 1821 and by 1831 had bought Gramercy Farm, occupying 22 acres (9 hectares) between Third and Fourth avenues and 20th and 22nd streets. He then subdivided the land into 108 lots, with 42 set aside for a private park to be held in perpetuity by the residents of the surrounding 66 lots. The result was Gramercy Park, a patch of green that became one of the most pleasant small spaces in Manhattan. Ruggles was active in promoting the creation of Union Square, one of the city's first public parks, and he was also a commissioner of the Croton Aqueduct and a longtime trustee of Columbia College.

Samuel B. Ruggles

Kenneth T. Jackson

rum. See Sugar.

Rumsey, Mary Harriman (*b* 17 Nov 1881; *d* 18 Dec 1934). Philanthropist and political adviser. The eldest of six children of the railroad magnate Edward H. Harriman, she graduated from Barnard College, for which she was a trustee from 1911 until her death. She founded the Junior League in 1901 and was its chairman until 1904. In 1910 she married the sculptor Charles Cary "Pad" Rumsey. In 1920 she formed the Welfare Council to bring together overlapping social agencies in New York City; this later became the Community Council of Greater New York. She persuaded her brother W. Averell Harriman to go to Washington, D.C., in 1933 to help restructure the National Recovery Administration. Later he largely attributed his having pursued a career in government to her influence. Although she usually lived with her three children in suburban Sands Point, Long Island, shortly before her death she lived with Frances Perkins in Washington, D.C., where the two worked to pass the Social Security Act.

Kenneth T. Jackson

running. Organized footraces were held in New York City in the early nineteenth century. The first cash prize was won in 1835 by Louis Bennett, who emphasized his half-Senecan background by competing under the name Deerfoot while wearing a loincloth and a feather headdress: he covered the distance of 10 miles (16 kilometers) in 56 minutes. By 1850 "pedestrianism" had become something of an obsession. Large prizes were offered to professional runners, who competed under

New York City Marathon 1970–2009

Year	Men's Winner	Nationality	Time	Women's Winner	Nationality	Time	Total Runners
1970	Gary Muhrcke	United States	2:31:38	no finisher			127
1971	Norman Higgins	United States	2:22:54	Beth Bonner	United States	2:55:22	245
1972	Sheldon Karlin	United States	2:27:52	Nina Kuscsik	United States	3:08:41	284
1973	Tom Fleming	United States	2:21:54	Nina Kuscsik	United States	2:57:07	406
1974	Norbert Sander	United States	2:10:09	Kathrine Switzer	United States	2:25:45	527
1975	Tom Fleming	United States	2:19:27	Kim Merritt	United States	2:46:14	534
1976	Bill Rodgers	United States	2:10:10	Miki Gorman	United States	2:39:11	2090
1977	Bill Rodgers	United States	2:11:28	Miki Gorman	United States	2:43:10	4823
1978	Bill Rodgers	United States	2:12:12	Grete Waitz	Norway	2:32:30	9875
1979	Bill Rodgers	United States	2:11:42	Grete Waitz	Norway	2:27:33	11,533
1980	Alberto Salazar	United States	2:09:41	Grete Waitz	Norway	2:25:41	14,012
1981	Alberto Salazar	United States	2:08:13	Allison Roe	New Zealand	2:25:29	14,496
1982	Alberto Salazar	United States	2:09:29	Grete Waitz	Norway	2:27:14	14,308
1983	Rod Dixon	New Zealand	2:08:59	Grete Waitz	Norway	2:27:00	15,193
1984	Orlando Pizzolato	Italy	2:14:53	Grete Waitz	Norway	2:29:30	14,590
1985	Orlando Pizzolato	Italy	2:11:34	Grete Waitz	Norway	2:28:34	16,705
1986	Gianni Poli	Italy	2:11:06	Grete Waitz	Norway	2:28:06	20,502
1987	Ibrahim Hussein	Kenya	2:11:01	Priscilla Welch	Great Britain	2:30:17	22,523
1988	Steve Jones	Great Britain	2:08:20	Grete Waitz	Norway	2:28:07	23,463
1989	Juma Ikangaa	Tanzania	2:08:01	Ingrid Kristiansen	Norway	2:25:30	24,996
1990	Douglas Waikihuri	Kenya	2:12:39	Wanda Panfil	Mexico	2:30:45	25,797
1991	Salvador Garcia	Mexico	2:09:28	Liz McColgan	Great Britain	2:27:32	26,900
1992	Willie Mtolo	South Africa	2:09:29	Lisa Ondieki	Great Britain	2:24:40	28,656
1993	Andres Espinoza	Mexico	2:10:04	Uta Pippig	Germany	2:26:24	28,140
1994	German Silva	Mexico	2:11:21	Tegla Loroupe	Kenya	2:27:37	31,129
1995	German Silva	Mexico	2:11:00	Tegla Loroupe	Kenya	2:28:06	29,000
1996	Giacomo Leone	Italy	2:09:54	Anuta Catuna	Romania	2:28:18	29,000
1997	John Kagwe	Kenya	2:08:12	Franziska Rochat-Moser	Switzerland	2:28:43	31,400
1998	John Kagwe	Kenya	2:08:45	Franca Fiacconi	Italy	2:25:17	32,398
1999	Joseph Chebet	Kenya	2:09:14	Adriana Fernandez	Italy	2:25:06	32,503
2000	Abdelkhader El Mouaziz	Morocco	2:10:09	Ludmila Petrova	Russia	2:25:45	29,930
2001	Tesfay Jifar	Ethiopia	2:07:43	Margaret Okayo	Kenya	2:24:21	24,057
2002	Rogers Rop	Kenya	2:08:07	Joyce Chepchumba	Kenya	2:25:56	32,560
2003	Martin Lel	Kenya	2:10:30	Margaret Okayo	Kenya	2:22:31	35,286
2004	Hendrick Ramaala	South Africa	2:09:28	Paula Radcliffe	Great Britain	2:23:10	37,257
2005	Paul Tergat	Kenya	2:09:30	Jelena Prokopcuka	Latvia	2:24:41	37,597
2006	Marsilon Gomes dos Santos	Brazil	2:09:58	Jelena Prokopcuka	Latvia	2:25:05	38,368
2007	Martin Lel	Kenya	2:09:04	Paula Radcliffe	Great Britain	2:23:09	39,265
2008	Marsilon Gomes dos Santos	Brazil	2:08:43	Paula Radcliffe	Great Britain	2:23:56	37,899
2009	Meb Keflezighi	United States	2:09:15	Derartu Tulu	Ethiopia	2:28:52	43,741

Compiled by David White

such colorful names as the American Deer, the Welsh Bantam, and the Yankee Clipper; one runner who called himself the Grand American Union ran in an outfit bearing the Stars and Stripes. A popular event was the six-day race, which was run continuously and usually indoors. Prizes were as high as $30,000 and competitors covered upwards of 400 miles (640 kilometers). At one six-day race in 1888 George Littlewood ran 623.75 miles (1003.6 kilometers), setting a record that lasted for nearly a century (it was broken in New York City in 1984, when Yannis Kouros covered 635 miles and 1023 yards, or 1022.8 kilometers, at a six-day race on Randalls Island). A race of about 35 miles (56 kilometers) from Stamford, Connecticut, to New York City in 1896 was won by John McDermott, who later that year won the Boston Marathon. Between November 1908 and April 1909 four professional and five amateur marathons were run in and around the city. The last of these was the Marathon Derby, run on a dirt track at the Polo Grounds, where in a steady rain the Frenchman Henri St. Yves handily defeated some of the greatest runners in the world in a time of 2:40:50. The Millrose Athletic Association, formed as the Wahna Athletic Association by employees of Wanamaker's department stores, held its first meet in Madison Square Garden in 1914.

The New York Road Runners Club was formed in 1958 by a small group of dedicated runners and grew into a large organization when running became widely popular during the 1970s. On 13 September 1970 it organized the first running of the New York City Marathon: 127 runners started the course, which was run entirely in Central Park. The president of the club, Fred Lebow, later persuaded the city to have the course of the marathon run through each of the five boroughs beginning in 1976, with the starting line in Staten Island at one end of the Verrazano–Narrows Bridge and the finish line in Central Park near Tavern on the Green. In the early twenty-first century the New York City Marathon, held annually on the first Sunday in November, is one of the largest marathons in the world, with more than 40,000 finishers and drawing on average more than two million spectators.

The 2002 creation of the Armory Track and Field Center and the National Track and Field Hall of Fame in the Fort Washington area of upper Manhattan provided the city with one of the best indoor track facilities in the world and made it a national center of high school and collegiate track. Central Park and Prospect Park remain important centers of recreational running in New York City. In Central Park many runners train at the reservoir, which is surrounded by a dirt track with a perimeter of 1.58 miles (2.54 kilometers); races are frequently run on the main paved road in the park, which has a perimeter of 6.03 miles (9.7 kilometers) and is closed to motor vehicles for much of the week during the summer. The New York Road Runners Club on East 89th Street sponsors group runs and meetings on athletic topics, as well as a race in Central Park almost every weekend throughout the year, drawing on average between 3000 and 6000 participants. The organization also puts on many races outside of Central Park, including the New York City Half Marathon, which runs each year from the park through Times Square and down the West Side Highway, as well as a half marathon in each of the five boroughs.

Robert Hillenbrand, David White

Runyon [Runyan], **(Alfred) Damon** (*b* Manhattan, Kan., 3 Oct 1880; *d* New York City, 10 Dec 1946). Journalist and short-story writer. He worked for newspapers in Colorado before moving to New York City in 1910. In 1911 he began covering sports for the *New York American,* owned by William Randolph Hearst. Runyon took on a wide range of assignments, working as a foreign war correspondent, crime reporter, and feature writer for Hearst's syndicated news empire, accumulating a daily readership of over 10 million. Recognized at his peak as "America's Premier Journalist," Runyon became famous for short stories recounting the misadventures of petty criminals, gamblers, and the women who loved them. This "hard-boiled" writing style, with its use of slang and its depiction of sordid events, became known as Runyonesque. Many of Runyon's works were transformed into film and theater productions, including Frank Loesser's musical *Guys and Dolls* (1950), and Frank Capra's film *Lady for a Day* (1933). After his death in 1946, an airplane scattered Runyon's ashes over Broadway, and the Aqueduct Racetrack in Queens dedicated a horse race to his memory.

Cecilia Magnusson

Ruppert, Jacob. See Jacob Ruppert Brewery.

Russell Sage Foundation. Charitable organization formed in 1907 by Olivia Sage and named after her late husband, a prominent financier. Encouraged by her friend and adviser Robert de Forest, president of the Charity Organization Society, she gave the foundation a broad mandate to improve social and living conditions in the United States that allowed it to become a leader in the reforms of the Progressive era. Her original endowment of $10 million was increased by $5 million on her death in 1918. Among those who served the foundation during its early years were de Forest (first chairman of the board); John Glenn of the Charity Organization Society of Baltimore (general director); Louisa Lee Schuyler, founder of the New York State Charities Aid Association; and Gertrude Rice, a founder of the Charity Organization Society of New York (all original board members); Mary Richmond, a dominant figure in the Charity Organization Society (director of the Charity Organization Department); and Luther Gulick, organizer of the Camp Fire Girls (director of the Department of Child Hygiene). During its early years the foundation sought to promote the new profession of social work and to develop practical applications of social welfare theories. The foundation donated $1.2 million to the Committee on the Regional Plan between 1921 to 1932 to conduct a comprehensive survey of the metropolitan region and an additional $500,000 to promote adoption of the committee's recommendations. From 1913 the headquarters were at Lexington Avenue and 22nd Street. As part of a major reorganization the foundation in 1948 shifted its focus toward the funding of social science research and sold its main building to the Catholic archdiocese. The foundation continues to support research in fields ranging from the means of escaping poverty to the success rates of second-generation immigrants, and has an active publications program. In 2010 the offices of the foundation were at 112 East 64th Street, former headquarters of the Asia Society.

Melissa Smith Clayton

Russians. New York City was the principal point of entry at the time of the first large-scale immigration of Russians to the United States, which began in the 1880s and continued until the outbreak of World War I. About 60 percent of these immigrants were Jews who spoke Yiddish. Townspeople without specific trades, called *luftmenschen,* arrived soon after the assassination of Tsar Alexander II in 1881, which the Russian government and populace used as a pretext for subjecting Jews to persecution and pogroms. Many of the first immigrants were also fleeing poverty and seeking better economic conditions in the United States; a large number settled on the Lower East Side in Manhattan and across the East River in Williamsburg. They found employment in clothing factories, in the fur business, and in the building trades as bricklayers, carpenters, house painters, and house wreckers. A sense of Russian identity among Jews and non-Jews was sustained by the publication of *Novoe russkoe slovo* (1910–), the oldest and most widely read Russian-language newspaper outside the homeland. The Russian Social-Democratic Society was formed in the city in 1891 and became the basis for a Russian division of the American Socialist Party. Its aggressively leftist newspaper *Novyi mir* (1911–20, 1927–38) included on its editorial staff Leon Trotsky, who lived in the Bronx in early 1917 before returning to Russia to join Lenin in leading the Bolshevik Revolution. During the "Red Scare" of 1919–20 Russian immigrants were generally assumed to be communist agitators, and many were arrested and deported.

In the early decades of the twentieth century the city was a center of religious activity for Russians of various faiths. It became the headquarters of the Russian Orthodox Church in North America in 1905, and the headquarters of all three groups into which the church split as a result of political changes in Russia (the Metropolia, later the Orthodox Church in America; the Moscow Patriarchal Exarchate; and the Russian Orthodox Synod Abroad). Among the earliest and largest organizations was the Russian Orthodox Christian Immigrant Society of North America (1908), which for many years occupied a five-story building on East 14th Street and provided shelter and social services to immigrants. Basic and advanced adult education was available through the Russian Collegiate Institute (1919), the Russian Technical Institute (1920), and the Russian-American Technicum (1924). The Russian Student Fund (1921) provided assistance to students in American colleges and universities.

A second group of Russians settled in the city during the early 1920s and was largely made up of political exiles forced out of their country by the Bolshevik Revolution. Many of these immigrants were professionals (lawyers, doctors, engineers, professors), businesspeople, members of the clergy, performing artists, and wealthy aristocrats. While some of the professionals were able to retrain themselves and continue their work, others worked as taxi drivers, watchmen, and house painters and in retail sales; some became restaurant managers, shop owners, and hotel managers. The best-known existing landmark from this period of immigration is the Russian Tea Room on 57th Street in Manhattan. Russians who settled in New York City in the late 1940s and early 1950s included refugees from the Bolsheviks who had spent the interwar years in Europe, as well as "displaced persons" who had escaped from the Soviet Union during World War II. Although these immigrants were from social and economic backgrounds similar to those of earlier immigrants, they found it easier to secure skilled work. Their Russian-language skills were valued by U.S. and international government agencies during the cold war, and they entered professions such as interpreting, translating, and teaching. This group of immigrants launched the first Russian literary and public affairs quarterly outside Russia, *Novyi zhurnal* (1942), and formed the Association of Russian-American Scholars (1947) to promote scholarly research and publications, as well as several organizations dedicated to political change in the Soviet Union and the United States.

The popular image of Russian Americans as communist prevailed even though many of the immigrants were fiercely anticommunist. Among the best-known Russian immigrants from these years was Alexander Kerensky, who settled in New York City in 1940; in 1949 he formed the League to Fight for National Freedom. In the 1970s and 1980s the Soviet Union allowed many Jews to emigrate, and of these the largest number settled in New York City, specifically in Brighton Beach. As Russian became the dominant language in the neighborhood and signs in the Cyrillic alphabet were hung from the facades of its shops and restaurants, Brighton Beach replaced the Lower East Side as the principal Russian neighborhood in the city. The Society of New Russian Immigrants, an educational and cultural organization, was formed in 1975. In the 1990s, after the breakup of the Soviet Union, another wave of immigration followed. In the early twenty-first century Russians constituted the 10th largest group of newcomers to New York City; in 2007 more than 72,000 New Yorkers had been born in Russia.

Of the prominent Russians who have lived in New York City many have been artists and musicians, including the composer Igor Stravinsky, the pianist Vladimir Horowitz, the choreographer and founder of the New York City Ballet George Balanchine, the sculptor Louise Nevelson, and the artistic director of the American Ballet Theatre Mikhail Baryshnikov.

Paul Robert Magocsi, *The Russian Americans* (New York: Chelsea House, 1981)

Paul Robert Magocsi

Russian Tea Room. Restaurant at 150 West 57th Street next to Carnegie Hall in Manhattan, opened in 1927 by several former members of the Russian Imperial Ballet as a meeting place for Russian émigrés and later expanded to a full-size restaurant by its proprietor, Sammy Kaye. On Kaye's death in 1967 control of the restaurant passed to his widow, Faith Stewart-Gordon, who continued to operate it until 1996 when she sold it to businessman Warner LeRoy. After a $36 million, four-year renovation, the Russian Tea Room reopened, only to close in July 2002, after its owner declared bankruptcy. Its most recent incarnation opened under the direction of Gerald Lieblich in 2006. The decor of the restaurant is meant to evoke a Russian Christmas before the Bolshevik Revolution and includes dark green walls, samovars, and Christmas decorations. A number of films have been made there, among them Woody Allen's *Manhattan.* The restaurant's clientele has included such well-known figures as George Balanchine, Leonard Bernstein, Anita Loos, and Harold Clurman.

Rachel Sawyer

Russwurm, John B(rown) (*b* Port Antonio, Jamaica, 1 Oct 1799; *d* Liberia, 17 June 1851). Newspaper editor, abolitionist, and government official. After moving with his father to Maine he graduated from Bowdoin College in 1826. He moved to New York City in the following year and helped to found *Freedom's Journal,* the country's first black-owned newspaper, which he published first with Samuel E. Cornish and from late 1827 by himself. His despair over what he saw as the grim future of blacks in the United States led him to accept a position in the Liberian Department of Education in February 1829, a decision that caused a scandal among blacks in the city. Russwurm spent the rest of his life in Liberia.

Graham Hodges

Rustin, Bayard Taylor (*b* West Chester, Pa., 17 March 1912; *d* New York City, 24 Aug 1987). Civil rights activist. Brought up as a Quaker, he embraced communism during the 1930s before turning to socialism during the 1940s. After being imprisoned for refusing to serve in World War II he devoted himself to pacifism and was an aide to Martin Luther King, Jr., from 1955 to 1960. He helped to organize the March on Washington that drew 200,000 participants in 1963 and a school boycott in New York City on 3 February 1964 involving 464,000 students. Believing that racial oppression was due primarily to economic injustice, he sought to form a coalition led by blacks, white liberals, and workers. He favored cooperation with the federal government and supported the domestic and international policies of President Lyndon B. Johnson, including the Vietnam War. For his approach to these issues he was criticized by many black nationalists, whom he steadfastly opposed; he later maintained that their criticism was also due to his homosexuality. Rustin lived for many years in the Chelsea neighborhood in Manhattan. In 1983 Bayard Rustin High School for the Humanities opened at 351 West 18th Street.

Kevin Kenny

Rutgers, Henry (*b* near New York City, 7 Oct 1745; *d* New York City, 17 Feb 1830). Landholder and philanthropist. A descendant of Dutch immigrants who settled in New York City in 1636 and prospered as brewers, he graduated from King's College in 1766 and became active in politics, serving in the state assembly as a Jeffersonian Republican and political ally of Aaron Burr. He was a colonel during the American Revolution and in 1811 helped raise funds for the construction of Tammany Hall. He also gave land and funds to his own Dutch Reformed church, to Presbyterian and Baptist churches, and to schools for children of the poor. He became president of the Public School Society in 1828. At the time of his death Rutgers's estate in Chatham Square was one of the most valuable in Manhattan. Rutgers University in New Jersey is named in his honor.

Elaine Weber Pascu

Rutgers v. Waddington. Case decided in 1784 in which a state law called the Trespass Act of 1783 was overturned. The act allowed people whose premises had been occupied by the British during the American Revolution to recover damages, and Mrs. Elizabeth Rutgers invoked its provisions in filing suit for £8000 against Joshua Waddington, a British merchant who during the war had lived in her brewery in Maiden Lane. Alexander Hamilton successfully argued for the defendant before the mayor's court that the act was a violation of the Articles of Confederation and of international law. The case helped to establish the principle of judicial review.

Julius Goebel, ed., *The Law Practice of Alexander Hamilton,* vol. 1 (New York: Columbia University Press, 1964)

Peter Eisenstadt

Ruth, Babe [George Herman] (*b* Baltimore, 6 Feb 1895; *d* New York City, 16 Aug 1948). Baseball legend. The son of Kate and George Herman, Sr., Ruth was the first of eight children, but only he and his sister Mamie survived childhood. In 1902, unable to financially support their children, Ruth's parents gave over legal custody of their son to Catholic missionaries at the St. Mary's Industrial School for Boys in Baltimore. Ruth played on the St. Mary's baseball team, garnering the attention of professional scouts. The Baltimore Orioles, a Minor League subsidiary of the Boston Red Sox, signed Ruth to his first professional baseball contract at the age of 19. Teammates referred to Ruth as "the newest babe" of Jack Dunn, the Orioles owner who took over legal guardianship of his young acquisition. Over the next six years he developed into an ace pitcher and a feared hitter, leading Boston to three World Series titles. In the winter of 1919 Red Sox owner Harry Frazee sold the rights to Ruth to New York Yankees co-owner Jacob Ruppert for $150,000 and a $350,000 loan to jump-start Frazee's career as a Broadway producer. Ruth's sale to the Yankees marked a shift in the fortunes of the Red Sox and the Yankees that continued until 2004, when the Red Sox won their first World Series in over 85 years. The Yankees, previously of minor significance in professional baseball, became arguably the most well-known sports franchise in the world and won 26 World Series titles during the Red Sox 86-year championship drought. The Red Sox and Yankees also developed a heated rivalry after the Ruth transaction that continued into the twenty-first century as the Yankees success and the Red Sox failures were attributed to the "Curse of the Bambino," one of Ruth's many nicknames. With the Yankees Ruth switched from being a pitcher to playing right field so he could focus on his hitting. The results were astounding as Ruth's popularity and home run–hitting ability, coupled with the team's newfound success, led to a dramatic increase in attendance that allowed the Yankees, which had previously shared a stadium with the New York Giants at the Polo Grounds, to build Yankee Stadium, nicknamed the "House That Ruth Built," in the Bronx in 1923. Ruth remained with the Yankees until 1935, leading the team to its first four World Series titles and setting the single-season home run record in 1929 with 60 home runs, a mark that stood until another Yankee, Roger Maris, topped it in 1961. Ruth's legend and popularity stemmed as much from his personality and activities off the field as from his home run prowess. Sportswriter Bill Broeg noted that "to try to capture Babe Ruth with cold statistics would be like trying to keep up with him on a night out." Ruth's annual income from endorsements was greater than his contract with the Yankees. Babe was also known for his hearty appetite, late-night partying, and love of children, to whom he frequently paid hospital visits. Less than a year after leaving the Yankees, Ruth retired from baseball following a brief stint with the Boston Braves. In the last year of his career Ruth had a falling-out with the Yankees and then the Braves as both franchises refused to hire him as their manager. Having finished his career with 714 home runs, 2217 runs batted in, a .342 batting average, and a 94–46 record as a pitcher, Ruth became one of five members of the inaugural class of the National Baseball Hall of Fame. In 1938, still hoping to manage a Major League Baseball team, Ruth joined the Brooklyn Dodgers as a first-base coach, but when a managerial opening the next season was given to Leo Durocher instead of Ruth, the Babe left the game for good. Ruth died of throat cancer in 1948 at Memorial Hospital in New York City. An estimated 100,000 mourners lined the streets around St. Patrick's Cathedral on the day of his funeral service. Ruth was survived by his second wife, Claire, and his daughter Dorothy, whom he had adopted with his first wife. He is buried at Gate of Heaven Cemetery in suburban Hawthorne in Westchester County. Ruth remains the single most revered athlete and personality in all of American sports to this day. His nicknames included the Babe, the Sultan of Swat, the Great Bambino, and the Home Run King.

Robert W. Creamer, *Babe* (New York: Simon and Schuster, 1974); Marshall Smelser, *The House That Ruth Built* (New York: Quadrangle, 1975); Lawrence S. Ritter and Mark Rucker, *The Babe: A Life in Pictures* (New York: Ticknor and Fields, 1988)

RWDSU. See Retail, Wholesale and Department Store Union.

Ryan, Thomas Fortune (*b* Lovingston, Va., 17 Oct 1851; *d* New York City, 23 Nov 1928). Businessman. Orphaned and impoverished as a youth, he arrived in New York City in 1870 and formed an investment syndicate that dominated the transportation franchises in the city through the Metropolitan Traction Company (formed in 1886, reorganized in 1902 as the Metropolitan Securities Company). Essentially he consolidated the city's various street railway firms into a single entity. He also controlled the State Trust Company, investigated in 1900 by banking authorities, and the Equitable Life Assurance Company, investigated in 1905 by the state legislature of New York. After withdrawing from the Metropolitan Traction Company in 1906 he became embroiled in many legal actions when it was placed under receivership in the following year; among these was an investigation by the Public Service Commission into charges of bribery, overcapitalization, and fraudulent accounting. He was also a founder of the American Tobacco Company, dissolved as a monopoly in 1911 by the U.S. Supreme Court. Ryan was best known during his life for his wealth and his questionable business practices. He lived at 60 Fifth Avenue and had a country house in Suffern, New York.

Theresa Collins

Ryan, William F(itts) (*b* Albion, N.Y., 28 July 1922; *d* New York City, 17 Sept 1972). Congressman. After working as a lawyer he was elected to the U.S. Congress in 1960 from the West Side, the first reform Democrat elected to public office from the city. Labeled a radical and a firebrand by opponents, he remained in office for six terms and consistently worked for civil rights, peace, social justice, and the environment. His first vote was to end funding for the House Un-American Activities Committee. Ryan was one of the first elected officials to speak out against the Vietnam War and in 1964 went to Mississippi to investigate the disappearance of three civil rights workers. In 1965 he was an unsuccessful mayoral candidate. Having won renomination in 1972 against Bella S. Abzug, whose own congressional seat had been eliminated by redistricting, he died before the general election.

Andrew Wiese

S

Sage [née Slocum], **(Margaret) Olivia** (*b* Syracuse, N.Y., 8 Sept 1828; *d* New York City, 4 Nov 1918). Philanthropist. She worked as a schoolteacher in Syracuse, New York, and moved to New York City when she married the financier Russell Sage in 1869. On the death of her husband in 1906 she inherited $65 million but continued to live modestly on Fifth Avenue near what is now Rockefeller Center. At the age of 77 she embarked on a career in large-scale philanthropy; in 1907 she formed the Russell Sage Foundation. Her giving totaled more than $80 million, much of it going to New York City and the Northeast.

Ruth Crocker, *Mrs. Russell Sage: Activism and Philanthropy in Gilded Age and Progressive Era America* (Bloomington: Indiana University Press: 2006)

Melissa Smith Clayton

Sage, Russell (*b* Oneida, N.Y., 4 Aug 1816; *d* Lawrence, near Cedarhurst, N.Y., 22 July 1906). Financier. Successful in business as a young man, he was elected to Congress as a Whig in 1852 and later joined with Jay Gould in building the railroads. After moving to New York City he helped to make "puts" and "calls" popular on the stock market. Shrewd and conservative, he lent money on an immense scale and amassed a fortune worth $70 million; most of it was given by his wife, Olivia Sage, to such charities as the Young Men's Christian Association (YMCA), the Young Women's Christian Association (YWCA), Women's Hospital, the American Museum of Natural History, and the Metropolitan Museum of Art, and to the Russell Sage Foundation, which she organized in 1907 and which continues to operate in New York City in the early twenty-first century.

James E. Mooney

Said, Edward (*b* Jerusalem, 1 Nov 1935; *d* New York City, 25 Sept 2003). Literary critic and political activist. Perhaps best known for his book *Orientalism* (1978), he was an outspoken critic of Western conceptions about the East, particularly of Western attitudes toward Palestine. A professor of comparative literature at Columbia University, Said lived and worked in New York City for several decades. He never taught politics of the Middle East, but he was a vocal defender of the State of Palestine both at Columbia University and throughout the United States, speaking to many publications such as the *New York Times*.

Marlena Slowik

sailing. Although commercial and naval vessels regularly plied New York City's harbor from the time of the arrival of the Dutch until the end of the age of commercial sail, yachting and other forms of leisure sailing were not popular and organized in the city until the 1840s. The city's first and best-known yachters were the brothers John Cox, Robert, and Edwin Stevens, who as boys soon after 1800 began sailing small boats, including a catamaran called *Double Trouble*. John Cox Stevens founded the New York Yacht Club in 1844, and a year later the club ran the first yacht race in U.S. history under rules that its members drafted to prevent collisions and encourage a fair contest. The race course was close to a tour of the harbor. The 10 boats started from anchor 3 miles (4.8 kilometers) up the Hudson River, near the Stevens family's estate at Hoboken, New Jersey; sailed across the upper bay to a mark near Owl's Head, off Bay Ridge; and then sailed south through the Narrows to Southwest Spit, near Sandy Hook. There the boats reversed the course, with a last leg near the Battery before the finish at Hoboken. This 40-mile (64.4-kilometer) course was used in most of the club's races until after the Civil War. Another course took the boats out into the Atlantic and around Sandy Hook Lightship or Scotland Lightship. The ships sailed mostly within sight of thousands watching from the bluffs of Weehawken, Bay Ridge, or Staten Island or the promenades at the Battery.

Initially, most racing boats were about 60 feet (18.3 meters) in length and were polished-up versions of either the Sandy Hook pilot schooner or the typical Hudson River trading vessel, the North River sloop. They had two things in common: they were usually steered by their owners, most of whom were skilled sailors, and they had the traditional local features of shallow draft and retractable fins, called centerboards, that could be pulled up to avoid running aground on shoals and rocks. After the Civil War, however, the boats of the New York Yacht Club's racing fleet became much bigger and more extreme, with unstable hulls under large sails that were barely kept under control by 30 or more professional sailors. Few owners or other amateur sailors had the skill and strength needed to manage these boats. The notorious capsize in 1876 of the 141-foot (43-meter) schooner *Mohawk* with the loss of six lives stimulated a return to safer vessels.

Among small craft the most popular racing boat was the sandbagger, a thrilling 20- to 25-foot (6.1- to 7.6-meter) open boat kept upright by satchels of sand that the sailors carried from side to side. Where yacht club racing was governed by written rules and judicial-like procedures, sandbagger racing disputes were often settled by fistfights. A few of the New York Yacht Club's best racing sailors were sandbagger alumni. Although yacht racing was largely a male sport, women did sail and were eligible for associate membership in the New York Yacht Club beginning in 1894. As one indication of the growth of the sport of sailing in New York City, membership in the New York Yacht Club grew from nine in 1844, to 483 in 1860, to 2135 in 1901.

Staten Island became the sailing center in 1869 when the New York Yacht Club moved its headquarters from Hoboken to Clifton (the club later had a clubhouse at Stapleton). The club was known for rich owners who handed control of their expensive yachts over to professional captains. Nearby was a very different kind of organization, the first U.S. yacht club that required that boats be run entirely by amateur (corinthian) sailors. Founded in 1871, the Seawanhaka Corinthian Yacht Club had its clubhouse at Tompkinsville, Staten Island, and held its races in New York Harbor before it moved to Oyster Bay, Long Island, in 1892.

Another popular sailing center was across the Narrows in Brooklyn. The Brooklyn Yacht Club was founded on Gowanus Creek in 1857, and in 1866 it spun off the Atlantic Yacht Club, at Bay Ridge. Both clubs later moved south of the Narrows to the shores of Gowanus Bay, where they thrived for many years. The first ocean race to Bermuda was cosponsored and started by the Brooklyn Yacht Club in 1906. Brooklyn sailors also kept boats on Sheepshead Bay and Jamaica Bay, where the Canarsie Yacht Club was founded in 1887.

Serious yachting came relatively late to Manhattan when the Columbia Yacht Club was founded at 86th Street on the Hudson River in 1867. Later came the Harlem Yacht Club on the Harlem River (1883). In 1901 the New York Yacht Club built a new clubhouse well away from the water in midtown Manhattan. The needs of its members during the sailing season were served by the club's 11 waterside outposts, called stations, in ports between New Jersey and Nantucket Island. As an indication of how widely the sport had spread from its New York City origins, only four stations were within city limits: one at Whitestone, Queens; two on Manhattan on the Hudson and East rivers; and another that in some years was at Bay Ridge and other years at Stapleton, Staten Island.

As New York Harbor became more crowded with commercial traffic, many yacht clubs shut down or moved their clubhouses and races to Long Island Sound or New England. In 1899 the New York Yacht Club began to hold the eliminations to choose its representative in America's Cup races in Newport, Rhode Island, even though the races themselves continued to be sailed off New York City for 21 years.

After 1900 the city's most active sailing area was City Island, in the Bronx, where there were anchorages, boatyards, sailing schools, and yacht clubs, including the City Island Yacht Club (founded in 1905) and its neighbor, the Harlem Yacht Club, which had moved up from Manhattan. Racing continued to be held at City Island and at Staten Island, Brooklyn, and Queens throughout the twentieth century. The sport returned to Manhattan in the 1960s with the opening of sailing schools, the arrival of charter boats, and the founding of South Street Seaport (which began the annual MAYOR'S CUP race). The city's first new yacht club in years was founded in 1987 when the Manhattan Yacht Club opened near South Street Seaport. Renamed the Manhattan Sailing Club and relocated to North Cove, in 2007 it continued to sponsor many training programs and races, leaving New York Harbor once again speckled with white sails.

John Parkinson, Jr., *The History of the New York Yacht Club* (New York: New York Yacht Club, 1975); John Rousmaniere, *History of the New York Yacht Club* (New York: New York Yacht Club, 2008)

John Rousmaniere

Sailors' Snug Harbor. Retirement home in Livingston in Staten Island. It was created by a bequest of Robert Richard Randall (*d* 1801), a resident of Manhattan who made a fortune in the maritime industry, as a home to care for "aged, decrepit, and worn-out sailors." The trustees of the bequest, who included the rector of Trinity Church and the minister of the First Presbyterian Church, funded the project by leasing 20 acres (8 hectares) of farmland left by Randall at Washington Square North and Fifth Avenue. In 1833 the home opened with 27 residents, and by 1900 it housed 1000. It was one of the best-funded charitable institutions in the United States and an innovator in care for the aged. The years after World War II saw a gradual decline in enrollment, and legal battles with the New York City Landmarks Commission caused the property to be sold to New York City in 1975. The home was moved in 1976 to Sea Level, North Carolina, where in 2007 about 50 residents continued in the institution. The trustees began a new stipend program to sustain eligible sailors in their own environment. The former site in Snug Harbor was taken over by the Snug Harbor Cultural Center in 1976.

Barnett Shepherd, *Sailors' Snug Harbor, 1801–1976* (New York: Snug Harbor Cultural Center/Staten Island Institute of Arts and Sciences, 1979; repr. 1994); Gerald J. Barry, *The Sailors' Snug Harbor: A History, 1801–2001* (New York: Fordham University Press, 2000)

Barnett Shepherd

St. Albans. Neighborhood in southeastern Queens, bounded to the north by Hollis Avenue, to the east by Springfield Boulevard, to the south by Merrick Boulevard, and to the west by Farmers Boulevard. A syndicate of developers from Manhattan bought the Francis farm on Linden Boulevard in 1892 and laid out streets and building lots. A railroad station opened along Linden Boulevard on 1 July 1898, and a post office was built in April 1899, when the population stood at 600. The section of Linden Boulevard beyond the railroad station was paved in July 1912. The Lenox Development Company in 1916 promoted a tract now covering 35 blocks east of Farmer's Boulevard on 195th and 196th streets and 115th Road. The St. Albans Golf Club opened in 1919 along Merrick, Linden, and Baisley boulevards. Between 1924 and 1926 a few hundred small one-family houses were built by several firms, including Blattmacher–Porth, Richmond Homes, St. Albans Gardens Homes, and Mezik Homes. Addisleigh Park was developed overlooking the golf course in 1926 by the Burfrey Realty Company: its half-timbered and stucco houses stood on lots 40 by 100 feet (12 by 30 meters), and each sold for $13,000 or more. Development slowed during the 1930s as land was used up and the Depression worsened. The golf course closed during World War II and became the site of a large naval hospital that was eventually converted by the Veterans Administration into an extended care center. During the 1940s prominent black athletes and musicians moved to Addisleigh Park, notably Lena Horne, Count Basie, Fats Waller, Milt Hilton, Illinois Jacquet, Ella Fitzgerald, Roy Campanella, and Jackie Robinson. The neighborhood was racially integrated in the 1950s and 1960s, but in the early 1970s St. Albans became almost exclusively African American. Apartment buildings were built nearby, among them Merrick Park Gardens (1952) and the Addisleigh (1960). A large number of black immigrants settled in the neighborhood and its environs during the 1980s, almost half from Jamaica and the rest from Haiti, Guyana, Trinidad and Tobago, and the United Kingdom. The economic status of the neighborhood is middle class and the character proudly suburban. In 2008 the Addisleigh Park Civic Organization succeeded in having the neighborhood down-zoned and began pursuing designation as a historic district.

Vincent Seyfried

St. Anthony of Padua. Shrine church of the Roman Catholic Archdiocese of New York. It is located at 155 Sullivan Street in Manhattan. Established in 1859, it remains the oldest parish serving Italian American immigrants in the United States. Its first home was a former Methodist sanctuary at 149 Sullivan Street. The current building (designed by Arthur Crooks) was dedicated on 10 June 1888.

Joseph Ditta

St. Augustine's Episcopal Church. Formerly known as All Saints Free Church and completed in 1828, it was begun as a mission by students of the General Theology Seminary. Located at 290 Henry Street, it was once the parish of poet Edgar Allan Poe. Still intact are two small unventilated rooms above the nave's balcony in the rear of the church, referred to as the "slave gallery." This cramped space separated formerly enslaved Africans and indentured servants from other worshippers. The congregation, once predominantly white, is nearly all African American early in the twenty-first century.

Celedonia Jones

St. Bartholomew's Church. Name given to several Episcopal churches occupied successively by a congregation established in 1835 on Lafayette Place and Great Jones Street. The congregation was one of the wealthiest and most fashionable in New York City when it moved in 1872 to Madison Avenue and 44th Street. In the late nineteenth century and the early twentieth the pastors reshaped "St. Bart's" into a model "institutional church" supporting a wide range of educational and social services. In 1918 the congregation moved to a church in the Romanesque style designed by Bertram Grosvenor Goodhue on Park Avenue at 50th Street, which incorporated the portals designed by McKim, Mead and White for the church on Madison Avenue. Members of the church vestry proposed during the 1980s to raise money by replacing the Community House on 50th Street (1927) with a high-rise office tower. Their application was twice refused by the municipal Landmarks Preservation Commission, a decision that was upheld by the U.S. Supreme Court (1991). The low, spacious church of St. Bart's remains an anomaly in a neighborhood of skyscrapers.

Peter J. Wosh

St. Denis, Ruth (*b* Englewood, N.J., 20 Jan 1879; *d* Hollywood, 21 July 1968). Dancer. She received her professional training in New York City and worked as a "skirt dancer." Featured in 1904 by David Belasco in the revue *Madame DuBarry,* she developed an exotic dance that became known as the Radha, which she performed on a tour of Europe in 1906–7. From 1909 to 1914 she worked in New York City, where with Ted Shawn she formed Denishawn, the premier American dance company until the 1930s. Among the many dancers who trained with the company were Doris Humphrey, Martha Graham, and Charles Weidman.

Suzanne Shelton, *Divine Dancer: A Biography of Ruth St. Denis* (Garden City, N.Y.: Doubleday, 1981)

Peter M. Rutkoff, William B. Scott

St. Elizabeth, Church of. Roman Catholic Church at 268 Wadsworth Avenue in northern Manhattan. Founded in 1869, it was originally housed at 4381 Broadway in a church designed by Napoleon Le Brun and funded by James Gordon Bennett. The church on Wadsworth Avenue, which sits atop a hill, was designed

by Robert J. Reiley in 1927 and in the early twenty-first century was central to the large Dominican population of upper Manhattan.
Kate Lauber

St. Francis College. Catholic school at 180 Remsen Street. Originally limited to boys, it was opened in 1859 at 300 Baltic Street in Brooklyn by the Franciscan Brothers and offered instruction on all levels from elementary school to college. By 1884, when it was authorized to grant degrees, it had expanded to Smith and Butler streets. In 1902 the lower divisions split off to form St. Francis Academy. The college became coeducational with the admission of nuns in 1953; lay women were admitted from 1969. It moved in 1963 to its present site, formerly the headquarters of the Brooklyn Union Gas Company. In 2008 the school had about 2400 students, including 2000 who attended full time. St. Francis College is the oldest Catholic school in Brooklyn.
Gilbert Tauber

Saint-Gaudens, Augustus (*b* Dublin, 1 March 1848; *d* Cornish, N.H., 3 Aug 1907). Sculptor. The son of a French shoemaker and a working-class Irishwoman, he lived from 1848 to 1860 in lower Manhattan. He moved to 22 Washington Place in 1880, remaining there until 1890. His first public commission, *Admiral David Glasgow Farragut* (1881, Madison Square Park), was a collaboration with Stanford White that set a standard for American sculptors: the first major public work in the country influenced by a French beaux-arts aesthetic, it strove for an ideal of integrating sculpture, architecture, and landscape to promote urban harmony. He had a studio at 148 West 36th Street from 1884 until his death and lived at 51 West 45th Street from 1890 to 1897. Among his municipal commissions were *Robert Randall* (1884, Sailors' Snug Harbor) and *Diana* for the tower of Madison Square Garden (1894, Philadelphia Museum of Art),

Memorial to William Tecumseh Sherman by Augustus Saint-Gaudens, ca 1905

both with White; *Peter Cooper* (unveiled 1897, Cooper Square); and *William Tecumseh Sherman* (1903, pedestal by Charles Follen McKim; Grand Army Plaza, Manhattan). Private commissions included angels for St. Thomas Church (1877, destroyed), decorations for the mansions of Cornelius Vanderbilt II (1883, Metropolitan Museum of Art) and the publisher Henry Villard (1883, 451 Madison Avenue), tomb reliefs for the importer David Stewart (1883, Green-Wood Cemetery, Brooklyn), and bronze bas-relief portraits of many prominent New Yorkers. Saint-Gaudens drew unprecedented international attention to American sculpture, especially through his public works.

Kathryn Greenthal, *Saint-Gaudens: Master Sculptor* (New York: Metropolitan Museum of Art, 1985); Burke Wilkinson, *Uncommon Clay: The Life and Works of Augustus Saint-Gaudens* (New York: Harcourt Brace Jovanovich, 1985); Michele H. Bogart, *Public Sculpture and the Civic Ideal in New York City, 1890–1930* (Chicago: University of Chicago Press, 1989)

Michele H. Bogart

St. George. Neighborhood on the northeastern shore of Staten Island (2009 pop. 7500) bounded on the north and east by the Upper New York Bay, on the south by Tompkinsville, and on the west by New Brighton. Richmond Terrace and Bay Street are main streets. St. George is the government center, the transportation hub, and the most densely populated neighborhood in Staten Island.

During the British occupation of Staten Island between 1776 and 1783 an earthwork fort was built at the top of today's Fort Hill. New York State built a quarantine station on the waterfront in 1799. In 1815 Governor Daniel D. Tompkins purchased farms in the area, laying out the streets of Tompkinsville and establishing steam ferry service to Manhattan. The western portion of early Tompkinsville is part of St. George. Tompkins enlarged the Van Buskirk farmhouse, which faced Fort Place, living in it until his death in 1825, at which time it was demolished. In 1835 portions of the Tompkins estate and other farms west of it were acquired by Thomas E. Davis, a New York City developer. Large lots were laid out along the shore and hillside to create the fashionable resort of New Brighton. The first Catholic church on Staten Island, St. Peter's, was organized in 1839; the present building was completed in 1903. The Brighton Heights Reformed Church was built in 1863 (destroyed by fire in 1996; new building constructed in 1997). In 1868 a portion of the former quarantine site was taken over by the U.S. Lighthouse Service. The neighborhood was considered part of New Brighton until 1886 when Erastus Wiman, a local entrepreneur, consolidated ferry lines and rail routes along the east and north shores and created a terminal where the two lines came together; he then named the community near the terminal St. George after George Law, an investor in the project. Between 1886 and 1888, near the ferry slips, Wiman's Staten Island Amusement Company offered athletic events, an illuminated fountain, and spectacular pageants.

After Staten Island's consolidation with New York City in 1898 St. George grew rapidly. Curtis High School, named after George William Curtis, opened in 1904. Municipal ferry service began in 1905. Carrère and Hastings designed a new ferry terminal (destroyed by fire in 1947), Borough Hall (1906), a branch of the New York Public Library (1907), and the Richmond County Courthouse (1919). The Staten Island Institute of Arts and Sciences moved into its new museum at 75 Stuyvesant Place in 1919. In 1936 the lighthouse service was taken over by the U.S. Coast Guard, which operated it until 1967.

The opening of the Verrazano–Narrows Bridge in 1964 and of the Staten Island Expressway led to development of the interior and the decline of the neighborhood. Commercial property remained vacant and important institutions moved out. In the mid-1990s, however, the waterfront, which commands fine views of Manhattan, was redeveloped and the community began to revive. A large ferry repair facility and a public esplanade were built on the former U.S. Coast Guard site, and St. George was designated a historic district in 1994. In the early twenty-first century building and renovation continue: the Richmond County Bank Ballpark opened in 2001; the Staten Island September 11 Memorial on the esplanade from the ferry terminal to Jersey Street was dedicated in 2004; the St. George Theatre, a 1929 movie and vaudeville palace, was restored in 2004; and major renovation of the Staten Island Ferry Terminal was completed in 2005. In the early twenty-first century the population of St. George was economically and racially diverse; many residents were young professionals who commuted by ferry to Manhattan.

Edna Holden, "The Cosmopolitan Period," *Staten Island: A Resource Manual for School and Community* (New York: Board of Education of the City of New York, 1964); "St. George Historic District," designation report (New York: New York City Landmarks Preservation Commission, 1994)

Barnett Shepherd, Carol V. Wright

St. George Hotel. Hotel erected in Brooklyn Heights in 1884 by William Tumbridge. By 1930 it comprised eight buildings bounded by Hicks, Henry, Clark, and Pineapple streets; contained 2632 rooms (the most of any hotel in New York City); and had a grand ballroom, an indoor saltwater swimming pool, and a rooftop for dining and dancing. The hotel's busiest years were during and just after World War II because of Brooklyn's role as the country's major port of embarkation for soldiers en route to Europe. During the 1980s the St. George was in decline and the owners converted two wings into cooperative residential units. A 1995 fire destroyed the single building that was still operating as a hotel. By 2007 the remaining buildings had been converted to other uses, including a dormitory for local university students.

Stephen Weinstein

St. George's Episcopal Church (i). Episcopal church at 16th Street and Stuyvesant Square, formed as a chapel of Trinity Church in 1752 and made independent in 1811. From early on it emphasized the Protestant nature of the Episcopal Church. Under the leadership of William Rainsford (1850–1933) it was a leader at the end of the nineteenth century in the institutional church movement, which believed that institutions should help support community members, offering such services to the community as sewing classes, soup kitchens, and fitness and health programs. The financier J. P. Morgan was for decades its most influential parishioner. During the mid-1970s it formed a united parish with Calvary Church and the Church of the Holy Communion; the building continues to be used for worship services.

Robert Bruce Mullin

St. George's Episcopal Church (ii). Church built in 1746 in Flushing where Episcopal services were held from 1704. During the nineteenth century the parish established important educational institutions, including the Academy (1803) and the Flushing Institute (1828). Later St. George's moved to a Gothic Revival church known for its grand interior (1854, on Main Street between 38th and 39th avenues). Parishioners undertook ambitious missionary work and helped to establish Episcopal churches in Bayside, College Point, Whitestone, Queens Village, and Fresh Meadows. During the late 1980s they organized a ministry program for the growing Chinese community in Flushing.

Peter J. Wosh

St. George's Square. Square located at the intersection of Pearl, Cherry, Frankfort, and Dover streets. In existence in the 1770s, it was extended in 1816 at the same time that new houses and lots at Pearl and Cherry streets were added. Improvements included one of the first iron gas lamps in the city. The name was changed to Franklin Square in 1817 in honor of Benjamin Franklin. The square ceased to exist when construction began on the approaches to the Brooklyn Bridge in the 1870s.

Lisa Keller

St. George Ukrainian Catholic Church. Church located at 30 East Seventh Street; it was designed by Apollinaire Osadca in the Historicist style and completed in 1977.

Sharon Wilkins

St. George's Episcopal Church (i) and Stuyvesant Square, 1905

St. Ignatius Loyola, Church of. Roman Catholic church at 980 Park Avenue, home to the largest mechanical action pipe organ in the city. Founded in 1851 as the St. Lawrence O'Toole Church, the parish was taken over by Jesuits in 1866; its lavish Baroque building, designed by Schickel and Ditmars, was dedicated in 1898. Jacqueline Kennedy Onassis was baptized at St. Ignatius Loyola and her funeral was held there in 1994; the funeral for the singer Aaliyah was held at the church in 2001. The following year, Edward M. Cardinal Egan halted a $3 million renovation that would have moved the altar closer to the pews, removed the communion rail, and expanded the sanctuary, all in accordance with reforms of the Second Vatican Council; Egan was concerned about maintaining the church's historical tradition. Minor renovations were completed in 2008.

Kate Lauber

St. James Cathedral. Roman Catholic cathedral church of the Diocese of Brooklyn, at 250 Cathedral Place, built in a neo-Gothic style under the leadership of Peter Turner and dedicated by Bishop John Connolly in 1823. It is the oldest church in the Diocese of Brooklyn, the third-oldest Catholic church in New York City, and the sixth-oldest Catholic church in New York State. When the Diocese of Brooklyn separated from the Archdiocese of New York in 1853 St. James became its procathedral. The first bishop to administer the cathedral was John Loughlin, who served from 1853 to 1891.

Margaret M. McGuinness

St. James Church. Prominent nineteenth-century Catholic parish at 32 James Street. Built in the Greek Revival style and dedicated in 1836, the architect is unknown; scholars have questioned its attribution to Minard Lafever. Also in 1836, the first branch of the Ancient Order of the Hibernians, an Irish Catholic fraternal group, was organized at St. James. Alfred E. Smith, who grew up on the Lower East Side and became governor of New

Franklin Square (formerly St. George's Square), 1856

York, was an altar boy at the church, which was restored by the Hibernians after major structural problems with its roof threatened its closure in 1983.

Kate Lauber

St. James Hotel. Hotel built during the 1860s at 26th Street and Broadway. It was one of several elegant hotels, including the Fifth Avenue Hotel, the Grand, and the Gilsey, that were clustered near Madison Square, then the city's most fashionable district. In 1864 Confederate conspirators set fire to the hotel and other buildings in the neighborhood; it sustained only minor damages. In the late nineteenth century the St. James catered mostly to personages of the local theaters; in 1897 it was replaced by the St. James Building, which was designed by Bruce Price and housed many architects' offices.

Andrew Wiese

St. John's Evangelical Lutheran Church. Church at 79–83 Christopher Street between Seventh Avenue and Bleecker Street; it is built of painted brownstone and metal in a Romanesque style and has a cupola in a Federal style. Completed in 1821 for the congregation of the Eighth Presbyterian Church, it was sold in 1857 to St. John's Evangelical Lutheran Church, a German Lutheran congregation organized in 1855.

Alana Erickson Coble

St. John's Park. See Hudson Square.

St. John's University. Roman Catholic institution opened in 1870 by the Vincentian Fathers at the request of the first bishop of Brooklyn, John Loughlin. Originally called St. John's College, under its first president, John T. Landry, it occupied a building on Willoughby Street and Lewis Avenue in Brooklyn. The college awarded its first baccalaureate degree in 1881 and opened a separate seminary at Lewis Avenue and Hart Street in 1891. After being chartered as a university in 1906 it added a law school (1925), a college of pharmacy (1929), and a downtown division on Schermerhorn Street (1929). In 1936 the school purchased the Hillcrest Golf Club in Jamaica (Queens), and in 1954 it began construction of a new campus there (completed in 1956). It assumed control of Notre Dame College of Staten Island in 1971 and closed the school on Schermerhorn Street. St. John's purchased the former College of Insurance in 2001 to reestablish a downtown Manhattan campus. In the early twenty-first century the school completed several major projects, including the 2003 addition of dormitories at its Queens, Manhattan, and Staten Island campuses. Its basketball team has one of the highest winning percentages in intercollegiate basketball history.

Frederick Ernst Hueppe, *"The Radiant Light": A History of Saint John's College* (New York: C. H. Helmken for St. John's University, 1956)

Matthew J. Brennan

St. John the Divine. See Cathedral of St. John the Divine.

St. Joseph's College. Four-year Catholic college, opened in 1916 at 286 Washington Avenue in Brooklyn as a women's college by the Sisters of St. Joseph. It moved to 245 Clinton Avenue in 1918 and became coeducational in 1970; a branch campus opened in Patchogue, New York, in 1979. In 2006 there were 1087 students enrolled at the main campus and 3798 at the branch. The college has a predominantly lay faculty and offers preprofessional programs in business, education, law, and health administration.

Gilbert Tauber

St. Luke's Hospital. Private hospital formed by Episcopalians in 1846. It stood at Fifth Avenue and 54th Street before moving in 1896 to 113th Street and Amsterdam Avenue, where it occupied five buildings. Additions to the hospital were built in 1906 and 1933. At the request of the U.S. Army in January 1942 it collaborated with Roosevelt Hospital in planning a field hospital with 750 beds called the Second Evacuation Hospital; this was deployed 5 miles (8 kilometers) from Omaha Beach in Normandy on 17 June 1944. The hospital became affiliated with the College of Physicians and Surgeons at Columbia University in the early 1950s, expanded in 1954 and 1957, and entered into an affiliation with Women's Hospital in 1965. Throughout the 1970s it responded to the changing needs of the community by expanding its clinic programs and its emergency room facilities. It also became well known for its research and for such medical innovations as the first open-heart surgery in New York City (1955). The hospital merged with Roosevelt Hospital in 1979 to form St. Luke's–Roosevelt Hospital Center, which had 1076 beds in 2010.

John Petit West, *Surgeons and Surgery: St. Luke's Hospital* (New York: Woodhaven, 1978)

Andrea Balis

St. Luke's–Roosevelt Hospital Center. Hospital formed in 1979 by the merger of two of the oldest and largest hospitals in New York City. It serves the West Side of Manhattan from 34th Street to 142nd Street. The merger of St. Luke's Hospital and Roosevelt Hospital made it possible to consolidate some services. At the time of the merger both institutions were teaching affiliates of the College of Physicians and Surgeons at Columbia University, and this function continued uninterrupted. Facilities added after the merger include the Kathryn and Gilbert Miller Health Care Institute for the Performing Arts at Roosevelt Hospital (the only full-service center for performing-arts medicine in New York City and the largest in the nation) and the largest center for AIDS at any private hospital in New York City. In 2010 the hospital had 1076 beds.

Andrea Balis

St. Mark's Church in the Bowery. Episcopal parish church at East 10th Street and Second Avenue in the East Village. Its site, formerly occupied by Peter Stuyvesant's family chapel, is reportedly the oldest in continuous use by any Christian congregation in the city. The building was completed in 1799; a steeple in a Greek Revival style was added in 1828, a Georgian interior in later years. During the mid-1960s the St. Mark's Poetry

St. Mark's Church in the Bowery, ca 1910

Project was established to explore aesthetic and social concerns. The interior was restored after a serious fire in 1978, and stained-glass windows in a striking abstract design by Harold Edelman were installed in the balcony in 1982. St. Mark's in the Bowery is the second-oldest church in the city, after St. Paul's Chapel. The churchyard contains Stuyvesant's grave.

Memorials of St. Mark's Church in the Bowery (New York: Thomas Whittaker, 1899)

J. Robert Wright

St. Mark's German Lutheran Church. Church on East Sixth Street just east of Second Avenue. In 1904 the excursion vessel General Slocum, chartered by the congregation, burned; more than 1000 people died, most of them women and children and members of the church, which closed soon after the tragedy. In 1940 the church became the Sixth Street Community Synagogue.

St. Mary's Episcopal Church, Manhattanville. Church located in Harlem at 521 West 126th Street. After the Dutch Reformed church (erected in East Harlem in the eighteenth century), St. Mary's became the second church established in Harlem (circa 1823). T. E. Blake and the architectural firm of Carrère and Hastings completed the present stone structure in 1909. It was the first church in the Episcopal Diocese to abolish pew rentals. The porch of the church houses the vault of Jacob and Hannah Schieffelin, the church's land donors and Manhattanville's principal founders. Granted landmark status in 1998, St. Mary's remains Harlem's oldest congregation in continuous existence.

Sharon Wilkins

St. Michael's Church. Episcopal parish church at 99th Street and Amsterdam Avenue in Manhattan, founded in 1807. The present building, designed by Robert W. Gibson in a Byzantine Romanesque style and built of Indiana limestone with a square bell tower 160 feet (50 meters) high, opened in 1891 and became known for its interior and its stained-glass windows by Louis Comfort Tiffany (installed mostly between 1893 and 1900, restored 1989–90). The seven lancet windows in the chancel (1895), which depict the victory of St. Michael in Heaven, are widely considered Tiffany's ecclesiastical masterpiece in glass. St. Michael's grew under the direction of its ninth rector, Frederick Hill (1976–92), during a period of recovery on the Upper West Side that began about 1980.

J. Robert Wright

St. Moritz Hotel. Hotel at 50 Central Park South, on the east side of Sixth Avenue. Designed by Emery Roth and built by the Harper organization (representing Harris H. Uris and Percy Uris), it was completed in October 1930, standing 38 stories tall with 1000 rooms, and was named for the resort in the Swiss Alps. The Bowery Savings Bank took over the hotel in 1932 and then sold it to the Engadine Corporation, led by S. Gregory Taylor. In 1950 the hotel redecorated and redesigned its rooms, and from the following year it housed the Café de la Paix, said to be the first sidewalk restaurant in New York City. The hotel also housed Rumpelmayer's, a well-known tea and pastry shop decorated by the German American interior designer and artist Winold Reiss. Donald Trump bought the St. Moritz in 1985 only to sell it three years later to Alan Bond, an Australian entrepreneur. Bond gave the hotel up to his lender, F. A. I. Insurances, which ran it until 1998, when Ian Schrager bought it. Schrager in turn sold it in 1999 to Millennium Partners, which remodeled the old hotel and turned it into the flagship of the Ritz–Carlton chain. The top dozen floors were transformed (by Millennium Partners in conjunction with Schrager) into luxury condominiums. In 2002 the hotel reopened as the Ritz–Carlton New York, Central Park, with 259 rooms, including 47 suites.

W. Parker Chase, *New York: The Wonder City* (New York: Wonder City, 1931); Steven Ruttenbaum, *Mansions in the Clouds: The Skyscraper Palazzi of Emery Roth* (New York: Balsam, 1986)

Allen J. Share

St. Nicholas Greek Orthodox Church. Church formerly located at 155 Cedar Street under the shadow of the World Trade Center; it was destroyed in the terrorist attacks of 11 September 2001. Founded in 1916 at a hotel at Greenwich and Liberty Streets, the church moved into the Cedar House tavern in 1919 when five families raised $25,000 to buy and convert the building. Although it was promised a place in the redeveloped Ground Zero site, the church remained homeless in 2010 as planning and negotiations for Ground Zero stalled.

Kate Lauber

St. Nicholas Kirche. First German Catholic church in New York City, founded in 1833 on East Second Street by Johann Stephen Raffeiner, a wealthy Austrian priest. In 1842 he abandoned the parish because of disputes with the congregation; in the same year the church was formally recognized by the diocese. Raffeiner's successor, Gabriel Rumpler, appointed by Bishop John Hughes, left in 1844 after battling church members and trustees to form the Most Holy Redeemer Church on East Third Street, which became the leading German Catholic church in the city. St. Nicholas Kirche then declined in importance.

Stanley Nadel

St. Nicholas Magazine. Monthly children's magazine launched by Roswell Smith of the publishing house of Charles Scribner in November 1873. It became highly successful under its first editor, Mary Mapes Dodge, who assembled a staff of illustrators that included Palmer Cox, Arthur Rackham, Reginald Birch, and Thomas Nast and attracted contributions from leading writers, including stories by Louisa May Alcott and Rudyard Kipling (later published as *The Jungle Book*), as well as Mark Twain's *Tom Sawyer Abroad*, which it serialized. In 1880 Smith formed the Century Company to publish the most popular selections from the magazine as books; in 1884 Theodore Low De Vinne, one of the city's finest printers, was engaged to work for both the magazine and Century. At Dodge's death in 1905 William Fayal Clarke, a member of the staff for many years, was chosen to replace her. He successfully continued her policies, but the magazine declined after he resigned in 1927. *St. Nicholas Magazine* left the city after being sold in 1930 and ceased publication in June 1943.

Alice M. Jordan, "Good Old St. Nicholas and Its Contemporaries," *From Rollo to Tom Sawyer* (Boston: Horn Book, 1948), 131–43

Michael Joseph

St. Nicholas Russian Orthodox Cathedral. Church established on the Lower East Side in the early 1890s. The Reverend Alexander Hotovitzky traveled to Russia in 1900 and obtained 5000 rubles from Czar Nicholas II to build a church at 15 East 97th Street; designed by John Bergesen and built in 1901–2, the Muscovite Baroque structure featured five impressive domes and became a cathedral in 1905 when the seat of the American diocese was transferred to New York City from San Francisco. The 1917 Russian Revolution resulted in a conflict over the cathedral's leadership; during the 1920s the noncommunist Russian Orthodox Church Outside Russia, housed at 75 East 93rd Street, was founded. In 1952 the Supreme Court overruled a state law requiring the cathedral to be run by the American separatist movement, and in 2007 the two churches were reunited. The church was designated a landmark in 1973.

Kate Lauber

St. Nicholas Hotel. Hotel built in 1853 at Spring Street and Broadway. Constructed of white marble, containing 600 rooms, and employing more than 300 staff, it was one of the world's largest hotels and eclipsed the Astor House as the most luxurious hotel in New York City. Even as the wealthy gradually moved north of Houston Street, the hotel continued to attract exclusive guests and residents, largely because of the 1853–54 world's fair and the increasing cost of private homes and servants. During the draft riots of

1863 Mayor George Opdyke abandoned City Hall for more commodious headquarters in the hotel.

Andrew Wiese

St. Patrick's Cathedral. Roman Catholic cathedral church of the Archdiocese of New York, on 50th Street and Fifth Avenue in Manhattan. It was built by the architect James Renwick during the administration of Archbishop John Hughes. Although it was estimated that building the cathedral would take eight years when work began in 1859, the project took longer because of its interruption by the Civil War. During construction St. Patrick's Old Cathedral on Prince and Mott streets was destroyed by fire (1866) and then rebuilt and rededicated by John Cardinal McCloskey (1868), who also dedicated the new cathedral on its completion on 25 May 1879; the final cost of construction was $1.9 million. McCloskey appointed William Quinn, vicar of the archdiocese, as the first pastor of the new cathedral. The archbishop's house and the rectory were added from 1882 to 1884, and the school opened in 1882. Major additions to St. Patrick's were completed under Archbishop Michael Corrigan. The building of the spires began in 1885 at a cost of $200,000. Funds for building the Chapel of St. John were donated to the cathedral by Corrigan, who also began construction of the Lady Chapel in 1901, completed during the tenure of John Cardinal Farley. In 1945 the exterior of the cathedral was renovated extensively at a cost of more than $3 million. Later improvements included the great rose window, bronze doors on the Fifth Avenue side of the cathedral, and an elevator to the choir loft. The cathedral was visited by Popes Paul VI (1964) and John Paul II (1979). Funeral masses held there of notable people include those for Governor Alfred E. Smith (1920), baseball player Babe Ruth (1948), and Senator Robert F. Kennedy (1968). St. Patrick's Gothic exterior is 400 feet (120 meters) long and 174 (53 meters) wide and seats about 2400. The church is visited each year by hundreds of thousands of tourists.

St. Patrick's Cathedral, 1923

Leland A. Cook, *St. Patrick's Cathedral* (New York: Quick Fox, 1979)

Margaret M. McGuinness

St. Patrick's Day Parade. The first St. Patrick's Day parade in New York City was held in 1762 by Irishmen in a military unit recruited to serve in the American colonies. Military units continued to organize the parade each year until after the War of 1812, when local Irish fraternal and beneficial societies began sponsoring the event. In the early nineteenth century the parade was a relatively simple affair in which the members of individual Irish societies joined together at their meeting rooms and moved in a procession toward St. Patrick's Old Cathedral, St. James Church, or one of the many other Roman Catholic churches in the city. The size of the parade increased after 1851, as individual societies merged under a single grand marshal. In keeping with the parade's military origins, soldiers marched at the head, followed by the Irish societies of the city. In the 1850s the Irish 69th Regiment (now the 165th Infantry) became the parade's primary escort unit and the Ancient Order of Hibernians its chief sponsor. Other major participants in the parade have included the 30 Irish county societies and various Emerald, Irish-language, and Irish nationalist societies. Floats, automobiles, and exhibits are not permitted in the parade, in which more than 150,000 marchers take part each year. Attendance at the St. Patrick's Day Parade has become a tradition among politicians of various ethnic backgrounds and political leanings. The route is designated on Fifth Avenue from 44th Street to 86th Street.

John T. Ridge

St. Paul's Chapel. A "chapel of ease" completed in 1766 at Broadway and Fulton Street for Anglicans living beyond convenient walking distance of Trinity Church. It was designed by Thomas McBean in the Georgian style and was often used for extraordinary ceremonies, including a thanksgiving service for George Washington on 30 April 1789 after his inauguration as president; his customary pew in the north aisle remains a popular tourist attraction. The chapel is the oldest public building in continuous use in Manhattan and its last remaining colonial church. St. Paul's was directly across the street from the World Trade Center, but when the twin towers collapsed during the terrorist attacks of 11 September 2001, the church did not suffer any structural damage. For almost a year after the attacks, St. Paul's served as the primary center for recovery operations, and the sanctuary was filled 24 hours a day with exhausted firefighters, police officers, and construction workers. It now houses a permanent exhibition about the recovery efforts; it also holds regular services, weekday concerts, and occasional lectures and provides shelter for the homeless.

Peter J. Wosh

St. Paul's Chapel, Columbia University. Chapel of Columbia University in Morningside Heights. Built during 1904–7, the chapel was a part of McKim, Mead and White's master plan for the university. Philanthropists Olivia Egleston Phelps Stokes and Caroline Phelps Stokes funded the project in 1903 on the condition that their nephew, architect Isaac Newton Phelps Stokes, be given the commission. The church's Northern Italian Renaissance exterior is redbrick and limestone to match the rest of the campus; the interior is Byzantine in style. The central dome rises 91 feet (27.7 meters). The chapel was designated a landmark in 1966. In the early twenty-first century it hosted services for faiths ranging from Baptists to Buddhists, as well as the concert series Music at St. Paul's.

Kate Lauber

St. Paul the Apostle, Church of. Victorian Gothic church at 405 West 59th Street, dedicated in the mid-1890s. In addition to an impressive exterior with 114-foot (34.7-meter) towers, this sanctuary is known for its interior, including ecclesiastic art and mosaic floors designed by Bertram Goodhue. Rev. Isaac Thomas Hecker helped to lay the foundation for the parish in the late 1850s when he organized the Paulist Fathers, or the Missionary Society of St. Paul the Apostle. Hecker is also credited with developing the first national Catholic magazine, *Catholic World.* Subsequently, this publishing enterprise became the Paulist Press.

Sharon Wilkins

St. Peter's Church. Episcopal church in the Bronx. Its beginnings may be traced to 1693 when Episcopalians in what is now the Bronx began meeting for worship. They erected a church in 1700 and received a minister from the Society for the Propagation of the Gospel in 1702. Generally St. Peter's chose to follow the rites of the High Church, retaining the Anglo-Catholic sacraments and liturgical traditions. Several of its rectors became bishops, notably Samuel Seabury (1729–96). By the mid-nineteenth century its wealthy congregation was concentrated in Throgs Neck. A new church in the Gothic Revival style at

2500 Westchester Avenue was designed by Leopold Eidlitz and opened in 1855. St. Peter's continued to occupy this structure into the early twenty-first century.

Peter J. Wosh

St. Peter's Church [Lutheran]. Church of the Evangelical Lutheran Church in America completed in 1977 and erected in the Citigroup Center (619 Lexington Avenue). Designed by Stubbins and Associates, the modern interior incorporates furnishings by Vignelli Associates as well as sculpture commissioned from Louise Nevelson. Long recognized for its substantial music ministry, a tradition established by the Reverend John Garcia Gensel, St. Peter's continues to be a sanctuary for musicians and the general public. Music association meetings, lectures, concerts, and jazz were among St. Peter's outreach and programs in the early twenty-first century.

Sharon Wilkins

St. Peter's Church [Roman Catholic]. Oldest Roman Catholic church in the state and city of New York, located at 22 Barclay Street. The cornerstone for the first St. Peter's was laid in 1785. Early parishioners included Elizabeth Ann Seton (1774–1821), who converted to Catholicism and was the first American to be canonized a saint (1975); and Pierre Toussaint (1766–1853), a black slave from Haiti and a major financial supporter of St. Peter's. Because of the rapidly growing parish, a larger church was needed, and in 1836 the cornerstone was laid on the same site for the current St. Peter's, designed by John R. Haggerty and Thomas Thomas in Greek Revival style. From 1800 to 1940 it operated the nation's first free parochial school. The congregation was largely Irish in the 1880s and Polish and Ruthenian in the 1920s; eventually many parishioners worked in the area but did not live there. The congregation was small in the 1960s but attracted many new members among residents of Battery Park City after 1990. The building was designated a landmark in 1965.

Located just north of Ground Zero, St. Peter's was greatly affected by the terrorist attacks on the World Trade Center on 11 September 2001: the roof was damaged when the landing gear from one of the planes fell on it; after Father Mychal Judge, the firefighters' chaplain, was killed in the North Tower, his body was carried into St. Peter's and placed before the altar; and the church became one of the major staging areas after the disaster, being used to house workers and volunteers and to store bandages, gas masks, boots, hoses, and cans of food.

St. Peter's Church: The Oldest Catholic Parish in New York State (New York: Parish of St. Peter, n.d.); Leo Raymond Ryan, *Old Saint Peter's: The Mother Church of Catholic New York (1785–1935)* (New York: United States Catholic Historical Society, 1935); Ellen Tarry, *The Other Toussaint: A Post Revolutionary Black* (Boston: Daughters of St. Paul, 1985)

Mary Elizabeth Brown, Ernest L. Osborne

St. Philip's Episcopal Church. Church formed in 1809 by a group of black parishioners who withdrew from Trinity Church on Wall Street because of its discriminatory practices. Located in Manhattan's Tenderloin District, its first rector (1812) was Peter J. Williams, Jr., an abolitionist and activist. Over several years, rising racism and neighborhood tensions resulted in periodic vandalism and destruction of church property. These conditions caused progressive black churches like St. Philip's to seek safer spiritual spaces in less contentious areas. In 1910 the congregation relocated to Harlem at 204 West 134th Street. Under the leadership of Rector Hutchins Chew Bishop, St. Philip's Church was rededicated on 25 March 1911. The design team included Vertner W. Tandy, the first registered black architect in New York State. During this time, St. Philip's purchased 10 apartment buildings on 135th Street that were previously restricted to whites. The presence of a major black congregation that owned property helped to pave the way for black migration from downtown to Harlem. In 1940 structural improvements were required, and Tandy was again called upon to coordinate the design. The church was granted New York City landmark status in 1993.

Sharon Wilkins

St. Raphael's Catholic Church. See Sts. Cyril and Methodius Church and St. Raphael's Church.

St. Raymond's Cemetery. Roman Catholic cemetery laid out in 1856 beside the Church of St. Raymond at Castle Hill and East Tremont avenues in the Bronx. In 1877 a noncontiguous parcel of more than 60 acres (24 hectares), with its main gate at Whittemore and East Tremont avenues, was added; this became known as Old St. Raymond's when another noncontiguous parcel of roughly the same size, with its main gate at Lafayette Avenue and East 177th Street, was added in 1954. Among the well-known figures buried at St. Raymond's are Francis P. Duffy, Billie Holiday, and "Typhoid Mary" (Mary Mallon). The cemetery was where the ransom was delivered in connection with the kidnapping of the son of Charles Lindbergh in 1932.

Howard Kaplan

St. Regis. Hotel erected in 1904 at 2 East 55th Street. Designed in a beaux-arts style by Trowbridge and Livingston and containing 316 rooms in 19 stories, it was intended to replace the Waldorf–Astoria as the city's most elegant hotel. The hotel was one of the first in the city that was a skyscraper, a structure that until that time had been used primarily for offices; it was also one of the first hotels in its neighborhood, in which mansions were soon displaced by fashionable shops and businesses. The hotel was designated a landmark in 1988. The St. Regis is among the most elegant and costly hotels in New York City, with prices beginning at more than $800 a night in 2010. It also has floors dedicated to condominium residency. Among the well-known residents have been Salvador Dalí, John Lennon, and Yoko Ono.

Andrew Wiese

Sts. Cyril and Methodius Church and St. Raphael's Church. Croatian Roman Catholic church formed in 1913 by Irenej Petricak, a Franciscan priest, at 552 West 50th Street in Manhattan. It was bought, renovated, and sustained with funds donated by parishioners. Missionary sisters joined the parish in 1922 to prepare children for the sacraments and teach them folksongs, the Croatian language, and the kolo dance, and a church hall opened as a religious, educational, and national center. During World War II the church became a center of opposition to the communist government in Yugoslavia and a staunch supporter of the Croatian independence movement. The church in 1971 set up a Croatian center at 40th Street and 10th Avenue; in 1974 the congregation moved to larger quarters near the center, at St. Raphael's Catholic Church at 502 West 41st Street. The former parish of St. Raphael's was organized in 1886; its redbrick church was designed in Gothic style by George H. Streeton and built in 1902. It served the Irish population of Hell's Kitchen and during World War II was home to many Italians who lived in the community. New York City political figure Daniel Patrick Moynihan was a member of St. Raphael's. When the Archdiocese of New York authorized Sts. Cyril and Methodius to relocate to St. Raphael's, three names were adopted to honor the church's past and its present (symbols of the rise of Christianity, Cyril and Methodius are considered to be patrons and protectors of Eastern Europe). The church served as a center of relief efforts during the Bosnian War, and in the early twenty-first century it oversaw the Cardinal Stepinac Croatian School.

Frances Kraljic, Sharon Wilkins

St. Stanislaus Bishop and Martyr Parish. Roman Catholic church founded in 1872 at St. Mark's Place and Third Avenue on the Lower East Side. It was the mother church of later Polish congregations in New York

City. In the early 1950s the parish began a steady decline as young Polish Americans left the neighborhood. It is located at 101 East Seventh Street.

James S. Pula

St. Stanislaus Kostka Vincentian Fathers Church. Polish Catholic church at 607 Humboldt Street in Greenpoint, Brooklyn. Built circa 1890, the church features two asymmetrical spires and accommodates the largest Polish Catholic congregation in the borough. In the early twenty-first century the Polish character of the neighborhood was reflected in the church's cross streets, Humboldt Street and Driggs Avenue, which were renamed Lech Walesa Place and Pope John Paul II Plaza.

Kate Lauber

St. Thomas Church. Episcopal parish church at Fifth Avenue and 53rd Street in Manhattan, formed in 1823. During the late nineteenth century parishioners first carried flowers used in the Easter service to St. Luke's Hospital (then at Fifth Avenue and 54th Street), thus beginning the tradition of an Easter parade along Fifth Avenue. The current building, designed in a French Gothic Revival style by the firm of Cram, Goodhue and Ferguson, is built of Kentucky limestone and was consecrated in 1916. A boarding school to train choirboys was added in 1919 and in 1989 moved to a 14-story building for 50 students at 202 West 58th Street; in the early twenty-first century this was the only school of its kind affiliated with a church in the United States. Under John Andrew, the rector from 1972 until 1996, attendance on Sundays rose to about 1450. The church has many notable features, including the statues on the facade completed in 1963; the 21-bell chime in the great tower; and the statue of Our Lady of Fifth Avenue, which was dedicated in a joint service by many of the city's church leaders on 17 January 1991. Also notable is the ornate reredos, which stands 80 feet (24 meters) tall, is pierced by three stained-glass windows, and features rows of statues that center on an empty cross, a symbol of the Resurrection.

George E. Demille, *Saint Thomas Church in the City and County of New York,* 1823–1954 (Austin, Tex.: Church Historical Society, 1958); J. Robert Wright, *Saint Thomas Church Fifth Avenue* (Grand Rapids, Mich.: William B. Eerdmans/New York: Saint Thomas Church Fifth Avenue, 2001)

J. Robert Wright

St. Thomas More, Church of. English-style Country Gothic church at 65 East 89th Street, originally established in 1870 as Blessed Disciple Episcopal Church. In 1950 ownership was transferred to the Roman Catholic Church of St. Thomas More. The parish serves Manhattan's Carnegie Hill neighborhood on the Upper East Side. In the early twenty-first century its sanctuary remained one of the oldest church properties on the East Side of Manhattan. The church gained national recognition as the site of the memorial mass for John Fitzgerald Kennedy, Jr., in 1999.

Sharon Wilkins

St. Vincent de Paul Society. Charity organization. On 23 April 1833 six laymen gathered in Paris, France, to follow Saint Vincent de Paul's example of personal charity. St. Louis, Missouri, organized the first U.S. "conference," or local unit, in 1845; one formed in the Archdiocese of New York in 1847 and in the Diocese of Brooklyn in 1855. New York Vincentian Henry J. Anderson, M.D., collaborated with Levi Silliman Ives to establish the Catholic Protectory, an institution for youth, in 1863. New York created the first U.S. district council (1857) and hosted the first general assembly (1864). Vincentian Thomas M. Mulry reached out to the National Conference of Charities and Corrections, speaking before that group in 1884, and served as the first president of the society's U.S. Supreme Council (1915). National President T. Raber Taylor (1969–75) brought women into the organization. Both dioceses have

St. Stanislaus Kostka, 2009

offices to coordinate Vincentian activities, New York City's at 1011 First Avenue and Brooklyn's at 191 Joralemon Street. The 2006 national annual report counted 16 conferences with 556 members in New York City and 61 conferences with 422 members in Brooklyn raising money and performing personal service, their work's value estimated at $1.5 million and $3.2 million, respectively.

Mary Elizabeth Brown

St. Vincent's Home for Homeless Newsboys. Forerunner of Mount Loretto–Mission of the Immaculate Virgin.

St. Vincent's Hospital and Medical Center of New York. Roman Catholic hospital in Manhattan, located on the corner of West 11th Street and Seventh Avenue. Opened by the Sisters of Charity of New York in 1849 on 13th Street between Third and Fourth avenues, it housed 30 patients at the outset and 70 by 1852. The first administrator was Mary Angela Hughes, who left when elected superior general of the Sisters of Charity in 1855; she returned to the hospital as its head administrator in 1861. In 1856 the hospital moved into a building at its current site that had earlier housed St. Joseph's Half Orphan Asylum. Costs were defrayed through private contributions, patient fees, and public appropriations. Catholic laywomen organized one of the most successful fund-raising efforts at the Crystal Palace in 1856. In 1880 a group of prominent Catholic laymen organized St. Vincent's Advisory Board; its first chairman was Eugene Kelly, nephew of Mary Angela Hughes and Archbishop John Hughes. Katherine Sanborne, a New York Hospital School of Nursing graduate, opened a school of nursing in 1892 with eight students. Additions were continually made in Manhattan: the Cardinal Spellman Pavilion (1941), the Alfred E. Smith Memorial Building (1950), the John J. Rascob Building (1952), the John A. Coleman Pavilion (1983), and the George Link, Jr., Pavilion (1988).

In 1975 St. Vincent's fell under the joint sponsorship of the Archdiocese of New York and the Sisters of Charity, and in 1977 it became a teaching affiliate of the New York Medical College. In 2000 St. Vincent's merged with Brooklyn's Catholic Medical Center to form Saint Vincent Catholic Medical Centers (SVCMC); this organization filed for bankruptcy in 2005. In order to regain solvency, SVCMC sold off several hospital locations under its umbrella in 2006. The hospital's specialties include cardiac surgery, oncology, and obstetrics, and it is the designated provider for the U.S. Family Health Plan (an option within TRICARE, which provides medical benefits for military personnel and their families) in New York State and New Jersey. The hospital is designated a "level one" trauma center, a "level three" neonatal intensive care unit, and an AIDS center by New York State. It is also noted for its cystic fibrosis, cardiovascular, and cancer centers, as well as its Chinatown outreach program. St. Vincent's emergency room served as the primary admitting station for those injured in the terrorist attacks of 11 September 2001.

Matthew J. Brennan

Saks Fifth Avenue. Firm of clothing retailers. It began in 1902 as a store on 34th Street near Herald Square opened by Andrew Saks (1847–1912), who had been born in Baltimore, worked as a newsboy and peddler in Washington, D.C., and operated men's stores in several cities. With Bernard Gimbel, a grandson of the founder of Gimbel's, his son Horace Saks agreed to a merger arrangement in 1923 under which Gimbel's bought out Saks's store; this enabled Horace Saks in 1924 to open a lavish store on Fifth Avenue catering to the wealthy. On the death of Saks in 1925 Adam Gimbel became the president of the business, which he expanded according to Saks's plans. After changing hands several times and going public in 1996, the firm was bought in 1997 by the department store consolidator Proffitt's, based in Birmingham, Alabama. Despite an investigation of the company's accounting practices in early 2005 by the Securities and Exchange Commission, Saks Fifth Avenue has set a standard for elegance for generations of shoppers and remains one of the best-known retailers in the world.

Leslie Gourse

salad-oil swindle. Notorious incident that occurred in 1963, involving the securities firm Ira Haupt and Company. After accepting warehouse receipts as collateral, the firm approved loans to a salad-oil company in New Jersey for which it traded commodities futures. When futures prices for soybean and cottonseed oil declined, the firm discovered that the receipts had been forged; the salad-oil company declared bankruptcy. Ira Haupt could not repay millions of dollars in loans taken to cover the declining futures prices and was liquidated in late November by the New York Stock Exchange, which covered the losses of the firm's 20,700 customers and set up a trust fund to pay for similar liquidations in the future.

Norman C. Miller, *The Great Salad Oil Swindle* (New York: Coward–McCann, 1965)

Mary E. Curry

Salisbury, Harrison E(vans) (*b* Minneapolis, Minn., 14 Nov 1908; *d* near Providence, R.I., 5 July 1993). Newspaper editor, reporter, and essayist. He began his career in 1930 at the United Press in Minneapolis, became head of its bureau in London during World War II, and worked after the war as a foreign editor. He joined the *New York Times* in 1949 and reported from the Soviet Union for five years. In 1955 he won a Pulitzer Prize for a series of stories about the country written after his return to New York City. He was promoted to national news editor of the *Times* in 1962 and assistant managing editor in 1964;

Andrew Saks's department store on Herald Square, forerunner of Saks Fifth Avenue

in 1966 he became the first U.S. journalist to report from North Vietnam, outraging the administration of Lyndon B. Johnson by reporting that contrary to official claims, Vietnamese civilians had been bombed. In 1970 he became the first editor of the "op-ed" page, and after retiring from the newspaper he retraced Mao Zedong's "long march" of 1934, which became the subject of *The Long March* (1985), one of his more than two dozen books.

Michael Green

Salmagundi Club. Club formed in 1871 by a group of artists and their patrons, incorporated in 1880 as the Salmagundi Sketch Club. Its members rented a brownstone at 14 West 12th Street from 1895 until 1917, when they bought a brownstone at 47 Fifth Avenue (designated a national landmark in 1974). Women were first admitted in 1973. In 2007 there were more than 600 members. The club holds a number of events open to the public, including exhibitions of members' work and competitions for nonmembers; it also sponsors lectures, demonstrations, and sketch classes and has a reference library. The building reputedly has the only remaining stoop on Fifth Avenue.

James E. Mooney

Salomon, Haym (*b* Leszno, Poland, *ca* 1740; *d* Philadelphia, 6 Jan 1785). Patriot and financier. After moving to New York City he opened a brokerage and became a patriot. Imprisoned during the British occupation as a spy, he was released on parole to serve as an interpreter for Hessian troops, whom he encouraged to desert; after being freed he was arrested again, confined to the Provost prison, and condemned to death. He escaped to the American lines and traveled to Philadelphia, where he gave large sums to finance the patriot cause and died nearly penniless.

Laurence R. Schwartz, *Jews and the American Revolution: Haym Salomon and Others* (Jefferson, N.C.: McFarland, 1987)

James E. Mooney

Salomon Brothers. Firm of investment bankers. Its forerunner was a small brokerage opened on Exchange Place in the 1880s by Ferdinand Salomon, a German immigrant. The firm of Salomon Brothers and Hutzler, formed at 80 Broadway in 1910 by his sons Arthur Salomon, Percy Salomon, and Herbert Salomon and by Morton Hutzler, began after World War I to trade securities of the U.S. government, which remained its chief source of income for the next half century. The headquarters moved to 60 Wall Street in 1922, and by the mid-1920s Arthur Salomon was a leading financier on Wall Street, one of few who did not need an appointment to meet with J. P. Morgan. By underwriting bonds for Swift and Company in 1935 the firm was the first to break the "Wall Street strike" (the refusal of investment bankers to underwrite securities to protest regulations of the New Deal). Among those who led the firm during the 1940s and 1950s were Benjamin Levy (1888–1966) and Rudolph Smutny (1897–1974), whose aggressive style of management led to his replacement in 1957 by William Salomon (*b* 1914).

The firm was reshaped by several men who joined it as partners during the 1950s, including Sidney Homer, Gedale B. Horowitz, Henry Kaufman (1927–2000), John Gutfreund (*b* 1929), and William Simon (*b* 1927; later secretary of the treasury under President Gerald R. Ford). William "Billy" Salomon became the first managing partner of the firm in 1963. By the late 1960s the firm made "block trades" involving unprecedentedly large amounts of stock. In 1970 it moved its headquarters to 1 New York Plaza (near Battery Park City) and became known as Salomon Brothers. The firm helped to end a fiscal crisis in the city in 1975 by underwriting more than $1 billion in bonds of the Municipal Assistance Corporation. After William Salomon retired, he was succeeded in 1978 by Gutfreund, who in 1981 oversaw a $550 million merger with the Phibro Corporation (a commodities firm formed in the city in 1892 by Julius and Oscar Philipp): this provided the capital that allowed Salomon Brothers to become the largest firm of securities underwriters by the mid-1980s. Its prosperity was imperiled in August 1987 by revelations that illegal bids had been made for Treasury securities, leading to the resignation of some of the firm's most important officials, including Gutfreund. Salomon Brothers employed many people who later managed or founded other leading financial companies, including Mayor Michael Bloomberg, who worked at Salomon until 1981. In 1997 Smith Barney, a subsidiary of Travelers Group, merged with Salomon Brothers to form Salomon Smith Barney. In 1998 Travelers and Citicorp combined to become Citigroup Inc., with headquarters at 399 Park Avenue. The name Salomon Smith Barney was dropped after what was known as the 2003 global settlement agreement and several stock fraud claims against the bank.

James Bradley, Meryl Cates

saloons. On saloons generally, see BARS, TAVERNS, AND SALOONS; the type of saloon offering entertainment in the nineteenth century is discussed in the entry CONCERT SALOONS.

Salvadorans. Few Salvadorans lived in New York City until the mass migration occasioned by the 1979 civil war in El Salvador. In the following two decades the number of Salvadorans in the city increased from 7260 to more than 100,000, many living in Far Rockaway, Jamaica, Flushing, and upper Manhattan. Newer immigrants tended to be urban working class, employed as factory workers, domestic workers, carpenters, and gardeners. A few were granted political asylum, though under a 1990 law they were given "temporary protected status" from deportation. In the early 1990s fewer than 15,000 Salvadorans had acquired legal residency, and most remained fearful of deportation. Because of their long workdays Salvadorans enjoy few voluntary associations. Soccer clubs and Salvadoran restaurants called *pupuserias* offer a place for social gatherings. In the early twenty-first century four of the top 10 cities with the most residents born in El Salvador were in the Greater New York area.

Sarah Mahler

Salvation Army. Charitable organization formed in 1878 in England by William Booth (1829–1912). It began as an evangelical Christian movement for the urban working class and poor and had titles, ranks, brass bands, and uniforms modeled on those of the British military. A small corps was set up in Philadelphia in 1879, but the first authorized missionary to the United States was George Scott Railton, who disembarked at Battery Park in March 1880 with seven women "soldiers." From this time to 1905, New York City was the national headquarters of the organization. The corps sought spiritual salvation of the "fallen, degraded, and forsaken" at meetings held outdoors and in rented halls, where large crowds were drawn by popular tunes and hymns, parades, bands, and the testimony of the repentant. The organization focused almost exclusively on evangelism during its early years and met with some opposition. By the late 1880s it sponsored several charitable endeavors, including shelters for "fallen women" and homeless men and assistance by women members to families in slums. In 1890 large cities in 35 states had 410 corps. During the same year Booth published *In Darkest England and the Way Out,* which described how the organization's doctrines could be applied practically and marked the shift of the organization almost entirely toward social work.

During the next 25 years the Salvation Army became widely known and respected in the United States for its efficient administration of many services. At its workingmen's hotels (temporary shelters opened in the 1890s in New York City; Chicago; San Francisco; Buffalo, New York; and Newark, New Jersey) a bed, a wash, and a meal were made available to men for 11 cents or two hours' work at the shelter or at a woodyard. These hotels inspired industrial homes, where homeless or unemployed men (often alcoholic) were employed to salvage and repair used clothing, which was resold at low prices to the poor. Rescue homes helped prostitutes and desperate women, and prison brigades helped prisoners and former prisoners. By 1895 the American branch of the organization was the largest and most successful overseas mission and had its own national headquarters at 120 West 14th Street. Booth named several of his children and their spouses national commanders in the United States. He and his son Bramwell were sometimes considered rigid and autocratic for dictating from London without understanding the needs of the army in the United States. A schism occurred in 1896, when Booth's son Ballington, national commander from 1887 to 1896, and his wife resigned to form the Volunteers of America. Booth's son-in-law Frederick Booth–Tucker became the national commander in 1896 and held the post until 1904, when Booth's daughter Evangeline took over; her tenure ended in 1934.

World War I marked the heyday of the Salvation Army in the United States. Its "lassies" baked doughnuts, wrote letters, sewed, and provided other services for U.S. troops in Europe. Public contributions to its welfare projects increased greatly, and eventually the organization became a beneficiary of fund drives by the Community Chest and the United Way. By the 1920s it operated 26 homes for unwed mothers that provided prenatal care, delivery and recovery services, infant care, and an adoption service. As the organization grew it became decentralized, and in 1920 the United States was divided into four independent territories. The tremendous extent of homelessness and unemployment during the Depression put a severe strain on resources, and the organization gradually declined in importance as its mix of services and evangelizing came to be perceived as outmoded and as the government assumed a greater role in social welfare. During World War II it joined with the Red Cross, the Young Men's and Young Women's Christian Associations, and other groups to form the United Service Organizations, which provided a range of personal services to U.S. troops. After the war the industrial homes were superseded by adult rehabilitation centers, which provided both men and women with shelter, food, clothing, medical care, psychiatric counseling, meaningful work, and vocational training, as well as practicing Christian evangelism. Rescue homes disappeared as the stigma attached to unwed mothers diminished, and the Salvation Army opened maternity and general hospitals, day-care centers, and residences for young working women. A rescue home opened in 1892 on the Lower East Side eventually became Booth Memorial Hospital and Medical Center.

In the 1990s the Salvation Army was the single largest charitable organization in the country. In 2007 it had 46 social programs, which provided aid to children and adults in more than 35 halls in the New York City metropolitan area, which is part of its Eastern Territory. Among its services are emergency disaster relief, aid to poor families and teenagers, housing for the elderly, and unemployment and missing persons bureaus. Because of its widely recognized social services, the Salvation Army is often thought to be primarily an agency for social welfare, but it is also a Christian denomination with 1.5 million adherents in 90 nations.

William H. Tolman and William Hull, *Handbook of Sociological Information with Special Reference to New York City* (n.p.: n.pub., 1894); Edward H. McKinley, *Marching to Glory: The History of the Salvation Army in the United States of America, 1880–1980* (New York: Harper and Row, 1980); Edward H. McKinley, *Somebody's Brother: A History of the Salvation Army Men's Social Service Department, 1891–1985* (Lewiston, N.Y.: Edwin Mellen, 1986)

Jane Allen

Sampson, William (*b* Londonderry [now in Northern Ireland], 17 Jan 1764; *d* New York City, 28 Dec 1836). Lawyer. Exiled as an Irish nationalist, he settled in New York City in 1806, where, as a Protestant, he remained active in promoting the welfare of Irish Catholic immigrants and articulating his nonsectarian vision. In his law practice he championed individual rights: among his cases was one establishing the principle that Catholic priests should not have to divulge information revealed in confession. Sampson ridiculed excessive reliance on English common law and promoted reform and codification of the law to meet American needs. He unsuccessfully argued against English precedents in defending the Journeymen Cordwainers, a trade union indicted for conspiracy. He was also a skilled stenographer who published reports of the city's more engrossing trials. His flamboyant eloquence and whimsy in argument furthered public interest in the law.

See also Irish Republicanism.

Mariam Touba

Sanborn fire insurance maps. Maps designed to show insurance agents potential fire hazards in more than 12,000 U.S. cities and towns. D. A. Sanborn opened the National Insurance Diagram Bureau in New York City in 1867; it took the name Sanborn Map Company in 1902, and the company headquarters moved to Pelham, in Westchester County, in 1907. The maps, produced until the late 1960s, detailed the size, use, and materials of individual buildings and are an important tool for researchers such as historians, architects, geographers, and environmentalists. In the early twenty-first century the company is based in Colorado and is a leader in the GIS and photographic survey fields.

sandhogs. Slang term that refers to the underground miners and construction workers responsible for excavating and building the foundations of most of New York City's bridges and skyscrapers as well as all its tunnels—including the subways, sewer system, and freshwater supply tunnels. Their earliest work in New York City was doing caisson excavation for the Brooklyn Bridge, beginning in 1870. During that project, the rate of decompression sickness ("the bends") among sandhogs was so high that excavation for the construction of the tower on the Manhattan side stopped 30 feet (9 meters) above the bedrock, leaving the tower to rest on sand. In 1916 a 28-year-old sandhog named Marshall Mabey was working on a subway tunnel under the East River when the pressure differential sucked him through a hole in the side of the tunnel and through 12 feet (3.7 meters) of riverbed, shooting him above the East River on a geyser four stories high, an accident he survived without major injury. The advent of more sophisticated technology, such as air compression systems and tunnel boring machines, helped to make the work of sandhogs safer, but it remains dangerous, a factor that contributes to sandhogs' high wages. Because the urban mining projects in which sandhogs are involved often span decades, it is not uncommon for several generations of a family to work together as sandhogs, passing the occupation's extensive folklore from parent to child. Since 1969 hundreds of sandhogs have been at work on the largest capital construction project in city and state history, water tunnel no. 3, which will stretch 60 miles (96.5 kilometers) into the Catskills and deliver up to 1.5 billion gallons of water to New York City daily.

Rowan Moore Gerety

Sandy Ground. Neighborhood in southwestern Staten Island, centered at Bloomingdale Road between Rossville and Charleston. Settled in 1830s as the first free black community in New York State and perhaps the nation, it was known as Harrisville and then as Little Africa before being given its current name because of the poor quality of its soil. Only a few descendants still live in the area. The early settlers included a few local families along with oystermen from New Jersey, Delaware, Virginia, and Maryland, who were attracted by the rich oyster beds in the area and by business opportunities not available in the South. The area was served by the Underground Railroad, and the Zion African Methodist Episcopal Church (1850) at Bloomingdale and Woodrow roads became a community center. Food crops and farm animals were kept near well-maintained homes on large plots, and relations with white neighbors were cordial. As the oyster beds of Raritan Bay became overworked many oystermen moved their operations to the Arthur Kill; when these oyster beds were condemned in 1916 some residents turned to well digging, ironworking, smithing, and midwifery. Homes fell into disrepair and a fire in 1964 destroyed many dwellings. New housing developments stand near the church; the small museum run by the Sandy Ground Historical Society, which was formed in 1979, is visited by thousands of schoolchildren every year. The neighborhood was listed on the National Register of Historic Places as an archaeological site in 1982. Most blacks moved as real estate prices rose but return to attend church services and to affirm their historical connection.

Howard R. Weiner

Sandy Hook. Narrow sandspit 5 miles (8 kilometers) long just off the New Jersey shore at the entrance to Lower New York Bay, regarded as the outer limit of the Port of New York. It resembles a fishhook curving inward from the sea and pointing toward Lower Manhattan, which is 17 miles (27 kilometers) to the north. Between Sandy Hook and Coney Island lies a broad sandbar, in some places perilously close to the surface, and large vessels must stay within the few hundred yards of the Main–Gedney Ship Channel. Only experienced harbor pilots who know the location of every sandbar may navigate large ships past Sandy Hook and into the Narrows and Upper New York Bay.

Kenneth T. Jackson

Sandy Hook Pilots. Organization whose members board arriving ships to guide them safely through the Lower Bay and the Narrows or the waterways around the west side of Staten Island. It was created in 1895 by the legislatures of New York and New Jersey to end open competition among the fleet of individually owned schooners then in use. The legislation was in part brought about by the disastrous blizzard of 1888 that caught vessels offshore, destroying 12 of the 17 schooners then active, with heavy loss of life. The pilots operate out of a base in the Rosebank section of Staten Island. Modern pilot vessels are stationed 7 miles (11.3 kilometers) off Rockaway and Sandy Hook in the vicinity of the Ambrose Channel Light. The pilots are transferred to ships by smaller motor launches; they guide the ships into the Upper Bay where docking pilots employed by the tugboat companies take over. Pilots stationed at City Island bring ships through the East River from Long Island Sound, and Hudson River pilots board ships at Yonkers to take them up the river as far as the Port of Albany.

Norman J. Brouwer

San Gennaro Festival. Annual festival held in mid-September along Mulberry Street in Manhattan, organized from 1926 and perhaps earlier by a men's club and mutual benefit society of immigrants from southern Italy. The food offered at the festival has become more international as immigrants from many countries have settled in New York City and taken up the vending trade. The festival is not primarily a religious one, but a statue of San Gennaro (Januarius), the patron saint of Naples, is still enshrined on an outdoor altar to preside over the affair. In 1997, after years of rumors about Mafia involvement, several members of the Genovese crime family were convicted of extortion in connection with the festival. Allegations of Mafia involvement have continued into the twenty-first century, and gentrification in Little Italy has led to further conflict concerning the festival, with many residents complaining about noise and litter.

Mary Elizabeth Brown

Sanger [née Higgins]**, Margaret (Louise)** (*b* Corning, N.Y., 14 Sept 1879; *d* Tucson, Ariz., 6 Sept 1966). Activist and birth control advocate. She trained as a nurse before marrying architect William Sanger in 1902, and in 1910 she moved with her family to Manhattan, where she embraced radical politics and bohemian culture and lived successively at 135th Street in Hamilton Heights, Post Avenue near Dyckman Street (from 1914), and 236 West 14th Street (from 1917). While working as a visiting nurse and midwife for poor families in the Lower East Side she saw the suffering inflicted on women by unwanted pregnancies and became convinced that it would be alleviated only by making contraceptives widely available. Defying state and federal "Comstock laws," she advocated contraception in her journal the *Woman Rebel* (1914) and published explicit information on contraceptive methods and sexuality in her pamphlets *Family Limitation* (1914) and *What Every Girl Should Know* (1916). She helped to coin the phrase "birth control" and with her sister Ethel Byrne opened the first birth control clinic in the country at 46 Amboy Street in Brownsville in Brooklyn on 16 October 1916. It printed advertisements in English, Italian, and Yiddish and served more than 400 women before being closed by the police on 25 October. The two sisters were arrested and convicted of violating state laws prohibiting the distribution of contraceptives and information about them. Byrne was sentenced to 30 days in the workhouse in Blackwell's Island, and Sanger to 30 days in the Queens County Penitentiary, where she gave lectures on birth control to her fellow inmates. In 1918 the New York State Court of Appeals upheld Sanger's conviction but allowed physicians to prescribe contraceptives to women to cure or prevent disease.

In 1921 Sanger formed the American Birth Control League at 104 Fifth Avenue. On 13 November a riot nearly broke out after police removed her from the stage of Town Hall. In seeking the support of physicians, she fought for legislation giving them the exclusive right to dispense contraceptives. Divorced in 1920, Sanger then married J. Noah Slee, a millionaire who supported her work, and on 2 January 1923 opened the Birth Control Clinical Research Bureau (later renamed the Margaret Sanger Bureau) at 17 West 16th Street, a facility staffed by such women physicians as Hannah Stone (1893–1941), who provided gynecological services as well as contraceptives. For some time Sanger lived in an apartment above the bureau, which gathered detailed statistics on the effects of contraceptives on women's health. At the urging of Catholic leaders the bureau was raided on 15 April 1929 by the police, who seized its medical records. Outraged at this violation of the confidentiality of patients' records, the medical establishment rushed to Sanger's defense, and charges against her were dropped. In 1939 the American Birth Control League combined with the Clinical Research Bureau to become the Birth Control Federation of America, renamed the Planned Parenthood Federation of America in 1942.

By 1938, the year in which she wrote an autobiography, Sanger was dismayed with the increasingly conservative male leadership of the birth control movement, which shifted its focus from female empowerment toward "child spacing" and infertility. She remained an active supporter of Planned Parenthood but retired to Tucson. In 1952 concerns about overpopulation and global stability led her to help form the International Planned Parenthood Federation. She also encouraged the research that led to the development of the first birth control pill in the early 1960s.

David M. Kennedy, *Birth Control in America: The Career of Margaret Sanger* (New Haven: Yale University Press, 1970); Linda Gordon, *The Moral Property of Women: A History of Birth Control Politics in America*, 3rd edn. (Urbana: University of Illinois Press, 2002); Ellen Chesler, *Woman of Valor: Margaret Sanger and the Birth Control Movement in America* (New York: Simon and Schuster, 2007)

Esther Katz

Sanitary Commission. See U.S. Sanitary Commission.

Sanitary Report of 1866. The *Report on the Sanitary Condition of the City* was published in 1866 by the Citizens' Association of New York. It led to the establishment of the Metropolitan Board of Health, which later became the New York City Department of Health. The report presented the high costs of disease through a detailed inspection of the city's health districts. Organized by a committee of the city's political and commercial elites, such as Hamilton Fish, John Jacob Astor, Jr., August Belmont, and Robert Roosevelt, the report brought to public attention the horrifying conditions of life in the rapidly expanding city. Its medical committee was also composed of some of the leading physicians in the city, including Valentine Mott, Austin Flint, Stephen Smith, and Willard Parker.

The "introductory statement" to the report noted that "when pestilential diseases visit this city, the impotence of the existing sanitary system" is exposed. "The people are panic-stricken, while the interests of commerce suffer by the *insensible loss of millions.*" Underlying the report was a belief that "Public Health is Public Wealth." In general, the tone of the report was patronizing toward the poor, the most obvious victims of disease, explaining their suffering as a result of personal habits such as ignorance and lack of cleanliness. However, the report also said that diseases can be stopped "if the laws of public hygiene have sway . . . and sanitary regulation" is practiced. The report marked a milestone in public health for it laid out the proposition that the city had no more important responsibility than the protection of the well-being of its citizens.

John Duffy, *A History of Public Health in New York,* vol. 2 (New York: Russell Sage, 1974); Charles E. Rosenberg, *The Cholera Years: The United States in 1832, 1849, and 1866* (Chicago: University of Chicago Press, 1987)

Molly Rosner

sanitation. Colonists were responsible for disposing of their own waste in New Amsterdam. In 1657 the Common Council forbade the disposal of offensive materials in the streets (including dirt and animal carcasses), established proper dumping sites, and required residents to clean the streets in front of their homes. Efforts to ban the emptying of privies in the streets were made as early as 1658 but for years remained unsuccessful. Most sewers were simply open or closed ditches for draining surface water; they often overflowed after becoming clogged with solid wastes and the contents of illegally connected privies, cesspools, and sinks. During the 1670s cartmen were granted a monopoly over their trade in exchange for hauling away household refuse, which residents set out once a week. The city's sanitation code was often ignored, and waste ranging from garbage to sewage was disposed of in the streets, attracting pigs, dogs, and rats. Slaughterhouses were banned within the city limits by the Common Council in 1676, but those on the outskirts were soon engulfed by the growing city. Rotting carcasses and entrails continued to be dumped in the streets. The first public sewer, built in 1703, emptied into the waterways around the city.

During 1784–85 the city appointed three street commissioners to oversee the work of cartmen and also so-called scavengers who picked through solid wastes for reusable materials. For the next century responsibility for street cleaning and waste collection was assumed by a succession of public and private ventures. Political ties figured in the awarding of contracts, and the city often took over for contractors who performed inadequately. The thoroughness of disposal depended on a fluctuating market for different kinds of refuse (ash, street sweepings, manure, garbage, and rubbish). Unsalvageable materials were loaded onto scows and dumped at sea, a practice that from the 1850s drew criticism as waste clogged sections of the harbor and washed ashore in resort communities. A large, decentralized network of sewers was haphazard; disposal for the entire city became possible only when a constant supply of water was provided by the Croton Aqueduct after 1842. Campaigns for sanitary reform, bolstered by the widespread belief that decaying garbage and filth released poisonous vapors that caused disease, led to the formation of the Metropolitan Board of Health in 1866. The board assumed control of street cleaning and waste collection and also won the cooperation of the courts and the police in enforcing an ordinance prohibiting slaughterhouses south of 40th Street. In 1870 the board was replaced by the Department of Health, which in the same year banned all slaughterhouses between Second and 10th avenues and by 1877 had largely confined 52 of these establishments to two areas, one bounded by 41st Street, 10th Avenue, 40th Street, and the Hudson River, the other by 47th Street, the East River, 43rd Street, and First Avenue. In 1877 the first chemically treated wastewater facility in the United States opened at Coney Island.

Waste collection and street cleaning were handled by the Metropolitan Board of Police from 1872 until the Department of Street Cleaning was formed in 1881. Political patronage remained an obstacle to effective service until 1895, when George E. Waring, Jr., was appointed commissioner. He reorganized the department along military lines, minimized political influence in employing workers, stressed sweeping by hand rather than with machines, and dressed street sweepers in white uniforms, earning them the nickname "white-wings." Waring also revolutionized waste disposal and temporarily suspended ocean dumping. Although experiments with incineration and the landfilling of garbage had been conducted as early as 1870, only in 1896 did Waring implement a system of salvaging solid wastes: garbage was boiled down for greases and fertilizers by a private firm on Barren Island, ash and street sweepings were used as fill in dumps and low-lying areas, and rubbish (wood, paper, rags, bottles, and metals) was reclaimed by scavengers for a fee paid to the city.

Sanitary conditions improved steadily. Manure and dead horses disappeared from the streets as automobiles became popular, and public education campaigns helped to make littering socially unacceptable. After World War I salvaging became less profitable as inflation rose and synthetic materials were introduced. Garbage reduction and rubbish reclamation companies defaulted on their contracts, leading the city to resume ocean dumping. The Department of Street Cleaning

"Street Arabs Taking a Foot-bath," Harper's Weekly, *3 August 1872*

was renamed the Department of Sanitation in 1929 and given new jurisdiction over sewers (until 1938) and centralized control over all street cleaning and solid waste disposal functions throughout the city. This centralization brought about the first significant improvements in sewage treatment in the 1930s; federal aid was used during the New Deal to build an enormous sewage treatment plant on Wards Island and upgrade existing plants.

When ocean dumping of garbage was outlawed by the U.S. Supreme Court in 1934, the city had 22 incinerators and more than 80 inland dumps, but most of these were expensive to operate and soon became inadequate. The Uniformed Sanitationmen's Association was formed in 1935. In 1938 the sanitation commissioner William F. Carey launched a vigorous campaign to reduce costs by using vast sanitary landfills, which he argued were cheaper than incinerators and created usable property out of wetlands. His plan met with opposition, and between 1938 and 1940 he was engaged in a debate with citizens' groups and the parks commissioner, Robert Moses, over plans to fill in parts of Jamaica Bay. He agreed to limit operations there but extended landfills elsewhere, which soon became the city's principal disposal method. Beginning in 1946 plans were made to build more incinerators; few were completed owing to high construction costs and opposition from neighborhoods near proposed sites, and a landfill opened at Fresh Kills in Staten Island as a temporary facility in 1948. The sewage system was also expanded.

To ensure that streets were kept clean, several measures were adopted in the 1950s: alternate-side-of-the-street parking, mechanical sweepers, monitoring of service in each block, and collection of household waste two to five days a week. In 1975 the "Scorecard Cleanliness Program" was implemented to grade the condition of streets and sidewalks on a scale from "filth" to "acceptably clean." That year, 71.3 percent of all streets and sidewalks earned an "acceptably clean" rating. The city's physical appearance declined in part because of public service cutbacks stemming from the fiscal crisis of the 1970s. In 1980 street and sidewalk conditions reached an all-time low, with only 53 percent qualifying as "acceptably clean."

In March 1986 the North River Wastewater Treatment Plant began advanced preliminary treatment of wastewater that eliminated, for the first time in the city's history, the daily discharge of raw sewage into the Hudson River. Located on a 28-acre (11.3-hectare) reinforced concrete platform between 137th and 145th streets west of the West Side Highway, the plant initially suffered from design flaws and emitted higher-than-permitted levels of hydrogen sulfate. Concerned neighbors organized West Harlem Environmental Action and joined forces with the Natural Resources Defense Council in suing the city to mitigate odors and address related environmental and social justice concerns.

In 1987 a barge named *Mobro 4000* traveled roughly 6000 miles (9656 kilometers) from Islip, Long Island, to Central America and back to Brooklyn, New York, in search of a disposal location for 3100 tons (2812 metric tons) of residential trash, commonly called municipal solid waste. The barge received sensationalized media coverage and was turned away by officials in dozens of countries who feared that it contained hazardous material. The New York City Department of Sanitation agreed to burn the barge's contents at its Southwest Brooklyn incinerator. In 1989 the city mandated municipal recycling to extend the lifecycle of Fresh Kills, then the largest sanitary landfill in the world at approximately 2200 acres (890 hectares).

Street sweeper with handcab

In 1992 Mayor David N. Dinkins appointed Emily Lloyd as the city's first female sanitation commissioner. Incineration of municipal solid waste within city limits ended after a 1994 U.S. Supreme Court ruling, which mandated the testing of ash for the presence of hazardous materials, proved too costly. In 1996 Mayor Rudolph W. Giuliani announced that the city would close Fresh Kills, its last remaining landfill, by the end of his term in December 2001. To replace Fresh Kills, the city hired national solid waste management firms to export, for the first time ever, all of its trash to disposal facilities outside of the five boroughs.

The shift from municipal to corporate disposal was one of the most dramatic and costliest public works infrastructure realignments in the city's history. Within six years (1996–2001) the century-old trend toward the centralization of disposal under one municipal agency was reversed. City trash became interstate commerce and was shipped by tractor trailer, rail, and barge to dozens of landfills and incinerators in states all over New England, the South, and the Midwest. Privatization also effectively doubled the annual operating budget of the Department of Sanitation from $590 million in 1997 to more than $1 billion in 2002.

The disproportionate clustering of commercial waste transfer stations (WTS) needed to export trash in the South Bronx and the Brooklyn neighborhoods of Red Hook, Greenpoint, and Williamsburg resulted in a wave of environmental justice activism. Roughly 40 percent of the city's WTS in the late 1990s were located in Brooklyn, with most located north of the Williamsburg Bridge near the Newtown Creek Wastewater Treatment Plant, the largest on the East Coast. The South Bronx contained a high concentration of WTS plus dozens of private recycling and salvage yards that, when combined with the city's mammoth meat, fruit, and vegetable market, resulted in millions of tractor trailer trips each year through densely populated streets. Community coalitions such as Neighbors against Garbage (NAG), Groups against Garbage (GAGS), and Organization of Waterfront Neighborhoods (OWN) formed to fight the placement of WTS in low-income, immigrant, white ethnic, Latino, and African American communities. Pressure from activists forced the city to adopt a policy of borough equity in the placement of WTS and the reduction of trash transport by diesel trucks.

Although Fresh Kills stopped receiving municipal solid waste ahead of schedule in March

Sanitation dump on the East River, ca *1937*

2001, it reopened the day after the terrorist attacks on the World Trade Center of 11 September 2001 to receive debris from Ground Zero. Fresh Kills became a staging ground for recovery efforts with 132 acres (53.4 hectares) set aside for government officials to sort through material brought from lower Manhattan and another 48 acres (19.4 hectares) for burial. Mayor Michael Bloomberg announced in 2003 that Fresh Kills would be transformed into a park twice the size of Central Park, complete with a memorial for victims of 9/11.

In 2006 the Department of Sanitation collected 12,000 tons (10,886 metric tons) of municipal solid waste and swept 6000 miles (9656 kilometers) of roads, the equivalent distance from New York City to Los Angeles and back, daily. That same year the department had 9701 employees, 2230 collection trucks, 450 mechanical sweepers, and 200 operational facilities that ranged from section stations and repair shops to marine transfer stations. In 2007 the department achieved a recycling diversion rate of 32 percent and the highest level of cleanliness in history, with a 94.3 percent "acceptably clean" rating. The department's operating budget for 2007 was just under $1.2 billion. In addition to street cleaning, waste collection, and recycling, the department is also responsible for removing snow and enforcing the city's health and administrative code to deter littering and illegal dumping.

In 2008 the Department of Environmental Protection (DEP) maintained more than 6000 miles (9656 kilometers) of sewer pipes and operated 14 wastewater treatment plants throughout the five boroughs that handled a total of 1.4 billion gallons (5.3 billion liters) of sewage each day. That same year the DEP's Bureau of Wastewater Treatment had 1900 employees, an annual operating budget of $262 million, and an annual capital budget of $114 million.

John Duffy, *A History of Public Health in New York City* (New York: Russell Sage Foundation, 1968, 1974); Martin V. Melosi, *The Sanitary City: Urban Infrastructure in America from Colonial Times to the Present* (Baltimore: Johns Hopkins University Press, 2000); Benjamin Miller, *Fat of the Land: Garbage in New York the Last Two Hundred Years* (New York: Four Walls Eight Windows, 2000); Julie Sze, *Noxious New York: The Politics of Urban Health and Environmental Justice* (Cambridge, Mass.: MIT Press, 2007)

Steven H. Corey

San Juan Hill. Former neighborhood on the Upper West Side of Manhattan, bounded to the north by 64th Street, to the east by Amsterdam Avenue, to the south by 57th Street, and to the west by the Hudson River. Dutch settlers named the area Bloemendael or Bloomendal, which was changed to Bloomingdale by the English after 1664. Shantytowns built by Irish immigrants covered some parts by the middle of the nineteenth century. The name San Juan Hill may refer to the black veterans who moved to the area after the Spanish–American War, or to the street brawls that often erupted there, many of them interracial. In the early twentieth century the neighborhood became the center of black life in New York City, and its theaters and clubs played an important role in the development of ragtime and early jazz. Several musicians lived there, including the bandleader Benny Carter and the pianist Thelonious Monk, after whom the intersection of 63rd Street and West End Avenue is named. The neighborhood was also the setting for Leonard Bernstein's musical *West Side Story* (1957). In 1956 it was designated as the site of Lincoln Center for the Performing Arts. Construction of the complex displaced more than 1500 families, most of them black and Puerto Rican, and other tenements were demolished to make way for a branch of Fordham University, expensive new housing near Broadway, and new housing for the elderly farther west. The area attracted a number of immigrants from the Dominican Republic, the United Kingdom, China, Israel, and France in the 1980s, by which time the southern reaches were considered part of Clinton and the name San Juan Hill became obsolete.

Peter Salwen, *Upper West Side Story: A History and Guide* (New York: Abbeville, 1989)

Mario A. Charles

San Remo. Cooperative apartment building at 145–146 Central Park West completed in 1930 on the site of a hotel with the same name. The 1929 Multiple Dwelling Law allowed architect Emery Roth to design a 27-story twin-towered Italian Baroque skyscraper that has appealed to the rich and famous throughout its history.

Eric Robinson

Santería. Religion incorporating Roman Catholicism and the religion of the West African Yoruba people, developed in Cuba by slaves under Spanish rule. Leaders, or *babalawos*, make divinations through seashell readings; prescribe herbal medicine, baths, and potions; and call for sacrifices to appease deities known as *orishas*. Candles, beads, oils, and plaster statues of Catholic saints are sold in botánicas in the Bronx, Brooklyn, and East Harlem. Followers had conflicts with the American Society for the Prevention of Cruelty to Animals over the practice of sacrifice: during a raid on 23 May 1980 three goats and 18 chickens were retrieved from an apartment on East 146th Street in the Bronx. Among the leaders of Santería was Oba Ifa Morote, who founded Santería in the city. A babalawo born in Cuba in 1903, he moved to New York City in 1946 and became known as Padrino.

Joseph Murphy, *Santería: An African Religion in America* (Boston: Beacon, 1988); Steven Gregory, *Santería in New York City: A Study in Cultural Resistance* (New York: Routledge, 1999)

Walter Friedman, Marjorie Harrison

Sardi's. Restaurant opened in 1921 in a brownstone at 246 West 44th Street by Vincent Sardi and his wife, Eugenia Sardi; its first customers included prominent figures in the silent-film industry. In 1926 the restaurant moved to the Shubert Building at 234 West 44th Street, next to the *New York Times.* Vincent Sardi, Jr., son of the original owner, took over the restaurant in 1946. In 1950 a practice began for which

Sardi's became famous: its patrons gave a standing ovation to the cast of a show that had just opened, and the members of the cast dined late into the evening while awaiting the arrival of reviews in the next morning's newspapers. In 1985 Vincent Sardi, Jr., sold the restaurant to three partners who encountered financial troubles and closed it on 30 June 1990. The restaurant was then reacquired by Sardi and reopened on 1 November. Sardi's is frequented by actors, producers, theatergoers, and tourists and offers a low-cost "actor's menu" available to members of Actors' Equity. Many who enjoyed the discount when they were young and struggling have returned the favor by visiting Sardi's after they have achieved success. The walls of the restaurant are adorned with hundreds of caricatures of well-known customers.

Marjorie Harrison

Sarnoff, David (*b* Minsk [now in Belarus], 27 Feb 1891; *d* New York City, 12 Dec 1971). Entrepreneur. He worked as a telegraph operator for Marconi Wireless Telegraph Company and claimed for many years that from his station atop Wanamaker's department store in 1912 he was one of several radio operators who received and transmitted information about the sinking of the *Titanic* and its survivors. This story has been contested, however. In 1926 at the Radio Corporation of America (RCA) he formed the National Broadcasting Company (NBC), the first centralized broadcasting network. He bought a house in 1937 at 44 East 71st Street. After introducing the first American public television broadcast in New York City at the World's Fair in 1939 he led a team of scientists that developed color television. He is buried in Kensico Cemetery in Westchester County.

Kenneth Bilby, *The General: David Sarnoff and the Rise of the Communications Industry* (New York: Harper and Row, 1986)

JillEllyn Riley

Sarony, Napoleon (*b* Quebec, 9 March 1821; *d* New York City, 9 Nov 1896). Photographer and lithographer. Sarony moved to New York in the early 1830s, working as a lithographer for Currier and Ives before starting his own business with Henry Major in 1846. Sarony opened his first photography studio in 1865 and quickly gained notoriety for his portraits of public figures like Mark Twain, Oscar Wilde, and Sarah Bernhardt. Sarony pioneered the practice of paying his subjects to sit for pictures and then selling the reproductions; Sarony's session with Bernhardt cost him $1500. In 1883 Sarony sued the Burrow-Giles Lithographic Company for copyright infringement following its unlicensed use of his Oscar Wilde portrait in an advertisement for Ehrich Brothers department store. Following an appeal, in 1884 the Supreme Court ruled in favor of Sarony, thereby upholding the power of Congress to extend copyright protection to photography. In his later years Sarony would found the Kit Kat Club with a group of notable artists including Charles Yardley Turner and Edward Moran. He is buried in Brooklyn's Green-Wood Cemetery.

Ben Silk

Satmars. Members of a Hasidic sect founded in Hungary. After the Holocaust many of them emigrated from Eastern Europe and settled in Brooklyn, chiefly around Bedford Avenue in Williamsburg; their rebbe, Joel Teitelbaum (1887–1979), settled in the city after emigrating to the United States in 1946. Most members speak Yiddish and are strongly oriented toward their community. The men dress in broad-brimmed black fur hats and wear beards and often *peyes* (long sidelocks), married women shave their heads, and children are segregated by sex from an early age. The Satmars form the largest Hasidic group in New York City, and one of the most religiously uncompromising. With an estimated following of 120,000 members in the early twenty-first century, they set themselves apart from other Hasidim and are vehemently opposed to Zionism.

Lisa Gitelman

Saturday Review. Literary journal launched in August 1924 as the *Saturday Review of Literature* by Henry Seidel Canby, a former literary editor of the *Saturday Evening Post;* the name was shortened to *Saturday Review* in 1951. The magazine attracted such distinguished writers as Ezra Pound and remained under Canby's direction until 1936. Under Norman Cousins (from 1940) circulation increased from 20,000 to nearly 660,000; he resigned in 1971 after the magazine was sold to a group of investors. The *Saturday Review* was briefly issued as four separate magazines called the *Saturday Review of Society,* the *Saturday Review of Science,* the *Saturday Review of the Arts,* and the *Saturday Review of Education;* these foundered and in 1973 were bought by Cousins, who merged them with his own magazine, the *World,* to form the *Saturday Review of the World.* Circulation continued to decline and in 1983 the magazine was bought by a firm in Columbia, Missouri, which changed the format and added interviews with celebrities. After circulation dwindled to less than 150,000 the magazine was bought by General Media in 1987. As of 2003, it had ceased to exist.

Eric Wm. Allison

Savage [Fells], **Augusta (Christine)** (*b* Green Cove Springs, Fla., 1892/1900; *d* New York City, 27 March 1962). Sculptor. After moving to New York City in 1921 she studied with George Brewster at Cooper Union. She went to Europe in 1930 on a grant from the Julius Rosenwald Fund and produced such works as *Gamin,* a bust of her young nephew that captured the youthful energy of the Harlem Renaissance. On her return in 1932 she opened the Savage Studio of Arts and Crafts at 163 West 143rd Street, aimed at younger artists. Her heroic sculpture *The Harp* adorned the entrance to the Contemporary Arts Building at the World's Fair of 1939–40. She later retired to Saugerties in the Catskill Mountains, where she became an assistant to a commercial mushroom grower. Savage is considered the most important sculptor of the Harlem Renaissance and one of the earliest African American artists to depict black physiognomy sympathetically.

Augusta Savage and the Art Schools of Harlem (New York: Schomburg Center for Research in Black Culture, 1989)

Edmund Gaither

Savannah. First steamship to cross the Atlantic Ocean. Designed by Moses Rogers and built in 1819 in New York City, it weighed 300 tons and had sails in addition to a steam engine. Known as the "elegant steam ship" for its luxurious passenger accommodations, it was nonetheless unable to attract passengers or cargo on transatlantic voyages: potential customers were alarmed that a fire burned continuously onboard to generate power. The ship sailed on 22 May 1819 from Savannah, Georgia, and went as far as Saint Petersburg, Russia, before returning home. The owners declared bankruptcy; the vessel was converted into a sailing ship and sank off Fire Island in 1821.

Frank O. Braynard

savings and loan associations. The precursors of modern savings and loan associations were the English building societies of the 1780s, which were cooperative ventures of limited duration: they existed only long enough to provide sufficient credit for each member to build or buy a home. In 1836 the Brooklyn Building and Mutual Loan Association was organized to provide credit to home buyers. In the 1850s, however, savings and loan associations were restructured as permanent institutions. New ones were formed, but their rate of failure was so high that a bill was introduced in the New York state legislature in 1856 to revoke all their charters. In 1875, New York State took responsibility for auditing the performance of savings and loan associations and issuing annual reports of their condition; scrutiny was tightened in the 1890s after the collapse of the "nationals" (associations with offices in many areas of the country). The Land Bank of the State of New York was formed in 1915 to provide a central credit facility for savings and loans, issuing bonds to raise funds that could be borrowed by its members.

During the Depression falling real-estate values and the inability of home owners to meet their mortgage payments damaged the system and led to passage of the Federal Home Loan Bank Act (1932) and the National Housing Act (1934). By the end of World War II, savings and loan associations had been revitalized, making substantial contributions to the postwar building boom through the provision of long-term, fully amortized residential mortgages.

Congressional legislation to deregulate banking in 1980 and 1982 freed savings and loans from restrictions on the interest rates they could pay and expanded the kinds of loans and investments they could make. Among other things, it allowed them to provide checking accounts and to make commercial loans. It also imposed Federal Reserve System reserve requirements.

A legacy of long-term mortgage loans funded by short-term deposits proved, however, too heavy a burden for most associations when they were exposed to the unprecedented levels and high volatility of interest rates in the early 1980s. Through the 1980s, many associations supported by federal deposit insurance engaged in excessive risk-taking. By the end of the decade, Congress found it necessary to close large numbers of insolvent associations and to restructure the regulatory framework. Associations with little or no capital were closed or acquired by other institutions, and their depositors bailed out. The number of savings and loan associations declined at the national level from about 4000 in 1980 to fewer than 900 in the first decade of the twenty-first century. In New York City, there had been 39 in 1980; only two remained in the early twenty-first century.

Alan Tecki, *Mutual Savings Banks and Savings and Loan Associations: Aspects of Growth* (New York: Columbia University Press, 1968); Gerald Hanweck and Bernard Shull, *Interest Rate Volatility* (Chicago: Irwin Professional Publishing, 1996)

Bernard Shull

Greenwich Savings Bank, Sixth Avenue and 16th Street, 1899

savings banks. In 1816, a group of businessmen led by John Pintard and Thomas Eddy made a proposal to the state legislature of New York that would have established the Bank for Savings as the first savings bank in the United States. They envisioned the bank as encouraging "provident habits" among workers. Strong opposition in the legislature to banks of any kind delayed chartering until 1819, by which time savings banks had been formed elsewhere. The New York bank was finally incorporated with sponsorship by the Society for the Prevention of Pauperism in the City of New York and was modeled after English banks that were established for similar reasons. Managed by a self-perpetuating board of trustees, the bank adhered to its founding principles by encouraging the establishment of other savings banks. The Greenwich Savings Bank opened in 1833. Savings banks became the fastest-growing financial intermediaries of the first half of the nineteenth century. However, between 1825 and the Civil War, savings banks shifted their focus from philanthropy to profit, and their portfolios from low-risk investments such as government securities to corporate stock, mortgages, and other types of loans. Some commercial banks formed savings banks as profit-making ventures; among those that did was the bank of Butchers and Drovers which opened the Bowery Savings Bank and immediately took possession of all of its deposits. By 1860 there were 19 savings banks in New York City, with total deposits in excess of $40 million. The number of savings banks in New York State grew at a slower rate after the Civil War. A peak of 140 was reached in 1910. From the Civil War to the Depression, savings bank deposits grew with the population and workers' incomes. During the 1930s, savings banks proved more stable than commercial banks and gained a reputation for conservative management and stability; they benefited from inclusion in the new system of federal deposit insurance. Also to their advantage was the formation of the Savings Bank Trust Company in New York City in the early 1930s as a cooperative organization to provide liquidity and other financial assistance to its members.

Congressional legislation to deregulate banking in 1980 and 1982 freed savings banks, as it did other depository institutions, from restrictions on the interest rates they could pay and on the investments they could make. Among other things, it gave federal sanction to the provision of checking accounts and commercial loans by savings banks. It also imposed Federal Reserve System reserve requirements.

Deregulation measures continued through the end of the twentieth century, and facilitated the emergence of savings banks as full-service banking institutions. These reforms sparked organizational changes, including conversions from mutual to stock organization and from state to federal charter; they also generated a series of mergers. In early 2006, only 53 savings banks remained in New York State, of which 27 were in New York City. Few, like Emigrant Savings Bank and Dime Savings Bank, retained the names that reflected their original purpose and clientele.

Alan Teck, *Mutual Savings Banks and Savings and Loan Associations: Aspects of Growth* (New York: Columbia University Press, 1968); Alan L. Olmstead, *New York City Mutual Savings Banks, 1819–1861* (Chapel Hill: University of North Carolina Press, 1976)

Bernard Shull

Savoy Ballroom. Dance hall. It opened at 596 Lenox Avenue (between 140th and 141st streets) on 12 March 1926 and was advertised as the "world's most beautiful ballroom." Because it also sponsored dog races it was sometimes known as "the track." In the 1930s and 1940s the managers of the hall promoted band battles and dance contests in which many popular dance steps evolved, among them the Lindy hop. The ornate ballroom could accommodate as many as 1000 people, and patrons of all races were admitted. By the time the hall closed in 1958, nearly 250 big bands had played there, including those of Duke Ellington, Benny Goodman, Fletcher Henderson, and Chick Webb. The mood of competition and innovation at the Savoy is evoked by Edgar Sampson's composition *Stompin' at the Savoy* (1934).

Kathy J. Ogren

Scalamandré. Firm of textile manufacturers formed in New York City in 1929 by Franco and Flora Scalamandré. In the mid-1990s its factory in Long Island City was the only family-run mill operating in the city and one of the few left in the United States. It housed dye vats, equipment used in wallpaper manufacturing, hand-operated looms, and extensive archives. Best known for its reproductions and classical designs, the company produced three-quarters of its textiles in the city. Scalamandré has undertaken projects for the White House, the World Trade Center, the Old Merchant's House, and the Metropolitan Opera.

Christina Plattner

scandals and corruption. Cycles of corruption, scandal, and reform have occurred throughout the history of New York City. One of the earliest scandals involved the collector of the Port of New York, Samuel Swartwout, who during the administration of President Andrew Jackson stole $1 million in customs receipts from the U.S. Customs House and fled the country, embarrassing the Democratic Party. The biggest scandal of the nineteenth century involved William M. "Boss" Tweed, the superintendent of public works in New York City and the dominant figure in TAMMANY HALL. In 1871, after the county auditor had died, an official hostile to Tweed became the new auditor and turned over to the *New York Times* documents revealing that Tweed had collected bribes from contractors and shared them with the other three members of what came to be known as the TWEED RING: Mayor A. Oakey Hall, Comptroller Richard B. Connolly, and Parks Commissioner Peter Barr Sweeny. These and other revelations encouraged prominent merchants and bankers in the city to organize the Committee of Seventy, which undertook to elect officials committed to "reform." In 1872 a slate of reform candidates swept the municipal elections and William F. Havemeyer became mayor. Tweed was tried, convicted, and imprisoned; he died in the Ludlow Street jail.

At the turn of the century, Reverend Charles H. Parkhurst and state legislative investigating committees led by J. S. Fassett, Clarence Lexow, and Robert Mazet alleged that under Tammany Hall the police were corrupt and offered protection to prostitution. These allegations helped the reform candidates William L. Strong and Seth Low to win the mayoral elections of 1894 and 1901, respectively. In 1907 John Ahearn, borough president of Manhattan, was embroiled in a paving scandal and removed from office by Governor Charles Evans Hughes.

During the administration of Mayor James ("Jimmy") Walker in the early 1930s, investigations led by Samuel Seabury revealed widespread corruption in the municipal and county governments, ultimately leading Walker to resign. After Fiorello H. La Guardia won the mayoralty on a reform platform in 1933, regulatory procedures were tightened and municipal corruption declined. Although Tammany Hall was weakened, in the 1940s it served as a base for the "Ahearn crowd," a group that allegedly controlled rackets on the Lower East Side. During the mayoralty of William O'Dwyer in the 1940s, the organized-crime figure FRANK COSTELLO exerted great influence on local politics. To avoid having his career destroyed, O'Dwyer resigned and accepted an appointment as the U.S. ambassador to Mexico. James Marcus, water commissioner under Mayor John V. Lindsay (1966–73), was accused of corruption in connection with a contract to clean and repair the Jerome Park Reservoir. In the late 1980s, a highly publicized scandal in the Parking Violations Bureau implicated the borough president of Queens, Donald Manes, who took his own life. In the early twenty-first century the most notable case of public corruption concerned BERNARD KERIK, police commissioner under Rudolph W. Giuliani.

Seymour Mandelbaum, *Boss Tweed's New York* (New York: John Wiley and Sons, 1965); Warren Moscow, *The Last of the Big Time Bosses* (New York: Stein and Day, 1971); David Hammack, *Power and Society: Greater New York at the Turn of the Century* (New York: Russell Sage Foundation, 1982)

Martin Shefter

Schaefer Brewing. See F AND M SCHAEFER BREWING.

Schapiro, Meyer (*b* Siauliai, Lithuania, 23 Sept 1904; *d* New York City, 3 Mar 1996). Art historian. After immigrating to New York City at age three, he became immersed in the world of art, as a frequent visitor to the Brooklyn Museum and as the only child in Ashcan painter Johan Sloane's class at the Hebrew Settlement House in Brownsville, where he lived. He graduated from Columbia University in 1924 with a degree in philosophy and art history, the two fields that would coalesce in his many theories on art. Four years later Schapiro began teaching at Columbia and continued to do so long after his official retirement in 1973. In 1954 he, along with Irving Howe, Milton Kramer, and several other New York intellectuals, founded *Dissent* magazine, targeting liberal social democrats unhappy with the presidential administration. In 1974, for his 70th birthday, 12 leading artists (including Jasper Johns, Roy Lichtenstein, Robert Rauschenberg, and Andy Warhol) made lithographs, silk-screen prints, and etchings to sell and fund the endowment of a chair in Schapiro's name at Columbia, which was established in 1978. His teaching captured all genres of art, mingling an American approach with a European intellectual (often Marxist) foundation and an emphasis on psychoanalysis. Schapiro, whose former students and friends included Robert Motherwell, Jacques Lipchitz, and Willem de Kooning, was known for bringing to the United States an intellectual understanding of European works by the likes of Picasso, Braque, and Miró. Columbia University erected a hall in his memory and the Brooklyn Museum dedicated a wing to him. He and his wife lived in Greenwich Village for almost 60 years.

Cecilia Magnusson

Schechter, Solomon (*b* Focşani, Romania, 7 Dec 1850; *d* New York City, 15 Nov 1915). Educator. He studied in Vienna and Berlin, taught at Cambridge University and the University of London, and traveled to Cairo, where he discovered 50,000 Hebrew and Arabic manuscripts. At the age of 50 he moved to New York City; there he became president of the Jewish Theological Seminary and helped to establish the Conservative branch of Judaism, and he was soon widely considered the country's leading Jewish scholar. He lived at 512 West 122nd Street.

James E. Mooney

Schechter Poultry Corp. v. United States. Case decided by the U.S. Supreme Court on 27 May 1935, in which the court struck down the National Industrial Recovery Act (NIRA), a cornerstone of the New Deal. Known as the "sick chicken" case, it was brought by the A. L. A. Schechter Poultry Corporation and the Schechter Live Poultry Market in Brooklyn, slaughterhouses operated by the Schechter brothers, who had been convicted in 1934 of selling diseased chickens and violating the wages and hours stipulated in NIRA's live poultry code. The ruling was overturned when the court ruled that the statute had unconstitutionally delegated legislative powers to the executive and that the Schechters' business, as intrastate commerce, was not subject to federal regulation.

Walter Friedman

Schick, Béla (*b* Boglár, Hungary, 16 July 1877; *d* New York City, 6 Dec 1967). Pediatrician. He received a medical degree in 1900 from Karl Franz University in Graz, Austria, where he also studied the principles of immunity with Clemens von Pirquet; in 1905 the two published *Serum Sickness,* which began the medical field of allergy. Schick later proved that diseases following bouts of scarlet fever are allergic in nature, and in 1913 he developed the Schick test for diphtheria. He moved to New York City in 1923 to become the chief pediatrician for Mount Sinai Hospital and later was the director of pediatrics at Seaview Hospital (Staten Island) and Beth El Hospital (Brooklyn). He married Catherine Fries in 1925 and in 1927 was elected a fellow of the New York Academy of Medicine. For many years Schick lived and maintained an office at 17 East 84th Street; toward the end of his life he lived in an apartment building at 1045 Park Avenue.

Antoni Gronowicz, *Béla Schick and the World of Children* (New York: Abelard–Schuman, 1954)

Anthony Gronowicz

Schieffelin, William (Jay) (*b* New York City, 14 April 1866; *d* New York City, 29 April 1955). Reformer. A great-great-grandson of John Jay, he earned a PhD in chemistry from the University of Munich in 1889 and entered his family's pharmaceutical business. He served on the Committee of Seventy that nominated William L. Strong and helped him to defeat Tammany Hall in the mayoral election of 1894, and on the Fusion Committee that elected John Purroy Mitchel to the mayoralty in 1913. As the chairman of Citizens Union from 1909 to 1941 he advocated reforms such as a short ballot, nonpartisan elections, a judiciary free from political interference, the abolition of unnecessary county offices, proportional representation, and equitable reapportionment of the state legislature. In 1931 he organized the Committee of One Thousand, which prevailed on the state legislature to investigate the administration of Mayor James J. Walker.

Bernard Hirschhorn

Schiff, Dorothy (*b* New York City, 11 March 1903; *d* New York City, 30 Aug 1989). Newspaper publisher, granddaughter of Jacob Schiff. With little business experience she became vice president of the *New York Post* in 1939 when George Backer, second of her four husbands, bought the newspaper. After they divorced she eventually became the publisher, named James A. Wechsler as the editor, and transformed the newspaper into a liberal tabloid that crusaded against McCarthyism. During a printers' strike in the winter of 1962–63 her anger at being shut out of negotiations led her to break with the New York City Publishers Association and resume publication. After losing money for many years she sold the *Post* to Rupert Murdoch in 1977. Her ashes lie in a mausoleum at Salem Fields in Brooklyn.

Jeffrey Potter, *Men, Money and Magic: The Story of Dorothy Schiff* (New York: Coward, McCann and Geoghegan, 1976); Marilyn Nissenson, *The Lady Upstairs: Dorothy Schiff and* The New York Post (New York: St. Martin's, 2007)

Michael Green

Schiff, Jacob (Henry) (*b* Frankfurt am Main, 10 Jan 1847; *d* New York City, 25 Sept 1920). Banker and philanthropist, grandfather of Dorothy Schiff. The son of Moses and Clara Schiff, he emigrated to the United States from Germany in 1865, became wealthy on Wall Street, and was a partner in the firm of Budge, Schiff from 1867 to 1872. In 1870 he took U.S. citizenship. He revisited Germany but returned to New York City in 1875 after accepting an offer from Abraham Kuhn to join the banking firm of Kuhn, Loeb; on 6 May he married Solomon Loeb's daughter Theresa Loeb. He helped the firm to become one of the most respected on Wall Street and was its senior partner by 1885. An expert in railroad reorganizations and industrial underwriting, he acted as an adviser during the reorganization of the Union Pacific Railroad in the 1890s and later advised its chairman, Edward H. Harriman, during a struggle with James J. Hill for control of the Northern Pacific Railroad (1901). Schiff was a vice president of the city's chamber of commerce; he also helped to form Montefiore Hospital (of which he was president) and the Jewish Theological Seminary, established the department of Semitic literature at the New York Public Library, and supported the Henry Street Settlement, Columbia University, Barnard College, and Jewish charities and schools around the world. He lived at 965 Fifth Avenue.

Mary E. Curry

schist. See Manhattan schist.

Schlesinger, Arthur M., Jr. (*b* Columbus, Ohio, 15 Oct 1917; *d* New York City, 28 Feb 2007). Historian and intellectual. A prolific writer, scholar, unapologetic liberal, and Democratic activist, Schlesinger also served in the administration of John F. Kennedy as a special assistant and intellectual mentor to the Kennedy family. He was the author of more than 20 books and was twice the recipient of both the Pulitzer Prize and the National Book Award. Although Schlesinger was long associated with Harvard University, from which he graduated in 1938 and where he taught history from 1946 until 1961, in 1966 he became the Albert Schweitzer Professor of Humanities at the City University of New York, a post he held until 1994, when he retired from teaching. Upon settling in Manhattan in the 1960s, he lived in a town house at 171 East 64th Street, later moving to a building in the East 50s where he housed an estimated 13,000 books that filled the apartment that he shared with his wife as well as another one that he used as his study.

Valerie Paley

Schlesinger, Benjamin (*b* Kriukai, Lithuania, 25 Dec 1876; *d* Colorado Springs, 6 June 1932). Labor leader. He immigrated to the United States in 1891 and settled in Chicago, where he took up cloakmaking. As a representative of the cloakmakers' union he traveled to New York City in 1900 to attend the first convention of the International Ladies' Garment Workers' Union (ILGWU), of which he was elected president in 1903. Defeated for reelection in 1904, he became the manager of the cloakmakers' union in New York City. In 1907 Schlesinger became the business manager of the *Jewish Daily Forward;* he also served again as president of the ILGWU (1914–23, 1928–32).

Robert D. Parmet

Schneerson, Menachem (Mendel) (*b* Nikolaev, Ukraine, 14 April 1902; *d* New York City, 12 June 1994). Seventh rebbe (leader) of the Chabad–Lubavitch branch of Hasidim. After studying mathematics and engineering at the University of Berlin and the Sorbonne, Schneerson, with his wife Chaya Mushka—daughter of the sixth Lubavitch rebbe Yosef Yitzchak Schneersohn—moved to New York City in 1941 when the Nazis invaded France. They settled with his father-in-law in Crown Heights, Brooklyn, where the world headquarters of the Lubavitchers became located at 770 Eastern Parkway. Schneerson developed outreach programs for the Lubavitch movement, and upon his father-in-law's death in 1950 he became the seventh rebbe. Under his leadership the Lubavitch movement expanded exponentially. During the 1980s many Lubavitchers began to identify Schneerson as the messiah. Lubavitchers were divided on the question of Schneerson's identity, and other orthodox Jewish groups criticized him for messianic behavior. During his weekly drive to Queens to visit his father-in-law's grave in Montefiore Cemetery, a car in his motorcade struck and killed a Guyanese child. Violence and rioting erupted in Crown Heights, fueled by preexisting racial tensions between Lubavitchers and Afro-Caribbean residents. A group of black men killed a visiting Hasidic student in retaliation. Schneerson suffered a stroke in March 1992; as his health declined, debate on his messianic identity raged. Schneerson, who was childless and left no successor, is buried in Montefiore Cemetery in Queens.

Kate Lauber

Schneiderman, Rose (*b* Saven, near Chelm, Poland, 6 April 1882; *d* New York City, 11 Aug 1972). Labor activist. Her family moved to New York City in 1890, and she joined the labor movement while still in her teens. In 1906 she became vice president of the New York Women's Trade Union League and in 1917 she was elected its president, a position she held until her retirement in 1949; from 1926 to 1950 she also led the National Parent Organization. During her long tenure she both organized many of the lowest-paid and most severely exploited workers in New York City and trained a new generation of working-class organizers. She spent much of the second decade of the twentieth century helping to organize unions for immigrant women who worked at manufacturing garments, paper boxes, gloves, hats, and artificial flowers. Famed for her power as a speaker, she won national attention for a speech in 1911 chastising wealthy New Yorkers for their indifference after the Triangle Shirtwaist fire, in which 146 women lost their lives. In the 1920s she turned to organizing laundry workers, beauty parlor workers, and hotel chambermaids, many of whom were black and Puerto Rican. An ardent suffragist, she led the industrial section of the state's Woman Suffrage Party in 1916–17 and was nominated for the U.S. Senate by the American Labor Party in 1920. She also fought throughout her career for legislation to improve wages, hours, and working conditions. In 1933 she was the only woman named by President Franklin D. Roosevelt to the labor advisory board of the National Recovery Administration; in this capacity she wrote the regulatory codes for every industry in which women workers predominated. In 1937 she was named secretary of labor of New York State, remaining until 1943. After her retirement in 1949 Schneiderman continued to attend union functions and annual memorials for the victims of the Triangle Shirtwaist fire.

See also American Federation of Labor.

Annelise Orleck

Schoenfeld, Gerald (*b* New York City, 22 Sept 1924; *d* Manhattan, 25 Nov 2008). Theater executive. After serving in World War II, he graduated from New York University law school. In 1957 Schoenfeld and his high school friend Bernard B. Jacobs became the primary lawyers for the Shubert Organization. By the early 1970s Jacobs and Schoenfeld ran the organization at 225 West 44th Street, and in 1972 Schoenfeld became chairman and head of the nonprofit Shubert Foundation. At a time when the organization and Broadway were suffering, the two men were credited with reviving commercial theater in New York City by producing the major hit shows of *Pippin* (1972), *Equus* (1974), and *A Chorus Line* (1975) and cleaning up the Times Square area. In 2005 the Plymouth Theater at 236 West 45th Street was renamed the Gerald Schoenfeld Theater.

Jessica Montesano

Schomburg, Arthur [Arturo] **(Alfonso)** (*b* San Juan, 24 Jan 1874; *d* Brooklyn, 10 June 1938). Bibliophile. Schomburg, educated in Santurce (Puerto Rico) and St. Croix, moved to New York City in April 1891, where he became active in the Puerto Rican and Cuban independence movements. He developed friendships with John Edward Bruce, James Weldon Johnson, and W. E. B. Du Bois, and settled in Harlem. He was recognized as a bibliophile and a historian of Africa and its people: elected secretary and treasurer of the Negro Society for Historical Research in 1911, he amassed a large collection of books, pamphlets, prints, paintings, and photographs in the following years; he also helped to form the Negro Book Exchange and became acquainted with the civil rights activist Joel E. Spingarn. He eventually moved to Brooklyn, but he maintained close ties to Harlem and was active in the Harlem Renaissance. He kept his collection in his home before selling it in May 1926 to the New York Public Library for $10,000. He was then curator-in-chief of the collection from January 1932 until his death and continued to buy material for it, often with his own funds. Most of the collection later became the nucleus of the Schomburg Center for Research in Black Culture. Toward the end of his life he also helped Fisk University to form a black history collection.

Elinor DesVerney Sinnette, *Arthur Alfonso Schomburg: Black Bibliophile and Collector* (Detroit: Wayne State University Press, 1989)

Rodger C. Birt

Arthur A. Schomburg

Schomburg residence, 2009

Schomburg Center for Research in Black Culture. National research center of the New York Public Library at 515 Malcolm X Boulevard in Manhattan. It originated as the collection of Arthur Alfonso Schomburg, a Puerto Rican of African descent who built a collection of black history. He sold his collection to the library in 1926 and worked as its curator at the 135th Street branch from 1932 until his death in 1938. Although it lacked an endowment and funding from the city was sparse, the collection gradually attracted wide interest. In 1972 it was designated as a Research Library of the New York Public Library system and received an infusion of federal, state, municipal, and private funds to enlarge and catalogue its collections. It opened a new building in 1980 and added space for public programming. In 2009 it housed more than 10 million items including books, newspapers, photographs, prints, music, and manuscripts. The center also offers public lectures and mounts exhibitions.

Robert Sink

Schomburg Library, 2009

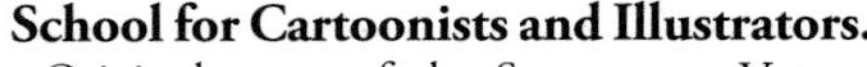

School for Cartoonists and Illustrators. Original name of the School of Visual Arts.

School for Democracy. Precursor to the Jefferson School of Social Science.

School of American Ballet [SAB]. Official school of New York City Ballet (NYCB). In 1933 Lincoln Kirstein asked choreographer George Balanchine to establish a ballet school and company where American dancers would be instructed by the world's best teachers to perform new repertory. Balanchine agreed and developed the School of American Ballet, which served as the training ground for his dancers and was the first step toward creating the new company. On 2 January 1934 the school opened in Midtown East with 32 students. Through the 1930s and 1940s its students performed in the early incarnations of what would become NYCB; in the mid-1950s the school relocated to Manhattan's Upper West Side. In 1963 SAB received a Ford Foundation grant that helped it become a national organization and allowed its dancers and faculty to travel around the country recruiting and distributing scholarships. Stanley Williams, former dancer of the Royal Danish Ballet, joined the faculty in 1964 and received much recognition as an instructor of male dancers, attracting the likes of Rudolf Nureyev, Peter Martins, and Mikhail Baryshnikov to his classes. In that same year Alexandra Danilova, leading ballerina of the Ballets Russes de Monte Carlo, also became a faculty member. She taught variation classes for women and established the school's annual year-end Workshop Performance, in which the most advanced students performed publicly in professionally staged ballet works. In the twenty-first century, the Workshop Performance is attended by the heads of many ballet companies, including NYCB, to choose several students to join their companies. In 1969 SAB moved to rented studios at the Julliard School's new Lincoln Center headquarters, close to the New York State Theater, home of NYCB. Upon Balanchine's death in 1983 Martins became the school's chairman of faculty and the company's co–ballet master in chief. SAB and NYCB share the same artistic leadership in order to guarantee that the school's students develop into the dancers that the company needs to maintain Balanchine's aesthetic, style, and vision. In 1987 SAB became the 11th constituent of Lincoln Center for the Performing Arts, and in 1991 it moved to Lincoln Center's Samuel B. and David Rose Building. The custom-built facility has dance studios and a residence hall that allows SAB to house the majority of its nonlocal advanced students for the first time in its history. Martins then began a tuition-free boys program to increase male enrollment in the school's Children's Division, where students are as young as six years old. In 1997 Kay Mazzo, alumnus of SAB and NYCB, became co-chair of faculty at the school. With each year, current dancers and alumni of NYCB form a larger number of the SAB's faculty, many of whom worked with Balanchine. Alumni of the school and the company, including Maria Tallchief, Suzanne Farrell, and Jock Soto, often instruct, choreograph new works, or begin other schools and companies. In the twenty-first century about 90 percent of the NYCB's roster trained at SAB; other students have become members of leading national and international dance companies.

Frank Nestor

School of Interior Decoration. Original name of the New York School of Interior Design.

School of Visual Arts. Private art school at 209 East 23rd Street in Manhattan. It was opened in 1947 as the School for Cartoonists and Illustrators by Silas H. Rhodes, who remained as the school's chairman of the board until his death in 2007, and illustrator Burne Hogarth. From the outset the school sought to assemble a faculty consisting entirely of working artists, art directors, photographers, designers, and filmmakers. In 1956 it took its current name, added programs in art history and the humanities, and expanded its vocational curriculum. The school, which in the twenty-first century has an enrollment of 3500 students, awards the bachelor of fine arts degree in advertising, animation, cartooning, computer art, film and video, fine arts, graphic design, illustration, interior design, photography, and visual and critical studies. The graduate program, begun in 1983, offers a master of fine arts degree in painting, drawing, sculpture, art criticism and writing, art education, art therapy, computer art, design, digital photography, illustration as visual essay, photography, and video and related media. The School of Visual Arts operates six student galleries as well as a professional gallery in Chelsea and also offers international programs.

Linda Elsroad

schools. New York City has one of the most complicated educational systems in the nation.

Its public schools enroll more than one million students and include institutions of every size and type, from giant high schools to elite secondary facilities to which admission is by standardized test scores. The city also boasts the largest parochial system in the United States, mostly Catholic but including many Orthodox and Hasidic Jewish institutions as well. Furthermore, it has more private schools than any other U.S. city. Many are small, expensive, and overwhelmingly white, but their availability and variety enables the city to retain a higher percentage of affluent families than is the case in other U.S. municipalities. Mayor Michael Bloomberg, who took office in 2002, made education the issue on which he expected ultimately to be judged. He took over the Department of Education and moved its headquarters to the old Tweed Courthouse just behind City Hall. Test scores improved over the next half dozen years, but schooling remained unequal throughout the region early in the twenty-first century.

See also Catholic schools, Independent schools, and Public schools.

Kenneth T. Jackson

Schrafft's. Chain of restaurants that began in 1898 as a candy and ice cream shop opened by Frank Garrett Shattuck on the site now occupied by Macy's; the candy and ice cream were supplied by William Schrafft and Sons of Boston. By 1910 Shattuck owned a number of shops and had added a luncheon menu. Schrafft's became known as a genteel meeting place where ladies ate before attending a matinee or after shopping. The restaurants continued to operate after Shattuck's death in 1937, and by 1950 they numbered more than 50 in New York City. Schrafft's began to decline in the 1960s, and its last branch closed in the 1980s.

Howard Kaplan

Schuetzen Park. Popular amusement park in Queens, opened on 16 May 1870 on 7 acres (3 hectares) at the southeast corner of Broadway and Steinway Street in Long Island City. The area was heavily German; the name refers to target shooting, a favorite attraction in amusement parks of the period. The park also had a hotel, picnic grounds, bowling alleys, dancing pavilions, taverns, and eventually movie theaters; it became a popular venue for outings by churches, labor unions, and political groups. It was irreparably damaged by Prohibition and the advent of the automobile and closed in 1924. The land was sold for residential and retail development.

Vincent Seyfried

Schultz, Dutch [Flegenheimer, Arthur] (*b* Bronx, 6 Aug 1902; *d* Newark, N.J., 24 Oct 1935). Racketeer and extortionist. By the mid-1920s, he was a bartender and took advantage of Prohibition to become a major figure in organized crime in New York City. He formed a gang, cornered the beer market in the Bronx, and seized control of numbers rackets in Harlem. Violent and erratic, he was fond of reading about himself in the newspapers. He also exploited a connection to Tammany Hall: his patron was James Hines, the Democratic district leader for lower western Harlem and Morningside Heights. Hines was later convicted of protecting Schultz. In 1935, Schultz proposed to several associates in Murder Incorporated, including Lucky Luciano and Meyer Lansky, that they assassinate the federal prosecutor Thomas E. Dewey, who was preparing a case against him. After his plan was rejected he declared his intention of carrying out the assassination himself. He was shot and mortally wounded soon after, on the orders of crime figures from Murder Incorporated who disapproved of his plans. He survived for nearly two days in the hospital where his wife staged a deathbed conversion to Catholicism for the purpose of establishing a proprietary claim over his two other undivorced wives. Schultz is buried in Gate of Heaven Cemetery in Westchester County.

Paul Sann, *Kill the Dutchman! The Story of Dutch Schultz* (New York: Arlington House, 1971)

Robert W. Snyder

Schuman, William (Howard) (*b* New York City, 4 Aug 1910; *d* New York City, 15 Feb 1992). Composer. In high school he formed a jazz ensemble in which he played the piano, the violin, the clarinet, the saxophone, and the banjo and occasionally sang. In 1933 he entered Teachers College (BS 1935); he then joined the faculty at Sarah Lawrence College (1935) and earned an MA from Columbia University (1937). His Symphony no. 3, which had its world premiere on 17 October 1941, won the first New York Music Critics Circle Award and made him a national figure. *A Free Song,* a cantata to a text by Walt Whitman, was given its premiere on 26 March 1943 and later won the first Pulitzer Prize in music. In 1945 he resigned from Sarah Lawrence to become director of publications for G. Schirmer; within the year he became president of the Juilliard School of Music. At Juilliard he merged the Institute of Musical Art with the Juilliard Graduate School, while remaining active as a composer of works such as the score for Martha Graham's *Judith.* In January 1962 he became president of Lincoln Center for the Performing Arts. His tenure was marked by the introduction of concerts in the city's schools and of the Young People's Concerts by the New York Philharmonic. He resigned in 1969 to return to composing. Schuman was honored in 1985 with a special Pulitzer Prize for the entire body of his work, which includes the frequently performed orchestral work *New England Triptych* (1956), *George Washington Bridge* for concert band (1950), concertos for violin, viola, cello, and piano, choral works, and music for the theater and films.

Flora Rheta Schreiber and Vincent Persichetti, *William Schuman* (New York: G. Schirmer, 1954); Christopher Rouse, *William Schuman Documentary: Biographical Essay, Catalogue of Works, Discography, and Bibliography* (New York: Theodore Presser, 1980)

Allen J. Share

Schurz, Carl (*b* Liblar [now in Germany], 2 March 1829; *d* New York City, 14 May 1906). Statesman, writer, and newspaper editor. He moved to New York City in 1852 as an exiled student leader of the abortive revolution of 1848, then settled in Wisconsin and rose to national prominence within the Republican Party. He gave two speeches at Cooper Union that became well known: one attacking Stephen A. Douglas, Abraham Lincoln's opponent for the presidency (1860), the other seeking public support for emancipating the slaves (1863). He served in the U.S. Senate from Missouri and in President Rutherford B. Hayes's cabinet before returning in 1881 to New York City, where he lived successively in Washington Heights, on East 68th Street, and from 1887 at 175 West 58th Street. He was the editor of the *Evening Post* until 1883 and the chief editorial writer for *Harper's Weekly* from 1892 to 1898. In 1902 he bought a home at 24 East 91st Street from his friend Andrew Carnegie. He led the Civil Service Reform Association of New York from 1893 to 1906 and played a vital part in mayoral elections. To the end of his life he remained active in local and national politics. The park in which Gracie Mansion is situated is named for him.

Hans Trefouse, *Carl Schurz: A Biography* (Knoxville: University of Tennessee Press, 1982)

Edward T. O'Donnell

Carl Schurz

Schuyler, George (Samuel) (*b* Providence, R.I., 25 Feb 1895; *d* New York City, 31 Aug 1977). Journalist and social commentator. Known as the Sage of Sugar Hill, he was one of the most influential intellectuals of the Harlem Renaissance. Despite an early interest in socialism, he drifted to the political right. He later gained notoriety as a congressional candidate of the Conservative Party against Adam Clayton Powell, Jr.

Jeffrey B. Ferguson, *The Sage of Sugar Hill: George S. Schuyler and the Harlem Renaissance* (New Haven: Yale University Press, 2005)

Kenneth T. Jackson

Schuyler, Louisa Lee (*b* New York City, 26 Oct 1837; *d* Highland Falls, N.Y., 10 Oct 1926). Philanthropist and reformer. As the corresponding secretary of the Women's Central Association of Relief (1861–65) she worked closely with the U.S. Sanitary Commission to care for Union soldiers and recruited the assistance of Gertrude Stevens Rice, Grace Hoadley Dodge, and Josephine Shaw Lowell. She formed the State Charities Aid Association (1872), of which she was a leader until her death, and the Bellevue Training School for Nurses (1873), the first institution of its kind in the United States. In 1907 she became a director of the Russell Sage Foundation, and in 1915 she launched the National Committee for the Prevention of Blindness.

Sarah Henry Lederman

Schuyler, Montgomery (*b* Ithaca, N.Y., 19 Aug 1843; *d* New Rochelle, N.Y., 16 July 1914). Journalist, editor, and architectural critic. He began at the *World* in the 1860s and then moved to the *New York Times* where he remained an editorial writer and critic until 1907. He was also an editor at *Harper's Weekly* and wrote for numerous magazines, including *Architectural Record,* where he promoted the advancement of American architecture, especially in the new form of the skyscraper.

Montgomery Schuyler, *American Architecture and Other Writings,* ed. William H. Jordy and Ralph Coe (Cambridge, Mass.: Harvard University Press, 1961)

Peter L. Donhauser

Schuylerville. Neighborhood in the eastern Bronx, bounded to the north by the intersection of East Tremont Avenue and the Bruckner Expressway, to the east by East Tremont Avenue, to the south by Route 95 and St. Raymond's Cemetery, and to the west by the Hutchinson River Parkway. The area was settled about 1840 by Irish stonemasons, gardeners, and laborers who worked on estates in Throgs Neck. In the early twenty-first century it consists mostly of one-family houses and remains largely unchanged since 1920. Many who live in the neighborhood consider themselves residents of Throgs Neck.

Gary D. Hermalyn

Schwartz, Delmore (David) (*b* New York City, 8 Dec 1913; *d* New York City, 11 July 1966). Poet and short-story writer. Of Romanian background, he lived in Brooklyn until his family moved in 1921 to an apartment building on 179th Street in Washington Heights. He attended George Washington High School and then New York University (BA in philosophy 1935). His modernistic, largely autobiographical poems include "Shenandoah" (1941) and "Genesis, Book 1" (1943), which capture the life and customs of Jewish immigrants in New York City. *The World Is a Wedding* (1948) is a collection of stories portraying the Jewish middle class in New York City during the Depression.

James Atlas, *Delmore Schwartz: The Life of an American Poet* (New York: Farrar, Straus and Giroux, 1977)

Robert Morrow

science. During the eighteenth century science in New York City was largely derivative of European traditions, ideas, and institutions. Scientific books and instruments were lacking, local scientific institutions were inadequate, and the popular attitude toward science was on the whole one of indifference. The indebtedness to Europe was exemplified by the career of the New York scientist Cadwallader Colden, who received his medical education in London and sent most of his scientific papers there for publication by the Royal Society. After 1750 conditions in the city gradually began to improve with the formation of the Society for the Promotion of Arts, Agriculture, and Economy (1764) and the King's College Medical School (1767), and the launching of a campaign for the New-York Hospital (1771), but science and medicine suffered during the seven years of British occupation occasioned by the American Revolution.

The King's College Medical School was the only place in New York City where science was taught and where any research was taking place until the Society for Promoting Agriculture, Arts, and Manufactures was formed in 1791 by Samuel Latham Mitchill, a professor of natural history, chemistry, and agriculture at Columbia College and a central figure in the scientific community in the city for many years: he was the editor of the first medical journal in the United States (the *Medical Repository,* 1797), a member of the U.S. House of Representatives (from 1801), the first occupant of the chair of chemistry at the College of Physicians and Surgeons (1807), and a founder of the New-York Literary and Philosophical Society (with DeWitt Clinton and David Hosack, 1814) and the Lyceum of Natural History (1817, serving as president until 1823). In the early decades of the nineteenth century scientific and medical societies in the city continued to enjoy little general support. The New-York Literary and Philosophical Society was ineffective (dissolved in 1834), and the medical profession was crippled by internal feuding. The Lyceum of Natural History was the only institution to achieve even modest success; it published a journal from 1823 and moved into its own building in 1835, which it was forced to sell in 1844. On the whole science and learning were far healthier in Philadelphia, notwithstanding its economic and political decline after 1800.

In the years after the Civil War the condition of science in New York City improved. After the natural history collections of the Lyceum were destroyed by fire in May 1866, a campaign to raise funds for a museum of natural history was begun by a small group of patricians working in conjunction with the city. In 1871 the state legislature agreed to provide $30,000 a year to maintain the new museum, and the city provided land to the west of Central Park between 77th and 81st Streets; President Ulysses S. Grant formally opened the American Museum of Natural History in June 1874. During the same period Columbia experienced rapid growth, and by 1900 it was the center of academic scientific research in the United States. Under the leadership of Frederick Barnard (1809–89) it added a school of mines and formed an affiliation with the College of Physicians and Surgeons. The faculty of the School of Mines included Thomas Egleston (1832–1900), John Strong Newberry (1822–92), and Charles F. Chandler (1836–1925), who was largely responsible for the rapid growth of the school into a center of scientific research (he was also a president of the city's Board of Health and a founder in 1876 of the American Chemical Society).

Although science in New York City in the final decades of the nineteenth century was increasingly controlled by professionals, avocational scientists were catered to by such groups as the Torrey Botanical Club, the Linnaean Society of New York, the West Side Natural History Society, the New-York Microscopical Society, the Hulst Botanical Club of Brooklyn, the New York Mineralogical Club, the Bronx Society of Arts and Sciences, and the New York Mathematical Society. The New York Botanical Garden, formed by Nathaniel Lord Britton (1859–1934) under the auspices of the Torrey Botanical Club, opened in 1896 on 500 acres (200 hectares) of land in the Bronx and soon began a sustained program of scientific research. The New York Zoological Society was organized with public and private support in 1895 by George B. Grinnell (1849–1938), a prominent explorer and conservationist who as secretary of the society ensured that the New York Zoological Park would serve an educational function and adhere to principles of wildlife conservation.

Science in the city was eventually dominated by Columbia and the American Museum of Natural History. Academic PSYCHOLOGY developed largely through the efforts of James McKeen Cattell, professor of psychology at Columbia from 1891 to 1917 and editor of *Science* and *Popular Science Monthly.* At Columbia he was responsible for the appointment to the faculty of the philosopher John Dewey and had many students who became influential psychologists (among them, Edward L. Thorndike, whose later work at Teachers College emphasized the connections in learning between stimulus and response); his influence also extended to the New School for Social Research, where John B. Watson taught during the 1920s, and his interest in statistics gave American psychology a bias toward quantification. Other prominent psychologists in the city included Harry Stack Sullivan (1892–1949), founder of the journal *Psychiatry,* and Karen Horney (1885–1952), who taught at the New School and in 1941 helped form the Association for the Advancement of Psychoanalysis.

About the turn of the twentieth century Columbia and the American Museum of Natural History reached an agreement that proved particularly fruitful for ANTHROPOLOGY and the related fields of ethnology and folklore. Franz Boas joined the museum in 1896 as an assistant curator of ethnology; appointed professor of anthropology at Columbia in 1899, he reoriented the discipline in the United States from an evolutionary perspective to a relativistic and contextual one emphasizing empirical fieldwork. At Barnard College Ruth Benedict studied Zuni culture and as a result of studies undertaken as part of the war effort published *The Chrysanthemum and the Sword: Patterns of Japanese Culture* (1946), which became widely influential. Margaret Mead (1901–78), who like Boas and Benedict saw anthropology as the comprehensive study of culture, focused in such earlier works as *Coming of Age in Samoa* (1928) on the importance of adolescence, child rearing, and sex roles in the cultural patterning of human behavior; in her later studies on enculturation she adopted photography as a methodological tool, introduced biological processes in the analysis of culture, and stressed the importance of interactions between mother and infant. For 45 years she was a central figure at the American Museum of Natural History, where her work resulted in 44 books and more than 1000 articles and monographs. Ashley Montagu (1905–99), who received his doctorate in anthropology from Columbia in 1937, reached a large audience with his writings, in which he argued against the usefulness of race as an anthropological concept and tied together the cultural and biological branches of anthropology. The influence of Boas and the adherents of the brand of anthropology associated with Columbia and Barnard College was furthered through such organizations as the American Anthropological Association, the American Ethnological Society (formed in New York City in 1842 by Albert Gallatin), and the American Folklore Society and through such publications as the *Journal of American Folklore,* edited by both Boas (1908–24) and Benedict (1925–40).

In the late nineteenth century natural history became transformed into academic BIOLOGY. There was also a growing perception that medical therapeutics depended on advanced scientific research. Against this background the Rockefeller Institute for Medical Research was founded in 1901 by John D. Rockefeller, whose desire to establish a medical research institute had been made more immediate by the sudden death from scarlet fever of his grandson. To enable the scientific staff to pursue original research untrammeled by teaching demands, the institute remained independent from the university medical schools in the city. By 1910 there were 30 laboratory scientists at Rockefeller and eight physicians at its associated hospital; the scientific staff edited the *Journal of General Physiology* and the *Journal of Experimental Medicine* and played a leading role in opposing an antivivisection campaign being waged at the time. The director of the institute from 1901 to 1935 was Simon Flexner, professor of pathology at the University of Pennsylvania, during whose tenure many important scientific discoveries were made, including the application of physical chemistry to living tissues by Jacques Loeb, studies of blood antigens by Karl Landsteiner, and the crystallization of the tobacco mosaic virus by Wendell Stanley (1904–71).

The American Museum of Natural History continued to flourish. Carl Akeley (1864–1926) went to Africa in 1909 and 1921 on behalf of the museum and returned with the elephants and gorillas that became the centerpieces for its African Hall. Roy Chapman Andrews (1884–1960), an expert on cetaceans who joined the museum in 1906, studied whales and whaling in the Dutch East Indies in 1909. In 1916 he became interested in the theory advanced by Henry Fairfield Osborn that Asia was the origin of reptilian and mammalian life, and after raising funds from John D. Rockefeller and J. P. Morgan he led five major expeditions to central Asia, where he uncovered many fossil specimens of early mammals and dinosaurs, demonstrated that Outer Mongolia was the oldest area of continuously dry land, and found implements dating back 20,000 years. His spectacular discovery of dinosaur eggs in the Gobi Desert in 1928 gave the museum an international reputation in the popular press. Andrews was later a vice director (1931–34) and director (1935–42) of the museum.

At the Rockefeller Institute studies were reoriented toward the investigation of life at the cytological level by Flexner's successor Herbert S. Gasser (1888–1963), a professor of physiology at Cornell University who won the Nobel Prize in 1944 for his studies of the electrophysiology of nerve impulses. He was himself succeeded in 1953 by Detlev W. Bronk, who in 1956 announced that the institute would become a graduate university with doctoral programs in the biological sciences. During these years many scientists at Rockefeller received the Nobel Prize: John Northrop (1891–1987) and Wendell Stanley in 1946 for research on the crystallization of enzymes, Fritz Lipmann (1899–1986) in 1953 for his discovery of coenzyme A, Joshua Lederberg in 1958 for work on the genetic material in bacteria, Gerald Edelman (*b* 1929) in 1972 for determining the chemical structure of immunoglobulins, David Baltimore in 1975 for research on the interaction between tumor viruses and the genetic material of the cell, and R. Bruce Merrifield (1921–2006) in 1984 for synthesizing peptides.

Columbia played a prominent role in the development of PHYSICS as an academic discipline. By 2009, 24 Nobel Prizes in physics had been awarded to its faculty and former students. Among these were prizes to Enrico Fermi in 1938 for work on neutron bombardment, I. I. Rabi in 1944 for his studies of molecular beams, Tsung-Dao Lee (*b* 1926) in 1957 for his demonstration that the conservation of parity was not applicable to weak interactions, James Rainwater (1917–86) and Aage Bohr (1922–2009) in 1975 for their research into the structure of the atomic nucleus, and Jack Steinberger, Melvin Schwartz, and Leon Lederman in 1988 for their discovery of muon neutrinos and electron neutrinos.

New York City early became a center for applied science and technology, and especially for electrical engineering. Thomas Edison worked in the city from April 1869, where he effected improvements to stock tickers and devised methods of sending multiple messages over a single wire. Elmer Sperry, an entrepreneur who worked in Brooklyn and formed the Sperry Gyroscope Company, concentrated on innovations to the electric streetcar and the automobile. Nikola Tesla moved to New York City in 1884 and worked on alternating-current dynamos, transformers, and motors; he gave remarkable demonstrations of electrical phenomena that impressed local audiences, and made and lost several fortunes. Edwin H. Armstrong and Lee De Forest, two pioneers in radio transmission, fought each other for many years over patent infringement. De Forest invented the triode in 1906 and Armstrong, who had studied with Michael Pupin at Columbia, soon after invented the triode feedback (regenerative) circuit and later was an innovator in frequency-modulation (FM) radio transmission. Chester F. Carlson perfected a dry copying process in his laboratory in a rented room in Astoria, where the first successfully photocopied image was made in October 1938. At Bell Telephone Laboratories (which was based in New York City before moving to New Jersey in 1947) the scientists William Shockley (1910–89), Walter Brattain (1902–87), and John Bardeen (1908–91) discovered that germanium crystals containing impurities were highly efficient rectifiers of alternating current. In 1948 Shockley invented the transistor by combining solid-state rectifiers to amplify electrical current, effecting a revolution in electronics by allowing for the miniaturization of radios and computers. Shockley, Brattain, and Bardeen received the Nobel Prize in 1956. Charles Townes (*b* 1915), who was associated with Columbia from 1948 after working at Bell Laboratories, used Shockley's work in solid-state physics to develop the maser in 1953. Theodore Maiman developed a maser using visible light; the first laser was constructed in 1960. Research proceeded rapidly during the 1980s: at a meeting in the city in 1987 of the American Physical Society scientists described superconductors effective at 90 kelvin (−183 degrees Celsius, −362 degrees Fahrenheit), thus presaging the practical application of superconductivity.

In the twenty-first century New York City continues to be a center for science research, studies, and employment, especially at New York University, Columbia University, City College of New York, New York–Presbyterian Hospital, and Memorial Sloan-Kettering Cancer Center. These institutions and others focus on topics such as global warming, stem cell research, and robotics. Columbia University researchers, for instance, developed models for predicting the city's future through the years 2030 and 2100 showing possible increases in sea level due to global warming. The nonprofit New York Stem Cell Foundation on Amsterdam Avenue works to further stem cell research, inform the public about developments, and build better facilities for equipment and resources. Honeybee Robotics Spacecraft Mechanisms Corporation is based in New York City and is responsible for creating and supplying robotic mechanisms for industrial and exploration purposes, and Mount Sinai School of Medicine has an entire department dedicated to robotic oncology.

Simon Baatz, *Knowledge, Culture, and Science in the Metropolis: The New York Academy of Sciences, 1817–1970* (New York: New York Academy of Sciences, 1990)

Simon Baatz, Danielle Molinski

Science and Society. Quarterly journal of Marxist thought and analysis launched in New York City in the fall of 1936 by left-wing intellectuals. It had no official affiliation with or funding from any political party. Its early readership included many in the nonacademic political left, and the initial editorial board included scholars from New York University, the Massachusetts Institute of Technology, and Harvard University, along with an associated group of British scientists who wrote critically on such subjects as Lysenkoism. Columbia University professor Bernhard J. Stern was the journal's mainstay for its first two decades. The journal's main subject matter was Marxism in all of its ramifications: in art, education, literature, science, linguistics, political economy, mathematics, and in such aspects of history as slavery, the Reconstruction era, and the American and French Revolutions. The cold war directly affected the magazine, as several of its editors were forced out of their teaching positions. Subscriptions declined, and many former writers abandoned Marxism or were fearful of connections with a left-wing magazine. Nikita Khrushchev's disclosure of Stalin's crimes in 1956 prompted contributors to recognize the greater complexity of Marxist concepts. The English translation of Marx's 1844 *Economic and Philosophical Manuscripts* in the mid-1960s also encouraged new left academics to submit a wider range of essays and reviews. Articles on the ideological and political concerns of the Third World appeared in the journal, along with such issues as feminism, ecology, civil rights and liberation struggles, often contributed by younger scholars. In the twenty-first century its offices were at 451 West Street.

David Goldway, "Fifty Years of Science & Society," *Science and Society* 50.3 (Fall 1986); David F. Price, "Theoretical Dangers: The FBI Investigation of Science & Society," *Science and Society* 68.4 (Winter, 2004–5)

See also Communism, McCarthyism.

Marvin E. Gettleman

Scorsese, Martin (Marcantonio Luciano) (*b* Queens, 17 Nov 1942). Filmmaker. He grew up in Little Italy in Manhattan and during the early 1960s attended New York University, where he earned a graduate degree in the film school (MFA 1969). His first major film was *Mean Streets* (1972), a tale of petty gangsters on the Lower East Side. He earned national renown for *Taxi Driver* (1976), a violent, haunting study of a tormented taxicab driver's search for redemption in a deteriorating New York City. His later films offer an unusual, fascinating, and often controversial picture of the city. They include *New York, New York* (1977), a nostalgic story of a jazz musician; *Raging Bull* (1980), based on the life of the prizefighter Jake La Motta; the eccentric comedy *After Hours* (1985); the short film "Life's Lessons," part of the triptych *New York Stories* (1989); *Goodfellas* (1990), an epic of organized crime; an adaptation of Edith Wharton's *The Age of Innocence* (1993); and *Gangs of New York* (2002).

James Bradley

Scots. Until the 1760s most Scottish settlers in colonial New York were Lowlanders. One of the first to achieve prominence was Richard Nicolls, a member of the Scottish gentry appointed by James, Duke of York, to seize New Netherland and set up English colonial headquarters there. Scots played an important role in a rebellion led by Jacob Leisler in 1689 (suppressed in 1691 by Captain Kidd, a native of Greenock). After the Act of Union in 1707 Scotland was allowed to trade with the American colonies. Archibald Kennedy (1685–1763), a British colonial official, moved to the city in 1710 and later served on the city's council (1721–32), and a number of Scots were New York colonial governors: Robert Hunter of Ayrshire took office in 1710, followed by William Burnet in September 1720 and John Montgomerie in April 1728. James Alexander of Stirling, an exile of the Jacobite rebellion of 1715, attacked Governor William Cosby in pamphlets published by John Peter Zenger; this helped lead to Zenger's trial, in which Alexander briefly served as a counsel for the defense until he was removed from the roll of attorneys. A charity organization known as the Scots Society, formed in 1744, became a forerunner of the St. Andrew's Society (1756), later the most important organization of its kind in the city.

Intellectual life in colonial New York City was enriched by graduates of the University of Edinburgh who moved to the city to teach and continue their studies in theology, medicine, and philosophy. Philip Livingston and William Alexander helped to form King's College (now Columbia University) in 1754. Founders of its medical school (1767) included James Smith and John van Brugh Tennent (graduates of Edinburgh) and Peter Middleton. Cadwallader Colden of Dunse was lieutenant governor from August 1760 to June 1775, his tenure interrupted by the brief terms of several governors. Scots were largely responsible for introducing Presbyterianism to the city. In 1761 John Mason (1734–92) of Linlithgowshire moved to the city to lead the Scottish Presbyterian Church on Cedar Street. He and his son John Mitchell Mason were among the most important ministers of the time. Archibald Laidlie gave the first sermon in English to a Dutch Reformed congregation, and Charles Inglis became a prominent figure in the Episcopal Church. Highlanders settled in the city increasingly after the end of the Seven Years' War in 1763. Some were exiles of the Jacobite rebellions, but most sought relief from poverty and high rents in Scotland. They often faced discrimination in the colony, as many were Catholic and spoke Gaelic.

During the American Revolution Scots were suspected of remaining loyal to the Crown. Those in the city were more evenly divided in their allegiances than those in other parts of the colonies. The Presbyterian clergy supported the Revolution; Highlanders who had settled recently in the city were usually Loyalists, as were merchants, many of whom continued to do business throughout the war. A number of Highlanders joined the patriot cause: under Donald McLeod in June 1775 they presented a petition to the state legislature promising to serve the colonies if they were allowed to wear their traditional dress, which had been outlawed in Scotland in 1745. Of the 21 members of the St. Andrew's Society, 11 were Loyalists. The merchant Robert Bruce remained loyal; his brother Peter Bruce, also a merchant, became a revolutionary. Alexander MacDougall helped to organize the Sons of Liberty in the city, was a general in the Continental army, and served in the Continental Congress. Alexander McDonald, a Highlander who had fought in the Seven Years' War, secretly recruited 100 men on Staten Island to fight for the British.

There were 22,006 people of Scottish birth or descent in the city in 1790. Scottish gardeners and landscapers were well known, among them Grant Thorburn, who moved to the city in 1794 from Dalkieth and later wrote his memoirs under the pseudonym Laurie Todd. During the same year Jane (Jeffrey) Renwick, the subject of Robert Burns's poems "I Gead a Waefu' Gate Yestreen" and "When First I Sae Jeannie's Face," made her way to the city, where Renwick Street was named for her (her grandson was the architect James Renwick). Scots were active in financial affairs and several helped to form the Bank of New York. Archibald Gracie of Dumfries led the Chamber of Commerce from 1800 to 1825, and Isabella Graham and her daughter Joanna Bethune organized the Sunday school movement in the city. Scottish national holidays were celebrated, among them Hogmanay (New Year's Eve) and St. Andrew's Day (30 November), and as early as 1820 the St. Andrew's Society held a banquet on 25 January to honor Burns's birth. By the 1820s a number of taverns and boarding houses were popular among Scots, including the Caledonian House on Gold Street, John O'Groat's House on Essex Street, the Waverly House on Fulton Street, the Burns House on Liberty Street, and the Weaver's Arms and Tavern on Hudson Street. At the first meeting of the Highland Society of New York in 1836 such traditional games as throwing the heavy hammer, putting the heavy stone, and caber tossing were held; quoits and curling also were popular.

The Scottish population grew especially after the English lifted their ban on the emigration of craftspeople in 1825. Many skilled laborers, especially textile workers and stonecutters, moved to the city, where at mid-century stonemasons' wages were two to three times higher than in Britain. Nearly a fifth of Scottish workers were in the building trades at this time, and many of them became active in such labor organizations as the New York Union Society of Journeymen House Carpenters. In 1835 James Gordon Bennett, Sr., produced the first issue of the *New York Herald* in his apartment on Wall Street. A number of Scottish publications were also launched, among them the *Scottish-Patriot* (1840–42; later renamed the *Scottish Journal of Intelligence and Literature*), the *Scottish American*, a journal published from 1857 to 1925, and the *Scotsman and Caledonian Advertiser* (1874–76). The Caledonian Club (1861) sponsored traditional games. Many Scottish business leaders became philanthropists, among them James Lenox, who donated the Lenox Library to the city in 1870; Archibald Russell, who formed the Five Points Mission; John M. Kennedy, who donated the Public Charities Building; Alexander Robertson, who built a school for poor children that bears his name; and Andrew Carnegie, a native of Dunfermline, who gave away most of his fortune. A statue of the novelist Sir Walter Scott was installed on the Central Park Mall in 1872, the 100th anniversary of his birth; a statue of Burns facing this was added in 1880 (both were the work of John Steel of Edinburgh). The first golf course in the metropolitan area, St. Andrew's, was laid out in suburban Yonkers, New York, in 1887 by John Reid of Dunfermline and Robert Scott.

During six weeks in the spring of 1887, an especially difficult year in Scotland, 2000 Scots sailed to the city seeking work. The number of Scottish immigrants increased again in the 1930s and 1940s, but Scots accounted for an ever declining share of the city's population. One native of Scotland who achieved renown as a baseball player was Bobby Thomson, who hit a memorable home run to win the National League pennant for the New York Giants in 1951. Helen MacInnes, a resident of the city, wrote many spy novels. James B. "Scotty" Reston (*b* Scotland, 1909; *d* 1995) joined the *New York Times* in 1940 and twice won the Pulitzer Prize. Early in the twenty-first century Scottish organizations in the city included the St. Andrew's Society and the American–Scottish Foundation, with offices at Lenox Hill, and the New York Caledonian Society, which operated from the Second Presbyterian Church at 96th Street and Central Park West.

Walter Friedman

Scott, Winfield (*b* Laurel Branch, Va., 13 July 1786; *d* West Point, N.Y., 29 May 1866). General. A hero of the War of 1812, he became known as "Old Fuss and Feathers." On his return from the Mexican War in 1848 he was given a rousing reception in New York City. He settled in Manhattan in 1852 when a group of friends led by Senator Hamilton Fish bought him a four-story brownstone at 24 West 12th Street (now the Scott House National Historic Landmark). During the same year he sought the presidency as a Whig but was soundly defeated by Franklin Pierce, the Democratic candidate. Scott maintained his home on 12th Street until his death.

James Bradley

sculpture. Sculpture in colonial New York City was limited to ornaments of various kinds until a number of commissions were given for public statues in the late eighteenth century. Beaux-arts sculptures treating civic themes remained popular until World War I, when changing attitudes and increasing numbers of private commissions allowed sculptors to develop new styles and treat a greater range of subjects.

1. To 1920

In New Amsterdam and colonial New York gravestones, architectural ornaments, shop signs, and figureheads were typical sculptural forms. The first public sculptures in the city were executed by Joseph Wilton (1722–1803), sculptor for George III. One depicted the king (1770, formerly at Bowling Green) and the other William Pitt the Elder, commemorating his role in repealing the Stamp Act (1770, formerly at Wall and William streets). A mob toppled the statue of George III after the Declaration of Independence was read in July 1776, and British soldiers retaliated by decapitating the statue of Pitt in November.

After the Revolutionary War a bronze statue of the lawyer James Watt (1830, Metropolitan Museum of Art) was commissioned from Robert Ball Hughes (1806–68), who in April 1835 made the first marble statue in the United States, a portrait of Alexander Hamilton for the New York Merchants' Exchange (destroyed during the Great Fire in December). A larger marble monument to John Wells was commissioned from John Frazee (1790–1852) for St. Paul's Chapel (1824). A gallery of busts modeled on masks of Thomas Jefferson and other leaders was executed by John Henri Isaac Browere (1790–1834). A group of merchants led by the shipping magnate James Lee raised subscriptions for an equestrian statue of George Washington in 1852. Cast in bronze by Henry Kirke Brown (1814–86) and John Quincy Adams Ward, it was raised in Union Square in 1856.

Soldiers from the city who were killed in the Civil War were commemorated by monuments such as Ward's Seventh Regiment Memorial (1869, Central Park at West 69th Street). Other war memorials include the bronzes *Army* and *Navy* (1901) by Frederick MacMonnies for the Soldiers' and Sailors' Arch (designed by John Duncan) at Grand Army Plaza in Brooklyn; the Soldiers' and Sailors' Monument (1902,

Equestrian statue of Washington by John Quincy Adams Ward, east side of Union Square at Fourth Avenue, ca *1870*

89th Street and Riverside Drive) by Charles W. Stoughton (1860–1944), Arthur A. Stoughton (1867–1955), and Paul M. DuBoy; and *Admiral David Glasgow Farragut* (1881, Madison Square Park) and *William Tecumseh Sherman* (1902, Grand Army Plaza) by Augustus Saint-Gaudens with Stanford White. Only a few memorials depicted black soldiers. Ward's *Freedman* (1863, Metropolitan Museum), a bronze statue of a stern, powerful black man who has broken his shackles, was never made into a public monument. Bronze statues depicting critics of slavery include *William H. Seward* (1876, Madison Square), by Randolph Rogers (1825–92); *William Earl Dodge* (1885, Bryant Park), *Horace Greeley* (1890, City Hall Park), and *Henry Ward Beecher* (1891, Columbus Park, Brooklyn) by Ward; and *Horace Greeley* (1892, 32nd Street between Broadway and Sixth Avenue) by Alexander Doyle (1857–1922). The small plaster statuettes by John Rogers (1829–1904) helped to interest a large middle-class audience in American sculpture; his sometimes controversial subjects include *Fugitive's Story* (1869, New-York Historical Society) and *Slave Auction* (1879, New-York Historical Society).

Civic and ethnic pride inspired Irish, Italian, and German groups in the 1870s and 1880s to donate statues of well-known figures from their native countries. In Central Park this included *Giuseppe Mazzini* (1876, West Drive at 68th Street) by Giovanni Turini (1841–99), *Ludwig von Beethoven* (1884, the Mall) by Henry Baerer (1837–1908), and *Robert Burns* (1880, the Mall) by Sir John Steel (1804–91). During these years sculptors became well respected, and better training became available in the city at Cooper Union, the National Academy of Design, and the Art Students League, and in Paris at the École des Beaux-Arts and in ateliers. Typical of the era were MacMonnies's *Nathan Hale* (1890, City Hall Park, bronze), Saint-Gaudens's *Richard Randall* (1884, Sailors' Snug Harbor, bronze) and *Admiral David Glasgow Farragut.* Sculptors often collaborated with such architects as White and Richard Morris Hunt, whose ideal of a beautiful city required monuments and architectural sculpture and influenced public sculpture for the next quarter century. Inspired by the gift from France of Frédéric-Auguste Bartholdi's *Statue of Liberty* (1886) and by a sculptural program celebrating cultural unity at the World's Columbian Exposition of 1893 in Chicago, the city's elite sponsored programs of public art expressing the ideals of civic harmony, patriotism, civilization, and good government.

The National Sculpture Society (NSS) was formed in May 1893 and became associated with the Municipal Art Society and the Fine Arts Federation (FAF), organizations dedicated to beautifying New York City. Members of the NSS took part in public sculpture projects such as the temporary Dewey Arch at the intersection of Broadway, Fifth Avenue, and 24th Street (1899). With their supporters they also sought to ensure that prime locations were used only for works that met with their approval, and they worked to prevent citizens' groups from placing what they believed were poorly executed portraits of well-known Italians, Irish, and Germans on various sites in Manhattan. Controversy attended the raising of the Columbus Monument (1892, Columbus Circle) by Gaetano Russo, and in 1898 the NSS and the FAF prevented the city from placing the Heine Memorial Fountain (1900,

Lorelei Fountain in Joyce Kilmer Park in the Bronx, commemorating Heinrich Heine's "Die Lorelei," 1899

Judith Weller, The Garment Worker *(1984), 2009*

Joyce Kilmer Park) by Ernst Herter (1846–1917), a gift from the Arion Society, on a site at 58th Street and Fifth Avenue (now occupied by Pulitzer Fountain [1916] by Thomas Hastings [1860–1929] and Karl Bitter). Republican politicians were especially eager to sponsor sculpture for public buildings: their commissions included *Four Continents* (1907) by Daniel Chester French and 12 limestone statues of ancient and contemporary commercial seafaring powers for the cornices of the U.S. Custom House. The government also commissioned allegorical sculptures as an important tool for educating the public, especially immigrants. Complex sculptural programs like those of the Brooklyn Institute of Arts and Sciences and the New York City Hall of Records (1907) were aimed at hastening assimilation.

During the second decade of the twentieth century, some sculptors, including Abastenia St. Leger Eberle and Saul Baizerman, depicted workers and common people. The only public works by women were Anna Hyatt Huntington's *Joan of Arc* (1915, Riverside Drive and 93rd Street), the only statue of a woman erected in the city at the time; and Gertrude Vanderbilt Whitney's Washington Heights–Inwood War Memorial (1922, Broadway between 167th and 168th streets). Disputes over public sculpture remained heated: there were conflicts over the Maine Memorial (1913, Columbus Circle) and the Firemen's Memorial (1913, Riverside Drive and 100th Street) by H. Van Buren Magonigle (1867–1935) and Attilio Piccirilli (1868–1945), and a fierce controversy over MacMonnies's *Civic Virtue* (1922, Queens Boulevard at Union Turnpike), which signaled the breakdown of public support for large sculptures funded by the government.

During the 1920s the number of commissions increased for sculptures of children and animals for private gardens. Sculpture of a far more irreverent sort was produced by Marcel Duchamp, who settled in New York City in June 1915 and became a leader of the dadaist movement. One of his particularly notorious pieces was a urinal that he titled *Fountain* and signed with the name "R. Mutt"; it was rejected by the Society of Independent Artists for its inaugural exhibition in 1917.

2. After 1920

After World War I works still emphasized the beaux-arts ideals of civic virtue and public heroism, but to some critics they appeared increasingly ponderous, cluttered, and outmoded, and modernism gradually influenced change. The first welded metal sculptures were produced in the 1930s, and Chaim Gross became a well-known proponent of direct carving. Little public sculpture was created in the city during the Depression. From 1925 to 1950 a group of private developers led by John D. Rockefeller, Jr., commissioned major figurative and decorative sculptures for Rockefeller Center. The first phase of building was during 1931–40: two oversized, free-standing, figural sculptures of mythic Greek figures were erected, the streamlined and elegant *Prometheus* by Paul Manship (1934, gilded bronze, lower level of plaza) and the geometric and overpowering *Atlas* by Lee Lawrie (1937, bronze, 630 Fifth Avenue); Isamu Noguchi's sculpture *News* (1939–40, stainless steel casting, 50 Rockefeller Center Plaza) was installed over the entrance of the Associated Press Building. After 1945 there were several attempts to erect a major war memorial; although widely supported, all failed because of insufficient funds. A number of peace memorials were erected at the United Nations headquarters (1947–53), and a small number of traditional, heroic memorial sculptures were constructed with private funds, as at Central Park South and Seventh Avenue, where a group of statues depicts Latin American heroes; among the best-known is Huntington's *José Martí* (1959, bronze).

Apart from public memorials, sculpture after World War II was highly diverse. Among the first sculptors to incorporate surrealist elements was Joseph Cornell, who became internationally known for his assemblages of varied objects such as news clippings, toys, and maps contained in small boxes. In 1941 Jacques Lipchitz settled in the city and concentrated on autobiographical subjects in such works as *Mother and Child II* (1941–45, bronze). Duchamp returned to the city in 1942, and between 1945 and 1950 Herbert Ferber launched his career as a surrealist. During the 1950s abstract expressionists were influential. The most important was David Smith, whose works of welded steel expressed a concern with universal themes common to the art of the postwar era. In the 1960s minimalism became popular; Carl Andre, Donald Judd, Robert Morris, and Tony Smith created work that consisted chiefly of geometric elements that could be manufactured on the basis of the artist's instructions.

During the 1960s and 1970s abstract styles dominated public art. A zoning ordinance known as the "plaza law" (1961) required that developers of new buildings provide an open forecourt at street level, a particularly appropriate place for sculpture. At the Chase Manhattan Bank Plaza, Noguchi executed *Sunken Garden* (1961–64, granite and basalt rocks in a glass enclosure). After a decade Jean Dubuffet's whimsical piece *Group of Four Trees* (1972, fiberglass over aluminum) was added to the plaza. Modern abstract sculpture by already famous artists was also chosen for Lincoln Center (1962–68), a part of the urban redevelopment of the Upper West Side. Alexander Calder's *Le Guichet* (1963, steel painted black) marks the entrance to the New York Public Library for the Performing Arts, and Henry Moore's *Reclining Figure* (1965, bronze) rests in the reflecting pool between Avery Fisher Hall and the Vivian Beaumont Theater.

In 1967, 29 contemporary sculptures were placed throughout Manhattan in an exhibition titled *Sculpture in Environment.* Bernard (Tony) Rosenthal's *Alamo* (1966–67, Astor Place, Corten steel painted black) remained permanently installed on city property. In 1968 Noguchi's rhombohedral sculpture *Red Cube* (1968, welded steel and aluminum) was installed in front of 140 Broadway. Pablo Picasso's *Bust of Sylvette* (1968, sandblasted concrete and basalt), enlarged from a small maquette by the artist, stands 36 feet (11 meters) high in the open area between the three towers of a residential complex at New York University Plaza designed by I. M. Pei (1966, north of Houston Street between Mercer Street and La Guardia Place). In 1971 Doris Freedman formed and directed the Public Arts Council (later known as the Public Art Fund), a private organization that continues to provide temporary displays of public sculpture in a variety of locations.

The World Trade Center (1962–77, Minoru Yamasaki) commissioned Masayuki Nagare's abstract work *World Trade Center Plaza Sculpture* (1967–72, Swedish granite over a steel armature) and Fritz Koenig's *Sphere* for the Plaza Fountain (1968–72, bronze), a work intended to symbolize the idea of peace through trade. Calder's *World Trade Center Stabile* (1969–71, installed 1974, steel painted red) was placed at the entrance to the center on West Street but was moved several times because of construction. James Rosati's *Ideogram* (1967–73, stainless steel), commissioned from a model executed in 1962, was the most successful of the exterior pieces. A notable interior relief by Louise Nevelson, *Sky Gate New York* (1977–78, lobby of 1 World Trade Center, wood painted black), was intended to convey the experience of seeing the city at night. All were destroyed in the terrorist attacks of 11 September 2001 except the Koenig. Its crushed remains served as one of the first memorials to the attack. Louise Nevelson Plaza (1977, Maiden Lane, William Street, and Liberty Street) was also altered after 9/11, with the site redesigned to accommodate security concerns and the seven Nevelson sculptures rearranged accordingly. Alan Sonfist's *Time Landscape* (1965–78, La Guardia Place, plantings) is a garden of flora indigenous to Manhattan before colonization.

By the end of the 1970s contemporary public sculptors addressed function as well as aesthetics. Postmodern buildings became more colorful and ornamental and less dependent on public sculpture to enliven their spaces. A zoning ordinance in 1981 rewarded developers for including interior spaces with public amenities other than art. The same year Richard Serra's *Tilted Arc* (1981, Corten steel), a large, curved wall-like sculpture commissioned by the U.S. General Services Administration, was installed at Federal Plaza. In 1989 after a bitter controversy and questionable procedures, federal officials replaced the sculpture with benches and planters.

Fritz Koenig's Sphere *(1971), recovered from the World Trade Center site, 2009*

The developers of the Equitable Life Assurance Center (787 Seventh Avenue) also took a functional approach to public sculpture when they commissioned Scott Burton to redesign the building's public spaces (1985–86) with marble benches, tables, and planters. Battery Park City (1987–89) in lower Manhattan commissioned individual projects by Richard Artschwager, R. M. Fischer, and Ned Smyth along the esplanade that provided an amalgam of street furniture and art. Open areas at the southern and northern coves were developed by artists, architects, and landscape architects such as Stanton Ekstut, Mary Miss, Susan Child, Cesar Pelli, Scott Burton, Siah Armajani, and M. Paul Friedberg. In 1983 a new law allocated 1 percent of the city's construction budgets to art. Among the early works commissioned under the program was Donna Dennis's *Dreaming of Far Away Places: The Ships Come to Washington Market* (1988, Public School 234, 300 Greenwich Avenue, steel), a fence depicting ships in the harbor that appear to sail around the schoolyard. Since 1986 the Metropolitan Transit Authority has commissioned a variety of pieces of contemporary art for the city's subways and railroad lines. Tom Otterness's *Life Underground* (2001, 14th Street and Eighth Avenue) is one of the most notable and popular sculpture projects.

Margot Gayle and Michele Cohen, *Manhattan's Outdoor Sculpture: The Art Commission and the Municipal Art Society Guide* (New York: Prentice Hall, 1988); Michele H. Bogart, *Public Sculpture and the Civic Ideal in New York City, 1890–1930* (Chicago: University of Chicago Press, 1989); Harriet F. Senie, *Contemporary Public Sculpture: Tradition, Transformation, and Controversy* (New York: Oxford University Press, 1992); Tom Eccles, Dan Cameron, and Katy Siegel, *Plop: Recent Projects of the Public Art Fund* (London: Merrell, 2004); Marvin Heiferman, ed., *City Art: New York's Percent for Art Program* (London: Merrell, 2005)

Michele H. Bogart (§1), Harriet F. Senie (§2)

Seabury, Samuel (*b* New York City, 22 Feb 1873; *d* East Hampton, N.Y., 7 May 1958). Jurist and reformer. He graduated from New York Law School in 1893 and was admitted to the New York State Bar Association in 1894. He was elected to a municipal court judgeship at age 28 as a candidate of Citizens Union. He then served on the New York Supreme Court from the age of 33 as a supporter of William Randolph Hearst and was elected to the court of appeals as a Progressive in 1914. He made an unsuccessful run for governor in 1916 and went into private practice after his defeat, becoming a wealthy trusts and estate lawyer. He reentered public life in 1930 to investigate the magistrates' courts. During the following year he uncovered evidence of illegal private business activity by magistrates, the alteration of court records, the sale of judgeships, and the harassment of innocent women by police vice squads allied with dishonest bail bondsmen and lawyers. In May 1930 Governor Franklin D. Roosevelt called on Seabury to investigate charges of incompetence against Manhattan district attorney Thomas T. C. Crain; he wrote a critical report but nonetheless recommended that Crain be retained. The state legislature then appointed him counsel to a joint committee formed to investigate the city's government. His staff assembled more than 60,000 pages of evidence, most of which was later shredded on Seabury's orders. The most spectacular testimonies were made public, including Sheriff Thomas Farley's description of his "wonderful tin box" of cash and Mayor James J. Walker's admission that he had received large "beneficences" from friends; Walker resigned in late 1932 while his dismissal hearing was in progress. In 1933 Seabury pushed for the fusion committee to nominate mayoral candidate Fiorello H. La Guardia, a staunch opponent of Tammany Hall. On 1 January 1934 La Guardia took the oath of office in Seabury's town house. Seabury is buried in Trinity Church Cemetery at 153rd Street and Amsterdam Avenue.

Herbert Mitgang, *The Man Who Rode the Tiger: The Life and Times of Judge Samuel Seabury* (Philadelphia: J. B. Lippincott, 1963)

Frank Vos

Sea Gate. Neighborhood in southwestern Brooklyn (2000 pop. *ca* 5200), lying on a peninsula at the western end of Coney Island

Aerial view of Sea Gate, 2009

Sea Gate, 2009

and bounded to the north by Coney Island Creek, to the east by West 37th Street, to the south by the Atlantic Ocean, and to the west by Norton's Point. Also known as West End and located in the town of Gravesend (1654–1894); Norton's Point was named after Mike Norton, a Coney Island landowner and state senator. Soon after ferry service from the Battery in Manhattan was introduced in the 1850s, Norton's Point became popular, especially among sports enthusiasts hoping to escape the censure of religious reformers and the restrictions of the police. After the Civil War a colony of misfits, criminals, and disgruntled veterans camped out there amusing themselves with illegal prizefights and dogfights. The area was placed under the control of the land commissioners of Gravesend and remained largely uninhabited until it was bought in 1888 by William K. Ziegler, president of the Royal Baking Powder Company. The Sea Gate Association, formed in 1892, was modeled on a plan for a restricted upper-class neighborhood proposed by Alrick Man, president of the Sea Beach Railroad; it retained control of future development and installed gates at Surf and Mermaid avenues and a fence 12 feet (3.7 meters) high to keep out intruders and visitors to Coney Island. The Atlantic Yacht Club clubhouse (1866), a destination for prestigious yachting races, was designed by Frank Cornell but burned in 1934. From 1909 until 1915, the Brooklyn Marathon ran on February 12 from Prospect Park to Sea Gate and returned. In 2009 there were about 900 houses in the 43 blocks of the neighborhood, which remained entirely separate from Coney Island. Since World War II, the population has been primarily Orthodox Jewish, mostly Hasidic. Only a few small stores can be found in Sea Gate, with most shopping outside its fence; the association has provided its own police protection since 1940. Well-known buildings include a chapel and two houses designed by Stanford White and a lighthouse (1890) 85 feet (26 meters) high at Norton's Point. Until his death in 1997 Frank Schubert was the official lighthouse keeper appointed by the U.S. Coast Guard. Among the unusual homes in Sea Gate is an all steel house designed by William van Alen and owned by Peter Spanakos, a former Golden Gloves champion. Other famous former residents have been Governor Al Smith, opera singer Beverly Sills, and authors Joseph Heller and Isaac Bashevis Singer.

Norman Blacher, *Sea Gate: A Private Community within the Confines of New York City* (New York: Sea Gate Association, 1955); Stephen Weinstein, "The Nickel Empire: Coney Island and the Creation of Urban Seaside Resorts in the United States" (diss., Columbia University, 1984); Kenneth Jackson and John Manbeck, eds., *The Neighborhoods of Brooklyn* (New Haven: Yale University Press, 2nd edn 2004)

Stephen Weinstein

Seagram Building. Landmarked office building at 375 Park Avenue, designed by Ludwig Mies van der Rohe and erected from 1954 to 1958; it is the headquarters of the firm of Joseph E. Seagram and Sons. Mies van der Rohe used only a quarter of the site to avoid having to comply with a zoning requirement (1916) that a tall building occupying its entire lot must have a setback design: his plan called for a slab-shaped building with a bronze exterior standing on a public plaza. Although the building had less space for rent than was usual, investors were attracted by the beauty of the exterior, the plaza, and the Four Seasons, a restaurant on the ground floor designed by Philip Johnson. The international acclaim that the building received prompted the city to pass a resolution in 1961 encouraging the construction of office buildings with amenities such as public plazas.

Mary Beth Betts

Seal of the City of New York. The Seal of the City of New York is affixed to official documents, publications, and stationery and depicted on buildings and other structures, vehicles, and the city flag. The first seal was granted by the duke of York to the Corporation of New York in 1664, to be used for the sealing of warrants, writs, executions, patents, grants, and other public acts. The symbol of the Imperial Crown was removed from the seal in 1783 and replaced by a federal eagle soaring over the northern hemisphere. By the early twentieth century the seal had suffered many variations and historical inaccuracies. To mark the 250th anniversary in 1915 of the English capture of New Amsterdam from the Dutch, the Associates of the Art Commission designed an official flag and conducted research for a historically correct seal to be executed by the sculptor Paul Manship. The new seal was blazoned on a flag of blue, white, and orange (the historic colors of the Netherlands) that was first raised at City Hall on 14 June 1915. In 1977 the City Council changed the date on the seal from 1664 to 1625, the year the Dutch founded New Amsterdam—though the first Dutch settlers arrived in 1624 and the town was incorporated as New Amsterdam in 1653. The seal depicts a shield crossed with the vanes of a windmill (representing the first source of energy in Manhattan); on the shield are a beaver (the chief commodity of the fur trade) and barrels of flour (recalling the milling industry). On one side of the shield stands a sailor named Dexter (representing the port and shipping), dressed in knee breeches and holding a lead plummet for sounding channels, with a cross-staff (a navigating instrument used to measure latitude) draped across his right shoulder; opposite the shield to his left an Algonquin Indian named Sinister, a member of the Lenape tribe, holds a single curved bow, the weapon of the coastal tribes. Both figures stand on a laurel branch. The border of the seal consists of a laurel wreath, the heraldic symbol of triumph, and the legend "Sigillum Civitatis Novi Eboraci" (sometimes omitted). The seal is maintained by the office of the city clerk; the Municipal Archives hold previously used designs along with the seals of the five boroughs and other variations used by municipal departments. Unofficial use of the seal

Seal of the City of New York (revised in 1977)

on any vehicle is subject to a fine of $25 or imprisonment not exceeding 10 days.

John Buckley Pine, *Seal and Flag of the City of New York* (New York: G. P. Putnam's Sons, 1914)

Gordon Hyatt

Seamen's Church Institute. Church for seafarers formed in 1834 and affiliated with the Episcopal Church. It began as a floating chapel in the Gothic Revival style and became known among seamen as the "doghouse on a raft" and later simply as the "doghouse." From 1907 to 1968 it occupied a large facility at 25 South Street. The most durable of the many organizations formed during the mid-nineteenth century to promote the welfare of men and women of the sea, it operates a facility on Water Street in lower Manhattan, as well as a large clubhouse at Port Newark in New Jersey.

Norman J. Brouwer

Seaside. Neighborhood in southern Queens, lying on the Rockaway Peninsula and centered on Beach 103rd Street; it is part of Rockaway Beach. The area became a resort after the New York, Woodhaven and Rockaway Railroad opened a station in 1880 at Beach 102nd and Beach 103rd Streets. Seasonal bungalows lined the side streets. Thousands of visitors frequented local bathhouses and amusements, including the Wainwright and Smith bathhouses and the Ferris wheel at 103rd Street; a large amusement complex called Steeplechase and bathhouses between 98th and 100th streets; the iron pier and bathhouses at 105th Street; and the scenic railway, carousel, and hotel between 103rd and 104th streets. The resorts largely disappeared after World War II. Rockaways Playland, opened in 1901 as the L. A. Thompson Amusement Park, closed after the 1985 season. Playland's roller coaster was featured in *This Is Cinerama* (1952). Two publicly assisted middle-income projects opened between 102nd and 108th streets in the 1960s: Surfside Park and Dayton Towers West. The Queens Library began serving the summer visitors in the 1920s and opened a new building in 1979.

Vincent Seyfried

Sea View Hospital. See New York City Farm Colony–Seaview Hospital Historic District.

SEBCO. See South East Bronx Community Organization.

Second Avenue subway. The two-track Second Avenue subway (SAS) will ultimately link 125th Street with Hanover Square. First proposed in 1929 and again in 1951, it was not built despite the demolition of the Second and Third Avenue elevated lines (1942 and 1955, respectively), which caused overcrowded conditions on the East Side's remaining rapid transit route, the Lexington Avenue subway (4/5/6 trains). In 1968 the initial capital plan of the Metropolitan Transportation Authority (MTA) included the SAS. Construction began in 1972; portions were constructed in East Harlem and near the Manhattan Bridge, but work was stopped in 1975 because of New York City's fiscal crisis. MTA resurrected the SAS project in 1996 after analyses of alternatives clearly demonstrated its need. After required environmental and design work was performed, construction of the first of four phases began again in April 2007.

Andrew Sparberg

Second Bank of the United States. Federal bank formed in 1816 in Philadelphia to alleviate difficulties in financing the War of 1812. A branch in New York City opened in October 1817 at 65 Broadway in Manhattan (later moved to Wall Street) and had capital assets of $2.5 million, more than any other bank in the city. The constitutionality of the bank was affirmed by the U.S. Supreme Court in *McCulloch v. Maryland* (1819). A requirement that state and local banks redeem their notes at the Second Bank, imposed by Nicholas Biddle (1786–1844), its president from 1823, was strongly opposed; there was also resentment that the bank attracted a disproportionate share of deposits by the federal government. The bank was entangled more thoroughly in politics than the First Bank of the United States had been, and after the "bank war" of the early 1830s its charter was allowed to expire in 1836. Its dissolution freed commercial banks from competition and enabled the city to become the undisputed capital of commercial banking.

Ralph H. Catterall, *Second Bank of the United States* (Chicago: University of Chicago Press, 1903)

James Bradley

Secor, John. Alias of William M. "Boss" Tweed while he was a fugitive.

Seeger, Alan (*b* New York City, 22 June 1888; *d* Belloy-en-Santerre, France, 4 July 1916). Poet. He grew up in Staten Island and lived in Mexico City for several years after his father's import-export business failed; in 1902 he and his brother returned to New York City to attend the Hackley School in suburban Tarrytown. Seeger attended Harvard University 1906 to 1910, where he befriended journalist John Reed. After graduation he returned to New York City, did odd jobs, and wrote poetry. He moved to Paris in 1912 and joined the French Foreign Legion. During World War I his poetry was published in the Atlantic Monthly and he was a war correspondent for the New Republic and the New York Sun. In 1916 his poem "I Have a Rendezvous with Death" appeared in the *New Republic;* that summer Seeger was killed in action during the bloody Somme offensive. He was awarded the Croix de Guerre and Medaille Militaire after his death; *Poems by Alan Seeger* (1916) and *Letters and Diary of Alan Seeger* (1917) were published posthumously. Folksinger Pete Seeger is Seeger's nephew.

Kate Lauber

Seeger, Pete (Peter) (*b* Patterson, N.Y., 3 May 1919). Folksinger and political activist. Although he was born in Putnam County, traveled widely, and settled permanently upstate, he is intimately identified with New York City. A banjo and guitar player and singer since youth, after dropping out of Harvard University in 1938 he usually lived in the city until he and his wife moved to near Beacon, New York, in the 1950s. He taught folk singing at the Dalton School, regularly performed at Town Hall and Lewisohn Stadium and on New York radio stations, and led hootenannies at Carnegie Hall. Seeger was a member of the Almanac Singers, a New York City–based group that, after changing its name to the Weavers, recorded with Folkways Records (founded in the city by Moses Asch and Marian Distler), won international fame, founded the folk music revival, and inspired opponents to the Vietnam War. "Where Have All the Flowers Gone?" "Turn, Turn, Turn," and his other well-known songs have both memorable melodies and often political messages. Seeger's career was all but ended in 1955 by a controversy over his ties to the Communist Party. Although a media blacklist ended his national prominence as a performer, he continued to sing at folk concerts and festivals until he was in his 80s. A pioneer environmentalist, in the late 1960s he spearheaded the effort to build the replica Hudson River sloop *Clearwater,* which often sailed off the city with crews of youngsters learning marine biology. In 2008 a television show on public broadcasting emphasized Seeger's New York City roots, and a year later he was a featured singer alongside Bruce Springsteen at a show in Washington, D.C., preceding the inauguration of President Barack Obama.

John Rousmaniere

Segal, George (*b* New York City, 26 Nov 1924; *d* South Brunswick, N.J., 9 June 2000). Sculptor. Born to Russian immigrants, he spent his childhood in the Bronx, and attended Stuyvesant High School. His family later moved to South Brunswick, New Jersey, where they farmed chickens. Segal's first medium was painting. He exhibited at the Hansa Gallery in New York City, an artist cooperative where abstract expressionism flourished. Segal cemented his reputation when he began to swathe people in plaster-infused bandages and freeze these forms amid quotidian objects to create minimalist tableaux. He salvaged objects from Manhattan and New Jersey for his tableaux. Though linked to the pop art movement, Segal's sculptures defied classification. In 1980 he cast *Gay Liberation,* a bronze of two same-sex couples commissioned by the Mildred Andrews Fund to commemorate the Stonewall Rebellion. Homosexual residents of Greenwich Village resented the homogeneity of the white, youthful figures, while heterosexuals resented the presence of a gay rights monument in their neighborhood. Such outrage halted installation in Christopher Park until 1992. Segal was represented by the Sidney Janis Gallery for most of his career. His work appears in the collections of the Metropolitan Museum of Art, the Guggenheim, the Whitney, and the Museum of Modern Art.

William C. Seitz, *Segal* (New York: Harry N. Abrams, 1972); Phyllis Tuchman, *George Segal* (New York: Abbeville Press, 1983)

Clare Richfield

Seixas, Gershom Mendes (*b* New York City, 15 Jan 1746; *d* New York City, 2 July 1816). Rabbi. He became the rabbi of SHEARITH ISRAEL in 1768 and extended his ministry to Jews in outlying areas. During the American Revolution he settled briefly in Philadelphia, returning to New York City in 1784. A strict observer of Orthodox traditions, he promoted the Hebrew language; he was also the first rabbi to use English for services and took part in religious exchanges, giving sermons to Christian congregations and inviting Christian ministers to his congregation. One of his Thanksgiving sermons at St. Paul's was published as a pamphlet that the *Daily Gazette* recommended to "every pious reader, whether Jew or Christian" (23 December 1789). Seixas formed the charitable organization Hebra Hasad Va-Amet and was a trustee of Columbia College. He is buried at New Bowery Cemetery of Shearith Israel.

James E. Mooney

Seligman. See J. AND W. SELIGMAN.

Seligman, Joseph (*b* Baiersdorf, Bavaria, 22 Nov 1819; *d* New Orleans, La., 28 April 1880). Banker, father of E. R. A. Seligman. With two of his brothers, Jesse Seligman (1827–94) and William Seligman (1822–1910), he formed a clothing firm in 1846 with headquarters at 5 William Street, which supplied uniforms for the Union army. He also negotiated more than $200 million in foreign loans to support the Union cause and was a financial adviser to Presidents Abraham Lincoln, Ulysses S. Grant, and Rutherford B. Hayes. He worked in the family's banking firm of J. and W. Seligman and Company, was a founder with Felix Adler of the New York Society for Ethical Culture, and was active in politics. In addition to working in business he supported the Hebrew Orphan Society and Mount Sinai Hospital, served on the Board of Education, and helped to plan the city's first elevated rapid transit. His son Isaac Newton Seligman (1855–1917) became the head of J. and W. Seligman in 1894.

Ross L. Muir and Carl J. White, *Over the Long Term: The Story of J. and W. Seligman and Company* (New York: J. and W. Seligman, 1964)

Joyce Mendelsohn

seltzer. Artificially carbonated water. After effervescent mineral water was discovered in upstate New York in the 1780s, samples were taken to New York City for experiment to re-create the effervescence by such prominent scientists as Samuel Latham Mitchill and Valentine Seaman (1770–1817). Artificially carbonated water, then called soda water, was made at the City Hotel by Noyes Darling and first served in the city at the TONTINE COFFEE HOUSE in 1809. With George Usher and Joseph Boston, Darling became a leading manufacturer of soda water. The soda-water industry developed mostly in the city, where the Englishman John Matthews (1808–70) made many innovations; he learned the trade in England, moved to the United States in 1832, and a few years later bought a factory at First Avenue and 26th Street where he formed the John Matthews Apparatus Company. During the following decades the business became tremendously successful in selling soda water, bottles, glasses, tubes, pumps, generators, and hundreds of Matthews's designs for soda fountains. When he retired in 1865 the firm was the undisputed national leader in the industry and renowned worldwide (it merged with the American Soda Fountain Company in 1891, became independent again in 1914, and closed in the 1920s). Soda water became known mostly as seltzer and was popular among Jews because it complemented rich foods included in kosher diets; it was often called *Belchwasser* or Jewish champagne.

During the 1870s soda fountains became popular attractions in drugstores and department stores, and such establishments as Hudnut's in the Herald Building were known for their marble soda fountains; the price of a glass of seltzer gave rise to the expression "two cents plain." Egg creams, a confection sold at candy stores, were made with seltzer, chocolate syrup, and milk (but neither eggs nor cream). During the first half of the twentieth century seltzer became widely popular and its production became an important business in the city. The most prosperous firm was for many years the Good Health Seltzer Company on the Lower East Side. Companies in Brooklyn included Bensonhurst Seltzer and Jacob Goldberg and Sons. Seltzer was distributed in glass siphon bottles by "seltzer men," who made seltzer that they delivered to homes by wagon and truck. When carbonated water and mineral water became popular again in the 1970s, such soft drink companies as Canada Dry, White Rock, and Schweppes began making seltzer. Home delivery was reintroduced in the 1980s by such manufacturers as Gimme Seltzer in Long Island City and Havana Dry in the Bronx. The Canada Dry Bottling Company in Queens distributed seltzer under the brand names of Cott, Hoffman's, Kirsch, and Good Old Times Seltzer. In the early twenty-first century New York City is the largest seltzer and mineral-water market in the country.

James Bradley

Sendak, Maurice (Bernard) (*b* Brooklyn, 10 June 1928). Illustrator and writer. He grew up in Brooklyn, where at age nine he wrote and illustrated his first stories; he later worked for the toy store F. A. O. Schwarz. After producing the illustrations for Ruth Krauss's book *A Hole Is to Dig,* he left the store in 1952 to concentrate on writing and illustrating children's books. In 1963 his book *Where the Wild Things Are* won the Caldecott Medal, the highest award for children's literature, and became an instant classic; it was made into a movie in 2009. In his book *In the Night Kitchen* (1970) he recast the city's skyline as a row of kitchen utensils and containers dating from the 1930s, drawn in a homey style. He lived in Greenwich Village until 1972, when he moved to Connecticut. Sendak has illustrated more than 70 books, written and illustrated 17, and won many awards for excellence in children's book illustration.

Selma G. Lanes, *The Art of Maurice Sendak* (New York: Harry N. Abrams, 1980)

Michael Joseph

Seneca Village. Manhattan's first known community of African American real property owners, settled in 1825. Located between 82nd and 89th streets and Seventh and Eighth avenues, Seneca Village was a community numbering more than 250 people, with three churches, several cemeteries, and a school. African Americans owned more than half the households. An early example of racial harmony, this multiethnic community, which also included Irish and German immigrants and possibly some Native Americans, lived peaceably. Seneca Village was razed in 1857 to make way for Central Park.

Kathleen Benson, Celedonia Jones, Diane Jones Randall, Sharon Wilkins

Senegalese. In the late 1970s and 1980s severe droughts and economic crises in Senegal brought immigrants to New York City. Most spoke only Wolof, the principal language of Senegal. They were from the peanut farming region of Diourbel and belonged to a Muslim sect called the *mourids* known for its work ethic. Many drew on their experience as street vendors in Senegal to set up successful peddling businesses on city streets, buying scarves, sunglasses, watches, handbags, and T-shirts by the case in Chinatown and selling them in midtown and Greenwich Village. In the mid-1980s it was estimated that some Senegalese vendors earned $100 a week (compared with an annual per capita income in Senegal of $460), spent about $60 a week on inexpensive hotel rooms in Manhattan or apartments in the outer boroughs, and sent home as much as $45 a month. In the early twenty-first century Senegalese remained active street traders.

B. Kimberly Taylor

Sensation show. Controversial art exhibit at the Brooklyn Museum. Fully entitled *Sensation: Young British Artists from the Saatchi Collection,* the show ran from 2 October 1999 through 9 January 2000 and was previously shown in London and Berlin. When the show arrived in Brooklyn, animal-rights groups protested works by Damien Hirst that incorporated animal carcasses, while Catholic groups were outraged by Chris Ofili's painting *The Holy Virgin Mary,* which depicted a black Madonna with one breast made from resin-covered elephant dung surrounded by pictures of female genitalia cut from pornographic magazines. Mayor Rudolph Giuliani fought to have the show closed and threatened to withhold the museum's municipal funding, and the U.S. House of Representatives passed a resolution to end federal funding for the museum. The New York Civil Liberties Union, along with Hillary Rodham Clinton, then Giuliani's opponent in the New York senate race, defended the museum. A federal judge ultimately ordered all funding to be restored, and the exhibit was shown as planned.

Kate Lauber

September 11 [9/11]. Day in 2001 on which two jet aircraft purposefully flew into the World Trade Center (WTC) twin towers, destroying them and killing thousands of people. It is the worst terrorist attack ever committed on U.S. soil.

At 8:00 a.m. on Tuesday, 11 September 2001, American Airlines Flight 11 took off from Boston's Logan Airport, bound for Los Angeles; at 8:29 it turned sharply to the left, followed the Hudson River toward New York City, and at 8:46 a.m. flew into 1 WTC, the North Tower, at 470 miles per hour. United Flight 175 left Boston at 7:58, also headed to Los Angeles, crossed into New Jersey, and then turned nearly 180 degrees and crashed into the South Tower (2 WTC) at 9:02 at 560 miles per hour. Each plane had been hijacked by several men carrying knives and box cutters; wounding or killing the crews, they took control of the planes using skills they had learned in part at flying schools in the United States. Together with a third team, which sent a plane crashing into the Pentagon that day, and a fourth, whose mission was thwarted when passengers crashed the plane in the countryside near Pittsburgh, the hijackers were members of Al-Qaeda, a network of Islamic radicals who sought vengeance for American and other Western incursions into Muslim lands. It is believed they chose the WTC as a target because it symbolizes Western capitalism and secularism and American worldwide economic influence.

When the planes hit, about 12,000 people were in or near their offices or preparing for meetings in the North and South Towers. The first plane—a Boeing 767 loaded with fuel for a transcontinental flight—hit the north face of that tower between the 92nd and 98th floors, sending engine parts into structural columns in the core. Jet fuel caught fire and burned through the insulation protecting the horizontal floor trusses, generating heat that softened the trusses and the vertical supports in the core and in the building's perimeter. These held for more than an hour and a half, permitting thousands of people who worked on the 90th floor and below to rush down stairways and escape.

The South Tower, which was the first to collapse, was also hit by a fully fueled 767, but at a higher speed, piercing the building between the 78th and 84th floors. Rubble and fire blocked everyone above the 77th floor from escaping via the stairwells. By 9:45 fires had spread through at least five floors, and the horizontal trusses began to sag. Firefighters were headed up the stairs to rescue survivors when the structure collapsed at 9:59 a.m.; the descending floors cascaded downward to the concourse level and below. The 17 minutes between attacks on the buildings had given people the opportunity to escape; the death toll was 700. Then at 10:28 the North Tower collapsed, killing 1344 people, mostly on the floors above the impact.

The force of the collapse was devastating. Ten stories of the South Tower were later found in the lower basement; they had compacted into a dense pancake 6 feet (2 meters) high. Twenty floors of the North Tower were found in a basement area, compressed to 10 feet (3 meters) in height. As the two towers fell, pieces smashed into nearby buildings, including 4, 5, 6, and 7 WTC and the Marriott Hotel; a dozen structures beyond the WTC super block were badly damaged, including St. Nicholas Greek Orthodox Church, a block away, which was smashed to the ground, and 90 West Street, a 23-story structure that burned for a day and a half.

Twin towers from the Brooklyn Promenade, 11 September 2001

World Trade Center site from the roof of the World Financial Center, November 2001

It was originally feared that as many as 6000 had died in the attack, but the final tally was estimated at 2749 (the exact number has never been determined), including 343 firefighters and 70 police killed in both towers, and the 92 passengers and crew on Flight 11 and the 65 on Flight 175. In addition, several thousand survivors, rescuers, and others suffered significant long-term health damage caused by inhaling the air around the site, which was contaminated with smoke from fires, toxic dust and suspended debris from the buildings' collapse, and exhaust from cleanup equipment.

Cleanup proceeded slowly, in part in the hope that survivors would be found in the rubble, but only 21 were finally rescued. All debris was not removed from the 16-acre (6.5-hectare) site—called Ground Zero—until June 2002. The cleanup effort was also complicated by the need to protect the WTC "bathtub"—the 70-foot-deep (21.3-meter) hole in which the buildings had been constructed that was surrounded by a 3000-foot-long (914-meter-long) waterproof "slurry" wall that prevented water from the nearby Hudson River from seeping into the foundation.

It was difficult to determine why the towers fell, in part because the various investigations were not well organized and were poorly funded. Investigations that were completed indicated that thicker fireproofing on the floor trusses would have delayed their buckling, and if the trusses had been stronger, they might have held the outside structure and the core longer. However, because of the intense heat of the fire from burning jet fuel, most studies concluded that the collapse could not have been prevented.

The 9/11 attacks had a profound effect on the New York metropolitan region. In addition to the human toll, which included thousands of people exhibiting symptoms of post-traumatic stress disorder five to six years after the attacks, the city lost more than 15 million square feet (1.4 million square meters) of office space and 100,000 jobs. For months, the streets of lower Manhattan were quiet and had a heavy police and military presence; a distinctive smell pervaded everyplace south of Chambers Street.

At the same time the attack resurrected the career of Mayor Rudolph Giuliani, who was then in the last months of his second term and whose popularity had been declining. In the immediate aftermath of 9/11, he became a national hero—calm in the face of disaster, reassuring to those who thought the city was doomed, and compassionate in his evocation of loss. He was particularly sympathetic to the families of the more than 400 firefighters and police officers who died in the performance of their duties.

But the effects went beyond the loss of lives, buildings, and jobs. Soon after the attack, tighter airport security systems were established, improved building codes for tall buildings were created, and additional efforts to monitor people entering the United States were undertaken. Concluding that Al-Qaeda leader Osama bin Laden had orchestrated the events of 9/11 and that he was hiding in Taliban-controlled Afghanistan, the United States and Britain invaded Afghanistan in the fall of 2001. Congress passed the USA PATRIOT Act of 2001 and other legislation that expanded the president's powers to "fight terrorism." The administration of George W. Bush then asserted that Iraq was part of the "terrorist network" and invaded that country in 2003. In November 2002 Congress created the semi-independent 9/11 Commission, which issued a final report in July 2004 that criticized the Central Intelligence Agency, the Federal Bureau of Investigation, and other federal agencies for failing to take actions that could have averted the disaster.

New York City eventually recovered from the attack, with its economy and popularity as a business and tourist site, and its real estate market, rebounding. Plans for rebuilding the World Trade Center site include a memorial

After 9/11, memorials like this one, the Marsh and McLennan Memorial at 1166 Avenue of the Americas, were created to remember victims of the attacks

in honor of those who died, as well as five new skyscrapers and a museum (see World Trade Center and National September 11 Memorial and Museum).

James Glanz and Eric Lipton, *City in the Sky: The Rise and Fall of the World Trade Center* (New York: Times Books, 2003); 9/11 Commission (National Commission on Terrorist Attacks upon the United States), *9/11 Commission Report* (2004), http://www.9-11commission.gov/report/911Report.pdf; National Institute of Standards and Technology, *Investigation of the World Trade Center Disaster* (2005), http://wtc.nist.gov; 9/11 Public Discourse Project, *Final Report on 9/11 Commission Recommendation* (2005), http://www.9-11pdp.org/press/2005-12-05_report.pdf; Jonathan M. Samet, Alison S. Geyh, and Mark J. Utell, "The Legacy of World Trade Center Dust," *New England Journal of Medicine* 356 (31 May 2007), pp. 2233–36

Jameson W. Doig, Kenneth T. Jackson, Lisa Keller

Serbs. Economic refugees from Serbia immigrated to the United States in the late nineteenth century to work in factories, steel mills, and mines in the Midwest, but a number settled in New York City. A small Serb, Croat, and Slovenian colony took shape along Ninth and 10th avenues between 21st and 40th streets, and in 1914 the famed physicist Michael Pupin formed the central committee of Srpska Narodna Odbrana (Serbian national defense). Although small in number the city's Serbian community supported a daily newspaper, *Srbski Dnevnik,* between 1911 and 1932. The quota system imposed in 1924 suspended Serbian immigration until the communist takeover of Yugoslavia in 1946 led to an influx to the United States of war prisoners, refugees, Serbian nationalists, and German collaborators. After the Yugoslavian dictator Marshal Josip Broz Tito opened his country's borders in 1963, many Serb professionals, including physicians, architects, and engineers, as well as students, immigrated to the United States and settled in New York City. Many Serbs also worked in real estate and construction. The most vital Serbian institution in the city was the Serbian Cathedral of St. Sava, built by Richard Upjohn in 1855 at 20 West 26th Street and bought from the Episcopalians in 1942. Nikola Tesla, the scientist and inventor, lived in New York City for 40 years and died at the New Yorker Hotel. In the early twenty-first century an estimated 40,000 people of Serbian ancestry lived in the city, with large communities in Ridgewood and Astoria.

Marc Ferris

Serpico, (Francesco Vincent) Frank (*b* Brooklyn, 14 April 1936). New York City police officer. He was the most feared, hated, and controversial policeman in New York City in the late 1960s. Working as a plainclothes detective, he went public about police corruption, revealing bribery and kickbacks that eventually led to the formation in 1970 of the Knapp Commission, which investigated and exposed the corruption. Serpico became the first police officer in history to testify openly about systemic police corruption and payoffs and received numerous death threats after testifying. A year after appearing before the commission, Serpico was shot in the face during a raid on a suspected drug deal in Brooklyn. The bullet entered his cheek and lodged at the top of his jaw. Fellow officers did not come to his aid, nor did they call headquarters to report that an officer had been shot. One month after receiving the New York City Police Department's highest honor, the Medal of Honor, he retired in 1972. He lived in Europe for many years, and his story was turned into a best-selling book, which in turn became the movie *Serpico* (1973) starring Al Pacino.

Frank Dyer

servants. See Domestic servants.

Sesame Workshop. Nonprofit corporation formed in 1968 by Joan Ganz Cooney and Lloyd Morrisett to develop educational television programs for children. It was a pioneer in educational programming techniques and an outgrowth of a research project by Cooney called "The Potential Uses of Television in Preschool Education" for the Carnegie Corporation. Formerly known as the Children's Television Workshop, it changed its name in 2000. It became especially well known for *Sesame Street,* a program for two- to five-year-olds that eventually won more than 50 Emmy Awards and a Peabody Award and was shown in 90 countries. *Sesame Street* proved so successful that it funded many of the other projects by the Sesame Workshop. Other television series that the workshop created include *3-2-1 Contact, Square One, Ghostwriter,* and *The Electric Company.* It also developed *Sesame Street Magazine* and expanded into print and electronic educational materials, home video, and software. Its programming and other media are designed to teach basic reading and writing, mathematics, and science to a young audience. The programming has also addressed children with learning disabilities and bilingual education. The offices are at 1 Lincoln Plaza in Manhattan.

Gladys Chen

Seton [née Bayley]**, Elizabeth Ann** (*b* Staten Island, 28 Aug 1774; *d* Emmitsburg, Md., 4 Jan 1821). First American-born saint. The daughter of the physician Richard Bayley, as a child she spent her summers at Cragdon, her grandparents' home in Edenwald (now Seton Falls Park in the Bronx). She married the successful merchant William Magee Seton in 1794. Her involvement with social work led her to form the Society for the Relief of Poor Widows and Children in 1797. After the premature death of her husband (1803) she converted to Roman Catholicism (1805) and was baptized at St. Peter's Church (Barclay Street). Ostracized by her Protestant family and friends, she moved with her five children to Baltimore in 1808 to open a school for girls. After taking her vows before the bishop, she formed in 1809 in Emmitsburg, Maryland, the American Sisters of Charity, the first Roman Catholic religious order in the United States; it was modeled after the Daughters of Charity, formed by St. Vincent de Paul in Paris during the sixteenth century to assist the poor. Although Seton did not return to New York City, the Sisters of Charity opened the Roman Catholic Orphan Asylum there in 1817. Seton was beatified in 1963 and canonized on 14 September 1975. The rectory of the Shrine of St. Elizabeth Bayley Seton is at 7 State Street in lower Manhattan, the site where Seton's family once lived. Among the other entities that bear her name are Seton Falls Park at West 233rd Street and Baychester Avenue in the Bronx, Bayley Seton Hospital at 75 Vanderbilt Avenue in Staten Island, and the Elizabeth Seton Campus of Iona College in the Bronx.

Bernadette McCauley

settlement houses. Houses that provided social services for the poor in urban areas. What is believed to be the first settlement house, Toynbee Hall, was formed in a slum in East London in 1884 by the vicar Samuel A. Barnett, who hoped to bridge class lines by having men with university education live and work in poor neighborhoods to improve the health, education, housing, and living conditions of working people. Stanton Coit (1857–1944), an American, lived briefly at Toynbee and in August 1886 set up the first settlement house in the United States in a tenement at 146 Forsyth Street on the Lower East Side. Originally open only to men and called the Lily Pleasure Club, it was renamed the Neighborhood Guild in 1887. It was soon followed by a women's settlement across the street when Jean Fine and the medical student Jane Robbins rented an apartment and invited girls' clubs to meet there during the winter of 1888–89. Later in 1889 the College Settlement opened nearby on Rivington Street and in its charter announced that it would provide a setting where "educated women" could live among "working people" for their "mutual benefit and education." Coit's settlement was renamed University Settlement in 1891 and from that time accepted both men and women as workers or residents; this became the common pattern, although women predominated among both residents and leaders. University

Settlement continued to function at 184 Eldridge Street.

Settlement houses in the United States retained many of the characteristics of their British counterparts: they were situated in poor neighborhoods and sought to improve the community as a whole; they often cooperated with charitable organizations but set themselves apart from them by stressing betterment through individual effort rather than philanthropy; and they helped primarily the working poor rather than the destitute. In other ways American settlement houses developed differently in response to unique conditions. The large number of immigrants to the United States produced a more heterogeneous and mobile population in New York City than in London, as well as a greater strain on the supply of housing and on educational, medical, and recreational resources. Settlement workers typically lived in neighborhoods where the local population had diverse religious and cultural backgrounds and seldom spoke English. Most American settlements came to be staffed by women who held college degrees but found the professions closed to them. Influenced by the Social Gospel movement, a Protestant effort to establish "the kingdom of God on earth through social reform," they saw settlement work as a socially acceptable way to apply their skills. But although some settlements drew financial support from religious groups and resembled missions, the importance of the religious element declined over time.

The settlement was an institution marked by adaptability and change. Programs constantly shifted to reflect the interests of residents, large organizations opened branches and smaller ones were absorbed, and their addresses were only temporary. The number of settlements in the city was 18 in 1897 and 89 in 1911 (of which 23 were in Brooklyn and 66 in Manhattan), not all providing living accommodations for those who worked there or offering a full range of programs. Four were umbrella organizations that coordinated neighborhood work; three were instruction centers offering classes in a single area such as music or housekeeping. About half gave religious instruction, and one of these had the stated objective of "winning children to its clubs and classes and to Christ." The typical settlement in the city offered meeting rooms for clubs, recreation and summer camp programs, kindergartens, health clinics, dramatic presentations, concerts, exhibits, debates on important issues, milk stations for infants, and classes in housekeeping, English, citizenship, carpentry, needlework, art, and music. At their peak the largest settlements had a few dozen residents and several times that number of part-time volunteers.

The College Settlement and University Settlement were among the best-known institutions of their kind. The Henry Street Settlement, formed by Lillian Wald and Mary Brewster, had 46 residents by 1911, of whom 41 were women. Incorporated in 1903 for the "usual settlement purposes," it was the first settlement to have a visiting nurse service. By 2008 it had expanded to eight buildings. Greenwich House, incorporated in 1902 as the Cooperative Social Settlement Society, was formed in a tenement on Jones Street and moved during World War I to permanent quarters at 27 Barrow Street. One of the first settlements in Greenwich Village, it reflected the interests of Mary Simkhovitch, its head resident from 1902 to 1946, by placing a special emphasis on music and the improvement of housing. It ultimately had 10 locations and offered drug and alcohol treatment and counseling services in addition to pottery and music programs. Hartley House was formed in 1897 at 413 West 46th Street in Manhattan under the auspices of the Association for Improving the Condition of the Poor and incorporated in 1903. It emphasized free baths and workrooms for women and a large playground for their children. The settlement continued into the twenty-first century to run a family day-care program. Hudson Guild, incorporated in 1895 at 441 West 26th Street by John L(ovejoy) Elliott (1868–1942) to "teach the ethics of social organization," benefited from the support of the New York Society for Ethical Culture. It was known for the well-regarded work of its affiliate the Hudson Guild Theatre, at 441 West 26th Street in Manhattan. Union Settlement, opened by the Alumni Club of Union Theological Seminary at 202 East 96th Street in the summer of 1895, moved frequently and operated out of several different apartments on East 104th and 105th streets.

Some reform-minded artists used the settlement as an instruction center. The violinist David Mannes and his wife, the pianist Clara Damrosch Mannes, taught at the Music School Settlement on the Lower East Side and then formed the Music School Settlement for Colored People in 1911. They soon devoted their energies to the David Mannes Music School, which they formed in 1916. Few settlements worked hard at racial integration. Branches set up in African American neighborhoods included the Lincoln Settlement (1908), at 105 Fleet Place in the 11th ward of Brooklyn, and the Stillman Branch for Colored People (1906), a branch of the Henry Street Settlement formed in an apartment in the West 60s in Manhattan. Greenwich House on the Lower West Side helped to conduct and publish several studies of African Americans living in New York City, including those of Mary White Ovington, but it did not set up a separate facility for them.

Settlements offering religious instruction were typically run by individual churches, with which they identified themselves openly. One of the largest, Amity Baptist Church and Settlement House, was formed in 1896 on West 54th Street to illustrate "true Christian living and to work for the religious and social well-being of the neighborhood." By 1911 it had 16 resident workers and 24 volunteers. Nondenominational Protestant religious instruction was offered by Christodora House, formed in 1897 by C. I. MacColl and Sara Carson on the Lower East Side "for the physical, social, intellectual, and spiritual development of the people in the crowded portions of the city." Through the efforts of Anna Hempstead Branch (1875–1937) the Poet's Guild was formed there in 1920 to sponsor readings and issue publications. From 1928 to 1948 the settlement occupied its own building on Tompkins Square (145 Avenue B at Ninth Street). It assumed the status of a foundation in 1981 and became known as Christodora Inc.

Settlements in New York City provided the basis for many national reform movements. Lillian Wald worked with Robert Hunter and J. G. Phelps Stokes of University Settlement to form a state child labor committee in 1902, and all three joined with other settlement workers to support the establishment in 1912 of a children's bureau in the U.S. Department of Labor. Mary Simkhovitch helped to form the Women's Trade Union League in 1903 and in the 1930s fought for a program of federally subsidized housing. Henry Moskowitz, a protégé of Wald and the head resident of the Down Town Ethical Society Settlement, worked for many municipal reforms, was a founder in 1909 of the National Association for the Advancement of Colored People (NAACP), and ran for Congress in 1912.

By World War I the impulse underlying the establishment of settlements had begun to weaken. Immigration had declined and women found more careers open to them. As social work became professionalized and the state and federal governments offered more social services, settlement houses lost their distinctiveness and became simply one part of a large network. Nonetheless, they continued to flourish. A 1935 survey counted 80 settlements operating in New York City, with 55 of them in Manhattan (of which half were on the Lower East Side) and 15 in Brooklyn. Of these 80 settlements, four had begun operation in the 1880s, 25 in the 1890s, 18 between 1900 and 1909, 22 between 1910 and 1919, and eight in the 1920s. By 1942 settlements no longer merited a separate entry in the city's Directory of Social Agencies and were included as part of "Recreation, Group Work and Neighborhood Centers." Only about one-fifth of those listed retained the word "settlement" in their name, and most had converted their residents' housing quarters to other uses. By the early twenty-first century the settlement had been redefined; now a neighborhood center staffed by professional social workers, it continued to provide meeting spaces for clubs and offered a variety of services in child care, recreation, drug and alcohol counseling, music and art education, and employment training.

Albert J. Kennedy et al., *Social Settlements in New York City: Their Activities, Policies and Administration* (New York: Columbia University Press, 1935)

Betty Boyd Caroli

Seven Arts. Monthly magazine of literature and opinion launched in 1917 by James Oppenheim (1882–1932), who engaged Waldo Frank and Van Wyck Brooks as his associate editors and benefited from the patronage of Mrs. A. K. Rankine. The magazine promoted art as a regenerative social force and dwelled on topics of interest to the intelligentsia of Greenwich Village, especially cultural criticism, pacifism, and psychoanalysis. Its emphatic opposition to American participation in World War I led to the financial collapse of *Seven Arts* after one year in print.

James Oppenheim, "The Story of the Seven Arts," *American Mercury* 20 (1930), 156–64

Jan Seidler Ramirez

Seventh-day Adventists. Christian denomination born from the Millerite movement of the 1840s and formally organized in 1863. One of the fastest-growing religions in the world, in 2008 the church had more than 150 congregations in the five boroughs, almost half of them in Brooklyn. Adventist churches in New York City served a vast number of ethnic groups, including Asians, Latinos, West Indians, West Africans, Hungarians, and Ukrainians. Black members had a presence in the city as early as 1904; in 2008 the largest congregation in Manhattan, Ephesus Seventh-day Adventist Church at 101 West 123rd Street, was largely African American and had more than 1000 members. The Gothic building was designed by John Rochester Thomas and constructed in 1887 as the Second Collegiate Church of Harlem; after Ephesus moved there in 1930 the church's interior and its distinctive 37-foot (11.3-meter) spire were partially destroyed by fire in 1969; the steeple was not rebuilt until 2006. The Boys Choir of Harlem was founded at Ephesus in 1968. In the early twenty-first century Spanish-language churches in upper Manhattan and the Bronx served the city's Latino Adventist population; West Indian congregations met in South Brooklyn, including the Eglise Adventiste Gethsemane on Empire Boulevard, which served French-speaking Haitians; and the Queens Ghanaian Church in Ozone Park and the Staten Island Korean Seventh-day Adventist Church furthered the church's diversity and breadth in New York City.

Kate Lauber

Veterans' Room (designed by Louis Comfort Tiffany), Seventh Regiment Armory, ca *1890*

Seventh Regiment. Regiment formed in 1847, known as the "silk stocking regiment." Its forerunner was a volunteer militia of four companies formed in 1806 to safeguard New York Harbor from attacks by British frigates. The members developed their own rules, elected their own officers, supplied their own arms, and designed and bought their own uniforms. The regiment was chosen to serve as the Marquis de Lafayette's honor guard during his visit to New York City in 1824–25 and took the name National Guard in honor of Lafayette's Garde Nationale in Paris. It won many honors during the War of 1812 and played a vital role in defending the city during riots of the nineteenth century. In 1847 the regiment was reorganized and took its current name. By the 1860s it had more than 1000 members and had outgrown its armory at Tompkins Square. The city provided a square block at Park Avenue and 66th Street. The regiment established the New Armory Fund, which received private contributions from members and from individuals, banks, and insurance companies. One of its veterans, Charles W. Clinton, designed the three-story administration building containing the regimental and company rooms. A one-story drill shed stretching 300 feet (90 meters) to Lexington Avenue was added at the rear, its massive truss system designed by the Delaware Bridge Company and modeled after the train shed of

Drill hall of the Seventh Regiment Armory, 1885

Thomas Nast's depiction of the departure of the Seventh Regiment for the Civil War, 19 April 1861

the first Grand Central Depot. The cornerstone was laid on 13 October 1877, and on completion of the building in 1879 a fair was held inside to raise money for the interior decoration; President Rutherford B. Hayes presided over the opening ceremonies, and during three weeks $140,000 was raised, bringing the construction budget of the armory to $600,000. The regiment engaged the leading decorating firms to design the public rooms on the first story and the individual company rooms on the second. The best-known of these firms, Louis C. Tiffany and Associated Artists, designed the Veterans' Room and the library; other work was executed by the firms of Alexander Roux, Herter Brothers, Pottier and Stymus, Kimbel and Cabus, and Leon Marcotte. The interiors were completed by 1881 and remain some of the finest surviving examples of American interior design of the time.

Designated a National Historic Landmark in 1986, the armory remains privately owned and is a military facility for the 107th Support Group of the New York National Guard. It also houses other military organizations, a tennis club, a rifle club, and a public restaurant; presents exhibitions of art and antiques; and serves as a shelter for homeless women. In late 2001 the armory became the 9/11 National Guard Center, providing support for those affected by the terrorist attacks on the World Trade Center. As of 2008 the building was undergoing a massive renovation after having been the only New York venue named on the World Monuments Fund's list of the 100 most endangered sites in the world.

Lisa Weilbacker

79th Street Boat Basin. See Boat basins.

sewers. Most cities historically had little or no underground sewage systems until the nineteenth century, and New York City was no different. In the seventeenth century and for most of the eighteenth kitchen slops were generally poured on the ground or emptied into cesspools, and sewage was collected in pails and dumped into the river. What is now Broad Street in Manhattan was originally a brook that the Dutch widened into a canal and then paved over for a road to create the city's first "common sewer," primarily designed to carry off storm water. As the city grew during the late eighteenth century, a network of sewer pipes made first of wood and later of stone and brick expanded, but without a coherent plan. Criticism of the system increased during the early nineteenth century, when the city's population neared 300,000, real estate development disrupted the island's natural drainage, backyard privies overflowed, and riverbanks became reeking cesspools. The completion of the Croton Aqueduct in 1842 aggravated the problem by increasing the flow of water in the already overburdened sewers. Wealthy householders further contributed by installing the city's first water closets and flushing their effluent into the storm sewers.

Although some thought was given to converting sewage into fertilizer, the abundant water carried through the Croton Aqueduct made it easier to float away the city's wastes through underground pipes. Following a cholera epidemic in the mid-1800s, the Croton Aqueduct Department (1849) was given responsibility for building a comprehensive sewer system. Seventy miles (112 kilometers) of sewers were constructed from 1850 to 1855, yet the Association for Improving the Condition of the Poor estimated that three-quarters of the city's 500 miles (800 kilometers) of streets lacked sewers. The Metropolitan Health Board (1866) greatly expanded the system and by the early 1890s New York City had 464 miles (747 kilometers) of sewers, more than any U.S. or European city except Chicago. In 1894 half the residents of the city's tenements lived in houses with flush toilets, and by 1902 the city had more than 1400 miles (2240 kilometers) of sewers, and most newly constructed tenements had private flush toilets.

After an elaborate system of sewer lines was constructed in the city, the Metropolitan Sewerage Commission (1910–14) turned its attention to the problem of sewage disposal. Each day a flood of sewage from six million residents flowed directly into New York Harbor. Recommendations by the commission for a sophisticated system of collection and purification were often reiterated, but in 1930 the city was still pouring 1.3 million gallons (4.9 million liters) of raw sewage into the harbor every day. The growing urgency of the problem and the availability of public works funds during the New Deal finally led to the construction of seven sewage treatment plants, the first opening on Coney Island in 1935. When it was discovered in 1942 that seven facilities could treat only about half of the city's sewage, a master plan was drawn up that recommended a system of 14 plants. The Interstate Sanitation Commission ordered the city in 1948 to hasten the pace at which the plants were being constructed. Three more plants opened in 1952, but by 1962 one-quarter of the city's sewage still went untreated. The last two of the 14 plants, North River (on the Hudson at 137th Street in Manhattan) and Red Hook (in Brooklyn), did not open until 1986 and 1987. With all its plants operating the system was able to handle the nearly 1.7 billion gallons (6.4 billion liters) of sewage carried every day through 6200 miles (9975 kilometers) of pipe, but it did not end the pollution of the waters surrounding the city. Six of the largest plants operated at or above capacity in 1991, and odors emanating from the Newtown Creek plant in Brooklyn and the North River plant in Manhattan caused resentment among local residents, who argued that the facilities had been deliberately placed in poor neighborhoods. Plants with purification processes that met specific requirements continued to dump final-stage sewage precipitate at sea until 1992, when the practice was banned. In the early twenty-first century the New York City Water Board oversees sewers.

Joseph Duffy, *A History of Public Health in New York City, 1866–1966* (New York: Russell Sage

Foundation, 1974); Jon C. Teaford, *The Unheralded Triumph: City Government in America, 1870–1900* (Baltimore: Johns Hopkins University Press, 1984)

See also Sanitation, Pollution.

Sandra Opdycke

sewing machines. New York City played a role in developing the sewing machine when Walter Hunt, a resident of the city, invented a mechanized device in 1834 that made a lock stitch with sewing thread. The region became a leading center for the manufacture of sewing machines soon after the sewing machine itself was invented in 1846 by Elias Howe of Boston. Isaac M. Singer formed I. M. Singer and Company in 1851 with Edward Clark, a lawyer who took charge of finances, and opened his main office in Manhattan, where production facilities were moved in the following year. Singer took out 20 patents between 1851 and 1863; with his competitors (among them several firms in the city such as Grove and Baker, and Wheeler and Wilson) he set up the Sewing Machine Combination in 1856, the first patent pool in the country, which lasted until 1877. Although his machines were the only ones that could stitch continuously, they sold poorly at first, prompting Clark to launch a marketing system that was one of the most innovative in the country. The firm was one of the first to have its own distribution network and developed techniques for promoting, repairing, and financing durable goods. It both responded to the demand of the rapidly growing apparel industry in the city and persistently developed the household market: during the mid-1850s the company headquarters featured lavish showrooms where young women demonstrated the use of sewing machines. In 1863 the firm was renamed the Singer Manufacturing Company. The sewing machine and the availability of textiles allowed the average family to own more clothing than even the wealthy had been able to own just one generation earlier. The primary manufacturing operation was moved to a factory complex opened in 1873 in Elizabethport, New Jersey. By 1875 the firm was the largest manufacturer of sewing machines in the world. It moved into a building designed by Ernest Flagg and completed at 561 Broadway in lower Manhattan in 1904; the Singer Tower (also designed by Flagg) was completed at 149 Broadway in 1908.

From the 1880s New York City solidified its position as the center of the garment industry in the United States. Specialized devices such as the buttonhole machine made manufacturing more efficient by allowing for an increased division of labor and a reduction in the skills that each worker required. Because the sewing machine was compact and had low power requirements, it was often operated by women both in sweatshops and in the home (where work was paid for by the piece, often at exploitative rates). From the 1950s the use of the household machine declined, largely as a result of the increasing numbers of women who worked outside their homes. The garment industry itself had declined sharply in the area by 2008.

Darwin H. Stapleton

Shaarey Zedek. Conservative synagogue opened in 1839 by Polish Jews who seceded from B'nai Jeshurun. The congregation prospered during the nineteenth and early twentieth centuries and had two branches, one in a remodeled Quaker meetinghouse on Henry Street on the Lower East Side and the other in a building in an exuberant Moorish style on 118th Street in Harlem. Shaarey Zedek moved to the Upper West Side during the 1920s.

Jenna Weissman Joselit

Shahn, Ben(jamin) (*b* Kaunas, Lithuania, 12 Sept 1898; *d* New York City, 14 March 1969). Painter and illustrator. After settling in Brooklyn with his family in 1906 he worked for a lithographer and attended New York University and the City College of New York. He left school to study at the National Academy of Design and the Art Students League, then traveled in Europe during the 1920s and returned to New York City in 1929. His series of 25 gouache paintings depicting the trial of Sacco and Vanzetti was exhibited at the Downtown Gallery in 1932. In the same year he assisted Diego Rivera in painting a mural at Rockefeller Center (later destroyed). During the 1930s he worked as a photographer for the Resettlement Administration and as a muralist for projects sponsored by the federal government in New York and New Jersey; during World War II he designed posters for the Office of War Information. Although his graphic depictions of socially relevant subjects angered many conservative politicians and critics, he was chosen to represent the United States (along with Willem de Kooning) at the Venice Biennale in 1954.

Bernarda Bryson Shahn, *Ben Shahn* (New York: Harry N. Abrams, 1972)

Patricia Hills

Shakespeare in the Park. Ongoing seasonal theater company (also known as Shakespeare in Central Park; New York Shakespeare Festival). Since 1962 the Public Theater has staged productions of Shakespeare plays each summer in the Delacorte Theater in Central Park, typically two or three plays with runs of several weeks each. The performances are free and open to the public, and they bring about 80,000 New Yorkers and tourists to the open-air theater every summer. An outgrowth of Public Theater, the Shakespeare Workshop was founded by Joseph Papp and produced free outdoor performances of Shakespeare's works starting in 1954. The workshop productions were staged all over the city at first, moving to a lawn adjacent to Central Park's Turtle Pond in 1957. The company then moved to the Delacorte Theater, where it has remained. The inaugural production there

Home of Shakespeare in the Park, Delacorte Theater and Belvedere Castle, 2009

Free Summer Season Productions of Shakespeare in the Park (New York Shakespeare Festival)

Year	Productions
1956	Julius Caesar, The Taming of the Shrew
1957	Macbeth, Two Gentlemen of Verona, Romeo and Juliet
1958	Othello, Twelfth Night
1959	Julius Caesar
1960	Henry V, Measure for Measure, The Taming of the Shrew
1961	A Midsummer Night's Dream, Richard II
1962	The Merchant of Venice, The Tempest, King Lear
1963	As You Like It, The Winter's Tale, Antony and Cleopatra
1964	A Midsummer Night's Dream, Hamlet
1965	Troilus and Cressida, Love's Labour's Lost, Coriolanus
1966	All's Well That Ends Well, Portluck!*
1967	King John, The Comedy of Errors
1968	Romeo and Juliet, Henry IV (Part I and Part II)
1969	Twelfth Night
1970	Henry VI (Part I and Part II), Richard III
1971	Timon of Athens, Two Gentlemen of Verona, Cymbeline
1972	Hamlet, Ti-Jean and His Brothers,* Much Ado about Nothing
1973	As You Like It
1974	Pericles, The Merry Wives of Windsor
1975	Hamlet, The Comedy of Errors
1976	Henry V
1977	Threepenny Opera,* Agamemnon*
1978	All's Well That Ends Well, The Taming of the Shrew
1979	Othello
1980	Pirates of Penzance*
1981	The Tempest, Henry IV (Part I)
1982	Don Juan,* A Midsummer Night's Dream
1983	Richard III, Non Pasquale*
1984	Henry V, The Golem*
1985	Measure for Measure, The Mystery of Edwin Drood*
1986	Twelfth Night, Medea*
1987	Richard II, Two Gentlemen of Verona, Henry IV (Part I)
1988	Much Ado about Nothing, King John
1989	Titus Andronicus, Twelfth Night, Cymbeline
1990	The Taming of the Shrew, Richard III, Romeo and Juliet (Spanish)
1991	Henry V, Othello, A Midsummer Night's Dream (Portuguese), The Tempest (Spanish)
1992	The Comedy of Errors, As You Like It, Woyzeck*
1993	Wings,* Measure for Measure, All's Well That Ends Well
1994	Richard II, The Merry Wives of Windsor, Two Gentlemen of Verona
1995	The Merchant of Venice, The Tempest, Troilus and Cressida
1996	King Lear, Henry V, Timon of Athens
1997	Henry VIII, Antony and Cleopatra
1998	Macbeth, Cymbeline, Pericles
1999	The Taming of the Shrew, Hamlet
2000	The Winter's Tale, Julius Caesar
2001	The Seagull,* Measure for Measure, Othello
2002	Twelfth Night
2003	Henry V, As You Like It, The Two Noble Kinsmen
2004	Much Ado about Nothing, Richard III
2005	As You Like It, Two Gentlemen of Verona
2006	Macbeth, Mother Courage and Her Children*
2007	Romeo and Juliet, A Midsummer Night's Dream
2008	Hamlet, Hair*
2009	Twelfth Night, The Bacchae*

* Plays marked with an asterisk were not written by Shakespeare.

Compiled by Frank Nestor

starred James Earl Jones and George C. Scott, and many famous stage and film actors since then, including Meryl Streep, Kevin Kline, Denzel Washington, and Natalie Portman, have gotten their start in Shakespeare in the Park or performed there later.

Rowan Moore Gerety

Shalom Aleichem Houses. Cooperative housing project at Sedgwick Avenue and 238th Street in the Bronx, organized in 1927 by the Yiddishe Cooperative Heim Gesellshaft (an offshoot of the Workmen's Circle). Named for the prominent Yiddish writer, the building contained artists' studios, an auditorium, meeting rooms, and housing for 240 families; many of the residents were artists, performers, and writers. The cooperative failed financially in 1929, but its members maintained the organization after the property was taken over, and they defeated the landlord's attempts to evict unemployed tenants in 1932. The residents continued to operate the meeting rooms, auditorium, cooperative kindergarten, and Yiddish schools until the 1960s.

Stanley Nadel

Shanker, Albert (*b* Queens, 14 Sept 1928; *d* New York City, 22 Feb 1997). Labor leader. He grew up in New York City, attended Stuyvesant High School and the University of Illinois, and did graduate work at Columbia University. After becoming a substitute teacher in 1952 he took an interest in the Teachers' Guild and after 1959 worked as a union official full time. He helped to form the United Federation of Teachers (UFT) in 1960, played an important role in securing its collective bargaining election, and was elected its president in 1964. He consistently argued that as professionals teachers deserve adequate pay and the authority to make decisions, and during the 1960s and 1970s he led several strikes to secure higher wages and an effective grievance procedure. In 1968 he led the UFT in a bitter strike after 19 school employees, including 13 teachers, were transferred involuntarily by the Ocean Hill–Brownsville School Board, which sought greater control over its staff. Charges of racism and anti-Semitism were traded, and Shanker was sentenced to 15 days in prison for defying a court order; his position was strengthened after the teachers were reinstated, and during the 1970s he made the UFT a powerful force in politics and extended membership in it to a group of assistants to classroom teachers known as paraprofessionals. He became president of the American Federation of Teachers in 1974 and served in this position until his death. Shanker also continued to lead the UFT until January 1986. In 1975 he led the UFT in a plan to save the city from bankruptcy by using pension funds to buy bonds of the Municipal Assistance Corporation.

Philip Taft, *United They Teach: The Story of the United Federation of Teachers* (Los Angeles: Nash, 1974); Richard Kahlenberg, *Tough Liberal: Albert Shanker and the Battles over Schools, Unions, Race and Democracy* (New York: Columbia University Press, 2007)

Irwin Yellowitz

shantytowns. There were many shantytowns during the 1870s and 1890s throughout New York City. More than 20 were built during the Depression, and these attracted a great deal of attention. Named Hoovervilles after President Herbert Hoover, they had about 2000 residents, most of them men, during the 1930s. The largest was the Hard Luck Town at Ninth Street and the East River, which housed about 450 men in 1933. The best-known Hooverville, set up after the Lower Reservoir was drained to make way for the Great Lawn, was variously called Hoover Valley, Shanty Village, Shack Town, Squatters Village, and Forgotten Man's Gulch. Twenty-two men were arrested for vagrancy in July 1931 after residents of Fifth Avenue complained about the "hobos" sleeping in Central Park; a sympathetic judge suspended their sentences and sent the men back to the park after giving $2 of his own money to each one. By the autumn of 1932 there were 17 shacks in the area, each furnished with chairs, beds, and a chimney. There was also a shack known as the Rockside Inn, built by unemployed bricklayers of brick with an inlaid roof. One well-known resident was Ralph Redfield, an unemployed vaudeville performer who charged visitors a fee to watch him walk a tightrope stretched across the shantytown. His act inspired Robert Nathan's novel *One More Spring*, which was made into a motion picture in 1935 and became the basis for Al Jolson's successful musical *Hallelujah I'm a Bum*. After World War II public intolerance of shantytowns increased. Between the late 1980s and mid-1990s those near Columbus Circle, Tompkins Square Park, the Port Authority Bus Terminal, the United Nations, and the base of the Manhattan Bridge were razed, forcing many of the city's 25,000 homeless to seek shelter elsewhere.

Roy Rosenzweig and Elizabeth Blackmar, *The Park and the People: A History of Central Park* (Ithaca, N.Y.: Cornell University Press, 1992)

See also HOMELESSNESS.

Chad Ludington

"A Scene in Shantytown, New York," from the New York Daily Graphic, *4 March 1880, the first halftone photograph printed in a newspaper*

Sharpton, Al(fred Charles, Jr.) (*b* Brooklyn, 3 Oct 1954). Minister and civil rights activist. He began preaching at the age of four and soon was touring as the "wonder boy preacher." He attended Samuel J. Tilden High School in Brooklyn and attended Brooklyn College from 1973 to 1975. In 1964 he was ordained, preached at the World's Fair, and toured with the gospel singer Mahalia Jackson. In the late 1960s he became a follower of Adam Clayton Powell, Jr., and in 1969 he was appointed youth director of Operation Breadbasket, a group led by Jesse Jackson for which he spent two years organizing boycotts and demonstrations to force businesses to employ blacks. In 1971 he formed an offshoot of the organization called the National Youth Movement. He met the singer James Brown in 1973, and for the next eight years he worked variously as the manager of Brown's singing tours and for the National Youth Movement, at the same time forging political connections in the black community of New York City. In 1978 he was an unsuccessful candidate for the state senate. He worked as a community activist in the early 1980s and first became widely known in 1987, when he led protests after the racially motivated murder of a black man in Howard Beach and served as an adviser to Tawana Brawley, a young black woman whose allegations that she had been raped by white men in upstate New York became a cause célèbre. Sharpton's reputation suffered when an investigation found that Brawley's charges were baseless; he was later ordered to pay $65,000 in damages to Steven A. Pagones, who was accused in the case. Sharpton's image was further damaged when he was accused of financial impropriety in the National Youth Movement (for which he was later acquitted), and it was revealed that he had worked with the Federal Bureau of Investigation to avoid being prosecuted for his connections with boxing promoter Don King. He regained notoriety in 1991 when he was stabbed in Bensonhurst while protesting the 1989 murder of a 16-year-old black boy; he also led protests in Crown Heights after the 1991 riots there. In 1992 Sharpton mounted a campaign for the Democratic nomination for the U.S. Senate in which he cultivated a moderate image, avoided an acrimonious debate indulged in by his three opponents, and won about 15 percent of the vote. He was again a candidate for the Senate in 1994, losing the Democratic primary to Senator Daniel Patrick Moynihan; he ran unsuccessfully for mayor in 1997 and for president in 2004. Sharpton organized effective large-scale protests after the 1999 police killing of unarmed West African immigrant AMADOU DIALLO in the Bronx and the 2006 police killing of Sean Bell in Queens; in the early twenty-first century he remains an active figure in politics and civil rights, in the city and nationally.

Greg Robinson

Shea, William A(lfred) (*b* New York City, 21 June 1907; *d* New York City, 2 Oct 1991). Lawyer. He grew up in Washington Heights and graduated from New York University. After several years of work for the Democratic Party in Brooklyn and for insurance companies, he entered private law practice in 1941. He was founding partner of the Shea and Gould law firm. He is best known for having restored National League baseball to New York City after the departure of the Dodgers and the Giants in 1957. His efforts led to the formation of the New York Mets in 1962, and the team's new ballpark in Flushing was named Shea Stadium in his honor in 1964.

James Bradley

Shearith Israel. First Jewish congregation in North America, formed in 1654 in New Amsterdam by a small group of Sephardim from Recife, Brazil, seeking refuge from the Inquisition. The congregation was initially denied permission by both the Dutch and the British to build a house of worship; legal impediments were gradually removed and by 1729 it built its first synagogue on Mill Street, which remained

Shearith Israel graveyard, 2009

in continuous use for almost a century. Shearith Israel was for many years the most important institution in the Jewish community: it supervised the preparation of kosher food, educated Jewish children, provided charity for the poor, adjudicated internal disputes, and supervised all Jewish marriages and burials. It ceased to be the city's only synagogue in 1825, when several Ashkenazim seceded to form B'nai Jeshurun after becoming disgruntled by what they considered an undemocratic system for distributing communal honors; this schism inspired the formation of 27 other congregations before the Civil War. By 1833 the city's Jewish population moved northward, and the synagogue moved to Crosby Street and then to 19th Street. In 1897 it moved to Central Park West and 70th Street. Designed by Arnold Brunner, the new building was said to be inspired by Greco-Roman synagogues discovered in the Mediterranean basin during the late nineteenth century. In the early twenty-first century Shearith Israel remained a vital center of Jewish religious life in New York City.

Jenna Weissman Joselit

Shea Stadium. Municipally owned stadium at Flushing Meadows–Corona Park in Queens, opened 17 April 1964 as the new home of the New York Mets baseball team. Named for William A. Shea, a lawyer instrumental in helping New York City to regain a National League baseball team in 1962, it seated 55,101. It was also home to the New York Jets from 1964 until 1983. It was designed by Praeger–Kavanagh–Waterbury as one of the largest stadiums at the time. The Mets inaugurated Shea Stadium with a 4–3 loss to the Pittsburgh Pirates. In 1975 Shea was the home field for the New York Mets and the New York Yankees as well as the New York Jets and the New York Giants — the first and only time to date that a single stadium has hosted two baseball and two football teams. Shea has hosted college football, soccer, boxing, and wrestling events, as well as concerts and mass gatherings. In 1965 the Beatles played the first large-scale outdoor stadium concert in the United States at Shea, with 55,000 fans attending the half-hour-long performance; in 1982 The Who drew a crowd of 70,346. Pope John Paul II held a Mass at the stadium in 1979 for nearly 60,000 people. After the terrorist attacks of 11 September 2001, Shea Stadium was used as a relief center where rescue workers provided food, supplies, and shelter for people in need. In 2006 city officials announced that a new municipal stadium would be built, and on 28 September 2008 the Mets played their final game in Shea. It was dismantled by February 2009, and the site is now part of the parking lot of the new Citi Field.

Steven A. Riess, Anne Epstein

Sheen, Fulton (John) (*b* El Paso, Ill., 8 May 1895; *d* New York City, 9 Dec 1979). Catholic bishop and radio and television personality. Ordained a priest of the diocese of Peoria, Illinois, on 20 September 1919, he joined the faculty of the Catholic University of America in 1926 but found his true vocation a few years later as a preacher. His weekly broadcasts on NBC Radio's "The Catholic Hour" (1930–52) and later his television program *Life Is Worth Living* (1952–57), which reached 30 million people, made him the best-known Catholic priest in the United States. The author of 93 books, Sheen received into the Catholic Church such notable converts as the journalists Heywood Broun and Louis Budenz, Congresswoman Clare Boothe Luce, and Henry Ford II. In 1950 he moved to New York City when he was appointed the national director of the Society for the Propagation of the Faith (an international fund-raising organization for Catholic missionaries), eventually raising more than $200 million. The following year he was appointed an auxiliary bishop of New York, but he later clashed with Cardinal Francis Spellman over the financial management of the Society for the Propagation of the Faith. Although Rome sided with Sheen, Spellman banned him from the pulpit of St. Patrick's Cathedral and ended his television career. In 1966 Sheen was named the bishop of Rochester, New York, but resigned after three unhappy years. He returned to New York City, was appointed a titular archbishop, and spent the remaining 10 years preaching throughout the world. He wrote *Treasure of Clay: The Autobiography of Fulton J. Sheen* (1980).

D. P. Noonan, *The Passion of Fulton Sheen* (New York: Dodd, Mead, 1972); Thomas C. Reeves, *America's Bishop: The Life and Times of Fulton J. Sheen* (San Francisco: Encounter Books, 2001)

Thomas J. Shelley

Sheep Meadow. Clearing in Central Park between 66th and 69th streets, occupying 15 acres (6 hectares) of relatively flat land. It was set aside as a parade ground (named the Green) by the principal designer of the park, Frederick Law Olmsted, to meet a requirement imposed in 1857 that proposed designs for the park must include an area for military exercises. Although the National Guard used the grounds for this purpose in 1864, a state law passed later that year banned military drills in the park. The way was then clear for the introduction of a flock of 150 sheep, a crook-carrying shepherd, and a Victorian sheepfold. During the next six decades the area was also the site of such recreational activities as dancing, baseball, and lawn tennis. In 1934 Parks Commissioner Robert Moses exiled the sheep to Prospect Park in Brooklyn and converted the sheepfold into the restaurant Tavern on the Green. During the 1960s and 1970s a succession of rallies and concerts destroyed much of the grass, reducing the area to a dustbowl. Part of the field was then fenced in, replenished with new topsoil and sod, and installed with drainage systems. Loud noise and team sports were prohibited in 1986. The meadow was renovated yet again starting in November 2000 when the Central Park Conservancy installed a new irrigation system; it reopened in April 2001. The lush lawn and skyline views of Sheep Meadow make it one of the park's most popular and picturesque attractions.

Robert Sanger Steel

Sheepshead Bay. Neighborhood in southeastern Brooklyn (2000 pop. circa 63,000), overlooking an ocean inlet of the same name to its south and bordered to the north by Marine Park, to the east by Shell Bank Creek, to the south by Manhattan Beach, and to the west by Gravesend. The area was the site of a large Canarsee Indian village and remained undeveloped for more than a century and a half after the English settled Gravesend in 1645 only a short distance to the northwest. The Wyckoff–Bennett residence (1766) is one of the most striking of the extant Dutch farmhouses in Brooklyn. In the early nineteenth century a cluster of wooden shacks took shape around the inlet, which provided a sheltered anchorage for small boats. Shortly after the Civil War the village began to attract visitors from the city during the summer, who were drawn by the cool sea breezes and the seafood that had become a local specialty. Although two hotels were built, there was no permanent growth until 1877 when a farm of 50 acres (20 hectares) by the bay was subdivided and developed. The same fate soon befell other farms, and by the end of the century the village had some 400 houses served by stores, churches, and a post office. During the 1870s John Y. McKane, the notorious political "boss" of Gravesend, facilitated the extension of several railroads and boulevards to Coney Island, making the whole southern shore more accessible than it had been before. Meanwhile, the Coney Island Jockey Club opened the Sheepshead Bay Race Track on a site of 2200 acres (1000 hectares). This was replaced in 1915 by the Sheepshead Speedway, which was demolished in 1923; the site was then subdivided into small building lots and developed.

Greenlawn Colony in Sheepshead Bay, 1992

Sheepshead Bay, 1992

In 1931 the city took title to the area around the basin as the first step toward revitalizing it. Aging structures on stilts above the water were restored, and Emmons Avenue was widened. When work was completed in the summer of 1937 the *Brooklyn Eagle* characterized the renovated neighborhood as "clean, tidy and practically odorless." The character of the neighborhood changed again after 1954 as wooden houses were replaced by six- and seven-story redbrick apartment buildings for middle-income residents. By 1960 Sheepshead Bay was the fastest-growing community in Brooklyn. It became widely known as the center of recreational fishing in New York City, and a number of private boats moored at its 10 piers and used it as a port from which to launch cruises for bluefish, snappers, and striped bass. In the 1980s the city announced new development plans for Sheepshead Bay that provided for the improvement of the piers, private residential and retail construction, an esplanade along Emmons Avenue, and a park and ferry landing at the foot of Knapp Street; these plans remained unrealized several years later. The population of the neighborhood in the early twenty-first century was mostly Italian and Jewish, though there were increasing numbers of people from Asia and the Caribbean Islands. In the neighborhood and its environs there was considerable settlement by immigrants from the former Soviet Union, China, India, Pakistan, Vietnam, Israel, the Philippines, Poland, and Guyana.

Ellen Fletcher

shellfish. A great variety of shellfish inhabit the varied estuarine environments around New York City, especially the glacially created outwash plain of Jamaica Bay and the terminal moraine landscape of the northern shore of Queens and Staten Island. The many species of bivalves include the American Oyster (*Crassostrea virginica*), the Hard-Shelled Clam (*Mya arenaria*), the Surf Clam (*Spisula solidissima*), the Razor Clam (*Ensis directus*), the Blue Mussel (*Mytilus edulis*), the Periwinkle (*Littorina littorea*), and the Channeled Whelk (*Busycon canaliculatum*). Other common invertebrates are the Blue Crab (*Callinectes sapidus*), the Common Spider Crab (*Libinia emarginata*), the American Lobster (*Homarus americanus*), young Sand Shrimp (*Crangon septemspinoa*), and the Fiddler Crab (*Uca pugnax*), which is usually found in salt marshes. New Yorkers during the eighteenth and nineteenth centuries were great shellfish-eaters, but by the early twenty-first century the waters had been overharvested and polluted by industrial and residential development, and shellfish remained unsafe to eat.

See also Oysters.

John T. Tanacredi

Sheridan, Martin (Joseph) (*b* Bohola, County Mayo, Ireland, 28 March 1881; *d* New York City, 27 March 1918). Track and field athlete. After emigrating to the United States in 1900 he joined the New York Police Department and became a detective. He trained at the New York Athletic Club and competed in the Olympic Games of 1904 (St. Louis) and 1908 (London), winning two gold medals, one silver medal, and one bronze; in unofficial games at Athens in 1906 he won three gold medals and two silver medals, a performance exceeding that of any national team. He competed in nine events and excelled in the shot put, discus, broad jump, long jump, pole vault, and stone and javelin throws. During a career lasting 16 years he set 16 world records and won 12 national championships in the United States and 30 in Canada. In 1918 the Police Department named for him its highest award for valor. Sheridan is buried in Calvary Cemetery in Queens.

John J. Concannon

Sheridan Square. Triangular park in Greenwich Village bounded by West Fourth Street, Washington Place, and Barrow Street and named for the legendary Civil War cavalry general Philip Henry Sheridan. Originally part of an Indian settlement called Sappokanican, the triangle was created when two estates were divided and was paved as part of a public road in 1830. During the late twentieth century the triangle served as a traffic safety island and was often filled with illegally parked cars and trucks. In 1981 a community group led by Vera Schneider formed the Sheridan Square Triangle Association to create a garden on the site, which it succeeded in doing the following year. The site was officially transformed from street to parkland in 1989 when it was added to New York City Department of Parks and Recreation oversight. The Sheridan Square Triangle Association, however, fully funds the park and maintains it with volunteer gardeners.

Kate Lauber

sheriff. Chief civil law enforcement office of New York City. Until 1943 positions as volunteer and paid county sheriffs were awarded to political supporters. Mayor Fiorello H. La Guardia consolidated the offices and created the first salaried sheriff's office in the United States subject to civil service. On 12 July 1990 the sheriff became a mayoral appointee. The sheriff executes mandates issued by city courts and is authorized to make civil arrests under court orders; the office is within the Department of Finance.

Neal C. Garelik

Sherry Netherland Hotel. Hotel built in 1927 at 59th Street and Fifth Avenue. Designed by the firm of Schultze and Weaver and containing 525 rooms in 40 stories, it was erected at one of the country's most distinguished addresses as the first graceful skyscraper hotel in the area. It was largely a residential hotel, advertised as "more than a place to live . . . a new way of living." Like other hotels of the time the Sherry Netherland became known for its opulent interiors and elegant appointments and helped to make luxury high-rise apartments fashionable.

Andrew Wiese

Sherry's. Restaurant and apartment hotel opened in 1890 at Fifth Avenue and 37th Street by Louis Sherry, the owner of a confectionery shop near the Metropolitan Opera House that expanded into a home catering service for the wealthy. A competitor of Delmonico's, the restaurant was the site of many elaborate parties, including a breakfast that followed the wedding of Consuelo Vanderbilt to the duke of Marlborough in 1895, and a dinner given by Herbert Barnum Seeley for men only that was raided by the police because of the presence of a nude female dancer. Delmonico's soon moved uptown and Sherry followed on 10 October 1898, opening diagonally across the street from it a 12-story restaurant and apartment hotel designed by Stanford White at the southwest corner of Fifth Avenue and 45th Street. At its new site it continued to stage outlandish events, including a dinner for the New York Riding Club at which diners ate on horseback. Sherry's closed on 17 May 1919. The building survived for a time as the Guaranty Trust Company of New York.

Allen Churchill, *The Upper Crust: An Informal History of New York's Highest Society* (Englewood Cliffs, N.J.: Prentice Hall, 1970)

Rohit T. Aggarwala

Shinn, Everett (*b* Woodstown, N.J., 7 Nov 1876; *d* New York City, 1 May 1953). Painter. After beginning his career as an artist and reporter in Philadelphia, he moved in 1897 to New York City where he worked for the *New York World* and later for *Harper's Weekly.* He initially painted urban street scenes, but after a trip to Paris in 1900 he turned his attention to the theater and society in New York City. Eventually he came to prefer a realist style, which he used to depict the life of the working class. In 1908 he took part in an exhibition of The Eight at the Macbeth Gallery. He also executed murals for the Stuyvesant Theatre (1907) and the Plaza Hotel (1945) and was active as a playwright, a costume designer, and an art director for motion pictures. In 1912 he formed the Waverly Street Players, a theatrical group that performed out of his home at 112 Waverly Place in Greenwich Village. The life of Eugene Witla, the central character in Theodore Dreiser's novel *The Genius* (1915), was purportedly based on Shinn's early career.

Edith DeShazo, *Everett Shinn, 1876–1953: A Figure in His Times* (New York: Clarkson N. Potter, 1974)

Carol Lowrey

shipbuilding. The first ship built in New York City probably was Adriaen Block's *Onrust* in 1614, and as the city developed to become the busiest port in the world early in the nineteenth century, it supported a vibrant shipbuilding and repair industry. The normalization of commerce after the American Revolution led Forman Cheeseman, Samuel Ackerly, Thomas Vail, and other shipbuilders to operate yards along the East River in lower Manhattan. The New York Navy Yard (later the New York Naval Shipyard, popularly called the Brooklyn Navy Yard) opened in 1806. The navy's first steam warship, the *Demologos,* was built there in 1814 by Adam and Noah Brown with machinery provided by Robert Fulton. As trade expanded after the War of 1812, a mile of new shipyards opened on the East River. By the 1850s, considered the golden age of wooden shipbuilding, there were 31 yards in Manhattan and Brooklyn, with a total of 2313 employees. Robert Greenhalgh Albion's *The Rise of New York Port* (1939) estimated that in 1855 a total of 96 companies (including builders, sailmakers, riggers, and rope works) depended on ship construction on the East River.

The East River yards were famous for the quality of their work, called "the standard for nearly all ports in the commercial world" by the naval architect John W. Griffiths in 1851. The most renowned shipbuilder was William H. Webb, who in 1840 took over a yard founded by his father, Isaac, extending from East Fifth Street to East Seventh Street. Webb is best remembered for the clipper ship *Young America,* the ironclad *Dunderberg,* and the packet *Charles H. Marshall,* which was the last square-rigged sailing ship built in New York City when it was launched in 1869. William H. Brown started out building crude canal boats for the Erie Canal and moved on to more complex vessels, including the yacht *America,* pilot boats, Hudson River passenger boats, and oceangoing steamers for the Collins line. Of the 55 large ships built in New York City in 1850, Brown built seven at his yard at the foot of 12th Street on the Manhattan side of the East River. In 1855 his name was on a list of New Yorkers worth more than $100,000.

Sailing ships in the mid-nineteenth century were usually designed by carving or laying up small models using principles based largely on experience and known as rules of thumb. More scientific theories developed by John W. Griffiths, John Scott Russell, and other thinkers were known but not widely applied. The most important innovation was the sharp, hollow bow that appeared during the 1840s and 1850s on such vessels as the clipper ship *Rainbow,* designed by Griffiths, and pilot boats designed by George L. Steers, who in 1851 placed such a bow (among other innovations) on the racing yacht *America,* built under his supervision at William H. Brown's yard. As an example of increasing specialization, John Ericsson's ironclad *Monitor* was outfitted at the Continental Iron Works in Greenpoint, Brooklyn, in 1862, with machinery from another company and a rotating gun turret constructed by Novelty Iron Works in Manhattan.

The *Monitor* was one of relatively few iron hulls built in New York City, which declined as a shipbuilding center after the Civil War largely because it was located some distance from ironworks. Iron shipbuilding was more common along the Delaware River. The yard of John Englis in Greenpoint built the last large wooden hulls in the area. The steamship *City of Vera Cruz* in 1874 was the last for oceangoing service, and the Hudson River steamboat *Adirondack* in 1896 was the last for inland waters. By the end of the nineteenth century shipbuilders in New York City either turned to steel or specialized in wooden construction of yachts. Propulsion machinery was provided locally. Fletcher, Harrison (later W. and A. Fletcher), the city's most renowned engine builder, was first situated on West Street and later moved to suburban Hoboken, New Jersey, which became a shipbuilding center. Many of these firms also built steam engines, boilers, and other machinery for use ashore.

As the East River yards declined after the Civil War, shipyards were opened in New Jersey, on Staten Island and nearby Shooter's Island, and on the banks of the Harlem River. After the turn of the twentieth century several builders of relatively small vessels set up shop on City Island, off the Bronx, many of them specializing in high-quality yacht construction. Henry B. Nevins founded a yard on City Island in 1907. From the 1920s through the 1950s the Nevins Yacht Yard, working closely with the naval architecture firm Sparkman and Stephens, built hundreds of wooden yachts, including the yawl *Bolero* and the America's Cup winner *Columbia*. The yachts built by Nevins and other City Island yards (including Jacobs and Minneford) were more expensive than yachts built in New England and elsewhere and were the most advanced. Because of their experience with wooden construction long after most large shipyards moved to steel and iron, Nevins and other yacht yards were chosen by the U.S. Navy and other navies to build minesweepers during World War II and the cold war. When most yachts began to be built of fiberglass and aluminum, Nevins and similar yards closed down or were converted to service operations.

The Staten Island Shipbuilding Yard, later owned by Bethlehem Steel, was the only important shipbuilding firm in the city to survive the 1930s and was a major builder of destroyers during World War II. Other shipyards on the Harlem River and in Brooklyn turned out patrol crafts, tugs, and barges, while battleships, aircraft carriers, and cruisers were built in the Brooklyn Navy Yard (both the battleship *Arizona,* which sank with 1100 sailors at Pearl Harbor, and the battleship *Missouri,* on whose deck the Japanese formally surrendered on 2 September 1945, were built at the Brooklyn Navy Yard). But the long history of New York City shipbuilding was coming to an end. The Navy Yard closed in 1966, and Todd Shipyards and Bethlehem Steel closed 20 years later.

Robert Greenhalgh Albion, *The Rise of New York Port, 1815–1860* (New York: Charles Scribner's Sons, 1939; repr. 1970); John Rousmaniere, *The Low Black Schooner: Yacht America, 1851–1945* (Mystic, Conn: Mystic Seaport Museum Stores, 1987); Edwin L. Dunbaugh and William duBarry Thomas: *William H. Webb, Shipbuilder* (Glen Cove, N.Y.: Webb Institute of Naval Architecture, 1989); Phillip Lopate, *Waterfront: A Journey around Manhattan* (New York: Crown, 2004); John Rousmaniere, *In a Class by Herself: The Yawl* Bolero *and the Passion for Craftsmanship* (Mystic, Conn.: Mystic Seaport, 2006)

John Rousmaniere, William duBarry Thomas

shoes, boots, and leather. The tanning pits used to cure leather in New York City were concentrated as early as 1680 in the Swamp, a section of lower Manhattan near the East River and the Brooklyn Bridge. The pits were considered a nuisance and were moved to Maiden Lane and William and Gold streets, names later used in the marketing of leather goods. Tanneries were small operations that relied mostly on local hides and skins; leather for shoe and boot soles was imported from Britain. By 1813 these stocks were no longer adequate for the demands of shoe, saddlery, and harness manufacturers, and as a result tanners, especially those in the Catskill Mountains, sought out Latin American hides. According to the federal census of 1810 there were nine tanneries in Manhattan and six in Brooklyn; they used lighter skins for shoe and boot uppers and darker, hemlock-tanned ones for soles. By the 1840s and 1850s the brokers who bought and sold this sole leather were clustered in the Swamp under such names as Gideon Lee, Charles M. Leupp, and Thorne, Watson, Corse and Company. Shoe factories in the city before the Civil War were small and were not mechanized and usually stood near the leather brokers, who also provided sole leather to firms in New Jersey, Philadelphia, and Massachusetts. In 1860 about 70 percent of the firms in the metropolitan area were in Manhattan, and the 5500 workers in the leather industry accounted for 5 percent of the city's labor force in manufacturing. Leather manufacture was transformed during the war by new technology and an increased demand for leather goods.

Between 1860 and World War I the city's leather industry expanded. It employed 20,000 workers, about 3 percent of those in manufacturing, and in 1913 footwear accounted for 53 percent of employment in the leather industry in New York City, ranking the city among the five largest shoe centers in the country; it was known especially for its fine women's shoes. Although the factories in Brooklyn were fewer in number than those in Manhattan, they were larger and employed about two-thirds of the city's shoe workers. Several firms in the city came to dominate the national market. Shoes of higher quality were made possible by the Goodyear welt machine, which was invented by Charles Goodyear, Jr. (1833–96) and improved the method of attaching uppers to soles. The shoe firm of John H. Hannan (*b* 1849) in Brooklyn, one of the largest in the country, was among the first to use trademarks, national advertising, and its own retail stores to increase sales. Hannan also helped to organize the United Shoe Machinery Company in 1899, of which he was vice president until 1907, and became the first president of the National Boot and Shoe Manufacturers Association in 1904. Mark Hoyt (1834–96), the youngest child in a well-known family of tanners, helped in 1893 to form the United States Leather Company, a firm known as the "leather trust" and based in the city.

Bolstered by the presence of the fashion industry in Manhattan, leather manufacturers remained strong and employed more than 31,000 workers in the decade after World War II; a third of these produced footwear, another third produced such items as handbags, and more were employed in Manhattan than in Brooklyn. From the mid-1960s the leather industry declined as the number of imported shoes increased and consumers turned to less expensive canvas and rubber footwear. The number of leather workers fell from 19,000 in 1967 to 5800 in 1988, representing about 2.5 percent of the city's manufacturing sector. Handbags and other small leather goods accounted for almost 60 percent of the labor force; there were fewer than 1000 shoe workers, and only one firm employed more than 100. In the early twenty-first century the number of leather workers

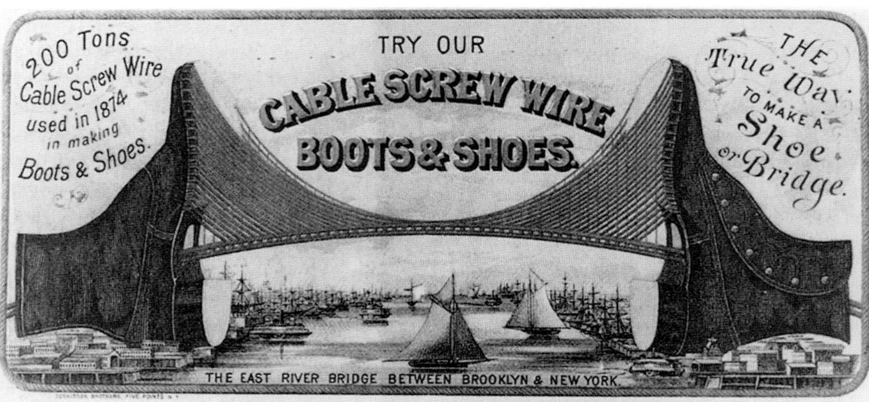

Advertisement for Donaldson Brothers' cable screw wire boots and shoes, ca *1875*

continued to decline; as a capital of fashion the city nonetheless remained an important center for products requiring skilled labor and fresh ideas.

Frank W. Norcross, *A History of the New York Swamp* (New York: Chiswick, 1901); Charles H. McDermott, *A History of the Shoe and Leather Industries of the United States* (Boston: John W. Denehy, 1918); Edgar Malone Hoover, *Location Theory and the Shoe and Leather Industries* (Cambridge, Mass.: Harvard University Press, 1937)

James L. Wiles

Sholem Aleichem [Rabinowitz, Sholem] (*b* Pereyaslavl, Russia [now Pereyaslav–Khmelnitski, Ukraine], 3 March 1859; *d* New York City, 13 May 1916). Writer, sometimes called "the Jewish Mark Twain." The pen name that he used—Sholem Aleichem—is a Hebrew greeting meaning "peace be with you." His stories of Jewish life in eastern Europe were popular in the United States, though his attempts to write for an American immigrant audience were largely unsuccessful when he lived in New York City (1906–7, 1914–16). His funeral, which took place in the city, was attended by more than 100,000 mourners, and after his death he was venerated as an icon of European Yiddish culture. Sholem Aleichem's works have been extensively translated into English, and the Broadway musical *Fiddler on the Roof* was based on his stories about Tevye and Dairyman. A system of secular Yiddish schools and a cooperative apartment complex in the Bronx are named after him.

Joseph and Frances Butwin, *Sholom Aleichem* (Boston: Twayne, 1977)

Jeffrey Shandler

Shooters Island. Island off the northwestern shore of Staten Island in the Kill van Kull. It has a land area of 51 acres (21 hectares), of which one-third lies in New Jersey and the rest in New York State. The island was popular for duck hunting during colonial times, and during the American Revolution it was a haven for spies. In the late nineteenth century it became a shipbuilding center: the Townsend Downey Shipyard launched Kaiser Wilhelm's yacht *Meteor* from the island in 1907. The industry declined after World War I and, after a brief revival during World War II, the island was abandoned. In the early twenty-first century it was covered with derelict piers, dry docks, and rotting debris. Five species of heron and other sea birds are found on Shooters Island, which is protected as a wildlife sanctuary. The New York Audubon Society is in charge of wildlife research on the island.

Gerard R. Wolfe

shopping malls. Regional shopping malls were developed throughout Greater New York after 1970. The three largest malls in the five boroughs are the Queens Center at Queens and Woodhaven boulevards, King's Plaza in Mill Basin in Brooklyn, and the Staten Island Mall in Heartland Village. There are smaller malls in Manhattan, which lack the large parking lots of their counterparts in the outer boroughs: A&S Plaza at Sixth Avenue and 33rd Street, the World Financial Center at Battery Park City, Manhattan Mall at 34th Street and Broadway, Trump Tower at Fifth Avenue and 56th Street, Citicorp Center at 53rd Street and Lexington Avenue, and the Time Warner Center at Columbus Circle. The largest malls in the region tend to be in the suburbs, especially Paramus and Jersey Gardens in New Jersey, White Plains and Palisades in New York, and Stamford in Connecticut.

Richard Kobliner

Shop Rite. Name used from the 1950s by several supermarkets in New York City and its environs belonging to the Wakefern Cooperative, a group formed by several small grocers in New Jersey to counter the proliferation of large grocery chains. The supermarkets grew rapidly during the 1950s and 1960s by using such innovative techniques as maintaining butcher departments and stocking frozen foods and nonfood items. In 1968 a group within the Wakefern Cooperative broke away to form the chain known as Pathmark. As of 2008 Shop Rite and the Wakefern Corporation had a revenue of more than $7.5 billion.

Chad Ludington

Shor, Toots [Bernard] (*b* Philadelphia, 6 May 1903; *d* New York City, 23 Jan 1977). Restaurateur. He attended the Drexel Institute and the Wharton School of Business, worked as a salesman, and in 1930 moved to New York City. In 1940 he opened the first of several restaurants named Toots Shor's Restaurant at 51 West 51st Street. The establishment, which featured a circular bar, became popular with tourists and celebrities such as Joe DiMaggio, Mickey Mantle, Red Smith, Jack Dempsey, Frank Gifford, Frank Sinatra, and Jackie Gleason. Shor was big, social, loud, and brash and often insulted customers, notably the football player Joe Namath and the film producer Louis B. Mayer. In 1959 he sold the lease on the original restaurant, and in the following year he opened a new one with virtually identical decor at 33 West 52nd Street; he later opened a restaurant at 5 East 54th Street that was less successful than the two earlier ones had been. At the time of his death Shor operated three restaurants, at 1 Penn Plaza, 64 West 52nd Street, and 44 East 43rd Street.

Eric Wm. Allison

Shore Acres. Neighborhood in northeastern Staten Island lying on a bluff overlooking the Verrazano–Narrows Bridge and bounded to the north by Harborview Place, to the east by Upper New York Bay, to the south by Von Briesen Park, and to the west by Bay Street; it is near Fort Wadsworth. The land belonged to the estate of Henry Alexandre during the nineteenth century and was developed in the 1930s by Cornelius G. Kolff, an entrepreneur who lived at 15 Harbor View Place South. Known for its views inland and toward the Narrows, Shore Acres is an exclusive residential neighborhood. The principal street is Sea Gate Road.

Barnett Shepherd

Short, Bobby [Short, Robert Waltrip] (*b* Danville, Ill., 9 Sept 1915; *d* New York City, 21 March 2005). Cabaret singer and pianist. He was already an experienced child singer and pianist by the time he first broached the New York jazz scene at the age of 12; but not until 1968, following a busy career performing in nightclubs throughout the United States and in Europe, did he begin appearing at the intimate Café Carlyle (Madison Avenue at 76th Street), which would remain his principal venue for 37 years. He spent half of each year performing there, sometimes backed by a swing band but more often seated at the piano (assisted by a drummer and bass player) accompanying his own gravelly baritone in rhythmically precise, perfectly enunciated song interpretations. His repertoire focused on classic popular songs by Cole Porter, George Gershwin, and their ilk, but he also quietly championed works by underappreciated African American songwriters such as composer James P. Johnson and lyricist Andy Razaf, whose "Guess Who's in Town?" served as his virtual theme song. Short became a fixture of high-society entertainment that connected the Harlem style of Cab Calloway to the hyper-refined elegance of modern nightclub culture.

Bobby Short and Robert Mackintosh, *Bobby Short: The Life and Times of a Saloon Singer* (New York: Clarkson Potter, 1995)

James M. Keller

Shrine of St. Elizabeth Ann Seton. Roman Catholic complex at 7–8 State Street, Manhattan. Seton lived at number 8 from 1801 to 1803. Number 7 (the James Watson House, built 1793–1806) became the Church of Our Lady of the Rosary in 1883. In 1964 a new church incorporating a shrine to Seton replaced number 8, and number 7 became its rectory.

Joseph Ditta

Shubert Organization. Theater syndicate formed in the late nineteenth century in Syracuse, New York, by Sam S. Shubert (?1877–1905), Lee Shubert (?1875–1953), and J(acob) J. Shubert (?1879–1963), the sons of immigrants from East Prussia. After operating theaters in upstate New York for several years they began in 1900 to work in New York City and to present light theatrical entertainment. Soon they controlled the Herald Square Theatre on Broadway and 35th Street, the Casino Theatre on Broadway and 39th Street, and the Lyric Theatre on 42nd Street. Sam Shubert was generally considered the head of the firm, which came into conflict with the Theatrical Syndicate, a powerful organization operated by Marc Klaw and Abraham Erlanger. After Sam Shubert was killed in a railroad accident, most expected his brothers to sell their business to Klaw and Erlanger; instead, they expanded it, and by the late 1920s they owned more than 100 theaters around the country. Among those in the city were the Shubert Theatre (1913) and the Broadhurst Theatre (1917), both on 44th Street; the Booth Theatre (1913) on 45th Street; and the Ethel Barrymore Theatre (1928) on 47th Street (all of which the organization retained into the early twenty-first century). Some of their most successful presentations included the summer revue *The Passing Show* (1912–22), *Artists and Models* (1923), and *The Student Prince* (1924). Performers who were associated with the organization included Alla Nazimova, Al Jolson, Ethel Barrymore, the team of Olsen and Johnson, and Carmen Miranda. Jacob Shubert's son John Shubert (1908–62) ran the company during the 1950s, followed by a great-nephew of the Shubert brothers, Lawrence Shubert Lawrence, Jr. (1916–92). In the 1970s the company produced plays under the direction of its chairman Gerald Schoenfeld (1924–2008) and its president Bernard Jacobs (1916–96). Productions during the 1970s and 1980s included *Ain't Misbehavin'* (1978), *Cats* (1982), and *Jerome Robbins' Broadway* (1989). As of 2004 the Shuberts owned and operated 16 Broadway theaters and had produced more than 500 comedies, melodramas, musicals, operettas, and revues. They had offices at 234 West 44th Street above the Sam H. Shubert Theatre in what had once been Lee Shubert's living quarters, the entrance to which was on Shubert Alley (which runs west of Broadway from 44th Street to 45th Street next to the Shubert and Booth theaters).

Jerry Stagg, *The Brothers Shubert* (New York: Random House, 1968); Brooks McNamara, *The Shuberts of Broadway* (New York: Oxford University Press, 1990)

Brooks McNamara

"sick chicken case." See SCHECHTER POULTRY CORP. V. UNITED STATES.

Sickles, Daniel E(dgar) (*b* New York City, 20 Oct 1819; *d* New York City, 3 May 1914). Legislator and Civil War general. As a state senator from New York City he sponsored legislation in 1855 authorizing the acquisition of the land that became Central Park. From 1856 to 1861 he represented the city in the U.S. House of Representatives as a Democrat. His most notable act during his tenure was killing Philip Barton Key (a son of Francis Scott Key) for allegedly having an affair with Sickles's wife; in a bizarre trial Sickles became the first defendant in the United States acquitted on grounds of temporary insanity. At the request of the governor of New York he raised a volunteer brigade during the Civil War. Promoted to major-general, he played an important role at the Battle of Gettysburg in 1863 when his controversial moves on 2 July resulted in many casualties, as well as the loss of his own leg. In later positions in the United States and abroad he was often accused of incompetence and impropriety. After returning to the city he was elected to another term in Congress (1893–95). Bankrupt and separated from his family, Sickles spent the rest of his life in Manhattan where he died in his home at Fifth Avenue and 19th Street.

W. A. Swanberg, *Sickles the Incredible* (Gettysburg, Pa.: Stan Clark Military Books, 1992); Thomas Kenneally, *American Scoundrel: The Life of the Notorious Civil War General Dan Sickles* (New York: Nan A. Talese, 2002)

James Bradley

sidewalks. New York City's first official pedestrian way was established in 1672, when the Mayor's Court ordered that "a Strooke or foot path" be laid on Pearl Street. Before long, slightly elevated walkways to the sides of streets were constructed to allow citizens to proceed unhindered by the hogs, sewage, wagons, and rough cobblestones that made the city's streets dangerous to pedestrians. After the American Revolution, the Common Council passed several acts regarding walking spaces. By 1817 sidewalks were required to be paved with flat stones or bricks, and newly paved streets were required to have footpaths of specified width (streets 40 and 60 feet [12 and 18 meters] wide were required to have footpaths 10 and 16 feet [3 and 5 meters] wide, respectively). Although a sidewalk was the city's property, maintenance was the duty of the owners of adjacent property.

The law barred carriages, wheelbarrows, horses, and obstructive wood piles and coal bins from sidewalks. The accidents receiving the most attention were caused by falling building materials. "Brickbats, rafters, and slates are showering down in every direction," Philip Hone wrote in his diary in 1839, during one of the city's first construction booms. "There is no safety in the sidewalks, and the head must be saved at the expense of soiling the boots." By 1894 the city had enough safe sidewalks for James W. Blake and Charles B. Lawlor to write the song that became New York City's anthem, promising that, "East Side, West Side, all around the town," even a child could "trip the light fantastic on the sidewalks of New York." But pedestrians continued to be harmed. The death of a Barnard College student in 1979 due to falling building materials caused the Buildings Department to launch periodic crackdowns on inadequate sidewalk scaffolding.

As the length of New York City sidewalks approached 13,000 miles (20,921 kilometers), ultimate responsibility for sidewalks remained unsettled until 2003, when three amendments to Section 7 of the New York City Administrative Code unequivocally charged property owners with the responsibility of keeping sidewalks abutting their properties "in a reasonably safe condition" and requiring them to carry liability insurance. Even as sidewalks were covered, other dangers appeared. In 2008 there were 592,130 trees in city streets, enough to cause damage to an estimated 22,229 sidewalks. The city paid $321.2 million in legal settlements during 2003–8 for accidents.

Sidney I. Pomerantz, *New York: An American City, 1783–1803: A Study in Urban Life* (Port Washington, N.Y.: I. J. Friedman, 2nd edn 1965); *Records of New Amsterdam, 1653–1674,* vol. 6, ed. Berthold Fernow (Baltimore: Genealogical Publishing, 1976); Kathleen Lucadamo, "Falling through the Cracks," *New York Daily News,* 9 March 2009

John Rousmaniere

Siegel–Cooper. Firm of retailers, based in Chicago, occupying a store on Sixth Avenue between 18th and 19th streets in New York City. Known as the "big store," it had 18 acres (7 hectares) of floor space and was the largest department store in the city at its opening in 1896; it stood in the heart of the LADIES' MILE. In addition to a vast selection of merchandise the store provided such amenities as a post office, a dental parlor, a theater, an art gallery, and a nursery. In 1903 the management published one of the first newspapers for employees, *Thought and Work.* The store relied on elaborate advertising gimmicks and high-volume sales but also promoted its elegance and fashionable address with the slogan "Meet Me at the Fountain," referring to its huge centerpiece fountain with a replica of Daniel Chester French's statue *Republic.* Siegel–Cooper declared bankruptcy in 1915.

Elaine S. Abelson

Sigel, Franz (*b* Sinsheim, Baden, 18 Nov 1824; *d* New York City, 22 Aug 1902). Soldier, editor, and public official. He moved to the United States after the German Revolution of 1848 and in May 1852 settled in New York City where he worked as a tobacconist, surveyor, draftsman, and musician. With his father-in-law, Rudolph Dulon, he formed the German-American Institute in 1855; he also taught in the city's public schools and at the German Turner Society, belonged to the Fifth New York Militia, and wrote for the *New Yorker Staats-Zeitung* and the *New York Times.* In August 1857 he moved to St. Louis to teach at the German–American Institute. When the Civil War broke out he joined the Union army and became a major-general after fighting in several campaigns. He returned to New York City after the war and in 1869 worked for the Brooklyn Steamship and Emigration Company and the Metropolitan Railway Company. In June 1870 he was appointed internal revenue collector for the ninth New York district by President Ulysses S. Grant. Elected to one term as register of the city in 1871, he served during Grover Cleveland's presidency as chief clerk in the county clerk's office (May 1885 to June 1886) and pension agent for the New York district (March 1886 to May 1889). After retiring from politics Sigel published the *New Yorker Deutsches Volksblatt* and edited the *New York Monthly* from 1897 to 1904. An equestrian statue of him was dedicated at 106th Street and Riverside Drive in 1907, and a park bounded by 158th Street, the Grand Concourse, 153rd Street, and Walton Avenue in the Bronx was named for him.

Stephen D. Engle, *Yankee Dutchman: The Life of Franz Sigel* (Fayetteville: University of Arkansas Press, 1993)

Stephen D. Engle

Silicon Alley. A takeoff on California's Silicon Valley area that refers to high-technology, multimedia, and Internet companies located in Manhattan. Initially, the term referred to areas of Chelsea, the garment district, So-Ho, Flatiron, and parts of lower Manhattan where high-tech firms began to congregate in the early 1990s. Attracted by lower rents, the city's pool of creative talent, and the proximity to major media, advertising, and publishing firms, those firms expanded rapidly as the Internet boom took off from 1995 to 2001. New York City technology firms became the country's third largest recipient of venture capital, and employment in the newer media hit 140,000 according to a 2000 estimate. The collapse of Internet and tech stocks after March 2001 and the terrorist attacks of 11 September 2001 produced massive layoffs. The sector began to recover in 2005, thanks to nearly ubiquitous Internet usage, a booming Internet advertising market, and massive investments by major media, telecommunications, and advertising companies in newer media. Estimates of the industry's employment vary widely, as government statistics lump many new media jobs into other industries and media sectors, but in 2006 the *City Journal* estimated that Internet and high-tech firms employed about 80,000 to 100,000 people in New York City, producing an annual payroll of $8 billion.

George Winslow

silk stocking district. Loose term usually applied to the congressional district that includes the Upper East Side of Manhattan and sometimes to state and local legislative districts in the same area. First recorded in 1897, the name arose because of the concentration of wealthy residents along Fifth and Park Avenues and nearby streets, making the district the wealthiest in the United States. The richest people in the world, such as Andrew Carnegie, Cornelius Vanderbilt, and John D. Rockefeller, built homes there in the early twentieth century. Gracie Mansion is the last of many grand homes in the area. Because of decennial redistricting the boundaries of the congressional district have changed repeatedly, as has the number by which the district is designated (successively eighteen, seventeen, fifteen, and fourteen). Representatives from the district have exerted a disproportionately large influence in Washington, D.C., because of their prominent constituents. In general they have exemplified the liberal, patrician brand of Republicanism with which the district has long been associated. John V. Lindsay represented the district from 1959 to 1965 before his election as mayor; Edward I. Koch, who also later was mayor, became in 1968 the first Democrat to represent the district in 34 years. After Koch was elected mayor in 1977 the district was represented by Bill Green, a liberal Republican. Redistricting brought about by the federal census of 1990 enlarged the district and diluted its liberal Republican character, and in 1992 Green was defeated by a Democrat, Carolyn B. Maloney.

Andrew Sparberg

Silk Stocking Regiment. See Seventh Regiment.

Sills, Beverly [Silverman, Belle] (*b* Brooklyn, 25 May 1929, *d* Manhattan, 2 June 2007). Opera singer and administrator. At the age of three she was named Brooklyn's "Miss Beautiful Baby 1932." As a child she performed in the first radio advertisement to include singing, and in 1947 she made her debut as a soprano with the Philadelphia Civic Opera. With the New York City Opera she sang the role of Rosalinde in Johann Strauss's *Die Fledermaus* in 1955, Baby Doe in the Douglas Moore opera *The Ballad of Baby Doe* in 1959, and Cleopatra in Handel's *Giulio Cesare* in 1966, which was considered her break-out role. Nicknamed "Bubbles" for her effervescent personality, in 1975 she also began performing at the Metropolitan Opera. In 1979 she became the general director of the New York City Opera and devoted herself to the position full time after retiring from the stage in the following year. She became a managing director of the Metropolitan Opera in 1991. In 1994 she became chairwoman of the Lincoln Center for the Performing Arts, a position she held for eight years. In 2002 she became chairwoman for the Metropolitan Opera, and she retired in 2005.

B. Kimberly Taylor

silver. The first goldsmith recorded in New Amsterdam was Jeuriaen Blanck, Sr., in 1643, but he may not have practiced his craft in the colony. Only after the 1664 English conquest, when silver coin, bullion, and outmoded plate became widely available, was there enough wealth to support several smiths. The first silversmith who was not from the Netherlands was Bartholomew LeRoux (1663–1713), a Huguenot refugee who settled in the city in 1687. He trained his son John, another son, Charles (1689–1745), who was the silversmith for the Common Council from 1720 to 1743, and Peter Van Dyck (1684–1750). Charles LeRoux in turn trained succeeding generations of apprentices. Between 1723 and 1745 the city supported as many as 23 silversmiths. By 1750 about 60 silversmiths worked in the city, of whom 32 were of Dutch heritage, 10 French Huguenot, and seven English. They produced a wide range of objects, usually in the prevailing English fashion; they also developed distinctive forms like the brandywine bowl, as well as an ornamental vocabulary encompassing meander wire, cut-card work, and cast appliqués. Silversmiths in New York City used distinctive marks, such as the trefoil of Gerrit Onckelbag, the stylized initials of Peter Van Dyck, and the conjoined initials of Cornelius Vander Burch. During the mid-eighteenth century silversmiths in the city kept abreast of

Brandywine bowl by Gerrit Onckelbag, ca *1710*

international fashions by importing silver and plated wares and engraved designs and by employing British and European silver workers who had settled in the city, among them Daniel Christian Fueter, a Swiss Moravian, who worked from 1754 to 1769, and his chaser John Anthony Beau of Geneva, Switzerland. British designs predominated in the products of such mid-century silversmiths as Myer Myers, who won commissions from churches, synagogues, and prominent families.

The production of silver declined during the American Revolution as patriots including Myers sought safety in Philadelphia, New Jersey, and Connecticut. After the Revolution international neoclassicism was quickly adopted by the city's silver workers, among them Daniel Van Voorhis (1751–1824) and Ephraim Brasher (1744–1810), who seamed sleek surfaces from rolled or "flatted" sheet silver and decorated them with bright-cut engraving and beading. During the early decades of the nineteenth century the silver trade reorganized, as smaller manufacturers stopped selling their wares directly to customers, instead supplying them to retailers who often advanced capital to buy bullion and also shared in any profits. Large firms dominated by mid-century. In 1855 the firm of William Gale and Son employed 65 men and 10 boys; its competitors, Charles Wood and Jasper W. Hughes, employed 60 men, 20 women, 10 boys, and 15 girls. Products were distributed throughout the Midwest and the South. In 1851 the firm of Tiffany and Company made an exclusive arrangement with a leading silversmith, John Chandler Moore, to make hollowware pieces. Moore's son Edward C. Moore directed the manufactory. After the Civil War Tiffany and Company secured much of the luxury trade, particularly for objects in the "testimonial ostentatious" style. During the late nineteenth and the early twentieth centuries the industry consolidated and many plants left Manhattan. Silver continued to be hand wrought in the studios of such silver workers as the German-born Peter Müller-Munk (1904–67) and the jeweler Marie Zimmermann (1878–1972) and in classes at the Craft Students League.

Deborah Dependahl Waters

Silver Beach. Neighborhood in the eastern Bronx, lying on a bluff near the tip of Throgs Neck overlooking the East River. The land was used as a lookout during the American Revolution. A farm in the area owned by the Stephenson family was sold in 1795 to Abijah Hammond, who built a mansion (later the offices of the Silver Beach Garden Corporation). In the 1920s the Peters and Sorgenfrei families formed Silver Beach Garden (named for the color of the beach at low tide), a summer colony of bungalows that were later adapted for year-round use; most of the streets were named for flowers and trees found on the Hammond estate. Residents owned their houses but rented the land until 1972 when they joined together to buy it. In the early twenty-first century there are 350 small houses lying along narrow lanes. The neighborhood is not easily accessible, and its policy of requiring any prospective owners to have three current residents as references has insulated the area from change.

Gary Hermalyn and Robert Kornfeld, *Landmarks of the Bronx* (New York: Bronx County Historical Society, 1990)

Gary D. Hermalyn

Silver Lake. Neighborhood in northeastern Staten Island, comprising the area around Silver Lake Park. In the late nineteenth century the area now occupied by the park was a popular resort for boating, fishing, picnics, and ice skating and the site of a hotel. The lake once supported a thriving ice-harvesting business. The main thoroughfare is Victory Boulevard, where there are several attractive one-family houses. All of the neighborhood is at high elevation, giving sweeping views to the north. The recreation area is maintained by the parks department and has a golf course, tennis courts, and walking trails; it is also the site of summer concerts. Beneath the lake in giant tanks is the main reservoir for Staten Island's water supply from the Catskills.

Marjorie Johnson

Silverstein, Larry A. (*b* New York City, 30 May 1931). Real estate developer and investor. He became involved in real estate with his father, Harry G. Silverstein, and then brother-in-law, Bernard Mendik, establishing Silverstein Properties and buying their first building in 1957. After splitting with Mendik in 1977 Silverstein bought several Manhattan buildings throughout the 1970s and 1980s, and also made a winning bid to construct 7 World Trade Center, to the north of the World Trade Center, for the Port Authority of New York. In January 2001 Silverstein, via Silverstein Properties and Westfield America, made a $3.2 billion bid for the lease to the World Trade Center. His bid was accepted on 24 July 2001, the first time in the building's 31-year history that it had changed management. Less than two months later the terrorist attacks of 11 September decimated the area. Silverstein declared his intent to rebuild but ran into several disputes with insurers over whether the attack constituted one or two occurrences. A settlement was made in 2004 for $4.55 billion. An agreement was reached in April 2006 with the port authority, and Silverstein retained the rights to build three office towers.

Benjamin Yakas

Simkhovitch [née Kingsbury]**, Mary (Melinda)** (*b* near Boston, 8 Sept 1867; *d* New York City, 15 Nov 1951). Famed settlement house founder. She was educated in Massachusetts and Berlin and in 1899 married Vladimir G. Simkhovitch. In 1902 she formed the Cooperative Social Settlement Society on Jones Street, later known as Greenwich House; she was its head resident until 1946. By the 1930s she concentrated on national housing reform; she led the Public Housing Conference from 1932 to 1943 and was vice chairman of the New York City Housing Authority from 1934 to 1947.

Betty Boyd Caroli

Simon, Kate [Grobsmith, Kaila] (*b* Warsaw, 5 Dec 1912; *d* New York City, 4 Feb 1990). Writer. In 1917 she moved to New York City with her mother and younger brother to join her father, who had settled there in 1914. After growing up near 178th Street and Lafontaine Avenue in the Bronx she earned a bachelor's degree from Hunter College. She wrote a number of books about the city, including *New York Places and Pleasures: An Uncommon Guidebook* (1959), which became a best seller; *New York* (1964, illustrated with photographs of the city by Andreas Feininger); and *Fifth Avenue: A Very Social History* (1978). Among her autobiographical works are *Bronx Primitive: Portraits in a Childhood* (1982), *A Wider World: Portraits in an Adolescence* (1986), and *Etchings in an Hourglass* (1990).

Allen J. Share

Simon, (Marvin) Neil (*b* New York City, 4 July 1927). Playwright. He was born in the Bronx and attended DeWitt Clinton High School and New York University. In 1948 he quit his job as a mailroom clerk at the Warner Brothers offices in Manhattan to become a sketch writer for the *Phil Silvers Arrow Show* (1948), contributed sketches to the Broadway revue *Catch a Star* (1955), and collaborated with his brother Daniel on the revue *New Faces of 1956*. His first full-length play was *Come Blow Your Horn* (1961). During the following decades he wrote more than a dozen comedies set in New York City, including *Barefoot in the Park* (1963), *The Odd Couple* (1965), and *Prisoner of Second Avenue* (1971), all of which were adapted for film, television, or both. Simon is known for writing about growing up in working-class New York City neighborhoods, especially in his autobiographical trilogy, *Brighton Beach Memoirs* (1983), *Biloxi Blues* (1985), and *Broadway Bound* (1986). The follow-up to these plays, *Lost in Yonkers* (1991), received a Tony Award for best play as well as a Pulitzer Prize. He won the Mark Twain Prize for American Humor in 2006.

Sara J. Steen

Simon, Paul (*b* Newark, N.J., 13 Oct 1941). Singer and songwriter. He grew up in Forest Hills in Queens, graduated from Queens College, and briefly attended Brooklyn Law School. From 1964 to 1971 he belonged with

Art Garfunkel to a duo known as Simon and Garfunkel that forged a distinctive genre known as folk-rock: among their well-known songs is "The 59th Street Bridge Song (Feelin' Groovy)" (1966). After embarking on a career as a soloist he continued to maintain a residence in New York City and gave several concerts there, including one at Radio City Music Hall in April 1987 and another in Central Park on 15 August 1991 before an audience of 750,000. He also performed with Garfunkel in Central Park in September 1981. In February 2009 Simon and Garfunkel performed in New York City at the recently renovated Beacon Theatre, and in October of that year they sang together again at Madison Square Garden for the 25th anniversary of the Rock and Roll Hall of Fame, into which they were inducted in 1990.

Simon and Schuster. Firm of book publishers, formed in 1924 by Richard L. Simon (1899–1960) and Max Lincoln Schuster (1897–1970) in a three-room office at 37 West 57th Street. Its first title was a crossword puzzle book that became a best seller. A paperback division called Pocket Books began operations in 1939. Over the years the firm published such writers as William Shirer, Joseph Heller, Joan Didion, Margaret Atwood, John Gregory Dunne, Larry McMurtry, and Anthony Burgess. It also became noted for its aggressive advertising. In 1975 the firm was acquired by Gulf and Western Industries, which later became Paramount Communications. After Paramount was in turn acquired by Viacom, Simon and Schuster in 1994 took over all the publishing operations of Viacom worldwide. In 2009 Simon and Schuster maintained its headquarters at 1230 Sixth Avenue in Rockefeller Center.

Peter Schwed, *Turning the Pages: An Insider's Story of Simon and Schuster* (New York: Macmillan, 1984)

See also Book publishing.

James Bradley

Simplicity Pattern Company. Firm of pattern makers formed in New York City in 1927 by James J. Shapiro. Specializing in simple designs sold at low prices, it opened a foreign subsidiary in 1928 and a large manufacturing plant in Michigan in 1931 and soon became the largest pattern company in the world. In 1998 the company was acquired by Conso Products Company. In 2009 the firm's executive offices were at 2 Park Avenue in Manhattan.

Marc Ferris

Sinatra, Frank [Francis Albert] (*b* Hoboken N.J., 12 Dec 1915; *d* Los Angeles, 14 May 1988). Singer and actor. His first big break came in 1935 when he won first prize on the popular radio show *Major Bowes Amateur Hour* at the Capitol Theater (1645 Broadway) with the Hoboken Four. In 1942 Sinatra opened at the Paramount Theater (1501 Broadway) to an enthusiastic crowd of teenaged "bobbysoxers," ushering in the era of "Sinatramania." Throughout his career Sinatra performed at theaters throughout New York City, including the Paramount Theater and Madison Square Garden. He played the role of Chip in the 1949 film *On the Town,* which featured the song "New York, New York" and was filmed partly on location in the city. His version of the theme from the Martin Scorsese film *New York, New York* (1980) became one of his signature songs, as well as an unofficial anthem for the city. Patsy's Italian Restaurant in Manhattan, a well-known favorite of Sinatra's, commemorates his birthday by offering a menu of his favorite dishes, and in 2009 on the anniversary of his death they displayed 15 never before exhibited photos of Sinatra.

Caleb Smith, Meryl Cates

Sinclair, Upton (*b* Baltimore, 20 Sept 1878; *d* Bound Brook, N.J., 25 Nov 1968). Novelist and social activist. The son of southern gentry whose fortunes suffered during the Civil War, he moved with his family to New York City at age 10. Before graduating from City College of New York (1897) and Columbia University (1901) he supported himself by churning out dime novels for the Manhattan firm Street and Smith and short stories for New York pulp magazines and newspapers. A founding member of the Intercollegiate Socialist Society in New York, Sinclair often addressed class inequality and corporate corruption in his writings. His first novel, *Springtime and Harvest,* was published in 1901, but he did not achieve commercial success until the publication of his renowned work *The Jungle* in 1906. A "muckraking" investigative novel, it exposed the labor practices and unsanitary conditions of the U.S. meatpacking industry, greatly affecting many Americans, including President Theodore Roosevelt, who pushed the passage of the Pure Food and Drug Act and Meat Inspection Act through Congress in 1906. Another of his novels, *The Metropolis* (1908), examined the economic extremes in New York City society. Sinclair continued to write novels such as *King Coal* (1917), *The Profits of Religion* (1918), and *Oil!* (1927), fortifying his status in American literature as an investigative activist who inspired change. Sinclair's last work was an autobiography published in 1962.

Anthony Arthur, *Radical Innocent: Upton Sinclair* (New York: Random House, 2006)

Joseph Breen

Singer, Isaac Bashevis [Zinger, Yitskhok] (*b* Leoncin, near Warsaw, Poland, 14 July 1904; *d* New York City, 24 July 1991). Novelist and short-story writer. The son of a Hasidic Orthodox rabbi, he immigrated to New York City in 1935 to flee anti-Semitism. Already a published author, Singer began his career in the city working for the Yiddish-language newspaper *Forverts.* He is most well known for his mythical and gothic short stories and novels, written almost exclusively in Yiddish and primarily focused on the Eastern European Jewish tradition. He won the Nobel Prize for literature in 1978. Among the more than three dozen books he wrote are *The Family Moskat* (1950), *The Magician of Lublin* (1960), *The Golem* (1969), *Enemies, A Love Story* (1972), and *Yentl the Yeshiva Boy* (1983), which was made into the movie *Yentl.* Singer was a longtime resident of the Upper West Side of Manhattan where he lived in the Belnord Apartments located at 225 West 86th Street.

Sarah Brafman

Singer, Isaac M(erritt) (*b* Pittstown, N.Y., 27 Oct 1811; *d* Torquay, England, 23 July 1875). Sewing machine inventor. After several years in upstate New York, where he trained as a machinist and cabinetmaker in Oswego, he moved first to New York City and then to Boston. There he unsuccessfully promoted a device to carve wooden printer's type and became aware of Elias Howe's sewing machine. In 1851 he returned to New York City where his firm I. M. Singer and Company opened an office and facilities to manufacture sewing machines. Howe sued for patent infringement, and even though Singer was ordered to pay royalties, his firm quickly became the leader in its field in the United States and prospered. The business made Singer a wealthy man, and he lived in a mansion on Fifth Avenue. He had many children with several women–some of whom he never married. Singer remained active in the business until he moved to Europe in 1863 after he was arrested for bigamy. When he died his estate was worth about $13 million, and his many wives and close to two dozen children battled for years in court over its settlement.

Ruth Brandon, *Singer and the Sewing Machine: A Capitalist Romance* (Philadelphia: Lippincott, 1977; repr. New York: Kodansha America, 1996)

Darwin H. Stapleton

Singer Building. The architect Ernest Flagg built three structures for the Singer Manufacturing Company, all on Broadway in lower Manhattan. The first was a 10-story beaux-arts office building, completed in 1896 at 149 Broadway. The second structure, the Singer Loft Building (also known as the Little Singer Building) was completed in 1904 at 561–3 Broadway. The ornate, French-inspired design featured an innovative use of materials, especially steel, recessed glass, and terra-cotta. The facade was suspended from the structural elements, foretelling the curtain walls found in many postwar skyscrapers. The third structure, the Singer Tower, was completed in 1908. It was an ornate skyscraper 612 feet (186.5

meters) tall, which was added to the original Singer Building at 149 Broadway. It was the first tower designed after zoning laws were passed limiting the height of new buildings relative to the area that they covered and to their frontage along the street. With the Woolworth Building (Cass Gilbert, 1913) it helped to make setbacks and terraces standard elements in the design of skyscrapers in Manhattan during the following decades. The Singer Tower was the tallest building in the world for 18 months. In 1968 it became the tallest building ever demolished, to make way for the U.S. Steel Building (Skidmore, Owings and Merrill, 1972) and remained so until the destruction of the World Trade Center towers on 11 September 2001.

Susan Lyman, *The Story of New York* (New York: Crown, 1964); Barbaralee Diamonstein, *The Landmarks of New York* (New York: Harry N. Abrams, 1988)

James O. Drummond, Caleb Smith

single-room occupancy hotels. See SROs.

Singleton, Anne. Pseudonym under which Ruth Benedict published poetry.

Sing Tao. Daily Chinese-language newspaper launched in 1965. Aimed at immigrants, businesspeople, and students, it covers Chinese communities worldwide and offers articles on leisure, finance, tourism, medicine, and entertainment. The New York City office publishes five editions covering New York City, Boston, Philadelphia, Washington, D.C., and Chicago. In 2003 it claimed a circulation of 50,000 in New York City and was one of four major Chinese-language newspapers in the United States. About 80 percent of its readers speak Cantonese and 20 percent Mandarin. Often categorized as more sensationalistic than its competitors, *Sing Tao* is owned by a parent company in Hong Kong with offices worldwide.

Jacqueline Lalley

Sisters of Charity of Mount St. Vincent. Roman Catholic women's order formed in New York City in 1846. Its original members belonged to the American Sisters of Charity (formed in 1809 by Elizabeth Ann Seton in Emmitsburg, Maryland) who first worked in New York City in 1817 at the Roman Catholic Orphan Asylum. The first superior was Elizabeth Boyle (1788–1861), and the first motherhouse was at McGowan's Pass in what is now Central Park. The order conducted much of the Catholic Church's charitable work in child care, health care, and education in the city. They earned a reputation as effective nurses during cholera epidemics in 1832 and again in 1849, when they opened their first hospital, St. Vincent's Hospital, in Manhattan. The motherhouse was moved to Mount St. Vincent in Riverdale in 1859. During the Civil War the order volunteered to operate St. Joseph's Military Hospital at McGowan's Pass. In 1868 the members opened St. Mary's Female Hospital in Brooklyn (reorganized to provide general care as the Hospital of the Holy Name in 1909 and transferred to the Daughters of Wisdom in 1955). They also opened several schools and formed the New York Foundling Home (1869) and the College of Mount St. Vincent (1901). On Staten Island the order established several other health services, later combined as the Sisters of Charity Services Corporation. The order continues to operate as a constituent community of the Federation of Sisters of Charity in the Vincentian–Setonian Tradition.

Sister Marie De Lourdes Walsh, *The Sisters of Charity of New York, 1809–1959* (New York: Fordham University Press, 1960)

Matthew J. Brennan

Sisters of Mercy. Roman Catholic women's order formed in 1831 in Dublin by Mary Catherine McAuley to serve the poor. It established a branch in Pittsburgh in 1843 before opening another in New York City in 1845 under Mary Agnes O'Connor, who was persuaded to move to the city from England by Bishop John J. Hughes. In 1848 the order took over the former convent of the Sisters of the Sacred Heart on the corner of Houston and Mulberry streets and renamed it St. Catherine's Convent of Mercy. During the following years it focused on the care, training, and placement of immigrant women. In 1855 nuns of St. Catherine's under Mary Vincent Haire established the Sisters of Mercy in the Convent of St. Francis of Assisi in a brick house at Jay and Chapel streets in Brooklyn.

Kathleen Healy, ed., *Sisters of Mercy: Spirituality in America, 1843–1900* (New York City: Paulist Press, 1992)

Melissa M. Merritt

69th Regiment. Military unit privately formed in 1848 in New York City, although the A Company traces its roots to the American Revolution. It joined the New York Militia (now the New York National Guard) in 1849. At the outset the regiment consisted largely of Irish Americans, and it became the military escort of the St. Patrick's Day parade in 1851 (a status that it retained in the twenty-first century). During the Civil War the regiment fought in the battles of Bull Run, Antietam, and Appomattox and suffered huge losses; General Robert E. Lee nicknamed it the "Fighting 69th." As part of the 42nd Division of the American Expeditionary Forces in World War I it fought with distinction in the Battle of the Argonne Forest; the regiment's service, especially that of military chaplain Francis P. Duffy, was celebrated in the film *The Fighting 69th* (1940). During World War II the regiment served in the Pacific theater, fighting on Makin, Saipan, and Okinawa. It was one of the first to respond to the terrorist attacks on 11 September 2001, losing several members during rescue operations. After 11 September the regiment guarded the U.S. Military Academy at West Point as well as the city's bridges and tunnels before it was sent to Iraq in 2004, where it suffered further casualties. In 2008 the regiment was deployed to Afghanistan. Since 1904 the 69th has been based at the armory at 68 Lexington Avenue.

William Francis Stanton Root, *The 69th Regiment in Peace and War* (New York: Blanchard, 1905)

See also Armories, Irish Brigade.

Eleanor Hannah, Kate Lauber

Skidmore, Owings and Merrill. Firm of architects, begun in 1935 as the partnership of Louis Skidmore (1897–1962) and Nathaniel Owings (1903–84), later joined by John Ogden Merrill (1896–1975). The firm prospered with commissions from corporations and government, adding four partners in 1949, including Gordon Bunshaft as chief designer. Lever House (completed 1952), a slab-shaped office tower on slender supports at Park Avenue and 52nd Street, introduced European modernism to the United States as the first glass-faced commercial building in the city. Its prismatic shape, contrasting with setback skyscrapers, and open space at its base helped to promote new zoning regulations in 1961. Bunshaft was also responsible for Manhattan House (1950), the Manufacturers' Trust Company bank branch at 43rd Street and Fifth Avenue (1954), Chase Manhattan Plaza (1961), the Library and Museum at Lincoln Center (1965), and 9 West 57th Street (1984), among other buildings. Later, other partners including David Childs, Raul de Armas, Michael McCarthy, Marilyn Taylor, and Roger Duffy designed institutional, civic, and conspicuous office buildings such as Liberty Plaza (1974); Olympic Tower (1976); Park Avenue Plaza (1981); the Citicorp Building, Queens (1990); Worldwide Plaza (1990); the Time Warner Center (2004); and 7 World Trade Center (2006). Current work includes the Penn Station Restoration Project at the Farley Post Office, condominiums in Manhattan House, and the World Trade Center site. The firm is also well known for its hospitals and several structures at John F. Kennedy Airport.

Carol Krinsky

Skinner, Otis (*b* Cambridge, Mass., 28 June 1858; *d* New York City, 4 Jan 1942). Actor. He left school at age 16 to become an insurance clerk and resolved on a stage career after seeing *The Hunchback of Notre Dame* at the Lyceum Theatre. Assisted by a referral from his father's friend P. T. Barnum, Skinner was hired by a Philadelphia theater in 1877. He made his first New York appearance in a traveling production of *Coriolanus* at the Grand Opera House in 1879. Later that year he moved to New York City and appeared in a Kiralfy brothers production at Niblo's Garden. This was followed by a 10-week engagement with Edwin Booth's company, the first in a succession of prominent companies (including those of Augustin Daly and Helena Modjeska) to engage Skinner's services over the next 15 years. During this period Skinner was frequently on tour and played various kinds of roles, both leads and character parts; playwright George Middleton later described his style as "flamboyant and scene-filling, like rich claret running over everything." By 1894 he was a star in his own right and launched his own touring company. His greatest success came in 1911 as the beggar Hajj in *Kismet,* a romantic drama that ran for one year at the Knickerbocker Theater in New York City; he also excelled in Shakespearean roles. His daughter, Cornelia Otis Skinner, became an author and actress.

Otis Skinner, *Footlights and Spotlights* (Indianapolis: Bobbs–Merrill, 1924); George Middleton, *These Things Are Mine* (New York: Macmillan, 1947)

Susan Kriete

Skyscraper Museum. Private, nonprofit educational corporation located in Manhattan's Battery Park City at 39 Battery Place. It was founded in 1996 to celebrate New York City's architectural heritage and to examine the individuals and circumstances that have shaped the city's skyline. The museum's inaugural show was titled *Downtown New York* and ran from April through December of 1997 at one of the museum's previous Manhattan locations, 44 Wall Street. The museum was also located briefly at 110 Maiden Lane in Manhattan but had to move because of its proximity to the site of the terrorist attacks of 11 September 2001 at the World Trade Center.

Marlena Slowik

skyscrapers. New York City is inextricably associated with skyscrapers.

1. 1870–1916

The demand for tall office buildings arose during the 1860s as the commercial district along Broadway between the Battery and City Hall became more congested, and as large businesses, among them insurance and communications firms, sought more impressive and larger corporate headquarters.

Skyscrapers were made possible by technological advances, especially the passenger elevator, used successfully in the late 1850s. As the first office building to include elevators in its initial design, the Equitable Building (1868–70, Gilman and Kendall with George B. Post; demolished), eight stories tall, opened the age of the skyscraper. By 1875 the city had several 10-story buildings, notably the Western Union Building (1872–75, Post; demolished) at Broadway and Dey Street and the Tribune Building (1873–75, Richard Morris Hunt; demolished) at Nassau and Spruce streets, both of which had a mansard roof and a tower. The 1880s saw the construction of such massive commercial blocks as Temple Court (1881–83, Silliman and Farnsworth; enlarged 1890) at Beekman and Nassau streets, which has twin towers. The Produce Exchange (1881–84, Post; demolished) overlooking Bowling Green, innovative in its "modified Renaissance" design, incorporated iron-framed inner court walls that were a forerunner of skeleton construction.

A cluster of skyscrapers had formed next to City Hall Park with the completion of the ebulliently ornamented Potter Building (1883–86, N. G. Starkweather) on Park Row and the mansarded, neo-Romanesque New York Times Building (1888–89, Post; altered). Using as its structural base the iron-framed floors of the newspaper's old five-story building (1857–58, T. R. Jackson), the new Times Building at the intersection of Park Row, Spruce, and Nassau streets combined load-bearing walls with cage framing. The narrow, 11-story Tower Building (1888–89, Bradford L. Gilbert; demolished) at 50 Broadway introduced full skeleton, or skyscraper, construction to the city: the metal frame carried both walls and floors, allowing the walls to be reduced in thickness and the site to be used more efficiently. The Pulitzer, or World, Building at Park Row and Frankfort Street (1889–90, Post; demolished), known for its gilded dome, was less innovative structurally, but with a reported height of 309 feet (94 meters) it was briefly the city's tallest building.

The word *skyscraper* came into common usage during the 1890s when skeleton construction was widely adopted, building methods were refined, and competition intensified to build ever higher buildings. The steel-skeleton–framed Manhattan Life Building (1893–95, Kimball and Thompson; demolished) at 66 Broadway was the city's first skyscraper erected on pneumatic caisson foundations. Others soon followed, among them the American Surety Building (1894–96, Bruce Price; enlarged 1921) at 100 Broadway, an elegant, columnlike tower of 21 stories. R. H. Robertson, who designed the 23-story American Tract Society Building (1894–95) at Nassau and Spruce streets with a distinctive arcaded top, set a new height record with his formidable 30-story Park Row Building (1896–99). Neoclassical designs with three-part facades also became fashionable and were used in such distinctive buildings as the Bowling Green Offices (1895–98, W. and G. Audsley; altered), decorated with crisp Grecian motifs, and the slablike Empire Building (1897–98, Kimball and Thompson) south of Trinity Church at Broadway and Rector Street. Standing 13 stories tall, the Bayard Building (1897–99) at 65–69 Bleecker Street was designed by Louis Sullivan with slender, structurally revealing piers and lush, fluid ornamentation (it was Sullivan's only work in New York City). The Broadway Chambers Building (1899–1900), a colorful brick- and terra-cotta–clad tower across from City Hall Park, was the first of several stunning skyscrapers in New York City designed by Cass Gilbert.

During the first decade of the twentieth century skyscrapers were built in areas beyond lower Broadway. At 21 stories the Flatiron Building (1901–3, D. H. Burnham and

Skyscrapers in midtown along 42nd Street, ca *1940*

Company), just south of Madison Square, was the tallest building north of the financial district. Designed to conform to its triangular site, it was likened to the bow of a "monster ocean steamer" by the photographer Alfred Stieglitz. The neo-Gothic Trinity and U.S. Realty buildings (1904–7, 1906–7, Francis Kimball) were erected north of Trinity Church Yard on Broadway. As the Broadway subway neared completion (opened 1904), the Times Tower (1903–5, Eidlitz and McKenzie; altered 1966) was built on a midtown site that soon became known as Times Square. Elegant skyscrapers were also erected in lower Manhattan: the neo-Gothic West Street Building (1906–7, Cass Gilbert), which set a new standard of opulence, as well as the neoclassical Whitehall Building at Battery Place and West Street (1902–3, Henry Hardenbergh; 1909–11, Clinton and Russell) and the flamboyant City Investing Company Building (1906–9, Kimball; demolished) at Broadway and Cortlandt Street. As the narrow streets off Broadway became more densely built up, the loss of light and air emerged as an increasingly serious problem. A solution was offered by Ernest Flagg, who determined that adequate light and air would be let in if a skyscraper tower, no matter how high, occupied only 25 percent of its site. He demonstrated the effectiveness of this principle in his needlelike Singer Tower (1906–8; demolished), which at 47 stories was the tallest building in the city. But not for long: the Metropolitan Life Tower (1907–9, Napoleon Lebrun and Sons) on Madison Square, modeled after the Campanile of San Marco in Venice, was three stories higher.

The last unregulated office buildings were completed about the time of World War I, among them the new Equitable Building (1913–15, Ernest Graham and Associates), which rose 38 stories and was said to cast a noonday shadow four blocks long; the colossal Municipal Building (1909–14, W. M. Kendall of McKim, Mead and White), at Chambers and Centre streets; and the romantic neo-Gothic Woolworth Building (1910–13, Cass Gilbert), which had a mounted tower and with a height equal to 60 stories remained the world's tallest commercial building until 1930. The design of skyscrapers was transformed in 1916 when the city passed a zoning law restricting the height and bulk of buildings.

2. 1916–1995

A formula called the "zoning envelope" required that upper stories be stepped back above a prescribed level. A tower of unlimited height was allowed over only 25 percent of the site. These regulations produced the "setback" or "wedding cake" profiles (some with a slender tower) that dominated design until the next major zoning change in 1961. During the 1920s architects developed an aesthetic of simple, sculptural mass expressed in pyramidal forms clad in brick or stone; early examples of the setback style were the Shelton Hotel (1924, Arthur Loomis Harmon) and the New York Telephone Building at 140 West Street (1923–25, Ralph Walker). Fueled by national prosperity and easy financing, the volume of construction increased in the second half of the 1920s. This increase coincided with the peak of art deco design to produce a spate of modernistic skyscrapers. Most activity took place in midtown Manhattan. Within a few blocks of Grand Central Terminal rose the Chanin, Chrysler, Lincoln, Graybar, Fred F. French, and Daily News buildings, while projects such as Rockefeller Center and the Empire State Building opened up new areas distant from transportation centers. Speculation drove up land prices and led to the construction of taller towers. Downtown in the financial district several structures of 50 to 70 stories were shoehorned into narrow sites, among them the Bank of Manhattan Company and the Cities Service buildings. The race to build ever taller buildings resulted in the Chrysler Building (1930; 1046 feet, or 319 meters) and the Empire State Building (1931; 1250 feet, or 381 meters). Between 1920 and 1935 the amount of office space in the city nearly doubled, from 74 million square feet (7 million square meters) to 138 million square feet (13 million square meters); at least two-thirds of this amount was in speculative construction. Skyscrapers also accommodated hotels, apartments, and even hospitals. Most high-rise buildings in the outer boroughs were residential, although a number of office towers were built in Brooklyn.

Construction virtually ceased during the Depression and World War II, and when it resumed, the new aesthetic of the International Style was firmly established. Both external and internal design changes were made possible by advances in curtain-wall technology, air conditioning, and other mechanical and structural systems. The United Nations Secretariat (1947) and the corporate headquarters Lever House (1952, Gordon Bunshaft) and the Seagram Building (1958, Ludwig Mies van der Rohe) on Park Avenue established the prismatic glass box as the modern paradigm. Unlike older buildings that usually filled their lots, these were sited away from the street in plazas. Acclaimed by planners, the "tower-in-the-plaza" arrangement was encouraged by the zoning law of 1961, a sweeping revision that imposed a maximum volume for a building based on a multiple of the area of the lot, known as the floor area ratio (FAR); bonus floors could be added by including public spaces and amenities. Under the new code in the 1960s and 1970s sheer metal and glass shafts such as those on Sixth Avenue at Rockefeller Center proliferated. Skyscrapers of the 1960s were often big and bland; the construction of the Pan Am Building exploited the air rights above Grand Central Terminal to create 2.4 million square feet (222,960 square meters) of floor space.

Chrysler Building, 2009

Redevelopment in lower Manhattan did not begin until the Chase Manhattan Bank built its new headquarters, designed by Bunshaft, in 1960. During the late 1960s large speculative buildings on Water Street boxed in the skyline along the East River. On Broadway the Singer Tower became the tallest building ever demolished, making way for 1 Liberty Plaza (1974). Plans for the World Trade Center, announced in 1964, called for twin towers of 110 stories (as built, the North Tower was 1368 feet [417 meters] and the South Tower was 1362 feet [415 meters] tall). Designed by Minoru Yamasaki

Tallest Buildings in New York City

Name	Year Completed	Height, feet / (meters)[1]	Floors	Address	Architect or Architectural Firm
One World Trade Center[2] (North Tower)	1972	1368 / (417)	110	One World Trade Center	Minoru Yamasaki of Yamasaki and Associates
Two World Trade Center[2] (South Tower)	1973	1362 / (415)	110	Two World Trade Center	Minoru Yamasaki of Yamasaki and Associates
Empire State Building	1931	1250 / (381)	102	350 Fifth Ave.	Shreve, Lamb and Harmon Associates
Bank of America Tower	2009	1200 / (366)	54	One Bryant Park	Cook + Fox Architects, Gensler
Chrysler Building	1930	1046 / (318.9)	77	405 Lexington Ave.	William van Alen
New York Times Tower	2007	1046 / (318.8)	52	620 Eighth Ave.	Renzo Piano Building Workshop; FXFOWLE Architects
American International Building	1932	952 / (290)	66	70 Pine St.	Clinton and Russell
Trump Building (40 Wall St.)	1930	927 / (283)	70	40 Wall St.	H. Craig Severance and Yasuo Matsui; Shreve and Lamb
Citigroup Center	1977	915 / (279)	59	153 East 53rd St.	Hugh Stubbins and Associates; Emery Roth and Sons
Trump World Tower	2001	861 / (262)	72	845 United Nations Plaza	Costas Kondylis and Partners
GE Building	1933	850 / (259)	70	30 Rockefeller Center	Raymond Hood
CitySpire Center	1987	814 / (248)	75	150–156 West 56th St.	Murphy / Jahn, Inc. Architects
One Chase Manhattan Plaza	1961	813 / (248)	60	1 Chase Manhattan Plaza	Skidmore, Owings and Merrill LLP
Condé Nast Building (4 Times Square)	1999	809 / (247)	48	4 Times Square Plaza	FXFOWLE Architects
MetLife Building (Pan Am Building)	1963	808 / (246)	59	200 Park Ave.	Emery Roth and Sons
Bloomberg Tower	2005	806 / (246)	54	731 Lexington Ave.	Cesar Pelli and Associates
Woolworth Building	1913	792 / (241)	57	233 Broadway	Cass Gilbert
One Worldwide Plaza	1989	778 / (237)	50	825 Eighth Ave.	Skidmore, Owings and Merrill LLP
Carnegie Hall Tower	1991	757 / (231)	60	152 West 57th St.	Cesar Pelli and Associates
383 Madison Ave.[3]	2001	755 / (230)	47	383 Madison Ave.	Skidmore, Owings and Merrill LLP
AXA Center	1986	752 / (229.2)	54	787 Seventh Ave.	Edward Larrabee Barnes Associates
One Penn Plaza	1972	750 / (228.6)	57	250 West 34th St.	Kahn and Jacobs
1251 Ave. of the Americas (Exxon Building)	1971	750 / (228.6)	54	1251 Sixth Ave.	Harrison and Abramovitz
Time Warner Center[4]	2004	750 / (228.5)	55	10 Columbus Circle	Skidmore, Owings and Merrill LLP

1. Antenna masts are not included in height; spires and architectural details are included in height.
2. Destroyed in the terrorist attacks of 11 September 2001.
3. Formerly Bear Stearns world headquarters.
4. Includes both towers.

Sources: Emporis.com, "The World's Building Website," http://www.emporis.com; SkyscraperPage.com, http://skyscraperpage.com

Compiled by Frank Nestor

and completed in 1973, the complex added 10 million square feet (929,000 square meters) of office space just before a downturn of the real estate market that persisted until the late 1970s.

Changing tastes and technology dictated new forms and styles in skyscrapers of the 1980s. Reacting against the anonymity of modernist slabs and spurred by the theories of postmodernism, many architects revived historical references and lavish ornamentation. Masonry cladding was used in the headquarters of American Telephone and Telegraph (1978–84, Philip Johnson; now the Sony Building) and the Heron Tower (1987, Kohn Pedersen Fox); others such as the Carnegie Hall Tower (1990, Cesar Pelli) reflected the character of an adjacent landmark or neighborhood. With the demand for "smart buildings" wired for computers and for large floor areas of 30,000 to 40,000 square feet (3000 to 4000 square meters), buildings became bulkier. Sites at the edges of the dense business districts permitted such buildings, among them the four giants of the World Financial Center (1985–88, Pelli) at Battery Park City and the full-block development of Worldwide Plaza (1989, Skidmore, Owings and Merrill; David Childs) west of Eighth Avenue between 49th and 50th streets. Other towers more centrally situated, such as the headquarters of the Morgan Bank on Wall Street (1988, Kevin Roche), were able to achieve the same expanded volume by using the air rights of adjacent low-rise buildings or landmarks. Special zoning incentives made the West Side of midtown Manhattan especially attractive to developers. From 1978 to 1991 more than 59 million square feet (6 million square meters) of commercial space was constructed in Manhattan. In 1990 New York City had 25 of the 100 tallest buildings in the world.

3. Since 1995

A real estate recession during the first half of the 1990s put a stop to most high-rise construction. High vacancy rates in older office buildings, especially in lower Manhattan, led to the beginning of widespread conversion of "Class B" properties into apartments and condominiums. A few significant office towers and some mixed-use projects, all in midtown, were started in the late 1990s, including a cluster around Times Square and the Time Warner Center at Columbus Circle (2004, SOM).

After the destruction of the World Trade Center on 11 September 2001, many people predicted that the era of tall towers in New York City was over. But the desire to occupy the sky and exploit the value of Manhattan land returned with the post-9/11 economic recovery, with something of a renaissance of high-profile design: most significant were several media company headquarters, including the Time Warner Center, Hearst Tower (2006, Foster and Partners, Norman Foster), the New York Times Tower (2006, Renzo Piano Building Workshop, Renzo Piano and FXFOWLE), and the mixed-use Bloomberg Tower (also called One Beacon Court; 2005, Pelli Clarke Pelli).

The market for luxury apartments also expanded, and for the first time residential towers matched or exceeded the number of stories (if not the height in feet) of office buildings or major hotels. The residential Trump World Tower (2001, Costas Kondylis) pioneered new heights with a 72-story, 861-foot (262-meter) dark-glass prism that was nearly indistinguishable from a corporate office tower, and in the early 2000s, numerous mixed masonry and glass apartment blocks stretched taller than 55 stories. Signature towers by world-famous architects became a marketing strategy for some developers, as exemplified by the curvy, inventive Beekman, designed by Frank Gehry for Forest City Ratner (2010, Gehry Partners), rising 76 stories on a lower Manhattan lot near the foot of the Brooklyn Bridge. Another iconic, but controversial Gehry tower, dubbed "Miss Brooklyn," was designed to culminate the ensemble planned above the Atlantic Yards, a mega-project of Forest City Ratner.

One of the most important innovations in high-rise design in the late 1990s and early 2000s was the green building movement and the embrace of LEED (Leadership in Energy and Environmental Design) standards. America's first "green" skyscraper was 4 Times Square, also known as the Condé Nast Building (1999, FXFOWLE), conceived as a demonstration of "best practices" by the Durst Organization and its architect Fox and Fowle. A few photovoltaic solar panels were the only signal on the facade of a dramatic new type of commercial architecture, for most of the features of high-performance and energy-efficient design were manifest in the mechanical systems. By 2006 a crop of green towers, including the Hearst and Times buildings, 7 WTC, and most notably the Bank of America Tower at One Bryant Park (2009, Cook + Fox) established sustainable design as the sine qua non for quality buildings, as well as for retrofits.

Bank of America Building, 2009

Residential high-rises were slower to adopt LEED standards, but an exemplary experiment was instituted by the Battery Park City Authority, which in 2000 mandated rigorous green guidelines for all new buildings. Completed in 2003 the Solaire was the first LEED-rated high-rise apartment in the United States. By 2009 every remaining site in Battery Park City had a new green building either recently completed or under construction, and the new world headquarters of Goldman Sachs (2009, Pei Cobb Freed) completed the build-out of the master plan of the World Financial Center. Rebuilding of the office towers at the World Trade Center was under way in 2010, but only infrastructure and one building had been started.

Paul Goldberger, *The Skyscraper* (New York: Alfred A. Knopf, 1981); Robert A. M. Stern et al., *New York 1900* (New York: Rizzoli, 1983) and *New York 1930* (New York: Rizzoli, 1987); Sarah Bradford Landau and Carl W. Condit, *Rise of the New York Skyscraper, 1865–1913* (New Haven: Yale University Press, 1996); Carol Willis, *Form Follows Finance* (New York: Princeton Architectural Press, 1995)

Sarah Bradford Landau (§1),
Carol Willis (§2, §3)

slang. From the early nineteenth century life in New York City has inspired the formation of slang words and phrases. The wealthy were known in the 1840s as the *Upper Ten (Thousand)*; many lived on Fifth Avenue and by 1850 were known as *Avenoodles,* which played on the local pronunciation of "avenue" as two syllables. In the 1880s *Astorbilt* (a form combining Astor and Vanderbilt) became a generic surname for the wealthy. The words *ritz* and *ritzy* and the phrase *puttin' on the ritz* were inspired by the high style of the Ritz hotels. During the 1890s the wealthy were often called the *Four Hundred* in newspapers, after the society figure Ward McAllister remarked that Mrs. William Astor limited her guest list to 400 names. Chorus girls, often called *Dumb Doras* from 1890, accompanied *sugar daddys* (1905), who took them to late-night dinners of champagne and lobster at *lobster palaces* in Times Square. From the Cockney use of the verb *to hook,* meaning to solicit for prostitution, the noun *hooker* was formed in the 1840s; the term was later reinforced by the reputation of brothels in Corlear's Hook, where residents were known as "Hookers." About this time the terms *O.K., shyster,* and *smart aleck* came into use in the city. From the 1860s being *sent up the river* meant going to Sing Sing Prison, which stood on the Hudson River at Sing Sing, now known as Ossining. Pesky, loud-mouthed newsboys in the city prompted the phrase *go peddle your papers,* meaning "get lost."

In the 1880s *hokey pokey* came to mean "penny serving of ice cream" rather than simply "trickery"; the ice cream vendor became known as the *hokey-pokey man.* Some newspapers in the city gained a reputation for *yellow journalism,* a term associated with circulation battles between the *New York World* and *New York Journal,* both of which published the comic strip "The Yellow Kid." *Skyscraper* was coined in the 1880s, and its adoption was influenced by the spectacle of tall buildings in New York City. The phrase *to do a Brodie* (or *to take a Brodie*) was inspired by the claim of Steve Brodie, a saloonkeeper from the Bowery, that he had dived from the Brooklyn Bridge in 1886. *Hot dogs,* introduced at Coney Island about 1890, were perhaps so named because according to urban folklore they were made with dog meat. New York City was always a destination for tourists, and gawking tourists became known as *rubberneckers* in the 1890s. At the beginning of the twentieth century the elevated lines, or *els,* were so crowded that the hours when most people traveled to and from work became known as *rush hours;* many riders stood clinging to overhead straps, inspiring the word *straphanger.* About this time the word *breadline* came into use, after Fleischmann's bakery began giving bread and coffee to the poor each night at the side door of its shop on Broadway at 10th Street.

By 1915 country residents of upstate New York were called *appleknockers,* after a putative method of harvesting apples by knocking them down with long sticks; the name of the town of Herkimer, New York, inspired the term *Herkimer Jerkimer,* meaning both a hick and a jerk. Nightlife after World War I focused on the activities of *café society,* a name first used in a gossip column and popularized by *Herald Tribune* columnist Lucius Beebe in the 1930s. As it became fashionable and respectable in the city for society members to live in apartment buildings, those younger members who had apartments were called *cliff dwellers,* and older ones who still lived in their mansions on Murray Hill were known as *cave dwellers.* The 1928 Broadway musical *Whoopee!* helped to make popular the expression *makin' whoopee* for risqué behavior, including that of the *butter-and-egg man,* a big spender in nightclubs, who was so named because he seemed to have become wealthy in the dairy business. The term *G-string* came into use in the 1930s in the city's burlesque theaters and derives from the name of a loincloth used by an American Indian male. Young men and women of little means sunbathed at *tarpaper beach,* the tarred and graveled rooftops of city apartment buildings. *Dumbbell* tenements in the city were named for the shape of their floor plan. *Yuppies,* a term coined in New York City in 1983, came to symbolize the 1980s, just as *hipsters* became identified with early twenty-first century New York City, especially Brooklyn.

Irving Lewis Allen, *The City in Slang: New York Life and Popular Speech* (New York: Oxford University Press, 1993)

Irving Lewis Allen

slaughterhouses. See Meatpacking.

slavery. Slavery was introduced in Manhattan by the Dutch, who settled 11 African men there in 1626 and three women in 1628, all of whom had been captured during war. The Dutch West India Company was among the foremost slave traders in the world but provided only a few Africans to New Netherland, where slaves commanded lower prices than in the Caribbean. Most slaves in New York before the 1650s were taken by Dutch or French privateers from Spanish or Portuguese ships. Initially the company, the main employer in the colony, used slaves for projects such as building Fort Amsterdam, laying roads, carrying merchandise, and providing domestic services such as cooking and laundering. During these years slaves were married in church and their children were registered with the company. As the settlement became established and public works slackened, the need for slaves diminished and the 11 men of the first cargo petitioned for their freedom. On 25 February 1644 they and their wives received their conditional release in return for services on demand and lifelong payments due annually in cash or kind. The company surrendered none of its claims to service, shifted living costs to the petitioners, and bound to service their children, born and unborn; it later freed some of the nearly two dozen people affected by this arrangement, and a comparable number were freed privately by 1664 when the English took control of the colony. At this time at least 9 percent of the 8000 settlers were Africans, both slave and free.

The Articles of Capitulation formalizing the surrender of the Dutch to the English in 1664 preserved all the property rights that they recognized, and the ownership of slaves was transferred to the English, who soon institutionalized slavery by endorsing it as a system of property rights in the Laws of 1665, the first legal code in the colony. Slaves were classified as chattel bound to serve involuntary, indefinite, and heritable tenure, and their marriages were no longer recognized as legal. American Indians and Africans were enslaved, but the laws made "slaves" synonymous with "Negroes," and the Iroquois Confederacy, the Hurons, and the Delawares made pacts with the English to return runaways. To help keep peace the colonial governor Edmund Andros prohibited the enslavement of Indians from local tribes in 1679; others continued to be enslaved until the 1740s.

White working men protested the increasing use of slaves in shops, along the docks, and in skilled and unskilled trades, and eventually municipal licensing ordinances banned Africans from driving wagons and selling goods in public markets. The restrictions mostly affected free blacks, since slaves continued to be employed in these ways by their masters. Restrictions on slavery were proposed as early as the 1680s. Many people resented the power of the Royal African Company (chartered in 1672), which had a monopoly in the slave trade: a tax was levied on the importation of slaves, though smuggling made this ineffective. By the beginning of the eighteenth century about 14.2 percent of the New York City population was black. The number of slaves entering the port was 225 between 1701 and 1704, and 185 between 1710 and 1712; all were from Africa, and unlike those who had entered on earlier shipments from the West Indies, they had no experience with slavery. Between 1700 and 1774 the city legally admitted about 6800 slaves, 2800 of whom were from Africa. Slave markets at the foot of Wall Street were named after prominent families involved in slave trading, including the Crommelins, Schuylers, Van Zandts, and Waltons. Other families that made profits legally and illegally in the slave trade were the Beekmans, Crugers, Livingstons, Philips, Van Hornes, and Van Cortlandts.

Slaves did have a few rights: for instance, people who willfully killed or maimed slaves were punished under a law passed in 1686, but the purpose of most laws was to control rather than to protect slaves. A set of laws passed in 1702 prohibited slaves from escaping, taking part in conspiracies or insurrections, trafficking in stolen goods, assembling in groups larger than three, bearing arms, and traveling without permission. In 1705 the state assembly declared baptism ineffective for slaves and from the following year endorsed conversion to Christianity. Local ordinances barred slaves from various activities. Despite such legislation slaves often stole, gambled, drank, evaded curfew, and disturbed the peace; less frequently they committed serious crimes

Free Blacks and Slave Populations of New York, Kings, Queens, Richmond, and Westchester Counties, 1790–1820

	1790		1800		1810		1820	
	Slaves	Free Blacks	Slaves	Free Blacks	Slaves	Free Blacks	Slaves	Free Blacks
New York	2,369	1,101	2,868	3,499	1,686	8,137	518	10,368
Kings	1,432	46	1,479	332	1,118	735	879	882
Queens	2,309	808	1,528	1,431	809	2,354	559	2,648
Richmond	759	127	675	83	437	274	532	78
Westchester	1,419	357	1,259	482	982	948	205	1,638
Total	8,288	2,439	7,809	5,827	5,032	12,448	2,693	15,614
Total Black Population	10,727		13,636		17,480		18,307	
Slaves as Percentage of Black Population	77.3		57.3		28.8		14.7	

Source: U.S. Bureau of the Census, *Census of Population* 1790, 1800, 1810, 1820

Compiled by James Bradley

such as assault, battery, murder (usually of whites), and arson. After a time in which the number of slaves increased dramatically, recently arrived Africans led an uprising on the night of 6 April 1712, in which eight whites were killed and more than 20 others seriously injured. In addition fires were set in the east ward, although only a few outbuildings burned and property damage was light. Twenty-five blacks paid for the incident with their lives. During the same year and again in 1730 more laws were passed to tighten the control of slaves.

The separation of husbands from wives and of parents from their children was a principal cause of hardship. Slave families in New York City seldom shared one household. Mothers and young children lived together, but men were housed separately. Visiting privileges were granted for Sundays, but husbands and wives frequently negotiated weeknight meetings, usually at the woman's quarters. Often men were denied visits and violence resulted; in 1741 Roosevelt Quack was kept from seeing his wife, the governor's cook, and burned the governor's house. The separation of mothers and children at sale, especially beyond visiting distance, was also a source of great distress.

Slaves recognized and respected their own family unions regardless of law, and kinship networks developed early. The proximity of houses to each other also encouraged networks for friendship and recreation. Some slaves organized theft rings such as the Geneva Club of the 1730s; members conspired with whites and caroused with them in notorious taverns where they held private celebrations. Some celebrations were public, but carnivals such as Pinkster and Election Day that were held by rural blacks were restrained in Manhattan, perhaps because officials feared that they could not assure public safety.

Between 1730 and 1740 at least 1429 slaves were brought to the city. By 1741 the ratio of men to women had become imbalanced: because of the growing use of slaves in business, the number of men for every 100 women rose from 99 in 1731 to 120 in 1741. On 18 March 1741 a slave uprising began that lasted more than six months and resulted in massive property damage. The seat of royal government was destroyed by fire, including the governor's residence and the rest of Fort George on the southwestern tip of Manhattan; other homes and businesses burned during the following three weeks. The only death was that of a soldier at the fort. An investigation led by Justice Daniel Horsmanden of the supreme court blamed a conspiracy of slaves aided by white accomplices for the fires, and trials on various charges resulted in the execution of 30 black men, two white men, and two white women, as well as the deportation of 72 blacks. Misgivings arose almost immediately that the punishments had exceeded the crimes, and the episode remained controversial. In the 1740s the proportion of slaves in the population peaked at 20.9 percent.

Just before the American Revolution New York City was second only to Charleston, South Carolina, among urban centers of slavery. There were 3137 African Americans in Manhattan, about 14.3 percent of the population, and the number grew during the war as thousands of runaways and Loyalists' slaves flooded Manhattan, hopeful for freedom that had been promised by the British. Many bore arms against patriots who owned slaves. The local Black Brigade was housed at several sites, including 18 Broadway and 10 Church Street, and distinguished itself variously as the Royal African Regiment and the Ethiopian Regiment in battles in New York State and New Jersey. Many slaves won their freedom from one side or the other during the war. Nearly 5000 blacks sailed away from the United States with the British in the evacuation of the city in November 1783.

In the decades after the Revolution the effects of national liberty eventually eroded slavery in New York City. Large numbers of white workers who moved to the city forced gradual emancipation, but like many others they refused to extend civil rights to blacks, who were omitted from legislation passed by the state in 1785. There were 2369 slaves in the city in 1790.

The first step toward ending slavery in New York City was an act of 1799 that declared free the children of slaves born on or after 4 July but required that these children remain servants to their mother's owner until they reached the age of 25 for women and 28 for men. The law also called for granted freedom to slaves born before that date at the age of 24 for women and 28 for men and required the registration of children indentured to their masters until the age of manumission. A law passed in 1809 recognized the legality of marriages between slaves and prohibited for the first time the forced separation of slave families. In 1817 the state legislature and Governor Daniel D. Tompkins agreed to abolish slavery in New York on 4 July 1827, a date followed by two days of singing, parades, and fireworks. Complete abolition was not achieved until 1841, when the state rescinded provisions allowing nonresidents to hold slaves for as long as nine months. Slavery nonetheless remained a part of the economy in New York City until the Civil War. The slave states had strong economic ties to the city, which the *New York Times* described as "the spot most tainted by Southern poison." Blacks lived in fear of the notorious "blackbirders," who until the war seized victims from the streets for sale in the South. Other hardships also persisted for former slaves, who had to eke out a living amid racial hostility that flared into such violent incidents as the draft riots of 1863.

Edgar J. McManus, *Negro Slavery in New York* (Syracuse, N.Y.: Syracuse University Press, 1966)

See also Abolitionism.

Thomas J. Davis

sliver buildings. Term used in New York City during the late 1970s and early 1980s to describe tall, slender apartment buildings on small parcels in mid-block, built by real estate developers when the city's residential housing market was at its peak. The structures rose as high as 30 stories, usually contained only one apartment on each floor, and could be as narrow as 22 feet (7 meters). They were especially common on the Upper East Side. Sliver buildings were criticized for disrupting the visual harmony of low-rise residential streets, and after a campaign by activists the city's zoning laws were amended in 1983 to prohibit their construction in designated areas of the city, including the Upper East Side. Some examples of sliver buildings are 350 East 86th Street, 344 East 63rd Street, and 266 East 78th Street.

Rebecca Read Shanor

Sloan, John (French) (*b* Lock Haven, Pa., 2 Aug 1871; *d* Hanover, N.H., 7 Sept 1951). Painter. Brought up in Philadelphia, he studied with Robert Henri, who encouraged him to paint in a realist style. He joined Henri in New York City in 1904 and worked for several magazines as a freelance illustrator while completing a series of etchings depicting life in the city (including *New York City Life,* 1905–6) and various paintings. With Henri in 1908 he organized an exhibition at the Macbeth Galleries of eight realist and independent painters; he also helped to organize the Exhibition of Independent Artists in 1910. He took part in the Armory Show of 1913 and in the first exhibition of the Society of Independent Artists in 1917 and was also a president of the society. Sloan was a socialist candidate for the state assembly in 1910, and in 1912 he joined the staff of the radical publication *The Masses,* edited by Max Eastman. He did his best illustrations for the magazine but resigned in 1916 over a policy dispute and eventually left the Socialist Party. During the 1920s and into the 1930s he was an influential teacher at the Art Students League. The Whitney Museum of American Art held a retrospective exhibition of Sloan's work in 1952.

David W. Scott and E. John Bullard, *John Sloan, 1871–1951* (Washington, D.C.: National Gallery of Art, 1971)

Patricia Hills

Sloane. See W. and J. Sloane.

Sloppy Louie's. Fish restaurant. Louis Morino opened it in 1930 on South Street by the Fulton Fish Market. Fishers and fishmongers made up the restaurant's earliest clientele.

Workers and executives from the financial district soon joined them, creating something of a cross-class lunchtime utopia. When Joseph Mitchell published his famous profile of the restaurant, "Up in the Old Hotel," in the *New Yorker* in 1952, tourists began to seek out the place for its fresh fish and cantankerous servers. As the restaurant's fame and popularity grew, some complained that its sloppiness had become contrived for the benefit of out-of-towners and that the rudeness of the servers had become inauthentic. The restaurant closed in 1998.

Daniel Levinson Wilk, "Rough Service at Sloppy Louie's," *New-York Journal of American History* 67:1 (2008)

Daniel Levinson Wilk

Slovaks. The first Slovaks in New York City were immigrants from the Austro-Hungarian Empire who settled around 14th Street and Second Avenue in 1848. In the 1880s Slovak communities took shape in the 70s and 80s between York and Third Avenues and in Long Island City, Astoria, and Sunnyside in Queens, and in Greenpoint in Brooklyn, particularly the section bounded by Newtown Creek, the East River, Grand Street, and McGuinness Boulevard. The first Slovak organization in the city, Živena (1883), was absorbed in 1887 by the St. John the Baptist Society. A large number of organizations soon followed, by the early 1890s including the Catholic Ženská Jednota (Women's Union, 1892), St. Catherine's Society for Slovak Women, the Social Society of St. Francis, St. Peter's Society, and the St. Matthew's and St. Joseph's Society. These were joined in 1905 by the Central Slovak National Council and in 1915 by the Slovenská Telovičná Jednota Sokol (Slovak Gymnastic Union Falcon). National Slovak organizations also opened branches in the city, among them the Prvý Bednársky Výpomocný Spolok (First Cooper's Benefit Society, 1888), the Slovak Evangelical Union (a Lutheran organization, 1893), the Slovak Calvinist Union (1894), Národný Slovenský Spolok (National Slovak Society), Jednota (Union), and the American Fund for Czechoslovak Relief (founded 1948). A Slovak American Cultural Center was formed in the city in 1968.

Religious institutions included the St. Elias Greek Catholic parish (1883) and three Roman Catholic churches: the Church of St. Elizabeth of Hungary (1891), the Church of St. John Nepomucene (1895), and the Church of the Holy Family (1895). The Holy Trinity Evangelical Lutheran parish began in lower Manhattan in 1902. Slovaks also launched a number of local newspapers, notably *Slovák v Amerike* (1889–), *Newyorský denník* (New York Daily, 1895–1974), and *Slobodný orol* (Free Eagle, 1900–1904), published by Jozef Kossalko. The Slovak population in the city exceeded 10,000 by 1910 and increased sharply after the formation of Czechoslovakia in 1918.

The issue of Slovak independence sharply divided the local community, with one group supporting Tomáš Masaryk and the ideal of one democratic Czechoslovak state, while others argued that only through independence could the Slovaks avoid being taken advantage of by the Czechs. By 1970 Slovaks in the city accounted for more than 1 percent of the total population, and in 1977 they numbered 85,000. Among the prominent members of the Slovak community were the writer Thomas Bel, the journalist John Sciranka, the social leader Daniel Sustek, the actress Pauline Novomeská, and the editor and political leader Andrew J. Valusek.

Vrastislav Busek and John Shintay, *The Czechs and Slovaks of New York* (Cicero, Ill.: Czechoslovak National Council of America, 1969); Mark Stolarik, *Immigration and Urbanization: The Slovak Experience* (New York: AMS, 1989)

Edward Kasinec

Slovenes. The Slovenes, a southern Slavic people, first emigrated from the Austro-Hungarian Empire and settled in Greater New York at the end of the nineteenth century. Because they were typically of peasant background, their earliest occupations were in the straw-hat industry in New York City. During the 1920s and 1930s some Slovenes were successful in establishing hat-manufacturing firms in the city. Other entrepreneurs opened groceries, bars, bakeries, craft shops, travel agencies, and shipping companies. Some of these firms evolved into banks. Community life focused on the Slovenian parish of St. Cyril (Franciscan Fathers), formed in July 1916. Mutual assistance organizations included the League of Slovenian Americans, founded in the early 1970s, and singing and dramatic societies. The Society for Slovene Studies was established in 1973 at Columbia University as a national association of American scholars, devotees, and supporters. In 1979 it began sponsoring the journal *Slovene Studies.* Among the notable Slovenian leaders who have lived or worked in New York City are the writer and political activist Louis Adamic (1899–1951), the musician Anton Schubel (1899–1965), and the editor and community leader Frank Sakser (1859–1937). Sakser was also the founder and publisher of *Glas naroda* (the People's Voice), published between 1893 and 1963.

John Arnez, *Slovenci v New Yorku* (New York: Studia Slovenica, 1966)

Edward Kasinec

SLP. See Socialist Labor Party.

smallpox. Viral infectious disease that is easily transmitted from person to person. Epidemics of smallpox have wreaked havoc from the colonial period well into the nineteenth century. The disease had a high mortality rate and left its survivors with disfiguring scars along the exposed parts of the body. One of the most devastating smallpox epidemics of the colonial period was one lasting three months in the late summer and autumn of 1731 when 5 to 8 percent of New York's 10,000 inhabitants were killed. During this epidemic a smallpox inoculation was first used in Manhattan, beginning a debate between proponents and opponents of vaccination that lasted in some fashion into the late twentieth century. By the mid-eighteenth century smallpox visited the city almost annually. Lazarettos or quarantine hospitals were established by the city during the nineteenth century on remote Blackwell's Island (1828) and North Brother Island (1880) to care for smallpox patients and more importantly to remove them from the healthy population. By 1850 smallpox accounted for 25.4 of every 1000 deaths in New York City. The settlement in the city of immigrants from countries such as Ireland, Great Britain, and Germany in the early to mid-nineteenth century, followed by eastern Europeans and Italians between 1880 and 1924, became the most frequent vector of smallpox. Many immigrants and anti-vaccinationists distrustful of American medicine avoided the inoculations sponsored by the Public Health Department, creating a susceptible reservoir for the continued spread of the disease. Mandatory vaccination laws during the late nineteenth century, better screening methods, and educational programs that explained the importance of smallpox prevention helped bring about the decline of the disease by the beginning of the twentieth century. It was eventually eradicated by vaccination programs from the 1920s to the 1940s aimed at children entering the public schools, as well as efforts by the World Health Organization from the 1950s to the 1980s.

John Duffy, *Epidemics in Colonial America* (Baton Rouge: Louisiana State University Press, 1953; repr. 1979); John Duffy, *A History of Public Health in New York City* (New York: Russell Sage Foundation, 1968, 1974)

Howard Markel

Smalls' Paradise. Harlem jazz club, opened in 1925 on Seventh Avenue and 135th Street by Ed Smalls. It seated about 1500 and was famous for its Sunday night after-hours jazz sessions. The club featured performances by such musicians as Willie "the Lion" Smith, Fletcher Henderson, and James P. Johnson, as well as elaborate floor shows and singing waiters. It attracted leading figures of the Harlem Renaissance, including Countee Cullen and Carl Van Vechten. Smalls' operated under the same name until 1986, when it closed.

Marc Ferris

Smith, Alfred E(manuel) (*b* New York City, 30 Dec 1873; *d* New York City, 4 Oct 1944). Four-term New York governor and presidential candidate. The son of second-generation immigrants, Smith was born at 174 South Street and attended St. James Parochial School but left shortly before graduation following his father's death. If he had not been forced to support his mother and sister, Smith might have become an actor. He possessed a nearly photographic memory and a quick wit. He worked at the Fulton Fish Market and other blue-collar jobs before he entered politics as a protégé of saloonkeeper Thomas F. Foley, a Tammany Hall district leader who sent Smith to the New York Assembly in 1904. During these years he lived at 83 Madison Street (1900–1901, now the site of the St. James Convent) and 28 Oliver Street (1904–9) before moving to 25 Oliver Street (1909–24).

In Albany, Smith discovered that the legislature was dominated by the Republican Party, a result of an 1894 change in the state constitution that denied New York City the representation to which it was entitled. The legislature also refused to grant home rule to the city, depriving city officials of the right to decide the most basic issues of local government and imposing the social mores of upstate Protestants on the Catholic and Jewish majority by banning baseball and closing bars on Sundays. The split between upstate and downstate also divided the Democrats in the legislature between upstate reformers like Franklin D. Roosevelt and Tammany men who followed the leadership of Charles F. "Silent Charlie" Murphy. Smith became a Tammany leader in the assembly and helped impeach and remove Democratic governor William Sulzer after he had broken with Murphy.

While he was publicly reviled as a "machine" man by both Republicans and upstate Democrats, Smith was personally very popular with members of both parties. He had an open mind about social and economic reforms and made friends with reformers like Frances Perkins. In the aftermath of the Triangle Shirtwaist fire in 1911, he helped persuade the reformers to support the appointment of a legislative commission to investigate working conditions in the state's factories. Co-chaired by Smith and State Senator Robert F. Wagner, the Factory Investigating Commission held hearings throughout the state and later helped pass dozens of laws that dramatically increased government protection for workers, including restrictions on child labor and a 54-hour week for female workers.

Smith was elected sheriff of New York County in 1915 and president of the Board of Aldermen in 1917. He was narrowly elected as governor in 1918, helped by the influenza epidemic that held down the upstate vote. Although the legislature considered Smith an "accidental" governor, he acted vigorously. He opposed the legislature's plan to ratify the federal prohibition amendment, demanding that it be submitted to a popular vote. Smith appointed a Reconstruction Commission to recommend changes to achieve "a full realization of democracy." One of the major recommendations was a government reorganization program that expanded the power of the governor, giving him control of a streamlined bureaucracy, power to set the state's fiscal priorities through an executive budget, and a longer term. Social worker Belle Moskowitz, who had recommended the commission, became its secretary; Robert Moses was chief of staff. Moskowitz would become Smith's closest political adviser. Smith appointed Perkins to the State Industrial Commission, the highest state office that had been held by a woman. Smith also spoke out strongly on civil liberties, condemning the assembly's expulsion of its four socialist members during the Red Scare in 1919–20 and vetoing legislation that gave the state broad power to curb dissent. Smith was narrowly defeated for reelection in the Warren Harding landslide of 1920.

Smith was reelected governor in 1922, but Republicans succeeded in thwarting many of his proposals, including public ownership and development of water power and the construction of public housing. By appealing directly to the public, however, he won approval for a series of bond issues to undertake an extensive public works program that included the construction of new state hospitals and psychiatric facilities and the expansion of the state park system. State education spending multiplied and made up almost half of the budget by the time he left office in 1928.

In 1928 Smith became the first Catholic to be nominated for president on a major party ticket. Four years earlier his religion had been an issue during the Democratic convention at Madison Square Garden, and he and William Gibbs McAdoo had struggled fruitlessly for the nomination for 103 ballots. Smith chose Franklin Roosevelt to run for governor in an effort to bolster his support among New York Protestants, but he lost in a landslide to Herbert Hoover following a campaign that included many ugly attacks on his religion.

Alfred E. Smith's campaign poster for the Democratic National Convention, 1924

Soon after Smith's defeat he returned to the city and took up residence on Fifth Avenue. He became president of the corporation that built the Empire State Building. Although Smith initially supported Roosevelt's candidacy for the 1932 Democratic presidential nomination, the two men disagreed over strategy, and Smith made a last-minute bid for the nomination. Four years later Smith attacked the New Deal and endorsed the Republican nominee for president; however, he was an early critic of Adolf Hitler and publicly supported Roosevelt against the isolationists as the country prepared for war.

During his final decades Smith undertook many charitable projects, gave lectures, and was active in the Catholic Church; he also gave his name to a public housing development, the Alfred E. Smith Houses, which was built near his birthplace. His statue stands in one of the courtyards of the Smith Houses.

Paula Eldot, *Governor Alfred E. Smith: The Politician as Reformer* (New York: Garland, 1983); Robert F. Wesser, *A Response to Progressivism: The Democratic Party and New York Politics* (New York: New York University Press, 1986); Christopher M.

Finan, *Alfred E. Smith: The Happy Warrior* (New York: Hill and Wang, 2002)

Christopher M. Finan

Smith, Bessie [Elizabeth] (*b* Chattanooga, Tenn., 15 April 1895; *d* Clarksdale, Miss., 26 Sept 1937). Singer. She began her career in 1912 as a dancer with Moses Stokes's traveling show and toured with the Theatre Owners Booking Agency and the Liberty Belles. She sang with Charlie Taylor's Band in New York City in 1920 and with the revue "How Come?" in 1923. Her recording career began when Clarence Williams and Frank Walker of Columbia Records persuaded her to record "Down Hearted Blues" (1923); her subsequent collaborations with Louis Armstrong, Fletcher Henderson, and Tommy Ladnier sold millions of copies. She achieved a level of popularity unusual for a jazz and blues singer; Carl Van Vechten, a white patron of the Harlem Renaissance, promoted her work among white intellectuals and leaders in entertainment. She made her debut on Broadway in *Pansy* (1929) and performed in the revue "League of Rhythm" in 1936 at the Apollo Theater. Smith is remembered for her rich, expressive voice and her dramatic stage presence. Many of her songs describe the experiences of southern African American migrants, especially the struggles of African American women to adjust to urban life in the North. Langston Hughes considered her songs exemplars of the creativity inherent in African American vernacular culture.

Chris Albertson, *Bessie Smith: Empress of the Blues* (New York: Schirmer, 1975)

Kathy J. Ogren

Smith [née Keogh]**, Betty** [Elizabeth] **(Wehner)** (*b* Brooklyn, 15 Dec 1896; *d* Shelton, Conn., 17 Jan 1972). Novelist. She grew up in Williamsburg, Brooklyn, and in 1921 moved to Ann Arbor, Michigan, where she studied journalism and literature and husband George Smith pursued his law degree. She also studied playwriting at the Yale School of Drama (1931–34). During the Depression, she worked for the Federal Theatre Project in New York City while living at 63 Richmond Street in Brooklyn. She relocated with the project to Chapel Hill, North Carolina, in 1936. Though she wrote more than 40 plays, she is best known for her novel *A Tree Grows in Brooklyn* (1943; film version, 1945), a coming-of-age story set in Williamsburg, Brooklyn, that had sold more than 2.5 million copies into the twenty-first century. Her later works include *Tomorrow Will Be Better* (1948), *Maggie Now* (1958), and *Joy in the Morning* (1963).

Irina Ikonsky

Smith, David (Roland) (*b* Decatur, Ind., 6 March 1906; *d* near Bennington, Vt., 23 May 1965). Sculptor. He arrived in New York City in 1926, studied painting at the Art Students League during 1927–32, and began welding metal sculptures in his studio at the Brooklyn Terminal Iron Works in 1933. In 1938 he moved to Bolton Landing in upstate New York. His *Hudson River Landscape* (1951, welded steel), inspired by frequent train trips along the Hudson into New York City, is at the Whitney Museum of American Art. His last works, in stainless steel, are characterized by an unusual finish, first polished and then abraded, creating abstract marks that reflect the light around them. His work is usually discussed in the context of abstract expressionism. Major retrospectives of his work were held at the Museum of Modern Art (1957) and at the Solomon R. Guggenheim Museum (1969, 2006).

Harriet F. Senie

Smith, Red [Walter Wellesley] (*b* Green Bay, Wis., 25 Sept 1905; *d* Stamford, Conn., 15 Jan 1982). Sportswriter. He studied journalism at the University of Notre Dame (graduated 1927) and began his career at the *Milwaukee Sentinel,* the *St. Louis Star,* and the *Philadelphia Record.* In 1945 he moved to New York City to write a sports column for the *New York Herald Tribune* that was soon syndicated in 90 newspapers. After the dissolution of the *Herald Tribune* and its successor, the *World Journal–Tribune,* Smith in 1971 joined the *New York Times,* for which he wrote a column until the end of his life. Smith strove for simplicity in his writing and disdained hyperbole, sentimentality, and cliché. He avoided both the tendency to lionize athletes and the "wiseguy" style affected by many urban sportswriters. Although he wrote about virtually all sports, he was especially fond of baseball, football, boxing, and horse racing and disliked basketball. He won a Pulitzer Prize for commentary in 1976. Collections of his writings include *Out of the Red* (1950), *Views of Sport* (1954), *The Best of Red Smith* (1963), and *The Red Smith Reader* (1982).

Ira Berkow, *Red: A Biography of Red Smith* (New York: Times Books, 1986)

Smith, Stephen (*b* near Skaneateles, N.Y., 19 Feb 1823; *d* Montour Falls, N.Y., 26 Aug 1922). Surgeon and public health official. A graduate of the College of Physicians and Surgeons (1850), he was an attending surgeon at Bellevue Hospital from 1854 to 1896, and from 1861 to 1872 he taught surgery and anatomy at Bellevue Hospital Medical College. His leadership of the campaign to establish the Metropolitan Board of Health (1866) is regarded as one of the most notable achievements in the history of public health in New York City and the United States; he was a member of the board from 1868 to 1875. Smith designed the plan for Roosevelt Hospital (1866) and promoted improvements at Bellevue Hospital. He edited the *New York Journal of Medicine* and founded the American Public Health Association. His book *The City That Was* (1911) describes his numerous battles to improve public health in New York City. He lived for many years at 300 Central Park West.

Allen J. Share

Smith, Tony (*b* South Orange, N.J., 23 Sept 1912; *d* New York City, 26 Dec 1980). Architect, painter, and sculptor. He studied at the Art Students League during 1933–36 and worked briefly as an apprentice to Frank Lloyd Wright before pursuing a 20-year career as an architect and painter. From 1960 he worked as a sculptor and became an important figure in the development of minimalist sculpture. From 1962 on Smith taught at Hunter College, which in his honor installed *Tau* (1965–80, welded steel painted black) at the southwest corner of 68th Street and Lexington Avenue. In 1998 the Museum of Modern Art mounted a career retrospective of his work.

Robert Storr, *Tony Smith: Architect, Painter, Sculptor* (New York: Museum of Modern Art/Harry Abrams, 1998)

Harriet F. Senie

Smith, William, Jr. (*b* New York City, 25 June 1728; *d* Quebec, 3 Dec 1793). Loyalist lawyer and historian. After attending Yale College he was admitted to the bar and with William Livingston in 1752 published a digest of colonial laws enacted between 1691 and 1751. A central figure among lawyers, he was an influential contributor to the *Independent Reflector* and the *Occasional Reverberator.* He became known for *The History of the Province* (1757), the first published history of the province of New York. Appointed chief justice of the province in 1763, he became a member of the provincial council in 1767 and helped to organize the Whig Club. Smith moved to England during the evacuation of the British in 1783; he was later the chief justice of Canada.

Leslie F. S. Upton, *The Loyal Whig: William Smith of New York* (Toronto: University of Toronto Press, 1969)

James E. Mooney

Smith, Willie "the Lion" [William Henry Joseph Bonaparte Bertholoff] (*b* Goshen, N.Y., 25 Nov 1897; *d* New York City, 18 April 1973). Pianist and composer. He grew up in Newark, New Jersey, and began playing the piano at the age of six. In his teens he played professionally in the saloons of New York City and Atlantic City, New Jersey; took part in many "cutting contests" in Harlem; performed at various Harlem venues, including

Leroy's, the Rhythm Club, Pod's and Jerry's, and the Hoofer's Club; and worked occasionally as a cantor. A decorated veteran of the 350th field artillery serving in World War I in France, he earned his nickname "the Lion" for bravery. He was called a "musician's musician," but his popularity with the general public increased when Artie Shaw and Tommy Dorsey performed his arrangements and compositions. He recorded for Decca in 1935; among his recordings for Commodore in 1939 was "Echoes of Spring," a work inspired by a park in New York City. He toured Europe in 1949 and played as a soloist and accompanist and with bands in nightclubs, revues, and theaters across the United States until the end of his career. A pioneer of ragtime, Harlem stride (along with James P. Johnson and Fats Waller), and jazz and blues piano, Smith was one of the most distinctive figures in the music of the HARLEM RENAISSANCE. With George Hoefer he wrote *Music on My Mind: The Memoirs of an American Pianist* (1964).

Kathy J. Ogren

Snider, Duke [Edwin Donald] (*b* Los Angeles, Calif., 19 Sept 1926). Baseball player. Known as the "Duke of Flatbush," he was the star home-run hitter for the Brooklyn Dodgers during the team's heyday from 1947 to 1957 when it frequently played and lost to the New York Yankees in the World Series. He played center field and batted third in a lineup that included Jackie Robinson, Pee Wee Reese, and Roy Campanella and helped lead Brooklyn to its only championship in 1955 against the Yankees. Snider moved with the team to Los Angeles after the 1957 season and they won the World Series in 1959. He returned east to play for the New York Mets for one season in 1963 before finishing the final year of his career in San Francisco. He was elected to the National Baseball Hall of Fame in 1980.

Joshua Robinson, David White

Snook, John Butler (*b* London, 16 July 1815; *d* Brooklyn, 1 Nov 1901). Architect. His most innovative building was the department store of A. T. Stewart at Broadway and Chambers Street (1845–46, with Joseph Trench), the first of its kind in the world. Intended as an elegant palace for the consumer, it had an exterior of marble and plate glass. He also designed hotels, among them the Metropolitan (1850–52), that had elaborate decorations and superior heating and ventilating systems; their lavish interiors inspired the construction of luxury hotels throughout the country. By 1855 he used cast iron for the facade of a building (examples of his cast-iron buildings still stand at 65 Greene Street and 287 Broadway). Well-known buildings by Snook include the Grand Central Depot (1869–71, demolished in 1903 for the construction of Grand Central Terminal) at 42nd Street and Park Avenue and the William H. Vanderbilt Houses (1879–82) on Fifth Avenue between 51st and 52nd streets.

Mary Beth Betts

Snug Harbor Cultural Center. Center for the performing and visual arts at 1000 Richmond Terrace in Staten Island. It opened in 1976 on a site of 83 acres (34 hectares) formerly occupied by Sailors' Snug Harbor and now New York City parkland. The site contains 28 historic buildings (dormitories, residences, a chapel, a library, and a music hall) that were constructed between 1831 and 1917 by such prominent architects as Minard Lafever, Robert W. Gibson, William Jallade, and the firm of Carrère and Hastings and offer fine examples of Greek Revival, Italianate, Second Empire, and beaux-arts architecture; two of the buildings retain their High Victorian interior decoration. The cultural center houses numerous cultural organizations, including the Staten Island Children's Museum, the Staten Island Botanic Garden, the Art Lab, the Noble Maritime Collection, and many community arts organizations. The Samuel I. Newhouse Center for Contemporary Art exhibits work by artists from the region. Private artists' studios are provided, and musical, dramatic, and dance performances take place throughout the year. The site is listed on the National Register of Historic Places.

Barnett Shepherd

Snyder, Ruth (*b* 1895; *d* Ossining, N.Y., 22 Jan 1928). Murderer. In the hope of collecting a life insurance policy worth $95,000 she tried seven times to kill her husband, Albert Snyder, the art editor of the magazine *Motor Boating*, by methods that included gassing him in his sleep and poisoning his whiskey. She succeeded on 20 March 1927 by hitting him with a sash weight, muzzling him with chloroform, and strangling him with picture wire. Both she and her companion, a traveling corset salesman named Henry Judd Gray, confessed to the crime during the police investigation, although each sought to assign most of the blame to the other. The two were executed at Sing Sing Prison. A photograph of Snyder's electrocution taken surreptitiously and published on the front page of the *Daily News* became legendary in tabloid photojournalism.

John Kobler, *The Trial of Ruth Snyder and Judd Gray* (Garden City, N.Y.: Doubleday, Doran, 1938)

Norris Randolph

soap and toiletries. In its early history New York City became a leading manufacturing and distribution center for soaps and toiletry products. As the major Atlantic port and largest U.S. city, Manhattan combined ready access to basic and specialized raw materials with a huge consumer market.

Soap making is a branch of the chemical industry traditionally connected with candle manufacture. During the colonial period a few artisans established shops in Manhattan, and in rural districts people made soap at home; fine soaps were imported from Europe. Since tallow rending and other aspects of the process often produced unpleasant odors, from 1796 the city restricted soap and candle manufacturing to the residential outskirts; workshop production also required substantial space for boiling and presented fire and chemical hazards.

Larger-scale, scientific soap manufacture took root in New York City in the first decade of the nineteenth century, primarily along the lower West Side. In 1806 William Colgate established a small factory on Dutch and John streets, and in 1809 David Williams opened a factory on Greenwich Street near Barclay Street that later became known as Enoch Morgan's Sons. Other soap and candle firms of the time included J. C. Hull's Sons (1780); Benjamin T. Babbitt (1836); James Buchan; Johnson, Vroom and Fowler; D. S. and J. Ward; J. D. and W. Lee; Holt and Horn; Patrick Clendenen; John Alsop; C. W. Smith and Company; John Taylor and Sons; W. G. Browning and Company; Lee A. Comstock; John Buchanan; George F. Penrose; John Ramsey; John Kirkman; and John Sexton.

By 1845 the introduction of steam power, an expanded knowledge of chemistry, and the discovery of new vegetable and animal oils helped the industry to grow and diversify. One distinct branch that developed was the manufacture of "fancy toilet soaps," an industry that bore some relation to cosmetics. Soaps of this kind were made in the United States from imported oils, perfumes, and coloring agents and competed successfully with similar products from Europe before 1850. Noted makers of fancy soaps at mid-century included Thomas Jones, John Lindmark, Levi Beals, John Wyeth, James Mackey, John Ramsey, William White and Company, Robert Reed, John B. Breed, J. M. de Ciphlet, F. F. Gouraud, August Grandjean, and Eugene Roussel. Other specialized products included laundry and shaving soaps and scouring soaps and powders.

In 1847 the firm of Colgate moved its manufacturing operations to Jersey City, New Jersey, where it maintained an important industrial presence (eventually as COLGATE–PALMOLIVE) until 1988; it continued to maintain offices on John Street in Manhattan. Despite this departure and others like it, soap factories in New York City continued to increase in size and number to the end of the nineteenth century. The number of people employed in the industry in Manhattan grew from 229 in 1840 to 1371 in 1900. Eighty to 90 firms were engaged in the soap business in the 1890s, of which about 20 were important manufacturers, such as Enoch Morgan's Sons, Benjamin T. Babbitt, James S. Kirk and Company, Charles S. Higgins, and D. S. Brown and Company. Many of their products became nationally known, among them Enoch Morgan's Sapolio soap and two products made by Babbitt: Babbitt's Best Soap and, later, Bab-O.

After consolidation in 1898, the chemical industries expanded to the outer boroughs and the metropolitan region. Firms in the New York City area accounted for one-sixth of all the soap production in the United States in 1900 and for nearly one-quarter by 1919. The share of manufacturing in Manhattan, however, decreased. By 1922 there were 207 soap factories in the region employing 10,231 workers. The largest factories were on the western bank of the Hudson River and on Staten Island, where PROCTER AND GAMBLE built a huge facility at Port Ivory in 1907. Others operated in Brooklyn and Long Island City.

Several trends contributed to the departure of many soap manufacturers from Greater New York after the late 1920s. New forms of technology had created additional demands for space and equipment, and the cost of land, labor, energy, and taxes in the region had risen. The industry became concentrated in a few large national and international firms that produced not only soap and toiletries but foods, paper goods, chemicals, cosmetics, and other items. Although there were more than 30 soap manufacturers in the metropolitan region as late as 1956, from that time the number and production of soap firms declined sharply. By 1991 both Colgate–Palmolive and Procter and Gamble had shut down their local operations.

Samuel Mitchell, comp., *The Case of the Manufacturers of Soap and Candles in the City of New York* (New York: John Buel, 1797); Mabel Newcomer, "The Chemical Industry," *Regional Survey,* vol. 1a, *Chemical, Wood, Metal, Tobacco, and Printing Industries* (New York: Regional Plan of New York and Environs, 1927); Richard B. Stott, *Workers in the Metropolis* (Ithaca, N.Y.: Cornell University Press, 1990)

Charles L. Sachs

soccer. Soccer in New York City has been especially popular among college students and immigrants. In 1873 Columbia University adopted English soccer rules for collegiate play, and the school was a founding member of the first Intercollegiate Soccer Association, formed in 1905. Van Cortlandt Park in the Bronx was an early venue for soccer matches. The United States Soccer Association (formed 1913) staged its first tournament for the U.S. Challenge Cup in Brooklyn between two local teams composed of Irish immigrants. New York City had a team in the first professional soccer league in the United States, the American Soccer League (1923), which during the 1950s broadcast some of its games on television. The formation in 1971 of the New York Cosmos of the North American Soccer League marked the return of professional soccer to the city; in the same year the league moved its headquarters to Manhattan. The team played its home games at Downing Stadium on Randalls Island and had on its roster the most popular player in American soccer, Randy Horton. It won the league championship in 1972 and in 1975 signed the famed Brazilian soccer star Pelé, who drew huge crowds and made the Cosmos the most important franchise in U.S. soccer. The team moved to Yankee Stadium in 1976 and then to Giants Stadium at the Meadowlands in New Jersey. Pelé retired in 1977, but the Cosmos continued to dominate the league, qualifying for the playoffs every year between 1975 and 1984. The Cosmos left the league in 1985, and both the team and the league disbanded soon after. Columbia remained a force in intercollegiate soccer: it won several Ivy League championships and finished fourth in the tournament of the National Collegiate Athletic Association in 1979 and second in 1983. The center of amateur soccer in New York City is the Metropolitan Oval in Maspeth; founded in the 1920s by immigrants from central Europe, later it also became the site of spirited competition between teams from other parts of the world, notably South America. In 1994 the New York and New Jersey area was named as the site for a Major League Soccer team. Initially known as the Empire Soccer Club, the MetroStars, as they were later named, was one of the first 10 teams in the league. In 2006 an Austrian energy drink producer bought the team, renaming it Red Bull New York (the Red Bulls); they played in Giants Stadium in East Rutherford, New Jersey. The state-of-the-art, soccer-specific Red Bull Arena is slated to open in 2010 in Harrison, New Jersey.

Rohit T. Aggarwala

social clubs. Usually groups with regular meeting places, or clubhouses, that admit new members on the basis of nomination and election by existing members. Although there were political, fraternal, artistic, literary, and athletic groups in New York City during the colonial and early Federal periods, social clubs were not formed until later, and they numbered only three by the late 1830s: the Union Club (1836), which represented the city's oldest families; the Hone Club (1836); and the Kent Club (1838), which was for lawyers. The number increased markedly during the following decades with the formation of the Century Association (1846), the Lotos Club (1870), the Salmagundi Club (1871), and the Lambs (1874). The Knickerbocker Club was formed in 1871 by 18 members of the Union Club dissatisfied with its new, more liberal admissions policy: they sought to associate with "men of good will and common aspirations," by which they meant members of established Dutch and English families (the founders of the Knickerbocker nevertheless included two Jews: Moses Lazarus and August Belmont). In some cases what motivated the formation of a new club was a political orientation (the Hone Club supported the Whigs between the 1830s and the Civil War, the Manhattan Club the Democrats, and the Union League the Republicans); ethnicity, especially among the city's large German population (which founded the Allemania Club, the German Club, and the Harmonie Club); or a common interest in literature, theater, the arts, or sports such as rowing, sailing, and tennis. Virtually all the clubs modeled themselves after the English gentleman's club and were governed in similar fashion, with an executive committee and subordinate committees concerned with finance, membership, the clubhouse, and the library. By the last quarter of the nineteenth century New York City was second only to London in the number of its clubs (more than 100) and club memberships (about 50,000). All the members were white men, three-quarters were married, and half were bankers or businessmen. A study of club life in 1871 found that half the members descended from only about 20 families and that each man usually held several memberships, perhaps belonging to a university club, a tennis or yachting club, and a literary club. Prominent clubs formed about the turn of the twentieth century include the Players (1888), the Montauk Club in Brooklyn (1889), the Metropolitan Club (1891), the Brook (1903), and the Friars Club (1904).

Social clubs in New York City declined in number after the 1920s, as the automobile became increasingly important, members moved to the suburbs, and social patterns changed. Clubs such as the Athenaeum and the New York Club disappeared. By the late twentieth century social clubs came to adopt a defensive posture, often fearful of lawsuits over such matters as sexual and ethnic discrimination and challenges to their tax-exempt status. Some clubs sought to avoid publicity at any cost: perhaps the most reticent was the Knickerbocker.

After World War II the term social club took on a new meaning, as immigrants from Cuba, the Dominican Republic, Honduras, and other Latin American countries opened informal clubs, generally unlicensed, that served alcohol and provided musical entertainment. Nevertheless, early in the twenty-first century New York City had the most social, literary, and university clubs of any U.S. city.

See also UNIVERSITY CLUBS, WOMEN'S CLUBS.

James E. Mooney

Social Gospel. Christian doctrine seeking to address social ills, also known as social Christianity and Christian socialism. It developed during the late nineteenth century and became especially popular in New York City. Adherents emphasized the doctrine of the kingdom of God and called for the conversion to Christianity of both individuals and social institutions. The many theorists and practitioners of the doctrine included Washington Gladden, Josiah Strong, Richard T. Ely, Charles M. Sheldon, Jane Addams, and Reverdy C. Ransom. The best-known advocate in the city was Walter Rauschenbusch, a pastor of the Second German Baptist Church at the edge of Hell's Kitchen who became a passionate defender of the poor; his book *Christianity and the Social Crisis* (1907) was central to the Social Gospel movement.

Paul M. Minus, *Walter Rauschenbusch: American Reformer* (New York: Macmillan, 1988)

Randall Balmer

socialism. New York City became a national center of socialism during the nineteenth century. Between the late 1820s and the 1840s utopian socialism became a tenet of the city's labor movement. Drawing on the ideas of the Welsh reformer Robert Owen, his son Robert Dale Owen, Frances Wright, and Thomas Skidmore, radical workers sought to abolish inheritance, distribute property more equitably, and educate children in state boarding schools. A small group of German immigrants, some of whom had worked with Karl Marx and Friedrich Engels, introduced Marxist socialism in New York City during the 1840s; after the Civil War they joined with such radical reformers as Victoria Woodhull and Tennessee Claflin to form a branch of the International Workingmen's Association (IWA), which collapsed in 1876 owing largely to German members' strong sympathy for trade unions and discomfort with radical reformers. The Socialist Labor Party, the first socialist party in the United States, was formed in 1877. In the city it appealed to German workers and conducted nearly all its business in German. With the IWA it introduced Marx's ideas to important trade unionists in the city, including Samuel Gompers.

During the 1890s Daniel DeLeon became the leader of the Socialist Labor Party and steered it toward an uncompromising and revolutionary brand of socialism. Tension arose in the party over his dogmatism and his hostility toward trade unions (the leaders of which he condemned as "labor lieutenants of capitalism"). Jewish workers led by Morris Hillquit and Abraham Cahan, editor of the *Jewish Daily Forward,* were especially opposed to DeLeon's policies and joined with trade unionists in 1901 to form the Socialist Party of America (SPA). Soon after, socialism reached its peak strength in both the city and the rest of the nation. Under Hillquit's leadership the branch of the party in the city stressed immediate reforms and allied itself closely with trade unionism. It built firm ties to the garment workers who supported socialist political candidates. Socialism also attracted leading artists and intellectuals, who saw it as an effective challenge to stultifying Victorian conventions and hypocrisies; among those who joined the party were the painter John Sloan, the novelist Theodore Dreiser, the intellectual Max Eastman, the journalists Walter Lippmann and John Reed, and the reformers Florence Kelley, Frances Perkins, and W. E. B. Du Bois. Intellectuals in Greenwich Village published the magazine *The Masses;* the local branch of the SPA published the *Call,* a daily newspaper with a large circulation. The party offered adult education at its own school, the Rand School of Social Science. Meyer London, a member of the SPA, was elected to the U.S. House of Representatives in 1914 from the Lower East Side and won reelection in 1916 and 1920. In 1917 voters there and in the Bronx and Brooklyn supported Hillquit in the mayoral election and helped to elect 10 socialists to the state assembly, five to the city's Board of Aldermen, and one to a municipal judgeship.

The party was crippled by its opposition to the country's entrance into World War I. Members split into factions supporting and opposing the war, and *The Masses* was shut down by the federal government. The party became divided after the Bolshevik Revolution of 1917 caused some members to abandon socialism for communism; the division was deep and bitter in the city, where Hillquit led socialists opposed to communists. Between 1918 and 1921 socialist candidates continued to win strong support among Jewish workers. Norman Thomas, the best-known American socialist of the 1920s and 1930s, was a candidate for mayor of New York City in 1925 and 1929 and a member of Mayor Fiorello H. La Guardia's charter revision committee in 1934. Another leading socialist in the city was Max Shachtman (1904–72), editor of the Trotskyist journals the *Militant* and *New International.*

Competition between socialists and communists nearly destroyed the International Ladies' Garment Workers' Union during the 1920s and the Fur and Leather Workers' Union during the 1930s, and by the end of the 1920s socialism seemed a spent force in the city. It revived during the Depression, and in 1933 Hillquit won more than 100,000 votes as the mayoral candidate of the SPA. In 1936 a faction that refused to embrace communism formed the Social Democratic Federation (SDF) after splitting off from a faction of the SPA that sought to form a revolutionary front with communists; the SDF launched a journal, the *New Leader.* Socialism became a fringe movement after trade unions and Jewish workers left the SPA to support the New Deal and join the American Labor Party.

After World War II those who remained loyal to the SPA devoted themselves to fighting communism, and the journal *Dissent* was launched in 1955 by a small group of intellectuals in the city to preserve socialist ideas, remaining in operation into the 1990s. The emergence of the New Left in the 1960s caused much division among socialists. The League for Industrial Democracy, a group concentrated in New York City, helped to form Students for a Democratic Society in 1962. Social Democrats USA, organized in 1972, soon adopted conservative positions on many issues. One of few remaining socialist groups in the city in the early twenty-first century was the Democratic Socialists of America, formed in 1982 by Michael Harrington.

David A. Shannon, *The Socialist Party of America: A History* (New York: Macmillan, 1955); Irving Howe, *World of Our Fathers: The Journey of the East European Jews to America and the Life They Found and Made* (New York: Harcourt Brace Jovanovich, 1975); Sean Wilentz, *Chants Democratic: New York City and the Rise of the American Working Class, 1790–1850* (New York: Oxford University Press, 1984)

Melvyn Dubofsky

Socialist Labor Party [SLP]. Political party formed in 1877, largely by German-speaking immigrants. It was the first party in the United States to advocate Marxist socialism. The party was especially strong in New York City, where there was a large community of German immigrants. In 1886 it took an active part in Henry George's mayoral campaign. Under the leadership of Daniel DeLeon, after 1890 the branch in the city adopted English as its official language. The party split in 1901 after DeLeon alienated many supporters, including German Americans, Jewish immigrants, and members of trade unions. Ruled with an iron hand by DeLeon until his death in 1914, the party moved increasingly toward the political fringe in the city. It nevertheless remained active into the twenty-first century, with members idolizing DeLeon and nominating candidates for local, state, and national office.

Glen Seretan, *Daniel DeLeon: The Odyssey of an American Marxist* (Cambridge, Mass.: Harvard University Press, 1979)

Melvyn Dubofsky

Socialist Party of America [SPA]. Political party formed in Indianapolis in 1901 that built a large following in New York City among eastern European Jewish workers. The party's most prominent leaders in the city, Morris Hillquit and Meyer London, were engaged as attorneys by the garment workers' unions, which endorsed the party and aggressively sought votes for its candidates. London was elected to the U.S. House of Representatives from the Lower East Side in 1914, 1916, and 1920; Hillquit won more than 22 percent of the vote in the mayoral election of 1917. Largely Jewish districts elected five socialists to the Board of Aldermen, one to a municipal judgeship, and several to the state assembly. In April 1920 five socialists from the city were expelled from the state assembly; two were reelected in November but denied their seats after the election, marking the decline of the party's influence. Throughout the 1920s the garment workers' unions continued to endorse the party, which maintained support among Jewish voters but was severely weakened by opposition from conservatives and competition from the Communist Party. The party during the 1930s was reduced to a small faction, as members joined the Democratic and American Labor parties to support the New Deal. It survived in the city largely through the efforts of such leaders as Norman Thomas, Michael Harrington, and Irving Howe and journals such as the *New Leader* and *Dissent.*

David A. Shannon, *The Socialist Party of America: A History* (Chicago: Macmillan, 1955); Irving Howe, *World of Our Fathers* (New York: Harcourt Brace Jovanovich, 1975); Charles Leinenweber, "Socialists in the Streets: The New York City Socialist Party in Working-Class Neighborhoods, 1908–1918," *Science and Society* 41 (1977), 152–71

Melvyn Dubofsky

Social Science Research Council. Independent association of scholars that conducts interdisciplinary research in the social sciences and on public policy. It was formed in New York City in 1923 by professors from the University of Chicago and occupied offices in the tower of Grand Central Terminal. In the early 1970s it moved to 605 Third Avenue at 40th Street. The council has a rotating membership of some 300 social scientists who are assisted by a professional staff of 15. They study such diverse subjects as the urban underclass, the learning process, the Latino community, international relations, and research methods. The council sponsors workshops, seminars, conferences, and summer training institutes: one series of meetings held during 1982–85 led to the formation of the Committee on New York City, dedicated to scholarly study of the city and its culture, politics, and economy. In the early twenty-first century the council continued to develop new initiatives on major issues of public concern, including the social effect of AIDS and the structure of humanitarian emergencies.

Samuel Z. Klausner and Victor M. Lidz, *The Nationalization of the Social Sciences* (Philadelphia: University of Pennsylvania Press, 1986)

Marjorie Harrison

social work. New York City became a center for the development of professional social work during the nineteenth century. The Association for Improving the Condition of the Poor was formed in 1843, and in 1882 Josephine Shaw Lowell and others formed the Charity Organization Society, a federation of private relief organizations. Under Lowell the society practiced what it called scientific philanthropy: it developed a central listing of relief recipients and a network of "friendly visitors" who investigated and counseled relief applicants. Although the society originally relied on volunteers, it increasingly turned to paid caseworkers, who were seen as more reliable and better qualified. Out of its Summer School of Philanthropy (1898), a program to train social workers, evolved the New York School of Social Work (later renamed the Columbia University School of Social Work), the first such school in the nation. From 1891 the society also published the *Charities Review,* which later became the leading social work periodical the *Survey.*

While the Charity Organization Society emphasized the role of casework in social work, SETTLEMENT HOUSES emphasized the role of social reform. The Lower East Side was the site of the first settlement house in the United States, opened in 1886 and later named University Settlement. In the early twentieth century the Russell Sage Foundation sought to promote the new profession of social work and to develop practical applications of social welfare theories. During 1909–28 Mary Richmond wrote case histories for use as teaching guides, organized summer institutes for caseworkers and supervisors, and published the influential books *Social Diagnosis* (1917) and *What Is Social Casework?* (1922), which defined the skills involved in casework and helped to elevate professional standards. The foundation also provided office space for a number of emerging national professional organizations such as the American Association of Social Workers. Francis H. McLean, another employee of the foundation, encouraged cities to form councils of private welfare agencies that could coordinate their activities; in 1925 the Welfare Council was organized as such an agency, partially supplanting the Charity Organization Society, which soon experienced overwhelming competition from public welfare programs.

Both public and private local social agencies were inadequate to face the problems of the Depression, leading the federal government to assume responsibility. Many New Yorkers contributed to the development of federal welfare programs under President Franklin D. Roosevelt, and as the field of social work expanded, many of the leading activists, schools, and professional associations emerged in the city. In 1939 the Charity Organization Society and the Association for Improving the Condition of the Poor merged to form the Community Service Society. Neva Deardorff worked for the Research Bureau of the Welfare Council of Greater New York during 1927–46, demonstrating the value of statistical analysis and sociological data for social work planning. She then helped to form and direct the Health Insurance Plan of Greater New York, a precursor of health maintenance organizations. The American Association of Social Workers was founded in 1922 by Deardorff, David Holbrook, William Hodson, and Dorothy Kahn. In 1920 Holbrook became the head of the American Association for Organizing Family Social Work (based in the city), and in 1925 he joined the National Social Work Council, an organization that provided a forum for other national social work agencies (he remained there for more than 20 years). In 1922 Hodson became the head of the Division of Child Welfare Legislation at the Russell Sage Foundation and later of its Division of Social Legislation; he led the private Welfare Council (1925) and the first state-level public assistance program (1931) and campaigned for federal relief programs, which he also helped to formulate. In 1934 he became the city's commissioner of public welfare. Walter Mott West led the American Association of Social Workers from 1927 to 1942, during which time the organization shaped federal welfare policies; in 1938 Kahn became an assistant to West. As the associate editor from 1930 of the *Survey,* Gertrude Springer called attention to the growing role of the federal government in social welfare. Jane Hoey, Hodson's assistant at the Welfare Council, became the head of the Bureau of Public Assistance of the Social Security Administration in 1935. After World War II Kahn directed the Health and Welfare Council (also in New York City), and during 1950–55 she led the Social Welfare Section of the Department of Social Affairs at the United Nations.

Because of the growing importance of the federal government in financing social programs, many national social welfare organizations moved to Washington, D.C., but in the early twenty-first century New York City remains a center for innovation and education in social work. Social work programs are offered at Columbia University (1898), Fordham University (1929), New York University (1955), Hunter College (1958), and Yeshiva University (1959).

Roy Lubove, *The Professional Altruist: The Emergence of Social Work as a Career, 1880–1930* (Cambridge, Mass.: Harvard University Press, 1965); Walter I. Trattner, *From Poor Law to Welfare State: A History of Social Welfare in America* (New York: Free Press, 1974; 4th edn 1989); Judith Ann Trolander, *Professionalism and Social Change: From the Settlement House Movement to Neighborhood Centers, 1886 to the Present* (New York: Columbia University Press, 1987)

Judith Ann Trolander

society. More than in Boston, Philadelphia, or Charleston, the upper class in New York City has been based on wealth. The legitimacy and longevity of elite society depended on a delicate balance between on one hand exclusiveness and isolation, and on the other hand a willingness to defer to the elite on the part of the community at large. Within society a sense of kinship was important, traditionally determining the choice of school, camp, dancing class, and college, as well as admission to clubs, membership in charity and cultural boards, and invitations to social events. All these distinctions were based originally on success in business and government, the two areas that saw the first changes for the declining old families of the establishment. Later came the disturbance in the careful balance between community leadership and the once-acceptable separation of classes into enclaves.

The group that dominated New Amsterdam consisted of old Dutch families. Their sense of aristocracy was based on wealth held in land originally granted by the Dutch West India Company and later by the colonial governments in which the leadership group was powerfully well represented. The manorial system of land ownership along the Hudson River and on Long Island was as close as the northern colonies came to an aristocracy. Another source of early strength among these leaders was wealth earned from mercantile trade, usually wholesale and seldom retail, to which a social stigma was long attached. When the British gained control in 1664 they did not displace the social leaders, whom they joined in business partnerships, church congregations, and marriages. Cadwallader Colden, a colonial governor of New York, described this society as based first on the landed gentry of the large baronial holdings, second on the lawyers, and last on the merchants, but there was mixing of these categories. They held the major royal government offices in the legislative and judicial branches and were close allies of both British- and American-born members of the executive branch. They also controlled land grants, military contracts, and lucrative franchises. Although there were internal competitions for leadership, as among the Livingston, De Lancey, and other factions, the upper class continued to exercise power no matter which of the contending groups prevailed. The class became a cosmopolitan one of great ethnic variety, with the great Dutch families joined by French Huguenots (the Jays and De Lanceys), English and Scots (the Barclays and Waltons), and Germans (the Beekmans). Together they founded the New York Chamber of Commerce (1768), the Society of New York Hospital, Trinity Church, King's College, and similar institutions.

This group faced difficulties with the coming of the American Revolution, during which the British army occupied the city from 1776 to 1783. When the troops left, so did many Loyalists for maritime Canada and for England. Many new fortunes were built and new families replaced the departing Loyalists, but they still faced the task of fitting in among the great social families that had remained in New York City or returned there from exile. The social sovereignty of these colonial families was ended by 1810, when their withdrawal from commerce and government had become apparent and many of the great manorial estates had been broken up. It was about this time, at the beginning of the new nation and the end of the brief tenure of the Federalists, that the old patrician group in its confusion turned toward exclusivity for the first time.

The new patrician society was a combination of old New Yorkers and people from New England. Many members of the new families were merchant bankers who became active in public affairs because they appreciated the need for close ties between finance and government. They often held local political office, first as Federalists and then as Republicans (notably the Clintons, Lewises, and Livingstons). The aristocrats had been superseded by the bourgeoisie of the marketplace, whose standards for admission were more flexible, and the tension between the old families and the new gave vitality to the social life of New York City.

The amalgam of families that led the city supported its existing charities and founded new ones, as the city attracted new residents from the countryside and immigrants from Ireland and Germany. In the years preceding the Civil War society managed to assimilate the new fortunes without changing its accustomed patterns. Social events and other functions were largely the province of men, who looked after their business interests during the day and established ancillary clubs and hereditary societies. The pace of change at mid-century featured the emergence of the social arbiter: Isaac Brown was the first in a series that came to include Ward McAllister and Harry Lehr.

During the Civil War fortunes were made by such entrepreneurs as J. P. Morgan, John D. Rockefeller, Jim Fisk, and Jay Gould, and after the war the change in society was dramatic. The old guard was pushed aside by the new, and the latest old guard sought solace in clubs and in the creation of yet more hereditary societies where family lines remained important. In such clubs members could meet, dine, and do business with the new elite.

New millionaires who did not have the properly matured credentials and were thus unwelcome in more established society were attracted to the idea of the "Four Hundred," a guest list prepared by McAllister for Mrs. William Astor. (The number of names was in fact 273, said to be the number of guests that could be accommodated in her ballroom.) This inner circle of society included only half a dozen people with intellectual or artistic interests, and the Four Hundred were rarely involved in cultural gatherings. One member of the group, Mrs. Winthrop Chanler, who had been brought up in Rome in an artistic family and found New York City to be prim and dull, wrote that the Four Hundred "would have fled in a body from a painter, a musician, or a clever Frenchman." The Four Hundred was a group dominated by determined women seeking newspaper publicity for the Rockefellers, Dodges, Morgans, and Schiffs. But because its membership was continually changing, it did provide an entrée into society for those with manners, patience, and money.

Social events and functions in New York City took place in what newspapers called the "Magic Parallelogram" (between 14th and 59th streets and between Third and Sixth avenues) during a period called the Gilded Age, after an 1875 novel by Mark Twain and Charles Dudley Warner. It was Twain who published the joke "In Boston they ask, How much does he know? in Philadelphia, Who were his parents? in New York, How much is he worth?" The period lasted for half a century, during which fashionable society drew the attention of an avid public fed by society writers and gossips. In 1887 this group was given a sort of codification when the *Social Register* appeared with fewer than 2000 New Yorkers listed. In an age of excesses, few were as outrageous as the costume ball given by Bradley Martin during the winter of 1896–97, an expensive event described in five pages of agonizing detail in the Hearst newspapers. Criticism of the party for its ostentation was widespread and fierce, driving the stunned Martins into permanent exile in England. The incident seemed to confirm Henry Adams's remark that American society was the first to go from barbarism to decadence without passing through civilization.

The Four Hundred was succeeded between the world wars by café society, a vacuous collection of poseurs, playboys, heiresses, and party-givers from Hollywood, Paris, and London. It was the sort of crowd that could appreciate Oscar Wilde's comment about society that "to be in it is merely a bore, but to be out of it is simply a tragedy." The man who named café society, Maury Henry Biddle Paul, known as Cholly Knickerbocker, was from Philadelphia, where his critics said that he came from the wrong branch of each of the four distinguished families that constituted his name. In 1921 he divided society into two lists, distinguishing café society from the old guard. Each list had 50 names, and only two families were represented in both: the Drexels, with mother in the old guard and son in café society; and the Vanderbilts, with three older ladies including "the Dowager Mrs. Vanderbilt" on the old list and an alcoholic man and a divorced woman on the new. Knickerbocker lived long enough to see the celebrities whom he disdained replace the members of café society whom he had celebrated in his lists and newspaper columns, never realizing that they were all celebrities in the first place and that he had helped make them so.

After World War II society in New York City was in tatters. Social secretaries had a difficult time finding eligible escorts for the few remaining assemblies and balls. The survival of society was also threatened by divorce, indifference to cultural and charitable affairs, and the move to the suburbs and beyond. Public attention focused on music and sports instead of society names. In his novels Tom Wolfe epitomized a time when the scramble for wealth and power was not only accepted but revered. The new members of the elite held lavish parties in such grand institutions as the Metropolitan Museum of Art, which some facetiously called "Club Met." Any relation between this group and what used to be thought of as class was purely coincidental.

Dixon Wecter, *The Saga of American Society: A Record of Social Aspiration, 1607–1937* (New York: Charles Scribner's Sons, 1937; repr. 1970); Frederick Cople Jaher, *The Urban Establishment: Upper Strata in Boston, New York, Charleston, Chicago, and Los Angeles* (Urbana: University of Illinois Press, 1982); Louis Auchincloss, *The Vanderbilt Era: Profiles of a Gilded Age* (New York: Charles Scribner's Sons, 1989)

James E. Mooney

Society for the Prevention of Crime. Reform organization formed in 1878. In its early years it was led by Howard Crosby and focused on helping the police arrest gamblers and prostitutes, as well as saloonkeepers who violated the Sunday closing laws. After Crosby's death in 1891 leadership of the society was assumed by Charles H. Parkhurst, pastor of the Madison Square Presbyterian Church, who adopted a more provocative style, touring saloons and brothels in disguise to prove that vice flourished in New York City under police protection. During his tenure the society was widely known as the "Parkhurst society." Detectives employed by it uncovered evidence of protected vice in the city, which led to the appointment of a committee of the state senate to investigate police blackmail and corruption in Tammany Hall; the committee was known as the Lexow Committee, after its chairman, Clarence Lexow of Nyack, New York. The resulting scandal led to the defeat of Tammany Hall and the election of a reform administration in 1894. The society declined in power and influence after Parkhurst resigned as its president in 1908, and it disbanded after the repeal of Prohibition.

Timothy J. Gilfoyle, "The Moral Origins of Political Surveillance: The Preventive Society in New York, 1867–1918," *American Quarterly* 38 (1986), 637–52

Warren Sloat

Society for the Prevention of Cruelty to Children. Children's advocacy organization formed in New York City in December 1874 (incorporated in 1875 as the New York Society for the Prevention of Cruelty to Children) by Elbridge T. Gerry (1837–1927) and John D. Wright. With Henry Bergh (1811–88) of the American Society for the Prevention of Cruelty to Animals, Gerry prosecuted the adoptive parents of Mary Ellen MacCormack (or Wilson) for having severely beaten her; this was the first case of child abuse brought before the city's courts. The society, also known during its founder's lifetime as the Gerry Society, sought out and rescued abused children and was given law enforcement powers in 1881. In the early twenty-first century it has offices at 161 William Street in Manhattan and runs programs that include parenting classes, counseling services for abused children, and training in how to recognize and report child abuse.

Alana Erickson Coble

Society for the Propagation of the Gospel. Religious organization incorporated by royal charter in 1701 with the aim of settling ministers of the Church of England in America. Because of the multidenominational character of New York City, the city and its environs were an important focus for the society, and missionaries in the area established churches in Manhattan, Queens, Westchester, and Staten Island. The society sought to endow churches, set parish boundaries, provide rectories and glebes (plots of farmland controlled by parishes), and secure public support for the Church of England. The society supplemented the salaries of the clergy until the American Revolution; it also aggressively pursued the conversion of blacks and American Indians. Elias Neau, a missionary from France, operated an innovative school for catechizing slaves in New York City from 1704 until his death in 1722. From 1706 the society supported charity schools in the city to provide rudimentary religious and literary instruction, and in 1754 it was instrumental in founding King's College (later Columbia University), from which the church hoped to obtain a supply of well-educated young men eager to enter the ministry. Throughout the colonial period the society remained controversial; non-Anglicans especially were wary of its missionary program and of its political and social influence. The withdrawal of the Society for the Propagation of the Gospel from the colonies during the Revolution was followed by the establishment of the American Episcopal Church as an independent entity in 1783.

Frank J. Klingberg, *Anglican Humanitarianism in Colonial New York* (Philadelphia: Church Historical Society, 1940); Henry Paget Thompson, *Into All Lands: The History of the Society for the Propagation of the Gospel in Foreign Parts, 1701–1950* (London: Society for Promoting Christian Knowledge, 1951)

Peter J. Wosh

Society of the Friendly Sons of St. Patrick in the City of New York. Charitable and fraternal body formed in 1784 to assist needy Irish immigrants; it is the oldest continuously functioning Irish organization in New York City. In its early years the society had both well-to-do Catholics and Protestants as members and later became predominantly Catholic, although its charitable activities remained ecumenical. Its annual St. Patrick's Day Dinner remained an important social event for prominent local residents of Irish descent through 2008. Its offices are at 80 Wall Street.

Richard C. Murphy and Lawrence J. Mannion, *The History of the Society of the Friendly Sons of St. Patrick in the City of New York, 1784–1955* (New York: Society of the Friendly Sons of St. Patrick in the City of New York, 1962)

William D. Griffin

Society of Umbra. Group of writers that formed in 1962 on the Lower East Side. As one of the founders, Tom Dent, put it, Umbra was "a vehicle for the expression of the bitterness and the beauties of being Afro-American." Major members included Dent, Steve Cannon, Al Haynes, David Henderson, Calvin C. Hernton, Joe Johnson, Norman Pritchard, Lenox Raphael, Ishmael Reed, Lorenzo Thomas, James Thompson, and Brenda Walcott. They conducted writing workshops, gave poetry readings, and published *Umbra* magazine, with Dent, Henderson, and Hernton as editors. The workshops met Friday evenings and often ended at Stanley's Bar on East 12th Street and Avenue B, an informal center of the Harlem artistic and jazz community. The group splintered after only two years and two issues of *Umbra,* partly because of disagreement between members who saw themselves primarily as activists and those whose main concern was writing. Umbra has been called "the first post–civil rights Black literary group" that established "their own voice distinct from, and sometimes at odds with, the prevailing white literary establishment" and a forerunner to the Black Arts literary movement of the mid-1960s and early 1970s started in Harlem by LeRoi Jones (Amiri Baraka) and others.

Calvin Hernton, "Umbra: A Personal Recounting—A Lower East Side Cultural Group of the 1960s," *African American Review,* "Lower East Side Retrospective" (Winter 1993); Aldon Lynn Nielsen, *Black Chant: Languages of African-American Postmodernism* (Cambridge: Cambridge University Press, 1997)

Advertisement for Blakely's Blizzard Soda

soft drinks. The manufacture of soft drinks in New York City began in 1809, when chemist Noyes Darling brought soda water to the popular Tontine Coffee House on Wall Street. Flavored soda water came to prominence after the Civil War. Dr. Brown's Cel-Ray Tonic (named for its celery flavor) was introduced in 1869; eventually distributed nationwide, it continued to be made into the early twenty-first century. During the 1870s soda fountains drew customers to drugstores and department stores, and such establishments as Hudnut's in the Herald Building were known for their marble soda fountains. Bottled soft drinks became popular in the last quarter of the nineteenth century, and the city became the site of more than 100 soft drink factories producing such brands as Imperial Inca Cola, John Morgan ginger ale, Golden Key mint sodas, and Centennial root beer. Cream, celery, and coffee sodas were developed and widely sold in the city. The firms of Pepsi-Cola, Seven-Up, and Coca-Cola made and distributed their products in the city from the 1930s, and for a time Canada Dry and Pepsi-Cola had their headquarters there. The city ceased to dominate the industry after several large soft drink companies were formed elsewhere between 1900 and 1950; nonetheless, by the mid-1950s the city had 250 soda factories and soft drink sales exceeding $70 million. In 1988 more than 120 million cases of soft drinks were consumed in the city. The American Natural Beverage Corporation achieved success with Soho Natural Soda, and in addition to its own products the Canada Dry Bottling Company in College Point distributed such local brands as Best Health Natural Soda and Dr. Brown's. Pepsi-Cola headquarters is now in suburban Westchester County.

John J. Riley, *A History of the American Soft Drink Industry, 1807–1957* (Washington, D.C.: American Bottlers of Carbonated Beverages, 1958)

James Bradley

SoHo. Neighborhood in lower Manhattan, bounded to the north by Houston Street, to the east by Crosby Street, to the south by Canal Street, and to the west by Sixth Avenue; the name stands for "south of Houston." The hilly area originally contained a path used by the Weckquasgeek Indians to travel the length of Manhattan; this later became Broadway. Slaves granted their freedom by the Dutch West India Company in 1644 moved to the area and formed the first settlement of free blacks in Manhattan; there were also some white settlers. The land was used mostly for farming until the end of the eighteenth century. At that time city planners decided to cover the polluted and foul-smelling canal that formed the southern boundary of the neighborhood, using local hills as landfill. The leveled countryside soon became suitable for development, and by 1825 the neighborhood was the most densely populated in Manhattan. Its streets were lined with shops and elegant three- and four-story houses, mostly built of red brick in the Greek Revival and Federal styles. John Jacob Astor owned much of the land around Canal Street, and the residents were among the wealthiest and most renowned in the city.

In the mid-nineteenth century many large retail and wholesale firms moved in, including Lord and Taylor, Tiffany, and E. V. Haughwout. Broadway was dominated by expensive hotels, as well as stores built of marble, brownstone, and cast iron; casinos, theaters, music halls, and brothels lined the side streets. An influx of businesses caused the residential population to decline by a quarter between 1860 and 1865, as buildings were demolished to make way for factories, warehouses, and offices. The neighborhood became known for dry goods, china, glass, silks, satin, lace, ribbons, furs, and tobacco. To glorify their enterprises, ambitious business leaders commissioned four- to six-story buildings with elaborate ornamentation. Most of these structures were made from cast iron, which was favored for its strength and versatility and became incorporated into a unique architectural technique developed in the neighborhood (see Cast-iron architecture). Stores and factories (including some that housed sweatshops) had facades in the Victorian Gothic, neo-Grec, Italianate, and Second Empire styles and were carefully painted and decorated with colorful striped awnings. The ground floor often had high windows and a vast interior for displays; upper stories contained offices, storage, and manufacturing areas.

SoHo, 2009

A thriving commercial center until 1890, the neighborhood became depressed after the turn of the century as fashionable businesses moved uptown to Fifth Avenue. Local buildings were ill suited to modern industry, and by 1959 the neighborhood was a commercial slum known as "hell's hundred acres." With the proposed Lower Manhattan Expressway, many businesses left the area. Between 1960 and 1970 artists seeking low rents and space for large works defied zoning laws and converted vacant warehouses into studios, galleries, and living quarters. There was a large colony of artists in the neighborhood by 1971, and with other residents they persuaded the city to change the zoning laws governing warehouses. An area of 26 blocks was designated a historic district by the New York City Landmarks Preservation Commission in 1973. After it was revitalized in the 1970s and 1980s, the neighborhood became the newly fashionable site of boutiques, performance centers, galleries, restaurants, bars, and shops. Many artists who had reclaimed the neighborhood from its former state of neglect found themselves unable to afford the increasing rents brought about by gentrification. After the terrorist attack on the World Trade Center on 11 September 2001, many shops, museums, and galleries left the district, but in 2004 Bloomingdale's opened a branch in the neighborhood, and many other upscale shops followed. In the early twenty-first century SoHo remains one of the most commercially vibrant neighborhoods in the city. Many cast-iron buildings house small publishing, graphic design, and manufacturing firms; some artists continue to inhabit spacious lofts with high ceilings.

Joyce Gold

SoHo News. Alternative weekly newspaper launched by Michael Goldstein in 1973 and published until 1982. Described as the "alternative to alternative papers," it was inspired by an alternative art movement in SoHo in the mid-1970s. The newspaper focused on the arts but also offered news and opinion pieces as well as reviews and listings in a format similar to that of the *Village Voice.* It distinguished itself from other newspapers by publishing articles from a range of political perspectives. Between 1978 and 1980 it was owned by the Associated News Group of London, publishers of the *Daily Mail.* The *SoHo News* ceased publication in 1982 after incurring cumulative losses of $6 million.

Amanda Aaron

Soldiers' and Sailors' Monument. Monument at 89th Street and Riverside Drive in Riverside Park, standing 100 feet (30 meters) tall in the center of an esplanade 100 feet wide lined with cannons. The first step toward erecting the monument was taken in 1893 when the city established a board of commissioners to propose a means of honoring fallen soldiers. The original proposal was for a monument at Grand Army Plaza at 59th Street and Fifth Avenue, but because of objections from the Municipal Art Commission the present site was chosen instead. The cornerstone was laid on 15 December 1900, with Governor Theodore Roosevelt officiating. Work was completed in 1902 although the monument never received its finishing touch: bronze statues intended to sit in five niches in the polished marble interior chamber. In 1976 the monument was declared a city landmark.

For illustration see Riverside Park.

Kenneth T. Jackson

Solomon R. Guggenheim Museum. Museum opened in 1939 by the mining tycoon Solomon R. Guggenheim. It began as a collection of works by such modern artists as Wassily Kandinsky, László Moholy-Nagy, Paul Klee, and Amedeo Modigliani amassed between 1929 and 1937 for Guggenheim by the baroness Hilla Rebay von Ehrenwiesen. By 1937 Rebay became the curator of the collection, which was held by the Solomon R. Guggenheim Foundation and placed on public display as the Museum of Non-Objective Painting on East 54th Street. Under Rebay's direction the museum became a forum for young artists and exhibited the work of modern artists including Kandinsky and Moholy-Nagy. At her urging Guggenheim commissioned a new building from Frank Lloyd Wright in 1943. A site was acquired on Fifth Avenue between 88th and 89th streets, and in 1948 the collection was moved temporarily into a town house at 1071 Fifth Avenue. After Guggenheim's death in 1949 his nephew Harry F. Guggenheim became the chairman of the foundation; in 1952 the museum took its current name and Guggenheim replaced Rebay with James Johnson Sweeney, a former curator at the Museum of Modern Art, who added sculpture to the collection and documented it more systematically. The new building, opened in October 1959, was Wright's only important commission in the city. It is shaped like a spiral that is narrowest at its base and is built entirely of hand-plastered concrete, inside and outside, over a steel frame. Inside the building, around a large, central space, a curved ramp leads upward from street level through the height of the building, allowing exhibitions to be mounted in one virtually continuous line; Wright intended for visitors to begin at the top and move downward. Thomas Messer, appointed director in 1960, continued Sweeney's policies and secured the Justin K. Thannhauser Collection, which was housed in separate galleries adjacent to the original building and opened in 1972. In 1992 a controversial new 10-story wing opened adjacent to the original building: designed by Gwathmey Siegel and Associates, it incorporates gallery, storage, and office space. In the same year the museum opened a branch in SoHo, in a building constructed for John Jacob Astor in 1881–82 at 575 Broadway near Prince Street; it closed in 2001. Director Thomas Krens, appointed in 1988, generated controversy by reinterpreting the exhibition program beyond traditional art-historical boundaries with shows such as *The Art of the Motorcycle* (1998), *Giorgio Armani* (2001), and *Brazil: Body and Soul* (2002). Krens also oversaw the expansion of the museum abroad, most notably to Bilbao, Spain, in a celebrated building designed by Frank Gehry (1997). Krens left as director in 2006 but remained head of the museum's parent institution, the Guggenheim Foundation.

Joan M. Lukach, *Hilla Rebay: In Search of the Spirit in Art* (New York: George Braziller, 1983)

Peter L. Donhauser

Soloveitchik, Joseph [Dov] (*b* Pruzhany [now in Belarus], 27 Feb 1903; *d* Brookline, Mass., 8 April 1993). Rabbi and philosopher. The son of a rabbi, he moved to Boston in 1932 with his wife, where he founded the Maimonides School, the first Jewish day school in New England. In 1941 he joined the faculty of Yeshiva University in Manhattan, where he became the preeminent teacher of the Talmud in North America and ordained about 2000 rabbis, more than any other seminary teacher in the United States. Orthodox leaders around the world queried him about how to apply Jewish law to modern problems. His annual lectures, which lasted two to five hours, attracted thousands of listeners and were regarded as the major annual academic event for American Orthodoxy.

Kenneth T. Jackson

Sondheim, Stephen (Joshua) (*b* New York City, 22 March 1930). Lyricist and composer. He lived in the San Remo apartment building on Central Park West between 74th and 75th streets in Manhattan until his parents divorced when he was 10 years old. Sondheim then moved to Bucks County, Pennsylvania, with his mother. While living there he met producer, playwright, and lyricist OSCAR HAMMERSTEIN II, who would become his mentor. Hammerstein tutored and instructed him in the ways of musical composition until Sondheim left to attend Williams College and later Princeton University. After having difficulty finding work Sondheim made his Broadway debut as a lyricist for the Leonard Bernstein musical *West Side Story* (1957). He next wrote lyrics for the musical *Gypsy* (1959) and received billing for the first time as a composer and a lyricist in *A Funny Thing Happened on the Way to the Forum* (1962), starring Zero Mostel. The success and royalties of these three shows, which all became films, gained Sondheim the freedom to choose his endeavors, and from 1965 onward he insisted on both composing and writing lyrics for his projects. For a year in the late 1960s he created a series of word puzzles in *New York* magazine with cryptic clues, such as anagrams, involving humor and cleverness to hide the true meaning of the clue and its answer. Some critics believed his love of word games related to the intricacy and complexity of his lyrics. By the mid-1970s he established himself as one of the most daring and imaginative composers at that time with his next three productions: *Company* (1971), *Follies* (1972), and *A Little Night Music* (1973) showed Sondheim's ability to break with and honor tradition as well as utilize multiple musical styles. All three shows won Tony Awards for best score in their respective years. His song "Send in the Clowns" from *A Little Night Music* eventually made its way into the mainstream and won a Grammy Award for song of the year. From 1973 to 1981 he served as president of the Dramatists Guild during which time he produced *Pacific Overtures* (1976) and *Sweeney Todd* (1979), the latter winning Sondheim another Tony Award. *A Little Night Music* and *Sweeney Todd* are performed in opera houses around the world. In 1985 his musical *Sunday in the Park with George* (1984) won a Pulitzer Prize for drama. He continued to produce works through the 1990s and 2000s, and in 2008 *Gypsy* and *Sunday in the Park with George* enjoyed successful Broadway revivals. That same year Sondheim received a special Tony Award for lifetime achievement.

Frank Nestor

songs. The first song to feature New York City in its title was probably the "New York Patriotic Song," written by Charles Dibdin and published about 1799. The "Castle Garden March (circa 1820) and "New York, Oh What a Charming City" (1831) were other early songs published as sheet music. After the Civil War, songs about the city began to appear in larger numbers. Many paid tribute to specific places (notably Broadway and the Bowery), such as "Walking down Broadway" (1868), "The Broadway Opera and the Bowery Crawl" (1871), "Strolling on the Brooklyn Bridge" (1883), and "The Bowery" (1892). In 1894 Charles B. Lawlor and James W. Blake wrote the first enduring song about the city, "The Sidewalks of New York," which portrayed its flourishing Irish population. Many laudatory "anthems" were written in the late nineteenth and early twentieth centuries in praise of the city's vitality and diversity, including "In Good Old New York Town" (1899), Victor Herbert's "In Old New York" (1906), "Take Me Back to New York Town" (1907), and the best-known of the time, George M. Cohan's "Give My Regards to Broadway" (1904). By contrast Charles K. Harris's "The City Where Nobody Cares" (1908) and H. Altman's "Die Nyu-Yorker Tiern" (New York Tears, 1910) portrayed the city as a cruel place.

During the first half of the twentieth century a number of songs appeared about neighborhoods in New York City, such as "Chinatown, My Chinatown" (1905), "Nestin' Time in Flatbush" (1917), and "(We'll Have) Manhattan" (Richard Rodgers and Lorenz Hart, 1925) as well as Irving Berlin's "Easter Parade" (1933) and "Slumming on Park Avenue" (1937), about the wealthy enclaves of midtown and Fifth Avenue. The Yiddish theater and its English-language equivalents offered songs about life in the tenements, notably "Second Hand Rose (from Second Avenue)" (1921) and "My Yiddisha Mama" (1925). Broadway and Times Square were featured in the lachrymose "There's a Broken Heart for Every Light on Broadway" (1915) and the exuberant "42nd Street" (1932) and "Lullaby of Broadway" (1935). The neighborhood most often treated in songs of the 1920s and 1930s was Harlem, which like the Bowery and Broadway before it came to symbolize the effervescence of the city. There were quasi-operatic and extended orchestral works, such as George Gershwin's *opera scena 121st Street* (1925) and William Grant Still's ballet *Lenox Avenue* (1937), and popular songs such as Berlin's "Puttin' on the Ritz" (1929) and "Harlem on My Mind" (1936). The Savoy Ballroom, the best-known dance hall in Harlem, was immortalized in "Stompin' at the Savoy" (1934) and "The Joint Is Jumpin'" (1937). Duke Ellington, a resident of Harlem, wrote the songs "Drop Me Off in Harlem" (1933), "Harlem Speaks" (1935), "Harlem Air Shaft" (1940), and "Take the 'A' Train" (in collaboration with his partner Billy Strayhorn, 1941) as well as the extended orchestral work *Harlem (A Tone Parallel to Harlem)* (1952).

Songs about New York City continued to be written in great numbers during the middle decades of the twentieth century, including Vernon Duke's "Autumn in New York" (1934), "New York, New York" (Betty Comden, Adolph Green, and Leonard Bernstein, 1945), "52nd Street Theme" (1948), "I Love a New Yorker" (1950), and "Manhattan Spiritual" (1958). After 1960 compositions ranged from the lighthearted "59th Street Bridge Song" (1966) by Paul Simon and Art Garfunkel and "Boy from New York City" (1964) to the wistful "On Broadway" (1962) and "Spanish Harlem" (1960) and the fierce rap song "New York, New York" (1984) by Grandmaster Flash and the Furious Five. Several country musicians wrote vitriolic songs such as "I Wouldn't Live in New York City (If They Gave Me the Whole Damn Place)" (1970) and "I Hate New York" (1983). The theme song (John Kander and Fred Ebb) from Martin Scorsese's film *New York, New York* (1977) attained a popularity that transcended the usual limitations of the genre and was made the city's official song by Mayor Edward I. Koch in 1983. As the birthplace and primary home of hip-hop, New York City also became the subject of countless rap songs from the 1980s onward.

Until the dawn of hip-hop, the outer boroughs have been a much more infrequent subject of songs. John Philip Sousa wrote a well-known march about a resort in Brooklyn, "Manhattan Beach March" (1893), and depicted Luna Park in his song "I've Made My Plans for the Summer" (1907). Songs about the Bronx included "On the Banks of the Bronx" (1919) and "Bronx Express" (1922). Many hip-hop artists have made songs about their neighborhoods, often becoming identified with a particular borough, such as the Notorious B.I.G. and Jay-Z with Brooklyn, Afrika Bambaataa and Grandmaster Flash with the Bronx, and Run-D.M.C. and Nas with Queens.

Floyd M. Henderson

Cover for New York Mud, *sheet music by Will L. Randolph, 1874*

Songs and Compositions Inspired by New York City (selective list)

GENERAL
The Aldermanic Board (1885), Edward Harrigan, David Braham
Alice (1990), Ian Hunter
All Alone on Christmas (1990), Steve Van Zandt
All the Critics Love U in New York (1983), Prince
All the Way from New York (1992), Wilson Phillips
All the Way to New York City (2006), Rosie Thomas
America (1968), Paul Simon
American Boy (2008), Estelle
American Tune (1973), Paul Simon
Am I Ever Gonna Fall in Love in New York City? (1978), Grace Jones
Amity (1998), Elliott Smith
And It Rained All Night (2006), Thom Yorke
Anniversary (2007), Suzanne Vega
Another Hundred People (1970), Stephen Sondheim
Another Lonely Night in New York (1984), Robin Gibb
Another Rainy Day in New York City (1976), Chicago
Arthur's Theme (Best That You Can Do) (1981), Christopher Cross, Burt Bacharach, Carole Bayer Sager
As I Was Walking in New York One Day (*ca* 1836), W. H. Parker
At the Zoo (1968), Paul Simon
Au Revoir Poland, Hello New York (1964), Albert Hague, Marty Brill
Autumn in New York (1934), Vernon Duke
The Babies on Our Block (1879), Edward Harrigan, David Braham
Back in N.Y.C. (1974), Tony Banks, Phil Collins, Peter Gabriel, Steve Hackett, Mike Rutherford
Back of a Truck (2001), Regina Spektor
Big Apple (1978), Danny Joe Brown, Dave Hlubek
Big Apple Dreamin' (1973), Alice Cooper
Boss Tweed (1945), Sigmund Romberg, Dorothy Fields
Boy From New York City (1964), John Taylor
The Brave Old City of New York (1971), Helen Miller, Eve Merriman
Bulletproof Weeks (2007), Matt Nathanson
Cab (2005), Train
Cabbies on Crack (1993), The Ramones
Cell Phones Ringing (in the Pockets of the Dead) (2006), Willie Nile
China (1992), Tori Amos
Christmas in the City (1997), Mary J. Blige
City Love (2001), John Mayer
City of Blinding Lights (2004), U2
City Song (2003), David Ippolito
The City Where Nobody Cares (1908), Charles K. Harris
Cobwebs (2008), Ryan Adams
Cold Hands from New York (1993), Gordon Lightfoot
Comin' Home (1974), Paul Stanley, Ace Frehley
Conquering New York (1955), Leonard Bernstein, Betty Comden, Adolph Green
A Country Boy Can Survive (1981), Hank Williams, Jr.
Covered in Rain (2003), John Mayer
Cradle and All (1995), Ani DIFranco
C.R.E.A.M. (1994), Wu-Tang Clan
Croton Water Celebration (1842), George P. Morris, Sidney Pearson
Daddy Don't Live in That New York City Anymore (1975), Walter Becker, Donald Fagen
Darlin' of New York (1969), Bill and Patti Jacob
The Daughter of Rosie O'Grady (1918), Monty C. Brice, Walter Donaldson
Daughters of the SoHo Riots (2005), Matt Berninger
Dawn of a New Day (Song of the New York World's Fair) (1939), George Gershwin, Ira Gershwin
Desolation Row (1965), Bob Dylan
Diamonds and Rust (1975), Joan Baez
Dirty Blvd. (1989), Lou Reed
Doin' It (1996), LL Cool J
Don't Be Upset (2005), Jeffrey Lewis
Do the New York (1931), Jack P. Murray, Barry Trivers, Ben Oakland
Down and Out in New York City (1973), Bodie Chandler, Barry de Vorzon
Down in the Depths on the 90th Floor (1936), Cole Porter
Downtown (1964), Tony Hatch
Do You Miss New York? (2006), Dave Frishberg
Dream Like New York (2008), Tyrone Wells
Dropping Some N.Y.C. (1990), Chan Kinchla, Bob Sheehan, John Popper
Easter Parade (1933), Irving Berlin
The East Side and the West Side (1925), J. D. McCarthy
Egg Cream (1996), Lou Reed
88 Christopher Street (1999), Dirt Bike Annie
Eleanor Put Your Boots On (2006), Alex Kapranos, Nick McCarthy
11:11 (2003), Rufus Wainwright
Empire State (1982), Lindsey Buckingham, Richard Dashut
Empire State Building (1996), Randy Newman
Empire State Express (1965), Son House
Empire State Halo (1997), Echo and the Bunnymen
Empire State of Mind (2009), Jay-Z
Englishman in New York (1987), Sting
Every Street's a Boulevard in Old New York (1953), Jule Styne, Bob Hilliard
Eyes of a New York Woman (1968), B. J. Thomas
Eyes of a New York Woman (1968), Thomas Pynchon, Jeff Ogden
Face Down at Folk City (1985), Maggie Roche, Suzzy Roche, Terre Roche
Faded Flower of Broadway (2006), Willie Nile, Frankie Lee
Fairytale of New York (1987), Jem Finer, Shane MacGowan
Famous Blue Raincoat (1971), Leonard Cohen
53rd and 3rd (1976), Dee Dee Ramone
First Snow on Brooklyn (2003), Ian Anderson
14th Street (2003), Rufus Wainwright
Frank Mills (1967), James Rado, Gerome Ragni, Galt MacDermot
Girl from New York City (1965), Brian Wilson, Mike Love
Girls of New York (1925), Seymour Firth, Lee Edwards, R. F. Carroll
Give It Back to the Indians (1939), Richard Rodgers, Lorenz Hart
Glad Tidings (1970), Van Morrison
A Glance at New York (1848), English Burton
Good Fortune (2000), P. J. Harvey
Good Night, New York (?1991), Julie Gold
The Great Four Hundred (1890), Edward Harrigan, David Braham
The Great New York Police (1922), George M. Cohan
Hard Times in New York Town (1961), Bob Dylan
A Heart in New York (1981), Benny Gallagher, Graham Lyle
Hello New York (1976), Ronnie Britton
Hudson River (1928), Henry Myers, Henry Sullivan
I Can't See New York (2002), Tori Amos
Idiot Kings (1996), Soul Coughing
I Gotta Get Back to New York (1933), Richard Rodgers, Lorenz Hart
I Guess the Lord Must Be in New York City (1969), Harry Nilsson
I Happen to Like New York (1930), Cole Porter
I Hate New York (1983), Hank Williams, Jr.
I Have a Friend at Chase Manhattan Bank (1975), Jack Bussins
I Have Grown to Love New York (1943), Vernon Duke, Howard Dietz
(I Like New York in June), How About You? (1941), Ralph Freed, Burton Lane
I'll Take New York (1987), Tom Waits
Illume (9/11) (2003), Stevie Nicks
I Love a New Yorker (1950), Ralph Blane, Harold Arlen

(continued)

Songs and Compositions Inspired by New York City (selective list) (*Continued*)

I'm Never Going Back to New York City (1983), Bruce Donnelly, Joey Harris
I'm Waiting for the Man (1967), Lou Reed
In a Brownstone Mansion (1962), Sal Kaplan, Edward Eliscu
In Gay New York (1896), Hugh Morton, Gustave Kerker
In Good Old New York Town (1899), Paul Dresser
In Old New York (1906), Victor Herbert
In the Cage (1974), Tony Banks, Phil Collins, Peter Gabriel, Steve Hackett, Mike Rutherford
In the Flesh (1977), Chris Stein, Deborah Harry
Into the Fire (2002), Bruce Springsteen
Isle de Blackwell (1878), Edward Harrigan, David Braham
It's a Lovely Night on the Hudson River (1937), Richard Lewine, Ted Felter
I Wanna Go to City College (1946), Sammy Fein, George Marion, Jr.
I Wouldn't Live in New York City (If They Gave Me the Whole Damn Place) (1970), Buck Owens
I Wouldn't Trade You (2000), Jessica Molaskey, John Pizzarelli
J'ai rêvé New York (1974), Yves Simon
Jazzhattan Suite 1967 (1967), Oliver Nelson
Just Across from Jersey (1883), Edward Harrigan, David Braham
The Killing of Georgie (Part I and II) (1976), Rod Stewart
Knickerbocker Quadrilles (1843), published by Firth and Hall
Lady Cab Driver (1999), Prince
The Lady Is a Tramp (1937), Richard Rodgers, Oscar Hammerstein
La Vie Bohème (from *Rent*) (1994), Jonathan Larson
Leaving New York (2004), Peter Buck, Mike Mills, Michael Stipe
Let's Take a Walk around the Block (1934), Harold Arlen, Yip Harburg, Ira Gershwin
A Letter to the New York Post (1991), Public Enemy
Lightning Strikes (Not Once but Twice) (1980), The Clash
Little Old New York (1923), Victor Herbert, Gene Buck
Little Tin Box (1959), Sheldon Harnick, Jerry Bock
Living for the City (1973), Stevie Wonder
Lonely Town (1945), Betty Comden, Adolph Green, Leonard Bernstein
Lonesome in New York (1954), Jerry Herman
Lost and Found (1986), Ray Davies
Lua (2004), Conor Oberst
Lullaby on New York (1975), Aztec Two-Step
Made in N.Y.C. (2001), The Casualties
Maggie Murphy's House (1890), Edward Harrigan, David Braham
Manhattan Transfer (1926), Manning Sherman, Arthur Herzog, Jr.
Me and Julio Down by the Schoolyard (1972), Paul Simon
Minnie the Moocher (1931), Irving Mills, Cab Calloway
Mona Lisas and Mad Hatters (1972), Elton John
Morph the Cat (2006), Donald Fagen
Motorcycle Drive By (1997), Stephan Jenkins
Move Over, New York (1964), Walter Marks
My Best Girl's a New Yorker (1895), John Stromberg
My Blue Manhattan (2004), Ryan Adams
My Name's La Guardia (1959), Jerry Bock, Sheldon Harnick
My Personal Property (1968), Cy Coleman, Dorothy Fields
Myriad Harbour (2007), Carl Newman
Native New Yorker (1977), Sandy Linzer, Denny Randell
New Amsterdam (1979), Elvis Costello
New Killer Star (2003), David Bowie
New New York (1930), Arthur Schwartz, Howard Dietz
New New York (2002), The Cranberries
New York (*ca* 1800), P. Landren Duport
New York (1925), R. H. Bonnell
New York (1928), George M. Cohan
New York (1943), Nathan Goodman, Irene Shannon
New York (1944), Mario Castelnuovo-Tedesco, Arthur Guiterman
New York (1959), Tommy Wolfe, Fran Landesman
New York (2000), U2
New York (2004), Ja Rule
New York (2005), AZ
New York, New York (1945), Leonard Bernstein, Betty Comden, Adolph Green
New York, New York (1983), Nina Hagen
New York, New York (1984), Grandmaster Flash and the Furious Five
New York, Oh What a Charming City (1831), I. A. Gairdner
New York, You've Got Me Dancing (1988), performed by Andrea True Connection
New York After Dark (1937), Vernon Duke, Ted Fettner
New York Afternoon (1976), Richie Cole
New York Ain't New York Any More (1925), Billy Rose, Lew Brown
New York Blues (1952), Duke Ellington
The New York Boy (*ca* 1825)
New York Boy (1966), Neil Diamond
New York Central (*ca* 1965), Son House
A New York Christmas (2002), Rob Thomas
New York City (1972), John Lennon
New York City (2000), Peter Malick
New York City (2007), Paul van Dyk, Austin Leeds
New York City Boy (1999), Neil Tennant, Chris Lowe
New York City Cops (2001), Julian Casablancas/The Strokes
New York City Rhythm (1975), Marty Panzer, Barry Manilow
New York Cliché (1978), Rob Fremont, Doris Willens
The New Yorker (*ca* 1920), Edwin Franco Goldman
New Yorkers (1911), George M. Cohan
The New York Fireman (*ca* 1836), A. Yates
New York Forever (1903), Nicholas Biddle, Ben J. Jerome
New York from the Air (1975), Hank Beebe, Bill Heyer
New York Groove (1975), Russ Ballard
New York Hippodrome (1915), John Philip Sousa
New York (Hold Her Tight) (1986), Restless Heart
New York Is a Woman (2007), Suzanne Vega
New York Isn't Such a Bad Old Town (1912), Jean Schwartz, William Jerome
New York Is Rockin' (1995), Curtis Stigers, Willie Nile
New York Is So Exciting (1983), Glen Moore
New York Is the Same Old Place (1922), Victor Herbert, B. G. DeSylva
New York Mining Disaster 1941 (1967), Barry Gibb, Robin Gibb
New York Minute (1989), Don Henley, Danny Kortchmar, Jai Winding
New York Patriotic Song (1799), Mr. Dibdin
New York Profiles (1952), Norman Dello Joio
New York Rhapsody (1931), George Gershwin
New York's a Lonely Town (1965), Pete Andreoli, Vince Poncia
New York's Alright If You Like Saxophones (1981), Fear
New York Serenade (*ca* 1800), Dr. G. K. Jackson
New York Serenade (1925), George Gershwin, Ira Gershwin, P. G. Wodehouse
New York Serenade (1973), Bruce Springsteen
New York Serenading Waltz (*ca* 1800), Peter Weldon
New York's in Love (1987), David Bowie
New York '69 (1975), Hank Beebe, Bill Heyer
New York Skyline (1977), Garland Jeffries
New York's My Home (1946), Gordon Jenkins
New York's Not My Home (1976), Jim Croce
New York Society (*ca* 1922)
New York Song (1902), Malcolm Lang
New York State of Mind (1975), Billy Joel

(continued)

Songs and Compositions Inspired by New York City (selective list) (*Continued*)

New York Taxi (1977), Harry Belafonte, Fitzroy Alexander
New York Tendaberry (1969), Laura Nyro
New York Times (1978), Cat Stevens
New York Town (1896), Gilmore and Leonard
New York Town (1927), Morrie Riskind, Howard Dietz, Henry Souvaine, Jay Gorney
New York Town for Mine Boys (1903), H. H. Niemeyer, Stanley Murphy
New York U.S.A. (1964), Serge Gainsbourg
The Night Maloney Landed in New York (1889), Joseph Flynn
Nothing Can Ever Happen in New York (1927), James F. Hanley, Eddie Dowling
N.Y.C. (1977), Martin Chanin, Charles Strouse
N.Y.C. (2008), Kevin Rudolf
N.Y.C. (There's No Need to Stop) (2006), The Charlatans
N.Y.C. Ghosts & Flowers (2000), Lee Ranaldo
N.Y.C. Man (1996), Lou Reed
N.Y.C. Weather Report (2004), John Ondrasik
N.Y. Electric (2003), Ian Bavitz
N.Y. Trip (2008), The Cure
Off to See New York (1927), Alfred Nathan, George Oppenheimer
The Oldest Established (Permanent Floating Crap Game in New York) (1950), Frank Loesser
Once Upon a Time in New York City (1988), Barry Mann, Howard Ashman
One New York (1896), Stafford Waters
Only in New York (2002), Jeanine Tesori, Dick Scanlan
The Only Living Boy in New York (?1969), Paul Simon
Only Right Here in New York City (1975), Hank Beebe, Bill Heyer
On the Ferry (1922), Emerson Whitmore
On the Hudson (*ca* 1920), Edwin Franko Goldman
An Open Letter to N.Y.C. (2005), Beastie Boys
Our New York (1939), Sigmund Spaeth
Paddy Duffey's Cart (1881), Edward Harrigan, David Braham
Penthouse Serenade (1931), Will Jason, Val Burton
People Who Died (1980), Jim Caroll, Brian Linsley, Stephen Linsley, Terrell Winn, Wayne Woods
Poses (2001), Rufus Wainwright
Poster Girl (2005), Billy Mann, Rasmus Bahncke, René Tromborg (performed by the Backstreet Boys)
Queensboro Bridge (2004), David Mead
Queens Is (2000), LL Cool J
Q.U.-Hectic (1995), Mobb Deep
Rhinestone Cowboy (1974), Larry Weiss
Riding on the Elevated Railroad (*ca* 1895), Sam Devere
Rockin' Around in N.Y.C. (1980), Marshall Crenshaw
Safe in New York City (2000), AC/DC
Seeing New York in the Rubber-Neck Hack (1904), Paul West, John W. Bratton
Shattered (1977), Keith Richards, Mick Jagger
She Is the Belle of New York (1894), Hugh Morton, Gustave Kerker
She Reads the New York Papers Every Day (1902), Paul West, John W. Bratton
Sidewalks of New York (1894), Charles B. Lawlor, James W. Blake
Skylines and Turnstiles (2002), My Chemical Romance
Snowin' in Brooklyn (1984), Ferron
Song for Sharon (1976), Joni Mitchell
The Song of New York (1903), Frank Damrosch
Sophie in New York (1983), Steve Allen
So They Call It New York (1972), Don Pippin, Steve Brown
Streets of New York (2003), Alicia Keys
Streets of New York (2006), Willie Nile
The Streets of Old New York (1914), Jeff Branen, Arthur Lange
Sunday in New York (1959), Portia Nelson
Sunday in New York (1963), Carroll Coates, Peter Nero
Sunday Night in New York (1935), Charles Tobias, Charles Newman, Maury Mencher
Take Me Back to New York Town (1907), Andrew B. Sterling, Harry Von Tilzer
Taking in the Town (1890), Edward Harrigan, David Braham
Talkin' New York (1961), Bob Dylan
Tammany (1905), Vincent P. Bryan, Gus Edwards
Tenement Symphony (1941), Sid Kuller, Ray Golden
(Theme from) New York, New York (1980), John Kander, Fred Ebb
There's a Boat Dat's Leavin' Soon for New York (1935), George Gershwin, Ira Gershwin
There's Nothing New in Old New York (1927), Harry Akst, Benny Davis
Thro' the Streets of New York City (1838), C. E. Horn
'Tis My Home, Dear Old New York (Spirit of New York) (1930), Hugh Ross
Typical New Yorkers (1979), Ted Simons, Elinor Giggenheimer
Up on the Hudson Shore (1913), Jean Schwartz, Joseph W. Herbert, Harold Atteridge
Uptown, Downtown (1981), Stephen Sondheim
What New York Swells Are Coming To (*ca* 1871)
When New York Was New York (1937), George M. Cohan
When They Get Through with Reform in New York (*ca* 1900)
When You're Far Away from New York Town (1963), Arthur Schwartz, Howard Dietz
Where I'm From (1993), Digable Planets
Where Is My Little Old New York? (1924), Irving Berlin
Where the Hudson River Flows (1925), Richard Rodgers, Lorenz Hart
The World I Know (1995), Ed Roland, Ross Childress
Wouldn't Have You Any Other Way (N.Y.C.) (2006), Elton John
Yeah! New York (2003), Yeah Yeah Yeahs
You Discover You're in New York (1943), Leo Robin, Harry Warren
You'll Never Be Poor in New York (1971), Jule Styne
You're in New York Now (1973), Matt Dubey, Dean Fuller

STATUE OF LIBERTY

Give Me Your Tired, Your Poor (1949), Irving Berlin
Miss Liberty (1949), Irving Berlin
The Most Expensive Statue in the World (1949), Irving Berlin
She Will Be Standing in the Harbor (1943), Carmen Lombardo, John Jacob Loeb
Statue of Liberty (1978), XTC
Ten Million Men and a Girl (1942), John Redmond, Jim Cavanaugh, Jack Edwards

MANHATTAN

Better in Manhattan (2006), Casey Dienel
First We Take Manhattan (1986), Leonard Cohen
I'll Sink Manhattan (1989), John Flansburgh, John Linnell
A Latin Tune, a Manhattan Moon, and You (1940), Jimmy McHugh, Al Dubin
Love Letter to Manhattan (1950), Harold Rome
Macy's Day Parade (2000), Billie Joe Armstrong, Mike Dirnt, Tré Cool
Manhattan Hymn (1923), Christopher Condie
Manhattan Lullaby (1932), Michael H. Cleary, Max Lief, Nathaniel Lief
Manhattan Madness (1931), Irving Berlin
Manhattan Mary (1927), B. G. DeSylva, Lew Brown, Ray Henderson
Manhattan Melodrama (1931), Richard Rodgers, Lorenz Hart
Manhattan Merry Go Round (1936), Pinky Herman, Gustav Haenschen
Manhattan Mood (1942), Harold Adamson, Peter DeRose
Manhattan Rag (*ca* 1929) performed by Irving Mills and His Hotsy Totsy Gang

(continued)

Songs and Compositions Inspired by New York City (selective list) (*Continued*)

Manhattan Serenade (1928), Louis Atler (lyrics added 1942 by Harold Adamson)
Manhattan Spiritual (1958), Billy Maxted
Manhattan Square Dance (1948), David Rose
Manhattan Walk (1928), Bert Kalmar, Herbert Stothart, Harry Ruby
Marching Bands of Manhattan (2005), Ben Gibbard
May in Manhattan (1960), Tom Romano, Ruth Cleary Patterson
Melody of Manhattan (1976), Ronnie Britton
Monday in Manhattan (1935), Richard Himber, Elliott Grennard
Movie House in Manhattan (1948), Richard Lewine, Arnold B. Horwitt
Oh My! How We Pose (Sixth Avenue) (*ca* 1884), Edward Harrigan, David Braham
On a Roof in Manhattan (1932), Irving Berlin
Say, Young Man from Manhattan (1930), Vincent Youmans, Clifford Grey
Seventh Avenue (1993), Rosanne Cash, John Leventhal
She's a Latin from Manhattan (1935), Richard Rodgers, Lorenz Hart
Silver Bells (1950), Jay Livingston, Ray Evans
Take Me Back to Manhattan (1930), Cole Porter
Vineyards of Manhattan (1929), Arthur Schwartz, Agnes Morgan
(We'll Have) Manhattan (1925), Richard Rodgers, Lorenz Hart

LOWER MANHATTAN

Alphabet Town (1995), Elliott Smith
Ann Street (1921), Charles Ives
Avenue C (2006), Barry Manilow
Baxter Avenue (1886), Edward Harrigan, David Braham
The Belle of Avenoo A (1895), Safford Waters
Belle of Avenue B (*ca* 1922)
Belle of 14th Street (*ca* 1871)
The Bowery (1981), Charles B. Hoyt, William Gaunt
The Bowery Bum (1929), Benny Samberg
Bowery Lass (*ca* 1820)
Bowery Serenade (1942), Eddie DeLange, Johnny Brooks
Castle Garden March (*ca* 1820), E. Riley
Castle Garden Schottische (1852)
Chelsea (1998), Counting Crows
Chelsea Avenue (2004), Patti Scialfa
Chelsea Girls (1967), Lou Reed, Sterling Morrison
Chelsea Hotel (1999), Dan Bern
Chelsea Hotel No. 2 (1974), Leonard Cohen
Chelsea Morning (1969), Joni Mitchell
Chinatown (1982), Joe Jackson
Chinatown, My Chinatown (1906), William Jerome, Jean Schwartz
Down Where the East River Flows (1930), Vincent Youmans, Harold Adamson, Clifford Grey
8 Million Stories (1984), Kurtis Blow
59 Chrystie Street (1989), Beastie Boys
I'm a Vamp from East Broadway (1920), Irving Berlin, Bert Kalmar, Harry Ruby
I'm Something on Avenue A (1925), George Gershwin
It's a Windy Day on the Battery (1917), Sigmund Romberg, Rida Johnson Young
Lower East Side (1988), U.K. Subs
The Luckiest Guy on the Lower East Side (1999), Stephin Merritt
Ludlow Street (2007), Suzanne Vega
Minnie the Moocher's Wedding Day (1925), Harold Arlen, Ted Koehler
Moon over Mulberry Street (1935), Raymond B. Egan, Harry Tierney
Mulberry Springs (1886), Edward Harrigan, David Braham
My Pearl's a Bowery Girl (1894), William Jerome, Andrew Mack
Nolita Fairytale (2007), Vanessa Carlton
Only a Bowery Boy (1894), Charles B. Ward, Gussie L. Davis
Pell Street (1933), Emerson Whitmore
Second Avenue and 12th Street (1956), Vernon Duke, Ogden Nash
Second Hand Rose (from Second Avenue) (1921), Grant Clarke, James F. Hanley
Wall Street Wail (1930), Duke Ellington

GREENWICH VILLAGE

Bleecker and MacDougal (1965), Fred Neil
Bleecker Street (1961), John Dooley
Bleecker Street (1963), Paul Simon
Bottom End of Bleecker Street (1967), Tom Sankey
Christopher Street (1953), Leonard Bernstein, Betty Comden, Adolph Green
Down at the Village (1928), Ray Perkins, Max Lief, Nathaniel Lief
Down Greenwich Village Way (1922), Albert Von Tilzer, Neville Fleeson
Down in Dear Old Greenwich Village (*ca* 1928)
Greenwich Village (1917), John Murray Anderson, A. Baldwin Sloane, Philip Bartholmae
Greenwich Village (1918), Jerome Kern, P. G. Wodehouse
Greenwich Village Folk Song Salesman (1967), Tom T. Hall
Greenwich Village Follies (1976), Ronnie Britton
A Greenwich Village Tragedy (1922), Emerson Whitmore
Greenwich Village U.S.A. (1960), Jeanne Bargy, Frank Gehrecke, Herb Cory
MacDougal Blues (1990), Kevn Kinney
Market Day in the Village (1936), Ralph Benatzky, Irving Caesar
On Union Square (1886), Edward Harrigan, David Braham
Positively 4th Street (1965), Bob Dylan
Rose of Washington Square (1920), Ballard MacDonald, James F. Hanley
Sullivan Street (1993), Adam Duritz, David Bryson
Sullivan Street Flat (1975), Ronnie Britton
The Sunny Side of Thompson Street (1893), Edward Harrigan, David Braham
Tenth and Greenwich (1971), Melvin Van Peebles
Washington Square (1930), Cole Porter
Washington Square (1950), Clay Warnick, Mel Tolkin, Lucille Kallen
Washington Square (1975), Ronnie Britton

MIDTOWN AND UPTOWN

The A-1 Belle of Madison Square (*ca* 1871), J. A. Hardwick
At the Roxy Music Hall (1938), Richard Rodgers, Lorenz Hart
Belle of Murray Hill (1899), Willis Clark, Maurice Levy
Carnegie Blues (1945), Duke Ellington
Central Park West (1960), John Coltrane
Chimes of St. Patrick's (1922), Emerson Whitmore
Christmas on Riverside Drive (1982), August Darnell
Confessions to a Park Avenue Mother (I'm in Love with a West Side Girl) (1960), Jerry Herman
Conversation on Park Avenue (1946), Willie "the Lion" Smith
Easter Parade (1933), Irving Berlin
The 59th Street Bridge Song (1966), Paul Simon
52nd Street (1978), Billy Joel
52nd Street Theme (1948), Thelonious Monk
45th and Broadway (1922), Gene Buck, Dave Stamper
42nd Street (1932), Al Dubin, Harry Warren
42nd Street and Broadway Strut (1922), Albert Von Tilzer, Neville Fleeson
42nd Street Blues (1977), David Langston Smyrl
Grand Central Station (2004), Mary Chapin Carpenter
Hollywood, Park Avenue, and Broadway (1933), Ray Henderson, Lew Brown
Incident on 57th Street (1973), Bruce Springsteen
The Joint Is Really Jumpin' Down in Carnegie Hall (1943), Roger Edens, Ralph Blaine, Hugh Martin
L.S.A. All the Way (Lincoln Square Academy March) (1966), Leonard Kirby, Gregory Paul Deutsch
Lullaby of Birdland (1952), George Shearing, George Weiss
Madison Avenue (1979), Ted Simons, Elinor Guggenheimer

(continued)

Songs and Compositions Inspired by New York City (selective list) (*Continued*)

Meet Me under the Maple Tree in Radio City (1942), Frank Turner, Charles Wynn
Memories of Madison Square Garden (1935), Richard Rodgers, Lorenz Hart
Park Avenue's Going to Town (1936), Edgar Fairchild, Milton Pascal
Park Avenue Strut (1929), Phil Baker, Maury Rubens, Moe Jaffe, Harold Atteridge
San Juan Hill (1942), Duke Ellington
She Lives on Murray Hill (1882), Edward Harrigan, David Braham
Sixth Avenue Heartache (1988), Jakob Dylan, Jim Snider
Slumming on Park Avenue (1937), Irving Berlin
Stairway to the Stars (Park Avenue Fantasy) (1935), Mitchell Parish, Matt Melneck, Frank Signorelli
Tenth Avenue Freeze Out (1975), Bruce Springsteen
Times Square (1922), Emerson Whitmore
Times Square (1922), Jerome Kern, Anne Caldwell
Times Square Dance (1940), Sammy Fain, Jack Yellen
Tin Pan Alley (1953), Sammy Fain, Jack Yellen
Uptown Girl (1983), Billy Joel
Way Out West (on West End Avenue) (1937), Richard Rodgers, Lorenz Hart
West End Avenue (1974), Stephen Schwartz
When Love Beckoned (in 52nd Street) (1939), Cole Porter
Yuletide, Park Avenue (1946), Harold Rome

FIFTH AVENUE

Breakfast at Tiffany's (1996), Deep Blue Something
Fifth Avenue (1868), William H. Lingard
Fifth Avenue (1901), George V. Hobart, A. B. Sloane
Fifth Avenue (1949), Gordon Jenkins, Tom Adair
Fugitive From Fifth Avenue (1949), Richard Stutz, Nat Hilson
Lady From Fifth Avenue (1937), Walter G. Samuels, Leonard Whitcup, Teddy Powell
Lament on Fifth Avenue (1957), Claire Richardson, Paul Rosner
On Double Fifth Avenue (1927), Abel Baer, Sam Lewis, Joe Young
South Fifth Avenue (1881), Edward Harrigan, David Braham

BROADWAY

Angel of the Great White Way (1937), Elton Box, Desmond Box, Don Pelosi, Paddy Roberts
Belle of the Gay White Way (1909), Charles Shackford
Better Than Broadway (1980), Tom Savage
Boogaloo down Broadway (1967), Jesse James
Broads of Broadway (1926), Gitz Rice, Paul Porter
Broadway (1913), Lew Brown
Broadway (1921), Hank Hawkins, G. E. Johnson
Broadway (1927), B. G. DeSylva, Lew Brown, Ray Henderson
Broadway (1929), Con Conrad, Sidney D. Mitchell, Archie Gottler
Broadway (1930), Percy Weinrich, Harry Clarke
Broadway (1940), Henry Woode, Teddy McRae, Bill Bird
Broadway (1959), Jule Styne, Stephen Sondheim
Broadway (1980), The Clash
Broadway (1980), Stephen Lemberg
Broadway, Broadway (1978), Charles Strouse, Lee Adams
Broadway, My Street (1971), John Kander, Fred Ebb
Broadway, New York (1979), Ann Harris
The Broadway, Opera, and Bowery Crawl (1871), Philip Stoner, Giuseppe Operti
Broadway Baby (1971), Stephen Sondheim
Broadway Baby (1980), Jim Wise, George Harrison, Robin Miller
Broadway Belle (1908), Julian Eltinge, Ted Snyder
Broadway Belles (1919), Arthur J. Jackson, Herbert Spencer
Broadway Blossom (1945), Morton Gould, Betty Comden, Adolph Green
Broadway Blues (1920), Arthur Swanstrom, Carey Morgan
Broadway Caballero (1941), Henry Russell
Broadway Conga (1938), Walter Hirsch, Ernest Lecuona
Broadway Dandy (*ca* 1871)
Broadway Follies (1981), Walter Marks
Broadway Girl (1904), Grace Leonard, Joe Nathan
Broadway Glide (1912), A. Seymour Brown, Bert Grant
Broadway Gypsy (1928), Rob Merwin, Frank Galassi
Broadway Honeymoon (1913), Collin Davis, Joe E. Howard
Broadway Indian Chief (1909), William J. McKenna
Broadway Indians (1923), Gene Buck, Dave Stamper
Broadway Jamboree (1937), Jimmy McHugh
Broadway Lady (1933), Sam H. Stept, Bud Green
Broadway Lights (1939), Enoch Light, Jimmy Eaton, Terry Shand
Broadway Love Song (1949), Jay Gorney, Jean Kerr, Walter Kerr
Broadway Mastery (1927), Jimmy Duffy, Clarence Gaskill
Broadway Melody (1929), Arthur Freed, Nacio Herb Brown
Broadway Melody of 1974 (1974), Tony Banks, Phil Collins, Peter Gabriel, Steve Hackett, Mike Rutherford
Broadway Moon (1939), Al Koppell, Terry Shand
A Broadway Musical (1978), Charles Strouse, Lee Adams
Broadway of My Heart (1971), Skip Redwine, Larry Frank
Broadway Reverie (1931), Gene Buck, Dave Stamper
Broadway Rhythm (1929), Bob Jaffe, Millard G. Thomas
Broadway Rhythm (1933), Arthur Freed, Nacio Herb Brown
Broadway Rose (1920), Eugene West, Otis Spencer
Broadway's Gone Hawaii (1937), Mack Gordon, Harry Revel
Broadway's Gone Hillbilly (1934), Lew Brown, Jay Gorney
Broadway Sights (1835), N. H. Latham
Broadway Swell and Brooklyn Belle (*ca* 1927), J. D. Kelly
Broadway to Madrid (1926), Morris Hamilton, Grace Henry
Broadway Waltzes (1949), George W. Warren
The Call of Broadway (1927), Maury Rubens, Jack Osterman, Ted Lewis
Don't Blame It on Broadway (1913), Sal Young, Harry Williams, Bert Grant
Forty Five Miles from Broadway (1905), George M. Cohan
From Broadway to Main Street (1923), Harry Archer, Harlan Thompson
Funky Broadway (1966), Arlester Christian
Girl I Met on Broadway (*ca* 1871), J. Currie
Give My Regards to Broadway (1904), George M. Cohan
Goodbye Broadway, Hello France (1917), Francis Reisner, Benny Davis, Billy Baskette
Hang Up Your Hat on Broadway (1933), Bernard Grossman, Dave Sylvester
Howdy Broadway (1926), Richard Rodgers, Lorenz Hart
I Beg Your Pardon Dear Old Broadway (1911), Irving Berlin
Indians Along Broadway (1920), Benjamin H. Burt
It's Getting Dark on Old Broadway (1922), Louis A. Hirsch, Gene Buck, Dave Stamper
The Lady from Broadway (1935), Dave Oppenheim, Max Rich
The Light Dies Down on Broadway (1974), Tony Banks, Phil Collins, Peter Gabriel, Steve Hackett, Mike Rutherford
Lullaby of Broadway (1935), Al Dubin, Harry Warren

(*continued*)

Songs and Compositions Inspired by New York City (selective list) (*Continued*)

Milkmaids of Broadway (1930), Alma Sanders, Monte Carlo
Nights on Broadway (1977), Barry Gibb, Robin Gibb, Maurice Gibb
Old Broadway (1906), Joseph E. Howard, Charles K. Harris
On Broadway (1885), Sydney Rosenfeld
On Broadway (1962), Barry Mann, Cynthia Weil, Jerry Lieber, Mike Stoller
On Broadway after Three (1897), Walter De Frece, Edmund Francis
On the Proper Side of Broadway on a Saturday P.M. (1902), Cobb and Edwards
Pearl of Broadway (1927), Jerome Kern, Bert Kalmar, Harry Ruby
Please Don't Monkey with Broadway (1939), Cole Porter
A Side Street Off Broadway (1927), Edgar Fairchild, Henry Meyers
1617 Broadway (1956), Jerry Bock, George Weiss, Larry Holofcener
Slaves of Broadway (1928), Ray Perkins, Max Lief, Nathaniel Lief
Take Me Back to Broadway (1907), James O'Dea, A. Payson Caldwell
That's Broadway (1944), Gene Herbert, Teddy Hall
Theme from Mr. Broadway (1964), Dave Brubeck
There's a Broadway Up in Heaven (1935), Edward J. Lambert, Gerald Dolin
There's a Broken Heart for Every Light on Broadway (1915), Howard Johnson, Fred Fisher
Turn Me Loose in Broadway (1952), Vernon Duke, Ogden Nash
Up Broadway (1900), J. Hoyt Toler
Waiting for a Broadway Stage (*ca* 1871), Bobby Newcomb
Walking Down Broadway (1870), William Lingrad, Charles E. Pratt
What Would Become of New York Town If Broadway Wasn't There? (1910), Sterling, Costello, Kerry Mills
When a Fella Meets a Flapper on Broadway (1929), Irving Caesar, Philip Charig
Wouldn't You Like to Be on Broadway? (1947), Kurt Weill, Langston Hughes
You Can Have Broadway (1906), George M. Cohan

CENTRAL PARK

Big Back Yard (1945), Sigmund Romberg, Dorothy Fields
Carousel in the Park (1944), Sigmund Romberg, Dorothy Fields
Central Park (*ca* 1920), Edwin Franko Goldman
Central Park 'n' West (1981), Ian Hunter
Central Park on a Sunday Afternoon (1975), Hank Beebe, Bill Heyer
In Central Park (1927), Harold Orlob, Iving Caesar
In the Center of Central Park (1942), Peter Tinturin
Listening to the Music Up in Central Park (1869), George Leybourne
On the Mall (1923), Edwin Franko Goldman
Romanzo di Central Park (1900), Charles Ives
Saturday in the Park (1972), Robert Lamm (performed by Chicago)
Saturday Night in Central Park (1948), Richard Lewine, Arnold B. Horwitt
Sunday in the Park (1937), Harold Rome
Through Central Park (*ca* 1870), William Lingard
Winter in Central Park (1929), Jerome Kern, Oscar Hammerstein

HARLEM

Across 110th Street (1972), Bobby Womack
Blue Belles of Harlem (1945), Duke Ellington
Bojangles of Harlem (1936), Jerome Kern, Dorothy Fields
Boys from Harlem (1939), Duke Ellington
Christmas Night in Harlem (1934), Mitchell Parish, Raymond Scott
Come to Harlem (1932), Al Wilson, Charles Weinberg, Ken Macomber
Deep Harlem (1929), Joe Jordan, Homer Tutt, Henry Creamer
Deep in the Heart of Harlem (1964), Clyde McPhatter
Doin' the Uptown Lowdown (1933), Mack Gordon, Harry Revel
Don't Forget 127th Street (1964), Charles Adams, Lee Strouse
Drop Me Off in Harlem (1933), Duke Ellington, Nick Kenny
Echoes of Harlem (1936), Duke Ellington
Everybody's Happy in Jimtown (1928), Fats Waller, Andy Razaf
Formal Night in Harlem (1936), Francis K. Shuman, Johanny Farro, Jules Loman
Happy Heaven of Harlem (1929), Cole Porter
Harlem (1927), Ford Dabney, Jo Trent
Harlem (A Tone Parallel to Harlem) (1952), Duke Ellington
Harlem Air Shaft (1940), Duke Ellington
Harlemania (1930), Richard Rodgers, Lorenz Hart
Harlem Blues (1922), W. C. Handy
Harlem Bolero (1937), Benny Davis, J. Fred Coors
Harlem Congo (1934), Chick Webb
Harlem Dan (1933), Alexander Hill
Harlem Drag (1928), R. Arthur Booker, Walter Bishop
Harlem Flat Blues (1929), Duke Ellington
Harlem Follies (1980), Stephen H. Lemberg
Harlem Holiday (1932), Harold Arlen
Harlem Lullaby (1932), Margot Hillham, Willard Robinson
Harlem Madness (1929), Milton Ager, Jack Yellen
Harlem Mania (1932), Donald Heywood
Harlem Moon (1931), Mann Holiner, Alberta Nichols
Harlem Nocturne (1939), Dick Rogers, Earle M. Hagan
Harlem on My Mind (1933), Irving Berlin
Harlem River Chanty (1925), Richard Rodgers, Lorenz Hart
Harlem Sandman (1943), Harold Adamson, Jule Styne
Harlem's Goin' to Town (1936), Joseph Elly
Harlem Shuffle (1963), Bobby Relf, Earl Nelson
Harlem Speaks (1933), Duke Ellington
Harlem's Poppin' (1940), Maceo Pinkard, William Tracey
Harlem Streets (1972), Micki Grant
Harlem Symphony (1932), James P. Johnson
Harlem Twist (1928), Fud Livingston, Chauncey Morehouse
Harmony in Harlem (1938), Irving Mills, Duke Ellington, Johnny Hodges
Headin' For Harlem (1927), James Hawley, Eddie Dowling
High Up in Harlem (1939), Jerome Kern, Oscar Hammerstein
Home to Harlem (1933), Ray Henderson, Lew Brown
I Dreamt I Dwelt in Harlem (1941), Robert B. Wright, Jerry Gray, Ben Smith, Leonard B. Ware
I'm Slapping Seventh Avenue with the Sole of My Shoe (1938), Duke Ellington
It Was a Sad Night in Harlem (1936), Al Lewis, Helmy Kresa
Jumpin' at the Woodside (1938), Count Basie
Jungle Nights in Harlem (1927), Duke Ellington
A Night in Harlem (1962)
Old Man Harlem (1933), Hoagy Carmichael, Rudy Vallee
On My Way to Harlem (1994), Coolio
121st Street (1925), George Gershwin
Puttin' on the Ritz (1929), Irving Berlin
Shades of Harlem (1957)
Song of Harlem (1929), Frank Marcus, Bernard Maltin
Spanish Harlem (1960), Jerry Lieber, Phil Spector
Spanish Harlem Incident (1963), Bob Dylan
The Spell of Those Harlem Hights (1932), Al Wilson, Charles Weinberg, Ken Macomber
Stompin' at the Savoy (1934), Edgar Sampson
Sugar Hill Penthouse (1945), Duke Ellington
Take a Trip to Harlem (1930), Eubie Blake, Andy Razaf

(*continued*)

Songs and Compositions Inspired by New York City (selective list) (*Continued*)

Take the "A" Train (1941), Duke Ellington, Billy Strayhorn
There's a Boy in Harlem (1938), Richard Rodgers, Lorenz Hart
Underneath the Harlem Moon (1932), Mack Gordon, Harry Revel
Uptown (1962), Barry Mann, Cynthia Weil
Uptown Downbeat (1936), Duke Ellington
Uptown Saturday Night (1974), Tom Scott, Morgan Ames
What Harlem Is to Me (1935), Andy Razaf, Russell Wooding, Paul Danniker

BROOKLYN

The Belles about the Flat Bush (1785)
Born and Bred in Brooklyn (Over the Bridge) (1923), George M. Cohan
Brooklyn (1983), Scott McLary, Dorothy Chansky
Brooklyn (1999), Mos Def
Brooklyn (2002), Jesse Malin
Brooklyn (Owes the Charmer under Me) (1972), Walter Becker, Donald Fagen
Brooklyn Baseball Cantata (1940), George Kelinsinger, Mike Stratton
Brooklyn Blues (1987), Barry Manilow
Brooklyn Boogie (1944), Louis Prima
Brooklyn Bridge (1947), Jule Styne, Sammy Cahn
Brooklyn Bridge (2005), Darren Hanlon
Brooklyn Dodger Strike (1981), Bob Brush, Martin Chanin
The Brooklyn Ferryman (*ca* 1836), W. H. Parker
Brooklyn Girls (1981), Robbie Dupree
Brooklyn Girls (2008), Charles Hamilton
Brooklyn Go Hard (2008), Jay-Z
Brooklyn Polka (1944), Zeke Manners
Brooklyn Roads (1968), Neil Diamond
Brooklyn's Finest (2007), Jay-Z
Brooklyn Zoo (1995), Ol' Dirty Bastard
By the Beautiful Sea (1914), Harold R. Atteridge, Harry Carroll
Coney Island (1930), Richard Rodgers, Lorenz Hart
Coney Island (1957), Mel Tormé
Coney Island (2001), Ben Gibbard
Coney Island, U.S.A. (1964), Jack Lawrence, Stan Freeman
Coney Island Baby (1976), Lou Reed
Coney Island Boat (1954), Dorothy Fields, Arthur Schwartz
Coney Island's Shore (*ca* 1871), Johnny Delfield
Danny by My Side (Brooklyn Bridge) (1891), Edward Harrigan, David Braham
Down on Coney Island, W. Warren Bentley
Hail, Brooklyn (*ca* 1920), Edwin Franko Goldman
I'm Gonna Hang My Hat on a Tree in Brooklyn (1944), Dan Shapiro, Milton Pascal, Phil Charig
In a Little "Jernt" in Greenpernt (1936), "Gowanus Canal"
I've Made My Plans for the Summer (1907), John Philip Sousa
Just over the Brooklyn Bridge (1993), Art Garfunkel
Leave Us Go Root for the Dodgers, Rogers (1942), Dan Parker, Bud Green
Lighters Up (Welcome to Brooklyn) (2005), Lil' Kim
Lovecraft in Brooklyn (2008), John Darnielle
Manhattan Beach (1893), John Philip Sousa
Miss Euclid Avenue (1961), Jerry Herman
Moon over Brooklyn (1946), Jason Matthews, Terry Shand
Nestin' Time in Flatbush (1917), P. G. Wodehouse
No Sleep 'til Brooklyn (1986), Beastie Boys
Ode on Science (1840), E. C. Embury (dedicated to the Trustees of the Brooklyn Collegiate Institute)
Red Dragon Tattoo (1999), Chris Collingwood, Adam Schlesinger
Rene and George Magritte with Their Dog after the War (1983), Paul Simon
Respiration (1998), Black Star
Strolling on the Brooklyn Bridge (1883), George Cooper, Joseph Skelly
Take Me Down to Coney Island (1897), Gustave Kerker, Hugh Morton
Token Back to Brooklyn (2002), John Flansburgh, John Linnell
A Tree Grows in Brooklyn (1944), Moe Jaffe
Two Orphans (Brooklyn Theater Fire) (*ca* 1922), C. A. Fuller

THE BRONX, QUEENS, STATEN ISLAND

Alfie from the Bronx (1984), Toy Dolls
Bedstuy Parade and Funeral March (2004), Mos Def
Bronx (1986), Kurtis Blow
Bronx Express (1922), Creamer and Layton
The Bronx Is Beautiful (1984), Robert Klein
Bronx Tale (1995), Fat Joe
Christmas in Hollis (1987), Russell Simmons, Daryl McDaniels
Don Jose from Far Rockaway (1952), Harold Rome
Here Come the Yankees (1967), Bob Bundin, Lou Stallman
I Love the New York Yankees (1981), Paula Lindstrom
Meet the Mets (1961), Ruth Roberts, Bill Katz
On the Banks of the Bronx (1919), William Le Baron, Victor Jacobi
Riker's Island (1991), Cocoa Tea
Rockaway Beach (1977), Dee Dee Ramone
So Long, Astoria (2003), Kris Roe
South Bronx (1987), Boogie Down Productions
The Tremont Avenue Cruisewear Fashion Show (1973), Jerry Livingston, Mark David

SUBWAYS

Don't Sleep in the Subway (1967), Tony Hatch, Jackie Trent
GG Train (1959), Charles Mingus
A Month of Subways (1949), Johnny Mercer, Robert E. Dolan
Old Man Subway (1933), Robert Russell Bennett, Owen Murphy, Robert A. Simon
The Rumble of the Subway (1923), Vincent Youmans, William Carey Duncan, Oscar Hammerstein, Herbert Stothart
Subway Directions; Ride through the Night (1961), Jule Styne, Betty Comden, Adolph Green
Subway Dream (1971), Helen Miller, Eve Merriam
Subway Rag (1958), Buster Davis, Steven Vinaver
Subway Rider (1980), Micki Grant
Subway Song (1948), Richard Lewine, Arnold B. Horwitt
The Subway Sun (1928), Ray Perkins, Max Lief, Nathaniel Lief
Subway Train (1973), New York Dolls
Third Avenue El (1956), Michael Brown
Up in the Elevated Railway (1954), Sigmund Romberg, Leo Robin

Compiled by Andrew A. Kryzak, Marc Ferris

Son of Sam. Nickname of serial killer David (Richard) Berkowitz (*b* 1 June 1953). He was also referred to as the .44 caliber killer. Berkowitz was born in Brooklyn and adopted by two hardware store owners, Nathan and Pearl Berkowitz. He was raised at 1105 Stratford Avenue in the Bronx. Between July 1976 and August 1977, Berkowitz terrorized New York City as he fatally shot five women and one man and wounded seven others in eight incidents across the Bronx, Brooklyn, and Queens. He targeted young women sitting in parked cars with male companions, and police mounted a massive manhunt. Berkowitz left notes at crime scenes and sent an open letter to *New York Daily News* columnist Jimmy Breslin signed "Son of Sam." On 10 August 1977 police arrested Berkowitz outside of his apartment at what was then known as Pine Hill Towers at 35 Pine Street in Yonkers (a building now identified as Horizon Hill at 42 Pine Street). Berkowitz admitted to having committed all of the shootings; his defense lawyers claimed that he was told to commit the acts by his neighbor's demon-possessed Labrador retriever. He was found guilty and sentenced to six consecutive life terms. The

"Son of Sam law," passed by the state legislature of New York to limit the ability of convicted criminals to profit from accounts of their crimes, was declared unconstitutional by the U.S. Supreme Court in 1991.

Anne Epstein

Sontag, Susan (*b* New York City, 16 Jan 1933; *d* New York City, 28 Dec 2004). Writer, critic, and film and theater director. She attended the University of California, Berkeley, and the University of Chicago (BA 1951); Harvard University (MA 1954, English; MA 1955, philosophy); Oxford University; and the Sorbonne. In 1959, after arriving in New York City, where she would live for the rest of her life, she began to write and publish her first essays and works of fiction. She gained fame in 1966 with the publication of *Against Interpretation,* a collection of provocative analyses of art and culture. The book broadcast her abiding interest in popular culture and her willingness to address it with the same seriousness she gave to high art. Throughout her career Sontag explored the ways in which new cultural realities influence our ability to address human suffering, in such books as *On Photography* (1977), *Illness as Metaphor* (1978), *AIDS and Its Metaphors* (1989), and *Regarding the Pain of Others* (2003). Her works of fiction included *In America* (2000), winner of the National Book Award.

Sontag expressed her convictions through lifelong activism. From 1987 to 1989 she served as president of the American Center of PEN, the international writers' organization dedicated to freedom of expression. Her focus on human rights led to clashes with both left-wing and right-wing critics. She opposed the Vietnam War; she also opposed the Soviet Union's domination of Eastern Europe and, later, Serbia's invasion of Bosnia. Sontag published 17 books, including fiction, plays, monographs, and essays, and directed four films and numerous theater pieces. Her penthouse apartment in the Chelsea neighborhood of Manhattan, where she lived until her death, contained a library of more than 15,000 books.

Helen Graves

Sony Corporation of America. Technology company. Based in New York City, it is a U.S. subsidiary of Sony Corporation that is headquartered in Tokyo. Located at 550 Madison Avenue, the company employed about 120 people locally and more than 33,000 worldwide in 2009.

Jessica Montesano

Sorge, Friedrich A(dolf) (*b* Bethau, near Torgau [now in Germany], 9 Nov 1828; *d* Hoboken, N.J., 26 Oct 1906). Communist activist. After taking part in the German Revolution of 1848, he moved to New York City in 1852 and became the leading proponent of Marxism in the United States. In the city he helped to form the Kommunisten Klub (1857), which drew its members from among well-educated German radicals who sought to abolish private property, and the Socialist Party for New York City and Vicinity (1868), a forerunner of the Socialist Party of America. With other German exiles he played a prominent role in the International Workingmen's Association and was the leader of its general council when it was transferred to the city in 1872. In 1877 he moved to suburban Hoboken, New Jersey, where he promoted the eight-hour workday and organized textile workers. Sorge gradually turned away from the American socialist movement and came to favor a more moderate approach to workers' issues.

Kevin Kenny

Sorosis. Club for women formed in New York City in 1868 by Jane Cunningham Croly; it was one of the first women's clubs in the United States. The impetus behind its formation was the decision by the New York Press Club, which was mostly male, to bar women reporters from a function honoring Charles Dickens's visit to Manhattan. Croly invited several distinguished women to meet for social and intellectual companionship. During lunches held twice a month from September to June at Delmonico's restaurant, the poets Alice Cary and Phoebe Cary, the businesswoman Madame Demorest, the reporter Anne Field, and the novelist Sara "Fanny Fern" Willis Parton discussed contemporary issues. The group soon attracted other ambitious women, including the physician Anna Manning Comfort and the Universalist minister Phebe Hanford, and became one of the most influential women's clubs in the country. It regularly entertained guests from outside the city, among them Louisa May Alcott, Maria Mitchell, and the anthropologist Alice Fletcher; it also pressed for scholarships, better opportunities for women (such as admission to Columbia University), the reform of women's fashion, and the establishment of other women's clubs. It continues to assert a collective concern about social inequities.

Karen J. Blair, *The Clubwoman as Feminist: True Womanhood Redefined, 1868–1914* (New York: Holmes and Meier, 1980), 15–31

Karen J. Blair

Sotheby's. Auction house. Its forerunner was the firm of Samuel Baker, a bookseller in London who first held an auction of rare books in 1744. At his death in 1778 the business was taken over by his partner George Leigh and his nephew John Sotheby and renamed Leigh and Sotheby. Under Sotheby's son Samuel Sotheby the firm became the leading auctioneer of books in London by the 1840s; it often acquired art objects in estate sales but passed them on to Christie's. Eventually renamed Sotheby, Wilkinson and Hodge, the firm was sold in 1908 to a group of investors led by Montague Barlow, who in 1913 held the first auction of paintings. By 1924 the firm took the name Sotheby and rivaled Christie's in importance. It opened a branch in New York City in 1954, which it merged in 1964 with the Parke–Bernet Galleries, the most important art auctioneer in the city until after World War II, to form Sotheby Parke Bernet. In 1983 the firm, including its branches, took its current name. New York City Sotheby's operates a real estate business dealing in expensive properties as well as an auction house at 1334 York Avenue specializing in art and antiques. In 2000 Sotheby's bought the auction house where it had been a tenant for 20 years for $11 million and launched a $140 million expansion; two years later, after a price-fixing scandal that landed its chair in jail, it sold the auction house for $175 million to a real estate developer who agreed to lease it back to the company. In 2008, after tussles with the developer, Sotheby's repurchased the building for $468 million.

Frank Herriman, *Sotheby's: Portrait of an Auction House* (New York: W. W. Norton, 1981); Thomas E. Norton, *100 Years of Collecting in America: The Story of Sotheby Parke Bernet* (New York: Harry N. Abrams, 1984)

Eric Wm. Allison

Sothern, E(dward) H(ugh) (*b* New Orleans, 6 Dec 1859; *d* New York City, 28 Oct 1933). Actor. He built a distinguished career as the leading actor at the Lyceum Theatre in New York City before marrying the actress Julia Marlowe (1866–1950) in 1904; the two formed an acting company and won acclaim for their performances of Shakespeare, to which they brought a light, modern approach that placed them among the most popular Shakespearean actors of their time. After Marlowe's retirement in 1924, Sothern continued to perform until 1927.

David J. Weiner

Sotomayor, Sonia (*b* Bronx, N.Y., 25 June 1954). Lawyer. She was the first Latina and the third woman to serve on the U.S. Supreme Court. Her parents came to New York City from Puerto Rico, and Sotomayor was raised in the Bronxdale Houses, a public housing project in the east Bronx, and then in Co-op City in the northeast Bronx. Her mother, a nurse, became the sole breadwinner of the family after Sotomayor's father died. She was educated in Catholic schools, Blessed Sacrament in the Soundview section of the Bronx and Cardinal Spellman High School, and was valedictorian at both. In 1976 she graduated from Princeton University, where she became a student activist promoting issues of concern to Latinos, including the hiring of Latino professors. She graduated in 1979 from Yale Law School and was admitted to the New York bar in 1980. She was first a prosecutor in the Manhattan district attorney's office and then entered private practice in the law firm of Pavia and Harcourt. In 1991 President George H. W. Bush nominated her to the U.S. District Court for the Southern District of New York, where she served from 1992 to

1998. In 1998 she joined the Court of Appeals for the Second Circuit, a position that she held from 1998. In May 2009 she was nominated to the Supreme Court by President Barack Obama to replace retiring justice Daniel H. Souter; the Senate confirmed her nomination and she assumed office in August.

Karen E. Markoe

Soundview. Neighborhood in the southeastern Bronx, bounded to the north by Westchester Avenue, to the east by Soundview Avenue, to the south by Soundview Park, and to the west by the Bronx River. Despite the name it is closer to the East River than to the Long Island Sound (at the time the neighborhood was developed, maps showed the upper East River as part of Long Island Sound). The area was mostly farmland until the Lexington Avenue subway was completed along Westchester Avenue in 1920; later one- and two-family houses were built. In 1937 the City of New York took title to 93 acres (38 hectares) along the Bronx River that was later designated Soundview Park but remained swampy and mostly undeveloped. Before World War II the population was largely Jewish. The construction of the Bruckner Expressway in the 1960s spurred the development of middle-income high-rise housing and low-income housing projects, including the Soundview Houses. In the 1970s Robert Moses proposed that the entire population of the southern Bronx should be moved to new housing in Soundview Park and the most dilapidated housing in the southern Bronx demolished; his plan was never carried out. By the 1980s the population of Soundview was largely black and Latin American. Among immigrant groups moving to the area in the 1980s more than a quarter were from the Dominican Republic; others were from Jamaica, Guyana, and Ecuador. In 1999 the area gained notoriety as the site of the Amadou Diallo shooting at 1157 Wheeler Avenue.

Gary D. Hermalyn

Sousa, John Philip (*b* Washington, D.C., 6 Nov 1854; *d* Reading, Pa., 6 March 1932). Bandmaster. After leaving the U.S. Marine Band to form his own ensemble in 1892, he recruited 19 musicians from the defunct Gilmore Band and moved his operations to New York City, where his band maintained its offices and usually ended its rigorous tours. He lived with his family in several hotels in the city and occupied a suite on the top story of Carnegie Hall from 1892 until 1914, when he bought a house on Long Island. For many years associated with Coney Island, he played several summer engagements at Manhattan Beach, and in 1907 he wrote and dedicated to Luna Park the words and music for the song "I've Made My Plans for the Summer," which concerns a young woman who declines a proposal of marriage so that she can instead spend her vacation at Coney Island. At least two of Sousa's marches were inspired by New York City: "Manhattan Beach March" (1893) and "New York Hippodrome" (1915). In 1933 American Legion Post no. 1112 in the city renamed its chapter after Sousa, and in 1959 John Philip Sousa Junior High School opened at 3750 Baychester Avenue in the Bronx.

Souvenir book, Sousa and His Band: Golden Jubilee Tour, *1928*

Paul E. Bierley, *John Philip Sousa: American Phenomenon* (Englewood Cliffs, N.J.: Prentice Hall, 1973)

Marc Ferris

South Beach. Neighborhood in northeastern Staten Island, bounded to the north by the Staten Island Expressway, to the east and south by Lower New York Bay, and to the west by Dongan Hills. It is on the site of Oude Dorp, a Dutch community built in 1661 near the foot of Ocean Avenue. Although no trace of the community remains, seventeenth-century reports of the Dutch West India Company mention 12 to 14 families and a blockhouse. From the 1880s to the 1920s the beach was a resort, with hotels, beer gardens, bathing pavilions, shooting galleries, Ferris wheels, theaters, and dance halls. On weekends during the summer as many as 100,000 visitors would travel to the beach by boat or train. By 1891 there at least 25 hotels. The Bachmann Hotel had a theater that in 1906 became the Happyland Amusement Park; in 1917 bathing was declared unsafe and the amusement park was destroyed by fire. The beachfront was renovated by the Works Progress Administration in 1935; the 2.5-mile-long (4-kilometer-long) South Beach–Franklin Delano Roosevelt boardwalk is the fourth largest in the world. Recreation facilities have since replaced the amusement parks. A roller hockey rink was installed in 1995, and a new playground in 1996. The elaborate *Fountain of the Dolphins* sculpture, featuring fiber-optic cables that illuminate water jets, was added in 1998. In 2006, 4 acres (1.6 hectares) of wet woods and marshland were designated as a South Beach Blue Belt by the New York City Department of Environmental Protection.

Long known as an Italian neighborhood, South Beach is characterized by a high rate of homeownership, carefully tended gardens, and well-attended churches, especially the Church of the Holy Rosary on South Lane. In the 1960s a number of blacks and Latinos moved into the neighborhood, which has become increasingly diverse. Important local institutions include the South Beach Psychiatric Center (dedicated in 1973), the North Campus of the Staten Island University Hospital, and the Giuseppe Mazzini Senior Citizens' Center.

Howard R. Weiner

South Bronx. Imprecise term used after 1950 to designate an area of shifting boundaries in the southwestern Bronx. At first applied only to Mott Haven and Melrose, by 1975 it came to include the area along the Cross Bronx Expressway and later Fordham Road as well. The widespread use of the name has done much to obscure the diversity of the neighborhoods making up the South Bronx, which many local residents do not regard as being a neighborhood itself.

South Brooklyn. Obsolete and imprecise term applied to the southern parts of the city of Brooklyn about 1855 and including what are now known as Red Hook, Carroll Gardens, and Park Slope.

South Brooklyn Railway. Freight railway subsidiary of the Metropolitan Transit Authority, operating between Second Avenue and Fort Hamilton Parkway in Sunset Park. Brooklyn Rapid Transit opened the line on 13 January 1900 for freight services between Bush Terminal and Coney Island. On 28 February 1907 the railway acquired the lease for the tracks on McDonald Avenue from the Brooklyn Heights Railroad, which had in turn acquired the rights in 1899 from the Long Island Rail Road. The line interchanged freight with the Long Island Rail Road and the New Haven Rail Road at Parkville (Avenue I and McDonald Avenue) and with the New York Dock Railway at Second Avenue and 37th Street. The cessation of freight interchange at Parkville after Conrail was formed in 1976, along with the poor condition of track along McDonald Avenue, prompted the railway on 1 February 1978 to abandon all track south of Fort Hamilton Parkway.

Jay Bendersky, *Brooklyn's Waterfront Railways* (Uniondale, N.Y.: Meatball, 1988)

John Fink

South Brother Island. Island in the western arm of the East River, at the entrance to Long Island Sound. Comprising 7 acres (3 hectares), it is officially part of Bronx County. The island and its neighbor, North Brother Island, (located one-third of a mile, or half a kilometer, to the east), were originally called the *Gezellen*, the Companions, by the Dutch. South Brother Island was once the property of brewer Jacob Ruppert, who was also the owner of the New York Yankees. He built his summer home on the island in 1894, but in 1907 it was destroyed by fire. The island remained in Ruppert's hands until the late 1930s. It then passed through several owners until acquired by the City of New York. It was sold in 1975 for a mere $10 to Hampton Scows, Inc., a sand company, but little was done to develop the island. In the fall of 2007 the city repurchased it for approximately $2 million for development as a wildlife sanctuary. The acquisition of the island was supported by several preservation organizations, including the Wildlife Conservation Society, the Point Community Development Corporation, the Public Land Trust, and the federal government. The now uninhabited and densely overgrown island has long been home to a variety of nesting bird colonies, including herons, egrets, and cormorants.

Gerard R. Wolfe

South East Bronx Community Organization [SEBCO]. Group founded in the autumn of 1968 by community leaders in Hunts Point and Longwood North to halt their neighborhood's decline. Their leader was Father Louis R. Gigante, a Roman Catholic priest then assigned to St. Athanasius Church, which is at the center of the redevelopment area. Using a combination of public and private funds, SEBCO concentrated on the rehabilitation of existing housing. By 2009 SEBCO Development Inc., as it became known, had developed more than 6000 units of affordable and low-income housing, including condominiums, cooperatives, and private houses, and managed more than 3000 units of low-income and senior citizen housing; it employed more than 300 people. It also provided supportive community services such as senior citizen meals, after-school tutoring, and computer training. Peter Cantillo, an expert in affordable urban housing, succeeded Gigante in 2007.

Kenneth T. Jackson

Southfield. Former administrative district in southeastern Staten Island, bounded to the north by Arthur Kill Road and Richmond Road, to the east by the Narrows and Lower New York Bay, to the south by the Atlantic Ocean, and to the west by Gifford's Lane; it comprised Stapleton, Clifton, Rosebank, Old Town, South Beach, Dongan Hills, Midland Beach, New Dorp, Oakwood, Richmondtown (the seat), and parts of Great Kills and Eltingville. The area was variously known as South Division and South Quarter; the area encompassing it and Westfield was sometimes called Southside. In 1860 Middletown was formed from a part of the northwestern section along with a bordering part of the town of Castleton. The district was abolished when New York City was consolidated in 1898.

Marjorie Johnson

South Jamaica. Name sometimes applied to an area in southern Queens bounded to the north by the Long Island Railroad, to the east by Merrick Boulevard, to the south by the Belt Parkway, and to the west by the Van Wyck Expressway. In colonial times a race course ran around Beaver Pond (Beaver Road and 158th Street). For most of the nineteenth century the area was covered by vast farms and isolated farmhouses. St. Monica's Roman Catholic Church opened in 1857 (160th Street); abandoned in 1973 and landmarked in 1979, it collapsed in 1998. Prospect Cemetery on 159th Street had burials from 1668; the chapel was built in 1857. The Jamaica Racetrack opened in 1894 on a large tract south of Baisley Boulevard and east of New York Boulevard. Several small developments grew up after 1900, including Talfourd Lawn, Jamaica Heights, Jamaica Park, and Jamaica Falls. Streets opened in the 1920s and hundreds of modest one-family houses were built; by World War II there was no vacant land, and the population was largely African American. The South Jamaica Houses, 440 units in 11 buildings, opened in 1940; an additional 598 units in 16 buildings were completed in 1954 (South Road to 109th Avenue, 159th to 168th Streets). The racetrack closed in August 1959, after Aqueduct Raceway was renovated, and was demolished in 1960; in December 1963 Rochdale Village was built on the site. With 5860 units it was the largest middle-income cooperative in the nation. Two smaller apartment complexes are Baisley Park Houses and Cedar Manor Houses. The rest of the housing consists of detached frame houses of two and a half stories each on lots measuring 25 by 100 feet (8 by 30 meters). In the 1980s the neighborhood attracted many immigrants from Jamaica and Guyana, and to a lesser extent from Haiti, Trinidad and Tobago, the Dominican Republic, and Colombia. South Jamaica is the largest African American neighborhood in Queens. Many residents are public employees. The York College (founded in 1966) campus on 160th Street south of the railroad was designed by Gruzen Partnerships in 1973 and completed in 1986. Baisley Pond (originally a collection pond of the Brooklyn Water Works) and Baisley Park remain the most attractive natural features.

Vincent Seyfried

South Ozone Park. Neighborhood in south central Queens, bounded to the north by Rockaway Boulevard, to the east by the Van Wyck Expressway, to the south by the Belt Parkway, and to the west by Aqueduct Racetrack. Aqueduct, named for the Brooklyn water system's conduit, opened in 1894; it was renovated in 1959. Until 1908 the area was occupied mostly by truck farms and there were few roads. David P. Leahy, a real estate agent from Brooklyn, built a development south of Rockaway Turnpike between 131st and 140th streets that he named South Ozone Park in 1909 and promoted so successfully that by 1913 there were almost 100 houses. Initially, sole access to the neighborhood was provided by a trolley on Rockaway Turnpike. Eventually, hundreds of detached one-family houses were built along new streets, especially during the 1920s. The neighborhood became largely Italian and Irish. By 2009 immigrants from Guyana accounted for almost 30 percent of all the population. Others came from Jamaica (20 percent), Haiti, the Dominican Republic, and Trinidad and Tobago.

Vincent Seyfried

South Street Seaport. District on the Lower East Side of Manhattan between Maiden Lane

South Street Seaport, 1878

South Street Seaport, ca *1897*

and Dover Street that was the center of the port from 1815 to 1860. The area was favored by sea captains because it was sheltered from the prevailing westerly winds and from ice that floated down the Hudson River; winds blowing off the shore also facilitated departure from berths there. The original shorefront road was Pearl Street, apparently named for its oyster-shell surface. During the eighteenth century the shoreline was extended with landfill, and a new shorefront road was built (later named Water Street), followed by Front Street and later by South Street in the early nineteenth century. South Street became known worldwide for its proximity to moorings in the harbor: bowsprits and jib booms projected nearly to the buildings across the street that housed the businesses of merchants, ship chandlers, sailmakers, and figurehead carvers, as well as boarding houses, saloons, and brothels. Evangelical organizations attempted to restore respectability and propriety to the often rowdy neighborhood. After 1880 the area began to decline, in part because adequate space to develop facilities was lacking and in part because the water was too shallow to accommodate steam-powered vessels. By the 1930s most of the open piers were covered, as large ships calling at New York City berthed on the West Side of Manhattan and in Hoboken, New Jersey. In 1966 a citizens' group led by Peter and Norma Stanford formed the Friends of the South Street Maritime Museum. Inspired by the restoration of the waterfront in San Francisco, they gathered a fleet of historic ships and obtained landmark designation for the buildings in the area; the South Street Seaport Museum opened in 1967. In 1973 two blocks were condemned by the city and leased to the museum, and another block was acquired for a state maritime museum that was eventually abandoned.

In 1979 development of the South Street Historic District was undertaken by the Rouse Company of Columbia, Maryland, which had rebuilt the historic Quincy Market District in Boston. The project required major investment by the firm, support from the city and the state, the surrender of some properties by the museum, and federal funding in the form of an Urban Development Action Grant. The first section of the district, opened in 1983, consisted of a modern market building on the site of the Fulton markets and two restored blocks of historic buildings; the second, opened in 1985, was a three-story shopping mall pier called Pier 17 built into the East River on the former site of the slip used by the Fulton Fish Market. By the 1990s the South Street Seaport Museum had assembled one of the world's largest collections of historic ships, renovated a large area of landmark buildings south of Fulton Street for exhibit space and storage of collections, and supplemented its own collection of ship models and marine art by purchasing the extensive former holdings of the Seamen's Bank for Savings.

After two expansions the South Street Seaport District extends from the south side of Burling Slip at the foot of John Street north to the Brooklyn Bridge and from the East River west to Pearl Street. The Rouse Company development of 1979–1983 involved three blocks between Burling Slip and Beekman Street. Development of the remaining blocks to the north between Beekman Street and the bridge proceeded more slowly, in part because of the presence of Fulton Fish Market dealers in many of the landmark buildings. Vacant lots in these blocks were largely replaced by modern sympathetic construction, beginning with new headquarters for the Seamen's Church Institute of the Port of New York, which opened on Water Street in May 1991. The move of the Fulton Fish Market to Hunts Point in the Bronx in November 2005 opened the way for renovation and reuse of the remaining landmark buildings in the district.

The Rouse Company properties in the South Street Seaport were acquired in 2004 by the real estate investment trust General Growth Holdings, which published plans for extensive changes to the district's riverfront. Piers 15 and 16 to the south continued to serve as berthing for the museum's historic ships and visiting vessels, the latter also providing pedestrian access to Pier 17. The original wooden Pier 15 dating from the late 1800s fell into disrepair and was eventually condemned by the city and removed; the museum installed a temporary floating pier, with plans for building a permanent replacement. The city's parks department also plans to use the inland open spaces lately serving as parking lots at Burling Slip and Peck Slip: the former to provide a playground for children from the growing residential community, and the latter to be repaved with granite paving stones centering on a maritime-related sculpture and landscaping.

Norman J. Brouwer

South Street Seaport, 2009

South Woodhaven. Obsolete name for the neighborhood in Queens now known as Aqueduct.

Soyer, Moses (*b* Borisoglebsk, Russia, 25 Dec 1899; *d* New York City, 4 Sept 1974). Painter, twin brother of Raphael Soyer. After immigrating to the United States in 1912, he studied at Cooper Union, the National Academy of Design, the Ferrer Art School, and the Educational Alliance. His first solo exhibition was held in 1929, and during the 1930s he taught at several art schools in New York City and was employed by the Federal Art Project of the Works Progress Administration. Primarily a painter of portraits and figures, he worked in the naturalistic style of his brother but never received as much critical acclaim.

Patricia Hills

Soyer, Raphael (*b* Borisoglebsk, Russia, 25 Dec 1899; *d* New York City, 4 Nov 1987). Painter, twin brother of Moses Soyer. After immigrating to the United States in 1912, he studied at Cooper Union, the National Academy of Design, and the Art Students League. He had his first exhibition in New York City in 1929 and during the Depression taught classes at the John Reed Club, to which he belonged; he also taught at the Art Students League, the New School for Social Research, and the National Academy of Design. In the late 1930s he was a member of the American Artists' Congress. His compassionate, naturalistic paintings of homeless men in the Depression were critically acclaimed; the Metropolitan Museum of Art and the Whitney Museum of American Art bought many of these works, including *Office Girls* (1936). During the 1950s he was an important member of a group of realists who published the periodical *Reality: A Journal of Artists' Opinions,* which defended realism and figurative painting. He later painted subdued portraits of street people and of his friends, including the poet Allen Ginsberg. The Whitney Museum of American Art held a retrospective exhibition of Soyer's work in 1967.

Lloyd Goodrich, *Raphael Soyer* (New York: Harry N. Abrams, 1972)

Patricia Hills

SPA. See Socialist Party of America.

Spanish–American War. Military conflict from April to December 1898 between the United States and Spain over Pacific and Caribbean islands, including the Philippines, Guam, Cuba, and Puerto Rico. In February 1898 the USS *Maine* battleship, which had been constructed at the Brooklyn Navy Yard in 1888, blew up off the coast of Cuba. While the cause of the explosion was unknown, New York City newspaper editors, particularly William Randolph Hearst of the *New York Journal* and Joseph Pulitzer of the *New York World,* readily blamed the Spanish government and sensationalized the event in order to outsell their competitors, giving birth to a style of investigative reporting later known as yellow journalism. New York State provided more than 12,000 soldiers from 12 regiments to meet President William McKinley's call for troops in April.

David White

Spanish Harlem. Name commonly used for El Barrio.

Spanish-language press. Spanish-language publications in New York City fall into three categories: the exile press, the immigrant press, and the native press. The first Spanish or bilingual newspapers appeared in the early nineteenth century published by anticolonials agitating for Cuban and Puerto Rican separation from Spain through annexation to the United States or independence. Antillean liberation and other concerns of the exile community were promoted by some 25 newspapers—beginning with *El Mensajero* (1828) and *El Mercurio de Nueva York* (1828) and ending with the official organ of the Cuban Revolutionary party, *Patria* (1892), launched by José Martí and Sotero Figueroa. *La Aurora*, *Cultura Proletaria,* and *El Porvenir* emerged out of workers' organizations connected to the cigar industry. The immigrant and native presses appeared in the early twentieth century. Connecting the homeland with emerging barrios in the city, in 1901 the Puerto Rican political leader Luis Muñoz Rivera published the bilingual newspaper *Puerto Rican Herald*. The general-interest newspaper *La Prensa* appeared weekly from 1913 and daily from 1918; other important newspapers included the radical *Grafico* (weekly, 1926–31) and the literary *Revista de Artes y Letras* (monthly, 1933–45). Newspapers published by the sociocultural, professional, and political organizations that structured the Latino neighborhoods, such as the *Boletín de la Liga Puertorriqueña e Hispana* (1927), emphasized the community's civic role. The large-scale influx to New York City from Puerto Rico in the late 1940s and later from the Dominican Republic, Cuba, and other Latin American countries gave rise to several mass-circulation newspapers, including the tabloid *El Diario* (1948), which merged with *La Prensa* to form *El Diario–La Prensa* (1963); this achieved a circulation of more than 100,000 and was the largest of the papers in the twenty-first century. *Noticias del Mundo* was launched as a daily newspaper in 1980. By this time Spanish-language newspapers tended to be published by firms not owned by Latin Americans: *El Diario–La Prensa* was published by Gannett Newspapers from 1981 to 1989 and *Noticias del Mundo* by a branch of the Unification Church.

Nicolas Kanellos, with Helvetia Martell, *Hispanic Periodicals in the United States, Origins to 1960: A Brief and Comprehensive Bibliography* (Houston, Tex.: Arte Publico Press, 2000); Virginia Sánchez Korrol, *From Colonia to Community: The History of Puerto Ricans in New York City* (Berkeley: University of California Press, 2004)

Michael Lapp, Virginia Sánchez Korrol

sparrows. See House Sparrow.

Spartan Association. Political gang in the Bowery. It was organized in 1840 by the radical Democrat Mike Walsh and was the first gang to become active in local politics. The gang joined with the insurgent "shirtless" Democrats who banded together after a depression and the collapse of the Workingmen's Party and used violent tactics to wrest power from the party's leadership. Its exploits included taking over the nominating conventions of Tammany Hall and invading Whig campaign headquarters.

Michael Walsh, *Sketches of the Speeches and Writings of Michael Walsh, including His Poems and Correspondence* (New York: T. McSpedon, 1843)

Joshua Brown

Spartan Braves and Spartan Hornets. African American amateur basketball teams formed by Robert L. Douglass in Harlem in 1919. The teams competed locally until 1923 and were the predecessors of the HARLEM RENAISSANCE.

speech. The speech of New York City is regarded as distinctive by both phoneticians and nonspecialists. The first trained phonetician to study it was E. H. Babbitt (1896), who taught at Columbia University. C. K. Thomas, who taught at Cornell, and Allen F. Hubbell (1950), a lifelong resident of the city, relied on speech samples elicited in controlled circumstances. For his pivotal 1966 study William Labov asked questions of sales clerks in department stores. A number of conclusions may be drawn from the work of these linguists. First, although in the nineteenth century the accent characteristic of New York City was called a "Bowery accent" and in the twentieth it became associated with Brooklyn, in fact it arises from social class and not from a neighborhood, even though the two are closely allied. Most New Yorkers show some trace of the local accent, except for those isolated by their wealth and social status from the rest of the city. Second, some New York City elements have been discerned elsewhere. A. J. Liebling remarked on similarities with the common speech of New Orleans; the word *spoil* has been transcribed as *spile* in several other American regions, and it is not known to what extent the speech of New York City before the advent of phonetic transcription and sound recording was heard to differ from the speech of other parts of the country. Third, linguists regard as unprovable and unlikely the common surmise that the speech of New York City is an amalgam of elements from several foreign accents (for example that the devoicing of dentals may be traced to Irish, the slurring together of words to Italian, and the so-called hard [g] to Yiddish).

Like many distinctive local accents the speech of New York City has low prestige in the estimation of those who hear it and those who speak it, and providing speech therapy to New Yorkers to eliminate their local accent has long been a profitable line of work. By the early twenty-first century the speech traditionally associated with New York City was infrequently heard, not because it was being assimilated to a general American accent or because of speech therapists, but because it was evolving into a new but still distinctive form.

Allen F. Hubbell, *The Pronunciation of English in New York City: Consonants and Vowels* (New York: King's Crown, 1950); William Labov, *The Social Stratification of English in New York City* (Washington, D.C.: Center for Applied Linguistics, 1966)

George A. Thompson, Jr.

Spellman, Francis (Joseph) (*b* Whitman, Mass., 4 May 1889; *d* New York City, 2 Dec 1967). Cardinal. A graduate of Fordham College and of the North American College in Rome, he was ordained a priest of the Archdiocese of Boston on 14 May 1916 and became auxiliary bishop of Boston in 1932. On 15 April 1939 he was appointed the sixth archbishop of New York by the newly elected Pope Pius XII, a close friend. During his 28 years as archbishop, Spellman showed himself to be a skillful administrator. He modernized and centralized the structure of the archdiocese, refinanced its debt, formed 45 new parishes, created a system of diocesan high schools, and spent almost $600 million on expanding Catholic educational and charitable facilities. He was made a cardinal on 18 February 1946.

Spellman played a significant role on both the national and international scenes. In October 1939 he was instrumental in persuading President Franklin D. Roosevelt to appoint a "personal representative" to the Vatican. As the Catholic vicar for the armed forces during World War II he became the best-known Catholic prelate in the country and was recognized as a symbol of Catholic patriotism. His visits to the troops overseas attracted much media attention, especially a mystery-shrouded trip to Rome through neutral Spain in 1943. In 1949 he confronted Eleanor Roosevelt over her opposition to federal aid for parochial schools and accused her of anti-Catholic bigotry. He cultivated strong ties to the Jewish community and supported the establishment of the state of Israel. In 1945 he inaugurated the annual Alfred E. Smith Dinner (a major event in the political calendar of the city) and maintained a close relationship with its chairman, the Jewish philanthropist Charles H. Silver. He created the Spanish Apostolate to provide Puerto Ricans and others with Spanish-speaking priests.

Spellman was, however, also a controversial figure. During the cold war he was an outspoken critic of communism. In 1949 he blamed a strike at Calvary Cemetery on communists and employed seminarians as gravediggers to break the strike, an action that appalled many trade unionists. His presence at an address by Senator Joseph R. McCarthy in New York City on 4 April 1953 was widely interpreted as a gesture of support. On the other hand he sheltered progressive biblical scholars in his seminary from reactionary theological critics. He was responsible for the presence at the Second Vatican Council of Father John Courtney Murray, S.J., who was a principal architect of the *Declaration on Religious Freedom* and *Nostra Aetate,* the decree regarding Judaism and other non-Christian religions. Both documents received Spellman's strong support. In his last years Spellman was often an uncritical proponent of American intervention in Vietnam, equating it with World War II. A conservative churchman, he represented a synthesis of Catholic orthodoxy and American patriotism that had eluded liberal American Catholic leaders in the late nineteenth century.

Robert I. Gannon, *The Cardinal Spellman Story* (Garden City, N.Y.: Doubleday, 1962); John Cooney, *The American Pope: The Life and Times of Francis Cardinal Spellman* (New York: Times Books, 1984); Gerald P. Fogarty, S.J., "Francis J. Spellman: American and Catholic," *Patterns of Episcopal Leadership,* ed. Gerald P. Fogarty, S.J. (New York: Macmillan, 1988)

Thomas. J. Shelley

Spence–Chapin Adoption Agency. An agency formed in 1943 by the merger of the Spence and Chapin nurseries for children. The Spence nursery was formed in 1895 by Clara Spence as an organization for crippled and tubercular children, and by 1915 it had evolved into an adoption agency called the Spence Alumnae Society; the Chapin nursery began in 1910 when Alice Chapin and her husband, a pediatrician, first took in abandoned infants. Spence–Chapin was an innovator in using the techniques of social work in the adoption process. It began placing children from racial minority groups in 1946, an effort that led to the formation of the Harlem–Dowling Children's Service in 1969.

Stephen Weinstein

Spencer Estate. Neighborhood in the eastern Bronx. The land once belonged to an estate of 129 acres (52 hectares) owned by Robert Morris, who sold it in 1856 to William Spencer. The original estate extended over parts of what are now Country Club and Pelham Bay Park. Palmer Cove, a small inlet nearby in Eastchester Bay, is widely described in records dating from the American Revolution as a point of reference, a boundary marker, and a place for mooring boats.

John McNamara, *McNamara's Old Bronx* (New York: Bronx County Historical Society, 1989)

Gary D. Hermalyn

Spence School. All-girls' independent school. Clara B. Spence, one of whose many sponsors was the Carnegie family, opened

Miss Spence's School for Girls in 1892 on West 48th Street for 10 young women. For 31 years Spence developed an all-encompassing and progressive curriculum for girls, which included studies ranging from politics to the arts and emphasized the importance of charity and etiquette. In 1932 the school merged with the Chandor School. In the twenty-first century the Spence School enrolls approximately 680 students at its two campuses: grades 5 through 12 are located at 22 East 91st Street on Manhattan's Upper East Side (opened 1929), and kindergarten through grade 4 are at 56 East 93rd Street (opened 2003).

Richard Schwartz, Cecilia Magnusson

Sperry, Elmer (Ambrose) (*b* Cortland, N.Y., 12 Oct 1860; *d* Brooklyn, 16 June 1930). Inventor and manufacturer of modern navigation technology. At the age of 20 he formed the Sperry Electrical Illuminating and Power Company in Chicago, and while living in Brooklyn he formed Sperry Products (precursor of modern-day organizations such as Sperry Rand and Sperry Univac). He was responsible for a number of gyroscope-based inventions used in aviation and marine navigation, including the Gyrocompass, the Gyrostabilizer, and the Gyro Automatic Pilot. His instrument for finding defective rails improved safety on the New York Central Railroad between New York City and Chicago. Sperry bequeathed $1 million to local branches in Brooklyn and Queens of the Young Men's Christian Association, which sponsored a visit that he made as a teenager to the 1876 Philadelphia Exposition and which determined the direction of his career. He is buried in Green-Wood Cemetery in Brooklyn.

Thomas Parke Hughes, *Elmer Sperry: Inventor and Engineer* (Baltimore, Md.: Johns Hopkins University Press, 1971)

Val Ginter

Spingarn, Joel E(lias) (*b* New York City, 17 May 1875; *d* New York City, 26 July 1939). Literary critic and civil rights activist. Born to Viennese and English immigrant parents, he was one of four sons raised in New York City where his father, who had built a successful wholesale tobacco business, was a senior member of the New York State Chamber of Commerce. Spingarn attended the Collegiate Institute of New York City and City College before earning a BA in literature from Columbia University in 1895, where, after a year at Harvard University, he also earned his doctorate in 1899; he was the youngest in his class at age 24. That same year, Spingarn accepted a position as a professor of comparative literature at Columbia that lasted until 1911. He was dismissed that year by the university after drafting a resolution of support for long-time professor Harry Thurston Peck, who had been released by the university in a breach-of-promise suit. The controversy at Columbia marked the end of his engagement in the academic field. A few years later Spingarn was elected as a member on the Executive Committee for the recently formed National Association for the Advancement of Colored People (NAACP). He became the group's second president and served as chairman of its board until his death. In 1914 he established the Spingarn Medal to be awarded annually to an African American of outstanding achievement; some notable winners include W. E. B. Du Bois, Ernest Just, George Washington Carver, Paul Robeson, Jackie Robinson, Martin Luther King, Jr., Langston Hughes, Rosa Parks, Jesse Jackson, Maya Angelou, and Oprah Winfrey. His brother Arthur Spingarn also served as legal counsel for the NAACP and was its president until 1966.

Garrett Felber

Spirit of the Times. Weekly newspaper founded by William T. Porter in New York City on 10 December 1831. It was the first comprehensive sporting journal in the United States and helped to mark the city as a national center for sport. The newspaper soon merged with the *Traveller* but was reestablished independently in 1835. Financial troubles compelled Porter to relinquish ownership in 1842; he remained the editor until 1856. In its first years of publication the newspaper reprinted many articles from British periodicals but increasingly published contributions of sporting news, essays, and fiction from American writers. It focused on horse racing and also covered swimming, rowing, baseball, boxing, cricket, field sports, foot racing, and winter sports. In his editorials Porter wrote tirelessly of the value of recreation and exercise for men, women, and children. With George Wilkes in 1856 he launched *Porter's Spirit of the Times;* after Porter's death in 1858 Wilkes parted with the new editors and founded *Wilkes' Spirit of the Times* on 10 September 1859. *Porter's Spirit of the Times* lasted until late 1859, the *Spirit of the Times* until 1861, and *Wilkes' Spirit of the Times* until 1902.

Francis Brinley, *Life of William T. Porter* (New York: D. Appleton, 1860); Frank Luther Mott, *A History of American Magazines,* vol. 1, *1741–1850* (New York: D. Appleton, 1930), 480–81; Frank Luther Mott, *A History of American Magazines,* vol. 2, *1850–1865* (Cambridge, Mass.: Harvard University Press, 1938), 204

George B. Kirsch

Spitzer, Eliot Laurence (*b* New York City, 10 June 1959). Lawyer and politician. Born and raised in the Riverdale section of the Bronx, he attended the Horace Mann School and graduated from Harvard Law School in 1984. Spitzer joined the Manhattan district attorney's office in 1986 and became chief of the labor racketeering unit, where he investigated organized crime. A Democrat, in 1998 he was elected state attorney general in New York and served for eight years, aggressively investigating Wall Street; in 2004 he sued New York Stock Exchange chairman Richard Grasso over Grasso's $190 million compensation package. Spitzer successfully ran for governor in 2006; in March 2008 he was implicated as a client of a prostitution ring and resigned his office. Spitzer lived at 985 Fifth Avenue, in a building owned by his father, real estate developer Bernard Spitzer.

Kate Lauber

Spofford Juvenile Center. Secure youth detention facility in the Bronx, at 1221 Spofford Avenue in Hunts Point. Designed by the firm of Kahn and Jacobs, it opened in 1957 as the Bronx Youth House for Boys. In its early years the center suffered from such severe problems as drug dealing on the premises, sex offenses, suicides, and assaults, but the situation improved after 1979 when the newly created Department of Juvenile Justice instituted better case management, the provision of social services after release, improved medical programs, and extended school days. Spofford, however, continued to deteriorate physically and was vacated in 1998 while detainees were divided among the Horizon Juvenile Center in Mott Haven (Bronx), the Crossroads Juvenile Center in Brownsville (Brooklyn), and the Vernon C. Bain prison barge, which was temporarily leased from the Department of Correction. The Spofford building was reopened in 1999 as the Bridges Juvenile Center, an intake and admissions facility for boys and girls.

Mishi Faruqee, *Rethinking Juvenile Detention in New York City* (New York: Correctional Association Juvenile Justice Project, 2002); Malikah J. Kelly, *10 Reasons New York City Should Close the Spofford Youth Jail* (New York: Correctional Association Juvenile Justice Project, 2004)

Val Ginter

sport fishing. The Hudson River estuary and the ocean waters off Sandy Hook became known as superb fishing grounds during colonial times. The largest fish ever taken in the waters of Manhattan with rod and reel was a drum weighing more than 70 pounds (31.7 kilograms) pulled from the Harlem River in 1844 near Macomb's Dam; anglers in rowboats took striped bass weighing up to 50 pounds (23.7 kilograms) from the shoals and tide rips of Hell Gate. The waters off Liberty Island and Robbins Reef provided bluefish, striped bass, weakfish, and blackfish (tautog). Weakfish were plentiful in the Narrows and Gravesend Bay; the Kill van Kull and the Arthur Kill were also prime fishing grounds for striped bass and weakfish.

Children, the old, and the poor fished off the docks of Manhattan for porgies, flounder, and small striped bass. Only the hardy fished for sharks measuring up to 14 feet (4.2 meters) that frequented the waters of Manhattan until the late 1890s. The development of steam-powered vessels brought easy access to the rich Atlantic fishing grounds between Long Island and New Jersey, and the ocean-fishing steamboat excursion, introduced in 1819, quickly became popular as an inexpensive family outing.

Water pollution caused by industrialization during the nineteenth century diminished the aesthetic pleasure of angling and contributed to a decline in the number and variety of fish in the waters off Manhattan. Small ports along the cleaner waters of Sheepshead Bay, Canarsie, Great Kills, and towns in New Jersey around Sandy Hook eventually attracted most of the city's anglers. These areas gained a decisive advantage with the advent of powerboats, which were cheaper to operate, required smaller docking facilities, and were capable of traveling to local bays, inlets, and even ocean grounds. By the 1920s powerboats dominated charter-boat and party-boat operations in the metropolitan area. After World War II such services declined as a growing number of anglers bought their own boats. Fishing around Manhattan improved somewhat after mid-century, owing partly to major efforts at reducing industrial and sewage pollution. In the early twenty-first century fine catches of striped bass could be made in the East River near the United Nations, and schools of feeding bluefish occasionally drew charter boats and party boats into the harbor; freshwater lakes and rivers in the outer boroughs also attracted anglers.

William Zeisel

sports. Sports in New York City are as dynamic, cosmopolitan, and ever changing as their surroundings. They have helped to shape the economy of the city, its social arrangements, its architecture, and even its politics.

1. Colonial Period and Early Nineteenth Century

The Dutch settlers of New Amsterdam indulged their love of physical activity by pursuing a variety of outdoor amusements, including tavern sports, ICE SKATING, and LAWN BOWLING, which from the seventeenth century was played on Bowling Green at the foot of Broadway. The English introduced new sports to the city; the most important was HORSE RACING, which began in 1665 when the first English governor, Richard Nicolls, offered a silver cup for a race to be held each spring and autumn. The growth of sport in the eighteenth century was stimulated by the cosmopolitan nature of the city and the emergence of a wealthy aristocracy. During the American Revolution and its aftermath sporting activities declined, largely because of their association with the colonial aristocracy, gambling, and violations of the Sabbath. A low point for sport was reached in 1802, when thoroughbred horse racing was banned in New York State; harness races were nevertheless held on Third Avenue from the early nineteenth century. The return of legalized thoroughbred racing in 1820 marked the beginning of a period of renewed growth in sporting activity, one different from those that preceded it in that the complexity of urban life now made it difficult for New Yorkers to engage in sport informally and spontaneously; instead they relied on voluntary associations and entrepreneurs.

Thoroughbred racing was the first sport to benefit from this trend. In 1821 wealthy New Yorkers formed a jockey club and built the Union Course in Jamaica, and during the next quarter-century New York City and its environs became the national center of the sport. The growing popularity of harness racing led to the formation in 1825 of the New York Trotting Club and the building of a racecourse at Centerville on Long Island. One of the reasons for the emergence of harness racing as the leading spectator sport in antebellum New York City was the ability of those who controlled the sport to appeal to the growing middle class in the city, which the wealthy traditionalists who controlled thoroughbred racing were unable to do. There were also clubs for ROWING, CRICKET, racquet sports, gymnastics, SAILING, and shooting by 1850, and for 21 sports in all by 1870.

The first organized BASEBALL club in the city, the Knickerbockers, was formed in 1845. Other teams followed in the 1850s; there were a dozen in Manhattan and Brooklyn by 1855 and about 100 several years later. The explosion in the number of clubs led residents of Manhattan and Brooklyn in 1857 to form the National Association of Base Ball Players to clarify and codify the rules of the game. Although the association did not allow ballclubs to pay their players, the Brooklyn Excelsiors paid their star pitcher James Creighton as early as 1860 and other clubs soon followed. Baseball was now being described as the "national pastime" and in the 1860s became a competitive, commercialized, professional spectator sport. Entrepreneurs were quick to capitalize on the desire of the public to attend the contests of leading teams. In 1862 William Cammayer built the first enclosed baseball park, the Union Grounds, at Lee Avenue and Rutledge Street in Brooklyn, and his success led in 1864 to a similar venture, the Capitoline Grounds, at Halsey Street and Marcy, Putnam, and Nostrand avenues; the cost of admission, at first fixed at 10 cents, rose to 50 cents by 1870. By 1867 Brooklyn and New York City had three professional teams. Baseball remained popular as a participatory sport, but games between the best professional clubs attracted the attention of both spectators and the press.

2. Late Nineteenth Century and Early Twentieth: Sport, Politics, and Society

Interest in sports in New York City increased dramatically after the Civil War. New Yorkers became acquainted with TENNIS and formed organizations such as the NEW YORK ATHLETIC CLUB (1868) to promote sports with which they were already familiar. Athletic clubs made it easy for their members to practice a variety of sports, especially track and field.

College FOOTBALL enjoyed popularity in the city during the late nineteenth century, although games between local schools attracted less attention than those between schools from out of town that staged their games in the city to attract more fans. These included the annual Thanksgiving Day game between Yale and Princeton, which drew crowds of more than 30,000 in the 1890s, and that between Army and Notre Dame in the second decade of the twentieth century.

Baseball remained the most popular middle-class sport. At least one major league team was based in Manhattan or Brooklyn throughout the late nineteenth century, except for the years 1878–82. At the same time the dominant position of local teams eroded as the sport became popular throughout the country, and only a few teams from Greater New York won the championships of the National League and the American Association during the nineteenth century. After John McGraw became the manager of the New York Giants in 1902 the city regained its advantage, and in the next 88 years there was no period longer than five years during which at least one team from the city did not play in the World Series.

In the late nineteenth century a common thread linked baseball, thoroughbred racing, and BOXING, which became popular for the first time: politicians played an important role in all of them. Almost all the owners of baseball clubs in the city had connections with the Democratic Party and Tammany Hall. They were therefore able to secure preferential treatment from the city for their teams, to receive proprietary information on developments in mass transit, and to protect themselves against competitors. Boxing, a product of the boisterous masculine culture of the saloon and the political club, had an even stronger political element: it was the emergence of the professional politician before the Civil War that had enabled it to grow in the first place. John L. Sullivan, the last of the bareknuckle champions, fought several of his most memorable bouts in Manhattan and Brooklyn between 1881 and 1884, during which the local area became a center for boxing both with and without gloves. In the

1890s political bosses like John Y. McKane and Big Tim Sullivan sponsored fights and used their political influence to ensure that the police would cooperate at a time when boxing was subject to severe legal restraints. Politicians were also engaged in horse racing: some like Richard Croker of Tammany Hall raced thoroughbreds, others owned racetracks. The strange alliance between politicians and wealthy owners of racehorses was based on mutual interest. Both groups favored the legalization of on-track betting and bitterly opposed off-track betting, which they believed would lower attendance at the racetrack and tarnish the image of the sport.

The growth of sport in the nineteenth century was aided by the increasingly accepted view that athletics contributed to individual health, morality, and character. This position, first articulated before the Civil War by sportswriters and other journalists, was drawn on by the end of the century by reformers who infused it with the rhetoric of evolutionary theory and progressive education. The result was the formation of organized youth sport programs directed by adults, the most important of which was the Public School Athletic League (1903). Aided by prominent business, education, and sports leaders, the league provided sports programs for about 100,000 students annually. After 1900 an increasing number of working-class, ethnic, and black athletic clubs were formed in New York City. Most lacked financial resources and athletic facilities and consequently relied on public parks. Although many were short-lived and all had problems, there were reportedly 700 small athletic clubs in the city in 1914 that catered largely to underprivileged youths.

3. Between the World Wars: The Growth of Sport as a Business

The economic prosperity that followed World War I gave a renewed impetus to sport and especially to baseball. Attendance at baseball games was also helped by the legalization in 1919 of Sunday baseball, which for two decades local ballclubs had sought and Sabbatarians had successfully opposed. The legislation affected both the size and composition of baseball crowds: games played on Sunday regularly drew more than 20,000 spectators, which for the first time included large numbers of working-class fans. All three local teams prospered during the 1920s. The Brooklyn Dodgers were financially sound although for the most part their play was mediocre; the Giants remained the dominant team in the National League; and the New York Yankees began a period of remarkable success when they purchased the contract of Babe Ruth from the Boston Red Sox in 1920 for $125,000, one of several transactions by the Yankees and the Giants that illustrated how teams playing in the largest market in the country could strengthen their positions by buying players from poorer clubs. The presence of Ruth was soon felt at the gate, as the Yankees attracted nearly 1.3 million spectators in 1920, a new record and more than twice the attendance of the preceding year. Ruth's home runs and his appeal continued to draw fans, and from 1921 to 1930 the Yankees made more than $3 million in profit. Sunday baseball combined with the popularity of Ruth led to the construction of Yankee Stadium, which opened in 1923. The Yankees had been evicted in 1922 from the Polo Grounds, which they had shared since 1913 with the Giants, by the Giants' owner Charles Stoneham (1876–1936), who wanted to keep for himself the lucrative Sunday dates and feared that Ruth's presence would make his team a secondary attraction at its own park. The spacious new ballpark testified to the growth and prosperity of professional sport, and its steel and concrete were a symbol of permanence.

The interwar years were the high point for college football in New York City, which nonetheless failed to generate the enthusiasm or draw the crowds that it did elsewhere. New Yorkers also showed little interest in professional football until the formation in 1925 of the New York Giants by Tim Mara. The team was not an immediate financial success, but in December of its first season more than 70,000 spectators at the Polo Grounds saw the Giants play against Red Grange and the Chicago Bears. In the following year Grange and his agent, Charles Pyle, asked permission from Mara and the National Football League (NFL) to form another team in New York City; when the request was denied they formed the American Football League, which ceased operations after one year. Other attempts in the next 20 years to challenge the NFL were all based on the assumption that a successful franchise in New York City was a necessity, and each new league sought to put a team in Yankee Stadium that would be identified with the baseball Yankees. Although Mara resisted efforts by entrepreneurs to challenge his team in its own market, he did allow the NFL to establish teams in Brooklyn and Staten Island. These teams posed no threat to Mara, who dominated football in the city and by the 1930s had built a solid foundation for both the Giants and the sport in general.

The popularity of boxing rose dramatically in New York City about this time. The sport won a new respectability after having been used to train soldiers during World War I, and professional boxing, which had been made illegal in 1900, was legalized by the Walker Act in 1920. Although boxing remained centered in ethnic and working-class neighborhoods and clubs, it now attracted the interest of the middle and upper classes as well. Championship fights took place sometimes in large ballparks but more often in indoor arenas, such as St. Nicholas Garden and especially Madison Square Garden, which became profitable for the first time after it was leased in 1920 to Tex Rickard. An important venue for sport since the late nineteenth century, when it was the site of racewalking competitions and six-day bicycle races, Madison Square Garden now attracted a new clientele as Rickard presented fights with such popular boxers as Jack Dempsey. It was somewhat paradoxical that as boxing gained respectability and championship fights became as much social events as athletic events, the sport came increasingly under the control of organized crime. A particularly strong hold on the sport was exerted by Frankie Carbo, who for two decades from the mid-1930s used force and intimidation to determine who fought and at times even who won.

Another sport strongly identified with Madison Square Garden was basketball, a sport popular since the turn of the century with youth groups in immigrant neighborhoods. By the 1920s some of these groups had evolved into professional teams, although they remained based in their communities and had an ethnic focus. College basketball had a wider appeal, as was made clear in 1931 when a crowd filled Madison Square Garden for a program of three college games organized by local sportswriters at the behest of Mayor James J. Walker for the benefit of the city relief fund. In 1934 the sportswriter Ned Irish (1905–82) began promoting college games at Madison Square Garden in which local teams often faced powerful opponents from other parts of the country, and in 1938 a group of sportswriters organized the National Invitation Tournament (NIT). Madison Square Garden also became the home of the professional basketball team the New York Knickerbockers (formed 1946) and of two professional ice hockey teams, the New York Americans (1925–42) and the New York Rangers (formed 1926).

4. After World War II: Increased Mobility and the Spread of the Suburbs

The decade between 1947 and 1956 was a high point for baseball in New York City, during which local clubs won 16 pennants. The city was also the focus during the struggle for racial integration of the game: Jackie Robinson, signed by the Brooklyn Dodgers to a minor league contract in October 1945, in 1947 became the first African American player in the major leagues since 1884 and in the next 10 years was the most visible symbol of the success that the Dodgers enjoyed. In the following years the team remained in the forefront of racial integration and had the most black players. The Giants became integrated when they signed Monte Irvin and Hank Thompson in 1949, followed by Willie Mays in 1951; the Yankees drew criticism for not having an African American player until Elston Howard joined the team in 1955. Most residents of the city and especially of Brooklyn approved of integration and were proud of the role that their teams played in bringing it about.

Madison Square Garden in 1950 was a leading center for college basketball: games there drew more than 600,000 fans, and City College of New York won the championships of the NIT and the National Collegiate Athletic Association. There were nevertheless persistent rumors that college games were rigged, and in 1951 investigations by the district attorney of Manhattan, Frank Hogan, found them to be true. Thirty-two players from seven schools in Greater New York were arrested for "point shaving," or deliberately reducing the margin of victory in their games to accommodate bettors. The country found the fact that college sports could be corrupted to be shocking and distasteful, and the scandal fueled a climate of suspicion and mistrust that was only worsened by the onset of McCarthyism. New York City came under heavy criticism, which, owing to the ethnic background of some of the players connected with the scandal, was often expressed in anti-Semitic terms. When players from other parts of the country were eventually implicated, the image of a uniquely sinful New York City was belied, but by then the revelations had done irreversible damage: the powerful college basketball programs in the metropolitan area were destroyed, Madison Square Garden was no longer a financial force in the sport, and the NIT became a tournament of secondary importance.

The heyday of baseball in the city was abruptly brought to an end in 1958, when the president of the Dodgers, Walter O'Malley (1903–79), moved his team to Los Angeles after the City of New York refused his request to replace Ebbets Field with a new ballpark. With the encouragement of O'Malley the owner of the Giants, Horace Stoneham (1903–90), moved his team to San Francisco. The departure of the Dodgers and the Giants quickly disabused their fans of the idea that the owners of teams were civic-minded philanthropists more concerned about their cities than about their pocketbooks.

Professional football was at the same time gaining in popularity. The football Giants moved in 1956 from the Polo Grounds to Yankee Stadium and in the same year won the NFL championship for the first time in a decade. Football in general and the Giants in particular were the greatest beneficiaries of the departure from the city of two of its baseball teams; the Giants won a divisional title in each of the next two years (losing an exciting championship game to the Baltimore Colts in overtime in 1958), and their performance along with the colorful personalities of such players as Sam Huff and Frank Gifford made them popular among those who worked in advertising. This new affinity between a leading team and the advertising business was instrumental in strengthening the link between television and professional football. In 1960 a new organization called the American Football League established a franchise in New York City known first as the New York Titans and from 1963 as the New York Jets. The team played in the Polo Grounds until 1964, when it moved to Shea Stadium.

New Yorkers moved quickly to replace the baseball teams they had lost. There was some discussion of having an existing team move to New York City; a more serious effort was that of Branch Rickey and the lawyer William A. Shea in 1959 to form not only a new team but an entire new league. The owners of existing ballclubs were fearful that this venture, the Continental Baseball League, might offer serious competition and that the U.S. Congress might revoke an exemption from the antitrust laws that organized baseball had long enjoyed. To avert these possibilities they voted to expand their own leagues and to award a franchise to New York City beginning in 1962. The new team, the New York Mets, played for two years in the Polo Grounds before moving in 1964 to Shea Stadium in Flushing Meadow, where the city had proposed several years earlier to build a stadium for the Dodgers. The site had the advantages of being accessible both by subway and by automobile, which had become the mode of transportation fans most often used to get to sporting events. The Mets became popular in the 1960s despite their fabled ineptitude.

The formation of new leagues in various sports brought a number of new clubs to the metropolitan area. The New York Nets (basketball) and the New York Islanders (ice hockey) both chose to play not in the city but at Nassau County Coliseum in Uniondale, on Long Island. There were several reasons for this: it would have been difficult to find an existing venue in the city and economically unfeasible to build a new one; it was unlikely that the teams could have found enough fans in the city to be financially successful, given the entrenchment of the Rangers and of the Knickerbockers (who owing to their success in the late 1960s and early 1970s had become one of the most popular teams in the history of the city); the Nets and the Islanders were offered generous financial incentives to locate in Uniondale, much as teams in earlier years had been offered similar incentives by cities; and Nassau Coliseum was easily accessible to the well-off residents of the suburbs who had come to constitute the majority of spectators at indoor sporting events.

Although Long Island was a challenge to the city, a more formidable one was presented by New Jersey. In 1976 work was completed in East Rutherford, only 5 miles (8 kilometers) from midtown Manhattan, on the Meadowlands Complex, which eventually included a racetrack, a basketball arena, and a football stadium. In the same year the stadium was occupied by the Giants, after whom it was named. In 1984 the Jets also moved to the Meadowlands: their president, Leon Hess, had long been dissatisfied by having to share Shea Stadium with the Mets and was drawn by the larger seating capacity at Giants Stadium. Even after the Giants and the Jets left for New Jersey, most of their fans continued to perceive them as representing the city, and the name of the city remained a part of the team names. During the following decades the Meadowlands became an important venue for basketball (after the Nets moved there) and especially for horse racing, and the New York Cosmos of the North American Soccer League, a short-lived attempt at a professional soccer league, played their home games at Giants Stadium between 1977 and 1984 (see Soccer).

Several important athletic facilities were built in New York City during the 1960s and 1970s. A new Madison Square Garden opened in 1968 atop Pennsylvania Station. The National Tennis Center, near Shea Stadium, replaced the Forest Hills Tennis Stadium in 1978 as the site of the US Open Tennis Championship, better known as the US Open, which had been held in Forest Hills since 1915. In the early 1970s the City of New York agreed to refurbish Yankee Stadium, which was deteriorating. The cost of the renovation was originally estimated at $24 million but in the end rose to more than $100 million; this was a financial disaster at a time when the city could ill afford one, and it was compounded by an unfavorable lease negotiated in 1973 with the owner of the Yankees, George Steinbrenner, according to which the team paid only a small portion of its large revenue to the city as rent.

5. Participatory Sports

Public parks, playgrounds, and gymnasiums have long made New York City a center of participatory sports, although the demand for athletic facilities has continually exceeded the supply. It was in the playgrounds of the city that a number of leading basketball players learned to play, and the sport became influenced in its evolution by the "city game," a leaping, athletic style of play favored by African American youths in the 1950s and 1960s.

Running became widely popular in the city in the 1970s and 1980s. The New York City Marathon, first staged in Central Park in 1970 with 127 entrants, by 2008 had nearly

40,000, as well as prize money for the leading finishers, corporate sponsorship, and a television contract. The major impetus underlying the growth of the marathon was the decision in 1976 to have its route run through all five boroughs; this made it the only sporting event linking the entire city and brought it enormous popularity. The best-known participant during the first two decades of the marathon was the Norwegian runner Grete Waitz, who between 1978 and 1988 won the women's division of the race nine times.

New York City is the site of the main offices of Major League Baseball (as well as the offices of both its leagues), the National Football League, the National Basketball Association, and the National Hockey League.

David Quentin Voigt, *American Baseball,* vol. 3 (University Park: Pennsylvania State University Press, 1983); Melvin L. Adelman, *A Sporting Time: New York City and the Rise of Modern Athletics, 1820–1870* (Urbana: University of Illinois Press, 1986); Neil J. Sullivan, *The Dodgers Move West* (New York: Oxford University Press, 1987); Steven A. Riess, *City Games: The Evolution of American Urban Society and the Rise of Sports* (Urbana: University of Illinois Press, 1989)

See also Bicycling, Curling, Fencing, Fox hunting, Sport fishing, Stickball, Surfing, and Swimming.

Melvin L. Adelman

Sports Illustrated. Weekly magazine launched in 1954 by Henry R. Luce. At the outset it was directed at an affluent, adult, mostly white male readership and featured stories on hunting, sailing, skiing, skin diving, and swimming. Over the years its coverage expanded to include team sports and its readership became more diverse. Circulation increased between 1954 and 1990 from 450,000 to 3.8 million, and the regular cover price increased from 25 cents to $2.69. *Sports Illustrated* has consistently crusaded to clean up abuses in sports: it attacked the role of organized crime in boxing during the 1950s and gambling and the use of steroids during the 1980s. In 1989 the magazine launched an offshoot called *Sports Illustrated for Kids.* The annual swimsuit issue, first published in 1964, became the most popular issue. In 2009 the magazine was owned by Time Warner and was read by more than 23 million people every week.

William Jaspersohn, *Behind the Scenes at Sports Illustrated* (Boston: Little, Brown, 1983)

Benjamin Yakas, Randy Roberts

sportswriting. New York City became the hub of sportswriting early in the nineteenth century. Journalists in the city both capitalized on the growing popularity of sports and helped to accelerate and stimulate it. Such weekly and monthly journals as the *Spirit of the Times, Porter's Spirit of the Times, Wilkes' Spirit of the Times,* and the *New York Clipper* were instrumental in promoting horse racing, prizefighting, and baseball in the city. Other publications important to the growth of commercialized sports were the *New York Sporting Magazine,* the *United States Sporting Magazine,* the *National Police Gazette,* and such newspapers as the *New York Herald,* the *Brooklyn Eagle,* the *New York American,* the *New York Post,* and the *New York Times.* A daily newspaper launched in 1839 as the *Sunday Morning Visitor* and later that year renamed the *Sunday Morning Weekly* covered horse racing extensively; in 1897 it became the *Morning Telegraph.* Richard Kyle Fox of the *National Police Gazette* and James Gordon Bennett, Jr., of the *Herald* used sports coverage to increase circulation, and their success led other daily newspapers in New York City to follow.

By the 1880s and 1890s most daily newspapers in New York City assigned a reporter exclusively to sports and set aside a page for sports coverage. The space allotted more than doubled between 1890 and 1920, and the sports page grew into a sports section. Journalists such as Grantland Rice, Paul Gallico, Ring Lardner, Damon Runyon, Westbrook Pegler, Heywood Hale Broun, Arch Ward, and Frank Graham generated interest in sports by promoting their virtues. In the 1920s the *New York Times* carried news about the World Series and major prizefights on its front page, and Captain Joseph Medill Patterson, a publisher of the *Chicago Tribune* and later the publisher of the *Daily News,* began a national amateur boxing tournament known as the Golden Gloves. After World War II one of the best-known sportswriters in the city was Red Smith, who wrote for the *New York Herald Tribune* (1945–67) and the *New York Times* (1971–82). In 1954 the publisher Henry R. Luce launched *Sports Illustrated* in New York City as a weekly magazine that also emphasized participatory sports such as hunting, sailing, skiing, skin diving, and swimming. Longer essays appeared in the *New Yorker,* which published the work of A. J. Liebling (on boxing), Roger Angell (on baseball), Audax Minor (on horse racing), and Herbert Warren Wind (on golf). Sportswriting in New York City was affected by the rise of radio and television, which made fans less dependent on print as a source of information about sports. Newspapers and magazines shifted their focus to the events taking place off the field: contract negotiations, disputes between players and owners, labor conflicts, drug problems, and racial strife. Now with the growth of Internet sports coverage and blogs, up-to-the-minute information and updates are available with videos and instant alerts.

Melvin L. Adelman, *A Sporting Time: New York City and the Rise of Modern Athletics, 1820–1870* (Urbana: University of Illinois Press, 1986)

Randy Roberts

Sprague, Frank J(ulian) (*b* Milford, Conn., 25 July 1857; *d* New York City, 25 Oct 1934). Inventor and entrepreneur. He studied electrical engineering at the U.S. Naval Academy (1874–78), did electrical work at the Brooklyn Navy Yard, and settled in Manhattan in May 1883, where as an employee of Thomas Edison he studied the new concept of electric traction. He left the firm in the following year to form the Sprague Electric Railway and Motor Company, which produced a successful motor manufactured by the Edison Machine Works. In an effort to apply electric power to the city's elevated railroads, in 1885 he built a short elevated test track at 29th Street and continued his experiments on a larger scale using the branch of the Manhattan Elevated Railroad on 34th Street. Despite promising demonstrations, by the end of 1886 he was unable to convince the officials of the elevated lines (including Jay Gould of the Manhattan Elevated Railway) of the merits of electric traction. But in 1888 he developed a large-scale electrified streetcar system in Richmond, Virginia, the first of its kind in the country, and the advantages of his system for streetcars became obvious. By 1890 there were more than 100 electric street railways either in operation or under construction in the United States, and Sprague supplied the equipment to about half of them. His firm merged with Edison's in 1889 to form the Edison General Electric Company, for which he became a consulting engineer, but he came into conflict with Edison and resigned in 1890. After forming the Sprague Electric Elevator Company in the following year he developed efficient passenger elevators for the city's tall buildings. As early as 1890 he proposed a four-track underground electric railroad for the city, a plan that was rejected. He also continued his efforts to interest the directors of the elevated lines in electric traction, without success until his innovative multiple-unit system of train control was introduced in Chicago; this led to contracts to install his system on other elevated lines, including the Brooklyn Elevated Railway.

Sprague sold his elevator company to the firm of Otis Elevator in 1900 and the Sprague Electric Company to General Electric in 1902. Having taken an interest in automatic railroad signaling, he formed the Sprague Safety Control and Signal Corporation in 1906. He was instrumental in electrifying the city's steam railroad terminals and from 1903 to 1908 was a member of the commission responsible for electrifying Grand Central Terminal. A president of the New York Electrical Society, he continued to work as an engineer and entrepreneur until the end of his life.

Allen J. Share

Sprague, Joseph (*b* Leicester, Mass., 25 July 1783; *d* Brooklyn, 12 Dec 1854). Mayor of Brooklyn. He moved to Brooklyn in 1809 to market the textile-mill supplies that his family manufactured in Leicester, Massachusetts. In 1834 he was instrumental in obtaining a city charter for Brooklyn, and he later advocated the annexation of Williamsburgh and Bushwick. Elected mayor of Brooklyn in 1843 and 1844, he introduced municipal street cleaning.

Ellen Fletcher

Spring Creek. Neighborhood in east central Brooklyn, bounded to the north by Linden Boulevard, to the east by Fountain Avenue, to the south by the Belt Parkway, and to the west by Pennsylvania Avenue. It is sometimes said to extend into Canarsie and Howard Beach and to be part of East New York and New Lots. The area saw a period of growth in the 1950s when several large housing projects were built; the best-known, built in the 1970s, is now called Spring Creek Towers (or Starrett City). The neighborhood was given its name in 1973 by Sebastian Leone, borough president of Brooklyn, at the suggestion of several local organizations. In later years development was hampered by large amounts of garbage fill, pollution in the canals of Spring Creek and Jamaica Bay, noise from Kennedy Airport, and the proximity of a sewage treatment plant. In the 1980s a large number of Latin Americans and blacks from the Caribbean settled in Spring Creek and its environs, principally from the Dominican Republic, Jamaica, and Guyana. A small commercial area lies along Pennsylvania Avenue between Linden Boulevard and Flatlands Avenue. At 888 Fountain Avenue stands the Brooklyn Developmental Center, a residential facility for the developmentally delayed run by the Brooklyn Developmental Disabilities Office of the Office of Mental Retardation and Developmental Disabilities. The center is dominated by the Spring Creek Towers in the southeast corner, a public housing project in the northeast corner, and a large industrial park in the east.

Ellen Marie Snyder-Grenier

Spring Creek Towers. Housing development in east central Brooklyn formerly known as Starrett City (and often still referred to as such). Located on a 153-acre (60-hectare) site along Jamaica Bay, the development is bounded to the north by Vandalia and Flatlands avenues, to the east by Schenck Avenue, to the south by the Belt Parkway, and to the west by Louisiana Avenue; it is bisected by Pennsylvania Avenue. It is the largest federally funded housing project in the United States, composed of 46 apartment buildings containing 6000 apartments, and it has its own private police force, post office, and power plant. Construction began in 1972, although the project was first conceived in 1964 by the union group United Housing Foundation, which wanted to create affordable cooperatives. The development was built under the state's Mitchell–Lama limited-profit housing program and was designed by Herman J. Jessor and known as Twin Pines Village until the Starrett Corporation assumed control. When it opened in 1975, quotas were used to fill two-thirds of the apartments with whites; when the National Association for the Advancement of Colored People (NAACP) filed a class-action suit against Spring Creek, the management defended the necessity of quotas to maintain racial integration and prevent white flight. In 1988 the U.S. Supreme Court upheld the decisions of lower courts that the quotas were illegal, and Spring Creek abandoned the system. In the early twenty-first century about 10 percent of the residents were white. During a real estate boom in 2006 Clipper Equity made a $1.3 billion bid for the development, and many feared that its 14,000 residents would be priced out of their apartments by the new owner. City, state, and federal officials blocked the sale, and in 2008 Spring Creek's owners agreed to sell only to a buyer who would keep the development in the Mitchell–Lama program and retain other subsidies for 20 years; the new buyer would be able to build an additional 1000 apartments.

Kate Lauber

Springfield Gardens. Neighborhood in southeastern Queens, bounded to the north by St. Albans, to the east by Laurelton, to the south by John F. Kennedy International Airport, and to the west by Farmers Boulevard. The area was settled about 1660. Farms were built during the eighteenth century southward from what is now Montefiore Cemetery to Rockaway Boulevard by Dutch farmers from Brooklyn, among them the Higbies, the Hendricksons, and the Nostrands, and by British such as the Bedells and the Baylises. A gristmill opened as early as 1750 at the mouth of Springfield Pond and 147th Avenue and was operated successively by millers named Cornell, Abraham Higbie (1815 to about 1855), and D. H. Simonson (1855 to at least 1873). To the south were vast meadows extending to Jamaica Bay. During the American Revolution local farmers were required to provide firewood for the British army, but no troops were stationed there. The City of Brooklyn in 1854 built a conduit along what is now Sunrise Highway to obtain water from the brooks in the area and in Nassau County; this was extended to Springfield in 1858, and a brick pumping station was built in 1885 at the northern edge of the pond. The farm of John W. Decker was put up for sale in December 1910, and his sons formed the Decker Realty Company to develop Springfield Gardens North. Ornamental brick pillars and trellises were erected opposite the railroad station. Dozens of streets and hundreds of houses were built between 1920 and 1930, and the population rose from 3046 to 13,089. William Schabehorn, a builder from Brooklyn, erected more than 1000 one- and two-family houses. About 1932 the construction of the Springfield Boulevard sewer destroyed the pond and its feeder stream; the city filled in the pond during the 1930s for Springfield Park. Lack of funds curtailed efforts in 1985 to designate a historic district of eighteenth-century houses. During the 1980s Springfield Gardens and its environs attracted many immigrants from Caribbean nations, including Jamaica (accounting for almost half of all immigrants at the time), Haiti, and Guyana. In 2007 the population was 42,000, and several rezoning measures were adopted by the City Planning Commission to allow for single-family homes to be converted into or rebuilt as two-family homes. The neighborhood retains much of its original character, and families are known to live in their homes for many years and even for more than one generation. Baisley Pond Park is a favorite of locals, with 110 acres (44.5 hectares) of green space.

Spuyten Duyvil Creek. Narrow tidal channel about 1 mile (1.5 kilometers) long separating Manhattan Island from the Bronx and connecting the Harlem and Hudson Rivers. Before the arrival of the Dutch in the early seventeenth century the area was explored briefly in 1609 by Hendrik (Henry) Hudson and his ship *Halve Maen* (Half Moon). The region had been home to the Lenape Indians, who enjoyed plentiful fishing and hunting along the creek that they called *Shorakapok*. In 1669 Johannes Verveelen began ferry service across the creek at about the point where Broadway and West 231st Street now intersect. Four years later Frederick Philipse built the first bridge over the creek, which he named the Kings Bridge, at the present site of West 230th Street and Marble Hill Avenue, in the area that came to be called Kingsbridge. Another bridge, called the Farmer's Free Bridge because Verveelen's ferry charged a toll, was erected by farmer/landowner Jacob Dyckman in 1759. It was later destroyed by George Washington's retreating Continental Army during the American Revolution. Dyckman's house at Broadway and West 204th Street is a designated landmark and the only surviving eighteenth-century farmhouse in Manhattan.

The Dutch named the creek Spuyten Duyvil in 1647, and the meaning of this name has

New York City Squares in the Nineteenth Century

Name	Street Boundaries*	Current Use	Notes
Abingdon Square	8th Ave., 12th St.	Park	Existed before 1850
Bloomingdale Square	53rd–57th St., Eighth–Ninth Ave.	Nonexistent	Existed before 1850
Chatham (Kimlau) Square	Oliver St., Worth St., Broadway	Park	Existed before 1850
Cooper Square	Cooper Square, Seventh St.	Park	Existed before 1850
Duane Square	Hudson St., Duane St.	Park	Existed before 1850
Foley Square	Foley St., Duane St., Centre St.	Park	Existed before 1850
Gramercy Square	17th–22nd St., Park Ave. South, Second Ave.	Square	Existed before 1850; referred to as both park and square; private
Great/Delancey Square	Grand St., Broome St., Third St., Essex St.	Nonexistent	Existed before 1850
Greeley Square	32nd–33rd St., Broadway, Sixth Ave.	Park	Existed before 1850
Hamilton Square (i)	Winthrop St., Dow St., Eliza St., Margaret St.	Nonexistent	Existed before 1850
Hamilton Square (ii)	66th–69th St., Third–Fifth Ave.	Nonexistent	Existed before 1850
Hanover Square	Pearl St., Hanover St.	Nonexistent	Existed before 1850
Harlem Square	Sixth–Seventh Ave., 117th–121st St.	Nonexistent	Existed before 1850
Harry Howard Square	Canal St., Mulberry St., Baxter St.	Square	Existed before 1850
Herald Square	Broadway, 34th–36th St.	Park	Existed before 1850
Hudson Square	Hudson St., Laight St., Varick St., Beach St.	Nonexistent	Existed before 1850
Jackson Square	Eighth St., Greenwich Ave.	Park	Existed before 1850
Kilpatrick (Randolph) Square	St. Nicholas, Seventh Ave., 116th–117th St.	Square	
Lincoln Square	Broadway, 66th St.	Square	
Longacre (Times) Square	Broadway, Seventh Ave., 45th–47th St.	Square	

(continued)

been the subject of speculation and discussion ever since. A number of translations have been proposed of the seventeenth-century Dutch *spuitendei duyvil*, the most likely being "spouting devil," which probably referred to the strong spoutlike effect of the currents in the narrow waterway during storms. The once popular "to spite the devil" is no longer accepted (*spuyten* was erroneously thought to mean "to spite"). This interpretation was attributed to Walt Whitman, who in his famous *History of Old New York* recounts the story of a trumpeter who, against local inhabitants' admonitions, insisted on swimming across the rough waters during a violent thunderstorm "to spite the devil."

By the mid-nineteenth century it became clear that the creek, with its turbulent, rocky, and unpredictable waters, needed to be developed into a dependable navigable waterway. In 1876 the New York State Legislature asked the Army Corps of Engineers to begin construction of the Harlem River Shipping Canal, which was completed in 1895. As a result, the Marble Hill section was severed from Manhattan and became an island. In 1914 the creek bed was partially filled in and Marble Hill was then physically attached to the Bronx—a situation that caused confusion and annoyance to the people of Marble Hill, who found themselves unwilling residents of the Bronx. After years of prolonged protest, a compromise was reached when the "orphan" neighborhood was again declared legally part of the borough of Manhattan.

With the completion in 1923 of the Harlem River Ship Canal, the older sections of Spuyten Duyvil Creek were covered over and the western section excavated and straightened, providing a direct, safer, and more navigable waterway. The distance between the Hudson River and Long Island Sound was thus shortened by 14 miles (22.5 kilometers). Spanning the Harlem River Ship Canal near the Hudson River are the Henry Hudson Bridge and a swing bridge used by Amtrak mainly for its long-distance trains to and from Pennsylvania Station.

Gerard R. Wolfe

Spuyten Duyvil neighborhood. Neighborhood in the northwestern Bronx, bounded to the north by Riverdale, to the east by Kingsbridge, to the south by the Harlem River Ship Canal, and to the west by the Hudson River. It began to develop and grow in the second half of the nineteenth century after the completion of the New York and Hudson River Railroad (now the Hudson Division of the Metro-North Commuter Railroad). In the early twenty-first century commuter trains operated by Metro-North stopped regularly at the Spuyten Duyvil station, on the north side of the ship canal. Residential development continued in the 1920s and increased markedly in the 1950s through the 1980s with the construction of high-rise apartment buildings, many of which were converted into cooperatives and condominiums. Affluent families were drawn to the area by its scenic steeply sloped hills and views of the Hudson River and by the proximity to the upscale communities of Riverdale and Fieldston.

In the center of the Spuyten Duyvil neighborhood is Henry Hudson Park, where a 16-foot-tall (5-meter-tall) bronze statue of Henry Hudson (by Karl Gruppe) stands atop the 100-foot-tall (30-meter-tall) Doric-style Henry Hudson Memorial Column (by Walter Cook). The landmark monument was erected in 1912 by public subscription after the Hudson–Fulton Celebration of 1909; the statue, however, was not installed until 1938.

John McNamara, *History in Asphalt: The Origin of Bronx Street and Place Names* (New York: Bronx County Historical Society, 1978); John McNamara, *McNamara's Old Bronx* (New York: Bronx County Historical Society, 1989)

Gerard R. Wolfe

squares. Public spaces that serve as centers for commercial activities; they are important in the formation of civic identity and as places for popular political, commercial, and social expression. Unlike traditional European cities, New York City has numerous tiny squares but few large ones, a reflection of the commonly held belief in Manhattan that land was too valuable to be kept as open space, which was a frequently debated issue.

In the seventeenth century the city gained legal jurisdiction over all unowned land on Manhattan Island; some space was reserved as open, but most was sold to raise revenue. The 1811 Commissioners' Plan made some provision for preserving open land, providing for a market, reservoir, and parade ground but no additional public parks or

New York City Squares in the Nineteenth Century (*Continued*)

Name	Street Boundaries*	Current Use	Notes
Madison Square	Fifth Ave., Broadway, 23rd–26th St.	Park	Existed before 1850
Manhattan Observatory Square	Eighth–Ninth Ave., 77th–81st St.	Park	Existed before 1850
Mission Square	Park St., Worth St., Mission Pl.	Park	Existed before 1850
Mt. Morris (Marcus Garvey) Square	Fourth Ave., Sixth Ave., 120th–124th St.	Park	Existed before 1850
Reservoir Square (Bryant Park)	Sixth Ave., 40th–42nd St.	Park	Existed before 1850
St. George's (Franklin) Square	Pearl St., Cherry St., Frankfort St., Dover St.	Nonexistent	
Schuyler (Straus) Square	West End, Broadway, 106th St.	Park	Originally named Bloomingdale, changed to avoid confusion with the original defunct Bloomingdale Square
Sheridan Square	Barrow St., Grove St., Seventh Ave.	Square	
Sherman Square	Broadway, Amsterdam, 70th–71st St.	Park	Existed before 1850
Stuyvesant Square	15th–17th St., Rutherford Pl., Perlman Pl. (bisected by Second Ave.)	Park	Existed before 1850
Tompkins Square	Ave. A, Ave. B, Seventh–10th St.	Park	Existed before 1850
Union Square	14th–17th St., Broadway	Park	Existed before 1850
Verdi Square	Broadway, Amsterdam, 72nd–73rd St.	Park	Existed before 1850
Washington Square	Waverly Pl., Fourth St., MacDougal St., Wooster St.	Park	Existed before 1850

*Addresses in twenty-first century may differ.

Compiled by Lisa Keller

squares. It did leave five areas open with no special designation for future use: Bloomingdale Square, Hamilton Square, Manhattan Observatory (Place), Harlem Marsh, and Harlem Square, constituting more than 150 acres (60.7 hectares); by the end of the nineteenth century all had disappeared except for Manhattan Observatory, of which only a small portion remained in 2008. Decisions regarding public space usage were guided by the strong desire of city leaders to promote commercial development, keep real estate values high, and rely on the "large arms of the sea" surrounding Manhattan to provide fresh air.

By the 1830s rising population density, frequent epidemics, increasing prosperity, and the desire for a more beautiful city led officials to create additional open spaces for public enjoyment. In order to do this at a time of soaring real estate prices, officials used the practice of condemning land intended for public use, purchasing it, and then assessing local landholders for the costs of the purchase; they justified this by claiming that property values would increase with squares and parks nearby (which did not always occur). By 1850 there were 29 major squares in the city, of which none existed as squares in 2008: nine were eliminated, and the remainder became parks that were often reduced in size. In the second half of the nineteenth century civic and sanitary improvement groups lobbied intensely to create more open space, which resulted in the conversion of many squares into parks. Unlike traditional squares, parks are subject to specific regulations regarding what activities can occur in them. After 1870 jurisdiction for open spaces including squares was placed under the Department of Public Parks.

The city had few traditional squares in the twenty-first century, as most of the original ones became parks, were absorbed by street improvements, or were sold off for commercial purposes. There were many very small, fractionally sized squares, whose irregular or triangular shapes were a result of the conversion of small slivers of property left over from road widening or development. The commissioners of 1811 foresaw this, referring to them as the "children of necessity." In 2008 there were 89 areas designated by the Department of Parks and Recreation as squares, comprising approximately 20 acres (8 hectares): five in the Bronx, 33 in Queens, 21 in Brooklyn, 29 in Manhattan, and one in Staten Island.

Straus Square, 2009

New York City Squares in 2008, by Borough

Borough and Name	Acreage
Bronx	
Benjamin Gladstone	0.20
D'Onofrio	0.38
Hutton	0.10
McKinley	0.12
Monsignor Del Valle	0.42
Brooklyn	
Albee	0.01
Archie Ketchum	0.06
Arlington	0.01
Bartel–Pritchard	1.17
Beattie	0.01
Corporal Wiltshire	0.05
Cutinella	0.08
Father Giorgio	0.01
Fraser	0.67
Freedom	N/A
Gravesend	0.06
Harold Cohn Memorial	0.07
Heffernan	0.03
J. W. Person	0.06
Lady Moody	0.05
Lithuania	0.02
Macri	0.57
McDonald	0.06
Meucci	0.04
Sgt. Joyce Kilmer	N/A
Todd Memorial	0.04
Manhattan	
Abingdon	0.22
Alexander Hamilton/ Johnny Hartman	N/A
A. Philip Randolph	0.07
Dorrence Brook	0.04
Duarte	0.45
Father Demo	0.07
Father Duffy	0.08
Father Fagan	0.05
Finn	0.10
Foley	1.92, including park
General Worth	0.08
Greeley	0.14
Harry Howard*	N/A
Herald	0.04
Jackson	0.23
Kimlau (Chatham)	0.09
Lafayette	0.02
Lincoln*	N/A
Little Red	N/A
McCarthy	0.04
McKenna	0.24
Mitchel	0.77
Montefiore	0.34
Peretz	0.19
Roosevelt	0.04
St. James	0.04
Sheridan*	
Sherman	0.001
Stuyvesant	3.93
Times*	N/A
Verdi	0.05
Worth	0.08
Queens	
Albert E. Short	0.01
Alexander Grey	0.01
Athens	0.90
Capt. Malcolm Rafferty	0.10
Carl R. Sohncke	0.04
Catholic War Veterans	0.01
Charles J. Steinmann	0.20
Columbus	0.10
Corporal Ruoff	0.05
Chappeto	1.23
Daniel Carter Beard Memorial	0.66
David O'Connell	0.06
Dwyer	0.03
Elmer Studley	0.02
Father Reilly	0.03
Freedom	0.33
Hollis Veterans	0.02
Jabez E. Dunningham	0.01
Jewish War Veterans Memorial	N/A
Legion	0.05
Leonard	0.06
Lt. Clinton Whiting	0.05
Lithcult	0.07
Live Barclay	0.05
McKenna	0.01
Private Edward Gordon	0.80
Private Edward McKee	0.06
Private John Dwyer	0.03
Sgt. Colyer	0.10
Strippoli	0.06
Vincent Daniels	0.25
Veterans	0.10
Veterans Memorial	0.47
Staten Island	
Egbert	0.11

*Not listed by Parks Department but exists on maps.

Notes: N/A = Not Available. Square designations and sizes are according to the New York City Department of Parks and Recreation in 2008. Some properties are also referred to as triangles. A number of nineteenth-century squares that still exist are not listed because they were officially named parks.

Compiled by Lisa Keller

I. N. Phelps Stokes, *The Iconography of Manhattan Island 1498–1909* (1926; repr. New York: Arno Press, 1967)

Lisa Keller

squeegee men. Individuals who solicit money from drivers at red lights or stuck in traffic by cleaning windshields. They became synonymous with petty crime in New York City during the 1980s. In 1994 Mayor Rudolph Giuliani embarked on a major initiative to remove squeegee men from New York City's streets, arguing that their presence created an environment of disorder that allowed more serious crime to flourish. His campaign succeeded in removing most from the streets, although they reemerged in the early twenty-first century during the economic recession.

Anne Epstein

Squibb. Firm of pharmaceutical manufacturers. It was formed in 1858 in Brooklyn as E. R. Squibb and Company by Edward Robinson Squibb (1819–1900), a physician who advocated pure drug formulations and who developed at the Brooklyn Naval Hospital a process for making consistently pure ether. The firm specialized in anesthetics, including ether, chloroform, and cocaine. Taken over by Theodore Weicker and Lowell M. Palmer, it was incorporated in New York City in 1905; it established the Institute for Medical Research in 1938 in New Brunswick, New Jersey, and became a leader in pharmaceutical research. During World War II the firm helped to develop penicillin in a consortium led by the government. After being acquired in 1952 by the Olin, Mathiesin Chemical Corporation, it retained its name but moved its manufacturing operations from Brooklyn to New Jersey in 1956; it became independent in 1968 and then acquired Beech-Nut Life Savers. In 1989 Squibb merged with Bristol–Myers to form Bristol–Myers Squibb, with headquarters at 345 Park Avenue. In 2007 it had global sales of $17.9 billion and more than 43,000 employees.

Lawrence G. Blochman, *Doctor Squibb: The Life and Times of a Rugged Idealist* (New York: Simon and Schuster, 1958)

David J. S. King

Squier, Miriam. See Leslie, Miriam.

Sri Lankans. The first major wave of Sri Lankan immigrants to New York City was in the late 1960s. They settled on northern Staten Island, were mainly professionals (many were physicians), and belonged to Sri Lanka's Sinhala ethnic majority. On 2 October 1971 the Sri Lankan Association of New York had its inaugural meeting at 630 Third Avenue, where the Permanent Mission of Sri Lanka to the United Nations remained in the twenty-first century. In 1980 Staten Island was estimated to be home to about 450 Sri Lankans. In the mid-1980s Sri Lankan immigration patterns shifted to the Tamil peoples, a minority ethnicity, which caused tensions within the Sri Lankan immigrant community when the civil war ended in 2000. The early 1990s saw a wave of undocumented immigrants who found work at the sex shops around Times Square. Of the 488 Sri Lankans who migrated legally to New York City between 1990 and 1994, almost a quarter moved to Staten Island. In 2000 an estimated 3000 Sri Lankans lived in Staten Island. Their community was served by Sri Lankan restaurants, a Buddhist temple, and a cluster of grocery stores centered around Victory Boulevard in the Tompkinsville neighborhood. As an ethnic group, Sri Lankans have focused their efforts on cultural activities and community organizations. In 2009 New York City's Sri Lankan immigrant community was estimated at 5000 people.

Jessica Montesano

SROs [single-room occupancy hotels]. Cheap lodgings with communal bathrooms and sometimes kitchens that became prevalent in New York City after World War II. Along with "flophouses" they were an important form of housing for the poor, especially around the Bowery. A number of hotels were converted to SROs, among them the Endicott Hotel on Columbus Avenue between 81st and 82nd streets, which became the largest SRO in the city. Residents were usually single men, at first mostly transient workers, then pensioners. Eventually SROs became notorious for drug and alcohol abuse among their tenants, and several buildings were demolished because of code violations or were simply abandoned. During the late 1970s and 1980s a large number of SROs were converted to housing for the affluent (including the Endicott); of the 150,000 SRO units in the city, more than 30,000 were lost during 1975–81, and about 100,000 units were lost by 1990. Many of the residents were forced to live in the streets. Under pressure from the courts, the city in 1982 began to use SROs to house families; by 1987 more than 5300 families were housed in 60 hotels, often in deplorable conditions and at high cost. In 1985 the City Council imposed a moratorium on the conversion, alteration, and demolition of SROs, but the state court of appeals overturned the legislation in 1989.

Starting in the late twentieth century the New York City Department of Housing Preservation and Development implemented programs to improve significantly the quality of SROs. They offered financial incentives to not-for-profit organizations to rehabilitate the buildings or construct new ones; these had to meet new minimum standards for rooms and to provide handicapped accessibility. New units included studios with kitchenettes and private bathrooms. Old buildings were renovated and put under new management, which provided supportive services to assist tenants in various ways, such as finding employment. These building also had community spaces for recreation. Two SROs that were converted are the Kenmore (23rd Street) and the Holland (42nd Street).

Robert A. Slayton, Lisa Keller

stables. Stables were common in New York City as long as HORSES were the primary means of transport. In 1896 there were 4649 stables housing 73,746 horses, which were used to pull private carriages, horsecars, omnibuses, firefighting equipment, and delivery wagons. Wealthy families built private stables for their horses and carriages, usually close enough to their residences for convenient access yet far enough away to shield them from noise and odor; the less wealthy boarded their horses and equipment in large commercial stables. Stables were also maintained by riding schools and academies. The five schools in the city in 1887, all near Central Park, together boarded more than 900 saddle horses. At the time an estimated 300 saddle horses were kept in private stables. Large peddler stables for the horses and equipment of delivery and peddler services were also common throughout the city. Soon after the turn of the twentieth century horses gradually gave way to streetcars, automobiles, trucks, and buses. In 1917 the operation of horsecars ended. The disappearance of horses left behind many stable buildings; many were demolished, and some were converted into parking garages and factories. Rows of stables called *mews* were often converted into distinctive and highly sought-after residences, such as Washington Mews in Greenwich Village. The CLAREMONT RIDING ACADEMY in Manhattan closed in 2007 after being the oldest continuously operated stable in the city. By 2008 the remaining working stables included several in Hell's Kitchen for Central Park carriage horses and the police department mounted unit at Pier 76. A handful of riding facilities remained open to the public: Kensington Stables at Prospect Park in Brooklyn, Forest Equine Center at Forest Park in Queens, the Bronx Equestrian Center at Pelham Bay Park and the Riverdale Equestrian Center at Van Cortlandt Park in the Bronx, and the Seguine Equestrian Center in Staten Island.

John Duffy, *A History of Public Health in New York City,* vol. 2, *1866–1966* (New York: Russell Sage Foundation, 1974)

Craig D. Bida

Stadt Huys. Tavern at Pearl Street and Coenties Alley, converted into the first town hall of New Amsterdam in 1653. The building served as the town hall until 1699 and was eventually demolished. Its site was investigated in 1979 during the city's first large-scale archaeological excavation.

Nan A. Rothschild

stage design. Until the mid-nineteenth century stage designs generally consisted of stock scenery: painted flats and backdrops depicting generic interiors and exteriors were slid on and off the stage in parallel tracks. After the Civil War the emergence of New York City as the theatrical center of the country coincided with the emergence of studios engaged in building and painting scenery. The scene painter became a significant theater artist, especially with the introduction of gas lighting on the stage, which provided a brighter illumination that required more detailed and sophisticated scene painting. Most scenic artists remained obscure until Charles Witham (1842–1926), who created the decor for Edwin Booth's long-running production of *Hamlet* (1864) in the city, as well as for many other productions with Booth, Augustin Daly, Edward Harrigan, and Dion Boucicault. Booth opened his own theater in New York City in

Livery stables on Grand Street, ca *1865*

1868 with *Romeo and Juliet,* and critic William Winter rhapsodized over the "reality and nearness" of the "picturesque Italian streets, luxurious gardens, gay and bright interiors, and the solemn, cypress-shaded precincts of the tomb." Witham was also largely responsible for replacing the painted flats and backdrops with free-standing units and flown scenery and introducing the three-walled box set to depict interiors.

The new approaches to decor necessitated more cumbersome, long, and noisy scene changes, thus prompting innovations in stage technology. The most ambitious were associated with Steele MacKaye (1842–94). His Madison Square Theatre opened in 1880 and included an elevator stage—two stages on top of one another that could be moved up and down, thereby allowing a new scene to be set on the offstage unit while another scene was being played. The trend toward mechanized spectacle was epitomized by the 1899 Broadway production of *Ben Hur* which was complete with a chariot race utilizing real horses on treadmills.

By the turn of the twentieth century painted scenery had largely given way to three-dimensional settings with real props. The most noted exponent of this new approach to stage design, now called *photographic realism,* was the producer and director David Belasco, who became widely known for his attention to detail and fondness for reproducing real environments onstage, most famously for *The Governor's Lady* (1912), for which he purchased fixtures from a popular restaurant to fashion a faithful reproduction of its interior. Belasco was among the first to exploit the new medium of electric light to create realistic effects, as in a four-minute sequence in a production of *Madame Butterfly* (1905) that simulated a sunset and then a sunrise.

A combination of changing aesthetics and economic concerns in the years before World War I drove Belasco's realism from favor. Largely influenced by European designers and the theoreticians Adolph Appia and Edward Gordon Craig, a movement toward simplification and abstraction known as the "new stagecraft" overtook American design. Although the most spectacular forerunner of the trend was a 1912 production by the German director Max Reinhardt of *Sumurun,* the movement is generally dated to the production in 1915 of Anatole France's *The Man Who Married a Dumb Wife,* produced by the New York Stage Society at Wallack's Theater and designed by Robert Edmond Jones (1887–1954). The commercial legitimacy of the simplified, abstracted setting was established by Jones's subsequent work with the Provincetown Players and with the director Arthur Hopkins on a series of plays by Shakespeare on Broadway featuring the Barrymores. The new stagecraft was further developed by Lee Simonson (1888–1967) in productions of the Theatre Guild and in Broadway productions by Norman Bel Geddes (1893–1958), who was largely responsible for eliminating footlights and revamping lighting systems in several Broadway theaters. Still more changes, especially in the use of color, were wrought by the Austrian-born designer Joseph Urban (1872–1933), who began designing sets for Florenz Ziegfeld's *Follies* in 1915 and also designed for the Metropolitan Opera and Broadway. Modern dance played an important role in the development of stage design, and although dance and theater had different scenic and aesthetic needs, many designers worked in both media.

By the end of World War I the stage designer was established as an important artist. Local 829 of the United Scenic Artists joined the American Federation of Labor in 1918, and designers received prominent credit in theater programs. The next few decades saw a struggle between a popular demand for naturalism and the aesthetic pull of abstraction, symbolism, and constructivism. The naturalist school was exemplified by the tenement facade designed by Jo Mielziner (1901–76) for Elmer Rice's *Street Scene* (1929); Bel Geddes's design for Sidney Kingsley's *Dead End* (1935), complete with water in the orchestra pit representing the East River; and the re-creation by Howard Bay (1912–86) of a tenement on the Lower East Side that burst into flames in a production of Arthur Arent's *One Third of a Nation* (1936) by the Living Newspaper of the Federal Theatre Project. At the other extreme such plays as Clifford Odets's *Waiting for Lefty* (1935) and Thornton Wilder's *Our Town* (1938) virtually did away with scenery, using the bare stage and the theater itself as a set (an idea revived in 1975 in the design by Robin Wagner [*b* 1933] for *A Chorus Line*). The musical developed its modern form during the 1920s and 1930s, and lavish, innovative scenery became the norm. Revolving sets, elevators, rolling platforms, and masses of scenery became the trademark of such designers as Albert Johnson (1910–67) and Vincente Minnelli (1910–86). Many later developments in stage design were made possible by innovations in lighting during the 1930s, especially those of Jean Rosenthal (1912–69), who broadened the function of lighting design to encompass not merely illumination but also the subtle evocation of mood and even of rhythm and movement.

In the 1940s there emerged a distinctly American style generally known as poetic realism, most closely associated with the later designs of Mielziner and the plays of Tennessee Williams. Visually the style was characterized by fragmented settings and soft, dreamlike images often enhanced by the use of scrims. Arthur Miller's *Death of a Salesman* (1949) and Williams's *A Streetcar Named Desire* (1947), both designed by Mielziner, are classic examples of this style. Oliver Smith (1918–94) bridged the world of theater and dance while carrying poetic realism and fantasy into the musicals of the 1950s. His works included *Brigadoon* (1947) and *My Fair Lady* (1956), as well as several influential ballets, among them *Rodeo* and *Fall River Legend* (1948). The 1950s saw a move away from realism and toward structural and symbolic designs that emphasized theatricality; the stage regained a sense of being a stage rather than a re-creation of another place. Among the first stage designers to move in this direction was Rouben Ter-Arutunian (1920–92). Another was Isamu Noguchi (1904–88), who worked closely with the choreographer Martha Graham from 1935 and developed a sculptural style of stage design. These innovations culminated in the mid-1960s in the work of Ming Cho Lee (*b* 1930), whose designs for the New York Shakespeare Festival at the Delacorte Theater in Central Park and for the New York City Opera made scaffolding, emblematic scenery, textured materials, and collage the basic vocabulary of American design for the next two decades. At the same time Merce Cunningham and other modern and postmodern choreographers engaged visual artists as stage designers such as Robert Rauschenberg, Jasper Johns, and Andy Warhol. In the 1980s work by the artists David Hockney and David Salle and even the architect Frank Gehry appeared on the stages of the Brooklyn Academy of Music and the Metropolitan Opera House. On the other hand the choreographer Twyla Tharp tended to rely on designers who worked principally in the theater, notably Jennifer Tipton (*b* 1937), who shaped modern lighting practice, and Santo Loquasto (*b* 1944), whose costumes influenced fashion design.

Stage design was strongly influenced by avant-garde theater and in particular by theatrical minimalism. Environmental theater, characterized by stage settings that surround the audience, was made popular with the production in 1968 of *Dionysus in 69* by Richard Schechner's Performance Group in a converted garage in SoHo. This iconoclastic approach influenced Eugene Lee's design in 1974 for the Broadway production of *Candide.* The theater artist Richard Foreman developed idiosyncratic conceptual settings at his loft theater in SoHo in the 1970s as well as for Joseph Papp's revival in 1976 of *The Threepenny Opera* at the Vivian Beaumont Theater. At the same time Robert Wilson conceived grandiose settings for such works as Philip Glass's opera *Einstein on the Beach* (1976), which was staged at the Brooklyn Academy of Music and the Metropolitan Opera.

The 1980s saw a trend toward lavish productions with elaborate settings, as in *Cats* (1983) and *Phantom of the Opera* (1988), both British imports by Andrew Lloyd Webber, and *Miss Saigon* (1990), by Claude-Michel Schönberg and Alain Boublil. Tony Walton (*b* 1934) devised more elegant spectacles for such shows as *Grand Hotel* (1989) and *Guys and Dolls* (1992). The arrival of Disney Theatrical Productions on Broadway with *Beauty and the Beast* (1994) merged the style of Disney animation with Broadway spectacle. Disney's 1998 production of *The Lion King* injected the avant-garde aesthetics of director Julie Taymor—particularly an inventive use of puppets—into the visual spectacle. At the same time a postmodern approach to design emerged in opera and Off Broadway, particularly in the work of the designers John Conklin (*b* 1937), George Tsypin (*b* 1954), and Adrianne Lobel (*b* 1955) and also in that of James Clayburgh (*b* 1949) for the avant-garde Wooster Group. The new approach was typified by a multiplicity of incongruous, competing, and conflicting images that made for a historical and stylistic eclecticism. Postmodern designs such as Tsypin's for *Henry IV, Parts 1 and 2* (1992), directed by JoAnne Akalaitis at the Public Theater, made wide-ranging references to diverse periods of art and architecture, to other productions, and to themselves. Others, such as those of the Wooster Group, "deconstruct" the stage by merging onstage and offstage space, often by using video and sound to separate performer, voice, and image and by combining simple and technologically advanced elements and objects in an almost random and unfocused way within the performing space.

The Wooster Group's use of video and digital technology had a profound effect on newer experimental groups such as Elevator Repair Service, Collapsable Giraffe, and Radio Hole, which tend to incorporate such technology into their productions—frequently staged in converted industrial spaces—in almost mundane and offhand ways, reflecting the pervasive presence of technology in twenty-first century life. Meanwhile, digitally projected imagery and large-scale video imagery have become increasingly common on Broadway and in some Off-Broadway productions. Because such decor is projected or exhibited on flat screens behind the actors, it is surprisingly similar to Baroque scenery in its spatial relationships. But the imagery used seems closer to that found in computer games and digital animation. While most new technologies are developed for other media, they ultimately find their way into theater either as part of the scenic spectacle or as a means of controlling scenery, lights, and sound.

Barnard Hewitt, *Theatre U.S.A., 1668 to 1957* (New York, McGraw–Hill, 1959); Mary Clarke and Clement Crisp, *Design for Ballet* (New York: Hawthorn, 1978); Arnold Aronson, *American Set Design* (New York: Theater Communications Group, 1985); Orville K. Larson, *Scene Design in the American Theater from 1915 to 1960* (Fayetteville: University of Arkansas Press, 1989); Mary C. Henderson, *The City and the Theatre: The History of New York Playhouses* (New York: Back Stage Books, 2004)

Arnold Aronson

Stagg Town. Seventeenth-century name for an area also known as LITTLE AFRICA.

stair streets. Streets composed of steep staircases built in areas too hilly for cars. Also known as *step streets,* they are open only to pedestrians and were given names such as Bradley Terrace, 166th Stair Street, and Step Street. About 90 percent of the city's stair streets are in the Bronx, particularly in Riverdale, along the Grand Concourse ridge, and in Highbridge; West 230th Street is a stair street that stretches across several blocks from Irwin Avenue to Netherland Avenue. Stair streets were also built in upper Manhattan, Staten Island, and Bay Ridge and Highland Park in Brooklyn. Apartment buildings abutting these streets often have entrances from a landing to an upper story.

Gary D. Hermalyn

Stair street west of Broadway above 231st Street in the Bronx, early 1990s

stamp and coin dealers. Collectors and dealers of stamps and coins frequent New York City from around the world for its conventions, shops, and auctions. Gimbel's in Herald Square was known for its large stamp and coin department as early as the late 1940s. In the early twenty-first century the major purveyors of stamps were H. R. Harmer and Company and Robert Siegel; coin dealers included Harmer Rooke, Manfred Tardella and Brooks, and Stack's. Important organizations in the city include the Philatelic Foundation (70 West 40th Street) and the American Numismatic Society (96 Fulton Street), which maintains a museum and research library.

Rachel Shor

Standard and Poor's. Firm of financial publishers formed by the merger of Poor's Publishing Company and the Standard Statistics Company in 1941. It is commonly known as S&P. The origins of the firm may be traced to the publications of Henry Varnum Poor (1812–1905), who issued *History of Railroads and Canals of the United States* in 1860 and in 1867 formed a corporation to publish annually a "Manual of the Railroads and Canals of the United States." Poor's *History* was the most valuable financial source of its day and is considered the precursor of financial and investment publications in the United States. Standard Statistics Company was begun in 1913 as Standard Statistics Services by Luther Blake. In 1957 S&P introduced the S&P 500 stock price index, which became the most widely accepted barometer of the market. A subsidiary of McGraw–Hill from 1966, S&P rates bonds and commercial promissory notes and issues more than 50 financial publications. In 1975 the firm suspended ratings of New York City bonds in response to the reluctance of major underwriters to help the city sell or roll over its debts. By 2007 more than $4.8 trillion was benchmarked to the S&P 500. Its offices are located at 55 Water Street in lower Manhattan.

Hugh C. Sherwood, *How Corporate and Municipal Debt Is Rated: An Inside Look at Standard and Poor's Rating System* (New York: John Wiley and Sons, 1976)

James D. Norris

Standard Oil. Huge multinational trust dissolved by the U.S. Supreme Court in 1911. Incorporated in 1870 in Cleveland as the Standard Oil Company under John D. Rockefeller, it grew to control virtually every aspect of the industry. The activities of the trust, which in 1885 relocated to 26 Broadway in Manhattan (Ebenezer L. Roberts, architect), came increasingly under attack with the passage of the Sherman Antitrust Act (1890), Ida M. Tarbell's exposé in *McClure's Magazine* (1902–4), and the antitrust efforts of Presidents Theodore Roosevelt and William Howard Taft. In 1911 the U.S. Supreme Court ordered it broken into separate entities. The company remained headquartered at 26 Broadway, which was enlarged in 1895 (Kimball and Thompson), and again in 1920–28 (Carrère and Hastings; and Shreve, Lamb and Blake). Although Standard Oil no longer occupies the building, the main lobby still displays plaques bearing the names of the trust's principal officers.

Margaret Latimer

Stapleton. Neighborhood in northeastern Staten Island bounded to the north by Grant Street, to the east by Upper New York Bay, to the south by Vanderbilt Avenue, and to the west by St. Paul's Avenue and Van Duzer Street. It consisted at first of farmland; Cornelius Vanderbilt spent his youth on a farm facing the bay on a site now occupied by the Paramount Theatre on Bay Street. In its early years the area was the commercial center of Southfield Township (it became part of the incorporated village of Edgewater in 1866). The Seamen's Retreat, a hospital for sailors, was built in 1831 on a site of 40 acres (16 hectares). In the following year land was acquired from the Vanderbilts and streets were laid out by William J. Staples (1807–83), a merchant and entrepreneur from Manhattan after whom the neighborhood was named, and Minthorne Tompkins (1807–81), a son of Vice President Daniel D. Tompkins. The two established ferry service to Manhattan and advertised their newly created village in 1836. The availability of spring water led several German American breweries to establish themselves in the area in the nineteenth century: the Bachmann Brewery (1851) and the Bechtel Brewery (1853) merged in 1911 to form the Bachmann–Bechtel Brewing Company, which operated until 1920; the Rubsam and Horrmann Atlantic Brewery Company (1871) was bought by Piels in 1953 and closed in 1963. By 1884 Staten Island Rapid Transit extended its tracks along the waterfront from the foot of Vanderbilt Avenue to Tompkinsville Landing and to ferry facilities in St. George; direct passenger ferry service from Stapleton to Manhattan was discontinued in 1886. The Village Hall (1889) in Tappen Park was designed by Paul Kuhne (1850–1903), a resident of Stapleton. Seamen's Retreat became successively the U.S. Marine Hospital, the U.S. Public Health Service Hospital, and the Bayley Seton Hospital, the largest employer in the area. In 2007 the Salvation Army purchased the property and began developing it for residential and community recreational uses. The waterfront was filled in on the east side of Bay Street. Municipal piers built by New York City in the 1920s were never fully exploited: several were used as the first foreign trade zone in the United States (1937–42), as the New York Port of Embarkation by the U.S. Army and the U.S. Navy (1942–45), and again as a foreign trade zone after World War II, but by 1950 only two piers were in use, and in the 1970s these were demolished. Stapleton Houses, a housing project sponsored by New York State, opened in 1962, providing 693 subsidized apartments on land formerly belonging to the Seamen's Retreat. A new and controversial homeport for the U.S. Navy was constructed and opened in 1990; this closed in 1994.

Among the notable buildings in Stapleton are simple Greek Revival houses from the 1830s at 364 and 390 Van Duzer Street, 60 William Street, and 92 Harrison Street; several historic churches, including St. Paul's Episcopal (1870, designed by Edward Tuckerman Potter), First Presbyterian Church (1887, Josiah C. Cady), Immaculate Conception Church (1908), and Trinity Lutheran Church (1913, Upjohn and Conable); and the Staten Island Savings Bank (1925, Delano and Aldrich). In the 1980s Stapleton attracted immigrants from India, Liberia, China, Jamaica, and Trinidad and Tobago, and to a lesser extent the Philippines, Guyana, Korea, and Nigeria. The neighborhood in the early twenty-first century was a residential and commercial center inhabited by urban professionals and blue-collar workers, including blacks, Italians, Armenians, and Latin Americans.

Barnett Shepherd

Stapleton Heights. Neighborhood in northeastern Staten Island near the western boundary of Stapleton along St. Paul's Avenue. It is an area of large houses and lots, and many of the residents have views of the Narrows and the Verrazano–Narrows Bridge. Early efforts to restore the area were promoted by the Mud Lane Society (named after the street that later became St. Paul's Avenue). Notable buildings in the neighborhood include 368 St. Paul's Avenue (designed by Paul Kuhne, a resident of Stapleton, for Adolf Baudenhausen of the Rubsam and Horrmann Brewery) and 387 St. Paul's Avenue, an elaborate Queen Anne house (built for the daughter of George Bechtel, the owner of Bechtel Brewery).

Barnett Shepherd

Starin, John Henry (*b* Sammonsville, N.Y., 27 Aug 1825; *d* New York City, 21 March 1909). Congressman. He was involved in lighterage within the Port of New York and operated freight and passenger boats on the Hudson River and Long Island Sound and ferries to Staten Island and New Jersey. Starin was also active in the excursion trade, developing a number of picnic grounds and amusement areas to which residents of the city were transported by his fleet of steamboats and excursion barges. When his activities were at their peak in the late 1800s, he is believed to have had the largest fleet of boats under private ownership in the world. Starin, a Republican, served in the U.S. House of Representatives from 1877 to 1881. He was well-known for his generosity, organizing giant annual picnic excursions at his own expense for New York City's Civil War veterans and their families, police and firefighters, newsboys and bootblacks, and women and children of the Five Points Mission. In 1893 he agreed to serve on New York City's Transit Commission. When the construction of further elevated railroads above the avenues of Manhattan was put to a vote that required unanimity, Starin cast the only opposing vote, effectively killing the proposal and bringing about the shift to subway construction.

Norman J. Brouwer

Starrett City. See Spring Creek Towers.

Starrett Corporation. Firm of general contractors, incorporated in 1922 as Starrett Brothers and later renamed Starrett Brothers and Eken. One of the most successful firms of its kind in the city, it was directed by Paul Starrett (1866–1957) and William A. Starrett (1877–1932), two of five brothers working as builders, often in bitter competition. In the 1920s it erected many skyscrapers, including the Empire State Building, which was finished 45 days ahead of schedule and $5 million under budget. Starting in the 1930s the firm concentrated on such housing complexes as Parkchester in the Bronx (1938–42), Stuyvesant Town (1943), and Peter Cooper Village (1945–47). Andrew J. Eken (1882–1965), a partner, became president in 1938 and was chairman from 1955 to 1961. As developers the Starrett Corporation built Starrett City (1976, Herman J. Jessor), a community for 6000 families in eastern Brooklyn, now called Spring Creek Towers, and the Jacob K. Javits Center in Manhattan (1986). In 2008 the company owned and managed about 7000 apartments, both market rate and government assisted, in the metropolitan area.

Carol Willis

state attorney general. Elected office possessing broad powers to investigate and prosecute wrongdoing when local authorities cannot or will not act. The office has intervened in a wide range of cases in New York City. In 1894 it investigated charges of cruelty and neglect in the city's insane asylums; its report resulted in their takeover by the state. After prosecuting widespread election fraud in the city in 1899 it supervised elections there for decades and sought to remove Mayor George B. McClellan from office because of electoral fraud in 1905. Under the Donnelly Act (1899) the attorney general prosecuted illegal monopolies and trusts and in 1908 broke up the American Ice Company of New York. It gained sweeping powers of investigation and enforcement in the securities industry through the Martin Act, a "blue sky" law passed in 1921 that in the 1980s was extended to cover the conversion of apartments and lofts into condominiums and cooperatives. During the

1930s the attorney general prosecuted racketeering in construction and among laundries and dry cleaners. The office also gained broad authority to prosecute consumer fraud and regulate charities. After the Knapp Commission presented its report on police corruption to the mayor in 1972, a deputy attorney general was appointed to investigate and prosecute cases of corruption in the city's criminal justice system. In 1986 another special prosecutor investigated the fatal beating of several black men in HOWARD BEACH. When ELIOT SPITZER was elected attorney general in 1998, he redefined the office and expanded the definition of consumer fraud, serving two terms and gaining the nickname "the Sheriff of Wall Street" for his hawkish investigation and reform of the city's financial institutions.

James D. Folts

State Communities Aid Association. Private agency formed in New York City in 1872 by Louisa Lee Schuyler as the State Charities Aid Association to monitor and reform asylums, hospitals, almshouses, and other public welfare institutions. It recruited volunteers from the Women's Central Association of Relief and the U.S. Sanitary Commission. Under the leadership of Homer Folks, general secretary from 1893 to 1947, the association won reforms in housing, child and maternal welfare, foster care, juvenile justice, public health, and unemployment benefits. The association surveyed all state institutions, but it focused its efforts on New York City and maintained its headquarters there. It took its current name in 1967 and moved the office of its executive secretary to Albany, New York, in 1985.

Walter I. Trattner, *Homer Folks: Pioneer in Social Welfare* (New York: Cambridge University Press, 1968)

Sarah Henry Lederman

state courts. See COURTS, §2.

Staten Island. Borough at the juncture of Upper New York Bay and Lower New York Bay, it has long been the most geographically separate, economically homogeneous, and politically self-conscious of the city's five boroughs. It encompasses 60 square miles (155 square kilometers) and resembles an elongated diamond with a length of 13.9 miles (22 kilometers) between St. George and Tottenville and a width of 7.3 miles (12 kilometers) between Fort Wadsworth and Howland Hook. It is the third-largest borough in area but the least populous and least densely populated; in 2008 it contained only 6 percent of the population of New York City. Within its political boundaries are several smaller islands, uninhabited in the early twenty-first century: Prall's Island and the Island of Meadows, which are natural features; Hoffman Island and Swinburne Island, which are man-made; and Shooters Island, which lies partly in Staten Island and partly in New Jersey. Guarding the Atlantic gateway to the metropolitan region, Staten Island (Richmond County, formerly known as the Borough of Richmond) is the southernmost borough of New York City. It is the borough farthest removed from Manhattan, separated at its closest point by a 5-mile (8-kilometer) stretch of water, without direct tunnel, bridge, or subway linkage, traversed only by a world-famous passenger ferry (see STATEN ISLAND FERRY) that covers the distance in 25 minutes. Staten Island is connected to Brooklyn by the Verrazano–Narrows Bridge (1964), a suspension bridge with a main span of 4600 feet (1400 meters). The northern shore of Staten Island is separated from the Bayonne Peninsula by the Kill van Kull and the lower expanse of Newark Bay; the eastern shore borders the Upper New York Bay and the Narrows, a waterway 1 mile (1.6 kilometers) wide between Fort Wadsworth and Bay Ridge, the closest part of any other borough; the southern shore runs along Lower New York Bay and the edge of the Atlantic to the head of Raritan Bay; and the western shore runs parallel to the shoreline of New Jersey along the Arthur Kill (Staten Island Sound), at a distance often less than 500 feet (150 meters). Staten Island is connected to New Jersey by four bridges: to Elizabeth by the Goethals Bridge (1928) and an unnamed railroad lift bridge (1959), to Perth Amboy by the Outerbridge Crossing (1928), and to Bayonne by the Bayonne Bridge (1931), which crosses the Kill van Kull from Port Richmond. A ridge of seven rocky hills extending from the ferry landing at St. George diagonally to the center of the island at Richmondtown afforded sites for estates and institutions from the 1830s. Todt Hill, at 409 feet (125 meters), is the highest natural point on the eastern seaboard south of Maine. The marshy western shore of the island is bisected by the broad tidal entrance of the Fresh Kills, which drains the borough's northeastern hills and central Greenbelt, and in 1948 became the setting for the city's principal garbage dump, which from the 1980s until it closed in 2001 was the world's largest sanitary landfill. The borough has long been linked culturally and economically with the northern coast of New Jersey, particularly the industrial centers of Elizabeth, Perth Amboy, Carteret, Woodbridge, and Bayonne. During the Civil War the island's western and northern shores became important parts of the maritime and industrial service corridor for the developing city. Historic features and archaeological remains on Staten Island are abundant: there are more structures dating from the seventeenth century to the early nineteenth than in any other part of the city.

1. To 1860

During the sixteenth century and the early seventeenth the island was inhabited by Raritans and related Algonquin peoples of the Lenape (Delawarean) tribe, who referred to the land as Aquehonga Manacknong and Eghquaons. The first recorded exploration by a European was that of Giovanni da Verrazano, who in 1524 anchored in the Outer Bay and sailed through the Narrows. Henry Hudson's explorations of the North River in 1609 led to the establishment of trade at the mouth of the river by the Dutch, who named the island Staten Eylandt for the States General, the governing body of the Netherlands. In the 1620s Dutch settlement was concentrated at the southern tip of Manhattan. Three attempts were made to settle on Staten Island under the sponsorship of the patroons David Pietersen De Vries (1639–41) and Cornelis Melyn (1642–43; 1650–55, with Baron van der Capellan toe Ryssel). Each became the seat of conflict and was destroyed during the Dutch–Indian Wars waged by Governors Willem Kieft and Peter Stuyvesant. The first permanent settlement was made in 1661 by a

Population of Selected Towns in Staten Island, 1790–1890

	Castleton	Middletown	Northfield	Southfield	Westfield
1790	805	N/A	1,021	855	1,154
1800	1,056	N/A	1,377	932	1,198
1820	1,527	N/A	1,980	1,012	1,616
1830	2,204	N/A	2,171	975	1,734
1840	4,275	N/A	2,745	1,619	2,326
1850	5,389	N/A	4,020	2,709	2,943
1860	6,778	6,243	4,841	3,645	3,985
1870	9,504	7,589	5,949	5,082	4,905
1880	12,679	9,029	7,014	4,980	5,289
1890	16,423	10,577	9,811	6,644	8,258

NA = Not Available.

Note: Population figures for towns were not included in the census of population of 1810.

Compiled by James Bradley

Amboy Road in Staten Island, 2009

small group of Dutch Walloon and Huguenot families at Oude Dorp, just south of the Narrows near South Beach. From this beginning and well into the 1750s the island's population retained a distinctive cultural and linguistic mix, which included a strong French Huguenot presence. Throughout the colonial period European settlers were fairly evenly divided among Dutch, Huguenot–Walloon, and English immigrants and descendants, with a substantial, growing minority (10 to 13 percent) of Africans, most of whom were slaves.

After the Dutch surrendered New Netherland to the English in 1664, Staten Island became part of the province of New York and was initially incorporated along with Westchester and all of Long Island (including Brooklyn and Queens) into the county of Yorkshire. In 1670 the provincial governor made a renewed treaty and final purchase agreement for the island with the local Indians, most of whom left soon after. To encourage colonial settlement, the English resurveyed the 18 lots of Oude Dorp (which they also called Dover or Old Town) and added 22 new lots along the beach to the south, which became known as the "New Lots of the Old Town," or New Dorp.

When the colony of New York was divided into 10 counties in 1683, Staten Island, Shooters Island, and the Island of Meadows were designated the county of Richmond, named for the residence and dukedom of James, brother of Charles II, in Yorkshire. Land patents were granted in multiples or portions of 80 acres (32 hectares), usually for rectangular lots along the coastline or inland waterways. By 1708 the entire island had been divided into at least 166 modest farmshares and two manorial estates: the Manor of Bentley, belonging to Captain Christopher Billopp, which encompassed 1600 acres (650 hectares) in the southwestern section (opposite the Amboys); and the manor kept by the colonial governors Francis Lovelace and Thomas Dongan, which covered 5100 acres (2065 hectares) and dominated the north-central hills. By 1687–88 the English had divided the county into four administrative precincts that to some extent followed natural features: these were the North, South, and West divisions, and Dongan's estate, known as the "Lordship or Manner of Cassiltown." These divisions in 1788 became the townships of Northfield, Southfield, Westfield, and Castleton.

The population of Staten Island grew from 727 in 1698 to 2847 in 1771. The island supported a productive coastal, agricultural economy that included farming, fishing, shipping, piloting, maritime trade, the milling of flour and lumber, and trades such as blacksmithing and cooperage. In 1729 the county seat was established at Richmond, a hamlet at the crossroads near the island's geographic center at the head of the Fresh Kills. Although it had barely a dozen buildings, it remained the only village on the island until after the War of 1812. During the eighteenth century small settlements arose near ferry landings, meeting places, and other sites of commercial activity, including what later became Port Richmond, New Brighton, and Woodrow. Licenses were granted for about 10 ferry crossings to points in New Jersey, Long Island, and Manhattan, allowing for frequent travel and communication with Manhattan and the towns of northern New Jersey, which served as the market centers for farm and fishery produce and goods from the island.

The strategic position of Staten Island at the entrance to New York Harbor was important in the American Revolution. In July 1776 the island became the primary ground for landing and staging troops for the Battle of Brooklyn in August, the largest battle of the entire war; Staten Island was also the site of a futile peace conference on 11 September. Although predominantly Tory in sentiment, Staten Islanders were hard-pressed to fulfill their obligation to supply and house the troops, who sometimes numbered 30,000, or 10 times the resident population. Staten Island was occupied by the British throughout the war, after which it was virtually deforested; its county government buildings and a number of churches were also destroyed. The island became the point of departure for the British on 25 November 1783.

After the revolution the population rose slowly but steadily, from 3835 in 1790 to 4564 in 1800. Despite local protest the state of New York in 1799 moved the quarantine station, used for isolating passengers and seamen with contagious diseases, from Governors Island to new buildings on the northeastern shore of Staten Island. Between 1807 and the end of the War of 1812 improvements were made to the fortifications in the harbor, and a signal flag system was established between the forts at the Narrows, the Upper Bay, and the Navy Yard in Brooklyn. Development from 1815 to 1820 was spurred by the rise of New York City as the national metropolis and the inception of steam ferry service. Daniel D. Tompkins, the governor of New York from 1807 to 1816 and a longtime resident of Staten Island, promoted several developments, establishing a ferry line linked to a cross-island turnpike and stagecoach system, which provided an improved route between New York City and Philadelphia, and a suburban village planned on a grid surrounded by hillside villas (Tompkinsville, 1814–15). The industrial complex and settlement of Factoryville was built in 1819. During the 1820s the population grew at a rate almost twice that of each of the three preceding decades. In response to a declining extractive shell fishery, the island's watermen initiated a system of oyster cultivation and trade, which became the basis of a major metropolitan food industry.

The island's population increased by 54 percent during the 1830s, to 10,960, and by 69 percent during the 1850s, to 25,492, as many sought out the island for summer retreats away from the dangers and discomforts of Manhattan, especially after the epidemics of yellow fever and cholera during the 1820s and 1830s and the Great Fire of 1835. A romantic suburb and hotel resort was founded in New Brighton in 1834–35; other development included Stapleton (1833–34), Elliotville (1836), Clifton and Rossville (1837), and Port Richmond (*ca* 1838). The island also became the setting for institutions, particularly maritime philanthropies and health care facilities: Sailors' Snug Harbor (1831–33) and Seamen's Retreat (Clifton, 1834–37) were monumental complexes; Mariners' Family Asylum (Stapleton, 1854) and the Society for Seamen's Children (Port Richmond, 1849) were more modest in conception and design. On the southern shore wealthy residents of New York City and New England such as Frederick Law Olmsted made experimental farms. Oystering and shipping along the eastern seaboard linked Staten Island closely with the southern states, especially Maryland and Virginia, where the island's mariners introduced methods of shellfish cultivation and distinctive vessel types. White merchants and planters with business interests in Manhattan also patronized the island's fashionable hotels and hillside villas. About 1840 free black watermen from Snowhill, Maryland, moved to Staten Island with their families to escape restrictive laws and established the community of Sandy Ground near Prince's Bay.

Many Irish and German immigrants who sailed across the North Atlantic in the late 1840s settled on Staten Island. Stapleton, Castleton Corners, and Kreischerville (1854) became a prominent center of German-language culture and industries. The majority of Irish immigrants settled in Factoryville and other areas of manufacturing on the northern shore; lesser numbers took up small-scale farming and village trades near Richmond, Rossville, and Graniteville. Staten Islanders in 1857–58 opposed the expansion of the state quarantine station, which they burned to the ground after their protests were ignored. The station was eventually transferred to an offshore floating hospital and then to Hoffman and Swinburne islands (1873).

2. After 1860

In 1860 a railroad between Clifton and Tottenville opened and hamlets formed near railroad depots (later Dongan Hills, Oakwood, Eltingville, Annadale, Huguenot, and Richmond Valley); that year a new township, Middletown, was created in the northeastern section of the island from parts of Castleton and Southfield. During the Civil War, Staten Island became a major military encampment and training ground, and influential abolitionists lived in Elliotville and New Brighton. Riots against the draft broke out in Tompkinsville, Stapleton, New Brighton, and Factoryville between 14 and 20 July 1863, coinciding with similar riots in Manhattan.

In 1866 Edgewater (including Tompkinsville, Stapleton, and Clifton), Port Richmond, and New Brighton became the first villages to be formally incorporated, followed by Tottenville in 1869. By 1870 there were only 33,029 inhabitants, making Staten Island smaller than the section of Westchester later designated the Bronx. An 1871 committee led by Olmsted reported that the lack of development in Richmond County was due to poor ferry service and a belief that malaria was prevalent. The committee recommended stricter supervision of the ferries, a system for managing natural watersheds, and improvements to highways and parks, including a central public common 4 miles (6.4 kilometers) long. Most of these proposals were ignored, but improvements made to utilities and transportation by the developer Erastus Wiman (1834–1904) spurred growth in the 1880s and 1890s. Rail and ferry services were consolidated and unified in 1880. The Staten Island Railway (1860) was expanded to double tracks and extended in 1884 to St. George, where a combined rail and ferry terminal was constructed in 1886. Two new branch lines were added, one along the northern shore in 1887 that crossed the first permanent bridge to New Jersey (1889), the other along the eastern shore to South Beach (1892). Wiman and his associates sought to establish suburbs, estates, heavy industry, popular resorts, and mass entertainment. Staten Island gained telephone service in 1882 and electric trolley lines between 1892 and 1896. Housing developments were built at St. George, Arlington, Elm Park, Livingston, Fort Wadsworth, Arrochar, Rosebank, Giffords, and Meiers Corners. Suburban temperance communities at Westerleigh (Prohibition Park) and New Dorp met with immense success. Large amusement parks were built at Midland Beach and South Beach. The city's industrial and business elite continue to build mansions on the hills and organize private clubs, schools, and sporting associations. Manufacturing expanded in the north and east at Port Richmond, Mariners Harbor, Elm Park, West Brighton, and Stapleton. The company villages of Linoleumville and Kreischerville dominated the sparsely populated shore of the Arthur Kill, and major factories appeared as far south as Prince's Bay and Tottenville. Several institutions for aiding poor children were established, among them Mount Loretto, a mission for homeless newsboys in Prince's Bay (1882); St. Michael's Home, a large Catholic orphanage in Greenridge (1884); and Seaside Hospital in New Dorp Beach (1886).

Most residents of Staten Island favored closer connections with New York City. In a nonbinding referendum in 1894 they voted four to one in favor of consolidation with the city. When the new charter took effect in 1898 George Cromwell became the first president of the borough of Richmond, the four village and five town governments were disbanded, and the townships became designated as wards. Consolidation accelerated development on Staten Island: between 1880 and 1930 the population rose from 12,702 to 41,815. By 1900 immigrants had moved in: Italians in Rosebank, South Beach, and West Brighton; Hungarians, Poles, and Slavs in factory villages on the western shore, including Linoleumville and Kreischerville; and Scandinavians near the shipyards of Mariners Harbor and at Great Kills. Small Jewish communities developed in parts of Port Richmond, New Brighton, and Tompkinsville; Greeks took up truck farming in Bull's Head, Greenridge, and New Springville; and southern blacks joined the small local African American communities in Tompkinsville and Stapleton, West Brighton, and Sandy Ground.

A new borough hall was constructed between 1904 and 1906 and a civic center in St. George. By 1905 the ferry system, schools, police, fire protection for the northern and eastern shores, and most other primary services were

Last pair of working oxen in New York City, La Tourette Farm in Staten Island, 1904. Photograph by Edward Wenzel

run by the city, which also took over and expanded the old County Almshouse (renamed the New York City Farm Colony) in the south central hills, and erected Sea View Hospital (1913), for many years the largest tuberculosis sanitarium in the world. A pipeline laid under the Narrows brought pure water from the Catskill Mountains to the island's Silver Lake Reservoir in 1917. By 1921, when virtually every government facility had been transferred out of Richmondtown (except the county jail), 67 percent of the 116,531 inhabitants of the borough were concentrated in a belt 2 miles (3 kilometers) wide across the eastern and northern shores, about one-sixth of the total land area. An aggressive program of road construction improved internal circulation and opened new areas for subdivision. Between 1907 and 1919, Sunnyside, Giffords, and parts of Tottenville were developed. This served as a prelude to the bigger boom of the 1920s, which swept the island in anticipation of a planned system of bridges to New Jersey and a promised direct subway connection with the city, for which ground was broken in St. George and Brooklyn in 1923. Groups of modest, detached one-family houses were built at Randall Manor and Shore Acres, on Lighthouse, Todt, and Emerson hills, and along Hylan Boulevard (1924–27), the broad artery along the southern shore between Dongan Hills and Great Kills. Staten Island was promoted as a "borough of homes," much like Queens. By the end of the decade the borough had its first four-family duplexes and apartment buildings, concentrated in St. George, New Brighton, and Silver Lake.

As the volume and scale of activity in the port of New York swelled, industry expanded along the shores of the Arthur Kill and the Kill van Kull. Procter and Gamble established its manufacturing and distribution center for the East Coast of the United States at Port Ivory in 1907. The shipyards at Mariners Harbor and Shooters Island became known nationally during World War I. Local factories produced chemicals, paint, metals, textiles, tools, and building materials. After the war the federal government converted the estate of William H. Vanderbilt at New Dorp Beach into Miller Field, an air defense station and training ground (1919).

Industrialization of the lower harbor and the spread of bungalow and immigrant working-class development diminished the island's desirability for the wealthy. The last of the great resort hotels closed before World War I, and during the 1920s most estates were sold to institutions or developers for subdivision. In 1918 Wagner College moved from Rochester, New York, to Bellevue, the former estate of Sir Edward Cunard, and later absorbed into its campus the estate of William Greene Ward and a tract previously owned by Jacob Vanderbilt.

The opening of three bridges (the Goethals Bridge and the Outerbridge Crossing in 1928, and the Bayonne Bridge in 1931) and a new local span over the Fresh Kills (1931) improved commercial access to the island, just as the onset of the Depression devastated local manufacturing and ended work on the subway tunnel to Brooklyn. The failure to complete the tunnel under the Narrows or a bridge in its place delayed development for a generation, and the population rose slowly during the 1930s and 1940s; only after 1964, when the Verrazano–Narrows Bridge opened, did the growth rate equal the level achieved during the 1920s. The Depression brought hardship to the island. For many, relief was provided by massive public works projects, which left a legacy of parks, schools, and amenities. Important projects built on Staten Island by the Temporary Emergency Relief Administration and the Works Progress Administration included many parks, schools, cultural institutions, and public facilities, among them the Staten Island Zoo (Barrett Park, 1930s), the museum of the Staten Island Historical Society (1950s), La Tourette Golf Course (1920s), Clove Lake Park (1930s), Silver Lake Golf Course (1920s), the George Cromwell Recreation Center (1930s), the Goodhue playground and pool, the Franklin D. Roosevelt Boardwalk (1930s), an addition to the hospital of the U.S. Public Health Service (1930s), murals for Borough Hall, the high schools at Tottenville and New Dorp, and an addition to Curtis High School. To stimulate commerce the city established a foreign trade zone at the piers in Stapleton (1937–38). The Great Kills Wetlands were used for landfill (1938), on which Great Kills Park was later built.

In 1940 the population of the borough, 174,441, still had the highest proportion of native-born residents in the city (74 percent). World War II renewed military activity on Staten Island and invigorated the shipyards and other industries. The U.S. Army took over the piers in Stapleton, established the Staten Island Area Station Hospital in New Dorp Beach and Halloran General Hospital (converted in 1947 into Willowbrook State School), and built barracks in Fox Hills. A few residential developments also went up, including the island's first public housing project (in Port Richmond, 1943). The population grew after the war, and in 1946 Robert Moses revived and modified a plan for arterial parkways and bridges that was approved between 1954 and 1958. Development during the 1950s and early 1960s reflected the increasing prominence of the automobile and the growing divergence between the older, densely settled northern shore, and the southernmost 70 percent of the island. Seven public housing projects were built in Stapleton, West New Brighton, Mariners Harbor, South Beach, Castleton Corners, Dongan Hills, and New Brighton between 1950 and 1964. A section of Fresh Kills was first used as a city landfill in 1948; the project site was greatly expanded in 1951. Passenger rail lines on the northern and eastern shores were abandoned in 1953. The village business districts along the main streets of small towns were replaced by supermarkets and shopping centers along Hylan

Staten Island Borough Hall (left) and Richmond County Courthouse (both designed by Carrère and Hastings), Richmond Terrace, ca *1957*

Boulevard and near the center of the island. The College of Staten Island, now a branch of the City University of New York, opened in 1956.

The opening of the Verrazano–Narrows Bridge on 21 November 1964 allowed for "quick and easy access" to the rest of the city, with 19,000 unbuilt acres (7700 hectares) for development. Planners forecast a doubling of population, to 500,000, within 20 years. During the 1970s, when population declined in every other borough, Staten Island was among the fastest-growing counties in the state. The population according to the census of 1980 was 352,029, a gain of almost 20 percent for the decade; the figure 10 years later, 378,977, which local officials criticized as an undercount, indicated a growth rate of 7.7 percent, still by far the highest in the city. There was a net growth of more than 22,000 housing units on the island between 1980 and 1990, and this trend accelerated over the next decade: by 2000, 23,000 more new housing units had been added (up 14 percent) as the population reached 443,728—a gain of 17.1 percent, higher than any other borough in the city.

The apportionment of municipal costs and services became matters of intense public debate in the 1970s. A comprehensive development plan sponsored by the city for South Richmond (1971) was opposed by residents of the island and rejected by the state assembly in 1973. More traditional zoning was adopted by the City Planning Commission in the same year. The spread of semidetached housing, garden apartments, townhouses, and multistory condominiums across the interior and southern sections of the island redistributed the population toward its geographic center. During the 1970s the last privately owned truck farms were sold, and many factories and institutional complexes were abandoned or moved. The year 1975 marked the end of the five-cent ferry fare to Manhattan (increased to 25 cents), the partitioning of the island into three community districts along new east–west lines, and the official renaming of the borough from Richmond to Staten Island.

From the 1970s into the twenty-first century, the population remained predominantly white (about 77.6 percent, according to the census of 2000), even as increasing numbers of blacks (9.7 percent of the population in 2000), Hispanics (12.1 percent), and Asians (5.7 percent) became apparent. In 2000, 16.4 percent of the population was foreign born, with the largest immigrant groups from Italy, Mexico, China, the Philippines, and India. In the early twenty-first century Staten Island remained a residential borough with the highest proportion of owner-occupied housing (more than 64 percent in 2000), single family owner-occupied housing (47 percent), and car ownership in the city. The economy was service-oriented, directed to local market needs; health services and social assistance were the largest sector, followed by retail trade. Only 39 percent of the labor force was employed on the island. Many residents commuted to Manhattan, often to work for the uniformed city services and municipal government. Manufacturing continued to decline (Procter and Gamble closed its factory at Port Ivory in 1991; Sun Chemical in 2007), but maritime industries survived along the northern, eastern, and western shores. In 1990 the U.S. Navy opened Homeport–Stapleton, but in 1993 a presidential review committee found the facility unnecessary; the naval station was decommissioned and closed the following year. Plans to reactivate the Howland Hook Marine Terminal, a 187-acre (76-hectare) facility of the Port Authority of New York and New Jersey largely vacant since 1986 and unoccupied since 1991, were finally realized in 1996; it then became the fastest-growing marine terminal in New York Harbor. The Port Authority purchased Procter and Gamble's former Port Ivory property in 2001, adding 124 acres (50 hectares) to the terminal site. In April 2007 the Arthur Kill Bridge, closed since 1991, was reopened to freight rail line service, providing direct rail access to the container terminal, Pratt Industries' Visy Paper recycling plant in Travis (opened in 1996), and other industrial businesses on the west shore.

Residents became increasingly concerned with issues of development, land use, and the environment: pollution from refineries and other industries in New Jersey, traffic congestion, inadequate transportation and sewerage, high transit fares and tolls, and the continuing operation at Fresh Kills of the only active landfill in New York City, more than a decade after the city had agreed to close it. The abolition of the city's Board of Estimate in 1990 and the concomitant reduction in power of the borough presidency intensified feelings of resentment toward the city, and in November 1990 residents voted overwhelmingly in a referendum to create a special commission to examine the feasibility of seceding from New York City and establishing Staten Island as a separate municipality. In 1993 the Charter Commission on Staten Island Secession presented a favorable report on the issue and prepared a draft charter for an independent city of Staten Island, which was approved by 65 percent of the borough's voters in November 1993. The matter was opposed by city officials and, although approved by the state senate, remained blocked by the assembly, which refused to permit a vote without a home-rule message from the city. The call for secession brought attention to Staten Island concerns from new city and state government administrations that had benefited from island voter support in the mid-1990s. Local elected officials introduced legislation in the City Council and the state legislature to close the Fresh Kills landfill by 2002, an effort actively supported by the governor, mayor, and borough president. The landfill received the last barge of trash on 22 March 2001, but it was temporarily reopened six months later, until June 2002, to process the debris from Ground Zero during the recovery effort after the September 11 terrorist attacks. Master planning to transform the 2200-acre (890-hectare) Fresh Kills site into a world-class park began in 2003, and a park administrator was appointed in 2006. When completed in about 30 years, the result of one of the world's largest reclamation projects, the new park will double the size of the Greenbelt and increase the borough's public open space to more than 30 percent of its land mass.

In 1997 the ferry fare, raised from 25 to 50 cents per round trip in 1990, was eliminated altogether, to coincide with the introduction of the gold MetroCard, permitting free transfers between all transit buses and subways in the city. As part of the effort to revitalize the St. George waterfront and civic center, a 7171-seat baseball stadium was built on the former railroad site next to the Staten Island Ferry terminal for the Staten Island Yankees, a Minor League Baseball team brought to the island in 1999; the stadium opened in June 2001. Major rehabilitation of the island's beaches and restoration of the South Beach boardwalk began in 1994. More dramatically, concern with overdevelopment led to significant downzoning to reduce the density of new construction and preserve the traditional residential character of island neighborhoods by limiting construction of multifamily or semidetached housing. Between 1987 and 2002, more than 16,000 acres (6475 hectares), predominantly on the south shore, were downzoned through the efforts of community groups and the borough president. In July 2003 the mayor established the Staten Island Growth Management Task Force, co-chaired by the borough president and director of city planning, which issued a comprehensive report at the end of the year. At the same time, the borough president introduced six related downzoning initiatives covering 4554 acres (1843 hectares) in mid-island and the north shore. The task force's recommendations for lower-density growth management were adopted by the City Council in August 2004.

Staten Island lost nearly 270 residents in the 11 September 2001 terrorist attacks on the World Trade Center. Of the more than 1200 victims who were city residents, 16 percent lived on Staten Island. On the third anniversary of the attacks, the Staten Island 9/11 Memorial, designed by Masayuki Sono, was dedicated, located next to the ferry terminal, overlooking the harbor and lower Manhattan.

Staten Island is served by three colleges: Wagner College (1929), the College of Staten

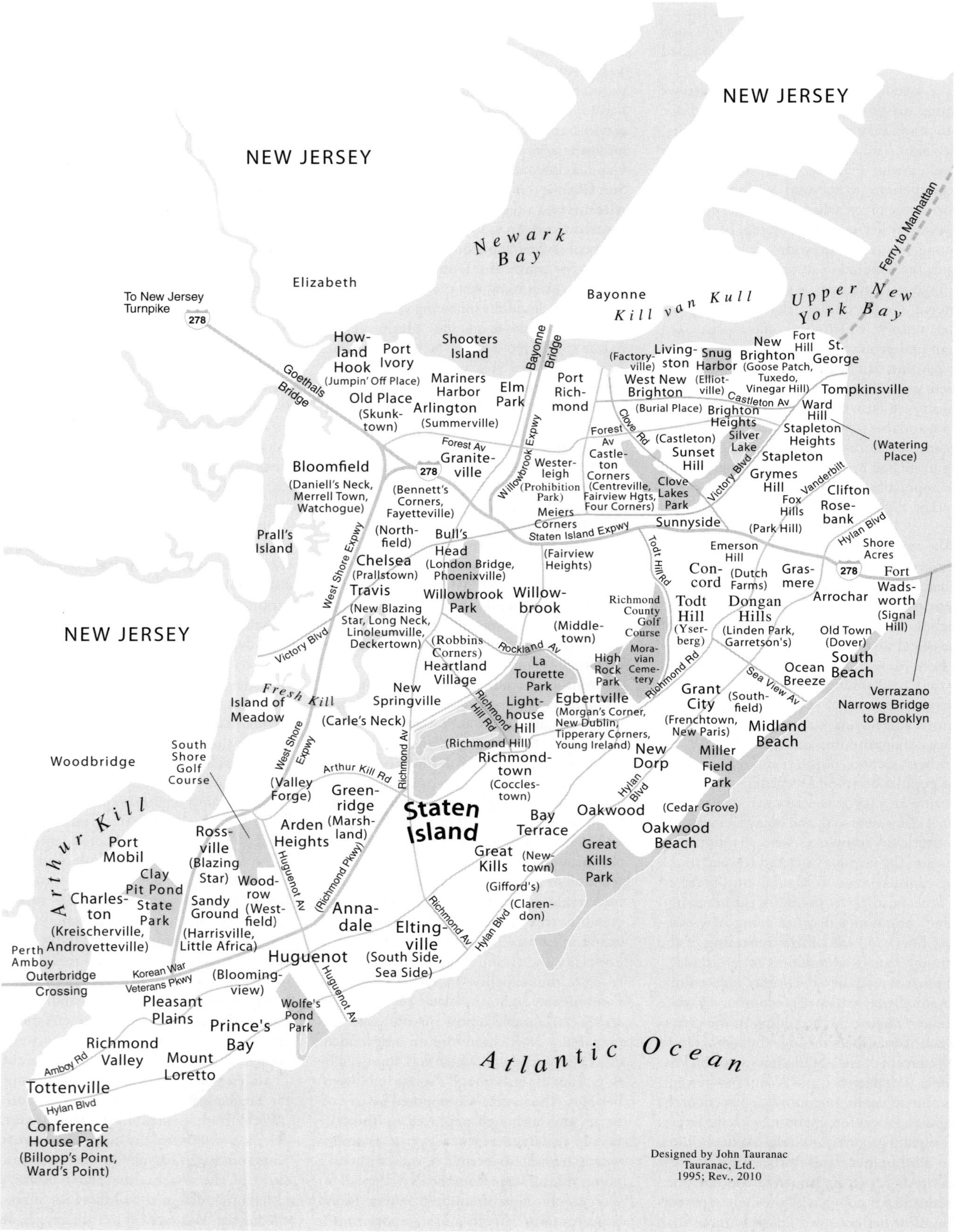

NEW JERSEY

NEW JERSEY

Newark Bay

Elizabeth

To New Jersey Turnpike
278

Bayonne
Kill van Kull
Upper New York Bay
Ferry to Manhattan

Goethals Bridge
Howland Hook (Jumpin' Off Place)
Port Ivory
Shooters Island
Bayonne Bridge
(Factoryville)
Livingston
Snug Harbor (Elliotville)
New Brighton (Goose Patch, Tuxedo, Vinegar Hill)
Fort Hill
St. George
Old Place (Skunktown)
Mariners Harbor
Arlington (Summerville)
Elm Park
Port Richmond
West New Brighton (Burial Place)
Castleton Av
Tompkinsville
Brighton Heights
Ward Hill
(Watering Place)
Forest Av
Willowbrook Expwy
Clove Rd
Forest Av
Castleton Corners (Centreville, Fairview Hgts, Four Corners)
(Castleton)
Sunset Hill
Silver Lake
Stapleton Heights
Stapleton
278
Graniteville
Westerleigh (Prohibition Park)
Clove Lakes Park
Victory Blvd
Bloomfield (Daniell's Neck, Merrell Town, Watchogue)
(Bennett's Corners, Fayetteville)
Meiers Corners
Grymes Hill
Vanderbilt
Fox Hills
Clifton
Rosebank
Sunnyside
(Park Hill)
Hylan Blvd
Staten Island Expwy
Prall's Island
(Northfield)
Bull's Head (London Bridge, Phoenixville)
West Shore Expwy
Chelsea (Prallstown)
(Fairview Heights)
Todt Hill Rd
Emerson Hill
Shore Acres
Concord
(Dutch Farms)
Grasmere
278
Fort Wadsworth (Signal Hill)
Travis (New Blazing Star, Long Neck, Linoleumville, Deckertown)
Willowbrook Park
Willowbrook
Richmond County Golf Course
Todt Hill (Yserberg)
Dongan Hills (Linden Park, Garretson's)
Arrochar
Old Town (Dover)

NEW JERSEY

Victory Blvd
(Robbins Corners)
Heartland Village
(Middletown)
Rockland Av
High Rock Park
Moravian Cemetery
La Tourette Park
Richmond Rd
South Beach
Ocean Breeze
Sea View Av
Verrazano Narrows Bridge to Brooklyn
Fresh Kill
Island of Meadow
New Springville
(Carle's Neck)
Richmond Hill Rd
Lighthouse Hill
Egbertville (Morgan's Corner, New Dublin, Tipperary Corners, Young Ireland)
Grant City (Frenchtown, New Paris)
(Southfield)
Midland Beach
Woodbridge
South Shore Golf Course
West Shore Expwy
Arthur Kill Rd
Richmond Av
(Richmond Hill)
Richmondtown (Coccles-town)
New Dorp
Miller Field Park
(Valley Forge)
Greenridge (Marshland)
Hylan Blvd
Arthur Kill
Port Mobil
Rossville (Blazing Star)
Arden Heights
Staten Island
Bay Terrace
Oakwood
(Cedar Grove)
Oakwood Beach
Clay Pit Pond State Park
Charleston (Kreischerville, Androvetteville)
Sandy Ground (Harrisville, Little Africa)
Woodrow (Westfield)
Huguenot Av
(Richmond Pkwy)
Annadale
Great Kills
(Newtown)
(Gifford's)
Great Kills Park
(Clarendon)
Richmond Av
Hylan Blvd
Eltingville (South Side, Sea Side)
Perth Amboy
Outerbridge Crossing
Korean War Veterans Pkwy
Huguenot
(Bloomingview)
Huguenot Av
Pleasant Plains
Wolfe's Pond Park
Prince's Bay
Richmond Valley
Amboy Rd
Mount Loretto
Tottenville
Hylan Blvd
Conference House Park (Billopp's Point, Ward's Point)

Atlantic Ocean

Designed by John Tauranac
Tauranac, Ltd.
1995; Rev., 2010

Island (1976), and a campus of St. John's University (1971). It is also the site of many parks, museums, historic houses, a zoo, a botanical garden, two highly ambitious landmark historic cultural facilities (Historic Richmond Town and Snug Harbor Cultural Center), a section of the Gateway National Recreation Area, and three major environmental preserves: the Greenbelt (1984), the largest park in New York City at 2500 acres (1012 hectares), operated by the city; Clay Pit Ponds State Park; and Mount Loretto State Preserve (2006).

Charles W. Leng and William T. Davis, *Staten Island and Its People: A History, 1609–1929* (New York: Lewis Historical Publishing, 1930); Shirley Zavin, *Staten Island: An Architectural History* (New York: Staten Island Institute of Arts and Sciences, 1979); Charles L. Sachs, *Made on Staten Island: Agriculture, Industry, and Suburban Living in the City* (New York: Staten Island Historical Society, 1988); *Staten Island: Economic Development and the State of the Borough Economy* (New York: Office of the State Deputy Comptroller for the City of New York, 2005 [Report 14-2005])

Charles L. Sachs

Staten Island Academy. Private, coeducational primary and secondary school opened in 1862 as the Methfessel Institute by Anion Methfessel, a German-educated teacher of language education who sought to establish a boys' boarding school with a strong emphasis on language training. In 1864 the school became Staten Island Academy and Latin School. After a series of mergers with other schools during the 1930s it moved to its present location on Todt Hill and in 1951 took its current name.

Richard Schwartz

Staten Island Advance. Daily newspaper, launched in 1886 as the *Richmond County Advance* (published weekly) by the printer John J. Crawford and the businessman James C. Kennedy. It later became the *Daily Advance* before taking its current name. The *Advance* was one of the first business establishments on Staten Island to use electricity and commercial telephones. It surpassed nine early competitors as its circulation rose from 4500 in 1910 to 80,000 on weekdays and 92,000 on Sundays in the mid-1990s. In 1922 the *Advance* was bought by S. I. Newhouse; between 1924 and 1958 Newhouse acquired 11 newspapers, with the *Advance* becoming the flagship of the Newhouse Group. After many years at two locations in West Brighton, the newspaper moved to its present site in Grasmere in 1960. Richard E. Diamond, Newhouse's nephew, became publisher in 1979. A 1986 "Centennial Edition" was the largest weekday paper ever published in New York City and an important chronicle of Staten Island history. Another special edition, "Guide 2001," examined every aspect of Staten Island life, including its new diversity. In 2002 the *Advance* launched a redesigned newspaper printed on a state-of-the-art German press. Caroline Diamond Harrison succeeded her father as publisher in 2004. The *Advance* continues as a community newspaper and a sponsor of special events for athletes, women, volunteers, and firefighters. Its stories about neighborhoods, ethnic groups, transportation, and the environment record and mirror the concerns of Staten Islanders.

Howard Weiner

Staten Island Ferry. Ferry route connecting Battery Park, Manhattan, with St. George, Staten Island, over a distance of 6.2 miles (10 kilometers). The earliest charters for sail service between Manhattan and Staten Island date from 1713; the first steamboat was used in 1817. In 1884 the Baltimore and Ohio Railroad acquired a number of existing lines and operated the ferry until 1905, when it was taken over by the city government. Large steamboat double-enders were used between 1857 and 1981 to accommodate passengers and vehicles. These were replaced by diesel-powered ships that could carry as many as 6000 passengers; boats that took automobiles were reduced to a limited schedule. Even after the opening in 1964 of the Verrazano–Narrows Bridge between Brooklyn and Staten Island the ferry remained a lifeline for a large commuting population, operating 365 days a year, 24 hours a day. The ferry trip became a favorite with tourists for its unsurpassed views of the harbor, the Statue of Liberty, and lower Manhattan. It also remained popular because of its low fare: until 1974 a one-way ride cost five cents. From that time only round-trip tickets were sold, successively for 10 cents (to 1976), 25 cents (to 1989), and 50 cents until the fare

Staten Island Ferry Terminal, 2009

Staten Island Ferry approaching the Staten Island Ferry Terminal, ca *1937*

was eliminated altogether in 1997. On 8 September 1991 a fire severely damaged the Whitehall terminal in Manhattan, and a terminal nearby maintained by the U.S. Coast Guard was temporarily used as a substitute. A ferry accident in October 2003 horrified the city: the *Andrew J. Barberi* crashed into a concrete pier at the St. George terminal at full speed, killing 11 people and injuring scores of others; the pilot had fallen asleep and was later convicted of manslaughter. Three new boats were launched in 2005–6, and in 2005 a new Whitehall terminal was constructed, while the St. George terminal underwent extensive renovation and expansion. Increased security after the terrorist attacks of 11 September 2001 and new ferry and terminal expenditures led operating costs for the system to more than double in the early twenty-first century. In 2008 the ferry carried more than 19 million passengers, or 65,000 passengers per weekday. Cars were prohibited after 9/11.

Theodore Scull, *Staten Island Ferry* (New York: Quadrant, 1982)

Arthur G. Adams

Staten Island Historical Society. Organization chartered by New York State in 1856. It sponsored meetings and lectures in its first decade but then lay dormant until 1900, when another charter was drawn up focusing on the preservation of historic landmarks. In 1920 the society was reorganized and in 1922 absorbed the Staten Island Antiquarian Society (formed in 1915), acquiring in the process the Billiou–Stillwell–Perine House (circa 1660) at 1476 Richmond Road in Dongan Hills, the oldest house on Staten Island and the second-oldest in New York City. Under the direction of Loring McMillen (1908–91) and with the assistance of the Works Progress Administration, the society opened the Historical Museum at Richmondtown in 1935 and launched a campaign to save artifacts and records of daily life and culture in the area. It purchased Voorlezer's House in 1939 and other buildings nearby in the hopes of restoring the entire village as a museum. Government support for this purpose was first sought in the 1950s; in 1958 the society deeded its property at Richmondtown to the City of New York in exchange for partial operating support. Historic Richmond Town is now administered on behalf of the city by the society, which maintains its headquarters there. In addition the society owns the Sylvanus Decker Farm in New Springville (10 acres [4 hectares]), the last remaining farm on Staten Island, acquired by bequest in 1955; the Judge Jacob Tysen House, purchased from the trustees of Sailors' Snug Harbor in 1970; a library and archive of local history; a photography collection of more than 50,000 images, including the Alice Austen Collection; and about 80,000 artifacts.

Barnett Shepherd

Staten Island Museum. Founded in 1881 as the Natural Science Association of Staten Island, it is New York City's only general-interest museum housing the arts, natural sciences, and local history. Each year more than 65,000 visitors go to the museum and participate in its programs. It has been instrumental in the founding of many other cultural organizations on Staten Island such as the Staten Island Botanical Garden and the Staten Island Zoo. As of 2009 it has secured almost $16 million in City Capital funds for opening the first major art museum in Staten Island. It is located at 75 Stuyvesant Place.

Jessica Montesano

Staten Island Railway [SIR]. Electrified rapid transit line operating exclusively on Staten Island, connecting the St. George Ferry Terminal to Tottenville at the island's southern end. The 14-mile (23-kilometer), double-tracked route has 22 stations and functions primarily to bring island commuters to and from the ferry terminal. Until the 1980s the SIR also hauled freight between Staten Island and New Jersey.

The SIR began in 1860 when Cornelius "The Commodore" Vanderbilt built a new rail line from Vanderbilt's Landing (now Clifton) to Tottenville. The SIR soon controlled the ferries connecting Staten Island to Manhattan, but an 1871 explosion on a ferry docked in Manhattan killed 68 people and sent the SIR into receivership. In the 1880s the Baltimore and Ohio (B&O) Railroad, looking to gain a railhead in New York City, provided financial backing to the SIR and financed expansions from Clifton to St. George, west along the north shore to Howland Hook, and from Clifton to South Beach. The new venture was named the Staten Island Rapid Transit Railroad Company, the first application of the term *rapid transit.* Ferry service to Manhattan was moved to the present location at St. George in 1898; after financial difficulties in the late 1890s, the B&O bought out the SIR and its Manhattan ferries in 1899. A 1901 ferry accident forced the B&O to relinquish the boat operations (1905) and concentrate on running Staten Island's rail lines, which now included a bridge over Arthur Kill to Cranford, New Jersey, for interchange of freight with mainline railroads.

In 1925 the B&O electrified the entire SIR passenger operation, using third rail and new subway-type cars designed to operate on Brooklyn–Manhattan Transit Corporation (BMT) subway routes as well. That same year construction started on a tunnel under the Narrows to connect the SIR to the BMT's Fourth Avenue subway, but work soon ground to a halt, never to be reinstated. Blame for never building this tunnel has often been placed on New York Mayor John F. Hylan (because of his earlier quarrels with the BMT), on the assumption that Hylan obstructed the work because the BMT stood to benefit from the tunnel. Another theory is that Alfred E. Smith, governor of New York in 1925, had a hand because he owned considerable Pennsylvania Railroad (PRR) stock. (The B&O was PRR's main competitor between New York City and Washington, D.C.) Beginning in the 1930s, the SIR embarked on the elimination of its many street grade crossings; the last one was completed in the 1970s. In 1947 the New York City Board of Transportation bought Staten Island's local bus route operator, cut fares to five cents, and in the process took away 60 percent of the SIR's patronage. In 1953 the SIR dropped passenger trains on its North Shore and South Beach branches, leaving the St. George–Tottenville route as its only passenger line. In 1959 the SIR completed a new lift bridge over Arthur Kill. On 1 July 1971 the B&O sold the SIR to the Metropolitan Transportation Authority, which created a subsidiary, the Staten Island Rapid Transit Operating Authority (SIRTOA), to run the railway. In 1973 a fleet of 52 R-44 subway cars replaced the 1925 fleet; later expanded to 64, the fleet continued to provide rapid transit service on Staten Island in the early twenty-first century. In the 1990s the line reverted to its old name of Staten Island Railway. Since the 1990s fares and transfers have integrated into the New York City Transit Authority's tariffs, and since 1997 the MetroCard system has enabled SIR riders to utilize Staten Island's buses, as well as subway and bus connections in all other boroughs, for no additional fare after riding the ferry from St. George.

Andrew Sparberg

Staten Island Yankees. Baseball team. It is a part of the New York–Penn League and

McNamara Division of Minor League Baseball's Class A (short season). Originally called the Watertown (New York) Indians, a farm team affiliated with the Cleveland Indians, the team moved to Staten Island and became affiliated with the New York Yankees in 1999. The newly named Staten Island Yankees played at the College of Staten Island Baseball Complex from 1999 to 2000 before moving to the new 7171-seat Richmond County Bank Ballpark in 2001. The "Baby Bombers" won division and league titles in 2000, 2002, 2005, 2006, and 2009 and have sent former players to the New York Yankees, including Jason Anderson (2003), Chien-ming Wang (2005), and Robinson Canó (2005).

Mary Elizabeth Brown

Staten Island Zoo. The Staten Island Zoological Society was formed in 1933 to develop a zoo in Clarence T. Barrett Park in northern Staten Island. A Works Progress Administration project, the zoo was completed in 1936 on an 8-acre (3.2-hectare) estate willed to the city by Mrs. Edward E. Hardin; it consisted of one redbrick building. Carl F. Kauffeld, curator of reptiles, led the zoo in exhibiting every kind of rattlesnake known in the United States. The zoo was the first American facility to employ a full-time female veterinarian, Dr. Patricia O'Connor, in 1942. Expanded in 1969 with a children's center, the zoo was modernized throughout the 1980s, winning accreditation from the American Association of Zoological Parks and Aquariums in 1988. The zoo, which is owned by the city and funded by the Department of Cultural Affairs, opened the Carl F. Kauffeld House of Reptiles in 2007. Known for its reptile collection and educational mission, the zoo received more than 300,000 visitors annually early in the twenty-first century.

Kate Lauber

State University of New York, Campuses in New York City, by Date of Founding

SUNY Health Science Center at Brooklyn (SUNY Downstate Medical Center), 1860 (4-year/graduate, Brooklyn)
Maritime College, 1874 (4-year/graduate, Bronx)
Fashion Institute of Technology, 1944 (4-year/graduate, Manhattan)
College of Optometry, 1970 (Graduate, Manhattan)
Empire State College,* 1971 (4-year/graduate, Manhattan)

*Only the college's Harry Van Arsdale, Jr., Center for Labor Studies is located in New York City.

State University of New York [SUNY]. Statewide system of higher education formed in July 1948. Four of its affiliates are in New York City: the Fashion Institute of Technology (227 West 27th Street, Manhattan), the College of Optometry (33 West 42nd Street, Manhattan), the Health Science Center at Brooklyn (Downstate Medical Center, 450 Clarkson Avenue), and the Maritime College (Fort Schuyler, Bronx). Empire State College, which specializes in distance learning, offers specialized programs in New York City, including the Harry Van Arsdale, Jr., School for Labor Studies at 325 Hudson Street, Manhattan; one program in Brooklyn at 177 Livingston Street; one program in Staten Island at 500 Seaview Avenue; and various special and fine arts programs.

Sixty Four Campuses: The State University of New York to 1985 (Albany: State University of New York Press, 1985)

Selma Berrol, Lisa Keller

Statler Hotel. See New York's Hotel Pennsylvania.

Statue of Liberty. Monument in Upper New York Bay. First proposed in 1875 by the French statesman Édouard de Laboulaye as a gift from France to the United States commemorating liberty and friendship between

Liberty Island, 2009

the two nations, it was completed by 1880 at a workshop in France by the sculptor Frédéric-Auguste Bartholdi, who chose Bedloe's Island (from 1956 Liberty Island) as the site of the monument. The American Committee for the Statue, composed largely of members of the Union League Club, solicited contributions to pay for the design and construction of the pedestal and selected an architectural plan submitted by Richard Morris Hunt, who had earlier designed the Tribune Building and the Lenox Library. To supplement the funds raised by the committee, the readers of the *World* contributed more than $100,000 in 1885, which made it possible for the pedestal to be finished and the statue assembled over a metal framework designed by Gustave Eiffel. The statue was dedicated on 28 October 1886 and soon became one of the most widely recognized landmarks in the world. Its symbolic association with New York City and particularly with its immigrants was heightened in 1903 when Emma Lazarus's poem "The New Colossus" was inscribed on a bronze tablet laid in the pedestal.

In 1956 the U.S. Congress approved the plans of several prominent New Yorkers and others to assist the National Park Service (NPS) in enlarging the base of the statue and opening a museum within it. In 1965 President Lyndon B. Johnson administratively joined neighboring Ellis Island to the Statue of Liberty, and the two became known as the Statue of Liberty National Monument. In 1982 President Ronald Reagan appointed Lee Iacocca to head a private-sector effort to raise funds for the restoration of both sites. The resulting Statue of Liberty–Ellis Island Foundation contributed more than $100 million to the statue's repair, which began in 1984; in July 1986 the refurbished statue reopened to the public in a gala celebration of its centennial. In 1984 it was designated by the United Nations as a World Heritage Site.

The statue received more than five million visitors annually in the early twenty-first century. After the destruction of the World Trade Center on 11 September 2001, the NPS closed Liberty Island for 100 days. Visitors were again able to enter the statue's base and museum on 3 August 2004, following a $20 million fire safety and security upgrade, but they were barred from access to the interior of the statue above the pedestal's observation deck. New York congressman Anthony Weiner pushed for years for the crown to be reopened, and on 4 July 2009 the NPS reopened the crown through a ticketing and reservation system that restricts the number of visitors.

Walter Hugins, *Statue of Liberty National Monument: Its Origin, Development and Administration* (Washington, D.C.: U.S. Department of the Interior, National Park Service, 1958); Barbara Blumberg, *Celebrating the Immigrant: An Administrative History of the Statue of Liberty National Monument, 1952–1982* (Boston: U.S. Department of the Interior, National Park Service, North Atlantic Regional Office, 1985); Richard Seth Hayden and Thierry W. Despont, *Restoring the Statue of Liberty: Sculpture, Structure, Symbol* (New York: McGraw–Hill, 1986)

Barbara Blumberg

steam. The Common Council of New York City in December 1878 granted a franchise to Francis B. Spinola to lay pipes under the streets of Manhattan and form a company to supply hot air or steam. The franchise was bought in 1879 by Wallace C. Andrews, who formed a company called the Steam Heating and Power Company of New York (incorporated 24 July 1879). The New York Steam Company, formed on 26 July 1880, became a rival and Andrews bought a controlling interest in it. On 19 September 1881 the companies merged to form the New York Steam Company, which opened headquarters at 16 Cortlandt Street and dug its first pipelines under the direction of chief engineer Charles Edward Emery. The American Steam Company offered keen competition until one of its pipes burst and hurled 3 tons (2.7 metric tons) of lampblack onto Maiden Lane. In March 1882 the New York Steam Company provided service for its first customer, the United Bank Building (88–92 Broadway). Steam heat soon became popular because it made heating plants for each building unnecessary. By the end of 1882 the company had 62 customers around Wall Street served by its boiler plant, which stood in the block bounded by Dey, Greenwich, Cortlandt, and Washington streets; in 1886 it had 350 customers and 5 miles (8 kilometers) of mains. A second boiler plant was opened at Madison Avenue and 58th Street, mainly for elegant homes, including those of Seth Low and Frederick Gallatin. The company bought some steam from Consolidated Gas (later Consolidated Edison), which by 1932 had six boiler plants and a network of pipes extending from the Battery to 97th Street. In 1959 the New York Steam Company was absorbed by Consolidated Edison.

In August 1989 a steam pipe burst near Gramercy Park, killing three people, injuring dozens, and spewing asbestos. Consolidated Edison removed asbestos from its 1800 manholes over steam mains, many of which it inspected and refurbished in 1991. More than a dozen smaller explosions have occurred since then, including a severe explosion in July 2007 that killed one person and injured more than 30. About 1800 buildings in the city relied on steam for heat and for power to run air-conditioning compressors in 2007, down from 2200 in 1989. In the early twenty-first century more than 100 miles (160 kilometers) of pipes under Manhattan provided steam for heat and power to hundreds of office and residential buildings.

Alana Erickson Coble

Steffens, (Joseph) Lincoln (*b* San Francisco, 6 April 1866; *d* Carmel, Calif., 6 Aug 1936). Journalist. He settled in New York City in 1892. As a reporter at the *Evening Post* covering the police and finance he was required by his editor E. L. Godkin to suppress his gift for story-telling. He became the city editor in 1897 of the *Commercial Advertiser* and the managing editor in 1901 of *McClure's,* where he made his reputation with the series "The Shame of the Cities" (1902–3), written on the eve of a municipal election. He was disappointed by the outcome of the voting, in which the reformist mayor Seth Low failed to win a second term. In 1906 he left *McClure's* for the *American,* and in 1908 he joined the staff of *Everybody's.* His autobiography (*The Autobiography of Lincoln Steffens,* 1931) includes compelling descriptions of immigrant neighborhoods in the 1890s, accounts of Theodore Roosevelt's frenetic career as president of the Police Board, and recollections of his own friendly rivalry with Jacob A. Riis, whom he once outdid by stealing files from the police. Steffens lived at 42 Washington Square South. He spent his last years in California.

Justin Kaplan, *Lincoln Steffens: A Biography* (New York: Simon and Schuster, 1974); Robert Stinson, *Lincoln Steffens* (New York: Frederick Ungar, 1979)

Robert Stinson

Steichen, Edward [Eduard Jean] (*b* Luxembourg, 27 March 1879; *d* West Redding, Conn., 25 March 1973). Photographer. In 1900 he became associated with Alfred Stieglitz, who published his soft-focus photographs in the magazine *Camera Work.* While living in France in 1906–14 he provided drawings by Auguste Rodin and Henri Matisse for exhibit at the Little Galleries of the Photo-Secession in New York City. His experience in aerial photography, acquired in the U.S. Army in 1917–19, helped to give a hard-edged, industrial quality to his work. He was chief photographer for Condé Nast's publications from 1923 to 1937, and he did portraits for the magazines *Vogue* and *Vanity Fair* of Greta Garbo and Paul Robeson. From 1924 he also worked for the J. Walter Thompson agency, which paid him $15,000 a year to advertise commercial products and the services of nonprofit organizations in New York City. He produced a series of skyline photographs during the 1930s that included a low-angle shot of the George Washington Bridge (1931), a montage of Rockefeller Center (1932), and a multiple exposure of the Empire State

Building (1932). During World War II he was placed in command of photography for the U.S. Navy. He returned to New York City after the war and became the director of the photography department at the Museum of Modern Art (1947–62), where he encouraged many photographers with highly acclaimed exhibitions such as *The Family of Man* (1955). He wrote *Edward Steichen: A Life in Photography* (1963).

Dennis Longwell, *Steichen: The Master Prints, 1894–1914: The Symbolist Period* (New York: Museum of Modern Art, 1978); Patricia A. Johnston, *Real Fantasies: Edward Steichen's Advertising Photography* (Berkeley: University of California Press, 2000)

Barbara L. Michaels

Stein, Clarence S(amuel) (*b* Rochester, N.Y., 19 June 1882; *d* New York City, 7 Feb 1975). Architect and housing reformer. Educated at the École des Beaux-Arts, he began his career in New York City working for Bertram Goodhue. He was a theorist, promoter, and practitioner of regional and community planning, the chairman of the New York State Commission on Housing and Regional Planning (1923–26), and an active member of the Regional Planning Association of America. Stein's most important works in New York City include Sunnyside Gardens in Queens (1924), the Fieldston School (1929), Temple Emanu-El (with Robert Kohn, 1929), the Phipps Garden Apartments I and II (1931, 1935), and Hillside Homes (1932). *Toward New Towns for America* (1951) summarizes his ideas and accomplishments.

Rosalie Genevro

Steinbeck, John (Ernst) (*b* Salinas, Calif., 27 Feb 1902; *d* New York City, 20 Dec 1968). Novelist. He moved to New York City in 1925 and worked for six weeks as a laborer on the construction of Madison Square Garden and then as a reporter for the *American.* He moved from Brooklyn to the Parkwood Hotel at 38 Gramercy Park North in Manhattan and began work on a book of stories set in New York City, for which he could not find a publisher; surviving stories that may have been written for the book include "East Third Street" and "The White Sister of Fourteenth Street." After returning to California in 1926 he began to write seriously and had his first success with *Tortilla Flat* (1935), followed by *Of Mice and Men* (1937), a novella about the friendship between two migrant workers, and *The Grapes of Wrath* (1939), about the mass migration of poor farmers from the Dust Bowl to California during the Depression (Pulitzer Prize 1940). In 1941 he returned to New York City and lived in the Bedford Hotel on East 40th Street; he moved in 1943 to 330 East 51st Street. After working for the federal government as a writer during World War II, he lived at East 37th Street (1945), 175–77 East 78th Street (1946–48), East 52nd Street (1949), and 206 East 72nd Street, where he remained for 13 years. His best-known later works include *Cannery Row* (1945), a biting critique of the greed of modern civilization, and *East of Eden* (1952), a partly autobiographical novel reflecting his newfound faith in humanity's ability to choose good over evil. He also wrote the scripts for the film versions of several of his stories, as well as scripts intended expressly for films, including *The Forgotten Village* (1941) and *Viva Zapata!* (1952). In 1962 he received the Nobel Prize for literature.

Jackson J. Benson, *The True Adventures of John Steinbeck, Writer* (New York: Viking, 1984)

Anthony Gronowicz

Steinbrenner, George (*b* Rocky River, Ohio, 4 July 1930; *d* Tampa, Fla., 13 July 2010). Owner of the New York Yankees. During his ownership the team grew from a $10 million franchise to the first professional sports team valued at more than $1 billion. After failing in a bid to buy the Cleveland Indians for a reported $9 million in 1971, Steinbrenner bought the Yankees two years later with a group of investors for $8.7 million. Between 1973 and 2008 he changed managers 20 times and general managers 11 times, feuded with players and the media, and became known as "the Boss" on account of his hands-on approach to managing the franchise. He pled guilty to making illegal contributions to Richard M. Nixon's reelection campaign in 1974 and was suspended by Baseball Commissioner Bowie Kuhn for nine months (reduced from two years); he was later pardoned by President Ronald Reagan. In 1990 he was banned from baseball for life on account of financial contractual issues with player Dave Winfield but was reinstated in 1993 and returned to the franchise less involved with day-to-day operations of the team.

Steinbrenner is also known for "spending money to make money," driving up player salaries, and setting a new precedent for competitive contracts. This philosophy helped turn the Yankees into a winning franchise in the late 1970s when they won the 1977 and 1978 World Series with such high-paid stars as Jim "Catfish" Hunter and Reggie Jackson. With the largest payroll in baseball the team again won the World Series in 1996, 1998, 1999, and 2000, and in the early twenty-first century Steinbrenner continued to pay high prices for the game's best players. He was the first baseball team owner to sell cable television rights and oversaw the creation of the Yankees Entertainment and Sports (YES) Network, which began broadcasting in 2002. Outside of baseball he invested in six Broadway shows between 1967 and 1988, hosted the New York City–based television show *Saturday Night Live* in 1990, was characterized in several seasons of the iconic New York television series *Seinfeld,* and appeared in Visa commercials with Yankee shortstop Derek Jeter and manager Joe Torre in the early twenty-first century. After 2006 Steinbrenner lived in Florida, and his sons Hal and Hank took responsibility for running the franchise. Nonetheless, he returned to the Bronx for the 2008 All-Star Game and spearheaded the construction of a new Yankee Stadium, which opened in 2009.

Frank Dyer

Steinem, Gloria (*b* Toledo, Ohio, 25 March 1934). Writer and activist. After graduating from Smith College in 1956 she moved to New York City to write for the satirical political magazine *Help!* "I Was a Playboy Bunny," an article she wrote for *Esquire* in 1963 based on her "undercover" assignment as a waitress at the Playboy Club in Manhattan, brought her to national attention. After attending a meeting in 1968 of the radical women's group the Redstockings she became an outspoken advocate of the women's movement. She wrote a political column for the magazine *New York* and took part in the presidential campaign of Eugene J. McCarthy (1968) and the mayoral campaign of Norman Mailer (1969). In January 1972 she launched the feminist magazine *Ms.,* which initially appeared as an insert in *New York;* her affiliation with *Ms.* continued after it changed ownership in 1987. She also remained active in the National Organization for Women and Voters for Choice. Steinem's published writings include *Outrageous Acts and Everyday Rebellions* (1983) and *Revolution from Within: A Book of Self-Esteem* (1992), a best seller that aroused controversy in the women's movement for what some saw as its equivocal commitment to feminism. By 2009 she had lived in New York City for more than half a century.

Marjorie Harrison

Steinway and Sons. Firm of piano makers, formed in New York City in 1853 by Henry Steinweg, who had been a piano maker in Seesen, Germany, since the 1830s, and his children, Theodore, Doretta, Charles, Henry, Jr., William, and Albert; the family changed its name to Steinway in 1866. In 1860 the firm opened an enormous, modern piano factory on 53rd Street and Fourth Avenue (now Park Avenue) in Manhattan. The master builders behind the extraordinary Steinway piano were Henry Steinway, Jr., and Theodore Steinway: they combined the techniques in piano building then current with many of their own innovations, improving the cast-iron plate, the fan-shaped overstrung pattern, and the action. Their younger brother William Steinway set out to establish for the Steinway piano a reputation as the finest piano ever made, a symbol of

Steinway and Sons, ca 1862

success and refinement for the middle class. The piano was entered in several international exhibitions and won prizes throughout Europe. William sponsored the debuts in New York City of Anton Rubinstein at Steinway Hall on 14th Street in 1872 and Jan Ignace Paderewski in 1892. He advertised his instrument as the "standard piano of the world." Between 1870 and 1873 William bought a tract of 400 acres (160 hectares) along the northwestern shore of Queens, and during the next decade he built a spacious factory and a town with a church, a library, a kindergarten, and a public trolley line. He became so affluent and influential in fashionable society that when he died in 1896 the mayor ordered the flags on all city buildings flown at half staff, and his funeral oration was delivered at Liederkranz Hall by Carl Schurz. After his death the business continued under the control of three nephews: Charles H. Steinway, aged 39, the head of the firm; Frederick Steinway; and Henry Ziegler.

Interior of the Steinway factory, 2009

Frederick took charge of the firm in 1919 and during the 1920s expanded production in Queens and Hamburg. In its peak year, 1926, the firm manufactured 6000 grand pianos; it also continued to assemble cases for Duo-Art player pianos under contract to the Aeolian Piano Company. A new Steinway Hall was built on West 17th Street in Manhattan in 1925 at a cost of $3 million.

Sales of pianos in the United States collapsed in 1927, owing to a troubled economy and competition from the radio and the phonograph. Frederick Steinway died during the summer; the new president of the firm was William's youngest son, Theodore E. Steinway. Devastated by the Depression and heavily in debt, the firm interrupted production from 1931 to 1933. In 1939 the employees voted to join Local 102 of the United Furniture Workers. Wood and metal were scarce during World War II and could not be spared for luxury items like pianos. Instead the firm manufactured CG-4A troop-carrying gliders, employing 1200 people, mostly older men and young women working in shifts. In Hamburg the Steinway factory was seized as enemy property by the Nazis to manufacture beds for air-raid shelters and wooden aircraft decoys.

Exhausted by the Depression and the war, Theodore E. Steinway in 1955 relinquished control of Steinway and Sons to his 40-year-old son, Henry Z. Steinway, who consolidated dispersed factory buildings into one site on Riker Avenue in Queens and worked with the union leadership to avoid costly strikes. The firm was successful during his tenure, and in 1972 he sold it to the Columbia Broadcasting System (CBS). In 1985 CBS, short of cash because of an attempted corporate takeover, sold the firm to Robert and John Birmingham, private investors from Boston, thus making Steinway again a family business. In 1985 Steinway was purchased by Kyle Kirkland and Dana Messina, and in 1996 it became a public company traded on the New York Stock Exchange. In 2006, 550 factory employees made 2000 grand pianos and 500 uprights. Henry Z. Steinway, the last Steinway family president, died in 2008.

Richard Lieberman, *Steinway and Sons* (New Haven: Yale University Press, 1995)

Richard K. Lieberman

Steinway Hall. Concert hall, built by the piano makers Steinway and Sons in 1866 as a promotional adjunct to their showroom at 71–73 East 14th Street. A lavish auditorium that had superb acoustics and seated 2000, it was the site of readings by Charles Dickens in 1867, of concerts in 1867 honoring the 25th anniversary of the New York Philharmonic, and of Anton Rubinstein's American debut in 1872. After the hall was sold in 1923, Steinway and Sons opened a new concert hall at 109 West 17th Street in 1925 that looked more like a museum than a piano showroom, with a small 240-seat concert hall. The building was sold in 1955 to the Manhattan Life Insurance Company. Steinway bought the building back in 1999.

Theodore E. Steinway, *People and Pianos: A Century of Service to Music: Steinway and Sons, New York, 1853–1953* (New York: Steinway, 1953); Richard K. Lieberman, *Steinway and Sons* (New Haven: Yale University Press, 1995)

Marc Ferris and Richard K. Lieberman

Stella, Frank (Philip) (*b* Malden, Mass., 12 May 1936). Artist. He became interested in abstract art while in his teens, attended Princeton University (BA in history 1958), and moved to New York City to become a painter. Inspired by the innovative work of Jasper Johns, he executed a series of austere paintings composed of solid-colored symmetrical stripes. In December 1959 four of his paintings were included in an exhibition at the Museum of Modern Art entitled *Sixteen Americans*. His works *Coney Island* (1958) and *The Marriage of Reason and Squalor* (1959), and his renowned black-stripe paintings, marked a transition from abstract expressionism to minimalism. He had his first retrospective exhibition at the Museum of Modern Art at a remarkably young age, in 1970. His *Exotic Bird* series then helped inspire the advent of pattern and decoration painting and graffiti art. He also created three-dimensional art forms, including freestanding sculptures for public spaces and architectural works such as band shells and pavilions. In 2007 the Metropolitan Museum of Art presented an outdoor rooftop exhibition of Stella's sculptural work. He worked out of a studio in Manhattan's East Village at 126–128 East 13th Street until 2005.

Robert Sanger Steel

Stella, Joseph [Giuseppe] (*b* Muro Lucano, Italy, 13 June 1877; *d* Queens, 5 Nov 1947). Painter. He immigrated to the United States in 1896 and settled in New York City, where he studied at the Art Students League and the New York School of Art. In an early series of realist drawings he recorded immigrant life on the Lower East Side. After a trip to Paris in 1911–12 he used color abstraction to depict such symbols of the modern city as Coney Island, the Brooklyn Bridge, skyscrapers, and subways. Stella lived in Williamsburg in Brooklyn from 1916 to 1917, and between travels to Europe he maintained studios at 451 West 24th Street in Manhattan (1923), 2431 Southern Boulevard in the Bronx (1935), 33-15 Crescent Boulevard in Astoria (1942), and 104 West 16th Street in Manhattan (1943). His paintings are held at the Museum of Modern Art and the Whitney Museum of American Art.

Barbara Haskell, *Joseph Stella* (New York: Whitney Museum of American Art, 1994)

Judith Zilczer

Stella D'Oro Biscuit Company. Firm of bakers formed in 1930 by the Italian immigrants Joseph Kresevich and his wife Angela. It began as a bakery on Bailey Avenue in the Bronx offering authentic Italian anisette toast cookies, breadsticks, and egg biscuits and within a year took its current name. After struggling through the Depression and World War II it enjoyed prosperity as its products became popular in the city, particularly in Italian neighborhoods. The headquarters were moved to 237th Street in Kingsbridge in 1947, and a factory was opened on the same street. During the late 1950s the firm became one of the country's most prominent bakers. It remained family-owned until it was acquired by Kraft in 1992. In late 2005 the company was sold to Brynwood Partners, a private equity firm. In 2009 it was closed.

James Bradley

Stengel, Casey [Charles Dillon] (*b* Kansas City, Mo., 30 July 1890; *d* Glendale, Calif., 29 Sept 1975). Baseball player and manager. As an outfielder for the Brooklyn Dodgers (1912–17), the Pittsburgh Pirates (1917, 1919), and the New York Giants (1921–23), he achieved a lifetime batting average of .284. He then worked for the Dodgers as a coach (1932–34) and manager (1934–36). Between 1948 and 1960 he managed the New York Yankees, winning 10 pennants and seven World Series. He became the first manager in 1962 of the New York Mets, which over the next four seasons finished last each year in the National League and compiled an overall record of 194 wins and 452 losses. Stengel was a consummate showman: while playing for the Pirates he tipped his cap to a hostile crowd, revealing a bird that flew out from under it, and as the manager of the Mets he used colorful malapropisms to divert the attention of the fans and the press from the ineptness of his players. He was elected to the National Baseball Hall of Fame in 1966.

Robert W. Creamer, *Stengel* (New York: Dell, 1985)

Harold S. Wechsler

Stern, Isaac (*b* Kremenets, Ukraine, 21 July 1920; *d* New York City, 22 September 2001). Violinist. After growing up and receiving musical training in San Francisco, he first performed in New York City in 1937. His third appearance in the city, at Carnegie Hall in January 1943, brought him recognition as a musician of the first rank. He performed around the world and made many recordings of both concertos and chamber music from the classic and modern repertories. In 1944 he played with the New York Philharmonic Orchestra, directed by Artur Rodzinski. In 1960 he became president of the Carnegie Hall Corporation and served in the office for more than 30 years. He led the campaign to save the hall from demolition and helped the city to purchase it and turn it into a landmark. The main concert hall was renamed the Isaac Stern Auditorium in 1997.

George A. Thompson, Jr.

Stern College for Women. Four-year college opened in 1954 at 245 Lexington Avenue in Murray Hill as a division of Yeshiva University, and the first Jewish liberal arts college for women in the United States. The school has a core curriculum that includes both the liberal arts and Jewish studies. Most of its more than 1000 students study for one year in Israel.

Erica Judge

Stern's. Department store. It began in 1867 as a small dry-goods shop selling dress material, laces, and silk, opened at 367 Sixth Avenue in Manhattan by four German immigrant brothers: Isaac, Louis, Bernard, and Benjamin Stern. They moved in 1877 to larger quarters along "Ladies' Mile" at 110 West 23rd Street; their store was the largest department store in the city until 1910. It employed uniformed doormen to greet members of the carriage trade and it also priced some of its merchandise for working-class customers. It moved in 1911 to a building at 42nd Street and Fifth Avenue with an elegant cast-iron facade, where it remained until the firm ceased its operations in the city in 1969.

Leslie Gourse

Stettheimer, Florine (*b* Rochester, N.Y., 19 Aug 1871; *d* New York City, 11 May 1944). Painter. She studied in New York City at the Art Students League and in Germany during an eight-year stay in Europe. On returning to the city in 1914 she established with her sisters Ettie and Carrie a salon attended by avant-garde artists such as Marcel Duchamp. While living at Alwyn Court on 57th Street in 1932 she designed the sets and costumes for the opera *Four Saints in Three Acts* by Virgil Thomson and Gertrude Stein. She later moved to Sixth Avenue and 40th Street. Stettheimer's richly ornamented, colorful paintings satirize art and society in New York City in the 1920s and 1930s.

Hilton Kramer, "Florine Stettheimer's Distinctive Vision of Society," *New York Times,* 16 March 1980, §1, pp. 33, 41

Betty Kaplan Gubert

Sets by Florine Stettheimer for original production of Four Saints in Three Acts *(music by Virgil Thomson, text by Gertrude Stein), Hartford, Connecticut, 1934*

Steuben Society. Organization formed in New York City in 1919 to honor the Prussian military leader Baron Friedrich Wilhelm von Steuben (1730–94). Its formation was intended to improve German American relations and emphasize the loyalty of German Americans in the aftermath of World War I. During the early 1930s the society took a forthright stance against Nazism in both Germany and the United States. After World War II Steuben societies were formed in Germany. Steuben parades modeled after those on St. Patrick's Day and Pulaski Day were held annually on Fifth Avenue after 1958, the year considered by many to be the 275th anniversary of the first immigration by Germans to the United States. The Steuben Society of America maintains its headquarters at 6705 Fresh Pond Road in Ridgewood, Queens.

Albert Bernhardt Faust, *The German Element in the United States* (New York: Steuben Society, 1927)

Kevin Kenny

Steuer, Max David (*b* Humenné [now in Slovakia], 6 Sept 1870; *d* Jackson, N.H., 21 Aug 1940). Lawyer. With his family in 1876 he moved from Austria to New York City, where his father found work in the garment trade. After winning academic honors at Public School 15 and City College of New York, he earned a degree from Columbia Law School in 1903. As attorney general of the city court he became known for his extraordinary memory and fierce style in conducting cross examinations; he was widely considered a peerless trial lawyer for successfully defending politician Harry Daugherty, banker Charles Mitchell, the owners of the Triangle Shirtwaist factory, and such organized-crime figures as Johnny Torrio. Steuer helped to negotiate the first industry-wide contract for female garment workers and was a delegate to the state constitutional convention of 1938.

George J. Lankevich

Stevens, Harry M(ozley) (*b* Derby, England, 14 June 1855; *d* New York City, 3 May 1934). Sports concessionaire and caterer. After attending a baseball game in Columbus, Ohio, in early 1887 he was inspired by the idea of scorecards with advertising printed on the back. Within four years he was selling such cards at major and minor league parks across the country. In 1894 he moved to New York City and obtained exclusive rights for a concession at the Polo Grounds, where he expanded his sales to include snack foods. He also began catering large events at hotels, exhibitions, and outdoor events and eventually acquired the rights for the dining room in Madison Square Garden. His business nevertheless continued to focus on serving food at outdoor sporting events. In 1901 he introduced what soon became standard fare for such venues: peanuts, soda, and hot dogs, earning him the title "Hot Dog King." In 1925 he incorporated his business under his name and had concessions at the five major league baseball parks in New York City and Boston.

Edward T. O'Donnell

Susan Smith McKinney Steward

Steward, Susan McKinney [Susan Maria Smith] (*b* Brooklyn, 18 March 1847; *d* Brooklyn, 7 March 1918). Born in Crown Heights, Susan Maria Smith became the first African American woman to earn a medical degree in New York State. Trained as an organist as a child, Steward taught music in Washington, D.C., and New York in order to pay for her medical studies. She attended New York Medical College for Women from 1867 to 1870, specializing in homeopathic medicine and pediatrics, and graduated as class valedictorian. In 1871 she married William G. McKinney, a Methodist minister who died in 1894. In 1896 she married Theophilus Gould Stewart, an army chaplin. She is buried in Green-Wood Cemetery in Brooklyn.

Sherrill D. Wilson

Stewart, A(lexander) T(urney) (*b* Ireland, *ca* 1802; *d* New York City, 10 April 1876). Retailer. Brought up in Ireland by his maternal grandfather, he studied for the ministry and moved to New York City where he taught school. On 1 September 1823 he opened a small dry-goods shop at 283 Broadway, later marrying the landlord's daughter Cornelia Clinch, and on 21 September 1846 he opened a lavish building designed by John Snook at 280 Broadway between Reade and Chambers streets. Known as the Marble Palace (a term first used in the *New York Herald,* 18 September 1846), this was the first commercial building with a marble facade; it had a domed atrium, mahogany cabinets, and lavish fixtures, and the store offered "free entrance" (allowing customers to browse rather than be attended to constantly by a patron), low markups, and set prices on a large variety of goods. In 1862 Stewart built the larger Iron Palace, on Broadway between Ninth and 10th streets, believed to be the first building in the city with a cast-iron front; it eventually occupied the entire block and became one of the largest iron structures in the world. During the 1860s Stewart was the wealthiest resident of the city and the most prominent importer, taxpayer, and home owner in the United States, living in a marble mansion at Fifth Avenue and 34th Street. His business had gross sales of $50 million in 1865 (primarily from wholesale trade), with domestic and European offices, warehouses, and factories. He avidly collected art and real estate in Manhattan, founded and planned suburban Garden City (Long Island), and maintained ties with the Tweed Ring and the administration of President Ulysses S. Grant. He died childless, and his estate was mismanaged by his attorney Henry Hilton. In 1878 Stewart's body was exhumed and ransomed (it remains unclear whether the body was recovered), and in 1884 the Marble Palace was converted to offices.

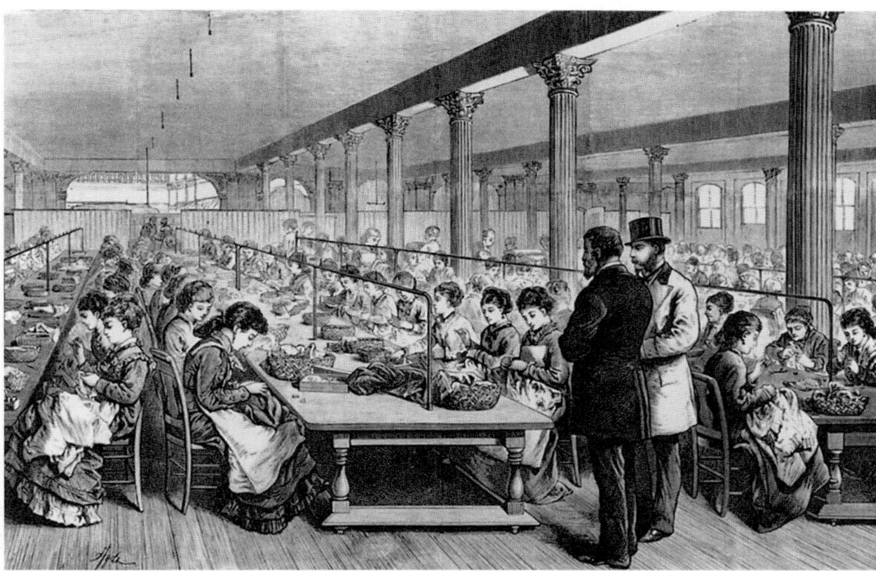

Sewing room at A. T. Stewart's store at Broadway and Tenth Street, 1875

A. T. Stewart's cast-iron building on Broadway, between Ninth and Tenth streets

Stephen N. Elias, *Alexander T. Stewart: Forgotten Merchant Prince* (Westport, Conn.: Praeger, 1992)

David B. Sicilia

Stewart, Ellen (*b* Alexandria, La., 7 Nov 1918). Founder of La MaMa Experimental Theatre Club, one of the oldest and most influential Off-Off-Broadway theaters. Stewart came to New York from Chicago in 1950 and began working as a clothing designer at Saks Fifth Avenue, though racial tensions and health problems eventually forced her to resign. She went on to work as a freelance designer for firms such as Bergdorf Goodman and Lord and Taylor. She lived in Morocco for a time before returning to New York and founding La MaMa in a basement at 321 East Ninth Street. Pushed from building to building by unfriendly neighbors and city zoning officials (Stewart got into trouble with the city more than once for staging performances without a license), in 1961 she moved La MaMa to its current location at 74A East Fourth Street.

Under Stewart's direction, La MaMa was instrumental in fostering the development of new playwrights, presenting original works by Sam Shepard and Lanford Wilson and staging the U.S. premiere of Harold Pinter with a production of *The Room* in 1962. Stewart also toured La MaMa plays throughout Europe and the Middle East.

Patrick Barrett

stickball. A form of baseball that developed in the early twentieth century in the streets of New York City. Each neighborhood had its own rules and traditions; many had teams of nine players and used parked cars or "sewers" (manhole covers) as bases. In different versions of the game, the pitcher threw the ball to the batter on one bounce, the batter hit the ball after tossing it in the air himself, or the pitcher would try to hit a strike zone drawn on a wall behind the batter. Equipment usually consisted of an old broomstick and a "spaldeen," a pink rubber ball made by the Spalding Company. An increase in playgrounds, organized sports, and vehicular traffic led to a post–World War II decline in stickball's popularity; interest in the game revived in the 1960s and 1970s, especially among adults who remembered the game from their childhood. In 1968 residents of East 111th Street in Manhattan held a stickball reunion in memory of a neighbor, a gathering that became an annual event. Sponsored by Budweiser beginning in 1975, it became known as the Budweiser Old Timers Stickball Reunion and drew people from across the nation who had grown up in the neighborhood. For a few summers in the mid-1970s three-sewer stickball was featured in a festival of street games sponsored by the Parks Department to celebrate the sporting heritage of the city. In 1983 and 1984 Spalding sponsored a stickball exhibition on West 60th

Street in Manhattan, in which baseball stars, celebrities, and members of the Police Athletic League took part. Newman Avenue in Clason Point was renamed Stickball Boulevard in 1987. In the early twenty-first century stickball remained popular with adults, as organizations like the Major Stick Ball League, the East Harlem Stickball League, and the New York Emperors Stickball League continued to schedule games and crown champions.

Joseph S. Lieber, Ben Silk

Stickley, Gustav [Gustave] (*b* Osceola, Wis., 9 March 1858; *d* Syracuse, N.Y., 20 April 1942). Furniture manufacturer, home designer, and publisher. He entered the furniture business at age 18 and started a furniture company in 1883 with his younger brothers; the Stickley Brothers Company, in Susquehanna, Pennsylvania, produced reproductions of colonial, Windsor, and other styles of chairs. In 1898 Stickley formed the Gustave Stickley Company (later dropping the "e" from his first name) and introduced his first Arts and Crafts furniture, which was characterized by straight lines, plain surfaces, and sturdy construction. He was strongly influenced by the work of William Morris and other members of the British Arts and Crafts movement. In 1901 he began publishing the *Craftsman,* a magazine devoted to the ideals of the Arts and Crafts movement and to publicizing his furniture and home designs; he dedicated the first issue to William Morris.

In 1905 Stickley moved his furniture showrooms and publishing business from Syracuse, N.Y., to 29 West 34th Street in New York City, expanding to 41 West 34th Street in 1908. That year he began purchasing land in suburban Morris Plains, N.J., and in 1909 he started construction of Craftsman Farms, which he intended as a working farm and school for boys that would offer both academic and manual training. In 1913 he leased a 12-story building at 6 East 39th Street, which he called the Craftsman Building. It housed his furniture showroom, the offices of the *Craftsman,* and a restaurant that served produce grown on Craftsman Farms. Financial problems arose, however, as Stickley expanded his business, tastes changed, and the war began in Europe. In 1915 he filed for bankruptcy; the *Craftsman* ceased publication in 1916.

Mary Ann Smith, *Gustav Stickley, The Craftsman* (New York: Dover, 1992); David Cathers, *Gustav Stickley* (London: Phaidon Press, 2003)

Catherine Mathis

Stieglitz, Alfred (*b* Hoboken, N.J., 1 Jan 1864; *d* New York City, 13 July 1946). Photographer. He was educated in New York City before going to Berlin to study engineering, which he soon abandoned for photography. After returning to New York City in 1890, he worked briefly in a photoengraving business and eagerly pursued amateur photography. During the next two decades he produced a group of atmospheric street and waterfront scenes, one of the best known being *The Hand of Man* (1902). He was active in the Camera Club of New York and became the editor of *Camera Notes.* Soon after, he formed the Photo-Secession, a group of photographers dissatisfied with the dominant styles in pictorial photography. Members exhibited their work in "291," a gallery on Fifth Avenue that he directed. He also published the elegant journal *Camera Work* with the hope of introducing advanced European photography in the United States and encouraging the development of American photographic art. With the help of Edward Steichen he exhibited and published the work of Picasso, Matisse, and Constantin Brancuşi. Eventually he promoted the work of a group of American modernist painters, first at An Intimate Gallery and then at An American Place. After 1915 he resumed making photographs, producing portraits of several friends who were artists; these included many images of Georgia O'Keeffe, whom he later married. *Equivalents,* a series of photographs of the sky near his summer home on Lake George, New York, and photographs of skyscrapers taken from his rooms in suite 3003 of the Hotel Shelton (525 Lexington Avenue) attest to his contradictory feelings toward New York City, which he both hated and loved. He lived from 1898 to 1918 at 1111 Madison Avenue, from July 1918 to the end of 1922 at 114 East 59th Street, for 10 years beginning in 1924 at the Hotel Shelton, from the autumn of 1936 to October 1942 at 405 East 54th Street, and from October 1942 to the end of his life at 59 East 54th Street.

Doris Bry, *Alfred Stieglitz, Photographer* (Boston: Museum of Fine Arts, 1965); Dorothy Norman, *Alfred Stieglitz: An American Seer* (New York: Random House, 1973); Sarah Greenough and Juan Hamilton, *Alfred Stieglitz: Photographs and Writings* (Washington, D.C.: National Gallery of Art, 1983); Waldo Frank et al., eds., *America and Alfred Stieglitz: A Collective Portrait* (New York: Doubleday, Doran, 1934; repr. Millerton, N.Y.: Aperture, 1989)

See also Photography.

Naomi Rosenblum

Still, Clyfford (*b* Grandin, N.D., 30 Nov 1904; *d* Baltimore, 23 June 1980). Artist. In 1945 he was introduced to Peggy Guggenheim, who gave him a solo exhibit at her Art of This Century gallery in 1946. He had solo exhibits in 1947, 1950, and 1951 at the Betty Parsons Gallery in Manhattan. In New York City in 1948 he and other artists including Mark Rothko developed the school known as the Subjects of the Artist. Still lived in the city for most of the 1950s. In 1980 he had an exhibition at the Metropolitan Museum of Art. After his death the Metropolitan Museum continued to maintain a collection of his work. He was known for his abstract expressionist style.

Jessica Montesano

Stimson, Henry L(ewis) (*b* New York City, 21 Sept 1867; *d* Huntington, N.Y., 20 Oct 1950). Secretary of state. He passed the bar in New York State in 1891 and spent his early career in New York City. In 1906 he was appointed U.S. attorney of the Southern District of New York by President Theodore Roosevelt, who supported him when he sought, unsuccessfully, the governorship of New York in 1910. He served from 1911 to 1913 as secretary of war under President William Howard Taft and from 1929 to 1933 as secretary of state under President Herbert Hoover. Although a Republican he was again secretary of war under President Franklin D. Roosevelt from 1940 to 1945. During 1918–27 and 1933–40 Stimson lived and practiced law in New York City.

Godfrey Hodgson, *The Colonel: The Life and Wars of Henry Stimson, 1867–1950* (New York: Alfred A. Knopf, 1990)

See also Espionage.

Elliot S. Meadows

stock exchanges. See American Stock Exchange, Consolidated (Stock and Petroleum) Exchange, and New York Stock Exchange.

Stokes, I(saac) N(ewton) Phelps (*b* New York City, 11 April 1867; *d* Charleston, S.C., 18 Dec 1944). Architect, historian, philanthropist, and housing reformer. The eldest of nine children of Helen L. Phelps and Anson Phelps Stokes, Sr., whose families had long been involved in charities and reform in New York City, he graduated from Harvard College (1891) and then studied architecture and housing design at Columbia University and in Paris from 1894 to 1897. With his friend John Mead Howells (1868–1959) he won a competition in 1897 for the design of the University Settlement House (184 Eldridge Street). The two opened a firm that received many New York City commissions, including Horace Mann Hall at Teachers College (1901, Broadway and 120th Street), the former building of the Royal Insurance Company (1906, 84 William Street), St. Paul's Chapel (1907, Columbia University), and the Open-Air Pulpit at St. John the Divine (1916, Amsterdam Avenue and 112th Street). The two men amicably dissolved their partnership in 1917.

Stokes was also known for his work to improve housing for the poor, and as a member of the New York State Tenement House Commission he was the author with Lawrence Veiller of the Tenement House Law of 1901, which raised the standards for multiple dwellings in New York City. In addition he designed two "model tenements for Negroes," the Tuskegee (1902) and the Hampton (1911), both on the West Side of Manhattan. As a director of the Phelps Stokes Fund he supervised its housing activities and gave advice on the development of publicly subsidized housing programs during the 1920s and 1930s. He was also a pioneer in historic preservation and was instrumental in saving the facade of the Bank of the United States on Wall Street (1823; later the Assay Office), which was later installed at the Metropolitan Museum of Art. A collector of prints and maps documenting the city's history, he produced a monumental illustrated reference work in six volumes, *The Iconography of Manhattan Island* (1915–28), which remains an important research tool.

Deborah S. Gardner

Stokes [née Pastor]**, Rose (Harriet)** (*b* Augustow, Poland, 18 July 1879; *d* Frankfurt, Germany, 20 June 1933). Writer and political activist. She settled in Cleveland with her family in 1890. After moving to New York City in 1903 she became a reporter for the *Jewish Daily News* and married James Graham Phelps Stokes, a resident of the University Settlement House. They became active in the Socialist Party, and she later took part in the hotel and restaurant workers' strike of 1912 and helped organize garment workers. Stokes wrote articles for the *Masses,* the *Century,* and the *Independent* and gave lectures in support of Margaret Sanger, Emma Goldman, and Elizabeth Gurley Flynn. Her play *The Women Who Wouldn't* was produced in 1916. Convicted under the Espionage Act in March 1918, she served two years in prison in Missouri before her case was dismissed on appeal.

Martha Foley

Stone, Harlan Fiske (*b* Chesterfield, N.H., 11 Oct 1872; *d* Washington, D.C., 22 April 1946). Chief justice of the United States. He graduated in 1898 from Columbia Law School, where he was later a professor (from 1902) and dean (1910–23). During his early career his conservative instincts and wariness of government made him sympathetic toward judges who invoked the sacredness of property to nullify state and federal measures regulating business. After serving briefly as attorney general under President Calvin Coolidge he was appointed in 1925 to the U.S. Supreme Court. By this time his skepticism toward regulation was outweighed by his belief in judicial restraint, as a result of which he often found himself aligned with Justices Oliver Wendell Holmes and Louis Brandeis in dissents against a majority inclined to invalidate laws governing the private economic sector. Among his best-known dissents was his opinion in *United States v. Butler* (1936), which overturned the Agricultural Adjustment Act, a law inspired by the New Deal. On this occasion he sarcastically reminded his fellow justices that judges were not the "only agency of government that must be assumed to have the capacity to govern." After becoming chief justice in 1941 he helped move the court toward greater activism in protecting civil liberties.

Alpheus T. Mason, *Harlan Fiske Stone: Pillar of the Law* (New York: Viking, 1956)

Frederick S. Voss

Stonewall Riots. Protests widely regarded as having launched the contemporary gay liberation movement. In the early morning hours of 28 June 1969 police raided the Stonewall Inn, which was a dancing bar in Greenwich Village frequented by gay men, lesbians, and transvestites. Since gay bars were illegal, the Stonewall was set up as a "bottle club" where "members" paid to have liquor served to them from their private bottles; in turn, they were free to slow dance with each other undisturbed. To protect his patrons, Mafioso owner Tony Lauria paid a monthly kickback to the police in the Sixth Precinct, who agreed to notify the bar before conducting a raid. In the 1960s raids were frequent at gay bars and were relatively uneventful because they were typically conducted by local precincts that were taking such kickbacks. The raid on the Stonewall, however, was different because it was intended to close down an illegal bond operation that Lauria was running. When the bust took place it involved a federal agent, two undercover detectives from the Fifth Precinct, six Public Morals Officers, and an inspector from the Department of Consumer Affairs. Resistance was fierce largely because there had been no prior notification. People spilled out into Sheridan Square, and patrons and passersby attacked police with bottles, rocks, and even a firebomb. On the first night, 13 people were arrested and 4 patrolmen were injured. During the next two nights similar acts of resistance took place throughout the area. The block of Christopher Street where the bar stands is now named Stonewall Place, and the annual gay pride celebration is dated to coincide with the anniversary of the Stonewall Rebellion.

Martin Bauml Duberman, *Stonewall* (New York: E. P. Dutton, 1993); David Carter, *Stonewall: The Riots that Sparked the Gay Revolution* (New York: St. Martin's Press, 2004)

Paul M. McNeil

Stork Club. Nightclub at 3 East 53rd Street, opened in 1929. Owned by Sherman Billingsley, it was frequented by the gossip columnist Walter Winchell, who sat at table no. 50 in the Cub Room, often with his friend Damon Runyon, and described the club as "the New Yorkiest place in New York." The Stork Club was a well-known venue for celebrity seekers for three decades, hosting, for instance, J. Edgar Hoover, John and Jacqueline Kennedy, the Roosevelts, and the duke and duchess of Windsor. It shut down in 1965.

James E. Mooney

Stover, Charles B(unstein) (*b* Riegelsville, Pa., 14 July 1861; *d* New York City, 25 April 1929). Park commissioner. He was trained as a Presbyterian minister and in the 1890s became known as a reformer on the Lower East Side, working out of University Settlement. A distinguished advocate for parks and playgrounds, he was the city's park commissioner from 1910 to 1914. During his tenure he built 30 playgrounds; planted 250 Lombardy poplars on Delancey Street; reclaimed 10 acres (4 hectares) of land along Riverside Drive (using stones from the boring of the Catskill Aqueduct through Manhattan); was instrumental in establishing Seward Park and Jacob Riis Park; led the opposition to elevated trains; and supported causes as varied as sailors' rights and municipal ownership of the subways. Late in his term he disappeared for more than three months, prompting a nationwide search that ended when he mailed his resignation from Cincinnati. When he reappeared in January 1914, he maintained that he had been touring

The Stonewall Inn, 2009

cities in the South. Stover spent his last years developing a summer camp in Beacon, New York, for University Settlement.

James Kirke Paulding, *Charles B. Stover: His Life and Personality* (New York: International Press, 1938)

Jeffrey Scheuer

Stranahan, James S(amuel) T(homas) (*b* Peterboro, near Oneida, N.Y., 25 April 1808; *d* Saratoga, N.Y., 3 Sept 1898). Businessman and public official. He settled in Brooklyn in 1844 and made his fortune working as a railroad contractor and building docks in Brooklyn, particularly the Atlantic Basin. As president of the park board of Brooklyn from 1860 to 1882 he led the effort to develop Prospect Park. When a financial discrepancy was discovered, he left the board and reconciled the accounts with his own funds. He also backed the construction of the Brooklyn Bridge and the consolidation of New York City in 1898.

John J. Gallagher

Strand. Largest bookstore in New York City and among the largest used book stores in the world. It is famous for its collection of rare books, publishers' overstock, and review copy books and has more than 2.5 million volumes on its shelves. The Strand was founded in 1927 by Ben Bass, one of 48 bookstores on New York City's "book row" and the only one that survived into 2009. When the founder's son, Fred Bass, took over the store's management in 1956, it moved to its present location at Broadway and 12th Street, where it has grown to occupy 55,000 square feet (5110 square meters) on five floors. The store also operates a 15,000-square-foot (1394-square-meter) annex on Fulton Street in the financial district and two outdoor kiosks: one bordering Central Park at Fifth Avenue and 60th Street and one on the Manhattan side of the tram to Roosevelt Island. Excluding the annex and the kiosks, the Strand boasts 23 miles (37 kilometers) of books measured along its shelves, although it has kept its slogan—"18 miles of books"—for marketing reasons.

Rowan Moore Gerety

Strand Theater [Brooklyn]. Historic movie theater at the northeast corner of Fulton Street and Rockwell Place. Designed by architect Thomas W. Lamb, it was called the Brooklyn Strand to distinguish it from the Strand in Manhattan, which Lamb also designed. After opening 30 August 1919 the Brooklyn Strand became part of a hub including the Majestic, a playhouse, and the Orpheum, a vaudeville venue. Lamb designed the Strand's exterior to resemble a classical temple with two-story Ionic columns topped by a colored frieze and entablature. The lobby, with a 60-foot-high (18-meter-high) ceiling, contained two staircases, furniture, and a fountain, all in marble. Red and yellow walls and columns of black and gold marble graced the lobby. The Strand had a deep stage, space for a 25-piece orchestra, and was used for live performances as well as movies; it could accommodate 3500 patrons. With the advent of sound movies the Strand became the first theater in Brooklyn equipped with Vitaphone projectors and speakers and in 1927 presented Al Jolson's *The Jazz Singer,* one of the early "talkies." In the late 1920s newer movie theaters supplanted the Strand, which became a second-run house and then in 1959 a 52-lane bowling alley. Early in the twenty-first century a variety of businesses and studios occupied the building, which New York City owned and planned to continue developing as a cultural center.

Cathy Alexander

Strasberg, Lee [Strassberg, Israel] (*b* Budzanów [now Budanov, near Terebovlya, Ukraine], 17 Nov 1901; *d* New York City, 17 Feb 1982). Theater director. He studied acting at the American Laboratory Theatre before joining the Theater Guild as a stage manager and actor. In collaboration with Harold Clurman and Cheryl Crawford he formed the Group Theatre in 1931 and directed several productions during the theater's 10 years of operation. In 1948 he joined the faculty of the Actors Studio, located at the Old Labor Stage at 432 West 44th Street, becoming its artistic director in 1951. Over the next 30 years Strasberg taught the Method, his influential and controversial approach to acting based on the teachings of Konstantin Stanislavsky, which stressed the actor's use of life experiences. Among his students were Marlon Brando, Marilyn Monroe, and Paul Newman. Strasberg is buried at Westchester Hills Cemetery in Westchester County, N.Y.

Cindy Heller Adams, *Lee Strasberg: The Imperfect Genius of the Actors Studio* (Garden City, N.Y.: Doubleday, 1980)

D. S. Moynihan

Stratton, Charles Sherwood. (*b* Bridgeport, Conn., 4 Jan 1838; *d* Middleboro, Mass., 15 Jul 1883). Performer. The diminutive Charles Stratton, better known as "Tom Thumb," came to the attention of P. T. Barnum at the age of four, when he reportedly weighed 25 pounds and was a mere 15 inches tall. The child of average-sized parents, he apparently suffered from an endocrine or pituitary irregularity. Barnum, recognizing Stratton's gift for mimicry and performance, renamed the child Tom Thumb and taught him to sing and impersonate famous characters, claiming to audiences that he was 11 years old.

Stratton's Tom Thumb performances at the American Museum on lower Broadway caught the public fancy. He toured the United States with Barnum and was taken to Europe, where he was granted an audience with Queen Victoria, returning to America as a celebrity. In February 1863, Stratton married Mercy Lavinia Warren Bump (or Bumpus), a woman of his own size. Lavinia's trousseau was displayed in the show windows of Lord and Taylor before the wedding, which took place in Grace Episcopal Church and was attended by thousands. He died of a stroke at the age of 45, having grown by the time of his death into a portly gentleman standing three feet four inches tall. During his adult life he developed a taste for racing yachts and distinguished company.

P. T. Barnum, *The Life of P. T. Barnum by Himself* (New York: Redfield, 1855); P. T. Barnum, *Struggles and Triumphs or, Forty Years Recollections of P. T. Barnum, Written by Himself* (1869 and later editions); "The Autobiography of Countess Lavinia Warren [Stratton] Magri," manuscript at the New-York Historical Society

Jean Ashton

Strattonport. Name used for a section of College Point in the early nineteenth century. A grant for 900 acres (365 hectares) near Flushing was given by the Dutch in 1645 to William Lawrence, whose descendants sold 320 acres (130 hectares) of land near what is now College Point Boulevard and 25th Avenue to Eliphalet Stratton in 1789. Half the property was sold to John Flammer in 1851 for development. In 1867 College Point, Strattonport, and Flammersburg became the Village of College Point.

Vincent Seyfried

Straus, Nathan (*b* Otterberg [now in Germany], 31 Jan 1848; *d* New York City, 11 Jan 1931). Merchant and philanthropist, brother of Oscar Straus. The son of a European revolutionary, he immigrated with his family in 1854 to Columbus, Georgia, where his parents became wealthy in the cotton trade. The fam-

Nathan Straus

ily lost its holdings during the Civil War and moved in 1865 to New York City, where Nathan entered Packard Business College (graduated 1866). He joined his father and his brother Isidor Straus in the family china and crockery business, L. Straus and Sons, which eventually became one of the largest of its kind in the country. With his brother he later acquired R. H. Macy and Company and entered into a partnership with the merchant Abraham Abraham to form Abraham and Straus; these two department stores were soon among the largest in the United States.

Nathan's philanthropic activities were wide-ranging. To alleviate illness among immigrants from drinking unprocessed milk, the principal health problem in the city, he formed a pasteurization laboratory in 1892 for distributing milk to poor children in New York and other cities. During the coal strike of 1892–93 he distributed cheap coal to the poor, and in 1894 he provided food and shelter to thousands hurt by the depression. After his brother's death aboard the *Titanic,* Nathan retired from business and devoted himself to philanthropy. During World War I he established a fund for war orphans and distributed free milk, bread, and coffee at Battery Park to returning soldiers. In 1923 he was named the greatest contributor to the city in the 25 years following its incorporation. Straus was the commissioner of parks for the city (1889–92), the president of the Board of Health (1898), and the president of the American Jewish Congress (1918–24). He lived at 27 West 72nd Street. A square is named for him at the intersection of Rutgers Street, Essex Street, East Broadway, and Canal Street on the Lower East Side.

Edward T. O'Donnell

Straus, Oscar S(olomon) (*b* Otterburg, Bavaria, 23 Dec 1850; *d* New York City, 3 May 1926). Lawyer and public official. A member of the German immigrant family that by the 1880s rose to own Macy's and Abraham and Straus, he left the family business to his elder brothers, Isidor Straus and Nathan Straus, and became a lawyer. He was ambassador to Turkey under President William Howard Taft and became the first Jewish member of a presidential cabinet when he was appointed secretary of commerce and labor by President Theodore Roosevelt. In 1912 he ran unsuccessfully for the governorship of New York State. He played an important role in forming the American Jewish Committee, the American Jewish Historical Society, and the Baron de Hirsch Fund.

Naomi W. Cohen, *A Dual Heritage: The Public Career of Oscar S. Straus* (Philadelphia: Jewish Publication Society, 1969)

Jeffrey S. Gurock

Stravinsky, Igor (*b* Oranienbaum, Russia, 17 June 1882; *d* New York City, 6 April 1971). Composer. He first visited New York City in 1925 and conducted the New York Philharmonic in Carnegie Hall. He also recorded some pianola rolls at the Aeolian studios. Later years included tours throughout the United States, during which he conducted his own works, and several more appearances in New York City. He moved to the United States in 1939 and became a citizen in 1945. In 1969 a frail Stravinsky moved to New York City, where he lived in the Essex House on Central Park South. He died in a newly purchased apartment at 920 Fifth Avenue a little over a week after moving in. One funeral service for him in the city was followed by another in Venice, Italy, where he was buried in the island cemetery of San Michele.

Stephen Walsh, *Stravinsky: A Creative Spring* (New York: Alfred A. Knopf, 1999), and *Stravinsky: The Second Exile* (New York: Alfred A. Knopf, 2006)

Frank Scaturro

Strawberry Fields. Memorial garden in Central Park at 72nd Street and Central Park West dedicated to John Lennon, the former member of the Beatles who was slain in front of his home at the nearby Dakota apartment building on 8 December 1980. The City Council established the memorial in 1985 and named the tear-shaped parcel after the song "Strawberry Fields Forever," written by Lennon and fellow Beatle Paul McCartney. Funded primarily by Lennon's widow, Yoko Ono, the 2.5-acre (1-hectare) memorial was designed by the landscape architect Bruce Kelly, who included donations of plants from nations around the world, symbolizing Lennon's dream of world peace. A circular mosaic inscribed with the word *Imagine,* the title of another Lennon composition, was donated by the city of Naples, Italy, and incorporated into the pavement of the main walkway. Crowds gather there each year on the anniversary of his death. Memorial gatherings have also been held at the site to honor other musicians, as were candlelight vigils after the terrorist attacks of 11 September 2001.

Robert Sanger Steel

streetcars. Street railways were constructed beginning with the New York and Harlem Railroad in 1832, to replace stagecoach routes. This pioneering railroad followed Fourth and Madison avenues using horses to pull a railroad-like coach on iron tracks, which provided passengers with a smoother ride, and the horses with an easier task, than stagecoaches on bumpy and unpaved streets. Stage companies converted their lines to rail and reincorporated (Sixth Avenue in 1851, Second and Third avenues in 1853, Eighth Avenue in 1855, Ninth Avenue in 1859, and Seventh Avenue in 1864, as well as many crosstown routes); by the 1880s lower Manhattan was a gridiron of street railways. Streetcars used before 1890 were small, slow, and horse-drawn, resulting in slow and crowded service, coupled with the sanitation problem of horse droppings on pavements. The shortcomings of horse traction led to searches for better propulsion. CABLE CARS, introduced on Amsterdam Avenue north of 125th Street in 1885, were the first forays into mechanical traction—cars were pulled by long cables made of braided iron and hemp ("ropes") that rested

Trolley cars on Nostrand and Atlantic avenues in Brooklyn, ca *1895*

Brooklyn Railroad

on pulleys and moved at a steady speed of 9 miles (14.5 kilometers) an hour. Each car was run by a "gripman" who operated a grip (or "plough") that protruded below the car, passed through a slot between the rails, and gripped the cable. Although cable cars were better than horse traction, they were expensive to build and operate; loose cable strands could snag on the car grip and cause the car to be dragged forward and smash into cars ahead of it, and a cable lasted only a few months. These shortcomings soon gave way to electric streetcars, which first appeared in 1886 in Richmond, Virginia, and Scranton, Pennsylvania. New York City soon embraced this new mode of travel, which was faster than cable cars and safer and cheaper to operate. Electric cars replaced Broadway's cable line in 1901, and the last cable line, in Brooklyn Heights, was discontinued in 1909.

The conversion of the cable rails to electricity was complicated by a municipal ordinance prohibiting overhead wires in Manhattan (only Washington, D.C., had a similar law); the streetcars in that borough used an underground conduit power system in which a buried third rail was connected to the streetcar using a plough that protruded through a slot between the rails, similar in appearance to the older cable cars. Some Manhattan streetcar lines were able to use the former cable slot to install a third rail. Outside of Manhattan, streetcars used the more common overhead wire power system with a trolley pole connecting to the car.

In 1890 there were roughly 24 street railway firms in New York City, which then consisted of Manhattan and the Bronx. Each firm had one main route or a branch, but from that time the Metropolitan Street Railway syndicate consolidated operations; it acquired the large Third Avenue Railway System in 1899 and achieved a virtual monopoly in those two boroughs, controlling a network extending from South Ferry to The Bronx and into Westchester County. Metropolitan bought larger cars, integrated short lines to form long routes, and extended transfer privileges. Until 1904 the volume of traffic was enormous, but business diminished as the subway system developed. In the panic of 1907 Metropolitan declared bankruptcy and was forced to relinquish the Third Avenue system, which controlled the entire Bronx and Upper Manhattan network as well as six key Manhattan routes on and south of 125th Street. In December 1911 the remainder of the old Metropolitan syndicate was reorganized as the New York Railways Company, which controlled most Manhattan routes. In an effort by the firm to maintain the formerly lucrative downtown routes that it could not afford to electrify, it bought battery-operated cars and developed five crosstown lines. One curiosity was a horse-car operation on Bleecker Street that continued until 1917.

When the City of Brooklyn became part of New York City in 1898, an already-large streetcar network was added to the picture. Like Manhattan it had evolved from horsecars to electric power in the 1890s; the Brooklyn Rapid Transit Company (BRT), formed in 1896, soon controlled virtually all elevated railway and surface streetcar systems in its namesake borough, and extended some streetcar routes into adjacent portions of Queens and over the Brooklyn Bridge to a terminal at Park Row. Queens was also home to a group of small and localized streetcar operators—Steinway Railway, Manhattan and Queens Traction, Long Island Electric Railway, New York and Queens County Railway, and New York and North Shore Traction. The BRT and its 1923 successor, the Brooklyn-Manhattan Transit Corporation (BMT) remained firmly committed to streetcars; in 1930 only a handful of buses were found among Brooklyn's huge surface route network. BMT management helped the U.S. streetcar industry develop new streamlined President's Conference Committee (PCC) streetcars in the early 1930s; the first PCC fleet, 100 cars, entered service on the Smith Street–Coney Island Avenue route on 1 October 1936.

Staten Island had electric streetcars from 1892 until 1934. Richmond Railways was the dominant operator until the 1920s, when buses began running on the island. In January 1934 the last Staten Island streetcar operated, replaced by buses of the Tompkins Bus Corporation and Staten Island Coach Company.

In 1919 the city's streetcar system peaked at 1344 miles (2162 kilometers), and streetcars carried more passengers than both the elevated lines and the subways. Patronage fell in the 1920s with the advent of the automobile and development of buses. After 1934 Mayor La Guardia's administration established a firm pro-bus surface transit policy, which put streetcar lines on borrowed time. Fifth Avenue Coach Company had acquired New York Railways in 1926 and converted the entire system, beginning with the Madison Avenue route, to buses in 1935–36, making Manhattan all-bus except for six Third Avenue Railway lines. The latter company, which also operated all Bronx surface routes, signed a franchise agreement in 1940 requiring bus conversion by 1960; its last Manhattan streetcars, on 125th Street and Amsterdam Avenue, ran 29 June 1947; its last Bronx cars, on Tremont Avenue, Southern Boulevard, and Boston Road, ran 22 August 1948. In 1938 the La Guardia administration stopped the BMT's attempt to use a U.S. government loan to acquire 500 more new PCC streetcars for Brooklyn; in 1940 New York City as part of the subway system unification inherited the BMT's entire Brooklyn bus and streetcar network, which ensured that Brooklyn streetcars would be completely converted to buses. On 31 October 1956 the last Brooklyn streetcar lines operated, on Church and McDonald avenues. In Queens most streetcar routes were converted to bus by 1939; exceptions were the BMT's routes extending from Brooklyn (converted to buses in 1949–50), and Steinway Railway's Queensboro Bridge line, which closed 7 April 1957 and was New York's last streetcar route.

Mark H. Rose, Vincent Seyfried, Andrew Sparberg

street games. For centuries children in New York City have adapted streets, empty lots, fire hydrants, stoops, rooftops, fire escapes, curbs, and walls for use in their games. According to the writer Gene Schermerhorn, in nineteenth-century New York City the game of marbles was played in a large ring 4 to 5 feet (1.3 to 1.5 meters) across, marked out on smooth, hard dirt. As open space disappeared, the ring became smaller, and by the 1880s children had difficulty finding a place in which to play. By the early twentieth century the game was relegated to the strip of earth between the street and sidewalk nicknamed "the boulevard." Marbles were not well adapted to asphalt and concrete and gave way to the game of skelly (also called skelsies, skully, killsies, loadsies, caps, bottle caps, or dead man, depending on the neighborhood), in which players flicked bottle caps (or other kinds of plastic caps weighted with tar, orange peels, wax, or melted crayons) along a board of nine or 13 squares chalked on asphalt or concrete. Games such as boxball used sidewalk squares as boundaries. Stoopball was played by throwing a ball against a stoop and using the dimensions of the curb and street to measure runs; in STICKBALL manhole covers often marked the bases. The ball commonly used in these games was the *spaldeen,* named for its manufacturer, Spalding. Distinctive variations of age-old games also developed in the city. Johnny on the Pony, traceable to ancient Greece and known as buck buck in other cities, may have been named for the fire hydrant, locally known as the Johnny pump. Players divided into two teams; one player, usually the heaviest, leaned against a fire hydrant or lamppost, and the others on the team held on to that player's waist, forming a human chain that the other team sought to break by jumping on their opponents' backs. An elaborate version of tag known as ring-a-leavio had a "jail" and was sometimes played in teams. Hopscotch was often called potsy.

During the Depression street rhymes in Harlem were collected by members of the Federal Writers Project of the Works Progress Administration, including Ralph Ellison. The largest collection of games and rhymes was amassed during the 1930s and 1940s by Esther and Oscar Hirschman, who wrote under the names Ethel and Oliver Hale. They recorded many versions of such activities as ball games, hopscotch, and jump rope (not only double Dutch but double Irish, double Jewish, French Dutch, and French Fried), in addition to documenting favorite rhymes and pranks. Titled "From Sidewalk, Gutter and Stoop," their 1000-page manuscript was acquired by the New York Public Library. About this time the term *pushmobile* became popular for a kind of scooter fashioned from a roller skate and an orange crate. By the turn of the twenty-first century street games were seen less frequently in the city owing to television, video games, and a commercialized toy industry; those that have persisted continue to evolve as the urban environment changes.

Amanda Dargan, Steven Zeitlin

street life. New York City has long been known for the vibrancy of its street life. In colonial times business was often conducted outdoors. Stocks were traded near a buttonwood tree between 68 and 70 Wall Street until 1792, when brokers formed the New York Stock Exchange. Indoor floor traders retained trading conventions from the street, including the use of pits and a system of hand gestures to call bids. The Curb Exchange conducted business alongside Broad Street until 1921, when it moved to a building at 78 Trinity Place. Before 1841 meats and vegetables had to be sold in public MARKETS rather than private shops. STREET VENDORS sold corn, gingerbread, crullers, roasted peanuts, baked pears in syrup, apple cider, mint, kindling, shoelaces and suspenders, brooms, and newspapers; chimney sweeps, ragmen, bootblacks, junkmen, chair and umbrella repairers, and knife sharpeners offered their goods and services. Various merchants and craftspeople used distinctive signs, many of which saw continued use in the early twenty-first century, including striped barber poles, cutouts of oversized keys (used by locksmiths) and pistols (by gun shops), three gilt balls (by pawnshops), and a mortar and pestle (by pharmacies). As late as the 1850s HOGS roamed along Sixth Avenue and were often retrieved by their owners with lassos made of clothesline.

As congestion increased, public peace and safety became serious issues. Ordinances were passed to eliminate public nuisances, among them kite-flying, which was banned south of 14th Street at mid-century. Order was strictly kept on the streets of wealthy sections: in 1898 the writer E. S. Martin noted that a "respectable Murray Hill street" was like "the abode of the departed . . . nobody in the side streets; nothing going on" compared with the "life, action, and social activity everywhere" else in the city. The streets of the Lower East Side, for instance, teemed with activity. Clotheslines were strung between tenements until being banned about 1900. As vacant lots disappeared, children playing STREET GAMES were often fined for disorderly conduct; while absorbed in play many were also killed by traffic. Teenaged boys developed SLANG words to describe interruptions of their games, including *flash* for a slow-moving vehicle, *butcher wagon* for an ambulance, and *stoolie, moose, crab-turtle, hotcakes,* or *gorilla* for a person who chased them or complained about their activities.

Seeking to eliminate "unnecessary noises," the city banned street cries in 1908, a measure that met with little success. In many parts of the city during the 1920s and 1930s old-clothes peddlers still sought their wares by crying out "Buy cash! Buy!" and waving a folded newspaper to attract attention; they then sold their goods to secondhand clothing dealers concentrated in the "market" at the end of Elizabeth Street. On Belmont Avenue in the Bronx Italian vendors sold watermelons and Jewish vendors sold roasted potatoes, taffy apples, knishes, and boiled chickpeas (*arbes*). In an effort to clear the streets of pushcarts, organ grinders, and children at play Mayor Fiorello H. La Guardia built PLAYGROUNDS, PARKS, and indoor markets, over the protests of what he called "penthouse slummers." In the 1920s, as work began on skyscrapers and other tall structures, construction sites attracted many

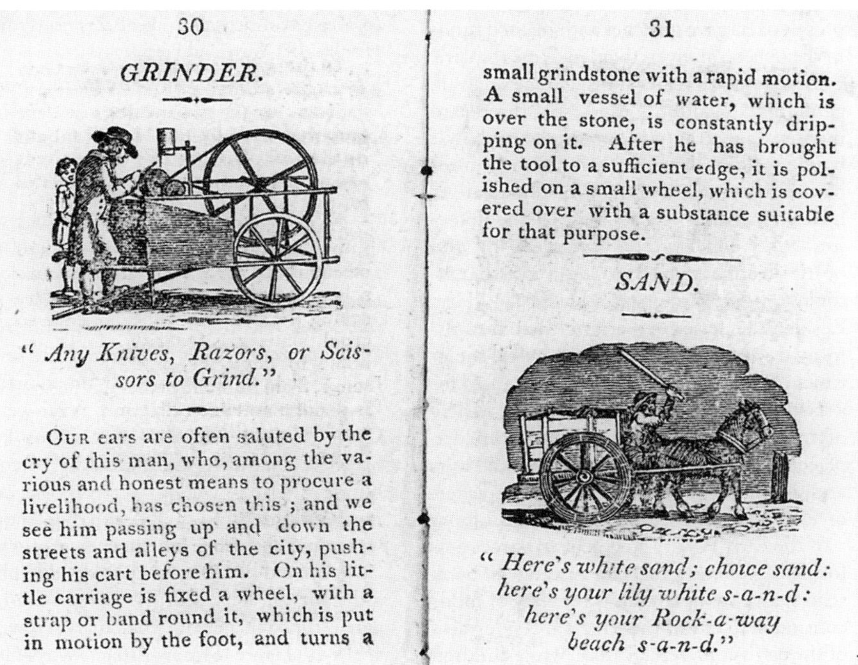

30

GRINDER.

"Any Knives, Razors, or Scissors to Grind."

OUR ears are often saluted by the cry of this man, who, among the various and honest means to procure a livelihood, has chosen this; and we see him passing up and down the streets and alleys of the city, pushing his cart before him. On his little carriage is fixed a wheel, with a strap or band round it, which is put in motion by the foot, and turns a

31

small grindstone with a rapid motion. A small vessel of water, which is over the stone, is constantly dripping on it. After he has brought the tool to a sufficient edge, it is polished on a small wheel, which is covered over with a substance suitable for that purpose.

SAND.

"Here's white sand; choice sand: here's your lily white s-a-n-d: here's your Rock-a-way beach s-a-n-d."

Pages from The Cries of New York *(1812), engraving by Alexander Anderson* spectators. The builders of Rockefeller Center were among the first to cut portholes in the fence around the site to accommodate "sidewalk superintendents."

As Chinatown became increasingly congested after 1965, even the smallest spaces along its streets were put to use. Vendors sold traditional foods from carts along Canal Street; shoe repairers, watchmakers, diviners, and fish sellers worked on the sidewalks; crowds stopped to watch candy makers transform discs of sugar into "dragon's moustaches"; greengrocers worked in trucks trimming vegetables. In Columbus Park elderly men met to practice tai chi and play *juk kay,* elderly women to chat and mind young children. Handwritten charms to stop children from crying were sometimes taped to lampposts, and mirrors were mounted over doorways and windows to ward off evil. During the Chinese New Year teams representing martial-arts clubs wore lion costumes and danced along the streets to bring good luck. In the early twenty-first century vendors hawking counterfeit designer purses also lined Canal Street.

The 1970s and 1980s saw renewed efforts to control street activities. About 1972 the *Guide to the New York City Noise Control Code* described the NOISE level in the city as "an aural state of siege"; enforcement of this code was usually selective. During the 1980s and 1990s the city cracked down on book vendors along Cooper Square, St. Mark's Place, Second Avenue, and Sixth Avenue in Greenwich Village. West African vendors were forced from Fifth Avenue in 1988; they moved to 125th Street and were disbanded again by Mayor Rudolph Giuliani in 1994. Many relocated to the Malcolm Shabazz Harlem Market on 116th Street. Street preachers and religious proselytizers gave speeches and solicited funds in the streets, many of them in Times Square. Efforts were also made to discourage sidewalk gambling operations, especially three-card monte and shell games. Some neighborhoods banned clotheslines, satellite dishes, birdbaths, and recreational and commercial vehicles. Attention also focused on the homeless, who collected redeemable cans and bottles from garbage bins and built shantytowns on vacant lots in the East Village. Residents of devastated neighborhoods transformed vacant lots into small estates, sometimes using rubble to build *casitas,* named for a style of country house in Puerto Rico; these often became meeting places for men displaced from social clubs by rising rents. Parks and sidewalks were also popular with players of "speed" chess, checkers, and backgammon.

In the early twenty-first century street performers, leafleters, bicycle messengers, book sellers, and vendors selling a variety of foods continued to crowd the streets and sidewalks of the city's commercial areas, while children played catch or STICKBALL, bicycled, and jumped rope alongside men playing dominoes

A game of dominos in the Bronx, 2009

in residential neighborhoods: what writer Jane Jacobs called the "street ballet" of New York City remained alive and well.

Alfred Kazin, *A Walker in the City* (New York: Harcourt, Brace, 1951); Benjamin Albert Botkin, ed., *New York City Folklore: Legends, Tall Tales, Anecdotes, Stories, Sagas, Heroes and Characters, Customs, Traditions, and Sayings* (New York: Random House, 1956); Amanda Dargan and Steve Zeitlin, *City Play* (New Brunswick, N.J.: Rutgers University Press, 1990); Barbara Kirshenblatt-Gimblett, "Ordinary People, Everyday Life: Folk Culture in New York City," *Urban Life: Readings in Urban Anthropology,* ed. George Gmelch and Walter P. Zenner (Prospect Heights, Ill.: Waveland Press, 1995)

Barbara Kirshenblatt–Gimblett

street numbering. See HOUSE NUMBERING AND STREET NAMING.

streets and highways. The original configuration of streets in New Amsterdam (1625) at the southern tip of Manhattan Island closely resembled that of a Dutch medieval city: narrow streets enclosed blocks with solid frontages, and a waterway penetrated the settlement at the Heere Graft (now Broad Street). Originally land extended only as far west as Greenwich Street and as far east as Pearl Street, but landfill was soon added to create building space. Wall Street was the city's northern limit until the city expanded northward during the late seventeenth century.

Streets and blocks were developed haphazardly for the next century. Several roads to agricultural villages and small market towns—such as Heere Straat–Broad Way–Great Georges Road, Kings Way–Great Post Road–Albany Post Road, Kingsbridge Road, Bloomingdale Road, Bowery Lane–Boston Post Road, and Flatbush Road—followed Indian and animal trails. They were progressively enlarged as they became the city's major transportation corridors.

Roads were paved gradually, usually through assessments against the owners of abutting property. Most of the street names of the early settlement had a literal meaning. For example, Stone Street was the first paved street, and Maiden Lane led to a favorite laundry spot in the river. The first commissioners of streets and roads were named in 1798.

Improvised expansion of the road network came to an end in 1811 with the adoption of the Commissioners' Plan, which called for streets to be arranged in a strict gridiron formation and numbered, with standardized block and lot sizes. The width of the east–west cross streets was fixed at 60 feet (18 meters) between building lines, and that of the roadway in the center at about 34 feet (10 meters); the north–south avenues were 100 feet (30 meters) wide. These dimensions were set at a time when there was no mechanical street transportation, few people owned horse carriages, and buildings were not expected to reach beyond a height of two or three stories. It was believed that the heaviest traffic would run east and west between the maritime facilities on both sides of the island, and therefore the cross streets were spaced close together. This prediction proved incorrect, and unlike the avenues the cross streets became regarded as suitable for low-density developments and light traffic.

The grid was extended as the city grew northward, and the natural topography was leveled so that valuable land would not be lost. Streets were cut through hills, rocks, and marshes by laborers who lived in shantytowns that were pushed forward in advance of the work area; the northern end of Manhattan Island was reached early in the twentieth century. The rectilinear pattern gave New York City its basic urban image, besides satisfying the original intent of creating convenient building lots for development and sale. The north–south avenues proved capable of accommodating ever growing traffic, except at chronic points of flow convergence along the spine of Manhattan, where the columns of the elevated railway obstructed movement below, and until traffic overloads became common in the second half of the twentieth century.

The other boroughs used the same basic grid, developing land in sections without adopting an overall plan; the results at the seams frequently were awkward triangular lots, confusing intersections, and patches of unused land. Most small settlements and farms disappeared with the construction of tenements and one-family housing; however, the larger established centers and the original pattern of their streets remained. Some of the old villages can still be traced in the configuration of street and lot lines.

In 1860 a commission was appointed to decide whether to complete the Commissioners' Plan of 1811 above 155th Street. Its duties were taken over in part by the Central Park Commission, which evaluated future patterns for Fort Tryon, Inwood, and their environs and had jurisdiction over the western half of the Bronx, and in part by the newly created Park Department in 1871. After consolidation of the greater city (1898), the Board of Estimate and Apportionment was given the right to approve street and park plans. Its chief engineer, Nelson P. Lewis (1902–20), was active in advocating orderly circulation systems and planning in advance of development, in contrast to political officials, who thought only in terms of the city's immediate needs. A request to the New York City Improvement Commission (1903) to prepare a comprehensive plan for the city brought no results; the Committee on the City Plan (1914) was the first to conceive the city as part of a region.

The gridiron pattern proved well suited to New York City: when one channel becomes congested, traffic can be diverted to one or more parallel routes, and the grid could accommodate widely differing types of buildings, from private homes to heavy industrial plants, as well as projects like the company town of Steinway (1877), the planned community of Sunnyside Gardens (1924), and Rockefeller Center (1932). In some parts of New York City curvilinear or diagonal streets and special interior networks were built for sizable developments, including villagelike enclaves such as Forest Hills Gardens (1913), Parkchester (1938), Stuyvesant Town (1947), Peter Cooper Village (1947), Fresh Meadows (1949), Co-op City (1968–70), Roosevelt Island (1974), Starrett City (1976), Battery Park City (1982), and Riverside South.

The "superblock," an area with no internal streets to which access is gained from without or underground, is a modification of the grid's scale that found many applications in the city: examples include the campus of Columbia University, the Jacob K. Javits Convention Center, Battery Park City, Rockefeller Center, Lincoln Center, parts of Roosevelt Island, Jamaica Center, and various hospitals, transportation terminals, housing projects, and industrial enclaves.

As traffic increased during the second half of the nineteenth century, better streets and highways needed to be developed. The design of Central Park (1857), for example, was characterized by controlled access, transverse roads beneath the park to carry crosstown traffic, and attention to the aesthetics of movement. Parkways, inspired by the grand boulevards of Paris, were also introduced at this time. Built as extensions of the parks system, they had well-delineated lanes divided by strips landscaped with trees, grass, and other plantings and were intended not for everyday traffic but for strolling and horse carriages, and later for bicycles. Frederick Law Olmsted was one of the leading advocates of parkways, the most prominent example of which in New York City is Eastern Parkway (1871–74). Others include Western Boulevard (now upper Broadway, 1868–1904), Ocean Parkway (1869–76), Riverside Drive (1872–1902), the Mosholu, Pelham, and Crotona parkways (1884), Park Avenue (1888–1927), the Grand Concourse (1892–1909), and Queens and Northern boulevards (1922). The advent of motor vehicles led to the introduction of a new type of parkway, intended primarily to facilitate the enjoyment of fast motion; the foremost early example in New York City and vicinity was the Bronx River Parkway (1906–23).

The Regional Plan of New York and Its Environs (1927–31) provided a comprehensive vision of a modern transportation system: it encompassed an area with a radius of 50 miles (80 kilometers), reflecting the true size of the metropolis. The principal features of its proposed highway system were a squarish metropolitan loop surrounding the core, with principal internal routes (four east–west and four north–south), routes radiating to the periphery, and distant circumferential bypasses. The plan strove to provide efficient paths between the many important centers of the region. A number of facilities were later completed in the plan's approximate locations, but without achieving the clear order envisioned by the original plan.

Between 1924 and 1972 Robert Moses built 17 parkways and 14 expressways in the city and in Nassau, Suffolk, and Westchester counties. He completed virtually the entire city's highway network, except for the Miller Elevated Highway (popularly known as the West Side Highway), the Harlem River Drive, and the FDR Drive. He also built bridges and parks to which his highways provided the best access. The city could not operate within a rubber-tire–dominated region and country without this system. Brooklyn and parts of Queens constitute the largest "island" in terms of urban territory and number of people in the United States that is surrounded but not crossed by expressways and parkways.

Although New York City achieved one of the most extensive networks of urban highways during the 1950s, it was among the first cities to limit highway expansion during the 1960s and 1970s. The only major highway projects completed during these years were the Bruckner interchange (1973) and the Staten Island West Shore Expressway (1976, now also known as Pearl Harbor Memorial Expressway), after which no limited-access highways or any new arterials were constructed, with the exception of West Street (Route 9A), which replaced a part of the elevated Miller Highway that collapsed in 1973 due to neglected maintenance.

Many highways proposed for New York City have generated extensive debate but were never built, such as the Lower Manhattan Expressway (researched from 1940 to 1969), the Richmond Expressway–Parkway (1941–88), the Mid-Manhattan Expressway (1946–69), the Cross-Brooklyn Expressway (1955–69), the Oyster Bay–Rye crossing of Long Island Sound (1967–72), Westway (1972–90), and a number of other local extensions and connections.

Limited-access expressways and parkways tend to surround each borough and connect the city to the regional and national road system. Since many of these are old, in places the pavement has deteriorated, physical elements and geometry are obsolete, and safety features are inadequate. No new construction of this type can be anticipated, however, so a principal task of the city is to gain the maximum utility from these existing alignments. Congestion is chronic on most sections of this network, which suffers from the fact that long-distance motor vehicle traffic along the eastern seaboard is compelled to cross the city via the Verrazano–Narrows and George Washington bridges because of the presence of the Atlantic Ocean.

The middle tier of New York City roadways consists of major and minor arterials. These are the real workhorses of each borough, and they frequently follow historical alignments. Substantial improvements are difficult because the roadways are fronted by intensive development. In Manhattan this middle tier consists of the avenues, Broadway, and certain principal cross streets. In the Bronx some of the principal arteries are Broadway, Jerome Avenue, and the Grand Concourse. Queens has the Queens, Astoria, Northern,

Kissena–Parsons, and Rockaway boulevards, among others. In Brooklyn examples are Flatbush, Atlantic, Fourth, Union, and Pennsylvania; and Staten Island is served by Victory and Hyland boulevards, Forest and Richmond avenues, and Bay Street.

Of the almost 6000 miles (almost 9700 kilometers) of streets and roadways found in New York City, the overwhelming majority are local service and collector streets. The concerns at this level are pavement repairs, adequate drainage, keeping through traffic out of neighborhoods, and efficient trash collection and snow removal. A new program affecting the use and character of local streets is "traffic calming," which aims to improve the livability in neighborhoods by discouraging through traffic and slowing down all vehicular movement through the use of speed humps, changes in street direction, pavement textures, narrowing of roadways, and other restraints. In the early twenty-first century bicycle lanes were added to many streets in Manhattan.

Robert A. Caro, *The Power Broker: Robert Moses and the Fall of New York* (New York: Alfred A. Knopf, 1974); Henry Moscow, *The Street Book: An Encyclopedia of Manhattan's Street Names and Their Origins* (New York: Fordham University Press, 1978); Sigurd Grava, "The Bronx River Parkway: A Case Study in Innovation," *New York Affairs* 7, no.1 (1981), 15–23; David N. Dunlap, *On Broadway: A Journey Uptown over Time* (New York: Rizzoli, 1990)

See also Paving.

Sigurd Grava

street vendors. People selling a wide variety of items have always found a thriving market on New York City's streets, contributing to the economic vitality of the city. Vendors over the past three centuries have sold everything from food to clothing to household goods. As early as 1691 New York City started to regulate vendors as part of an effort to regulate streets, instituting a rule intended to limit street selling to two hours after public markets closed. That regulation, as well as others intending to limit the practice, was not successful, as the growing population demanded more goods. In the nineteenth century the city began to sell licenses to street vendors (a practice that has continued into the early twenty-first century). In the nineteenth century popular vendors included "hot corn girls," who sold roasted corn on the cob near the Five Points in Manhattan; "Apple Marys," who peddled apples in the financial district; and "ole clothes men," who walked through the city trading clothes from wagons they pulled behind them. In particular, the Lower East Side, which had the densest concentration of people during the second half of the nineteenth century, was especially popular with vendors: Hester, Rivington, and Orchard streets were thronged daily with crowds.

By the early twentieth century the city designated areas especially for street vendors, including spaces under the ramps of the Williamsburg, Manhattan, and Queensboro bridges. City Hall legalized pushcart markets to alleviate food shortages during World War I, even as it decreased the number of licenses for itinerant vendors. In the 1920s pushcarts supplied fresh fruits and vegetables, pickles, soda water, used clothes, and all variety of merchandise and ethnic foods, bringing in approximately $50 million annually. Street markets—totaling about 60 citywide in the 1920s—fanned out across the city and expanded into Brooklyn, Queens, and the Bronx. Throughout the twentieth century businesses increasingly pressured the city to limit or stop street vendors, complaining that they lowered shop sales, created nuisances on streets, and blocked traffic. Mayor Fiorello H. La Guardia made an effort to put an end to pushcart peddling in New York City during the 1930s and 1940s, closing more than 40 street markets and trying unsuccessfully to outlaw itinerant pushcart vending. To replace the outdoor markets he had closed, the city built nine market buildings.

From the late twentieth into the early twenty-first century, New York City tightened the rules for street selling, including issuing strict guidelines regarding the number of licenses it would issue and raising the fees for these licenses. The police routinely issued summons for violations and confiscated goods. Only First Amendment vendors (those selling articles that could be deemed acts of expression) could operate without a license. Nonetheless, vendors remained on city streets, including hundreds of those with hot dog carts—a city icon. The wait for general vending licenses (nonfood) could be as long as 25 years, so the number of unlicensed vendors could be two or three times the number of licensed ones. In the early twenty-first century most street vendors were recent immigrants, predominantly from Latin America, South Asia, West Africa, and the Middle East. As of 2009 there were approximately 3000 permits granted to food vendors, with much public debate about increasing the number of licenses. Increasingly, street fairs, which require closing off large sections of avenues, have become the new home of street vendors. These are well-organized weekend events approved by the city in which hundreds of vendors sell food and goods, paying fees to the city to do so.

Rowan Moore Gerety

Streisand, Barbra [Barbara] **(Joan)** (*b* Brooklyn, 24 April 1942). Singer and actress. She spent her childhood in Williamsburg, Brooklyn, attending Beis Yakov Jewish School. She began her career singing on local television programs and in such nightclubs as the Bon Soir and the Blue Angel in Manhattan. After signing a contract with Columbia Records she made her debut on Broadway in a supporting role in *I Can Get It for You Wholesale* (1962); she became well known in the leading role of *Funny Girl* (1964) and won an Academy Award for her performance in the film version in 1969. In 1978 Streisand and Neil Diamond released their popular duet "You Don't Bring Me Flowers." The two performers had previously sung together in their school choir while students at Brooklyn's Erasmus High School. Streisand produced, directed, and acted in several motion pictures, including *Yentl* (1983) and *The Prince of Tides* (1991). In addition to having released number-one albums in each of the past four decades, Streisand is the only person to have won an Oscar, Tony, Emmy, Grammy, Golden Globe, Cable Ace, and Peabody Award as well as the American Film Institute's Life Achievement Award. One of the highest selling female solo artists of all time, she had released 50 gold records and 30 platinum records as of 2008.

Bernie Ardia, *Barbra Streisand in New York City: A Self Guided Tour of Landmark Locations in the Career of Barbra Streisand* (Outskirts Press, 2007)

David J. Weiner

Striker's Bay [Stryker's Bay]. Section of the former neighborhood of Bloomingdale, bounded to the north by 99th Street, to the east by Central Park West, to the south by 81st Street, and to the west by the Hudson River. It was named for Jacobus Strijker, a magistrate of the Court of New Amsterdam who in 1764 owned a mansion at what is now 96th Street; his descendants lived there for many years. Throughout the nineteenth century the area attracted such residents as Edgar Allan Poe (during summers in the 1840s) and Valentine Mott, a surgeon who owned a house on a parcel of 11 acres (4.5 hectares) covering what is now the area between 93rd and 96th streets. Like other sections of the Upper West Side, Striker's Bay disappeared during a period of rapid growth in the late nineteenth century when its buildings were razed to make way for new residential development.

James Bradley

strikes. Since 1677, when 12 carters faced criminal prosecution for opposing government-regulated hauling rates, New Yorkers have participated in strikes to win employer concessions and improve their working conditions. In 1741 bakers withheld their services to protest the high price of wheat. After the American Revolution artisans employed the rhetoric of liberty to defuse accusations of conspiracy as they organized. In the 1830s numerous strikes by tailors, dockworkers, construction workers, carpenters, and others gave New York City's working class a reputation for radicalism. In 1853 striking African American waiters won a 25 percent wage increase, inspiring their white colleagues to also fight for better pay. Long Island Rail Road car painters went on strike in Queens in 1886. In many instances strikers were met with violence, as when Brooklyn trolley workers clashed with state militia in 1895. Newsboys won concessions from publishing titans in 1899, overcoming great odds. Ten years later "the uprising of the 20,000" primarily Jewish women disrupted the city's garment industry for months, an example of militant unions organizing immigrants during the Progressive era. Strikes diminished after the 1919 Red Scare but reemerged as organizing won legal protections during the New Deal and gained popularity amidst the Great Depression. After World War II strikes gripped New York City following years of government-controlled wages. With tugboat pilots, teamsters, longshoremen, and others on picket lines, fuel and many other necessities were in short supply. In the face of the city's looming fiscal crisis during the 1970s and 1980s, some public employees, including teachers, police officers, and transport and sanitation workers, walked off their jobs despite the 1967 Taylor Law that prohibited them from striking. Taxi drivers, newspaper staff, theatrical stagehands, nurses, and building service workers are among the many other New Yorkers who have struck in recent decades, as lately as 2009.

Joshua B. Freeman, *Working Class New York: Life and Labor since World War II* (New York: New Press, 2000)

Eric Robinson

Strivers' Row [King Model Houses]. Group of 1891 row houses in Harlem on West 138th and 139th streets between Seventh and Eighth avenues. The 130 houses, which stand in four elegant rows along two blocks, were the brainchild of developer David H. King, Jr., who had gained acclaim as the builder of the Old Times Building, Madison Square Garden, and the base of the Statue of Liberty. King acquired the property to create a residential community. Originally, the houses were called the King Model Houses. The name Strivers' Row was coined to reflect the aspirations of "common folk" and prominent African Americans who moved to Harlem after World War I. Some of New York City's leading architects were commissioned to construct parts of the development, including McKim, Mead and White (north side, West 139th Street), Bruce Price and Clarence S. Luce (south side, West 139th Street; north side, West 138th Street), and James Brown Lord (south side, West 138th Street). The houses incorporated different styles (Georgian and neo-Italian Renaissance) but also contained similar materials and features. A novel feature still in existence is the private alleyway. Now used for parking, these private spaces allowed homeowners to discreetly receive deliveries and stable and care for horses. Strivers' Row has been home to many notable African Americans, including Adam Clayton Powell, Jr., Eubie Blake, W. C. Handy, Lincoln Perry (Stepin Fetchit), Harry Wills, Samuel T. Battle, Scott Joplin, Vertner Tandy, Noble Sissle, and Bill "Bojangles" Robinson.

Strivers' Row, 2009

Kathleen Benson, Celedonia Jones, Sandra Opdycke, Diane Jones Randall, Sharon Wilkins

Strong, George Templeton (*b* New York City, 26 Jan 1820; *d* New York City, 21 July 1875). Lawyer and diarist. His father, George Washington Strong, was a prominent New York City lawyer. Strong graduated from Columbia University in 1838 and in 1844 became a partner in his father's law firm, Strong, Bidwell and Strong, where he specialized in real estate and probate law. He was a trustee of Columbia for 20 years and helped to found its School of Law. During the Civil War he was treasurer of the U.S. Sanitary Commission (a predecessor to the American Red Cross), and he also helped to found the Union League Club. In 1872 he became comptroller of Trinity Church, where he was a member and vestryman from 1847 to 1870. Strong served as president of the Philharmonic Society and the Church Music Association. He is best known for his meticulously kept diary, which he began as a student at Columbia. The 2250-page diary contains detailed accounts of everyday life in the city from 1835 to 1875. Strong died in his home at 113 East 21st Street and is buried at Trinity Church Yard; President Ulysses S. Grant attended his funeral, and John Jacob Astor was a pallbearer. His diary was edited and published in four volumes in 1952; the original diary is held by the New-York Historical Society.

Kate Lauber

Strong, Josiah (*b* Naperville, Ill., 19 Jan 1847; *d* New York City, 28 April 1916). Religious leader and reformer. A leader of several reform organizations based in New York City, he encouraged social involvement as a practical expression of social Christianity. With Washington Gladden, Walter Rauschenbusch, and Lyman Abbott he edited the *Kingdom,* the most influential journal of the Social Gospel movement. He wrote five books on social reform, including *Our Country* (1885), a blending of social Christianity and Darwinian theory that sought to expose urban injustices and attribute corruption to wealth. Strong led the American Evangelical Alliance from 1886 to 1898 and the League for Social Service from 1898 to 1904 and also helped to form the Federal Council of Churches in the city in 1908. He lived in Greenwich, Connecticut.

Eileen W. Lindner

Strong, William L(afayette) (*b* Richland County, Ohio, 22 March 1827; *d* New York City, 2 Nov 1900). Mayor. After becoming a millionaire as a merchant and banker, he was elected mayor as a reform Republican with the backing of independents and the chamber of commerce and the grudging support of the Republican boss, Thomas C. Platt. He took office in 1895 and appointed Theodore Roosevelt police commissioner. Strong's school reforms, nonpartisan distribution of patronage, and enforcement of Sunday blue laws cost him reelection, and he left office in 1897.

Andrew Wiese

Stuart, Robert Leighton (*b* New York City, 21 July 1806; *d* New York City, 12 Dec 1882). Businessman, philanthropist, and art patron. With his brother Alexander Stuart he formed the sugar-refining firm of R. L. and A. Stuart on Greenwich Street in 1828, which by mid-century used innovative steam-based methods to produce more than 40 million pounds of sugar a year. He was a member of the Century Association (1859) and the Union Club (1863) and a president of the American Museum of Natural History (1872–81). A devout Presbyterian, he was president of Presbyterian Hospital (1880–82) and contributed to the construction of two churches on Fifth Avenue. His home at 154 Fifth Avenue housed an extensive collection of American and European art and a library of 15,000 volumes that he bequeathed to the Lenox Library.

Donna Ann Grossman

Studio 54. Discotheque named for its location at 254 West 54th Street in Manhattan. Originally built as the Gallo Opera House in 1927, the theater served as a television and radio stage for the Columbia Broadcasting System (CBS) from the 1950s to 1976. Reopening as Studio 54 in 1977, the club became the center of New York City nightlife, attracting such patrons as Andy Warhol, Truman Capote, Liza Minnelli, Cher, and Halston, and it received extensive press coverage. Known for its decadence and abandon, Studio 54 closed when its owners were convicted of tax evasion and sentenced to prison in 1979. Mark Fleishman owned the club during the 1980s, and it became a venue for rock concerts during the 1990s. The Roundabout Theater acquired the venue in 1998, staging such Broadway revivals as *Cabaret, A Streetcar Named Desire,* and *Threepenny Opera.* The second floor of the theater remained a nightclub.

Irina Ikonsky

Studio Museum in Harlem. Museum at 144 West 125th Street dedicated solely to the art and artifacts of black America and other cultures of African origin. Incorporated in 1967 as a studio for artists, it began a permanent collection that by 2007 numbered more than 10,000 items, including paintings by Romare Bearden and Jacob Lawrence as well as textiles and photographs. The only black museum accredited by the American Association of Museums and the custodian of the collection of black and Latin American art maintained by New York State, it sponsors exhibitions, lectures, and workshops and continues to provide studio space for artists. In 2005 the museum was one of 406 New York City arts institutions to receive part of a $20 million grant from the Carnegie Corporation of New York that helped expand and renovate the museum, including a new auditorium and additional gallery space.

Betty Kaplan Gubert

Sturges, Jonathan (*b* Southport, Conn., 24 March 1802; *d* New York City, 28 Nov 1874). Merchant, art patron, and philanthropist. After moving to New York City in 1821 he joined the mercantile firm of Luman Reed and in 1836 assumed control of the firm of Reed and Sturges at 125–27 Front Street. Known for his comprehensive collection of American art, he helped to form the Century Association (1847); the New-York Gallery of the Fine Arts (1844–58), of which he was president; and the Union League Club (1863), of which he became president in 1864.

Timothy Anglin Burgard

Stuyvesant, Peter [Petrus] (*b* Friesland, the Netherlands, 1610; *d* New York City, February 1672). Director general of New Netherland. The son of a minister, he joined the military and was eventually appointed governor of Curaçao before receiving his commission as director general of New Netherland from the States General. He sailed into New Amsterdam with a fleet of four vessels in 1647 and took up residence in the governor's house in Fort Amsterdam (now the site of the U.S. Custom House). Some of his first ordinances dealt with religious observance and the sale of intoxicants on Sundays. He soon rebuilt

Peter Stuyvesant, ca *1660 (artist unknown)*

the church at Fort Amsterdam and served as a church warden. In this position he forbade all religious observances except those of the Dutch Reformed Church and sought to prevent Jews and Quakers from entering the colony. Both of these attempts failed, however, helping to further the city's reputation for tolerance.

In 1651 he bought a farm bounded by what are now 17th Street, the East River, Fifth Street, and Fourth Avenue. Around 1655, using his salary of 250 guilders a month, he built an elegant home called White Hall (in his day also called Stuyvesant's Great House), at what is now the intersection of Whitehall and State streets; he bought the property in 1658 and made it his official residence. During his tenure he improved relations with English colonies, fostered commerce, regulated internal affairs, allowed the formation of municipal government for New Amsterdam, and removed Swedish settlements from the Delaware River. After surrendering to the English in 1664 he withdrew from public affairs and retired to his farm, where he spent the rest of his life at the manor house (now the site of Stuyvesant Street). He was buried beneath the chapel of the house, now the site of St. Mark's Church in the Bowery.

Anna Crouse and Russel Crouse, *Peter Stuyvesant of Old New York* (New York: Random House, 1954)

James E. Mooney

Stuyvesant Heights. Neighborhood in northwestern Brooklyn covering 12 blocks in the heart of Bedford–Stuyvesant founded in 1640 by Peter Stuyvesant. It is bounded to the north by Macon Street, to the east by Stuyvesant Avenue, to the south by Chauncey Street, and to the west by Tompkins Avenue, bordering on Weeksville (1838). Dutch farmers owned the land when streets were gridded in 1835, naming them after American heroes. Brick houses rose in 1870 for German and Irish residents. In 1870 Stuyvesant Heights became the first home for St. John's College. Most of the one-family brownstones and row houses lining the streets were built in the 1890s. During the 1930s Depression, African Americans moved into the community and white residents moved out. Designated a historic district in 1971, the area became known for its strong commitment to preservation. Among its many landmarks are the Mount Lebanon Baptist Church and the John and Elizabeth Truslow House. Stuyvesant Heights has always been residential: its population is middle class and overwhelmingly African American, with a large number of immigrants from Guyana, Jamaica, and Barbados. In the early twenty-first century it remained a mixed community of professionals.

Andrew Dolkart, ed., *Guide to New York City Landmarks* (New York: Preservation Press, National Trust for Historic Preservation, 1992)

James Bradley, John Manbeck

Stuyvesant High School. Public high school, named for Peter Stuyvesant, opened in 1904 on East 23rd Street as a "manual training school for boys"; in 1907 it was destroyed by fire and moved to East 15th Street. Conceived as part of the reform program of Superintendent of Schools William H. Maxwell, the school was intended to prepare children of immigrants for careers in science. Between 1909 and 1934 this goal was reaffirmed by its second principal, the physicist Ernst R. von Nardroff. The school became coeducational in 1969. In September 1992 it moved to a new building in Battery Park City, constructed at a cost of $150 million. At the time it had about 2700 students, of whom 51 percent were Asian, and about 100 teachers. The students at Stuyvesant are admitted by special examination and live throughout the city. Each year many are recipients of the Westinghouse Science Talent Award, which is the focus of an informal competition with the Bronx High School of Science.

During the terrorist attacks of 11 September 2001 the school, which was 400 meters from the World Trade Center site, was evacuated as smoke entered the building, though there was no physical damage to the structure. The building was then used as a base of operations for rescue and recovery workers until 9 October while students attended classes in two shifts at Brooklyn Technical High School.

Many renowned scientists and physicians have attended Stuyvesant High School, including two recipients of the Nobel Prize: Joshua Lederberg (physiology and medicine, 1958) and Roald Hoffmann (chemistry, 1981). Other famous alumni include the architectural critic Lewis Mumford, the film actor James Cagney, the jazz pianist Thelonious Monk, and the screenwriter Joseph Mankiewicz.

Stephan F. Brumberg, *Going to America, Going to School: The Jewish Immigrant Public School Encounter* (New York: Praeger, 1986)

Joshua Lederberg

Stuyvesant Square. Neighborhood on the East Side of Manhattan, bounded to the north by 18th Street, to the east by First Avenue, to the south by 14th Street, and to the west by Third Avenue. The land was sold by Peter Gerard Stuyvesant to New York City in 1836 for five dollars, on the condition that it become a park. Improvements to the 4-acre (1.6-hectare) lot were slow to come: in 1846 an iron railing was erected around it, and in 1847 it was graded and designated a park. It was officially opened in 1850, complete with fountains and landscaping. As German, Irish, Jewish, Italian, and Slavic immigrants moved into the area, it became an important neighborhood gathering place. Over the next century many improvements were made, the most significant in the 1930s and 1980s. St. George's Episcopal Church was built at 209 East 16th Street in 1856; the Friends Meeting House and Seminary was constructed at 15th Street and Rutherford Place in 1860. Other institutions in the neighborhood include Beth Israel Medical Center and the High School for Health Professions and Human Services, which was previously Stuyvesant High School. Area residents included artist Reginald Marsh, attorney Hamilton Fish, Tammany boss Charles Murphy, and Czech composer Antonín Dvořák, who has a monument in the park. Stuyvesant Square was designated a historic district in 1975.

Lisa Keller

Stuyvesant Town. Housing development in Manhattan, covering 18 blocks and bounded to the north by 20th Street, to the east by Avenue C, to the south by 14th Street, and to the west by First Avenue. Built during 1943–47 for $112 million by the Metropolitan Life Insurance Company (along with Peter Cooper Village immediately to the north), it was the beneficiary of a new state law to encourage private firms to rebuild slum districts. Both developments were built to replace tenements in the old Gashouse District and were initiated by Robert Moses under the guidance of Mayor Fiorello H. La Guardia. The architects were Irwin Clavan and Gilmore Clarke, who designed 35 redbrick buildings of 13 to 14 stories each, containing 8756 rent-stabilized apartments; tree-lined walkways complemented the sparse architecture, and a park with a fountain lay at the center of the development. When the first apartments opened in 1947, they attracted more than 11,000 applicants, most of them World War II veterans. All were white, young, and married: single people, unmarried couples, and African Americans were barred during the tenure of Frederick H. Ecker as chairman of Metropolitan Life from 1936 to 1950. Almost 100 organizations and individuals protested these restrictions during a hearing of the City Council before the contract to establish

Stuyvesant Town, 2009

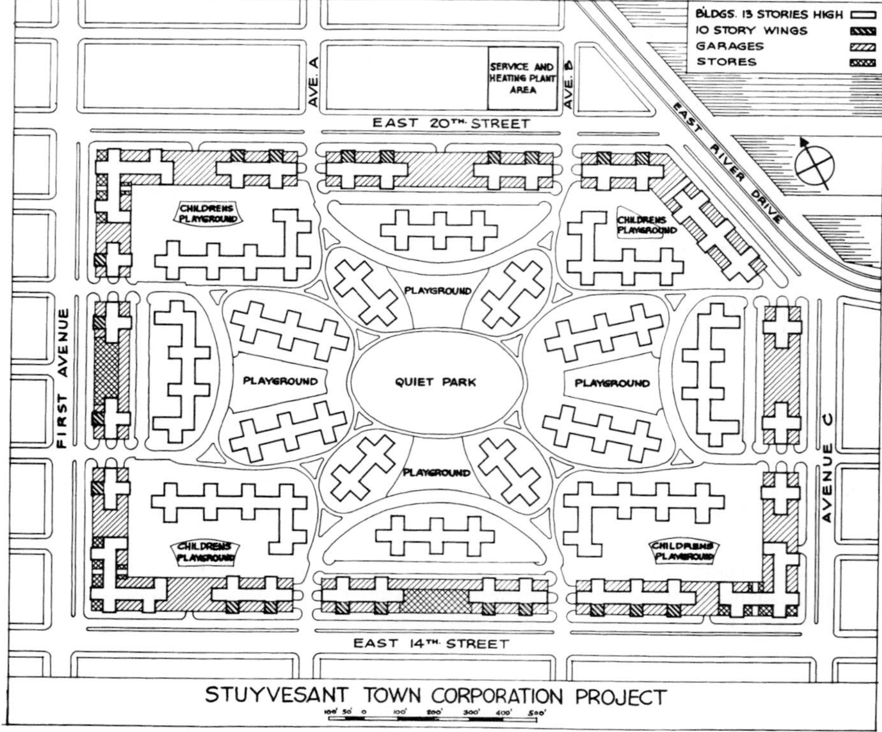

Plan for Stuyvesant Town, ca *1943*

Stuyvesant Town was signed. The courts upheld the rental policy until the company changed it voluntarily in August 1950; in October 1950 three black families moved in. By the end of the twentieth century the population became ethnically more diverse, with growing numbers of Dominican, Puerto Rican, and Chinese residents. Stuyvesant Town has always been considered a desirable address; typically thousands of applicants were on its waiting list in part because rents were lower than comparable buildings elsewhere. In October 2006 Metropolitan Life sold Stuyvesant Town and Peter Cooper Village to the real estate firm Tishman Speyer Properties for $5.4 billion, a record-high price for such a transaction. In 2010 they defaulted on their payments, and creditors took over the property.

B. Kimberly Taylor

Styne, Jule [Stein, Jules] (*b* London, 31 Dec 1905; *d* New York City, 20 Sept 1994). Composer and producer. Educated in the Midwest, he moved to New York City in the mid-1930s. He wrote several successful Broadway shows, including *High Button Shoes* (1947), *Gentlemen Prefer Blondes* (1949), *Gypsy* (1959), and *Funny Girl* (1964), as well as film scores. Among the works inspired by New York City are the show *The Kid from Brooklyn* (1946) and the songs "It Happened in Brooklyn" (1947) and "Ev'ry Street's a Boulevard in Old New York" (1953).

Theodore Taylor, *Jule: The Story of Composer Jule Styne* (New York: Random House, 1979)

Marc Ferris

submarines. The first submarine in New York Harbor probably was one nicknamed "the Intelligent Whale" that sank while it underwent trials in 1872 at the Brooklyn Navy Yard (officially the New York Naval Shipyard). Not long afterward the Irish American submarine pioneer John Holland tested model subs at Coney Island and built several full-sized boats in New York and Brooklyn shipyards. Two were financed by a group of Irish exiles who hoped to use them against the British; one was called the Fenian Ram and was a failure, like others built by him and his peers. In the 1920s and early 1930s the navy yard was charged by the U.S. Navy to develop new types of diesel engines for submarines that were built elsewhere. During the two world wars rescuers brought hundreds of survivors from ships sunk by German submarines to the city; most were put up at the Seamen's Church Institute at 25 South Street. During World War II steel antisubmarine nets were extended across the Narrows from Coney Island to Staten Island to prevent German submarines from invading the harbor. Other than participating in naval revues, U.S. submarines were not often seen in the harbor after 1945. When the Brooklyn Navy Yard was closed down in 1966, one reason given by Defense Secretary Robert McNamara was that it lacked the capability to build modern nuclear submarines.

Gary E. Weir, *Building American Submarines, 1914–1940* (Washington, D.C.: Naval Historical Center, 1991); Norman Friedman, *U.S. Submarines through 1945* (Annapolis, Md.: Naval Institute Press, 1995); Leah Robinson Rousmaniere, *Anchored within the Vail: A Pictorial History of the Seamen's Church Institute* (New York: Seamen's Church Institute, 1995)

John Rousmaniere

Subtreasury of the United States. Defunct agency for collecting federal taxes. It was an arm of the subtreasury system (formed in 1846 as part of the independent treasury overseen by the assistant treasurer of the United States) and was responsible for collecting and disbursing two-thirds of the nation's revenues; it was also the representative of the U.S. Treasury on Wall Street. From 1862 to 1925 the headquarters were at the Federal Hall National Memorial on the corner of Wall and Nassau streets. Among the well-known heads of the agency were John A. Dix (1798–1879), later governor of New York; John A. Stewart (1822–1926), a banker who formed the U.S. Trust Company; and Thomas C. Acton (1823–1909), later president of the Bank of New Amsterdam. By the mid-1920s the functions of the subtreasury were taken over by the Federal Reserve Bank of New York.

James Bradley

suburbs. Although New York City is the most densely populated municipality in the United States (2009 density of pop. 26,800 per square mile [43,130.4 per square kilometer]), universally symbolized by the towering skyline of Manhattan, the city's suburbs are older, larger, and more sprawling than those of any other city in the world. In 2000 the urbanized region comprised not only 8 million inhabitants in the city itself but an additional 14 million in 27 adjacent counties in New York, New Jersey, and Connecticut, for a metropolitan total of 22 million.

Brooklyn Heights was the world's first commuter suburb, transformed between 1815 and 1835 from a sleepy rural village into a middle-class bedroom community. Regular steam ferry service to New York City (then consisting only of Manhattan) began in 1814, and in the following year the *Brooklyn Star* predicted that Brooklyn Heights would become "a favorite residence for gentlemen of taste and fortune." Additional ferry lines soon expanded the commuting possibilities, and by 1860 the various ferries across the East River were carrying 100,000 passengers every working day.

Railroads had an even greater effect on suburban growth. Commuter travel in the region by steam railroad began in 1832, and by 1837 the New York and Harlem Railroad offered service to 125th Street. Additions to this same line led to White Plains and central Westchester by 1844. Meanwhile, the New York and New Haven Railroad along Long Island Sound reached New Haven, Connecticut, in 1843, and the Harlem River line toward Albany, New York, reached Peekskill in 1849. In the following decade real estate developments were constructed in Rye, Tarrytown, and New Rochelle. The northbound railroads opened up Westchester County (including what later became the Bronx), largely replacing the steamboats that had run to Yonkers and Peekskill.

At the same time the Long Island Rail Road and the New York and Flushing Railroad enabled former residents of Manhattan to commute from the east. By bringing villages in Queens County within an hour of the business district in the late 1850s, the railroads carried an influx into Newtown, Maspeth, and Flushing. On the other side of the Hudson River, Jersey City was the hub of a combined ferry and rail route that enabled commuters to traverse the 16 miles (25 kilometers) from South Orange, New Jersey, to New York City in less than an hour. Because of this route Llewellyn Park, the world's first picturesque suburb, was developed in the eastern foothills of the Orange Mountains in the decade before the Civil War. Conceived by Llewellyn S. Haskell, a prosperous drug merchant, and planned by Alexander Jackson Davis, the most prolific architect of his generation, the suburb was notable for its use of two features unprecedented in residential development: the curvilinear road and the central open space. The most ambitiously planned suburb of the nineteenth century was Garden City, about 20 miles (30 kilometers) east of Manhattan in Nassau County. The inspiration of the merchant A. T. Stewart and his long-time architect John Kellum, Garden City was unusual for its large lots and wide streets. Because Stewart chose to rent rather than sell the houses, the community did not prosper until the twentieth century.

By 1900 New York City had more suburbs than any other place in the world, as thousands of businesspeople chose opulence over the polyglot ambience of the city. Every morning hundreds of trains from northern and eastern New Jersey pulled into Hoboken, discharging passengers who then embarked on a 10-minute ferry ride to Manhattan. From southern and eastern Brooklyn and from Nassau County steam locomotives brought passengers to Atlantic Avenue in Brooklyn, where they had easy access to the financial district. Meanwhile, Westchester County became the first large suburban area. At the turn of the twentieth century the three major passenger railroads running along the Hudson, the Harlem River Valley, and Long Island Sound were carrying 118,000 commuters a day into Grand Central Terminal. The population of Westchester doubled three times in successive 20-year periods—1850–70, 1870–90, and 1890–1910—by the end of which it had 283,000 residents. Most of the development was actively encouraged by the railroads, which developed communities, promoted the advantages of suburban living, and offered frequent, reliable service. Indeed, commuter service from the city's northern suburbs in the late nineteenth century was almost as good as it would be in the twenty-first century.

The suburban shift accelerated after World War II, aided by a national mania for the automobile and by federal policies that favored private transportation. By 1970 more than 2200 square miles (5700 square kilometers) had been urbanized, about five times the area urbanized in 1920 even though the population had only doubled. Because suburban residents in the twentieth century rejected annexation by New York City, unlike their predecessors in what became the city's outer boroughs, the metropolitan region became highly fragmented: in 1960 the political scientist Robert C. Wood identified within the region more than 1400 separate suburban governments and taxing authorities.

Employment followed the same path as population. As late as 1920 Manhattan, the Bronx, Brooklyn, and Queens and Newark and Jersey City in New Jersey accounted for about 80 percent of the employment in what was later designated the New York–Northern New Jersey–Long Island Consolidated Metropolitan Statistical Area. Most of the rest was in satellite cities that were well served by rail lines, such as Yonkers and White Plains in Westchester, and Paterson and Passaic in New Jersey. By 1970, however, more than half the employment in the region was outside the old urban core. Even so, early in the twenty-first century New York City remained unique in the United States for the dominance of the central city.

Kenneth T. Jackson, *Crabgrass Frontier: The Suburbanization of the United States* (New York: Oxford University Press, 1985)

Kenneth T. Jackson

Subway Hero. See Autrey, Wesley.

subways. Serious consideration was given to building a rapid transit system in New York City as early as the 1860s, when the streets of Manhattan were choked with slow-moving traffic. Many proposals were made, most inspired by the first subway in the world, which opened in London in 1863. After delays in construction due to expense, political squabbling, and technological obstacles, the first segment of an experimental elevated line along Greenwich and Ninth avenues to 30th Street opened to passengers on 3 July 1868. Its success led elevated lines to be built with private capital and operated under long-term franchises in other parts of Manhattan and in the Bronx and Brooklyn. A pneumatic subway on 312 feet (100 meters) of track built illegally under Broadway near City Hall was demonstrated to the public in 1870 but for lack of legislative and financial support was not expanded. In the early 1890s proposals were made for adding rapid transit lines to keep pace with the city's growth. There was widespread interest in building an underground system using new electric motors, but private companies were unwilling to risk investing in such a project.

A plan allowing a subway to be built with city funds was overwhelmingly approved in a referendum in 1894; a public rapid transit board was formed and laid out the route, which ran from a point near City Hall to 42nd Street, then west to Times Square, and then north along Broadway to 96th Street, where the line divided. One branch continued along Broadway to 242nd Street, the other along Lenox Avenue and under the Harlem River to the central Bronx. Bids were solicited in 1900; the contract, awarded for $35 million to the Rapid Transit Subway Construction Company, leased the subway to the contractor for 50 years. The contractor was required to set the fare at five cents, to pay as annual rent the interest on the municipal bonds as well as a sinking fund of 1 percent to amortize the bonds, and to equip and operate the lines at its own expense. In 1902 the Interborough Rapid Transit Company (IRT) was formed to operate the subway and was awarded a second contract to build a line running south from City Hall under Broadway and the East River to downtown Brooklyn. The first segment opened on 27 October 1904 and was widely praised. The entire system, in operation by 1908, was the first in the world to have four-track service (separate express and local tracks in each direction).

Even before the IRT opened its first line, demands arose to extend routes throughout the metropolitan area, and a bitter struggle ensued over the best way to do so. Trains were overcrowded and the rapid transit companies were unwilling to undertake vast expansion. The city hoped to alleviate overcrowding in older neighborhoods and encourage settlement in less congested ones, and members of the Board of Estimate and the state public service commission led by Manhattan Borough President George McAneny drew up a plan for building as many lines as possible. On 19 March 1913 they approved the "dual system," under which rapid transit lines controlled by the IRT and the Brooklyn Rapid Transit Company (BRT) were expanded and organized as two networks. The two companies added 123 miles (197 kilometers) of routes and more than doubled the capacity of the rapid transit system at a cost of $302 million, more than had been spent on any other public works project in U.S. history at the time. Each company was granted a 49-year lease to operate its new lines and was permitted to charge a five-cent fare. Most track in outlying areas was built on elevated supports to save money.

In 1913 the city's rapid transit system carried 810 million passengers; by 1930, with the addition of the dual-system lines, it carried 2.49 billion. Under the dual-system plan the original subway line in Manhattan grew to include two north–south lines on the East and West sides joined by a shuttle under 42nd Street. These lines were connected in the Bronx to the Jerome Avenue, White Plains Road, and Pelham lines. In Brooklyn the original subway was connected to the Nostrand Avenue and New Lots lines; and in Queens a line was built to Corona (later extended to Flushing). The BRT was given a lease for a loop under lower Manhattan and a trunk line running under Broadway from lower Manhattan to midtown. Among the lines joined to this trunk were the Astoria line in Queens and the Fourth Avenue, Culver, West End, Sea Beach, and Brighton lines to southern Brooklyn. The BRT and IRT provided joint service on the Astoria and Flushing lines. The Myrtle Avenue line was improved, the BRT received the right to operate a line along 14th Street to Canarsie, and the Broadway elevated line was extended to Jamaica. Despite rising construction and operating costs Mayor John F. Hylan refused to allow an increase in fares, leading the BRT to fall into bankruptcy between 1918 and 1923, when it was reorganized as the Brooklyn–Manhattan Transit Corporation (BMT).

During the 1920s additional plans were discussed. Some proposed to extend the IRT and BMT networks and others to build an independent system. In 1925 Hylan, who fiercely opposed the private operators, won approval for the Independent Subway System (IND), which added 59 miles (94 kilometers) of routes that were entirely underground except for a short stretch in Brooklyn. Trunk lines built under Sixth and Eighth avenues in Manhattan had connections to lower Manhattan and across 53rd Street; feeder lines were built to northern Manhattan and under the Grand Concourse and Queens Boulevard. A line was built to Flatbush, another replaced the old Fulton Street elevated line, and one was also built between Brooklyn and Queens (this was the first in the city that did not cross into Manhattan). The IND, which opened its first line in 1932 and its last in 1940, provided faster, more convenient service than other lines to many areas and encouraged development along Queens Boulevard. Between the world wars there was more development in the areas served by the dual-system and independent system lines than in other parts of the city.

The Transport Workers Union (TWU) successfully fought for salary increases and better working conditions from the 1930s. As the IND lines attracted more passengers, the financial problems of the BMT and IRT intensified. The IRT declared bankruptcy in 1932, and in 1940 the city bought the operating rights, equipment, and some properties from the companies, paying $175 million to the IRT and $161.5 million to the BMT; operation of their networks was assumed by the Board of Transportation, which ran the IND.

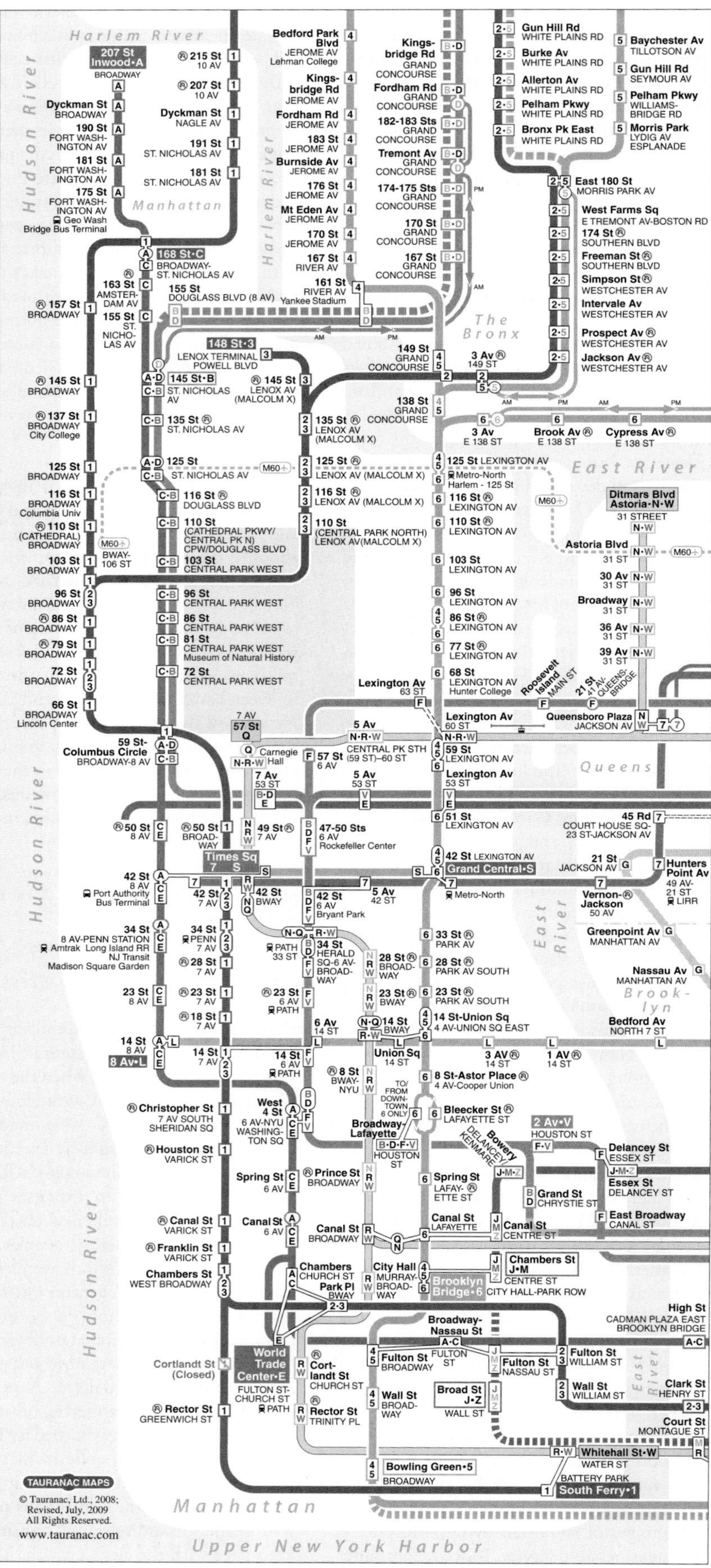

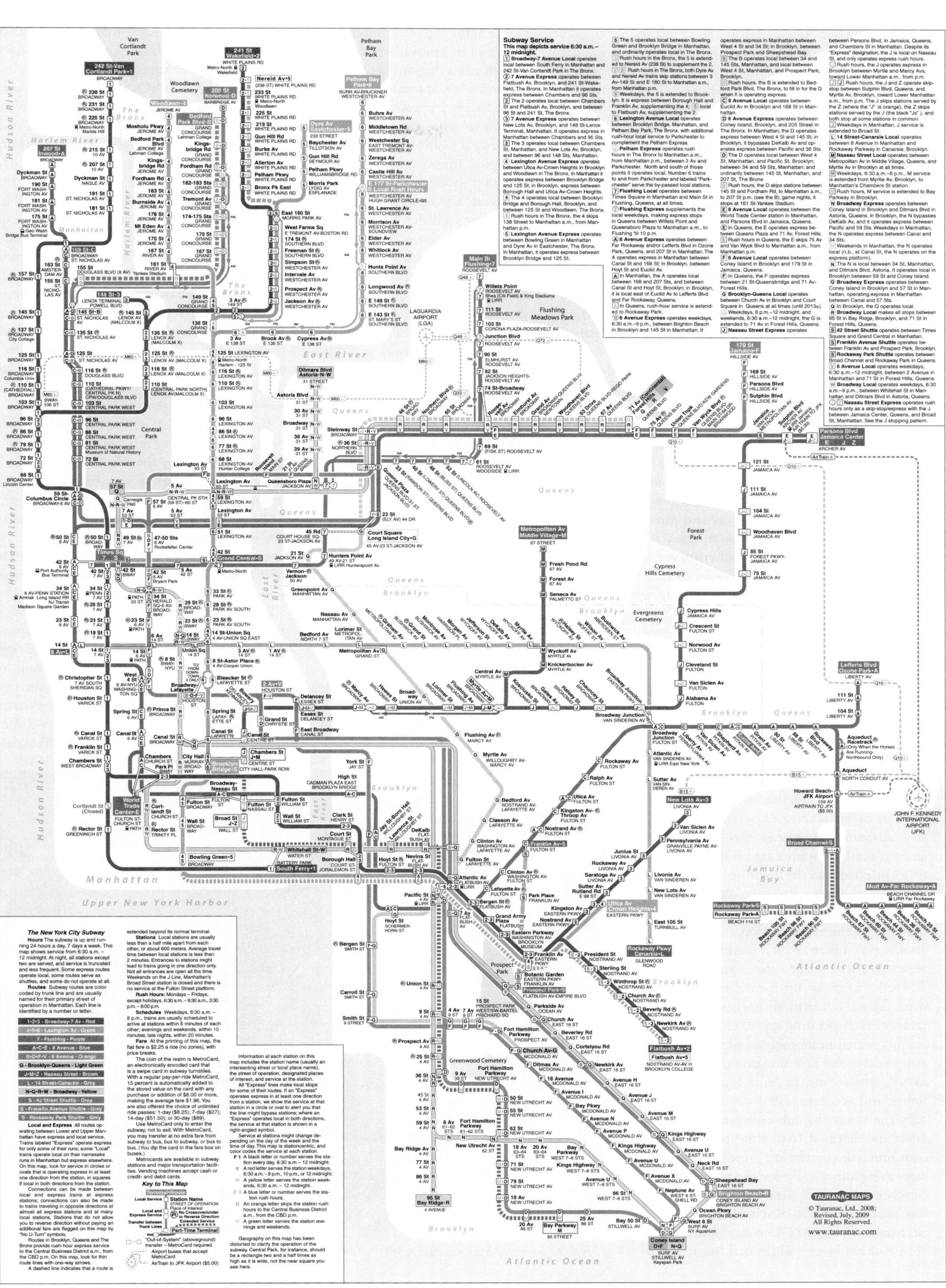
Subway Service
This map depicts service 6:30 a.m. – 12 midnight.
1 Broadway-7 Avenue Local operates local between South Ferry in Manhattan and 242 St-Van Cortlandt Park in The Bronx.
2 7 Avenue Express operates between Flatbush Av, Brooklyn, and 241 St-Wakefield, The Bronx. In Manhattan it operates express between Chambers and 96 Sts.
2 The 2 operates local between Chambers St and Flatbush Av, Brooklyn, and between 96 St and 241 St, The Bronx.
3 7 Avenue Express operates between New Lots Av, Brooklyn, and 148 St-Lenox Terminal, Manhattan. It operates express in Manhattan between Chambers and 96 Sts.
3 The 3 operates local between Chambers St, Manhattan, and New Lots Av, Brooklyn, and between 96 and 148 Sts, Manhattan.
4 Lexington Avenue Express operates between Utica Av-Crown Heights in Brooklyn and Woodlawn in The Bronx. In Manhattan it operates express between Brooklyn Bridge and 125 St; in Brooklyn, express between Borough Hall and Utica Av-Crown Heights.
4 The 4 operates local between Brooklyn Bridge and Borough Hall, Brooklyn, and between 125 St and Woodlawn, The Bronx.
4 Rush hours in The Bronx, the 4 skips 138 Street to Manhattan a.m., from Manhattan p.m.
5 Lexington Avenue Express operates between Bowling Green in Manhattan and Dyre Av in Eastchester, The Bronx. In Manhattan, it operates express between Brooklyn Bridge and 125 St.
5 The 5 operates local between Bowling Green and Brooklyn Bridge in Manhattan, and ordinarily operates local in The Bronx.
5 Rush hours in the Bronx, the 5 is extended to Nereid Av (238 St) to supplement the 2.
5 5 Rush hours in The Bronx, both Dyre Av and Nereid Av trains skip stations between 3 Av-149 St and E 180 St to Manhattan a.m., from Manhattan p.m.
5 Weekdays, the 5 is extended to Brooklyn. It is express between Borough Hall and Franklin Av, supplementing the 4; 5 local to Flatbush Av, supplementing the 2.
6 Lexington Avenue Local operates between Brooklyn Bridge, Manhattan, and Pelham Bay Park, The Bronx, with additional rush-hour local service to Parkchester to complement the Pelham Express.
6 Pelham Express operates rush hours in The Bronx to Manhattan a.m., from Manhattan p.m., between 3 Av and Parkchester. North and south of those points it operates local. Number 6 trains to and from Parkchester and labeled "Parkchester" serve the by-passed local stations.
7 Flushing Local operates between Times Square in Manhattan and Main St in Flushing, Queens, at all times.
7 Flushing Express supplements the local weekdays, making express stops in Queens between Willets Point and Queensboro Plaza to Manhattan a.m., to Flushing 'til 10 p.m.
A 8 Avenue Express operates between Far Rockaway and/or Lefferts Blvd in Ozone Park, Queens, and 207 St in Manhattan. The A operates express in Manhattan between Canal St and 168 St; in Brooklyn, between Hoyt St and Euclid Av.
A In Manhattan, the A operates local between 168 and 207 Sts, and between Canal St and Hoyt St, Brooklyn; in Brooklyn, it is local east of Euclid Av to Lefferts Blvd and Far Rockaway, Queens.
A In Queens, rush-hour service is extended to Rockaway Park.
B 6 Avenue Express operates weekdays, 6:30 a.m.–9 p.m., between Brighton Beach in Brooklyn and 145 St in Manhattan. It operates express in Manhattan between West 4 St and 34 St; in Brooklyn, between Prospect Park and Sheepshead Bay.
B The B operates local between 34 and 145 Sts, Manhattan, and local between West 4 St, Manhattan, and Prospect Park, Brooklyn.
B Rush hours, the B is extended to Bedford Park Blvd, The Bronx, to fill in for the D when it is operating express.
C 8 Avenue Local operates between Euclid Av in Brooklyn and 168 St in Manhattan.
D 6 Avenue Express operates between Coney Island, Brooklyn, and 205 Street in The Bronx. In Manhattan, the D operates express between West 4 St and 145 St; in Brooklyn, it bypasses DeKalb Av and operates express between Pacific and 36 Sts.
D The D operates local between West 4 St, Manhattan, and Pacific St, Brooklyn; between 34 and 59 Sts, Manhattan; and ordinarily between 145 St, Manhattan, and 207 St, The Bronx
D Rush hours, the D skips stations between 145 St and Fordham Rd, to Manhattan a.m., to 207 St p.m. (see the B); game nights, it stops at 161 St-Yankee Stadium.
E 8 Avenue Local operates between the World Trade Center station in Manhattan, and Parsons Blvd in Jamaica, Queens.
E In Queens, the E operates express between Queens Plaza and 71 Av, Forest Hills.
E Rush hours in Queens, the E skips 75 Av and Van Wyck Blvd to Manhattan a.m., from Manhattan p.m.
F 6 Avenue Local operates between Coney Island in Brooklyn and 179 St in Jamaica, Queens.
F In Queens, the F operates express between 21 St-Queensbridge and 71 Av-Forest Hills.
G Brooklyn-Queens Local operates between Church Av in Brooklyn and Court Square in Queens at all times (until 2013±).
G Weekdays, 8 p.m.–12 midnight, and weekends, 6:30 a.m.–12 midnight, the G is extended to 71 Av in Forest Hills, Queens.
J Nassau Street Express operates between Parsons Blvd, in Jamaica, Queens, and Chambers St in Manhattan. Despite its "Express" designation, the J is local on Nassau St, and only operates express rush hours.
J Rush hours, the J operates express in Brooklyn between Myrtle and Marcy Avs, toward Lower Manhattan a.m., from p.m.
J J Rush hours, the J and Z operate skip-stop between Sutphin Blvd, Queens, and Myrtle Av, Brooklyn, toward Lower Manhattan a.m., from p.m. The J skips stations served by the Z (where the "J" is orange), the Z skips stations served by the J (the black "Js"), and both stop at some stations in common.
J Weekdays in Manhattan, J service is extended to Broad St.
L 14 Street-Canarsie Local operates between 8 Avenue in Manhattan and Rockaway Parkway in Canarsie, Brooklyn.
M Nassau Street Local operates between Metropolitan Av in Middle Village, Queens, and Myrtle Av in Brooklyn at all times.
M Weekdays, 6:30 a.m.–8 p.m., M service is extended from Myrtle Av, Brooklyn, to Manhattan's Chambers St station.
M Rush hours, M service is extended to Bay Parkway in Brooklyn.
N Broadway Express operates between Coney Island in Brooklyn and Ditmars Blvd in Astoria, Queens. In Brooklyn, the N bypasses DeKalb Av, and it operates express between Pacific and 59 Sts. Weekdays in Manhattan, the N operates express between Canal and 34 Sts.
N Weekends in Manhattan, the N operates local (n.b., at Canal St, the N operates on the express platform).
N The N is local between 34 St, Manhattan, and Ditmars Blvd, Astoria. It operates local in Brooklyn between 59 St and Coney Island.
Q Broadway Express operates between Coney Island in Brooklyn and 57 St in Manhattan, operating express in Manhattan between Canal and 57 Sts.
Q In Brooklyn, the Q operates local.
R Broadway Local makes all stops between 95 St in Bay Ridge, Brooklyn, and 71 St in Forest Hills, Queens.
S 42 Street Shuttle operates between Times Square and Grand Central in Manhattan.
S Franklin Avenue Shuttle operates between Franklin Av and Prospect Park, Brooklyn.
S Rockaway Park Shuttle operates between Broad Channel and Rockaway Park in Queens.
V 6 Avenue Local operates weekdays, 6:30 a.m.–12 midnight, between 2 Avenue in Manhattan and 71 St in Forest Hills, Queens.
W Broadway Local operates weekdays, 6:30 a.m.–9 p.m., between Whitehall St in Manhattan and Ditmars Blvd in Astoria, Queens.
Z Z Nassau Street Express operates rush hours only as a skip-stop/express with the J between Jamaica Center, Queens, and Broad St, Manhattan. See the J stopping pattern.
The New York City Subway
Hours The subway is up and running 24 hours a day, 7 days a week. This map shows service from 6:30 a.m. – 12 midnight. At night, all stations except two are served, and service is truncated and less frequent. Some express routes operate local, some routes serve as shuttles, and some do not operate at all.
Routes Subway routes are color coded by trunk line and are usually named for their primary street of operation in Manhattan. Each line is identified by a number or letter.
1•2•3 - Broadway-7 Av - Red
4•5•6 - Lexington Av - Green
7 - Flushing - Purple
A•C•E - 8 Avenue - Blue
B•D•F•V - 6 Avenue - Orange
G - Brooklyn-Queens - Light Green
J•M•Z - Nassau Street - Brown
L - 14 Street-Canarsie - Grey
N•Q•R•W - Broadway - Yellow
S - 42 Street Shuttle - Grey
S - Franklin Avenue Shuttle - Grey
S - Rockaway Park Shuttle - Grey
Local and Express All routes operating between Lower and Upper Manhattan have express and local service. Trains labeled "Express" operate express for only some of their runs; some "Local" trains operate local on their namesake runs in Manhattan but express elsewhere. On this map, look for service in circles or ovals that is operating express in at least one direction from the station, in squares if local in both directions from the station.
Connections can be made between local and express trains at express stations; connections can also be made to trains traveling in opposite directions at almost all express stations and at many local stations. Stations that do not allow you to reverse direction without paying an additional fare are flagged on this map by "No U-Turn" symbols.
Routes in Brooklyn, Queens and The Bronx provide rush-hour express service to the Central Business District a.m., from the CBD p.m. On this map, look for thin route lines with one-way arrows.
A dashed line indicates that a route is extended beyond its normal terminal.
Stations Local stations are usually less than a half mile apart from each other, or about 600 meters. Average travel time between local stations is less than 2 minutes. Entrances to stations might lead to trains going in one direction only. Not all entrances are open all the time. Weekends on the J Line, Manhattan's Broad Street station is closed and there is no service at the Fulton Street platform.
Rush Hours: Mondays – Fridays, except holidays, 6:30 a.m. – 9:30 a.m., 3:30 p.m. – 8:00 p.m.
Schedules Weekdays, 6:30 a.m. – 8 p.m., trains are usually scheduled to arrive at stations within 5 minutes of each other; evenings and weekends, within 10 minutes; late nights, within 20 minutes.
Fare At the printing of this map, the flat fare is $2.25 a ride (no zones), with price breaks.
The coin of the realm is MetroCard, an electronically encoded card that is a swipe card in subway turnstiles. With a regular pay-per-ride MetroCard, 15 percent is automatically added to the stored value on the card with any purchase or addition of $8.00 or more, making the average fare $1.96. You are also offered the choice of unlimited ride passes: 1-day ($8.25); 7-day ($27); 14-day ($51.50); or 30-day ($89).
Use MetroCard only to enter the subway, not to exit. With MetroCard, you may transfer at no extra fare from subway to bus, bus to subway, or bus to bus. (You dip the card in the fare box on buses.)
Metrocards are available in subway stations and major transportation facilities. Vending machines accept cash or credit- and debit cards.
Key to This Map
Terminal•Route
Local Service
Station Name
STREET OF OPERATION
Place of Interest
Local and Express Service
No Crossover/under to Reverse Direction
Transfer between Trunk Lines
Extended Service
Part-Time Terminal
"Out-of-System" (aboveground) transfer – MetroCard required
Airport buses that accept MetroCard
AirTrain to JFK Airport ($5.00)
Information at each station on this map includes the station name (usually an intersecting street or local place name), the street of operation, designated places of interest, and service at the station.
All "Express" lines make local stops for some of their routes. If an "Express" operates express in at least one direction from a station, we show the service at that station in a circle or oval to alert you that the line might bypass stations; where an "Express" operates local in both directions, the service at that station is shown in a right-angled symbol.
Service at stations might change depending on the day of the week and the time of day. This map is stationcentric, and color codes the service at each station.
F 1 A black letter or number serves the station every day, 6:30 a.m – 12 midnight.
V A red letter serves the station weekdays, 6:30 a.m. – 9 p.m., 10 p.m., or 12 midnight.
N A yellow letter serves the station weekends, 6:30 a.m. – 12 midnight.
Z 5 A blue letter or number serves the station rush hours.
D An orange letter skips the station rush hours to the Central Business District a.m., from the CBD p.m.
G A green letter serves the station evenings and weekends.
Geography on this map has been distorted to clarify the operation of the subway. Central Park, for instance, should be a rectangle two and a half times as high as it is wide, not the near square you see here.
Hudson River
Harlem River
Manhattan
The Bronx
Queens
Brooklyn
East River
Upper New York Harbor
Jamaica Bay
Atlantic Ocean
Central Park
Prospect Park
Forest Park
Flushing Meadows Park
Van Cortlandt Park
Pelham Bay Park
Woodlawn Cemetery
Cypress Hills Cemetery
Evergreens Cemetery
Greenwood Cemetery
LAGUARDIA AIRPORT (LGA)
JOHN F. KENNEDY INTERNATIONAL AIRPORT (JFK)
TAURANAC MAPS
© Tauranac, Ltd., 2008;
Revised, July, 2009
All Rights Reserved.
www.tauranac.com

In 1941 the Dyer Avenue railroad line in the Bronx was incorporated into the subway system. The annual number of subway passengers reached 2.5 billion in 1947 and then declined until the 1970s. In 1948 the fare was raised to 10 cents. The New York City Transit Authority was formed by the State of New York in 1953 to operate the subway and the public bus system. The fare was raised to 15 cents on 25 July, requiring the introduction of tokens. By this time sections of the subway, some more than 50 years old, had fallen into disrepair because maintenance and capital renewal were inadequately funded. The transit authority used the proceeds from the sale of bonds approved in 1951 to replace subway cars and improve the physical plant. This plan had been approved by the voters largely because they assumed that it called for building a subway along Second Avenue. In 1956 the subway system absorbed the Long Island Rail Road's Rockaways railroad line in Queens.

Led by Michael J. Quill, the TWU went on strike in 1966 after failing to draw up a new contract with mayor-elect John V. Lindsay. It eventually won wage settlements and provisions for early retirement that inflated the operating costs of the transit authority, and in 1966 the fare was raised to 20 cents to compensate for these costs and for the decreasing number of passengers. The Metropolitan Transportation Authority (MTA) took control of the transit authority in 1968 and made plans to build lines to northeastern and southeastern Queens and under Second Avenue in Manhattan. Ridership continued to decline as people moved to the suburbs and relied on automobiles and as employment in the city fell by more than 600,000 between 1969 and 1977, by which time the number of riders was fewer than one billion for the first time in many years. The system also lost a large amount of revenue to "fare beaters," who entered stations without paying and sometimes inserted into the turnstiles foreign coins that were the same size as tokens, as well as counterfeit tokens known as slugs (a problem that led to the introduction in 1986 of the "bull's-eye" token, which could be counterfeited only with great difficulty; see People's Token). To make up for reduced revenues from fares the transit authority required increases in its operating subsidies, which eventually covered more than 40 percent of operating costs. The fare was raised successively to 30 cents (1970), 35 cents (1972), 50 cents (1975), and 60 cents (1980).

By the 1980s the subway system had seriously deteriorated. As crime became more common, the perception grew that the subways were unsafe. Passengers were also intimidated by graffiti, panhandling, and homeless people. Richard Ravitch, who became chairman of the MTA in 1979, suspended construction of any additional lines and focused on repairing aging facilities and reversing decay. As a result of innovative financial practices and pressure on the state legislature, the transit authority saw its annual capital budget for the subways increased from less than $300 million to more than $1 billion. Between 1982 and 1991 nearly $11 billion was committed to capital improvements. Under this capital program 4168 subway cars were overhauled, as were track, signals, power systems, maintenance facilities, and stations (often with the assistance of MTA Arts for Transit). By the early 1990s all subway cars were air conditioned. The system also bought 1775 new cars (all with air conditioning and surfaces resistant to graffiti). Under David L. Gunn, president of the transit authority, the management of the city's subway and bus system improved. An exhaustive effort to combat graffiti began with the removal from service of the most seriously vandalized cars and the protection of subway yards with barbed wire. During the early 1980s the subways again carried more than one billion passengers a year, and the number rose with improvements in service. In addition the New York City Transit Police Department was expanded and improved, and crime on the subways declined. Although subsidies to the MTA rose, so did operating costs; the fare was raised to 75 cents in 1981, 90 cents in 1984, $1 in 1986, $1.15 in 1990, and $1.25 in 1992.

After two five-year capital programs from 1982 to 1991, the MTA continued to raise capital funds from a variety of sources to continue the rebuilding of the subway system, as well as the bus network operated by MTA New York City Transit (the new name given to the transit authority by MTA in the mid-1990s). More than $45 billion was allocated to the agency's capital program between 1982 and 2009. In addition, in 1994 the MTA introduced the MetroCard to replace tokens; it also introduced free subway–bus transfers in 1997 and provided monthly, weekly, and daily discount MetroCards. The base fare on the system remained the cost of a single ride, and it was increased to $1.50 in 1995 and $2.00 in 2003. In 2008 the farebox operating ratio, that is, the fare's share of the cost of operating the New York City Transit subway and bus systems, was 58 percent (the balance came from subsidies from various levels of government). The improvements in service resulting from the capital program together with the free subway–bus transfers and fare discounts led to large increases in subway (and bus) ridership. In 1991 annual subway ridership had bottomed out at 995 million, but by 2007 it had increased to 1.56 billion.

The terrorist attacks of 11 September 2001 disrupted subway service by destroying the no. 1 station under the World Trade Center complex. The station was rebuilt and reopened ahead of schedule in September 2002. MTA and other agencies implemented a number of efforts to improve transit service to lower Manhattan, including the rebuilding of the Fulton Street station complex near the site of the World Trade Center.

In the early twenty-first century subways remain the most important form of transportation for millions of New Yorkers. In 2008 more than 66 percent of those traveling to Manhattan's central business district during peak hours used subways, and the system continued to run twenty-four hours a day throughout the year. On an average weekday

City Hall Subway Station, ca *1940s*

in 2008 there were 5.1 million subway trips. The city's rapid transit system was the most extensive in the world, with 714 miles (1142 kilometers) of track along 244 miles (390 kilometers) of routes; the longest line, the "A" line, is 32.4 miles (52.1 kilometers) long. The system was also one of the largest in the number of passengers it carried—fourth in the world in 2006 after Tokyo, Moscow, and Seoul; there were 26 lines, 468 stations, and 6241 subway cars in use. Portions of three of the original elevated lines remained, all in Brooklyn (along Myrtle Avenue, Broadway, and Franklin Avenue). Into the twenty-first century improvements to the system continued: in 2007 construction began once again on a subway under Second Avenue, and the Flushing line was being extended from Times Square to Manhattan's far West Side.

Brian J. Cudahy, *Under the Sidewalks of New York: The Story of the Greatest Subway System in the World* (Brattleboro, Vt.: Stephen Greene, 1979); Clifton Hood, *722 Miles: The Building of the Subways and How They Transformed New York* (New York: Simon and Schuster, 1992); Peter Derrick, *Tunneling to the Future: The Story of the Great Subway Expansion That Saved New York* (New York: New York University Press, 2001)

Peter Derrick

Sudanese. The first Sudanese to come to New York City was the Reverend Sayed (Satti) Magid Mohammed, who arrived in 1903 to spread Islam. He maintained a base on West Street in Little Syria, the city's first Arab neighborhood. Working closely with the Black Muslim Elijah Mohammed, he is said to have been responsible for the conversion to Islam of an estimated 120,000 Americans. Since the 1940s Sudanese immigration to New York City has been steady; some have come to pursue higher education, some to escape the military regime that took power in the coup d'état of 1989, and some to evade the precipitous devaluation of the Sudanese pound. New Sudanese immigrants are educated; they tend to work as livery and taxicab drivers until they can begin practicing their professions. Among Sudanese professionals are doctors, engineers, architects, teachers, college professors, and translators. Sudanese residential and commercial neighborhoods include Coney Island Avenue, Cortelyou Road, and Avenue C, in Brooklyn, and Jamaica, in Queens. Most Sudanese New Yorkers are Muslim, though they rarely associate with the city's larger Arab community except in mosques. Their own mosque, Masjid Al-Ihsan, is on Fulton Street, in Brooklyn. The first local Sudanese club, the Sudanese American Organization, was started by Mohammad Eisa, who arrived in 1942. More recently the Sudanese American Association (SAA) was established in 2006; it seeks to foster an appreciation of popular and traditional Sudanese culture among Sudanese émigrés and other Americans. In 2007 SAA helped produce a day-long festival of Sudanese music and dance on Central Park's Summerstage, a milestone event for the city's 10,000 Sudanese.

Paula Hajar

sugar. The first sugar refinery in New York City was opened on Liberty Street in 1730 by Nicholas Bayard. Most raw sugar was imported to the colonies from overseas, and the city was soon a center of sugar refining, largely because of the port and the high local demand for sugar. The industry attracted such prominent families as the Livingstons, Bayards, Cuylers, Roosevelts, Stewarts, and Van Cortlandts. The Rhinelander family built a sugar refinery near Rose, Duane, and William streets in 1763, and in 1799 the firm of Edmund Seaman and Company began operating the city's first sugar boiler, on Pine Street. William Havemeyer and Frederick C. Havemeyer, former employees of Seaman, opened the refinery of Wm. and F. C. Havemeyer in 1805 on Vandam Street. In 1857 they helped to form Havemeyer, Townsend and Company on South Third Street in Williamsburg, where undeveloped land, a deep-water harbor, and abundant cheap labor soon attracted other refineries. When it opened, Havemeyer's refinery had a daily capacity of 300,000 pounds (more than 136,000 kilograms) of raw sugar—more than all other New York City refineries combined. By the 1870s the figure was more than one million pounds (about 450,000 kilograms) a day, and Havemeyer's firm was employing 1000 workers for each shift.

After the sugar industry in the Gulf states was destroyed during the Civil War, sugar refining became concentrated in New York City, where the port had become the largest in the country, the transportation system was extensive, and banks were numerous. Sugar refining was the city's most profitable manufacturing industry from 1870 until World War I: 59 percent of the country's imported raw sugar was processed there in 1872, and 68 percent in 1887. In addition to the firms of the Havemeyers, several others in the city were successful, among them Wintjen, Dick and Schumacher (led by William Dick), Dick and Meyer, DeCastro and Donner in Brooklyn (with two refineries), the Greenpoint Sugar Refining Company, and Brooklyn Sugar Refining.

Because of intense competition, refineries in the city tried to fix prices in 1882. Their failure to do so led Henry O. Havemeyer in 1887 to form the Sugar Refineries Company (known as the Sugar Trust) to control the price of sugar and the labor pool. The trust consolidated most of the major refiners in Brooklyn, including Havemeyers and Elder, DeCastro and Donner, Brooklyn Sugar Refining, Dick and Meyer, and Moller, Sierck. After being ruled illegal in 1891 by the state supreme court, the Sugar Trust was reorganized by Havemeyer, who incorporated the American Sugar Refining Company in New Jersey and retained headquarters in the city on Wall Street. In 1900 Havemeyer eliminated the little remaining competition in the region by consolidating the surviving refineries in the city into the National Sugar Refining Company of New Jersey. The American Sugar Refining Company was the most important firm of the Sugar Trust, and the loose

Arbuckle's Sugar Company, 1934

network of companies controlled by the Havemeyers dominated the U.S. sugar industry, accounting directly and indirectly for 98 percent of national production by 1907. From that year the American Sugar Refining Company engaged in a protracted legal battle with the federal government over its control of the trust, during which its share of the cane market fell from 53 percent to 32 percent. The struggle ended with a settlement in 1922 that allowed the firm to remain intact but forced it to refrain from unfair business practices; as competition revived, the firm ceased to dominate the industry.

After the Depression the sugar refining industry declined in the city as modern technology and alternatives to sugar were introduced. Most refineries in the area were closed or destroyed by fire. The National Sugar Refining Company maintained its executive offices on Wall Street until 1982. The American Sugar Refining Company dominated the industry; its principal trademark was and is Domino. Ownership of the company, then known as Amstar, changed hands in 1984 and 1986, and in 1988 it was bought by Tate and Lyle. It opened headquarters at 1251 Sixth Avenue and in 1990 had more than $1 billion in sales, the highest among sugar companies in the United States. In 1992 the firm changed its name to Domino Sugar Corporation. In the mid-1990s Domino was one of the 500 largest companies in the country, maintained offices in the city, and made Domino sugar at the original refinery of Havemeyers and Elder. The Domino factory closed in 2004, ending a century of New York City's domination of the sugar industry; it was a victim of changing food tastes, pressure for lower labor costs, high real estate prices, and foreign competition. The neon sign for the factory defines the waterfront site, and in 2007 parts of the site were designated historic landmarks.

Paul A. Vogt, *The Sugar Refining Industry in the United States* (Philadelphia: University of Pennsylvania Press, 1906)

James Bradley, Rowan Moore Gerety

Sugar Hill. Neighborhood in Manhattan, lying within Harlem and bounded to the north by 155th Street, to the east by Edgecombe Avenue, to the south by 145th Street, and to the west by Amsterdam Avenue. Originally rural farmland, the area evolved into a residential enclave with the arrival of the Eighth Avenue Elevated Railway in 1879 and the subsequent construction of the subway in 1904, attracting middle- and upper-class whites. By 1919 wealthy members of the black community had relocated to the neighborhood, which earned the nickname Sugar Hill for the perceived "sweet life" of its new residents. During the first half of the twentieth century many prominent figures lived at 409 Edgecombe Avenue, including the poet and literary critic William Stanley Braithwaite and such leaders of the National Association for the Advancement of Colored People as W. E. B. Du Bois, Walter White, Thurgood Marshall, and Roy Wilkins. Although it is situated a few blocks north of 155th Street, the landmarked 555 Edgecombe Avenue, which housed many prominent jazz musicians, including Count Basie and Coleman Hawkins, is considered an integral part of Sugar Hill's heritage. Like those of many other city neighborhoods, its fortunes declined during the second half of the twentieth century. In the early twenty-first century, however, Sugar Hill became a diverse and vibrant area, with attractive apartment buildings, elegant town houses, and two mansions. The neighborhood is also home to St. Nick's Jazz Pub, formerly Lucky's Rendezvous and one of the oldest continuously operating jazz clubs in Harlem. Much of the area is encompassed within the Hamilton Heights–Sugar Hill Historic District and its northwest and northeast extensions.

Michael C. Repka

Sugar Hill, 2009

sugar houses. As many as half a dozen sugar houses, also known as sugar bakeries or refineries, were erected in lower Manhattan during the eighteenth century to process molasses imported by local merchants from the West Indies. Typically four or five stories high and built of massive granite blocks, they were the most foreboding structures in the city and tangible symbols of its lucrative commerce with distant slave plantations. During the Revolutionary War, two sugar houses were used by the British as prisons for captured Americans: Livingston's, on Crown (now Liberty) Street, and Van Cortlandt's, which stood on the northwest corner of Trinity Church Yard. Hundreds of men at a time were often confined in these buildings, without adequate food, water, ventilation, or sanitation. Typhus and other diseases ran rampant, and as many as 10 bodies a day were reportedly removed for burial. The longest-surviving sugar house was Cuyler's (later Rhinelander's), on Rose Street, which was demolished in 1892. Although two of its windows have been preserved as memorials to the Americans who died in captivity, there is no evidence that the British ever used it as a prison.

Edwin G. Burrows

Sullivan, Big Tim [Timothy D(aniel)] (*b* New York City, 23 July 1863; *d* New York City, 13 Aug 1913). Famed ward boss. Born at 125 Greenwich Street, he grew up from the age of four in the poor Irish tenements of the Five Points, a neighborhood in Manhattan at that time. As an adult he embarked on careers in business and politics, skillfully using each to support the other. From 1904 he was an owner of the Sullivan–Considine vaudeville circuit, which included the Dewey Theater on 14th Street and the Gotham Theater on 125th Street and by 1907 had become a lucrative national chain of more than 40 theaters. He was also a business partner of William Fox and Marcus Loew in the incipient nickelodeon business and made successful investments in entertainments at Coney Island, racetracks (including Metropolitan Racetrack near Jamaica), and athletic clubs.

With the backing of Tammany Hall, Sullivan represented the Bowery in the state assembly (1886–93), the state senate (1893–1902, 1908–12), and the U.S. Congress (1902–6).

One of the most powerful and colorful figures in the city at the turn of the twentieth century, Sullivan assembled a political machine that ruled lower Manhattan for 25 years. He combined the traditional tactics of the machine with his influence in the worlds of commercialized leisure and organized crime. At his huge summer "chowders" he staged theatrical entertainments and amateur athletic contests and gave shoes and food to his constituents; he also offered employment, social services, and legal protection to both ordinary citizens and key figures in the flourishing vice economy of the Lower East Side. He was accused by the police lieutenant Thomas Byrnes and the Episcopal bishop Henry Codman Potter of having profited from prostitution and gambling. Despite this he helped expand the franchise to the poor, the transient, and the homeless and became one of the most powerful individuals in the state. With the young reformer Frances Perkins, in 1911 he fought successfully to limit to 54 hours a week the amount of time women could work in factories in New York State; he also wrote a number of tenement reform bills, as well as the so-called Sullivan Law (1911), the state's first effort at gun control, and was a strong supporter of woman suffrage and organized labor. Sullivan's unique record of legislative achievement in many ways foreshadowed the future direction of the Democratic Party. In 1913 he was declared insane, apparently a victim of tertiary syphilis. He was killed by a train while visiting his brother Patrick in suburban Eastchester; his funeral on the Bowery, which drew as many as 75,000 onlookers, was one of the largest in the city's history.

Proceedings of the Legislature of the State of New York on the Life, Character and Public Service of Timothy D. Sullivan (Albany, N.Y.: J. B. Lyon, 1914)

Daniel Czitrom

Sullivan, Ed(ward Vincent) (*b* New York City, 28 Sept 1901; *d* New York City, 13 Oct 1974). Television host and journalist. Born in Harlem and brought up in Port Chester, New York, he graduated from high school and worked as a sportswriter for the *Port Chester Daily Item.* During the 1920s he reported for several newspapers, including the *New York Evening Mail,* the *Morning Telegraph,* and the *Leader,* and in 1929 he replaced Walter Winchell as the Broadway columnist for the *New York Evening Graphic.* He also worked as a master of ceremonies for a number of vaudeville shows, radio programs, and benefits. During World War II he organized shows in Madison Square Garden for the Army Emergency Relief Fund and the American Red Cross. In 1948 the Columbia Broadcasting System (CBS) made him the host of its weekly television variety program *Toast of the Town,* which eventually became *The Ed Sullivan Show.* For the next 23 years the program made him one of the most powerful people in the entertainment business. An astute judge of talent, he introduced to American television such performers as Humphrey Bogart, Jackie Gleason, Maria Callas, Rudolf Nureyev, Elvis Presley, and the Beatles. He also featured animal acts, magicians, and oddities. In 1959 he led a variety troupe on a tour of the Soviet Union. Sullivan vigorously supported charities and medical causes and spoke out against bigotry and fraud. In honor of his 20th year in television CBS in 1967 renamed its studio on Broadway and 53rd Street in his honor. In 1993 the Ed Sullivan Theater became home to the *Late Show with David Letterman.* Throughout most of his career Sullivan and his wife, Sylvia Weinstein, occupied a suite in Delmonico's Hotel at 59th Street and Park Avenue.

Robert Sanger Steel

Sulzberger, Arthur H(ays) (*b* New York City, 12 Sept 1889; *d* New York City, 11 Dec 1968). Newspaper publisher. He attended Columbia University, served in the U.S. Army, and in 1917 married Iphigene Ochs. In the following year he joined the *New York Times,* owned by his father-in-law, Adolph Simon Ochs, and in 1919 he became a vice president. He was named publisher on Ochs's death in 1935, and in the same year his wife acquired a controlling interest in the newspaper. With the assistance of the general manager, Julius Ochs Adler (Ochs's nephew), he made important changes, naming Anne O'Hare McCormick foreign affairs columnist, modernizing the printing plants, and adding a crossword puzzle and sections on food and fashion. By making a large commitment of money and staff to covering World War II at a time when other newspapers were cutting back on the space they devoted to news, he helped the *Times* to maintain its leadership position. He retired in 1961. Sulzberger lived at 5 East 80th Street from 1928 until 1952 and then at 1115 Fifth Avenue to the end of his life.

B. Kimberly Taylor

Sulzer, William (*b* Elizabeth, N.J., 18 March 1863; *d* New York City, 6 Nov 1941). Governor and legislator. A graduate of Columbia University, he practiced law in New York City before his election to the state assembly as a Democrat in 1888. He became speaker of the assembly in 1893 and in 1894 was elected to the U.S. House of Representatives from the eleventh congressional district of Manhattan (the East Village). During his 17 years in office he chaired several important committees. In 1912 he was elected governor of New York with the support of Tammany Hall, but he turned on boss Charles Francis Murphy and refused to accept Tammany Hall recommendations for patronage appointments. For that offense he was removed from office by the state legislature, technically on the grounds that records of his campaign contributions and expenditures had been falsified, a common offense at the time. Sulzer was the only governor ever to be impeached in New York State. Until the end of his life, Sulzer lived at 118 Washington Place and continued to practice law from his office at 115 Broadway.

James Bradley

Summerville. Disused name for the eastern part of OLD PLACE.

Sunday schools. The Sunday school movement was begun about 1781 by Robert Raikes in Gloucester, England. At first the aim was not to provide religious instruction but rather, more broadly, to better poor children's lives. Many churches initially opposed Sunday schools because they considered teaching a desecration of the Sabbath. Raikes's efforts became known in New York City, Boston, and Philadelphia, and in 1792 an evening Sunday school for adults was opened on Mulberry Street in Manhattan by Isabella Graham (1742–1814), who welcomed blacks and whites. Katy Ferguson's School for the Poor, in New York City, was opened in 1793 for blacks and whites, children and adults, by Catherine Ferguson (?1779–1854), a former slave. Gilbert S. Coutant's Sunday school also began in 1793 in what was then Bowery Village. With her daughter Joanna Graham Bethune and her son-in-law Divie Bethune (1771–1824), Graham opened a school in what is now Chinatown in 1803; in 1814 she and her daughter opened another school, in Greenwich Village, for women and children of all races. On 24 January 1816 a group of women including Joanna Graham Bethune organized the interdenominational Female Union for the Promotion of Sabbath Schools, later known as the New York Female Sunday-School Union. The New York Sunday-School Union was formed under the direction of Eleazer Lord (1788–1871), the clergyman John M. Mason, and the bishop Richard Varick in February 1816; it merged with the New York Female Sunday-School Union in the late 1820s to form the New York Sunday-School Union.

A number of innovations in the curriculum and organization of Sunday schools occurred during that decade. In 1820 advocates in the city urged the formation of a national society, a proposal that was realized when the American Sunday-School Union was organized in Philadelphia in 1824. Because Sunday school teachers were often inexperienced volunteers, training was offered by the New York Sunday-School Union, which inspired similar efforts by the national union. The New York Sunday-School Union also produced the first uniform system of lessons, a year-long series of Bible verses accompanied by "Judson's Questions," written by Albert Judson, a New Yorker, and distributed nationally. The system was adopted by the national union in 1872 and explained in the *American Sunday-School Magazine* by

John Hall (1829–98), a clergyman in New York City. The national union promoted the establishment of free public schools so that Sunday schools could concentrate exclusively on religious training. By the 1870s it won the endorsement of churches after demonstrating that Sunday-school teachings were based on the Bible. Among its supporters were such prominent New Yorkers as Samuel Bradhurst Schieffelin (1811–1900); Robert Lenox Kennedy (1822–87, president of the union, 1873–82); and Morris K. Jesup (president, 1896–1908). The New York Sunday-School Union was renamed the New York Sunday School Association in 1876 and had an office at 1 Madison Avenue until 1923; the national union had a branch at 156 Fifth Avenue until 1958.

Edwin Wilbur Rice, *The Sunday-School Movement, 1780–1917, and the American Sunday-School Union, 1817–1917* (Philadelphia: American Sunday-School Union, 1917); Anne M. Boylan, *Sunday School: The Formation of an American Institution, 1790–1880* (New Haven: Yale University Press, 1988)

Alana Erickson Coble

Sunnyside (i). Neighborhood in northwestern Queens, lying within Long Island City and bounded to the north by the Sunnyside Yards, to the east by Calvary Cemetery and 51st Street, to the south by the Long Island Expressway, and to the west by Van Dam Street. The area is named for a roadhouse built on Jackson Avenue to accommodate visitors to the Fashion Race Course in Corona during the 1850s and 1860s. South of Jackson Avenue the Fitting, Gosman, Heiser, Lowery, and Van Buren families owned farms that were eventually subdivided in the 1880s and 1890s. A small hamlet was built between Northern and Queens Boulevards and became known as Sunnyside. The Pennsylvania Railroad in 1901 adopted a plan to lay out a large railroad yard nearby, connected by tunnels to Manhattan. Most of the land was low-lying and boggy and therefore cheap; from 1902 to 1905 agents of the railroad gradually bought up all the land south of Northern Boulevard between 21st and 43rd streets. The entire area was leveled and the swamps filled in between 1907 and 1908, and the Sunnyside Yards opened in November 1910 (now used by Amtrak, the Long Island Railroad, and New Jersey Transit). The remaining land south of Skillman Avenue was dry but uninhabited. The Queensboro Bridge opened in 1909 and from it was built Queens Boulevard, which ran to the center of the borough through Sunnyside, where streets were built along the boulevard. The population grew rapidly after the elevated line opened in 1917, and many attractive apartment buildings with art deco touches and rows of attached houses were erected in the 1920s. SUNNYSIDE GARDENS (1924–28), one of the nation's first planned communities, featured landscaped interior courts and was hailed for its innovative design by such scholars of urban life as Lewis Mumford (a onetime resident). During the following years the neighborhood became middle class and lower middle class, and largely Irish. In the 1940s and 1950s its large apartments enticed many artists and writers and their families to leave their cramped quarters in lower Manhattan, and the area became known as the "maternity ward of Greenwich Village." Sunnyside during the 1980s attracted immigrants from Korea, Turkey, and Romania, and in the 1990s and 2000s Mexicans arrived in growing numbers. The Irish flavor persists, however, evidenced by the annual St. Patrick's Day Parade on Skillman Avenue.

Vincent Seyfried

Sunnyside (ii). Neighborhood in northeastern Staten Island, bounded to the north by Clove Lakes and Silver Lake parks, to the east by Grymes Hill and Fox Hills, and to the west by Castleton Corners. The name is derived from that of a boarding house that stood from 1889 on Clove Road at what is now Richmond Turnpike. Maps from the time of the American Revolution identify houses and gardens, including those of the Vanderbilts. Ice harvesting and the pumping of spring water were important activities in the nineteenth century. The Solheim Swedish Home for the Aged was built in the neighborhood in 1909. During the following decades the intersection of Clove Road and Victory Boulevard became busy and congested, in part because of traffic generated by Wagner College and the College of Staten Island, which moved to Willowbrook in 1993. The Michael J. Petrides School on the old College of Staten Island site is a comprehensive K–12 school and opened in 1995. Two large apartment buildings called the Fountains were built in 1968; a facility of the Health Insurance Plan was built in 1988. The neighborhood was disrupted in the mid-1970s as water mains and sewerage were installed to replace a system of artesian wells and natural drainage. Sunnyside is often cited as an exemplar of the change of Staten Island from an area of goat farms, trolleys, marshes, and two-lane roads to one of houses on small plots and busy traffic. Clove Lakes Park, designated a Forever Wild Nature Preserve by the New York City Department of Parks and Recreation, remains one of the finest open spaces in the city. The borough's first Hindu Temple is located at 1318 Victory Boulevard.

Howard R. Weiner

Sunnyside Gardens. Planned community in northwestern Queens, bounded to the north by 43rd Street and to the south by 51st Street; it covers 77 acres (30 hectares) and about 16 blocks. Influenced by the English garden city movement, the City Housing Corporation built Sunnyside Gardens between 1924 and 1928 for middle-income families under the direction of architects Clarence S. Stein and Henry Wright, who designed it according to ideals of "health, open space, greenery, and idyllic community living for all." One-, two-, and three-family attached brick houses with slate roofs, gables, and porches were constructed around open center courts with tree-lined pathways and private and communal flower gardens designed by Marjorie Cautley, one of the first female landscape architects in the United States. Garages were provided on the edges of the neighborhood near the railroad. A private park opened adjacent to the railroad. In the 1930s the beautiful art deco Phipps Gardens Apartments were built. Well-known residents have included the architectural critic Lewis Mumford, the painter Raphael Soyer, and entertainers Rudy Vallee, Perry Como, and Judy Holliday. During the Depression in the 1930s half the residents lost their homes to foreclosure. Marshals seeking to evict homeowners often met spirited resistance. The community was regulated by 40-year covenants limiting alterations and protecting the open spaces, but when the covenants expired in the 1960s, some residents fenced their rear yards, breaking up the courtyards. In 1974 the Department of City Planning designated Sunnyside Gardens a Special Planned Community Preservation District (together with Fresh Meadows, Parkchester, and the Harlem River Houses) to protect the original design. The Sunnyside Gardens Conservancy was formed in 1981 to restore the neighborhood to its original graciousness, and it had the neighborhood listed on the National Register of Historic Places in 1984. In 2007 the Landmarks Preservation Commission designated Sunnyside Gardens and Phipps Gardens as a historic district.

Patricia A. Doyal

Sunset Hill. Neighborhood in northeastern Staten Island, bounded to the north by West Brighton, to the east by Silver Lake, to the south by Bard Avenue, and to the west by Clove Road. The area was part of West New Brighton until the 1920s, when its streets were laid out in a grid and it was given its present name. The Tyler–Gardiner mansion (circa 1840), a landmark, was the home during the Civil War of Julia Gardiner, widow of President John Tyler; according to local reports youths tore town a Confederate flag that she displayed in the yard. The population is middle class, the housing consists of one-family houses, and there is shopping on Forest Avenue.

Marjorie Johnson

Sunset Park. Neighborhood in southwestern Brooklyn, bound by Bay Ridge to the south, Park Slope to the north, and Borough Park to the east. Until the 1960s the northern section was considered part of Gowanus and the southern section part of Bay Ridge; the area was renamed in the late 1960s for a local park built by the city in the 1890s. Development began in the 1830s and GREEN-WOOD CEMETERY was laid out in 1839 as one of the first rural cemeteries in the nation. Many Irish immigrants settled in the area during the 1840s. Improvements in transport spurred development in a section south of 36th Street, leading to industrial growth. After 1870 brick and brownstone row houses replaced wood houses. Polish, Norwegian, and Finnish immigrants settled in the area during the 1880s and 1890s, followed at the turn of the twentieth century by Italians, many of whom worked along the docks. Bush Terminal, a complex of piers, warehouses, and factory lofts, was built by Irving T. Bush in 1890, and industry expanded immensely during the early twentieth century. The Brooklyn Army Terminal was built in 1919. By the 1930s and 1940s several factors contributed to the decline of the neighborhood: the Depression, the cessation of the Third Avenue elevated line, and the construction (1941) and widening of the Gowanus Expressway, which separated the industrial sections of the neighborhood from its residential sections. After World War II many white residents moved to the suburbs, and many Puerto Ricans moved in and found work on the waterfront and in factories. Decline worsened from the 1950s to the 1970s: the maritime industry moved to New Jersey, and the Brooklyn Army Terminal was deactivated in the 1970s. With local, state, and federal aid the economy improved during the 1970s, and the 1980s saw a commercial revival and an influx of immigrants from Latin America, China, and the rest of Asia. A large number of new immigrants settled in the neighborhood in the 1980s; one-quarter were from China, with roughly an equal number from the Dominican Republic, and smaller numbers from Guyana, Ecuador, India, Vietnam, Colombia, Jordan, and Poland. The Brooklyn Army Terminal reopened as a light industrial center in 1987, and Bush Terminal was converted into an industrial park. Businesses owned by Latin Americans between 35th Street and 60th Street along Fifth Avenue include bodegas, restaurants, and stores selling clothing, records, and jewelry. In the 1990s Eighth Avenue became known as "Brooklyn's Chinatown," as it became home to the city's third largest Chinese community. Sunset Park is also the home of the Basilica of Our Lady of Perpetual Help, the largest church in Brooklyn.

Ellen Marie Snyder-Grenier

SUNY. See STATE UNIVERSITY OF NEW YORK.

Surdna Foundation. Philanthropic foundation established in 1917 by John Emory Andrus, who was the mayor of Yonkers, the director of the New York Life Insurance Company in the early 1900s, and a four-term congressman. The foundation had several programs in areas including organizational capacity building and the arts. In 1989 the third and fourth generations of the Andrus family board established programs in Environment and Community Revitalization; programs in Effective Citizenry and the Arts were added in 1994 and the Nonprofit Sector Support Program in 1997. In the early twenty-first century its offices were located at 330 Madison Avenue.

Jessica Montesano

surfing. Surfing in New York City was practiced in 1912 by Duke Kahanamoku of Hawaii, winner of a gold medal in swimming at the Olympic Games, and Joe Ruddy of Rockaway, also the winner of an Olympic medal. Surfing was made popular by the local lifeguard Mickey McManamon in the 1950s, as well as by the singing group the Beach Boys and the film *Endless Summer.* By the mid-1960s surfers could be found throughout the Rockaways. Their favorite spots were 92nd Street (known as Chicken Bone Beach), 111th Street, and 72nd Street, where in 1968 surfers protested a ban on the sport at local beaches. Although the ban was lifted, demands that a beach be designated for surfing went unfulfilled. Among the early surfboard builders was Tony Michaels, who produced surfboards in the back room of his father's garment factory. In the early 1980s Tom Sena of the Rockaway Beach Surf Shop began manufacturing and selling surfing equipment of high quality.

James Breslin, Peter Maguire

Surrogate's Court. Municipal building at 31 Chambers Street in Manhattan. Designed in an eclectic French Renaissance style by John R. Thomas, it was built during 1899–1911 and originally known as the Hall of Records. The granite building houses the city archives in addition to the Surrogate's Court and is an impressive monument to civic virtue. The interior lobby, finished in Siena marble, emulates the foyer of Jean-Louis Garnier's Opéra in Paris; the courtrooms on the fifth floor are finished in English oak and mahogany. In 1963 the building took its current name. The exterior was designated a landmark in 1966, the interior in 1976. It became a National Historic Landmark in 1977. The court handles cases involving the affairs of decedents, including the probate of wills and the administration of estates, as well as adoptions.

Brooke J. Barr

Survey Associates. Publisher for charitable causes. It began as the National Publication Committee of the Charity Organization Society in 1891. During the same year it launched *Charities Review* (soon renamed *Charities*), a journal that eventually merged with the publications *Commons,* which issued reports about settlement house activities, and *Jewish Charity* to form *Charities and the Commons;* Paul U. Kellogg (1879–1958) became the editor in 1909. Inspired by his work in cataloguing social conditions for the Pittsburgh Survey, he renamed the journal the *Survey* and with his brother Arthur Kellogg (1878–1934) made it and its illustrated companion, *Survey Graphic,* the most influential publications of their kind. The organization took its current name after becoming independent of the

Surrogate's Court, 1938

Charity Organization Society in 1912. Survey Associates published reports about housing, recreation, renewal, and industrial conditions in the city before ceasing operations in 1952.

Alana Erickson Coble

sustainable design. See Green buildings.

Sutton, Percy E. (*b* San Antonio, Tex., 24 Nov 1920; *d* New York City, 26 Dec 2009). Attorney and civil rights activist. A World War II veteran and member of the Tuskegee Airmen, he attended Brooklyn Law School, opened a Harlem law office with his brother Oliver in 1953, and represented Nation of Islam Minister Malcolm X and other controversial figures. He served as New York City branch president of the National Association for the Advancement of Colored People (NAACP) and cofounded the John F. Kennedy Democratic Club with fellow Harlemite Charles B. Rangel. He served in the New York State Assembly before becoming Manhattan Borough President (1966–77). When the famed Apollo Theater fell into bankruptcy in 1980, Sutton purchased it to return stability to this important institution and the commercial district of West 125th Street. He was instrumental in the successful mayoral campaign of David N. Dinkins and cofounded the information technology company Synematics.

Diane Jones Randall

Sutton, Willie [William Francis, Jr.] (*b* Brooklyn, 30 June 1901; *d* Spring Hill, Fla., 2 Nov 1980). Bank robber. He began robbing banks in 1927 and was soon nicknamed "the actor" because of the elaborate costumes and disguises he used. He escaped from prison in 1932 and again in 1948. In 1952 he was recognized on a subway in New York City and sentenced to 17 years in prison for stealing $64,000 from a bank in Queens. He was paroled from the Attica State Correctional Facility in 1967. Sutton was often quoted for having explained that he robbed banks because "that's where the money is." It is estimated that his thefts amounted to $2 million.

Melissa M. Merritt

Sutton Place. Neighborhood on the East Side of midtown Manhattan, between 53rd and 59th streets east of First Avenue, encompassing Sutton Place South and Sutton Place, respectively, from 53rd to 59th streets, which becomes York Avenue north of 59th Street. The original name for all three streets was Avenue A. It is named after Effingham B. Sutton, the entrepreneur who developed the area about 1875. Before World War I tenements, rundown brownstones, and a brewery covered the area. It was perhaps most famous as the home of the gang known widely through films as the Dead End Kids, but after Mrs. William K. Vanderbilt and Anne Morgan moved there in 1920, the neighborhood was gradually transformed into a secluded cluster of expensive private houses and exclusive apartment buildings; its success led to the development of other expensive residential enclaves along the East River at Beekman Place and East End Avenue. The buildings along the east side of the neighborhood are constructed atop the Franklin D. Roosevelt East River Drive, which runs under two apartment buildings between 54th and 56th streets and under a town house at 58th Street. Residents from 56th to 59th streets have access to landscaped backyards built on the drive by the city as compensation for the loss of access to the river occasioned by the construction of the drive; three vest pocket parks lie between these private yards at the ends of 56th, 57th, and 58th streets.

Owen Gutfreund, Andrew Sparberg

Swamp. An area in lower Manhattan encompassing Gold, Frankfort, Pearl, Water, and Ferry streets. It became the site of tanning pits during colonial times and was soon the center of the city's leather industry, which was attracted by the freshwater that flowed into the area from the Collect and by the proximity of the district to the docks along the East River. Although the pond was covered over by 1811, the Swamp remained the site of the city's leather district.

Frank W. Norcross, *A History of the New York Swamp* (New York: Chiswick, 1901); Lucius F. Ellsworth, *Craft to National Industry in the Nineteenth Century: A Case Study of the Transformation of the New York State Tanning Industry* (New York: Arno, 1975)

See also Shoes, boots, and leather.

Richard C. Wiles

Swedenborgians. Members of the Church of the New Jerusalem (or New Church); they are Christians who follow the teachings of the Swedish scientist turned theologian Emmanuel Swedenborg (1688–1772) and share his vision of Heaven and Hell and his assertion that a spiritual "last judgment" took place in 1757. Swedenborg, who simply wanted his writings (known to his followers as the "Third Testament") to be studied by university scholars, did not intend to make a separate church, but the novelty of his ideas inevitably created a following that would coalesce into the New Church.

After congregations were formed in England, and then in Philadelphia and Boston in the 1780s, Joseph Russell, an English immigrant, organized a branch in New York City in 1792. Swedenborgianism, as it was called, was avidly promoted during 1795–96 by the Anglican clergyman William Hill, who refused to break with the Anglican Church. A group formed in 1805 by Edward Riley, who settled in the city after emigrating from England, met at 16 Chambers Street before moving to larger quarters on James Street in 1807. Among its members were the bookseller James Chesterman and the poet Samuel Woodworth. In 1816 the city's first affiliated Swedenborgian church, the Association of the City of New York for the Dissemination of the Doctrines of the New Jerusalem Church, was formed by 26 men including Chesterman, who became the treasurer, and Woodworth, who became the secretary. The church met at the Mount Vernon School on Broadway until 1821, when it bought a large building on Pearl Street. One of the first mystical sects that flourished in the United States, the church attracted many intellectuals during the first half of the nineteenth century and was closely connected with such movements as mesmerism, transcendentalism, and spiritualism. In 1838 a schism reduced the congregation to a small group that sold the building on Pearl Street and held services at the Lyceum on Broadway near Prince Street.

The church attracted new members after George Bush, a professor of philosophy at New York University, gave lectures throughout the city and became the pastor in 1847. A larger building was erected on three plots of land at 114 East 35th Street, bequeathed to the church by Chesterman; the church was dedicated in 1859 and became highly influential during the next century. Among those who attended were the editor and writer John Bigelow, Henry James (father of the writer), the statesman William H. Seward, and the writer and lecturer Helen Keller. By 1932 the building was enlarged and the church offered Sunday services, a monthly lecture series, and a Sunday school. During the 1950s there were about 160 members and 75 students enrolled in the school. By the turn of the twenty-first century the Church of the New Jerusalem had declined to a few dozen active members.

Marguerite Beck Block, *The New Church in the New World: A Study of Swedenborgianism* (New York: Henry Holt, 1932)

Robert Ellwood

Swedes. The first known person of Swedish ancestry in New York City was Jonas Bronck, who was born in Copenhagen to Swedish parents and settled in 1639 in what is now the Bronx. Mons Pieterson, a Swede or Swedish-speaking Finn, helped to lay out Harlem, which was cleared in 1661 by a group of settlers that included Swedes. During English rule few Swedes moved to the city, and most settled in Manhattan. They numbered about 100 in 1835, and in 1836 the country's first Scandinavian mutual-aid society, Svenska Societen, was formed with 22 members. Swedes and other Scandinavians took part in religious services at the Bethel Ship (1845), a German Lutheran church aboard a German ship moored at Pier 11 at the foot of Liberty Street on the Hudson River; the church remained under the leadership of Olof Gustaf Hedstrom (1803–77) for 30 years and received financial assistance from Jenny Lind when she visited New York City in 1850. The first Swedish newspaper in the country, *Skandinaven,* was published from 1851 to 1853 by Anders Gustaf Obom (1812–81), also known as Napoleon Berger. Land shortages and compulsory military service in Sweden in the mid-nineteenth century led many Swedes to emigrate. Thousands passed through the city before settling elsewhere in the United States; those who remained were often merchants, carpenters, and longshoremen, among them John Ericsson and a crew that included six other Swedes who built the ironclad warship the *Monitor* at a private yard in Greenpoint.

Between 1860 and 1870 the city's Swedish population rose from about 800 to 3000, and Swedish enclaves developed on the East Side and what is now Cobble Hill in Brooklyn. Gustavus Adolphus Church, the city's first Swedish Lutheran church, opened in 1865 at 155 East 22nd Street. In 1872 the Immanuel Swedish Methodist Episcopal Church was formed on Dean Street near Fifth Avenue in Brooklyn by members of the Bethel Ship congregation, and eventually Swedish Congregational and Baptist churches followed. The Swedish-language weekly newspaper *Nordstjernan* (The North Star) began publication in 1872 from offices at 108 Park Row; it later moved to 4 West 22nd Street. The Swedish-American Athletic Society of Brooklyn was organized during the 1880s at 267 Sixth Avenue and lasted until 1974. Among the Swedish singing groups in Brooklyn were the Lyran Singing Society of Brooklyn (143 West 44th Street) and the Swedish Glee Club (142 Schermerhorn Street), which remained well known into the 1930s. Many Swedes worked on the Brooklyn Bridge and after 1900 in the Brooklyn Navy Yard, where they were supervised by Carl J. Mellin, a Swedish engineer. They formed the American Society of Swedish Engineers (1888), which established the annual John Ericsson Award, and the children of Swedish immigrants often became engineers and building contractors. Women found work as domestic servants. Among the social welfare organizations formed toward the end of the century were the Swedish Aid Society of New York (1891–1906), which had offices in Brooklyn and Manhattan and found employment for 20,000 Swedes, and the Kallman Home for Children in Brooklyn (1898–1964). Periodicals included the socialist weekly newspaper *Arbetaren* (1896–1928) and the magazine *Valkyrian* (1897–1909).

In 1900 there were 28,320 Swedes in the city, including 14,695 in Brooklyn and 10,936 in Manhattan. Several institutions were opened in the early twentieth century, among them the Scandinavian Young Women's Home (Fridhem) at 149 Portland Avenue in Brooklyn (1902–50), the Swedish Hospital on Rogers Avenue in Brooklyn (24 June 1906, moved to 1350 Bedford Avenue about 1940, closed in 1979), and the Swedish Augustana Home for the Aged (1908–61) at 1680 60th Street in Brooklyn. The Swedish Chamber of Commerce of the USA (1906) set up offices at Rockefeller Center and published the *American Swedish Monthly;* as the Swedish-American Chamber of Commerce, it remained active into the twenty-first century. The United Swedish Societies of Greater New York (138 Third Avenue in Manhattan) was formed in 1911 to promote awareness of Swedish heritage, and the American Scandinavian Foundation (1911; 127 East 73rd Street in Manhattan), which included among its founders Emil F. Johnson (1864–1953), a public health inspector who devised a means of controlling the quality of the city's milk supply, published the *American Scandinavian Review,* a literary quarterly journal. The cartographer Andrew G. Hagstrom (1890–1957) settled in the city in 1909 and opened a mapmaking business in 1916 that soon became widely known.

In 1930 there were 37,200 Swedish immigrants and 24,500 of their children in the city. Most lived in Sunset Park, southern Brooklyn near Hamilton Avenue, and Bay Ridge, some in the northern Bronx, Forest Hills Gardens, and Sunnyside Gardens, and about a quarter in Manhattan. During the following years the number of Swedish immigrants declined as the Swedish economy improved, and few children of immigrants remained in Swedish neighborhoods. In 1980 about 3000 Swedish immigrants lived in the city, which had the country's second-largest concentration of Swedish Americans, after Chicago. The Swedish Seamen's Church, at 5 East 48th Street, remained in operation into the early twenty-first century. In 1996 the Swedish consulate and New York City Parks Department began sponsoring the Swedish Midsummer Celebration in Battery Park City. Scandinavia House (38th Street at Park Avenue) opened in 2000. Well-known Swedes in New York City have included the merchant and banker Svante Magnus Svensson (later Swenson; 1816–96); John A. Johnson (1865–1938), who with his sons operated a construction company that built two-family houses and apartment buildings in Bay Ridge; David L. Lindquist (1874–1944), who helped the Otis Elevator Company to develop its first modern elevator; the tenor Jussi Björling (1911–60), who performed regularly at the Metropolitan Opera for 22 years; the actress Greta Garbo (1905–90), who lived on East 52nd Street until her death; and Marcus Samuelsson (*b* 1970), a chef who operated the restaurant Aquavit (65 East 55th Street).

Alana Erickson Coble

Sweet'N Low Factory (Cumberland Packing Corporation). Artificial sweetener plant. Founder Benjamin Eisenstadt owned a diner across from the Brooklyn Navy Yard on Cumberland Street. After World War II the restaurant business declined, so Eisenstadt converted his diner to the manufacture of teabags. He and his wife had the idea of putting sugar in similar small packets, and in 1957 the firm created a sugar substitute, a combination of saccharin, dextrose, and cream of tartar, also sold in small packages. Recalling a favorite song based on the Tennyson poem "The Princess: Sweet and Low," Eisenstadt named the product Sweet'N Low. The business prospered, occupying additional buildings inside the navy yard industrial park and worldwide. In the twenty-first century the company headquarters are still at 2 Cumberland Street in Brooklyn.

Rich Cohen, *Sweet and Low: A Family Story* (New York: Farrar, Straus and Giroux, 2006)

Cathy Alexander

swill milk. Term used in the nineteenth century to describe milk from cows fed on distillery waste that was then adulterated with water, chalk, eggs, flour, and other ingredients that increased the volume and masked the adulteration. Swill-milk dairies were noted for their filthy conditions and overpowering stench, caused by the close confinement of hundreds (sometimes thousands) of cows often standing in their own manure in narrow stalls and suffering from a range of diseases. In the 1850s such conditions proliferated in dairies in and around New York City. Swill milk became the focus of periodic reform crusades in the early 1840s, 1850s, and 1860s. The most notable effort began in May 1858, when *Frank Leslie's Illustrated Newspaper* did a landmark exposé of regional dairies that caused widespread public outrage in the city and nationally. With the advent of refrigeration, low-cost train transportation, and more vigorous pure food laws in the 1860s and later, the dairy industry gradually moved out of the city.

Jared Day

swimming. Swimming became a popular activity in New York City during the nineteenth century, owing partly to the crowded conditions of tenement housing. As early as 1817 two private marine baths were anchored off the Battery. After the Civil War concern about public health and sanitation mounted, and municipal funding was set aside for swimming and bathing facilities. Fifteen free-floating baths were installed in the Hudson and East Rivers in Manhattan, Brooklyn, and the Bronx between 1890 and 1910, and dozens of public bathhouses were built by 1912. The Coney Island Polar Bear Club was formed in 1903 by fitness enthusiast Bernarr Macfadden, and its members began a long-running tradition of swimming in the ocean on the coldest days of the year. The many accidents suffered by swimmers off the piers led bathhouses to open swimming facilities and offer swimming lessons during the early

Astoria Pool, 1936

twentieth century. Indoor pools were built throughout the city after the Croton Aqueduct was completed in 1842, and the construction of the subways provided access to beaches at Coney Island and the Rockaways.

The city's indoor and floating pools had deteriorated by the early twentieth century, and only two outdoor municipal pools existed when Robert Moses became parks commissioner in 1934. As the adjacent rivers became polluted by irresponsible development and waste disposal, Moses transformed the city's swimming facilities when he built 11 municipal pools in 1936. That summer Moses opened one pool a week, to great fanfare, beginning 24 June with Hamilton Fish Park on the Lower East Side. Moses loved to swim, and he made sure that the pools were attractive in their design. Each complex had modern bathhouses, and most contained three pools that were open from 10:00 a.m. to 10:30 p.m.; demand became so great that the hours were extended to midnight. Adults could swim for 20 cents and children for 10; in the mornings, admission was free for children younger than 14. Moses's new pools held a combined capacity of 49,000 people; more than 1.6 million New Yorkers in all five boroughs swam in them that summer, and the Astoria Pool in Queens became the site of the swimming and diving trials for the Olympic Games in Berlin.

Moses also worked to create cleaner beaches that were more accessible for swimming. He reconstructed Orchard Beach in the Bronx in 1938 and built a grand bathhouse; he acquired Manhattan Beach on Coney Island from the federal government, opening it in 1955, and he made improvements at Jacob Riis Park (1936–38) and the Rockaway beaches (1938–39) in Queens and South Beach (1955) in Staten Island. Moses also took control of three existing floating pools in Manhattan and strung them together on the Hudson River off 93rd Street in 1938; they closed in 1942. He launched a program of free swimming lessons called Learn to Swim in 1938; in the early twenty-first century, 7000 children participated in the program each summer. During Mayor John Lindsay's administration (1966–73), underserved neighborhoods gained access to swimming pools in the form of mini-pools and swimmobiles, which were portable. In the early 1970s, 19 new pools were constructed around the city, and the Moses-era pools were renovated during the 1980s. New complexes in Chelsea and Flushing Meadows added to the city's facilities, which in 2008 boasted 34 outdoor pools, 12 indoor pools, and 19 mini-pools.

Competitive swimming in New York was refined as a sport between 1900 and 1925, and such organizations as the New York Athletic Club and the New York Women's Swimming Association assembled large swim teams. Some of the first world records were set by swimmers from the city, including Charles M. Daniels (1907), Gertrude Ederle (1922, 1925), Walter Spence (1926), and Eleanor Holm (1932). A number of swimmers have swum great distances in the waters of New York. Byron Sommers in 1927 swam around Manhattan Island, a distance of 28 miles (45 kilometers), in eight hours and 56 minutes, a record that stood until Diana Nyad completed the swim in seven hours and 57 minutes in 1975. The fastest official time around Manhattan is six hours and 32 minutes, completed by Tobie Smith in 1999. In 1961 Palmer Donnelly became the first person to swim around Staten Island, in 25 hours; he repeated his feat in 1979. The swim around Manhattan became a more popular event during the 1980s, and some swimmers completed a double swim around the island (Julie Ridge in 1983) and even a triple swim (Stacy Chanin in 1984). In 1988 Skip Storch set a distance record by swimming 153 miles (246 kilometers) down the Hudson River from Albany, New York, to the Statue of Liberty.

During the early 1990s interest in the traditional swim around Manhattan declined, and the Manhattan Island Foundation was formed in 1993 to revive interest in swimming in New York City's waters; proceeds from its Manhattan Island Marathon Swim support the parks department's Learn to Swim program. In the twenty-first century the organization also hosted swims around Governor's Island and from Manhattan to Brooklyn underneath the Brooklyn Bridge; new studies were undertaken in 2008 to determine the "swimmability" of the Hudson River, the cleanliness of which improved after the Clean Water Act of 1972. At the city's beaches the Polar Bear Club's annual New Year's Day swim in Coney Island remained a popular

Lasker Pool, Central Park, 2009

event in the early twenty-first century. Hundreds of swimmers charge into the cold waters of the Atlantic Ocean, some dressed in wetsuits, some in sequins, and some in American flags. Amidst calls to connect New Yorkers to the city's long-obscured waterfront and polluted rivers, floating swimming pools have resurfaced, recalling the city's nineteenth-century floating baths. The Floating Pool Lady, a pool constructed on an old barge, was completed in 2007 and moored off of Brooklyn Bridge Park. It moved to Hunts Point in the Bronx during the summer of 2008, where it will remain for three years, serving a community district that does not have a single public pool.

Ann L. Buttenwieser: "Awash in New York: A Chronicle of the City's Floating Baths," *Seaport Magazine* 18 (1984), 12–19; Hilary Ballon and Kenneth T. Jackson, eds., *Robert Moses and the Modern City: The Transformation of New York* (New York: W. W. Norton, 2007)

Amanda Aaron, Kate Lauber

Swinburne Island. The smaller of two artificial islands off the eastern shore of Staten Island (the other is HOFFMAN ISLAND), it has an area of 2.5 acres (1 hectare). Originally named Dix Island, it was renamed to honor John Swinburne, a Civil War military surgeon. In the 1900s the island housed a hospital and quarantine station that treated arriving immigrants suspected of having infectious diseases. During World War II Swinburne Island was the site of a training facility for the U.S. Merchant Marine. Early in the twenty-first century it was managed by the National Park Service and was part of the Gateway National Recreation Area. Closed to visitors, it is home to large colonies of nesting wading birds.

Gerard R. Wolfe

Swingline. Firm of staple and stapler manufacturers, formed in 1925 on the Lower East Side by Jack Linsky as the Parrot Speed Fastener Company. In the late 1920s it began manufacturing staples that were glued together in rows (known as "frozen wire staples"), an innovation at a time when staples were still being inserted into a stapler one at a time or held together with sheet metal. Eventually the firm also introduced the first anti-jam stapler, the Tot 50 automatic stapler, which sold more than 100 million units, and electronic staplers and became a leader in the cartridge stapling technology used in electronic copiers. In 1991 it became part of ACCO USA, a manufacturer of office products and supplies based in Wheeling, Illinois. Swingline is the largest manufacturer of staples and staplers in the world. Its facility in Long Island City, Queens, topped with an enormous neon sign that was visible from Shea Stadium, shut down in 1999 when manufacturing moved to Mexico. The factory was temporarily occupied by the Museum of Modern Art from 2002 to 2004 while it was renovating its Manhattan building.

Rich Scheinin

Swing Street. Popular nickname in the 1930s and 1940s for 52ND STREET between Fifth and Sixth avenues and the site of many jazz clubs.

Swinton, John (*b* Edinburgh, 12 Dec 1829; *d* Brooklyn, 15 Dec 1901). Labor activist and editor. With only a modest formal education and an apprenticeship as a printer, he immigrated to Canada in 1843 and in 1850 arrived in New York City; there he worked as a printer and briefly attended New York Medical College. By the mid-1850s his participation in the abolitionist movement drew him to Kansas, where in 1857 he joined John Brown's raid at Osawatomie. On returning to New York City he worked successively for the *New York Times* (chief of the editorial staff, 1860–70) and the *Sun* (1870–75; chief editorial writer, 1875–83). During most of this time he lived at 124 East 38th Street. His career as a labor activist began in January 1874, when he witnessed the Tompkins Square Riot, in which unemployed workingmen who had gathered at a peaceful rally were attacked and beaten by police. That autumn he was the unsuccessful mayoral candidate of the Socialist Labor Party, and he became a regular speaker at labor rallies. In October 1883 he began his own weekly labor organ, *John Swinton's Paper,* published at 21 Park Row and widely recognized as the finest publication of its kind. Refusing to confine himself to any one movement, Swinton called on the nation's workers to work together for economic and social justice in the face of growing corporate power. His newspaper was influential in Henry George's mayoral campaign of 1886. In 1887 he ceased publishing the newspaper because of financial difficulties and rejoined the editorial staff of the *Sun,* where in spite of going blind in 1889 he worked until his death. Swinton's published writings include *John Swinton's Travels* (1880) and *Striking for Life* (1894).

Marc Ross, "John Swinton, Journalist and Reformer: The Active Years, 1857–1887" (diss., New York University, 1969)

Edward O'Donnell

Swope, Herbert Bayard (*b* St. Louis, 5 Jan 1882; *d* New York City, 20 June 1958). Journalist. As a reporter for the *New York World* in 1912 he investigated police corruption and helped to implicate Lieutenant Charles Becker in the murder of the gambler Herman Rosenthal. He became the city editor in 1916 and in the following year filed reports from Germany that won him the first Pulitzer Prize for reporting. As the executive editor of the *World* (1920–29) he developed the feature later known as the "op-ed" page and led sensational crusades against local slumlords and the Ku Klux Klan. Under his direction the *World* was known for its public-spirited liberalism, support of the progressive elements in the Democratic Party, and often dramatic investigative reporting.

Alfred Allen Lewis, *Man of the World: Herbert Bayard Swope: A Charmed Life of Pulitzer Prizes, Poker, and Politics* (New York: Bobbs–Merrill, 1978)

Steven H. Jaffe

Sylvia's. Restaurant in Harlem. Established in 1962 by Herbert and Sylvia Woods, the

Sylvia's, 2009

location at 328 Lenox Avenue originally seated 35 people. In the early 1980s Sylvia's son Van Woods expanded the restaurant to seat about 450 people. In 1992 he launched Sylvia's Food Products, which were distributed nationally. In 1997 Sylvia's opened a second restaurant in Atlanta, Georgia. In the early twenty-first century Sylvia's occupies most of a city block and features catering and banquet facilities in addition to the restaurant. As of 2008 Sylvia had written three cookbooks and the restaurant remained in the Woods family.

Jessica Montesano

Symphony Space. Performing arts center. Located at 95th Street and Broadway, it sponsors music, dance, film, literature, and theater programs and performances. Founded by Isaiah Sheffer in 1977, since 1980 it has maintained its commitment to art-based educational initiatives for children and adults in New York City and nationally through the distribution of programs via recording, radio broadcastings, and touring. It has a studio room and two theaters, the Peter Jay Sharp Theatre and the Leonard Nimoy Thalia, and annually hosts 125 performances, attracting more than 100,000 patrons.

Stephanie Miller

Symphony Space, 2009

synagogues. Jewish houses of worship. Manhattan alone has more than 150 current and former synagogue structures, and hundreds more dot neighborhoods throughout the five boroughs. New York's first synagogue, the earliest in North America, was established in the late seventeenth century by Shearith Israel, the congregation that emerged from the original settlement of Sephardic Jews in New Amsterdam in 1654. A makeshift "Jews' Synagogue" existed by 1695, and the first synagogue building was erected in 1729 on Mill Street (now South William Street). It served the congregation for more than a century and was the sole synagogue and only Jewish institution of the community until 1825. Shearith Israel later followed the uptown movement of New York Jews, building three successive synagogues, the last in 1897 on Central Park West at 70th Street, where the congregation remains in the twenty-first century. The 1897 building foresaw a Jewish future for the Upper West Side but also looked back to the colonial origins of New York Jewry. In addition to the main sanctuary, the building contains a smaller worship space called the Little Synagogue, which replicates the interior of the original Mill Street building.

In 1825 the establishment of B'nai Jeshurun, formed by a disaffected group of Shearith Israel members, signaled the breakup of the monolithic "synagogue community" and the advent of a "community of synagogues." B'nai Jeshurun was the city's first Ashkenazic-rite congregation and dedicated its first synagogue, a former church on Elm Street, in 1826. As immigration from central Europe intensified, the Jewish population of New York City multiplied from just 500 in 1820 to some 40,000 by 1860. During these years no fewer than 20 new synagogues were founded in the neighborhood of lower Manhattan known as Kleindeutschland, including Ansche Chesed (established 1828 as an offshoot of B'nai Jeshurun), Rodeph Sholom (1842), Shaaray Tefila (1845, also split from B'nai Jeshurun), and Ahawath Chesed (1846). In 1847 Shaaray Tefila dedicated a new Romanesque Revival synagogue on Wooster Street designed by Leopold Eidlitz, who is often called the first Jewish architect in the United States. In 1850 Ansche Chesed built a Gothic Revival synagogue on Norfolk Street designed by Alexander Saeltzer; it is the oldest surviving synagogue structure in New York City. Rodeph Sholom built its Rundbogenstil synagogue on Clinton Street in 1853; in 2009 it housed the Chatam Sofer congregation. Many of these congregations followed Shearith Israel's lead in moving uptown, through a series of ever more upscale locations. B'nai Jeshurun built new synagogues repeatedly: on Greene Street in 1851, on 34th Street in 1865, on Madison Avenue and 65th Street in 1885, and finally its current home on West 88th Street in 1918.

After the Civil War synagogues throughout the country were built as monuments to Americanization, most often designed in an opulent Islamic Revival style and in the religious fashion of Reform Judaism. The first Reform congregation in New York City, Emanu-El (see Temple Emanu-El), had been established in 1845. After using spaces in two refurbished churches, it built its luxurious new "temple" in 1868 on Fifth Avenue at 43rd Street. Designed by Leopold Eidlitz and Henry Fernbach, the neo-Islamic building became a landmark of post–Civil War New York City. Other monumental temples of the time include two more designed by Fernbach: Shaaray Tefila on West 44th Street (1869) and Ahawath Chesed at Lexington Avenue and 55th Street (1872) (known in the twenty-first century as Central Synagogue and extensively restored after a 1998 fire). Also in this category were Ansche Chesed at Lexington Avenue and 63rd Street (1873), Beth Elohim in Brooklyn (1876; Keap Street Temple), B'nai Jeshurun on Madison Avenue near 65th Street (1885), and Zichron Ephraim on East 67th Street near Third Avenue (1890) (Park East Synagogue). Arnold Brunner was the architect responsible for Beth El on Fifth Avenue at 76th Street (1891), Shaaray Tefila on West 82nd Street (1894) (West End Synagogue), and Shearith Israel on Central Park West (1897). Of these nineteenth-century structures, only Central Synagogue, Keap Street, West End Synagogue, Park East, and Shearith Israel were still extant in the late 2000s—the latter two still in the hands of their original Orthodox congregations. Such monumental uptown synagogues continued to be built through the early decades of the twentieth century, the most notable being the new Temple Emanu-El, built during 1928–30 on Fifth Avenue at the corner of 65th Street. An awe-inspiring structure, it is known as the "cathedral synagogue" of New York City.

The restored Eldridge Street Synagogue, one of the city's most historic houses of worship

The most prolific period of synagogue building in New York City came with the mass immigration of eastern European Jews from 1881 to 1914, when more than two million Jews arrived in the United States. Most of them settled in the city and formed an immigrant enclave on the Lower East Side of Manhattan. The neighborhood would become home to hundreds of immigrant congregations, making the synagogue, or *shul,* a ubiquitous institution of Jewish neighborhoods. According to one estimate, more than 500 shuls were established on the East Side during this period, of which about 60 occupied their own buildings, including several converted churches. Most of the myriad immigrant shuls were founded as hometown societies (a *landsmanshaft*), and their typical home was either a rented space, a "storefront shul," or a small structure of its own, often a renovated tenement, or *tenement shul.* The first Russian Jewish congregation in New York City appeared as early as 1852 with the establishment of Beth Hamedrash on Bayard Street. Its offshoot, Beth Hamedrash Hagadol, later acquired its own synagogue building, converting a former Baptist church on Norfolk Street in 1885. Two years later the original congregation, renamed K'hal Adas Jeshurun, completed the first major synagogue structure of the immigrant community. Located on a narrow side street south of Canal Street, the impressive edifice came to be known as the Eldridge Street Shul. Designed in an eclectic Revival style with pronounced neo-Islamic elements, it was reminiscent of the uptown temples of the same era. The 1887 structure was reopened in 2007 after 20 years of renovation work as the Museum at Eldridge Street (although it also still functions as an Orthodox synagogue). Besides Beth Hamedrash Hagadol and Eldridge Street, other extant downtown shuls include Anshe Ilya, better known as the Forsyth Street Shul (built in 1895 with a row of built-in storefronts on its Delancey Street side, now owned by a Spanish church); B'nai Israel Kalwarie, known as the Pike Street Shul (built in 1903 and now a Chinese church); the Bialystoker Shul on Willett Street (an 1826 church converted in 1905 and still in use by the congregation); and the former Anshe Slonim on Norfolk Street (originally built in 1850 as Ansche Chesed).

The second-generation Jews in the city were innovators of the "synagogue-center," or combined synagogue and community center, and helped spur a nationwide movement. Fondly called a "shul with a pool," the synagogue-center had its roots in the institutional church, the late nineteenth-century Reform temple, the Young Men's and Young Women's Hebrew Associations, and other institutional trends of the Jewish community. Two early exemplars in New York City were established by modern Orthodox congregations in 1917: the Institutional Synagogue, founded by Rabbi Herbert Goldstein and located on West 116th Street in Harlem, and the Jewish Center, founded by Rabbi Mordecai M. Kaplan and built on West 86th Street on the Upper West Side. Kaplan would later leave the Jewish Center, moving a block away on 86th Street to establish the first Reconstructionist synagogue, the Society for the Advancement of Judaism, in 1922. The synagogue-center concept would find its widest expression in the middle-class Jewish communities of the outer boroughs. In Brooklyn, which was rapidly becoming the borough with the largest Jewish population (100,000 in 1905, increasing to 567,000 in 1917, 740,000 in 1923, and reaching a peak of 974,765 in 1937), the prototypical synagogue-center was the Brooklyn Jewish Center (BJC), built in 1920–22 by a Conservative congregation on Eastern Parkway in Crown Heights. Throughout the 1920s dozens of new congregations were founded in Brooklyn, and nearly all followed the example of BJC, building well-appointed synagogue complexes with names such as Flatbush Jewish Center, East Midwood Jewish Center, and Ocean Parkway Jewish Center. The trend was so compelling that even the venerable Reform congregation of Brooklyn, Union Temple, built a new "Temple House" in 1926, still in use at its Grand Army Plaza location. Similarly, in 1929 Beth Elohim added a center to its 1909 temple on Garfield Place. The Bronx saw the founding of the Bronx Jewish Center and the Intervale Jewish Center; and the Rego Park Jewish Center and Forest Hills Jewish Center, among others, were established in Queens. In the twenty-first century many of these prewar structures are still in use by their congregations, although the BJC was acquired by the Lubavitcher Hasidic community and turned into a boys' school (yeshiva).

In the decades after World War II many New York Jews left the city for the suburbs

Conservative Synagogue, 2009

Shearith Israel, 2009

where hundreds of new congregations were formed and new suburban synagogue-centers built. Also after the war Holocaust survivors in the city rebuilt their lives, and charismatic leaders reasserted orthodoxy for a new generation. Unlike more liberal Jews eager to escape to suburbia, the Orthodox tended to stay in the urban environment, so the postwar period saw a spate of new Orthodox shuls, both modern and traditionalist, established within the city bounds. For example, Congregation Kehilath Jacob, founded in the 1940s on West 79th Street, came to be known as the Carlebach Shul, after Rabbi Naphtali Carlebach took over in 1950; from 1967 his son, folksinger Shlomo Carlebach, turned the Upper West Side shul into a center of hippie-styled neo-Hasidism. More traditional Hasidic enclaves had earlier emerged in the Brooklyn neighborhoods of Boro Park, Crown Heights, and Williamsburg, where synagogues flourished. Perhaps the best known is the synagogue and school complex at 770 Eastern Parkway that was the seat of the Lubavitcher Rebbe; the building's Tudor style has been replicated by Lubavitch institutions around the world. Yet another traditionalist enclave in Brooklyn was established by Sephardic Jews, primarily of Syrian origin, along Ocean Parkway. Two of their leading synagogues were Shaare Zion, designed by Morris Lapidus in 1958, and *Beth Torah,* designed by Richard Foster in 1969. At the same time, more modern Orthodox Jews were establishing new congregations farther uptown. In 1964 the Lincoln Square Synagogue was founded under Rabbi Shlomo Riskin and built a structure in 1970 with a sanctuary designed as a theater-in-the-round by Hausman and Rosenberg. The Hebrew Institute of Riverdale was founded in 1971 and built its current synagogue on the Henry Hudson Parkway in 1980. In 1973 Rebbetzn Esther Jungreis founded Hineni, an outreach organization whose mass gatherings were modeled after Billy Graham revivals. A new center was established in 1982 with the construction of the Hineni Heritage Center on West End Avenue.

In the second half of the twentieth century old structures were revitalized by new congregations. From the Jewish counterculture of the 1960s a desire emerged for a less formal synagogue and a more intimate and spiritual community called a *havurah.* Ultimately, the havurah movement influenced the mainstream synagogue, as when a dying Ansche Chesed—built in 1928 as a synagogue-center at the corner of West End Avenue and 100th Street—was revived in the 1980s by several *havurah*-style *minyanim* (prayer groups) that began to use its premises and reenergized the synagogue. Nearby B'nai Jeshurun underwent a similar revitalization as Rabbi Marshall Meyer (1985–93) began to attract young Jews to its West 88th Street synagogue. By the mid-1990s B'nai Jeshurun was attracting a standing-room-only crowd to its Friday night service, then held in a neighboring church as the original building was being restored. In a new spin on an old practice, several other nontraditional congregations began to use church spaces for their services. Congregation Beth Simchat Torah (CBST), New York's gay and lesbian synagogue, was founded in 1973 at the Holy Apostles Church on Ninth Avenue in Chelsea. In 1992, following the arrival of Rabbi Sharon Kleinbaum, it held a Yom Kippur service in the Jacob Javits Convention Center for 2200 worshippers. Though based in the Westbeth artists' complex on Bethune Street, CBST holds its Friday night service in the same church in which it was founded. The trend also includes Hadar, an egalitarian Orthodox *minyan,* and Romemu, a Jewish Renewal group, both meeting in Upper West Side churches. A new Upper East Side congregation, Or Zarua, thought it was purchasing an old church building until it discovered that the 1890 structure had originally been a synagogue. In 2001–2, the congregation rebuilt the East 82nd Street synagogue according to a modern design by Henry Wollman. Perhaps the most compelling story of renewal belongs to the 1850 Ansche Chesed synagogue on Norfolk Street. After serving a series of Jewish congregations, it was abandoned by 1974. Later acquired by the Spanish sculptor Angel Orensanz, the building became the Orensanz Center for the Arts; in addition to serving as a cultural venue, it has been home to the Shul of New York since 1997. New York Jews expend tremendous energy in building new homes for an ever-evolving Judaism, and in the twenty-first century their synagogues demonstrate both Jewish survival and civic integration.

Gerard Wolfe, *The Synagogues of New York's Lower East Side* (New York: New York University Press, 1978); Abraham Karp, "Overview: The Synagogue in America—A Historical Typology," *The American Synagogue: A Sanctuary Transformed,* ed. Jack Wertheimer (Cambridge: Cambridge University Press, 1987), 1–34; David Kaufman, *Shul with a Pool: The "Synagogue-Center" in American Jewish History* (Hanover, N.H.: University Press of New England, 1999); David Dunlap, *From Abyssinian to Zion: A Guide to Manhattan's Houses of Worship* (New York: Columbia University Press, 2004); Jonathan Sarna, *American Judaism: A History* (New Haven: Yale University Press, 2004)

David Kaufman

Syrians and Lebanese. Syrians began immigrating to the Americas in the late 1870s. Among the reasons often cited are inspiration from American missionaries and educators, wanderlust, family competition, and Ottoman conscription. Those who emigrated were mostly Christian mountain villagers—Maronites, Antiochian Orthodox, and Melchites, as well as many Protestants—but a large minority were urbanites from the cities of Tripoli, Zahle, Aleppo, Damascus, Homs, and Haifa. They first settled in lower Manhattan around Rector and Washington streets, an area that became known as Little Syria. Many of the early Syrian immigrants began as peddlers and soon accumulated enough capital to establish their own businesses, 383 of which were listed in the 1908 Syrian Business Directory. These businesses, which included groceries, import–export firms that often dealt in Madeira lace and Oriental rugs, and factories producing lingerie, kimonos, and other dry goods, were largely family run, employing local Syrians and supplying peddlers and Syrian businesses throughout the nation. The Bardwil, Haddad, Barsa, Tadross, and Trabulsi families were among the most prominent in these businesses. By the 1920s some "merchant princes" had factories in South America and East Asia. (In the early twenty-first century none of these original businesses remained, the progeny of the first immigrant generation having abandoned the family firms either to work in other businesses or to enter other professions. In fact, roughly half the members of the Salaam Club, a businessmen's fraternity dating to 1945, were in other professions.) There were 15,000 Syrians in the city by 1924, when quotas were imposed. In 1940 the community was displaced by the construction of the Brooklyn–Battery Tunnel. By that time Brooklyn and especially the stretch of Atlantic Avenue from Court Street to the water had became the community's new commercial center. Later Syrians moved to Park Slope and Bay Ridge, but Atlantic Avenue continued to be the heart of Arab New York.

Though the early immigrants identified strongly with their religious sects, they also formed new nonsectarian organizations such as the Syrian Ladies Aid Society (1907), the Damascus Masonic Lodge (1908), and the Syrian Young Men's Association (1934), all of which continued to operate in the early twenty-first century. Among the early leaders of the community were the Syrian physician Rizq George Haddad and the philanthropist Salim Malouk, a linen importer who had a shop on Fifth Avenue. One beneficiary of Malouk's generosity was al-Rabitah al-Qalamiyya (the Pen League; formed 1920), a group of Syrian émigré writers led by Kahlil Gibran, Amin Rihani, and Elia Abu Madi; its members' experiments with Western literary forms revolutionized Arabic poetry in the Arab world. Between 1890 and 1940 Syrians in the city published 51 Arabic-language periodicals (two-thirds of the country's total). The most influential of these was *Al-Hoda* (The Guidance), launched in 1898 by Naoum Mokarzel, who with his brother Salloum counseled the community on assimilation and championed Arab independence abroad. Readership of Arabic-language newspapers declined in the 1930s, primarily because of the freeze on immigration and because the American-born generation did not learn to read Arabic.

By the 1940s Syrians were becoming part of the American mainstream, as evidenced by their abandonment of arranged marriages, the employment of women outside the home and outside the family business, and growing aspirations to higher education. A large number were joining American Protestant and Roman Catholic churches or modifying their own Eastern rites, and 80 percent of the third generation of Syrian Americans in New York City were marrying non-Syrians. By the 1960s most Syrians and Lebanese were keeping their ethnicity private, with unusually strong family ties. Syrian–Lebanese culture continued to be expressed in food and music and at weddings and in *haflis,* large parties featuring Arabic dancing and performances by such musicians as the singers Hanan and Kahraman and the drummer and humorist Eddie Kochak, creator of the Ameraba (American Arabic) style of music.

New waves of Syrian, Lebanese, and other Arab immigrants began arriving after quotas were lifted in 1965. Lebanon's civil war (1975–90) accelerated Lebanese immigration. At least half the newcomers were Muslim. The new immigrants were more likely than their turn-of-the-century forerunners to be drawn from the professional classes. (New immigrants, for example, swelled the membership of the New York City chapter of the Arab American Medical Association.) While some of the immigrants planned to return to Lebanon when peace was restored, others came intending to stay. Families settled in Bay Ridge; eventually a strip of Bay Ridge's Fifth Avenue would be dotted with Arabic signage for restaurants and a variety of Arab stores and agencies, though none of the businesses yet rivaled those on Atlantic Avenue, where Rashid Music, Sahadi's Gourmet Deli, and the Damascus Bakery continued to serve the city (and the nation) by the end of the twentieth century. Manhattan drew young professionals who worked in engineering, computers, and banking, an important economic sector in Beirut. Some Lebanese became active in the city's alumni chapters of the American University of Beirut and Beirut University College. Most continued to be deeply interested in the future of Lebanon. Though they reinvigorated Arabic churches and neighborhoods, interaction between the new immigrants and the American-born Syrian–Lebanese took time to develop. One local institution that was an early bridge was St. Nicholas Home for the Aged, a nonsectarian facility that was opened in 1982 on Ovington Avenue in Bay Ridge by descendants of the first immigrants; its board represents the spectrum of Arab religious and national groups. In the 1980s new national organizations, such as the American Arab Anti-Discrimination Committee and the Arab American Institute, helped Syrians and Lebanese reframe their ethnic identities.

The twenty-first century saw the birth of new Arab American organizations, some spurred on by the anti-Arab backlash after the terrorist attacks of 11 September 2001. Among the new groups are the Arab American Family Support Center in downtown Brooklyn (established in 1994) and the Arab American Association of Bay Ridge (established in 2001), both multiservice advocacy groups; the Network of Arab American Professionals (established in 2000 as an outgrowth of the Union of Arab Students Associations); and the Kahlil Gibran International Academy (established in 2007), a bilingual Arabic public school in Boerum Hill. Since 2004 Lebanese Heritage Day has been celebrated annually in the rotunda of Brooklyn's Borough Hall, giving the city's Lebanese added visibility as they present their food and music to the public and honor individuals from the community, while the Lebanese cedar flag flies from the top of Brooklyn's Borough Hall. In the new millennium there were an estimated 80,000 Syrian and Lebanese Christians and Muslims living in New York City.

There is a roughly equal number of Syrian Jews in the city. Syrian Jews began arriving at the beginning of the twentieth century with the first wave of Syrian Christians; they came from Damascus, Homs, and especially Aleppo (Halab). They initially settled on the Lower East Side with Jews from Europe but quickly established their own enclaves in Brooklyn, first in Williamsburg and later in Flatbush and Midwood. Their institutions along Ocean Parkway and Kings Highway include yeshivas, community centers, residences for the elderly, and synagogues representing Aleppo, Damascus, Lebanon, and Egypt. Syrian Jews have prospered in the import–export trade, particularly in clothing and electronics. They have much in common linguistically and culturally with other Syrians and Lebanese, but politically they identify with other Jews in the city rather than with other Syrians.

Prominent Syrian and Lebanese Americans include the Metropolitan Opera singer Rosalind Elias; former secretary of health and human services Donna Shalala (a former president of Hunter College); Oscar-winning actor F. Murray Abraham; fashion designers Reem Acra, Norma Kamali, and Joseph Abboud; Broadway actress Kathy Najimi; Off-Broadway playwright Betty Shamieh (*Roar,* 2004, *Chocolate in Heat,* 2001); and theater and film director Julie Taymor (*The Lion King,* 1998).

Lucius Hopkins Miller, *Our Syrian Population: A Study of the Syrian Communities of Greater New York* (n.p. [?New York]: n.pub., n.d. [?1903]); Kathleen Benson and Philip Kayal, eds., *A Community of Many Worlds: Arab Americans in New York City* (New York: The Museum of the City of New York/ Syracuse: Syracuse University Press, 2002)

Paula Hajar

Szold, Henrietta (*b* Baltimore, 21 Dec 1860; *d* Jerusalem, 13 Feb 1945). Scholar and political activist. The first woman enrolled at the Jewish Theological Seminary, she worked as an editor and translator in German, English, and Hebrew on such books as Louis Ginzberg's *The Legends of the Jews* (1908–38) and the American Jewish Yearbook. A member of the Federation of American Zionists, she helped to form Hadassah, the first women's Zionist group, in 1912 in New York City, and was its president until 1926. Szold worked as a nurse in Palestine between 1912 and 1926, helped to organize the American Zionist Medical Unit, and directed the Youth Aliyah program from 1933.

Janet Frankston

T

tabloids. Newspapers with pages about half as large as a broadsheet and a large number of illustrations. Tabloid newspapers exerted an important influence on journalism in New York City between the world wars. The prototype for the genre was the *Daily News,* launched in 1919 by Joseph Medill Patterson and Robert McCormick, which had a terse, lively reporting style and coverage that emphasized crime, sex, scandal, sports, and gossip; its circulation reached 400,000 by 1922. The success of the *Daily News* inspired other newspapers to imitate its formula. Among the most prominent were the *Daily Mirror,* published by William Randolph Hearst, and the *New York Evening Graphic,* published by Bernarr Macfadden. By 1926 the three newspapers had captured more than 1.5 million readers, only a few of whom had been won over from the existing daily newspapers; most were immigrants and their children who had not been regular newspaper readers at all. The circulation of the *Daily News* reached 1.3 million on weekdays by 1930 and more than three million on Sundays by 1940, and in 1942 the *New York Post* adopted the format. Effectively exploiting class, racial, and ethnic tensions, tabloids had an important influence on advertising and magazines, which freely borrowed such devices as "confession" stories, suggestive headlines, and lurid photographs. Although critics dismissed them as vulgar and sensational, the tabloids expressed a shrewd awareness of working-class life not found in the more traditional press. The tabloid style remains a central element in print and broadcast journalism, especially in New York City. Three of the four major daily newspapers in the city in 2008 were tabloids: the *Daily News,* the *New York Post,* and *New York Newsday.*

Simon Michael Bessie, *Jazz Journalism: The Story of the Tabloid Newspapers* (New York: E. P. Dutton, 1938)

Daniel Czitrom

Takami, Toyohiko Campbell (*b* Kumamoto, Japan, 1875; *d* Brooklyn, 17 May 1945). Physician. In 1891 he left Yokohama as a "captain's boy" on an English steamship, which he abandoned when it docked in New York City. He worked as a mess-boy at the Brooklyn Navy Yard; studied English and the Bible at a Sunday school in Brooklyn; and with the support of Nancy E. Campbell, an American missionary, attended private preparatory schools in Massachusetts and New Jersey before attending Lafayette College, Brooklyn Polytechnic Institute, Columbia University, and Cornell University Medical College (graduating in 1916). In 1907 he formed the Japanese Mutual Aid Society, serving as its president until 1918. He maintained a private practice near Fort Greene Park, was chief of dermatology at Cumberland Hospital, helped to establish Japanese immigrant organizations, and was the president of the Japanese Association from 1930 until 1933, as well as an active leader in Christian church organizations.

Mitziko Sawada

Takamine, Jokichi (*b* Ishikawa Prefecture, Japan, 1854; *d* New York City, 22 July 1922). Chemist. In 1880 he was sent by the Japanese government to study in England; on his return to Japan he set up the first artificial-fertilizer business there. After traveling to the United States several times he assumed a research position at a distillery in Chicago where he shortened the distillation process by introducing an artificial fungus culture. In suburban Clifton, New Jersey, he established the Takamine Research Center, where he perfected a digestive medicine, Taka Diastase, and was the first chemist to extract a hormone (epinephrine) in pure form. He married in 1887 and built an elaborate mansion at 334 Riverside Drive. Takamine was a founding member of the Nippon Club in 1905, a vice president of the Japan Society in 1907, and a founding member and four-term president of the Japanese Association of New York.

Kiyoshi Karl Kawakami, *Jokichi Takamine: A Record of His American Achievements* (New York: W. E. Ridge, 1928)

Mitziko Sawada

Tallapoosa Point. Name formerly used for a section of the northeastern Bronx lying south of Eastchester Bay in what is now Pelham Bay Park. It was once a privately owned island that in colonial times became attached to the mainland through silting. In the 1890s a German political group, the Tallapoosa Club, leased it as a summer headquarters. Its rocky shores, inclining toward Long Island Sound, made the area a favorite spot for boating and fishing until the 1960s, when it was buried by a refuse dump used by New York City. Proposals in the 1970s that the new hill should be used as a ski slope were generally ignored.

Lloyd Ultan

Tamiris [Becker]**, Helen** (*b* New York City, 24 April 1905; *d* New York City, 4 Aug 1966). Dancer, choreographer, and teacher. A pupil of Michel Fokine and Rosina Galli, she formed the School of American Dance in 1930 and Tamiris and Her Group, an all-female company. Her modern dances in the 1930s and 1940s, including *Walt Whitman Suite, Cycle of Unrest,* and *How Long, Brethren?* reflected her concern with social issues. She was involved in the Concert Dancers' League, which was formed to fight the city's prohibition against Sunday dance concerts. Tamiris organized the Dance Repertory Theatre (1930–31) and was instrumental in the Federal Theatre Project (sponsored from 1936 to 1939 by the Works Progress Administration) and its offshoot, the Federal Dance Project. In 1937 she helped form the American Dance Association, which had the goal to protect the economic interests of dancers and promote educational opportunities. Between 1944 and 1955 Tamiris provided choreography for 14 Broadway musicals, including *Up in Central Park* (1945; film version 1948), *Annie Get Your Gun* (1946), *Inside U.S.A.* (1948), *Touch and Go* (1949; Tony Award for choreography), *Fanny* (1954), and *Plain and Fancy* (1955). With her husband, Daniel Nagrin, she formed the Tamiris–Nagrin Dance Company in 1960.

Norma Adler

Tammany Hall. Manhattan political organization formed in 1788 in New York City as the Society of St. Tammany or Columbian Order, in response to the city's more exclusive clubs. Initially most of its members were craftsmen; they adopted Tamanend, a legendary Delaware chief, as their patron and used pseudo-Indian insignia and titles (the lowest ranks were known as braves, the council members as sachems). Meetings were held in a hall on Spruce Street from 1798 to 1812 and in another at Nassau and Frankfort streets from 1812 to 1868.

In the early nineteenth century the society supported Aaron Burr, Martin Van Buren, and such progressive policies as universal male suffrage, lien laws to protect craftspeople, and the abolition of imprisonment for debt. It was soon riddled with graft, scandals, and internal conflicts of which the most notable was a struggle in 1835 between the Locofocos and the conservative old guard. The leaders expanded their political base by helping immigrants to survive, find work, and quickly gain citizenship; the organization also opposed anti-Catholic and nativist movements of the day, thus earning loyalties that endured for generations. During the mid-nineteenth century Mayor Fernando Wood furthered his career through the society, as did William M. "Boss" Tweed (the insigne of his volunteer fire company, a tiger, became the society's symbol). In 1868 the society moved into its "wigwam" on East 14th Street near Third Avenue, where it was the host of the Democratic National Convention during the same year.

Tammany Hall did not become a disciplined political machine until it came under the direction of John Kelly (1872–86), the first of 10 successive Irish American bosses; it is said that he found the society a horde and left it an army. He introduced a system of organization in which assembly district leaders elected a leader—an unsalaried, extralegal commander of operations. They also appointed precinct captains whose job it was to help families in their neighborhoods during times of emergency, to find them work, to ease any problems they had with the law, and to make sure that they voted. Although ballot boxes were often stolen on election day, most victories by candidates allied with Tammany Hall were achieved through year-round attention to voters' needs and interests. Because the boss controlled nominations to elective offices, he had the last word in the discretionary appointments made by successful candidates for municipal office and used this power to reward loyal district leaders and supporters and to punish dissenters. Political integration of different ethnic groups varied widely. From mid-century Irish men dominated Tammany Hall and virtually monopolized district leaderships, remaining in power despite the changing population of their neighborhoods. Many Jews and Germans were admitted to the Tammany Society and were chosen to be state legislators, congressional representatives, and judges. The growing Italian population was largely ignored, and when the number of black voters in Harlem became significant, the neighborhood was subdivided and reallocated to adjacent districts with white majorities. Richard Croker, the boss from 1886 to 1902, retained Kelly's system but delegated decisions about patronage to local leaders more than Kelly had done.

After consolidation in 1898 the primacy of Tammany Hall depended on gaining the cooperation of Democrats in the outer boroughs. Those in Brooklyn opposed the organization until John McCooey became the leader of Kings County in 1909. He was a longtime friend of Croker's successor, Charles F. Murphy. One result of their collaboration was the nomination of two mayoral candidates from Brooklyn, William J. Gaynor in 1909 and John F. Hylan in 1921. In state government during these years politicians allied with Tammany Hall sponsored progressive labor laws and opposed Prohibition and censorship. Murphy promised the suffrage leader Carrie Chapman Catt that his organization would do nothing to prevent women from gaining the right to vote; women were later allowed to be district co-leaders but rarely had a voice in decisions. After Murphy's death the leaders decided to replace Mayor Hylan with James J. Walker, a member of Tammany Hall and a state senator. Their efforts were successful owing largely to the support of Edward J. Flynn, the leader in the Bronx, and to an effective campaign against Hylan by Governor Alfred E. Smith; after winning the Democratic primary they swept the November elections.

The machine received money and "kickbacks" from many sources: municipal suppliers, real estate interests, aspirants for judgeships, and businessmen bidding for transit franchises and pier leases. Legal fees and brokerage commissions were funneled to politically active lawyers and insurance agents, and generous campaign contributions were often made by such wealthy families as the Lehmans and the Strauses. Members of the inner circle profited from "honest graft," successful speculations based on confidential information about plans for schools and public works. As George Washington Plunkitt, a sachem who died a millionaire, declared, "I seen my opportunities and I took 'em."

Tammany Hall reached its zenith in 1928. Smith was a powerful and widely respected governor; Walker was an extraordinarily popular mayor; and George W. Olvany, a college graduate, was the boss. A new building was completed in 1929 on Union Square at 17th Street, and during this period even reformers had few criticisms of Tammany Hall. But the organization's fortunes soon changed. Investigations of civic corruption by Samuel Seabury led to Walker's resignation in 1932. John F. Curry, Olvany's successor, sought to block Franklin D. Roosevelt's presidential nomination, allowing Flynn, no longer an ally of Tammany Hall, to become the strongest link between the Democratic White House and the city. In 1933 Mayor John P. O'Brien, the incumbent and a loyalist chosen by Curry, finished last in a three-way mayoral election won by Fiorello H. La Guardia, who led a coalition opposed to Tammany Hall that remained in place for 12 years. Unable to meet mortgage payments, the sachems sold their building to Local 91 of the International Ladies' Garment Workers' Union in 1943. By the time the Democrats recaptured the mayoralty in 1945, Tammany Hall had virtually ceased to exist, although politicians bred in the organization continued to flourish into the 1950s and beyond.

Louis Eisenstein and Elliot Rosenberg, *A Stripe of Tammany's Tiger* (New York: R. Speller, 1966); Alfred Connable and Edward Silberfarb, *Tigers of Tammany: Nine Men Who Ran New York* (New York: Holt, Rinehart and Winston, 1967)

See also DEMOCRATIC PARTY.

Frank Vos

Tannenbaum, Frank (*b* Brod, Galicia, 4 March 1893; *d* New York City, 1 June 1969). Historian. After moving from a farm near Great Barrington, Massachusetts, to New York City in 1906 he joined the Industrial Workers of the World. In 1914 he was imprisoned for almost a year on Blackwell's Island for disturbing the peace by leading homeless men into churches to demand financial assistance and work. He received a PhD in economics in 1927 from the Brookings Institution and began teaching at Columbia in 1935, becoming a full professor of Latin American history in 1945. He founded and directed the interdisciplinary University Seminars at Columbia, which grew from five seminars in 1945 to more than 90 by 2008. Tannenbaum's published writings on Latin America were numerous. He also wrote on crime and prison reform, the labor movement, and race relations and edited the book *A Community of Scholars: The University Seminars at Columbia* (1965).

Joseph Maier and Richard W. Weatherhead, *Frank Tannenbaum: A Biographical Essay* (New York: Columbia University, 1974)

See also UNEMPLOYMENT MOVEMENTS.

Bernard Hirschhorn

tap dancing. The origins of tap dancing in New York City may be traced to the Five Points of the 1840s, where the African dances of blacks and the jigs and clog dances of the Irish exerted a reciprocal influence. Early tap dancers included the black minstrel Master Juba (William Henry Lane) and his white rival, Master John Diamond, who in 1844 faced each other in a competition at John Tryon's Amphitheater that Master Juba won. During the last third of the nineteenth century, black vaudevillians further refined the tap style, which was more rhythmic and looser than most other dances in vogue at the time.

The successful musical *Shuffle Along* (1921) by Flourney Miller, Aubrey Lyles, Noble Sissle, and Eubie Blake, which opened at Daly's Music Hall on 63rd Street, helped to establish tap dancing on the Broadway stage. In 1923 *Runnin' Wild* (also by Miller and Lyles) opened at the Colonial Theater and featured the Charleston, a fusion of tap and ballroom dancing that became immensely popular. Tap dancing was now important to the success of Broadway revues. The first great proponent of tap dancing was BILL "BOJANGLES" ROBINSON. After several years on the vaudeville circuit, he performed at clubs in Harlem and then appeared in *Blackbirds of 1928* by Lew Leslie and Will Vodery. He later danced in other Broadway shows and revues and eventually moved to Hollywood. Robinson's success inspired many tap dancers during the 1930s, among them Honi Coles, King Rastus Brown, Peg Leg Bates (who tapped on one leg), and such duos as Buck and Bubbles (Ford Lee Washington and John Washington Bubbles), Chuck and Chuckles (Charles Green and James Walker), and Stump and Stumpy (James Cross and Harold Cromer). The brothers Fayard and Harold Nicholas, who regularly performed their acrobatic tap dances at the Cotton Club and the Apollo Theater during the early 1930s, appeared on Broadway in Florenz Ziegfeld's *Follies* (1936) and in *Babes in Arms* (1937), by Richard Rodgers and Lorenz Hart.

Although tap remained essentially a black art form during the 1930s and 1940s, there were many important white tap dancers as well, including Fred Astaire, Ruby Keeler, and Gene Kelly. Clarence "Buddy" Bradley taught tap to white students and introduced creative tap choreography. Tap dancers and their students frequented the Hoofers Club, a studio, rehearsal space, and social center that remained open at all hours and was situated at the rear of a pool hall next to the Lafayette Theatre at 131st Street and Seventh Avenue. The influence of tap was seen in the dance scenes of musicals and films and in such popular dances as the Lindy hop. During the 1940s and early 1950s groups such as the Four Step Brothers remained popular, and tap dancing was incorporated into the routines of such performers as Sammy Davis, Jr., and the members of the Hines family, who performed as Hines, Hines, and Dad (Gregory, Maurice, Jr., and Maurice, Sr.). Will Gaines and Groundhog Gaines and other performers developed a less refined and more improvisational subgenre known as bebop tap, which was influenced by recent developments in jazz and in turn influenced jazz drumming.

The popularity of tap dancing declined as that of rock-and-roll increased during the 1950s, and as dance critics focused their attention on ballet and modern dance. Interest was eventually renewed, in part by a revival on Broadway in 1969 of Vincent Youmans's musical *No, No, Nanette,* which has several tap dance numbers. In the following years several plays, musicals, and revues included tap dancing, among them *The Wiz* (1975, choreography by Geoffrey Holder), *Bubblin' Brown Sugar* (1976), and *Eubie!* (1978). Innovative dancers such as Jane Goldberg performed at the Brooklyn Academy of Music, and a number of dance schools offered instruction in tap, including the Ned Williams School of Dance, the Professional School of Dance (led by Henry LeTang), the Dance Theatre of Harlem, and the American Ballet Center. The Jerry Ames Tap Dance Company was the first professional ensemble in the United States devoted exclusively to tap and premiered in New York City in 1976; it combined elements of tap with others drawn from jazz, modern dance, and even ballet. Other notable groups included the American Tap Dance Orchestra (led by Brenda Bufalino), the Jazz Tap Ensemble (led by Linda Dalley), and Manhattan Tap. During the twentieth and early twenty-first centuries tap dancing was featured occasionally at such clubs as Smalls' Paradise, the Red Rooster, Northern Lights, and the Cat Club in Greenwich Village.

Rusty E. Frank, *Tap!: The Greatest Tap Dance Stars and Their Stories* (New York: William Morrow, 1990)

Marc Ferris

Tapia, Carlos (*b* Ponce, Puerto Rico, 27 Dec 1885; *d* New York City, 31 July 1945). Reformer and social activist. A grocer by trade, he worked with other Puerto Rican community activists to form Democratic clubs in Brooklyn between 1900 and 1919. Known as nationality clubs, these offered cultural and athletic programs and social services in addition to dispensing patronage. Often called upon to defend the fledgling Puerto Rican community, Tapia believed that by taking part in the electoral process, Puerto Ricans in New York City could achieve progress for themselves as well as play a role in deciding the political future of their homeland. Public School 120 in Brooklyn was named for him in 1965.

Virginia Sánchez Korrol

Tappan, Lewis (*b* Northampton, Mass., 23 May 1788; *d* Brooklyn, 21 June 1873). Businessman and abolitionist. He moved to New York City in 1828 to join his brother Arthur (*b* Northampton, 22 May 1786; *d* New Haven, Conn., 23 July 1865), who had moved to the city in 1826 and established the *New York Journal of Commerce* in 1827; the two had a successful partnership as silk jobbers under the name Arthur Tappan and Company from 1828 to 1841. Lewis established the Mercantile Agency, the first commercial credit-rating institution in the United States and a forerunner of Dun and Bradstreet. In the late 1820s the brothers became active in religious and social reform and led movements for stricter observance of the Sabbath and the cessation of mail delivery on Sunday. They also promoted the free church movement and financed a number of bible, tract, Sunday school, mission, and education societies in the antebellum city. Lewis Tappan broke with the American Colonization Society, which sought to repatriate freed slaves to Africa, and with his brother formed the American Anti-Slavery Society (1833), which urged the immediate abolition of slavery. The Tappans' uncompromising resistance to slavery angered many, and in 1834 Lewis Tappan's home at 40 Rose Street was ransacked by an anti-abolitionist mob. The brothers were instrumental in introducing the revivalist Charles G. Finney to the city and built the Broadway Tabernacle for his use in 1836. In 1840 they formed the American and Foreign Anti-Slavery Society, one of the leading abolitionist organizations in the city. After Arthur Tappan's business failed in 1842 the brothers helped to found the anti-slavery American Missionary Society (1846), and by the early 1850s both had retired from business to devote themselves to philanthropy. They resisted the Fugitive Slave Act of 1850 by helping the Underground Railroad to carry slaves to freedom in the North. Lewis Tappan wrote *The Life of Arthur Tappan* (1870).

Bertram Wyatt-Brown, *Lewis Tappan and the Evangelical War against Slavery* (Cleveland: Case Western Reserve University Press, 1969)

Peter J. Wosh

Tarbell, Ida M(inerva) (*b* Erie County, Pa., 5 Nov 1857; *d* Bridgeport, Conn., 6 Jan 1944). Journalist. After graduating from Allegheny College she taught for a few years, traveled, and in 1894 joined the staff of *McClure's,* where she wrote about Napoleon, Abraham Lincoln, and John D. Rockefeller; in the years after 1901 she produced 19 articles and the book *A History of the Standard Oil Company* (1904), which exposed the firm's ruthless practices. With several other members of *McClure's,* including Lincoln Steffens and Ray Stannard Baker, she acquired control of *American Magazine* and for a time wrote about tariff reform. Increasingly mistrustful of politics, she declined an appointment to the tariff commission from President Woodrow Wilson, and in the book *The Business of Being a Woman* (1912) she questioned the causes of woman suffrage and militant feminism. After investigating conditions in factories and Henry Ford's production methods, she strongly endorsed the scientific management planner Frederick W. Taylor. She lived at 40 West Ninth Street before retiring to Connecticut. Tarbell wrote an autobiography, *All in a Day's Work* (1939).

Ida Tarbell

Kathleen Brady, *Ida Tarbell: Portrait of a Muckraker* (Pittsburgh: University of Pittsburgh Press, 1989)

James E. Mooney

target companies. Groups of volunteers operating as firefighters and at times militia. The first target companies in New York City were formed in the 1830s by volunteer firefighters devoted to target practice; the earliest known by name were the Baxter Blues and the Black Joke Volunteers. Unlike the state militia, in which members often served their enlistment of seven years without ever firing their weapons, target companies such as the Pocahontas Guards assembled "the best shooters in the city" for frequent target excursions. Despite casual discipline they were probably at least as effective militarily as militia units of the time. By 1850 it was estimated that the companies had 10,000 members, a large number of whom had volunteered for the Mexican War. Some companies were formed by members of ethnic and political groups, such as the Asmonean Guard (Jewish), the American Rifles (nativist), and the Meagher Guards (Irish), and by employees of factories, foundries, and shipyards. Most target companies reportedly were democratic in selecting their officers and enforcing rules, but prosperous members often contributed for uniforms, weapons, and meals, and sometimes their largesse resulted in their being chosen as officers. Like the volunteer fire department, many target companies were allied with the Democratic Party and Tammany Hall. The Black Joke Engine Company sponsored the Baxter Blues and the Black Joke Volunteers, who by disobeying orders from the Common Council not to march in a parade for the presidential candidate James K. Polk in 1844 caused the engine company to be temporarily disbanded. Americus Engine Company no. 6 took over the equipment of the Black Joke Volunteers and was led to target practice as the William M. Tweed Guards (named after its foreman, later infamous as Boss Tweed). The *New York Times* observed that almost all politicians in Tammany Hall were leaders of target companies, which they found invaluable as bases of power.

Many companies' target excursions became drunken feasts at which the arms most in use were pocket pistols drawn during quarrels. One of the companies known for its social activity, the Shandley Legion, distributed its prizes by lottery, to the disgust of the few members who were skilled marksmen. Some companies were even named for their love of feasting, among them the Chowder and Epicurean guards; others had frivolous names such as the First Ward Magnetizers and Nobody's Guard.

Political maneuvering led to the only large-scale review of the companies, the Target Parade of 1857. At the height of Mayor Fernando Wood's dispute with the state legislature over control of the city police, the target companies formed two divisions and were led by the fire commissioner Henry Wilson in a parade down Broadway reviewed by the mayor; 2700 men took part. Frivolous companies marched alongside units such as the Peterson Guards, who had been invited to West Point to perform for the U.S. Military Academy. A month after the parade, supporters of Mayor Wood made an unsuccessful effort to join the companies into a city army.

When the Civil War began in 1861 men of all classes turned to the target companies for instruction. The companies did not enlist as units, but they contributed most of the men for the Fire Zouaves and other regiments such as the Jackson Guard (supported by Tammany Hall) and the Garibaldi Guard. Most New Yorkers expected the war to end quickly, and when it lengthened and turned into a war that would end slavery, many Irish workers became resolute Copperheads. President Abraham Lincoln's attempt to draft them in July 1863 brought about a revolt, and Black Joke Volunteers led an attack on the local conscription office. Entire companies of the volunteer fire department deserted out of sympathy with the rioters, but many others worked to control arson and violence throughout a week of disruption. During the first two days reporters thought they discerned among the rioters a well-organized cadre armed with military rifles. These roughly clad but expert marksmen at one point routed 150 Zouaves.

The treachery of some volunteer firefighters led to the dissolution of some target companies in 1865. In the following year a report of the police commissioner recommended that target excursions be outlawed, but the companies still had enough support from Tammany Hall to defeat a bill prohibiting civilian parades under arms. Membership reached its peak after the Civil War as companies recruited many former soldiers. Nearly all had become social clubs, and newspaper descriptions of their parades were no longer respectful: the *Times* alleged that the companies blackmailed saloonkeepers, politicians, and employers. A huge "target excursion" provided the cover for opposition to the Orange parade of 1871, which ended in a bloody riot. Discipline broke down among the National Guard defending the marchers; without orders, troops fired into the crowd lining the street. The disaster brought efforts to improve discipline and marksmanship in the militia. The National Rifle Association, formed later that year, was intended both to improve the skills of the militia and to put the popularity of target excursions to the service of the National Guard.

Russell S. Gilmore

Tasti D-Lite. Frozen dessert franchise. Founded in 1987 in New York City, the company sells diet frozen desserts in more than 100 flavors. In 2007 the company was acquired by a New York City private equity firm and became Tasti D-Lite LLC. In the early twenty-first century there were more than 60 independently owned and operated Tasti D-Lite locations in New York City.

Jessica Montesano

tattooing. The first mechanized tattoo shop in New York City was opened in 1875 at 11 Chatham Square by Samuel F. O'Reilly, who had invented the electric tattoo machine after observing that Thomas Edison's electric engraving pen could be modified to introduce ink into skin with speed and accuracy. The rowdy atmosphere of Chatham Square and the Bowery nurtured O'Reilly and his innovation, and he accepted two apprentices: Charlie Wagner, who took over the tattoo shop on O'Reilly's death in 1908 and went on to develop his own version of the tattoo machine, and to start a small tattoo supply business; and Ed Smith, who designed dozens of sheets of tattoo designs for the trade. During the first few decades of the twentieth century, performers at dime museums on the Bowery visited Wagner's shop regularly. These early "canvas backs" helped to boost the reputation of both Wagner and tattooing, and Chatham Square soon became a worldwide tattoo center, attracting more than a dozen tattooers from as far away as Japan.

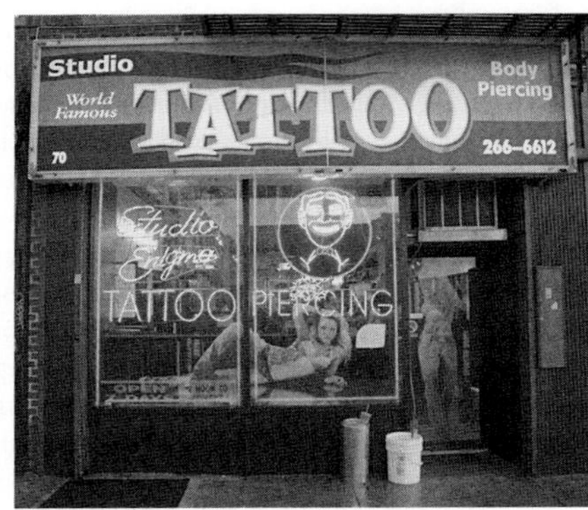

Tattoo parlor, 2009

Usually operating out of cramped booths in local barber shops, tattooers in Chatham Square decorated the skin of the day laborers who congregated in the area and of those who visited the Bowery in search of amusement. Among the most noted tattooers were Bob Wicks at 9 Chatham Square; Millie Hull at 16 Bowery, the only female tattooer in New York City; and Willie Moskowitz at 12 Bowery, a barber who had learned tattooing from Wagner and was known for his speed. Moskowitz's sons Stanley and Walter inherited his tattoo business and moved with him to 52 Bowery, just off Chatham Square. They were the last tattooers to work on the Bowery and among those who were forced to retire from their locations in Coney Island and 48th Street on 1 November 1961, when tattooing in New York City was banned because of an outbreak of hepatitis. In March 1997 the ban was lifted, and two years later the South Street Seaport Museum hosted an exhibition titled *American Tattoo: The Art of Gus Wagner* at the same time that the American Museum of Natural History presented *Body Art: Marks of Identity,* which featured tattooing. In the early twenty-first century there were numerous tattoo parlors throughout the five boroughs, including the notable Andromeda on St. Marks Place and Red Rocket Tattoo on West 36th Street.

Michael McCabe, *New York City Tattoo: The Oral History of an Urban Art* (Honolulu, Hawaii: Hardy Marks Publications, 1997)

Michael McCabe

Tavern on the Green. Restaurant in Central Park at West 67th Street. Originally a sheepfold built in 1870 and designed by Jacob Wrey Mould, it was converted into a restaurant in 1934 by order of the parks commissioner Robert Moses when the park was renovated. Overlooking the gardens of Central Park and filled with stained-glass windows, including one by Louis Comfort Tiffany, it offered a rustic setting rare in central Manhattan. In the 1950s the designer Raymond Loewy added the Elm Room (later called the Park Room) to the front of the building. In 1962 Restaurant Associates took over the business from its original manager, Arthur Schleiffer. After the restaurant closed in 1974, the lease was acquired by Warner LeRoy, who undertook extensive renovations: the Crystal Room and the Terrace Room were added, along with 14 sand-carved mirrors and 45 chandeliers. The restaurant reopened in 1976 and soon became a popular locale for weddings, opening-night parties, and political fund-raisers. In 2009 the city decided not to renew the lease with LeRoy, and the restaurant went bankrupt and closed; the furnishings were auctioned off in January 2010. Tavern on the Green has been a backdrop for several films and marks the finish line of the New York City Marathon.

Marjorie Harrison

taverns. See Bars, taverns, and saloons.

taxes. In the early years of New Amsterdam, Peter Stuyvesant financed his government primarily by a tax on liquors. An uncooperative public often stymied other efforts to raise revenue, notably an ill-fated property tax to pay off a debt. Under British rule minor taxes on property in New York City were levied for various municipal functions including public works and relief, a pattern that continued after independence and well into the nineteenth century. The creation of the comptroller's office in 1801 helped facilitate the city's taxing powers.

New York City did not pass its first important tax legislation until 1859, when it established a comprehensive system for the assessment and collection of property taxes. There were three commissioners of taxes and assessments, each appointed by the mayor, whose deputies set out every September to appraise property, both real (fixed assets like land and buildings) and personal (financial assets and material items like jewelry). Citizens were given four months in which to challenge assessments. Once the books were closed the assessments were brought before the Board of Aldermen, which set a rate of taxation according to the city's needs each year: the rate for every $100 in assessed valuation ranged from $0.42 in 1830 to $2.94 in 1875.

The city's system of taxation was widely criticized for being inequitable. Personal property taxes were valued lower than real estate taxes (45 percent lower in 1860), even though they were believed to be greater in worth. When William H. Vanderbilt died it was estimated that $40 million of his personal estate was taxable, but he had paid only $500,000 during his lifetime. The city managed to close the differential between personal property and real property rates to 22 percent by 1896, but still only 21,000 of the city's nearly two million inhabitants paid personal property taxes that year. The city's tax commissioner acknowledged in 1891 that his office was able to collect taxes only from "the widows and the orphans," because their personal property was documented in the surrogate's office.

With minor variations the system remained intact until the Depression. With the city on the brink of bankruptcy and having to resort to bank loans to pay its debts, it became obvious that the tax system was inadequate: property owners, who supplied more than 80 percent of the city's revenues, simply lacked the means to finance city government on their own. As a result an agreement was reached with the city's financial institutions, known as the "Bankers' Agreement," under which the city committed tax revenues to pay off bank loans and imposed a new tax on utilities to provide unemployment benefits. The agreement was in effect from 1 January 1934 to 31 December 1937 and curtailed the city's taxing and discretionary powers.

Other taxes were adopted during this period as well. In 1934 the city established a business tax of less than 1 percent and a sales tax of 2 percent. The sales tax was intended to be an emergency measure only, but it was eventually raised to 4 percent and remained in place into the early twenty-first century. In the following decades the city added taxes on hotel rooms, parimutuel betting, automobiles, theater tickets, gross payrolls, and other items. An income tax, begun in 1966, applied both to residents and to nonresidents who earned income in the city. Initially those subject to the income tax were required to file a separate tax return with the city, until in 1975 the state of New York began collecting the tax on the city's behalf. With the growth in new taxes, the proportion of the city's revenues accounted for by the property tax fell steadily, from 70 percent in the 1950s to 55 percent in the early 1970s. Meanwhile, the commuter tax on suburban residents was repealed in 1999.

Major changes in the city's property tax system were made in 1982, when the state passed a law establishing four classes of property for taxation: one-, two-, and three-family houses; apartment buildings (essentially cooperatives and condominiums); utilities; and commercial property. Each class of property had a different ratio of assessed valuation to market value, a formula that worked to the advantage of homeowners in the outer boroughs. (In the mid-1990s homeowners owned 32.5 percent of the city's property but paid 11.5 percent of its property taxes, while owners of cooperatives and condominiums paid much more.) Property taxes became a contentious political issue during the budget crises of the 1990s, when some observers called for a more equitable system that would generate more revenue.

Like all municipalities in New York State, New York City depends on the legislature for the power to tax. In the mid-1990s the city raised more than $18 billion a year in taxes, of which 43 percent was derived from property taxes, 19 percent from income taxes, 13 percent from sales taxes, 6 percent from corporate taxes, and 19 percent from other taxes. The city is generally regarded as a highly taxed jurisdiction: in 2007 the income tax rate ranged from 2.9 percent to 3.6 percent.

Edward D. Durand, *The Finances of New York City* (New York: Macmillan, 1898)

James Bradley

taxicabs. Taxicabs became a popular mode of transport for New York City residents in 1907, when slow-moving vehicles powered by batteries weighing 800 pounds (360 kilograms) that had been in use since 1899 were replaced with gas-powered ones. The new taxicabs were equipped with taximeters to halt widespread fare gouging. Drivers became more assertive: 5000 held a strike in November 1907 calling for better wages and the right to unionize. By 1909 there were six major "fleets" employing hundreds of drivers, as well as thousands of independent owner–drivers. In the same year the city government appointed inspectors to monitor taxicabs, and in 1913 it fixed the cost of a taxi ride at 50 cents a mile (30 cents a kilometer), a figure lower than the prevailing average.

In the early 1920s the taxi business was largely unregulated and controlled by automobile manufacturers and owners of large fleets: General Motors, the Ford Motor Company, and the Checker Motors Corporation offered easy credit to fleets seeking to purchase automobiles and sometimes set up fleets of their own. Large owners sought to drive out small ones by discounting their fares and advocating high bond requirements; reformers accused the city of ignoring corruption and complained of taxicabs that were dangerous, dirty, and uninsured. In response, the police department took control of licensing in 1923, on the grounds that taxicabs were often used in burglaries, holdups, and bootlegging; by this time there were 16,000 licensed taxicabs in the city. The new licensing requirements were lax, and cab driving remained open to all. The large fleets that controlled the business were increasingly competitive, and rate wars worsened in 1925, with some fleets lowering fares by 50 percent. In the same year the first women became licensed drivers, and the police department gained control over the licensing of taxi drivers through its newly formed Taxicab Commission.

The Depression led to a huge increase in the number of taxi drivers in New York City (75,000 operating 19,000 vehicles in 1933) and an upsurge in labor strife. Average weekly pay dropped from $26 in 1929 to $15 in 1933. Loan sharks, racketeers, and corruption were rampant: in 1932 an investigation by the Taxicab Commission revealed that the Checker Cab Company, which owned Parmalee, the largest taxi fleet in New York City, had bribed Mayor

James J. Walker, and further inquiries contributed to Walker's resignation. The Haas Act (1937) established a system of medallions, or official taxicab licenses, available for $10 and limited in number to 13,566. Considered a compromise between the owners of large fleets and the independent drivers, the law in fact created a new monopoly, as the owners of medallions became a powerful bloc intent on limiting access to the trade.

For many years most taxi drivers were Jewish, Italian, and Irish immigrants, and except during World War II almost all were men. Taxi drivers developed the image of being amiable cynics with an encyclopedic knowledge of the city who were eager to express their opinions on almost any subject. Efforts to unionize drivers in the city by the International Brotherhood of Teamsters, the Taxi Workers Union, the United Mine Workers, the American Federation of Labor–Congress of Industrial Organizations (AFL–CIO), and local unions between 1934 and 1957 met with little success. Bitter strikes shut down the business in 1934, 1939, 1949, 1956, and 1965, and the fleets retaliated by locking out and dismissing drivers and by calling in replacements. Vehicles were burned and rallies were held in Times Square and on Fifth Avenue, and striking drivers blocked avenues, squares, and bridges. The strike in 1965 resulted in an election supervised by the National Labor Relations Board in which the Taxi Workers Union, an affiliate of the AFL–CIO led by Harry Van Arsdale, was chosen to represent the city's drivers.

By the 1960s attrition reduced the number of medallion taxicabs in the city to 11,300. Special medallions for veterans of World War II were never issued because of political opposition from the unions and independent drivers. In 1967 the city ordered all medallion cabs painted yellow, which further increased the value of a license. By the late 1960s, 10 percent of the taxicab drivers in New York City were women. Drivers were often the victims of violent crimes, and bulletproof partitions were installed between the front and back seats of taxicabs in 1967.

The limited number of medallions, and medallion drivers unwilling to go to certain neighborhoods, gave rise to a number of private livery, or "gypsy," services. Unlike medallion cabs the gypsies could offer their services only to passengers who had requested them by telephone, a restriction often disregarded. Gypsy services operated primarily in black neighborhoods: the largest of these was Black Pearl Livery in Brooklyn. The Taxi and Limousine Commission reported in 1971 that although gypsy drivers earned only about a third of what medallion drivers did, gypsy services were much-needed enterprises in the inner city: they employed nearly 13,000 drivers in metropolitan New York City, of whom 58 percent were black and 39 percent Puerto Rican.

The trade experienced an influx of black, Middle Eastern, and Latino drivers in the 1970s, and of Russian Jews, Haitians, and South Asians in the 1990s. A survey by the Taxi and Limousine Commission found that 1991 applicants for licenses were 42.8 percent South Asian, 11.2 percent African, 7.6 percent Caribbean, 7 percent Middle Eastern, and 6.8 percent Russian; 10.5 percent were born in the United States. Starting in 1983, these changing demographics resulted in a mandatory orientation program consisting of 20 hours of classroom instruction for new drivers starting in 1983.

In 1979 the fleets won the right to impose a surcharge of 50 cents a ride between 8 p.m. and 6 a.m. The cost of medallions rose to $136,000 by 1989; in the same year a survey showed that drivers who leased their taxicabs earned between $21,000 and $31,000 from tips and a percentage of their fares (these drivers paid for their own gasoline), that owner–drivers averaged more than $40,000, and that only 30 percent of the city's drivers worked full time. Dangers continued to accompany the job. In 1993 alone a rash of armed robberies and murders cost the lives of 41 livery drivers and four yellow-cab drivers.

In 2006 the New York City Labor Council recognized the Taxi Workers Alliance as a "work center," the first such designation of independent contractors. Under the leadership of Bhairavi Desai, the alliance then boasted about 7000 members. It successfully negotiated a sizable pay increase in 2004. The Ford Crown Victoria continued to be the workhorse of the taxicab industry into the twenty-first century.

Taxi driving in New York City has been the subject of several anecdotal memoirs, including *Hacking New York* (1930) by Robert Hazard and *My Flag Is Down: Diary of a New York Taxi Driver* (1948) by James Maresca, and it figures prominently in Martin Scorsese's film *Taxi Driver* (1976). One well-known former taxi driver is Danny Sullivan, who worked in the city during the early 1970s and won the Indianapolis 500 in 1985.

Charles Vidich, *The New York Cab Driver and His Fare* (Cambridge, Mass.: Shenkman, 1976); Biju Mathew, *Taxi! Cabs and Capitalism in New York City* (New York: New Press, 2005); Graham Russell Gao Hodges, *Taxi! A Social History of the New York City Cabdriver* (Baltimore: Johns Hopkins University Press, 2007)

Graham Hodges

taxpayers. Term used to mean one- and two-story buildings that yield sufficient commercial or residential rent to pay real estate taxes until landlords can undertake more intensive and more profitable development. After the collapse of the real estate market in 1929, taxpayers became a common means of "land banking" and kept land productively available to the urban economy, but the term did not come into popular use until after the Depression. One of the best-known and most distinctive taxpayers in New York City is Pomander Walk on the Upper West Side of Manhattan, a two-row mews of very small town house apartments that extends from 94th Street to 95th Street between Broadway and West End Avenue. Its developer, Thomas Healy, and the architectural firm of King and Campbell obtained the model for its layout from the popular play *Pomander Walk* (1911), which takes place in a mythical suburb of London at the time of George III. Healy had hoped to build a high-rise hotel with 600 rooms, but by the time construction began in 1921 the hotel project was no longer feasible. Much construction during the real estate expansion of the 1980s took place on sites that had been developed as taxpayers during the Depression.

Elliot Sclar

Taylor, Billy (*b* Greenville, N.C., 24 July 1921). Jazz pianist and composer. He began playing piano professionally after graduating from Virginia State College with a BS in music in 1942. His first professional gig was playing piano for Ben Webster's Quartet on 52nd Street in New York City. He became the house pianist at Birdland, a famous jazz venue in midtown Manhattan, where he performed with the likes of Miles Davis, Charlie Parker, and Dizzy Gillepsie and was a protégé of jazz pianist Art Tatum. In 1958 he became the musical director of the National Broadcasting Company (NBC) program *The Subject Is Jazz,* the first-ever television series about jazz music. During the 1960s the Billy Taylor Trio was a regular feature at the Hickory House on West 55th Street in Manhattan. In 1964 Taylor founded New York City's Jazzmobile, which provides arts education programming via special projects, concert series, and workshops. One of his most famous songs is "I Wish I Knew How It Would Feel to Be Free," composed in 1954, which became associated with the civil rights movement of the 1950s and 1960s, and which was covered most famously by Nina Simone. In the early twenty-first century Taylor held over 20 honorary doctoral degrees and was the recipient of two Peabody awards, a National Endowment for the Arts (NEA) Jazz Masters Award, an Emmy Award, and a Grammy Award.

Benjamin Yakas

Taylor, Cecil (Percival) (*b* New York City, 15 March 1933). Pianist. After growing up in Corona, Queens, and studying at the New England Conservatory, he made his debut in 1956 at the Five Spot in New York City and recorded the albums *Jazz Advance* (1956), *Looking Ahead* (1958), and *The New Breed* (1961). Influenced by Thelonious Monk, he soon forged a percussive and often violently atonal style that owed something to the keyboard works of Igor Stravinsky, Béla Bartók, and Karlheinz Stockhausen. His performances and recordings with the drummer Max Roach secured his reputation as the most uncompromising member of the jazz avant-garde. For many years he lived in a loft at 58 West 31st Street.

Marc Ferris

Taylor [Cooney], **Laurette** (*b* New York City, 1 April 1884; *d* New York City, 8 Dec 1946). Actress. In 1912 she achieved success in the play *Bird of Paradise,* as well as in *Peg o' My Heart,* written by her second husband, J. Hartley Manners, who later wrote a number of unsuccessful plays in which she appeared. After his death she became reclusive but then returned to Broadway in 1938 for a revival of Sutton Vanes's *Outward Bound.* Known for her radiance, she won critical acclaim for her profound characterization of Amanda in Tennessee Williams's *The Glass Menagerie* (1945), a role that she continued to play until near the end of her life.

Marguerite Courtney, *Laurette* (New York: Atheneum, 1968)

David J. Weiner

Taylor, Moses (*b* New York City, 11 Jan 1806; *d* New York City, 23 May 1882). Industrialist and financier. Born at Broadway and Morris Street, he was the son of John Jacob Astor's business manager. In 1821 he began an apprenticeship to G. G. and S. S. Howland, a leading trader in products from Latin America; he formed his own company at 44 South Street in 1832 for importing Cuban sugar. In 1837 he was made a director of City Bank, which became a treasury for his business empire, as did the Manhattan and Metropolitan insurance companies and Farmers' Loan and Trust. After 1841 he invested aggressively in gas lighting companies in the city, including the Manhattan Gas Light Company, and in 1853 he became a director of the Lackawanna Iron and Coal Company, a producer of rails. He also recognized the importance of anthracite coal to New York City and from 1854 was a director of the Delaware, Lackawanna and Western Railroad, a producer and carrier of coal. During the same year he was made the treasurer of the New York, Newfoundland and London Electric Telegraph Company, which after five attempts linked New York City and London by transatlantic cable (1866). By 1855 the customs duties of Moses Taylor and Company were the second highest in the nation, after those of A. T. Stewart's department store. Taylor became the president of City Bank in 1856 (remaining until 1882), and as the chairman of the loan committee of the New York Clearing House he gave strong financial support to the federal government during the Civil War. By 1865 he controlled the entire gas lighting industry in the city. After the transatlantic cable began operating in 1866 he controlled the American side and became a director of the Western Union Telegraph Company, which had a monopoly on the telegraph industry in the United States. He became a vice president of Lackawanna Iron and Coal in 1872 and in the 1870s arranged for its conversion to the Bessemer process in steel production. At his death he left an estate worth $40 million. Taylor was perhaps the most important businessman in New York City between 1840 and 1880. His varied investments in trade, lighting, communication, and finance were instrumental in making the city a national and international center of business.

Daniel Hodas, *The Business Career of Moses Taylor: Merchant, Finance Capitalist, and Industrialist* (New York: New York University Press, 1976)

See also Citibank.

Joan L. Silverman

Taylor, Paul (*b* Pittsburgh, 29 July 1930). Dancer and choreographer. He moved to New York City in 1952 to study at the Juilliard School, danced with the companies of Merce Cunningham and Pearl Lang, and in 1955 began to perform his own choreography and became a soloist with Martha Graham, for whom he originated the roles of Aegisthus in *Clytemnestra* and Hercules in *Alcestis.* His concert *Seven New Dances* at the 92nd Street Young Men's and Young Women's Hebrew Association in 1957 became legendary as an exploration of extremes: ordinary movement and stillness, ordinary sounds and quiet. To a degree these concerns continued to color his work. In 1961 he left Graham to devote himself fully to his own company, which performed in New York City and toured consistently into the next century. He provided choreography to scores by many modern composers and commissioned designs from several well-known artists. A number of distinguished dancers performed in his company, including Bettie de Jong, Carolyn Adams, Dan Wagoner, Twyla Tharp, and Cliff Keuter. In 1989 he received the Mayor's Award of Honor for Art and Culture and was elected an honorary member of the American Academy and Institute of Arts and Letters. The tension in Taylor's work between light and dark, athleticism and wit, and the lovely and the sinister has created an unusually provocative body of work. One of his most popular and most musical dances is *Aureole* (1962). His published writings include *Private Domain* (1987).

Don McDonagh, *The Complete Guide to Modern Dance* (Garden City, N.Y.: Doubleday, 1976); Marcia B. Siegel, *The Shapes of Change: Images of American Dance* (Boston: Houghton Mifflin, 1979)

Robert Seder

Taylor Law [Public Employees' Fair Employment Act]. New York State statute. Named for labor researcher George W. Taylor, it authorizes a governor-appointed Public Employment Relations Board to resolve contract disputes for public employees, while also curtailing their right to strike. Mediation and binding arbitration are intended to give voice to unions, while work stoppages are made punishable with fines and jail time. The United Federation of Teachers and the Uniformed Sanitationmen's Association challenged the Taylor Law soon after its 1967 inception. Following a 2005 strike, Roger Toussaint, president of the Transport Workers Union Local 100, was incarcerated for three days as a result of a Taylor Law ruling.

Eric Robinson

Teachers College. Graduate school of education. It was founded in 1887 at 654 East 11th Street (9 University Place) by the philanthropist Grace Hoadley Dodge and the philosopher Nicholas Murray Butler as the New York School for the Training of Teachers. The impetus for the school was the rapid increase in New York City of poor immigrant children, whom it aimed to serve through social services and innovative methods of education. In 1892 it took its present name and received its permanent charter. The need for additional space and a gift of $100,000 from George Vanderbilt prompted the founders in 1894 to move the school to its present location on West 120th Street between Broadway and Amsterdam Avenue, making it the first of many academic institutions to settle in Morningside Heights. Constructed of brick and red sandstone, the original building dominated a rocky hilltop otherwise occupied only by farms, squatters, and the Bloomingdale Insane Asylum. Soon after Columbia University moved its campus to the same neighborhood in the mid-1890s, the two institutions entered into an academic alliance. Their agreement of 1898 provided the college with access to the university's faculty and empowered it to grant degrees in the university's name, while permitting it to retain its legal and financial independence. After the turn of the twentieth century, the college embraced the educational philosophy of pragmatism promoted by faculty member and Progressive reformer John Dewey, and it expanded and diversified its curriculum to include emerging fields such as psychology, sociology, health, and nutrition. In later years it focused special attention on research programs, urban education, increasing educational access and achievement for disadvantaged youth, and advanced classroom technology. Among the better-known alumni are Shirley Chisholm, the first African American woman to serve in the U.S. Congress; Norman Cousins, author and editor of the *Saturday Review;* Thomas H. Kean, chairman of the National Commission on Terrorist Attacks upon the United States (also known as the 9/11 Commission); artist Georgia O'Keeffe; and sex therapist Ruth Westheimer. In the early twenty-first century it enrolls more than 5000 students from 80 different countries.

Robert Sanger Steel

Teachers Insurance and Annuity Association–College Retirement Equities Fund [TIAA–CREF]. Nonprofit financial institution formed in New York City in 1918 as the Teachers Insurance and Annuity Association by the Carnegie Foundation for the Advancement of Teaching, with an endowment of $1 million from the Carnegie Corporation of New York. It began as a pension and insurance organization that offered life insurance and retirement plans to professors and other employees of colleges and universities. Both employers and employees contribute to the pension, which the employees may take with them from one institution to another. In the 1930s the association began to invest in mortgage loans and became a leader in investing pension assets in mortgages and real estate. The high inflation that followed World War II severely eroded the purchasing power of fixed-income investments, and in response the association formed the College Retirement Equities Fund and took its current name. The fund invested in common stocks and offered a variable annuity, a method of managing retirement savings and income that was considered radical at the time but was later adopted by many other companies and pension plans. Group life and disability insurance was added in the 1950s, and eligibility for individual life insurance was extended to public school teachers in 1989. In the early twenty-first century TIAA–CREF manages approximately $400 billion in assets, with more than 3.5 million customers at 15,000 colleges, universities, research organizations, and independent schools throughout the nation. Its headquarters are at 730 Third Avenue.

William C. Greenough, *It's My Retirement Money, Take Good Care of It: The TIAA–CREF Story* (Homewood, Ill.: Irwin, 1990)

Carolyn Kopp

teachers' unions. Teachers in New York City first organized in 1913, and in 1916 they formed the Teachers' Union, an affiliate of the American Federation of Teachers (AFT). Because teachers were split among many societies, the union was not recognized as their bargaining agent but nonetheless effectively defended and advanced their interests. During the early 1930s the union was divided by a struggle among its officers, many of them socialists, and a growing faction led by communists. In 1935 the communist faction took over, and the former leaders left to organize the Teachers' Guild. In 1940 the AFT expelled the Teachers' Union and recognized the Teachers' Guild as the city's local. During the next 20 years the guild grew stronger but did not represent most teachers, and in 1960 it merged with a large segment of the High School Teachers' Association to form the United Federation of Teachers (UFT) under the direction of Charles Cogen. It held a strike, the first in the history of the school system, on 7 November 1960 for a collective bargaining election promised by the Board of Education; the election was finally held in December 1961 and was won by the UFT, which proved highly effective, conducting strikes in April 1962 and September 1967 that resulted in higher salaries, better working conditions, and a workable grievance procedure.

The UFT made a number of gains under Albert Shanker, who succeeded Cogen as president in 1964 and became a major figure in the local labor movement. Efforts to decentralize the school system led to a major crisis in 1968 when the local school board in the largely black Ocean Hill–Brownsville district ordered the transfer of 13 teachers and six other school employees, of whom 18 were white. Despite intense pressure 10 of the teachers continued to oppose their involuntary transfer, and this led to a conflict over teachers' contractual rights and community control of schools that culminated in three strikes by the UFT and a citywide political and racial crisis. The final settlement largely upheld the position taken by the UFT, and the teachers were reinstated. Strengthened by its role in the conflict, the UFT also helped to save the city from bankruptcy during its fiscal crisis by urging the trustees of the Teachers' Retirement System to buy bonds of the Municipal Assistance Corporation. Shanker was succeeded by Sandra Feldman in 1986. On Shanker's death in 1997, Feldman replaced him as president of the AFT while remaining as the leader of the UFT. In 1998 Randi Weingarten succeeded her as president of the UFT. In 2007 home child-care providers joined the union, bringing the UFT's membership in the early twenty-first century to more than 200,000.

Philip Taft, *United They Teach: The Story of the United Federation of Teachers* (Los Angeles: Nash, 1974); Richard Kahlenberg, *Tough Liberal: Albert Shanker and the Battles over Schools, Unions, Race, and Democracy* (New York: Columbia University Press, 2007)

Irwin Yellowitz

technology. During the seventeenth century commercial activity in New York Harbor encouraged the growth of technology. Shipbuilding employed local blacksmiths and carpenters, who fashioned raw materials into vessels. Wind and water provided the power for many other trades that developed near the harbor: millers used waterwheels and windmills to grind grain for bread and for export goods such as beer and flour; sawmills and paper mills also used these sources of power. A system of apprenticeship evolved in the trades that was reminiscent of the medieval European guilds. By the eighteenth century emerging technology in New York City reflected increased wealth. Bricklayers were active as brick became an increasingly common substitute for wood. Silversmiths made engraved silver plates; coppersmiths made kettles, stills, and maritime instruments; and pewterers made ornate goblets and candlesticks.

At the same time New Yorkers made plans to build turnpikes and canals to tap the natural resources of the nation's interior and to serve new markets. Many saw transportation as the most promising area for investment, because unlike commerce or manufacturing it seemed relatively safe and long-lived. Water travel gained in importance during the early nineteenth century: the *North River Steamboat,* built by ROBERT FULTON, marked the beginning of steamboat service, with regular trips between Albany, New York, and New York City; and the Erie Canal was completed in 1825, linking Albany to Lake Erie at Buffalo and granting New York City access to national markets. Many western cities sought to tie into the canal, while eastern cities sought to compete with New York City by other means: among these were Baltimore, which built a railroad to the Ohio River, and Philadelphia, which set out to establish a connection with Pittsburgh and therefore the Ohio River by canal, turnpike, rail, and inclined plane.

Europeans who immigrated to the United States during the nineteenth century brought with them knowledge of technological advances related to textiles, steam engines, daguerreotype photography, railroads, telegraphs, and ocean steamers. By 1840 the American interest in technology was highly visible in New York City: Samuel F. B. Morse made critical contributions to photography and TELEGRAPHY at the University of the City of New York (now New York University); John B. Jervis invented a device to improve locomotive cornering. The city's most important role in railroad development was as a source of capital for the extraction and smelting of iron ore, the laying of track, and the manufacture of engines and rolling stock. Railroad promoters made New York City the eastern terminus of the four great antebellum railroad lines.

Much of the groundwork for the city's basic services and utilities was laid during the mid-nineteenth century. The CROTON AQUEDUCT, which carried abundant water from outside the city limits to private and public facilities, was constructed during 1837–42. Sewers were dug for storm drainage and wastewater, and mains were laid to deliver gas to homes and offices. Paved city streets were continually torn up so that new mains could be laid and new buildings constructed. Of all the technological developments occurring in New York City, the farthest-reaching were centrally generated electricity and TELEPHONY: businesses in the city provided the money that enabled THOMAS EDISON and Alexander Graham Bell to capitalize on their inventions. At his laboratory in Menlo Park, New Jersey, Edison developed a high-resistance filament bulb that made electrical lighting economically competitive with gas lighting. In 1882 he placed the first commercial generating station on Pearl Street in the heart of the financial district, offering four months of free service to prospective customers. Edison also worked on the microphone device of the telephone for Western Union, which attempted to patent a telephone on the same day as Bell in 1876. In 1879 the firm contested Bell's patent in court: under a settlement Western Union received $3 million from Bell Telephone to withdraw from telephony and sold to Bell its sets and Edison's patent for the microphone.

During the nineteenth and early twentieth centuries, New York City was a center of manufacturing, in part because the many southern European immigrants who lived there provided a large supply of labor. Most of the factories were powered by steam engines and built near railroad terminals connected to the waterfront. The city acquired its reputation as a garment center during these years. The early twentieth century also saw many developments in transportation, as the automobile became popular and Americans began moving to the suburbs. SUBWAYS were a technologically impressive achievement, as were the Lincoln and Holland tunnels and the George Washington Bridge, which made parts of neighboring states more accessible. During the 1960s and later years entrepreneurs in the city financed influential ventures elsewhere and helped to fuel the technological revolution around the country, making substantial investments in the development and manufacture of technologically advanced microelectronic equipment, lasers, computers, and pollution-control equipment.

In the late twentieth and early twenty-first centuries, New York City residents embraced the vast new electronics technologies that arose, including various digital technologies, cellular phones, "smartphones," and MP3 players. Wireless Internet access became available in many New York City cafés, restaurants, colleges, universities, and hotels. The New York City College of Technology, a division of the City University of New York, offered close to 60 degree and certificate programs related to technology in areas such as applied mathematics, architectural technology, computer systems, and communication design. Forums and organizations such as Government Technology and the New York City Department of Information Technology and Telecommunications (DoITT) oversaw how the city used current and emerging technologies and the way in which it delivered such services to the general public. DoITT was intended to improve the government's technological efficiency and make any communications clear and comprehensible. Public information services were available through the 311 Citizen Service Center, a citywide customer service organization that provided nonemergency government services and around-the-clock online information about city services and information. In addition, DoITT offered the NYC Media Group, made up of one broadcast television station, five cable stations, and an FM radio station, all featuring information about culture, government, history, and lifestyle.

Robert Greenhalgh Albion, *The Rise of New York Port, 1815–1860* (New York: Charles Scribner's Sons, 1939; repr. 1970); Matthew Josephson, *Edison: A Biography* (New York: McGraw–Hill, 1959); Alan I Marcus and Howard P. Segal, *Technology in America: A Brief History* (New York: Harcourt Brace Jovanovich, 1989)

Alan I. Marcus, Danielle Molinski

telegraphy. The telegraph was invented in the 1830s by Samuel F. B. Morse, a professor of art at the University of the City of New York, with the help of Leonard Gale, a fellow professor, and Alfred Vail, a mechanic and former student from Morristown, New Jersey. The first functional line was built in 1844 between Washington, D.C., and Baltimore by the federal government and operated for a time by the U.S. Post Office. After Congress refused to buy patent rights and establish a permanent postal telegraph system, entrepreneurs acquired rights from Morse and his partners to build lines between major U.S. cities. In January 1846 the first sections of a network connecting New York City with Philadelphia, Boston, Buffalo, St. Louis, and New Orleans became operational. The location of the city on the eastern seaboard and its role as the major financial and shipping center in the nation helped to make it the heart of the U.S. telegraph network. Telegraph companies chartered in New York State seeking to consolidate lines and link them to New York City benefited from liberal incorporation laws passed by the state legislature. As a result these companies led the reorganization of the industry during the 1850s, when many small, regional companies were taken over by a few conglomerates such as the Western Union Telegraph Company, which controlled the most important lines west of New York City, and the American Telegraph Company (formed by Cyrus Field, Peter Cooper, and others), which bought enough eastern companies and links to the planned transatlantic cable to dominate the telegraph market in most states on the Atlantic coast. In 1857 representatives from American Telegraph, Western Union, and four other companies met in the city to sign a cartel agreement known as the "treaty of six nations," which carved the market into clearly defined territories. Western Union abrogated the agreement in 1860 when it won a government subsidy to build a transcontinental telegraph; the completion of this system and government subsidies acquired during the Civil War gave Western Union a competitive advantage, and by 1866 it had almost gained a monopoly by obtaining control of its major competitors, including American Telegraph. About this time it moved its headquarters from Rochester, New York, to the American Telegraph Building at 145 Broadway in New York City.

In the decade after the Civil War the city remained the national center for telegraphy. New telegraph companies made their headquarters there, thus gaining access to funds for laying lines and to advanced technology that would reduce their construction costs and make them competitive with the national system operated by Western Union. Many inventors including THOMAS EDISON settled in the metropolitan area and helped to develop long-distance technology and a distinct urban telegraph industry. The first urban telegraph system, the fire alarm telegraph, was developed in Boston, but in the decade after the Civil War most services and companies evolved in New York City.

The Gold and Stock Telegraph Company installed the first stock tickers at the New York Stock Exchange in 1868 and soon offered market quotations for other exchanges in the city. It also adapted its printing telegraphs to provide communication banks, linkages between courthouses and lawyers' offices, and private lines connecting homes, offices, and factories. Gold and Stock was in competition with several firms; in an effort to control the expansion of its commercial news services outside New York City, Western Union signed an exclusive contract with the Associated Press for the transmission of news and used the local American District Telegraph Companies in major cities and towns to deliver messages. It acquired these local companies in 1901 and combined them into the alarm company that later became known as ADT. The American District Telegraph Companies, the first of which was organized in New York City in 1871, used message boxes connecting homes and businesses with a central station to provide a number of urban telegraph services, including private burglar and fire alarms. Fire and burglar alarms were also an important business of such other firms in the city as the Holmes Burglar Alarm Company, which offered the first major private security service; the Gamewell Fire-Alarm Telegraph Company, which installed most of the municipal fire and police alarm systems in the nation during the rest of the nineteenth century; and American District. Fire and burglar alarm services became separate from telegraphy in the twentieth century.

Western Union continued to dominate the long-distance telegraph industry into the twentieth century even as the telegraph was gradually supplanted by the telephone and the radio. In the decades after World War II telegraphy was superseded by other telecommunications, and Western Union moved to suburban New Jersey and reduced its operations.

Alvin F. Harlow, *Old Wires and New Waves: The History of the Telegraph, Telephone, and Wireless* (New York: D. Appleton Century, 1936); Robert Luther Thompson, *Wiring a Continent: The History of the Telegraph Industry in the United States, 1832–1866* (Princeton, N.J.: Princeton University Press, 1947); Paul B. Israel, *From the Machine Shop to the Industrial Laboratory: Telegraphy and the Changing Context of American Invention, 1830–1920* (Baltimore: Johns Hopkins University Press, 1992)

For a discussion of wireless telegraphy see RADIO.

Paul Israel

telephony. The first licenses granted by the American Bell Telephone Company in New York City date from 27 August 1877, and a primitive telephone device was placed on the market soon after. The Metropolitan Telephone and Telegraph Company was formed in 1878, when a central switching office opened in Manhattan, serving 271 subscribers. The only competitor of American Bell in the early years of telephony in New York City was a subsidiary of WESTERN UNION; this firm abandoned the field in 1879, and within a year the Metropolitan Telephone and Telegraph Company expanded service beyond Manhattan. New York Telephone was organized in 1896 and absorbed the Bell operations for New York City. Over time AMERICAN TELEPHONE AND TELEGRAPH (AT&T) acquired a controlling interest in New York Telephone, which in 1909 consolidated six regional companies serving New York State, northern New Jersey, and parts of Pennsylvania. In 1927 operations in New Jersey were taken over by New Jersey Bell, and in the same year transatlantic service was established between New York City and London. In 1984 AT&T divested itself of its regional operating companies to comply with the settlement in 1981 of an antitrust suit. New York Telephone then became a subsidiary of NYNEX along with New England Telephone and other, smaller regional subsidiaries. By 1990 New York Telephone employed nearly 50,000 people, served 9.2 million access lines (connections between the customer and the central switching office, excluding coin and private lines), and handled nearly 106 million telephone calls a day through almost 100 million miles (160 million kilometers) of cable, including calls for new services in data transmission and cellular telephones. Through various acquisitions during the late 1990s, NYNEX eventually became part of Verizon Communications, with headquarters at 140 West Street.

Verizon Building, 2009

Robert W. Garnet, *The Telephone Enterprise: The Evolution of the Bell System's Horizontal Structure, 1876–1909* (Baltimore: Johns Hopkins University Press, 1985)

See also TECHNOLOGY.

George David Smith

television. During the 1930s the nation's two leading radio networks, the Columbia Broadcasting System (CBS) and the National Broadcasting Company (NBC), operated experimental television stations in New York City. NBC's parent company, Radio Corporation of America (RCA), aggressively promoted the new technology, with television being the centerpiece of RCA's pavilion at the World's Fair of 1939–40 in the city. NBC also telecast President Franklin D. Roosevelt's remarks opening the fair. In May 1939 NBC aired the first sports telecast, a Columbia–Princeton baseball game at Baker Field, but reception was poor. Concerns about uneven transmission standards and the cost of receivers inhibited sales, but at the end of 1941 three stations operating in New York City served about 5000 set owners. Promotion declined during the war years, and the city's stations remained on the air but had limited schedules. Soon after the war, however, regular telecasts began on four networks: CBS, NBC, Du Mont (ceased operations in 1955), and the American Broadcasting Company (ABC), each of which owned stations in New York City. Several independent stations were formed as well, including WPIX (1948; owned by the *Daily News*). Like the city's other non-network channels, WPIX relied heavily on sporting events and old movies.

The long-awaited television boom arrived in the late 1940s; a February 1949 survey indicated that 40 percent of all American television set owners lived in Greater New York. The city dominated early television in other ways; in particular, all the networks were based there. Up until 1951 all network programs originated from New York City, which had an ample supply of theatrical performers, who were especially suited for live broadcasts. Network executives assumed that viewers preferred live broadcasts, and the more cost-effective method of videotaping programs did not become available until the late 1950s. But the city's reign over television did not last. In October 1951 *I Love Lucy* debuted on CBS. Although set in New York City, the show was filmed in California, and its great popularity demonstrated that viewers had no bias against filmed series. Filmed Westerns, private detective series, and situation comedies displaced much of the mostly live, New York–based programming. New York City also never had enough studio space to overcome southern California's advantages as a production center. In early 1965 all but 10 of the 96 entertainment programs aired in evening prime time by the three networks were produced in the Los Angeles area. During the 1977–78 season only one network prime time series was shot in New York City.

But New York City was not entirely abandoned; the network variety program remained a New York City product into the 1960s. The most durable, CBS's *The Ed Sullivan Show*, ran for more than two decades (1948–71). Sullivan, a former columnist for the *New York Graphic* and *New York Daily News*, had an eye for spotting and luring talent to his Sunday night program. A variation on the variety program was NBC's *The Tonight Show*, which aired late at night on weekdays. From 1954 to 1972 *The Tonight Show* usually originated from New York City, as did many non-network talk shows and several late evening network efforts, including shows hosted by the comedian David Letterman and the long-running *Saturday Night Live* (premiered 1975). NBC's popular situation comedy *The Cosby Show* (1984–92) was videotaped in a studio in Queens, and the fictional Huxtable family lived in Brooklyn.

During the 1990s the city became a common setting for network programs. Twenty series in the fall of 1997 took place in New York City, including the cable series *Sex and the City* and *The Sopranos*, and the NBC show *Friends*. NBC also produced a succession of popular *Law & Order* dramas that were filmed in the city. Other city-centered programs, such as *NYPD Blue* and *Seinfeld*, were mostly produced in and around Hollywood. Many long-running soap operas, however, were filmed in Manhattan. The networks continued to produce most of their news programs, including their newscasts, in New York City. NBC's *Today Show*, a morning information program, originated from the network's Rockefeller Center studios. Competing programs on ABC, CBS, and the Fox News Network were also based in the city.

The growing popularity of cable during the 1980s and 1990s robbed the networks of about half of their evening audience. These new

Television Shows Set in New York City (selective list)

Name	Years in New York City
DAYTIME AND LATE NIGHT TALK/VARIETY	
The Caroline Rhea Show	2002–3
The Colbert Report	2005–
The Daily Show[1]	1996–
The Ed Sullivan Show	1948–71
Fridays	1980–82
Late Night with Conan O'Brien	1993–2009
Late Night with David Letterman	1982–93
Late Night with Jimmy Fallon	2009–
The Late Show with David Letterman	1993–
Live with Regis and Kelly[2]	1988–
The Milton Berle Show	1948–55
The Rosie O'Donnell Show	1996–2002
Saturday Night Live[3] [SNL]	1975–
Saturday Night Live with Howard Cosell	1975–76
The Tonight Show Starring Johnny Carson	1962–72
The Tony Danza Show	2004–6
The View	1997–
MORNING NEWS AND TALK, SOAP OPERAS, GAME SHOWS, AND NEWS	
All My Children	1970–
Another World	1964–99
As the World Turns	1956–
Cash Cab	2005–
Chain Reaction	2006–7
Dateline NBC	1992–
The Early Show	1999–
Emeril Live	1997–
Entertainment Tonight	1981–
Fox and Friends	1998–
Good Day New York	1988–
Good Morning America	1975–
Guiding Light	1952–2009
Jeopardy!	1964–78
Martha	2005–
Maury [The Maury Show]	1991–
Nightline	1979–
One Life to Live	1968–
Password; Million Dollar Password[4]	1961–67; 2008–
Power of Ten	2007–8
Rachael Ray	2006–
Real Sports with Bryant Gumbel	1995–
Sesame Street	1969–
Swans Crossing	1992
Today [The Today Show]	1952–
Total Request Live [TRL]	1998–2008
20/20	1978–
The Tyra Banks Show	2007–
Where in the World Is Carmen San Diego?	1991–96
Where in Time Is Carmen San Diego?	1996–98
PRIMETIME REALITY, COMEDY, AND DRAMA	
All in the Family	1971–79
America's Next Top Model	2003–4, 2008
The Amos 'n Andy Show	1951–53
Animal Precinct	2002–
The Anne Sothern Show	1958–61
The Apprentice	2004–6, 2007
Archie Bunker's Place	1979–83
Baretta	1975–78
Barney Miller	1975–82

Name	Years in New York City
Beauty and the Beast	1987–90
Becker	1998–2004
The Bedford Diaries	2006
Bewitched	1964–72
The Black Donnellys	2007
Blind Justice	2005
Bored to Death	2009–
Bosom Buddies	1980–84
Bridget Loves Bernie	1972–73
The Bronx Zoo	1987–88
Brooklyn Bridge	1991–93
Brooklyn South	1997–98
Cagney and Lacey	1982–86
Car 54, Where Are You?	1961–63
Caroline in the City	1995–99
Cashmere Mafia	2008
Castle	2009–
Central Park West	1996
Chappelle's Show	2003–6
City Guys	1997–2001
Conviction	2006
Cosby	1996–2000
The Cosby Mysteries	1994–95
The Cosby Show	1984–92
The Critic	1994–95
CSI: NY	2004–
Damages	2007
The Danny Thomas Show [Make Room for Daddy]	1953–57; 1957–64
The Days and Nights of Molly Dodd	1987–91
The Dick Van Dyke Show	1961–66
Diff'rent Strokes	1978–86
Dirty Sexy Money	2007–9
Dr. Kildare	1961–66
Eischied	1979–80
Ellery Queen	1975–76
The Equalizer	1985–89
Everybody Hates Chris	2005–9
Fame	1982–87
Family Affair	1966–71; 2002–3
Felicity	1998–2002
Fired Up	1997–98
Fish	1977–78
Flatbush	1979
Foley Square	1985–86
Friends	1994–2004
Fringe	2008–
Futurama	1999–2003
The George Carlin Show	1994–95
The Goldbergs	1949–56
Gossip Girl	2007–
Grounded for Life	2001–5
Heroes	2006–
The Honeymooners	1955–56
How I Met Your Mother	2005–
I Covered Times Square	1950–51
I Love Lucy	1951–57
Jake in Progress	2005–6
The Jeffersons	1975–85

(*continued*)

Television Shows Set in New York City (selective list) (*Continued*)

Name	Years in New York City
The Job	2001–2
The Joey Bishop Show	1961–65
Johnny Staccato	1959–60
The Jury	2004
Just Shoot Me!	1997–2003
Kate and Allie	1984–89
The King of Queens	1998–2007
Kojak	1973–78
Law and Order	1990–2010
Law and Order: Criminal Intent	2001–
Law and Order: Special Victims Unit	1999–
Law and Order: Trial by Jury	2005
Less Than Perfect	2002–
Life on Mars	2008–9
Lipstick Jungle	2008–9
Living Single	1993–98
Lotsa Luck	1973–74
Love Monkey	2006
Love, Sidney	1980–83
Mad about You	1992–99
Mad Men	2007–
Madigan	1972–73
Man against Crime	1949–56
Man from U.N.C.L.E.	1964–68
Mary Kay and Johnny	1947–50
McCloud	1970–77
Melba	1986
Mickey Spillane's Mike Hammer	1984–87
Mr. and Mrs. North	1952–54
Mr. District Attorney	1951–52
My Little Margie	1952–55
Naked City	1958–63
The Nanny	1993–99
Nero Wolfe	1981
New Amsterdam	2008
NewsRadio	1995–99
New York News	1995
New York Undercover	1994–98
Night Court	1984–91
Nurse	1981–82
Nurse Jackie	2009–
The Nurses	1962–65
N.Y.P.D.	1967–69
NYPD Blue	1993–2005
The Odd Couple	1970–75
On Our Own	1977–78
Paper Dolls	1984
The Parent 'Hood	1995–99
Park Place	1981
The Patty Duke Show	1963–66
Penthouse Party	1950–51
Popi	1976
The Real World	1992, 2002
Related	2005–6
The Reporter	1964
Rescue Me	2004–
Rhoda	1974–78
The Robbins Nest	1950
Ryan's Hope	1975–89
Seinfeld	1989–98
Serpico	1976–77
704 Hauser	1994
Seventh Avenue	1977
Sex and the City	1998–2004
Shaft	1973–74
Silver Spoons	1982–87
Spin City	1996–2002
Sports Night	1998–2000
The Street	2000
Tarzan	2003
Taxi	1978–83
The Ted Knight Show	1978
That Girl	1966–71
That's Life	1998
That Wonderful Guy	1949–50
The Thin Man	1957–59
Third Watch	1999–2005
13 Queens Boulevard	1979
30 Rock	2006–
Throb	1986–88
Tonight on Broadway	1948–49
The Trials of O'Brien	1965–66
The Trouble with Tracy	1970–71
Tru Calling	2003–5
The Two of Us	1981–82
Ugly Betty	2006–
The Unusuals	2009
Valentine's Day	1964–65
Veronica's Closet	1997–2000
The Wayans Bros.	1995–99
Welcome Back, Kotter	1975–79
Welcome to New York	2000–1
What I Like about You	2002–6
Will and Grace	1998–2006
Without a Trace	2002–9
Working Girl	1990
CHILDREN'S PROGRAMS AND CARTOONS	
Cousin Skeeter	1998–2003
The Electric Company	1971–77; 2009–
Gargoyles	1994–97
Ghostwriter	1992–95
The Real Ghostbusters	1986–91
Sesame Street	1969–
The Spectacular Spider-Man	2008–
Spider-Man: The Animated Series	1994–98
Teenage Mutant Ninja Turtles	1987–96; 2003–
Wizards of Waverly Place	2007–

1. Hosted by Craig Kilborn, 1996–98. Jon Stewart became host in January 1999 and the show became known at *The Daily Show with Jon Stewart.*
2. Previously titled *Live with Regis and Kathie Lee*, 1988–2000.
3. Originally titled *Saturday Night*, 1975–77.
4. Update of original series.

Source: "Current NYC Productions," http://www.nyc.gov/html/film/html/locations/current_nyc_productions.shtml

channels often proved immensely profitable, and many cable channels elected to operate out of New York City. The city remained a significant programming source for the Public Broadcasting Service (PBS). The popular PBS children's series *Sesame Street* (premiered 1969; still running in the early twenty-first century), was a New York–based production; set in a fictional New York City neighborhood, it had a decidedly urban look. Although the Public Broadcasting Act of 1967 discouraged a centralized programming authority, WNET (Channel 13), which covers the New York metropolitan area and whose transmitter is on the Empire State Building, was a major supplier of series to PBS stations. It distributed the well-regarded British miniseries *The Forsythe Saga* in the late 1960s and subsequently produced the arts anthology *Great Performances.*

New York City's commercial channels in the powerful very high frequency range were 2 (CBS), 4 (NBC), 5 (Fox), 7 (ABC), and 9 (independent). The networks owned their profitable outlets; indeed, they contended that their New York City stations helped to make up for losses occasionally incurred from other network operations. The major profit center of New York City stations beginning in the 1960s was the evening newscast. News programs, despite high salaries paid to some on-air talent, actually cost less than the rights to rerun the more popular old network series; moreover, stations could keep any sales of advertising time. Not surprisingly, the length of early evening newscasts grew from 15 to 120 minutes, though critics could find little of substance added to the programs. Early in the twenty-first century New York City remains the headquarters of all four major television networks (ABC, CBS, NBC, and Fox).

James L. Baughman

Temple Ansche Chesed. Conservative synagogue, opened in 1876 by a traditional German-speaking congregation on 86th Street and Third Avenue in Yorkville; it was initially known as Chebra Ansche Chesed. The congregation moved successively to East 112th Street in Harlem (during the 1890s) and to a stately brick temple designed by Edward I. Shire on 114th Street and Seventh Avenue (1907), where it flourished under the direction of Jacob Kohn. By the 1920s many Jews had left the neighborhood for the Upper West Side, and after languishing for a number of years the synagogue moved to a new building designed by Edward I. Shire and erected in 1927 at 100th Street and West End Avenue. The facilities there included a sanctuary for a congregation of more than 1500 and a community house containing classrooms, a library, an auditorium, and a social hall. After World War II the congregation declined as the surrounding neighborhood changed; it prospered again when the Upper West Side revitalized after the 1970s.

Jenna Weissman Joselit

Temple Emanu-El. The first Reform congregation in New York City, formed in 1845 as a *Cultus Verein,* or German literary society, and incorporated as a congregation within 10 years. It initially occupied rented rooms and remodeled church buildings on the Lower East Side. By 1868 a synagogue in a Moorish style was erected on Fifth Avenue and 43rd Street, where the congregation remained for nearly 60 years. As the neighborhood became commercial, the congregation moved farther up the East Side, sold its building to the developer Joseph Durst for $7 million, merged with Beth El, another prominent Reform congregation, and moved to Fifth Avenue and 65th Street in 1927, where an art deco synagogue designed by Robert D. Kohn, Clarence Stein, Charles Butler, and Bertram Goodhue was built in limestone. One of the largest synagogues in the world, Temple Emanu-El was built with seating for 2500 in a sanctuary ornamented with dazzling stained-glass windows and colorful mosaics in a Viennese Secessionist style. A community house was built on an adjacent site to accommodate a wide range of educational and social activities; several architectural elements from Beth El were incorporated into the design, among them a Tiffany window. Temple Emanu-El remains one of the most prominent Reform congregations in the United States.

Jenna Weissman Joselit

Temple Israel. Reform Jewish synagogue. Founded in 1870 by German Jews as Congregation Hand in Hand, Temple Israel's first location was on East 125th Street. The congregation was traditional and quickly established a religious school called the Gates of Learning. By 1876 the congregation was in its third location on 116th Street between First and Second avenues. The first permanent rabbi, Maurice H. Harris, was appointed in 1882; that same year the congregation became Temple Israel of Harlem. As the congregation grew, it moved to a former church at 125th Street and Fifth Avenue, to a limestone building at 120th Street and Lenox Avenue (still standing), to 91st Street and Broadway, and finally to 112 East 75th Street. In 2006 David Gelfand became the fifth rabbi of Temple Israel.

Jessica Montesano

Temple of Dendur. Ancient Nubian sanctuary dedicated to Isis from circa 15 BCE at the Metropolitan Museum of Art. Donated in 1965 to the United States by the Egyptian government in gratitude for assistance in constructing the Aswan Dam, it was reassembled in a spacious new wing at the museum, specially designed for it by Roche Dinkeloo and Associates and opened in 1978, after alternative proposals to place it near the Potomac River in Washington, D.C., were rejected.

Peter L. Donhauser

Ten American Painters. Group of impressionist and figurative artists formed in 1898 by Thomas Dewing, Childe Hassam, Willard Leroy Metcalf, Robert Reid, Edward Simmons, John Henry Twachtman, and Julian Alden Weir (from New York City) and Frank Weston Benson, Joseph Rodefer De Camp, and Edmund Charles Tarbell (from Boston). When Twachtman died in 1902 William Merritt Chase was elected to take his place. Until 1918 the group held yearly exhibitions in New York City, usually at the Durand–Ruel Gallery or the Montross Gallery.

Patricia Hills

Tenderloin. Nightclub district in Manhattan during the 1880s, bounded to the north by 42nd Street, to the east by Fifth Avenue, to the south by 24th Street, and to the west by Seventh Avenue. The name allegedly was coined by police captain Alexander Williams, sometimes known as the Czar of the Tenderloin, who was reported to have said that after his transfer from an obscure precinct to his new command, he was going to enjoy eating tenderloin after years of rump steak. During the Lexow Committee investigations, Williams denied that the name referred to better living in the district because of extortion payments made to the police by legitimate and illegitimate businesses in the area. Known as Satan's Circus by reformers, the district contained the greatest concentration of saloons, brothels, gambling parlors, dance halls, and "clip joints" in the city. It is now the site of the Empire State Building, the garment district, and Herald Square.

Linda Elsroad

Tenement House Law Act of 1901. See Housing.

tenements. The construction of multiple-unit residential buildings called tenements began in the mid-nineteenth century, providing compact rental housing at $2 to $3 a room a month for poor and working-class immigrants living and working in lower Manhattan. Tenements were inspired by "rookeries," a name applied to warehouses, mansions, churches, and breweries in the fourth ward that were converted in the 1830s so that each floor housed many families in small, cramped, poorly ventilated rooms. The first tenements built by speculators were spartan, functional buildings erected on standard lots 25 feet (8 meters) wide and 100 feet (30 meters) deep: each building had four stories, four apartments to a floor, and dark, unventilated interior rooms connected like railroad cars (hence the expression "railroad apartment"). Many buildings had no indoor running water, and there was a communal privy in a cellar vault or in the backyard. Often a second tenement known as a "double house" went up in the backyard.

The regulation of construction began just after the Civil War, when middle-class citizens began to view the tenements as a social and health menace. In 1867 the state legislature enacted the first legislation in the United States to improve living conditions. The law defined a tenement house as a multiple dwelling, required landlords to provide a privy and a fire ladder for every 20 tenants, and established the maximum proportion of a lot that could be covered by a building, a minimum area for rear courts, and standards for the open-air ventilation of interiors. Throughout this period, apartments were designed with a front room, or "parlor," and two inner sleeping chambers barely 10 feet (3 meters) square, and privies began to be placed in a subterranean vault where the effluvial stench became so powerful that it contributed to concerns about cholera.

By the late 1870s the housing stock contained roughly 21,000 rookeries and railroad apartments. The Association for Improving the Condition of the Poor sought to improve the living conditions in these buildings. In 1878 the publication *Plumber and Sanitary Engineer* conducted a competition for the best new design for a tenement. The architect James E. Ware won the contest with the "dumbbell" design, which was intended to raise hygienic standards by providing ventilation and light for interior rooms. The design was so named because the building resembled a dumbbell when seen from above: between the front and back rooms the exterior walls were indented, creating air shafts of nearly 10 by 13 feet (3 by 4 meters) between adjacent buildings that extended from the ground to the roof. The tenements had interior toilets with plumbing, vents to guard against sewer gas, two rear bedrooms, each 6.5 feet by 8 feet (2 by 2.25 meters), a kitchen of 7.5 feet by 10.5 feet (2.5 by 3 meters), and a living room of 8.5 feet by 13 feet (2.5 by 4 meters), for a total area in each apartment of 293 square feet (27 square meters). The interior rooms were ventilated by horizontal air shafts 4 feet (1.5 meters) long and a 2-foot (60-centimeter) indentation formed by the dumbbell. Reformers incorporated these designs into the Tenement House Law of 1879, introducing a clause that forbade the construction of rooms removed from a source of outside air.

During the 1880s many real estate developers installed sinks and stationary tubs in the hallways, where they could be ventilated by horizontal, "studded" (embedded) shafts, 5 feet (1.5 meters) long, that were square or octagonal. Soon sanitary regulation and the rising cost of brick construction caused the studded shafts to be replaced by a single shaft, or "light well," 2 feet (60 centimeters) square and 30 feet (9 meters) deep. Architects also repositioned stairways and hallways in the indentation of the dumbbell to avoid the layout of a railroad apartment, which had the stairs at the front, and installed extra shafts to ventilate toilets, hallways, and interior rooms. In rough accordance with the law of 1879, nearly 20,000 dumbbell buildings went up in Manhattan and the Bronx between 1880 and 1900; nearly one-third of these were in Yorkville and Harlem, and thousands more were on the Lower East Side.

At the end of the nineteenth century, five-story tenement houses were designed for 20 families, housing perhaps 100 residents, not including boarders. Upwards of 200 licensed "flophouses" with nearly 18,000 bunks lined the Bowery and Oliver, Chatham, and Mulberry streets. Many people lived in basements subject to tidal seepage, and thousands lived in the 2379 rear houses counted in the census of 1897. Apartments with two rooms had no closets: tenants hung their clothing from nails that they tacked into recesses in the walls 6 inches (15 centimeters) deep. Bedrooms had no space for washbasins or bureaus, and kitchens were rarely large enough for people to sit around the four sides of a table. The lack of privacy led families to develop a strict hierarchy, particularly regarding children. Only one-third of the city's tenements had running water, and in some blocks it was lacking altogether. Only 306 of the 255,033 persons living on the Lower East Side had bathrooms in their apartments, and most East Siders continued to use a vault privy or one at school even as hallway toilets became standard. In 1893 there were 12,434 persons in the Italian slum of Centre Street, where the typical apartment had two rooms, each housing two persons, and was rented for $4.60 a month. Only 2 percent of all families there had toilets on their level, and most shared with their neighbors a backyard or vault privy that was "mucked out" by hand (hygienically advanced "school sinks" were ostensibly flushed once a day). Although most working-class families had three rooms (including a dark inner bedroom), during the 1890s health inspectors found that in dilapidated buildings on Allen, Orchard, and Baxter streets entire families lived in a single room.

Miserable conditions in the tenements prompted the reformers Jacob A. Riis, Lillian Wald, Felix Adler, Simon Baruch, and Alfred E. Smith to take action. The Tenement House Committee of the Charity Organization Society, led by Robert De Forest but run by Lawrence Veiller, launched investigations and mounted exhibits that indicted the dumbbell tenement and led to the passage of the Tenement House Law of 1901. Buildings constructed before that date are still referred to as "old law" tenements. The law required that buildings have side courts 4 feet (1.33 meters) wide and backyards 11 feet (3.5 meters) deep, which meant that a building could cover no more than 72 percent of a standard lot; one room had to have an area of at least 120 square feet (11 square meters) and none could be smaller than 70 square feet (6.5 square meters), which made the traditional lot size impractical for the development of mass housing. The law also created a Tenement House Department to administer improvements in upwards of 83,000 "old law" structures and enforce "new law" standards on buildings under construction in the outer boroughs.

Around the turn of the twentieth century, a wave of new immigrants arrived in the city, and in response to the heightened demand for housing the department sought to improve the conditions in the "old law" buildings rather than shut them down. It focused on Manhattan and Brooklyn, bringing up to code 331,168 previously undocumented inner rooms and 96,079 rooms with no ventilation. The development of "new law" buildings and steam-heated apartments in the outer boroughs by the late 1920s decreased the population of the Lower East Side by nearly 250,000, and throughout lower Manhattan landlords boarded up thousands of "old law" buildings with vacancy rates of 15 to 30 percent. As the housing market moved to the outer boroughs, thousands of old structures were removed and major public works projects were executed: Sixth and Seventh avenues were extended, Allen Street was widened, and the notorious stretch of "old law" tenements between Chrystie and Forsyth streets was leveled.

The Multiple Dwellings Law (1929) required that landlords install toilets, fire retardants, and ventilation for inside rooms, and the commissioner of tenement housing Langdon W. Post bolstered the law with radical revisions, notably a six-month limit on the installation of fire retardants and an amendment that expanded the definition of legal ownership to include mortgage holders: as a result landlords and local banks threatened to abandon the 68,000 "old law" tenements that remained standing in the early 1930s. With the aid of New Deal subsidies for slum clearance, Mayor Fiorello H. La Guardia razed nearly 9500 buildings beginning in 1934. The end of the Depression brought a sharp increase in the occupancy of "old law" buildings, and La Guardia eased the enforcement of the Multiple Dwellings Law. After World War II the city's construction coordinator Robert Moses, who believed that the poor should move into public housing, used federal funds granted under Title I of the Housing Act of 1949 to demolish "old law" buildings on the Lower East Side between the Brooklyn Bridge and 23rd Street and to build projects such as the Corlears Hook Houses (1955). Social reformers and architects in the mid-1960s explored various possibilities in tenement renovation. Attempts were made at "gut rehabilitation" of remaining tenements, but the buildings proved difficult to repair and nearly impossible to bring up to code. About 200,000 tenement units remained scattered throughout the city at the end of the twentieth century, with the largest concentration in lower Manhattan between Houston and Delancey streets and west of Sarah D. Roosevelt Park, a neighborhood of Chinese immigrants adjacent to Chinatown. At 97 Orchard Street the Lower East Side Tenement Museum (opened in 1988) preserves the interior of a typical "old law" residence.

Robert W. De Forest and Lawrence Veiller, eds., *The Tenement House Problem* (New York: Macmillan, 1903); Anthony Jackson, *A Place Called Home: A History of Low-Cost Housing in Manhattan* (Cambridge, Mass.: MIT Press, 1976)

Joel Schwartz

tennis. Tennis was introduced to the United States in 1874 by Mary Outerbridge, who oversaw the construction of the first lawn court at the Staten Island Cricket and Baseball Club. The growing popularity of the sport led to the formation in New York City on 21 May 1881 of the United States National Lawn Tennis Association (USNLTA), known from 1920 as the United States Lawn Tennis Association (USLTA) and from 1975 as the United States Tennis Association (USTA).

The first courts in Manhattan opened in Central Park in 1881. Although primarily for the wealthy, tennis attracted players from all economic and racial groups, and local clubs were organized according to language, ethnicity, and class. Initially the USNLTA had no African American clubs or players. The centers for local tennis were the Crescent Athletic Club, bounded by New York Bay, First Avenue, 83rd Street, and 85th Street in Bay Ridge, and the West Side Tennis Club in Manhattan, which began as an all-male club on Central Park West in 1892 and moved successively to 238th Street and Broadway (1898), 117th Street and Morningside Drive (1902), and Forest Hills (1914, and remaining into the twenty-first century). The National Indoor Championship was played in the city from 1900 until 1940 and again from 1946 to 1963. In 1902 the Crescent Athletic Club competed for the Davis Cup against players from Great Britain. Robert LeRoy, a student at Columbia University, became the first national intercollegiate champion from the city in 1904. The West Side Tennis Club in Forest Hills was the site of American defenses of the Davis Cup (from 1914), as well as the United States Open tennis championships (US Open) from 1915 to 1920 and again from 1924 to 1978, when the championship was first held at Louis Armstrong Stadium in Queens. (After its relocation, the US Open became the fourth of the Grand Slam tournaments after the Australian Open, the French Open, and Wimbledon.) Much of the growth of the club from World War I to 1950 was overseen by Julian Myrick, a resident of New York City who was also a president of the USNLTA.

Church and club teams were formed by black immigrants from the West Indies, who also helped to establish the Cosmopolitan Tennis Club (at 138th Street and Convent Avenue in Harlem) and the predominantly black American Tennis Association in 1916. Two black players, Gerald Norman and Reginald Weir, competed in several indoor events sponsored by the USNLTA at the Seventh Regiment Armory. The National Public Parks championships began in 1923 and inspired the construction of most of the 550 public courts in the city. In 1938 Don Budge, champion of the USLTA, played against the African American champion Jimmy McDaniels in an exhibition at the Cosmopolitan Tennis Club. Althea Gibson received her training at the public courts on 155th Street in Harlem; with the help of Sarah Palfrey, another New Yorker, in 1950 she became the first black member of the West Side Tennis Club, and in 1957 she won Wimbledon and the national championship and became the first African American player to be generally recognized as world champion. Another well-known player of the 1950s from New York City was Dick Savitt. In 1968 the national indoor championship of the USLTA adopted an open format, allowing both amateurs and professionals to compete. Vitas Gerulaitis, a New Yorker who attended Columbia, won major world tournaments during the 1970s; John McEnroe, who grew up in Douglaston, Queens, dominated the sport in the 1980s.

Lawn tennis

By the 1990s the US Open was broadcast on television worldwide from the Billie Jean King National Tennis Center in Flushing Meadows Corona Park; the New York Junior Tennis League operated on public courts and schoolyards and was the largest league of its kind in the United States. In 1997 the US Open introduced the largest outdoor tennis stadium in the world, Arthur Ashe Stadium, which seats 22,547 spectators and features five restaurants and two players' lounges. Louis Armstrong Stadium was then downgraded to court number two in the complex and for the tournament. In 2006 the US Open became the first major tennis tournament to implement the use of instant replay.

Robert Minton, *Forest Hills* (Philadelphia: J. B. Lippincott, 1975)

Arthur Ashe, Meghan Lalonde

Tenth Street Studio Building. Building erected in 1857 at 15 10th Street, between Fifth and Sixth avenues, to house artists' studios, the first such building in the United States or Europe. The address was renumbered 51 West 10th Street in 1866. The building was commissioned by the businessman James Boorman Johnston and designed by Richard Morris Hunt, the first American architect trained at the École des Beaux-Arts. Its symmetrical plan incorporated a large central exhibition gallery two stories high surrounded by 25 studios. In the early years tenants included Frederic E. Church and Albert Bierstadt, both prominent members of the Hudson River School; Winslow Homer (in the 1870s); and William Merritt Chase, who painted cosmopolitan subjects of everyday life as well as landscapes. An annex was added at 55 West 10th Street in 1873. Although a few well-known artists remained into the twentieth century, the building became antiquated and was inhabited mostly by illustrators, art teachers, and photographers. It was sold by Johnston's descendants in 1920 and after several changes of ownership was demolished in 1956.

Annette Blaugrund, "The Tenth Street Studio Building: A Roster, 1857–1895," *American Art Journal* 14, no. 2 (spring 1982), 64–71

Annette Blaugrund

term limits. Since its founding, New York City has limited its mayors to two four-year terms, either by tradition or by law. Advocates of term limits argue that having limited years in office prevents the corruption associated with career politicians. The opposition counters that term limits keep those with valuable experience from continuing their work and fulfilling their goals. After the terrorist attacks of 11 September 2001, Mayor Rudolph Giuliani asked for several extra months in office in order to ease the transition between mayors, but Michael Bloomberg nevertheless was elected in November 2001 and took office in January 2002, per the usual procedures. As Bloomberg approached the end of eight years in office, he petitioned for a measure from the City Council to rescind term limits. In 2008 the council voted to allow Bloomberg to run for mayor for a third term; he won the election in November 2009.

Penelope Gelwicks

terra-cotta. Glazed or unglazed ceramic made from clay was used in New York City during the late nineteenth and early twentieth centuries to ornament masonry and to make curtain walls. It was introduced in the city in 1853 as a cheaper substitute for cut stone. Early examples include the Trinity Building by Richard Upjohn (1851–53, demolished), which used material from the Hudson River Pottery and Terra Cotta Works, and the Cooper Union Building by Fredrick A. Petersen (1853–58, extant). The material for this building was manufactured by Tolman, Hathaway and Stone in Worcester, Massachusetts. Recent research shows that this company supplied terra-cotta for numerous buildings on the East Coast, some of which still survive. In 1853 James Renwick engaged a local sewer pipe factory owned by Alexander Young to manufacture terra-cotta cornices and window surrounds for the Tontine Building, the St. Denis Hotel, and three houses on Ninth Street. These projects were successfully completed but met with opposition from stonecutters and masons, who feared that terra-cotta would endanger their livelihood and helped to keep it out of the city for many years. The terra-cotta industry flourished in other parts of the country, and in 1877 the Chicago Terra Cotta Company supplied unglazed, reddish terra-cotta for use on two buildings in New York City: the Braehm Residence (1877, George B. Post) and the Morse Building at 12 Beekman Street (1879, Silliman and Farnsworth). The fireproof qualities of the material were put to use in the Potter Building at 38 Park Row (1883–86, N. G. Starkweather). Its owner, Orlando B. Potter, was committed to fireproof construction after a fire destroyed his previous building on the site. Potter was instrumental in founding the first local terra-cotta manufacturer to achieve success, the New York Architectural Terra Cotta Company, in Long Island City, in 1886 (offices built in 1892 with terra-cotta trim at 42-10 Vernon Boulevard). Another local supplier in the 1890s was B. Kreischer and Sons, a brick-making firm in Charleston, Staten Island. Polychrome glazed terra-cotta in blues, whites, yellows, and greens was introduced in 1906 by McKim, Mead and White in the Madison Square Presbyterian Church (Madison Avenue at 24th Street, demolished 1913) but did not become popular for two decades. A wide range of glazes was developed about 1925, including metallic lusters, vivid yellows, and shades of lime green and lavender characteristic of art deco; the McGraw–Hill Building (1931, Hood, Godley and Fouilhoux), at 330 West 42nd Street, was decorated with horizontal bands of blue-green. Other buildings in the city that used terra-cotta ornament include the Bayard Building (1898, Louis Sullivan), the Flatiron Building (1901–3, D. H. Burnham), the Alwyn Court Apartments (1909, Harde and Short), the Audubon Theatre and Ballroom (1912, Thomas W. Lamb), the Woolworth Building (1913, Cass Gilbert), 2 Park Avenue (1927, Ely Jacques Kahn), the Pythian Temple at 135 West 70th Street (1927, Thomas W. Lamb), and 235 East 22nd Street (1928, George and Edward Blum). After the International Style was introduced by Henry Russell Hitchcock and Philip Johnson in 1932 in an exhibition at the Museum of Modern Art, architects abandoned the kind of exuberant ornamentation to which terra-cotta was suited, and its use diminished during the 1930s. Terra-cotta regained popularity in the twenty-first century and is being used in both its glazed and unglazed forms as a cladding or "rainscreen" for tall buildings. Renzo Piano is the architect who has been most involved with this renewed interest; his New York Times Tower (2007) used 250,000 glazed clay rods to create a screen on this skyscraper's facade.

Gary F. Kurutz and Mary Swisher, *Architectural Terra Cotta of Gladding, McBean* (Sausalito, Calif.: Windgate, 1989); Andrew S. Dolkart and Susan Tunick, *George and Edward Blum: Texture and Design in New York Apartment House Architecture* (New York: Friends of Terra Cotta Press, 1993); Susan Tunick, *Terra Cotta Skyline: New York's Architectural Ornament* (New York: Princeton Architectural Press, 1997)

Susan Tunick

terrorism. Because of its size and importance, New York City has often been a target of terrorists. An explosion on 30 July 1916 killed seven people, when munitions bound for England and France exploded on Black Tom Island. A claims commission ruled in 1939 that the Black Tom explosion was an act of saboteurs of the imperial German government. Thirty people were killed in an unsolved attack on Wall Street on 16 September 1920, when a horse-drawn wagon exploded across from the New York Stock Exchange; Bolsheviks were suspected, but no arrests were made. A disgruntled former employee of Consolidated Edison named George P. Metesky became known as the Mad Bomber after he terrorized New York City with 33 homemade bombs that he planted around the city between 1940 and 1956. Fifteen people were injured. During the 1960s and 1970s a wave of political terrorism swept the United States, and left-wing terrorists attacked several targets in the city. Many were the headquarters of corporations such as Mobil Oil, General Telephone and Electronics, and International Business Machines; other targets were governmental or institutional, including the Federal Office Building. The city's most notable terrorist incident of the 1970s was accidental. On 6 March 1970 an explosion demolished a town house at 18 West 11th Street in Greenwich Village, killing three people, including Theodore Gold, a student at Columbia University. Two women were seen fleeing the explosion, one of whom was Cathlyn Wilkerson, whose father owned the town house. Wilkerson and Gold were members of the Weathermen, a violent radical faction of the left-wing group Students for a Democratic Society. Sixty sticks of dynamite and 30 blasting caps were found in the ruins, leading the police to conclude that the building was being used as a bomb factory.

From the 1970s into the mid-1980s several violent attacks were staged on businesses and institutions in the city by advocates of independence for Puerto Rico, in particular by the group Fuerzas Armadas de Liberación Nacional (FALN). In early 1975 the FALN claimed responsibility for a bomb that exploded at Fraunces Tavern and killed four people, and in 1977 and 1978 the group planted pipe bombs at the headquarters of several major corporations in New York City and at the New York Public Library; it also planted incendiary devices that set off fires at La Guardia, Kennedy, and Newark airports. In 1982 it bombed the lobbies of several financial firms on Wall Street and of the headquarters of the New York Police Department. The FALN also remains the main suspect in the unsolved bombing of the Trans World Airlines terminal at La Guardia Airport on 29 December 1975, which killed 11 people. Other Puerto Rican nationalist groups also attacked targets in New York City: one occupied the Statue of Liberty on 25 October 1977, and another bombed Pennsylvania Station in 1980.

On 26 February 1993 a car bomb exploded in an underground parking garage beneath the World Trade Center, killing six people and closing both towers for several weeks. Four Egyptians arrested in connection with the bombing were identified as followers of the Muslim cleric Sheik Omar Abdel-Rahman, who had been exiled from Egypt and was then living in the United States. In late June the Federal Bureau of Investigation arrested eight other Egyptian and Sudanese followers of Abdel-Rahman on charges of plotting to bomb

Ground Zero, site of the World Trade Center attack in 2001, shown in 2009

several targets in the city, including the United Nations, the tunnels between Manhattan and New Jersey, and the Javits Federal Office Building and to assassinate the secretary general of the United Nations, Boutros Boutros-Ghali, as well as Egyptian President Hosni Mubarak and New York Senator Alfonse D'Amato. Abdel-Rahman himself was charged as the ringleader of the terrorist group. In 1994 the four main suspects in the bombing of the World Trade Center were convicted on nearly all charges.

The most famous and destructive of terrorist attacks on New York City—and the United States—occurred on 11 September, when two hijacked airliners crashed into both towers of the World Trade Center, resulting in at least 2749 deaths. The hijackers were members of Al-Qaeda, a network of Islamic radicals, who had been training for the attack for years. In the years after 2001, the New York Police Department enhanced its own anti-terrorist activities and began stationing its operatives in multiple locations around the world in order to help prevent more terrorist attacks on American soil.

See also Civil defense, Counterterrorism, September 11, and World Trade Center.

Rohit T. Aggarwala, Kenneth T. Jackson

Terry, William (Bill) (*b* 30 Oct 1898, Atlanta; *d* 9 Jan 1989, Jacksonville, Fla.). New York Giants baseball player and manager; member of National Baseball Hall of Fame. Originally the team's first baseman, Terry became manager as well in June 1932. He retired from playing after 1936 but was the Giants manager through 1941. In 1930 he amassed 254 hits and his batting average was .401. As Giants manager, Terry won three pennants (1933, 1936, 1937) and one World Series (1933).

Andrew Sparberg

Tesla, Nikola (*b* Smiljan, near Gospic, Croatia, 10 July 1856; *d* New York City, 7 Jan 1943). Physicist, electrical engineer, and inventor. He moved to New York City in 1884 to work for the Edison Machine Works and in the following year joined Westinghouse in Pittsburgh, where he was the leading advocate of alternating electric current in the debate over its merits relative to direct current. In 1889 he built a laboratory at South Fifth Avenue (now La Guardia Place), which he then moved to 46 East Houston Street; there he demonstrated his best-known invention in 1898, a device known as the "Tesla coil" that contributed to the development of broadcasting. Having gained great wealth and prominence from his inventions, Tesla lived at the Waldorf-Astoria, dined at Delmonico's, and was acquainted with John Jacob Astor IV, J. P. Morgan, and Mark Twain, but he died a debt-ridden recluse at the Hotel New Yorker. His memoir *My Inventions: The Autobiography of Nikola Tesla* was published posthumously in 1982.

Margaret Cheney, *Tesla, Man Out of Time* (Englewood Cliffs, N.J.: Prentice-Hall, 1981)

Val Ginter

T. G. I. Friday's. Restaurant and bar opened on 15 March 1965 on First Avenue and East 63rd Street by Alan Stillman, a perfume and flavor salesman, on the site of a neighborhood bar called the Good Tavern. Generally regarded as the world's first "singles bar," it inspired many imitators in the neighborhood, notably Maxwell's Plum and Mister Laff's. By the time the original location closed in 1994, it had given rise to 294 franchises throughout the world.

Kenneth T. Jackson

Thalia Movie Theater. Movie theater at West 95th Street between Broadway and West End Avenue, occupying the basement of the former Astor Market building (opened in 1915). Originally the site of the Sunken Garden Restaurant, it was converted in 1931 by Raymond Irrera and Ben Schlanger into a theater seating 292 and using many architectural innovations. The long, narrow parabolic reverse floor, dipping in the center and sloping up toward the edges, was invented by Schlanger to provide each seat with the same view of the screen and soon became standard in the construction of movie theaters nationwide. The Thalia offered mainly foreign films initially but added Hollywood films in 1955. Under the direction of Richard Schwartz it became exclusively a revival house by 1977. After years of neglect it closed in 1987, the victim of a struggle for the ownership of the old market building as well as the decline of revival houses. Refurbished by local businesspeople, the Thalia reopened in 1993, its original architecture and *art moderne* interior intact, and it remained one of few repertory movie theaters in New York City. After being closed once again in the mid-1990s, the theater reopened on 13 April 2002 at 250 West 95th Street. A part of Symphony Space, it is called the Leonard Nimoy Thalia at Symphony Space.

Isabelle Kaplan

Thanksgiving Day Parade. See Macy's Thanksgiving Day Parade.

Tharp, Twyla (*b* Portland, Ind., 1 July 1941). Dancer and choreographer. She graduated from Barnard College in 1963 and danced with the Paul Taylor Dance Company from 1963 to 1965, when she formed her own modern dance company. Since then she has choreographed over 125 dances for her own company and others, including the Joffrey Ballet, American Ballet Theatre (where she was Artistic Associate), New York City Ballet, Mikhail Baryshnikov, ice skater John Curry, Martha Graham Dance Company, Paris Opera Ballet, and the Royal Ballet. Tharp's loose-limbed, impudent, high-energy style includes elements from jazz, modern dance, and ballet. Her dances include *Tank Dive* (1965), *Eight Jelly Rolls* (1971), *Deuce Coupe* (1973), *Sue's Leg* (1975), *Push Comes to Shove* (1976), *The Catherine Wheel* (1981), *Nine Sinatra Songs* (1982), *Brahms/Handel* (1984), and *In the Upper Room* (1986). Tharp choreographed for five Hollywood films, among them *Hair* (1978), *Amadeus* (1984), and *White Nights* (1985). Her Broadway shows include *When We Were Very Young* (1980), *Singin' in the Rain* (1985), *Movin' Out* (2002), and *Come Fly Away* (2010). Among her numerous awards and grants are the National Medal of Arts, a Tony Award, two Emmy Awards, and a Drama Desk Award.

Norma Adler

Tharpe [née Nubin], **Rosetta** (*b* Cotton Plant, Ark., 20 March 1915; *d* Philadelphia, 9

Oct 1973). Gospel singer and guitarist. She is known for popularizing gospel music among audiences outside of African American churches. After moving to New York City in 1934, Tharpe made a number of pioneering recordings for Decca Records that blended gospel and jazz styles. Her albums drew harsh criticism from gospel aficionados, but they were wildly popular among secular audiences. Her performance in Cab Calloway's 1938 fall revue at the Cotton Club (then segregated) is thought to be the first performance of gospel music for a white audience.

Rowan Moore Gerety

theater. The history of theater in New York City reflects the city's dominance as the cultural hub of the United States. No other city has been able to support such an ensemble of richness.

1. Colonial Period and Early Republic (1699–1798)

During the first half of the eighteenth century, theater in the city was confined to amateur productions presented in venues such as the New Theatre (better known as the Theatre in Nassau Street), which opened in 1732 in a house owned by Rip Van Dam, president of the Common Council. The first confirmed professional performance in the city took place there on 5 March 1750, when an English company led by Walter Murray and Thomas Kean produced *Richard III.* Murray and Kean continued at the Theatre in Nassau Street until July 1751; when they left for Williamsburg, Virginia, the theater was leased to Robert Upton, who had been sent by the London theatrical manager William Hallam to ascertain whether the city could support continued theatrical activity. Although there is no record of Upton's scouting report, a British troupe billed as the London Company of Comedians and led by Hallam's brother Lewis arrived in the city in the summer of 1753. When it left for Philadelphia in March 1754, the Theatre in Nassau Street ceased operation.

The company returned to New York City in 1758 under the leadership of David Douglass. In addition to managing the London Company (soon renamed the American Company of Comedians) Douglass embarked on a building campaign that led to the construction of a theater on Cruger's Wharf (1758) and the Theatre in Beekman Street (1761), as well as the Theatre in John Street (1767), which became the best-known playhouse in New York City and remained so until the Park Theatre on Park Row was built in 1797–98. During the American Revolution all professional production ceased, and the only theatrical activity in the city was amateur drama presented for the entertainment of British troops. By 1785 the American Company returned from wartime exile in the West Indies, and theater in the city began a period of expansion and popularity.

Theaters within the Present Boundaries of New York City, by Date of Founding

Corbett Tavern,[1] Broadway and Exchange Place, *ca* 1732
Playhouse on Broadway, Broadway north of Beaver Street, *ca* 1732
New Theatre,[2] 1732–54
Theater on Cruger's Wharf,[3] Cruger's Wharf near Dock and William streets, 1758–?59
Theater in Beekman Street, Beekman (Chapel) Street near Kid Street, 1761–64
Theater in John Street, John Street near Broadway, 1767–97
Rickett's Amphitheatre, Greenwich Street,[4] from 1795
Park Theatre,[5] Park Row, 1798–1848
Theater in Mount Vernon Gardens, Broadway between Leonard and Franklin streets, 1800–1803
Grove Theatre,[6] Madison (Bedlow) Street and Catherine Street, 1804–5
Lyceum Theatre, Broadway between Warren and Chambers streets, 1808–9
Broadway Circus, 1812–14
Washington Hall,[7] Broadway and Houston Street, 1812–1945
Anthony Street Theatre, Worth (Anthony) Street near Broadway, 1814–21
Pantheon, Mercer Street between Houston and Prince streets, 1821–22
African Grove Theatre, Church Street between Duane and Anthony streets, from 1821
City Theatre, 15 Warren Street near Broadway, 1822–23
Niblo's Garden Theatre, Broadway and Prince Street, 1822–46
Unnamed African theater, Greene Street and Bleecker Street, 1823
Chatham Garden Theatre, Chatham Street off Pearl Street, 1824–32
Lafayette Theatre, Canal Street between Thompson and Laurens streets, 1825–29
Vauxhall Garden Theatre, Lafayette Place between Broadway and Bowery, 1826–55
Bowery Theatre, 48 Bowery between Bayard and Canal streets, 1826–1929
Richmond Hill Theatre, Varick Street between Charlton and Vandam streets, 1831–49
National Theatre,[8] Church Street between Leonard and Franklin streets, 1833–41
Bowery Amphitheatre,[9] 37–39 Bowery between Bayard and Canal streets, 1833–66
Franklin Theatre, 175 Chatham Street between James and Oliver streets, 1835–54
Broadway Theatre, 410 Broadway at Canal Street, 1837
(Second) City Theatre, Broadway and Ann Street, 1837
Olympic Theatre,[10] 444 Broadway between Howard and Grand streets, 1837–54
Chatham Theatre,[11] Chatham Street between James and Roosevelt streets, 1837–60
Castle Garden Theater, Battery Park, 1839–55
Barnum's American Museum and Lecture Room, Broadway and Ann Street, 1841–65
Apollo Rooms, Broadway between Canal and Walker streets, 1842–51
Palmo's Opera House,[12] 39–41 Chambers Street behind City Hall Park, 1844–76
Astor Place Opera House, Astor Place, 1847–53
Mechanics Hall, 472 Broadway near Grand Street, 1847–57
Broadway Theatre, 326 Broadway, 1847–59
Niblo's Theatre,[13] Broadway and Prince Street, 1849–95
Coliseum, 448 Broadway between Howard and Grand streets, 1850s
Minerva Rooms, Broadway and Grand Street, 1850s
Old Stuyvesant Hall, Broadway between Bleecker and Bond streets, 1850–60
Brougham's Lyceum,[14] Broadway and Broome Street, 1850–69
Tripler Hall,[15] Broadway at Bond Street, 1851–67
Deutsches National Theatre, 53 Bowery, 1853
Crystal Palace, Bryant Park (Reservoir Square), Sixth Avenue and 42nd Street, 1853–58
St. Charles Theatre, 17–19 Bowery, 1853–54
Chinese Rooms to Barnum's New American Museum,[16] 539 Broadway between Spring and Prince streets, 1853–68
Fellow's Opera House and Hall of Lyrics, 444 Broadway between Howard and Grand streets, 1854–66
White's Opera House, 49 Bowery, 1854–?70
Academy of Music,[17] East 14th Street between Irving Place and Third Avenue, 1854–1926
Kelly and Leon's, 720 Broadway near 12th Street, 1855–1870s
Laura Keene's Varieties to Olympic Theatre,[18] Broadway between Houston and Bleecker streets, 1856–80
Buckley's Hall, Broadway between Prince and Houston streets, 1856–81
Atlantic Gardens, 50 Bowery, 1856–1911
Henry Wood's Marble Hall, 561 Broadway near Houston Street, 1857–59
Hoym's Theatre,[19] Bowery and Spring Street, from 1858

(*continued*)

Theaters within the Present Boundaries of New York City, by Date of Founding (*Continued*)

New Bowery Theatre, Bowery between Canal and Hester streets, 1859–66
Irving Hall, Irving Place and 15th Street, 1860–88
Wallack's Theatre, 728 Broadway at 13th Street, 1861–1901
Park Theatre, 383 Fulton Street, Brooklyn, 1863–98
Das Neue Stadt Theatre, 45–47 Bowery, 1864–72
New York Stadt Theatre,[20] 43 Bowery, 1864–1910
Grand Street Theatre, Grand and Crosby streets, 1865–66
Lucy Rushton's Theatre,[21] Broadway and Waverly Place, 1865–81
Broadway Athenaeum,[22] 734 Broadway, 1865–84
Theatre Comique, 514 Broadway between Spring and Broome streets, 1865–84
Fifth Avenue Theatre,[23] southwest corner of Fifth Avenue and 24th Street, 1865–1908
Fourteenth Street Theatre, West 14th Street between Sixth and Seventh avenues, 1866–1911
Steinway Hall, 109 East 14th Street, 1866–1925
Daly's Theatre, 1221 Broadway between 29th and 30th streets, 1867–1920
Pike's Opera House,[24] northwest corner of Eighth Avenue and 23rd Street, 1868–1960
Booth's Theatre, southeast corner of Sixth Avenue and 23rd Street, 1869–83
Harlem Music Hall, Third Avenue at 130th Street, 1870–85
Koster and Bial's,[25] West 23rd Street between Sixth and Seventh avenues, 1870–1924
Madison Square Garden,[26] 26th to 27th streets between Fifth and Madison avenues, 1870–1925
Union Square Theatre, Broadway and Fourth Avenue, 1870–1936
Brooklyn Theatre,[27] Johnson and Washington streets, Brooklyn, 1871–90
Neuendorff's Germania Theater, 1872–81
New Park Theatre, 932 Broadway from 21st to 22nd streets, 1873–82
Chickering Hall, Fifth Avenue and 18th Street, 1875–1902
San Francisco Music Hall, Broadway and 28th Street, 1875–1907
Eagle Theatre,[28] Sixth Avenue between 32nd and 33rd Streets, 1875–1909
Third Avenue Theatre,[29] Third Avenue between 30th and 31st streets, from 1875
Pendy's Gayety Theatre,[30] Third Avenue between 125th and 126th streets, 1877–79
Daly's Fifth Avenue Theatre, northwest corner of Broadway and 28th Street, 1877–1930
Brighton Theatre,[31] 1239 Broadway between 30th and 31st streets, 1878–1915
Das Thalia Theater, 1879–88
Aberle's Theatre,[32] East Eighth Street between Broadway and Fourth Avenue, 1879–1904
Miner's Bowery Theatre, 169 Bowery, from 1879
Broadway Theatre,[33] southwest corner of Broadway and 41st Street, 1880–1929
Metropolitan Opera Hall, Broadway between 41st and 42nd streets, 1880–1965
Das Star Theater, 1881–83
Miner's Eighth Avenue Theatre, Eighth Avenue between 26th and 27th streets, 1881–1902
Tony Pastor's New 14th Street Theatre, East 14th Street between Irving Place and Third Avenue, 1881–1928
Oriental Theatre,[34] 104 Bowery, 1882–98
Wallack's Theatre, northwest corner of Broadway and 30th Street, 1882–1918
Casino Theatre, southeast corner of Broadway and 39th Street, 1882–1930
Temple Theatre,[35] 141 West 23rd Street, 1883–?1900
Herald Square Theatre, northeast corner of Broadway and 35th Street, 1883–1914
Metropolitan Opera House, Broadway to Seventh Avenue between 39th and 40th streets, 1883–1966
Theatre Comique,[36] 125th Street between Third and Lexington avenues, 1885–93
Lyceum Theatre, Fourth (Park) Avenue between 23rd and 24th streets, 1885–1902
F. F. Proctor's Theatre,[37] Driggs Avenue and South Fourth Street, Brooklyn, from 1886
Théâtre Français,[38] 14th Street west of Sixth Avenue, from 1886
Criterion Theatre, Fulton Street near Grand Street, Brooklyn, 1886–95
Amberg Theatre, 11 Irving Place at 15th Street, 1888–93
Berkeley Theatre, 19 West 44th Street, from 1888
Amphion Theatre, Bedford Avenue between South Ninth and South 10th streets, Brooklyn, 1888–1913
Hyde and Behman's Theatre, Adams Street between Fulton and Myrtle streets, Brooklyn, 1888–?1915
Broadway Theatre,[39] southwest corner of Broadway and 41st Street, 1888–1929
Chinese Theatre, 5 Doyers Street, 1890s
The Gayety (Gaiety), Broadway and Throop Street, Brooklyn, from 1890
Harrigan's Theatre,[40] West 35th Street off Sixth Avenue, 1890–1932

(*continued*)

2. Lower Broadway, the Bowery, and the Park (1798–1850)

At the beginning of the nineteenth century the Park Theatre dominated dramatic activity in the city. Under the management of William Dunlap (an art critic, playwright, theater historian, and early manager) and then Stephen Price and Edward Simpson, the Park engaged some of the most accomplished actors from England, encouraged American-born actors, and introduced New Yorkers to Italian opera. The Park had no serious competition until 1824, when a theater was erected nearby in the Chatham Gardens on Park Row between Duane and Pearl streets. The building of new and in some cases larger theaters continued (the Bowery Theatre, Vauxhall Garden Theatre, Niblo's Garden and Theatre), and theaters began to concentrate on Broadway and the Bowery. The same period saw the beginnings of the "star system" in American theater, as stage actors from England sought fame in the new country, and managers in New York City tried different means of filling their new theaters. The first English star was George Frederick Cooke, engaged by Dunlap in 1810 to stimulate attendance at the Park; he was followed by such well-known performers as Edmund and Charles Kean, Charles Mathews, William Conway, William Charles Macready, and Charles Kemble and his daughter Fanny.

During the 1820s a popular and aggressively democratic theater emerged as laborers and recent transplants from rural areas began to patronize the theater in larger numbers and enjoyed early melodramas, foreign and American; "Yankee" plays that appealed specifically to their tastes; the performances of American-born stars like James Hackett, George H. Hill, and Dan Marble, known for their wry humor in Yankee roles; and the performances of Edwin Forrest and Charlotte Cushman, both renowned for their displays of raw emotional power. The following decades saw the emergence of native-born stars like E. L. Davenport, Lawrence Barrett, Laura Keene, Lester Wallack, John Brougham, Matilda Heron, and E. A. Sothern and theatrical dynasties like those of the Jeffersons, the Drews, the Barrymores, and the Booths. By the early 1830s popular theaters for working-class audiences complemented those customarily patronized by high society. The new theaters furnished the fare demanded by the masses, whom they further accommodated by reducing admission prices (75, 50, and 37-and-a-half cents). Theaters like the Park and Burton's remained bastions of the elite, but the Bowery, the National, and the Chatham were for the working classes. Thus while Knickerbocker society appreciated the talents of the Kembles at the Park during the 1832–33 season, the masses flocked to the Bowery to see George Gale in the spectacular melodrama *Mazeppa*.

During the 1840s many popular entertainment forms evolved and flourished. Minstrelsy, descended from the songs and dances performed in the 1830s by Thomas D. "Jim Crow" Rice and other entertainers, attracted New Yorkers in such numbers that it rivaled the legitimate stage. Variety—the raunchy precursor of the more genteel vaudeville—catered to all-male audiences in museums, saloons, and concert halls. Circuses occupied any vacant lot large enough to hold them; panoramas (giant landscapes or other spectacular scenes painted on canvas) were shown in buildings built especially for their viewing; and dime museums displayed their assorted oddities to thousands each day. For about the first half of the nineteenth century no attempt was made to centralize the theaters, so they remained scattered throughout Manhattan. There were small clusters of theaters at Park Row, on Broadway between City Hall and Houston Street, and on the lower Bowery, while roughly half a dozen theaters were in the regions west of Broadway (including three African American theaters, one of which helped to foster the career of Ira Aldridge, the first famous black actor in the United States).

3. Lower Broadway and the Bowery to Astor Place (1850–75)

It was not the legitimate theater but the minstrel show that was instrumental in the evolution of the first theater center in New York City. In the 1850s and 1860s a belt of minstrel halls developed along Broadway, extending from Fellow's Opera House at 444 Broadway to a minstrel hall in Hope Chapel just south of Waverly Place. This concentration of theaters was a harbinger of a district that developed around Union Square during the last quarter of the nineteenth century. Theatrical impresarios in Brooklyn had difficulty competing with their counterparts in Manhattan. The first Brooklyn Academy of Music was not built until 1861, followed by the Park Theatre in 1863 (opposite City Hall on Fulton Street). Frederick and Sarah Conway managed the Park from 1864 until 1871, when they opened the Brooklyn Theatre. Both of their theaters housed repertory companies and presented performances by Sothern, James O'Neill, Kate Claxton, John Gilbert, and Lillian Russell.

By the middle of the nineteenth century the economic centralization of the American theater had already become evident. The success of *Uncle Tom's Cabin,* which ran for more than 300 performances at the National Theatre in 1853–54, and the ensuing mania for "Tom shows" that swept both the city and the nation, signaled a new preoccupation with long runs in the American theater that persisted into the twenty-first century. Although some managers were at first skeptical about the long run, they were quickly persuaded by the success of *The Black Crook.* Based on a melodrama by Charles M. Barras, this show ran for 475 performances from 1866 and was important in the evolution of the musical.

Theaters within the Present Boundaries of New York City, by Date of Founding (*Continued*)

Carnegie Hall, 154 West 57th Street, from 1891
Manhattan Opera House,[41] 315 West 34th Street between Broadway and Seventh Avenue, 1892–1901
Bedford Avenue Theatre, Broadway and Bedford Avenue, Brooklyn, 1892–1903
Weber and Fields' Broadway Music Hall, West 29th Street west of Broadway, 1892–1911
Knickerbocker Theatre,[42] 1396 Broadway at northeast corner of 38th Street, 1893–1930
American Theatre,[43] 260 West 42nd Street at Eighth Avenue, 1893–1932
Empire Theatre, 1430 Broadway between 40th and 41st streets, 1893–1953
International Theatre,[44] 5 Columbus Circle, 1893–1954
Irving Place Theatre, 11 Irving Place at 15th Street, 1893–1985
Harlem Music Hall, 125th Street between Seventh and Eighth avenues, from 1894
Olympia Theatre,[45] Broadway between 44th and 45th streets, 1895–1935
Proctor's Pleasure Palace,[46] 58th Street between Lexington and Park avenues, from 1895
Grand Palace Theatre, Lexington Avenue and 43rd Street, 1896–1910
Murray Hill Theatre,[47] Lexington Avenue between 41st and 42nd streets, 1896–1950
Montauk Theatre, 587 Fulton Street, Brooklyn, 1899–1906
Victoria Theatre,[48] northwest corner of West 42nd Street and Seventh Avenue, 1899–1935
Henry McCaddin Memorial Theatre, Berry Street near South Third Street, Brooklyn, 1900–?15
Republic Theatre,[49] 207 West 42nd Street, from 1900
Circle Theatre,[50] 1825 Broadway at Columbus Circle, 1901–54
Folly Theatre Broadway, Graham and Flushing avenues, Brooklyn, 1902–9
New Amsterdam Theatre,[51] 214 West 42nd Street, from 1903
Hudson Theatre,[52] 139 West 44th Street, from 1903
Lyric Theatre,[53] 213 West 42nd Street, 1903–96
Lyceum Theatre, 149 West 45th Street, from 1903
Liberty Theatre,[54] 234 West 42nd Street, from 1904
Wallack's Theatre,[55] 254 West 42nd Street, from 1904
Hippodrome, Sixth Avenue between 43rd and 44th streets, 1905–39
Colonial Theatre, 1887 Broadway at 62nd Street, 1905–77
Majestic Theatre,[56] Fulton Street between Rockwell and Ashland places, Brooklyn, from 1905
Astor Theatre,[57] 1537 Broadway at 45th Street, 1906–82
Manhattan Opera House,[58] 311 West 34th Street, from 1906
Belasco Theatre,[59] 111 West 44th Street, from 1907
Maxine Elliott's Theatre, 109 West 39th Street, 1908–59
Brooklyn Academy of Music, 30 Lafayette Street, Brooklyn, from 1908
Orpheum Theatre, 126 Second Avenue, from 1908
Century Theatre, Central Park West between 62nd and 63rd streets, 1909–30
Comedy Theatre, 108 West 41st Street, 1909–42
Gaiety Theatre,[60] 1547 Broadway between 45th and 46th streets, 1909–82
Jefferson Theatre, East 14th Street between Third and Fourth avenues, *ca* 1910–20
Lunt–Fontanne Theatre,[61] 205 West 46th Street, from 1910
Thirty-Ninth Street Theatre,[62] 119 West 39th Street, 1910–26
Winter Garden Theatre, 1634 Broadway between 50th and 51st streets, from 1911
George M. Cohan's Theatre, 1482 Broadway at 43rd Street, 1911–38
Playhouse Theatre, 137 West 48th Street, 1911–68
Helen Hayes Theatre,[63] 210 West 46th Street, 1911–82
Cort Theatre, 148 West 48th Street, from 1912
Helen Hayes Theatre,[64] 238 West 44th Street, from 1912
Eltinge Theatre,[65] 236 West 42nd Street, from 1912
Forty-Eighth Street Theatre, 157 West 48th Street, 1912–55
Palace Theatre, 1564 Broadway at 46th Street, from 1913
Booth Theatre, 222 West 45th Street, from 1913
Longacre Theatre,[66] 222 West 48th Street, from 1913
Shubert Theatre, 225 West 44th Street, from 1913
Forty-Fourth Street Theatre,[67] 216 West 44th Street, 1913–45
Princess Theatre,[68] 104 West 39th Street, 1913–55
Charles Hopkins Theatre,[69] 155 West 49th Street, 1914–87
Sam H. Harris Theatre,[70] 226 West 42nd Street, 1914–96
Lewisohn Stadium,[71] 136th to 138th streets between Amsterdam and Convent avenues, 1915–66

(*continued*)

Theaters within the Present Boundaries of New York City, by Date of Founding (*Continued*)

Folksbiene Playhouse, 175 East Broadway, from 1915–1980s
Harry De Jur Playhouse,[72] 466 Grand Street, from 1915
Plymouth Theatre,[73] 236 West 45th Street, from 1917
Bijou Theatre, 217 West 45th Street, 1917–82
Morosco Theatre, 222 West 45th Street, 1917–82
Broadhurst Theatre, 235 West 44th Street, from 1917
Henry Miller's Theatre,[74] 124 West 43rd Street, from 1918
Selwyn Theatre,[75] 229 West 42nd Street, from 1918
Central Theatre,[76] 1567 Broadway at 47th Street, from 1918
Belmont Theatre,[77] 125 West 48th Street, 1918–51
Vanderbilt Theatre,[78] 128 West 48th Street, 1918–54
Apollo Theatre,[79] 223 West 42nd Street, 1920–96
Times Square Theatre,[80] 219 West 42nd Street, from 1920
Ritz Theatre,[81] 233 West 48th Street, from 1921
Music Box Theatre, 239 West 45th Street, from 1921
Nederlander Theatre,[82] 208 West 41st Street, from 1921
The Town Hall, 123 West 43rd Street, from 1921
Ambassador Theatre, 215 West 49th Street, from 1921
Forty-Ninth Street Theatre,[83] 235 West 49th Street, 1921–40
Klaw Theatre,[84] 251 West 45th Street, 1921–54
New Century Theatre,[85] 932 Seventh Avenue between 58th and 59th streets, 1921–62
Provincetown Playhouse, 123 MacDougal Street, 1921–2009
Earl Carroll Theatre,[86] 753 Seventh Avenue at 50th Street, 1922–90
Imperial Theatre, 249 West 45th Street, from 1923
Martin Beck Theatre,[87] 302 West 45th Street, from 1924
Broadway Theatre,[88] 1681 Broadway at 53rd Street, from 1924
Richard Rodgers Theatre,[89] 226 West 46th Street, from 1924
Cherry Lane Theatre, 38 Commerce Street, from 1924
Steinway Hall, 109 West 57th Street, from 1925
Eugene O'Neill Theatre,[90] 230 West 49th Street, from 1925
Biltmore Theatre,[91] 261 West 47th Street, from 1925
August Wilson Theatre,[92] 245 West 52nd Street, from 1925
Elysee Theatre,[93] 202 West 58th Street, 1925–85
Brooks Atkinson Theatre,[94] 256 West 47th Street, from 1926
Yiddish Art Theatre,[95] 189 Second Avenue at 12th Street, from 1926
Paramount Theatre, 1501 Broadway, 1926–65
Waldorf Theatre,[96] 116 West 50th Street, 1926–68
President Theatre,[97] 247 West 48th Street, 1926–88
John Golden Theatre,[98] 252 West 45th Street, from 1926
New Yorker Theatre,[99] 254 West 54th Street, from 1927
Royale Theatre,[100] 242 West 45th Street, from 1927
Ed Sullivan Theatre,[101] 1697 Broadway between 53rd and 54th streets, from 1927
St. James Theatre,[102] 246 West 44th Street, from 1927
Majestic Theatre, 245 West 44th Street, from 1927
Neil Simon Theatre,[103] 250 West 52nd Street, from 1927
Ziegfeld Theatre,[104] northwest corner of Sixth Avenue and 54th Street, 1927–66
Century Theatre,[105] 235 West 46th Street, from 1928
Ethel Barrymore Theatre, 243 West 47th Street, from 1928
George Abbott Theatre,[106] 152 West 54th Street, 1928–70
Kaufmann Concert Hall, Lexington Avenue at 92nd Street, from 1929
Mark Hellinger Theatre,[107] 237 West 51st Street, from 1930
Center Theatre,[108] Sixth Avenue between 48th and 49th streets, 1932–54
Radio City Music Hall, Sixth Avenue at 49th Street, from 1932
City Center,[109] 131 West 55th Street, from 1943
New Dramatists, 424 West 44th Street, from 1949
Circle in the Square, 189 Bleecker Street, from 1951
Lucille Lortel Theatre,[110] 121 Christopher Street, from 1954
Sheridan Square Playhouse, 99 Seventh Avenue South, 1958–96
Sullivan Street Playhouse, 181 Sullivan Street, from 1958
Delacorte Theatre, Central Park near West 81st Street, from 1962
St. Clement's Church,[111] 423 West 46th Street, from 1962
Lincoln Center for the Performing Arts, Broadway between 62nd and 66th streets, from 1962

(*continued*)

The breakdown of the traditional stock company, which had been the standard producing unit since before the American Revolution, and the advent of the combination company (a company formed for the run of one play and then disbanded) created a need for a new industry. Unlike the stock company, which was self-contained and produced scenery, costumes, and properties in its own shops, the combination company was transient, with neither theater nor shop facilities, and was forced to rely on businesses formed specifically to cater to its complex needs. A growing number of actors seeking work created a demand for agents; increased competition among theaters and the consequent demand for better publicity generated a market for the theatrical printer and the bill poster; and the sheer increase in the size of the theatrical community supported many new hotels and restaurants. During the 1870s the coalescence of these enterprises in one area, Union Square, created the first theater district in the city.

4. Union Square (1875–1900)

In the late nineteenth century the Union Square neighborhood was the site of appearances by such leading performers as the Booths, Adelaide Ristori, John McCullough, George L. Fox, Helena Modjeska, Maurice Barrymore, Mary Anderson, Henry Irving, and Ellen Terry. Among the theaters where they performed were the Fourteenth Street Theatre, the Union Square Theatre, and Wallack's Theatre, on Broadway at 13th Street. The area around Union Square was also a center of venues for popular entertainments: the Palace Garden, a pleasure garden on West 14th Street near Sixth Avenue; the Hippotheatron, on East 14th Street, which housed equestrian shows and in the 1870s the famous menagerie of P. T. Barnum; a hall on East 14th Street near Irving Place where Dan Bryant's Minstrels appeared; one of the city's largest panoramas, the Battle of Gettysburg, on Fourth Avenue between 18th and 19th streets; two of the most popular dime museums in the city, Huber's (on East 14th Street adjacent to Lüchow's) and Bunnell's Museum (on the northwest corner of Broadway and Ninth Street); and several small-time variety theaters. The best-known theater in New York City devoted exclusively to popular entertainment was the New Fourteenth Street Theatre of Tony Pastor, which was widely renowned as the birthplace of vaudeville; it was regarded as having the best, most wholesome variety entertainment in the city and the widest array of stars, which included the vaudevillians Russell, May Irwin, Nat Goodwin, the team of Harrigan and Hart, Denman Thompson, Pat Rooney, and Sophie Tucker. The Academy of Music, on the corner of East 14th Street and Irving Place, was built expressly for opera (as only three other theaters in the city before it had been). Meanwhile, the Park Theatre in Brooklyn achieved its greatest success under the management of Colonel

William E. Sinn (1875–95). When the Brooklyn Theatre was destroyed in 1876 by what was then the worst theater fire in U.S. history (295 died), Sinn and others improved their shows, and there was a boom in the construction of theaters in Brooklyn during the 1880s and 1890s.

By 1900 the city's legitimate theaters established themselves along the streets around Long Acre Square (now Times Square). The area surrounding Union Square was given over to dime museums, film studios (including the Biograph Studios at 11 East 14th Street), and movie theaters, while Second Avenue below 14th Street had become the locus for Yiddish theater. At the same time the theater increasingly underwent structural changes: not only had the stock system been displaced by the combination company and the theater become a thriving, lucrative industry, but the actor-manager in the mold of Brougham, Wallack, William Mitchell, and William Burton had been supplanted by the producer. Businessmen like A. M. Palmer, Marc Klaw, Abraham Erlanger, Charles and Daniel Frohman, and the brothers Sam S., Lee, and J(acob) J. Shubert were astute entrepreneurs with little or no stage experience. A turning point was marked in 1896 when the firm of Klaw and Erlanger, which controlled or leased many theaters nationwide, joined forces with the producer Charles Frohman, the booking agent Al(bert) Hayman, and two theater owners from Philadelphia, S. F. Nixon and J. F. Zimmerman, to standardize chaotic booking practices. The result was the Theatrical Syndicate, which soon held a monopoly on American theater production.

5. Times Square (after 1900)

By 1904 it was estimated that the Theatrical Syndicate controlled more than 500 theaters and had a virtual stranglehold on American theater, employing a blacklist to keep both the acting profession and independent theater owners in line. Although a few theater professionals were courageous enough to challenge the power of the Theatrical Syndicate (among them Harrison Grey Fiske, Minnie Maddern Fiske, and David Belasco), there were no serious threats to its monopoly until the early twentieth century, when the Shubert brothers built a theatrical empire in direct opposition to it. Compared with the Theatrical Syndicate the Shuberts at first appeared to be the benevolent saviors of American theater, but as they continued to acquire theaters, it became apparent that they were creating an organization as powerful and monopolistic as the syndicate had been, and that they used similar tactics. After the death in 1905 of Sam S. Shubert in a train wreck, his brothers continued to work together; by 1925 they controlled the legitimate theater. But the influence of the Shuberts was minimal in Queens, Staten Island, and the Bronx, where professional theater was not standard fare. Repertory companies

Theaters within the Present Boundaries of New York City, by Date of Founding (*Continued*)

Public Theatre,[112] 425 Lafayette Street, from 1967
Theatre 80 St. Marks, 80 St. Mark's Place, from 1967
Theater at Madison Square Garden, Eighth Avenue at 32nd Street, from 1968
The Kitchen, 512 West 19th Street, from 1971
Circle in the Square Theatre, 253 West 50th Street, from 1972
George Gershwin Theatre,[113] 222 West 51st Street, from 1972
Minskoff Theatre, 1515 Broadway between 44th and 45th streets, from 1972
Marquis Theatre, 1535 Broadway at 45th Street, from 1986
Hilton Theatre,[114] from 1998

1. Corbett Tavern and the Playhouse on Broadway may have been the same; sources differ.
2. May have been at Pearl (Queen) Street and Maiden Lane (Garden Street), but more likely on Nassau Street between Maiden Lane and John Street. The building stood until 1765, though it was used as a theater only until 1754.
3. In business only for a short time; the owner, David Douglass, had neglected to obtain permission for the theater and left for Philadelphia, returning in 1761 to open a theater on Beekman Street.
4. At Broadway and Exchange Alley until 1797.
5. Originally known as the New Theater in the Park.
6. Later known as the Covent Garden Theatre.
7. Known as Charley White's Opera House from 1860.
8. Originally the Italian Opera House, 1833–36.
9. Known as Das Alte Stadt Theater, 1854–64.
10. Also known as Mitchell's.
11. Also known as Purdy's New National Theatre.
12. Known as Burton's Chambers Street Theatre from 1848.
13. Replaced Niblo's Garden Theatre, which had burned in 1846, on same site.
14. Later known as Wallack's Lyceum.
15. Also known as Metropolitan Hall and by various other names from 1854–59; known as Winter Garden from 1859.
16. Known as Barnum's, 1865–68.
17. Building housed the Palladium nightclub in the mid-1990s; demolished by New York University in 1998.
18. Became the Olympic in 1863.
19. Known as Tony Pastor's Opera House 1865–75, People's Theatre 1883–1901, and Yiddish Theatre from 1902.
20. Known as the Windsor, 1878–1910.
21. Later known as the New Theatre Comique.
22. Various names, including Lucy Rushington's (1865), the Globe (1870), and the Theatre Comique (1881).
23. Known as the Madison Square Theatre from 1877.
24. Later known as the Grand Opera House.
25. Also known as Old Koster and Bial's.
26. Also known as Gilmore's Garden, P. T. Barnum's Hippodrome.
27. Destroyed by fire 1876; rebuilt 1879.
28. Known as the Standard (1878–97) and Manhattan Theatre (1897–1909).
29. Also known as the American; became a movie theater in 1909.
30. Also known as Tony Pastor's.
31. Also known as the Bijou Theatre from 1883.
32. Also known as the Germania Theatre.
33. Known as the Metropolitan Concert Hall (1880–88).
34. Also known as the National, Adler's Theatre, the Columbian Theatre, the Roumanian Theatre, and by other names.
35. Became Proctor's Theatre in 1889.
36. Also known as the Harlem Theatre.
37. Known as the Novelty Theatre (1886–88,) Blaneys (1902–4), and the Novelty (from 1904).
38. Known as Haverley's (1879) and Fourteenth Street Theatre (1886); became a movie theater 1908.
39. Became a movie theater and vaudeville house 1913.
40. Became the Garrick Theatre in 1895.
41. Later known as Koster and Bial's New Music Hall.
42. Known as Abbey's Theatre, 1893–96.
43. Became a movie theater in 1911.
44. Known as the Majestic until 1908, then by various names until 1944. Became a television studio 1949.
45. Later known as the Criterion.
46. Also known as Proctor's 58th.
47. Site of the Socony–Mobil Building; may have been demolished earlier.
48. Became a movie theater 1915; known as the Rialto from 1916.

(*continued*)

Theaters within the Present Boundaries of New York City, by Date of Founding (*Continued*)

49. Known as the Belasco (1900–1910); converted to a Minsky's Burlesque in 1931; became the Victory, a movie theater, in 1942; restored as a main stage and reopened 1995 as New Victory Theatre.
50. Became a movie theater in 1917.
51. Became a movie theater in 1937, but resumed operation as a main-stage theater from 1997 under a lease with Walt Disney Theatrical Productions.
52. Controlled by the Columbia Broadcasting System (1934–37) and the National Broadcasting Company (1950–59), used as a movie theater 1967–80 and a nightclub 1980–83. Used as a conference center and auditorium for adjacent hotel since 1987.
53. Became a movie theater in 1934.
54. Became a movie theater in 1933, through 1980s. In 2000 Madame Tussaud's Wax Museum was built on the site, retaining the building's exterior structure.
55. Known by various names until 1924, as Wallack's (1924–31), and as the Anco (from 1940). Became a movie theater in 1931, interior gutted 1988.
56. Became a movie theater in 1942; abandoned in 1968. Acquired by Brooklyn Academy of Music in 1987 and returned to service as a main-stage theater. Known from 1999 as the BAM Harvey Lichtenstein Theatre.
57. Became a movie theater in 1925, closed 1972; demolished 1982.
58. Known as the Stuyvesant until 1910.
59. Became a Minsky's Burlesque in 1932; renamed the Victoria in 1943; became a movie theater in 1943; demolished 1982.
60. Later known as Manhattan Center. Acquired by Unification Church 1976.
61. Originally at 1555 Broadway. Known as the Globe until 1958; used as a movie theater from 1932–57.
62. Also known as Nazimova's.
63. Known as the Folies Bergère April–Oct 1911; as the Fulton Theatre until 1955.
64. Known as the Little Theatre (until 1931), Times Hall (1931–63), and Winthrop Ames Theatre (1963–82).
65. Became a movie theater in 1942. Entire building moved 200 feet (61 meters) east of original location in 1998 to become lobby and facade of AMC Empire 25 multiplex. Interior destroyed.
66. Used for radio and television, 1943–53.
67. Originally Weber and Fields' Broadway Music Hall. Basement was the site of the Stage Door Canteen, 1941–43.
68. Was the Labor Stage briefly in the late 1930s; became a movie theater in 1933.
69. Known as the Candler (until 1916), and as Cohan and Harris (until 1921); became a movie theater in the 1930s.
70. Known as the Punch and Judy until 1926; showed movies as the World Theatre from 1933. Became the Embassy 49th Street Theatre in 1982.
71. Part of City College. Demolished 1973.
72. Also known as Henry Street Playhouse.
73. Known as the Gerald Schoenfeld Theatre from 2005, after the chairman of the Schubert Organization from 1972–2008.
74. Became a movie theater 1969; later the site of the nightclubs Xenon (1978) and Shout.
75. Became a movie theater in 1934. Returned to use as a main stage in 2000. Known as the American Airlines Theatre from 2000.
76. From 1921 through 1957, alternated movies and live theater; operated as a movie theater alone through 1988. Lobby became Roxy Deli; auditorium became dance club. Auditorium demolished 2005 to make way for W Hotel.
77. Originally known as the Norworth.
78. Used as a radio studio, 1939–53.
79. Known as the Bryant until 1938; showed films 1938–78; became the Academy cabaret 1987.
80. Used as movie theater, 1933–97.
81. Used as radio studio, 1943–65. Dark through 1969, it reopened in 1971. Bought by Jujamcyn in 1981 and renovated in 1989. Known as the Walter Kerr Theatre from 1990.
82. Known as the National Theatre until 1959, later as the Billy Rose Theatre.
83. Became a movie theater in 1938.
84. Known as the Avon Theatre from 1929.
85. Known as Jolson's 59th Street Theatre until 1934; used as a movie theater 1934–37; known as the New Century from 1944; acquired by the National Broadcasting Company 1954. Demolished 1962.
86. Used as a nightclub 1933–39. Acquired by Woolworth's 1939; interior demolished. Razed 1990.
87. Known as the Al Hirschfeld Theatre from 2003.
88. Known as B. S. Moss's Colony until 1930 and B. S. Moss's Broadway until 1939. Bought by the Shuberts in 1939, who turned it into a legitimate house.
89. Known as the Forty-Sixth Street Theatre until 1990.
90. Known as Forrest Theatre (1925–45) and Coronet Theatre (1945–59).
91. Known as the Samuel J. Friedman Theatre from 2008.
92. Built as the Guild Theatre; renamed the Virginia in 1982; known since 2005 as the August Wilson.
93. Known originally as the Golden; became a movie theater in 1936; later a film and television studio.

(*continued*)

like the Brooklyn Comedy Company visited the Jamaica Opera House, but entertainment consisted largely of musical evenings, balls, amateur theatrical productions, and lectures. The Bronx Theatre opened in 1908, the first of many vaudeville houses situated on or near East 149th Street, an area known as the Hub.

During these years there was a growing dissatisfaction among actors with their working conditions, particularly with regard to rehearsals, which were unpaid and unlimited; moreover, actors often found themselves stranded on the road without sufficient funds to pay for their train fare back to New York City. The theater managers at first refused to redress the actors' grievances, and the phrase "starve the actors out" became their rallying cry. The managers' attitude changed only when the actors went on strike moments before curtain time on 6 August 1919, and a contract between the managers and Actors' Equity was signed on 6 September.

While the economic structure of the professional theater was moving toward centralized control, an upheaval of similar magnitude was occurring in American dramaturgy. During the early years of the twentieth century the work of the European Realists and of the native dramatists James A. Herne, Augustus Thomas, Clyde Fitch, William Vaughn Moody, Eugene Walter, and Ned Sheldon created a demand for psychological realism and for drama that was more socially aware than its nineteenth-century predecessors had been. This change in attitudes did not endanger traditional melodrama or escapist works, but it altered the climate on Broadway. In the 1920s audiences took a growing interest in plays by Henrik Ibsen, George Bernard Shaw, Anton Chekhov, Sean O'Casey, and Luigi Pirandello, on Broadway as well as in the avant-garde theaters of Greenwich Village. New York City was visited by the Moscow Art Theatre (led by Konstantin Stanislavsky), the Comédie Française, the well-known Chinese actor Mei Lan-fang, the Spanish Art Theatre, Austrian director Max Reinhardt, Habima (a troupe from Israel), and the Italian star Elenora Duse. A remarkable number of young American playwrights came to prominence in the 1920s, among them Elmer Rice, George S. Kaufman, Marc Connelly, Maxwell Anderson, Paul Green, Sidney Howard, and Robert E. Sherwood. Eugene O'Neill saw 14 of his plays produced during the decade, including *Beyond the Horizon* (1920–21), *Anna Christie* (1921–22), and *Strange Interlude* (1927–28), all of which won the Pulitzer Prize, as well as *The Emperor Jones* (1921), *The Hairy Ape* (1922), and *Desire under the Elms* (1925).

During the 1920s artists who had been prominent in the experimental theater of the 1910s began to work on Broadway, thus infusing it with some of the experimental spirit that had been generated in Greenwich Village. The Theatre Guild, which had begun in 1914 as the Washington Square Players to provide an alternative to the mainstream theater (see §6, below), emerged as a major Broadway producer, and regular performances were given of such innovative works as O'Neill's *Mourning Becomes Electra* (1931) and *Strange Interlude* (1928), Elmer Rice's expressionistic work *The Adding Machine* (1923), John Howard Lawson's *Processional* (1925, which the author called a "jazz symphony of American life"), Georg Kaiser's *From Morn to Midnight* (1912), and Ernst Toller's *Man and the Masses* (1924). Yet the experimental spirit did little to dampen the popular taste for entertainments that challenged neither the conventions of the stage nor the mind of the viewer: garish revues like Florenz Ziegfeld's *Follies* (1912), Earl Carroll's *Vanities* (1924), and the Shuberts' *Passing Shows* retained their popularity in the early 1920s; vaudeville remained in fashion until the end of the decade; and racy melodramas, saccharine comedies, and other innocuous fare in the vein of *Lightnin'* (1925, by Winchell Smith and Frank Bacon), *Rain* (1922, by John B. Colton and Clemence Randolph, after the short story by W. Somerset Maugham), *The Bat* (1926, by Avery Hopwood and Mary Roberts Rinehart), and *Abie's Irish Rose* (1922, by Anne Nichols) continued to set records for long runs.

During the same years the American musical moved away from the stereotyped romantic characters, formulaic plots, and fairyland settings of the comic operas of Victor Herbert, Rudolph Friml, and Sigmund Romberg. In musicals like *Show Boat* (1927), by Jerome Kern and Oscar Hammerstein II, and *Of Thee I Sing* (1931), by George Gershwin, and in Gershwin's opera *Porgy and Bess* (1935), more serious subjects were addressed, the musical numbers advanced the dramatic action, and the characters sang songs that expressed their personalities. Vincent Youmans, Cole Porter, Richard Rodgers, and Lorenz Hart also wrote works in the 1920s that established new goals and standards for musical comedy. Economically the 1920s were a peak for the theater, and the 1927–28 season still stands as the most successful in New York City's history: 264 shows opened in 76 Broadway theaters. This prosperity was, however, short-lived, as the "talkies," introduced in 1926–27, siphoned audiences away from burlesque and other live theater, and the Depression severely curtailed production. By the 1930–31 season only 187 shows opened in 64 theaters, and the signs of a decline in production were evident.

Along with widespread poverty the Depression brought unemployment to 5000 actors in the city and roughly 25,000 theater workers nationwide. The theater became politicized as leftist organizers saw that drama could be used as an ideological weapon. In New York City capitalism underwent stinging critiques at the hands of the Workers' Laboratory Theatre, the German-language company the Proletbuhne, the Theatre Collective, the Theatre Union, and the Group Theatre, which gave the American theater not only the playwright Clifford Odets but also the actors Morris Carnovsky, Ruth Nelson, Franchot Tone, John Garfield, and Lee J. Cobb; the directors Harold Clurman and Elia Kazan; Lee Strasberg, founder of the Actors' Studio; and Stella Adler, founder of her own acting school. The Depression also prompted the federal government to become a theatrical producer through its Federal Theatre Project. Formed under the auspices of the Works Progress Administration and administered by Hallie Flanagan, a drama professor and director of the Experimental Theatre at Vassar College, the project set as its central goal the reemployment of theater people who were on relief rolls. To this end it began a number of ventures ranging from regional theaters to an experimental theater wing to popular entertainments. Although the Federal Theatre Project was national, New York City was the site of its largest branch, which encompassed a Black Theatre wing, a troupe called the Living Newspaper that produced social documentaries, and offices that functioned as a national service center for the project. The *Federal Times Magazine* was published and distributed there, and the offices also housed a play-reading center and a bibliographic service. More important, some of the best-known works of the project were originated in the city, including *It Can't Happen Here* (1936, after the novel by Sinclair Lewis; adapted by Lewis and John C. Moffitt), *One Third of a Nation* (1938, by Arthur Arent), and *Triple A Plowed Under* (1936, the writing of which was supervised by Arent).

The 1940s and 1950s were a contradictory period in American theater. During World War II the New York City stage was dominated by escapist froth (*Arsenic and Old Lace*, 1941, by Joseph Kesselring; *My Sister Eileen*, 1940, by Joseph Fields and Jerome Chodorov; *Harvey*, 1944, by Mary C. Chase; *Life with Father*, 1939, by Howard Lindsay and Russel Crouse) and patriotic dramas (*Candle in the Wind*, 1941, and *Storm Operation*, 1944, by

Theaters within the Present Boundaries of New York City, by Date of Founding (*Continued*)

94. Known as the Mansfield Theatre until 1960.
95. Became Village East Cinema in 1992.
96. Became a movie theater in 1933; used for shops from 1941.
97. Originally the Edyth Totten, known by various names until 1956. Part of Mamma Leone's restaurant until 1988.
98. Known as the Theatre Masque until 1937.
99. Known as the Gallo Theatre until 1943, used for radio and television by the Columbia Broadcasting System from 1943. Later the site of the nightclubs Studio 54 (1977–80) and the Ritz (1989–96). Known as Studio 54 from 1998. Acquired by the Roundabout Theater Company in 2003 after a successful revival of Cabaret was staged there.
100. Known as the Bernard B. Jacobs Theatre from 2005.
101. Known as Hammerstein's until 1931; used for radio and television by the Columbia Broadcasting Company from 1936. Renamed for Ed Sullivan 1967.
102. Known as Erlanger's Theatre until 1932.
103. Originally known as the Alvin Theatre.
104. Used as a television studio, 1955–63.
105. Originally known as Billy Rose's Diamond Horseshoe.
106. Known as the Craig Theatre until 1934; the Adelphi (1934–39); the Fifty-Fourth Street Theatre (1939–65).
107. Used as a movie theater until 1934. Known as the Hollywood until 1936 and the Fifty-First Street Theatre until 1949; leased (from 1989), then sold to the Times Square Church in 1991.
108. Showed films as the RKO Roxy and RKO Center until 1934.
109. Built as meeting hall for the Ancient and Accepted Order of Nobles of the Mystic Shrine 1923.
110. Originally the Theatre de Lys.
111. Built in 1872 as the Faith Chapel of the West Presbyterian Church, used since 1920 as an Episcopal parish church. Interior reconfigured in 1962 as small proscenium theater.
112. Founded as the Shakespeare Workshop 1954; housed in the former Astor Library building on Lafayette Street from 1967.
113. Known as the Uris Theatre until 1983.
114. Opened in 1998 as the Ford Center for the Performing Arts on the location of the Lyric Theatre, retaining the Lyric's 42nd Street and 43rd Street facades.

Sources: Ruth C. Dimmick, *Our Theatres To-Day and Yesterday* (New York: H.K. Fly, 1913); Mary C. Henderson, *The City and the Theatre: New York Playhouses from Bowling Green to Times Square* (Clifton, N.J.: James T. White, 1973); John W. Frick and Carlton Ward, eds., *Directory of Historic American Theatres* (New York: Greenwood, 1987); Timothy J. Gilfoyle, *City of Eros: New York City, Prostitution and the Commercialization of Sex, 1790–1920* (New York: W. W. Norton, 1992); Jodé Susan Millman and Sandy Millman, *Seats New York: 180 Seating Plans to New York Metro Area Theaters, Concert Halls, and Sports Stadiums* (New York: Limelight Editions, 2008); "The Internet Broadway Database," http://www.ibdb.com

Compiled by Alana J. Erickson, Andrew A. Kryzak

Maxwell Anderson; and the classic of the genre, *Watch on the Rhine,* 1941, by Lillian Hellman). After the war American playwriting experienced a renaissance, which for a short time seemed to presage a second flowering of native dramaturgy. Among the high points of this period were the production of O'Neill's *The Iceman Cometh* (1946) and *Long Day's Journey into Night* (1956) and of the early plays of Arthur Miller (*All My Sons,* 1947; *Death of a Salesman,* 1949; an adaptation of Ibsen's *An Enemy of the People,* 1950; *The Crucible,* 1953; *A Memory of Two Mondays* and *A View from the Bridge,* 1955), Tennessee Williams (*The Glass Menagerie,* 1945; *A Streetcar Named Desire,* 1947; *Summer and Smoke,* 1948; *The Rose Tattoo,* 1951; *Camino Real,* 1953; *Cat on a Hot Tin Roof,* 1955; *Orpheus Descending,* 1957; *Sweet Bird of Youth,* 1959), and William Inge (*Come Back Little Sheba,* 1950; *Picnic,* 1953; *Bus Stop,* 1955; *The Dark at the Top of the Stairs,* 1957). At the same time the playwriting careers of Odets, Hellman, and William Saroyan declined.

The economic troubles besetting New York City theater that had begun in the mid-1920s continued in the 1940s and 1950s. Fewer shows opened each year in fewer active Broadway houses, and it took longer to make back the "nut" (the income needed to recoup the cost of mounting a production). Opportunities for productions other than musicals continued to dwindle as the costs of producing even a small-cast comedy or drama soared. But musical comedy thrived during this period, largely because it was increasingly favored by the public: librettos continued to improve, themes became generally more substantial, and the production of *Oklahoma!* (1943), by Rodgers and Hammerstein, heralded a greater synthesis of libretto, score, and dance. During the succeeding decades nonmusical comedies were gradually displaced as the longest-running shows on Broadway by musicals (*My Fair Lady,* 1956, by Alan Jay Lerner and Frederick Loewe; *Annie,* 1977, by Charles Strouse and Martin Charnin; *Hello, Dolly!,* 1964, by Jerry Herman; *Fiddler on the Roof,* 1964, by Jerry Bock and Sheldon Harnick; *Grease,* 1974, by Jim Jacobs and Warren Casey), which soon gained recognition as the economic bedrock of Broadway.

The early 1960s introduced Broadway audiences to two playwrights who were influential in shaping theater in New York City. Edward Albee was controversial and often esoteric (*Who's Afraid of Virginia Woolf?* 1962; *Tiny Alice,* 1964; *A Delicate Balance,* 1966); Neil Simon was popular and extremely prolific: during the 1960s alone his output encompassed *Come Blow Your Horn* (1961), the book for *Little Me* (1962), the book for *Sweet Charity* (1962), *Barefoot in the Park* (1963), *The Odd Couple* (1965), *The Star-Spangled Girl* (1966), *Plaza Suite* (1968), and the book for *Promises, Promises* (1968).

Manhattan's theater fared better than that in the other boroughs. Although Brooklyn had been part of the vaudeville subway circuit until the late 1920s, by the mid-twentieth century its legitimate theater barely existed. The Brooklyn Center for the Performing Arts opened at Brooklyn College in 1955, and smaller venues like the Billie Holiday Theatre in Bedford–Stuyvesant were founded in subsequent decades. The Brooklyn Academy of Music, refurbished in the 1960s, remained at the center of Brooklyn theater—and at the forefront of New York City's alternative theater—into the early twenty-first century. Stage performance in Queens, Staten Island, and the Bronx was largely displaced by movie theaters and was left to college theater programs and local troupes, like the Selma and Max Kupferberg Center at Queens College and the Lehman Center for the Performing Arts at Lehman College in the Bronx. After being shuttered for years, the St. George Theatre in

Broadway Theaters, by Seating Capacity

Theater	Estimated Seating Capacity (including wheelchairs)	Year Opened
George Gershwin, 222 West 51st St.	1,935	1972
Hilton, 213 West 42nd St.	1,829	1998
New Amsterdam, 214 West 42nd St.	1,801	1903
Broadway, 1681 Broadway	1,763	1924
Palace, 1564 Broadway	1,740	1913
St. James, 246 West 46th St.	1,710	1927
Majestic, 247 West 44th St.	1,650	1927
Marquis, 1535 Broadway	1,611	1986
Minskoff, 200 West 45th St.	1,597	1973
Winter Garden, 1634 Broadway	1,529	1911
Lunt–Fontanne, 205 West 46th St.	1,505	1910
Shubert, 225 West 44th St.	1,465	1913
Imperial, 249 West 45th St.	1,445	1923
Neil Simon, 250 West 52nd St.	1,445	1927
Richard Rodgers, 226 West 46th St.	1,319	1924
Al Hirschfeld, 302 West 45th St.	1,292	1924
Nederlander, 208 West 41st St.	1,232	1921
August Wilson, 245 West 52nd St.	1,222	1925
Broadhurst, 235 West 44th St.	1,160	1917
Ambassador, 219 West 49th St.	1,120	1921
Eugene O'Neill, 230 West 49th St.	1,108	1925
Ethel Barrymore, 243 West 47th St.	1,096	1928
Longacre, 220 West 48th St.	1,095	1913
Cort, 138 West 48th St.	1,084	1912
Gerald Schoenfeld, 236 West 45th St.	1,081	1917
Bernard B. Jacobs, 242 West 45th St.	1,080	1927
Vivian Beaumont,* 150 West 65th St.	1,080	1965
Brooks Atkinson, 256 West 47th St.	1,069	1926
Belasco, 111 West 44th St.	1,043	1907
Music Box, 239 West 45th St.	1,013	1921
Walter Kerr, 219 West 48th St.	947	1921
Lyceum, 149 West 45th St.	924	1903
Studio 54,254 West 54th St.	922	1927
John Golden, 252 West 45th St.	806	1927
Circle in the Square, 235 West 50th St.	776	1972
Booth, 222 West 45th St.	768	1913
American Airlines, 227 West 42nd St.	740	1918
Biltmore, 261 West 47th St.	650	1925
Helen Hayes, 240 West 44th St.	597	1912

*Only theater not in the theater district that houses productions qualified for Tony Awards

Sources: Internet Broadway Database, http://www.ibdb.com; The Shubert Organization, http://www.shubertorganization.com/; Nederlander Producing Company of America on Broadway, http://www.nederlander.com/Broadway.html

Compiled by Frank Nestor

Longest-Running Broadway Shows,* by Original Performance Run (as of 6 September 2009)

Show	Original Performance Run	Opening and Closing Years
Phantom of the Opera	8,987	1988–
Cats	7,485	1982–2000
Les Misérables	6,680	1987–2003
A Chorus Line	6,137	1975–90
Oh! Calcutta! (Revival)	5,959	1976–89
Beauty and the Beast	5,461	1994–2007
Chicago (Revival)	5,316	1996–
Rent	5,124	1996–2008
The Lion King	4,808	1997–
Miss Saigon	4,097	1991–2001
42nd Street	3,486	1980–89
Grease	3,388	1972–80
Mamma Mia!	3,264	2001–
Fiddler on the Roof	3,242	1964–72
Life with Father (play)	3,224	1939–47
Tobacco Road (play)	3,182	1933–41
Hello, Dolly!	2,844	1964–70
My Fair Lady	2,717	1956–62
Hairspray	2,641	2002–9
Avenue Q	2,534	2003–9
The Producers	2,502	2001–7
Wicked	2,422	2003–
Cabaret (Revival)	2,378	1998–2004
Annie	2,377	1977–83
Man of La Mancha	2,328	1965–71
Abie's Irish Rose (play)	2,327	1922–27
Oklahoma!	2,212	1943–48
Smokey Joe's Café	2,036	1995–2000
Pippin	1,944	1972–77
South Pacific	1,925	1949–54

*All shows are musicals unless noted.
Source: Ernio Hernandez, "Long Runs on Broadway," http://www.playbill.com/celebritybuzz/article/75222.html
Compiled by Frank Nestor

Staten Island was restored in 2007 and staged music, theater, and opera productions.

By the late twentieth century the cost of Broadway shows had reached an average of $8 million, a successful run of 60 to 65 weeks was required to reimburse investors, and ticket prices ran as high as $100 a seat. The mainstream theater had grown increasingly dependent on revivals, spectacle, and imports from Britain (especially those by Andrew Lloyd Webber) and on such promotional and sales devices as package tours, "two-fers," and half-priced tickets from the "TKTS" booths in Times Square and on Wall Street. While detractors viewed these developments as symptoms of weakness and even impending doom, its supporters saw them as signs of the theater's ability to adapt to changing economic and artistic currents. In 1990–91 Broadway theaters drew 7.36 million spectators. Because tourists accounted for a high percentages of Broadway audiences, ticket sales slumped after the terrorist attacks of 11 September 2001, but by 2005 they had risen to record-breaking figures. During the 2007–8 Broadway season more than 12 million people attended performances, including 36 new productions. Broadway grossed about $937 million, a slight decline from the previous year due to a 2007 stagehand strike that darkened theaters for more than two weeks. Notable new productions included Tom Stoppard's Tony Award–winning winning trilogy *The Coast of Utopia* (2002, Broadway debut 2006), and Tracy Letts's *August: Osage County* (2007), which won the Pulitzer Prize for drama and the Tony Award for best play in 2008.

6. Alternative Theater: Art Theater, Off-Broadway, Off-Off-Broadway

By the second decade of the twentieth century many alternative theaters and companies flourished in the progressive environment of Greenwich Village. The Washington Square Players, formed in Greenwich Village in 1914 by Philip Moeller, Helen Westley, and Lawrence Langner, had the stated goal of producing "plays of artistic merit." After staging 62 one-act plays and six full-length plays the group was disbanded in 1918 and reorganized as the Theatre Guild, which became one of the leading production institutions in New York City, instrumental in introducing Americans to the plays of Shaw, Ibsen, Leonid Andreyev, Maurice Maeterlinck, and August Strindberg and in producing plays by O'Neill, Saroyan, Sherwood, Rice, and Philip Barry. The Theatre Guild was also one of the first American theater companies to exhibit the style of theater design known as the new stagecraft, which was practiced by Robert Edmond Jones and Lee Simonson. The Provincetown Players were established in 1915 as a playwrights' company presenting the works of Susan Glaspell, Theodore Dreiser, Edna St. Vincent Millay, and Green, but their most notable achievement was their advocacy of O'Neill and their staging of many of his early plays (first in a makeshift theater on a wharf in Provincetown, Massachusetts, and later in a small theater at 133 MacDougal Street). The Neighborhood Playhouse began in the Henry Street Settlement on the Lower East Side; it was endowed in 1915 by Alice and Irene Lewisohn and produced not only experimental playscripts (by O'Neill and Shaw, among others) but also avant-garde dance and music. During the 1920s actress and director Eva Le Gallienne established a company run on a strict repertory system (1926–31), which entailed a nightly change of bill and a nightly rotation of scenery. During the following decades alternative theater was for the most part confined to the agitprops (propaganda plays) and socially aware dramas of the Group Theatre and other left-wing troupes. The American Negro Theater was formed in 1940 and performed at the Schomburg Library on 135th Street; Sydney Poitier, Ruby Dee, and Harry Belafonte were affiliated with it. Like one of its predecessors, the Lafayette Players (formed in 1915 by Anita Bush), it was criticized for imitating Broadway.

The next important phase of alternative theatrical activity in New York City began on 24 April 1952, when Williams's *Summer and Smoke* opened at the Circle in the Square, an event widely regarded as marking the beginning of Off Broadway. When the production was reviewed by Brooks Atkinson, drama critic for the *New York Times,* public attention became focused on theater below 42nd Street, and Off Broadway was discovered, legitimated, and made economically viable. The cost of producing on Broadway had grown prohibitive, which meant that fewer new scripts could be staged; the increased conservatism of audiences and backers had severely limited production concepts and all but stifled creativity; and producers were using only experienced actors. In opening the Circle in the Square, its founders, José Quintero and Theodore Mann, were fighting the fiscal, artistic, and political conservatism of mainstream theater.

During the 1950s and early 1960s the commercialism of Broadway led to the formation of other companies (the Living Theatre of Julian Beck and Judith Malina, the New York Shakespeare Festival of Joseph Papp, the Phoenix Theatre) and individual playhouses (the Sullivan Street Playhouse, the Public Theater, the Theatre de Lys, and the Cherry Lane). In an environment that encouraged experimentation, such young, progressive artists as Beck and Malina, Quintero, Geraldine Page, George C. Scott, Peter Falk, Ellis Rabb, Jason Robards, and Dustin Hoffman tested their talents and ideas; scripts considered too risky for Broadway were staged; and a second hearing was given to some artists who were in danger of being forgotten (such as O'Neill and Williams). This nurturing milieu provided backing and a suitable environment for staging "small" musicals like *Little Mary Sunshine* (1959) and *The Fantasticks,* which ran for more than 17,000 performances (1960–2002) at the Sullivan Street Playhouse. The formation in 1967 of the Negro Ensemble Company was a landmark in attempts to forge an autonomous black theater. It staged works by such leading African American playwrights as Lorraine Hansberry, James Baldwin, LeRoi Jones (later known as Amiri Baraka), Douglas Turner Ward, Ed Bullins, Lonne Elder, and Charles Gordone. Other black companies such as AMAS Rep symbolized more than simply an alternative to the mainstream values of Broadway: they enabled blacks to enter the ranks of theatrical producers, dramatically represented black life, and in general promoted the goal articulated by W. E. B. Du Bois, that there should be a theater "about, by, for, and near" African Americans.

In the 1960s political, social, and artistic upheaval created the environment for yet another form of alternative theater, Off Off Broadway. Theatrical radicals rejected the professionally trained actor, the classics, conventional relations between actor and audience, the star system, and even the role of the playwright and the primacy of the script. The Caffe Cino, a small coffeehouse at 31 Cornelia Street, is generally acknowledged as the place where Off Off Broadway began. In 1958 the proprietor, Joe Cino, invited performers and writers to present their work; among those who did were the writers Jean-Claude van Itallie, Lanford Wilson, and Sam Shepard. The Caffe Cino closed when the proprietor took his own life in 1967, but other venues opened and continued to offer a forum for experimental work (Ellen Stewart's La MaMa Experimental Theatre Club, the Judson Poets' Theatre, Theatre Genesis). In the decades that followed, the rebellion inherent in Off Off Broadway became embodied in the iconoclasm and political activism of the Living Theatre; in ex-

Caravan Theatre, 1937

periments with the relation of actor to audience and with the creation of performance "environments" by Richard Schechner and the Performance Group; in the improvisational ensemble work of Joseph Chaikin and the Open Theater; in the use of masks and puppets and the public protests of the Bread and Puppet Theater; in Allan Kaprow's happenings; and in the high "camp" of Charles Ludlam's Ridiculous Theatrical Company.

By the 1980s alternative theater in New York City had grown more fragmented, eclectic, and private, encompassing black, Latin American, gay, and lesbian theater and artists and ensembles as diverse in their ideologies and aesthetics as Robert Wilson, JoAnne Akalaitis, Ethyl Eichelberger, Richard Foreman, Lee Breuer, the Wooster Group, Split Britches, and Michael Kirby's Structuralist Workshop. The alternative theater generated the most influential American playwrights of the 1970s and 1980s. Although their works were routinely produced on Broadway, the playwrights Lanford Wilson and August Wilson nevertheless created many of them for the Circle Repertory Theatre and the Yale Repertory Theatre, respectively. David Mamet generally premiered his plays Off Broadway—when they were performed in New York City at all. Shepard, whom many critics considered the most talented playwright of his generation, had his work produced in a prominent theater in New York City (*Operation Sidewinder* at the Vivian Beaumont Theater in Lincoln Center in 1970), but during the 1970s and 1980s he did not have his work produced even once in a Broadway theater. In the late twentieth and early twenty-first centuries festivals offered important theatrical venues: the New York International Fringe Festival was founded in 1997, and in 2008 it presented 1300 performances at more than 20 venues; the Summer Play Festival began in 2004, and in 2008 it began a partnership with the Public Theater. By offering low ticket prices, festivals were able to attract young theatergoers. Other alternative companies tried to broaden theater audiences: the critically acclaimed company Waterwell offered free tickets to veterans and high school students.

In the early twenty-first century the lines between Broadway and Off Broadway began to blur; many successful musical productions were staged Off Broadway and moved to Broadway in an effort to recoup investments. *Avenue Q* (2003), *Spring Awakening* (2006), and *Grey Gardens* (2006) garnered critical success Off Broadway and moved to Broadway within a year, each later winning Tony Awards. In 2008 tax-exempt Off-Broadway institutions had taken control of five Broadway theaters, further confusing the distinction. Off-Off-Broadway productions were more difficult to track, as the characteristics of this brand of theater made it nebulous and resistant to classification; about 1700 such productions were staged in 2006–7, for example.

7. The Business of the Theater

A variety of businesses and organizations in New York City help to mount theatrical productions and support the many people who work in the theater. Labor is by far the major resource used in theatrical production. In the early twentieth century the considerable growth in the number, size, and type of productions and the increasing role of technology led to the formation of theatrical unions and societies to establish contractual guidelines. A century later, theater owners and producers did business with many such organizations; which ones are involved in a given production will depend on the type of production (play, musical, opera, revue) and on the size and location of the theater. The principal unions and associations include the Dramatists Guild, which represents authors; Actors' Equity Association (which, along with six other performers' unions, is affiliated with the Associated Actors and Artistes of America), for professional actors and stage managers; the Society of Stage Directors and Choreographers; the United Scenic Artists of America, to which most scenic, costume, and lighting designers belong, along with scenic, mural, display, and diorama artists; Wardrobe Supervisors and Dressers, Local 764; the International Alliance of Theatrical Stage Employees, of which Local 1 in Manhattan represents all carpenters, stagehands, electricians, sound technicians, and property crewmen; Treasurers and Ticketsellers, Local 751; Porters and Cleaners-Service Employees in Amusement and Cultural Buildings, Local 54; the International Union of Operating Engineers, Local 30, for those who maintain heavy equipment, such as heating and air-conditioning engineers; Ushers and Doormen; the Association of Theatrical Press Agents and Managers; and the American Federation of Musicians, Local 802. In response to difficulties posed by these performers' and technicians' unions, after 1910 producers and theater owners formed their own association; this has undergone several reorganizations and changes of name and is now known as the League of American Theaters and Producers, a voluntary body with headquarters in the city.

Goods and services used in the theater are provided by many businesses in the metropolitan area, including builders and suppliers of scenery, lighting and sound equipment, costumes, and makeup. Traditionally these businesses were situated in and around the theater district, where "walk-in" business accounted for much of their trade, but over the years many moved out of Manhattan because of rapidly rising real estate costs and a lack of suitable space. The difficulty of moving goods in and out of midtown was especially troublesome for scenic studios, which deal in large, bulky items, and the majority of these studios relocated outside of Manhattan. Most production suppliers nonetheless chose to remain near Broadway because of the necessity of maintaining a connection with the theater district, no matter how tenuous.

Theater's growth in the late nineteenth century begat the rise of theatrical agents and managers. Agents advise, represent, and promote performers, playwrights, directors, and other creative artists; they arrange bookings in venues ranging from Broadway theaters to small cabarets, negotiate terms and contracts, and mediate disputes. Although in the early twenty-first century some agents operated independently and with only a few clients, large organizations like the William Morris Agency had thousands. Theatrical managers differ from agents in that they often provide their clients with legal and financial guidance.

Lucille Lortel Theatre, 2009

Theatrical publishing encompasses play publishers' and authors' representatives as well as trade and general-interest magazines and newspapers. The acting versions of most plays and the scores of most musicals are published by companies based in New York City. In the early twenty-first century Samuel French and the Dramatists Play Service remained leading publishing houses for nonmusical properties; musicals were controlled by Tams Witmark, Music Theater International, and the Rodgers and Hammerstein Music Library. These companies maintained the sole authority to charge royalty fees and to release plays for production in stock, educational, and amateur theaters throughout the world. All funds collected were apportioned by prior agreement between the publishing houses and their authors.

The first theatrical periodical in the city was the weekly newspaper the *Thespian Mirror,* published for a brief period in 1805. It was followed by hundreds of magazines and newspapers devoted to the theater, including the weekly general-interest newspapers the *New York Clipper* (1853–1924) and the *New York Dramatic Mirror* (1879–1922); the monthly magazine *Theater Arts* (1916–64), which was noted for publishing the complete texts of new plays; *New Theater* (1934–37), the mimeographed monthly organ of the Workers Theaters of U.S.A. and the Workers Dance League; and the *New York Review* (1909–31), a weekly trade newspaper issued by the Shubert Organization as a vehicle to combat the Theatrical Syndicate. Leading periodicals in the early twenty-first century included *TDR* (The Drama Review), a quarterly journal devoted to performance theory from an anthropological perspective; *American Theater,* a monthly forum for news, features, and opinions; *TCI* and *Live Design,* monthly magazines on technical aspects of the theater; and the weekly trade publications *Backstage* and *Variety.* The influential publication *Best Plays and Year Book of the Drama in America,* first compiled in 1919 by Burns Mantle, contains a detailed overview of every play produced in New York City the preceding year as well as condensations of the 10 best.

Bookshops devoted to the performing arts once doubled as informal gathering places for professionals in the theater, as at Brentano's Literary Emporium in the nineteenth century. In the early twenty-first century, as chain bookstores drove small, specialized bookshops out of business, the Drama Book Shop persevered: the city's oldest extant store for theatrical books and periodicals, it set up shop in 1923 on a card table in the lobby of the ANTA Theater. Web sites such as Playbill.com stepped in to replace some aspects of bookstores as centers of information about the theater world.

8. Acting and Theater Schools

The American Academy of Dramatic Arts, formed in New York City in 1884, was the first school in the United States to provide professional training in acting. In the early twenty-first century most colleges and universities in the city had offerings ranging from informal courses to doctoral programs; among the most notable were the Juilliard School, the Graduate School at City University of New York, and the Tisch School of the Arts at New York University. Most acting schools were founded by noted practitioners in the field, including Strasberg (the Actors Studio), Adler (the Stella Adler Conservatory of Acting), Herbert Berghof and Uta Hagen (HB Studio), and Sanford Meisner (the Neighborhood Playhouse School of the Theater). Certificates in acting were granted by the American Academy of Dramatic Arts, the Circle in the Square Theater School, and the American Musical and Dramatic Academy.

Thomas Allston Brown, *A History of the New York Stage* (New York: Dodd, Mead, 1903); Alfred L. Bernheim, *The Business of the Theatre: An Economic History of the American Theatre, 1750–1932* (New York: Actors' Equity Association, 1932); Mary C. Henderson, *The City and the Theatre: New York Playhouses from Bowling Green to Times Square* (Clifton, N.J.: James T. White, 1973); Mary C. Henderson, *Theater in America* (New York: Harry N. Abrams, 1986); Stephen Langley, *Theatre Management in America* (New York: Drama Book Publishers, 1974; rev. 1990 as *Theatre Management and Production in America: Commercial, Stock, Resident, College, Community, and Presenting Organizations*)

John W. Frick, Martha S. LoMonaco

theater architecture. The first of more than 1000 theaters in New York City was perhaps the New Theatre (also known as the Theatre in Nassau Street), built by English colonists about 1732. A theater district took form in 1798 when the Park Theatre was erected across from City Hall Park. Its facade was designed in a neoclassical style by the French-born architect Joseph François Mangin, who later helped to design City Hall. Little survives of the early theaters, but drawings and photographs suggest that their exteriors were designed according to the architectural fashions of the day. The facades of the Chatham Gardens Theatre (1824) and the New York Theatre (1826; later the Bowery Theatre) were built in the Greek Revival style and could easily have been mistaken for those of churches. As the city expanded to the north, theaters were built along Broadway, the most fashionable avenue, and became well known. The center of the theater district moved successively to Canal Street, Union Square, Madison Square, and Herald Square; there were also German music halls on the Bowery, theaters for Yiddish productions on Second Avenue, theaters and opera houses in Harlem, and a theater district in downtown Brooklyn. Most nineteenth-century theaters were narrow and semicircular; two balconies, one directly above the other, were supported by slender cast-iron columns, while enclosed two-tiered boxes flanked the stage. Theaters with elaborate neoclassical designs were common, such as Haverly's Theatre (1866; later the 14th Street Theatre). Edwin Booth's Theatre (1869) on 23rd Street had a facade in a French style with an enormous mansard roof. Harrigan's Theatre (1890; later the Garrick Theatre) on West 35th Street had a facade in the beaux-arts style.

The theater district moved to what is now called Times Square in 1895, when Oscar Hammerstein opened the Olympia theater complex on Broadway at 45th Street, and during the next three decades about 85 theaters were built in the blocks between Sixth and Eighth avenues from 39th Street to Columbus Circle. All were built for impresarios who produced their own shows and sometimes their own plays with companies of actors under contract. These theaters were both auditoriums and business offices, designed to be symbols of the impresarios and their productions. Many of the upstairs offices were attached to handsome living and sleeping quarters that often acted as venues for seduction. Hammerstein, David Belasco, Daniel Frohman, Winthrop Ames, Henry B. Harris, and Charles Dillingham had theaters built to their specifications and engaged architects who specialized in designing theaters. Commissions were given to many architects, including J. B. McElfatrick and Son, George Keister, Herts and Tallant, Thomas W. Lamb, V. Hugo Koehler, C. Howard Crane, Carrère and Hastings, Warren and Wetmore, and Harry Creighton Ingalls.

The grand beaux-arts designs popular in the late nineteenth century were used into the early years of the twentieth. The Republic Theatre (Albert E. Westover, 1899; now the Victory Theatre), built for Hammerstein on West 42nd Street, is the only remaining theater on Broadway with an interior in the nineteenth-century style; sculpted *putti* look down at the audience from the rim of the ceiling dome. In Frohman's New Lyceum Theatre (1902–3), Herts and Tallant introduced cantilevered balconies to eliminate columns that obscured the view of the stage in the orchestra and the first balcony; they also gave the theater one of the most heavily ornamented facades in the city and an elaborate interior decorated with murals, bronze statues, and unusual lighting fixtures (featuring hundreds of electric bulbs across the ceiling instead of a chandelier). The New Amsterdam Theatre (Herts and Tallant, 1902–3), built for the "Theatrical Syndicate" of Marc Klaw and Abraham Erlanger, remains the finest art nouveau theater in the city. For Dillingham's Globe Theatre (1909–10; now the Lunt–Fontanne Theatre), Carrère and Hastings, the architects of the New York Public Library, designed a monumental, classic beaux-arts facade.

Changes in audiences, entertainment, and technology led to changes in theater design. Second balconies were eliminated in the early twentieth century as patrons of the cheapest seats abandoned the theater for the movie palaces. Interest in "little theater," which consisted of dramatic productions in intimate spaces, led to the restrained neo-Georgian style of Belasco's Stuyvesant Theatre (George Keister, 1906; now the Belasco Theatre) and Ames's Little Theatre on West 44th Street (H. C. Ingalls, 1912; now the Helen Hayes Theatre), both designed to recall the privacy of drawing rooms in Georgian mansions. The Stuyvesant has Tiffany fixtures, a paneled ceiling, and murals by Everett Shinn over the proscenium arch. After World War I, theaters were built for several impresarios, among them Henry Miller, Martin Beck, Irving Berlin, Sam Harris, and the members of the Theatre Guild. Most were built for one of two organizations: the Shuberts, producers who built theaters in Times Square and across the nation for lease to producers or in concert with them, and the Chanins, major developers in the city who built six theaters in three years. Between 1916 and 1927 both organizations gave most of their commissions to Herbert J. Krapp, who was known for designing similar theaters with fine acoustics and sightlines, handsome plasterwork, and minimal ornamentation. He designed simple theaters that often had to fit awkward spaces, such as the Ambassador Theatre (1923), which had an angled entrance. The Plymouth and Broadhurst theaters were intended to be simpler versions of the adjoining Shubert and Booth theaters (Henry B. Herts, 1912): they have inexpensive brick and terra-cotta facades and plasterwork in the Adam style. Some of Krapp's simplest facades for the Shuberts are those of the Ritz Theatre (1919–20) and the Imperial Theatre (1923), which were designed to support signboards. For the Chanins he designed the Majestic Theatre, the Royale Theatre, and the Theater Masque (now the Golden Theatre) in 1926–27 in a Spanish-Moorish style executed in simple brickwork with stone trim on the facades.

The Shuberts and the Chanins, both families of immigrants, softened the distinction between the orchestra and the balconies, which was a vestige of class distinction in English theaters; they also replaced separate entryways with a single entrance for all ticket holders, as in the Shuberts' Broadhurst and Plymouth theaters (Krapp, 1917). As the Shuberts strengthened their hold on Broadway theater, an area along West 44th and 45th streets between Seventh and Eighth avenues came to be known informally as "Shubert Alley." The Chanins introduced the "stadium plan" in their 46th Street Theater (Krapp, 1924–25; now the Walter Kerr Theatre), in which the balcony, cantilevered over the lobby rather than the orchestra, merged with the orchestra into an undifferentiated space. Boxes flanking the stage, which had often been reserved for royalty in English theaters, gradually diminished in size and importance: in the Ethel Barrymore Theater (Krapp, 1928) they were entirely ornamental and contained no seats.

Theaters ceased to be built on Broadway during the Depression, and only five were built in the following half-century (others were built at Columbus Circle and Lincoln Center). The American Place, the Uris Theatre (now the Gershwin Theatre), the Circle in the Square Theatre, and the Minskoff Theatre were built after a zoning resolution was passed to encourage the construction of theaters in new office buildings in Times Square. Despite strong public opposition led by Actors' Equity, the Marquis Theatre was built in the Marriott Marquis Hotel on Broadway between 45th and 46th streets, which replaced five theaters (the Folies Bergère, later known as the Fulton Theatre and then as the Helen Hayes Theatre; the Astor Theatre; the Gaiety Theatre; the Bijou Theatre; and the Morosco Theatre). More than 40 of the original theater buildings in Times Square were demolished during the late twentieth century. Many of the remaining ones have been designated landmarks by the city or the federal government, and most are protected by the special listing of the New York City Planning Commission.

Mary C. Henderson, *The City and the Theatre* (Clifton, N.J.: James T. White, 1973); Randolph Williams Sexton and Ben Franklin Betts, eds., *American Theatres of Today: Illustrated with Plans, Sections, and Photographs of Exterior and Interior Details* (New York: Architectural Books, 1927–30; repr. Vestal, 1977)

See also Movie theaters.

theater criticism. Daily reviews first appeared in New York City when regular theaters opened there in the eighteenth century. Authors writing for the *Daily Advertiser* and the *Gazette of the United States* under the names "Candour" and "Criticus" reviewed plays staged in the John Street Theatre, and by 1796 a circle of daily critics was established in the city. In the beginning of the nineteenth century Washington Irving wrote lively review letters under the name Jonathan Oldstyle for the *Morning Chronicle,* and William Coleman frequently contributed long articles on the theater to the *New York Evening Post.* After 1829 William Leggett carried on Coleman's tradition of providing substantial theater criticism and became the critical champion of Edwin Forrest. In the 1840s plays were reviewed by Edgar Allan Poe for the *Broadway Journal* and the *Evening Mirror* and by Walt Whitman for the *Brooklyn Eagle* (of which he was also the editor). They did not use pseudonyms, unlike many nineteenth-century reviewers including William Winter, who wrote as "Mercutio" for the *Albion* in the early 1860s, and Andrew Carpenter Wheeler, the most influential reviewer just after the Civil War, who wrote for the *New York Weekly Leader* as "Trinculo" and later for the *New York World* and the *Sun* as "Nym Crinkle"; by the 1870s pseudonyms were rarely used. Winter dominated criticism in the city for several decades, writing under his own name as the drama critic for the *New York Tribune* (where he remained until 1909). Henry James, who was not affiliated with any one newspaper, became well known in 1865–69 and 1874–75 for his writings on European theater. The end of the century saw the rise of a new group of critics receptive to modern drama: J. Ranken Towse of the *New York Post* (1874–1927), James Gibbons Huneker of the *New York Recorder* and later the *New York Advertiser* and the *Sun,* Edward August Dithmar of the *New York Times* (1884–1901), known for his advocacy of the playwright Clyde Fitch, and Alan Dale, perhaps the most influential critic, who wrote for the *Evening World* (1887–95), the *New York Evening Journal* (1897–1915), and the *New York American* (1913–21). Critics sometimes came into conflict with producers eager for good reviews, as James Metcalfe of *Life* did with the Theatrical Syndicate.

The leading critics of the 1920s included such talented writers as Robert Benchley, George Jean Nathan, Gilbert W. Gabriel, John Mason Brown, Stark Young, Heywood Broun, Alexander Woollcott, and Joseph Wood Krutch. Perhaps the best-known was Brooks Atkinson, who began reviewing for the *New York Times* in 1926 and remained there until 1960 (except for a few years in the 1940s); he was the first president of the New York Critics' Circle (formed in 1935). During the same years pressure increased on critics to ensure the commercial success of plays in the city by providing positive reviews. In general they acquiesced, and from 1923 to 1950 *Variety* calculated scores based on how often each critic's favorable reviews were followed by success at the box office. The early 1940s were marked by confrontations between on the one hand the producers Jacob and Lee Shubert and on the other Woollcott and Walter Winchell. In an effort to prevent theater managers from denying entry to their productions to reviewers who they thought would be antagonistic, the state legislature passed a bill prohibiting the practice in 1941. The most important critics after World War II were Atkinson, Howard Barnes, and later Walter Kerr of the *New York Herald Tribune* and John Chapman of the *Daily News;* others who had considerable influence included Robert Coleman (the *Daily Mirror*), Louis Kronenberger (*PM*), Robert Garland (the *Journal-American*), Richard Watts (the *New York Post*), William Hawkins (the *New York World-Telegram*), and Ward Morehouse (the *Sun*). The ability of critics to make or break a show caused such widespread concern by the late 1940s that the first "paid preview" was offered in 1952 to curtail their power. This financially "opened" the show before the reviews appeared, and allowed time for publicity to work by word of mouth.

Apart from Atkinson reviewers of plays on Broadway paid little attention to the emerging theater of Off Broadway, and consequently there developed in the early 1960s a separate group of critics who specialized in it, among them Jules Novick and Erika Munk of the *Village Voice.* As the number of daily newspapers diminished (only three remained by 1967) the power of each critic increased commensurately. Public disputes arose between Howard Taubman of the *New York Times* and David Merrick, and in 1968–69 between Kerr, later at the *Times,* and Joseph Papp. A new generation of Broadway critics became prominent in the 1970s and early 1980s, and many of them remained so into the 1990s: Edwin Wilson of the *Wall Street Journal,* Howard Kissel and Martin Gottfried of *Women's Wear Daily,* Frank Rich of the *New York Times,* Clive Barnes of the *Times* and the *New York Post,* John Beaufort of the *Christian Science Monitor,* and Douglas Watt of the *Daily News.* Reviews on television and radio became more common but lacked the influence of those in newspapers. A number of weekly and monthly magazines continued to provide important reviews, among them the *New Yorker* (Edith Oliver, Brendan Gill, and Mimi Kramer), *New York* (John Simon), *Time* (William A. Henry III), *Newsweek* (Jack Kroll), the *Nation,* and the *New Republic.*

By the end of the century regular television and radio reviewing had almost disappeared and only a few newspapers and magazines offered regular reviews and fewer had specific full-time reviewers on their staff. The most influential of these were Ben Brantley at the *New York Times,* Clive Barnes at the *New York Post,* Eric Grode at *The Sun,* and Michael Feingold at the *Village Voice.*

As the reviews in the print media declined in number, electronic reviewing increased in importance. In the opening years of the new century, regular reviewing was provided by major booking Web sites such as nytheatre.com (Martin Denton) and theatermania.com (Brian Scott Lipton), and more significantly by individual Web sites. A few of these, such as Jonathan Kalb's hotreview.org, offered electronic reviews in a traditional format, but more operated as interactive blogs, mixing reviews with other material and encouraging ongoing conversations about productions. A pioneer in blog reviewing was Terry Teachout, the *Wall Street Journal* reviewer, who established the Weblog *About Last Night* in 2003 where he also provided connections to more than 20 other stage blogs, such as George Hunka's *Superfluities* (established 2003) and Garrett Eisler's *The Playgoer* (established 2005).

Montrose J. Moses and John Mason Brown, eds., *The American Theatre as Seen by Its Critics, 1752–1934* (New York: Cooper Square, 1967); Lehman Engel, *The Critics* (New York: Macmillan, 1976)

Marvin Carlson

Theater Row. Complex of small Off-Broadway theaters on 42nd Street between Ninth and 10th avenues. Initiated in 1976 under the auspices of the 42nd Street Development Corporation and the New York State Urban Development Corporation, in the early twenty-first century it consists of the Acorn, Beckett, Clurman, Kirk, Lion, and Studio theaters, each renovated after several improvement phases from earlier burlesque or moderately sized, legitimate show houses.

Peter L. Donhauser

Theatre Guild. Organization of theater producers. Known initially as the Washington Square Players, it was formed in 1914 by amateurs including the patent lawyer Lawrence Langner (1890–1962), the directors Edward Goodman and Philip Moeller (1880–1958), the actresses Helen Westley (1879–1942) and Ida Rauh, and the bookseller Albert Boni; they sought to present intellectual plays of artistic merit as an alternative to the glossy revues popular on Broadway at the time. The group took its current name in 1918 and in 1920 mounted the American premiere of George Bernard Shaw's *Heartbreak House.* It moved in 1925 to its own theater at 243 West 52nd Street, designed by Norman Bel Geddes, where it presented plays by Shaw, Robert E. Sherwood, Maxwell Anderson, William Saroyan, and S. N. Behrman; it also presented most of Eugene O'Neill's plays on Broadway, including *Marco Millions* (1927) and *Strange Interlude* (1928), which was so long that a dinner intermission was required after the fifth act. Among the actors and actresses that the guild engaged regularly were Katherine Cornell, Eva Le Gallienne, Judith Anderson, Judy Holliday, and Joseph Schildkraut. It cast Alfred Lunt and Lynn Fontanne in Ferenc Molnar's *The Guardsman* in 1924, and the two later appeared together in 18 other productions. Sets, lighting, and costumes were designed by Lee Simonson (1888–1967). The guild sold season subscriptions and by the mid-1920s had more than $600,000 in working capital each season. In 1931 it bought the Westport Country Theatre in Connecticut. During the 1920s and 1930s Langner, Westley, Simonson, Moeller, the financier Maurice Wertheim (1886–1950), and Theresa Helburn (1887–1959) made up the board of directors.

Financial pressure during the Depression led the guild to offer more commercial productions, which nonetheless introduced a new level of artistry to Broadway. Such musicals as *Porgy and Bess* (1935) and *Oklahoma!* (1943) were praised for their innovativeness. After 1939 Helburn was the executive director and Langner and his wife, Armina Marshall (1895–1991), were administrators. The guild produced dramatic plays for the *Theatre Guild of the Air* on radio and *The U.S. Steel Hour* on television and also made motion pictures, the best-known being *The Pawnbroker* (1961). In 1972 the Theatre Guild and its subsidiary American Theatre Society won a special Tony Award for its service to touring companies. The guild's presentation of *Golda* (1977) on Broadway was successful, as was its 1996 production of *State Fair.* For many years, it handled subscription series for the Shubert Organization in New York City and elsewhere through the American Theatre Society. Run from offices on Central Park West (having vacated the Theatre Guild building at 226 West 47th Street), it operated the Theatre at Sea cruises (est. 1975).

See also Theater, §§5, 6.

Alana Erickson Coble

Theatrical Syndicate. A trust formed in 1896 by the theater producers Marc Klaw, Abraham Erlanger, and Charles Frohman, the booking agent Al(bert) Hayman, and two theater owners from Philadelphia, S. F. Nixon and J. F. Zimmerman. It was intended to bring order to the chaotic booking practices of the time and by 1903 controlled legitimate theater production throughout the United States. In New York City only a few independent producers, including David Belasco, Harrison Grey Fiske, and Minnie Maddern Fiske, successfully challenged the syndicate; the Shubert brothers finally broke its monopoly in 1916.

Don B. Wilmeth

The Gates. Public art installation created in Central Park in 2005. Designed by artists Christo and Jeanne-Claude, the exhibit was made up of a series of metal gates with saffron-colored fabric spread across them. The artists were inspired by the fact that the park had no gates. Spread out over 23 miles (37 kilometers) of walkways in the park, 503 gates were installed, each of them 16 feet (1.8 meters) tall, transforming the experience of walking through the park. The exhibit was installed on 12 February 2005 and removed by 11 March 2005, during which time millions of people visited the park.

Jessica Montesano

Theosophists. The Theosophical movement, organized to explore ancient wisdom, comparative religion, and science, was founded in New York City by the Russian aristocrat Helena Blavatsky and Henry Steel Olcott, a lawyer and journalist. Together they explored the occult and lived at 302 West 47th Street, which became known as the Lamasery, where they sponsored well-attended lectures and parties. They formed the Theosophical Society in September 1875, with Olcott as president and Blavatsky as corresponding secretary. She wrote *Isis Unveiled* (1877), and in 1879 the two moved to India. After the deaths of Blavatsky and Olcott, Theosophy survived in New York City, influencing occultism and a number of artists, including Nicholas Roerich. In the early twenty-first century the society's branches in the city were the Theosophical Society at 240 East 53rd Street and Theosophy Hall at 347 East 72nd Street. The Roerich Museum, dedicated to the work of Nicholas Roerich, is located at 107th Street and Riverside Drive.

Bruce F. Campbell, *Ancient Wisdom Revived: A History of the Theosophical Movement* (Berkeley: University of California Press, 1980)

Robert Ellwood

Thomas'. Baking company. Founder Samuel Bath Thomas (1855–1919) left England for New York City in 1874 and opened his own bakery shop at 163 Ninth Avenue in 1880. In addition to regular breads, the bakery sold English muffins, a new type of baked good in the United States. During the following decades other stores began buying English muffins from him, deliveries increased to outside New York City, and Thomas opened more bakeries. After his death his daughters and nephews inherited and incorporated the business into S. B. Thomas. In the early twenty-first century Thomas' is owned by George Weston Bakeries, which sells bagels, breads, and multiple flavors of English muffins under the brand name.

Jessica Montesano

Thomas, Andrew J(ackson) (*b* New York City, 1875; *d* New York City, 25 July 1965). Architect. He distinguished himself by developing the community of Jackson Heights for the Queensboro Corporation and became known as a designer of garden apartments set in full-block, open-court plans. In 1920 he completed the Homewood Garden Apartments for the City and Suburban Homes Company (17th Avenue and 73rd Street, Brooklyn) and Linden Court. Thomas's later projects included the Dunbar Apartments in central Harlem (1926–28) for John D. Rockefeller, Jr., buildings in Woodside and Astoria for the Metropolitan Life Insurance Company, the Thomas Garden Apartments at 840 Grand Concourse in the Bronx (1928), and the Dunolly Gardens in Jackson Heights (1939). He wrote *Industrial Housing* (1925).

Marjorie Pearson

Thomas, Dylan (Marlais) (*b* Swansea, England, 27 Oct 1914; *d* New York City, 9 Nov 1953). Poet and performer. Well known in Britain for his intensely personal verse and readings in a ringing voice, the Welsh poet found a new audience in 1950 when he came to New York City at the invitation of John Malcolm Brinnin, director of the Poetry Center at the Young Men's and Women's Hebrew Association (now the 92nd Street Y). Thomas's national tour of 40 universities was a financial and critical success, and he returned to America in 1952 and twice in 1953. New York City at first intimidated Thomas: "I would never get used to the speed, the noise, the utter indifference of the crowds, the frightening politeness of the intellectuals, and, most of all, those huge phallic towers, up & up & up, hundreds of floors, into the impossible sky." He came to enjoy the city, however, socializing with Allen Ginsberg, E. E. Cummings, and other poets and writers. He usually lived at the Hotel Chelsea at 222 West 23rd Street and spent evenings at the White Horse Tavern, 567 Hudson Street, and other bars. Thomas recorded poems and prose pieces for the new Caedmon record label at Steinway Hall, 109 West 57th Street. On his last visit, in declining health and extremely agitated, Thomas was injected with morphine, fell into a coma, and died on 9 November 1953 at St. Vincent's Hospital. His body was returned to Wales for burial.

Paul Ferris, ed., *The Collected Letters of Dylan Thomas* (London: J. M. Dent, 1985); Peter Thabit Jones and Aeronwy Thomas, "Dylan Thomas Walking Tour of Greenwich Village, New York, " http://www.dylanthomas.com/media/pdf/j/m/Dylan_Thomas_Walking_Tour.pdf

John Rousmaniere

Thomas, Franklin A(ugustine) (*b* Brooklyn, 27 May 1934). Lawyer and foundation executive. Educated at Columbia University (BA 1956, LLB 1963), he worked in New York City as a lawyer for the Federal Housing and Home Finance Agency (1963–64), as an assistant U.S. attorney (1964–65), and as an attorney with the police department (1965–67). He was the president and chief executive officer of the Bedford Stuyvesant Restoration Corporation (1967–77). As president of the Ford Foundation (1979–96) he focused on domestic poverty, problems of refugees and immigrants, and leadership in state government. Since 1996, Thomas has worked as a consultant for TTF Study Group, a nonprofit organization working with development in South Africa. He also was hired as chair of the September 11th Fund to aid victims of the 9/11 attacks.

Shan Jayakumar

Thomas, Lowell (Jackson) (*b* Woodington, near Greenville, Ohio, 6 April 1892; *d* Pawling, N.Y., 29 Aug 1981). Broadcaster and writer. In 1930 he was made the broadcaster of the first daily network news program on radio by William S. Paley of the Columbia Broadcasting System (CBS), and until 1976 he worked for both CBS and the National Broadcasting Company (NBC). He traveled widely and often gave reports at remote locations from which radio broadcasts had never before been made. He was also the narrator of *20th Century-Fox Movietone News,* a founder of Capital Cities Communications, and the author of more than 50 books, the best known of which was *With Lawrence in Arabia* (1924). His broadcasts and many of his other writings were done in collaboration with Prosper Buranelli, a former feature writer for the *New York World.* At the end of his career he was the host of the television series *Lowell Thomas Remembers* for the Public Broadcasting System (PBS) and of *The Best Years,* a daily syndicated radio series about the accomplishments of well-known people in their later years; he also wrote an autobiography, *Good Evening Everybody: From Cripple Creek to Samarkand* (1976). Thomas's was the longest continuous career of any reporter in radio.

Judith Adler Hennessee

Thomas, Norman (Mattoon) (*b* Marion, Ohio, 20 Nov 1884; *d* Huntington, N.Y., 19 Dec 1968). Political leader. His family moved to Lewisburg, Pennsylvania, and he attended Bucknell University and then Princeton University, where he graduated in 1905 as the valedictorian of his class. He next moved to New York City and enrolled at Union Theological Seminary where he was influenced by Henry Sloane Coffin; he became the minister of the East Harlem Presbyterian Church on 116th Street between Second and Third avenues in 1911 and in 1917 helped to form the National Civil Rights Bureau (later the American Civil Liberties Union). In 1918 he was pressured by church officials and community members to resign his pastorate because he opposed World War I and belonged to the Socialist Party. After leaving East Harlem he moved with his wife to East 17th Street and entered politics, unsuccessfully seeking election as mayor in 1925 and 1929, state senator in 1926, alderman in 1927, borough president of Manhattan in 1931, and president of the United States in every campaign between 1928 and 1948 (his strongest showing was in 1932 when he received more than 2 percent of all presidential votes cast). A visit to Europe and the Soviet Union in 1937 led him to abandon notions of importing socialism based on the Soviet model, but he remained a committed socialist and peace activist. He formed the Keep America out of War Committee in the city in 1938 but was forced to reassess pacifism by the Spanish Civil War and Nazism; he became an outspoken critic of the internment of Japanese citizens and later protested against nuclear weapons. In 1943 he moved with his family to 20 Gramercy Park. Thomas was at the forefront of American activism during the 1950s and 1960s, protesting McCarthyism and the Korean and Vietnam wars. Toward the end of his life he lived in suburban Cold Spring Harbor, New York, but continued to work in Manhattan and make national speaking tours.

Harry Fleischman, *Norman Thomas* (New York: W. W. Norton, 1969); W. A. Swanberg, *Norman Thomas: The Last Idealist* (New York: Charles Scribner's Sons, 1976)

Chad Ludington

Thomas, Theodore (Christian Friedrich) (*b* Esens [now in Germany], 11 Oct 1835; *d* Chicago, 4 Jan 1905). Conductor and violinist. He arrived in New York City in 1845 and in 1854 became a violinist with the Philharmonic Society. On 29 April 1859 he made his debut as a conductor at the New York Academy of Music, and he then had a distinguished career as the conductor of the Brooklyn Philharmonic Society (1862–91), his own ensemble the Thomas Orchestra (1869–88), and the New York Philharmonic Society (1877–78, 1879–91). He was one of the first orchestral conductors in New York City to popularize German classical music, which he performed at such events as the summer concerts in Central Park (1868–75). As the conductor of the American Opera Company (1886–87), which experienced financial difficulties, he suffered exhaustion from his competition with the rival conductors Anton Seidl and Frank and Peter Damrosch, and in 1891 he moved to Chicago.

Ezra Schabas, *Theodore Thomas: America's Conductor and Builder of Orchestras* (Champaign: University of Illinois Press, 1989)

Nancy Shear

Thomashevsky, Boris (*b* Ukraine, 12 May 1868; *d* New York City, 9 July 1939). Yiddish theater actor. Thomashevsky is considered by most critics to be the greatest actor of the Yiddish theater, which thrived in New York City from the late nineteenth through the early twentieth centuries. An immigrant from the Ukraine with no formal voice training, he learned about music from listening to fellow workers in a cigarette-manufacturing sweatshop who sang tunes from Yiddish productions. By the time he was 13, Thomashevsky, a forceful tenor, was touring with Yiddish theater companies, singing and acting. He performed with many companies; at its peak there were a dozen based in New York City and as many as 200 traveling to cities where Jewish immigrants had settled. He produced the first Yiddish Shakespeare plays in New York City, including *King Lear, Othello,* and *Hamlet;* his repertoire also included *Faust, Salome,* and *Parsifal,* as well as popular productions dealing with common issues of immigrant life, such as *The Singing Rabbi.* During the first two decades of the twentieth century, Thomashevsky packed the Yiddish theaters. He also made several movies, including the acclaimed *Bar Mitzvah* in 1935. More than 30,000 people attended his funeral in 1939.

Stefan Kanfer, *Stardust Lost: The Triumph, Tragedy, and Mishugas of the Yiddish Theater in America* (New York: A. A. Knopf, 2006)

Lisa Keller

Thomas Y. Crowell Company. Firm of book publishers formed in 1876 by Thomas

Young Crowell at 744 Broadway. It published little fiction, focusing instead on specially bound gift editions as well as religious and inspirational titles. With its publication in 1886 of *Roget's Thesaurus* it also developed a strong list of reference books, and in the same year it established a children's list that eventually became a leader among book publishers. Crowell remained autonomous after being acquired in 1968 by Dun–Donnelly Publishing Company; in 1979 it became an imprint of Harper and Row.

Eileen K. Cheng

Thompson, Kay (*b* St. Louis, 9 Nov *ca* 1903; *d* New York City, 2 July 1998). Actress and author. See Eloise.

Thomson, Virgil (Garnett) (*b* Kansas City, Mo., 25 Nov 1896; *d* New York City, 30 Sept 1989). Composer and critic. After early study in Kansas City and then with Edward Burlingame Hill at Harvard, he studied the organ and counterpoint with Nadia Boulanger from 1919 to 1921 in Paris, where he took up residence. His opera *Four Saints in Three Acts* (1933), to a libretto by Gertrude Stein, was staged on Broadway for 48 performances in 1934 with an all-black cast and launched his career. After the fall of Paris in 1940 he moved to New York City, where he spent the rest of his life at the Chelsea Hotel on 23rd Street. In addition to composing he wrote acerbic, witty, and often controversial music criticism for the *New York Herald Tribune* from 1940 to 1954. His second opera to a libretto by Stein, *The Mother of Us All,* was first performed in 1947 at Columbia University; *Lord Byron,* his last opera, was given its premiere at the Juilliard School in April 1972. Thomson's music is characterized by a fondness for Americana, a conception of harmony that owes something to the French impressionists, and an aphoristic quality reminiscent of Erik Satie. Among his compositions inspired by New York City are *The Mayor LaGuardia Waltzes* (1942), *Crossing Brooklyn Ferry* (1958), and *Metropolitan Museum Fanfare* (1969).

Barbara L. Tischler

Thorndike, Edward L(ee) (*b* Williamsburg, Mass., 31 Aug 1874; *d* Montrose, near Croton-on-Hudson, N.Y., 9 Aug 1949). Psychologist. He attended Wesleyan College and Harvard University and in 1898 received his PhD from Columbia University for a dissertation on animal psychology, a subject that he was among the first to study scientifically. In 1899 he joined the faculty of Teachers College at Columbia; he became a full professor there in 1904 and the director of the division of psychology of the Institute of Educational Research in 1922. His belief that measurement was the key to scientific progress in education and psychology led him to devise several tests that were later used to assess intelligence and evaluate handwriting, drawing, and reading. He wrote many basic texts in the field of educational psychology, helped design intelligence tests for the U.S. Army during World War I, and published more than 500 books and articles on behavior, education, intelligence, and the learning process. Thorndike was also a president of the American Psychological Association, the American Association for the Advancement of Science, and the New York Academy of Science. He remained at Columbia until his retirement in 1940.

Geraldine M. Jonçich, *The Sane Positivist: A Biography of Edward L. Thorndike* (Middletown, Conn.: Wesleyan University Press, 1968)

Sandra Opdycke

Thorne's Neck. Former name of the peninsula in Queens later known as Willets Point.

311. New York City's nonemergency hotline. The idea of the hotline was first launched in Baltimore and was introduced in New York City by Mayor Michael Bloomberg in 2003. The individual phone numbers for various city agencies were consolidated into one phone number through which people could be connected to agencies specific to their complaints or inquiries, in an effort to avoid overlapping jurisdictions among city government departments. While offering a more organized system for handling citizens' phone calls on all nonemergency, city-related matters, the system also allowed for Bloomberg to gauge the performance of the city officials responsible for helping callers, as well as of the organization of the city's services. In 2008 the system received on average 15,000 calls a day through 375 operators, who worked out of centers in lower Manhattan and Long Island City. It has been hailed as one of Bloomberg's greater contributions throughout his mayoralty.

Cecilia Magnusson

Throg(g)s Neck. Neighborhood in the northeastern Bronx, lying on a peninsula overlooking Long Island Sound to the north and east and the East River to the south. The area was called Vriedelandt by the Dutch and derives its current name from John Throckmorton, an Englishman whom the Dutch allowed in 1642 to settle a colony in the area; the colony was eventually driven out by American Indian uprisings. The peninsula was mapped as Frockes Neck in 1668, and General George Washington wrote of Frogs Neck in his journal during an invasion of 4000 redcoats and Hessians in 1776. In the nineteenth century the area became the site of estates and farms where Irish immigrants worked as servants and tenant farmers. The construction from 1833 to 1856 of Fort Schuyler drew laborers, stonemasons, and other craftsmen and their families to the area, which in the late part of the century became a fashionable summer resort. When all of what is now the Bronx became part of New York City in 1895, the expanding transit lines spurred an influx of Italian farmers and tradesmen. Old landowners sold out to developers, and soon rows of private houses covered what had been cultivated estates. Fort Schuyler ceased being an active military installation in 1932 and then became the campus for the cadets of the New York State Maritime College. The neighborhood changed again in 1961 when the Throgs Neck Bridge was completed, and the Throgs Neck, Cross Bronx, and Bruckner expressways ended its comparative isolation. Throgs Neck has several beach clubs and marinas, and a diverse housing stock that includes modest middle-class housing, expensive beachfront condominiums such as White Beach, former summer resorts such as Silver Beach and Edgewater Park that have been converted to cooperative ownership, and Throgs Neck Houses, begun in 1953 as one of the first low-income housing projects in the city. In 2006 the population was about 22,000 residents, mostly of Italian, Irish, and German ancestry. In the early twenty-first century many first-generation Italian immigrants remained in the neighborhood.

John McNamara, *History in Asphalt: The Origin of Bronx Street and Place Names* (New York: Bronx County Historical Society, 1984); John McNamara, *McNamara's Old Bronx* (New York: Bronx County Historical Society, 1989)

John McNamara

Throgs Neck Bridge. Steel suspension bridge spanning the East River between Throgs Neck in the Bronx and Bayside in northern Queens. Designed by Othmar H. Ammann and built at a cost of $92 million by the Triborough Bridge and Tunnel Authority, it was built to relieve traffic congestion on the Bronx–Whitestone Bridge, 2 miles (3 kilometers) to the west. It opened on 11 January 1961 and was used by an average of 63,000 vehicles a day during its first year. The bridge has six lanes, a main span of 1800 feet (549 meters) between two towers 360 feet (110 meters) high, and a total length of 13,410 feet (4087 meters). The bridge is an important element in a system of highways that connect New Jersey, upstate New York, New England, and Long Island. In the mid-1980s a controversy occurred when the Metropolitan Transportation Authority (MTA) intended to use South Korean steel to reconstruct the roadway of the bridge. After several "Buy American" protests by union workers and their supporters, the MTA purchased steel from domestic mills. Usage of the bridge expanded early in the twenty-first century to an average of more than 100,000 vehicles a day.

Rebecca Read Shanor

Thumb, Tom. See Stratton, Charles Sherwood.

Thurber, James (Grover). (*b* Columbus, Ohio, 18 Dec 1894; *d* New York City, 2 Nov 1961). Humorist and cartoonist. After attending Ohio State University he worked on newspapers in Columbus and Paris. In 1926 he moved to New York City to work for the *Evening Post.* He soon left to join the staff of the *New Yorker,* for which he provided humorous stories and drawings. He began drawing cartoons for that magazine when his colleague E. B. White discovered Thurber's cartoons in the trash and submitted them for publication. He collaborated with White on the book *Is Sex Necessary?* (1929) and with Elliot Nugent on the play *The Male Animal* (1940), which had two runs on Broadway. He had quarters at 65 West 11th Street in 1928–29 and from that time lived mostly at the Algonquin Hotel at 59 West 44th Street. From the autumn of 1935 until the summer of 1936 he lived at 8 Fifth Avenue. Among Thurber's many books are *My Life and Hard Times* (1933), *Men, Women and Dogs* (1945), and the *Years with Ross* (1957), recollections of working at the *New Yorker.* His short story "The Secret Life of Walter Mitty" (1939) inspired the motion picture. He wrote the children's books *Many Moons* (1943) and *The White Deer* (1945) as well as the Broadway play *A Thurber Carnival* (1960), in which he starred as himself.

James E. Mooney, Max Seppo

TIAA–CREF. See Teachers Insurance and Annuity Association–College Retirement Equities Fund.

Photographer Andreas Feininger's view of a ticker-tape parade

ticker-tape parades. Parades given in New York City to honor heroes, champion athletes, pioneers of air and space travel, political leaders, soldiers, and sailors. The parades begin at the Battery at the southern end of Manhattan. Those honored ride in open limousines or on parade floats up lower Broadway, the "canyon of heroes," to City Hall where the mayor hosts a reception. Spectators shower confetti and shredded paper, and in the past ticker tape, on the parade. (Ticker tape, invented in 1867, was a 1-inch-wide ribbon of paper on which ticker machines recorded telegraphed stock quotes; its use was discontinued in the 1960s.) Contemporary accounts of the earliest parades describe the cascade of ticker tape as a spontaneous gesture by office workers. Grover A. Whalen, chairman of the mayor's reception committee (1919–53), recognized the promotional value of ticker-tape parades and established them as a function of municipal government. From 1919 to the present, the mayor has decided who will receive a ticker-tape parade.

During the 1920s it became customary to hail arriving heads of state with a ticker-tape parade. The city started a tradition of recognizing champion athletes with the parade for the U.S. Olympic team on 6 August 1924. The legendary reception on 13 June 1927 for Charles Lindbergh's solo transatlantic flight, one of 17 parades for achievements in aviation, made the ticker-tape parade famous around the world. From 1945 to 1965 the city staged 130 ticker-tape parades, more than half of them welcoming heads of state, usually at the request of the U.S. Department of State. During this cold war period, many parades featured men and women of the armed services. By the mid-1960s there had been so many ticker-tape parades that they came to be seen as routine. Mayor John V. Lindsay, elected in 1965, ended the practice of greeting heads of state with ticker-tape parades but kept the tradition alive for celebrating the success of the U.S. Apollo space program (10 January to 13 August 1969) and the World Series–winning Mets baseball team (20 October 1969). The number of parades dropped considerably during the last decades of the twentieth century, though parades still celebrated sports champions, war veterans, and noted individuals, such as Pope John Paul II (1979) South African leader Nelson Mandela (1990), astronaut John Glenn (1998), and baseball player Sammy Sosa (1998).

There have been numerous recipients of more than one ticker-tape parade, including sea captain George Fried (1926 and 1929), golfer Bobby Jones (1926 and 1930), Admiral Richard E. Byrd (1927 and 1930), the aviators Amelia Earhart (1928 and 1932) and Wiley

Ticker-Tape Parades, 1886–2009

1886–95

28 Oct 1886, Dedication of the Statue of Liberty

29 April 1889, Centennial of George Washington's inauguration as first president of the United States

1896–1905

30 Sept 1899, Adm. George Dewey, hero of the Battle of Manila during the Spanish–American War

1906–15

18 June 1910, Theodore Roosevelt, former president of the United States, on his return from an African safari

1916–25

9 May 1917, Joseph J. C. Joffre, marshal of France

8 Sept 1919, Gen. John J. Pershing, commander in chief, American Expeditionary Force in World War I

3 Oct 1919, Albert and Elizabeth, King and Queen of the Belgians

18 Nov 1919, Edward Albert, Prince of Wales

19 Oct 1921, Gen. Armando V. Diaz, chief of staff of the Italian army

21 Oct 1921, Adm. Lord David Beatty, commander of the British and Allied fleets in World War I

28 Oct 1921, Ferdinand Foch, marshal of France, commander of the Allied armies in World War I

18 Nov 1922, Georges Clemenceau, premier of France during World War I

5 Oct 1923, David Lloyd George, prime minister of Great Britain during World War I

6 Aug 1924, U.S. Olympic athletes on their return from the Paris games

1926–35

16 Feb 1926, Capt. George Fried and the crew of the steamship *President Roosevelt* for rescuing the crew of the British freighter *Antinoe*

27 May 1926, Gustaf Adolf and Louise, Crown Prince and Princess of Sweden

23 June 1926, Lt. Cmdr. Richard E. Byrd and Floyd Bennett for the first flight over the North Pole

2 July 1926, Bobby Jones, British Open champion

27 Aug 1926, Gertrude Ederle, first woman to swim the English Channel

10 Sept 1926, Mille Gade Corson, first mother and second woman to swim the English Channel

18 Oct 1926, Marie, Queen of Romania

13 June 1927, Charles A. Lindbergh for the first solo nonstop transatlantic flight

18 July 1927, Double parade for two separate transatlantic flights: one by Cmdr. Richard E. Byrd, Lt. George O. Noville, Bernt Balchen, and Bert Acosta; and the other by Clarence D. Chamberlin and Charles A. Levine

11 Nov 1927, Ruth Elder, first woman to attempt a transatlantic flight, with pilot George Haldeman

20 Jan 1928, William T. Cosgrave, president of Ireland

30 April 1928, Capt. Hermann Koehl, Maj. James Fitzmaurice, and Baron Guenther von Huenefeld for the longest westward transatlantic flight

4 May 1928, Prince Ludovico Potenziani Spada, governor of Rome

6 July 1928, Amelia Earhart, first woman to complete a transatlantic flight, with pilots Wilmer Stultz and Louis E. Gordon

16 Oct 1928, Dr. Hugo Eckener and the crew of the dirigible *Graf Zeppelin* for the first commercial transatlantic flight

28 Jan 1929, Capt. George Fried, Chief Officer Harry Manning, and the crew of the steamship *America* for rescuing the crew of the Italian freighter *Florida*

4 Oct 1929, Ramsay MacDonald, prime minister of Great Britain

29 April 1930, Henry Lewis Stimson, secretary of state, and U.S. delegates returning from the London Naval Disarmament Conference

26 May 1930, Marquis Jacques de Dampierre and family, descendants of the Marquis de Lafayette, passengers on the maiden voyage of the French ocean liner *Lafayette*

11 June 1930, Dr. Julio Prestes de Albuquerque, president-elect of Brazil

18 June 1930, Rear Adm. Richard E. Byrd for his first Antarctic expedition and flight over the South Pole

2 July 1930, Bobby Jones, British Open champion

3 Sept 1930, Capt. Dieudonné Costes and Maurice Bellonte for the first nonstop transatlantic flight from Paris to Long Island

2 July 1931, Wiley Post and Harold Gatty for their flight around the world (eight days, 15 hours, 51 minutes)

2 Sept 1931, Olin J. Stephens, Jr., and the crew of the *Dorade*, winners of transatlantic yacht race from Newport, Rhode Island, to Plymouth, England

22 Oct 1931, Pierre Laval, premier of France

26 Oct 1931, Henri Philippe Pétain, marshal of France

30 Nov 1931, Dino Grandi, foreign minister of Italy

20 June 1932, Amelia Earhart for the first solo transatlantic flight by a woman

21 July 1933, Italian Air Marshal Italo Balbo and the crews of 24 seaplanes for their flight from Rome to Chicago

26 July 1933, Wiley Post for the first solo flight around the world (seven days, 18 hours, 49 minutes)

1 Aug 1933, Pilots Amy Johnson and Capt. James A. Mollison, the first married couple to fly the Atlantic

1936–45

3 Sept 1936, Jesse Owens and members of the U.S. Olympic team on their return from the Berlin games

15 July 1938, Howard Hughes and crew for their record-breaking flight around the world (three days, 19 hours, eight minutes)

5 Aug 1938, Douglas "Wrong Way" Corrigan for his flight from New York to Ireland instead of his "intended" destination of California

27 April 1939, Olav and Martha, Crown Prince and Princess of Norway

1 May 1939, Rear Adm. Alfred W. Johnson, officers and men of the Atlantic Squadron of the U.S. Fleet

19 June 1945, Gen. Dwight D. Eisenhower, supreme commander of the Allied Expeditionary Force in World War II

27 Aug 1945, Gen. Charles de Gaulle, president of the Provisional Government of France

13 Sept 1945, Gen. Jonathan M. Wainwright, hero of the Battles of Bataan and Corregidor in World War II

9 Oct 1945, Fleet Adm. Chester W. Nimitz, commander in chief of the navy's Pacific Fleet in World War II

27 Oct 1945, Harry S. Truman, president of the United States

14 Dec 1945, Fleet Adm. William F. Halsey, Jr., commander of the navy's Third Fleet in World War II

1946–55

15 March 1946, Winston Churchill, prime minister of Great Britain during World War II

23 Oct 1946, Delegates to the first plenary session of the General Assembly of the United Nations

25 Oct 1946, Col. Clarence S. Irvine, commander of the B-29 *Dreamboat*, and his crew for their Honolulu-to-Cairo flight over the North Pole

13 Jan 1947, Alcide De Gasperi, premier of Italy

7 Feb 1947, Harold Alexander, viscount of Tunis, field marshal of the British armies in World War II, and governor-general of Canada

(*continued*)

Ticker-Tape Parades, 1886–2009 (*Continued*)

2 May 1947, Miguel Alemán, president of Mexico
9 June 1947, Willie Turnesa, British amateur golf champion, and fellow members of the victorious American Walker Cup team
5 Nov 1947, Officers and crew of the French warship *Georges Leygues* for bringing rare French tapestries for exhibition at the Metropolitan Museum of Art
18 Nov 1947, Friendship Train bearing gifts and supplies from the United States to Europe
9 March 1948, Eamon De Valera, former prime minister of Ireland
7 July 1948, Rómulo Gallegos, president of Venezuela
3 Feb 1949, French Gratitude Train bearing gifts from France to the United States in appreciation of the Friendship Train
19 May 1949, Gen. Lucius D. Clay, military governor of Germany and commander of the Berlin airlift
23 May 1949, Eurico Gaspar Dutra, president of Brazil
11 Aug 1949, Elpidio Quirino, president of the Philippines
19 Aug 1949, Connie Mack on his 50th year as manager of the Philadelphia Athletics baseball team
16 Sept 1949, 48 European journalists in celebration of Freedom of the Press Day during their U.S. tour
4 Oct 1949, Raymond A. Garbarina Memorial Post 1523 for winning the American Legion Drum and Bugle Corps national championship
17 Oct 1949, Jawaharlal Nehru, prime minister of India
21 Nov 1949, Mohammad Reza Pahlevi, shah of Iran
17 April 1950, Gabriel González Videla, president of Chile
28 April 1950, Adm. Thomas C. Kinkaid, hero of World War II naval battles and retiring commander of the navy's Eastern Sea Frontier and the Atlantic Reserve Fleet
8 May 1950, Liaquat Ali Khan, prime minister of Pakistan
9 May 1950, Fernando Casas Alemán, governor of Mexico City Federal District
10 May 1950, Ten foreign mayors attending the 18th annual U.S. Conference of Mayors
2 June 1950, Fourth Marine Division Association veterans of Pacific Battles in World War II
4 Aug 1950, Robert Gordon Menzies, prime minister of Australia
22 Aug 1950, Lt. Gen. Clarence R. Huebner, commander of U.S. Armed Forces in Europe
31 Aug 1950, William O'Dwyer upon his resignation as mayor of the City of New York
3 April 1951, Vincent Auriol, president of France
20 April 1951, Gen. Douglas MacArthur
9 May 1951, David Ben-Gurion, prime minister of Israel
24 May 1951, U.S. Army Fourth Infantry Division, Eighth Regimental Combat Team: the first NATO troops to be sent overseas
25 June 1951, Galo Plaza Lasso, native New Yorker and president of Ecuador
17 Sept 1951, Sir Denys Lowson, 623rd lord mayor of London
28 Sept 1951, Alcide De Gasperi, premier of Italy
8 Oct 1951, New York National Guard's 165th Infantry Regiment on its centennial
29 Oct 1951, 50 wounded United Nations veterans of the Korean War
13 Nov 1951, Women in the armed services
17 Jan 1952, Capt. Henrik Kurt Carlsen for his heroic attempt to save his sinking ship, the SS *Flying Enterprise*
7 April 1952, Juliana, Queen of the Netherlands, and Prince Bernhard
14 May 1952, Mayors of 250 cities attending the 20th annual U.S. Conference of Mayors
7 July 1952, U.S. Olympic team send-off to the Helsinki games
18 July 1952, Commodore Harry Manning, Chief Engineer William Kaiser, and crew of the SS *United States* for setting a new transatlantic speed record
18 Dec 1952, Lt. Gen. Willis D. Crittenberger, retiring commander of the First Army
30 Jan 1953, Vice Adm. Walter S. Delany, commander of the navy's Eastern Sea Frontier and the Atlantic Reserve Fleet
3 April 1953, Metropolitan New York Combat Contingent, the first U.S. Army troops to return from the Korean War
24 April 1953, Gen. James A. Van Fleet, retired commander of the United Nations ground troops in Korea
26 May 1953, New York City departments and units of the armed services to commemorate the 150th anniversary of the laying of the cornerstone for City Hall
21 July 1953, Ben Hogan, British Open champion
1 Oct 1953, José Antonio Remón, president of Panama
20 Oct 1953, Gen. Mark W. Clark, retiring commander of U.S. forces in the Far East
26 Oct 1953, Maj. Gen. William F. Dean, hero of Taejon and prisoner of war for three years during the Korean War
2 Nov 1953, Paul I and Frederika, King and Queen of Greece
5 Nov 1953, Lt. Gen. James H. Doolittle and marching units from the armed forces in observance of the 50th anniversary of powered flight
21 Dec 1953, 144 convalescing Korean War veterans from the New York metropolitan area
1 Feb 1954, Celâl Bayar, president of Turkey
31 March 1954, 4000 New York City firefighters in observance of Firemen's Day
22 April 1954, Veterans of the 45th "Thunderbird" Infantry Division on their return from the Korean War
1 June 1954, Haile Selassie, emperor of Ethiopia
26 July 1954, Geneviève de Galard-Terraube, a nurse known as the Angel of Dienbienphu for staying with wounded French soldiers in Vietnam
2 Aug 1954, Syngman Rhee, president of South Korea
27 Sept 1954, New York Giants, National League champions
28 Oct 1954, William V. S. Tubman, president of Liberia
19 Nov 1954, Lt. Gen. Withers A. Burress, retiring commander of the First Army
31 Jan 1955, Paul Eugène Magloire, president of Haiti
1 March 1955, New York Chapter of the American Red Cross to kick off their 1955 fund-raising campaign
15 April 1955, 3000 New York City firefighters in observance of Firemen's Day
11 Aug 1955, Order of the Knights of Pythias
4 Nov 1955, Carlos Castillo Armas, president of Guatemala
9 Dec 1955, Luis Batlle Berres, president of Uruguay

1956–65

12 March 1956, Giovanni Gronchi, president of Italy
23 May 1956, Sukarno, president of Indonesia
30 Aug 1956, 3000 volunteer firefighters attending the 84th annual convention of the New York State Firemen's Association
2 May 1957, 62 U.S. Navy and Marine veterans of World War II and the Korean War
13 May 1957, Ngo Dinh Diem, president of South Vietnam
2 July 1957, Capt. Alan J. Villiers and the crew of the replica ship *Mayflower II*
11 July 1957, Althea Gibson, Wimbledon women's champion

(*continued*)

Ticker-Tape Parades, 1886–2009 (*Continued*)

21 Oct 1957, Elizabeth II, Queen of the United Kingdom of Great Britain and Northern Ireland, and Prince Philip, Duke of Edinburgh
20 May 1958, Van Cliburn, first winner of Moscow's International Tchaikovsky piano competition
20 June 1958, Theodor Heuss, president of the Federal Republic of Germany
23 June 1958, Carlos P. García, president of the Philippines
27 Aug 1958, Rear Adm. Hyman G. Rickover, Cmdr. William R. Anderson, and crew of the *Nautilus*, the first nuclear submarine
29 Jan 1959, Dr. Arturo Frondizi, president of Argentina
10 Feb 1959, Willy Brandt, mayor of West Berlin
13 March 1959, José María Lemus, president of El Salvador
20 March 1959, Sean T. O'Kelly, president of Ireland
29 May 1959, Baudouin I, King of the Belgians
11 Sept 1959, Beatrix, Princess of the Netherlands
14 Oct 1959, Adolfo López Mateos, president of Mexico
4 Nov 1959, Sékou Touré, president of Guinea
9 March 1960, Carol Heiss, Women's Olympic figure-skating champion
11 April 1960, Dr. Alberto Lleras Camargo, president of Colombia
26 April 1960, Charles de Gaulle, president of France
2 May 1960, Mahendra Bir Bikram Shah Dev and Ratna Rajya Lakshmi Devi Shah, King and Queen of Nepal
5 July 1960, Bhumibol Adulyadej and Sirikit, King and Queen of Thailand
14 Oct 1960, Frederick IX and Ingrid, King and Queen of Denmark
19 Oct 1960, Senator John F. Kennedy, Democratic presidential nominee
2 Nov 1960, Dwight D. Eisenhower, president of the United States, and Vice President Richard M. Nixon, Republican presidential nominee
11 May 1961, Habib Bourguiba, president of Tunisia
14 July 1961, Mohammad Ayub Khan, president of Pakistan
22 Sept 1961, Manuel Prado Ugarteche, president of Peru
13 Oct 1961, Gen. Ibrahim Abboud, Sudanese leader
27 Oct 1961, Capt. Thomas J. Walker, crew and builders of the USS *Constellation*, the world's largest aircraft carrier
1 March 1962, Lt. Col. John H. Glenn, Jr., first American to orbit the earth
16 March 1962, Ahmadou Ahidjo, president of Cameroon
22 March 1962, Sylvanus Olympio, president of Togo
5 April 1962, João Goulart, president of Brazil
12 April 1962, New York Mets, new National League baseball team
16 April 1962, Mohammad Reza Pahlevi, shah of Iran, and Empress Farah
25 May 1962, Félix Houphouët-Boigny, president of the Ivory Coast
8 June 1962, Archbishop Makarios III, president of Cyprus
14 June 1962, Roberto F. Chiari, president of Panama
1 April 1963, Hassan II, King of Morocco
22 May 1963, Maj. L. Gordon Cooper, Jr., *Mercury* astronaut who orbited the earth 22 times
10 June 1963, Dr. Sarvepalli Radhakrishnan, president of India
10 Sept 1963, Mohammad Zahir Shah and Homaira, King and Queen of Afghanistan
4 Oct 1963, Haile Selassie, emperor of Ethiopia
16 July 1964, Crews of sailing vessels participating in Operation Sail
3 Sept 1964, Staten Island's Mid-Island All-Stars, Little League World Series champions
8 Oct 1964, Diosdado Macapagal, president of the Philippines
29 March 1965, Maj. Virgil I. Grissom and Lt. Cmdr. John W. Young, *Gemini III* astronauts
19 May 1965, Park Chung Hee, president of South Korea
1 June 1965, 4500 firefighters celebrate the 100th anniversary of New York City's first professional fire department

1966–75

10 Jan 1969, Lt. Col. Frank Borman, Lt. Col. William A. Anders, and Capt. James A. Lovell, Jr., *Apollo 8* astronauts, the first people to see the far side of the moon
13 Aug 1969, Neil A. Armstrong, Col. Buzz Aldrin, and Lt. Col. Michael Collins, *Apollo 11* astronauts, for the first manned moon landing
20 Oct 1969, New York Mets, World Series champions

1976–85

6 July 1976, Crews of sailing vessels participating in Operation Sail for the United States bicentennial
19 Oct 1977, New York Yankees, World Series champions
19 Oct 1978, New York Yankees, World Series champions
3 Oct 1979, Pope John Paul II
30 Jan 1981, U.S. hostages released from Iran after 444 days in captivity
15 Aug 1984, U.S. Olympic medal winners from the Los Angeles games
7 May 1985, Vietnam War veterans

1986–95

28 Oct 1986, New York Mets, World Series champions
20 June 1990, Nelson Mandela, African National Congress leader
10 June 1991, Persian Gulf War veterans
25 June 1991, Korean War veterans
17 June 1994, New York Rangers, Stanley Cup champions

1996–2009

29 Oct 1996, New York Yankees, World Series champions
17 Oct 1998, Sammy Sosa, Chicago Cubs baseball player who broke the single-season home-run record
23 Oct 1998, New York Yankees, World Series champions
16 Nov 1998, Senator John Glenn and fellow crew members of the U.S. space shuttle *Discovery*
29 Oct 1999, New York Yankees, World Series champions
30 Oct 2000, New York Yankees, World Series champions
5 Feb 2008, New York Giants, Super Bowl champions
6 Nov 2009, New York Yankees, World Series champions

Compiled by Kenneth Cobb, edited by Frank Nestor

Post (1931 and 1933), Dwight D. Eisenhower (1945 and 1960), French president Charles de Gaulle (1945 and 1960), Italian premier Alcide De Gasperi (1947 and 1951), Ethiopian emperor Haile Selassie (1954 and 1963), astronaut John Glenn (1962 and 1998), the New York Mets (1962, 1969, and 1986), and the New York Yankees (1977, 1978, 1996, 1998, 1999, and 2000). The largest ticker-tape parade, as measured by the amount of paper collected by the Sanitation Department, took place on 1 March 1962 for astronaut John Glenn. It resulted in 3474 tons (3152 metric tons) of scrap paper along the 7-mile (11-kilometer) route through the city (longer than the traditional route from the Battery to City Hall). Of parades confined to lower Broadway, Douglas "Wrong Way" Corrigan (5 August 1938, who flew to Ireland

Ticker-tape parade for Major General William F. Dean, 26 October 1953

instead of California) and Howard Hughes (15 July 1938, after his record-breaking flight around the world) were the champions of paper usage, at 1900 and 1800 tons (1724 and 1633 metric tons), respectively. Parades in the twenty-first century average about 50 tons (45 metric tons) of scrap paper.

Kenneth R. Cobb

tides and currents. New York Harbor challenges navigators with its flow of tidal currents, as the water level rises and falls approximately 5 feet (1.5 meters) every six and a half hours (and more during the spring tides that arrive with the full moon). Every hour, hundreds of millions of gallons of water flow in the harbor, from or back to three large bodies of water: the Atlantic Ocean through Ambrose Channel, the Hudson River off the Battery, and Long Island Sound through the East River. A prolonged, strong south wind can push even more water into the harbor, and a brisk northerly will blow water out—in both cases changing water depth and disrupting the tide's schedule and velocity.

The most dangerous tidal currents are at the aptly named Hell Gate, where the East River turns sharply toward Long Island Sound. The area already had that name and was a graveyard of ships in 1670, when a mariner, Daniel Denton, wrote that "there runneth a violent stream both upon flood and ebb, and in the middle lieth some islands of rocks, which the current sets so violently upon, that it threatens present shipwreck; and upon the flood is a large whirlpool, which continually sends forth a hideous roaring." Even though the boulders were dynamited in the late 1800s, Hell Gate's currents continue to run as fast as 5 to 6 knots (5.8 to 6.9 mph), often swirling violently.

The water moves less quickly and more straightly in the main part of the two rivers. In the Hudson, the flow usually runs 10 percent faster on the ebb, when it carries freshwater out of the great inland watershed, than it does on the flood, which carries saltwater all the way to Albany. Off the Battery, where the Hudson and the East rivers meet, the currents can be risky to navigate. Two hours after high water, the ebb current out of the East River meets the flow out of the Hudson in an intricate, confusing pattern that the *U.S. Coast Pilot* calls "the Spider." It can push unwary ships down onto Governor's Island.

River currents were quickened in the early 1800s when the construction of wharves and piers, and the dumping of vast amounts of garbage and human waste, constricted the Hudson and especially the East River, where flow sped up by more than half a knot. Currents were further accelerated by dredging harbor channels from the normal average depth of 20 feet (6.1 meters) at low tide to at least 40 feet (12.2 meters) to accommodate ocean liners, and (in the early twenty-first century) to more than 60 feet (18.3 meters) in order to allow the biggest container ships to enter and leave the harbor safely.

Meanwhile, knowledge of currents and tides advanced with the development of current-recording buoys, satellite imaging, and computer modeling. The New York Harbor Observing and Prediction System (NYHOPS) at the Stevens Institute of Technology employs these and other tools in enhancing both navigation and port security, while also managing emergencies. After the emergency landing of U.S. Airways Flight 1549 on the Hudson off 48th Street on 15 January 2009 (the "Miracle on the Hudson"), NYHOPS advised New York City's Office of Emergency Management, the New York Fire Department, and the National Transportation Safety Board concerning the environmental conditions surrounding the slowly sinking airplane as it drifted down the river on an ebb tide. The system's advice to deploy rescue vessels south of the landing site and then to pull the plane to the west side of the Battery, where currents were then weakest, helped lead to the rescue of all 155 people on board the plane and the recovery of the aircraft.

Robert Greenhalgh Albion, *Rise of New York Port, 1815–1860* (New York: Scribner, 1939); Stevens Institute of Technology, The Center for Maritime Systems, "NY/NJ Coastal Observing and Forecasting System," http://hudson.dl.stevens-tech.edu/maritimeforecast

John Rousmaniere

Tiemann, Daniel F(awcett) (*b* New York City, 9 Jan 1805; *d* New York City, 18 June 1899). Mayor. A paint dealer and member of Tammany Hall, he became known as a Democratic alderman and almshouse governor before winning the mayoral election of 1858, in which he called attention to the outrageous excesses of his opponent, Fernando Wood. While in office he reorganized the Board of Education and set up an efficient government based on honesty. He did not receive his party's nomination again.

James E. Mooney

Tiffany, Louis Comfort (*b* New York City, 18 Feb 1848; *d* New York City, 17 Jan 1933). Artist and designer. He was born at 57 Warren Street. As a young man he studied painting in New York City and Paris and pursued a career in the decorative arts rather than enter his father's business, Tiffany and Company. He soon became one of the most innovative designers of the American Aesthetic movement. During the late 1870s he and his rival, John La Farge, revolutionized the production of stained glass. By 1881 they were granted patents for a kind of opalescent glass with inherent tonal gradations, textures, and densities that could be used for detailing rather than enamels. In 1879 Tiffany opened his own firm, Louis C. Tiffany and Associated Artists, which decorated the interiors of mansions and private clubs. In 1893 he built a factory in Queens that produced Favrile, a line of organically shaped objects free blown from integrally colored glass that was often iridescent; these items were widely exhibited in Europe and gained him international recognition. This factory became known as Tiffany Studios, which in the early twentieth century produced decorative light fixtures, metalwork, enamelware, ceramics, and jewelry that were sold from his showroom in Manhattan, as well as thousands of windows, many of which remained in their original settings into the twenty-first century. For many years Tiffany lived at 27 East 72nd Street; his last home was at 19 East 72nd Street. A wide range of his work is displayed by the Metropolitan Museum of Art, and many of his lamps are held by the New-York Historical Society. One of his surviving interiors is the restored Veterans' Room of the Seventh Regiment Armory on Park Avenue.

Robert Koch, *Louis C. Tiffany, Rebel in Glass* (New York: Crown, 1964); Hugh F. McKean, *The "Lost" Treasures of Louis Comfort Tiffany* (New York: Doubleday, 1980); Alastair Duncan, Martin Eidelberg, and Neil Harris, *Masterworks of Louis Comfort Tiffany* (New York: Harry N. Abrams, 1989); Martin Eidelberg, Alice Cooney Frelinghuysen, et al., *The Lamps of Louis Comfort Tiffany* (New York: Vendome Press, 2005)

Alice Cooney Frelinghuysen

Tiffany and Company, 2009

Tiffany and Company. Firm of jewelers at 727 Fifth Avenue in Manhattan, formed on 21 September 1837 as Tiffany and Young by Charles L. Tiffany (1812–1902) and John B. Young. At the outset it sold stationery and fancy goods at 237 Broadway. When Jabez Ellis became a partner in 1841, the firm changed its name to Tiffany, Young and Ellis and began selling jewelry and silver from Europe; it soon manufactured jewelry in gold (from 1848) and silver (from 1851). In 1853 Tiffany bought out Young and Ellis, and the name became Tiffany and Company. As its business expanded, the firm moved successively to 271 Broadway (1847), 550 Broadway (1854), Union Square (1870), the corner of 37th Street and Fifth Avenue (1905), and its present location (1940). Under the direction of Edward C. Moore (1827–91), Paulding Farnham (1859–1927), and George Frederick Kunz (1856–1932) the firm achieved international recognition for its innovative designs (particularly of Japanesque-inspired silver) and elaborate diamond and enameled jewelry, and for its collection of rare gemstones. On Tiffany's death in 1902 his son Louis Comfort Tiffany became vice president and artistic director of the company, and from 1907 to 1933 a department manufactured and sold his jewelry and enamels. Walter Hoving (1897–1989) took over the firm in 1955 and worked with such talented designers as Jean Schlumberger (1907–87), Donald Claflin (1931–79), Angela Cummings (*b* 1944), Elsa Peretti (*b* 1940), and Paloma Picasso (*b* 1949). Tiffany and Company was bought in 1979 by Avon Products. During the tenure of William R. Chaney (*b* 1932) the firm was sold by Avon in 1984 and expanded nationally and internationally. Truman Capote's novella *Breakfast at Tiffany's* (1958), later made into a film, helped to make Tiffany the most famous jewelry store in the United States.

Joseph Purtell, *The Tiffany Touch* (New York: Random House, 1971); Charles and Mary Grace Carpenter, *Tiffany Silver* (New York: Dodd, Mead, 1984); John Loring, *Tiffany's 150 Years* (New York: Doubleday, 1987)

Janet Zapata

Tilden, Samuel J(ones) (*b* New Lebanon, N.Y., 9 Feb 1814; *d* Yonkers, N.Y., 4 Aug 1886). Governor, lawyer, and presidential candidate.

Samuel J. Tilden

After his admission to the bar in 1841, he practiced law with Andrew Haswell Green and had one of the earliest and most successful corporate practices in New York City. He first gained political prominence when he directed an attack on the Tweed Ring: elected governor as a reformer in 1874, he continued his crusade against corruption and was nominated for the presidency by the Democrats in 1876. He lost to Rutherford B. Hayes in a stolen election; a dispute surrounding the electoral vote was resolved in Hayes's favor by a commission in which Republicans formed a majority. Tilden was praised by supporters for his principles but criticized by others as indecisive. His bequest of his large book collection for the establishment of a public library was long delayed in the courts, but ultimately led to the formation of the New York Public Library. He lived at 15 Gramercy Park.

Alexander C. Flick, *Samuel Jones Tilden: A Study in Political Sagacity* (New York: Dodd, Mead, 1939); Keith Ian Polakoff, *The Politics of Inertia: The Election of 1876 and the End of Reconstruction* (Baton Rouge: Louisiana State University Press, 1973)

Jerome Mushkat

Tile Club. Social organization formed in 1877 by 12 artists and writers, among them the painters Winslow Homer and J. Alden Weir and the journalist William Mackay Laffan. It held informal weekly meetings for a decade. Inspired by the aesthetic movement, its members painted white tiles and later plaques 8 inches (20 centimeters) square, experimenting with a range of subject matter and styles. They also published articles on their activities in *Scribner's* and the *Century* that helped to popularize tile painting. Later members of the club included William Merritt Chase and Augustus Saint-Gaudens. Most of the club's tiles were destroyed by fire in 1881, and the group disbanded in 1887. Surviving examples of their work were collected by the Guild Hall Museum in East Hampton, New York.

Carol Lowrey

Time. Magazine launched by Henry R. Luce and Briton Hadden in New York City in February 1923. It was the nation's first successful "news magazine." Initially relying on the *New York Times* and Walter Lippmann's editorials in the *New York World, Time* summarized and interpreted the week's news. Its dependence on New York City newspapers was reinforced when Luce and Hadden, in a money-saving gesture, tried to publish the magazine in Cleveland during 1925–27 and found that Cleveland's newspapers proved inadequate sources on national and international events. Despite *Time*'s New York City base, the magazine's core readership consisted of middle-class Americans living in smaller cities and towns whose demand for national and international news was largely unmet by their hometown papers, which stressed local news. For such readers, *Time*'s distinctive voice—sometimes irreverent, usually omniscient—created the sensation of "being in the know." *Time*'s circulation rose sharply during the 1930s and 1940s, when economic upheaval and global conflict greatly complicated the task of staying informed. By then, *Time* had its own reporters, though it was said that their stories were heavily edited. During the 1950s *Time* was commonly considered the single most influential national news medium. Its importance declined beginning in the 1960s as television news provided small-town Americans with a national news agenda. The magazine's bias toward the Republican Party and intervention in Vietnam soured some readers, to the advantage of rival *Newsweek*. During the late twentieth century *Time*'s editors labored to reposition the publication. It stopped trying to summarize the week's news, and much international news was dropped in favor of more stories on domestic trends and interpretative pieces. In the early 2000s the magazine's circulation was approximately 3.4 million.

James L. Baughman

Timely Publications. Original name of Marvel Comics.

Times Square. A section of midtown Manhattan centered at the intersection of Broadway and Seventh Avenue. Known as Long Acre Square before 1904, the area was the site of William H. Vanderbilt's American Horse Exchange and was an important commercial center. Between 1830 and 1860 the Astor family built a neighborhood there that remained exclusive until the 1890s. "Silk hat" brothels opened at the turn of the century, served discreetly by carriages and cabs. The area was renamed after the turn of the century when the *New York Times* erected a new building nearby on 43rd Street. To commemorate the new site publisher Adolph Ochs staged a New Year's Eve spectacular that began a tradition continuing into the twenty-first century. During the early years of the twentieth century Times Square became the main transfer point for north–south traffic in the new subway system, and its importance grew after Grand Central Terminal opened at 42nd Street and Fourth Avenue in 1913, further helping to focus commercial activity in midtown Manhattan.

By the time of World War I most legitimate theaters had moved to Times Square from the former entertainment districts along the Bowery to East 14th Street and along Broadway from 42nd Street to Union Square; vaudeville, the music business (known as Tin Pan Alley), dance halls, and cabarets were concentrated in the streets nearby. Hotels like the Astor and the Knickerbocker and restaurants like Rector's thrived. The entertainment newspaper *Variety* had its offices in the neighborhood, and there was ceaseless activity in trade associations such as the Actors' Equity Association, in the Lambs and Friars clubs, and in the many local bars and gathering places. During the 1920s the number of visitors increased, owing partly to large-scale tourism and business travel and partly to the decline of religious and moral strictures against various amusements. In 1927–28 a record was set when 264 shows were produced in 76 theaters. The Palace Theatre at 47th Street and Broadway was the center of vaudeville, and the neighborhood also became a staging area for the touring companies of Broadway shows. Several journalists were closely associated with the area, among them Walter Winchell and Damon Runyon, whose columns were nationally syndicated.

The neighborhood changed dramatically after the stock market crash of 1929. Few new theaters were built, and during the Depression many existing ones were converted into cheap "grinder" houses that offered continuous showings of sexually explicit films. The Palace became a movie theater, and the premieres of motion pictures replaced the openings of Broadway shows as the focus of entertainment. Burlesque shows were introduced by the Minsky brothers and other promoters; cheap restaurants, peep shows, taxi dance halls, penny arcades, and dime museums also opened. There was an increasing array of commercialized sex, including that offered by unemployed women and men who became prostitutes along 42nd Street. At the same time Tin Pan Alley had produced more than half a million songs, and many of the entertainments developed in Times Square became known nationally through the efforts of the major broadcasting companies and Hollywood studios, which had offices there.

The interruption to Broadway theatrical productions brought on by World War II

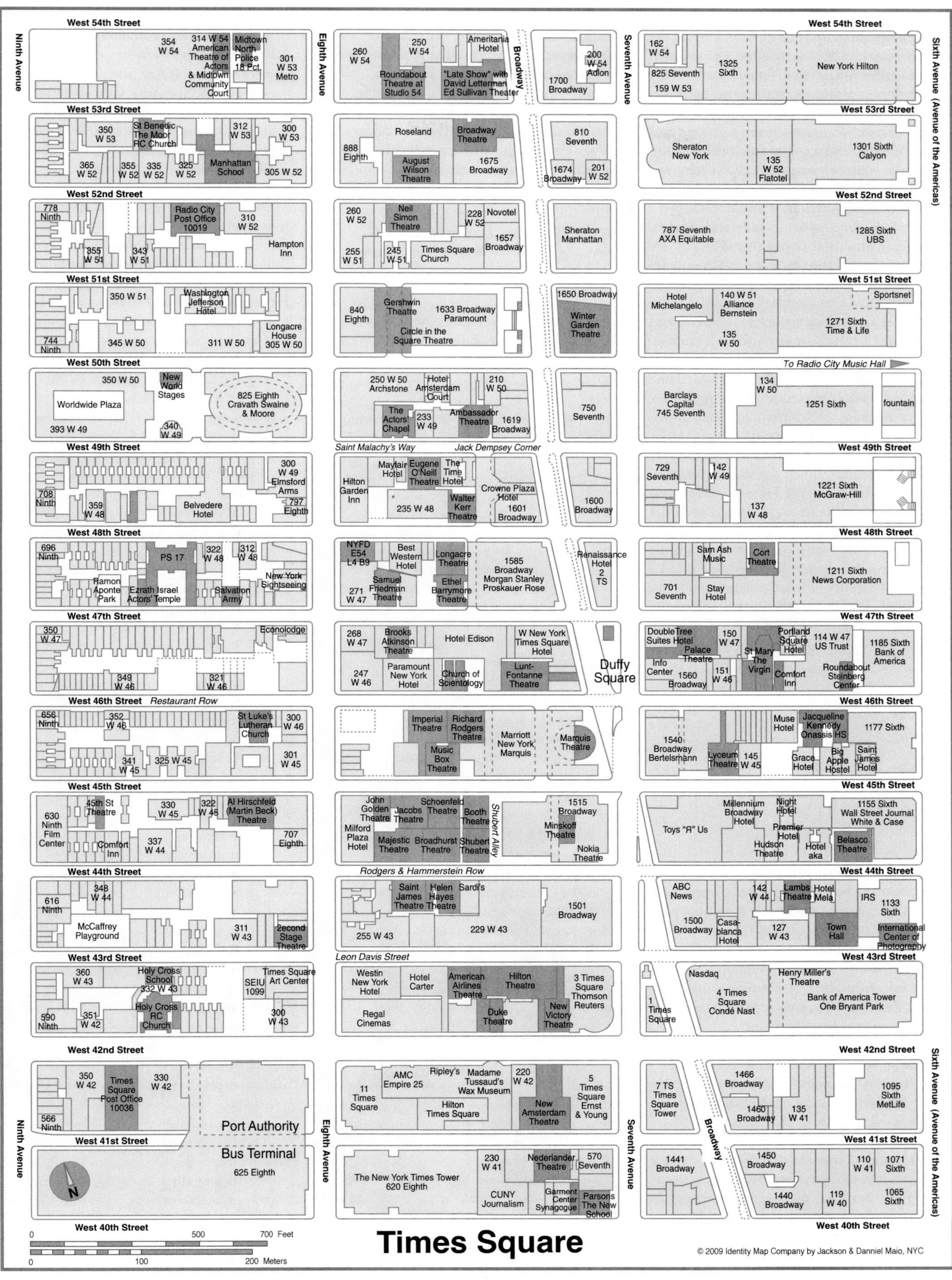

West 54th Street
Ninth Avenue
354 W 54
314 W 54 American Theatre of Actors & Midtown Community Court
Midtown North Police 18 Pct.
301 W 53 Metro
Eighth Avenue
260 W 54
250 W 54
Ameritania Hotel
Roundabout Theatre at Studio 54
"Late Show" with David Letterman Ed Sullivan Theater
Broadway
200 W 54 Adlon
1700 Broadway
Seventh Avenue
162 W 54
825 Seventh
159 W 53
1325 Sixth
New York Hilton
Sixth Avenue (Avenue of the Americas)
West 53rd Street
350 W 53
St Benedict The Moor RC Church
312 W 53
300 W 53
365 W 52
355 W 52
335 W 52
325 W 52
Manhattan School
305 W 52
Roseland
Broadway Theatre
888 Eighth
August Wilson Theatre
1675 Broadway
810 Seventh
1674 Broadway
201 W 52
Sheraton New York
135 W 52 Flatotel
1301 Sixth Calyon
West 52nd Street
778 Ninth
Radio City Post Office 10019
310 W 52
355 W 51
343 W 51
Hampton Inn
260 W 52
Neil Simon Theatre
228 W 52
Novotel
1657 Broadway
255 W 51
245 W 51
Times Square Church
Sheraton Manhattan
787 Seventh AXA Equitable
1285 Sixth UBS
West 51st Street
350 W 51
Washington Jefferson Hotel
744 Ninth
345 W 50
311 W 50
Longacre House 305 W 50
840 Eighth
Gershwin Theatre
1633 Broadway Paramount
Circle in the Square Theatre
1650 Broadway
Winter Garden Theatre
Hotel Michelangelo
140 W 51 Alliance Bernstein
135 W 50
Sportsnet
1271 Sixth Time & Life
West 50th Street
To Radio City Music Hall
350 W 50
New World Stages
Worldwide Plaza
825 Eighth Cravath Swaine & Moore
393 W 49
340 W 49
250 W 50 Archstone
Hotel Amsterdam Court
210 W 50
The Actors' Chapel
233 W 49
Ambassador Theatre
1619 Broadway
750 Seventh
Barclays Capital 745 Seventh
134 W 50
1251 Sixth
fountain
West 49th Street
Saint Malachy's Way
Jack Dempsey Corner
300 W 49 Elmsford Arms
708 Ninth
359 W 48
Belvedere Hotel
797 Eighth
Hilton Garden Inn
Maytair Hotel
Eugene O'Neill Theatre
The Time Hotel
235 W 48
Walter Kerr Theatre
Crowne Plaza Hotel 1601 Broadway
1600 Broadway
729 Seventh
142 W 49
137 W 48
1221 Sixth McGraw-Hill
West 48th Street
696 Ninth
PS 17
322 W 48
312 W 48
Ramon Aponte Park
Ezrath Israel Actors' Temple
Salvation Army
New York Sightseeing
NYFD E54 L4 B9
Best Western Hotel
Longacre Theatre
Samuel Friedman Theatre
271 W 47
Ethel Barrymore Theatre
1585 Broadway Morgan Stanley Proskauer Rose
Renaissance Hotel 2 TS
Sam Ash Music
Cort Theatre
701 Seventh
Stay Hotel
1211 Sixth News Corporation
West 47th Street
350 W 47
Econolodge
349 W 46
321 W 46
268 W 47
Brooks Atkinson Theatre
Hotel Edison
W New York Times Square Hotel
247 W 46
Paramount New York Hotel
Church of Scientology
Lunt-Fontanne Theatre
Duffy Square
DoubleTree Suites Hotel
Info Center
Palace Theatre
150 W 47
1560 Broadway
151 W 46
St Mary The Virgin
Portland Square Hotel
Comfort Inn
114 W 47 US Trust
Roundabout Steinberg Center
1185 Sixth Bank of America
West 46th Street
Restaurant Row
656 Ninth
352 W 46
St Luke's Lutheran Church
300 W 46
341 W 45
325 W 45
301 W 45
Imperial Theatre
Richard Rodgers Theatre
Music Box Theatre
Marriott New York Marquis
Marquis Theatre
1540 Broadway Bertelsmann
Lyceum Theatre
145 W 45
Muse Hotel
Jacqueline Kennedy Onassis HS
Grace Hotel
Big Apple Hostel
Saint James Hotel
1177 Sixth
West 45th Street
630 Ninth Film Center
45th St Theatre
330 W 45
322 W 45
Al Hirschfeld (Martin Beck) Theatre
Comfort Inn
337 W 44
707 Eighth
Milford Plaza Hotel
John Golden Theatre
Jacobs Theatre
Schoenfeld Theatre
Booth Theatre
Shubert Alley
Majestic Theatre
Broadhurst Theatre
Shubert Theatre
1515 Broadway
Minskoff Theatre
Nokia Theatre
Toys "Я" Us
Millennium Broadway Hotel
Night Hotel
Premier Hotel
Hudson Theatre
Hotel aka
Belasco Theatre
1155 Sixth Wall Street Journal White & Case
West 44th Street
Rodgers & Hammerstein Row
616 Ninth
348 W 44
McCaffrey Playground
311 W 43
2econd Stage Theatre
Saint James Theatre
Helen Hayes Theatre
Sardi's
255 W 43
229 W 43
1501 Broadway
ABC News
1500 Broadway
Casablanca Hotel
142 W 44
Lambs Theatre
Hotel Mela
127 W 43
Town Hall
IRS
1133 Sixth
International Center of Photography
West 43rd Street
Leon Davis Street
360 W 43
Holy Cross School 332 W 43
Times Square Art Center
SEIU 1099
Holy Cross RC Church
590 Ninth
351 W 42
300 W 43
Westin New York Hotel
Hotel Carter
American Airlines Theatre
Hilton Theatre
3 Times Square Thomson Reuters
Regal Cinemas
Duke Theatre
New Victory Theatre
1 Times Square
Nasdaq
4 Times Square Condé Nast
Henry Miller's Theatre
Bank of America Tower One Bryant Park
West 42nd Street
350 W 42
Times Square Post Office 10036
330 W 42
566 Ninth
Port Authority Bus Terminal
625 Eighth
AMC Empire 25
Ripley's
Madame Tussaud's Wax Museum
220 W 42
11 Times Square
Hilton Times Square
New Amsterdam Theatre
5 Times Square Ernst & Young
7 TS Times Square Tower
1466 Broadway
1460 Broadway
135 W 41
1095 Sixth MetLife
West 41st Street
The New York Times Tower 620 Eighth
230 W 41
Nederlander Theatre
570 Seventh
CUNY Journalism
Garment Center Synagogue
Parsons The New School
1441 Broadway
1450 Broadway
1440 Broadway
119 W 40
110 W 41
1071 Sixth
1065 Sixth
West 40th Street
N
0 500 700 Feet
0 100 200 Meters
Times Square
© 2009 Identity Map Company by Jackson & Danniel Maio, NYC

removed the last real check on the descent of Times Square into a zone for vice. During the war soldiers on leave made the area a haven for hustlers (male and female) and other purveyors of erotic entertainment. Attempts during the 1950s to check the growth of disreputable businesses through zoning had little effect. The continuing proliferation of cheap rooming houses, hotels, cafeterias, bars, adult bookstores, peep shows, and arcades was depicted in John Schlesinger's film *Midnight Cowboy* (1968) and Martin Scorsese's film *Taxi Driver* (1976).

Efforts during the 1980s and 1990s to redevelop the area met with success, and by the early twenty-first century Times Square was more successful, attractive, opulent, and brilliantly lit than in any previous decade. The once grimy 42nd Street pornographic shops and theaters had given way to Madame Tussaud's Wax Museum, giant multiplex movie theaters, child-oriented emporiums, and hugely successful musicals. Most notably, new skyscrapers throughout Times Square made the neighborhood the media capital of the world. The *New York Times* itself relocated to an impressive new tower between 40th and 41st Streets along Eighth Avenue, and high-tech billboards made the area easily visible from commercial aircraft descending into La Guardia Airport. Times Square continues to advertise itself as "the crossroads of the world" and the "Great White Way."

William R. Taylor, ed., *Inventing Times Square: Commerce and Culture at the Crossroads of the World, 1880–1939* (New York: Russell Sage Foundation, 1991); Lynne B. Sagalyn, *Times Square Roulette: Remaking the City Icon* (Cambridge, Mass.: MIT Press, 2001)

See also Bartholdi Inn, Broadway, New Year's Eve, Outdoor advertising, Theater, and TKTS.

William R. Taylor

time standardization. As the commercial and scientific hub of the United States, New York City played a major role in establishing standard time zones. Before 1883 every community ran according to its own local time: in New York City a time ball atop the Western Union Building at Broadway and Dey Street descended precisely at noon, and sailors referred to another ball at the U.S. Custom House and the South Street Seaport. An early campaign for time standardization was led by William F. Allen, a railroad engineer from New York City who was the head of the American Railway Association, and Frederick A. P. Barnard and J. K. Rees, two prominent scientists at Columbia University who tried to have a national standard time law enacted by the U.S. Congress; Barnard was also instrumental in having meteorological and astronomic observations coordinated to a standard time. Time standardization was first put into effect by railroad engineers, who depended on strict timetables to establish schedules and avoid collisions. Allen edited the *Traveller's Official Guide,* a collection of railway timetables and trade information, and formulated a four-zone plan that railroads adopted at noon on Sunday 18 November 1883 without benefit of federal or state law. There was little opposition in New York City, but other parts of the nation objected strenuously to the new time zones.

Michael O'Malley, *Keeping Watch: A History of American Time* (New York: Viking, 1990)

Michael O'Malley

Time Warner. Entertainment conglomerate formed by a merger of Time Inc. and Warner Communications Inc. in 1990. Time Inc. became successful by publishing a succession of innovative and profitable magazines, notably *Time* (1923), *Fortune* (1930), *Life* (1936), *Sports Illustrated* (1954), and *People* (1974). All were based in New York City. After working out of various midtown sites, including the Chrysler Building and Rockefeller Center, in 1960 Time Inc. moved into an office tower at Rockefeller Center (1271 Avenue of the Americas). In 1970, three years after the death of Henry R. Luce, Time Inc. entered cable television, securing a controlling interest in Sterling Communications, which provided cable service for the lower half of Manhattan. The firm inaugurated a premium cable service, Home Box Office (HBO); subscribers paying an additional fee could view recent films and live events. With access to a satellite relay system beginning in 1976, HBO offered its

Time Warner Building, 2009

service nationally and became the leading pay cable outlet. By 1988 cable activities constituted 41 percent of Time Inc.'s revenues, but a large cash flow made the company vulnerable to a hostile takeover. In a bold if defensive gesture, in 1990 Time Inc. paid $15 billion in stock for Warner Communications Inc., a giant filmmaking, cable, and book publishing concern; Time Warner became the largest entertainment conglomerate in the world. Despite the firm's massive debt from the Warner purchase, Chairman of the Board Gerald Levin made still more acquisitions. In 1995 Time Warner purchased the substantial broadcast-cable properties of Ted Turner. Five years later, the Internet provider AOL bought Time Warner. Although a friendly merger, it was poorly timed. The value of AOL stock, which had been used to pay for the acquisition, collapsed, and Levin fell from power. His successor struggled to placate investors who wanted to break up the conglomerate. In 2004 the company moved to the $1.7 billion Time Warner Center on Columbus Circle; the magazine operations continued at Rockefeller Center.

James L. Baughman

Time Warner Center. Mixed-use building located at 10 Columbus Circle. It was designed by David Childs and Mustafa Kemal Abadan of the architecture firm Skidmore, Owings and Merrill. The project faced nearly 15 years of delays spearheaded by opponents like Jacqueline Kennedy Onassis, who believed that a building there would cast a shadow on Central Park. The project hung in limbo until 2000, when the Coliseum, the building that formerly occupied the site, was demolished and construction started. In 2003 it became the first major construction project to be completed after the terrorist attacks of 11 September 2001. It occupies nearly half of Columbus Circle, consisting of two 750-foot (229-meter) towers connected by a multistory atrium with a facade that curves to echo the traffic circle in front. The center includes the headquarters of Time Warner Inc., upscale shops, hotel and restaurant space, a Cable News Network (CNN) studio, residential units, performance space, and other office space.

Anne Epstein

Tin Pan Alley. Name applied originally to a district in New York City in which composers and music publishers were concentrated from the 1890s to the 1950s, and by extension to the style of their music and to the popular music business generally; the term may derive from the tinny sound of the pianos played by song pluggers. During the 1890s the corner of Broadway and 14th Street was the focus of the popular music business. After the eminent publishers M. Witmark and Sons moved uptown in the late 1890s, the focus shifted successively to West 28th Street between Broadway and Sixth Avenue; during 1903–8 to West 42nd Street, where many large publishers had their offices; during 1911–19 to the vicinity of the Exchange Building at 145 West 45th Street, which housed many smaller publishers; and during the 1920s to an area near 49th Street where the Brill Building was erected in 1931 at 1619 Broadway, although the music district extended as far south as West 42nd Street and as far north as West 56th Street.

Tin Pan Alley innovated music marketing and production. In the early days of music publishing the industry was dispersed across the country; such established firms as Oliver Ditson of Boston and Lee and Walker of Philadelphia issued many kinds of music, which they publicized and distributed with little business acumen. Songwriters of the time, including Stephen Foster, George Root, Will S. Hays, and James Bland, wrote melodies rooted in English and American folk traditions, supported by simple harmonies and set to lyrics that expressed the values of rural America. During the 1880s a new group of publishers and songwriters emerged, many of them of eastern European and Jewish origin, and the industry changed dramatically after Charles K. Harris's song "After the Ball" (1892) sold nearly five million copies in the 1890s and nearly 10 million altogether. New songs were now expertly promoted and aggressively advertised in newspapers and magazines, on the back covers of the sheet music of older songs, and by hired song pluggers who played them on city streets and in theaters, department stores, and retail music shops. Noted singers and unknown organ grinders alike received stipends for publicizing new songs, publishers readily altered pieces to suit the needs of any entertainer, and free copies went to everyone likely to perform the music in public. To advance their music, publishers in Tin Pan Alley also staged musicals and invested in theaters and vaudeville circuits. During the 1920s, when sheet music sales began to decline, the industry began producing recordings and promoting them on the radio. The advent of motion pictures with sound during the 1930s made possible the filming of musicals and helped bring songs to a wider public.

Through the early years of the twentieth century the best-known songwriters in Tin Pan Alley included Charles Harris, Jean Schwartz ("Bedelia," 1903), George M. Cohan ("Give My Regards to Broadway," 1904), Paul Dresser ("My Gal Sal," 1905), and Harry Von Tilzer ("Wait 'Till the Sun Shines, Nellie," 1905). Between 1910 and 1940 publishers enlisted a generation of younger composers, including Irving Berlin, Fats Waller, Jerome Kern, George Gershwin, Cole Porter, Duke Ellington, and Richard Rodgers and lyricists such as Ira Gershwin, Lorenz Hart, and Oscar Hammerstein II. Although they worked in the same idiom as their older colleagues, their music was more original and their lyrics more sophisticated. During the 1950s and 1960s Tin Pan Alley failed to compete with new styles of music, such as the rock-and-roll of Elvis Presley, the protest folk songs of Peter, Paul and Mary, and country music, and New York City accordingly ceased to dominate the popular music business. Nevertheless, the best-known songs of Tin Pan Alley remain in the repertory into the twenty-first century, inspiring films, television productions, and theatrical revivals, and many new songs and Broadway shows draw on their stylistic conventions.

David A. Jasen, *Tin Pan Alley: The Composers, the Songs, the Performers, and Their Times* (New York: Donald I. Fine, 1988); Nicholas E. Tawa, *The Way to Tin Pan Alley: American Popular Song, 1866–1910* (New York: Schirmer, 1990)

Nicholas E. Tawa

Tipperary Corners. Obsolete name of Egbertville.

Tishman, David (*b* New York City, 1889; *d* New York City, 18 June 1980). Real estate developer. With his father, Julius Tishman, he built luxury apartment buildings on the Upper West Side between 1910 and 1920, 17 similar buildings on the Upper East Side between 1922 and 1929, and several office buildings and lofts in the garment district. The city's most prominent and successful developer by the late 1930s, he survived the Depression and built the first postwar office tower in Manhattan (1947, 445 Park Avenue). In 1957 he completed the Tishman Building, a skyscraper at 666 Fifth Avenue between 52nd and 53rd streets that became the headquarters of his firm, which was taken over during the 1960s by his sons Robert Tishman and Alan Tishman, his nephew John Tishman, and his son-in-law Jerry Speyer.

Marc A. Weiss

Titanic. Steamship that sank in 1912 on its maiden voyage from England to New York City. New York banker J. Pierpont Morgan held the controlling interest in the International Mercantile Marine Co., which owned the RMS *Titanic.* Of the 74 passengers from the city, at least 24 died, including millionaires John Jacob Astor IV and George Widener, and two maids, Julia Barry and Ida Livija Ilmakangas. Twelve victims were buried in New York City. The ship was to dock at Chelsea Piers, on the Hudson near 18th Street. Instead, more than 700 survivors were brought by the liner *Carpathia* to Pier 54, at 12th Street, and were treated at St. Vincent's Hospital.

There are four permanent *Titanic*-related monuments in the city. The official *Titanic* Memorial is a 60-foot (18-meter) lighthouse that was placed on the roof of the 12-story

Seamen's Church Institute building at 25 South Street in 1915. Its green light guided ships into the harbor until 1968, when the building was torn down and the lighthouse was moved to the corner of Water and Fulton streets. At the Battery is a monument to maritime wireless telegraph operators who lost their lives at sea; at the top of the list is Jack Phillips, the *Titanic*'s radio operator. Set into Central Park's retaining wall at Fifth Avenue and 91st Street is a bronze plaque memorializing William Thomas Stead, an English journalist who was on his way to a peace congress at Carnegie Hall. (The plaque is a copy of one at the London Embankment.) The Straus Park and Memorial Fountain, at 106th Street between Broadway and West End Avenue, memorializes Ida and Isidor Straus, who had lived nearby at 2745 Broadway. A former congressman and an officer at the R. H. Macy and Abraham and Straus department stores, Straus declined to enter a lifeboat until all women and children were saved, and his wife of 41 years refused to leave without him. The monument, designed by H. Augustus Lukeman, is called *Memory*. Its inscription reads, in part, "'Lovely and pleasant were they in their lives and in their death they were not divided.' II Samuel 1:23."

The most authoritative account of the loss of the *Titanic* remains *A Night to Remember* (1955), by Walter Lord, who lived at 116 East 68th Street. His large collection of *Titanic*-related artifacts is now at the National Maritime Museum in Greenwich, England. The loss of the *Titanic* became a landmark in American journalism, according to *New York Times* columnist Russell Baker, who in his memoir *The Good Times* (1989) wrote that the *Times* maintained an overstaffed newsroom of more than 100 reporters as late as the 1960s because the paper's owners always resolved to be prepared "to cover the story when the *Titanic* sinks."

John Rousmaniere

TKTS. Discount theater ticket service (pronounced Tee-Kay-Tee-Ess). At the behest of the New York City mayor's office and with the cooperation of the League of American Theaters and Producers, the Theater Development Fund (TDF) opened a discount ticket booth in Times Square's Duffy Square in 1973 with the hope that it would boost sagging theater ticket sales. With a Parks Department construction trailer, TKTS began selling day-of theater tickets at a 25 to 50 percent discount, modeled after Joe LeBlang's cut-rate ticket service during the 1920s and 1930s at Gray's Drugstore. TKTS was immediately successful and broke even within two months. As of 2007 TKTS had sold nearly 50 million tickets to productions on and off Broadway and to music and dance events in New York City, generating $1.2 billion in returned revenue for city theaters. A $2.50 service charge per ticket funds the daily operations of the three TKTS booths in Duffy Square, South Street Seaport, and downtown Brooklyn. TKTS has helped to make TDF the largest performing arts foundation in the country and has led to the establishment of similar services nationally in Boston, Chicago, Pittsburgh, Philadelphia, Denver, and San Francisco and internationally in London, Sydney, and Toronto.

TKTS, 2009

Rowan Moore Gerety

TLC Beatrice International Holdings. International holding company. It was based at 9 West 57th Street, specializing in grocery products and food distribution. Formed in 1987, when Reginald F. Lewis bought Beatrice International Foods for $985 million, it became the largest black-owned firm in the United States from 1989 to 1999. At its highest point TLC Beatrice grossed over $2.1 billion in sales. Its operations consisted mainly of the former overseas operations of Beatrice International Foods, which became a subsidiary of Conagra. Most of the subsidiaries made well-known brands of ice cream, desserts, beverages, and snacks in western Europe; the firm also had interests in Thailand, Puerto Rico, and Canada. After Lewis's death in January 1993, the firm came under the control of his heirs. In 1997 TLC Beatrice sold off its food distribution business, which had constituted the vast majority of its revenues, and in 1999 the rest of the company was liquidated.

Gilbert Tauber, Nathan Morgante

tobacco. Trade in tobacco began in New Amsterdam and flourished after the British took control of the colony. During the eighteenth century tobacco was brought north from the Chesapeake River and prepared for export to Europe, becoming the third most lucrative export crop for the colony, after cotton and flour. It was also grown on small plantations in Manhattan and Brooklyn but was never a major crop, as the quality was considered not as good as Virginia tobacco, a dominant export. The growth in snuff and pipe tobacco consumption led French Huguenot immigrant Pierre Lorillard to open the first large snuff factory in 1760. Its snuff mill was in a rural area now part of the northern Bronx (the site of the Bronx Botanical Garden), but most snuff mills were in Manhattan, including those of Isaac de Voe and Daniel Snowhill.

In the early nineteenth century the firm of G. B. Miller, later known as H. J. Mickle and Sons, was a major producer of chewing tobacco. The federal census of 1840 lists more than 200 workers in Manhattan's tobacco business. By 1846 the city was the principal point of entry for Caribbean cigars, an increasingly valuable import during the first half of the nineteenth century: city directories listed 44 importers. By the mid-nineteenth century most pipe and chewing-tobacco businesses had moved to the South, while most snuff manufacturing was in Middlesex County, New Jersey. In New York City, small shops around Chatham Square specialized in cigars; immigrants from Cuba, Spain, England, the Netherlands, and Germany worked in this growing industry. After the Civil War domestic cigar making became more popular as import duties on foreign tobacco increased, and New York City became the largest cigar-making center in the United States. In 1870 about 144 million cigars were produced annually in Manhattan (eight times as many as in 1863), and more than 5500 men and women were employed by more than 1000 cigar-making establishments.

During the late 1860s the introduction of the cigar mold enabled workers with much less skill to roll reasonably uniform cigars, resulting in significant expansion of the industry. By 1881 at least 17 employers had more than 250 workers each, with more than 1500 workers in each of the three largest firms: Kerbs and Spiess, Straiton and Storm, and Lichtenstein Brothers. At the same time about 1700 small shops were situated in the city, as well as an indeterminate number of "tenement manufacturers" who rented tenements in which families lived and worked as cigar makers. German immigrants and east European Jews accounted for the bulk of employees. In the 1870s new unions fought for higher pay for cigar workers. During the height of the industry's growth cigar making was concentrated in two sections of Manhattan: around Chatham Square, an immigrant area, and north of 50th Street, where large numbers of Germans and Bohemians settled. In Brooklyn the industry was smaller, with only a few firms employing more than 100 workers.

By the twentieth century continued mechanization changed the industry. The increasing need for space and capital investment made the city much less desirable to cigar manufacturers, and many firms moved to Lancaster County, Pennsylvania, or farther south. Some remaining firms became part of the American Cigar Company of New York City, a cigar trust formed in 1901 by James B. Duke. Over the next six years the trust was joined by some of the largest firms (including Powell and Smith; Kerbs and Spiess; Wertheim and Schiffer; Hirshorn, Mack and Company; and Straiton and Storm), but it was less successful than trusts in the tobacco trade and in cigarette manufacturing. By World Ward II few cigars were manufactured in the city and none in major factories.

The decline of cigar making was largely due to the rise of the cigarette industry during the 1880s. Centered in Manhattan and Jersey City, New Jersey, the industry was dominated by Duke and the firm of P. Lorillard. By the 1890s cigarette production was mechanized and the workforce was ethnically heterogeneous: young women operated cigarette-rolling machines in large factories employing an average of more than 500 workers. In 1911 six large cigarette factories throughout Manhattan dominated the industry, with a large facility owned by Lorillard in Jersey City overlooking the Hudson River. A number of New York City firms, including Goodwin and Company, Kinney Tobacco, Lorillard, and the Continental Tobacco Company, merged and became the Consolidated Tobacco Company of Jersey City, which dominated the cigarette and "plug" (chewing-tobacco) markets nationwide from 1904 until a court order in 1911 forced the dissolution of the trust into three firms (Lorillard, American Tobacco, and Ligett and Myers).

New York City was the largest metropolitan market for cigarettes and a source of cheap female labor until the 1920s, when more than 30 percent of all North American cigarettes were still manufactured in the metropolitan area. The Depression reduced the size of the region's cigarette industry. By 1963 only about 200 people in Greater New York were employed in the tobacco industry. The city remained a center of corporate headquarters for tobacco conglomerates such as Philip Morris, American Brands (successor to the American Tobacco Company), and Lorillard. By the early 1990s there were no longer any tobacco, cigarette-making, or cigar-making facilities in the region.

After the 1960s opposition to tobacco use increased significantly, resulting in more laws restricting advertising, requiring notices of health dangers, and eventually limiting places where smoking could occur. New York City benefited from the 1998 Tobacco Master Settlement Agreement and received more than $1.8 billion as of 2007, a quarter of the annual payments made to New York State. The city used the payments to fund antismoking campaigns in schools and around the city. In 2002 the city increased the cigarette tax from eight cents per pack to $1.50, making New York City home to the country's most expensive pack of cigarettes. More dramatically, in 2003 a citywide ban on smoking in restaurants and bars took effect. Despite a backlash centered on smokers' rights and fears over diminished business in restaurants and bars, the ban is considered a success.

Dorothee Schneider, Rowan Moore Gerety

Tobagonians. Tobagonian immigration is discussed in the entry Trinidadians and Tobagonians.

Tobin, Austin J(oseph) (*b* Brooklyn, 25 May 1903; *d* New York City, 8 Feb 1978). Public official. After graduating from Holy Cross College in 1925 he joined the Port of New York Authority in 1927 and earned a law degree from Fordham University in 1928. Appointed executive director of the authority in 1942, he assembled a skilled, politically independent staff and during the next three decades oversaw the development of La Guardia, John F. Kennedy, and Newark Liberty airports; the creation of the massive bus terminal in Manhattan and of container ports in Newark–Elizabeth, New Jersey; the modernization of the Port Authority Trans-Hudson (PATH) transit system; and the construction of the World Trade Center. He retired in 1972.

Jameson W. Doig, *Empire on the Hudson: Entrepreneurial Vision and Political Power at the Port of New York Authority* (New York: Columbia University Press, 2001)

Jameson W. Doig

Todt Hill. Neighborhood in north central Staten Island. It is centered at a hill near the intersection of Todt Hill Road and Ocean Terrace that rises 410 feet (125 meters) above sea level and is the highest point on the Atlantic Coast of the United States south of Maine. The area was initially called Yserberg ("iron hill") by Dutch settlers, for the iron in the local serpentine rock, and was eventually renamed for a burial ground at the foot of the hill (now Moravian Cemetery). Large open-pit mines were operated from 1830 to 1885; some were eventually covered by the large golf course of the Richmond County Country Club. In 1928 St. Francis Seminary was built on a lot of 44 acres (17 hectares) north of the golf course. Architect Ernest Flagg built many houses of the native rock, including his own on a side of the hill (now a city landmark). Eventually the golf course and the seminary became part of the Greenbelt, a nature preserve that also includes 140 acres (57 hectares) to the south covered by Moravian Cemetery and the cemetery of the Vanderbilt family, as well as some other private land; the Greenbelt has many marked trails and a study area at High Rock Conservation Center (formerly a Girl Scout camp). The area was the primary filming location for the movie *The Godfather* (1972). In the early twenty-first century Todt Hill was one of the wealthiest neighborhoods in Staten Island and the site of Staten Island Academy, a prestigious private day school. Buttonwood Road is typical of its elegant, tree-lined streets.

Marjorie Johnson

toiletries. See Soap and toiletries.

tokens. Coin issued by various New York City institutions to be used in place of money. The city's first token was issued under Governor Francis Lovelace (1668–73). It depicted Cupid and Psyche (a rebus on the name Lovelace) and on the reverse an eagle on a regulated fesse (the crest of the Lovelace arms) within the inscription "New Yorke in America." The merchants Talbot, Allum and Lee issued large numbers of tokens in 1794 and 1795. The Theatre at New York token shows an image of the First Park Theatre copied from Longworth's Directory of 1797. "Hard-times tokens" circulated after the panic of 1837; during the Civil War, nearly 100 different merchants in the city issued tokens. In the late 1800s tokens were issued by amusement arcades on Coney Island. When the dime fare on the subways increased to 15 cents in 1953, brass tokens were introduced; to discourage hoarding when fares were increased, the design was altered on five subsequent occasions. Subway tokens were phased out at midnight, 13 April 2003, in favor of the electronic MetroCard.

John M. Kleeberg, "The New Yorker in America Token," *Money of Pre-Federal America,* ed. John M. Kleeberg (New York: American Numismatic Society, 1992), 15–57; John M. Kleeberg, "The Theatre at New York," *The Token: America's Other Money,* ed. Richard G. Doty (New York: American Numismatic Society, 1995), 19–64

See also People's Token.

John M. Kleeberg

tolls. Many of the connections between New York City's five boroughs, and all of the crossings to New Jersey, require the payment of a toll. There are no toll roads within New York City. The first toll bridge in the city was King's Bridge (1693), at Manhattan's northern end, which charged a toll until 1759. Other early city toll bridges were Coles Bridge (1795), across the East River at 129th Street, and the first Macomb's Dam Bridge (1813), which crossed the Harlem River at 155th Street. The first modern toll facility in the city was the Brooklyn Bridge (1883). Horse-drawn vehicles were charged 10 cents, riders on horseback paid five cents, and pedestrians were charged a penny. The toll for pedestrians was later dropped, and a 10-cent fee was added for automobiles. Similar charges were levied on the Williamsburgh Bridge (1903), the Manhattan Bridge (1909), and the Queensboro Bridge (1909). However, while all four of the East River crossings charged tolls, bridges across the Harlem River were free, as were crossings elsewhere in the city. This prompted Mayor William Gaynor in 1911 to halt the collections of the tolls on the four East River bridges.

In the 1920s and 1930s tolls were used on new bridges and tunnels. The revenues collected by these new tolls fueled the growth of two giant public benefit corporations—the Port Authority of New York and the Triborough Bridge and Tunnel Authority. The Port Authority collects tolls on all of the links between New York City and New Jersey, including two tunnels, the Holland (1927) and the Lincoln (1937), as well as four bridges: Goethals (1928), Outerbridge Crossing (1928), Bayonne (1931), and George Washington (1931). The Triborough Bridge and Tunnel Authority also collects tolls within the city on two tunnels, Midtown (1940) and Brooklyn–Battery (1950), plus seven bridges: Henry Hudson Memorial (1936), Triborough (1936), Marine Parkway–Gil Hodges Memorial (1937), Bronx–Whitestone (1939), Cross Bay–Veterans Memorial (1939), Throgs Neck (1961), and Verrazano–Narrows (1964).

Toll collection changed dramatically in 1993 with the introduction of E-ZPass, an electronic toll-collection technique pioneered by a consortium of New York toll authorities and agencies in Pennsylvania and New Jersey. The technology quickly spread nationwide and prompted new debates about variable pricing policies that had previously been impractical, such as congestion pricing, off-peak discounts, and rush-hour surcharges.

Owen Gutfreund

Tombs. Name commonly applied to the Manhattan Detention Complex at 125 White Street, the third prison to occupy the same general site. It is derived from the design for the first building, which was inspired by a photograph of an Egyptian tomb that appeared in a book on the Middle East written by John L. Stephens in 1837. Construction of the prison was made necessary by the city's growing population, the decrepit condition of the Bridewell near City Hall, and the inconvenient location of the penitentiary at Bellevue. The new prison proved inadequate: it had too few cells (200, of which 50 were reserved for women), and because it was built on a swampy landfill near the canal connecting the Hudson and East rivers, it soon began to sink; the same happened to a new building constructed in 1902, which was replaced in 1941. For decades the prison received widespread attention for its deplorable conditions and became a symbol of much that was wrong in correctional institutions. A renovation of the South Tower was completed in 1983, and construction of the North Tower, connected by a footbridge, was completed in 1990. Between 2001 and 2006 the facility was temporarily named the Bernard B. Kerik Complex after the former corrections commissioner who became police commissioner and later was indicted on corruption charges. The Tombs is now a modern facility that has a capacity for 900 inmates.

Charles Sutton, *The New York Tombs: Its Secrets and Its Mysteries,* ed. James B. Mix and Samuel A. Mackeever (New York: United States Publishing, 1874; repr. Montclair, N.J.: Patterson Smith, 1973)

See also Jails.

Joseph P. Viteritti

Tompkins, Daniel D. (*b* Fox Meadow [now Scarsdale], N.Y., 21 June 1774; *d* Staten Island, 11 June 1825). Governor and vice president of the United States. He graduated from Columbia College in 1795, practiced law in New York City, and became a Tammany Hall organizer. Elected governor of New York State in 1807 and thrice reelected, he achieved several reforms during his tenure, notably a commitment by the state to abolish slavery by 1827. During the War of 1812 he resolutely supported President James Madison's policies against legislative opposition, mobilized an unprepared militia, and raised money for the war effort by backing loans with his own credit; he also supervised the ceding of land and construction of forts on the islands of New York Harbor and, as the commander of the third military district, oversaw the mobilization of the civilian work crews that fortified the city in 1814. His founding that same year of a village called Tompkinsville

The Tombs, 1941

on Staten Island marked the beginning of the island's integration into Greater New York; even while serving as President James Monroe's vice president from 1817 to 1825, he spent much of his time developing this property. His Richmond Turnpike Company built the thoroughfare across the island now known as Victory Boulevard and, with the launching of the *Nautilus* in 1817, began the first steamboat ferry service to Manhattan and later the first towing service in the harbor. In 1824 he was the host in Staten Island of the start of the Marquis de Lafayette's triumphant tour of the United States. His last years were marred by ill health and political and financial embarrassment occasioned by his protracted struggle for compensation for his wartime expenditures and unsettled accounts. Tompkins is buried in the churchyard of St. Mark's Church in the Bowery, where a bust was unveiled in 1939. Tompkins Square was named for him in 1833; Tompkins Street was eventually obscured by the FDR Drive.

Ray W. Irwin, *Daniel D. Tompkins: Governor of New York and Vice President of the United States* (New York: New-York Historical Society, 1968)

Mariam Touba

Tompkins Square, 2009

Tompkins Square. Neighborhood bordering Tompkins Square Park, bounded to the north by 10th Street, to the south by Seventh Street, to the east by Avenue B, and to the west by Avenue A. Originally called Clinton Square, the park was the remnant of a large area designated a market in the 1811 Commissioners' Plan. In 1834 John Jacob Astor sold the 10.5-acre (4.2-hectare) swamp (used for snipe hunting) to New York City for $93,000. Named after New York Governor Daniel D. Tompkins, the square was first opened in 1834; it was landscaped and fenced, and it featured walkways and a fountain. The neighborhood, known as the Dry-Dock before the Civil War, became the new 17th ward, a dense population center for immigrants and new businesses. St. Brigid's, on the northwest corner, served Irish residents; the large number of Germans gave rise to the area's nickname, Kleindeutschland. A monument was erected in the square to honor the more than 1000 Germans—all local residents—killed in the GENERAL SLOCUM disaster in 1904. In the 1860s a radical transformation occurred when the square was converted into a parade ground. But in the 1870s it became a park again, hosting concerts, fireworks, and military parades. Political protest occurred in the 1870s: the 1874 "Blood or Bread" Riot involved police clashing with unemployed demonstrators, and in 1877 a meeting of people sympathetic to striking railroad workers was held (violence was averted).

In the twentieth century Tompkins Square continued to serve as a local recreation ground for the large immigrant community that surrounded it, increasingly Italians, Jews, Poles, and Ukrainians. In the 1980s it became a camping ground for the homeless and a gathering place for drug dealers; their eviction in 1988 precipitated one of the last violent demonstrations in the square. The park was renovated once again in the 1990s, and the neighborhood became increasingly gentrified in the early twenty-first century.

Lisa Keller, *Triumph of Order: Democracy and Public Space in New York and London* (New York: Columbia University Press, 2008)

Lisa Keller

Tompkins Square Riot. Name given to two riots on the Lower East Side of Manhattan, the first on 13 January 1874 and the second on 6 August 1988. See RIOTS.

Tompkinsville. Neighborhood in northeastern Staten Island lying along the eastern shore south of the terminal for the Staten Island Ferry at St. George. The oldest village in eastern Staten Island, it was a landing where early explorers replenished their water supply and was known in colonial times as the Watering Place; a settlement was established there next to the quarantine station in 1815 by Daniel D. Tompkins, who built a dock at the foot of Victory Boulevard and initiated steam ferry service to New York City in 1817. He named several streets after his children: Arietta Street (now Victory Boulevard), Griffin Street, Hannah Street, Sarah Ann Street (now part of Van Duzer Street), and Minthorne Street. A fleet of the U.S. Coast Guard was based there in the early nineteenth century and shared quarters with a regional lighthouse depot. In 2008 the population was Italian, Latin American, and black. The center of the village is a commercial area around Tompkinsville Park where a statue was placed to honor heroes of World War I and two smaller markers commemorate Tompkins and the Watering Place.

Barnett Shepherd

tongs. Secret Chinese protective associations that operate legal and illegal enterprises and employ youth gangs to control gambling, drug dealing, and extortion. Wars between tongs took place during periods of rapid expansion and internal power struggles in Chinatown. From 1910 to 1930 the young "soldiers" of the Hip Sing and On Leung tongs fought each other in the streets. Gangs sponsored by tongs became strong again in the 1960s, when there was a new influx of Chinese immigrants. By the 1980s tongs were outnumbered by other street gangs, which undertook their own enterprises, expanded into Chinese communities outside Manhattan, and increasingly engaged in violence to assert their authority against other gangs sponsored by tongs. Although such gangs as the Ghost Shadows became known citywide through sensational accounts in the press, their activities were largely confined to Chinese communities.

Betty Lee Sung, *Gangs in New York's Chinatown* (Washington, D.C.: Department of Health, Education and Welfare, 1977)

Joshua Brown

Tontine Coffee House. Building erected in 1793 at the corner of Wall and Water streets. In 1796 it became the headquarters of the New York Insurance Company. The 21 members of the company's board of directors

Tontine Coffee House

assigned values to slaves, ships, houses, and effects to form a tontine, a financial arrangement in which each member received a share of profit that increased as the number of participants was reduced by death. The tontine asserted that its actions would "have a tendency to advance the mercantile interest in particular and promote the general welfare of the State." Its first president was Archibald Gracie, whose home on the East River later became the official residence of the mayor.

Anthony Gronowicz

Tony Award. Award presented annually by the American Theater Wing, an educational and service organization of theater professionals, for distinguished achievement on Broadway. It was established in 1947 to honor the actress and director Antoinette "Tony" Perry (1888–1946), who at the time of her death was the head of the board of directors of the organization. The Tony Award is given to outstanding performers, plays, playwrights, and designers in both dramatic plays and musicals.

Martha S. LoMonaco

Topps Company. Chewing gum and baseball card manufacturers. Formed as Topps Chewing Gum in 1938, it was headquartered initially in Williamsburg before moving in 1946 to Bush Terminal at 36th Street. (The factory at Bush Terminal closed in 1965.) In 1947 the firm introduced Bazooka bubble gum, which became its first important success; Major League Baseball cards followed in 1951. The firm enjoyed tremendous prosperity in the late 1980s, when baseball cards became collector's items. In August 1989 it sponsored a baseball card auction at Hunter College that attracted national attention and yielded more than $1.5 million in receipts. The undisputed leader in sports trading cards, Topps became a publicly traded company and in 1994 moved its headquarters to 1 Whitehall Street.

James Bradley

Torres, Edwin (*b* New York City, 7 Jan 1931). Judge and novelist. Born to Puerto Rican parents, he lived as a child at 107th Street and Madison Avenue in Spanish Harlem and graduated from Stuyvesant High School and City College of New York. After serving in the navy overseas he attended Brooklyn Law School, working as a waiter to support himself. In 1958 he became the city's first Puerto Rican assistant district attorney. In 1977 he became a criminal court judge. In 1975 he published *Carlito's Way,* a novel about a small-time cocaine hustler during the 1940s, 1950s, and 1960s that was one of the first fictional works to deal with Puerto Ricans' experience in the city after World War II. *Q&A* (1976), a novel drawn from Torres's experience as a prosecutor and defender, and the sequel to *Carlito's Way, After Hours* (1979), were made

Tony Awards for Best Musical and Best Play

Year	Best Musical	Best Play
1948	(None awarded)	Mister Roberts
1949	Kiss Me, Kate	Death of a Salesman
1950	South Pacific	The Cocktail Party
1951	Call Me Madam	The Rose Tattoo
1952	The King and I	The Fourposter
1953	Wonderful Town	The Crucible
1954	Kismet	The Teahouse of the August Moon
1955	The Pajama Game	The Desperate Hours
1956	Damn Yankees	The Diary of Anne Frank
1957	My Fair Lady	Long Day's Journey into Night
1958	The Music Man	The Dark at the Top of the Stairs, Sunrise at Campobello
1959	Redhead	J.B.
1960	The Sound of Music, Fiorello!	The Miracle Worker
1961	Bye Bye Birdie	Becket
1962	How to Succeed in Business without Really Trying	A Man for All Seasons
1963	A Funny Thing Happened on the Way to the Forum	Who's Afraid of Virginia Woolf?
1964	Hello, Dolly!	Luther
1965	Fiddler on the Roof	The Subject Was Roses
1966	Man of La Mancha	Marat/Sade
1967	Cabaret	The Homecoming
1968	Hallelujah, Baby!	Rosencrantz and Guildenstern Are Dead
1969	1776	The Great White Hope
1970	Applause	Borstal Boy
1971	Company	Sleuth
1972	Two Gentlemen of Verona	Sticks and Bones
1973	A Little Night Music	The Championship Season
1974	Raisin	The River Niger
1975	The Wiz	Equus, Same Time Next Year
1976	A Chorus Line	Travesties
1977	Annie	The Shadow Box

(*continued*)

Tony Awards for Best Musical and Best Play (*Continued*)

1978	Ain't Misbehavin'	Da
1979	Sweeney Todd	The Elephant Man
1980	Evita	Children of a Lesser God
1981	42nd Street	Amadeus
1982	Nine	Nicholas Nickleby
1983	Cats	Torchsong Trilogy
1984	La Cage Aux Folles	The Real Thing
1985	Big River	Biloxi Blues
1986	The Mystery of Edwin Drood	I'm Not Rappaport
1987	Les Misérables	Fences
1988	The Phantom of the Opera	M. Butterfly
1989	Jerome Robbins' Broadway	The Heidi Chronicles
1990	City of Angels	The Grapes of Wrath
1991	The Will Rogers Follies	Lost in Yonkers
1992	Crazy for You	Dancing at Lughnasa
1993	Kiss of the Spider Woman	Angels in America: Millennium Approaches
1994	Passion	Angels in America: Perestroika
1995	Sunset Boulevard	Love! Valour! Compassion!
1996	Rent	Master Class
1997	Titanic	The Last Night of Ballyhoo
1998	The Lion King	Art
1999	Fosse	Side Man
2000	Contact	Copenhagen
2001	The Producers	Proof
2002	Thoroughly Modern Millie	The Goat, or Who Is Sylvia?
2003	Hairspray	Take Me Out
2004	Avenue Q	I Am My Own Wife
2005	Spamalot	Doubt
2006	Jersey Boys	The History Boys
2007	Spring Awakening	The Coast of Utopia (Part 1: Voyage)
2008	In the Heights	August: Osage County
2009	Billy Elliot the Musical	God of Carnage
2010	Memphis	Red

Compiled by Michelle Hutt and Emily Johnson

into motion pictures in 1990 and 1993, respectively. In 2005 *Carlito's Way* was made into the motion picture *Carlito's Way: Rise to Power.* As a state supreme court justice in New York City (1980–2007) Torres maintained a reputation for toughness. In 2008 he was appointed to the New York State Athletic Commission.

Chad Ludington

Toscanini, Arturo (*b* Parma, Italy, 25 March 1867; *d* New York City, 16 Jan 1957). Conductor. He conducted the world premieres of Giacomo Puccini's *La bohème* (Turin, 1896) and Ruggiero Leoncavallo's *Pagliacci* (Milan, 1892), as well as the Italian premieres of works by Richard Strauss and Claude Debussy. In 1908 he became the artistic director of the Metropolitan Opera, a position he retained until 1915. In 1926 he was a guest conductor of the New York Philharmonic, which under his direction became one of the leading orchestras in the world and made its first European tour (1930); he was made music director in 1933. He became well known for his performances of Beethoven, Brahms, Verdi, and Wagner. He gave his final concert on 29 April 1936. In the following year he was named conductor of the NBC Symphony Orchestra. The orchestra became known worldwide through its radio broadcasts and its recordings for RCA Victor. Toscanini retired to home in Riverdale in the Bronx after its last concert, on 4 April 1954 at Carnegie Hall.

Arturo Toscanini conducting the NBC Symphony Orchestra, ca *1937*

Harvey Sachs, *Toscanini* (Philadelphia: J. B. Lippincott, 1978); Joseph Horowitz, *Understanding Toscanini: How He Became an American Culture-God and Helped Create a New Audience for Old Music* (New York: Alfred A. Knopf, 1987)

Allen J. Share

Tottenville. Neighborhood in southwestern Staten Island, bounded to the north by the Arthur Kill and Mill Creek, to the south by Raritan Bay, and to the west by the Arthur Kill; it is the most southerly part of New York City and New York State. The land was first inhabited by the Delaware or Lenape Indians, whose burial sites and artifacts were found near Ward's Point. The first European settler was Captain Christopher Billopp, an English naval officer who in 1678 was given 1200 acres (486 hectares) by the British government; he built a stone house called Bentley Manor and before 1700 operated a ferry across the Arthur Kill to carry travelers to Philadelphia after they crossed into Staten Island from Manhattan along King's Highway (now Richmond and Amboy roads). Ferry service was continual until the Outerbridge Crossing was built in 1927. The local economy was closely linked to that of Amboy (now Perth Amboy), New Jersey, and was composed of agriculture, mining, and oyster farming. The Totten family owned land in the area during the eighteenth century. Colonel Christopher Billopp, a great-grandson of the first settler, actively supported the British during the American Revolution, and after the war all his land was confiscated. Bentley Manor became known as the Conference House, after an unsuccessful peace conference held there in 1776 between Lord Howe and Benjamin Franklin, John Adams, and Edward Rutledge.

The deep water of the Arthur Kill was well suited to fishing and water transport, and the waterfront flourished in the early nineteenth century as freight and passenger boats docked there on their way to Manhattan. The Staten Island Railroad built a line to the area from St. George in the 1860s. The Atlantic Terra Cotta Company, the primary manufacturer of architectural terra-cotta ornaments, built a factory on the Arthur Kill in 1897; it became one of the largest employers on Staten Island and remained in operation until the early 1930s. There were eight boatyards in the neighborhood in 1898 (the best-known of which was Brown and Ellis), but after 1900 they declined as steel replaced wood in ship construction.

The Nassau Smelting and Refining Company built a plant in 1900 on the Richmond Valley line. In 1915 state officials banned the harvesting of oysters and clams in Raritan Bay because of pollution. Oyster harvesting was allowed to resume in the 2005 season. The smelting works was bought by Western Electric in 1931; in 1971 it became a metal recycling plant and was renamed the Nassau Recycling Corporation. In the early twenty-first century the contaminated site was undergoing remediation.

The shopping and business area of Tottenville is on Main Street; in the 1990s and early twenty-first century many houses in the Federal and Victorian styles remained there and along Amboy Road, and a second commercial center began to emerge at the north end of the community, along Page Avenue west of Amboy Road. During this period there was also housing construction southeast of Hylan Boulevard. In 2003 the Tottenville Historical Society was created. Conference House Park lies along the shore and contains two designated landmarks: Conference House and Biddle House. There are seven small marinas serving commercial and sport fishermen. The population remained predominantly white into the early twenty-first century.

Marjorie Johnson

tour boats. See Excursion boats.

Tourian, Leon Elisee (*b* Üsküdar, Turkey, 1881; *d* New York City, 24 Dec 1933). Archbishop. Ordained in 1903, he was made bishop in 1913, and upon his arrival in New York in 1931 he was named the archbishop of the Armenian Apostolic Diocese of North America. His vocal support of Soviet hegemony over the republic of Armenia was resented by members of the Armenian Revolutionary Federation (known as Dashnags), and during a Christmas Mass he was fatally stabbed at the altar of the Holy Cross Church of Armenia (580 West 187th Street in Manhattan); he was later interred in the church. When nine Dashnags were found guilty of the murder in July 1934, thousands of the party's members left the diocese to form independent parishes.

Harold Takooshian

tourism. Tourists visited New York City in increasing numbers after 1820, when improvements in transportation made travel faster, cheaper, and more comfortable. Journeys through the United States often began in the city, a terminus of major steamship companies. Most tourists first saw the city from the harbor, framed by a number of islands to the east and the Hudson to the north; wharves extended the length of the waterfront, and masts and steeples defined the skyline. By 1850 the city was known for its effervescence and cosmopolitan character. The shopping, entertainment, and jostling crowds on Broadway were noted by many, including Charles Dickens, who visited the city in 1842, and the Scottish publisher William Chambers, who found the hotels on Broadway to be more like palaces than commercial enterprises. The city did little to promote tourism, and guidebooks, pamphlets, and newspapers were among the few resources for planning itineraries. About the turn of the century the Royal Blue Line offered tours of Manhattan and Brooklyn in its nine electric buses; tours of the waterfront were given by sightseeing boats such as the *Halcyon* and the *Tourist,* which sailed from Battery Park. By the mid-1920s viewing the city's skyscrapers was a popular activity. Soon after its completion in 1931 the Empire State Building (often called the "eighth wonder of the world") became a symbol of the city and a destination for most tourists: during the first year one million people rode the elevator to the top, at a cost of a dollar each. Transformed by electricity, Broadway at night was considered by Philippe de Rothschild in 1930 and other Europeans to be a spectacle unmatched in the world. The city's art galleries, museums, concert halls, and theaters also drew many visitors. In 1935 the city formed the New York Convention and Visitors' Bureau to build tourism into a major industry.

By the mid-twentieth century tourism was an important part of the city's economy. Sightseeing excursions around Manhattan were introduced in 1945 by the Circle Line, which by 1991 had carried more than 45 million passengers. Mayor John V. Lindsay promoted the city as "fun city" in the 1960s. In 1971 the Visitors' Bureau under Charles Gillett launched the "Big Apple" promotional campaign, which became one of the most successful ventures of its kind. At the end of the 1980s the city remained the world's most popular city to visit. The Empire State Building alone had about two million visitors a year. Other popular attractions included Central Park (where rides in horse-drawn carriages were especially popular), Dyckman House (the only surviving eighteenth-century farmhouse in Manhattan), the United Nations, McSorley's Old Ale House, the Russian Tea Room, and the Cloisters, the medieval branch of the Metropolitan Museum of Art, which overlooks the Hudson from Fort Tryon Park.

Before the 11 September 2001 terrorist attacks, tourists were drawn to lower Manhattan to enjoy dining at Windows on the World on the 107th floor of the North Tower of the World Trade Center or to take in the spectacular views of the metropolis from the observation deck on the 107th floor of the skyscraper's South Tower. In the immediate aftermath of the attacks, visitors to the city continued to be drawn to the World Trade Center site, but now they came to both see and contemplate what no photograph or television image could convey as well as to pay their respects. Both before and after the attacks, the World Trade Center site was the primary tourist destination in lower Manhattan. The Tribute WTC Visitor Center, a project of the September 11th Families Association located at 120 Liberty Street opposite the World Trade Center site, opened to the public on 18 September 2006. The center functioned as what New York Governor George E. Pataki called an "interim destination" for visitors and tourists until the National September 11th Memorial and Museum opened. Lower Manhattan has other attractions for tourists, including the Skyscraper Museum, the New York City Fire and Police museums, the Lower East Side Tenement Museum, the South Street Seaport Museum, the Museum of American

Double-decker tour bus, 2009

Financial History, and the Museum of Jewish Heritage—A Living Memorial to the Holocaust.

The aftermath of the 9/11 attacks saw a modest decline in tourism (which had already fallen off slightly in 2000 due to the economic downturn), but by 2003 tourism already had surpassed the level of 1999. This happened in part because the city acted immediately to retain and attract tourists and visitors. A patriotic tourism campaign was launched with "Paint the Town Red, White and Blue" hotel and theater packages. A television campaign promoted the theme "Everyone has a New York dream. Come find yours," spotlighting celebrities engaged in activities in the city they had supposedly always dreamed of doing. In 2007 an estimated 46 million tourists visited New York City, according to NYC & Company, New York City's official marketing, convention, and tourism organization. Of that number 37.1 million were domestic visitors, while 8.76 million came from other nations—making New York City the number-one port of entry into the United States for foreign visitors. Visitor spending totaled $24.71 billion in 2006, and tourism generated $16 billion in wages, supported 368,179 jobs, and generated $6.24 billion in taxes that year. At the end of February 2008 there were 73,333 hotel rooms in the city, and the occupancy rate for 2007 was 86.5 percent.

Bayrd Still, *Mirror for Gotham: New York as Seen by Contemporaries from Dutch Days to the Present* (New York: New York University Press, 1956); Mary Dawn Earley, comp., "A New York Visitors' Book," *New York, N.Y.: An American Heritage Extra,* ed. David G. Lowe (New York: American Heritage, 1968), 134–37; John A. Jakle, *The Tourist: Travel in Twentieth-Century North America* (Lincoln: University of Nebraska Press, 1985); Jan Morris, *Among the Cities* (New York: Oxford University Press, 1985), 259–81; Jan Morris, *Manhattan '45* (New York: Oxford University Press, 1986, 1987); *Tourism's Economic Impact on New York City, 1989* (New York: New York Convention and Visitors Bureau, n.d. [1990])

Allen J. Share

Touro College. Private coeducational institution at 27–33 West 23rd Street in Manhattan, founded by Bernard Lander in 1971. It offers undergraduate programs in the liberal arts, general studies, health studies, and Jewish studies; a law school was added in 1980. The college is nonsectarian but requires that students in the liberal arts division earn credits in Hebrew and Jewish studies. As of 2008 the college enrolled approximately 17,500 students at 28 locations domestic and abroad, although the majority are in New York City.

Rachel Sawyer

Toussaint, Pierre (*b* St.-Marc, St.-Domingue [now Haiti], 27 June 1766; *d* New York City, 30 June 1853). Philanthropist and candidate for sainthood. Born a slave in St.-Domingue, he moved to New York City in 1797 with the family of the French colonist Jean-Jacques Bérard. Toussaint supported the Bérard family with earnings he received while working as a hairdresser for New York City society women. He was freed on 2 July 1807 and later purchased freedom for his fiancée, Juliette Noël, whom he married on 5 August 1811 at St. Peter's Church (16 Barclay Street). He gave financial assistance to Catholic orphanages and to the clergy. He housed refugees of the French and Haitian revolutions, welcomed the indigent into his home, and helped a number of people purchase their way out of slavery. He was buried at St. Patrick's Old Cathedral cemetery on Mott Street. The Pierre Toussaint Guild was established in New York in the 1950s. In 1990 Toussaint's remains were removed from the cemetery of St. Patrick's Old Cathedral and placed in the crypt under the altar of St Patrick's Cathedral on Fifth Avenue. On 17 December 1996 Pope John Paul II proclaimed him "venerable," a necessary step toward canonization, or sainthood.

Michel S. Laguerre

Towers Nursing Home. Nursing home located at 455 Central Park West (at 106th Street) during the NURSING-HOME SCANDALS of the 1970s. In 1955 Bernard Bergman opened Towers Nursing Home in a Charles Haight–designed building modeled on a French château, which had originally housed the New York Cancer Hospital. By the mid-1970s the facility was one of the largest in a Bergman-operated network of 37 nursing homes facing state and federal fraud charges, and Bergman himself was eventually convicted of Medicaid fraud and bribery. As a result of the scandals, Towers Nursing Home was closed in 1974.

Eric Hollingsworth

Town Hall. Four-story building at 123 West 43rd Street in Manhattan housing a concert hall of the same name. Designed in a Georgian Revival style by the firm of McKim, Mead and White, it was built during 1919–21 by the League of Political Education for public meetings, lectures, and concerts. From the outset the hall was a popular forum for debates on a wide range of social and political issues. Ann Blaksley Bliss contributed funds to buy the site in the rapidly developing theater district. The concert hall, renowned for its superb acoustics, has been the setting for performances by Richard Strauss, Sergei Rachmaninoff, Dizzy Gillespie, and Joan Sutherland.

Rebecca Read Shanor

Townsend Harris High School. Public high school in Queens, opened in 1906 as a three-year school for boys called Townsend Harris Hall on the campus of City College in Manhattan, with which it was affiliated. It was named for an influential merchant and diplomat who also established the Free Academy (which later became City College). The school offered free tuition to its selectively admitted students, who in early years were frequently immigrants and the sons of immigrants. Notable graduates included the bacteriologist Jonas Salk and the writer Herman Wouk. The school closed in 1942. In 1984 it reopened as a four-year, coeducational school affiliated with Queens College.

Rachel Shor

Town Shop. Lingerie store on the Upper West Side that specializes in bra fitting. Located on Broadway near 82nd Street since 1936, it began as a dry-goods store on Sixth Avenue near 53rd Street and at one point expanded to four locations throughout the city. The business was established by Samuel Koch in 1888 and was transformed into a lingerie emporium by his daughter-in-law Selma Koch, who began working in the shop in 1928. She focused on customer service and gave every woman individual attention, claiming that almost 80 percent of her customers were wearing the wrong bra size before visiting Town Shop. Her knack for sizing, usually with a look rather than a tape measure, gained her loyal customers and national celebrity status. She was interviewed on National Public Radio in 2002 and appeared on the New York City–based *Rosie O'Donnell Show* to discuss her field of expertise. Koch died in 2003; her obituary in the *New York Times* stated that "she was 95 and a 34B." Her son and grandson continue to run the store.

Holly Cronin

toys and games. Until the mid-nineteenth century, the majority of toys in the United States were imports from Germany. Many of the earliest domestic toymakers were based in New York City, including F. and R. Lockwood (154 Broadway), makers of printed wooden game boards; J. Ruthven and Son (14 John Street), metal, wood, and ivory turners who made whistles, balls, chessmen, and blocks; and Boardman and Hart (6 Burling Slip), pewterers who manufactured miniature utensils and table settings. After moving to New York City from Rhode Island, several members of the Crandall family emerged as the city's most prominent toymakers between 1845 and 1915. The most renowned was Jesse A. Crandall, who in a shop at 73 Fulton Street made wooden hobby horses, sleds, and early bicycles called velocipedes. Other outstanding toymakers were the McLoughlin Brothers, who opened a store at 24 Beekman Street in 1855 and sold paper dolls and dollhouses, toy books, lithographed wooden toys, board games, and blocks. After the Civil War more elaborate toys helped to free U.S. toymakers from the domination of European imports. The Buckman Manufacturing Company in Brooklyn sold a "Brooklyn toy steam engine," and the Union Manufacturing Company of Brooklyn manufactured cast-iron boats, fire engines, and steam-powered toy factories that included lathes and grindstones. One of the country's largest makers of "clockwork," or windup, toys was R. J. Clay's Automatic Toy Works, which secured patents for a creeping doll and a crying doll. Althof, Bergmann and Company, formed in 1867, advertised 177 tinplate toys and miniatures in its catalogue in 1874. The first department store to open a section devoted to toys was R. H. Macy in 1875. With the growing commercialization of Christmas, toy stores rapidly increased in number across the city. Some of the largest included Hinrich's at 29–33 Park Place, Hubbell and Ward at 21st Street and Broadway, E. Ridley and Sons at 309 Grand Street, and F. A. O. Schwarz, which opened a store at 42 East 14th Street in 1880.

To sell their products, most nineteenth-century American toymakers relied on catalogues or middlemen. Edward I. Horsman and Company, which manufactured dolls, also imported toys and acted as a wholesale agent for small U.S. makers. George Borgfeldt at 425 Broome Street helped to change the way toys were sold by opening a sample house where manufacturers exhibited their products to retailers. His system was a forerunner of the toy convention, which eventually made New York City the center of the toymaking business and also made the middleman unnecessary. Perhaps the city's most lasting contribution in the field of toymaking was the teddy bear, named after President Theodore Roosevelt, whose nickname was Teddy. It was introduced in 1902 by Morris Michtom, the owner of a cigar and novelty store in Brooklyn, who in the following year formed the Ideal Toy and Novelty Company. By 1906 the teddy bear was so popular that Ideal was also a maker of dolls, and through Michtom's nationwide marketing efforts it became the world's largest. The city was also the original location of the Lionel Train Company, a maker of model railroad sets formed in 1903 by Joshua Lionel Cowen (the firm moved to New Haven, Connecticut, in 1910). In 1916, 68 toy companies in the city organized a trade group called the Toy Manufacturers of the USA (now the Toy Manufacturers of America) with headquarters at 200 Fifth Avenue; in later years the group expanded its headquarters to 1107 Broadway and developed a degree program in toy design at the Fashion Institute of Technology. The city's most successful toy magnate was Louis Marx, an innovator in mass production and mass marketing who formed Marx Toys in 1921 and took advantage of the boycott of German goods occasioned by World War I to build it into the world's largest toymaker by the late 1920s. In 1972 Marx sold the firm to the Quaker Oats Company for $52 million.

After World War II plastic became the most widely used material in toy manufacturing. Many firms in New York City maintained showrooms and corporate headquarters at 200 Fifth Avenue and other locations but moved their manufacturing elsewhere, sometimes under contract. Among the toymakers that continued to manufacture in the city in the 1950s were Ideal (at 184-10 Jamaica Avenue in Hollis), Palmer Plastics (at 31 Stone Avenue in Brooklyn), and the Automatic Toy Company (at 77 Alaska Street in Staten Island). Popular toys and games developed in the city included the "action figure" G. I. Joe, Mr. Potato Head (by toy inventor George Lerner), and the board games Scrabble and Parcheesi. The number of toy factories in the city declined after the 1950s, and those that remained were small. In 1987 there were 45 plants that made dolls and stuffed toys, with a total employment of 1500. In the early twenty-first century the doll makers that remained in the city included the well-known firms of Alexander at 615 West 131st and Goldberger at 538 Johnson Avenue in Brooklyn.

Marshall McClintock and Inez McClintock, *Toys in America* (Washington: Public Affairs Press, 1961)

Marc Ferris

trade associations. In New York City associations to promote the business interests of various merchants were formed during the earliest days of the colony. Among the first were the Society for the Promoting of Arts, Agriculture, and Economy, in the Province of New York (1764) and the Marine Society (1770). The New York Cheap Transportation Association (1873), later renamed the New York Board of Trade and Transportation, rivaled the Chamber of Commerce (1768) in its influence over the development of the city. Most of its members were merchants in wholesale and import commerce who sought to reduce their transportation costs, and in 1904–6 they supported congressional investigations of the rate structures used by the railroads. These investigations led to the passage in 1906 of the Hepburn Act, which significantly increased the power of the Interstate Commerce Commission to regulate railroad rates. The Retail Dealers Protective Association was formed by 1899. Other associations of small businesses included the Neighborhood Cleaners Association, the New York Association of Women Business Owners, the Dairy Council of Metropolitan New York, the Downtown–Lower Manhattan Association, the Boot and Shoe Travelers Association of New York (which sponsored a semiannual trade show that continues in the early twenty-first century), the Box Manufacturers Association of Greater New York, the Business Committee on Midtown Traffic, and the Chinese Merchants Association.

Joseph F. Bradley, *The Role of Trade Associations and Professional Business Societies in America* (University Park: Pennsylvania State University Press, 1965)

Donald R. Stabile

traffic. The control of traffic and proper management of street space started slowly in New York City. During the eighteenth century carts traveling northward along the road that is now Broadway were required to give way to those traveling southward. In the second third of the nineteenth century, the city's booming business and manufacturing base made traffic much worse. Heavy horse wagons, carriages, omnibuses and horse trams, riders, pushcarts, porters, and pedestrians formed a chaotic mix, each mode moving at its own speed with no traffic lanes, no rules, no signs, no insurance, and no oversight. There were also no formal procedures for handling accidents and collisions, and it was not uncommon for disputes to be settled by physical means (drivers always carried whips and knives).

The constant stream of vehicles and the wet layer of horse manure made street crossing hazardous for pedestrians, so the newly formed Police Department (1845) stepped in and created the Broadway Squad to help people across. A pedestrian bridge was built across Broadway near Fulton Street in the years after the Civil War, but it was not much used. Bicyclists presented a new challenge during the 1890s, and Police Commissioner Theodore Roosevelt formed the Bicycle Squad, called the Scorchers, to keep order on the streets. They were soon also charged with the responsibility of controlling motor vehicles, which became increasingly difficult because offenders had to be apprehended and fined on the spot.

The arrival of automobiles in New York City was greeted with great expectation and relief because a car was smaller than a horse and wagon, it was more maneuverable, it moved faster, it could back up, and it did not leave any waste (air pollution was not discovered for many decades). However, the number and speed of motor vehicles soon overwhelmed the capacity of streets to accommodate them. Some of the principal arteries were made dark and dangerous by the building of elevated rail structures with a forest of columns in the middle of roadways (the last elevated railway in Manhattan's core was removed in the 1950s). The Mounted Division of the Police Department, with a peak number of 800 men, formed the core of the Traffic Squad.

In 1908 Police Commissioner Theodore Bingham started to define and enforce traffic rules—keep to the right, pass on the left, and signal turns and stops. A system of summonses for traffic violations was instituted in 1910. Eventually police officers were posted at street intersections to direct competing flows of traffic; they were aided by stop-and-go mechanical devices known as semaphores from 1915 into the 1930s. In 1919 the first crude electric traffic signal with large lights was introduced on Fifth Avenue. Placed atop 16-foot-high (4.9-meter-high) control towers in the middle of the street, 50 such signals were erected throughout the city. The system of red-amber-green lights was confusing until the standard railroad code was adopted in 1924. The signals placed on Fifth Avenue during the 1920s were handsome art deco structures in bronze. The late 1920s and 1930s was a period of major tunnel, bridge, and highway construction in the city, accompanied by a growth in street traffic volumes. The standard electric traffic signal was developed, and in 1934 there were 7700 of them in the city. A significant improvement in 1914 brought the synchronization of lights between intersections. Traffic engineering and management became recognized as a profession after World War II, largely in response to the rise of the automobile and the shift of freight transport from rail to trucking.

The Police Department was almost entirely responsible for traffic control until many of its duties were given over to the newly formed Department of Traffic in 1950. Commissioner Thomas T. Wiley (1950–61) initiated a number of control programs, including strict parking rules and the installation of the first parking meters. To free up streets and generate revenue, the city also built parking garages, the first of which opened in Flushing in 1954. The streets in Manhattan were the first in the city to be marked for one-way traffic, which improved carrying capacity and safety, and during the 1950s and 1960s almost all the avenues were converted to one-way traffic (the last were Madison and Fifth avenues in 1966). The program was soon extended to the other boroughs as well. Wiley's successor, Henry A. Barnes (1962–68), was effective in gaining support for the Traffic Department. Computerized signals that took traffic loads into account from minute to minute were introduced in the early 1960s, and the first exclusive bus lanes were designated along Livingston Street in Brooklyn and Victory Boulevard in Staten Island in 1963. The "Barnes Dance," a pedestrians-only signal phase in all directions, was tried at some critical intersections in the early 1950s but did not become widespread.

During the 1960s the first national, state, and local laws were passed to clean the air of pollutants produced by internal combustion and diesel engines, including carbon monoxide and ozone (two types of emissions for which New York City was soon identified as a "nonattainment" area, or an area that exceeded accepted levels of certain pollutants) and particulates. In the early 1970s the State Implementation Plan for air quality was formulated, which constituted basic guidelines for traffic control and urban development, and it became mandatory for developers to write environmental impact statements assuring that their proposed projects would not result in unacceptable levels of congestion and air pollution. In 1969 a consolidated Transportation Administration was formed; this agency was eliminated after a few years, and most of its functions were transferred in 1977 to the New York City Department of Transportation, which in turn assigned responsibility for street operations to its bureaus of traffic and parking violations and established its own uniformed force of traffic enforcement agents (mostly parking control). Bus lanes were added at the inbound lanes of the Lincoln Tunnel (1970) and the Long Island Expressway (1971); a transitway was implemented on 49th and 50th streets (1979), followed by one along Madison Avenue (1981). Plans to establish pedestrian malls failed on Madison Avenue (1971–73) but succeeded on Nassau Street in lower Manhattan (1969), 165th Street in Jamaica Center, and Fulton Street in Brooklyn (1984).

By the early 1990s it was estimated conservatively that traffic delays cost the local economy $7 billion a year; lines at the gateways to the city extended for miles every day during the morning hours, and accidents were numerous. The speeds in midtown Manhattan usually ranged on the avenues from 12 to 15 miles per hour (19 to 24 kilometers per hour), and on the cross streets from 9 to 12 miles per hour (14 to 19 kilometers per hour). During the worst periods traffic crawled at 2.5 miles per hour (4 kilometers per hour) throughout the area.

Unlike most urban areas that have a clearly distinguishable inward flow of traffic in the morning and an outward flow in the late afternoon, central Manhattan fills up in the early morning and remains nearly saturated until the theaters let out late at night. The bridges and tunnels to the island of Manhattan, being completely full and generating lines during the morning, act as metering devices for vehicular entry. Because of this, many motorists now arrive earlier or later, thus extending the duration of the overload period (often to 14 hours) and increasing the total volume of daily entries nevertheless. The battle for space is waged among pedestrians, bicyclists, private automobiles, delivery and repair vans, minibuses, taxicabs, commuter vans, trucks, public delivery vehicles, buses, emergency vehicles, and limousines. In addition, the streets and highways carry a considerable volume of traffic that neither originates nor terminates in the city (20 percent of the flow in the core). Intersections are vulnerable to gridlock, a term coined to describe the blockage of traffic flow in all directions caused by vehicles caught in intersections when traffic lights change. Heavy truck traffic on city streets remains a major problem because there is no freight delivery by rail within or across the city, barges are used very little, motor vehicles are becoming larger, designated truck routes create controversies, and high tolls in the westbound direction only on the Verrazano–Narrows Bridge force additional movement on city streets. Space along curbs in Manhattan is rarely available for parking or standing, off-street facilities are expensive, and many motorists park, stand, or stop illegally, thus further reducing already limited street carrying capacity. Traffic congestion hinders the movement of fire trucks and ambulances (fire lanes are not always clear of other vehicles). Manufacturing and distribution operations in the city are also impeded by traffic congestion — the principal source of the estimated economic losses — and many production establishments left the city during the second half of the twentieth century. It was estimated in 2006 that the total economic loss to the city caused by traffic congestion, delays, and uncertainty amounted to more than $13 billion per year. Business organizations have asserted that traffic congestion is no longer just an inconvenience but a "significant drag" on the city's and region's economy. Considerable nonmotorized traffic also complicates traffic flow. Bicycles are used by commuters and messengers, but attempts to create bicycle lanes have met with little success, in part because they reduce the amount of space available to other types of traffic. In central districts walking is frequently the best means of reaching destinations on time (residents of New York City walk more than residents of any other American city).

The city's traffic control responsibility since the 1990s has reverted almost entirely to the Police Department. In 1996 the Parking Enforcement District was established within the Police Department, and movement control was assumed almost entirely by regular police. The handling of tickets for noncriminal moving violations (not parking) and the collection of fines was taken over by the Traffic Violations Bureau of the New York State Department of Motor Vehicles. The New York City Department of Transportation became the sole owner and caretaker of city streets, traffic signals, street lights, and parking meters, not the enforcer of traffic regulations or planner of long-range transportation programs.

The city uses various methods to alleviate traffic congestion, such as marking off loading zones at curbside (as well as red zones for buses), establishing truck routes (of doubtful utility), providing pedestrian crossing elements (zebras or black and white stripes to distinguish walking areas, signals, fences), and striping boxes in heavily traveled intersections in which motorists may be fined for stopping ("Don't Block the Box!") as well as applying discretion in ticketing double-parked vehicles. In 2004 a new effort established nine "Thru Streets" in midtown to expedite cross-town movements by banning almost all turns and giving time for pedestrian crossing. The introduction of electronic "E-ZPasses," in 1991, which allow vehicles to move through toll gates without stopping, has improved flow at these facilities. Additional bus lanes (for example on Fulton Street in Brooklyn and the Staten Island Expressway) have reduced the space available for cars and trucks but improved the movement of public service vehicles. This program is to be expanded by introducing bus rapid transit (BRT) priority arrangements on several arterials in each borough. In general the city's efforts to limit traffic congestion do not include efficient land-use planning, although sectorial and district plans are produced as needed. Streets and highways are no longer being built, and it is not possible to create additional lanes. Repair and maintenance have high priority, as do attempts to achieve greater capacity and safety with the current streets. Most parking garages and lots are now in the outer boroughs where the overall traffic situation resembles the "normal" conditions in most U.S. cities.

By 2008 more than 1.8 million motor vehicles were registered in New York City, a number that had remained practically unchanged for a decade. Many city residents, however, registered their cars outside the city. Meanwhile, 3.3 million residents hold driver's licenses. Each day 810,000 vehicles enter Manhattan south of 60th Street; this number was 650,000 in 1978. Motor vehicles accumulated a total of 51 million vehicle-miles on the streets of New York City each day. The Gowanus Expressway near the Brooklyn–Battery Tunnel experienced the largest traffic overloads in the city, with rush hour lines lasting six hours or more. In 2003 it was estimated that an average traveler in the metropolitan area was delayed 49 hours each year; this number was 34 hours in 1993. The highest daily traffic volume, about 300,000 vehicles per day, was found on the George Washington Bridge; this number represents the practical capacity of the bridge and is as high as can be found anywhere in the country. Among New York City highways, the Brooklyn–Queens Expressway (at the Kosciuszko Bridge) carried 199,000 vehicles almost every day in 2008. Among major surface arterials, the Queens Boulevard (in Elmhurst, including service roads) recorded 79,000 vehicles daily. By 2007 severe traffic accidents dropped in the city, and the number of traffic fatalities, reflecting national trends, changed from about 450 in 1996 to less than 300 annually. Between 2000 and 2006 about 160 pedestrians were killed annually by motor vehicles, compared with 952 in 1929. The city has 11,800 signalized intersections, 1.3 million traffic signs, and more than 300,000 streetlights. The average commuting time to work for New York residents is the highest in the country, at 39 minutes; 12 percent of Staten Islanders commute for 90 minutes or more.

See also Streets and highways and Parking.

Sigurd Grava

Trains Meadow. Former name of Jackson Heights. From colonial times the area was mostly lowlands with a few meadows and farms. In 1915 the Board of Estimate abolished Trains Meadow Road and adopted a street grid, making the development of Jackson Heights possible.

Vincent Seyfried

transatlantic cable. Following a series of failures, the New York, Newfoundland, and London Telegraph Company, headed by capitalist entrepreneur Cyrus W. Field, successfully laid down more than 1000 miles (1600 kilometers) of underwater cable for the first transatlantic cable communication. On 17 August 1858 U.S. President James Buchanan and Queen Victoria of Great Britain successfully communicated via cable. Nationwide celebrations followed, with none more elaborate than those in New York City, where activities continued for more than a month. The official day of celebration in New York City was 1 September 1858. The morning began with services at Trinity Church and the disembarkment at Castle Garden by Field and many of the sailors who had placed the cable. The ensuing procession, including bands and extensive fanfare, headed from the Battery to the Crystal Palace at 42nd Street and Fifth Avenue, where numerous speeches and commemorations took place. Napoleon Sarony captured the day's events with lithographs. The celebration ultimately proved somewhat premature and costly, as the cable communication technology soon faltered, and the bonfires and fireworks for the occasion ignited a fire that razed City Hall. In 1866 Field and other entrepreneurs renewed their efforts with longer-lasting results.

David White

transportation. See Aviation, Buses, Cable cars, Elevated railways, Ferries, Heliports, Railroads, Streetcars, Subways, and Taxicabs.

Transportation Alternatives. Advocacy organization promoting bicycling, walking, and public transit in New York City. Founded in 1973, it fought the city for less dependency on automobile transportation and has since worked on campaigns in five areas: car-free parks, pedestrian advocacy and traffic calming, bicycling, safe streets, and "sensible transportation." In 1993 it began publishing the quarterly *Reclaim* magazine. In the early twenty-first century its headquarters are located at 127 West 26th Street.

Jessica Montesano

Transport Workers Union of America [TWU]. Union of transit workers formed in 1934 and based in New York City. Within three years it had 30,000 members and contracts with the Interborough Rapid Transit Company (IRT), the Brooklyn–Manhattan Transit Corporation (BMT), and the city's major bus and trolley companies. After becoming an affiliate of the Committee for Industrial Organization in 1937 it organized transit workers in other cities and airline and railroad workers. In New York Irish workers initially accounted for half the membership, but later declined in number. When New York City took over the IRT and BMT in 1940, Mayor Fiorello H. La Guardia refused to engage in collective bargaining or sign union contracts, but the TWU successfully pressured the city to continue discussions about working conditions and grievances. In the following years it set a precedent for other civil service unions by gradually expanding its role. In 1941 it shut down most bus lines in Manhattan for 12 days. The union was often at the center of controversy because of its close ties to the Communist Party, its support for the American Labor Party, and the sharp comments of its president, Michael J. Quill. In 1948 Quill broke with the Communist Party and, after a bitter factional struggle, so did the union. It regained the bargaining rights that it had lost under Mayor La Guardia after lending strong support to mayors William O'Dwyer and Robert F. Wagner.

In 1954 the TWU signed a contract with the New York City Transit Authority, an agency set up in 1953 to run the buses and subways. From this time into the early 1960s the union won only modest wage gains for its members, resulting in a week-long wildcat strike by subway motormen in December 1957. On failing to reach a contract agreement with Mayor-elect John V. Lindsay, the TWU called a strike of workers on city-run lines on 1 January 1966. The union was widely criticized for crippling the city, and nine of its leaders were imprisoned, but after 12 days the walkout ended with terms highly favorable to the workers. Quill died soon afterward; his successors, including Matthew Guinan and John E. Lawe, were neither as skillful nor as prominent as he had been. Opposition groups sprung up within Local 100, the main unit of the TWU in the city, based on the fact that they were unhappy with its diminished militancy and the underrepresentation of African Americans in its leadership. In 1980, after winning control of the Local 100 Executive Board, they called a strike of bus and subway workers that lasted for 11 days. Under the Taylor Law heavy fines were imposed on workers for illegally striking, but these fines were partially offset by the gains they made in the walkout.

By the late 1980s, opposition groups once again were challenging incumbent leaders, including Sonny Hall, Lawe's successor as Local 100 president and head of the national TWU. In elections in 2000, members of the New Directions caucus took over all the major posts in Local 100, with Roger Toussaint becoming its president. A more militant stand toward management and greater rank-and-file involvement culminated in a three-day strike in December 2005 that threw the city into chaos just before Christmas. In an era when public employee strikes had become extremely rare, the TWU again proved itself exceptional in its willingness to take militant action to advance its members' interests.

Joshua B. Freeman, *In Transit: The Transport Workers Union in New York City, 1933–1966* (New York: Temple University Press, 2001)

Joshua B. Freeman

Trans World Airlines [TWA]. Formed in 1928 as Transcontinental Air Transport, it offered the first transcontinental service by air and rail from Greater New York. In 1934 it flew Mayor Fiorello H. La Guardia from Newark Airport in New Jersey to Floyd Bennett Field in Brooklyn to satisfy the implied guarantee of his flight ticket that he would be offered transport into the city. The airline lobbied to develop what is now La Guardia Airport. It is well known for its terminal at Kennedy Airport, designed by Eero Saarinen and completed in 1960. Until the 1980s TWA was the second-largest international carrier in the United States. In 1988 it moved its headquarters from midtown Manhattan to suburban Mount Kisco, New York. In 1994 it moved the headquarters to St. Louis while maintaining large operations at Kennedy and La Guardia airports. After financial difficulties TWA filed for bankruptcy in 2001 and was bought by American Airlines. The final TWA flight was on 1 December 2001.

Robert J. Serling, *Howard Hughes' Airline: An Informal History of TWA* (New York: St. Martin's, 1983); Robert Rummel, *Howard Hughes and TWA* (Washington, D.C.: Smithsonian Institution Press, 1991)

Travelers. One of the country's largest providers of property and casualty insurance products, formerly based in New York City at 55 East 65th Street in Manhattan as the Travelers Group. The Travelers Group merged in 1998 with Citicorp to become Citigroup. In 2002 the Travelers property and casualty insurance business was spun off as a stand-alone company to become Travelers Property and Casualty Corp., a predecessor company of the Travelers Companies, now based in St. Paul, Minnesota. A forerunner of Travelers Group was Primerica Corporation, from which it evolved after a series of mergers. In 2007 the Travelers Companies reacquired its red umbrella trademark, a logo once prominent at 388 Greenwich Street in Manhattan.

Janet Frankston

Travis. Neighborhood in west central Staten Island bounded to the north by Meredith Avenue and Victory Boulevard, to the east by the William T. Davis Wildlife Refuge and Main Creek, to the south by Fresh Kills, and to the west by the Arthur Kill. The area was the site of an Indian village and was renamed many times after being settled by Europeans. Developed as Jersey Wharf and known as New Blazing Star during the American Revolution, it was an important connecting point for ferries to New Jersey. One ferry operated from 1757 by Jacob Fitz Randolph and then for several decades by John Mersereau was a segment of a short route connecting Manhattan and Philadelphia: a road led from the area to the Port Richmond Ferry, from which passengers could travel to Manhattan and Bergen Point, New Jersey. During the following decades the area and the local settlement were known variously as Travisville (in the early nineteenth century, after the local property owner Captain Jacob Travis), Long Neck (during the Civil War, because of its peninsular configuration), and Deckertown (after a local family). In 1873 the American Linoleum Company opened a factory and workers' cottages on a tract of 300 acres (120 hectares) near the docks. Much of the early workforce was imported from England, where the process of rolling ground cork and oxidized linseed oil into a floor covering had been developed. Success led to rapid expansion, and the area became known as Linoleumville. The firm was an innovator in the development of decorative and inlaid styles of linoleum; surfaces for battleships, railroad cars, and large institutions; and linoleum-making machinery. In the early twentieth century the factory had 700 employees, or half the population of Linoleumville. The firm was sold in 1928 and ceased operations in 1931. Residents then voted to rename the village Travis. In later years the relative isolation of the area was disrupted by the building of the West Shore Expressway, of new housing, and of the Teleport, a fiber-optics network and business complex. Important institutions in the neighborhood include the Church of St. Anthony of Padua, which serves a largely Polish and Slavic congregation; a volunteer fire company; and an equestrian group. An Independence Day Parade inaugurated in 1911 continues to be held into the twenty-first century. Travis's location near the chemical factories of nearby New Jersey can lead to poor air quality, which was somewhat improved in the early twenty-first century by the closing of the Fresh Kills landfill.

Charles L. Sachs, *Made on Staten Island* (New York: Staten Island Historical Society, 1985); "Travis: A Brief History" (1987) [unpubd, New York Public Library, St. George Branch]

Howard R. Weiner

Treadwell Farm. Designated historic district on the Upper East Side of Manhattan, bounded to the north by 62nd Street, to the east by Second Avenue, to the south by 61st Street, and to the west by Third Avenue. The area was once the farm of Peter Van Zandt and William Beekman and is named for the fur merchant Adam Treadwell, who in 1815 bought Van Zandt's parcel, on which he built his own farm. After his death in 1852 his daughter Elizabeth bought Beekman's parcel. Luxurious brownstones and row houses were erected in the 1860s and 1870s. The neighborhood was designated a historic district in 1967; among its landmarks is Trinity Baptist Church (1931). Well-known residents have included Walter Lippmann, Tallulah Bankhead, and Eleanor Roosevelt.

James Bradley

Tree of Hope. Tree formerly situated at the corner of 131st Street and what is now Adam Clayton Powell Boulevard. It symbolized the promise that many black artists found in Harlem and was believed to have the power to bring good luck; however, it fell victim to urban renewal and was cut down in 1934. A few months later a second tree on the same site was donated by the entertainer Bill "Bojangles" Robinson, who had a brass plaque embedded in the sidewalk bearing the inscription "The Original Tree of Hope / Beloved by the People of Harlem / You asked for a tree of hope, so here 'tis, Best wishes," along with his signature. The brass plaque was later stolen, and the second tree, also cut down, was replaced in 1972 by an interpretive sculpture by Algernon Miller of lavender, black, red, and green. A portion of the original Tree of Hope remains a fixture at the Apollo Theater.

Emilyn L. Brown

trees. More than five million trees grow in New York City, covering about one-quarter of the land area in tree canopy. When Henry Hudson arrived in 1609, Manhattan was a wilderness full of American Chestnuts, Red Oaks, White Oaks, and Canadian Hemlocks; Inwood Hill Park at the northern tip of the island contains the last piece of original forest in the borough. Native Red Oak and Tulip trees grow at the park, and forest restoration teams battle the invasive Norway Maple. The Bronx River Forest features Pin Oak and River Birch trees, and Forest Park in Queens contains the largest continuous oak forest in the United States. Trees on New York City's streets also play an important role in residents' quality of life. A survey by the Parks Department in 2007 tried to quantify the dollar value of street trees, finding that they provided residents with a total annual benefit of $122 million, including increased property values and positive environmental effects such as carbon dioxide absorption. Of the total number of street trees in 2006 (592,130—a 19 percent increase from 1996), 41 percent are in Queens, followed by Brooklyn (24 percent), Staten Island (17 percent), the Bronx (10 percent), and Manhattan (8 percent). Of the 168 species identified, the top 10 accounted for 74 percent of street trees: London Planetree, Norway Maple, Callery Pear, Honeylocust, Pin Oak, Littleleaf Linden, Green Ash, Red Maple, Silver Maple, and Gingko. The Asian Longhorned Beetle, an invasive insect from China that probably arrived in untreated packing crates, presents a twenty-first century threat, infesting and killing trees across the boroughs.

Kate Lauber

Tremont. Neighborhood in the west central Bronx bounded to the north by East 182nd Street and Bronx Park South, to the east by the Bronx River and the Boston Road, to the south by Claremont Park, Mount Eden Avenue, and Mount Eden Parkway, and to the west by the Grand Concourse. It includes several smaller neighborhoods, including Claremont, Mount Eden, and Mount Hope. The area was farmland when the New York and Harlem Railroad opened a station in 1841 that soon became the center of a village. The name Upper Morrisania was used until the postmaster, Hiram Tarbox, discovered that it was being confused with that of a neighboring town, Morrisania; in the 1850s he renamed his office Tremont for three hills in the area (Fairmount, Mount Eden, and Mount Hope). Growth hastened after improvements were made to the transit system in the 1890s: a trolley line along Tremont Avenue that served the railroad station in the west, a new subway station to the east in West Farms, and an extension of the Third Avenue elevated line running between the two stations. In 1897 the borough hall, designed by George B. Post, opened in Crotona Park at Tremont and Park avenues. In the late nineteenth and early twentieth centuries apartment buildings replaced one-family frame houses and Tremont Avenue became a thriving shopping district. Jews accounted for most of the population; there were also many Italians and Irish who moved from crowded neighborhoods in Manhattan. In 1934 the borough offices were moved to the new Bronx County Building on 161st Street, but other city offices continued to occupy Borough Hall until it was abandoned in 1965; fire destroyed the building in 1968. Other city agencies occupied the Bergen Building on Arthur Avenue. In the early 1950s there was strong opposition to plans for the Cross Bronx Expressway, which called for the demolition of homes and the bisecting of the neighborhood. After the expressway opened in 1955 the population became increasingly black and Latino. Arson was common in the early 1970s, but at the same time the construction of the innovative scatter-site housing project Twin Parks helped the neighborhood to slowly stabilize. About one-third of the immigrants who settled in Tremont in the 1980s were Dominican; there were also many immigrants from Jamaica, Guyana, Honduras, Ecuador, and Guatemala. The late 1990s saw an increased number of Puerto Rican immigrants in the region. By the early twenty-first century, much of the devastated existing housing was rehabilitated or replaced with new dwellings. Tremont Avenue has remained a thriving local commercial thoroughfare.

Lloyd Ultan, *The Beautiful Bronx, 1920–1950* (New Rochelle, N.Y.: Arlington House, 1979)

Lloyd Ultan

Tresca, Carlo (*b* Sulmona, Italy, 9 March 1879; *d* New York City, 11 Jan 1943). Labor leader and revolutionary. He moved from Italy to the United States in 1904 and for more than a decade after his arrival edited several radical newspapers and led striking workers in Italian immigrant communities throughout the East. During 1912–16 he became well known as a labor agitator for the Industrial Workers of the World. He moved his newspaper *L'Avvenire* in 1913 from Steubenville, Ohio, to New York City where his militant activities and flamboyant personality quickly made him a leader among the city's radicals. He was a key figure in the defense of Ferdinando Sacco and Bartolomeo Vanzetti, for whom he mobilized support from 1920 until their execution in 1927. In the early 1920s he attacked the fascist government in Italy in his newspaper *Il Martello*. His arrest and conviction for sending "obscene" matter (a book on birth control) through the mail was engineered by the State Department, the Federal Bureau of Investigation, and the postal authorities at the behest of Benito Mussolini's government and led to his imprisonment for four months in a federal penitentiary in 1925; a protest campaign waged by his friends and political associates in New York City defeated efforts by the government to deport him to Italy. An opponent of Stalinism, he supported the anarchists during the Spanish Civil War (1936–39) and served on the commission led by John Dewey in 1937 that found Leon Trotsky innocent of the conspiracy charges leveled against him by Joseph Stalin. From 1941 he fought efforts of communists and prominent former fascists to infiltrate the Mazzini Society and the Italian–American Victory Council, both of which had large followings in New York City. Tresca was assassinated outside the office of *Il Martello* on Fifth Avenue and 15th Street. Although many associates believed that the murder was instigated by the communist Vittorio Vidali or by Generoso Pope, publisher of *Il Progresso*, it is more likely to have been the work of a member of the Mafia named Frank Garofalo, who acted to avenge a personal insult.

Dorothy Gallagher, *All the Right Enemies: The Life and Murder of Carlo Tresca* (New Brunswick, N.J.: Rutgers University Press, 1988); Nunzio Pernicone, *Carlo Tresca: Portrait of a Rebel* (New York: Palgrave Macmillan, 2005)

Nunzio Pernicone

Triangle Shirtwaist fire. The worst factory fire in the history of New York City occurred on 25 March 1911 in the Asch Building at the northwest corner of Washington and Greene streets where the Triangle Shirtwaist Company occupied the top three of 10 floors. Five hundred women were employed there, mostly Jewish and Italian immigrants between the ages of 13 and 23 who were working on the Sabbath out of economic necessity. To keep the workers at their sewing machines, the proprietors locked the doors leading to the exits. The fire began shortly after 4:30 p.m. in the cutting room on the eighth floor and spread rapidly, fed by thousands of pounds of fabric. Panicked workers rushed to the stairs, the freight elevator, and the fire escape. Most on the eighth and 10th floors escaped, but dozens on the ninth floor died, unable to force open the locked exit door. The rear fire escape collapsed, killing many and eliminating an escape route for others. Some tried to slide down elevator cables but lost their grip. Many more, their dresses on fire, jumped to their deaths from open windows. Engine Company 72 and Hook and Ladder Company 20 of the Fire Department arrived within minutes, but firefighters were hindered by the bodies of victims who had already jumped. Fire Department ladders extended only to the sixth floor, and life nets broke when panicked workers jumped in groups of three and four. Additional companies were summoned by four more alarms transmitted in rapid succession.

In fewer than 15 minutes, 146 women died. Although there was widespread revulsion and rage over the working conditions that had contributed to the fire, many defended the right of shop owners to resist government safety regulations, and some in government insisted that they were at any rate powerless to impose it. The owners of the company were charged with manslaughter and later acquitted, but in 1914 a judge ordered them to pay damages of $75 to each of the families of 23 victims who had sued. The Factory Investigating Commission of 1911 gathered testimony, and later that year the city established the Bureau of Fire Investigation under the direction of Robert F. Wagner, which gave the Fire Department additional powers to improve factory safety. The event crystallized support for efforts to organize workers in the garment district and in particular for the International Ladies' Garment Workers' Union. A witness to the event was Francis Perkins, who became Franklin D. Roosevelt's secretary of labor. The first woman appointed to a cabinet post, she remained in that post throughout the New Deal years. The Triangle Shirtwaist fire remains one of the most vivid symbols for the American labor movement of the need for government to ensure a safe workplace.

Triangle fire plaque, 2009

Triangle Building, 2009

Leon Stein, *The Triangle Fire* (Philadelphia: J. B. Lippincott, 1962); David Von Drehle, *Triangle: The Fire That Changed America* (New York: Atlantic Monthly, 2003)

Donald J. Cannon

Tribeca. Neighborhood in lower Manhattan occupying a trapezoidal parcel bounded to the north by Canal Street, to the east by Broadway, to the south by Murray Street, and to the west by the Hudson River; the name was adopted by real estate developers in the mid-1970s and stands for the "triangle below Canal." Once used as farmland by Dutch settlers, the area was included in a large tract granted in 1705 by Queen Anne to Trinity Church, which built St. John's Chapel on Varick Street in 1807 and several years later laid out St. John's Park on an adjacent lot bounded by what are now Laight Street, Varick Street, Ericsson Place, and Hudson Street; the park could be used only by the wealthy families living in Hudson Square, the surrounding neighborhood of elegant brick houses. A fruit and produce market called Bear Market opened in 1813 at the western edge of the neighborhood along Washington, Vesey, and Fulton streets and became an important wholesale and retail supplier of food to the city. Among the products sold were locally grown fruits and vegetables, wild game, and imported meats, cheeses, and caviar. The neighborhood remained mostly residential until increased shipping and commerce in lower Manhattan attracted businesses during the 1840s and soon made the area a major point of transfer. During the mid-nineteenth century the eastern section was the center of the textile and dry goods industry: five- and six-story buildings with marble, sandstone, and cast-iron facades were built to house stores, factories, and storage facilities. After the Civil War St. John's Park became the site of the freight depot of the New York Central and Hudson River Railroad. The site of the depot is now the exit of the Holland Tunnel.

Bear Market became known as Washington Market, and the name was eventually applied to the entire neighborhood. During the 1880s warehouses were built to accommodate mercantile exchanges dealing in butter, cheese, and eggs. By 1939 the market stretched from Washington Street to West Street and had a greater volume of business than all the other markets in the city combined. It remained vital until the early 1960s when fruit and produce markets moved to Hunts Point in the Bronx and city planners approved the Washington Market Urban Renewal Project, leading to the demolition of many old buildings to make way for high-rise housing, office buildings, and educational facilities. Among these were Independence Plaza (1975) on Washington Street, a 40-story apartment building for middle-income tenants, the Borough of Manhattan Community College (1980) to the west, and Washington Market Park (1983) to the south. Factories and warehouses were converted to residential lofts, many of which became the homes of artists. The Tribeca Film Festival was founded in 2002 by Robert De Niro, Jane Rosenthal, and Craig Hatkoff as a response to the terrorist attacks on the World Trade Center of 11 September 2001. It was conceived as a way to foster the economic and cultural revitalization of lower Manhattan through an annual celebration of film, music, and culture. In the early twenty-first century Tribeca is a fashionable residential neighborhood with an affluent population. The streets are lined with shops, art galleries, bars, and restaurants.

Joyce Gold

Tribeca Film Festival. Film festival spearheaded in 2002 by actor Robert De Niro in the wake of the terrorist attacks of 11 September 2001. It was part of an initiative to economically and culturally revitalize the Tribeca area, for which it is named. (*Tribeca* stands for "triangle below Canal [Street]"; the area is directly north of the World Trade Center site.) The participation of De Niro, who has appeared in some of the most acclaimed movies made in New York City, helped lead to the festival's success. Occurring annually in the spring, by 2008 the festival had attracted more than two million attendees and was estimated to have generated more than $425 million in economic activity for New York City.

Jessica Montesano

Triborough Bridge. See Robert F. Kennedy Memorial Bridge.

Triborough Bridge and Tunnel Authority. Municipal agency responsible for financing, constructing, and maintaining bridges and tunnels in New York City. Its origins date to the 1920s when the city made plans to build a major crossing over the East River at 125th Street in Manhattan. Construction of the Triborough Bridge began at the site on 25 October 1929, during the same week the stock market crashed. Construction was soon halted when investors were unwilling to purchase municipal bonds. In early 1933 Robert Moses, chairman of the New York State Emergency Public Works Commission, initiated state legislation that formed the Triborough Bridge Authority as an alternative source of funds. The authority was structured as an independent public-benefit corporation empowered to sell revenue bonds to the Reconstruction Finance Corporation (RFC) and later the Public Works Administration; once all debts were retired, it was to be dismantled and the bridge turned over to the city. The bridge opened in 1936 and during its first year generated $2.72 million in tolls. Its unexpected success made the authority's bonds attractive in the private market: Moses persuaded the RFC to resell the bonds, which were bought quickly. He then transformed the authority into a permanent, multipurpose agency capable of refinancing its bonds to take on new projects. Once restructured, the authority became a model of fiscal resourcefulness and political independence. It built the Bronx–Whitestone Bridge and the Brooklyn–Battery Tunnel, then took its current name. It also assumed control of the Queens–Midtown Tunnel and acquired or built the New York Coliseum, the Eastside Airline Terminal, several parkway approaches, and five more bridges, including the Verrazano–Narrows Bridge (opened in 1964). The authority's political and fiscal powers were curtailed in 1968 when Governor Nelson A. Rockefeller removed Moses as its chairman and merged the authority with the financially troubled regional subway, rail, and bus authorities to form the Metropolitan Transportation Authority (MTA). Eventually, its receipts from tolls and other sources came to provide almost 80 percent of the total income of the MTA. During the early twenty-first century the nine crossings of the former Triborough Bridge and Tunnel Authority carry 300 million vehicles a year and generate $1 billion in revenues annually.

Robert A. Caro, *The Power Broker: Robert Moses and the Fall of New York* (New York: Vintage, 1975)

David C. Perry

Trilling, Lionel (Mordecai) (*b* New York City, 4 July 1905; *d* New York City, 5 Nov 1975). Literary critic. He attended Columbia University (BA 1925, MA 1926, PhD 1938) where he joined the faculty in 1938 and remained for the rest of his career. His first book, a study of Matthew Arnold (1939), marked him as a critical scholar of the first rank, and he soon emerged as a leader of the liberal intellectual community in New York City. Although he disdained the bitter ideological struggles that divided his peers, his criticism nonetheless reflected ideological concerns: his only novel, *The Middle of the Journey* (1947), is a fictionalized account of the retreat from communism by his friend Whittaker Chambers, and in such critical works as *The Liberal Imagination* (1950) he explored the ambiguity of conventional political ideals. Trilling's criticism had a decisive effect on the self-critical, antitotalitarian liberalism of the 1950s, and as a teacher and mentor he influenced figures as diverse as Norman Podhoretz and Norman Mailer.

Stephen L. Tanner, *Lionel Trilling* (Boston: Twayne, 1988)

Peter Eisenstadt

Trinidadians and Tobagonians. Immigrants from the West Indian nation of Trinidad and Tobago first settled in New York City about 1900 and numbered several thousand by the early 1950s. Most then lived in Harlem or Bedford–Stuyvesant. Although often skilled, they were usually denied employment in their trades and consequently did menial and unskilled industrial work outside their neighborhoods. Before the 1930s Trinidadians and Tobagonians formed the Trinidad Benevolent Association and the Tobago Benevolent Society. In the 1930s they also formed the United Mutual Insurance Company, which for decades was the largest black insurance company with headquarters in New York City. Charles Augustin Petioni, a physician, was the best-known leader of the community. Immigration increased markedly with the passage of the Hart–Celler Act in 1965 and continued into the early twenty-first century. The new immigrants included both blacks and East Indians (each group accounts for about 40 percent, respectively, of the population of Trinidad and Tobago). In the mid-1990s the number of Trinidadian and Tobagonian nationals in the metropolitan region was estimated at 150,000. In 2000 they were eighth on the list of new immigrant groups in the city, and more than 88,000 residents of Trinidadian and Tobagonian ancestry had been born outside of the United States. In the early twenty-first century both blacks and East Indians from Trinidad and Tobago lived in the black neighborhoods of Brooklyn, as well as in racially integrated neighborhoods throughout the city; East Indians were especially numerous in Richmond Hill. Most Trinidadians and Tobagonians were unskilled or clerical workers; others worked as technicians and managers and in business and other professions. Black Trinidadians have had a noticeable impact on the city's cultural life through the musical genres calypso and soca, and through their participation in the West Indian carnival on Labor Day in Brooklyn, which they were instrumental in creating in the late 1960s. Indo-Trinidadian organizations in the city include the Sanatana Dharma Maha Sabaha of the West Indies.

Calvin B. Holder, "The Causes and Composition of West Indian Immigration to New York City, 1900–1952," *Afro-Americans in New York Life and History* 11 (1987); Veronica Udeogalanya, *A Comparative Analysis of Caribbean Immigrants Admitted into the United States, 1985–1987* (New York: Medgar Evers College, Caribbean Research Center, 1991)

Calvin B. Holder

Trinity Church. Anglican church. It was formed by royal charter from King William III on 6 May 1697; the first service was conducted on 13 March 1698 in a new church at Broadway and Wall Street. In 1705 Queen Anne granted the church land extending from Fulton Street to Christopher Street that became known as the Queen's Farm. The Charity School (now Trinity School) opened at the church in 1709, the parish granted land for King's College (now Columbia University) in 1754, and it founded a school for freed blacks in the late 1700s. Chapels were added around the city; St. Paul's Chapel (1766, Broadway and Fulton Street) became the best-known. Trinity Church was destroyed by fire in 1776, and a replacement building was consecrated in 1790 but demolished after structural problems became evident in 1839. A new Gothic Revival church designed by Richard Upjohn opened in 1846.

The parish adapted to meet the needs of its members, founding a home for the elderly called St. Margaret's House, the John Heuss House for the homeless and mentally ill, and a cemetery and mausoleum at 155th Street. Income from the Queen's Farm enabled the parish to contribute to 1700 churches and religious institutions of different denominations; Trinity later gave about two-thirds of the land to the city and to various religious institutions. Some of the land was sold, and Trinity Real Estate managed the parish's remaining commercial properties. The chapels of St. Augustine, the Intercession, and St. Luke became independent churches in 1976; other chapels closed, and St. Cornelius's on Governors Island was given to the federal government in 1987.

During the terrorist attacks of 11 September 2001, debris knocked over a huge and ancient sycamore tree at St. Paul's Chapel; the roots were used in a sculpture by Steve Tobin and displayed next to Trinity Church. The church's organ was also damaged by debris; a new organ was installed in 2003. In 2006 the church's bell tower was redesigned to accommodate 12 change-ringing bells, a gift of British philanthropist Martin Faulkes. Trinity Church and St. Paul's have had many well-known members, including William Kidd, John Jay, and Alexander Hamilton. Among those buried in the churchyard are Francis Lewis, a signer of the Declaration of Independence; Hugh Williamson, a signer of the U.S. Constitution; and Robert Fulton. Because Trinity Church owns more than 5 million square feet (464,000 square meters) of commercial office space in lower Manhattan, it has long been regarded as one of the wealthiest parishes in the world.

Morgan Dix, *A History of the Parish of Trinity Church in the City of New York* (New York: G. P. Putnam's Sons [vols. 1–4], Columbia University Press [vol. 5], Rector Churchmen and Vestrymen at the Parish of Trinity Church in the City of New York [vol. 6], Seabury [vol. 7], 1898–1978)

Phyllis Barr

Trinity Church Cemetery and Mausoleum. Last active cemetery in Manhattan. Part of Trinity Church parish, it was established in 1842 on 23 acres (9.3 hectares) of naturalist John James Audubon's estate, bounded by 153rd and 155th streets, Riverside Drive, and Amsterdam Avenue. Audubon is buried at the cemetery, along with Charles Dickens's son Alfred Tennyson Dickens, Albert Gallatin, Clement Clarke Moore (author of the poem "A Visit from St. Nicholas"), and actor Jerry Orbach. In 2008 former mayor Edward I. Koch bought a much-coveted burial plot in the cemetery for $20,000.

Kate Lauber

Trinity School. Private, coeducational elementary and secondary school founded by royal charter in 1709 in Manhattan as a charity school and directed by the headmaster William Huddleston (the first licensed lawyer in the colonies). Classes were held at Trinity Church until 1717; in 1749 the first school building was constructed near Rector Street. In the nineteenth century the school became a private institution along the English model with mostly middle-class students, moving to Varick Street, 14th Street, Eighth Avenue and 33rd Street, Longacre Square, Madison Avenue near 59th Street, West 45th Street, and its present location, on West 91st Street. Trinity is the oldest continuously operating educational institution in New York City.

Richard Schwartz, Peter L. Donhauser

Tri-State Regional Planning Commission. Planning organization. It was a source of much praise and considerable criticism during its 21 years of operation, from 1961 to 1982. The commission was born in a crisis—the imminent abandonment of the money-losing, privately owned commuter rail lines serving the region. New York's governor at the time, Nelson Rockefeller, invited his counterparts from New Jersey and Connecticut to a summit meeting on 30 August 1961, where they announced the formation of the Tri-State Transportation Committee. They selected Dr. William J. Ronan, Governor Rockefeller's personal secretary, to chair the committee, and invited J. Douglas Carroll, Jr., the nation's leading expert in urban travel demand analysis, to direct its technical activities. Rockefeller's grand plan for the committee was to convert it into an interstate transportation commission that would take control of the bus, subway, railroad, and toll highway facilities in the region, absorbing the Port Authority of New York and the Triborough Bridge and Tunnel Authority. Though he succeeded in gaining the approval of the New York and Connecticut legislatures, his plan was rejected twice in the New Jersey legislature, in 1963 and 1964.

With this setback Rockefeller concentrated his efforts on New York State, creating the Metropolitan Transportation Authority in 1965. New Jersey and Connecticut agreed to join New York in establishing the Tri-State Regional Planning Commission, with Carroll as its executive director. The agency's responsibilities grew as planning requirements for federal funding were increased. In the Great Society era of the 1960s, the federal government encouraged metropolitan planning organizations (MPOs) to support programs that went beyond transportation; as a result the commission, as the official MPO for the region, became responsible for creating plans for housing, open space, and other governmental functions, in addition to transportation. Federal agencies made funds available for planning in these functional areas but also imposed planning requirements through the MPOs as a condition for receiving federal assistance.

While many factors led to the agency's dissolution in 1982, the unpopularity of many of these federal programs in the suburbs was an important source of conflict. Counties and localities felt that they did not have an adequate voice in the affairs of the commission. With the election of a conservative U.S. president in 1980, hope ended that the federal government might intervene and stem the growing tide for dissolution. Connecticut voted to terminate its participation in the commission, leaving New York and New Jersey to scramble for a bi-state solution. That was not to happen, and the agency was dissolved on 30 June 1982. For the New York State portion of the metropolitan area, the official MPO became the New York Metropolitan Transportation Council.

George Haikalis

trolleys. See Streetcars.

Trotsky, Leon [Bronstein, Lev (Davidovich)] (*b* Yanovka [now in Ukraine], 26 Oct 1879; *d* Mexico City, 21 Aug 1940). Revolutionary. After being expelled from France and Spain he settled with his wife and two sons in January 1917 in New York City, where they lived for a short time in a three-room apartment at 1522 Vyse Avenue in the Bronx. He was welcomed enthusiastically by the city's Russian expatriates and joined Nikolai Bukharin in producing the newspaper *Novyi Mir* (New World), which was printed in the basement of a building at 77 St. Mark's Place; he was also a popular speaker at gatherings of workers and antiwar activists. Trotsky left the city in March 1917 and made a two-month journey to Russia to join the Bolshevik Revolution.

Kevin Kenny

trucking. Everything that a New Yorker consumes or uses arrives in the city, at least part of the way and certainly on the "last mile," by motor truck. Of all the large cities in North America, save for Boston, New York City has the smallest percentage of goods delivered by rail (1 percent), which, together with water and pipeline transport, in most cities remains the most efficient mode for moving large volumes of cargo.

In some respects, freight operations in New York City are primitive, lacking overall coordination and advanced goods-handling methods (for example, large containers to all destinations, direct rail access, double-stack movements, or large tandem trailers). The job gets done, however, largely because of trucks and vans. Intricate and effective coordination mechanisms among shippers, carriers, and receivers function as business enterprises to make the freight move, almost entirely through private operators using public roadways. These individual enterprises range from national companies with thousands of units to individuals with vans moving their own goods. The integrated carriers, such as United Parcel Service and Federal Express, are special cases that set an example. The carriers operate independently to deal with their own tasks; they expect the government to provide the infrastructure but otherwise not to interfere. The operations are not regulated or controlled, and public agencies have no direct role, except for street traffic rules (including size and weight limits) and safety regulations (including drivers' work practices). The activity operates at a metropolitan level, with political boundaries having little significance (except for the registration of vehicles and taxation), which is particularly the case in the metropolitan region. No regular process exists for recording what and how much moves where, but estimates can be made. Thus, for example, the total annual freight volume generated in the city plus the five nearby counties is 392 million tons, of which 263 million tons are associated with the city. Trucks carry the bulk of it, but they are registered and garaged mostly outside the city.

Rail cargo systems have atrophied in the metropolitan region, and the largest modern freight rail cars cannot even enter the city. The nearest crossing of the Hudson River is near Albany, New York; there are no efficient freight or container yards; and clearances are not adequate. But even if more freight could be brought in by rail, it would still have to be distributed locally by truck. The continental goods-carriage systems effectively stop on the west side of the river, and internal access has to be gained from the many active nodes there. Marine cargo operations have mostly moved to Port Elizabeth and Port Newark in New Jersey. Distribution centers relying on trucks have assumed a major role in freight handling and they, too, are now located primarily west of the Hudson. All of these generate heavy vehicular volumes. Air cargo is growing in volume and is particularly time-sensitive and valuable, thus relying entirely on truck feeders. The congestion around John F. Kennedy International Airport is an economic drain for many of these carriers.

The critical trucking tasks in New York City are the distribution of consumer goods, the moving and storage of household items, the supply of offices and institutions, and the transport of materials to construction sites, as well as sufficient access by repair and maintenance vehicles. Responsiveness to immediate needs is the dominant objective, and vans and trucks can do that well; however, they face various complications in the city: on-time delivery is more important than a full load, so trucks frequently are almost empty; most enterprises are in fierce competition, so they insist on having full control of their own supply operations, resulting in duplication of effort and lack of cooperation; the city is crisscrossed by waterways, and each bridge and tunnel—almost all of which have width and height restrictions affecting the entry of large vehicles—can become a bottleneck for trucks; illegal parking by passenger cars is prevalent in some busy districts, so goods delivery is impeded by blocked access and lack of loading space; construction equipment, parades, and motorcades can disrupt normal operations; much of the regional highway network consists of parkways, so trucks must use overcrowded local streets and arterials. As trucks become larger and heavier, they damage old pavements; the trucks in turn are easily damaged by potholed roadways. The most common damage that trucks sustain in the city is the loss of side-view mirrors because of tight clearances.

Above all, there is the persistent congestion of streets and highways in the city. Although the trucking industry suffers direct economic effects from congestion, it also contributes to it because of the high number of trucks in the regular traffic stream and the fact that they are not easily maneuverable and need to get as close as possible to their loading locations. Truckers in New York City are reluctant to leave their vehicles and cargo out of sight even briefly, and the busiest shopping streets tend to have a solid row of double-parked trucks during the early part of each working day, when stores are restocked. Certain road sections—such as the Cross Bronx Expressway, the Long Island Expressway in Queens, the Gowanus Expressway, and the Brooklyn–Queens Expressway—can be counted on to be always overloaded, but chronic congestion is found throughout the city on the larger arteries that touch high-intensity areas (such as the several business districts, Hunts Point Market, and the Brooklyn waterfront) and at gateways.

The principal effort by the municipal government to assist truck operations is a truck route program extending over some 1000 miles (1600 kilometers). A few major expressways and arterials are designated as through routes and allow 53-foot-long (16-meter-long) trailers. Most of the network consists of local truck routes that reach all districts. All cargo vehicles are required to stay on this system and leave it only at the closest point to a local delivery. The program is effective, except for inadequate signage, some drivers who are unfamiliar with the system, and temporary obstructions. But many of the traffic improvements and controls on streets that expedite the operations of private cars, buses, pedestrians, and bicycles (for example, special lanes, turn restrictions, bus stops, privileged parking permits, reserved spaces, and exclusive lanes) are seen by truckers to be at the expense of trucks and other working vehicles.

The costs that result from congestion and other difficulties are tangible. The delivery of a ton of goods or a parcel in New York City is more expensive than in any other North American city. Surcharges are routinely imposed. The most common complaint by city truckers is the high number of traffic and parking summonses that they receive, which is nonetheless considered a normal cost of doing business in the city. Some firms have employees working full time to get tickets dismissed. Also, truckers may have to pay various tolls in the city, which add up, with other charges, in the ledgers of truck operators.

An "external" trucking-related problem is the fact that truck movements along the eastern seaboard of the United States tend to cross New York City, thus overloading the George Washington and Verrazano–Narrows bridges. Three out of every five eastbound goods vehicles on the George Washington Bridge have destinations east and north beyond the city. Because the tolls on the Verrazano–Narrows Bridge are collected only in the western direction, westbound truckers avoid them by utilizing, for example, Canal Street, thus exacerbating traffic conditions across Manhattan.

Congestion has contributed materially to the disappearance of manufacturing from the city. The only remaining large manufacturing component is the garment industry in midtown Manhattan, which is serviced entirely by motor and hand trucks. This is an example of a traditional manufacturing and marketing activity housed in a fixed environment (buildings, elevators, and streets) that cannot accommodate modern transport and access operations.

Trucking activity in any city is associated with several environmental and community issues that are secondary to their primary business of moving freight; the effects of these are particularly obvious in New York City. Motor truck operations have a reputation for environmental pollution, largely because of diesel engines, which generate nitrogen oxides and small particulate matter (soot) from their exhausts and are noisy if not properly controlled. The noise affects the livability of many neighborhoods, and vibrations from several large units operating near buildings can be destructive. There are also safety and security issues. Truck-related accidents are feared in residential areas. Hijacking of trucks (particularly those loaded with liquor or clothes) was a common occurrence, but this practice has been brought under control because of rooftop identification numbers, better communications among law enforcement personnel, and the fact that vehicles and drivers are now equipped with advanced communications and surveillance systems. Nevertheless, three-person crews are frequently employed for moving valuable cargo in the city. The New York City Police Department is also aware that trucks can be used to blow up strategic targets, as was the case in the 1993 terrorist attack on the World Trade Center.

All other nonmanufacturing activities of the city have to live with the chronic frictions and inefficiencies affecting the trucking industry. Demands for relief and improvement have always been a part of the civic and business debate. Effective programs are difficult to implement: for instance, rail-freight access could be created by building a cross-harbor tunnel to Brooklyn, but the cost could amount to more than $7 billion. Truck routes could be expanded, but there are only a few places where truck volumes would fill dedicated lanes adequately; exclusive "freightways" do not appear to be feasible. Nighttime deliveries could be practiced more, but most small establishments cannot afford to engage another shift of personnel during off-hours. Deliveries could be consolidated and district distribution centers built, but both would require direct and strong city action, the granting of monopoly rights to some enterprises, or the enforcement of cooperative arrangements. None of these approaches is feasible, given the institutional characteristics of the industry. Large vehicles (18-wheelers, for example) could be banned from all city streets, but this might create even larger inefficiencies. Trucks could be ferried along and across waterways on barges, but this might slow down operations because of complicated on- and off-movements. Off-street loading spaces could be built every few blocks in business districts, but land acquisition costs would be prohibitive, ownership and management responsibilities would be contested continuously, and delivery people would probably avoid them anyway. Some parkways could be opened to small trucks and vans, but excess capacity to be used for working vehicles is rare.

Estimates indicate that by the year 2030 the freight volume in the region will grow by 50 percent because of population increases, expansion of business activity, and changing distribution patterns. The existing street and highway network cannot absorb this additional load. In the short run, work hours will have to be extended; in the long run, consolidation and prioritization of movements may became mandatory.

Sigurd Grava

Trumbull, John (*b* Lebanon, Conn., 6 June 1756; *d* New York City, 10 Nov 1843). Artist. Born to a prominent family, he graduated from Harvard and fought in the American Revolution before traveling to London to study with Benjamin West. In 1804 he moved to New York City and became the guiding force behind the American Academy of the Fine Arts, serving as its president (1817–35). Guided by a belief that the fine arts are essential to national welfare, he advocated hanging American portraits and historical paintings beside works by old masters and generally favored the works of his contemporaries. Although criticized by young artists for his conservatism, he was widely regarded for his talent. In 1816 he received a commission for four murals for the rotunda of the U.S. Capitol. He executed idealized, patriotic scenes drawn from the Revolution

Irma B. Jaffe, *John Trumbull: Patriot-Artist of the American Revolution* (Boston: New York Graphic Society, 1975); Helen A. Cooper, *John Trumbull: The Hand and Spirit of a Painter* (New Haven, Conn.: Yale University Art Gallery, 1982)

Carrie Rebora Barratt

Trump, Donald (John) (*b* Queens, 14 June 1946). Real estate developer. The son of Fred Trump, an important developer and owner of residential housing in the outer boroughs of New York City, he attended the University of Pennsylvania and then entered his family's business. In 1974 he took an option to buy the Penn Central Railroad yards on the Upper West Side and announced plans for what later became known as Trump City, a large development of luxury apartments and mixed-use facilities. In 1976 he received the first tax abatement under the city's new business-incentive program to purchase the distressed Commodore Hotel near Grand Central Station and refurbish it as the Grand Hyatt. In the 1980s he purchased the Plaza Hotel at 59th Street and Fifth Avenue. A number of his projects during the 1980s proved controversial because of the ways in which he allocated funds. He used tax abatements to finance Trump Tower, a lavish skyscraper on Fifth Avenue serving as the organization's headquarters and also containing offices, stores, and condominiums; he built a number of luxury apartment complexes in midtown Manhattan and on the Upper East Side, including Trump Plaza at Third Avenue and 63rd Street, as well as several gambling casinos in Atlantic City, New Jersey; and he bought a football team (the New Jersey Generals) and the Eastern Airlines shuttle (which he renamed the Trump Shuttle). Because his investments were highly leveraged, the collapse of the real estate market in the late 1980s forced him to renegotiate nearly $2 billion in debt and divest himself of various holdings, including the air shuttle (bought by U.S. Air). In the 1990s he continued to work on various developments, including a scaled-down version of Trump City that was renamed Riverside South in 1991. In 2001 the Trump World Tower, a residential skyscraper across from the United Nations headquarters, was completed. In addition to his vast real estate holdings Trump became known for his flamboyant personality. In 2003 he began producing and hosting the reality television show *The Apprentice,* which takes place in New York City and for which Trump received a star on the Hollywood Walk of Fame.

Marc A. Weiss

"trunk mystery." Incident in 1871 that began when a baggage master discovered a nude female corpse in a trunk measuring 3 by 3 by 2 feet (90 by 90 by 60 centimeters) at the Hudson River Depot on Saturday, 26 August. The body was identified as that of Alice Augusta Bowlsby, a 19-year-old unmarried woman from Paterson, New Jersey. An investigation revealed that she had been impregnated by a man named Walter Conklin, who arranged for Jacob Rosenzweig to perform an abortion. After accidentally killing Bowlsby, Rosenzweig sought to conceal the evidence by sending her corpse to Chicago; he was sentenced to seven years in prison, and Conklin took his own life. The case fueled campaigns to outlaw abortion.

James C. Mohr, *Abortion in America: The Origins and Evolution of National Policy, 1800–1900* (New York: Oxford University Press, 1978)

Mary Elizabeth Brown

Truth, Sojourner [Baumfree, Isabella] (*b* Hurley, N.Y., *ca* 1797; *d* Battle Creek, Mich., 26 Nov 1883). Abolitionist. Born a slave, she was separated from her parents in 1810 after being sold to a farmer in New Paltz, New York. With a slave named Thomas she had five children including a son, Peter, who was sold to a planter in Alabama despite a state law (1788) prohibiting the sale of slaves out of state. She fled her owner in 1826 and with the help of Quakers undertook a lawsuit that resulted in the return of her son. Freed under state law in 1827, by 1829 she settled with her children in New York City, where she worked as a domestic servant and sometimes attended the Mother African Methodist Episcopal Zion Church at 156 Church Street. She maintained that she took the name Sojourner Truth after hearing a voice in 1843 calling on her to testify against the sins of slavery. She then left the city to travel throughout New England, where she met such noted abolitionists as William Lloyd Garrison, Frederick Douglass, and Wendell Phillips; they invited her to speak at abolitionist gatherings, where she described the experiences of women slaves and the destruction of black families under slavery. The eloquence and religious tone of her speeches became a powerful tool for abolitionists committed to "moral suasion," the policy of attacking slavery by revealing its evils through moral argument. Truth became one of the best-known abolitionists in the country, and by 1850 she was acquainted with such leaders of the woman suffrage movement as Lucretia Mott and Elizabeth Cady Stanton. She spoke at many women's rights conventions, among them the Fourth Annual Women's Rights Convention in New York City (1853). She often called on white women to recognize black women as sisters, who had much in common as mothers. During the Civil War she nursed black troops, worked in a freedmen's community in Arlington, Virginia, and in 1864 was invited to Washington, D.C., to consult with President Abraham Lincoln about the fate of emancipated blacks; she later unsuccessfully petitioned the U.S. Congress to pass a bill allowing freedmen to claim homesteads on public land in the West.

Jacqueline Bernard, *Journey toward Freedom: The Story of Sojourner Truth* (New York: W. W. Norton, 1967); Margaret Washington, ed., *Narrative of Sojourner Truth* (New York: Vintage, 1993)

Thelma Foote

tuberculosis. Infectious disease that usually affects the lungs. Once known as consumption or the "white plague," it became an unfortunate hazard of life in New York City in colonial days, and for most of its history little could be done to combat it. The disease was long thought to be hereditary rather than contagious, and even Robert Koch's discovery in 1882 of the microbe that causes tuberculosis met with some hostility among the local medical community. In 1897 Health Commissioner Hermann M. Biggs made the reporting of tuberculosis cases to the Health

Department mandatory. At that time tuberculosis was one of the leading killers of New Yorkers; about 12,000 new cases occurred that year, and the disease was responsible for about one of every four deaths of people between the ages of 15 and 65. By 1904 the number of cases had tripled. Privately practicing physicians were hesitant to report their tubercular patients to the Health Department for fear of initiating their forcible removal to a sanitarium or quarantine hospital and of losing paying patients in economically difficult times. Despite this reluctance a strong public health campaign was mounted by such local officials as Biggs, T. Mitchell Prudden, William H. Park, and Lawrence Veiller. The Health Department opened the first municipal clinic for tuberculosis in the United States in 1904, and efforts at education, prevention, and isolation helped contribute to the decline of the disease by the late 1930s. Several chemotherapeutic agents that cured tuberculosis were developed between 1944 and 1952.

A further decline was brought about by municipal programs beginning in the 1950s and lasting into the 1980s that provided daily nursing and medical attention to the city's urban poor and others with the disease. During the late 1960s the New York City Department of Health spent more than $41 million each year on tuberculosis treatment and prevention programs. As a result of these efforts, new cases of the disease declined steadily each year between 1960 and 1978. Basking in the glow of overconfidence and changing budget priorities, however, the city began to execute massive funding cuts for almost every public health program, especially those directed at tuberculosis control. Added to this volatile mix were two decades of increasing numbers of homeless New Yorkers, the dismantling of psychiatric and public hospitals, the rise of AIDS, and the boom in immigration from nations where tuberculosis is common. Each of these factors helped to create a situation one infectious disease expert labeled a "tuberculosis time bomb." In 1979 the decades-long decline in tuberculosis in New York City came to an end, and by 1992 the case rate ballooned to almost three times what it had been in 1979. More striking, doctors established that once released from the hospital only 11 percent of tuberculosis patients completed their six-month course of medication and that one of every three newly diagnosed cases in the city was resistant to many of the drugs used to treat the disease. In response, the Health Department unrolled a massive anti-tuberculosis campaign, including neighborhood screening programs, directly observed therapy (DOT) clinics, improved health care in the city's jails, and for noncompliant patients a special quarantine facility. The price tag for these interventions was more than $1 billion. By 2008 the tide had turned in New York City. In the years following the epidemic's peak in 1992, multidrug-resistant cases of the disease fell by 91 percent in the city, and the overall case rate fell from a high of 49.8 cases per 100,000 to 16.6 cases per 100,000. Nevertheless, this incidence remained almost three times the nationwide rate of 5.8 cases per 100,000.

C.-E. A. Winslow, *The Life of Hermann Biggs* (Philadelphia: Lea and Febiger, 1929); John Duffy, *A History of Public Health in New York City* (New York: Russell Sage Foundation, 1968, 1974); René Dubos and Jean Dubos, *The White Plague: Tuberculosis, Man, and Society* (New Brunswick, N.J.: Rutgers University Press, 1987)

Howard Markel

Tucker, Richard [Ticker, Reuben] (*b* Brooklyn, 28 Aug 1913; *d* Kalamazoo, Mich., 8 Jan 1975). Singer. Trained as a cantor in Brooklyn, he gained fame as a lyric tenor specializing in classical Italian repertory. He was a star at the Metropolitan Opera from the time of his debut in *La Gioconda* in January 1945. He was known for the quality of his voice and technique. He died during a concert tour with his friend Robert Merrill. The Richard Tucker Music Foundation aids the careers of American opera singers.

George A. Thompson, Jr.

Tudor, Antony [Cook, William] (*b* London, 4 April 1908/9; *d* New York City, 19 April 1987). Choreographer. He provided choreography for the Ballet Rambert in London before leaving Britain for New York City in 1939 to join the Ballet Theatre, which had just been formed. For the company's first season in January 1940 he revived three of his earlier ballets: *Jardin aux lilas* (1936), *Dark Elegies* (1937), and *Judgment of Paris* (1938). Tudor gained wide recognition for his explorations of psychological themes, especially in such works as *Pillar of Fire* (1942) and *Romeo and Juliet* (1943).

David Vaughan

Tudor City. Apartment complex located in Manhattan between 40th and 43rd streets and First and Second avenues. It was New York City's largest residential construction project when the Fred F. French Company began building in 1927; it included nine apartment buildings and 4500 residents by 1932. Promoted as an urban enclave with moderately priced housing, most of the buildings face parks between East 42nd and East 43rd streets or between East 41st and East 42nd streets. French oriented the building this way to eliminate East River views, because slaughterhouses occupied the land directly to the east of Tudor City before the construction of the United Nations in the 1940s. Ownership of Tudor City changed hands several times before most of the buildings became cooperatively owned in the 1980s. The 11 apartment buildings range from 11 to 32 stories and are notable for designs including gargoyles and protrusions of limestone. The complex includes two public parks, two private parks, a church, and a few businesses. New York City's Landmarks Preservation Commission declared Tudor City a historic district in 1988. In 2008 there were approximately 5000 residents.

Ben Silk

tugboats. Tugboats began running in New York Harbor shortly after the initial voyage of Robert Fulton's *North River Steamboat* in 1807. The steamboats transported people and pulled barges between New York City and Albany, cutting the travel time from four days to 36 hours. The steamboat *Nautilus* towed a large ship through New York Bay in 1818, the first recorded tug in the harbor; many tugs were equipped with towing bitts in the years to follow. The steam towing business opened up in 1824 with the revocation of Fulton's steamboat ferry monopoly and the opening of the Erie Canal a year later, leading to large increases in steamboat efficiency and affordability and the quantity of harbor and river towing. During the 1840s coal began to replace wood as fuel for steamboats. Irish immigrants played a large roll in tug operation during the era, with two such immigrants founding McAllister Tugging and the Moran Company, two of the largest tugging firms in New York City. During the Civil War, the Union army bought roughly 50 tugs from the New York City area to implement its Anaconda Plan to blockade southern ports. After the Civil War the army auctioned off its remaining tugs, and propeller tugs began to replace the old side-wheel tugs; both of these factors led to an increase in the number of tugboats in the harbor, which reached around 600 by 1900. During the 1920s many tugs converted to diesel power, though the less efficient steam tugs remained on the harbor into the 1960s.

The first tugboat unions developed during the 1880s as small independent entities segregated by the type of work its members performed. In the years before World War I many of these unions combined to become the Marine Workers Affiliation of the Port of New York. This group went on strike for three

Tugboat, 2009

days in 1918 until President Woodrow Wilson ordered arbitration; the strike led to union gains in power and effectively set up a closed shop. During the early 1930s Captain William Bradley organized the Harbor Tugboatmen's Union, which became the International Longshoremen's Association (ILA) Local 333, the dominant tugboat union in New York City. From 1946 to 1988 the ILA organized at least six harborwide tugboat strikes, each lasting between 10 and 88 days and crippling harbor commerce. During this period the volume of work for tugs in New York Harbor fell as trucking cut into tugboat business, commerce on the Hudson River declined, companies shifted their shipping to less expensive ports on the East Coast, and newer ships were less dependent on tugs for propulsion in the harbor. The power of ILA Local 333 and its membership fell after 1988, and seven of the largest tugboat companies recruited replacement crews, some from around the country, to replace the ILA members on their tugs. New York City tugboat commerce continues in the twenty-first century, with tugs transporting oil and waste and doing other jobs around the harbor.

George Matteson, *Tugboats of New York: An Illustrated History* (New York: New York University Press, 2005)

Ben Silk

Tully, Alice (Bigelow) (*b* Corning, N.Y., 11 Sept 1902; *d* New York City, 10 Dec 1993). Musician and philanthropist. Granddaughter of an early president of Corning Glass Works, she earned a reputation as a concert singer during the 1930s but left a more enduring mark as a patron of the arts. She promoted many musicians at salon concerts in her rambling, art-filled apartment high in the Hampshire House on Central Park and supported numerous musical organizations, often anonymously. She largely underwrote the construction of the concert hall at Lincoln Center that bears her name—it opened in 1969—and for many years chaired the board of the Chamber Music Society of Lincoln Center, which makes its home there. In 1970 she received the Handel Medallion, New York City's highest cultural award.

Albert Fuller, *Alice Tully: An Intimate Portrait* (Urbana and Chicago: University of Illinois Press, 1999)

James M. Keller

tunnels. Beneath the land and waterways of New York City lie 161 miles (259 kilometers) of tunnels. Of this total, the subway accounts for 137 miles (220 kilometers); four vehicular tunnels, two railroad tunnels, and the tunnels of the Port Authority Trans-Hudson Corporation (PATH) account for 24 miles (39 kilometers). Plans for an underwater tunnel were first developed in 1807, but the technology necessary to build tunnels through the mud and silt of riverbeds was not perfected until the late 1860s. The first attempt to construct a tunnel under the Hudson River was made in 1874 by Colonel DeWitt C. Haskin, who broke ground in Hoboken, New Jersey, for a tunnel to Morton Street in lower Manhattan. Several financial setbacks caused the project to be abandoned in 1892 after 2000 feet (600 meters) of tunnel beneath the Hudson had been constructed. In 1902 William Gibbs McAdoo took over the project, formed the New York and New Jersey Railroad (later known as the Hudson and Manhattan Railroad), and completed the tunnel along with one parallel to it, as well as a pair of tunnels between Cortlandt Street in Manhattan and Exchange Place in Jersey City. The tunnels opened in 1908–9 and later became part of the PATH system. Under the East River the piano maker William Steinway began construction in 1892 of the Steinway Tunnels (the oldest surviving tunnels entirely within the five boroughs), which were two trolley tunnels connecting 42nd Street in Manhattan with Queens that opened in 1907 and were converted to accommodate subways in 1915; these tunnels are now part of the No. 7 subway. The first subway tunnels in the city, the Broadway line of Interborough Rapid Transit (IRT), were constructed during 1900–1906 through the rocky center of Manhattan from City Hall to the northern tip of Manhattan; this project included tunnels close to the street surface in most areas but deep in the ground between 157th and Dyckman Streets because of hilly topography.

As the city's subway network expanded to provide multiple interborough routes, 13 double-track rail tunnels were built between 1908 and 1933 under the Harlem River, the East River, and Newtown Creek. During 1904–10 the Pennsylvania Railroad built two tunnels—a double one beneath the Hudson River and a quadruple one beneath the East River—both running to Pennsylvania Station; the East River tunnels also carry Long Island Rail Road (LIRR) trains. The first underwater vehicular tunnel was the Holland Tunnel, opened in 1927 beneath the Hudson River and connecting Canal Street in lower Manhattan with Jersey City in New Jersey; its ventilation system became a model for subsequent vehicular tunnels worldwide. The Lincoln Tunnel, opened in 1937, connects midtown Manhattan at West 40th Street with Weehawken, New Jersey, and at first had a single tube, to which parallel tubes were added to the north in 1945 and to the south in 1957. East River vehicular tunnels were built in 1940 (the Queens–Midtown Tunnel) and 1950 (the Brooklyn–Battery Tunnel).

During the early 1970s two new tunnel projects were started and then aborted because of the city's 1975 fiscal crisis. The Second Avenue Subway, first proposed in 1929, was built at Chatham Square, between 99th and 105th streets and between 110th and 120th streets before the tunnels were sealed. A fourth subway tunnel between Queens and Manhattan connecting East 63rd Street with Long Island City, which also included a lower level for the LIRR, was built but was unused until 1989 because of lack of connections to existing Queens subways. First opened to serve one new station in Long Island City (Queensbridge/21st Street), it was connected to the Queens Boulevard line in 2001, permitting through train service via 63rd Street between Manhattan and Queens stations. In the early twenty-first century the city's improved economic fortunes required an expansion of mass transit tunnels to accommodate new subway and commuter rail routes, and several new projects were under construction or in the final design phase, including the Second Avenue subway between 63rd and 96th streets; an extension of the No. 7 subway westward from 41st Street and Seventh Avenue (part of Times Square Station) to 34th Street and 11th Avenue; improvements to subway service in lower Manhattan; LIRR East Side access; and a second pair of New Jersey Transit rail tunnels to midtown Manhattan, terminating at 34th Street and Seventh Avenue immediately north of Penn Station.

Carl W. Condit, *American Building: Materials and Techniques from the First Colonial Settlements to the Present* (Chicago: University of Chicago Press, 1968); Norval White and Elliot Willensky, eds., *AIA Guide to New York City* (New York: American Institute of Architects, New York Chapter, 1967; 3rd edn San Diego: Harcourt Brace Jovanovich, 1988)

Rebecca Read Shanor, Andrew Sparberg

Tunney, Gene [James Joseph] (*b* New York City, 25 May 1897; *d* Greenwich, Conn., 7 Nov 1978). Boxer. He grew up in a working-class Irish Catholic family in Greenwich Village, where he dropped out of school at age 15 to work as an office clerk. He practiced boxing at the Greenwich Village Athletic Club and turned professional in 1915. After winning the post-Armistice light heavyweight championship in Paris, he resumed his professional career, briefly holding the American light heavyweight championship in 1922 before losing it to Harry Greb and regaining it the following year. On 23 September 1926 he defeated Jack Dempsey for the world heavyweight title, which he successfully defended against Dempsey in the controversial "long count" fight of 22 September 1927 in Chicago. He later became a prominent businessman.

Steven A. Riess

Turks. Turkish-speaking Muslims from the Ottoman Empire settled in New York City in the late eighteenth century and numbered 1401 in 1900. By 1940 the figure had reached 17,663, although many were not ethnic Turks. During these years the city's Turks occupied a low position on the economic ladder. Some settled along Rivington and Forsythe streets in lower Manhattan and supported such clubs as the Turkish Aid Society on Theriot Avenue in

Unionport (dominated by Cypriot Turks) and the Turkish Cultural Alliance at 856 Broadway in Williamsburg (mostly Anatolian). After World War II many Turkish physicians, scientists, and engineers left for the United States, and especially for New York City, where the United Nations became the anchor of the local Turkish community. In 1977 the Turkish government bought 821 United Nations Plaza at First Avenue and 46th Street, which among other organizations houses the Turkish Consulate, the Turkish mission to the United Nations, and the Federation of Turkish-American Societies (formed in 1956). Turks in the early twenty-first century were dispersed throughout the five boroughs, with large concentrations in Brighton Beach, Sunnyside, and Richmond Hills in Queens.

Most of the metropolitan area's 70,000 to 100,000 ethnic Turks represent the wealthier classes of their home country. Many drive taxicabs, own filling stations and import–export firms, and work in restaurants. Few intend to return to Turkey. They take part in many groups, including the Turkish Women's League, the Turkish Cultural Alliance, and the Turkish Music Society of New York. The predominant religion is a secular brand of Islam: Anatolian Turks worship at the Fatih Mosque at 89-11 Eighth Avenue, Turkestanians at 2302 West 13th Street, and Crimean Turks at 4509 New Utrecht Avenue (all in Brooklyn). For several years Turkish law forbade Turks who took citizenship of another country to inherit property or exercise other property rights in Turkey. These laws were amended in 1985 to allow for dual citizenship, an arrangement that most Turkish-Americans found agreeable. In the early 1990s the Federation of Turkish-American Societies fought to change the use of the English term *Turkey* to its Turkish counterpart, *Türkiye* (though it was largely unsuccessful), and the city government designated as Turkish-American Week the week closest to 19 May, the Turkish Youth and Sport Holiday. The most prominent Turkish-American in the city was Ahmet Ertegun, a founder of Atlantic Records and an owner from 1970 to 1985 of the soccer team the New York Cosmos. More than 15,000 people reported Turkish ancestry in 2000.

Marc Ferris

Turner Corporation. Construction firm formed in 1902 as the Turner Construction Corporation by the engineer Henry C. Turner (1893–1954); it was originally based in Brooklyn. The firm was the first to use the Ransome method of building construction (using concrete reinforced by steel bars, rather than wood frames and masonry), and in its early years it built several notable structures, including the factory of the Robert Gair Company (the largest concrete structure until that time), the stairways for the first subway station in New York City, and Bush Terminal in Brooklyn. It eventually became one of the nation's largest builders of commercial, industrial, residential, and government buildings. During World War I the firm built several industrial buildings throughout the city, including the U.S. Army Supply Base and the U.S. Navy Fleet Supply Base in Brooklyn. Other famous city buildings constructed by the Turner Corporation include those of Bloomingdale's, Tiffany and Company, and the New-York Historical Society, and the Lexington Hotel, the Port Authority Bus Terminal, Lincoln Center for the Performing Arts, United Nations Plaza, and the current Madison Square Garden. In 2006 the New York Yankees and Tishman Speyer awarded Turner the contract to construct the new Yankee Stadium in the Bronx.

James Bradley

Turnverein. German educational society formed on 6 June 1850 by 36 exiles of the German Revolution of 1848, modeled on a society formed in Germany by Friedrich Ludwig Jahn to promote health and physical education among young men. Soon an important political institution, it supported labor unions and abolitionism. During the 1850s it helped to establish good relations between Americans and German immigrants and defended German Americans against Know-Nothings. In 1861 it organized the 20th New York Volunteer Regiment (also known as the United Turner Rifles), which distinguished itself during the Civil War in 1861 and was also the main body for assimilating Germans into American society during the Civil War and Reconstruction. From the end of the nineteenth century it focused on physical culture, and in 1891 a women's section was formed. The society was weakened by anti-German sentiment during World War I and by a sharp reduction in the number of German immigrants. During the late 1920s it adopted English as its official language to broaden its membership. Weakened further by the stock market crash of 1929 and World War II, it did not regain financial stability until after the war. In September 1986 it merged with the Mount Verein Turners and dedicated a new building in Throgs Neck.

Stephen D. Engle

Turtle Bay. Neighborhood on the East Side of Manhattan (2000 pop. *ca* 20,000), bounded to the north by 53rd Street, to the east by the East River, to the south by 43rd Street, and to the west by Lexington Avenue. It was named for the Deutal Bay farm, which originally covered 86 acres (35 hectares) of land surrounding a cove, shaped like a knife blade (*deutal* in Dutch), that contained turtles. Initially an area of small farms and country houses, Horace Greeley and Edgar Allan Poe lived there. The cove was filled in after the Civil War and brownstones were built, many of which were converted to tenements and rooming houses during the late nineteenth century to house European immigrants who worked in breweries, factories, and slaughterhouses by the river. Turtle Bay Gardens and Beekman Place were built in the 1920s (as some brownstones were converted to town houses), followed by the United Nations in the 1950s; United Nations Park stands on what was once Turtle Bay. Most of the housing consists of luxury apartment buildings, renovated brownstones, and town houses. The population is mostly young and affluent and includes many diplomats. East 49th Street between Second and Third avenues is officially named Katharine Hepburn Place after the actress who purchased one of the town houses in 1932. Other well-known residents have included the writer Kurt Vonnegut and the composers Irving Berlin and Stephen Sondheim.

Edmund T. Delaney, *New York's Turtle Bay, Old and New* (Barre, Mass.: Barre, 1965)

Val Ginter

Tuxedo. Name formerly applied to New Brighton.

TWA. See Trans World Airlines.

Twain, Mark [Clemens, Samuel (Langhorne)] (*b* Florida, Mo., 30 Nov 1835; *d* Redding, Conn., 21 April 1910). Novelist and short-story writer. He began a career as a journalist in 1862 and went on his first lecture tour in 1866, speaking about his experiences in Hawaii, where he had been a travel correspondent for the *Union* (based in Sacramento, California). His first book, *The Innocents Abroad* (1869), an account of a boat trip to the Mediterranean, made him nationally well known. In 1871 he moved to Hartford, Connecticut. During this period Twain wrote his best-known works: *The Adventures of Tom Sawyer* (1876), a novel modeled on his childhood experiences living on the Mississippi River; *The Prince and the Pauper* (1881), a historical romance for children; *Life on the Mississippi* (1883), about his experiences as a riverboat captain in the 1850s; *Adventures of Huckleberry Finn* (1884), a companion to *Tom Sawyer;* and *A Connecticut Yankee at King Arthur's Court* (1889). He formed his own subscription firm (1884) that issued *Huckleberry Finn* as its first publication and invested heavily in the Paige typesetting machine. Both ventures failed, leaving him bankrupt in 1893–94. To pay his debts Twain sent his family to Europe and spent the winter in a single room at the Players Club (of which he was a charter member). In 1895 he embarked on a five-year speaking tour of the world, and in 1900 he returned with his family to New York City, where he was welcomed as a hero. The family rented an apartment at 14 West 10th Street and lived at Wave Hill in Riverdale (from 1901) and 21 Fifth Avenue (1904–8). Twain frequented the Century, the Lotos, and the Metropolitan clubs, particularly enjoying his walks up Fifth Avenue to the mansion of his friend Andrew Carnegie on 92nd Street. He retired to a small farm in Redding, Connecticut, in 1908.

Justin Kaplan, *Mr. Clemens and Mark Twain* (New York: Simon and Schuster, 1966)

Anthony Gronowicz

Tweed, William M(agear) "Boss" (*b* New York City, 3 April 1823; *d* New York City, 12 April 1878). Political leader. His middle name was almost certainly Magear (his mother's maiden name) but is often given incorrectly as Marcy. Born in his family's home at 1 Cherry Street (now the site of the approaches to the Brooklyn Bridge in Manhattan), he left school at age 11 to learn chair making from his father and was later apprenticed to a saddler; he also studied bookkeeping for a time, was a clerk at a mercantile office in the city, and worked as a bookkeeper and later a partner in brush shops at 206 and 357 Pearl Street. He married Mary Jane C. Skaden on 18 September 1844, and they lived for two years with her family at 193 Madison Street. Standing about 6 feet (1.8 meters) tall and weighing nearly 300 pounds (136 kilograms), Tweed was famous for his free and easy manners, ample-though-coarse humor, and jovial swagger. In 1848, at the invitation of state assemblyman John J. Reilly, he helped to form a new fire company, no. 6; it was named the Americus Engine Company and its symbol was a fierce Bengal tiger, later adapted by Tweed for Tammany Hall. He became the foreman in 1849 and through the company, which was known as the Big Six, was introduced to municipal politics. After unsuccessfully seeking election as a Democratic assistant alderman in 1850, he won a seat in the following year as an alderman representing the seventh ward.

In 1852 Tweed joined his brother Richard in the family's chair-making business and was elected to the U.S. House of Representatives. After serving a single term he was appointed to the Board of Education and in 1856 to the Board of Supervisors of New York County. By 1858 he was a member of the general committee of Tammany Hall and the undisputed leader of the seventh ward. He and his well-trained ward heelers, district leaders, and block captains built a power base by courting Catholics and helping to feed, clothe, and shelter immigrants and the poor at a time when there were few agencies to help. Although he had little knowledge of the law, he was certified as a lawyer by his friend George Barnard in 1860 and opened a practice at 95 Duane Street. Despite his defeat in the election for sheriff in 1861 he was an astute politician. Shortly after the election he was named chairman of the Democratic General Committee of New York County, and on 1 January 1863 he was chosen to lead the general committee of Tammany Hall. He earned the nickname "Boss" after becoming grand sachem of the society in April. He then formed a smaller executive committee, which eventually wielded much more power than the general committee, and had himself appointed deputy street commissioner. In the following year he bought a controlling interest in the New York Printing Company, which became the city's official printer, and was paid lavishly for the work it performed. He also bought the Manufacturing Stationers' Company, which sold supplies to the city at inflated prices, and used his law practice to extort large sums that were disguised as legal fees for services rendered.

Tweed began wearing a large diamond in his shirtfront and turned to real estate to invest the enormous sums that he received in the form of kickbacks. Among his properties was a fashionable brownstone at 41 West 36th Street that he bought in 1866, and by the late 1860s he was one of the city's largest landowners. About this time he helped Jay Gould and Jim Fisk in their battle with Cornelius Vanderbilt for control of the Erie Railroad. Elected to the state senate in 1867, he pushed the Erie Classification Bill through the state legislature to legalize stock issued fraudulently by Gould and Fisk; they rewarded him with a large block of stock and a seat on the board of directors. Recognizing that he needed the support of his constituents to remain in power, he prevailed on the municipal government to provide more orphanages, almshouses, and public baths; helped to set up the Manhattan Eye and Ear Hospital; introduced a bill in the state legislature to fund parochial schools; sought to increase state appropriations to private charities; and fought for greater home rule for New York City. He also made himself the commissioner of public works. As the chairman of the senate committee on cities he oversaw the passage of a new charter for the city in 1870 that replaced the Board of Supervisors with a new Board of Audit. This body, consisting essentially of a group of associates known as the Tweed Ring, siphoned off staggering amounts of money from the many bond issues that were passed, and from 1869 to the end of 1871 the city's debt tripled and municipal taxes climbed accordingly.

Tweed owned a mansion at Fifth Avenue and 43rd Street and a stable on 40th Street where he kept his carriages and sleighs. By 1871 he was on the board of directors of the Harlem Gas Light Company, the Brooklyn Bridge Company, and the Third Avenue Railway Company and was president of the Guardian Savings Bank. To keep control of their own fortunes and funds belonging to the city, he and his confederates organized the Tenth National Bank. He also widened Broadway and fought to preserve a site for the Metropolitan Museum of Art in Central Park.

His fortunes soon changed, owing partly to the efforts of Thomas Nast, who exposed the corruption of Tweed and his associates in a series of cartoons. Evidence of the ring's corruption was passed to the *New York Times,* which published a series of damning articles from 8 July 1871, and in August Tweed began transferring his real estate holdings and other investments to family members. After his reelection as chairman of the general committee of Tammany Hall, he was served with an arrest warrant on 26 October; he nonetheless won reelection as a state senator in November and planned to return to Albany until his criminal indictment and arrest in December. At the end of the month he was deposed as grand sachem and expelled from the Tammany Society. His trial began on 7 January 1873 and ended in a hung jury. At a second trial, begun on 19 November, he was convicted on 204 of 220 counts, ordered to pay a fine of $12,750, and sentenced to 12 years in prison. When asked his occupation by prison officials, he replied, "Statesman." He was released after a year when a judge ruled the sentence excessive but was immediately rearrested on a civil charge and imprisoned on Ludlow Street. On 4 December 1875 he escaped to New Jersey during a visit to his family at 647 Madison Avenue. A civil trial in February 1876 ended in a judgment of $6 million against him. Using the alias John Secor, he fled to Florida and Cuba before reaching Spain, where the authorities sent him back to the city. He was returned to prison on 23 November. Toward the end of 1877 he disclosed many details of the ring's activities to a special committee of the Board of Aldermen. After Tweed's death from pneumonia in prison, Mayor Smith Ely refused to fly the flag at City Hall at half-staff.

Alexander B. Callow, Jr., *The Tweed Ring* (New York: Oxford University Press, 1966); Leo Hershkowitz, *Tweed's New York: Another Look* (Garden City, N.Y.: Anchor/Doubleday, 1977); Oliver E. Allen, *The Tiger: The Rise and Fall of Tammany Hall* (Reading, Mass.: Addison–Wesley, 1993); Kenneth D. Ackerman, *Boss Tweed: The Rise and Fall of the Corrupt Pol Who Conceived the Soul of Modern New York* (New York: Carroll and Graf, 2005)

See also Charter, Scandals and corruption, and Target companies.

Allen J. Share

Tweed Courthouse. Municipal building in Manhattan. In 1858 architect John Kellum designed the building for a site where an eighteenth-century almshouse had stood. The city's Board of Supervisors appropriated about $13 million for construction between 1862, when William M. "Boss" Tweed became the board's president, and 1871, when investigations into corruption toppled Tweed. The city completed the classical Victorian structure of gray Massachusetts marble in 1878 and used it as a courthouse until 1926, then as offices, and since 2002 as headquarters for the Department of Education. It is both a national and city landmark (1974, 1984).

Alexander B. Callow, Jr., *The Tweed Ring* (New York: Oxford University Press, 1966), 197–206; John G. Waite, Nancy A. Rankin, and Diana S. Waite, *Tweed Courthouse: A Model Restoration* (New York: W. W. Norton, 2006)

Mary Elizabeth Brown

Tweed Ring. Corrupt group of politicians associated with TAMMANY HALL who controlled the government of New York City during the 1860s. Its leader, William M. "Boss" Tweed, was influenced by the dictatorial style of Mayor Fernando Wood and the notorious Common Council of the early 1850s, known as the Forty Thieves. From 1866 to 1871 the ring controlled Tammany Hall, the municipal government, the county government, the judicial system, the governorship, and the Board of Audit, which supervised all city and county expenditures after its formation by the charter of 1870 (a reform document supported by Tweed that gave the city home rule). In manipulating the board Tweed was aided by Mayor A. Oakey Hall, Comptroller Richard B. Connolly, and Peter B. Sweeny, head of the Department of Public Works. In July 1871 the *New York Times* charged that the ring had defrauded the city of millions of dollars; these allegations, along with mounting taxes and rising municipal bonded debt, swept the Tweed Ring from power and disgraced its members.

Alexander B. Callow, Jr., *The Tweed Ring* (New York: Oxford University Press, 1966); Leo Hershkowitz, *Tweed's New York: Another Look* (Garden City, N.Y.: Anchor/Doubleday, 1977); Kenneth D. Ackerman, *Boss Tweed: The Rise and Fall of the Corrupt Pol Who Conceived the Soul of Modern New York* (New York: Carroll and Graf Publishers, 2005)

Jerome Mushkat

20th Century Limited. Express passenger train of the New York Central Railroad, running from Boston and New York City to Chicago in 15.5 hours and inaugurated on 15 June 1902 by George Henry Daniels, a patent medicine salesman turned passenger agent. The train followed the "water level route," which consists of the shores of Lake Michigan, Lake Erie, the Erie Canal, and the Hudson River, and traveled through Albany. It offered a barber shop, secretarial services, and onboard telephone in addition to the legendary red carpet treatment at its terminals. The train traveled as many as seven sections, of which the first to depart was called the Advance 20th Century. In 1938 the train was redesigned in a streamlined style by Henry Dreyfuss and until 1958 only Pullman cars were used, some of which carried passengers through to Los Angeles. Over the years such notables as Joan Crawford, William Randolph Hearst, J. P. Morgan, and Theodore Roosevelt rode the Century, and it became an institution in passenger rail travel. Service ceased on 2 December 1967; Amtrak's Lake Shore Limited follows a similar route.

Edward Hungerford, *The Run of the Twentieth Century* (New York: New York Central Lines, 1930); Lucius M. Beebe, *20th Century: The Greatest Train in the World* (Berkeley, Calif.: Howell-North, 1962); Karl R. Zimmerman, *20th Century Limited* (Minneapolis, Minn.: MBI, 2003)

Val Ginter

twenty-four-dollar purchase. Transaction in which William Verhulst, governor of New Netherland, reportedly bought the island of Manhattan from Indians of the Wappinger Confederacy for 60 guilders' worth of trading goods (equivalent to $24), satisfying a Dutch law requiring settlers to buy their land from the Indians. The sale is said to have taken place by the end of the summer of 1626 and is usually credited to Verhulst's immediate successor, Peter Minuit. No deed of sale survives; a clever fake remains on file in the state archives at Albany.

James E. Mooney

"21" Club. Restaurant at 21 West 52nd Street, between Fifth and Sixth avenues. Opened in 1922 as a speakeasy by Jack Kriendler and Charles Berns and popularly known as Jack and Charlie's, it was the most expensive and fashionable of the nightclubs that served alcohol during Prohibition. It became famous for a secret door to a wine cellar (in the basement of 19 West 52nd Street) that let it hide 2000 crates of wine from police raids. It changed addresses several times, moving from Greenwich Village to Washington Place to 49th Street to its current address. In addition to costly drinks, the establishment offered unusually good food and had a dance floor and orchestra; it was much favored by members of Café Society and aging celebrities. The "21" Club was renovated in 1987 and remained one of the city's most popular restaurants in the early twenty-first century.

James E. Mooney

Twin Parks. Housing project on several sites in the central Bronx; it includes Twin Parks West, which lies along Webster Avenue south of Fordham Road, and Twin Parks East, along Southern Boulevard south of the Bronx Zoo. The project was the result of a study sponsored during 1966–67 by the J. M. Kaplan Fund on scatter-site high-rise housing for people of low and middle incomes. Construction was largely subsidized by the New York State Urban Development Corporation. The development was named for Bronx and Crotona parks and included new schools and community centers in Tremont, West Farms, and Belmont. Most of the buildings were designed by such young architects as Richard Meier and were completed between 1973 and 1975.

Gary D. Hermalyn

Twin Towers. See WORLD TRADE CENTER and SEPTEMBER 11.

Two Bridges. Housing project on the Lower East Side of Manhattan, covering 10 blocks between the Manhattan and Williamsburg bridges and bounded to the north by Cherry Street, to the east by Montgomery Street, to the south by South Street, and to the west by Market Slip. Completed in 1967 at a cost of $44 million, it has more than 1400 units in several towers and three-story buildings. Drugs and crime afflicted Two Bridges in the 1980s but later decreased through the efforts of various community organizations. It has traditionally been an immigrant neighborhood, first populated by Europeans, then peoples from Latin America and, into the twenty-first century, the Chinese. In 2003 it was added to the National Register of Historic Places. The area slowly began to improve during the early twenty-first century.

James Bradley

Typhoid Mary. Nickname of Mary Mallon (*b* 23 Sept 1869; *d* New York City, 11 Nov 1938), a carrier of typhoid fever. She was first recognized as a healthy carrier in 1904 after an outbreak of the disease in a household in suburban Oyster Bay, New York, where she was employed as a cook. For the next three years she continued to work as a cook in several residences, until she was traced to one on Park Avenue and institutionalized at Riverside Hospital on North Brother Island (1907–10). She was released after promising not to work as a cook and to report regularly to the city's Department of Health. But she promptly disappeared and for the next five years worked in restaurants, hotels, and resorts in and around New York City, sometimes under an assumed name. In February 1915 she caused a serious outbreak of typhoid fever at Sloane Hospital for Women. In the following month she was apprehended and reinstitutionalized on North Brother Island, where she spent the rest of her life. In all, she was implicated in 47 cases of typhoid fever and three deaths.

Judith Walzer Leavitt, *Typhoid Mary: Captive to the Public's Health* (Boston: Beacon Press, 1996)

Allen J. Share

U

UDC. See URBAN DEVELOPMENT CORPORATION.

Uhl, Anna Behr (*b* Würzburg [now in Germany], 13 Feb 1815; *d* New York City, 1 April 1884). Newspaper publisher. She lived in Niagara County before moving to New York City where with her husband Jacob Uhl, a printer, she bought the small weekly newspaper *New Yorker Staats-Zeitung*. Under their direction it began publishing daily and achieved influence in local and national affairs. She was the sole manager from her husband's death in 1852 until her marriage in 1859 to her assistant Oswald Ottendorfer (*b* Moravia, 26 Feb 1826; *d* 15 Dec 1900). Known for their philanthropy, the two made donations to the German Hospital, the Astoria House for Aged Women, and the Ottendorfer Branch of the New York Public Library.

James E. Mooney

UHT. See UNITED HEBREW TRADES.

UJA. See UNITED JEWISH APPEAL.

Ukrainian Museum. Museum at 222 East Sixth Street in Manhattan, founded in 1976 by the Ukrainian National Women's League of America. The folk art collection of more than 4000 items contains regional costumes, needlework, and textiles including kilims (flat, woven rugs with traditional designs), as well as ceramics, woodwork, metalwork, and *pysanky* (traditionally decorated Ukrainian Easter eggs). Most objects date from the late nineteenth century and the early twentieth. The museum also has a photographic archive of the past 100 years of Ukrainian immigration to the United States.

Carol V. Wright

Ukrainians. Ukrainian immigration to the United States began in the late 1870s, mostly from economically depressed mountainous border districts between Austrian Galicia and the Subcarpathia and Presov region of Hungary. After passing through the Port of New York, the majority of immigrants went to work as miners in the anthracite region of northeastern Pennsylvania, where they became known as Ruthenians. In 1894 political differences with immigrants from Subcarpathia led the Galicians to form the Rusky Narodny Soiuz (now the Ukrainian National Association) and many other organizations. As national consciousness spread during the late nineteenth and early twentieth centuries, immigrants from Austrian Galicia and Bukovina adopted the new national name Ukrainian; immigrants from Subcarpathia continued to use the name Ruthenian.

Ukrainian cultural institutions developed slowly in New York City because of the transitory character of the city's early Ukrainian immigrants. Although small localized societies like the Sisterhood of St. Olga (1898) and the Brotherhood of St. Nicholas (1899) were organized, community life among Ukrainians in the city did not flourish until 1905, the year that the city's Ukrainians, virtually all of whom were Byzantine rite Catholics (Uniates), purchased a Baptist chapel at 322 East 20th Street in Manhattan; this was refurbished and named St. George's Ukrainian Catholic Church. When the first Ukrainian bishop, Soter Ortynsky, arrived in 1907, his first pontifical Mass in the United States was celebrated in St. George's Church. The parish moved to 24 East Seventh Street in 1911, when a larger church was purchased from a Methodist congregation. St. George Church and the surrounding neighborhood became a major hub for Ukrainian Americans in New York City.

Immigrants to the United States from Galicia, who feared Polish rule, dramatically increased in number after World War I. They developed organizations to protect their cultural and religious traditions, encourage Ukrainians to become loyal citizens of the United States, and work toward an independent, democratic Ukraine. In the 1920s the means of achieving these goals became a source of serious conflict among Ukrainian Americans in New York City, as communists, socialists, monarchists, and nationalists struggled for support. The postwar period also saw the establishment of the Ukrainian Autocephalous Orthodox Church in the United States and the arrival of Bishop John Theodorovich from eastern Ukraine (1924); the first parish, St. Vladimir's, was organized in 1926 at 334 East 14th Street in Manhattan.

In the 1930s about 50,000 Ukrainian Americans lived in New York City. St. George's Catholic Church, the community's largest institution, had a membership of more than 1000 families, and the Orthodox Church of St. Vladimir had 225 families. Periodicals such as the *Ukrainian Quarterly* (beginning 1944), published by the Ukrainian Congress Committee of America, were launched after World War II to provide Americans with reliable information about the Ukraine. After the war Ukrainians from displaced-persons camps in Europe refused to return to their homeland while it was under the control of the Soviet regime. Assisted by volunteer agencies, about 100,000 Ukrainians immigrated to the United States and nearly 15,000 settled in metropolitan New York. Most were college graduates and professionals from urban areas, whose transition to the United States was aided by well-established Ukrainian American urban communities. As a group they were instrumental in organizing scholarly societies such as the American branches of the Shevchenko Scientific Society and the Ukrainian Academy of Arts and Sciences. Ukrainian Americans in New York City numbered more than 100,000 in the early twenty-first century, forming the largest community outside Ukraine. They were then the 13th largest group of newcomers.

Wasyl Halich, *Ukrainians in the United States* (Chicago: University of Chicago Press, 1937; repr. New York: Arno, 1970); Myron B. Kuropas, *The Ukrainians in America* (Minneapolis: Lerner, 1972)

Bohdan P. Procko

unbuilt projects. Over the centuries, hundreds of plans proposed for New York City have not been realized because of political, technological, or financial obstacles. Many of the more grandiose schemes have been related to transit, and a number of projects that did not succeed influenced later projects that did. A bridge over the Hudson River was first proposed in 1805. The plan called for a timber pontoon crossing designed by Colonel John Stevens that would extend for more than 1 mile (1.6 kilometers) between Hoboken (New Jersey) and West 11th Street in Manhattan. An underground rapid transit system for the city was proposed as early as 1866 by the engineer Egbert L. Viele, who intended to build an arcade 15 feet (4.6 meters) beneath Broadway, through which trains powered by steam locomotives would transport passengers from the Battery to Harlem. This project was defeated by William M. "Boss" Tweed, who feared that it would end the kickbacks that he received from the city's surface transport companies. But several features of Viele's plan were resurrected by William Barclay Parsons, who designed the Broadway line for the Interborough Rapid Transit company when the city finally built a subway some 40 years later: among these were the basic route of the system and Viele's innovative four-track arrangement, which allowed for separate express and local trains in each direction.

In 1868 Andrew Haswell Green invited British artist Benjamin Waterhouse Hawkins to create dinosaur models for a proposed Paleozoic Museum in Central Park. Hawkins, who had built full-size dinosaur models based on skeletal findings for the 1854 Crystal Palace Exhibition in London, traveled to New York City, set up a studio in the park, and got to work on a 39-foot (12-meter) hadrosaur. However, by 1871 Hawkins had run afoul of Tweed and his Tammany cohorts, who had taken control of the park. Tweed sent his thugs to Hawkins's studio, where they smashed his models and buried them somewhere in the park; the museum remained unbuilt, and the remains of the models were never found.

The demand for housing occasioned by immigration in the late nineteenth century and the early twentieth inspired several proposals for planned developments. Among those that failed was Utopia, intended as a cooperative town in north central Queens for Jews from the Lower East Side. The developers acquired land in 1905 and received a loan from the New York Mortgage and Security Company to grade the streets and stake out lots, but they abandoned their plan when they were unable to secure more funds.

Several large-scale unbuilt projects date from the 1930s and 1940s. The original plan for the Empire State Building would have given midtown Manhattan an unusual airport: it provided for special mooring facilities for dirigibles near the top of the skyscraper, on the 102nd story, and lounges, ticket agencies, and baggage rooms on the 86th. Although two blimps briefly made contact with the "mooring mast" in 1931, the fanciful scheme was abandoned, and the facilities on the 86th and 102nd stories became observation decks open to the public. A plan for a bridge between Battery Park in Manhattan and Hamilton Avenue in Brooklyn was put forth in 1939 by Robert Moses and a design was submitted by Othmar H. Ammann. The bridge was vigorously opposed by residents and politicians, and the Brooklyn–Battery Tunnel was built instead. The United Nations in 1946 considered building its headquarters in Flushing Meadow Park in Queens, and designs for a complex were drawn up by the architects Wallace K. Harrison, Louis Skidmore, and Aymar Embury II. The organization eventually rejected Queens in favor of its current site in Manhattan when the land was donated by John D. Rockefeller, Jr.

In 1960 Buckminster Fuller, inventor of the geodesic dome, and Shoji Sadao designed a climate-controlled transparent dome that would stretch over midtown Manhattan, covering 50 blocks; the materials would be lifted into place by helicopter. Fuller thought the dome's construction costs would be offset by savings in energy bills and the elimination of snow-removal costs. Fuller also envisioned a redevelopment plan for Harlem that involved high-rise structures built above existing buildings, thus preventing residents from being displaced during construction; seen in the context of Moses's urban renewal plans of the 1960s, it might not have been a bad idea. Several years earlier, Fuller had created a domed stadium at the request of Walter O'Malley, owner of the Brooklyn Dodgers, although many believed that O'Malley never wanted the stadium and was already planning the team's move to Los Angeles.

One project that accomplished more for the city through its failure than it would have through its success was a plan to construct an expressway through lower Manhattan. Outlined on the city's official map from 1941 to the late 1960s, the plan virtually froze development along a path 2.5 miles (4 kilometers) long while community groups campaigned against it, and as a result much of the unique cast-iron architecture of SoHo was preserved. Other proposals were defeated much more quickly, including one in 1957 to demolish Carnegie Hall and build a skyscraper in its place. Among the more contentious development projects of the 1970s and 1980s was Westway, proposed in 1972 as a replacement for the crumbling West Side Highway between the Battery and 42nd Street. The plan called for extensive landfill along the Hudson and construction of a park, an incinerator, and a bus depot. Opponents of the project argued that it would damage the quality of the air and the ecology of the Hudson, and they eventually prevailed in the courts. Plans for Westway were terminated in 1989. In the first decade of the twenty-first century, plans for a grandiose Guggenheim Museum in lower Manhattan and for a huge stadium for the New York Jets professional football team failed to reach fruition.

Rebecca Read Shanor, *The City That Never Was: 200 Years of Plans That Might Have Changed the Face of New York* (New York: Viking, 1988)

Rebecca Read Shanor

unemployment movements. Protests by the unemployed in New York City date back to the colonial period. When an American embargo on shipping in 1808 put many sailors out of work, the affected workers led protests in the streets, displaying placards demanding work or bread. Eventually the city responded by setting them to work leveling Murray Hill with shovels: this was the first public works relief project in the United States. In 1837 an angry crowd shouting slogans of the Working Men's Party and the Locofocos mobbed a flour warehouse owned by Eli Hart at Broadway and Washington Street to demand that the city provide relief. Rallies of the unemployed in 1854 attracted large numbers of mechanics and laborers to meetings in Tompkins Square Park and City Hall Park; after months of demonstrations the city announced that construction of Central Park would soon begin, giving work to thousands of laborers. During a severe economic depression in the 1870s many thousands of the unemployed turned out for rallies, speeches, and parades at which they decried temporary soup lines offered by private charities as insufficient and demanded more public works projects. A committee on safety threatened to seize food for the hungry and forward to the city any bills that it received; flyers were circulated in English and German, and French immigrants who had taken part in the revolution of 1848 and the Paris Commune argued that workers were entitled to public works projects. In response Mayor William F. Havemeyer ordered a large number of police officers to attack a peaceful rally in Tompkins Square Park and arrest labor leaders.

The city charter was amended in 1893 to forbid "outdoor relief," or direct food subsidies and rent relief for the unemployed. This attempt to curb unemployment failed, and with each succeeding economic crisis protests by the unemployed increased. During the depression of 1913 they invaded churches to protest the inadequacy of private charity and the need for public works. Under the leadership of the Industrial Workers of the World (IWW) and the young organizer Frank Tannenbaum, they demanded a minimum wage on public works projects, an eight-hour day, and a public employment bureau. The largest movement of the unemployed was formed during the Depression. The socialist organizer David Lasser in 1935 formed the Workers' Alliance of America, which later cooperated with programs of the New Deal. During this period councils of the unemployed and the Workers' Alliance of America sought to reshape public policy and attitudes. Following the example of the IWW, this movement emphasized the dignity of workers and criticized any relief system that threatened to make outcasts of aid recipients. Hospitals first reported deaths from starvation in 1931, and the unemployed soon raided stores, warehouses, and delivery trucks. In Harlem and other working-class neighborhoods residents mobilized to protect the indigent from being turned out into the streets by organizing rent strikes and forcibly resisting evictions.

By the 1960s movements of the unemployed had been largely superseded by movements for welfare rights. Groups advocated a guaranteed income, helped welfare recipients to file grievances and to obtain subsidies for furniture and clothing, and engaged in picketing and sit-ins at welfare offices; many of their most militant leaders were women. The National Welfare Rights Organization in New York City had 4030 members before the movement faded in 1969.

Frances Fox Piven and Richard A. Cloward, *Poor People's Movements: Why They Succeed and How They Fail* (New York: Pantheon, 1977); Franklin Folsom, *Impatient Armies of the Poor: The Story of Collective Action of the Unemployed, 1808–1942* (Niwot: University Press of Colorado, 1991)

Kathleen Hulser

United Nations Children's Fund [UNICEF]. Agency formed in 1946 as the United Nations International Children's Emergency Fund to help children in Europe and China recover from World War II. It became a permanent agency of the United Nations in 1953, focused on Asia, Africa, the Middle

East, and Latin America. The principal activities of the organization include providing food, clean water, health care, and education to children and women, especially in regions affected by natural and other disasters, and promoting self-sufficiency through long-term development. Its offices are at 3 United Nations Plaza in Manhattan.

Shan Jayakumar

Unificationists. Members of the Family Federation for World Peace and Unification (formerly the Holy Spirit Association for the Unification of World Christianity, and commonly the Unification Church), formed in 1954 in Korea by the evangelist Sun Myung Moon; also sometimes called Moonies (considered derogatory by members). The church was registered in New York City on 4 October 1972. In 1975 it bought the former New Yorker Hotel (4 West 43rd Street), which became its national headquarters and a center for its world mission. Moon was also rumored to control the Manhattan Studios at 311 West 34th. The unificationists published three newspapers: the *New York City Tribune* (1976–91), the anti-communist *Noticias del mundo* (1980–), and the *Sae Gae Times* (1982–). Moon gave a number of public addresses in the city, including a "God Bless America" celebration at Yankee Stadium in 1976. He also conducted a marriage ceremony at Madison Square Garden in 1982 for more than 2000 couples (many of whom he had brought together), an event intended to promote world peace. During the same year he stood trial in the city for tax evasion; he was convicted and served a 13-month prison term in Danbury, Connecticut. The Unification Church had about 3000 members in the city in 1992 and operated two churches in Manhattan (one in Harlem) and one each in Brooklyn, the Bronx, Queens, and Staten Island. In 2008 Moon appointed his youngest son, Hyung Jin Moon, to be the new leader of the Unification Church and the worldwide Unification movement; his daughter In Jin Moon heads the U.S. church and Lovin' Life Ministries, based in New York City. In the early twenty-first century the church's headquarters remained at 4 West 43rd Street.

Irving Louis Horowitz, ed., *Science, Sin, and Scholarship: The Politics of Reverend Moon and the Unification Church* (Cambridge, Mass.: MIT Press, 1978)

Walter Friedman

Uniformed Sanitationmen's Association. Labor union, formally known as Local 831 of the International Brotherhood of Teamsters. Formed in 1935 by John J. DeLury, it became the first union recognized by the city as an exclusive bargaining agent for its members in August 1958. From 2 to 10 February 1968 it called a strike that halted garbage collection and left more than 110,000 tons (99,790 metric tons) of refuse on the sidewalks and streets. In 2007 the Uniformed Sanitationmen's Association secured a contract for roughly 6500 workers in the Department of Sanitation that included a 17 percent wage increase and a new paid holiday (Martin Luther King, Jr., Day).

Steven H. Corey

Union Carbide. Chemical manufacturers. It was formed in 1898 as the Union Carbide Company on 42nd Street by entrepreneurs from Chicago soon after the discovery of acetylene, merged in 1917 with Carbon Corporation (formed in 1876), and took its current name in 1922. Soon one of the country's most prosperous chemical and plastics manufacturers, it developed the electric battery, the refrigerator, various carbon and metal products, and antifreeze. For decades it was among the most profitable firms in New York City, and it had more than a dozen plants and offices there by the 1950s. In 1960 the firm built a 52-story skyscraper at 270 Park Avenue designed by the firm of Skidmore, Owings and Merrill. Union Carbide left the city for suburban Connecticut in the early 1980s. On 6 February 2001 the Dow Chemical Company acquired Union Carbide.

James Bradley

Union Club. Men's social club formed in 1836. It met in a building at 343 Broadway from 1837 and made several moves over the next century: in 1842 to the former home at 376 Broadway of its member William B. Astor, in 1850 to 691 Broadway, in 1855 to a building at Fifth Avenue and 21st Street (the first building in the city designed as a clubhouse), in 1903 to Fifth Avenue and 51st Street (where it occupied a building designed by Cass Gilbert and John du Fais), and in 1933 to 101 East 69th Street (designed by Delano and Aldrich). The Union Club is one of the oldest and most prestigious clubs in New York City, and many of the younger clubs are descended from it.

James E. Mooney

Union League Club. Club formed in 1863 to support the Union cause in the Civil War. It evolved to include a library and gallery of art and military trophies. The first three clubhouses were at 26 East 17th Street (1863), at Madison Avenue and 26th Street (1868, the Jerome Mansion), and at Fifth Avenue and East 39th Street (1881). Early functions included the raising and sponsorship of black regiments in the Civil War and the organizing of events such as the Sanitary Fair. In 1870 members of the club were involved in establishing the Metropolitan Museum of Art; the club also helped found the American Red Cross and build the Statue of Liberty. Less than a decade after its founding the club had a membership of 1400, the largest in New York City. In 1931 the architectural firm of Morris and O'Connor designed a new clubhouse in a neo-Georgian style at 37th Street and Park Avenue in Murray Hill. The club began admitting women in the 1980s.

James E. Mooney

Union Place. Name applied during the 1820s to Cypress Hills.

Union Porcelain Works. Pottery manufacturer. It was opened in 1863 by Thomas C. Smith at 300 Eckford Street in Greenpoint, near the East River. The mainstay of its business was a heavy, white porcelain used for hotel chinaware and house trimmings. It became internationally known for a number of large-scale pieces designed by the sculptor Karl L. H. Müller for the Centennial Exposition in Philadelphia in 1876. The Union Porcelain Works ceased operations about 1922. Examples of its work are displayed at the Metropolitan Museum of Art.

Alice Cooney Frelinghuysen, *American Porcelain, 1770–1920* (New York: Metropolitan Museum of Art, 1989)

Alice Cooney Frelinghuysen

Unionport. Neighborhood in the eastern Bronx, bounded to the east by Westchester Creek, to the west by the Bronx River, to the south by Castle Hill and Soundview, and to the north by Westchester Avenue. The first area of development was near a port along Westchester Creek that is no longer used. Throughout the nineteenth century the housing consisted mostly of one-family frame houses, many of which remained into the twenty-first century. In 1851 the Village of Unionport was settled west of Westchester Avenue between Westchester Creek and what became Castle Hill Avenue; the streets were numbered, the avenues lettered from A to E. The village was annexed to New York City in 1895, and the streets and avenues were renamed (after early settlers) so that they would not be confused with those of surrounding neighborhoods. The extension of the Lexington Avenue subway in 1920 led to the construction of a few brick apartment buildings. In the 1960s several streets were obliterated when an interchange was built connecting the Bruckner Expressway, the Cross Bronx Expressway, and the Hutchinson River Parkway. In the early twenty-first century the population was mostly Latin American.

John McNamara, *McNamara's Old Bronx* (New York: Bronx County Historical Society, 1989)

Gary D. Hermalyn

unions. See Labor.

Union Square. Park and neighborhood in Manhattan bounded by 14th Street to the

Union Square, 2009

south, 21st Street to the north, Third Avenue to the east, and Sixth Avenue to the west. It was one of the few open spaces designated on the 1811 grid mapping out Manhattan. It was used as a potter's field until 1815 when the graves were removed and an iron fence erected. At that time the oval-shaped area became known as Union Place because it lay at the conjunction of several roads, some of them at unusual angles. Much of the surrounding land was purchased by real estate developer Samuel B. Ruggles, who campaigned for the open space to become a public square in the 1830s, and in 1833 it was purchased by the city. Union Square became a highly desirable residential area, as wealthier residents moved north to avoid the increasingly dense population in lower Manhattan. The park, filled with a grand fountains and walks, opened in 1839 and quickly became the center for civic celebrations of all kinds, such as the grand opening of the Croton water system in 1842. It was one of the first areas to have gaslights in the 1840s, and by the 1850s it was surrounded by more than 40 hotels in the neighborhood. In 1854 the Academy of Music opened at 14th Street at the southeast corner of the square. Numerous Civil War parades and rallies were held at Union Square, including one that attracted more than 100,000 in support of the Union cause.

By the 1860s the neighborhood was also changing into a commercial hub featuring the most desirable stores. In 1862 A. T. Stewart opened his great cast-iron department store, and by the 1870s, when Tiffany's opened, the park was redesigned and refurbished according to plans by Frederick Law Olmsted and Calvert Vaux. The fashionable shopping district later known as the Ladies' Mile started at Union Square and continued up Broadway. Toward the end of the nineteenth century the nature of the square changed as the wealthy continued to move uptown, followed by a commercial exodus of the more expensive retail establishments. The square was transformed into a manufacturing district, as evidenced by the presence in the 1880s of six sewing machine companies. The nation's first Labor Day was celebrated in the square on 5 September 1882, and from that time the square became a working-class meeting place. Also in the 1880s electric lights were installed in Union Square, and in the 1890s the first cable car ran along Broadway on its west side.

By the early twentieth century the area was filled with booksellers and inexpensive clothing stores such as Kleins and Ohrbach's. The square was taken apart during subway construction and the establishment of an extensive underground concourse in the 1920s. Numerous political and protest meetings were held in Union Square by permit, including those of the Industrial Workers of the World and various unions, such as those of garment workers. Many unions, such as the International Ladies' Garment Workers' Association and the Amalgamated Clothing Workers of America, established headquarters around the square, as did the American Civil Liberties Union. Labor rallies attracted large crowds during the 1930s, such as one on May Day 1937 that drew 70,000, but by the 1950s such meetings became scarce. The square emerged again as a place of political meeting and protest during the 1960s, such as when young men burned their draft cards to protest the Vietnam War. By the 1970s Union Square had become neglected and the area run down; the park was popular with drug dealers and homeless people. But a turnaround started during the 1980s, followed by 20 years of major improvements of the square, as new residential and commercial construction transformed the area around it. Many of the old buildings were declared historic, the park was cleaned up and redesigned, and by the twenty-first century the square and the neighborhood had once again become an attractive and popular

Memorial in Union Square, ca *15 September 2001*

area. Although Union Square is no longer usable for public meetings, it has retained its reputation as a place for public expression, and many memorials are set up casually there. For instance, after the destruction of the World Trade Center towers by terrorists on 11 September 2001, the square became a magnet for people who wanted to place expressions of remembrance. It is also the home to a greenmarket four days a week and a large holiday fair.

Statues in Union Square include ones of George Washington (Henry Kirke Brown, 1856), Abraham Lincoln (Brown, 1868), the Marquis de Lafayette (Frédéric-Auguste Bartholdi, 1876), and the Independence Flagstaff (Anthony de Francisci, 1926).

Lisa Keller

Union Theological Seminary. Seminary established in Lenox Hill in 1836 by New School Presbyterians. Originally named the New York Theological Seminary, its founders eschewed strict adherence to confessional standards, embraced revivalism, and emphasized the experiential aspects of the Reformed tradition. The seminary attracted such respected figures as Edward Robinson, Henry Boynton Smith, and Philip Schaff and became affiliated with the United Presbyterian Church in the United States of America in 1870. It resumed its independence in 1892 after the church tried and suspended Charles A. Briggs, a faculty member who was one of the first biblical critics. By the time it moved in 1910 to a Gothic quadrangle just north of Columbia University in Morningside Heights, the seminary was nondenominational. Among its faculty were many distinguished theologians, including Arthur Cushman McGiffert, Henry Sloane Coffin, Henry P. Van Dusen, Reinhold Niebuhr, Paul Tillich, Robert T. Handy, and Raymond E. Brown. In the 1970s it became known as a center of liberal theology after James H. Cone and Beverly Wildung Harrison joined the faculty. In the early twenty-first century Union Theological Seminary remained known for its ecumenism and theological inclusiveness.

Robert T. Handy, *A History of Union Theological Seminary in New York* (New York: Columbia University Press, 1987)

Randall Balmer

Unisphere, 2009

Unisphere. Large, hollow, stainless-steel globe in Flushing Meadows–Corona Park. It was designed by landscape architect Gilmore D. Clarke and built and donated by U.S. Steel as the symbol of the World's Fair of 1964–65, with its theme "Peace through Understanding." The largest globe in the world, it is 140 feet (42.7 meters) tall, has a diameter of 120 feet (36.6 meters), and is estimated to weigh 900,000 pounds (400,000 kilograms). In 1994 the globe and its surroundings, including its reflecting pool and fountains, were renovated at a cost of $3 million. In 1995 it was designated a New York City landmark.

Unitarian Universalists. Unitarian Universalism stems from the formerly separate Unitarian and Universalist churches. Such Universalists as John Murray gave sermons in New York City as early as 1795, and in 1796 a Universalist church opened in reaction against the Calvinistic concept of arbitrary salvation and damnation. Unitarianism in New York City began in earnest after William Ellery Channing of Boston gave a sermon to a small gathering in the city after the ordination of Jared Sparks in Baltimore in May 1819.

Later in the same year a Unitarian church was formed as the First Congregational Church of New York City (later renamed All Souls Church). The congregation was mostly from New England and rejected the traditional doctrine of the Trinity. A meetinghouse was built on Chambers Street, and the congregation engaged as its minister William Ware, the brother of Henry Ware, of Cambridge, Massachusetts. He served the church for 15 years and later became well known for his novels about the Roman Empire. His successor was Henry Whitney Bellows, who took over after graduating from the Harvard Divinity School. During his 43-year career Bellows became known nationally for his sermons and for his work as the president of the U.S. Sanitary Commission during the Civil War. All Souls Church counted among its members the writers Herman Melville, William Cullen Bryant, and Catharine Sedgwick and the illustrator Nathaniel Currier.

With the blessing of the First Church a second church opened farther uptown in 1825; this became known as the Church of the Messiah and later the Community Church of New York City. Among its ministers were Minot Savage and Robert Collyer, both known for their oratory, and later the social activists John Haynes Holmes and Donald Harrington. Unitarian societies were organized in Brooklyn in 1833 and Staten Island in 1852. There were eventually seven Universalist churches in Manhattan, including one in Harlem and another called the Church of the Divine Paternity (1838) at 160 Central Park West, which for a time was led by Edwin Chapin; it was later renamed the Fourth Universalist Society. The All Souls Universalist Church of Brooklyn opened in 1845.

After Bellows's death All Souls Church was led successively by the hymn writer Theodore Chickering Williams, the social reformer Thomas Slicer, and William Laurence Sullivan, a former Catholic priest who had become a Unitarian after the papal decrees on infallibility. Under Sullivan, All Souls Church wrote President Woodrow Wilson a letter of support at the beginning of World War I; the Community Church under Holmes, a pacifist, never supported the war. All Souls moved to a building at 80th Street and Lexington Avenue in 1932 during the tenure of Minot Simons, Sullivan's successor. In the following years the church was led by Laurance I. Neale, a layman appointed minister by the congregation, Walter Donald Kring, and F. Forrester Church.

The American Unitarian Association and the Universalist Church of America merged to form the Unitarian Universalist Association in 1961. In the mid-1990s the Community Church was known for its political activism; All Souls was known for its conservatism in religious matters and its social activism (it was one of the largest churches on the East Side seeking social reform). Only two Universalist congregations have survived into the twenty-first century: All Souls at 80th and Lexington and the Fourth Universalist Society at 76th and Central Park West. A third remaining church, All Souls Universalist Church of Brooklyn, merged in 1998 with the Bethlehem United Church to become All Souls Bethlehem Church, a congregation that, in the early twenty-first century, represented Unitarian Universalism, the United Church of Christ, and the Disciples of Christ.

Walter Donald Kring, *Liberals among the Orthodox: Unitarian Beginnings in New York City, 1819–1839* (Boston: Beacon, 1974); Walter Donald Kring, *Henry Whitney Bellows* (Boston: Unitarian Universalist Association, 1979)

Walter Donald Kring, Colin J. Davis

United Association of Plumbers. Labor union. Its international organization is dominated by its branch in New York City, known initially as Local 2 and later renamed Local 463. Well-known members in the city have included George Meany, head of the American Federation of Labor–Congress of Industrial Organizations (AFL–CIO). The headquarters of the union are at 21 East 26th Street.

United Baltic Appeal. Organization formed in New York City in 1966 to promote independence in the Baltic countries and preserve their culture. It sponsors seminars, festivals, and internships, maintains a library and a speakers' bureau, and produces *BATUN News,* a semimonthly publication devoted to current events in the Baltic countries, relevant activities at the United Nations, and organizational news. After Estonia, Latvia, and Lithuania became independent in 1991, the organization evolved into an information center. In the early twenty-first century the Baltic Association to the United Nations (BATUN), a division of United Baltic Appeal, continued to work on behalf of the three nations. The organization is based in the Bronx.

Vladimir Wertsman

United Brotherhood of Carpenters. Labor union formed in New York City in 1881 by Peter J. McGuire. It was preceded by a number of unions formed by carpenters in the early nineteenth century. The union fought aggressively for the eight-hour workday and eventually dominated the carpentry trade. In the early twenty-first century the union represented carpenters, cabinetmakers, millwrights, pile drivers, latherers, framers, floor layers, roofers, drywallers, and workers in the forest-products industry and related industries.

Robert A. Christie, *Empire in Wood: A History of the Carpenters' Union* (Ithaca, N.Y.: Cornell University Press, 1956), 102–36

Colin J. Davis

United Cerebral Palsy of New York City. Charitable organization formed in 1946 by parents in New York City to help their children with cerebral palsy. As the incidence of prenatal cerebral palsy decreased, the group began to serve people with other developmental disabilities, including mental retardation. The expansion of its goals led to a tripling of its size during the 1980s. United Cerebral Palsy of New York City maintains a network of affiliates throughout the world. Its headquarters are at 105 Madison Avenue.

Sandra Opdycke

United German Trades [Vereinigte Deutsche Gewerkschaften]. German central labor body formed in New York City in the early 1880s and associated with the new German labor and socialist newspaper *New Yorker Volkszeitung.* In 1882 it joined the Central Labor Union, an ethnically diverse labor organization that became one of the most powerful in the city, and in 1888 it sponsored the United Hebrew Trades, the first major Jewish labor organization.

Stanley Nadel

United Hatters, Cap and Millinery Workers International Union. Labor union formed in 1934 when the United Hatters of North America and the United Cloth Hat, Cap and Millinery Workers International Union combined their operations. The merger was brought about by a desire on the part of the unions to end their jurisdictional battles during a slump in the hat trade occasioned by the Depression. The New Deal caused further consolidation in New York City and elsewhere, and by 1947 the union had 45,000 members, more than two-thirds of all workers in the industry. Over the next 25 years production rapidly shifted overseas and membership dropped by two-thirds. Its survival threatened, the union merged with the Amalgamated Clothing and Textile Workers of America in 1981.

Donald Robinson, *Spotlight on a Union: The Story of the United Hatters, Cap and Millinery Workers International Union* (New York: Dial, 1948); David Bensman, *The Practice of Solidarity: American Hat Finishers in the Nineteenth Century* (Urbana: University of Illinois Press, 1985)

Ronald Mendel

United Hebrew Charities. Confederation of five German Jewish relief associations formed in 1874 to help eastern European Jewish immigrants adjust to the United States; among its supporters were Jacob Schiff and Adolph Lewisohn. It had an immigration bureau that represented Jewish immigrants arriving at Ellis Island, and it established an employment bureau on the Lower East Side as well as a loan fund. It also offered vocational training to the children of immigrants; scholarships were tendered to students enrolling in the Hebrew Technical Institute. While newcomers sought work or business opportunities, they could obtain free lodging, food, and medical services. The organization also provided burial care without charge and operated the National Desertion Bureau, which addressed the major problem of fathers deserting their families. It was the sponsor for the Industrial Removal Office and the Jewish Immigrant Information Bureau, which worked to persuade recent immigrants to leave the city for other parts of the country by offering them employment and better housing. By 1917 the United Hebrew Charities was absorbed into the Federation of Jewish Philanthropies of New York.

Jeffrey S. Gurock

United Hebrew Trades [UHT; Fareynikte yidishe geverkshaftn]. Federation of predominantly Jewish trade unions formed in 1888 by 80 radical intellectuals in New York City. It was modeled after the United German Trades. The federation encouraged the spread of labor unionism by organizing new unions, directing strikes, negotiating with employers, interceding on behalf of workers, and helping immigrant employees gain membership in the unions of the American Federation of Labor. In 1909 it planned a strike by shirtwaist makers that gave rise to mass strikes in the garment industry, and it mustered material and public support for striking cloak makers in the following year. Only 5000 workers belonged to the 41 member locals in 1909, but by 1913 it had grown to more than 200,000 members in 107 locals. The UHT sponsored the Trade Union Immigration Bureau to channel immigrants into the unionized branches of their trades; it also took part in the labor-oriented relief committee for the devastated Jewish populations of eastern Europe after World War I, and it aided the Jewish trade union federation in Palestine from the 1920s. As Jewish membership fell in the affiliated unions, the United Hebrew Trades declined in importance, maintaining only a tenuous existence by the late twentieth century.

Harry Lang and Morris C. Finestone, eds., *Gewerkschaften* (New York: United Hebrew Trades of the State of New York, 1938); Aaron Antonovsky, *The Early Jewish Labor Movement in the United States* (New York: YIVO Institute for Jewish Research, 1961); Morris U. Schappes, "The Political Origins of the United Hebrew Trades, 1888," *Journal of Ethnic Studies* 5 (1977)

Daniel Soyer

United Hospital Fund. Charitable organization formed in New York City in 1879 as the Hospital Saturday and Sunday Association to collect charitable donations for the treatment of indigent patients as well as to promote economy in hospital management. The fund took its present name in 1916, expanded its operations throughout the city in 1920, and in 1935 awarded its first grants to women's hospital auxiliary committees. In addition to its own charitable contributions, the fund is an agent for the Greater New York Fund. In 2007 the United Hospital Fund awarded $2.42 million in grants.

Brian Greenberg

United House of Prayer for All People. Christian Pentecostal denomination founded in 1919 in Massachusetts and incorporated in 1927 in Washington, D.C., by Bishop Charles Manuel "Sweet Daddy" Grace (?1881–1960); in New York City the United House of Prayer for All People is located at Frederick Douglass Boulevard between 124th and 125th streets in Harlem. It is known for its "shout band," the McCollough Sons of Thunder Brass Band, which has worked with David Byrne and played at Carnegie Hall, Lincoln Center, and the White House, among other venues.

Sharon Wilkins

United Independent Broadcasters. Original name of the Columbia Broadcasting System.

United Insurance Company of the City of New York. Firm of insurers, organized under a deed of settlement on 3 April 1787 as the first insurance company in New York City. It received a charter from the state legislature in 1798 to provide fire, marine, and life insurance, as well as property insurance for goods and buildings. The name was changed in 1806 to the Mutual Assurance Company, and in 1809 the firm was reorganized as a stock company. In 1846 it was given the name Knickerbocker Fire Insurance Company, by which it became well known. It was dissolved in 1890.

Robert J. Gibbons

United Irish Counties Association. Federation of Irish organizations formed in New York City in 1904. Based in the Bronx, the association has delegates from the 32 county societies and from two other fraternal organizations and provides a forum for Irish Americans to discuss political matters. Its annual *Feis* (cultural festival) draws thousands of participants and features competitions in Gaelic recitation and traditional music and dance.

See also Irish.

John J. Concannon

United Irishmen [United Irish Society]. Political organization formed in Belfast in 1791 in support of an independent Ireland. Although it began mainly as a Presbyterian movement, Catholics joined from 1795, making this the only time in Irish history when substantial representation from the two religious groups worked together to bring about change. In 1798 its activities culminated in a futile rebellion that led to the execution, imprisonment, or forced emigration of many members. Of those imprisoned, several of the most prominent later moved to New York City, including Thomas Addis Emmet, William James MacNeven, Michael Hora, and William Sampson. There they formed the Irish Emigrant Society and became active members of the Friendly Sons of St. Patrick; they also began a tradition of stimulating support in the city for Irish independence.

William McGimpsey

United Jewish Appeal [UJA]. Philanthropic organization formed in 1939. Its aims were to rescue Jews from distressed lands and resettle them in Israel, and to support Jewish communities around the world through educational, rural settlement, and other programs. In 1974 the UJA combined its fund-raising activities with those of the Federation of Jewish Philanthropies. In 1999 the UJA merged with the Council of Jewish Federations and United Israel Appeal to create a large umbrella organization named United Jewish Communities, representing 155 Jewish federations and 400 independent Jewish communities in North America. In 2009 the organization changed its name to the Jewish Federations of North America; it is based in Manhattan.

United Nations. International organization located on the East Side of Manhattan, bordering the East River and extending from 42nd to 48th streets. Its aim is to promote global peace, security, and economic development; the basic structure was agreed to in 1944 at the Dumbarton Oaks Conference. New York City was chosen as the site of the organization despite strong competition from San Francisco, Boston, and Philadelphia, in part because it was the preferred site of the first secretary general, Trygve Lie, and in part because the Soviet Union threatened to boycott the organization if it were on the West Coast. In its early years, several arms of the

United Nations, 2009

United Nations were established in temporary sites in and around the city: at Hunter College in the Bronx (now Lehman College), on the grounds of the World's Fair of 1939–40 at Flushing Meadows Park, and in an old gyroscope factory at Lake Success, New York. In 1946 John D. Rockefeller, Jr., donated to the United Nations 17 acres (7 hectares) of land in Turtle Bay that he had purchased from William Zeckendorf for $8.5 million. The city agreed to contribute $5 million toward clearing the land of its slaughterhouses, cattle pens, and tenement houses; to resettle 270 residents; and to give the United Nations street and waterfront rights. In the following year an international team of architects led by Wallace K. Harrison began construction. The 39-story Secretariat Building (1950) includes the domed General Assembly Hall, the Conference Building, and the Dag Hammarskjöld Library. More than 190 member states have missions to the United Nations in New York City. The city provides police protection for diplomats and grants tax exemptions to diplomats and property of missions to the United Nations. The grounds of the organization are not considered part of the United States and are not bound by any national, state, or city laws; the organization has its own security service and fire unit, which coordinate with the New York City police and fire departments. Although the United Nations was the focus of some troubled politics during the cold war, its relations with its host city have on the whole been harmonious; in addition to drawing about half a million tourists each year and raising revenue, the organization has helped New York City to maintain its international prominence. The United Nations has about 5000 employees in the city.

See also BRIARWOOD.

Lauren Markoe

United Negro College Fund. Nonprofit organization formed on 13 May 1944 at the Waldorf–Astoria Hotel by several private black colleges. Its principal organizer was Frederick Douglass Patterson, president of the Tuskegee Institute, which in 1943 had a tiny endowment and a deficit of $50,000. Under Patterson and William J. Trent, Jr., the fund raised $100,000 during its first campaign; half was contributed by the Julius Rosenwald Fund and the General Education Board, the other half by various colleges. Crucial support came from John D. Rockefeller, Jr., who gave money and offered to use his influence on the fund's behalf. Headquarters were set up in New York City, which was chosen for its importance as a financial center. In the early twenty-first century the United Negro College Fund had 39 member colleges, administered more than 400 scholarship and internship programs, and helped more than 60,000 students each year.

Eric Wm. Allison

United States. Passenger liner weighing 53,329 gross tons, designed by the naval architect William Francis Gibbs. Known for its speed and safety and built during the decline of passenger ships, it had the capacity to hold 1928 passengers. It broke all Atlantic speed records on its maiden voyage, embarking from New York City on 3 July 1952 and arriving in Bishop Rock, England, three days, 10 hours, and 40 minutes later, making the trip in 10 fewer hours than the record previously held by the *Queen Mary.* As most transatlantic passenger services were taken over by airplanes, in 1969 the SS *United States* was retired and docked in Philadelphia. Norwegian Cruise Line purchased it in 2003 with hopes of restoring it as a cruise ship, but the company abandoned the plans in 2009 and put the ship up for sale. In March 2010 it was reported that despite a nonscrapping provision in the original terms of sale, bids were being accepted from scrappers.

Frank O. Braynard

United States Attorney's Office. The United States attorney is an official of the U.S. Department of Justice who prosecutes federal cases and represents the United States in civil and criminal litigation in New York City and its environs. The first U.S. attorney in New York City was Richard Harison, appointed on 26 September 1789, whose first victory resulted in a net gain to the federal government of $95; most of his cases were admiralty decisions. In April 1814 the Southern District of New York was formally created, with a jurisdiction that extended to Albany, and the Northern District was formed for the rest of the state. Imprecise lines of administration and difficulties in communication before the Civil War helped to make the U.S. attorney for the Southern District of New York virtually independent. The growth of the Port of New York led to the formation on 25 February 1865 of the Eastern District, consisting of Long Island (including Brooklyn and Queens) and Staten Island. During the late nineteenth century cases dealing with equity, bankruptcy, and crime accounted for the bulk of the caseload. U.S. attorneys in the city remained highly independent and were often nationally known, even after the U.S. Department of Justice was formed on 1 July 1870. Among the most visible New York U.S. attorneys during this period were William Price (1834–49), who looted the office, as well as several future cabinet officers: Edwards Pierrepont (1875, later attorney general), Elihu Root (1883–86, later secretary of war and secretary of state), and Henry L. Stimson (1906, later secretary of war). The Southern District failed to win convictions against Samuel J. Tilden on income tax charges (1876–81) and Harry Daugherty for malfeasance while serving as attorney general of the United States (1922–23). It did, however, handle 25,728 criminal cases between 1927 and 1930, of which 23,167 dealt with violations of the 18th Amendment (which established Prohibition). In 1951 the office won the case of *Dennis v. United States* (341 U.S. 494) before the U.S. Supreme Court. The office of the Eastern District refuted a claim by the Good Humor company that it invented the ice-cream pop (1932); argued the case of *Schechter Poultry Company v. United States* (1935) before the U.S. Supreme Court, which ended in the overturning of the National Industrial Recovery Act of 1933; and brought Rudolf Abel to trial for espionage (1957). Among those who launched political careers after serving as U.S. attorney were Thomas E. Dewey in the 1930s and Rudolph W. Giuliani in the 1980s, who both mounted vigorous efforts against organized crime. In the mid-1990s and into the early twenty-first century, New York City remained the busiest area of federal litigation in the country. Under the leadership of U.S. Attorney Mary Jo White, who began serving in 1993, the office added to its successful track record of major international terrorism prosecutions and investigations, including the 1993 bombing of the World Trade Center, the 1998 bombings of the U.S. embassies in East Africa, the indictment of Osama bin Laden, and the attacks of 11 September 2001. In the early twenty-first century the U.S. attorney had offices at 1 St. Andrew's Plaza (Southern District) and 225 Cadman Plaza East (Eastern District).

George J. Lankevich

United States Life Insurance. Firm of insurers. It was formed with $100,000 in capital in 1850, at a time when New York City was emerging from a cholera epidemic. The first president of the firm was Frederick Sheldon, and the first home office was at 27 Wall Street. In 1852 the firm moved to larger offices at 40 Wall Street, and by the turn of the century it had $20 million in life insurance policies in force. It weathered the Depression and World War II with conservative business practices. In 1952 more than 70 percent of its outstanding stock was purchased by the Continental Insurance Company, which in turn sold a large number of shares to the Continental Assurance Company. This restructuring was followed by tremendous expansion. In 1966 United States Life sponsored the formation of its parent company, U.S. Life Holding Corporation, of which it became the largest among many subsidiaries. In the early twenty-first century, United States Life Insurance had its headquarters at 125 Maiden Lane in Manhattan.

Chad Ludington

United States Trust. Bank chartered in 1853 as a specialist in trusts for individuals and corporations. During an era when stock portfolios were increasingly used to build wealth, it was the first institution of its kind in the country. The bank had offices at 45 Wall Street for more than a century before moving in 1989 to 114 West 47th Street, which remained its headquarters into the early twenty-first century. Bank of America acquired United States Trust as its private wealth management arm in 2006.

Nancy V. Flood

universities. See COLLEGES AND UNIVERSITIES.

University Building. Structure erected in 1833–36 on the northeastern corner of Washington Square by the University of the City of New York (now New York University). Its principal designer was James Dakin, who was assisted by Ithiel Town, Alexander Jackson Davis, and two professors at the university. Built of white marble in the English Collegiate Gothic style, the building had a symmetrical plan comprising a central chapel flanked by wings terminating in four corner towers. The building was effectively the first artists' enclave in Greenwich Village: from the outset the upper stories were specifically set aside as artists' studios, and over the years there were more than 60 tenants, including Samuel F. B. Morse (1835), Eastman Johnson (1858–72), and Winslow Homer (1861–71). The building was demolished in 1894 to make way for a new campus and commercial buildings.

Annette Blaugrund

University Club. Private club founded in 1865 by alumni of Harvard, Yale, and Columbia as a private social and intellectual group. It first held meetings at Columbia University's Law School and later moved to a town house at 26th Street and Madison Avenue. In 1899 it moved to its present location at 1 West 54th Street, along Fifth Avenue, in an Italian Renaissance Revival structure designed by McKim, Mead and White. Standing seven stories tall behind a three-story facade, the building has been described by the critic Paul Goldberger as McKim's best surviving work and by Harmon Goldstone of the Landmarks Commission as one of the great buildings of the city. After its move the club began maintaining a library and one of the largest private art collections in New York City. In 1980 the building was added to the National Register of Historic Places; in 1987 the club admitted its first female members. In the early twenty-first century the club had more than 4000 active members.

Jessica Montesano

university clubs. In New York City university clubs became an important force in the latter half of the nineteenth century, usually as an outgrowth of alumni associations. In 1865 Harvard became the first university to have quarters given over to a club in the city. The UNIVERSITY CLUB was formed in the same year, and its membership was open to degree holders from colleges and universities and the military and naval academies, as well as recipients of honorary degrees. Toward the end of the nineteenth century, clubs were formed by the alumni of different schools, including Yale and Princeton universities. Typically university clubs were especially attractive to recent graduates, who then gravitated toward other clubs in the city as their careers and interests became more clearly focused. More university clubs were established during the first half of the twentieth century despite the wars and the Depression, during which some clubs shared facilities and even memberships (as Yale and Princeton did during World War I). With suburbanization and different patterns of family living, all but the most select clubs saw a decline in membership and activity by members in the clubhouses between 1970 and 2000, although the clubs continued to be used for business and social purposes at lunchtime. After the turn of the twenty-first century, with the general revival of urban living, the clubs once again began to prosper.

James E. Mooney, Kenneth T. Jackson

University Heights. Neighborhood in the northwest Bronx, lying on a ridge and bounded to the north by Fordham Road, to the east by Jerome Avenue, to the south by Burnside Avenue, and to the west by the Harlem River. Originally part of Fordham Manor, the area was known as Fordham Heights at the time of the American Revolution. Small forts above the Harlem River formed part of the British defenses of New York City and were the site of several skirmishes. A few fine estates were built during the mid-nineteenth century. The area was renamed University Heights after New York University moved most of its operations there from Greenwich Village in 1894. For the next 80 years the university dominated the neighborhood, much of which was covered by the campus and its many residential buildings. The HALL OF FAME FOR GREAT AMERICANS (1901) was dedicated on campus and became a popular attraction. The opening of the Jerome Avenue elevated line (1918) and the Grand Concourse subway (1933) spurred the construction of apartment buildings: University Avenue became one of the prime residential streets in the borough. Children and grandchildren of European immigrants moved to the area from Manhattan and soon accounted for most of the population.

During the 1960s and 1970s many older residents moved to the suburbs and the population became predominantly Latin American and black. The university sold its campus to the city in 1973 to be used by Bronx Community College. Many apartment buildings south of the campus were abandoned by their landlords and ravaged by fire. Many of the immigrants who settled in University Heights in the late twentieth century were Dominican, and there were large numbers of Jamaicans and Guyanese, as well one of the largest concentrations of Vietnamese and Cambodian refugees in New York City. The University Heights Bridge, which connects the neighborhood to upper Manhattan, celebrated its centennial in 2008.

Peter Derrick

University of the City of New York. Original name of NEW YORK UNIVERSITY.

University Parish of St. Joseph. Roman Catholic parish. It was founded in 1829 as St. Joseph's Church. Located at 371 Avenue of the Americas, its Greek Revival building was designed by John Doran and built during 1833–34. Reverend Thomas Farrell began the Academia movement at the parish. The church was restructured in 2005; renamed the University Parish of St. Joseph, in the early twenty-first century it served the Catholic communities of Cooper Union, New School, New York University, and Pace University.

Kate Lauber

University Settlement. First settlement house in the United States, opened in 1886 at 146 Forsyth Street on the Lower East Side as the Lily Pleasure Club (a boys' club) by Stanton Coit (1857–1944), a divinity student influenced by the Social Gospel movement and the structure of Toynbee Hall in London. It was renamed the Neighborhood Guild in 1887 and took its current name in 1891. In 1898 the rapidly growing settlement moved to 184 Eldridge Street, where it has continued to focus on the needs and acculturation of immigrants on the Lower East Side, serving various educational, civic, recreational, social service, and research functions. A model for more than 400 settlements in New York City and elsewhere, University Settlement has been responsible for a number of innovations later adopted by community and government organizations, including kindergartens, branch libraries, and public baths. It was also a hub of political reform from which leaders such as Charles B. Stover, Carl Schurz, Robbins Gilman, Nicholas Murray Butler, and Seth Low campaigned for safer tenements, better working and sanitary conditions, parks and playgrounds, and the abolition of child labor. Over time the settlement has developed a health clinic, cultural and antipoverty programs, a senior citizens' center, an early mental health clinic, day care, youth counseling, and classes in home management. The University Settlement has a summer camp that opened in Beacon, New York, in 1911. Eleanor Roosevelt taught dance at the settlement, which Franklin

D. Roosevelt called a "landmark in the social history of the nation."

Jeffrey Scheuer, *Legacy of Light: University Settlement's First Century* (New York: University Settlement, 1985)

Jeffrey Scheuer

Upjohn, Richard M(ichell) (*b* Shaftesbury, England, 7 March 1828; *d* New York City, 3 March 1903). Architect. He moved to New York City with his family as an infant; he later worked in his father's firm, Richard Upjohn and Sons, and helped to design many buildings in the city, among them Trinity Church Wall Street (1846), Mechanics Bank (one of the first buildings using rolled-iron beams, 1854), Trinity School (1895), and Madison Square Presbyterian Church (1904). He also designed the main entrance gate at Green-Wood Cemetery (1838).

James E. Mooney

Upper East Side. Neighborhood in Manhattan, bounded to the north by 96th Street, to the east by the East River, to the south by 59th Street, and to the west by Fifth Avenue. Synonymous with wealth since the early twentieth century, its first permanent structures were large frame houses lining the East River; many residents attended St. James Church (Episcopal) at 71st Street and Madison Avenue (1810), the oldest surviving building in the neighborhood. Hamilton Park was planned in 1811 as an English residential square and consisted of two sections, one bounded by 68th Street, Fourth Avenue, 66th Street, and Fifth Avenue, the other by 69th Street, Third Avenue, 68th Street, and Fourth Avenue. Until the 1840s most of the neighborhood was common land and pastures. The settlement extended as far east as 66th Street and Lexington Avenue in 1851 and as far north as Madison Avenue and 86th Street in 1860, by which time the opening of Central Park gave it a distinct identity. Transportation was provided by omnibuses until horsecar service on rails was extended along Madison Avenue after the Civil War. Streets were laid through Hamilton Park in 1868, and the German Hospital went up at Fourth Avenue and 77th Street in the following year. The area soon became known as Lenox Hill.

Construction of the Metropolitan Museum of Art on Fifth Avenue began in 1880, and there was scattered development along the avenue as the museum took shape. In 1878 and 1880 elevated lines were opened along Third and Second avenues, respectively, which were soon lined with brownstones; most residents were immigrants from Germany, Ireland, and Bohemia. In 1888 Fourth Avenue was renamed Park Avenue, about the same time that Louis Comfort Tiffany, Josiah M. Fiske, Herman O. Armour, and other magnates built palatial homes on or just off Fifth Avenue. The elegant status of the area was confirmed when Caroline Astor had a château built at Fifth Avenue and 65th Street in 1893, and by 1900 such wealthy industrialists as the Schermerhorns, the Vanderbilts, and the Rhinelanders were moving into the area and building opulent townhouses. A luxury apartment building at 998 Fifth Avenue designed by the firm of McKim, Mead and White (completed in 1912) became a model for developments along Madison Avenue, where row houses were demolished or had their lower floors converted into elegant shops; Park Avenue attracted wealthy residents after the railroad tracks running along it were buried by the New York Central Railroad between 42nd and 96th streets. West of Park Avenue many stables and carriage houses were erected, as were exclusive clubs like the Metropolitan Club (1 East 60th Street), the Harmonie Club (6 East 60th Street), the Knickerbocker Club (2 East 62nd Street), the Colony Club (62nd Street and Park Avenue), and the Union Club (69th Street and Park Avenue). Apartments became fashionable after World War I.

The Lexington Avenue Interborough Rapid Transit Company subway was completed through the area in 1918, by which time the neighborhood had a large population of immigrants from central and eastern Europe. Yorkville, centered at 86th Street between Lexington and Second avenues, was for many years the focus of German cultural activity in the city and a center of both Nazi and anti-Nazi activity and propaganda throughout the 1930s; a Hungarian section of Yorkville around Second Avenue and 80th Street underwent a marked increase in population after the Hungarian Revolution of 1956; and First Avenue between 67th and 74th streets was known as "Czech Broadway." The Second Avenue elevated was razed in 1940; the Third Avenue elevated line was razed in 1956, leading to luxury apartment house construction all through the neighborhood. Real estate prices rose after 1970, and brownstones became highly desirable. Since the 1980s, well-to-do immigrants have moved to the Upper East Side from China, the United Kingdom, the Philippines, France, Israel, India, Ireland, Iran, and Brazil.

In the early twenty-first century the Upper East Side is still the heart of the Silk Stocking District. Its postal zone, 10021, is perhaps the wealthiest in the United States. No single demographic group predominates: there are Christians and Jews, a few Puerto Ricans and Latin Americans to the north, and even a few remaining Germans, Czechs, and working-class residents, who live east of Lexington Avenue. One prominent mansion from the turn of the twentieth century, that of Henry Clay Frick, covers the block between 69th and 70th streets and Fifth and Madison avenues. It is now a museum devoted to Frick's art collection. Another surviving estate, at 91st Street and Fifth Avenue, was the home of Andrew Carnegie and is now the Cooper–Hewitt Museum.

Anthony Gronowicz

Upper Manhattan Empowerment Zone. Area in upper Manhattan designated for economic revitalization. In 1994 President Bill Clinton designated El Barrio, central Harlem, parts of Washington Heights, and Inwood as the Upper Manhattan Empowerment Zone, one of nine "empowerment zones" in the nation to receive federal and state tax incentives and financial assistance for fledgling business investment. The program offered reimbursement for broker fees if businesses relocated to main thoroughfares in upper Manhattan, tax breaks for hiring residents of the empowerment zone, and low-rate loans to encourage new investment in underserved neighborhoods. In the first 10 years of operation, the Upper Manhattan Empowerment Zone invested $159 million in revitalizing neighborhoods and attracting businesses north of 96th Street. By the early twenty-first century, upper Manhattan had become one of the fastest-growing residential areas in New York City. The numbers of housing units, population, and median income level were all rising at high rates. From the standpoint of goods and services, however, upper Manhattan had more underserved households than the rest of Manhattan.

Penelope Gelwicks

Upper New York Bay. Center of New York Harbor, at the northern end of a route 17 miles (27 kilometers) long that leads from open ocean to the mouth of the Hudson River at the southern tip of Manhattan Island. The waterway continues northward from Lower New York Bay, passing through the Narrows into Upper New York Bay. Upper New York Bay is at its widest at the confluence of the Hudson and East rivers and the Kill van Kull. Kill van Kull opens into Arthur Kill on the north side of Staten Island, and it then becomes its western boundary and the passageway leading south to the Port Newark–Elizabeth Marine Terminal. Most container traffic that once used the piers of Brooklyn and Manhattan shifted to that New Jersey facility by 1990. To the east, in Brooklyn, is another of the bay's commercial tributaries, the Gowanus Canal. Upper New York Bay is 5 miles (8 kilometers) long from the Battery to Staten Island and 4 miles (6.5 kilometers) wide from Brooklyn to New Jersey; it may be seen almost in its entirety from the Staten Island Ferry. At the entrance to Upper New York Bay a number of sights are clearly visible, including the striking Manhattan skyline, Liberty Island, and the Statue of Liberty; just to the west is Ellis Island, as well as New Jersey's growing commercial panorama, from

Bayonne to Hoboken; and to the southwest, close to Staten Island, is the former Coast Guard base, Governors Island, with its many historic landmarks.

Gerard R. Wolfe

Upper West Side. Largely residential neighborhood in Manhattan (2000 pop. *ca* 250,000) between the Hudson River to the west and Central and Morningside parks to the east, and running north from 59th Street to 125th Street. (By another definition, the area ends at 110th Street and does not include Morningside Heights.) Called Bloemendaal ("flowering valley") by Dutch and Flemish settlers, under the British the area was known as "the End" or "the West End" and was the site of farms and country homes. The Battle of Harlem Heights was fought on 16 September 1776 on land that is now part of Barnard College at 118th Street. After the Revolution the property of many Tories was confiscated and villages formed, among them Harsenville (near the present 71st Street), Striker's Bay (near 90th), Bloomingdale Village (near 100th), and Manhattanville (at 125th). Outings by sleigh and carriage up the Bloomingdale Road (now Broadway) were popular. The Bloomingdale Insane Asylum was built on farmland now part of Columbia University. Edgar Allan Poe spent summers in Bloomingdale, where he composed "The Raven" in 1844. George Pope Morris's poem "Woodman, Spare That Tree" (1848) was inspired by an encounter in Striker's Bay.

Development of the area did not commence in earnest until after trolley service was introduced in 1878, followed a year later by the opening of the Ninth Avenue El (which was shut down in 1940). To add to the area's appeal, in the 1880s numbered avenues were given more romantic names: Eighth Avenue above 59th Street was renamed Central Park West, Ninth became Columbus Avenue, 10th was first called Holland and finally Amsterdam, and 11th and 12th were renamed West End Avenue and Riverside Drive. Businesses and tenements were built on Columbus and Amsterdam, row houses went up on cross streets, and Riverside Drive, Broadway, and finally Central Park West became well known for their large apartment houses. The most fashionable avenue was, and remains, Central Park West. What has been called the avenue's "distinctive silhouette" began to appear when the city's first grand luxury apartment house, the Dakota, opened on 72nd Street in 1884; it was so named because it was remote from the most populated part of the city. Standing in similar splendid isolation was the American Museum of Natural History at 79th Street. Central Park West attracted more construction around the turn of the twentieth century, including the New-York Historical Society, the New York Society for Ethical Culture Hall, the Second Church of Christ Scientist, the intimate Hotel des Artistes, Congregation Shearith Israel (the new home of the city's oldest Jewish congregation), and several commanding apartment buildings. Development was so sporadic at first that the West Side Tennis Club maintained five clay tennis courts on Central Park West at 89th Street before moving to Forest Hills, Queens. A German American Jewish social organization, the Progress Club, built its clubhouse on the lot in 1903. Later came the avenue's four famous twin-tower apartment buildings built during the 1930s: the Century (25 Central Park West), the Majestic (116 Central Park West), the San Remo (145 Central Park West), and the El Dorado (300 Central Park West). These and other large apartment buildings received such care over the decades that even during the great building boom of the late twentieth century, only two of them were torn down and replaced.

The extension of the Interborough Rapid Transit subway line (now the Nos. 1, 2, and 3 trains) up Broadway in 1904 opened the Upper West Side to serious development, which was later bolstered when the Independent line (the A, B, C, and D trains) was built under Central Park West in the 1930s. The large neighborhood took on a distinctive identity: mostly middle and working class, ethnically mixed (with a large African American population until it moved to Harlem in the 1920s), and popular among people in the arts, the theater, literature, commerce, sports, and politics. The area became famous for its social tolerance and political activism.

After World War II the Upper West Side declined as entire districts were seized by crime, poverty, drugs, and disease. The writer Theodore H. White wrote in his memoir, *In Search of History,* that after living in war-torn Europe, he did not fear walking outside at night until he moved to Central Part West at 84th Street in 1953. There were riots and gang wars like those in the play and film *West Side Story,* filmed in the early 1960s in the slums that were soon razed for housing, for Lincoln Center, and for Fordham University's Manhattan campus. Another, less successful urban renewal project of that time was the 17-building Frederick Douglass Houses that Robert Moses built between 100th and 104th streets.

During the 1970s the city and developers proposed a redevelopment plan along the bank of the Hudson called Westway. It was rejected for environmental and financial reasons, and Donald Trump and other developers proposed transforming the railroad yards near 72nd Street into an immense commercial–residential complex. (The 16-building project, much trimmed and known as Trump Place or Riverside South, was under completion in the early twenty-first century.) As crime decreased in the 1980s, the Upper West Side became a desirable residential area. Real estate prices rose, and developers built luxury apartment towers. Efforts were also made to protect classic buildings. In 1990 the West Side/Central Park West Historic District between 59th and 86th streets was given landmark status.

In the late twentieth century, a large number of immigrants settled in the neighborhood, about one-fifth from the Dominican Republic and a smaller number from Haiti, the United Kingdom, China, Canada, the Middle East, and France. The Upper West Side's historic diversity is visible also in its houses of worship, including B'nai Jeshurun and Lincoln Square Synagogue, First Baptist Church, Holy Trinity Lutheran Church, the Cathedral of St. John the Divine, Corpus Christi Church, the New York Buddhist Church, the Manhattan Temple of the Church of Jesus Christ of Latter-Day Saints, and the Interchurch Center, home of the National Council of Churches.

Bounded by three large parks, the Upper West Side also contains many smaller green areas, including Damrosch Park at 62nd Street, the Straus Park and Memorial Fountain at 106th Street, the largely McKim, Mead and White–designed campus of Columbia University at 116th Street, and Sakura Park at 122nd Street. The area's historic access to the water by ferries and boating clubs along the Hudson is now limited to the 79th Street Boat Basin. Besides Columbia, there are many other educational institutions in the Upper West Side, including Trinity, Collegiate, Calhoun, and St. Hilda's and St. Hugh's; the Juilliard and Manhattan schools of music and the arts; Fordham University; Barnard College; and Jewish and Union Theological Seminaries.

John Rousmaniere

Urban, Joseph (*b* Vienna, Austria, 26 May 1872; *d* Yonkers, New York, 10 July 1933). Architect and stage designer. Trained in Vienna, he was part of the turn-of-the-century Jugendstil movement, which applied modernist principles to architecture and theatrical design. Immigrating in 1911 to the United States, where he first designed sets for the Boston Opera, Urban was brought to New York City in 1914 by Flo Ziegfeld to design the Ziegfeld Follies. From then until his death in 1933, Urban worked in architecture, theater, and film, creating striking stage designs for the Metropolitan Opera and the Broadway stage. Productions included the annual Ziegfeld Follies revues, the Metropolitan Opera's presentations of, among others, *Don Giovanni, Parsifal, Lohengrin, The Tales of Hoffman, Faust,* and *Don Carlo,* and musical comedies ranging from *The Garden of Paradise* (1914) to *Rio Rita* (1927) and *Whoopee* (1928). In the early 1920s he was hired as a set and lighting designer for William Randolph Hearst's Cosmopolitan Pictures, where his design work included *Heliotrope* (1920), *Enchantment* (1921),

Buried Treasure (1922), *The Young Diana* (1922), and *Under the Red Robe* (1923).

Urban was an important ambassador for European innovations in theatrical design, bringing the so-called "new stagecraft" to the United States and laying the groundwork for the more radical modernist work of the middle years of the century. His sophisticated designs, distinguished by intense color and innovative use of light, were influential during the 1920s and 1930s. The color "Urban blue," named for him, is still in use.

Although some of Urban's architectural commissions were in Florida (for example, Mar-A-Lago, the home of Marjorie Merriweather Post, and the Palm Beach Bath and Tennis Club) and elsewhere in the United States, his most important architectural work was done in New York City, where he designed the original building for the New School for Social Research (on West 12th Street), the Central Park Casino (later destroyed), the Ziegfeld Theatre (on Sixth Avenue), and the William Randolph Hearst Building on the corner of 57th Street and Eighth Avenue.

Randolph Carter and Robert Reed Cole, *Joseph Urban: Architecture, Theatre, Opera, Film* (New York: Abbeville Press, 1992); Arnold Aronson, et al., *Architect of Dreams: The Theatrical Vision of Joseph Urban* (New York: Columbia University, 2000)

Jean Ashton

Urban Development Corporation [UDC]. Public authority formed in 1968 by the state legislature of New York to initiate, finance, construct, and manage building projects of all kinds. It was empowered to override local zoning ordinances and building codes, issue building permits, sell $1 billion in tax-exempt bonds (later increased to $2 billion), lend and grant money to subsidiaries, take land by condemnation, and sell, lease, and retain real property. The corporation had a mandate to stimulate the economy of New York State, provide employment, increase the housing stock, and construct public facilities; it was soon perceived as a powerful vehicle for promoting development in New York City. The first head of the UDC, Edward J. Logue, used its broad powers to launch more than 100 housing projects comprising 32,000 units statewide, as well as many nonresidential projects. At Roosevelt Island and elsewhere the corporation undertook the first developments of new towns under public auspices since the New Deal.

In 1975 the UDC became the first major issuer of municipal bonds since the Depression to default on its obligations. Its insolvency was caused by a depressed real estate market; a "fast-track" construction process that allowed problems to go undetected, thus escalating construction costs; high-risk financing techniques; a cutoff of federal aid; and the revocation of a state commitment to guarantee its loans. When the extent of its financial troubles became apparent at the end of February, the corporation had $134.5 million in short-term debt coming due and needed $370 million to complete projects comprising more than 20,000 residential units. The corporation was eventually rescued by the Savings Bank Association, the Property and Liability Insurance Fund, and a group of commercial banks, but its long-term debt of more than $1 billion did not regain its investment-grade credit rating. The staff was cut by 75 percent, Logue was replaced in 1975 by Richard Ravitch, and the corporation turned away from public housing and toward economic development. In 1976 it aided Donald Trump's development of the Grand Hyatt Hotel by purchasing construction materials on his behalf, thus freeing Trump from the sales tax. Similar methods were used to subsidize the renovation of the Marriott–Marquis Hotel in Times Square, the South Street Seaport, and a brewery in Brooklyn. After Ravitch was replaced in 1977 by Richard Kahan, the corporation took over the development of Battery Park City, which had been long delayed and encumbered by debt, as well as of the New York City Convention Center (later named the Javits Convention Center); it also helped to convert the Federal Archives Building in Manhattan, renovate the Farberware plant in the Bronx, and develop Fordham Plaza. After a prison bond referendum was defeated in 1981, it began to finance and construct prisons. In 1995 the UDC was renamed the Empire State Development Corporation. In 2002, after the terrorist attacks of 11 September 2001 on the World Trade Center, a new subsidiary of the corporation was formed, the LOWER MANHATTAN DEVELOPMENT CORPORATION, and was given primary responsibility for coordinating the reconstruction of the area.

Owen D. Gutfreund

Urban League. See NATIONAL URBAN LEAGUE.

urban psychology. Specialty in the behavioral sciences that focuses on the study of the effect city living has on individuals. The KITTY GENOVESE MURDER of 13 March 1964 in Kew Gardens, where 38 witnesses ignored the screams of the murdered woman because they "just did not want to get involved," led several New York City psychologists to test different theories of whether such noninvolvement is a product of city life. These included Stanley Milgram's field experiments on "stimulus overload," Philip Zimbardo's tests of anonymity and deindividuation, Harry Kaufmann's surveys on cognition, and Bibb Latane and John Darley's lab experiments on "diffusion of responsibility." Milgram's now-classic 1970 essay "The Experience of Living in Cities" enunciated and defined the new specialty of urban psychology, which has since become a vibrant new specialty.

Harold Takooshian

Urey, Harold C(layton) (*b* Walkerton, Ind., 29 April 1893; *d* La Jolla, Calif., 6 Jan 1981). Nobel Prize–winning scientist. He joined the faculty of Columbia University in 1929 and during the next 15 years he taught, wrote a number of books, and edited the *Journal of Chemical Physics.* He won the Nobel Prize in chemistry in 1934 for discovering deuterium and was later responsible for separating isotopes of uranium for the atomic bomb project. Urey eventually left Columbia for the University of Chicago.

James E. Mooney

Uris Buildings Corporation. Real estate development firm formed by brothers Percy Uris (*b* New York City, 19 Aug 1899; *d* Palm Beach, Fla., 20 Nov 1971) and Harold Uris (*b* New York City, 26 May 1905; *d* Palm Beach, Fla., 28 March 1982). It built luxury apartment towers in Manhattan before the Depression and 17 office towers containing more than 13 million square feet (1.2 million square meters) of space after World War II. It also built the New York Hilton at Rockefeller Center (1963), headquarters for J. C. Penney (1964) and International Telephone and Telegraph (1961), and office buildings at 60 Broad Street (1962), 1290 Sixth Avenue (1962), and 55 Water Street (1972). It became the largest publicly owned real estate firm in the country; after Percy's death, Harold sold it to the National Kinney Corporation in 1973. Uris Hall at the Graduate School of Business of Columbia University is named for Percy Uris.

Marc A. Weiss

U.S. Custom House [Alexander Hamilton U.S. Custom House]. Erected in 1907 at Bowling Green on the site of Fort Amsterdam (demolished 1790) and Government House (demolished 1815), it housed the offices of the Collector of Customs of the Port of New York, the headquarters of Custom Collection District no. 10, and several other customs and federal departments until 1973 when the Customs Service moved into the World Trade Center. The Custom House building is an imposing, monumental granite structure designed by Cass Gilbert in a beaux-arts style replete with maritime, commercial, and national symbols. Forty-four Corinthian columns surround the building, each with the head of Mercury, the god of commerce, and a dolphin or seashell in its capital. The facade is further embellished by statues. Four figures by Daniel Chester French represent the continents of Asia, Europe, Af-

U.S. Custom House, 1938

rica, and North America. The 12 statues along the cornice depict the commercial centers of the ancient and modern worlds: Greece, Rome, Phoenicia, Genoa, Venice, Spain, Holland, Portugal, Denmark, Germany, England, and France. The attic balustrade is broken by a giant cartouche bearing the seal of the United States. This is flanked by winged female figures of war and peace and topped by a federal eagle. Murals by Reginald Marsh decorate the walls of an interior rotunda. The building was designated a National Historic Landmark in 1976. In October 1994 it became the site of the George Gustav Heye Center of the National Museum of the American Indian. In the early twenty-first century it also houses the U.S. Bankruptcy Court for the Southern District of New York.

Mollie Keller

U.S. Customs Service. Arm of the Department of Homeland Security charged with collecting duties on goods entering the United States. Established by the fifth act of the First Congress of the United States in 1789, it provided the largest part of the government's revenue before the income tax was imposed in 1913, and it remained the second-largest source of revenue supporting the federal government into the early twenty-first century. The Customs Service was placed under the direct supervision of the nation's first Treasury secretary, New Yorker Alexander Hamilton. In the first year that the service was in operation, the Port of New York was the largest of 59 collection districts in 11 states, and the service accounted for the largest federal presence in the city. It employed a collector, a naval officer (or deputy collector), and a cadre of inspectors, surveyors, weighers, measurers, and crews for revenue-cutters (small boats used by customs officers to carry them to ships in the harbor). The Customs Service collected $2 million in revenue during its first year, and by 1835 it had paid down the national debt accumulated during the Revolution and before the ratification of the Constitution.

The removal of a customs collector for embezzlement in 1798 marked the beginning of a long period of corruption, which was encouraged by the sheer size of the port and the large volume of goods passing through it, and essentially institutionalized by the excesses of the spoils system under President Andrew Jackson. Apart from Moses Grinnell, whose honesty cost him the collectorship in 1870, all collectors and many subordinates between 1829 and 1877 used their positions to enrich themselves. The corrupting influence of the service even tainted prominent New Yorkers: Samuel Swartwout, scion of an old Dutch family, fled to England in 1838 with $1 million obtained illegally from the Customs Service; Philip Hone, whose diaries commented on society in New York City, asked that his son succeed him as a naval officer (deputy collector) so that his family could recoup the fortune that it had lost in the panic of 1837.

In 1853 the Port of New York was collecting almost three-quarters of all customs revenue in the country, and 700 vacant positions at the Custom House in the city attracted 27,000 applicants. Chester A. Arthur was the customs collector from 1871 to 1878 before becoming president of the United States. He was sympathetic toward the spoils system, ignored the corrupt activities in his office, and allegedly earned income as a customs collector that was several times greater than what he earned as a lawyer: by one account he made $50,000 a year from 1871 to 1873. (At the same time the customs collector Herman Melville brought home $4 a day to supplement his income from writing.)

Many attempts at federal reform found the Custom House in the city an inviting target. There were sporadic plans to make the operations of the Customs Service in the city more professional and rational, but all failed until the investigations in 1877 of the Jay Commission (led by John Jay, a descendant of the chief justice). The report of the commission inspired President Rutherford B. Hayes to dismiss Arthur and institute the civil service reforms approved during the administration of President Ulysses S. Grant, including competitive examinations and the freeing of all offices from political patronage. After 1879, when the first examinations were held in New York City, the reputation and performance of the Custom House improved markedly. The Pendleton Act (1883), passed during Arthur's presidency, reestablished the Civil Service Commission and ensured that there would be no return to the old ways.

A more prudent and professional service proved essential in the twentieth century, as the Customs Service was increasingly called on to enforce notions of morality as well as trade laws. Customs agents had the primary responsibility for enforcing the restrictive Chinese Immigration Act (1882), which predated the formation of the Immigration and Naturalization Service. Between 1915 and 1917 customs agents monitored belligerent ships, searched for contraband, and impounded arms and matériel purchased by foreign nations. When Congress declared war on 7 April 1917 the customs collector Dudley Malone impounded the 27 German and Austrian ships then in port and interned the 1100 enemy aliens aboard. During Prohibition customs officers worked with the Federal Bureau of Investigation to seize illegal alcohol: they not only had to search foreign ships in the harbor for forbidden spirits but also to watch out for and interdict small boats ferrying cases of liquor ashore from mother ships floating in the "rum rows" 3 miles (5 kilometers) off the coast of New Jersey. The Customs Service also worked with the U.S. Post Office to enforce pornography laws: in 1933 its agents confiscated as obscene rotogravure reproductions of the frescoes in the Sistine Chapel and copies of James Joyce's *Ulysses.* In 1945 the service began to focus on interdicting illegal exports of arms and high technology.

During the nineteenth century, the Custom House frequently moved throughout lower Manhattan to meet the growing volume of work under its jurisdiction. By the early 1890s the 55 Wall Street location proved inadequate, and Congress authorized the construction of a new Custom House, which was to be located at Bowling Green, the same location as the original Dutch Custom House and the first U.S. Custom House. The contract was awarded to Cass Gilbert, a prominent young New York City architect. In 1907 the Custom House was relocated to 1 Bowling Green, a historical structure now known as the Alexander Hamilton U.S. Custom House. In 1973 the U.S. Custom House relocated to the newly built 6 World Trade Center, with satellite offices at the John F. Kennedy (JFK) Airport and the piers in Brooklyn and with 1500 employees working for the agency. Unhindered by the need for search warrants, it continued to examine goods and passengers entering New York City from abroad and to enforce federal laws governing the importation of controlled substances, forbidden foods, and counterfeit currency. In 2008 it collected $5.9 billion in revenue at JFK Airport, the Port of New York, and the Port of New Jersey.

After the World Trade Center was destroyed by the terrorist attacks of 11 September 2001, Custom House officials and offices were relocated throughout the metropolitan area. The subsequent creation of the Department of Homeland Security in the fall of 2002 led to a dramatic reorganization of federal law enforcement agencies. The new U.S. Customs and Border Protection agency, created on 1 March 2003, adopted a number of new responsibilities, such as the inspectional functions of the former U.S. Immigration and Naturalization Service, the U.S. Border Patrol in its entirety, and the Plant Protection and Quarantine programs from the Animal and Plant Health Inspection Service (APHIS) in the Department of Agriculture. Though this department is centrally based in Washington, D.C., in the early twenty-first century the New York City field office included offices at the 1 Bowling Green location.

Carl E. Prince and Mollie Keller, *The U.S. Customs Service: A Bicentennial History* (Washington, D.C.: U.S. Department of the Treasury, 1989); Anne Saba, "History of the U.S. Customs Service at the Port of New York," http://www.oldnycustomhouse.gov/history

Mollie Keller, Janos Marton

US Open (tennis). Tennis tournament. The first United States Open tennis championships, or US Open, were held in Newport, Rhode Island, in 1881 and were exclusively for amateur men; a separate tournament was held for amateur women. In 1915 the tournament relocated to the West Side Tennis Club in Forest Hills, Queens, and was played there until 1921, before moving to Philadelphia. In 1924 the tournament moved back to the West Side Tennis Club, and in 1968 the inaugural season of the "open era" of tennis began there, meaning all players (professional or amateur) were eligible to compete. That same year the tournament combined the separate men's and women's tournaments and held them simultaneously. The tournament continued to be held in Forest Hills until 1978, when it moved to its permanent location at Flushing Meadows–Corona Park in Flushing, Queens, known as the Billie Jean King National Tennis Center. Until 1997 the main court and matches were played at Louis Armstrong Stadium within this tennis complex. However, in 1997 Arthur Ashe Stadium, named after the 1968 US Open champion, was opened. This became the largest outdoor tennis venue in the world, with a seating capacity of 24,000; Louis Armstrong Stadium became the location of court number two. In 2005 all courts in the center were given blue inner courts and green outer courts, in an attempt to make the ball more visible to the audience.

The US Open is the fourth and final tournament of tennis's "Grand Slams," following the Australian Open, the French Open, and Wimbledon, all of which are regulated by the International Tennis Federation. It is annually held in August and September over a two-week period and consists of championships in men's and women's singles and doubles, and mixed doubles. It is the only tournament of the Grand Slam that features final-set tiebreakers; the other events continue play in the final set until a winner is determined. In 2006 the US Open became the first Grand Slam to use instant replays for challenging disputed calls.

See also Tennis and Arthur Ashe Stadium.

Meghan Lalonde

US Open Men's Singles Championship Results

Year	Champion	Runner-Up	Year	Champion	Runner-Up
1881	Richard D. Sears (R)	William E. Glyn	1904	Holcombe Ward (L)	William J. Clothier
1882	Richard D. Sears (R)	Clarence M. Clark	1905	Beals C. Wright (R)	Holcombe Ward
1883	Richard D. Sears (R)	James Dwight	1906	William A. Larned (R)	Beals C. Wright
1884	Richard D. Sears (R)	Howard A. Taylor	1907	William A. Larned (R)	Robert LeRoy
1885	Richard D. Sears (R)	Godfrey M. Brinley	1908	William A. Larned (R)	Beals C. Wright
1886	Richard D. Sears (R)	R. Livingston Beeckman	1909	William A Larned (R)	William J. Clothier
1887	Richard D. Sears (R)	Henry W. Slocum, Jr.	1910	William A Larned (R)	Thomas C. Bundy
1888	Henry W. Slocum, Jr. (R)	Howard A. Taylor	1911	William A. Larned (R)	Maurice E. McLoughlin
1889	Henry W. Slocum, Jr. (R)	Quincy Shaw	1912	Maurice E. McLoughlin (R)	Wallace F. Johnson
1890	Oliver S. Campbell (R)	Henry W. Slocum, Jr.	1913	Maurice E. McLoughlin (R)	Richard N. Williams
1891	Oliver S. Campbell (R)	Clarence Hobart	1914	Richard N. Williams (R)	Maurice E. McLoughlin
1892	Oliver S. Campbell (R)	Fred H. Hovey	1915	William M. Johnston (R)	Maurice E. McLoughlin
1893	Robert D. Wrenn (L)	Fred H. Hovey	1916	Richard N. Williams (R)	William M. Johnston
1894	Robert D. Wrenn (L)	Manliff Goodbody	1917	R. Lindley Murray (L)	Nathaniel W. Niles
1895	Fred H. Hovey (R)	Robert D. Wrenn	1918	R. Lindley Murray (L)	William T. Tilden
1896	Robert D. Wrenn (L)	Fred H. Hovey	1919	William M. Johnston (R)	William T. Tilden
1897	Robert D. Wrenn (L)	Wilberforce Eaves	1920	William T. Tilden (R)	William M. Johnston
1898	Malcolm D. Whitman (R)	Dwight F. Davis	1921	William T. Tilden (R)	William M. Johnston
1899	Malcolm D. Whitman (R)	J. Parmly Paret	1922	William T. Tilden (R)	William M. Johnston
1900	Malcolm D. Whitman (R)	William A. Larned	1923	William T. Tilden (R)	William M. Johnston
1901	William A. Larned (R)	Beals C. Wright	1924	William T. Tilden (R)	William M. Johnston
1902	William A. Larned (R)	Reginald F. Doherty	1925	William T. Tilden (R)	William M. Johnston
1903	Hugh L. Doherty (R)	William A. Larned	1926	Rene Lacoste (R)	Jean Borotra

(*continued*)

US Open Men's Singles Championship Results (*Continued*)

Year	Champion	Runner-Up	Year	Champion	Runner-Up
1927	Rene Lacoste (R)	William T. Tilden	1968	Arthur Ashe (R)	Tom Okker
1928	Henri Cochet (R)	Francis T. Hunter	1969	Rod Laver (L)	Tony Roche
1929	William T. Tilden (R)	Francis T. Hunter	1970	Ken Rosewall (R)	Tony Roche
1930	John H. Doeg (L)	Francis X. Shields	1971	Stan Smith (R)	Jan Kodes
1931	H. Ellsworth Vines (R)	George M. Lott, Jr.	1972	Ilie Nastase (R)	Arthur Ashe
1932	H. Ellsworth Vines (R)	Henri Cochet	1973	John Newcombe (R)	Jan Kodes
1933	Fred Perry (R)	John H. Crawford	1974	Jimmy Connors (L)	Ken Rosewall
1934	Fred Perry (R)	Wilmer L. Allison	1975	Manuel Orantes (L)	Jimmy Connors
1935	Wilmer L. Allison (R)	Sidney B. Wood	1976	Jimmy Connors (L)	Bjorn Borg
1936	Fred Perry (R)	J. Donald Budge	1977	Guillermo Vilas (L)	Jimmy Connors
1937	J. Donald Budge (R)	Baron Gottfried von Cramm	1978	Jimmy Connors (L)	Bjorn Borg
			1979	John McEnroe (L)	Vitas Gerulaitis
1938	J. Donald Budge (R)	C. Gene Mako	1980	John McEnroe (L)	Bjorn Borg
1939	Robert Riggs (R)	S. Welby van Horn	1981	John McEnroe (L)	Bjorn Borg
1940	Donald McNeill (R)	Robert Riggs	1982	Jimmy Connors (L)	Ivan Lendl
1941	Robert Riggs (R)	Francis Kovacs II	1983	Jimmy Connors (L)	Ivan Lendl
1942	Frederick R. Schroeder, Jr. (R)	Frank Parker	1984	John McEnroe (L)	Ivan Lendl
1943	Lt. Joseph R. Hunt (R)	Seaman Jack Kramer	1985	Ivan Lendl (R)	John McEnroe
1944	Sgt. Frank Parker (R)	William F. Talbert	1986	Ivan Lendl (R)	Miloslav Mecir
1945	Sgt. Frank Parker (R)	William F. Talbert	1987	Ivan Lendl (R)	Mats Wilander
1946	Jack Kramer (R)	Tom Brown, Jr.	1988	Mats Wilander (R)	Ivan Lendl
1947	Jack Kramer (R)	Frank Parker	1989	Boris Becker (R)	Ivan Lendl
1948	Richard A. Gonzales (R)	Eric W. Sturgess	1990	Pete Sampras (R)	Andre Agassi
1949	Richard A. Gonzales (R)	Frederick Schroeder	1991	Stefan Edberg (R)	Jim Courier
1950	Arthur Larsen (L)	Herbert Flam	1992	Stefan Edberg (R)	Pete Sampras
1951	Frank Sedgman (R)	E. Victor Seixas, Jr.	1993	Pete Sampras (R)	Cedric Pioline
1952	Frank Sedgman (R)	Gardnar Mulloy	1994	Andre Agassi (R)	Michael Stich
1953	Tony Trabert (R)	E. Victor Seixas, Jr.	1995	Pete Sampras (R)	Andre Agassi
1954	E. Victor Seixas, Jr. (R)	Rex Hartwig	1996	Pete Sampras (R)	Michael Chang
1955	Tony Trabert (R)	Ken Rosewall	1997	Patrick Rafter (R)	Greg Rusedski
1956	Ken Rosewall (R)	Lewis Hoad	1998	Patrick Rafter (R)	Mark Philippoussis
1957	Malcolm J. Anderson (R)	Ashley J. Cooper	1999	Andre Agassi (R)	Todd Martin
1958	Ashley J. Cooper (R)	Malcolm J. Anderson	2000	Marat Safin (R)	Pete Sampras
1959	Neale Fraser (L)	Alejandro Olmedo	2001	Lleyton Hewitt (R)	Pete Sampras
1960	Neale Fraser (L)	Rodney Laver	2002	Pete Sampras (R)	Andre Agassi
1961	Roy Emerson (R)	Rodney Laver	2003	Andy Roddick (R)	Juan Carlos Ferrero
1962	Rodney Laver (L)	Roy Emerson	2004	Roger Federer (R)	Lleyton Hewitt
1963	Rafael Osuna (R)	Frank Froehling, III	2005	Roger Federer (R)	Andre Agassi
1964	Roy Emerson (R)	Fred Stolle	2006	Roger Federer (R)	Andy Roddick
1965	Manuel Santana (R)	Cliff Drysdale	2007	Roger Federer (R)	Novak Djokovic
1966	Fred Stolle (R)	John Newcombe	2008	Roger Federer (R)	Andy Murray
1967	John Newcombe (R)	Clark Graebner	2009	Juan Martin del Potro (R)	Roger Federer

Abbreviations: R, right-handed; L, left-handed

Source: http://2009.usopen.org/en_US/about/history/mschamps.html?promo=topnav

US Open Women's Singles Championship Results

Year	Champion	Runner-Up	Year	Champion	Runner-Up
1887	Ellen Hansell (R)	Laura Knight	1896	Elisabeth Moore (R)	Juliette Atkinson
1888	Bertha L. Townsend (R)	Ellen Hansell	1897	Juliette Atkinson (R)	Elisabeth Moore
1889	Bertha L. Townsend (R)	Lida D. Voorhes	1898	Juliette Atkinson (R)	Marion Jones
1890	Ellen C. Roosevelt (R)	Bertha L. Townsend	1899	Marion Jones (R)	Maud Banks
1891	Mabel Cahill (R)	Ellen C. Roosevelt	1900	Myrtle McAteer (R)	Edith Parker
1892	Mabel Cahill (R)	Elisabeth Moore	1901	Elisabeth Moore (R)	Myrtle McAteer
1893	Aline Terry (R)	Augusta Schultz	1902	Marion Jones (R)	Elisabeth Moore
1894	Helen Hellwig (R)	Aline Terry	1903	Elisabeth Moore (R)	Marion Jones
1895	Juliette Atkinson (R)	Helen Hellwig	1904	May Sutton (R)	Elisabeth Moore

(*continued*)

US Open Women's Singles Championship Results (*Continued*)

Year	Champion	Runner-Up
1905	Elisabeth Moore (R)	Helen Homans
1906	Helen Homans (R)	Maud Barger-Wallach
1907	Evelyn Sears (L)	Carrie Neely
1908	Maud Barger-Wallach (R)	Evelyn Sears
1909	Hazel Hotchkiss (R)	Maud Barger-Wallach
1910	Hazel Hotchkiss (R)	Louise Hammond
1911	Hazel Hotchkiss (R)	Florence Sutton
1912	Mary Browne (R)	Eleonora Sears
1913	Mary Browne (R)	Dorothy Green
1914	Mary Browne (R)	Marie Wagner
1915	Molla Bjurstedt (R)	Hazel Hotchkiss Wightman
1916	Molla Bjurstedt (R)	Louise Hammond Raymond
1917	Molla Bjurstedt (R)	Marion Vanderhoef
1918	Molla Bjurstedt (R)	Eleanor E. Goss
1919	Hazel Hotchkiss Wightman (R)	Marion Zinderstein
1920	Molla B. Mallory (R)	Marion Zinderstein
1921	Molla B. Mallory (R)	Mary K. Browne
1922	Molla B. Mallory (R)	Helen Wills
1923	Helen Wills (R)	Molla B. Mallory
1924	Helen Wills (R)	Molla B. Mallory
1925	Helen Wills (R)	Kathleen McKane
1926	Molla B. Mallory (R)	Elizabeth Ryan
1927	Helen Wills (R)	Betty Nuthall
1928	Helen Wills (R)	Helen J. Jacobs
1929	Helen Wills (R)	Phoebe Holcroft Watson
1930	Betty Nuthall (R)	Anna McCune Harper
1931	Helen Wills Moody (R)	Eileen Bennett Whitingstall
1932	Helen H. Jacobs (R)	Carolin A. Babcock
1933	Helen H. Jacobs (R)	Helen Wills Moody
1934	Helen H. Jacobs (R)	Sarah H. Palfrey
1935	Helen H. Jacobs (R)	Sarah H. Palfrey Fabyan
1936	Alice Marble (R)	Helen H. Jacobs
1937	Anita Lizana (R)	Jadwiga Jedrzejowska
1938	Alice Marble (R)	Nancye Wynne
1939	Alice Marble (R)	Helen H. Jacobs
1940	Alice Marble (R)	Helen H. Jacobs
1941	Sarah Palfrey Cooke (R)	Pauline Betz
1942	Pauline Betz (R)	A. Louise Brough
1943	Pauline Betz (R)	A. Louise Brough
1944	Pauline Betz (R)	Margaret Osborne
1945	Sarah Palfrey Cooke (R)	Pauline Betz
1946	Pauline Betz (R)	Patricia Canning
1947	A. Louise Brough (R)	Margaret Osborne
1948	Margaret Osborne duPont (R)	A. Louise Brough
1949	Margaret Osborne duPont (R)	Doris Hart
1950	Margaret Osborne duPont (R)	Doris Hart
1951	Maureen Connolly (R)	Shirley J. Fry
1952	Maureen Connolly (R)	Doris Hart
1953	Maureen Connolly (R)	Doris Hart
1954	Doris Hart (R)	A. Louise Brough
1955	Doris Hart (R)	Patricia Ward
1956	Shirley J. Fry (R)	Althea Gibson
1957	Althea Gibson (R)	A. Louise Brough
1958	Althea Gibson (R)	Darlene R. Hard
1959	Maria Bueno (R)	Christine Truman
1960	Darlene R. Hard (R)	Maria Bueno
1961	Darlene R. Hard (R)	Ann Haydon
1962	Margaret Smith (R)	Darlene R. Hard
1963	Maria Bueno (R)	Margaret Smith
1964	Maria Bueno (R)	Carole Caldwell Graebner
1965	Margaret Smith (R)	Billie Jean Moffitt
1966	Maria Bueno (R)	Nancy Richey
1967	Billie Jean Moffitt King (R)	Ann Haydon Jones
1968	Virginia Wade (R)	Billie Jean King
1969	Margaret Smith Court (R)	Nancy Richey
1970	Margaret Smith Court (R)	Rosemary Casals
1971	Billie Jean King (R)	Rosemary Casals
1972	Billie Jean King (R)	Kerry Melville
1973	Margaret Smith (R)Court	Evonne Goolagong
1974	Billie Jean King (R)	Evonne Goolagong
1975	Christine Marie Evert (R)	Evonne Goolagong
1976	Christine Marie Evert (R)	Evonne Goolagong
1977	Christine Marie Evert (R)	Wendy Turnbull
1978	Christine Marie Evert (R)	Pam Shriver
1979	Tracy Austin (R)	Chris Evert Lloyd
1980	Chris Evert Lloyd (R)	Hana Mandlikova
1981	Tracy Austin (R)	Martina Navratilova
1982	Chris Evert Lloyd (R)	Hana Mandlikova
1983	Martina Navratilova (L)	Chris Evert Lloyd
1984	Martina Navratilova (L)	Chris Evert Lloyd
1985	Hana Mandlikova (R)	Martina Navratilova
1986	Martina Navratilova (L)	Helena Sukova
1987	Martina Navratilova (L)	Steffi Graf
1988	Steffi Graf (R)	Gabriela Sabatini
1989	Steffi Graf (R)	Martina Navratilova
1990	Gabriela Sabatini (R)	Steffi Graf
1991	Monica Seles (L)	Martina Navratilova
1992	Monica Seles (L)	Arantxa Sanchez-Vicario
1993	Steffi Graf (R)	Helena Sukova
1994	Arantxa Sanchez-Vicario(R)	Steffi Graf
1995	Steffi Graf (R)	Monica Seles
1996	Steffi Graf (R)	Monica Seles
1997	Martina Hingis (R)	Venus Williams
1998	Lindsay Davenport (R)	Martina Hingis
1999	Serena Williams (R)	Martina Hingis
2000	Venus Williams (R)	Lindsay Davenport
2001	Venus Williams (R)	Serena Williams
2002	Serena Williams (R)	Venus Williams
2003	Justine Henin-Hardenne (R)	Kim Clijsters
2004	Svetlana Kuznetsova (R)	Elena Dementieva
2005	Kim Clijsters (R)	Mary Pierce
2006	Maria Sharapova (R)	Justine Henin-Hardenne
2007	Justine Henin (R)	Svetlana Kuznetsova
2008	Serena Williams (R)	Jelena Jankovic
2009	Kim Clijsters (R)	Caroline Wozniacki

Abbreviations: R, right-handed; L, left-handed.

Source: http://2009.usopen.org/en_US/about/history/wschamps.html

Compiled by Frank Nestor

U.S. Sanitary Commission. Organization formed in 1861 by the Unitarian minister Henry Whitney Bellows and the urban sanitation expert Elisha Harris, both directors of the Women's Central Association of Relief in New York City, along with two physicians, W. H. Van Buren of the College of Physicians and Surgeons and Jacob Harsen of the New York Lint and Bandage Association. The four traveled to Washington, D.C., in May to assess the preparedness for the Civil War of the U.S. Medical Bureau. Convinced that the bureau was incapable of maintaining the health of Union soldiers, they chartered the sanitary commission, approved by executive order of President Abraham Lincoln on 13 June, to organize the national distribution of sanitary information and material relief to Union soldiers. Bellows was president of the commission and George Templeton Strong its secretary; members of the executive committee, including Van Buren, Oliver W. Gibbs, Cornelius Agnew, and Charles J. Stille, met in New York City every day of the war except Sundays. The general secretary of the commission was Frederick Law Olmsted, who from his office in Washington, D.C., oversaw the gathering of statistics, the implementation of dietary reforms to prevent scurvy, and construction of the first pavilion hospitals to prevent contagion. Largely through the efforts of the Women's Central Association of Relief, the commissioners raised more than $15 million to buy supplies and pay teamsters, doctors, nurses, and cooks. The commission succeeded in restructuring the outmoded U.S. Medical Bureau and in promoting public health measures that reduced mortality and greatly eased soldiers' suffering, but Olmsted's position eventually was undermined by political rivalry with Secretary of War Edwin Stanton and the U.S. Medical Bureau, and by competition with the Christian Commission, a private evangelical aid society formed in New York City in November 1861. He resigned in August 1863, after which the influence of the commission declined; it was officially terminated by Bellows in April 1878. Information gathered by the U.S. Sanitary Commission during the Civil War helped further the work of the International Red Cross (1863); the Public Health Association, formed in New York City by Harris in 1872; and the American Association of the Red Cross (1881).

William Quentin Maxwell, *Lincoln's Fifth Wheel: The Political History of the United States Sanitary Commission* (New York: Longmans, Green, 1956); Jane Turner Censer, ed., *The Papers of Frederick Law Olmsted,* vol. 4, *Defending the Union: The Civil War and the U.S. Sanitary Commission, 1861–1863* (Baltimore, Md.: Johns Hopkins University Press, 1986)

Sarah Henry Lederman

U.S. Ship Canal. See Harlem River Ship Canal.

U Thant Island. See Belmont Island.

Utopia. Proposed neighborhood in north central Queens, covering a tract of 50 acres (20 hectares) east of 164th Street between Jamaica and Flushing. The land was acquired in June 1905 by the Utopia Land Company, which planned to build a cooperative town for Jews from the Lower East Side. The streets were named for those on the East Side, including First and Second avenues and Ludlow, Hester, Division, and Essex streets; there were to be several industries and a large cooperative store. The developers received a loan from the New York Mortgage and Security Company to grade the streets and stake out lots, but abandoned their plan after they were unable to secure more funds. Although the development was never realized, it inspired the name of Utopia Parkway.

Vincent Seyfried

Valachi, Joseph [Cago, Joe] (*b* New York City, 22 Sept 1903; *d* El Paso, Tex., 3 April 1971). Organized-crime figure and informer. He was born and brought up in East Harlem and was a low-ranking criminal in the Mafia under the name Joe Cago. While serving a term in Atlanta Federal Prison in 1962 he became convinced that he was marked for execution by Vito Genovese, the head of an organized-crime family in New York City, and decided to reveal what he knew of the Mafia to the U.S. Department of Justice, becoming the first person ever to violate the Mafia's code of silence. He later testified on the same subject before an investigatory committee of the U.S. Senate (September–October 1963) and wrote an account of 300,000 words, which although of questionable accuracy on some points provides extensive information on organized crime. Valachi made current the term *Cosa Nostra,* insisting that the word *Mafia* was used only by outsiders. He died while serving a sentence of life imprisonment for murder.

Peter Maas, *The Valachi Papers* (New York: HarperCollins, 2003)

See also ORGANIZED CRIME.

Warren Sloat

Valentine, David T(homas) (*b* Eastchester, N.Y., 15 Sept 1801; *d* New York City, 25 Feb 1869). Public official and publisher. After moving to New York City in 1815 he worked as a grocer's clerk and through political contacts became the clerk of the marine court in 1826, deputy clerk of the Common Council in 1830, and clerk of the council in 1842. In 1841 he compiled and published the first edition of his *Manual of the Corporation of the City of New York,* a compendium of historical material with illustrations. The book proved popular and Valentine published an annual edition until 1867. The other major title published under Valentine's name, *History of the City of New York* (1863), was actually the work of his aide William I. Paulding.

Stephen Weinstein

Valentine, Lewis J(oseph) (*b* Brooklyn, 19 March 1882; *d* ?New York City, 16 Dec 1946). Police commissioner. During the administration of Mayor John Purroy Mitchel (1914–18) he took part in raids by "confidential" squads on brothels and gambling joints being protected by corrupt policemen. From July 1926 to December 1928 he led a similar squad that was formed shortly after the election of Mayor James J. Walker. Appointed police commissioner by Mayor Fiorello H. La Guardia in September 1934, he caused an immediate controversy when he publicly ordered his officers to "muss up" professional criminals. He retired in September 1945. Valentine was credited with greatly improving the efficiency, honesty, and morale of the police force. He wrote a memoir, *Night Stick* (1947).

George A. Thompson, Jr.

Valentine's Manual. See VALENTINE, DAVID T.

Valentine–Varian House. Historic house at 3266 Bainbridge Avenue in the Bronx. The two-story structure was built about 1758 of local fieldstone with wood details by Isaac Valentine, a blacksmith and farmer. It was sold in 1791 to Isaac Varian and remained in his family until 1905. Bought in 1965 by the Bronx County Historical Society, it was moved across the street from its original site, restored as the society's headquarters, and designated a city landmark in 1966. The Valentine–Varian House is the only remaining house that once lined the Boston Post Road and is one of few of its style that survives in the Bronx.

Eric Wm. Allison

Valentino, Rudolph [di Valentina d'Antonguolla, Rodolfo Alfonzo Raffaello Pierre Filibert Guglielmi] (*b* Castellanata, Italy, 6 May 1895; *d* New York City, 23 Aug 1926). Silent-film actor and sex icon. Born to a middle-class Italian family in the year cinema was invented, he left home at a young age, going first to Paris and ultimately to New York City in 1913. He started out working as a waiter, dancer and, reportedly, gigolo. After earning some fame in New York City as a taxi dancer at Maxim's, he ventured to California, where his sex appeal and stage presence earned him appearances in 14 major silent films (during the last seven years of his life), such as *The Four Horseman of the Apocalypse* (1921) and *The Sheik* (1921). Valentino became a Hollywood celebrity, bearing such nicknames as the Great Lover. He died abruptly in New York City after surgery for appendicitis and ulcers; his funeral was attended by more than 100,000 mourners—most of them women, who allegedly began rioting in the streets.

Cecilia Magnusson

Vallee, Rudy [Vallée, Hubert Prior] (*b* Island Pond, Vt., 28 June 1901; *d* North Hollywood, Calif., 3 July 1986). Singer. Brought up in Vermont and Maine, he taught himself to play the saxophone at an early age and changed his forename in honor of his favorite saxophonist, Rudy Wiedoeft. He played in several bands while attending Yale University (bachelor's degree in philosophy, 1927) and in 1928 formed the Connecticut Yankees, a dance band that performed at the Heigh Ho Club in New York City. He achieved success soon after he began singing over the radio station WABC in February 1928. For the next 10 years his variety show, *The Fleischmann's Yeast Hour* (*The Royal Gelatin Hour* from 1936 to 1939), broadcast on Thursday evenings, was heard by millions of listeners. He sang such tunes as "My Time Is Your Time" and "I'm Just a Vagabond Lover," amplifying his singing voice with a hand-held megaphone. In addition to his radio programs he frequently performed at the Villa Vallee (which later became the Copacabana) at 10 East 60th Street. He also appeared on stage and in several Hollywood films. Although his popularity faded after World War II, he enjoyed a revival in the 1960s as an actor in the Broadway and screen versions of *How to Succeed in Business without Really Trying.* His published writings include *Vagabond Dreams Come True* (1930), *My Time Is Your Time: The Story of Rudy Vallee* (1962), and *Let the Chips Fall* (1975).

Robert Sanger Steel

Van Anda, Carr (Vattel) (*b* Georgetown, Ohio, 2 Dec 1864; *d* New York City, 28 Jan 1945). Newspaper editor. He studied mathematics at Ohio State University and spent 16 years at the *Sun.* In February 1904 he joined the *New York Times* as its managing editor and quickly distinguished himself when his staff became the first to cover the destruction of the Russian fleet by Japan in 1904–5. He gained further recognition for the newspaper's coverage of the sinking of the *Titanic* in 1912 and of World War I, which he charted with such acumen that his reporters often reached the scene of battle before the armies did. He also published detailed accounts of the discoveries of the North and South poles and of the theories of Albert Einstein (whose error in transcribing an equation he once detected). His knowledge of Egyptian hieroglyphics led him to expose a forgery that had misled Egyptologists into believing that King Tutankhamen had been assassinated. An indefatigable worker, Van Anda retired from the *Times* in 1925 and spent the rest of his life studying science.

Harrison Salisbury

Van Arsdale, Harry (Jr.) (*b* New York City, 23 Nov 1905; *d* Queens, 16 Feb 1986). Labor leader. The son of an electrician, he joined Local 3 of the International Brotherhood of Electrical Workers in 1925 and became its business manager in 1933, a position he held until 1968. An innovator, he expanded his local into allied fields; developed Electchester, a cooperative workers housing project in Queens; and led a strike that won construction electricians a 25-hour workweek. In 1959 he was elected the first president of the New York City Central Labor Council of the American Federation of Labor and Congress of Industrial Organizations (AFL-CIO), making him the city's most powerful labor leader. His influence peaked during the 1960s when he formed a close alliance between the

900,000-member council and Governor Nelson A. Rockefeller and Mayor Robert F. Wagner. Van Arsdale played an important role in the unionization of public employees, hospital workers, and taxi drivers (serving as the first president of their union) and intervened on behalf of labor in many strikes. Well-known in business circles, he pressed for public works spending and served on many state, local, and federal boards. He remained head of the Central Labor Council until his death.

Gene Ruffini, *Harry Van Arsdale, Jr.: Labor's Champion* (Armonk, N.Y.: Sharpe, 2003)

See also American Federation of Labor.

Joshua B. Freeman

Van Cortlandt, Philip (*b* New York, 21 Aug 1749; *d* Croton-on-Hudson, N.Y., 5 Nov 1831). Political and mercantile leader; son of Pierre Van Cortlandt. He served as an officer in the American Revolution, became a founding member of the Society of the Cincinnati, and was a commissioner of forfeiture for the Southern District, in which capacity he was responsible for the breakup and sale of confiscated Loyalist holdings in New York City and surrounding counties. He later served in the U.S. Congress (1793–1809). Although his family continued to engage in regional and international commerce on a large scale, its political influence waned after the death in 1812 of Vice President George Clinton.

Louis E. DeForest, *The Van Cortlandt Family* (New York: Historical Publication Society, 1930); Jacob Judd, comp., *Van Cortlandt Family Papers* (Tarrytown, N.Y.: Sleepy Hollow Restorations, 1976–80)

Jacob Judd

Van Cortlandt, Pierre (*b* New York City, 21 Jan 1721; *d* Croton-on-Hudson, N.Y., 1 May 1814). Political and mercantile leader; grandson of Stephanus Van Cortlandt. He was a member of the general assembly (1768–74) and served on every major provincial council and congress during the revolutionary period before assuming the presidency of the Committee of Safety. Under Governor George Clinton he was the first lieutenant governor of New York State, from 1778 to 1795. He accompanied George Washington on his triumphal entry into the city in November 1783.

Jacob Judd, comp., *Van Cortlandt Family Papers* (Tarrytown, N.Y.: Sleepy Hollow Restorations, 1976–80)

Jacob Judd

Van Cortlandt, Stephanus (*b* New Amsterdam, 7 May 1643; *d* New York City, 25 Nov 1700). Mercantile and political leader. The son of Oloff Stevense Van Cortlandt (circa 1610–84), who was stationed in New Amsterdam in 1638 as a soldier employed by the Dutch West India Company and soon began a career as a merchant, he became the first native-born mayor of New York City in 1677. In addition to expanding the family's overseas trading operations he opened a brewery, as well as a sugar mill that is believed to have been a notorious prison when the British occupied New York City during the American Revolution. His sister Catherine (1652–1730) married into the Philipse family, as did his brother Jacobus (1658–1739), whose branch of the family became associated with the lands now making up Van Cortlandt Park.

Jacob Judd, comp., *Van Cortlandt Family Papers* (Tarrytown, N.Y.: Sleepy Hollow Restorations, 1976–80)

Jacob Judd

Van Cortlandt Park. Public park in the northwestern Bronx, occupying 1122 acres (454 hectares). It is the fourth largest park in New York City. Originally a part of the estate of the Philipse family, the land was sold to Jacobus Van Cortlandt on his marriage in 1691 to Eva Philipse, daughter of Frederick Philipse I. The Van Cortlandt mansion was built of stone in 1748 by Frederick Van Cortlandt, grandson of Oloff Stevense Van Cortlandt, and was at various times during the American Revolution the headquarters for General George Washington and General William Howe; it is now near Broadway and West 242nd Street and is the oldest house in the Bronx. Vault Hill nearby holds the family gravesites. In 1776 Augustus Van Cortlandt, the city recorder, moved the municipal records to his father's vault there to hide them from the British army. Indian Field in the northeast section of the park marks the graves of the Stockbridge Indians who fought on the American side in the Revolution and fell in a

First, 23rd, and 71st regiments camping in Van Cortlandt Park, 1917

Van Cortlandt Park, Mill Pond

battle with Hessians and Tories in 1778. The first Croton Aqueduct, built in the 1840s, forms a walkway, as does the right-of-way of the Putnam Division of the New York Central Railroad (1881–1984). The park's most popular area, the Parade Ground (opened in 1888), was originally used by the National Guard and is now a center for baseball, football, soccer, cricket, and hurling. Members of the Van Cortlandt family lived in the mansion continuously until 1889, when they sold the building and the surrounding lands to the city for a public park. In 1895 the Van Cortlandt Golf Course became the first municipal golf course in the nation, followed by the Mosholu Golf Course nearby. Playgrounds and a stadium were added in the 1930s and a large swimming pool complex opened in 1970. Despite the intrusion of the Henry Hudson and Mosholu parkways and the Major Deegan Expressway in the 1930s and 1940s, the park still has a bird sanctuary, two nature walkways, a bridle path, the nation's leading cross-country track, picnic areas, and a tree and shrub nursery maintained by the parks department.

Lloyd Ultan

Van Dam, Rip (*b* Albany, *ca* 1660; *d* New York City, 10 June 1749). Merchant and interim governor. After moving to New York City at the age of 20 he became a prominent shipbuilder and trader. He gained notoriety by resisting the restrictions on trade imposed by Governor Richard Coote, earl of Bellomont, against which he and other merchants petitioned the king of England. From 1693 to 1696 he held a seat on the Board of Aldermen and in 1699 he was elected to the provincial assembly, where he became the leader of the opposition party. Lord Cornbury appointed him in 1702 to the provincial council, of which he eventually became president. He served as interim governor of the colony of New York from 1731 (on the death of Governor John Montgomerie) until his replacement in the following year by the king's appointee William Cosby, with whom he had a bitter dispute after refusing to surrender half the salary he had earned as governor. During legal proceedings in 1733 he was expelled from the provincial council by Cosby, who was then near death, and while he fought to regain his position the council named as acting governor George Clarke; Van Dam maintained that he was still a member of the council and that his seniority entitled him to the governorship. When armed conflict seemed imminent, orders arrived in 1736 from England naming Clarke the lieutenant governor. Van Dam never held another political office.

Edward T. O'Donnell

Vanderbilt, Cornelius (*b* Staten Island, 27 May 1794; *d* New York City, 4 Jan 1877). Entrepreneur, grandfather of industrialist William K. Vanderbilt. He attended school in Port Richmond on Staten Island until the age of 11, when he went to work on his father's lighter in New York Harbor; he later bought a boat and set up a passenger and freight ferry service between Staten Island and Manhattan. During the 1830s he lived on Stone and Madison streets and East Broadway. After assembling a small fleet of vessels that worked around New York City, he offered service to Albany and undercut his competitors. A millionaire by 1846, he built a mansion on Staten Island and a townhouse on Washington Place that became his principal residence. He captured most of the traffic to California during the gold rush by reducing the fare between New York City and San Francisco. At about age 70 he merged three railroad lines operating between the city and points upstate into an efficient line offering dependable service; he then formed one of the largest transportation networks in North America. During the panic of 1873 he paid dividends as usual and issued contracts to build Grand Central Terminal that led to the employment of thousands of workers. By the end of his life Vanderbilt had a fortune of more than $100 million, most of which he left to family members. He also gave money to the Church of the Strangers in New York City, where a friend was pastor.

See also Aviation and Railroads, §1.

James E. Mooney

Vanderbilt, Gloria (Morgan) (*b* New York City, 20 Feb 1924). Fashion designer, painter, actress, and writer. She was born an heiress to the dynasty founded by her great-great-grandfather, the financier Commodore Cornelius Vanderbilt, and when her father died in 1925 she inherited a trust fund of about $4 million. At the age of 10 she became the focus of one of the nation's most notorious child custody cases when her parental aunt, Gertrude Whitney, accused her mother of neglect and sued for custody. After a highly publicized trial, during which she was widely referred to as the "poor little rich girl," she was turned over to Whitney's care. As an adult she embarked on successful careers as a painter, actress, writer, and fashion designer while remaining active as a member of fashionable society. Beginning in the 1970s, she licensed the use of her name on a variety of fashion items—eyeglasses, perfume, and clothing—and later appeared in television commercials promoting her products. Vanderbilt attracted considerable media attention for her marriages: successively, to the Hollywood agent Pasquale di Cocco (1942), the conductor Leopold Stokowski (1945), the film director Sidney Lumet (1956), and the writer Wyatt Cooper (1963). In 1996 she published *A Mother's Story,* a book about the suicide of her son.

Robert Sanger Steel

Vanderbilt, William K(issam) (*b* Staten Island, 12 Dec 1849; *d* Paris, 22 July 1920). Industrialist and sportsman; grandson of Cornelius Vanderbilt. With his brothers Cornelius and George he was educated by private tutors and at schools in Switzerland. He later worked for the Hudson River Railroad and by 1877 was a vice president of the New York Central and Hudson River Railroad; after six years he left to direct other railroads owned by his family. His marriage to Alva Ertskin Smith in 1875 helped him to gain acceptance in elite circles; they were divorced in 1895 and in 1903 he married Anna (Harriman) Sands Rutherfurd. After his brother Cornelius's death in 1899 he left many of his positions in the railroads to manage the family's immense holdings; in 1903 he resigned as executive director of the New York Central and allowed direction of it to pass to the Pennsylvania Railroad, but he retained control through ownership. An avid sportsman, he sailed in the America's Cup race and owned many Thoroughbred racehorses. Vanderbilt also established the Vanderbilt Clinic, supported the Metropolitan Opera Company and Columbia University, and collected paintings that he bequeathed to the Metropolitan Museum of Art.

Louis Auchincloss, *The Vanderbilt Era: Profiles of a Gilded Age* (New York: Macmillan, 1989)

James E. Mooney

Van der Donck, Adriaen (*b* Breda, Dutch Republic, *ca* 1618; *d* New Netherland, 1655). Popular representative. After studying law at Leiden University, he took a position as *schout,* or law officer, at Rensselaerswijck, a fief within the Dutch colony of New Netherland that surrounded present-day Albany, New York. Three years later he moved south, where Peter Stuyvesant, director-general of New Amsterdam, was facing conflict with its residents. Stuyvesant had followed the orders of the West India Company, which ran New Netherland for profit rather than as a settlement colony, and the residents were demanding rights as Dutch citizens. Van der Donck, the only lawyer in the colony, became their leader, writing petitions to the States General, appealing to ancient authorities and to new principles and rights. Stuyvesant arrested him and threatened to try him for treason. On his release, Van der Donck led a delegation to The Hague, where he spent four years presenting the case of New Netherland and arousing popular interest in the colony. He did not achieve his ultimate aim—having the government take control of the colony to strengthen it before the English could invade—but the States General did grant New Amsterdam a municipal charter. Thus, when the English took over in 1664, many Dutch features remained in effect in New York City, ensuring that it would develop along a different trajectory from that of other cities in British North America. Van der Donck returned to New Netherland in 1653 where he made his home on a tract of land north of Manhattan that he had received in 1645 in payment for negotiating an Indian treaty. His unofficial title of *yonkheer,* or young landowner, eventually transferred to the land, and it is to this that the city of Yonkers owes its name.

Russell Shorto, *The Island at the Center of the World* (New York: Doubleday, 2004); Jaap Jacobs, *New Netherland: A Dutch Colony in Seventeenth Century America* (Boston: Brill, 2005)

Russell Shorto

Vanderlip, Frank A(rthur) (*b* Aurora, Ill., 17 Nov 1864; *d* New York City, 29 June 1937). Banker. As an assistant secretary of the Treasury from 1897 to 1901, he arranged the Spanish–American War Loan. His work caught the attention of James Stillman, the president of National City Bank, who in 1901 made him its vice president, a position he retained until he became president in 1909. He helped to plan the Federal Reserve System and in 1911 formed the National City Company, a nationwide bank holding company and securities affiliate of the National City Bank that was not subject to the restrictions of the National Bank Act. His most important achievements were the establishment of branches overseas, beginning in Buenos Aires in 1914, and the acquisition in 1915 of the branches of the International Banking Corporation in the Far East. A volunteer during World War I, he led the War Savings Certificates Committee from 1917 to 1918. A group led by James A. Stillman (son of James Stillman) and William Rockefeller forced him to resign in 1919. He lived in suburban Scarborough-on-Hudson, New York.

Frank A. Vanderlip, with Boyden Sparkes, *From Farm Boy to Financier* (New York: D. Appleton Century, 1935)

Joan L. Silverman

Van Der Zee, James (Augustus) (*b* Lenox, Mass., 29 June 1886; *d* Washington, D.C., 15 May 1983). Photographer. He became interested in photography while still in his teens and moved in 1905 to New York City. In 1916 he opened his first photography studio on 135th Street near Lenox Avenue in Harlem. During the 1920s Van Der Zee was closely associated with several figures in the Harlem Renaissance and worked as Marcus Garvey's official photographer (1921–24). He moved his studio first to 2069–77 Seventh Avenue and then to 272 Lenox Avenue, where he continued to take portraits. Retired and forced into poverty, he was rediscovered at the age of 82. He was the largest individual contributor to the Metropolitan Museum of Art's 1967 photographic exhibition *Harlem on My Mind,* which documented life in Harlem; the exhibition opened in January 1969 and brought him international recognition. In 1970 the Metropolitan added 60 of his prints to its permanent collection, and an institute was formed in his name to promote the work of young minority photographers. Van Der Zee received the first Pierre Toussaint Award from the New York Archdiocese in 1978.

Reginald McGhee, *The World of James VanDerZee: A Visual Record of Black Americans* (New York: Grove, 1969); Deborah Willis-Braithwaite, *VanDerZee, Photographer, 1886–1983* (New York: Harry N. Abrams, 1998)

Rodger C. Birt

Van Doren, Carl (Clinton) (*b* Hope, Ill., 10 Sept 1884; *d* Torrington, Conn., 18 July 1950). Literary critic, historian, and editor, brother of literary critic Mark Van Doren. He attended Columbia University in 1908 to complete work on his PhD and in 1911 accepted a teaching position there in American literature and history. After working briefly as the headmaster of the Brearley School in 1916–18, he was the literary editor of the *Nation* in 1919–22. Van Doren became an influential literary figure in New York City by supporting young, modern writers. His published writings include an authoritative biography of Benjamin Franklin (1938).

Robert Morrow

Van Doren, Mark (Albert) (*b* Hope, Ill., 13 June 1894; *d* Torrington, Conn., 10 Dec 1972). Literary critic; brother of Carl Van Doren. After receiving his PhD at Columbia in 1920 he joined his brother as a member of the university's English department until 1959. A gifted and influential professor, he taught for 39 years: his students included the poet John Berryman and the writer and Trappist monk Thomas Merton. He wrote fiction and criticism, and received the Pulitzer Prize for his poetry in 1940. Van Doren's published writings include critical studies of John Dryden (1920) and Nathaniel Hawthorne (1949), several books of poetry, novels, and a play, and *Liberal Education* (1943). A teaching award at Columbia is given each year by the students in his honor.

Mark Albert Van Doren, *The Autobiography of Mark Van Doren* (New York: Harcourt, Brace, 1958)

Robert Morrow

Vanity Fair. Name used by four magazines published in New York City. The first appeared from 1859 to 1863, and the second was a glossy publication inspired by such pulp magazines as *Police Gazette.* The third and best-known was published for more than 20 years by Condé Nast, who acquired the rights to the name for $3000, bought out the magazine *Dress* (a competitor of his own fashion magazine *Vogue*), and from 1913 published *Dress and Vanity Fair;* he sought a wide readership by covering fashion, the arts, and sports as well as humorous pieces. His dissatisfaction with the first four issues of the magazine led him to engage Frank Crowninshield, an editor of eclectic tastes. The magazine, known by its abbreviated name, published the work of Robert Benchley, Dorothy Parker, Robert E. Sherwood, Donald Ogden Stewart, Clare Boothe, John Peale Bishop, Edna St. Vincent Millay, Edmund Wilson, Gertrude Stein, Aldous Huxley, Noël Coward, Ferenc Molnar, Tristan Tzara, and Colette. It was difficult for *Vanity Fair* to retain its readers during the Depression, and in an effort to broaden its appeal Crowninshield began to publish articles by Walter Lippmann and engaged Jay Franklin and Henry Pringle as members of the editorial staff in 1932. The magazine was nevertheless merged with *Vogue* in 1936. A fourth magazine named *Vanity Fair* was introduced by Condé Nast Publications in March 1983 and as of 2009 had a circulation of more than 1.1 million.

American Humor Magazines and Comic Periodicals (Westport, Conn: Greenwood, 1987)

Brenda Wineapple

Van Nest. Neighborhood in the central Bronx, bounded to the north by Park Avenue and the Esplanade, to the east by Bronxdale Avenue, to the south by East Tremont Avenue, and to the west by Bronx River Parkway. The first European settlers were members of the family of Pieter Pietersen Van Neste, who settled in the area in 1647. A railroad station was built to accommodate visitors to the Morris Park Racecourse. The area remained farmland until the 1870s, when it was divided into 1700 lots for development by the Van Nest Land Improvement Company. A nexus of trolley lines nearby in West Farms led to the construction of one-family frame houses; the streets were named for members of the Van Neste family. The first apartment buildings were constructed in the 1920s. In addition to a large Italian and Irish population, in the 1980s Van Nest and its environs attracted some new immigrants from Jamaica, the Dominican Republic, Guyana, India, and China. After 2000 it still consisted of single-family homes, although many had been converted into apartments.

Nicholas DiBrino, *Morris Park Racecourse* (New York: Bronx County Historical Society, 1977); John McNamara, *McNamara's Old Bronx* (New York: Bronx County Historical Society, 1989)

Gary D. Hermalyn

Van Vechten, Carl (*b* Cedar Rapids, Iowa, 17 June 1880; *d* New York City, 21 Dec 1964). Critic and novelist. He graduated from the University of Chicago and worked as a music critic for the *New York Times* and the *New Music Review;* he was also a photographer and patron of Harlem Renaissance artists. After 1920 he abandoned criticism for fiction. An avid collector of books and memorabilia, he donated the Van Vechten Collection of books and manuscripts to the New York Public Library. Van Vechten's published writings include the novel *Nigger Heaven* (1926), an autobiography (1932), *Fragments from an Unwritten Autobiography* (1955), and *Between*

Friends (1961). For many years he lived on Central Park West.

James E. Mooney

Van Wyck, Robert A(nderson) (*b* New York City, 1849; *d* Paris, 13 Nov 1918). Mayor. A graduate of Columbia Law School, he was elected judge of the City Court in 1889 and became its presiding judge. He was nominated for mayor in 1897 by Richard Croker, the leader of Tammany Hall, and prevailed against divided opposition to become the city's first mayor after the great consolidation of the five boroughs into one huge municipality. While in office he engaged in questionable practices: he was accused of accepting $500,000 of stock in the American Ice Company but cleared of any wrongdoing by Governor Theodore Roosevelt in 1900. Such scandals became the focus of the election of 1901, in which Van Wyck was defeated by the Republican reformer Seth Low. He lived at 135 East 46th Street.

James E. Mooney

Varela, Felix (*b* Havana, 1788; *d* St. Augustine, Fla., 18 Feb 1853). Religious and political reformer. He taught from 1811 to 1820 at San Carlos Seminary in Cuba, where he modernized the curriculum and wrote a number of texts, and was ordained a Roman Catholic priest in 1812. An advocate of republicanism and Cuban independence, he served in the Spanish legislature, the Cortes, until 1823. As a political refugee he moved to New York City in 1824 and continued to promote republicanism and Cuban independence through the newspaper *El Haberno*. He became a diocesan vicar general, wrote articles, edited a number of short-lived Catholic newspapers, published a children's catechistic periodical, and defended Catholicism against nativism. In 1825 he became the pastor of Christ Church, holding services in the basement of the Church of St. Peter until 23 March 1827, when services were moved to Christ Protestant Episcopal Church at 41 Ann Street. Eventually the congregation divided into two branches; Varela became the pastor of one that he named the Church of the Transfiguration, which occupied the former Reformed Scots Presbyterian Church on Chambers and Park streets after a rededication on 31 March 1836. Varela financed the church with his own money, as most of the congregants were poor residents of the Five Points. In 1850 he moved for health reasons to St. Augustine, but he continued to aid the parish financially until his death. The parish is now at 23–29 Mott Street.

Helen McCadden and Joseph McCadden, *Father Varela: Torch Bearer from Cuba* (New York: United States Catholic Historical Society, 1969)

Mary Elizabeth Brown

Varèse, Edgar(d Victor Achille Charles) (*b* Paris, 22 Dec 1883; *d* New York City, 6 Nov 1965). Composer. He moved to New York City in December 1915 and formed the International Composers' Guild in 1921. Many of his major compositions were given their first performances in the city, including *Hyperprism* (1922–23) for winds and percussion, *Ionisation* (1931) for percussion ensemble, *Density 21.5* (1936) for solo flute, and *Nocturnal* (1961) for soprano, bass chorus, and small orchestra. After failing in the 1930s to gain a large following for his music, which he termed "organized sound," he turned his attention to early music; in 1943 formed the Greater New York Chorus, which he led until 1947; and taught at Columbia University in 1948. In the 1950s he gained critical recognition for his work with electronic music and in particular for his compositions *Déserts* (1954), for chamber orchestra and tape, and *Poème électronique* (1958), for tape alone. During his last years he lived at 189 Sullivan Street. Varèse's music is often uncompromisingly dissonant and yet accessible because of its colorful instrumentation, which relies heavily on brass and percussion.

Fernand Oullette, *Edgar Varèse* (New York: Orion, 1968)

Barbara L. Tischler

Varian, Isaac L(eggett) (*b* New York City, 25 June 1793; *d* Peekskill, N.Y., 10 Aug 1864). Mayor. An ally of Tammany Hall, he was known for his honest character as an alderman and mayor during the 1830s and early 1840s. A dispute over his selection as the chairman of a meeting of Tammany Hall in the autumn of 1835 led to the formation of the Locofocos, an egalitarian faction of the Democratic Party.

James E. Mooney

Varick, James (*b* Newburgh, N.Y., 1750; *d* New York City, 22 July 1827). Religious leader. A shoemaker and the father of four children, he joined the John Street Methodist Episcopal Church but became disillusioned by the racism of white congregants. After withdrawing in 1796 he helped to form a congregation that became legally established in 1801. He was ordained in 1820 while leading efforts to form the African Methodist Episcopal Zion Church, of which he was elected bishop in 1822 and 1826. He was also an advocate for racial equality for African Americans in New York City; he was active in the New York African Society for Mutual Relief, founded in 1808, and served as vice president of the New York African Bible Society, founded in 1817.

Benjamin F. Wheeler, *The Varick Family* (Mobile, Ala.: n.pub., 1906)

Dennis C. Dickerson

Varick, Richard (*b* Hackensack, N.J., 25 March 1753; *d* Jersey City, N.J., 30 July 1831). Mayor. He moved to New York City in 1775 and enlisted as a captain in the Continental army, where he was an aide-de-camp to Benedict Arnold from 1777 to 1780; he later was cleared of complicity in Arnold's treasonous activities and in 1781 became George Washington's secretary. He was the city's recorder from 1784 to 1789, the speaker of the state assembly in 1787–88, and the state attorney general in 1788–89. In 1789 he helped to codify the state's statutes and as a Federalist was appointed mayor by Governor George Clinton. Republicans later criticized his use of marketing and tax-licensing fees, and he was swept out of office in 1801 after a bitter campaign. A street in lower Manhattan is named after him.

David William Voorhees

Variety. Weekly publication. Launched in 1905 by Sime Silverman to cover the vaudeville circuit, it later expanded to include coverage of motion pictures, radio, and television. The publication was controlled by Silverman's descendants until 1990, when Gerard A. Byrne became the publisher. In 1987 *Variety* was acquired by Reed Business Information, a division of Reed Elsevier. As of 2008 the magazine had a circulation of more than 31,000 and covered entertainment worldwide, including theater, home video, and cable television. It is known for a breezy, jargony style of writing and in particular for such memorable headlines as "Wall Street Lays an Egg" (30 October 1929) and "Sticks Nix Hick Pix" (17 July 1935).

Laura Gwinn

varnishes. See Paints, dyes, and varnishes.

vaudeville. Popular American entertainment in the nineteenth and early twentieth centuries. Entertainment in nineteenth-century New York City appealed to specialized audiences: opera attracted the middle and upper class, minstrel shows and melodramas the middle class, and variety shows in concert saloons the working class. After the Civil War, with the population expanding in both numbers and diversity, producers wanted to attract wider audiences and gain bigger profits. Vaudeville's broad appeal in the post–Civil War era came from its attempt to attract both men and women from different economic and social groups by presenting everything from minstrel shows to comedians to dancers in dedicated theaters. The first vaudeville performer was Tony Pastor, a singer in concert saloons during the Civil War who experimented with different formats into the 1870s. In 1881 he moved his operations to a theater in Tammany Hall (near Union Square in the heart of the theater district), where he reworked old variety shows to preserve their vitality but removed what he called their "cigar-smoking and beer-drinking accompaniment." Soon his audiences ranged from newsboys to middle-class women and leaders of Tammany Hall.

From the 1880s to the 1920s theaters were grand and alcohol was usually banned, contributing to vaudeville being the most popular form of theater in the United States. It attracted performers who worked in other forms of popular entertainment, including variety shows, minstrelsy, melodrama, the street performances of the Bowery, and eventually motion pictures and television; material was adapted for vaudeville from these genres (Pastor was especially influenced by the theater of the Bowery), and music was often provided by musicians from Tin Pan Alley. Managers of vaudeville theaters cultivated audiences that included men and women, native-born and immigrant, from the working class and the middle class, but they were often segregated racially, as was typical of the era. B. F. Keith and E. F. Albee, circus managers from New England, were among the first to plan nationwide tours for which they helped to develop a particularly wholesome form of vaudeville. They opened the first of their many theaters in the city on Union Square in 1893 and in 1900 established a national booking system with headquarters in the city. Despite strikes by performers in a union called the White Rats in 1900 and 1916–17, Keith's office eventually controlled nearly all the most highly sought-after bookings. Times Square became the heart of vaudeville in the city in 1913 after Albee opened the Palace Theatre at 47th Street and Seventh Avenue; the theater soon became the center of Keith's operations, which ran a booking office upstairs.

At this time New York City was the national center of vaudeville. Links from the city to transport lines across the country were useful in planning national tours, and many booking agencies made their headquarters in the city, which was often the first stop on the tours. There were vaudeville theaters in virtually every part of the city, ranging from celebrated ones in Times Square, to those catering to an entire borough (the Royal Theater and the National Theatre in an area known as the Hub in the Bronx), to small theaters in residential neighborhoods (Loew's Avenue B Theatre on the Lower East Side and Fox's Folly Theatre in Williamsburg). A "subway circuit" took shape along subway lines to the outskirts of the city and ran from the Fordham Theatre (owned by Keith) in the Bronx to the Albee Theatre and other points in Brooklyn. Acts by nationally known performers (or their imitators) could tour within the city for weeks. Many performers including Eddie Cantor and Sophie Tucker lived in the city and began their careers singing and dancing on street corners and on the stages of minor theaters. The chances of becoming successful in vaudeville were slim, but performers were attracted by the possibility of achieving national renown and earning high salaries (as much as $2500 a week in 1915). Many who became successful were immigrants and members of the working class.

Mainstream culture was changed immensely by vaudeville, which offered a commercial venue for ethnic cultural forms. Offerings were broad and included such songs as "My Yiddisha Mama" (performed by Tucker) and "Maggie Cline, the Irish Queen." Performances before mixed audiences of songs like "Cyclonic Eva Tanguay" and demonstrations of strength by Eugene Sandow and others helped to break down Victorian notions of propriety. African American performers such as Eubie Blake and Bert Williams used vaudeville bookings to build their careers and their artistic influence and paved an important path in the entertainment industry.

With the onset of the Depression and the increasing popularity of sound motion pictures, the Palace became a movie house in 1932 and theatrical vaudeville in New York City ceased. Former vaudeville performers such as Groucho Marx, Fanny Brice, and James Cagney adapted their routines to musical theater, radio, film, and television.

Robert W. Snyder, *The Voice of the City: Vaudeville and Popular Culture in New York* (New York: Oxford University Press, 1989)

See also THEATER, §§4–5.

Robert W. Snyder

Vaux, Calvert (*b* London, 20 Sept 1824; *d* Brooklyn, 18 Nov 1895). Landscape designer and architect. He moved to the United States in 1850 to work with Andrew Jackson Downing, a collaboration that lasted until Downing's death in 1852. After moving to New York City in 1856, Vaux worked with Frederick Law Olmsted to win the city competition to design Central Park. The two would later design Prospect and Fort Greene parks. After this partnership ended in 1872 Vaux began his own architecture practice. An adherent of reformist ideas current among his contemporaries, he undertook commissions for the Metropolitan Museum of Art, the American Museum of Natural History (with Jacob Wrey Mould), the townhouse of Samuel J. Tilden in Gramercy Park, and several lodging houses and industrial schools for the Children's Aid Society. Vaux drowned under mysterious circumstances in Gravesend Bay in 1895. His book *Villas and Cottages* (1857) details an array of his domestic architecture and helped shape an ideal of American domesticity for decades.

Rick Beard

Vega, Bernardo (*b* Cayey, Puerto Rico, 14 Jan 1885; *d* San Juan, Puerto Rico, June 1965). Cigar worker (*tabaquero*), political activist, editor, writer. In 1899 he participated in the formation of La Federacion Libre de Trabajadores (the Free Federation of Workers), the first large-scale organization of the working class in Puerto Rico. In 1915 he became a charter member of La Socialista (the Socialist Club), which had been recently founded in his hometown of Cayey. In 1917 he carried this leftist perspective to New York City, where the dialectics of nationalism and socialism mingled with that of colonial liberation for a complex discourse that appeared in local Spanish newspapers and commentaries. From 1927 to 1931 he edited the weekly Spanish-language newspaper *El Grafico,* and in 1948 he led the Hispanic division of Henry A. Wallace's presidential campaign. In the 1950s Vega returned to Puerto Rico, where he led the island's independence movement. In the late 1940s Vega wrote his memoirs, *Memoirs of Bernardo Vega: A Contribution to the History of the Puerto Rican Community in New York,* but the book was not published until 1977.

Linda Delgado

Veiller, Lawrence (Turnure) (*b* Elizabeth, N.J., 7 Jan 1872; *d* New York City, 30 Aug 1959). Housing reformer. Soon after graduating from City College of New York, he became the most important figure in housing reform in the United States. An ardent critic of the dumbbell, or "old law," tenements that were built throughout the city after 1879, he led a campaign for a new tenement code in 1901 requiring that designs include an open court, thus providing more light and air to back rooms that had once opened onto narrow airshafts. As the deputy commissioner of the New York City Tenement House Department (1902–4) and secretary of the Tenement House Committee of Charity Organization (1900–1901), and as an organizer of the National Housing Association (1910) and its first director, he transformed the housing-reform movement from a series of local efforts into a national project managed by professionals. In 1921 he played an important role in drafting the Standard Zoning Law of the U.S. Department of Commerce, which with minor modifications was adopted by most communities during the following 10 years. Toward the end of his career Veiller was often criticized by younger experts for relying heavily on restrictive legislation rather than public action to ensure the quality of housing.

Roy Lubove, *The Progressives and the Slums: Tenement House Reform in New York City, 1890–1917* (Pittsburgh: University of Pittsburgh Press, 1962)

Stanley Buder

vendors. See STREET VENDORS.

Vereinigte Deutsche Gewerkschaften. See UNITED GERMAN TRADES.

Verplanck, Gulian C(rommelin) (*b* New York City, 6 Aug 1786; *d* New York City, 18 March 1870). Writer and political leader. Born to a wealthy family from the Hudson River

Valley, he graduated from Columbia College in 1801. For his role in the commencement riot of 1811 at Columbia he received a stiff fine in mayor's court from DeWitt Clinton, provoking him to write a number of satirical pieces on Clinton and his associates under the name Abimelech Coody. In 1818 Verplanck published "The Bucktail Bards," political satire aimed at Clinton, and he became well known for writing political pamphlets. He was also a biographer, literary critic, and student of religion and served in the state assembly (1820–23), the U.S. Congress (1825–33), and the state senate (1838–41). In 1834 he narrowly lost the first direct mayoral election, in which he ran as a Whig. Verplanck helped to form the Century Association and was its president from 1857 until 1864 when he was forced to step down because of his affiliation with the Copperheads.

Evan Cornog

Verrazano [Verrazzano]**, Giovanni da** (*b* Val di Greve, Italy, *ca* 1485; *d* ?West Indies, *ca* 1528). Navigator. On behalf of France he led an expedition to the northeastern coast of North America in 1524 trying to find the Northwest Passage to Asia; he traveled from Cape Fear in North Carolina to Cape Breton of Nova Scotia and was the first European known to sail into New York Harbor and Narragansett Bay. He made note of the Hudson River. He met native tribes such as the Narragansett and sailed along Staten Island, Long Island, and Block Island on the same voyage, claiming the territory he discovered for France. The Verrazano–Narrows bridge across the Narrows, where he lay anchor on his journey, was completed in 1964 and is named for him. In 1909 a bronze statue of him was dedicated at Battery Park after the city's Italian community, spurred by Carlo Barsotti, editor of *Il Progresso Italo-Americano,* contributed funds for its creation. It is believed that Verrazano was eaten by cannibals in the West Indies.

James E. Mooney, Henry B. Cooper

Verrazano–Narrows Bridge. Suspension bridge across the NARROWS between Staten Island and Brooklyn, opened in November 1964. It is named for the Italian explorer GIOVANNI DA VERRAZANO, who sailed into the bay in 1524, probably the first European to see New York Harbor. A bridge across the Narrows had been proposed for more than 80 years and planned for nearly 15 when construction began in September 1959. The project was put in motion by Robert Moses, chairman of the Triborough Bridge and Tunnel Authority, who overcame opposition that was particularly intense in the Bay Ridge section of Brooklyn because of the displacement of some 8000 residents. The bridge was the 66th in New York City over navigable waterways and the last of eight in the city designed by the Swiss engineer Othmar H. Ammann. Its towers are 623 feet (190 meters) tall and rest on steel and concrete caissons sunk into man-made islands of sand; the anchorages are concrete wedges more than 100 feet (30 meters) tall set into the ground at Fort Hamilton in Brooklyn and Fort Wadsworth in Staten Island. The roadway has two levels and is suspended from four steel-wire cables with a diameter of 36 inches (91 centimeters). Computers were used to calculate the stresses to which all parts of the bridge would be subjected while the roadbed sections were hoisted into place and anchored to the cables. On its opening day Moses called the bridge a "triumph of simplicity and restraint." In the following years it spurred considerable development in Staten Island. The toll plaza in Staten Island is the starting point for the New York City Marathon. By 2009 the bridge was being crossed each day by 200,000 vehicles, and it had become a commercial colossus, generating more than $1 million every 24 hours.

Sharon Reier, *The Bridges of New York* (New York: Quadrant, 1977)

Ellen Fletcher

vest pocket parks. Small parks, often built on vacant lots wedged between buildings. They became popular in New York City when open space became scarce in the 1960s. Many of the parks were developed with funds from the city, state, and federal governments and were used as parks only until the lots were built on. Often they were built at the urging of community groups and charitable organizations: examples include the Clinton Community Garden at 48th Street between Ninth and 10th avenues and the Dream Street Park at Lexington Avenue and 124th Street, a result of the efforts of the Creative Arts Workshop for Homeless Children. In a few cases private endowments for construction and maintenance gave rise to small parks that endured, such as Paley Park at 53rd Street between Fifth and Madison avenues, and Greenacre Park at 51st Street between Second and Third avenues. Vest pocket parks exist as sitting areas, community gardens, and playgrounds for neighborhoods that have little open space. The Liz Christie Garden at Houston Street and Second Avenue in Manhattan, which dates back to the early 1970s, is the oldest operating community garden in the city.

Jonathan Kuhn

Veterans Administration (VA) medical centers. Veterans honorably discharged from the armed forces receive medical care from three facilities in New York City operated by the Department of Veterans Affairs (formerly the Veterans Bureau, then the Veterans Administration, or VA). The Bronx VA Medical Center, opened in 1922 in an abandoned orphanage, moved in 1981 to a facility at 130 West Kingsbridge Road with 350 beds, including 120 beds in a skilled nursing unit. The Brooklyn VA Medical Center, originally the Manhattan Beach Veterans Administration Hospital, occupies a complex with 1000 beds that was built in 1950 at the southern end of Brooklyn facing the Narrows at Fort Hamilton. It also administers the VA Extended Care Center in St. Albans in Queens (opened in 1974), formerly the St. Albans Naval Hospital, which has 425 beds and offers skilled nursing and intermediate

Varrazano–Narrows Bridge, 2009

care. The facilities in the Bronx and Brooklyn conduct research and offer a range of services including dental care. The New York Department of Veterans Affairs Medical Center (1954) at First Avenue and 24th Street in Manhattan was one of 150 centers built by the Veterans Administration nationwide in the 1950s. It has 492 beds (a large addition was completed in the early 1990s), is affiliated with the New York University School of Medicine, and is recognized for its research. The center provides emergency surgery and other medical care, has one of the few units in the veterans' health care system for the treatment of AIDS, receives referrals for open-heart surgery from other centers throughout the Northeast, and has a strong rehabilitation program.

Sandra Opdycke

Veterans Affairs, U.S. Department of. For a discussion of hospitals maintained by this department and by its predecessor, the Veterans Administration, see VETERANS ADMINISTRATION (VA) MEDICAL CENTERS.

Viacom. Entertainment and communications firm formed in 1970 by the Columbia Broadcasting System (CBS) to comply with federal regulations preventing networks from owning cable television systems. Over the years the firm acquired such cable systems as Showtime/The Movie Network, Nickelodeon, and MTV, as well as television and radio stations. After a long takeover attempt by the investor Carl Icahn, the firm was bought in March 1987 by National Amusements, a chain of movie theaters owned by Sumner Redstone. Viacom in March 1994 acquired Paramount Communications along with one of its most valuable properties, the Madison Square Garden sports and entertainment complex (including the New York Knickerbockers and the New York Rangers), which it then resold in August of the same year for $1.1 billion. As of 2008 Viacom was based at 1515 Broadway in Times Square. Among its subsidiaries are the noted book publishers Macmillan and Simon and Schuster.

James Bradley

Victory Arch. Monument erected in 1919 at the urging of Mayor John F. Hylan to honor the city's war dead. Originally intended as a patriotic gesture in support of U.S. involvement in World War I, it remained unfinished at the time of the November 1918 armistice and was reenvisioned as a victory monument. It stood on a site straddling Fifth Avenue at 24th Street formerly occupied by the Dewey Arch, by which it was partly inspired. The 100-foot-tall (30-meter-tall) memorial was modeled after the tripartite Arch of Constantine in Rome and included an honor court with allegorical figures of Peace, Justice, Power, and Wisdom. Relief panels commemorated American military, industrial, service, and patriotic contributions to the war. Architect Thomas Hastings used wood and plaster for the memorial, assuming that the arch would subsequently be rebuilt in a more permanent form. Arguments over who was to receive the commission and who was to pay for it doomed completion of the project, and the arch was eventually razed.

Kenneth T. Jackson

Viele, Egbert Ludoricus (*b* Waterford, N.Y., 17 June 1825; *d* New York City, 22 April 1902). Cartographer and civil engineer. After graduating from the U.S. Military Academy and serving in the Mexican War, he drafted plans for Central Park. The Greensward plan of Frederick Law Olmsted and Calvert Vaux was chosen through a competition, but Viele contended that the others had copied his own plans for the park. He also filed suit for compensation for the plans he was hired to create before the competition was announced. He was awarded $8000. Despite this rocky start, Viele was appointed the chief engineer for the park's construction in 1856. He also engineered Prospect Park in Brooklyn, another project of Olmsted and Vaux. He joined New York's Seventh Regiment and served as the captain of the Engineer Corps during the Civil War. During the war he authored *Handbook for Active Service,* a volume that was popular with both Confederate and Union soldiers. After resigning from military service in 1863, he moved back to New York City. He was appointed president of the city's parks department in 1884, and also served in the U.S. Congress. He mapped the city's natural waterways and soil deposits in great detail. The Viele Map, published in 1874, is still referenced by engineers and architects today.

Penelope Gelwicks

Egbert L. Viele

Viking Press. Firm of book publishers formed in 1925 by Harold K. Guinzburg and George S. Oppenheim at 30 Irving Place. It developed a reputation for both literary excellence and distinction in design, benefiting especially from the expertise and distinguished list that it acquired by taking over B. W. Huebsch's imprint during its first year. Among the writers whom it published were D. H. Lawrence, John Steinbeck (*The Grapes of Wrath,* 1939), James Joyce (first American edition of *Finnegans Wake,* 1939), Lillian Hellman, Arthur Miller (*Death of a Salesman,* 1949), Rebecca West, Malcolm Cowley, and Saul Bellow. In 1975 the firm was acquired by Penguin Books, which retained Viking as a hardcover imprint. Viking Penguin is at 375 Hudson Street in Manhattan.

See also BOOK PUBLISHING.

Eileen K. Cheng

Village Gate. Nightclub. For 36 years it operated as a two-level nightclub at the corner of Bleecker and Thompson streets in Greenwich Village. Art D'Lugoff opened the club in 1958 in the basement of 160 Bleecker Street. Patrons entered the original basement club through a large metal gate on Thompson Street, which gave the venue its name. D'Lugoff later purchased the street and upper levels of the building, which became known as the Terrace Café and the Top of the Gate, respectively. Countless jazz, folk, rock and roll, poetry, and comedy greats gave debuts and seminal performances on all levels of the venue, including Nina Simone, Thelonious Monk, Miles Davis, Stan Getz, Art Blakey, Aretha Franklin, The Byrds, Allen Ginsberg, Woody Allen, Bill Cosby, and "National Lampoon's Lemmings," a comedic musical revue that featured John Belushi, Chevy Chase, and Christopher Guest. Because of rising costs, the loss of a preferential rent rate, and the unwillingness of big stars to play small venues, the Village Gate shut down in 1994. A CVS Pharmacy opened in the lower level that same year, and in 2008 a new music venue called Le Poisson Rouge opened in the upper level. The old Village Gate sign remains.

Breanne Scanlon

Village Vanguard. Jazz club. Located at 178 Seventh Avenue South between West 11th Street and Waverly Place in Greenwich Village, it was originally opened on Charles Street by Max Gordon (1903–89), a Lithuanian immigrant, as a night club. In 1957 the Vanguard adopted an all-jazz policy. The club has pristine acoustics because of its unusual triangular shape. Its unpretentious atmosphere in a small basement room creates an intimate ambience conducive to improvisation. The club attracted the best jazz artists of the time, including Miles Davis and Charles Mingus.

It has also been the recording site for more than 100 jazz titles, including classic albums by Sonny Rollins, Bill Evans, and John Coltrane. While many jazz clubs closed as jazz began to wane in popularity during the 1960s, the Vanguard continued to thrive, becoming a venue for the avant-garde. The Vanguard Jazz Orchestra, led for 25 years by Thad Jones and Mel Lewis, performed at the Vanguard every Monday night from 1966 to 2008. Gordon remained the owner of the club until his death, when his wife, Lorraine Gordon, took over the club's management.

Max Gordon, *Live at the Village Vanguard* (New York: St. Martin's, 1980)

Kathy J. Ogren, Nicholas Kelly

Village Voice. Weekly newspaper launched on 26 October 1955 by the publisher Ed Francher along with his editor Dan Wolf, the columnist Norman Mailer, and the writer John Wilcox; it occupied offices on University Place in Greenwich Village. Intended as a countercultural response to the "vulgarities of McCarthyism," it covered life in Greenwich Village, reformist politics in New York City, the civil rights and peace movements, and culture, especially Off-Broadway theater and the avant-garde. Jules Feiffer joined the staff in 1956 as its first editorial cartoonist. The *Voice* attracted a national readership as an exponent of "new journalism," which eschewed any pretense of journalistic objectivity and emphasized advocacy reporting. In the late 1960s it became an innovative leader in investigative journalism, particularly through the work of Jack Newfield, who revealed corruption among officials in city government and executives; this coverage made the *Voice* an important force in electoral and reform politics. It also covered the arts, including film reviews by Andrew Sarris and opinion pieces by such writers as Nat Hentoff. The newspaper was acquired successively by Carter Burden (1970), Clay Felker, publisher of *New York* (1974), Rupert Murdoch (1977), and Leonard Stern (1985, for more than $55 million). In the 1980s it moved its offices to Broadway near Union Square. The *Voice Literary Supplement,* an insert launched in 1981 and published 10 times a year, was made available by subscription in 1989. Among those who have contributed to the *Voice* are the writers Alexander Cockburn, Richard Goldstein, Eliot Fremont-Smith, Erika Munk, Ellen Willis, Joe Conason, and James Ridgeway and the cartoonists Mark Alan Stamaty and Stan Mack. In 1991 the newspaper moved its offices to 33 Cooper Square. In the early twenty-first century its circulation was about 250,000.

Kevin Michael McAuliffe, *The Great American Newspaper: The Rise and Fall of the "Village Voice"* (New York: Charles Scribner's Sons, 1978)

Marjorie Harrison

Villard, Oswald Garrison (*b* Wiesbaden, Germany, 13 March 1872; *d* New York City, 1 Oct 1949). Newspaper publisher and civil rights advocate. Grandson of abolitionist William Lloyd Garrison, founder of the *Liberator,* and son of Henry Villard, a newspaperman turned railroad owner. In 1881 he bought the *New York Evening Post* and the *Nation.* When his son joined the *Post* in 1897, he resolved to make both newspapers worthy followers of the *Liberator,* and under his leadership in the early twentieth century they became staunch advocates of civil rights. In 1909 he played an important role in forming the National Association for the Advancement of Colored People: he wrote the call for the National Negro Conference held in New York City on 31 May and 1 June, where the plans for a permanent organization were formulated. With Rollo Ogden, editorial page editor of the *Post,* he made the newspaper progressive and anti-imperialist. During World War I he was attacked for being insufficiently anti-German. When the war ended, he sold the *Post,* which was in debt, and turned his attention to the *Nation,* which he continued to edit until his retirement in 1933. Villard was a member of the Cosmopolitan Club in New York City, an interracial group. A consistent pacifist, in later years he opposed World War II. Villard's published writings include *Some Newspapers and Newspaper-Men* (1923), *Prophets True and False* (1928), *Our Military Chaos* (1939), and a biography of John Brown (1943).

Michael Green

Villard houses. Six brownstone houses built in 1882–83 on property that was purchased by the railroad magnate Henry Villard on Madison Avenue between 50th and 51st streets. The architect Joseph M. Wells of McKim, Mead and White skillfully organized the houses around a central courtyard to create the appearance of an Italian palazzo. Villard reserved the largest house for himself, but his residency was cut short when he declared bankruptcy in 1883 and the house was purchased by Whitelaw Reid. In 1980 the property was sold to Harry B. Helmsley, who preserved some of the interiors as part of the Helmsley Palace Hotel. The northern wing of the courtyard, not part of the hotel, is the home of the Municipal Art Society, the Architectural League, and an urban bookstore.

William C. Shopsin, *The Villard Houses* (New York: Viking, 1980)

Elliott B. Nixon

Vincent Astor Foundation. Charitable organization formed in 1948 by Vincent Astor (1891–1959). During his lifetime the foundation annually contributed about $175,000 to such organizations as the Astor Home for Children in Rhinebeck, New York; the New York Public Library; and New York Hospital. His widow, Brooke Astor, became the head of the foundation in 1960. Under her leadership the foundation focused exclusively on making donations in New York City in such diverse fields as animal care, botanical gardens, community economic development, health care, homelessness, housing development, historic preservation and church renovation, vocational education, and zoos. Between 1969 and 1985 the foundation's annual giving averaged $7 million and included grants from its principal, which surpassed $100 million in 1972 but was reduced to $20 million by 1985, when the trustees agreed to make grants only from the foundation's income and to focus on projects in literacy and housing. The foundation had authorized grants totaling approximately $200 million when it closed in 1997.

Brooke Astor, *Twenty-five Years of Giving in New York: The Vincent Astor Foundation* (New York: Vincent Astor Foundation, 1985)

Kenneth W. Rose

Vinegar Hill (i). Name formerly applied to New Brighton.

Vinegar Hill (ii). Neighborhood in northwestern Brooklyn (2009 pop. *ca* 5000), bounded to the north by the East River, to the east by the Brooklyn Navy Yard, to the south by Sands Street, and to the west by Bridge Street; it was once called Irishtown. A large tract of land was bought from the Sands brothers in 1800 by John Jackson, who named part of it Vinegar Hill after the battle waged in 1798 during the Irish Revolution. The neighborhood was only eight square blocks. Sands Street, the main artery, was adjacent to the navy yard and in its heyday was lined with bars, gambling dens, and brothels. During World War II industries in the neighborhood prospered. The population was working class and lived in nineteenth-century row houses. After the war major industrial firms in the area included Brillo (makers of steel wool) and Boorum and Pease. The Commandant's House, a city, state, and National Historic Landmark and once home to Commander Matthew C. Perry, was built in 1805. It housed the commandant of the Brooklyn Navy Yard from 1806 until its conversion to a private residence in 1966, when the navy yard was decommissioned. In the twenty-first century Vinegar Hill remains a quaint neighborhood with few stores or restaurants.

Stephen Weinstein

Viñoly, Rafael (*b* Montevideo, Uruguay, 1944). Architect. By age 20 he was a founding partner of Estudio de Arquitectura, one of the largest design studios in Latin America.

In 1978 he moved to the United States and briefly guest-lectured at Harvard University Graduate School of Design. A year later he moved to New York City where in 1983 he founded Rafael Viñoly Architects PC, with offices also in London and Los Angeles. His first big project in the city was the John Jay College of Criminal Justice (1988), and he later worked on projects like Jazz at Lincoln Center (2004) and the Brooklyn Children's Museum (2008). A recipient of several prestigious awards for his international projects, Viñoly was chosen in 2008 to design the New York University campus in Abu Dhabi to be opened in 2012.

Cecilia Magnusson

Visiting Nurse Service of New York [VNSNY]. Voluntary home care agency. The largest not-for-profit home care agency in the United States, it was formed in 1944 when the nursing services of the Henry Street Settlement acquired independent status and moved to 107 East 70th Street. Since that time, VNSNY has provided a variety of services for the acute and chronically ill, mothers and newborns, children and adolescents, mentally ill, hospice patients, and the elderly in their homes. Continuing in its founder Lillian Wald's tradition of social reform and political activism, the VNSNY's Center for Home Care Policy and Research was created in 1993. In 2005, with a budget of more than $900 million, the staff of 2450 nurses made more than two million home visits to more than 115,000 people.

Healing at Home: Visiting Nurse Service of New York, 1893–1993 (New York: Visiting Nurse Service of New York, 1993)

Karen Buhler-Wilkerson

Vitagraph Company. Open-air, rooftop motion picture studio opened in 1898 by American Vitagraph in the Morse Building at 140 Nassau Street. The film *Burglar on the Roof* was produced at the studio during its first year. In 1900 the company moved its offices to 110–16 Nassau Street and then opened a glass-enclosed studio in 1906 at 15th Street and Locust Avenue in Flatbush. Under the ownership of J. Stuart Blackton, Albert E. Smith, and William Rock, the facilities expanded rapidly between 1906 and 1915. Warner Brothers purchased American Vitagraph in 1925 and used the studio for many of its Vitaphone short subjects before closing it in 1939; it continued to process film there even after the National Broadcasting Company (NBC) bought the studio in 1952 and began using it for color television broadcasts. Interiors of Elia Kazan's *On the Waterfront* (1954) were shot in the studio. Part of the facility was bought by Yeshiva University in 1962, although NBC continued to use sections of it into the 1990s.

Charles Musser

Vladeck, Baruch Charney [Charney, Baruch] (*b* Dukora, Belarus, 1886; *d* New York City, 1938). Journalist and public official. Well known as a revolutionary orator in Russia, he arrived in the United States in 1908 and settled permanently in New York City in 1916. He worked first as the city editor and from 1918 as the general manager of the *Jewish Daily Forward.* From 1917 to 1921 he served on the Board of Aldermen, representing Williamsburg as a socialist. He was the host of a weekly radio program that the *Forward* had on WEVD and led the Jewish Labor Committee from its founding in 1934; in the same year he was appointed to the New York City Housing Authority. In 1937 he was elected as a candidate of the American Labor Party to the City Council, where he led the coalition supporting Mayor Fiorello H. La Guardia. In recognition of his interest in public housing, a housing project on the Lower East Side bears his name.

Daniel Soyer

Vogue. Weekly magazine launched in 1892 by Arthur Turnure and Harry McVickar. Intended for the elite of New York City, it was first edited by Josephine Redding; McVickar left shortly after 1900. The magazine increasingly emphasized fashion, and circulation rose steadily, reaching 25,000 by 1907. During the same year Turnure died and Marie Harrison, his sister-in-law, became the editor. In 1909 the magazine was bought by Condé Nast. Under Edna Woolman Chase from 1914 it became the leading publication in fashion, known for its sleek look. In addition to news about fashion it published innovative art and photography and experimented with new color techniques, types of paper, and methods of reproduction. In 1936 it absorbed Nast's unprofitable magazine *Vanity Fair,* and Frank Crowninshield, a former editor of *Vanity Fair,* joined its staff. Jessica Daves succeeded Chase in 1948, and after Nast's company became part of Advance Publications (led by S. I. Newhouse) Diana Vreeland left *Harper's Bazaar* to take over as the editor in 1962. She herself was succeeded in 1971 by Grace Mirabella, who added features about fashion for working women and saw circulation rise to more than 1.2 million, which is still the level in the early twenty-first century. In 1988 S. I. Newhouse, Jr., appointed Anna Wintour as the editor of the magazine; she set out to reach a younger audience. In 2009 the documentary film *The September Issue* presented an insider's view of Wintour and others working on the September 2007 issue of the U.S. edition of *Vogue* (at the time, the largest issue ever published, with more than 800 pages). In the twenty-first century the magazine was published in 19 countries, with circulation of about 1.3 million.

Caroline Seebohm, *The Man Who Was Vogue: The Life and Times of Condé Nast* (New York: Viking, 1982); Norberto Angeletti and Alberto Oliva, *In Vogue: The Illustrated History of the World's Most Famous Fashion Magazine* (New York: Rizzoli, 2006)

Mary Ellen Zuckerman

Voorhees Technical Institute. Private postsecondary school formed in 1881 as the New York Trade School by the architect Richard T. Auchmuty (1831–93). Specializing at first in the building and mechanical trades, it benefited from the financial support of Auchmuty and J. P. Morgan and from a charter granted by the state legislature in 1892; by 1900 it was able to expand its offerings to include blacksmithing, tailoring, tinsmithing, gas fitting, printing, and electrical engineering. After World War I the most popular courses were in automobile mechanics, plumbing and heating, electrical engineering, and sheet metal work. The school moved to Second Avenue between 66th and 67th streets in 1930 and added new programs in air conditioning and lithography. Veterans of World War II brought enrollment to a peak of 4106 in 1949. In 1961 the school began offering associate degrees and changed its name in honor of the industrialist and trustee Enders M. Voorhees. It moved to 450 West 41st Street in 1963. After discontinuing its apprenticeship program in the following year, it was absorbed in 1971 by the New York City Community College of Applied Arts and Sciences, which maintained the campus until 1987 and in the same year gave the name Voorhees Hall to its own engineering technology building at 186 Jay Street in Brooklyn.

Marc Ferris

Vorse (O'Brien), Mary Heaton (*b* New York City, 11 Oct 1874: *d* Provincetown, Mass., 14 June 1966). Journalist and feminist. One of a number of radical authors attracted to the Greenwich Village of the early 1900s, Vorse published her first novel, *The Breaking-In of a Yachtsman's Wife,* in 1908. A member of the Liberal Club and Heterodoxy Club, an early feminist organization, Vorse became known as one of the best labor journalists of her time, writing on child and general labor issues and infant mortality. In New York City, she wrote for *The Masses,* where she served as an editor until its closing in 1918; she also wrote for the *New Masses,* the *New Republic, Harper's,* and other publications. Vorse wrote 18 works of fiction, which were widely read at the time. An active member of the woman suffrage movement, Vorse was influential in the founding of the Woman's Peace Party in 1915. In the same year she was one of the founding members of the Provincetown Players, a group of radical poets and playwrights whose work centered around Greenwich Village.

Nathan Morgante

Vreeland [née Dalziel], **Diana** (*b* Paris, *ca* 1905; *d* New York City, 22 Aug 1989). Fashion editor and socialite. She moved to New York City with her family at the beginning of World War I and married Reed Vreeland at St. Thomas Church on 1 March 1924. From 1936 she wrote a fashion column called "Why Don't You?" for *Harper's Bazaar,* and she was the fashion editor of the magazine from 1937 to 1962. She and her husband mixed in the highest social circles, and she was well known for hosting parties in her red-themed apartment at 550 Park Avenue, where she entertained friends that included Cole Porter, Andy Warhol, Oscar de la Renta, and Jacqueline Onassis. She exerted a profound influence on American fashion as the editor of *Vogue* from 1962 to 1971 and as a consultant to the Costume Institute of the Metropolitan Museum of Art from 1971 to 1989. She wrote her autobiography, *D.V.,* in 1984. She is considered as one of the inspirations for Lauren Weisberger's best-selling 2003 novel *The Devil Wears Prada* and Meryl Streep's character in the 2006 film.

Caroline Rennolds Milbank

WABC. Radio station. It began broadcasting as WJZ in October 1921 from Newark, New Jersey, under the auspices of Westinghouse; within a few months it opened a studio at the Waldorf–Astoria in Manhattan. In 1924 the station was purchased by the Radio Corporation of America and moved to Aeolian Hall on 42nd Street, from where it broadcast news, entertainment, sports, and coverage of political events, including the Democratic National Convention of 1924. When the National Broadcasting Company was formed in 1926, WJZ became the flagship station for its Blue Network. It was acquired in 1943 by Edward J. Noble and renamed WABC. When rock and roll became popular in the 1960s, WABC was known as an innovator, in its brand of programming known as "top 40," characterized by a limited playlist (consisting only of the 40 best-selling records); and in its staff of disc jockeys whom the station heavily advertised as "personalities," its frequent contests and promotions, and its policy of broadcasting selections requested by listeners (mostly teenagers). By 1968 the station had captured 25 percent of the radio audience in the metropolitan area, a huge share in a highly competitive market. Its best-known disc jockey was perhaps Bruce Morrow, known as Cousin Brucie. Competition from stations on the FM band prompted a change to an all-talk format in February 1982. Since then, WABC has often been accused of a conservative bias in its commentators, though the station maintains that its shows are driven by ratings, not a political agenda. WABC broadcasts at a frequency of 770 kHz.

Erik Barnouw, *The Tower of Babel: A History of Broadcasting in the United States* (New York: Oxford University Press, 1966); Bruce Morrow and Laura Baudo, *Cousin Brucie: My Life in Rock 'n Roll Radio* (New York: William Morrow, 1987)

JillEllyn Riley, Rachel Sawyer

Wadleigh High School. Secondary school opened in 1897 as Girls' High School on East 12th Street; the first public high school for girls in Manhattan. It took its current name in 1900 to honor Lydia F. Wadleigh (?1818–88), the superintendent of Normal College (later Hunter College) and an advocate of public schools for girls. In 1902 Wadleigh High School moved to 114th Street west of Seventh Avenue, where it remained until it closed in 1954. In the early twenty-first century the building was occupied by Wadleigh Secondary School for Performing and Visual Arts.

Erica Judge

Wagner, Robert F(erdinand) (Bobby) (*b* New York City, 6 Jan 1944; *d* San Antonio, Tex., 15 Nov 1993). Public official. Son of Mayor Robert F. Wagner (ii) and grandson of Senator Robert F. Wagner (i), he was educated at Harvard College (BA 1965) and Princeton University (MPA 1969). He was a member of the City Council (1973–77), and from 1977 to 1984, via appointments by Mayor Edward Koch, he served as chairman of the City Planning Commission and then as deputy mayor for policy (and chairman, Health and Hospitals Corporation). From 1986 to 1989 he was president of the New York City Board of Education. After leaving government service in 1989, he was vice chairman of Louis Harris Research, chairman of the Citizens Union, and an adjunct professor at Columbia University.

Jameson W. Doig

Wagner, Robert F(erdinand) (i) (*b* Nastätten, Germany, 8 June 1877; *d* New York City, 5 May 1953). Senator, father of Robert F. Wagner (ii). He immigrated to the United States and settled in New York City in 1886. His political career began in Yorkville, where he joined the Tammany Society. He won election to the state assembly in 1904 and the state senate in 1908 and was a justice of the New York State Supreme Court from 1918 to 1926. After gaining the support of Tammany Hall, he was elected to the U.S. Senate in 1926. In office he became known as a leading spokesman for urban liberalism and the New Deal: he sponsored the National Labor Relations Act of 1935, the Social Security Act of 1935, and the Public Housing Act of 1937.

See also Civil service unions and Factory Investigating Commission.

Chris McNickle

Wagner, Robert F(erdinand) (ii) (*b* New York City, 20 April 1910; *d* New York City, 12 Feb 1991). Mayor, son of Robert F. Wagner (i) and father of Robert F. "Bobby" Wagner. He graduated from Yale College, Yale Law School, and Harvard Business School and was elected to the state assembly (1938–41), resigning to join the Army Air Corps and serve in North Africa during World War II. Under Mayor William O'Dwyer he served as tax commissioner (1945–47) and commissioner of housing and buildings (1947–49). He was elected borough president of Manhattan (1950–53) on the Democratic and Liberal lines, and in 1953 he was elected mayor of New York City as a Democrat, winning reelection in 1957 by a landslide after an unsuccessful campaign for the U.S. Senate in 1956 against Jacob K. Javits. In 1961 Democratic officials opposed his reelection after he split with Carmine DeSapio, leader of Tammany Hall; but with support from Herbert H. Lehman, Eleanor Roosevelt, and other reformers, he won a decisive victory in the Democratic primary against Arthur Levitt and then won the general election against his Republican opponent, Louis Lefkowitz. His wife, Susan Edwards Wagner, died during his third term, and citing the claims on him of his sons he declined to seek a fourth term. In 1969 he ran for mayor again, narrowly losing the Democratic nomination to Mario Procaccino in a four-way primary.

Robert F. Wagner (ii), 1954

As mayor Wagner launched the largest municipal public housing program in the nation and authorized city workers to establish unions with formal powers. He prided himself on his commitment to everyday people, appointed blacks and Puerto Ricans to senior municipal positions, approved local legislation forbidding racial discrimination in housing (1957), and installed the first black Democratic Party leader in New York City (J. Raymond Jones, 1964). Critics accused him of indecisiveness; supporters applauded his subtle effectiveness and his unusual ability to forge consensus on controversial issues.

Chris McNickle, *To Be Mayor of New York* (New York: Columbia University Press, 1993)

Chris McNickle

Wagner College. Private four-year liberal arts college in Staten Island, on a wooded campus of 86 acres (35 hectares) atop Grymes Hill and overlooking New York Harbor. It was founded in Rochester, New York, in 1883 as the Rochester Lutheran Proseminary and was associated with the Evangelical Lutheran Church in America. In 1884 the college was refounded as Wagner Memorial Lutheran College. Owing in part to the influence of Frederic Sutter, a prominent German Lutheran pastor in Staten Island from 1907 to 1971, it moved in 1918 to the Cunard estate in Staten Island and was rededicated in honor of George Wagner, whose father helped to finance the first campus. In its early years at the new location the college was a six-year German gymnasium with 16 students and one professor, which prepared young men for a bilingual German-English ministry. Women were first admitted in 1933. The school was renamed Wagner Lutheran College in 1952 and retained its Lutheran affiliation into the twenty-first century. In 1959 it took its current name as an indication of its desire to be a liberal arts college open to the general public. Wagner began recruiting more aggressively in the 1980s and undertook improvements in its computer and athletic facilities. In the early twenty-first century Wagner enrolled about 2000 undergraduate students and offered programs in the arts, business, literature, law, finance, and the health professions; about 300 students were enrolled in graduate programs in business, nursing, education, and bacteriology. The campus architecture is an eclectic blend of neo-Gothic halls, mansions, cottages, and modern buildings.

Miriam Zeller Cross, "Brief History of Wagner Lutheran College" (unpubd ms, New York Public Library, St. George branch)

Howard R. Weiner

waiters. Until the early nineteenth century waiters in New York Cit usually worked as specialized servants in rich households or in inns and taverns that also ran on a household scale. But before even the Civil War, Delmonico's, Astor House, Howard House, and the St. Nicholas, Metropolitan, and Fifth Avenue Hotels had scores, even hundreds, of employees on staff. At the ends of their shifts, many of these waiters went across town to working-class saloons and neighborhoods.

Unlike other members of the working class, waiters retained personal connections to customers, acting stately, buffoonish, casually rude, sexual, or invisible according to customers' tastes. These tastes shifted over time; for example, minstrel-like black waiters slowly fell out of favor over the course of the twentieth century, and sexy white female waiters gained popularity. Rituals of service such as uncovering dishes, uncorking bottles, and receiving tips gave form to these relations, as did offers of preferred tables, friendlier smiles and conversation, better cuts of meat, and other extra services. Customers returned tips, business advice, and a level of respect often lacking in other service jobs. In the 1930s diners also began to lend their support to waiters' labor unions.

During the nineteenth century the Hotel and Restaurant Employees Union (HRE, then Hotel Employees and Restaurant Employers Union [HERE], and recently joined with the Union of Needletrades, Industrial, and Textile Employees Union [UNITE HERE]) was dominated by bartenders. Despite multicity strikes in 1853 and 1893, the majority of waiters in New York City and elsewhere remained unorganized, whether they worked for big companies or family restaurants. Through the early twentieth century unions affiliated with the Industrial Workers of the World organized competing unions with little lasting success; their combative approach made it difficult to cultivate support among customers. Victory came to New York City's waiters' unions in the 1930s after a spell of domination by the Dutch Schultz mob was broken by District Attorney Thomas E. Dewey. Communist organizers Jay Rubin and Michael Obermeier took control of several New York locals of hospitality workers, including Local 1, a sometimes corrupt union of waiters. In a series of strikes and negotiations that lasted into the 1940s, they forced most large, established employers of waiters to recognize their unions. HERE and its New York locals lost their communist affiliations soon afterward but remained a force in the labor movement. Through much of the twentieth century female waiters built particularly strong locals and used them as incubators of female leadership. At the same time, the huge number of restaurants in New York City, the traditional transience of waiters trying to break into other careers, and the questionable immigration status of many waiters made it difficult to maintain union dominance or protect the rights of workers. The struggle between union waiters and antiunion employers in the city continues.

Dorothy Sue Cobble, *Dishing It Out: Waitresses and Their Unions in the Twentieth Century* (Champaign: University of Illinois Press, 1992); Matthew Josephson, *Union House, Union Bar: The History of the Hotel and Restaurant Employees International Union, AFL-CIO* (New York: Random House, 1956); Daniel Levinson Wilk, "Cliff Dwellers: Modern Service in New York City, 1800–1945" (diss., Duke University, 2005)

Daniel Levinson Wilk

Wakefield. Neighborhood in north central Bronx, bounded by Westchester County, East 233rd Street, and the Bronx River. Initially part of Eastchester, the land was surveyed in 1855 and named for the estate where George Washington was born. Shortly after its incorporation as a village it was annexed to New York City in 1895. Growth hastened during the 1920s after the Interborough Rapid Transit extended its subway to White Plains Road, where a local shopping district soon took shape. Wakefield was one of the first areas of the Bronx to attract large numbers of immigrants after immigration was liberalized in 1965. Almost all the immigrants who settled there in the 1980s were blacks from the Caribbean, and of these nearly two-thirds were from Jamaica; many of the rest were from Guyana, the United Kingdom, and Antigua–Barbuda. The neighborhood is an ethnically diverse area of one- and two-family houses with some apartment buildings, as well as industrial facilities near the Bronx River.

Lloyd Ultan

Wald, Lillian (D.) (*b* Cincinnati, 10 March 1867; *d* Westport, Conn., 1 Sept 1940). Public health nurse, reformer, and settlement worker. Wald grew up in Rochester, New York, and moved in 1889 to New York City to attend the New York Hospital School of Nursing. In 1893 she and Mary Brewster, her comrade from nursing school, devised a plan to live in the Lower East Side and care for sick neighbors in their homes. Their expanding activities in the neighborhood led to the formation in 1895 of the Henry Street Settlement. As the first modern public health nurse, Wald was instrumental in securing reforms in health care, education, recreation, industry, and housing. She worked with the Metropolitan Life Insurance Company to establish a nationwide insurance payment scheme for home nursing care that provided more than one billion home visits between 1909 and 1952. In 1912 she was responsible for the creation of the first national nursing service in the United States, the American Red Cross Public Health Nursing Service. With Robert Hunter and J. G. Phelps Stokes she helped to form a state Child Labor Committee in 1902; she also helped found the New York Women's Trade Union League in 1903 and the Children's Bureau in the U.S. Department of Labor in 1912. Wald persuaded Columbia University in 1910 to establish the first university department of nursing. In 1933 she retired from the Henry Street Settlement and moved to her country home in Westport, Connecticut, where she died in 1940. In 1971 a bronze bust of Wald was placed in the Hall of Fame for Great Americans at New York University.

Marjorie N. Feld, *Lillian Wald: A Biography* (Chapel Hill: University of North Carolina Press, 2008)

Karen Buhler-Wilkerson

Walden School. Private elementary and secondary school opened in 1914 on East 60th Street as the Children's School by the progressive educator Margaret Naumburg. It changed its name in 1917 and moved to 88th Street and Central Park West in 1933. A student of Freudian psychology, Naumburg rejected formalist education and stressed the emotional side of learning and the need to unleash children's innate curiosity. Students at the school were encouraged to express themselves through the arts and to call teachers by their first names (a practice extended even to the prominent educators Lewis Mumford and Ernst Bloch). The school merged with the New Lincoln School in 1988 to form the New Walden–Lincoln School, which closed in 1991.

Alfonso J. Orsini

Waldensians. Adherents of a sect formed in the late twelfth century by dissident Catholics dedicated to apostolic poverty. New York City became the site in the 1890s of one of the few congregations formed by them in the United

States. Many of the Waldensian immigrants were of Italian origin. The congregation was formerly at 2 East 82nd Street in Manhattan, with denominational offices at the Interchurch Center. The Waldensians no longer have a space in the city.

Giorgio Tourn et al., *You Are My Witnesses: The Waldensians across Eight Hundred Years* (Turin: Claudiana, 1989)

Mary Elizabeth Brown

Waldheim. Name formerly applied to a development in downtown Flushing, bounded to the north by Sanford Avenue, to the east by Murray Street and 156th Street, to the south by Rose Street, and to the west by Kissena Boulevard. The area was once the site of Allan MacDonald's estate of 10 acres (4 hectares), which was bought in June 1903 by the Wallace–Appleton Company. The thick woods in the area inspired the name of the development, where the wealthy built large houses on lots of 40 by 100 feet (12 by 30 meters). In 1916 the developers declared bankruptcy, and the name ceased to be used because of anti-German sentiment.

Vincent Seyfried

Waldo, Samuel Lovett (*b* Windham, Conn., 6 April 1783; *d* New York City, 16 Feb 1861). Collaborator with William Jewett in the most successful portraiture partnership of the era. He trained at the Royal Academy and in 1809 settled in New York City. With Jewett, who became his apprentice in 1814 and his partner in 1817, he painted many portraits and attracted the support of wealthy patrons in New York City. The prolific association lasted until 1854, when Jewett retired to Bergen Hill, New Jersey.

Carrie Rebora Barratt

Waldorf=Astoria. Hotel that first opened on Fifth Avenue between 33rd and 34th streets and then later on Park Avenue. It originally consisted of two separate hotels designed by Henry J. Hardenbergh and erected by feuding cousins: the Waldorf (1893, 11 stories), built by William Waldorf Astor on the site of his father's mansion, and the Astoria (1897, 16 stories), built by John Jacob Astor IV on the site of his mother's mansion to the north. German Renaissance details unified the facades of the two buildings, and they functioned as a unit and were connected by a corridor, hence the original hyphen in the name Waldorf–Astoria, which later became the double hyphen. The opulently furnished hotel had about 1300 rooms and was the largest and grandest hotel in the city during the 1890s. Its 40 public rooms provided members of elite society with an alternative to holding social events in their own homes, and tourists and local residents often watched fashionable ladies pass through Peacock Alley, the corridor to the main entrance on 34th Street.

In 1929 the first Waldorf–Astoria was demolished to allow for construction of the Empire State Building, and the present 47-story building was built on the block between Park and Lexington avenues and between 49th and 50th streets. Designed by the firm of Schultze and Weaver in a restrained art deco style, it opened in 1931 and was the world's largest and tallest hotel at the time. In 1949 the Hilton Hotels Corporation assumed management of the hotel. Famous residents of the Waldorf=Astoria have included Herbert Hoover (after his presidency), Cole Porter, and Prince Rainier and Princess Grace of Monaco. It is the only hotel to have been the residence of three five-star generals: Dwight Eisenhower, Douglas MacArthur, and Omar Bradley. In 1982–88 the Waldorf=Astoria underwent extensive interior restoration; it was recognized as a New York City landmark in 1993. In the twenty-first century it contains three restaurants, five lounges, a fitness center and spa, 40 function rooms, and 1416 guest rooms, including 181 rooms in its upper section, a "boutique hotel" known as the Waldorf Towers. It remains one of the world's largest art deco buildings.

An enduring legacy of the original Waldorf Hotel is the Waldorf salad, a mixture of apples, grapes, celery, and mayonnaise (walnuts were added later) created between 1893 and 1896 by the hotel's maître d'hôtel, Oscar Tschirky.

James Remington McCarthy, *Peacock Alley: A Romance of the Waldorf-Astoria* (New York: Harper and Brothers, 1931); Henry B. Lent, *The Waldorf-Astoria: A Brief Chronicle of a Unique Institution Now Entering Its Fifth Decade* (New York: Hotel Waldorf-Astoria Corporation, 1934); Frank Crowninshield, ed., *The Unofficial Palace of New York: A Tribute to the Waldorf-Astoria* (New York: Hotel Waldorf-Astoria Corporation, 1939)

May N. Stone

Walker, James J(ohn) (*b* New York City, 19 June 1881; *d* New York City, 18 Nov 1946). Mayor. Born at 110 Leroy Street in Manhattan, Walker attended St. Joseph's Parochial School, St. Francis Xavier, and New York Law School. At the insistence of his father, a former district leader associated with Tammany Hall, he gave up a career as a songwriter to become a lawyer. He was elected to the state assembly (1909) and the state senate (1914). As the floor leader (1921–25) he oversaw the passage of Governor Alfred E. Smith's progressive legislation while personally promoting bills to legalize prizefighting and Sunday baseball. George W. Olvany, leader of Tammany Hall, and Edward J. Flynn, leader of the Bronx, chose Walker to oppose Mayor John F. Hylan in the election of 1925; meanwhile, the Democratic Party leaders of Brooklyn, Queens, and Staten Island remained loyal

James J. Walker

to Hylan. Walker won the ensuing primary with Smith's help and then swept the general election. Slim, elegant, and always ready with a wisecrack, "Jimmy" Walker became a symbol of the jazz age. During his first term he appointed an incorruptible police commissioner, unified the city hospitals, and argued successfully before the U.S. Supreme Court for the preservation of the nickel subway fare. While mayor he continued to live in his childhood home in Greenwich Village at 6 St. Luke's Place. In the mayoral election of 1929 he overwhelmingly defeated Fiorello H. La Guardia. He ultimately caused his own downfall by secretly accepting large sums of money from businessmen seeking municipal contracts and by conducting an affair with the actress Betty Compton, whom he later married. Investigations by Samuel Seabury (1930–32) resulted in formal charges against him and a hearing before Governor Franklin D. Roosevelt. On 1 September 1932 Walker resigned and left for Europe. He planned to seek vindication at the polls in November, but he lost the support of Tammany Hall after the Roman Catholic hierarchy intervened. He returned to New York City and lived at 132 East 72nd Street. In 1940 La Guardia appointed him an impartial arbitrator for the garment industry. About 1944 Walker moved to 120 East End Avenue, where he remained until the end of his life.

Gene Fowler, *Beau James: The Life and Times of Jimmy Walker* (New York: Viking, 1949)

Frank Vos

Walker, Madame C. J. [Breedlove, Sarah] (*b* Delta, La., 23 Dec 1867; *d* Irvington, N.Y., 25 May 1919). African American businesswoman. From 1905 she sold a beauty cream and hair products marketed to African American women; her business savvy helped her become one of the most prominent entrepreneurs at the time. She moved to New York City in 1914 and bought a Harlem townhouse at 108–10 West 136th Street, where she lived and operated a beauty salon. After her death the business was taken over by her daughter A'lelia Walker (1885–1931), who became one of the wealthiest women in Harlem and sponsored grand functions for musicians, actors, and writers on 136th Street, at 80 Edgecombe Avenue in Sugar Hill, and at her villa in suburban Westchester County; Langston Hughes wrote that A'lelia Walker's death, more than any other event, marked the end of the Harlem Renaissance.

Marc Ferris

Walker, Ralph Thomas (*b* Waterbury, Conn., 28 Nov 1889; *d* 17 Jan 1973). Architect. He served an apprenticeship, studied at the Massachusetts Institute of Technology, and worked in several places before moving in 1916 to New York City, where after World War I he joined the firm of McKenzie, Vorhees, and Gmelin (renamed Vorhees, Gmelin, and Walker in 1926). During the 1920s he designed monumental art deco skyscrapers in lower Manhattan for such clients as Western Union and the New York Telephone Company. Among his most important works were the Barclay-Vesey Building at 140 West Street (1926) and a tower for Irving Trust at 1 Wall Street with subtle faceting and a limestone exterior. A leading figure in architecture from the mid-1920s, he was a well-known writer on contemporary building, an editor of the architectural journal *Pencil Points,* and a president of the American Institute of Architects; the institute in 1957 named him Architect of the Century. After World War II he produced innovative designs for research centers and received large commissions from various institutions and corporations. Walker also developed a photographic process used in the motion-picture projection technique called Cinerama.

Carol Willis

walking tours. The earliest recorded walking tours in New York City occurred in the middle of the nineteenth century and amounted to little more than sensational excursions into the city's poorest quarters, particularly the Five Points. Well-known visitors often took such tours, including Charles Dickens during his visit to the city in 1842, an experience he described in his work *American Notes.* Abraham Lincoln, on his 1860 visit to speak at Cooper Union, also toured the Five Points, as did a group of senators in 1883 as part of an investigation into the status of American workers. In the early twentieth century the city's leading guide was Chuck Connors, a colorful character who led well-heeled customers, including Sir Thomas Lipton and members of the German royal family, on sensationalized "slumming" tours of Chinatown and the Lower East Side.

Walking tours of a more reputable sort, taking as their theme the architecture, history, and culture of New York City, became regular features in the mid-1950s. In 1955 the Municipal Art Society established the first series of walking tours, many of which were led by the architectural historian Henry Hope Reed. In 1975 architectural historian Gerard Wolfe published *New York: A Guide to the Metropolis; Walking Tours of Architecture and History,* a work which quickly became the leading guidebook for walking tours.

As interest in walking tours soared in the 1980s and 1990s—a growing number of institutions, including the Lower East Side Tenement Museum and the 92nd Street Young Men's Hebrew Association (YMHA), and private companies such as Big Onion Walking Tours and Joyce Gold Historical Tours, began offering an ever-widening range of tours. These included ethnic excursions on the Lower East Side, tours of pubs in Greenwich Village, nature walks in Central Park, and architectural studies of lobbies in midtown, as well as tours on themes such as ghosts, sex, food, crime, and politics. Steady increases in tourism and public interest in New York City history in the 1990s and 2000s led to continued growth of the industry. By 2009 more than 50 independent operators and companies and 20 institutions offered 100 public walking tours per week in warmer months, not to mention hundreds of excursions for private groups.

Seth Kamil and Eric Wakin, *The Big Onion Guide to New York City: Ten Historic Tours* (New York: New York University Press, 2002); Gerard R. Wolfe, *New York: Fifteen Walking Tours; An Architectural Guide to the Metropolis,* 3rd edn (New York: McGraw-Hill Professional, 2003)

Edward T. O'Donnell

Wallabout. An obsolete name for a neighborhood in northwestern Brooklyn, bounded to the north by the East River, to the east by Nostrand Avenue, to the south by Park Avenue, and to the west by Grand Avenue. Local Native Americans called the area Rennegackonck after a small creek that fed into the bay; it was later named Waal-bogt (meaning "bend in the inner harbor") by Dutch settlers. Walloons settled in 1637 on 335 acres (135 hectares) of land bought by Joris Jansen de Rapalje. During the American Revolution tens of thousands of Continental soldiers were imprisoned aboard the *Jersey* and dozens of other rotting British prison ships moored in Wallabout Bay; the conditions were horrible and thousands of soldiers died. In 1801 the federal government built the Brooklyn Navy Yard, of which a section at Flushing and Clinton avenues was sold to the City of Brooklyn in 1890 to form the Wallabout produce market; this remained in operation until the beginning of World War II. Most of the neighborhood is now occupied by the Brooklyn Navy Yard in the twenty-first century.

Edwin G. Burrows, *Forgotten Patriots: The Untold Story of American Prisoners during the Revolutionary War* (New York: Basic, 2008)

Stephen Weinstein

Wallace Foundation. Charitable organization with headquarters in New York City formed in 2003 when the DeWitt Wallace–Reader's Digest Fund and the Lila Wallace–Reader's Digest Fund were merged. It focuses on three areas: education, afterschool learning, and the arts. DeWitt and Lila Acheson Wallace, founders of the Readers Digest Association, established several family philanthropies in the 1950s that evolved into the current Wallace Foundation. In the early twenty-first century its offices were at 5 Penn Plaza.

Waller, Fats [Thomas Wright] (*b* New York City, 21 May 1904; *d* Kansas City, Mo., 15 Dec 1943). Pianist and composer. The son of an assistant pastor at the Abyssinian Baptist Church in Harlem, he began his career in 1918 by winning a talent contest at the Roosevelt Theatre. He performed at rent parties in the 1920s and commemorated their lively ambience in the song "The Joint Is Jumpin'" (1937); he was also a resident organist at the Lincoln Theatre and played in many nightclubs and at the Apollo Theater. He enjoyed considerable success on Broadway, notably with *Hot Chocolates* (1929). Waller recorded his own material and versions of other popular songs in a distinctive, humorous style. His best-known songs, many with lyrics by Andy Razaf, include "Ain't Misbehavin'" (1929), "Honeysuckle Rose" (1929), and "Jitterbug Waltz" (1942). From 1939 to the end of his life he lived at 147-15 Village Road in Jamaica, Queens. He died of pneumonia near Kansas City, Missouri, on a cross-country train trip.

Kathy J. Ogren

Wall Street. A small street in lower Manhattan that runs for less than a mile (1.6 kilometers) between Broadway and the East River along what was originally the northern edge of New Amsterdam. About 1653 a small wooden wall was built there as protection against possible attacks by the Indians, the New Englanders, or the British. The weak wall was never tested in battle before the British demolished it in 1699. The street itself later became famous when its junction with Broad Street became the site of the New York Stock Exchange. Wall Street eventually became synonymous with high finance, and the term came to refer not so much to the narrow street itself as to a type of business.

Wall Street, 2009

Wall Street has been the site of one major tragedy. On 16 September 1920, just as the bells of Trinity Church struck noon, a terrorist bomb exploded beside J. P. Morgan and Company at 23 Wall Street, killing 33 persons, mostly clerks and stenographers, and injuring more than 400. Those responsible were never identified, but scars from the explosion remain visible in the stonework of the Morgan Guaranty Trust Company. The attack on the World Trade Center of 11 September 2001 took place just a few blocks from the corner of Broadway and Wall Street. In the first decade of the twenty-first century, and especially after the global financial meltdown that began in 2008, Wall Street became even more famous around the world for its association with investment banking and sophisticated financial instruments that only experts could begin to understand. Much of the activity took place far from lower Manhattan, but the term "Wall Street" was continuously invoked as a synonym for high finance and excessive risk taking.

Kenneth T. Jackson

Wall Street Journal. Daily newspaper. Its forerunner was the *Customer's Afternoon Letter,* a bulletin about stock activity printed five days a week by Charles Henry Dow (1851–1902) and Edward Jones (1856–1920), who from 1882 operated a financial news service in a basement at 15 Wall Street. The current name dates to 1889. Initially the newspaper sold for 2 cents a copy, consisted of four pages, and published only railroad and crop conditions and Dow's index of leading stock prices. By the late 1890s the circulation reached 7000. In 1902 Dow sold the publication to C(larence) W(alker) Barron, who increased the length to 20 pages and added news correspondents in major cities. Circulation rose from 18,750 in 1920 to 52,000 in 1928 but fell to less than 30,000 during the Depression. Among the most influential writers was Bernard Kilgore (1908–67), a reporter who moved to New York City from San Francisco in 1932 and was known for describing complex economic issues in clear, simple terms (in several press conferences President Franklin D. Roosevelt referred reporters to his work). Under Kilgore's leadership in later years coverage was broadened, and in 1957 the *Journal* became the first national daily business newspaper with a circulation of more than half a million. Robert Feemster, who worked for the *Wall Street Journal* from 1933 to 1962, took a more aggressive approach to promotion. Strong leadership was provided by a number of managing editors, including William Henry Grimes and Warren Phillips, as well as Ed Coney, whose articles about corruption on Wall Street in the early 1960s were the first in the *Journal* to win a Pulitzer Prize; he also introduced the column "Heard on the Street," in which Daniel Dorfman investigated a speculative frenzy on Wall Street during the late 1960s. Under William F. Kirby, Fred Taylor, and Larry O'Donnell in the 1970s the newspaper placed its emphasis on the basics of business and economics. During Ronald Reagan's presidency the editors became the country's leading defenders of "supply-side" economics. In late 1982 a reporter, R. Foster Winans, leaked inside information from forthcoming columns to the stockbroker Peter Brant; Winans was sentenced to 18 months in prison but the *Journal* suffered no loss of credibility. By 1991 the *Wall Street Journal*'s circulation had grown to about two million. In addition to its main edition, it publishes the *Asian Wall Street Journal* (1976) and the *Wall Street Journal Europe* (1983). In 2007 News Corporation, headed by Rupert Murdoch, acquired the newspaper for $5 billion from the Bancroft family. The paper has undergone many changes, including the addition of photographs. In the twenty-first century worldwide circulation remained around two million and the *Journal* had about a million subscribers to its online newspaper.

Edward E. Scharff, *Worldly Power: The Making of the Wall Street Journal* (New York: Beaufort, 1986)

Walter Friedman

Walsh, Mike [Michael] (*b* Cork, Ireland, 4 May 1810; *d* New York City, 17 March 1859). Political leader. As the head of the Spartan Association in the Bowery and the editor of a radical newspaper, the *Subterranean,* he became a critic of capitalism and a defender of workers. After years as an insurgent in the Democratic Party, he was elected to the state assembly in 1846, where he unsettled his colleagues with his reform proposals and flamboyance. Elected to the U.S. Congress in 1852, he joined with southerners seeking to foster an alliance between slaveholding planters and northern workers. This decision along with his abiding racism undermined his radical populism. After leaving office in 1855 Walsh drank heavily and drifted in and out of New York City on various business ventures.

Sean Wilentz

Wanamaker's. Firm of retailers. Originally based in Philadelphia, it expanded to New York City in 1896 when John Wanamaker (1838–1922) purchased the six-story "Iron Palace" on Broadway between Ninth and 10th streets from Hilton, Hughes and Company, along with the stocks, stables, and goodwill of the late A. T. Stewart. Reopened as Wanamaker's on 16 November 1896, it was soon one of the leading department stores in the city. On 24 September 1907 Wanamaker dedicated an adjacent 14-story emporium (1905), which had 32 acres (13 hectares) of retail space, an auditorium with 1300 seats, and a huge restaurant. The two buildings were linked by the three-tiered "Bridge of Progress." Wanamaker's was sold in 1955 and destroyed by fire, just before its scheduled demolition, on 14 July 1956.

David B. Sicilia

W. and J. Sloane. Firm of carpet and furniture retailers. It began in 1853 as a modest shop selling carpets and "floor cloth," opened at 245 Broadway by William Sloane (1810–79), a young Scottish weaver who had moved to New York City in 1834. After building the business himself he was joined for about a decade by his brother John Sloane. William Sloane bought a fine collection of Oriental rugs during the Centennial Exposition in Philadelphia in 1876, sold them to wealthy customers in New York City, and moved his shop farther up Broadway. He later contracted with a weaving firm in India and was the only dealer in Oriental rugs in the United States to have his own East Asian supplier. After his death his nephew, also named William Sloane, took over the business and made it the best-known and most exclusive rug store in the city. In 1891 an upholstery and decorating department was added. The store followed the carriage trade uptown and maintained several addresses on Fifth Avenue; later it opened branches throughout the country. In 1985 Sloane's began to suffer financially and in the following year it closed its store in Manhattan.

Leslie Gourse

Warburg, Felix M(oritz) (*b* Hamburg, Germany, 14 Jan 1871; *d* New York City, 20 Oct 1937). Philanthropist; brother of Paul M. Warburg. Born to a leading Jewish family of bankers, he moved to the United States in 1894. He became a partner of Kuhn, Loeb and Company in 1897 and remained with the firm to the end of his life. He is best known for his support of more than 50 philanthropic organizations, including the Educational Alliance, the Henry Street Settlement, the Juilliard School, the New York Association for the Blind, the Symphony Society, and Teachers College. In 1917 he was a founder of the Federation for the Support of Jewish Philanthropies; he was its first president and later its chairman. Warburg was also a prominent spokesman for American Jewry. His mansion at 1109 Fifth Avenue is now the site of the Jewish Museum.

Ron Chernow, *The Warburgs: The Twentieth Century Odyssey of a Remarkable Jewish Family* (New York: Random House, 1993)

Theresa Collins

Warburg, Paul M(oritz) (*b* Hamburg, 10 Aug 1868; *d* New York City, 24 Jan 1932). Banker, brother of philanthropist Felix M. Warburg. He was simultaneously a partner of the firm of M. M. Warburg in Hamburg and the firm of Kuhn, Loeb and Company in New York City. In 1907 he began publishing his views on monetary reform, and in 1911 he helped to draft the plan for a central bank sponsored by Senator Nelson W. Aldrich. He became the vice chairman of the original Federal Reserve Board in 1914 but resigned in 1918 after one term so that his German origin would not be an issue affecting his reappointment. In 1921 he formed the International Acceptance Bank (merged in 1928 with the Bank of Manhattan Company). During the spring of 1929 Warburg often warned of an impending worldwide economic disaster because of excessive credit in the United States.

James P. Warburg, *The Long Road Home: The Autobiography of a Maverick* (Garden City, N.Y.: Doubleday, 1964); Ron Chernow, *The Warburgs: The Twentieth Century Odyssey of a Remarkable Jewish Family* (New York: Random House, 1993)

Theresa Collins

Ward, John Quincy Adams (*b* Urbana, Ohio, 29 June 1830; *d* New York City, 1 May 1910). Sculptor. While most of his peers studied neoclassical sculpture in Europe, he moved to New York City in 1861 to perfect his technique and obtain commissions for public monuments in bronze. His *Indian Hunter,* considered an exemplar of realism and artistic excellence, was the first statue by an American to be installed in Central Park (completed 1866, unveiled 1867); its success led to many other commissions in the city and elsewhere. Before 1890 he enjoyed a virtual monopoly on public commissions in the city, where his works included the Seventh Regiment Memorial (1869), *Shakespeare* (1870), and *The Pilgrim* (1884) for Central Park; *George Washington* (1883, Wall and Nassau streets); *William Earl Dodge* (1885, Bryant Park); *Memorial to Alexander Lyman Holley* (1889, Washington Square Park); *Horace Greeley* (1890, City Hall Park); *Henry Ward Beecher* (1891, Columbus Park, Brooklyn); and *Integrity Protecting the Works of Man* (1903, with Paul Wayland Bartlett), the pediment of the New York Stock Exchange. His work helped to establish a professional standard in sculpting and encouraged commissions in unprecedented numbers. He lived for many years at 119 West 52nd Street.

Lewis I. Sharp, *John Quincy Adams Ward, Dean of American Sculptors* (Newark: University of Delaware Press, 1985); Michele H. Bogart, *Public Sculpture and the Civic Ideal in New York City, 1890–1930* (Chicago: University of Chicago Press, 1989)

Michele H. Bogart

Ward Hill. Neighborhood in northeastern Staten Island, lying on a hill overlooking New York Harbor and New Jersey. It is named for Caleb T. Ward, who bought the hill in 1826 and in 1844 built a brick and stucco mansion in the Greek Revival style with a two-story portico and Ionic columns. Located at 141 Nixon Avenue, it became known as the Caleb T. Ward House and was designated a landmark in 1978. Elegant houses surround the hill; the population includes many professionals. The area is mainly residential, with shops nearby in Tompkinsville and Stapleton. It is about a mile from the ferry terminal.

Marjorie Johnson

wards. Governor Thomas Dongan's charter of 1686 divided New York City into six wards: North, East, West, South, Dock, and Out. A seventh ward was added in 1731 and given the name Montgomerie, after Governor John Montgomerie. In 1791 the Common Council voted to replace the names of the wards with numbers.

For two centuries the ward was the smallest political unit of New York City. Each ward elected an alderman and an assistant alderman to the Common Council, and in the seventeenth and eighteenth centuries also such lesser officials as tax assessors, tax collectors, and constables. After 1800 the city experienced an explosive growth in population, and wards increasingly became centers of political power and sometimes corruption. New wards were added as the city expanded northward or as the population density of older wards required their subdivision: the

Growth of the Ward System, 1683–1895

(Wards from which parts were taken to form other wards are given in parentheses.)

1683 North, East, West, South, Dock, and Out wards
1731 Montgomerie Ward
1791 Wards assigned numbers to replace original names
1803 Eighth and ninth wards
1808 Tenth ward
1825 Eleventh and twelfth wards
1827 Thirteenth ward (tenth), fourteenth ward (sixth and eighth)
1832 Fifteenth ward (ninth)
1835 Sixteenth ward (twelfth)
1837 Seventeenth ward (eleventh)
1846 Eighteenth ward (sixteenth)
1850 Nineteenth ward (twelfth)
1851 Twentieth ward (sixteenth)
1853 Twenty-first ward (eighteenth), twenty-second ward (nineteenth)
1873 Twenty-third and twenty-fourth wards (annexed territory of lower Westchester)
1895 Territory annexed from Westchester County added to twenty-fourth ward

Compiled by Edward T. O'Donnell

city had 17 wards in 1845 and 22 by 1853. Tammany Hall emerged by 1850 as an organized political "machine," an important element of which was the ward boss, or ward heeler, often a saloonkeeper who functioned as the local provider of patronage, dispenser of cheer and charity, and vote gatherer. The ward boss gained more power as the city expanded its efforts in the areas of police and fire protection, sanitation, and street and sewer construction, creating patronage positions that the ward boss could trade for votes. Wards were more than political units: many were notable for their wealth or poverty, culture, crime, ethnic makeup, population density, or economic activity. In the nineteenth century 15 of the 22 wards in Manhattan occupied the area south of 14th Street, the center of the city's economic activity and its most densely populated area. When the ward system was at its height in 1855, the state census showed that whereas the proportion of foreign-born inhabitants in the city was 52 percent, the figures for individual wards ranged from 34 and 41 percent in the "American" wards (the ninth and the 15th) to 70 percent in those with large numbers of immigrants (the fourth and the "bloody ould" sixth). The fifth, sixth, and eighth wards were home to most of the city's free blacks.

By 1850 critics of municipal government focused on the ward system as the primary source of corruption and inefficiency. To begin with they noted the unequal representation on the Common Council brought about by great differences in the population of individual wards. Although wards were never uniform either in population or in area, the city's growth after 1800 had led to unprecedented disparities: wards uptown were larger in area than those downtown, and the most heavily populated ward in 1855, the 17th, had more than 15 times as many inhabitants as the least heavily populated, the second (at the heart of the business district downtown). Reformers also condemned ward politics. From their perspective ward politicians were too parochial, too committed to "bargain and sale" as the basic principle of conducting public business, and too concerned with their own neighborhoods rather than the city as a whole. Implicit in this attack was a desire on the part of the reformers to reduce the power of ethnic and working-class leaders of Tammany Hall.

In the end reformers failed in their broader goal of reducing the influence of Tammany Hall, but they did succeed in eroding and finally eliminating the ward system and the unequal representation that characterized it. New charters in 1853 and 1857 replaced the wards with districts, which were used to elect members of both the state legislature and the bicameral City Council but otherwise had a smaller administrative role than the wards did. Although politically vestigial after 1857, ward boundaries were maintained, largely for the purposes of administering public schools and conducting the state and federal censuses. In 1871 a new law organized the public school system under a single superintendent, a board of education, and 25 boards of ward trustees, who were laypeople appointed by the Board of Education. The addition to the city in 1874 of a part of Westchester County gave the city its last two wards. In 1896 a group of reformers led by Nicholas Murray Butler of Columbia University succeeded in eliminating the ward trustees and centralizing the school system. From this time wards were politically insignificant, but they were never formally abolished, and the city charters continued to define their boundaries until 1938, when the charter for the first time made no reference to wards at all.

Brooklyn also used the ward system. At the time of its incorporation as a city in 1834 its charter divided the city into nine wards, each of which elected one representative for a two-year term to a board of aldermen. In addition to constituting the city's legislative branch, aldermen were responsible for administering certain functions within their wards, such as employing street cleaners and raising the funds with which to pay them, and acting as justices of the peace in criminal proceedings. Brooklyn was divided into 19 wards by its charter of 1857 and into 25 by that of 1877; at the time of its incorporation into New York City in 1898 it had 32 wards.

James F. Richardson

Wards Island. An island of 255 acres (103 hectares) at the northern end of the East River; it is legally part of Manhattan. Purchased from the Indians in 1637 by the Dutch governor-general Wouter van Twiller, it was sold as farmland after the American Revolution to the brothers Jasper and Bartholomew Ward. After the island was acquired by the city in 1955 it was used successively for a potter's field, a hospital for destitute immigrants, an auxiliary immigration station, and the City Asylum (an early mental institution). The asylum later became the Manhattan State Hospital and then the Manhattan Psychiatric Center; one of its buildings is now occupied by a men's shelter. The island became the site in 1937 of one of the largest sewage disposal plants in the world, and later of the training school for the city's fire department. Much of the island is now a park, accessible from Manhattan by a footbridge over the Harlem River. Wards Island is connected by landfill to Randalls Island and is traversed by the Triborough Bridge and the Hell Gate Bridge. The island is also home to Wards Island Park, with popular athletic fields, picnic areas, and spectacular views.

Gerard R. Wolfe

Ware, James E. (*b* New York City, 12 July 1864; *d* New York City, 4 April 1918). Architect. After receiving his education in New York City he worked in the office of R. G. Hatfield. In 1878 he designed a model tenement that won a competition sponsored by the magazine *Plumber and Sanitary Engineer;* based on the railroad apartment, this had a floor plan shaped like a dumbbell, with a corridor between front and rear rooms that allowed for airshafts. The design became the model for the Tenement House Act of 1879. His design for tenements surrounding a courtyard won second place in a competition sponsored by the Improved Housing Council in 1896; it was built as the First Avenue Estate in 1900 and helped to inspire the "new law" of 1901 requiring that lots for tenements measure at least 100 feet (30 meters) square. Ware also designed the Osborne (1885) at West 57th Street and Seventh Avenue, one of the city's first high-rise apartment buildings.

Richard Plunz, *A History of Housing in New York City* (New York: Columbia University Press, 1990)

Edward A. Eigen

warehouses. New York City became a center of warehousing in its earliest days. The Dutch West India Company began construction of five stone warehouses shortly after the settlement of New Netherland, on what is now Whitehall Street between Bridge and Stone streets. During the late seventeenth century several buildings were used as warehouses on Great Queen Street (now Pearl Street), and in 1797 a warehouse constructed on Furman street between Cranberry and Orange streets was operated by Jonathan Thompson. By the early nineteenth century warehousing districts emerged on South Street and along the East River in Brooklyn to meet the demands of the area's growing port traffic. In conjunction with the dredging of the Atlantic Basin in Brooklyn, the Atlantic Warehouses were constructed in 1844 at the initiative of Colonel Daniel Richards. The increased use of steam-powered vessels, which navigated the western part of the harbor more effectively than sail ships, encouraged the growth of warehousing on the Lower West Side of Manhattan. By 1850 there were as many warehouses in this district as around South Street.

Federal regulations enacted in 1842, 1846, and 1854 that exempted export goods from customs duties encouraged the use of bonded warehouses, and New York City accounted for more than half of all goods kept in such warehouses in the United States during the second half of the nineteenth century. At the same time the storage of household goods grew in importance in the city. John Morell introduced systematic business practices to warehousing and became a prominent figure in the development of the trade. After his warehouse was destroyed by fire in 1881, warehouses constructed of fire-resistant materials became increasingly common in Manhattan. Warehousing activity began shifting from Manhattan to Brooklyn as the cost of property rose and traffic became more congested. Major warehousing complexes emerged in Brooklyn with the founding of Bush Terminal by Irving T. Bush in 1895 and of the New York Dock Company in 1901, and most warehouses in New York City became concentrated along the shoreline in Brooklyn between the Brooklyn Bridge and Bush Terminal. From about 1950 warehousing shifted steadily to New Jersey because of the rise of container shipping and the land required for single-story warehouses, which were replacing multistory warehouses.

New York City retained a huge inventory of warehouses through the early twenty-first century, although their use was often varied. Some were converted into retail or wholesale centers, housing, artistic developments, small manufacturing centers, or even historically preserved sites. The New York City Department of Consumer Affairs mandates that a person or business must have a storage warehouse license if storing consumers' goods for compensation. The self-storage industry is exempt.

David F. Mitch

Warhol, Andy [Warhola, Andrew] (*b* Pittsburgh, 6 Aug 1928; *d* New York City, 22 Feb 1987). Painter and filmmaker. He graduated from the Carnegie Institute in 1949 and moved to New York City, where he dropped the last letter of his surname. For about six years he gained success as a freelance commercial artist for clients ranging from Glamour to I. Miller Shoes, living in a townhouse on Lexington Avenue with his mother. From 1960 Warhol found acclaim as an artist, experimenting with comic-strip motifs and using the silkscreen process to produce repetitive images in *Campbell's Soup Cans* (1962) and portraits of Marilyn Monroe, Jacqueline Kennedy, and Elvis Presley. He was considered a leader in the pop art movement. In 1963 he opened a studio called the Factory on 47th Street where he used methods of mass-production to make silk-screened images; he later moved operations to 33 Union Square West. He also made experimental films—about 650 between 1963 and 1968—including *Sleep* (1963), a six-hour film depicting writer John Giorno sleeping; *Empire* (1964), an eight-hour film of the the Empire State Building; and *The Chelsea Girls* (1966), which was considered controversial for its eroticism.

Warhol cultivated fame and eccentricity, wearing a silver wig and attracting legions of followers to his Factory. In 1968 Warhol was shot by writer Valerie Solanas in 1968 and recuperated for a year; in 1969 he launched *Interview* magazine. In 1971 a social exhibition, "Portraits of the 70s," filled the fourth floor of the Whitney Museum of American Art. During the 1980s Warhol supported several young artists, including Keith Haring and Jean-Michel Basquiat; a collaboration with Basquiat produced Warhol's first hand-painted work in years. In 1984 he gave his original films to the Museum of Modern Art for a collaborative project with the Whitney Museum of American Art to preserve, catalogue, and rerelease them. Warhol died from complications following gall bladder surgery at New York Hospital–Cornell Medical Center; his memorial service at St. Patrick's Cathedral attracted over 2000 people. Warhol is famous for his comment that in the future everyone would be "famous for fifteen minutes."

James E. Mooney, Kate Lauber

Waring, George E(dwin), Jr. (*b* Pound Ridge, N.Y., 4 July 1833; *d* New York City, 29 Oct 1898). Agriculturist, sanitary engineer, street-cleaning commissioner, and author. He studied "scientific agriculture" at the model farm of James Jay Mapes near Newark, N.J. (1853), and managed Horace Greeley's farm in Chappaqua, N.Y. (1855–57); he became "agricultural engineer" of Central Park in August 1857. To counteract waterlogged soil, he buried cylindrical drainage-tile lines throughout the park; he also installed the four elm rows that framed the Mall. During the Civil War he served as a major in the Garibaldi Guards (the 39th New York Volunteers)

Jacob A. Riis, Colonel George E. Waring, Sanitation Supervisor *(ca 1895)*

and as a colonel in 4th Missouri Cavalry. After the war he eventually gained prominence as an authority on household sanitation and town sewerage. His pioneering system of small-pipe sanitary sewers, first built in Memphis in 1880, was widely adopted despite engineering controversy. In 1881 he reworked the plumbing of the White House in Washington, D.C., and shortly thereafter did the plumbing of the Villard house in New York City at the northeast corner of Madison Avenue and 50th Street. Appointed New York City commissioner of street-cleaning by reform mayor William L. Strong in January 1895, he transformed a lackluster department into a merit-based, white-uniformed force—the famous White Wings—that got the city's streets "really clean" for the first time in history; he also attempted the nation's first systematic waste recycling system. Waring contracted yellow fever while studying sanitary conditions in Cuba for President William McKinley after the Spanish–American War and died in New York City. Altogether, he wrote 15 books, including three European travel accounts, and compiled the massive *Report on the Social Statistics of Cities* (1886, 1887) for the United States Census Bureau.

Martin V. Melosi, *The Sanitary City: Urban Infrastructure in America from Colonial Times to the Present* (Baltimore: Johns Hopkins University Press, 2000)

Jon A. Peterson

War Memorials. Monuments that mark wars and those who served or died in them. The city's (and nation's) first memorial, located at St. Paul's Chapel, was dedicated in 1776 to General Richard Montgomery, first officer to fall in the Revolution. Like much civic sculpture of its time, it was produced in France, and embodied the heroic iconography of late eighteenth-century Europe. Two early influential works were J. G. Batterson's 1857 General Worth funerary obelisk and crypt at Madison Square and the 1856 equestrian statue of Washington by Henry Kirke Brown and J. Q. A. Ward in Union Square, the first of the nation's memorials to adapt imperial scale and imagery to American ideals. Notable early Civil War funerary columns include the Irish Brigade memorial at Calvary Cemetery (1865) by John G. Draddy; the tribute to the Union Hebrew dead at Salem Fields; and the city's memorial on Battle Hill (1865) by Draddy and Batterson. These works helped legitimize new forms of memorial iconography, including the blessing of angels, ethnic mottos and symbols, strong decorative programs, realistic soldier statuary, lists of battles fought, and bas-relief narratives of war.

American memorial imagery took a new direction in Ward's Seventh Regiment Memorial (1869). His iconic rendering of the common soldier (*The Sentry*) on a solitary pedestal was widely emulated in both North and South, and thereafter the naturalistic hero figure remained integral to the American war memorial until the 1930s. Other notable Civil War tributes include John Duncan's Soldiers' and Sailors' Arch at Grand Army Plaza in Brooklyn, with its beaux-arts bronze sculptural groups of the *Army* and *Navy* (1901) by Frederick MacMonnies; and the Soldiers' and Sailors' Monument (1902) in Riverside Park by Stoughton and Stoughton and Paul M. DuBoy, modeled on the ancient Athenian Choragic Monument of Lysicrates. A pair of collaborative works by Augustus St. Gaudens and architect Stanford White, of Admiral David Glasgow Farragut (1881) at Madison Square Park, and of William Tecumseh Sherman (1902) in Manhattan's Grand Army Plaza, brought an unprecedented aesthetic and spiritual refinement to the hero figure and his setting, and so became an inspiration for the statues and memorials that apotheosized the American World War I remembrance after 1918.

World War I memorials include ten "Doughboys"; six female Victory and Angel statues bestowing the blessings of Peace and Hope; the Ridgewood Tholos bas-reliefs of Anton Schaaf; and the *Dawn of Glory* (1923) by Pietro Montana. The language of sacrifice and immortal memory were joined in these tributes to decoration and detail, and an emotional honesty about the American hero in warfare. These formal works were complemented by a new, popular embrace of public works memorials, and especially tree memorials. Seven thousand such trees were planted with memorial plaques in Brooklyn alone, and memorial groves rose in Central Park, Pelham Bay Park, and Hero's Park in Staten Island.

The era of 1918–32 saw the fading of nineteenth-century European monumentality. It also marked the last sustained effort to create an American war memorial canon and mythos of ideals, memory, and exaltation of purpose. These trends would be short-lived, however, as the influence of European modernism through the 1930s replaced naturalism and the figure with abstract and minimalist form, and the city, at the behest of Robert Moses, sought to limit impending World War II memorials to an approved design, one per borough. Only the Brooklyn tribute (1948, Constable and Gilmore et al., with sculptor Charles Keck) was ever completed according to his plan. Many traditional, small, deeply felt neighborhood shrines subsequently appeared after the Korean armistice in 1953.

Reflecting a decline in civic, political, and artistic support for the memorial arts, few major tributes materialized after the federally sponsored East Coast Memorial in Battery Park (1963), by William Gehron and Gilbert Seltzer, with sculptor Albino Manca. Three more recent works have sought to reimagine the war memorial using a postmodern vocabulary. The Korean War Veterans Memorial (1993) by Mac Adams enlarges the soldier figure to enormous size, rendering him as a cartoon-like cutout, *The Universal Soldier,* while nearby at the National Merchant Mariners Memorial (1991) by Marisol, a tableau of shipwrecked sailors combines with kinetic art, as a drowning man stretches out his hand for help while the tide submerges and resurrects him twice each day. At the Vietnam Veterans Memorial (1985), by William Britt Fellows and Peter Wormser, a Manhattan corporate plaza is combined with an ancient votive way, memorial stele, and a hallowed precinct for communion with the fallen. This is also the last city tribute utilizing language to evoke a deepened understanding of war, sacrifice, and forgiveness. More than a quarter of all monuments in New York City parks, 270, are war memorials, ranging from plaques to statues to arches.

Donald Martin Reynolds, *Monuments and Masterpieces: Histories and Views of Public Sculpture in New York City* (New York: Macmillan, 1988); Cal Snyder, *Out of Fire and Valor: The War Memorials of New York from the Revolution to 9-11* (Piermont, N.H.: Bunker Hill, 2005)

Cal Snyder

Warner–Lambert. Firm of pharmaceutical manufacturers. Formed in Philadelphia in 1856 as the William R. Warner Company, a maker of pharmaceuticals and cosmetics, it was taken over in 1908 by Gustavus A. Pfeiffer and Company, makers of patent medicine in St. Louis. It moved its headquarters and manufacturing facilities to New York City in 1916 and expanded by acquiring other companies, including the cosmetics firms Hudnut and DuBarry. In 1938 it established the Warner Institute for Therapeutic Research in New York City. Elmer Holmes Bobst became the president of the firm in 1945. He acquired the firm Lambert, manufacturer of the oral antiseptic Listerine (1955); the Emerson Drug Company, manufacturer of Bromo-Seltzer (1956); Smith Brothers, American Optical, Schick Shaving, the American Chicle Company (1962), and Parke, Davis and Company (1970). The firm changed its name in 1970 to Warner–Lambert Pharmaceutical Company and merged with Pfizer in 2000.

David J. S. King

wars. See American Revolution, Civil War, Spanish–American War, World War I, and World War II.

Warwick Hotel. Thirty-six-story hotel at the corner of 54th Street and Sixth Avenue in Manhattan, built in 1927 by William Randolph Hearst as an elegant retreat for the actress Marion Davies. At the time it was one of the tallest apartment hotels in the world. Over the years residents of the hotel have included Cary Grant, who lived on the 27th floor at intervals during the 1960s, and the Beatles, who favored the hotel because it lacked a large lobby and offered privacy. With its purchase in 1980 it became part of the Warwick International Hotels chain and was renamed Warwick New York Hotel.

Kenneth T. Jackson

Washington, George (*b* Bridges Creek, near Fredericksburg, Va., 22 Feb 1732; *d* Mount Vernon, Va., 14 Dec 1799). First president of the United States and commander in chief of the Continental army. He briefly visited New York City in February 1756, in May 1773, and in June 1775 shortly before taking command of the Continental army. During his defense of Manhattan against the British in 1776 his headquarters were at the Mortier House (at the present site of Charlton Street between Varick and MacDougal streets) and at the Morris–Jumel Mansion. The campaign proved disastrous when his forces were routed in the Battle of Long Island (26–31 August) and again in the loss of Fort Washington (16 November), and he retreated with the remainder of his forces across New Jersey. On Evacuation Day (25 November 1783) he returned triumphantly to the city to observe the final departure of British troops, and he bade an emotional farewell to his officers at Fraunces Tavern on 4 December. He returned to the city just before his inauguration at Federal Hall as the first president of the United States on 30 April 1789, took up residence on Cherry Street, and from February to August 1790 lived in larger quarters at 39 Broadway, where his wife, Martha, supervised a household that included 21 servants, among them seven slaves. After the national capital was moved to Philadelphia, he left New York City for the last time in October 1790. Washington's name is borne by more than a dozen of the city's streets and avenues, several neighborhoods, and two bridges. Statues depicting him are at Federal Hall and Union Square, and an arch honoring him stands in Washington Square Park. The earliest known use of the term *New Yorker* in a published work is contained in a letter that he wrote in 1756.

Robert I. Goler

Washington Bridge. Bridge spanning the Harlem River between West 181st Street in Manhattan and University Avenue in the Bronx, originally called the Harlem River and Manhattan Bridge. Designed by Charles C. Schneider and Wilhelm Hildebrand under the direction of William McAlpine and William Hutton, it was built of steel, cast iron, and wrought iron, with arched masonry approaches, and was the first arched bridge to use plated girders. When the bridge opened in 1889 it was referred to as the "glory of the Harlem River" and was considered one of the finest steel arched bridges in the United States. The bridge was named in 1889, the year of its completion, to commemorate the centenary of George Washington's inauguration. The Washington Bridge is the third-oldest standing bridge in New York City, after the High Bridge and the Brooklyn Bridge.

Joseph Deplasco, "Spanning the Centuries: The Washington Bridge over the Harlem River," *Bronx County Historical Society Journal* 26 (1989), 1–8

Gary D. Hermalyn

Washington Heights. Neighborhood in northern Manhattan, bounded to the north by Dyckman Street, to the east by the Harlem River, to the south by 155th Street, and to the west by the Hudson River. Two ridges run north and south through it; during the American Revolution the Continental army erected Fort Washington on the summit of the western ridge at what is now Fort Washington Avenue between 181st and 186th streets. Outlying forts included Fort Tryon in what became Fort Tryon Park, Cock-Hill Fort on Inwood Hill, and Fort George at what is now 192nd Street and Audubon Avenue; these were captured by British and Hessian forces after a battle in 1776. Most of the area was poor farmland, sometimes called Harlem Heights in the eighteenth century. It soon became a choice location for country estates of wealthy New Yorkers because of its spectacular views, and by the 1870s it was known by its current name. Although some estates were sold for development in the late nineteenth century, much of the area was rural as late as 1900.

In 1904 the Broadway subway line reached 157th Street in the southern end of Washington Heights; by 1906 it passed through the neighborhood to points farther north. Rapid development followed and several major complexes were built, including Columbia–Presbyterian Medical Center, museums and scholastic institutions at Audubon Terrace, and Yeshiva University. In 1912 the Polo Grounds stadium was built near the Harlem River between 155th and 157th Streets beneath Coogan's Bluff. Inexpensive apartment buildings were added in the southern and eastern sections, more expensive ones in the west and the north; eventually Broadway divided poor and working-class areas to the east from middle-class areas to the west. This division persisted even as the ethnic composition of the neighborhood changed. The southern boundary was not so clearly defined: in the 1930s it was at times placed as far south as 135th Street, while some white residents placed it farther north to distinguish the neighborhood from Harlem. The Eighth Avenue subway was completed on the west side of the neighborhood in 1932.

Washington Heights appealed to many residents because of its convenient transit, plentiful housing, and parks (developed on land formerly occupied by estates). A large number of Greeks and Irish settled there, as did many Jews, who increased in number during the Nazi regime. During the 1930s and 1940s such right-wing groups as the Christian Front and Irish gangs defaced synagogues and assaulted Jewish youths. The number of anti-Semitic incidents declined after World War II owing to increased policing, interfaith cooperation, and the forceful condemnation of attacks on Jews and synagogues voiced by local Christian leaders.

By the early 1960s many Irish and Jews had left the neighborhood, which became predominantly black, Puerto Rican, and Cuban. It was the site in 1965 of the assassination of Malcolm X, who was shot while addressing a rally at the Audubon Ballroom. After the mid-1960s Dominicans increased in number, but they had little political power because most tended to abstain from U.S. politics. No neighborhood in New York City attracted more immigrants in the 1980s than Washington Heights. Almost all were Latin American, and more than three-quarters were Dominican. By 1990 the Dominican community in Washington Heights and Inwood was the largest in the United States. District lines were redrawn in 1991 to give Dominicans a better chance of being represented on the City Council, and in the same year Guillermo Linares became the first elected official of Dominican ancestry in the United States.

In the mid-1990s problems evident in many neighborhoods were especially acute in Washington Heights: poverty, overcrowded schools and housing, entrenched drug trading accompanied by a high murder rate in the southern and eastern sections, and troubled relations between residents and the police (in the summer of 1992 there were several days of rioting when a police officer fatally shot a drug dealer). The neighborhood nevertheless retained a bustling business district, and the parks remained intact. The site of the assassination of Malcolm X was incorporated into an 11-story building housing a biotechnology research center affiliated with Columbia University, retail space, and a community mental health clinic. By the latter part of the 1990s vigorous policing, changes in the drug trade, and an increased sense of stability in the neighborhood reduced crime. In the twenty-first century Dominicans remain prominent in the heights but are noticeably more integrated into the politics and government of the city. At the same time, increased safety and a tight housing market have brought new residents and substantial white gentrification to the area. In 2007 the neighborhood was depicted in the musical *In the Heights,* which depicted the area as a striving, vigorous neighborhood defined by its Latinos and Latinas.

Reginald Pelham Bolton, *Washington Heights, Manhattan: Its Eventful Past* (New York: Dyckman Institute, 1924); Ira Katznelson, *City Trenches: Urban Politics and the Patterning of Class in the United States* (Chicago: University of Chicago Press, 1981); Beth Rosenthal and David Rubel, *A Community in Transition: State of Current Resources and Needs* (New York: Northern Manhattan Improvement Corporation, 1989)

Robert W. Snyder

Washington Irving High School. Secondary school opened in 1902 as the Commercial High School for Girls at 36 East 12th Street. It took its current name in 1906 and moved to 40 Irving Place in 1913. The last remaining single-sex public high school in New York City, it began admitting boys in the autumn of 1986 and changed its focus from nursing, secretarial studies, and child care to international studies and foreign languages. Distinguished alumnae of Washington Irving High School include the actress Claudette Colbert and the fashion designer Norma Kamali. In 2010s its enrollment was around 1500 students.

Erica Judge

Washington Market. Market built in 1812 on Washington, Fulton, and Vesey streets. The country's largest food market by 1858, it was condemned in 1859 because it caused traffic jams and was unregulated and rife with corruption. At the end of the Civil War a separate wholesale produce market emerged and ran about a dozen blocks north of Vesey Street to North Moore Street. The market on Washington, Fulton, and Vesey streets was rebuilt in 1883–84, became primarily a retail market, and was remodeled in 1915 and again in 1935; the retail section was closed by the city in 1956, and the wholesale market was demolished and replaced by the Hunts Point Market in the Bronx in 1967.

Suzanne R. Wasserman

Washington Square Park. Public park in Manhattan, bounded by Waverly Place (Washington Square Park North), University Place (Washington Square Park East), West Fourth Street (Washington Square Park South), and MacDougal Street (Washington Square Park West). The area was once a marsh fed by Minetta Brook near a Sappokanican Indian settlement and was used from 1797 to 1826 as a potter's field and as a place for public hangings. In 1827 the city acquired the land for a public park, and exclusive development hastened in the surrounding community. After the parks department was established in 1870, Washington Square was improved: monuments were erected to Giuseppe Garibaldi in 1888 east of the Central Fountain and to Alexander Lyman Holley in 1890 west of the fountain; and a temporary arch commemorating the inauguration of George Washington, erected in 1889, was replaced in 1895 by a permanent arch designed by Stanford White. Sculptures by Hermon MacNeil and Alexander Stirling Calder depicting Washington as the commander in chief were added about 20 years later. The park was bisected by Fifth Avenue until the 1960s, when the through-street and bus turnaround were closed off and a fountain became a public meeting place where folk musicians and other performers entertained local residents, students at New York University, and tourists from around the world. In December 2007 the parks department began a multiyear reconstruction project; the plans included increased green space, restoration of the fountain and several monuments, and construction of an outdoor stage.

Emily Kies Folpe, *It Happened on Washington Square* (Baltimore: Johns Hopkins University Press, 2002)

Jonathan Kuhn

Washington Square Park, 2009

Washington Square United Methodist Church. Romanesque Revival church designed by Charles Hadden and built before the Civil War at 135 West Fourth Street. Its 1901 Odell organ was not electrified but rather retained the rare original console (tubular pneumatic action). The church was called the "Peace Church" for its stance against the Vietnam War; it was also known for its support of New York City's gay community. Paul M. Abels, its pastor from 1973 to 1984, was the first openly gay minister of a major Christian congregation in the United States, and in 1985 the church was the first site of the Harvey Milk School for lesbian and gay youth. In 2004 the congregation sold the building, which converted into apartments.

Sharon Wilkins

Wasserstein, Wendy (*b* New York City, 18 Oct 1950; *d* New York City, 30 Jan 2006). Playwright. She grew up in Flatbush and on the Upper East Side, graduated from Mount Holyoke College, and studied at the Yale School of Drama. Her works gave voice to a generation of successful, well-educated women who struggled to fit into a man's world and weren't always successful in their personal lives. She wrote autobiographical essays for the magazine *New York Woman* and also contributed to *Harper's* and *Harper's Bazaar.* Her first successful plays, *Uncommon Women and Others* (1977) and *Isn't It Romantic* (1984), were drawn from childhood experiences. Wasserstein is best known for *The Heidi Chronicles* (1989), which won a Pulitzer Prize and a Tony Award for best play in 1989, and *The Sisters Rosensweig* (1992), in which the main characters are based on herself and her family. Other Broadway plays included *An American Daughter* (1997) and *Old Money* (2000). She also adapted a screenplay, *The Object of My Affection* (1998); wrote children's books, including *Pamela's First Musical* (1996); and personal essays, including *Bachelor Girls* (1990) and *Shiksa Goddess: Or, How I Spent My Forties* (2001).

Janet Frankston

Watchogue. Name applied to Bloomfield before the 1870s. The area was called Merrell Town during the early nineteenth century, after Ike Merrell, who owned a large farm known for its magnificent oak trees. A conjectural etymology is that after several trees were stolen, the farm became known as Watch Oak Farm, and that the name was soon used for the entire settlement and eventually became corrupted to Watchogue.

James Bradley

water. The drinking water system of New York City may be its most valuable capital asset. In 2009 the system supplied an average of 1.1 billion gallons of water a day to roughly nine million residents of the city and neighboring counties. In its current form the system includes an upstate watershed of nearly 2000 square miles (5200 square kilometers), 19 collecting reservoirs, 346 miles (557 kilometers) of aqueducts and tunnels, and 5814 miles (9355 kilometers) of distribution mains and pipes. This extensive network, in which water is transported almost exclusively by gravity, has been the envy of municipal water providers around the world and is recognized as an engineering marvel.

1. Early Sources of Water

During the colonial period, American Indians and Dutch and English settlers drew

Standpipe, 2009

water from clear ponds and streams and from freshwater wells on Manhattan Island. Clean water was plentiful for those living in what later became the city's other boroughs. But by the time of the American Revolution New Yorkers were struggling to secure an adequate supply of pure water. From the eighteenth to the mid-nineteenth century residents of Manhattan relied principally on four sources for their water supply. One was the Collect, a pond occupying 48 acres (19 hectares), with wetlands lying to its south, around what is now Foley Square. By the 1780s, however, its water quality had begun to decline because of the dumping of garbage and waste from tanneries and other industries. Not surprisingly its use as a water supply fell off, and in 1803 the city began filling it in.

Local wells were another early water source. The first public well was sunk by the English in 1666 at the fort on Manhattan's southern tip. Reliance on underground supplies increased throughout the eighteenth century, and by 1809 the city had 249 pump-operated public wells. Residents also drew on private wells. As early as the mid-eighteenth century, however, some wells had already been contaminated by seepage from cesspools and street runoff. Among the more interesting of the well-water ventures was the Manhattan Company, originally envisioned by public officials as a provider of pure waters from north of the city. The company's founders, including Aaron Burr, obtained a state charter for a water company in 1799, which, not incidentally, allowed it to establish banking operations. The company's water supply purposes were never realized: its primary source was a modest existing well near the Collect, the mostly wooden mains reached only a small portion of the city's residents, and the water quality was poor. But the financial component of the company evolved into what later became the Chase Manhattan Bank.

Natural springs furnished a third water supply from colonial times through the mid-1800s. A popular source was the Tea Water spring, whose pump was located just east of the present Chinatown. For decades this source provided high-quality water for drinking and cooking. Affluent New Yorkers purchased this water from private dealers whose "Tea Water Men" carted it around in large casks and sold it by the bucket. By the 1780s water from the Tea Water spring had dropped in quality, but it was still considered the best on Manhattan Island until the arrival of waters from upstate in 1842. Cisterns, or tanks for collecting rainwater, served as a fourth water source during this period. Although sometimes relied upon for drinking, water from household cisterns was used primarily for bathing, cleaning, and other domestic chores. As urban activities increased, cistern water quality deteriorated from dust and cinder fallout. Still, in an effort to help meet the needs of firefighting, the city built 40 public cisterns between 1817 and 1829.

2. The Croton System

By the 1830s the inadequacies of the city's patchwork supply had become apparent, and most residents still relied on well water. By this time the connection between bad water and typhoid fever, yellow fever, and cholera epidemics had been made; in 1832 more than 3500 New Yorkers perished in a cholera outbreak. The need for water for fire protection also reached a crescendo after fires in 1776 and 1828 and the Great Fire of 1835, which leveled 20 blocks and destroyed nearly 700 buildings. In 1835 the Common Council placed the issue before the voters, who approved by a 3–1 margin a referendum calling for damming the Croton River in Westchester County and funneling the collected water to a desperate city. Under state authorization, city officials raised construction funds and authorized water commissioners to acquire land and water rights outside city limits for a new water system. In 1842 the Croton Aqueduct was put into service, which carried water more than 40 miles (64 kilometers) to a receiving reservoir, now the site of the Great Lawn in Central Park. The arrival of pristine water from the Croton Reservoir triggered the great water celebration of 1842, complete with parades, fireworks, music, and fountains shooting plumes of water 50 feet (15 meters) into the air.

For the next 75 years an expanding Croton system was the main source of water for residents of Manhattan. In the 1840s many New Yorkers who had not yet connected their residences and businesses to the Croton supply were opening fire hydrants without authorization to draw water for their daily needs. The widespread installation of private baths, fixed washbasins, and flush toilets beginning in the 1850s, along with a continuing upswing in population, led to mounting water usage. The original Croton system was unable to keep pace with the growing demand. One result was the construction of a new and larger receiving reservoir in Central Park, completed in 1862. (This reservoir, now surrounded by a popular running track, was taken out of service in 1991.) From 1866 to 1911 the city dammed new water sources in Putnam and Westchester counties and linked them to the Croton system. Ultimately, 12 new reservoirs had been placed in service: Boyd Corners (1873), Middle Branch (1878), East Branch (1891), Bog Brook (1892), Titicus (1893), West Branch (1895), Amawalk (1897), Muscoot (1905), New Croton (1905), Cross River (1908), Croton Falls (1911), and Diverting (1911). In 1890 the New Croton Aqueduct was put into operation. Mostly an underground pressure tunnel, it provided more than three times the capacity of the original aqueduct.

By the time this system was completed, the city had already outgrown it, as population increased dramatically, the Bronx was annexed, and the city's consolidation in 1898 brought the number of residents to almost 3.5 million. Consolidation, among other benefits, helped head off water problems in the newly incorporated boroughs. Queens and Staten Island had historically derived their water from underground wells. But by the time of consolidation these sources were inadequate. The only remnant of their service is the former Jamaica Water Supply Company, now city-owned, which has wells that in 2007 were providing a portion of the water consumed by about 100,000 residents of southeastern Queens. The Bronx relied on local sources until the completion of the Croton system, which eventually supplied the borough with nearly all its water. In Brooklyn, residents depended mostly on local wells and cisterns until 1859, when its Ridgewood public water supply system began delivering stream-fed surface waters collected on the southern shore of Long Island. By the late nineteenth century the rapid growth of Brooklyn strained the Ridgewood supply, and many wells were being polluted by the intrusion of seawater. Brooklyn in fact voted to join New York City in part to tap into its enviable supply of upstate water.

3. The Catskill and Delaware Systems

The continuing search for new water sources led planners to the Catskill Mountains, as far as 125 miles (201 kilometers) north of Manhattan. At first some officials proposed that the city obtain water from the Catskills by contracting with a private firm, the politically influential Ramapo Water Company. The city's comptroller, Bird S. Coler, successfully opposed the plan on the grounds that it would be too expensive and would leave the city dependent on private interests. Instead the state legislature passed a law in 1905 creating a new public board of water supply, with broad authority to condemn land and build new reservoirs and aqueducts. Construction of the huge Catskill system began in 1907, and by 1917 clean mountain water from the Catskills was flowing into all five boroughs.

The centerpiece of the system was the Ashokan collecting reservoir (placed into service in 1915) on Esopus Creek in Ulster County, a facility holding at full capacity more water than all the reservoirs in the Croton system combined. The city also began operating three distribution and storage reservoirs for the Catskill system: the Kensico and the Hillview in Westchester County (1915) and the Silver Lake Reservoir (1917) on Staten Island (later replaced by underground storage tanks). Water flowed from the Ashokan to the Hillview through the Catskill Aqueduct (92 miles [148 kilometers]), which included grade-level, covered trenches and a circular tunnel with a diameter of 14 feet (4.3 meters) that plunged 1100 feet (335 meters) beneath the surface of the Hudson River near Storm King Mountain. Construction of the Catskill system ended shortly after a second reservoir, the Schoharie, at the intersection of

Ashokan Reservoir, 1916

Schoharie, Delaware, and Greene counties, was placed into service in 1926. Like the Croton system before it, the Catskill system had a profound effect on upstate communities in the watershed. To make way for the Ashokan Reservoir, for example, seven villages were submerged, their nearly 2000 residents resettled, and about 2800 bodies reinterred. This pattern was repeated to a lesser degree during the construction of the Schoharie Reservoir and the city's Delaware system reservoirs. In part because of these contentious beginnings, relations between watershed communities and New York City were strained.

Even after the Catskill system was completed, demand for water in the city continued to rise. As early as 1921 the Board of Water Supply was looking to the Delaware River watershed, in the western Catskills, as a new source. New Jersey and Pennsylvania asserted that the Delaware was an interstate waterway and objected to a diversion of its water by New York. But in 1931 the U.S. Supreme Court allowed the city to withdraw as much as 440 million gallons (1666 million liters) a day from the Delaware River, as long as it maintained flows to protect downstream fisheries and downriver water systems in New Jersey and Pennsylvania. Under a later modification of this ruling, the city was permitted to increase its daily withdrawals to 800 million gallons (3028 million liters). Financial woes delayed the start of construction of the new Delaware system until 1937. The first of its reservoirs, the Rondout in Ulster and Sullivan counties, was put into regular service in 1951. To deliver water from the Delaware system the city constructed a new aqueduct 85 miles (137 kilometers) long from Rondout to the Hillview Reservoir. This aqueduct was bored through deep rock, 300 to 1000 feet (90 to 300 meters) below ground level. The city next brought into service the Neversink (Sullivan County) Reservoir in 1953 and the Pepacton (Delaware County) Reservoir in 1955. In 1964 it began drawing water from the Cannonsville Reservoir in Delaware County, the final piece of the giant Delaware system and the last reservoir added to the city's water supply network.

Early in the twenty-first century, the roughly 580 billion gallons (2196 billion liters) in the three reservoir systems at full capacity could theoretically satisfy the city's drinking water demand for an entire year, when the city derived 10 percent of its water from the Croton system, 40 percent from the Catskill system, and 50 percent from the Delaware system. Water from the Croton reservoirs travels through the New Croton Aqueduct into the Jerome Park Reservoir in the northern Bronx; both the aqueduct and the reservoir are directly linked to the city's trunk mains. Waters from the Catskill and Delaware aqueducts ordinarily pass through the Hillview Reservoir just north of the city limits in Yonkers before entering water tunnels no. 1 (1917) and no. 2 (1936), which also feed into trunk mains. The trunk mains in turn carry water into smaller distribution mains that connect to service lines running into private homes and apartment buildings. About one-fourth of the city's water mains that were in service in 2009 had been installed before 1930 and were made of unlined cast iron; these mains accounted for the bulk of the most disruptive of the 600 or so water-main breaks (usually small) that were occurring annually throughout the city. At the beginning of the twenty-first century the city had been replacing about 60 miles (96.5 kilometers) of water mains every year.

4. Recent Developments

The newest addition to the water network is city tunnel no. 3, which will increase the system's capacity to deliver water throughout all five boroughs, enhance reliability, and allow officials to inspect and repair tunnels nos. 1 and 2 for the first time since they went into service in the first decades of the twentieth century. The tunnel is being constructed in stages, with the first stage, completed in 1998, running 13 miles (20.9 kilometers) from the Hillview Reservoir through the Bronx and northern Manhattan into Queens. Stage 2, connecting the new tunnel in Queens to Brooklyn and Staten Island, is expected to be placed into service in 2013. At a projected total cost of more than $6 billion, the tunnel is among the largest capital building projects in the city's history. Digging for the third water tunnel began in 1970, and the entire project is not expected to be completed before 2025. During the first 37 years of construction, more than 5000 tunnel workers, called SANDHOGS, worked on the project, including at least 24 who lost their lives during excavation and tunnel building.

More than 170 years after officials began developing the upstate water system, the city continues to confront two persistent water-related challenges. The first is the availability of an adequate supply. Between 1960 and 1990, during which time the consumption of water from the upstate reservoirs increased by more than 25 percent, the city experienced three severe droughts (1963–67, 1980–81, and 1985). These prompted city managers to step up water conservation activities beginning in the mid-1980s. Measures included more sophisticated leak-detection efforts and implementation of a local law allowing only water-saving toilets, showerheads, and other plumbing fixtures to be sold or installed in New York City. At the same time the city began a long-term program to place water meters in individual homes and apartment buildings so that property owners would pay for the amount of water actually used rather than flat rates. In part as a result of such initiatives, total city water consumption fell from an average of 1.5 billion gallons (5.7 billion liters) a day in 1990 to an average of 1.1 billion gallons (4.2 billion liters) a day by 2007. Since the late 1980s two leaks in portions of the concrete-lined Delaware Aqueduct in Ulster and Orange counties have been sending between 15 and 36 million gallons (56.8 and 136.3 million liters) of water a day to the surface, according to city estimates. City officials have maintained that there is little risk of a near-term tunnel failure, but with concerns growing they began contingency planning and preparatory work for aqueduct repair in 2004. In addition, global warming also poses serious long-term risks for the city's water supply. According to climate scientists, rising temperatures will mean more days over 90 degrees, greater demand for water during hot summer months, disruptive changes to precipitation patterns in the watershed region, and increased evaporation from city reservoirs, all of which—along with projected increases in city population—are likely to strain existing supplies in the coming decades.

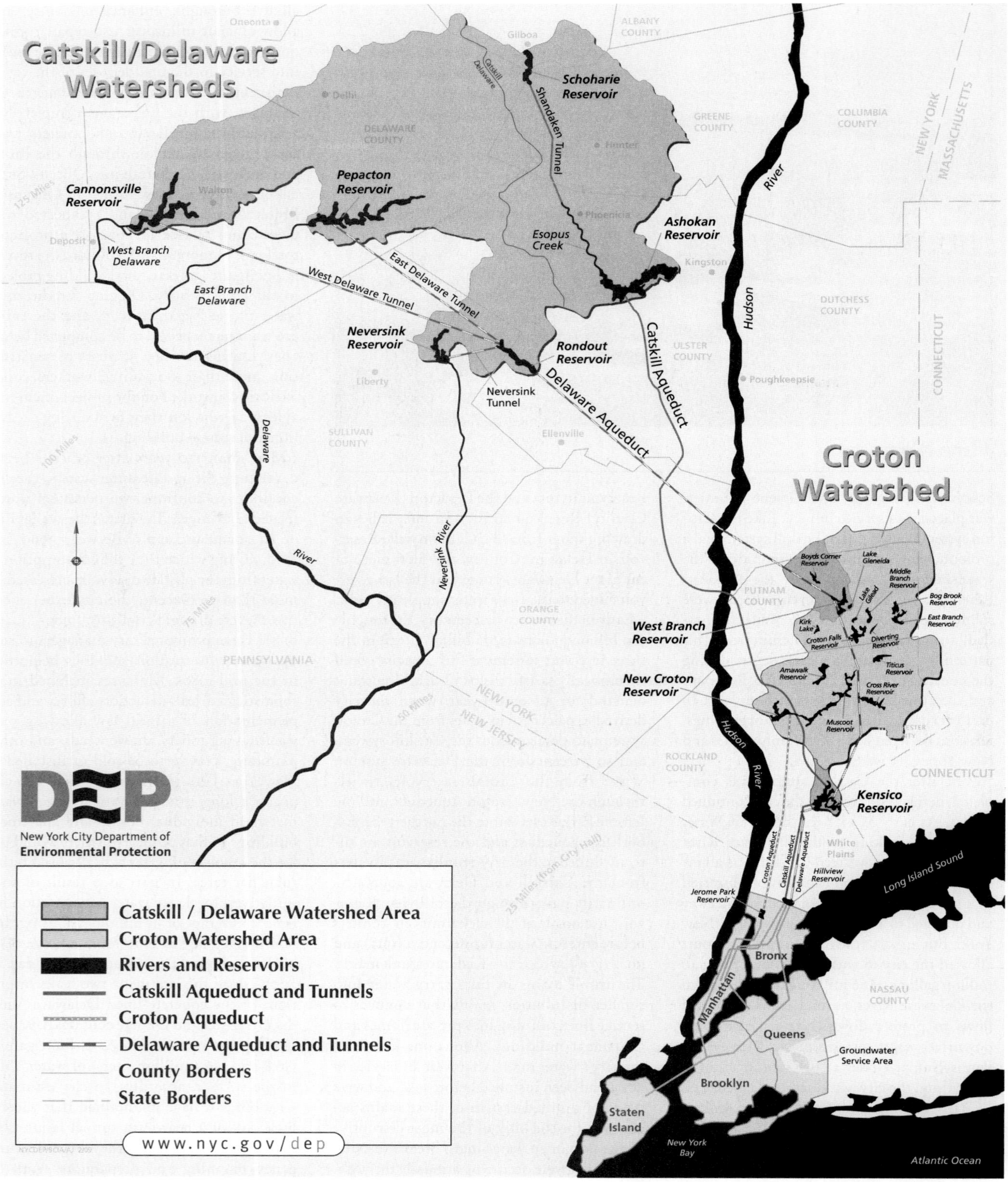

The second recurring issue is that of water purity. Historically, drinking water from the city's upstate reservoirs has been high in quality and has consistently met federal and state health standards. But increased residential and commercial development, especially in the Croton watershed, has contributed significant storm-water runoff into rivers and streams that feed the upstate reservoirs. In addition, by the early 1990s more than 100 sewage plants were discharging treated wastewaters into watershed tributaries. As a result of these and other conditions, water quality in some reservoirs had begun to slip. To help protect against waterborne disease, the city agreed in 1998 to construct a large filtration plant to cleanse water from the Croton system. Filtration of Croton system water had

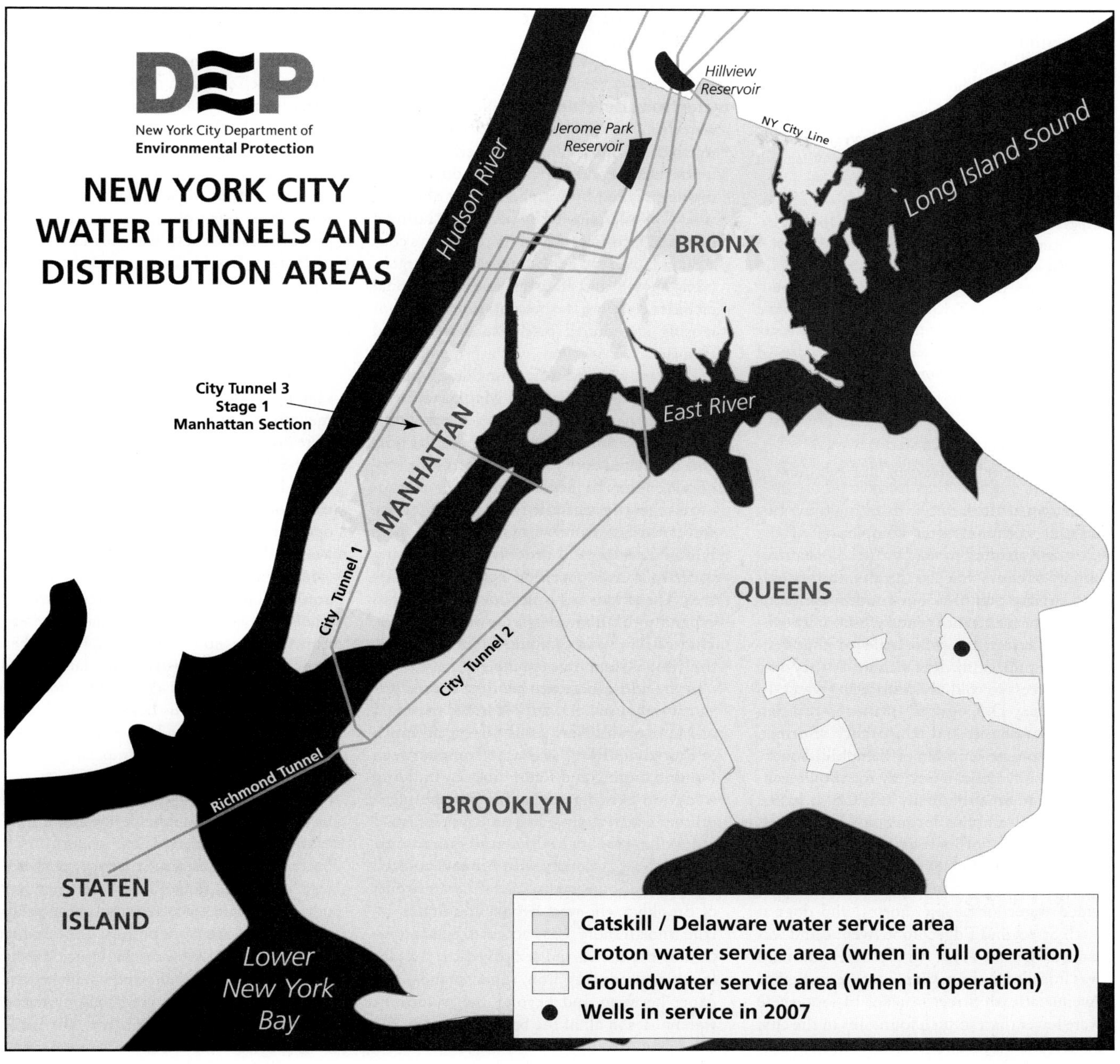

been contemplated for decades before the U.S. Environmental Protection Agency (EPA) determined in the early 1990s that Croton filtration was necessary for city compliance with the federal Safe Drinking Water Act. Still, the siting of the plant at the Mosholu Golf Course in Van Cortlandt Park was controversial. The projected cost of the facility, originally estimated at $660 million in 1998, had jumped to approximately $2.8 billion a decade later. The city expects that the plant, designed to treat up to 290 million gallons (1098 million liters) of water a day by filtering microbiological contaminants, will also alleviate intermittent problems with color, odor, and taste and enhance the dependability of the Croton supply. The facility was scheduled to begin operating in 2012.

In an effort to prevent pollution at its source and stave off filtration for the much larger Catskill and Delaware systems, the city in the early 1990s began efforts to implement a watershed protection strategy. In 1992 city environmental protection commissioner Albert Appleton launched a cooperative program with upstate farmers to reduce agricultural runoff into watershed tributaries. By 2008 more than 450 participating farms had implemented best management practices. But an upstate coalition objected to new city rules governing other watershed activities and sued to block their implementation. In 1997 city, state, and watershed stakeholders signed a milestone accord, brokered by Governor George Pataki, that bridged the impasse. The upstate-downstate watershed agreement provided for the city's acquisition from willing sellers of critical land parcels around reservoirs and tributaries, for city-funded upgrades to watershed sewage plants, and for the application of new rules governing storm-water discharges and other polluting activities in the watershed. New partnership programs to benefit watershed communities were also funded as part of the city's 10-year, $1.5-billion watershed protection initiative. In response to the city's commitment to implementing these and other programs and to continuing to meet water-quality standards, the EPA granted the city a filtration waiver for the Catskill and Delaware systems. The EPA issued a 10-year renewal of that waiver, adding additional requirements, in 2007. By then the costs to construct massive filtration facilities for the Catskill and Delaware systems had been estimated at $10 billion or more, providing a further incentive for successful implementation of the watershed protection approach.

Edward Wegmann, *The Water Supply of the City of New York: 1658–1895* (New York: John Wiley and Sons, 1896); Charles H. Weidner, *Water for a City: A History of New York City's Problem from the Beginning to the Delaware River System* (New Brunswick, N.J.: Rutgers University Press, 1974); Diane Galusha, *Liquid Assets: A History of New York City's Water System* (Fleischmanns, N.Y.: Purple Mountain, 1999); Gerard T. Koeppel, *Water for Gotham: A History* (Princeton, N.J.: Princeton University Press, 2000); Stanley Greenberg, *Waterworks: A Photographic Journey through New York's Hidden Water System* (New York: Princeton Architectural, 2003)

See also Water tanks and towers.

Eric A. Goldstein, Mark A. Izeman

water fountains. Public drinking fountains became common after completion of the Croton Aqueduct in 1842 brought a plentiful supply of clean water to the city. Individuals and private organizations funded fountains during the nineteenth century, especially temperance reformers, who believed that residents would drink less alcohol if they had ready access to cold, fresh drinking water. In 1888 Henry D. Cogswell (1820–1900), a San Francisco dentist and temperance reformer, built an ornate fountain in Tompkins Square Park. The American Society for the Prevention of Cruelty to Animals (ASPCA) installed dozens of fountains for people and animals from the time of its founding in 1866. The Hooper Fountain (1894), funded at the bequest of newspaperman John Hooper, provided water for people, horses, and dogs at 155th Street and Edgecombe Avenue and was landmarked in 1992. An ice water fountain was installed at the main post office on Eighth Avenue at 34th Street in 1880. In 1906 there were fewer than 50 such fountains in the city. Robert Moses installed fountains in city parks after he became parks commissioner in 1934; by the early twenty-first century parks contained more than 2400 fountains, although a survey in 2000 found many inoperable and needing repair.

Water fountain, 2009

Kate Lauber

waterfront development. New York City's waterfront developed in a pattern similar to that in most North American cities (with the exception of Chicago): dock building augmented by warehouses for shipping (1647–1980s), followed by peripheral railroad lines and factories (1846–1911), highways constructed over or replacing railroad tracks (1898–1950s), and housing and recreational facilities (1980s to the present) supplanting or reusing abandoned piers, warehouses, and factories.

The first wave of waterfront development began on the East River in Manhattan with the construction of Schreyer's Hook Dock near today's South Street Seaport. The port and its related activities were the city's economic engine. In 1814 Robert Fulton inaugurated regularly scheduled steam ferry service to Manhattan from what is now known as Fulton Landing in Brooklyn, introducing waterfront transportation activities to that area. The advent of steam allowed the port to expand to Manhattan's West Side along the Hudson River and catapulted New York City to national shipping supremacy.

In the mid-nineteenth century streets, private warehouses, and docks formed the edges of Manhattan below 42nd Street and much of Brooklyn's East River waterfront between Fulton Landing and Red Hook. By building tracks on existing streets behind the piers, railroads such as the Hudson River Railroad (opened in 1846 on Manhattan's 12th Avenue linking New York City with Albany) boosted commerce. Soon tracks lined the waterfronts of Brooklyn, the west Bronx, and Staten Island's north shore. Easy access to transportation by both land and sea paved the way for factories producing iron, sugar, pianos, and paper between and beyond the waterfront warehouses in all of the boroughs except the Bronx.

Twentieth-century technological improvements added another stratum and a new structure to the city's waterfront. Given the need to accommodate the widespread use of cars and trucks after World War I, the Hudson River and East River shorelines provided cheap land and minimal disruption for building highways. Construction on East River Drive began in 1929, followed two years later by the elevated West Side Highway. Expansion of this system continued on the periphery of Manhattan, Brooklyn, and portions of Queens and the Bronx into the 1950s.

During the Great Depression the federal government financed public housing projects along the water; shipping activities had moved elsewhere. From the Vladeck Houses on Manhattan's Lower East Side (1940) to Red Hook in Brooklyn and Queensbridge in Queens (1937), subsidized housing provided jobs and apartments with waterfront views. This pattern expanded into the Bronx in the 1970s with the construction of the state-subsidized Harlem River Park Towers on the Harlem River.

In the 1960s containerization caused the decline of the city's port economy and opened the door to higher class housing and recreational use of the waterfront. The needs of huge deep-draft ships rendered the city's narrow finger piers obsolete. In addition, jet aircraft created a new land use in the marshes of Jamaica Bay in Queens and the Long Island Sound waterfronts, reduced passenger ship travel, and left even more piers useless.

Between 1960 and 1980, despite city studies encouraging growth at the edge, the combination of vain hope for port revival and a sagging economy caused waterfront development to come to a virtual standstill. But there were inroads in upscale housing. The opening of the Verrazano–Narrows Bridge (1964) caused a single-family housing boom along the shores of Staten Island. A private developer used state Mitchell–Lama funds to build Waterside on the East River in Manhattan (1965), and the state created 92 acres (37 hectares) of landfill to begin Battery Park City (1968). In 1977 the city Landmarks Preservation Commission formed the Fulton Ferry Landing Historic District, the state opened a small park, and artists moved into former warehouse lofts. Thus began the slow transformation of the area between the Brooklyn and Manhattan bridges into an office and residential community.

By the early twenty-first century, helped by a combination of public policy and a robust economy, New York City's waterfront has been largely transformed into a residential/recreational resource. The Waterfront Revitalization Plan (1982) required public access in any new waterfront project. The demise of the controversial Westway building project by 1990 was followed by city and state investment in a 5-mile-long (8-kilometer-long) waterfront park on the Hudson River from the Battery to 59th Street that includes the reuse of many outmoded piers. In place of Manhattan's once vibrant port economy, private developers sought financing for luxury apartment houses and offices designed by architects such as Richard Meier and Frank Gehry. Donald Trump's Riverside South opened on platforms above the former Hudson River Railroad yard. In Queens, a César Pelli–designed high-rise apartment tower initiated the redevelopment of Queens West. Under the aegis of the Port Authority of New York and New Jersey, the city, and the state, a former landing for freight bound to and from Long Island became Gantry Plaza Park. More luxury apartment towers with accompanying parkland were in the works from Queens West northward along the East River. In Brooklyn, old warehouses on the Red Hook peninsula were transformed into mixed-use housing, shops, and light manufacturing businesses. In 2006 the city's

Department of Planning rezoned 134 blocks along the Williamsburg/Greenpoint East River waterfront from manufacturing to residential. Thus began the transformation of Brooklyn's vacant, industrial waterfront into luxury housing with required low-income components and parkland. On Piers 1–6, built by the Port Authority of New York and New Jersey in 1950 to replace turn-of-the-century shipping facilities, the city and state made plans for an innovative 1.3-mile (2.1-kilometer) park running from Atlantic Avenue to the Manhattan Bridge.

Ann L. Buttenwieser, *Manhattan Water-Bound: Manhattan's Waterfront from the Seventeenth Century to the Present* (Syracuse, N.Y.: Syracuse University Press, 1999); Phillip Lopate, *Waterfront: A Journey around Manhattan* (New York: Crown, 2004); Robert A. M. Stern, *New York 2000: Architecture and Urbanism between the Bicentennial and the Millennium* (New York: Monacelli Press, 2006)

Ann L. Buttenwieser

Waterfront Priest [Corridan, John M.] (*b* New York City, 15 June 1911; *d* New York City, 1 July 1984). Reformer, priest, and teacher. He was born in Harlem, attended New York University's School of Commerce, and then studied theology, becoming a Jesuit priest in 1945. Subsequently appointed the associate director of the Xavier Institute of Labor Relations on West 16th Street, he encountered rampant corruption among longshoremen on the docks, where gangsters, with the cooperation of union officials, often took kickbacks for jobs. His exposure of the corruption led to congressional hearings and the formation of the watchdog Waterfront Commission in 1953. He became known as the Waterfront Priest, which is also the title of a 1955 biography by *New York Times* reporter Allen Raymond. The role of Father Barry in the classic film *On the Waterfront* was loosely based on Corridan. He went on to teach economics and theology and served as hospital chaplain in Brooklyn from 1967 until 1981.He is buried in Jesuit Cemetery in Auriesville, Montgomery County, New York.

Nicholas Kelly

Watering Place. Name applied in colonial times to Tompkinsville.

Waters, Ethel (*b* Chester, Pa., 31 Oct 1896; *d* Los Angeles, 1 Sept 1977). Singer. She moved to Harlem during World War I. Her first performance in New York City came with a one-week engagement at the Lincoln Theater followed by an appearance in *Hello, 1919!* at the Lafayette Theater in Harlem. She made her debut on Broadway in 1927 as the lead in the all-black production *Africana,* written by Earl Dancer and Donald Heywood. In 1933 the songwriter Irving Berlin heard her sing "Stormy Weather" at the Cotton Club and invited her to act in his play *As Thousands Cheer;* she made many appearances on stage, in films, and on television during the next three decades. She is best known for her performances of the songs "Dinah" (recorded in 1926); "Black and Blue" (1929), by Andy Razaf, Fats Waller, and Harry Brooks; "Harlem on My Mind" (1933), by Berlin; and "Stormy Weather" (1933), by Harold Arlen. She sang with the evangelist Billy Graham from 1960 to 1975. Waters was one of the first black singers to achieve widespread popularity and also among the first to blend jazz and popular music. With Charles Samuels she wrote *His Eye Is on the Sparrow* (1951).

Loren Schoenberg

water tanks and towers. Elevated water storage and distribution devices. New York City is one of very few large U.S. cities that primarily depend on gravity to distribute water through rooftop water tanks. The city's water supply does not have sufficient pressure to lift water to upper stories of taller buildings. Because pressure increases with height, structures taller than seven stories have rooftop storage tanks that are fed by pumps and that feed the building below by gravity.

The first large water tank is believed to be one put up in 1800 by Aaron Burr's Manhattan Company on Chambers Street. With Doric columns and a statue of Oceanus, this freestanding iron and masonry 132,600-gallon (501,945-liter) tank stood 15 feet (4.5 meters) above the street and was fed from a well by a 3.5-foot-diameter (1-meter-diameter) standpipe and a horse-driven pump. The company was soon making a profit providing water to clean city streets and to suit the needs of 1400 home subscribers. By 1830 an elevated tower almost twice as large and charged by a steam pump was erected at Broadway and 13th Street. After water began to flow into the city through aqueducts from Croton and other upstate reservoirs in the 1840s, water pressure was sufficient to supply the typical low building. The Highbridge Water Tower, with a height of 185 feet (56.3 meters) and capacity of 47,000 gallons (177,814 liters), was built in 1872 at 174th Street and Amsterdam Avenue to provide hilly northern Manhattan with water that crossed the Harlem River over the High Bridge Aqueduct. The Highbridge Water Tower still stands.

Water tower, 2009

The technology and appearance of water tanks have changed little over the years. Lower buildings still are not required to have them. Most tanks are constructed like barrels, with wooden staves, while some are made of steel. Most wooden tanks contain 5000 to 10,000 gallons (18,927 to 37,854 liters) of water, need regular maintenance, are covered to keep birds out of the water, and usually are replaced about every 25 years. The city had only two manufacturers and servicers in 2007, Isseks Brothers, founded in 1890, and the Rosenwach Tank Company, founded in 1896. The city is expected to continue to be dependent on its distinctive tanks and towers until (and if) pumps are installed throughout the city's water system.

J. N. Hazelhurst, *Towers and Tanks for Water Works* (New York: Wiley, 1901)

John Rousmaniere

waterways. The waterways of New York City were the reason for the city's founding and an important asset in its growth and development. Their rich marine life was a source of food to the Indians and early colonists. Henry Hudson wrote eloquently of the ample, sheltered harbor, and the early Dutch colonists took advantage of its deep, ice-free waters. The strategic importance of New York Harbor was recognized by the British, who before the Battle of Long Island in the late summer of 1776 were able to assemble in the protected waters of Lower New York Bay a gigantic fleet of 32 men-o'-war and 400 supply ships, as well as their huge army of 32,000 (at the time this was the largest gathering of warships in history). After the American Revolution and well into the twentieth century the harbor was crisscrossed by an extensive network of ferries. The port's strategic importance prompted the government to build defensive forts along the major waterways leading into the harbor. The Brooklyn and Manhattan docks remained important in world commerce until after World War II, when the growth of container shipping redirected most traffic to New Jersey, especially Port Newark–Elizabeth and to a lesser extent the western shore of the Hudson River. Some commercial shipping remained along the waterfront in Brooklyn between Erie Basin and Brooklyn Heights.

Over the years the waterways of New York City became polluted and the marine life virtually disappeared. Efforts by the city and surrounding communities in the 1970s and

1980s to control the dumping of raw sewage and toxic waste produced favorable results, and many of the fish species returned. In the early twenty-first century the Hudson River remained an important link for waterborne traffic to points as far upstate as Albany; among the vessels that navigated its waters were the Staten Island Ferry, excursion boats to the Statue of Liberty and Ellis Island, and around Manhattan, water taxis, new and faster ferry lines to Queens and New Jersey, a few tourist boats from the South Street Seaport, and private passenger yachts.

New York Harbor has 65 square miles (168 square kilometers) of inland waterways and 772 miles (1242 kilometers) of direct shoreline, of which more than 580 miles (933 kilometers) are within the corporate boundaries of New York City. The most important commercial waterways are Lower New York Bay, Upper New York Bay, and Newark Bay; the tidal estuaries Kill van Kull, Arthur Kill, Gowanus Canal, and, in the East River, Newtown Creek, an oily and polluted tidal inlet 4 miles (6.5 kilometers) long that separates Brooklyn from Queens; Long Island Sound (an important means of access to the harbor, connecting the Atlantic Ocean with the East River); and the Hudson River. Other waterways include Gravesend Bay, Jamaica Bay, Flushing Bay, Little Neck Bay, and Raritan Bay, the tidal estuary Harlem River (including Spuyten Duyvil Creek), the Hackensack River, the Passaic River, the Raritan River, the Bronx River, Rockaway Inlet, the Gowanus Canal (not a canal but a drab, polluted tidal tributary of Gowanus Bay within the Upper Bay, adjacent to Erie Basin), and several creeks, rivulets, inlets, and small streams.

Gerard R. Wolfe

Watson, John B(roadus) (*b* Greenville, S.C., 9 Jan 1878; *d* New York City, 25 Sept 1958). Psychologist. He was a professor of experimental and comparative psychology at Johns Hopkins University (1908–22). In 1913 he announced the principles of behaviorism, stressing the predominant role of training and environment in shaping human behavior and minimizing the importance of heredity. His belief that external "reinforcements" rather than heredity or inner character determine human actions drew considerable criticism from many who saw his approach as overly mechanistic. He nevertheless continued to advance his theories, drawing support from his own experiments as well as from the work of Edward L. Thorndike at Columbia University, B. F. Skinner at Harvard University, and Ivan Pavlov in Russia. His contentious and highly publicized divorce and remarriage led to his dismissal from Johns Hopkins in 1922. He then moved to New York City, where he entered the growing field of advertising and used behavioral principles to analyze what motivated consumers; he rose rapidly in the field and in 1924 became a vice president at the firm of J. Walter Thompson. In the late 1920s he also resumed his scholarly work: he gave lectures part time at the New School for Social Research, conducted new experiments in the field of child psychology, and published many articles. Watson became a vice president in 1934 of the William Esty Company, an advertising agency, where he remained until his retirement in 1945.

Sandra Opdycke

Watson, Jr., Thomas J. (*b* Dayton, Ohio, 14 Jan 1914; *d* Greenwich, Conn., 31 Dec 1993). Businessman. He moved to Manhattan in 1937 to work as a salesman for International Business Machines (IBM). In 1952 he was elected president of the company and four years later became its chief executive officer, succeeding his father. Watson, Jr., oversaw the transformation of IBM's typewriters to computers and seemed to recognize early the importance of electronics. He also moved IBM's headquarters out of Manhattan, relocating them in Armonk, New York. He stepped down as chairman and CEO in 1971, though he remained a member of the company's board until 1984. From 1979 to 1981 he took a leave from IBM to serve as the U.S. ambassador to the Soviet Union, advocating for nuclear arms reduction. *Fortune* magazine called him the "greatest capitalist who ever lived."

Thomas J. Watson, Jr., and Peter Petre, *Father, Son & Co: My Life at IBM and Beyond* (New York: Bantam, 1990)

Jessica Montesano

Wavecrest. Southwestern section of Far Rockaway in southeastern Queens, bounded to the north by the tracks of the Rockaway subway line, to the east by Beach 20th Street, to the south by the Atlantic Ocean, and to the west by Beach 32nd Street. The land was purchased in 1878 by Charles H. Cheever and an association of investors from Manhattan. It consisted of 80 acres (32 hectares) of upland and was enclosed as an exclusive park with lodges and gate entrances. Building began in 1880, with the "cottages" originally ranging in value from $5000 to $50,000. The owners were obviously wealthy: railroad presidents, insurance executives, and investors from Wall Street. After World War I the estates were broken up, streets laid out, and apartment buildings erected. The name is obsolete except for use by a few stores and the housing development Wavecrest Gardens.

Vincent Seyfried

Wave Hill. Estate and public garden on 28 acres (11 hectares) overlooking the Hudson River in Riverdale in the Bronx. A gray stone mansion built in 1843 by the lawyer William Lewis Morris was purchased as a summer home by the publisher William Henry Appleton in 1866, who added greenhouses and exotic gardens and during the summers of 1870 and 1871 rented the estate to the family of Theodore Roosevelt. The financier George W. Perkins acquired the property in 1893, assembled a large wooded parcel around it, and in 1910 added an underground recreation building with a bowling alley. He rented the stone house to Mark Twain (1901–3) and then to Bashford Dean, an ichthyologist at the

Wave Hill, 1965

American Museum of Natural History (1909); Dean built the Armor Hall as a private museum adjoining the main building. After Perkins died in 1920 his wife Evelina Ball Perkins lived in Glyndor, a smaller house on the property. The stone house was later rented to the conductor Arturo Toscanini (1942–45) and to the British delegation to the United Nations (1950–56). At the suggestion of parks commissioner Robert Moses, the Perkins and Freeman families in 1960 deeded Wave Hill to the City of New York, which made it into a botanical garden and nonprofit center for the study of the arts and nature.

Michele Herman

weather. The weather in New York City is controlled largely by the jet stream, a strong westerly wind that meanders across the middle latitudes of North America at an altitude of 25,000 to 45,000 feet (7600 to 13,700 meters), usually passing north of the city over northern New York State and southern Quebec but occasionally dipping as far south as the Carolinas. Its movement causes the confluence of warm, moist air from the tropics and cold, dry air from the polar regions. Low and high pressure systems, carried by the jet stream, move through the metropolitan area quickly in winter and more slowly in summer. The primary storm track runs from the Great Lakes and down the St. Lawrence Valley to the Atlantic provinces of Canada after sweeping through Quebec, New York State, and New England, its storm systems usually lasting only a few days and accompanied by fronts that bring shifting winds and a change of weather.

A second important storm track carries storms from the Gulf of Mexico and the Southeast up the Atlantic seaboard from the Carolinas to Maine, including northeasters in winter and tropical storms and hurricanes in summer and autumn. These systems rarely last more than 24 to 36 hours but supply much of the city's precipitation, which amounts to an annual average of 44.12 inches (1122.6 millimeters) and is spread fairly evenly throughout the year: an average of 3.38 inches (85.9 millimeters) falls each month in winter, 3.91 inches (99.3 millimeters) in spring, 3.68 inches (93.5 millimeters) in summer, and 3.74 inches (95.0 millimeters) in autumn. The driest month is February, with 3.13 inches (79.5 millimeters), and the wettest is March, with 4.22 inches (107.2 millimeters), when air from the warming south clashes with Arctic air. About 28.8 inches (73.2 centimeters) of snow falls each year, and snowstorms producing 10 inches (25.4 centimeters) or more occur about once every three to four years. Humidity varies widely, averaging 72 percent at 7:00 a.m. and 56 percent at 1:00 p.m. annually at the Central Park Observatory.

Proximity to several rivers and the Atlantic Ocean causes wind speeds to be higher than those in many landlocked areas. According to the anemometer at the Central Park Observatory, which stands 68 feet (20.7 meters) above ground level, the average wind speed is 9.4 miles (15 kilometers) an hour; the windiest month is March, the calmest ones are July and August, and the prevailing direction is northwest from November to April and southwest from May to October. Arctic blasts from the Canadian tundra can lower the temperature to less than 0°F (−17.8°C), and southwest winds can drive it above 100°F (37.8°C). The average annual temperature is 54.5°F (12.5°C), and average winter and summer temperatures differ by 45.3°F (25.2°C), from 31.5°F (−0.3°C) in January to 76.8°F (24.9°C) in July. During the coldest period of the year, from about 10 December to 4 March, the average temperature is 38°F (3.3°C) or colder, and during the warmest period, from about 7 June to 12 September, the average is 70°F (21.1°C) or warmer. The temperature–humidity index, a measure of human comfort, often rises above 75 in summer.

The climate of the metropolitan area warmed and cooled after the end of the last ice age (about 12,000 B.P.). A "climate optimum," or period of warmth, occurred about 5000 B.P. and was followed by fluctuations in temperature. After 1000 C.E. a period of cooling culminated in the "little ice age" between 1650 and 1850, when temperatures were about 2° to 3°F (1.1° to 1.7°C) cooler than those of the early twenty-first century. The severest winters of the eighteenth century were those of 1740–41 and 1779–80. During both, the Hudson and East rivers froze over, and in the winter of 1779–80 (known as "the hard winter") New York Bay became so solidly frozen for five weeks that the British were able to drag heavy cannon over it to fortify outposts against American attacks.

Extreme weather included hurricanes. On 3 September 1821 the center of the Cape May–Long Island Hurricane passed over part of the city near Jamaica Bay, blowing down thousands of trees in the metropolitan area. The high tide, estimated at 9 feet (2.7 meters) above normal, set a record and caused flooding at the Battery and in much of downtown Manhattan. This was the first indication of a hurricane coming up the coast from North Carolina. According to one report, "Everywhere, so far as heard from outside the Capes and in the Chesapeake Bay, the wind blew with great fury, producing an almost unprecedented heavy sea." The storm capsized a ferry boat in Philadelphia, killing 20 people. Within a few hours thousands of New York City roofs were blowing off houses, and hundreds of ships were dragging anchor or snapping their cables. In the hurricane's dangerous right-hand sector lay the approaches to New York City, where many vessels were approaching the city in the great funnel between New Jersey and Long Island with no knowledge that they were sailing into a storm. This storm drove the ship *Elizabeth* ashore at Fire Island, killing the American writer Margaret Fuller Ossoli.

The first continuous series of weather observations in the city was made by William Laight and his son Henry Laight at various places in lower Manhattan between 1788 and 1836; a trustworthy series was undertaken in 1822 by the U.S. Army Hospital at Fort Columbus on Governors Island, and from 1826 to 1863 the academies Union Hall in Jamaica and Erasmus Hall in Flatbush gathered information about the weather for the New York State Regents.

By the mid-nineteenth century the first weather maps were printed in New York City's newspapers. The city opened the Central Park Observatory and began collecting data in 1869, and a federal weather station was opened in lower Manhattan by the U.S. Signal Service in 1870; this was taken over in 1891 by the U.S. Weather Bureau. During the coldest month of the nineteenth century, January 1857, the average temperature was 19.7°F (−6.8°C), the East River froze solid, and Long Island Sound was icebound for 30 days. A storm known as the "cold storm" struck on 18 January and continued through the next day, leaving 12 inches (30.5 centimeters) of snow as temperatures hovered at about 0°F (−17.8°C) before dropping to −9°F (−22.8°C) on 24 January. In September 1882 two tropical storms dropped 15.44 inches (392.2 millimeters) of rain in the area in 13 days.

The city's best-known storm, the blizzard of 1888, began a few minutes after midnight on 12 March when rain changed to snow; the temperature dropped to 6°F (−14.4°C), a gale-force wind rose, and 21 inches (53.3 centimeters) of snow fell, most of it during a period of 16 hours. Enormous drifts caused most activities to be suspended until the morning of 15 March, and the East River froze over. Hundreds of power and telephone lines were toppled, leading the utilities to lay new lines beneath the street. Successive storms in March 1896 dropped 30.5 inches (77.5 centimeters) of snow, the largest amount recorded for one month.

The first decades of the twentieth century witnessed many severe storms. On 8–9 October 1903 a dissipating tropical storm dropped 11.63 inches (295 millimeters) of rain. During a coastal storm on 1 March 1914 the extremely low barometric pressure of 28.37 inches (960.7 millibars) was recorded. The severest winter of the modern period was that of 1917–18: the average temperature was 25.7°F (−3.5°C), with a low of −13°F (−25.0°C) in December, −4°F (−20.0°C) in January, and −6°F (−21.1°C) in February; New York Harbor became clogged by ice floes, and 27.3 inches (69.4 centimeters) of snow fell in December and January. The earliest snowflakes observed by a weather reporter occurred on 10 October 1925. In

February 1934 the average temperature was 19.9°F (−6.7°C), only 10 days had a maximum above 32°F (0°C), and there was a freeze every night. On 9 February a temperature of −15°F (−26.1°C) was recorded at the Central Park Observatory. Summers were unusually hot during the 1930s, and on 9 July 1936 the temperature reached 106°F (41.1°C). When the western edge of the Long Island–New England Hurricane swept the city on 21 September 1938, the barometer dropped to 28.62 inches (969.2 millibars), and 4.05 inches (102.9 millimeters) of rain fell. The wind blew at 35 miles (56 kilometers) an hour, a gust of 80 miles (128 kilometers) an hour was recorded by an anemometer 454 feet (138 meters) above the Battery, and the tide surging in from Long Island Sound rose 9 feet (2.7 meters) in the East River, causing flooding; most subways stopped running, and power outages were widespread.

Extreme weather conditions continued to visit the city occasionally. In a severe storm that began on 26 December 1947, snow fell at a rate of 2.8 inches (7.1 centimeters) an hour during part of the afternoon; it drifted during the evening and at night, when the wind rose to 30 miles (48 kilometers) an hour. By the next day 26.4 inches (67.1 centimeters) of snow had fallen, and traffic was immobilized for three days; the winter brought 63.2 inches (160.5 centimeters) of snow, setting a record. During the "great Appalachian wind storm" on 25 November 1950 the wind speed averaged 26.6 miles (42.6 kilometers) an hour for 24 hours. A sustained wind of 70 miles (112 kilometers) an hour was recorded, a gust of 90 miles (144 kilometers) an hour hit Idlewild Airport, and high tides closed La Guardia Airport. On 15 October 1954 a gust of 113 miles (181 kilometers) an hour was recorded by an anemometer 484 feet (147 meters) above the Battery during Hurricane Hazel, the center of which passed over Pennsylvania.

Drought conditions during the 1960s forced the city to restrict the use of water. Between 1961 and 1966 precipitation averaged only 80 percent of normal: it fell to 0.14 inches (3.6 millimeters) during the driest month (October 1963), and in December 1964 the reservoirs fell to 26 percent of capacity (compared with a normal figure of 73.2 percent of capacity). The driest year was 1965, with only 26.09 inches (738.9 millimeters) of precipitation. On 9–10 February 1969 a snowstorm dropped 20.2 inches of snow (51.3 centimeters) at John F. Kennedy Airport (which was completely shut down), 16.1 inches (40.9 centimeters) at La Guardia Airport, and 15.3 inches (38.9 centimeters) in Central Park. Snow was not cleared from outlying areas of the city for days, leading critics to name the storm "Mayor Lindsay's storm," with political repercussions.

In 1972 there were 67.03 inches (1702.6 millimeters) of precipitation, or 152 percent of the normal amount, yet over the winter of 1972–73, only 2.8 inches (7.1 centimeters) of snow fell in Central Park; on 6–7 February 1978 and 11–12 February 1983 storms produced 17.7 inches (45.0 centimeters) of snow total. Barometer readings reached a high of 31.08 inches (1052.2 millibars) on 12 February 1981, when a large anticyclone covered the Northeast.

One of the city's notable weather events was the winter of 1993–94, when snow and ice remained on the ground for more than two months, from 29 December to 8 March, and snowfall totaled 53.4 inches (135.6 centimeters). The greatest single storm that year of 12.8 inches (32.2 centimeters), on 11–12 February, left the winter's maximum depth of 22.0 inches (30.5 centimeters) on the ground. December averaged 0.7°F (0.4°C) above normal, January 5.9°F (3.3°C) below normal, February 3.0°F (1.7°C) below normal, and March 1.7°F (0.9°C) below normal. The winter's lowest temperature of −2.0°F (−18.9°C) occurred on 19 January. Although records were not set for snow or cold, the persistence of icy streets and sidewalks heightened the impression of an unusually hard winter.

Unusual weather patterns became frequent. Air pollution over the city caused temperature inversions that trapped heat radiated from buildings and paved surfaces, allowing temperatures to build and remain higher than those in surrounding suburbs, especially at night. Twenty of the 30 summer months between 1980 and 1989 had temperatures above average (in the warmest, August 1980, the average was 80.3°F, or 26.8°C), leading some observers to wonder whether a global warming trend was beginning. July 1999 was New York City's hottest month on record, with an average temperature of 81.4°F (27.4°C), well above the July average of 77.2°F (25.1°C). The temperature was over 90°F (32.2°C) on 18 days, 11 of them consecutive. On two nights in July 1999 the temperature never dropped below 86°F (30°C).

New York City has always experienced extremes, but they seemed especially dramatic in the late twentieth and early twenty-first centuries. The city's highest recorded temperature was 102°F (38.9°C), in July of 1966; the lowest was −4°F (−20°C), in January of 1994. Snowflakes fell on the city on 9 May 1977. When the city's temperature rose to 72°F (22.2°C) on 6 January 2007, many blamed global warming.

Climatic Guide for New York City, New York and Nearby Areas, Climatology of the United States, no. 40–30 (Washington, D.C.: Weather Bureau, U.S. Department of Commerce, 1958); David M. Ludlum, "New York Weather Highlights," *Weatherwise* 14 (1961), 63–67, 78–79; David M. Ludlum, *Early American Hurricanes, 1492–1870* (Boston: American Meteorological Society, 1963); *Local Climatological Data, 1993, New York, Central Park, New York* (Asheville, N.C.: National Climatic Data Center, National Oceanic and Atmospheric Administration, 1994); John Rousmaniere, *After the Storm* (New York: McGraw–Hill, 2002); Christopher C. Burt and Mark Stroud, *Extreme Weather: A Guise and Record Book* (New York: W. W. Norton, 2007)

David M. Ludlum, John Rousmaniere

Weaver, [Susan] **Sigourney (Alexandra)** (*b* New York City, 8 Oct 1949). Actress. The daughter of *The Today Show* creator Sylvester "Pat" Weaver, she studied acting at Stanford University and the Yale School of Drama. She started her career in New York City Off-Off-Broadway and made her film debut in Woody Allen's *Annie Hall* (1977). Her work in Ridley Scott's *Alien* (1979) immediately earned her recognition in Hollywood. She has since starred in plays in New York City, including *Hurly Burly* (1984), *The Merchant of Venice* (1987), *The Mercy Seat* (2002), and *Crazy Mary* (2007). Weaver, a three-time Academy Award nominee, continues to support and participate in the Off-Off-Broadway community alongside her husband Jim Simpson, director of the Flea Theater in Tribeca. Though she spends part of her time in Los Angeles, she defines herself as a New Yorker.

Cecilia Magnusson

Weavers. Folk-singing group formed in 1948 by Pete Seeger (*b* 1919), Lee Hays (1914–81), Ronnie Gilbert (*b* 1926), and Fred Hellerman (*b* 1927). They first performed in Greenwich Village. They became popular for incorporating traditional folk songs, contemporary topical and political songs, ballads, and love songs into their repertory; they also blended folk tunes and harmonies with the rhythms of modern popular music. In 1950 the group made its first hit recording, "Good Night, Irene" by Leadbelly; by 1953 it had sold more than four million records. "If I Had a Hammer," by Hays and Seeger, became one of the group's most popular songs. Supporters of civil rights and opponents of the cold war, the Weavers often allied themselves with the causes of the Communist Party and were persecuted by the Federal Bureau of Investigation. At the height of their popularity they were blacklisted from national television and nightclubs in New York City; their subsequent inability to obtain bookings forced them to disband in 1953, though they reformed in 1955. After Seeger left in 1958 to begin a career as a soloist, the group continued without him until 1963. The original members gave a reunion concert at Carnegie Hall in November 1980 that was shown on public television as *Wasn't That a Time* in 1982. Seeger continued his solo career and his advocacy of social change and became a strong supporter of such environmental causes as protecting the Hudson River. In the 1980s Gilbert resumed singing to give concert tours with the singer, feminist, and social activist Holly Near. Although they sang together for only a short time, the Weavers had a tremendous influence on the repertory and performance styles of American folk music.

David K. Dunaway, *How Can I Keep from Singing: Pete Seeger* (New York: McGraw–Hill, 1981)

Barbara L. Tischler

Webb, Chick [William Henry] (*b* Baltimore, 10 Feb 1909; *d* Baltimore, 16 June 1939). Drummer and leader of the Chick Webb Orchestra, one of the most popular swing bands of the 1930s. As a drummer he was admired for his speed, power, drive, tonal shadings, breaks, dynamic control, and showmanship. At the Savoy Ballroom in Harlem, where his orchestra was the house band, Webb wrote the song "Stompin' at the Savoy" (1934) with Edgar Sampson. The following year the singer Ella Fitzgerald joined the band.

Douglas Henry Daniels

Webb, William H(enry) (*b* New York City, 19 June 1816; *d* 30 Oct 1899). Son of shipbuilder Isaac Webb, co-owner of Webb and Allen shipyard on Lewis Street between Fifth and Seventh avenues, he apprenticed with his father's firm and trained abroad in Europe. Upon his father's death in 1840, Webb returned to New York City to run the shipyard. With his ability to integrate both artful design and careful construction into his vessels, he became one of the most respected naval architects of the nineteenth century. By the mid-1800s Webb and Allen employed 400 workers and produced fast clipper ships, such as the great *Young America* (1853), and packet ships, including the *Guy Mannering* (1849), which sailed between Liverpool and New York City. Webb built the ironclad warship USS *Dunderburg* (1865) for the Union navy during the Civil War. In 1889 he established and endowed the Webb Institute of Naval Architecture in suburban Glen Cove, N.Y.

Edwin L. Dunbaugh and William D. Thomas, *William H. Webb: Shipbuilder* (Glen Cove, N.Y.: Webb Institute of Naval Architecture, 1989)

Joseph Breen

Webb and Bell. Shipbuilding firm. Eckford Webb (1825–93) was one of the first shipbuilders to leave Manhattan for Greenpoint in Brooklyn as shipbuilding became a burgeoning industry in the area. He founded the firm near Newton Creek in 1850, and George W. Bell became a partner in 1856. Webb and Bell became famous for building the wooden caissons for the Brooklyn Bridge, stipulating payment in advance for the $100,274.51 bill. As the shipbuilding industry declined during the late nineteenth century, the firm focused on manufacturing oil and paint.

Kate Lauber

Weber, Max (*b* Bialystok, Russia, 18 April 1881; *d* Great Neck, N.Y., 4 Oct 1961). Painter, sculptor, and printmaker. He emigrated from Russia in 1891 and was a pupil of the noted educator Arthur Wesley Dow at the Pratt Institute. From 1905 he studied abroad: his teachers included Henri Matisse, who persuaded him to embrace modernism. After returning to New York City in 1909 he organized an exhibition in the following year of Henri Rousseau's work at Alfred Stieglitz's gallery "291." Inspired by the modern city, he produced abstract paintings (1914–15) and sculpture. He taught at the Clarence White School of Photography (1914–18) and from 1918 focused on themes of Jewish religious life. Weber developed an influential theory of the fourth dimension, a concept of a higher spiritual reality that transcended the physical world of appearances. He also wrote *Cubist Poems* (1913) and *Essays on Art* (1916). The Whitney Museum of American Art features some of his works.

Percy North, *Max Weber: American Modern* (New York: Jewish Museum, 1982)

Judith Zilczer

Weber and Fields. Team of comedians. It consisted of Joe (Joseph M.) Weber (*b* New York City, 11 Aug 1867; *d* Los Angeles, 10 May 1942) and Lew Fields (*b* New York City, 1 Jan 1867; *d* Beverly Hills, Calif., 20 July 1941), who first performed together as youths in small variety houses on the Bowery. The two specialized in knockabout routines performed in German dialect: Weber, short and stubby, was a foil to Fields, who was tall and bullying. In 1885 they formed a company presenting musical variety shows; this lasted until September 1896, when they became the proprietors of Weber and Fields Broadway Music Hall. There they presented burlesques and travesties of current theatrical productions, and the hall soon became a leading center of American theatrical activity. In 1904 the two ended their partnership; they resumed it in 1912 when they opened Weber and Fields New Music Hall and ended it again when this venture failed. Later they pursued independent careers and occasionally appeared together in vaudeville.

William Green

Webster Hall. Rental hall and later a nightclub at 119–125 East 11th Street between Third and Fourth avenues. It opened in 1886 as a hall for hire. Although it was rented for charitable and society events, it was better known for the labor unions, liberal groups, and radicals, such as Margaret Sanger and Emma Goldman, who used it for lectures, meetings, and rallies. The Progressive Labor Party and the Amalgamated Clothing Workers of America formed at Webster Hall. Starting in the 1910s, outlandish masquerade balls, the most notorious of which were sponsored by the socialist magazine *The Masses,* earned Webster Hall the nickname the Devil's Playhouse. By the late 1950s it had been converted into a recording studio for RCA Victor Records. Elvis Presley, Frank Sinatra, and Julie Andrews recorded there, as did the casts of *Hello, Dolly!* and *Fiddler on the Roof.* In the 1980s Webster Hall reemerged as a nightclub known as the Ritz. It is used early in the twenty-first century as a club and concert venue, again under its historic name, and was designated a city landmark in 2008.

Melissa Baldock

Wechsler, David (*b* Lespedi, Romania, 12 Jan 1896; *d* New York City, 2 May 1981). Psychologist. After studying with leading psychologists at universities in New York, London, and Paris, Wechsler completed his PhD in psychology in 1925 at Columbia University. In 1932 he became chief psychologist at Bellevue Psychiatric Hospital in Manhattan, a world leader among clinical psychology programs. Wechsler is best known for the debut in 1939 of his revolutionary Bellevue–Wechsler Intelligence Scale, which changed the procedure for calculating the intelligence quotient (IQ) and went beyond one IQ score to offer a 15-score "profile" of a person's abilities. He published *The Measurement of Adult Intelligence* in 1939. Since that year, the revised and expanded Wechsler test series has become a gold standard for assessing the mental abilities at three age levels: preschoolers, children, and adults. Wechsler's many awards from the American Psychological Association (APA) include clinical psychology (1960), school psychology (1973), and the APA Distinguished Professional Contribution Award in 1973.

Harold Takooshian

Wedtech scandal. Widely publicized political scandal involving a machine shop formed in 1965 by John Mariotta as the Welbilt Electronic Die Corporation at 595 Girard Avenue in the Bronx. The firm's efforts to employ members of minority groups qualified it for the "no-bid" programs of the Small Business Administration, and during the early 1980s it won an army contract for $32 million; eventually it grew into a business handling a total of $250 million in military contracts. In 1983 the firm changed its name to the Wedtech Corporation and became publicly owned. An investigation in 1984 uncovered evidence of bribery, influence peddling, misstatements made to shareholders, and the theft of millions of dollars by the firm's officers. The firm declared bankruptcy, and federal charges led to the convictions of Mariotta and about 20 government officials, including Bronx congressman Mario Biaggi and borough president Stanley Simon. Some convictions were reversed on appeal in view of the fact that star witness and former Wedtech president Anthony Guariglia had committed perjury.

Marilyn W. Thompson, *Feeding the Beast: How Wedtech Became the Most Corrupt Little Company in America* (New York: Scribner, 1990); James Traub, *Too Good to Be True: The Outlandish Story of Wedtech* (New York: Doubleday, 1990)

Val Ginter

Weegee [Fellig, Arthur H.] (*b* Zloczow, Austria [now in Poland], 12 June 1899; *d* New York City, 26 Dec 1968). Press photographer. He immigrated to the United States in 1920 and settled in New York City, where he joined Acme Newspictures in 1924. A freelance photographer from 1935, he concentrated on violent crime, accidents, and fires. In 1938 he became the only press photographer permitted to have a police radio in his automobile, a device that gave him an advantage over his competitors. Around 1940 he adopted his nickname (probably derived from the Ouija board) while working for the newspaper *PM.* He self-consciously played on his notoriety, calling himself "Weegee the Famous." He published *Naked City* (1945), a collection of his photography that later inspired a film version that took his career to Hollywood. He also made portraits of celebrities and world leaders, worked on assignment for glossy magazines, including *Vogue,* and later in his life sold his work to the Museum of Modern Art.

Weegee's New York: Photographs, 1935–1960 (New York: Schirmer–Mosel, 1982)

Madeline Rogers

Weeksville. Former neighborhood in Brooklyn, bounded to the north by Fulton Street, to the east by Ralph Avenue, to the south by Eastern Parkway, and to the west by Troy Avenue. The area was settled by blacks shortly after the abolition of slavery in New York State in 1827 and grew during and after the Civil War. It was named for James Weeks, a settler who moved there from Virginia in 1838; his property was formerly part of the vast estate of the Lefferts family. Susan Smith McKinney-Steward, the first black female physician in New York State and the third in the nation, was born in 1847 in the neighborhood, which was first shown on a map in 1849; the main street was Schenectady Avenue south of Atlantic Avenue. The residents sheltered many of the black victims of the New York City draft riots in 1863, and several soldiers who fought with the New York regiments of the United States Colored Troops came from this district. The area was once the site of the Howard Colored Orphanage Asylum, the Zion Home for Aged Relief, and the African Civilization Society. It lost its identity during the rapid growth of Brooklyn after the completion of the Brooklyn Bridge in 1883. From about 1968 the name Weeksville was revived, amid a growing interest in local history, historic preservation, and black heritage. The Hunterfly Road Houses, a city landmark at 1698–1708 Bergen Street, are the only surviving houses of a group built parallel to a seventeenth-century road. The Bethel Tabernacle African Methodist Episcopal Church (1847) and the Berean Missionary Baptist Church (1851) still serve the neighborhood; Colored School no. 2 (1847) became Public School 243 (the Weeksville School).

Harold X. Connolly, *A Ghetto Grows in Brooklyn* (New York: New York University Press, 1977); Joan Maynard and Gwen Cottman, *Weeksville Then and Now* (New York: Society for the Preservation of Weeksville and Bedford–Stuyvesant History, 1983)

Joan Bacchus Maynard, Craig Steven Wilder

Weeksville, 2009

WeightWatchers. Weight-loss company. Founded in the early 1960s by Brooklyn native Jean Nidetch, the company grew out of the weekly support group meetings that Nidetch had with her friends about how to best lose weight. The company's strategy is to promote a healthy lifestyle, rather than dieting, as a way to achieve sustained weight loss. As part of the program, participants are encouraged to attend support group meetings. The Web site WeightWatchers.com was launched in 1999 and is based in New York City. In 2005 Weight Watchers International moved it headquarters to the MetLife Building at 11 Madison Avenue.

Jessica Montesano

Weill, Kurt (Julian) (*b* Dessau, Germany, 2 March 1900; *d* New York City, 3 April 1950). Composer. On 13 April 1933 his musical *The Threepenny Opera* premiered on Broadway, closing after 13 performances. With his wife, the actress and singer Lotte Lenya, he fled Nazi Germany and arrived in New York City on 10 September 1935; the two lived at the St. Moritz Hotel (50 Central Park South) before moving to an apartment at 231 East 62nd Street. During his years in New York City Weill wrote a number of successful musicals for the Broadway stage: *Knickerbocker Holiday* (1938), set in New Amsterdam; *One Touch of Venus* (1943, lyrics by Ogden Nash); *Street Scene* (1946, lyrics by Langston Hughes), set in a rundown neighborhood in New York City; *Love Life* (1948); and *Lost in the Stars* (1949). He bought a house in Rockland County in 1941 but continued to spend much time in the city. After his death *The Threepenny Opera* enjoyed great success, and the New York City Opera incorporated *Street Scene* into its repertory.

David Drew, *Kurt Weill: A Handbook* (Berkeley: University of California Press, 1989)

Marc Ferris

Weill Medical College of Cornell University. Medical school. Originally Cornell University Medical College, it was opened by the board of trustees of Cornell University in New York City on 14 April 1898, on the grounds of Bellevue Hospital. In 1900 it moved to a new building on First Avenue and 28th Street. The first graduating class of 58 students included 10 women. In 1912 the college became affiliated with New York Hospital; the two institutions agreed on 14 June 1927 to build the New York Hospital–Cornell Medical Center on York Avenue between 67th and 68th streets, which began receiving patients on 1 September 1932. In 2009 the school had 400 students who received clinical training at New York Hospital and other affiliated hospitals.

Comprehensive Medical Care and Teaching: A Report on the New York Hospital-Cornell Medical Center Program (Ithaca, N.Y.: Cornell University Press, 1967)

Adele A. Lerner

Weitling, Wilhelm (*b* Magdeburg [now in Germany], 5 Oct 1808; *d* New York City, 25 Jan 1871). Revolutionist. A tailor by trade, he was a prominent socialist during the 1840s. After fleeing Germany for Paris in 1837 he immigrated to the United States at the invitation of the Sozialreformassoziation, a radical German organization in New York City; there he formed the revolutionary group Befreiungsbund in 1846. An adherent of the labor theory of value, he proposed a labor exchange bank where workers would receive notes worth the value of their work. Unlike some of his contemporaries he shrank from encouraging open class warfare and saw communism and Christianity as compatible ethical systems. For this stance and his tendency to concentrate on problems of exchange rather than those pertaining to the mode of production, he was bitterly criticized by Karl Marx and Friedrich Engels but nonetheless became a popular and influential figure among radicals in New York City. He went to Germany for the revolution of 1848 and in 1850 returned to the city where he launched the German newspaper *Die Re-*

publik der Arbeiter (*The Workers' Republic*), formed the nationwide socialist organization Arbeiterbund (the Workingmen's League), and led the German labor council. After the Arbeiterbund collapsed and his newspaper ceased publication in 1855, he largely abandoned politics to work as a tailor and care for his family.

Kevin Kenny, Stanley Nadel

welfare. For a discussion of welfare in New York City see POVERTY.

Welfare Hospital for Chronic Disease. Name used from 1939 to 1942 by COLER–GOLDWATER SPECIALTY HOSPITAL AND NURSING FACILITY.

Welfare Island. Name applied between 1921 and the 1970s to ROOSEVELT ISLAND.

Welles, (George) Orson (*b* Kenosha, Wis., 6 May 1915; *d* Los Angeles, 10 Oct 1985). Actor and director. After growing up primarily in Chicago, he moved to New York City in 1934, living at 319 West 14th Street in Manhattan until 1937. He toured in Off-Broadway productions and eventually established himself by directing unconventional interpretations of classic plays. In 1936, while working for the Federal Theater Project of the Works Progress Administration, he directed a modern version of *Macbeth* with an all-black cast; in 1937 he directed the "labor opera" *The Cradle Will Rock.* Welles and John Houseman formed the Mercury Theater in the same year. *Time* magazine proclaimed the 23-year-old Welles the "wonder boy" of Broadway in 1938. Aside from directing and acting, he and the Mercury Theater also had a radio show; their 1938 broadcast of H. G. Wells's *The War of the Worlds* was believed by some listeners to be an actual report of a Martian invasion. After 1940 Welles worked primarily as a director and actor. He moved to California in 1939 and became widely known for his films, including *Citizen Kane* (1941).

Frank Brady, *Citizen Welles: A Biography of Orson Welles* (New York: Scribner, 1989)

Max Seppo

Welsh. There were few Welsh residents in New York City in colonial times. Among them was Francis Lewis (1713–1802), an officer during the American Revolution and a signer of the Declaration of Independence; his son Morgan (1754–1844) became governor of New York in 1804. In 1790 Welsh immigrants accounted for 2.3 percent of the city's population. Poor harvests during the 1790s drove hundreds from Wales across the Atlantic, and the number increased after 1817 when estates in Wales were consolidated and rents and population there began to increase. Many of the Welsh who moved to the city settled near English and Scottish immigrants on the West Side and were accepted because they were British, literate, and Protestant. Welsh men often entered the building trades and quickly sought citizenship; they usually joined the Republican Party because it opposed the expansion of slavery before the Civil War and because the Democratic Party was dominated by the Irish. Welsh women became homemakers and domestic servants. Welsh immigrants were often evangelical and opened several chapels; these grew slowly because there was a shortage of ministers, the population was transient, quarrels broke out between denominations, and some members were attracted to other churches. Welsh societies were formed in 1801 by Congregationalists and in 1806 by Baptists but disbanded within a few years. After moving to the city in 1836 William Rowlands (*b* 10 Oct 1807; *d* 27 Oct 1866) revitalized the Calvinistic Methodist congregation, which moved in 1859 to a new building on 13th Street and in 1913 to 155th Street; he also launched the monthly publication *Y Cyfaill* (The Friend) and the weekly *Y Drych* (The Mirror), which by mid-century were moved to the larger Welsh center at Utica, New York.

There were 935 Welsh residents in Manhattan and 338 in Brooklyn in 1855. The minister Robert D. Thomas reported in 1872 that only half the Welsh population spoke Welsh and about a tenth attended Welsh services or took part in *gymanfas* (preaching and singing meetings) or *eisteddfods* (singing and poetry competitions). The St. David Society of the State of New York absorbed older benefit societies in 1886. Immigration decreased gradually after 1900, when there were 1686 Welsh immigrants (who had 2750 children), and more rapidly after 1914; by 1940 there were only 1296 Welsh inhabitants in the city. The Calvinistic Methodist Church in the United States merged with the Presbyterian Church in 1919, leading many former members of the congregation in the city to attend Welsh-language services at the Rutgers Presbyterian Church on 73rd Street. In the early twenty-first century the Welsh Congregational Church of New York still holds monthly services at Rutgers Presbyterian.

In March the St. David Society of New York celebrates the birthday of St. David (the patron saint of Wales) with songs and honors such distinguished Welsh Americans as Samuel Ellis, who once owned Ellis Island (his heirs sold it to New York State in 1808), and Charles Evans Hughes, the son of a Welsh Baptist minister, who became governor of New York, secretary of state under President Warren G. Harding, and chief justice of the United States.

David Maldwyn Ellis

Werblin, Sonny [David A(braham)] (*b* New York City, 17 March 1910; *d* New York City, 21 Nov 1991). Entrepreneur. He worked as a copy boy at the *New York Times* and then as an office worker at Music Corporation of America (MCA). He became a booking agent at MCA in 1934; he soon represented such performers as Johnny Carson, Elizabeth Taylor, Frank Sinatra, and Jackie Gleason. After becoming president of MCA in 1958, he led a group of investors that bought the football team the New York Titans in March 1963, which was renamed the New York Jets. In 1965 he retired from MCA to devote himself to the team, and in the same year he signed the quarterback Joe Namath to a three-year contract for $427,000, an enormous sum at the time. He also named Weeb Ewbank as head coach and general manager and built a team that won the Super Bowl in 1969. Before the beginning of the football season in 1968 he was bought out by his partners, including Leon Hess and the banker Townsend Martin, who resented the power that he wielded over the organization. Werblin took over Madison Square Garden in 1977 and also owned a share in the racetrack at Monmouth Park in New Jersey.

Janet Frankston

Wertham, Fredric (*b* Munich, Germany, 20 Mar 1895; *d* Kempton, Pa., 18 Nov 1981). Psychiatrist. He crusaded against comic books in the 1950s and argued in congressional testimony that they caused juvenile delinquency. His 1953 book *Seduction of the Innocent,* based on interviews with young offenders who said that they read comics, was scientifically flawed because he did not interview a control group of nondelinquents. Wertham studied medicine in Europe and became interested in Freudian theory. He immigrated to the United States in 1922 and moved to New York City in 1932 to direct a new psychiatric clinic for the city court system. He later became a professor of psychiatry at New York University, senior psychiatrist at the New York City Department of Hospitals, and director of a mental hygiene clinic in Harlem for mostly poor and African American patients. His article "Psychological Effects of School Segregation" was submitted as evidence in the litigation that led to the Supreme Court's 1954 decision in *Brown v. Board of Education.* Wertham first linked media entertainment to crime in his 1941 book *Dark Legend* about a young murderer who lived in a fantasy world fueled by movies, radio plays, and comics. Wertham's luridly illustrated and polemical *Seduction of the Innocent* was excerpted in *Reader's Digest* and *Ladies' Home Journal,* thereby expanding his influence. His 1954 testimony before Senator Estes Kefauver's committee investigating juvenile delinquency made a particular impact because of his medical credentials. *Seduction of the Innocent* attacked Western, science fiction, and superhero comics. It condemned the eroticization of violence as well as the "subtle atmosphere of homoeroticism which pervades the adventures of the mature Batman and his young friend Robin." Wertham's advocacy, and particularly his Senate testimony, motivated the industry to create a Comics Code Authority, whose standards for a code seal of approval essentially killed the crime and horror genre.

Fredric Wertham, *Seduction of the Innocent* (New York: Rinehart, 1953); Marjorie Heins, *Not in Front of the Children: "Indecency," Censorship, and the Innocence of Youth* (New Brunswick, N.J.: Rutgers University Press, 2007)

Marjorie Heins

West, Mae [Mary Jane] (*b* Brooklyn, 17 Aug 1892; *d* Los Angeles, 22 Nov 1980). Actress and playwright. After making a successful debut as Baby Mae during an amateur night at the Royal Theater on Fulton Street in Brooklyn, she performed in 1911 at the Columbia Theatre on Broadway and in Ned Wayburn's production of *A la Broadway and Hello Paris.* Her distinctive manner, characterized by double entendres and suggestive movements and dress, both glorified and parodied conventional sexuality. In 1918 West incorporated her own version of the "shimmy," which she learned at black jazz clubs and cafés in Chicago, into her role as Mamie Dyne in Rudolf Friml's *Sometime.* Unable to find roles to her liking, she began to write her own plays. Her first, *Sex* (1925), was rejected by J. J. Shubert, so she produced the play herself. It opened at Daly's Theatre in 1926, and despite a ban on advertising it ran for 40 weeks until it was shut down by the Society for the Suppression of Vice. She was convicted on charges of "corrupting the morals of youth" and spent eight days in jail on Welfare Island. West's later Broadway plays included *The Wicked Age* (1927), in which she exposed the corruption of beauty contests, and *Diamond Lil* (1928), her most successful work, in which she portrayed a saloon singer on the Bowery in the 1890s. In 1932 she accepted a contract from Paramount Pictures and moved to Los Angeles. She is buried with her family in Brooklyn's Cypress Hill Cemetery.

Chad Ludington

West, Nathanael [Weinstein, Nathan Wallenstein] (*b* New York City, 17 Oct 1903; *d* near El Centro, Calif., 23 Dec 1940). Novelist. The son of Lithuanian immigrants, in 1926 after graduating from Brown University he changed his name to Nathanael West. He was introduced to a circle of writers for the *New Yorker* by a college classmate and brother-in-law S. J. Perelman. Working as a night manager at the Kenmore Hotel at East 23rd Street, he wrote his novel *Miss Lonelyhearts* (1933), which was set in Depression-era New York City. In 1933 he left New York City to pursue screenwriting in Hollywood, where he underwent periods of unemployment and wrote his highly acclaimed novel *The Day of the Locust* (1939). West died in an automobile crash and is buried in Mount Zion Cemetery in Queens.

Frank Morrow

Westbeth. Complex of several buildings in lower Manhattan, bounded to the north by Bethune Street, to the east by Washington Street, to the south by Bank Street, and to the west by West Street. Designed by Cyrus L. W. Eidlitz and others and built from 1880 to 1900, the buildings were used for research by the American Bell Telephone Company. The vacuum tube, the condenser microphone, and the transistor were all invented there. After the firm moved to New Jersey, the J. M. Kaplan Fund helped to convert the buildings into artists' housing in 1965; this marked the first conversion of industrial lofts into residential space on a large scale. The inner court as redesigned by Richard Meier and Associates is notable for its stark geometry and semicircular egress balconies.

John Voelcker

West Brighton (i). Name by which West New Brighton is sometimes known.

West Brighton (ii). Neighborhood in southwestern Brooklyn, bounded to the north by Neptune Avenue, to the east by Ocean Parkway, to the south by the Atlantic Ocean, and to the west by Stillwell Avenue; south of Surf Avenue stretches a network of narrow walks that were once crammed with restaurants, cheap hotels, carousels, roller coasters, saloons, and amusement stands. The name was most widely used during the late nineteenth century, when the blocks between West 10th and West 16th streets were among the most notorious in the nation and the first houses were built in an area known as the Gut along West First, Second, and Third streets. African Americans who worked at racetracks nearby and Jewish peddlers at the shore settled in the neighborhood. Substandard one- and two-story frame houses remained until the 1950s, when the land was cleared under urban renewal programs and used for more than 15 apartment buildings of 23 stories each, including Trump Village and the Warbasse Houses. The New York Aquarium, built in 1957 at West Eighth Street, became an important research center and tourist attraction. The 1980s saw an influx of immigrants from the Soviet Union. The hub of the neighborhood is a shopping center in Trump Village at West Fifth Street. In the early twenty-first century, recreational attractions included the ocean, the beach, Seaside Park, which offered summer concerts, and a small part of the amusement district of Coney Island.

Martha Munzer and Helen Vogel, *Block by Block: Rebuilding City Neighborhoods* (New York: Alfred A. Knopf, 1973)

Stephen Weinstein

Westchester Square. Neighborhood in the east central Bronx, centered at an intersection of the same name. English colonists from Connecticut established a village there in 1654 that was the first European settlement in what is now the Bronx. Called Oostdorp (east village) by the Dutch, it was formally acquired in 1664 by Great Britain and renamed West Chester; the settlers solidified their claims with the Indian treaty of 1692. In the following year an Anglican church was founded that is now known as St. Peter's Episcopal Church. The hamlet became a river port on Westchester Creek, and sea captains and sailors made up a sizable part of the Anglican and Quaker community. In 1776 the village suffered a weeklong cannonade from British and Hessian forces, but the Continental army dismantled a bridge over the creek, forcing the enemy to detour to Pell's Point. Fort Schuyler was built on Throgs Neck in the 1840s, and new families, chiefly Irish Catholics, settled in the area as builders, laborers, and stonemasons. During the Civil War rioters invaded the village in 1863 to destroy draft records, unaware that these were safe in Fort Schuyler. The twentieth century brought subway lines, streetcars, and buses to the area, which changed into a busy hub of commerce. In the twenty-first century the neighborhood remains an important junction, with thriving businesses, banks, shops, churches, schools, and hospitals.

John McNamara, *History in Asphalt: The Origin of Bronx Street and Place Names* (New York: Bronx County Historical Society, 1984); John McNamara, *McNamara's Old Bronx* (New York: Bronx County Historical Society, 1989)

John McNamara

West End Collegiate Church. Dutch Reformed Church in a landmark 1892 building located at 370 West End Avenue and 77th Street. Part of the oldest continually operating church corporation in the country, which was established in New Amsterdam around 1628, the Flemish-style structure, designed by Robert W. Gibson with Tiffany windows, was built during the Upper West Side residential building boom of the 1880s. It remains allied, though not institutionally affiliated, with the Collegiate School for Boys located next door at 241 West 77th Street.

Peter L. Donhauser

Westerleigh. Neighborhood in north central Staten Island bounded to the north by Forest Avenue, to the east by Manor Road, to the south by Watchogue Road, and to the west by Wooley Avenue. It was first developed in 1887 by the National Prohibition Campground Association, which purchased 25 acres (10 hectares) of land and opened Prohibition Park. The University Temple was built in 1891; an auditorium seating 4000, it attracted such nationally known speakers as William Jennings Bryan before being destroyed by fire in 1903. In 1892 the area took its present name. The Westerleigh Collegiate Institute, a private secondary school, opened in 1895. Many local streets were named for prohibitionists and for states that voted for Prohibition. In the 1890s Westerleigh was a close-knit, upper-class neighborhood with narrow streets and one-family houses, many of which were built during the decade. Well-known residents included Isaac Funk, the editor of the *Funk and Wagnalls Encyclopedia;* the poet Edwin Markham; and the etiquette writer Amy Vanderbilt. The center of the neighborhood is Westerleigh Park; there is no commercial section. Landmarks include Westerleigh Park and its octagonal bandstand (built 1923, renovated 1990); the Immanuel Union Church; and 208 Neal Dow Avenue, a house designed by Ernest Flagg. The Westerleigh Improvement Society (1893) is one of the oldest neighborhood associations in the city.

Barnett Shepherd

Western Electric Company. Firm of telecommunications equipment manufacturers, incorporated in 1915 in New York City as a wholly owned subsidiary of American Telephone and Telegraph (AT&T). It was a successor to a concern based in Chicago that since 1882 had developed, manufactured, engineered, installed, and maintained telephone equipment and systems for AT&T and its operating companies. The firm was important in enabling AT&T to dominate American telephony and remain technologically advanced. It was also the research arm of the American Bell Telephone Company until the formation of Bell Laboratories in 1925. For many decades the company had offices on the east side of Broadway just south of City Hall Park. In 1984 AT&T was divested of its regional operating companies, and the functions of Western Electric were absorbed by the operating companies and various business units of AT&T.

George David Smith

Western Union Company. Firm established in 1851 as the New York and Mississippi Valley Printing Telegraph Company and based during its early years in Rochester, New York. It expanded rapidly by means of agreements with several railroads, which provided rights of way and lines in exchange for trained operators and priority service for railroad messages. Renamed the Western Union Telegraph Company in 1856, the firm soon commanded the most important western routes. During the 1850s liberal incorporation laws passed by the state legislature of New York allowed it to take over many small, regional companies and in doing so to reorganize the industry. With five other companies, including the American Telegraph Company, it made an agreement in 1857 to divide the market into clearly defined territories; Western Union abrogated the agreement in 1860 by obtaining a government subsidy to build a transcontinental telegraph, which by garnering large government subsidies during the Civil War gave the firm a competitive advantage. By 1866 it had acquired control of its major competitors and moved its headquarters to 145 Broadway in New York City.

After the Civil War the capitalist Jay Gould became the most formidable competitor of Western Union by building his own company that combined telegraph lines from his railroad empire with those of small companies. In 1871 Western Union acquired the Gold and Stock Telegraph Company and operated it as a subsidiary that remained the most important commercial news and market-reporting company to the end of the nineteenth century. Gould's unrelenting competition allowed him to gain control of Western Union in 1881; his consolidation of the industry reduced opportunities for small telegraph operators and led them to strike in 1883, without success. Western Union entered into exclusive agreements to transmit news for the Associated Press and messages through the national network of American District Telegraph, which it reorganized in 1901 into the alarm company that came to be known in the late twentieth century as ADT. At the same time the near-monopoly in telegraphy achieved by Western Union faced a new challenge from the long-distance telephone network of American Telephone and Telegraph, which briefly acquired control of Western Union in 1909; antitrust action soon led to the separation of the two firms. After World War II telegraphy was largely supplanted by other systems, but Western Union continued to be an important telecommunications company until the early 1980s, launching the first communications satellite and establishing one of the first electronic mail services. Later in the decade the firm abandoned most of its communications business and concentrated on financial services, including money transfers (which it began in 1871) and priority message services such as "mailgrams," an overnight mail service introduced in 1970. In 1996 the company moved its headquarters from Paramus, New Jersey, to Colorado.

Robert Luther Thompson, *Wiring a Continent: The History of the Telegraph Industry in the United States, 1832–1866* (Princeton, N.J.: Princeton University Press, 1947); Edwin Gabler, *The American Telegrapher: A Social History, 1860–1900* (New Brunswick, N.J.: Rutgers University Press, 1988); Paul B. Israel, *From the Machine Shop to the Industrial Laboratory: Telegraphy and the Changing Context of American Invention, 1830–1920* (Baltimore: Johns Hopkins University Press, 1992)

See also Technology.

Paul Israel

Westervelt, Jacob Aaron (*b* Tenafly, N.J., 20 Jan 1800; *d* New York City, 21 Feb 1879). Shipbuilder and mayor. For about 50 years he had a shipbuilding firm on the East River that produced about 200 seagoing vessels. Considered honest but weak during his term as mayor from 1852 to 1854, he introduced reforms and reorganized the police department but was widely criticized for the filthy condition of the streets.

James E. Mooney

West Farms. Neighborhood in the central Bronx, bounded to the north by Bronx Park, to the east by the Bronx River, to the south by Hunts Point, and to the west by Southern Boulevard; some of those who live east of the Bronx River also consider themselves residents of the neighborhood. From about 1812 the area was the site of paint, glass, pottery, and bleaching factories; flour mills; a sawmill; and coal yards. A large area around it was incorporated as a town in 1846 and initially named Ten Farms before being renamed for its location west of the village of Westchester. From the Civil War to the 1930s the area was a thriving river port. In 1874 the town was annexed to New York City and became part of the Annexed District, or North Side. After the subway was extended to White Plains Road, apartment buildings were constructed and shops opened; several of these were replaced during a renewal project of the 1960s. In the early twenty-first century the population is mostly Latin American, and some manufacturing and commerce continue to exist in the neighborhood.

John McNamara, *McNamara's Old Bronx* (New York: Bronx County Historical Society, 1989)

Gary D. Hermalyn

Westfield. Former administrative district in southwestern Staten Island, bounded to the north by Fresh Kills and Richmond Creek, to the east by Gifford's Lane, to the south by Lower New York Bay, and to the west by the Arthur Kill; towns within its boundaries included Tottenville, Pleasant Plains, Prince's Bay, Woodrow, Kreischerville, Rossville, Greenridge, Annadale, and parts of Eltingville and Great Kills. The district was established after the American Revolution. It was variously called West Division and West Quarter, and the area encompassing it and Southfield was sometimes called Southside. The seat was Richmondtown, in Southfield. The district was dissolved when New York City was consolidated in 1898.

Marjorie Johnson

West Flushing. Original name of Corona.

Westies. Irish-American gang based in the Hell's Kitchen neighborhood on the west side of Manhattan. It was notorious for violent crimes mostly from the 1950s to the mid-1980s, although some sources say they have continued influence into the twenty-first century. The extent and coherence of the gang may have been exaggerated by law enforcement officials. Operating mostly from the docks of the West Side, its members successfully engaged in gambling and drug dealing until links with the Mafia led to internal rivalries and assassinations.

T. J. English, *The Westies: Inside the Hell's Kitchen Irish Mob* (New York: G. P. Putnam's Sons, 1990; repr. New York: St. Martin's Griffin, 2006)

Joshua Brown

West Jamaica. Original name of Dunton.

Westminster Kennel Club. Oldest dog club in New York and the best known in the nation. A group of sportsmen formed the club in 1877 "to increase the interest in dogs, and thus improve the breeds, and to hold an Annual Dog Show in the city of New York." The club is named after the Westminster Hotel in Union Square where its founders would often meet. The club's first show in 1877 featured 1201 dogs and drew an estimated 20,000 spectators to the second and third days of the competition at the Hippodrome (popularly known as Gilmore's Gardens). The show has taken place every year since, making it the second longest running annual sporting event in the United States behind the Kentucky Derby. In 1884 the competition began to be judged by officials from the American Kennel Club, an organization partially established by members of the Westminster Kennel Club and Kennel Club of Philadelphia to oversee their dog shows. Some degree of showmanship and celebrity marked the show's early years: J. P. Morgan's dogs competed with entrants claiming the Queen of England, the czar of Russia, and General Custer as their dogs' former owners or breeders. The Best in Show award was first given in 1907 to a Smooth Fox Terrier named Ch. (Champion) Warren Remedy; she would win again in 1908 and 1909 and remains Westminster's only three-time champion. Dogs must advance from the breed and group levels before becoming one of the seven finalists vying to become crowned Best in Show. As of 2008 the show featured more than 2600 dogs competing in 169 breeds. As of 2010, 45 terriers—more than twice as many as any other group—have been crowned Best in Show. All four Madison Square Gardens have hosted the event, which has been televised nationally since 1948.

Ben Silk

West New Brighton. Neighborhood in north central Staten Island sometimes referred to as West Brighton. The main streets include Richmond Terrace on the waterfront, Castleton Avenue, and Forest Avenue; Broadway and Jewett Avenue run north to south. The area was originally the site of a hunting lodge built in the late seventeenth century by Governor Thomas Dongan on his manor facing the Kill van Kull. The Kruzer–Pelton House, a rambling stone farmhouse at 1262 Richmond Terrace, and the Scott–Edwards House at 752 Delafield Avenue, were also built during the colonial period. The first factory was established near Richmond Terrace and Broadway in 1819 by Barrett, Tileson and Company of Maine; it was reorganized in 1825 as the New-York Dyeing and Printing Establishment for cleaning and dyeing cloth. Factoryville was an early name for the area, and the brick buildings, smokestacks, and pond of the factory were long the principal features. By 1840 a commercial area had developed on Richmond Terrace and Broadway near the factories and the ferry landing at Castleton. Nathan Barrett left the New-York Dyeing and Printing Establishment in 1851 and formed Barrett, Nephews and Company, which opened a factory on Forest Avenue; this merged in 1890 with New-York Dyeing and Printing, and the operations of the new firm were consolidated at Broadway, where operations continued until 1932. A post office opened in 1871 and used the name West New Brighton (after New Brighton, an earlier and wealthier suburb). The C. W. Hunt Company, a manufacturer of heavy coal-handling equipment used in ports worldwide, built a plant in 1872 near Richmond Terrace and Van Street; this became the largest factory in Staten Island before closing during the 1930s. Tompkins Department Store opened in 1877 and became the largest retail establishment in Staten Island. Calvary Presbyterian Church was formed in 1894, followed by the Church of the Sacred Heart in 1898. Castleton Avenue was extended to Port Richmond in 1911 and became the principal commercial street; the newspaper the *Staten Island Advance* had its offices at 1267 Castleton Avenue from 1913 to 1960. In 1936 the former estate of the Barrett family was made the site of the Staten Island Zoo. The local Young Men's Christian Association opened on Broadway in the 1950s. West Brighton Plaza, a complex of 400 apartments subsidized by the federal government, opened in 1962. The population of West New Brighton in 2008 was largely Italian, Irish, black, and Latin American. There were ship repair facilities on the waterfront and a wooded residential area on the southern boundary near the zoo. The West New Brighton Local Development Corporation and the Neighborhood Housing Services invigorated the community during the early twenty-first century. Lawrence C. Thompson Park and its swimming pool occupy part of the site once occupied by the New-York Dyeing and Printing factory.

Staten Island: A Resource Manual for School and Community (New York: Board of Education of the City of New York, 1964)

Barnett Shepherd

West Nile virus. Virus discovered in Uganda in 1937; its first known case in the United States was in New York City in 1999. It can be carried by birds and spread by mosquitoes and has been known to cause severe human meningitis (the inflammation of the membranes that surround the spinal cord and brain) and encephalitis (the inflammation of the brain itself). Since 1999 the infectious West Nile virus has been detected in humans, animals, and mosquitoes in all states. In 2007, 18 New Yorkers contracted the disease; three of them died.

Jessica Montesano

West Side Highway. Popular name variously applied to the highways along the Hud-

West Side Highway, 1938

son River in Manhattan (New York State Route 9A). The name was first used for the Miller Elevated Highway (1931–48), an elevated structure along West Street and 12th Avenue that originally extended from Rector Street to 72nd Street. In its early years the highway was noted for its artwork, which included cast-metal reproductions of the seal of New York City, but it suffered from heavy traffic and deferred maintenance. On 15 December 1973 a loaded dump truck plunged through a pothole near the Gansevoort Market, and the highway was closed south of 57th Street on the southbound side and 46th Street on the northbound side. Repairs were delayed as the city and state made plans to build Westway. Most of the elevated structure was demolished in stages from 1976 to 1989; through the West Side Highway Replacement Project (1985–2001), the elevated segment between 59th Street to 72nd Street was rebuilt and remained in use, while the at-grade roads previously beneath the highway south of 59th Street were rebuilt into an at-grade urban arterial. The road was renamed for baseball player Joe DiMaggio in 1999.

The name West Side Highway is often (incorrectly) applied to the Henry Hudson Parkway, which runs north from 72nd Street over the Henry Hudson Bridge and through the Bronx to the Westchester county line. It was built in the 1930s as part of Robert Moses's West Side Improvement Project, which included the construction of Riverside Park, and is noted for its graceful curves and riverside views. The section of the Henry Hudson within Manhattan was also closed for a time in the 1970s owing to deterioration from lack of maintenance, but was repaired and restored to use in its entirety in 2001.

Rohit T. Aggarwala

West Side Tennis Club. Tennis organization formed on 22 April 1892. The 13 founders rented ground for three tennis courts on Central Park West between 88th and 89th streets. They charged a $10 initiation fee and a $10 annual fee. By the end of the first season the membership had reached 43 and two additional courts had been built, and in 1897 the club was designated the sponsor of the Metropolitan Matches of the United States National Lawn Tennis Association (USNLTA; later renamed successively the United States Lawn Tennis Association and the United States Tennis Association). In 1902 the club, now with 102 members, moved to Morningside Heights, where it rented eight courts for $20 each from Mrs. John Drexel. The club moved again in 1908 to 238th Street and Broadway, where it rented two city blocks and built 12 grass courts and 15 clay courts, as well as a two-story shingled clubhouse. In 1911 the club was invited by the USNLTA to stage the matches for the Davis Cup with Great Britain, for which the daily attendance exceeded 3000. The club then bought 10 acres (4 hectares) of land in Forest Hills, in Queens; after the 1913 Davis Cup matches were played at the old club, the best of the turf was excavated and taken to the new one in Forest Hills. In 1915 the new club at Forest Hills became the site of the nationals, called the U.S. Open, which had been held at Newport, Rhode Island, since 1881. The West Side Tennis Club was also the site of many concerts by artists including Frank Sinatra, the Beatles, Jimi Hendrix, the Rolling Stones, Bob Dylan, the Who, Diana Ross, and the Boston Pops. In 1978 the U.S. Open left Forest Hills and moved to Flushing Meadows.

Robert Minton, *Forest Hills: An Illustrated History* (Philadelphia: J. B. Lippincott, 1975)

Eric Wm. Allison

Westway. Controversial building project. It was introduced in 1972 by political and business leaders, who proposed to demolish the aging West Side Highway and build in its place a six-lane highway extending from the Battery to 42nd Street (with the portion north of Battery Park City placed underground), an incinerator, a bus depot, and a park; the name of the project was conceived by Deputy Mayor John E. Zuccotti. The plan won the support of Mayor Abraham D. Beame, Governor Hugh L. Carey, and Nelson A. Rockefeller, leaders of business and labor, and groups such as the Regional Plan Association. Opponents led by Marcy Benstock and the New York Clean Air Campaign argued that the proposed road would harm air quality and marine life, and that minority groups would receive an insufficient share of the construction work entailed by the project. In the first of many court hearings, Judge Thomas P. Griesa of the Federal District Court ruled on 1 April 1982 that the U.S. Army Corps of Engineers had violated environmental requirements, and he ordered federal and state officials not to expend funds on Westway. On 30 March 1989 Governor Mario M. Cuomo, originally a supporter of the project, recommended that commercial development along the planned route be banned. Westway was effectively canceled when federal officials instructed the city and state on 10 August 1990 to repay funds that had been advanced to purchase rights of way.

Paul Ramon Pescatello, "Westway: The Road from New Deal to New Politics" (diss., Cornell University, 1986)

Mark H. Rose

wetlands. Ecosystems that are both terrestrial and aquatic where the water table is usually at or near the surface and periodic saturation determines soil development, plant life, and animal life. From colonial times wetlands were believed to harbor disease and were thus considered nuisances that needed to be controlled; this attitude and the pressure to develop land around New York City led most of the wetlands in the area to be drained, dredged, filled, and built on. This trend was reversed during the 1960s as scientists demonstrated the importance of wetlands as immensely productive habitats sustaining diverse wildlife populations and as natural means of flood control and water purification. Over the objections of landowners, federal protection was extended to most American wetlands by the mid-1970s, including many of those remaining in the five boroughs. In 1975 the New York State legislature passed the Freshwater Wetlands Act, requiring the Department of Environmental Conservation (DEC) to map wetland sites of more than 12 acres (5 hectares) and to prevent any construction injurious to them. Under the state's Hudson River Estuary Management Act (1987) the DEC began mapping a focused area encompassing the city's Hudson River wetlands in an effort to prevent further loss, improve state regulatory authority, and restore and enhance wetlands. These protections had limitations in New York City's industrial harbor, however; in 1990 Exxon spilled more than 500,000 gallons of oil into the Arthur Kill of Staten Island, devastating the area's wetlands. The marshes were slowly restored, and funds from a 1994 agreement with the tanker company provided resources for acquisition of undeveloped wetlands for preservation. In 2008 the Harbor Herons Wildlife Complex on Staten Island's western shore encompassed more than 2000 acres (809 hectares) of tidal and freshwater marshes, a pond, creeks, and four islands; the area, home to the largest breeding population of colonial water birds (birds that gather in colonies) in the northeastern United States, was designated a State Bird Conservation Area in 2001. Although in the early twenty-first century the Department of Parks and Recreation has jurisdiction over 4500 acres (1821 hectares) of wetlands, these areas remain vulnerable. Some of the largest wetlands are in the Jamaica Bay Wildlife Refuge, a preserve of more than 9000 acres (3642 hectares) of land and water known for its salt marshes and shore birds. Despite legislative protections and a growing awareness among New Yorkers about the importance of the city's wetlands, Jamaica Bay's salt marshes are shrinking by about 40 acres (16 hectares) annually.

Steven D. Garber, *The Urban Naturalist* (New York: John Wiley and Sons, 1987)

See also Birds, Fauna, Flora, Port of New York, Shellfish, and Waterways.

Steven D. Garber, Kate Lauber

Whalen, Grover A(loysius) (*b* New York City, 2 June 1886; *d* New York City, 20 April 1962). Public official. He oversaw many ticker-tape parades as chairman of the mayor's reception committee (1919–53); as commissioner of the Department of Plant and Structures he was the principal figure behind the formation in 1924 of the municipal broadcasting system WNYC. Appointed police commissioner by Mayor James J. Walker in December 1928, he served for 18 months, during which he zealously pursued communist organizations. In 1935 he became president of the New York World's Fair Corporation. He was featured on the cover of *Time* magazine on 1 May 1939. Whalen wrote *Mr. New York: The Autobiography of Grover Whalen* (1955).

Kenneth R. Cobb

Wharton [née Jones]**, Edith (Newbold)** (*b* New York City, 24 Jan 1862; *d* St.-Brice-sous-forêt, near Paris, 11 Aug 1937). Novelist. Related to the most prominent families in New York City, she was born at 14 West 23rd Street and spent much of her life in Europe; Lenox, Massachusetts; and Newport, Rhode Island. After the death of her father in 1882, she moved to 28 West 25th Street until her marriage to Edward "Teddy" Robbins Wharton in 1889; in 1891 she bought a house at 884 Park Avenue, though by then she spent little time in New York City. A close friend of Henry James, she was known for portrayals of New York City in which her characters negotiated the boundaries of conventional places and custom. Six of her books—*The House of Mirth* (1905), *The Custom of the Country* (1913), *The Age of Innocence* (1920; for which she won the Pulitzer Prize in 1921), *Old New York* (1924; containing four novellas spanning the 1840s to 1880s), *Hudson River Bracketed* (1929), and *The Gods Arrive* (1932)—were set in the city and treated the contradictions of its elite at a time when genteel insularity was ceding to the extremes of the Gilded Age.

Jeff Finlay, Dianna Ng

Wheeler [née Thurber]**, Candace** (*b* Delhi, N.Y., 24 March 1827; *d* New York City, 5 Aug 1923). Writer and decorator. In 1844 she married Thomas Wheeler, a successful businessman and one of the founders of the National Academy of Design. She became central to the promotion of the decorative arts in the United States, wrote many engaging articles promoting interior and exterior home decorating and gardening, helped to form the Society of Decorative Artists and the Associated Artists, and was both the director of the Women's Building at the World's Columbian Exposition in Chicago in 1893 and the head of the Women's Art Committee. Her principal home was "Nestledown," a house built in 1854 in Hollis, Queens, that until 1932 stood on the south side of Liberty Avenue between 186th and 187th streets. There she entertained such writers and artists as William Cullen Bryant, James Russell Lowell, Frank R. Stockton, Mark Twain, William Merritt Chase, John Burroughs, Albert Bierstadt, and Eastman Johnson. Wheeler's published writings include *Content in a Garden* (1901), *History of Embroidery in America* (1921), and her autobiography, *Yesterdays in a Busy Life* (1915).

Vincent Seyfried

Whig Party. Political party organized in 1834 that supported tariffs and internal improvements. It was the party of the middle and upper classes. The party elected five mayors between 1837 and 1850, owing much of its success to economic troubles, support from nativists, and divisions within the Democratic Party, its major opponent. The most influential Whig newspaper was the *New York Tribune,* edited by Horace Greeley. By embracing nativism, the Whigs ultimately helped to strengthen the Democrats, who developed a broad base of support among immigrants. The Whig Party remained an important force in city politics until it disintegrated in the 1850s.

Evan Cornog

White, Alfred T(redway) (*b* Brooklyn, 28 May 1846; *d* Harriman State Park, Orange County, N.Y., 30 Jan 1921). Housing reformer. As a student at Rensselaer Polytechnic Institute he became interested in building affordable model tenements for workers. After graduating he joined his father in a prosperous importing firm in Brooklyn and traveled frequently to London where he visited innovative model housing projects. His first effort, the Tower and Home Buildings, opened in Brooklyn in 1877 at the corner of Baltic and Hicks streets; modeled on houses built by Sir Sidney Waterlow in London and intended for well-paid and "respectable" workers, it had rents that guaranteed investors a return of 5 percent a year. White undertook several other projects that later influenced the work of City and Suburban Homes. He was also a member of several municipal commissions and was associated with a number of campaigns to improve tenements, including one to enforce building codes. As a trustee of the Russell Sage Foundation in 1920 he supported Charles Dyer Norton's efforts to draw up a regional plan, leading to the publication of the *Regional Plan of New York and Its Environs* in 1929 and 1931.

Anthony Jackson, *A Place Called Home: A History of Low Cost Housing* (Cambridge, Mass.: MIT Press, 1976)

See also Limited-dividend housing.

Stanley Buder

White, Clarence H(udson) (*b* West Carlisle, near Newark, Ohio, 7 April 1871; *d* Mexico City, 8 July 1925). Photographer. He produced some of his finest work in Ohio, where he supported himself by working as a grocer's bookkeeper. After moving to New York City in 1906 he became an influential teacher and formed the Clarence H. White School of Photography in 1914; among his pupils were Doris Ullman, Laura Gilpin, Paul Outerbridge, and Anton Bruehl. A leading member of the Photo-Secession of Alfred Stieglitz, White helped to form the Art Center, an organization for designers, and the Pictorial Photographers of America, a national organization for amateurs.

Bonnie Yochelson

White, E(lwyn) B(rooks) (*b* Mount Vernon, N.Y., 11 July 1899; *d* Brooklin, Maine, 1 Oct 1985). Essayist. *New Yorker* editor Harold Ross invited him to write for the publication in 1925; he wrote the columns "Talk of the Town" (1926–38) and "Notes and Comment" (with James Thurber). After writing the column "One Man's Meat" for *Harper's* from 1938 to 1943 he returned to the *New Yorker* in 1945, where he remained for the next 30 years. In 1959 he helped William Strunk, Jr., a professor at Cornell, to revise *The Elements of Style,* a guide to prose writing that became widely used and sold more than 10 million copies. After retiring he moved to Brooklin, Maine. White is best known for his children's stories, especially *Stuart Little* (1945) and *Charlotte's Web* (1952); he also wrote a book about New York City, *Here Is New York* (1949). His wife, Katharine Angell White, was the first fiction editor at the *New Yorker.*

Janet Frankston

White, Stanford (*b* New York City, 9 Nov 1853; *d* New York City, 25 June 1906). Architect. He was born at 110 East 10th Street. In 1878 he traveled to Europe to complete his education. When he returned he joined McKim, Mead and Bigelow as a specialist in drafting and interior design. In 1879 he became a partner in the firm, then called McKim, Mead and White, where he became known as the "master of effects." He admired European antiquities and bought many, which he often incorporated into the interiors of his new buildings. During a second trip to Europe he began to formulate a style based on the symmetrical styles of the Italian Renaissance. Named the "free classical" style in 1887, this combined features of several European styles. Primarily Italian in form, many of White's buildings were made of tawny Roman brick and decorated with terra-cotta ornaments. In his free time he also designed book covers, picture frames, and bases for statues and even decorated the city for public celebrations; a temporary arch that he designed for a parade commemorating George Washington's inauguration along Fifth Avenue was later rebuilt in stone and set in Washington Square.

At the height of his career in the 1890s White lived sumptuously, in part from the income that he earned by importing boatloads of antiquities that he sold to clients for their grand homes. He had a studio in the tower of Madison Square Garden and for a time lived in a rented house at 121 East 21st Street and in rooms at 22 West 24th Street. By the mid-1890s he had abandoned the free classical style for the popular styles of the École des Beaux-Arts that adapted the styles of well-known European buildings; he later returned to the free classical style.

One of the most prolific architects of the late nineteenth century, White produced many designs, some drawn on table napkins. During the early 1890s he was diagnosed with renal disease, and for the rest of his life he visited doctors and sought cures in spas and bottled water. His public and private life became so lavish that he fell deeply in debt. In 1905 he was forced to relinquish his partnership and become a salaried employee. He was quite ill when he was shot and killed on the roof garden of Madison Square Garden by Harry K. Thaw, a wealthy man from Pittsburgh who suspected White of romantic involvement with his wife, Evelyn Nesbit. After a long, sensational trial, Thaw was sent to a mental institution and then allowed to go free.

Charles C. Baldwin, *Stanford White* (New York: Dodd, Mead, 1931); Leland M. Roth, *McKim, Mead and White* (New York: Harper and Row, 1983); Paul R. Baker, *Stanny* (New York: Free Press, 1989)

Mosette G. Broderick

White, Walter (Francis) (*b* Atlanta, 1 July 1893; *d* New York City, 21 March 1955). Writer and civil rights leader. He graduated from Atlanta University in 1916 and in 1918 was appointed the assistant secretary of the National Association for the Advancement of Colored People (NAACP) by James Weldon Johnson, whom he succeeded as its executive secretary in 1931. He expanded the number of branches of the association, increased its membership to more than half a million, and helped to form the NAACP Legal Defense and Educational Fund. Because of his fair skin, blond hair, and blue eyes he was often thought to be white, which helped him to investigate 41 lynchings and eight race riots. During World War II he was a special correspondent in Europe for the *New York Post* (1943–45). He played an important role in preparing the NAACP for its victory in the school desegregation case *Brown v. Board of Education* (1954). White wrote two novels and three works of nonfiction, among them *A Man Called White* (1948).

R. L. Harris, Jr.

Whitehall Street Armed Forces Induction Center. Draft induction center. Located in the U.S. Army Building at 39 Whitehall Street in lower Manhattan, it was the largest draft induction center in the United States beginning with the peacetime drafts after World War II until 1972, when it closed. Frequent protests against the war in Vietnam took place there in the 1960s and 1970s, and hundreds of arrests included such celebrities as Dr. Benjamin Spock, Allen Ginsberg, Susan Sontag, and Jane Jacobs. Radical groups detonated bombs inside and outside of the building in 1968 and 1969, although no one was injured in either blast. The musician Arlo Guthrie described being "*in*-jected, *in*-spected, *dee*-tected, *in*-fected, *nee*-glected, and *see*-lected" at the center in his 1969 song "Alice's Restaurant Massacree."

Caleb Smith

White Horse Tavern. Tavern built in 1880 at the corner of Hudson and West 11th streets in Greenwich Village. A designated landmark and one of the few wood-framed buildings remaining in the city, it was a speakeasy throughout Prohibition and a seamen's bar until the late 1940s, when it was frequented by the Welsh poet Dylan Thomas, who stayed at the Chelsea Hotel during his visits to New York City. By the time of his death in 1953 the tavern had become a popular meeting place for young writers and artists, with a room dedicated to Thomas's memory. The tavern figures prominently in Jane Jacobs's influential book, *The Death and Life of Great American Cities* (1961).

Ann Charters

Whiteman, Paul (*b* Denver, 28 March 1890; *d* Doylestown, Pa., 29 Dec 1967). Bandleader. After moving to New York City in 1920 he organized a dance band that played at the Palais Royale. He gained popularity through his performances in Florenz Ziegfeld's *Follies* and his recording of *Whispering* (1920), the first disc to sell a million copies. During the 1920s he was the first important figure to incorporate jazz elements into popular music, and he used the nickname the "King of Jazz." In 1924, at Aeolian Hall on West 42nd Street, he gave a concert called "An Experiment in Modern Music"; this featured his own arrangements, which incorporated elements of jazz into concert music, along with the first performance of *Rhapsody in Blue* by George Gershwin. He helped to develop the role of the modern arranger by relying on the orchestrations of Ferde Grofé; he also worked with the arranger Bill Challis and performed with the cornetist Bix Beiderbecke, the saxophonist Frank Trumbauer, the bandleaders Tommy and Jimmy Dorsey, the violinist Joe Venuti, the xylophonist Red Norvo, and the singer Bing Crosby, who performed with him between 1926 and 1930 as one of the Rhythm Boys. After his popularity declined in the 1930s Whiteman worked in films and radio, and in 1943 he became the music director of the Blue Network (later the American Broadcasting Company). For many years he owned a farm in New Jersey. Whiteman is best known for introducing an attenuated brand of jazz to a wide audience and for influencing big-band arrangements.

Loren Schoenberg

Whitepot. Outdated name used until 1910 to mean Rego Park and Forest Hills Gardens. It comes from the Dutch *Whiteput,* which means "hollow creek." In colonial times the Furman, Springsteen, and Boerum families owned farms along what is now Yellowstone Boulevard and Whitepot Road (now 66th Avenue). During the American Revolution British troops under General William Howe were stationed around the Dow Van Duyn House at what is now the intersection

White Horse Tavern, 2009

of Woodhaven Boulevard and 67th Avenue. The old Whitepot School House stood for years at Woodhaven Boulevard and 66th Avenue. As the area was developed, the name Whitepot became disused.

Vincent Seyfried

White Russians [White Ruthenians]. Name sometimes used before 1945 for BELARUSIANS.

Whitestone. Neighborhood in north central Queens, bounded to the north by the East River, to the east by Clearview Expressway, to the south by Bayside Avenue and 29th Avenue, and to the west by Whitestone Expressway. The area was settled in 1645. During the American Revolution the British burned the house near 152nd Street and Seventh Avenue of the patriot Francis Lewis (a signer of the Declaration of Independence). In 1838 or 1839 Walt Whitman probably taught in a building on the west side of 11th Avenue between 12th and 13th streets, and the neighborhood was renamed Clintonville in the 1840s for DeWitt Clinton. John D. Locke, a manufacturer of tinware and copperware, moved to the area from Brooklyn in 1853 to build a large stamping works; many of his workers moved with him, and by 1860 the population reached 800. A Methodist church started in 1850, the first school opened in 1857, and the area was incorporated as a village in April 1869. A number of wealthy New Yorkers built mansions along the East River in the 1880s and 1890s. At the foot of 152nd Street and the foot of Clintonville Street were picnic parks that served steamboat excursion parties from Manhattan and Brooklyn. Stimmel's and Duer's parks had hotels, bars, dancing pavilions, and baseball grounds; crowds were often rowdy and drunken, and the resorts were closed during Prohibition. The Shore Acres Realty Company built a development called Beechhurst at the eastern end of the village in 1906, and in 1909 the trolley was extended to the area, linking it with Flushing and Bayside. During a period of rapid development in the 1920s the southern section was enlarged; streets were laid out and houses built on former farmlands. Railroad service ended during the Depression, but the right of way was used for the Belt Parkway, which was completed in 1938 and provided access to the Bronx–Whitestone Bridge (1939). After World War II a large apartment complex was built on the shore between 162nd Street and the Throgs Neck Bridge. Much of Whitestone is upper middle class; the original village and the area south of the parkway are covered by houses and tree-lined streets. The population in the early twenty-first century was around 40,000.

Vincent Seyfried

Whitman, Walt(er) (*b* West Hills, N.Y., 31 May 1819; *d* Camden, N.J., 26 March 1892). Poet. One of nine children in a family of farmers, he taught in a one-room schoolhouse briefly before pursuing a career in journalism. Working as an editor and printer in Brooklyn (1840–45), he also submitted poems and short stories to prominent journals like the *Democratic Review,* which published his first poem, "Death in the Schoolroom," in August 1841. In 1842 he left his position as the editor of the *Long Islander* to take charge of the *Aurora.* During the same year he lived in a boardinghouse at 12 Centre Street in Manhattan. He soon returned to Brooklyn, where he spent much of his career. He became the editor of the *Brooklyn Daily Eagle* in 1846, but resigned in 1847 over his support for the Free Soil Party. In 1849 he built a house at 106 Myrtle Avenue in Brooklyn and remained there for three years; he later lived at 142 Skillman Street (1854–55) and 107 Portland Avenue (1859–63). Much of his work is devoted to an appreciation of New York City, which he called "the great place . . . the heart, the brain, the focus." Celebratory images suffuse his articles about the city for *Life Illustrated* (1853) and his poems in his life's work, *Leaves of Grass* (1855), including "A Broadway Pageant," "Give Me the Splendid Silent Sun," "Crossing Brooklyn Ferry," and "Mannahatta I," a paean to the city's growth. He attributed the inspiration for his slim volume of poetry to "my life in Brooklyn and New York, absorbing a million people for fifteen years, with an intimacy, eagerness, an abandon, probably never equaled." His unrivaled passion for the city—its streets, bars, boardinghouses, and lower classes—was remembered more than 100 years later by the urban planner Lewis Mumford, who said: "Wherever one goes in New York, whether one knows it or not, one walks in the steps of Walt Whitman."

Walt Whitman

Joseph J. Rubin and Charles H. Brown, *Walt Whitman of the New York Aurora* (State College, Pa.: Pennsylvania State University Press, 1950); Gay Wilson Allen, *The Solitary Singer: A Critical Biography of Walt Whitman* (New York: Macmillan, 1955); Justin Kaplan, *Walt Whitman: A Life* (New York: Simon and Schuster, 1980); Paul Zweig, *Walt Whitman: The Making of the Poet* (New York: Basic Books, 1984); Jerome Loving, *Walt Whitman: The Song of Himself* (Berkley: University of California Press, 1999)

Jeff Finlay, Barbara Jackson

Whitney, Gertrude Vanderbilt (*b* New York City, 9 Jan 1875; *d* New York City, 18 April 1942). Sculptor and arts patron. The daughter of Alice Claypoole Gwynne and Cornelius Vanderbilt II, she was a student at the Brearley School and a debutante. After her marriage to Harry Payne Whitney, with whom she had three children, she confounded the expectations of her social position to become a sculptor in 1900. Her work was in a traditional figurative style but her sympathies were with liberal artists; she studied with James Earle Fraser at the Art Students League before taking a studio at 19 MacDougal Alley in 1907 and joining the artistic community in Greenwich Village. She bought four paintings from the historic exhibition of The Eight in 1908. She leased the town house attached to her studio (8 West Eighth Street) in 1912 and converted it into the Whitney Studio, an exhibition space that opened in 1914; in 1918 she established the Whitney Studio Club, a meeting place and gallery for young artists spurned by dealers. After World War II she received many commissions for public monuments, exhibited widely, and continued to support hundreds of artists, opening the Whitney Studio Galleries in 1928. After her personal collection was rejected by the Metropolitan Museum of Art she founded the Whitney Museum of American Art in 1930 at 8–14 West Eighth Street. Examples of Whitney's public sculptures in the city are the Washington Heights War Memorial (1921, Broadway and 168th Street) and a statue of Peter Stuyvesant (1936, Stuyvesant Square). She is buried at Woodlawn Cemetery in the Bronx.

B. H. Friedman, *Gertrude Vanderbilt Whitney* (Garden City, N.Y.: Doubleday, 1978)

Avis Berman

Whitney, Richard (*b* Beverly, Mass., 1 Aug 1888; *d* Short Hills, N.J., 5 Dec 1974). Financier. The son of a bank president in Boston, he attended Harvard University before taking a seat on the New York Stock Exchange at the age of 23. He became the principal brokerage agent for J. P. Morgan and Company and rose to national prominence during the crash of 1929, when he temporarily stabilized prices by buying stocks for large banks. Elected to the first of four terms as president of the exchange in 1930, he became a symbol of conservative elements who opposed regulatory reform. In 1938 his brokerage firm declared bankruptcy, and investigators discovered that he had embezzled money from a number of customers. He pleaded guilty to embezzlement and served a sentence at Sing Sing Prison. The scandal surrounding Whitney had long-lasting effects on Wall Street by inaugurating a period of new leadership and regulatory reform at the New York Stock Exchange.

George Winslow

Whitney, William Collins (*b* Conway, Mass., 5 July 1841; *d* New York City, 2 Feb 1904). Financier. After graduating from Yale University he studied law and opened a practice in New York City where he had a house at 2 West 57th Street. A Democrat opposed to the Tweed Ring, he supported Grover Cleveland in the presidential election of 1884 and was secretary of the navy from 1885 to 1889. He returned to Manhattan where he helped to finance utilities and the Metropolitan Street Railway Company. After taking up horse breeding in Lexington, Kentucky, and Saratoga, New York, he won the English Derby and in 1902 published *The Whitney Stud,* a horse-breeding guide. At the end of his life Whitney had 10 residences, including a mansion designed by McKim, Mead and White at Fifth Avenue and 68th Street.

James E. Mooney

Whitney Museum of American Art. First museum devoted to American art of the twentieth century. It was founded in 1930 by Gertrude Vanderbilt Whitney, who promoted living artists neglected by museums and commercial galleries. After her collection of nearly 500 objects was refused by the Metropolitan Museum of Art in 1929, Whitney established her own museum with Juliana Rieser Force as the director. It occupied four town houses (8–14 West Eighth Street) and opened to the public on 18 November 1931. Contemporary and historical works were bought, and biennial and annual invitational exhibitions featured artists from all areas of the country. Hermon More was appointed director in 1948, and during his tenure the museum moved to 22 West 54th Street. He was succeeded in 1958 by Lloyd Goodrich, who oversaw the construction of a gray granite building designed by Marcel Breuer and Hamilton Smith at 945 Madison Avenue, where the museum moved in 1966. Under the direction of John I. H. Baur from 1968 to 1974, Jean and Howard Lipman donated about 200 pieces of sculpture: they became the museum's most important benefactors after the Whitney family. Thomas N. Armstrong III, director from 1974 to 1990, expanded and broadened the permanent collection. Under his direction, the Whitney partnered with the Museum of Modern Art on a massive project to research, catalogue, preserve, and screen the films of Andy Warhol. Subsequent directors have included David A. Ross (1991–97), Maxwell Anderson (1998–2003), and Adam Weinberg (2003–). The Whitney has the largest and most comprehensive collection of its kind: among its 8500 objects are works by every important American artist active in the twentieth century to the present. It has unrivaled holdings by such artists as Alexander Calder, Edward Hopper, and Reginald Marsh, as well as many examples of Charles Burchfield, Stuart Davis, Jasper Johns, Gaston Lachaise, Georgia O'Keeffe, John Sloan, David Smith, and Frank Stella. The Whitney Biennial remains one of the most significant surveys of contemporary American art. In March 2008 cosmetics executive and Whitney chairman Leonard A. Lauder donated $131 million to the museum, the largest gift in its history, before resigning his post. In May 2008, after unsuccessful attempts to expand the Breuer Building, the Whitney released plans for a second museum; designed by architect Renzo Piano, it would be on Gansevoort Street in the meatpacking district, near the redeveloped High Line. As of 2010 work on the new building had not yet begun.

Avis Berman, *Rebels on Eighth Street: Juliana Force and the Whitney Museum of American Art* (New York: Atheneum, 1990)

Avis Berman

Whyte, William H(ollingsworth) "Holly," Jr. (*b* West Chester, Pa., 1 Oct 1917; *d* New York City, 12 Jan 1999). Writer and editor. After graduating from Princeton University and serving with the U.S. Marine Corps, he became an editor of *Fortune* magazine in 1946. Whyte was best known for his essays and books on business and American popular culture, including *The Organization Man* (1956). Starting in the 1960s, Whyte's love of New York City drew him into urban planning as a reformer, researcher, and mentor to other urban planners such as Jane Jacobs. Whyte spent 16 years walking city streets unobtrusively observing and using stop-motion photography to examine how people behave in public spaces. Through this he developed a study of street life called the Street Life Project, and much of this research contributed to his 1988 book, *City: Rediscovering the Center.* For example, he observed that the corner of 59th Street and Lexington Avenue outside Bloomingdale's had the most daytime pedestrian traffic, and that having vendors on the street tended to increase sales in local stores, particularly if the vendors and carts sold food. In 1969 he edited New York City's Master Plan and acted as a consultant on many building and zoning projects. He helped develop vest-pocket parks and contributed to the design of the modern Bryant Park. Whyte was a distinguished professor at Hunter College of the City University of New York.

Albert LaFarge, ed., *The Essential William H. Whyte* (New York: Fordham University Press, 2000)

Harold Takooshian

Wilder case. Court case filed in 1973 against New York City for foster-care abuses. Since the nineteenth century, New York City's foster-care system had contracted private agencies to care for children, and laws allowed these mostly Jewish and Roman Catholic charities (90 percent in 1972) to give preference to children of their own faith. An African American girl named Shirley Wilder entered the foster-care system in 1972, at age 13, and was rejected by countless agencies based on her Protestant beliefs. With nowhere to go, she was forced into the care of the Dickensian reformatory at Hudson, New York, which was for children convicted of criminal offenses. There she was raped and put into solitary confinement when she tried to fight back. At 14, having been refused contraceptives by the Catholic foster agency, she became pregnant. That same year lawyer Marcia Lowry took up Wilder's case of neglect and abuse; she asked the courts to declare the entire statutory basis for the provision of child-welfare services in New York City unconstitutional. Drawn out for many years, the case finally ended on 22 January 1999 and was settled in her favor; three weeks earlier Wilder had died from AIDS.

Jessica Montesano

wildlife. See Fauna.

Wildlife Conservation Society. Organization promoting zoology and conservation research and education, formerly known as the New York Zoological Society. Established in 1895 by Andrew Haswell Green, Henry Fairfield Osborn, and Theodore Roosevelt, among others, the society opened the New York Zoological Park, later known as the Bronx Zoo, in 1899. In 1902 the society took over management of the New York Aquarium, later building a new facility in Coney Island. In the late twentieth century, it took over three of the city's zoos, renovating and reopening them: the Central Park Zoo (1988), the Prospect Park Zoo (1992), and the Queens Zoo (1993). The society took its current name in 1993 to reflect its emphasis on international conservation. In 2008 it began a dual-degree program with Fordham University, offering a master's degree in Teaching Adolescence Conservation Life Science.

Kate Lauber

Willets Point. Enclave of 75 acres (30 hectares), in the shadow of Citi Field, the Mets stadium, in northern Queens. *Willets Point* was at one time the name applied to the entire 150-acre (61-hectare) Fort Totten peninsula. The area was known in the eighteenth century as Thorne's Neck, after its owner, Jacob Thorne; the land was acquired in turn by William Wilkens, David Ousterman, Charles Willets (1829), and the federal government (1857). A movement in the U.S. Congress to erect a fort opposite Fort Schuyler in the Bronx, which began when the government took title to the property, was hastened by the outbreak of the Civil War; construction began in 1862. But the invention of rifled bores in cannon made stone forts obsolete, and work was abandoned. In 1864–65 Grant Hospital treated members of the Union Army at the fort. At the behest of President William McKinley the fort was renamed in August 1898 to honor Brigadier General Joseph G. Totten, director of the Bureau of Seacoast Defense in the Department of War. In *The Great Gatsby* (1925), F. Scott Fitzgerald referred to the neighborhood as the Valley of Ashes. Early in the twenty-first century, Willets Point was also known as the Iron Triangle because of its concentration of about 250 auto-parts and repair shops.

Kenneth T. Jackson

William A. Read. Forerunner of the investment banking firm DILLON, READ.

William Cullen Bryant High School. Secondary school opened in 1889 as Long Island City High School in Smithsonian Hall at Vernon Boulevard and Fourth Street in Queens; it was the first public high school in the borough. The school moved in 1890 to the Munson Building on Astoria Avenue. In 1904 it merged with Woodside High School, moved to a new building at Academy and Reddee streets, and was renamed in honor of the poet and editor. It offered three courses of study: academic, commercial, and manual training. In 1939 it moved to 48-10 31st Avenue in Long Island City. In the early twenty-first century William Cullen Bryant High School had about 3600 students.

Erica Judge

William Morrow and Company. Firm of book publishers formed in 1926 by William Morrow at 303 Fifth Avenue. It attracted many popular authors and soon achieved success by publishing best sellers such as James Hilton's *Lost Horizon* (1935). During its early years the firm became known for the relative youth of its executives. In 1967 Morrow became a subsidiary of Scott, Foresman, and Company, which sold it in 1981 to the Hearst Corporation. In the twenty-first century it is an imprint of HarperCollins, a subsidiary of News Corporation. Among the notable books published by the firm over the years are *Coming of Age in Samoa* (1928) by Margaret Mead, *The Shoes of the Fisherman* (1963) by Morris West, *The Jewel in the Crown* (1967) by Paul Scott, *The Peter Principle* (1969) by Lawrence J. Peter and Raymund Hull, *Zen and the Art of Motorcycle Maintenance* (1974) by Robert M. Pirsig, *The Cider House Rules* (1985) by John Irving, more than 150 books by Erle Stanley Gardner (including the Perry Mason series), and the children's novels of Beverly Cleary.

See also BOOK PUBLISHING.

Eileen K. Cheng

Williams, Alexander S. (*b* Fairfax, Nova Scotia, 9 July 1839; *d* New York City, 25 March 1917). Corrupt police captain. During the 1880s and 1890s he enjoyed good relations with gamblers and procurers and was responsible for the evolution of the TENDERLOIN. Known as the "clubber" for his harsh justice, he retired with a house on East 10th Street, an estate in Connecticut, and a yacht.

Joseph P. Viteritti

Williams, Bert [Austin, Egbert] (*b* Antigua, 12 Nov 1874; *d* New York City, 4 March 1922). Comedian, singer, and dancer. After beginning his career in minstrel shows, he met his partner, George Walker. Billed as "Two Real Coons," they first performed in Manhattan in 1896 and later became renowned in vaudeville. In black theater at the turn of the twentieth century they made the cakewalk popular and perfected comic routines in which Williams was "Jonah Man," the foil to Walker's dandy, much like the "Little Tramp" of his contemporary Charlie Chaplin. Williams and Walker later formed a troupe and presented the musicals *In Dahomey* (1903), *Abyssinia* (1906), and *Bandana Land* (1908). As their fame increased, they were instrumental in the creation of the first black actor's union, the Negro Society. After illness led to Walker's retirement in 1909, Williams performed briefly in vaudeville, but by 1912 he was headlining Florenz Ziegfeld's *Follies* with W. C. Fields and George M. Cohan. An international star who also made recordings and films, he was identified by his mournful signature song "Nobody." Although he was black, Williams was forced to perform in blackface so that his appearance would conform to racial stereotypes; he believed that the makeup limited the range of his roles, and he became sorrowful and bitter. Fields called him "the funniest man I ever saw, and the saddest man I ever knew." He spent the end of his life at 2309 Seventh Avenue. He is buried in Woodlawn Cemetery in the Bronx.

Ann Charters, *Nobody: The Story of Bert Williams* (New York: Macmillan, 1970)

Robert W. Snyder

Williams, Tennessee [Thomas Lanier] (*b* Columbus, Miss., 26 March 1911; *d* New York City, 25 Feb 1983). Playwright. He grew up in Mississippi and St. Louis and after college moved to New York City in the late 1930s. There he lived at the Royalton Hotel, the Hotel Shelton (on 44th Street at the East River), and the West Side Young Men's Christian Association; he worked as a waiter at the Beggar Bar in Greenwich Village, as an elevator operator in the San Jacinto Hotel (on Madison Avenue), and as an usher in the Strand Theatre (on 47th Street and Broadway). His first play to be staged on Broadway was *The Glass Menagerie,* which in 1945 was named the best play of the year by the New York Drama Critics' Circle; the same award was given to his play *A Streetcar Named Desire* (1947), as was the Pulitzer Prize. His later works were also critically successful, including *The Rose Tattoo* (1951, Tony Award for best play and playwright), *Cat on a Hot Tin Roof* (1955, New York Drama Critics' Circle Award, Pulitzer Prize), and *The Night of the Iguana* (1961, New York Drama Critics' Circle Award). From 1948 to the early 1950s he lived at 235 East 58th Street; in his later years he spent periods at 15 West 72nd Street (1965–68), 145 West 55th Street (mid-1960s), 400 West 43rd Street (for three years from 1978), and the Hotel Élysée, at 54–60 East 54th Street (where he died). Along with Arthur Miller and Eugene O'Neill he ranks as America's most important and influential playwright. His lyrical dramas are frequently set in the American South and feature vulnerable yet vibrant characters in search of love, sexual fulfillment, compassion, and dignity in a callous world. His *Memoirs* were published in 1975.

A. J. Devlin, *Conversations with Tennessee Williams* (Jackson: University of Mississippi Press, 1986); Ronald Hayman, *Tennessee Williams: Everyone Else Is an Audience* (New Haven: Yale University Press, 1993)

Martha S. LoMonaco

Williamsbridge. Neighborhood in the north central Bronx, centered on Gun Hill Road and bounded to the north by East 233rd Street, to the east by Edenwald, to the south by the neighborhood of Pelham Parkway, and to the west by the Bronx River. It was named for a bridge built over the Bronx River in colonial times by John Williams, a local farmer. The area saw several battles and skirmishes during the American Revolution. A route to Manhattan was first provided in 1841 by the New York and Harlem Railroad. After Interborough Rapid Transit extended its subway to White Plains Road, the population grew rapidly in the 1920s as Italian, Jewish, and black families moved in. The neighborhood became predominantly black in the 1960s. Almost all the immigrants who settled there in the 1980s were blacks from the Caribbean. Most were from Jamaica and many of the rest were from Guyana, the United Kingdom, Antigua–

Barbuda, and the Dominican Republic. In the early twenty-first century Williamsbridge remained a largely residential area of one-family houses; there was also a low-income development, the Gun Hill Houses.

Lloyd Ultan

Williamsburg(h). Neighborhood in northwestern Brooklyn (2008 pop. *ca* 121,000), bounded on the east by the Queens County line, on the south by Flushing Avenue, on the west by the East River, and on the north by North 15th Street, then along McCarren Park's western and southern edges to the Brooklyn–Queens Expressway at Bayard Street. Originally part of the Dutch village of Boswijck, the area was chartered in 1660. On marshy land along the East River between what are now South Seventh Street and North First Street the first European settler, Jean Mesurolle of Picardy, built a farm that according to legend was a favorite boarding place of Captain Kidd. A number of Dutch, French, and Scandinavian farmers and African slaves settled in the area in 1663. A hamlet sometimes known as Cripplebush remained isolated until speculators took an interest in land up the East River from the city of Brooklyn. From 1800 Richard M. Woodhull offered ferry service from Corlear's Hook in Manhattan to the foot of what is now North Second Street; hoping to develop a town for those working in Manhattan, he bought a parcel of 13 acres (5.3 hectares) around the ferry landing and named it for Jonathan Williams, the surveyor of the area, but he declared bankruptcy in 1806 after selling only a few lots. Speculation increased after roads were built to replace roundabout tracks used by farmers. In 1818 David Dunham (who became known as the "father of Williamsburgh") opened a steam ferry and lent money to the new development, which was incorporated as the Village of Williamsburgh in 1827 and soon attracted industry; in 1852 it had a population of 31,000 and was incorporated as a city. Later its mayor, Abraham J. Berry, proposed that it be consolidated with Brooklyn; in 1855 his plan was enacted and the final "h" was dropped from the name of the neighborhood (it remains in the name of the Williamsburgh Savings Bank, which has a landmark building on Broadway).

The neighborhood became a fashionable suburb for industrialists and professionals of German, Austrian, and Irish descent. There were hotels, beer gardens, and exclusive clubs; the German section lay along Montrose Avenue and Meserole and Scholes streets. Docks, shipyards, factories, distilleries, taverns, mills, and foundries stood along the waterfront, where some of the largest industrial firms in the nation were built: the Pfizer Pharmaceutical Company (1849), Astral Oil (later Standard Oil), Brooklyn Flint Glass (later Corning Glassware), and the Havemeyers and Elder sugar refinery (later Amstar), once the largest establishment of its kind in the world.

The population grew from 105,000 in 1900 to 260,000 in 1920, a peak for recent years. After the Williamsburg Bridge opened in 1903 thousands of Jews from eastern Europe moved to the neighborhood from the Lower East Side. Lithuanian, Polish, and Russian Orthodox enclaves also developed, as did an Italian one between Bushwick and Union avenues. In July 1903 near North Eighth and Havemeyer streets hundreds of Italian residents, many from the village of Nola, held the first annual celebration in the city of a festival called the dancing of the *giglio*. Coldwater flats and six-story tenements replaced brownstones, and by 1917 the neighborhood had some of the most densely populated blocks in the city. During the early 1930s many businesses in the neighborhood declared bankruptcy and many prosperous residents left. The Jewish community continued to grow, and a large number of Jewish refugees escaping Nazism moved in and formed Hasidic synagogues and schools; there were more than 20 sects from different parts of Europe, including the large Satmar sect from Hungary and Romania, led by its rabbi Joel Teitelbaum. Manufacturing, which employed more than a million people in the city in 1950, attracted many Puerto Ricans during the following decade.

About this time scores of decaying buildings were demolished to make way for enormous public housing projects. In 1957 the construction of the Brooklyn–Queens Expressway bisected the neighborhood and destroyed more than 2200 units of low-income housing. Looting and arson left blocks of abandoned buildings, factories, and warehouses, but some housing was renovated in the 1980s. Although Pfizer and other businesses remained in the neighborhood, by 1990 manufacturing employment had decreased sharply. By this time Puerto Ricans, Dominicans, and other Latin Americans constituted about half the population, with Dominicans alone accounting for more than half the immigrants who settled in the neighborhood during the 1980s. Far smaller numbers arrived from Israel, Poland, Ecuador, and China. The neighborhood was largely overcrowded and poor, and housing remained inadequate; Latin American families often shared cramped apartments, as did Hasidic families.

A trickle of artists and musicians in the 1970s became a stream in the 1980s and early 1990s. Refugees from rising East Village rents, hipsters squatted in empty factory lofts and initiated a club scene in the vicinity of the L train stop at Bedford and North Seventh Street in Northside. The Hasidim continued to dominate Williamsburg's southernmost section, with Lee Street as their main shopping district. Latinos occupied Southside, too, and also East Williamsburg. The Polish enclave, an offshoot of Greenpoint's larger Polish community, persisted in Northside. The Italian community continued in northeastern Williamsburg.

Legacies of the waterfront's heavy industrial past also remained. In the 1990s the U.S. Superfund cleaned some pollution, but in the early twenty-first century more persists in the neighborhood. Numerous waste transfer stations still line the river, including one that handles radioactive materials, but development and gentrification proceed. The city's May 2005 rezoning plan has reclassified some industrial areas as residential. At the same time, increasing rents and new construction have displaced some longtime residents and artists. The rezoning plan, encompassing Williamsburg north of the bridge and Grand Street and west of Keyspan's natural gas facility and all of Greenpoint, provides for parks and a waterfront esplanade, permits to build high-rise apartments along the East River (when affordable housing is also developed), and retention of some light manufacturing and mixed-use zones. In June 2007, as the number of new building and demolition permits soared, the National Trust for Historic Preservation named Brooklyn's industrial waterfront an endangered historic district.

Henry Stiles, *The Civil, Political, Professional, and Ecclesiastical History of the County of Kings and the City of Brooklyn, 1683–1884* (New York: W. W. Munsell, 1884); George Kranzler, *Williamsburg: A Jewish Community in Transition* (New York: Philipp Feldheim, 1961); Victor Lederer and the Brooklyn Historical Society, *Images of America: Williamsburg* (Charleston, S.C.: Arcadia, 2005)

Judith Berck, Cathy Alexander

Williamsburg Bridge. Steel suspension bridge spanning the East River between Delancey Street on the Lower East Side and Marcy Avenue in Williamsburg. It was designed by Leffert L. Buck and opened in December 1903 as an alternative to the overburdened Brooklyn Bridge. During construction in 1902, Commissioner of Bridges Gustav Lindenthal employed Henry Hornbostel to improve the aesthetics of the structure. Hornbostel added ornamental detail to the towers and other sections of the bridge and designed the approach in Manhattan. The bridge remained primarily the work of Buck, however, and was criticized almost from the moment the plan was unveiled for its graceless form. The second bridge over the East River, it was constructed in seven years (half the time it took to build the Brooklyn Bridge) and was the longest and heaviest suspension bridge in the world and the first suspension bridge with towers made entirely of steel. It is 7308 feet (2229 meters) long, with a main span of 1600 feet (488 meters) suspended from four steel cables, each 1.5 feet (0.5 meter) thick. Steel latticework, called stiffening trusses, extends between the anchorages, giving the bridge great strength (as well as its ungainly appearance). The deck of the bridge supports two subway tracks and four flanking traffic lanes. In the early twentieth century the bridge was seen as a passageway to a new life in Williamsburg by thousands of Jewish immigrants fleeing the slums of the Lower East Side.

Sharon Reier, *The Bridges of New York* (New York: Quadrant, 1977)

Rebecca Read Shanor

Williamsburgh Daily Times. Original name of the Brooklyn Times–Union.

Williamsburgh Savings Bank. Savings bank chartered in Brooklyn in 1851, and acquired by the Republic National Bank of New York in 1987. Best known for its buildings, it occupied rented quarters in Williamsburgh until 1867, when it bought a site at 175 Broadway and held a design competition for its headquarters. The winning entry, submitted by George B. Post, called for a four-story building of limestone, sandstone, and marble, designed in a Classical Revival style with a monumental arched portico and an ornate cast-iron railing along the sidewalk. Construction began in 1870 and was completed in 1875; additions were made by the firm of Helmle, Hubery, and Hudswell in 1905 and by Helmle and Huberty in 1925, among them a dome crowned with an ornate lantern and a delicate weathervane. The bank bought land in 1926 at 1 Hanson Place, behind the Brooklyn Academy of Music and across the street from a terminal of the Long Island Rail Road (now demolished), and engaged the firm of Halsey, McCormick, and Helmer to design a skyscraper, which was built between October 1927 and 1 May 1929 and became known as one of the most elegant examples of a modern structure combining Romanesque and Byzantine elements. At 512 feet (156 meters) the tallest structure in Brooklyn, it was built with setbacks at the 13th and 26th stories accented by rounded arches and terra-cotta bands. Symbols of thrift were carved into the base in bas-relief; a four-faced clock, the largest in the world at the time, and a gilded dome recalling the one at 175 Broadway were also added. The interior was decorated in exquisite detail: polychrome mosaics were installed in the elevator lobby, which was separated from the marble banking room by ornate cast-iron gates; in the banking room the ceiling was built to a height of 63 feet (19 meters), three windows 40 feet (12 meters) tall were installed overlooking Hanson Place, and a mural of Brooklyn was painted on the rear wall. The city granted landmark status to the building at 175 Broadway in 1966 and to the one at 1 Hanson Place in 1977.

Eric Wm. Allison

Williamsburg Trust Company. Commercial bank in Brooklyn. Until 1922 its main branch was a building that is now the Holy Trinity Cathedral of the Ukrainian Autocephalous Orthodox Church in Exile.

William T. Davis Wildlife Refuge. First wildlife sanctuary in New York City. It was dedicated in 1929 and occupies 260 acres (105 hectares) of the Greenbelt in New Springville, near the center of Staten Island. The area was once farmland; its artesian wells, connected to the Fresh Kills Creek, supplied the island with water in the 1880s. A preservationist movement led by the National Audubon Society and William Thompson Davis, a naturalist and one of the founders of the Staten Island Institute of Arts and Sciences, prevailed on the New York City Parks Department to take over 52 acres (21 hectares) of the area in 1928. Davis paid for a fence to be built around much of the area to halt the hunting of waterfowl and pheasants. In 1955 the area was enlarged to its current size. The refuge harbors a wide range of habitats, as well as tidal marshland, freshwater wetlands, and woodlands. Opened in 1999, the United for Wildlife Rehabilitation and Education Center, located at the wildlife refuge, seeks to care for sick, injured, and orphaned wildlife and return them to the wild.

James Bradley

Willis Avenue Bridge. Four-lane bowstring truss swing bridge spanning the Harlem River, connecting First Avenue and 125th Street in Manhattan with Willis Avenue and 132nd Street in the Bronx. Intended to relieve traffic on the Third Avenue Bridge and designed by the engineer Thomas C. Clarke (who also designed the Third Avenue Bridge), it opened on 23 August 1901. The bridge measures 3212.5 feet (979 meters) in length, including approaches, and has a clear height of 25.1 feet (7.65 meters).

Rebecca Read Shanor

Willkie, Wendell (Lewis) (*b* Elwood, Ind., 18 Feb 1892; *d* New York City, 8 Oct 1944). Lawyer and presidential candidate. He lived at 1010 Fifth Avenue in 1929 when he began work with Judge John Weadcock as the general counsel for Commonwealth and Southern Corporation, a public utility holding company. Named president of Commonwealth and Southern in 1933, he became a prominent critic of President Franklin D. Roosevelt, particularly regarding public power. He resigned from the company in 1940 when he was nominated as the Republican candidate for the presidency. A moderate who rejected his party's conservative orthodoxy, he won the nomination in part because of early backing from the *New York Herald Tribune.* Soundly defeated by Roosevelt, he returned to private law practice in 1941 and became a partner of the firm of Willkie, Owen, Otis, and Reilly. Willkie remained active in politics and philanthropy in the city during his remaining years. He died at Lenox Hill Hospital.

Steve Neal, *Dark Horse: A Biography of Wendell Willkie* (Lawrence: University Press of Kansas, 1989)

James Bradley

Willowbrook. Neighborhood in south central Staten Island, lying near the Staten Island Expressway. Until development began in the 1960s it was sparsely populated farmland named for the brook that flowed through the area into the Fresh Kills. The main roads are Bradley Avenue and Forest Hill Road; the Center for Basic Research at 1050 Forest Hill Road opened in 1964 and is known worldwide for its research into the causes of mental retardation and other developmental disabilities. For many years the neighborhood was the site of the Willowbrook State School; after it ceased operations the campus was taken over in 1993 by the College of Staten Island.

Barnett Shepherd

Willowbrook State School. School for the mentally disabled in Staten Island, formally known as the Richmond Complex of the Staten Island Developmental Center. It occupied a parcel of 375 acres (151.9 hectares) on Willow Brook Road purchased in 1938 as the intended site of the New York State Department of Mental Hygiene; plans changed with the outbreak of World War II, and in 1942 the land became the site of Halloran General Hospital, the nation's largest hospital for wounded soldiers. Under the control of the Veterans Administration from 1947 to 1951 the hospital admitted mentally retarded and disabled civilians, including infants. In 1952 it was reclaimed by New York State. The hospital often received severely retarded children from other state institutions, and its population increased rapidly during the 1950s. By 1963 the facility, designed for 4200 residents, had more than 6000. The situation caused a public outcry as well as a class-action suit in 1972 against Governor Nelson A. Rockefeller, and on 30 April 1975 Judge Orrin Judd ordered the population to be reduced to 250 and the remaining residents to be transferred to other, less restrictive environments, preferably group homes. A legal and bureaucratic struggle ensued that resulted in the closing of Willowbrook in 1987. In 1989 the City University of New York acquired the property for use as a campus of the College of Staten Island.

David J. Rothman and Sheila M. Rothman, *The Willowbrook Wars* (New York: Harper and Row, 1984)

Rachel Shor

Wilson, (Harvey) Earl (*b* Rockford, Ohio, 3 May 1907; *d* Yonkers, N.Y., 16 Jan 1987).

Columnist. In 1942 he began writing a gossip column about nightlife in New York City called "It Happened Last Night" that appeared six times a week in the *New York Post;* by the time he retired in 1983, about 200 newspapers carried his column. Wilson specialized in interviews with starlets; he never used his column to critique the city's culture or express his political opinions. While living in Manhattan, Wilson and his wife, Rosemary, known to his readers as "B.W." (for Beautiful Wife), lived in an apartment on West End Avenue.

Judith Adler Hennessee

Wilson, Edmund (*b* Red Bank, N.J., 8 May 1895; *d* Talcottville, near Rome, N.Y., 12 June 1972). Critic. He graduated from Princeton University in 1916 and after his discharge from the army in August 1919 sought a literary career in New York City. He soon moved to West 16th Street, where he remained until 1921. Wilson worked as a freelancer for *Vanity Fair* and the *New Republic,* of which he became literary editor. In the 1920s through the 1940s he had several residences in the city: 3 Washington Square North (1921–25), 229 West 13th Street (1925–29; building later renumbered), 224 West 13th Street (from 1929), 314 East 53rd Street (1933–35), 2 Lexington Avenue (early 1940s), and 14 Henderson Place (1944–45). His novel *I Thought of Daisy* (1929) depicted intellectual life in Greenwich Village; he also wrote *Axel's Castle* (1931), an influential study of literary modernism, and *To the Finland Station* (1940), perhaps the finest American treatment of the roots of communism. In his later work, much of which appeared in the *Nation,* he offered his analysis of writers both well known and obscure. He also wrote treatises on such diverse subjects as the Civil War, the Dead Sea Scrolls, and the purported evils of the income tax.

Lawson Bowling, Benjamin Yakas

Wiman, Erastus (*b* Churchville, Ontario, 21 April 1834; *d* Staten Island, 9 Feb 1904). Businessman and writer. He worked as a printer's apprentice and commercial editor for the *Toronto Globe* before joining Dun, Barlow, and Company, an American mercantile reporting agency, in 1860. The firm transferred him to New York City in 1866 and made him its general manager in 1880. In 1882 he teamed with Jay Gould to found the Great Northwestern Telegraph Company, which gained a near monopoly over Canada's telegraph services. In 1884 and 1885 he took control of the Staten Island ferry and the Staten Island Railway Company while funding a railway bridge to New Jersey. Wiman built an amusement park dubbed Erastina, made Buffalo Bill's Wild West show a hit, and in 1885 bought the New York Metropolitans, a professional baseball team, and unsuccessfully tried to transplant the team to Staten Island. He also worked to popularize Canadian sports such as lacrosse and cricket and led expeditions of New York City socialites to Montreal's winter carnival. Wiman met financial ruin in 1893; the following year Dun laid charges of forgery against him. (He was acquitted.) An 1897 run for councilman of Greater New York was unsuccessful. In addition to numerous pamphlets, he published a memoir, *Chances of Success: Episodes and Observations in the Life of a Busy Man* (1893).

Mike Woodsworth

Winchell [Winschel], **Walter** (*b* New York City, 7 April 1897; *d* Los Angeles, 20 Feb 1972). Columnist. He worked for a number of newspapers as a drama critic before launching his gossip column "On Broadway" in the *New York Daily Mirror,* in which he carried out personal vendettas against politicians and personages in show business and coined such words as "storked" and "Reno-vated"; the column was eventually syndicated in 50 states and 11 foreign countries. He also gave weekly radio broadcasts. He lived at 870 Seventh Avenue during the early 1930s before moving to the St. Moritz Hotel at 50 Central Park South, where he remained for many years. A feud with the entertainer Josephine Baker contributed to the decline of his popularity after 1950. Originally a strong supporter of Franklin D. Roosevelt, Winchell moved increasingly to the political right in his later years. He wrote a memoir, *Winchell Exclusive* (1975).

Neal Gabler, *Winchell: Gossip, Power and the Culture of Celebrity* (New York: Alfred A. Knopf, 1994)

James E. Mooney

Windels, Paul (*b* Brooklyn, 7 Dec 1885; *d* Norwalk, Conn., 15 Dec 1967). Lawyer. He graduated from Columbia College (1907) and Brooklyn Law School (1909) and served as counsel to the State Bridge and Tunnel Commission (1918–30), corporation counsel of New York City (1934–37), and chairman of the City Traffic Commission (1937–40). A Republican leader in Brooklyn, Windels was an important adviser to Fiorello H. La Guardia, for whom he provided essential financial backing and party support. He played a critical role in La Guardia's presidency of the Board of Aldermen (1920) and in his mayoral victories.

Thomas Kessner, *Fiorello La Guardia and the Making of Modern New York* (New York: McGraw–Hill, 1989)

Neal C. Garelik

Windows on the World. Restaurant. Opened in 1976 by Joe Baum, the 50,000-square-foot (4645-square-meter) restaurant and bar was located on the 106th and 107th floors of the North Tower of the World Trade Center. It had a glass-enclosed observatory and outdoor observation deck. Notable for its views of the city and gourmet cuisine, it underwent a $25 million renovation after the 1993 terrorist bombing of the World Trade Center. In 2000 it was the highest-grossing restaurant in the United States, with revenue of $37 million. It was destroyed during the terrorist attacks of 11 September 2001.

See also September 11.

Jessica Montesano

Windsor Hotel fire. One of the worst hotel fires in the history of New York City. It occurred on the afternoon of 17 March 1899 at the six-story Windsor Hotel on Fifth Avenue between 46th and 47th streets, known for many years as one of the most elegant hotels in the city. The fire broke out in one of the sitting rooms in the second story after a guest lit a cigar and then threw the match out the window, igniting a set of lace curtains. Although the fire spread rapidly, many guests were initially unaware of the danger because the cries of the staff were drowned out by the St. Patrick's Day parade proceeding along Fifth Avenue. Spectators eventually noticed the fire and pulled an alarm. Low water pressure hindered firefighters' efforts, and many guests jumped from upper-story windows. Within a few hours the hotel was destroyed; 33 people were killed and 52 injured, and property losses were estimated at $1 million.

Jonathan Aspell

Windsor Terrace. Neighborhood in northwestern Brooklyn, bounded to the north by Seventh Avenue and Prospect Park Southwest (formerly Coney Island Road), to the east by Prospect Park Southwest, and to the south and west by Green-Wood Cemetery. Once covered by John Vanderbilt's farm, the area was sold to developers in 1849 and became the village of Windsor Terrace in 1851. It remained a small settlement at a crossroads until 1900, when row houses were built throughout the area; many of these were occupied by Irish American workers, and a few continued to be occupied for several decades by descendants of the original owners. The gentrification of Park Slope in the 1980s led to a modest increase in the development of real estate, including several condominiums. The area remained predominantly Irish Catholic, with several neighborhood bars such as Farrell's (opened in 1933) on Prospect Park West.

John J. Gallagher

Winfield. Former neighborhood in northwestern Queens, bounded to the north by Queens Boulevard, to the east by the New York Connecting Rail Road, to the south by Mount Zion Cemetery and Maurice Avenue, and to the west by New Calvary Cemetery; it is considered part of Woodside. A hamlet was built in May 1854 by the developers from Manhattan G. G. Andrews and J. F. Kendall and named after General Winfield Scott, a hero of the

Mexican War. The Long Island Rail Road was extended to the area in 1861 and in 1870 Queens Boulevard was laid out, providing a route to Long Island City and Manhattan. The intersection of Shell Road (now 45th Avenue) and Queens Boulevard became the center of the community. A factory built of brick was used to manufacture Singer sewing machines and later metal coffins before World War I, when it became the Moisant aircraft factory. The neighborhood lay at the junction of the North Side Division and the Main Line of the Long Island Rail Road and about 1900 became known as Winfield Junction; the railroad station closed in 1929. Most of the housing consisted of small wooden-frame houses. The name Winfield became disused after the World War II.

Vincent Seyfried

Wingate. Neighborhood in north central Brooklyn (2009 pop. *ca* 12,000), lying east of Prospect–Lefferts Gardens and south of Crown Heights; it is bounded to the north by Empire Boulevard, to the east by Troy Avenue, to the south by Winthrop Street, and to the west by Nostrand Avenue. The area was long known as Pig Town for its many pig farms until it was renamed for General George Wingate High School, built on Kingston Avenue in 1954. The period between 1920 and World War II saw the gradual appearance of detached and semidetached houses and walk-up apartment buildings. On Miami, Palm, and Tampa courts during the 1920s an enclave of two-story town houses was erected: these had their entrances perpendicular to the street, facing each other across interior gardens that formed courtyards. The population in the early twenty-first century consisted mostly of eastern Europeans, Irish, and Caribbeans, with an enclave of Orthodox Jews in the northern section. The main commercial areas were on Nostrand Avenue and Empire Boulevard. There were also 8 acres (3 hectares) of parkland: Wingate Playground, Alexander Metz Playground, and All Boys Athletic Field.

Elizabeth Reich Rawson

Wise, Stephen S(amuel) (*b* Eger, Hungary, 17 March 1874; *d* New York City, 19 April 1949). Religious and political leader. Known for his skills as a speaker and organizer, he became a leader of the American Zionist movement and helped to form the Free Synagogue in New York City (1907) and the Jewish Institute of Religion (1921); he also directed the American Jewish Congress (1922). He achieved prominence for his work in municipal reform with his friend John Haynes Holmes, minister of the Church of the Messiah. From 1929 the two mounted a campaign to expose corruption in the government of Mayor James J. Walker; their efforts were vindicated in 1933 by the findings of the Saber Investigatory Commission.

Stephen Wise

Carl H. Voss, ed., *Stephen S. Wise, Servant of the People* (Philadelphia: Jewish Publication Society of America, 1969); Melvin I. Urofsky, *A Voice That Spoke for Justice: The Life and Times of Stephen S. Wise* (Albany: State University of New York Press, 1982)

Henry Feingold

WNYC. Public radio station. It includes the noncommercial radio stations WNYC-AM (820 kHz; began broadcasting 17 July 1924) and WNYC-FM (93.9 MHz; 1943). It was formed as part of the Department of Plant and Structures at the initiative of its commissioner Grover A. Whalen, originally for emergency communication. WNYC-AM was the first municipally owned noncommercial radio station in the United States. It flourished from 1934 under the administration of Mayor Fiorello H. La Guardia, who gave broadcasts every Sunday that drew large audiences. As manager of the station he appointed Seymour N. Siegel and Morris S. Novick, who developed a unique brand of programming that included classical music, news, and public affairs. Herman Neuman, music director from 1924 to 1969, inaugurated *The Masterwork Hour,* which began in 1929 as the first radio program of recorded classical music ever broadcast and continued into the 1990s, and the *American Music Festival,* an annual celebration of American music aired between Lincoln's and Washington's birthdays, first presented in 1939. A television production unit set up in 1949 to make short educational films for commercial stations led to the launch of WNYC-TV; its schedule in the following decades came to include documentaries and interviews on local affairs, hearings of city agencies, programs of the Public Broadcasting System, and programs of independent production companies to which the stations leased airtime.

Severe budget cuts in the 1970s led to the formation in 1979 of the WNYC Foundation, which by the early 1990s provided three-quarters of the operating budget of the system. Mayor Rudolph Giuliani cut WNYC from its sister television station in 1995, and the station was sold to the WNYC Foundation in 1997, becoming an independent not-for-profit operation. In 2008 the station moved from its longtime home in the Municipal Building to 160 Varick Street, near the Holland Tunnel. In the early twenty-first century the station remained the flagship station of National Public Radio in the area and included notable local shows such as *The Leonard Lopate Show, The Brian Lehrer Show,* and *Soundcheck.*

Benjamin Yakas, Kenneth Cobb

Wolfe, Thomas (Clayton) (*b* Asheville, N.C., 3 Oct 1900; *d* Baltimore, 15 Sept 1938). Novelist. He graduated from the University of North Carolina at Chapel Hill and studied playwriting at Harvard University before moving to New York City in 1923. He obtained a job at New York University (NYU) the following year and moved to the Hotel Albert on University Place, teaching English composition at Washington Square College. He completed the manuscript of *Look Homeward, Angel,* a semiautobiographical novel that is considered his masterpiece, in the spring of 1928, and Maxwell Perkins (1884–1947), the prominent editor of Fitzgerald and Hemingway at Charles Scribner's Sons, agreed to publish it. Perkins cut between one-fourth and one-third of the enormous manuscript and released it in 1929 to positive reviews. Wolfe became a literary celebrity; he resigned from NYU in 1930 and spent a year in Paris on a Guggenheim Fellowship. After living at various places in Manhattan he moved to Brooklyn Heights in 1931 but returned to Manhattan in 1935, eventually settling at the Chelsea Hotel. Scribner's also published *From Death to Morning* in 1935, which included "Only the Dead Know Brooklyn," a story narrating an encounter between two New Yorkers on a subway platform. During his years in New York City he wrote *Of Time and the River* (1935) and *The Story of a Novel* (1936). Two novels, *The Web and the Rock* (1939) and *You Can't Go Home Again* (1940), as well as a collection of short stories and chapters of an unfinished novel, were published posthumously. Wolfe described New York City as the "ecstatic Northern city." He died of complications from pneumonia at age 37.

David Herbert Donald, *Look Homeward: A Life of Thomas Wolfe* (Cambridge, Mass.: Harvard University Press, 2003)

Anthony Gronowicz, Kate Lauber

Wolfe, Tom [Thomas Kennerly, Jr.] (*b* Richmond, Va., 2 March 1931). Journalist and novelist. He received a BA from Washington and Lee University in 1951 and a PhD in

American Studies at Yale University in 1957. He first worked as a journalist at the *Washington Post* and then joined the *New York Herald Tribune* in 1962. He wrote for the paper's Sunday supplement, which became *New York Magazine.* During the 1960s Wolfe honed a style that used literary techniques more commonly seen in fiction writing. He wrote idiosyncratic pieces for *New York* and *Esquire;* under *New York* editor Clay Felker in 1965 he blasted the *New Yorker,* writing a profile of its venerable, reclusive editor William Shawn titled "Tiny Mummies! The True Story of the Ruler of 43rd Street's Land of the Walking Dead!" His first book, *The Kandy-Kolored Tangerine-Flake Streamline Baby* (1965), was a collection of such pieces; Wolfe continued to comment on New York City life in *Radical Chic & Mau-Mauing the Flak Catchers* (1970), part of which detailed a party for the Black Panthers given by Leonard Bernstein in his Park Avenue apartment. Wolfe made the transition from journalist to novelist in 1984–85 when his first novel, *The Bonfire of the Vanities,* was published in serial form by *Rolling Stone;* it was published as a book in 1987. The novel, a successful and controversial satire, presented New York as a city obsessed with money, sex, and power. In the early twenty-first century Wolfe, who lives on the Upper East Side of Manhattan, continues to publish novels and nonfiction.

Kate Lauber

Woman's Journal. Weekly newspaper launched in Boston in 1870. It became the official organ of the National American Suffrage Association in 1910 and moved to New York City in 1917. Editors for the newspaper included Mary A. Livermore, Lucy Stone, Henry B. Blackwell, Alice Stone Blackwell, and Virginia Roderick; the editorial board was composed of such distinguished abolitionists as Julia Ward Howe and William Lloyd Garrison. The *Woman's Journal* ceased publication in 1931.

Sandra Roff

woman suffrage. The right of women to vote. Although historians tend to characterize American suffragism as a middle-class phenomenon, the movement in New York City always had a more complex character. The first New York City Woman Suffrage Association was formed in 1870 by such elite women as the physician Clemence Lozier, the writer Lillie Devereux Blake, and Charlotte Wilbour, the president of Sorosis, one of the first women's clubs. Suffragists in the city were drawn to the cause of the many wage-earning women there. During a campaign in 1893–94 to have the issue of woman suffrage included at the state constitutional convention, wealthy and well-placed women from the city, including Josephine Shaw Lowell, Mary Putnam Jacobi, and Olivia Sage, argued before the legislature that upper-class women would provide responsible leadership for the masses of female voters. After this campaign failed, many of these suffragists turned to local politics, especially mayoral elections at the end of the century, and supported such reform candidates as Seth Low.

The class heterogeneity of the suffrage movement in the city and these experiences with political activism helped to produce a more modern style of activism, which eventually spread through the national suffrage movement. In 1907 Harriot Stanton Blatch formed the Equality League of Self Supporting Women, which recruited wage-earning women and adopted such tactics as mass parades and outdoor meetings. At Blatch's invitation the English suffragist leader Emmeline Pankhurst visited New York City, where audiences filled Carnegie Hall and Cooper Union to hear her speak. Blatch's style of activism attracted a great deal of publicity. By 1913 the largest suffrage parades in the country were held along Fifth Avenue, conducted with military precision and complete with banners and viewing stands for local politicians.

Carrie Chapman Catt, a former president of the National American Woman Suffrage Association, also focused her attention on the movement in New York City, where in 1909 she organized many small societies into the New York City Woman Suffrage Party. She condemned the corruption of urban political machines but used their tactics to organize members of her own party and deploy them in election districts throughout the city (by 1917 there were half a million members). Under intense pressure from suffragists, the state legislature in 1913 authorized a referendum in 1915 on whether women should vote in New York State. The city was the center of the campaign; suffragists there had a weekly newspaper that they hawked in the streets, and by November 1915 they reported spending $25,000, holding 5000 outdoor meetings and reaching 60 percent of the city's voters. The referendum was nonetheless defeated by 85,000 votes in the city and 200,000 statewide. Suffrage activists immediately embarked on a second campaign in which supporters in the city held fewer rallies but spent six times as much money as they had in 1915. Aware of mounting concern over World War I, organizers presented suffrage as an issue related to women's capacity for national service. More than money and patriotism, political support made the difference. Late in the referendum Tammany Hall let it be known that it would not oppose the suffrage measure. As a result, not only did the referendum pass in New York City, where suffrage leaders had assumed the opposition of immigrant voters, but the city accounted for the margin of victory for the whole state. And just as New York City carried the state, New York State carried the country, because its congressional delegation was now obligated to the votes of women as well as men, helping to ensure the passage of the Nineteenth Amendment to the U.S. Constitution in 1920.

See also Feminism.

Ellen Carol DuBois

Women's City Club of New York. Activist organization formed by suffragists in 1915. Its early leaders included Mary Garrett Hay, Katharine Bement Davis, Mary E. Dreier, Belle Moskowitz, Frances Perkins, Eleanor Roosevelt, Genevieve Earle, and Dorothy Kenyon. After women were given the right to vote in New York State in 1917, membership reached several thousand and the organization bought a mansion on Park Avenue designed by Stanford White. During the Depression membership fell and the organization began occupying rented space in mid-Manhattan. In the early twenty-first century it has offices at 307 Seventh Avenue and a membership of more than 800. It addresses public policy issues such as health-care reform, affordable housing, and government transparency and accountability.

Elisabeth Israels Perry

women's clubs. Some of the first women's clubs in New York City were formed during the antebellum period and the Civil War and were devoted to such causes as temperance, abolitionism, suffrage, and charity and relief. Sorosis, formed in 1868, became influential and inspired many women to undertake social, intellectual, and civic activities in their own clubs throughout the nation. These were in their heyday from the late 1860s until the late 1920s. Members were usually married, middle-class white women who had time for meetings and committee work, but some groups were formed on the basis of shared work experiences, religious convictions, and interests by women of almost every age, class, race, and ethnic background. In 1890 Sorosis invited 63 delegates from clubs in 17 states to form an alliance for mutual aid, which became known as the General Federation of Women's Clubs. Women also formed alumnae associations; patriotic societies; organizations for municipal and legislative reform; neighborhood improvement groups; girls' clubs; networks for workers and professionals; trade unions; suffrage and antisuffrage organizations; benevolent societies; sororities; groups devoted to such topics as health, music, drama, painting, and conservation; and auxiliaries to men's fraternal organizations, secret societies, and lodges.

Branches of statewide and national organizations have often found support in New York City, where their local branches contribute time and money, provide leadership and ideas, and sponsor regional, national, and international conferences: the elections and resolutions of some have led to changes in government policy, including child labor laws, the creation of juvenile courts, and compulsory schooling. Many national women's organizations have their headquarters in the city, including in the twenty-first century Hadassah, the Daughters of Cincinnati, the National Association of Women Artists, the National Council of Jewish Women, the National Council of Women of the United States, the Women's National Republican Club, the Women's Auxiliary to the American Institute of Mining Engineers, and the Women's City Club of New York. Organizations formerly based in the city include the International Sunshine Society, the International Woman's Peace Society, the American Birth Control League, the Girls' Service League of America, the Lucy Stone League, the Medical Women's National Association, the National Consumers' League, the National Florence Crittenton Mission, and the National Emergency Committee of Near East Relief.

Karen J. Blair, *The Clubwoman as Feminist: True Womanhood Redefined, 1868–1914* (New York: Holmes and Meier, 1980)

Karen J. Blair

Women's Hotel. Original name of the Park Avenue Hotel.

women's hotels. For several decades a number of hotels in New York City offered supervised housing to young females. The first women's hotel in the city was built in the 1870s and lasted only two months. The heyday of women's hotels was between 1940 and about 1974, when a directory listed 16 such establishments in Manhattan. Most of the residents were recent graduates of high school or college who had moved to the city to work, attend secretarial or other trade schools, or try breaking into show business. The Barbizon (1927), at Lexington Avenue and 63rd Street, was the most exclusive women's hotel and the best known; fictionalized by Sylvia Plath in her novel *The Bell Jar,* it had a swimming pool, a health club, a library, daily maid service, music studios, and an eighteenth-floor lounge with a terrace. Its residents included Grace Kelly, Candice Bergen, and Joan Crawford. The East End Hotel for Women was similarly elite, as was the Allerton, built in 1923. Originally intended for women looking for something more upscale than a boardinghouse but homier than a hotel, the Allerton housed physicians, politicians, decorators, lecturers, and store managers, who enjoyed the high-class amenities such as sewing rooms and ballrooms. Other hotels included the Martha Washington, the Webster Apartments, and the Young Women's Towne House.

Many parents agreed to have their daughters live in the metropolis only on the condition that they remain in protective surroundings. The hotels asked prospective residents to give references (the Barbizon required that one be a clergyman) and had strict rules and curfews; men were allowed only in designated lounges on the first floor or semiprivate "beau rooms." The length of a woman's stay at a hotel could range from a single day to many years: several of the original residents of the Barbizon remained for more than half a century. In 1973 the New York Commission on Human Rights deemed segregation by sex in public accommodations illegal, although hotels could legally segregate by sex if most of their guests were permanent. Webster Apartments, now The Webster, continues to house working women but also includes working college students and interns. The Barbizon admitted men in 1981 after determining that doing so was a financial necessity. In 2002 it completed conversion to luxury condominiums and was renamed the Melrose Hotel. When the Allerton was bought in 1997 its women-only restriction was lifted and the hotel was renamed the Habitat Hotel. Some more modest women's hotels operated by the Salvation Army and the Young Women's Christian Association remain in operation into the twenty-first century, as does St. Mary's Residence.

Aleeza Lubin, Jacqueline Lalley

Barbizon Hotel

Women's House of Detention. Detention center for women awaiting trial, designed in an art deco style by the firm of Sloan and Robertson and built in 1931 at Greenwich Avenue and 10th Street on the former site of the Jefferson Market Prison. It drew strong opposition from the surrounding neighborhood because the shouts of inmates could be widely heard, so it was demolished in 1973–74, at a time when correctional facilities were placed away from populated areas. The site was later used for the Jefferson Market Garden.

Nancy V. Flood

women's magazines. As early as 1794 a magazine for women, the *New York Weekly Magazine,* was published in Manhattan. Others soon followed, including the *Lady's Weekly Miscellany* (1805–8) and the *Ladies' Literary Cabinet* (1819–22). As the city became a center of dressmaking and pattern manufacturing during the mid-nineteenth century, fashion publications were introduced there, among them Frank Leslie's *Ladies' Gazette of Fashion and Fancy Needlework* (1854–57), *Mme. Demorest's Mirror of Fashion* (1860–65), and *Harper's Bazaar* (1867–), which in addition to news about fashion printed pictures and serials. When national magazines supported by advertising became common in the late nineteenth century, the city eclipsed Philadelphia as the largest national center of women's magazine publishing. *Vogue* (1892–), which chronicled the activities and fashions of the city's elite, was bought by Condé Nast in 1909 and under the direction of Edna Woolman Chase became the nation's most important fashion journal. Others that became influential during the first decades of the twentieth century were the *Delineator* (1873–1937), the *Woman's Home Companion* (1874–1957; edited by Gertrude Battles Lane, 1911–41), *McCall's* (1876–2001), *Ladies' Home Journal* (1883–), *Good Housekeeping* (1885–), and the *Pictorial Review* (1899–1939). Advertising played an important role in the growth of these periodicals, especially that for clothing and cosmetics. The 1930s saw the introduction of *Mademoiselle* (1935–) and *Glamour* (1939–), and the homemaking magazines *Family Circle* (1932–) and *Woman's Day* (1937–). Among the most successful editors at mid-century were Otis L. Wiese (*McCall's,* 1928–58), Herbert Mayes (*Good Housekeeping,* 1942–58; *McCall's,* 1958–61), and John Mack Carter (*McCall's,* 1961–65; *Ladies' Home Journal,* 1965–74; and *Good Housekeeping,* 1975–).

Under the direction of Helen Gurley Brown from 1965, *Cosmopolitan* (1886–) shifted its focus to advise young women about sexual liberation. *Essence* (1970–) was intended for middle-class black women, and *Ms.* (1972–), edited by Gloria Steinem and published by Patricia Carbine, was one of the first feminist publications with commercial backing and nationwide circulation. By the early 1970s *Good Housekeeping, McCall's, Ladies' Home Journal, Family Circle, Woman's Day, Redbook* (1903–), and *Cosmopolitan* dominated the market, and all were edited in New York. Several magazines were introduced in the late 1980s, including *New York Woman* (1987–), *Lear's* (1988–94), and *Mirabella* (1989–2000), a fashion magazine for older women launched by Grace Mirabella after she was dismissed as the editor of *Vogue.* In the twenty-first century New York City continued to be the dominant center for women's magazines.

Mary Ellen Zuckerman

Women's House of Detention, 1943

Women's Political Union. Name after 1910 of the Equality League of Self Supporting Women.

Women's Wear Daily. Fashion trade newspaper. It was established in 1910 by Edmund W. Fairchild and initially covered only trade news; from 1913 its headquarters were at 7 East 12th Street in Greenwich Village. A bureau in Paris was eventually operated by John B. Fairchild, grandson of the founder, who became known for his irreverence toward respected designers. In 1960 he took over and expanded the parent company, Fairchild Publications. Under his direction *Women's Wear Daily* began to treat a range of topics, including film, books, society, and gossip, and became known for enhancing or diminishing the reputations of the famous, for whom it coined the term "beautiful people." Fairchild promoted some designers and pointedly ignored others. In 1970 he promoted mid-length skirts by ensuring that women wearing skirts of other lengths would not be photographed for the newspaper. Circulation reportedly doubled to 800,000. Although it remains the only daily publication of the fashion industry and is virtually required reading in not only the garment industry but also social and artistic circles, its circulation was down to 162,730 in 2007. However, in the twenty-first century it also reaches readers through its Web site, WWD.com, which includes the day's paper, blogs, a calendar, classified ads, and other services.

Katie Kelly, *The Wonderful World of Women's Wear Daily* (New York: Saturday Review Press, 1972)

Leslie Gourse

Wong Chin Foo [Huang Qijgfu] (*b* China *ca* 1851; *d* after 1898). Civic leader and journalist. He moved to New York City in 1874 and was known as a compelling bilingual lecturer on Chinese customs and religion. As part of a cross-country lecture tour arranged by Madame Helena Blavatsky, founder of the Theosophical Society, Wong spoke at Steinway Hall in 1877. He was advertised as a Buddhist missionary, despite his own refutation of this description. Instead, his address confronted the stereotypes of the Chinese, which he attributed to Christian missionaries, who, he said, were propagating misinformation to obtain donations. His weekly newspaper, the *Chinese American* (Hua Mei Xin Bao), featuring articles in both English and Chinese, was launched in New York City in 1883 but lasted for only nine months. He also wrote articles for the *Atlantic Monthly, Harper's Weekly, Chautauqua, Cosmopolitan,* and the *North American Review.* In 1884 he founded the first Chinese American voters' association in the United States and advocated for political representation. In 1892 he became the founder and secretary of the Chinese Equal Rights League, the first Chinese civil rights organization in the country. In 1893 Wong left New York City for Chicago, where he reestablished his weekly newspaper and founded another Chinese Equal Rights League.

Dianna Ng

Wood, Alfred M. (*b* 19 April 1828; *d* ?Germany, 25 Jan 1871). Mayor of Brooklyn. During the Civil War he commanded the 14th Regiment of the New York State Militia and was wounded and captured in 1861 during the First Battle of Bull Run. Eventually discharged, he returned to serve as mayor of Brooklyn from 1864 to 1866.

Jerome Mushkat

Wood, Fernando (*b* Philadelphia, 14 Feb 1812; *d* Hot Springs, Ark., 14 Feb 1881). Mayor. During his early career he was a businessman, real estate speculator, and member of the U.S. Congress (1841–43). As mayor during 1855–57 and 1859–61 he became a prototypical "boss," the model for William M. "Boss" Tweed. While in office he was praised by immigrants and the poor and criticized by members of Tammany Hall, Republicans, and business leaders. He proposed innovative programs to improve the city but few passed because of the scandals surrounding him (he was convicted of defrauding investors during the gold rush), his dictatorial methods, and his reputation for politicizing the police. The state legislature, controlled by Republicans, revised the municipal charter and stripped him of his power in 1857. Scorned by Tammany Hall, he formed his own organization, Mozart Hall, and defended home rule. Before 1861 he was the city's chief defender of slavery in the South, owing to both the city's dependence on the cotton trade and his own racism. He made a notorious suggestion in 1861 that New York City become a "free city" and during the Civil War walked a fine line between loyalty and treason, eventually becoming the city's leading Copperhead. In 1867 he was again elected to the U.S. Congress, where he served to the end of his life.

Jerome Mushkat

Woodhaven. Neighborhood (2009 pop. *ca* 40,000) in southwestern Queens, bordering Cypress Hills and bounded to the north by Park Lane South, to the east by 106th and 107th streets, to the south by Atlantic Avenue, and to the west by the Brooklyn line. The area was settled in the eighteenth century and the early nineteenth by members of the Ditmars, Lott, Wyckoff, Suydam, and Snediker families. A racetrack called Union Course was built in 1821 between 78th and 82nd streets south of Jamaica Avenue; races were held there as late as 1868, often between the horses of plantation owners from the South and those of wealthy northerners. Another track, the Centerville, opened in 1825 east of Woodhaven Boulevard and south of Rockaway Boulevard and was the subject of lithographs produced in the 1850s by Currier and Ives. The area was developed as a workers' village by John R. Pitkin, who moved to Long Island from Connecticut in 1835 to build a manufacturing center in East New York. He abandoned his plan during the depression in 1837 and turned to promoting his village, Woodville, in the 1850s after persuading the railroad in 1850 to build a station. In 1853 he launched a newspaper and the few inhabitants voted to change the name of the village to Woodhaven.

A shoe factory opened in 1854, and development increased after a tinware factory was built in 1863 by Charles Lalance and Florian Grosjean, Frenchmen who improved the process of tin stamping. The factory eventually covered 11 acres (4.5 hectares). Grosjean, who managed the factory, invited French workers and built company housing. During the 1880s and 1890s the stamping works dominated the village, employing 2100 workers; it also had a feeder steel mill in Harrisburg, Pennsylvania, and branches in Chicago and Boston and supplied mess kits for soldiers during the Spanish–American War. Several residential developments were built at the end of the century: Ozone Park (1882–90), Brooklyn Hills (1889), and Forest Parkway (1900). After elevated lines reached Liberty Avenue (1915) and Jamaica Avenue (1917), thousands of Italians and Irish moved to new housing in the neighborhood, which was well known after Schmidt's Candies opened on Jamaica Avenue near 94th Street. The actress Mae West once lived on 88th Street near 98th Avenue and sang at the Union Course Tavern on nearby 78th Street. The redbrick building of the stamping works remained until 1955; in 1984–85 its former clock tower became a bank, and the site of the factory was used for a shopping mall. After 1970 the neighborhood attracted African Americans, Latin Americans, and immigrants from Guyana, Jamaica, and China. In 2009 Woodhaven was 45 percent Hispanic, 29 percent white, 14 percent Asian, and 5 percent African American, and its character remained suburban.

Vincent Seyfried

Woodhull, Caleb S. (*b* New York City, 26 Feb 1792; *d* Port Jefferson, Long Island, 16 July 1866). Mayor. He was elected mayor as a Whig in 1849 against divided Democratic opposition. Among his concerns were designating more public squares and controlling the 750 sites in the city where meat was processed. During the 1849 Astor Place Riot, his house and the Astor Place Opera House were targets of vandals.

James E. Mooney

Woodhull [née Claflin], **Victoria** (*b* Homer, Ohio, 23 Sept 1838; *d* Bredon's Norton, Worcestershire, England, 9 June 1927). Reformer. Born to poverty, she began her career as a spiritualist and in 1868 moved to New York City, where she became a leader of the American branch of the International Workingmen's Association and edited a reform newspaper. With her sister Tennessee Claflin (1843–1923) she published *Woodhull and Claflin's Weekly,* a widely circulated reform journal, and they ran the first women's brokerage firm. In the spring of 1870 Woodhull announced her candidacy for president of the United States. She was a lecturer at venues such as the Cooper Institute. In 1871 she became the first woman to address the U.S. Congress on women's suffrage, and she made an unsuccessful and well-publicized attempt to vote in New York during the 1871 election. She was formally nominated for the presidency at Apollo Hall near Madison Square on 10 May 1872 by the new Equal Rights Party, with Frederick Douglass as her running mate (although Douglass was not present and never accepted the nomination).

A supporter of "free love" (the doctrine that the state should not interfere with sexual relations), she attacked sexual hypocrisy, most notoriously when in the early 1870s she exposed the adulterous triangle between Henry Ward Beecher, Theodore Tilton, and Elizabeth Tilton. Her actions cost her the acceptance of respectable society, her sanity, and her residence in the United States. She moved to England in 1877.

Altina Waller, *Reverend Beecher and Mrs. Tilton: Sex and Class in Victorian America* (Amherst: University of Massachusetts Press, 1982); Louise Beachy Underhill, *The Woman Who Ran for President: The Many Lives of Victoria Woodhull* (New York: Penguin, 1995)

Ellen Carol DuBois, Kate Lauber

woodlands. A large part of the New York City metropolitan area was once covered by woodlands, where coniferous and deciduous forests thrived in the rich local soils and coastal temperate climate of the region. Most of the original woodlands were destroyed as the city grew, but a few trees survived alongside buildings, in parks, and in vacant lots; in later years species adapted to the harsh city environment were planted for decoration. Much of the city is classified as an open forest (that is, the crowns of trees are not contiguous) and as an urban forest. A few modified stands of native deciduous forest survive in Inwood, Fort Tryon, Riverside, High Bridge, and Central parks in Manhattan; the New York Botanical Garden and Van Cortlandt and Pelham Bay parks in the Bronx; the Gateway National Recreation Area and Kissena, Cunningham, Forest, and Flushing Meadows–Corona parks in Queens; Prospect Park in Brooklyn; and the William T. Davis Wildlife Refuge and Great Kills, High Rock, Willowbrook, New Springville, and Blue Heron Pond parks in Staten Island. Remnants of native temperate evergreen forest are found in parts of Staten Island. There the dominant species is the needle-leaved pitch pine, which thrives in poor, acidic, sandy soils prone to drought and fire; in the absence of fire such areas generally become oak forests.

Steven D. Garber, *The Urban Naturalist* (New York: John Wiley and Sons, 1987)

Steven D. Garber

Woodlawn. Neighborhood in the north central Bronx, bounded to the north by the city of Yonkers, to the east by the Bronx River Parkway, to the south by Woodlawn Cemetery, and to the west by Van Cortlandt Park. It was settled after the railroad was extended and Woodlawn Cemetery was laid out in 1863. The village was established in 1873 by George Updyke on the former farm of Gilbert Valentine. Also known as Woodlawn Heights, it is a neighborhood mostly of one- and two-family houses with some apartment buildings, and has a predominantly Irish and Italian population. Many residents describe the neighborhood as having a suburban feel.

Gary D. Hermalyn

Woodlawn Cemetery. Four-hundred-acre (160-hectare) nonsectarian cemetery in the Bronx near the Westchester County border, bounded to the north by East 233rd Street, to the east by Webster Avenue, to the south by East 211 Street and Bainbridge Avenue, and to the west by Jerome Avenue. It was laid out in the rural style in 1863 by James C. Sidney. After the ceremonious burial of Admiral David Farragut in 1870 Woodlawn became a favorite cemetery for prominent New Yorkers. Many mausoleums, some very large, were designed by important architects, including James Renwick, Stanford White, Louis Comfort Tiffany, John Russell Pope, and Richard Morris Hunt. Because approval of the management was required for each new monument, the cemetery compiled a large collection of plans for structures and the grounds. In 2006 this collection was donated to Columbia University's Avery Architectural and Fine Arts Library. There have been more than 300,000 interments in Woodlawn Cemetery. Little space remains for burials, but facilities include new community mausoleums, a crematorium, and columbariums. Among those buried at Woodlawn Cemetery are songwriters Irving Berlin, Duke Ellington, and W. C. Handy; writer Herman Melville; dancers Vernon and Irene Castle; publisher Joseph Pulitzer; musician Miles Davis; Mayor Fiorello H. La Guardia; and members of the prominent Belmont, Goelet, Gould, and Whitney families.

Edward Streeter, *The Story of Woodlawn Cemetery* (New York: Woodlawn Cemetery, 1972); Edward F. Bergman, *Woodlawn Remembers: Cemetery of American History* (Utica, N.Y.: North Country, 1988)

Edward F. Bergman, John Rousmaniere

Woodlawn Heights. Alternative name for Woodlawn.

Woodrow. Neighborhood in south central Staten Island, lying north of the Richmond Parkway. It was a sparsely settled area of woodland and small farms until one-family houses were built during the 1970s. The early Methodist bishop Francis Asbury preached in the area in 1771, and a Methodist church was established there in 1787; the Woodrow United Methodist Church at 1075 Woodrow Road (1842) has white clapboard siding, a Greek Revival portico, an Italianate bell tower, and an adjoining cemetery and parsonage (1850). The main thoroughfares are Woodrow Road and Foster Road.

Barnett Shepherd

Woods, Granville T. (*b* Columbus, Ohio, 23 April 1856; *d* New York City, 30 Jan 1910). Engineer and inventor. He invented at least 15 improvements to make railroad travel safer and more effective, including a complete electric railway system developed in 1892 and operated at Coney Island. Sometimes known as the "Black Thomas Edison," he received many patents over his lifetime for his inventions.

Celedonia Jones

Woodside. Neighborhood in northwestern Queens, adjoining Long Island City. The area was settled in the late seventeenth century by Joseph Sackett. During the American Revolution a dry ridge known as the Narrow Passage lay near what is now Woodside Avenue and 37th Avenue and provided a route for troops and couriers; high ground that is now the site of Public School 11 was used by the British as a bivouac area and lookout. Between 1830 and 1860 John Kelly, William Schroeder, Gustav Sussdorf (all of Charleston, South Carolina), and Louis Windmuller moved to the area and built mansions. The name is derived from a series of articles titled "Letters from Woodside" written by Kelly's son, the newspaperman John Andrew Kelly. In 1861 the railroad was extended to the area, providing a connection to Manhattan. A village was developed in 1867 by Benjamin W. Hitchcock, who laid out streets and sold lots; his success encouraged other developers during the 1870s and 1880s. The population rose from 1355 in 1875 to 3878 in 1900; many moved to the area after trolley lines were extended in 1895 and a trolley terminal was built (later the Tower Square Shopping Center). More houses were erected after the extension of the elevated line in 1917, and the last open land disappeared during a period of rapid development in the 1920s. A large number of Irish families moved to the neighborhood from cramped quarters in Manhattan.

After World War II some older housing in Woodside was replaced by apartment buildings, notably Big Six Towers on Queens Boulevard and 60th Street, a cooperative housing development sponsored by New York Typographical Union no. 6. Woodside Houses, a 1357-unit public housing project, opened on 22 acres (8.9 hectares) in 1949. The large Irish population was complemented during the 1980s by immigrants from China, Colombia, Korea, Mexico, Ecuador, and the Dominican Republic, and to a lesser extent from India, the Philippines, Guyana, Peru, and Ireland. Roosevelt Avenue and Northern Boulevard are the neighborhood's principal commercial thoroughfares. In the early twenty-first century Woodside retained its special appeal because it had several subway lines, including one (No. 7) with the first rush-hour express stop in Queens. Green space in the neighborhood comes mostly from two cemeteries, St. Michael's to the north and New Calvary to the south.

Vincent Seyfried, Kenneth T. Jackson

Woodstock. Neighborhood in the southern Bronx, bounded to the north by the Boston Road, to the east by Jackson Avenue, to the south by East 160th Street, and to the west by Cauldwell Avenue. It was populated from the 1860s to the 1920s chiefly by Germans, who formed several political and social clubs and singing societies that became well known (the Woodstock branch of the New York Public Library is one of few buildings remaining from this time). The neighborhood became the site in 1904 of the first public high school in the Bronx, Morris High School. In the early twenty-first century the population is growing but remains mostly black and Latin American.

John McNamara, *McNamara's Old Bronx* (New York: Bronx County Historical Society, 1989)

Gary D. Hermalyn

Woollcott, Alexander (Humphreys) (*b* Phalanx, N.J., 19 Jan 1887; *d* New York City, 23 Jan 1943). Theater critic. He began his career as an obituary writer for the *New York Times* (1910) and helped to organize the ALGONQUIN ROUND TABLE. As a theater critic for the *New York Herald,* the *Sun,* and the *New York World* (1922–28) he wielded enormous power; his reviews often determined whether a play would succeed or fail. He is considered a pioneer of drama criticism for having freed the critic from the obligation to placate theater owners by reviewing all productions favorably. In his later career he became nationally known through his columns for the *New Yorker* and the radio program *The Town Crier* (on the stations of the Columbia Broadcasting System, 1929–43) for his flamboyance, outspokenness, and intimate although biting style, as well as for his sometimes mawkish enthusiasms. Woollcott lived from 1922 to 1927 at 412 West 47th Street, from 1927 to 1936 at 450 East 52nd Street, and toward the end of his life at 10 Gracie Square and 2 West 55th Street.

Edwin Hoyt, *Alexander Woollcott: The Man Who Came to Dinner* (New York: Abelard–Schuman, 1944; repr. 1968)

Brenda Wineapple

Woolsey, John Munro (*b* Aiken, S.C., 3 Jan 1877; *d* New York City, 4 May 1945). Federal judge. He graduated from Yale University and Columbia Law School and practiced in New York City until 1929 when President Herbert Hoover appointed him a U.S. District Court judge for the Southern District of New York. In 1933 he ruled in favor of Random House's right to publish James Joyce's controversial novel *Ulysses,* which had been withheld from publication because of what were deemed explicit and allegedly obscene descriptions. Woolsey concluded that Joyce had tried with "astonishing success to show how the stream of consciousness with its ever-shifting kaleidoscopic impressions" helps to reveal the "life and behavior" of the characters and that the novel was not obscene. The state appellate court upheld Woolsey's decision, and *Ulysses* was finally published legally in the United States. The decision was a landmark for freedom of the press in the United States.

David White

Woolworth, F(rank) W(infield) (*b* Rodman, near Adams, N.Y., 13 April 1852; *d* Glen Cove, N.Y., 8 April 1919). Businessman. After attending a business school in Watertown, New York, he learned in 1878 of a retail store where each item was priced at five cents. He then opened a "five-cent store" in Utica, New York, that failed. Convinced that a store with a larger selection of merchandise would succeed, he opened one in Lancaster, Pennsylvania, where some goods were sold for 10 cents. This store, the first "five and ten," prospered, and he opened many others. In 1886 he moved his headquarters to New York City to be closer to the offices of his suppliers. The firm rented a small office at 104 Chambers Street, and he lived with his family in Brooklyn. In 1896 he opened his first store in New York City, at 17th Street and Sixth Avenue. He built a 30-room mansion for himself in 1901 at 990 Fifth Avenue, near the homes of many other wealthy merchants. In 1911 he erected the Woolworth Building, the tallest structure in the world, on Broadway and Park Place in lower Manhattan. This neo-Gothic skyscraper was derided as a "cathedral of commerce," but Woolworth took the term as a compliment and began using it himself. At his death there were more than 1000 stores in the Woolworth chain, and his personal fortune was estimated at $65 million. He is buried at Woodlawn Cemetery in the Bronx.

James Brough, *The Woolworths* (New York: McGraw–Hill, 1982)

Rohit T. Aggarwala

Woolworth Building. Office building located at 233 Broadway, on the corner of Park Place in Manhattan, across from City Hall Park. It has 55 stories and is approximately 792 feet (241 meters) tall; it was the tallest building in the world from its completion in 1913 until 1929, when the Chrysler Building surpassed it. The graceful neo-Gothic building was designed by Cass Gilbert of the firm McKim, Mead and White as the new corporate headquarters for the five-and-dime stores. Woolworth paid the $13.5 million price tag in cash, more than half going toward the cost of the land. The construction consists of a masonry and terra cotta covering of a steel frame designed by engineer Gunvald Aus. Because no buildings of comparable height had ever been constructed, the design of the Woolworth Building took into account many safety precautions. The tower is built with portal braces to protect against excessive wind in a manner similar to bridge construction. The elevators underwent excessive safety testing that included dropping elevator cars filled with eggs and bottles to test the "air cushion." The building was entirely self-sufficient; it contained its own power plant, air conditioning, barber shop, restaurant, doctor's office, and swimming pool. The lobby features a three-story arcade entrance with gold-veined marble, glass mosaics, large frescos titled "Commerce" and "Labor," as well as 12 marble busts of individuals including Gilbert and Woolworth. Known as "the Cathedral of Commerce," the building opened to great fanfare on 24 April 1913. The Venator Group (the former F. W. Woolworth Company) sold the building to the Witkoff Group in 1998.

Woolworth Building, 1913

Gail Fenske, *The Skyscraper and the City: The Woolworth Building and the Making of Modern New York* (Chicago: University of Chicago Press, 2008)

Ellen Fletcher, Anne Epstein

Wooster Group. Performance group. Known for avant-garde productions with unique staging and the inclusion of video and sound, the group originally took form in 1975 as an offshoot of the Performance Group. Led by Elizabeth LeCompte, Jim Clayburgh, Willem Dafoe, Spalding Gray, Libby Howes, Peyton Smith, Kate Valk, and Ron Vawter, it first became known as the Wooster Group in 1980. Self-described as a company focusing on innovative staging of both modern and classic texts, found materials, films and videos, dance and movement, multitrack scoring, and an architectonic approach to theater design, the group has been a leading player in experimentation with multidisciplinary performance.

The group's unconventional style grew in part out of the "Happenings" of the 1960s—experimental theater events that usually took place in lofts, basements, and other small spaces and generally involved improvisation and audience participation. The Wooster Group's founders were also influenced by the concept of "intermedia," as set forth in the eponymous 1965 essay by artist Dick Higgins. The group was among the first performance companies to move into SoHo during the Fluxus art movement of the 1960s, basing themselves in a former metal-stamping flatware factory christened the Performing Garage and located at 33 Wooster Street at a time when the area was still zoned for manufacturing. It also performed at venues like St. Ann's Warehouse in Brooklyn and the Public Theater. In the early twenty-first century the group serves as the resident theater company of the Jerome Robbins Theater in the Baryshnikov Arts Center at 450 West 37th Street.

Some of the Wooster Group's most famous and controversial productions include *Frank Dell's the Temptation of St. Antony* (1987); *Brace Up!* (1990), a vaudeville adaptation of Chekhov's *Three Sisters*; *Fish Story* (1994); *To You, the Birdie! (Phèdre)* (2002); Eugene O'Neill's *The Emperor Jones* (2006); and Molière's *The Misanthrope* (2007).

Patrick Barrett

Workingman's School. Original name of the Ethical Culture Fieldston School.

Workmen's Circle [Arbeter Ring]. Fraternal order for Jewish laborers founded on socialist principles as a mutual-aid society in 1892 and reorganized as a national order in 1900. For many years, beginning about 1912, its headquarters were in the Forward Building at 175 East Broadway. The membership remained centered in New York City, where the order provided material assistance to members, took part in the labor movement, undertook cultural projects, and opened children's schools that offered instruction in the Yiddish language, Jewish history, and socialism. Membership peaked in 1925 at nearly 85,000 and then slowly declined. In 1915 Workmen's Circle helped found the city's Folksbiene Yiddish Theatre, which worked under the auspices of the organization until 1998. In the early twenty-first century it is the only remaining professional Yiddish theater group in the country and one of only four worldwide. In 2000 Workmen's Circle entered its second century; the national headquarters are at 45 East 33rd Street.

Daniel Soyer

Works Progress Administration [Work Projects Administration; WPA]. Federal emergency employment and relief agency established in 1935 by President Franklin D. Roosevelt. Its initial appropriation of $4.8 billion represented more than half the total federal budget. The agency was closely associated with New York City from its inception, and much of its activity was centered there. Its national director, Harry Hopkins, had experience working in a settlement house in Manhattan and with the Association for Improving the Condition of the Poor; he also had led the New York State Temporary Emergency Relief Administration and between 1933 and 1935 the Federal Emergency Relief Administration and the Civil Works Administration, both forerunners of the WPA. Moreover, New York was the only city to have a local organization that stood on an equal footing with state organizations: Mayor Fiorello H. La Guardia gained this special treatment for the city because of his influence with Roosevelt and Hopkins, the innovative work relief projects developed by private and public welfare agencies in the city during the Depression, and the city's huge welfare burden (as the home of nearly 7 percent of all Americans on relief in 1935). By 1936 the WPA was spending about $20 million a month in the city, or one-seventh of all the funds being spent nationally; from 1935 to 1939 it had a labor force that fluctuated between 100,000 and 245,000, but because of insufficient funding it still could not provide work for all the able-bodied residents of the city who sought it: about 100,000 were on general relief when the agency was at its peak in 1936. The first local director of the WPA was General Hugh Johnson, who served only briefly. During the crucial period 1936–40 the local director was Colonel Brehon B. Somervell of the Army Corps of Engineers. The agency was renamed the Work Projects Administration in 1939.

Two-thirds of those employed by the WPA in the city worked on construction and engineering projects. In 1937–38 projects sponsored by the agency accounted for 60 percent of all construction in the city; among its developments were La Guardia Airport, the lower portion of the FDR Drive and the South Shore Drive in Brooklyn, 255 playgrounds, and 17 municipal swimming pools. The agency also refurbished Jacob Riis Park, Orchard Beach, and other beaches; developed 5000 acres (2000 hectares) of new parks, including one at a former dump and ash heap in Queens that became the site of the World's Fair of 1939–40; repaired 2000 miles (3200 kilometers) of streets and highways; demolished 5500 decaying structures to make way for public housing projects in Williamsburg, on the Lower East Side (the First Houses), and elsewhere; and built and repaired many schools, clinics, hospitals, municipal markets, and police and fire stations.

The remaining third of those employed by the WPA in the city were engaged in white-collar and professional work, which provided many services not available to residents even during the prosperous 1920s: these included adult education classes and preschool day care at 28 centers, screening and X-rays for tuberculosis for 400,000 urban residents, and dental services for the poor. Because the city had more actors, artists, musicians, and writers than any other place in the United States, it also had the largest program administered by the Federal Arts Project, between 1936 and 1938 accounting for nearly half of the 5000 people employed by artists' projects nationwide. The Federal Theatre in the city employed more than 4000 actors, dramatists, directors, and stagehands in 1938. It produced classics, new plays, and social documentaries by a troupe called the Living Newspaper; companies affiliated with it produced plays for children, marionette shows, radio plays, and German, black, and Yiddish theater. John Houseman and Rose McClendon, joint directors of the New York Negro Theatre Project, staged an all-black *Macbeth* adapted by Orson Welles, and a Yiddish *King Lear* enjoyed the longest run of any production mounted by the WPA in the city. The Federal Writers' Project engaged many writers in the city, of whom some had already been published but had fallen into disfavor (Maxwell Bodenheim and Anzia Yezierska) and others were young and largely unknown (John Cheever and Ralph Ellison). The writings supported by the project ranged from the guidebooks *New York Panorama* (1939) and *New York City Guide* (1939) to Richard Wright's novel *Native Son* (1940). The Federal Art Project supported such painters as Raphael Soyer, Stuart Davis, and Jackson Pollock, as well as sculptors, printmakers, photographers, and teachers. Murals painted under the auspices of the WPA may be seen at the New York Public Library on Fifth Avenue and 42nd Street, at Harlem Hospital, and at many municipal buildings. Berenice Abbott took thousands of photographs of New York City while associated with the project, some of which appeared in *Changing New York* (1939). Some 2000 musicians in the city belonged to groups sponsored by the Federal Music Project, including a symphony orchestra and jazz, swing, and dance bands; these performed in theaters, on the radio, and in parks.

In 1938 and 1939 the Un-American Activities Committee and an appropriations subcommittee of the U.S. House of Representatives investigated the Federal Arts Project, focusing in particular on writers, actors, and artists in the city. Members of the committees charged that the projects were dominated by communists. In 1939 the Federal Theatre was eliminated, and the other arts projects were drastically curtailed. The WPA ceased operations on 1 February 1943. In its seven and a half years the WPA in New York City provided income for 700,000 workers and their dependents, an amount equal to a quarter of the city's total population.

Jane D. Matthew, *The Federal Theatre, 1935–1939* (Princeton, N.J.: Princeton University Press, 1967); Jerre G. Mangione, *The Dream and the Deal: The Federal Writers' Project, 1935–1943* (Boston: Little, Brown, 1972); Barbara Blumberg, *The New Deal and the Unemployed: The View from New York City* (Lewisburg, Pa.: Bucknell University Press, 1979)

Barbara Blumberg

World Council of Churches [WCC]. Organization of nearly 350 churches in more than 120 countries, formed in Amsterdam in August 1948 after years of planning; its members include Anglican, Protestant, Old Catholic, Eastern Orthodox, and Oriental Orthodox churches. The council brings together theologians and church leaders to discuss issues and promote unity among Christian groups. The WCC United Nations Liaison Office is at the United Nations headquarters in New York City; the WCC U.S. office was in the Interchurch Center Building at 475 Riverside Drive until January 2010, when the office was closed.

Thomas E. Bird

World Financial Center. Commercial development, owned by Brookfield Properties Corporation, built on 14 acres (5.7 hectares) of landfill in Battery Park City, bounded to the north by Vesey Street, to the east by West Street, to the south by Albany Street, and to the west by the Hudson River. Rights for commercial development in the area were won in a lawsuit by the firm Olympia and York, which engaged César Pelli as the architect. His design, adapted to a master plan prepared in 1979 by Battery Park City Associates and the firm of Cooper, Eckstut, called for four postmodern towers ranging from 33 to 51 stories in height and containing 8 million square feet (743,200 square meters) of space. Ground was broken in December 1981 and construction completed in 1988. The complex includes the Winter Garden atrium, a vaulted glass and steel structure 120 feet (37 meters) high that houses restaurants and shops, and the Courtyard, a landscaped park covering 2.5 acres (1.4 hectares) along the North Cove yacht harbor, both of which are often used for performances and events. Tenants of the four towers include Dow Jones, Merrill Lynch, American Express, and the New York Mercantile Exchange (NYMEX). Various components of the development, especially the Winter Garden, were damaged in the terrorist attacks of 11 September 2001 but were later restored.

Eric Wm. Allison, Cecilia Magnusson

Winter Garden atrium in the World Financial Center, 2009

world's fairs. New York City was the site of world's fairs in 1853–54 (the first in the United States), 1939–40, and 1964–65. The iron and glass Crystal Palace (Georg Carstensen and Karl Gildemeister, architects) opened on 14 July 1853 immediately west of the Croton Reservoir in what is now Bryant Park. President Franklin Pierce spoke at the opening. Modeled after 1851's Great Exhibition at the Crystal Palace in London, the "Exhibition of the Industry of All Nations" featured 5272 exhibits of agricultural and industrial products and artworks from the United States and 22 other nations. Although paid attendance exceeded one million, the sponsors were left $300,000 in debt when the exhibition closed on 1 November 1854. The Crystal Palace burned in 1858.

The 1939 fair was in Flushing Meadow, a tidal expanse covering 1216 acres (492 hectares) along the Flushing River. Used for dumping by the Brooklyn Ash Removal Company since 1910, the site was known locally as the Corona Dumps. Parks Commissioner Robert Moses supported the fair as a way to transform the site into Flushing Meadow Park. Groundbreaking was on 29 June 1936. Mounds of refuse were leveled, and water mains, sewers, and streets were installed. Also built in conjunction with the fair were the Bronx–Whitestone Bridge, the Whitestone Expressway, the Grand Central and Cross Island parkways, the Queens Boulevard line of the Independent subway (extended to Kew Gardens on 31 December 1936), Willets Point stations for the Interborough Rapid Transit and the Long Island Rail Road, La Guardia Airport, and the Bowery Bay sewage treatment plant. Grover A. Whalen headed the nonprofit corporation, which issued $27,829,500 in 4 percent bonds due in 1941 backed by receipts from concessions, rents, and admissions (75 cents for adults, 25 cents for children), with all profits dedicated to construction of Flushing Meadow Park. New York City contributed $26.7 million to the fair, the federal government \$3 million, New York State \$6.2 million, and foreign governments about \$30 million. A board of design under Stephen A. Voorhees and Robert D. Kohn's "theme committee" prescribed standards for buildings and artwork. Notable statuary created for the fair included *Four Freedoms* by Leo Friedlander, *Speed* by Joseph E. Renier, *George Washington* by James Early Fraser, and *Chassis Fountain* by Isamu Noguchi. The fair opened on 30 April 1939, the 150th anniversary of George Washington's inauguration (ostensibly the rationale for the fair). The symbol was the Trylon and Persiphere (Harrison and Fouilhoux, architects), a futuristic structure that housed "Democracity" (designed by Henry Dreyfuss). Scattered across seven zones—amusement, communications, community interests, food, government, production and distribution, and transportation—were exhibits by 60 countries, the League of Nations, 33 states and territories (including Puerto Rico), federal agencies like the Works Progress Administration, and the City of New York (designed by Aymar Embury II, the building later housed an ice-skating rink, the United Nations, the city's exhibit for the 1964 fair, and the Queens Museum of Art).

A large number of consumer and industrial products were introduced to the public at the fair, including Lucite, television (the Radio Corporation of America), air conditioning (in the Carrier Corporation's igloo-shaped pavilion), color film (Kodak), nylon stockings (E. I. du Pont de Nemours), and diesel engines (in the Railroad Building). Especially popular attractions included Billy Rose's Aquacade in the New York State Pavilion; the Heinz Foods Pavilion (where visitors received a pickle-shaped pin as a souvenir); the Ford Motor Company's "Road of Tomorrow"; *Mickey's Surprise Party,* an animated film shown by the National Biscuit Company; the Life-Savers Parachute Tower, standing 250 feet (75 meters) high and later moved to Coney Island; American Telephone and Telegraph, where visitors could place free long-distance telephone calls; demonstrations of a robot by Westinghouse; the 21 model homes in the "Town of Tomorrow"; and above all "Futurama," a depiction of the world in 1960 by General Motors designed by Norman Bel Geddes, where visitors received a pin inscribed "I have seen the future."

Despite its optimistic, utopian tone, the fair reflected and was beset by the political turmoil of its time. After the outbreak of World War II the theme of the fair changed from "Building the World of Tomorrow" to "For Peace and Freedom." The Soviet Union's pavilion featured a statue of a worker 70 feet (21 meters) tall (dubbed "Joe the Worker" by fairgoers) and a model of the Moscow subway; it was demolished after the nonaggression pact between Joseph Stalin and Adolf Hitler and the site became "American Common," the scene of patriotic rallies. On 4 July 1940 a bomb exploded at the British Empire Exhibition, killing two members of the police department's bomb squad. The Japanese Pavilion, intended as a permanent structure, was set afire by vandals after Pearl Harbor. The fair was a financial disappointment: total attendance was 44.9 million, well short of the projected 100 million; only about 40 cents of each dollar invested was repaid. The highest daily attendance of 550,962 came on closing day, 26 October 1940.

After World War II Flushing Meadow Park did indeed open, maintaining landscape architect Gilmore Clarke's site plan, as did the 1964–65 World's Fair, "Peace through Understanding." Robert Moses was president of the World's Fair Corporation, which leased the park from the city and issued \$29.8 million in bonds. The city also lent \$24 million (never repaid). Major construction projects connected with the fair included widening the Grand Central Parkway and the Whitestone Expressway, extending the Van Wyck Expressway, and building Shea Stadium. The symbol of the fair was the UNISPHERE, erected by U.S. Steel, Gilmore Clarke designer. Unlike the first fair, it lacked the sponsorship of the Bureau of International Expositions. Even so, exhibitors included 80 countries, the federal government, 24 states, New York City, and 50 corporations. President Lyndon B. Johnson attended the opening, which also attracted civil rights protests led by James Farmer of the Congress of Racial Equality. Moses called the fair an "Olympics of Progress" and saw to it that the trials for the Olympic Games of 1964 were held in conjunction with the fair. Major attractions included "Futurama II" by General Motors, modeled after the popular exhibit from the first fair and depicting the world in 2064, the film *To Be Alive* shown by Johnson's Wax, demonstration models of the Picturephone at the American Telephone and Telegraph Pavilion, computers at the International Business Machines Pavilion, and the Panorama of New York City, a three-dimensional scale model in the New York City Pavilion showing every building in the five boroughs. The surprise of the fair was the popularity of the Belgian waffle. Walt Disney designed four exhibits, each featuring audio-animatronics: the Magic Skyway for Ford (the company introduced the Mustang at the fair), the "Carousel of Progress" for General Electric, "Great Moments with Mr. Lincoln" for the state of Illinois, and "It's a Small World" for Pepsi-Cola, with proceeds going to the United Nations International Children's Emergency Fund (UNICEF) (the latter three were reinstalled in Disneyland). The fair attracted more than 27 million visitors in 1964 (22 April to 18 October) and 24 million in 1965 (21 April to 17 October). It ran a deficit of about \$21 million, repaying about 40 cents for each dollar invested. The city rededicated Flushing Meadows–Corona Park on 3 June 1967. Left standing were the Unisphere, the Singer Bowl (later Louis Armstrong Stadium, now the site of the U.S. Tennis Center), the Port Authority Heliport (now Terrace on the Park), the Hall of Science, and the New York State Pavilion (designed by Philip Johnson, and abandoned for decades), the Federal Pavilion (abandoned, then finally demolished), and various statuary and a time capsule. The Aquacade became a public pool named for Gertrude Ederle, but the parks department closed the pool and allowed it to decay; it was demolished in 1996. The Panorama of New York City in the Queens Museum is periodically updated.

Jeffrey A. Kroessler

World Trade Center. Complex of seven buildings in lower Manhattan, including two 110-story skyscrapers (the twin towers), constructed by the Port Authority of New York and New Jersey. The two towers collapsed and the other buildings were damaged or destroyed in the terrorist attacks of 11 September 2001 (9/11) (see SEPTEMBER 11).

The complex was built as part of a massive urban renewal project of the Port Authority. Planning for a world trade center began in the late 1950s, when David Rockefeller and other business leaders sought ways to revitalize the downtown area. In 1958 they proposed the creation of a "world trade and financial center," and the Port Authority joined forces with them in 1961. The Port Authority's interest was based in part on the desire to enhance the region's role in world trade and to commit large sums to nonrail projects, making the agency less vulnerable to demands that it take control of the money-losing commuter railroads in the region. New York State and New Jersey approved the trade center with the stipulation that the Port Authority take control of the Hudson and Manhattan (H&M) Railroad and operate that bankrupt but crucial bi-state commuter line. In the spring of 1962 the port agency was committed both to constructing the trade center and to modernizing the old commuter line, now renamed the Port Authority Trans-Hudson Corporation (PATH). Progress on the trade center was delayed because of lawsuits brought by private realty interests that did not want competition for tenants from a large governmental office building, and by some of the 325 merchants who would be displaced from the site.

In 1962 the Port Authority engaged Minoru Yamasaki as its architect. The first building opened in 1970, but the towers and the plaza were not completed until 1976; the last building was completed in 1988. As construction went forward, projected costs rose—from an initial \$355 million to \$600 million in 1967, to \$800 million in the 1970s; when the last building was completed in 1988, total costs were more than \$1 billion. During construction, five streets were closed, 164 buildings demolished, and 1.2 million cubic feet (34,000 cubic meters) of earth removed and used for landfill that eventually created 23.5 acres (9.5 hectares) for Battery Park City.

The World Trade Center (WTC) site occupied 16 acres (6.5 hectares) near the Hudson River, bounded to the north by Vesey Street, to the east by Church Street, to the south by Liberty Street, and to the west by West Street. When finished, it included 10 million square feet (929,000 square meters) of usable space, surpassing the Pentagon as the largest office complex on earth, and it had its own zip code, 10048. The complex rose above an enormous underground shopping concourse and was best known for its two towers, which displaced the Empire State Building as the world's tallest building. For more than two decades the WTC towers were the dominant structures associated with Manhattan's image as a forest of skyscrapers. A public observation deck on the 107th floor of the South Tower was a popular tourist attraction and afforded a magnificent view of the New York City skyline and the surrounding harbor. Each tower, which featured load-bearing steel walls rather than the steel-cage construction typical of modern skyscrapers, had an area of 4 million square feet (371,600 square meters), a height of 1250 feet (381 meters), and a base length of 400 feet (122 meters). They transformed the skyline of the city, especially at night when they were lit from within. The smaller buildings of the complex surrounded an enormous plaza modeled after St. Mark's Square in Venice.

The complex was often criticized as architecturally unimaginative, although unlike many postwar "glass boxes," the towers gave the impression of being metallic sculptures that glistened and floated weightlessly over the tip of Manhattan; because of narrow windows and projecting metal piers, the glass in the towers disappeared behind aluminum-clad steel. Famous worldwide, the towers were, to many people, not only beautiful but also a defining presence in the city skyline. They attracted a number of daredevils, including Philippe Petit, who in 1974 walked between the two towers on a steel cable (the documentary of this feat, *Man on Wire,* was released in 2008), and George Willig, a mountain climber from Queens, who scaled the South Tower in 1977 in 3.5 hours.

On 26 February 1993 terrorists set off a car bomb in an underground parking garage beneath the center, killing six people. Both towers were closed for several weeks after the explosion. In 1994 the four main suspects in the bombing were convicted on nearly all charges.

Then, on 11 September 2001, two jet aircraft hijacked by members of the terrorist organization Al-Qaeda flew directly into the twin towers, destroying them and killing an estimated 2749 people, including 343 firefighters and 70 police officers, as well as the passengers and crew onboard the two planes. It was the worst terrorist attack ever committed on U.S. soil. By 10:30 a.m., both towers had collapsed.

World Trade Center, 1973

The "Survivors' Staircase," World Trade Center, 11 September 2008

Later that day, 7 World Trade Center also collapsed. The Marriott Hotel, nearby St. Nicholas Greek Orthodox Church, and 3 World Trade Center were destroyed during the collapse of the towers, and other nearby structures were badly damaged. The remaining three WTC buildings around the plaza were so devastated that they were eventually razed. Although several thousand people managed to escape from the towers before they collapsed, only 21 people were found alive in the rubble. Removal of 1.8 million tons of debris from the area, which came to be called Ground Zero, was not completed until May 30, 2002. (For a full account of the attacks, see SEPTEMBER 11.)

Immediately after the attacks the Port Authority of New York and New Jersey and the City and State of New York began taking steps to reconstruct the WTC site and to memorialize the victims. From the beginning, however, the plans for reconstruction were beset by conflict among the parties involved in the process, budget problems, and security concerns. In November 2001 Governor George Pataki, in consultation with Mayor Rudolph Giuliani, created, the LOWER MANHATTAN DEVELOPMENT CORPORATION (LMDC) to plan and coordinate the rebuilding. Its recommendations for future public and private development in lower Manhattan were adopted in July 2002 but met with so much negative reaction from the public that the plans were abandoned. The LMDC then held an international design and planning competition, to which more than 400 teams responded. In December 2002 seven teams of designers exhibited their entries at the World Financial Center. The final choice of design was controversial, but ultimately, in February 2003 Governor Pataki announced that the Studio Daniel Libeskind proposal, called *Memory Foundations,* would provide the basis for a master redevelopment plan. The centerpiece of the plan was to be the 1362-foot-tall (415-meter-tall) "Freedom Tower" with an antenna rising to the symbolic height of 1776 feet (541 meters). This building was redesigned by architect David Childs of Skidmore, Owings and Merrill after a public debate over the issue and later renamed One World Trade Center. In 2006 the building was yet again redesigned in light of New York Police Department concerns about the building's security, creating more construction delays. As of 2010 One World Trade Center had a projected opening date of 2013.

7 World Trade Center, 2009

Silverstein Properties became a critical partner in all WTC activities in July 2001, when it became a 99-year leaseholder of buildings 1, 2, 3, 4, and 5 and the retail space in the complex. In what was called the world's richest real estate deal at the time, the lease was worth $3.2 billion. Although Libeskind's master plan was still in place, Silverstein Properties selected its own architects for its buildings. In September 2006 Silverstein announced that Norman Foster, Richard Rogers, and Fumihiko Maki would be the architects for 2, 3, and 4 WTC, respectively. That same year, the Port Authority assumed responsibility for One World Trade Center, which had originally been part of the Silverstein leasehold. Silverstein Properties also completed construction of 7 WTC, a 52-story, 1.6-million-square-foot (148,645-square-meter) office building that opened in May 2006. In June 2007 JPMorgan Chase announced it would erect its investment banking headquarters at 130 Liberty Street, just south of the WTC site where the Deutsche Bank Building had stood.

Another part of the WTC master plan was a new transportation hub. The first of three temporary PATH railroad stations was opened in November 2003. The Port Authority hired architect Santiago Calatrava to design the new hub, which began construction in September 2005. Work was delayed because of revisions, reengineering, security concerns, and high costs, and projections in 2010 placed possible completion of this project no earlier than 2014, but possibly later.

The *Memory Foundations* plan also provided for memorial and cultural buildings and open spaces dedicated to those killed in the 1993 and 2001 terrorist attacks. In June 2003 the LMDC invited interested parties to submit ideas for the 600,000 square feet (55,742 square meters) available for the projects. By September more than 110 responses had been received, and four institutions were selected in June 2004 to be part of a performing arts center; by 2010 the Joyce International Dance Theater was the only arts group in consideration. The plans from the architects originally chosen for this—Frank Gehry and the Norwegian firm Snøhetta—were dropped after concerns were raised by 9/11 families and their supporters. The museum was then redesigned by New York City architectural firm Davis Brody Bond. The performing arts center, which is under the jurisdiction of the City of New York, was given $50 million in 2010 by the LMDC to build the underground support structure for the 1000-seat theater, but in 2010 the project continued to face budgetary and construction challenges and only infrastructure was complete.

The 9/11 memorial was the subject of an international design competition won by Michael Arad and Peter Walker in 2004. Their design, called *Reflecting Absence,* was significantly altered to reduce construction costs (once estimated at more than $1 billion) and to address security concerns. The outdoor memorial—which will include pools, parapets, and a planted plaza—is part of the National September 11 Memorial and Museum slated for a public dedication on the 10th anniversary of the towers' destruction, 11 September 2011; it is projected that the core and shell of the plaza-level museum pavilion will be finished, but the museum itself will not be open at that time. In late 2012 or 2013 the full pavilion and underground museum are projected to be open.

As of 2010 the WTC site remained largely empty of buildings although construction work continued. Of the above-ground buildings, only One World Trade Center was under construction; Silverstein Properties was planning how to proceed with buildings 2, 3, and 4 given the economic downturn of the time. In March 2010 Silverstein Properties and the Port Authority had developed a framework for how the three building sites might be developed. Although billions of dollars had been spent, it was uncertain if and when all of these buildings would be completed.

Anthony W. Robins, *Classics of American Architecture: The World Trade Center* (Englewood, Fla.: Pineapple/Omnigraphics, 1987); Angus Kress Gillespie, *Twin Towers* (New Brunswick, N.J.: Rutgers University Press, 1999); Jameson W. Doig, *Empire on the Hudson: Entrepreneurial Vision and Political Power at the Port of New York Authority* (New York: Columbia University Press, 2001); James Glanz and Eric Lipton, *City in the Sky: The Rise and Fall of the World Trade Center* (New York: Times Books, 2003)

Jameson W. Doig, Anthony W. Robins, Alex Garvin, Lisa Keller

World War I. The outbreak of war in Europe in August 1914 sparked an initial economic contraction in the United States as overseas trade diminished. To avert a financial panic, the New York Stock Exchange closed for four and a half months. Ultimately, New York City financial institutions, especially J. P. Morgan, played an instrumental role in financing the war effort of Great Britain and France. One of the lasting legacies of the war would be the rise of the city as the unparalleled financial capital of the world, surpassing London. Similarly, defense orders revived a sluggish economy and much of the trade with European belligerents passed through New York Harbor.

New Yorkers were divided over whether the United States should enter the war against Germany. Much of the city's business and financial elite were prominent supporters of the preparedness movement and pressed President Woodrow Wilson to take a more aggressive stand against German actions. During the summer of 1915 many joined Mayor John Purroy Mitchel in preparing for military service by attending as civilians a summer army training camp established at Plattsburgh, New York, and staffed by army officers. In sharp contrast, strong sentiment existed among the city's large German and Irish populations opposing intervention. They were joined by socialists and many labor leaders who saw the conflict as a struggle between imperialist powers in which workers had no stake. Peace organizations, often attracting the support of Progressive reformers, pressed Woodrow Wilson in 1915 and 1916 to maintain American neutrality and for the United States to act in the role of mediator between the major belligerents.

After Congress declared war in April 1917, many former opponents embraced the war effort, fostering deep divisions in the Socialist Party, the labor movement, and the intellectual community. For instance, Walter Lippmann, founding editor of the *New Republic,* embraced the war, while Randolph Bourne continued to dissent. Emma Goldman and Alexander Berkman delivered a series of speeches in New York City urging young men to avoid the draft and were tried and convicted in federal court for disrupting the war effort. The depth of antiwar sentiment in the city after the U.S. entry into the conflict can be gauged by the tenor of the 1917 municipal election. Mitchel ran a reelection campaign for mayor advocating support of the war effort and accused Tammany's candidate John F. Hylan and socialist Morris Hillquit of disloyalty. Although Hylan had initially opposed the United States' entrance into the war, he ignored the conflict during his campaign, but Hillquit ran on an antiwar platform that opposed conscription and publicly stated his refusal to buy Liberty Bonds. Mitchel suffered a humiliating defeat by Hylan. Meanwhile, the extent of antiwar sentiment was reflected in the strong support for Hillquit, who received 22 percent of the vote.

Federal authorities suppressed many radical organizations, individuals, and publications based in the city, including *The Masses.* The New York Board of Education demanded that teachers abandon antiwar activism and even dismissed several for lukewarm support of the war effort. Government propaganda, employers, public-school teachers, and neighbors often pressured New Yorkers to purchase Liberty Bonds used to finance the war. Columbia University mandated faculty support of the war effort and dismissed several dissenting professors. Anti-German sentiment was reflected by such actions as the banning of all German works from its repertoire by the Metropolitan Opera in the city. Nonetheless, the city was spared the worse excesses of vigilante activity aimed at German Americans, radicals, and antiwar opponents common in other parts of the country. Moreover, the city served as headquarters for a new organization established to fight for dissenters and conscientious objectors, the National Civil Liberties Bureau, which evolved into the American Civil Liberties Union.

Several New York National Guard units compiled distinguished combat records. The 69th New York regiment, renamed the 165th regiment, became part of the 42nd Division and saw action in the Aisne Marine and Meuse Argonne. Father Francis P. Duffy, regimental chaplain for this unit, was an inspirational figure whose wartime service would be commemorated in a public statue erected in Times Square and a Hollywood film, *The Fighting 69th* (1940). The U.S. Army deployed the African American, Harlem-based 15th National Guard regiment to France, where it was renamed the 369th and attached to the French army; the regiment acquired a notable combat record. Most New Yorkers fought as conscripts, and a disproportionate number served with the 77th Infantry Division, one of the first big units deployed to France.

The war led to a reallocation of the city's manufacturing to war production, especially in the case of the garment industry. The demand for labor improved the bargaining power of labor unions, and the war brought substantial growth in recognition, and access to federal officials, for Sidney Hillman and the Amalgamated Clothing Workers of America. Nearly four of five U.S. soldiers were deployed overseas from the Port of New York and nearby Hoboken. Most war material bound for Europe passed through the port, severely taxing both the railroad network and port facilities.

The announcement of the armistice on 11 November 1918 provoked celebration in all five boroughs. Waves of returning troops passed through the city in 1919, and public officials staged major victory parades for the 77th Division and other returning units. The Hylan administration planned to build a major memorial in Central Park, but instead over the course of the 1920s and 1930s scores of smaller statues, memorial tablets, and memorials were dedicated in all five boroughs. Many returning veterans of World War I joined the newly created American Legion and organized posts throughout the city. Although the legion was conservative in orientation, the Willard Straight Post in Manhattan had a liberal cast that eventually forced a confrontation with the national organization. World War I spawned a new civic holiday, Armistice Day, that was widely observed in the city. For several decades Armistice Day was marked by a brief service suspension of the city's subway system for two minutes on the 11th hour.

Edwin R. Lewinson, *John Purroy Mitchel: The Boy Mayor of New York* (New York: Astra, 1965); Stephen L. Harris, *Harlem Hell Fighters: The African-American 369th Infantry in World War I* (Washington, D.C.: Brassey's, 2003); Richard Slotkin, *Lost Battalions: The Great War and the Crisis of American Nationality* (New York: Henry Holt, 2005)

G. Kurt Piehler

World War II. Memories of World War I shaped how New Yorkers responded to the rise of Nazi Germany, fascist Italy, and imperial Japan during the 1930s. Many financial and business elites who had embraced intervention in World War I were disillusioned by the legacy of this conflict and thus opposed the United States' entrance into World War II before the Japanese attack on Pearl Harbor on 7 December 1941. The isolationist America First organization had an active branch within the city, and most New Yorkers of German, Irish, and Italian descent opposed intervention in another European war. The pro-Nazi Bund attracted several thousands adherents in the 1930s and staged a number of public rallies and street demonstrations. Most New Yorkers of German descent did not embrace the Bund, but several mainstream German civic organizations participated in public programs with the Bund in the early 1930s. The continued hostility of the city's Irish community toward Britain dimmed that group's concern over the threat the Nazis posed to the British. Benito Mussolini's fascist regime drew considerable support within New York City's Italian community, and even Mayor Fiorello H. La Guardia, a fierce anti-Nazi throughout his years as mayor, remained relatively silent on fascism, even after Mussolini ordered an invasion of Ethiopia.

The city served as an important center for anti-fascist activity soon after Adolf Hitler came to power in 1933. The Jewish War Veterans and the American Jewish Congress mobilized much of the city's large Jewish community and other anti-Nazi opponents to support a boycott of German goods. In the 1930s the American Community Party made significant headway in enlisting New York City liberals and socialists to support the common front against fascism. The city sent a large contingent to fight with the Abraham Lincoln Brigade during the Spanish Civil War. It also served as a refuge for many German Jewish exiles fleeing the Nazi regime, with many settling in Washington Heights in Manhattan. The New York City–based Rockefeller Foundation played a significant role in aiding German intellectuals in resettling in the United States, and many made the city their home.

Even before the United States entered the war, New Yorkers were conscripted in the nation's first peacetime draft. New York City units of the National Guard were placed in federal service in October 1940, and the 27th Division was eventually deployed to Hawaii in 1942 and later saw combat at Saipan in 1944. The U.S. declaration of war on 8 December 1941 prompted a series of measures by city and federal officials to secure access to key transportation, industrial, and utilities facilities. The city initiated elaborate civil defense plans and dimmed most streetlights—although the city never was attacked from the air. As New York City was a major port, the threat of German submarines to U.S. merchant ships proved significant, especially in 1942. The U.S. Coast Guard took extraordinary measures to secure the harbor from sabotage, and together with the U.S. Navy eventually drove German submarines away from the U.S. coast.

More than one million New Yorkers served in the armed forces during World War II, and the city served as home to several major army, naval, and air bases, including Governors Island, Brooklyn Navy Yard, Fort Hamilton, Fort Totten, and Floyd Bennett Field. At least two-thirds of the personnel, equipment, and supplies destined for the European theater of occupation passed through the Brooklyn docks. As it had during World War I, the city served as a crucial staging area for troops departing overseas. To entertain these servicemen and servicewomen, many civic organizations sponsored special programs. The American Theater Wing organized one of the most distinctive endeavors, the Stage Door Canteen, a free club for Allied soldiers, which provided them with a place to dance, eat, and watch performances staged by the New York theater community.

The transition from a peacetime economy to a wartime footing led to a drop in unemployment. Ultimately, New York City factories, especially those associated with the shipbuilding and garment industries, made a major contribution to the war effort, with military contracts valued at approximately $18.8 billion awarded between June 1940 and September 1945. Membership in unions soared during the war, and the city achieved a full employment economy that sharply reduced the number of individuals receiving relief.

Wartime inflation, especially the price of food and housing, buffeted New York City's poor and working class. New York was one of the last major cities to have the federal Office of Price Administration implement rent control to keep a check on skyrocketing real estate prices. Gasoline rationing as well as limits on automobile production resulted in the city subways carrying a record number of passengers. Although city residents endured food rationing, and many other items were either unavailable or in short supply, the rising wages of most workers sparked a wave of consumer spending in entertainment, restaurants, and the consumer goods that remained available. New York City did not see the exponential population growth experienced by many industrial centers, such as Detroit and Los Angeles, that worsened race relations in those cities. However, despite the leadership of La Guardia and his reputation as an advocate for civil rights, the city did experience a major race riot. In August 1943 an incident of alleged police brutality involving a black serviceman on leave sparked a wave of looting and several deaths in Harlem.

The announcement of the end of the war on 14 August 1945 led to spontaneous celebrations throughout the city. Thousands crowded Times Square, and the New York Stock Exchange closed for two days. New York City served as the port of arrival for many troops returning from overseas, including the 82nd Airborne Division, which was greeted by a giant victory parade in 1946. Many returned veterans used the benefits accorded to them to purchase homes in suburban communities after the war, fostering a mid-century decline in the city's population.

Dominic J. Capeci, *The Harlem Riot of 1943* (Philadelphia: Temple University Press, 1977); Timothy J. Holian, *The German-American and World War II: An Ethnic Experience* (New York: Peter Lang, 1996); Peter N. Carroll and James Fernandez, eds., *Facing Fascism: New York and the Spanish Civil War* (New York: Museum of the City of New York/NYU Press, 2007)

G. Kurt Piehler

Worldwide Plaza. Building complex that occupies an entire city block bounded by 49th and 50th streets and Eighth and Ninth avenues in Clinton, formerly the site of the third Madison Square Garden (1925–66). It consists of a pinkish beige condominium building (39 stories) and office tower (49 stories), connecting structures, and an underground movie theater, all designed by David Childs of Skidmore, Owings and Merrill and developed by William Zeckendorf, Jr., at a cost of $650 million. The complex was completed a year after the stock market crash of 1987, adding 1.5 million square feet (139,000 square meters) of office space to an already glutted market. Agents nevertheless succeeded in signing the prestigious advertising firm of Ogilvy and Mather and the law firm of Cravath, Swaine and Moore to long-term leases. Because the city wished to encourage the westward movement of offices from the more crowded central spine of Manhattan, Worldwide Plaza has more floor space than would have been allowed in east midtown.

Kenneth T. Jackson

WPA. See Works Progress Administration.

W. R. Grace and Company. Firm of chemical manufacturers. It began as a firm of guano suppliers in Peru and received its current name when William Russell Grace moved his operations to 110 Wall Street in Manhattan in 1866. The firm expanded by building a diverse network of trade between North America and the western coast of South America. In 1882 the Merchant Line was introduced, offering the first regular transportation by ship between Manhattan and the western coast of South America; renamed the Grace Line after steamships were put into service in 1893, it dominated the route for half a century before being sold in 1969. By the beginning of the twentieth century the firm had many commercial and industrial ventures in Latin America, including railroad construction, sugar processing, rubber extraction, and nitrate mining; on its sugar estate in Paramonga, Peru, it developed a process for producing paper from bagasse, a fibrous residue from the manufacture of sugar. With Pan American Airlines it formed Pan American Grace Airways (Panagra) in 1928, the first international airline to offer flights between the United States and South America. The firm maintained its central operations in Peru until 1945, when under the direction of J. Peter Grace it focused on manufacturing chemicals in the United States. It bought the Dewey Almy Chemical Company and the Davison Chemical Company in 1954, expanded in North America and Europe, and by the 1970s had divested itself of nearly all of its Latin American operations. In 1974 the firm moved to a skyscraper at 41 West 42nd Street designed by Skidmore, Owings and Merrill. The headquarters were moved to Florida in 1991.

Mira Wilkins, *The Maturing of Multinational Enterprise: American Business Abroad from 1914 to 1970* (Cambridge, Mass.: Harvard University Press, 1974); Lawrence A. Clayton, *Grace: W. R. Grace & Co.: The Formative Years, 1850–1930* (Ottawa, Ill.: Jameson, 1985)

Lawrence A. Clayton

Wright, Bruce McMarion (*b* Princeton, N.J., 19 Dec 1918; *d* New York City, 24 March 2005). Judge. He served for 25 years in the civil and criminal courts of Manhattan. Best known for his vigorous defense of the Eighth Amendment, Wright believed that setting bail beyond the economic means of a defendant, or for any reason other than ensuring the defendant's return to court, violated the Constitution. This earned him the enmity of police officers and politicians and the nickname Turn 'Em Loose Bruce, coined by the Patrolmen's Benevolent Association. Wright was also a critic of racism in the judiciary, even criticizing other African American judges for accepting or replicating their white peers' prejudice against minority defendants. Some found his outspokenness unbecoming to his position, but as Wright wrote in his book *Black Robes, White Justice* (1987), "Prejudice must be publicly attacked by all who oppose it, even and especially if one is a judge."

Daniel Levinson Wilk

Wright, Richard (Nathaniel) (*b* near Natchez, Miss., 4 Sept 1908; *d* Paris, 28 Nov 1960). Writer. The son of sharecroppers, he migrated north to Chicago during the Depression, where he worked menial jobs. The self-taught Wright, who showed writing genius from an early age, began contributing to radical literary magazines affiliated with the Communist Party, soon joining the party itself in 1932. He was also hired by the Works Progress Administration's Writers' Project. In 1937 he moved to New York City to 235 West 26th Street and became the Harlem editor of the Communist Party newspaper the *Daily Worker.* There he befriended the writer Ralph Ellison. After writing the *Guide to Harlem* (1937), he drew the public's attention with a collection of novellas, *Uncle Tom's Children* (1938), which depicts an African American man's struggle to live with dignity in the face of racism. His following novel, *Native Son* (1940), tells the story of Bigger Thomas, a young African American man in 1930s Chicago who accidentally kills a white woman. *Native Son* was almost universally acclaimed by critics and became an international best seller—with 215,000 copies sold in its first three weeks—making Wright the first best-selling African American writer in U.S. history.

In 1944 Wright renounced the Communist Party because of its lack of focus on improving the conditions of African Americans and its dogmatic political program. In the following year he published *Black Boy,* an autobiographical novel about growing up in the South. During the early 1940s he lived at 175 Carlton Avenue, Lefferts Place, Washington Place, and his last New York City residence, 13 Charles Street. Shortly after the end of World War II he moved to Paris. There, Wright befriended Jean-Paul Sartre and Albert Camus, and in 1953 he wrote the existentialist novel *The Outsider* (1953). He also published five works of nonfiction, including *White Man, Listen!* (1957); a collection of short stories; and several other novels.

During the McCarthy era the federal government targeted Wright as a communist and revoked his passport, despite his break with and public denunciation of the Communist Party in 1944. In 1960 he fell ill, was admitted to a hospital in Paris, and died shortly after. His ashes reside in the Père Lachaise Cemetery in Paris. *American Hunger,* the continuation of *Black Boy,* was published posthumously in 1977. The Black Power movement of the 1960s sparked a refocus on *Native Son* as powerful social criticism, and today the novel is widely regarded as a classic of American literature.

Addison Gayle, *Richard Wright: Ordeal of a Native Son* (Garden City, N.Y.: Doubleday, 1980); Hazel Rowley, *Richard Wright: The Life and Times* (New York: Henry Holt, 2001)

Anthony Gronowicz

Wright, Theodore S(edgwick) (*b* near New York City, 1797; *d* 25 Nov 1847). Pastor and abolitionist. He received his education at the African Free School and Princeton Theological Seminary, becoming the first black graduate of a divinity school in the United States, and in 1827 he took over as pastor of the First Colored Presbyterian Church (later Shiloh Presbyterian Church). He toured the northern and western states, giving lectures under the auspices of the New England and New York antislavery societies, and became an outspoken critic of the "back-to-Africa" movement, maintaining that it undermined abolitionism and the status of free blacks. He denounced the American Colonization Society (1817) and proclaimed his commitment to abolishing slavery through political means. After helping to form the American Anti-Slavery Society in 1833 he withdrew after disagreeing with a faction devoted to "moral suasion," a policy of attacking slavery by revealing its evils through moral argument; he helped to form the American and Foreign Anti-Slavery Society in 1840 and urged the passage of a federal law abolishing slavery. A member of the Liberty Party, he served on the committee that nominated James G. Birney as a presidential candidate in 1844. Wright was also vice president of the Phoenix Society of New York City (1833), a lyceum for young black men; a director of the New York Vigilance Committee, formed in 1835 to help fugitive slaves and rescue blacks who had been kidnapped and sold in the South; and president of Phoenix High School (1836), a private school for gifted black youths.

Thelma Foote

Wriston, Walter B(igelow) (*b* Appleton, Wis., 3 Aug 1919; *d* New York City, 19 Jan 2006). Banker. After graduating in 1941 from Wesleyan University, Wriston completed a master's degree at Tufts's Fletcher School of Law and Diplomacy (1942) and then served 38 months in the U.S. Army during World War II. He began work at Citibank in 1946 as a branch auditor. When he went to the foreign division in 1955, Citibank had only 61 overseas offices. After George Moore became bank president in 1959, Wriston was put in charge of foreign offices, with the goal of placing Citibank facilities in promising locations on every continent. By 1969 a network of 578 offices operated in 78 nations. Moore's ambition to transform Citibank into a "global financial services institution" was being realized. Wriston became executive vice president of Citibank in 1960, president and CEO in 1967, and chairman from 1970 until his retirement in 1984.

Wriston constantly prodded his top officers to move women, minorities, and foreigners into top positions. A lifelong advocate of laissez-faire capitalism, he fought against controls restraining the geographic expansion of banks and the scope of permissible financial services. President Jimmy Carter, signing the Depository Institutions, Deregulation and Monetary Control Act of 1980, praised Wriston for being "a leading spokesman for reform" of the financial system. He was hailed for running the most admired bank in the world and recognized as the most influential banker in the world. A 1982 Gallup poll of businessmen rated Wriston the most admired of all business leaders.

George S. Moore, *The Banker's Life* (New York: Norton, 1979); Phillip C. Zweig, *Wriston* (New York: Crown, 1995)

Benjamin J. Klebaner

Writers Guild of America, East [WGAE]. Union formed in 1954 to represent radio, television, and motion picture writers east of the Mississippi River. Among its forerunners were the Authors League of America (1912) and the Screen Writers Guild (1921), which became threatened by the political climate after World War II and the rapid development of television. After intense negotiation and reorganization the Authors League of America divided into two branches in 1954 (the Authors Guild and the Dramatists Guild), and the Writers Guild of America, which was composed of eastern and western divisions, became the union for all other writers. In addition to negotiating contracts with producers, the Writers Guild offers writing fellowships, a script registration service, and various programs for members and the general public. WGAE became affiliated with the AFL–CIO in 1989. In 2006 its membership was nearly 4000. In the early twenty-first century its headquarters were at 555 West 57th Street.

Geoffrey Cowan, *See No Evil: The Backstage Battle over Sex and Violence on Television* (New York: Simon and Schuster, 1979)

Grai St. Clair Rice

Wurster, Catherine Bauer (*b* Elizabeth, N.J., 11 May 1905; *d* Marin County, Calif., 21 Nov 1964). Reformer. She was active in the late 1920s in the Regional Planning Association of America and became an advocate for improved low-income housing. In several books and articles she argued that governmental subsidies offered a more effective means of financing housing than tax exemptions, which she believed had failed as a source of aid in New York City during the 1920s. A protégée and later mistress of Lewis Mumford, she worked with Senator Robert F. Wagner and leaders of housing and labor organizations in 1936–37 to draft national legislation for public housing; her efforts led to the formation of the U.S. Housing Authority (1937). Wurster taught at Harvard University until 1950 and at the University of California at Berkeley until her accidental death while hiking on a mountain. She wrote *Modern Housing* (1934).

Roy Lubove, *Community Planning in the 1920s: The Contribution of the Regional Planning Association of America* (Pittsburgh: University of Pittsburgh Press, 1962)

Mark H. Rose

Wurster, Frederick W. (*b* Plymouth, N.C., April 1850; *d* Brooklyn, June 1917). Last mayor of Brooklyn. A businessman, he served from 1896 until the consolidation of New York City in 1898.

Ellen Fletcher

W. W. Norton and Company. Firm of book publishers, formed in 1923 as the People's Institute of Publishing Company by William Warder Norton. It set out to publish books that would appeal to both general and academic readers and became especially well known for its strong lists in psychology (including the works of Sigmund Freud), music, economics, and literature. In 1930 it established its college department, which became one of its most profitable divisions by publishing such standard college texts as *The Norton Anthology of English Literature,* and other "Norton anthologies." Over the years the firm published such widely read titles as *The Ugly American* (1958) by William Lederer and Eugene Burdick, *Present at the Creation* (1969) by Dean Acheson, *Helter Skelter: The True Story of the Manson Murders* (1974) by Vincent Bugliosi, and *The Mismeasure of Man* (1981) by Stephen Jay Gould. Norton is the only major U.S. publisher owned entirely by its employees and one of few to have avoided a takeover by a larger firm. Its offices are at 500 Fifth Avenue, and it publishes as many as 400 books annually.

See also Book publishing.

Eileen K. Cheng

Wyckoff House. Historic house in Brooklyn, on Clarendon Road near Ralph Avenue. It was built about 1652 and may be the oldest house in New York City. The house is named for Pieter Claesen Wyckoff, an indentured servant who in 1637 was taken from the Netherlands to America, where he became a successful farmer and magistrate and one of the wealthiest men in the region. His descendants lived in the house until 1902. Bought by a family foundation in 1961, the house became the first official landmark in New York City in 1965, was donated to the city in 1970, and was restored in 1982. A modest dwelling with pine floors, shingled walls, and a steeply pitched roof, Wyckoff House contains artifacts and furniture representative of colonial life.

Jonathan Kuhn

Wyckoff House

Xavier High School. Jesuit school for boys located at 30 West 16th Street in Manhattan, formed in 1847 by John Larkin (1801–58). Initially it occupied the Holy Name Church at Elizabeth and Walker streets. After the church was destroyed by fire in January 1848, the school moved to St. James Church and then to a rented building at 77 Third Avenue. In 1850 it took over its current site and was renamed the College of St. Francis Xavier. For many years the school offered both secondary and college-level courses. In 1913 its college charter was transferred to Brooklyn College, but its college division closed in 1920. In 2004 the first lay headmaster was appointed. In 2008 the school caused some neighborhood controversy in a dispute over real estate air rights in the area behind the school along 15th Street. In the early twenty-first century the school had a student population of about 950.

Gilbert Tauber

Xavier Institute of Industrial Relations. Catholic labor school opened in 1934 at the College of St. Francis Xavier on West 16th Street in Manhattan. The school trained men and women working in several industries in New York City to organize unions free of communist influence. Like many other Catholic labor schools throughout the United States it was directed by members of the Society of Jesus, and it offered classes taught by representatives of labor and business. These classes covered the ethics of labor-management relations, the rights and responsibilities of labor, contract negotiation, the practices of shop stewards, and public speaking; several courses were designed specifically for workers in government and the trades. Philip A. Carey, director of the school from 1940 to 1989, was prominent in business, advised the labor leader Harry Van Arsdale, Jr., and belonged to the War Labor Board (during World War II), the New York State Commission for Human Rights (1963), and the New York State Public Employment Relations Board (from 1968). John M. Corridan, associate director of the school from 1947 to 1957, became known as the city's Waterfront Priest. Xavier Institute closed in 1989.

Brenda Parnes

yachting. See Sailing.

Yale Club. Club formed in 1897 by an active local Yale University alumni association. Its 22-story clubhouse on Vanderbilt Avenue at 44th Street, designed by James Gamble Rogers and completed in 1915, is very close to Grand Central Terminal at the end of the railroad line from the northern subways and from New Haven, Connecticut. It contains the usual complement of dining rooms, library and reading rooms, and sporting and sleeping facilities. All these amenities were shared with the Princeton Club during World War I, when many members were in uniform overseas. In the early twenty-first century the club had about 11,000 members.

James E. Mooney

Yalow, Rosalyn Sussman (*b* New York City, 19 July 1921). Nobel laureate and nuclear physicist. She excelled in chemistry at Walton High School in the Bronx and in physics at Hunter College. She did a teaching assistantship at the University of Illinois, where she was the only female faculty member at the College of Engineering. After completing her PhD and marrying fellow student Aaron Yalow, she returned to New York City in 1945 and began teaching at Hunter College. Yalow joined the Bronx Veterans Administration Hospital full time in 1950, where she did research in radioactivity and endocrinology with Sol Berson; she also worked as a researcher and professor at various medical schools in New York City. She was a developer in the 1950s of the radioimmunoassay, a technique for the precise measurement of biological substances. Yalow was the first female recipient of the Albert Lasker Award, and in 1977 she was the second woman to win the Nobel Prize in physiology or medicine. Yalow makes her home in Riverdale in the Bronx, where she has lived since 1950.

Olga S. Opfell, *The Lady Laureates: Women Who Have Won the Nobel Prize* (Metuchen, N.J.: Scarecrow, 1978)

Rachel Shor

Yankee Stadium. Home of the New York Yankees baseball team, nicknamed "The House That Ruth Built," referring to baseball legend Babe Ruth, who played for the Yankees after 1919. A new stadium opened in 2009, replacing the original, which opened in 1923 under the ownership of Tillinghast L'Hommedieu Huston and Jacob Rupert. Situated at 161st Street and River Avenue in the Bronx, the original stadium had a seating capacity of 67,224. It was the first ballpark to be called a stadium and the first built with a triple deck, at the expense of $675,000 for the land and $2.5 million for the stadium itself, which included a special fortified concrete created by Thomas Edison. The famous facade that circled the stadium was constructed of copper and was unpainted until the 1960s. The first game at the original Yankee Stadium was held on 18 April 1923 against the Boston Red Sox; the Yankees won, 4–1.

The original stadium hosted 37 World Series, numerous boxing events and college football games, four Major League All-Star games (1939, 1960, 1977, and 2008), and three papal masses (including one by Pope Benedict XVI on 20 April 2008). The New York football Giants were also tenants of the stadium from 1956 but left in 1973. Originally, the foul lines were a short 280 feet (85.3 meters) to left field and 295 feet (89.9 meters) to right field. But the distance to center field was deep, 490 feet (149.3 meters), so that the playing area was among the largest in the league. During the stadium's first season 20 inside-the-park home runs were hit, and attempts to hit a baseball out of the stadium remained unattainable (with the possible exception of one hit by Josh Gibson during a Negro Leagues game in 1934). Only Mickey Mantle came close when he hit a home run that rang off the white-fenced facade. In 1928 the stadium went through its first major renovation, extending its third layer of grandstand seating. Lights were added in 1946, and in 1959 it became the first stadium to unveil an electronic scoreboard. Nonetheless, the stadium remained largely unchanged until the 1960s.

The original owners of the New York Yankees and Yankee Stadium, Huston and Rupert, sold both in 1945 for $2.8 million. In 1953 the stadium was acquired by Arnold Johnson, owner of the Kansas City Athletics, for $6.5 million. Johnson then sold the land and adjacent parking lots to the Knights of Columbus for $2.5 million while maintaining his ownership of the stadium itself. In 1955 Johnson sold the controlling interest of only the stadium to John Cox for an undisclosed sum. Cox, an alumnus of Rice University, gave Yankee Stadium to his alma mater in 1962 while the Knights of Columbus maintained ownership of the land. In 1971 the City of New York forced Rice to sell the stadium for $2.5 million via eminent domain, allowing the city to acquire the property as a public place with the intention of modernizing the stadium. The Yankees had complained numerous times to Rice University about the deteriorating condition of the stadium and the need for renovation. By 1972 the city had also acquired the land from the Knights of Columbus and paid the Yankees $24 million for the stadium with an agreement to lease it back after renovation. The Yankees signed a 30-year lease with the city and closed the stadium after the 1973 season to begin a two-year renovation, with costs eventually reaching $100 million. The Yankees played the 1974–75 seasons at neighboring Shea Stadium in Queens, home of the New York Mets.

In 1976 Yankee Stadium reopened with a capacity of 56,866 and slightly altered dimensions, which were shifted in 1985 and 1988 to 318 feet (96.9 meters) to left field, 399 feet (121.6 meters) to left-center, 408 feet (124.4 meters) to center field, 385 feet (117.3 meters) to right-center, and 314 feet (95.7 meters) to right field, where they remained until its final game in 2008. Among the renovations to the original stadium was the relocation of Monument Park, an outdoor museum commemorating famous Yankee ballplayers. The first monuments were placed within the field of play until the 1976 renovation moved them behind the left-center field fence. The monuments honor Yankee legends, including Babe Ruth, Joe DiMaggio, Mickey Mantle, Lou Gehrig, and Yogi Berra, and one non-Yankee, Jackie Robinson. Other changes included the removal of several steel columns that obstructed views, removal of the stadium's original roof and facade, and the lowering of the playing field while increasing the slope of lower stands, which resulted in improved sight lines for fans. The iconic facade was replaced by an exact replica that stretched across the scoreboard and through the outfield. The exterior of the stadium also changed dramatically as three escalator towers were added.

During the 1980s Yankees owner George Steinbrenner began a campaign for a new Yankee Stadium, and in 2001 Mayor Rudolph Giuliani approved a tentative agreement for the construction of a new stadium across the street from the original. Ground was broken on 19 August 2006, the 58th anniversary of Babe Ruth's death; the estimated cost of construction was $1.6 billion, half of which would be paid for by city and state taxpayers as the land remained the property of the City of New York. This price tag made the new stadium the most expensive professional sports venue in the United States. During construction of the new stadium, a worker named Gino Castignoli, a Boston Red Sox fan, buried a replica David Ortiz jersey in the cement of the visitors' dugout as an attempt to reverse the "Curse of the Bambino," a hex allegedly attached to the Boston Red Sox after Babe Ruth was sold to the Yankees. Co-workers reported Castignoli, and he was forced to help remove the jersey in a widely publicized ceremony before the stadium's completion.

The final game at the original Yankee Stadium was played on 21 September 2008, when the Yankees defeated the Baltimore Orioles, 7–3, and failed to make the postseason. Following the game, Yankee captain Derek Jeter delivered an impromptu speech saying goodbye to the Yankee home for the past 85 years.

On 8 November 2008 former Yankees Scott Brosius, David Cone, Jeff Nelson, and Paul O'Neill, members of the 1998 championship team, joined 60 Bronx children in ceremoniously digging up home plate and the pitcher's mound from the original Yankee Stadium and transporting them across the street to the new stadium. Demolition of the old stadium began in March 2009, with plans to complete the process in 2010.

The new stadium opened for its first exhibition game against the Chicago Cubs on 3 April 2009 and hosted its first regular season games to the Cleveland Indians on 16 April. The Yankees won the first game over the Cubs, 7–4, but lost the regular season opener to the Indians, 10–2. During its first season of operation, the new Yankee Stadium developed a reputation as a "hitter's ballpark" while breaking the single-season record for most home runs hit in a stadium with 216. As was true after the opening of the stadium in 1923, the Yankees followed the opening of the new Yankee Stadium with their 27th World Championship, in 2009.

Designed by Populous (HOK Sports), the new Yankee Stadium was intended to closely resemble the original. The exterior facade is constructed of 11,000 pieces of Indiana limestone, granite, and cement, and the interior features a similar white frieze facade that circles the upper level. The dimensions of the new field are identical to those of the old stadium, with the exception of a shortened backstop. Monument Park was also moved and placed behind the center field wall in the new stadium. The new stadium features 59 luxury boxes (compared with 19 in the old stadium), more restrooms, 25 fixed concession stands and 112 movable ones, and restaurants. The new stadium's capacity is significantly reduced, however, seating 52,325 (including standing room), more than 4000 fewer than the previous stadium. The first eight rows of seats in the lower level of the new stadium are called "Legends Suites" and rank among the highest priced tickets in professional sports. The average ticket was more than $500 in 2009, with the highest reaching nearly $3000 for a single seat. Because of the price, the Legends Suites were notoriously difficult to sell during the opening season, and during televised games the empty seats behind home plate were visible to a national audience, a situation that Yankees owner Steinbrenner called "embarrassing."

Michael Benson, *Ballparks of North America: A Comprehensive Historical Reference to Baseball Grounds, Yards and Stadiums, 1845 to the Present* (Jefferson, N.C.: McFarland, 1989)

See also New York Yankees.

Meghan Lalonde

yellow fever. An acute and often fatal viral infection carried by the mosquito *Aedes aegypti.* It was one of the diseases most feared by New Yorkers in the late eighteenth and early nineteenth centuries. It was brought to American shores chiefly by ships originating from the endemic yellow fever locales of the West Indies and South America.

The first recorded epidemic of yellow fever in New York City was in 1702, followed by more severe ones in 1731, 1742, and 1743. Between 1791 and 1821 yellow fever epidemics plagued the city almost annually; the most severe occurred in 1798. During much of this time most physicians believed the disease to be caused by foul, polluted, or marshy air tainted with the yellow fever miasma. Others blamed the filthy conditions of the streets, tenement districts, and the intemperate poor. Yellow fever epidemics prompted massive clean-up efforts in New York City, with varying degrees of success. During the first decades of the nineteenth century they also inspired the empowerment of the city's Board of Health to order strict quarantine regulations, destroy public nuisances, and force mass evacuations. These strong emergency powers were supported by New Yorkers not only out of fear of a deadly epidemic, but also to protect the economic interests of the busy port.

By 1825 yellow fever was all but eliminated in the northeastern United States, although it continued to plague the ports of the Gulf and the southern Atlantic coast for decades. The occasional case of yellow fever discovered at the Staten Island Quarantine Station would be immediately isolated and methods of disinfection applied to the ship in question. In 1858 the station was destroyed by angry residents living nearby who feared the spread of the disease to their homes; it was rebuilt in the following year. With the discoveries of the Yellow Fever Commission, led by Walter Reed of the U.S. Army during 1898–1900, the mosquito carriage of yellow fever was finally confirmed and better means of prevention were developed.

F. H. Garrison, "The Destruction of the Quarantine Station in 1858," *Bulletin of the New York Academy of Medicine,* n.s. 2 (1926), 1–5; John Duffy: *A History of Public Health in New York City* (New York: Russell Sage Foundation, 1968, 1974)

Howard Markel

Yellow Hook. Name applied to Bay Ridge until 1853.

yellow journalism. A sensational form of journalism. It originated from 1895 in New York City with two competing newspapers, Joseph Pulitzer's *New York World* and William Randolph Hearst's *New York Journal.* The term was inspired by a comic-strip character called "the Yellow Kid" that was published in different and competing versions by the two newspapers. Yellow journalism at the time was characterized by profuse illustrations, entertainment features, and popular "crusades," all devices introduced by Pulitzer and soon adopted by Hearst, who also became known for his bold headlines, disregard for facts, and flamboyant Sunday magazines. Reporters for the newspapers included Richard Harding Davis, Stephen Crane, and Sylvester Scovel; among the editors were Arthur Brisbane and Bradford Merrill. After more than 250 Americans died when the battleship Maine exploded and sank, the *Journal* blamed the Spanish and offered a reward of $50,000 for the arrest of those responsible. The circulation of the *Journal* reached one million on the day the reward was offered, and that of the *World* reached five million a week later when Pulitzer sent a team of divers to search the sunken hull of the ship. The militarist sentiment provoked by the yellow press spread throughout the nation and persuaded President William McKinley to declare war on Spain. During the war, competition between the two newspapers reached a peak, as both dispatched correspondents to Cuba and drew attention to Spanish atrocities. In the twenty-first century the term can still be used to refer to publications that overdramatize the news or are unethical or biased in the way they present the news.

W. A. Swanberg, *Citizen Hearst: A Biography of William Randolph Hearst* (New York: Charles Scribner's Sons, 1961); Joyce Milton, *The Yellow Kids* (New York: Harper and Row, 1989); David Nasaw, *The Chief: The Life of William Randolph Hearst* (Boston: Houghton Mifflin, 2000)

Julian S. Rammelkamp

Yemenis. Immigrants from Yemen who created two communities in New York City, Jewish and Muslim. The majority of Yemeni Jews live in Borough Park, Brooklyn; a small number are in Flatbush. Most are blue-collar workers. There are four Yemeni synagogues, all in Borough Park; the best-known is Congregation Ohel Shalom at 45th Street and 12th Avenue, established in the 1920s. Yemeni Jews began settling in New York City at the beginning of the twentieth century. Immigration was never more than a trickle until 1967, when there was a large influx of Yemenis from Israel. In the early 1990s more Yemeni Jewish families arrived from the greatly reduced Jewish community still living in Yemen.

Yemeni Muslim men began moving to New York City in the late 1960s, and many more came after the first Gulf War. In time they became one of the city's most visible Arab groups, especially around Court Street and Atlantic Avenue in Brooklyn, where they founded Masjid Al-Farouq on Atlantic Avenue, and opened several coffeehouses. In 1972 they founded the now defunct Yemeni American Benevolent Association and the Club of Yemeni Immigrants to provide financial assistance, employment, and housing referrals to new arrivals. Many first-generation Yemenis owned or worked in supermarkets, newsstands, candy stores, and restaurants on and around Atlantic Avenue; their children became police officers, city workers, teachers, lawyers, and hospital workers. The Almontaser Restaurant on Court Street, among the best known, is one of several restaurants owned by the Almontaser family. The Yemeni American Association (est. 2005) served Yemenis for a time with English classes, counseling, tutoring, and cultural activities; it was one of the founding members of New York's Arab Heritage Week, celebrated each July.

Celebrations in the Muslim Yemeni community center on music and poetry performances by such local artists as Muhammad Ha il. Although the melodies of Muslim and Jewish men are the same, the words are taken from their respective religious traditions; women's music is, however, identical across the two communities. There is little mingling between Yemeni Jews and Muslims day to day, but they occasionally attend each other's cultural events. In the early twenty-first century estimates of the number of Yemenis in the city ranged between 10,000 and 25,000.

Paula Hajar

Yeshiva University

Yeshiva University. Incorporated under the auspices of Orthodox Jews, it began in 1886 as Yeshiva Etz Chaim, a small elementary yeshiva for boys formed by immigrant Orthodox Jews on the Lower East Side who wished to shield students from Americanization by giving them an education in an eastern European tradition. The Rabbi Isaac Elchanan Theological Seminary (RIETS), formed in 1897, provided students with advanced Talmudic training, and by 1903 it graduated the first Orthodox rabbis trained in the United States according to eastern European precepts. During the next decade students complained that RIETS was failing to instill in them the pedagogic and pastoral skills necessary for the modern pulpit and was preparing them inadequately for leading congregations of Jews born to immigrant parents; others who did not plan to become practicing rabbis felt deprived of the education needed in business and the professions. Strikes by students in 1906 and 1908, supported by some local Orthodox Yiddish newspapers, ultimately moved the directors of the school to appoint Bernard Revel as its first permanent president (1915–19, 1923–40). In addition to merging the two schools, upgrading secular studies, and modernizing the rabbinical curriculum he articulated a philosophy that came to be known as Torah Umada, which stressed the value to Orthodox Jews of worldly knowledge; he also oversaw the formation in 1915 of the Talmudical Academy (the first American Orthodox Jewish high school) and the building of a campus for the newly formed Yeshiva College in Washington Heights in 1929. Revel's successor Samuel Belkin (1943–75) focused on practical applications of the same ideas, as the school grew to include several campuses and was incorporated as a university in 1946. Stern College, the first women's college run by Orthodox Jews, was formed in 1954 under his auspices. During a period of expansion in the 1950s the university sought to attract a more diverse student population, and a Jewish studies program was introduced for undergraduates with a limited background in the field. Soon after becoming president in 1976 Norman Lamm made the university financially stable and oversaw the development of the Benjamin N. Cardozo School of Law and the Sy Syms School of Business. He also began to formulate a vision of Torah Umada for a new generation of Orthodox Jews.

By the early twenty-first century Yeshiva University had approximately 7000 students at its four campuses in New York City: in Washington Heights, the undergraduate college for men, the graduate schools of Judaica and social work, and RIETS; in the Morris Park area of the Bronx, the Albert Einstein College of Medicine and the Ferkauf Graduate School of Psychology; in Greenwich Village, the Benjamin N. Cardozo School of Law; and in Murray Hill, the undergraduate colleges for women and the institute for graduate Jewish education. In 2003 Yeshiva inaugurated its first lay president, attorney and Jewish communal leader Richard M. Joel, who continued Yeshiva's long-standing religious-secular educational mission and challenged students to be more actively involved in serving Jewish communities around the United States.

Jeffrey S. Gurock, *The Men and Women of Yeshiva: Higher Education, Orthodoxy, and American Judaism* (New York: Columbia University Press, 1988); Norman Lamm, *Torah Umada: The Encounter of Religious Learning and Worldly Knowledge in the Jewish Tradition* (Northvale, N.J.: Jason Aronson, 1990)

Jeffrey S. Gurock

Yiddishe Tageblatt. One of the first Yiddish-language daily newspapers in the world, launched in 1885 by Kasriel H. Sarasohn and published at 185–187 East Broadway. It was politically conservative but did not become affiliated with any political party; it supported Orthodox and Zionist causes in its editorials. In 1928 *Der Yiddishe Tageblatt* merged with *Der Morgen Zhornal.*

Mordecai Soltes, *The Yiddish Press: An Americanizing Agency* (New York: Teachers College, Columbia University, 1924; repr. 1950); Charles A. Madison, *Jewish Publishing in America: The Impact of*

Jewish Writing on American Culture (New York: Sanhedrin, 1976)

Seth Kamil

Yiddish theater. New York City was the site of the first Yiddish theater production in the United States, a production of Avrom Goldfadn's *Koldunya; or, The Witch* at Turn Hall on the Bowery in 1892. Professional, secular Yiddish-language theater was then an innovation even in eastern Europe, the homeland of most Yiddish-speaking Jews. For this reason many performers and audiences first became acquainted with Yiddish theater on the Lower East Side, which through mass migration was rapidly becoming the largest Yiddish-speaking settlement in the United States, and New York City remained an important center of Yiddish theater for the next century.

A Yiddish theater district developed in Manhattan on and around the Bowery and later on Second Avenue, eventually including the Rumanian Opera House and the Oriental, National, Thalia, Windsor, Grand, People's, and Poole's theaters. By 1914 a typical season was marked by the residence of some 14 companies in the metropolitan area, including Brooklyn and the Bronx. New York City was also the headquarters for troupes touring the United States and eastern Europe and for related businesses: cabarets, sheet-music publishers, record companies, film studios, and radio stations. Streets and cafés in theater districts were thronged and sociable; the Yiddish press printed reviews, editorials, and gossip, and scripts were published for reading and for amateur productions. Theatrical unions organized in the city, beginning with Local 1 of the Hebrew Actors Union in 1887. The Yiddish theater was an important community institution: plays offered entertainment and escape, portrayals of immigrant life, and political forums. Translations of the classics introduced immigrants to world literature; translations of Broadway hits helped them to adjust to a new culture. The wide range of theatrical genres included music-hall revues, costume operettas, domestic melodramas with music, and serious drama influenced by the theatrical avant-garde. Successful performers were leading figures in the community who commanded fierce loyalty. Among the best-known in the early years were the comic actor Sigmund Mogulesko, the romantic baritone Boris Thomashevsky, the dramatic actors Jacob Adler and David Kessler, and the actresses Keni Liptzin, Bertha Kalich, Sara Adler, and Bessie Tomashevsky. Works for the stage were written by such playwrights as Goldfadn, "Professor" Moshe Ish-HaLevi Hurwitz, Joseph Lateiner, and Shomer (Nahum Meyer Shaikevich), and at a high literary level by Sholom Aleichem and Jacob Gordon; these were accompanied by the music of such composers as Alexander Olshanetsky, Joseph Rumshinsky, and Sholem Perlmutter. Almost all the major writers and composers for the Yiddish stages of the world lived for at least part of their lives in New York City.

The Yiddish theater had a sizable effect on the development of the mainstream theater. Such innovations in repertory and technique as naturalism, expressionism, "art theater," and Stanislavskian Method acting were introduced on the Yiddish stage before they reached the English-language stage, and the Yiddish avant-garde was often reviewed in the intellectual English-language press. Although after World War I the Yiddish theater was hurt by a restricted flow of immigration, movement away from the old neighborhoods where theaters were situated, and Americanization, another generation of stars came to prominence: Celia Adler, Jacob Ben-Ami, Joseph Buloff, Pesach Burstein, Bertha Goldstein, Samuel Goldenburg, Jennie Goldstein, Jacob Jacobs, Aaron Lebedev, Mikhel Mihhalesko, Moyshe Oysher, Molly Picon, Ludwig Satz, Rudolph Schildkraut, Maurice Schwartz, Menashe Skulnik, and Herman Yablokoff. There were new popular playwrights such as Z. Libin, H. Kalmanovitch, Max Gabel, William Segal, Anshel Shor, and Isidore Zolatrevsky, and composers such as Sholem Secunda. There was also a new art-theater movement. Theaters in New York City including the Yiddish Art Theatre (1918–50) of Schwartz, the Jewish Art Theatre (1918–20) of Ben-Ami, and the Arbeiter Teater Farband (1925–39) performed ambitious repertory by David Pinski, Peretz Hirschbein, H. Leivick (Leivick Halpern), Osip Dimov (Joseph Perlman), and Sholem Asch. Between 1935 and 1939 the Theatre Project of the Works Progress Administration sponsored several Yiddish troupes, some in New York City.

Adolf Hitler and Joseph Stalin destroyed the Old World sources of Yiddish culture and Yiddish speakers. By 1950 audiences were severely diminished by continuing acculturation, movement to the suburbs, the ascendance of Hebrew over Yiddish, and television. The average age of performers and spectators rose while the number of performances and new scripts each season steadily diminished. The Yiddish theater came to be characterized increasingly by limited runs and by matinees offered for the convenience of the elderly. Nevertheless, into the 1990s almost every season offered at least one musical comedy (generally based in a midtown theater), often a touring company from Israel or elsewhere, and revues in theaters, community centers, and retirement homes around the city. Productions were mounted occasionally by the Yiddish National Theatre (sponsored by the Hebrew Actors Union), as was a new production each year by the semiprofessional company the Folksbiene, the oldest continually performing Yiddish company in the world. Amateur groups continued to give readings and performances, and WEVD broadcast radio programs in Yiddish. The leading performers included Bruce Adler, Mina Bern, Miriam Kressyn, Jack Rechseit, Eleanor Reissa, Symour Rexite, and Mary Soreanu.

In the early twenty-first century an increased interest in ethnicity has fostered new approaches to the Yiddish theater. To make Yiddish productions more widely accessible, simultaneous translation devices are employed, and English is frequently interpolated into dialogue and lyrics. Bilingual shows like *The Golden Land* and *Songs of Paradise* have attracted spectators who speak no Yiddish at all. The traditions of Yiddish theater are sustained by professional and amateur productions (often in translation), film revivals, and academic courses. The Yiddish theater retains a romantic resonance for many American Jews, including those who have never seen it, and has become integrated into their images of their forebears as well as their culture.

Nahma Sandrow, *Vagabond Stars: A World History of Yiddish Theater* (New York: Harper and Row, 1972); Stefan Kanfer, *Stardust Lost: The Triumph, Tragedy, and Meshugas of the Yiddish Theater* (New York: Alfred A. Knopf, 2006)

Nahma Sandrow

Yiddish writing and publishing. New York City became an important center of Yiddish literary and cultural activity in the late nineteenth century. The traditional vernacular of Ashkenazic Jewry, Yiddish served Jewish immigrants as a means of maintaining ties with their central and eastern European heritage. The use of Yiddish also fostered a sense of community among immigrants and their descendants, who forged a distinctive American Yiddish culture. In 1870 the first American Yiddish newspaper was launched in New York (*Di Yidishe Tsaytung*), followed in 1871 by the first periodical (*Di Post*). Newspapers and periodicals published the work of authors such as Jacob Levi Sobol, whose volume of Yiddish and Hebrew verse *Yisroel der alter* (1877) was the first book of Yiddish literature published in the United States. From 1881 to 1914 the mass emigration of eastern European Jews increased the number of Yiddish speakers in the United States and made New York City a major center of Yiddish literary activity; the Yiddish press flourished during this period. By 1915 the city had five major daily newspapers catering to a range of immigrant political and cultural sensibilities: *Forverts*, *Der Morgen Zhornal*, *Der Yiddishe Tageblatt*, *Der Tog*, and *Di Varheyt*. During the 1880s and 1890s the first school of American Yiddish literature emerged, reflecting the national and class consciousness of Jewish immigrants. Working-class poets such as Joseph Bovshover, David Edelstadt, Morris Rosenfeld, and Morris Vinchevsky, who later became known as the "sweatshop poets," wrote verses that exhorted working-class Jews to take part in the labor movement. In 1898 Rosenfeld became the first American Yiddish writer to achieve fame outside the immigrant community when a collection of his poems was published in English.

A number of established European Yiddish writers settled in the city during this period, among them Eliakum Zunser, who wrote lyrics in a familiar, vernacular idiom; Shomer (Nahum Meyer Shaikevich), a notoriously prolific author of sensational potboilers; and Abraham Reisin, an author, editor, and cultural activist. Sholem Aleichem visited the city twice in the first two decades of the century but failed to achieve the level of acclaim that he had in eastern Europe. In the first decade of the twentieth century the first modernist school of Yiddish literature emerged. Known as the "Yunge," the group included the poets Mani-Leyb, Moyshe-Leyb Halpern, Reuben Iceland, and Zisha Landau, who in the journals *Yugnt, Literatur,* and *Shriftn* championed a literature of artistic self-consciousness and personal voice. During this period publishers of Yiddish books began to issue a wide range of titles for general audiences. Works of political activism, popular education, trade unionism, literary criticism, and Jewish history and culture were issued by commercial presses (notably the Hebrew Publishing Company) and later by cultural organizations (such as the WORKMEN'S CIRCLE and the Yiddish Cultural Congress).

American secular Yiddish publishing was most extensive between the world wars. Yiddish was an especially important vehicle for leftist writers who united briefly under the name of "Protetpen" in the 1920s. The secular Yiddish school movement generated a body of children's literature in the 1920s and 1930s under such imprints as Farlag Matones, Kinderbukh, and Arbeter-ring. After World War I a group of poets known as the Inzikhistn (introspectivists) emerged under the leadership of A. Leyeles (Aaron Glanz), Yankev Glatshteyn, and N. B. Minkoff. In the journal *Inzikh* the group promoted Yiddish as a cosmopolitan language and presented aesthetically and psychologically expressive, idiosyncratic literature. Major works of world literature were also translated into Yiddish: the translator and poet Yehoash (Solomon Bloomgarten) rendered the entire Hebrew Bible (1937) in a modern, literary style and also translated Longfellow's *Hiawatha* and Omar Khayyám's *Rubáiyát.* Although Yiddish literature reached its greatest heights in the United States in the genre of poetry, during the first half of the twentieth century New York City was also the home of such important critics as Sh. Niger (Samuel Charney), Moses J. Olgin (Novomisky), Kalman Marmor, and playwrights and novelists including Sholem Asch, Jacob Gordon, Peretz Hirschbein, David Ignatoff, H. Leivick (Leivick Halpern), Leon Kobrin, Joseph Opatoshu, L. Shapiro, and Isaac Raboy. Asch's major novels were translated into English, making him the only one of these authors to find a following beyond the Yiddish-reading public.

Yiddish literature and cultural activity were profoundly affected by the genocide of European Jews during World War II. After the war hundreds of collaborative memorial books (or *yizker-bikher*) were published commemorating the Jewish communities that had been destroyed. Secular Yiddish cultural activity declined during the following decades. A noteworthy exception was Isaac Bashevis Singer, who gained a wide readership when his prose works were translated into English. Two major serial publications continued to be printed into the twenty-first century: *Forverts,* which first appeared in 1897 and became a weekly newspaper in 1983, and *Di Zukunft,* a monthly cultural and literary journal first issued by the Socialist Labor Party in 1892.

New York City remains the largest and most important center of Yiddish literature and culture in both the United States and the world. Yiddish culture is increasingly centered in the large community of Hasidim and other observant Jews who settled in the city after World War II. In addition to daily newspapers (*Der Algemeyner Zhurnal* and *Der Yid*) some Hasidic groups publish instructional and devotional literature in Yiddish. Secular books and journals are published by the Central Yiddish Cultural Organization (CYCO), the League for Yiddish, the Workmen's Circle, the YIVO Institute, and Yugntruf (Youth for Yiddish). Important Yiddish reference works published in the city include Yiddish-English dictionaries compiled by Alexander Harkavy (1898–1928) and Uriel Weinreich (1968), a Yiddish thesaurus by Nahum Stutchkoff (1950), and the *Algemeyner entsiklopedye* (begun in the 1940s, never completed).

Irving Howe, *World of Our Fathers* (New York: Harcourt Brace Jovanovich, 1975)

Jeffrey Shandler

Yidishe Tog. Yiddish-language daily newspaper, launched in 1914 by Judah Magnes, Herman Bernstein, Bernard Semel, and Morris Weinberg and published at 183 East Broadway. Under the slogan "The Newspaper of the Yiddish Intelligentsia" it became known for its fine writing and liberal, nonpartisan politics. Its circulation reached 81,000 in 1916 but declined in later years, despite the absorption of *Die Warheit* in 1919. After years of editorial conflict a six-month strike in 1941 nearly caused the newspaper to cease operations. In 1953 *Der Yidishe Tog* merged with *Der Morgen Zhornal.*

Mordecai Soltes: *The Yiddish Press: An Americanizing Agency* (New York: Teachers College, Columbia University, 1924; repr. 1950)

Seth Kamil

YIVO Institute for Jewish Research [Yidisher visnshaftlekher institut]. Jewish research institute. Founded in 1925 in the Lithuanian city of Vilnius (then in Poland), it opened a branch in New York City at 425 Lafayette Street, which became its headquarters in 1940. YIVO is one of the foremost institutes devoted to the study of the history and culture of Jews in the modern world, especially eastern Europe and the United States. It maintains an archive and a multilingual library that holds the world's largest collection of Yiddish publications. It also offers instruction in Yiddish and graduate-level courses in Jewish studies, issues a number of scholarly publications, and sponsors conferences and public programs. In 1993 YIVO sold its building at Fifth Avenue and 86th Street in Manhattan and in the following year acquired the former headquarters of the American Foundation for the Blind, two four-story neo-Georgian structures on West 16th Street between Fifth and Sixth avenues. In 2000 YIVO celebrated its 75th anniversary with the grand opening of its fifth American home, the Center for Jewish History at the 16th Street location.

Daniel Soyer

YMCA [Young Men's Christian Association]. International, interdenominational Christian organization formed as a prayer group in London in 1844 by George Williams and dedicated to community evangelism and the moral and intellectual development of young men. After spreading through England it opened a branch in Boston in 1851. A YMCA reading room in New York City was established at 659 Broadway in 1852 by George H. Petrie, a merchant who became acquainted with the organization at the Crystal Palace exhibition in London in 1851. Initially the organization focused on street-corner evangelism, missionary efforts, Sunday schools, Bible classes, and relief for the sick and the poor; it also offered temporary boarding facilities. It gradually became more secular as it opened libraries and introduced educational programs. In 1857 the branches in New York City and Brooklyn began offering classes in music, foreign languages, and gymnastics. Membership was denied to African Americans, who were encouraged to organize separate branches; one of the first opened in the city in 1866 (others were opened in Washington, D.C., and Harrisburg, Pennsylvania). Segregation remained the policy of the YMCA until after the Commission on Interracial Co-operation of the YMCA was formed in 1919. The "uptown" branch undertook interracial community work in 1930.

In the twenty-first century the YMCA offers sports, child care, and international programs and operates gymnasiums and residences. It maintains branches in Chinatown, Chelsea,

Harlem, and midtown and on West 63rd Street in Manhattan; on Castle Hill in the Bronx; in Flatbush, Prospect Park–Bay Ridge, Twelve Towns, Bedford–Stuyvesant, Greenpoint, and downtown Brooklyn; in Bayside, Flushing, Long Island City, Highland Park, and central and eastern Queens; and at Broadway and South Shore in Staten Island. The YMCA of Greater New York was located at 5 West 63rd Street in Manhattan. As of 2009 the YMCA had 21 million members nationwide.

C. Howard Hopkins, *History of the YMCA in North America* (New York: Association Press, 1951)

Melissa M. Merritt

YM-YWHAs [Young Men's and Young Women's Hebrew Associations]. Name used in New York City for nonsectarian cultural, educational, and recreational centers for adults and children that are known elsewhere in North America as Jewish Community Centers (JCCs). The associations originated in the nineteenth century as social and literary societies, at the same time that Jewish settlement houses such as the Educational Alliance (1889) were promoting Americanization through educational and social activities. The first YMHA in New York City was formed in 1874 and became known as the 92nd Street Y; the first YWHA dates to 1902. By the early twentieth century these associations offered social, religious, educational, and recreational programs for both immigrants and the native-born. A number of YMHAs opened during the early part of the century, followed by several centers formed by the YWHA in 1943–44 in underserved parts of the city: Coney Island, East Flatbush, Canarsie, and Upper Williamsburg in Brooklyn; and East Tremont, Bronx River, and Mosholu in the Bronx. From 1945 to 1957 a successor to the YWHA called the Jewish Association for Neighborhood Centers (JANC) operated these YM-YWHAs, as well as others in Little Neck and Flushing, and the Emanu-El Midtown YM-YWHA (1903).

The Associated YM-YWHAs of Greater New York was formed in 1957 by the Federation of Jewish Philanthropies to build new centers by soliciting Jewish support and funds from throughout the metropolitan area. The new organization absorbed all units of the JANC, the JCC of the Rockaways, the Shorefront YM-YWHA in Brooklyn, and the East Bronx YM-YWHA, and by 1980 it was operating 10 facilities in the city and Westchester County. Because of financial constraints in 1991 it closed the operations in Far Rockaway and Flushing and set up its remaining centers as autonomous units.

Among the independent YM-YWHAs in New York City are the Recreation Rooms and Settlement (1898), the Hebrew Educational Society (Brooklyn, 1899), the Jewish Community House of Bensonhurst (1906), the Riverdale YM-YWHA (1909), Bronx House (1911), the Boro Park YM-YWHA (1912), the YM-YWHA of Washington Heights and Inwood (1916), the JCC of Staten Island (1926), the Central Queens YM-YWHA (1938), and the Sephardic Community Center (Brooklyn, 1981). All continued to offer services in the twenty-first century.

Elinor K. Bernheim and Irving Brodsky, *Jewish Association for Neighborhood Centers: A Final Report, 1942–1958* (New York: Jewish Association for Neighborhood Centers, 1958)

Steven W. Siegel

Yonah Schimmel Knish Bakery. Bakery and restaurant that makes and sells knishes, an eastern European Jewish specialty food made from potatoes, flour, sometimes kasha (buckwheat groats), and various seasonings or flavorings. They are baked in rounds about 4 to 5 inches (10 to 13 centimeters) in diameter and 3 to 4 inches (8 to 10 centimeters) in height. The shop, located at 137 Houston Street on the Lower East Side, was founded in 1910 and is said to be the oldest continuing knish bakery in New York City.

York, Duke of (*b* St. James Palace, England, 14 Oct 1633; *d* St. Germain-en-Laye, France, 6 Sept 1701). Proprietor of New York under English rule, for whom the province was named. He wrote a set of laws (1665) that sanctioned religious toleration but not representative government; in 1683 he allowed the creation of an assembly. On the death of his brother, King Charles II in 1685, he ascended to the English throne as King James II, and New York became a royal rather than a proprietary colony. In 1688 he abolished the assembly when New York became part of the Dominion of New England. He was deposed during the Glorious Revolution (1688–89), after which residents of New York led by Jacob Leisler temporarily overthrew his colonial government (see Leisler's Rebellion).

Cynthia A. Kierner

York College. College of the City University of New York. Established in 1966, it occupies a campus in South Jamaica in Queens. By the early twenty-first century it enrolled nearly 6000 full- and part-time undergraduate students.

Selma Berrol

Yorkville. Neighborhood on the Upper East Side of Manhattan. Originally a rural village centered at 86th Street and Third Avenue, it is now bounded to the north by 96th Street, to the east by the East River, to the south by 72nd Street, and to the west by Central Park. An Indian trail once ran along what later became the Post Road and is now Third Avenue between 83rd and 89th streets. The hamlet arose between the farmlands of Harlem and the settlement of New Amsterdam. Hazzard's roadhouse at 84th Street and the Post Road was the first stop for coaches carrying passengers from the Hell Gate Ferry at the end of 86th Street. The New York and Harlem Rail Road was extended in 1834 to 86th Street and Fourth Avenue (renamed Park Avenue in 1888) and soon after to Harlem. Every half-hour, horse-drawn cars carried passengers for a fare of 12½ cents from Prince Street to the neighborhood. There was a stagecoach terminus at Third Avenue and 86th Street. By 1850 Yorkville was a predominantly German neighborhood that remained 1.5 miles (2.5 kilometers) from the northern edge of the city but was included in the 19th ward, which stretched from 40th to 86th streets. After the Civil War squatters' shacks were replaced by two-story houses for the wealthy, who between the 1880s and 1920s moved to new luxury apartments on Madison, Fifth, and Park avenues. Brownstones and tenements became multifamily dwellings with shops on the ground floor and two apartments on each floor above. The Third Avenue elevated line began service on 30 December 1878 between South Ferry and 129th Street; the Second Avenue elevated line was completed in August 1879. During the next two years the neighborhood became more ethnically diverse. Irish immigrants moved there during a period of growth aided by the construction of the Croton Reservoir, and in 1885 a third of the population was Irish born.

During the early years of the twentieth century the largest groups were Irish, Germans, Hungarians, Jews, Czechs, Slovaks, and Italians; 86th Street, the center of the neighborhood, had shops, restaurants, and bakeries, many of them German. The Irish section was circumscribed by 81st and 85th streets and Lexington and Fifth avenues. Jews lived on Second Avenue, blacks on 79th Street, and Puerto Ricans in the 90s east of Lexington Avenue. Gracie Mansion (1799–1804), near the northern end of Carl Schurz Park, became the mayor's official residence in 1942. After World War II the neighborhood began to lose its ethnic character. The dismantling of the Third Avenue elevated line in 1955 spurred the demolition of many brownstones, and their central and eastern European residents moved to the suburbs. Eventually the character of Yorkville became increasingly changed by gentrification and markedly less European. In the 1980s a *Turnverein*, or German gymnastics society, at 86th Street and Lexington Avenue and Mozart Hall on 86th Street between Second and Third avenues were demolished to make way for expensive high-rise apartment buildings. The 1990s and 2000s continued this trend, with even more high-rises taking the place of Yorkville's low-rise walkups. The Rhinelander mansion at 72nd Street and Madison Avenue, home to the most influential German family in nineteenth-century Yorkville, was occupied by the Polo Ralph Lauren flagship store in 2010.

Anthony Gronowicz

Young, Art(hur Henry) (*b* Orangeville, Ill., 14 Jan 1866; *d* New York City, 29 Dec 1943). Cartoonist. Brought up in rural Illinois, he studied art with J. H. Vanderpoel at the Art Institute in Chicago, publishing cartoons on the side to help pay his tuition. By 1888 he was in New York City, where he continued his training at the Art Students League with J. Carroll Beckwith and Kenyon Cox. His emerging political consciousness was influenced by Eugene V. Debs, whose local lectures he attended. He published a book of his drawings, *Hell up to Date,* in 1893 and satirized capitalism, militarism, and the middle class in such diverse periodicals as the *Judge, Puck, Collier's,* the *Call,* the *Nation,* William Randolph Hearst's newspaper the *Evening Journal,* and publications of the Industrial Workers of the World. An associate of leading radicals in Greenwich Village, he was an original editor of *The Masses* in 1911 and remained on its board until it ceased publication in 1917. He later published his work in the *Liberator* and the *New Masses.* Young's cartoons were scalding depictions of bloated businessmen attempting to crush the American proletariat. He coined the term "Ashcan School" and wrote *Art Young: His Life and Times* (1939). He lived for many years at 9 East 17th Street.

Jan Seidler Ramirez

Young, Lester "The Prez" Willis (*b* Woodville, Miss., 27 Aug 1909; *d* New York City, 15 March 1959). Jazz saxophonist. He came to New York City from Kansas City in 1936 as a tenor saxophonist with Count Basie's band. Young had a smooth, sparse playing style; he met mixed reviews from critics but proved a strong influence on a cohort of younger saxophonists like Dexter Gordon and Stan Getz. He is also well known for his collaborations and close friendship with Billie Holiday and is responsible for her nickname Lady Day. While in New York City during the first half of the 1940s, Young briefly started his own band and played freelance until rejoining Basie in 1943. In 1946 he began a 12-year gig playing for Jazz at the Philharmonic. In 1957 he delivered one of his finest performances for the landmark television show *The Sound of Jazz,* recorded live from their 59th Street studios; it was a duet with Holiday on her "Fine and Mellow" at a time when both were in declining health.

Rowan Moore Gerety

Young Ireland. Obsolete name of EGBERTVILLE.

Young Lords. Radical mainland Puerto Rican organization that emerged in New York City in 1969. It consciously fashioned itself after the Black Panther Party (BPP) and championed the independence of Puerto Rico. The Young Lords called themselves socialists, and their political worldview borrowed from variants of Marxism and third world revolutionary nationalist theories. The group published a bilingual revolutionary newspaper called *Palante.*

In New York City the Young Lords led a series of militant, media-savvy campaigns with a community service aspect akin to the BPP's survival programs, which included a free breakfast program for poor children. The group's aim was to alleviate the most visible manifestations of the new poverty in U.S. cities: chronic unemployment, lack of health care, childhood lead poisoning, poor sanitation, drug addiction, hunger, racism, and police brutality. The organization's most famous campaign was its garbage dumping protests, which forced the city to conduct regular trash collections in East Harlem. A quieter victory was its anti–lead poisoning campaign, which the *Journal of Public Health* deemed instrumental in the passage of anti–lead poisoning legislation in New York City during the early 1970s. At Lincoln Hospital in the Bronx the Young Lords led a dramatic 12-hour occupation of one of the hospital's buildings to protest deplorable conditions. Their actions eventually led to the creation of one of the principal acupuncture drug treatment centers in the western world.

Although commonly associated with New York City activism, the group first emerged in Chicago as a reformed gang. The primary architect of the gang's political conversion was its chairman, Jose Cha Cha Jimenez, who transformed the Young Lords into the BPP's Puerto Rican counterpart. The Chicago Young Lords inspired the formation of sister organizations in other cities, the most influential of which was in New York City where a group of college-educated Puerto Rican radicals established a much more politically sophisticated chapter of the organization that renamed itself the Young Lords Party (YLP). The core founders of the New York City group were affiliated with the City University of New York, State University of New York at Old Westbury, and Columbia University. They include Juan Gonzales, who writes for the *Daily News*; Pablo Guzman, currently of WCBS-TV in New York; Sonia Ivani; Felipe Luciano, a former WNBC-TV New York news anchor; Miguel Melendez; Iris Morales, currently a filmmaker and director of the Union Square Awards; Denise Oliver; Juan Ortiz; and David Perez.

Johanna Fernandez

Young Men's and Young Women's Hebrew Associations. See YM-YWHAs.

Young Men's Christian Association. See YMCA.

Yunqué, Edgardo Vega (*b* Ponce, Puerto Rico, 20 May 1936; *d* New York City, 26 Aug 2008). Novelist. He moved to New York City at age 13 in 1949, when his father, a Baptist minister, took over a Spanish-speaking congregation in the South Bronx. He served as a radio operator in the air force, attended New York University, and helped found the Clemento Soto Vélez Cultural Center on the Lower East Side as a home for theater artists, dancers, and visual artists. Yunqué wrote many novels, the most famous of which was *No Matter How Much You Promise to Cook or Pay the Rent You Blew It Cauze Bill Bailey Ain't Never Coming Home Again* (2003). Reflecting the author's own teenage years in a Puerto Rican and Irish neighborhood in the Bronx, it is a tale of two families, one Irish and one Puerto Rican, and their interactions over many decades.

Kenneth T. Jackson

YWCA of the USA. National organization of Young Women's Christian Associations (YWCAs) that had its origins in several independent local associations of the late nineteenth century. Formed in various U.S. cities, these associations were intended to meet the physical, intellectual, and spiritual needs of young women. Although they were often rooted in the religious revivals of the time, by the turn of the twentieth century most had evolved into more secular entities. One of the first associations began in New York City in 1870 as an offshoot of the Ladies' Christian Union and provided young women who moved to the city from rural areas with a variety of services relating to employment, housing, recreation, education, religion, and health, as well as travelers' aid, cafeterias, and free libraries. A local association was formed in Brooklyn in 1888. With the assistance of Grace H. Dodge, in 1906 these urban associations merged with a network of evangelically oriented groups based on college campuses; the new organization set up its national board in New York City and took its current name.

During the early twentieth century the YWCA adopted the principles of the Social Gospel and became active in public affairs. It conducted studies of conditions for working women and stressed leadership training. Programs for African Americans, immigrants, and adolescents were also developed. Edith Terry Bremer (1885–1964) oversaw the association's work in immigrant communities through its international institutes, and after devising an experimental program in Manhattan in 1910 she promoted institutes in other cities and in Brooklyn. In 1915 the YWCA adopted a policy that permitted racial segregation in local associations; Eva del Vakia Bowles (1875–1943), a member of the staff of the national board, oversaw programs for African American women and girls. The YWCA also fostered the development of organizations such as the National Board of Travelers Aid Societies (1917; later the National Association of Travelers Aid Societies), the National Federation of Business and Professional Women's Clubs (1919), and the United Service Organizations (1941). In 1920 a YWCA opened in Queens. Elizabeth Ross Haynes became the first black member of the national board in 1924. In 1933 Bremer created the National Institute of Immigrant Welfare (the predecessor of the American Council for Nationalities Service), and most international institutes became autonomous. YWCA racial segregation ended in 1946 when the association's national convention voted unanimously to integrate all facilities. In the early twenty-first century there were more than 2.6 million members.

Mary S. Sims, *The Natural History of a Social Institution: The Young Women's Christian Association* (New York: Woman's Press, 1936); Sims, *The YWCA: An Unfolding Purpose* (New York: Woman's Press, 1950); Helen Bittar, "The YWCA of the City of New York, 1870 to 1920" (Ph.D. diss., New York University, 1979)

See also HARLEM YWCA.

Nancy Marie Robertson

Z

Zabar's. Gourmet delicatessen in Manhattan located at 2245 Broadway at 80th Street. Opened by Louis Zabar in 1939 it gained prominence in the 1960s when his sons Stanley and Saul Zabar were joined in the enterprise by Murray Klein. In the mid-1970s it added kitchenware items. Known for its reasonable prices and extensive choices, the business remained in the family and expanded into adjacent buildings. In the early twenty-first century Zabar's employed more than 250 people and was frequented by more than 35,000 customers a week. Eli Zabar, Louis's youngest son, began a separate franchise of Eli's and E.A.T. in 1973, located on the Upper East Side.

Jessica Montesano

Zagat Survey. Company founded in 1979 by Tim and Nina Zagat that publishes consumer survey–based information in city and nationwide guidebooks. The Zagat annual guides cover hotels, restaurants, shopping, nightlife, and lifestyle; each entry is based on 30-point scales in categories such as service, food, cost, and facilities. In the early twenty-first century the guidebooks continue to be available and widely used. Zagat headquarters are at 4 Columbus Circle.

Jessica Montesano

Zeckendorf, William (*b* Paris, Ill., 1905; *d* New York City, 30 Sept 1976). Real estate developer who led the firm of Webb and Knapp. In 1946 he assembled the land for the site of the United Nations and sold it to the Rockefeller family for $8.5 million. He then became for the next 20 years the city's best-known real estate developer, owing largely to the distinctive designs of his chief architect, I. M. Pei. Zeckendorf focused mostly on large hotels and office buildings and at various times owned the St. Regis Hotel and the Graybar and Chrysler buildings; he also took an active role in urban renewal projects financed by the federal government during the 1950s. With Pei he planned three residential renewal projects in Manhattan: Park West Village, a development covering 23 acres (9 hectares) on the Upper West Side and accommodating 2500 families; Kips Bay Plaza near the United Nations; and Lincoln Towers, a complex of 4000 apartments adjoining Lincoln Center for the Performing Arts. Zeckendorf also built one of the nation's first large suburban shopping centers — Roosevelt Field on Long Island. Zeckendorf's willingness to embark on risky projects took its toll, and in 1965 Webb and Knapp declared bankruptcy. His son William Zeckendorf, Jr., became a prominent developer during the 1980s, building Worldwide Plaza on the former site of Madison Square Garden and Zeckendorf Towers across from Union Square.

Marc A. Weiss

Zenger, John Peter (*b* Germany, 1697; *d* New York City, 28 July 1746). Printer. His work helped establish freedom of the press in the United States. He moved to New York City in 1710 and from 1711 to 1719 worked as an apprentice in William Bradford's printing shop at 81 Pearl Street. After a stint as a journeyman he set up as a printer of works in Dutch and English and lived on Smith Street (now William Street) near Maiden Lane from 1726 until 1734, when he moved to Broad Street. During the early 1730s he became known for criticizing the colonial government in his newspaper the *Weekly Journal.* He published this new paper on behalf of James Alexander and Lewis Morris, two men whose ambitions were being frustrated by the new Governor Cosby. Arrested for seditious libel in 1734, Zenger was imprisoned for almost a year at City Hall before his trial, in which he was defended by Andrew Hamilton after his first two lawyers were disbarred by a pro-Cosby court. Hamilton defended Zenger by arguing that the articles Zenger published criticizing Cosby were not libel if the facts printed in them were indeed true and published for the public good. Found not guilty by the jury, Zenger resumed his printing business and published an account of the trial in the *Journal* and in the pamphlet *A Brief Narrative* (1736), which was widely reprinted in America and abroad. His case set a precedent for the American interpretation of libel and the protection of freedom of speech. Zenger was then appointed public printer for New York and New Jersey. During his imprisonment his wife Anna continued publication of the *Weekly Journal,* only missing one issue, that of the week her husband was arrested. At the end of his life he was plagued by financial problems; his wife and children continued his newspaper.

Eric Foner, *The Story of American Freedom* (New York: W. W. Norton, 1998)

James E. Mooney

Ziegfeld, Florenz(, Jr.) (*b* Chicago, 15 March 1867; *d* Los Angeles, 22 July 1932). Impresario. He grew up in Chicago and managed vaudeville tours in Europe and the Far West before marrying Billie Burke, while maintaining an intimate relationship with the French actress Anna Held, for whom he produced seven musicals, including *Papa's Wife* (1899) and *Miss Innocence* (1908). When in New York City during the 1890s he usually stayed at the Netherland Hotel (781 Fifth Avenue); after 1907 he had a permanent suite in the Ansonia Apartments (2107 Broadway). He was best known for producing revues designed to "glorify the American girl," including 21 Follies (1907–25, 1927, 1931), *The Century Girl* (1916) and *Miss* (1917) at the Century Theatre, and *Midnight Frolics* (1915–22), which was presented at late-night dinner theaters. He also produced a number of musical comedies in which Eddie Cantor and Marilyn Miller played the leading roles, among them *Sally* (1920), *Whoopee* (1928), and *Show Boat* (1927). Ziegfeld eventually moved to Hollywood to advise Samuel Goldwyn on motion pictures based on the Follies.

Marjorie Farnsworth, *The Ziegfeld Follies* (London: Davies, 1956); Charles Higham, *Ziegfeld* (New York: W. H. Allen, 1973); Randolph Carter, *The World of Flo Ziegfeld* (New York: Praeger, 1974)

Barbara Cohen-Stratyner

Ziegfeld Follies. Extravagant Broadway theater revue from 1907 to 1931 created by impresario Florenz Ziegfeld, Jr. Modeled on the Parisian Folies Bergère, it combined elements of vaudeville, comedy, dance, and musical theater featuring headline performers such as Fanny Brice, Will Rogers, W. C. Fields, Bert Williams, Norma Shearer, Eddie Cantor, Billie Burke (Ziegfeld's wife), and Anna Held (Ziegfeld's lover), who is said to have first proposed the Follies idea to him. For most of their run the Follies were performed at the New Amsterdam Theatre with flamboyant costumes — often made of gauzy chiffon and resplendent feathers — by designer sensation Lady Duff-Gordon and flashy sets by Viennese-trained Joseph Urban. A risqué offshoot of the Follies, the Midnight Frolic, staged at the nightclub venue atop the New Amsterdam, featured scantily dressed beauties parading along Urban's glass runway and revolving stage. Ziegfeld died in 1932 but the Follies and the Frolic were celebrated in the MGM movie *The Great Ziegfeld* (1936), starring William Powell and Myrna Loy.

Peter L. Donhauser

Ziff-Davis. Firm of magazine publishers formed in 1927 by William B. Ziff (1898–1953), who in his early career had established an advertising agency on Park Avenue called W. B. Ziff and Company (1920), and a magazine publisher, E. C. Auld Company (1923), which launched such publications as *Ziff's Magazine* (a humorous periodical later renamed *America's Humor*). The new firm published many titles, including *Modern Bride* and *Car and Driver.* Ziff himself was a popular author whose book *The Coming Battle of Germany* (1942) became a best seller. In the 1980s Ziff-Davis sold many of its existing magazines and entered the business of computer publishing. It became the nation's leader in the field, publishing such magazines as *PC Magazine, PC Week,* and *Computer Shopper.* In June 1994 the firm put its assets up for sale; these were purchased in October of that year by the investment firm of Forstmann–Little and Company. In 2002 the firm changed ownership and was renamed Ziff Davis Media; it filed for bankruptcy in 2008, from which the company emerged after restructuring.

James Bradley

zoning. The impetus for zoning legislation in New York City came from the Fifth Avenue Association, which about 1900 sought to protect the carriage trade and exclude loft buildings and the garment industry. Others who favored zoning were residents concerned by the size of skyscrapers such as the Equitable Building (120 Broadway) and reformers who wanted to build a well-planned, healthy city by dividing land according to use, controlling the density and configuration of buildings, and providing for adequate light and air. The state legislature gave the city permission in 1914 to adopt a zoning resolution, and the Board of Estimate responded by establishing the Building Heights and Restrictions Commission, which formulated in its final report on 2 June 1916 a zoning plan that was adopted by the board at the end of the year. The plan allowed for a maximum population of 55 million in the city and outlined modifications of its traditional pattern of development: a system of mapped districts of height, area, and use was to control the rate of development; adequate light and air and proper building density were to be maintained by designing new buildings to fit an imaginary envelope determined by the size of their lots and their location on a block; each district was assigned a maximum streetwall height (the height of a building allowed at the street lot line); building setbacks were made to conform to an angle of light plane (later called the sky exposure plane); skyscrapers were allowed by the tower regulation to be of any height as long as they occupied no more than 25 percent of the area of their lots; and yard and building coverage regulations were imposed (specifying the proportion of a lot that could be built up). The guidelines adopted in the city soon became a model for zoning ordinances throughout the nation.

Zoning in New York City changed after World War II, when the *Plan for the Rezoning of New York* (1950) appeared. It drew heavily on European modernist principles of town planning and recommended widely spaced skyscrapers set in large blocks resembling parks (super blocks). Its authors intended to limit the population of the city to about 11 or 12 million by imposing a density control called floor area ratio (FAR), under which the size of a lot and its location determined the size and height of the building that could be erected on it. The regulations set forth in the plan were adopted by the city in 1961, superseding those of 1916. Developers were given incentives to build arcades, plazas, and other open spaces accessible to the public under a plan that became known as tower-in-the-park zoning, of which Co-op City in the Bronx and the office towers on the west side of Sixth Avenue in midtown Manhattan were examples. Within 10 years of its approval by the city this form of zoning had proved inflexible and incompatible with the traditional pattern of attached building in the city. The Planning Commission modified the regulations of 1961 by establishing special districts (35 were created by 1990) as well as a system of special permits, which allowed greater flexibility of design for large-scale developments, especially in midtown Manhattan. In keeping with a traditional public concern for enough daylight in midtown, the Midtown Zoning Regulation of 1982 set a standard for the amount of daylight in new buildings and the public space of the street. The Quality Housing and Contextual Zoning Regulations (1988–90) promoted the construction of housing in keeping with the character of older neighborhoods.

The most important zoning development in the 1990–2010 period was the replacement of manufacturing districts with areas open to residential development. The sharpest changes came in the meatpacking district of Manhattan and the Williamsburg and Greenpoint neighborhoods of Brooklyn, when gritty factories gave way to dense, luxury residential development.

Stanislaw J. Makielski, Jr., *The Politics of Zoning: The New York Experience* (New York: Columbia University Press, 1966)

Michael Kwartler

zoos. New York City's five zoos are spread across the boroughs. The Bronx Zoo, by far the largest, the Central Park Zoo, Prospect Park Zoo, and Queens Zoo are all managed by the Wildlife Conservation Society, formerly known as the New York Zoological Society. The Staten Island Zoo is managed by the city.

Zorach [née Thompson], **Marguerite** (*b* Santa Rosa, Calif., 25 Sept 1887; *d* Brooklyn, 27 June 1968). Painter. After marrying the painter and sculptor William Zorach (1912) she took part in the Armory Show (1913) and the Forum Exhibition of Modern American Painters (1916). Her paintings were influenced by European fauvism and cubism and characterized by bold color, expressive brushwork, and simplified form. She was the director of the Society of Independent Artists (1922–24) and the first president of the New York Society of Women Artists (1925) and was also active as a textile artist.

Roberta K. Tarbell, *Marguerite Zorach: The Early Years, 1908–1920* (Washington, D.C.: Smithsonian Institution Press for the National Collection of Fine Arts, 1973); Marilyn Friedman Hoffman, *Marguerite and William Zorach: The Cubist Years, 1915–1918* (Manchester, N.H.: Currier Gallery of Art, 1987)

Carol Lowrey

Zorach, William (*b* Jurbarkas, Lithuania, 28 Feb 1887; *d* Bath, Maine, 15 Nov 1966). Sculptor and painter. After living in Paris he moved in 1912 to New York City and settled in Greenwich Village. He and his wife, Marguerite Thompson Zorach, exhibited paintings at the Armory Show in 1913 that were considered wildly modern. In 1917 he took up sculpture and abandoned all painting except watercolors in 1922. Many of his works are large figures of children, animals, lovers, and biblical figures sculpted in granite, marble, onyx, or wood in a primitive style. His *Spirit of the Dance* (1932) was installed at Radio City Music Hall. For

New York City Aquariums, Wildlife Centers, and Zoos

Name	Year Opened	Size (Acres)	Number of Animals
Central Park Zoo* (Manhattan)	1864, remodeled 1934, renovated then reopened in 1988	5	130 species
New York Aquarium* (Brooklyn)	1896	14	over 8000
Bronx Zoo* (Bronx)	1899	265	over 4500
Staten Island Zoo (Staten Island)	1936, renovated in 1969 and throughout the 1980s	8.5	over 858
Prospect Park Zoo* (Brooklyn)	1935, renovated then reopened in 1993	11	almost 400
Queens Zoo* (Queens)	1968, renovated then reopened in 1992	11	

*Wildlife Conservation Society Institution

Sources: Wildlife Conservation Society Web site and each zoo's respective Web site

Compiled by Frank Nestor

several years Zorach lived with his family at 17 West Ninth Street and kept a studio at 2 West 15th Street; from 1939 both home and studio were at 271 Hicks Street in Brooklyn.

Alana Erickson Coble

Zoroastrians. Members of a Persian religion founded in the sixth century BCE by the prophet Zoroaster. Most of the world's Zoroastrians live in Iran or in India (where they are known as Parsis), and those who emigrate are in general well-educated professionals. In the late nineteenth century a number of Zoroastrian students moved to New York City to study at Columbia University, where in 1895 a professorship in Zoroastrian scriptures was established under A. V. Williams Jackson. Most of the students left the city after their studies, and in 1992 the university discontinued the program. Iranian Zoroastrians established a presence in the city in the 1920s, when the Soroushian family operated a retail carpet business; Philip Lopate's novel *The Rug Merchant* (1987) is loosely based on the family's story. Some Indian Zoroastrians settled in the city after the Immigration Act of 1965, and Iranian Zoroastrians increased in number after the Iranian revolution of 1979. Zoroastrians in New York City have not developed lasting religious institutions, but both Parsi and Iranian Zoroastrians from the metropolitan area support the Zoroastrian Association of Greater New York, also known as the Dar-e-Mehr (path of compassion), in suburban New Rochelle in Westchester County. Maintaining the Zoroastrian tradition in New York City is complicated by small numbers, low birthrates, and long prayer services held in the ancient language of Avestan. Another obstacle to the long-term survival of the religion in New York City is that orthodox Zoroastrians reject converts. In the early twenty-first century fewer than 200,000 Zoroastrians were active worldwide, and fewer than 1000 lived in the New York metropolitan area.

Marc Ferris

Zukofsky, Louis (*b* New York City, 23 Jan 1904; *d* Port Jefferson, N.Y., 12 May 1978). Poet. Born on the Lower East Side, he graduated from Columbia University in 1927. During the Depression he worked for the Works Progress Administration at Columbia University, the radio station WNYC, and the New York Arts Project. He later worked as a freelance editor and substitute high school teacher and taught English at Brooklyn Polytechnic Institute from 1947 until his retirement in 1966. Influenced by Ezra Pound and later by the objectivists, he wrote poetry that was intensely passionate and went unpublished for most of his life. His 800-page epic *"A,"* which begins with a description of a concert at Carnegie Hall and includes many references to the history and life of New York City, took 50 years for him to complete. Zukofsky lived at 135 Willow Street in Brooklyn, spent some time at 77 Seventh Avenue, and moved to Long Island in 1972.

Marc Ferris

NOTES ON THE CONTRIBUTORS

An asterisk denotes "deceased."

Amanda Aaron (MA New York University) lives and works in New York City.

Susan Aaronson (PhD Johns Hopkins University) is an associate research professor of international affairs at George Washington University in the Elliott School of International Affairs and the School of Business. She has authored books on trade, investment, business, and human rights.

Elaine S. Abelson (PhD New York University) is an associate professor in history and urban studies as well as a senior lecturer to graduate faculty at The New School.

Alan David Aberbach (PhD University of Florida) is a former professor and current director of the Seniors Program at Simon Fraser University's Harbour Centre Campus in Vancouver. He is the author of several books, including *The Ideas of Richard Wagner: An Examination and Analysis*, 2nd edn. (2003).

Joan Acocella (PhD Rutgers University) is a dance critic and staff writer for the *New Yorker*. She is the recipient of a Guggenheim Fellowship.

Arthur G. Adams is the founding president of the Hudson River Maritime Center in Kingston, New York, and the vice president of the Steamer Alexander Hamilton Society. He is an editor of *The Hudson River in Literature: An Anthology* (1988) and a coauthor of *Railroad Ferries of the Hudson* (1987).

Melvin L. Adelman (PhD University of Illinois) teaches at Ohio State University specializing in the history of American sports.

Norma Adler (JD Northeastern University) has edited and written for numerous dance and theater publications.

Emery E. Adoradio (JD American University; MA History, New York University) is the senior attorney for the Complex Crimes Unit in the Hennepin County Attorney's Office, Minneapolis. Previously he was the executive director of the Police Corruption Commission in New York City and an assistant district attorney in the New York County District Attorney's Office for 10 years.

Rohit T. Aggarwala (PhD Columbia University) is a former special assistant at the Federal Railroad Administration in Washington, D.C. He is currently the director of the New York City Mayor's Office of Long-Term Planning and Sustainability.

Irving Lewis Allen (PhD University of Iowa) is a professor emeritus of sociology at the University of Connecticut, Storrs. He is the author of *The City in Slang: New York Life and Popular Speech* (1995) and *Unkind Words: Ethnic Labeling from Redskin to WASP* (1990).

Jane Allen is a former program officer at the IRI Research Institute in Stamford, Connecticut.

Cathy Alexander is an independent historian.

Eric Wm. Allison (BA Columbia College) is a former professor at the Pratt Institute and a resident of Brooklyn.

Marc D. Angel (PhD Yeshiva University) is rabbi emeritus of the Congregation Shearith Israel, the historically Spanish and Portuguese synagogue of New York City. He is also the former president of the Rabbinical Council of America and the founder of the board of Sephardic House. His books include *The Rhythms of Jewish Living: A Sephardic Approach* (1989).

Thea Arnold (PhD Binghamton University) is a parent mentor advocate at Southern Tier Independence Center in Ithaca, New York.

Arnold Aronson (PhD Drama, New York University) is a professor of theater at Columbia University and the author of *Looking into the Abyss: Essays on Scenography* (2005).

Marc H. Aronson (PhD New York University) is an editor at HarperCollins. His dissertation was on William Crary Brownell and publishing at the end of the nineteenth century.

Arthur Ashe* (BS University of California, Los Angeles) won the US Open Tennis Championship at Forest Hills in 1968 and was the author of *The Hard Road to Glory: A History of the African American Athlete* (1988).

Arten Ashjian (MA Theology, Harvard University Divinity School) is a former instructor of Armenian church history and liturgics at St. Nersess Armenian Seminary in New Rochelle, New York, where he was honored in 2008 on the 60th anniversary of his ordination.

Jean Ashton (PhD Columbia University, MLS Rutgers University School of Library and Information Studies) is executive vice president and library director of the New-York Historical Society.

Jonathan Aspell (MBA Boston University) works in the broadcasting industry in Tampa, Florida.

John C. Aubry is an associate secretary and archivist for the College Board.

Simon Baatz (PhD University of Pennsylvania) is a professor of history at John Jay College of Criminal Justice in New York City and the author of *Knowledge, Culture, and Science in the Metropolis: The New York Academy of Sciences, 1817–1970* (1990).

Ellen D. Baer (RN, PhD, Fellowship in the American Association of Nurses) is a professor emerita of nursing at the University of Pennsylvania, where she held the Hillman Term Professorship in Nursing. She is an associate director of the Center for the Study of the History of Nursing at the University of Pennsylvania.

David A. Balcom (PhD City University of New York) is the associate vice chancellor and the vice president for board relations at the University System of Maryland. He was formerly director of development for the Lawyers' Committee for Civil Rights under Law in Washington, D.C.

Maurita Baldock (MA New York University, MLS Pratt Institute) is the curator of manuscripts for the New-York Historical Society.

Melissa Baldock (MS Historic Preservation, Columbia University) is the Kress/RFR Fellow for Historic Preservation and Public Policy at the Municipal Art Society of New York.

Andrea Balis is professor of history and interdisciplinary studies at John Jay College of Criminal Justice.

Randall Balmer (PhD Princeton University) is a professor of American religious history at Barnard College. He is an editor at *Christianity Today* and the author of numerous books on religion in America.

Sally Banes (PhD New York University) is the Marian Hannah Winter Professor Emerita of Theater History and Dance Studies at the University of Wisconsin–Madison. She authored *Greenwich Village 1963: Avant-garde Performance and the Effervescent Body* (1993) and *Subversive Expectations: Performance Art and Paratheater in New York, 1976–85* (1998).

Rudolf Baranik* studied painting at the Art Institute of Chicago, at the Art Students League, and in Paris. He taught at the Art Students League and at the Pratt Institute, where he was a professor emeritus.

Barbara Barker (MFA University of Texas at Austin) was a professor and head of the Dance Department at the University of Minnesota until her retirement in 1998. She is the author of *Ballet or Ballyhoo: The American Careers of Maria Bonfanti, Rita Sangalli and Giuseppina Morlacchi* (1984) and editor of *Bolossy Kiralfy: Creator of Great Musical Spectacles* (1988).

Brooke J. Barr (PhD Yale University) completed her dissertation, "Past Surfaces: History and Theory of Landmark Preservation in New York City, 1945–1989," in 1996.

Phyllis Barr (MPhil and MA History, New York University) is president of Corporate Culture Marketing by Barr Consulting Services in Manhattan. She is a certified archivist, records manager, and historian. She also served as director of archives of the Parish of Trinity Church in New York City.

Carrie Rebora Barratt (PhD City University of New York) is the curator of American paintings and sculpture and manager of the Henry R. Luce Center for the Study of American Art at the Metropolitan Museum of Art.

Patrick Barrett (BA Columbia University) is an assistant editor for *The Encyclopedia of New York City*, 2nd edn.

Paul Barrett* (PhD University of Illinois) was a professor and chair of the Humanities Department at the Illinois Institute of Technology in Chicago. He was the author of *The Automobile and Urban Transit: Public Policy in Chicago, 1900–1930* (1983).

James L. Baughman (PhD Columbia University) is the director of the School of Journalism and Mass Communication at the University of Wisconsin–Madison. His books include *Same Time, Same Station: Creating American Television, 1948–1961* (2007) and *The Republic of Mass Culture: Journalism, Filmmaking, and Broadcasting in America since 1941* (2005).

Marcia Bayne-Smith (PhD Columbia University), formerly a professor of health and physical education at Queens College, is a professor in the Urban Studies Department at Queens College. She specializes in issues of teen pregnancy and immigrant health.

Thomas D. Beal (PhD State University of New York, Stony Brook) is an assistant professor of American history and urban studies at the State University of New York, Oneonta. His focus is on New York City, urban history, and nineteenth-century social and economic history.

Rick Beard (PhD Emory University) is the former chief operating officer of the New-York Historical Society and former director of the Abraham Lincoln Presidential Library and Museum in Springfield, Illinois.

Elizabeth Beirne (PhD Fordham University, BA Mercy College) is an editor, a writer, and an associate professor of philosophy at the College of Mount St. Vincent in New York.

Trudy E. Bell (MA New York University) is a freelance science journalist and independent scholar. She was an editor for *Scientific American*, a founding senior editor for *Omni*, and a senior editor for *IEEE Spectrum*. She has coauthored two books and more than 250 articles on science and technology.

Martha S. Bendix (BA Allegheny College) has worked as the public relations director for the Newark Museum in New Jersey and as an editor, feature writer, and columnist for the *Staten Island Advance*.

Gerald Benjamin (PhD American government, Columbia University) is Distinguished Professor of Political Science at the State University of New York (SUNY) and dean of the College of Liberal Arts and Sciences at SUNY New Paltz. He has written numerous books on New York state and local government.

Kathleen Benson is a project manager at the Museum of the City of New York.

Judith Berck (MFA Creative Nonfiction, University of Iowa) is a freelance writer whose articles have appeared in the *New York Times* and the *Washington Post*. She is the author of *Children in Crisis* (1994) and since 1999 has been a direct vendor for Intel Corporation and Microsoft Corporation with her company Judith Berck, Inc.

Ben Berger (BA Columbia University) is an assistant editor for *The Encyclopedia of New York City*, 2nd edn.

Ira Berger is a magazine editor, the curator of a book and oral history collection on jazz, and a writer of articles on jazz.

Edward F. Bergman was a professor in and chairman of the Environmental, Geographic, and Geological Sciences Department at Lehman College and the author of several books, including *The Spiritual Traveler: New York City: The Guide to Sacred Spaces and Peaceful Places* (2001) and *A Geography of the New York Metropolitan Region* (1975).

Edward A. Berlin (PhD Musicology, City University of New York) is a scholar of ragtime and the author of many books on the subject, including *Ragtime: A Musical and Cultural History* (1980).

Avis Berman (MA Rutgers University) has directed the Oral History Program of the Roy Lichtenstein Foundation since 2001. She is the author of *Rebels on Eighth Street: Juliana Force and the Whitney Museum of American Art* (1990) and coauthor of *Edward Hopper's New York* (2005).

Greta Berman (PhD Columbia University) is a professor of art history at the Juilliard School and the author of *The Lost Years: Mural Painting in New York City under the Works Progress Administration's Federal Art Project, 1935–1943* (1975).

Iver Bernstein (PhD Yale University) is a professor of American culture studies and history at Washington University in St. Louis and the author of *The New York City Draft Riots: Their Significance for American Society and Politics in the Age of the Civil War* (1990).

Selma Berrol (PhD City University of New York) is professor emerita of history at Baruch College, where she also served as chair of the department and the assistant dean of liberal arts. She is the author of *Immigrants at School: New York City, 1898–1914* (1967) and *Getting Down to Business: Baruch College in the City of New York* (1989).

Mary Beth Betts (MPhil Graduate School and University Center, City University of New York) is the director of research at the New York City Landmarks Preservation Commission. She was previously an associate curator of architectural collections at the New-York Historical Society.

Craig D. Bida (BA Yale University) is a former urban planner for the New York City Department of Housing Preservation and Development. He writes on urban and rural issues, focusing on the effects humans have on the natural world.

Eugenie Ladner Birch (PhD and MS Urban Planning, Columbia University) is a codirector of the Penn Institute for Urban Research at the University of Pennsylvania and a chair and professor at the Department of City and Regional Planning there.

Thomas E. Bird (PhD Princeton University) is a professor of Slavic and Eastern European languages at Queens College as well as a historian at the St. Nicholas Society of the City of New York.

Rodger C. Birt (PhD Yale University) is a professor of American studies and humanities at San Francisco State University. He has written numerous articles on photography and New York City.

Elizabeth Blackmar (PhD Harvard University) is a history professor at Columbia University. Her publications include *The Park and the People: A History of Central Park* (1992), coauthored with Roy Rosenzweig.

Karen J. Blair (PhD State University of New York, Buffalo) is a professor of history at Central Washington University and the author of *The Clubwoman as Feminist: True Womanhood Redefined, 1868–1914* (1980).

Annette Blaugrund (PhD Columbia University) is a former director of the National Academy Museum and School of Fine Arts and continues to write and lecture on subjects in American art at international venues.

Jack Blicksilver* (PhD Northwestern University) was professor emeritus of economic history at Georgia State University and author of *Defenders and Defense of Big Business in the United States, 1880–1900* (1985).

Alexander Bloom (PhD Boston College) is a professor of American history at Wheaton College. He is the author of *Prodigal Sons: The New York Intellectuals and Their World* (1986) and "The Social and Intellectual Life of the City," in *New York: Culture Capital of the World, 1940–1965* (1988).

Jonathan D. Bloom is a historian and the executive director of the Workers Defense League in New York City.

Barbara Blumberg (PhD Columbia University) is a professor of history at Pace University and the author of *The New Deal and the Unemployed: The View from New York City* (1979) and *Celebrating the Immigrant: An Administrative History of the Statue of Liberty National Monument* (1985).

Stuart M. Blumin (PhD University of Pennsylvania) is professor emeritus of American history and director of the Cornell in Washington program at Cornell University. He is the author of *The Emergence of the Middle Class: Social Experience in the American City, 1760–1900* (1989) and the editor of *George G.*

Foster: New York by Gas-Light, and Other Urban Sketches (1990).

Michele H. Bogart (PhD University of Chicago) is professor of art history at Stony Brook University and vice president of the Fine Arts Federation of New York. She is the author of *The Politics of Urban Beauty: New York and Its Art Commission* (2006) and *Public Sculpture and the Civic Ideal in New York City, 1890–1930* (1997).

Patricia U. Bonomi (PhD Columbia University) is professor emerita of history at New York University and author of *A Factious People: Politics and Society in Colonial New York* (1971), *The Lord Cornbury Scandal: The Politics of Reputation in British America* (1998), and *Under the Cope of Heaven: Religion, Society, and Politics in Colonial America* (2003).

Lawson Bowling (PhD and MPhil Columbia University) is a professor of history at Manhattanville College, specializing in twentieth-century subjects.

Mary B. Bowling (MLS Columbia University, BA Case Western Reserve University) is a consulting archivist. She is a former curator of manuscripts at the New York Public Library, archivist and supervisory museum curator at the Edison National Historic Site, and manuscript librarian at Columbia University's Rare Book and Manuscript Library.

Elizabeth Bradley is the manager of programs at the Dorothy and Lewis B. Cullman Center for Scholars and Writers, the New York Public Library. She is the author of *Knickerbocker: The Myth That Made New York* (2008).

James Bradley is a freelance journalist and writer based in Brooklyn.

Sarah Brafman (BA History, Columbia University) is a contributor to *The Encyclopedia of New York City*, 2nd edn.

Barry Bragg (PhD University of Wisconsin) is a volunteer researcher with the Canadian Museum of Civilization.

James D. Bratt (PhD Yale University) is a professor of history at Calvin College, specializing in religion in America and colonial America. He is director for the Calvin Center for Christian Scholarship and coeditor of *Perspectives: A Journal of Reformed Thought*.

Frank O. Braynard* (MA Columbia University) was a maritime historian and founder of the South Street Seaport Museum. He authored many books on maritime history, including *S.S. Savannah* (1963) and *The Elegant Steam Ship* (1988) and was a consultant to *Great Liners* (1978).

Charles Brecher (PhD Political Science, City University of New York) is the research director for the Citizens Budget Commission and a professor of public and health administration in the Robert F. Wagner Graduate School of Public Service at New York University. He is a coauthor of *Power Failure: New York City Politics and Policy since 1960* (1993) and *Privatization and Public Hospitals: Choosing Wisely for New York City* (1995).

Joseph Breen is an assistant editor for the *Encyclopedia of New York City*, 2nd edn., and attends Yale University.

Matthew J. Brennan (BA University of Massachusetts–Amherst) is a graduate student at the City University of New York studying religion and the history of physical fitness culture in the United States.

James Breslin is a contributor to *The Encyclopedia of New York City*, 2nd edn.

Richard Briffault (JD Harvard University) is the Joseph P. Chamberlain Professor of Legislation at Columbia Law School. He is the author of numerous publications on law.

Mosette G. Broderick (PhD Columbia University) is a clinical associate professor of art history at New York University and writes on nineteenth- and twentieth-century architecture and urbanism. She is the author of "Fifth Avenue" in *Grand American Avenues* (1994).

Norman J. Brouwer is a maritime historian and was the curator of ships at the South Street Seaport Museum. He is also the author of *The International Register of Historic Ships* (1985).

Emilyn L. Brown (MLS Pratt Institute, MA Columbia University) is an archivist and administrative fellow at Harvard College Library. She is an archival consultant for Abyssinian Baptist Church and previously worked for the African Burial Ground Project.

Joshua Brown (PhD Columbia University) is the executive director at the American Social History Project's Center for Media and Learning and a professor in the PhD program in history at City University of New York, where he is also the codirector of the New Media Lab. He received a Guggenheim Fellowship in 2010.

Mary Elizabeth Brown (PhD Columbia University) is the archivist for Marymount Manhattan College. She also assists in the archives of the Center for Migration Studies. She is the author of *Italian Immigrants and the Catholic Church in the Archdiocese of New York, 1880–1950*.

Stuart Bruchey (PhD John Hopkins University) is the Allan Nevins Professor Emeritus of American Economic History at Columbia University and author of numerous works on U.S. economic history.

Stephan F. Brumberg (EdD Harvard University) is the program head of the Educational Leadership Program at the School of Education at Brooklyn College, City University of New York, where he is also a professor of education.

Roy S. Bryce-Laporte (PhD University of California, Los Angeles) was the John D. and Catherine T. MacArthur Professor of Sociology and Anthropology, Emeritus, from 1989 to 2000. He has conducted extensive research on the African diaspora and Caribbean migration.

Peter G. Buckley is an associate professor on the faculty of humanities and social sciences at the Cooper Union. His dissertation was titled "To the Opera House: Culture and Society in New York City, 1820–1860."

Stanley Buder (PhD University of Chicago) is professor emeritus of history at Baruch College and the Graduate Center, City University of New York. His books include *Visionaries and Planners: The Garden City and the Modern Community* (1990) and *Capitalizing on Change: A Social History of American Business* (2009).

Karen Buhler-Wilkerson* (RN, PhD University of Pennsylvania) was a professor emerita and historian of health care at the University of Pennsylvania's School of Nursing and the author of *No Place Like Home: A History of Nursing and Home Care in the United States* (2001).

John Bull* was a field associate for the American Museum of Natural History and the author of many ornithological works, including *Birds of New York State* (1974) and the *Macmillan Field Guide to the Birds of North America: Eastern Region* (1985).

Timothy Anglin Burgard (MPhil Columbia University) is the Ednah Root Curator-in-Charge of the American Art Department for the Fine Arts Museums of San Francisco and is a former curator at the New-York Historical Society. He is also the author of *Mr. Luman Reed's Picture Gallery: A Pioneer Collection of American Art* (1990).

Edwin G. Burrows is professor of history at Brooklyn College of the City University of New York. He is a coauthor of *Gotham: A History of New York City to 1898* (1998), which won the Pulitzer Prize, and *Forgotten Patriots: The Untold Story of American Prisoners during the Revolutionary War* (2008).

Clarissa L. Bushman (MBA Columbia University) is a former professional dancer and investment banker. She now teaches at Stuyvesant High School in Manhattan.

Inea Bushnaq is the editor and translator of *Arab Folktales* (1986). She has worked in publishing in both Europe and New York City and now is a freelance writer and teaches part time in the New York public school system.

Jon Butler (PhD University of Minnesota) is dean of the Graduate School of Arts and Sciences at Yale University, where he is also the Howard R. Lamar Professor of American History. He is the author of several books, including *Becoming American: The Revolution before 1776* (2000).

Ann L. Buttenwieser is an urban planner and historian and an adjunct professor at Columbia University. She is the author of *Manhattan Water-Bound* (1999) and *Governors Island: The Jewel of New York Harbor* (2009). She was instrumental in creating the first floating pool in New York City.

Bernadette G. Callery (PhD School of Library and Information Science, University of Pittsburgh; MS Library Science, University of

Chicago) is a museum librarian at the Carnegie Museum of Natural History.

Kerry Candaele (PhD Columbia University) is head of Battle Hymns Productions, LCC, a production company based in Vince, Los Angeles. He is the author of two books on U.S. history and several articles in academic periodicals.

Vincent J. Cannato (PhD Columbia University) is associate professor of history at the University of Massachusetts, Boston, and the author of *American Passage: The History of Ellis Island* (2009) and *The Ungovernable City: John Lindsay and His Struggle to Save New York* (2001).

Donald J. Cannon* (PhD Fordham University) was professor of history at St. Peter's College; an adjunct professor in fire science at John Jay College, City University of New York; the editor of *Heritage of Flames: The Illustrated History of Early American Firefighting* (1977); and a coauthor, with Glenn Corbett, of *Historic Fires of New York City* (2005).

Marvin Carlson is the Sidney E. Cohn Distinguished Professor of Theatre Studies and Comparative Literature at the City University of New York Graduate Center.

Betty Boyd Caroli (PhD New York University) is a former professor of history, philosophy, and political science at Kingsborough Community College. She is the author of several books on America's First Ladies.

Marion R. Casey (PhD New York University) is associate editor at Glucksman Ireland House at New York University and a senior archivist at Archives of Irish America at New York University. She is the coeditor, with J. J. Lee, of *Making the Irish American: History and Heritage of the Irish in the United States* (2006).

S. D. R. Cashman is a freelance writer and the author of several books on U.S. history, a subject that he has taught at the University of Manchester in England, at New York University, and at Adelphi University, where he was also a dean.

Graciela M. Castex (EdD Columbia University) is an associate professor of sociology and social work at Lehman College, City University of New York. She is also a coauthor of *Encounters in Diversity: A Social Work Reader.*

Meryl Cates (BA Dance and Journalism, Purchase College, State University of New York) is a freelance journalist in New York City specializing in dance and the arts.

Jonathan G. Cedarbaum (JD Yale University Law School; MPhil History, Yale University) was formerly a partner at Wilmer, Cutler, Pickering, Hale and Dorr, LLP, in Washington, D.C.

Mario A. Charles (MSLIS Pratt Institute; MS Education Administration, Baruch College) is an associate professor and a former head librarian at the College of New Rochelle's Mother Irene Gill Memorial Library, Rosa Parks Campus.

Ann Charters (PhD Columbia University) is a professor of English at the University of Connecticut and the author of several books on Jack Kerouac and the beat writers.

George Chauncey, Jr. (PhD History, Yale University), is professor of history at Yale University. He is author of *Gay New York: Gender, Urban Culture, and the Makings of the Gay Male World, 1890–1940* (1994).

Gladys Chen (BA Columbia College) was born in New York City and studied political science and biology.

Eileen K. Cheng (PhD Yale University) is a professor in the graduate studies in Women's History Department at Sarah Lawrence College. She is the author of *The Plain and Noble Garb of Truth: Nationalism and Impartiality in American Historical Writing, 1784–1869* and of multiple articles and book reviews.

Barbara A. Chernow (PhD Columbia University) is associate editor of *The Papers of Alexander Hamilton* (1969–1977) and coeditor of the *Columbia Encyclopedia*, 5th ed. (1993) and the *Datapedia of the United States: American History in Numbers*, 4th ed. (2007).

Charlie Chin is an independent performer, composer, and writer. He is a former community education director at the New York Chinatown History Project, Center for Community Studies.

James Ciment (PhD City University of New York) is the general editor of *Postwar America: An Encyclopedia of Social, Political, Cultural, and Economic History* (2006).

Lawrence A. Clayton (PhD Tulane University) is a professor and former chair of the History Department at the University of Alabama and the author of *W. R. Grace & Co., Los Años Formativos, 1850–1930* (2008).

Melissa Smith Clayton is a former archivist for the Rockefeller Archive Center and served as the director of advancement research for Marymount College before joining March of Dimes Birth Defects Foundation in 2000 where she is director of major gifts support services.

Kenneth Cobb is assistant commissioner to the New York City Department of Records and Information Services.

Alana Erickson Coble (PhD Columbia University) is an independent scholar and a previous deputy managing editor of *The Encyclopedia of New York City*, 1st ed. She published *Cleaning Up: The Transformation of Domestic Service in Twentieth Century New York City* (2006).

Peter A. Coclanis (PhD Columbia University) is an associate provost and Albert R. Newsome Professor in the History Department at the University of North Carolina at Chapel Hill. He books include *The Atlantic Economy during the Seventeenth and Eighteenth Centuries* (2005).

Gerald Leonard Cohen (PhD Columbia University) is a professor of German at the Missouri University of Science and Technology (formerly University of Missouri–Rolla) in the Department of Arts, Languages, and Philosophy.

Barbara Cohen-Stratyner (PhD New York University) is the Judy R. and Alfred A. Rodenburg Curator of Exhibitions for the New York Public Library for the Performing Arts. She is the author of the *Biographical Dictionary of Dance* (1982) and a former editor of *Performing Arts Resources.*

Theresa Collins is an associate research professor at Rutgers University School of Arts and Sciences in the History Department as well as an associate editor for the Thomas A. Edison Papers. She is a coauthor of *Thomas Edison and Modern America: An Introduction with Documents* (2002).

John J. Concannon is a former *Newsweek* journalist and author. He is the national historian and national press officer for the Ancient Order of Hibernians in America as well as the author and compiler of *The Irish Directory* (1983) and *The Irish-American Who's Who* (1984).

Robert P. Cook (PhD Ecology, City University of New York) is a wildlife biologist with the National Park Service and has worked since 1980 to restore amphibian and reptile populations in New York City.

Terry A. Cooney (PhD State University of New York, Stony Brook) is the current dean of the College of Liberal Arts at Towson University in Maryland and the author of *The Rise of the New York Intellectuals:* Partisan Review *and Its Circle* (1986).

Henry B. Cooper is a graduate of Columbia University.

Henry S. F. Cooper, Jr., wrote about space exploration for the *New Yorker* for more than three decades and has published eight books on the subject. He is a trustee and past chairman of the New York Society Library in New York City and is also the president of Otsego 2000, an environmental organization in Cooperstown, New York.

Cynthia Copeland (BA John Jay College of Criminal Justice) is a former public educator with the Office of Public Education and Interpretation of the African Burial Ground and is a founder of *ZuZu*, a multicultural children's newspaper published in New York City.

Glenn P. Corbett, associate professor of fire science at John Jay College of Criminal Justice, is the technical editor of *Fire Engineering.* He is a coauthor, with Donald Cannon, of *Historic Fires of New York City* (2005) and, with Francis L. Brannigan, of *Brannigan's Building Construction for the Fire Service*, 4th edn. (2007).

Michael R. Corbett is an architectural historian, a cultural resource consultant, and a writer in Berkeley, California. He worked for the New York City Landmarks Preservation Commission from 1988 to 1990.

Francesco Cordasco* (PhD New York University) was a professor of education at Montclair State College (now Montclair State University) and the author of works on American history such as *Medical Education in the United States* (1980).

Steven H. Corey (PhD New York University) is a professor and chair of the Urban Studies Department at Worcester State College in Massachusetts. He served as research curator at the New York Public Library for the exhibit *Garbage? The History and Politics of Trash in New York City*.

Evan Cornog (PhD Columbia University) is former associate dean of academic affairs in the School of Journalism at Columbia University. He also served as press secretary to New York City mayor Edward I. Koch from 1982 to 1983.

William S. Cottam (PhD University of Utah) is the former director of the Church of Jesus Christ of Latter-Day Saints Institute of Religion and a former bishop of the church in New York City.

Edward Countryman (PhD Cornell University) is a Distinguished Professor in the Clements Department of History at Southern Methodist University. He is author of *A People in Revolution: The American Revolution and Political Society in New York, 1760–1790* (1981) and *The Empire State* (2001).

Holly Cronin (BA Columbia University) is a deputy managing editor for *The Encyclopedia of New York City*, 2nd edn.

Robert Emmett Curran (PhD Yale University) is professor emeritus of history at Georgetown University and the author of the *Bicentennial History of Georgetown University* (1993).

Mary E. Curry (PhD American University) is a business historian who has worked for the National Portrait Gallery in Washington, D.C.; the Winthrop Group in Cambridge, Massachusetts; and Wells Fargo Investigative Services of New York. She is the author of *Creating an American Institution: The Merchandising Genius of J. C. Penney* (1993).

Daniel Czitrom (PhD University of Wisconsin–Madison) is a professor of history at Mount Holyoke College. He has published *Rediscovering Jacob Riis: Exposure Journalism and Photography in Turn-of-the-Century New York* (2008, with Bonnie Yochelson) and is working on *Mysteries of the City: Politics, Culture, and New York's Underworld in Turn-of-the-Century America*.

Phyllis Dain (DLS, Columbia University) is professor emerita of Library Service at the School of Library Service at Columbia University. She is the author of *The New York Public Library: A History of Its Founding and Early Years* (1972) and editor with John Y. Cole of *Libraries and Scholarly Communication in the United States: The Historical Dimension* (1990).

Douglas Henry Daniels (PhD University of California, Berkeley) is a professor in black studies and history at the University of California, Santa Barbara. His publications include *Lester Leaps In: The Life and Times of Lester "Pres" Young* (2002) and *One o'Clock Jump: The Unforgettable History of the Oklahoma City Blue Devils* (2005).

Mimi Gisolfi D'Aponte (PhD City University of New York) is professor emerita of theater at Baruch College and City University of New York Graduate Center. She is also the author of *Teatro Religioso e Rituale della Penisola Sorrentina e la Costiera Amalfitana* (1984).

Amanda Dargan (PhD University of Pennsylvania) is a folklorist who works at City Lore, Inc., where she is the editor of CARTS catalogue and a coeditor of CARTS Newsletter. She is also the author with Steve Zeitlin of *City Play* (1990).

Colin J. Davis (PhD State University of New York, Binghamton) is a professor of history at the University of Alabama, Birmingham. He books include *Waterfront Revolts: New York and London Dockworkers, 1946–1961* (2003) and *Power at Odds: The 1922 National Railroad Shopmen's Strike* (1997).

Thomas J. Davis (PhD Columbia University, JD University of Buffalo) is a professor of history and law at Arizona State University. He is the author of *A Rumor Revolt: The Great Negro Plot in Colonial New York* (1985) and, with Michael Conniff, *Africans in the Americas: A History of the Black Diaspora* (1994).

Harriet Davis-Kram (PhD City University of New York) is an adjunct professor of American history at Queens College, specializing in the history of women, labor, immigration, and New York City.

Jared Day is a visiting professor of history at Carnegie Mellon University in Pittsburgh. He is the author of *Urban Castles: Tenement Housing and Landlord Activism in New York City, 1890–1943* and coauthor (with Joe Trotter) of the forthcoming *Race and Renaissance along Three Rivers: The African American Experience in Pittsburgh since World War II*.

Gloria Deák is the author of *American Views: Prospects and Vistas* (1976), *Picturing America, 1497–1899* (1988), *William James Bennett, Master of the Aquatint View* (1988), and *Picturing New York* (2000).

James Deaville (PhD Northwestern University) is an associate professor of music in the School for Studies in Art and Culture at Carleton University.

GraceAnne A. DeCandido is an instructor through Rutgers University's School of Communication and Information online and a former executive editor of *School Library Journal*. She is the principal of Blue Roses Consulting, which specializes in writing, editorial consulting, and Web content planning and provision.

Gerald F. De Jong (PhD University of Wisconsin) is a former professor emeritus of history at the University of South Dakota and the author of *The Dutch in America, 1609–1974* (1975) and *The Dutch Reformed Church in the American Colonies* (1978).

Ormonde de Kay* was a freelance writer, poet, and former articles editor of *Horizon* magazine. He authored books on world history, biographies of famous Americans for young readers, and many historical and biographical articles in various magazines.

Linda Delgado is the coeditor with Felix V. Matos Rodriguez of *Puerto Rican Women's History: New Perspectives* (1998) and the editor of the *Ethnic Reporter*. She is currently the director at the Center for Ethnic Race Studies in New York City.

Jane DeLuca (MS, RN University of Rochester) is a former instructor in the Biology Department at Stonehill College.

Briana Dema (BA Columbia University) is an assistant editor for *The Encyclopedia of New York City*, 2nd edn.

Peter Derrick (PhD New York University) is archivist at the Bronx Historical Society. He is the author of *Tunneling to the Future: The Story of the Great Subway Expansion That Saved New York* (2001) and editor of the *Bronx County Historical Society Journal*.

Samuel Devons* (PhD Cambridge University) was professor emeritus of physics at Columbia University.

Dennis C. Dickerson (PhD Washington University) is the James M. Lawson, Jr., Professor of History at Vanderbilt University. His writings focus on African American religious history, labor, and the civil rights movement. He is author of *Out of the Crucible: Black Steelworkers in Western Pennsylvania, 1875–1980* (1986).

Joseph Ditta (MLIS) is a reference librarian at the New-York Historical Society and the author of *Gravesend, Brooklyn* (2009).

Michael N. Dobkowski (PhD New York University) is a professor of religious studies at Hobart and William Smith Colleges. He is author of *The Tarnished Dream: The Basis of American Anti-Semitism* (1979) and *Jewish American Voluntary Organizations* (1986).

Jameson W. Doig is Senior Scholar and Professor Emeritus in the Woodrow Wilson School and Department of Politics at Princeton University. He is the author of *Empire on the Hudson: Entrepreneurial Vision and Political Power at the Port of New York Authority* (2001) and a coauthor of *New York: The Politics of Urban Regional Development* (1982).

Andrew S. Dolkart is an architectural historian and preservationist and holds the James Marston Fitch Professorship in Historic Preservation at the Columbia University School of Architecture, Planning, and Preservation. His books include *Morningside Heights: A History of Its Architecture and Development* (1998) and *The Row House Reborn: Architecture and Neighborhoods in New York City, 1908–1929* (2009).

Peter L. Donhauser teaches history at the Trinity School in New York City. He is completing a dissertation on the architects Herts and Tallant.

George Dorris (PhD Northwestern University) is a dance historian and contributor to many New York–area journals of dance. He retired as associate professor of English at York College of the City University of New York.

Susan J. Douglas (PhD Brown University) is the Catherine Neafie Kellogg Professor, the Arthur F. Thurnau Professor, and department chair of the Department of Communications at the University of Michigan. She is also the author of *The Mommy Myth: The Idealization of Motherhood and How It Has Undermined Women* (2004).

Patricia A. Doyal (MA Queens College, MS Syracuse University) is a former assistant professor at Baruch College and a former library director for the Institute of Public Administration in New York City.

Joe Doyle (MA History, New York University) is a former columnist for *Seaport Magazine* and the former editor of *Work History News*.

Matthew P. Drennan is Visiting Professor of Urban Planning at the University of California, Los Angeles, and professor emeritus of city and regional planning at Cornell University. He is author of *The Information Economy and American Cities* (2002).

Jesse Drucker is a staff reporter at the *Wall Street Journal*.

James O. Drummond (PhD New York University) is a professor of history at Philadelphia Biblical University. His dissertation was titled "Transportation and the Shaping of the Physical Environment in an Urban Place: Newark 1820–1900."

Melvyn Dubofsky (PhD University of Rochester) is Distinguished Professor Emeritus of history and sociology at the State University of New York, Binghamton. His books include *We Shall Be All: A History of the Industrial Workers of the World* (1974) and *Hard Work: The Making of Labor History* (2000).

Ellen Carol DuBois (PhD Northwestern University) is a professor of history at the University of California, Los Angeles. Her books include *Harriet Stanton Blatch and the Winning of Woman Suffrage* (1997), *Woman Suffrage and Women's Rights: Essays* (1997), and *Feminism and Suffrage: The Emergence of an Independent Women's Movement in America, 1848–1869* (1977).

Vivian Ducat (MA Columbia University) is a producer of digital multimedia and documentary video and film and has worked with the Lower East Side Tenement Museum, the New-York Historical Society, and Harlem Hospital.

David Dunbar is the founder of CITYterm, an academic program for high school students, and the coeditor with Kenneth T. Jackson of *Empire City: New York through the Centuries* (2005).

James Duplacey (BA University of New Brunswick) writes about sports and culture. He has published many books, including *A Century of Hockey Heroes: 100 of the Greatest All-Time Stars* (2000).

Seymour Durst* (BA University of Southern California) was a real estate investor in New York City, an author, and the founder of the Old York Library (now the Seymour B. Durst Old York Library).

Frank Dyer is a former sports writer in New York City.

Martin Ebon* worked for the U.S. Office of War Information during World War II for the Foreign Policy Association and for the *Voice of America*. He was the author of more than 70 books, ranging from *World Communism Today* (1948) to *KGB: Death and Rebirth* (1994).

Brenda Edmands (MFA University of Southern Maine) is a lecturer and faculty tutor in the English Department at the University of Southern Maine.

Susan Edmiston is a native of New York City who lives in the San Francisco Bay area. She is a freelance writer and the author of *Literary New York: A History and Guide* (1976).

Edward A. Eigen (PhD Massachusetts Institute of Technology) is an assistant professor in the Department of History and Theory at Princeton University, as well as its departmental representative.

Fred Eisenstadt* studied architecture and worked in the management of a computer network for the City of New York.

Peter Eisenstadt (PhD New York University) is the editor in chief of *The Encyclopedia of New York State* and was the managing editor of the first edition of *The Encyclopedia of New York City*.

Nan Ellin (PhD Columbia University) is the planning program director in the School of Geographical Sciences and Urban Planning at Arizona State University. She is also an associate professor in the department and the author of *Postmodern Urbanism* (1995).

David Maldwyn Ellis (PhD Cornell University) retired from his position as an emeritus professor of history at Hamilton College. He is the author of *New York State and City* (1979).

Robert Ellwood (PhD University of Chicago) is Distinguished Emeritus Professor of religion at the University of Southern California. His books include *Campus Secrets: College Tales of Love and Loathing, Fear and Favor* (2007) and *Many Peoples, Many Faiths: Women and Men in the World Religions*, 9th edn. (2008).

Linda Elsroad (MA Columbia University) is a former student services administrator for the Bank Street College of Education (1982–91).

Michael Emery is former professor of journalism at California State University. He specialized in Middle East reporting and coauthored *The Press and America*, 7th edn. (1992).

Stephen D. Engle (PhD American History, Florida State University) is a professor in the History Department at Florida Atlantic University. His publications include *The American Civil War: This Mighty Scourge of War* (2003).

Anne Epstein (BA Barnard College) is a project editor for *The Encyclopedia of New York City*, 2nd edn.

Robert Ernst* (PhD Columbia University) was professor emeritus of history at Adelphi University and the author of *Rufus King: American Federalist* (1968), *Weakness Is a Crime: The Life of Bernarr Macfadden* (1991), and *Immigrant Life in New York City, 1825–1863* (1994).

Alice Fahs (PhD New York University) is an associate professor of history at the University of California, Irvine. She is author of *The Imagined Civil War: Popular Literature of the North and South, 1861–1865* (2002).

Talia Falk (BA English, Columbia University, JD Harvard University) is a contributor to *The Encyclopedia of New York City*, 2nd edn.

Henry Feingold (PhD History, New York University) is a professor emeritus at Baruch College specializing in American Jewish history and holocaust studies. His most recent work is titled *Silent No More: Saving the Jews of Russia. The American Jewish Effort, 1967–1989* (2007).

Garrett A. Felber worked at the Institute for Research in African-American Studies at Columbia University with Professor Manning Marable.

Johanna Fernandez (PhD Columbia University) is professor at Baruch College, City University of New York. She is currently working on a book on the Young Lords Party, the Puerto Rican counterpart of the Black Panther Party.

Marc Ferris (MA University of Massachusetts, Amherst) has taught history at City College of New York and Pace University. He is a freelance contributor to many journals, magazines, and newspapers.

Corinne T. Field (PhD Columbia University) is an adjunct professor at the University of Virginia specializing in women and work in nineteenth-century New York City.

Peter Field (PhD Columbia University) is a professor of American history at Canterbury University in New Zealand. He recently published *Ralph Waldo Emerson: The Making of a Democratic Intellectual* (2003).

Albert Figone (PhD) is a former professor emeritus of sports history and psychology at Humboldt University. He is the author of numerous publications and a regular contributor to the *Journal of Sport and Social Issues*.

Christopher M. Finan (PhD American History, Columbia University) is president of the American Booksellers Foundation for Free Expression. He is the author of *Alfred E. Smith: The Happy Warrior* (2002) and *From the Palmer Raids to the PATRIOT Act: A History of the Fight for Free Speech in America* (2007).

John Fink, a native of Brooklyn and a subway aficionado, is a historian specializing in railroads and central European topics.

Anita Finkel* (PhD University of California, Los Angeles) was the editor and publisher of the *New Dance Review* and an editor at *Collier's Encyclopedia*. She also taught at the University of California at Los Angeles.

Jeff Finlay (PhD New York University) was an administrator at the American Studies Crossroads Program, which is sponsored by Georgetown University.

Ellen Fletcher is a writer and interpretive planner focusing on the history of New York Harbor. Her writing includes *South Street: A Photographic Guide to New York's Historic Seaport* (1977).

Richard W. Flint (MA Cooperstown Graduate Programs, State University of New York) is the executive director of the Howard County Historical Society in Ellicott City, Maryland. He is a past president of the Circus Historical Society.

Nancy V. Flood is the managing editor (2005–8) of *The Encyclopedia of New York City*, 2nd edn.

Martha Foley is an archivist and was an associate producer of the documentary *Rebel Girl* (1993). She is the former curator of the Elizabeth Gurley Flynn Collection at the Tamiment Collection of New York University and is parish archivist at Grace Church in Brooklyn.

James D. Folts (PhD University of Rochester) is head of researcher services at the New York State Archives in Albany. He is the author of *Cohocton, New York, 1794–1994* (1994).

Nancy Foner, Distinguished Professor of Sociology at Hunter College and the Graduate Center of the City University of New York, is the author of *From Ellis Island to JFK: New York's Two Great Waves of Immigration* (2000) and *In a New Land: A Comparative View of Immigration* (2005).

Thelma Foote* (PhD Harvard University) was associate professor in the Department of History and the African-American Studies program at the University of California, Irvine, and author of *Black and White Manhattan: The History of Racial Formation in Colonial New York City* (2004).

Stanford M. Forrester is a freelance writer.

Ella M. Foshay, formerly curator of painting and sculpture at the New-York Historical Society, is an art historian and author of *Mr. Luman Reed's Picture Gallery: A Pioneer Collection of American Art* (1990).

Gino Francesconi (MA New York University) established the first archive at Carnegie Hall in 1986 and opened the Rose Museum at Carnegie Hall in 1991, where he is director.

Luis H. Francia is an adjunct professor of Asian Pacific American Studies at New York University. He is also a poet, critic, and journalist who has published in the *Village Voice* and the *Daily News*. He is the author of *The Arctic Archipelago and Other Poems* (1992).

Wayne Franklin (PhD University of Pittsburgh), professor of English and director of American Studies at the University of Connecticut, is the author of *The New World of James Fenimore Cooper* (1982) and *James Fenimore Cooper: The Early Years* (2007).

Janet Frankston Lorin (MS Columbia University) is a reporter for Bloomberg News in New York City. She previously worked for the *Atlanta Journal-Constitution*, the *Akron Beacon Journal*, and the Associated Press, Newark bureau.

Steve Fraser (PhD Princeton University) is a former vice president and executive editor of Basic Books and an executive editor at Houghton Mifflin. He is the author of *Labor Will Rule: Sidney Hillman and the Rise of American Labor* (1991).

John W. Freeman (BA Yale University) is a former associate editor and reviewer for *Opera News* (1960–2000). He is the author of *The Metropolitan Opera Stories of the Great Operas* (1984) and a coauthor of *The Golden Horseshoe* (1965) and *Toscanini* (1987).

Joshua B. Freeman (PhD Rutgers University) is a professor of history at Queens College and the Graduate Center, City University of New York. His books on the history of labor include *Working-Class New York: Life and Labor since World War II* (2001).

Alice Cooney Frelinghuysen is the Anthony W. and Lulu C. Wang Curator of American Decorative Arts at the Metropolitan Museum of Art. She is the author of *American Porcelain, 1770–1920* (1989) and *Louis Comfort Tiffany and Laurelton Hall: An Artist's Country Estate* (2006).

John W. Frick (PhD New York University) is a professor of theater history and dramatic literature at the University of Virginia. He is the author of *New York's First Theatrical Center: The Rialto at Union Square* (1985).

Robert Friedel (PhD Johns Hopkins University) is a professor of the history of technology and science and environmental history at the University of Maryland. He is the author of *A Material World* (1988).

Walter Friedman (PhD Columbia University) is a research fellow at the Harvard Business School. He is also a coeditor of *Business History Review* and a former deputy managing director for *The Encyclopedia of New York City*, 1st edn.

Erik J. Friis* was the editor of *Scandinavian Review* and director of publications for the American-Scandinavian Foundation for 25 years. He was also the publisher of the *American-Scandinavian Bulletin* and the book series *Library of Nordic Literature*.

William Lee Frost is the president and treasurer of the Lucius N. Littauer Foundation.

John Gaber (PhD Urban Planning, Columbia University) is alumni professor for the Community Planning Program at Auburn University. He has published many articles on ethnographic research methods and ethnic enterprises.

Edmund Gaither (MFA Brown University) is director and curator of the Museum of the National Center for Afro-American Artists in Boston.

John J. Gallagher is a writer, historian, and lecturer in Brooklyn, New York. He is also the author of *The Battle of Brooklyn, 1776* (1991).

Wendy Gamber (PhD Brandeis University) is a professor of history at Indiana University. She is the author *The Boardinghouse in Nineteenth-Century America* (2007).

Steven D. Garber (PhD Rutgers University) has taught biology at many universities and worked as a biologist at the American Museum of Natural History and the New York City Department of Parks and Recreation. He heads the consulting firm Worldwide Ecology and is the author of *The Urban Naturalist* (1987).

Deborah S. Gardner (PhD Columbia University) was the first managing editor of *The Encyclopedia of New York City*, 1st edn. She is special assistant to the provost at Hunter College.

Neal C. Garelik is the president and a principal of Excel Global Security and was senior managing director of the Garment Center Economic Security Council.

William M. Gargan (MA and MS Columbia University) is the language and literature bibliographer at the Brooklyn College Library. He is also a coauthor, with Sue Sharma, of *Find That Tune: An Index to Rock, Folk-Rock, Disco and Soul in Collections* (1988).

Bradford Garnett is a real estate consultant in New York City and Westchester County.

Alex Garvin is president and chief executive officer of Alex Garvin and Associates, Inc., a New York–based urban planning consulting firm, and an adjunct professor of urban planning and management at Yale University. He has served as deputy commissioner of New York City Housing and City Planning.

Carol Gayle (MA Columbia University) is an associate professor and chair of the Department of History at Lake Forest College. She is also associate director of the Graduate Program in Liberal Studies.

Margot Gayle is an expert on cast-iron architecture and a founding member of the Friends of Cast Iron Architecture. She is the recipient of the New York City Mayor's Doris Freedman Award (1986), the Landmarks Conservancy Lucy Moses Award (1990), and the Municipal Arts Society Jacqueline Kennedy Onassis Medal (1997).

Charles Gehring (PhD Indiana University) has been the director of the New Netherlands Project since 1987. He is a Fulbright Scholar and the author of numerous articles on the Hudson River Valley and the colonial Dutch.

Penelope Gelwicks (BA King's College) is a licensed New York City tour guide and writes essays about life in the city.

Rosalie Genevro is the executive director of the Architectural League of New York.

Eugenia Georges (PhD Columbia University) is professor and chair of anthropology at Rice University. She is the author of *The Making of a Transitional Community: Migration, Development and Cultural Change in the Dominican Republic* (1990).

Donald F. M. Gerardi (PhD Columbia University) is Emeritus Professor of History and Religious Studies at Brooklyn College, City University of New York. His published work has focused on eighteenth-century Anglo-American religion.

Rowan Moore Gerety (BA Columbia University) graduated in 2007 and is a project editor for *The Encyclopedia of New York City*, 2nd edn.

Marvin E. Gettleman (PhD Johns Hopkins University) is a professor emeritus of history at Polytechnic University and a former member of the editorial board of *Science and Society*.

Robert J. Gibbons (PhD Yale University) is the former executive director of the International Insurance Foundation. He is now a partner in Debevoise and Plimpton LLP.

Ann C. Gibson is a former assistant archivist at Chase Manhattan Bank.

Timothy J. Gilfoyle (PhD Columbia University) is a professor of history at Loyola University, Chicago. He is the author of *City of Eros: New York City, Prostitution and the Commercialization of Sex, 1790–1920* (1992) and *A Pickpocket's Tale: The Underworld of Nineteenth-Century New York* (2006).

Juliana F. Gilheany (PhD New York University) has taught at Fordham University, New York University, and Manhattan College.

Paul A. Gilje (PhD Brown University) is the George Lynn Cross Research Professor of History at the University of Oklahoma and the author of *Rioting in America* (1996) and *The Road to Mobocracy: Popular Disorder in New York City, 1763–1834* (1987).

Russell S. Gilmore (PhD American History, University of Wisconsin) is former director of the Harbor Defense Museum in Brooklyn and the author of *Guarding America's Front Door: Harbor Forts in the Defense of New York City* (1983) and *Hard at Play: Leisure in America, 1840–1940* (1992).

Val Ginter (BS Northwestern University, MA State University of New York) has taught at Kingsborough Community College, City University of New York, and LaGuardia Community College, City University of New York. He is the author of *Manhattan Trivia: The Ultimate Challenge* (1985).

Lisa Gitelman (PhD Columbia University) is an associate professor of media studies at Catholic University and has worked on the Thomas A. Edison Papers Project.

James Glass (JD) is a former president of the Marshall Chess Club in New York City.

Joyce Gold has headed the Joyce Gold History Tours of New York for 30 years. She has authored two guidebooks: *From Windmills to the World Trade Center: A Walking Guide to Lower Manhattan History* (1982) and *From Trout Stream to Bohemia: A Walking Guide to Greenwich Village History* (1988).

Joanne Abel Goldman (PhD State University of New York, Stony Brook) is an associate professor of history at the University of Northern Iowa.

Eric A. Goldstein (LLM New York University School of Law) is New York City environment director at the Natural Resources Defense Council (NRDC) and an adjunct professor at New York University School of Law.

Robert I. Goler (MA Case Western Reserve University) is the former curator of decorative and industrial arts at the Chicago Historical Society. He is the author of *Capital City: New York after the Revolution* (1987) and the editor of *Federal New York: A Symposium* (1990).

David L. González is a reporter for the *New York Times*.

Evelyn Gonzalez is professor and chair of the History Department at William Paterson University of New Jersey. She is the author of *The Bronx* (2004).

Lynn D. Gordon (PhD University of Chicago) is an associate professor of history at the University of Rochester. She is the author of *Education and Professions* (2002).

Elliott J. Gorn (PhD Yale University) is history professor at Brown University and author of *Dillinger's Wild Ride: The Year That Made America's Public Enemy Number One* (2009) and *Mother Jones: The Most Dangerous Woman in America* (2001).

Brenda Dixon Gottschild (PhD New York University) is a dance critic, professor, and performer focusing on Afrocentric and postmodern dance and professor emerita of dance at Temple University.

Leslie Gourse* was a freelance writer on culture for newspapers and magazines. She wrote many books on famous jazz musicians and on New York City, including *The Best Guided Walking Tours of New York City* (1989).

Chandler B. Grannis* was the editor in chief of *Publishers Weekly* and was later a contributing editor.

Martha W. Grannis has been a freelance copy editor.

James Grant is the editor of *Grant's Interest Rate Observer* and the author of *Bernard Baruch: The Adventures of a Wall Street Legend* (1983).

Sigurd Grava* was professor emeritus of urban planning at Columbia University and served as a planning and transportation consultant in some 25 countries. Among his many works is *Urban Transportation Systems: Choices for Communities* (2003).

Helen Graves (BA Princeton University) is the former director of the Academy of American Poets.

Barbara Grcevic (JD Brooklyn Law School) is a court attorney in the Brooklyn Criminal Court Law Department. She is the author of the New York State Women's Bar Association's first written history and the author of the history of the Brooklyn Women's Bar Association.

Ashbel Green (MA Columbia University) is a native of New York City and was a senior editor and vice president for Knopf Publishing Group at Random House.

Michael Green is a doctoral candidate in American history at Columbia University, where he is researching the ideology of the Republican Party during the Civil War.

William Green (PhD Columbia University), professor of English at Queens College, is the author of many books and articles on theater and drama. He is also a past president of the International Federation for Theatre Research.

Brian Greenberg (PhD Princeton University) is the Jules L. Plangere Jr. Professor of American Social History at Monmouth University. He has contributed to several other encyclopedias and published widely on social and labor history in the United States.

Cheryl Greenberg is the Paul E. Raether Distinguished Professor of History at Trinity College in Hartford, Connecticut, where she researches and teaches African American history and race and ethnicity. Her most recent book is *Troubling the Waters: Black-Jewish Relations in the American Century* (2006).

Larry A. Greene (PhD Columbia University) is a professor of History at Seton Hall University where he is also a former director of the Multicultural Program. He is the author of articles published in *The Encyclopedia of the Harlem Renaissance* (2004), *The Encyclopedia of American Economic History* (1980), and several periodicals.

William D. Griffin (PhD Columbia University) is a professor of history at St. John's University specializing in Irish and military history. He is also the author of *The Book of Irish Americans* (1990).

Gerald N. Grob (PhD Northwestern University) is Henry E. Sigerist Professor of the History of Medicine Emeritus at the Institute for Heath, Heath Care Policy, and Aging Research at Rutgers University. He is the author of *The State and the Mentally Ill*.

Nancy Groce is a research associate and former curator at the Smithsonian Center for Folklife and Cultural Heritage. She is an ethnomusicologist and the author of *New York: Songs of the City* (1999).

Carol Groneman (PhD University of Rochester) is professor of history emerita at John Jay College of Criminal Justice and the Graduate Center of the City University of New York. Her historical research focuses on immigration, cities, and female sexuality.

Anthony Gronowicz (PhD University of Pennsylvania) is a former professor at Borough of Manhattan Community College. He also was the Green Party candidate for the New York City mayoral election in 2005 and is still active in the party.

Donna Ann Grossman did her graduate work at Columbia University.

Robert S. Grumet is a retired National Parks Service archaeologist and the author of *Native American Place Names in New York City* (1981). He is currently a senior research associate with the McNeil Center for Early American Studies at the University of Pennsylvania.

Betty Kaplan Gubert is a retired director of general research and reference at the Schomburg Center for Research on Black Culture of the New York Public Library. She has edited and compiled numerous works on black culture.

Allen C. Guelzo (PhD University of Pennsylvania) is the Henry R. Luce Professor of the Civil War Era and professor of history at Gettysburg College. His books include *Lincoln's Emancipation Proclamation: The End of Slavery in America* (2004).

Jeffrey S. Gurock (PhD Columbia University) is Libby M. Klaperman Professor of Jewish History at Yeshiva University and the author of *Judaism's Encounter with American Sports* (2005).

Owen Gutfreund (PhD Columbia University) is associate professor of urban affairs and planning at Hunter College, City University of New York. He is the author of *Twentieth Century Sprawl: Highways and the Reshaping of the American Landscape* (2004).

Laura Gwinn (MFA Columbia University) is a freelance writer and public relations professional.

Mona Hadler (PhD Columbia University) is a professor of art history at Brooklyn College and the City University of New York Graduate Center. Her work focuses on abstract expressionist painters and sculptors.

Paula Hajar (EdD Harvard University Graduate School of Education) is an educator and activist in New York City's Arab American community. Her doctoral dissertation was titled "Arab Immigrant Parents and American Schoolpeople: An Ethnography of a Cross-Cultural Relationship." She is a cofounder of the Bronx Charter School for Better Learning.

George Haikalis is the president of the Institute for Rational Urban Mobility, Inc.

David C. Hammack (PhD Columbia University) is a Haydn Professor of History at Case Western Reserve University. His publications include *Power and Society: Greater New York at the Turn of the Century* (1983).

Ian Hancock (PhD London University) has represented the Romani people in the United Nations and the United States Holocaust Memorial Council. He is a professor of linguistics at the University of Texas–Austin, where he also founded the Romani Archives and Documentation Center.

Eleanor Hannah (PhD University of Chicago) is a former professor of American history at the University of Minnesota–Duluth. She specializes in social and cultural history at the turn of the twentieth century.

R. L. Harris, Jr. (PhD Northwestern University) is a professor of Afro-American history at the Africana Studies and Research Center of Cornell University. He is the author of more than 40 articles and chapters in academic journals and books.

Marjorie Harrison did graduate work at Columbia University.

C. Lowell Harriss (PhD Columbia University) is professor emeritus of economics at Columbia University. His publications include *The American Economy: Principles, Practices, Policies* (1953).

Gabriel Haslip-Viera (PhD) is an associate professor of sociology and the director of the Latin American and Latino Studies program at City College of New York. His publications include *Latinos in New York: Communities in Transition* (1996) and *Crime and Punishment in Late Colonial Mexico City, 1692–1810* (1999).

Constantine G. Hatzidimitriou (PhD Columbia University) is a senior administrator with the New York City Department of Education and adjunct professor at St. John's University. He has published articles on Byzantine and modern Greek history.

William J. Hausman (PhD University of Illinois) is Chancellor Professor of Economics at the College of William and Mary and chair of the department. He is a coauthor of *Global Electrification: Multinational Enterprise and International Finance in the History of Light and Power, 1878–1978* (2008).

Pamela W. Hawkes (MArch University of California–Berkley) is an architect with Ann Beha Associates in Boston. She specializes in historic preservation.

Barbara Haws (MA New York University) is the archivist and historian for the New York Philharmonic.

Mary Hedge (MA Georgetown University) is a graduate of the program in archival management at New York University and was the historian and archivist for American Express.

Anthony Heilbut (PhD Harvard University) writes on music, including gospel music. His publications include *The Gospel Sound: Good News and Bad Times* (1971) and *Thomas Mann: A Biography* (1985).

Alexander Heilner is a photojournalist and visual artist who lives in Prospect Heights, Brooklyn, and teaches at the Maryland Institute College of Art in Baltimore. His landscape photographs, videos, and other projects have appeared in exhibitions and publications throughout the United States and internationally.

Marjorie Heins (JD Harvard University) directs the Free Expression Policy Project and is the author of *Not in Front of the Children: "Indecency," Censorship, and the Innocence of Youth* (2007), *Sex, Sin, and Blasphemy: A Guide to America's Censorship Wars* (1998). She was a fellow at the Brennan Center for Justice (2004–7) at New York University.

Steven Heller is cofounder and cochair of the MFA Design as Author program at the School of Visual Arts in New York City. He was the art director of the *New York Times* for more than 30 years and is still a regular contributor there.

Clara J. Hemphill is the founding editor of InsideSchools.org, a resource for New York City parents. She also is a contributor to *New York Newsday*, where she shared a Pulitzer Prize in 1991.

Benjamin Hemric is a contributor to *The Encyclopedia of New York City*, 2nd edn.

Floyd M. Henderson (PhD University of Kansas) is emeritus professor of geography and planning at the State University of New York, Albany, and the author of numerous publications.

Judith Adler Hennessee is an author and journalist who contributes to several national magazines. She is the former media columnist for *Manhattan, Inc.*

Gary D. Hermalyn (PhD Columbia University) is the executive director of the Bronx County Historical Society and president of the History of New York Project. He has produced 147 publications and has served as a Centennial Historian of New York City.

Michele Herman (MFA Columbia University) is a freelance writer who specializes in subjects relating to New York City. She contributes regularly to *Metropolis*, the *Sun*, and various other publications.

Thomas M. Hilbink (PhD New York University) is an assistant professor of legal studies at the University of Massachusetts–Amherst. He specializes in American law, politics, and social movement history and theory.

E. G. Hill* (graduate degree, Royal Academy of Dramatic Arts) was a professor emeritus of drama and oratory at Dartmouth College.

Robert Hillenbrand is an instructor and chairman of special education in the Teacher Education Division at Felician College and former head track coach at Northern Highlands Regional High School in Allendale, New Jersey.

Patricia Hills is a professor of art history at Boston University. She has written multiple books and essays on nineteenth- and twentieth-century American art, African American artists, and art and politics. Among her publications are *Modern Art in the USA: Issues and Controversies of the 20th Century* (2001) and *Painting Harlem Modern: The Art of Jacob Lawrence* (2009).

Lee R. Hiltzik (PhD State University of New York, Stony Brook) is chief archivist and university archivist for the Rockefeller Archives. He specializes in the history of science and Rockefeller University's institutional history.

Bernard Hirschhorn (PhD Columbia University) has been the Chairman of the Social Studies Department at Fiorello H. La Guardia High School of Music and Art and Performing Arts, editor of the urban history issue of the *Magazine of History*, and the author of a number of articles and a biography of Richard S. Childs.

Graham Hodges is the George Dorland Langdon, Jr., Professor of History at Colgate University. His published works include *Root and Branch: African Americans in New York and East Jersey, 1613–1863* (1999) and *Taxi: A Social History of the New York City Cabdriver* (2007).

Calvin B. Holder (PhD Harvard University) is a professor of history at the College of Staten Island. He specializes in immigration and ethnic groups in American history.

Eric Hollingsworth is a former research data specialist at Weill Cornell Medical College.

Harold Holzer is senior vice president for external affairs at the Metropolitan Museum of Art in New York City. He is the author of more than 30 books on the Abraham Lincoln era.

Joel Honig is a contributor to the *Dictionary of American Biography*, the *Dictionary of American History*, and the annual supplement to the *Book of Knowledge*.

Clifton Hood (PhD Columbia University) is professor of history at Hobart and William Smith Colleges and the author of *722 Miles: The Building of the Subways and How They Transformed New York* (1993).

Kim Hopper (PhD Columbia University) is a professor of clinical sociomedical sciences at the Mailman School of Public Health at Columbia University. He is also a research scientist at the Nathan S. Kline Institute for Psychiatric Research and a founder of the Coalition for the Homeless.

Joseph A. Horrigan is the vice president of communications and exhibits at the Pro Football Hall of Fame. He is the author of *The Official Pro Football Hall of Fame Answer Book* (1993).

Raymond D. Horton (PhD Columbia University) is the Frank R. Lautenberg Professor of Ethics and Corporate Governance at the Columbia University Business School. He is a former president of the Citizens Budget Commission and the author, with Charles Brecher, of *Power Failure: New York City Politics and Policy since 1960* (1993).

Elizabeth Hovey (PhD Columbia University) taught at La Guardia Community College. Her dissertation was titled "Stamping Out Smut: The Enforcement of Obscenity Laws, 1872–1936."

Anne H. Hoy (MA New York University) is an author and editor of works of photography and art history. She is a former curator of the International Center of Photography and managing editor of the *Art Bulletin*.

Lee Hudson (PhD University of Texas, Austin) is a deputy commissioner at the New York City Commission on Human Rights and was a community liaison and founding director of the Mayor's Office for the Lesbian and Gay Community (1983–90). She coauthored with Steve Hogan *Completely Queer: The Gay and Lesbian Encyclopedia* (1998).

Deborah Huisken is a leadership coach and former editor and publisher of *Hoppin'*, an international newsletter devoted to the Lindy Hop.

Kathleen Hulser is a public historian at the New-York Historical Society, where she has mounted numerous exhibitions.

Leon Hurwitz (PhD Syracuse University) is a professor emeritus of political science at Cleveland State University. His published works include *Historical Dictionary of Censorship in the United States* (1985) and *Contemporary Perspectives on European Integration: Attitudes, Nongovernmental Behavior, and Collective Decision Making* (1980).

Yarema Hutsaliuk (PhD Syracuse University) studied military history at Columbia University and was the public affairs officer for the 369th Regiment of the New York National Guard and the 15th Regiment, New York Guard.

Michelle Hutt (BA Columbia University) studied archaeology and American history.

Gordon Hyatt (BFA) is a documentary film producer and former president of the Associates of the Art Commission (1986–88).

Irina Ikonsky (BA Columbia University) graduated in 2009.

Paul Israel (PhD Rutgers University) is a research professor at Rutgers University and the director and general editor of the Thomas A. Edison Papers Project.

Maurice Isserman (PhD University of Rochester) is the James L. Ferguson Professor of History at Hamilton College. His published works include *America Divided: The Civil War of the 1960s* (2000) and *Fallen Giants: The History of Himalayan Mountaineering from the Age of Empire to the Age of Extremes* (2008).

Mark A. Izeman is a senior attorney for the Urban Program at the Natural Resources Defense Council. He is the author of *The New York Environment Book* (1990).

Ira Jacknis (PhD University of Chicago) is a research anthropologist at the Phoebe A. Hearst Museum of Anthropology at the University of California, Berkeley. A specialist in the history of anthropology, he is the author of *The Storage Box of Tradition: Kwakiutl Art, Anthropologists, and Museums, 1881–1981* (2002).

Barbara Jackson (MA University of Illinois) recently retired as English department chair at Blind Brook High School in Westchester County.

Kenneth T. Jackson is the Jacques Barzun Professor of History and Social Sciences at Columbia University and the editor of this encyclopedia.

Kevan Jackson (BA Dartmouth, MBA Columbia) spent several years as a music agent and is currently a vice president at Westwood One. He lives with his family in Manhattan.

Steven H. Jaffe (PhD Harvard University) is an independent historian. He is former senior projects manager at the New-York Historical Society and was senior historian at the South Street Seaport Museum.

David James (PhD University of Pennsylvania) is a professor in the Department of Cinema at the University of Southern California. His published works include *Stan Brakhage: Filmmaker* (2006).

Shan Jayakumar is an architect, photojournalist, and writer based in New York City and was educated at Columbia and Cambridge universities.

David R. Johnson (PhD) is a professor of history and vice provost at the University of Texas–San Antonio. He is the author of *Policing the Urban Underworld* (1979), *American Law Enforcement: A History* (1981), and *Illegal Tender* (1995).

Emily Johnson (BA Columbia University) graduated with a degree in English in 2010.

Marjorie Johnson is a contributor to the *Staten Island Historian* and a long-time volunteer in the Staten Island Historical Society library. She is a coauthor of *The Swaim–Tysen Family of Staten Island, New York, New Jersey, and the Southern States* (1984).

Peter J. Johnson has been employed by the Rockefeller family since 1976. He is a coauthor of several books on the Rockefeller family.

Steven Johnson is the former manager of the Bronx Zoo Library and a supervising archivist and librarian for the New York Zoological Society (now the World Conservation Society).

Celedonia Jones served as Manhattan Borough Historian from 1997 to 2006 and also served on the Legislative Committee of the Association of Public Historians of New York State. He is a member of the Archivists Round Table of Metropolitan New York and was named 1998 Centennial Historian by the mayor of New York City.

Susanna A. Jones (MPhil Columbia University) is the current head of school at Holton-Arms School in Bethesda, Maryland, and the former head of school at the Ethel Walker School in Simsbury, Connecticut.

Thai Jones is a PhD student in the history department at Columbia University. He is the author of *A Radical Line: From the Labor Movement to the Weather Underground, One Family's Century of Conscience* (2004).

Jenna Weissman Joselit (PhD Columbia University) holds the Charles E. Smith Chair in Judaic Studies at the George Washington University Columbian College of Arts and Sciences. Her books include *Our Gang: Jewish Crime and the New York Jewish Community, 1900–1940* (1983) and *The Wonders of America: Reinventing Jewish Culture 1880–1950* (1994).

Michael Joseph is the rare book librarian in special collections and University Archives at Rutgers University and was previously a rare books librarian at the New-York Historical Society, where he helped to develop a research collection of early children's books.

Jacob Judd is a professor emeritus of history at the Herbert H. Lehman College and Graduate Center, City University of New York. He is the author of several publications, including *Colonial America: A Basic History* (1998).

Erica Judge (BA University of Virginia) is a native of New York City who worked for the U.S. Foreign Service.

Matthew Kachur is a writer and editor who has written widely on history and current events for a variety of audiences, especially younger readers.

Seth Kamil (MPhil Columbia University) is the director of Big Onion Walking Tours, a company that writes about and gives tours of New York City neighborhoods. He is the author of *Tripping Down Memory Lane: Walking Tours on the Jewish Lower East Side* (2000).

Nathan Kantrowitz is a former director of demographic studies, social planning, and education at the New York City Planning Department.

Howard Kaplan is a writer who contributes to the *Daily News* and other publications.

Isabelle Kaplan is retired from the Isabelle Kaplan Center for Languages and Cultures at Bennington College and does consultanting work.

James S. Kaplan (JD Columbia University) is a lawyer who also leads walking tours of New York City neighborhoods. He is the author of *New York Walks* (1992).

Edward Kasinec (PhD Columbia University) is the Chief of the Slavic and Baltic Division of the New York Public Library and author of numerous publications.

Philip Kasinitz (PhD New York University) is a sociology professor at Hunter College and the City University of New York Graduate Center. He is the author of *Becoming New Yorkers: Ethnographies of the "New" Second Generation* (2004).

Esther Katz (PhD New York University), adjunct associate professor of U.S. history and a senior research scholar at New York University, is the director of the Margaret Sanger Papers Project and editor of *The Selected Papers of Margaret Sanger* (2003–8).

Montana Katz (PhD Columbia University) is the author of *Get Smart: A Woman's Guide to Equality on Campus* (1988) and *The Gender Bias Prevention Book: Helping Girls and Women to Have Satisfying Lives and Careers* (1996).

David Kaufman (PhD Brandeis University) is the Robert and Florence Kaufman Chair in Jewish Studies at Hofstra University. He is the author of *Shul with a Pool: The "Synagogue-Center" in American Jewish History* (1999).

Peter Keepnews (BA Grinnell College) is a staff editor at the *New York Times* specializing in jazz music.

James M. Keller (MPhil Yale University), a musicologist and journalist, is program annotator of the New York Philharmonic and the San Francisco Symphony. From 1990 to 2000 he was the music editor at the *New Yorker*.

Lisa Keller (PhD Cambridge University) is associate professor of history at Purchase College, State University of New York. She is the author of *Triumph of Order: Democracy and Public Space in New York and London* (2009) and executive editor of *The Encyclopedia of New York City*, 2nd edn.

Mollie Keller is an independent historian who has worked as a researcher, writer, archivist, planner, and curator for clients ranging from the U.S. Customs Service to local historical societies.

Brian Kellow is the features editor of *Opera News* and the author of three books: *Can't Help Singing: The Life of Eileen Farrell* (1999), *The Bennetts: An Acting Family* (2004), and *Ethel Merman: A Life* (2007).

Nicholas Kelly (BA Columbia University) graduated with a degree in history.

Kevin Kenny (PhD Columbia University) is a professor of history at Boston College. He is the author of *The American Irish: A History* (2000).

Barry Kernfeld (PhD Cornell University) is a jazz scholar and musician as well as archivist for Pennsylvania State University.

K. Austin Kerr is a professor emeritus of history at Ohio State University. He is the past president of the Ohio Academy of History and the author of *American Railroad Politics, 1914–1920: Rates, Wages, and Efficiency* (1968), and several other publications.

Thomas Kessner is a professor of history at the Graduate School and University Center, City University of New York, and the author of *Capital City: New York City and the Men behind America's Rise to Dominance, 1860–1900* (2003), *Fiorello H. La Guardia and the Making of Modern New York* (1989), and *The Golden Door: Italian and Jewish Immigrant Mobility in New York City, 1880–1915* (1977).

Joy M. Kestenbaum (MA New York University Institute of Fine Arts) is the former Art Librarian for Purchase College. She has also taught in the School of Architecture and Fine Arts of the New York Institute of Technology.

Edward F. Keuchel (PhD Cornell University) is a professor emeritus of history at Florida State University and the former director of the Reichelt Oral History Program at Florida State University. He is the author of *American Economic History: From Abundance to Constraint* (1989).

Madhulika S. Khandelwal (PhD Carnegie–Mellon University) is an associate professor of urban studies and the director of the Asian/American Center at Queens College.

Cynthia A. Kierner (PhD University of Virginia) is a professor of history at George Mason University and author of *Traders and Gentlefold: The Livingstons of New York, 1675–1790* (1992).

Illsoo Kim immigrated to the United States from Korea in 1970. He is the author of *New Urban Immigrants: The Korean Community in New York* (1981).

David J. S. King (PhD Johns Hopkins University) is a freelance translator. He has also written children's books such as *Jelly Everywhere!: As Retold to His Daughter* (2007).

Vitaut Kipel is the director of the Belarusian Institute of Arts and Sciences in New York City. He has been affiliated with the New York Public Library for several decades.

George B. Kirsch (PhD Columbia University) is a professor of history at Manhattan College and the author of *The Creation of American Team Sports: Baseball and Cricket, 1838–72* (1989).

Barbara Kirshenblatt-Gimblett (PhD Indiana University) is a professor of performance studies at the Tisch School of the Arts at New York University and an affiliated professor in the Hebrew and Judaic Studies Department at New York University. She is a coauthor of *Image before My Eyes: A Photographic History of Jewish Life in Poland, 1864–1939* (1977).

Benjamin J. Klebaner is a professor of economics at City College of New York and a former associate editor of the *Journal of Money, Credit and Banking* (1975–79). He is the author of *American Commercial Banking: A History*.

John M. Kleeberg (DPhil Oxford University, JD New York University School of Law) served as curator of modern coins and currency at the American Numismatic Society from 1990 until 2000. He now practices law in New York City.

Christopher Klemek is an assistant professor of history at George Washington University. He co-curated a Rockefeller Foundation Exhibition at the Municipal Art Society and coedited the accompanying publication *Block by Block: Jane Jacobs and the Future of New York* (2008).

Amie Klempnauer (MA Union Theological Seminary) wrote the thesis "A Perfectly Normal Place: Eco-Justice and the Church in Fernald, Ohio" for her degree.

Margaret M. Knapp (PhD City University of New York) is a professor of theater and an administrator at Arizona State University. She writes on American theater history and American musical theater.

Richard Kobliner, a researcher, consultant, writer, and teacher, is affiliated with several professional organizations of American historians, as well as with the Association of Teacher Educators and the National Council for Social Studies.

Gerard Koeppel (BA Wesleyan University) is an independent historian. He is the author of *Water for Gotham: A History* (2000) and *Bond of Union: Building the Erie Canal and the American Empire* (2009).

Carolyn Kopp (MA University of California, Los Angeles) is the former archivist of Teachers Insurance and Annuity Association, College Retirement Equities Fund.

Anne E. Kornblut (BA Columbia College) is a political journalist for the *Washington Post*. She has also worked at the *New York Daily News*, the *Boston Globe*, and the *New York Times*.

Virginia Sánchez Korrol (PhD State University of New York, Stony Brook) is professor emerita of Puerto Rican and Latino studies at Brooklyn College, City University of New York. Her publications include *From Colonia to Community: The History of Puerto Ricans in New York* (1994) and *Latinas in the United States: A Historical Encyclopedia* (2006).

Hadassa Kosak (PhD City University of New York) is an associate professor of history at Stern College for Women at Yeshiva University. She is the author of *Cultures of Opposition: Jewish Immigrant Workers, New York City, 1881–1905* (2000).

William C. Kostlevy (PhD University of Notre Dame) is an associate professor of history and political science at Tabor College. He has served as archivist and special collections librarian for Asbury Theological Seminary and is the author of the *Historical Dictionary of the Holiness Movement* (2001).

Frances Kraljic (PhD New York University) is the chair of the Department of History, Philosophy, and Political Science at Kingsborough Community College. He is the author of *Croatian Migration to and from the United States, 1900–1914* (1978).

Elizabeth J. Kramer (JD New York University School of Law) graduated from Yale University and is a former adjunct instructor of legal writing at Brooklyn Law School. She is a former Assistant U.S. Attorney at the U.S. Attorney's Office in Brooklyn.

Susan Kriete is a reference librarian in the Department of Prints, Photographs, and Architectural Collections at the New-York Historical Society.

Walter Donald Kring* was the minister of the Unitarian Church of All Souls in New York City from 1955 to 1978 where he was also minister emeritus.

Carol Krinsky is a professor of art history at New York University's College of Arts and Science and the author of several books. She is the past president of the Society of Architectural Historians.

Jeffrey A. Kroessler (PhD Urban History, City University of New York Graduate Center, MS Queens College) is an associate professor in the Lloyd Sealy Library at John Jay College. He is the author of *New York, Year by Year* (2002) and *The Greater New York Sports Chronology* (2009).

Andrew A. Kryzak, a native New Yorker, is a history student at Columbia University.

Jonathan Kuhn (MA Columbia University) is the director of art and antiquities in the New York City Department of Parks and Recreation.

Mark Kurlansky is the author of *Nonviolence: Twenty-five Lessons from the History of a Dangerous Idea* (2006).

Michael Kwartler (MArch Cooper Union, MS Columbia University) is an architect, an urban designer, and the president of the Environmental Simulation Center, Ltd. He is also a fellow of the American Institute of Architects.

Chibu Lagman, a native of the Philippines, has conducted research on the Filipino community in New York City.

Michel S. Laguerre is a professor and the director of the Berkeley Center for Globalization and Information Technology at the University of California, Berkeley. He is the author of several books, including *Urban Multiculturalism and Globalization in New York City* (2003) and *Global Neighborhoods: Jewish Quarters in Paris, London, and Berlin* (2008).

Mark Laiosa (MS New York University) is a lifelong resident of the Bronx, a creator of numerous works, and former interim arts director at WBAI-FM in New York City.

Jacqueline Lalley (MFA Vermont College) is a communications consultant for nonprofit organizations and a contributing writer for publications including the *Onion* and *Rejected: Tales of the Failed, Dumped, and Canceled* (2008).

Meghan Lalonde (BA Purchase College) majored in journalism and is studying law.

Sarah Bradford Landau (PhD New York University) is a professor emerita of art history at New York University. She is the author of *Rise of the New York Skyscraper, 1865–1913* (1996), with Carl W. Condit, and *George B. Post, Architect: Picturesque Designer and Determined Realist* (1998). She is a former member of the New York City Landmarks Preservation Commission.

George J. Lankevich is professor emeritus of history at City University of New York and has published more than 20 volumes of history, including *New York City: A Short History* (2002).

Michael Lapp (PhD Johns Hopkins University) is the author of several publications, including "The Rise and Fall of Puerto Rico as a Social Laboratory, 1945–1965," *Social Science History* (Summer 1995).

Margaret Latimer (PhD Columbia University) has worked for several decades in the fields of urban and social history. She directed the Brooklyn Rediscovery program, a decade-long effort by the National Endowment for the Humanities.

Kate Lauber (MSLIS, Long Island University; BA Columbia University) is a librarian.

Peter L. Laurence (PhD University of Pennsylvania) is graduate director and assistant professor of architecture and architectural and urban history at Clemson University. His current research and recent publications focus on Jane Jacobs and the history of urban design.

Joshua Lederberg* (PhD Yale University) was a professor and president emeritus of Rockefeller University. He received a Nobel Prize for his work in bacteriology.

Sarah Henry Lederman (PhD Columbia University) is a history teacher at the Dalton School in Manhattan.

Roland Legiardi-Laura (BA Hampshire College) is a poet, a board member of the Nuyorican Poets Café, and a documentary filmmaker. His films include the work *Azul*.

Adele A. Lerner (MLS Columbia University) is the founder and archivist of the New York Hospital–Cornell Medical Center and the author of *An Introduction to the Medical Archives of the New York Hospital–Cornell Medical Center* (1976).

Steven A. Levine works as an archivist for the LaGuardia and Wagner Archives at LaGuardia Community College, City University of New York.

Erwin Levold (PhD Wayne State University) is a senior research archivist at the Rockefeller Archive Center in New York State. He specializes in the history of science.

Laura J. Lewison (MBA Columbia College) spent three years running a clinical research program in a pediatric intensive care unit at a children's hospital in Dallas.

Joseph S. Lieber (JD University of Michigan) is an Upper West Side native and a coauthor of *Frommer's Europe 2004* (2003). He now practices law in Boston.

Richard K. Lieberman is a professor of history at LaGuardia Community College, City University of New York, and the director of the LaGuardia and Wagner Archives. He is the author of *Steinway and Sons* (1995).

Eileen W. Lindner (PhD Union Theological Seminary) is the deputy general secretary for research and planning of the National Council of the Churches of Christ in the United States of America.

Charles H. Lippy held the LeRoy A. Martin Distinguished Professorship of Religious Studies at the University of Tennessee at Chattanooga in 2008. He is the author of *Faith in America: Changes, Challenges, New Directions* (2006) and *Do Real Men Pray? Images of the Christian Man and Male Spirituality in White Protestant America* (2005).

Arun Peter Lobo is deputy director of the Population Division of the New York City Department of City Planning. He has written on census survey methods, immigrant settlement patterns, and the demographic effect of immigration.

Martha S. LoMonaco (PhD New York University) is the resident director of theater studies and theater historian at Fairfield University. She specializes in theater history and performance.

Aileen Laura Love (BA Columbia University) is a medical student at Albert Einstein College of Medicine and is involved in Doctors against Drunk Driving. She is also a freelance writer and has been an associate editor for *Parenting* magazine.

John Lowe was formerly at the Gustave E. von Grunebaum Center for Near Eastern Studies at the University of California, Los Angeles.

Carol Lowrey (PhD City University of New York) is the curator of the permanent collection at the National Arts Club in New York City. She has also authored numerous articles and catalogues on American impressionism.

Aleeza Lubin (MA American Studies, Columbia University; BA History, York University; BEd University of Toronto) has researched contemporary social issues, particularly the changes in dating norms in the twentieth century.

James W. Lucas is a New York City–based lawyer, businessman, and Mormon historian. He is the author of "Mormons in New York City" in *New York Glory: Religions in the City* (2001) and a contributor to *City Saints: Mormons in the New York Metropolis* (2004).

Chad Ludington (PhD Columbia University) is assistant professor of history at the University of North Carolina State University and specializes in European intellectual history and the history of food and drink.

David M. Ludlum* (PhD Princeton University) was a well-known weather historian and founded and was editor of the magazine *Weatherwise*. He authored the *American Weather Book* (1982).

Michael A. Lutzker is a former associate professor of history at New York University and former codirector of the Graduate Program in Archival Management and Historical Editing there.

Bruce C. MacIntyre (PhD City University of New York) is a professor and the director of the Conservatory of Music at Brooklyn College. He has written numerous books and articles on Viennese classical music.

William C. MacKay (BA Drew University) is an editor of many works, such as Edwin Denby's *Dance Writings* (1998).

Richard Magat, former communications director of the Ford Foundation and retired president of the Edward W. Hazen Foundation, is a senior fellow at Community Resource Exchange. He is the author of *Unlikely Partners: Philanthropic Foundations and the Labor Movement* (1998).

Cecilia Magnusson (BA Barnard College) graduated in 2009 with a concentration in French. She is a project editor for *The Encyclopedia of New York City*, 2nd edn.

Paul Robert Magocsi (PhD Princeton University) is a professor of history and political science at the University of Toronto and author of more than a dozen books on east central Europe and immigration of people from this area to the United States.

Peter Maguire (PhD Columbia University) is a visiting assistant professor of history at Bard College. He is also a board member for the Oral History Project at Columbia University.

Harold Eugene Mahan (PhD University of Wisconsin–Madison) is a professor of American studies at Crossroads College (formerly Minnesota Bible College).

Sarah Mahler (PhD Columbia University) is the Director of the Transnational and Comparative Studies Center at Florida International University.

David Major has been a senior planner for the water supply system in New York City and the program director for global environmental change at the Social Science Research Council.

John Manbeck is professor emeritus of Kingsborough Community College and worked as Brooklyn Borough Historian from 1993 to 2002. He has written and collaborated on several books about Coney Island and the history of Brooklyn.

Nora L. Mandel (MA Harvard University) has worked for New York City, New York State, the federal government, and various nonprofit organizations.

Paul J. Maranti, Jr. (PhD Johns Hopkins University), is a professor of accounting at Rutgers Business School. He is a coauthor of *The Institute of Accounts: Nineteenth-Century Origins of Accounting Professionalism in the United States* (2004).

Alan I. Marcus (PhD University of Cincinnati) is a professor and the head of the History Department at Mississippi State University. He specializes in the history of technology and agriculture.

Tina Margolis is a freelance writer and researcher in New York City.

John F. Mariani (PhD Columbia University) is author of *America Eats Out* (1991), *The Encyclopedia of American Food and Drink* (1999), and, with Galina Mariani, *The Italian-American Cookbook* (2000).

Howard Markel (MD University of Michigan, PhD Johns Hopkins University) is the George E. Wantz Distinguished Professor of the History of Medicine, professor of pediatrics and communicable diseases, professor of history, professor of health management and policy, professor of psychiatry, and director of the Center for the History of Medicine at the University of Michigan. He is the author of *Quarantine! East European Jewish Immigrants and the New York City Epidemics of 1892* (1997) and *When Germs Travel: Six Epidemics That Invaded America since 1900* (2004).

Arnold Markoe (PhD New York University) is a former professor at Brooklyn College.

Karen Markoe (PhD Columbia University) is a professor of history at Maritime College of the State University of New York and a coeditor of *The Scribner Encyclopedia of American Lives: 2003–2005* (2006).

Lauren Markoe (MA Georgetown University) is a native of the Bronx and a journalist.

Janos Marton (JD Fordham Law School) lives in Brooklyn and practices civil rights law.

Martin E. Marty (PhD University of Chicago) is the Fairfax M. Cone Distinguished Service Professor Emeritus at the University of Chicago, specializing in late nineteenth- and twentieth-century American religion.

Renee D. Mastrocco (MA New York University) is the senior and campus archivist for Rockefeller University.

Catherine Mathis (MBA University of Minnesota) is senior vice president of corporate communications at the New York Times Company.

Cathy Matson is professor of history at the University of Delaware and director of the Program in Early American Economy and Society in Philadelphia. She is author of publications on the economy and political economy of North America from 1600 to 1815.

Antonia S. Mattheou (MA New York University) is an archivist and historian of Huntington, New York. She is the author of *Tracing Your Greek Ancestry: Reference to Cyprus* (1992).

Paul H. Mattingly (PhD University of Wisconsin) is a professor of history and the director of the Public History Program at New York University.

Daniel May has worked in the archives of the Metropolitan Life Insurance Company.

Joan Bacchus Maynard* (BA Empire College, State University of New York) was the executive director of the Society for the Preservation of Weeksville and Bedford–Stuyvesant History and a trustee of the National Trust for Historic Preservation.

Michael McCabe is a cultural anthropologist specializing in the history of tattooing in New York City. He is the author of *New York City Tattoo: The Oral History of a Forgotten Past* (1995).

Bernadette McCauley (PhD Columbia University) is an associate professor of history at Hunter College.

Kathleen McDermott (JD Suffolk University Law School) is a partner at Morgan, Lewis and Backius, LLP in the FDA/Healthcare Regulation Practice.

Richard McDermott is a New York City writer and researcher.

Mary McDonald (MPhil New York University) formerly taught at New York University.

William McGimpsey, born in County Down, Ireland, is an environmental engineer and a member of many Irish American organizations.

Margaret M. McGuinness is a professor and chair of the Department of Religion at La Salle University.

Harlow McMillen (MA Union College) is a public schoolteacher in New York City, a former editor of *Staten Island Historian* and the author of *A History of Staten Island, New York during the American Revolution* (1976).

Paul M. McNeil is vice dean at the School of Continuing Education at Columbia University.

Brooks McNamara is a professor emeritus of performance studies at the Tisch School of the Arts at New York University.

John McNamara* was an authority on Bronx history. His publications include *History in Asphalt* (1993).

Catherine McNeur is a doctoral candidate in history at Yale University writing a dissertation titled "The 'Swinish Multitude' and Fashionable Promenades: Battles over Public Space in New York City, 1815–1859."

Chris McNickle (PhD Chicago) is an independent scholar and author of *To Be Mayor of New York: Ethnic Politics in the City* (1993).

Elliot S. Meadows (BA Columbia College) is a former manuscript reference assistant at the New-York Historical Society and a former computer programmer.

Joseph F. Meany, Jr. (PhD Fordham University), is the former senior historian at the New York State Museum.

David E. Meerse (PhD University of Illinois) taught American history at the State University of New York. He is former Stated Clerk, New York City Presbytery, and is now Interim General Presbyter, Missouri Union Presbytery, Presbyterian Church U.S.A.

Abigail Mellen (PhD New York University) is a professor of history at Rutgers University, teaching the history of Western civilization.

Ronald Mendel is the senior lecturer in American social and economic history at the University of Northampton. He authored *A Broad and Ennobling Spirit: Workers and Their Unions in the Late Gilded Age, New York and Brooklyn, 1886–1898* (2003).

Joyce Mendelsohn was the first director of education at the Lower East Side Tenement Museum and taught courses on New York City history and architecture at the New School. Her works include *The Lower East Side, Remembered and Revisited: History and Guide to a Legendary New York Neighborhood* (2001) and *Touring the Flatiron: Walks in Four Historic Neighborhoods* (1998).

Jean Ulitz Mensch is an independent historian.

David Ment (PhD History of Education, Columbia University; MS Columbia University School of Library Science) is archivist/curator of the Board of Education collection at the New York City Municipal Archives.

Melissa M. Merritt (PhD University of Pittsburgh) is an assistant professor of philosophy at Georgia State University.

Rohanna Mertens is a New York City–based photographer who works for newspapers, magazines, and international nonprofit organizations. She has photographed for various nongovernmental organizations, including Operation Smile, ACCION International, AmeriCares, and Save the Children in more than 20 countries in Latin America, Africa, and Asia.

John T. Metzger (PhD Columbia University) has taught urban studies at the City University of New York, advised the urban poverty program of the Ford Foundation, and worked on oral history projects of Mayors Abraham Beame and Edward Koch.

Barbara L. Michaels (PhD City University of New York) writes and lectures on the history of art and photography.

Jerry Mikorenda (MA Syracuse University) is a writer living in Northport, New York. His work has appeared in the *New York Times*, *Newsday*, the *Boston Herald*, and the *San Francisco Chronicle*.

Caroline Rennolds Milbank (BA Bennington College) is the author of *New York Fashion: The Evolution of American Style* (1989) and *Couture: The Great Designers* (1985).

Page Putnam Miller (PhD University of Maryland) is a former professor of history at the University of South Carolina and the former director of the National Coordinating Committee for the Promotion of History.

Stephanie Miller (BA Columbia University) graduated in 2007 and is an elite archer.

Esther Mipaas (MA New York University) is a freelance photographer and writer on local history and architecture. She is a coauthor of *Bridges of Central Park* (1990).

Paul J. Miranti, Jr., is an associate professor of accounting at the School of Business at Rutgers, the State University of New Jersey. He is the author of *Accountancy Comes of Age: The Development of an American Profession, 1886–1940* (1990).

David F. Mitch is currently professor of economics at the University of Maryland, Baltimore County. He is a coeditor of *Origins of the Modern Career* (2004).

Raymond A. Mohl (PhD New York University) is a professor of history at the University of Alabama–Birmingham. His publications include *Urban Policy in Twentieth Century America* (1993), *The New African American Urban History* (1996), and *The Making of Urban America*, 2nd edn. (1997).

Danielle Molinski (BA Purchase College) majored in journalism and premedicine.

John Mollenkopf is a Distinguished Professor of Political Science and Sociology at the Graduate Center of the City University of New York and directs its Center for Urban Research.

Carolyn Monastra (MFA Yale University) is a professional photographer who lives in Brooklyn and maintains a studio in Long Island City. In addition to her commercial ventures she is an active exhibiting artist and a professor of photography.

Jessica Montesano (BA Columbia University) is a project editor for *The Encyclopedia of New York City*, 2nd edn.

James E. Mooney (PhD Clark University) is a former librarian of the New-York Historical Society and authored *National Index of American Imprints through 1800* (1969).

Richard E. Mooney is a former member of the editorial board of the *New York Times*.

Nathan Morgante (BA History, Columbia University) graduated in 2009.

Robert C. Morris* (PhD History, University of Chicago) was director of the National Archives–Northeast Region and the author of *Reading, 'Riting, and Reconstruction: The Education of Freedom in the South, 1861–1870* (1981) and "Educational Reconstruction" in *The Facts of Reconstruction: Essays in Honor of John Hope Franklin* (1991).

Frank Morrow is a graduate of Yale College and Harvard University Law School.

Robert Morrow studied acting at HB Studio in New York and has since formed the acting troupe Naked Angels.

Jane E. Mottus (PhD New York University) is the executive associate to the dean of natural and social sciences at Lehman College and author of *New York Nightingales: The Emergence of the Nursing Profession at Bellevue and New York Hospital, 1850–1920* (1981).

Richard J. Moylan (JD New York Law School) has been employed at the Green-Wood Cemetery since 1972 and its president since 1986.

D. S. Moynihan (PhD New York University) is a playwright and director. He has taught theater at Sarah Lawrence College and has been a creative director of the Shubert Organization.

Robert Bruce Mullin (PhD Yale University) has been a professor of history and a subdean of academic affairs for the Society for the Promotion of Religion and Learning.

John M. Murrin is a professor emeritus of history at Princeton University, a past president of the Society for Historians of the Early American Republic, and a coauthor of *Liberty, Equality, Power: A History of the American People*, 5th edn. (2007).

Jerome Mushkat (PhD Syracuse University) is a professor emeritus of history at the University of Akron and the author of *The Reconstruction of the New York Democracy, 1861–1875* (1981) and *Tammany: The Evolution of a Political Machine* (1971).

Charles Musser is a professor of film studies at Yale University. His books include *Edison Motion Pictures, 1890–1900: An Annotated Filmography* (1997).

David F. Musto is a professor of child psychiatry at Yale University and the curator of historic scientific instruments at the Peabody Museum. He is the author of *The American*

Disease: A History of Drug Use and Policy in the United States (1987).

Stanley Nadel (PhD Columbia University) has been a professor of history at Southwest Missouri State University and Southwestern Oklahoma State University and is the author of various articles on nineteenth-century German American and Jewish history.

Robin Nagle (PhD Anthropology Columbia University) is anthropologist-in-residence for New York City's Department of Sanitation. She also directs the Draper Program at New York University, where she teaches anthropology and urban studies. She is the author of *Picking Up* (2009) and cofounder of New York City's Sanitation Museum.

David Nasaw is the Arthur M. Schlesinger Jr. Professor of History at the Graduate Center of the City University of New York and the author of *Andrew Carnegie* (2006).

Robert M. Neer is a doctoral student at Columbia University and has been a historian, author, blogger, attorney, and entrepreneur.

Dale L. Neighbors (BA New York University) has been the curator of photography at the New-York Historical Society and is now the chief archivist at the Museum of Sex in Manhattan.

Joan Nestle is a cofounder of the Lesbian Herstory Archives of New York City and author of two volumes of memoirs, *A Restricted Country* (1987) and *A Fragile Union* (1998), about her life in the New York lesbian and gay communities from the 1950s through the 1990s.

Frank Nestor (BA Columbia University) graduated in 2010 and is a project editor focusing on charts and tables for *The Encyclopedia of New York City*, 2nd edn.

John L. Neufeld is professor of economics at the University of North Carolina, Greensboro. He has authored a number of publications on the history of the U.S. and modern electric utility industry.

Dianna Ng (BA Columbia University) is a medical student at New York University's School of Medicine. She was an assistant editor for *The Encyclopedia of New York City*, 2nd edn.

Becky M. Nicolaides (PhD Columbia University) is a research scholar at the Center for the Study of Women at the University of California, Los Angeles, and taught history and urban studies and planning at the University of California, San Diego. She is the author of *My Blue Heaven: Life and Politics in the Working-Class Suburbs of Los Angeles, 1920–1965* (2002).

Katarzyna Nikhamina (BA Columbia University) works as a paralegal in the Manhattan District Attorney Office.

Barbara J. Niss (MA New York University) is the archivist of the Mount Sinai Medical Center. She is a coauthor of *Teaching Tomorrow's Medicine Today: The Mount Sinai School of Medicine, 1963–2003* (2005).

Elliott B. Nixon* (JD Harvard University) practiced maritime law in New York City for more than 40 years. He also gave architectural tours of the city.

Claire E. Nolte (PhD Columbia University) is professor of history at Manhattan College. In addition to numerous articles on Czech history and culture, she is the author of *The Sokol in the Czech Lands to 1914: Training for the Nation* (2002).

James D. Norris has been a professor of history and dean of the College of Liberal Arts and Sciences at Northern Illinois University.

Victoria Núñez (PhD American Studies, University of Massachusetts) is a professor of education at Brooklyn College, City University of New York, who writes and publishes in the areas of Latina studies and women's studies.

Edward T. O'Donnell (PhD Columbia University) is an associate professor of history at the College of the Holy Cross.

Kathy J. Ogren (PhD Johns Hopkins University) is a professor of history at the Johnston Center at the University of Redlands. She specializes in late nineteenth- and twentieth-century social and cultural history of the United States, with emphasis on jazz and American culture.

Chauncey G. Olinger, Jr., is the president of the New York City–based National Institute of Social Sciences.

Robert A. Olmsted (BA Cornell University) is a civil engineer and an expert in transportation history. He retired in 1989 as an assistant director of planning for the Metropolitan Transportation Authority.

Michael O'Malley (PhD University of California–Berkley) is an associate professor of history and the associate director of the Center for History and New Media at George Mason University. His focus is on money and value in nineteenth-century America.

Sandra Opdycke (PhD Columbia University) is the associate director of the Institute for Innovation in Social Policy at Vassar College. She is the author of numerous works on American history, including *No One Was Turned Away: The Role of Public Hospitals in New York City since 1900* (2000).

Annelise Orleck (PhD New York University) is the chair of the Jewish studies program at Dartmouth College. She has written many books on American and Jewish American history, including *The Soviet Jewish Americans* (2001).

Alfonso J. Orsini (PhD Teachers College, Columbia University) is the director of the Western International School of Shanghai and a coeditor of *Colors of Excellence: Hiring and Keeping Teachers of Color in Independent Schools* (2003).

Ernest L. Osborne is a contributor to *The Encyclopedia of New York City*, 2nd edn.

Robert A. Padgug (PhD Harvard University) has been a director of health policy and government affairs at Empire Blue Cross Blue Shield in New York City. He is the author of many articles on health-care financing, health-care policy, and HIV/AIDS.

Valerie Paley (MPhil Columbia University) is the founding editor of the *New-York Journal of American History* and historian for special projects at the New-York Historical Society.

Charles Palms (JD) has been the chairman of the board of the Bedford–Stuyvesant Family Health Center. He has also worked with the Bedford Stuyvesant Restoration Corporation since 1969.

Lisa Papandrea is a graduate of Columbia University with a degree in civil engineering.

Robert D. Parmet (PhD Columbia University) is a professor of history at York College. He is the author of *The Master of Seventh Avenue: David Dubinsky and the American Labor Movement* (2005) and *Labor and Immigration in Industrial America* (1981), and a coauthor of *American Nativism, 1830–1860* (1971).

Brenda Parnes (PhD New York University) is the regional advisory officer for New York City for the New York State Archives.

Elaine Weber Pascu (PhD Northern Illinois University) is an editor and the director of the papers of Albert Gallatin and Thomas Jefferson.

Marjorie Pearson (MPhil City University of New York) has been the director of research at the New York City Landmarks Preservation Commission.

James Penton is a theater director and information technology specialist based in Chicago.

Nélida Pérez has been the librarian and archivist of the Centro de Estudios Puertorriqueños at Hunter College.

Nunzio Pernicone is an associate professor of history at Drexel University. He is the author of *Carlo Tresca: Portrait of a Rebel* (2005).

Patricia A. Perito is the library director for the Town of Pelham Public Library in Westchester County, New York.

Edwin J. Perkins (PhD Johns Hopkins University) is a professor emeritus at the University of Southern California. He is the author of numerous works on U.S. economic and business history, including *Wall Street to Main Street: Charles Merrill and Middle Class Investors* (1999).

David C. Perry (PhD Syracuse University) is a professor of planning and design and the director of the Great Cities Institute at the University of Illinois–Chicago. He is a coeditor, with Wim Wiewel, of *Global Universities and Urban Development: Case Studies and Analysis* (2008).

Elisabeth Israels Perry (PhD University of California, Los Angeles) is a professor of women's studies and history at Saint Louis University. She is the author of *We Have Come to Stay: American Women and Political Parties, 1880–1960* (1999).

Jon A. Peterson (PhD Harvard University) is a professor emeritus of history at Queens

College, City University of New York, and author of *The Birth of City Planning in the United States, 1840–1917* (2003).

G. Kurt Piehler (PhD Rutgers University) is an associate professor of history at the University of Tennessee, the author of *Remembering War the American Way* (1995), and a consulting editor to the *Oxford Companion to American History.*

Joe Piscina is a contributor to *The Encyclopedia of New York City,* 2nd edn.

David Pitt is a former *New York Times* editor and reporter. In 1994 he joined the United Nations Secretariat, where he wrote extensively on development issues and spent nearly 10 years as chief speechwriter for the executive director of UNICEF. He began fencing in 1965 at Salle Santelli and was national over-40 foil champion in 1997 and 16th at the World Veteran Championships in Hungary in 1999.

Christina Plattner (MS Columbia University) is a preservation planner who writes about neighborhood history, historic and archaeological resources, land use, and urban design for environmental impact statements.

Richard Plunz is a professor of architecture at Columbia University and the author of *A History of Housing in New York City* (1990).

Jane R. Pomeroy has been a letterpress printer and has published articles in the *Proceedings of the American Antiquarian Society, Printing History,* and *Imprint.* Her book *Alexander Anderson (1775–1870), Wood Engraver and Illustrator: An Annotated Bibliography* received the 2007 Ewell L. Newman Book Award.

Alex Poole (AM Brown University, MSLS University of North Carolina at Chapel Hill) is a doctoral student in information science at the University of North Carolina at Chapel Hill.

Marjory Potts is a writer and film producer based in Martha's Vineyard. She produced a documentary about Frances Perkins called *You May Call Her "Madam Secretary."*

William S. Pretzer (PhD Northern Illinois University) is associate professor of history and director of the Museum of Cultural and Natural History at Central Michigan University.

Bohdan P. Procko (PhD University of Ottawa) is a professor emeritus of Villanova University specializing in Ukrainian history.

James S. Pula (PhD Purdue University) is a professor of history and vice chancellor at Purdue University North Central specializing in Polish and American history.

Gail Radford (PhD Columbia University) is an associate professor of history at the State University of New York at Buffalo. She is the author of *Modern Housing for America: Policy Struggles in the New Deal Era* (1996).

Ronald Rainger specializes in the history of biology, anthropology, and other sciences. He is a coauthor of numerous books, including *The American Development of Biology* (1991).

Jan Seidler Ramirez (PhD Boston University) is chief curator and director of collections for the National September 11 Memorial and Museum in New York City. She has also served as vice president and museum director of the New-York Historical Society and as a curator and associate director for the collections at the Museum of the City of New York.

Julian S. Rammelkamp (PhD Harvard University) is a professor emeritus of history at Albion College and the author of *Pulitzer's* Post-Dispatch, *1878–1883* (1967).

Arnold Rampersad (PhD Harvard University) is a professor of English at Stanford University. His publications include *The Art and Imagination of W. E. B. DuBois* (1976); *The Life of Langston Hughes* (2 vols., 1986, 1988); *Days of Grace: A Memoir* (1993), coauthored with Arthur Ashe; *Jackie Robinson: A Biography* (1997); and *Ralph Ellison* (2007).

Diane Jones Randall (MS Columbia University) is a former managing editor of *The Manhattan African-American History and Culture Guide.* She was an editor at Reader's Digest for 19 years and is currently an editorial director at NBC Universal's iVillage.

Norris Randolph is a freelance writer and former editor at the *Saturday Evening Post* and *Good Housekeeping.* He has written about crime and criminals for *Esquire, New York,* and the *New England Monthly,* for which he was a contributing editor.

Philip Ranlet is an adjunct associate professor of history at Hunter College. He is the biographer of historian Richard B. Morris and the author of *The New York Loyalists,* 2nd edn. (2002).

Nina Rappaport is an architectural critic, curator, and educator. She is the author of *Support and Resist: Structural Engineers and Design Innovation* (2007) and has contributed articles to numerous architectural publications.

Susan Rather (PhD University of Delaware) is an associate professor of art history at the University of Texas–Austin. She publishes on early twentieth-century sculpture.

Alan R. Raucher (PhD University of Pennsylvania) is a professor of history at Wayne State University.

Elizabeth Reich Rawson is a former curator of collections and curator of exhibitions for the Brooklyn Historical Society and is now a consultant to historical museums.

John Recchiuti (PhD Columbia University) is a professor of history and the director of the American studies program at Mount Union College.

Henry Hope Reed (BA Harvard University) is the author of *The Golden City* (1959) and *The United States Capitol: Its Architecture and Decoration* (2007). He is a proponent of tradition in civic design.

Hilda Regier (MA University of Iowa) is a freelance writer. She has led the Chelsea Neighborhood Associations and was Chair of the Manhattan Community Board 4 from 1981 to 1983.

David M. Reimers (PhD University of Wisconsin) is a professor emeritus at New York University and a coauthor, with Frederick M. Binder, of *All the Nations under Heaven: A Racial and Ethnic History of New York City* (1995).

Claudio Iván Remeseira (MA Columbia University; BA University of Buenos Aires) is a writer and journalist who specializes in Latino studies. He was adjunct assistant professor of social and political theory at the School of Social Sciences, University of Buenos Aires. He is the author of *Hispanic New York: A Sourcebook* (2010).

Michael C. Repka (BA Columbia University) is a research technician at Memorial Sloan–Kettering Cancer Center.

Susan M. Reverby (PhD Boston University) is a professor of women's studies at Wellesley College.

Nancy Reynolds, a former dancer with the New York City Ballet, is the author of *Repertory in Review: 40 Years of the New York City Ballet* (1977) and *No Fixed Points: Dance in the Twentieth Century* (2003).

Grai St. Clair Rice (MFA Columbia University) has been director, screenwriter, editor, and researcher for a number of documentary and narrative projects in New York City. She was also an adjunct professor of screenwriting at Ramapo College.

James F. Richardson (PhD New York University) has been a professor of history at the University of Akron.

Clare Richfield (BA Barnard College) works as a research associate at the New-York Historical Society.

John-Paul Richiuso (MA New York University) is an archivist and has worked for the Staten Island Institute of Arts and Sciences–Museum of Staten Island.

John T. Ridge is the author of *Sligo in New York: The Irish from County Sligo* (1991).

Steven A. Riess (PhD University of Chicago) is a professor of history at Northeastern Illinois University. He is the author of *Sport in Industrial America, 1850–1920* (1995).

JillEllyn Riley (PhD University of California, Los Angeles) is an editor and a former assistant curator for radio at the Museum of Broadcasting.

Marju Rink-Abel (MS Columbia University) is the president of the Estonian American National Council, Inc., and the compiler of several bibliographies of sources on Estonia.

Robert C. Ritchie (PhD University of California, Los Angeles) is the H. T. and Jessie Chua Distinguished Professor of Engineering and chair of the Department of Materials Science and Engineering at the University of California–Berkley. He is the author of

Captain Kidd and the War against the Pirates (1986).

Lawrence S. Ritter* (PhD University of Wisconsin) specialized in the history of baseball and was the author of *The Glory of Their Times: The Story of the Early Days of Baseball Told by the Men Who Played It* (1985).

Steve Rivo has been a writer and researcher and has worked as the producer of *New York*, a film series of documentary history of New York City.

Randy Roberts is Distinguished Professor of History at Purdue University. He has written biographies of Jack Dempsey, Jack Johnson, John Wayne, and Oscar Robertson, as well as studies of the Mike Tyson trial, sports in America since 1945, and the war in Vietnam.

Nancy Marie Robertson (PhD New York University) is an associate professor of history and philanthropic studies as well as the director of women's studies at Indiana University–Purdue University Indianapolis. She is the author of *Christian Sisterhood, Race Relations, and the YWCA, 1906–46.*

Anthony W. Robins (MA Courtauld Institute of Art) is an author, lecturer, and tour guide in New York City. He has been the director of education and programs at the Municipal Art Society and the deputy director of research and director of survey at the New York City Landmarks Preservation Commission.

Eric Robinson (BA Haverford College) works at the library of the New-York Historical Society and is a member of Local 2110 of the United Auto Workers.

Greg Robinson (PhD New York University) is a professor of history at the University of Quebec–Montreal specializing in the history of Asian Americans and Asian Canadians.

Joshua Robinson (BA Columbia University) is a freelance writer for the *New York Times.*

Howard Rock is professor of history emeritus at Florida International University. He is the author of *Cityscapes: A History of New York in Images* (2001) and *Artisans of the New Republic: The Tradesmen of New York City in the Age of Jefferson* (1979).

Clara Rodríguez (PhD Washington University–St. Louis) is a professor of sociology at the College at Lincoln Center in Fordham University. She is the author of *Heroes, Lovers, and Others: The Story of Latinos in Hollywood* (2004).

Sandra Roff (MA University of Pennsylvania; MLS Pratt Institute) is professor and college archivist at Baruch College, City University of New York. She is a coauthor of *From the Free Academy to CUNY: Illustrating Public Higher Education in New York City, 1847–1997* (2000).

Elizabeth Barlow Rogers is an author and the president of the Foundation for Landscape Studies. From 1980 until 1995 she served as the founding president of the Central Park Conservancy and between 2001 and 2005 was the founding director of garden history and landscape studies at the Bard Graduate Center in New York City.

Madeline Rogers (MA New York University) has been the director of educational programs at the South Street Seaport Museum and is a former assistant managing editor of the *Daily News.*

Mary Ann Romano (PhD New York University) is an adjunct assistant professor of sociology at Malloy College.

Kenneth W. Rose (PhD Case Western Reserve University) is the assistant director of the Rockefeller Archive Center, specializing in twentieth-century American history and race relations.

Mark H. Rose (PhD Ohio State University) is a professor of history at the Dorothy F. Schmidt College of Arts and Letters at Florida Atlantic University focusing on twentieth-century social and policy bases in the United States.

Naomi Rosenblum (PhD Graduate Center, City University of New York) is the author of *A World History of Photography* (1989) and *A History of Women Photographers* (1994), a book that was followed by a traveling art exhibit. In 1998 she and her husband received the Infinity Award for Lifetime Achievement at the International Center for Photography.

Fay Rosenfeld (JD New York University) is the senior assistant dean of student affairs at the Hofstra University School of Law.

Roy Rosenzweig* (PhD Harvard University) was a professor of history and the director and chair of the Center for History and New Media at George Mason University. He was a pioneer of digital technology and new media.

David Rosner is a professor of history and ethics in the Sociomedical Science and History Department at the Mailman School of Public Health at Columbia University.

Molly Rosner (MA American Studies, Wesleyan University) wrote the thesis "Growing Apart(ment): A Social and Cultural History of the Apartment on the Upper West Side" for her degree. She is currently in the Oral History Masters of Art Program at Columbia University.

Nan A. Rothschild (PhD New York University) is an adjunct professor of archaeology in the Anthropology Department at Columbia University. She is an expert on New York City archaeology and recently published *Colonial Encounters in a Native American Landscape: The Spanish and Dutch in North America* (2003).

Morton Rothstein is a professor emeritus of history at the University of California–Davis.

John Rousmaniere is a writer, historian, and sailor who has written several books on a variety of topics related to New York City, including law, insurance, finance, and sports.

Donald S. Rubin is the senior vice president of investor relations at McGraw–Hill Companies.

Ellis Rubinstein is the president and chief executive officer of the New York Academy of Sciences. Previously, he served as editor of science for the Association for the Advancement of Science's magazine.

Peter M. Rutkoff (PhD University of Pennsylvania) is a professor of American studies at Kenyon University. He focuses on American and African American culture.

Charles L. Sachs is the senior curator at the New York Transit Museum and a former chief curator at the Staten Island Historical Society. His publications include *Made on Staten Island: Agriculture, Industry, and Suburban Living in the City* (1988) and *Blessed Isle: Hal B. Fullerton and His Image of Long Island, 1897–1927* (1991).

Harrison Salisbury* (BA University of Minnesota) was a reporter at the *New York Times* and the first editor of the op-ed page; he won a Pulitzer Prize in 1955.

Joseph J. Salvo is director of the Population Division at the New York City Department of City Planning. He is a former president of the Association of Public Data Users, serves on the Census Advisory Committee of Professional Associations, and is a Fellow of the American Statistical Association.

Peter Salwen is the author of *Upper West Side Story: A History and Guide* (1989).

James Sanders is an architect, writer, and filmmaker. He cowrote the award-winning *New York: A Documentary Film* and the companion volume *New York: An Illustrated History* (1999). He is a frequent contributor to the *New York Times,* and his design work has been featured in *House Beautiful*, *Architectural Digest*, and *Interiors.*

Nahma Sandrow (DFA Yale Drama School) writes and lectures on Yiddish theater. She has been a professor of English at Bronx Community College and won an Outer Critics Circle Award for her 1984 Off-Broadway musical *Kuni-Leml.*

Gene Santoro is a music and film critic for the *Nation* and the *New York Daily News.* He is the author of several essay collections, including *Stir It Up* (1997).

Mike Sappol (PhD Columbia University) is a medical historian for the U.S. Library of Medicine. He is the author of *A Traffic of Dead Bodies: Anatomy and Embodied Social Identity in 19th Century America* (2002).

Mitziko Sawada (PhD New York University) is a visiting professor emerita of history and dean of multicultural affairs at the University of Massachusetts–Amherst. She focuses on social history of the United States, including race issues, immigration, and the Asian American experience.

Rachel Sawyer (BA Touro College) is a managing editor for the North Jersey Newspaper Company.

Claude M. Scales III (JD Harvard University) is an attorney in New York City and has worked as counsel to the firm of Gilbert, Segall and Young.

Breanne Scanlon is a graduate student in the Public History Program at New York University. Her research interests include urban and local history and the history of popular music.

Frank Scaturro (JD University of Pennsylvania) founded the Grant Monument Association in 1994 to draw public attention to the disrepair of Grant's Tomb in New York City. Since 2005 he has served as counsel for the Senate Judiciary Committee on Senator Arlen Specter's staff. He is the author of *President Grant Reconsidered* (1999).

Lois Scharf has taught American history at Case Western Reserve University. She is the author of *To Work, to Wed: Female Employment, Feminism, and the Great Depression* (1980).

Barnet Schecter is an independent scholar and the author of *The Battle for New York: The City at the Heart of the American Revolution* (2002) and *The Devil's Own Work: The Civil War Draft Riots and the Fight to Reconstruct America* (2005).

Seth M. Scheiner is professor emeritus in the History Department at Rutgers University.

Rich Scheinin is the religious, ethics, and music writer for the San Jose *Mercury News*. He is the author of *Field of Screams: The Dark Underside of America's National Pastime* (1994).

Kenneth A. Scherzer (PhD Harvard University) is a professor of history at Middle Tennessee State University. He is the author of *The Unbounded Community: Neighborhood Life and Social Structure in New York City, 1830–1875* (1992).

Jeffrey Scheuer (MPhil Columbia University) has been published in the *New York Times* and the *Washington Post*. He is the author of *The Big Picture: Why Democracies Need Journalistic Excellence* (2007).

Arline H. Schneider (MA New York University, MLS Pratt Institute) is the director of archives for the Equitable Life Insurance Society of the United States.

Dorothee Schneider is a professor of history at the University of Illinois Urbana–Champaign. She is the author of *Trade Unions and Community: The German Working Class in New York City, 1870–1900* (1994).

Loren Schoenberg is a jazz musician and historian based in New York City. He is the executive director of the Jazz Museum in Harlem.

David Schorr (LLB and JSD Yale University) is a professor of law at Tel Aviv University.

Ellen W. Schrecker (PhD Harvard University) is a professor of American history at Yeshiva University. Her publications include *Cold War Triumphalism: Exposing the Misuse of History after the Fall of Communism* (2004), *The Age of McCarthyism: A Brief History with Documents* (2002), and *Many Are the Crimes: McCarthyism in America* (1998).

David Schuyler (PhD History, Columbia University) is the Arthur and Katherine Shadek Professor of the Humanities and professor of American studies at Franklin and Marshall College. He is author of *The New Urban Landscape* (1986) and *A City Transformed: Redevelopment, Race, and Suburbanization in Lancaster, Pennsylvania, 1940–1980* (2002). He has also coedited three volumes of *The Papers of Frederick Law Olmsted.*

Joel Schwartz* (PhD University of Chicago) taught history at Montclair State University and wrote *The New York Approach: Robert Moses, Urban Liberals and Redevelopment of the Inner City* (1992).

Richard Schwartz is a former dean of students at Columbia Grammar and Preparatory School.

Joseph Sciorra (PhD University of Pennsylvania) is a coauthor of *R.I.P.: Memorial Wall Art (Street Graphics/Street Art)* (2002).

Elliott Sclar (PhD Tufts University) is director of the Center for Sustainable Urban Development and professor of urban planning and international affairs at Columbia University. His publications include *You Don't Always Get What You Pay For: The Economics of Privatization* (2000).

David Scobey (PhD Yale University) is the Donald W. and Ann M. Harward Professor of Community Partnership at Bates College and an associate professor of architecture at the University of Michigan. He is the author of *Empire City: Politics, Culture, and Urbanism in Gilded-Age New York* (1989).

William B. Scott (PhD University of Wisconsin–Madison) is a professor of history at Kenyon College. He specializes in American intellectual and social history, with a focus on the South.

Robert Seder* was a theatrical lighting designer, playwright, and teacher at the Bard College Institute for Writing and Thinking.

Harriet F. Senie is a professor of art history at City College and the City University of New York Graduate Center and a board member of the Fine Arts Federation. She is the author of *The "Tilted Arc" Controversy: Dangerous Precedent?* (2002) and *Contemporary Public Sculpture* (1992), as well as a coeditor of *Critical Issues in Public Art* (1998).

Max Seppo graduated from Trinity High School in New York City in 2010.

Vincent Seyfried (MA Fordham University) is the author of numerous histories of street railways, the Long Island Rail Road, and Queens. He is a resident and historian of Garden City, Long Island.

Wendy Shadwell* was the Curator of Prints Emerita at the New-York Historical Society.

Jeffrey Shandler (PhD Columbia University) is a professor of Jewish Studies at Rutgers University and the author of *Adventures in Yiddishland: Postvernacular Language and Culture* (2005).

Rebecca Read Shanor (MS Columbia University) is the author of *The City That Never Was: 200 Years of Fantastic and Fascinating Plans that Might Have Changed the Face of New York* (1988).

Allen J. Share is a former professor at the University of Louisville. He is the author of *Cities in the Commonwealth: Two Centuries of Urban Life in Kentucky.* He is an associate editor of *The Encyclopedia of New York City*, 2nd edn., and served as a consulting editor to both *The Encyclopedia of Louisville* and *The Encyclopedia of Kentucky.*

Noël Shaw is a writer and filmmaker living in New York City. Under the name Dionisio Velasco he works as a freelance writer for several publications.

Leyli Shayegan (MA Political Science, City University of New York), born in Iran, immigrated to the United States as a child. She is the assistant director of Teachers College Press, Teachers College, Columbia University.

Nancy Shear is a writer, lecturer, and broadcaster and the president of Nancy Shear Arts Services. She was also an orchestra librarian for 20 years, working with the Philadelphia Orchestra and other organizations.

Martin Shefter is a professor of government at Cornell University. He is the author of *Political Crisis/Fiscal Crisis: The Collapse and Revival of New York City* (1985) and *Political Parties and the State: The American Historical Experience* (1994). He is also the editor of *Capital of the American Century: The National and International Influence of New York City* (1993).

Thomas J. Shelley (PhD Church History, Catholic University of America) is a priest with the Archdiocese of New York and a professor of church history at St. Joseph's Seminary and of historical theology at Fordham University.

Barnett Shepherd (MDiv Union Theological Seminary, MA Indiana University) is an independent historian and the former executive director of the Staten Island Historical Society (1981–2000). He is the author of *Sailors' Snug Harbor, 1801–1976* (1979), *Tottenville, the Town the Oyster Built* (2008), and a coauthor, with Lois Mosley, of *Sandy Ground Memories* (2003).

Rachel Shor is the pen name of a former instructor of English at York College and the former bibliography editor of *Funk and Wagnalls New Encyclopedia.*

Russell Shorto is the author of *The Island at the Center of the World: The Epic Story of Dutch Manhattan and the Forgotten Colony That Shaped America* (2004). He is also the director of the John Adams Institute in Amsterdam.

Bernard Shull (PhD University of Wisconsin) is a professor emeritus in the Department of Economics at Hunter College of the City University of New York and a special consultant to National Economic Research Associates, Inc.

David B. Sicilia (PhD Brandeis University) is an associate professor of history at the University of Maryland and a coauthor of *The Greenspan Effect* (2000).

Fred Siegel is a professor of history at the Cooper Union for Science and Art. He is the author of *The Future Once Happened Here: New York, L.A., D.C., and the Fate of America's Big Cities* (1997) and a coauthor of *The Prince of the City: Giuliani, New York, and the Genius of American Life* (2005).

Harry Siegel, a coauthor of *The Prince of the City: Giuliani, New York, and the Genius of American Life* (2005), is the assistant managing editor of POLITICO.

Steven W. Siegel (BS Cornell University) has been the library director and archivist at the 92nd Street Y. He is also the author of *Archival Resources* (Jewish Immigrants of the Nazi Period in the USA) (1978).

Sheldon C. Silberstein (BS) is a freelance writer specializing in the history of technology. He has taught science and done editorial work for various scientific and technical publications.

Ben Silk is a graduate of the University of Washington in St. Louis and an assistant editor of *The Encyclopedia of New York City*, 2nd edn.

Joan L. Silverman (PhD New York University) contributed to *Citibank, 1812–1970* by Harold van B. Cleveland and Thomas F. Huertas, and is a former officer of Citibank.

Barry Singer is the author of *Black and Blue: The Life and Lyrics of Andy Razaf* (1993).

Robert Sink has been an archivist and records manager at the New York Public Library.

Susan M. Sivard is a PhD candidate at Columbia University and has been a research associate at the New-York Historical Society.

Jeff Sklansky (PhD Columbia University) is an associate professor of American intellectual and cultural history at Oregon State University and the author of *The Soul's Economy: Market Society and Selfhood in American Thought, 1820–1920* (2002).

Kathryn Kish Sklar is Distinguished Professor of History at the State University of New York, Binghamton. She is the author of *Catharine Beecher: A Study in American Domesticity* (1973) and *Florence Kelley and the Nation's Work: The Rise of Women's Political Culture, 1830–1900* (1995). She is also a coeditor of *Women's Rights and Transatlantic Anti-Slavery in the Era of Emancipation* (2007).

Richard Skolnick (PhD Yale University) is a professor of history at City College of New York specializing in American history.

Robert A. Slayton (PhD Northwestern University) is a professor of history at Chapman University, where he specializes in twentieth-century U.S. history. He is the author of *Empire Statesman: The Rise and Redemption of Al Smith* (2001).

Warren Sloat is a writer specializing in American history. He is the author of *Battle for the Soul of New York: Tammany Hall, Police Corruption, Vice and Reverend Charles Parkhurst's Crusade against Them, 1892–1895* (2002) and *1929: America before the Crash* (1979).

Marlena Slowik is a student at the University of Chicago.

Caleb Smith is a writer, teacher, and tour guide in New York City. He is also an intrepid urban explorer: over a two-year period he documented a 500-mile walk along every single street in Manhattan. He is a project editor for *The Encyclopedia of New York City*, 2nd edn.

George David Smith (PhD Harvard University) is the president of the Winthrop Group and a clinical professor at the Stern School of Business, New York University. He is the author of *Anatomy of a Business Strategy: Bell, Western Electric, and the Origins of the American Telephone Industry* (1985) and *From Monopoly to Completion: The Transformations of Alcoa, 1888–1986* (1988).

Robert Smith (PhD Columbia University) is an associate professor of sociology, immigration studies, and public affairs at Baruch College and the Graduate Center, City University of New York. He is the author of *Mexican New York: Transnational Worlds of New Immigrants* (2006).

John B. Snook* was a supporter and docent at the New-York Historical Society and the author of *Going Further: Life-and-Death Religion in America* (1973).

Cal Snyder works in the Center for Biodiversity and Conservation at the American Museum of Natural History. He is the author of *Out of Fire and Valor: The War Memorials of New York from the Revolution to 9/11*.

Robert W. Snyder (PhD New York University) is an associate professor of American studies and journalism at Rutgers University–Newark. He is the author of *The Voice of the City: Vaudeville and Popular Culture in New York* (1989).

Ellen Marie Snyder-Grenier is the former chief curator at the Brooklyn Historical Society and the author of *Brooklyn! An Illustrated History* (2004).

Louis N. Sorkin is an entomologist and arachnologist at the American Museum of Natural History.

Daniel Soyer (PhD New York University) is an associate professor for graduate studies at Fordham University. He is the author of *Jewish Immigrant Associations and American Identity in New York, 1880–1939* (1997) and a coauthor of *My Future Is in America: Autobiographies of Eastern European Jewish Immigrants* (2006).

Jeanne Field Spallone is a descendant of John Bowne, a graduate of the University of Connecticut, and a probate judge in Deep River, Connecticut.

Edward K. Spann* (PhD New York University) was a professor of history at Indiana State University and the author of award-winning books about New York City history, including *Ideals and Politics: New York Intellectuals and Liberal Democracy, 1820–1880* (1972) and *The New Metropolis: New York City, 1840–1857* (1981).

Andrew Sparberg (MPA New York University), former assistant manager for resource planning for the Long Island Rail Road, is now the director of the Railway Electronics Program at TCI College of Technology. He also conducts subway tours for the New York Transit Museum.

A. M. Sperber* was the author of *Murrow: His Life and Times* (1987).

Donald R. Stabile (PhD University of Massachusetts) is a professor of economics at St. Mary's College of Maryland, the author of *Prophets of Order: The Rise of the New Class, Technocracy and Socialism in America* (1984), and a coauthor of *The Public Debt of the United States: An Historical Perspective, 1775–1988* (1991).

Darwin H. Stapleton is a historian who has been an educator and archival administrator. He has published widely in the history of American technology and science and urban history.

Robert Sanger Steel (MA Columbia Teachers College) taught New York City history as a summer instructor at Teachers College (1997–98) and currently teaches social studies at Rye High School in Rye, New York.

I. Steen (PhD New York University) is an associate professor of history at the State University of New York, Albany.

Sara J. Steen (BA New York University) was associate editor of the reference series *Contemporary Theatre, Film, and Television* and is now publications editor at the Institute of International Education.

Kayla Soyer Stein (BA Oberlin College) is a freelance writer.

Stephen A. Stertz (PhD University of Michigan) retired from work at the Bronx Historical Society after 25 years. He teaches history at Mercy College.

Robert Stinson (PhD Indiana University) is a professor emeritus of history at Moravian College. He is the author of *Lincoln Steffens* (1979), *The Long Dying of Baby Andrew* (1983), and *The Faces of Clio* (1987).

May N. Stone (MLS and Master of Historic Preservation, Columbia University) is a reference librarian at the New-York Historical Society. She wrote her master's thesis on historic preservation in the design of the Hotel Pennsylvania.

Richard Stott (PhD Cornell University) is an associate professor of history at George

Washington University and the editor of *History of My Own Times, or the Life and Adventures of William Otter, Sen.* (1995). He specializes in social and cultural history, labor history, immigration, and ethnicity.

Roy Strickland is the director of the Master of Urban Design Program at Taubman College of Architecture at the University of Michigan. He is the former associate editor of the *Harvard Architecture Review.*

Richard Sylla (PhD Harvard University), professor of economics at New York University's Stern School of Business, is the author (with Sidney Homer) of *A History of Interest Rates* (2005). He is also a trustee of the Museum of American Finance.

Harold Takooshian (PhD City University of New York) is a social psychologist on the faculty of Fordham University since 1975 where he is professor of organizational leadership and psychology.

Tao Tan (BA Columbia University) is a contributor to *The Encyclopedia of New York City,* 2nd edn.

John T. Tanacredi is a professor at Dowling College and the chair of the Earth and Marine Sciences Department.

G. Thomas Tanselle is the vice president of the John Simon Guggenheim Foundation and an adjunct professor of English at Columbia University.

Gilbert Tauber (MA Hunter College) is an urban planner and historian and a coauthor of *The New York City Handbook* (1966).

John Tauranac is a cartographer and writes on the history and architecture of New York City. He designed the iconic New York City subway map.

Nicholas E. Tawa (PhD Harvard University) is an associate professor emeritus of music at the University of Massachusetts, Boston. He is the author of many articles and books on American music, among them *Art Music in American Society* (1987), *The Way to Tin Pan Alley* (1990), and *From Psalm to Symphony: A History of Music in New England* (2001).

B. Kimberly Taylor is a freelance writer living in Greenwich Village. She has written for the *New York Times, New York Newsday, Our Town,* and the *Manhattan Spirit.*

Durahn A. B. Taylor (PhD Columbia University) is a history professor at Pace University in Pleasantville specializing in the development of Harlem politics during the administrations of Franklin D. Roosevelt. He has contributed articles about Harlem's political leaders to *The Encyclopedia of African-American Culture and History* (1996).

William R. Taylor teaches history. He is the author of *In Pursuit of Gotham: Essays on the Commerce and Culture of New York* (1992) and the editor of *Inventing Times Square: Commerce and Culture at the Crossroads* (1991).

William duBarry Thomas is a member of the Steamship Historical Society of America and the author of *William H. Webb, Shipbuilder* (1989).

George A. Thompson, Jr. (PhD New York University), is the librarian for English and American literature at New York University's Bobst Library and the author of *Key Sources in Comparative and World Literature: An Annotated Guide to Reference Materials* (1982).

Richard H. Timberlake is a professor emeritus of economics at the University of Georgia.

Barbara L. Tischler (PhD Columbia University) is an adjunct assistant professor of art education at Teacher's College, Columbia University. She is the author of *An American Music: The Search for an American Musical Identity* (1986).

Marilyn Tobias (PhD New York University) is a historian and writer. She is the author of *Old Dartmouth on Trial: The Transformation of the Academic Community in Nineteenth-Century America* (1982).

Maria Torres-Guzmán (PhD Stanford University) is associate professor of bilingual education at Teachers College, Columbia University. She is a coeditor of *Imagining Multilingual Schools: Languages in Education and Glocalization* (2006), with Ofelia Garcia and Tove Skutnabb-Kangas.

Mariam Touba is a reference librarian at the New-York Historical Society.

Louis P. Tremante (PhD Iowa State University) is an expert in environmental history, rural life, and peri-urban agriculture. He is an academic adviser for the University of Chicago.

Donald Tricarico (PhD New School for Social Research) is a professor of sociology at the City University of New York, Queensborough. His research specialization is Italian American life in New York City.

Thorin Tritter (PhD Columbia University) has taught history at LaGuardia Community College, Queens College, and Princeton University.

Judith Ann Trolander (PhD Case Western Reserve University) is a professor of history at the University of Minnesota, Duluth, and the author of *Professionalism and Social Change: From the Settlement House Movement to Neighborhood Centers, 1886 to the Present* (1987) and *Settlement Houses and the Great Depression* (1975).

Marion Archer Truslow (PhD New York University) is chair of the History Department at Rabun Gap–Nacoochee School, Rabun Gap, Georgia.

Susan Tunick (MFA Bennington College) is an artist and president of the Friends of Terra Cotta. She has written numerous articles and books on terra-cotta and other related forms of architectural ceramics.

Lloyd Ultan is a professor of history at the Edward Williams College of Fairleigh Dickinson University. He is the author of *The Beautiful Bronx (1920–1950)* (1979) and *Legacy of the Revolution: The Valentine–Varian House* (1983) and a coauthor of *The Bronx in the Innocent Years, 1890–1925* (1991). He is also a founding editor of the *Bronx County Historical Society Journal.*

John Vickrey Van Cleve (PhD University of California, Irvine) is a professor of history at Gallaudet University and the editor of the *Gallaudet Encyclopedia of Deaf People and Deafness* (1987). He is also the author of *A Place of Their Own: Creating the Deaf Community in America* (1989).

David Vaughan, archivist of the Merce Cunningham Dance Company, is the author of *Frederick Ashton and His Ballets* (1976) and of *Merce Cunningham/Fifty Years* (1997).

Joseph P. Viteritti is the Blanche D. Blank Professor of Public Policy and director of the graduate program in urban affairs at Hunter College, City University of New York. He is the author of *When Mayors Take Charge: School Governance in the City* (2009), *Choosing Equality: School Choice, the Constitution, and Civil Society* (1999), and *Across the River: Politics and Education in the City* (1983).

John Voelcker has lived in New York City for 25 years and worked at a variety of publications and online media.

David Q. Voigt is a professor of sociology and anthropology at Albright College and the author of *The League That Failed* (1998) and *Baseball: An Illustrated History* (1995).

David William Voorhees (PhD New York University) is the director and editor of the Jacob Leisler papers project at New York University.

Frank Vos* (MA Columbia University) was the chairman of an advertising agency in New York City. He formerly taught at the University of Connecticut.

Frederick S. Voss has worked as a historian for the permanent collection and a curator of the Time Collection at the National Portrait Gallery, Smithsonian Institution. He is the author of *Portraits of the Presidents* (2000).

Eric Wakin is the Lehman Curator for American History at the Columbia University Rare Book and Manuscript Library. He is the author of *Anthropology Goes to War: Professional Ethics and Counterinsurgency in Thailand* (1992) and a coauthor of guidebooks for Big Onion Walking Tours and Lonely Planet Publications.

Samuel Walker is a professor emeritus of criminal justice at the University of Nebraska. His interests include police accountability issues and U.S. presidents and civil liberties, from Woodrow Wilson through George W. Bush.

Bennett H. Wall* (PhD University of North Carolina) was a professor emeritus at the University of Georgia and author of several books, including *Growth in a Changing Environment: A History of Standard Oil Company (New Jersey), 1950–1972* and the *Exxon Corporation, 1972–1975* (1988).

Sarah Wansley (BA Columbia University) is an assistant editor of *The Encyclopedia of New York City,* 2nd edn.

Susan Ware is the author of several books on women and feminism, including *Notable American Women: Completing the 20th Century* (2004) and *Still Missing: Amelia Earhart and the Search for Modern Feminism* (1993).

Suzanne R. Wasserman (PhD New York University) is a historian and filmmaker whose works include *Thinger in Guyana* and *Brooklyn: Among the Ruins*. She is the director of the Gotham Center for New York City History at the City University of New York, Graduate Center, and a coauthor of *Life on the Lower East Side: Photographs by Rebecca Lepkoff, 1937–1950* (2006).

Deborah Dependahl Waters (PhD University of Delaware), senior curator, Decorative Arts and Manuscripts, Museum of the City of New York, has organized numerous exhibitions on New York decorative arts and cultural history, including examinations of New York silver, the furniture of Duncan Phyfe and his contemporaries, Jews in early New York, and Catholics in nineteenth- and twentieth-century New York.

Naomi Wax is a freelance writer and editor in New York City.

Harold S. Wechsler (PhD Columbia University), professor of education at New York University, is the author of *The Qualified Student: A History of Selective College Admission in America* (1977), *Jewish Learning in American Universities: The First Century* (1994), and *Access to Success in the Urban High School: The Middle College Movement* (2001).

Marilyn E. Weigold (PhD) is a professor of history and associate chair of the History Department at Pace University. Her books include *The Long Island Sound: A History of Its People, Places, and Environment* (2004) and *Silent Builder: Emily Warren Roebling and the Brooklyn Bridge* (1984).

Lisa Weilbacker (MS University of Pennsylvania) is the former curator of the seventh regiment armory and is an architecture historian for the Putnam County Historical Society.

David J. Weiner, former editor of *The Video Source Book*, is a freelance writer and producer of jazz and theater music recordings.

Howard R. Weiner (PhD New York University) is the chair of the History Department at the College of Staten Island and has been a Fulbright Professor at the University of Rome.

Stephen Weinstein (PhD Columbia University) has contributed entries to the *Dictionary of American Biography* and is the author of the *Random House Pro Football Dictionary* (1993) and the *Random House Pro Baseball Dictionary* (1994).

Judith Weisenfeld is professor of religion at Princeton University. She is the author of *Hollywood Be Thy Name: African American Religion in American Film, 1929–1949* (2007) and *African American Women and Christian Activism: New York's Black YWCA, 1905–1945* (1997).

Marc A. Weiss (PhD University of California, Berkeley) is a former staffer with the U.S. Department of Housing and Urban Development and the author of *The Rise of the Community Builders: The American Real Estate Industry and Urban Land Planning* (1987).

Vladimir Wertsman (MLS Columbia University) graduated from law school in Romania. He has worked at the Brooklyn Public Library, the Donnell Foreign Language Library, and the Mid-Manhattan Library and is now the head of the Publishers and Multicultural Materials Committee of the Ethnic Materials Round Table of the American Library Association.

Robert F. Wesser is a retired professor of history and public policy at the State University of New York.

David White (BA Columbia University) is a deputy managing editor for *The Encyclopedia of New York City*, 2nd edn. He has completed three New York City marathons.

Andrew Wiese (PhD Columbia University) is a professor of American history at San Diego State University and the author of *Places of Their Own: African American Suburbanization in the Twentieth Century* (2004).

Craig Steven Wilder (PhD Columbia University) is professor of history at the Massachusetts Institute of Technology. He is the author of *A Covenant with Color* (2000) and *In the Company of Black Men* (2001).

Sean Wilentz is the Sidney and Ruth Lapidus Professor in the American Revolutionary Era in the History Department of Princeton University.

James L. Wiles (PhD Harvard University) is a professor emeritus in economics at Stonehill College. He has written on the leather and shoe industries for the *Handbook of American Business History* (1990).

Richard C. Wiles (PhD Clark University) is an emeritus professor of social studies and economics at Bard College and the editor of *Hudson Valley Regional Review*.

Daniel Levinson Wilk (PhD Duke University) is assistant professor of American history at the Fashion Institute of Technology. He has written about the business, labor, and cultural history of apartment houses, elevators, hotels, railroads, restaurants, and skyscrapers.

Sharon Wilkins is the deputy Manhattan historian for the office of the Manhattan Borough President.

Marilyn Thornton Williams* (PhD New York University) is the author of *Washing "The Great Unwashed": Public Baths in Urban America* (1991) and was a devoted scholar and educator.

Carol Willis (MPhil Columbia University) is the founder, director, and curator of the Skycraper Museum in Manhattan. She is an adjunct associate professor at the Graduate School of Architecture, Planning, and Preservation at Columbia University.

Don B. Wilmeth (PhD University of Illinois) is a professor emeritus of theater, speech, and dance at Brown University and the former curator of the H. Adrian Smith Collection of Conjuring Books and Magicana. He coedited the *Cambridge Guide to American Theatre* (1993).

Sherrill Wilson (PhD New School for Social Research) is an urban anthropologist with the African Burial Ground Project. She is a lecturer and writer on the topic of Africans in northern colonial cities.

Sule Greg C. Wilson (MA New York University) is an archivist, a writer, an educator, and a folklorist and the author of *The Drummer's Path: Moving the Spirit with Ritual and Traditional Drumming* (1992). He has written for the *Washington Post*, the *Village Voice*, *Icarus*, *Attitude*, *Small Press*, *Banjo Newsletter*, and *Rhythm Music Magazine*. He has also recorded for Rounder Records and other independent labels.

Robert B. Winans (PhD New York University) is a professor emeritus of English at Gettysburg College. In his retirement he has written and published scholarly articles on the history of banjo music and African American instrumental music.

Brenda Wineapple (PhD University of Wisconsin, Madison) is a professor of English at Union College in Schenectady, New York, and the author of *White Heat: The Friendship of Emily Dickinson and Thomas Wentworth Higginson* (2008). She regularly writes for the *New York Times*, the *Los Angeles Times*, and the *Nation*.

George Winslow is the author of *Capital Crimes* (1999) and is a freelance writer covering the news media, white-collar crime, and financial issues.

Allis Wolfe (PhD Graduate School and University Center, City University of New York) is the archivist at the Bank of New York Mellon and has written on women's role in the history of labor.

Gerard R. Wolfe (PhD Union Institute and University) is the director of arts and liberal studies at the University of Wisconsin–Milwaukee. He was an early originator of architectural/historical walking tours of New York City and environs.

Nancy Woloch (PhD Indiana University) teaches history at Barnard College and is the author of several books on women in history, including *Women and the American Experience* (4th edn., 2006).

Mike Woodsworth is a graduate student in history at Columbia University.

James A. Wooten is a professor of law at the State University of New York, Buffalo.

Arthur J. Worrall (PhD Indiana University) is a emeritus faculty member at Colorado State University and the author of *Quakers in the Colonial Northeast* (1980).

Peter J. Wosh (PhD New York University) is an associate professor and director of the archives program at New York University. He is author of *Covenant House: Journey of a Faith-Based Charity* (2004) and *Spreading the Word: The Bible Business in Nineteenth-Century America* (1994).

Carol V. Wright (PhD) is the author of two books in the Blue Guide series: *New York* and *Museums and Galleries of New York*.

J. Robert Wright (DPhil Oxford University) is the St. Mark's in the Bowery Professor of Ecclesiastical History at the General Theological Seminary, New York City. He is a fellow of the Royal Historical Society and of the Society of Antiquaries, both of London, and is the official historiographer of the Episcopal Church. His publications include *The Church and the English Crown, 1305–1334* (1980) and *Saint Thomas Church Fifth Avenue* (2001).

Benjamin Yakas (MS Columbia University) is a freelance journalist in New York City specializing in the arts. He has worked for WNYC public radio and the Gothamist, a daily blog.

Victor Fell Yellin* (PhD Harvard University) was a professor of music at New York University and wrote operas, chamber music, choral pieces, and many scholarly articles during his career.

Irwin Yellowitz is a professor emeritus at City College of New York in the History Department. He is also the president of the New York Labor History Association and a member of the American Labor Studies Center.

Richard Yeselson (MA University of Pennsylvania) has planned corporate campaigns and investigated corporations for the United Steelworkers of America and the Industrial Union Department of the AFL–CIO. He is a research fellow for UNITE HERE, a union advocacy group.

Bonnie Yochelson (PhD New York University), a consulting curator at the Museum of the City of New York, is a professor of photography at the School of Visual Arts. She has written extensively on the history of photography, including the book *Rediscovering Jacob Riis: Exposure Journalism and Photography in Turn-of-the-Century New York* (2007).

George D. Younger* was an adjunct professor at Union Theological Seminary and executive minister of the American Baptist Churches of New Jersey. He authored several books, including *The Church and Urban Power Structure* (1963).

Charles Yrigoyen, Jr. (PhD Temple University), is a longtime writer, clergyman, professor, and chaplain serving the United Methodist Church as the general secretary of the General Commission on Archives and History. He has written numerous books about the history of Methodism.

Renqiu Yu (PhD New York University) is a professor of East Asian history at Purchase College and author of *To Save China, To Save Ourselves: The Chinese Hand Laundry Alliance of New York* (1992).

Liavon Yurevich (PhD), native of Minsk, is the author and compiler of more than 16 books on the Belarusian émigré literature and history and is a librarian for the New York Public Library.

Sharon Zane is a New York City oral historian and recently published a book on the growth and maturation of Lincoln Center.

Janet Zapata, a historian of jewelry and silver, is the former archivist at Tiffany and Co. and a consultant to Christie's. She is also a columnist for *Jewelers' Circular—Keystone*, a regular contributor to the magazine *Antiques*, and the author of *The Jewelry and Enamels of Louis Comfort Tiffany* (1993) and *Jeweled Garden: A Colorful History of Gems, Jewelry, and Nature* (2006).

Shirley Zavin (PhD) is an art and architectural historian and preservationist for New York City's Landmarks Preservation Commission.

William Zeisel (PhD History, Rutgers University) has authored and coauthored numerous books on immigration, censorship, urban history, and black history.

Steven Zeitlin (PhD University of Pennsylvania) is the founder and director of City Lore in New York City and the author, with Amanda Dargan, of *City Play* (1990).

Judith Zilczer is a curator emerita at the Hirshhorn Museum and Sculpture Garden in Washington, D.C. She is the author of many articles and catalogues, including *"The Noble Buyer": John Quinn, Patron of the Avant-Garde* (1978) and *The Advent of Modernism: Post-Impressionism and North American Art, 1900–1918* (1986).

Mary Ellen Zuckerman (PhD Columbia University) is an associate professor of marketing at the State University of New York, Geneseo. She is the author of *Sources on the History of Women's Magazines, 1792–1960* (1991) and a coauthor, with John Tebbel, of *The Magazine in America, 1741–1990* (1991).

ILLUSTRATION CREDITS

Special thanks go to photographers Alexander Heilner, Michael Lorenzini, Rohanna Mertens, and Carolyn Monastra.

Abbott, George: New-York Historical Society; Abingdon Square: New-York Historical Society; Abyssinian Baptist Church: Lisa Keller; Academy of Music: New-York Historical Society, Bracklow Collection; advertising: New-York Historical Society; AirTrain: Alexander Heilner; Algonquin Hotel: New-York Historical Society, George P. Hall Collection; Alice Austen House: Carolyn Monastra; almshouses: Museum of the City of New York, Jacob A. Riis Collection; alternative press: New-York Historical Society; American Academy of Dramatic Arts: Alexander Heilner; American Anti-Slavery Society: New-York Historical Society; American Ballet Theatre: New York Public Library for the Performing Arts, Dance Collection; American Indians: New-York Historical Society; American Museum of Natural History: New-York Historical Society; American Numismatic Society: New-York Historical Society; American Revolution: New-York Historical Society; Amsterdam News: Schomburg Center for Research in Black Culture, New York Public Library, and the Astor, Lenox, and Tilden foundations; Apollo Theater: Lisa Keller; Apthorp Apartments: Lisa Keller; Arabs: Alexander Heilner; architecture: New-York Historical Society; architecture: Alexander Heilner; architecture: Lisa Keller; armories: New-York Historical Society, McKim, Mead and White Collection; armories (three images): New-York Historical Society, Hall Collection; Arthur Ashe Stadium: Alexander Heilner; Art Students League: New-York Historical Society; Aspinwall, William Henry: New-York Historical Society; Astor House: New-York Historical Society, Bracklow Collection; Atlantic Basin: Alexander Heilner; Atlantic Yards: Alexander Heilner; Audubon, John J.: New-York Historical Society; automats: New York City Municipal Archives.

bagels: Lisa Keller; bakeries: Alexander Heilner; bakeries: Museum of the City of New York; Bankers Trust Company: New-York Historical Society, Hall Collection; Bank of New York: Alexander Heilner; Bank Street College of Education: Carolyn Monastra; Barnard College: Lisa Keller; Barnum, P. T.: New-York Historical Society; bars, taverns, and saloons: New-York Historical Society, Bagoe Collection; Bartow–Pell Mansion: Lisa Keller; Baruch, Bernard: New-York Historical Society; Baruch College: New-York Historical Society, Hall Collection; baseball: New-York Historical Society; Bath Beach: Grai St. Clair Rice; bathhouses: Grai St. Clair Rice; bathhouses: New-York Historical Society; Battery Park: New York City Municipal Archives, La Guardia Collection; Battery Park: Alexander Heilner; Battery Park City: Alexander Heilner; Bayonne Bridge: Grai St. Clair Rice; beaches: Lisa Keller; Beals, Jessie Tarbox: New-York Historical Society; Beame, Abraham: New York City Municipal Archives; Bedford–Stuyvesant: Alexander Heilner; Beecher, Henry Ward: New-York Historical Society; beer halls: New-York Historical Society; Bellevue Hospital: New-York Historical Society, Hall Collection; Belmont, August: New-York Historical Society; Bensonhurst: New-York Historical Society, Bracklow Collection; Bensonhurst: Camilo José Vergera; Berlin, Irving: New-York Historical Society; Bernstein, Leonard: New York Public Library for the Performing Arts, Music Division; Bethesda Fountain (both images): Alexander Heilner; Bialystoker Synagogue: Alexander Heilner; bicycling: New York City Municipal Archives; bicycling: Alexander Heilner; Blake, Eubie: Helen Armstead-Johnson Photograph Collection, 1921, Schomberg Center for Research in Black Culture, New York Public Library, and the Astor, Lenox, and Tilden foundations; blizzard of 1888: New-York Historical Society; Bloomingdale Insane Asylum: New-York Historical Society, Hall Collection; Bloomingdale's: New-York Historical Society; Bly, Nellie: New-York Historical Society, Hall Collection; Board of Education: Alexander Heilner; boat basins: Alexander Heilner; bodegas: Alexander Heilner; Boerum Hill: Alexander Heilner; Bowery Theatre: New-York Historical Society; Bowling Green: New-York Historical Society; brewing and distilling: New-York Historical Society; bridges: Lisa Keller; bridges: Alexander Heilner; Brighton Beach: New-York Historical Society, Hall Collection; Broadway: New-York Historical Society; Bronx: Lisa Keller; Bronx (map): John Tauranac, Tauranac, Ltd.; Bronx River: New-York Historical Society; Bronx Zoo: Lisa Keller; Brooklyn: New-York Historical Society; Brooklyn (map): John Tauranac, Tauranac, Ltd.; Brooklyn Academy of Music: Alexander Heilner; Brooklyn Borough Hall: Alexander Heilner; Brooklyn Bridge: Alexander Heilner; Brooklyn Cyclones: Alexander Heilner; Brooklyn Heights: New-York Historical Society, Hall Collection; Brooklyn Historical Society: Alexander Heilner; Brooklyn–Manhattan Transit Corporation: Collection of Brian J. Cudahy; Brooklyn Museum: Alexander Heilner; Brooklyn Navy Yard: New-York Historical Society, World War II Collection; Brooklyn Navy Yard: Lisa Keller; brownstones: New-York Historical Society; Bryant, William C.: New-York Historical Society; Bryant Park: New York City Municipal Archives; Burr, Aaron: New-York Historical Society; buses: Museum of the City of New York; Butterick, Ebenezer (both images): New-York Historical Society.

Cadman Plaza: Alexander Heilner; Calyo, Nicolino: New-York Historical Society; Canal Street: Alexander Heilner; Cantor, Eddie: New-York Historical Society; Cardozo, Benjamin: New-York Historical Society; Carnegie, Andrew: New-York Historical Society, Bracklow Collection; Carnegie Hall: Alexander Heilner; Carroll, Earl: New-York Historical Society, Browning Collection; Carroll Gardens: Alexander Heilner; cartooning: New-York Historical Society; Caruso, Enrico: New York Public Library for the Performing Arts, Music Division; cast-iron architecture: Lisa Keller; cast-iron architecture: New-York Historical Society; cast-iron architecture: Lisa Keller; Castle Clinton: New-York Historical Society, Hall Collection; Castle Hill: New-York Historical Society; Castle Williams: Alexander Heilner; Cathedral of St. John the Divine: Carolyn Monastra; Catt, Carrie: New-York Historical Society; cemeteries: Grai St. Clair Rice; cemeteries: Alexander Heilner; Central Park (maps): John Tauranac, Tauranac Ltd.; Central Park (both images): Alexander Heilner; Central Park Casino: New-York Historical Society; Central Park West: Lisa Keller; Charlotte Gardens: Camilo José Vergara; Chatham Square: New-York Historical Society; Chelsea Market: Alexander Heilner; Chelsea Piers: New York City Municipal Archives; Chelsea Piers: Alexander Heilner; chess: Grai St. Clair Rice; chess: Alexander Heilner; child labor: Museum of the City of New York, Jacob A. Riis Collection; Children's Aid Society: Museum of the City of New York, Jacob A. Riis Collection; children's book publishing: New-York Historical Society; Childs: New-York Historical Society; Chinatown: Melissa M. Merritt; Chinatown: Alexander Heilner; Chinese: New-York Historical Society; choruses: New-York Historical Society; Christodora House: Alexander Heilner; churches: Carolyn Monastra; Church of St. Brigid: Alexander Heilner; Church of the Transfiguration (ii): Grai St. Clair Rice; Citi Field: Alexander Heilner; City College of New York: New-York Historical Society, Bracklow Collection; city halls: New-York Historical Society, Hall Collection; civic associations: New-York Historical Society; Cleopatra's Needle: New-York Historical Society, Bracklow Collection; Clinton, DeWitt: New-York Historical Society; Cloisters: New-York Historical Society, Fifth Avenue Coach Collection; Cobble Hill: Alexander Heilner; Cole, Thomas: New-York Historical Society; colleges and universities: New-York Historical Society; Colonnade Row: New-York Historical Society, Bracklow Collection; Colored American: New-York Historical Society; Colored Orphan Asylum: New-York Historical Society; Columbia University (both images): New-York Historical Society; Columbus Circle: New-York Historical Society, Hall Collection; commercial banks: New-York Historical Society, Hall Collection; commercial banks: Museum of the City of New York, Byron Collection; commercial banks: Alexander Heilner; Comstock, Anthony: New-York Historical Society; concert saloons: New-York Historical Society, Geographic Collection; Coney Island: New-York Historical Society; Coney Island: Alexander Heilner; Coney Island: New-York Historical Society, Hall Collection; Congregationalists: New-York Historical Society; Convent of the Sacred Heart: New-York Historical Society, Hall Collection; Cooper, Peter: New-York Historical Society; cooperatives: New-York Historical Society; Cooper Union: New-York Historical Society; Cornell, Katharine: New York Public Library, Performing Arts Research Center; corners and panics: New-York Historical Society,

Peters Collection; Corrigan, Michael A.: New-York Historical Society; cosmetics: Carolyn Monastra; Costello, Frank: New York City Municipal Archives, La Guardia Collection; courthouses: New York City Municipal Archives; courthouses (two images): Alexander Heilner; courts: New-York Historical Society, Peters Collection; Croker, Richard: New-York Historical Society; Croton Aqueduct: New-York Historical Society; Crystal Palace: New-York Historical Society, Peters Collection; Cunningham, Merce: Gerda Peterich / New York Public Library for the Performing Arts, Dance Collection; curling: New-York Historical Society, Peters Collection; Currier and Ives (both images): New-York Historical Society.

Dakota: New-York Historical Society; Dakota: Lisa Keller; D. Appleton: New-York Historical Society; Davis, Miles: Schomburg Center for Research in Black Culture, New York Public Library, Astor, Lenox, and Tilden foundations; Dead Man's Curve: New-York Historical Society, Hall Collection; delicatessens: Grai St. Clair Rice; Delmonico's: New-York Historical Society; Dewey Arch: New-York Historical Society, Hall Collection; Diamond District: Grai St. Clair Rice; Dinkins, David N.: New York City Municipal Archives; Ditmas Park: Grai St. Clair Rice; Domino Sugar Plant: Alexander Heilner; Downing, Andrew Jackson: New-York Historical Society; draft riots: New-York Historical Society, Peters Collection; Dreiser, Theodore: New-York Historical Society; Du Bois, W. E. B.: Schomburg Center for Research in Black Culture, New York Public Library, and the Astor, Lenox, and Tilden foundations; Dunham, Katherine: Schomburg Center for Research in Black Culture, New York Public Library, and the Astor, Lenox, and Tilden Foundations; Durand, Asher B.: New-York Historical Society.

East River: New-York Historical Society; Ebbets Field: New-York Historical Society; Educational Alliance: Lisa Keller; El Barrio: New York City Municipal Archives; Eldridge Street Synagogue: Grai St. Clair Rice; elevated railways: New-York Historical Society; elevators: New-York Historical Society, Bella C. Landauer Collection; Ellington, Duke: New York Public Library for the Performing Arts, Music Division; Ellis Island: Alexander Heilner; Empire State Building: New-York Historical Society, Browning Collection; engineering: New-York Historical Society; Equitable Building: Alexander Heilner.

Fashion Institute of Technology: Alexander Heilner; FDR Drive: New York City Municipal Archives; Federal Hall: Alexander Heilner; Fieldston: Grai St. Clair Rice; Fifth Avenue: Carolyn Monastra; fire escapes: Alexander Heilner; firefighting: New-York Historical Society, Bracklow Collection; firefighting: New-York Historical Society; firefighting: Lisa Keller; firefighting: Carolyn Monastra; firefighting: Alexander Heilner; Fish, Preserved: New-York Historical Society; Five Points: New-York Historical Society; Flagg, Ernest: New-York Historical Society, Hall Collection; Flatbush: Grai St. Clair Rice; Flatiron Building: New-York Historical Society, Bracklow Collection; Flatlands: New-York Historical Society, Bracklow Collection; Floyd Bennett Field: Alexander Heilner; Flushing: New York City Municipal Archives; Flushing Meadows–Corona Park: Alexander Heilner; football: New-York Historical Society; Fordham: New-York Historical Society; Forest Hills: New-York Historical Society; Fort Amsterdam: New-York Historical Society; Fort Greene: Alexander Heilner; Fort Hamilton: New-York Historical Society; Fort Schuyler: Lisa Keller; Fort Wadsworth: Carolyn Monastra; foundlings: Museum of the City of New York, Jacob A. Riis Collection; Fraunces Tavern: Alexander Heilner; Freedom's Journal: Schomburg Center for Research in Black Culture, New York Public Library, and the Astor, Lenox, and Tilden foundations; French, Daniel Chester: Grai St. Clair Rice; Fulton, Robert: New-York Historical Society; Fulton Ferry: New-York Historical Society; Fulton Fish Market: New York City Municipal Archives; Fulton Fish Market: New York City Municipal Archives.

gambling: New-York Historical Society, Peters Collection; gambling: New York City Municipal Archives, La Guardia Collection; Gansevoort Farmers' Street Market: New-York Historical Society; Garibaldi, Giuseppe: New-York Historical Society, Bracklow Collection; garment district: Grai St. Clair Rice; Garvey, Marcus: Schomburg Center for Research in Black Culture, New York Public Library, and the Astor, Lenox, and Tilden foundations; General Slocum: Alexander Heilner; geology: New-York Historical Society; George Washington Bridge: Alexander Heilner; Gibson, Charles Dana: New-York Historical Society; glassmaking: New-York Historical Society; Goethals Bridge: New York City Municipal Archives; Gompers, Samuel: New-York Historical Society; Goodyear, Charles: New-York Historical Society; Gotham Court: New-York Historical Society, Lawrence Collection; government and politics: New-York Historical Society, Hall Collection; government and politics: New-York Historical Society; Governors Island (both images): Alexander Heilner; Gowanus Canal: Alexander Heilner; Grace Church: Alexander Heilner; graffiti: Meghan Lalonde; Gramercy Park: Grai St. Clair Rice; Gramercy Park Hotel: Alexander Heilner; Grand Army Plaza (i): New-York Historical Society, Hall Collection; Grand (Boulevard and) Concourse: New-York Historical Society; Grand Central Terminal: New-York Historical Society, Hall Collection; Grand Central Terminal: Alexander Heilner; Grand Union Hotel: New-York Historical Society; Grant's Tomb: Lisa Keller; Gravesend: Alexander Heilner; Great Atlantic and Pacific Tea Company (all images): New-York Historical Society; Great Fire: New-York Historical Society; Green, Andrew Haswell: New-York Historical Society; Greenpoint: Alexander Heilner; Greenwich Village (map): Identity Map Company; Green-Wood Cemetery: New-York Historical Society, Hall Collection; Green-Wood Cemetery: Lisa Keller; grid plan: New-York Historical Society.

Hall, A. Oakey: New-York Historical Society; Hall of Fame for Great Americans: New-York Historical Society; Hamilton Grange: Lisa Keller; Hansberry, Lorraine: Schomburg Center for Research in Black Culture, New York Public Library, and the Astor, Lenox, and Tilden foundations; Happy Land Fire (both images): Lisa Keller; Harlem: New-York Historical Society; Harlem Hellfighters: Schomburg Center for Research in Black Culture, New York Public Library, and the Astor, Lenox, and Tilden foundations; Harlem River Houses: Rohanna Mertens; Harlem River Ship Canal: New-York Historical Society; Havemeyer, William F.: New-York Historical Society; Hayes, Helen: Grai St. Clair Rice; Hearst Building and Tower: Carolyn Monastra; Hell's Kitchen: New-York Historical Society; Henry Street Settlement: Lisa Keller; Hepburn, Katharine: New York Public Library for the Performing Arts, Billy Rose Theater Collection, Astor, Lenox, and Tilden Foundations; Herald Square: New-York Historical Society, Hall Collection; High Bridge: New-York Historical Society, Hall Collection; High Line: Alexander Heilner; Hippodrome: New-York Historical Society, Hall Collection; Hispanic Society of America: New-York Historical Society; Holiday, Billie: Schomburg Center for Research in Black Culture, New York Public Library, and the Astor, Lenox, and Tilden foundations; homelessness: New-York Historical Society, Lawrence Collection; homelessness: New York City Municipal Archives; Homer, Winslow: New-York Historical Society; Horne, Lena: Schomburg Center for Research in Black Culture, New York Public Library, and the Astor, Lenox, and Tilden foundations; horse racing: New-York Historical Society; hospitals (both images): New-York Historical Society; hotels (two images): New-York Historical Society; hotels: Alexander Heilner; Houdini, Harry: New-York Historical Society; housing: New-York Historical Society, Hall Collection; Hudson River: New-York Historical Society; Hudson River School: New-York Historical Society; Hudson Yards: Alexander Heilner; Hughes, Langston: Morgan and Marvin Smith / Schomburg Center for Research in Black Culture, New York Public Library, and the Astor, Lenox, and Tilden foundations; Humphrey, Doris: New York Public Library for the Performing Arts, Dance Collection; Hunter, Alberta: Schomburg Center for Research in Black Culture, New York Public Library, and the Astor, Lenox, and Tilden foundations; Hurston, Zora Neale: Schomburg Center for Research in Black Culture, New York Public Library, and the Astor, Lenox, and Tilden foundations; Hylan, John F.: New York City Municipal Archives.

ice harvesting: New-York Historical Society; ice skating: New-York Historical Society; immigration: New-York Historical Society; Impellitteri, Vincent R.: New York City Municipal Archives; India House: New-York Historical Society, Bracklow Collection; Interchurch Center: Lisa Keller; Inwood: New-York Historical Society, Bracklow Collection; Irish Hunger Memorial: Alexander Heilner; Irving, Washington: New-York Historical Society.

Jacob K. Javits Convention Center: Alexander Heilner; jails: Museum of the City of New York, Jacob A. Riis Collection; jails: New York City Municipal Archives; jazz: Carolyn Monastra; jazz: Alexander Heilner; Jefferson Market: New-York Historical Society; Jews: Alexander Heilner; Jews: New-York Historical Society; John Jay College of Criminal Justice: Alexander Heilner; J. P. Morgan: New-York Historical Society, Hall Collection; Jumel, Stephen: New-York Historical Society, Lawrence Collection; Junior's: Alexander Heilner.

Kahn, Otto H.: New-York Historical Society; Katz's Delicatessen: Alexander Heilner; Keens Chophouse: New-York Historical Society; Kensington: Alexander Heilner; Kew Gardens: New-York Historical Society, Ingalls Collection; King, Rufus: New-York Historical Society; King Manor: Alexander Heilner; Kingsbridge: New-York Historical Society, Bracklow Collection;

Kiralfy, Imre: New-York Historical Society; Kleindeutschland: New-York Historical Society, Hall Collection; Koch, Edward I.: New York City Municipal Archives; kosher foods: Museum of the City of New York; kosher foods: New-York Historical Society.

Lafayette Theatre: Schomburg Center for Research in Black Culture, New York Public Library, and the Astor, Lenox, and Tilden foundations; La Guardia, Fiorello H.: New York City Municipal Archives, La Guardia Collection; La Guardia Airport: New-York Historical Society; La Guardia Airport: Alexander Heilner; Lansky, Meyer: New York City Municipal Archives; Lee, Spike: Alexander Heilner; Lever House: Rohanna Mertens; libraries: New-York Historical Society, Hall Collection; lighthouses: Museum of the City of New York, Jacob A. Riis Collection; lighthouses: New-York Historical Society; Limelight: Lisa Keller; Limón, José: New York Public Library for the Performing Arts, Dance Collection; Lindsay, John V.: New York City Municipal Archives; Lippmann, Walter: New-York Historical Society; Long Island Rail Road: New-York Historical Society, Hall Collection; Long Island University: Alexander Heilner; lotteries: New-York Historical Society, Bella C. Landauer Collection; Lower East Side: Grai St. Clair Rice; Lower East Side: Lisa Keller; Lutherans: New-York Historical Society; Lying-In Hospital: New-York Historical Society.

Macombs Dam Bridge: New-York Historical Society; Madison Square: New-York Historical Society, Hall Collection; Madison Square Garden (both images): New-York Historical Society, Hall Collection; magazines: New-York Historical Society, Browning Collection; Manhattan: Alexander Heilner; Manhattan (map): John Tauranac, Tauranac Ltd.; Manhattan: New-York Historical Society, Thomas Airviews; Manhattan (map): Identity Map Company; Manhattan: Alexander Heilner; Manhattan Beach: New-York Historical Society, Hall Collection; Manhattan Bridge: New-York Historical Society, Hall Collection; marble cemeteries: Alexander Heilner; marinas: Grai St. Clair Rice; markets (both images): New-York Historical Society; Martyrs' Monument: Alexander Heilner; Matthews, Victoria Earle: Schomburg Center for Research in Black Culture, New York Public Library, and the Astor, Lenox, and Tilden foundations; McAdoo, William: New-York Historical Society; McDougall, Alexander: New-York Historical Society; McKim, Mead and White: New-York Historical Society; McSorley's Old Ale House: Alexander Heilner; meatpacking: New York City Municipal Archives; Mercantile Library Association: New-York Historical Society, Bracklow Collection; Merchant's House Museum: Alexander Heilner; Merman, Ethel: Billy Rose Theatre Division, The New York Public Library for the Performing Arts, Astor, Lenox and Tilden Foundations; Metro-North Commuter Railroad: Grai St. Clair Rice; Metropolitan Museum of Art: New-York Historical Society; Metropolitan Museum of Art: New-York Historical Society, Hall Collection; Metropolitan Opera: New York City Municipal Archives; Middle Village: Grai St. Clair Rice; midtown: Alexander Heilner; Mitchel, John Purroy: New-York Historical Society; Montauk Club: New-York Historical Society, Hall Collection; Moore, Clement Clarke: New-York Historical Society; Morgan Library and Museum: Alexander Heilner; Morris, Gouverneur: New-York Historical Society; Morris High School: New-York Historical Society, Hall Collection; Morris–Jumel Mansion: Lisa Keller; Morse, Samuel F. B.: New-York Historical Society; Mount Vernon Hotel Museum and Garden: Rohanna Mertens; Mulberry Bend: Museum of the City of New York, Jacob A. Riis Collection; Municipal Building: New-York Historical Society, Hall Collection; Museum of Arts and Design: Lisa Keller; Museum of Jewish Heritage: Alexander Heilner; Museum of the Moving Image: Carolyn Monastra; museums: New-York Historical Society; musical instrument manufacture: New-York Historical Society; Muslims: Grai St. Clair Rice.

Nast, Thomas (both images): New-York Historical Society; Nathan's: Alexander Heilner; National Academy of Design: New-York Historical Society; National Debt Clock: Alexander Heilner; nativism: New-York Historical Society; Nesbit, Evelyn Florence: New-York Historical Society; New Dorp: Carolyn Monastra; newsboys: New-York Historical Society; newspapers (two images): New-York Historical Society; newspapers: Grai St. Clair Rice; Newtown Creek: Alexander Heilner; New Utrecht: New-York Historical Society, Nash Collection; New York and Harlem Railroad: New-York Historical Society; New York Herald Tribune: New-York Historical Society, Peters Collection; New-York Historical Society: New-York Historical Society; New-York Historical Society: Lisa Keller; New York Life Insurance Company: New-York Historical Society, Browning Collection; New York Mercantile Exchange: New-York Historical Society; New York Palace: New-York Historical Society; New York Produce Exchange: New-York Historical Society; New York Public Library: New-York Historical Society, Hall Collection; New York Public Library (two images): New-York Historical Society; New York Stock Exchange: New-York Historical Society; New York Stock Exchange: Alexander Heilner; New York Times: New-York Historical Society, Hall Collection; New York Times: Carolyn Monastra; New York University: Alexander Heilner; New York Water Taxi: Alexander Heilner; Niblo's Garden: New-York Historical Society; Novelty Ironworks: New-York Historical Society.

Odets, Clifford: Billy Rose Theatre Division, The New York Public Library for the Performing Arts, Astor, Lenox and Tilden Foundations; O'Dwyer, Paul: New York City Municipal Archives; O'Dwyer, William: New York City Municipal Archives; Olmsted, Frederick Law: New-York Historical Society, Hall Collection; Outcault, R. F.: New-York Historical Society, Bella C. Landauer Collection; oysters: New-York Historical Society.

Paine, Thomas: New-York Historical Society; parades: New-York Historical Society; parades: Meghan Lalonde; Parkchester: Lisa Keller; Parker, Charlie: Schomburg Center for Research in Black Culture, New York Public Library, and Astor, Lenox and Tilden foundations; Parkhurst, Charles H.: New-York Historical Society; parking: Alexander Heilner; parks (both images): Alexander Heilner; Park Slope: Grai St. Clair Rice; PATH and PATH Station: Alexander Heilner; paving: New York City Municipal Archives; Pelham Bay Park: New York City Municipal Archives, La Guardia Collection; Pennsylvania Station: New-York Historical Society, Bracklow Collection; Pennsylvania Station: New-York Historical Society, Hall Collection; Pete's Tavern: Alexander Heilner; Peter Luger Steak House: Alexander Heilner; phrenology: New-York Historical Society; Phyfe, Duncan: Museum of the City of New York, Gift of Mrs. J. Bertram Howell; Pintard, John: New-York Historical Society; pizza: Alexander Heilner; playgrounds: Museum of the City of New York, Jacob A. Riis Collection; Plaza Hotel: New-York Historical Society; Plymouth Church of the Pilgrims: New-York Historical Society, Hall Collection; Poe Cottage: New-York Historical Society; police: New-York Historical Society; police (two images): Alexander Heilner; Polo Grounds: New-York Historical Society; Pomander Walk: Lisa Keller; Port of New York: New-York Historical Society; Port of New York: Museum of the City of New York; Post, George B.: New-York Historical Society; post offices: New-York Historical Society, Hall Collection; post offices: New-York Historical Society; potter's fields: Museum of the City of New York, Jacob A. Riis Collection; poverty (both images): New-York Historical Society; Powell, Adam Clayton, Jr.: Schomburg Center for Research in Black Culture, New York Public Library, and the Astor, Lenox, and Tilden foundations; Presbyterians: New-York Historical Society, Hall Collection; Price, Leontyne: Schomburg Center for Research in Black Culture, New York Public Library, and the Astor, Lenox, and Tilden foundations; Prohibition: New-York Historical Society; prostitution: New-York Historical Society; public housing: New York City Municipal Archives; public schools: New-York Historical Society, Hall Collection; public schools: Alexander Heilner.

Quakers: New York City Municipal Archives; Queens (map): John Tauranac, Tauranac, Ltd.; Queensboro Bridge: Alexander Heilner; Queens Borough Public Library: New York City Municipal Archives.

radio: New York City Municipal Archives; radio: New-York Historical Society; Radio City Music Hall: New York City Municipal Archives; railroads: New-York Historical Society; Ravenswood: New-York Historical Society; RCA Corporation: New-York Historical Society, Bella C. Landauer Collection; RCA Corporation: New-York Historical Society; recycling: Carolyn Monastra; Red Hook: Alexander Heilner; religion: Grai St. Clair Rice; revivalism: Museum of the City of New York, Byron Collection; R. H. Macy: Museum of the City of New York, Byron Collection; Richmondtown: Carolyn Monastra; Riis, Jacob A.: New-York Historical Society; riots (both images): New-York Historical Society; Riverbank State Park: Alexander Heilner; Riverside Park: Carolyn Monastra; Riverside Park: New-York Historical Society; Robinson, Bill "Bojangles": New York Public Library for the Performing Arts, Dance Collection; Rockefeller Center: Lisa Keller; Roosevelt, Eleanor: New-York Historical Society; Roosevelt, Theodore: Lisa Keller; Roosevelt Island: Alexander Heilner; Roosevelt Island: New York City Municipal Archives; Roosevelt Island Tramway: Rohanna Mertens; Rosenberg case: Lisa Keller; Roxy Theater: New-York Historical Society; Ruggles, Samuel B.: New-York Historical Society.

Saint-Gaudens, Augustus: New-York Historical Society, Hall Collection; St. George's Episcopal Church (i): New-York Historical Society; St. George's Square: New-York Historical Society; St. Mark's Church in the Bowery: New-York Historical Society, Hall Collection; St. Patrick's Cathedral: New-York Historical Society, Hall

Collection; St. Stanislaus Kostka Vincentian Fathers Church: Alexander Heilner; Saks Fifth Avenue: New-York Historical Society, Hall Collection; sanitation: New-York Historical Society; sanitation (two images): New York City Municipal Archives; savings banks: Museum of the City of New York, Byron Collection; Schomburg, Arthur: Schomburg Center for Research in Black Culture, New York Public Library, and the Astor, Lenox, and Tilden foundations; Schomburg, Arthur: Lisa Keller; Schomburg Center for Research in Black Culture: Lisa Keller; Schurz, Carl: New-York Historical Society; sculpture : New-York Historical Society, Bracklow Collection; sculpture: New-York Historical Society; sculpture: Carolyn Monastra; sculpture: Alexander Heilner; Sea Gate (both images): Alexander Heilner; Seal of the City of New York: New York City Municipal Archives; September 11 (two images): Copyright Michael Lorenzini; September 11: Alexander Heilner; Seventh Regiment: New-York Historical Society, McKim, Mead and White collection; Seventh Regiment (two images): New-York Historical Society; Shakespeare in the Park: Alexander Heilner; shantytowns: New-York Historical Society; Shearith Israel: Alexander Heilner; Sheepshead Bay (both images): Grai St. Clair Rice; shoes, boots, and leather: New-York Historical Society, Bella C. Landauer Collection; silver: Museum of the City of New York; skyscrapers: New-York Historical Society; skyscrapers (two images): Alexander Heilner; Smith, Alfred E.: New-York Historical Society, Browning Collection; soft drinks: New-York Historical Society; SoHo: Alexander Heilner; songs: New-York Historical Society; Sousa, John Philip: New-York Historical Society, Bella C. Landauer Collection; South Street Seaport (two images): New-York Historical Society; South Street Seaport: Alexander Heilner; squares: Lisa Keller; stables: New-York Historical Society; stair streets: Grai St. Clair Rice; Staten Island: Carolyn Monastra; Staten Island (two images): New-York Historical Society; Staten Island (map): John Tauranac, Tauranac Ltd.; Staten Island Ferry: Alexander Heilner; Staten Island Ferry: New York City Municipal Archives; Statue of Liberty: Alexander Heilner; Steinway and Sons: New-York Historical Society; Steinway and Sons: Carolyn Monastra; Stettheimer, Florine: New York Public Library for the Performing Arts; Steward, Susan McKinney: Schomburg Center for Research in Black Culture, New York Public Library, and the Astor, Lenox, and Tilden foundations; Stewart, A. T. (both images): New-York Historical Society; Stonewall Riots: Alexander Heilner; Straus, Nathan: New-York Historical Society; streetcars (both images): New-York Historical Society; street life: New-York Historical Society; street life: Lisa Keller; Strivers' Row: Lisa Keller; Stuyvesant, Peter: New-York Historical Society; Stuyvesant Town: Alexander Heilner; Stuyvesant Town: New York City Municipal Archives, La Guardia Collection; subways (all maps): John Tauranac, Tauranac Ltd.; subways: New York City Municipal Archives; sugar: New-York Historical Society; Sugar Hill: Lisa Keller; Surrogate's Court: New York City Municipal Archives; swimming: New York City Municipal Archives; swimming: Alexander Heilner; Sylvia's: Lisa Keller; Symphony Space: Lisa Keller; synagogues (all images): Lisa Keller.

Tarbell, Ida: New-York Historical Society; tattooing: Alexander Heilner; telephony: Alexander Heilner; tennis: New-York Historical Society; terrorism: Alexander Heilner; theater: New York City Municipal Archives; theater: Alexander Heilner; ticker-tape parades: New-York Historical Society; ticker-tape parades: New York City Municipal Archives; Tiffany and Company: Lisa Keller; Tilden, Samuel J.: New-York Historical Society; Times Square (map): Identity Map Company; Time Warner Center: Lisa Keller; TKTS: Alexander Heilner; Tombs: New York City Municipal Archives; Tompkins Square: Alexander Heilner; Tontine Coffee House: New-York Historical Society; Toscanini, Arturo: New York City Municipal Archives; tourism: Alexander Heilner; Triangle Shirtwaist fire (both images): Lisa Keller; tugboats: Alexander Heilner.

Union Square: Alexander Heilner; Union Square: Copyright Michael Lorenzini; Unisphere: Alexander Heilner; United Nations: Alexander Heilner; U.S. Custom House: New York City Municipal Archives.

Van Cortlandt Park (both images): New-York Historical Society; Verrazano–Narrows Bridge: Alexander Heilner; Viele, Egbert Ludoricus: New-York Historical Society.

Wagner, Robert F. (ii): New York City Municipal Archives; Walker, James J.: New-York Historical Society; Wall Street: Alexander Heilner; Waring, George E., Jr.: New-York Historical Society; Washington Square Park: Lisa Keller; water: Alexander Heilner; water: New York City Municipal Archives; water (both maps): New York City Department of Environmental Protection; water fountains: Alexander Heilner; water tanks and towers: Alexander Heilner; Wave Hill: New York City Municipal Archives; Weeksville: Alexander Heilner; West Side Highway: New York City Municipal Archives; White Horse Tavern: Alexander Heilner; Whitman, Walt: New-York Historical Society; Wise, Stephen: New-York Historical Society; women's hotels: New-York Historical Society; Women's House of Detention: New York City Municipal Archives; Woolworth Building: New-York Historical Society; World Financial Center: Alexander Heilner; World Trade Center: New York City Municipal Archives; World Trade Center: Michael Lorenzini; World Trade Center: Alexander Heilner; Wyckoff House: New-York Historical Society.

Yeshiva University: New-York Historical Society.

INDEX

Page references to encyclopedia articles are in **boldface.** *References to illustrations are in italic. Neighborhoods are identified by borough with the two-letter abbreviations BX (Bronx), BK (Brooklyn), MN (Manhattan), QN (Queens), and SI (Staten Island). Numbered streets are alphabetized as if they were written out. An alphabetical index of the various tables of detailed historical information about the city is included here as the entry "City information tables." Page references to tables appear in* ***bold italic.***